PENGUIN REFERENCE

# The Penguin Guide to Punctuation

R. L. Trask was born in western New York State in 1944. For some years he pursued a career in chemistry in the USA and in Turkey. In 1970 he came to England and switched to linguistics, obtaining his Ph.D. from the University of London in 1983. He taught linguistics at the University of Liverpool from 1979 to 1988, since when he has taught in the School of Cognitive and Computing Sciences at the University of Sussex. His special interests are historical linguistics, grammar and the Basque language. He is the author of a number of books, including *A Dictionary of Grammatical Terms in Linguistics*, *Language Change*, *Language: The Basics*, *A Dictionary of Phonetics and Phonology*, *Historical Linguistics*, *The History of Basque*, *The Penguin Dictionary of English Grammar* and *Mind the Gaffe*. He is tired of reading poorly punctuated work, and he hopes this book will help.

# The Penguin Guide to PUNCTUATION

R. L. Trask

PENGUIN BOOKS

PENGUIN BOOKS

Published by the Penguin Group
Penguin Books Ltd, 80 Strand, London WC2R 0RL, England
Penguin Group (USA) Inc., 375 Hudson Street, New York, New York 10014, USA
Penguin Books Australia Ltd, 250 Camberwell Road, Camberwell, Victoria 3124, Australia
Penguin Books Canada Ltd, 10 Alcorn Avenue, Toronto, Ontario, Canada M4V 3B2
Penguin Books India (P) Ltd, 11 Community Centre, Panchsheel Park, New Delhi – 110 017, India
Penguin Group (NZ), cnr Airborne and Rosedale Roads, Albany, Auckland 1310, New Zealand
Penguin Books (South Africa) (Pty) Ltd, 24 Sturdee Avenue, Rosebank 2196, South Africa

Penguin Books Ltd, Registered Offices: 80 Strand, London WC2R 0RL, England

www.penguin.com

First published 1997
35



Set in 11.5/15.5pt Monotype Bembo
Typeset by Rowland Phototypesetting Ltd, Bury St Edmunds, Suffolk
Printed in England by Clays Ltd, St Ives plc



ISBN-13: 978–0–140–51366–0

# Table of Contents

# Acknowledgements

I am indebted to Lisa Wale, Max Wheeler, Richard Coates, Margaret Crowther and an anonymous reader for their valuable comments on earlier drafts of this book, and to Lisa Wale for providing many of the examples, and to Donald Wilson for a splendid job of copy-editing. Any remaining shortcomings are my own responsibility.

## To the Reader

The book in your hand is a textbook, and it is written for people who find punctuation difficult. If you're not too sure where commas ought to go, if you're puzzled by colons and semicolons, if hyphens and apostrophes are something of a mystery to you, then this book is for you.

The book starts at the beginning and assumes no knowledge of punctuation at all. Each punctuation mark is introduced in turn; its proper use is described with the aid of lots of examples; wherever possible I give you some simple rules for checking your punctuation.

The space devoted to each punctuation mark reflects the degree of difficulty that most people have with it. For example, apostrophes and bracketing commas, which between them probably account for about half of all punctuation mistakes, receive a great deal of discussion, while question marks are dealt with much more briefly, since hardly anybody finds them difficult.

A notable feature of the book is its inclusion of many examples which are badly punctuated. These are always marked with an asterisk (*), and the text explains in each case what is wrong. All of the most frequent punctuation mistakes are treated in this way.

The punctuation described here is the style which is currently the norm in Britain and the Commonwealth. Standard American usage differs in a few respects; in these cases, American usage is also described, but examples of specifically American punctuation are always marked as follows: (A). If you are writing expressly for an American audience, you should follow the American norms.

The book also covers a few topics which are not strictly aspects of punctuation, such as the proper use of capital letters, of contractions and abbreviations and of diacritics. The last chapter goes on to explain the proper way to handle titles, footnotes, references and bibliographies, and it also covers the punctuation of personal and business letters.

Since many people these days do most of their writing at a keyboard, and especially with a word processor, this book also explains the proper use of italics, boldface, small capitals and the special characters available on a word processor.

Chapter 1

# Why Learn to Punctuate?

Why should you learn to punctuate properly? After all, many people have made successful careers without ever learning the difference between a colon and a semicolon. Perhaps you consider punctuation to be an inconsequential bit of decoration, not worth spending your valuable time on. Or perhaps you even regard punctuation as a deeply personal matter – a mode of self-expression not unlike your taste in clothes or music.

Well, punctuation is one aspect of written English. How do you feel about other aspects of written English? Would you happily write *pair* when you mean *pear*, because you think the first is a nicer spelling? Would you, in an essay, write *Einstein were a right clever lad, 'e were*, just because that's the way people speak where you come from? Would you consider it acceptable to write *proceed* when you mean *precede*, or vice versa, because you've never understood the difference between them? Probably not – at least, I hope not.

Yet it is quite possible that you do things that are every bit as strange and bewildering when you punctuate your writing. Perhaps you use commas in what we shall soon see are surprising places, merely because you think you might pause there in speech. Perhaps you use semicolons where you should be using colons, because you've never quite understood the difference between them. Or perhaps, if you're really committed to punctuation as self-expression, you just stick in whatever punctuation takes your fancy, because it's *your* piece of work, and so it ought to have *your* punctuation.

The problem with poor punctuation is that it makes life difficult for the reader who needs to read what you've written. That reader shouldn't have to make allowances for your personal tastes in spelling and grammar: she expects to see standard English spellings and standard English grammatical forms. And the same is true for punctuation: she is most unlikely to know what your personal theories of punctuation are, and she won't be interested in them. She'll only be interested in understanding what you've written, and she's going to have trouble understanding it if it's badly punctuated.

When we speak English, we have all sorts of things we can use to make our meaning clear: stress, intonation, rhythm, pauses – even, if all else fails, repeating what we've said. When we write, however, we can't use any of these devices, and the work that they do in speech must be almost entirely handled by punctuation. Consequently, written English has developed a conventional system of punctuation which is consistent and sensible: every punctuation mark has one or more particular jobs to do, and every one should be used always and only to do those jobs. If your reader has to wade through your strange punctuation, she will have trouble following your meaning; at worst, she may be genuinely unable to understand what you've written. If you think I'm exaggerating, consider the following string of words, and try to decide what it's supposed to mean:

> We had one problem only Janet knew we faced bankruptcy

Have you decided? Now consider this string again with differing punctuation:

> We had one problem: only Janet knew we faced bankruptcy.
>
> We had one problem only: Janet knew we faced bankruptcy.
>
> We had one problem only, Janet knew: we faced bankruptcy.
>
> We had one problem only Janet knew we faced: bankruptcy.

Are you satisfied that all four of these have completely different meanings? If so, perhaps you have some inkling of how badly you can confuse your reader by punctuating poorly. What is the reader supposed to make of some feeble effort like this?

> ★ We had one problem only, Janet knew we faced bankruptcy.

(Remember, an asterisk is used to mark a sentence which is poorly punctuated, or which is otherwise defective.)

Bad punctuation does not require an enormous effort to put right. If you work carefully through this book, then, providing you think carefully about what you're writing as you write it, you will undoubtedly find that your punctuation has improved a great deal. Your readers will thank you for it ever after.

Chapter 2

# The Full Stop, the Question Mark and the Exclamation Mark

## 2.1 The Full Stop

The **full stop** (.), also called the **period**, presents few problems. It is chiefly used to mark the end of a sentence expressing a statement, as in the following examples:

> Terry Pratchett's latest book is not yet out in paperback.
> I asked her whether she could tell me the way to Brighton.
> Chinese, uniquely among the world's languages, is written in a logographic script.
> The British and the Irish drive on the left; all other Europeans drive on the right.

Note how the full stops are used in the following article, extracted from the *Guardian*:

> The opening of Ken Loach's film *Riff-Raff* in New York casts doubt on Winston Churchill's observation that the United States and Britain were two countries separated by a common language. In what must be a first, an entire British film has been given sub-titles to help Americans cut

through the thick stew of Glaswegian, Geordie, Liverpudlian, West African and West Indian accents. With the arrival of *Riff-Raff*, English as spoken by many British citizens has qualified as a foreign language in the US. Admittedly, the accents on the screen would present a challenge to many people raised on the Queen's English. But it is disconcerting to watch a British film with subtitles, not unlike watching Marlon Brando dubbed into Italian.

There is one common error you must watch out for. Here is an example of it (remember, an asterisk marks a badly punctuated sentence):

> ★ Norway has applied for EC membership, Sweden is expected to do the same.

Can you see what's wrong with this? Yes, there are two complete statements here, but the first one has been punctuated only with a comma. This is not possible, and something needs to be changed. The simplest way of fixing the example is to change the comma to a full stop:

> Norway has applied for EC membership. Sweden is expected to do the same.

Now each statement has its own full stop. This is correct, but you might consider it clumsy to use two short sentences in a row. If so, you can change the bad example in a different way:

Norway has applied for EC membership, and Sweden is expected to do the same.

This time we have used the connecting word *and* to combine the two short statements into one longer statement, and so now we need only one full stop at the end.

Here are some further examples of this very common error:

★ Bangladesh is one of the world's poorest countries, its annual income is only $80 per person.

★ The British are notoriously bad at learning foreign languages, the Dutch are famously good at it.

★ The proposal to introduce rock music to Radio 3 has caused an outcry, angry letters have been pouring into the BBC.

★ Borg won his fifth straight Wimbledon title in 1980, the following year he lost in the final to McEnroe.

All of these examples suffer from the same problem: a comma has been used to join two complete sentences. In each case, either the comma should be replaced by a full stop, or a suitable connecting word should be added, such as *and* or *while*.

In Chapter 4, I'll explain another way of punctuating these sentences, by using a semicolon.

Full stops are also sometimes used in punctuating abbreviations; this is discussed in Chapter 7.

### Summary of full stops

- **Put a full stop at the end of a complete statement.**
- **Do not connect two statements with a comma.**

## 2.2 The Question Mark

A **question mark** (**?**) is placed at the end of a sentence which is a direct question. Here are some examples:

What is the capital of Wales?
Does anyone have a pen I can borrow?
Who told you that?
In which country did coffee originate?

If the question is a direct quotation, repeating the speaker's exact words, a question mark is still used:

'Have you a pen I can borrow?' she asked.
'How many of you have pets at home?' inquired the teacher.

But a question mark is **not** used in an indirect question, in which the speaker's exact words are not repeated:

She asked if I had a pen she could borrow.
The teacher asked how many of us had pets at home.

Here only a full stop is used, since the whole sentence is now a statement.

The question mark also has one minor use: it may be inserted into the middle of something, inside parentheses, to show that something is uncertain. Here are two examples:

The famous allegorical poem *Piers Plowman* is attributed to William Langland (?1332–?1400).

The Lerga inscription fascinatingly contains the personal name *Vmme Sahar* (?), which looks like perfect Basque.

The question marks on the poet's birth and death dates indicate that those dates are not certain, and the one in the second example indicates that the reading of the name is possibly doubtful.

### Summary of question marks

- **Use a question mark at the end of a direct question.**
- **Do not use a question mark at the end of an indirect question.**
- **Use an internal question mark to show that something is uncertain.**

## 2.3 The Exclamation Mark

The **exclamation mark** (!), known informally as a *bang* or a *shriek*, is used at the end of a sentence or a short phrase which expresses very strong feeling. Here are some examples:

What a lovely view you have here!

That's fantastic!
Johnny, don't touch that!
Help!
Good heavens!
Aaarrgh!

Examples like these are quite normal in those kinds of writing that try to represent ordinary speech – for example, in novels. But exclamation marks are usually out of place in formal writing. Using them frequently will give your work a breathless, almost childish, quality.

An exclamation mark is also usual after an exclamation beginning with *what* or *how*:

What fools people can be!
How well Marshall bowled yesterday!

Note that such sentences are exclamations, and not statements. Compare them with statements:

People can be such fools.
Marshall bowled very well yesterday.

You can also use an exclamation mark to show that a statement is very surprising:

After months of careful work, the scientists finally opened the tomb. It was empty!

It is also permissible to use an exclamation mark to draw attention to an interruption:

On the (rare!) occasion when you use a Latin abbreviation, be sure to punctuate it properly.

Otherwise, you should generally avoid using exclamation marks in your formal writing. Don't write things like this:

★ Do not use exclamation marks in formal writing!
★ In 1848, gold was discovered in California!

Don't use an exclamation mark unless you're certain it's necessary – and **never** use two or three of them in a row:

★ This is a sensational result!!!

This sort of thing is all right in personal letters, but it is completely out of place in formal writing.

### Summary of exclamation marks

- **Don't use an exclamation mark unless it's absolutely necessary.**
- **Use an exclamation mark after an exclamation, especially after one beginning with *what* or *how*.**

## 2.4 A Final Point

Note that a full stop, a question mark or an exclamation mark is **never** preceded by a white space. Things like the following are **wrong**:

* How well has Darwin's theory stood up ?

A sentence-final punctuation mark is always written next to the last word of the sentence.

## 2.5 Fragments

A **fragment** is a word or a phrase which stands by itself but which does not make up a complete sentence. Fragments are very common in ordinary speech, in advertisements and even in newspapers. They may be used **very** sparingly in formal writing; when used, they should be followed by a full stop, a question mark or an exclamation mark, as appropriate:

Will the Star Wars project ever be resumed? Probably not.

We need to encourage investment in manufacturing. But how?

Can England beat Australia? Absolutely!

The judicious use of fragments can add vividness to your writing, and they are quite acceptable in writing which is somewhat informal. But don't overdo them: if you use too many fragments, your work will become breathless and disjointed.

# Chapter 3
# The Comma

The **comma** (,) is very frequently used and very frequently used wrongly. In fact, the rules for using commas are really rather simple, though complicated by the fact that the comma has four distinct uses. To begin with, **forget** anything you've ever been told about using a comma 'wherever you would pause', or anything of the sort; this well-meaning advice is hopelessly misleading. In this book, the four uses of the comma are called the **listing comma**, the **joining comma**, the **gapping comma** and **bracketing commas**. Each use has its own rules, but note that a comma is never preceded by a white space and always followed by a white space.

## 3.1 The Listing Comma

The **listing comma** is used as a kind of substitute for the word *and*, or sometimes for *or*. It occurs in two slightly different circumstances. First, it is used in a list when three or more words, phrases or even complete sentences are joined by the word *and* or *or*; we might call this construction an *X, Y and Z list*:

The Three Musketeers were Athos, Porthos and Aramis.
Hungarian is spoken in Hungary, in western Rumania, in northern Serbia and in parts of Austria and Slovakia.
You can fly to Bombay via Moscow, via Athens or via Cairo.
Lisa speaks French, Juliet speaks Italian and I speak Spanish.
We spent our evenings chatting in the cafés, watching the sun set over the harbour, stuffing ourselves with the local crabs and getting pleasantly sloshed on retsina.

Note that in all these examples the commas could be replaced by the word *and* or *or*, though the result would be rather clumsy:

The Three Musketeers were Athos and Porthos and Aramis.
Hungarian is spoken in Hungary and in western Rumania and in northern Serbia and in parts of Austria and Slovakia.
You can fly to Bombay via Moscow or via Athens or via Cairo.
Lisa speaks French and Juliet speaks Italian and I speak Spanish.
We spent our evenings chatting in the cafés and watching the sun set over the harbour and stuffing ourselves with the local crabs and getting pleasantly sloshed on retsina.

Observe that you can connect three or more complete sentences with listing commas, as in the Lisa/Juliet example above. Note the difference here:

> Lisa speaks French, Juliet speaks Italian and I speak Spanish.
>
> ★ Lisa speaks French, Juliet speaks Italian.

Remember, you must **not** join two complete sentences with a comma, but three or more complete sentences may be joined with listing commas plus *and* or *or*.

Note also that it is not usual in British usage to put a listing comma before the word *and* or *or* itself (though American usage regularly puts one there). So, in British usage, it is **not** usual to write

> (A) The Three Musketeers were Athos, Porthos, and Aramis.

This is reasonable, since the listing comma is a substitute for the word *and*, not an addition to it. However, you **should** put a comma in this position if doing so would make your meaning clearer:

> My favourite opera composers are Verdi, Puccini, Mozart, and Gilbert and Sullivan.

Here the comma before *and* shows clearly that Gilbert and Sullivan worked together. If you omit the comma, the result might be confusing:

> ★ My favourite opera composers are Verdi, Puccini, Mozart and Gilbert and Sullivan.

Here, the reader might possibly take Mozart and Gilbert as the pair who worked together. The extra comma removes the problem.

A listing comma is also used in a list of modifiers which all modify the same thing. This time there will usually be no *and* present at all, but again such a comma could be replaced by *and* without destroying the sense:

This is a provocative, disturbing book.
Her long, dark, glossy hair fascinated me.

Try replacing the commas by *and*:

This is a provocative and disturbing book.
Her long and dark and glossy hair fascinated me.

The sense is unchanged, though the second example, at least, is much clumsier without the commas.

Observe the difference in the next two examples:

She gave me an antique ivory box.
I prefer Australian red wines to all others.

This time there are no commas. It would be wrong to write

★ She gave me an antique, ivory box.
★ I prefer Australian, red wines to all others.

Why the difference? In these examples, a listing comma cannot be used because there is no list: the word *and* cannot possibly be inserted:

★ She gave me an antique and ivory box.

★ I prefer Australian and red wines to all others.

The reason for the difference is that the modifiers this time do not modify the same thing. In the first example, *ivory* modifies *box*, but *antique* modifies *ivory box*, not just *box*. In the second example, *Australian* modifies *red wines*, not just *wines*.

So the rules are clear:

- **Use a listing comma in a list wherever you could conceivably use the word *and* (or *or*) instead. Do not use a listing comma anywhere else.**
- **Put a listing comma before *and* or *or* only if this is necessary to make your meaning clear.**

## 3.2 The Joining Comma

The **joining comma** is only slightly different from the listing comma. It is used to join two complete sentences into a single sentence, and it **must** be followed by a suitable connecting word. The connecting words which can be used in this way are *and*, *or*, *but*, *while* and *yet*. Here are some examples:

Norway has applied to join the EC, and Sweden is expected to do the same.

You must hand in your essay by Friday, or you will receive a mark of zero.

Britain has long been isolated in Europe, but now she is beginning to find allies.

Billions of dollars have been hurled into the Star Wars projects, yet we appear to have nothing to show for this colossal expenditure.

A dropped goal counts three points in rugby union, while in rugby league it only counts one point.

Remember, as I pointed out in section 2.1, you **cannot** join two sentences with a comma unless you also use one of these connecting words. All of the following examples are therefore **wrong**:

* ★ Bangladesh is one of the world's poorest countries, its annual income is only $80 per person.
* ★ The British are notoriously bad at learning foreign languages, the Dutch are famously good at it.
* ★ The proposal to introduce rock music to Radio 3 has caused an outcry, angry letters have been pouring into the BBC.
* ★ Borg won his fifth straight Wimbledon title in 1980, the following year he lost in the final to McEnroe.

Joining two complete sentences with a comma in this way is one of the commonest of all punctuation errors, but one of the easiest to avoid if you pay a little attention to what you're writing. Either you must follow the comma with one of the connecting words listed above, or you must replace the comma with a semicolon, as explained in Chapter 4 below.

Note also that most other connecting words **cannot** be preceded by a joining comma. For example, the connecting words *however*, *therefore*, *hence*, *consequently*, *nevertheless* and *thus* cannot be used after a joining comma. Hence the following examples are also **wrong**:

★ Saturn was long thought to be the only ringed planet, however, this is now known not to be the case.
★ Two members of the expedition were too ill to continue, nevertheless the others decided to press on.
★ Liverpool are five points behind the leaders, therefore they must win both their remaining games.

Sentences like these once again require, not a comma, but a semicolon, as explained in Chapter 4.

The rule is again easy:

- **Use a joining comma to join two complete sentences with one of the words *and, or, but, yet* or *while*. Do not use a joining comma in any other way.**

## 3.3 The Gapping Comma

The gapping comma is very easy. We use a gapping comma to show that one or more words have been left out when the missing words would simply repeat the words already used earlier in the same sentence. Here is an example:

Some Norwegians wanted to base their national language on the speech of the capital city; others, on the speech of the rural countryside.

The gapping comma here shows that the words *wanted to base their national language*, which might have been repeated, have instead been omitted. This sentence is equivalent to a longer sentence like this:

> Some Norwegians wanted to base their national language on the speech of the capital city; others wanted to base it on the speech of the rural countryside.

Here is another example, which contains both listing commas and gapping commas:

> Italy is famous for her composers and musicians, France, for her chefs and philosophers, and Poland, for her mathematicians and logicians.

(Here I have inserted a listing comma before *and* for the sake of clarity.)

Gapping commas are not always strictly necessary: you can leave them out if the sentence is perfectly clear without them:

> Italy is famous for her composers and musicians, France for her chefs and philosophers, and Poland for her mathematicians and logicians.

Use your judgement: if a sentence seems clear without gapping commas, don't use them; if you have doubts, put them in.

## 3.4 Bracketing Commas

**Bracketing commas** (also called **isolating commas**) do a very different job from the other three types. These are the most frequently used type of comma, and they cause more problems than the other types put together. The rule is this: a **pair** of bracketing commas is used to mark off a weak interruption of the sentence – that is, an interruption which does not disturb the smooth flow of the sentence. Note that word 'pair': bracketing commas, in principle at least, always occur in pairs, though sometimes one of them is not written, as explained below. Look carefully at these examples of bracketing commas:

These findings, we would suggest, cast doubt upon his hypothesis.

Schliemann, of course, did his digging before modern archaeology was invented.

Pratchett has, it would seem, abandoned Rincewind the wizard to the ravages of the Discworld.

Darwin's *Origin of Species*, published in 1859, revolutionized biological thinking.

The Pakistanis, like the Australians before them, have exposed the shortcomings of the England batting order.

Rupert Brooke, who was killed in the war at the age of twenty-eight, was one of our finest poets.

We have been forced to conclude, after careful study of

the data, that the proposed correlations, in spite of their obvious appeal, do not stand up.

In each case a weak interruption has been set off by a pair of bracketing commas. (The last example has two weak interruptions.) Now notice something important: in every one of these examples, the weak interruption set off by bracketing commas could, in principle, be removed from the sentence, and the result would still be a complete sentence that made good sense. Try this with some of the examples:

These findings cast doubt upon his hypothesis.
Pratchett has abandoned Rincewind the wizard to the ravages of the Discworld.
The Pakistanis have exposed the shortcomings of the England batting order.
We have been forced to conclude that the proposed correlations do not stand up.

This is **always** the case with bracketing commas, and it gives you a simple way of checking your punctuation. If you have set off some words with a pair of bracketing commas, and you find you can't remove those words without destroying the sentence, you have done something wrong. Here is an example of wrong use, taken from Carey (1958):

★ Yet, outside that door, lay a whole new world.

If you try to remove the words *outside that door*, the result is ★ *Yet lay a whole new world*, which is not a sentence. The problem here is that *outside that door* is not an interruption at all: it's an essential part of the sentence. So, the bracketing commas shouldn't be there. Just get rid of them:

Yet outside that door lay a whole new world.

Here is another example:

★ She groped for her cigarettes, and finding them, hastily lit one.

This time, if you try to remove the words *and finding them*, the result is ★ *She groped for her cigarettes hastily lit one*, which is again not a sentence. The problem is that the interruption in this sentence is only the sequence *finding them*; the word *and* is not part of the interruption, but an essential part of the sentence. So move the first comma:

She groped for her cigarettes and, finding them, hastily lit one.

Now check that the interruption has been correctly marked off:

She groped for her cigarettes and hastily lit one.

This is a good sentence, so you have now got the bracketing commas in the right places.

Since bracketing commas really do confuse many people, let's look at some further examples:

★ Stanley was a determined, even ruthless figure.

What's wrong here? Well, that comma can't possibly be a listing comma, a joining comma or a gapping comma; therefore it must be intended as a bracketing comma. But where is the interruption it is trying to bracket? It can't be the three words at the end: ★ *Stanley was a determined* is so much gibberish. In fact, the weak interruption here is the phrase *even ruthless*, and the bracketing commas should show this:

> Stanley was a determined, even ruthless, figure.

This is perfect, since now the bracketed interruption can be safely removed:

> Stanley was a determined figure.

Sometimes this very common type of mistake will not disturb your reader too much, but on occasion it can be utterly bewildering:

> ★ The Third Partition of Poland was the last, and undoubtedly the most humiliating act in the sorry decline of the once-powerful kingdom.

Here the sequence before the comma, *The Third Partition of Poland was the last*, seems to make sense by itself, but unfortunately not the sense that the writer intends. With only one comma, the reader will surely assume the writer means 'The Third Partition of Poland was the last [partition of Poland]', will go on to assume that the word *undoubtedly* begins another statement, and will be left floundering when she abruptly comes to a full stop instead of a verb. The essential second bracketing comma removes the problem:

> The Third Partition of Poland was the last, and undoubtedly the most humiliating, act in the sorry decline of the once-powerful kingdom.

Here is another example of a type which often causes trouble:

> The people of Cornwall, who depend upon fishing for their livelihood, are up in arms over the new EC quotas.

As always, we could in principle remove the bracketed interruption to produce a sensible sentence:

> The people of Cornwall are up in arms over the new EC quotas.

But note carefully: this sentence is talking about *all* the people of Cornwall, and not just some of them, and hence so was the original sentence. The weak interruption in the original sentence is merely adding some extra information about the people of Cornwall. Now consider this different example:

> The people of Cornwall who depend upon fishing for their livelihood are up in arms over the new EC quotas.

This time there are no bracketing commas because there is no interruption: now we are not talking about *all* the people of Cornwall, but only about *some* of them: specifically, about the ones who depend upon fishing for their livelihood. Here the phrase *who depend upon fishing for their livelihood* is not an interruption but an essential part of the sentence, and hence it receives no bracketing commas.

The difference illustrated by the last two examples is the difference between what are called *restrictive* (or *defining*) *relative clauses* and *non-restrictive* (or *non-defining*) *relative clauses*. A restrictive clause is required to identify what is being talked about, and it never receives bracketing commas. A non-restrictive clause is not required for identification, but only adds further information, and it always receives bracketing commas. Here are some further examples of the difference. First, some non-restrictive clauses:

> Margaret Thatcher, who hated trains, refused to consider privatizing the railways.
>
> The rings of Saturn, which can be easily seen with a small telescope, are composed of billions of tiny particles of rock.
>
> Bertrand Russell struck up a surprising friendship with D. H. Lawrence, whose strange ideas seemed to fascinate him.
>
> Noam Chomsky is the originator of the innateness hypothesis, according to which we are born already knowing what human languages are like.

Observe that, in each case, the non-restrictive clause bracketed by commas could be removed without destroying the sense. Each of these clauses merely adds more information about Margaret Thatcher, the rings of Saturn, D.H. Lawrence and the innateness hypothesis, and this extra information is not required to let the reader know who or what is being talked about.

The next few examples illustrate restrictive clauses:

The pictures which are being sent back by the Hubble Space Telescope may revolutionize our understanding of the universe.

The Russian scholar Yuri Knorosov has provided an interpretation of the Mayan inscriptions which is now generally accepted.

Because of problems with the test, all the people who were told they were HIV-negative are being recalled.

Anybody who still believes that Uri Geller has strange powers should read James Randi's book.

Here, without the restrictive clauses, the reader would not know which pictures, which interpretation or which people are being talked about, and that *anybody* in the last example would make no sense at all, and so there are no bracketing commas.

Observe that a proper name always uniquely identifies the person or thing being talked about, and hence a proper name never receives a restrictive clause (with no commas) in normal circumstances:

* I discussed this with Johanna Nichols who is a specialist in Caucasian languages.

Here the clause following the proper name *Johanna Nichols* must be set off by a bracketing comma. The only exception is the special case in which a proper name is preceded by *the* to indicate that we are talking about some particular stage in time:

> The Napoleon who retreated from Moscow was a sadder and wiser man than the Napoleon who had previously known only unbroken triumph.

Finally, note that the word *that* can *only* introduce a restrictive clause, and so a relative clause with *that* can never take bracketing commas:

> ★ The European powers, that were busily carving up Africa, paid no attention to the boundaries between rival ethnic groups.

If this relative clause is intended to identify the European powers under discussion, then the commas should be removed; if, however, the sentence is meant to be about the European powers generally, the commas are correct but the *that* must be changed to *which*.

Sometimes a weak interruption comes at the beginning or at the end of its sentence. In such a case, one of the two bracketing commas would logically fall at the beginning or the end of the sentence – but we **never** write a comma at the beginning or at the end of a sentence. As a result, only one of the two bracketing commas is written in this case:

> All in all, I think we can say that we've done well.

I think we can say that we've done well, all in all.

When the weak interruption *all in all* comes at the beginning of the sentence, it has only a following comma; when it comes at the end, it has only a preceding comma. Compare what happens when the interruption comes in the middle:

I think we can say that, all in all, we've done well.

Now the interruption has two bracketing commas. Regardless of where the interruption is placed, it could be removed to give the perfectly good sentence *I think we can say that we've done well.*

Here are some further examples of weak interruptions that come at the beginning or at the end.

At the beginning:

Having worked for years in Italy, Susan speaks excellent Italian.

Unlike most nations, Britain has no written constitution.

Although Mercury is closer to the sun, Venus has the higher surface temperature.

After capturing the Aztec capital, Cortés turned his attention to the Pacific.

And at the end:

The use of dictionaries is not allowed, which strikes me as preposterous.

The pronunciation of English is changing rapidly, we are told.

The Rose Parade is held in Pasadena, a suburb of Los Angeles.

Once again, the words set off by a single bracketing comma in these examples could be removed to leave a good sentence. Check this for yourself.

There are a number of common words which typically introduce weak interruptions containing complete sentences. Among the commonest of these are *although*, *though*, *even though*, *because*, *since*, *after*, *before*, *if*, *when* and *whenever*. Weak interruptions introduced by these words are usually rather long, and therefore they most often come at the beginning or at the end of a sentence. Some examples:

Although Australian wines are a fairly new phenomenon, they have already established a formidable reputation.

After the Roman legions withdrew from Britain, the British found themselves defenceless against Irish and Viking raids.

If there are any further cuts in funding, our library will be severely affected.

Hitler could never have invaded Britain successfully, because their excellent rail system would have allowed the British to mass defenders quickly at any beachhead.

Columbus is usually credited with discovering America, even though the Vikings had preceded him by several centuries.

There is just one case in which you might find yourself apparently following all the rules but still using bracketing commas wrongly. Consider the following example, and try to decide if the comma is properly used:

> Note that in each of these examples, the material set off by commas could be removed without destroying the sentence.

The comma in this example is clearly not a listing comma, a joining comma or a gapping comma. Is it a bracketing comma? Try removing the words before the comma:

> The material set off by commas could be removed without destroying the sentence.

This appears to be a good sentence, and so you might think that the original example was correctly punctuated. But it is not. The problem is that the original sentence was an instruction to notice something, and the words *Note that* are therefore an essential part of the sentence, not part of the interruption. The interruption, quite clearly, consists only of the words *in each of these examples*. When we tried to remove the first seven words, we got something that was a sentence, purely by accident, but a sentence in which the original meaning had been partly destroyed. The original attempt at punctuating was therefore wrong, and it must be corrected by adding the second bracketing comma around the interruption:

> Note that, in each of these examples, the material set off by commas could be removed without destroying the sentence.

Now the interruption marked off by the bracketing commas can be safely removed without wrecking the sense of the sentence:

> Note that the material set off by commas could be removed without destroying the sentence.

Therefore, when you are checking your bracketing commas, make sure that the words enclosed in commas really do make up an interruption, and do not include an essential part of the sentence.

In many cases a weak interruption does not absolutely require bracketing commas. Thus either of the following is fine:

> Shortly before the war, he was living in Paris.
> Shortly before the war he was living in Paris.

With or without the bracketing comma, this sentence is perfectly clear. Sometimes, however, the bracketing comma is absolutely essential to avoid misleading the reader:

> ★ Just before unloading the trucks were fired upon.

Here the reader naturally takes *Just before unloading the trucks* as a single phrase, and is left floundering as a result. A bracketing comma removes the difficulty:

Just before unloading, the trucks were fired upon.

The best way to avoid problems of this sort is, of course, to read what you've written. Remember, it is **your** job to make your meaning clear to the reader. The reader should not have to struggle to make sense of what you've written.

Here are the rules for using bracketing commas:

- **Use a PAIR of bracketing commas to set off a weak interruption which could be removed from the sentence without destroying it.**
- **If the interruption comes at the beginning or the end of the sentence, use only one bracketing comma.**
- **Make sure the words set off are really an interruption.**

## 3.5 Summary of Commas

There are four types of comma: the **listing comma**, the **joining comma**, the **gapping comma** and **bracketing commas**.

A listing comma can always be replaced by the word *and* or *or*:

Vanessa seems to live on eggs, pasta and aubergines.
Vanessa seems to live on eggs and pasta and aubergines.

Choose an article from the *Guardian*, the *Independent* or *The Times*.
Choose an article from the *Guardian* or the *Independent* or *The Times*.

Stanley was an energetic, determined and even ruthless figure.

Stanley was an energetic and determined and even ruthless figure.

A joining comma must be followed by one of the connecting words *and*, *or*, *but*, *yet* or *while*:

The report was due last week, but it hasn't appeared yet.

The motorways in France and Spain are toll roads, while those in Britain are free.

A gapping comma indicates that you have decided not to repeat some words which have already occurred in the sentence:

Jupiter is the largest planet and Pluto, the smallest.

Bracketing commas always come in pairs, unless one of them would come at the beginning or the end of the sentence, and they always set off a weak interruption which could in principle be removed from the sentence:

My father, who hated cricket, always refused to watch me play.

We have a slight problem, to put it mildly.

If you're not sure about your commas, you can check them by using these rules. Ask yourself these questions:

1. Can the comma be replaced by *and* or *or*?
2. Is it followed by one of the connecting words *and*, *or*, *but*, *yet* or *while*?

3. Does it represent the absence of repetition?
4. Does it form one of a pair of commas setting off an interruption which could be removed from the sentence?

If the answer to all these questions is 'no', you have done something wrong. Try these questions on the following example:

> The publication of *The Hobbit* in 1937, marked the beginning of Tolkien's career as a fantasy writer.

Can that comma be replaced by *and* or *or*? No – the result would make no sense. Is it followed by a suitable connecting word? No – obviously not. Have some repeated words been left out? No – certainly not. Is it one of a pair? Not obviously, but maybe the interruption comes at the beginning or the end. Can the words before the comma be safely removed? No – what's left is not a sentence. Can the words after the comma be removed? No – the result would still not be a sentence.

We get the answer 'no' in every case, and therefore that comma shouldn't be there. Get rid of it:

> The publication of *The Hobbit* in 1937 marked the beginning of Tolkien's career as a fantasy writer.

Try another example:

> Josie originally wanted to be a teacher, but after finishing university, she decided to become a lawyer instead.

Let's check the first comma. Can it be replaced by *and* or *or*? Certainly not. Is it followed by a suitable connecting word? Yes, it's followed by *but*. So the first comma looks okay at the moment. Now the second comma. Can it be replaced? No. Is it followed by a connecting word? No. Does it stand for a repetition? No. Is it one of a pair? Possibly – but can we remove the words set off by the pair of commas? Let's try:

> Josie originally wanted to be a teacher she decided to become a lawyer instead.

This is clearly wrong. Is there an interruption at the end of the sentence?

> Josie originally wanted to be a teacher, but after finishing university.

This is even worse. (It does make sense of a sort, but the wrong sense.) There's something wrong with that second comma. Try getting rid of it:

> Josie originally wanted to be a teacher, but after finishing university she decided to become a lawyer instead.

This makes perfect sense, and it obeys all the rules. The comma after *teacher* is a joining comma, but that second comma was a mistake.

In fact, there's another way of fixing this sentence. The words *after finishing university* actually make up a weak interruption. So you can, if you prefer, put a pair of bracketing commas around these words:

> Josie originally wanted to be a teacher, but, after finishing university, she decided to become a lawyer instead.

Check that this new version is also correct by removing the words set off by the pair of bracketing commas:

> Josie originally wanted to be a teacher, but she decided to become a lawyer instead.

This is a good sentence, so the version with three commas is also correct. Remember, you don't **have** to set off a weak interruption with bracketing commas, as long as the meaning is clear without them, but, if you do use bracketing commas, make sure you use both of them.

In sum, then:

- **Use a listing comma in a list where *and* or *or* would be possible instead.**
- **Use a joining comma before *and, or, but, yet* or *while* followed by a complete sentence.**
- **Use a gapping comma to show that words have been omitted instead of repeated.**
- **Use a pair of bracketing commas to set off a weak interruption.**

Finally, the use of commas in writing numbers is explained in section 9.8.

Chapter 4

# The Colon and the Semicolon

## 4.1 The Colon

The **colon** (:) seems to bewilder many people, though it's really rather easy to use correctly, since it has only one major use. But first please note the following: the colon is **never** preceded by a white space; it is **always** followed by a single white space in normal use, and it is **never**, **never**, **never** followed by a hyphen or a dash – in spite of what you might have been taught in school. One of the commonest of all punctuation mistakes is following a colon with a completely pointless hyphen.

The colon is used to indicate that what follows it is an explanation or elaboration of what precedes it. That is, having introduced some topic in more general terms, you can use a colon and go on to explain that same topic in more specific terms. Schematically:

More general: more specific.

A colon is nearly always preceded by a complete sentence; what follows the colon may or may not be a complete sentence, and it may be a mere list or even a single word. A colon is not normally followed by a capital letter in British usage, though American usage often prefers to use a capital. Here are some examples:

> Africa is facing a terrifying problem: perpetual drought.
> [Explains what the problem is.]
>
> The situation is clear: if you have unprotected sex with a stranger, you risk AIDS.
> [Explains what the clear situation is.]
>
> She was sure of one thing: she was not going to be a housewife.
> [Identifies the one thing she was sure of.]
>
> Mae West had one golden rule for handling men: 'Tell the pretty ones they're smart and tell the smart ones they're pretty.'
> [Explicates the golden rule.]
>
> Several friends have provided me with inspiration: Tim, Ian and, above all, Larry.
> [Identifies the friends in question.]
>
> We found the place easily: your directions were perfect.
> [Explains why we found it easily.]
>
> I propose the creation of a new post: School Executive Officer.
> [Identifies the post in question.]

Very occasionally, the colon construction is turned round, with the specifics coming first and the general summary afterwards:

> Saussure, Sapir, Bloomfield, Chomsky: all these have revolutionized linguistics in one way or another.

Like all inverted constructions, this one should be used sparingly.

While you're studying these examples, notice again that the colon is never preceded by a white space and never followed by anything except a single white space.

You should **not** use a colon, or any other mark, at the end of a heading which introduces a new section of a document: look at the chapter headings and section headings in this book. It is, however, usual to use a colon after a word, phrase or sentence in the middle of a text which introduces some following material which is set off in the middle of the page. There are three consecutive examples of this just above, in the second, third and fourth paragraphs of this section.

The colon has a few minor uses. First, when you cite the name of a book which has both a title and a subtitle, you should separate the two with a colon:

> I recommend Chinnery's book *Oak Furniture: The British Tradition*.

You should do this even though no colon may appear on the cover or the title page of the book itself.

Second, the colon is used in citing passages from the Bible:

> The story of Menahem is found in II Kings 15:14–22.

Third, the colon may be used in writing ratios:

Among students of French, women outnumber men by more than 4:1.

In formal writing, however, it is usually preferable to write out ratios in words:

Among students of French, women outnumber men by more than four to one.

Fourth, in American usage, a colon is used to separate the hours from the minutes in giving a time of day: *2:10*, *11:30* (A). British English uses a full stop for this purpose: *2.10*, *11.30*.

Observe that, exceptionally, the colon is **not** followed by a white space in these last three situations.

Finally, see Chapter 10 for the use of the colon in formal letters and in citing references to published work.

## 4.2 The Semicolon

The **semicolon** (;) has only one major use. It is used to join two **complete** sentences into a single written sentence when all of the following conditions are met:

1. The two sentences are felt to be too closely related to be separated by a full stop;
2. There is no connecting word which would require a comma, such as *and* or *but*;
3. The special conditions requiring a colon are absent.

Here is a famous example:

> It was the best of times; it was the worst of times.

A semicolon can always, in principle, be replaced either by a full stop (yielding two separate sentences) or by the word *and* (possibly preceded by a joining comma). Thus Dickens might have written:

> It was the best of times. It was the worst of times. **or**
> It was the best of times, and it was the worst of times.

The use of the semicolon suggests that the writer sees the two smaller sentences as being more closely related than the average two consecutive sentences; preferring the semicolon to *and* often gives a more vivid sense of the relation between the two. But observe carefully: the semicolon **must** be both preceded by a complete sentence and followed by a complete sentence. Do **not** use the semicolon otherwise:

> ★ I don't like him; not at all.
> ★ In 1991 the music world was shaken by a tragic event; the death of Freddy Mercury.
> ★ We've had streams of books on chaos theory; no fewer than twelve since 1988.
> ★ After a long and bitter struggle; Derrida was awarded an honorary degree by Cambridge University.

These are all **wrong**, since the semicolon does not separate complete sentences. (The first and last of these should have only a bracketing comma, while the second and third meet the requirements for a colon and should have one.) Here are some further examples of correct use:

> Tolkien published *The Hobbit* in 1937; the first volume of *The Lord of the Rings* followed in 1954.
>
> The Cabernet Sauvignon grape predominates in the Bordeaux region; Pinot Noir holds sway in Burgundy; Syrah is largely confined to the Rhône valley.
>
> Women's conversation is cooperative; men's is competitive.

If a suitable connecting word is used, then a joining comma is required, rather than a semicolon:

> Women's conversation is cooperative, while men's is competitive.

A semicolon would be impossible in the last example, since the sequence after the comma is not a complete sentence.

Note, however, that certain connecting words **do** require a preceding semicolon. Chief among these are *however, therefore, hence, thus, consequently, nevertheless* and *meanwhile*:

> Saturn was long thought to be the only ringed planet; however, this is now known not to be the case.
>
> The two warring sides have refused to withdraw from the airport; consequently aid flights have had to be suspended.

Observe that in these examples the sequence after the semicolon **does** constitute a complete sentence. And note particularly that the word *however* must be separated by a semicolon (or a full stop) from a preceding complete sentence; this is a very common mistake.

There is one special circumstance in which a semicolon may be used to separate sequences which are not complete sentences. This occurs when a sentence has become so long and so full of commas that the reader can hardly be expected to follow it without some special marking. In this case, we sometimes find semicolons used instead of commas to mark the most important breaks in the sentence: such semicolons are effectively being used to mark places where the reader can pause to catch her breath. Consider the following example:

> In Somalia, where the civil war still rages, western aid workers, in spite of frantic efforts, are unable to operate, and the people, starving, terrified and desperate, are flooding into neighbouring Ethiopia.

This sentence is perfectly punctuated, but the number of commas is somewhat alarming. In such a case, the comma marking the major break in the sentence may be replaced by a semicolon:

> In Somalia, where the civil war still rages, western aid workers, in spite of frantic efforts, are unable to operate; and the people, starving, terrified and desperate, are flooding into neighbouring Ethiopia.

Such use of the semicolon as a kind of 'super-comma' is not very appealing, and you should do your best to avoid it. If you find one of your sentences becoming dangerously long and full of commas, it is usually better to start over and rewrite it, perhaps as two separate sentences:

> In Somalia, where the civil war still rages, western aid workers, in spite of frantic efforts, are unable to operate. Meanwhile the people, starving, terrified and desperate, are flooding into neighbouring Ethiopia.

In any case, don't get into the habit of using a semicolon (or anything else) merely to mark a breathing space. Your reader will be perfectly capable of doing his own breathing, providing your sentence is well punctuated; punctuation is an aid to understanding, not to respiration.

## 4.3 The Colon and the Semicolon Compared

Since the use of the colon and the semicolon, although simple in principle, presents so many difficulties to uncertain punctuators, it will be helpful to contrast them here. Consider first the following two sentences:

> Lisa is upset. Gus is having a nervous breakdown.

The use of two separate sentences suggests that there is no particular connection between these two facts: they just happen to be true at the same time. No particular inference can be drawn, except perhaps that things are generally bad. Now see what happens when a semicolon is used:

Lisa is upset; Gus is having a nervous breakdown.

The semicolon now suggests that the two statements are related in some way. The likeliest inference is that the cause of Lisa's annoyance and the cause of Gus's nervous breakdown are the same. Perhaps, for example, both are being disturbed by building noise next door. (Remember, a semicolon connects two sentences which are related.) Now try it with a colon:

Lisa is upset: Gus is having a nervous breakdown.

This time the colon shows explicitly that Gus's nervous breakdown is the reason for Lisa's distress: Lisa is upset **because** Gus is having a nervous breakdown. (Remember, a colon introduces an explanation or elaboration of what has come before.)

Consider another example:

I have the answer. Mike's solution doesn't work.

Here we have two independent statements: my answer and Mike's solution may possibly have been directed at the same problem, but nothing implies this, and equally they may have been directed at two entirely distinct problems. Now, with a semicolon:

I have the answer; Mike's solution doesn't work.

The semicolon shows that the two statements are related, and strongly implies that Mike and I were working on the same problem. Finally, with a colon:

I have the answer: Mike's solution doesn't work.

This time the use of the colon indicates that the failure of Mike's solution is exactly the answer which I have obtained: that is, what I have discovered is that Mike's solution doesn't work.

If you understand these examples, you should be well on your way to using colons and semicolons correctly.

### Summary of colons and semicolons

- **Use a colon to separate a general statement from following specifics.**
- **Use a semicolon to connect two complete sentences not joined by *and, or, but, yet* or *while.***

## Chapter 5
# The Apostrophe

The **apostrophe** (') is the most troublesome punctuation mark in English, and perhaps also the least useful. No other punctuation mark causes so much bewilderment, or is so often misused. On the one hand, shops offer ★ *pizza's*, ★ *video's*, ★ *greeting's cards* and ★ *ladie's clothing*; on the other, they offer ★ *childrens shoes* and ★ *artists supplies*. The confusion about apostrophes is so great, in comparison with the small amount of useful work they perform, that many distinguished writers and linguists have argued that the best way of eliminating the confusion would be to get rid of this troublesome squiggle altogether and never use it at all.

They are probably right, but unfortunately the apostrophe has not been abolished yet, and it is a blunt fact that the incorrect use of apostrophes will make your writing look illiterate more quickly than almost any other kind of mistake. I'm afraid, therefore, that, if you find apostrophes difficult, you will just have to grit your teeth and get down to work.

## 5.1 Contractions

The apostrophe is used in writing **contractions** – that is, shortened forms of words from which one or more letters have been omitted. In standard English, this generally happens only with a small number of conventional items, mostly involving verbs. Here are some of the commonest examples, with their uncontracted equivalents:

| | |
|---|---|
| it's | it is *or* it has |
| we'll | we will *or* we shall |
| they've | they have |
| can't | can not |
| he'd | he would *or* he had |
| aren't | are not |
| she'd've | she would have |
| won't | will not |

Note in each case that the apostrophe appears precisely in the position of the omitted letters: we write *can't*, not ★ *ca'nt*, and *aren't*, not ★ *are'nt*. Note also that the irregular contraction *won't* takes its apostrophe between the *n* and the *t*, just like all other contractions involving *not*. And note also that *she'd've* has two apostrophes, because material has been omitted from two positions.

It is not wrong to use such contractions in formal writing, but you should use them sparingly, since they tend to make your writing appear less than fully formal. Since I'm trying to make this book seem chatty rather than intimidating, I've been using a few contractions here and there, though not as many as I might have used. But I advise you **not** to use the more colloquial contractions like *she'd've* in your formal writing: these things, while perfectly normal in speech, are a little too informal for careful writing.

Such contractions represent the most useful job the apostrophe does for us, since, without it, we would have no way of expressing in writing the difference between *she'll* and *shell*, *he'll* and *hell*, *can't* and *cant*, *I'll* and *ill*, *we're* and *were*, *she'd* and *shed*, *we'll* and *well*, and perhaps a few others.

A few words which were contractions long ago are still conventionally written with apostrophes, even though the longer forms have more or less dropped out of use. There are so few of these that you can easily learn them all. Here are the commonest ones, with their original longer forms:

| | |
|---|---|
| o'clock | of the clock |
| Hallowe'en | Halloweven |
| fo'c's'le | forecastle |
| cat-o'-nine-tails | cat-of-nine-tails |
| ne'er-do-well | never-do-well |
| will-o'-the-wisp | will-of-the-wisp |

Some generations ago there were rather more contractions in regular use in English; these other contractions are now archaic, and you wouldn't normally use any of them except in direct quotations from older written work. Here are a few of them, with their longer forms:

| | |
|---|---|
| 'tis | it is |
| 'twas | it was |
| o'er | over |
| e'en | even |

There are other contractions which are often heard in speech. Here are a few:

| | |
|---|---|
| 'Fraid so. | 'Nother drink? |
| I s'pose so. | 'S not funny. |

It is, of course, never appropriate to use such colloquial forms in formal writing, except when you are explicitly writing about colloquial English. If you do have occasion to cite or use these things, you should use apostrophes in the normal way to mark the elided material.

In contemporary usage, there are a few unusual phrases in which the word *and* is written as *'n'*, with two apostrophes (**not** quotation marks); the commonest of these is *rock 'n' roll*, which is always so written, even in formal writing. One or two more of these are perhaps acceptable in formal writing, such as *pick 'n' mix* and possibly *surf 'n' turf* (this last is a cute label for a particular type of food). But don't overdo it: write *fish and chips*, even though you may see *fish 'n' chips* on takeaway shop signs or even on restaurant menus.

Contractions must be carefully distinguished from **clipped forms**. A clipped form is a full word which happens to be derived by chopping a piece off a longer word, usually one with the same meaning. Clipped forms are very common in English; here are a few, with their related longer forms:

| | |
|---|---|
| gym | gymnasium |
| ad | advertisement |
| pro | professional |
| deli | delicatessen |
| hippo | hippopotamus |
| bra | brassière |
| tec | detective |
| flu | influenza |
| phone | telephone |
| copter | helicopter |
| cello | violoncello |
| gator | alligator |
| quake | earthquake |

Such clipped forms are **not** regarded as contractions, and they should not be written with apostrophes. Writing things like *hippo'*, *bra'*, *'cello* and *'phone* will, not to mince words, make you look like an affected old fuddy-duddy who doesn't quite approve of anything that's happened since 1912. Of course, some of these clipped forms are still rather colloquial, and in formal writing you would normally prefer to write *detective* and *alligator*, rather than *tec* and *gator*. Others, however, are perfectly normal in formal writing: even the most dignified music critic would call Ofra Harnoy's instrument a *cello*; he would no more use *violoncello* than he would apply the word *omnibus* to a London double-decker.

**Important note**: Contractions must also be carefully distinguished from *abbreviations*. Abbreviations are things like *Mr* for *Mister*, *lb.* for *pound(s)*, BC for *before Christ* and *e.g.* for *for example*. Their use is explained in section 7.2.

Finally, there are a few circumstances in which apostrophes are used to represent the omission of some material in cases which are not exactly contractions. First, certain surnames of non-English origin are written with apostrophes: *O'Leary* (Irish), *d'Abbadie* (French), *D'Angelo* (Italian), *M'Tavish* (Scots Gaelic). These are not really contractions because there is no alternative way of writing them.

Second, apostrophes are sometimes used in representing words in non-standard forms of English: thus the Scots poet Robert Burns writes *gi'* for *give* and *a'* for *all*. You are hardly likely to need this device except when you are quoting from such work.

Third, a year is occasionally written in an abbreviated form with an apostrophe: *Pío Baroja was a distinctive member of the generation of '98*. This is only normal in certain set expressions; in my example, the phrase *generation of '98* is an accepted label for a certain group of Spanish writers, and it would not be normal to write ★ *generation of 1898*. Except for such conventional phrases, however, you should always write out years in full when you are writing formally: do **not** write something like ★ *the '39–'45 war*, but write instead *the 1939–45 war*.

## 5.2 Unusual Plurals

As a general rule, we **never** use an apostrophe in writing plural forms. (A plural form is one that denotes more than one of something.) Hence the things that those shops are selling are *pizzas*, *videos*, *fine wines*, *cream teas* and *mountain bikes*. It is absolutely **wrong** to write ★ *pizza's*, ★ *video's*, ★ *fine wine's*, ★ *cream tea's* and ★ *mountain bike's* if you merely want to talk about more than one pizza or video or whatever. The same goes even when you want to pluralize a proper name:

She's trying to keep up with the Joneses.
There are four Steves and three Julies in my class.
Several of the Eleanor Crosses are still standing today.

Do **not** write things like ★ *Jones's*, ★ *Steve's*, ★ *Julie's* or ★ *Eleanor Cross's* if you are merely talking about more than one person or thing with that name.

In British usage, we do not use an apostrophe in pluralizing dates:

This research was carried out in the 1970s.

American usage, however, does put an apostrophe here:

(A) This research was carried out in the 1970's.

You should **not** adopt this practice unless you are specifically writing for an American audience.

In writing the plurals of numbers, usage varies. Both of the following may be encountered:

If you're sending mail to the Continent, it's advisable to use continental *1*s and *7*s in the address.
If you're sending mail to the Continent, it's advisable to use continental *1*'s and *7*'s in the address.

Here, the first form is admittedly a little hard on the eye, and the apostrophes may make your sentence clearer. In most cases, though, you can avoid the problem entirely simply by writing out the numerals:

If you're sending mail to the Continent, it's advisable to use continental ones and sevens in the address.

An apostrophe is indispensable, however, in the rare case in which you need to pluralize a letter of the alphabet or some other unusual form which would become unrecognizable with a plural ending stuck on it:

Mind your *p*'s and *q*'s.
How many *s*'s are there in *Mississippi*?
It is very bad style to spatter *e.g.*'s and *i.e.*'s through your writing.

Without the apostrophes, these would be unreadable. So, when you have to pluralize an orthographically unusual form, use an apostrophe if it seems to be essential for clarity, but **don't** use one if the written form is perfectly clear without it. (Note that I have italicized these odd forms; this is a very good practice if you can produce italics. See Chapter 9.)

## 5.3 Possessives

An apostrophe is used in a possessive form, like *Esther's family* or *Janet's cigarettes*, and this is the use of the apostrophe which causes most of the trouble. The basic rule is simple enough: a possessive form is spelled with *'s* at the end. Hence:

| | |
|---|---|
| Lisa's essay | England's navy |
| my brother's girlfriend | Wittgenstein's last book |
| children's shoes | women's clothing |
| the aircraft's black box | somebody's umbrella |
| a week's work | my money's worth |

This rule applies in most cases even with a name ending in *s*:

| | |
|---|---|
| Thomas's job | the bus's arrival |
| James's fiancée | Steve Davis's victory |

There are three types of exception. First, a plural noun which already ends in *s* takes only a following apostrophe:

| | |
|---|---|
| the girls' excitement | my parents' wedding |
| both players' injuries | the Klingons' attack |
| the ladies' room | two weeks' work |

This is reasonable. We don't pronounce these words with two esses, and so we don't write two esses: nobody says ★ *the girls's excitement*. But note that plurals that don't end in *s* take the ordinary form: see the cases of *children* and *women* above.

Second, a name ending in *s* takes only an apostrophe if the possessive form is not pronounced with an extra *s*. Hence:

| | |
|---|---|
| Socrates' philosophy | Saint Saens' music |
| Ulysses' companions | Aristophanes' plays |

Same reason: we don't say ★ *Ulysses's companions*, and so we don't write the extra *s*.

The final class of exceptions is pronouns. Note the following:

| | |
|---|---|
| He lost his book | Which seats are ours? |
| The bull lowered its head. | Whose are these spectacles? |

**Note** in particular the spelling of possessive *its*. This word never takes an apostrophe:

★ The bull lowered it's head

This is **wrong, wrong, wrong** – but it is one of the commonest of all punctuation errors. I have even met teachers of English who get this wrong. The conventional spelling *its* is no doubt totally illogical, but it's none the less conventional, and spelling the possessive as *it's* will cause many readers to turn up their noses at you. The mistake is very conspicuous, but fortunately it's also easy to fix – there's only one word – so learn the standard spelling. (There is an English word spelled *it's*, of course, and indeed I've just used it in the preceding sentence, but this is not a possessive: it's the contracted form of *it is* or of *it has*. And there is **no** English word spelled ★ *its'* – this is another common error for *its*.)

The same goes for possessive *whose*: this cannot be spelled as ★ *who's*, though again there is a word *who's*, a contraction of *who is* or of *who has*, as in *Who's your friend?* or *Who's got a corkscrew?*

Note, however, that the indefinite pronoun *one* forms an ordinary possessive *one's*, as in *One must choose one's words carefully*.

There is a further point about writing possessives: when you add an apostrophe-*s* or an apostrophe alone to form a possessive, the thing that comes before the apostrophe *must* be a real English word, and it must also be the *right* English word. Thus, for example, something like ★ *ladie's shoes* is impossible, because there is no such word as ★ *ladie*. Moreover, a department in a shoeshop could not be called ★ *lady's shoes*, because what the shop is selling is *shoes for ladies*, and not ★ *shoes for lady*, which is meaningless. The correct form is *ladies' shoes*. (Compare *that lady's shoes*, which is fine.)

Finally, while we're discussing clothing departments, observe that there is at least one irritating exception: though we write *men's clothing*, as usual, we write *menswear* as a single word, with no apostrophe. By historical accident, this has come to be regarded as a single word in English. But just this one: we do **not** write ★ *womenswear* or ★ *childrenswear*. Sorry.

Chapter 6

# The Hyphen and the Dash

## 6.1 The Hyphen

The **hyphen** (-) is the small bar found on every keyboard. It has several related uses; in every case, it is used to show that what it is attached to does not make up a complete word by itself. The hyphen must **never** be used with white spaces at both ends, though in some uses it may have a white space at one end.

Most obviously, a hyphen is used to indicate that a long word has been broken off at the end of a line:

> We were dismayed at having to listen to such inconse-
> quential remarks.

You should avoid such word splitting whenever possible. If it is unavoidable, try to split the word into two roughly equal parts, and make sure you split it at an obvious boundary. Do not write things like:

| ★ incons-<br>equential | ★ inconseque-<br>ntial | ★ inconsequent-<br>ial |
|---|---|---|

The first two of these are not broken at syllable boundaries, while the third is broken into two very unequal pieces. If you are in doubt as to where a word can be split, consult a dictionary. Many good dictionaries mark syllable boundaries to show you where words can be hyphenated. Some publishers even bring out hyphenation dictionaries containing no other information. Best of all, many word processors will perform hyphenation automatically, and you won't have to worry about it. In any case, note that a hyphen in such a case must be written at the end of its line, and not at the beginning of the following line.

The hyphen is also used in writing compound words which, without the hyphen, would be ambiguous, hard to read or overly long. Here, more than anywhere else in the whole field of punctuation, there is room for individual taste and judgement; nevertheless, certain principles may be identified. These are:

1. Above all, strive for clarity;
2. Don't use a hyphen unless it's necessary;
3. Where possible, follow established usage.

On this last point, consult a good dictionary; Collins or Longman is recommended, since the conservative Chambers and Oxford dictionaries frequently show hyphens which are no longer in normal use.

Should you write *land owners*, *land-owners* or *landowners*? All are possible, and you should follow your judgement, and

British usage generally favours rather more hyphens here than does American usage; nevertheless, I prefer the third, since it seems unambiguous and easy to read, since it avoids the use of a hyphen and since this form is confirmed by Longman and Collins as the usual one (while Chambers, predictably, insists on the hyphenated form).

What about *electro-magnetic* versus *electromagnetic*? Collins and Longman confirm that only the second is in use among those who use the term regularly, but Oxford clings stubbornly to the antiquated and pointless hyphen.

On the other hand, things like ⋆ *pressurecooker*, ⋆ *wordprocessor* and ⋆ *emeraldgreen* are impossibly hard on the eye; reference to a good dictionary will confirm that the established forms of the first two are *pressure cooker* and *word processor*, while the last is *emerald green* or *emerald-green*, depending on how it is used (see below).

The hyphen is regularly used in writing so-called 'double-barrelled' names: *José-María Olazábal*, *Jean-Paul Gaultier*, *Claude Lévi-Strauss*, *Philip Johnson-Laird*. However, some individuals with such names prefer to omit the hyphen: *Jean Paul Sartre*, *Hillary Rodham Clinton*. You should always respect the usage of the owner of the name.

Now here is something important: it is usually essential to hyphenate compound modifiers. Compare the following:

She kissed him good night.
She gave him a good-night kiss.

The hyphen in the second example is necessary to show

that *good-night* is a single compound modifier. Without the hyphen, the reader might easily be misled:

★ She gave him a good night kiss.

Here the reader might be momentarily flummoxed into thinking that she had given him some kind of *'night kiss'*, whatever that means. Here are some further examples:

Her dress is light green.
She's wearing a light-green dress.

This book token is worth ten pounds.
This is a ten-pound book token.

She always turned up for the parties at the end of term.
She always turned up for the end-of-term parties.

This essay is well thought out.
This is a well-thought-out essay.

Her son is ten years old.
She has a ten-year-old son.

Use hyphens liberally in such compound modifiers; they are often vital to comprehension: *a light-green dress* is not necessarily *a light green dress*; *our first-class discussion* is quite different from *our first class discussion*; *a rusty-nail cutter* is hardly the same as *a rusty nail-cutter; a woman-hating religion* is utterly different from *a woman hating religion*; and *a nude-review producer* is most unlikely to be *a nude review producer*! You can mislead your reader disastrously by omitting these crucial hyphens: *She always turned up for the end of term parties* does not appear to mean the same as the hyphenated example above (example adapted from Carey 1958: 82). So make a habit of hyphenating your compound modifiers:

| | | |
|---|---|---|
| a long-standing friend | *not* | ★ a long standing friend |
| well-defined rules | *not* | ★ well defined rules |
| a copper-producing region | *not* | ★ a copper producing region |
| a low-scoring match | *not* | ★ a low scoring match |
| little-expected news | *not* | ★ little expected news |
| a green-eyed beauty | *not* | ★ a green eyed beauty |
| a rough-and-ready approach | *not* | ★ a rough and ready approach |
| a salt-and-pepper moustache | *not* | ★ a salt and pepper moustache |
| a far-ranging investigation | *not* | ★ a far ranging investigation |
| her Swiss-German ancestry | *not* | ★ her Swiss German ancestry |
| her new-found freedom | *not* | ★ her new found freedom |
| the hang-'em-and-flog-'em brigade | *not* | ★ the hang 'em and flog 'em brigade |

The correct use or non-use of a hyphen in a modifier can be of vital importance in making your meaning clear. Consider the next two examples:

The earliest known hominid was *Homo habilis*.
The earliest-known hominid was *Homo habilis*.

These do not mean the same thing at all. The first means that, of all the hominids we know about, *H. habilis* was the earliest one to exist (but not necessarily the first one we knew about). The second means that, of all the hominids, *H. Habilis* was the first one we knew about (but not necessarily the first one to exist). Effectively, the first sentence includes the structure [*earliest*] [*known hominid*], while the second includes the structure [*earliest-known*] [*hominid*]. Again, these two sentences would be pronounced differently, but the pronunciation difference is lost in writing; hence accurate punctuation is essential if you are not going to mislead your reader utterly. Punctuation is not a matter for personal taste and caprice, not if you want your readers to understand what you've written. (As it happens, the first statement is true, but the second one is false.)

A compound modifier may also require a hyphen when it appears after the verb. Here is a splendid example from Carey (1958): *Her face turned an ugly brick-red* appears to mean something very different from *Her face turned an ugly brick red*.

Old-fashioned usage, especially in Britain, favours excessive hyphenation, producing such forms as *to-day*, *co-operate*, *ski-ing*, *semi-colon* and even *full-stop*; such hyphens are pointless and ugly and should be avoided. Much better are *today*, *cooperate*, *skiing*, *semicolon* and *full stop*: don't use a hyphen unless it's doing some real work.

Prefixes present special problems. *She's repainting the lounge* seems unobjectionable, but *She's reliving her childhood* is possibly hard to read and should perhaps be rewritten as *She's re-living her childhood*. And *She re-covered the sofa* [= 'She put a new cover on the sofa'] is absolutely essential to avoid confusion with the entirely different *She recovered the sofa* [= 'She got the sofa back']. The chemical term meaning 'not ionized' is routinely written by chemists as *unionized*, but, in some contexts, you might prefer to write *un-ionized* to avoid possible confusion with the unrelated word *unionized* 'organized into unions'. Use your judgement: put a hyphen in if you can see a problem without it, but otherwise leave it out. Here are a few examples of good usage:

| | | |
|---|---|---|
| miniskirt | *but* | mini-aircraft |
| nonviolent | *but* | non-negotiable |
| prejudge | *but* | pre-empt |
| antisocial | *but* | anti-aircraft |

The hyphen is written only when the word would be hard to read without it: ★ *nonnegotiable*, ★ *preempt*. As always, consult a good dictionary if you're not sure.

Observe, by the way, that a prefix must **not** be written as though it were a separate word. Thus all the following are **wrong**:

★ post war period ★ non communist countries
★ mini computer ★ anti vivisectionists

There are three cases in which a hyphen is absolutely required after a prefix. First, if a capital letter or a numeral follows:

| | |
|---|---|
| non-EC countries | un-American activities |
| pre-Newtonian physics | anti-French feeling |
| post-Napoleonic Europe | pre-1500 English literature |

Second, if the prefix is added to a word which already contains a hyphen:

| | |
|---|---|
| non-bribe-taking politicians | his pre-globe-trotting days |
| non-stress-timed languages | an un-re-elected politician |

Your reader cannot be expected to take in at a glance some indigestible glob like ⋆ *his preglobe-trotting days* or ⋆ *an unre-elected politician.*

Third, if the prefix is added to a compound word containing a white space. In this case, the white space itself must be replaced by a hyphen to prevent the prefixed word from becoming unreadable:

| | | |
|---|---|---|
| seal killing | *but* | anti-seal-killing campaigners |
| twentieth century | *but* | pre-twentieth-century music |
| cold war | *but* | our post-cold-war world |

Again, your readers will not thank you for writing something like ⋆ *antiseal-killing campaigners* or ⋆ *our postcold-war world* (or, still worse, ⋆ *our postcold war world*, a piece of gibberish I recently encountered in a major newspaper). Who are these campaigners who kill *antiseals*, whatever those might be, and what is a *war world* and what is special about a *postcold* one?

In any case, do not go overboard with large and complex modifiers. The cumbersome *anti-seal-killing campaigners* can easily be replaced by *campaigners against seal killing*, which is much easier to read.

Finally, the hyphen has one rather special use: it is used in writing pieces of words. Here are some examples:

The prefix *re-* sometimes requires a hyphen.
The suffix *-wise*, as in 'moneywise' and 'healthwise', has become enormously popular in recent years.
The Latin word *rex* 'king' has a stem *reg-*.

Only when you are writing about language are you likely to need this use of the hyphen. If you do use it, make sure you put the hyphen at the correct end of the piece-of-a-word you are citing – that is, the end at which the piece has to be connected to something else to make a word. And note that, when you're writing a suffix, the hyphen must go on the same line as the suffix itself: you should not allow the hyphen to stand at the end of its line, with the suffix on the next line. Word processors won't do this automatically, and you will need to consult your manual to find out how to type a *hard hyphen*, which will always stay where it belongs.

There is, however, one very special case in which you might want to write a piece of a word in any kind of text. Consider the following example:

Pre-war and post-war Berlin could hardly be more different.

There is another way of writing this:

> Pre- and post-war Berlin could hardly be more different.

This style is permissible, but observe that the now isolated prefix *pre-* requires a hyphen, since it is only a piece of a word.

The same thing happens when you want to write a piece of a word which is not normally hyphenated, in order to avoid repetition:

> Natalie is studying sociolinguistics and psycholinguistics.

This can also be written as follows:

> Natalie is studying socio- and psycholinguistics.

The use of the hyphen in writing numerals and fractions is covered in Chapter 9.

## 6.2 **The Dash**

The **dash** (–) is the long horizontal bar, noticeably longer than a hyphen. Few keyboards have a dash, but a word processor can usually produce one in one way or another. If your keyboard can't produce a dash, you will have to resort to a hyphen as a stand-in. In British usage, we use only a single hyphen to represent a dash - like this. American usage, in contrast, uses two consecutive hyphens -- like this (A). Here I must confess that I strongly prefer the American style, since the double hyphen is far more prominent than a single one and avoids any possibility of ambiguity. If you are writing for publication, you will probably have to use the single hyphen; in other contexts, you should consider using the more vivid double hyphen. In any case, you will be very unlucky if your word processor can't produce a proper dash and save you from worrying about this.

The dash has only one major use: a **pair** of dashes separates a strong interruption from the rest of the sentence. (A strong interruption is one which violently disrupts the flow of the sentence.) Again, note that word 'pair': in principle, at least, dashes come in pairs, though sometimes one of them is not written. (Remember that the same thing is true of bracketing commas, which set off weak interruptions.) Here are some examples:

An honest politician – if such a creature exists – would never agree to such a plan.

The destruction of Guernica – and there is no doubt that the destruction was deliberate – horrified the world.

When the Europeans settled in Tasmania, they inflicted genocide – there is no other word for it – upon the indigenous population, who were wiped out in thirty years.

If the strong interruption comes at the end of the sentence, then of course only one dash is used:

The Serbs want peace – or so they say.

In 1453 Sultan Mehmed finally took Constantinople –

> and the Byzantine Empire disappeared from the map for ever.
>
> There was no other way – or was there?

In the case in which the original sentence is never resumed after the interruption, only one dash is used:

> John, do you suppose you could – oh, never mind; I'll do it.

This sort of broken sentence is only found in representations of conversation, such as you might find in a novel; it is never appropriate in formal writing.

Finally, in the rare case in which a sentence is broken off abruptly without being completed, a single dash is also used:

> General Sedgwick's last words to his worried staff were 'Don't worry, boys; they couldn't hit an elephant at this dist–'.

Note that, in this case, the dash is written solid next to the unfinished piece-of-a-word which precedes it. (If the sentence merely tails off into silence, we use, not a dash, but an ellipsis; see section 9.6.)

When a dash falls between the end of one line and the beginning of the next, you should try to ensure that the dash is placed at the end of the first line and not at the beginning of the second, if you can. Most words processors will not do this automatically, however, and it will require some fiddling.

The dash is also used in representing ranges of numbers, and occasionally also other ranges. A representation of the form *X–Y* means 'from *X* to *Y*' or 'between *X* and *Y*'. Here are some examples:

Steel contains 0.1–1.7% carbon.
These fossils are 30–35 million years old.
The London–Brighton vintage car rally takes place on Sunday.
The declaration of the Rome–Berlin axis led to the use of the label 'Axis powers' for Germany and Italy.

Do **not** write things like this:

★ Steel contains from 0.1–1.7% carbon.
★ Steel contains between 0.1–1.7% carbon.

These are terrible, since the sense of 'from' or 'between' is already included in the punctuation. If you prefer to use words, then write the words out in full, with no dashes:

Steel contains from 0.1 to 1.7% carbon.
Steel contains between 0.1 and 1.7% carbon.

And, of course, do not tangle up these two constructions:

★ Steel contains between 0.1 to 1.7% carbon.

A construction of the form ★ *between X to Y* is always wrong. Similarly, do **not** write things like this:

★ She was living in Rome from 1977–83.

Instead, write the dates out in full:

She was living in Rome from 1977 to 1983.

That's all there is to know about the dash. Use the dash carefully: overuse of dashes will give your writing a breathless and disjointed appearance. And don't use a dash for any purpose other than setting off a strong interruption or marking a range: the dash is **never** used in place of a hyphen, after a colon or after a heading. It is not used to introduce a direct quotation, except sometimes in novels, but this is not a usage you should imitate.

There is one last point, very trivial. In a certain style of writing which is now felt to be antique and genteel, an extra-long dash is occasionally used to represent the omission of several letters from a word or a name. The exceedingly genteel Victorian novelists often wrote *d—n* in place of *damn*, and even *Go to the d—l!* instead of *Go to the devil!* Such usages strike us as comical now, and few writers today would hesitate to write out such mild oaths in full (but compare the related use of asterisks in section 9.10 for the coarser words). Some Victorians, not wanting to set their fictional narratives in any identifiable location, also wrote things like *At the time, I was living at B— in the county of S—*. This quaint affectation is now dead.

# Chapter 7
# Capital Letters and Abbreviations

## 7.1 Capital Letters

Capital letters are not really an aspect of punctuation, but it is convenient to deal with them here. The rules for using them are mostly very simple.

(**a**) The first word of a sentence, or of a fragment, begins with a capital letter:

> The bumbling wizard Rincewind is Pratchett's most popular character.
> Will anyone now alive live to see a colony on the moon? Probably not.
> Distressingly few pupils can locate Iraq or Japan on a map of the world.

(**b**) The names of the days of the week, and of the months of the year, are written with a capital letter:

> Next Sunday France will hold a general election.
> Mozart was born on 27 January 1756.
> Football practice takes place on Wednesdays and Fridays.

However, the names of seasons are **not** written with a capital:

> Like cricket, baseball is played in the summer.

Do not write ★ . . . *in the Summer.*

(**c**) The names of languages are always written with a capital letter. Be careful about this; it's a very common mistake.

> Juliet speaks English, French, Italian and Portuguese.
> I need to work on my Spanish irregular verbs.
> Among the major languages of India are Hindi, Gujarati and Tamil.
> These days, few students study Latin and Greek.

Note, however, that names of disciplines and school subjects are **not** capitalized unless they happen to be the names of languages:

> I'm doing A levels in history, geography and English.
> Newton made important contributions to physics and mathematics.
> She is studying French literature.

(**d**) Words that express a connection with a particular place must be capitalized when they have their literal meanings. So, for example, *French* must be capitalized when it means 'having to do with France':

> The result of the French election is still in doubt.
> The American and Russian negotiators are close to agreement.

There are no mountains in the Dutch landscape.

She has a dry Mancunian sense of humour.

(The word *Mancunian* means 'from Manchester'.)

However, it is not necessary to capitalize these words when they occur as parts of fixed phrases and don't express any direct connection with the relevant places:

Please buy some danish pastries.

In warm weather, we keep our french windows open.

I prefer russian dressing on my salad.

Why the difference? Well, a danish pastry is merely a particular sort of pastry; it doesn't have to come from Denmark. Likewise, french windows are merely a particular kind of window, and russian dressing is just a particular varietyof salad dressing. Even in these cases, you can capitalize these words if you want to, as long as you are consistent about it. But notice how convenient it can be to make the difference:

In warm weather, we keep our french windows open.

After nightfall, French windows are always shuttered.

In the first example, *french windows* just refers to a kind of window; in the second, *French windows* refers specifically to windows in France.

(**e**) In the same vein, words that identify nationalities or ethnic groups must be capitalized:

The Basques and the Catalans spent decades struggling for autonomy.

The Serbs and the Croats have become bitter enemies.
Norway's most popular singer is a Sami from Lapland.

(An aside: some ethnic labels which were formerly widely used are now regarded by many people as offensive and have been replaced by other labels. Thus, careful writers use *Black*, or *Afro-Caribbean*, not *Negro*, in Britain (but *African-American*, not *Black*, in the USA); *native American*, not *Indian* or *red Indian*; *native Australian*, not *Aborigine* (though *Aboriginal* is still just about acceptable, but probably not for long). You are advised to follow suit.)

**(f)** Formerly, the words *black* and *white*, when applied to human beings, were never capitalized. Nowadays, however, many people prefer to capitalize them because they regard these words as ethnic labels comparable to *Chinese* or *Indian*:

The Rodney King case infuriated many Black Americans.

You may capitalize these words or not, as you prefer, but be consistent.

**(g)** Proper names are always capitalized. A proper name is a name or a title that refers to an individual person, an individual place, an individual institution or an individual event. Here are some examples:

The study of language was revolutionized by Noam Chomsky.
The Golden Gate Bridge towers above San Francisco Bay.

There will be a debate between Professor Lacey and Doctor Davis.

The Queen will address the House of Commons today.

Many people mistakenly believe that Mexico is in South America.

My friend Julie is training for the Winter Olympics.

Next week President Clinton will be meeting Chancellor Kohl.

Observe the difference between the next two examples:

We have asked for a meeting with the President.

I would like to be the president of a big company.

In the first, the title *the President* is capitalized because it is a title referring to a specific person; in the second, there is no capital, because the word *president* does not refer to anyone in particular. (Compare *We have asked for a meeting with President Wilson* and ★ *I would like to be President Wilson of a big company*.) The same difference is made with some other words: we write *the Government* and *Parliament* when we are referring to a particular government or a particular parliament, but we write *government* and *parliament* when we are using the words generically. And note also the following example:

The patron saint of carpenters is Saint Joseph.

Here *Saint Joseph* is a name, but *patron saint* is not and gets no capital.

There is a slight problem with the names of hazily defined geographical regions. We usually write *the Middle East* and

*Southeast Asia*, because these regions are now regarded as having a distinctive identity, but we write *central Europe* and *southeast London*, because these regions are not thought of as having the same kind of identity. Note, too, the difference between *South Africa* (the name of a particular country) and *southern Africa* (a vaguely defined region). All I can suggest here is that you read a good newspaper and keep your eyes open.

Observe that certain surnames of foreign origin contain little words that are often not capitalized, such as *de*, *du*, *da*, *von* and *van*. Thus we write *Leonardo da Vinci*, *Ludwig van Beethoven*, *General von Moltke* and *Simone de Beauvoir*. On the other hand, we write *Daphne Du Maurier* and *Dick Van Dyke*, because those are the forms preferred by the owners of the names. When in doubt, check the spelling in a good reference book.

A few people eccentrically prefer to write their names with no capital letters at all, such as the poet *e. e. cummings* and the singer *k. d. lang*. These strange usages should be respected.

(**h**) The names of distinctive historical periods are capitalized:

London was a prosperous city during the Middle Ages.
Britain was the first country to profit from the Industrial Revolution.
The Greeks were already in Greece during the Bronze Age.

(**i**) The names of festivals and holy days are capitalized:

We have long breaks at Christmas and Easter.

During Ramadan, one may not eat before sundown.
The feast of Purim is an occasion for merrymaking.
Our church observes the Sabbath very strictly.
The children greatly enjoy Hallowe'en.

(**j**) Many religious terms are capitalized, including the names of religions and of their followers, the names or titles of divine beings, the titles of certain important figures, the names of important events and the names of sacred books:

An atheist is a person who does not believe in God.
The principal religions of Japan are Shinto and Buddhism.
The Indian cricket team includes Hindus, Muslims, Sikhs and Parsees.
The Lord is my shepherd.
The Prophet was born in Mecca.
The Last Supper took place on the night before the Crucifixion.
The Old Testament begins with Genesis.

Note, however, that the word *god* is **not** capitalized when it refers to a pagan deity:

Poseidon was the Greek god of the sea.

(**k**) In the title or name of a book, a play, a poem, a film, a magazine, a newspaper or a piece of music, a capital letter is used for the first word and for every significant word (that is, a little word like *the*, *of*, *and* or *in* is not capitalized unless it is the first word):

I was terrified by *The Silence of the Lambs.*
*The Round Tower* was written by Catherine Cookson.
Bach's most famous organ piece is the *Toccata and Fugue in D Minor.*
I don't usually like Cher, but I do enjoy 'The Shoop Shoop Song'.

**Important note**: The policy just described is the one most widely used in the English-speaking world. There is, however, a second policy, preferred by many people. In this second policy, we capitalize only the first word of a title and any words which intrinsically require capitals for independent reasons. Using the second policy, my examples would look lke this:

I was terrified by *The silence of the lambs.*
*The round tower* was written by Catherine Cookson.
Bach's most famous organ piece is the *Toccata and fugue in D minor.*
I don't usually like Cher, but I do enjoy 'The shoop shoop song'.

You may use whichever policy you prefer, so long as you are consistent about it. You may find, however, that your tutor or your editor insists upon one or the other. The second policy is particularly common (though not universal) in academic circles, and is usual among librarians; elsewhere, the first policy is almost always preferred.

(I) The first word of a direct quotation, repeating someone

else's exact words, is always capitalized if the quotation is a complete sentence:

> Thomas Edison famously observed, 'Genius is one per cent inspiration and ninety-nine per cent perspiration.'

But there is no capital letter if the quotation is not a complete sentence:

> The Minister described the latest unemployment figures as 'disappointing'.

(**m**) The brand names of manufacturers and their products are capitalized:

> Maxine has bought a second-hand Ford Escort.
> Almost everybody owns a Sony Walkman.

**Note**: There is a problem with brand names which have become so successful that they are used in ordinary speech as generic labels for classes of products. The manufacturers of *Kleenex* and *Sellotape* are exasperated to find people using *kleenex* and *sellotape* as ordinary words for facial tissues or sticky tape of any kind, and some such manufacturers may actually take legal action against this practice. If you are writing for publication, you need to be careful about this, and it is best to capitalize such words if you use them. However, when brand names are converted into verbs, no capital letter is used: we write *She was hoovering the carpet* and *I need to xerox this report*, even though the manufacturers of *Hoover* vacuum cleaners and *Xerox* photocopiers don't much like this practice, either.

**(n)** Roman numerals are usually capitalized:

> It is no easy task to multiply LIX by XXIV using roman numerals.
> King Alfonso XIII handed over power to General Primo de Rivera.

The only common exception is that small roman numerals are used to number the pages of the front matter in books; look at almost any book.

**(o)** The pronoun *I* is always capitalized:

> She thought I'd borrowed her keys, but I hadn't.

It is possible to write an entire word or phrase in capital letters in order to emphasize it:

> There is ABSOLUTELY NO EVIDENCE to support this conjecture.

On the whole, though, it is preferable to express emphasis, not with capital letters, but with italics, as explained in Chapter 9.

It is not necessary to capitalize a word merely because there is only one thing it can possibly refer to:

> The equator runs through the middle of Brazil.
> Admiral Peary was the first person to fly over the north pole.
> The universe is thought to be about 15 billion years old.

Here the words *equator, north pole* and *universe* need no capitals, because they aren't strictly proper names. Some people choose to capitalize them anyway; this is not wrong, but it's not recommended.

The use of capital letters in writing certain abbreviations and related types of words, including the abbreviated names of organizations and companies, is explained in the next section; the use of capital letters in letter-writing and in the headings of essays is explained in Chapter 10.

There is one other rather rare use of capital letters which is worth explaining if only to prevent you from doing it by mistake when you don't mean to. This is to poke fun at something. Here is an example:

> The French Revolution was a Good Thing at first, but Napoleon's rise to power was a Bad Thing.

Here the writer is making fun of the common tendency to see historical events in simple-minded terms as either good or bad. Another example:

> Many people claim that rock music is Serious Art, deserving of Serious Critical Attention.

The writer is clearly being sarcastic: all those unusual capital letters demonstrate that he considers rock music to be worthless trash.

This stylistic device is only appropriate in writing which is intended to be humorous, or at least light-hearted; it is quite out of place in formal writing.

The use of unnecessary capital letters when you're trying to be serious can quickly make your prose look idiotic, rather like those content-free books that fill the shelves of the New Age section in bookshops:

> Your Eidetic Soul is linked by its Crystal Cord to the Seventh Circle of the Astral Plane, from where the Immanent Essence is transmitted to your Eidetic Aura . . .

You get the idea. **Don't** use a capital letter unless you're sure you know why it's there.

## Summary of capital letters

### Capitalize

- **the first word of a sentence or fragment**
- **the name of a day or a month**
- **the name of a language**
- **a word expressing a connection with a place**
- **the name of a nationality or an ethnic group**
- **a proper name**
- **the name of a historical period**
- **the name of a holiday**
- **a significant religious term**
- **the first word, and each significant word, of a title**
- **the first word of a direct quotation which is a sentence**
- **a brand name**
- **a roman numeral**
- **the pronoun *I***

## 7.2 Abbreviations

An **abbreviation** is a short way of writing a word or a phrase that could also be written out in full. So, for example, you might write *Dr Kinsey* instead of *Doctor Kinsey*. Here *Dr* is an abbreviation for the word *Doctor*. Likewise, the phrase *for example* can sometimes be abbreviated to *e.g.*

Abbreviations must be clearly distinguished from *contractions*, which were discussed in section 5.1. The key difference is that an abbreviation does not *normally* have a distinctive pronunciation of its own. So, for example, the abbreviation *Dr* is pronounced just like *Doctor*, the abbreviation *oz.* is pronounced just like *ounce(s)* and the abbreviation *e.g.* is pronounced just like *for example*. (True, there are a few people who actually say 'ee-jee' for the last one, but this practice is decidedly unusual.) A contraction, in contrast, *does* have its own distinctive pronunciation: for example, the contraction *can't* is pronounced differently from *cannot*, and the contraction *she's* is pronounced differently from *she is* or *she has*.

Abbreviations are very rarely used in formal writing. Almost the only ones which are frequently used are the abbreviations for certain common titles, when these are used with someone's name: *Mr Willis*, *Dr Livingstone*, *Mrs Thatcher*, *Ms Harmon*, *St Joan*. (Note that the two items *Mrs* and *Ms* are conventionally treated as abbreviations, even though they can be written in no other way.) When writing about a French or Spanish person, you may use the abbreviations for the

French and Spanish equivalents of the English titles: *M. Mitterrand*, *Sr. González*. (These are the usual French and Spanish abbreviations for *Monsieur* and *Señor*, equivalent to English *Mister*.) Observe that each of these abbreviations begins with a capital letter.

Other titles are sometimes abbreviated in the same way: *Prof. Chomsky*, *Sgt. Yorke*, *Mgr. Lindemann*. However, it is usually much better to write these titles out in full when you are using them in a sentence: *Professor Chomsky*, *Sergeant Yorke*, *Monsignor Lindemann*. The abbreviated forms are best confined to places like footnotes and captions of pictures.

Note carefully the use of full stops in these abbreviations. British usage favours omitting the full stop in abbreviations which include the first and last letters of a single word, such as *Mr*, *Mrs*, *Ms*, *Dr* and *St*; American usage prefers (A) *Mr.*, *Mrs.*, *Ms.*, *Dr.* and *St.*, with full stops. Most other abbreviated titles, however, require a full stop, as shown above.

A person's initials are a kind of abbreviation, and these are usually followed by full stops: *John D. Rockefeller*, *C. Aubrey Smith*, *O. J. Simpson*. Increasingly, however, there is a tendency to write such initials without full stops: *John D Rockefeller*, *C Aubrey Smith*, *O J Simpson*. And note the rare special case illustrated by *Harry S Truman*: the *S* in this name never takes a full stop, because it's not an abbreviation for anything; President Truman's parents actually gave him the middle name *S*.

Two other common abbreviations are *a.m.* ('before noon') and *p.m.* ('after noon'): *10.00 a.m.*, *six p.m.* These are always acceptable. Note that these are not capitalized in British usage (though American usage prefers (A) *10:00 AM* and *six PM*, with small capitals and no full stops).

Also usual are the abbreviations *BC* and *AD*, usually written in small capitals, for marking dates as before or after the birth of Christ:

> According to tradition, Rome was founded in 753 BC.
> The emperor Vespasian died in AD 79. **or**
> The emperor Vespasian died in 79 AD.

It is traditional, and recommended, to write *AD* before the date, but nowadays it is often written after.

Non-Christians who do not use the Christian calendar may prefer to use *BCE* ('before the common era') and *CE* ('of the common era') instead. This is always acceptable:

> According to tradition, Rome was founded in 753 BCE.
> The emperor Vespasian died in 79 CE.

All four of these abbreviations are commonly written in small capitals, and you should follow this practice if you can; if you can't produce small capitals, use full-sized capitals instead.

Note also that, when an abbreviation comes at the end of a sentence, only one full stop is written. You should **never** write two full stops in a row.

Many large and well-known organizations and companies have very long names which are commonly abbreviated to a set of initials written in capital letters, usually with no full stops. Here are a few familiar examples:

| | |
|---|---|
| BBC | British Broadcasting Corporation |
| ICI | Imperial Chemical Industries |
| FBI | Federal Bureau of Investigation |
| RSPCA | Royal Society for the Prevention of Cruelty to Animals |
| NATO | North Atlantic Treaty Organization |
| MIT | Massachusetts Institute of Technology |
| TUC | Trades Union Congress |

These and some others are so famous that you can safely use the abbreviated forms without explanation. But don't overdo it – not every reader will recognize *IRO* as the International Refugee Organization, or *IOOF* as the Independent Order of Odd Fellows (an American social and charitable organization). And, if you're writing for a non-British readership, you'd better not use the abbreviated forms of specifically British institutions, such as the *TUC*, without explaining them. If you are in doubt, explain the abbreviation the first time you use it. (Note that a few of these were formerly written with full stops, such as *R.S.P.C.A.*, but this tiresome and unnecessary practice is now obsolete.)

A few other abbreviations are so well known that you can use them safely in your writing. Every reader will understand what you mean by *GCSE examinations* (*GCSE* = *General Certificate of Secondary Education*), or by *DDT* (*dichlorodiphenyltrichloroethane*), or by *IQ* (*intelligence quotient*), or by *FM radio* (*FM* = *frequency modulation*). Indeed, in some of these cases, the abbreviated form of the name is far more familiar than the full name.

Otherwise, however, you should try to avoid the use of abbreviations in your formal writing. The frequent use of unnecessary abbreviations will make your text irritating and hard to read. So, you should write *four ounces* (**not** *4 oz.*), *80 miles per hour* (**not** *80 mph*), *the Church of England* (**not** *the C of E*), *the seventeenth century* (**not** *C17* or *the 17th cent.*) and *the second volume* (**not** *the 2nd vol.*). It is far more important to make your writing easy to read than to save a few seconds in writing it.

There is one exception to this policy. In scientific writing, the names of units are always abbreviated and always written without full stops or a plural *s*. If you are doing scientific writing, then, you should conform by writing *5 kg* (**not** *5 kilogrammes*, and certainly not ★ *5 kg.* or ★ *5 kgs.*), *800 Hz* (**not** *800 Hertz*) and *17.3* $cm^3$ (**not** *17.3 cubic centimetres*).

There are a number of Latin abbreviations which are sometimes used in English texts. Here are the commonest ones with their English equivalents:

| | |
|---|---|
| e.g. | for example |
| i.e. | in other words |
| *viz.* | namely |
| *sc.* | which means |
| *c.* | approximately |
| *cf.* | compare |
| *v.* | consult |
| etc. | and so forth |
| *et al.* | and other people |

The rule about using these Latin abbreviations is very simple: **don't use them**. Their use is only appropriate in special circumstances in which brevity is at a premium, such as in footnotes. It is very poor style to spatter your page with these things, and it could be disastrous to use them without being quite sure what they mean. If you do use one, make sure you punctuate it correctly. Here is an example. The recommended form is this:

> Several British universities were founded in the Victorian era; for example, the University of Manchester was established in 1851.

The following version is not wrong, but it is poor style:

> Several British universities were founded in the Victorian era; e.g., the University of Manchester was established in 1851.

But this next version is disastrously wrong, because the punctuation has been omitted:

> ★ Several British universities were founded in the Victorian era e.g. the University of Manchester was established in 1851.

Using a Latin abbreviation does not relieve you of the obligation of punctuating your sentence. Again, if you avoid Latin abbreviations, you won't get into this sort of trouble.

The abbreviation *c.* 'approximately' is properly used only in citing a date which is not known exactly, and then usually only if the date is given in parentheses:

The famous Basque cemetery of Argiñeta in Elorrio (*c.* AD 883) shows tombs with sun-discs but no crosses.
Roger Bacon (*c.* 1214–94) was known as 'the Admirable Doctor'.

Here the use of *c.* shows that the date of the cemetery and the date of Bacon's birth are not known exactly. If neither birth date nor death date is known for sure, then each is preceded by *c.*

Outside of parentheses, you should usually avoid the use of *c.* and prefer an English word like *about* or *approximately*:

The city of Bilbao was founded in about 1210.

Do not write '. . . *in* c. *1210*'.

The abbreviation *etc.* calls for special comment. It should **never** be used in careful writing: it is vague and sloppy and, when applied to people, rather offensive. **Do not** write something like this:

* Central Africa was explored by Livingstone, Stanley, Brazza, etc.

Instead, rewrite the sentence in a more explicit way:

Central Africa was explored by Livingstone, Stanley and Brazza, among others. **or**
Central Africa was explored by several Europeans, including Livingstone, Stanley and Brazza.

If you *do* find yourself using *etc.*, for heaven's sake spell it and punctuate it correctly. This is an abbreviation for the Latin phrase *et cetera* 'and other things', and it is pronounced ET SETRA, and **not** ★ EK SETRA. Do **not** write ghastly things like ★ *ect.* or ★ *e.t.c.* Such monstrosities make your writing look hopelessly illiterate. Again, if you avoid Latin abbreviations, you won't fall into such traps.

Finally, for the two further (and highly objectionable) Latin abbreviations *ibid.* and *op. cit.* see section 10.3.

Observe that it is usual to write most Latin abbreviations in italics, but this is not strictly essential, and many people don't bother.

There has recently been a fashion in some circles for writing Latin abbreviations without full stops, and you may come across things like *ie* and *eg* in your reading. I consider this a ghastly practice, and I urge you strongly not to imitate it. (Note, however, that *et al.* has only one full stop, since *et* 'and' is a complete word in Latin.)

One final point: very many people who should know better use the Latin abbreviation *cf.*, which properly means 'compare', merely to refer to published work. It is now very common to see something like this:

> ★ The Australian language Dyirbal has a remarkable gender system; *cf.* Dixon (1972).

This is quite wrong, since the writer is not inviting the reader to *compare* Dixon's work with anything, but only to consult that work for more information. Hence the correct form is this:

The Australian language Dyirbal has a remarkable gender system; see Dixon (1972).

This widespread blunder is a signal reminder of the danger of using Latin abbreviations when you don't know what they mean. Far too many writers fall into this trap, and write *i.e.* when they mean *e.g.*, or something equally awful. If you *must* use a Latin abbreviation, make sure you're using the right one. In most circumstances, though, you are best advised to avoid these abbreviations: almost every one of them has a simple English equivalent which should usually be preferred.

## Summary of abbreviations

- **Do not use an abbreviation that can easily be avoided.**
- **In an abbreviation, use full stops and capital letters in the conventional way.**
- **Do not forget to punctuate the rest of the sentence normally.**

## Chapter 8
# Quotation Marks

## 8.1 Quotation Marks and Direct Quotations

The use of **quotation marks**, also called **inverted commas**, is very slightly complicated by the fact that there are two types: **single quotes** (' ') and **double quotes** (" "). As a general rule, British usage prefers single quotes for ordinary use, but double quotes are also very common; American usage insists upon double quotes. Usage in the rest of the world varies: double quotes are preferred in Canada and Australia, and perhaps also in New Zealand, while single quotes are perhaps more usual in South Africa. As we shall see below, the use of double quotes in fact offers several advantages, and this is the usage I recommend here. You may find, however, if you are writing for publication, that your editor or publisher insists upon single quotes. If you are using a word processor, though, you may find that your printer produces single quotes which are all but invisible, in which case double quotes will make life easier for your readers.

The chief use of quotation marks is quite easy to understand: a **pair** of quotation marks encloses a **direct quotation**

– that is, a repetition of someone's exact words. Here are some examples:

> President Kennedy famously exclaimed, 'Ich bin ein Berliner!'
>
> Madonna is fond of declaring, 'I'm not ashamed of anything.'
>
> 'The only emperor,' writes Wallace Stevens, 'is the emperor of ice cream.'

Look closely at these examples. Note first that what is enclosed in quotes must be the exact words of the person being quoted. Anything which is not part of those exact words must be placed outside the quotes, even if, as in the last example, this means using two sets of quotes because the quotation has been interrupted. (The commas in the last example set off a weak interruption, as usual; their presence has nothing to do with the quotation.) And note something else which is very strange: the first comma in the last example comes *inside* the quotes, even though it is not part of the quotation. This makes no sense, and it contradicts the usual principles of punctuation, but for some reason this illogical style has become almost universal in English. I don't like it, and I would very much prefer to put that comma *outside* the quotes, where it belongs, as follows:

> 'The only emperor', writes Wallace Stevens, 'is the emperor of ice cream.'

But, if you do this, you will find most of the world lined up against you. See below for more on this topic.

Otherwise, however, you should not put quotes around anything other than a word-for-word quotation. Consequently, the following example is **wrong**:

> * Thomas Edison declared that 'Genius was one per cent inspiration and ninety-nine per cent perspiration.'

Here the passage inside the quotes transparently does not reproduce Edison's exact words. There are three ways of fixing this. First, drop the quotes:

> Thomas Edison declared that genius was one per cent inspiration and ninety-nine per cent perspiration.

Second, rewrite the sentence so that you can use Edison's exact words:

> According to Thomas Edison, 'Genius is one per cent inspiration and ninety-nine per cent perspiration.'

Third, move the quotes so that they enclose only Edison's exact words:

> Thomas Edison declared that genius was 'one per cent inspiration and ninety-nine per cent perspiration'.

All three of these are perfect, since only Edison's exact words are enclosed in quotes.

Now notice something else which is very important: a quotation is set off by quotation marks **and nothing else**. A sentence containing a quotation is punctuated exactly like any other sentence apart from the addition of the quotation marks. You should **not** insert additional punctuation marks into the sentence merely to warn the reader that a quotation is coming up: that's what the quotation marks are for. Here are some common mistakes:

★ President Nixon declared: 'I am not a crook.'
★ President Nixon declared:– 'I am not a crook.'

The colon in the first is completely pointless, while the startling arsenal of punctuation in the second is grotesque. (Remember, a colon can never be followed by a hyphen or a dash.) Here is the style I recommend:

President Nixon declared 'I am not a crook.'

Adding more dots and squiggles to this perfectly clear sentence would do absolutely nothing to improve it. No punctuation mark should be used if it is not necessary.

Nevertheless, very many people prefer to put a comma before an opening quote, as follows:

President Nixon declared, 'I am not a crook.'

I consider such commas to be unnecessary, since they do no work at all, but most publishers insist upon them. If you are writing for publication, then, you will probably find yourself obliged to use them.

On the other hand, the presence of quotation marks does not remove the necessity of using other punctuation which is required for independent reasons. Look again at these examples:

> According to Thomas Edison, 'Genius is one per cent inspiration and ninety-nine per cent perspiration.'
>
> 'The only emperor,' writes Wallace Stevens, 'is the emperor of ice cream.'

The commas here are bracketing commas, used as usual to set off weak interruptions; their presence has nothing to do with the presence of a quotation, which is itself properly marked off by the quotation marks.

Here is another example:

> Mae West had one golden rule for handling men: 'Tell the pretty ones they're smart, and tell the smart ones they're pretty.'

The colon here is **not** being used merely because a quotation follows. Instead, it is doing what colons always do: it is introducing an explanation of what comes before the colon. It is merely a coincidence that what follows the colon happens to be a quotation.

This last example illustrates another point about quotations: the quotation inside the quote marks begins with a capital letter if it is a complete sentence, but not otherwise. Look once more at two versions of the Edison sentence:

> According to Thomas Edison, 'Genius is one per cent inspiration and ninety-nine per cent perspiration.'

> Thomas Edison declared that genius was 'one per cent inspiration and ninety-nine per cent perspiration'.

The first quotation is a complete sentence and therefore gets an initial capital letter; the second is not a complete sentence and hence receives no capital.

There is one situation in which the use of single quotes instead of double quotes can be rather a nuisance. This is when the quotation contains an apostrophe, especially near the end:

> Professor Cavendish concludes that 'The Turks' influence on the Balkans has been more enduring than the Greeks' ever was.'

Since an apostrophe is usually indistinguishable from a closing quote mark, the reader may be momentarily misled into thinking that she has come to the end of the quotation when she has not. This is one reason why I personally prefer to use double quotes:

> Professor Cavendish concludes that "The Turks' influence on the Balkans has been more enduring than the Greeks' ever was."

With double quotes, the problem goes away.

Things can get a little complicated when you cite a quotation that has another quotation inside it. In this rare circumstance, the rule is to set off the internal quotation with the *other* type of quotation marks. So, if you're using double quotes:

> The Shadow Employment Secretary declared, "Describing the unemployment figures as 'disappointing' is an insult to the British people."

And if you're using single quotes:

> The Shadow Employment Secretary declared, 'Describing the unemployment figures as "disappointing" is an insult to the British people.'

Naturally, you'll be asking what you should do if you have a quotation inside a quotation inside a quotation. My answer: you should rewrite the sentence. Otherwise, you will simply lose your reader in a labyrinth of quotation marks.

If you have a long quotation which you want to display indented in the middle of the page, you do not need to place quotes around it, though you should make sure that you identify it explicitly as a quotation in your main text. Here is an example cited from G. V. Carey's famous book on punctuation, *Mind the Stop* (Carey 1958):

> I should define punctuation as being governed two-thirds by rule and one-third by personal taste. I shall endeavour not to stress the former to the exclusion of the latter, but I will not knuckle under to those who apparently claim for themselves complete freedom to do what they please in the matter.

It would not be wrong to enclose this passage in quotes, but there is no need, since I have clearly identified it as a quotation, which is exactly what quotation marks normally do. No punctuation should be used if it's not doing any work.

Occasionally you may find it necessary to interrupt a quotation you are citing in order to clarify something. To do this you enclose your remarks in **square brackets** (never parentheses). Suppose I want to cite a famous passage from the eighteenth-century French writer Alexis de Tocqueville:

> These two nations [America and Russia] seem set to sway the destinies of half the globe.

The passage from which this sentence is taken had earlier made it clear which two nations the author was talking about. My quotation, however, does not make this clear, and so I have inserted the necessary information enclosed in square brackets.

Some authors, when doing this, have a habit of inserting their own initials within the square brackets, preceded by a dash. Thus, my example might have looked like this:

> These two nations [America and Russia – RLT] seem set to sway the destinies of half the globe.

This is not wrong, but it is hardly ever necessary, since the square brackets already make it clear what's going on.

There is one special interruption whose use you should be familiar with. This happens when the passage you are quoting contains a mistake of some kind, and you want to make it clear to your reader that the mistake is contained in the original passage, and has not been introduced by you. To do this, you use the Latin word *sic*, which means 'thus', again enclosed in square brackets and immediately following the mistake. The mistake can be of any kind: a spelling mistake, a grammatical error, the use of the wrong word, or even a statement which is obviously wrong or silly. Here are some examples, all of which are meant to be direct quotations:

> We have not recieved [*sic*] your letter.
>
> The number of students are [*sic*] larger than usual.
>
> The All Blacks won the match with a fortuitous [*sic*] try in the final minute.
>
> The last dinosaurs died about 60,000 years ago [*sic*].

(The word *received* is misspelled; the form *are* has been used where *is* is required; the word *fortuitous*, which means 'accidental', has been used where *fortunate* was intended; the last statement is grotesquely false.) Note that the word *sic* is commonly italicized, if italics are available. And note also that *sic* is **not** used merely to emphasize part of a quotation: it is used only to draw attention to an error.

If you *do* want to emphasize part of a quotation, you do so by placing that part in italics, but you must show that you are doing this. Here is a sentence cited from Steven Pinker's book *The Language Instinct*:

> Many prescriptive rules of grammar are *just plain dumb* and should be deleted from the usage handbooks [emphasis added].

Here my comment in square brackets shows that the italics were not present in the original but that I have added them in order to draw attention to this part of the quotation. In Chapter 9 we shall consider the use of italics further.

If you want to quote parts of a passage while leaving out some intervening bits, you do this by inserting an **ellipsis** (...) (also called a **suspension** or **omission marks**) to represent a missing section of a quotation. If, as a result, you need to provide one or two extra words to link up the pieces of the quotation, you put those extra words inside square brackets to show that they are not part of the quotation. If you need to change a small letter to a capital, you put that capital inside square brackets. Here is an example, cited from my own book *Language: The Basics* (Trask 1995):

> Chelsea was born nearly deaf, but . . . she was disastrously misdiagnosed as mentally retarded when she failed to learn to speak . . . [S]he was raised by a loving family . . . [but] only when she was thirty-one did a disbelieving doctor . . . prescribe for her a hearing aid. Able to hear speech at last, she began learning English.

Naturally, when you use an ellipsis, be careful not to misrepresent the sense of the original passage.

Finally, there remains the problem of whether to put other punctuation marks inside or outside the quotation marks. There are at least two schools of thought on this, which I shall call the *logical view* and the *conventional view*. American usage adheres closely to the conventional view; British usage prefers the logical view, but, as we shall see, with one curious exception.

The logical view holds that the only punctuation marks which should be placed inside the quotation marks are those that form part of the quotation, while all others should be placed outside. The conventional view, in contrast, insists on placing most other punctuation marks inside a closing quote, regardless of whether they form part of the quotation. Here are three sentences punctuated according to the logical view; the second is taken from Pullum (1984), of which more below:

> 'The only thing we have to fear', said Franklin Roosevelt, 'is fear itself.'
>
> Bolinger never said 'Accent is predictable'; he said 'Accent is predictable – if you're a mind-reader.'
>
> The Prime Minister condemned what he called 'simple-minded solutions'.

And here they are punctuated according to the conventional view:

> 'The only thing we have to fear,' said Franklin Roosevelt, 'is fear itself.'
>
> Bolinger never said, 'Accent is predictable;' he said, 'Accent is predictable – if you're a mind-reader.'
>
> The Prime Minister condemned what he called 'simple-minded solutions.'

Note the placing of the comma after *fear* in the first example, of the semicolon after *predictable* in the second, and of the final full stop in the third. These are not part of their quotations, and so the logical view places them outside the quote marks, while the conventional view places them inside, on the theory that a closing quote should always follow another punctuation mark.

Which view should we prefer? I certainly prefer the logical view, and, in a perfect world, I would simply advise you to stick to this view. However, it is a fact that American usage clings grimly to the conventional view, and you will find it very difficult to persuade an American publisher to refrain from changing your logical punctuation. British usage, in contrast, generally prefers the logical view, but with one inconsistent and bizarre exception: British publishers normally insist on putting a comma inside closing quotes, even when it logically belongs outside. Hence a British publisher will usually insist on the conventional style with my Roosevelt example above, but on the logical style with the other two. This is mysterious, but it's a fact of life.

The linguist Geoff Pullum, a fervent advocate of the logical view, once got so angry at copy-editors who insisted on reshuffling his carefully placed punctuation that he wrote an article called 'Punctuation and human freedom' (Pullum 1984). Here is one of his examples, first with logical punctuation, as it would usually be printed in Britain:

> Shakespeare's play *Richard III* contains the line 'Now is the winter of our discontent'.

This is true. Now try it with conventional punctuation, as preferred in the USA:

> Shakespeare's play *Richard III* contains the line 'Now is the winter of our discontent.' (A)

This is strictly false, since the line in question is only the first of two lines making up a complete sentence, and hence does not end in a full stop, as apparently suggested by the conventional punctuation:

> Now is the winter of our discontent
> Made glorious summer by this sun of York.

The same point arises in the General Sedgwick example cited in Chapter 6:

> General Sedgwick's last words to his worried staff were 'Don't worry, boys; they couldn't hit an elephant at this dist–'.

Here, putting the full stop inside the closing quotes, as required by the conventionalists, would produce an idiotic result, since the whole point of the quotation is that the lamented general didn't live long enough to finish it.

You may follow your own preference in this matter, so long as you are consistent. If you opt for logical punctuation, you will have the satisfaction of knowing that you are on the side of the angels, but you should also expect some grim opposition from the other side.

## 8.2 Scare Quotes

The use of quotation marks can be extended to cases which are not exactly direct quotations. Here is an example:

> Linguists sometimes employ a technique they call 'inverted reconstruction'.

The phrase in quote marks is not a quotation from anyone in particular, but merely a term which is used by some people – in this case, linguists. What the writer is doing here is *distancing* himself from the term in quotes. That is, he's saying, 'Look, that's what they call it. I'm not responsible for this term.' In this case, there is no suggestion that the writer disapproves of the phrase in quotes, but very often there *is* a suggestion of disapproval:

> The Institute for Personal Knowledge is now offering a course in 'self-awareness exercises'.

Once again, the writer's quotes mean 'this is *their* term, not mine', but this time there is definitely a hint of a sneer: the writer is implying that, although the Institute may *call* their course 'self-awareness exercises', what they're really offering to do is to take your money in exchange for a lot of hot air.

Quotation marks used in this way are informally called **scare quotes**. Scare quotes are quotation marks placed around a word or phrase from which you, the writer, wish to distance yourself because you consider that word or phrase to be odd or inappropriate for some reason. Possibly you regard it as too colloquial for formal writing; possibly you think it's unfamiliar or mysterious; possibly you consider it to be inaccurate or misleading; possibly you believe it's just plain wrong. Quite often scare quotes are used to express irony or sarcasm:

> The Serbs are closing in on the 'safe haven' of Goražde.

The point here is that the town has been officially declared a safe haven by the UN, whereas in fact, as the quote marks make clear, it is anything but safe. Here's another example:

> Sharon made dozens of 'adult films' before getting her Hollywood break.

The phrase 'adult films' is the industry's conventional label for pornographic films, and here the writer is showing that she recognizes this phrase as nothing more than a dishonest euphemism.

It is important to realize this distancing effect of scare quotes. Quotation marks are **not** properly used merely in order to draw attention to words, and all those pubs which declare *We Sell 'Traditional Pub Food'* are unwittingly suggesting to a literate reader that they are in fact serving up microwaved sludge.

Some writers perhaps take the use of scare quotes a little too far:

> I have just been 'ripped off' by my insurance company.

Here the writer is doing something rather odd: she is using the phrase 'ripped off', but at the same time she is showing her distaste for this phrase by wrapping it in quotes. Perhaps she regards it as too slangy, or as too American. Using scare quotes like this is the orthographic equivalent of holding the phrase at arm's length with one hand and pinching your nose with the other.

I can't really approve of scare quotes used in this way. If you think a word is appropriate, then use it, without any quotes; if you think it's not appropriate, then don't use it, unless you specifically want to be ironic. Simultaneously using a word and showing that you don't approve of it will only make you sound like an antiquated fuddy-duddy.

## 8.3 Quotation Marks in Titles

A couple of generations ago, it was the custom to enclose all titles in quotation marks: titles of books, titles of poems, titles of films, titles of newspapers, and so on. This usage, however, has now largely disappeared, and the modern custom is to write most titles in italics, as explained in Chapter 9. But in academic circles, at least, it is still usual to enclose the titles of articles in journals and magazines in quotes, as well as the titles of chapters in books – hence my reference above to Geoff Pullum's article 'Punctuation and human freedom'. In British usage, however, we **always** use single quotes for this purpose, though American usage usually prefers double quotes here too.

It is still not exactly wrong to refer to a newspaper as 'The Guardian', or to a book as 'Uncle Tom's Cabin', but it is certainly old-fashioned now, and my advice is to use italics rather than quotation marks, except perhaps when you are writing by hand.

## 8.4 Talking About Words

There is one very special use of quotation marks which it is useful to know about: we use quotation marks when we are talking about words. In this special use, all varieties of English normally use only single quotes, and not double quotes (though some Americans use double quotes even here). (This is another advantage of using double quotes for ordinary purposes, since this special use can then be readily distinguished.) Consider the following examples:

Men are physically stronger than women.
'Men' is an irregular plural.

In the first example, we are using the word 'men' in the ordinary way, to refer to male human beings. In the second, however, we are doing something very different: we are not talking about any human beings at all, but instead we are talking about the *word* 'men'. Placing quotes around the word we are talking about makes this clear. Of course, you are only likely to need this device when you are writing about language, but then you should certainly use it. If you think

I'm being unnecessarily finicky, take a look at a sample of the sort of thing I frequently find myself trying to read when marking my students' essays:

> * A typical young speaker in Reading has done, not did, and usually also does for do and dos for does.

I'm sure you'll agree this is a whole lot easier to read with some suitable quotation marks:

> A typical young speaker in Reading has 'done', not 'did', and usually also 'does' for 'do' and 'dos' for 'does'.

Failure to make this useful orthographic distinction can, in rare cases, lead to absurdity:

> The word processor came into use around 1910.
> The word 'processor' came into use around 1910.

If what you mean is the second, writing the first will create momentary havoc in your reader's mind. (The second statement is true; the first is wrong by about seventy years.) Here we have a particularly clear example of the way in which good punctuation works: in speech, the phrases *the word processor* and *the word 'processor'* sound quite different, because they are stressed differently; in writing, the stress difference is lost, and punctuation must step in to do the job.

Printed books usually use italics for citing words, rather than quotation marks. If you are using a keyboard which can produce italics, you can use italics in this way, and indeed this practice is preferable to the use of quotes. See Chapter 9 for more on this. In one circumstance, though, italics are not possible: when we are providing brief translations (or *glosses*, as they are called) for *foreign* words. Here's an example:

> The English word 'thermometer' is derived from the Greek words *thermos* 'heat' and *metron* 'measure'.

This example shows the standard way of mentioning foreign words: the foreign word is put into italics, and an English translation, if provided, follows in single quotes, with **no other punctuation**. Observe that neither a comma nor anything else separates the foreign word from the gloss.

You can even do this with English words:

> The words *stationary* 'not moving' and *stationery* 'writing materials' should be carefully distinguished.

In this case, it is clearly necessary to use italics for citing English words, reserving the single quotes for the glosses.

## Summary of quotation marks

- **Put quotation marks (single or double) around the exact words of a direct quotation.**
- **Inside a quotation, use a suspension to mark omitted material and square brackets to mark inserted material.**
- **Use quotation marks to distance yourself from a word or phrase or to show that you are using it ironically.**
- **Place quotation marks around a word or phrase which you are talking about.**

Chapter 9
# Miscellaneous

## 9.1 Italics

Most word processors can produce **italics**, which are slanted letters – *like these*. If you can't produce italics, the conventional substitute is to use underlining – like this. Italics have several uses.

Most commonly, italics are used for emphasis or contrast – that is, to draw attention to some particular part of a text. Here are some examples:

The Battle of New Orleans was fought in January 1815, two weeks *after* the peace treaty had been signed.

According to the linguist Steven Pinker, 'Many prescriptive rules of grammar are *just plain dumb* and should be deleted from the usage handbooks' [emphasis added].

Standard English usage requires '*in*sensitive' rather than '*un*sensitive'.

Lemmings have, not two, but *three* kinds of sex chromosome.

The first two examples illustrate emphasis and the last two illustrate contrast. This is the standard way of representing emphasis or contrast; you should not try to use quotation marks or other punctuation marks for this purpose.

Another use of italics, as explained in Chapter 8, is to cite titles of complete works: books, films, journals, musical compositions, and so on:

> We saw a performance of the *Messiah* on Saturday.
>
> Chomsky's book *Syntactic Structures* revolutionized linguistics.
>
> Spielberg won his Oscars for *Schindler's List*.

An exception: the names of holy books are usually *not* written in italics. Thus, we write about the (Holy) Bible and the (Holy) Koran, with no italics. Don't ask me why.

Note, however, that we do not use italics when citing a name which is only a conventional description:

> Dvořák's ninth symphony is commonly known as the *New World* symphony.

Here the label 'Dvořák's ninth symphony' is not strictly a title, and hence is not italicized.

A third use of italics is to cite foreign words when talking about them. Examples:

> The French word *pathétique* is usually best translated as 'moving', not as 'pathetic'.
>
> The German word *Gemütlichkeit* is not easy to translate into English.

The Sicilian tradition of *omertà* has long protected the Mafia.

At Basque festivals, a favourite entertainment is the *sokamuturra*, in which people run in front of a bull which is restricted by ropes controlled by handlers.

Related to this is the use of italics when using foreign words and phrases which are not regarded as completely assimilated into English:

Psychologists are interested in the phenomenon of *déjà vu*.

This analysis is not in accord with the *Sprachgefühl* of native speakers.

If you are not sure which foreign words and phrases are usually written in italics, consult a good dictionary.

As explained in Chapter 8, it is also quite common to use italics when citing English words that are being talked about, as an alternative to single quotes:

The origin of the word *boy* is unknown.

Note the spelling difference between *premier* (an adjective meaning 'first' or 'most important') and *premiere* (a noun meaning 'first performance').

Finally, italics are used in certain disciplines for various specific purposes. Here are two of the commoner ones. In biology, genus and species names of living creatures are italicized:

The earliest known member of the genus *Homo* is *H. habilis*.

The cedar waxwing (*Bombycilla cedrorum*) is a familiar American bird.

Note that a genus name always has a capital letter, while a species name never does.

Second, names of legal cases are italicized:

The famous case of *Brown* v. *Board of Education* was a landmark in American legal history.

In this case, note that the abbreviation *v.*, which stands for *versus* ('against') stands in roman type, not in italics. Note also that the American abbreviation is *vs.*:

(A) The famous case of *Brown* vs. *Board of Education* was a landmark in American legal history.

**Special note**: If you have a sentence containing a phrase which would normally go into italics, and if for some reason the entire sentence needs to be italicized, then the phrase that would normally be in italics goes into ordinary roman type instead. So, if for some reason my last example sentence needs to be italicized, the result looks like this:

*The famous case of* Brown *v.* Board of Education *was a landmark in American legal history.*

## 9.2 Boldface

**Boldface** letters are the extra-black ones – **like these**. Most word processors can produce these. They have only a few general uses.

First, they are used for chapter titles and section headings, exactly as is done in this book.

Second, they are used for the captions to illustrations, tables and graphs.

Third, they are sometimes used to provide very strong emphasis, as an alternative to italics. In this book I have used them in this way very frequently – probably too frequently:

> A colon is **never** followed by a hyphen or a dash.

Finally, boldface is often used to introduce important new terms. Again, I have been doing this regularly in this book: the name of each new punctuation mark is introduced in boldface.

The judicious use of boldface can provide variety and make a page more attractive to the eye, but it is never essential. If you can't produce boldface, use ordinary roman type for chapter and section headings and captions, and italics for emphasis and important terms. If you do use boldface, don't overdo it.

## 9.3 Small Capitals

**Small capitals** are just what they sound like: THEY LOOK LIKE THIS. They have only one common use: certain abbreviations are commonly written in small capitals. In particular, the abbreviations BC and AD are usually so written:

> Alexander the Great died in 323 BC.
> Charlemagne was crowned in Rome on Christmas Day, AD 800.

Recall too that American usage prefers to write the time of day with small capitals:

> (A) The earthquake struck at 6:40 AM.

In British usage, this would appear as follows:

> The earthquake struck at 6.40 a.m.

A few publishers have recently adopted the practice of putting *all* abbreviations in small capitals, but this is not something you should imitate.

Many word processors can produce small capitals; if you can't produce them, use full capitals instead:

> Alexander the Great died in 323 BC.

Very occasionally, small capitals are used for emphasis, but it is usually preferable to use italics for this, or even boldface.

## 9.4 Parentheses

**Parentheses** (**( )**), also called **round brackets**, always occur in pairs. They have one major use and one or two minor uses.

Most commonly, a pair of parentheses is used to set off a strong or weak interruption, rather like a pair of dashes or a pair of bracketing commas. In the case of a strong interruption, very often it is possible to use either dashes or parentheses:

> The destruction of Guernica – and there is no doubt that the destruction was deliberate – horrified the world.
>
> The destruction of Guernica (and there is no doubt that the destruction was deliberate) horrified the world.

As a rule, however, we prefer parentheses, rather than dashes or bracketing commas, when the interruption is best regarded as a kind of 'aside' from the writer to the reader:

> On the (rare!) occasion when you use a Latin abbreviation, be sure to punctuate it correctly.
>
> The battle of Jutland (as you may recall from your school days) put an end to Germany's naval threat.
>
> The Basque language is not (as the old legend has it) exceedingly difficult to learn.

We also use parentheses to set off an interruption which merely provides additional information or a brief explanation of an unfamiliar term:

The number of living languages (currently about 6000, by most estimates) is decreasing rapidly.

The *bodegas* (wine cellars) of the Rioja are an essential stop on any visit to northern Spain.

The royal portraits of Velázquez (or Velásquez) are justly renowned.

The German philosopher Gottlob Frege (1848–1925) laid the foundations of formal logic and of semantics.

In the last two examples, the phrases in parentheses merely provide an alternative spelling of the painter's name and the birth and death dates of the philosopher. In all these examples, neither dashes nor bracketing commas would be possible, except that you might conceivably use dashes in the first. Note also the way I introduce each new punctuation mark in this book.

It is possible to put an entire sentence into parentheses, or even a series of sentences, if they constitute an interruption of an appropriate type:

It appears that 33% of girls aged 16–18 smoke regularly, but that only 28% of boys in this age bracket do so. (These figures are provided by a recent newspaper survey.)

Note that a sentence in parentheses is capitalized and punctuated in the normal fashion.

Do not overdo parentheses to the point of stuffing one entire sentence inside another:

> ★ The first-ever international cricket match (very few cricket fans are aware of this) was played between Canada and the United States in 1844.

This sort of thing is very common in the writing of those who neither plan their sentences ahead nor polish their writing afterward. If you find you have done this, rewrite the sentence in some less overcrowded way:

> Very few cricket fans are aware that the first-ever international cricket match was played between Canada and the United States in 1844. **or**
>
> The first-ever international cricket match was played between Canada and the United States in 1844. Very few cricket fans are aware of this.

Parentheses may also be used to represent options:

> The referees who decide whether an abstract should be accepted will not know the name(s) of the author(s).
>
> The (french) horn is an unusually difficult instrument to play.

The point of the last example is that the names *french horn* and *horn* denote the same instrument.

Finally, parentheses are used to enclose numerals or letters in an enumeration included in the body of a text:

> A book proposal prepared for a potential publisher should include at least (1) a description of the content, (2) an identification of the intended readership, (3) an

> explanation of why the book will be necessary or valuable and (4) a comparison with any competing books already in print.

Observe that, in contrast to what happens with dashes and bracketing commas, we **always** write both parentheses:

> He was smitten by a *coup de foudre* (as the French none too romantically put it).

Occasionally you may find yourself placing one set of parentheses inside another. Sometimes this is unavoidable, but you should avoid it whenever possible, since it makes your sentence hard to follow.

## 9.5 Square Brackets

There is only one common use for **square brackets** ([ ]). As was explained in Chapter 8, square brackets are used to set off an interruption within a direct quotation; refer to that chapter for details.

Very occasionally square brackets are used for citing references; see Chapter 10.

Specialist fields like mathematics and linguistics use square brackets for certain purposes of their own, but these are beyond the scope of this book.

## 9.6 The Ellipsis

The **ellipsis** (. . .), also called the **suspension** or **omission marks**, has just two uses.

First, as was explained in Chapter 8, the ellipsis is used to show that some material has been omitted from the middle of a direct quotation; see that chapter for details.

Second, the ellipsis is used to show that a sentence has been left unfinished. Unlike the dash, which is used to show that an utterance has been broken off abruptly (recall the unfortunate General Sedgwick!), the suspension shows that the writer or speaker has simply 'tailed off' into silence, deliberately leaving something unsaid:

> Colonel García leered at the prisoner: 'We want those names now. If we don't get them . . .'
>
> San Francisco gets a major earthquake about every sixty years. It has been ninety years since the last one . . .

This second usage is more typical of journalistic prose than of formal writing; excepting only when you are citing a direct quotation which seems to require it, you should generally avoid the ellipsis in formal writing.

## 9.7 The Slash

The **slash** (/), also called the **oblique**, the **virgule**, the **stroke**, the **solidus** or the **shilling mark**, has several uses, all of them rather minor.

First, it is used to separate alternatives:

> Applicants must possess a good university degree in French and/or have worked for two years in a French-speaking country.
>
> Each candidate must bring his/her identity card.
>
> If your work is badly punctuated, your reader may quickly decide that s/he has better things to do.

This usage is rather hard on the eye, and it is usually preferable to write the alternatives out in full:

> Each candidate must bring his or her identity card.

This style is particularly frequent in job advertisements:

> The University of Saffron Walden wishes to appoint a lecturer/senior lecturer in media studies.

Second, the slash may be used to represent a period of time:

> The 1994/95 football season was marred by frequent scandals.
>
> This office is open Tuesday/Saturday each week.

Third, the slash is used, especially in scientific writing, to represent the word *per* in units:

The density of iron is 7.87 g/cm$^3$.

Light travels at 300,000 km/sec.

Fourth, the slash is used in writing fractions, as in ¾ or *3/4*; in this use, it is often called the **scratch**. (See the next section for usage.)

Fifth, the slash is used in writing certain abbreviations. Virtually the only one of these you will find outside of specialist contexts is *c/o* for 'care of' in addresses:

Write to me at Sylvia Keller, c/o Andrea Mason, 37 The Oaks, Plumtree, East Sussex BN17 4GH.

Finally, slashes are used to separate lines of poetry when a poem is written solid, instead of being set out line by line:

When you are old and grey and full of sleep/And nodding by the fire, take down this book/And slowly read of the soft look/Your eyes had once, and of their shadows deep. (W. B. Yeats)

## 9.8 Numerals, Fractions and Dates

The compound numerals from twenty-one to ninety-nine are written with hyphens:

France is divided into ninety-six departments.

Mozart was only thirty-five years old when he died.

No additional hyphens are used in writing larger numbers:

A leap year has three hundred and sixty-six days.
The maximum possible score with three darts is one hundred and eighty.

In formal writing, the numerals from one to twenty are almost always written out:

The American flag has thirteen stripes.
We have four candidates for president.

Do **not** write:

★ The American flag has 13 stripes.
★ We have 4 candidates for president.

Larger numbers, however, may be written with digits, if you prefer:

The bomb killed 37 people and injured over 200 others.
Writing was invented less than 6000 years ago.

It is, however, always acceptable to write out numbers up to ninety-nine, and in fact some publishers will insist upon this; if you are writing for publication, you should check:

The bomb killed thirty-seven people and injured over 200 others.

When writing a four-digit numeral in digits (other than a date), American writers never use a comma, but British writers usually do. Hence Americans write *2000 years* and *3700 people*, while Britons often write *2,000 years* and *3,700 people*.

I consider such commas completely pointless, and I don't use them myself, but others may insist that you do so. A five-digit or larger numeral always takes one or more commas: *53,000 refugees*, *170,000 cases of AIDS*, *2,760,453 patents*.

Naturally, we make an exception for addresses and other special cases, in which numerals are always written with digits:

I lived for years at 4 Howitt Road in Belsize Park.

Observe that it is bad style to start a sentence with a numeral: either the number should be written out, or the sentence should be rewritten:

* 650 MPs sit in Parliament.
Six hundred and fifty MPs sit in Parliament.
There are 650 MPs in Parliament.

Fractions are always written with hyphens:

Almost three-fourths of the earth's surface is water.
More than one-half of babies born are male.

But note the following case:

One half of me wants to take the job while the other half doesn't.

Here the phrase *one half* is not really a fraction at all.

In formal writing, a fraction is always written out. You should **not** write things like the following:

★ Almost ¾ of the earth's surface is water.

In writing a date, it is increasingly common today to use no commas:

It was on 18 April 1775 that Paul Revere made his famous ride.
On December 7 1941 the Japanese attacked Pearl Harbor.
She died on the last day of November 1843.

An older style, still acceptable, puts commas around the year:

It was on 18 April, 1775, that Paul Revere made his famous ride.
On December 7, 1941, the Japanese attacked Pearl Harbor.
She died on the last day of November, 1843.

You may use either fashion, so long as you are consistent.

**Important note**: In British usage, a date is written day-month-year, while American usage prefers month-day-year. Hence, Britons write *23 March*, while Americans write *March 23*. This is a potentially serious problem when we use the abbreviated style of writing dates often found in letters and business documents: to a Briton, *5/7/84* means *5 July 1984*, while to an American it means *May 7 1984*. If you are writing something that might be read on the other side of the Atlantic, therefore, it is best to write out a date in full, to avoid any misunderstanding.

## 9.9 Diacritics

**Diacritics**, often loosely called 'accents', are the various little dots and squiggles which, in many languages, are written above, below or on top of certain letters of the alphabet to indicate something about their pronunciation. Thus, French has words like *été* 'summer', *août* 'August', *ça* 'that' and *père* 'father'; German has *Wörter* 'words' and *tschüss* 'good-bye'; Spanish has *mañana* 'tomorrow' and *ángel* 'angel'; Norwegian has *brød* 'bread' and *frå* 'from'; Polish has *łza* 'tear', *źle* 'badly' and *pięć* 'five'; Turkish has *kuş* 'bird' and *göz* 'eye'; Welsh has *tŷ* 'house' and *sïo* 'hiss', and so on. When you are citing a word, a name or a passage from a foreign language which uses diacritics, you should make every effort to reproduce those diacritics faithfully. Fortunately, most word processors can produce at least the commoner diacritics.

You are most likely to need to do this when citing names of persons or places or titles of literary and musical works. The French politician is *François Mitterrand*, the Spanish golfer is *José-María Olazábal*, the Polish linguist is *Jerzy Kuryłowicz*, the Turkish national hero is *Mustafa Kemal Atatürk*, the town in the former Yugoslavia is *Goražde*, Wagner's opera is the *Götterdämmerung* and the French film is *Zazie dans le Métro*. So far as you can produce them, therefore, these are the forms you should use even when writing in English. But don't overdo it. If an accepted English form exists, use that: write *Munich*, not *München*, *Montreal*, not *Montréal*, *The Magic Flute*, not *Die Zauberflöte*.

In English, diacritics are not normally used, but they occur in three situations. First, many foreign words and phrases have been borrowed into English, and some of these are not yet regarded as fully anglicized. Such forms should be written with their original diacritics, and they should also be written in italics, if possible, to show their foreign status:

Lloyd George was the Tories' *bête noire.*
She was an artist *manquée.*
The *Wörter und Sachen* approach is favoured by some etymologists.

Many other such items have become so completely anglicized that they are now usually treated as ordinary English words. Hence, most people now write *cafe*, rather than *café*, *naive*, rather than *naïve*, and *cortege*, rather than *cortège*, and such words are not normally italicized in any case. If you are in doubt about these, you should, as always, consult a good dictionary.

Second, one particular diacritic, the **diaeresis** (¨), is very occasionally written in English to show that a vowel is to be pronounced separately. A familiar example of this is the name *Zoë*, but other cases exist. A few people write *coöperate*, rather than *cooperate*, and *aërate*, rather than *aerate*, but the spellings with the diaeresis are now decidedly old-fashioned and not recommended. Usage varies with the surname *Brontë*: all the members of this famous family spelled their name with the diaeresis, which should therefore perhaps be retained by the usual rule of respecting the preferences of the owner of a name, but many people nevertheless now write *Bronte*.

Third, a **grave accent** (`) is occasionally written over the letter *e* in the ending *-ed* to show that it is pronounced as a separate syllable. Thus we write *a learnèd scholar* or *an agèd man* to show that *learnèd* and *agèd* are each pronounced here as two syllables. Compare *I learned French at school* and *He has aged rapidly*, in which *learned* and *aged* are pronounced as single syllables.

For convenience, here are the names of the commoner diacritics:

| | |
|---|---|
| **á** | the **acute accent** |
| **à** | the **grave accent** |
| **â** | the **circumflex accent** |
| **ā** | the **macron** |
| **ă** | the **breve** |
| **č** | the **hachek**, or **wedge**, or **caron** |
| **ü** | the **diaeresis**, or **trema**, or **umlaut** |
| **ñ** | the **tilde** |
| **ç** | the **cedilla** |
| **å** | the **ring**, or **bolle** |
| **ą** | the **ogonek**, or **hook** |
| **ø** | the **slash**, or **solidus**, or **virgule** |

## 9.10 The Other Marks on Your Keyboard

Your keyboard contains a number of other characters, most of which are not properly punctuation marks at all, and very few of which are normally used in formal writing, except in certain specialist disciplines. Here are the ones which are found most commonly, or which can be produced with a word processor; such special symbols are often informally called **dingbats**:

**%** the **per cent sign**

**$** the **dollar sign**

**£** the **pound sign**

**¢** the **cent sign**

**#** the **hash mark** (in computer parlance, the 'pound sign')

***** the **asterisk** (in the US, informally called a 'bug')

**•** the **bullet**

**@** the **at sign**

**&** the **ampersand**, or **and sign**

**¶** the **paragraph mark**, or **blind**, or **pilcrow**

**§** the **section mark**

**||** the **parallel mark**

**^** the **caret**

**~** the **swung dash** (informally called the 'twiddle' or 'tilde')

**_** the **underbar**

**<** the **less-than sign**

> the **greater-than sign**

< > **angle brackets**

{ } **braces** (also called **curly brackets**)

« » **guillemets** (French quotation marks)

» « **reversed guillemets** (German quotation marks)

+ the **plus sign**

± the **plus-or-minus sign**

= the **equal sign**

\ the **backslash**

| the **pipe**

· the **centre(d) dot**

You will undoubtedly be familiar with the use of the per cent sign, the dollar sign and the pound sign:

> Over 40% of Australia is desert.
> The USA bought Alaska for only $3 million.
> This word processor costs £1800.

Note that we write £42.50, and **not** * £42.50p, and similarly for other currencies.

Most computer keyboards lack the pound sign, but it can usually be produced in one way or another. If you absolutely can't produce a pound sign, it has become conventional in computing circles to use the hash mark instead (hence its other name):

> This word processor costs #1800.

In American English, the hash mark is used informally to represent the word 'number' before a numeral, as in *look for*

# 27 (A). This is not usual in British English, and it is out of place in formal writing.

The asterisk is occasionally used to mark footnotes; see Chapter 10. It also has one other rather curious use: it is sometimes used to replace a letter in writing a word which is felt to be too coarse to be written out in full, as in *f**k*. This is a usage mostly found in newspapers and magazines, in which writers are often careful to avoid offending their very broad readership. In most other types of writing, such words are normally written out in full if they are used at all. (Compare the somewhat similar use of the dash in section 6.2.)

A bullet may be used to mark each item in an enumeration if numbering of the items is not thought to be necessary; look at the summaries at the ends of most of the earlier sections of this book.

The at sign is chiefly confined to business documents, in which it stands for 'at a price of . . . each':

200 shower units @ £42.50

It is also used in electronic mail addresses to separate a username from the rest of the address, as in my e-mail address:

larryt@cogs.susx.ac.uk

The ampersand represents the word 'and' in the names of certain companies and legal firms, as in the name *Barton & Maxwell, Solicitors*. Except when citing such a name, you should **never** use an ampersand in place of 'and' in formal writing, nor should you use a plus sign for this purpose. The word 'and' is always written out.

The paragraph mark and the section mark are occasionally used to represent the words 'paragraph' and 'section' when referring to some part of a work: *in ¶ 2, in § 3.1.* They are only appropriate when brevity is important, such as in footnotes; in your text, you should write these words out: *in paragraph two, in section 3.1.*

The remaining symbols in my list have various particular uses in specialist disciplines, and sometimes in dictionaries, but they have no function in ordinary writing.

## 9.11 Priority Among Punctuation Marks

As I hope you have gathered by now, punctuation marks are, in most cases, independent of one another. Each mark is inserted to do a particular job, and using one mark neither allows you to drop another one which is independently required nor permits you to insert one or two extra marks which are not needed. There are, however, a few exceptions.

First of all, we never write two full stops at the end of a sentence. Observe the following examples:

> Officially, the clocks will go back at 2.00 a.m.
> Leo Durocher never in fact made that famous remark 'Nice guys finish last.'

The abbreviation and the direct quotation already end in full stops, so no second full stop is written. Similarly, if a sentence would logically end in two question marks, only the first is written:

Who wrote the sonnet that begins 'How do I love thee?'

If a sentence-final quotation ends in a question mark or an exclamation mark, no full stop follows:

Pontius Pilate famously asked, 'What is truth?'

However, a question mark *is* written after a full stop if this is logically required:

Does the flight arrive at 7.00 a.m. or 7.00 p.m.?

You already know that the second of two bracketing commas or dashes is not written at the end of a sentence. This is because the comma or dash that would logically appear there is 'outranked' by the full stop or other mark that appears at the end of the sentence:

The Spaniards and the Canadians are close to war over fishing rights, it would appear.
We commonly assume that there are only two sexes – but could we be wrong?

In the same way, a comma that should logically appear is suppressed if a colon or a semicolon is present at the same position:

The planet Venus is a hellhole, as the Russian probes have revealed; no human could survive for a moment on its surface.
Only two groups are excluded from the French Foreign Legion, according to the rules: women and Frenchmen.

In these examples the second bracketing commas that would logically appear after the words *revealed* and *rules* are suppressed by the following colon and semicolon. Here is a useful rule of thumb: a comma is **never** preceded or followed by any other punctuation mark at all, except possibly by a quotation mark or by a full stop which forms part of an abbreviation.

Chapter 10

# Punctuating Essays and Letters

There are a few special points to be considered in writing essays, reports and articles, and in writing letters. We will consider these points in this chapter. There is in practice a good deal of variation in these matters, and the usages I recommend here are those which are common and generally acceptable. You may find, however, that your teacher, your university tutor, your business firm or your publisher insists upon some different usages from those I describe here. If so, you should, of course, conform to those requirements. Note that printed books and popular magazines sometimes depart from the normal usages in order to make their pages look attractive or eye-catching; you should leave such decisions to designers and layout editors, and not try to imitate them yourself.

## 10.1 Titles and Section Headings

The title of a complete work is usually centred near the top of the first page; if possible, it should be printed either in large letters or in boldface, or even in both. It should not be italicized or placed in quotation marks, and it should not have a full stop at the end. Any punctuation or italics which are required for independent reasons should be used normally; this includes a question mark at the end if the title is a question. If there is a subtitle, a colon should be placed at the end of the title proper; unless the title and the subtitle are both very short, it is best to use two lines.

There are two possible styles for capitalization: you may capitalize every significant word, or you may capitalize only those words which intrinsically require capitals, as explained in Chapter 7. (The first word should be capitalized in any case.) Here are some examples; I have used the second style of capitalization:

**The origin of Mozart's *Requiem***

**The imposition of English in Wales**

**Classroom discipline in Birmingham schools:**
**a case study**

**Football hooligans: why do they do it?**

**The parasites of the quaking aspen (*Populus tremuloides*)**

**'Thou unnecessary letter':**
**the history of the letter Z in English**

The quotation marks in the last example are used because the first phrase is a quotation from Shakespeare.

In a work which is very short (no more than five or six pages), it is rarely necessary to divide the work into sections.

Longer works, however, are usually best divided into sections which are at least named and possibly also numbered; numbers are recommended if there are more than two or three sections. Section headings are usually placed in boldface but in ordinary-sized type; they are not centred but placed at the left-hand margin. A section heading may be placed on a separate line (with a following blank line), or it may be placed at the beginning of a paragraph; only in the second case should there be a full stop at the end. Here is an example illustrated in each of the two styles:

> **3. The dictatorship of Primo de Rivera**
>
> In 1923, King Alfonso XIII handed over power to General Primo de Rivera, who immediately abrogated the Constitution, dissolved the Cortes and installed a brutal right-wing dictatorship . . . **or**
>
> **3. The dictatorship of Primo de Rivera.** In 1923, King Alfonso XIII handed over power to General Primo de Rivera, who immediately abrogated the Constitution, dissolved the Cortes and installed a brutal right-wing dictatorship . . .

Either style is acceptable. Note that the *first* paragraph after a title or a section heading is not indented; all following paragraphs should be indented.

If the work is very long, or if it consists of a number of points and subpoints (as is often the case with bureaucratic and business documents), then the sections may be further divided into subsections. In this case, you should certainly number all the sections and subsections, in the following manner (these passages are taken from John Wells's book *Accents of English*) (Wells 1982):

> **6. North American English**
>
> **6.1. General American**
>
> **6.1.1. Introduction**
>
> In North America it is along the Atlantic coast that we find the sharpest regional and social differences in speech . . .
>
> 6.1.2. The ***thought-lot*** **merger**
>
> A well-known diagnostic for distinguishing the northern speech area of the United States from the midland and southern areas is the pronunciation of the word *on* . . .

## 10.2 Footnotes

A **footnote** is a piece of text which, for some reason, cannot be accommodated within the main body of the document and which is therefore placed elsewhere. It is usual, and preferable, to place footnotes at the bottom of the page on which they are referred to, but this usually requires a great deal of fiddling about, unless you are lucky enough to have a word processor which arranges footnotes automatically. It is easier for the writer to put all the footnotes at the end of the document, but of course this makes life harder for the reader, who is obliged to do a lot of fumbling about in order to find the footnotes. **Exception**: If you are preparing a work for publication, then you must put all the footnotes on separate pages at the end of your document; such notes are called **endnotes**. But don't use endnotes in a document which will pass directly from your hands to the reader.

There are two main rules in the use of footnotes. First:

Do **not** use a footnote if you can possibly avoid it.

The overuse of footnotes will make your work laborious to read: a reader who finds herself constantly directed away from your text to consult footnotes will lose the thread of your writing and possibly lose her place altogether. The use of avoidable footnotes is self-indulgent and sloppy, and it is contemptuous of the reader. Academic writers in particular are often guilty of this kind of objectionable behaviour. Far too often I have wearily chased up a footnote only to find something like this at the end of the trail:

[7] This term is used in the sense of Halliday (1968). **or**
[23] As is commonly assumed. **or even**
[51] (1878–1941).

(The last example provides nothing but the birth and death dates of someone mentioned in the text.) Such trivial asides could easily be incorporated into the main text inside parentheses, and that's where they should be, if they're going to be present at all.

But **think** whether such information needs to be present at all. If the term being footnoted in the first of these examples is so obscure, why not merely explain it? What is your reader supposed to do if she doesn't recognize it – put your book down, go off to the library and find Halliday (1968), and read that book from cover to cover? You should make every effort to make your work a pleasure to read. Reading it should not be an epic struggle on the part of your hapless reader.

If you decide that a footnote is unavoidable, then the standard procedure is to flag it in the text with a superscript numeral at the point at which it is relevant:

> Let us consider the case of Algerian immigrants in Marseille, for whom a substantial number of case studies[6] are now available.

At the bottom of the page (one hopes), the reader will find your footnote:

> [6]I am indebted to Sylvette Vaucluse for kindly providing me with unpublished data from her own research, and to Sylvette Vaucluse and Jacqueline Labéguerie for illuminating discussions of these case studies. They are not to be held responsible for the use I make of the work here.

If you can't produce superscript numerals, then the alternative is to place the footnote numeral inside of parentheses or, preferably, square brackets:

> Let us consider the case of Algerian immigrants in Marseille, for whom a substantial number of case studies[6] are now available.

The second rule about footnotes is also a prohibition:

> Do **not** use a footnote merely to introduce a reference to work which you are citing.

The proper way to cite such references is explained in the next section.

If your footnotes are very few in number (and one hopes that they are), it is permissible to use symbols rather than numerals to flag them. The symbol most commonly used for this purpose is the **asterisk** (*):

> Let us consider the case of Algerian immigrants in Marseille, for whom a substantial number of case studies* are now available.

I do not recommend this, for two reasons. First, if you happen to be writing in a specialist field in which the asterisk is used for other purposes (as it is in mathematics and linguistics), then your reader may not immediately recognize what the asterisk is doing. Second, if you want to put more than one footnote on a page, you have a problem. Printed books sometimes trot out a startling array of further doodahs to mark additional footnotes, such as the **dagger**, or **obelisk**, or **obelus** (†) and the **double dagger**, or **diesis** (‡). Using these squiggles will at least force you to put your footnotes at the bottom of the page, but it is far better to use numerals.

A footnote should be as brief as possible, and here alone it is preferable to make liberal use of readily identifiable abbreviations, including those Latin abbreviations to which I objected so strongly in Chapter 7.

Footnotes at the bottom of the page must be set off in some way from the main text. The common way of doing this is to put the footnotes in a smaller typeface. If you can't do this, a horizontal line is permissible.

If a footnote is too long to fit at the bottom of its page, it may be continued at the bottom of the next page. When this starts to happen to you, though, you may well begin to wonder whether that footnote is really essential after all.

Don't use footnotes if you can avoid them.

## 10.3 References to Published Work

Especially in academic writing, it is frequently necessary to refer in your text to other work of which you have made use or to which you want to direct the reader's attention. There are several different systems for doing this, and they are not all equally good.

By far the best system is the **Harvard system**, also called the **author–date system**, and this is the one I recommend. In the Harvard system, you provide a reference in the form of the author's surname and the year of publication; this is enough to direct the reader to the list of full references in your bibliography. Like any brief interruption, the date is enclosed in parentheses, and the surname goes there too, unless it is a structural part of the sentence. Multiple references are separated by commas. Where necessary, a few words of explanation may also be placed inside the parentheses. Here are some examples:

A recent study (Barrutia 1992) has uncovered further evidence for this analysis.

Several earlier investigators (Wale 1967, Ciaramelli 1972, Mott 1974) reported just such a correlation.

These figures are cited from Curtis (1987), the most comprehensive treatment to date.

Roberts has developed this approach in a series of publications (1981, 1984, 1989).

This topic has been explored most thoroughly by Lumley (1984, 1985, 1987, 1988).

Very many investigators (for example, Scacchi 1980) have argued for the first view.

If your work includes references to two people with the same surname, use initials to distinguish them. For example, if you have both John Anderson and Stephen Anderson in your bibliography:

This approach is explored by J. Anderson (1995).

If you need to cite two or more works by the same author published in the same year, use the letters *a*, *b*, *c*, and so on, to distinguish them:

The significance of these observations is denied by several workers, including Goodlet (1990b), Shiels (1992) and White (1993a).

If you need to do this, then, of course, be sure you use the letters consistently right throughout your references and your bibliography. Finally, if you want to refer the reader to some specific pages of the work you are citing, put the page numbers after the date, with a colon intervening:

> For a description of this method, see Rogers (1978: 371–2).

Many people do not put a white space after the colon in this usage, but I prefer to do so. Some people use a comma instead of a colon, but the colon is much easier on the eye and avoids any possibility of ambiguity, so I recommend that you use a colon.

Very occasionally you may need to cite something which somebody else has told you personally, either in conversation or in a personal letter. You do it like this:

> This information has been provided by Jane Guest (personal communication).

In academic circles it is permissible to abbreviate *(personal communication)* to *(p.c.)*.

A second widely used system is the **number system**, which is particularly popular in some scientific circles. Here a reference takes the form merely of a number enclosed in square brackets:

> A recent study [17] has uncovered further evidence for this analysis.
>
> Several earlier investigators [5, 11, 23] reported just such a correlation.

This saves space, but it has several drawbacks: it gives the reader no clue as to what work is being cited, it obliges you to number all the items in your bibliography, it makes the citing of page numbers slightly awkward and it forces you to cite an author's name when that name is part of your sentence but to leave the name out otherwise. I don't like this system, and I don't recommend it, but you may at times find yourself obliged to use it.

There are several other ways of citing references, but they are all highly objectionable and should never be used. A few writers put complete references into the body of the text, which is both distracting to the reader and absurdly inefficient, especially when the same work is cited several times. Very many writers have the bad habit of putting references into footnotes and flagging them just like ordinary footnotes; not only does this practice clutter the page with pointless footnotes, but it wastes the reader's time by constantly sending her off to consult 'footnotes' which are nothing but references. Do **not** use footnotes for references.

Worst of all is the dreadful hotchpotch used by many scholars in arts subjects, in which references are presented sometimes in footnotes and sometimes in the text and are almost always incomplete and full of cryptic abbreviations which the reader has no hope of deciphering. If you spatter your work with unexplained exotica like *DCELC*, *REW* 1317, *Schuch. Prim.*, *Urquijo BSP IV, 137 ff.*, and so on, then no doubt the other eighteen specialists in your field will follow you, all right, but the rest of your readers will be helpless. Do **not** provide incomplete references, and do **not** use unexplained abbreviations. If you find that the use of some abbreviation is unavoidable, then explain it clearly, either the first time you use it, or, better still, in a list of abbreviations at the *beginning* of your work.

The perpetrators of such inexcusable obscurity have the further outrageous habit of citing references with the Latin abbreviations *ibid.* and *op. cit.* What do these mean? Well, *ibid.* means 'This is another reference to the last thing I cited; it's back there somewhere, maybe only a page or two, if you're lucky.' And *op. cit.* means 'This is another reference to the work by this author which I cited some time ago, and, if you want to know what it is, you can leaf back through twenty-five or fifty pages to find it, you miserable peasant.' (Technically, they mean 'in the same place' and 'in the work cited', but my explanations are far more honest.) **Don't use these ghastly things.** A writer who uses them is expressing utter contempt for the reader, and should be turned over to the Imperial Chinese Torturer for corrective treatment.

Use the Harvard system. It's vastly superior to everything else.

## 10.4 Bibliography

In any piece of written work in which you have cited references to published works, it is necessary to provide a **bibliography**, or list of references, at the end of your work.

You should provide only **one** such list. For some reason,

many people have acquired the curious belief that they should give *two* lists: one list of all the references in the order they occur, and a second alphabetical list, or something similar. This silly practice is a pointless waste of time and paper: there should be only one list of references, and the references in your text should direct the reader straight to that list, as explained in section 10.3 above.

The precise form of your bibliography may vary slightly, depending on what system you have used for citing references in your document. Here I shall assume that you have used the Harvard system, as recommended.

The bibliography is put into alphabetical order according to the surnames of the authors and editors you are citing. If you cite two authors with the same surname, put them in alphabetical order by their first names or initials. If you cite several different works by the same author, put them in date order, earliest to latest. If you have two or more works with the same author and the same date, use the *a*, *b*, *c* system described in the last section. When you cite multiple works by the same author, that author's name need be written out only once; for succeeding works, you can use an extra-long dash instead of repeating the name. A book with no author or editor is listed alphabetically by its title.

There are just three types of work which are very commonly cited in bibliographies: books, articles in books, and articles in journals. For each type, the form of the reference is slightly different, but, above all, the reference must be **complete**.

For a book, you must give the name(s) of the author(s) or editor(s), the date, the title, the place of publication and the name of the publisher. For an article in a book, you must give the name(s) of the author(s), the title of the article and the first and last pages, as well as full information on the book itself, as just described. For an article in a journal, you must give the name(s) of the author(s), the date, the title of the article, the name of the journal, the volume number and the first and last pages. Names of authors should be given just as they appear in their publications.

If you are citing two or more articles from a single book, you can put that book into your list as usual, and cross-refer each article to that book, as shown below.

There are several slightly different systems for arranging and punctuating references in a bibliography, almost all of them acceptable. They differ chiefly in whether they use full stops or commas to separate parts of the reference, in whether they put quotation marks around the titles of articles, and in where they place the date. I recommend full stops rather than commas, single quotation marks around titles of articles, and the placing of the date immediately after the author's name, and that is the system used in my examples below. Standard sources like *The MLA Style Guide* often recommend slightly different systems, and your tutor or publisher may insist upon one of these; in that case, you should fall into line, but make sure your references are complete.

Here is a sample bibliography; note that each item is

presented with what is called a 'hanging indent' (every line indented except the first):

Anderson, Henrietta. 1986. *A Study of Shoes*. New York: Cavalier Press.

— 1989a. *American Footwear: A Cultural History*. Boston: Institute for American Cultural Studies.

— 1989b. *The Rise and Rise of the Stiletto Heel*. New York: Cavalier Press.

Cannon, Felix (ed.). 1964. *European Footwear: A Collection of Readings*. Oxford: John Compton & Sons.

Ginsberg, Sylvie and Kate Bruton (eds). 1977. *If the Shoe Fits: Essays on the History of Footwear*. San Diego: Malibu Press.

Halliwell, C. N. 1990. 'The Irish brogue'. In C. L. James and P. T. Caldwell (eds). *British and Irish Footwear 1720–1880*. Dublin: Irish Academy of Arts. Pp. 173–203.

Institute for American Cultural Studies. 1978. *A Sourcebook on American Costume*. Boston: Institute for American Cultural Studies.

Jensen, Carla. 1964. 'The wellington boot'. In Cannon (1964), pp. 358–71.

Kaplan, Irene. 1983. 'The evolution of the stiletto heel'. *American Journal of Costume* 17: 38–51.

— 1990a. Review of Anderson (1989b). *American Journal of Costume* 24: 118–121.

— 1990b. 'The platform shoe and its influence'. *Boots and Shoes* 23: 154–178.

Maxwell, Catherine. 1982. 'The ski boot: practical footwear or fashion accessory?' *Boots and Shoes* 15: 1–37.

Maxwell, Catherine and Henrietta Anderson. 1981. 'The great American sneaker'. *Boots and Shoes* 14: 77–92.

Maxwell, George. 1964. 'Italian Renaissance footwear'. In Cannon (1964), pp. 105–138.

*Shoes and Boots: A Compendium.* 1950. London: British Museum.

Note carefully how these references are given. If you need to cite some other kind of work, such as a newspaper article, a sound recording, a film, a video, a radio or television broadcast or a CD-ROM, you should consult a comprehensive source such as *The MLA Style Manual*. However, so long as your reference is complete, you can't go too far wrong.

One further point. If you have to enter a title in your alphabetical list, ignore the words *the*, *a* and *an* at the beginning. So, a book entitled *A History of Footwear* would be listed under H, not under A, and the newspaper called *The New York Times* would be listed under N, not T.

If you are using the number system for citing references, then, of course, each item in your bibliography must be preceded by its number. You should still, however, put those items in alphabetical order. Many people who use the number system simply list the items in the order in which they occur in the text. This allows the reader to find a particular reference, all right, but she can no longer glance at your bibliography to see if particular authors or works are present. All readers will find this unhelpful, at best, and a university tutor is likely to be very annoyed.

## 10.5 Paragraphing

It is beyond the scope of this book to treat paragraphing in detail. Here I content myself with a few brief remarks.

Every piece of written work should be broken up into a series of reasonably small paragraphs, and each new paragraph should represent some kind of break, however small, in the continuity of the text. Some people have trouble with this, and tend to produce enormous paragraphs running to a whole page or more. This is very tiring for the reader and should be avoided. If you have this kind of problem, try studying the paragraphs in any longish section of this book; this may help you to get a grasp of where it is appropriate to start a new paragraph.

As remarked above, the first paragraph after a title or a section heading is not indented (again, look at the paragraphs in this book). Every succeeding paragraph should be indented; the tab key on any keyboard will do this for you.

For certain kinds of writing, such as technical reports and business letters, there is another format which is sometimes preferred. In this second format, every paragraph is separated from the next by a blank line, and no paragraphs are indented. This format uses more paper, and it is not normal in other types of writing.

## 10.6 Punctuating Letters

Letters require very little punctuation, apart from whatever is needed for independent reasons. The address on the envelope looks like this:

Joanna Barker
54 Cedar Grove
Brighton BN1 7ZR

There is no punctuation at all here. Note especially that the number *54* is not followed by a comma. In Britain, it was formerly common practice to put a comma in this position, but such commas are pointless and are no longer usual.

The same goes for the two addresses in the letter itself: your own address (the *return address*), usually placed in the top right-hand corner, and the recipient's address (the *internal address*), usually placed at the left-hand margin, below the return address:

168 Trent Avenue
Newark NG6 7TJ

17 March 1995

Joanna Barker
54 Cedar Grove
Brighton BN1 7ZR

Note the position of the date, and note that the date requires no punctuation.

In British English, the *greeting* is always followed by a comma:

Dear Esther, **or** Dear Mr Jackson,

In American usage, only a personal letter takes a comma here, while a business letter takes a colon:

Dear Esther, **but** (A) Dear Mr. Jackson:

If you are writing to a firm or an institution, and you have no name, you may use the greeting *Dear Sir/Madam.*

The *closing* always takes a comma:

Yours lovingly, **or** Yours faithfully,

Note that only the first word of the closing is capitalized. In British usage, it is traditional to close with *Yours sincerely* when writing to a named person but *Yours faithfully* when using the *Dear Sir/Madam* greeting, but this distinction is anything but crucial. American usage prefers *Yours sincerely* or *Sincerely yours* (A) for all business letters. Things like *Yours exasperatedly* are only appropriate, if at all, in letters to newspapers.

In a personal letter, of course, you can use any closing you like: *Yours lovingly*, *Looking forward to seeing you*, *It's not much fun without you*, or whatever.

# Bibliography

Achtert, Walter S. and Joseph Gibaldi. 1985. *The MLA Style Manual.* New York: The Modern Language Association of America.

Carey, G. V. 1958. *Mind the Stop: A Brief Guide to Punctuation*, 2nd edn. London: Penguin.

Pullum, Geoffrey K. 1984. 'Punctuation and human freedom'. *Natural Language and Linguistic Theory* 2: 419–25. Reprinted in Geoffrey K. Pullum, 1991, *The Great Eskimo Vocabulary Hoax and Other Irreverent Essays on the Study of Language*, Chicago: University of Chicago Press, pp. 67–75.

Trask, R. L. 1995. *Language: The Basics*. London: Routledge.

Wells, J. C. 1982. *Accents of English*, 3 vols. Cambridge: Cambridge University Press.

# Other Useful Works on Punctuation

Gowers, Sir Ernest. 1962. *The Complete Plain Words*. Harmondsworth: Penguin. Chapter 10: 'Punctuation'.

Jarvie, Gordon. 1992. *Chambers Punctuation Guide*. Edinburgh: Chambers.

# Index

# READ MORE IN PENGUIN

In every corner of the world, on every subject under the sun, Penguin represents quality and variety – the very best in publishing today.

For complete information about books available from Penguin – including Puffins, Penguin Classics and Arkana – and how to order them, write to us at the appropriate address below. Please note that for copyright reasons the selection of books varies from country to country.

**In the United Kingdom**: Please write to *Dept. EP, Penguin Books Ltd, Bath Road, Harmondsworth, West Drayton, Middlesex UB7 0DA*

**In the United States**: Please write to *Consumer Services, Penguin Putnam Inc., 405 Murray Hill Parkway, East Rutherford, New Jersey 07073-2136.* VISA and MasterCard holders call 1-800-631-8571 to order Penguin titles

**In Canada**: Please write to *Penguin Books Canada Ltd, 10 Alcorn Avenue, Suite 300, Toronto, Ontario M4V 3B2*

**In Australia**: Please write to *Penguin Books Australia Ltd, 487 Maroondah Highway, Ringwood, Victoria 3134*

**In New Zealand**: Please write to *Penguin Books (NZ) Ltd, Private Bag 102902, North Shore Mail Centre, Auckland 10*

**In India**: Please write to *Penguin Books India Pvt Ltd, 11 Community Centre, Panchsheel Park, New Delhi 110017*

**In the Netherlands**: Please write to *Penguin Books Netherlands bv, Postbus 3507, NL-1001 AH Amsterdam*

**In Germany**: Please write to *Penguin Books Deutschland GmbH, Metzlerstrasse 26, 60594 Frankfurt am Main*

**In Spain**: Please write to *Penguin Books S. A., Bravo Murillo 19, 1°B, 28015 Madrid*

**In Italy**: Please write to *Penguin Italia s.r.l., Via Vittorio Emanuele 45/a, 20094 Corsico, Milano*

**In France**: Please write to *Penguin France, 12, Rue Prosper Ferradou, 31700 Blagnac*

**In Japan**: Please write to *Penguin Books Japan Ltd, Iidabashi KM-Bldg, 2-23-9 Koraku, Bunkyo-Ku, Tokyo 112-0004*

**In South Africa**: Please write to *Penguin Books South Africa (Pty) Ltd, P.O. Box 751093, Gardenview, 2047 Johannesburg*

# READ MORE IN PENGUIN

## REFERENCE

**The Penguin Dictionary of Literary Terms and Literary Theory**
J. A. Cuddon

'Scholarly, succinct, comprehensive and entertaining, this is an important book, an indispensable work of reference. It draws on the literature of many languages and quotes aptly and freshly from our own' – *The Times Educational Supplement*

**The Penguin Dictionary of Symbols**
Jean Chevalier and Alain Gheerbrant, translated by John Buchanan-Brown

This book draws together folklore, literary and artistic sources and focuses on the symbolic dimension of every colour, number, sound, gesture, expression or character trait that has benefited from symbolic interpretation.

**Roget's Thesaurus of English Words and Phrases**
Edited by Betty Kirkpatrick

This new edition of Roget's classic work, now brought up to date for the nineties, will increase anyone's command of the English language. Fully cross-referenced, it includes synonyms of every kind (formal or colloquial, idiomatic and figurative) for almost 900 headings. It is a must for writers and utterly fascinating for any English speaker.

**The Penguin Guide to Synonyms and Related Words**
S. I. Hayakawa

'More helpful than a thesaurus, more humane than a dictionary, the *Guide to Synonyms and Related Words* maps linguistic boundaries with precision, sensitivity to nuance and, on occasion, dry wit' – *The Times Literary Supplement*

**The Penguin Book of Exotic Words** Janet Whitcut

English is the most widely used language today, its unusually rich vocabulary the result of new words from all over the world being freely assimilated into the language. With entries arranged thematically, words of Saxon, Viking, French, Latin, Greek, Hebrew, Arabic and Indian origin are explored in this fascinating book.

JMA DODD

PENGUIN REFERENCE

# The Penguin Dictionary of English Grammar

R. L. Trask was born in western New York State in 1944. Having come to England in 1970, he obtained his Ph.D. from the University of London in 1983. He taught linguistics at the University of Liverpool from 1979 to 1988, and then at the School of Cognitive and Computing Science (now the Linguistics and English Language Department) at the University of Sussex. His special interests are historical linguistics, grammar and the Basque language. He wrote a number of books, including *A Dictionary of Grammatical Terms in Linguistics, Language Change, Language: The Basics, The Penguin Guide to Punctuation, The Penguin Dictionary of English Grammar* and *Mind the Gaffe. How to Write Effective Emails*, one of the Penguin Writers' Guides series, was sadly his last book for Penguin as he died in 2004.

The Penguin Dictionary of

# ENGLISH GRAMMAR

R. L. Trask

PENGUIN BOOKS

PENGUIN BOOKS

Published by the Penguin Group
Penguin Books Ltd, 80 Strand, London WC2R 0RL, England
Penguin Group (USA) Inc., 375 Hudson Street, New York, New York 10014, USA
Penguin Group (Canada), 10 Alcorn Avenue, Toronto, Ontario, Canada M4V 3B2
(a division of Pearson Penguin Canada Inc.)
Penguin Ireland, 25 St Stephen's Green, Dublin 2, Ireland
(a division of Penguin Books Ltd)
Penguin Group (Australia), 250 Camberwell Road, Camberwell, Victoria 3124, Australia
(a division of Pearson Australia Group Pty Ltd)
Penguin Books India Pvt Ltd, 11 Community Centre, Panchsheel Park, New Delhi – 110 017, India
Penguin Group (NZ), cnr Airborne and Rosedale Roads, Albany, Auckland 1310, New Zealand
(a division of Pearson New Zealand Ltd)
Penguin Books (South Africa) (Pty) Ltd, 24 Sturdee Avenue, Rosebank 2196, South Africa

Penguin Books Ltd, Registered Offices: 80 Strand, London WC2R 0RL, England

www.penguin.com

First published 2000
27



Set in ITC Stone
Typeset by Rowland Phototypesetting Ltd, Bury St Edmunds, Suffolk
Printed in England by Clays Ltd, St Ives plc

# Preface

GRAMMAR is the study of word structure and sentence structure. Grammar has been pursued for centuries, and a number of different approaches have been developed and elaborated. These approaches differ to some extent in the analyses they recognize, and, inevitably, they differ also in their terminology.

Many of the most venerable traditional terms are still in use today, such as ADJECTIVE, TRANSITIVE VERB, DIRECT OBJECT and RELATIVE CLAUSE. Other traditional terms are now obsolete or at least old-fashioned, such as SUBSTANTIVE and NOUN CLAUSE. At the same time, important new terms, not used by our ancestors, have been introduced into the subject and have become indispensable; examples are DETERMINER, NOUN PHRASE, COMPLEMENT CLAUSE and SUBJECT RAISING.

Such change in terminology is natural and inevitable in any field of study. However, the existence today of several quite distinct approaches to the study of grammar has the unappealing consequence that grammarians of different persuasions use somewhat different terminology. For example, the proponents of transformational grammar attach great importance to the concepts they call DEEP STRUCTURE and SURFACE STRUCTURE, which are not even recognized in other approaches. And the authors of the QUIRK GRAMMARS of English employ a collection of innovating names for labelling types of adverbial, such as SUBJUNCT and ADJUNCT, terms used by no one else for this purpose.

Worse still, different grammarians sometimes use the same term in quite different senses. Examples of this include ADJUNCT, PARTICLE, CONJUNCT and COMPLEMENT, terms which can denote rather different things depending upon who is using them.

Irritating though it may be, this variation in terminology is not vast. Most grammarians today use much the same terminology as other grammarians, and the differences in usage are only an exasperating little nuisance, not a formidable obstacle to understanding.

The purpose of this book is to introduce our present-day grammatical terminology as clearly as possible. Virtually every significant term is entered and explained, usually with some examples to illustrate the use of the term. Competing and conflicting usages are carefully explained, and there are numerous cross-references to related terms.

This book treats only the terminology of grammar. Terms pertaining to the study of other areas of language, such as pronunciation, meaning and history, are not covered here. Punctuation is included, but only in its main points; for more detailed information, see *The Penguin Guide to Punctuation*. The focus throughout is on the grammar of English, but the dictionary nevertheless includes grammatical terms which are chiefly important in the grammatical study of other languages, such as ABLATIVE and GENDER.

R. L. Trask

# A

**abbreviation** A brief way of writing a word or a phrase that could also be written out in full, using only the letters of the alphabet and possibly full stops. Examples are *Dr* for *Doctor*, *Prof.* for *Professor*, *Capt.* for *Captain* and *lx* for *linguistics*. In British usage, an abbreviation that contains the first and last letters of the full expression, like *Dr*, does not take a full stop; in American usage, it does, and *Dr.* is preferred. Many abbreviations are derived from Latin equivalents for English words and phrases, such as *lb.* for *pound(s)*, *e.g.* for *for example*, *i.e.* for *in other words* and *et al.* for *and others*. An abbreviation does not normally have a distinct pronunciation of its own: we pronounce *Dr* as 'Doctor' and *e.g.* as 'for example'. But there are exceptions: the abbreviation *p.* for *pence* is sometimes pronounced 'pee'. However, saying 'ee-jee' for *e.g.* or 'eye-ee' for *i.e.* is eccentric. Some people extend the term 'abbreviation' to include ACRONYMS and INITIALISMS, but this use is neither usual nor recommended. An abbreviation must be distinguished from a clipped form (see under CLIPPING), which is not an abbreviation but a real word, and from a LOGOGRAM, which is not constructed from letters of the alphabet.

**ablative** In a language with CASE, a particular case-form which denotes 'from', 'away from' and sometimes also 'out of'. An example is Basque *-tik*: attached to *etxe*, 'house', this gives *etxetik*, 'from the house, away from the house, out of the house'. Note that the 'ablative' case of Latin has a variety of miscellaneous uses, of which 'ablative' in the strict sense is only one: for example, it serves to provide the objects of most prepositions and to provide ABSOLUTE CONSTRUCTIONS in that language.

**absolute comparative** A COMPARATIVE form used with no standard of comparison: *Whizzo washes whiter*; *the younger generation*. That is, there is no answer provided to questions like 'Whiter than what?' or 'Younger than who?'

**absolute construction** (also **nominative absolute**) A phrase which is linked to the sentence containing it only by meaning and intonation, with no grammatical link of any kind. In the following examples, the bracketed sequences are absolute constructions: [*The day being cloudy,*] *we decided to stay home*; *The two women* [*, their business concluded,*] *retired to the bar*. Compare the example *The two women, having concluded their business, retired to the bar*, in which the phrase enclosed in commas *is* overtly linked to the rest of the sentence by the participle *having*.

**absolute transitive** A label sometimes applied to a VERB which can appear in the construction called UNSPECIFIED OBJECT DELETION.

**abstract noun** A NOUN which denotes something which is not physical and cannot be touched, such as *happiness, absence, advice, beauty* or *history*. Sometimes the term is extended to include nouns denoting events and actions, such as *arrival, explosion* and *somersault*. Compare CONCRETE NOUN.

**acceptability** The degree to which a linguistic form is considered normal, usable and comprehensible by speakers. Acceptability judgements arise in at least three circumstances. First, speakers of differing geographical, social and educational backgrounds may genuinely differ in what they regard as normal and acceptable. Here are a few examples of variably acceptable pieces of English; the per cent sign indicates that what follows is normal and acceptable to some speakers but not to others: % *You need your hair cutting*; % *It ain't funny*; % *You have to really give it a go*; % *This road is terrible any more*; % *We have agreed a deal*; % *Having said that, there's another option*; % *This paper was written by Mike and myself*. Second, some pieces of English 'stretch' the ordinary rules to the point at which many speakers find it difficult to decide whether or not they are normal: % *Susie was seen by the students while enjoying themselves*; % *There's the woman that I didn't know if she was coming or not*; % *I phoned the woman that I met at the party up*. Third, certain pieces of English which clearly conform to the rules of English grammar present serious difficulties for mental processing, and may therefore be rejected: % *The book the professor the students who failed their exam complained about is hard to understand* (this means 'The book which the professor who the students who failed their exam complained about is hard to understand'); % *The horse shot from the stable collapsed* (this means 'The horse which was shot from the stable collapsed'); % *Flounder flounder badger badger flounder* (this last means '[Flounder which [other] flounder badger] [[themselves] badger [other] flounder]').

**accidence** An old-fashioned term for INFLECTION, now little used.

**accusative** In a language with CASE, a particular case-form which serves to mark the DIRECT OBJECT of a verb. For example, the Latin noun *puella*, 'girl', has the accusative form *puellam*, as in *Puellam vidit*, 'I saw the girl'. In Latin and some other case languages, the accusative also has some further miscellaneous functions. The label *accusative* is sometimes applied to the OBJECTIVE case of English, but this is not really appropriate, since the English objective case serves a large number of functions, of which the direct object is only one.

**accusative and infinitive** The traditional name for a certain construction, found in English and in some other languages, in which a verb is followed by a NOUN PHRASE in the OBJECTIVE or ACCUSATIVE case and an INFINITIVE – in English, an infinitive preceded by *to*. Examples: *She wants me to come home; I persuaded them to wait a little longer; Her coach advised her to work on her serve.*

**acronym** In the simplest case, a word constructed by combining the initial letters of the principal words in a phrase to produce something which can be pronounced as a word and which has the same meaning as the original phrase. Examples include *scuba* for *self-contained underwater breathing apparatus*, *laser* for *light amplification by the stimulated emission of radiation* and *NATO* for *North Atlantic Treaty Organization*. Some acronyms depart from the canonical pattern in various ways, such as *radar* for *radio detection and ranging*. Some people extend the term *acronym* to an INITIALISM, which is formed in the same way but cannot be pronounced as a word, such as *BBC*.

**active voice** The characteristic of a verb-form, or of the clause containing it, whose SUBJECT represents the ACTOR, the person or thing presented as most directly responsible for the action or state denoted by the verb. In English, an INTRANSITIVE verb can only appear in the active voice: *The sun rose at 6.30 this morning; Susie smiled knowingly*. A TRANSITIVE verb most commonly occurs in the active voice: *The Mongols sacked Baghdad; Susie wrote this book; We are eating our dinner; Mike will collect our clothes from the dry cleaner*. In all these cases, the subject (the noun phrase at the beginning of the sentence) represents the person or thing responsible for the action. But, by choosing our verb appropriately, we can sometimes present either of two entities as responsible for the action or state: *The play delighted Susie* means about the same as *Susie enjoyed the play*, but the first presents *the play* as the source of the enjoyment, while the second presents *Susie* in that role, yet both sentences are in the active voice. Compare PASSIVE VOICE.

**actor** A generalization of the concept of an AGENT to include any person or thing that is presented as chiefly responsible for the action or state denoted by a sentence. In all of the following sentences, *Susie* is an actor, but *Susie* is an agent only in the first: *Susie washed the car; Susie received a letter; Susie dreamt about Mike; Susie weighs 55 kilos; Susie earns over £30,000; Susie has blue eyes*.

**adjectival** A label applied to any word, phrase or other linguistic item which modifies a NOUN in the way that an ADJECTIVE does. In the following examples, the bold italic item is adjectival; *my* ***new*** *book* (an adjective phrase consisting only of an adjective); *a* ***very long*** *opera* (an adjective phrase containing a degree modifier and an adjective); *the roses* ***in your garden*** (a prepositional phrase); *a* ***copper-producing*** *region* (a participial phrase); *his* ***damn-your-eyes*** *attitude* (an entire sentence reduced to a modifier); *the woman* ***you were talking to*** (a relative clause). A few linguists would also apply the label *adjectival* to a noun modifying another noun, as in *a* ***security*** *van* and *a* ***plastic*** *cup*, but this use is not normal.

**adjectival passive** The PASSIVE PARTICIPLE of a verb functioning as an ADJECTIVAL, sometimes accompanied by additional modifiers. In the following examples, the bold italic sequences are adjectival passives: *a* ***newly discovered*** *fossil;* ***well-taught*** *children; a* ***ruined*** *city; an* ***uninhabited*** *island*. Most examples, like those just cited, involve the participles of TRANSITIVE verbs, but INTRANSITIVE verbs can also form adjectival passives: *a **vanished** civilization; their **long-departed** spirits.*

**adjective** The PART OF SPEECH that includes words like *big, happy, beautiful, interesting* and *sudden*. An adjective typically modifies a NOUN and denotes a temporary or permanent quality: for example, *a beautiful picture* is a picture which is distinguished from other pictures by being (permanently) beautiful, and *an exhausted player* is a player who is distinguished from other players by being (temporarily) exhausted. But this is not a definition, and some adjectives are different: for example, the adjective *mere*, as in *a mere child*, does not denote a quality of the child; the adjective *heavy*, when used as in *a heavy smoker*, does not denote a quality of the smoker, but rather of her habit; and the phrase *a counterfeit dollar* does not denote any kind of dollar at all, but only something designed to resemble a dollar, even though *counterfeit* is still an adjective.

A typical adjective exhibits the following properties:

1. It can be used in ATTRIBUTIVE position, as in *a(n) __ book*.
2. It can be used in PREDICATE position, as in *This book is __*.
3. It can be compared either with *-er, -est* or with *more, most*; *big, bigger, biggest; beautiful, more beautiful, most beautiful*.
4. It can take a DEGREE MODIFIER: *very big, too big, rather big, so big, exceedingly big*.

Many adjectives, however, fail to exhibit some of these properties, such as *awake, chief, topmost* and *final*, but these are still adjectives, because the properties that they do exhibit are typical adjective properties.

Note carefully that an English NOUN can also appear in attributive position, but in this position it remains a noun and does not become an adjective. For example, *red, short* and *expensive* are adjectives, in *a red dress, a short dress* and *an expensive dress*, but *cotton, maternity* and *cocktail* are nouns in *a cotton dress, a maternity dress* and *a cocktail dress*. Note the following differences, where an asterisk marks an ungrammatical expression: *This dress is expensive*, but **This dress is maternity*; *a more expensive dress*, but **a more maternity dress*; *a very expensive dress*, but **a very maternity dress*. Like adjectives, nouns can appear in attributive position, but they do not exhibit the other properties of adjectives.

**adjective clause** Another term for RELATIVE CLAUSE, now little used.

**adjective phrase (AP)** A PHRASE constructed around an ADJECTIVE as its HEAD. Examples: *as clever as Jan* (head adjective *clever*), *bigger than Chicago* (*bigger*), *very interesting* (*interesting*), *not sober enough to drive* (*sober*). A bare adjective, like *big* in *a big meal*, is also an adjective phrase, one consisting of the head adjective and no other material. Compare ADJECTIVAL.

**adjunct 1**. Any part of a sentence which could in principle be removed without leaving behind something which is ungrammatical. An adjunct is always an ADVERBIAL of some kind. In the sentence *I ran into Susie in town yesterday*, the phrases *in town* and *yesterday* are adjuncts, since either or both could be removed without producing ungrammaticality, but nothing else is an adjunct, since removing anything else would produce an ungrammatical result. Compare ARGUMENT.

**2**. In the QUIRK GRAMMARS, an adverbial forming part of the structure of its clause, such as the examples just given. In these grammars, the term contrasts with CONJUNCT, DISJUNCT and SUBJUNCT.

**adnominal** A label applied to any element which modifies or determines the HEAD noun within a NOUN PHRASE. In the example *that rather nice bottle of wine we had at Susie's*, the determiner *that*, the adjective phrase *rather nice*, the prepositional phrase *of wine* and the relative clause *we had at Susie's* are all adnominal elements attached to the head noun *bottle*.

**adposition** Any item which is either a PREPOSITION or a POSTPOSITION.

**adverb** The PART OF SPEECH containing words like *slowly*, *happily*, *suddenly*, *here*, *tomorrow*, *soon* and *elsewhere*. An adverb usually modifies a VERB or a VERB PHRASE and provides information about the manner, time, place or circumstances of the activity or state denoted by the verb or verb phrase.

Adverbs are traditionally divided into three classes according to the kind of meaning they have, though this classification has nothing to do with their grammatical behaviour. A MANNER ADVERB says something about the manner in which an action is performed (*carefully*, *eagerly*); most of these end in *-ly*, but a few don't, such as the *fast* of *Susie drives too fast* and the very formal *thus*, as in *She did it thus*. A TIME ADVERB says something about the time of an action: *yesterday, soon, often, always, never*. A PLACE ADVERB says something about the location or direction of an action: *here, somewhere, elsewhere, uphill, ahead*.

Most adverbs of manner can be modified by DEGREE MODIFIERS: *very slowly, rather carefully, too fast, quite suddenly*. And most adverbs of manner can also be compared with *more* and *most* (rarely with *-er, -est*): *more carefully, most commonly, faster*. Most other adverbs do not accept degree modifiers or comparison, but a few do: *quite soon, very often, more often*.

Traditional grammarians, who worked with too few parts of speech, had the bad habit of applying the label *adverb* to almost any word that gave them trouble, including degree modifiers, PARTICLES and a number of rather miscellaneous words of doubtful category. Most linguists no longer do this, but some dictionaries and other reference books continue this practice; therefore, when your dictionary tells you that some word is an 'adverb', you should be a little cautious about accepting this at face value.

English has a rather distinctive subclass of adverbs called SENTENCE ADVERBS, which function rather differently from ordinary adverbs.

**adverbial** A functional label applied to any linguistic item, of whatever category, that behaves like an ADVERB with respect to the rest of its sentence. An adverbial may be an ADVERB PHRASE (including a bare adverb), a BARE-NP ADVERBIAL, a PREPOSITIONAL PHRASE, an ADVERBIAL CLAUSE or a NON-FINITE VERB PHRASE. In the following example, each of the bracketed sequences is an adverbial: *Susie confessed to me* [*rather unhappily*] *that she would have to go* [*to London*] [*this week*] [*to see her solicitor*] [*because there are problems with her contract*]. In the *QUIRK GRAMMARS, adverbials are classified into CONJUNCTS (sense 2), DISJUNCTS (sense 2), ADJUNCTS (sense 2) and SUBJUNCTS.*

**adverbial clause** (also **adverb clause)** Any SUBORDINATE CLAUSE which behaves as an ADVERBIAL with respect to the rest of its sentence. An adverbial clause may express time, place, manner, cause, purpose, concession, condition or another circumstance. In the examples below, the adverbial clauses are bracketed.

Time: [*As soon as she finished work,*] *Susie rushed off to play bridge; Let's have a drink* [*before we go*]; *I've been sleeping better* [*since I changed jobs.*]

Place: *Susie takes her mobile phone* [*wherever she goes.*]
Manner: *Susie drives* [*better than Mike does.*]
Cause: *I missed my flight* [*because my train was late.*]
Circumstance: [*Since Monday is a holiday,*] *let's take a day trip.*
Concession: [*Even though it had been raining for days,*] *the cricket pitch was in perfect condition; We're out of rice,* [*though we do have some pasta.*]
Condition: [*If Susie gets back in time,*] *she can go with us.*

Some of these types are often given distinctive names, such as TEMPORAL (for time), CIRCUMSTANTIAL, CONCESSIVE or CONDITIONAL clauses.

**adverbial participle** An ADVERBIAL headed by a PARTICIPLE: one type of NON-FINITE VERB PHRASE. In the following examples, the bracketed sequences are adverbial participles: [*Encouraged by her success,*] *she persevered;* [*Arriving a little early,*] *I decided to take a stroll.*

**adverb phrase (AdvP)** A PHRASE built around an ADVERB as its HEAD. An adverb phrase functions in a sentence in much the same way as an adverb, and the simplest type of adverb phrase is in fact a bare adverb. Examples of adverb phrases are *slowly, now, very soon, rather hurriedly* and *as gracefully as a cheetah.*

**adverb preposing** The construction in which an ADVERB occurs at the beginning of its sentence, instead of inside the VERB PHRASE. Examples: *Carefully she decanted the wine; Suddenly she burst into laughter; Nervously she lit a cigarette.*

**AdvP** The abbreviation for ADVERB PHRASE.

**affirmative** The opposite of NEGATIVE. The label is most commonly applied to a statement which contains no negative item, such as *There are rings around Jupiter* and *Susie sipped her brandy*, but it might equally be applied to questions and commands containing no negative, such as *Are you coming to Mike's party?* and *Wash your hands!*

**affix** A BOUND MORPHEME which is grammatical in nature. Affixes are classified according to the position they occupy. A PREFIX precedes the stem it is attached to, like the *un-* of *unhappy*, while a SUFFIX follows its stem, like the past-tense marker *-ed* in *walked*. See these entries for more examples. In some languages, more unusual types of affix exist, such as INFIXES. The addition of an affix to a word is *affixation*.

**agent** The SEMANTIC ROLE borne by the (typically human) entity that is the conscious and deliberate instigator of an action. Not every sentence contains an agent, but, if an agent is present, then, in English, it must normally be the SUBJECT. For example, *Susie* is an agent in each of the following: *Susie put up the shelves; Susie lit a cigarette; Susie slapped Mike; Susie wrote this book*. If an agent is present but is not the subject, then we must use the PASSIVE VOICE and precede the agent with *by*, as in *This book was written by Susie*. See also PATIENT.

In cases like *Susie spilled her wine* (assuming the spilling was not deliberate), *Susie fell asleep* and *Susie dreamt about Mike, Susie* is not an agent, because the actions are not deliberate. It is for cases like these that the superordinate term ACTOR has been introduced.

**agentless passive** See under PASSIVE VOICE.

**agglutination** Building a word by combining MORPHEMES into sequences without altering the forms of those morphemes. Agglutination occurs to a certain extent in English. For example, starting with the morpheme *happy*, we can attach first the prefix *un-* to obtain *unhappy* and then the suffix *-ness* to obtain *unhappiness*. Ignoring its pointless spelling change, this last word exhibits all three morphemes in clear and unaltered form, and this is agglutination. Other examples of agglutination in English are *dog-catchers* (*dog* plus *catch* plus *-er* plus *-s*) and *baby-sitting* (*baby* plus *sit* plus *-ing*). But most English words with multiple morphemes are not constructed in such a simple way; instead, the morphemes undergo various changes of shape: for example, *child* plus *-s* yields *children*; *take* plus *-ed* yields *took*; *photograph* plus *-y* yields *photography*; *electric* plus *-ity* yields *electricity*; *destroy* plus *-(t)ion* yields *destruction* (pay attention to the pronunciation, not to the spelling).

In some languages, such as Turkish, Japanese and Swahili, almost all words are constructed by agglutination, and we call these agglutinating languages. In others, such as Latin, French, Russian and the Eskimo languages, agglutination is almost unknown, and most words are formed in the messy way illustrated by the last English examples above. Compare INFLECTION.

**agreement** (also **concord**) The grammatical phenomenon in which the *form* of a particular word or phrase is determined by the *form* of another word or phrase which is grammatically linked with it. For example, English requires *this book* but *these books*: the form of the determiner *this/these* must agree with the form of the noun *book/books* (singular or plural), and English further requires *This book is good* but *These books are good,* where the form of the verb *be* (*is/are*) must agree with the noun phrase *this book* (singular) or *these books* (plural). English has only a small amount of agreement, but many other languages have far more. Compare GOVERNMENT.

**alienable possession** The property of a POSSESSIVE in which the possessed represents something that could, in principle, be readily separated from the possessor. Examples: *Susie's cigarettes, my car, their house.* Compare INALIENABLE POSSESSION.

**allomorph** See under MORPHEME.

**alternation** Variation in the form of a single MORPHEME, depending on which other morphemes it occurs next to. For example, the morpheme {sane} has the allomorph /seɪn/ in *sane* and *insane*, but the allomorph /sæn/ in *sanity* and *insanity*; the morpheme {electric} has the allomorph /ɪˈlektrɪk/ in *electric* but the allomorph /ɪlekˈtrɪs/ in *electricity*; and the morpheme {leaf} has the allomorph /li:f/ in *leaf* but the allomorph /li:v/ in *leaves*.

**ambiguity** The presence in a single string of words of two or more sharply distinct meanings. A LEXICAL AMBIGUITY results only from the presence of a word with different meanings, as in *The sailors enjoyed the port.* A STRUCTURAL AMBIGUITY results from assigning different syntactic structures to the words, as in *Visiting relatives can be a nuisance, Old men and women are easily frightened, The chicken is too hot to eat* and *Anne likes horses more than Mark.* Complex cases are possible, as in *I saw her duck* and the classic *Janet made the robot fast.*

**anacoluthon** An abrupt change from one syntactic construction to another in the middle of an utterance, leaving the original construction incomplete. Example: *I think you ought to – well, do it your own way.*

**analogy** The extension of an existing grammatical pattern to new cases. New words entering the language routinely acquire their inflections by analogy with existing words: for example, the new noun *CD-ROM* has acquired its plural *CD-ROMs* by analogy with other nouns like *dog*, plural *dogs*, and the new verb *fax* has acquired its past tense *faxed* by analogy with other verbs like *wash*, past *washed*. But even existing words can change their forms by analogy. For example, the verb *melt* formerly had the participle *molten*, but today this form is confined to use as an ADJECTIVAL PASSIVE, as in *molten metal*, and the participle has otherwise changed to the regular form *melted*, as in *The sun has melted the ice* (not *. . . *molten the ice*), by analogy with other verbs. Analogy need not bring about greater regularity. The verb *catch* formerly had the regular past tense *catched*, but this has been replaced by irregular *caught*, apparently by analogy with *teach*, past *taught*, and some American varieties have altered the past tense of *dive* from *dived* to *dove*, by analogy with verbs like *drive*, past *drove*.

**analytic construction** Another name for a PERIPHRASTIC construction.

**analytic language** A language in which the form of each word is invariable, and all grammatical markers are independent words. Vietnamese is a perfect example of such a language, and Chinese and Hawaiian come very close. English is not so strongly analytic, but it does have a significant degree of analytical character. Compare English *I will have loved*, in which every morpheme except the ending *-ed* is an independent word, with its Latin translation *amavero*, in which all the morphemes are bound and the whole thing is a single word.

**anaphor** (also **pro-form**) An item with little intrinsic meaning or reference of its own which takes its interpretation from another linguistic item in the same sentence or discourse, its ANTECEDENT. In the sentence *I asked Jan to check the proofs, and she did it*, *she* is an anaphor with *Jan* as its antecedent, and *did it* is an anaphor with *check the proofs* as its antecedent. The relation between an anaphor and its antecedent is one of *anaphora*, also called BINDING, COREFERENCE or (rarely) CONSTRUAL: we say that an antecedent binds its anaphor, or that it corefers with it. An anaphor that precedes its antecedent is occasionally called a CATAPHOR; an example is *she* in *After she finished dinner, Susie lit* *a cigarette*. See the entry for ANTECEDENT for further examples, and compare EXOPHOR.

The labels NULL ANAPHOR or ZERO ANAPHOR are sometimes applied to a blank space which functions like an anaphor. In the example *Susie got up and took a shower*, the subject position of the verb *took* is empty (compare . . . *and she took a shower*). This is an example of a null anaphor, since we still understand the empty subject position as referring to *Susie*.

**animate** A label applied to a NOUN or a NOUN PHRASE which denotes a human being or a higher animal. Examples: *tiger, salesman, student, shark, my mother, the Marx Brothers, that cute little cocker spaniel, the woman you were talking to*. The opposite is INANIMATE.

**anomalous** Departing in some way from the ordinary rules of the language. When an attempted sentence violates the grammatical rules of the language, we usually describe it as *ungrammatical* or *ill-formed* rather than *anomalous*; see ILL-FORMED. More commonly, we apply the label (*semantically*) *anomalous* to a sentence which is grammatically perfect but impossible to interpret, like the following example, in which the hash mark (#) indicates the anomaly: *#Jezebel killed Ahab, but Ahab didn't die*. Here *Ahab died* is an intrinsic part of the meaning of *killed Ahab*, and so this sentence is incoherent, assuming only one Ahab is involved. Further examples of anomalous sentences are *#The square root of seven is green and squishy* and the celebrated *#Colourless green ideas sleep furiously*, in which words of incompatible meanings are combined.

Note that the following sentence is rather different: *Natalie enjoyed himself at the disco*. Here there is really no linguistic problem at all: it is merely that our experience of the world leads us to expect that a person called *Natalie* will be female. Nor is there any linguistic problem with this next example: *The capital city of the USA is Dallas*. This is not anomalous at all, but merely false.

**antecedent** 1. A linguistic expression which provides the interpretation for a second expression, an ANAPHOR, which has little intrinsic meaning of its own. Most commonly, an antecedent is a NOUN PHRASE. In the following examples, the first bold italic item is the antecedent and the second is the anaphor referring to it: *If you see* ***Susie****, give* ***her*** *my regards*; ***The children*** *ran to* ***their*** *mother*; ***Jan*** *rang to tell me* ***she'd*** *be* *late;* ***Most of my students*** *have submitted* ***their*** *essays;* ***Susie*** *injured* ***herself*** *playing hockey;* ***Susie and Natalie*** *showed* ***each other*** *their purchases*. Occasionally an antecedent follows its anaphor: *If you see* ***her****, give* ***Susie*** *my regards*. It is possible for the antecedent and the anaphor to be in different sentences, and even in utterances produced by two different people: Susie: *I ran into* ***Alice*** *today*. Mike: *How is* ***she*** *getting on in* ***her*** *new job?*

It is possible for an antecedent to belong to another category. Examples: *She asked me to* ***wash the car****, and I* ***did it*** (the antecedent is a verb phrase); *This job requires a* ***cordless*** *drill, but I don't have* ***such a*** *thing* (the antecedent is an adjective phrase); *I thought Susie was* ***in the library****, but I didn't find her* ***there*** (the antecedent is a prepositional phrase); *I've lost my favourite* ***earrings****, and I'll have to get some new* ***ones*** (the antecedent is the word *earrings*, which is only a piece of a noun phrase). The antecedent can even be a complete sentence, as in the following exchange: Susie: *Our budget is being cut*. Mike: *Where did you hear that?* Here the anaphor *that* refers to Susie's entire utterance.

**2.** See under CONDITIONAL SENTENCE.

**aorist** A label which has no specific meaning but which is conventionally applied to certain verb-forms in certain languages, most notably in ancient Greek, where the label is conferred upon a set of past-tense forms differing from the PERFECT.

**AP** The abbreviation for ADJECTIVE PHRASE.

**apodosis** (also **consequent**) See under CONDITIONAL SENTENCE.

**apostrophe** The punctuation mark [']. This has four functions.

**1.** It is used in writing a CONTRACTION to show the place of the omitted letters. Examples: *it's* for *it is* or *it has*; *she'll* for *she will*.

**2.** It is used in writing certain words which were formerly contractions, but are no longer regarded as such, such as *o'clock* and *cat-o'-nine-tails*.

**3.** It is used in writing most POSSESSIVES, as in *Jan's brother, children's shoes, my parents' wedding* and *two weeks' work*. But it is *not* used in writing the possessive forms of most PRONOUNS: *The bull lowered its head; Whose umbrella is this?; These books are hers*.

**4.** Though it is not normally used in writing PLURALS (see GREEN-

GROCER'S APOSTROPHE), it is used in writing the plurals of letters and other forms which would otherwise be difficult to read: *Mind your p's and q's*.

For more on its use, see chapter 5 of *The Penguin Guide to Punctuation*.

**appellative** An old-fashioned term for COMMON NOUN.

**appositive** A NOUN PHRASE which immediately follows another noun phrase of identical reference. Appositives are typically NON-RESTRICTIVE: the reference of the first noun phrase is clear, and the appositive serves only to add further information. In writing, an appositive of this sort must be set off by commas. The phrases set off by commas in the following examples are appositives of this sort: *Mexico City*[, *the largest city in the Americas*,] *suffers from fearful pollution*; *His newest book*[, *the last one in the trilogy*,] *concludes the saga*. In each case, removal of the appositive would leave a sentence which is both grammatical and sensible. But an appositive can also be RESTRICTIVE (required for identification of the reference of the first noun phrase). Such an appositive is not set off by commas in writing. An example is *Shelley* in the sentence *I'm writing a biography of the poet Shelley*. Here, removing *Shelley* would leave a result which is impossible to interpret: we would have no idea which poet was being referred to.

An appositive is said to be in apposition with the preceding phrase.

**appositive clause** Another name for a NON-RESTRICTIVE RELATIVE CLAUSE; see under RELATIVE CLAUSE.

**arbitrary control** See under CONTROL.

**archaism** A word or a form which was normal long ago but which has generally disappeared from the language and is used occasionally only for special effect. Examples include the *hath* of *What hath God wrought?* (Marconi's first trans-Atlantic radio message) and the *wilt*, *thou* and *thy* of *Wilt thou take this woman to be thy lawfully wedded wife?* (in one version of the marriage service).

**argument** A NOUN PHRASE whose presence in a sentence is absolutely required by the verb of that sentence. For example, in the sentence *The Mongols destroyed Kiev*, both *The Mongols* and *Kiev* are arguments, since the verb *destroy* requires these two slots to be filled, and leaving either empty would produce ungrammaticality. In contrast, all further phrases that might be added are optional, and not required to produce a grammatical result: *in the year 1240*, *out of revenge*, *angrily*, *at the command of the Great Khan*, and so on. These optional elements are ADJUNCTS. See VALENCY.

**article** A DETERMINER which has little meaning of its own but serves to indicate that the NOUN PHRASE containing it is definite or indefinite, specific or non-specific. English has two articles, the DEFINITE ARTICLE *the* and the INDEFINITE ARTICLE *a*(*n*). The definite article typically indicates that what its noun phrase denotes is either already known to the listener or easily guessable from the context: for example, *the girl* can usually only be used if the girl in question has already been identified earlier, while *the waiter* can be used if the scene has already been set in a restaurant, where the presence of a waiter would naturally be assumed. The indefinite article is used when its noun phrase does not meet these conditions: if we want to introduce a bus into the conversation for the first time, we must normally say *a bus*, unless the context has already made it clear that the presence of a bus is not surprising, as in *I had finished my shopping and was ready to go home, so I got on the bus*.

The English indefinite article does not distinguish between specific and non-specific interpretations. For example, *I'm looking for a cookery book* can equally mean 'I'm looking for a specific cookery book' or 'I'm looking for any old cookery book'.

**ascriptive sentence** A sentence in which a (temporary or permanent) quality is ascribed to somebody or something. In English, an ascriptive sentence is usually constructed with the COPULA *be*: *Susie is pretty*; *Susie is clever*; *Susie is Irish*; *Susie is drunk*. But sometimes we use *have* instead: *Susie has blue eyes*; *Susie has a temper*. In each case, some property (prettiness, inebriation, blue eyes, or whatever) is being attributed to Susie. Unlike an EQUATIONAL SENTENCE, an ascriptive sentence cannot be turned round: **Pretty is Susie*; **Drunk is Susie*.

**aspect** The GRAMMATICAL CATEGORY which indicates how the time-structure of the activity or state described by a sentence is viewed: as a structureless whole, as continuing over time, as a series of repetitions, as a habit, as beginning or ending, and so on. Aspect must be carefully distinguished from TENSE – grammatical *location* in time – even though the formal expressions of these two categories are often deeply intermingled in particular languages.

For example, the English sentences *I drank brandy, I was drinking brandy* and *I used to drink brandy* are all identical in tense – they are all in the past tense – but they differ in aspect: the first presents my brandy-drinking as an unanalysed whole, the second presents it as a continuing action, and the third presents it as a habitual activity.

Aspectual distinctions are mostly classified into two superordinate types: PERFECTIVE (no internal structure) and IMPERFECTIVE (some kind of internal structure), with the second subdivided into several more specific types. The English PERFECT is also often classed as an aspect, even though it is rather unusual among aspects. See these terms for more information.

**aspectual verb** A VERB which does not itself denote any particular action, event or state, but which serves to indicate that the action or state denoted by another verb or an adjective is beginning, continuing, ending or changing. Among our aspectual verbs are *start, begin, continue, keep* (*on*), *stop, quit, finish, become, get* (when this means 'become') and *turn*. Examples: *Susie started eating; Susie kept* (*on*) *driving; Susie quit smoking; Susie got angry; Susie turned ugly*.

**asterisk** The symbol *, conventionally placed in front of a string of linguistic material to show that it is ill-formed (ungrammatical), as in **She smiled me*.

**asyndeton** The joining together of two or more complete sentences without the use of a coordinating CONJUNCTION. Examples: *I came, I saw, I conquered; It was the best of times; it was the worst of times; The biologists have fossils; we linguists don't*. Such a construction is said to be asyndetic.

**atelic** A label applied to a verb or a sentence which denotes an activity or state which has no recognizable goal whose achievement would necessarily bring the activity or state to an end. Atelic verbs include *sleep* (as in *Susie is sleeping*), *speak* (as in *Susie speaks good French*) and *remember* (as in *I remember the summer of 1970*). The opposite is TELIC.

**attraction** The grammatical phenomenon in which a verb shows AGREEMENT, not with its logical subject, but with something else, typically something which is closer to it. An example is *I wonder if the right kind of supplies are being sent*, in which the plural verb-form *are* is agreeing, not with its logical (and singular) subject *kind*, but with the nearby plural noun *supplies*. Occasionally attraction occurs in the other direction: in the example *She is one of those people who is always critical of everybody else*, the verb should logically be *are*, since its subject is *people*, but *is* has been used to agree with *one*, which is further away.

**attributive** Inside a NOUN PHRASE, the position between the DETERMINER (if any) and the HEAD noun. In the following example, the blank indicates the attributive position: *a __ textbook*. In English, the attributive position may be filled either by an ADJECTIVE, like *new*, or by a NOUN, like *linguistics*. Compare PREDICATIVE.

**auxiliary** (in traditional grammar, **helping verb**) In English, one of a small set of items which have certain properties in common with verbs but which also exhibit some distinctive characteristics of their own. Most linguists regard the English auxiliaries as a subclass of VERBS, but a minority view sees them as forming an entirely distinct PART OF SPEECH.

Our auxiliaries are divided into two types: the PRIMARY AUXILIARIES *be* and *have*, plus the 'dummy' auxiliary *do*, and the MODAL AUXILIARIES *can, could, will, would, shall, should, may, might, must* and *ought* (*to*). The two SEMI-AUXILIARIES *need* and *dare* are anomalous, behaving sometimes like modals but at other times like LEXICAL VERBS (ordinary verbs); see this entry.

The auxiliaries share the following properties with lexical verbs:

**1.** They occupy the same position in the sentence, typically immediately after the SUBJECT: *Jessica bought a teddy-bear*; *Jessica should go home*.

**2.** They exhibit SEQUENCE OF TENSES: *Jessica says she drinks vodka*; *Jessica said she drank vodka*; *Jessica says she will come*; *Jessica said she would come*.

**3.** The primary auxiliaries (but not the modal auxiliaries) take the present-tense third-singular ending *-s* and form PARTICIPLES: *Jessica wants a drink*; *Jessica has finished her drink*; but not **Jessica cans speak French*; *Finishing her drink, Jessica stood up*; *Having finished her drink, Jessica stood up*; but not **woulding* or **oughting*.

The auxiliaries differ from lexical verbs in four respects:

**1**. Only auxiliaries allow NEGATION: *Jessica isn't smoking; Jessica shouldn't smoke*; but **Jessica smokes not / smokesn't.*

**2**. Only auxiliaries can undergo INVERSION with the subject: *Is Jessica smoking?; Should Jessica smoke?*; but **Smokes Jessica?*.

**3**. Only auxiliaries can appear in TAG QUESTIONS, a property sometimes called 'code': *Jessica smokes, doesn't she?; Jessica isn't smoking, is she?*; but **Jessica doesn't smoke, smokes she?*.

**4**. Only auxiliaries can receive EMPHATIC STRESS to contradict a preceding statement: if you say *Jessica isn't smoking* or *Jessica doesn't smoke*, I can contradict you with *Jessica IS smoking* or *Jessica DOES smoke*, but not with **Jessica SMOKES*.

These four properties are sometimes called the NICE PROPERTIES as a mnemonic. The 'dummy' auxiliary *do* is used whenever one of these four properties must be added to a sentence which contains no other auxiliary: *Jessica smokes; Jessica doesn't smoke; Does Jessica smoke?; Jessica smokes, doesn't she?; Jessica DOES smoke.*

# B

**back-formation** A particular type of WORD-FORMATION, or a word formed in this way. In back-formation, we take an existing word and remove from it a piece that *looks* like an affix, but really isn't, in order to obtain a new word. For example, the words *burglar*, *sculptor* and *editor*, which are borrowed from Old French or from Latin, all *sound* as though they contain the familiar agent suffix *-er*, as in *writer* and *singer*, and so we have removed this apparent suffix to obtain the previously non-existence verbs *burgle*, *sculpt* and *edit*. Other examples of back-formation are *pea* from earlier *pease* (which sounds like a plural, but originally wasn't) and *televise* from *television*.

**backshift** Another term for SEQUENCE OF TENSES.

**bahuvrihi** (also **headless compound**, **exocentric compound**) A type of COMPOUND in which neither element is a HEAD. For example, a *hatchback* is not a type of back, nor is it a type of hatch: it is a type of car. Other bahuvrihis are *redhead*, *hard-hat* and *highbrow* (all types of person) and *pickpocket*. Compare ENDOCENTRIC COMPOUND.

**bare infinitive** An infinitive not preceded by *to*. See under INFINITIVE.

**bare-NP adverbial** An ADVERBIAL which consists of a NOUN PHRASE with no preposition. Examples (in brackets): *Do it* [*this way*]; *Get started* [*the minute she arrives*]; *I've seen that* [*every place I've been*].

**base** In WORD-FORMATION, the form which is the direct source of another form. For example, *happy* is the base for forming all of *happily*, *unhappy* and *happiness*, while *unhappy* is the base for forming both *unhappily* and *unhappiness*.

**basic word order** In any given language, the order in which the major units of a sentence most commonly appear. Basic word order is commonly formulated in terms of the SUBJECT (S), the OBJECT (O) and the VERB (V). In English, the basic word order is SVO: *Susie kissed Natalie*. Other orders are unusual (*Natalie Susie kissed*) or impossible (**Kissed Natalie Susie*). But other languages are different: Japanese, Turkish and Basque are SOV; Welsh, Irish and Classical Arabic are VSO; Malagasy (in Madagascar) is VOS; and so on.

**benefactive** (also **beneficiary**) The SEMANTIC ROLE assigned to a NOUN PHRASE denoting a person who benefits from some action. In the following examples, *Susie* is a beneficiary: *I've knitted Susie a sweater*; *Mike has fixed the washing machine for Susie*. In some CASE languages, there is a specific *benefactive* case-form for expressing this.

**binding** Another term for anaphora; see under ANAPHOR.

**blending** A kind of WORD-FORMATION in which a word is constructed by combining arbitrary parts of two or more existing words. Examples include *smog* (*smoke* plus *fog*), *brunch* (*breakfast* plus *lunch*) and *rockumentary* (*rock* plus *documentary*). Occasionally all parts of both words are retained, as in *sexploitation* (*sex* plus *exploitation*) and *guesstimate* (*guess* plus *estimate*). A word constructed in such a way is a blend.

**blocking** The phenomenon in which a perfectly regularly formed word is prevented from existing by the existence of another word of identical meaning. For example, an English verb can usually take the suffix *-er* to denote the agent of that verb: *singer* from *sing*, *writer* from *write*, *smoker* from *smoke*, and so on. But *steal* does not yield **stealer*, because this is blocked by *thief*, and, while *curious* yields *curiosity*, *furious* does not yield **furiosity*, because this is blocked by *fury*.

**block language** The distinctive type of language used in public signs, typically consisting of PHRASES, rather than of complete SENTENCES. Examples: *No Parking*; *Left turn only*; *Stage door*; *EU passports*; *Birmingham and the North*; *Open Sundays*. Compare HEADLINE LANGUAGE.

**bold face** Dark type, **like this**. Boldface is used for highlighting, most obviously for headwords in dictionaries, as in this one.

**borrowing** Copying a word from one language into another language. English has borrowed vast numbers of words from other languages: *lettuce* from Latin, *virgin* from Norman French, *pretzel* from German, *cigarette* from modern French, *sherry* from Spanish, *ski* from Norwegian, *ombudsman* from Swedish, *retsina* from modern Greek, *tea* from Chinese, *algebra* from Arabic, *yogurt* from Turkish, *ukulele* from Hawaiian, *sushi* from Japanese, *pyjamas* from Hindi, *kangaroo* from the Guugu-Yimidhirr language of Australia, and countless others. Indeed, the modern English vocabulary is about seventy per cent borrowed, with Norman French, Latin and ancient Greek being the main donor languages. A borrowed word is called a LOANWORD.

**bound morpheme** A MORPHEME which cannot stand alone to make a word, but which must be combined with at least one other morpheme within a word. The most familiar type of bound morpheme is an AFFIX (a prefix or a suffix). Most affixes in English are grammatical in nature, like the prefixes *un-* (as in *uninteresting*) and *re-* (as in *rewrite*) and the suffixes *-ly* (as in *slowly*) and *-ness* (as in *happiness*). A few, though, are not really grammatical, like the *step-* of *stepmother* (which has nothing to do with the independent word *step*) and the *anti-* of *anti-war*. But our technical terms are largely constructed from another type of bound morpheme, the COMBINING FORMS (sense 2); see that entry.

**bracketing** A way of displaying the syntactic structure of a phrase or a sentence. Each syntactic unit which is recognized is enclosed within a pair of square brackets. For example, the phrase *the little girl* would be bracketed as follows: [[*the*] [[*little*] [*girl*]]]. This shows that the phrase consists of *little* plus *girl*, which form a unit *little girl*, which in turn combines with *the* to form the complete phrase. If the bracketed units are labelled to show what SYNTACTIC CATEGORY they belong to, the result is a labelled bracketing: [$_{NP}$[$_{Det}$*the*] [$_{N'}$[$_{A}$*little*] [$_{N}$*girl*]]]. This shows that *little* is an adjective, that *girl* is a noun, that *little girl* is of the category that linguists call an N-bar, that *the* is a determiner, and that the whole thing is a noun phrase.

# C

**calque** (also **loan-translation**) A word which is constructed by translating a word in another language piece by piece, or the process of forming a word in such a way. For example, Greek *sympathia* 'sympathy, compassion', which consists of *syn-* 'with' plus *pathia* 'feeling', was calqued into Latin as *compassio*, from *con-* 'with' and *passio* 'feeling'. English rarely forms calques, but one example is *it goes without saying*, calqued on French *il va sans dire*.

**canonical** A label applied to any pattern in a language which represents the most typical or usual pattern in some domain. For example, the canonical pattern for forming plurals in English is with *-s*, as in *books, islands* and *CD-ROMs*, even though there are exceptional plurals like *sheep, women, teeth* and *phenomena*.

**cardinal numeral** A counting number: any one of the linguistic items of the type *one, two, three, twelve, twenty-seven*, and so on. The English cardinal numerals exhibit some rather distinctive grammatical properties, and it is not easy to assign them to a PART OF SPEECH. Some linguists class them as DETERMINERS, others as ADJECTIVES, and still others as a separate category of their own. Compare ORDINAL NUMERAL.

**case** In some languages, an ending (or other modification) attached to a NOUN or to a NOUN PHRASE to express its relation to the rest of the sentence. In English, case is exhibited only by a few PRONOUNS: we say *I saw her* but *She saw me*, where *I* and *me*, and also *she* and *her*, are two different case-forms of the same pronoun.

Some other languages have far more in the way of case. Basque, for example, has about a dozen cases, and these are attached to all noun phrases. With *neska* 'the girl', for example, we have sentences like *Neska ikusi dut* 'I saw the girl', *Neskak ikusi nau* 'The girl saw me', *Neskari eman diot* 'I gave it to the girl', *Neskarekin joan naiz* 'I went with the girl', *Neskaren lagunak hemen daude* 'The girl's friends are here', and a number of others.

**case grammar** Any approach to grammatical description which stresses the importance of SEMANTIC ROLES. Case grammar was developed in the 1960s and is still favoured in some quarters today, though most practical grammars of English pay little attention to it.

**catachresis** A formal or old-fashioned term for MALAPROPISM.

**cataphor** See under ANAPHOR.

**catenative verb** A VERB which is commonly followed by another verb, often with the infinitival *to* intervening. Examples include *want* in *I want to go home*, *need* in *We need to draw up a budget*, *quit* in *Susie quit smoking*, and *start* in *She started to run*. Different linguists define the term somewhat differently, but note that a verb followed by a verb of purpose, such as *babysit* in *She babysat to earn extra money*, is not normally regarded as a catenative verb by anybody.

**causative** A construction meaning that somebody caused somebody else to do something. Given the simple sentence *I washed the car*, the most usual causative pattern in English is illustrated by *She made me wash the car*, though other patterns are possible, such as *She got me to wash the car*, and, in American English, *She had me wash the car*. Some (but not all) linguists would extend this label to cases like *I had my car repaired*, whose source is roughly *Somebody repaired my car*.

**circumstantial clause** Any ADVERBIAL CLAUSE expressing circumstance, such as the bracketed clause in [*Since the weather looks threatening*,] *let's forget about our picnic*.

**citation form** That form of a word which is conventionally used in naming it, talking about it or entering it in a dictionary, such as *dog*, *big* or *take*.

**clause** A grammatical unit consisting of a SUBJECT and a PREDICATE. There are two principal types of clause: a MAIN CLAUSE can possibly stand alone to make a sentence by itself, while a SUBORDINATE CLAUSE must be attached to another clause within a larger sentence. Every SENTENCE must contain at least one main clause, though a sentence may contain two or more main clauses, and in any case may additionally contain one or more subordinate clauses. For example, the sentence *Mike started making dinner* consists of a single main clause, while the sentence *Mike started making dinner and Susie tidied the lounge* consists of two main clauses connected by *and*, and the sentence *Mike started making dinner while Susie tidied the lounge* consists of a main clause plus a subordinate clause beginning with *while*.

A SIMPLE SENTENCE consists of a single main clause. A COMPOUND SENTENCE consists of two or more main clauses. A COMPLEX SENTENCE consists of one main clause plus one or more subordinate clauses. A COMPOUND-COMPLEX SENTENCE consists of two or more main clauses plus one or more subordinate clauses. See these entries for examples.

In traditional grammar, and still today for most linguists, a clause must contain a verb which is FINITE (marked for TENSE). In this view, the bracketed sequences in the following example would not be clauses, but only PHRASES within a single large clause: [*Having finished her dinner,*] *Susie settled down* [*to study*] [*in order to prepare for her exams*]. In some current theories of grammar, however, every verb must be assigned to its own clause, and hence all of the bracketed sequences would count as clauses.

**cleft** Any of various constructions in which some element of a sentence is removed from its normal position and certain extra words are added to highlight the cleft. The purpose of a cleft is to place the clefted element into FOCUS. For example, starting with the sentence *Mike wants a new car*, we can form an IT-CLEFT to focus either on *Mike* (*It's Mike who wants a new car*) or on *a new car* (*It's a new car that Mike wants*). Or we can form a WH-CLEFT (or PSEUDO-CLEFT) to focus on *a new car*: *What Mike wants is a new car* or *A new car is what Mike wants*.

**clipping** A type of WORD-FORMATION in which a short piece is extracted from a longer word and given the same meaning. Examples include *bra* from *brassière*, *gym* from *gymnasium*, *flu* from *influenza*, *cello* from *violoncello*, *phone* from *telephone* and *bus* from *omnibus*. A word formed in this way is a clipped form. A clipped form is a real word, and not an ABBREVIATION. A clipped form may continue to co-exist with its source word, like *gym* and *flu*, or it may largely or wholly displace its source word, like *bra* and *bus*.

**clitic** An element of a sentence which is less than an independent word but more than an AFFIX. A clitic is usually quite short, and it is fixed into a certain position from which it may not be moved. English is not rich in clitics, but the *'ll* of *I'll be right there* is perhaps best viewed as a clitic attached to the preceding *I*. French has many more clitics: for example, in *Il te le donnera* 'He'll give it to you', the pronouns *il* 'he', *te* 'you' and *le* 'it' are all clitics: they must occur directly before the verb *donnera* 'will give' and only in the order given. The material to which a clitic is attached is its host. For example, *I* is the host for *'ll* in *I'll*, and *donnera* is the host for the French clitics. A clitic which precedes its host, like the French ones, is a PROCLITIC, while a clitic which follows its host, like English *'ll*, is an ENCLITIC.

**closed class** A PART OF SPEECH which is small and which rarely accepts new members. English examples include PREPOSITION, DETERMINER and PRONOUN. The opposite is an OPEN CLASS.

**cognate object** A DIRECT OBJECT which merely repeats the meaning of its verb, such as *dream* in *I dreamt a wonderful dream last night* and *thoughts* in *I'm thinking terrible thoughts*.

**coherence** The property of a TEXT which hangs together in a readily intelligible manner, which 'makes sense'. For example, in response to the question *Is Susie coming to Mike's party?*, a coherent answer might be any of *Yes, I don't know, Susie is not speaking to Mike's girlfriend* or *Is the sun going to rise tomorrow?* But a response like *The specific gravity of mercury is 13.6* is unlikely to be coherent. Compare COHESION.

**cohesion** The use of linguistic devices to connect the elements of a TEXT. For example, in response to the question *Is Susie coming to Mike's party?*, the reply *She's looking forward to it* exhibits cohesion, in that *she* refers to *Susie* and *it* refers to *Mike's party*. Compare COHERENCE.

**collective noun** A NOUN which denotes a collection of individual persons or objects, such as *committee, team, government* and *herd*. In some varieties of English, including British English, a collective noun may be treated either as singular (if the whole group is being thought of as a unit) or as plural (if the group is being regarded as a collection of individuals): hence we may say *The committee has announced its decision* (the committee is regarded as a unit) or *The committee are divided on this issue* (the committee is regarded as a group of individuals). In other varieties, especially in American English, a collective noun is always treated as singular, and Americans say *The committee is divided on this issue*. Names of sports teams are treated differently in British and American English: a Briton says *Liverpool are playing Arsenal*, while an American says *Buffalo is playing Dallas*.

**colloquialism** A word or phrase which is typical of COLLOQUIAL SPEECH but not of formal speech or writing, such as *bummer* or *Get a life!*

**colloquial speech** Informal everyday speech, of the sort that everybody uses in relaxed circumstances. Colloquial speech is normal for all of us. It is not, in general, ignorant, vulgar or wrong; it is merely different from the sort of language we use in formal speech or writing, when we are being self-conscious and careful. A speaker who never used colloquial speech at all, but who used only formal English in all contexts, would be abnormal.

**colon** The punctuation mark [:]. This is almost always used after a complete sentence, and its function is to indicate that what follows is an explanation or elaboration of what precedes. Examples: *I propose the creation of a new post: School Executive Officer*; *I've found the problem: a faulty heating element*. A colon is never preceded by a white space, and it is never followed by a dash or a hyphen. For more on its use, see chapter 4 of *The Penguin Guide to Punctuation*.

**combining form** **1**. A special form taken by a word when it forms part of a larger word. For example, *piano* takes the combining form *pian-* in *pianist*. Native English words do not usually have distinctive combining forms.

**2**. An element, usually one taken from Latin or Greek, which never stands alone, but can only appear as part of a larger word. For example, *bibliophile* 'lover of books' consists of the combining forms *biblio-* 'book' and *-phile* 'lover'; neither of these can stand alone, but both recur in other formations, such as *bibliography* 'list of books' and *thermophile* 'heat-lover'. Most English technical terms are constructed from combining forms of this sort.

**comitative** The relation 'in the company of', usually expressed in English by the preposition *with*, as in *Susie went to the party with Dave*. Some CASE languages have a special case-form for this purpose.

**comma** The punctuation mark [,]. This has four uses.

**1.** A *listing comma* is used to connect the items in a list, except for the last two, which are connected by a CONJUNCTION like *and* or *or*. Example: *The Three Musketeers were Athos, Porthos and Aramis*.

**2.** A *joining comma* is used to join two complete sentences into a single sentence, and it must be followed by a connecting word like *and*, *or*, *but*, *while* or *yet* (but not *however*, which requires a SEMICOLON). Example: *A dropped goal counts three points in rugby union, while in rugby league it counts only one point*.

**3.** A *gapping comma* is used to show that certain words have been omitted instead of repeated. Example: *Larry decided to order the chicken pathia and Jan, the duck special*. (The omitted words are *decided to order*.)

**4.** A *pair* of *bracketing commas* is used to set off a weak interruption to a sentence, one which does not greatly interrupt its flow. Example: *She groped for her cigarettes and, finding them, hastily lit one*. (The weak interruption *finding them* could in principle be omitted without destroying the sentence.)

For more on the use of the comma, see chapter 3 of *The Penguin Guide to Punctuation*.

**command** The (functional) SENTENCE TYPE of any utterance used to issue instructions. This may be done by using an IMPERATIVE sentence: *Wash your hands!*; *Sit down!* But it can also be done by using other sentence types: *You must go home now* (with the DECLARATIVE form more typical of a STATEMENT); *Will you shut up?* (with the INTERROGATIVE form more typical of a QUESTION).

**comment** In some analyses of sentence structure, that part of a sentence which expresses new information, as opposed to the TOPIC, which expresses old information. For example, in reply to the question *What does Susie do?*, the reply *She's a publisher* consists of the topic *she* and the comment *is a publisher*. Not every sentence has a topic/comment structure.

**common gender** In a language with GENDER, the property of a noun which can be assigned to more than one gender, depending on what it refers to. For example, the French nouns *enfant* 'child' and *hypocrite* 'hypocrite' are masculine when referring to males but feminine when referring to females. Occasionally, though rather unnecessarily, the label is extended to English nouns which can denote people of either sex, like *teacher* and *doctor*, as opposed to those which mark sex, like *host/hostess* and *widow/widower*. Compare EPICENE.

**common noun** (formerly also **appellative**) An ordinary NOUN, one which denotes a class of things, such as *dog, pencil, explosion* or *happiness*. Compare PROPER NOUN.

**comparative** That form of an ADJECTIVE or an ADVERB which is constructed either with *-er* or with *more* and which serves to express a higher degree of the quality denoted by the base word. Examples are *bigger* from *big*, *worse* from *bad*, *more beautiful* from *beautiful* and *more carefully* from *carefully*. English also has a comparative of inferiority, constructed with *less*, as in *less interesting*. See DEGREE and ABSOLUTE COMPARATIVE, and compare POSITIVE, SUPERLATIVE.

**comparative clause** A CLAUSE attached to a COMPARATIVE. Examples, with the comparative clauses bracketed: *My ticket was more expensive* [*than I expected*]; *Mike is taller* [*than I am*]; *His latest film has been less successful* [*than his other films have been*]. When no VERB is present, the comparative expression is only a PHRASE, not a clause: *Mike is taller* [*than me*]; *His last film has been less successful* [*than his other films*]. Quite often, an EQUATIVE clause is classed as a comparative clause: *Susie drives as well* [*as I do*].

**competence** The abstract knowledge of your language which you have in your head; the knowledge which allows you to speak and to understand your language easily. Compare PERFORMANCE.

**complement** A label which is applied variously to several quite different things.

**1.** A subject complement is a phrase which follows a COPULA or a QUASI-COPULA and either modifies the subject or denotes something identical to the subject. Examples (in brackets): *Jan is* [*a senior administrator*]; *Susie became* [*a journalist*]; *The children were* [*very excited*]; *Susie is* [*in the shower*].

**2.** An object complement is a phrase which follows a DIRECT OBJECT and either modifies that object or denotes something identical to it. Examples (in brackets): *I consider hang-gliding* [*dangerous*]; Stage Coach *made John Wayne* [*a star*].

**3.** The complement of a lexical HEAD is a phrase which directly follows it and, in some broad sense, 'completes' it. Examples (in brackets): *Susie is fond* [*of chocolate*] (*of chocolate* is the complement of the adjective *fond*); *I am sorry* [*to tell you this*] (*to tell you this* is the complement of the adjective *sorry*); *Let's get a bottle* [*of wine*] (*of wine* is the complement of the noun *bottle*); *The cat is under* [*the bed*] (*the bed* is the complement of the preposition *under*; this is the same as the OBJECT of the preposition); *Susie has bought* [*a new car*] (*a new car* is the complement of the verb *bought*; this is the same as the DIRECT OBJECT of the verb); *She wants* [*to find a new job*] (*to find a new job* is the complement of the verb *wants*). The use of *complement* for *object* is now rather old-fashioned.

**4.** In some older approaches to grammar, the label *complement* is applied to every phrase following a VERB. In this approach, the sentence *I saw Lisa in town yesterday* contains three complements to the verb *saw*: *Lisa*, *in town* and *yesterday*.

**5.** In some recent theories of grammar, the label *complement* (of a verb) is applied to the entire VERB PHRASE containing that verb except for the verb itself. In this approach, the verb phrase *saw Lisa in town yesterday* consists of the verb *saw* and the complement *Lisa in town yesterday*. This usage is not normal in most circles.

**6.** Short for COMPLEMENT CLAUSE.

**complement clause** (also **complement**, for short) A CLAUSE which is introduced by a COMPLEMENTIZER (though this may sometimes be optionally omitted) and which is attached to a preceding noun, adjective or verb. In *The report that mobile phones cause memory loss has been challenged*, *that mobile phones cause memory loss* is a NOUN-COMPLEMENT CLAUSE attached to the noun *report*. In *I am sure that Susie is coming*, *that Susie is coming* is an adjective-complement clause attached to the adjective *sure*. In *My doctor says that I drink too much*, *that I drink too much* is a VERB-COMPLEMENT CLAUSE attached to the verb *says*. In the second and third of these, but not in the first, the complementizer *that* may be optionally omitted.

Note that a noun-complement clause is different from a RELATIVE CLAUSE, even though the two are often superficially similar. In *The reports that Ted is sending poison-pen letters are surprising, that Ted is sending poison-pen letters* is a noun-complement clause attached to the noun *reports*. But in *The reports that Ted is sending are surprising, that Ted is sending* is a relative clause attached to *reports*.

Note: traditionally, and still today for most linguists, a complement clause, like any clause, must be FINITE (marked for TENSE). Hence, in *Susie wants to see that new film*, the complement *to see that new film* is only a PHRASE, and not a clause. However, in some current theories of grammar, every verb must be assigned to its own clause, and so this complement would be regarded as a complement clause.

See also SENTENTIAL SUBJECT.

**complementizer** The PART OF SPEECH which includes the words which introduce COMPLEMENT CLAUSES, most commonly *that* and *whether* (and also *if*, when this means *whether*). Examples of use: *She said that she was coming; I don't know whether she's coming*.

**complex preposition** A PREPOSITION which consists of two or three words, such as *in spite of*, *in front of*, *out of* and *on top of*. In spite of their form, such items behave like simple prepositions.

**complex sentence** A sentence which contains at least one SUBORDINATE CLAUSE. In the following examples, the subordinate clauses are bracketed: *Susie said* [*that she would come*]; [*After Susie got up,*] *she took a shower; The scientists* [*who believe* [*that there may be life on Mars*]] *suspect* [*that it exists below the surface*]. Compare COMPOUND SENTENCE.

**composition** A slightly old-fashioned word for the formation of a COMPOUND.

**compound** A word constructed by combining two or more existing words. The meaning of a compound is not always predictable from the meanings of its component parts: for example, not every board which is black is a *blackboard*, and not every friend who is a girl is your *girlfriend*. The formation of a compound is compounding.

**compound sentence** A sentence which contains two or more MAIN CLAUSES but no SUBORDINATE CLAUSES. The clauses in a compound sentence are often connected by a CONJUNCTION like *and*, *or* or *yet*. In the following examples, the main clauses are bracketed: [*Susie smokes*] *but* [*Mike doesn't*]; [*The Turks captured Constantinople in 1453,*] *and* [*that was the end of the Byzantine Empire*]; [*It was the best of times;*] [*it was the worst of times*]; [*Susie wants a brandy,*] [*Mike wants a whisky,*] *and* [*Natalie would like a Cointreau.*] Compare COMPLEX SENTENCE.

**compound-complex sentence** A sentence which is both a COMPOUND SENTENCE and a COMPLEX SENTENCE: that is, it contains at least two MAIN CLAUSES and at least one SUBORDINATE CLAUSE. Example: *After she left university, Susie moved to London and her boyfriend followed her*.

**concessive clause** An ADVERBIAL CLAUSE which expresses the sense of *although*. Examples include the first clauses in *Although it had been raining for days, the cricket pitch was in perfect condition* and *Even though Susie speaks fluent Italian, she could not understand the Genoese dialect*.

**concord** Another term for AGREEMENT.

**concrete noun** A NOUN which denotes something which is physical and can be touched, such as *dog*, *plastic*, *grass* and *brother*. Compare ABSTRACT NOUN.

**conditional** In English, a traditional label for the MODAL AUXILIARY *would*, and also for *should*, when this does not express obligation. The name is given because sentences with these auxiliaries often seem to imply an unstated condition. For example, the sentence *I would like a drink* appears to imply something like 'if I had a choice', even though, in practice, this is merely a polite way of asking for a drink. This label is now considered somewhat old-fashioned. But certain other languages, such as French, do have a distinctive set of verb-forms called the *conditional*.

**conditional sentence** Any sentence of the form *if . . .* (*then*). There are two types. In an open conditional, the fulfilment of the condition is seen as a realistic possibility. Examples: *If Susie gets a promotion, she plans to buy a new car; You'll have to go outside if you want to smoke.* In a COUNTERFACTUAL, the condition is seen as contrary to fact. Examples: *If I spoke better French, I could get a job in Paris; If McClelland had been more aggressive, the American Civil War might have ended two years earlier.* In both cases, the clause with *if* is called the PROTASIS or ANTECEDENT, while the other clause is the APODOSIS or CONSEQUENT.

**conjoined** See under COORDINATE STRUCTURE.

**conjugation** **1**. Changing the form of a VERB for grammatical purposes. For example, the English verb *take* may appear as any of *take, takes, took, taken* or *taking*, depending upon its grammatical position.

**2**. In some languages (not including English), a class of verbs whose members change their forms in the same way for grammatical purposes. For example, Spanish has three conjugations: the *-ar* verbs, the *-er* verbs and the *-ir* verbs. Once you have learned how to make the forms of a single *-ar* verb, such as *amar* 'love', you can immediately make the forms of all other *-ar* verbs (apart from any which may be irregular), but you still have to learn the other two classes separately.

**conjunct** **1**. Any one of the items linked by a word like *and* with a COORDINATE STRUCTURE. Examples (in brackets): [*Susie*] *and* [*her parents*] are coming to dinner.

**2**. In the QUIRK GRAMMARS, a label applied to an ADVERBIAL which connects its sentence to neighbouring sentences, such as *moreover, nevertheless, finally* or *in addition*.

**conjunction** **1**. The PART OF SPEECH which can combine two or more linguistic items in a COORDINATE STRUCTURE, such as *and, or* and *but*. Examples: *Susie smokes and drinks; She is clever but careless; Would you prefer to stir-fry the vegetables or to make the salad?*

**2**. Another term for coordinate structure.

**consequent** See under CONDITIONAL SENTENCE.

**constituent** Any sequence of one or more words which functions as a grammatical unit within a sentence. See CONSTITUENT STRUCTURE.

**constituent structure** (also **phrase structure**) The type of structure typically exhibited by a sentence in English and in most other languages. Constituent structure is *hierarchical* in nature. The sentence consists of two or three smaller units, each of which consists of some still smaller units, each of which consists of some even smaller units, and so on, until we reach the smallest units, which we may take either as WORDS or as MORPHEMES.

Consider the sentence *The little girl hugged her dolly*. This consists of two large constituents, its IMMEDIATE CONSTITUENTS: *the little girl* and *hugged her dolly*. The first consists of two smaller constituents (its immediate constituents): *the* and *little girl*, with the second in turn consisting of *little* and *girl*. The second original constituent consists of *hugged* and *her dolly*, with the latter consisting of *her* plus *dolly*. The constituent structure of the whole sentence can be displayed by means of a BRACKETING: [[[*the*] [[*little*] [*girl*]]] [[*hugged*] [[*her*] [*dolly*]]]].

**construal** **1**. Another term for PARSING, now somewhat old-fashioned. We may say, for example, that in *She took off her jumper* the word *off* is construed with (forms a unit with) *took*, while in *She jumped off the pier* the word *off* is construed with *the pier*.

**2**. Another term for anaphora; see under ANAPHOR.

**construction** Any grammatical structure which occurs systematically in a language, or a particular instance of it. English examples include the CONTINUOUS, the PERFECT, TOPICALIZATION and PREPOSITION STRANDING.

**contamination** The process in which the form of a word is altered in a somewhat arbitrary way because of the influence of another word of similar form or meaning. An example is the alteration of *regardless*, in non-standard English, to *irregardless*, by contamination from *irrespectively*.

**continuous** (also **progressive**) A particular ASPECT form, a variety of the IMPERFECTIVE, which indicates that the action of the verb is, was or will be in progress or continuing over a period of time. In English, the continuous is expressed with the *be -ing* construction. Examples: *Susie is eating dinner; Susie was taking a shower when the phone rang; Susie will be vacationing in Hawaii this summer; Susie's car is being serviced; Susie is smoking a lot these days.*

**contraction** A short way of pronouncing, and writing, a series of two or more words. Examples include *can't* for *can not*, *she'll* for *she will*, and *we'd've* for *we would have*.

**control** The process by which a VERB PHRASE with no overt SUBJECT is interpreted as having some subject. For example, in *Susie wants to buy a new car*, the VP *buy a new car* has no overt subject, but we understand that its logical subject is *Susie*, the subject of *wants*, and we call this an instance of SUBJECT CONTROL. But, in *Susie persuaded me to buy a new car*, the understood subject of *buy a new car* is *me*, the object of *persuaded*, and we call this OBJECT CONTROL. Finally, in *Buying a new car is a good idea*, the VP *buying a new car* has no logical subject at all, and we call this ARBITRARY CONTROL.

**conversion** (also **zero-derivation**) A type of WORD-FORMATION in which a word is shifted from one PART OF SPEECH to another without any additions or changes. For example, the adjective *brown*, as in *a brown skirt*, can be converted into a verb, as in *brown the meat*, and into a noun, as in *The Cleveland Browns traditionally wear brown*, and the noun *smoke*, as in *no smoke without fire*, can be converted into a verb, as in *Susie smokes*, and then back into a noun, as in *Susie was having a smoke.*

**cooccurrence restriction** Any limitation on the ability of particular words or forms to occur together within a single sentence. A purely grammatical restriction is a DEPENDENCY, while one based on meaning is a SELECTIONAL RESTRICTION. See these entries.

**coordinate structure** (also **coordination**, **conjunction**) Any grammatical construction in which two or more grammatical units are connected (CONJOINED) with a conjunction like *and*, *or* or *yet*. Each of the units connected in a coordinate structure is a CONJUNCT (sense 1). In the following examples, the conjuncts are bracketed: *I'm having dinner with* [*Susie*] *and* [*her mother*]; *Would you like* [*coffee*] *or* [*tea?*];

*Diamonds are found [in Russia,] [in South Africa] and [in the Congo]; She polished the table [lovingly] and [with great care].*

If the conjunction is *or*, then the whole construction may be called a DISJUNCTION, and each of its conjuncts may be called a DISJUNCT (sense 1).

**copula** A special item, often a VERB, which serves to connect two parts of a sentence and to express either that the two parts denote the same thing or that the first has the property denoted by the second. The English copula is the verb *be*. The EQUATIONAL SENTENCE *Jan is my girlfriend* asserts that *Jan* and *my girlfriend* are the same person, while the ASCRIPTIVE SENTENCE *Jan is British* assigns the quality of Britishness to *Jan*. See also QUASI-COPULA.

**coreference** Another term for BINDING; see under ANAPHOR.

**corpus** A very large body of material produced by the speakers or writers of a particular language, these days typically held on a computer, and available for study. The scrutiny of corpora (this is the plural of *corpus*) has revolutionized both the study of language and the writing of dictionaries, since corpora allow us to obtain large samples of how a language is actually used by its speakers and writers. Linguistic investigations based upon corpora are corpus linguistics.

**correlative** **1**. A very general term for either a pair of items which work together to connect things in a sentence but are not adjacent. English examples include *both . . . and, either . . . or, neither . . . nor, not only . . . but also, as . . . as, more . . . than, rather . . . than* and *so . . . that.* Examples of use: *I'd rather be lucky than good; Susie both smokes and drinks; This book is so interesting that I can't put it down; Susie earns as much money as Mike does.*

**2**. In traditional grammar, a generic term including DEMONSTRATIVES, INTERROGATIVES and INDEFINITES. This second sense is now obsolete.

**count noun** A NOUN denoting something which can be counted, such as *dog, girl, occasion, birthday, link* and *arrival.* Compare MASS NOUN.

**counterfactual** See under CONDITIONAL SENTENCE.

**cranberry morpheme** A MORPHEME which occurs in only a single word, such as the *cran-* of *cranberry*, the *twi-* of *twilight* and the *-art* of *braggart*.

# D

**dangling participle** (also **hanging participle**) A PARTICIPLE which is not grammatically linked to the rest of its sentence, or at least not in an orderly manner. For example, in **Driving down the road, a deer leapt out in front of me*, the participial phrase *driving down the road* is dangling: if anything it appears to be linked (wrongly) to *a deer*. In **Having said that, there's another solution*, the participial phrase *having said that* is linked to nothing at all. Though they are not rare in speech, dangling participles are regarded as inappropriate in formal writing, and they should be avoided; they violate the SUBJECT-ATTACHMENT RULE.

**dash** The punctuation mark [–]. This is used to indicate that a sentence has been broken off without being completed: *General Sedgwick's last words to his worried staff were 'Don't worry boys; they couldn't hit an elephant at this dist– .'* A *pair* of dashes is used to set off a strong interruption to a sentence, one which violently disrupts its flow: *The destruction of Guernica – and there is no doubt that the destruction was deliberate – horrified the world.* For more on its use, see chapter 6 of *The Penguin Guide to Punctuation*. Compare HYPHEN.

**dative** In some languages with CASE, a case-form used to mark an INDIRECT OBJECT. For example, Basque has the dative case-ending -(*r*)*i*, as in *Liburua Anari eman diot* 'I gave the book to Ana', 'I gave Ana the book'. In traditional grammar, the label *dative* is sometimes applied very loosely to any indirect object, even to the English examples given above as translations.

**dative shift** A name sometimes given to the construction illustrated by *Susie showed Mike her photos*, as opposed to *Susie showed her photos to Mike*. Only some English verbs permit dative shift: for example, *Susie* *demonstrated her technique to Mike* does not permit **Susie demonstrated Mike her technique*.

**declarative** The (formal) SENTENCE TYPE commonly used to make a STATEMENT, or the MOOD assigned to a sentence or a verb-form which makes a statement presented as true. English has no special form for this, but the following are examples of declarative sentences: *Susie smokes*; *The war is over*; *Three students failed to sit the examination*; *I am not ready yet*.

**declension** In a language with CASE, the INFLECTION of a noun or other word for case, or the complete set of inflected forms of such a word, especially when presented as a model for other words showing similar forms. For example, the Latin word *amicus* 'friend' has the following declension:

| | Singular | Plural |
|---|---|---|
| Nominative | *amicus* | *amici* |
| Accusative | *amicum* | *amicos* |
| Genitive | *amici* | *amicorum* |
| Dative | *amico* | *amicibus* |
| Ablative | *amico* | *amicibus* |

**deep structure** In TRANSFORMATIONAL GRAMMAR, an abstract structure assigned to a sentence for analytical purposes. The deep structure of a sentence may be quite different from its SURFACE STRUCTURE. For example, the sentence *Jan seems to be happy* may be assigned a deep structure like this: [*Jan to be happy*] *seems*. Most other theories of grammar do not recognize deep structures.

**defective** Of a particular word, lacking some of the forms which a word of that class normally has. For example, the English verb *must* is defective. It has no past tense: *Today I must pay my bills*, but *Yesterday I ? pay my bills*. It also has no *-ing* form.

**defining** Another term for RESTRICTIVE.

**definite** A label applied to a NOUN PHRASE which denotes something which is either already known to the listener or reader or easily identifiable from the context. In the following examples, the bracketed noun phrases are definite. *We interviewed three men and a woman, and we decided to appoint* [*the woman*] (the woman has just been identified by the previous material); [*The moon*] *will rise around midnight* (there is only one moon, and everybody knows about it); *I can't recommend* [*this book*] (I am holding the book up, or pointing at it, or else I identified it a moment ago); [*My mother*] *is ill* (everybody has a mother, and the listener will expect me to have one); *What is* [*the capital of Bulgaria?*] (every country has a capital city); *I took a taxi to their place, but* [*the driver*] *got lost* (every taxi must have a driver). The opposite is INDEFINITE.

**definite article** A conventional label for the English DETERMINER *the*, or for a similar item in another language.

**degree** The GRAMMATICAL CATEGORY which expresses the degree to which some quality is present. English ADJECTIVES and ADVERBS commonly distinguish three degrees: the POSITIVE (the basic form), the COMPARATIVE (expressing a higher degree than is present in something else), and the SUPERLATIVE (expressing a maximal degree). The comparative is formed with *-er* or with *more*; the superlative is formed with *-est* or with *most*. Short words like *big* and *fast* tend to prefer *-er* and *-est*; longer ones like *beautiful* and *carefully* take *more* and *most*, though the rules for choosing are a bit complicated. Examples: *Mike is tall; Mike is taller than Ted; Mike is the tallest man I know; Natalie drives carefully; Natalie drives more carefully than Susie; Natalie drives the most carefully of anybody in Sussex*.

Finer distinctions of degree may be made with DEGREE MODIFIERS.

**degree modifier** That PART OF SPEECH, or a word belonging to this part of speech, which modifies an ADJECTIVE or an ADVERB and expresses the degree to which some quality is present. For example, in the frame *This book is* __ *expensive*, the blank can be filled by any of various degree modifiers, such as *very, too, so, rather, somewhat, exceedingly, moderately* or *impossibly*. Colloquial English permits some additional degree modifiers, such as *pretty, kind of, sort of, bloody* and a number of rather coarse items. Each of these indicates some degree of expensiveness. Traditional grammars and dictionaries often classify the degree modifiers as a subclass of adverb, but it is probably best to distinguish them.

**deictic category** Any GRAMMATICAL CATEGORY which 'points' in space or in time. For example, DEICTIC POSITION points in space; TENSE points in time; and PERSON points to the participants in a speech situation.

**deictic position** The GRAMMATICAL CATEGORY which distinguishes different degrees of distance from the speaker (and, in some languages, also from the hearer). English has a very simple system of deictic position: it distinguishes only a PROXIMAL 'close to the speaker' and a DISTAL 'far from the speaker', as in *this/these* versus *that/those* and *here* versus *there*. Some other languages make more elaborate distinctions, as does Spanish, with its three-way contrast: *aquí* 'here', *allí* 'just there', *ahí* 'over there'.

**deixis** Linguistic pointing. See DEICTIC CATEGORY.

**demonstrative** A DETERMINER or a PRONOUN which indicates distance away from the speaker (or, in some languages, from the hearer). English has only a two-way distinction between *this* (plural *these*) (close to the speaker) and *that* (plural *those*) (distant from the speaker). Some other languages make more elaborate distinctions.

**deontic modality** The area of MOOD or MODALITY concerned with permission, obligation and prohibition. For example, *must* is deontic when it means 'is obliged to', as in *We must finish this job by tomorrow*, and *may* is deontic when it means 'is permitted to', as in *You may use the car tonight*. Compare EPISTEMIC MODALITY.

**dependency** Any grammatical link between two different items in a sentence. Among the more important dependencies are SUBCATEGORIZATION, AGREEMENT and GOVERNMENT; see those entries.

**derivation 1.** A type of WORD-FORMATION in which a word is derived from another word by adding an AFFIX. English examples include *writer* and *rewrite* from *write*, *trans-Atlantic* from *Atlantic*, *frosty* and *defrost* from *frost*, and each of the steps involved in *nation* > *national* > *international* > *internationally*. Compare INFLECTION.

**2.** In TRANSFORMATIONAL GRAMMAR, the series of steps involved in converting a DEEP STRUCTURE into a SURFACE STRUCTURE.

**derivational morphology** The branch of MORPHOLOGY dealing with DERIVATION (sense 1).

**descriptivism** The policy of describing the facts of languages as we find them to be spoken, without introducing any value judgements of our own. All serious work in linguistics is descriptivist. Compare PRESCRIPTIVISM.

**determiner** The PART OF SPEECH, or a word belonging to this class, which typically forms the first element in a NOUN PHRASE and which limits the applicability of that noun phrase in some way. A determiner typically occurs in the blank in an incomplete noun phrase like __ *new book* or __ *new books*. Among them are *the, a(n), this, those, some, many, most, few, all, both, no, several, my* and *your*. Note that possessive items like *my* and *your* are strictly determiners, and not PRONOUNS, since they behave grammatically like determiners, and not like pronouns; nevertheless, some traditionally oriented books still label them (wrongly) as possessive pronouns.

The two English determiners *the* and *a(n)* have rather special functions and are often called ARTICLES: *the* is the DEFINITE ARTICLE and *a(n)* is the INDEFINITE ARTICLE.

Those determiners which indicate something about quantity, like *many, all, both* and *no*, are called QUANTIFIERS. A few linguists prefer to regard the quantifiers as a separate part of speech from determiners, but there is little basis for this.

Sometimes we find two determiners in a single noun phrase: *all my books, both my children*. In this case, the first of the two is often called a PREDETERMINER.

There is disagreement about the classification of the CARDINAL NUMERAL. These often behave like determiners, as in *three new books*. But they also occur together with other determiners, as in *these three new books*. Some linguists therefore regard them as POSTDETERMINERS, another special subclass of determiner.

See also ZERO DETERMINER.

**diachronic** Pertaining to the time element in language; involving change in a language over time. A diachronic approach to the study of a language is the study of its development over some period of time. Compare SYNCHRONIC.

**diacritic** (also, informally, **accent**) A mark placed above, below or on top of a letter to indicate something about its pronunciation. English makes only limited use of diacritics, but we sometimes write *Zoë*, *learnèd* or *Nestlé* to indicate that the marked vowel is a separate syllable. Many other written languages make very heavy use of diacritics.

**diaeresis** A mark, consisting of two dots placed above a vowel letter, to indicate that the vowel forms a separate syllable, as in *Zoë* or *naïve*.

**dialect** Any distinctive speech variety associated with the people in a particular geographical region (this is a *regional dialect*) or in a particular social group (this is a *social dialect*, or *sociolect*). English, like most languages, exhibits a number of regional dialects: people from London, Liverpool, Newcastle, Glasgow, New York, Chicago and Sydney (for example) all speak English somewhat differently. There are also social dialects: even in London, a taxi driver does not speak like a stockbroker. Even STANDARD ENGLISH is just one dialect of English, though it is a dialect with a very special status.

Note: in Britain, the term *dialect* denotes only the particular vocabulary and grammatical features of a speech variety, and it excludes accent, a particular type of pronunciation. In the USA, however, an accent is usually considered to be part of a dialect.

**digraph** A sequence of two letters representing a single sound, such as the *sh* in *fish* or the *th* in *think*.

**diminutive** (also **hypocoristic**) A modified form of a word which expresses small size, or, sometimes, merely affection. English usually forms diminutives by suffixing *-y* or *-ie*, often to a reduced form of the source word, as in *hanky* for *handkerchief*, *doggie* for *dog* and *Tommie* for *Thomas*. But we also use *-ette*, as in *statuette* and *kitchenette*.

**direct object** The GRAMMATICAL RELATION which most typically represents the person or thing receiving the action of the verb. In the following examples, the bracketed sequences are prototypical direct objects: *John hit* [*Bill*]; *Tamerlane defeated* [*Sultan Beyazit*]; *Susie painted* [*the bedroom*]. In the following further examples, the bracketed sequences are still grammatically direct objects, even though they are less typical: *Issagonis designed* [*the Mini*]; *Susie spotted* [*an intruder*]; *Susie bid* [*six spades*]; *Mike owns* [*400 board games*]; *Susie has* [*blue eyes*].

**direct question** A sentence which has the form of a question expecting an answer. Examples: *Are you going to Susie's party?*; *What is the capital of Latvia?*; *How many players are there in a baseball team?* Compare EMBEDDED QUESTION, and see RHETORICAL QUESTION.

**direct speech** Quoting someone's exact words. In writing, direct speech is enclosed within QUOTATION MARKS. Example: *'I'm fed up', Susie said.* Compare INDIRECT SPEECH.

**discontinuous constituent** A syntactic unit which is broken up into two separated pieces. Consider the sentence *A student who speaks Chechen turned up this morning*. Here the subject is *a student who speaks Chechen*, and this is a single grammatical unit, a NOUN PHRASE. But it is also possible to say, or write, *A student turned up this morning who speaks Chechen*. Here that noun phrase has been split into two separated pieces, *a student* and *who speaks Chechen*, and it is now a discontinuous constituent.

**discourse** A connected stretch of language of some size, such as a conversation or a lecture. Some linguists restrict the term to a piece of speech, preferring TEXT for a piece of writing.

**discourse marker** A word or a phrase which is linked weakly or not at all to an adjoining sentence and which serves chiefly to keep a conversation or a text flowing smoothly. Among the items commonly used in this way are *yes*, *so*, *of course*, *nevertheless*, and, of course, *well*.

**disjunct** **1**. Any of two or more items connected by *or*, as in *coffee or tea*.

**2**. In the QUIRK GRAMMARS, another name for a SENTENCE ADVERB, so called because a sentence adverb is very weakly linked grammatically to the rest of its sentence.

**disjunction** A COORDINATE STRUCTURE involving *or* or *either . . . or*. Examples: *Would you like coffee or tea?*; *On an attempted runout, a cricket umpire may make the call or ask the third umpire to adjudicate*; *The successful applicant will either be a native speaker of French or hold a degree in French*. The items connected by the *or* are DISJUNCTS.

**dislocation** A construction in which a NOUN PHRASE is moved out of its normal position to the beginning or the end of the sentence, while its normal position is occupied by a PRONOUN. If it is moved to the beginning, we have LEFT-DISLOCATION; if to the end, we have RIGHT-DISLOCATION. Two examples of left-dislocation: *Mike, he's a nice guy*; *Susie, I really like her*. Of right-dislocation: *She's a great person, Susie*; *I really hate it, this takeaway exam*. Compare TOPICALIZATION.

**distal** See under DEICTIC POSITION.

**distribution** The set of linguistic contexts in which a linguistic item or class of items can occur. For example, a typical ADJECTIVE can occur in the following contexts, among others: *a very __ book*; *This book is __*; *__ though this book is, it is too expensive*. Distribution is a major criterion in assigning linguistic elements to classes, such as assigning words to PARTS OF SPEECH.

**distributive** Any linguistic form which picks out the members of a group as individuals. A distributive often involves *each* or *apiece*. Examples: *There's enough wine for two bottles apiece* (every person in the group can have two bottles); *The children each received a present* (there was one present for each child).

**ditransitive verb** A VERB which takes two objects, such as *give*, *show* and *teach*. In the following examples, the two objects are bracketed: *She gave* [*me*] [*a kiss*]; *She showed* [*her girlfriend*] [*her flat*]; *She taught* [*us*] [*Latin*].

***do*-support** A name sometimes given to the use of the 'dummy' auxiliary *do*, which is used in English when an AUXILIARY is required but no other auxiliary is present. Examples, starting with *Susie smokes*; *Susie doesn't smoke*; *Does Susie smoke?*; *Susie smokes, doesn't she?*

**double genitive** A name sometimes given to the English construction illustrated by examples like *a friend of mine, a student of Chomsky's* and *that car of John's*. These are used to express the sense of the ungrammatical forms like **my a friend* and **John's that car*.

**double negative** Any construction in which two or more negative words occur in a single clause. Examples: *I didn't see nothing* (= *I didn't see anything*); *No football team can't win no championship without no defenders* (= *No football team can win a championship without defenders*). Such constructions are normal in most vernacular forms of English, and they were formerly accepted also in standard English, but, for some centuries now, they have been regarded as non-standard. But note that standard English does accept double negatives when both negatives are logically required, as in *You can't not go* (= *It is impossible for you not to go*).

The use of double negatives is called NEGATIVE CONCORD by linguists, and negative concord is standard in some other languages. For example, to express 'I don't regret anything', standard French requires *Je ne regrette rien*, literally 'I don't regret nothing', and, to express 'I didn't see anybody', standard Spanish requires *No he visto a nadie*, literally 'I didn't see nobody'.

It is a common error to suppose that a double negative is equivalent to a positive. For example, *I didn't see nobody* plainly does not mean 'I saw somebody', and nobody but a fool would think that it does. This merely happens to be a non-standard, but perfectly familiar and understandable, way of saying 'I didn't see anybody'.

**double passive** The construction in which passive verb-forms occur both in a matrix clause and in a complement clause. The result is often clumsy, as in *The city was allowed to be captured*. Sometimes it results in ungrammaticality, as in **The Duke was attempted to be killed*.

**double perfect** The construction in which two instances of perfect *have* appear within a single sequence of verbs. A typical example is *I would have liked to have seen that*. This construction is usually objectionable: it would be better to write either *I would like to have seen that* or *I would have liked to see that*, depending on whether the liking is in the present or the past. For example, you would write *I would like to have met Napoleon*, since **I would have liked to meet Napoleon* suggests, wrongly, that you had a chance to meet Napoleon, but you might write

*I would have liked to marry Gabriella*, meaning that marrying Gabriella would have pleased you at the time, though not necessarily now.

**dual** A grammatical form denoting exactly two of something. English has only a very few dual forms, notably *both*, *either* and *neither* (with more than two, we use *all*, *any* and *none*, respectively).

**dummy** (also **expletive**) A meaningless word which is grammatically required to fill a position which would otherwise be empty but which refers to nothing. The two common English dummies are *it* and *there*. Examples: *It's raining; It's obvious that she's interested; There's a wasp on your back; There are no tigers in Africa*. In each of these examples, the *it* or *there* refers to nothing at all, but is required to make the sentence grammatical. Compare *They've just had a baby – it's a girl* and *I looked in the bedroom, but I didn't find it there*, in which *it* refers to the baby and *there* means 'in the bedroom'.

The English AUXILIARY *do* is sometimes called a *dummy auxiliary*, since it is required only for grammatical purposes, as in *Mike doesn't smoke* and *Does Mike smoke?*

**durative** An ASPECT form which indicates that an action or a state of affairs persists unchanged over a period of time. English has no special form for this. In the past tense, we commonly use the simple past, as in *I waited for an hour*.

**dvandva** A type of COMPOUND in which each element has an equal claim to being considered the HEAD, as though the elements were joined by the word *and*. Examples: *Austria–Hungary, tragicomic, freeze-dry*.

**dynamic** (also **eventive**) A label applied to a verb, a verb-form, a predicate or a sentence expressing an action, a movement or a change. Examples: *Jan peeled the potatoes; Jan left the room; Jan turned bright red*. Compare STATIVE.

# E

**echo response** Any response to an utterance which largely repeats what has just been said. Examples: Susie: *Did you get the coriander?*; Mike: *Did I get what?*; Susie: *I saw Alice this morning*; Mike: *You saw Alice this morning*.

**ellipsis** The omission from a sentence of material which is logically required to complete its structure. Examples: *'Nough said* ('Enough said'); *Seems we have a problem* ('It seems we have a problem').

**embedded question (also indirect question)** A QUESTION which is not being asked directly, but which merely forms part of a larger sentence, which itself may or may not be a question. In the following examples, the bracketed sequences are indirect questions. *I don't know* [*what I should do*] (the whole sentence is a statement in which the direct question *What should I do?* is embedded); *Tell me who I should talk to* (a command embedding the direct question *Who should I talk to?*); *Can you tell me where I can find the lost-and-found office?* (a question embedding the direct question *Where can I find the lost-and-found office?*). Note that an embedded question has a different word order from a direct question. An embedded YES–NO QUESTION is introduced by *whether* or *if*: *I don't know if we can afford it* (the embedded question is *Can we afford it?*).

**embedding** The presence of one CLAUSE inside another, sometimes especially inside another clause of the same kind. Consider the following example: *The critics who declared that the book that I had written was rubbish have been embarrassed*. Here the relative clause *that I had written* is embedded within the larger complement clause *that the book that I had written was rubbish*, which in turn is embedded within the still larger relative clause *who declared that the book that I had written was* *rubbish*, which finally is embedded within the main clause making up the whole sentence. With clauses bracketed, the structure of the whole sentence is this: [*The critics* [*who declared* [*that the book* [*that I had written*] *was rubbish*]] *have been embarrassed*].

**emphasis** A broad and informal term for any way of attaching particular importance to some part of a sentence or an utterance. Linguists prefer the term FOCUS: see this term for examples.

**emphatic stress** The addition of stress to a part of a sentence in order to emphasize it. For example, instead of saying *The Scots invented golf*, we can say *The SCOTS invented golf*, with strong stress on *Scots*, in order to emphasize this word.

**empty morph** A piece of a word which contributes nothing to the meaning of a word but which is required to make the word easily pronounceable. An English example is the *-o-* found in words like *kissogram* (*kiss* plus *-gram*) and *stripogram* (*strip* plus *-gram*).

**enclitic** See under CLITIC.

**endocentric compound** A COMPOUND which denotes a particular type of what is denoted by its HEAD. Examples: an *armchair* is a type of chair; *sky-blue* is a kind of blue; and to *spray-paint* is one way to paint. Compare BAHUVRIHI.

**epicene** In a language with a GENDER system showing a correlation with sex, denoting a noun which is invariable in gender but which can take referents of either sex. For example, French *écrivain* 'writer' and *témoin* 'witness' are always masculine, even when referring to women, while *victime* 'victim' and *personne* 'person' are always feminine, even when referring to men. Compare COMMON GENDER.

**epistemic modality** The area of MOOD or MODALITY concerned with knowledge and belief. For example, *must* is epistemic when it means 'is undoubtedly', as in (on hearing the doorbell) *That must be Susie*, and *may* is epistemic when it means 'is possibly', as in *We may need some help*. Compare DEONTIC MODALITY.

**equational sentence** A sentence which asserts that two descriptions or names denote (or do not denote) the same person or thing. Examples: *Tony Blair is the British prime minister; Saturn is not the largest planet; My wife is my best friend.* An equational sentence can be turned around: *My best friend is my wife.* This is one type of copular sentence; compare ASCRIPTIVE SENTENCE.

**equative** A construction indicating that the DEGREE of one thing is equal to the degree of another thing, usually expressed in English with *as . . . as*, sometimes reinforced with further words like *just* or *every bit*. Examples: *Susie drives as well as I do; Mike is just as good a cook as I am; Susie speaks French every bit as fluently as Ted.*

**ergative verb** A verb which can be either INTRANSITIVE, in which case the thing undergoing the action is represented by the subject, or TRANSITIVE, in which case the thing undergoing the action is represented by the direct object and the subject denotes the person or thing causing the action. An example is *sink*: *The ship sank; The sub sank the ship*. English has many such verbs; among the others are *melt* (*The ice melted/The sun melted the ice*), *boil, dissolve, explode, freeze* and *collapse*.

The term is inappropriate and unfortunate, since the sense has nothing to do with the grammatical phenomenon linguists call 'ergativity', and it is not usual among linguists, but it has become conventional among teachers of English.

**ethical construction** Any construction which includes explicit reference to a person who is affected by the action (almost always adversely) but not directly involved in it. The most usual English form for this purpose is the preposition *on* followed by a pronoun. Examples: *The dog died on me; Jane's boyfriend walked out on her; They stole the car on us.*

**euphemism** A polite word or expression used in place of a blunter one in order to avoid giving offence. Examples include *pass away* for *die*, *wee* for *urinate* and *make love* for *copulate*.

**eventive** Another term for DYNAMIC.

**exception** A form or construction which does not obey the usual rules. English nouns usually form their plurals in *-s*, as with *girls* and *foxes*, but *children* and *teeth* are exceptions. Transitive verbs usually form passives, as in *Susie kissed Natalie* and *Natalie was kissed by Susie*, but *Susie weighs 45 kilos* is an exception, since **45 kilos is weighed by Susie* is not possible.

**exclamation** An utterance, especially a complete sentence, which expresses strong emotion: one kind of (functional) SENTENCE TYPE. In English, an exclamation usually has a distinctive structure, the EXCLAMATORY sentence type. Examples: *How well Thorpe batted yesterday!*; *What a lovely painting this is!* Compare these with ordinary statements: *Thorpe batted very well yesterday*; *This is a very lovely painting.*

**exclamation mark** The punctuation mark [!], placed at the end of an utterance which is an EXCLAMATION or which merely expresses strong emotion. Examples: *What a lovely day it is!*; *I can't believe it!* For more on its use, see chapter 2 of *The Penguin Guide to Punctuation.*

**exclamatory** The (formal) SENTENCE TYPE (or MOOD) represented by the distinctive sentence structure illustrated in *How beautiful it is!* This pattern is commonly used in making an EXCLAMATION.

**existential sentence** A sentence which asserts the existence or non-existence of something, either in general or in a specified location. English uses its *there is* construction for this purposes. Examples: *There's a wasp on your back*; *There are no tigers in Africa*; *There are billions of galaxies*; *There were no human beings in New Zealand before the Maoris arrived.*

**exocentric compound** Another term for BAHUVRIHI.

**exophor** A linguistic item which resembles an ANAPHOR but which points to something in the context in which the speaker finds herself, and not to the linguistic context. For example, if I hold up a book and say *This is a good book*, the item *this* is behaving as an exophor, since there is no earlier linguistic context for it to point to, but only the book in my hand.

**expletive** **1**. Another term for DUMMY.

**2**. A swear word, sometimes especially one which is inserted into the middle of a phrase as a meaningless emotional intensifier, as in *Where's that bloody cat?*

**external sandhi** See under SANDHI.

**extraction** Another term for an UNBOUNDED DEPENDENCY.

**extraposition** Any construction in which a (typically long) phrase is removed from its normal position and placed at the end of the sentence. For example, *That she is drunk is obvious* has an extraposed counterpart *It is obvious that she is drunk*. A slightly different example is represented by *A student who speaks Chechen turned up this morning* and its extraposed counterpart *A student turned up this morning who speaks Chechen.*

# F

**factive verb** A VERB which assumes that what follows it is true. For example, *realize* is a factive verb, and so *Susie realized that she had lost her keys* can only be said by someone who believes that it is true that Susie had lost her keys. Not all verbs are factive: *Susie suspected that she had lost her keys* does not assume that Susie had in fact lost her keys.

**false friend** A word in a foreign language which looks very much like a word in your own language but which has a very different meaning. For example, French *librairie* looks very much like *library*, but it means *bookshop*, and Spanish *competencia* looks like English *competence*, but it means *competition*.

**feminine** In some languages with GENDER, a gender class which shows some degree of correlation with female sex. Many European languages have such a gender class, but the correlation with female sex is usually rather weak. In French, for example, most nouns denoting females are grammatically feminine, but there are exceptions, such as *soprano* 'soprano', which is grammatically masculine, even though all sopranos are women. In any case, most feminine nouns in French denote things which have no sex at all, such as *maison* 'house', *moûtarde* 'mustard' and *découverte* 'discovery'.

English, of course, has no grammatical gender at all, and words like *she* and *duchess* are marked only for female sex, not for feminine gender.

**finite** (also **tensed**) A label applied to a verb-form or a clause which is marked for TENSE. With its paucity of verbal inflection, English is not the ideal language to illustrate the distinction between finite and non-finite forms, but here are some examples. In the PRESENT tense, only the third-person singular normally receives an overt marking for tense: the ending *-s*. So, for example, in *Susie smokes*, the verb-form *smokes* is finite. By analogy, then, the form *smoke* is also finite in *I smoke, you smoke* and *Both women smoke*, even though there is no overt marker of tense in these cases. In contrast, the identical-looking form *smoke* is not finite in cases like *You may smoke* and *Susie wants to smoke*, where *smoke* is the INFINITIVE. In the PAST tense in English, tense is marked rather more systematically, either by the ending *-ed* or by a change in the stem of the verb: *Susie enjoyed her holiday* (here *enjoyed* is finite); *Susie took her niece to the beach* (here *took*, the past tense of *take*, is finite). The opposite is NON-FINITE.

**first-person** The PERSON category which denotes the speaker and possibly also some people associated with the speaker. The English first-person PRONOUNS are *I/me* (singular) and *we/us* (plural). The singular pronoun *I/me* always means 'the speaker', as in *I need a holiday*. The plural pronoun *we/us* usually means 'the speaker plus somebody else associated with the speaker', as in *The boss wants us to finish this report by Friday*. In rare circumstances, *we/us* can mean 'the speakers', as when an American football crowd chant *We want a touchdown!*

**flection** An old-fashioned term for INFLECTION.

**floating quantifier** A QUANTIFIER which occurs later in a sentence than in its logical position. For example, instead of saying *All the students have submitted their essays*, we can say *The students have all submitted their essays*, in which the quantifier *all* has 'floated' away from its logical position.

**focus** That part of a sentence which represents the most important new information. Consider the sentence *Jan bought Larry a shirt*. Here nothing is obviously in focus. But we can place any part of the sentence into focus in speech by stressing it: *JAN bought Larry a shirt* (it was Jan, not somebody else, who bought it); *Jan BOUGHT Larry a shirt* (she got it by paying for it, not otherwise); *Jan bought LARRY a shirt* (the shirt was for Larry, not for someone else); *Jan bought Larry A SHIRT* (not a tie or a book). We can also focus on an element with a CLEFT construction: *It was a shirt that Jan bought Larry* (not a tie or a book).

**folk etymology** The process in which a word of obscure formation is altered in form in order to make it seemingly more transparent, if not always sensible. English examples include *Welsh rabbit* to *Welsh rarebit* (the motivation for *rabbit* is obscure), French *écrevisse* to *crayfish* (a crayfish is not a fish, but at least it lives in the water), and *asparagus* to regional *sparrowgrass* (asparagus is not grass, but at least it's a green plant).

**foreign plural** A PLURAL form of a NOUN which is not formed according to any native pattern, but which has been imported directly from a foreign language. English has dozens of these. Examples include *radii* for *radius* (from Latin), *phenomena* for *phenomenon* (from Greek), *concerti* for *concerto* (from Italian) and *kibbutzim* for *kibbutz* (from Hebrew). These often cause difficulties for English-speakers, who may have trouble remembering which form is the singular and which is the plural.

**form** The internal structure, or the physical shape, of a linguistic element, without regard for any meaning or function it may have.

**formal** **1**. Pertaining to FORM. For example, English makes a formal difference between *hung* and *hanged*, as in *We hung the picture in the lounge* and *We hanged the murderer in Tombstone*.

**2**. The label applied to an approach to the description of grammar which is fully explicit and mechanical, and often somewhat mathematical in appearance. For example, the statement S → NP VP is a formal way of saying 'A sentence may consist of a noun phrase followed by a verb phrase.' Formalisms of this type are much used in modern grammatical description and theory.

**formative** A grammatical MORPHEME. English examples include the past-tense marker *-ed* of *She played well*, the plural *-s* of *a swarm of bees* and the possessive *-'s* of *I met Susie's girlfriend*.

**fragment** An incomplete piece of a SENTENCE, used by itself. Fragments are normal and very frequent in speech. In each of the following exchanges, Mike's response is a fragment. Ted: *Where's Susie?* Mike: *In the library*. Ted: *Can England win the World Cup?* Mike: *Probably not*. In formal writing, however, fragments are usually out of place.

**free morpheme** A MORPHEME which can possibly stand alone to make a word all by itself, even though it may sometimes combine with other morphemes in a larger word. For example, the English morpheme *happy* is free, because it can stand alone to make the word *happy*, even though it can also combine with other morphemes to make larger words like *unhappy* and *happiness*. Compare BOUND MORPHEME.

**free relative** (also **headless relative**) A RELATIVE CLAUSE which has no HEAD and which occupies a noun-phrase position all by itself. In the following examples, the free relatives are bracketed: [*What we need*] *is a hot-air gun*; [*Whoever did this*] *is in trouble*; *We talked about* [*when we should retire*]. As you can see, an English free relative begins with a WH-word. In each case, there is an alternative which is an ordinary relative clause. In my examples, these would be *the thing that we need*, *the person who did this* and *the time when we should retire*.

Note that, in English, a free relative sometimes looks just like an EMBEDDED QUESTION. Consider the example *I saw what she put in the box*. When this means 'I saw the thing that she put in the box', it is a free relative. But, when it means 'I can answer the question "What did she put in the box?"', it is an embedded question.

**fronting** (also **preposing**) Any construction in which an element of a sentence which would commonly occur somewhere else is placed at the beginning of the sentence. For example, *There was a spider in the bath* has a fronted counterpart *In the bath there was a spider*, in which the prepositional phrase *in the bath* has been fronted. Likewise, *I have seldom seen such a mess* has a fronted counterpart *Seldom have I seen such a mess*, in which the adverb *seldom* is fronted; in this case, the auxiliary verb *have* must also be placed before the subject *I*. Finally, *I can't recommend this book* has a fronted counterpart *This book I can't recommend*, in which the direct object noun phrase *this book* is fronted; this last is TOPICALIZATION.

**full stop** (also **period**) The PUNCTUATION MARK [.]. In writing, this is placed at the end of a SENTENCE which expresses a statement. See almost any sentence in this book for an example. The full stop is also used in writing certain ABBREVIATIONS, such as *oz.* for *ounce(s)*, *Prof.* for *Professor*, *i.e.* for *in other words*, and *e.g.* for *for example*. See chapters 2 and 7 of *The Penguin Guide to Punctuation* for further information.

**function** A purpose to which a linguistic form or construction may be put. In linguistic analysis, it is essential to distinguish between form and function: these do not match up one to one, and often a single form can be used in several different functions, while a single function can be served by several different forms. For example, if I want to get somebody to sit down, I can use any of several formally quite different constructions: a command (*Sit down!*), a question (*Why don't you sit down?*), or even a statement (*You can sit down, you know*).

**functional grammar** Any approach to grammatical description which attaches great importance to the purposes to which grammatical forms are put, and not only to the forms themselves. A number of functional approaches have been developed; one of the most prominent is SYSTEMIC GRAMMAR.

**function word** Another term for GRAMMATICAL WORD.

**fusion** The grammatical phenomenon in which two or more morphemes are combined into a larger unit in such a way that no clear boundaries are visible between the morphemes. For example, in English, {foot} plus {Plural} yields *feet*, in which the two morphemes have fused into a single form. In the same way, {take} plus {Past} yields *took*.

**future** A TENSE which chiefly correlates with time later than the time of speaking. Romance languages like French, Spanish and Italian have a distinct future tense, though they do not always use their future tense for talking about future time. For example, 'I'm going to sing tonight' would in Spanish usually be expressed with present-tense *Voy a cantar esta noche*, not with future *Cantaré esta noche*. English, like most Germanic and Slavic languages, has no future tense at all. We have many ways of talking about future time, but all involve PRESENT-tense forms: *I go to London tomorrow*, *I'm going to London tomorrow*, *I'm going to go to London tomorrow*, *I'll go to London tomorrow*, *I must go to London tomorrow*, *I may go to London tomorrow*, and others. All of these express different views of a future event, but not one is a future tense.

**future-in-the-past** A VERB-form with the following interpretation: at some point in the past, the action is viewed as lying in the future.

Suppose that, last Tuesday, you said this: *Susie is going to quit her job*. Today you might say the following: *Susie was going to quit her job*. This last is a future-in-the-past.

**future perfect** A VERB-form which indicates that something which is in the future now will be in the past at some point in the future. English uses *will have* or *shall have* to express this. For example, if I say *I will have finished my essay by Friday*, this means that the essay is not finished now, but that I will finish it on or before Friday, so that on Friday I will be able to say *I have finished my essay*.

# G

**gap** The missing grammatical unit in an example of GAPPING.

**gapping** The construction in which a unit of a sentence is omitted, rather than repeated. Here is an example, in which the gapped unit is represented by *e*: *Jan ordered vegetable pathia and Larry* e *chicken dhansak*. Here the gap *e* represents a silent repetition of *ordered*. It is possible to have more than one gap in a single sentence: *Rod gave the museum a T-shirt and Elton* e e *a pair of glasses*. Here the two gaps represent *gave* and *the museum*.

**gender** A phenomenon found in some languages, though not in all, in which all NOUNS are divided into two or more classes requiring different AGREEMENT. French, for example, has two gender classes, traditionally called 'masculine' and 'feminine', though the labels are not entirely appropriate. In French, 'an old book' is *un vieux livre*, while 'an old house' is *une vieille maison*. Here both the determiner meaning 'the' and the adjective meaning 'old' vary in form according to the gender of the noun: masculine for *livre* 'book', feminine for *maison* 'house'. Spanish and Italian are similar to French, while German, Russian and Latin have three genders called 'masculine', 'feminine' and 'neuter'.

It is important to realize that gender is not the same thing as sex. In French, for example, gender has only a weak connection with sex: masculine nouns like *oiseau* 'bird', *vin* 'wine' and *soprano* 'soprano' have no particular connection with male sex, and feminine nouns like *moutarde* 'mustard', *découverte* 'discovery' and *sentinelle* 'sentry' have no particular connection with female sex.

In some other gender languages, gender exhibits no connection with sex at all. For example, the African language Swahili has eight genders, none of which shows any connection with sex, while the American language Navaho has at least ten genders, none of which has any connection with sex. In these other languages, gender is sometimes correlated with other categories, such as animacy, size or shape.

English, of course, has no grammatical gender at all. The familiar distinction among *he*, *she* and *it* is a matter of biology, not of gender. It is an error to speak of the difference between *he* and *she* as one of gender, or the difference between *duke* and *duchess*, or the difference between *Robert* and *Roberta*. These are purely distinctions of sex, not of gender.

**generative grammar** A kind of formal grammar of a language which is capable of listing all and only the grammatical sentences of that language in a purely mechanical way. That is, once a generative grammar has been constructed, it simply defines all the sentences of a language in a mindless, mechanical way, with no further human intervention, much as an algebraic equation defines all the points lying on a particular curve. The idea of generative grammars was introduced into linguistics by the American linguist Noam Chomsky in the 1950s; since then, Chomsky and others have developed and elaborated dozens of different kinds of generative grammars, the most famous being Chomsky's own TRANSFORMATIONAL GRAMMAR. But every kind of generative grammar requires a LEXICON (a set of words) and a set of rules for combining those words into permissible sentences, and generative grammars chiefly differ in the nature of the rules used and in the way the lexicon is organized. Generative grammars are of little or no use in the everyday study of language or grammar for most practical purposes, but they are often of great importance in addressing certain theoretical questions and in constructing computer programs intended to perform real-world tasks with language data.

Note that, in recent years, Chomsky and his followers have been applying the term *generative grammar* rather loosely to the kind of grammatical theorizing which they embrace, even though this work is no longer generative in the original sense of the term.

**generic** A NOUN or a NOUN PHRASE which denotes an entire class of things, rather than picking out an individual thing. Most ordinary nouns are generic in isolation: *dog, girl, wine, mystery, happiness*. Generic noun phrases can take any of several forms: *Dogs are closely related to wolves; The dog is closely related to the wolf; A dog is closely related to a wolf.*

**genitive** Another term for POSSESSIVE, often especially in a language which has a special CASE-form for this function.

**gerund** A form of a VERB which retains verbal properties but which turns the entire VERB PHRASE containing it into a NOUN PHRASE. In English, the gerund ending is *-ing*. Consider the verb *have*, and consider this example: *I enjoy having a drink in my hand*. Here *have* stands in its gerund form *having*, and *having* is exhibiting verbal properties: in this case, it takes the object *a drink*. The entire verb phrase *having a drink in my hand* is a noun phrase functioning as the object of the verb *enjoy*. In English, a verb phrase headed by a gerund can occupy any noun-phrase position. It can be a subject (*Killing foxes is a horrible pastime*), a direct object (as in the first example), a predicate nominal (*Edward's idea of foreplay is taking his socks off*), or the object of a preposition (*I don't believe in buying wine as an investment*). Compare VERBAL NOUN, and note the discussion there about distinguishing a verbal noun in *-ing* from a gerund.

***get*-passive** See under PASSIVE VOICE.

**given and new** One way of analysing the structure of a sentence, in terms of its information structure. Many (not all) sentences can be divided into two parts: one part expressing information already known to the hearer (the *given* or *old* information), and a second part expressing information which is not already known (the *new* information). Usually the given part comes first. For example, if I am giving a lecture on the geography of Africa, I might say *Africa has three major deserts*. Here *Africa* is the given information, while *has three major deserts* is the new information.

**gnomic** The ASPECT category of a statement which expresses a general or timeless truth. English generally uses the simple present for this purpose: *Water boils at 100°C*; *Rhubarb leaves are poisonous*.

**goal** The SEMANTIC ROLE which represents the person or place toward which some action is directed, such as *Susie* in *I'm sending Susie some flowers*.

**government** The grammatical phenomenon in which the *presence* of one item determines the *form* of another item linked to it. For example, in English any preposition requires its object to stand in the objective form if it is a pronoun: *with her*, not **with she*; *to us*, not **to we*; *between you and me*, not **between you and I*. We say that an English preposition *governs* objective case. Compare AGREEMENT.

**Government-and-Binding Theory** (also **principles-and-parameters approach**) A theory of grammar developed by Noam Chomsky and his colleagues in the 1980s, the direct successor of TRANSFORMATIONAL GRAMMAR.

**gradable** Of an ADJECTIVE or ADVERB, denoting a property which can be present to a greater or lesser degree. Gradable words permit DEGREE MODIFIERS like *more, most, very* and *rather*. Examples include *big* (*bigger*), *beautiful* (*most beautiful*), *slowly* (*very slowly*) and *interesting* (*rather interesting*). Not all adjectives and adverbs can do this: *alive* (**most alive*), *principal* (**very principal*), *topmost* (**rather topmost*), *immediately* (**very immediately*).

**grammar** **1**. The branch of linguistics dealing with the structures of words and sentences, commonly divided into MORPHOLOGY (word structure) and SYNTAX (sentence structure).

**2**. Any particular approach to this study. This is the sense found in labels like TRADITIONAL GRAMMAR and TRANSFORMATIONAL GRAMMAR.

**3**. A particular description of the grammatical facts of a language.

**4**. A book containing such a description.

**grammatical** **1**. Pertaining to GRAMMAR, especially in sense 1.

**2**. Another term for WELL-FORMED.

**grammatical category** Any category whose presence causes the words in a particular PART OF SPEECH to vary in form for grammatical reasons. Examples include PERSON, NUMBER, DEGREE, CASE and TENSE, though others exist. In English, pronouns distinguish person (*I, you, she*); nouns distinguish number (*dog/dogs*); adjectives distinguish degree (*big/bigger/biggest*); some pronouns distinguish case (*I/me*); and verbs distinguish tense (*take/took*). Compare SYNTACTIC CATEGORY.

**grammatical morpheme** A MORPHEME which has little or no meaning but which serves a grammatical function. English examples include *of*, *the*, the plural suffix *-s* and the past-tense suffix *-ed*. Compare LEXICAL MORPHEME.

**grammatical relation** Any one of the ways in which a NOUN PHRASE can be related to the rest of its sentence. Among the familiar grammatical relations are SUBJECT, DIRECT OBJECT, INDIRECT OBJECT and OBLIQUE OBJECT.

**grammatical word** (also **function word**) A word which has little or no meaningful content, but which has a grammatical function. English examples include *the*, *of*, *and* and the infinitival *to*. The preposition *to* is grammatical in *Jan gave her magazines to Pete*, as shown by the fact that it can be omitted without loss of meaning in the alternative *Jan gave Pete her magazines*.

**greengrocer's apostrophe** The non-standard use of the APOSTROPHE in writing a PLURAL, often seen in public signs like *Pizza's £2.99*. Standard English orthography does not normally permit apostrophes in plurals, and would require *Pizzas £2.99*.

**group genitive** The English construction in which the possessive *-'s* is added to the end of a NOUN PHRASE whose final word is not its HEAD. Examples include *The Queen of England's ancestors* (the ancestors belong to the Queen, not to England), *The Wife of Bath's Tale* (the tale belongs to the wife, not to Bath), and *the woman you were talking to's husband* (the husband belongs to the woman, not to the grammatical word *to*).

# H

**habitual** A particular ASPECT form, a variety of the IMPERFECTIVE, which indicates that the action named is customary, habitual or usual. Some languages have a specialized auxiliary verb for expressing habitual aspect, as does Spanish, with its verb *soler*. English has no such verb, and it expresses habitual aspect variously. In the present tense, the SIMPLE PRESENT form is used: *Susie smokes*; *I get up at 7.30*; *Koalas eat eucalyptus leaves*. Indeed, this is by far the most frequent function of the simple present. In the past tense, we most commonly use our *used to* construction: *Susie used to smoke*; *I used to get up at 7.30*; *Baseball games used to be played in the daytime*. This last often indicates that what was true in the past is no longer true today, but not necessarily so: if I have lost touch with Susie, then *Susie used to smoke* may be consistent with 'and she still does, for all I know'. But sometimes the past habitual is expressed with the simple past: *The Romans wore togas*; *Huge sabre-toothed cats ranged over Kansas at that time*; *The Mogul emperors practised Islam*.

**hanging participle** Another term for DANGLING PARTICIPLE.

**haplology** The process in which one of two consecutive identical or similar syllables is lost. For example, *library* is often pronounced in Britain as though it were *libry*, with loss of the first of the two syllables starting with /r/.

**head** That element in a PHRASE which determines the nature of the phrase. For example, the phrase *the little girl in the blue dress* clearly denotes a kind of girl, and not a kind of dress or a kind of blue. It is therefore a NOUN PHRASE, and its head is *girl*. Similarly, the phrase *as blue as the sky* denotes a kind of blue, and it is an ADJECTIVE PHRASE with the head *blue*.

**headless compound** Another term for BAHUVRIHI.

**headless relative clause** Another term for FREE RELATIVE.

**headline language** The rather special variety of English used in writing newspaper headlines. In the following examples, the first form illustrates headline language and the second ordinary English: *President denies misconduct* (*The President has denied misconduct*); *Universities feeling the pinch* (*Universities are feeling the pinch*); *PM to visit China* (*The Prime Minister is going to visit China*). Compare BLOCK LANGUAGE.

**headword** (also **lemma**) A word which is a main entry in a dictionary.

**hedge** An expression used to reduce your commitment to what you are saying, such as *I think, I suppose, I fancy, I would guess, I take it* or *it seems to me*.

**helping verb** Another term for AUXILIARY.

**historic present** The use of the PRESENT tense in a narrative.

**homograph** One of two or more words of different meaning which are spelled in the same way, regardless of whether they are pronounced the same or differently. For example, *bear* (the name of the large animal) and *bear* (the verb, as in *I can't bear this*) are homographs which are pronounced identically, while *lead* (the name of the metal) and *lead* (the verb, as in *The Mayor will lead the parade*) are homographs which are pronounced differently. Compare HOMOPHONE.

**homonym** A cover term including both HOMOPHONE and HOMOGRAPH.

**homophone** One of two or more words of different meaning which are pronounced in the same way, regardless of whether they are spelled the same or differently. For example, *bear* (the name of the large animal) and *bear* (the verb, as in *I can't bear this*) are homophones which are spelled the same, while *bare* ('naked') is a further homophone which is spelled differently. Compare HOMOGRAPH.

**hortative** A traditional label for a construction expressing an exhortation, represented in English by the *let's* construction, as in *Let's go* and *Let's see what's going on.*

**hybrid** A word constructed by combining MORPHEMES deriving ultimately from different languages. A familiar example is *television,* in which *tele-* 'far' derives from Greek while *vision* 'seeing' derives from Latin. Pedants sometimes object to such hybrid formations, but these are so well-established and so numerous that it is pointless to object to them: *speedometer* (English plus Greek), *megastar* (Greek plus English), *drinkable* (English plus French), *high school* (English plus Greek/Latin), and so on. New hybrids are coined freely: I recently encountered *techno-anorak* 'computer nerd', which elements derive from Greek and from an Eskimo language.

**hypercorrection** A mistake resulting from a confused attempt at avoiding another mistake. Here is an example. In many vernacular forms of English, it is normal to say *Him and me were there,* but standard English requires *He and I were there.* Vernacular speakers who have been taught to avoid their normal form may overcompensate by saying *This job was done by he and I,* even though standard English requires *by him and me*: this is hypercorrection.

**hyphen** The punctuation mark [-], which is shorter than a DASH. The hyphen has the following uses.

**1.** It must be used within a compound modifier, a phrase of two or more words which modifies a following noun. Examples: *a copper-producing region, a low-scoring match, her Swiss-German ancestry, her new-found freedom, a green-eyed beauty, a good-morning kiss, a salt-and-pepper moustache, a ten-year-old son.*

**2.** It may optionally be used in any COMPOUND word which would be hard to read without it. Examples: *land-owners, bounty-hunter, brick-red.* Often a white space is an alternative here.

**3.** It must be used after a PREFIX if the whole word would otherwise be hard to read. Examples: *pre-war, mini-computer, anti-vivisectionist, re-cover* ('put a new cover on'; compare *recover* 'get back').

**4.** It must be used, at the appropriate end, whenever a piece of a word is cited. Examples: *the prefix* re-, *the past-tense suffix* -ed, *pre- and post-war Berlin.*

**5**. It must be used whenever a word is broken at the end of a line.

For more information on the hyphen, see *The Penguin Guide to Punctuation*, section 6.1.

The hyphen should not be confused with the dash, and it should never follow a COLON.

**hypocoristic** Another term for DIMINUTIVE.

**hypotaxis** Another term for SUBORDINATION.

# I

**idiom** A fixed expression whose meaning is not guessable from the meanings of its parts. Examples include *let the cat out of the bag* (reveal a secret), *buy a pig in a poke* (commit oneself to a course of action without investigating), *a fish out of water* (a person struggling in an unfamiliar environment) and *kick the bucket* (die).

**ill-formed** (also **ungrammatical**) Of a sentence, not constructed in accordance with the grammatical rules of the language; not WELL-FORMED. All of the following are ill-formed in standard English, and probably in all varieties of English: **These dog are hungry*; **New book this is interesting*; **Susie wants buy a car*. The next examples, however, are ill-formed in standard English but well-formed in certain regional and social varieties of English: **NYPD Blue is a poor show any more*; **I ain't seen him today*; **I might could do it*; **Us is happy about it.*

In educational contexts, we are normally concerned only with well-formedness and ill-formedness in standard English, but even this issue is not always straightforward: see USAGE.

**immediate constituent** See under CONSTITUENT STRUCTURE.

**imperative** The (formal) SENTENCE TYPE (or MOOD) illustrated in English by the following distinctive sentence pattern: *Wash your hands!* This pattern commonly expresses a COMMAND. In English, an imperative usually has no overt subject (though *you* is understood as its subject), and the verb stands in its INFINITIVE (uninflected) form. In writing, an imperative is often punctuated with an EXCLAMATION MARK. Examples: *Wash the dishes!*; *Do your homework!*; *Don't smoke in the house!* It is possible, however, to put *you* into subject position, as in *You watch your mouth, young lady!*

It is best to reserve the label *imperative* for a sentence which has this form. It is possible, and normal, in English to use an imperative sentence for a function other than giving a command. For example, if you are going out to a film, I may say *Enjoy the film*, but this is not an order, only a hope. And, if we are following a recipe that calls for caraway seeds, and we've run out of them, I can say *Try cumin seeds*, and this is not an order, but a suggestion.

Likewise, it is possible to use another sentence form to give an order. Most obviously, an army officer can say to his men *I order you to hold your position*. This is certainly an order, yet it does not have the form of an imperative sentence: instead, it has the form of a DECLARATIVE sentence. Compare JUSSIVE.

**imperfect** A particular set of verb-forms, found in Romance languages like Spanish, French and Italian. The imperfect is PAST in tense and IMPERFECTIVE in aspect, and so it usually denotes an action which extended over a period of time in the past. There is no single English equivalent: for example, Spanish *bebía* may be translated as 'I was drinking', 'I used to drink' or even (in certain circumstances) 'I drank'.

**imperfective** The ASPECT category which indicates that the action of a verb is presented as having internal structure. The most familiar varieties of the imperfective in English are the CONTINUOUS and the HABITUAL. For example, corresponding to the perfective form *Susie drank vodka*, which expresses no internal structure, we have continuous *Susie was drinking vodka* and habitual *Susie used to drink vodka*, as well as other possibilities like the ITERATIVE *Susie kept (on) drinking vodka*. Compare PERFECTIVE.

**impersonal** A very general label for any construction in which the action described is assigned to no one in particular. English often uses the 'dummy' pronoun *it* for this purpose: *It is raining; It seems that we have a problem; It transpired that the councillors had been fiddling their expenses; It so happened that there was a doctor in the audience*. But other constructions exist: impersonal *they* in *A delicatessen is a place where they sell specialist foods*, impersonal *you* in *A delicatessen is a place where you buy specialist foods*, and impersonal *one*, as in *One must be very careful*. See also IMPERSONAL PASSIVE.

**impersonal passive** A sentence in the PASSIVE VOICE which attributes the action of the verb to no one in particular. In English, impersonal passives often begin with the dummy *it*: *it is thought that . . . , it is believed that . . . , it is said that . . .* Example: *It is often said that Basque is an exceedingly difficult language to learn.*

**inalienable possession** The property of a POSSESSIVE in which the possessed represents something that cannot reasonably be separated from the possessor. Examples: *Susie's parents, my eyes, Susie's name, France's history*. Unlike some other languages, English makes no distinction of form between this and ALIENABLE POSSESSION.

**inanimate** The label applied to a NOUN or a NOUN PHRASE which denotes something other than a human being or an animal. Plants, though living, are classed as inanimate. Examples: *tree, index, absence, my ancestry, the capital of Italy, the rest of the book*. Compare ANIMATE.

**inchoative** The ASPECT category which indicates that something is just beginning. Unlike some other languages, English has no particular form for this. We use a verb like *start* or *begin*, as in *It started to rain.*

**incorporation** The grammatical pattern in which a noun is combined with a verb to produce a complex verb. Incorporation is not common in English, but we do have complex verbs like *babysit* ('sit with a baby'), *house-hunt* ('hunt for a house') and *stargaze* ('gaze at stars').

**indefinite** A very general label applied to any linguistic form which refers to nobody and nothing in particular. English has the INDEFINITE ARTICLE *a*(*n*), several INDEFINITE PRONOUNS like *something* and *anybody*, and various other indefinite forms like *somewhere, somehow* and the *ever* of *Have you ever been in Paris?*

**indefinite article** The conventional name for the English determiner *a* (or *an*). This has two distinct uses. For example, *I'm looking for a house* can mean either 'I'm looking for a specific house (of which I know the identity but you don't)' or 'I'm looking for some house or other (perhaps one suitable for buying)'. The first is called the *specific* sense, the second the *non-specific sense*. Compare DEFINITE ARTICLE.

**indefinite pronoun** A PRONOUN which denotes nobody in particular. The English indefinite pronouns are *somebody, someone, something, anybody, anyone* and *anything*. The negative pronouns (*nobody, no one, nothing*) are sometimes also classed as indefinite pronouns.

**indicative** The MOOD category associated with an ordinary statement: *My wife is away; We have just returned from Prague; Oil is not soluble in water; Susie will be back shortly*. In English, as in most languages, the indicative has no special marking.

**indirect object** In traditional grammar, the GRAMMATICAL RELATION borne by a noun phrase which represents a grammatical OBJECT, distinct from a DIRECT OBJECT, which identifies the person or people indirectly affected by the action of the verb. Consider the sentences *Mike gave the books to Susie* and *Mike gave Susie the books*. Traditionally, *Susie* would be classed as an indirect object in both cases, contrasting with the subject *Mike* and the direct object *the books*. However, not all contemporary linguists would agree: in the first example, *Susie* looks very much like an ordinary object of a preposition, while, in the second, the existence of the passive *Susie was given the books by Mike* suggests that *Susie* is really a direct object. It is therefore not certain that English has any indirect objects, and different linguists hold varying views on the issue.

**indirect question** Another term for EMBEDDED QUESTION.

**indirect speech** (also **reported speech**) Reporting what someone has said without quoting the exact words. Example: *Susie said she was fed up*. Compare DIRECT SPEECH.

**infinitive** A particular verb-form, occurring in some but not all languages, which serves to express the verbal idea in its simplest form, without any marking for tense, aspect, mood, person or other grammatical categories. In English, the infinitive is the bare form of a verb, its dictionary form, the form which can immediately follow a MODAL AUXILIARY like *must* or *will* or which can follow the 'infinitival' particle *to*: *go, sleep, take, be, arrive, consider, decide* and so on. Because of the confusion noted in the next paragraph, this form is sometimes called the *bare infinitive* or the *base form*.

However, as a result of confusion, many people have gained the false impression that the infinitive of a verb consists of the bare infinitive preceded by the particle *to*, and as a result they believe that infinitives are forms like *to go*, *to sleep* and *to take*. This view is mistaken: that *to* does not form part of the verb at all, as is shown, for example, by the fact that *to* can readily be separated from a following infinitive by a phrase, as explained under SPLIT INFINITIVE. Still, this erroneous view is prominent, and therefore we sometimes find it convenient to speak of a sequence like *to go* as a TO-INFINITIVE.

**infix** An AFFIX which interrupts another MORPHEME. English has no true infixes, but the plural suffix *-s* behaves something like an infix in unusual plurals like *passers-by* and *mothers-in-law*.

**inflection** Changes in the form of a word for grammatical reasons. For example, the noun *dog* has just two inflected forms, *dog* and *dogs*, while the verb *take* has the five inflected forms *take*, *takes*, *took*, *taking* and *taken*. Compare DERIVATION (sense I).

**inflectional morphology** The branch of MORPHOLOGY dealing with the way in which words (LEXICAL ITEMS) change their forms for grammatical purposes. For example, *dog* may appear as either *dog* or *dogs*, depending on the context; *big* may appear as any of *big*, *bigger* or *biggest*; and *write* may appear as any of *write*, *writes*, *wrote*, *writing* or *written*. Compare DERIVATIONAL MORPHOLOGY.

**initialism** A word constructed by taking the initial letters of the important words in a phrase, producing something which cannot be pronounced as a word, but must be spelled out letter by letter. Examples: *BBC* (for *British Broadcasting Corporation*), *FBI* (for *Federal Bureau of Investigation*). Compare ACRONYM. Note that some people do not distinguish initialisms from acronyms, using *acronym* for both.

**instrument** The SEMANTIC ROLE which expresses the object with which some task is performed, such as *an old toothbrush* in *She scrubbed her brooch with an old toothbrush*. English usually expresses an instrument with the preposition *with*, as in the example, though occasionally it uses *by*, as in *She wrote this by hand*. Some other languages, such as Russian and Basque, have a distinct CASE-form for instruments, the *instrumental* case.

**instrumental** A label applied to a NOUN PHRASE which denotes the instrument or means with which some task is performed. English commonly uses the preposition *with* for this purpose: *She writes her letters with a fountain pen*. But other prepositions are sometimes possible: *I wrote this book on my Mac; I wrote this book in WordPerfect.*

**intensifier** Another (and rather inaccurate) term for DEGREE MODIFIER.

**intensive reflexive** A REFLEXIVE PRONOUN which does not occupy its own slot in the sentence but serves only to emphasize a noun phrase which is already present. An example is *myself* in *I myself did it* or *I did it myself*. These are merely emphatic ways of saying *I did it*, and they are different from a true REFLEXIVE, like *I saw myself in the mirror*.

**interfix** A piece of meaningless material inserted between a STEM and an AFFIX to produce a result which is easier to pronounce. An English example is the *-o-* which appears in formations like *kissogram* (*kiss* plus *-gram*) and *stripogram* (*strip* plus *-gram*).

**interjection** A word or phrase which, as a rule, occurs by itself, expresses emotion and does not form part of a sentence. English examples include *Ouch!*, *Damn!*, *Aaargh!*, *Whoopee!*, *My god!* and *Bloody hell!*, as well as a number of coarser expressions.

**internal sandhi** See under SANDHI.

**interrogative** The MOOD category assigned to a QUESTION, or the (formal) SENTENCE TYPE commonly employed for this purpose. Unlike some other languages, English has no special marking for questions, but we do construct most questions with a distinctive word order. Compare the word order of the (INDICATIVE) statement *Susie is drinking tea* with the word order of the YES–NO QUESTION *Is Susie drinking tea?* and the WH-QUESTION *What is Susie drinking?* Here both questions exhibit INVERSION.

**interrogative pronoun** A PRONOUN which asks a question. The English ones are *who*, *what* and *which*, as in these examples: *Who were you talking to?*; *What happened?*; *Which do you prefer?*

**intransitive** The label applied to a VERB which does not take a DIRECT OBJECT. Some English verbs are always intransitive and can never take an object; among these are *arrive, snore, elapse, hibernate* and *stroll*:

| | |
|---|---|
| *Susie arrived early.* | **Susie arrived the party early.* |
| *Susie was snoring.* | **Susie was snoring a racket.* |
| *Two hours elapsed.* | **Two hours elapsed my attention.* |
| *Bears hibernate.* | **Bears hibernate the winter.* |
| *Susie strolled along the shore.* | **Susie strolled the kids along the shore.* |

Many other verbs can be either transitive or intransitive; see LABILE VERB. Compare TRANSITIVE. The label *intransitive* is also applied to a verb phrase or a clause containing an intransitive verb.

Note that certain intransitive verbs can be followed by NOUN PHRASES which are not direct objects. For examples of these, see COPULA and QUASI-COPULA.

**inversion** Any construction in which the ordinary WORD ORDER is reversed, and particularly a case in which the order of the SUBJECT and an AUXILIARY verb is reversed (this is SUBJECT-VERB INVERSION). Consider the statement *Susie is buying a car,* in which the subject *Susie* precedes the auxiliary *is.* In the corresponding YES-NO QUESTION *Is Susie buying a car?*, the order of these two elements is inverted, and the same is true in the WH-QUESTION *What car is Susie buying?* Inversion also occurs in certain other circumstances. For example, *I have often wondered about that* undergoes FRONTING to produce *Often I have wondered about that,* but *I have seldom seen such a mess* has the fronted version *Seldom have I seen such a mess,* with inversion of *I* and *have.*

**inverted commas** Another name for QUOTATION MARKS.

**irrealis** A very general label for any grammatical form or construction which expresses some kind of unreality. English has no very systematic way of expressing unreality, but the irrealis is clearly expressed in COUNTERFACTUAL sentences; see under CONDITIONAL SENTENCE.

**irregular** A label applied to any linguistic item which does not behave in the way that is typical of items in its class. For example, the verb *watch* is REGULAR (*I watch her, I watched her, I have watched her*), while *see* is irregular (*I see her, I saw her, I have seen her*).

***it*-cleft** See under CLEFT.

**iterative** An ASPECT form, a variety of the IMPERFECTIVE, which indicates that an action is repeated a number of times. In English, the iterative is usually expressed with *keep* (*on*), as in *I keep* (*on*) *losing my keys* and *I kept* (*on*) *failing my driving test.*

# JK

**jocular formation** A word which is constructed purely as a joke and, as a rule, does not gain a place in the language. Examples include *wasm* ('an outdated doctrine', based on *ism*) and *monokini* ('bikini with no top', from *bikini* with replacement of the accidental syllable *bi-*, resembling the prefix *bi-* 'two', by *mono-* 'one').

**jussive** A traditional label for a verb-form or a sentence structure which expresses some kind of command. The jussive includes the ordinary IMPERATIVE, as in *Wash your hands!* But it also includes other structures, such as *Everybody pay attention* and *Let's go*. Sometimes the label is applied more narrowly to a command directed at someone other than the addressee, as in *Let them eat cake!*, when this is interpreted as an instruction to 'them', and not as an order to the addressee.

# L

**labile verb** A verb which can be either TRANSITIVE or INTRANSITIVE, with related meanings. English has many of these, divided into a number of subclasses. Examples: *Susie smokes Turkish cigarettes; Susie smokes; Susie undressed the children; Susie undressed; The sub sank the ship; The ship sank; Susie washed her bikini; This bikini washes easily; She swam the Channel; She swam slowly; Susie jumped the horse over the fence; The horse jumped over the fence; They are reprinting my book; My book is reprinting.*

**learnèd word** A word taken from a classical language. For example, instead of *breakable*, English often uses the Latin word *fragile*; instead of *dog*, we sometimes use the Latin word *canine*; instead of saying that a disease is *catching*, we often prefer the Latin word *infectious*.

**left-branching** Any grammatical construction in which elements are added to the left-hand end of something which is already present. Typical of some languages, such as Japanese and Basque, left-branching is unusual in English, but it does occur in the SAXON GENITIVE: *my mother's sister's neighbour's doctor's husband.* Compare RIGHT-BRANCHING.

**left-dislocation** See under DISLOCATION.

**lemma** A formal term for HEADWORD, preferred by the writers of dictionaries.

**lexeme** Another term for LEXICAL ITEM.

**lexical** Pertaining to words.

**lexical ambiguity** An AMBIGUITY which resides within a single word. An example is *port* in *The sailors enjoyed the port*. Here *port* can mean either 'city by the sea' or 'fortified wine'. Compare STRUCTURAL AMBIGUITY.

**lexical category** Another term for PART OF SPEECH.

**lexical entry** In an idealized formal grammar of a language, the information required to describe the behaviour of a single LEXICAL ITEM (word). For each lexical item, its lexical entry provides its part of speech, its pronunciation, its meaning, and all unpredictable or irregular details of its grammatical behaviour.

**lexical item** (also **lexeme**) A WORD considered as an item of vocabulary, apart from any variation in form it may exhibit for grammatical purposes. A lexical item is a word in the sense in which a dictionary lists words. For example, *dog* is a lexical item of English with the two grammatical forms *dog* and *dogs*, and *take* is a lexical item with the grammatical forms *take, takes, took, taking* and *taken*. Compare WORD-FORM.

**lexical morpheme** A MORPHEME which has dictionary meaning. Examples: *woman, green, decide, under*, the *bio-* of *biology* and the *step-* of *stepmother*. Compare GRAMMATICAL MORPHEME.

**lexicalization** The expression of a meaning by a single word. For example, in English, 'adult male equine' is lexicalized as *stallion*, 'adult female equine' as *mare*, and 'equine' as *horse*. However, while 'adult male bovine' is lexicalized as *bull* and 'adult female bovine' as *cow*, there is no lexicalization for 'bovine': we have no word to denote any bovine animal, parallel to *horse* for equine animals.

**lexical verb** (also **main verb**) Any VERB which is not an AUXILIARY. For example, in the sentence *I must have tried fifteen bookshops*, the lexical verb is *try*, while *must* and *have* are auxiliaries. Among the thousands of lexical verbs in English are *run, smile, die, elope, describe, explain, kill, tickle, grow* and *analyse*.

**lexicography** The writing of dictionaries. A writer of dictionaries is a *lexicographer*.

**lexicon** (also **lexis**) The set of words in a language, sometimes particularly together with their LEXICAL ENTRIES and with the rules for constructing words from other words. It is most usual to apply VOCABULARY to the words known by a person but *lexicon* to the words in a language.

**light verb** A VERB which has no meaning of its own but which serves merely to convert another word into a verbal form. The English verbs which can serve as light verbs are *do, make, have, give* and *take*. Examples of expressions involving a light verb: *do a dance, make a move, have a smoke, give a shrug* and *take a sip*. A sentence with a light verb often expresses a subtle nuance of meaning: for example, *Susie took a sip of her drink* does not mean quite the same as *Susie sipped her drink*. But note that these verbs can also serve as ordinary (not light) verbs, as with *make* in *Susie made a coffee table* and *give* in *Susie gave Natalie a present*.

**linking verb** Another term for COPULA or QUASI-COPULA.

**loan shift** A shift in the meaning of a word to accommodate a new concept acquired from speakers of another language. For example, in pagan England, *hell* meant 'pagan underworld' and *heaven* meant only 'sky', but the introduction of Christianity from abroad caused these words to lose their original meanings in favour of new Christian concepts.

**loan-translation** Another term for CALQUE.

**loanword** A word which is taken over by BORROWING; see that entry.

**locative** A word or form expressing location. English most commonly does this by using one of the prepositions *in, on* and *at*: *in the bedroom, on the table, at the pub*.

**logogram** (also **symbol**) A character which conventionally represents a word or a phrase without using the letters of the alphabet. Familiar examples include the symbols 5 for *five*, $ for *dollars*, @ for *at* and § for *section*. A logogram differs from a PICTOGRAM in that a pictogram is clearly meant to be a picture of what it represents while a logogram is not: a logogram is entirely arbitrary in form. Like a pictogram, a logogram is *not* an ABBREVIATION.

In a purely logographic writing system, such as that of Chinese, all words are written with logograms, and the total number of symbols required runs into the thousands. In the alphabetic English writing system, we don't strictly require any logograms at all, but we find the use of logograms convenient as a brief way of writing things that are either very frequent or rather long: most people prefer to write *£487*, with logograms, rather than to write out *four hundred and eighty-seven pounds*.

**long passive** See under PASSIVE VOICE.

**main clause** A CLAUSE which is capable of making a complete sentence by itself; a clause which is not a SUBORDINATE CLAUSE. A sentence always contains at least one main clause, and a SIMPLE SENTENCE consists only of a single main clause. In the simple sentence *Susie finished her drink*, the whole sentence is the main clause. In the COMPOUND SENTENCE *Susie cooked dinner, and Natalie did the washing-up*, there are two main clauses connected by *and*. See also MATRIX CLAUSE.

**main verb** Another term for LEXICAL VERB.

**major lexical category** (also **major part of speech**) A label for any PART OF SPEECH seen as especially important. Traditionally, the major classes were the four OPEN CLASSES of English: noun, verb, adjective, adverb. In much contemporary theorizing, however, the major classes are taken to be noun, verb, adjective and preposition.

**malapropism** (also **catachresis**) The use of the wrong word, often especially when another word of similar sound is intended. Examples: *He lay prostate on the floor* (intended *prostrate*); *The All Blacks scored a fortuitous try* (intended *fortunate*); *We have a mutual interest in this* (intended *common interest*).

**manner adverb** An ADVERB that answers the question 'how?' Examples: *slowly, carefully, rashly, enthusiastically, grudgingly*. An ADVERBIAL PHRASE that does the same is a *manner adverbial*: *with a sly expression, in hope, without hesitation*.

**marked form** See under MARKEDNESS.

**markedness** A difference in the status of two forms or constructions which exist side by side in a language but which exhibit a difference in complexity or applicability. One of these, the UNMARKED FORM, is the 'ordinary' or 'basic' form, while the other, the MARKED FORM, differs from the first in containing extra material or in being confined to special contexts.

For example, *cat* is unmarked, while its plural *cats* is marked by the suffix *-s*. Likewise, *lion* is unmarked, while the female *lioness* is marked by the suffix *-ess*, and *consistent* is unmarked in comparison with its negative *inconsistent*. The active sentence *The police arrested Susie* is unmarked with respect to its passive counterpart *Susie was arrested by the police*, which contains more material. Of the two plurals of *brother*, *brothers* is unmarked (used in most contexts), while *brethren* is marked (used only in certain religious contexts).

**masculine** In some languages with GENDER, a gender class which shows some degree of correlation with male sex. Many European languages have such a gender class, but the correlation with male sex is usually rather weak. In French, for example, most nouns denoting males are grammatically masculine, but there are exceptions, such as *sentinelle* 'sentry', which is grammatically feminine, even though most sentries are men. In any case, most masculine nouns in French denote things which have no sex at all, such as *livre* 'book' and *argent* 'money'.

**mass noun** (also **non-count noun**, **uncountable noun**) A NOUN which denotes something which cannot be counted, such as *wheat*, *sand* or *wine*. A mass noun cannot normally be counted or pluralized: **these wheats*, **two sands*. An exception occurs with SECONDARY RECATEGORIZATION: *these wines*.

**matrix clause** A clause which contains a SUBORDINATE CLAUSE within it. In the COMPLEX SENTENCE *The employees who were dismissed are suing the company*, the matrix clause is *The employees . . . are suing the company*, while the remainder is the subordinate clause (a RELATIVE CLAUSE) contained within it.

Does the subordinate clause itself form part of its matrix clause? Traditional grammarians usually answered 'no' to this question, but contemporary linguists more often prefer to answer 'yes'.

A matrix clause is often a MAIN CLAUSE, as in the example above, but it need not be: it can itself be a subordinate clause. In the sentence *The victim told police that the man who attacked her had had a beard*, the subordinate clause *who attacked her* is contained within the subordinate clause *that the man . . . had had a beard*.

**mediopassive** The construction in which an intrinsically TRANSITIVE verb is construed intransitively with a patient as its subject and receives a PASSIVE interpretation, even though the construction is not formally passive. Examples: *This fabric washes easily*; *My new book is selling well*. In these examples, somebody unspecified is washing the fabric and selling the book. In the past, only a few English verbs could appear in this construction, but, in contemporary English, most speakers are happy to accept many more verbs in it: *This wall will paint (up) pretty well*; *That carpet should hoover without much difficulty*; *This grass will cut easily enough*. Note that the mediopassive construction is usually only possible with an adverb phrase expressing ease or difficulty. A verb which can appear in the mediopassive is one kind of LABILE VERB. Note: the mediopassive has sometimes been called the MIDDLE, but this name is not recommended.

**metalanguage** A language used to talk about a language. For example, terms like *noun*, *transitive verb*, *relative clause* and *prepositional phrase* constitute part of the metalanguage we use for talking about English grammar.

**metanalysis** The process in which a sound is transferred from the end of one word to the beginning of the next word, or vice-versa. For example, the earlier *an ewt* has become *a newt*, while the earlier *a numpire* has become *an umpire*.

**metaphor** The use, for effect, of words which are not literally accurate but which call up a resemblance. For example, we may speak of a failing business as *a lame duck*, meaning that, like a lamed creature, it is unable to compete effectively with healthy competitors. A great deal of the grammar of any language is metaphorical in origin. For example, we say *in the morning*, as though a morning were a location.

**middle** A label which has been applied by grammarians to a very wide range of different things. Most commonly, perhaps, this term is used to mean either MEDIOPASSIVE or RELATIONAL VERB, though it has also been used in other senses.

**minor lexical category** (also **minor part of speech**) Any PART OF SPEECH which is not a MAJOR LEXICAL CATEGORY; see that entry.

**minor sentence** Any piece of speech or writing which does not have the form of a complete sentence but which is normal in context. Examples: *Why not do it now?*; *Any news?*; *All aboard!*; *No smoking*; *This way, please*; *As if I would know*.

**modal** (also **modal auxiliary**) Any one of the several English AUXILIARY verbs which serve to express aspects of MODALITY and which exhibit rather distinctive grammatical behaviour. The English modals are *may, might, can, could, will, would, shall, should, must* and the somewhat anomalous *ought*; the two verbs *dare* and *need* sometimes also behave like modals, and are then called SEMI-MODALS. Like other auxiliaries, the modals exhibit the NICE PROPERTIES; unlike the PRIMARY AUXILIARIES, however, the modals have only finite (tensed) forms, with no participles, gerunds or infinitives, and they also fail to take *-s* in the third-person singular: *She can do it*, not **She cans do it*.

**modality** A label for those aspects of meaning centring on possibility, probability, certainty, impossibility, permission, obligation and prohibition. In English, these notions are most commonly expressed by means of our MODAL auxiliaries, sometimes combined with *not*.

**modifier** Any word or phrase which limits the meaning of another word, usually the HEAD of the phrase containing both. For example, given the phrase *the dog*, we can introduce various modifiers to narrow its applicability: *the big dog, the new dog, the dog on the left, the dog I got for Christmas*, and so on. See PREMODIFIER and POSTMODIFIER for more examples, and compare SPECIFIER.

**mood** The GRAMMATICAL CATEGORY which correlates with the degree or kind of reality assigned by the speaker to what she is saying. Traditional grammarians recognize four or five moods: INDICATIVE (utterance presented as a fact), SUBJUNCTIVE (utterance presented as doubtful or unreal), IMPERATIVE (utterance presented as a command), OPTATIVE (utterance presented as a wish) and sometimes INTERROGATIVE (utterance presented as a question). This is because, in the classical languages

Latin and Greek, all but the interrogative are marked by distinctive verb-forms.

In English, however, we generally lack distinctive verb-forms for distinguishing moods, and the distinctions, where they are made at all, are made almost entirely by the use of different sentence structures:

Indicative: *Susie is being hired.*
Subjunctive: [*I suggest*] *that Susie* (*should*) *be hired.*
Imperative: *Hire Susie!*
Optative: *May Susie be hired.*
Interrogative: *Is Susie going to be hired?*

Only the subjunctive is very occasionally marked by distinct verb-forms; see SUBJUNCTIVE for details. All further distinctions of mood are made in English by adding words: *Susie will probably be hired*; *Maybe Susie will be hired*; *Surely Susie will be hired*; *I doubt that Susie will be hired.* Consequently, modern grammarians, instead of speaking of mood in English, often prefer to speak of (formal) SENTENCE TYPES.

**morph** **1**. Another term for ALLOMORPH; see under MORPHEME.

**2**. Any piece of a word we may want to talk about, sometimes including the whole word. We might speak of the *cran-* of *cranberry* as a morph, or the *-o-* of *kissogram*, or the entire word *took*.

**morpheme** The minimal unit of word structure. For example, *cat* consists of a single morpheme {cat}, *doghouse* consists of the two morphemes {dog} and {house}, *happiness* consists of the two morphemes {happy} and {-ness}, *rewrite* consists of the two morphemes {re-} and {write}, and *recrystallized* consists of the four morphemes {re-}, {crystal}, {-ize} and {-ed}. A particular morpheme may appear in more than one shape, depending on context; these variant forms are the morpheme's ALLOMORPHS (or MORPHS). For example, the morpheme {sane} has one allomorph in *sane* and *insane*, but a different one in *sanity* (listen to the pronunciations), and the negative prefix {in-} has several allomorphs in *insane, impossible* and *illegal*. See PORTMANTEAU MORPH, EMPTY MORPH.

**morphology** Word structure, or the study of word structure. Morphology is divided into two main areas: INFLECTIONAL MORPHOLOGY (the way in which words vary their shapes for grammatical purposes) and WORD-FORMATION (the construction of new words from the resources of the language). See these entries.

**morphosyntax** The link between MORPHOLOGY (word-form) and SYNTAX (sentence structure). For example, the English pronoun *he* must appear in the form *him* in certain syntactic positions: *We saw him*; *We gave it to him*. This is a morphosyntactic observation.

# N

**natural gender** An inappropriate label sometimes applied to English, which has no grammatical GENDER. English has a certain amount of sex-marking, as in *he* versus *she* and *duke* versus *duchess*. But sex is a matter of biology, while gender is a matter of grammar, and it is an error to confuse the biological sex-marking of English with the gender distinctions found in some other languages.

**negation** The use of a NEGATIVE element, especially of *not* or of a NEGATIVE AUXILIARY like *can't*.

**negative** An element which reverses the truth value of a statement, changing it from true to false or vice versa. The most familiar English negative is *not*: the truth value of *Susie will be there* is reversed in its negation *Susie will not be there*. Often *not* combines with an auxiliary to produce a NEGATIVE AUXILIARY. Several pronouns, adverbs and determiners also have negative senses: the pronouns *nobody, no one, nothing* and *none*, the adverbs *nowhere* and *never*, and the determiner *no*, as in *We have no wine*.
See also SEMI-NEGATIVE.

**negative auxiliary** The distinctive and sometimes irregularly constructed negated forms of the English AUXILIARIES, such as *don't, doesn't, can't, won't* and *mustn't*.

**negative concord** The technical term for a DOUBLE NEGATIVE.

**negative polarity item** An item which can only occur in certain contexts, notably negative sentences and questions. A good example is *any*: it is normal to say *We don't have any wine* and *Do we have any wine?*, but it is impossible to say **We have any wine*. Other examples are *ever* and *anything*.

**negative raising** The construction in which a negative element appears earlier in a sentence than is logically appropriate. For example, the common construction *I can't seem to find my keys* exhibits negative raising from *I seem unable to find my keys.*

**neologism** A word which has been recently coined. Some fairly recent English examples are *eco-friendly* 'not harmful to the environment' and *geopathic* 'pertaining to illnesses caused by radioactive rocks'.

**neuter** In some GENDER languages, a conventional label for a gender class exhibiting no correlation with sex.

**new** See under GIVEN AND NEW.

**NICE properties** A mnemonic for the four properties which distinguish AUXILIARY verbs from other verbs, as follows.

**1.** Auxiliaries alone can be negated: *She doesn't smoke; She wouldn't smoke; She's not smoking;* but not **She smokes not.*

**2.** Auxiliaries alone can be inverted: *Is she smoking?; Does she smoke?; May she smoke?;* but not **Smokes she?*

**3.** Auxiliaries alone exhibit *code*, the ability to allow a following verb phrase to be deleted: *Will she take the job? I think she should, and she probably will, but Mike thinks she can't.*

**4.** Auxiliaries alone can be emphasized: *She DOES smoke; She MUSTN'T smoke; She CAN smoke; She IS smoking.*

**nominal group** A syntactic unit which can combine with a DETERMINER to make a NOUN PHRASE. A typical nominal group can fill the blank in the following frame to make a good sentence: *The __ was/were nice*. Examples: *young lady, rest of the meal, other people, meal I had last night, puppies*. Linguists often apply the term *N-bar* to this category. Note that a few linguists use this term in a completely different way, sometimes as a synonym for noun phrase, but these other uses are not standard.

**nominalization** Any word or construction in which a linguistic unit belonging to another category is converted to a noun-like category. For example, the verb *arrive* can be nominalized into the noun *arrival*, and the adjective *absent* can be nominalized into the noun *absence*. But more complex examples exist. In *That she smokes surprises me*, the NOUN PHRASE *that she smokes* is a nominalization of the sentence *she smokes*; in *Lisa's going topless upset her father*, the noun phrase *Lisa's going topless* is a nominalization of the sentence *Lisa went topless*; and in *To quit your job would be a mistake*, the noun phrase *to quit your job* is a nominalization of the VERB PHRASE *quit your job*. A GERUND represents another kind of nominalization.

**nominative** In many languages with CASE, the case-form used to mark a grammatical SUBJECT, and sometimes for other purposes. In English, only a few pronouns distinguish case. For example, the first-person singular pronoun has nominative *I*, as in *I saw her*, as opposed to the OBJECTIVE form *me*, as in *She saw me*.

**nominative absolute** Another name for ABSOLUTE CONSTRUCTION.

**nonce form** A form which is created on a particular occasion and which does not find a lasting place in the language. Two examples are *disclude*, heard as the opposite of *include*, and *techno-anorak* for 'computer addict'.

**non-count noun** Another term for MASS NOUN.

**non-defining** Another term for NON-RESTRICTIVE; see under RESTRICTIVE.

**non-finite** A label applied to a verb-form which is not marked for TENSE and which cannot be the only verb in a clause. A typical English verb usually has the following non-finite forms: the PRESENT PARTICIPLE (ending in *-ing*), the PAST PARTICIPLE (usually ending in *-ed* or in *-en*), the INFINITIVE (with no ending), and the GERUND (also ending in *-ing*).

It is not always easy to distinguish non-finite forms from FINITE ones in English, because some finite forms carry no marking and are therefore identical to the infinitive. For example, in *I leave for work at 8.30*, the verb-form *leave* is finite, while in *I decided to leave for work*, *leave* is non-finite (it is an infinitive).

**non-past** Another name for the PRESENT tense in English.

**non-restrictive** See under RESTRICTIVE.

**notional definition** A definition based on meaning. TRADITIONAL GRAMMAR made heavy use of notional definitions, but these don't really work. The categories we work with in grammar are defined by their shared grammatical properties, not by their meanings. For example, the grammarians of the past often defined a NOUN as 'the name of a person, place or thing'. Well, *red* is certainly the name of a colour, and so by this definition it ought to be a noun – yet it is most commonly an adjective, as in *a red skirt*. In fact, nouns like *arrival* and *absence* are really no more the names of anything than is the verb *arrive* or the adjective *absent*: these words are nouns because they behave grammatically like nouns, and not because they are the names of something 'out there'.

**noun** The PART OF SPEECH which includes words like *dog, tree, niece, arrival, pursuit* and *number*. The easiest way to identify nouns is to consider the following frames: *The* __ *was nice*; *The* __ *were nice*. Any single word which can fill one of the blanks to produce a grammatical sentence (though not necessarily a sensible one) is a noun, because the grammar of English permits nouns, and only nouns, to fill such positions. So, for example, *spinach, girls, entertainment, kangaroo, police* and *torture* can fit into one of the blanks, and hence these words can be nouns in English – though the last one can also be a VERB. But the words *happy, with, slowly, admire* and *this* cannot fill either of the blanks, and so these words cannot be nouns.

The reason we needed two frames above is that English nouns distinguish NUMBER: that is, most nouns can be either SINGULAR or PLURAL. This is the only kind of INFLECTION exhibited by nouns in English; see NUMBER for discussion. In some other languages, nouns exhibit one or both of GENDER and CASE.

In the great majority of instances, the HEAD of a NOUN PHRASE is a noun.

**noun clause** A traditional label for any kind of SUBORDINATE CLAUSE which appears to occupy the position of a NOUN PHRASE. This label includes several rather different cases, as follows:

1. A VERB-COMPLEMENT CLAUSE: *Susie has decided that she will quit her job* (see under COMPLEMENT CLAUSE).

**2.** A SENTENTIAL SUBJECT: *That she is not here worries me.*
**3.** An EMBEDDED QUESTION: *I don't know what we should do.*
**4.** A FREE RELATIVE: *I want to find whoever did this.*

In most contemporary work, we avoid the term *noun clause* in favour of the more specific labels.

**noun-complement clause** See under COMPLEMENT CLAUSE.

**noun phrase (NP)** A syntactic unit which can serve as any GRAMMATICAL RELATION in a sentence, such as SUBJECT, DIRECT OBJECT or object of a PREPOSITION. A noun phrase may be of any size or degree of complexity, from one word to dozens of words. Here is a simple test. Any phrase which can fit into one of the following blanks to make a grammatical sentence is a noun phrase: __ *was nice;* __ *were nice*. So, all of the following are noun phrases: *she, Susie, the party, your sister's boyfriend, the women we met at Mike's party the other night, none of the people on the interview panel*.

A noun phrase is constructed around a NOUN or a PRONOUN as its HEAD. In my examples, the heads are *she, Susie, party, boyfriend, women* and *none*.

**noun used as adjective** An old-fashioned label for a NOUN used to modify another noun, such as the first noun in *bus station, pea soup* or *physics textbook*. The term is inaccurate and should not be used, since a noun in this position remains a noun and does not become an adjective.

**NP** The abbreviation for NOUN PHRASE.

**null anaphor** See under ANAPHOR.

**number** The GRAMMATICAL CATEGORY which relates to the number of countable objects in the world. In English, number is mainly important with NOUNS. An English noun usually exhibits a two-way distinction of number: a SINGULAR form, denoting one of something, and a PLURAL form, denoting two or more. As a rule, the singular form has no particular marking, while the plural form carries the suffix *-s* or *-es*. Example: *dog/dogs; box/boxes; amusement/amusements*. But a few dozen nouns form their plurals irregularly. Examples: *child/children; man/men; woman/women; tooth/teeth; mouse/mice; sheep/sheep; radius/*

*radii*; *phenomenon/phenomena*; *bacterium/bacteria*. (Note that *sheep* really does have singular and plural forms, even though these are identical: *This sheep is hungry*; *These sheep are hungry*.)

Some nouns are unusual in having only a singular form or only a plural form. Nouns which have only a singular form include *furniture*, *wheat*, *happiness*, *gratitude*, *knitting* and *rugby*. Nouns which have only a plural form include *police*, *cattle*, *oats*, *tweezers*, *pants*, *pliers* and *remains*; see PLURALE TANTUM. Still other nouns normally have only a singular form, and can be pluralized only in special senses; see SECONDARY RECATEGORIZATION.

An English noun must always appear either in a singular form or in a plural form. There is no possibility of avoiding the choice, even when it appears irrelevant. For example, it is far from clear that the distinction between one object and more than one is of any relevance to grain, but the grammar of English forces us to choose one form or the other, and so we make arbitrary choices: *wheat* is singular (and has no plural), while *oats* is plural (and has no singular).

**numeral** See CARDINAL NUMERAL, ORDINAL NUMERAL.

**object** Any of several different GRAMMATICAL RELATIONS. See DIRECT OBJECT, INDIRECT OBJECT, OBLIQUE OBJECT.

**object control** See under CONTROL.

**objective** In English, the CASE form used with certain pronouns to mark a non-subject. Only the following pronouns distinguish a NOMINATIVE form (the subject form) from an objective form: *I* (nominative)/*me* (objective); *he/him*; *she/her*; *we/us*; *they/them*; and, very marginally, *who/whom*. Other pronouns, like *you*, *it* and *what*, are invariable in form. The objective is sometimes called the ACCUSATIVE, but this name is not really appropriate.

**objective genitive** A POSSESSIVE phrase with *of* or *-'s* in which the thing possessed is interpreted as a logical object. For example, *the destruction of the city* is logically related to *destroyed the city*, and *the manager's dismissal* is in most cases related to *dismissed the manager*. Compare SUBJECTIVE GENITIVE.

**object of comparison** In English, the object of the preposition *than*, such as *China* in *India is growing faster than China* and *me* in *Susie is taller than me*. In English, there is little difference between an object of comparison and any other object of a preposition, though the same is not true of all languages.

**object of preposition** See OBLIQUE OBJECT.

**object raising** The construction in which the logical object of a subordinate clause appears as the surface subject of a main clause. For example, *To please Susie is hard* is more idiomatically expressed as *Susie* *is hard to please*. Here *Susie*, the logical object of *please*, appears as the surface subject of *is*.

**oblique object** (also **object of a preposition**) In English, the NOUN PHRASE which follows a PREPOSITION. Examples (in brackets): *before* [*the war*]; *in* [*the shower*]; *a bottle* [*of wine*]; *without* [*any assistance*]; *under* [*the bed*].

**open class** A PART OF SPEECH which is large and which accepts new members easily. In English, the open classes are NOUN, VERB, ADJECTIVE and ADVERB.

**optative** The MOOD category which expresses a wish. The only distinctive optative constructions in English are rather archaic: *Would that we were at home; May you be happy always*.

**ordinal numeral** Any number term of the form *first, second, third, fourth, fifth, twenty-seventh* or *three hundredth*. The English ordinals are usually classed as ADJECTIVES. Compare CARDINAL NUMERAL.

**orthographic word** Anything which is conventionally written with a white space at each end but no white space in the middle. For example, *dog, girl's, land-owners* and *thermonuclear* are all single orthographic words, while *ice cream, New Zealand* and *cocktail dress* are not, even though each of the last three is arguably a single word in some important sense – for example, each would receive an entry in the dictionary.

**orthography** A conventional way of writing a language, or the rules governing this. Most obviously, the orthography of English includes the conventions for spelling words, but the use of capital letters and of punctuation is also part of the orthography. For example, English orthography requires *precede* and *proceed*, while the spellings *preceed* and *procede* are not acceptable, and it requires the possessive to be spelled *its* and not *it's*.

# P

**paradigm** A list of the set of forms which can be assumed by a word for grammatical purposes. English has very little in the way of paradigms, but some other languages have far more. An example is Latin, one of whose paradigms is this: *amo* 'I love', *amas* 'you (singular) love', *amat* 's/he loves', *amamus* 'we love', *amatis* 'you (plural) love', *amant* 'they love'. Note how the Latin forms vary constantly, while the English paradigm distinguishes only *loves* from all the others.

**paradigmatic relation** The relation which holds among a set of linguistic items or forms which have the property that only one of them is present in a given case. For example, *I* and *me* are in a paradigmatic relation: in any circumstance in which one of them is required, the rules of English grammar require either one or the other to be present. Examples: *I did it*; *I'm American*; *She saw me*; *Can anybody lend me a fiver?* Compare SYNTAGMATIC RELATION.

**paraphrase** Either of two structurally different sentences which are related in meaning in the following way: if one of them is true, then the other must be true. Examples: *Susie bought a car from Mike/Mike sold a car to Susie*; *The Mongols sacked Kiev/Kiev was sacked by the Mongols*; *Susie is older than Natalie/Natalie is younger than Susie*.

Paraphrase is a useful way of distinguishing the meanings of an ambiguous sentence. For example, the two meanings of the ambiguous string *The target was not hit by many arrows* can be revealed by offering a paraphrase of each: *Few arrows hit the target* for one, and *Many arrows missed the target* for the other.

**parataxis** Juxtaposing two or more CLAUSES without the use of SUBORDINATION (or HYPOTAXIS). Example: *It was the best of times; it was the worst of times*. Some, but not all, authorities apply this term to cases in which the clauses are connected by *and* or a similar word: *It was the best of times, and it was the worst of times*. Note the difference in the following examples. Paratactic: *John and Esther got married, and then they bought a house*. Hypotactic: *After they got married, John and Esther bought a house*.

**parenthetical** An interruption, in the middle of a sentence, which is not grammatically connected to the rest of its sentence. In writing, a parenthetical is set off by a pair of dashes, by a pair of parentheses, or (if not too strong) by a pair of commas. The sequences set off in the following examples are parentheticals: *The destruction of Guernica – and there is no doubt the destruction was deliberate – horrified the world; Otto Jespersen (1860–1943) was one of the greatest linguists of the twentieth century; Bill Clinton, as they say in Arkansas, was a hard dog to keep on the porch.*

**parse** To analyse the grammatical structure of (a sentence). Parsing sentences was once a familiar classroom exercise in the teaching of English grammar in schools. Today this is no longer usual, but university students of linguistics and of English language are still expected to learn parsing, and so, in some traditions, are the learners of foreign languages.

**participial adjective** A word-form which is identical in form to the (present or past) PARTICIPLE of a verb but which functions as an ADJECTIVE. Examples (in brackets): [*missing*] *persons, a* [*smiling*] *face, a* [*loving*] *family, a* [*surprising*] *result, an* [*expected*] *visitor, a* [*delayed*] *appearance, a* [*vanished*] *civilization,* [*determined*] *investigators.*

**participial relative clause** (also **reduced relative clause**) A construction which resembles a RELATIVE CLAUSE but which contains a PARTICIPLE instead of a finite verb. In the following examples, the first member of the pair contains a participial relative clause, while the second contains an equivalent full relative clause. *The employees sacked by the company are going to court; The employees who were sacked by the company are going to court; The woman playing the flute is my wife; The woman who is playing the flute is my wife.*

**participle** A NON-FINITE form of a VERB with certain special functions. English has two participles: the PRESENT PARTICIPLE and the PAST PARTICIPLE; see these entries for more information.

**particle** **1**. Broadly, any grammatical word of invariable form, such as *of, and, the, to* or *up*.

**2**. Narrowly, a small word making up the second part of a PHRASAL VERB, such as the *up* of *make up*.

**partitive** A form meaning 'some of'. English usually expresses this with *of*, as in *some of the men* and *most of the men*. Some other languages have a distinct form for this.

**part of speech** (also **word class, lexical category**) Any one of the several classes into which the lexical items (words) of a language are divided on the basis of their grammatical behaviour. Languages differ in the parts of speech they possess. For English, this dictionary recognizes the following twelve parts of speech: NOUN, VERB, ADJECTIVE, ADVERB, PRONOUN, PREPOSITION, CONJUNCTION, DETERMINER, DEGREE MODIFIER, COMPLEMENTIZER, SUBORDINATOR, and the rather marginal INTERJECTION. A few grammarians regard AUXILIARY as a class distinct from *verb* and QUANTIFIER as a class distinct from *determiner*, but these further classes are not usual.

Words are assigned to parts of speech according to their grammatical behaviour. Most especially, we classify words according to their DISTRIBUTION (the positions in which they can occur), their INFLECTION (the way they change their forms for grammatical reasons), and their possibilities for DERIVATION (sense 1) (their ability to accept prefixes and suffixes in order to form other words). Unlike earlier grammarians, we do not try to classify words according to their meanings, since the meaning of a word is not at all a reliable guide to its grammatical behaviour.

Words are placed together in a single part of speech because they have important grammatical properties in common, but not all the words in a single part of speech necessarily have grammatical properties which are entirely identical: see SUBCATEGORIZATION.

In English, a single word must often be assigned to two or more parts of speech. For example, *kiss* is a noun in *Give me a kiss* but a verb in *Kiss me*, and *straight* is an adjective in *a straight line*, an adverb in *He can't walk straight*, and a noun in *Schumacher accelerated down the straight*.

A few words exhibit unique behaviour and cannot sensibly be assigned to any part of speech at all. English examples include the negative *not*, the polite *please* and the infinitival *to*, all of these being illustrated by the example *Please do not try to stand up*.

Desk dictionaries of English, though they have improved greatly in recent years, are still often rather old-fashioned and outdated in their part-of-speech labels. You should be a little careful about accepting dictionary labels at face value.

**passive voice** The construction in which the logical object of a verb becomes its grammatical subject, while its logical subject is either reduced to a PREPOSITIONAL PHRASE introduced by *by* or removed from the sentence altogether.

Consider the sentence *Madame Curie discovered radium in 1898*, which is in the ACTIVE VOICE. Here the logical subject *Madame Curie* is also the grammatical subject. This has two corresponding passive forms. The LONG PASSIVE, or passive with agent, is this: *Radium was discovered in 1898 by Madame Curie*, or, equally, *Radium was discovered by Madame Curie in 1898*. In this case, the logical subject appears after *by*. The SHORT PASSIVE, or AGENTLESS PASSIVE, is this: *Radium was discovered in 1898*. Here the logical subject is omitted.

In English, the passive voice is constructed by combining either the verb *be* or the verb *get* with the PAST PARTICIPLE of the lexical verb. As a rule, only the passive with *be* is found in formal English, and the passive with *get* (the *GET*-PASSIVE) is strictly informal. Compare the *be*-passive *England were beaten by Australia* with the *get*-passive *England got beat by Australia*.

As a rule, any TRANSITIVE verb can appear in the passive voice, but there are a few exceptions, like *have, fit* and *weigh*: *Susie has blue eyes*, but not **Blue eyes are had by Susie*; *That dress fits you*, but not **You are fitted by that dress*; *Susie weighs nine stone*, but not **Nine stone is weighed by Susie*. An INTRANSITIVE verb cannot normally appear in the passive at all, but see PREPOSITIONAL PASSIVE for an exception.

A construction formally identical to the passive occurs in English with the distinctive class of verbs called PSYCH-VERBS. Note also that a STATIVE construction often looks just like a passive in form, even though it is not passive.

**passive participle** Another name for the English PAST PARTICIPLE, when this is used in the PASSIVE VOICE.

**past** (also **preterite**) The usual name for a TENSE category which most typically refers to a time before the moment of speaking. English has only two tenses, the past and the PRESENT. With most English verbs, the past tense is marked by the suffix *-ed*, though a number of verbs have an irregular past tense. A past-tense form in English can be identified by its ability to co-occur with an adverb of past time, such as *yesterday*. Examples: (regular) *I washed the car yesterday*; *It rained yesterday*; *They delivered our furniture yesterday*; (irregular) *I saw Susie yesterday*; *I bought a car yesterday*; *We took the dog to the vet yesterday*; *I had a bad experience yesterday*; *I was busy yesterday*.

The forms illustrated above are examples of the SIMPLE PAST, in which no AUXILIARY is present. The simple past exhibits PERFECTIVE aspect. But it is possible to combine a past-tense form of the auxiliary *be* with a PRESENT PARTICIPLE in order to construct the past continuous: *Susie was smoking a cigarette*; *We were watching the cricket*. It is also possible to combine a past-tense form of the auxiliary *have* with a PAST PARTICIPLE in order to construct the PAST PERFECT: *Susie had finished her dinner*; *We had drunk the wine*.

English also has a special past-tense form to express HABITUAL aspect in the past: the *used to* construction, as in *I used to live in Liverpool*; *Susie used to smoke*.

The past tense does not always refer to past time. Consider the example *It's time you went to bed*. Here the past-tense form *went* refers to the immediate future, not to the past. And consider the example *If I spoke better French, I could get a job in Paris*. Here the past-tense form *spoke* refers to a hypothetical present, not to the past. This is an example of a COUNTERFACTUAL; see under CONDITIONAL SENTENCE.

**past anterior** A construction which indicates that one event preceded another in the past. English can express this either with the simple past or with the PAST PERFECT. For example, to show that I ate dinner and that Susie arrived (in that order) in the past, I can say either *I ate dinner before Susie arrived* or *I had eaten dinner before Susie arrived*.

**past participle** (also **perfect participle**) A particular NON-FINITE form of an English VERB. With a REGULAR verb, this form ends in *-ed* and is identical in form to the PAST tense: *loved*, *waited*, *decided*. With an IRREGULAR verb, it has any of a variety of forms, though it often ends in *-en*: *broken*, *written*, *spoken*, *seen*, *drawn*, *sat*, *put*. The past participle has several uses.

First, it combines with the AUXILIARY *have* to make the PERFECT forms of verbs: *I have seen her; I had finished dinner.* Second, it can be used as an ADJECTIVE: *boiled cabbage, dried tomatoes, a vanished civilization.* (Note: a few verbs use for this purpose a different form of the past participle from the ordinary one: *The metal has melted,* but *molten metal; I have mowed the grass,* but *new-mown hay.*) Third, it can be used in a PARTICIPIAL RELATIVE CLAUSE: *The fossils discovered by the Leakey family have revolutionized our understanding of human evolution.* Fourth, it can be used to construct the PASSIVE VOICE: *Fred Lieb was invited to write his autobiography.* In this last function, the participle is sometimes called the PASSIVE PARTICIPLE.

Compare PRESENT PARTICIPLE.

**past perfect** (also **pluperfect**) The English construction in which *had* is combined with the PAST PARTICIPLE of a verb. This is the past-tense form corresponding to the PRESENT PERFECT, and it often has a comparable meaning to the present perfect: it presents a state of affairs in the past resulting from an earlier event. For example, *I had finished the wine* commonly means 'There was no wine at the (past) time I am talking about, because I drank the last of it earlier.' However, the past perfect can also be used as a PAST ANTERIOR; see this entry.

The past perfect can also be used to express an unreal condition in the past. Example: *If the Germans had invaded the USSR in April, they might have captured Moscow.* Here the use of the past perfect *had invaded* indicates that the Germans did not in fact invade in April. This is an example of a COUNTERFACTUAL; see under CONDITIONAL SENTENCE.

**patient** The SEMANTIC ROLE borne by the entity which is directly affected by the action of the verb. In a TRANSITIVE sentence, a patient, if present, is usually the DIRECT OBJECT. In the following examples, the objects are patients: *Susie slapped Mike; Susie is repainting the bedroom; Susie stroked the cat; Susie is washing the car.* (But note that not all direct objects are patients: the objects are not patients in *Susie received a letter* or *Susie loves Natalie.*) In an INTRANSITIVE sentence, it is possible for the SUBJECT to be a patient: *The ship sank; The ice is melting; This bikini washes easily.* In the PASSIVE VOICE, the subject is commonly a patient: *Mike was stung by a bee; The Arndale Centre was bombed by the IRA.* See also AGENT.

**perfect** The English construction consisting of the auxiliary verb *have* followed by the PAST PARTICIPLE of a lexical verb. When *have* is in the present tense, the result is the PRESENT PERFECT; when *have* is in the past tense, the result is the PAST PERFECT. See these two entries. Most commonly, the perfect represents a state of affairs resulting from an earlier event, but it also has other uses.

**perfect infinitive** The traditional, but pointless, label for a sequence of *to* plus *have* plus the PAST PARTICIPLE of a verb. An example is *to have met* in *I would like to have met Napoleon*. The name is inappropriate, since such a sequence is neither an infinitive nor a grammatical unit of any kind. See INFINITIVE.

**perfective** The ASPECT form which indicates that the action of a verb is presented as an unanalysed whole, with no internal structure. English has no particular form for marking perfective aspect, which is the simplest of the aspect forms. In the past tense, the SIMPLE PAST is usual: *Susie washed the car*; *Susie sneezed*; *Susie bought a new house*; *Susie worked in London*. Compare imperfective forms like *Susie was washing the car* and *Susie used to work in London*, which do assign some kind of internal structure to the activity.

In the present tense, we usually use the SIMPLE PRESENT to express perfective aspect, though this is not the most frequent function of the simple present. Stage directions provide a good example: *Iago enters stage right*.

Commands and instructions usually also represent perfective aspect: *Wash your hands!*; *Cut along the dotted line*.

See IMPERFECTIVE for an account of how this differs from the perfective.

Note: the perfective should not be confused with the PERFECT. In spite of the unfortunate similarity of their names, the two are entirely distinct. Regrettably, many books on English grammar do confuse the two, and you should be prepared to encounter this confusion in your reading.

**perfect participle** Another name for the PAST PARTICIPLE.

**performance** The actual linguistic behaviour which you exhibit on particular occasions. Performance is often imperfect, since we all suffer from slips of the tongue, mishearings, memory lapses and other shortcomings, but such slips do not result from imperfect knowledge of the language. Compare COMPETENCE.

**period** The American name for the FULL STOP.

**periphrastic** A label applied to a grammatical form which uses two or more words to express something which might, in principle, be expressed with a single word. In English, the label is chiefly applied to verb-forms constructed with one or more AUXILIARY verbs plus a lexical verb: *have eaten, is eating, will have eaten, has been eating, must have been eating,* and so on. But it can also be applied to two-word comparatives like *more lovely* (as opposed to *lovelier*). The use of a periphrastic form is periphrasis.

**person** The GRAMMATICAL CATEGORY which distinguishes participants in a conversation. Like most languages, English distinguishes three persons. The *first person* represents the speaker and possibly other people associated with the speaker. The PRONOUNS are *I/me* (singular) and *we/us* (plural). The *second person* represents the hearer(s) and possibly other people associated with the hearer(s), and the pronoun is *you*. The *third person* represents everybody and everything else, and the pronouns are *he/him, she/her* and *it* (singular) and *they* (plural).

**personal pronoun** Any PRONOUN which carries an expression of PERSON. The English personal pronouns are *I/me, you, he/him, she/her, it, we/us* and *they/them.*

**phrasal genitive** The English construction in which both the preposition *of* and a POSSESSIVE appear. Examples: *a friend of Susie's, those colleagues of mine.*

**phrasal verb** A complex verb consisting of a simple verb and a PARTICLE, like *make up, take off, turn on, do up* and *put away*. A phrasal verb differs from a sequence of a verb and a preposition (a PREPOSITIONAL VERB) in four respects. Here *call up* is a phrasal verb, while *call on* is only a verb plus preposition.

**1.** The particle in a phrasal verb is stressed: *They called* up *the teacher,* but not **They called* on *the teacher.*

**2.** The particle of a phrasal verb can be moved to the end: *They called the teacher up,* but not **They called the teacher on.*

**3.** The simple verb of a phrasal verb may not be separated from its particle by an adverb: **They called early up the teacher* is no good, but *They called early on the teacher* is fine.

4. The particle of a phrasal verb may not undergo PIED-PIPING: **The teacher up whom they called* is no good, but *The teacher on whom they called* is fine.

**phrase** A sequence of one or more words which forms a single grammatical unit. There are five principal types of phrase in English: NOUN PHRASE, VERB PHRASE, ADJECTIVE PHRASE, ADVERB PHRASE and PREPOSITIONAL PHRASE.

**phrase structure** Another term for CONSTITUENT STRUCTURE.

**pictogram** A more-or-less pictorial symbol which is intended to represent a word or a phrase without the use of language. In a pictogram, the idea is that the picture should suffice to convey the intended meaning directly, so that it can be understood even by someone who does not know the local language. Pictograms are common today in public places like roads and airports. For example, a sketch of a telephone handset means *Telephones This Way*; a sketch of a leaping deer means *Caution: Deer Crossing the Road*; a sketch of an airplane with its nose in the air means *Flight Departures This Way*; and a sketch of car tyre tracks zigzagging wildly means *Danger: Slippery When Wet.* Compare LOGOGRAM.

**pied-piping** The construction in which a PREPOSITION is moved to the front of its clause, just before its object. Examples: *To whom were you speaking?*; *With what did they hit it?*; *The shop from which I bought my gloves*. As can be seen, this construction is rather formal in English; the more colloquial equivalents are *Who were you speaking to?*; *What did they hit it with?*; *The shop (which) I bought my gloves from*, with PREPOSITION STRANDING.

**place adverb** An ADVERB that answers the question 'where?' Examples: *here, nearby, somewhere, above*. An ADVERB PHRASE that does the same is a place adverbial: *somewhere nearby, high above, right there*.

**pleonasm** The use of words which duplicate each other's meanings. Examples: *three a.m. in the morning, a free gift, his talents are not limited only to music*. Such a formation is pleonastic.

**pluperfect** Another term for PAST PERFECT.

**plural** That form of a NOUN which normally denotes that more than one thing is being mentioned. The English plural is regularly formed with the suffix *-s* (sometimes spelled *-es*): *girl/girls*; *ashtray/ashtrays*; *kangaroo/kangaroos*; *fox/foxes*. But a few dozen nouns form their plurals irregularly: *child/children*; *woman/women*; *tooth/teeth*; *sheep/sheep*; *millennium/millennia*; and others.

Not all nouns have a plural form: for example, *furniture, wheat, dust, drunkenness* and *silverware* normally have only a singular form. But do not confuse these with nouns like *sheep* and *deer*, which have both singular and plural forms. It is merely that, with these last nouns, the plural is identical in form to the singular: *This sheep is hungry*; *These sheep are hungry*.

There are also nouns with a plural form only; see PLURALE TANTUM.

**plurale tantum** A NOUN which is invariably plural in form, even though it may be singular in sense. Examples include *oats, cattle, remains, pants, scissors, binoculars, pyjamas, shorts* and *tweezers*. Such nouns are awkward to count: we cannot say **a pants* or **a cattle*, and we must say instead *a pair of pants* and *a head of cattle*. The plural of *plurale tantum* is *pluralia tantum*.

**polar question** **1**. Another term for YES-NO QUESTION.

**2**. Any question which offers a choice between two possible answers, such as *Are these units metric or Imperial?*

**portmanteau morph** A single linguistic form which clearly consists of two or more MORPHEMES but which cannot be neatly divided up into an obvious sequence of morphemes. For example, while past-tense *loved*, as in *I loved it*, can easily be divided (segmented) into a verb-stem *love* plus a tense-suffix *-(e)d*, the past-tense *took*, as in *I took it*, cannot be neatly divided up in the same way, even though it plainly consists of the verb-stem *take* plus the past-tense marker. Hence *took* is a portmanteau morph.

**positive** The basic, or dictionary, form of an ADJECTIVE. Examples include *big, pretty* and *enormous*. Compare COMPARATIVE and SUPERLATIVE.

**possessive** (also **genitive**) That form of a NOUN PHRASE which indicates that it represents a possessor. This is most commonly done with the SAXON GENITIVE *-'s*: *Susie's cigarettes, my mother's car, the students' work*. Some PRONOUNS take irregular possessive forms: *my family, their clothes*. But the possessive can also be expressed with *of*, especially when the possessor is not alive: we prefer to say *the legs of the table*, rather than *the table's legs*, even though we prefer *the horse's legs* to *the legs of the horse*.

**possessive determiner** A DETERMINER which expresses possession, such as *my, your, his, our* or *their*: *my wife, your mother, his new car, our old friends, their fate*. Though traditional grammar classes these as PRONOUNS, they are not pronouns but determiners, since they behave like determiners and not like pronouns.

**possessive pronoun** **1**. A PRONOUN which expresses possession, such as *mine, yours, hers* or *ours*: *This is mine*; *Yours is ready*; *as nice as hers*; *Ours doesn't work*.

**2**. The traditional, but inaccurate, name for a POSSESSIVE DETERMINER.

**postdeterminer** A label sometimes applied to a DETERMINER which follows another determiner within a noun phrase. Examples are *two* in *these two books* and *these* in *both these books*.

**postmodifier** A MODIFIER which follows the word or phrase it modifies. In the following examples, the bracketed items are postmodifiers: *warm* [*enough*], *too hot* [*to eat*], *tired* [*of London*], *persons* [*unknown*], *a better man* [*than I am*], *a yacht* [*big enough to sleep 24 people*].

**postposition** A word which is similar in function to a PREPOSITION but which follows its object. Basque and Japanese are two languages which use postpositions, as in Basque *Jonen kontra* 'against John' and Japanese *Tookyoo de* 'in Tokyo'. English has the postposition *ago*, as in *five years ago*, as well as *notwithstanding*, which may be either a preposition or a postposition: *notwithstanding this decision* or *this decision notwithstanding*.

**PP** The abbreviation for PREPOSITIONAL PHRASE.

**predeterminer** A label applied to the first of two consecutive DETERMINERS, such as *both* in *both these books* and *all* in *all my children.*

**predicate** That part of the sentence which is not the SUBJECT, the part that contains the VERB and consists of a VERB PHRASE. In the following examples, the bracketed portion is the predicate: *My sister* [*is a nurse*]; *Susie* [*put the mayonnaise in the fridge*]; *The Red Arrows* [*often perform at public events*].

In a QUESTION or in another sentence involving FRONTING, the predicate may be discontinuous, or it may precede the subject: [*Who were*] *you* [*talking to?*]; [*Behind the President stood*] *a row of bodyguards*; [*Seldom have*] *I* [*seen such a mess*]. Compare *You* [*were talking to Mike*]; *A row of bodyguards* [*stood behind the President*]; *I* [*have never seen such a mess*].

**predicate complement** A phrase immediately following a COPULA or a QUASI-COPULA. Examples (in brackets): *Susie is* [*a businesswoman*] (noun phrase; this is a PREDICATE NOMINAL); *Susie turned* [*bright red*] (adjective phrase); *Susie is* [*in the shower*] (prepositional phrase).

**predicate nominal** A NOUN PHRASE which follows a COPULA, one type of PREDICATE COMPLEMENT. An example is *a businesswoman* in *Susie is a businesswoman.*

**predicative** A label applied to a linguistic element which appears inside a PREDICATE. For example, the adjective *red* is in predicative position in *This shirt is red.* Compare ATTRIBUTIVE.

**prefix** An AFFIX which precedes the material it is added to. Examples include the *re-* of *rewrite* and the *un-* of *unhappy*. Compare SUFFIX.

**premodifier** A MODIFIER which precedes the word or phrase it modifies. In the following examples, the bracketed items are premodifiers: [*very*] *interesting,* [*nearly*] *finished,* [*straight*] *into the hole,* [*red*] *wine*. Premodification is the norm in English with most kinds of modifiers, but see POSTMODIFIER for a number of exceptions.

**preposing** Another term for FRONTING.

**preposition** The PART OF SPEECH containing words like *in, to, with, under* and *beyond*. A preposition usually occurs inside a PREPOSITIONAL PHRASE, but in some circumstances it may instead appear in the construction called PREPOSITION STRANDING.

**prepositional adjective** (also **transitive adjective**) An ADJECTIVE which can or must be followed by a PREPOSITIONAL PHRASE. Examples, in which the adjective is the first word in each case: *proud of Susie, frightened of snakes, ready for anything, concerned about this.*

**prepositional passive** In English, a somewhat unusual instance of the PASSIVE VOICE in which the grammatical subject is logically the object of a PREPOSITION. Consider the sentence *George Washington slept in this bed.* Here the verb *sleep* is intransitive, and *this bed* is the object of the preposition *in*. Nevertheless, this sentence has a corresponding passive form: *This bed was slept in by George Washington*.

Other examples of prepositional passives are *My flowers have been trampled on by the children* and *This bridge has been walked across by generations of lovers*. The circumstances in which the prepositional passive is possible are somewhat obscure. Many or all speakers reject efforts like these: **The garden was raced across by the dog*; **This tree is lived under by a fox*; **Susie is lived with by Mike.*

**prepositional phrase (PP)** A PHRASE consisting of a PREPOSITION followed by a NOUN PHRASE, its OBJECT. In the following example, all the bracketed sequences are prepositional phrases: [*After the game,*] *several* [*of the players*] *went* [*into town*] [*with their wives*].

**prepositional verb** See under PHRASAL VERB.

**preposition stranding** The phenomenon in which a PREPOSITION is left without a following object. The preposition *to* is stranded in each of the following examples: *Who were you talking to?*; *The woman you were talking to is my boss*. Compare PIED-PIPING.

**prescriptivism** The policy of describing languages as we would like them to be, rather than as we find them. Typical examples of prescriptivist attitudes are the condemnation of PREPOSITION STRANDING and of the SPLIT INFINITIVE and a demand for *It's I* in place of the normal *It's* *me*. Prescriptivism was a prominent feature of TRADITIONAL GRAMMAR, and it is still widely embraced today among non-specialists in linguistics. Linguists recognize the influence of prescriptivism in society, and accept some forms of prescriptivism as appropriate in educational contexts, but they reject it as a basis for describing languages. Compare DESCRIPTIVISM.

**present** The usual name for a TENSE category which includes reference to the moment of speaking. English has only two tenses, the PAST and the present; the present might better be called the NON-PAST, since it covers both present and future (English has no distinct future tense), as well as timeless statements. With most English verbs, the present tense is marked by the suffix *-s* in the third-person singular but otherwise has no marking at all.

The simplest form of the English present is the SIMPLE PRESENT, in which no AUXILIARY is present. This has several functions, among which the following are important.

**1.** It expresses timeless truths: *Rhubarb leaves are poisonous; Mongooses kill snakes; Water boils at 100°C; Viruses take over their host cells' DNA*.

**2.** It expresses HABITUAL actions: *Susie smokes; I get up at 7.30; The Danes drink beer; Susie drives to work*.

**3.** Especially in stage directions, summaries and the like, it presents an action as an unanalysed whole (this is the present PERFECTIVE): *Antonio enters stage left; Mercutio and Tybalt fight, and Mercutio falls; The white rook gives check, and black interposes his bishop*.

**4.** Especially in reports of intellectual debates or issues which are seen as currently relevant, it is used to present the views of scholars or writers of the past: *Grice presents sixteen maxims of conversation, but Sperber and Wilson propose just one; Hardy sees little reason for optimism in human affairs; Einstein assures us that no matter can travel faster than light*.

**5.** Especially in informal speech and in certain kinds of fiction, it serves to present a narrative with more vividness than that provided by the past tense: *This guy walks into a bar with a dog and asks the bartender for two beers; The mortally wounded Caesar slumps to the ground, his life's blood oozing out of him*. This function is often called the HISTORIC PRESENT, and it is hardly ever found in formal writing.

The present CONTINUOUS is formed by combining a present-tense form of *be* with the PRESENT PARTICIPLE: *Susie is eating dinner; The children are playing in the garden*.

The PRESENT PERFECT is formed by combining a present-tense form of *have* with a PAST PARTICIPLE; see that entry.

For the use of the present tense in referring to future time, see FUTURE. Compare PAST.

**present participle** The *-ing* form of an English verb, though only when this is not used as a GERUND or as a VERBAL NOUN. The present participle combines with the auxiliary *be* to form the CONTINUOUS aspect: *Susie is eating*; *Susie was smoking a cigarette*. It can also occur in a PARTICIPIAL RELATIVE CLAUSE: *The woman wearing the white skirt is Susie*. It also occurs in certain COMPLEMENTS: *I saw Susie crossing the street*. Compare PAST PARTICIPLE.

**present perfect** The English construction consisting of a present-tense form of the auxiliary verb *have* plus the PAST PARTICIPLE of a lexical verb. Examples: *I have finished the wine*; *Susie has quit her job*; *The UN has voted to impose sanctions on Iraq*. The present perfect is strictly a present tense in English, not a past tense, and it cannot co-occur with an adverb of past time: **I have seen her ten minutes ago*; **I have seen a good film last night*. The present perfect has several functions, but its principal function is to denote a present state of affairs resulting from an earlier action. For example, *I have finished the wine* means 'There is no wine now, because I drank the last of it earlier'. Compare PAST PERFECT.

**preterite** Another name for a PAST-tense form, such as *enjoyed* in *Susie enjoyed her holiday* or *took* in *Susie took her niece to the beach*.

**primary auxiliary** See under AUXILIARY.

**principal parts** Those inflected forms of a VERB which are required to construct all or most of its forms. In English, these are three: the INFINITIVE, the PAST TENSE and the PAST PARTICIPLE. For regular verbs, which exhibit the pattern shown by *love, loved, loved*, only the first is strictly necessary. Irregular verbs, however, require all three: *take, took, taken*; *write, wrote, written*; *sing, sang, sung*; *teach, taught, taught*; *put, put, put*. For the exceptionally irregular verbs *be*, *have* and *do*, even the three principal parts do not suffice to predict all of the irregular forms.

**principles-and-parameters approach** Another name for GOVERNMENT-AND-BINDING THEORY.

**proclitic** See under CLITIC.

**pro-drop** The property of a language in which a sentence does not require an overt subject. Spanish is a pro-drop language: it is perfectly normal in Spanish to say *Viene* to mean 'He/She/It is coming'. English is not a pro-drop language, and **Is coming* is not a grammatical sentence.

**productivity** The degree to which a grammatical pattern can be used freely to construct new instances. Productivity is most familiar in connection with WORD-FORMATION. For example, the noun-forming suffix *-ness* is highly productive, since it can be used to coin new nouns almost at will: *user-friendliness, sexiness, crash-worthiness*. In contrast, the noun-forming suffix *-th* (as in *warmth*) is not productive at all: it cannot be used to coin a single new noun, and **bigth*, **happyth* and **sexyth* are all impossible. Intermediate degrees of productivity are possible. For example, the adjective-forming suffix *-less* is of medium productivity: we can coin *braless, moonless* and *paperless* (as in *the paperless office*), but other formations, such as *forkless, cigaretteless* and *rugless* sound odd or worse to most people.

The productivity of a pattern can change. Until recently, the adverb-forming suffix *-wise* was unproductive and confined to a handful of cases such as *likewise, clockwise, lengthwise* and *otherwise*. But today it has become highly productive, and we frequently coin new words like *healthwise, moneywise, clotheswise* and *romancewise* (as in *How are you getting on romancewise?*).

**pro-form** Any linguistic form which has little or no meaning or reference of its own but which takes its meaning from another linguistic form present in the same sentence or discourse. See PRONOUN or PRO-VP for two important kinds of pro-form.

**progressive** Another term for CONTINUOUS.

**prolepsis** The use of a modifier which only becomes appropriate through the action of a verb. An example is *green* in *paint it green*, since the thing being painted is not green until the painting is completed.

**pronoun** The PART OF SPEECH which includes words like *you, they, somebody, anything* and *who*. A pronoun is one kind of PRO-FORM; it is usually a single word (occasionally two words in English), and it forms a complete NOUN PHRASE all by itself. Logically, then, the term should be 'pro-NP', but the less accurate label *pronoun* is established. Pronouns can be divided into several subclasses:

1. PERSONAL PRONOUNS (like *me* and *she*).
2. INTERROGATIVE PRONOUNS (like *who* and *what*).
3. RELATIVE PRONOUNS (like *who* and *which*).
4. INDEFINITE PRONOUNS (like *somebody* and *anything*).
5. DEMONSTRATIVE pronouns (like *this* and *those*).
6. REFLEXIVE PRONOUNS (like *myself* and *themselves*).
7. RECIPROCAL PRONOUNS (like *each other* and *one another*).
8. POSSESSIVE PRONOUNS (like *mine* and *hers*).

See these entries, especially the last, since the term *possessive pronoun* is often wrongly used.

As a rule, a noun phrase built on a pronoun cannot contain any other material: **the happy I*, **the nice who* and **the other two anythings*, for example, are impossible. But there are a few exceptions: *little me, poor old you, what else, somebody nice, anything you like*.

**proper noun** A special kind of NOUN which is a name denoting a particular person, place or thing. In English, proper nouns are normally written with initial capital letters, and most proper nouns do not take an article. Examples: *Susie, Gwyneth Paltrow, Queen Elizabeth I, Dublin, Siberia, Never-Never-Land*. But proper nouns denoting historical periods and events, as well as certain others, often do take the article: *The Iron Age, The Industrial Revolution, The Meiji Restoration, The United States, The Hague*.

**proposition** The semantic content (meaning) of a statement. For example, the statement *Susie smokes* may be interpreted as saying 'The proposition *Susie smokes* is true', while its negation *Susie doesn't smoke* may be interpreted as saying 'The proposition *Susie smokes* is false.' Similarly, the YES–NO QUESTION *Does Susie smoke?* may be interpreted as meaning 'Is the proposition *Susie smokes* true?', and the WH-

QUESTION *Who smokes?* may be interpreted as meaning 'For which value of x is the proposition *x smokes* true?'

**pro-sentence** A single word which can take the place of a complete sentence. The most familiar English examples are *yes* and *no*. Here is an example. Jan: *Would you like some tobasco sauce?* Larry: *Yes*. Here Larry's response is equivalent to the sentence *I would like some tobasco sauce*.

**protasis** See under CONDITIONAL SENTENCE.

**pro-VP** A word or phrase which occupies the position of a VERB PHRASE but which has no meaning of its own, taking its meaning instead from another verb phrase, its ANTECEDENT. The two pro-VPs in English are *do it* and the more formal *do so*. In the example *I asked Susie to peel the potatoes, and she did it* (or . . . *she did so*), the pro-VP *do it* or *do so* is interpreted as *peel the potatoes*.

**proximal** See under DEICTIC POSITION.

**pseudo-cleft** See under CLEFT.

**psych-verb** A VERB expressing a psychological state, particularly one which, in English, is typically construed in the passive with a following preposition other than *by*: *be surprised at, be disgusted with, be excited about, be interested in*.

**punctual** The ASPECT category denoting an action which occupies only a moment of time. English has no special form for this. Mostly, we use the SIMPLE PAST for the purpose: *Susie sneezed; The bomb exploded*.

**punctuation** The conventional system of marks used in writing in order to display and clarify the structure of the text. The principal punctuation marks used in writing English are the FULL STOP, the QUESTION MARK, the EXCLAMATION MARK, the COMMA, the SEMI-COLON, the COLON, QUOTATION MARKS, the APOSTROPHE, the HYPHEN and the DASH. See these entries for summaries. For more information, see *The Penguin Guide to Punctuation*.

**purpose clause** A CLAUSE which expresses the purpose of an action. An example is the bracketed clause in the sentence *Susie bought a computer* [*so that she could work at home*]. For those linguists who recognize NON-FINITE clauses, the following example is also a purpose clause: *Susie is learning Spanish* [*to improve her job prospects*].

# Q

**quantifier** A DETERMINER which expresses a concept of quantity. Examples are *many, every, most, all, some, no* and *both*: *many people, most students, no book, both cars*.

**quantifier floating** The construction in which a QUANTIFIER occurs later in its sentence than is logically required. For example, *All the students have passed their exams* is equivalent to *The students have all passed their exams*, in which the quantifier *all* has 'floated' away from its noun phrase.

**quasi-copula** A verb which resembles a COPULA but which has semantic content. English examples include *seem*, as in *She seems happy*, and *become*, as in *She became famous*.

**question** A sentence expressed in a form which requires, or appears to require, an answer: one kind of (functional) SENTENCE TYPE. Two common types exist: YES–NO QUESTIONS, like *Is Susie coming?*, and WH-QUESTIONS, like *Who were you talking to?* But other types exist, such as *Is that a snark or a boojum?* (This is a POLAR QUESTION.) These are DIRECT QUESTIONS, and they represent the INTERROGATIVE mood. But English allows utterances which have the force of questions, even though they have the form of statements, such as *You're coming with us?* (uttered with rising intonation). In contrast, a RHETORICAL QUESTION has the overt form of a question, but expects no answer. See also EMBEDDED QUESTION, TAG QUESTION.

**question mark** The punctuation mark [?], which marks a direct question. Example: *What are you doing?* For more on its use, see section 2.2 of *The Penguin Guide to Punctuation*.

**question word** Another term for WH-WORD.

**Quirk grammars** A series of grammars of English written by Randolph Quirk and his colleagues. Though rather traditional in orientation, these grammars are informed by contemporary linguistic research. They introduce a certain amount of novel terminology.

**quotation marks** (also **inverted commas**) The pair of punctuation marks [' '] (*single quotes*) or [" "] (*double quotes*). These are chiefly used to set off DIRECT SPEECH, as in the example *'Can I help you?' she asked.* See chapter 8 of *The Penguin Guide to Punctuation* for more on quotation marks.

# R

**raising** Any construction in which a word or phrase which logically belongs in a SUBORDINATE CLAUSE appears instead in the MATRIX CLAUSE above it. See SUBJECT RAISING, OBJECT RAISING and NEGATIVE RAISING.

**raising verb** A VERB which can take a grammatical SUBJECT which is logically the subject of a following clause. A good example is *seem*. For example, the sentence *It seems that Jan is happy* can be expressed with the raised structure *Jan seems to be happy*, in which *Jan* has been raised from being the subject of *be* to being the subject of *seem*.

**reanalysis** A process in WORD-FORMATION in which an existing word is divided at a point at which historically no boundary exists, and one of the resulting pieces is removed and used to construct other words. For example, the word *hamburger* is historically derived from the city name *Hamburg*, but, in English, the word has been re-analysed into *ham* plus *-burger*, and the new element *-burger* has been used to coin further words like *cheeseburger*, *beefburger* and *vegeburger*.

**reciprocal** A form or construction which indicates that two or more people or things are acting upon one another in the same way. In English, reciprocal constructions are expressed with the RECIPROCAL PRONOUNS *each other* or *one another*. Examples: *Jan and I like to tease each other*; *The suspects have blamed one another for the crime*. Compare REFLEXIVE.

**reciprocal pronoun** A PRONOUN used in a RECIPROCAL construction. The English ones are *each other* and *one another*.

**recursion** The ability of a syntactic unit (a CONSTITUENT) to occur inside a larger unit of the same kind, and so on, without limit. Consider this sentence: *I'm reading a book about the reasons for the development of computers with the capacity for high-speed manipulation of virtual objects.* Here the prepositional phrase *of virtual objects* lies inside the large PP *for high-speed manipulation* . . . , which lies inside the PP *with the capacity for* . . . , which lies inside the PP *of computers* . . . , which lies inside the PP *for the development* . . . ; which lies inside the PP *about the reasons* . . .

**reduced relative clause** (or **reduced clause**) Another name for a PARTICIPIAL RELATIVE CLAUSE.

**reference** The relation that holds between a NOUN PHRASE and the non-linguistic object or objects it picks out. For example, in the sentence *That cat has ruined my geraniums*, both *that cat* and *my geraniums* refer to particular things in the world. See COREFERENCE.

**reference grammar** A book providing an orderly description of the grammatical facts of a language, designed for looking things up rather than as a practical textbook.

**reflexive** Any construction which indicates expressly that two NOUN PHRASES in a sentence refer to the same person(s) or thing(s). In English, a reflexive sentence contains a REFLEXIVE PRONOUN. Examples: *Susie cut herself; Susie saw herself in the mirror; Susie doesn't know what to do with herself.* A few verbs intrinsically require a reflexive object: *Susie prides herself on her cooking; Susie perjured herself.* See INTENSIVE REFLEXIVE.

**reflexive pronoun** Any PRONOUN ending in *-self* or *-selves*. The English ones are *myself, yourself, himself, herself, itself, ourselves, yourselves, themselves*. The reflexive pronouns occur both in true REFLEXIVE constructions and in the INTENSIVE REFLEXIVE construction.

**regular** A label applied to any linguistic item which behaves in the way that is typical of items in its class. For example, the verb *watch* is regular (*I watch her, I watched her, I have watched her*), while *see* is IRREGULAR (*I see her, I saw her, I have seen her*).

**relational adjective** An ADJECTIVE derived from a NOUN which carries no meaning beyond that of the noun but which merely serves to provide a form of the noun which can be used as a modifier. Examples include *telephonic* from *telephone* and *Glaswegian* from *Glasgow*. English makes little use of these, preferring COMPOUNDS instead: we prefer *Glasgow telephone system* to *Glaswegian telephonic system*. Languages in which compounding is poorly developed, such as the Romance and Slavic languages, often make heavy use of relational adjectives.

**relational verb** A superficially TRANSITIVE verb which denotes a relation between two things, such as *have, own, involve, want, need* or *deserve*. Examples: *Susie has blue eyes; Susie owns a Volvo; Susie deserves more consideration*. Relational verbs are often difficult or impossible to put into the PASSIVE VOICE: **Blue eyes are had by Susie; *More consideration is deserved by Susie*. Note: relational verbs have sometimes been called MIDDLE verbs.

**relative adverb** An ADVERB which introduces a RELATIVE CLAUSE. The English relative adverbs are *where, when, wherever* and *whenever*. Examples of use: *The place where I come from is very small; The day when I met Jan was the best day of my life; I take my laptop wherever I go*.

**relative clause** (also **adjective clause**) A type of SUBORDINATE CLAUSE which is attached to a HEAD noun within a NOUN PHRASE. The most familiar type is a RESTRICTIVE (or DEFINING) relative clause, which is required to identify what is being referred to. Example: *The restaurant (which) we visited last night was pretty good*. Here the relative clause is *(which) we visited last night* (the RELATIVE PRONOUN *which* is optional), and it is attached to the head noun *restaurant* within the noun phrase *the restaurant (which) we visited last night*. This relative clause is restrictive, since it is required for identification: without it, we would have only *The restaurant was pretty good*, which does not identify the restaurant under discussion.

In contrast, a NON-RESTRICTIVE (or NON-DEFINING) relative clause is not required for identification, but serves only to provide additional information. Consider this example: *Margaret Thatcher, who hated trains, always refused to privatize the railways*. Here the relative clause is *who hated trains*, attached to the head *Margaret Thatcher*. This relative clause is non-restrictive, since it is not required to identify Margaret Thatcher: it merely provides extra information.

See also the special case illustrated under SENTENTIAL RELATIVE CLAUSE.

**relative pronoun** A PRONOUN which introduces a RELATIVE CLAUSE. The English relative pronouns are *who* (with its rare variant *whom*), *whose* and *which*. The complementizer *that* can also introduce a relative clause; when it does, it is counted as a relative pronoun by some grammarians, but not by all.

In most cases, the use of a relative pronoun is optional in English, and informal speech favours its omission. In the following examples, the optional relative pronoun appears in parentheses: *The woman* (*who*) *you were talking to is my boss; The coffee machine* (*which*) *I bought for my wife was on special.* In the following further examples, the relative pronouns *who* and *whose* are obligatory, and may not be omitted: *The settlers who jumped the gun in Oklahoma grabbed the best land; The creature whose bones we are looking at lived over 200 million years ago.*

Compare RELATIVE ADVERB.

**reported speech** Another term for INDIRECT SPEECH.

**restrictive** (also **defining**) A label applied to a MODIFIER which is required to identify the thing being talked about. Take the noun phrase *the old man*, containing the modifier *old* (an adjective). This can be used in two different ways. Here is one way. *A young man and an old man walked into the shop. The old man took off his hat.* Here, clearly, *old* is required to identify the man referred to ('the old man, not the young one'), and so *old* is a restrictive adjective. But here is another way. *The 83-year-old Sinatra was gravely ill, and it was clear that the old man did not have long to live.* Here, of course, the identity of the man under discussion is already clear, and *old* is not required to identify him, and so it is in this case a NON-RESTRICTIVE (or NON-DEFINING) adjective.

For examples of restrictive and non-restrictive relative clauses, see under RELATIVE CLAUSE.

**retained object** A traditional name for a certain NOUN PHRASE in a certain construction. In the sentence *My wife gave me this book*, it is far from clear whether the DIRECT OBJECT is *me* or *this book*. When this sentence is converted to a PASSIVE, the result is *I was given this book by my wife*, in which *this book*, whose grammatical role is now obscure, is the retained object.

**rhetorical question** A QUESTION which is asked merely for effect, and which does not expect an answer. For example, if I say to you *Do I look like a fool?*, then I don't expect an answer: I am merely choosing a rhetorical way of saying *I am not a fool*.

**right-branching** Any grammatical construction in which elements are added to the right-hand end of something which is already present. Right-branching is typical of English, and it is illustrated by the following example: *This is the cat that killed the rat that ate the malt that lay in the house that Jack built*. Compare LEFT-BRANCHING.

**right-dislocation** See under DISLOCATION.

**right-node raising** The construction in which two beginnings share the same ending. Examples: *Jan prepared, and Marian served, the sandwiches; She is a bright, though careless, student; By day the Americans, and by night the British, poured bombs onto Germany*. Rare in speech, right-node raising is typical of formal writing. It should be used sparingly, since it can be difficult for the reader to process. Note that, when written, this construction requires two commas, as shown.

**root** The minimal form of a LEXICAL ITEM (a dictionary word). In native English words, a root is usually identical to the independent form of a word. For example, the word *dog* always keeps the same shape in inflected forms like *dogs* and in cases of WORD-FORMATION like *doggie* and *doghouse*. But some other languages are different. For example, the Latin verb *amare* 'love' has the root *am-*, which appears in all forms of the verb, such as *amamus* 'we love', *amabit* 's/he used to love', *amavero 'I shall have loved'*, amare *'to love'* and amatus *'loved'*. Compare STEM.

**rule** A statement of something which is generally true in a language. In linguistics, we apply the term *rule* only to a statement of what we observe to be true of somebody's speech: for example, 'an English noun normally forms its plural by suffixing *-s*'. However, among the proponents of PRESCRIPTIVISM, the label is applied to a statement of somebody's opinion about good usage, such as 'You shouldn't use a split infinitive.' You should not confuse these two senses.

# S

**sandhi** Any change in pronunciation, whether optional or obligatory, which occurs when two particular words or MORPHEMES occur consecutively. If the change occurs within a single word, we have INTERNAL SANDHI. For example, the negative prefix *in-* (as in *insane*) combines with *possible* to produce *impossible*. If the change occurs across a boundary between two words, we have EXTERNAL SANDHI. For example, the sequence *can't you* can optionally be pronounced as *canchoo*.

**Saxon genitive** See under POSSESSIVE.

**scope** That portion of a sentence which is included in the applicability of a QUANTIFIER or a NEGATIVE. For example, in *I didn't hide your vodka in the piano*, the negative has more than one possible scope, and the sentence is ambiguous. If the scope of the negative is *in the piano*, then the sentence means 'I hid your vodka, but not in the piano'. If the scope is *your vodka*, then the sentence means 'I hid something in the piano, but it wasn't your vodka'. If the scope is *hide*, then the sentence means 'I put your vodka in the piano, but not with the intention of hiding it'. If the scope is *I*, then the sentence means 'Somebody may have hidden your vodka in the piano, but it wasn't me'. To some extent, these different interpretations can be distinguished in speech by differing stress patterns.

**secondary recategorization** The phenomenon in which a word which normally belongs to one subcategory of its PART OF SPEECH is shifted to another subcategory, with different grammatical behaviour, with a shift in interpretation. For example, the English nouns *wine*, *coffee* and *intelligence* cannot be counted or pluralized in their central senses, but they can be counted and pluralized when recategorized to mean 'variety' (*Rhone wines*), 'measure' (*four coffees, please*), or 'embodiment' (*an alien intelligence*).

**second person** The PERSON category representing the addressee(s), and possibly also other people linked with the addressee(s). English, unusually, has only a single second-person pronoun, *you*. Many other languages have two or more second-person pronouns distinguishing number, sex, degree of intimacy, and other categories.

**selectional restriction** A limitation upon the ability of words to be combined which depends only on their meaning, and not on their grammatical nature. For example, *You have deceived my watermelon* is grammatically perfect, but it violates a selectional restriction: watermelons do not belong to the category of things that can be deceived. Compare SUBCATEGORIZATION.

**semantic role** Any one of several relations which a NOUN PHRASE may bear in its clause, classified from the point of view of the person or thing denoted by that noun phrase in the situation denoted by its clause, independently of its grammatical form. Among the most obvious semantic roles are AGENT, PATIENT, GOAL and INSTRUMENT, though many more are recognized by specialists. Any approach to grammar which places great emphasis upon the behaviour of semantic roles is a CASE GRAMMAR.

**semantics** The study of meaning. Semantics is not strictly part of grammar, but the dividing line between the two areas is often far from sharp.

**semi-auxiliary** A sequence of words containing a verb and having much the same function as an AUXILIARY but lacking the distinctive grammatical properties of auxiliaries (the NICE PROPERTIES). Familiar semi-auxiliaries include *have* (*to*), *be going* (*to*) and *be able* (*to*). Examples: *I have to go home*; *Susie is going to buy a new car*; *We won't be able to make the last train*.

**semicolon** The punctuation mark [;]. The semicolon connects two complete sentences when all the following conditions are met:

**1**. The two sentences are too closely related to be separated by a full stop (a period).

**2**. There is no connecting word which would require a comma, such as *and* or *but*.

**3**. The special conditions requiring a colon are absent. Examples: *Women's conversation is cooperative; men's is competitive. Tolkien published* The Hobbit *in 1937; the first volume of* The Lord of the Rings *followed in 1954*.

For more information, see *The Penguin Guide to Punctuation*, chapter 4.

**semi-modal** A conventional label for the two English verbs *need* and *dare*, which sometimes behave like MODAL auxiliaries but at other times like ordinary lexical verbs. For example, we can say either *I don't dare to do that*, in which *dare* is an ordinary verb, or we can say *I dare not do that*, in which *dare* is a modal.

**semi-negative** A label sometimes applied to an ADVERB which is not really negative at all but which behaves grammatically like a negative. Examples are *seldom, scarcely* and *hardly*. For example, *seldom* behaves like the negative *never* in cases like *Seldom have I seen such a mess* and *Never have I seen such a mess*, as opposed to the ordinary adverb *often*, as in *I have often seen such a mess*. In standard English, a semi-negative cannot occur together with a negative: *I can hardly see it*, but not **I can't hardly see it*.

**sentence** The largest grammatical unit whose structure is governed by rigorous grammatical rules. In English, a sentence always contains a SUBJECT (except in an IMPERATIVE sentence), and it always contains a PREDICATE. A sentence always contains at least one MAIN CLAUSE, and it may contain additional main clauses or SUBORDINATE CLAUSES. In writing, a sentence is written with an initial capital letter and a final full stop, question mark or exclamation mark. Examples: *The Vikings reached North America in the eleventh century*; *Who was the last Doge of Venice?*; *The students I've talked to tell me that they would prefer a takeaway exam*.

Sentences are variously classified; see SENTENCE TYPE.

It is important to realize that not every plausible UTTERANCE corresponds to a sentence: see FRAGMENT for examples of the difference. Speech makes heavy use of incomplete sentences, and informal writing may do the same. But formal writing normally consists entirely of complete sentences: this is one of the characteristics making it formal.

**sentence adverb** An ADVERB which does not merely modify a VERB or a VERB PHRASE, but which instead modifies the entire sentence containing it. Most commonly, a sentence adverb expresses the speaker's or writer's view of the likelihood, desirability or other characteristic of the state of affairs denoted by the rest of the sentence. Typical sentence adverbs include *probably, surely, certainly, undoubtedly, fortunately, unfortunately, frankly* and *hopefully*. Examples: *Susie will probably be coming* ('It is probable that Susie will be coming'); *Fortunately, Susie will be coming* ('It is fortunate that Susie will be coming'); *Surely Susie will be coming* ('I can't believe that she won't be coming'); *Hopefully Susie will be coming* ('I hope and expect that Susie will be coming'). Compare SUBJUNCT.

**sentence type** Any of the several types into which SENTENCES can be classified. If we classify sentences by their grammatical forms, there are four types in English: DECLARATIVE, INTERROGATIVE, IMPERATIVE and EXCLAMATORY. (These are traditionally classed as MOODS, even though English verbs do not vary for mood in the way that verbs do in some other languages.) If we classify them by their functions, there are again four types: STATEMENT, QUESTION, COMMAND and EXCLAMATION. Most typically, we use the declarative form for a statement, interrogative for a question, imperative for a command, and exclamative for an exclamation. However, we do not have to do this.

For example, *You will now sit down* has declarative form (it looks like a statement), but it can be used to issue a command. And *Boy, can Susie dance!* has interrogative form (it looks like a question), but it can be used as an exclamation. It is therefore essential, in classifying sentences, to distinguish form from function, since the two do not match up one to one in all cases.

**sentential relative clause** The construction in which a RELATIVE CLAUSE, instead of being attached to the HEAD NOUN inside an ordinary NOUN PHRASE, is attached to an entire sentence. Example: *The French and the Germans have refused to allow the sale of British beef, which has enraged British farmers*. Here the relative clause *which has enraged British farmers* is a sentential relative modifying the entire preceding sentence.

**sentential subject** The construction in which the subject position of a sentence is occupied by a complete sentence introduced by a

COMPLEMENTIZER *that* or *whether*. For example, *That Susie is drunk is obvious* shows the subject position of the main clause _ *is obvious* occupied by the sentential subject *that Susie is drunk*. See EXTRAPOSITION.

**sequence of tenses** (also **backshift**) A restriction on the choice of TENSE in a SUBORDINATE CLAUSE resulting from the choice of tense in a preceding MATRIX CLAUSE. For example, while we can say *Susie says that she is coming*, if we put the first verb into the past tense, we normally put the second verb into the past as well, producing *Susie said that she was coming*. Here *Susie said that she is coming* is somewhat unnatural, though not strictly ungrammatical: sequence of tenses is less rigid in English than in some other languages.

**short passive** See under PASSIVE VOICE.

**simple past** See under PAST.

**simple present** See under PRESENT.

**simple sentence** A SENTENCE which contains only one CLAUSE. Examples: *Susie will be here at eight o'clock*; *The King is dead*; *My brother-in-law wants to buy a new van*. Compare COMPOUND SENTENCE, COMPLEX SENTENCE.

**singular** The simplest form of an English NOUN, the form which is entered in a dictionary, such as *dog, tree, girl* or *spaghetti*. With a COUNT NOUN denoting a thing that can be counted, the singular is usually the form used to talk about exactly one of something: *one dog, a dog, that dog*. Here it contrasts with the PLURAL: *two dogs, those dogs, several dogs*. With a MASS NOUN denoting something that cannot be counted, the singular is usually the only form that exists at all, as with *spaghetti* and *flour*. But see PLURALE TANTUM for a class of exceptions. The GRAMMATICAL CATEGORY that distinguishes singular from plural is called NUMBER.

**specifier** A label sometimes applied to any grammatical word which specifies (delimits, identifies) the range of applicability of the phrase containing it. Consider the incomplete NOUN PHRASES _ *nylon shirt* and __ *nylon shirts*. We can complete these noun phrases by filling the blank with a DETERMINER which specifies something about which of all conceivable nylon shirts we have in mind: *a nylon shirt, the nylon shirt, this nylon shirt, any nylon shirt, some nylon shirts, most nylon shirts, all nylon shirts*, and so on. A determiner is therefore a specifier within a noun phrase.

Now consider the incomplete ADJECTIVE PHRASE __ *nice*. This time we can fill the blank with a DEGREE MODIFIER to indicate what degree of niceness we have in mind: *fairly nice, very nice, too nice, extremely nice, moderately nice, rather nice*, and so on. A degree modifier is therefore a specifier within an adjective phrase.

**split infinitive** A traditional but misleading label for a particular English construction. Consider the sentence *She decided to never touch another cigarette*. Here the sequence *to never touch* is an example of what is called a 'split infinitive'. Those who use the term believe that there is something wrong with separating the particle *to* from a following INFINITIVE like *touch*: they take the view that *to* is itself part of the infinitive, which they cite as *to touch*, and they object to breaking up this sequence with other material. But this view is quite wrong: the infinitive is a single word (here *touch*); the particle *to* is not part of the infinitive or part of the verb at all; and the sequence *to touch* is not a grammatical unit of any kind, as shown by the fact that it can be readily interrupted by other material.

**stacking** The 'piling up' of MODIFIERS. In the phrase *a pretty little white house*, the adjectives *pretty*, *little* and *white* are stacked on the head noun *house*, which is modified by each of them. In the more complex phrase *the finest Australian red wines*, the adjective *red* strictly modifies *wines*, while *Australian* modifies *red wines* and *finest* modifies *Australian red wines*.

**standard English** That particular variety of English which is regarded by educated people as appropriate for most types of public discourse, including most broadcasting, almost all publication, and virtually all conversation with anyone other than intimates. Standard English is the mother tongue of few people and is most commonly acquired only through formal education; consequently only the well educated normally acquire a good command of it. Standard English exists in both spoken and written forms, which at times may show interesting differences: for example, the form illustrated by *Much research has been done* is normal in standard written English but not in standard spoken English. Standard English can be spoken with almost any kind of regional accent, though some accents are regarded by some people as less appropriate than others for speaking standard English.

Standard English is not entirely uniform around the globe: for example, American users of standard English say *first floor* and *I've just gotten a letter* and write *center* and *color*, while British users say *ground floor* and *I've just got a letter* and write *centre* and *colour*. But these regional differences are few in comparison with the very high degree of agreement about which forms should count as standard. Nevertheless, standard English, like all living languages, changes over time: for example, standard English in the early nineteenth century required *My house is painting* and did not permit *My house is being painted*, while today it is the other way round. Because of this ceaseless change, there is at any given moment a noticeable degree of uncertainty and disagreement as to which usages should be accepted as standard. Here are some examples of usages whose status has recently been controversial: *She decided to never touch another cigarette*; *Hopefully we'll be there in time for lunch*; *I'm disinterested in opera*; *normalcy*.

It is important to realize that standard English is in no way intrinsically superior to any other variety of English: in particular, it is not 'more logical', 'more grammatical' or 'more expressive'. It is, at bottom, a convenience: the use of a single agreed standard form, learned by speakers everywhere, minimizes uncertainty, confusion, misunderstanding and communicative difficulty generally. But the social prestige of standard English is so great that mastery of it is now essential in a wide variety of careers.

**statement** The (functional) SENTENCE TYPE which expresses a proposition presented as true. A statement is normally made using the DECLARATIVE form: *Roses are red*; *Venus has no moons*; *I saw Mommie kissing Santa Claus*.

**stative** A label applied to a form or a construction which expresses a state of affairs, rather than an event. For example, *My window is broken* usually indicates a state of affairs (there is a hole in my window), and not the act of breaking the window. Especially in the past tense, English sentences can be ambiguous between stative and DYNAMIC interpretations. For example, *My window was broken* can be either stative (as in *My window was broken for a week*) or dynamic (as in *My window was broken by a hailstorm*); here only the second represents the PASSIVE VOICE.

**stative verb** A VERB which expresses a state of affairs, rather than an action or an event. Typical stative verbs include *know, want, believe, understand, fear* and *like*. In English, stative verbs cannot easily appear in the CONTINUOUS aspect: we cannot usually say **Lisa is knowing French, *Jan is liking Eric Clapton* or **I am believing you*.

**stem** In some languages, a form of a lexical item (a word) which typically cannot stand alone but to which affixes are added to produce word-forms. For example, the Latin verb *amare* 'love' has the root *am-*, from which are derived its several stems, such as the present stem *ama-* (as in *amat* 's/he loves'), the imperfect stem *amaba-* (as in *amabat* 's/he used to love', and the perfect stem *amavi-* (as in *amavit* 's/he loved'). Native English words do not usually make any distinction among roots, stems and word-forms. Compare ROOT.

**stranding** See PREPOSITION STRANDING.

**strong verb** A VERB which inflects by changing its stem vowel, such as *sing, sang, sung*. Compare WEAK VERB.

**structural ambiguity** An AMBIGUITY which involves assigning two (or more) grammatical structures to a string of words, as in *Visiting relatives can be a nuisance*. Compare LEXICAL AMBIGUITY.

**structuralism** An approach to describing the structure of languages which sees a language as an orderly structured system in which each element is defined chiefly by the way in which it is related to other elements. Structuralism was introduced by the Swiss linguist Ferdinand de Saussure in the early years of the twentieth century, and almost all approaches to linguistics since then have been structuralist. In the 1940s and 1950s, a particularly narrow version of structuralism was developed in the USA, and the term *structuralism* is sometimes used specifically to denote this kind of *American structuralism*. As a result, proponents of

GENERATIVE GRAMMAR sometimes use *structuralism* as a term of abuse for their predecessors, but, in the original sense of the term *structuralism*, generative linguistics is every bit as structuralist as its forerunners.

**subcategorization** The phenomenon by which the words belonging to a single PART OF SPEECH do not all behave grammatically in exactly the same way. Take verbs, and consider the following frames: (a) *Susie* __; (b) *Susie* __ *the cat*; (c) *Susie* __ *at the cat*; (d) *Susie* __ *me the book*; (e) *Susie* __ *she was coming*; (f) *Susie* __ *me she was coming*. Now try to insert the following past-tense verb-forms into the blanks: *smiled, chased, said, told, decided*. Quite apart from any awkward meanings that may arise, you will find that each verb fits into some of the blanks to make a grammatical sentence but not into the others. For example, *said* goes into (e) but not into (f), while *told* works the other way round. This is subcategorization: we want to assign all these words to the category *verb* because they all have important grammatical properties in common, but not all verbs behave in the same way.

All parts of speech exhibit subcategorization. For example, the preposition *from* can be followed by *under the chair*, as in *The cat ran out from under the chair*, but the preposition *to* cannot do this: **The cat ran in to under the chair* is not grammatical.

Compare SELECTIONAL RESTRICTION.

**subject** A particular GRAMMATICAL RELATION which may be borne by a NOUN PHRASE in a sentence. Most typically, the subject is the first noun phrase in the sentence and it represents the thing that the rest of the sentence 'is about', but this is not always true. Here are some typical examples, in which the subject is bracketed: [*Pratchett's Discworld novels*] *have sold millions of copies*; [*I*] *want to go home*; *Last week* [*a tropical storm*] *devastated Bangladesh*.

In the next examples, the subject is not the first noun phrase in the sentence: *This book* [*I*] *can't recommend*; *In the corner sat* [*a man in a dark cloak*].

In a sentence containing more than one CLAUSE, each clause has its own subject. Here is a simple example: [*Susie*] *told me that* [*Natalie*] *was ill*. Here *Susie* is the subject of the MAIN CLAUSE, while *Natalie* is the subject of the COMPLEMENT CLAUSE. The next example is more complex: [*The woman* [*you*] *were talking to*] *is my boss*. Here *you* is the subject of the RELATIVE CLAUSE *you were talking to*, while *the woman you were talking to* is the subject of the main clause. Hence one subject is contained within the other.

**subject-attachment rule** A rule of standard English by which the absent SUBJECT of a NON-FINITE phrase must be interpreted as identical to the subject of the higher clause containing it. Consider some examples: *Having finished her dinner, Susie opened a book*; *Before going out, Susie checked the back door*; *Wearied by the discussion, Susie left the meeting*. In all these cases it must be Susie, and only Susie, who finished dinner, who went out and who was wearied. Violation of this rule produces a DANGLING PARTICIPLE; see that entry.

**subject control** See under CONTROL.

**subjective genitive** A POSSESSIVE construction with *of* or *-'s* in which the possessed item represents the logical subject. For example, *Susie's arrival* is logically related to *Susie arrives*, and *the conquests of the Mongols* is related to *the Mongols conquered*. Compare OBJECTIVE GENITIVE.

**subject raising** The construction in which the logical subject of a subordinate clause appears on the surface as the subject of a higher clause. For example, in *It seems that Susie is happy*, *Susie* is both the logical subject and the grammatical subject of *be happy*. However, in the alternative form *Susie seems to be happy*, *Susie* has been raised to be the grammatical subject of *seem*.

**subject-verb inversion** See under INVERSION.

**subjunct** In the QUIRK GRAMMARS, a label applied to a kind of ADVERB or ADVERBIAL which does not modify a verb or a verb phrase in the usual manner but which modifies the entire sentence containing it. A subjunct is thus rather like a SENTENCE ADVERB, except that it does not express the speaker's attitude. Consider the adverb *strictly*. In the sentence *She treats her children strictly*, the word is an ordinary adverb (an ADJUNCT in the Quirk terminology). We can ask 'How does she treat her children?' and get the answer 'Strictly'. However, in the sentence *Dogs are strictly domesticated wolves*, the adverb does not describe the manner in which dogs are wolves: rather, it means something like 'The proposition "Dogs are domesticated wolves" is strictly true.'

**subjunctive** A label for a MOOD distinction which was prominent in English many centuries ago but which is now almost entirely gone. In modern English, the ancient subjunctive, marked by distinctive verb-forms and expressing doubtful reality or unreality, survives only marginally. The distinctive subjunctive forms are now confined to the verb *be* and to the third-singular forms of other verbs; they are still common in American English, while in British English they are confined to very formal styles. A subjunctive normally only follows a verb like *suggest, propose, demand* or *insist*. Examples, in which the subjunctive verb-forms are bracketed: *I suggest that she* [*refuse*] *the offer; They are demanding that she* [*reveal*] *her sources; I insist that they* [*be*] *freed.* These subjunctive forms contrast with the corresponding INDICATIVE (ordinary) forms – in my examples, *refuses, reveals* and *are*, respectively. Informal and moderately formal British English in fact uses the indicative forms in all cases. British English therefore loses the distinction, still always made in American English, between *I insisted that they were locked up* ('I asserted vigorously that they were already in jail') and *I insisted that they be locked up* ('I demanded that they should be put in jail').

To avoid this ambiguity, British (and other) speakers sometimes insert the MODAL *should*: *I insisted that they should be locked up*. As a result, some grammarians extend the label *subjunctive* to sequences like *should be locked up*, but not everyone would accept this extended usage.

**subordinate clause** A CLAUSE which cannot stand alone to make a complete sentence but which must form part of a larger clause, its MATRIX CLAUSE. The principal types of subordinate clause are the RELATIVE CLAUSE, the COMPLEMENT CLAUSE, the ADVERBIAL CLAUSE and the EMBEDDED QUESTION.

**subordinating conjunction** (also **subordinator**) The PART OF SPEECH containing the words which can introduce an adverbial clause. These include *when, whenever, although, after, if,* and a number of others. See ADVERBIAL CLAUSE for examples of use.

**subordination** (also **hypotaxis**) The use of SUBORDINATE CLAUSES.

**subordinator** Another term for SUBORDINATING CONJUNCTION.

**substantive** An old-fashioned word for NOUN.

**suffix** An AFFIX which follows the material it is attached to. Examples include the *-ness* of *happiness*, the *-ly* of *slowly* and the *-th* of *warmth*. Compare PREFIX.

**superlative** That form of an adjective or an adverb expressing the highest degree. For *big*, this is *biggest*; for *bad*, it is *worst*; for *beautiful*, it is *most beautiful*; for *slowly*, it is *most slowly*. Compare POSITIVE, COMPARATIVE.

**suppletion** The use of two or more different stems to construct the inflected forms of a word. Examples include *person/people*, *go/went* and *bad/worse*.

**surface structure** In TRANSFORMATIONAL GRAMMAR, the overt outward form of a sentence; the form which it actually has when used. This contrasts with its DEEP STRUCTURE, which may be very different in form.

**symbol** Another term for LOGOGRAM.

**synchronic** Pertaining to a language at a given point in time, with no attention to the development of the language over time. That point in time need not be the present: we can equally construct a synchronic description of contemporary English or of Elizabethan English. Compare DIACHRONIC.

**syncretism** The grammatical phenomenon in which two functionally distinct forms of a word are identical in form. For example, many English verbs distinguish the PAST from the PAST PARTICIPLE: *I saw her*, but *I have seen her*. But *love* does not distinguish these two in form: *I loved her*, but *I have loved her*. This is syncretism.

**syntactic category** Any one of the structural categories of linguistic objects which can be used in building sentences. Among the syntactic categories are the PARTS OF SPEECH like NOUN and ADJECTIVE, and several larger categories such as NOMINAL GROUP, NOUN PHRASE, VERB PHRASE and even SENTENCE (since a sentence may contain a smaller sentence within it). See the example presented under TREE DIAGRAM. Compare GRAMMATICAL CATEGORY.

**syntagmatic relation** The relation between linguistic items which are present at the same time in the same utterance or sentence. For example, in the sentence *Susie bought herself a new suit*, there is a syntagmatic relation between *Susie* and *herself* (which refer to the same person) and between *bought* and *a new suit* (the second being the DIRECT OBJECT of the first). Compare PARADIGMATIC RELATION.

**syntax** Sentence structure, or the study of sentence structure: one branch of GRAMMAR.

**Systemic Grammar** (also **Systemic-Functional Grammar**) A particular approach to the study of grammar developed chiefly by Michael Halliday and his colleagues in Britain. Systemic Grammar is a variety of FUNCTIONAL GRAMMAR: that is, it attaches great importance not only to linguistic forms but also to the functions which they serve. Accordingly, its grammatical descriptions typically involve considerable appeal to the purposes which language-users have in mind, and its proponents have particularly stressed its usefulness in the study of TEXTS.

# T

**tag question** A brief question which is tacked on to the end of a statement. English uses two different kinds of tag question, both of somewhat complex formation. Consider the statement *Susie is Irish*. One kind of tag question extends this statement so as to ask for explicit confirmation: *Susie's Irish, isn't she?* The other kind of tag usually forms only a RHETORICAL QUESTION not requiring a response: *Susie's Irish, is she?*

**telic** A label applied to a verb or a sentence which denotes an activity or state which has a recognizable goal whose achievement would necessarily bring the activity or state to an end. Telic verbs include *paint* (as in *Rembrandt painted* The Night Watch), *wash* (as in *Jan is washing her hair*), and *sack* (as in *The Mongols sacked Kiev*). The opposite is ATELIC.

**temporal clause** Any ADVERBIAL CLAUSE pertaining to time, such as one beginning with *when*, *whenever*, *after*, *before* or *while*. Examples (in brackets): [*When I was young,*] *television was in black and white*; [*After the French army was crushed in Serbia,*] *there was no effective Christian force between the Turks and the North Sea*; *I met my wife* [*while we were working in London*].

**tense** The GRAMMATICAL CATEGORY which correlates most closely with location in time. Like many other languages, English marks tense in verbs: *I see her* versus *I saw her*. English has only two tenses: the PAST tense and the other one, which is commonly called the PRESENT tense but which might more accurately be called the *non-past* tense or the *present/future* tense, since it generally expresses all times other than past time. Accordingly, the forms of English verbs usually come in pairs. Below are a few examples.

| Non-past | Past |
|---|---|
| *I see her.* | *I saw her.* |
| *I am watching her.* | *I was watching her.* |
| *I have met her.* | *I had met her.* |
| *I will visit her.* | *I would visit her.* |
| *I have been seeing her.* | *I had been seeing her.* |

If the relationship is not clear, try putting *I told you that . . .* in front of each. You should find that the past-tense form is far more natural than the non-past form in every case, because of SEQUENCE OF TENSES.

Unlike some other languages, English has no future tense. It is quite wrong to claim that forms involving *will* or *shall* are 'future': they are not future in tense merely because they often denote future time. See FUTURE for discussion. But some other European languages, such as Spanish, French and Italian, really do have three tenses, including a true future tense, and some non-European languages have more than three tenses.

**tensed** Another term for FINITE.

**text** A general term for any connected piece of speech or writing, such as a conversation, a lecture, a newspaper article or a book. Some linguists restrict the term to a piece of writing, preferring DISCOURSE for a piece of speech.

**thematic structure** The structure of a sentence seen from the point of view of the organization of the information it contains. The GIVEN AND NEW distinction is a familiar aspect of thematic structure, while TOPIC and FOCUS are others.

**third person** The PERSON category representing everyone and everything other than the speaker and the addressee and those people expressly linked with the speaker or the addressee. Practically all NOUN PHRASES are third-person: *she, they, the dog, my sister, Australian wines, Neptune, most first-basemen, beauty, the square root of seven,* and so on. In English, the only non-third-person noun phrases are the first-person pronouns *I/me* and *we/us* and the second-person pronoun *you.*

**time adverb** An ADVERB that answers the question 'when?' Examples: *tomorrow, soon, often, occasionally, always*. An ADVERB PHRASE that does the same is a time adverbial: *as soon as possible, next Thursday, whenever you like*.

***to*-infinitive** A traditional, but confused, label for a sequence consisting of the particle *to* followed by an infinitive. For example, in *Susie has decided to buy a new car*, the sequence *to buy* would be regarded as a *to-infinitive*. In reality, *to buy*, like other such sequences, is not an infinitive, nor is it a verb-form, nor is it a grammatical unit of any kind. See INFINITIVE and SPLIT INFINITIVE. Nevertheless, there is something of a tradition of using the *to-infinitive* as the CITATION FORM of an English verb, such as *to buy* for the verb *buy*. This somewhat eccentric use is not normal among linguists, is never found in dictionaries, and is not recommended.

**topic** That part of a sentence that names what the sentence is 'talking about'. Not every sentence has a topic, and, even in sentences that do have one, it may not be obvious out of context. Consider a simple example: Alice: *Where's Susie?* Mike: *She's in the library*. In Mike's response, it is clear that *she* (= *Susie*) is the topic, while the rest of his response is the COMMENT – that is, what is being said about her. See also TOPICALIZATION.

**topicalization** The construction in which a phrase is moved out of its ordinary position to the beginning of a sentence in order to serve as a TOPIC. Consider the following sentence: *I can't recommend this book*. It is possible to move the noun phrase *this book* to the front of the sentence in order to produce *This book I can't recommend*, in which *this book* is topicalized: that is, the new sentence is a comment about *this book*.

**traditional grammar** The name given to the entire body of grammatical description and investigation in Europe and North America before the rise of modern linguistics in the twentieth century. Traditional grammar is the kind of grammar that was taught in schools in the days when grammar was still taught in schools, and it is still the kind of grammar which is most often taught today in those few schools which teach it. While many of the insights and terms of traditional grammar have been accepted into contemporary linguistic work on grammar, others have been modified or rejected altogether as inadequate, while many new concepts and terms have been introduced.

Some contemporary work is still rather traditional in outlook, such as the QUIRK GRAMMARS, a series of grammars of English written by Randolph Quirk and his colleagues, but these works are none the less informed by more recent linguistic investigations.

**transformational grammar** An approach to the investigation of SYNTAX devised by the American linguistic Noam Chomsky in the 1950s, one version of GENERATIVE GRAMMAR. Transformational grammar is highly abstract and intended chiefly to serve certain theoretical purposes; it is not designed to serve as a framework for the practical teaching of language or of grammar, and it is not well suited to such purposes. For theoretical purposes, transformational grammar was largely displaced in the 1980s by Chomsky's newer GOVERNMENT-AND-BINDING THEORY.

**transitive** A label applied to a VERB which takes a DIRECT OBJECT. Some verbs are always transitive, and produce an ungrammatical result if used without an object. Among these are *destroy*, *assassinate*, *want*, *seduce* and *trigger*:

| | |
|---|---|
| *The Mongols destroyed Kiev.* | **The Mongols destroyed.* |
| *Sirhan assassinated RFK.* | **Sirhan assassinated.* |
| *Susie wants a new car.* | **Susie wants.* |
| *Susie seduced Natalie.* | **Susie seduced.* |
| *The bomb triggered an avalanche.* | **The bomb triggered.* |

Many other verbs can be either transitive or intransitive; see LABILE VERB. Compare INTRANSITIVE. The label *transitive* is also applied to a verb phrase or a clause containing a transitive verb.

**transitive adjective** Another term for PREPOSITIONAL ADJECTIVE.

**tree diagram** A pictorial way of displaying the syntactic structure of a sentence. Trees are widely used in the study of syntax, though proponents of different approaches to syntax may differ significantly in the way they draw their trees. The diagram below shows a typical tree structure for the sentence *The little girl hugged her doll*; the SYNTACTIC

CATEGORIES labelled are Det(erminer), A(djective), A(djective) P(hrase), N(oun), N(ominal) G(rou)p, N(oun) P(hrase), V(erb), V(erb) P(hrase) and S(entence).

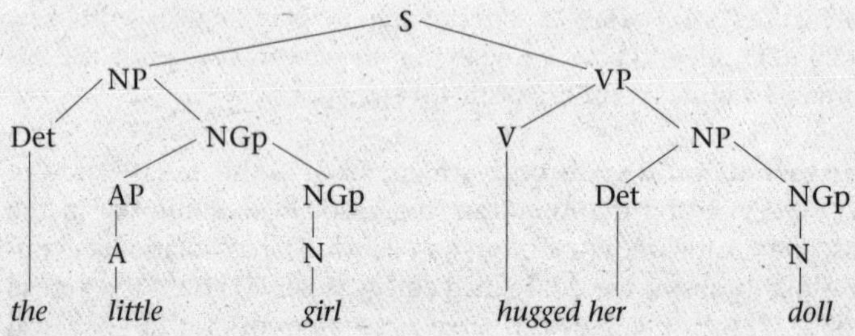


**typology** The classification of languages according to their structural properties, and not according to their ancestry. For example, in terms of ancestry, English is closely related to German and more distantly related to French, Russian and Greek, yet typologically it is in some ways rather more similar to the unrelated Chinese than to its relatives.

| Chinese: | Gěi | wǒ | yī | bēi | júzishuǐ | ba. |
|---|---|---|---|---|---|---|
| | *give* | *me* | *one* | *glass* | *orange juice* | *OK*? |

'Give me a glass of orange juice, OK?'
'How about a glass of orange juice?'

**unbounded dependency** (also **extraction**) Any grammatical structure in which an element of a sentence is removed from its ordinary or logical position and moved to the beginning of its sentence, possibly out of its clause altogether. Of the several unbounded dependencies in English, the formation of WH-QUESTIONS is the most familiar. The person or thing being asked about must be expressed by a suitable question word, such as *who* or *what*, and this word must be moved to the beginning of its sentence, no matter how far away this is from its logical position. Consider the following examples, in which the logical position of *who* is marked by *e*: *Who was Susie talking to* e*?*; *Who did Mike think Susie was talking to* e*?*; *Who did Natalie say Mike thought Susie was talking to* e*?*; *Who did Ted suspect that Natalie said Mike thought Susie was talking to* e*?* This can go on without limit in English: hence the name.

**uncountable noun** Another term for MASS NOUN.

**underlying form** An abstract representation of a linguistic form which is different from its surface form. For example, *won't* has the underlying form *will not*. A more elaborate example is *I can't seem to find my keys*, which may be said to have an underlying form of the approximate shape [*seem* [*not* [*I can find my keys*]]] – or, in English, *It seems to be the case that it is not the case that I can find my keys*. This last illustrates the meaning of the sentence more directly than the idiomatic surface form.

**understood** A very general label sometimes applied to any part of a sentence or an utterance which is logically required for interpretation but which is not overtly present, because its nature can be easily inferred from the context. Such elements arise in a variety of contexts; here are some examples. Alice: *Where's Susie?* Mike: *In the shower*. (Here *Susie is* is understood.) Alice: *Is Susie going to the concert?* Mike: *She doesn't want to*. (Here *go to the concert* is understood.) Mike: *Get yourself ready, Susie*. (Here the subject *you* is understood.)

**ungrammatical** Another term for ILL-FORMED.

**unmarked form** See under MARKEDNESS.

***un*passive** The English construction which looks in most respects like a PASSIVE VOICE, but in which the participle of the verb carries the prefix *un-*. Example: *Her arrival was unnoticed by the crowd*. This looks as if it ought to be the passive corresponding to **The crowd unnoticed her arrival*, but no such sentence is possible.

**unproductive** A label applied to a pattern of WORD-FORMATION which can no longer be used to create new words. An example is the noun-forming suffix *-th*, seen in *warmth* (from *warm*), *length* (from *long*) and *filth* (from *foul*). Today it is impossible to coin new words with this unproductive suffix: we cannot construct words like **bigth*, **sexyth* or **user-friendlyth*. Compare PRODUCTIVITY.

**unspecified object deletion** The construction in which an intrinsically transitive verb appears with no object, because the nature of the object is obvious or unimportant. For example, *smoke* can do this: we can say *Susie smokes Turkish cigarettes*, but equally we can say *Susie smokes*, in which the missing object is obviously 'cigarettes', or at least 'tobacco'. Other transitive verbs which can appear in this construction are *eat* (*Susie is eating*) and *read* (*Susie is reading*). The verbs which can appear in this construction constitute one kind of LABILE VERB. They are sometimes called ABSOLUTE TRANSITIVE verbs, meaning that they are logically transitive even when they appear with no overt direct object.

**usage** The manner in which a word or a construction is commonly used in a language. Descriptions of usage can be difficult, because usage in fact varies from region to region, from social group to social group, from person to person, and from context to context. Consequently, dictionaries of English, and sometimes also grammar books, frequently attach usage labels like 'chiefly American', 'informal', 'offensive', 'nautical', 'old-fashioned' and 'obsolete'.

A purely descriptive account of the language, as practised by professional linguists, will record and report those usages which are truly typical of the variety of English being examined (see DESCRIPTIVISM), regardless of what anybody thinks about them. However, an account of STANDARD ENGLISH, such as might be found in a textbook for learners or a guide to formal writing, must take a different tack: it must present those usages which are felt to be generally accepted as standard, and it must warn against usages not currently accepted as standard. But, since standard English – like every variety of every living language – is constantly changing, there will always be disagreements and uncertainties, even among specialists, as to which usages should be accepted as currently standard. This is why handbooks of good usage sometimes disagree with one another, and why they so often prefer to make recommendations rather than simply to lay down the law.

Here are two examples. Until the nineteenth century, the grammatical form illustrated by *My house is being painted* hardly existed in English, and the linguistic commentators of the day objected to it bitterly, condemning it as 'illogical' and 'monstrous', and demanding instead the traditional form **My house is painting*. Today, however, the once-offensive form is the only possibility in standard English, and no sane person would try to use the older form, which is now ungrammatical. Usage has changed.

Now, all contemporary handbooks of standard English will tell you to write *Shearer was replaced by Owen*, and to avoid the non-standard **Shearer was substituted by Owen*. However, observation reveals that the rejected second form is exceedingly common in the speech and writing of even well-educated people. In another generation or so, it may be that the authors of the handbooks will find themselves obliged to accept the second form as standard. That hasn't happened yet, but it may not be far away.

It is these ceaseless changes in usage which make it so difficult for us to decide just what exactly should be accepted as standard usage at any given moment. Since every new usage inevitably annoys some older or more conservative speakers, most handbooks will advise you to be conservative, to err on the side of caution, to avoid any usage, however widespread, which cannot yet be safely regarded as fully established in the standard language. But, of course, writers may genuinely differ on whether a given usage is now so established.

**utterance** A particular piece of speech produced by a particular person upon a particular occasion. It is important to distinguish an utterance from a SENTENCE, since an utterance very often does not correspond to a sentence. See FRAGMENT.

# V

**valency** The number of ARGUMENTS required by a verb. A monovalent verb like *smile* or *sleep* requires only one argument: *Susie smiled; Susie was sleeping*. A divalent verb like *slap* or *see* requires two arguments: *Susie slapped Mike; Susie saw Mike*. A trivalent verb like *give* or *show* requires three arguments: *Susie gave Mike a kiss; Susie showed Mike her new kitchen*. Using a verb with the wrong number of arguments produces an ungrammatical result: **Susie smiled Mike; *Susie slapped; *Susie showed her kitchen*. But quite a few English verbs exhibit variable valency, such as *melt* and *swim*. Examples: *The ice melted* (monovalent); *The sun melted the ice* (divalent); *Susie was swimming* (monovalent); *Susie swam the Channel* (divalent). See LABILE VERB.

**verb** The PART OF SPEECH which contains words like *see, arrive, sleep, discuss, shoot* and *take off*. Verbs are distinguished from other parts of speech by a number of properties, illustrated here by the verb *drink*.

**1**. A verb can be marked for TENSE: *I drink wine; I drank wine.*

**2**. A verb can usually be preceded by an AUXILIARY: *I have drunk wine; I am drinking wine.*

**3**. A verb is the HEAD of a VERB PHRASE: *drink wine; drinking wine in the garden; drunk wine the night before.*

**4**. A verb can form a GERUND in *-ing*: *Drinking wine every night is bad for you.*

**5**. A verb can form a PRESENT PARTICIPLE, in *-ing*, and a PAST PARTICIPLE, usually in *-ed* or *-en* but sometimes irregular (*drink* forms *drunk*): *I have been drinking wine; I have drunk too much wine.*

Verbs are divided into two groups: LEXICAL VERBS (which includes most verbs) and AUXILIARIES (which have some special properties). Lexical verbs are further divided into INTRANSITIVE and TRANSITIVE verbs, with certain unusual intransitive verbs further distinguished as COPULAS and QUASI-COPULAS. The PHRASAL VERBS of English constitute a somewhat distinctive subclass of lexical verbs.

**verbal noun** A NOUN which is derived from a verb, usually by adding an AFFIX, and which exhibits all the ordinary properties of nouns and none of the properties of verbs. A verbal noun can be pluralized or counted (sense permitting); it can occur in a noun phrase with a determiner, with adjectives and with prepositional phrases, just like any other noun. In English, verbal nouns are constructed with a variety of suffixes: *arrive* (verb)/*arrival* (noun); *decide/decision*; *realize/realization*; *destroy/destruction*; *fly/flight*; and others. Examples, with verbal nouns bracketed: *Her sudden [arrival] startled us*; *These thoughtless [decisions] are ruining our business*; *I'm looking for a [flight] to Tokyo*. It is possible for a verbal noun to be unaffixed and identical to its source verb, as in *return* (verb)/*return* (noun) and *attack/attack*.

It is also possible for a verbal noun to be formed with the suffix *-ing* used to make GERUNDS, and such a formation should not be confused with a gerund, even though many textbooks make this error. For example, in *Deliberately bowling bouncers is unfair*, the subject NP *deliberately bowling bouncers* contains the gerund *bowling*, which, like any gerund, retains its verbal properties, such as the ability to take objects and adverbs. However, in *This deliberate bowling of bouncers has to stop*, the subject NP *this deliberate bowling of bouncers* is not a gerund but a verbal noun, as shown by its nominal properties: taking determiners, adjectives and prepositional phrases.

**verb-complement clause** See under COMPLEMENT CLAUSE.

**verb phrase (VP)** A PHRASE consisting of a VERB and all the phrases linked grammatically to that verb except a SUBJECT. Here is a simple test for verb phrases (VPs): *Susie* __. Any sequence which can fill the blank to make a grammatical sentence will probably be a VP. Examples: *smiled*; *was washing the car*; *wants to buy a mobile phone*; *has told me that she's getting married*; *will be vacationing in Jamaica*.

It is possible for a VP to contain a smaller VP within it. For example, the VP *was washing the car* contains the smaller VP *washing the car*, and the VP *wants to buy a mobile phone* contains the smaller VP *buy a mobile phone*.

The PREDICATE of an English sentence is always a VP, though VPs can also occur in non-predicate positions. In the sentences *Wanting to try on some bikinis, Susie looked for the changing room* and *Having made her choice, she headed for the cash desk,* the two sequences before the commas are VPs but are not in predicate position.

**vocabulary** The set of words known by a particular person. We must distinguish between your *active vocabulary*, the words you use yourself, and your *passive vocabulary*, the additional words you understand but do not use. Your passive vocabulary is always bigger than your active vocabulary.

The passive vocabulary of a typical moderately well-educated speaker of English has been variously estimated between 50,000 and 250,000 words. For comparison, a good desk dictionary of English typically enters around 100,000 words. Compare LEXICON.

**vocative** A NOUN PHRASE used to address someone directly. In the examples *Susie, come here* and *Where do you think you're going, young man?*, the NPs *Susie* and *young man* are vocatives.

**voice** The GRAMMATICAL CATEGORY which deals with the way the noun phrases representing the participants in an event are assigned to GRAMMATICAL RELATIONS. English distinguishes only two voices, the ACTIVE VOICE and the PASSIVE VOICE, and these are distinguished only with TRANSITIVE verbs. In an active sentence, the grammatical subject represents the performer of the action, while in a passive sentence the subject represents the thing undergoing the action, and the performer is either expressed with a *by* phrase (the long passive) or removed from the sentence altogether (the short passive). For example, the active sentence *The Mongols sacked Kiev* has the long passive counterpart *Kiev was sacked by the Mongols*, as well as the short passive *Kiev was sacked.*

**VP** The abbreviation for VERB PHRASE.

**VP-deletion** The construction in which a VERB PHRASE which would duplicate a preceding verb phrase does not appear overtly in the sentence. Example: *Jan wants me to get my hair cut, but I don't want to.* This is equivalent to *. . . but I don't want to get my hair cut,* with the second occurrence of the verb phrase *get my hair cut* deleted.

**weak verb** In English, a VERB which forms both its past tense and its past participle by adding the suffix -*(e)d*. Examples: *love, loved, loved; wash, washed, washed; smoke, smoked, smoked*. Compare STRONG VERB.

**weather verb** A verb which denotes some kind of weather phenomenon and which, in English, normally permits no subject other than the dummy subject *it*. The weather verbs include *rain, snow, sleet, hail, thunder* and *freeze*, among others. Examples: *It's raining; It snowed last night; It's thundering; It's freezing today*.

**well-formed** (also **grammatical**) Of a sentence, constructed in accordance with all the grammatical rules of the language. For example, in standard English, *I haven't finished dinner* is well-formed, while **I hasn't finished dinner* and **I ain't finished dinner* are not well-formed (they are ILL-FORMED). The last one, however, is well-formed in many non-standard regional varieties of English. The rules governing well-formedness are not the same in all varieties of English; see RULE. See also ACCEPTABILITY.

**WH-cleft** See under CLEFT.

**WH-question** A QUESTION which uses a WH-WORD and which expects an answer other than *yes* or *no*. Examples: *What are you doing?; Where did you find that?; Why are you crying?* Compare YES–NO QUESTION.

**WH-word** (also **question word**) A word which asks a question. In English, these words are *who, what, which, where, when, why* and *how*.

**word** A term with several quite distinct senses, which must be carefully distinguished. An *orthographic word* is anything written with a white space at each end and no white spaces in the middle: *snowed, grammar, can't, re-election*. A *phonological word* is any sequence pronounced as a single unit: all of the preceding four examples plus *ice cream, no one* and *take off*. A LEXICAL ITEM is an item of vocabulary, a word in the sense in which a dictionary contains words; see that entry for more information. A WORD-FORM is any one of the several different forms a lexical item may assume for grammatical purposes; see that entry for more information.

For example, *take* and *took* are two different orthographic words (they are written differently), two different phonological words (they are pronounced differently), one lexical item (they are both forms of the lexical item *take*), and two different word-forms (they are different grammatical forms of *take*). In contrast, *bear* (the name of the animal) and *bear* (the verb, as in *I can't bear this*) are one orthographic word (they are written the same), one phonological word (they are pronounced the same), two lexical items (they must be entered separately in the dictionary), and two word-forms (one is a noun, the other a verb).

**word class** Another term for PART OF SPEECH.

**word-form** The particular form which a given lexical item assumes in a particular context for grammatical reasons. For example, the lexical item *dog* can appear either in the word-form *dog* or in the word-form *dogs*: *That dog is dangerous*; *Those dogs are dangerous*. Likewise, the lexical item *take* can appear in any of several word-forms: *take, takes, took, taking, taken*. Examples: *Shall we take an umbrella?*; *Susie takes an umbrella to work*; *I took an umbrella with me*; *We're all taking umbrellas*; *You should have taken an umbrella*. Compare LEXICAL ITEM.

**word-formation** The process of constructing new words from the existing resources of a language. The most important processes of word-formation in English are compounding (see under COMPOUND) and DERIVATION. Other significant processes include BACK-FORMATION, CLIPPING, REANALYSIS, BLENDING, and the coining of ACRONYMS and INITIALISMS. See PRODUCTIVITY, and compare BORROWING.

**word order** The order in which words and phrases occur within a sentence. The BASIC WORD ORDER of English is Subject-Verb-Object, as in *Susie wrote this book*, though other orders are possible in special circumstances, such as *This book Susie wrote*. The order of words within phrases is generally fixed, however: we must say *this new book*, and no other order is possible: **new this book*, **this book new*, **book new this*.

**yes–no question** (also **polar question**) A QUESTION which expects *yes* or *no* as an answer. Examples: *Are you coming with us?*; *Have you brushed your teeth?* In English, a yes–no question differs from the corresponding statement only in word order. For example, the statement *The Europeans have won the Ryder Cup* has the corresponding yes–no question *Have the Europeans won the Ryder Cup?*, in which the AUXILIARY *have* is moved to the beginning of the sentence; this is SUBJECT-VERB INVERSION (see under INVERSION). Compare WH-QUESTION.

**zero anaphor** See under ANAPHOR.

**zero-derivation** Another term for CONVERSION.

**zero determiner** A name given to the absence of a DETERMINER in certain NOUN PHRASES. Examples: *Susie, beer, French wines, contraband ivory, drugs, linguistics.* In the sentence *Susie always takes Australian wine to parties,* all three noun phrases have a zero determiner.

# The Penguin Guide to Punctuation

R. L. Trask

*The Penguin Guide to Punctuation* is indispensable for anyone who needs to get to grips with using punctuation in their written work. Whether you are puzzled by colons and semicolons, unsure of where commas should go or baffled by apostrophes, this jargon-free and succinct guide is for you.

- Contains precise definitions of every type of punctuation mark and shows how each should be used
- Provides numerous examples of good and bad usage
- Explains the correct use of capital letters, contractions and abbreviations, italics, boldface and the special characters available on computers
- Covers punctuation in footnotes, references, bibliographies and letters

'Excellent . . . covers almost every point that an editor needs' The Society of Freelance Editors and Proofreaders

'A concise and highly readable reference book . . . tightly-structured, with clear definitions of each type of punctuation' *Sunday Telegraph*

SECOND EDITION

# The Penguin Dictionary of English Idioms

Daphne M. Gulland and David G. Hinds-Howell

*Power napping*, the *Oprah effect*, *girl power* – these are just some of the recent figures of speech to have entered our language. The perfect guide to the idiosyncrasies of the English language, this best-selling dictionary has been completely revised for its second edition and includes hundreds of new idioms. It provides clear and concise definitions and explains how the idioms should be used. At the same time the dictionary's thematic arrangement makes it possible not only to study and compare all the idioms in a given subject area, but to match the right one to the right occasion.

- Gives full explanations of some 4,000 phrases
- Entries are grouped according to theme: for example, colours (*white as a sheet*), elements (*air-kissing*), life and death (*as pale as death*), clothes (*verbal handbagging*), war and peace (*eco-warrior*)
- Offers a clear example of usage for each idiom, using everyday speech
- Provides background information on the origins of certain expressions, such as *like the measles, nutty as a fruitcake*

# Roget's Thesaurus of English Words and Phrases

Edited by George Davidson

*Roget's Thesaurus* is the world's most famous and trusted word-finder and is the essential desk companion for anyone who wants to improve their command, creative use and enjoyment of the language. It remains, definitively, a writer's best friend and the key to inspirational and creative writing.

- Contains over a quarter of a million words and phrases arranged according to ideas and meaning
- Covers formal English, technical terms, slang and jargon
- Revised and updated to include hundreds of recently coined words and expressions – from *surrender monkey* to *pester power*, *broadband* to *mockney*
- Provides useful panels to mark groups of vocabulary, including signs of the zodiac, cocktails and phobias
- Over 32 million copies sold worldwide

'The indispensable guide to the English language' *Daily Express*

'One of the English language's greatest achievements' *Guardian*

PENGUIN REFERENCE

# THE PENGUIN GUIDE TO PLAIN ENGLISH

Harry Blamires, a graduate of University College, Oxford, was formerly Dean of Arts and Sciences at King Alfred's College, Winchester. He was Visiting Professor of English Literature at Wheaton College, Illinois, in 1987. The University of Southampton has awarded him a D.Litt. in recognition of his achievements as a writer. His total output of some thirty books includes fiction and theology, but he is widely known for his works of literary history and criticism. These include *A Short History of English Literature* (Routledge) and *Twentieth-Century English Literature* (Macmillan). For over three decades students in the USA and the UK have benefitted from his classic guide to Joyce's *Ulysses*, *The New Bloomsday Book*. More recently, in *The Cassell Guide to Common Errors in English*, he has shown how lively and entertaining the exploration of current usage can be.

HARRY BLAMIRES

# The Penguin Guide to Plain English

Express Yourself Clearly and Effectively

PENGUIN BOOKS

PENGUIN BOOKS

Published by the Penguin Group
Penguin Books Ltd, 80 Strand, London WC2R 0RL, England
Penguin Putnam Inc., 375 Hudson Street, New York, New York 10014, USA
Penguin Books Australia Ltd, 250 Camberwell Road, Camberwell, Victoria 3124, Australia
Penguin Books Canada Ltd, 10 Alcorn Avenue, Toronto, Ontario, Canada M4V 3B2
Penguin Books India (P) Ltd, 11 Community Centre, Panchsheel Park, New Delhi – 110 017, India
Penguin Books (NZ) Ltd, Cnr Rosedale and Airborne Roads, Albany, Auckland, New Zealand
Penguin Books (South Africa) (Pty) Ltd, 24 Sturdee Avenue, Rosebank 2196, South Africa

Penguin Books Ltd, Registered Offices: 80 Strand, London WC2R 0RL, England

www.penguin.com

First published 2000
19



Set in 9.75/12 pt Monotype Joanna
Typeset by Rowland Phototypesetting Ltd, Bury St Edmunds, Suffolk
Printed in England by Clays Ltd, St Ives plc

# Contents

INTRODUCTION

# What is Plain English?

'Sir, 'tis my occupation to be plain' says Kent to the king in Shakespeare's *King Lear*, as he all but despairs of persuading his master to face facts. And Kent is Shakespeare's chosen vehicle to represent the values of common sense and reason in a world toppling into lunacy. Kent's is the voice of healthy discernment in recognizing the difference between truth and falsehood, genuineness and corruption. Plainness is his pride. And in Shakespeare's *Richard III* this is how the villain Gloucester protests against misrepresentation of his character:

> Cannot a plain man live and think no harm,
> But that his simple truth must be abused
> By silken, sly, insinuating Jacks?

He postures as the plain man up against the showy, greasy tricksters who specialize in nods and winks and innuendoes. The 'plain' is again opposed to the bogus and the deceptive. And although we sometimes nowadays use the word 'plain' as the converse of 'beautiful', it remains a connotatively rich one. 'Plain living and high thinking are no more' Wordsworth complained in criticism of the worship of wealth and show corrupting contemporary life. Yet plainness does not generally imply austerity. When the words 'plain' and 'English' are taken into the expression 'plain English cooking', we are more likely to encounter roast beef and Yorkshire pudding, apple pie and cream, than the menu of the ascetic.

We are looking then for usage which is genuine and direct, unspoiled by any hint of the bogus or the pretentious, English which is clear and open as the day, which claims no special attention to itself but rather melts away into what it conveys. That should be the standard usage of speakers and writers. But we only need to open a newspaper or turn on the radio to realize that the prevailing verbal usage of our age falls short in numerous ways. That is the reason for the method of approach adopted in this book. Tidily explaining to readers how the English language should be used by a neat progression through the parts of speech, and the construction of clauses and sentences, can be illuminating. But it is not quite the same process as checking up at the coalface on the English that is actually used and uncovering where it goes wrong. I have taken heed of a wise popular saying, 'If it ain't broke, don't mend it.' That advice has always seemed to me to be peculiarly applicable to the business of writing books with an instructive purpose. And that is why I have believed that the most practically helpful starting-point for giving advice about how to write good English is from the mass of bad English with which we are surrounded.

I now have a collection of some 7,000 bad sentences, accumulated over the years from the press, the radio, commercial publicity and junk mail. Bringing this material to light enables us to discern where people go wrong in their use of English, not just occasionally but time after time. Where a bad practice turns up day after day in the newspaper, on the air and in the morning mail it ought to get proportionate attention and space in a book which specifically concentrates on the English we actually read, actually hear, actually use.

That is why this book abounds in examples. It does not take up a dogmatic position in relation to traditional grammar or to the revisionist grammars of the last few decades. It does not lay into the latest slang or get over-excited about split infinitives. It explores the English now in use with determined emphasis on the guide-lines we must follow if what we say and what we write is to be exactly what we mean.

For we are about a much more positive task than that of mere detection and correction of error. That in itself is not an inspiring activity. Nor does it win friends. 'Filthy famished correctioner' Shakespeare's Doll Tearsheet screams at the interfering Beadle. But correction can be salutary. 'Whom the Lord loveth He correcteth,' the Book of Proverbs tells us. And the positive aim here is to reveal how gratifying, indeed how stimulating it is to achieve that sustained level of correctness which marks 'plain English'. There is great satisfaction for all those who do not have to worry that what they write, or what they say when they speak in public, may not stand up to scrutiny on some point of style or usage.

For most people it is not a matter of mastering a lot of grammatical rules. It is rather a matter of learning to keep a clear head. Having read 'Glancing to the right, the church spire is visible above the rooftops', the grammarian will talk about the 'hanging participle', while the clear-headed reader will anyway protest mentally 'But the church spire is not glancing to the right.' In the same way, having read 'As the inheritor of an illustrious name in hunting, the threat to the sport came as a great shock', the grammarian will quite properly talk about 'misconnecting an appositional phrase', but the clear-headed reader can see anyway that it is nonsense to talk of a 'threat' as having 'an illustrious name in hunting', and will not need to refer to the grammatical rule book. Correct use of English depends so much on straight thinking and sheer common sense that it is possible in discussion of the subject to be selective and economic in the use of grammatical terminology. That is the policy in this book.

Some light can be shed on what constitutes 'plain English' if we take a preliminary look at a few of the obvious qualities it must have. Utterance that is plain is utterance that cannot be misunderstood. And utterance that cannot possibly be misunderstood will be precise. To be precise is to get exactly the right word. Precision ought not to be regarded as the preserve of pedants. Getting nearly the right word renders prose uncomfortable for the educated reader. Here we have an advertisement where a touch of cleverness misfires through failure to be precise.

> Five Alive, one of the most popular fruit drinks on the market, has developed a new tasty recipe that's an ideal accompaniment for any breakfast table.

Reading with proper attention, we sense at once that the word 'accompaniment' is ill-chosen. Tomato sauce might be a suitable accompaniment for fish and chips, and a piano might provide a suitable accompaniment for a singer, but a breakfast table does not need to be accompanied by a recipe. The writer's desire not to say the simple and direct thing, that 'the recipe makes a tasty drink for breakfast', instead of dragging in the notion of accompanying a table, merely makes for imprecision.

Plain English is never wasteful of words. If a thing can be said briefly, then so it should be. Great poets recognize this. Few sentences say as much as Shakespeare's 'To be or not to be; that is the question.' Not that compression so extreme fits all occasions. But the pointless piling-up of words degrades the words it wastes. Nevertheless, the notion that brief conversational idioms should be translated in print into long-winded utterance is widespread. Here is a report on the result of a test taken by nurses.

> The assessments were all successfully undertaken. The anticipated learning outcomes of each group member were substantially exceeded and are currently being expressed as part of the outcome profile for each of them.

Translated into English, this would read: 'They all did better than expected and their results are being recorded.'

The converse error of excessive thrift in the number of words used is perhaps much rarer. But it is possible to write without being long-winded and yet to produce wording that is stilted and strained. Here is a comment on the disposal of a locomotive by a railway preservation society.

> It is a year since its custodianship transferred to another society.

The use of the word 'custodianship' here sounds awkwardly affected. Why not: 'It is a year since it was handed over into the keeping of another society'?

There is of course a place for artificial vocabulary which confers a degree of dignity on what is said. But there are contexts where the avoidance of the most familiar and natural vocabulary merely seems emptily pretentious. Here is a piece from an article about a particular breed of dogs.

> It was apparent that with the enormity of their size, their slobbering habits and also their general dislike of the heat it was obvious that their preference would be an outside environment, which was certainly more practical for us.

We overlook the elementary error of repeating 'it was apparent' in 'it was obvious'. What concerns us here is the use of such expressions as 'the enormity of their size' (a bad error anyway, since 'enormity' does not mean magnitude but dreadfulness) and 'their preference would be an outside environment'. What it all amounts to is that 'because they are big and slobber and dislike heat, they would be better kept outside'. And that is how it should be put.

It should go without saying that plain English will be accurate in its use of words. Ensuring that your sentence makes the point you want to make clearly is a matter of clarifying your meaning mentally before you pen a word. Inaccuracy is not found only in long, awkward paragraphs. A brief and at first sight simple sentence, which to the superficial glance raises no problems, may not stand up to careful scrutiny in this respect. Here is a sentence from an article about collecting Old Master drawings.

> The history of collecting Old Master drawings in this country is of unrivalled distinction.

The reader wonders how a 'history' can be so distinguished. From the sentence that follows this one we learn of aristocratic collectors who indulged in this hobby. In short, the writer did not mean that the 'history' had unrivalled distinction, but that from earliest times collectors were distinguished people. What was really meant was: 'Distinguished aristocrats were early collectors of Old Master drawings in our country.'

In this matter of accuracy, the good writer will learn to play safe. We must fully understand every word we use and take no risks. Venturing outside the range of our understanding is dangerous. Sometimes avoiding what is simple and straightforward lures us into error. A misjudged attempt at distinctiveness in vocabulary can fail disgracefully. Even highbrow critics are not exempt from the temptation to be just a little too clever. Thus we find a literary reviewer writing:

> After a while exaggerated comic scenes mount up meaninglessly, and even the funniest feel belaboured.

Clearly what the writer wanted to convey was that the comic scenes seemed 'laboured', which means laboriously put together. The somewhat archaic verb to 'belabour' means to thrash, so the critic's sentence really means that the comic scenes seemed thrashed, which makes no sense at all.

There is another way of avoiding what is straightforward, when we pick up some ready-made but contrived expression where a simple sequence of familiar words would be better.

> He was awkward, stubborn and lazy to the extent that his parents finally lost patience with him.

This is a case in point. It is difficult to think of a sentence using the expression 'to the extent that' which would not be better without it. Nothing is gained here from avoiding the straightforward wording: 'He was so awkward, stubborn and lazy that his parents finally lost patience with him.'

Plain English will use words that are appropriate to the context. There will not be words which seem incongruously out of place. Even a fairly simple statement of fact may be marred in this respect. Here is a police officer reporting on the discovery of a dead body:

> At 7.0 p.m. last night officers attended some waste ground.

The word 'attended' may be standard in 'police-speak', but it is surely out of place here. It has too formal a ring and in any case conveys the wrong meaning. We might speak of 'attending' a wedding reception in a hotel, but not of 'attending' the hotel. To speak of attending 'waste ground' is a clumsy way of avoiding something very simple: 'Officers went to some waste ground.' Plain English will not furrow the brow of the reader by a hint of inappropriateness in the relation of word to word.

We cannot write plain English unless we keep a clear head. Here is a sentence from an article in a quality paper on the subject of body-piercing.

> With a tongue-stud, there are two main veins underneath the tongue and you have to make sure that you keep away from them.

There is a strange illogicality here. The two main veins underneath the tongue are there whether you are going to fix a stud in the mouth or not. 'With' is a problematic word in this respect. We shall see many instances of its misuse later in the book. What the writer means is: 'If you fit a tongue stud, you have to make sure that you keep away from the two main veins underneath the tongue.'

Plain English is easy on the ear. It reads fluently. There are occasions in poetry and in other imaginative literature when the writer may wish to exploit the unsettling, percussive power of words. But generally speaking, prose should flow smoothly. It should not unsettle the reader's response by jerkiness or by seemingly cluttered wording.

> 'School from Hell' headlines stereotyped children from the Ridings School in Halifax, young reporters from the Save the Children-backed Newcastle Children's Express News Agency told journalists at a recent seminar.

The thirteen-word pile-up as the subject of the verb 'told' unsettles the reader's attention. 'Young reporters from the Newcastle Children's Express News Agency' is surely long enough as the subject of the verb. To bolt on to that the words 'Save the Children-backed' is to apply a packed bale of straw to the camel's already fully loaded back. Where the situation is as desperate as this, use brackets: 'young reporters from the Newcastle Children's Express News Agency (backed by Save the Children) told journalists'.

If utterance is plain, it will not be complex. Whatever intricacies there may be in the message conveyed, the wording will not overtax our minds to sort it out. Here is a piece from a marketing journal about the European Monetary Union.

> The respondents, however, in spite of their doubts about the single currency, foresaw many benefits, including the elimination of the risks involved with currency exchange, the equalization of currencies, the reduced administration costs (e.g. in billing) and the psychological benefits attached because of a strengthening of the bonds between countries and it being evidence of a united European economic power.

The complexity here is not gross, but it is enough to make the sequence seem awkward. The reader senses a lack of cohesion. Too many bits seem to have been stuck together. Indeed, the passage asks to be broken up into its constituent parts. 'The correspondents had doubts about the single currency, but they foresaw many benefits. The risks taken in exchanging currencies would be removed, currencies would be equalized, administrative costs would be reduced, and, psychologically, bonds between countries would be strengthened by the existence of a united European economic power.'

Two general lessons could be learned from this little exercise. Where argument or reasoning is involved, a watch should be kept on paragraphing, to ensure that the force of individual points is not lost in the process of heaping them together. The second point is that replacing nouns by verbs often simplifies and clarifies meaning ('elimination' is replaced by 'could be removed', 'equalization' by 'equalized' and 'strengthening' by 'strengthened'). That kind of shift in usage will be thoroughly explored later in the book.

Plain English will never be muddled. Here is a travel article tempting us to visit the island of Corfu.

> From Odysseus through to the English poet and novelist Lawrence Durrell, the island has long been lauded for its glorious beaches, great rock formations along the west coast, picturesque villages and spectacular birdlife. Add to that the acres of silvery, ancient olive groves, and it is hard to believe that you are nearly at the end of the twentieth century.

We do not have doubts about what the writer is wanting to tell us here. But we wish she had actually said it, instead of leaving us to keep up a running process of mental correction as we read. 'From Odysseus to

Durrell, people have lauded Corfu' would make sense. 'From Odysseus to Durrell, the island has been lauded' does not. The word 'that' in 'Add to that', placed where it is, ought to refer to the long lauding of the island. But it doesn't. The writer has changed tack. Moreover, she immediately changes tack again. Adding olive groves to villages and birdlife does not make it difficult to believe that we are where we are in history. What the writer means is that the (unmentioned) tranquillity and remoteness of the scenery seem to belong to a past century. Clear articulation of a train of thought will leave no gaps in logic which the reader's mind has to jump over. The connecting expressions 'Add to that', 'and it is hard to believe' and 'Otherwise' all need to be replaced: 'From Odysseus through to the English poet Lawrence Durrell, people have long lauded the island for its glorious beaches, great rock formations along the west coast, picturesque villages and spectacular birdlife. Moreover, there are acres of silvery, ancient olive groves, and the peaceful atmosphere makes it hard for the visitor to remember that we are nearly at the end of the twentieth century.'

Finally, plain English has a directness which ensures that its meaning will never seem more complex than it is. It will never become convoluted by tangled syntax. Here we have an observation about the introduction of a new High Intensity Cruising Licence for vessels which have no permanent mooring, on our inland waterways.

> In an about-face British Waterways changed from claiming the new licence was due to the majority of continuous cruisers flouting the rules, causing mooring congestion at popular visitor moorings, and cost enforcement issues, to saying that this was part of the process to resolve the funding and arrears of maintenance problems.

To begin with, by 'the new licence was due to' the writer really means 'the introduction of the new licence was due to'. Too big a pile-up of participles and gerunds (ending in '-ing') is almost always clumsy. The basic construction chosen ('changed from claiming . . . to saying'), when complicated by 'due to flouting' and 'causing congestion' sinks under its own weight. The direct presentation of the items awkwardly joined would make reading far easier. 'BW has done a U-turn. They said the new licence was introduced because continuous cruisers flouted the rules, caused congestion at popular mooring sites and made enforcement of the regulations expensive. They now say that the new scheme helps towards the general costs of maintenance.' In the original there are three finite verbs only ('changed', 'was' and 'this was') surrounded by an entanglement of non-finite forms ('claiming', 'flouting', 'causing', 'saying', 'to resolve', 'funding'). In our corrected version there are eight finite verbs ('has done', 'said', 'was introduced', 'flouted', 'caused', 'made', 'say' and 'helps'). The change not only makes the passage more straightforward and easier to follow. It also makes the prose tauter and more vigorous.

## THE PLAN OF THIS BOOK

We have dipped our toes into the sea of carelessness that contemporary usage exemplifies. We have noticed dominant tendencies – tendencies to inflation, to inexactitude, to muddle and to illogicality. In all these directions, and in many others, variable degrees of erroneousness will be fully explored in the following chapters, as we systematically take stock of current usage.

### Part 1 The Words at Our Disposal

The focus of the earlier chapters of the book is upon our vocabulary. The English vocabulary is vast and varied. We must learn to be confident about which is the right word and which is the wrong word in any context. To that end the chapters in Part 1 are devoted to thorough exploration of words now commonly misused or over-used and to problems that can arise in maintaining accuracy in meaning when juxtaposing word with word. We then take a look at the peculiar character of the English language, examining the development of its extraordinarily rich vocabulary and considering some of the problems as well as the advantages that its resources present.

### Part 2 Arranging Words Correctly

Part 2 has a series of chapters more concerned with the build-up of sentences, the proper arrangement of words in rational utterance and the need for congruity and coherence in this respect. It is in this section that attention is given to the constructions that tend to trip us up, to the proper techniques for arguing a case, to the demands of sound logic, and to what it is that distinguishes good style from bad. The aim throughout this section is to ensure clear understanding of the various pitfalls besetting the would-be writer of good English today, and to show how they may be avoided.

## Part 3 Changing Fashions in Usage

Finally, in Part 3 the emphasis is upon verbal fashions and trends affecting current usage. Here the book explores the innovations of recent decades, samples trendy verbal practices, and looks into some of the liberties taken in current usage. There is emphasis throughout upon the evident need for new discipline to restore vitality to our utterance. The last chapter, in particular, focuses on contemporary usage in various spheres of business and public life.

PART 1

# The Words at Our Disposal

CHAPTER 1

# The Words to be Used

## SOME RISKY CONTEXTS

When are we most likely to feel a little dissatisfied with what we have just said? Which are those occasions when we feel for the right word and don't quite find it? When are we most likely to say 'You know what I mean?' One such occasion may arise when we are trying to explain a situation to someone else, or trying to argue a point. The process of explaining or arguing is one of the contexts in which the use of words is likely to present problems. By 'explaining or arguing' I do not have in mind any very abstruse reasoning processes. After all, we are involved in modest reasoning processes when we say 'That sunset seems to promise a fine day tomorrow.' And we may get involved in a fairly awkward search for the right words in the right order when a passing motorist asks us the way to a given street in a town riddled with one-way signs.

We have seen that to choose the right word is to choose the precise word, the appropriate and straightforward word. That ought to mean choosing the obvious word, the word that comes first to mind. But unfortunately that is not the case. What comes first to mind is often the currently most frequently used word. Now of course there is no point in trying to avoid use of the most frequently used word simply in order to be different. But fashionable habits establish some words widely and firmly in current usage to the neglect of others. And that has unfortunate consequences. In the first place, a given word is over-used while other words are too little used. In the second place, differences in connotation, sometimes slight, sometimes subtle, are thus lost. And thirdly, current speech is riddled with usages which excessive exploitation has rendered inaccurate. We shall consider various spheres of discourse in which the damage done to the connotation of crucial words makes difficulties for us.

Of course, things can go wrong in a more complex way than in the mere choice of words. Later on in the book we shall have to return to consider the contexts in which errors abound, with an eye on more complex problems of sentence structure and syntax.

## Reasoning

***cause, reason, reasonably***

Nowhere is it more necessary to select words carefully than in dealing with matters of cause and effect. In this respect a current bad habit is the careless use of the word 'reason'. In the contexts with which we are concerned 'reason' is best used of human motivation. If a man is hurrying to catch a train, the 'reason' for his haste may be that he wants to be home in time for dinner. If he meets an old friend who detains him, that is not the 'reason' why he misses the train, it is the 'cause' of his missing it. Thus when we read: 'Acne is on the increase among women . . . The reason is thought to be stress', we recognize that this should be: 'the cause is thought to be stress'. The error is a common one.

> The common reason for money to go unclaimed is shareholders failing to inform registrars of change of address . . . Another reason is cheques, delivered to the wrong address, lapsing because they are not cashed within six months.

This gives us two 'causes', not reasons. In correcting the passage it would be far better, as so often is the case, to base the wording neither on the noun 'reason' nor on the noun 'cause' but on use of the word 'because': 'Money often goes unclaimed because shareholders fail to inform registrars of change of address . . . It also may go unclaimed because cheques are delivered to the wrong address, are not cashed within six months and so lapse.'

> The company's difficulties were due to no other reason than inefficiency.

Similarly this would better be: 'Inefficiency was the sole cause of the company's difficulties.'

If 'reason' is a word that over-use has weakened, even more so is the word 'reasonably'. It is one of those adverbs which we throw about in conversation with little sense of precision. If we were more disciplined in our choice of words we should recall that the distinction between what is 'reasonable' and what is 'unreasonable' is a crucial one. But conversational freedom allows the word 'reasonably' to mean something like 'moderately' ('I'm reasonably certain about it') until its connotation deteriorates finally into something like 'rather' and we find in print: 'The details are reasonably sketchy at the moment.'

### *mean*

In dealing with matters of cause, result and effect, there is now a tendency to fall back too often on the word 'mean'. Throughout this book usage of the word in its strictest connotation is bound to be frequent. We must repeatedly observe that a given word 'means' this and does not 'mean' that. It is by a natural and logical development that we arrive at such conversational usages as 'That sky means there's rain ahead' or even the more idiomatic 'That fellow means business.' However, popular usage now drags the verb into contexts where it merely draws attention to the paucity of vocabulary in the writer's grasp.

> The hillside location of this hotel means there are wonderful views of the town and harbour.

The writer is here concerned, not with a matter of meaning, but with a matter of cause and effect. It would be much better to say: 'Because of its hillside location, this hotel has wonderful views of the town and harbour.' There is a similar causal function in the word 'mean' in:

> Recent developments in surgical practice mean that patients are not required to stay in hospital overnight.

Clearly it would be more precise to say: 'As a result of recent developments in surgical practice patients are not required to stay in hospital overnight.' And the following advice, given to young women about their appearance when they are going to be interviewed, stretches the idiomatic usage further.

> If in doubt, dress 'up' rather than 'down' – even if the job you're going for doesn't mean looking smart.

Our objection to the usage is that it over-uses a much over-used verb, and also that it is imprecise, when what is really meant is: 'even if the job you're going for doesn't require you to look particularly smart'. It is after all the possible 'requirement' presented by the employer or the post that is at issue.

***involve / involvement***

The verb to 'involve' is also being used to cover a variety of rational connections, causal and otherwise. Its connotation has developed interestingly. The Latin root ('volvere') meant to roll something about and is behind both our words 'revolve' and 'involve'. 'Involvere' came to mean to overwhelm or cover, used of clouds sweeping over the sky. So in English usage in the eighteenth century the poet William Cowper began his powerful poem about a castaway at sea with the lines:

> Obscurest night involved the sky,
> The Atlantic billows roared . . .

From meaning to roll things up, to enwrap, to envelop or entangle we can see how it has become the useful word we now know too well.

> The retirement package involved continued rent-free residence.

Here the word 'involve' is used to mean 'include'.

> The expedition would involve spending three weeks in an exposed position on the mountain.

Here the word 'involve' is used to mean 'necessitate'.

> Accepting the new post would have involved my whole family.

Here the word 'involve' is used to mean 'affect'.

> We could not consider the board's proposal without involving the whole work force.

Here the word 'involve' means 'consult'. This is a far cry from the notion of rolling up clouds in a stormy sky. It is a pity to weaken an already weakened word further. That is what we should say to ourselves before lightly using the word.

The popularity of the verb to 'involve' has now been matched by the popularity of the noun 'involvement'. If a project 'involves' collecting information, then collecting information is a necessary part of the project. People 'involved' in a project are significantly concerned and associated with it. When we read of the hope that a pretty but neglected waterway 'will see an increased local involvement' we recognize the same usage, but what can we make of the following?

> The case for one member, one vote involvement in future leadership elections is not just to provide democratic legitimacy but also as an incentive to join.

The writer here errs in trying to balance 'is not just to' with 'but also as' instead of with 'but also to'. But that grammatical lapse is not what we happen to be interested in just now. What is 'one member, one vote involvement'? The writer is trying to say: 'The case for using the one-member, one-vote system in future leadership elections is not only that it will be more democratically legitimate but also that it will encourage people to join the party.'

### *problem, solution, different*

The word 'problem' too readily springs to our lips these days. The current drift is towards increasingly indiscriminate use of it. We need not be over-fussy about this in conversation. We know now that when the waiter says 'No problem', he means that the cook will be only too happy to do the steak exactly as requested, and when the garage foreman says it, he means that he will deal immediately with the punctured tyre or the broken exhaust pipe. Sometimes the word seems to be superfluous.

> A government research study in 1995 pinpointed insufficient iron as a problem in the underfives.

The 'problem' is the 'insufficiency of iron'. Does the word 'problem' add anything here? 'Insufficiency' cannot be present anywhere without representing a 'problem'. All that is needed is: 'A government research study in 1995 pinpointed a deficiency of iron in the underfives.'

There is a graver current misuse than that.

> The problem that faced the police was the remote site.

At first sight, that is probably not a sentence that worries us. Even the sentence 'The remote site made access difficult' may seem acceptable. Yet, strictly speaking, it is not the remote site but the 'remoteness of the site' that makes access difficult. We see immediately that it would not be right to say 'The extremely aged man made questioning difficult' when what we mean is 'The extreme age of the man made questioning difficult.' The two sentences differ sharply in meaning. Precision in that kind of statement is the sign of a logical mind.

We also need to watch the tendency to use the word 'problem' as an adjective:

> Apparently beauty salons have been using this method for years to control problem skin.

We have heard of the problem of controlling problem children in schools. Presumably that usage ('problem children') stemmed from a psychologically convenient and politically correct desire not to define the children's idiosyncrasies too blatantly. It would appear that a similar tenderness has to be employed in defining defects in personal appearance. The young woman does not want to think of her skin as in any way imperfect, but she will gladly regard it as a 'problem'.

There is no doubt of our fondness nowadays for talking, wherever possible, in terms of 'problems' and 'solutions'. The latter word is even more misused than the former. Sometimes a 'solution' is posited seemingly without reference to a problem.

> We took the scooter to Spain last winter and found it a good solution to taking a large motorcaravan off site and parking in spots where a large vehicle could be an embarrassment.

This is a striking example of allowing the pen to move faster than the brain. What the writer means is: 'We found it a good alternative to taking the large motorcaravan off site.' Such misuse is not rare. Consider this notice about an art course.

> The course questions the notion of the book, and most students have different solutions.

Here the use of 'most' and 'different' is illogical. The question arises, 'different' from what? And what about the minority of students not represented by the word 'most'? Do they share a 'non-different', that is an identical view? Better start afresh: 'The course examines what a book should be, and the students air various views.' Unfortunately this misuse of 'different' is not rare either.

> I'm a part-time nurse in Saudi Arabia where architecture and furnishings are very different.

Different from what? The implication ('different from our own') must be spelt out. When we say 'Men and women are different' and then 'Men and women are different from dumb animals' we use the word 'different' in two recognized, but 'different' ways.

***convince, persuade, induce***
These words should be carefully differentiated. Historically 'convince' is a powerful word. Deriving from the notion of vanquishing, it is used to convey the idea of overcoming someone so completely in argument that acknowledgement of the truth in question is made. The emphasis therefore should be on acknowledgement of some fact or theory.

> When American expatriates Sara and Gerald Murphy discovered Antibes' sleepy seaside Hôtel du Cap in 1923, they convinced the owner to keep it open for them out of season with a minimal staff.

'Convinced' here should be 'persuaded'. To 'convince' someone of some truth should be carefully distinguished from 'persuading' them to act in a certain way. Of course there is an overlap of meaning. But it is the once powerful verb 'convince' that suffers deterioration of meaning when it is misused.

> Cadbury Garden Centre, near Bristol, aimed to convince gardeners to use more exotic plants.

This should be: 'aimed to persuade' or 'aimed to induce'.

## Evading and Preventing

***avert, avoid, forestall, obviate, preempt, prevent***
Closely related to the business of arguing in terms of cause and effect is the business of explaining how some consequence might be evaded or prevented. It will be made evident at many points in this book that bad usage often arises from failure to discriminate precisely between words which may have a slight overlap of meaning, but which nevertheless cannot be regarded as interchangeable. In discourse concerning evasion and prevention the danger is notable. Current practice seems to be to over-use the word 'avoid'. It is gradually taking over in the press and on the radio where there are other and better words to hand. When we consider the number and variety of these words, as illustrated above, we are bound to regret the excessive use of one of them.

> The driver's quick thinking avoided a major railway disaster.

This should read: 'averted a major railway disaster'. To 'avoid' something is to render it void, or of no effect. It can also mean to escape something or to have nothing to do with it. To 'avert' is to turn away. 'She averted her eyes in embarrassment', we say. Thus it means to deflect something from the course it is taking and therefore to ward off a possible development.

In the basic meaning of the verb 'avoid' the overlap with notions of preventing or averting is not sufficient to justify turning it into a verb virtually synonymous with either 'prevent' or 'avert'. Yet that is what has happened. This is not so much a question of correctness or incorrectness as of discrimination in the use of words. People who care for language will naturally not like to see subtle distinctions lost. We may 'avoid' a puddle in the road by stepping round it. We may 'avoid' paying income tax by various questionable means. But where evasion is less an issue than prevention, the word can be used very unhappily, as in the following.

> We had no criticism of the cab seats, which gave enough support to avoid fatigue.

As I read that, I get the image of cab seats narrowly escaping exhaustion. Surely 'to prevent fatigue' would be better.

> Remove each piece from the table one at a time . . . This avoids having to reconstruct the entire pattern.

Here, in instructions for practising decorative decoupage, there is an excellent chance to use a now neglected word especially appropriate where something is prevented by anticipatory action: 'This obviates having to reconstruct the entire pattern.'

A bad habit has lately developed of misusing the word 'preempt'. Although it has a special intransitive use in the game of Bridge, it properly means to acquire or appropriate beforehand. Someone might 'preempt' a deal at an auction by putting in a high offer in advance. But one does not 'preempt' someone else's announcement by getting in first with it. That is to 'anticipate' it. Nor can anyone 'preempt' the building of a motorway by organizing objections to it. That is to 'forestall' it. And again no one can 'preempt' some parallel claimant's case by accepting a low offer before that claimant's case comes up. That is to 'prejudice' it.

## Exchanging and Replacing

### ***substitute, exchange, usurp***

In words for exchanging and replacing we find a carelessness that causes not just a deterioration in meaning but sometimes an almost total reversal in meaning. That happens with the words 'substitute' and 'substitution'. To 'substitute' a player for an injured player is to replace the injured one by the 'substitute'. It is incorrect to speak of an injured player being 'substituted' by a reserve. Yet we often read or hear the blunder made.

> At the moment Katie tends to have a savoury dish followed by, say, a jam tart. This could be substituted for fresh fruit, yogurt or fromage fresh . . .

This nutritionist's advice is seemingly topsy-turvy. She says she wants to replace the child's fresh fruit and yogurt diet by a savoury dish and a jam tart. What she means is: 'This could be replaced by fresh fruit, yoghurt or fromage fresh.'

> More than 20 passengers . . . rode the service on July 11, with NWT having been advised to avoid the train being substituted by a taxi, which has occurred on several occasions this year.

The writer in the *Railway Magazine* has provided us with a similar topsy-turvy misuse of the verb 'substitute' along with another unfortunate use of 'avoid'. Get rid of the redundant 'with', omit the unnecessary 'avoid' and switch the wording round: 'More than 20 passengers . . . rode the service on July 11, NWT having been advised not to substitute a taxi for the train.'

Where 'for' is used along with a verb in such constructions as 'I exchanged my old bike for a new one' it is important to remember that what you exchange is what you part with and the thing 'for' which you exchange it is what you take possession of. If readers think this an utterly unnecessary warning, let them carefully read the following. It comes from a review of a book on Mary Robinson, the former President of the Irish Republic. The review makes the point that where the Irish were once known for their devotion to religious figures, they now appear to give that devotion to secular figures. The review concludes:

> But it is not clear that the Irish have done well in exchanging secular for religious sanctity.

This error, in a quality weekly, raises one's eyebrows. The writer has got it the wrong way round. What he means is: 'But it is not clear that the Irish have done well in exchanging religious for secular sanctity.' As so often, the word 'replace' could have been used: 'in replacing religious by secular sanctity'.

Before taking leave of the word, however, we should take note of an unfortunate new development. It is a construction that works like this:

> The committee have decided to exchange a new and revised brochure with their rather old-fashioned one.

In this sentence the clear mistake was to use 'with' at all. We do not exchange a new car 'with' our old one. We may exchange the old car 'for' a new one. In any case 'exchange' is surely not the best verb to use where the issue is a matter of replacement: 'The committee have decided to replace their rather old-fashioned brochure with a new and revised one.' Oddly enough, an alternative correction would be to use the so often misused verb 'substitute': 'The committee have decided to substitute a new and revised brochure for their rather old-fashioned one.'

Another verb of replacement now misused is the verb to 'usurp'.

> The friendship ended irrevocably in 1987, when Mr Milosevic championed the cause of the Kosovo Serbs and usurped his mentor.

To 'usurp' is to seize without proper authority some position to which one is not entitled. Thus a rebel may 'usurp' a throne, but he could not 'usurp' the king. The above should read: 'championed the cause of the Kosovo Serbs and usurped his mentor's position'.

## Repaying and Forbearing

### *reimburse, compensate, condone*

A category of verbs which can easily lure to error is the kind which affects two objects in different ways. The verb works directly on the object in such sentences as 'He stole a car.' The meaning there is complete. But there are verbs which affect two objects. In 'He gave his sister a book', the verb has both a direct object ('the book') and an indirect object ('his sister'). Though 'he' truly gave the book, it cannot be said that 'he gave his sister'. But there are verbs where this double effect is more complicated. From the sentence 'He paid the retailer five pounds' it would be correct to derive both the sentence 'He paid the retailer' and the sentence 'He paid five pounds.' Because the verb 'pay' and the verb 'repay' work thus, there is a temptation to try to make other verbs of paying work similarly. Thus a minister in the House of Commons spoke of 'reimbursing the cost' of an enterprise. One hears this error repeated on the radio. The announcer tells us that the National Health Service is to recoup the cost of treating road accident victims from insurance companies. There is determination to 'track down the money and reimburse it to the Health Service'. But money cannot be 'reimbursed'. To 'reimburse' is to repay someone, not to repay a sum. Thus the words 'it to' should be omitted in the above: 'track down the money and reimburse the Health Service'.

A comparably faulty use of the verb to 'compensate' occurs when it is treated as though it worked like the verb to 'pay'. We may 'pay someone five pounds' because we can either 'pay someone' or 'pay five pounds', but we cannot 'compensate someone five pounds' because, though we can 'compensate someone' we cannot 'compensate five pounds'.

> They are now working out how much he should be compensated.

Thus that statement on Radio 4 will not serve. Add the word 'by': 'They are now working out by how much he should be compensated.'

We can 'compensate' a person but not a sum of money. Conversely, however, we can 'condone' an offence but not the person who committed it. We hear on the radio:

> A lot of parents condone their truant children.

To condone is to forgive or overlook an offence, not a person. Thus this should be: 'A lot of parents condone their children's truancy.'

## Approving and Disapproving

***creative, dogmatic, pathetic***

Words of strong approval or strong disapproval acquire emotive force which sometimes gets out of hand. That is to say, speakers or writers latch on to them for giving vent to likes or dislikes with a rather loose awareness of their exact meaning. An instance is provided by the words 'creative' and 'creativity'. The precise connotation of such words requires us to use them of acts which produce something where nothing of the kind existed before. One thinks of the acts of creation recorded in the Book of Genesis. And so one feels a certain verbal discomfiture when one reads in a travel article of a Spanish township, 'It was here that the study of medicine and surgery was created.' Why not just 'began'? When one thinks of the kind of context in which the word 'creative' is properly at home, what comes most readily to mind is perhaps the towering genius of a Shakespeare or a Beethoven. But the word so conveniently arouses feelings of wonder that it gets bandied about in relation to all kinds of activities calling for our approval where, strictly speaking, true creation is not at issue. There are courses in 'Creative Cookery' and 'Creative Advertising', not to mention less publicized activities in 'Creative Accountancy'. We perhaps ought not to be too solemn about such usage. We naturally smile when we read 'Owing to the creativity of the weather this year, her garden has been subject to some confusion.' But there are plenty of misuses. Advertisements of vacant posts in various spheres, business or professional, would seem, by the wording of their demands for 'creativity' in their applicants, to be expecting some as yet unrecognized Botticelli or some mute inglorious Milton to emerge from suburbia and take the bait.

We have looked at the decay of a word through its positive connotation; let us look at the decay of a word through its negative connotation. The adjective 'dogmatic' takes its meaning from the noun 'dogma' used of a system of authoritative doctrines, especially religious doctrines. To assert such doctrines with due authority is to be 'dogmatic'. Now such assertiveness, especially in a liberal age, will be described as 'bigotry' by those who reject the doctrines. Gradually the word 'dogmatic' acquires overtones more and more pejorative. Thus, although even a recent dictionary defines the word 'dogmatic' objectively as 'forcibly asserted' or (of a person) 'prone to forcible assertion', it is scarcely possible now to use the word without a condemnatory implication.

> Today many teachers realize that there is little point in imposing dogmatic dress or disciplinary codes.

Here is a case in point. A 'code' is a conventionalized set of rules. The adjective 'dogmatic' therefore adds nothing to the strict connotation of the word, but the pejorative emotive resonance conveys that such codes are to be disliked.

A more remarkable degeneration of meaning has occurred in our use of the word 'pathetic', the adjective deriving from the noun 'pathos'.

Like the word 'pathetical' in Shakespeare, it was applied to persons or things which evoked or expressed genuine sympathy. In his *Life of Samuel Johnson* Boswell quotes a poetic tribute paid by Johnson on the death of his old friend, Robert Levett. Boswell declares that Johnson had such an affectionate regard for Levett 'that he honoured his memory with the following pathetic verses'. Thus at that time one might have praised an actress's sympathetic and moving performance in a tragedy by declaring it 'pathetic'. If that were said today, it would be more likely to mean that the acting was 'pitiably' bad.

### *derisory, derisive, abusive, nauseous*

Sad to say, there are cases of misuse of words which we find sanctioned by new dictionaries. Where there are adjectives which define human attitudes we generally distinguish between the attitude and the object at which it is directed. That is to say, a man may be described as being 'desirous' of something and the object of his desire as 'desirable'. Similarly a person may be described as 'contemptuous' and, if the object of the contempt merits the attitude, we say it is 'contemptible'. If I developed a bad habit of mixing up these two words and describing a thing as 'contemptuous' when I meant that it was 'contemptible', the pedants would rightly be unwilling to give me their support. But in fact that is exactly what has happened in connection with the verb to 'deride'. By all reasonable linguistic tradition, a person who derides is being 'derisory' or 'derisive' and the object of the derision is 'derisible'. My *Shorter Oxford English Dictionary* (1933 edition, reprinted with corrections 1947) presents all this clearly. Yet I find a new dictionary accepting the assumption that what is to be derided is 'derisory'.

Adjectives such as 'derisive' and 'decisive' are descriptive in the first place of human attitudes. So is the adjective 'abusive'. An 'abusive speech' is a speech full of abuse. Yet a speaker on BBC Radio 4, reporting on child-abuse, declared that 'people have been making their abusive claims for years'. Clearly a claim that there has been abuse cannot be called an 'abusive claim', any more than a protest against indecency could be called an 'indecent protest'.

A word misused in the same way as 'derisory' is the word 'nauseous'. What is 'nauseous' is nauseating. It causes nausea; it is repulsive and distasteful. Indeed the word has the connotative strength of 'loathsome'. Yet journalists regularly misuse the word.

> The first signs that Cardinal Hume was ill appeared when he began feeling nauseous at mealtimes a few weeks ago.

Thus *The Times* tells us that the Cardinal felt loathsome. He did not. He felt 'nauseated'. He was affected by nausea.

## Use of Fashionable Abstractions

### ***concept, value***

There are some abstract nouns found once in rigorous philosophical usage that are now so inappropriately exploited that they have become almost unusable. The word 'concept' has the same root as 'conceit' and means an idea or notion, something that the mind has 'conceived'. Yet just as the word 'idea' has been weakened in conversational usage ('the very idea!'), so now the word 'concept' has lost its anchorage in the realm of thought. Here is a statement about a new block of open-plan offices with café and shops:

> This concept of management on the move has been made possible by the design of Waterside.

Now the 'concept' of the change, that is the idea for the change, existed before anything was done about it. The 'concept' would have been exactly what it was, had nothing been done about it. It was the 'realization' of the concept that was made possible by the design of the building: 'The concept of management on the move has been realized in the design of Waterside.'

The word having been thus weakened, it becomes a way of muffling exact thought. Thus we get someone explaining the pains of having to sack employees.

> To tell them they're now on the scrap heap – I found that as a concept very difficult.

Again what the speaker meant was surely that the realization of the concept would be difficult. Merely to think about sacking people hurts no one. To correct the sentence, simply omit 'as a concept'.

What has happened to the word now is that it has achieved a life of its own as a kind of adjective. The AA tells us that 'special concept cars of the 21st century' will be an attraction at a show. And *The Times* captions an illustration 'Concept cars on show at the NEC, Birmingham'. So 'concept' now carries associations of the latest thing in design. Indeed we are reminded of what happened to the word 'designer' a few decades ago. Taken over as an adjective to describe an item of clothing, flaunting the designer's label, it came to mean 'trendy' in a desirable sense.

The word 'value' is a word with deep resonances for those who worry about moral or metaphysical issues. Consider how it is now abused.

> Modern, in that it uses environmentally friendly materials, the Monaco [kitchen] still had traditional construction values.

The kitchen 'still had traditional construction values'. Does that mean anything other than that it was 'well made'? The truth is that the word 'value' is often used, especially by advertisers, so as to be conveniently evasive of what particular benefits are supposed to accrue to the responsive readers. The word 'value' becomes an all-purpose way of praising without having to specify too clearly what you are praising.

> Epitomizing the Volkswagen approach to motorhome base vehicles, the L. T. shares the values Volkswagen have been building into leisure vehicles for decades.

## SOME VERBAL DISTORTIONS

### Reversals of Meaning

There is an odd, and fortunately rare, kind of misuse which causes not so much a deterioration in meaning as an almost total reversal in meaning. As we have seen, words for substituting and exchanging provide notorious examples of this.

#### *deceptively, availability*

Another glaring example is provided by the word 'deceptively' as used by estate agents. They will advertise a house as being 'deceptively spacious', intending to mean that it is really much more spacious than it appears to be at first sight. If a man is described as 'deceptively considerate', it is implied that though he appears to be considerate, that appearance is deceptive. On this reading a 'deceptively spacious' house would be one which appeared to be spacious, but in fact was not so. One wonders whether the word 'deceptively' can be rescued in contexts like these. For instance we read:

> Giles Turner held the lead on Mavis Davis, before Geoff Glazzard dislodged him with a deceptively fast round on his first ride, Hello Oscar.

Are we really to believe that Hello Oscar appeared to be running fast but that this was a *trompe l'œil* and he was really taking his time? Clearly the construction must be changed. One can hardly substitute 'dislodged him with a deceptively leisurely round'. It would not be very neat to substitute 'dislodged him with a round much faster than it seemed', but that is probably the best we can do.

A comparable kind of misuse threatens the word 'availability'. It too is in danger of suffering reversal of meaning.

> A real concern of AA members is the high cost of petrol, and its availability as rural petrol stations struggle to stay open.

Clearly the availability of petrol can never be a concern. It is the lack of petrol or the possible unavailability of petrol that is or might be a matter of concern. 'A real concern of AA members is the high cost of petrol, and the doubt whether it will continue to be available as rural petrol stations struggle to stay open.'

### *help, improve*

There is sometimes near-reversal of meaning in the use of words for improving, curing or helping. Here are two instances from magazines on the subject of restoring hair. The first is a caption:

> Hair-raising electrichogenesis, a process to help baldness, being launched at Manor House Hospital in North London.

The question arises whether helping baldness is the same thing as helping the man who is bald. Clearly the need is to get rid of baldness, which sounds as though it ought to be the opposite of 'helping' it. The passage should read: 'a process to help to cure baldness'. The second example seems to represent the same error:

> However, increasing intake of iron itself and vitamin C to aid iron absorption often fails to improve hair loss . . .

Again the question is whether to improve hair loss is the same thing as to improve the hair. A 'loss' is not something that needs to be 'improved', but to be repaired. So the sentence should end: 'often fails to repair the loss of hair'.

## Adjectives That Cannot be Qualified

Dissipation of meaning has its worst effects when the connotation of a once powerful word is virtually forgotten. There are adjectives which cannot be qualified. That is another way of saying that, if something is the very 'best', there cannot be anything 'more best'. The same is true of the word 'equal'. In *Animal Farm* George Orwell mocked totalitarian communist propaganda when the pigs amended the slogan 'All animals are equal' by adding the illogical form, 'but some are more equal than others.'

### *ideal*

Here is a case in point. An 'ideal' concept or article is one which cannot be improved upon.

> There could be no more ideal Christmas gift than a flight on Concorde.

The 'ideal' Christmas gift is the perfect or 'best' conceivable Christmas gift, and therefore the concept of a 'more ideal' one is inadmissible.

### *minimal*

> They feel there is everything to gain from keeping a start-up service on the go, however minimal.

Just as the 'minimum' is the least possible amount, so the word 'minimal' describes the smallest possible quantity. Thus there can be no degrees of minimality, and the words 'however minimal' do not make sense. If 'minimal' is kept, 'however' must go, and vice versa: 'They feel there is everything to gain from keeping a start-up service on the go, however small.'

### *normal*

A 'norm' is an average level qualitatively or quantitatively. Just as a certain level of achievement or behaviour cannot be described as 'more average' than another, so it cannot be described as 'more normal' than another. What the weather forecasters mean when they mistakenly promise us 'more normal' temperatures tomorrow is that the temperatures tomorrow will be 'nearer to the average' (or the 'norm') for the time of year.

### *perfect*

I find it hard to imagine a more perfect view.

If the speaker could imagine a 'more perfect' view, then the view in question would not be 'perfect'. What is 'perfect' cannot be improved upon.

### *true*

A statement is either true or false. If John is six feet tall, the statement 'John is five feet eleven' is not 'truer' than the statement 'John is five feet six.' Both statements are false.

Would it not be truer to admit that we can never guess at the workings of the divine mind?

This kind of rhetorical flourish, whatever it follows, is totally illogical. 'Truer' could be replaced by 'true', but the introduction of the word is unnecessary: 'Must we not admit that we can never guess at the workings of the divine mind?'

### *unique*

If something is 'unique' it is absolutely the only one of its kind. Therefore one cannot speak of anything being 'more unique' than other things, nor of something being 'very unique'. The word 'unique' is properly applied to a thing of which only one exists, yet the number of 'unique' opportunities now offered by the business world seems to be limitless.

## WORDS DAMAGED BY MISUSE AND OVER-USE

As in so many departments of life, fashion in language has a deleterious effect on usage, cheapening terms by misuse and then by over-use in too many different contexts. The most obvious kind of misuse is that which results from sheer error in understanding. One or two people make mistakes and others follow suit. We have shown how the words 'substitute' and 'substitution' have been confused with the words 'replace' and 'replacement', and now they are so widely misused that one is likely to be accused of pedantry if one draws attention to the error.

In many cases over-use cheapens words without damaging them to that extent. There is a gradual process of change in which can be traced the drift from the orthodox connotation. This chapter is much concerned with words which manifest that drift. We are considering the questions: What are the spoilt words of today, the words damaged by being misunderstood, and the words whose meaning is dissipated in lax over-use? It would take a very long list to contain them all. But we have already considered several in this chapter and we can pick out a few more of the most glaring examples. Over-use is not, of course, an arithmetically calculable matter. If you work in a restaurant, you and your colleagues may use the word 'table' thousands of times a year without affecting the meaning of the word in the slightest. Here we are concerned with the kind of over-use which weakens and distorts meaning.

***access***

We accept that, largely perhaps through the influence of the computer world, the noun 'access' has taken new life as a verb.

> It is part of our policy to present visual art to people who might not normally visit a gallery by accessing through other artforms.

My dictionary classifies 'access' as a transitive verb that requires an object. One 'accesses' a source of information on the internet. But in the sentence here we do not know what is being accessed nor who is accessing. The grammar suggests that 'our policy' is to help people 'by accessing' through other artforms. But in the back of the mind one guesses that it is the people who are being helped who will be able to 'access' something unspecified.

***address***

There are contexts where this is the exact word needed. Used of putting the appropriate directions on an envelope or of speaking formally to an audience, it is not replaceable. But the word is now being used where better words are available.

> At last the editor has addressed an issue which is of vital importance to all of us.

Thus people speak of addressing 'issues', 'situations', 'problems', and the like where they might better use verbs such as 'deal with', 'tackle', 'attend to', 'cope with' or even 'study'. I have just heard a BBC Radio 4 comment on a report about the treatment of cancer by the National

Health Service. The report found that the wealthy do better in this respect than the poor. The announcer spoke of the report as 'a catalogue of injustices that will have to be addressed'. The word 'addressed' is not happily used here of dealing with a 'catalogue'. There are mail-order firms that regularly address catalogues to potential customers. The usage has to be handled with care because there are contexts where it might easily lead to ambiguity.

> While the voluntary code of practice has been welcomed by park officials and rangers, Maryl Carr feels that it does not adequately address the increasing number of participants or their impact on other mountain users.

To speak of not adequately 'addressing' participants inevitably suggests a public 'address' from a platform. The mistake here needs to be analysed. To address a problem is one thing, and to address a crowd of participants is another thing. What the writer means is that the 'problem' of the increasing number of participants has to be 'addressed'. If the verb to 'address' is used, there can be no way of avoiding some such word as 'problem'.

### *alternate / alternative*

Basically the verb 'alternate' defines movement this way and that way, as of a pendulum. Thus day 'alternates' with night. The word can be used only of such balanced couples.

> This may be more so now that the Game Fair alternates between only four central sites . . .

If there are more than two variants, as here, then the word 'alternate' will not do. One must write: 'now that the location of the Game Fair varies between only four central sites'.

The word 'alternative' is even more frequently abused. 'Alternatives' are two mutually exclusive possibilities. When we choose between two possibilities, say going to the theatre or staying at home, we choose between two 'alternatives'. There can never be more than two alternatives. If a third possibility is presented to us, then the three possibilities become 'options'. More often than not the word 'alternative' is now being used as though it meant 'option'. This development has led to usages such as the following:

> ContiFlug is a relatively small airline. It offers a highly cost-effective alternative for commuter travel to Berlin.

The question arises: alternative to what? If there were only one other means of commuter travel to Berlin, the word might be appropriate. But often now, especially in advertising, the word is used too vaguely of a possibility which the advertiser wishes to recommend.

> The purpose of the advertising campaign is to present self-catering holidays as an attractive and economic alternative.

Clearly what we are really being offered here is again an 'option'. But the most satisfactory correction would be to use neither 'alternative' nor 'option': 'The purpose of the advertising campaign is to present self-catering holidays as attractive and economic.' After all, a self-catering holiday might be an attractive alternative to staying at home, but it would not be an economic alternative to staying at home.

There are usages which seem to remove from the word even the notion of an option.

> I wanted to create an alternative trading model.

There the word simply means 'fresh' or 'new'. And now we have to allow too for the fact that, in recent decades, novel movements which questioned the status quo and prevailing climates of opinion began to define their innovative life-styles as 'alternative', and the word has stuck.

***answer***

Shortly before she died Gertrude Stein is said to have muttered 'What's the answer?' and shortly afterwards to have added 'What's the question?' The partnership of the two nouns is such that to use the word 'answer' when there is no notion of a question, or even a problem in the background, is lax. Yet that is what happens.

> The real answer is periodically to have a thorough clean . . .

The recommendation that it may be a good idea to clean vehicles ought to be able to be made without turning it into an 'answer'.

***approach***

We know well enough when this word is exactly the right one, whether used of coming nearer to a physical position or making advances towards influencing someone. Too often neither notion is involved.

> Running a mobile snack-bar falls into two distinct approaches. You must decide whether you want to sell at the roadside or in a market.

The notion of falling into two 'approaches' when running a mobile snack-bar suggests a Road Traffic Accident. What the writer means is: 'There are two possible sites for a mobile snack-bar.'

> My actual manner of painting in gouache is not that different from my approach to oils.

If one wants to say that the manner or method used for one medium is similar to that used for another medium, why drag in the word 'approach'?

### *area*

The use of the word 'area' has been adopted in place of a wide range of possible options.

> The way peer pressure stimulates in children the demand for ever more unsuitable footwear is another area of concern.

One can think of many a word which would have saved the writer from this over-used word 'area'. The simplest correction would be to omit 'area of': 'demand for ever more unsuitable footwear is another concern'. But possible words such as 'matter', 'issue' and 'topic' also suggest themselves. Elsewhere we hear that 'Truancy is an area that must be looked into', where there would be no loss in substituting 'Truancy also must be looked into.'

> The committee will be responsible for areas such as funding, excursions and new members.

There is gross incongruity in labelling 'excursions' as one area and 'new members' as another. Again it would be better to substitute 'matters' for 'areas'.

### *aspect*

One of the situations in which the writer ought to pause and scratch the head is well illustrated here, where the writer is recommending the varied delights of exploring an area of waterways:

> For instance, canals, industrial history, wildlife, landscape, cycling or walking the towpaths, or many other aspects may appeal to you.

Canals, industrial history, wildlife, landscape, cycling and walking together represent a mixed bag. How many of them can properly be called 'aspects'? Probably none of them, so the expression 'many other aspects' is totally out of place. The first four of the items listed are really cited as topics of interest for possible study. The other two items, cycling and walking, are activities. The six items cannot be classed together as 'aspects'. The distinction between them must be made: 'For instance, the study of canals, industrial history, wildlife or landscape may appeal to you, or activities such as cycling or walking the towpaths.'

***ballot***

A 'ballot' is an instance of the practice of electing a representative by voting. We speak of the 'ballot paper' on which voters register their vote and the 'ballot box' into which the papers are consigned. Voters 'cast their votes'. They do not 'cast their ballots', a fact which ought to be conveyed to the news writers of the BBC.

> The Israelis are expected to cast their ballot early in the spring.

This should be either: 'The Israelis are expected to cast their votes' or: 'The Israelis are expected to hold their ballot.'

***challenge, challenging***

The words 'challenge' and 'challenging' have lost whatever overtones they once had of knightly encounters in the lists, meetings with pistols at dawn, or any other such desperate situations. Over-use of the word in business has emptied the word 'challenging' of resonance.

> We provide a challenging, unique environment where those with ability can realize their ambitions.

The same applies to the word 'challenge'. Over-use has rendered it null and void.

> PowerGen has continued to move ahead to new challenges during the year.

This, of course, is tantamount to saying nothing at all except that the firm still exists.

***component***

Feeling for the right word to apply to a bunch of supposedly related items, the mind may throw up such words as 'aspects', 'elements', 'features', 'attributes' and 'factors'. It is worthwhile to pause before plumping for one. The following is a piece of evolutionary theorizing on BBC Radio 4:

> We got to having a higher intelligence because shorter people had to be cleverer, they had to be faster on their feet, they had to adapt in different ways, and that may be one of the components in our progress.

The word 'component' (officially defined as 'a constituent part of something more complex') has strong technical and mechanical overtones, and is out of place in this human context. Why not: 'and that may have contributed to our progress'?

### *compromise*

A 'compromise' is a settlement between two parties in a dispute, by which they meet each other half way. In wider use it can therefore indicate a half-way meeting point between two opposing interests.

> We chose a 40 ft boat because it seemed a sensible compromise between the amount of living space aboard and running costs.

A boat cannot be a 'compromise' between living space and expenditure. A modest outlay might represent a compromise between heavy spending and sharp economy. A 40 ft boat might represent a compromise between an 80 ft boat and a 10 ft boat. There must be the relationship between the two elements of the 'compromise' that allows of a meeting point on the same plane. What the writer meant was: 'We chose a 40 ft boat, adjusting our wish for living space aboard by calculating the running cost.'

### *core*

Used for the central part of something, this word carries colourful overtones of what you find in the middle of an apple. Over-use in the business world is now reducing its connotation to the same diluted level as that of words like 'central', 'important' or even 'essential'. Where an employee might once have been allotted his 'main task', he is now given his 'core remit'.

### *credible / credibility*

These two words, like the words 'creed' and 'credulous', have to do with belief. A man who is 'credulous' is too ready to believe what he hears, accepts things on inadequate evidence, and is easily taken in. What is 'credible' is worthy of belief. The word has suffered lately from over-use in contexts where it is little more than a term of general approval, roughly equivalent to 'effective' or 'convincing'.

On European integration I don't find his attitude credible.

This is the equivalent of saying 'I don't agree with his attitude to European integration.' The same looseness affects the word 'credibility'.

The double lining is a guarantee of the jacket's credibility in wet weather.

Here 'credibility' presumably means 'reliability'.

### *decimate*

This word derives from Latin. The Latin verb was used of the practice of Roman generals to punish by killing every tenth man in a given force. There are two current misuses of the word. The one occurs when use of the verb implies that a body of people has been all but wiped out. In that case it is as though the meaning of the verb is that a body of troops or a section of some population has been reduced to a tenth of its original size, instead of to nine-tenths. The other misuse occurs when the word 'decimate' is seemingly confused with some other word such as 'devastate', as when a judge tells a criminal that he has 'decimated the lives of two whole families'.

### *diagnose*

An interesting case of changing usage is provided by the verb to 'diagnose'. The verb strictly means to identify something, most usually a physical condition. Thus the doctor may examine a patient and diagnose whooping cough. It is the condition that is diagnosed, not the patient. Yet over the past few years usage has veered confusingly. 'You should be properly diagnosed by your doctor' should be either: 'You should be properly examined by your doctor', or: 'Your condition should be properly diagnosed by your doctor.' It is now common to speak of someone having been 'diagnosed with epilepsy' when, strictly speaking, 'epilepsy has been diagnosed'.

### *emerge*

The verb 'emerge' carries its own clear meaning, but it is now being over-used as a means of avoiding the verb to 'occur' or to 'happen'.

> The most amazing escape from the Naïrobi carnage emerged yesterday when an Israeli team rescued a mother and her son from an upper floor in the 22-storey building.

No doubt the mother and her son 'emerged' from the building, but to describe the escape as emerging from the carnage is just careless usage.

***equate / equation***

Popularization of the word 'equation' has diluted its meaning. It is used as an alternative not just to 'problem', but to 'situation'. 'I've nothing new to add to the equation' apparently just means 'I've nothing to say on the subject.' Correspondingly the verb to 'equate' is in fashion.

> But sensual and sexy equate to two different things for me.

This simply means: 'are two different things'.

***factor***

Properly used of an element that contributes to some result, the word 'factor' suffers from the same loose treatment as 'aspect'.

> But the exact make-up of his [Schröder's] government was unclear last night because of the complicating factor of small parties which might not gain the 5 per cent needed for parliamentary representation.

Here the word 'factor' is a dead counter and the word 'complicating' not needed if the argument is simply presented: 'But the exact make-up of his Government was unclear last night because the small parties might not gain the 5 per cent needed for parliamentary representation.'

***focus***

The 'focus' in Latin is the hearth around which people gather. The word has been usefully adopted in the mathematical and scientific worlds. Now that the business world has discovered its usefulness, that usefulness is being destroyed.

> Nigel Woods, accounts director for the UK's fastest growing motivations group, MotivForce, says travel is often a more focused way of rewarding staff.

In what sense is the present of a holiday package 'more focused' than the present of a cheque or of private health care, or of any other of the perks that companies distribute? 'Focus' is a nice-sounding word with the air of some intellectual meat about it, of some clarity and resonance. But what the writer means is that 'travel is often a good way of rewarding staff'.

### *impact*

When a word has some dramatic thrust it is especially destructive to use it so as to deprive it of colour or force. Here the word 'impact' is used in a piece of advice about prettifying the home:

> To add impact, choose flowers that make a statement.

'Impact' is a powerful word, used of fatal crashes at high speed on the motorway, or of dramatic effects produced by some spectacle of rare impressiveness. The writer of the above, however, reduces the word to the level of any old piece of worn-out currency; then, to make things worse, trundles out the most hackneyed of current non-sayings, 'flowers that make a statement'.

### *instigate*

My dictionary definition of this verb is 'to bring about, as by incitement' and 'to urge on to some violent or unadvisable action'. The notion of stirring things up into a state of excitement attaches to the verb, which has been much used of fermenting rebellion. The word is now used increasingly as though it meant no more than 'initiate' or 'start'.

> His grandfather instigated the first public transport system in the city.

Here 'initiated' or 'started' would be better.

> He joined the society soon after going up to Cambridge, instigated by a former school friend.

Here 'encouraged' would be the right word.

### *materialize*

Something which 'materializes' takes on material form. Therefore the verb is used of things which become fact, which actually take place. Thus the word has been increasingly used of plans which 'come off', as we say. The usage is not favoured by the pedants. The modern tendency to use the verb as an alternative to the verbs to 'happen' or to 'occur' is regarded as lax and imprecise. As one looks at instances of its use one can see why. Here is a sentence from the controversy about student loans.

> Nor is there much evidence that the least affluent will be adversely affected. This claim was made when student loans were first introduced nearly a decade ago: it did not materialize in practice.

The trouble here is that a 'claim' is not something that might 'materialize'. A 'claim' of this kind may prove true or false, but if it is made about the future it is probably better called a 'forecast': 'This was forecast when student loans were first introduced nearly a decade ago: it did not happen.'

### *optimistic*

A descriptive term increasingly misused is the word 'optimistic'.

> The truth [about cancer] is far more optimistic: cancer is largely a preventable disease.

An 'optimistic' person is one who expects the best. The philosophical doctrine of 'optimism' holds that good will ultimately triumph over evil. 'Truth' can be neither optimistic nor pessimistic. It appears that the writer means 'The truth is far more encouraging', that is, productive of optimism rather than 'optimistic'.

### *option*

This word is being misused in the same way as 'alternative'.

> If you are one of the growing number of owners who are trying to give their pets the healthier option . . .

What this means is: 'If you are one of the growing number of owners who want to keep their pets healthy . . .' Use of the word 'option' should be restricted to contexts in which there are at least two possible courses of action from which one may be chosen. One cannot speak of the 'healthier option' in a context where no other option is mentioned.

### *potential*

What is 'potential' is possible but not yet actual, latent but not yet realized.

> We need to look at the present situation, where potential nannies need no qualifications for training.

'Potential nannies' is not a satisfactory usage. In a sense every girl is a 'potential nanny', just as she is a potential mother, wife, or wage-earner. 'Would-be nannies' is the simplest expression for aspirants to nannyhood.

### *pragmatic*

A 'pragmatic' attitude is an attitude adopted rather for its practical consequences than on any basis of principle or theory. Thus, in loose use, it refers to practical, everyday business.

> But in recent years the Princess has become the pragmatic and acceptable face of royalty at a time when other, younger members of the Royal Family have behaved in a manner which not only saddens the Queen, but also sullies the reputation of the monarchy itself.

The contrast between the Princess Royal's conduct and that of other members of the Royal Family might reasonably bring the word 'acceptable' into play, but the concept of the pragmatic as opposed to the theoretical is scarcely relevant. A better wording would be: 'the Princess has become the fitting and acceptable face of royalty'.

### *priority*

The list of words already 'spoilt' or in the process of being 'spoilt' must surely include this one (not to mention 'prioritize'). It is now thrown about far too freely. Here is a piece of advice to parents wondering whether to send their children to holiday camps.

> Your main priority is whether or not your child is going to be happy away from home.

Do we really need a 'priority' to be mentioned? What is lost if we write: 'You must first decide whether or not your child is going to be happy away from home'?

### *properly*

This is one of those words which we readily throw about in conversation: 'You haven't cleaned the car properly', 'He doesn't brush his hair properly.' The lax usage jars on the printed page.

> Old enamelware is now quite hard to find, but if hunted down properly can still be found at car boot sales.

Here the sense of appropriateness which the word should convey is absent. There is no issue of 'propriety' here. The word could be replaced by 'carefully' or 'keenly', or, better still, could be omitted.

### *prospective*

We find a boarding school advising 'prospective parents' to get in touch with the school secretary. But a 'prospective' parent is either a pregnant woman or the father of her child. The word is out of place here. The message is meant, not for prospective parents, but for prospective customers.

### *proverbial*

There is a point in the decay of a word's meaning at which the question arises whether the word is worth using at all. Does it add anything?

> She was the warmest, sweetest person you could ever meet, the proverbial prostitute with the heart of gold.

Now although there is no well-known 'proverb' about a prostitute, we recognize that the word here serves the purpose of conjuring up a certain stereotype exploited in literature. But what is the result when the word 'proverbial' is dragged further from any anchorage?

> You could have heard the proverbial pin drop as Kilbaha entered the arena for the jump-off.

It requires no great mastery of the English language to be familiar with the expression 'You could hear a pin drop.' Not to be able to use it without annotating it as though attention needed to be drawn to its hallowed position in our linguistic tradition is surely pretentious. It is like talking of 'the thin end of the proverbial wedge' or 'barking up the proverbial tree'.

### *scenario*

The 'scenario' is basically the plot of a stage play or film. The first person to use the word outside its theatrical context showed some imagination to inspired effect. The usage became fashionable. Over-use has now diluted its significance. It is done to death.

> Jane revels in major contracts, and starting from scratch is her ideal scenario.

The word gets applied to any sequence of events. We even hear 'Getting up late in the morning is his ideal scenario.' Thus the original connotation is dissipated.

***sector***

'Sector' meaning a part or subdivision has a geometrical basis. It has been much used in the expressions 'public sector' and 'private sector', but it is best not applied to groups of human beings. There is nothing to be gained from saying (rather ungrammatically) 'There is a sector of the police force who are racist' instead of 'Some policemen are racist.' The word is equally unhappily used in the following:

> This scheme represents a new era in reproductive medicine and helps certain sectors who before couldn't get treatment.

Why not: '... and helps certain people who before couldn't get treatment'?

***spectrum***

In the case of words such as 'concept' we have seen how a technical term may be taken over, quite usefully, for more general use, and then may suffer a gradual loss of definable meaning. This has begun to happen with the word 'spectrum'. Strictly it means the band of colours into which a prism resolves a beam of light. The image is useful, but we are beginning to hear the word applied more and more widely when people want to sum up a range of attitudes. Speaking for social workers, someone says 'Yet we deal with a spectrum of emotional issues in the course of our work', where 'spectrum' would be better replaced by 'range' or 'variety'.

***theme***

The word 'theme' is not perhaps a vivid word, but it is rich in association with accounts of symphonic movements in music and metaphorical sequences in poetry.

> But humiliation was the theme of Yeltsin's position in those days.

If we want to say that Yeltsin was being humiliated, do we need to drag in the word 'theme' at all?

***unnecessary***

Here again is a forceful word which ought not to be employed so as to weaken its connotation.

> Sight Savers International desperately needs your help to wipe out this cruel and unnecessary disease.

This illustrates the increasing tendency to misuse the word 'unnecessary'. The question of 'necessity' or its absence simply does not arise. What the writer means is: 'Sight Savers International desperately needs your help to wipe out this cruel and avoidable disease.'

### *vandalism*

This word is chosen as representative of abstract nouns ending in '-ism'. If one considers, say, the verb to 'colonize', it is matched by two distinct nouns, 'colonialism' and 'colonization'. 'Colonialism' is the abstract word for the theory and practice of colonizing, but any single act of colonizing itself represents 'colonization'. It would be a mistake to confuse the two words.

> His head chef at l'Oranger, the restaurant, has been arrested after the alleged theft of £1;500 and the vandalism of the restaurant, the night after he was sacked.

Here that mistake is made with the word 'vandalism'. To vandalize a building is to commit an act of 'vandalism', but the process of vandalizing a building is 'vandalization'. Here the sentence could read: 'has been arrested after the alleged theft of £1,500 and the vandalization of the restaurant', or: 'and the vandalizing of the restaurant'. Better still would be: 'has been arrested for allegedly stealing £1,500 and vandalizing the restaurant'.

### *virtually*

'Virtually' means 'in effect' as opposed to 'in fact'. We might say 'She was only a recently elected member of the committee but she was virtually in charge of everything.' But increasingly the word is being weakened.

> It was virtually sixty years ago that Edith Smith took the photograph.

There is no contrast here between what happened in effect and what happened in fact. To use 'virtually' to mean 'almost' or 'nearly' is bad enough. But here it means neither. What is meant is: 'It was about sixty years ago that Edith Smith took the photograph.'

CHAPTER 2

# The Right Words and the Wrong Words

Choosing the wrong word sometimes results from getting confused between two words which are very similar in sound or spelling. The mistake is even more likely to occur if the two words are also close in meaning. The extreme form of confusion between two words similar in sound is the 'malapropism', so called after the character Mrs Malaprop in Sheridan's play *The Rivals*. Mrs Malaprop declares that she would have no wish for a daughter of hers to be a 'progeny' of learning, when she clearly means 'prodigy'. She considers her niece Lydia to be by no means 'illegible' for a certain match, but she finds her 'as headstrong as an allegory on the banks of the Nile'. There is perhaps little need now to warn readers against confusing an 'allegory' with an 'alligator' or using 'illegible' instead of 'ineligible', but I have quite recently seen 'prodigy' misused where the word should have been 'protégée'. Of the many pairs of words which lend themselves to this confusion, observation suggests that the following deserve attention.

***abjure / adjure***

To 'abjure' is to renounce, often used of formal recantations. 'This rough magic / I here abjure' says Shakespeare's Prospero, when he renounces the practice of magic at the end of *The Tempest*. To 'adjure' is formally to command, earnestly to bind or appeal to ('His friends earnestly adjured him to take care of his health').

***abrogate / arrogate***

To 'abrogate' is to cancel, to repeal, officially to revoke. When Holofernes in *Love's Labour's Lost* seems to be about to tell a *risqué* tale. Sir Nathaniel warns him to 'abrogate scurrility'. The verb to 'arrogate', derived from a Latin verb meaning to adopt as a child, came to mean to assume to oneself rights to which one is not entitled. In *Paradise Regained* Milton attacks false philosophers who 'arrogate' all glory to themselves and none to

God. Thus an 'arrogant' person is one who unwarrantably lays claim to dignities, qualities or knowledge.

***accede / exceed***

To 'accede' is in the first place to enter upon an office ('He acceded to the throne'), and in the second to give assent to ('She acceded to my request for admittance'). The verb 'to exceed' means to be greater than, to surpass ('The total sum collected exceeded their wildest hopes').

***accessary / accessory***

Practice has now run these two words together. Historically 'accessary' (connected with the word 'access') is the word for someone who aids and abets in an offence, whether before or after the event. An 'accessory' (connected with the words 'accede' and 'accession') is an adjunct. Since the spelling 'accessory' has now for some time been accepted in place of 'accessary', a useful distinction has been lost.

***activate / actuate***

To 'activate' is to render active, used mainly of scientific processes, but sometimes used non-technically of launching a plan of action. To 'actuate' is also to set something going, but is used more generally to mean motivate ('Her proposal was actuated by the most generous intentions').

***adduce / deduce***

To 'adduce' an argument or a proposition is to bring it forward for consideration as evidence ('He adduced a series of instances to corroborate his case'). To 'deduce' is to derive a conclusion logically from some proposition or piece of evidence ('From the evidence before him he deduced that it was a case of murder').

***adverse / averse***

'Adverse' means hostile. We speak of 'adverse circumstances' when those circumstances are unfavourable to what we want to do. 'Averse' means personally disinclined. A nervous man may describe himself as 'averse to speaking in public'.

***affect / effect***

To 'affect' is to influence ('Coming across the work of Tolstoy affected his own ambitions as a writer') or to disturb ('Her son's distress affected her deeply'). To 'effect' is to bring about ('The teaching of Tolstoy effected a revolution in his thinking').

***allusive / elusive***

The verb to 'allude' means to refer to something indirectly or just to mention it. An 'allusion' therefore is a passing reference ('In the whole speech there was only the slightest allusion to his own desperate state of health'). The verb to 'elude' is to escape something or avoid it, very often something which ought not to be evaded ('For seven years he managed to elude the police'). The balancing noun 'elusion' is now obsolete. The adjective 'allusive' means rich in allusions and is often used of literary style. One might apply it to the prose of Joyce's *Ulysses*. The adjective 'elusive' refers to what easily escapes attention or is difficult to get hold of. It might be applied to the narrative content of Joyce's *Finnegans Wake*.

***ambiguous / ambivalent***

The element 'ambi', based on the Latin word for 'both', occurs for instance in 'ambidextrous', meaning equally skilled with both hands. Something which is 'ambiguous' is open to more than one interpretation, and the word is used primarily of statements, but also of actions. The word 'ambivalent' is not a synonymous alternative to 'ambiguous', as some writers seem to think. An attitude which is 'ambivalent' involves two different and perhaps conflicting emotions, not interpretations. ('There was ambivalence in her attitude to the man who had both aided and injured her.')

***amend / emend***

To 'amend' is to improve, make better. 'God amend us, God amend!' says Berowne in Shakespeare's *Love's Labour's Lost*. In the House of Commons efforts are made to 'amend' bills being put before members when they think an 'amendment' advisable. The verb to 'emend' is used in a more specialized way of correcting errors or making textual improvements in manuscripts and printed material. The correction is an 'emendation'.

***amoral / immoral***

The prefixes 'a-' and 'im-' cancel out the meaning of the word 'moral' in two different ways. What is 'immoral' transgresses moral laws and the word is used generally of unethical and corrupt behaviour. What is 'amoral' is totally outside the realm of the moral; behaviour or beliefs which accept no such measure of behaviour as the 'moral' and the 'immoral'. The prefix 'a-' signifies negation or privation just as 'in'- and 'un-' do. It is used nowadays in such words as 'asocial' and 'asymmetrical' as well as in the technical musical terms 'atonal' and 'atonality', of the absence of key in some twentieth-century compositions.

### *appraise / apprise*

To 'appraise' is to assess the value of something, to make an 'appraisal' of it. To 'apprise' is to inform. Thus 'The authorities could not act before they were appraised of the break-in' should be: '. . . before they were apprised of the break-in'.

### *assume / presume*

To 'assume' is to take something for granted ('As he had got engaged to the girl, we assumed that he would marry her'). It is also used of taking things up other than mentally ('He assumed the role of guardian'). Similarly there is an impersonal use ('The situation began to assume a threatening character'). In its most common use, 'presume' may be substituted for 'assume' ('Dr Livingstone, I presume'). Often, however, to 'presume' is arrogantly to take up a position to which one is not entitled. That is the case in Pope's celebrated couplet:

> Know then thyself, presume not God to scan,
> The proper study of mankind is man.

In legal usage an accused person is 'presumed' innocent until proved guilty.

### *authoritarian / authoritative*

The difference between these two words, both concerned with the exercise of authority, is that 'authoritarian' generally implies some exercise of authority which is undesirable, while 'authoritative' carries no such pejorative overtone. An 'authoritarian' government or management lays the law down from above without democratic consultation, and an 'authoritarian' personal manner is similarly inflexible. An 'authoritative' statement or action is one which carries the weight of due authority, such as for instance an announcement by the Prime Minister in Parliament.

### *baleful / baneful*

Both words now have a faintly archaic flavour. 'Bale' is evil, both in the sense of malignancy and in the sense of torment. 'Rome and her rats are at the point of battle' says Menenius Agrippa at the beginning of Shakespeare's *Coriolanus*, and adds 'The one side must have bale', meaning 'One or the other is going to come a cropper.' 'Bane' is death and destruction. Thus the two words 'baleful' and 'baneful' overlap in that they threaten misery. 'Baleful' became a literary word for sorrowful and miserable, and we still hear the expression 'baleful news'. 'Bane' means 'poison' in the word 'ratsbane'. Milton left us a memorable expression when he told how riches grow in hell, which naturally supplies the ideal environment for the 'precious bane'.

### *bathos / pathos*

As the word 'pathetic' properly refers to what arouses sympathy or pity, so the word 'pathos' is the power of arousing feelings of sympathy, pity or sorrow. It is used of works of literature and of oratory as well as of personal situations. Burns wrote:

> To make a happy fireside clime
> To weans and wife,
> That's the true pathos and sublime
> Of human life.

The word 'bathos' is used of any sudden switch from what is exalted and dignified to what is pedestrian and trivial. It is also used of attempts at pathos which are overdone or fail to come off.

### *beneficence / benevolence*

There is a subtle distinction between these two words. Where 'beneficence' is generosity in action, 'benevolence' is generosity of spirit. Thus it is an act of 'beneficence' for a benefactor to endow a new hospital, but the action stems from the benefactor's 'benevolence'.

### *biannual / biennial*

As 'annual' means occurring once a year, so 'biannual' means occurring twice a year. But a 'biennial' event is one that occurs every two years.

***carousal / carousel***

As to 'carouse' is to drink freely, so a 'carousal' is a drunken feast. (In pronunciation the stress is on the second syllable.) A 'carousel', originally a knightly tournament with racing horses, came to be used of a merry-go-round. Hence it is used for the revolving luggage conveyor at an airport and also for the circular tray into which slides are slotted and produced one by one for a projector.

***classic / classical***

A 'classic' is a work of art of the highest excellence which has stood the test of time. The word is used for something created which is of the first rank and must be regarded as definitive. Hence comes the less strict connotation of the adjective 'classic' exemplified in such statements as 'It was a classic case of parental negligence', where the word means little more than 'typical'. The word 'classical' was applied to the civilization of ancient Greece and Rome and to later forms of art and architecture that preserved the same tradition of formality and restraint. In this respect contrasts between 'classical' and 'romantic' styles were drawn. More recently the word 'classical' has come to be used of music belonging to serious traditional culture as opposed to ephemeral 'popular' music.

***complacent / complaisant***

To be 'complacent' is to be over-easily satisfied with things, and especially with one's self and with one's own achievements. It is to be unmoved by matters which really should cause concern, and thus the word is much used in criticism of political opponents. Conversationally 'complacent' means smug. The bachelor essayist Charles Lamb found nothing more distasteful than the 'complacency and satisfaction which beam in the countenances of new-married couples'. To be 'complaisant' is to be agreeably obliging, accommodating one's self readily to the requests and needs of others. In Buckingham's burlesque play *The Rehearsal* (1672), which satirizes contemporary drama, a Mr Smith avers that it's 'very complaisant to be of another man's opinion before knowing what it is'.

***complement / compliment***

These two words are often confused, both as verbs and as nouns. A 'compliment' is an appreciative or respectful tribute paid to someone. A 'complement' is basically a person or thing which completes something. We speak of a 'full complement' of staff or crew. The word is most commonly used of a person or thing which nicely balances or partners another. Thus in grammatical usage the word 'policeman' in the sentence 'My husband is a policeman' balances the subject 'My husband' and is therefore its 'complement'. 'Compliment' is the more frequently misused of the two words. We find new cutlery advertised as the 'perfect compliment' to a new china dinner service, where the word should be 'complement'. The parallel adjective 'complimentary' is similarly misused.

***comprise / consist***

The point to remember about this tricky couple of verbs is that 'consist' is intransitive. It cannot be followed by an object. It is most commonly followed by 'of': 'The company consisted of old-age pensioners.' (The rarer use of the words 'consist in' is exemplified in 'His filial devotion consists in visiting his mother once a year.') But to 'comprise' is a transitive verb. It takes an object ('The company comprised people of all ages'). What it amounts to is that 'to consist of' means 'to comprise'. To 'comprise', meaning to be made up of ('The choir comprised fifteen men and fifteen women'), covers the whole number (unlike the verb 'include').

> He will accept a company cheque from anywhere in the world as long as the shareholders are comprised principally of individuals from whom personal donations can be solicited.

This *Times* leader misuses the verb. (One should not say 'The members are comprised of' instead of 'comprise'.) Moreover, 'principally' cancels out the proper meaning of 'comprise', which covers the whole, not a part. The sentence should read: 'as long as the shareholders are composed principally of individuals'.

***connote / denote***

Both words are used in defining what words or signs mean. The word 'connote' is the more comprehensive of the two. If someone says 'She is a real lady' the expression 'real lady' implies notions of charm and grace associated with the aristocracy. The 'connotation' of the word includes all such implications. What a word 'denotes' is exactly what it literally stands for. But, used of signs other than words, 'denote' now has wider reference ('The fellow's sly smile may denote a degree of untrustworthiness').

***continually / continuously***

A matter that continually affects me does so repeatedly, but not unbrokenly. I might complain if my work were 'continually' interrupted by telephone calls. What happens 'continuously' is not something that recurs but something that is ceaseless ('She went to bed and slept continuously for ten hours').

***converse / inverse***

The word 'converse' is used of something which is the opposite of something already referred to. 'She is certainly not helping to support her mother; indeed the converse is probably the case.' This would mean that far from supporting her mother, it is likely that her mother is supporting her. In such a case, 'The converse is true' is the equivalent of 'The boot is on the other leg.' But the word 'converse' does not always bring in the notion of contradiction. It may introduce a reversal rather than a contradiction. 'She is of great assistance to her mother, and of course the converse is true' would mean that just as she helps her mother, so too her mother helps her. The word 'inverse' overlaps in meaning with 'converse' but is primarily used of what is turned upside down or reversed in order.

We hear winners listed in 'inverse order' when a judge announces the results of a race, reserving the name of the first to the last.

***council / counsel***

A 'council' is a body of people gathered together for consultation or administration. The members of the council ('councillors') are appointed or elected to direct the affairs of a given society or a given area of the country. 'Counsel' is advice or guidance, and hence the word is used too for the barrister who undertakes to advise clients and to pursue legal cases for them. Outside the legal profession a person giving advice is called a 'counsellor'. The verb to 'counsel', meaning to give advice or comfort, is used in the fields of psychology and social work. The expression 'to keep one's own counsel' means to be noticeably reticent over matters public or private when perhaps some opinion or revelation is being sought.

***defective / deficient***

What is 'defective' has a defect, and a 'defect' is a fault, a shortcoming. The word is much used of objects or materials that have not been manufactured without flaws, and of flawed ideas and schemes. A thing that is 'deficient' lacks something necessary to its completeness. It has an inadequacy. A socially clumsy person may be said to be 'deficient' in tact.

***definite / definitive***

Something which is clearly defined is said to be 'definite'. The word implies sureness and precision. 'We must have a definite answer' is a call for an end to vagueness or prevarication. The words 'a' and 'an' are called 'indefinite' articles because, unlike the 'definite' article 'the', they do not point to a specific subject. The word 'definitive' means conclusive and final. It is used of statements which put an end to doubt or controversy.

***defuse / diffuse***

To 'defuse' a situation is to remove the tension from it. The connection is obvious between this general meaning and the particular process of making a bomb safe by removing its 'fuse'. To 'diffuse' is to pour out, to scatter or to spread out in all directions. Thus the adjective 'diffuse' is used of ideas that lack clear focus and conciseness. The word 'diffuser' has a technical usage in relation to scattering light to reduce glare, and to dispersing sound waves in a radio.

***delusion / illusion***

A 'delusion' is a mistaken notion or belief ('She suffered from the delusion that her family were all against her'). An 'illusion' is a false or misleading appearance or perception ('Whether he had actually seen a ghost or whether what he saw was an illusion he could never decide').

***dependant / dependent***

A 'dependant' is someone who depends for their living on another. 'Dependant' is thus a noun. 'Dependent' is the matching adjective. A 'dependant' is 'dependent' on someone else for a living.

> Year-round travel insurance is provided without an additional cost to any cardholder, his or her spouse and dependant children.

This should read: 'dependent children'. Correspondingly we find an advertisement for 'Eurocamp Independant Holidays', which should be 'Independent Holidays'. Confusingly, the noun 'dependant' does not have a matching noun 'independant'. So a parliamentary candidate is called an 'Independent' and the newspaper is called '*The Independent*'.

***deprecate / depreciate***

To 'deprecate' something is to express earnest disapproval of it ('We strongly deprecated the movement's decision to resort to a public demonstration'). To 'depreciate' is to belittle or to reduce the value of something by criticism or ridicule. The verb is also used intransitively. As to 'appreciate' is to rise in value, so to 'depreciate' is to fall in value.

***discreet / discrete***

'Discreet' means careful and tactful in behaviour, and is used especially of being able to be trusted with confidences. The corresponding noun is 'discretion'. The Book of Common Prayer gave us the expression 'years of discretion' as representing the age at which the growing person can begin to exercise sober judgement. 'Discrete' (related by contrast to the word 'concrete') is used of separate parts that cannot be assembled together. It is quite erroneous for advertisers who seek sexual partnerships through the columns of *Private Eye* to propose 'discrete' contacts. Under such arrangements they would never meet.

***disinterested / uninterested***

The word 'disinterested' is more often used incorrectly than correctly. It does not mean 'uninterested'. 'Uninterested' negates 'interested' in the most common use of the word ('I am not interested/uninterested in ball games'). The word 'interest' has a special connotation in the sentence 'Smith is personally interested in the sale of the property', which conveys that Smith has a financial 'interest' in the matter, and may benefit or fail to benefit from the transaction. That is the usage which the word 'disinterested' negates. To be 'disinterested' in any matter is to be in no position either to benefit or to be disadvantaged by whatever transpires. 'Disinterest' is impartiality.

> We're told that growing children need a healthy diet, but how can you put this into practice when you're faced with a disinterested toddler?

Here the word should be 'uninterested'.

***dispense with / dispose of***

Basically, to 'dispense' is to distribute, and a 'dispensation' is an act of distributing. Its connection with the issuing of acts of papal pardoning in the Middle Ages is the root of the modern usage in which to 'dispense' is to exempt from some rule or obligation and therefore to do away with something and to manage without it. To 'dispose' something was basically to arrange it suitably, to settle it. ('My Author and Disposer' Milton's Eve calls Adam in a moment of wifely compliance.) To 'dispose of' a matter was to deal with it finally and thus to get rid of it. But whereas to 'dispense with' implies an attitude of removing what is superfluous or redundant ('After a successful operation for cataract, he was able to dispense with his glasses'), to 'dispose of' carries no such overtones ('He disposed of his country house and bought a town house').

The development in use of the corresponding nouns, 'dispensation' and 'disposition', is noteworthy. Whereas the noun 'disposition' is now chiefly used of a person's temperament or frame of mind (the arrangement of personal idiosyncrasies), the noun 'dispensation' tends to be used of the public system of administration (the ordering of its regulations). In T. S. Eliot's *Journey of the Magi* the three kings, having witnessed the newborn Jesus, return to their kingdoms 'no longer at ease here, in the old dispensation'.

***equable / equitable***

'Equable' means unvarying and uniform. A generally calm and placid person may be described as 'of an equable temperament'. 'Equitable' means fair and just. Where 'equable' relates to the word 'equality', 'equitable' relates to the word 'equity'.

***erupt / irrupt***

To 'erupt' is to break or burst out as a volcano does from time to time. (On the appearance of the Ghost in *Hamlet* Horatio foresees 'some strange eruption to our state'.) To 'irrupt' is suddenly and forcibly to break in, as an invading army might after besieging a stronghold.

***exclude / preclude***

To 'exclude' is the opposite of to 'include'. It is to keep out, to prevent from entering a place, or from taking part in an activity or celebration. The dictionary definition of to 'preclude' is 'to make impossible, especially beforehand'. It is used of disbarments made necessary by other factors ('Smith's parlous state of health precludes him from taking part').

> A consultative paper sent out to members [from Tory headquarters] excludes a Prime Minister Hague restoring the hereditary principle to the Lords.

The reporter used the wrong verb here: 'precludes restoration of the hereditary principle to the Lords by a Prime Minister Hague'.

***exhausting / exhaustive***

The verb to 'exhaust' means to draw off, to drain of resources, and therefore to empty and to weary. The word 'exhausting' is thus generally used to mean tiring, but we speak of 'exhausting' all possibilities in trying to find something lost. The word 'exhaustive' is a favourite word to use of investigations or books which thoroughly and comprehensively finish the task they were intended to deal with ('This book is an exhaustive account of the French Revolution').

***expedient / expeditious***

To 'expedite' is to push quickly forward some action or project, clearing away any obstacles. The word 'expeditious' is used with emphasis on the speed of such action ('At this crisis the demand for more troops called for an expeditious response'). The word 'expedient' is used with emphasis on the appropriateness of the action ('As his former wife remained on the same staff, he found it expedient to seek a new post elsewhere'). The emphasis on convenience produces an implicit contrast with action that is inconvenient but is dictated by principle and propriety. Thus politicians get accused of being motivated by 'expediency' rather than by principle.

***explicit / implicit***

What is 'explicit' is clearly and precisely expressed, leaving no room for doubt ('There was an explicit requirement that employees should wear formal dress'). What is 'implicit' is not directly stated in so many words but implied. The notice 'Thank you for not smoking' in a restaurant is an 'implicit' request that customers should not smoke. That request is 'implicit' in the notice.

***fallacious / fallible***

Something which is 'fallacious' contains a fallacy, an inaccuracy or a deception. The forbidden apple which Adam and Eve eat in Milton's *Paradise Lost* is described as the 'fallacious' fruit. To say something which is 'fallacious' is not necessarily to lie, because the speaker may not know that what is said is false; 'falsehood' is assumed to be dishonest, where a 'fallacy' may merely be a mistake. The word 'fallible' means liable to be deceived or to be erroneous. In Shakespeare's *Measure for Measure* the Duke advises Claudio, who faces a death-sentence, not to comfort himself 'with hopes that are fallible'.

### *fatal / fateful*

A 'fatal' event or decision is one which leads to disastrous consequences. A 'fatal' accident or a 'fatal' disease is one which causes death. (Lady Macbeth tells how the hoarse raven 'croaks the fatal entrance of Duncan' into the castle where he will be murdered.) The word 'fateful' is used of events or decisions which have momentous consequences, but which are not necessarily unfortunate. A person's decision to drive to a certain meeting might be described as 'fateful' if an accident en route proved 'fatal'. But similarly a woman's decision to seek work in a given firm might be described as 'fateful' if she there met her future husband.

### *febrile / frenetic*

It is helpful to remember how these two words are related to others. 'Febrile' is basically a medical term, the adjective formed from 'fever'. Thus it means 'feverish' and appropriately describes a person in a state of restlessness and discomposure. The word 'frenetic' is related to the words 'frantic' and 'frenzy'. So its associations are with madness rather than with physical illness. It will be seen that while 'febrile' implies a rather enfeebled restlessness, 'frenetic' implies frantic activity.

### *ferment / foment*

To 'ferment' is to cause fermentation and therefore to stir something up into an agitated condition. The word is often used of stirring up trouble. An agitator may be said to 'ferment' rebellion. To 'foment' is originally to bathe in warm healing water, hence to cherish, to encourage or to promote. Since it is sometimes used of promoting or encouraging the growth or development of what may be undesirable ('The failure of his application fomented his frustration') it may come near to 'ferment' in meaning.

### *fewer / less*

'Fewer' refers to number, whereas 'less' refers to bulk or amount. One rarely finds 'fewer' used where the word should be 'less'. But the converse error is still very common.

> If public transport were better, there would be far less people going about in cars.

There the word should be 'fewer'. 'Less people' would be people of smaller stature. It would be correct to say 'If public transport were better, there would be far less use of cars.'

> However, it is sad, to many of us who remember it, that the passing of time has caused less and less converted lifeboats and pontoons to be seen being boated by those less concerned with what their boat looked like, but more where they could take it.

The first two uses of 'less' are wrong: 'the passing of time has caused fewer and fewer converted lifeboats to be seen'.

### *fictional / fictitious*

Both words derive from the word 'fiction', used to classify imaginative works of literature, more especially in prose. Thus Jane Eyre is a 'fictional' character, not a person from real life. The expression 'fact or fiction' highlights the contrast between what is true and what is invented. So the word 'fictitious' carries the connotation not only of the invented, but also of the false as opposed to the genuine ('He carried on a correspondence with his mistress from a fictitious address').

### *flammable / inflammable*

These two words both mean susceptible to being inflamed or easily set on fire. Confusion can arise because in so many cases adding the prefix 'in-' to an adjective turns it into a negative. Thus the positive 'soluble' becomes the negative 'insoluble'. But the prefix 'in-' serves the same positive purpose in 'inflame' as it does in 'inspire'.

### *flaunt / flout*

These two words are confused in spite of the fact that their meanings are totally unrelated. To 'flaunt' something is to display it proudly and ostentatiously. Thus a rich man may be said to 'flaunt' his wealth, a glamorous actress may be said to 'flaunt' her charms. To 'flout' is to reject scornfully and arrogantly some authority, some regulation, or some code which one ought officially to accept and observe ('He flouted the firm's rules by smoking in the office').

### *gourmand / gourmet*

Both words refer to a person who is devoted to eating and drinking. But whereas 'gourmand' is used pejoratively of a gluttonous person who may shovel food away without much discrimination, 'gourmet' is used of a connoisseur with a cultivated and sophisticated taste for food and wine.

***heritage / inheritance***

Both words have to do with what is inherited. A man's 'inheritance' is what is handed on to him from his ancestors in the way of money, possessions, and such things as titles or family prerogatives. The word 'heritage' is used more generally for what is handed down from generation to generation, not only in the way of personal possessions, but also in the way of institutions and public properties, culture and knowledge.

***honorary / honourable***

Both words are obviously connected with the word 'honour'. What is 'honourable' is worthy of honour. What is 'honorary' is bestowed as an honour. Thus a university degree awarded as an honour and not as the result of any examination is an 'honorary' degree, and a post held without payment is an 'honorary' post. Confusion can arise because the abbreviation 'hon.' is widely used in more than one context. In parliamentary reference to the 'Hon.' Member for Bedford the abbreviation stands for 'honourable', whereas in a society's reference to the 'hon.' secretary the abbreviation stands for 'honorary'.

***imaginary / imaginative***

What is 'imaginary' is a product of the imagination in the sense that it has no real existence ('He is a hypochondriac whose ailments are largely imaginary'). What is 'imaginative' is the product of the imagination working creatively in the arts or in original thinking.

***immanent / imminent***

The word 'immanent' is used in philosophy to define what dwells or operates within. Thus God has been sometimes defined as 'immanent' within the universe rather than overlooking it. The word 'imminent' basically refers to something that overhangs as a lofty mountain may overhang a valley. From this sense of 'overhanging' it derives its most common meaning today of something immediately, and often threateningly, impending ('Little did we know that the explosion was imminent').

***immunity / impunity***

There is a slight overlap of meaning between these two words. The word 'immunity' is used medically of the body's ability to resist disease and more generally of freedom from legal obligations and from official restraints ('In return for agreeing to assist the authorities, the former criminal was granted immunity from prosecution'). 'Impunity' is exemption from charge or penalty and thus now describes a state of safety ('He ridiculed the authorities with impunity').

***imply / infer***

To 'imply' something is to convey it by what is said, perhaps indirectly. If a father informs his unemployed son that there is work to be had in a nearby firm, he is probably 'implying' that the son should go and apply for a job there. In fact the word 'imply' is rarely misused. What goes wrong generally is that the word 'infer' is used as though it meant the same as 'imply'. 'By every thing she said, she inferred that I was lazy' should be: 'she implied that I was lazy'. In modern usage to 'infer' is not to convey a message but to deduce one ('From his sickly appearance and lack of appetite I inferred that he was ill').

***inapt / inept***

A thing which is 'apt' is highly suitable to its purpose. Thus what is 'inapt' is inappropriate. The word is also used to mean unskilful, that is, lacking in aptitude. 'Inept' is originally the same word spelt differently but we tend to apply it to a degree of inappropriateness and lack of skill that implies clumsiness or stupidity ('It was inapt of him to miss his mother's funeral, and inept to imagine that no one would notice').

***informant / informer***

The history of these two words is curious. In present-day usage, an 'informant' is simply a person who conveys information, while an 'informer' is someone who lays information against another, bringing to light offences against the law. In the eighteenth century, however, the word 'informant' was used in this latter sense, and the word 'informer' could be used to mean one who animates and inspires. Thus in Pope we find 'Nature! informer of the human heart'.

### *ingenious / ingenuous*

An 'ingenious' person has skill and inventiveness, and the products of his cleverness are also 'ingenious'. The word 'ingenuous' once meant straightforward and candid but now indicates (especially when qualified as 'over-ingenuous') not mere lack of duplicity but rather over-simplicity, naivety and even gullibility.

### *junction / juncture*

A 'junction' is the point at which two things join, especially used of the place where a road or a railway line divides into two. The word 'juncture' is now generally used for a point in time at which the convergence of events creates a significant moment, perhaps a moment of crisis ('In the autumn he lost his job, and at this juncture his wife chose to leave him').

### *loathe / loath (loth)*

To be 'loath' or 'loth' to do something is to be reluctant, unwilling to do it ('I was loth to part with my collection of stamps'). The verb to 'loathe' means to detest. Because the spelling 'loath', for reluctant, is now more often used than the spelling 'loth', confusion with the verb 'loathe' occurs.

### *luxuriant / luxurious*

Both words are related to the word 'luxury'. The word 'luxuriant' is used to describe things (such as houses, artefacts, gardens, works of art) that are richly ornate and profusely decorative. The word 'luxurious' overlaps in meaning, but conveys more the sense of what indulges human appetite for ease and comfort, and for all that delights the senses ('In retirement he was able to live a luxurious life in luxuriant surroundings').

### *militate / mitigate*

Here the similarity in sound between the two verbs causes confusion in spite of the totally different meanings they convey. To 'militate' is to combat or oppose ('Our genteel upbringing militated against the call to go and work down the mines'). In fact the word is rarely misused. The verb to 'mitigate' means to soften or soothe ('His daughter's decision to come and live with him somewhat mitigated his grief at the loss of his wife'), but it gets used mistakenly in the place of 'militate'.

***momentary / momentous***

A moment is a short space of time and the word 'momentary' means brief, lasting for only a moment. The word 'moment' has another use in expressions such as 'a matter of great moment'. It is this use that is reflected in the word 'momentous', which means 'of great moment' or very important.

***nationalize / naturalize***

A business or an organization is 'nationalized' when it is taken under public ownership and becomes the property of the state. The word is not used of human beings who change their nationality. If someone of foreign birth seeks to become a citizen of their adopted country, the official process is known as becoming 'naturalized'.

***naught / nought***

Strictly speaking, where 'aught' means anything, 'naught' means nothing ('I tell you naught for your comfort' says the visionary voice to King Alfred in Chesterton's *Ballad of the White Horse*). 'Nought' is the digit which, oddly enough, we pronounce 'Oh' when making a telephone call. The spelling 'nought' is now used as a variant of 'naught'.

***obsolete / obsolescent***

Increasingly 'obsolescent' is being used where the word should be 'obsolete'. What is 'obsolete' is out of date, no longer in use or no longer fashionable. What is 'obsolescent' is becoming obsolete, gradually perhaps going out of date and ceasing to be of use.

***official / officious***

The adjective 'official' relates to an office and in particular to what issues authoritatively from it ('As an MP's secretary, she has an official permit to enter the House'). One may be called to attend an 'official' meeting or invited to an 'official' dinner. The word 'officious' has a pejorative connotation. It is applied to self-important people who are unnecessarily free with attention or advice.

***ostensible / ostentatious***

Here are two more related adjectives, like 'official' and 'officious', with vastly different overtones. What is 'ostensible' is apparent, plain to see.

Sometimes the word is used to distinguish what is seemingly apparent on the surface from what lies hidden beneath ('The ostensible purpose of the journey was to visit his aunt, but he had far more sinister motives'). The word 'ostentatious' implies showiness that is pretentiously extravagant ('He never concealed his wealth: indeed he was ostentatious enough to run two Rolls-Royces, each with its own chauffeur').

### *perspicacious / perspicuous*

The word 'perspicacious' (along with the noun 'perspicacity') is related to such words as 'perspective' and used to mean 'clear-sighted', but is now applied only to mental clear-sightedness and means penetrating or sharply perceptive. The word 'perspicuous', related to the word 'conspicuous', means transparently clear, and therefore, applied to people's thought or utterance, lucid and easily understood.

### *practical / practicable*

The word 'practical' often offsets the word 'theoretical' and means related to actual experience and the world of daily action. A 'practical' person will quickly respond to an emergency by doing what common sense would recommend. The word 'practicable' means strictly able to be put into practice, and is therefore used to express a strong recommendation for any plan or scheme that is as yet at the theoretical stage.

### *precipitate / precipitous*

In non-technical usage the verb to 'precipitate' is to bring something about too soon, over-hastily ('The quarrel in public precipitated a breakdown in their relationship'). The adjective 'precipitate' thus means overhasty or rash. The verb also means to hurl down from a height. 'Precipitous' means steep. The connection of both words with the word 'precipice' is what makes for confusion.

### *prerequisite / perquisite*

These two words have nothing in common except a number of identical letters. A 'prerequisite' is something required in advance, often used of conditions required by an employer ('A prerequisite of the appointment was that I should move into the area'). The word 'perquisite' (abbreviated to 'perk') is now used chiefly for benefits from employment additional to the salary, such as a waiter's tips or an executive's company car.

***prescribe / proscribe***

To 'proscribe' is officially to outlaw or prohibit some conduct or person. Words including the syllables 'scribe' or 'script' (from the Latin) are to do with writing. To outlaw a person was to publish his name publicly in writing, to 'proscribe' it. To 'prescribe' is to lay down authoritatively some regulation or, in medicine, some treatment or potion. Thus the doctor 'prescribes' medicaments for us and we take our 'prescription' to the pharmacist. There is a danger of misusing the words as 'diagnose' is now misused:

> I have been prescribed with a variety of medicines.

The word 'with' must go. Just as doctors diagnose illnesses and not patients, so too they prescribe medicines and not patients.

***presumptuous / presumptive***

The word 'presumptuous' is related to that usage of 'presume' which implies that someone is taking more for granted than they have the right to do ('It was highly presumptuous of him to gatecrash that very exclusive party'). The word 'presumptive' is related to the usage of 'presume' which is disinfected of all such overtones, and simply means highly probable. The 'heir presumptive' to the throne is the one who will succeed provided that no stronger claimant comes on the scene. In the United Kingdom if the monarch had a daughter as first-born child, she would be the 'heir presumptive' unless or until a brother was born. The 'heir apparent' is the heir who will definitely succeed, provided that death does not intervene.

***prevaricate / procrastinate***

To 'prevaricate', deriving from a Latin verb meaning to walk crookedly, is to deviate from the proper course and hence to be deceptive or evasive in action or speech. To 'procrastinate' is to postpone action, to put it off to another day. 'Procrastination is the thief of time' said the almost forgotten eighteenth-century poet Edward Young in his *Night Thoughts*.

***principal / principle***

People continue to be tripped up by the similarity of these two words. The adjective 'principal' means first in importance ('The resignation of the Chairman is the principal business of the meeting'). Thus we use the noun 'principal' of the person in charge of an institution. A 'principle' is a fundamental law or a basic proposition from which other deductions follow.

### *prone to / susceptible to*

The word 'prone', basically meaning bending forward or lying prostrate, flat on the face, came to mean having a natural inclination to do something. We stress the words 'to do'. A naughty child might be said to be 'prone' to telling lies. It would be less satisfactory to say that someone is 'prone to attacks of bronchitis'. That is where the word 'susceptible' is better. For where 'prone' means having an inclination to 'do' something, 'susceptible' means having an inclination to be responsive to something. Yet we read:

> My own limitations, of energy, time, or approach, make me always susceptible to behaving badly.

Bad behaviour does not come upon us from outside like the flu germ. It is something we do, not something we suffer: 'My own limitations make me always prone to behaving badly.'

### *recourse / resort*

If you 'resort' to something you turn to it in need, and what you turn to is your 'resort'. Thus Polonius tells Ophelia to lock herself away from Hamlet's 'resort'. The use of the word for a holiday destination was a natural development. Whereas 'resort' is both a noun ('That is our last resort') and a verb ('All else having failed, we had to resort to the use of force'), the word 'recourse' is a noun only. What a person resorts to is in fact his recourse. 'He resorted to force' and 'He had recourse to force' are two ways of saying the same thing.

### *remission / remittance*

Both words derive from the verb 'remit'. 'Remission' means forgiveness (the Bible speaks of the 'remission of sins') or release from some obligation or penalty. It is applied to the reduction of a term of imprisonment ('a remission of three years from the life sentence') and to a temporary period of abatement from a life-threatening disease. A different kind of obligation is finished off by a 'remittance', a payment that settles a debt.

***reversal / reversion***

'Reversal' means the act of reversing, physically going back on one's tracks, or coming up against something which stops one in one's desired progress ('The failure of her second novel to sell brought a reversal of all her ambitions'). The word 'reversion' is used of the return to an earlier condition or attitude ('In his latest poems we detect a reversion to the style of his earliest work'). It is also used legally of the part of an estate which is restored to the original testator or his heirs after the death of some temporary grantee.

***salubrious / salutary***

Both words are concerned with a healthy effect. While 'salubrious', meaning conducive to health, is used chiefly of spas and other resorts where climate may benefit health, 'salutary' is used much more widely of whatever promotes health or well-being. In its looser use, it means little more than 'beneficial' ('It might be salutary at this stage of the meeting to pause for reflection').

***sensibility / sensitivity***

The word 'sensible' most often means showing good judgement, but is also used more technically to mean capable of being sensed or perceived. It is from the latter connotation that the word 'sensibility' derives its meaning: the capacity to respond to emotional needs or aesthetic qualities. An art critic needs to be a person of cultivated 'sensibility'. The word 'sensitivity' is used generally of ready personal responsiveness. It is usually a tribute to call a person 'sensitive', but there is another usage where the word implies over-ready responsiveness which is 'touchy', the responsiveness of someone who is quick to take offence.

***sensual / sensuous***

Both words are concerned with the appeal to the senses or the responsiveness of the senses to what is physically attractive, but 'sensual' is pejorative; it is used of excessive indulgence in what appeals to the physical appetites. The word 'sensuous' is used of what properly appeals to the senses by its beauty and richness, especially perhaps in the aesthetic sphere, and of the sensitive human response to it. One might speak of the rich 'sensuous' appeal of a poet such as Keats or a composer such as Wagner.

### *stimulant / stimulus*

Anything that stimulates, whether physically or mentally, is a 'stimulus' in that it encourages or goads to action or to decision. But the word 'stimulant' is mostly restricted to use for drugs or other consumables, such as alcohol, coffee or tea, which at least temporarily revitalize the body or raise the spirits.

### *substantial / substantive*

These two words, both obviously connected with the word 'substance', overlap somewhat in meaning, but the overlap scarcely justifies the recent tendency to use only 'substantive' where 'substantial' would be equally or more appropriate. The word 'substantive' was the technical name of a noun. As an adjective it stresses therefore the independent and essential basis of whatever is referred to. The word 'substantial' has been more used to refer to the magnitude, the importance, the solidity of a thing. It also distinguishes what is actual and soundly based ('Substantial evidence was produced against him').

### *testament / testimony*

A 'testament' is a will. Because it testifies to the intentions of the testator, being indeed the expression of his 'will', the word has come to be used more generally of what can stand as a proof or attestation. It is at this point that the meaning of 'testament' overlaps with the meaning of 'testimony', which is most commonly used in law for the evidence of witnesses. It has become evident that people are using 'testament' where once they would have been inclined to use 'testimony':

> The tyre gouges on the roundabout bore testament to the frequency of accidents.

This is a case in point. The gouges really bear 'testimony', that is, witness to a fact as in a court of law.

### *titillate / titivate*

'Titillate' derives from a Latin verb meaning to 'tickle'. Hence its present meaning, to excite pleasure by some delightful gratification. It is used of comparatively trivial delights. One would not speak of being 'titillated' by a Beethoven symphony; one might of being 'titillated' by a delicious trifle or a nice new hat. 'Titivate' is a nineteenth-century word developed out of 'tidivate', that is to make tidy. It is used of the final touches to hair, to make-up or to dress, made just before appearing in company.

### *tortuous / torturous*

I have just heard on the radio a reference to the experience of a man who was kidnapped. There was emphasis on what he endured in 'several tortuous months' of imprisonment. Clearly the person who wrote the report thought that the word 'tortuous' was connected with the word 'torture'. But it isn't. The word the newswriter wanted was 'torturous', the adjective derived from 'torture'. The word 'tortuous' derives from the word 'tort'. It refers to what is twisted, winding or crooked, the reverse of direct and straightforward. Thus one might speak of someone having to make a 'tortuous' journey by some difficult and circuitous route. Coincidentally I read in the newspaper that it was inevitable that 'Danny Wilson's torturous season in charge of Sheffield Wednesday would take another debilitating twist.' Plainly the word here should be 'tortuous'.

### *tragedy / travesty*

A 'travesty' is an unworthy mockery of something, farcical in its extravagance. Yet we read this about a shrine to D. H. Lawrence in New Mexico, which is suffering from neglect.

> It's going to be lost to future generations, and that will be a travesty.

This appears to be one of those blunders which result from confusing two words that are similar in sound. Presumably the writer meant: 'and that will be a tragedy'.

### *trustful / trustworthy*

It seems surprising that anyone could confuse these words. Adjectives that end in '-ful', such as 'truthful' and 'fearful', convey the meaning 'full of truth' and 'full of fear'. Just so 'trustful' means 'full of trust'. By contrast, adjectives which end in '-worthy', such as 'praiseworthy' and 'blameworthy', mean 'deserving of praise' and 'deserving of blame'. Nevertheless, in a BBC Radio 4 discussion about the quality of treatment provided by the Health Service, we hear an educated voice declaring:

> I, as a patient, want to feel absolutely trustworthy about any one who attends to me.

She means that she wants to be able to be 'trustful', and she wants those who attend to her to be 'absolutely trustworthy'.

CHAPTER 3

# Words at Work

## COMBINING WORD WITH WORD

### Preserving Consistency

The 'right word' does not exist in isolation. What may seem to be the right word in the first half of the sentence may have to be questioned when we see what follows it. The exact combining of words is what guarantees clarity and precision. It is no use getting what seems to be the right word if you then attach to it something that is not precisely appropriate.

> Delay, even for a month, could be too late.

The sentence is a case in point. Delay can make some action or event 'too late'. But the delay in itself cannot be too late. It is whatever is delayed by delay that may be 'too late'. The delay is 'too long'. Similarly the sound beginning of the following sentence is thoroughly spoiled by the words at the end:

> It might be damaging to Mr Clinton to provoke a crisis which he might then lose.

When a 'crisis' arrives for a statesman, there may be grave dangers, whether political or physical. The person who faces a crisis may 'survive' it successfully or go under. But a 'crisis' is not a kind of competitive event which one might either 'win' or 'lose'. This straightforward collision of meanings between the subject of the sentence and what follows it is surprisingly common. Here is a sentence from a piece about the building of new railways in the nineteenth century.

> Parliamentary powers were passed in 1866.

'Powers' were not 'passed'. The writer means either that 'powers were taken' to do this or that, or that 'legislation was passed'.

It is perhaps when we are being conversational in our style that it is easiest to lose exact consistency of meaning.

> There are a few simple tips that if used with care should help your little problem quite nicely.

A 'tip', when it is not a gratuity given to a waiter or waitress, is a useful piece of advice. We do not, however, speak of 'using' such pieces of advice, but of 'following' them. And the desirable thing is not to 'help' a problem, but to solve it or get rid of it. Since the tone of the whole is conversational, we need not quibble about 'quite nicely', though it is not the most precise expression for the meaning required. We should correct to: 'There are a few simple tips that, if carefully followed, will help you in your little difficulty.' And if one is seeking a gem of thoughtlessness in this connection perhaps the following will do:

> Even today weather forecasting is difficult to predict.

That is the equivalent of saying 'Even today weather forecasting is difficult to forecast.' Nobody could possibly be interested in having forecasting predicted instead of the weather.

Simple, familiar words that are frequently on our lips may make an ill-assorted anarchic concoction if they are allowed to slide out unchecked.

> There is a clear funding gap which, if not resolved, will stunt future development of small businesses in London.

The way to deal with a 'gap' is to bridge it, not to 'resolve' it. And how can a 'gap', whether 'resolved' or not, 'stunt' future development of small businesses? A better sentence would be: 'There is a shortage of cash which, if not made up, will impede future development of small businesses in London.'

The word 'gap' has a metaphorical element here. And where metaphors are used, it is crucial not to mix them too glaringly.

> Throughout Central Europe the loss of monopoly on power reduced overnight the individual communist parties to an insignificant fraction in a blossoming political landscape.

The good writer would never speak of a 'fraction' in a 'blossoming landscape', any more than he would speak of a bunch of lilies in a quadratic equation.

Utterance at the political level too readily overstretches the meaning of words to the point where connotation collides with connotation.

> One of the most basic elements of US concern for any freed hostage is his or her privacy. Yesterday Mr Ronnegut violated that policy.

To begin with, a 'concern' is not a 'policy'. Secondly, a 'policy' is not something that can be 'violated'. A 'principle' might be 'violated' and a 'policy' might be 'abandoned'. Then again, the use of the words 'basic elements' is unnecessary. We may write: 'One of the basic US concerns for any freed hostage is his or her privacy. Yesterday Mr Ronnegut ignored that concern.'

## Preserving Coherence

The kind of verbal inconsistency we are investigating can lead to partial or total loss of coherence. Indeed it is possible to cancel out the meaning of a word by careless choice of a succeeding word or words. For instance, something which is 'inescapable' obviously cannot be avoided. It may be said that death is an 'inescapable' consequence of swallowing cyanide. Writing of a natural disaster, a journalist says:

> The inescapable conclusion is probably that most of the missing are dead.

Here the force of the word 'inescapable' is destroyed by the succeeding word 'probably'. Clearly, if the conclusion is a matter of probability only, then it is not 'inescapable'. In any case, the writer has sufficiently hedged his bets by use of the word 'most'. One of the two words should go, either 'inescapable' or 'probably'.

It is perhaps easiest to lose coherence when sentences are clogged with words. Nevertheless economy with words can sometimes have the same effect. Here is a sentence from an article on the nocturnal threat to cattle farms in Africa from hyenas.

> Often only a part of the victim was eaten and when found next morning had to be shot.

The sentence tells us that part of the animal was eaten, found next morning, and shot. But it was not the part that was eaten that was shot. It was the remaining uneaten part. Economy with words is the trouble here. What is needed is: 'Often only a part of the victim was eaten, and when the animal was found next morning it had to be shot.'

A similar miserliness with words leads to trouble in the following sentence. It is part of a plea for keeping sewage and other contamination away from our lakes.

> If we don't, we may have to forgo our favourite lakeside walks with kingfishers, dragonflies and water lilies.

We may take our country walks with our friend or with our dog, but we don't take them with kingfishers and water lilies. Some words must be inserted: 'our favourite lakeside walks and the glimpses of kingfishers, dragonflies and water lilies'. That is the kind of error produced by over-hasty writing. Journalists often work under pressure and their prose sometimes bears the mark of hasty composition. In the attempt to be concise and not to waste words they may transfer on to paper the freedoms which are proper only to conversation.

> She set about a rigorous training programme culminating in a 20-mile sponsored canoe from Lancaster to Preston.

This will not do in print. A training programme cannot culminate in a canoe. Nor, strictly speaking, is the canoe 'sponsored'. It was the ride in the canoe that was twenty miles long and was sponsored. That is a fairly crude example of the effects of over-compression. At a subtler level the error is not so easy to spot.

> Shareholders have angrily denounced the company's speedy receivership over the weekend.

The word 'receivership' means 'the condition of being administered by a receiver'. This is not in itself a condition that can be either speedy or tardy. What the writer means (and what the reader understands in spite of the illogicality) is that: 'Shareholders have angrily denounced the company's speedy recourse to receivership.' It was the decision that was over-hasty in the shareholders' eyes.

The risk of combining words together incoherently is especially strong with over-used words. The more a word is used, the weaker and vaguer its connotation becomes. The word 'problem' was cited in this connection in Chapter 1. Here is a sentence about dealing with antelopes in Kenya:

> Controlling these problems does not come under the heading of sport.

The 'problems' concern the business of 'controlling' antelopes and, in a very crudely conversational sense, the antelopes may 'be' problems. But however one looks at it, the difference is that antelopes have to be 'controlled' and that problems have to be 'solved', and you can no more 'control' a 'problem' than you can 'solve' an 'antelope'.

Another much used word, 'issue', also tends to such vagueness that precision gets lost in its use. Here is an observation on football tactics by a commentator:

> The issue of diving and over-reacting, basically cheating, needs to be quickly eradicated, probably using video technology.

There is more than one 'issue' here. To use the word 'basically' as the equivalent of 'in other words' is characteristic of what is now a general loose treatment of the word. But more serious is the claim that an 'issue' should be 'eradicated'. It is not the 'issue' which the writer really wants to be rid of, but the 'practice' of diving and over-reacting.

## Preserving Congruity in a Sequence

Loss of consistency and coherence occurs in improperly controlled accumulations of items. Track is lost of a crucial word because what follows it wanders away from accurate preservation of its meaning. Here is some publicity material from a major bank:

> This means that our income on retirement is likely to be based on pensions from a number of different sources. Each of these must be tracked down, calculated and taken into account for someone to build up an accurate picture of the kind of retirement they will enjoy.

The writer's first sentence focuses on the 'sources' of pensions. 'Each of these must be tracked down' makes sense, because 'these' means the 'sources' of the pensions. But to continue by saying that 'each of these' must be 'calculated' is totally incongruous. One does not 'calculate' a 'source'. A different subject is required for the verb 'calculate' and what follows. The mistake arises because the writer has used the word 'these' and then forgotten exactly what it refers to. Better avoid it: 'Each source must be tracked down, the pensions calculated and taken into account.'

Just as use of a pronoun such as 'this' or 'these' can bring about a lapse of congruity in word usage, a long parenthesis can produce the same danger.

> The moves towards allowing more of us to take control of our working environment – whether that means working for ourselves from home full-time or working for an employer from home two days a week – are coming true at last.

The long parenthesis causes the writer to forget what the subject of the sentence was. 'Moves' may lead to action. 'Moves towards' something may eventually get there. But 'moves' cannot be said to be 'coming true'. It would be better to get rid of the word 'moves': 'Plans towards allowing more of us to take control of our working environment . . . are being realized at last.'

It should be noted that it is when a sentence gets somewhat clogged with words (as by the introduction of the parenthesis in the sentence above) that the logical sequence from subject ('The moves') through verb ('are coming') to what follows ('true') may be defective.

> His combination of talent, daring, intelligence and dedication amounts to the most impressive sportsman of our time.

Here, for instance, the accumulation of the four words ('talent, daring, intelligence and dedication') clogs progress sufficiently for the sequence from subject ('His combination') through verb ('amounts to') to what follows ('the most impressive sportsman') to be upset. The writer would not have been tempted to write 'His combination amounts to the sportsman', but when divested of the verbal clogging around it, that is the basic construction used. A simple change of verb would correct the error: 'His combination of talent, daring, intelligence and dedication mark him as the most impressive sportsman of our time.'

## Avoiding Just the Wrong Word

If you fasten on just the wrong word, you put consistency and coherence at risk. Consider the following advertisement for insurance in a magazine for people with equestrian interests:

> A unique choice of cover for all the flexibility you need – from family ponies to competition horses.

It is less than exact to convey that the need for satisfactory insurance for a variety of activities or possessions can be summed up as a 'need for flexibility'. But then seemingly to define 'flexibility' as a category of beings ranging from family ponies to competition horses makes matters worse. What should be offered is: 'cover for whatever you need it for, from family ponies to competition horses'.

Where a metaphor is involved it is all too easy to attach the wrong word to it. An image which has lately become popular is that of a 'raft'. A 'raft' is a platform which floats and can usefully carry a load of items carefully arranged together. Hence we hear that the government is producing a 'raft of proposals' on this matter or that. That is a useful expression, if handled properly.

> The government has unveiled a raft of proposals.

Here it is mishandled. The writer has opted for the wrong initial verb, and the imagery breaks down. It might be appropriate to 'launch' a raft, but the picture of someone 'unveiling' a raft will not do.

There are words which can be used in different senses in different contexts. Exploiting double meanings can be a source of humour or, in poetry, of profundity. One might flippantly say 'The baby was delivered at eight o'clock in the morning, at the same time as the newspaper in fact.' There is always a risk for the writer in using any word which has the sort of double usages that are exploited there in the verb 'deliver'. For it is possible to call up the 'wrong' meaning unintentionally.

> A glass of wine and an introductory lecture will precede a special guided tour of the exhibition by gallery staff.

The verb 'precede' means to take place before in time. It also means to go before in movement. The glass of wine and the lecture 'precede' the guided tour in time. But the concept of people walking through the gallery on a guided tour is apt to bring the other meaning of 'precede' to mind, so that one pictures a procession headed by a glass of wine.

Even the shortest words can be used to exploit this kind of ambiguity. The word 'in' is made to do double duty in Dickens's celebrated account of the agitated Miss Bolo in *Pickwick Papers*, who 'went straight home, in a flood of tears and a Sedan chair'.

The writer has to take care not to allow an unintended ambiguity to intrude through lack of watchfulness.

> A summerhouse is a treat. People buy them as a self-indulgent present for their garden.

I assume that what the writer means here is that people give themselves a present by purchasing a summerhouse 'for' the garden ('People buy them for their garden as a self-indulgent present'). But the sentence fails to allow for the divergence in the usage of 'for' in 'He bought a wheelbarrow for the garden' and 'He bought a present for his wife.' By using the word 'present' the writer has unintentionally brought to mind the second usage, which makes it sound as though people buy presents for their gardens.

## Confusion Between Word and Fact

In a variety of ways word may be confused with fact, form with substance.

> The catalogue is packed with everything you need to keep your dog safe while in the car – for example harnesses for all sizes . . .

It may sound pedantic, but it has to be pointed out that the catalogue is not packed with harnesses or with any other bits of apparatus to keep a dog safe. The catalogue is packed only with 'information' about such items, in print, and perhaps in pictures too. There is no escape from including the necessary clarification: 'The catalogue is packed with details of everything you need . . .'

This mistake occurs at many different levels of literacy from the crude to the subtle.

> These walks are written by over twenty different authors.

That is an example of the mistake at a rather crude level. The sentence is from a review of a book giving routes for walks. It is not the walks that are 'written' but accounts of the walks. If the word 'written' is to be kept, then the missing verbal link must be supplied ('Accounts of these walks are written by over twenty different authors'). But of course it may be better to get rid of the verb 'written': 'These walks are described by over twenty different authors.' The mistake occurs quite often in accounts of books or other publications. There is confusion between speaking about the publication as a whole and speaking about the contents contained within it.

> In a survey of 100 wetland Sites of Special Scientific Interest a majority are beginning to suffer from eutrophication.

This is like saying of a history book 'The funeral of King Edward VII takes place in chapter seven.' The wetland sites are not suffering from eutrophication in the survey any more than King Edward VII is interred in the history book. The survey and the developments it reports are two different matters. All that is needed to correct this error is the insertion of a simple parenthetical expression such as 'we learn that' or 'it is revealed that' after the word 'Interest'. But even that need could have been obviated if the writer had not begun the sentence with the word 'In': 'A survey of 100 wetland Sites of Special Scientific Interest reveals that a majority are beginning to suffer from eutrophication.'

It is not only in accounts of books and in official reports that we find this error. The word 'news' is misused in similar fashion on the radio. We hear from the commercial world that a certain rather questionable financial deal, involving huge profits for the fat cats, has just been agreed. Then we are told that 'The Shadow Chancellor has condemned the news.' Clearly it is not the publicization of the facts ('the news') that angered the politician, but the facts recorded. After another such announcement of a possible scandal, the BBC reporter tells us 'The news is part of a continuing investigation' – which it plainly is not. The investigation is one thing, the news of the scandal another thing.

Confusion between statement and fact, between words and what they convey, lies behind many such errors. In the extreme case we read this on the subject of stag-hunting:

> Words such as biodiversity and Agenda 21 Local Plans are the way forward.

No one is likely to defend this as a justifiable verbal short cut. If the writer means that 'biodiversity' should be encouraged, then he should talk about it and not about the 'word'. Clearly to recommend certain 'words' as a 'way forward' is not going to get anyone very far.

## Keeping Connotation Intact

A peculiar form of misusing a single word occurs sometimes when a word is made to do duty in two different ways in the same sentence. The error can turn up in accounts of football matches.

> Wolverhampton's victory thrilled him, for it was his native city.

The victory was scored by a team of footballers. 'Wolverhampton', meaning that team, cannot in the same sentence mean the place. It is like saying 'Wolverhampton is a magnificent team with a fine town hall in the middle.' There is no escape from repeating the word: 'Wolverhampton's victory thrilled him, for Wolverhampton was his native city.' The error is not rare in the world of sport.

> Mr Scoular travelled to England every week to watch Liverpool, where he was a season-ticket holder.

The word 'where' gives the word 'Liverpool' a double usage which it cannot have. For the place 'where' Mr Scoular was a ticket-holder was not the same thing as the band of players he came to watch. 'Mr Scoular, a season-ticket holder, travelled to England every week to watch Liverpool.'

The same error can occur in speaking about the past. A confusion arises between the record and the reality.

> Even this building has a most fascinating history which is well worth reading.

The 'history' of what the building has been through is one thing and what you can read is another thing. It would be correct, but rather awkward to say: 'Even this building has a most fascinating history, which is well worth reading about.' Perhaps it should rather be: 'which is well worth knowing'. Not very different in category is the slip in the following recommendation for certain wines.

> Currently the range consists of three wines . . . , each of which has a recipe on the back that you can peel off and keep.

We may overlook the fact that it is the bottle and not the 'wine' which has a recipe 'on the back'. This, of course, represents a shift in meaning of the word 'wine'. More interesting is the shift in meaning of the word 'recipe'. First it is a real 'recipe' with advice about use of the wine. But a moment later it has become a piece of paper that you can 'peel off' the bottle. 'Currently the range consists of three wines . . . , and each bottle has a recipe on the back label which you can peel off and keep.'

These transitions in meaning, however, are less stark than the following:

> She immediately passes the information on to the social services, who leave at once to find the boy.

Now it may be argued that the person who received the information did indeed leave at once. But 'the social services' to whom the communication is sent is surely an organization with a substantial staff. They do not all 'leave at once'. If 'who' is to be kept, then 'leave' must be changed: 'who send someone at once to find the boy'.

## PERSONAL AND IMPERSONAL

A peculiar kind of inappropriateness can be found when words and images that should be personal in their connotation are used in contexts where the impersonal is required. We use of living creatures words and expressions inappropriate if applied to inanimate or abstract objects. We must not be too solemnly pedantic about this. Poets often rely upon fanciful applications of the personal idiom to the impersonal world. Shakespeare tells the winter wind that it is 'not so unkind/As man's ingratitude'. The poet Thomas Nashe tells how, in spring, 'the daisies kiss our feet', and Wordsworth declares that 'Earth fills her lap with pleasures of her own.' We do not protest that the wind can be neither kind nor unkind, that daisies have no mouths to kiss with, and that the earth lacks the kind of build which would grant it a lap.

Can 'plain English' prose, utilized for day-to-day communication, allow such liberties? There are indeed contexts in which the mixture causes us to smile rather than to criticize. We indulge weather forecasters as they personalize aspects of the climate. When the forecaster tells us that the 'rain will be reluctant to move away', or when she says that 'temperatures will struggle to get up to 15' we probably feel that she has as much right to this exercise of the 'pathetic fallacy' as the poet has. Our long struggles with weather encourage us to endow it with a will. We tend to nod in approval in mid-winter when the forecaster announces that 'there is a bit too much weather about today'. We may jib at the extension of the linguistic liberties, however, when the forecaster predicts 'more organized bands of rain'.

Temperatures may be allowed to 'struggle' and rain to be 'reluctant', but in colder prose argument is marred when such liberties are taken.

## Personal Verbs Misused

Here is a sentence from an article complaining of the decline of grouse on moorland and the problem of dealing with harriers:

> Other methods – translocation, disturbance prior to breeding, and removal of eggs – have all stumbled on the legal fence.

The metaphor of stumbling at a fence can be appropriately applied to any human experience of frustration. But 'stumbling' is essentially something that living beings do. To attribute the capacity to 'stumble' to a series of 'methods' of tackling a problem will not do. The sentence would more appropriately read: 'Other methods – translocation, disturbance prior to breeding, and removal of eggs – have all been rejected on legal grounds.' There is a comparable misapplication of personal vocabulary in this sentence from my morning paper:

> The Derby has become an occasion racked with self-doubt.

Neither a horse race nor an 'occasion' of any kind can suffer self-doubt. It is the people involved who may suffer so.

Some verbs are so frequently on our lips in a personal context that they slip too readily out when the context is decisively impersonal. A legal spokesman, speaking on BBC Radio 4 of defects in the prosecution service, argues the need for 'a system that can enjoy public confidence'. So accustomed are we to the expression 'enjoy public confidence' that it slips out here irrespectively of the fact that enjoyment is a human experience that no 'system' could feel. There is no advantage in not saying: 'a system that the public can trust'. There is a similar liberty taken in the following:

> A rise in interest rates will exert further pressure on the Bank of England to consider an emergency cut in interest rates.

My dictionary gives the meaning of 'exert' as 'to apply (oneself) vigorously, make a strenuous effort'. The bracketed 'oneself' indicates the propriety of using the verb for personal effort. A 'rise in interest rates' cannot make a strenuous effort. It is a pity to weaken the verb 'exert' by making it the equivalent of the more colourless verb 'put', which would be better used in the sentence we are looking at. The same issue arises with the verb 'achieve' in the following.

> The paper used with gouache is significant; different types achieve different qualities.

Paper is not capable of 'achieving' anything. The meaning is that different types of paper enable the artist to achieve different qualities.

A rather subtler question arises from a statement made on Radio 4:

> Cannabis should be allowed to be prescribed.

This is like saying 'Meat should be allowed to be eaten'. If one says 'It should be legal to prescribe cannabis', one is urging that doctors should be 'allowed' to do something, but this does not empower cannabis in any way. Although we are used to notices saying 'Smoking is not allowed', it is clearly better to avoid the converse instruction 'Cigarettes should be allowed to be smoked' as a variant of 'People may smoke.'

The issue arises again with the verb to 'enable'. It is better reserved for the personal field. 'The grant enabled us to finance the foreign tour' represents the personal usage. 'The whole discussion is about enabling a framework to be in place' represents the far less satisfactory, impersonal usage. Strictly speaking, a framework cannot be 'enabled' to 'be' anything. As material things such as cannabis ought not to be said to be 'allowed' privileges, so material things such as frameworks ought not to be said to be rendered capable of doing anything.

Before leaving this topic, we should note that there is one verb properly reserved for the activity of living beings which has long been used idiomatically of inanimate beings in certain contexts. It is the verb to 'see'. We use the word widely of actual vision and also of registering by the mind ('See what I mean?'). I doubt whether any pedants are shocked when someone writes 'The year 1945 saw the defeat of Germany' even though years are not gifted with either vision or mental understanding. But the acceptance of such an idiom does not justify extending its use into other and very different contexts. Here is an account of some horse trials.

> Twenty-four started over Keith Bristow's track . . . and some tricky related distances saw only five reach the jump-off.

The notion of 'related distances' witnessing or registering this or that number of successful riders strains the idiom too far. The same may be said of the following account of repairs to railway trucks.

> Despite experiments with aluminium doors, a programme of repairs to OBA open wagons sees the original wooden dropside doors replaced in kind.

Again there is no advantage in using the verb to 'see'. No verb other than 'replaced' is required: 'in a programme of repairs to OBA open wagons the original wooden dropside doors are replaced in kind'.

Like other metaphors, the verb to 'see', meaning to register, ought not to be used in a context where metaphors might collide. A newspaper headline about a speech made by an opposition spokesman in Serbia reads 'Dissenting voice seen as proof of split in Belgrade'. Since voices are heard and not seen, this particular use of the verb to 'see' ought to be avoided.

## Personal Terms Used Inappropriately

We suffer advertisers to take certain freedoms in this matter of using a personal vocabulary where it is strictly inapplicable.

> Sensitive skin needs treating with respect and understanding.

The advertiser purposely takes the regularly partnered words, 'respect' and 'understanding', out of their normal psychological milieu. Both respect and understanding are desirable human qualities most often directed towards other human beings. Here the advertiser treats them as proper attitudes to be taken up towards one's skin. The point made is valid enough, but we should observe that the more the two words 'respect' and 'understanding' are thus used, thus 'depersonalized' as it were, the more the resonances of human warmth and appreciation are dissipated.

Of course a writer has a perfect right consciously to mix the personal and the impersonal to comic effect, such as in:

> What self-respecting garden would be without a few bold clumps of Cornflower Blue Ball?

Just as one should be wary of attributing actions and processes proper to human beings to the inanimate, so one must be wary of describing the inanimate in inappropriate personal terms. The attempt to personalize the impersonal, even when consciously made, can easily fail to come off.

> A well-designed playground in a park or school can be a child's paradise, particularly if the ground is forgiving.

Presumably this means: 'particularly if the ground is soft to fall on'. Whatever allowances one makes for metaphorical experiment, the attempt to endow the earth with the capacity to forgive surely misses fire. There is a similar, if less stark, failure in the following sentence:

> Some private companies provide safe, well-organized camps during the holidays, of which Camp Beaumont is probably the most experienced.

The writer was trying not to waste words here, but the camp must not be said to be 'experienced'. Either persons must be involved: 'of which Camp Beaumont is probably in the most experienced hands' or the word 'experienced' must go: 'of which Camp Beaumont is probably the best run'.

We have in English a number of adjectives which can be used either personally or impersonally. The questions 'Are you comfortable in that chair?' and 'Is that a comfortable chair?' amount to the same thing. Either a human being or a chair can be said to be 'comfortable'. An 'innocent' child may be playing an 'innocent' game, and a 'naughty' child may be up to 'naughty' tricks. A 'wicked' man does 'wicked' deeds and a 'brave' man does 'brave deeds'. There is an old illustrated Yorkshire joke about a young hiker climbing over a gate into a field in which there is a bull. A farmer approaches and the young man addresses him: 'I say, farmer, is that bull safe?' The reply is 'A damn sight safer than you are.' This double application of the word 'safe' to the man's situation and to the threat from the animal is perfectly acceptable. We ask ourselves 'Is it safe?' or 'Am I safe?' in many a situation. But we cannot extend this freedom of duplicated reference to any word we choose. A journalist tells us of the discovery of something vitally important to the food industry:

> . . . a plant that provides sugars that can make non-fattening and guilt-free sweets and cakes.

To speak of sweets and cakes as 'guilt-free' is to make an unacceptable transfer of qualification from consumer to commodity. We may feel 'guilty' about eating too many chocolates, but the chocolates do not share the guilt.

What applies to personal descriptions applies too to personal definitions. In a statement about proposed legal reforms a spokesman on the radio committed himself to this:

> We have put into process measures that will be witnesses to our intention to put things right.

Imaginatively to describe, say, objects in a room in which a murder had been committed as 'witnesses' to the crime would be appropriate because of the emotional quality of the situation. But to define vague 'measures' thus is verbally insensitive. It would be better to write: 'We have put into process measures that will prove our intention to put things right.'

We turn to an example of the imprecision now affecting use of the word 'role'. It is not so long ago that respectable publishers spelt it 'rôle', as though it had not yet settled down fully in the English language. Now it is on everyone's lips. Correct usage requires one to limit it in application to human beings. They are the beings who can play 'roles' whether on the stage or in real life. Licence may be allowed to such expressions as 'the role of management today' because 'management' consists of human beings. But this, from a railway magazine, surely abuses the word:

> The managing director and general manager will continue to run the railways' daily role.

One may 'assume' a role, but scarcely 'run' one. And to apply to the machinery of the railway a word which should be rich in associations of theatrical performances by world-famous actors is woefully insensitive. But what we are concerned with is the sad tendency to use the word 'role' as though it meant 'function' and then, as here, as though it meant 'operation'. There is also use of the word as an adjective, especially in the expression 'role model'. Here again, provided that the words refer to some human being, the usage is unobjectionable. But there is the danger that it will be used simply to mean 'example'. That has happened in the following comment on the Politically Correct decision to reprint photographs of the great Victorian railway engineer Isambard Brunel and to blot out the cigar he habitually smoked.

> They think the cigar is an inappropriate role model for the young.

Brunel may be less useful as a 'role model' if he is represented with a cigar in his mouth, but to apply the expression to the cigar will not do.

## Favourite Personal Expressions Misapplied

It is all too easy to slip into use of some much used expression which is distinctly personal in a quite inappropriate impersonal context.

> Either end of the outside edge of the top berth is usually higher than the mattress in the hope of stopping its occupants from falling out when they turn over.

Human beings can take action 'in the hope' of achieving certain results. Indeed someone might design a berth in a certain way, as described here, 'in the hope' of preventing occupants from falling out. But we must not say that the 'berth' takes this or that form 'in the hope' of preventing occupants from falling out. We need mention of a person, directly or indirectly, to justify reference to 'hope'. The direct mention of a person would satisfy the purist: 'The designer made either end of the top berth higher than the mattress in the hope of preventing its occupants from falling out.' The less dogmatic stylist might be satisfied with the implicit reference to a human agent which use of the passive voice involves: 'Either end of the outside edge is usually made higher than the mattress in the hope of preventing its occupants from falling out.' Here one understands that, if something 'is made', a person is involved in the making.

Here is a rather more subtle confusion of the same kind:

> The course, she believes, has made the Bar more accessible to those from less privileged backgrounds, 'and that can only be good news for the depth and diversity of the legal system'.

What the writer means here is: 'that can only serve to improve the depth and diversity of the legal system'. And it is insensitive to equate the expression 'to bring good news to' with the expression 'to benefit' or 'to improve'. Only human beings can be sensitive to 'good news'. Good news cannot excite any response in the depth and diversity of a system. Nor can a system experience 'hope'.

> The railway is pinning its hopes that any outstanding work on *Ditcheat Manor* will be completed in time.

The sensitive reader jibs at the notion of a railway 'pinning its hopes' anywhere, but the attribution of human characteristics to railway systems attracts railway enthusiasts. Perhaps generations brought up on *Thomas the Tank Engine* are imbued with enthusiasm for an anthropomorphic railway.

> That month also saw the demise of *Caerphilly Castle*, which with 1,910,730 miles under its running plate, was withdrawn to be exhibited at the Science Museum, Kensington.

The writer here takes the familiar expression from the personal field ('A promising young writer, he had two successful novels under his belt'), and applies it to the engine, changing 'belt' to 'running plate'. The joke is taken. By contrast we finally cite an instance where flippancy fails.

> Every five years or so, London Fashion Week is supposedly about to meet its Maker.

The words about going to meet one's Maker have been a traditional euphemism for dying. Applied to anything other than human beings, they represent a failed flippancy in rather bad taste.

## READY-MADE USAGES

### Established Combinations

There are established combinations of words which come naturally to mind because they are so apt and useful. To speak of someone having a 'steady hand' or an 'infectious smile' can often enough be appropriate. To describe someone's hardships as a 'crippling burden' and an addition to them as a 'terrible blow' is to reach for very well-used expressions. That a combination of words is stereotyped does not prevent it from being genuinely usable. Some of the most useful and forceful such combinations have a metaphorical content. We speak of someone having received a 'bloody nose' when he has merely been rebuffed. There is only a metaphorical iciness about being in a 'cold sweat', having 'cold feet' or giving someone the 'cold shoulder'. And we move further still from literalness when we say things are 'in apple-pie order' or when we describe a grandiose creation as a 'white elephant'. The origin of the former is disputed, but the latter expression apparently dates back to a Siamese king who presented expensive white elephants to out-of-favour courtiers who couldn't afford to keep them.

But combinations establish themselves which lack spark or freshness and which are done to death by over-use. Habit then prevents the quick speaker or quick writer from using the dominant word in the combination without the other. We hear that someone is 'totally committed' to a project or 'thoroughly tired' of some involvement. Words such as 'totally' and 'thoroughly' (which the grammarians call 'intensifiers') increase the force of what is said, but so vaguely and colourlessly as to be little more than the equivalent of underlining or italicizing the words they accompany. Similarly we say something is 'completely useless' or someone is 'utterly stupid' and the words 'completely' and 'utterly', although they are in themselves meaningful words when properly used, in that context just exercise that function of intensifying the words 'useless' and 'stupid' without any connotative clarity.

When over-use leads to an automatic coupling of such words, then meaningful words are diluted of content, and are turned into colourless intensifiers. 'He's hopelessly inefficient', we say, and the word 'hopelessly' means no more than 'very' or 'thoroughly' would have meant. This does not just apply to adverbs such as 'utterly' and 'thoroughly' and 'hopelessly'. Adjectives too can be so over-used in certain combinations that they are deprived of content, and function only to lay emphasis on the words they are partnered with. When we read that some advertiser is offering us a 'unique opportunity' we understand that the opportunity is supposed to be a considerable one, but the word 'unique' does not convey anything clearer than that. Over-use has emasculated it.

The careful writer will always be on guard against falling back on words which serve only as counters for enhancing the importance of the words they accompany. Not every opportunity is a 'golden opportunity', not every failure a 'dismal failure'. Indeed it is even possible to 'beat a retreat' that is not 'hasty'.

There are, however, a couple of now much-used combinations which deserve attention. I have just heard a comment on a sportsman who surprised by suddenly achieving success after a string of mediocre performances. The commentator said he was 'shaking off his wooden-spoon reputation'. The image of the 'wooden spoon' is in popular use just now. In the early twentieth century the person who achieved the worst result in such organized competitive activities as whist drives would be presented with the 'booby prize'. The use of the word 'booby' for a silly person was clearly well established in the eighteenth century when

Fielding made his Lady Booby the absurd would-be seductress of innocent Joseph Andrews. The image of the 'wooden spoon', now more commonly used, has a curious history. The associations of insensitivity and comparative worthlessness which the word 'wooden' carries date well back. In Shakespeare's *Henry VI Part 1* the Earl of Suffolk writes off the king as 'a wooden thing'. It became the custom at Cambridge University to present a wooden spoon to the student who obtained the lowest marks in the Mathematical Tripos. From this derives the image now popular with journalists.

Imaginative inventiveness is revealed sometimes in adding to the stock of such expressions. Consider the expression 'golden handshake'. The two words 'golden' and 'handshake' are rich in associations which offset each other powerfully in the partnership. 'Golden' endows a concept with preciousness. The word 'handshake', used of a parting, can convey a deep pathos. In Shakespeare's *Troilus and Cressida* there is a fine image of how the parting handshake differs from the welcoming embrace.

> For time is like a fashionable host
> That slightly shakes his parting guest by the hand,
> And with his arms outstretched as he would fly,
> Grasps in the comer.

Put together the image of the golden gift and the limp parting handshake, and there is something which sums up a world of emotional complexities that victims of involuntary and half-voluntary redundancies experience.

The effectiveness of the expression 'golden handshake' has inspired further verbal partnerships. When an employing board is induced to give a new top manager a package of pecuniary benefits, the manager is said to have received a 'golden hello'. Similarly, a person may be appointed to a post in management or in the professions and granted pecuniary benefits (such as removal and resettlement costs) which must be repaid if the appointee stays less than two or three years in the post. The employee is then said to be held in 'golden handcuffs'. Moreover, I see now that a person employed at the top level of a major business who is given a lump sum and required to leave his lucrative post for a much more modest one is described as being brought down to earth in a 'golden parachute'. Journalists seeking an expression to convey an even rarer and more valuable gesture to a departing director have now spoken of a 'platinum handshake'.

## Familiar Metaphorical Expressions

A living language is rich in well-used phrases and expressions that have stood the test of time. We are always ready to fall back on them when they seem to meet our need. Using old biblical images, we may call a hypocrite a 'whited sepulchre' or a favourite child 'the apple of my eye'. We speak of something occurring 'at the drop of a hat' and of someone being 'at the end of their tether'. On occasions we feel that there is no equally expressive alternative to speaking of 'a pig in a poke' or 'a pain in the neck'. We have a stock of long-established metaphorical sayings to hand which we readily resort to. How we should miss the metaphor 'He has hit the nail on the head'! And that use of the verb 'hit' reminds us how fruitful certain basic verbs have been in supplying us with multifarious expressions. When someone gave us the expression 'hit the bottle', we gained a vivid way of saying something for which no crisp and neat alternative could be found. One could only match it in meaning by qualifying the verb to 'drink' ('heavily', 'continually', 'addictively') or by having recourse to terms like 'alcoholic' or 'dipsomaniac'. And how richly different from 'hitting the bottle' is 'hitting the roof', 'hitting the headlines', 'hitting the hay' or 'hitting the jackpot'.

We have other verbs which have supplied such expressions. The verb to 'drive' gives us 'drive a hard bargain', 'drive a coach and horses through', 'drive a point home' and 'drive a nail into someone's coffin'. The word 'run', as verb and noun, gives us 'run the gauntlet', 'run rings round', 'run the show' and 'the run of the house'. The best such metaphorical expressions have a colourfulness and a vividness which seem to make them indispensable. Where should we turn for an alternative when we want to say that someone is 'barking up the wrong tree'? This particular experience is typical in the way it encapsulates human experience. For it derives from hunting with dogs. The dog chases its prey but fails to identify the tree up which the animal has escaped. The saying is one of many associated with dogs, such as 'I have a bone to pick with you.' There the hostile struggle caused by giving one bone to two dogs to share is in the back of the mind. 'His bark is worse than his bite' is an apt description of someone who is superficially threatening or hostile but is unlikely to harm anyone in practice. When we want to criticize someone for playing a double game and trying to protect his own interests by keeping in with two opposing parties, we say 'He's trying to run with the hare and hunt with the hounds.'

Our stock of such sayings is rich in reference to animals. We advise someone who hesitates to grapple decisively with a problem to 'take the bull by the horns'. We talk about having 'backed the wrong horse' when we have made a costly misjudgement. Indeed horses seem to appear frequently in imagery about the limitations of the human lot. When all our best efforts fail to produce the desired effect on someone, we say 'You can take a horse to water, but you cannot make it drink.' We refer to effort wasted on a failing project that is beyond recovery as 'flogging a dead horse'. On the other hand, when someone is seemingly questioning or hesitant as some real benefit is offered, we tell him 'not to look a gift horse in the mouth'.

To understand the full meaning of that last example, we need to know that the expert judges the age of a horse by examining its teeth. Many of the most used traditional expressions of this kind are self-evident in meaning and indeed self-explanatory. We do not yet need to inquire how the expression 'I take off my hat to him' comes to mean I am full of respect for him. But even this seemingly most obvious expression will perhaps be less easy to understand as headgear disappears and fashions of courtesy change. Other sayings were self-evident in meaning at an earlier stage in history but might need to be explained to the youth of tomorrow. The origin of the expression 'to strike while the iron is hot', for acting at exactly the most propitious moment, was more immediately evident to the villager who passed the blacksmith's shop every day than it is to us now. Even the advice 'You must make hay while the sun shines' presupposes a knowledge of the farming year. But these sayings are not so far removed from our daily life as, for instance, the saying 'He has more than one string to his bow', which derives from the fact that the prudent archer would go into battle with a spare string. And when we talk of 'taking someone down a peg', meaning to dislodge them from their pretentiously assumed superiority, we are using imagery derived from the raising and lowering of flags on ships. There is a naval background too behind the expression 'show a leg', meaning 'bestir yourself'. It derives from the morning call to sailors to jump out of their hammocks.

Not all such sayings can be received as feelingly as they once could. When there is talk of some breadwinner 'bringing home the bacon' or of someone who has narrowly escaped disaster 'saving his bacon' we get the full force of it only by recalling how important once was the bacon preserved in the house for the family's food through the winter. Eating is in the background too in that most useful way of expressing doubt about the literal truth of what someone has said: 'You must take it with a pinch of salt.' The implication is that the thing cannot stand on its own without qualification. The degrees of obviousness in such sayings vary greatly. To 'save one's face', meaning to protect one's reputation, may be obvious enough, as is the expression for a rebuff, 'to shut the door in someone's face', but to 'face the music', meaning to face up to the dire consequences of one's mistakes, is not at all obvious. It has been suggested that the basis of the saying was the fact that an officer in the army who was guilty of some offence had to face the drums when the charges were formally put to him. We have no such explanation for the seemingly illogical saying 'He'll laugh on the other side of his face', meaning 'His rejoicing will be turned to disappointment.'

It will be noticed that many traditional sayings testify to the wisdom acquired through experience. They warn us against rash optimism ('One swallow does not make a summer'), against being deceived by outward appearances ('All that glisters is not gold'), against overvaluing seeming promise ('All her swans are geese'), against wanting too much of life ('She thinks she can have her cake and eat it'), and against thinking we can escape the consequences of our own mistakes ('He has made his bed and he must lie on it'). When we shrug our shoulders over some failed enterprise we quote (or misquote) Robert Burns:

> The best laid schemes [not 'plans'] o' mice an' men
> Gang aft a-gley.

So familiar is the quotation that it is only necessary to mention 'mice and men' together to make the point.

It is because of the homely wisdom and the moral guidance enshrined in such sayings that literary figures (and after-dinner speech-makers) can have fun in turning them upside down. G. K. Chesterton insisted that 'If a thing is worth doing, it's worth doing badly.' And, for one person, sad experience turned the comforting saying 'As one door closes, another opens' into 'As one door closes, another shuts.'

## Misuse of Metaphorical Expressions

What concerns us especially here is the proper use of common expressions. Unfortunately, vivid sayings can have their force dissipated by over-use. Moreover, sometimes over-use leads to misuse by people who hear them and fail fully to understand them. Let us consider some such cases.

### *begging the question*

Here is one striking case where a familiar expression is being widely misunderstood. We hear a speaker saying 'That begs the question whether first past the post is a fair electoral system' as though it meant 'That raises the question whether first past the post is a fair electoral system.' But strictly to 'beg the question' in controversy is to assume in argument a conclusion which is in fact at issue in the controversy. From this, by a natural development, derives the accepted practice of using to 'beg the question' to mean to evade the issue. The current habit of treating to 'beg the question' as meaning to 'raise the question' is thus inexcusable.

### *breathing down the neck*

When an athlete is closely pursued in a race so that the nearest rival seems to be challenging most strongly, we say that the challenger is 'breathing down the neck' of the one in front. The expression is useful quite outside the sports field. A candidate in a parliamentary election whose voting figures seem to be threatening his rival's position could be said to be 'breathing down his neck'. Using another metaphor from athletics, the challenger could be said to be close on his rival's heels. It is as well to keep such images clearly sorted in one's mind. On the eve of elections in Northern Ireland we heard a BBC Radio 4 spokesman declare of one candidate 'He's breathing heavily down Mr Trimble's heels.'

### *the end of the road*

Here is a saying which needs to keep its connection with human beings. The image of people 'reaching the end of the road' is a telling one. But what can we make of the following?

> Water gardens are still popular, but I think they have reached the end of the road.

The notion of gardens in progress along a road is absurd. The difference between good writers and bad is that good writers think about what they are saying, word by word, and image by image.

### *entering a minefield*

We find similar liberties taken with the expression 'to enter a minefield'.

> A divorce court faced with assessing the potential pension of a healthy man of 38, and then calculating how much of it his divorcing wife is entitled to, is entering a minefield.

The phrase is used here with a proper sense of its meaning. But one must question whether it is proper to speak of a 'divorce court' as entering a minefield. Surely the phrase is one that should be used only of a person or perhaps a vehicle. The reader will not easily picture the assembled personnel of a court aboard a tank or even a bus. Nevertheless, the above usage is far less unsatisfactory than the following:

> Once you start organizing walking expeditions for other people, you find that your bright idea can turn into a minefield of snarling legislative traps.

Here one is unhappy with the notion of the 'bright idea' turning into a minefield rather than leading one into a minefield. And what is buried in this minefield? Not explosives seemingly, but traps which 'snarl'. Users of motorways know all about the inconvenience of being 'snarled up'. But the threat of being locked into an entanglement simply does not fit with the 'minefield' image of being blown up by hidden explosives.

### *flash in the pan*

The old flintlock had a flashpan to hold the gunpowder. It was hit by a hammer when the trigger of the gun was pulled. The act of firing was a failure if there was a flash in the pan but no other result. Hence the use of this metaphor to describe the promising first display of seeming brilliance by someone who in fact produced nothing afterwards to justify the promise. We read in a piece on flat racing:

> Will they prove to be champions this year? Or just a couple of flashes in a notoriously volatile pan?

Again we see the need to have full understanding of the imagery we use. The word 'volatile' has come to mean changeable. Unless one accepts an insensitive connotation of the word as meaning 'unreliable', it could scarcely be applied to anything so solid as a flashpan.

### *a running sore*

In an article about the possibility of holding referendums on the subject of hunting, we read:

> Anything which did reach the statute book as a result would be a recipe for a 'running sore' with no final resolution.

It may be that the writer thought the quotation marks justified the freedom taken with the image of the running sore. But to speak of a 'recipe' for a sore introduces the smell of the kitchen into the pharmacy, and to suggest by use of the word 'resolution' that a sore should be 'resolved' rather than healed is equally incongruous.

### *stepping into the breach*

The word 'breach', familiar to us in its legal usage ('breach of promise') was used of a gap in fortifications through which a besieging enemy might make an entry. Thus Shakespeare's Henry V calls his men 'Once more unto the breach' outside the walls of Harfleur. The more general use of the phrase now is of taking over from a missing or injured person in an emergency:

> Emma Gibson . . . fell heavily on her feet. The subsequent injury to her knee kept her from riding her impressive heavyweight hunter Shelford Rupert. Fortunately, her friend Sam Fisher, who has not ridden him before, stepped into the breech, and went on to win.

Stepping into the 'breech' is rather a matter of getting dressed than of taking over in an emergency, for 'breech', like the more common form 'breeches', is a word for trousers.

### *striking a chord*

Where a familiar expression has a metaphorical content, it is important not to use it in such a way that incongruous metaphors collide.

> When companies blame the pound they know they are striking a politically sensitive chord on the back of which it is easier to push through measures that would otherwise seem draconian.

To speak of pushing through a measure 'on the back of' some forceful but not necessarily wholly relevant argument is an effective way of making the point desired. But the effect is destroyed, indeed swamped in humour, by the reader's need to picture first the 'striking' of a sensitive 'chord'. The struggle to conceive of something pushed through on the 'back' of this chord dissolves in farce.

***thin end of the wedge***

It is not a good idea to mutilate colourful idiomatic expressions. A 'wedge' is something solid shaped like a letter 'V', which can easily be inserted into a narrow space at the thin end. We speak of 'the thin end of the wedge' to define something seemingly slight which, if pushed further, will turn into something unwanted or threatening. It is one of those expressions which perfectly fits the case where the only alternative would be a clumsy circumlocution. Such expressions are valuable, and should not be lightly exploited.

> This is the end of the wedge for our town and the problem needs to be stamped on.

Unless the wedge is introduced from the thin end, we may point out, the threat that it represents would decrease rather than increase. We can't have the idiomatic wedge divested of its thin end. Moreover, though subversive movements perhaps need to be 'stamped on', problems do not call for that treatment.

***watch like a hawk***

One danger is that such established images as this one may float from the mouth so automatically that the demands of grammar, and even of common sense, are ignored. We readily say that some close observer watches like a hawk, but on BBC Radio 4 an eminent public figure declared:

> Prescribing practice should be watched like a hawk.

To speak of being watched like a hawk seems to put the leg into the wrong boot.

***the winning hand***

Here is another expression which is best kept for reference to human beings. To speak of someone having 'the winning hand' in some testing situation makes a point forcefully. We think of card games. We know that a player may recognize that he has in his hands a selection of cards likely to bring him victory. The image is useful because while the favoured player recognizes his good luck, the other players cannot see what he has in his hand. But we hear this from a speaker explaining why he chose to accept a certain post:

> The attractions of the job had the winning hand.

This is to waste a useful image in a context where half its meaning is lost. It is no more appropriate than to explain one's choice on the menu by saying 'The attractions of the profiterole had the winning hand.'

## Some Other Overdone Expressions

We have looked at a handful of established metaphorical expressions which readily come to mind when we are speaking or writing. It is now worth adding a few usages which have no metaphorical content but which are often misapplied.

***no exception***

An error of misuse which regularly occurs in the press and on the radio is represented by statements ending with the expression 'no exception'. The proper use of these words requires some generalization to be made ('Englishmen like their roast beef on Sundays, and John Smith is no exception'). Too often there is no appropriate generalization to which the expression may be appended.

> Cricket statisticians are oft-times a breed apart and Anandji Dossa is no exception.

Here there is no generalization to which an 'exception' could be made. The statement is that cricket statisticians are 'oft-times' a breed apart. This implies that they are not in all cases a breed apart. Therefore the question of an individual statistician being an 'exception' cannot arise. If the writer had said 'All cricket statisticians are a breed apart' then it would have been reasonable to point out that Dossa was no exception to this generalization. Yet one can find worse misuses of the exception than that one. Here is an advertisement:

> You rely on your horse's ability to respond to your commands. But your horse relies on you too, and your insurance is no exception.

One has to ask 'no exception to what?' The writer seems to assume that a generalization has been propounded on the subject of reliance to which not insuring a horse would be an exception. It is only by a process of imaginative detection that one deduces the existence of this fragile connection in the writer's mind.

### *in the event that*

An increasingly used construction that is generally better avoided is introduced by the expression 'in the event that'. It is a rather clumsy way of avoiding simple constructions.

> In the event of a breakdown or accident in the UK or Europe, help is just a phone call away.

Since firms are not usually shy of using the second person, one wonders why this did not begin 'If you have a breakdown or accident in the UK or Europe'. A similar question arises over this advertisement for an insurance company.

> New Disposal cover to help you with the costs in the event that your horse may lose its life.

In this case the writer is committed to use of the second person, openly referring to 'your' horse. So why not: 'New Disposal cover to help you with your costs, should your horse lose its life'?

### *least of all*

It is odd that this particular expression gets used when its opposite is required.

> Turks and Cypriots will find it difficult to agree about anything on that divided island, least of all about the current anniversary.

What the speaker meant was that the Turks and Cypriots will find it especially difficult to agree about the anniversary. If the opening of the sentence is kept ('Turks and Cypriots will find it difficult to agree') then what follows must be: 'most of all about the current anniversary'. That sounds a little clumsy. The better correction would be: 'Turks and

Cypriots will not readily agree about anything on that divided island, least of all about the current anniversary.'

### *few and far between*

One danger to be avoided is that of falling back on a familiar expression when in fact it merely wastes words.

> The number of vacancies there are is rather few and far between.

That is a comment on the employment situation made on the radio. 'Few and far between' is a telling expression where it is appropriately used, say of habitations in a largely unpopulated area. But here it slips from the speaker's tongue to fill time. In fact 'There are few vacancies' would say all that the speaker said, reducing the number of words from twelve to four, indeed saving two-thirds of them.

### *in terms of*

This expression means 'as represented by' and is properly used in such statements as 'In terms of public influence he counted for nothing.' It is now being used indiscriminately.

> They have no use for civil servants in terms of getting things done.

Here 'in terms of' simply means 'for'.

> In terms of the current controversy I have nothing to add.

Here 'in terms of' simply means 'about'.

CHAPTER 4

# The Make-up of the English Vocabulary

## THE HISTORICAL BACKGROUND

It is time to pause in our exploration of some of the vagaries of current English usage. For one cannot give close attention to choosing the right words without becoming aware of what a remarkably rich vocabulary English has. In order to understand why that is so, and also in order to understand what kind of variety it is that English has, it is necessary to look briefly at the historical development of the language.

### Roman Britain

The Britons inhabiting our country, who faced the first Roman invasions by Julius Caesar in 55 BC and then the actual conquest undertaken by the Emperor Claudius some ten years later, were Celts. The Romanization of the country, of which we still see so many reminders in our roads and in the scattered relics of houses, baths and temples, had its effect on the language spoken here. Many people must have used Latin. Natives who prospered and took advantage of Roman civilization in the form of centrally heated country houses no doubt had to use Latin from time to time. But whereas Latin replaced the Celtic language in Gaul, its use in England seems to have been limited to a small section of the population.

The Romans withdrew, the last troops finally leaving round about AD 410. There followed the invasion of Britain by tribes from Denmark and the Low Countries. These were Teutonic tribes defined by early historians as Jutes, Angles and Saxons. The Anglo-Saxons, as they came to be called, no doubt settled down with the Celts comfortably enough in certain areas. But elsewhere the Celts fiercely resisted the invaders and were gradually driven west to settle in Wales and Cornwall. Roman towns were destroyed and abandoned. A different kind of social order developed. The organization of life in tribes under various leaders gradually produced separate kingdoms, such as Northumbria, Mercia, Essex and Wessex. The relationship between the Anglo-Saxons and the Celts was such that very few words from Celtic were taken over into Anglo-Saxon. (If we want to find Celtic elements in our vocabulary, we must look chiefly to place names.) But, even before the Teutonic invaders came to England, their own languages had already been enriched by words from the language of the conquering Romans. And that enrichment continued after they settled here.

## The Old English Period

We speak of the years between about 450 and 1150 as the Old English period and the years between about 1150 and 1500 as the Middle English period. Old English, or Anglo-Saxon, was an inflected language. That is to say, nouns changed their endings according to their grammatical function in a sentence, as they do in German or Latin. In modern English we distinguish between 'The dog bit the man' and 'The man bit the dog' by word order alone. The biter comes before the verb and the bitten comes after. In inflected languages the distinction is made by a change in the form of the noun in question. Modern English retains just enough of the old inflexions in its pronouns for the principle to be easily understood. The differences in meaning between 'I gave her a book' and 'She gave me a book' are registered by the changes from 'I' to 'me' and from 'her' to 'she' as well as by the word order.

Inflexions, it appears, tend to disappear if the educated classes do not watch over them. We can see it happening in our own day as the distinction between 'who' and 'whom' is gradually being lost. Our dialects in particular tend to play fast and loose with inflexions. In Hampshire I once heard three workmen emptying a lorry of sand, and two of them were chaffing the third. 'Oh George, 'e don't get on with the girls. 'E don't like they, and they don't like 'e.' There we see the distinction between 'he' and 'him' being lost and the distinction between 'they' and 'them'.

The Old English period was a period of cultural development. The conversion of the country to Christianity began with the coming of St Augustine in 597. Some scholars claim that by the time Charlemagne called Alcuin from York to run his Palace School in 782, England had become the intellectual centre of Europe. Be that as it may, the crucial event in determining the future character of the English language was the Norman Conquest in 1066. From that point our country had a ruling class who spoke French. Not unnaturally natives found it useful to learn the language of their superiors. English became the language of the less educated and socially inferior people. It is worth recalling that our words for animals who were looked after by peasants, such as 'ox', 'cow', 'sheep', 'pig' and 'hog', are Anglo-Saxon, while when the animals reach the table to be eaten by the better off, the meat is defined in French as 'beef', 'mutton' and 'pork'.

## The Middle English Period

It was in the thirteenth century that English reasserted itself. Although French was still much used in the upper classes and in business and administrative circles, its preservation became increasingly a matter of social convention, no longer a natural inheritance of the mother tongue. For English was adopted more and more in general use among all classes. By the beginning of the fourteenth century English was understood by all. And here we must note that the English which had been in the care of the uneducated peasantry since the Norman Conquest had been freed from the pedantic oversight of the educated classes. Consequently it had largely lost its inflexions. The English of Chaucer may look strange to us at first sight, but, by comparison with it, the English of the Anglo-Saxons is a foreign language. To master it we are required to sit down and learn how to inflect (or to 'decline') the nouns, adjectives and pronouns, and how to conjugate the verbs. It is salutary for linguistic scholars and protectors of the purity of our language to recall that it made such progess when it was freed for a century or so from the control of the educated.

If the changes in our grammar consequent on the Norman Conquest were so beneficial, the changes in our vocabulary were equally so. We have seen how the Norman-French occupation left us with two words where we might have had only one in the case of 'cow' and 'beef', 'pig' and 'pork'. This enrichment of vocabulary, sometimes by duplication, sometimes as straight additions, came about in many areas. Words poured in, words to do with government (realm, sovereign, adjourn, alliance), words to do with nobility (duchess, countess, marquis, baron, squire), words to do with the Church (religion, theology, sacrament, communion), words to do with law (assize, plea, plaintiff, defendant). So too did words to do with the army and the navy, with food and fashions and social life, with art, medicine and learning. It is true that many native words were lost, but the new borrowings more than compensated, numerically speaking.

French is one of the European languages directly descending from Latin. When the words which came directly into English from Latin in the various periods of our history are added to the words which came indirectly into English from Latin through French, the double ancestry of modern English becomes evident. A basically Teutonic language which shares much of its vocabulary with German has acquired an immense vocabulary from Latin which it shares with French. Whether we ought to rejoice in Harold's defeat at the Battle of Hastings becomes a question hard to answer. Because of it the English language has become the richest in Europe, a language which can act as a bridge between the Teutonic races and the Latins.

## OUR DUAL VOCABULARY

### Homeliness and Sophistication

It is not surprising that so often our words from Latin carry a flavour of sophistication which our Anglo-Saxon vocabulary lacks. It is not surprising that our Anglo-Saxon vocabulary has an earthiness and a homeliness that our Latin vocabulary lacks. It is not surprising that when we want to be very friendly we use our Anglo-Saxon vocabulary, and when we want to be formal and dignified we use our Latin vocabulary. 'Can you call at our house next Tuesday' we say to a close friend. But when the formal occasion arises it's 'Mr and Mrs George Smith request the pleasure of your company at the wedding of their daughter Mary to . . .' The words 'request', 'pleasure', 'company' all derive from French and ultimately have Latin roots.

Certainly there is fascination in the dual vocabulary we enjoy. Philologists have contrasted the warm word 'darling' with the less touching word 'favourite', the homely word 'deep' with the dignified word 'profound', the intimate word 'lonely' with the resonant word 'solitary'. Such duplication does not always produce synonyms. Indeed the tendency was for duplicated terms which began as synonyms to drift apart in meaning. That is what happened with 'darling' and 'favourite'. And this drifting apart often produced subtle differentiations of meaning. Even where the meanings remained for dictionary purposes identical, the duplication allowed of subtle distinctions resonating in the overtones of the words. 'Sorrow' is an Anglo-Saxon word, 'misery' a Latin word. They have drifted apart in their emotive baggage. 'Hearty' and 'cordial' give us synonyms which strike the ear with very different resonance. 'We greeted him heartily' rings different mental bells from 'We saluted him cordially.' No one would suggest that there is much difference in meaning between the verb 'begin' and the word 'commence'. Even so we use the two words in different contexts.

It is risky to generalize about this drifting apart of native and parallel Latin words. Where, say, the word 'grasp' is a forceful word in its concrete sense ('He grasped the pole and hurled it in the air') and the parallel Latin words 'comprehend' and 'apprehend' are likely to be associated with getting hold of things with the mind rather than with the body, nevertheless we readily speak of 'grasping' new ideas and we used to refer regularly to the business of 'apprehending' criminals. Usage does not stand still in this respect. We now use the word 'heavy' chiefly in reference to physical weight. We use the word 'weighty' of both physical items and arguments. The Latin equivalent, 'ponderous', tends to be used only in a metaphorical sense of over-solemn personages. Yet I have just read a notice issued by the Midland Railway in 1875:

> This bridge is insufficient to carry weights beyond the ordinary traffic of the district, and the owners and persons in charge of Locomotive Traction Engines and other ponderous carriages are warned against passing over the bridge.

A century or so later that use of the adjective 'ponderous' can only be said to seem too ponderous.

Otto Jesperson pointed out that our native vocabulary seems to have been short of adjectives, with the result that we tend to shift from native nouns to foreign adjectives. He cites the noun 'mouth' and the adjective 'oral', the noun 'nose' and the adjective 'nasal', the noun 'eye' and the adjective 'ocular', the noun 'son' and the adjective 'filial'. The adjectives here have no native equivalents, unless we count the adjective 'nosey' (and what a homely, unsophisticated word that is). In cases where there has been recourse to foreign adjectives despite the existence of parallel native ones, the two words tend to drift apart in meaning. Thus 'timely' is not an exact synonym for 'temporal', and 'earthy', 'earthly' and 'earthen' differ each from each as well as from 'terrestrial'.

What most of us first think of when reference is made to the Latin half of our vocabulary is that mass of words which have at best a sophisticated, at worst an artificial flavour: words like 'speculate', 'cogitate', and 'meditate', which contrast with words like 'think', 'weigh' and 'brood'. We must not oversimplify this issue. 'She was always showing off' says what 'She continually conducted herself ostentatiously' says. But in practice we do not find ourselves asking whether we should use this word or that, 'drive' or 'impel', 'showy' or 'ostentatious'. A kind of instinct for what is appropriate operates.

Choosing the best word is not always a matter of choosing the native Anglo-Saxon word instead of the Latin borrowing. Our minds enter different linguistic worlds according to where we are, whom we are talking to, and what the occasion is. There is a time to say 'I told him to shut up' and a time to say 'I requested him to keep silent.' And however great the overlap between seeming synonyms, ingrained habits prevent us often from treating them as always interchangeable. We may speak interchangeably either of 'burying' someone or of 'interring' them, but we should never exclaim of someone, 'Oh, she's always got her head interred in a book!'

It should go without saying that it is the Latin part of our vocabulary that can trip us up most easily. All those words that end in '-ation', how easy it is to get one wrong. We are amused when someone is shown up picking the wrong one. We laugh aloud when *Private Eye* records how a speaker on the radio said 'The script evolved after three years of gesticulation', when he should have said 'after three years of gestation'. It is not just the slip-up that is funny, but the image produced of radio programme-makers devoting themselves for three years to 'gesticulation'.

## Monosyllables and Polysyllables

Very often the difference between the homely and the more sophisticated word can be measured in length. We tend to use shorter words (not always native Anglo-Saxon ones, of course) in the home than in public. When differences or tensions in relationships within the family or between close friends arise and are at issue, words such as 'vex' and 'fret', 'nag' and 'pester', 'badger' and 'taunt' come to our minds. But when the affairs of societies and institutions, political parties and public figures are involved, then words such as 'aggravate' and 'exacerbate', 'irritate' and 'exasperate', 'reproach' and 'discountenance' are more likely to be used. The first six words together contain eight syllables, the other six words together contain twenty syllables.

But the longer word is not always the more artificial and less vivid one. The Anglo-Saxon practice of forming abstract nouns by adding such endings as '-ship' and '-hood' has left us with some sturdy and vivid longer words such as 'friendship', 'fellowship' and 'courtship', 'motherhood', 'sisterhood' and 'brotherhood'. Here again, in the context of the family, there is a discrepancy in emotive power between the words 'fatherly' and 'fatherhood' on the one hand, and the Latinate 'paternal' and 'paternity' on the other, between 'brotherly' and 'brotherhood' on the one hand, and the Latinate 'fraternal' and 'fraternity' on the other.

The number of syllables in the words we use also affects the sturdiness of our utterance. A series of monosyllables can give a strikingly urgent and dramatic flavour to utterance. John Donne begins a celebrated poem with a line of ten monosyllables:

For God's sake, hold your tongue and let me love!

William Cowper manages two full lines of verse in monosyllabic words and there are sixteen of them:

Lord, we are few but Thou art near,
Nor short thine arm nor deaf thine ear.

In Shakespeare the proportion of polysyllables to monosyllables is often quite low. The line 'To be or not to be, that is the question' contains one two-syllable word to nine monosyllables. The lines 'Friends, Romans, Countrymen, lend me your ears / I come to bury Caesar, not to praise him' contain one three-syllable word, three two-syllable words and twelve monosyllables.

Uninhibited use of polysyllabic words does not necessarily produce nervelessness or spinelessness. No writer used our Latinate vocabulary more freely than Dr Johnson, but it is done with such care for exactness of meaning and for rhetorical balance that it pleases the ear at the same time that it stimulates the mind. Here he is defending Shakespeare against the charge that he ignored the old classical unities (of time, place and action) in the construction of his plays.

> He that, without diminution of any other excellence, shall preserve all the unities unbroken, deserves the like applause with the architect, who shall display all the orders of architecture in a citadel, without any deduction from its strength; but the principal beauty of a citadel is to exclude the enemy; and the greatest graces of a play, are to copy nature and instruct life.

To be able to use freely phrases like 'diminution of any other excellence' without sounding pedantic or pretentious indicates Johnson's mastery of the polysyllabic vocabulary. Such is the shaping of the prose that to replace 'without any deduction' by 'without taking away from' would not strengthen the passage. Similarly, to replace 'to exclude the enemy' by 'to keep the enemy out' would upset the balance. Such possible changes would merely introduce an alien aural element and disrupt the flowing rhythm.

There is a place for heavily Latinate diction. Johnsonese might sound incongruously artificial at the breakfast table among the family. It might sound very appropriate in a eulogy on a world figure from the lips of a distinguished diplomat at a state funeral.

## FOREIGN WORDS AND PHRASES

### French Words: Pronunciation

We have seen that our language has taken in words from Latin and French throughout its history. Yet we find in current English a number of words and phrases from these languages which retain their foreignness. In the case of words from the French accents are preserved in spite of the fact that English has no accents. Moreover, among the educated classes at least, the French pronunciation is preserved, or something like it. When French words were introduced in the past there was often a considerable space of time before the pronunciation got anglicized. We know that when the word 'oblige' came in from French in the sixteenth century, it was pronounced 'obleege', and indeed that pronunciation survived right up to the nineteenth century. In this connection it is interesting that we keep the French pronunciation in our use of the expression 'noblesse oblige' (literally 'nobility obliges'), which we quote, often ironically, in reference to the honourable and generous conduct which is expected of the aristocracy.

Anglicization, in respect of French accents, is happening all the time, if very slowly. Where 'rôle', which came in in the seventeenth century, has lost its accent during the last few decades, 'cliché', which came in last century, still keeps its accent. The word 'cortège' we sometimes see nowadays without its accent. Yet 'tête-à-tête' (a confidential conversation, literally 'head to head'), which came in during the seventeenth century, keeps its accents. The word 'café', a nineteenth-century importation, has preserved its accent and its pronunciation hitherto.

## Haute Cuisine and Haute Couture

'Café' is just one among many French words from the world of eating and drinking which have now established themselves in regular English usage. We use the French terms 'gourmet', 'gourmande' and 'bon viveur', for those who relish the delights of the table. No doubt the French preeminence in the world of what we call 'haute cuisine' ('high-class cookery') is responsible for this influence of the French language. At the restaurant we study the 'à la carte' ('according to the list') menu, from which we are free to select as we choose, and the 'table d'hôte' (literally 'the host's table') menu which contains a series of courses planned by the establishment at a quoted price. The first course may be called the 'hors d'œuvre' ('outside the work') and is supposed to consist of preparatory appetizers. If the word 'starters' seems now to be replacing 'hors d'œuvre', other French expressions at the table seem to hold their own. There are dishes such as 'pâté de foie gras' ('pâté of fat liver'), and a beefsteak cut from between the ribs is called 'entrecôte'. Our sweet dishes include a 'soufflé'. They also include a 'sorbet' and, accustomed as we are to adapting our pronunciation to suit the French, we give the word the French treatment, though in fact it comes from Turkish and is really the same word as 'sherbert'. There is a dessert called 'crème caramel', and a liqueur called 'crème de menthe' ('cream of mint').

We may add that the expression 'crème de la crème' ('cream of the cream') takes us right out of the restaurant. It stands for the very best of the best. Our inherited respect for the French as social superiors and arbiters of taste applies beyond the dining-room. Just as we speak of 'haute cuisine' so also we use the expression 'haute couture' for high-class dressmaking, another sphere of French preeminence. We used to call high society the 'haut monde' ('the high world') and the world of fashion the 'beau monde' ('the beautiful world'). We still preserve the French pronunciation of 'boudoir', 'massage' and 'coiffure'. In the wider world it is significant that when we wish to characterize an act of patronization and condescension we call it acting 'de haut en bas' ('from high to low'). The French language therefore, having the cachet or prestige of the upper class, comes in useful for veiling unmentionable items and practices in delicate terminology. When women want new underwear, they seek it in the 'lingerie' department. Their undress is their 'negligée' or their 'déshabillé'. We describe a woman's low-cut garment that exposes the bosom as 'décolleté'. When a married couple (or a pair of sexual partners) choose to live in cohabitation with a third person, the additional sexual partner of one of them, we call it a 'ménage à trois'. A comparable delicacy no doubt stands behind the now established practice of referring to hotel rooms that are fully equipped with washing and toilet facilities as 'en suite' (literally 'in sequence').

## Social Niceties

Our vocabulary for the intimate and the personal is rich in French terms. We use the expression 'en famille' for someone who is at home with his family. Another French expression, 'entre nous' ('between you and me'), serves us in the sphere of confidential intimacy. We even tend to preserve the masculine and feminine spellings of 'confidant' and 'confidante' for a very special friend who can be let into all our secrets. A delicate way of speaking of a communication which amounts to a love letter is to call it a 'billet doux' (literally a 'sweet note'). Delicacy of a different kind encourages us to speak of a 'faux pas' (literally a 'false step') when someone puts their foot in it, as we say, and we call a social blunder a 'gaffe'.

Somehow in the realm of social proprieties and social indiscretions recourse to French is habitual. We hear people use the expression 'comme il faut' ('as it should be') as a delicate way of pronouncing some practice thoroughly acceptable in the best circles. We speak of damage to a person's self-respect and personal sense of propriety as something which wounds their 'amour-propre' ('self-love'). The French expression 'lèse majesté' (meaning 'wounded majesty') is used for suffering presumptuous behaviour from inferiors against their 'betters'. We describe someone who is unconventional in behaviour and commits indiscretions as an 'enfant terrible' ('terrible child'). A 'contretemps' (literally something 'against the time') is an inopportune action or an awkward situation. A 'jeu d'esprit' ('playful act of the spirit') is a light-hearted pleasantry or a display of playful cleverness. The expression is used in apologetic excuse for a prank that may have misfired. A subtle use of the word 'frisson' has established itself: it comes into play in not very earnest conversation to define a shiver of delight that is too refined and evanescent to justify the use of the cruder English word 'thrill'.

It would be difficult to account on any other grounds than those of social one-upmanship for the use of 'en passant' as an alternative to 'by the way' or 'incidentally', though in fact the usage has its origin in the technicalities of moves in the game of chess. It is also difficult to account for the survival of 'nom de plume' when the English equivalent ('pen-name') matches it perfectly, and of the word 'soubriquet' for the English 'nickname'. The same may be said of 'carte blanche' ('blank paper'): to give someone a 'free hand' or a 'blank cheque' is the English equivalent. But we can perhaps understand why there are still those who fall back (often with a shrug of the shoulders) on French expressions such as 'faute de mieux' ('for want of something better'), 'tant mieux' ('so much the better') and 'tant pis' ('so much the worse'), where the French seems slightly less clumsy than the English. We find the French 'bête noire' ('black beast') a useful way of referring to what we regard as a pet aversion. The foreignness allows one to distance oneself from the expression of personal distaste.

The French verb 'savoir' ('to know') has given us the general expression 'savoir-faire' (literally 'to know how to do') for knowingness and tact. The colloquial word 'savvy' ('He's got plenty of savvy') for shrewdness and acuteness has the same derivation. So too has the phrase 'je ne sais quoi' ('I don't know what'), which has a touch of subtlety in its connotation. When we say of a work of art or a newly furnished room 'It has a je ne sais quoi', we generally imply that it has a touch of something indefinably special. By contrast, the common English versions of the 'don't-know-what' brand are half-humorous deprecatory expressions like 'thingumabob' and 'thingumajig'. They certainly seem to belong on a different social level.

## The Public Scene

In the military world the words 'aide de camp' are still used for an officer serving as a personal assistant to a senior officer. One of the dominant motivating principles behind acts of obedient self-sacrifice or heroism is the 'esprit de corps', pride in the company to which one belongs and fidelity to it. In the world of espionage and undercover work by the police we use the term 'agent provocateur' for a secret agent who is used, by disguise and deception, to provoke a suspected spy to reveal himself or a suspected criminal to commit an illegal act which confirms his guilt.

The words 'coup d'état' ('stroke of state') have long been the accepted expression for a sudden seizure of power which overturns an existing government, while a 'coup de grâce' ('blow of mercy') is the mortal blow that mercifully puts an end to the recipient's suffering. A 'laissez faire' policy is a 'let-them-get-on-with-it' policy of not interfering in other people's affairs, and therefore used of government policies that allow unrestricted freedom to commerce and industry. In the historical field we still refer to the end of the nineteenth century as the 'fin de siècle' ('end of the age'), thereby denoting a period of artistic decadence. And, suprisingly enough perhaps, we have never found an English alternative to the expression 'avant-garde' ('the vanguard') for the group of artists, composers, poets or figures in any cultural field whose work represents the latest thing in experiment and innovation. The 'pièce de résistance' is the most important and outstanding item, the one which brings a performance to a climax. We use the expression 'cause célèbre' ('celebrated case') to highlight the importance of a trial or controversy. We say someone is 'hors de combat' ('out of the fight') when they have retired from some struggle or are so placed that it is of no consequence to them. A 'trompe l'œil' ('deception of the eye') is a work of art or an artifact so realistic as to give an illusion of actuality. A 'double entendre' is a form of words which can be interpreted in two different ways, the one of them innocent, the other indecent.

Of longer French expressions, which we use because they so neatly sum up an attitude, the words 'receuiller pour mieux sauter', meaning to take a backward step in order to jump forward better, concisely hit off an attitude for which no equally brief phrase exists in English. Similarly there is a euphony about Voltaire's words 'pour encourager les autres' ('in order to encourage others'), which ensures its survival. The sentence

'Plus ça change, plus c'est la même chose' is an expressive way of saying 'The more things change, the more they remain the same.' The phrase 'Chacun à son gout' means no more than 'everyone to his taste' but is still used. People say 'Cherchez la femme' ('Look for the woman'), often not very seriously, when urging that attention be given to the possibility of a sex element or motive behind some mystery.

## Latin Abbreviations

We constantly use a number of abbreviations derived from Latin. A writer may insert the word 'sic' in parenthesis. Literally it means 'thus', but we use it to draw attention to something remarkable in what has just been said, more especially perhaps when quoting another source. It may draw attention to what is anomalous or dubious in the writer's eyes. On the other hand it may draw attention to something that confirms what the writer is saying. The abbreviation 'i.e.', standing for the Latin 'id est', means 'that is to say', and is useful when clarifying a point already made by words which amount to the same thing. The abbreviation 'e.g.', standing for 'exempli gratia' ('for example's sake') and meaning 'for example', is useful when providing an illustration which exemplifies and corroborates the point made. These two abbreviations are so established that people will use them in conversation ('Did he have anything more to say - e.g. about where he was on the night in question?'). Other Latin abbreviations include 'NB' ('nota bene'), meaning 'note well', drawing special attention to what follows. Certain abbreviations have been preserved in the religious field. There are the letters 'DV' ('Deo volente'), meaning 'God willing', once much used by Christian bodies advertising future events and anxious to draw public attention to the fact that all that may be planned from day to day could take place only with divine permission. Another abbreviation much used by the Church is 'RIP' ('requiescat in pace') meaning 'rest in peace'. The same Latin noun is used in the traditional greeting 'pax vobiscum', meaning 'peace be with you'. The letters 'IHS', originally of Greek derivation, were used from the fifteenth century to stand for 'Jesus Hominum Salvator' ('Jesus, the Saviour of Men').

Some Latin words have become so firmly established that one questions whether they ought still to be distinguished as not English. The Latin word 'passim', meaning 'in many or various places', is a convenient device used especially by academic writers, when the writer wishes to indicate that a given individual or topic is referred to, not once or twice, but at many points throughout the book. I have seen this word confused in print with the Latin word 'pace', which means 'by leave of'. When a writer wishes to make a polite nod towards some known authority with whom he is disagreeing, he may insert the parenthesis, '*pace* Dr Johnson', which conveys the message, 'in spite of what Dr Johnson says to the contrary' or 'if Dr Johnson will kindly allow me to dispute his judgement'. Clearly these two expressions economize in words wonderfully.

## Latin Expressions

The expression 'tabula rasa' is still in use (literally 'a clean slate' on which nothing has yet been written), though in fact the English expression a 'clean sheet' (unused writing paper) means neither more nor less. There are more useful Latinisms than that, many of a more technical kind. The Latin word 'quasi' means 'just as if' or 'just as though'. In English we have converted it into a prefix, so that a 'quasi-philosophical statement' would be a statement which passes itself off as philosophical without actually being so. One might, for instance, describe scientology as a 'quasi-religious' cult. The nearest simple English equivalent would be a 'seemingly religious' cult. The Latin expression 'a priori', meaning literally 'from the previous' is used adjectivally of a proposition that is being assumed from the beginning of an argument rather than deduced in the course of the argument. This expression came into use in England in the eighteenth century and is so well settled that the noun 'apriority' has been derived from it. Another expression used in arguing a case is 'ipso facto' (literally 'by that very fact'), which is said to introduce a point inexorably following from a point just made. The alternative form of this connecting link is 'eo facto' ('by that fact'), a slightly less forceful version. The expression 'sui generis' means 'of its own kind' and therefore sometimes 'peculiar' or even more loosely, 'unique'. It is not considered over-pedantic to use the expression 'sine qua non' (literally 'without which nothing') for an indispensable condition. The words 'status quo' are used for the existing state of affairs ('The agitators had no thought of rebellion, being anxious to preserve the status quo'). A 'quid pro quo' (literally 'something for something') is something given in exchange for some object or some advantage received ('His knighthood was a quid pro quo for his services to the party'). An interesting Latinism is preserved in the words 'pro rata' (an abbreviation of 'pro rata parte', literally 'according to what has been fixed in calculation') which means 'in proportion'. Universities award honorary degrees 'honoris causa' (literally 'for the sake of honour') in recognition of meritorious achievements.

Latinisms more likely to be used in a personal conversational context include 'mea culpa' ('my fault'), which constitutes an apology, and 'infra dig', an abbreviation of the Latin 'infra dignitatem', meaning 'beneath one's dignity' and applied to any suggestion for conduct which self-respect would not condone. And people used to be conversationally free and easy with the words 'non compos mentis' ('not master of one's mind') applied to mentally defective people. 'Inter alia' is sometimes used in place of the English 'among other matters', and likewise 'ceteris paribus' for the English 'other things being equal'. More difficult to spare would be the expression 'mutatis mutandis', a most economic way of saying something for which several words are needed in English. It is the equivalent of 'once the necessary changes have been made'.

## Legal Latin

There are Latinisms much used in legal affairs which have also been taken into general usage. The expression 'de jure', which means 'according to law', is usefully balanced by the expression 'de facto', meaning 'in actual fact'. Thus a man convicted of a 'mercy killing' might be described as a 'de jure' murderer but 'de facto' innocent. The expression 'prima facie', meaning 'at first sight', is used of assumptions made before full trial of a case. Thus a 'prima facie' case must be made by police and prosecuting counsel before a person charged with a crime can be sent before an assize court. The expression 'sub judice', literally meaning 'before a judge', is applied to matters still under judicial consideration. The fact that they have yet to be officially pronounced upon limits the right of general public comment. 'Ultra vires' (literally 'beyond strength') defines something which is legally outside the power of a person or an institution to affect or control. The word 'ultra' is used also in the expression 'nec et non plus ultra', roughly the equivalent of 'so far and no further'. 'Obiter dictum' (literally 'something said on the way, while travelling') was originally an expression of opinion given by a judge which was not essential to the judgment he was making, and therefore not binding or authoritative. Hence the words 'obiter dictum' or the plural 'obiter dicta' are used of some person's incidental remark or remarks. The words 'rigor mortis' ('rigidity of death') are in common use for the state of a corpse after stiffness has set in.

## Longer Latin Expressions

There are longer expressions, some of them quotations from great writers, which have been so much used that it may be necessary only to quote the first words of the saying for the rest to be understood. The words 'quot homines' will be understood to stand for 'quot homines, tot sententiae', literally 'how many men there are, so many opinions there are'. The English language does not have matching resources to make such complex comparisons so briefly. The words 'sic transit gloria mundi', meaning 'thus the glory of the world passes away', will be understood if the speaker merely says 'sic transit'. Similarly the words 'de mortuis nil nisi bonum', meaning 'only good things should be said of the dead', will be understood if only the words 'de mortuis' are said. The Latin poet Horace's famous line 'Dulce et decorum est pro patria mori', meaning 'How beautiful and honourable it is to die for one's country', comes into the same category. Wilfred Owen called one of his war poems 'Dulce et Decorum est', and in fact it is perhaps his most horrifying picture of men at the front. It includes a grim account of a soldier choking from a gas attack, whom his fellows fling on to a wagon, watching his 'white eyes writhing' in his hanging face. It was from Horace too that we gained the expression 'laudator temporis acti' ('praiser of days gone by'), used to describe someone who repeatedly compares the present unfavourably with an idealized past. Juvenal's line 'Orandus est ut sit mens sana in corpore sano', meaning 'One should pray to have a sound mind in a sound body' has left us an expression 'mens sana in corpore sano', a healthy mind in a healthy body, which has been cited as an educational ideal.

In many of the instances listed above the foreign expression has advantages of clarity and brevity as well as a peculiar neatness and forcefulness. If we take these advantages into account, we should certainly not think of condemning the introduction of foreign phrases into English prose. But over-use of such expressions, or use of them in inappropriate contexts, smacks of artifice and pedantry. There is always the risk that the writer or speaker who readily makes use of them will appear to be showing off.

## ARCHAISMS

The vocabulary of a language changes over the centuries. We have seen how English has acquired new words throughout the ages. It has also of course lost words. And sometimes words are half-lost, or nearly lost. They disappear from popular general use, but turn up from time to time either in special circles with strong traditionalist leanings, or in the utterance of knowledgeable people who find them useful and, perhaps, irreplaceable. Where words stand for things once part of the environment but which have now disappeared from daily life, it is natural that they should get lost. We come across such words, say in reading Shakespeare, and when we discover that they refer to items of dress or armour long since discarded, we find the loss quite understandable. But words are also lost, not because the things they stood for have gone from the modern scene, but because they have been replaced by other words. We read Hamlet's question, 'Woo't drink up eisel?' and learn from the glossary that 'eisel' is vinegar, so the question is 'Would you drink up vinegar?' However, quite apart from nouns, which may stand for things no longer used, or for things for which we now have other names, there are words which we class as 'archaisms' for another reason. They have ceased to be used altogether, or ceased to be used much in general parlance. They sound quaint. Such is the adverb 'eke', meaning 'also' or 'moreover'. As 'eek' it was a favourite word of Chaucer. He tells how the monk's bridle would jingle in the wind 'And eek as loude as dooth the chapel belle.' It is to be distinguished from the verb which we use in saying that someone 'eked out' a living on a poor croft. It is a useful word to cite as an instance because in James Joyce's *Portrait of the Artist as a Young Man* we meet a close friend of the hero Stephen, one Cranly, whose habit of using the word 'eke' adds comically to his ironic pose of scholarly solemnity.

There are words which have not entirely disappeared from current usage yet which carry an archaic flavour. This archaic flavour is not strong enough to prevent our use of the words, but it is strong enough for us to hesitate before using them for fear of sounding affected and pretentious. Thus we may hesitate before using 'albeit' instead of 'although'.

We should think twice before using the verb 'abide'. Similarly we may hesitate before using the impersonal word 'behove'. Perhaps that is a pity. 'It behoves me to give you a grave warning' lays emphasis on the duty and responsibility of the speaker, depersonalizing the rebuke. The comparable impersonal verb 'befit' remains in use, but is subtly different from 'behove'. What is 'befitting' is appropriate. What is 'behoveful' is needed, called for. Like 'befit', the word 'beholden' remains in use while carrying a faintly archaic air. 'I am greatly beholden to you' means 'I am greatly obliged, or indebted, to you.'

A few archaisms survive in common usage because they are found in memorable quotations. We still hear the expression 'hoist with his own petard', deriving from Shakespeare. Hamlet speaks of the irony of seeing an 'enginer Hoist with his own petar', that is struck by his own machine which is meant to blow a hole in a wall with gunpowder. This quotation has only recently been rendered disposable by the equally useful phrase about 'scoring an own goal'. Another interesting survival is the use of the word 'cudgel' when we say 'I must cudgel my brains', meaning struggle to remember. A cudgel was a stick that could be used for beating people. The noun has gone but the verb lingers on in this one expression.

There is possible cause for regret over the loss of a word from general parlance only where it is not replaceable. Here we may cite the gradual disappearance of the words 'whence' and 'whither'. 'Whence' is the equivalent of 'from where' and 'whither' is the equivalent of 'to where'. We have replaced 'Whence have you come?' by 'Where have you come from?' (the change adding a word). We have replaced 'Whither are you going?' firstly by 'Where are you going to?' and then by 'Where are you going?'

The word 'where' was once used in various compounds which have mostly ceased to be used. They include 'whereat', 'whereby', 'wherefore', 'wherefrom', 'whereof', 'whereto' and 'wherewithal'. We still use the words 'whereas', 'whereupon' and 'whereabouts'. We use the word 'wherewithal' in a semi-ironic tone of voice when we are short of cash ('I haven't got the wherewithal'). But otherwise it is chiefly in legal documents that the words survive. The usefulness of some of these words is made evident by the way lawyers fall back on them when seeking the maximum clarity of definition. It is also made evident when we ask ourselves what has replaced them. 'The means whereby I live' has to become 'The means by which I live.'

What applies to the word 'where' also applies, in different degrees, to the words 'there' and 'here'. We still say 'therefore' and sometimes 'thereby', but for 'therewith' and 'thereunder' we must turn to legal and other official documents. Such documents still depend on compounds of 'here', such as 'hereafter', 'hereat', 'hereby', 'herein', 'hereon', 'hereto', 'hereunder', 'hereunto', and 'herewith'. We continue to use 'hereabouts' as well as 'whereabouts' in conversation. The intensified forms, 'whereso-ever' and 'whensoever', like the forms 'whosoever' and 'whomsoever', are words which we associate now with lawyers and with past poets. When we read the poet Robert Herrick's famous lines,

> Whenas in silks my Julia goes,
> Then, then (me thinks) how sweetly flows
> The liquefaction of her clothes

we mentally accept 'whenas' and 'me thinks' as archaic poetic diction.

If we have any doubt about the value of the kind of compound here represented, we have only to study the prose of the King James Bible. When we read the words of Saint Paul in the King James Bible, 'Howbeit, whereinsoever any is bold, I am bold also', and we ask ourselves what we should now substitute for the word 'whereinsoever', we realize what a convenient word it was, and how many words it would take to replace it. For 'whereinsoever any is bold' really amounts to 'in whatever respects anyone is bold' or 'in whatever circumstances anyone is bold'. Checking up on two more recent versions, I find the words 'whereinsoever any is bold' multiplied to 'whatever anyone dares to boast of' and 'in whatever particular they enjoy such confidence'. It is perhaps a pity that we cannot rescue words so useful, but we must face facts. The discerning writer may be able to use an archaism from time to time, but clearly it is desirable to exercise restraint in that respect. People may get away with a lavish use of archaisms in the world of ceremonial officialdom. Anywhere else it will seem comic.

## AMERICANISMS

That usages should have come into English from America is no more surprising than that they have come into England from France. Where words and expressions are equally well established in both the US and the UK, no problem arises. In the UK we now all say 'OK' as naturally as the Americans. We speak about 'barking up the wrong tree' or 'burying the hatchet' without picturing an American scene. The relationship between British English and American English becomes significant only when two usages do not match. We feel uncomfortable when the American says 'gotten' where we would say 'got', but the American turns out to be using a now disused English form. There was dispute among nineteenth-century English scholars about what Shakespeare meant when, in the fencing scene between Hamlet and Laertes in *Hamlet*, the Queen says of Hamlet that he is 'fat and scant of breath'. A fat Hamlet was not what readers wanted. One scholar suggested that perhaps Richard Burbage had put on weight by the time he came to play the part. The matter was cleared up only when an English scholar, walking in rural New England, was told by a farmer's wife from whom he sought a drink that he looked 'fat'. 'Sweaty' was what she meant. The seemingly provincial usage had survived among the descendants of immigrants from Warwickshire.

Thus American usage may be as historically valid as British usage where the two differ. Moreover, the American usage may be the more vivid. The Americans say 'sidewalk' where we use the Latin word 'pavement'. Resistance to American importations has often been both ignorant and irrational. There was a time when the American fondness for saying 'I guess' was ridiculed, yet Chaucer was fond of the interjection. As for American pronunciation, the American vowel sound in words such as 'path', 'bath', and 'father' is said to be closer to Elizabethan pronunciation than current English pronunciations are. I have heard intelligent people reacting in mock horror to American use of the verb to 'enjoy'. The American waitress puts down the dish on the table and says 'Enjoy!' For us the verb to 'enjoy' is a transitive verb that requires an object. We do not say 'I enjoyed' but 'I enjoyed myself'. And my latest dictionary allows of no intransitive use. But it would be a mistake to criticize the American usage as 'incorrect', for the OED cites an archaic intransitive use of the verb, meaning 'to be in a joyous state, to rejoice' from the year 1549.

All one can say of current divergences between British and American English is that they are interesting rather than culturally significant. We are amused when an American air pilot announces that 'We shall be landing at Heathrow momentarily', for to us it suggests a stay too brief to allow of safe escape from the plane. Just as the Americans use 'momentarily' to mean 'in a few moments' time', so they use 'presently' to mean 'at present' ('I'm sorry, I'm afraid the manager is presently away from the office'), where we use it to mean 'very soon'.

Sometimes new specialized usages can misfire in the US as in the UK. Failure of sensitivity to accepted meanings can be unfortunate. A recent development in US medical circles involves the word 'emergent'. Because acutely sick patients are picked up from their homes or from the street by the Emergency Services, and because they then go into hospital through the Emergency Room, the habit has arisen of calling such patients 'emergent' patients. Here is a case where innovation has failed to recognize what the word 'emergent' means and must continue to mean, that is, coming into being or making an entry. Clearly the only patient in a hospital who might justifiably be called 'emergent' would be a new-born baby. It is obvious that not all American innovations are to be encouraged. I am told by a correspondent that in programmes for the Chicago Symphony Orchestra concerts the conductor Sir George Solti used to be said to be 'concertizing' abroad.

When, during a stay in the US, my wife went into a shop and asked for a 'reel of cotton', the shopkeeper showed his amusement by asking 'Are you going fishing?' She then learned that she should have asked for a 'spool of yarn'. When she was involved in conversation with our hosts on the subject of the kitchen equipment in the apartment provided for us, she happened to use the word 'toast-rack'. The word was unknown to our hosts. Friends asked to explain it tended to make conjectures in terms of mediaeval torture. Such differences merely testify to slightly different domestic habits in our respective countries. Try to locate an 'electric fire' in any American shop and you will almost certainly fail.

In some cases, where words differ, the American word is gradually driving out the English word. That is happening as 'diaper' replaces 'nappy', as 'truck' replaces 'lorry', as 'rare' (for a beefsteak) replaces 'underdone' and 'freight train' begins to replace 'goods train'. But plenty of interesting contrasting pairs of words remain. There is 'biscuit' and 'cookie', 'boot' (of a car) and 'trunk', 'windscreen' and 'windshield', 'petrol' and 'gas', a 'wage rise' and a 'wage raise', and 'sweets' and 'candies'.

PART 2

# Arranging Words Correctly

CHAPTER 5

# The Use of Verbs

The key to meaningful utterance is the verb. The verb transforms the indeterminate utterance 'the plumber' into the meaningful utterance 'Call the plumber.' You can utter nouns or pronouns by the dozen without making sense. 'Potatoes, peas, cabbage, carrots.' The nouns make meaningful utterance only if a verb is added or is understood. 'Please supply me with . . .' In earlier chapters we were concerned with the choice of words. Our subject was primarily the meaning of individual words. Here, however, we are more concerned with the way in which words can properly be arranged. And since the verb is a key element in the structure of utterance, good writing is impossible without correct use of verbs. Where we go wrong in the use of verbs is something we cannot afford to ignore. If we examine current error carefully, we shall find that a few false uses of the verb corrupt current usage widely. It is our task to examine these bad habits and show how they can be avoided.

## USE OF SINGULAR AND PLURAL

We say 'The bird sings sweetly' and 'The birds sing sweetly' and we do not think of the choice between the singular 'sings' and the plural 'sing' as a grammatical danger zone. Yet we may feel less confident in choosing between 'The choir is singing two madrigals' and 'The choir are singing two madrigals.'

## Collective Nouns

We have raised the question of the collective noun, the noun which, like the word 'choir', refers to a group or body of objects or people. Strictly speaking, it should in most cases take a singular verb, but one finds the rule broken wherever one turns.

> Our range of tiles have many different themes to choose from.
>
> Behind the small village are a range of mountains.
>
> A range of unique water-mixable mediums have been developed.

That is but a handful of examples from the world of magazines and devoted to the one collective noun 'range' alone. In each case the verb should be singular: 'Our range of tiles has many different themes'; 'Behind the village is a range of mountains'; 'A range of mediums has been developed.'

What applies to the word 'range' applies to other collective nouns. Yet it is easy to find specimens of error. Note the bracketed corrections in the following sentences.

> An impressive array of their paintings hang [hangs] on the walls.
>
> A selection of bars, tavernas and shops are [is] within easy walking distance.
>
> A rash of television designers have [has] erupted . . .
>
> The entire fleet of Mendip Rail-operated GB Class 59s were [was] on site.
>
> Her exhibition featured a mixture of hats; a combination of transparent, woven, flexible and solid fabric structures were [was] used.

One finds the same mistake being made with a variety of words like 'combination' that gather items together. But usage sometimes presents us with problems in this respect. The following is a piece about cabinet meetings.

> In the early 1970s, there were still an average of 60 meetings a year.

Technically the singular verb 'was' would seem to be required here to go with the singular word 'average', but it would be a rash pedant who would insist on that. The safest correction would be: 'there were still, on average, 60 meetings a year'. The same applies to the following sentence:

An average of 3.3 starlings were seen in each garden.

To 'correct' this by making the verb singular ('An average . . . was seen') would not do because it was not the average that was seen but the starlings. Far better would be to change the subject of the sentence and write: 'On average 3.3 starlings were seen in each garden.'

An interesting variation occurs naturally in the use of the word 'number'. In 'There was any number of reasons for them to perform below their best' the singular verb 'was' is correct, for the issue is a list of reasons. But no one would wish to press for 'was' instead of 'were' in the sentence 'A number of people were shouting outside and clamouring for admittance', where it is the behaviour of several individuals that is being described. Similarly, while it is correct to say 'The audience was small', it is also correct to say 'The audience were screaming and waving their hands.' In the former case 'the audience' is the whole body. In the latter case 'the audience' is the gathered individuals. (To say 'The audience were small' would convey that the people were of diminutive stature.)

This freedom in mixing singular and plural is accepted in such sentences as 'This group are all paid-up members of the society', where, in spite of the singular pronoun and noun – 'this group' – the plural verb is required by what follows.

## The Institutional Collective

The same distinction is regularly made in speaking of collective bodies such as the 'government' or the 'council'. Speaking of a collective decision, we say 'The government has decided to push the act through', but thinking of the body as a collection of individuals, we say 'The government are deeply divided on this issue.' Thus the following sentences need correction as indicated.

The authority plan [plans] a low-key promotion of the route.

Since then the museum have [has] funded two lots of restoration work.

The National Trust have [has] one other complete example, *Reliance*, which has been authentically restored.

The institutional collective, as used of football teams and the like, tends to take a plural verb. I hear of a match 'where Aston Villa meet Tranmere

Rovers' and I doubt whether one would often be likely to hear the equivalent of 'where Aston Villa meets Tranmere Rovers'. A rather different liberty is taken when the commentator makes this judgement:

> Seven defeats out of ten on Scottish soil tells its own story.

To make a pedantic correction here ('Seven defeats out of ten tell their own story') would be nit-picking. When a given series of events ('Seven defeats out of ten') is thus summed up as a single significant fact, the case for using the singular verb is strong. And when, moreover, the verb in question is part of a single well-worn expression ('it tells its own story'), the case is strengthened.

## Attracting the Wrong Verb

Sometimes a mistake is made when the noun in question can in no sense be called 'collective'.

> Detailed analysis of the cost of rehabilitation and the potential revenue were given.

What happens here is that the writer forgets that the subject of the sentence is the singular word 'analysis' because the word has been followed by the plurality of items, 'cost of rehabilitation' and 'potential revenue'. But the subject 'analysis' is what must govern the verb: 'Detailed analysis of the cost and the revenue was given.' This blunder all too often appears in print.

> It is the abiding interest in the countryside, its landscape and wild-life, its traditions, customs and crafts, that result in constant reinterpretation . . .

By the time the six items have been listed, 'countryside, its landscape and wildlife, its traditions, customs and crafts', the writer has completely forgotten that the subject of the sentence was the word 'interest', and that it must be followed by the verb 'results'.

We may define the process that leads to this error as 'attraction' in that the nearness of the listed nouns 'attracts' a plural verb. The fatal attraction can lure journalists in the most respectable broadsheets.

> The area of interests which can be labelled 'women only' have shrivelled dramatically.

The word 'interests' exercises the fatal attraction so that the journalist writes 'The area . . . have shrunk' instead of 'has shrunk'. And just as the plural noun 'interests' lures the writer astray there, so the singular noun 'subject' lures the writer astray below.

> The tensions among naval intelligence staff inside the building known as the Citadel was the subject of a recent report.

Surely the tensions 'were' the subject of a report. Here the writer might urge that he strays where the great have strayed in that the King James Bible includes the much quoted sentence 'The wages of sin is death.'

Perhaps the attraction towards the incorrectly singular verb is at its most subtle when the verb is made to precede the subject.

> On the evidence available there does not appear to be any legal grounds for intervention.

In saying 'there does not appear', the writer fails to anticipate that what is to come is a plural noun, 'grounds'. It may seem less natural to say 'there do not appear', but that is what is needed to introduce 'any grounds'. And it is presumably out of a desire not to sound too stilted that a journalist writes:

> Also in the redheads' hall of fame is singer Belinda Carlisle and actresses Shirley Maclaine and Julia Roberts.

Over-formal as it may sound to begin 'Also in the redheads' hall of fame are . . .', that is the correct wording.

## Plural Terms in Singular Units

Where the subject of a verb contains a plural noun but nevertheless represents a singular entity as a whole, the grammatical rule accords with common sense. The most obvious instance is in the case of titles. We say '*The Two Gentlemen of Verona* is one of Shakespeare's early plays.' It would be absurd to say '*The Two Gentlemen of Verona* are one of Shakespeare's early plays', making the verb plural because 'Two Gentlemen' are included in the subject that governs it. But that represents the matter very starkly. Consider the following sentence about some ancient standing stones in Cumbria.

> To the west along the valley is Long Meg and her daughters, memorial to an even more ancient presence.

Why is the singular verb 'is' correct here? Because 'Long Meg and her daughters' is the official name of the group of stones, and it is the location of that group that is being described. In a superficially similar sentence about real people the plural verb would be required ('To the west, down the road, live my friend Mrs Bean and her daughters'). We extend this freedom to have singular verbs to certain very familiarly partnered nouns. 'Bread and butter is good for you', we say, and even 'Bacon and eggs is my favourite meal.' Rhetorical tradition permits extension of this freedom to closely related pairs of nouns, as in Kipling's *Recessional* ('The tumult and the shouting dies').

## The Universal Singular

The universal singular is the construction used in such statements as 'The fox is a pest', where the formally singular noun stands for the species as a whole. The usage is familiar in daily talk. 'The mini-skirt is back in fashion' we say, referring to thousands and thousands of such garments. There is a danger that quick movements from use of the universal singular to use of the normal plural will upset the grammar.

> One of the good things about a television series is the interest they generate.

Obviously this shift from 'a television series' to the words 'they generate' will not do. One must stick with the universal singular: 'One of the good things about a television series is the interest it can generate.' It may be that this particular sentence goes astray because there is no recognizable plural form of 'series', but the error is found where that problem does not arise.

> The sleeve section is also made from EXEAT and they are wool-mix lined for extra warmth.

It is easy to slip thus from the universal singular 'section' to 'they' when the garments in general are being held in mind. The safest correction here would be to stick to the plural: 'The sleeve sections are also made from EXEAT and they are wool-mix lined for extra warmth.' Perhaps the slippage in the following section is less excusable.

> Another rarity was the large mirror on the outside wall; these steam up like the ones outside.

Although we are dealing with mirrors in general in the second half of the sentence, there is no excuse for the shift from the large 'mirror' to 'these'. The singular noun must be cancelled out: 'these mirrors steam up like the ones outside'.

### *none / either / neither / or*

These words appear to raise queries about the use of singular and plural. 'None' is basically the equivalent of 'no one'. Thus logic seems to guide us to think of it as singular. And indeed there are writers who always treat it so. But popular usage tends towards the plural. Thus Dryden, a classicist, left us the famous line, 'None but the brave deserves the fair', and we hear it misquoted as 'deserve the fair'. Schoolboys used to be made familiar with Macaulay's idealized summing-up of the probity of Roman political life in the days when Horatius kept the bridge.

> Then none was for a party,
> Then all were for the state.

That firm contrast between singular and plural for 'none' and 'all' tends to make sticklers for style uncomfortable with plural verbs after 'none'. However, from a writer as reliable as Oliver Goldsmith the OED quotes 'None of these however are known to us.' And the drift towards that usage today seems to be irresistible.

> None of those applicants who sent in their forms last year are required to re-apply.

It has seemingly become the mark of the pedant to prefer: 'is required to re-apply'.

The words 'either' and 'neither' match the words they refer to. Although it is obviously correct to say 'Neither Catholics nor Protestants were present at the ceremony', it is not correct to say 'Neither the bride nor the bridegroom were willing to be interviewed.' It should be: 'was willing to be interviewed'. Similarly 'Neither of us enjoy eating out' should be: 'Neither of us enjoys eating out.'

We have dealt with the permissive sportsman's 'team plural' used of football teams. It is improper, however, to extend too far the liberties granted by this collective. When we hear of two teams that 'neither side are much fancied for the title', we are bound to protest. 'Neither' is there singular. If two teams are competing, 'either' one or the other 'is' probably going to be victorious. If the match proves to be a draw, then 'neither is the winner'.

In such incorrect usages as 'Neither my father nor my mother were willing to help', the difficulty arises because the speaker or writer has just been dwelling mentally on the fact that two people failed to respond. That difficulty is not confined to the use of negatives like 'none' and 'neither'.

> For my style of working I find that top grade cartridge or hot pressed paper are best suited.

Here it is the force of the word 'or' that the writer ignores. She is mentally dwelling on the fact that two methods suit her. But 'or' separates the two items. When one says 'Paint or wall-paper is acceptable', one means that one or the other will serve. Logic demands the singular similarly in the above: 'I find that top grade cartridge or hot pressed paper is best suited.'

## USE OF THE INFINITIVE

The infinitive is used after certain verbs such as to 'wish', to 'decide', to 'help' and to 'advise'. In the sentences 'I wished to leave' and 'I decided to go', the infinitives 'to leave' and 'to go' act as objects of the verbs 'wished' and 'decided'. There are also cases where the infinitive acts as subject of a verb ('To postpone decision seemed to be the best policy'). We have the occasional usage in which the infinitive is used with the verb 'to be' both as subject and as complement: 'To work is to pray'; 'To know her was to love her.'

It is important not to try to use the infinitive construction after verbs which it cannot properly follow. We say 'I allowed him to go', 'I encouraged him to go' and 'I persuaded him to go', but this cannot be a model for any verb one chooses.

> The challenge now is to prevent mass migration, by supporting people to stay on their land and cultivate, fish, or raise cattle.

We do not say 'They supported their son to try for the university', but 'They supported their son in trying for the university.' So here, if 'supporting' is kept the end of the sentence should read: 'by supporting people in staying on their land and cultivating'. However, in view of the context of the sentence, which is taken from a charitable appeal for money, it would be clear enough to write: 'by enabling people to stay on their land'.

## Omission of *to*

In cases where the infinitive is properly placed, a tendency has developed of omitting the word 'to'. We find people saying 'I helped him move his house' instead of 'I helped him to move his house.' No doubt the practice of omitting 'to' is harmless enough in conversation. We ought not to get excited when someone says 'They are helping her cope with the problem', but in print that omission of 'to' can appear lax.

> The book suggests methods parents can try to help children master these basic skills.

> Parents can help their less buoyant offspring cultivate this ability.

In each of the above cases the restoration of 'to' is recommended: 'Parents can try to help their children to master these basic skills' and 'Parents can help their less buoyant offspring to cultivate this ability.' At present it is especially the case with the verb 'help' that this liberty is taken, but the thin-ended wedge is being slowly pushed further. It is a small step from 'Help her cross the road' to 'Encourage him eat his cereals.' If we too readily accept statements like 'I helped my daughter choose her engagement ring', may we soon be asked to accept 'I taught my daughter make mince pies'? For we can already read:

> A lost rail can force you bring stream-crossing skills into play.

This of course should be: 'force you to bring'. It should be added that English does have a few verbs which are properly followed by what grammarians call the 'bare' form of the infinitive (the infinitive without 'to'): 'We watched her *go*'; 'They made me *help*.'

## Infinitive Misused

Misuse of the infinitive tends to occur when it stands in close relationship to a noun. We should naturally say 'He hopes to succeed in this venture', following the verb to 'hope' with the infinitive 'to succeed'. But we should equally naturally say 'We had little hope of reviving him', following the noun 'hope' with the gerund 'of reviving'. But this does not mean that infinitives cannot ever have a proper dependence on a noun. There are numerous cases of such dependence. In the sentence 'There was no doubt of his determination to leave', the infinitive 'to leave' is directly attached to the noun 'determination'. Such sentences as 'They acknowledged her promise to take part', 'We saw their willingness to participate' and 'He welcomed our readiness to cooperate' give some idea of how common this use of the infinitive is. In each of those cases the infinitive is directly attached to a noun. We say 'I have a duty to go', 'She has an obligation to be there', and 'They have a strong claim to present.' In any of these cases use of the gerund would be out of the question ('duty of going', 'obligation of being there'). But there are certain nouns which, unlike these, sometimes seemingly offer a choice to the writer. Whereas 'We saw no reason to rejoice' is acceptable usage, 'We had a hundred reasons for rejecting the proposal' is equally respectable.

The escape from use of an ill-placed infinitive cannot always be best achieved by use of a gerund. Consider the following sentence:

> Today's Airbath International is founded on thirty years of market experience, with constant research and development to improve and refine the original unique idea.

The infinitives 'to improve and refine' cannot stand thus, unhappily connected to the nouns 'research and development'. The best way to make the infinitives usable is to introduce a participle on which they can depend: 'with constant research and development designed to improve and refine the original idea'.

> The models are complete with rubber feet to prevent them from slipping or scratching the table.

Here is another sentence which requires the same treatment. Since it would be clumsy to write 'complete with rubber feet for preventing them from slipping', the participle should be inserted: 'complete with rubber feet designed to prevent them from slipping'.

Perhaps one can safely say that the use of the infinitive presents us with one of the most obvious instances of a construction which can pass in conversation where it could not in print.

> It's a sheltered spot to sit in the sun and breathe in the scent of rosemary, sage and creeping thyme.

The wild card infinitive 'to sit' can get by in conversation. On paper the sentence must become: 'It's a sheltered spot where you can sit in the sun.' And in the following sentence the infinitive 'to try' should be avoided in print.

> Rowse has produced a twelve-page booklet that contains lots of tempting dishes to try.

Correct this by anchoring the infinitive: 'contains lots of tempting dishes for you to try'. A comparable liberty is taken in the following from a concert programme.

> The two Violin Rhapsodies are rare to find in performance.

If one wanted to be technical about this usage one would call it perhaps a 'constructional transfer'. Because the idiom 'hard to find' exists, therefore on the model of that the writer describes something as 'rare to find'. It is quite illogical, for though the process of finding something may indeed be 'hard', it is not that process but the thing found that may be 'rare'.

In conversational use of the infinitive there is a curious habit of substituting 'and' for 'to', more especially with the verbs 'come' and 'try'. 'Come and see me whenever you like' we say, instead of 'Come to see me whenever you like.' In the same way we say 'Try and do your best' instead of 'Try to do your best.' Obviously there is no point in trying to disparage usages so well established. But writers should be chary of transferring them from the world of conversation to the printed page.

## The Split Infinitive

One can scarcely leave the subject of the infinitive without reference to the vexed question of the split infinitive. There are linguistic issues which arouse great passion, and this is one of them. It is difficult to sympathize with those who would totally ban its use. There are times when it is tasteless. When President Nixon first faced questions about Watergate, he is reported to have told his staff 'I want you to all stonewall it.' Now clearly it would have been better to say 'I want you all to stonewall it.' But it is not difficult to assemble instances of the split infinitive which are unobjectionable.

> The steam will soften your skin, enabling you to gently remove any blackheads with tissue-covered fingers.
>
> You should be able to simply slot the new stud into the original mortices in these two beams.

It is difficult to see the point of replacing 'to gently remove' with 'gently to remove' and 'to simply slot' with 'simply to slot'.

## THE PRESENT PARTICIPLE

We turn now to consider the first of a group of constructions which probably cause more elementary grammatical upsets than any others in our language. They involve participles and the gerund. Our first concern is with that part of the verb which ends in '-ing'. There are two such forms to be distinguished, the gerund and the present participle. That is to say, we have to distinguish the use of the word 'singing' in the sentence 'Singing is my hobby' from its use in the sentence 'I heard father singing in the bath.'

In the first instance 'singing' functions as a noun. Though it is part of a verb, it is the subject of the sentence and functions just as a real noun would in 'Music is my hobby.' That is the gerund, sometimes conveniently called the 'verbal noun'. In the second instance 'singing' functions as an adjective. Though it is part of a verb, it functions just as a real adjective would, describing 'father'. That is a participle. Of course we should tend to put the real adjective before the noun, whereas the participle often follows it.

There are various ways in which the present participle can be misused. One can say of them, as one can say of certain misuses of the gerund, that at the worst these misuses represent a crude abuse of language. But at the other end of the scale the least serious misuses sometimes merely represent the difference between good style and a touch of amateurishness.

## Hanging Participles

The most common error in using the present participle is to leave it unconnected to a noun or pronoun. Thus disconnected, it is called a 'hanging' or 'dangling' or 'detached' participle.

> Reclining there in a deck chair on the lawn in the summer sunshine, the house had never looked so beautiful.

The mistake is easily made. 'Reclining' is the present participle and must agree with a noun or a pronoun. It would have been correct to write 'Reclining there on the lawn in the summer sunshine, we thought that the house had never looked so beautiful', because 'we' provides the pronoun for 'reclining' to agree with. As the sentence stands in the original, the writer declares that the house was reclining in a deck chair on the lawn.

> Listening to the Chancellor in full spate, his confidence seemed utterly disproportionate.

Exactly the same error is committed here. There is neither noun nor pronoun for the participle 'listening' to attach itself to. In strict grammatical terms, 'his confidence' is said to be listening. The participle must be properly anchored: 'Listening to the Chancellor in full spate, I found his confidence utterly disproportionate.'

### *being*

Perhaps the worst examples of this error are to be found when the participle is formed from the verb to 'be'.

> Being mid-winter, the central heating should have been left on when we went away.

That is typical of the trouble that beginning a sentence with 'being' can lead to. The sentence tells us that the central heating was mid-winter, and that it should have been left on. The sentence should begin: 'As it was mid-winter'. At its silliest this same mistake falsely links 'being' with the reader.

> Being an Irvine Walsh book, you can guess where that rash is located, and what happens every time it gets a good scratch.

Here is a reviewer telling you that you are an Irvine Walsh book, for that is what the grammar strictly conveys. There is no escape from something like: 'As it is an Irvine Walsh book'. The truth is that the good writer will always pause before beginning a sentence with 'being', and will pause again before finishing the sentence.

## Directions for Routes

We often find detached participles when writers are spelling out directions for routes, especially routes to be taken by walkers.

> Heading due east for a mile to Pen-y-bryn, there are wide views to the blue whalebacks of the Carneddau.

Here the wide views are said to be 'heading' due east. Such sentences can usually be corrected by introducing an appropriate personal pronoun to agree with the participle: 'Heading due east for a mile to Pen-y-bryn, you will have wide views to the blue whalebacks of the Carneddau.'

> Veering right at the junction of the paths, a magnificent panorama of hill and dale is opened up.

Here the magnificent panorama is said to veer right at the junction. Introduce a personal pronoun: 'Veering right at the junction of the paths, you will see a magnificent panorama of hill and dale.'

> Moving north of the border, the country turns wilder.

Here the country is said to move north. One could give the sentence the same treatment: 'you will find that the country turns wilder', but it would be just as natural to get rid of the troublesome participle: 'As you move north of the border, the country turns wilder.'

### *looking*

This is one of the participles with which the problem repeatedly arises.

> Looking out across its central grassy space, the place is much quieter these days.
>
> Looking downwards, the sea stretches out into the distance.
>
> Looking at the plan in detail, it seems too complicated.

In each case the participle 'looking' is unanchored. In strict grammatical terms we are told that the 'place' is looking out across the space, then that the 'sea' is looking downwards, and lastly that 'it' (the plan) is looking at itself. If 'looking' is kept, then there must be a pronoun to agree with it: 'Looking out across its central grassy space, we find the place much quieter.' Similarly we could have: 'Looking downwards, we see the sea stretching out into the distance' and 'Looking at the plan in detail, we find it too complicated.' But in each case the alternative correction would be to replace the participle 'looking': 'As we look out across its central grassy space, the place is much quieter'; 'As we look downwards'; and 'When we look at the plan in detail'.

### *using*

It is correct to say 'He removed the broken tile from the roof, using a step-ladder', because 'he' did indeed 'use' the ladder. But it is at best imprecise to say 'The broken tile was removed from the roof, using a step-ladder', because the 'broken tile' did not use the ladder. Nevertheless one can find that construction day after day in print in the press.

> Using proper firmness, most children over the age of two will sleep well.

It isn't the children who use proper firmness, as this tells us. The participle should go: 'If proper firmness is used, most children over the age of two will sleep well'.

> Using appropriate varieties, endive can be sown for much of the year.

Again endive must not be said to use varieties, as this sentence has it. And there is an excellent device for avoiding the grammatical trap. Drop the participle 'using' and substitute 'by the use of'.

## Employment Advertisements

A fairly recently established version of the hanging participle can be found in advertisements for industrial posts.

> Reporting to the Deputy Managing Director and liaising with the Sales and Marketing Directors, your responsibilities will be wide ranging.

It is not the 'responsibilities' that will report to the Managing Director and liaise with Sales and Marketing Directors. The sentence can make sense only if the pronoun 'you' is introduced and the sentence ends: 'you will have wide ranging responsibilities'. The specimen illustrates a very frequent error in the business world.

> Reporting to the Northern European Marketing Manager, the key responsibility will be development and implementation of channel marketing programmes.

Again the 'key responsibility' is said to have to report to the Marketing Manager. The advertisement should read: 'Reporting to the Northern European Marketing Manager, you will have the key responsibility for development and implementation of channel marketing programmes.' The error is made so frequently that one could quickly pile up further examples.

### *I / me*

Just as the personal pronoun 'you' is necessary in that kind of sentence, so the personal pronoun 'I' is needed in many sentences introduced by a participle.

> Writing at the end of a long hot summer, it is easy to forget that we had some cold times in the spring.

> Saying that, my personal favourites are La Prairie and Estée Lauder.

In these two sentences the personal pronoun is required to make sense of the opening participles: 'Writing at the end of a long hot summer, I find it easy to forget that we had some cold times in the spring'; 'Saying that, I personally favour La Prairie and Estée Lauder.' In matching an initial hanging participle with a personal pronoun, it is not always necessary to use the personal pronoun as subject of what follows.

> Standing in the glass-roofed, cobbled courtyard, the distinctive interior is reminiscent of Kew Gardens.

Here is a case in point. Instead of writing 'Standing in the glass-roofed, cobbled courtyard, I am reminded of Kew Gardens', it would here be technically quite correct to make sense of 'standing' by attaching it to 'me': 'Standing in the glass-roofed, cobbled courtyard, the distinctive interior reminded me of Kew Gardens.'

***generally speaking***

It would be wrong to leave this topic without drawing attention to various idiomatic uses of the present participle which seem to break the rules we have followed so far. For instance, we should accept the following sentences.

> Generally speaking, audiences here are poor.
>
> Strictly speaking, the fellow ought to be reprimanded.

These two expressions, 'generally speaking' and 'strictly speaking', have established themselves as detachable from the implicit pronoun ('Strictly speaking, I think the fellow ought to be reprimanded'). We have to accept that other such expressions could with popular use equally establish themselves as respectable. Is not the process happening in our hearing in the case of the participle 'looking'? Do we not hear educated people saying 'Looking at the idea objectively, it is impracticable', as though the idea were looking at itself?

## THE PAST PARTICIPLE

### The Passive Past Participle

There is an active and a passive form of the past participle. In 'Having heard you speak, I feel I must disagree with you' we see the active form 'having heard'. In 'Heard in silence, he soon finished his speech', we see the passive form 'heard'. Like the present participle, the past participle tends to get detached from any noun or pronoun that could make it grammatically acceptable. Errors are especially frequent in use of the passive past participle.

> Designed as part of a comprehensive series on the English counties, the author is deeply attached to his native area.

> Illustrated by beautiful colour photographs and useful sketch-maps, the reader will find delight in following in the author's footsteps.

It is curious that this particular grammatical error can often be found in book reviews. In the first sentence we never learn what it is that is 'designed' as part of a series. The wording really conveys that the 'author' is so designed. In the second sentence we never learn what it is that is 'illustrated' by photographs and sketch-maps. This time the actual wording conveys that the 'reader' is thus lavishly 'illustrated'. Participles resist being marooned. If deprived of their proper mooring, they will drift by the force of grammatical logic to an untenable attachment. If 'designed' and 'illustrated' are to be kept, then 'book' or some such word must follow somewhere: 'Designed as part of a comprehensive series on the English counties, the book reveals the author's deep attachment to his native area'; 'Illustrated by beautiful colour photographs and useful sketch-maps, the book will give delight to the reader who follows in the author's footsteps.'

There is a common version of this error which is not always easy to spot.

> Originally appointed by the monarch to oversee his affairs in the outposts of the kingdom, the Sheriff's role today is largely symbolic.

The writer begins the sentence ('Originally appointed') presumably assuming that the subject will be 'the Sheriff'. But the wording goes awry when we get to the 'Sheriff's role'. For it was not the 'role' but the Sheriff that the monarch 'originally appointed'. The Sheriff and his role must be differentiated: 'Originally appointed by the monarch to oversee his affairs in the outposts of the kingdom, the Sheriff today has a largely symbolic role.' We may call the mistaken construction here the 'possessive trap'. There is a subject involving a possessive, like 'Sheriff's role', and the writer proceeds as though the subject were really the Sheriff, and not the role.

Let us turn to a specimen of the blunder more veiled in words:

> Brought up in a family of singers and instrumentalists, his musical interests were the basis of many life-long friendships.

This wording conveys that somebody's 'musical interests' were brought up in a family of singers and instrumentalists. 'Brought up' must be attached where it belongs: 'Brought up in a family of singers and instrumentalists, he enjoyed life-long friendships on the basis of his musical interests.'

Sometimes we come across the hanging participle following a word such as 'if' or 'when'. In this usage the past participle can drift even further from any mooring.

> If confirmed, Mr Lader and his wife, Linda, are expected to continue running the annual Renaissance gatherings.

Since there is no other word for 'if confirmed' to attach itself to, this sounds as though Mr Lader and his wife will be allowed to continue their work provided that they submit to a certain religious ceremony. The best way out of this confusion is to sacrifice the participle and substitute a proper verb: 'If the appointment is confirmed'.

The same slip can occur after the word 'when'.

> The buffet had been laid out on sparkling white table-cloths. When removed, our hosts revealed that they were really trestle tables.

The strict literal sense here would surely be that the hosts made this revelation after they had 'removed'. It would also appear that the hosts identified themselves as trestle tables. Any correction would need to fill out the construction: 'When the table-cloths were removed, it was revealed that our hosts were using trestle tables.'

## The Active Past Participle

The active past participle is sometimes left as isolated from grammatical mooring as the passive. The following sentence takes us into the world of caravans and the caravan site.

> The installation of a microwave oven would be a boon and at no cost, having already paid the supplement to the site fee.

Here 'having paid' hangs in total isolation. The way to bring it into the sentence grammatically is to provide it with an anchorage: 'The installation of a microwave oven would be a boon and at no cost, the owner having already paid the supplement to the site fee.'

The active past participle suffers the same mistreatment as the passive one in that it can be left in seeming attachment to the wrong noun when the writer falls into the possessive trap.

> Alan's background is in civil engineering, having worked in the coal industry for twenty years.

Here Alan's background is said to have worked twenty years in the coal industry. The necessary correction can be very simply made: 'Alan has a background in civil engineering, having worked in the coal industry for twenty years.'

Perhaps the commonest version of this error is the misuse of the phrase 'having said that'.

> The site is vast and busy; but having said that, a quiet backwater can usually be found.

Here the 'quiet backwater' is said to have uttered. For though 'Having said that, I shall accept the plan' is correct, 'Having said that, the plan will do fine' is incorrect, since the plan did not speak. The ironical thing about this error, which is made day after day on the radio, is that the correct alternative is so rarely heard. 'That being said, the plan will do fine' is the obvious correction. An even shorter one is 'That said, the plan will do fine.'

## THE GERUND

The gerund is the part of the verb that is used as a noun. We use lots of gerunds in daily talk: 'Walking is good for you'; 'I love reading'; 'Too much talking tires her'; 'We have stopped going to the cinema.' These formations from the verbs to 'walk', to 'read', to 'talk' and to 'go' allow us to use the verbs as nouns, acting as subjects or objects to verbs proper.

### Gerunds After Prepositions

Gerunds can follow prepositions just as nouns can. Instead of 'You will succeed only by hard practice', one might say 'You will succeed only by practising hard.' We should notice the connection in meaning here between 'practising' and 'you'. 'I hoped to improve my holidays abroad by learning French' makes sense because 'by learning' is related to the word 'I'. 'By learning French, holidays abroad can be improved' will not do because 'holidays abroad' do not learn French. This is the first common misuse of that construction, to leave it unanchored.

> By paying his own way at Loughborough, it leaves more cash in the family pot to adopt a baby girl from Guatemala.

This is the error in crude form. 'By paying' cannot be attached to 'it'. All that needs to be done is to replace 'it' by 'he'. We turn to a slightly more complex version of the misuse.

> Time-tables and advance booking forms are available by sending an s.a.e. to the headquarters.

This will not do because neither time-tables nor booking forms can send stamped addressed envelopes. (It is necessary to make the further point that these items are 'available' whether anyone sends for them or not. They are 'obtainable' only on receipt of the applications.) Perhaps the shortest correct version here would be: 'Time-tables and advance booking forms will be sent from headquarters on receipt of an s.a.e.'

> A child who dislikes walking can be a problem, but by gentle coaxing and by insisting on leaving the car at home when taking him where he especially wants to go, he will gradually respond.

Here there is no proper 'subject' to make sense of the expressions 'by gentle coaxing' and 'by insisting on leaving the car at home'. As the wording stands, the two expressions attach themselves to the subject 'he', which relates back to 'child'. The one who does the coaxing must be mentioned: 'By gentle coaxing and by insisting on leaving the car at home when taking him where he wants to go, you will gradually get him to respond.'

Such mistakes are not hard to find. Indeed it is possible to find the same error muffled up in highbrow waffle. Consider the following from a book review.

> By repeating images, and multiplying visual fragments as a kind of marginal gloss on the text, our grasp on what it is that interests Jonathan Miller about a particular example builds up in stages.

We are here told that 'our grasp' is busily repeating images and multiplying visual fragments in the process of learning something or other. Either 'by repeating images and multiplying fragments' must go, or the phrases must be detached from our unwilling grasp and placed firmly where they belong: 'By repeating images, and multiplying visual fragments . . . Jonathan Miller builds up our grasp on what it is that interests him.' But alas, at the end of the reviewer's sentence one scarcely wants to know.

Failure to relate a gerund correctly to the noun to which it applies can sometimes cause it to drift towards a noun with which it has no connection. The following words from a speaker on BBC Radio 4 show the dangers of this possibility.

> After ordering my meal, the waiter started to gossip.

In strict grammatical terms this implies that the waiter ordered the meal.

***being***

A special caveat is needed about the use of 'being' as a gerund. 'Being young is not always an advantage.' Such sentences as that are proper and useful, though it should be pointed out that one could equally well use an infinitive and say 'To be young is not always an advantage.'

> Being a mass market marque means spare parts are never a problem.

It would be far better here to use the participle: 'The car being a mass market model, spare parts are never a problem.'

## The 'Gerciple'

There are matters of controversy in grammar, matters over which sometimes experts disagree. We approach one such now. Having acquainted ourselves with the participle, which acts like an adjective ('I found her reading') and the gerund, which acts like a noun ('She loves reading'), we must turn our attention to a form which tries to be both at the same time and fails satisfactorily to be either: 'She disliked me reading detective novels.' The word 'reading' there is a cross between a gerund (as in 'She disliked reading') and a participle (as in 'She found me reading'). Fowler called this misbegotten form the 'fused participle'. Because it tries to do the work of both gerund and participle, I have labelled it the 'gerciple'. There is logic in disallowing the construction. 'She disliked me reading detective novels' is improper because she did not dislike me at all. She disliked what I was doing. Thus it is that the correct thing to say is 'She disliked my reading detective novels.' We change the 'gerciple' into a genuine gerund, making it a verbal noun that is the object of 'disliked'.

Wherever one turns in the press today there are gerciples. But it is extremely difficult to find them in the work of good writers – not always impossible though. And have we not manufactured them ourselves? It would be a very bold writer who claimed never to have done so. For gerciples can appear at every level of impropriety from the grossly illiterate to the utterly excusable. We look first at the fondness for attaching gerciples to pronouns.

> Excuse me, I hope you don't mind me interrupting.

This should be: 'I hope you don't mind my interrupting.'

> The building remains more or less intact – thanks largely to it being listed.

This should be: 'thanks largely to its being listed'.

> The ride [in a car] is good: most bumps are swallowed without you even knowing they were there.

This should be: 'without your even knowing they were there'.

The expression 'difference between' tempts writers to illicit use of the gerciple. The following piece of parental advice illustrates the point.

> Make it clear there's a difference between you reading to him (sheer enjoyment for you both) and him learning to read (sometimes hard work).

The direct correction would simply adjust the pronouns: 'difference between your reading to him and his learning to read'.

We have corrected the sentences so far by turning the gerciples into genuine gerunds. This has meant turning 'me' into 'my', 'it' into 'its' and 'you' into 'your'. We face a different problem when the misuse involves a noun rather than a pronoun.

> If you don't mind long-term health-care becoming a means-tested service, then that's OK.

Technically this could be corrected by inserting an apostrophe: 'If you don't mind long-term health care's becoming a means-tested service'. But clearly that is intolerably awkward and clumsy. In such cases the construction must be changed: 'If you're quite happy for long-term health-care to become a means-tested service'.

It is frequently the case that clauses beginning with 'that' can rescue the writer from error in this context.

> In Britain there is a lay tradition of gifted naturalists undertaking the field work.

So here one gets rid of the gerciple 'naturalists undertaking', not by any apostrophe ('naturalists' taking') but by recourse to 'that': 'In Britain there is a lay tradition that gifted naturalists undertake the field work.'

> High tides up to 15 ft above normal were forecast, with the added risk of the hurricane stalling over the coast and dumping all its rain.

To correct by use of the possessive case is once more impracticable ('with the added risk of the hurricane's stalling'). Change the construction: 'with the added risk that the hurricane would stall over the coast and dump all its rain'.

This change is appropriate after those gerciples which tend to follow such words as 'risk', 'possibility', 'danger' and 'threat'. So 'the possibility of the whole staff being sacked' would not become 'the possibility of the whole staff's being sacked' but 'the possibility that the whole staff would be sacked'. Similarly 'the threat of all the union members coming out on strike' would become 'the threat that all the union members would come out on strike'. Thus the following comment on a stowaway cat on a flight in a Boeing 757 requires similar treatment.

> There was no danger of it being too cold for her during the flight.

Instead of correcting to 'danger of its being too cold', use 'that' again: 'There was no danger that she would be too cold during the flight.' And again here is a quotation from a letter displaying the same fault.

> Your report highlights the embarrassment which delays are already causing ministers, with the threat of the Jubilee Line not being completed in time for the public to visit the Millennium Dome.

Though 'the threat of the Jubilee Line's not being completed' would be correct, it would be clumsy. We need: 'with the threat that the Jubilee Line will not be completed'.

## SOME TROUBLESOME VERB FORMS

***may / might***

There are few problems with the form of the tenses of English verbs. We do not find ourselves confusing the present with the past tense by accident. The difficulties that do arise involve the conditional tenses. Above all there is slackness in the use of 'may' and 'might'. The rule is that where we are speaking in the present or future tense, we use the form 'may': 'I hope I may be able to come.' And where we are speaking in the past tense, we use 'might': 'I hoped I might be able to go.' It is not difficult to find this rule broken in print.

> Some parents worried that if they complained their children may be taken into care.

> If the information about the food poisoning had been acted upon without delay, the deaths may have been prevented.

> There had been a possibility that the locomotive may have gone abroad.

In each case 'may' should be 'might'. The rule is really a very simple one. Yet a news announcer speaks thus about a woman whose daughter has died of meningitis after an unfortunate delay in finding a hospital place for her.

> Her mother believes she may not have died if she could have had the treatment she required.

Plainly, once more, this should be: 'she might not have died if she could have had the treatment she required'.

The converse error, that of using 'might' where the present tense of the main verb requires 'may', is perhaps slightly less common.

> If you continue to work hard, you might get promotion.

> Try as we might, the DETR will give us no details.

In each case 'might' should be 'may'.

## Irregular Verb Forms

We have our irregular verbs (such as 'sing', 'sang', 'sung') but few of them cause us difficulties. It is interesting that we find writers today treating the verb to 'swing' as though it were exactly the same as 'sing' in this respect:

> Politically, the NUS swang decisively from the left to the pragmatic centre.
>
> The back-up teams swang into action.

Modern usage prefers 'swung'. Indeed my modern dictionary gives only 'swung' as possible. But the *OED* allows 'swang' as a rarity. We must observe that it is dangerous to assume that a verb will work exactly like a similar sounding one. 'Learnt' is an alternative to 'learned' as the past tense of to 'learn'. But there is no such alternative to the past tense of the verb to 'earn'.

> His pragmatism earnt him respect in Ulster.
>
> Her husband earnt yen in the Nippon Credit Bank in the City.

These sentences are incorrect. In each case 'earnt' should be 'earned'.

Some of our irregular verbs, however, provide us with choices in this respect. The past tense of 'weave' may be either 'weaved' or 'wove' and the perfect tense either 'I have weaved' or 'I have woven'. Other verbs too, whose irregular forms have been simplified through the years, offer us alternatives. The past tense of 'strive' should be 'strove' and the perfect tense 'I have striven'. Yet the past tense of 'thrive' may be either 'throve' or 'thrived' and the perfect tense either 'I have thriven' or 'I have thrived'.

### ***heave / hove***

The verb to 'heave' has either 'heaved' or 'hove' as the past and perfect forms. Publicity about a *Titanic* film on Channel 5 includes the sentence:

> Acting styles and accents fly in all directions, especially when the rascally Tim Curry hoves into view as a wicked steward/purser.

This is the same error as saying 'He sangs a song.' There is no English verb to 'hove'. The verb to 'heave' is used intransitively of a vessel moving. The only possible correction to the above would be: 'when the rascally Tim Curry heaves into view'.

### *lead / led*

Such words as 'hove' are not often on our lips. It is ironic that the main area of current error in the forms of verbs is to be found in one or two of our most commonly used verbs. The verb to 'lead' has the past tense 'led'. But because there is a noun 'lead' (the metal) which is pronounced exactly the same as 'led', the wrong spelling turns up for 'led' with remarkable frequency.

> My work with adults had lead us into many ventures.

> The workshop will be lead by Caroline E. Darl and Denise Allen.

In each case 'lead' should be 'led'.

### *lay / lie*

Overriding all other seeming difficulties with verb forms is the persisting confusion between the verbs to 'lay' and to 'lie'.

> The harassed parent only wants to lay drowsing in the sun.

> It's as good a place as any to lay for a couple of weeks in the sun.

> I just couldn't lay about the house eating cake.

In each case 'lay' should be 'lie'. 'Lay' is a transitive verb. It takes an object. A hen 'lays' an egg. A waitress 'lays' the table. No doubt the origin of the troublesome confusion lies in the fact that the verb to 'lie' has 'lay' as its past tense.

Is this a lost cause? I ask because, months after writing the above, I find the following in *The Times* report on Turkey after the earthquake:

> His wife, Aynur, cooks what she can on a camping stove and warms the milk for her ten-month-old baby, Ayae, who lays on a blanket under a tree.

The baby 'lies' on the blanket.

The converse error is just as common.

> When she took Vicki out in her pram, she would lie her on her side.

> First lie her on her back on a soft towel.

In each case 'lie' should be 'lay'. 'Lie' is an intransitive verb and cannot take an object.

### *sat, stood, sprawled*

A comparably frequent blunder in verb forms is the misuse of the past tenses of 'sit', 'stand', and 'sprawl'.

> I recently spent a week either sat by my phone or calling my answer machine from work.

The writer means that she spent a week 'sitting' by her phone. And once again the blunder is common. Within a few days I have come across the following two instances, the first from a radio presenter standing in for a celebrated presenter who is on holiday:

> It is a privilege to be sat in her seat.

And the second, according to my newspaper, from a QC addressing his Old Bailey jury:

> I don't suppose you want to be sat in here when there is an eclipse.

In each case 'sat' should be 'sitting'.

The verb to 'stand' is similarly mistreated

> He was stood there like a stuffed dummy.

The writer means that the fellow 'was standing' there like a stuffed dummy. Small wonder that a correspondent in *The Times* writes 'How I mourn the demise of "was sitting" and "was standing" in favour of the hideously inelegant "was sat" and "was stood".' It is not just a case of hideous inelegance, but of elementary grammatical error. We find the same treatment given to the verb to 'sprawl'. 'He was sprawled in front of the TV' should be 'He was sprawling'.

### *suit*

A rather silly practice has recently been cultivated in women's journals of inverting the proper usage of the verb to 'suit'.

> I'm going for a dressy evening look, as I feel Maureen will suit it.

In purchasing clothes the issue is what will suit the customer, not what will 'suit' the clothes. Subject and object are not here interchangeable. The clothes have no choice. The garments with the 'dressy evening look' cannot decide that they would rather clothe Maureen's friend than Maureen. There is no more sense in inverting the usage with the verb to 'suit' than there would be with, say, the verb to 'please'. No one has yet begun to write 'She greatly pleases this kind of holiday' instead of 'This kind of holiday greatly pleases her.'

CHAPTER 6

# The Fabric of the Sentence

## THE USE OF PRONOUNS

The main building blocks of utterance are nouns and verbs. But we frequently replace nouns by those convenient substitutes which we call 'pronouns'. We scatter our daily talk with pronouns. 'Where is it?', 'How is she?', 'Tell them to be quiet', 'That's the postman.' The words 'it', 'she', 'them' and 'that' are all pronouns. They function as nouns. They save us the trouble of saying 'Where is the newspaper?', 'How is your grandmother?', 'Tell the children to be quiet', or 'The noise at the door is made by the postman.' Stand-in words like these raise few problems in conversation where we know what nouns they are understudying. If you ask 'What is it?' with an unopened Christmas present in your hand, nobody is going to ask 'What do you mean by "it"?' And if you say 'Tell them to be quiet' as your youngsters are performing circus acts in the bedroom above, no one is going to ask you 'What do you mean by "them"?' But in print what the writer is getting at as he or she sprinkles pronouns over the page may sometimes not be clear.

### *it*

Nowhere is this more likely to occur than in the use of 'it'.

> You can never really know the limits of your body; it is always surprising.

What is 'it'? We can guess, but the writer doesn't tell us. For 'it' should refer back to something already referred to ('The tyre is flat; it must be punctured'). On this reading the writer is saying 'The body is always surprising.' But we know that she doesn't mean that. She means that discovering what the limits of your body are is always surprising. She should have said: 'it is always surprising to find out'.

That is the first of the problems raised in the use of pronouns. The reader always needs to know exactly what they refer back to. The good writer will never leave 'it' so placed that the reader is not absolutely certain what the word refers to. There should never be that moment of doubt in the reader's mind produced by a collision between the meaning suggested by the context and the meaning implicit in the grammar.

> Use a make-up sponge to sweep it over the face. Don't overload the sponge or it could look streaky.

Clearly the first 'it' refers to the make-up in use. But the reader's mind receives a little jolt from the second 'it'. The form of the sentence – the grammatical proximity of 'it' to sponge – suggests one meaning, then the brain rules it out as absurd. It can't after all be the sponge that may look streaky. It must be the face. These are reasoning processes which readers ought not to have to go through. The good writer will ensure that they don't have to. It's all a question of the primacy of concepts planted in the mind by the words.

> This is a lovely way to keep fruit for a couple of days. It's delicious for breakfast, lunch or tea.

Here is a case in point. The reader responds to a statement about a 'way' to keep fruit. That is the concept that has the primacy. But the reader is not allowed to continue to hold to the 'way' of keeping fruit as the subject of discourse. For the two words 'It's delicious' plainly refer, not to the way of keeping fruit, but to the fruit itself. Thus time after time it is by the misuse of pronouns that readers are jolted from following logical trains of thought by momentary mental doubts, quickly removed, but nevertheless interruptive.

***they / them***

The plural pronouns 'they' and 'them' must equally refer back to something previously mentioned.

> Introduce a friend to the AA, and both of you can choose a free gift. They include a travel rug, first-aid kit, sports bag . . .

To use 'they' to refer back to 'a free gift' is bad. Correction is needed: 'The gifts include a travel rug . . .'

Sometimes 'they' can be ill-used in that there seem to be two possible alternative nouns to which the word might refer back.

> People's ideas about the 50s and 60s tend to blur together – but they are really quite distinct from one another.

On first reading this one might assume that 'they' refers back to 'people's ideas'. But the context suggests that the writer meant not that people's ideas differ, but that the 50s differ from the 60s. So correction is needed: 'but the two periods are really quite distinct from one another'.

What applies to 'they' applies to 'them'.

> Under new proposals up to 200 car spaces may be lost with simply nowhere for them to go.

This conveys the message that there is nowhere for the spaces to go. Nothing has been said directly about 'cars'. The message is about the spaces they occupy. The cars must be specifically mentioned for 'them' to have a reference point: 'up to 200 parking spaces may be lost, leaving simply nowhere for the cars to go'.

***this***

'This is mine', we say. In relation to that usage the question may arise: What does 'this' refer to? The most common misuse of 'this' occurs when that question cannot be unambiguously answered.

> The railway would like to buy the old station building at Market Bosworth, which is used as a garage and workshop. Although it was on sale recently for around £200,000, this is beyond its present means, but it holds hope of some agreement. This may be difficult in the short term.

Here in three sentences are two uses of 'this' and two uses of 'it'. That 'it' was on sale does not trouble us. 'It' there is plainly the old station building. And that 'this' is beyond someone's means does not in itself trouble us. It is clearly the price quoted to which 'this' refers. But for the same sentence to state that 'it' was on sale at a price beyond 'its' present means and that nevertheless 'it' holds some hope will not do. Nor is the last 'this' happily related to what precedes it. The answer to all these problems is simply to economize on pronouns rather than on nouns, and to say: 'Although the station building was on sale recently for around £200,000, the price was beyond the railway's present means, but there is hope of some agreement, though reaching it may prove difficult in the short term.'

One of the facts that complicates the use of 'this' is the double application the word can have. In the one usage it refers back to a single noun, in the other usage to a complete clause. 'He had to take the examination in Physics yesterday. This is not one of his strong subjects.' There 'this' refers directly back to the one word in the previous sentence, 'Physics'. Now change the second sentence. 'He had to take the examination in Physics yesterday. This is unfortunate because he was not feeling well.' In that sentence 'this' refers back to the whole content of the previous sentence. When writing 'this' one should always check exactly what it is that it refers back to. There must be no ambiguity for the reader.

***he / him, she / her, I / me, we / us***

In turning to these personal pronouns we have to deal with a different kind of error, not so much the error of not making clear to whom the personal pronoun refers, but the error of getting confused between the two forms, subject and object, 'he' and 'him', 'she' and 'her', 'I' and 'me', 'we' and 'us'. When errors occur in this matter the likelihood is that 'him' is used where it should be 'he', that 'her' is used where it should be 'she', and that 'us' is used where it should be 'we'. (Yet, strangely enough, that tendency is reversed with the pronouns 'I' and 'me'.) In certain dialects one used to get the equivalent of 'they hated he' or 'he trusted she', but these are not common errors today. The rule to remember is that the forms 'him', 'her', 'me' and 'us' can never be used as subjects of a verb. Thus 'It is him who is to blame' should be 'It is he who is to blame' and 'We got on well together, him and me' should be 'We got on well together, he and I.' Similarly 'Mum is against him too: both her and Dad want me to leave him' should be 'both she and Dad want me to leave him'. Whereas it is correct to say 'It is we who are to blame', where 'we' is the subject of the verb 'are', it is correct to say 'It is us he blamed', where 'us' is the object of the verb 'blamed'. One has to turn to cheaper magazines to find the crudest such errors in print, and they often occur in letters from readers.

> I'm really interested in plants and have taken down lots of addresses for places me and my friend can visit in the spring.

This should read: 'lots of addresses for places I and my friend can visit'.

Alas, I had just written the sentence above about 'cheaper magazines' when my eye fell on a piece in *The Times*. The newspaper prints a tribute to Charlie Chaplin on the anniversary of his death which reads thus at one point:

> His childhood was unhappy and when Charles was five his mother sent he and half-brother Sydney to an orphanage.

This should be: 'sent him and half-brother Sydney to an orphanage'. The error is curious, for one could hazard a guess that the writer would in no circumstances have written 'His mother sent he to the grocer's shop'. What is it that happens to the human mind to upset it when pronouns are thus partnered with nouns?

There is only one error of this kind that is heard frequently in superficially cultivated circles. It is the misuse of 'I'. For in contrast with what obtains with the other pairs of personal pronouns, it is 'I' that is over-used and not 'me'. Somehow people have got the impression that it is always wrong to say 'you and me'. So we get such tortuous statements as 'They would never threaten you and I' instead of 'you and me'.

> Come immunization day, my mother couldn't get my brother and I jabbed fast enough.

Here is a typical case in print of 'I' used where 'me' would be correct. It is remarkable that people who would never think of saying 'My mother gave I a present' will readily say 'My mother gave my brother and I a present.'

> For you or I it would be an intolerably difficult decision to have to make.

The case after a preposition such as 'for' must always be 'me', 'him', 'her', 'us' or 'them'. It is curious that people are reluctant to commit themselves to the natural construction: 'for you or me'. How deeply this error has corrupted us may be gauged from Norman Lamont's account of how John Major, as Prime Minister, replied in the Commons to accusations of a split between the Chancellor and himself:

> It may be that many people would like to invent divisions between he and I, but there are none.

This should have been: 'divisions between him and me'.

### *who / whom*

This relic of Anglo-Saxon differentiation between the subject case and the object case is still troubling people.

There's a new couple down the road who I'd love to meet.

There's a man at work who I fantasize about.

You need to know who to contact.

In each of these three sentences 'who' should be 'whom', for in each case the pronoun is the object of a verb: 'whom I'd love to meet'; 'whom I fantasize about'; 'whom to contact'. 'Who' is appropriate only where the pronoun is the subject of the verb ('I want to know who lives there').

It is ironic that though the form 'whom' is used far less than it should be, yet people still manage to use it where they should not.

He refused to tell police whom he thinks is responsible for the guerrilla attack.

The pronoun ('whom') used here should not be regarded as the object of 'he thinks' but as the subject of 'is'. Many sentences are made on this pattern. There are two possible alternative corrections. We may change 'whom' to 'who': 'He refused to tell the police who he thinks is responsible'. Or we may make the pronoun the real object of 'thinks' by altering the verb 'is': 'He refused to tell the police whom he thinks to be responsible'. The same treatment could be given in the following case.

The ante-post market for the Sagitta 2000 Guineas has become lively after the winning debut at York last week of Stravinsky, the Aidan O'Brien colt whom many think will follow in the footsteps of his stable companion . . .

This must become either: 'the Aidan O'Brien colt who many think will follow in the footsteps', or: 'the Aidan O'Brien colt whom many think likely to follow in the footsteps'.

The relative pronoun 'whom' must refer back clearly to a noun (or pronoun), and it must be a noun used as a noun, not a noun used as an adjective.

I act for a small husband-and-wife partnership, both of whom are semi-retired and unlikely ever again to be liable to tax.

Here the words 'husband-and-wife' act as an adjective describing the partnership. Strictly speaking, neither husband nor wife has been mentioned as such. If the word 'whom' is to be kept, 'husband' and 'wife' must become genuine nouns: 'I work for a partnership of husband and wife, both of whom are semi-retired.'

## USING THE RIGHT PREPOSITIONS

Prepositions, those little words in the architecture of the sentence, are rather like the mortar that holds the bricks together in building. 'I went the cinema my friend the evening the twenty-fifth' is like a pile of loose bricks. When the prepositions are added ('I went *to* the cinema *with* my friend *on* the evening *of* the twenty-fifth') the bricks are fastened together in a meaningful fabric.

A word must be said about the label 'preposition'. In dealing with verbs in the last chapter we finally turned to the part of speech known as the gerund or the 'verbal noun'. The very expression 'verbal noun' can teach us a lot. If a verb can function as a noun from time to time, then basic grammatical labels must sometimes be taken with a pinch of salt. Indeed, the words we were taught at school to call 'prepositions' spend quite a lot of their time not being prepositions at all. Consider the word 'up', how variously it functions. One only has to compare 'He ran up a big hill' with 'He ran up a big bill' to realize that what he did in respect of the hill is very different from what he did in respect of the bill. In 'up a big hill', 'up' is indeed a preposition with a direct relationship to the noun 'hill'. In 'He ran up a big bill' 'up' is what is generally called a 'particle', determining the meaning of the verb 'ran'. This is not a special peculiarity of the word 'up'. 'The bus ran down the hill' might be compared with 'The bus ran down a pedestrian.' Again 'down' is a preposition in the first sentence and a particle (sometimes called an 'adverbial particle') in the second sentence.

What other forms of speech can the word 'up' become? Most commonly perhaps an adverb, as in sentences such as 'A storm suddenly blew up' or 'The winning number came up.' It can also become an adjective, for the railways used to speak of the 'up' line and the 'down' line according to whether the line was used for trains going towards London or away from London. And when we speak of the 'ups' and 'downs' of life we are using the word 'up' as a noun. Finally, in the sentence 'He upped and went away' we use the word 'up' as a verb.

We are here chiefly concerned with prepositions performing their proper prepositional function. As long as crude physical connections are at issue in such expressions as 'to the cinema' and 'with my friend', it is unlikely that the preposition used will be the wrong one. But of course prepositions are used to indicate connections less easily definable than those. And an observer of the way the English language is being used from day to day cannot avoid noticing an extreme carelessness in the choice of prepositions. This is not perhaps so much a matter of logic as of custom. When a reviewer in the *Daily Telegraph* writes 'Many people will be particularly interested by the more speculative pieces', the reader feels a jolt of mental discomfort. Traditional usage would surely require 'Many people will be particularly interested in the more speculative pieces.' Just as we say 'fascinated by' and 'attracted by', so we say 'interested in'.

Now it may be argued that many well-established uses of prepositions are simply the product of convention. But in a sense all verbal meanings are a matter of established convention. It may be agreed that some verbal conventions have more of a philological basis than others. Some verbal conventions are more important than others and no doubt certain verbal conventions are more purely 'conventional' than others. But is there some special reason for treating with indifference the conventions of usage affecting prepositions? I ask this because, so far as the spoken word is concerned, and if BBC Radio 4 is representative of general practice, then it would not be an exaggeration to say that there is an epidemic of prepositional anarchy around. A prominent symptom of the complaint is over-use of the preposition 'to'. There seems to be a campaign to turn it into an all-purpose preposition.

### to for *of*

> Remember too – that the secret to getting and staying physically active is to start at a level which is comfortable to you.

> We've discovered the secret to looking good for longer.

Here is evidence from the magazine world of how the usage 'secret of' is being neglected. In these two cases preference should surely be given to 'the secret of getting and staying physically active' and 'the secret of looking good'. Convention has established the usage 'the secret of success' matching the usages 'the riddle of the sands' and 'the enigma of the unsolved cypher'. The substitution of 'to' for 'of' after 'secret' appears to derive from the usage in such sentences as 'Detectives are searching for clues to the identity of the criminal.' By a familiar process of 'constructional transfer' the usage appropriate for 'clue' is applied to the word 'secret'.

And now I have just heard on the radio a speaker telling us that someone 'took a very different view to the whole affair'. Clearly it should be 'a different view of the whole affair'. What makes the mistake worse is the fact that there is a proper use of the expression 'view to' widely different in meaning from the expression 'view of'. One may say 'I bought the country cottage with a view to eventually retiring there.'

Again, I hear on the radio a well-spoken, well-educated woman give this reply to an interviewer: 'I don't know whether I'm the right person to ask that question to.' The established convention is that we ask a question 'of' someone, not 'to' someone, and therefore the speaker should have said 'I don't know whether I'm the right person to ask that question of.'

**to for *on***

And now someone has been speaking on Radio 4 about experimentation with GM crops, and insisting that there would be 'no detrimental effect to the environment'. But established convention requires us to speak of the effect 'on' the environment.

**to for *in***

> A former Manchester Ship Canal locomotive will celebrate its centenary by being painted to its original MSC livery.

We repaint things 'in' a given colour, not 'to' it: 'celebrate its centenary by being repainted in its original MSC livery'.

> The trick to drawing is measurement.

Even if we condone the dubious use of the word 'trick' (here roughly meaning what was meant above by 'secret'), it surely cannot be followed by 'to'. One might speak of the trick 'in' drawing, but 'trick' is the wrong word anyway.

**to for *for***

I read in *The Times* Diary:

> Charges of lack of sympathy to women have been successfully rebuffed by John Casey, Fellow of Gonville and Caius, Cambridge.

The preposition 'to' is again out of place after 'sympathy'. The sentence should read: 'Charges of lack of sympathy for women have been successfully rebuffed.'

### *to* for *with*

We now turn to a misuse which is increasingly damaging our verbal sensitivities, that is, the distinction between 'connected with' and 'connected to'.

> He believed Mr Pettit was connected to drugs.

Here is a clear misuse of 'to'. Mr Pettit may have been connected 'with' drugs, that is to say, he may have been associated 'with' people involved in the handling of drugs. An electric fire is connected 'to' the mains by a plug in a socket. The attachment of one thing 'to' another is a different matter from the association of one thing 'with' another. Cancer of the lung may be connected 'with' cigarette smoking, but cannot be said to be connected 'to' cigarette smoking. But to judge from the English of Radio 4 the habit of using 'connected to' where 'connected with' would be correct is widely prevalent. The word 'to' seems sometimes to have a compulsive grip on speakers. I have even heard a speaker take up a point by saying 'in connection to what we have been discussing' instead of 'in connection with what we have been discussing'.

Here is another case where 'to' appears at the expense of 'with':

> All chief constables have now been ordered to provide to the Home Office confidential reports on corruption in their forces.

It is not established English usage to speak of 'providing food to starving people', but to speak of 'providing starving people with food'. 'All chief constables have been ordered to provide the Home Office with confidential reports.'

### *to* for *after*

What looks like a further misuse of 'to' is displayed in a local journal.

> Then Tom, who has always hankered to run an evening paper, took over the editorship of the *North West Evening Mail* at Barrow.

The verb to 'hanker' actually derives from a verb meaning to 'hang about' and thus gathered its associations of being in search of something. In traditional usage the verb is followed by 'after', though 'for' is also sometimes used. There is no authority for 'to'. The correction is: 'Tom, who has always hankered after running an evening paper'.

### *to* for *from*

Most remarkable of all is this novel practice:

> Much of the decline [of village inns], however, dates to the introduction of greater competition on beer prices by the Thatcher government in the mid-80s.

Why not the established (and logical) 'dates from'?

### missing *to*

After the evidence above of over-use of the preposition 'to', it is ironic that we have to draw attention to a failing in the opposite direction. A lax habit is being cultivated in some quarters of omitting prepositions which are really indispensable.

> Some novels are hard to bid farewell.

To find this in print in a review is surprising. The once-fashionable, but quite illogical, ruling against ending a sentence with a preposition can hardly be said to excuse this. Inelegant as it may seem, we must have: 'Some novels are hard to bid farewell to.'

### *on* for *for*

Another over-used preposition today is 'on'. It appears in various contexts in substitution for various other prepositions.

> The Director outlines some of the implications on ministry as a whole.

We speak of implications 'for' ministry, not 'on' ministry. This again appears to be a case of constructional transfer. Because it is our practice to speak of the effects of an event 'on' someone or even the influence of an event 'on' someone, therefore the writer here assumes that one can speak of the implications of an event 'on' someone or something.

### *on* for *to*

> I wouldn't recommend it on anyone.

This is an even more extraordinary case of constructional transfer. Because we speak of imposing things 'on' people and, more idiomatically, of 'wishing' things 'on' people, the writer here assumes that one can speak of recommending things 'on' people. So we get the over-used preposition 'on' used where the even more over-used preposition 'to' would in fact be proper.

### *on* for *of*

> Economists said the data confirmed that the strong pound, the Asian financial crisis and a slowing domestic economy were taking heavy toll on the sector.

The more regular English usage is to take toll 'of'.

### *on* for *against*

Here is an even more remarkable misuse.

> The Government is continuing its campaign by stealth on the deluded middle classes who elected them.

A campaign 'on' vivisection is surely the same thing as a campaign 'about' vivisection, whether pro or con. Plainly there should be no such vagueness about the above sentence from the hunting lobby. The writer means to persuade us that the government is involved in a campaign 'against' the middle classes. No other word than 'against' would be right here.

### redundant *on*

As an extreme instance of the prepositional anarchy from which the media now suffer, let us consider the following passage from *The Times*.

> Hundreds of Ukrainian mercenaries are fighting alongside Sierra Leone's rebels who yesterday made good on their promise to burn Freetown, the capital, to the ground.

There are two idiomatic English usages of the words 'make good'. The one is represented by such statements as 'After a difficult start, he eventually made good', where 'made good' simply means 'succeeded'. The other usage is represented by such statements as 'He made good his pledge to cover all the cost' where 'made good' means 'faithfully kept', generally used of a promise duly fulfilled. The journalist above presumably meant just that: 'made good their promise to burn Freetown'. So what is the word 'on' doing there?

And here is a misplaced attempt to be colloquial:

> Atkinson, 47, of Kilburn, North London, had studied up on art and antiques . . .

'Up' and 'on' are alike out of place. If 'studied' is kept, they must both be removed.

### missing *on*

Here is Radio 4's announcement about the discovery of a black box after a plane crash.

> It sheds no light as to what caused the accident.

Light is shed 'on' the objects it illuminates, not 'as to' them.

### *off*

A local authority has sent a receipt for a parking fine.

> Received off . . . Mr Bloggs . . .

Is 'received from' now regarded in local government as an obsolete form?

### *for*

Perhaps 'for' is the common preposition most rarely misused, but the statement below provides an instance:

> Local Tory and Labour leaders share a fierce pride for their city.

This seems to be another case of constructional transfer. Because we speak of affection, fondness or love 'for' a city, the writer wrongly transfers this usage to the word 'pride'. The proper usage is: 'Local Tory and Labour leaders share a fierce pride in their city.'

Radio 4 has supplied another instance of such constructional transfer in a reference to 'a father who has an obsession for sport'. A person may be said to have a love 'for' sport, but we do not use 'for' after 'obsession'. Just as we say that someone is obsessed 'with' (or 'by') a hobby, so we say that someone has an obsession 'with' a hobby. But in the sentence quoted it is difficult to understand why the noun 'obsession' was used at all, instead of the verb: 'a father who is obsessed with sport'.

We are told by a voice on Radio 4 that a certain politician 'has no sympathy for this view'. English has two distinctive usages after the word sympathy. We say that we have sympathy 'with' a friend when we wish to indicate that we share her feelings or convictions in some respect. We say that we have sympathy 'for' the friend when we wish to indicate that we have understanding and fellow-feeling for her in her current situation. It is important not to confuse these usages. You may feel sympathy 'for' a stricken person, because you thereby enter into sharing that person's feelings, but you sympathize (more objectively) 'with' that person's viewpoint. The distinction may be a subtle one, but distinctions between usages have to match in subtlety the workings of the human mind. To lose the distinction in such cases as this is to jettison nuances which are a part of our heritage as thinking beings.

### *from . . . to*

One of the constructions which seems to cause people trouble is the use of 'from' and 'to' in such sentences as 'From saucepans to electric washers everything in the store seems too dear.' That sentence makes its point properly because 'saucepans' and 'electric washers' belong to the same series of items as goods on show in a particular shop. Thus 'everything' makes sense as summing them all up in a generalization about those items. But consider this:

> From frosty pinks to rosy hues, everyone will have a chance to look fashionably made up.

To define people as frosty pinks and rosy hues is not flattering. 'Everyone' here cannot be said to sum up that series of colours in making the generalization. The only possible sequence to 'From frosty pinks to rosy hues' would be something like 'all the colours were fashionable'.

Having looked at a case where a 'from . . . to' construction is improperly followed up, we should also look at a case where the 'from . . . to' construction is itself improperly handled.

> This action plan includes a wide range of activities from working with young offenders to those who suffer discrimination.

The 'from . . . to' construction here itself goes awry. There is no proper balance between what should be parallel items after 'from' ('working with young offenders') and 'to' ('those who suffer'). We need that balance: 'a wide range of activities from working with young offenders to helping those who suffer discrimination'.

### *from*

The preposition 'from' on its own is perhaps less often misused. But the following is noteworthy.

> While Tony Blair has reformed the Labour Party, making its policies more acceptable, the Conservative Party under William Hague has become unrecognizable from the party I used to support so enthusiastically.

We need to consider what prepositions can be properly used after 'unrecognizable'. We can say 'The building is unrecognizable from this distance', but plainly that is not the usage intended above. We can also say 'He is unrecognizable as the man who sold me the car.' And it would appear that this is the appropriate usage for the sentence above: 'The Conservative Party has become unrecognizable as the party I used to support.'

The word 'from' is used after certain verbs of prohibition. A person is prohibited or banned 'from' driving. But that does not justify a statement about Parliament having to decide 'which countries should be forbidden from receiving certain weapons'. We forbid people 'to' do this or that.

### *at*

Sometimes error or awkwardness results from rather thoughtlessly beginning a sentence with a preposition.

> At a meeting called last week by the President of the local Chamber of Trade over 130 people attended.

People do not attend 'at' a meeting. They attend the meeting. To correct this sentence while keeping the first words 'At a meeting' the verb 'attended' would have to go: 'over 130 people were present'.

It seems hazardous to begin a sentence with 'at'. Here a journalist is looking into the background of a newly revealed one-time spy:

> At the house in Kirkham Drive, Hull, where he has lived for the past three years, none of the neighbours knew about his cloak-and-dagger background.

Was it 'at' the house that nobody knew? Did the neighbours all gather there to oblige the journalist, allowing him to economize on prepositions? We cannot know.

There are a few verbs which are often followed by 'at'. We stare 'at' people and we marvel 'at' new inventions. In such cases the word is generally not dispensable even when the verb is passive. If I stare at you, then you are stared 'at', not just 'stared'. That is where the following touch of eloquence about the young goes astray.

> They don't want to be lectured, they don't want to be preached.

The only thing that can 'be preached' is a sermon. There is no alternative to: 'they don't want to be preached at'.

The conversational habit of omitting 'at' after certain verbs which require it should not be followed in print. Where 'It's a nice place to stay' might pass in conversation, in writing one would expect 'It's a nice place to stay at.'

> He reviews restaurants too, and makes most of them sound like places you wish you could eat.

Plainly this should be: 'most of them sound like places you wish you could eat at'. The notion of wanting to eat restaurants might seem unlikely to be often expressed in print, but in fact it is not rare.

> Penang has a mix of Chinese, Indian and Malay people, which, among other things, makes it a fantastic place to eat.

### *in* and *out*

A common malpractice with 'in' (as with 'at') is that of omitting it. A radio announcer, speaking of the plight of the sufferers from the Turkish earthquake, says that they are finding the emergency tents supplied to be 'places not fit to live' instead of 'not fit to live in'. It is only a living being who can logically be described as 'not fit to live'.

There is a temptation to use 'out' where it is superfluous – for example, 'There are two things you can separate out.' This means no more than 'There are two things you can separate.'

### *by*

At the beginning of this section we cited a misuse of 'by' after the word 'interested'. There is a similar lapse from established convention in a reference to

> Wives or girl friends . . . who don't understand why their partner is so concerned by being bald.

One might be upset, disturbed or moved 'by' something, but 'concerned' is followed by 'at': 'so concerned at being bald'. And another journalist seems equally at sea over the use of 'by':

> Nicholas Owen, of ITN, is in trouble with his friend Sophie Rhys-Jones, by comparing her with Diana, Princess of Wales.

Just as a criminal would not be jailed 'by' robbing a bank but 'for' robbing a bank, so Nicholas Owen must not be said to be in trouble 'by' anything he has done but 'for' comparing Sophie with Diana.

### *over*

We have various idiomatic usages of 'over'. In (a) 'She has changed over the years' the notion of duration is predominant. In (b) 'They exhibited great concern over the whole tragic affair' the word 'over' is the equivalent of 'about' or 'in respect of'. In (c) 'They discussed the latest news over lunch' the notion of simultaneity is present.

> What do you think of the government's handling over the whole affair?

In this question, put by a Radio 4 interviewer, the speaker seems to be trying to combine usage (a) with usage (b) in the same utterance. The effort does not come off. Usage (b) is appropriate only after certain words such as 'concern', 'worry' or 'disappointment' ('He expressed his disappointment over the whole discussion'). In this context the word 'handling' requires to be followed by 'of'.

### *with*

We come now to the treatment of the preposition whose misuse has run riot in contemporary journalism. Journalists, it seems, are prepared to force the preposition 'with' to do numerous jobs for which it is unfitted.

### the additive *with*

> She lives in London, with regular travels overseas.

We may accept that the comma after London makes clear that there is no question of cohabitation. Nevertheless since the proper use of 'with' would give us such sentences as 'She lives in London with her grandmother', it seems impossible to justify not writing 'She lives in London but/and travels regularly overseas.'

> We climbed and climbed with a sheer drop as one glanced out of the window.

Here again the word 'with' is asked to do an additive job it is unfitted for. The sentences 'We climbed with heavy rucksacks on our backs' and

'We climbed with great difficulty' show how 'with' should be used. Instead it here introduces an additional piece of information which, as before, might have been properly introduced by 'and': 'We climbed and climbed, and caught sight of a sheer drop as we glanced out of the windows.'

> The statement made clear that there was no agreement on interest rates, with governments likely to go their own way.

Once more 'with' is used improperly to add to the information given. The sentence should conclude: 'and governments were likely to go their own ways'.

There are times when the use of 'with' to add an appendage seems positively forced on the English tongue. Here we have a former ambassador on the subject of the Foreign Office.

> One of the great failures of the diplomatic service has been to cast off its image as bowler-hatted, pin-striped, chinless and with a fondness for champagne.

Why avoid the straightforward natural sequence here: 'cast off its image as bowler-hatted, pin-striped, chinless and fond of champagne'?

### the causal *with*

The misuse of 'with' for appending additional information is, however, a mild offence compared to the prevalent misuse of 'with' which treats it as having something in common with the word 'because'.

> As you say, with the noise, you could easily have been persuaded that the gear box was broken.

'With the noise' is here used to mean 'because of the noise'. One wonders what is the rational basis for using the word thus. For the causal element, in various degrees, now seems to intrude into the use of 'with' in many different contexts.

> With a mainly rural constituency it was no surprise when Paddy Ashdown joined the Countryside Alliance march through London.

Paddy Ashdown certainly did not join the march 'with' a rural constituency. He joined it, we are really being told, 'because' he has a rural constituency. Not that there is any need to introduce the word 'because' here. The participle could be used. 'Having a mainly rural constituency,

Paddy Ashdown not surprisingly joined the Countryside Alliance march through London.' This recourse to a participle will often correct misuse of 'with'.

> With trading pretty tough, don't expect a big profits advance this year.

Once more the 'causal' element is predominant in the connotation of 'with'. Yet there is no need to use 'because'. The participle will serve again: 'Trading being pretty tough, don't expect a big profits advance this year.'

Of course there are occasions when getting rid of the offensive 'with' may take much more trouble. Consider the following sentence about life in the Fens.

> Malaria was once a great problem, for example, and with few doctors and endemic poverty the local people often resorted to homemade remedies.

It is bad to combine endemic poverty 'with' few doctors as two equivalent possessions the locals had. The two items require separate verbs to indicate their proper connection 'with' the local people: 'Malaria was once a great problem, for example, and, having few doctors and suffering from endemic poverty, the local people often resorted to homemade remedies.'

### the causal / temporal *with*

There is a use of 'with' which is part-causal and part-temporal in its meaning.

> With Gordon's retirement, we have sought to make a few more changes within the team at Headquarters.

The words seem to combine the sense 'since Gordon retired' with the sense 'because Gordon has retired'. The most suitable correction would be: 'Now that Gordon has retired'.

> Now her childhood home is up for sale and, with both her parents dead, saying goodbye is going to be painful.

Here 'with' is used again to give both a temporal and a causal explanation, amounting to 'now that' they are dead and 'because' they are dead. But the participle construction could perfectly meet the need here: 'and, both her parents being dead, saying goodbye is going to be painful'. The same treatment can be given to the following:

> With Edith gone something had to be done about Jack.

Correct this to: 'Edith having gone, something had to be done about Jack.'

### *with* and participle

Some of the most unfortunate misuses of 'with' occur when the word is followed by a present participle.

> With the internet seeming to have an effect on many areas of our lives, it was probably only a matter of time before it was used to organize a railtour.

The causal force of 'with' should be differently obtained: 'Now that the internet seems to have an effect on many areas of our lives'.

Perhaps the most excruciating of all misuses of 'with' can be illustrated by the words of a *Times* correspondent from Washington:

> With it looking almost certain, barring new developments, that the required two thirds of the 100-member Senate will not remove Mr Clinton from office by voting to convict him on the two articles of impeachment, the disagreement among senators is over how quickly to rid themselves of the case.

What is meant here by 'With it looking almost certain' is 'Since it looks almost certain', and that is how it should read. The journalist is operating here on the same level as the person who could write 'With it being wet, I stayed inside' instead of 'Since it was wet, . . .'

Very often the bad combination of 'with' and a present or past participle can be more simply avoided.

> With the plc having increased its authorized share capital to £1,000,000, the relaunch will enable it to raise the money needed to rebuild the line.

All that needs to be done here to make the sentence a perfectly good one is to take out the word 'with': 'The plc having increased its authorized share capital to £1,000,000, the relaunch will enable it to raise the money needed.'

In a more complex sentence the same simple correction can often be made.

> The incumbents of Egremont Castle seemingly had problems providing male heirs, and with Richard de Lucy leaving no son, the superstition developed that no male heir would ever survive to inherit the castle.

If we take out the word 'with' and adjust the punctuation, we are left with a perfectly satisfactory sentence: 'The incumbents of Egremont Castle seemingly had problems in [*sic*] providing male heirs and, Richard de Lucy leaving no son, the superstition developed that no male heir would ever survive to inherit the castle.' This usage of the participle construction in a kind of parenthetical detachment from the rest of the sentence ('Richard de Lucy leaving no son') is one of the most neglected of all English constructions. It is the construction we recommended earlier in getting rid of the absurd hanging participle in 'Having said that, it looks like rain', which we replace by 'That being said, . . .

***without***

An ugly usage of the word 'without' has now established itself in the press.

> They hoped their partners would know what they wanted without them having to tell them.

This usage exploits what we have called the 'gerciple'. To correct it we must change the gerciple ('them having') into a proper gerund: 'without their having to tell them'. This is one of those cases where that correction can be made straightforwardly. The word 'them' becomes the possessive form 'their', and all is well. Unfortunately, where the error occurs, such a direct change is not always possible.

> Do not believe that Scotland can be given devolution without it then demanding independence.

Strictly speaking, the sentence would be correct if 'it' were changed to 'its': 'without its then demanding independence'. But that usage has an air of pedantic contrivance which we shy away from. Therefore it would be better to get rid of 'without': 'Do not believe that Scotland can be given devolution and not then demand independence.'

Dealing with bad usage of 'without' thus generally means getting rid of gerciples.

> If you, too, find it a trial of strength to pick up a saucepan full of cooked food and drain it without the contents disappearing down the sink, or dropping the pan, Boots has the answer.

This is a useful specimen because it shows the 'without' construction both ill used and properly used. It is correct to write of draining a saucepan 'without dropping the pan' because 'without dropping' is indeed what is meant. It is incorrect to speak of draining a saucepan 'without the contents . . .' because what is really meant is 'without the disappearing (disappearance) of the contents down the sink'. Since the use of the apostrophe ('contents' disappearing') is both awkward and ugly, the need for it must be removed: 'If you, too, find it a trial of strength to pick up a saucepan full of cooked food and drain it without losing the contents down the sink or dropping the pan, Boots has the answer.' The reader will notice that we have brought the two constructions into parallel: 'without losing the contents' and 'without dropping the pan'.

The advice to writers must be to exercise extreme caution whenever the impulse arises to use 'without' to introduce a phrase. Conversational idiom, I suppose, now allows such expressions as 'without anyone noticing' (instead of 'without anyone's noticing') and perhaps 'without trouble arising' (instead of 'without trouble's arising'). On paper, however, such constructions look bad. On the whole they do not appear in good books. And they are avoidable. They are replaceable without straining the language (which sentence is correct, where 'without the language being strained' would be incorrect).

***except***

This preposition is rarely misused, but error arises when one tries to use it as though it were a conjunction.

> You'll need to pay for these yourself, except if you're hard of hearing.

This instance of generosity on the part of BT is marred by the grammar in which it is expressed. The proper word to use here would be 'unless': 'You'll need to pay for these yourself, unless you're hard of hearing.' There is a construction 'except that' which can function as a conjunction and introduce a clause ('I would love to come along with you except that I have another engagement on the day'). But on its own 'except' must govern a noun or pronoun ('The whole family came except the baby').

CHAPTER 7

# Avoiding Grammatical Pitfalls

Our daily utterance in speech may contain a fair proportion of simple sentences or questions such as 'Dinner is ready' or 'What time shall I meet you?' But we also have a lot to say and to write which requires more complex arrangements of words. Daily life inevitably involves us in reasoning which complicates the way we handle words. By 'reasoning' I do not necessarily mean anything very sophisticated. We work through a simple pattern of reasoning when we say 'As a decorative scheme, it just doesn't come off' or 'I prefer the pink wallpaper to the blue one.' The intention here is to consider some of the lines of utterance which are a proportionately significant part of our daily conversation and which can be shown to lead our contemporaries frequently into error. For much of the error in the use of English today is concentrated in a handful of bad practices associated with certain frequently used constructions. When one studies current usage with a microscope, concentrating on the detection of error, one is surprised not just by how much of it there is, but by how limited it is in range. There is a handful of notable constructional defects and they turn up, in many different forms, day after day, by the thousand. Obviously there is a need to make clear what those errors are; and it should be helpful too to illustrate with what ingenious versatility they are committed. Then it becomes possible to look out for them.

As we express views about this or that, as we make plans, as we discuss matters of current interest, as we get involved in professional controversy, we naturally want to know what are the routes our thinking takes which are most hazardous to the preservation of accuracy. Which are the highways of reasoning and indeed the byways of passing reflection most littered with traps? Which are the much-used individual words which sign-post the way to the areas of stumbling and falling? That is at issue here and, at a slightly more sophisticated level, in the next chapter.

## FALSE PARALLELS

There are many usages in which item is related to item in such a way as to produce parallelism between them. We see this parallelism at its simplest in the relationship between 'John' and 'my solicitor' in the statement 'John, my solicitor, is ready to see you' or in the statement 'John is here as my solicitor.' The reader may be surprised to discover how much mismatching can be found in usages involving such parallelisms.

### Mismatches After *as*

We deal in the next chapter with misuse of 'as' in linking clause with clause ('They went home as soon as they could'). Here we are concerned with that superficially simple construction used when someone says 'As a doctor, I should advise a long rest.' So long as the words 'as a doctor' are firmly anchored to a subject such as 'I', all is well. Alas such simple connections are sometimes hard to find.

> As something of a steam enthusiast, it was good to see steam has now reached Mach 0.45.

There is no word later in the sentence to give meaning to the opening words 'as something of a steam enthusiast'. They require a matching noun or pronoun. Introduce either 'I' or 'me': 'As something of a steam enthusiast, I found it good to see that steam has now reached Mach 0.45', or: 'it pleased me to see that steam has now reached Mach 0.45'. A comparable failure to match the opening words appears in the following.

> As an international holiday resort, every type of cuisine can be found.

The words 'as an international holiday resort' are just forgotten. There is nothing to give them a meaning. A few words appended would provide the matching item needed: 'As an international holiday resort, every type of cuisine can be found in the town.' The words 'the town' provide the matching item for 'as an international holiday resort'.

Often there is a mismatch after 'as' that seems to result from sheer carelessness in writing, carelessness that a moment's thought would have forestalled.

> As the organization which represents the interests of the British-grown timber industry, I cannot let his article go unchallenged.

The writer surely did not intend to identify himself as an organization. He began his letter with something in mind that he then forgot. It would have been better to say at the beginning exactly what he was: 'As spokesman for the organization which represents the interests of the British-grown timber industry'.

There would seem to be a similar forgetfulness in this artist's comment on paintbrushes.

> The behaviour of the synthetic fibre is remarkably effective as a low-cost substitute for animal hair.

It is not 'the behaviour' that is effective as a substitute for animal hair, it is the synthetic fibre. One questions whether the word 'behaviour' is worth keeping: 'Synthetic fibre is remarkably effective as a low-cost substitute for animal hair.' If the original sentence looks like a version of the 'possessive trap', the following observation from the racecourse looks even more so.

> Bought at an auction in Mechelen, Belgium, as a three-year-old by Michael Whitaker, Pion's win pleased David Broome.

We are told here that Pion's 'win' was bought at an auction in Belgium as a three-year-old. So easy it is to slip into the 'possessive trap' and talk about a possession when you should be talking about the possessor. If the first part of the sentence is kept, the subject of the rest will have to be 'Pion': 'Pion pleased David Broome with his win.'

There is an even more common version of the 'possessive trap'.

> His association with Shackerstone, started 58 years ago as a railway junior, has continued ever since.

The strict grammarian will say that it was not 'his association' that started as a railway junior. 'He' started as a railway junior, but 'he' has not been mentioned. The writer is talking about his association and should not forget that. 'His association with Shackerstone, started 58 years ago when he was a railway junior, has continued ever since.'

## Mismatch After *although*

Like the word 'as', the word 'although' may be used to introduce a phrase in grammatical parallel. 'Although a heavy smoker, he survived to the age of ninety.' (The opening of the sentence is really an abbreviation of 'Although he was a heavy smoker'.) Care must be taken not to allow a mismatch between the two parts of the sentence.

> Although a strict vegetarian, his only daughter ate meat.

Strictly interpreted, this tells us that the strict vegetarian daughter ate meat. There is no other word than 'daughter' to give grammatical propriety to the words 'although a strict vegetarian'. The only way to rescue the sentence is to introduce the vegetarian and a second verb: 'Although he was a strict vegetarian, his only daughter ate meat.'

## Mismatches After Participles

Another source of mismatches is the misconnected participle. We have already seen such failures in looking at present and past participles. They are not hard to locate.

> Handmade by an experienced brushmaker, its Kolinsky sable hairs will hold a generous quantity of colour.

Are we to understand that the hairs were handmade by an experienced brushmaker, or that the entire paintbrush was so made? If the latter was intended, then the above requires correction: 'Handmade by an experienced brushmaker, the brush has Kolinsky sable hairs which hold a generous quantity of colour.'

> Originally designed in 1935 by John Adams, the war and its need for utility delayed wholesale production until 1946.

Here the burden of responsibility for the Second World War seems to be shifted from the shoulders of Adolf Hitler. For the war, we are told, was originally designed in 1935 by one John Adams. The only other possible noun for 'designed' to agree with would be 'production'. Correction involves supplying an appropriate noun to match the words 'originally designed'. This could be inserted towards the end of the sentence: 'the war and the consequent emphasis on utility products delayed production of the piece until 1946'. Alternatively, the sentence could be reworded: 'Originally planned in 1935 by John Adams, wholesale production of the piece was delayed until 1946 by the war and the need for utility.'

## Other Mismatches

Many mismatches are made simply by straightforward failure to parallel terms correctly. Sometimes a couple of words will serve to launch a sentence that explodes on take-off.

> Recent parents, our small patch of green had sadly become a wilderness of weeds.

We could allow 'Recent parents, we had no time for gardening', or even 'Recent parents, our neighbours allowed their garden to go to seed.' In each of these statements 'Recent parents' are identified ('we' and 'our neighbours'). But our writer identifies the small patch of green as 'recent parents'. What is meant is: 'As recent parents we had allowed our small patch of green to become a wilderness of weeds.' The longer the sentence, the more easily a mismatch of this kind can pass unnoticed.

> A devout practising Christian throughout his life, the calm of the village church at an early Sunday morning service provided a welcome respite from the hectic pressures of life in the City.

All that is needed here to transform slack writing into correct writing is the addition of the pronoun 'him' somewhere in the latter half of the sentence: 'A devout practising Christian throughout his life, the calm of the village church at an early Sunday morning service provided him with a welcome respite.' Without that 'him' there is nothing to make sense of the opening words 'A devout practising Christian'.

The world of advertising goes in for mismatching on a generous scale. The following is about pottery.

> Sleek and elegant in its simplicity, the clean lines still possess a contemporary modern quality.

What is 'it' that has this simplicity? 'It' cannot be the plural 'clean lines'. Yet those 'clean lines' are the only subject of the sentence, the only item under discussion. To correct the sentence one must either attach 'simplicity' to the clean lines: 'Sleek and elegant in their simplicity, the clean lines etc.' or change the subject of the sentence: 'Sleek and elegant in its simplicity, the pottery has clean lines that still possess a contemporary modern quality.'

## DRAWING COMPARISONS AND CONTRASTS

### Direct Similarities

#### *like*

In no area of statement on paper is there more error than in the making of comparisons and contrasts. Declaring similarities by using the word 'like', or declaring dissimilarities by using the word 'unlike' are processes which seem to bring out the worst in English penmanship. The most obvious failures occur when a comparison instituted by the word 'like' really fails to materialize. If we read 'Like most mothers, she soon tried to teach her child to speak', we recognize that the words 'like most mothers' introduce and define the word 'she'. But if we read 'Like most mothers, the demands of the children were a pressing preoccupation', we look in vain for the word which 'like most mothers' should introduce and define. It does not appear. The sentence illustrates the first kind of misuse of 'like', where the adjective 'like' (for it is usually an adjective) never acquires the noun which it should qualify.

The error is not rare. Consider the following sentence about collecting antiques.

> Like most of the treasured things we surround ourselves with, the fun is knowing their historical context.

The writer starts with the words 'Like most of the treasured things we surround ourselves with' and readers wait for the expected specimen. They await some sequence such as 'our favourite pictures are a constant delight'. But no such sequence appears. We never explicitly hear what these things are which are 'like most of the treasured things' we possess. Instead the writer talks about 'fun', which is not really a treasured piece of household equipment at all. If the opening of the sentence is kept, the conclusion must be totally changed: 'Like most of the treasured things we surround ourselves with, our antiques give delight as we explore their history.'

More common than such elaborately contrived excursions into error are the simple oversights of people who slip up in their use of a pronoun:

> These old horses love their work and, like humans who retire, it can be a shock to the system.

The natural sequence is always the best, and the natural sequence after 'like humans' would begin with 'they'. To introduce 'it' instead after 'like humans' is obviously going out of one's way in asking for trouble. The proper sequence would be: 'These old horses love their work and, like humans who retire, they can suffer a shock to the system.'

When the pedant starts to look for instances of bad usage following the word 'like', he is faced with a seemingly infinite variety. Here is a sentence recording that six kittens had been used in a year in a certain scientific research establishment.

> This was, like laboratories across Britain, the lowest level yet.

'This' presumably is the number cited. It is said to resemble laboratories across Britain. It would be difficult to think of a more disastrous placing of the word 'like'. Neither the number nor the 'level' can be said to be 'like' laboratories. If 'like' is to be kept, the subject of the sentence must be changed: 'This establishment, like laboratories across Britain, thus achieved the lowest level yet.'

The examples we have given may seem to be rather crude, and readers may well feel themselves totally immune from stumbling so badly. But skilled writers sometimes trip up with this same usage.

> Like a husband who has been caught in an adulterous affair, and who tries to repair his marriage with ever more expensive gifts, the relationship between politician and people has become demeaned.

Now indeed this accomplished writer of political diatribes in *The Times* excites our curiosity with his opening words. We are promised reference to someone who is behaving like an adulterous husband, vainly trying to compensate for his infidelities with boxes of chocolates and jars of perfume, chocolates first from Cadbury, then from Belgium, perfume first from Boots, then from Chanel. But alas this rather revolting individual is never named. It turns out that no one is 'like' him after all. What is like him is a 'relationship', and what could be more boring than that? Next time the writer should arrange his words differently: 'Like a husband who has been caught in an adulterous affair, and who tries to repair his marriage with ever more expensive gifts, the politician has demeaned his relationship with the people.'

## Other Misuses of *like*

We have dealt so far with failures to achieve correct matchings on either side of the word 'like'. But there is another current misuse of 'like' which is rapidly establishing itself.

> I'm making it sound like we didn't get on.

The correct version of this would be: 'I'm making it sound as though we didn't get on' (or: 'as if we didn't get on'). We find the misuse increasingly in print.

> I feel like my hair makes me look really young.
>
> You don't want to look like you're plastered with make-up.
>
> A body that doesn't look like it's swollen three sizes . . .
>
> As it sounds like you have under twenty per cent grey hair, it should give complete colour.

In each of the above cases 'like' should be replaced by 'as though' or 'as if'. The objection to 'like' used thus is that it is an adjective. 'She is like a mother to me'; 'The pie crust was like cardboard'; such sentences show the adjectival force of 'like' at its most direct. But the word 'like' as used in the faulty sentences above is made to function as a conjunction, hingeing on a verb and linking two clauses together. It links 'I feel' and 'my hair makes me look'; it links 'You don't want to look' and 'you're plastered'; it links 'A body doesn't look' and 'it's swollen'; it links 'it sounds' and 'you have'. This is a function that the adjective 'like' cannot perform.

A slightly different version of such misuse treats 'like' not as the equivalent of 'as though', but as the equivalent of 'as'.

> You get a bill a few weeks later like you would with a Visa.

The same judgement applies to this misuse. It treats 'like' as a conjunction, as a word that can link 'You get a bill' with 'you would with a Visa'. In the same way the substitution of 'as' for 'like' would correct the following sentences:

> *Raw Valley* drew in passengers like never before.

> When I first did Burghley, you could have taken a bold seven-year-old or, like I did, a slightly cobby 15.2 hh, and done well.

The question must be asked here whether this construction has sufficiently established itself to be pronounced acceptable. All one can say is that good writers are not using it.

### *as with*

The word 'like' is so over-used and so often misused that it is ironic to have to point to occasions when avoiding it leads to bad writing. Here we have a comment about 'Tudor Rose' dining trains.

> As with most services of this type, this is very popular.

It is a fairly safe piece of advice to writers to say that if they are just going to begin a sentence with 'as with' they are probably just about to make a blunder. Here the word should be replaced by 'like': 'Like most services of this type, this is very popular.'

> As with the Freud exhibition, Riley's show will include paintings.

The same correction should be made here: 'Like the Freud exhibition, Riley's show will include paintings.'

### *similar*

The word 'similar' (followed by 'to') suffers from the same laxity in usage as 'like'.

> The format will be similar to last year.

This not unusual carelessness requires a very simple correction: 'The format will be similar to last year's.' Short-circuiting a comparison in that way is an error that appears in many guises and at various levels of sophistication.

> The last time I wept was when my cat died. It was uncontrollable, short-term kind of reaction, similar to my father dying.

Here is a fairly crude specimen. The writer compares her misery to the death of her father, instead of to the misery she suffered on his death. She should have written: 'It was an uncontrollable, short-term kind of reaction such as my father's death caused.'

There are examples of this error at a more sophisticated level and they cannot be so easily dealt with.

> Great Eastern generated the fewest complaints, particularly commendable as its service complexity and density is similar to other commuter railways which show far worse figures.

This sentence puts the same error on show, though wrapped about with more words. Great Eastern's performance is being compared with other railways instead of with their performance. One may question too whether 'service complexity' is really a satisfactory equivalent of 'complexity of service', and whether the words 'particularly commendable' should not be more firmly attached to the rest of the sentence: 'Great Eastern generated the fewest complaints, a particularly commendable result, as the complexity and density of its service are similar to those of other commuter railways.' To get rid of the artificial 'those of', rewrite thus: 'a particularly commendable result in that, in the complexity and density of its services, it matches other commuter railways which show far worse figures'.

If two items resemble each other, they can be said to be 'similar'. A BBC news writer commits himself/herself to the absurd comment: 'Both reports are similar.' Since it would be impossible for A to be similar to B unless B were similar to A, the use of the word 'both' is out of place, and it should be omitted.

## Direct Contrasts

### *unlike*

Making direct contrasts by using the word 'unlike' is just as productive of error as declaring similarities by using the word 'like'. As is the case with so many misuses that we are examining, this abuse of 'unlike' appears at all levels of simplicity and sophistication.

> Unlike its rival, the Kenwood Chef, the top could be detached and used as a portable hand mixer.

There is the error at its simplest. The 'top' of the mixer, instead of the mixer itself, is said to be 'unlike its rival'. What is meant is: 'Unlike its rival, the Kenwood Chef, it has a detachable top that can be used as a portable hand mixer.'

One persistent version of the error appears in reference to dates.

> Unlike the late 1980s, the economy is starting to slow after the monetary squeeze applied by the Bank of England.

The pedant wonders why anyone should want to contrast 'the economy' with 'the late 1980s'. The only thing that could be properly contrasted with 'the late 1980s' would be another period, say, 'the 2000s'. If 'unlike' is kept, the sentence must be reshaped: 'The economy today, unlike that of the 1980s, is starting to slow.' The slip is not a rare occurrence.

> And, unlike the early 1980s, public finances are healthy enough not to need tightening.

Does the pressure of repeated occurrences of this construction require us to accept it? To anyone in whose mind the word 'unlike' persists in maintaining its adjectival status the idea is unacceptable. The acceptable pattern for these comparisons is 'Unlike 1980, 1990 had a hot summer.' The innovative pattern we are criticizing is represented by such statements as 'Unlike 1980, the weather is hot', where 'unlike 1980' hangs in the air, an incomplete utterance.

The misuse of 'unlike' in comparing dates may be bad, but there are far worse versions of the error. Consider this advertisement from an insurance company.

> Unlike many other plans, if you don't die during its 15-year term, you get a worthwhile cash sum to spend as you wish.

Your custom is sought by a kind assurance that you are 'unlike many other plans'. There is only one kind of sequence that could logically follow 'Unlike many other plans' and that is something that begins: 'this plan of ours' or words to that effect: 'Unlike many other plans, our plan ensures that if you don't die during its 15-year term, you get a worthwhile cash sum to spend as you wish.'

> Unlike the Labour Party, there is not a relationship between financial contributions and the control of policy.

This time there is no attempt to make clear what it is that is 'unlike the Labour Party'. To correct it that body will have to be mentioned: 'Unlike the Labour Party, the Conservative Party allows no relationship between financial contributions and the control of policy.'

Now let us turn to the error locked into a wordier and more complicated sentence:

> Unlike the angry response of western politicians, the Albanian villagers who survived the attack were muted, probably because they were still in shock after the butchery.

The 'Albanian villagers' were unlike the 'angry response' of our politicians, we are told. Only matching items can be drawn together by 'like' or pushed apart by 'unlike'. So the above should read: 'Unlike the angry response of western politicians, the response of the Albanian villagers who survived the attack was muted . . .'.

## Other Comparisons and Contrasts

***compared with***

Not all positive comparisons involve 'like' and not all negative comparisons involve 'unlike'. But the same error of failing to match like with like appears in a variety of constructions. When a man claiming descent from Sir Walter Ralegh was given a jail sentence, a newspaper made this comment:

> Compared with his alleged ancestor, whose tobacco was grown in Virginia, it was a moderate sentence. Sir Walter was executed for treason in 1618.

'Compared with his ancestor . . . it was a moderate sentence' illustrates the same failure in matching like with like as we have found above. The use of the apostrophe 's' could make the comparison valid ('Compared with his alleged ancestor's, it was a moderate sentence') but the more direct correction would be simply to alter 'it was a moderate sentence' to 'he received a moderate sentence'.

Sometimes the misused construction 'compared with' is used unnecessarily anyway.

> The prospect of an economic landline through euroland is adding to pressure on the currency, which has lost 7 per cent of its value against the dollar

> compared with its launch two months ago, and which fell to a new low this week.

The euro is said to have lost 7 per cent of its value 'compared with its launch', but its value cannot be compared with its launch, only with its value at the time of the launch. Yet there is no need for that kind of awkward precision. Simply scrap the construction 'compared with', for the real comparison is between value at one date and value at another. The end of the sentence should read: 'adding to pressure on the currency, which has lost 7 per cent of its value against the dollar since its launch two months ago'.

### *more than*

Making comparisons that involve 'more than' or just a comparative adjective ('bigger than') can produce similar problems. Here, for instance, a slip turns up in a travel piece.

> The food is described as an eclectic mix of Mediterranean and modern British, and is more authentically deserving of that description than many places.

The food, we are told, is better thus described than many other places. Unless the construction is changed there is no escape from: 'is more authentically deserving of that description than the food of many places'. But a writer may well prefer something less clumsy: 'more authentically deserving of that description than food you will find elsewhere'.

The mistake highlights the need for writers to ask themselves before making any comparisons: What exactly am I comparing with what? Failure to face that question squarely results in the error of missing the point in the sequence of thought.

> The Irish economy is growing at almost three times the rate of Britain.

Plainly the writer does not really mean to compare the Irish economy with Britain, but with Britain's economy. In this case the insertion of an apostrophe 's' will correct the error: 'The Irish economy is growing at three times the rate of Britain's.'

We turn to a slightly more subtle comparative misfire:

> Those facing redundancy today face a tougher time than in the previous recession.

This would be correct if those facing redundancy today were the same people who faced it in the previous recession. But they are not. So we cannot say that they are facing a tougher time than in the past. It would be correct, but clumsy, to write: 'Those facing redundancy today face a tougher time than their predecessors did.' It would be better to write: 'face a tougher time than was faced in the previous recession'. After all, the basic contrast is between periods of redundancy.

## Personal Likenesses

The kind of error we are dealing with always betrays a streak of illogicality. That is why one cannot accept the notion that it must be regarded as acceptable because so many people are guilty of it. Here, from the world of horse-racing, we have a comment on an expert.

> His knowledge of pedigrees would be the equal of any stud manager in Newmarket.

This error is another version of the 'possessive trap'. The false comparison between one man's knowledge and another man must be replaced by a contrast between one man's knowledge and another's. The apostrophe does the trick: 'His knowledge of pedigrees would be the equal of any stud manager's in Newmarket.'

That kind of false comparison cannot always be rescued by insertion of an apostrophe.

> She knows that the social skills acquired throughout her previous employment, not to mention her day-to-day legal experience, are a distinct advantage over full-time students.

The mistake is really the mistake made in 'Her pupils' skills are better than her children', where what is needed is to change 'children' to children's'. For the 'social skills' are not an advantage over 'full-time students', but over 'those of full-time students'. If an alternative correction is preferred, then it could be: 'She knows that the social skills acquired . . . give her a distinct advantage over full-time students.'

How widely the error is committed may be gauged from these two comments by a judge at the end of a trial.

> Your problems are no worse than hundreds of your fellow human beings who do not behave as you.

> No one hearing the evidence could fail to feel utter disgust at your life-style and others of your social circle.

The pedant is tempted to correct these two sentences with rather ugly additions ('Your problems are no worse than those of your fellow human beings' and 'utter disgust at your life-style and that of your social circle'). But correctness is not all. And evasion of the need to insert 'those of' and 'that of' is always better. We might recommend: 'You have faced no worse problems than hundreds of your fellow human beings' and: 'disgust at the life-style you and others of your social circle have adopted'.

### *different*

The trap which leads to misfires in comparisons operates in other contexts. The word 'different' sometimes lures the writer into it. We find the mistake in a piece on wildlife reserves in Russia.

> The brigade enforces strict regulations on the use of wildlife resources. Its work is very different from the brigades based in main trading centres such as Vladivostok.

The brigade's work must not be said to be different from other brigades, but from their work: 'Its work is very different from that of brigades based in main trading centres.'

> The layout of the boat was slightly different from the previous day's boat.

The layout of one boat must be contrasted with the layout of the other, but we can scarcely use the apostrophe 's' here ('very different from the previous day's boat's') because of the apostrophe already there in 'day's'. Recourse to the expression 'that of' smacks of artifice, so it would be better to recast the sentence: 'The boat was slightly different in layout from the previous day's boat.'

### *rather than*

The use of these words is especially productive of error. 'Rather than' is best followed by a construction that matches the construction preceding it. It is better to say 'I prefer to stay here rather than to go' than to say 'I prefer to stay here rather than going.' On these grounds we criticize the following sentence.

> If someone sustains personal injury while on holiday, through negligence or default of the hotel, and the hotel was booked through a tour operator, it's possible to sue the tour operator here rather than going to the difficulty of finding a lawyer in the USA.

The infinitive 'to sue' preceding 'rather than' should be matched by an infinitive after it: 'it's possible to sue the tour operator here rather than to go to the trouble of finding a lawyer in the USA'.

And here is another example of clumsy recourse to the gerund after 'rather than' where a matching infinitive is called for:

> As teeth became more complex it became advantageous to retain a permanent set rather than continually replacing them.

The sentence should read: 'it became advantageous to retain a permanent set rather than continually to replace them'.

Balancing what follows 'rather than' with what precedes it is not always a matter of rigid parallelism.

> Presumably this is because they want maximum profit now rather than plan for the long term future.

The proper correction here would be: 'they want maximum profit now rather than to plan for the future'. The infinitive can follow 'rather than' even though a balancing noun precedes it, because an infinitive can provide an object for certain transitive verbs ('They want to go') just as a noun can ('They want dinner').

It is alarming to find 'rather than' misused in a literary review of a new book.

> George Eliot's *Journals*, too, would have taken a better form at Oxford rather than they have at Cambridge.

A schoolchild would acquire red ink markings for this. 'Rather than they have' will not do. In fact 'rather' is simply redundant. Omit it.

### *than*

It is not uncommon to find the word 'than' grossly misused where it should not be used at all.

> More than twice as much was spent on tea than on coffee in 1968.

The construction 'twice as much' requires to be followed by 'as'. The word 'than' is totally out of place. Yet one finds the same error in the 'quality' press.

> A study of car prices by the European Commission found that some cars can cost half as much again in this country than in continental countries . . .

A schoolchild who wrote 'My lollipop cost twice as much than his' (instead of 'as his') would be rightly marked down. That is the mistake here. The sentence should read: 'cost half as much again in this country as in continental countries'. And I find this within a few lines in the same paper:

> A report soon to be published by the Organisation for Economic Co-operation and Development is expected to show that the gaps have widened between prices since its last report in 1995 and that goods and services are the most expensive in the UK than most comparable countries.

Again, a schoolchild who wrote 'My marks in Maths are the best than anybody's' would be taken to task. The sentence should read: 'goods and services in the UK are more expensive than in most comparable countries'.

And now I find a political correspondent writing thus of a public opinion poll:

> But nearly four times as many people would discourage others from voting for the Tories than would encourage them.

The journalist is mixing up two constructions. Either 'as many' must go ('four times more people would discourage others from voting for the Tories than would encourage them') or 'than' must go ('as would encourage them').

Logical breakdown can occur when a writer thus mixes up two constructions in the back of the mind.

> Jonathan hadn't been inside her cottage a matter of moments than she knew he was smitten by her lovely house.

The correct version here would be: 'Jonathan hadn't been inside her cottage a matter of moments before she knew he was smitten by her lovely house.' In the back of the writer's mind here was the construction

'No sooner had Jonathan entered her cottage than she knew he was smitten.' But this use of 'than' is firmly linked to the words 'No sooner had Jonathan entered'. It is logical to say 'No sooner did I enter than she left' because the comparative adjective 'sooner' is appropriately followed by 'than'. It is neither logical nor grammatical to say 'I hadn't been there a moment than she left.'

### *the same as*

This is another construction which requires a proper balance to be kept between the items compared. At the simplest level, no problem arises. In 'her hairdresser is the same as mine', 'her' is perfectly balanced by 'mine'. At a more complex level the same balance should be kept: 'She recited her multiplication tables at the same time as she helped with the washing-up.' There 'she recited' and 'she helped' are similarly balanced as grammatical parallels. But consider the following caption to a photograph in *The Times*.

> Drummer boys and Zulu warriors yesterday remember the fallen at the Battle of Isandhlwana 120 years ago in which British forces were overwhelmed on the same day as Britain's defence of Rorke's Drift.

Here the required parallelism is lost. We can correctly say 'They fought the battle on the same day as the reinforcements arrived', but it would be bad to say 'They fought the battle on the same day as the arrival of reinforcements.' 'They fought' can be paralleled by 'reinforcements arrived' but not by 'the arrival of reinforcements'. In the above sentence the error is well cushioned in words but the failure of balance is no less. The sentence should end: 'in which British forces were overwhelmed on the same day as Britain defended Rorke's Drift'.

### *such as*

The word 'such' may be followed by 'that' in statements asserting that something is a consequence of something else ('His anger was such that he sacked the fellow on the spot'). But where 'such' introduces a comparison, it must be followed by 'as' ('It was such a show as I have never seen before').

> This book is certainly entertaining and anecdotal, very funny in places as well as thought-provoking as the author covers such diverse subjects like the problems of access to open countryside, the history of Munros and other tick lists.

Here the word 'like' must be replaced by 'as'. The expression 'such like' is usable only as an idiomatic colloquial way of saying 'et cetera' ('He was always messing about with toy trains and buses, and such like').

## PUNCTUATION

### The Comma

Correct punctuation is achieved by close attention to meaning. That is especially applicable to the placing of commas. There is a big difference in meaning between 'He said nothing to make his lodger look guilty' and 'He said nothing, to make his lodger look guilty.' The addition of the comma transforms the meaning. Separate items may be linked falsely together if a comma is omitted where it is needed.

> Try not to panic and visit your GP if symptoms persist.

The word 'visit' and what follows it are too closely linked here to what precedes them. As the sentence stands, someone is being advised neither to panic nor to visit the doctor. Clearly that was not intended. The breath that a speaker would take after saying 'panic' needs to be represented by a comma: 'Try not to panic, and visit your GP if symptoms persist.'

> For games lessons we had to wear special togs and goal posts became a symbol of misery for me.

Once more too strong a link is established between the togs and the goal posts, which sound like two items to be worn. A comma must be inserted after 'togs'.

As lack of commas may connect material too closely to preceding words, it may result in failure to mark phrases that call for separation.

> They gathered around the table tasting delicacies and chatting amiably.

Again the natural break after 'table' must be marked by a comma. And quite often the appropriate degree of separation requires the use of commas at either end of a group of words.

> The conflagration had spread to the house next door and for the firemen the whole prospect was a very dangerous one.

The words 'for the firemen' need to be separated by commas at either end: 'and, for the firemen, the whole prospect was a very dangerous one'. It is important not to neglect the second comma in such constructions. Whether the two commas should be used in the case of a single word is now rather a matter of taste than of rule. 'The truth is, however, that not a single member agreed to the proposal.' There, the force of 'however', in announcing a matter seemingly out of line with what has preceded it, requires the prominence that the surrounding commas give. But in the sentence 'The pictures, too, gave me great delight' the intervention of the commas seems fussily interruptive, and they should be omitted.

## The Semicolon

The semicolon marks a slightly firmer break in the flow than the comma. The attempt to make a comma do more work than it is fitted to do is one of the faults in punctuation which do occur quite frequently.

> Recovering from the effects of bronchitis is never a quick process, it takes time.

Here the comma is inadequate. The separateness of the clause 'it takes time', which could be a sentence in itself, calls for something more than a comma. It would not be incorrect here to use a full colon, but because of the very close connection between the main clause and what follows, a semicolon will suffice. 'It' harks back to the subject of the sentence, 'Recovering'. This closeness of connection between the separated clauses is what determines the choice of semicolon. 'My husband gave me a necklace; my daughter gave me a box of chocolates.' That is correct, for although the subject of the first clause is 'My husband' and the subject of the second is 'my daughter', the sequence is so close that there is no need to use a colon.

## The Colon

The colon stands between the semicolon and the full stop in the forcefulness of the break it indicates.

> Lots of people spend hard-earned money on the lottery: very few of them ever benefit from it.

The contrast here between 'lots of people' and the 'few', and their respective experience makes the colon desirable. Very often the colon could be replaced by a full stop. It would be grammatically satisfactory here, but it would break up the prose too jumpily.

There is another and now perhaps more common use of the colon. It is placed after a general statement in order to introduce a series of specific instances. 'The board had twelve members in all: a chairman, a vice-chairman, a secretary and nine other elected representatives.'

## The Apostrophe

In the use of the apostrophe mistakes are made on every side. The apostrophe followed by 's' is required where single nouns are used in the possessive case ('Tom's book', 'the rainbow's end'). The general rule is that this applies even to nouns which already end in 's' ('St Thomas's church', 'Dickens's novels'). But this general rule is broken where it might produce an awkward sequence of letters. Thus we write 'Xerxes' rule', not 'Xerxes's rule'. Indeed in William Blake we find the lines 'What was the sound of Jesus' breath? / He laid his hand on Moses' law.' What happens with these special singular names is that they are treated as plural nouns ending in 's' are treated. ('The parent's attitude' refers to one parent; 'The parents' attitude' refers to more than one parent.)

The general rules are not all that difficult, yet retailers display notices for 'Potato's', 'Turkey's' and 'Newspaper's', and a stylish magazine reads:

> In fact, if her vegetables aren't cooked just so when she dines out, chef's had better be prepared for them to keep coming back until they get it right.

This mistake matches those of the retailers. The ordinary plural of a noun like 'chef' requires no apostrophe. The sentence illustrates the fact that apostrophes are more often put in where they are not wanted than missed out where they are wanted.

> Some of my mates' friends get on my wick. Can I dump them without chucking her too?

This is an interesting specimen of error. When we get to the end of the first sentence we assume that the writer is speaking of the friends of several mates ('my mates' friends'). Only after reading the second sentence do we realize that he has misplaced the apostrophe. There is only one 'mate', so he should have written: 'Some of my mate's friends'.

Mistakes are still frequently made with the words 'its' and 'it's'. The apostrophe is needed only when 'it's' is short for 'it is' ('It's time to go') or 'it has' ('It's disappeared'). Yet one reads in a gardening magazine:

> It's deep red flowers look quite different in full sun or shade.

This should be: 'Its deep red flowers look different'. I have before me a dozen sentences culled from recent journals all making this elementary mistake of inserting an apostrophe into the possessive 'its'. Perhaps more remarkably still, I have a letter from a garage drawing attention to the fact that my car is now three years old and needs an MOT.

> Of course, if any work is needed to get your vehicle through its' test, we won't start without your permission.

Trying to understand how this extraordinary form 'its'' came about, one can only conclude that someone remembers from schooldays that a word ending in 's' must have its apostrophe after the 's' ('Members' coats can be left in the cloakroom').

In forming plurals of words which normally do not have plurals the temptation to use apostrophes should be resisted.

> It was far too late for us to call on the Jones's.

That should be: 'to call on the Joneses'. The following illustrates a comparable error.

> . . . unless you know the basic do's and don'ts it can end up looking a mess.

The apostrophe is needed in 'don'ts' because 'don't' is the equivalent of 'do not'. It is not needed in 'dos' which is an idiomatic plural of 'do'. Comparably easy to find are instances of apostrophes inserted after numbers in recording dates or scores. It is quite wrong to write of 'the fashions of the 1960's' or of 'the 60's'. The apostrophes are not needed. We refer to 'the 1960s' and 'the 60s'. 'A building dating from the 1750's' should be 'A building dating from the 1750s'. Similarly we do not refer to 'a score of two 5's and two 3's' but 'of two 5s and two 3s'. It should go without saying that such headings as '51,516 Thank you's' are also improper.

## The Hyphen

Hyphens are used to knit words together into a single unit. In sentences such as 'The accommodation was rent-free' a noun ('rent') is tied to an adjective ('free'). 'Free' is one of a group of adjectives which are frequently used thus to form new adjectives ('pain-free', 'trouble-free'). The adjective 'dependent' is added to nouns in compounds such as 'insulin-dependent' and 'wheelchair-dependent'. In all these cases the hyphen is necessary. But it goes without saying that a compound which in its early days is hyphenated may become so established that the hyphen disappears. In my 1933 dictionary 'world-wide' is hyphenated. In my recent dictionary 'worldwide' is a single word. One should be wary of trying to initiate change in this respect. When in doubt, hyphenate. The same applies obviously to compounds in which prefixes are attached to nouns in such expressions as 'pre-Reformation history', 'post-Reformation history' and 'counter-Reformation movements'. All the compounds above function as adjectives. There are also prefixes attached to nouns which produce compound nouns, such as 'hyper-inflation' or 'pseudo-philosophy'.

There are compounds involving gerunds that function as nouns, such as 'jam-making' and 'bottle-washing'. It is helpful to distinguish these compounds from those which combine the noun with a present participle to form a kind of adjective, such as 'cancer-causing agents' and 'question-begging answers'. It is risky to experiment with this kind of formation.

> The lonely walk can be hard going, but there are no route finding problems.

If 'route finding' is used at all, then it should be hyphenated, but it would be better replaced by: 'there is no difficulty in finding the route'.

Compounds in which the noun is tied to a past participle also function as adjectives. Thus we speak of an 'air-cooled engine' and a 'family-run business'. We also have long-established compound adjectives made up of an adjective and a past participle, such as 'bald-headed', 'sure-footed' and 'long-legged'. When words are piled up together in impromptu combination, it is necessary to hyphenate them.

> This means that the jacket as a whole doesn't have the suit of armour like feel of a saturated double Ventile one.

There is no escape here from a sprinkling of hyphens: 'doesn't have the suit-of-armour-like feel'.

It is chiefly in the compounds made by fusing two nouns that problems arise. The recent fashion for making more and more of these compounds is fully explored in chapter 11. Here we are concerned with the proper use of the hyphen in such innovations.

> The material is notable for its durability and its frost resistance.

The two nouns 'frost' and 'resistance' thus combined in a compound noun technically need to be hyphenated together. However, we are now inundated with totally hyphenless compounds, in the literature of the business world especially. In one paragraph I read of 'a solutions strategy', 'implementation teams', the 'knowledge base', the 'service sectors', 'implementation activities' and 'Global Solutions teams'. In this area the battle for the adjective as well as for the hyphen seems to be already lost.

One must hope that it is still possible to resist the neglect of the hyphen in more general usage where accumulation of nouns is not an epidemic. However, I have recently seen references to 'British made beef', to a 'seven night cruise' and to the 'cat loving public', which seem to cry out for hyphens as the hunted hart for the waterbrooks.

There is, of course, a distinct use of the hyphen in print which merely indicates that a word has been split in two to preserve the neatness of the printed page. It is important to keep a watchful eye on such computerized hyphenation. Failure to do so, according to correspondents in *The Times*, has produced ambiguous combinations such as 'pronoun-cement', 'brains-canner', 'not-ables' and 'bed-raggled'.

CHAPTER 8

# Presenting a Case

The expression 'Presenting a Case' is used in its most general sense. You are presenting a case if you say 'In my opinion, the house is dingy as well as ugly.' That is reasoning at a very straightforward level, reasoning in which point is added to point. At a slightly more complex level of reasoning, you might say 'John will miss the bus if he doesn't hurry up.' That is reasoning by which a somewhat less obvious connection is established between two different points. From that level of directness to the level of sophistication at which managers or lawyers argue their cases, a few easily definable constructional patterns form the frameworks of reasoning.

We dealt in Chapter 1 with some of the words which can easily be misused in the reasoning process. There our concern was with the exact connotation of the words touched upon, and the importance of using the right ones. Here our concern is with the deployment of words used in reasoning. We are particularly concerned with the function of certain very frequently used terms which act as links or hinges in connecting point with point. Thus the expression 'as well as' established the link by which point was added to point in the sentence 'In my opinion, the house is dingy as well as ugly', and the word 'if' was the hinge on which point was connected with point in the sentence 'John will miss the bus if he doesn't hurry up.'

In the latter sentence the connection was established between two verbs, 'miss' and 'hurry up', each with its own subject. The word 'if' established the connection and is appropriately called a 'conjunction'. The clause 'if he doesn't hurry up' is a clause subordinate to the main clause 'John will miss the bus'. In respect of the interplay of point with point, the arrangement of words can easily go astray. That is so whether the related points are located within a single clause or in different ones.

We are to look now at the various constructions by which one point is related to another point in argument.

## ADDITION

The most straightforward of such constructions are those by which we add point to point cumulatively. The accumulation may be effected by direct aggregation ('I came, I saw, I conquered'), but more often we use linking terms. The simplest is the word 'and' ('I came and I saw'). But there are also much-used expressions such as 'besides', 'as well as' and 'in addition to'. (It should perhaps be added here that in literate English there is no place for the word 'plus' as a substitute for 'and'.)

### *and*

This is perhaps the most used of all link-words. A frequent mistake in the use of 'and' is introduction of what may be called the 'dual-function and'.

> Self-esteem builds up independence, self-reliance and also hikes up those resilience reserves.

The word 'and' here is introduced as though it is going to complete the sequence beginning 'independence, self-reliance' with another noun. Instead of which it introduces a sequence with a different construction. The word 'and' cannot serve two purposes at once. Unless the construction is changed, two 'ands' are needed, one to serve each purpose: 'Self-esteem builds up independence and self-reliance, and it hikes up those resilience reserves.' The following sentence goes astray similarly.

> Life is frustrating for all of us, but we cope using insight, patience, and by turning the other cheek.

The words preceding 'and' ('using insight, patience') lead us to expect a third noun ('using insight, patience, and common sense'). But in fact 'and' is used to connect 'using' with 'turning', while the other sequence ('insight', 'patience') is left hanging in the air. Correct either by using a second 'and': 'but we cope using insight and patience, and by turning the other cheek', or by introducing another verb: 'but we cope, using insight, showing patience, and turning the other cheek'.

When 'and' is used to link two items within a clause, care should be taken to ensure that there is no ambiguity. I read the following in my newspaper:

> Alan Clark, former minister and MP for Kensington and Chelsea, said the confrontation about the party's direction was 'deplorable'.

The reader abreast of current affairs would have had no difficulty here. But the forgetful or the ignorant would not know whether Alan Clark were still an MP or not. The words 'former minister and MP for Kensington' could stand if he had ceased to be an MP, but if the word 'former' applies only to the word 'minister', then another comma would be needed: 'former minister, and MP for Kensington'.

There is a tendency sometimes to insert what is really a redundant 'and' before a relative clause.

> The matter was recently the subject of a Parliamentary Question raised on our behalf by Eric Illsley MP and which resulted in an answer from the Secretary of State.

The word 'and' is here unnecessary and indeed awkward. Moreover, to say that the question 'resulted in' an answer is surely unnatural. The sentence should read: 'a Parliamentary Question raised on our behalf by Eric Illsley MP, which provoked an answer from the Secretary of State'.

***in addition to***

The various constructions we are here concerned with make the same requirement, namely that parallelism should be preserved between the items joined together by the linking expression chosen.

> In addition to his expertise as a wine-taster, Garrard was a skilful and far-seeing economist.

Here there is no exact parallelism between the two items which the expression 'in addition to' combines together. There must be a noun to balance 'expertise': 'In addition to his expertise as a wine-drinker, Garrard had great skill and far-sightedness as an economist.'

***along with***

Similar errors occur after 'along with' (and 'together with').

> Along with a complete redecoration of the premises we have added a new floor.

Since the 'redecoration' was not 'added', proper parallelism breaks down. If the construction is to be kept, there must be a noun to balance 'redecoration': 'Along with the redecoration of the premises, we have effected the construction of a new floor.' But obviously it would be much better to change the construction: 'We have both completely redecorated the premises and added a new floor.'

### *as well as*

The same rule about preserving parallelism applies to the use of 'as well as'. One could say 'He has a knife as well as a fork', where 'knife' balances 'fork'. One could say 'He has a habit of drinking too much as well as (of) smoking too much' where 'drinking too much' balances 'smoking too much'. But such parallels are not always preserved.

> The court was told that his route coincided with that of Miss Smith and that he was known to carry a knife on occasions, as well as having a collection of them.

It would be correct to say 'he was known to carry a knife as well as a cosh'. It would likewise be correct to say 'he was known to carry a knife as well as to take dope' where 'to take dope' matches 'to carry a knife'. There is no such parallelism in the sentence quoted. We should be able happily to break up such a sentence into the two balancing halves joined by 'as well as': 'he was known to carry a knife' and 'he was known to have a collection of them'. So the correct version would be: 'he was known to carry a knife on occasions as well as to have a collection of them'.

The temptation that writers succumb to when using 'as well as' is to follow it by a gerund. Whereas this is perfectly satisfactory if the gerund balances a previous one ('He was fond of fishing as well as shooting'), it is poor style to use it without such a parallel.

> He was a lively host and a brilliant raconteur as well as being an indefatigable public servant.

The word 'being' destroys the sequence and, ironically enough, is redundant anyway. It should be omitted.

### *not just / only . . . but also*

This is another construction whose function is to draw items together in parallel. 'It is not just beautiful, it is also valuable', we say, or 'It is not just raining, it is also very windy.' The relationship between 'beautiful' and 'valuable' or between 'raining' and 'very windy' is one where the parallelism intensifies a statement. The parallelism is crucial to the construction.

> The furniture is not just well-made, but also its design is up-to-the-minute.

The parallelism breaks down here because the sequence beginning 'not just well-made but also' is never completed. Instead a new subject and a new verb ('its design is') are brought in. The reading should be: 'The furniture is not just well-made, but also up-to-the-minute in design.'

What applies to 'not just' applies to 'not only'. There is need to preserve parallelism between what follows 'not only' and what follows 'but also'.

> The endangered gorilla families have found themselves in danger not only from the warring people, but have also had their habitats encroached on by refugees fleeing deep into the forests.

Again parallelism breaks down. It is like saying 'I bought not only a pound of butter but have also been given a free voucher for soap flakes.' The words 'not only from the warring people' need to be balanced: 'in danger not only from the warring people, but also from refugees fleeing deep into the forests and encroaching on their habitats'.

### *besides*

Once more we have a construction that draws items together in parallel and where sometimes due sequence breaks down.

> Besides a two-year guarantee the Pakka Jacket features an integral hood, studded stormflap over the full-length zip, side-adjusted hem, shaped back, hood drawcord tidies and extra arm extension.

There is stark incongruity here between the first item and the succeeding ones. The word 'besides' generally introduces an addition closely related to the other items ('Besides a flat in Mayfair, he has a country house in Gloucestershire'). But the sentence above is almost like saying 'Besides a flat in Mayfair, he has a sly expression and a sarcastic tongue.' There is no grammatical error, but the verb 'features', properly applied to the various aspects of the make-up of the garment, is incongruously applied to the two-year guarantee, as though it were also part of the fabric.

## ALTERNATION AND SEPARATION

The expressions we have touched upon link point with point accumulatively. We turn to expressions which link point with point so as to indicate distinctions of various kinds. Such is the word 'or' ('You can sleep upstairs or you can have a bed down here').

### *or*

There is a misuse of 'or' comparable to the misuse of 'and', which produces what we may call the 'dual-function or'.

> One can hire pedaloes, motorboats or try waterskiing.

It would be correct to write 'One can hire pedaloes, motorboats or water skis.' But 'or' cannot stand as the link to a third item that can be hired and at the same time serve as the link between hiring something and trying something. One 'or' must be allotted to each function: 'One can hire pedaloes or motorboats, or try waterskiing.'

### *apart from*

A converse construction to that serviced by 'in addition to' is the construction serviced by 'apart from'. We call it a 'converse' construction because that is what it ought to be. It separates where 'in addition to' combines. 'Apart from my youngest sister, we all love pancakes.' That represents the proper use of 'apart from', which distinguishes an exception from a general rule or statement. Unfortunately the construction is often used for the very opposite purpose.

> Apart from a huge fertile plain in the east, the centre of the island has a large mountainous backbone.

The fertile plain does not constitute an exception to a general statement about the island. No such statement has been made. Two facts are stated which need to be connected by 'and' or 'but': 'There is a huge fertile plain in the east, but the centre of the island has a large mountainous backbone.'

Sometimes 'apart from' is allowed to drift so far from its proper function that it stands for virtually the opposite of what it should stand for. Here is a recommendation for a camping stove.

> Apart from the ultralight weight, it's superbly made and the design is excellent.

Far from being a disadvantage, the ultralight weight is plainly an advantage. 'Apart from' is here being used, not to introduce an exception, but to introduce a further positive corroboration of the general drift. Scrap 'apart from' and change the construction: 'Ultralight in weight, the stove is also superbly made and the design is excellent.'

### *former / latter*

The word 'former' relates to the first of two things just mentioned and the word 'latter' to the second of the two. The word 'latter' should not be used when more than two items have been mentioned.

> Of the sitting-room, the dining-room and the study I thought the latter the best furnished.

That is strictly incorrect. Since it would be too strained to say 'I thought the last-named the best furnished', the wording should be: 'I thought the study the best furnished.'

> Some horses require a quiet corner and no changes to routine, others relish being stimulated. If your horse is the latter, stimulate his senses . . .

The words 'former' and 'latter' should refer back to nouns. It would be correct to say 'There is provision for the meat-eater and for the vegetarian: if you are the latter, please inform the housekeeper.' There 'if you are the latter' refers directly back to 'vegetarian'. It would be poor usage to say 'Some people are carnivores, others will not eat meat: if you are the latter, please inform the housekeeper' because there is no direct reference back to a single noun such as 'vegetarian'. In the sentence above ('If your horse is the latter') there is likewise no direct reference back to a single noun. If the word 'latter' is to be kept, the sentence should read: 'There is the horse which requires a quiet corner and a fixed routine, and the horse which relishes being stimulated. If your horse is the latter, stimulate his senses . . .'

## CAUSE AND EFFECT

The next group of terms to be investigated is a group of terms concerned with reasoning about cause and effect.

### *because*

The word 'because' has a clear function, yet is often misused. It is correct to say 'He left because he wanted promotion.' It is not correct to say 'His departure was because he wanted promotion.' The difference is that in the first sentence 'because' hinges properly on the verb 'left'. That is its proper function as a conjunction. In the second sentence 'because' is made to hang on the noun 'departure', which is grammatically inadmissible. Yet I read just such a sentence in a political piece about a recent public opinion poll.

> The growing gap between this pessimism and the stability of voting intentions is because the public is still giving the Government the benefit of the doubt.

One should not write 'The gap is because . . .' but 'The gap is caused by . . .' The simplest recipe for getting out of this bad habit is to shift back the verb 'is': 'There is this growing gap between pessimism and the stability of voting intentions because the public is still giving the Government the benefit of the doubt.'

What is virtually the same mistake may occur without the intervention of the verb 'to be'.

> The 34-year-old Ulsterman has always been interested in the media and during a three-month break because of injury from early May looked into the long-term future.

Just as it is improper to say 'His three-month break was because of injury', so it is not permissible to speak of a 'three-month break because of injury'. The correct version would be a 'three-month break caused by injury' or a 'three-month break due to injury'. All uses of 'because' on this pattern mark a writer badly.

Writers need also to be wary of 'because of'. The words often lead one into bad constructions.

> This is because of splinter groups coming down and attacking my home.

The gerciple ('splinter groups coming down') is unfortunate and unnecessary. The more straightforward construction is better: 'This is because splinter groups come down and attack my home.' And here is someone in *Cosmopolitan* explaining why it is always difficult to get over being rejected in love.

> But that's not because of her or him, that's because of oneself asking, 'What did I do wrong?'

The tongue-twisting 'because of oneself asking' could be technically corrected by making it even more of a tongue-twister ('because of oneself's asking'), but the reader deserves something more palatable, and of course more straightforward, than that: 'that is because one asks oneself "What did I do wrong?"'

Writers also need to be wary of what one might call 'causational overkill'.

> The reason she left him was because he was an alcoholic.

That is 'overkill'. Either 'the reason' must go ('She left him because he was an alcoholic') or 'because' must go ('The reason she left him was that he was an alcoholic'). The same kind of 'overkill' occurs at a conversational level in such sentences as:

> Just because he never goes out doesn't necessarily mean that he is ill.

This should be 'The fact that he never goes out doesn't necessarily mean that he is ill', which can be quite properly reduced to: 'That he never goes out doesn't necessarily mean that he is ill.'

> The highlighting is caused because each individual hair is lighter at the tip than at the shaft.

This is like saying 'His death was caused because he was ill.' The duplication represented by the two words 'caused because' is quite illogical. Clumsy as it may seem, if 'caused' is kept, then there is no escape from some such sentence as 'The highlighting is caused by the fact that each individual hair is lighter at the tip than at the shaft.'

### *due to*

This is one of the most ill-used constructions in general use today. 'Due to' is not interchangeable with 'because of'. We may write 'Because of the weather, the match was cancelled', but it would be incorrect to write

'Due to the weather the match was cancelled.' The reason is that 'due' is an adjective and, as such, has to agree with a noun. One can say 'The cancellation was due to the bad weather' because there 'due to' hinges on the word 'cancellation'. In this respect the misuse of 'due to' is as easily found as any misuse explored in this book.

> Due to the diversity of designs and number of bottles produced, it is still possible to pick up Lalique bargains.

> Due to the ever-increasing number of visitors, the company decided to appoint a full-time warden.

> Due to increased use of the locks several pounds were low, even though water was being back-pumped.

In each of these three sentences the words 'due to' are misused. In all cases they could be replaced by 'owing to' or 'because of'. Neither of these two constructions requires to be attached to a noun as 'due to' does. The consequent advice to writers is: Never start a sentence with 'due to' without first checking that it is going to be grammatically correct. In fact it very rarely is. Always consider 'owing to' or 'because of' as your alternative.

It is not only at the start of a sentence that the words 'due to' present risks for the writer.

> The Rail Tour has been put back to November 28 at the request of EWS due to initial problems with the loco.

The words 'due to' are again incorrectly used. It is the attempt to attach 'due' to a verb instead of a noun that is wrong. A 'postponement' might be 'due' to certain problems. But 'due to' cannot hinge on 'has been put back'. Again the words could happily be replaced by 'because of' or even 'owing to'.

There is a tendency to attach the word 'due' to the wrong word, thus producing a slight illogicality.

> The lower than normal number of birds seen could be due to last year's mild winter.

We have a subtle complaint here. When I say 'The top-storey flat makes access difficult', I really mean that the top-storeyness of the flat makes access difficult, or in other words, 'The fact that the flat is on the top storey makes access difficult.' Thus what the writer means in the sentence above is: 'The fact that a lower than normal number of birds are seen could be due to last year's mild winter.' 'The fact that' is a slightly clumsy construction, but what the writer is talking about is not 'the number' but 'the lower-than-normalness' of the number. We mentally bind adjective and noun tightly together in such familiar usages as 'The hot weather is due to an anti-cyclone', where the heat is what is due to the anti-cyclone. (The 'weather' is there, anti-cyclone or not.) But where the adjectival element is increased to 'The hotter than normal weather is due to an anti-cyclone', logic would seem to prefer: 'The abnormal heat is due to an anti-cyclone.'

Oddly enough, the word 'due' is misused in a totally different context from that of reasoning about cause and effect. I have just heard some advice given on a radio programme on the subject of Income Tax.

> If you're due some money back, you must apply at once.

But if money is due to you, that does not make you 'due' some money. Money can be 'due', or a railway train can be 'due'. That is the proper use of 'due'. Just as it would be improper to say 'It is five o'clock. You are now due a train to Paddington', so it is improper to say 'You are now due an income tax rebate.')

### *cause*

It was made clear above that care has to be taken to avoid attaching 'due' to the wrong word where a noun and an adjective are involved. The same problem arises with the verb to 'cause'.

> Dull hair can be caused by product build-up, chemical treatments, sun damage or environmental pollution, so it's not surprising so many of us suffer from it.

The 'hair' is not caused by any of these factors. It is the 'dullness' of the hair that is caused by them. The slight touch of illogicality represented by the above careless usage ('dull hair') will be avoided by good writers. Change the subject of the sentence: 'Hair can be made dull by product build-up.'

One can find even more awkward examples than the above of the way the verb to 'cause' can become detached from its proper mooring. Consider this remark about a railway viaduct.

> The lattice wrought iron structure is designed to minimize weight on the unstable ground caused by mining.

Just as the hair, whether dull or not, was not caused by product build-up, so too the ground, whether firm or not, was not caused by mining. One must spell out exactly what was caused by the mining. If 'caused by mining' is kept, then 'instability' must be mentioned. It is probably better to change the construction: 'The lattice wrought iron structure is designed to minimize weight on the ground rendered unstable by mining.'

## PURPOSE AND RESULT

Closely related to reasoning in terms of cause and effect is reasoning in terms of purpose and result.

### *in order that / to*

The words 'in order' can be followed by 'to' or by 'that'. It is not good to follow them by 'for'.

> The current account requires a balance of $2,000 in order for transactions to be free.

'In order' is really redundant here. One might say: 'in order that transactions may be free', but that would be clumsy. All one needs is: 'The current account requires a balance of $2,000 for transactions to be free.'

> In order for the AA to get to you as quickly as possible it would help if you have your membership card ready when phoning our call centres.

Again 'in order' is redundant. All one needs is: 'For the AA to get to you as quickly as possible'. The best correction would be: 'To enable the AA to get to you as quickly as possible'.

### *result*

Used as a verb or a noun, the word 'result' often introduces a bad construction.

> The failure to start on time resulted in them losing the title.

Reference has been made to the bad usage I have called the 'gerciple'. The verb 'result' all too often lures writers to use it. It would be correct to turn 'losing' into a genuine gerund ('resulted in their losing the title') but it would be equally satisfactory to use the verb 'cause' followed by an infinitive: 'caused them to lose the title'. The error is not rare. The following is advice to women on matters of style.

> Attempting to imitate may result in you not getting the look you wanted.

This time use of the genuine gerund is to be recommended: 'Attempting to imitate may result in your not getting the look you wanted.'

> The opportunity came about as a result of David reading an announcement of the Club's forthcoming cruise.

Here the same bad construction follows 'result' used as a noun. Again one can turn 'reading' into a genuine gerund: 'came about as a result of David's reading an announcement'. But the construction could be happily changed: 'The opportunity arose because David read an announcement'.

One can safely say that all writers should exercise extreme care in using the construction 'as a result of'. There is no shortage of evidence to support this advice.

> Premenstrual outbreaks can occur as a result of water retention putting pressure on both sides of the pore and follicle duct.

In this particular instance the option of converting the gerciple into a genuine gerund is not on offer ('as a result of water retention's putting pressure on'). Therefore the construction must be changed. And, as so often when this usage 'as a result of' faces us, the question arises: What is wrong with the word 'because' that people avoid it? It offers the most natural alternative here: 'Premenstrual outbreaks can occur because water retention puts pressure on both sides of the pore and follicle duct.'

Here is another, and very different, misuse of the verb 'result'.

> The dining room is a blue-grey violet that resulted by a happy accident.

The expression 'that resulted' normally occurs in such sentences as 'There was a tragic accident that resulted in two deaths.' The accident resulted in deaths. But the blue-grey violet did not 'result' in anything. It was itself the result. We would not say 'There were two deaths that resulted by a tragic accident.' Nor should we say that blue-grey violet 'resulted' by accident. We may correct here by turning the verb 'result' into a noun: 'The dining room is a blue-grey violet colour, the result of a happy accident.'

***resulting***

Writers should be wary of using the participle 'resulting'. It must keep the adjectival status it clearly has in such usages as 'The resulting conflagration destroyed the house.' There the word 'resulting' qualifies the noun 'conflagration'. It is lax usage to say: 'The house caught fire, resulting in its destruction' because 'resulting' cannot happily hinge on the whole previous clause.

> Many of the older oaks have been pollarded – the tops have been removed for a variety of uses, resulting in the growth of many almost horizontal branches.

What does the word 'resulting' qualify here? It does not qualify 'oaks' or 'tops' or 'uses'. Instead it is made to hinge on the whole of the previous part of the sentence. In short, it has been forced to do a job a participle is unfitted for. It is better not to use the participle: 'Many of the older oaks have been pollarded – the tops have been removed for a variety of uses, and many almost horizontal branches have grown as a result.'

It is rarely felicitous, though not incorrect, to use the word 'resulting' in such sentences as 'There was a party downstairs and the resulting noise was disturbing.' The construction has to be handled with extreme care.

> In Amsterdam there are literally thousands of cafés to choose from. The downside is that many of these rely on tourist trade and not regular customers, so the resulting meal can be very disappointing.

Clearly no meal should be said to be the result of reliance on the tourist trade. One cannot bypass the chef in the kitchen.

***in an effort to***

The words 'in an effort to' sometimes form a convenient alternative to other constructions expressing purpose ('in order that', 'so that'): 'He persevered in an effort to make money.' But, like 'so that' and 'because', 'in an effort to' must be connected with a verb (here 'persevered'). A journalist, writing of a plan to turn a sensational murder case into entertainment, speaks of:

> . . . the creation of five screenplays in an effort to make a drama that would not offend viewers.

This should be: 'five screenplays created in an effort to make a drama'. The grammatical mistake of linking 'in an effort' to the noun 'creation' is the same mistake made in linking 'because' to a noun in 'The exam failure was because of sheer laziness.'

## CONDITIONS

### *if*

The problems that arise with the word 'if' are similar to those arising with 'because'. It is correct to say 'He will die if he goes on smoking like that', because the word 'if' links directly with the verb 'will die'. It is incorrect to say 'Workers are threatening a strike if their demands are not met.' This will not do since, as is the case with 'because', it is incorrect to make the word 'if' hang on a noun like 'a strike'. The workers are definitely 'threatening' something, and the threat is there without any condition. It is the 'strike' that is conditional. Therefore it would be correct to say 'The workers are threatening to strike if their demands are not met.' For there the conditional 'if' is properly attached to the verb 'to strike'. Below we have a comment about a new Chairman of the Arts Council.

> His first task is to restore the Council's credibility if it is to survive.

This Radio 4 announcement illustrates the bad usage glaringly. The words 'if it is to survive' are made to hinge on the noun 'credibility'. Yet there is no such thing as a 'credibility if it is to survive'. If the words 'if it is to survive' are to be kept, a verb must be provided to make sense of them: 'His first task is to restore the credibility the Council will need if it is to survive.'

> The authorities are drawing attention to the possibly horrendous consequences if the worst predictions prove true.

Here again the clause 'if the worst predictions prove true' is anchored to the noun 'consequences', though a clause beginning with 'if' should always be anchored to a verb. In the sentence 'He will pay the price if the worst predictions prove true' we learn that someone will pay a price 'if' the worst predictions prove true. But in the sentence above the authorities are 'drawing attention' to something whether predictions prove true or not. The solution to the problem is to supply a verb for the 'if' clause to be anchored to: 'The authorities are drawing attention to the horrendous consequences that will follow if the worst predictions prove true.'

Another, less serious, misuse of 'if' is its replacement of 'whether' in indirect questions. This replacement has been gradually taking over. Here is a sentence about day nurseries.

> Your local authority's Early Years Advisor should be able to tell you if one exists in your area, if you're eligible for consideration and how long the waiting list is.

Not so very long ago this would have been: 'Your local authority's Early Years Advisor should be able to tell you whether one exists in your area, whether you're eligible for consideration amd how long the waiting list is.'

The new usage has established itself to such an extent that one can scarcely claim it to be incorrect. But the reader should note the pedant's (bracketed) preference in such cases as the following.

> You need to check if ('whether') management services are available.

> M. J. Street wondered if ('whether') the after-sales warranty would work when the vehicle battery failed.

It should always be remembered that an alternative conditional construction to the use of 'if' is represented by such sentences as 'Were it not raining, I should certainly go' instead of 'If it were not raining'. There are times when this usage is definitely called for.

> She was sentenced in the High Court to three months and told that her term would be higher if not for her ill health and her admission of guilt.

Here it would be better to write: 'her term would be higher were it not for her ill health and her admission of guilt'.

***unless***

The word 'unless' tends to be misused in the same way as 'if'. It is sometimes wrongly anchored. 'You will receive higher wages unless you insist on sticking to the restrictive practices' is correct, because the clause introduced by 'unless' hinges on the verb 'receive'. Receiving the higher wages is conditional on the employees' attitude. 'The management is offering higher wages unless the workers insist on sticking to their restrictive practices' is incorrect because it is not the act of 'offering' that will be obliterated if the men stick to their restrictive practices. The offer has been made. The simple correction that is needed is to supply the verb for 'unless' to hinge on: 'The management is offering to pay higher wages, unless the workers insist on sticking to their restrictive practices.'

When 'unless' is linked to a participle ('A child should not go out at night here unless accompanied by an adult') the writer must make sure that there is a proper link, like the link here between 'a child' and 'accompanied'.

> Because some medicines are designed to release their ingredients slowly, tablets should not be crushed unless directed by your doctor.

Here it is said that tablets must not be crushed unless they have been told to be crushed. The word 'directed' must be properly linked to a 'subject': 'Because some medicines are designed to release their ingredients slowly, you should not crush tablets unless directed by your doctor.'

Misuse of 'unless' is a matter of logic as much as of grammar:

> Unless your hair is quite thick, the style is most suited to those with even features.

This is like saying 'Unless you are too fat, roast turkey is the most popular Christmas dish.' The turkey's popularity does not depend on anyone's relative obesity. And if the hairstyle is most suited to women with even features, that is a fact independent of whether a given individual has thick hair or not. 'Unless' is out of place.

## DEPENDENCE AND INDEPENDENCE

### *depend / depending*

These words are used today with great laxity. The notion of reliance is present in the basic meaning of the word 'depend': 'He depends on farming for a living.'

> What kind of clothing you take with you will depend on the weather at the time.

The relationship here defined by 'depend' is not a matter of reliance. It is rather a matter of cause and effect. Where that is the case, one should use the words 'determined by': 'What kind of clothing you take with you will be determined by the weather at the time.'

> Some companies will charge more [interest on credit cards] depending on where you live.

Here the issue is not so much of dependence as of correspondence, so the better construction would be: 'Some companies will charge more interest according to where you live.' Thus in deciding whether to use 'depend', one should always consider what the relationship is that the word is supposed to define.

'Depending on' is an even more awkwardly mishandled expression.

> Depending on how long you have been a member, you may or may not be eligible for the hand-out.

This shows the risks of starting a sentence with 'depending on'. What is really meant is: 'Whether you are eligible for the hand-out will depend on how long you have been a member.'

***despite***

This word enables us to cancel out any question of either dependence or causation. 'Because it was fine, we took a walk.' That is positive causation. 'Despite the rain, we took a walk.' That removes any element of causation. The reader should notice that, whereas 'because' can be followed by a clause ('it was raining'), 'despite' is followed only by a noun ('despite the rain'). The attempt to make 'despite' introduce something more than a noun often leads to error.

> Despite his wife trying to dissuade him from the expedition, he determined to go through with it.

The inadmissible gerciple ('his wife trying') is easily avoided if one remembers that 'despite' should be followed by a noun: 'Despite his wife's attempts to dissuade him from the expedition, he determined to go through with it.'

> Despite the income from voluntary contributions having fallen, the treasurer is confident that the work will not suffer.

The same error occurs here. To avoid falling into it, the writer needs to pause before using 'despite' and ask the question whether 'although' or 'even though' would not be a better construction. Where 'despite' requires to be followed by a noun, 'even though' can introduce a clause ('Even though he was tired, he joined in'). Thus the above should be:

'Even though the income from voluntary contributions has fallen, the treasurer is confident that the work will not suffer.'

Of course, even if 'despite' is properly followed by a noun, it can be misused through a failure in logical sequence.

> Despite his detractors, Kitchener was responsible for laying the foundations of what was to become one of the best governed countries in the British Empire.

The writer here does not really mean that Kitchener got on with his job in spite of his detractors. What is meant is that this fact about him must stand in spite of what his detractors claim. The sentence illustrates the usefulness of asking oneself, before using 'despite', whether 'in spite of' would not be better. The sentence should begin: 'In spite of what his detractors say'.

## OTHER CONSTRUCTIONS

### *although*

Where 'although' is properly used, there is always an antithesis. 'Although she was over eighty years old, she picked up a hammer and hit the intruder on the head.' We do not expect old ladies of over eighty to pick up hammers and hit intruders on the head. If there is no such element of surprising contrast, then the word 'although' should not be used. Yet the death of an actor was announced thus on the radio:

> Although he was much loved by the public, he will be sadly missed by the acting profession.

'Although' is the wrong word here. The implication of using it is that popularity with the public normally alienates the acting profession. For it suggests that this particular combination of popularity with the profession as well as with the public represents a surprising reconciliation of opposites. What the BBC newswriter meant presumably was: 'He was much loved by the public and will be sadly missed by the acting profession.'

> Although we have to replace the odd tile after a windy day, everything else feels cosy.

This account of life in a country cottage errs in a slightly different way. The implicit contrast between living where tiles are blown off the roof and otherwise feeling cosy may justify the use of 'although', but the words 'everything else feels cosy' produce a disjointed effect. It is rather like saying 'Although we occasionally suffer from food-poisoning, everything else is eatable.' A possible correction might be: 'Although we have to replace the odd tile after a windy day, in all other respects the cottage is cosy.'

### *as*

This word is used in more than one function. Here we are concerned with its use in joining two clauses together. We see this use at its simplest in such sentences as 'The sun shone as the rain stopped', where it brings two statements together in a relationship. The relationship there is a matter of contemporaneity. (The sun shone at the time the rain stopped.) But in the sentence 'He did as he was told' the relationship is one of similarity. (He behaved in the way he was instructed to behave.) It is generally in sentences of the second kind that errors occur, that is, sentences defining some kind of likeness. The most obvious failures in this respect are in those sentences where the likeness is no real likeness. Such is the case in this BBC Radio 4 account of the effects of a tornado:

> The banana crop . . . has been completely flattened, as have other industries.

Clearly the verb 'flattened' cannot be applied to industries in general. Where the verb used in the main part of the sentence is so restricted in usage, the introduction of a parallel by 'as' cannot work. Either the verb 'flattened' must become a more general verb such as 'ruined', or the construction must be abandoned: 'The banana crop has been completely flattened, and other industries similarly damaged.'

Mishandling an 'as' clause can easily cause a more tangled confusion than that.

> Miss O'Donoghue, 54, admitted a crime born of passion as she attacked her former husband Bill Becket, 53, for 'leaving me penniless'.

This report of a court case makes it sound as though the defendant admitted the crime at the same time as she committed it. In fact the word 'as' is out of place: 'Miss O'Donoghue, 54, admitted that she committed a crime born of passion in attacking her former husband.'

There is a habit of taking an ungrammatical short cut after certain uses of 'as'.

> The Tories were not a selfish party, as they were caricatured.

This is really a short cut for: 'The Tories were not a selfish party as they were falsely pictured to be.'

The most common misuse of 'as' in this respect is its use in a bogus connection with the verb to 'know'.

> Ralph is one of the few grocers to specialize in cucurbits as the members of the pumpkin and squash family are known.

This should be 'as the members of the pumpkin and squash family are called'. In English we say 'Smith was called "Softy".' Therefore we can refer to '"Softy" as Smith was called'. But in English we do not say 'Smith was known "Softy"' and therefore we ought not to refer to '"Softy" as Smith was known'. The correct wording would be '"Softy" as Smith was known as'. No one is going to make that awkward statement. Therefore there is no alternative to '"Softy" as Smith was called.' It is incorrect, illogical and insensitive to misuse 'known' as it is now misused day after day by the press and the BBC.

## THE USE OF NEGATIVES

Positive statements and negative statements have to be carefully handled when closely combined in a single sentence. Consider the following sentence on the Government's proposals for lone parents' benefits:

> Its proposals were not coherent and a clumsy way in which to start Mr Blair's welfare reform initiative.

Our use of the word 'and' is such that 'She was not willing and helpful' means that she was neither willing nor helpful. On that basis the above sentence might at first sight be understood to be conveying that the Government's proposals were neither coherent nor a clumsy way in which to tackle the matter. No thoughtful reader would be likely so to misread it, but the construction is clumsy. In order clearly to confine the effect of the word 'not' to the part of the statement preceding 'and', the verb it affects must be repeated: 'Its proposals were not coherent and were a clumsy way in which to start Mr Blair's welfare reform initiative.'

An even more extraordinary mix-up between the negative and the positive occurs in this statement from a railway magazine:

> No major external structure modifications have been made during the rebuilding, the most noticeable being the large roof-mounted silencer and the bogie-mounted sandboxes.

This sounds like a contradiction in terms. One must assume that the 'noticeable' modifications referred to are not 'major'. On that assumption, the sentence is really the equivalent of saying 'No young people attended the performance, the most noticeable being a man of eighty.' If the second half of the sentence is to be rescued, it would probably be best to sacrifice the word 'major': 'Only minor structural modifications have been made during the rebuilding, the most noticeable being the large roof-mounted silencer.'

There are cases where the use of the negative should be avoided. It is more elegant to say 'Three people disapproved of the suggestion' than to say 'Three people did not approve of the suggestion.' In reporting views and attitudes, writers need to remember this.

> Only a quarter of the respondents don't feel satellite will ever challenge terrestrial TV.

Here it would be better to move the negative to where it really belongs in the recorded attitude of the respondents: 'Only a quarter of the respondents feel that satellite will never challenge terrestrial TV.'

A slightly more complicated version of this looseness appears in a comment on a report by the Waterways Ombudsman:

> Eight complainants did not show the internal complaints procedure had been completed.

Once more the negative needs to be shifted to where it belongs. As it stands, the sentence is a most uncomfortable way of trying to say: 'In eight cases the internal complaints procedure had not been completed.'

Our sense of logic is offended by double negatives. At its crudest the double negative cancels itself out. 'I don't want not to go', logically considered, would mean the same thing as 'I want to go.' By the same token the sentence 'She will never change her mind or say yes' means what it says, while 'She will never change her mind nor say yes' would appear to convey the message 'She will never change her mind and not say yes', that is, 'She will never change her mind and fail to say yes.' The truth is that double negatives have a respectable history in English literature. If we lay down strictly logical rules, then someone will come along with a quotation from Shakespeare to show that we are insensitive pedants. That being said, it is best to give logic the benefit of the doubt in making one's judgements.

> The dream of the moneyed country lover is shifting back to the green acres and privacy of the real countryside. But once there, they have no wish to farm nor to become the local squire.

Strictly speaking, logic here requires us to question the word 'nor'. The two items 'to farm' and 'to become the local squire' are equally what 'they' have no wish for. They have no wish for 'either' of them. In short: 'they have no wish to farm or to become the local squire'.

The placing of the word 'no' needs to be watched. It comes as a shock to hear on the radio the announcement:

> It's a No Vote of Confidence.

The vote was a vote and the word 'no' belongs elsewhere: 'a vote of No Confidence'.

There are certain words which are always followed by positive verbs. We do not say 'All the members did not turn up' but 'None of the members turned up.' Thus 'All the supporters we contacted could not have been more enthusiastic' would much better be 'All the supporters we contacted were very enthusiastic.' Sometimes a simple change in word order can improve usage in this respect. 'All twenty-five members of the family were never present together.' The awkwardness there is removed if we say: 'The twenty-five members of the family were never all present together.'

After the word 'any' the same rule against a following negative applies.

> From the beginning of April any member of staff will no longer be permitted to smoke in the office.

Here the proper usage would be: 'From the beginning of April no member of staff will be permitted to smoke in the office.' The tendency to break this rule occurs most often when the word 'any' is open-ended in referring to possible future developments.

> Any future changes in your income will not be taken into account in our calculations.

This should be: 'No future changes in your income will be taken into account'.

CHAPTER 9

# Good Style and Bad

## STYLE AND SUBSTANCE

We all want to write good English, and we believe that something called 'style' is involved. It will be good or it will not. Yet attempts to define good style are not easy to come by. On the contrary, great writers can be very dismissive of the matter. There is a recorded outburst on the subject by Matthew Arnold.

> People think that I can teach them style. What stuff it all is! Have something to say, and say it as clearly as you can. That is the only secret of style.

Is that all it amounts to? Can we not distinguish between the substance of a book and its style? May we not appreciate the one and dislike the other? No doubt we can think of writers in whose cases to think of separating content from style in discussion would seem almost absurd. Swift and Bunyan might be cited as examples. But there are writers who drive us to speak separately of style and content. There is a celebrated comment on Tennyson made by G. K. Chesterton: 'He could not think up to the height of his own towering style.' That implies that here is a writer, a poet, whose style markedly exceeds in quality what he has to say, so that the reader senses a lack of profundity underneath a loftiness of verbal bearing, a paucity of inner substance underneath an outer majesty that seems to cry out for a matching quality of thought.

Dr Johnson, who had so much to say on the subject of writers and writing, himself insisted in his *Life of Cowley* that 'Language is the dress of thought.' He clearly did not underestimate the importance of the substance. Nevertheless, in his *Life of Addison*, he spoke as though a writer might improve his or her style by modelling it on another's.

> Whoever wishes to attain an English style, familiar but not coarse, and elegant but not ostentatious, must give his days and nights to the volumes of Addison.

What is interesting here is that we have something like a definition of good style – or at least one brand of good style. It will be 'familiar' without being coarse and 'elegant' without being ostentatious. That is to say, if we may be so bold as to try to paraphrase Johnson, it will have a kind of natural simplicity which avoids vulgarity and a smooth dignity that avoids showiness. These qualities depend on two things: the appropriate choice of words and the appropriate arrangement of words. A twofold discipline is required of the good stylist, the discipline which forswears laxity and self-indulgence in the selection of words, and the discipline which forswears laxity and sloppiness in their arrangement.

## SIMPLICITY

### Avoiding Wordiness

Natural simplicity will avoid unnecessary wordiness. One of the first characteristics of good English is the economic use of words. It is not just a matter of not wasting words but also of using the most natural words available. There are certain words which bear the hallmark of unnecessary artifice.

> Recent correspondence regarding microwave ovens suggests it is time for a change concerning the provision of cookers in motorcaravans.

It would be good advice to any writer to say, 'If you are thinking of using the word "regarding", don't.' We do not write letters 'regarding' microwave ovens but 'about' microwave ovens. Likewise we do not say 'There has been a change "concerning" his attitude', but 'There has been a change "in" his attitude.' So the sentence should read: 'Recent correspondence about microwave ovens suggests that it is time to change the provision of cookers in motorcaravans.'

Economy in writing is much more than a matter of avoiding clumsy connecting words such as 'regarding' and 'concerning'. A correspondent with a feeling for English and a sense of humour has written thus to the press:

> The *Today* programme reported this morning that Tony Blair fears slippage in the time frame of the arms decommissioning process in Ulster. Well, I suppose that's better than a delay.

Of course, 'slippage in the time frame' means 'delay'. But alas, we regularly hear now that the 'time frame' or the 'time scale' allotted for some venture was too limited when what is meant is that someone tried to do something 'too quickly'. Here is a sentence from the world of caravanning:

> The gas locker easily accommodates two 6 kg propane or two 7 kg butane containers, which should keep most motor caravanners going for an adequate time span.

Plainly 'which should keep most motor caravanners going for an adequate time span' means 'which should last long enough for most motor caravanners'.

There seems to be something about this business of speaking on the subject of time – how long something takes or how much something is delayed – that stirs up the pot of verbosity.

> You should understand that any further delay in reaching a decision could well jeopardize the likelihood of maintaining a satisfactory level of public support for the whole venture.

In plain English this seems to mean: 'Postponing a decision could cost public support.' But just as we have to speak of 'time spans', 'time scales', and 'time frames' where once things were done slowly or quickly, so being acceptable or popular is now a matter of 'maintaining a satisfactory level of public support'.

Sometimes the choice of a single word or two sends a sentence spinning from the sphere of simple statement into the world of muddy pretentiousness.

> The fear of gas is firmly entrenched into the minds of virtually all sailors.

Why 'entrenched'? The word has, or ought to have, a powerful connotation from the picture of digging defensive positions in the stress of war. What purpose do hints of that connotation serve here? Does the sentence mean anything other than 'Most sailors fear gas'? Consider, too, the following:

> The HCS provide a much needed volunteer section input to the project.

On any list of overdone words 'input' would have to have a place. Is it needed here? And is the word 'section' needed either? Is a 'volunteer section input' anything more than 'volunteers'? What impulse towards wordiness is it that produces such excess? The following is another such instance.

> Building them in greater numbers is under review.

Surely this simply means 'They are thinking of building more.' Similarly the works manager who announced that results showed a 'product uptake curve' only meant that sales were up. And the employer who reported on an employee that he had 'an informal approach to time-tables' presumably meant that he was unpunctual.

## Formulas and Evasions

Sometimes wordiness is not so much a matter of picking up the wrong word here and adding the unnecessary word there, but of settling down to a bilious outflow of emasculated words that cushion the brain against thought and the heart against feeling:

> I should like to assure you that on our part we are determined to do our best to settle the matter to your satisfaction.

Clearly this means 'We shall do our best to meet your wishes.' One should be forewarned of coming excess by the opening words. It is a fairly safe piece of advice that if anyone in print would like 'to assure' you of something, then you are not about to receive a crisp announcement. 'I/We should like to assure you that' is only one of a group of introductory expressions that are presumably intended to soften up readers so that they respond more readily to what follows. These expressions have a personal flavour established by the initial 'We' or 'I' and sustained by the direct appeal to 'you' the reader. Other such formal introductory addresses include 'We are pleased to be able to announce that . . .', 'We are taking this opportunity to inform our customers that . . .', 'We believe it will be of interest to you to learn that . . .', and, most winning of all, 'As one of our most loyal and valued customers, you will no doubt be delighted to hear that . . .'

There are also introductory redundancies of a different kind, the impersonal ones. They are less winning. They do not cajole. They do not try to slide into intimacy with the reader. They do not attempt gently to gain the ear for a quiet word. Rather they clamber up to make a formal pronouncement before the face. Some of them retain a degree of restraint, such as 'It is felt that', 'It gives us great pleasure to record that' and even 'It is regretted that'. Others are more clamant and challenging' such as 'It is generally agreed that', 'It must be accepted that', 'It would not be claiming too much to assert that' and even 'It is surely obvious to everyone that'.

There is, of course, a brand of wordiness which has a purpose. The purpose may be to soften a blow, to make an announcement seem less shocking than it is. We are used to this kind of avoidance of the straightforward expression in talking about death. We say that so and so 'passed away'. A firm advising those in direct marketing about checking up on their lists of customers estimates that, while 12 per cent of the customers change their addresses, '3 per cent may be lost due to mortalities'. In short, they die.

The vocabulary of pregnancy and child-bearing was similarly wrapped about with verbiage in the Victorian age. A pregnant wife might be described as being 'in an interesting condition' and she and her husband might be said to be 'expecting a happy event'. In our own period verbal evasions tend to veil very different events. Industrial firms are said to be 'down-sizing' when they plan to dismiss large numbers of their staff. The process of adding to the numbers of unemployed is one of 'rationalization'. A recently sacked employee has ironically described himself as having suffered 'an involuntary career event'. This attitude of seeming tenderness towards employers is not always reciprocated by employers themselves. *The Times* city diarist gives us this information about a large firm:

> As the latest report and accounts reveals, 'as of December 31, 1998, 177 employees had been terminated'.

The finality of being 'terminated' contrasts with experiencing a passing 'career event'.

The sort of evasive style illustrated here is of course a speciality of political propaganda. At the time when news bulletins were filled with horror stories of the ethnic cleansing of Kosovo by Serbian troops, it was said that nearer home, in Serbia itself, the refugees were described as 'relocated transit Albanians' and their lot was to be 'rehoused as guests in Albanian homes'.

## NOUNS AND VERBS

### Recourse to Nouns

Since excessive wordiness often results from unnecessary recourse to nouns, it is worthwhile to explore fully the difference between English style heavily laden with nouns and English style heavily laden with verbs. But we must first note how uneconomic a too ready recourse to nouns – especially abstract nouns – can be.

> We shall continue to build on improvements in the efficiency of our operations, maximizing the potential for growth at home and for expansion in the global market-place.

We shall look carefully at the vocabulary of business later in the book. For the moment it is enough to observe that all we learn from this sentence could be learned from the simple statement: 'We shall do our best to be efficient and to expand our business at home and abroad.' This reduces the number of words in the original by about a third. And the nouns 'improvements', 'efficiency', 'operations', 'potential', 'growth' and 'expansion' have all gone.

Business reports abound in such wastage.

> The funding will provide us with the ability to deliver world class training to potential team members.

Whenever a writer is tempted to use such expressions as 'provide us with the ability', he or she should pause. All that is needed here is: 'The funding will enable us to deliver world class training to potential team members.' Just as 'to provide someone with ability to do this or that' is identical with 'to enable someone to do this or that', so there are many abstract nouns which can be attached to verbs in the business of manufacturing similar inflations. 'We are determined to give immediate consideration to the plan' should be: 'We are determined to consider the plan immediately.' 'The review should supply us with full awareness of the extent of the commitment that is required of us' should be: 'The review should inform us how far we need to be committed.'

Fondness for abstract nouns is now such that there are cases where a writer appears to have dragged one into the text by the scruff of the neck. Here is a claim from the nursing profession:

> We have finally taken our rightful place at the policy tables at federal and state level due to increasing public recognition of our essentiality.

That nurses are necessary to society is a fact we are not going to question. But can we not appreciate how important nurses are without talking about their 'essentiality'?

And I have just heard a speaker prophesying ill of likely future developments in the European Community:

> Such an eventuality would result in the gravest consequences for all of us.

This means 'If that happens, it would be bad for all of us.' Plainly the temptation to have recourse to established circumlocutions such as 'such an eventuality would result in' is wasteful.

## The Pile-up of Nouns

There is another aspect of the current over-fondness for nouns which has developed over recent decades. The fashion is to pile noun upon noun where once adjectives might have been more used. We find a breakfast cereal announcing itself thus:

> The superior high fibre wheat bran cereal.

The words 'fibre', 'wheat', 'bran' and 'cereal' are all nouns. There seems to be a willingness to expand lists of nouns indiscriminately. We hear of, say, a 'Barn Dance Revival Society', then of a 'Barn Dance Revival Society Conference' organized by a 'Barn Dance Revival Society Conference Coordinator'. The nouns are piled up with reckless abandon. The mind begins to long for an adjective as a thirsty man longs for drink in the desert.

The good writer will restrain the appetite for nouns. One of the excesses in this respect is that of forcing a noun into the garment of an adjective.

> These guidelines cover diet and other lifestyle factors that can help prevent cancer.

Notice what process produces a sentence like this. There is the noun 'life' and there is the noun 'style'. The two have been forced together as a new noun. But then this new noun is forced into an adjectival function by being jammed up against another noun 'factors'. The net result is not anything grossly tasteless, but the good writer is not satisfied merely to avoid the grossly tasteless. And the habit of jamming nouns together does not produce elegance. Consider this complaint about weather conditions that can produce flooding:

> There is evidence of some unsatisfactory forecasting and warning dissemination.

The objection here is not against bad grammar but against tortuous juxtaposition of nouns ill-fitted for mutual attachment ('forecasting and warning dissemination'). Reduction in the number of nouns would certainly make for improvement: 'It seems that forecasts and warnings were not made widely enough known.'

In this respect it is not always good style to use one word where two might have been used. 'Warning dissemination' is certainly not better English than 'dissemination of warnings'. The same may be said of the nouns in the following:

> Oil hydraulics have a number of advantages which include greater corrosion protection.

'Corrosion protection' in itself is scarcely a tenable concept. Nothing is to be gained from not saying: 'protection against corrosion'.

Perhaps even more tortuous is the mental process that produces this comment on the timber trade:

> The modern forestry, saw-milling and wood-processing industry has a good story to tell. It makes an important contribution to the economy by providing rural employment and contributes to the balance of payments by import substitution.

The expression 'import substitution' is grotesquely ill-chosen. If 'import substitution' made an acceptable combination, surely it would be more likely to mean substitution 'of' imports than substitution 'for' imports. Again verbal parsimony is misplaced, as it often is when it economizes on prepositions. The sentence should read: 'contributes to the balance of payments by replacing imports'.

## Using Nouns or Verbs

Over-use of nouns and under-use of verbs is a plague in much contemporary journalism, indeed in much contemporary prose of many kinds. Let us consider what are the characteristics of prose which is overladen with nouns, as opposed to prose which is fully laden, or indeed overladen, with verbs. For instance I read in a motoring magazine:

> Plans are in place to increase production of high top models.

The first seven words there include three nouns: 'plans', 'place' and 'production'. If we rewrite the sentence, replacing the nouns 'plans', 'place' and 'production' by verbs, it becomes 'We plan to produce more high top models.' The flavour of the latter sentence is less sophisticated and simpler.

We must not conclude that it is always better to sprinkle a paragraph with verbs rather than nouns. We need to take into account the kind of prose we are writing, its purpose and the readership it is intended for. To exemplify prose heavily laden with verbs perhaps no writer is more useful than Defoe. As a stylist he is simple and direct. His *Journal of the Plague Year*, published in 1722, is a supposedly first-hand account of the outbreak of the plague in London that occurred in 1665. Defoe would have been a child of four or five at the time, but he studied factual documentary accounts of the outbreak, and his book acquires a seeming authoritativeness from its sober direct reportage. Defoe always packed his fictional and semi-fictional work with descriptive and anecdotal detail. In the passage we quote he tells of a poor London citizen who lost his wife and all his children in the Plague. He decided to make for the country, taking two servants and an elderly relative with him. Arriving at a village he takes an empty house.

> After a few days he **got** a cart and **loaded** it with goods, and **carries** them down to the house; the people of the village **opposed** his driving the cart along, but with some arguings and with some force, the men that **drove** the cart along **got** through the street up to the door of the house. There the constable **resisted** them again, and would not **let** them be **brought** in. The man **caused** the goods to **be unloaden** and **laid** at the door, and **sent** the cart away; upon which they **carried** the man before a justice of the peace;

> that is to **say**, they **commanded** him to **go**, which he **did**. The justice **ordered** him to **cause** the cart to **fetch** away the goods again, which he **refused** to **do**; upon which the justice **ordered** the constable to **pursue** the carters and **fetch** them back, and **make** them **reload** the goods and **carry** them away, or to **set** them in the stocks till they **came** for further orders; and if they could not **find** them, nor the man would not **consent** to **take** them away, they should **cause** them to be **drawn** with hooks from the house-door and **burned** in the street.

For other purposes this might perhaps seem to have an excessive preponderance of verbs. But Defoe captures the urgency of the situation and something of the desperate frustration involved in trying to find safety. His flow of verbs renders the prose sinewy, home-spun and compelling, but neither elegant nor rhythmic.

By contrast let us look at the style of the historian Lord Macaulay. He concludes his *Essay on Warren Hastings* with a summary character study whose style abounds in resounding nouns.

> Those who look on his **character**, without **favour** or **malevolence** will pronounce that, in the two great **elements** of all social **virtue**, in **respect** for the **rights** of others, and in **sympathy** for the **sufferings** of others, he was deficient. His **heart** was somewhat hard. But though we cannot with **truth** describe him as either righteous or as a merciful **ruler**, we cannot regard without **admiration** the **amplitude** and **fertility** of his **intellect**, his rare **talents** for **command**, for **administration**, and for **controversy**, his dauntless **courage**, his honourable **poverty**, his fervent **zeal** for the **interests** of the **state**, his noble **equanimity**, tried by both **extremes** of **fortune**, and never disturbed by either.

The prose here is less taut, less plain, and less vigorous, but it has smoothness and some stateliness appropriate to the context. There is also a fine balance in the architecture of the prose and a rhythmic flow quite absent from Defoe's narrative.

## Current Over-use of Nouns

In our own age, generally speaking, the tendency is to over-use nouns heavily. This is the temptation which today's writer has to resist. It means that our prose is more likely to suffer from flaccidity than from jerkiness.

Contemporary prose is all too likely to lack vitality and force. At its most obvious the unnecessary preference for nouns can so easily be avoided.

> Health professionals yesterday urged the police to stop using CS spray to subdue psychiatric patients after research showed that it was a frequent occurrence.

We all know that a 'frequent occurrence' is something that often happens. Why do we translate 'after research showed that it often happened', which is the way we think, into 'after research showed that it was a frequent occurrence', which has become the way we write?

There seems to be a small glossary of abstract nouns labelled in our minds as 'for use in print'. Users feel that they must be dragged out and put on paper to prevent what they want to say from seeming too obvious or too easily comprehensible.

> The experts fear a worsening of the danger.

Now the person who put that into print would not have put it like that in conversation. To an acquaintance he would have said: 'The experts fear the danger will get worse.' What in speech 'gets worse' on paper becomes 'a worsening'.

> They can contemplate and accept the inevitability of its disappearance.

The person who wrote that would not have said it. He or she would have said 'They can see and accept that it must go.' In speech we recognize that something 'must go', whereas on paper we have to 'accept the inevitability of its disappearance'.

> Americans have long seen the Middle East, North Africa and sometimes even Western Europe as areas in which vigilance against such [terrorist] attacks is a permanent necessity.

Let us again try to imagine what happened in the mind and possibly even in speech before anything of this got put down on paper. Someone decided that there were areas 'where they would always have to watch out for terrorist attacks'. So the mental glossary of 'writable words' was ransacked and the recommended terms were brought into play. Instead of always having to watch out, there must be asserted the 'necessity' for 'vigilance'.

One begins to wonder whether press magnates encourage their

employees to translate from the language of thought and utterance into this laboured and inflexible idiom.

> A further sinister reinforcement of this attitude may be that smoking among older women has been found to be associated with relative thinness, a possibility that may not have been overlooked by observant teenage girls as well as the tobacco industry.

Older women who smoke tend to be thinner. Teenage girls notice that and so does the tobacco industry. The point is worth making, but do we really need all this stuff about 'reinforcement' of an 'attitude' and something being 'associated' with 'relative thinness' and a 'possibility' that some 'observant' people may not have overlooked?

Reaching for an abstract noun whenever one has something to say becomes a kind of ingrained habit. There was a news item on BBC Radio 4 about an incident in the Balkans in which bodies of Albanians were found, seemingly massacred by the Serbian Security Police. Various versions of what had happened were aired. On this issue the radio announcement ran:

> As the days passed the precise truth became less and less clear.

Why drag in this abstraction 'precise truth', when what the newswriter meant was that 'what had actually happened' became less and less clear as the days passed? There is a strange rooted objection in journalism to the use of such a natural English noun clause as 'what had happened'. If 'what was true' became ever more difficult to determine, that does not mean that 'truth' was becoming 'less clear'. It means that 'truth' was getting harder and harder to arrive at. But the reader will notice that, as we strive to make clear what should have been said, verbs come into play. We use such expressions as 'what had happened', 'becoming more difficult to determine', and 'getting harder and harder to arrive at'.

There is need for a campaign in English education against the over-use of nouns. Pick up any piece of publicity you receive through the post and you will find evidence of this. Today I read:

> Under self-assessment rules, the automatic penalty for the late submission of a tax return is £100.

Suppose we try to reduce the nouns there. 'Under self-assessment rules, you will be fined £100 if you send in your tax return late.' Instead of the noun 'penalty' we have the verb 'will be fined'. Instead of the noun 'submission' we have the verb 'send in'.

Children should be given exercises in schools in translating noun-ridden prose into verby prose. The earliest exercises could take the form of turning 'Our sole aim is your satisfaction' into 'We only want to please you.' Nothing is easier than turning up suitable specimens for this kind of exercise. Replaceable nouns are printed in bold type in what follows. Verbs introduced in their place are also in bold type.

> Our **intention** is to give the matter serious **consideration**.

This becomes:

> We **intend** to **consider** the matter seriously.

> **Consideration** must be given to organizational **developments** which could strengthen the **accountability** of senior management.

This becomes:

> We must **consider** how to **develop** our organization so as to **make** our senior managers more accountable.

> After a whole day of **negotiation** a settlement was arrived at which met with **acceptance** from both parties.

This becomes:

> After **negotiating** for a day, a settlement was reached which both parties **agreed** to.

> Greater customer **care** plus improved **support** for dealers were identified as key **benefits** behind one of the biggest **innovations** in the leisure vehicle industry.

This becomes:

> The leisure vehicle industry has **reformed** its practices so as to **care** more for customers and to **support** dealers better.

> There are too many **concentrations** of dangerous heavy metals in plants that are important **resources** for a wider **range** of waterbirds.

This becomes:

> Too often dangerous heavy metals are **concentrated** in plants that **help** to **sustain** many different waterbirds.

## Nouns Doubling as Verbs

We have been concerned here with nouns and verbs as words with contrasting functions. But the English language is rich in words which are both nouns and verbs. Look up a few simple nouns or a few simple verbs in a dictionary. Such nouns as 'love', 'force' and 'taste' are also verbs. Such verbs as 'drink', 'wash' and 'play' are also nouns. We think of 'give' as a verb and 'gift' as a noun, but the Scots have long used 'gift' as a verb. We think of 'author' as a noun, but the Americans use it as a verb. The temptation for writers to use an established noun as a verb or an established verb as a noun can scarcely be considered a practice alien to the language. We have been taking such liberties for a long time. Words as essentially nounlike in their form as 'condition', 'position', 'partition', 'requisition' and 'section' are all used as verbs. We can see this practice extended further and further in our own day. My latest dictionary gives 'rubbish' as a noun only, but we now often hear it used as a verb, meaning to disparage totally ('In an ironical outburst the leader of the Opposition rubbished the Government's new proposal'). There are even cases where an individual's career may furnish us with a new noun-turned-verb. It was during Mrs Thatcher's forceful premiership that the noun 'handbag' was turned into a verb expressive of aggressive diplomacy in action.

Experimentation with words can enrich the language. We have long been manufacturing new verbs from existing nouns and adjectives. 'My wife and I caravan all year round', I read. My older dictionary gives 'caravan' only as a noun; my newer dictionary gives it as a verb too. There are obvious advantages in not having to write 'My wife and I use our caravan all year round.' In the early days of the private car the word 'motor' was used of both the vehicle and the use of it. King George V was known to be fond of 'motoring' and Rowntrees successfully marketed 'motoring chocolate'.

It is true that sometimes verbs newly fashioned from nouns make readers squirm when they are first encountered.

> The Craft Movement Contemporary Craft Fair showcases the original work of more than 100 of the UK's best professional designer/makers . . .

Here is a case in point. The noun 'showcase' somehow seems too thoroughly 'nounish' to be so treated. Yet on reflection we realize that some seemingly most unlikely compound nouns such as 'time-table', 'soft-pedal' and 'steam-roller' have become useful verbs.

Where can we draw the line? I have heard an attempt to turn the noun 'nuance' into a verb: 'I think I should want to nuance that criticism a little.' Presumably this means 'I think I should want to give a subtle change to that criticism.' How free are we in this respect? Was the first person to use the word 'rubbish' as a verb charged with illiteracy? If we are so clever that we thus 'invent' a new verb, we must hope that it will catch on until those who at first squirm to read it begin to use it themselves. After all, what noun would totally resist being converted into a verb? The Victorian Age left us a tongue-twister in the form of a snatch of conversation between a lady and a workman repairing a pan:

> Are you aluminiuming it, man?
> No, I'm copper-bottoming it, mum.

And in conversation it is not only nouns that get turned into verbs. In Shakespeare's *Romeo and Juliet*, when Juliet annoys her father Capulet by resisting his demand that she should marry County Paris, Capulet accuses her of being too proud. She quibbles over the word 'proud' and Capulet loses his temper with her. 'Proud me no prouds' he says in rebuke, turning the adjective 'proud' temporarily into a verb and then temporarily into a plural noun.

## USE OF METAPHOR

The pursuit of simplicity and directness does not preclude colour and imagery. The judicious use of metaphor is crucial in the best writing. But metaphor misapplied damages style. And, once a seemingly appropriate metaphor has been seized on, it must be properly followed up. Here is a tribute to the old Nature Conservancy Council.

> Its official enthusiasm for local nature reserve designations on educational and recreational grounds has pumped life into official doorstep conservation.

Now to speak of 'pumping' life or 'breathing' life instead of just using a verb like 'strengthened' or 'revitalized' is to make sensible use of metaphor. But pumping life into a movement is one thing, and pumping life into 'doorstep conservation' is another thing. After all, 'wild life conservation' is conservation of wild life. And on that pattern 'doorstep conservation' would be conservation of doorsteps.

It tends to be with the introduction of fairly well-worn metaphors that writers trip up. We are so used to them that we lose sight of their metaphorical content. Consider this, for instance:

> Among the pantheon of great sporting clichés, the hoary old chestnut that luck is something you make for yourself has always seemed to me one of the more blatantly unsatisfactory.

The Pantheon was a circular temple in Rome. Its peculiarity was that it was dedicated, not to a particular god, but to all the gods. Thus the word has been taken up for a building in which a nation's dead heroes are commemorated. From that usage stems the use of the word for a place that houses the full tally of a nation's poets or artists. The writer of the above sentence may or may not have sensed that the word represents a place in which a number of beings are commemorated, but he assumes that he is free to use it to mean a repository for lots of items or indeed a kind of volume of quotations. This is to stretch the metaphor further than it will go. In other words it is to destroy the metaphor. We can accept the other metaphor, the 'hoary old chestnut', as standing for a sporting cliché. But to picture it taking its place in a pantheon is to turn a good metaphor into nonsense.

In the use of metaphor there must be appropriateness, restraint and consistency. These three requirements make for effective use of imagery. When the metaphorical use of the word 'pantheon' required us to treat a temple or a mausoleum as a thesaurus of quotations, there was a plain lack of appropriateness. One might argue that the imagery of the following sentence fails in respect of both restraint and consistency:

> I cannot believe that he [the Prime Minister] will choose to plunge into such an obvious elephant trap which would sour relations with the countryside up to and well beyond the next General Election.

We may or may not feel that it is over-stretching the image to parallel the passing of a new law with plunging into an obvious elephant trap. But, however that may be, we ought not to be asked to picture either the plunge or the trap 'souring' relations.

One ought not to go in for imagery whose effect on readers depends upon their not taking it too seriously; that is to say, not visualizing what is pictured. It is bad to rely on unresponsiveness by the reader to vivid metaphor, however well established.

> England's leading clubs are positioned today to make a gesture that could soothe the months of nagging warfare that have blighted British rugby since the introduction of professionalism.

Now if the writer had said 'a gesture that could put an end to the months of nagging warfare', we should not have complained. But the word 'soothe' is, or should be, a powerful metaphorical expression, and the sensitive reader balks at the idea of 'soothing' months. And just as we do not 'soothe' months, neither do we 'soothe' nagging warfare. This is what is meant by our demand for consistency in imagery.

When, quite justifiably, seeking to avoid the most obvious and most used verbs, the writer must take care not to use a verb with a metaphorical content that collides incongruously with its context.

> Saladin stopped Richard I from taking Jerusalem, sparking the decline of large-scale expeditions.

The image of 'sparking' derives presumably from starting a conflagration or an explosion. It would seem appropriate enough to the launching of an enterprise or to the outbreak of some catastrophic development such as a war, but surely it is not appropriate to an event which marks the beginning of a decline. One can only recommend a more colourless verb: 'starting the decline of large-scale expeditions'.

## WORD AND CONTEXT

We all know that words group themselves for us, not just according to their literal meanings, but according to the kind of context in which they are most often used. We read in a leaflet about some public meeting that 'Proceedings will commence with a statement from the Chairman.' The vocabulary does not strike us as odd. But if we were invited out to dinner with some close friends and our host turned to us as he received us and said 'Proceedings will commence with drinks in the drawing room', we should suspect him of being funny. The appropriate vocabulary for one situation is not the appropriate vocabulary for a very different situation.

Now we must not assume that transfer of vocabulary from its normally appropriate context into a seemingly inappropriate context is always a mistake. It may be intentionally done for a comic purpose, as we suggested with the host's greeting at the party. Samuel Beckett at one and the same time convulses us with laughter and wrings our hearts in his plays and in his novels by juxtaposing snatches of the familiar currencies of contemporary day-to-day usage with situations totally and tragically at loggerheads with the thrust and tone of what is said.

Indeed the forcing together of words from different areas of usage may be highly poetic in effect. Surely there is no more prosaic word in the English language than the word 'satisfactory'. We associate it with the dullest school reports on the most unexciting performances by the most pedestrian of achievers. Yet T. S. Eliot achieves a dramatic, indeed a climactic effect by his use of the word at the end of one section of *Journey of the Magi*, his poem about the coming of the three kings to Bethlehem on the birth of Christ. The poem begins in a conversational idiom as the journey is described, and one word seems to stick out at the end of the sixth line where the camels are described as 'galled, sore-footed, refractory'. The seemingly rather clumsy word resonates in the mind until, over twenty lines later, the speaker tells of the eventual arrival at Bethlehem and what they found there in the words 'it was (you may say) satisfactory'.

It takes a poet to make the word 'satisfactory' so powerfully evocative. We are unlikely to be inspired to comparable strokes of genius in our daily use of words. If we get the wrong word from the wrong context it is likely to be a defacement rather than an enrichment of our utterance. The careful speaker or writer uses words which meld happily together. We do not want business jargon in the privacy of the home. A police inspector, interviewed on the radio about a certain problem said:

> It's a question of getting the message down to that section of the police service which has an interface with the public.

The word 'interface', basically a scientific term for the surface which is common to two different contiguous things, has been found useful in the field of business organization, so useful that it has been over-used. It is now a 'vogue word'. But clearly it is out of place in the policeman's statement. If we cannot talk about the officers who come into personal contact with the public without introducing an 'interface' between them, we need some elementary instruction in the use of our language. It is this practice of dropping a decisively technical word into a humdrum sentence that needs to be disciplined. It introduces a linguistically alien element that discomfits the reader.

> The countryside is a complicated entity, in danger of being overlooked or taken for granted.

The word 'entity' is basically a philosophical term for something which has real and distinctive existence. Perhaps its nearest English equivalent would be 'beingness'. It is quite out of place in a sentence pleading for more attention to the preservation of the English countryside. Words such as 'complicated', 'entity' and 'danger' are weakened by usage which relies on the reader not to take any of them at their face value.

We move from the countryside to the garden for another experiment in verbal misplacement.

> People should experiment more with plants. They are unaware of the potential of their gardens, so they plant the norm.

The non-gardener may be so taken aback by this statement as to feel it necessary to check up in an encyclopaedia just to make sure that there is not a fast-spreading herbaceous perennial called 'norm'. After all, the word 'norm' we are accustomed to means the average level of achievement, the standard of action that can be expected as representing the average. It is not something that can be planted in a garden. To use the expression 'they planted the norm' to mean 'they put in the kind of thing that most people would' is again to introduce a verbally alien note.

The converse error of abusing familiar words that are associated with primal human experiences by exploiting them for commercial purposes is a commonplace of business publicity.

> All the members of our Board join me in urging you, as a valued shareholder, to look seriously at a new and exciting proposal which I am proud to be able to present to you.

Here our complaint is that familiar words are applied with an insensitivity to their genuine meaning that cheapens them. 'Valued', 'seriously', 'exciting' and 'proud' are thrown about like counters of little worth. The request to the reader to study something is what has to be conveyed. It is tasteless to wrap it around with the ambience of seriousness, excitement and personal pride.

It is in translations into English that the gravest misplacements of vocabulary can occur. Such misplacements can be a great source of humour. When we are told of them, we wonder whether they are not perhaps the stuff of fiction. But perhaps it is true that a Hong Kong tailor's shop displays a notice saying 'Ladies may have fits upstairs' and a Greek tailor's shop guarantees 'to execute customers in strict rotation'. And perhaps there really is a hotel in an Austrian ski resort where guests are requested 'not to perambulate the corridors in the hours of repose in the boots of ascension'. Periodically such specimens appear in the press and indeed they illuminate nuances and vagaries in our vocabulary.

It should go without saying in this matter of suiting the word to the context that what is appropriate in speech may be unsuitable on the printed page. Many a construction cited in this book for criticism might well be used in conversation without raising pedantic eyebrows. But there is a gossipy informality in our chatter that can look tasteless in print.

> Perhaps you're picking up on problems in their relationship and are feeling protective towards your friend.

The Agony Aunt must be allowed her due licence of informality, but this slangy construction 'to pick up on', meaning 'to take notice of' or 'to make something of', would be better replaced by some tasteful usage that is none the less homely, say: 'Perhaps you're dwelling too much on problems in their relationship.' But if readers feel indulgent towards the Agony Aunt's chatty idiom, they will be less inclined to look favourably on the following:

> Designers have already picked up on the potential of 'mood-enhancing' room fragrances.

Here the meaning is: 'Designers have already exploited the potential of "mood-enhancing" room fragrances.'

Certain readily used conversational expressions somehow have their constructional defects exposed when they are put into print. For instance we ask 'Was it just my imagination?' when we want to imply that perhaps what we are going to say is not factually correct but a guess on our part. Yet when this expression is put in print the literal meaning of the words is revealed in its bareness.

> Was it my imagination or were gardens in June neglected because of the bad weather?

It would be much better here to drop the colloquialism and say: 'Is my hunch correct, that gardens in June were neglected because of the bad weather?'

Such colloquialisms form quite a significant part of our daily conversations. Someone tells us something that fully confirms a perhaps controversial view that we have long held. 'Indeed', we say, 'that says it all!' But put that into cold print and advertise 'Furniture that says it all' and the expression suddenly has its absurdity revealed.

Words which carry only a slight metaphorical content when we use them in conversation may have that content strengthened when they are put into print. For instance, we might say 'That notion sounds absurd', and we are not thinking of the verb 'sound' in connection with noise of any kind. But put that in print and the effect is different.

> The notion of growing orchids in the bitter cold urban jungle of Chicago sounds as unlikely as snow falling in the desert.

When we have read words like 'cold urban jungle' we are mentally in a verbal world where things are felt. When we move on to expressions like 'snow falling in the desert' we are strengthened in our sense of the felt world, the world in which weather changes and snow may fall. As a result the word 'sounds' gets involved also in the world of sensation, and we think to ourselves that growing orchids and snow falling are both silent processes, and that 'notions' do not produce any sound at all.

## HYPERBOLE

Hyperbole is exaggeration indulged in for the sake of effect. It may be deliberate and effective. Poets use it unashamedly. In Shakespeare's *Macbeth*, when Macbeth has murdered Duncan and is horrified at the sight of his own bloodied hands, he cries:

> Will all great Neptune's ocean wash this blood
> Clean from my hand? No, this my hand will rather
> The multitudinous seas incarnadine,
> Making the green one red.

Here is hyperbole on the grand scale. Macbeth's notion that if he put his hand in the sea the world's oceans would turn red is imaginatively powerful precisely because its excess matches the enormity of the deed.

The worst kind of hyperbole is that which establishes itself by such frequent repetition that all novelty and force are lost. The most obvious of all hyperboles are those which we use daily in conversation. 'She's terribly late', we say, when in fact the element of terror is lacking. 'Terribly' has become a substitute for 'very'. 'My dear, it was absolutely devastating! The milkman failed to deliver on two successive days.' The potentially powerful words 'absolutely devastating' are used as little more than a substitute for 'inconvenient'.

Now conversation is one thing and the written word another thing. On paper, the cheapening of richly meaningful words by using them as so many counters to avoid repetition of 'very' or 'most' implies failure to think carefully. It also suggests poverty of imagination. Let us consider a few specimens.

> The hotel is close to a fabulous sandy beach.

The word 'fabulous' (from the word 'fable') strictly defines an imaginary beast such as the Minotaur or some other comparable creature or event with only legendary existence. Hence it is used to describe something so astoundingly remarkable as to be unbelievable or all but unbelievable. To describe someone as having 'fabulous wealth' would convey the possession of riches all but inconceivable. To throw the word around as an equivalent of 'very nice' is to dissipate its meaning. The same applies to the word 'fantastic'. An advertiser tells us that if we use certain dyes 'fantastic results are guaranteed'. The word 'fantastic' (from the word 'fantasy') is applied to beings and things conceived in the world of fancy rather than of reality. Again it is totally inappropriate to use the word thus. Closely related to the misuse of 'fabulous' and 'fantastic' is the misuse of 'incredible' and 'incredibly', words which also seem to belong more to the recounting of marvellous events than of day-to-day doings.

> The display of her work went down incredibly well.

Clearly again the word 'very' would do all that the now weakened word 'incredibly' can do.

The desire to give the highest degree of praise one can to efforts of this kind naturally breeds hyperbole. Here we have a comment on a horse trials event. The writer tells that no one is 'too big to give advice, when asked, or to share their ideals', and adds:

> It is eventing's greatest asset and creates such a good camaraderie amongst competitors, an ideal that I believe is unique to this sport.

Here the words 'ideal' and 'unique' seem to be brought into play chiefly because of the nice noise they make.

The specimens we have been looking at tend to arise from the desire to make something seem more remarkable than it is. By the use of hyperbole the writer exaggerates the emotional impact of what is said.

> Dr Jeff Sampson has just joined the Animal Health Trust as Canine Genetics Co-ordinator. This new post, sponsored by the Kennel Club, will help apply this exciting subject to the world of dog breeding.

Over-use of the word 'exciting' is not uncommon. In contexts like this it is apt to raise an ironic smile. Certainly the subject is one that dog-breeders will find 'interesting'. The writer gains nothing by using the word 'exciting', as though it meant no more than that. A similar, perhaps more justifiable, hyperbolic approach to the reader's feelings is made by the word 'horrifying' in the sentence:

> A horrifying number of pets are put to sleep because they can't be identified and their owners traced.

Just as words to do with stirring the reader's feelings tend to be hyperbolic, so too do words connected with suggestions of great size. It is easy to find examples of words such as 'tremendous', 'immense' and 'enormous' used where 'large' or 'big' would be more appropriate.

Hyperbole is not just a matter of using adjectives extravagantly. A different brand of hyperbole builds up an image in a word or two whose effect is quite disproportionate to what is needed. Here we have an advertiser's enthusiastic account of a new car.

> The sexy aristocrat of the open road. Sleek and swift. Purebred and powerful. With the body of a thoroughbred and the soul of a beast.

The world of cold prose seems to be left behind here. We are in the verbal world where Macbeth's bloodied hands could turn the world's oceans scarlet. The trouble is, however, that the AA journal is not designed for theatrical performance before a hushed and rapt audience. No doubt the psychologist could have some fun explaining the propaganda effect of words such as 'sexy' and 'aristocrat', with their associations of glowing beauty and social superiority, of words such as 'purebred' and 'thoroughbred', with their associations of high breed and grace on display in the fresh country air. And, lest it was all beginning to seem too cultivatedly high-class, there is the expression 'the soul of a beast' to raise associations of untamed power waiting to be unleashed.

Ours not to cavil or complain when the poetic souls of advertisers are let off their leash. But the imaginative efforts do not always come off. Witness the advertiser's question, put before recommending a skin treatment.

> Is your skin tight, tingly and throwing a tantrum?

One can give higher marks for ingenuity than for good taste here. To speak of 'throwing a tantrum' in connection with the conduct of skin is surely to go over the top.

CHAPTER 10

# Sound Logic

## BACK-REFERENCE

Good writing is logical. The relationship between logic and grammar is close. It is very often by a failure in grammar that a failure in logic occurs. That is one way of putting a crucial fact about good style. And the other way of putting it is this: It is often by a failure in logic that a failure in grammar occurs. Such is the interconnection between the two. It follows that we have already in this book had to criticize the choice or arrangement of words because of their illogicality. For instance, a common error which has both its logical and its grammatical aspects occurs when some such word as 'it' or 'this' is used without clarity as to what the word refers back to, and we cited cases in Chapter 6 that would exemplify this. At the crudest level this is a matter of making sure that such pronouns as 'it' and 'this' are properly anchored.

> All the work is done on anaesthetized animals. It is given a single injection and never wakes up.

The error assumes a grammatical character here. The singular 'it' is used where the plural 'they' is required.

But sometimes the failure in back-reference involves a different kind of lapse in the thought-process, which can only be described as illogical. Here is a journalist reporting on the restoration of a three-mile canal tunnel near Huddersfield:

> Sealed for more than fifty years, it has long been thought of as an impossible restoration.

Plainly 'it', as placed here, must refer back grammatically to the sealed tunnel. But no one has ever thought of the tunnel as a 'restoration', whether possible or impossible. When we say 'It has long been thought difficult to climb Mount Everest', 'it' refers forwards to the words 'to climb Mount Everest'. Using that construction, the journalist could have written: 'it has long been thought impossible to restore it', where the second 'it' refers properly back to the tunnel.

'It' is not the only pronoun that can introduce a failure in back-reference. Let us consider a notice seen in a shop in a tourist area:

> Will customers please leave their rucksacks and any other large baggage at the till. This is due to safety precautions.

The failure in grammar and logic here centres on the word 'this'. What is 'this'? If, as appears most likely, 'this' is the request itself to leave the baggage at the till, then it is not 'due to' safety precautions. Rather it 'is' a safety precaution. The better wording would have been: 'This is a safety precaution.'

We turn to a more complicated failure of logic involving the word 'this'.

> You often feel more depressed and alone, and probably quite angry that no one is making the effort to reach out to you. This leads to physical symptoms, hoping perhaps that you can get the attention and care you need that way.

The grammar suggests that the physical symptoms are 'hoping' for attention. The present participle 'hoping', lacking proper attachment, is required here to do an impossible job. What the writer means, I take it, is: 'This leads to physical symptoms, caused by the hope that they may win you the attention you deserve.'

An even more subtle case of faulty back-reference confuses concepts curiously:

> Salman Rushdie says what he most dislikes about his appearance is 'its infrequency'. Happily those who know him as a regular on the party circuit know this is not quite true.

The question arises: What is not quite true? As it stands, the diarist is telling us that Salman Rushdie did not quite tell the truth in saying that he disliked the infrequency of his appearances. But Rushdie's likes and dislikes are not at issue. All that the diarist is wanting to question is the word 'infrequency'. If the shape of the sentence is to be kept, it must end in some such statement as: 'Happily those who know him as a regular on the party circuit know that "infrequency" is not quite the right word.'

Faulty back-reference by misuse of a pronoun is a simpler error to correct than faulty back-reference involving a verb. When a passage includes some such back-reference as 'and that was what we did', it is important that the grammatical antecedents of the conclusion are appropriate. It is correct to say 'We were told to take our umbrellas, and that is what we did', because the words 'that' and 'did' refer back to the words 'take our umbrellas'. It is incorrect to say 'They planned a picnic for us, and that is what we did' because there is no proper connection between 'that is what we did' and 'they planned a picnic'.

> Society must be assured that anyone that comes to hospital for treatment is only discharged at the point where they are well and it's safe to do so.

Safe to do what? the reader wants to know. And here we come upon a typical instance of misusing the expression 'to do so'. Whereas it is correct to say 'I shall discharge you when it is safe to do so', because the words 'to do so' refer back to the word 'discharge', it is not correct to say 'You shall be discharged when it is safe to do so' because the back-reference of 'to do so' must involve an active not a passive verb: 'No one who comes to hospital for treatment will be required to leave before they are well and it is safe to do so' (i.e. 'to leave'). Oddly enough, it would be correct, though not elegant, to say 'You shall be discharged when it is safe to be so' (i.e. to be discharged). The verb to 'do' is so generalized in its meaning that this kind of failure is not rare.

> The Countrywide Holidays operating manual runs to 90 pages. A smaller company might not have the resources to do this.

Again the reader asks the question: to do what? The only verb to which the verb 'do' can refer back is the verb 'runs'. The pedantic logician would argue that what is said here is: A smaller company might not have the resources to run to 90 pages. But it is the manual that runs to 90 pages, not the Countryside Holidays company, however large. The writer is requesting the reader to thought-read: 'A smaller company might not have the resources to publish one so big.'

There is a similar lapse in this advice about simmering on a camp stove:

> It's not impossible, just so difficult that most users never learn to do it and don't often bother if they have.

If they have what? Again that is the question that arises. One might say 'I trust you have brought your raincoat: put it here if you have', because there 'if you have' refers back to 'brought your raincoat'. But it is not correct to say 'if you have' where there is no such clear use of a verb in the matching tense to refer back to. To keep 'if they have' the sentence above would have to read: 'It's not impossible, just so difficult that most users have never learned to do it and don't often bother if they have.' The alternative is to keep the first part of the sentence and change the ending: 'most users never learn to do it and don't often bother if they do'. Ending a sentence with words such as 'they have' or 'he has' requires the writer to check that what has gone before gives the words proper anchorage.

> Keen judges say the 26-year-old Mancunian is riding as well as he ever has.

In conversation this might pass. But there is no proper anchorage for 'he has', which requires 'ridden' if it is to make sense. Since there is no 'ridden' to refer back to, it must be inserted at the end: 'the 26-year-old Mancunian is riding as well as he has ever ridden'.

The risks involved in ending a sentence with 'they have' or 'he has' apply equally to ending a sentence with 'it will'. Here is a sentence about the placing of memorial plaques on the former London homes of famous people:

> The criteria are there to ensure the fame of the person concerned is lasting – in one or two cases it's obvious it will.

The question naturally arises – will what? We can say 'Perhaps rain will fall: I think it will' because 'will' recalls and reintroduces the rest of the verb, 'fall'. But we ought not to say 'There could be rain tomorrow: I think it will', because in that sentence there is no verb to be recalled to go with the auxiliary verb 'will'. The two parts of the sentence must match in this respect: 'The criteria are there to ensure the fame of the person is lasting – in one or two cases it obviously is.'

There are certain words which cannot generally be used except with some back-reference. The word 'others' is one such. Typical usage is represented by such sentences as 'Some like meat; others prefer vegetables.' It is true that sometimes the process is reversed and the word 'others' is balanced by a forward reference. The usage is rare in prose, because it has a somewhat artificial rhetorical quality, but there is a famous sonnet by Matthew Arnold, addressed to Shakespeare, that begins:

> Others abide our question. Thou art free.
> We ask and ask: Thou smilest and art still,
> Out-topping knowledge.

There 'others' is balanced by forward reference to the word 'Thou'.

> Sometimes artists have a very clear idea of what they want, but others may have an idea and be unsure how to resolve it.

Here there is no proper back-reference. One cannot balance 'sometimes' with 'others'. If 'others' is to be kept, then the sentence must begin: 'Some artists have a very clear idea of what they want.'

An instance of faulty back-reference is sometimes better seen as an instance of faulty forward-reference. Where two parts of a verb are joined by 'and', it is essential that the match is exact.

> That could, and has been, dismissed by Conservative Central Office as 'sour grapes'.

One could say 'That could, and I think will, help' because 'could' can be followed by 'help'. But the auxiliary 'could' cannot be followed by 'has been dismissed'. There is no escape from spelling out the first verb properly: 'That could be, and has been, dismissed by Conservative Central Office as "sour grapes".'

## INCONSEQUENTIALITY

All the illogical sentences quoted so far in this chapter called for collection which might have been defined in 'grammatical' terms. But of course it is possible to be extremely illogical while not erring grammatically. Not all the sentences criticized in this present section are faulty grammatically. Sometimes, in a perfectly grammatical sentence, a single ill-chosen word turns the logic of utterance upside down. In this respect we trespassed into the field of logic when illustrating in Chapter 3 how ill-chosen words in combination can produce inconsistency and incoherence. That is also at issue here. The following announcement was made on television.

> Louise Woodward will return home to restart the rest of her life.

There were two possible ways of making this announcement logically: either, 'Louise Woodward will return home to start the rest of her life', or 'Louise Woodward will return home to restart her life.' There was one thing that Louise could not do, and that was to return home and 'restart' the 'rest' of her life, because the 'rest' of her life had never been started, and what has not been started cannot be 'restarted'. QED. Words which place events in time (such as 'restart the rest of her life' above) have to be scrutinized for possible logical lapses. Here is one such:

> Jordan will be living on its nerves tomorrow when King Hussein, 63, undergoes a second bone marrow transplant at the Mayo Clinic in Minnesota in a last-ditch attempt to save him from last week's recurrence of lymphatic cancer.

A moment's thought could surely have prevented this illogicality. It is far too late to save someone from 'last week's recurrence' of a disease. The 'recurrence' has occurred, and that is that. The King can perhaps be saved from some of the possible consequences of the recurrence. It would appear that here the journalist's professional obsession with supposed compression led him astray. He wanted to avoid by way of abbreviation the obvious sequence: 'in a last-ditch attempt to save him from the effects of lymphatic cancer which became threatening again last week'. In fact the alteration of a single word ('from' to 'after') in his version would have given him the brevity he required with correctness thrown in as a bonus: 'undergoes a second bone marrow transplant at the Mayo Clinic in Minnesota in a last-ditch attempt to save him after last week's recurrence of lymphatic cancer'.

Placing events in time clearly sometimes strains the logical faculties. Here is a not uncommon misuse of 'when'. The sentence is about a hoarder who one day turned to crime.

> Cleaning the windows of a financial broker in the heart of Reading was when the turning point came.

It is correct to say 'It was a beautiful summer evening when the turning-point came' because 'when' properly relates to a time. It does not relate to a place such as Reading, or to an activity such as cleaning windows. If the activity were placed in time then 'when' could be used: 'He was cleaning the windows of a financial broker in the heart of Reading when the turning point came.'

There are certain words which tend to lure writers into illogicalities of various kinds. One is the word 'true'.

> The picture of political corruption in government circles there is increasingly true.

A picture cannot increase in truthfulness. Even if we take out the 'picture' and write 'The account of corruption there is increasingly true', the sentence would still be illogical. What changes with time is neither the picture nor the account, but the situation on the ground. The sentence should spell that out: 'The reported political corruption in government circles there is increasingly evident.'

Sometimes an ill-chosen descriptive word can collide in meaning with the word it qualifies. I turn to an advertisement for a mountaineering holiday. The advertisement is headed:

> Are you ready for the most fulfilling challenge of your life?

If someone faces a great challenge, whether it is of climbing a high mountain or running in a marathon, then to take it up and successfully accomplish the testing feat is what brings fulfilment. In short, answering a challenge successfully is what is 'fulfilling'. The challenge itself cannot be 'fulfilling'. In a way the two words 'fulfilling' and 'challenge' cancel each other out. To talk of a 'fulfilling challenge' is like talking of an 'answering question'. As the answer satisfies the question, so the fulfilment answers the challenge. Get the wrong combination of terms and the slide into illogicality is easy. A similar kind of misattachment relates two words in the following:

> Finding the right person to suit your need and budget can often be frustrating.

It is not 'finding' that is frustrating. What is frustrating is seeking and failing to find the right person. Logic requires: 'Trying to find the right person to suit your need and budget can be frustrating.'

> New figures were published yesterday showing an increase of one third in the amount of car travel over the past decade. Mr Strang said they demonstrated the need for change. 'Unless we alter some of these trends, they are not sustainable.'

Surely, if the trends are altered, then they become different trends. So the original trends cannot be 'sustainable' if such an alteration is made. The original trends fail to be sustained precisely because new trends have taken their place. The writer should not have used the construction beginning with 'unless'. What he meant was: 'We must alter these trends, because they are not sustainable.'

We see how logical clarity often depends on the careful selection of terms, especially where a choice between related terms has to be made. Here is a sentence from an article about the superstition that soil is best turned when the moon is in the 'barren' signs of Leo, Virgo, Aquarius or Gemini.

> Evidence of this technique is steeped in history and can be traced back as far as the ancient Greeks and Egyptians.

One wants to say 'but . . . but' at several points in this sentence. Is the practice of turning the soil at a certain time really a 'technique'? Then is it the 'evidence' that is steeped in history? One might justly say of an ancient castle 'Evidence shows that it is steeped in history.' The evidence establishes the fact. And is it the 'evidence' that is traced back? Rather the 'evidence' emerges from the act of tracing back. The sentence would be better without the word 'evidence': 'This practice is steeped in history and can be traced back as far as the ancient Greeks and Egyptians.'

There is a curious tendency to produce an illogical concertina effect when handling certain terms. Here is a comment on a World Cup match.

> An estimated worldwide television audience of one million watched Brazil take an early lead.

The question arises: Is an 'estimated audience of one million' really just the same thing as an 'audience estimated at one million'? An estimated audience is surely a concept rather than a crowd of people in an arena. It seems fair enough to say 'The estimated audience will number one million', but once the audience is a fact that use of 'estimated' is lax. It requires a minimum change in the wording to say: 'A worldwide television audience estimated at one million watched Brazil take an early lead.' A similar laxity appears in the use of the word 'predicted':

> However, Steve's predicted number of ten reached the first jump-off.

Surely the 'predicted number' is one thing, existing in the mind, and the horses that reached the jump-off are another thing, bodily active. What the sentence means is: 'As Steve predicted, ten competitors reached the first jump-off.'

In studying erroneous comparisons caused by misuse of the word 'like', as we did in Chapter 7, we were generally concerned as much with failings of logic as with failings of grammar. The worst instances of this misuse achieve a stark illogicality.

> Like all birds seen for the first time at very close quarters, there are surprises in store for those who might be familiar with gannets passing out to sea in their hundreds of thousands. It was the feet that took me by surprise when I first met the birds at such an intimate distance.

When we ask what it is that is 'like all birds', the passage gives us no answer. The seeming implication that surprises are 'like' all birds is clearly not intended. It is always a mistake to begin a sentence with the word 'like' unless one is absolutely clear what the resemblance is and what creatures or items it exists between. In fact the 'likeness' in the writer's mind here resides in the fact that very often birds look different when you get close up to them. This is a generalization for which use of the word 'like' is not needed. The writer should have started with that generalization. 'When you first see birds at very close quarters, their appearance can surprise you. Those familiar only with the sight of hundreds of thousands of gannets passing out to sea would be surprised to see them close up. It was the feet that surprised me.'

Rhetorical effect must not be bought by sacrificing grammatical and logical correctness. But slackness in construction following the word 'like' may appear at a much less obvious level. The following is from a passage on the demise of the Morse Code.

> Like the keyboard of a typewriter, the sequence of dots and dashes is delightfully random.

Is it proper to describe a typewriter keyboard as 'random'? Surely the machinery is such that everything about its construction and its functioning is planned to the last detail. The writer took an unjustifiable short cut in not saying 'Like the seeming arrangement of letters on the keyboard of a typewriter, the sequence of dots and dashes is delightfully random.'

There is another brand of illogicality which stems from making improper comparisons. Here is an advertisement for holdalls.

> They're available with fine leather handles to match the trim or with leather handles for rougher treatment.

Since no kind of 'treatment' has been mentioned, the reference to 'rougher' treatment is out of place. There can be no answer to the question: rougher than what? Since the alternatives are handles that match the trim or handles that can stand rough treatment, the point should be made without the comparative adjective: 'or with leather handles to stand rough treatment'. We see there how intertwined are the grammatical and the logical aspects of the misuse of 'or'.

Finally, we turn to a case where a sentence disintegrates. Whether we criticize it in terms of logic or of grammar, the issue is the same.

> He opened up Greenland, which wasn't well known topographically. The coastland, the mineral deposits and whether it was feasible to use it as an economic commodity were due to Watkins.

The first question is whether the coastland of any country or its mineral deposits can be said to be 'due to' a person. Clearly they cannot. The subject of the second sentence must be changed: 'Knowledge of the coastland and the mineral deposits . . . was due to Watkins.' The rest of the sentence seems to be almost untranslatable. In its basic structure it is the equivalent of 'whether it was going to rain was due to the forecaster'. To put it in grammatical terms, in no sentence can an opening clause beginning with an indirect question such as 'what is at stake' or 'who will be there' or 'whether it will rain' be followed by the adjective 'due'. A possible correction would be: 'Knowledge of the coastland, the mineral deposits and the possibility of developing them commercially was due to Watkins.'

## MISSING LINKS

There is a sometimes subtle kind of illogicality produced by mentally taking a short cut so that a statement is left with a link missing. What happens is that the mind of the writer moves too quickly for full control to be kept on the management of the words being used. The practice might well be called 'verbal leapfrog' or even 'mental leapfrog'. It is illustrated in the following sentence.

> During the mid-1920s he travelled throughout North America painting many commissions.

He may have painted landscapes or he may have painted portraits of distinguished people, but no one can paint 'commissions'. There is no escape from filling out the words: 'painting many commissioned pictures'.

Talking of 'commissions' seems to encourage this kind of carelessness.

> The commissions began to flood in, among them several high-profile pieces which demonstrate the young sculptor's impact in a relatively short space of time.

If an artist is commissioned to make a piece of sculpture, what he makes is a sculpture, not a 'commission'. The 'pieces' this artist made cannot be classed 'among' the commissions that flowed in. The sentence can be rescued by elimination of the words 'among them': 'The commissions began to flood in, some of them for high-profile pieces . . .'

A slightly different instance of confusion between the theoretical and the practical, another confusion caused by verbal leapfrog, occurs in this sentence:

> The contractors were behind schedule and completion of the line by 1871 had become unrealistic.

What had become 'unrealistic' was surely the 'plan' or the 'intention' to complete the line by 1871. No one would say 'My marriage in June of next year has become unrealistic' if what was meant was 'My wish to marry in June of next year has become unrealistic.'

There is a similar short cut in the following comment on women's part in secret work in the Second World War.

> Discrimination and poor training were the main complaints of the women who strove to interpret the Enigma codes and to track German submarines.

It is no more correct to say 'discrimination was a complaint' than to say 'the complaint was discrimination'. The complaint was 'against' discrimination. Either one must correct, somewhat clumsily, by directly supplying the missing link: 'Discrimination and poor training were the main subjects of complaint', or one must start again, perhaps replacing the noun 'complaint' by a verb: 'The women . . . complained mainly against discrimination and poor training.'

We are dealing with a kind of error, seemingly due to haste, which produces confusion of concepts. The mind moves so quickly that it leapfrogs a stage in the verbal process.

> Between 1900 and the late 1930s Siberian tigers plummeted to probably twenty or thirty.

This comes from a sad account of a species under threat of extinction. Clearly the tigers did not 'plummet'. The writer assumes that readers will mentally insert the missing word ('the number of Siberian tigers plummeted'), but it is the writer's business not to leave such gaps.

In conversation allowances can be made for a certain amount of verbal leapfrogging.

> Poor eating habits, such as too many snacks, pave the way for an unhealthy diet and possible weight problems.

We might not jib at that, said in our hearing, but in print it will not do. 'Too many snacks' do not constitute a 'habit', it is eating them that constitutes a habit. The point must be made: 'Poor eating habits, such as consuming too many snacks . . .'

A word which tends to encourage writers to make this particular mistake is the verb to 'include'.

> The charter is expected to include an increase in competitive tendering for council services.

A charter is a document. It contains clauses that state principles and make recommendations. No charter could 'include' anything other than such material. It certainly could not 'include' an increase in competitive tendering. What is meant is that the charter 'includes a recommendation for an increase in competitive tendering'. Let us turn to another example of such carelessness.

> As this was a very special occasion, all tickets were pre-booked and included a complimentary bottle of wine.

Obviously the 'tickets' did not 'include' bottles of wine. They supplied the right of admission to the dinner, but it was the dinner that 'included' the bottle of wine.

While we have questions of cost in mind, let us consider the following notice in a big store with a sale in progress. It was placed over a row of dresses.

> Up to half original price.

The verbal compression here produces a kind of contradiction. The writer who devised the notice had in mind that 'up to' half of the original cost was being defrayed for the benefit of customers. But if the reduction amounted to 'up to' half the original cost, then the maximum reduction on a dress costing £40 would be £20. In short £20 was the least that any customer might pay for a £40 item. No going lower than that – 'down to' half the original price.

Sometimes a missing link can leave a whole phrase floating away without any mooring. Here is an advertisement from a financial institution:

> At the risk of sounding like your parents, do you regularly contribute to a pension plan?

This is like saying 'At the risk of sounding like a beggar, can you lend me a few pounds?' There is no escape from mooring the phrase 'at the risk of sounding' to something in the rest of the sentence. We must know who is taking the risk. 'At the risk of sounding like your parents, we must ask you this. Do you regularly contribute to a pension plan?'

The reader will recognize that we are here often criticizing verbal habits which might be readily acceptable in conversation. Consider this advertisement:

> Double-glazed windows, doors or a conservatory are a major home improvement.

The mind leapfrogs over a step in the sequence of thought. It is the actual fitting of these new features that constitutes an 'improvement'. The 'improvement' resides in the fact that they are here today and they were not here last year. That is the definition of the improvement. If the double-glazed windows were fitted to a house while it was being built, then even the fitting of them would not represent an 'improvement'. And it is the use of the noun 'improvement' instead of the verb to 'improve' that causes the solecism: 'Fitting double-glazed windows, doors or a conservatory can greatly improve your house.' A similar excessive use of nouns has the same unfortunate effect in the following advertisement for climbing clothing:

> Its design combines the experience of world-class athletes and the expertise of our research and development teams.

Neither 'experience' nor 'expertise' is combined in the actual design. The design is rather the fruit of both experience and expertise. The verb 'combines' must give way to another: 'Its design embodies the experience of world-class athletes.'

As a tail-piece to our study of 'verbal leapfrog' we add the following prize specimen from the world of transport:

> To facilitate luggage, special facilities are provided.

There is a certain duplication in saying that 'facilities' are there to 'facilitate' something. We cannot allow the grave omission of a word giving proper meaning to the word 'facilitate': 'To facilitate the handling of luggage'. But if the word 'facilities' is to be kept then 'facilitate' must go. 'To expedite the handling of luggage' would perhaps best represent the meaning, but readers might prefer 'To simplify the handling of luggage'.

## WORD ORDER

A slight lapse in word order can mar the strict logicality of a sentence. One or two such lapses will categorize a writer as verbally clumsy. We have seen how desirable it is to take special care in placing 'only' or 'not only' in a sentence. To say 'The piano can only be placed opposite the window' when what is meant is 'The piano can be placed only against the window' is to place oneself as a writer only in the second class.

Another construction which requires particular care over word order is the use of 'both . . . and'.

> A rash of televisions have erupted, cheerfully egging their viewers on to radical change both in the house and garden.

This represents the most common slip in using 'both . . . and'. The writer has two alternatives here, either: 'radical change both in the house and in the garden', or: 'radical change in both the house and garden'. If 'both' comes before the word 'in', then 'in' must be repeated. If 'both' comes after 'in', then 'in' is not repeated. And 'have erupted' should be 'has erupted'.

Sometimes the failure with 'both . . . and' is more complex than that.

> The policy will not be easy to carry out both in respect of cost and how it will affect the environment.

To begin with, 'both' cannot be allowed to introduce one construction ('in respect of cost') while 'and' introduces a different construction ('how it will affect the environment'). We can allow 'both in respect of cost and in respect of its effect on the environment'. And in the right context we could allow 'both what it will cost and how it will affect the environment'. So long as the constructions following 'both' and 'and' match and balance each other, all is well. But in fact the above sentence has another grave error. One cannot follow the negative ('The policy will not be easy to carry out') by the words 'both' and 'and'. The negative construction requires 'either . . . or'. 'The policy will not be easy to carry out either in respect of the cost or in respect of the effect on the environment.'

Like the construction 'both . . . and', the construction 'either . . . or' requires careful attention to word order. It would be correct to say 'Either you attend the meeting or I shall go myself' where the alternatives are 'either you attend . . . or I go'. It would be incorrect to say 'You either attend the meeting or I shall go myself', because the first of the two alternatives is 'you attend', which must therefore be preceded by 'either'. 'You must either attend' would be a satisfactory alternative only in some such sequence as: 'You must either attend the meeting or resign.'

> It takes us just a day or two to complete any job. We can either do the work by mail order or you are welcome to stay on our free customer site.

Here we see the word 'either' misplaced. It is not a case of two alternatives that 'we' have ('We can either do the work by mail order or do it on our premises'). The alternatives are that 'we' do something or that 'you' do something. Therefore 'either' must precede 'we' as 'or' precedes 'you': 'Either we can do the work by mail order, or you are welcome to stay on our free customer site.'

There are times when a writer tries to rescue faulty word order by the use of commas.

> Mr Morris arrived on the island on Friday night and was travelling around in a taxi on Sunday, when the robbery took place, to familiarize himself with the area.

The comma before 'to' prevents the reader from gathering that the robbery was a means of familiarizing Mr Morris with the island. Nevertheless, this phrase ('to familiarize himself with the island') needs to be far closer to the place where it belongs ('travelling around in a taxi'). If the misplaced phrase were pushed back, the awkwardness would be removed. 'Mr Morris arrived on the island on Friday night and, to familiarize himself with the area, was travelling around in a taxi on Sunday when the robbery took place.'

The need thus to reposition a phrase at the end of a sentence recurs in the following.

> Remember that a UK provisional driving licence is unacceptable abroad and you cannot drive a car if you're 17 years old in most countries.

The placing of 'in most countries' almost suggests that a person's age may vary when travelling from country to country. The phrase would be much better placed earlier in the sentence: 'Remember that a UK provisional driving licence is unacceptable abroad and, in most countries, you cannot drive a car if you're 17 years old.' The Automobile Association seems to like to delay the arrival of crucial information.

> French motorway picnic areas featured mobile masseurs during the summer for stressed-out motorists, in an attempt to reduce road rage.

Again the last phrase should be pushed back in the sentence: 'In an attempt to reduce road rage, French motorway picnic areas featured mobile masseurs during the summer for stressed-out motorists.'

Even a small adverbial addition to a sentence, if wrongly placed, can make for uncomfortable reading.

> To the west of the house visitors can wander in the magnificent parkland at leisure, which contains woodland walks, deer parks and a profusion of wild flowers.

There is nothing grossly 'incorrect' here but the placing of 'at leisure' so far from the verb 'wander' is slightly awkward and causes an unnatural separation of the relative clause beginning 'which contains' from the noun 'parkland'. 'At leisure' would be better placed next to the verb: 'To the west of the house visitors can wander at leisure in the magnificent parkland.'

## EXACTITUDE

The good writer leaves no reader feeling that the meaning has been inexactly expressed. We are talking here about good style as opposed to criticizable style, not about mere correctness as opposed to error. Inexactitude is not just a matter of confusion existing where there ought to be clarity. There is a kind of inexactitude by which the reader is left feeling that really the surest words have not been used. Sometimes this is quite a subtle matter. Compare these two sentences.

> Following the right-hand path, the walker will soon come to a bridge across the river.
>
> Following its successful restoration, the monument has been moved to a new site.

The first sentence would not make any reader pause and ask: Is that the best way of putting it? But the second sentence makes the sensitive reader inwardly aware that the monument is not 'following' anything in the way that the walker would follow the right-hand path. So why not use the obvious 'after' instead of the journalist's favourite 'following'? And indeed, why not?

We dealt with bad use of the present participle in the appropriate place earlier in this book. Here, however, we are concerned with a question of logical sensitivity in the choice of words and constructions which is not always, though it often is, a matter of grammatical correctness. Here are another two sentences which call for comparison in this respect.

> The path meanders downhill for half a mile, eventually leading to a stile in the wall.
>
> In his haste Seth hadn't shut Martin's bag properly again, leading to Ros and Jack's unscheduled discovery.

Again, while sensitive readers find nothing in the first sentence to stir unease, the use of 'leading' in the second sentence makes them wonder whether the most precise word has been chosen. The 'path' led the way in the first sentence. What is it that is doing the 'leading' in the second sentence? To put it technically, the use of the participle 'leading' in relation to a whole clause ('He stormed out angrily, leading to a family quarrel') instead of in relation to a single noun or pronoun, whether grammatically defensible or not, is never a happy construction. And by 'happy' construction we mean one that is comfortably precise for the reader. The above sentence would be better without the word 'leading': 'In his haste Seth hadn't shut Martin's bag properly again, which brought about Ros and Jack's unscheduled discovery.'

A slightly more complex failure of precision involving the same construction is the following:

> Henry II granted the town its charter and right to hold a guild in 1179, making Preston one of the oldest boroughs in Britain.

Although we are dealing with the same construction here again, the degree of imprecision and the character of the reader's mental discomfort are different. When Henry II granted Preston its charter in 1179, he certainly did not thereby 'make' it one of the oldest boroughs in Britain. That is the achievement of history. Time was required. Now some readers may regard this as quibbling, but the attempt here is to sensitize people to the words they use. If you are sensitive to the proper meaning of the word 'make', then you will be mentally uncomfortable to see it ill-used. We can best recommend the simple, straightforward, natural wording: 'Henry II granted the town its charter and right to hold a guild in 1179, and so Preston is one of the oldest boroughs in Britain.'

There are certain words which seem to lure writers to imprecision. The word 'way' is a case in point.

> Campbeltown Heritage Centre is a fascinating way to learn about the cultural and industrial development of Kintyre.

To describe the centre as a 'way' to learn will not do. A given road may be the 'way' to town. A given technique may be the 'way' to learn the violin. In that sense to visit the centre and study its exhibits may constitute a helpful 'way' to learn more of the place.

> Trains provided a relaxing break from driving on the sometimes congested main roads and were a great way to see the country.

The trains were not a 'way' to see the country. Travelling on the trains may perhaps be said to have been such a 'way'.

Another word which lures writers to imprecision is the word 'any'. Since in itself it is a word of vague reference, it needs to be handled with care.

> In any event, any benefits from most of these proposals are bound to be in the long run.

This sentence might stand as a showpiece of minor laxities. To begin with, it is a pity to repeat the word 'any' so soon with a changing connotation. Secondly, there is a slight logical inadequacy in the new shorthand of writing 'any benefits from these proposals' when what is meant is 'any benefits that may accrue from these proposals'. It is the words 'that may accrue' which fully justify the use of 'any'. Thirdly, the main utterance, which amounts to 'any benefits are bound to be in the long run' misuses the verb to 'be'. We do not say 'the benefit will be' but 'the benefit will arise'. Fourthly, 'any benefits from most' is simply insensitive usage. The reading should be: 'In most cases, any benefits that may accrue from these proposals are bound to arise only in the long run.'

Sometimes imprecision results from careless use of 'when' or 'where'.

> Hindlimb lameness is more common than you realize, particularly when the onset is insidious and subtle and affects both hindlegs the same.

The subject is horses. The sentence illustrates a rather imprecise use of 'when'. Again it is the kind of usage which would be accepted in conversation. But lameness cannot be said to be more common 'when' the onset is insidious. If the word 'when' is to be kept, then what precedes it must be changed: 'You may be slow to recognize hindlimb lameness, particularly when the onset is insidious.'

The following sentence, however, errs more gravely.

> Often a coexisting front leg lameness detracts from an underlying problem behind – vets find that once they have resolved a problem in front, a hindlimb asymmetry then becomes apparent.

To 'detract' is to diminish. We might say of a statesman who has been found guilty of some minor lack of candour that 'it detracts from his high reputation'. The writer of the above does not surely mean that front leg lameness reduces the problem of the hindlimb asymmetry. Indeed it reveals it. What was meant was either: 'Often a coexisting front leg lameness derives from an underlying problem behind', or: 'Often a front leg lameness detracts attention from an underlying problem behind.'

## AMBIGUITY

It is possible to write a sentence, on the surface grammatically correct, which nevertheless leaves room for more than one interpretation. Very often this results from use of a pronoun the reference of which is not clear.

> About 15 per cent of kidney transplants in Britain are now provided by living donors, although the level is only half that in Scandinavia and the United States.

Here the pronoun 'that' might be construed in two different ways. In speech the meaning would be determined by the kind of intonation and emphasis placed on the word. The meaning might be (1): that the level of transplants from living donors is twice as high in Scandinavia and in the United States as it is in Britain. Alternatively the meaning might be (2): that the level of transplants from living donors is twice as high in Britain as it is in Scandinavia and the United States. It all depends on how you utter the word 'that'. If, as I suspect, sentence (1) gives us the intended meaning, the reading could be confirmed by moving the pronoun 'that' so as to make its reference unambiguous: 'About 15 per cent of kidney transplants in Britain are now provided by living donors, although that level is only half what it is in Scandinavia and the United States.'

A degree of ambiguity sometimes arises from the fact that some present participles are adjectives in their own right. We say 'That was a very moving story', and the word 'moving' is separate in our minds from the verb to 'move'. Such adjectives seem to drift slightly away from their grammatical mooring in the verbs they derive from. When we say 'I visited him on the following day', the verb to 'follow' is not really in our minds. We think of 'following' as an alternative to 'next'. One case where the adjective has drifted notably from the verb is that of the word 'retiring'. 'She is of a retiring disposition' we say, and we do not mean that she is in the habit of repeatedly signing off from her jobs. Thus, when a bank labels a section of a marketing leaflet 'Retiring Women', we are apt to think of ladies who demurely make themselves scarce, instead of ladies on the verge of retirement.

Where a word has two very different meanings ambiguities can be intentionally produced for comic purposes. The notice 'Refuse Tip' placed at the entrance to a field means something different from the advice 'Refuse tip' given to a waitress. The fact that an 'ocean liner' sails the ocean, whereas a 'bin liner' is placed inside a bin illustrates the complexity of the relationship between the first noun and the second. A 'family wrecker' destroys families but a 'family butcher' does not murder them. (If we were stricter in our use of hyphens we should apply them to 'bin-liner' and to 'family-wrecker'.) Sometimes the simplest word can operate in ways so distinctive that careless use can go disastrously wrong. *Private Eye* managed to get a photograph of an advertisement in which use of the word 'better' proves unintentionally hilarious.

> TRY OUR HEALING SERVICE. . . You won't get better!

With almost any other verb than to 'heal' this use of 'better' would have been unexceptional. 'Try our laundering service. You won't get better.' But with the verb to 'heal' a different meaning asserts itself.

Another special kind of problem can arise in making comparisons. If one writes 'These people give their children more attention than their garden', then the reader knows exactly what it means. But if one writes 'The Browns give their children more attention than their neighbours', the reader may wonder whether the neighbours are getting less attention from the Browns than the Browns' children, or are giving less attention to their children than the Browns are giving. A humorist might detect a hint of that kind of ambiguity in the following.

> Somehow the Hungarians have managed to keep their buildings and countryside in better condition than most of their contemporaries.

The context does not encourage misreading, but in controversy it is just that kind of sentence that an enemy might purposely misread. In this pattern of comparison the safeguard against ambiguity is to add a verb: 'Somehow the Hungarians have managed to keep their buildings and countryside in better condition than most of their contemporaries do.'

## LISTING IN SEQUENCE

The logical mind is always offended by failure to preserve due sequence in listing items. It frequently happens in devising plans or programmes in the world of business, or indeed of leisure and cultural activities, that a writer has to formulate a series of points in sequence. The framework of the list may be a single sentence. At the other extreme a single sentence may introduce a series of linked propositions. In either case the successive items in the list must be presented in matching sequence. We touched upon elementary grammatical aspects of this matter when use of the word 'and' was explored in Chapter 8.

At its crudest, failure to preserve due sequence results in such sentences as:

> We enjoyed ourselves bathing in the sea, playing in the sand, and a beautiful picnic tea.

Due sequence is broken by the third item, which should match the other grammatically: 'bathing in the sea, playing in the sand, and eating a beautiful picnic tea'. A slightly more complex instance of this kind of lapse is represented in this sentence from the world of waterways.

> The range of crafts considered by the Guild is diverse: to date this includes boat builder, cooper, cast ironware manufacturer, boaters' clothes maker, ropework and fender making, and woodcarving.

The first four items in the list are craftsmen, but the last three ('ropework and fender making and woodcarving') are crafts. Either 'crafts' must become 'craftsmen' and the last three must become 'rope-worker, fender-maker and woodcarver', or the first four in the list must become crafts: 'boat-building, cooperage, cast ironware manufacturing, boaters' clothes-making'.

In all kinds of listing the relationship between the items listed must justify their being assembled together.

> Telling people anything really contentious is always grounds for not telling them until you really have to. Stag nights, football matches, visits to mothers-in-law, requests to mind the children and shopping trips are just a few examples that spring to mind.

That is a straightforward case of failure in logical continuity. The trouble is that none of the items cited is in fact an 'example' of telling people something contentious. We can see what the writer wanted to say, but he or she did not say it. 'One always tends to put off mentioning a possibly contentious matter such as planning to go to a stag night or a football match, or dealing with requests to visit mother-in-law, mind the children or go shopping.' It is worth noting that in total this version saves four words.

We are concerned now with a much more sophisticated kind of listing than these sentences represent, but the basic danger of not preserving due sequence is just the same. We take as a specimen a document produced by the Campaign for Freedom to Roam.

> Our ten points make up a comprehensive plan which we urge the Government to adopt . . . The ten points are as follows:

- Freedom to roam – a new law to enable the public to walk over mountain, moor, heath, down and common land in England and Wales.
- Restrictions – the freedom is restricted to protect wildlife, farming and other interests.
- Enter at own risk – walkers take responsibility for their own safety with occupier's liability reduced.
- Code of Practice – for walkers, to provide education on how best to behave.
- Wardens and by-laws – where necessary . . .
- No access to back gardens, cornfields or farmyards . . .
- Dogs – no automatic right to roam for dogs.
- No compensation – top legal advice makes it clear that the Government need not pay compensation to landowners.
- No payment for access – access to be free of charge for walkers . . .
- Wilful obstruction – it will be an offence for landowners wilfully to obstruct access where parliament has said it must be freely available.

The failure here to preserve a semblance of continuity is comprehensive. One has only to cite the first words of each 'point' to see how incongruous the list is: 'Freedom to roam', 'Restrictions', 'Enter at own risk', 'Code of Practice', 'Wardens and by-laws', 'No access', 'Dogs', 'No compensation', 'No payment', 'Wilful obstruction'. Perhaps the writer made a crucial error in listing the items as 'points'. They might have been presented as a series of 'demands'. Thus a common construction could have been repeated throughout: 'There should be freedom to roam . . . The freedom should be restricted to protect wildlife . . . Entry should be at the walkers' own risk . . . Walkers should adopt a Code of Practice . . . There should be wardens and by-laws . . . There should be no access to back gardens . . . Dogs would have no automatic right to roam . . . There should be no compensation . . . There should be no payment for access . . . Wilful obstruction by landowners would be illegal.'

The sort of grammatical and logical anarchy represented above can be found frequently enough in the business world.

How *Renewal* can support you as a retailer:

- Enjoy healthy profits . . .
- A high percentage repeat purchase
- High quality attractive packaging
- No quibble money back guarantee if your customers are not satisfied.

Again a common pattern must be adopted. If an initial sentence begins with 'How' ('How to remain healthy in middle life') it must be succeeded by phrases which in each case could connect directly with that introductory formula ('By taking regular exercise . . . By drinking alcohol only in moderation . . . By not over-working . . .'). Thus, if the initial sentence is kept in the above declaration, then it must be logically followed up in the same way: 'How *Renewal* can support you as a retailer: By ensuring that you enjoy healthy profits . . .' But it would probably be better to scrap the word 'How' and begin more directly: '*Renewal* can give you these advantages as a retailer: Healthier profits . . .' and so on.

PART 3

# Changing Fashions in Usage

CHAPTER 11

# Innovation Good and Bad

Language is a changing medium. Even the meanings of individual words may be transformed within a few decades. New inventions inevitably make demands on language. The word 'mouse' is probably used more often today to refer to the computer device than to refer to the household pest. The word 'tape' is perhaps more commonly used of a device we put into our recording apparatus than of a strip of material. We have of course dealt with changes in usage at many points in this book. We have been compelled to do so by the need to illustrate what goes wrong in current practice. In this chapter, however, we turn our attention to developments in usage which do not necessarily call for blue-pencilling. They include innovations which have enriched the language, providing vividly expressive terms in contexts where traditional vocabulary can supply nothing to match them.

## COMPOUNDS

The last few decades have seen a vast increase in our use of compounds. Each decade adds to our vocabulary in that respect. The Second World War gave us 'blackout' and 'hitch-hike'. The developing needs of the office world have given us 'clipboard', 'polyfile' and 'word-processor', and now the general adoption of computers has supplied 'inkjet', 'desktop', 'internet', 'disk-drive' and 'web-site'. We speak of a 'test-tube' baby, and the words would have meant nothing a few decades ago. The words 'hitman', 'frog-man', 'front-man' and 'con-man' are twentieth-century coinages. The world of film-making has given new life to the word 'bit', colloquially used of a minor role in the compound 'bit-part'. I have heard a failing performer on the race-track described as being 'reduced to a bit-part straggler'.

Most popular compounds are self-explanatory. When we speak of 'ring-fencing' an issue, refer to someone's 'know-how', or describe a policy as a 'catch-all' solution, the expressions are not likely to be misunderstood. But when we first hear the expression 'squeaky-clean', used of someone who is above reproach, we perhaps need to have the expression explained. Apparently it comes from hairdressing salons, where hair may be washed so thoroughly that wet strands will squeak when rubbed. There is imaginative insight behind many such innovations in the first place. The sense of humour is often operative too, as in the use of the compound 'joined-up' to mock the elementary level of thinking attained by some public figures.

Just glancing thus at the productivity in new compounds today, one wonders how novel is the escalation in hyphenation. Taking down from the bookshelves volumes from past literature and turning the pages in search of hyphens proves surprisingly unfruitful. Oddly enough, only in the work of one of the simplest of early stylists, John Bunyan, does a quick search yield a harvest. *The Pilgrim's Progress* is peopled with such figures as 'Mr Money-love', 'Mr Fair-speech', 'Lord Time-server', 'Lord Turn-about' and 'Mr Facing-both-ways'. The time is perhaps right for a Ph.D. thesis on 'The Hyphen in English Prose'.

Be that as it may, the intention here is to draw attention to how rich and varied has been the production of compounds during the last century.

## VARIETIES OF COMPOUNDS

### The *Hag-ridden* Variety

It is fashionable to add to the stock of compounds used for a descriptive purpose. We look here at those in which a noun is tied to a past participle to produce a kind of compound adjective. We use a fund of such compounds conversationally, declaring people 'bone-headed', 'rubber-necked' or 'toffee-nosed'. There is nothing new in the practice itself. And there has been considerable grammatical freedom exercised in forming the compounds. 'Hand-made' pottery is made 'by' hand and 'tailor-made' clothing 'by' the tailor, while 'home-baked' cakes are made 'in' the home, a 'house-proud' woman is proud 'of' her house and a 'self-inflicted' wound is inflicted 'by' the self. In many recently developed compounds the relationship between the two partnered elements extends that degree of flexibility even further.

> These cookers are safety-checked and come with a three-month guarantee.

Here the meaning of 'safety-checked' is 'checked for safety'.

> She explained that I would have to fill out a detailed questionnaire and be risk-assessed before I could be considered for cover.

If I am to be 'risk-assessed', I am to be 'assessed for risk'. We now happily accept the complex relationships between noun and participle represented in such partnerships, and we extend such usages freely, speaking of 'government-sponsored' initiatives and 'welfare-focused' legislation.

Where does one draw the line? Perhaps at the following usage:

> Clarins' formulations are dermatologically and allergy-tested.

The curious relationship between 'allergy' and 'tested' ('tested in respect of possible allergic reactions') is made even less acceptable by being cheek-by-jowl with the grammatically clear relationship between 'dermatologically' and 'tested'.

Even in the case of well-established compounds, the logical basis may be problematic. We hear people speak of a 'Norland-trained' nanny, and we recognize that the Norland Institute did the training. But when we are told that the new kitten has been 'house-trained' we know that the house did not do the training. And again, when we hear that the toddler has been 'potty-trained', we know that the potty did not do the training. Moreover, the 'potty-trained' toddler is habituated to doing something in the potty which the 'house-trained' kitten is specifically trained not to do in the house. Such discrepancies abound in the field of compounds. Although a 'council-built' house is a house built by a council, in the words 'a purpose-built' structure the relationship between noun and participle is totally different in effect. But these expressions do not worry us on grammatical grounds as, for instance, the following does:

> We intend to pass on these bargain-priced motorhomes to our customers.

Such expressions as 'highly-priced' and 'cheaply-priced' apply a qualification to the verb 'priced' which is rationally and grammatically acceptable. The noun 'bargain' cannot operate thus.

## The *Deep-seated* Variety

Usage today abounds in compounds that attach an adverb to a past participle. There are terms for personal characteristics such as 'high-handed', 'hard-headed', 'tight-fisted', 'long-winded', 'near-sighted', 'flat-chested', 'heavy-handed', 'large-hearted' and 'soft-spoken'. There are colourful and economic compounds such as 'red-handed' and 'back-dated', 'hard-bitten' and 'soft-centred'. In many cultural and commercial activities descriptive compounds of this kind proliferate to meet practical needs. Thus, for instance, the fashion trade relies on compounds such as 'high-necked', 'long-sleeved', 'double-breasted', and 'wide-brimmed'.

## The *Mind-boggling* Variety

Compounds using a noun and a present participle (or gerund) are just as familiar. We speak of 'life-saving' equipment and 'labour-saving' devices, of 'back-breaking' jobs and 'nerve-racking' trials. We define difficult issues as 'mind-boggling' and pernicketiness in argument as 'hair-splitting' or 'nit-picking'. Compounds such as 'mouth-watering', 'eye-catching', 'face-saving', 'time-consuming', 'life-threatening', 'record-breaking' and even 'cringe-making' are very much part of living conversation. For the most part these are used adjectivally, but there are compounds such as 'square-bashing' and 'foot-slogging' that are used chiefly as nouns.

Novelists, of course, have long produced extempore compounds without any intention of adding permanently to the language. One reads of a 'cigar-smoking tycoon' and a 'gin-loving reprobate'. And we must hope that some of the business world's instances of the device are intended to be ephemeral.

> But Ms Trotter Betts hit out at 'process re-engineering programmes', which have reduced nursing output.

All of us alter the way we do things from time to time, if it's only the way we lay the table or the route we take to work, but we do not think of ourselves as being occupied in process re-engineering programmes. However, vapid as such usages may be, they do not worry us on grammatical grounds, as does the following:

These shade-growing plants prefer dappled light.

At this the mind boggles. The concept of a plant which grows shades instead of leaves and flowers is alarming. But by no species of grammatical jugglery can 'shade-growing' mean 'shade-loving'.

It is not desirable to try to give a comparative form to adjectival compounds of this kind.

We must encourage the companies to take a more risk-taking approach.

Nothing is gained by not saying: 'We must encourage the companies to take more risks.'

## The *Wide-ranging* Variety

What applies to compounds made from a noun and a participle ('risk-taking'), applies also to compounds made from an adverb and a participle such as 'far-seeing', 'long-standing', 'long-suffering', and 'wide-ranging'. The compounds cannot be happily qualified thus: 'We need more wide-ranging talks.' Better re-write: 'We need to range more widely in our talks.'

## The *High-profile* Variety

The same advice is needed for use of this other adjectival compound, manufactured of adjective and noun. There are well-established compounds such as 'first-rate', 'last-minute', 'old-time', 'top-grade' and even 'top-hole'. But no one has tried to intensify these adjectives by speaking of someone being 'more top grade' or 'topper grade' than someone else. Yet, regrettably, one now hears someone described as 'very high profile' and a suggestion made that 'a more low-key approach' is needed to a certain problem.

Nineteenth- and twentieth-century developments added to the stock of compounds using 'single' and a noun: 'single-decker', 'single-parent', 'single-track' and 'single-entry'. Though these are used adjectivally, there are comparable compounds using 'double' that make nouns ('double-time', 'double-talk') or verbs ('double-check', 'double-park').

## The *Reader-friendly* Variety

We turn to compounds in which the noun is partnered with an adjective. The form very usefully extends the old practice represented by hyphenless compounds such as 'footloose', 'headstrong' and 'seaworthy'. There are highly economic usages such as 'computer-literate', 'publicity-conscious', 'labour-intensive' and 'market-sensitive'. Advertisers produce self-explanatory compounds such as 'crease-resistant' and 'fade-resistant'. These expressions do not strain the language as does publicizing a food for kittens as 'nutrient-dense' and recommending a beauty treatment for 'blemish-prone' skin.

One may quibble too about the following:

> Completely dishwasher-safe, a pack of two coffee cups and saucers costs £15.

A certain grammatical licence is required to describe crockery as 'dishwasher-safe' when what is meant is that the cups and saucers will not drop to pieces as the dishwasher performs its proper function. We have the word 'waterproof' and have extended that usage in such expressions as 'fire-proof' and 'burglar-proof'. The terms 'dishwasher-proof', 'oven-proof' and 'microwave-proof' all make sense.

> It is machine-washable, quick-drying, and will see off light showers and wind.

Here we have in the same sentence a perfectly natural compound ('quick-drying') and a combination of noun and adjective ('machine-washable') which defies logical interpretation.

The habit of forming compounds by adding the word 'friendly' to a noun is well established. We hear of a 'child-friendly' environment, of a 'customer-friendly' approach in business. The usage is convenient but it ought not to be reversed (as it was in advising parents how to make children 'school-friendly'), and like other such compounds, it ought not to be used so as to extend already existing compounds, as it is in this letter to the press from the Breast-feeding Promotion Group.

> While our objective is a breast-feeding-friendly environment, our counsellors are committed to meeting parents' individual needs.

The tongue-twister 'breast-feeding-friendly' pushes compound-construction too far.

Where 'friendly' is attached to a noun, it generally has a human connotation. Where the relationship is between things inanimate, the notion that they can operate readily together without modification or adaptation is conveyed by the word 'compatible'. Thus we get references to computers as 'IBM-compatible'.

## The *Junk-mail* Variety

We turn to compounds which involve two nouns. The Second World War gave us 'Home-Guard' and the establishment of the Welfare State gave us 'home-help'. On the pattern of the older compound 'junk-shop' we have gained the useful words 'junk-food' and 'junk-mail'. The word 'junk' of course retains its pejorative connotation. And there is a certain aural crudity about such double-noun partnerships as 'space-walk', 'disc-jockey', 'bodice-ripper' and 'block-buster'. These compounds seem to retain their hyphens, where 'lifestyle' does not.

Glancing at a fifty-year-old dictionary, I find lots of now-popular compounds missing, such as 'egghead', 'ego-trip' and 'puppy-fat'. The old dictionary gives some general compounds of 'twin' such as 'twin-brother', 'twin-sister' and 'twin-born', and also some technical compounds such as 'twin-plane', 'twin-axis' and 'twin-screw', but it apparently predates the regular use of the terms 'twin-bed', 'twin-set', 'twin-track' and of course 'twin-tub'. To take another source of compounds, 'side', most of those we use today were well-established in this source too but, oddly perhaps, not that most useful word 'side-effect'. Colloquial practice has since given us 'side-kick' and transformed a 'sideboard' from a piece of sturdy furniture to a hirsute section of the male face.

More common, however, than the partnered nouns functioning as nouns are those functioning as adjectives. Some of these, such as 'knee-jerk', represent lively developments. But, alas, there is now a plague of partnered nouns used as vapid pseudo-adjectives.

> We know that losing excess body fat is good news, as are a healthy diet, regular exercise, effective stress-management strategies, and medication if necessary.

The compound 'stress-management', consisting of two nouns, performs an adjectival function here in relation to the noun 'strategies'. The two partnered nouns 'body' and 'fat' are given no hyphen, 'body' being given a kind of adjectival function in relation to 'fat'.

The juxtaposing of two nouns is an increasing practice in contemporary usage, and we shall explore the practice further in the next chapter. Indeed, the juxtaposition of noun with noun is now such a regular practice that the question arises: 'When is a compound not a compound?' To which the answer derived from experience would appear to be: 'When the writer omits a hyphen.'

> The interior of the main saloon follows a similar design theme.

There is evidence that the two nouns 'design' and 'theme' are entering into a stable relationship. And here is a tempting invitation to customers interested in fancy tiles:

> Come to our showroom where our helpful staff will be pleased to assist with your queries, design or theme concepts.

In this case we are faced not so much with a stable relationship as with a *menage à trois*. The noun 'design' is mentally conjoined with the noun 'concepts', and the noun 'theme' enters into the same partnership.

## The *Wall-to-wall* Variety

It is possible for a clever compound that sums up a topical notion to get out of date through changing fashions. In the fifties, sixties and seventies the smart home had wall-to-wall carpeting in its rooms. Thus 'wall-to-wall' became a useful and colourful expression to apply to any plan or attitude that was comprehensive: 'We can't afford wall-to-wall supervision for our staff.' In the nineties the fashion for wall-to-wall carpeting was replaced by the fashion for wooden floorboards and this colloquial use of 'wall-to-wall' disappeared.

Compounds which bind three words together are not new to the language. Early in the twentieth century the compounds 'ready-to-wear' and 'off-the-peg' were applied to ready-made suits at a time when bespoke tailoring was beginning to go out of fashion. We have some usefully vivid and economic expressions such as 'hand-to-mouth', 'face-to-face' and now 'eyeball-to-eyeball'. The compounds 'hit-and-run' and 'hit-and-miss' are surely irreplaceable. We now hear books called somewhat inelegantly 'no-holds-barred' biographies. And after the murder of a television personality the BBC announced:

Staff have been offered round-the-clock grief counselling.

Of the nine words there, five are involved in compounds; three constitute a triple compound and two ('grief counselling') a dual pseudo-compound.

The manufacture of triple compounds can achieve a no-squirm-spared inelegance:

We've got a quality-of-life policing strategy which has got several legs.

That is police-speak. The compound 'quality-of-life' is an empty term of approval, applicable to almost anything. And to follow the dry verbal artifice of the 'quality-of-life policing strategy' by saying that it 'has got several legs' is to achieve a masterpiece of bathos.

## Some Wilder Compounds

In addition to the various forms of compound using the participle of verbs there are a few which use the naked verb in the fashion of 'time-share'. There is something peculiarly unattractive about this kind of combination, but its usefulness is obvious.

I decided to job-share when I had my second child.

The fashion for this usage was set, one imagines, by the expression 'flat-share', which has now bred 'work-share' as well as 'job-share'. More useful and readily acceptable than these have been the now established and unhyphenated verbs 'brainwash' and 'headhunt'. In all these cases the noun is the object of the verb. One shares work or a flat. If that grammatical connection were generally maintained, then to 'force-feed' would presumably mean to cater for the police. But the freedoms exercised in the verb-based compound are wild. We read an advertisement for cosmetics pressing the case for 'leave-in conditioners', and there is advice in an article on decoupage to 'use a wipe clean surface'.

Occasionally an invention that offends one's literary sensibility may at the same time arouse a sneaking admiration for its brevity, as when someone in direct marketing deals with the problem of the 'gone-aways', the addressees who have moved, gone on holiday, or died. There is a similar concentration in the following now popular usage:

> Both were demonstrative people and touchy-feely by nature.

Fortunately it seems to be the case that, when the seemingly worst horrors of compound-manufacture are perpetrated, there is at least a hint of humour in the air.

> Ask anyone who's been docu-soaped and they will tell you it's like placing a ferret in your trousers.

There are worse horrors even than that to be found in the magazine world.

> Hear how other parents unwind and grab some me-time in the midst of their busy, busy lives.

## English Prefixes and Suffixes

The twentieth century was also fruitful in adding to the stock of compounds using native prefixes and suffixes.

### *up / down*

We have long-established compounds using the prefix 'up' ('upbraid', 'uphold') and the prefix 'down' ('downfall', 'downright'). Additions now include 'update', 'upmarket' and 'downmarket'. The verb to 'download' is used in the computer world, the word 'upfront' in business. And there too the verb to 'downsize' has acquired ominous overtones through its use in connection with reorganizations that involve cutting staff. The 'downside' of any plan or action is the disadvantages it may involve. And although, in conducting music, the downbeat is the emphatic one and the upbeat the relaxed one, popular usage has reversed this in making 'upbeat' stand for the positive and the cheerful, and 'downbeat' stand for the depressed and unexciting.

Current uses of 'up' as a suffix include 'carve-up' and 'stitch-up', which seems to have taken the place of 'frame-up'. The development of rocketry has popularized 'count-down'. The colloquialisms 'put-down' (for a humiliating rebuff) and 'climb-down' are economic simplifiers.

### *in / out*

An 'in-depth' study involves intensive research. The Automobile Association speaks of 'in-vehicle' devices. An 'in-house' project is one which involves only the employees of a given institution and is conducted within its boundaries. The compound 'out-house' has been used, not of a shed in the garden or an earth-privy at the bottom of the backyard, which used to be its meaning, but of BBC projects involving contracts with outsiders.

The prefix 'out' used with verbs has a distinct connotation: to 'outlive', 'outdo', 'outrun' or 'outstrip'. The meaning of the prefix is consistent. It is a matter of beating others in some exercise, not of turning them 'out' of some premises. When we read that in the Christmas sales 'men have outshopped women', we recognize the standard usage, however infelicitous. But then we read in a railway magazine that a certain engine has been 'outshopped' from a repair shed, and there is no linguistic justification for that usage. To describe an engine as being 'outshopped' (turned out of the repair shed) is like describing a recovered patient as being 'out-hospitalled'.

The world of protest has given us 'sit-in', indulging laziness has made an adjective of 'drive-in', and buying a car has given us 'trade-in'. A person who opts out of things is a 'drop-out'. A 'fade-out' gradually removes a scene from view. More vulgarly, a 'cop-out' is a failure or an escape from some responsibility.

### *over*

Here is another prefix which can be misused. When we use it in such words as 'overeat', 'oversimplify' and 'overstrain', our meaning is that something is being done to excess. There are dozens and dozens of such compounds in recent dictionaries. We now add it to any word we choose, adjectives ('over-explicit', 'over-indulgent', 'over-sceptical') and verbs ('over-supply', 'over-insure', 'over-tire'). Yet in the gardening world, where the verb to 'over-water' means to provide with too much water, we find the following:

> A cool porch is an ideal place to overwinter tender shrubs.

No doubt in the English climate it would be possible to supply tender plants with too much winter, but clearly that is not the meaning here. What makes the usage utterly unnecessary is that in fact we do use the verb to 'winter' (without any prefix) of looking after farm animals appropriately during the cold season.

Using 'over' as a suffix, we compress verbs and adverbs ('I shall need to think it over') into hyphenated nouns ('It will need a bit of a think-over'). The more established compounds of this kind ('hangover', 'pushover', 'flyover', 'walkover', 'takeover') have shed their hyphens.

### *on / off*

Something which is 'on-line' is directly related to the central project in question, and in the political field, the compound 'on-message' describes statements by MPs and party members which are fully in accord with official party policy. We now hear 'on-target' used as an adjective. 'On' is used in the compound 'hands-on', which is descriptive of immediate practical experience of some technical machinery.

The prefix 'off' occurs in the verb to 'off-load' and in the adjective 'off-peak'. The fashion for skiing has added the compound 'off-piste'. 'Off' as a suffix appears in speaking of giving someone a 'tip-off' and in the word 'spin-off' for a by-product. Air-travel has given us the compound 'lift-off'. If we buy something too expensively, we call it a 'rip-off'. To speak of giving a 'brush-off' to someone whose approach is unwelcome illustrates the imaginative quality of such images, recalling as it does the flicking away of an unsightly crumb or piece of hair from a smart suit.

### *-ism / -ist*

These common suffixes are much used in social polemic. We have long had words such as 'anarchism/t' and 'imperialism/t'. The development of liberal ideologies of recent decades has given us 'racism/t', 'sexism/t', and 'ageism/t'. The word 'abolitionist' came into use in connection with the abolition of slavery and has been used more recently in controversy about the House of Lords. Public controversy has given us 'environmentalist' and 'anti-abortionist', 'unilateralist' and 'devolutionist'. New compounds are readily thrown off in argument. One hears an opponent of proportional representation described as a 'first-past-the-post-ist'.

### *-free*

'Carefree' goes back to the mid-nineteenth century, and 'fancy-free' almost as far. The suffix is now added indiscriminately. There is talk of 'traffic-free' areas and 'stress-free' jobs, 'meat-free' diets and 'car-free' existence, not to mention phases of life that are 'child-free' and others that are 'oldie-free'.

### *-wise*

The word 'otherwise' has been matched in such words as 'contrariwise' and 'lengthwise'. We now hear and read innovative developments of this practice of adding the suffix 'wise'.

> Cost-wise I recommend the bus route; comfort-wise I recommend the railway.

This kind of running coinagery, which some people go in for in conversation, is economic but neither elegant nor grammatically impeccable. When one sees it in print, one feels uncomfortable:

> Celeb-wise, Gwyneth Paltrow, Sharon Stone and Cameron Diaz are setting the standard at the moment.

Which means that these celebrities are setting the standard 'hairwise'.

### *wrong-*

The old compounds 'wrongdoer' and 'wrong-headed' have been joined by 'wrong-foot'. Deriving from the game of tennis, in which a player can make the kind of shot which would put the opponent off-balance, it has proved a conveniently colourful way of defining an action which inconveniences an opponent or a rival.

### *-babble*

This is now used colloquially, added pejoratively to 'techno', 'psycho' and 'pharmaco' as a term for the specialist chatter of the respective experts when viewed as so much hot air.

## Latin and Greek Prefixes and Suffixes

### *ante- / post-*

These two prefixes, meaning 'before' and 'after', have been long with us. The word 'antecedent' dates back to the fourteenth century. Used more concretely, the prefix appears in 'antechamber', then in 'anteroom', for a room leading to a more important apartment. On the pattern of the word 'ante-natal' we now have 'ante-nuptial'. It has sometimes been convenient to extemporize with 'ante' in conversation so that words such as 'ante-decimalization' and 'ante-devolution' are born. The prefix 'post' occurs as early as the thirteenth century in the word 'postern' for a back door; the words 'posterior' and 'posthumous' date from the seventeenth century. Although we have several uses of the English prefix 'after' in such words as 'afternoon' and 'aftermath', they are now not nearly so numerous as the words prefixed by 'post' ('post-natal', 'post-war') to which we constantly add ('post-modern', 'post-Thatcher').

***anti- / pro-***

These two prefixes, meaning 'against' and 'for' respectively, are much used in general vocabulary and in scientific vocabulary. In the case of 'anti-' many of the new additions ('anti-abortion', 'anti-semitic', 'antidepressant' and 'antifreeze') testify to social and technological changes. Political developments add to the stock of words with these prefixes and suffixes. Just as we have 'pro-European' and 'anti-EMU', so we hear talk of 'anti-single-currency' attitudes and 'anti-proportional-representation' views. There are, of course, far more words in our language that begin with 'pro', but the recent tendency in use of the prefix has been to hyphenate it. People will declare themselves 'pro-euthanasia' or 'pro-devolution'. The compound 'pro-life' is used by the 'anti-abortionist' campaigners.

***cyber-***

This root, from a Greek word meaning to steer or to govern, has given us the words 'cybernate' (meaning to control with a servomechanism) and 'cybernetics' for the branch of science concerned with control systems. In the computer world it has given us compounds, serious and less serious, in connection with use of the internet. We hear of 'cyberspace', of 'cyberporn', of 'cyberphobia', of 'cybershopping' on the internet, of 'cybercodgers' addicted to the internet and of 'cyberchondriacs' who obsessively try to find treatments for their ailments there.

***contra-***

This prefix, standing for what is against or contrary, early used in such words as 'contradict' and 'contravene', has been less used lately, perhaps because the prefix 'anti-' serves a similar purpose. However, the nineteenth century gave us 'contraceptive' and 'contraception' and now the word 'contrasuggestive' has been used of personalities inclined to oppose prevailing and accepted views. We have a new use in 'contraflow', for the movement of traffic on a motorway.

### *flexi-*

The prefix 'flexi' derives from a Latin verb meaning to 'turn'. Hence the word 'flexible' means easily bent and therefore adaptable and variable. The compound 'flexitime' was introduced for the system by which employees are allowed a degree of freedom over the disposition of their hours of attendance at work provided that they serve the agreed minimum.

### *hyper-*

Of the two Greek prefixes, 'hyper' and 'hypo', the former refers to what is above normal or excessive, and the latter to what is below normal or inadequate. Parallel terms are not numerous in common speech, but in medicine there are the parallels 'hyper-thyroidism' and 'hypo-thyroidism', meaning respectively over-production and under-production of thyroid hormones. The popularity of the Latin prefix 'super' has perhaps restrained the development of new compounds with 'hyper', but we use the words 'hyper-inflation', 'hyper-tension' and 'hyper-sensitive'. Computer experts speak of the 'hypertext' and 'hyper-media'. In some cases compounds with 'hyper' duplicate compounds with 'super' ('hypermarket', 'hypersonic'). The colloquial verb 'hype', meaning to make exaggerated claims in publicity, and the parallel noun, derive from this prefix.

### *inter-*

This prefix, meaning between or among, has been used of late years to add scores of words to the already extensive list. Words such as 'Interpol', 'interface', 'intergalactic', 'intergovernmental', 'internet' and 'inter-nuclear' show how widely it has been used.

### *maxi- / mini-*

We took the words 'maximum' and 'minimum' directly from Latin to mean the most and the least. Although the word 'maxidress' (abbreviated to 'maxi') has been used of a full-length woman's dress, new compounds with 'maxi' are chiefly ephemeral coinages thrown off by advertisers (a 'maxi' savings account). But 'mini' has been well used since the 1960s fashion for the 'miniskirt', and the production of the small car by the Austin/Morris combine.

### *mega-*

This prefix, deriving from Greek, means huge or powerful. It gave us such words as 'megaphone', 'megalithic' and 'megalomania'. It has been a useful prefix in various sciences and technologies ('megahertz' and 'megawatt'), and then too in the world of computing. Recently it has been used colloquially as a popular way of conveying the grandeur or importance of something: a 'mega-match' or a 'mega-star'.

### *micro-*

This Greek prefix, meaning small, gave us established words such as 'microcosm' and 'microscope' and they have been added to in 'microlight', for a small aircraft, and 'microfiche', for a card holding miniaturized print, as well as in more specialized terms such as 'microchip' and 'microdot'.

### *multi- / omni-*

The prefix 'multi' derives from the Latin adjective meaning 'much' or 'many'. The 'multistorey' car park, the 'multistage' rocket, the 'multinational' business and 'multimedia' activities, all these compounds have now generally shed their hyphens. We read of a 'multi-million' pound campaign, and the hyphen survives.

In the case of the prefix 'omni' (from the Latin word for 'all' or 'every') the old compounds 'omnipotent' and 'omniscient' have been added to by such words as 'omnicompetent' and 'omnidirectional'.

### *non-*

This prefix, the Latin word for 'not', is used to nullify what follows. The word 'nondescript' goes back to the seventeenth century and the word 'nonpareil' to the fifteenth. In our own day the practice of prefixing a word with 'non' ('non-alcoholic', 'non-infectious') amounts to a runaway habit. We invent the words as we need them, presuming on an attitude of non-objection on the part of our non-pedantic friends.

### *-phile / -phobe*

An interesting development has been the tendency to use the Greek suffixes 'philia' for love of and 'phile' for lover of a movement or a programme, where the Latin prefix 'pro' has been more commonly used (as in the 'pro-life movement'). A foreign enthusiast for things British is sometimes called an 'Anglophile'. Thus we speak of a political supporter of closer ties with Europe as a 'Europhile'. Correspondingly there is the tendency to use the Greek suffix 'phobia' or 'phobe' for hatred or disapproval of a movement or programme, where once the Latin prefix 'anti' might have been used. Thus we speak of 'homophobia' for the disapproval of homosexual practices and of a 'homophobe' for a person so disapproving. Those highly critical of European union do not call themselves 'Europhobes', which somehow has a distasteful air of wholesale negativity, but call themselves by the anodyne word 'Eurosceptics' instead.

### *pre-*

This prefix (from the Latin 'prae') is in continual use. Whereas it used to be confined to historical references ('pre-Reformation' and 'pre-Restoration'), it has become handy for general use over a shorter term ('pre-Welfare State' and 'pre-decimal currency').

### *pseudo-*

Meaning false or bogus, 'pseudo', long used in the word 'pseudonym', is now prefixed depreciatively to any adjective of choice: 'pseudo-Bohemian', 'pseudo-Elizabethan', 'pseudo-Georgian' and 'pseudo-modern'. The noun 'pseud' is applied colloquially to someone scorned for their charlatanry.

### *retro-*

The words 'retrograde' and 'retrospect/ive' have long been in our language. In his astrological work *A Treatise on the Astrolabe* Chaucer uses the word 'retrograd', meaning 'moving in a direction contrary to the order of the signs'. In Shakespeare's *All's Well That Ends Well* Helena tells Parolles that he must have been born under Mars when the planet was 'retrograde', because he goes so much backward when he fights. So the word came into general use for taking backward steps. 'Retrospective' dates back to the seventeenth century. The space behind the high altar in a cathedral is the 'retrochoir'. The prefix has been used in anatomy and pathology as the converse of 'intro', and meaning 'situated behind' ('retro-ocular' and 'retro-uterine'). On this basis the word 'retrofit' has now come into use for the business of fitting parts to aircraft and other vehicles after they have already been in use. The prefix 'retro' is therefore to hand and in a piece in *The Times* Libby Purves uses the words 'retrophobia' and 'retro-dread' of current attitudes harking back to the evils of Nazism and the Second World War. She gives the words a somewhat within-quotes flavour by half-seriously also coining the word 'yesterphobia'. Thus it becomes difficult to draw the line between innovative compounds with a future and one-off compounds tossed out as *jeux d'esprit*, to add spice and not to be taken too seriously. For instance, in the same article Libby Purves ingeniously coins the word 'unthinkabilia' for those matters raised when people 'think the unthinkable'. The word 'memorabilia', for things worthy of being remembered, is clearly related to the word 'memorable'. It might consequently seem reasonable to treat other words ending in 'able' comparably. But one must exercise discipline in making such coinages. To try to treat 'deplorable' as 'memorable' has been treated would not give us words worth having, except perhaps for comic purposes. Neither 'deplorability' nor 'deplorabilia' would fill a gap in our vocabulary.

***super-***

Our language abounds in words with this prefix ('superficial', 'supercilious') and modern technology has given us 'supersonic'. From the days of the so-called 'supercinemas' of the interwar years and the 'supermarkets' of the post-war world, the prefix has come into use as an intensifier of quality that could be applied to anything in the advertisement world and the media world. Thus we have 'superglue', 'supergrass', 'superstar' and 'superfine'.

## TRENDY USAGE

### Euphemisms

There are areas of usage in which fashion changes from century to century, and others in which fashion changes from decade to decade. In areas where delicacy has required oblique terms to be used in polite conversation changes in fashion have been fairly frequent. When an inoffensive but evasive word is used in place of a word which might be considered in some way crude or offensive, we call it a euphemism. An early euphemism for a lavatory was the word 'privy' which dates from the fourteenth century. Since it meant 'private' and then 'private room' it was perhaps a more respectable word than the sixteenth-century word 'jakes' (to which Shakespeare seems to have intended an oblique reference when he used the name 'Jaques' for his somewhat sour philosopher in *As You Like It*).

When Sir John Harington, a courtier, equipped Queen Elizabeth I with a water-closet, it marked the beginning of an age in plumbing. But it was not until the mid-eighteenth century that the word 'water-closet' came into use. It is of course euphemistic in that 'closet' means any small room and the use of 'water' does not openly indicate what the closet contained. Indeed the word 'lavatory' was already in use for an apartment containing apparatus for washing. The addition of the lavatory pan to the wash basin was a logical development. The word 'water closet' had a long life. Early in the twentieth century it was in common use, and the letters 'WC' were printed on toilet doors. But already there had been squeamish Victorians whose euphemism for a visit to the lavatory was 'going to see Mrs Jones' or 'Aunt Jones'. Gradually the term 'WC' gave place to the word 'lavatory'. The double function of the apartment in question was convenient verbally. Indeed for a long time the hostess's welcoming question to a guest, 'Would you like to wash your hands?' was considered to be a polite way of asking 'Do you want to relieve yourself?' But eventually the word 'lavatory' began to seem too crude and direct and the word 'toilet' came into competition with it, though never in the 'best circles'. It has taken over on the public scene. It was in the sixties and seventies that the word 'loo' began to be used in conversation. Its origin is in doubt. The suggestion has been made that it comes from the French word for a water-closet – 'lieux d'aisance' ('place of easement'). Whether seriously or not, it has also been suggested that 'loo' is short for 'Waterloo'. Be that as it may, colloquially it is now the most used term.

An interesting euphemism for sexual intercourse came into use in the earlier part of the twentieth century. The press used it, and it was used in the law courts. To ask a defendant whether he or she had been 'intimate' with a partner was to ask whether the two had had sex. This extremely evasive euphemism became even more absurd when the noun 'intimacy' was used in the divorce courts: 'They went up to a hotel bedroom, m'lud, and intimacy took place.'

Sometimes a shift in usage is intentionally encouraged by lobby groups in order to corroborate a desired change in public attitudes. The most notable instance of this is the use of the word 'gay' by the homosexual community. Fashionable colloquial expressions, such as 'pansy', 'queer', 'poof' and 'nancy-boy', all expressed a disdain that the homosexual community was determined to counter.

## Colloquial Fashions

It is not only in the realms of the sexual and the lavatorial that verbal fashions change quickly. They change quickly too in the sphere of usage where new words hover uncomfortably between the category we call 'slang' and the category of respectable usage. One such word is the verb to 'scarper', meaning to depart quickly, to beat a hasty retreat. The general resonance of the word suggests a less than respectable getaway by a person leaving a mess behind. The word appears to have taken the place of a verb popular in Victorian usage which I cannot find in my recent dictionary, the verb to 'levant', meaning to bolt or abscond, used especially of betting men who got away without paying.

Today's trendy words will not necessarily be tomorrow's trendy words. To call attractive young girls 'dollybirds' or 'teenyboppers' nowadays would be to hark back to the sixties, and people no longer talk of 'beatniks' or 'groupies'. Moreover, such is the force of fiction, that sometimes yesterday's supposedly trendy words were in fact little used. For instance, the novels of P. G. Wodehouse preserve an upper-class idiom from the early twentieth century which was perhaps always more used in fiction than in fact. Indeed the act of using the idiom comically in fiction rendered expressions unusable in real conversation, except ironically and within metaphorical quotation marks. Only thus would one declare someone to be 'a bit of a bounder', someone's performance to be 'top-hole' or some welcome suggestion to be 'topping'.

But there are colloquialisms less subject to literary mockery that have a real life for a time. If one reads, say, Anthony Powell's *A Dance to the Music of Time*, which recaptures the England of the inter-war years, one will find terms, then trendy, which have since gone out of use. Where, earlier in the century, English people had visited the 'picture house' and the Americans had visited the 'movies', by the thirties middle-class English people talked of going to the 'flicks' (a word formed from the 'flickering' of the early screens). At the same time a favourite word for denigrating a venture or a business was to call it a 'ramp', meaning that it was a swindle, where twenty years later it would have been called a 'racket'. Today popular usage seems to be replacing these terms by the word 'scam'. In the inter-war years the colloquial expression for mockingly mimicking and satirizing famous people was to 'take off'. The Lord Chancellor in Gilbert and Sullivan's *Iolanthe* perhaps stuck a pipe in his mouth and 'took off' the Prime Minister, Stanley Baldwin. But forty or fifty years later the comedian would 'send up' the Prime Minister of the day.

An interesting twentieth-century development has been the use of the word 'chic'. It came into English in the nineteenth century to mean artistically stylish. Then it began to be used of stylishness and elegance in women's fashions. The noun 'chic' was correspondingly used of modish good taste. But colloquial use of the word outside the world of women's fashions later gave it a rather disparaging edge. For instance, in more recent decades, an attitude of political radicalism which was assumed by a well-to-do middle-class person might be dismissed as 'radical chic'. This implied that the radicalism was assumed as a fashionable pose rather than bred of real experience and deep conviction. And now past fashions can be implicitly discredited by calling them 'retro-chic', while firm resistance to fashion is called 'anti-chic'.

Among the words temporarily fashionable among trend-setters in the post-war world was 'camp', meaning affected and effeminate, vulgarly artificial and showy, used especially of homosexuals. It is an interesting word because it seems to have derived from a fictional tetralogy by the novelist L. H. Myers, *The Near and the Far*, published novel by novel between 1929 and 1940. Although the story is set in sixteenth-century India, that is merely a convenient background for Myers's reflections on the world he knew. And he presented a satirical study of contemporary Bloomsbury in the homosexual Prince Daniyal's Pleasaunce of the Arts, a remote camp of pleasure houses and a hotbed of scandal. 'Everybody in the Camp was always ready to do a friend a bad turn.' The word 'camp' appears to have been taken up by the chattering classes of the period.

An odd colloquial innovation of the sixties was the German word 'kitsch', introduced into voguish patter to mean something tawdry and vulgar, over-consciously modish. Applied at first to art and literature, it became the trendy word for dismissively devaluing attempts to catch up with the fashion in furniture and decoration.

In fashionable social circles the increasing habit of resorting to psychiatrists for treatment and advice led to the need for frequent conversational reference to 'psychiatrists'. A comical habit grew of avoiding the taxing series of syllables, and mentally distancing oneself from the psychological need by referring to a psychiatrist as a 'trick cyclist'. Later the word 'shrink' (derived from 'head-shrinker') took over.

Representing a different level of culture the word 'teddy-boy' came into use in the 1950s. In the early post-war years certain fashions imitative of the Edwardian age replaced what had been the fashions for men in the 1930s. For instance, suit jackets were much longer and looser-fitting, and trousers were narrower. There was a cult among youth to push the Edwardian style to extremes. Hence the name 'teddy-boys' was applied to groups of delinquent and roisterous teenagers and young men. Gradually the word came to stand for youths given to violence and criminality.

The same sub-culture gave us the word 'streetwise', a neat term to describe people, especially young people, who are wise in the ways of the street, which means that they are adept at keeping afloat in an environment that may be poor, unsavoury and criminal. The words 'street credibility', now colloquially 'street-cred', refer to awareness of the style and understanding needed to be at home in the urban counter-culture.

The worlds of the media, of pop music and of fashion supply an ever-changing colloquial vocabulary ('rock', 'rap', 'hip', 'grunge', 'grotty', 'glitch', 'glitzy', etc.) only some of which is taken into general usage.

The world of public life and politics has enriched colloquial vocabulary. Slang words readily become acceptable when they prove to serve a useful purpose. They may be widely taken up because they so exactly encapsulate a concept for which there is no easy alternative expression. Such is the case with the word 'freebie', standing for something provided without charge. Earlier in the twentieth century the abbreviation 'perk' was formed from the noun 'perquisite' to stand for the kind of incidental benefit that a person might gain from a certain employment. Thus waiters' and waitresses' tips were regarded as 'perks'. The word has been used for company cars and benefits such as private health contributions provided by certain employers. But the word 'freebie' has come to stand for treats provided, not so much by employers, as by interested parties anxious to gain influence. Thus, where 'perks' belong to the business world, 'freebies' belong to the political world, the world where Members of Parliament or of local councils may be treated to trips abroad.

During the nineties the fashionable vocabulary of political journalism was affected by the growth of the propaganda industry in the service of governments and political parties. We have been accustomed to use of the word 'spin' in the expression 'spinning a yarn', used of too-ready talkers telling a tale without overmuch scrupulousness as to facts. Hence the word 'spin' was adopted for the propaganda poured out by the publicity experts. The experts themselves began to be called 'spin-doctors'. And because of the sheer weight of the government propaganda machine and the irresistible direction it is supposed to exercise on MPs in the Party, the compound 'control-freaks' was used of its key manipulators.

## OVER-USE OF FAMILIAR PHRASES AND EXPRESSIONS

In recent decades there has been heavy over-use of certain originally highly expressive phrases and expressions, most of which have a metaphorical content. It is because they are so expressive that we too often have recourse to them. But as a result their force is dissipated. No doubt the first person in our age to speak of throwing something 'out of the window' instead of merely 'throwing it out' achieved quite a rhetorical effect. (Though one is inclined to ask whether the speaker was really brought up to use the window for this purpose.) But now that the expression has caught on so that everyone speaks of throwing things out of windows instead of getting rid of them or abolishing them, the expression scarcely makes an impact. Familiarity breeds contempt.

***at the end of the day***

So too now, when we hear someone beginning a sentence, 'Well, at the end of the day', we are inclined to yawn. The phrase 'at the end of the day' is of course used metaphorically in that the reference to fading daylight is introduced because as night falls the day's business has to be tied up. The implication is that the point has arrived at which what is said is final and brings doubt and controversy to an end. Thus the expression 'at the end of the day' has gradually taken over as a substitute for 'finally' or 'ultimately'. The trouble is that it now seems to stand for so many different expressions, such as 'when all is said and done', 'to cut a long story short', 'when push comes to shove', 'what it all amounts to', or even 'to give you my honest opinion'. The speaker or writer should weigh such other possible options before using an expression now so over-used.

### *the level playing field*

Other currently fashionable expressions of this kind derive their metaphorical content from the sports field. Again, though useful and colourful expressions, they are now grossly over-used. People demand 'a level playing field' when they want to ensure that there is no bias favouring the one side or the other where there is competition between the two. Thus we hear a government minister express his determination to play fair in looking at the competing interests of gas, oil and coal:

> Our aim is to put all fuels on a level playing field.

The image of a playing field is quite out of place in such a context. The concept of coal, oil and gas – a solid, a liquid and a vapour – in competition over an area of ground is simply unpicturable. In any case, it is perhaps surprising that this image has become so popular when in games such as football the two competing teams change places in the middle of the game, so that neither can reap the advantage of a field sloping this way or that.

### *moving the goal posts*

It is more understandable that this expression from the football field has become so popular. As a metaphor for unfairly changing the conditions under which rival sides compete, interfering in mid-career with the very standards and criteria by which winner is to be distinguished from loser, the expression is a useful one.

### *kick for the long grass*

We are beginning to hear this expression rather often too. Kicking a ball off the pitch into the long grass at the side is a temporary expedient for getting out of a testing position. Thus it makes a satisfactory image for an expedient move that sidelines an immediate problem for the time being.

### *blow the whistle*

Another useful expression deriving from the sports field is 'to blow the whistle on'.

> The British Marine Industries Federation has already blown the whistle on the decline in the number of inland boaters, attributing it largely to the industry's inability to attract the younger generation.

This quotation excellently exemplifies how a colourful expression can gradually be deprived of its usefulness. When the referee blows the whistle on the football field, he does so to draw attention to some foul or inappropriate behaviour by one of the players, thus temporarily putting a stop to the game. A crucial element in what the expression conveys is the notion of bringing to light some misdeed before the eyes of the public. But the writer of the above sentence has fastened merely on the notion of drawing attention to something, irrespectively of whether it involves anything improper. When enough people have used the expression 'blow the whistle on' merely to mean 'draw attention to', then a useful enrichment of the language will have been dissipated.

***the name of the game***

Another popular expression which comes from the sports field is less easy to account for. We hear the pronouncement 'that's the name of the game' spoken with some solemnity. In most contexts it appears to mean nothing more than 'that's what matters', 'that's the essential point'. It is a way of laying heavy emphasis on some judgement. But we also hear it used in a more explanatory sense to mean 'Yes, that is what is involved' or 'That is what you should expect.' Thus the reply to 'I've lost two thousand on the Stock Market' might well be 'Well, that's the name of the game.' There are times when use of the idiom seems to represent a way of saying nothing at all.

> Sound project management is clearly the name of the game.

The word 'clearly' rings a bell of challenge here.

***the bottom line***

An expression which, surprisingly enough, seems to overlap in meaning with 'that is the name of the game' is 'that is the bottom line'. Clearly we are in a different field of imagery here. The expression appears to derive from the world of accountancy. The last line on a balance sheet shows the final profit or loss made by the business concerned. But in other fields the last line of a document is apt to finalize matters with the central point to which argument or discussion has led. The expression is to be avoided simply because it has been cheapened by over-use to the point at which it becomes little more than a verbal gesture. As used by some people it is almost the equivalent of exclaiming 'That's that!' or indeed of emphatically saying 'Amen'. I found this at the end of an earnest article about preserving the Cumbrian environment: 'The bottom line is Cumbria.' There, as elsewhere, the expression seems to be enunciated with the flourish proper to proclaiming a credo.

### *raising awareness and profiles*

We nowadays hear of special occasions organized to 'raise awareness' of this problem or that, this affliction or that. Where once one would have said 'Its purpose is to draw attention to the lifeboat service', we now hear 'Its purpose is to raise awareness of the lifeboat service.' A slightly stronger version of drawing attention is represented by 'raising the profile'.

> The primary objectives are to raise the profile of dogs, and to act as a guide to prospective owners – allowing them to make an informed choice on the pet that will best suit their lifestyle.

To 'raise the profile', it appears, is not only to draw attention to, but also to increase the importance or significance of. But surely, whatever one writes about, one writes in the hope of drawing attention to it and increasing its significance in the eyes of the reader. As for the rest of the sentence, time was when one might choose or make a choice. Now one has to make an 'informed choice'. The insult to our intelligence implicit in the suggestion that, without the help offered, we should naturally make uninformed choices is hard to bear. Why not 'The aim is to rouse interest in dogs, and to help prospective dog owners to choose the right pet'? That reduces the number of words from thirty-five to nineteen.

### *make a statement*

There are some familiar expressions which have become substitutes for thought, and this is one of them.

> Black gingham curtains with an overstuffed heading filled with wadding make a huge and expensive statement.

> A Victorian decoupage screen makes a bold statement at the head of a bateau-lit bed.

> Strong sharp shapes are young and make a style statement.

What does all this amount to? Is anything at all said here except that the curtains, the decoupage screen, and strong sharp shapes are good things? Yet the statements abound. We have a 'huge' and 'expensive' one, a 'bold' one, and a 'style' one. So too we have flowers that make statements in gardening magazines and gyrations that make statements in the rock world. Here a controversial new production of Wagner or Shakespeare 'makes a statement', and there a seemingly haphazard collection of junk masquerading as sculpture 'makes a statement'. The literate mind demands an end to the making of statements. But the idiom seems to have bred its offshoots. We read in a magazine:

> Kate Butner shows you how to turn a lamp into a style statement.

Plainly this piece of legerdemain is of doubtful value if the transformation is complete and the source of light is lost.

### *what it's all about*

We should also like to hear no more of what this or that is 'all about'. We hear a comment on the thorny question of how the National Health Service should deal with mentally unstable individuals who might pose a threat to others. 'Treatment should not be about coercion.' This means that coercion should not lightly be used in treating patients, whatever their condition. Abuse of the word 'about' in this way is now an epidemic. We hear such monstrosities as 'Good relationships are all about being yourself' and 'Conservatism is all about being able to make choices.' People use the words 'it's all about' as simply a clumsy way of conveying that they think this or that is important without actually making a coherent statement.

### *window of opportunity*

This is currently a popular expression, over-used to an embarrassing extent. The trouble is that, in fact, the image of the 'window' scarcely adds anything to the concept 'opportunity', which in itself refers to something that opens up the view to a future possibility. In earlier decades of the last century the favourite image was not 'window' but 'avenue'.

***sing from the same hymn-sheet***

This expression has caught on for urging people in a common enterprise to make sure that they are of one mind in what they convey. Since it hints at the chaos produced when a church congregation tries to render two different hymns at the same time, it has forcefulness, but it is over-used.

CHAPTER 12

# Current Liberties and Constraints

## FREEDOM WITH TRANSITIVE/ INTRANSITIVE VERBS

During the last few decades liberties have been taken in the use of transitive and intransitive verbs, that is with verbs which normally take an object ('like' in 'I like ice-cream') and verbs which do not take an object ('sleep' in 'He sleeps on the couch'). The area of usage we are touching on is one which is like a minefield for the pedagogue. The reason is that historically English usage has allowed such freedoms from time to time that it is dangerous for one to lay down the law. It is easy enough to give examples of comparatively recent changes. In my fifty-year-old *Shorter Oxford English Dictionary* the verb to 'resume' is given only as 'transitive' and no instance of an intransitive use is supplied. Thus it is that fifty years ago one would have said 'The meeting was resumed.' Now we tend to say 'The meeting resumed.' Presumably the English teacher of the inter-war years would have been justified in correcting that as a grammatical error.

### Established Liberties

The freedom long exercised with certain verbs may be illustrated by the way we use the verb to 'show'.

> Some of Paul's work was already showing at a Glasgow gallery.

We accept this as an alternative to 'Some of Paul's work was already being shown at a Glasgow gallery.' The following sentence extends that freedom:

> The Andrews' London home in Hyde Park could rent for £1,000 a week.

We substitute 'could rent' for 'could be rented', a practice also applied to the verb to 'sell'. 'The picture was sold for £500' might become 'The picture sold for £500.' Just as this usage seems to be particularly favoured in the relevant trading circles, so the same freedom is adopted by specialists in other areas. Let us turn to the world of horsemanship.

> It looks enormous from the road, though fences jump deceptively easily off a sharp rise.

We know, of course, that it is the horses that do the jumping while the fences remain at rest. But we have always played this trick of verbal reversal. We 'tuck' a notecase away in our pocket and say 'See – the notecase tucks away neatly.' And I see that the Wine Society advertises red wines 'that are drinking beautifully now'. Where do we draw the line with this practice? Usage is very arbitrary. You will hear or read 'The organ was playing as we entered the church', but you will not hear or read 'The violin was playing as we entered the concert hall.' Instead it would be 'The violinist was playing'. The organ appears to be the only instrument that is allowed to play itself. (Is this because the player is hidden away in an organ-loft?)

## More Questionable Liberties

The difficulty in laying down the law in this matter can be illustrated by the following sentence in which a mother tells what happened when she dressed up her little girl:

> I noticed how she transformed to suit the costume.

The pedant's first impulse is to want to 'correct' this. My modern dictionary allows only a transitive use of the verb to 'transform'. On that basis the reading ought to be either: 'she was transformed' or: 'she transformed herself'. But in fact the *OED* quotes a sixteenth-century intransitive use of the verb and adds 'now rare'.

A comparable but converse instance is provided by the verb to 'vanish'. Here is a piece about a painting by Canaletto.

> And the delicate steeples which needle the horizon of the eighteenth-century city are mostly vanished in the modern photo, destroyed and never subsequently rebuilt.

Modern practice is to treat the verb to 'vanish' as intransitive only. So my later dictionary defines it. Yet the *OED* cites a fifteenth-century transitive use, meaning 'to cause to disappear'. Thus there is precedent for the converse freedoms exercised with the normally transitive verb 'transform' and the normally intransitive verb 'vanish'. It is plain that it would be foolish to be free with the words 'correct' and 'incorrect' when dealing with this particular matter of usage. All one can do is to call attention to what is happening.

> France warred on these neighbours through the 1790s, while trying to recover internal order and reconstruct.

To 'construct' is a transitive verb and to 'reconstruct' is too. But the writer here has taken with the verb to 'reconstruct' the freedom which traditional usage allows with the verb to 'recover'. You can 'recover' your balance and, if you have been ill, you can just 'recover'. Very well then, the verbal libertarian may ask, why should not a state, after a period of turmoil, just 'reconstruct'? And while we are on this subject, do we have the right to criticize an advertisement using 'erect' as 'reconstruct' was used?

> Tents that erect in thirty seconds.

We may itch to correct this to 'Tents that can be erected in thirty seconds', but again past literature can provide instances of the verb used intransitively. The following sentence too may strike one as improper:

> Motorists shun from flattening animal casualties in daylight.

Checking up in a recent dictionary, I find that the verb to 'shun' is labelled 'transitive'. In that case, one might 'shun' something, but not 'shun from' it. But once more recourse to the *OED* reveals that the verb was used intransitively 400 years ago.

We turn to a now more established though very questionable freedom taken with certain verbs.

> Two years ago fashion editors were eulogizing on the chain store's new chic.

This sentence exemplifies what is today probably the most common and regrettable laxity in use of transitive verbs. To 'eulogize' is to praise enthusiastically. There is no justification at all for the word 'on'. The editors 'were eulogizing the chain store's chic'. The habit of thus treating a transitive verb of speaking as though it had to be intransitive is wholly regrettable. Even when popular usage seems to have established the practice, the purist will feel uncomfortable with it.

> He comes across as refreshingly unacademic even when expounding upon complex subjects.

Although a recent dictionary would justify this, the insertion of the word 'upon' is totally unnecessary. It would be better to write: 'even when expounding complex subjects'. But the habit of inserting these redundancies grows apace. We have sentences such as 'The speaker expanded on the new plan of action', as though the speaker increased in size before his audience. There are appropriate verbs for this context, such as to 'expatiate' or to 'enlarge'.

One wonders to what novelties this practice may lead. I have just heard a radio commentator ask whether a certain political development has 'depleted from' a party's reputation. Perhaps he meant to say 'detract from'. To 'deplete' is firmly transitive and means to empty or exhaust.

## Unacceptable Liberties

We have been criticizing the unnecessary intrusion of the words 'on' and 'upon' after verbs which are better treated as transitive. Here is a specimen of the converse error.

> This plant hunter embarked his perilous journey.

This should read: 'embarked on his perilous journey'. For while in its intransitive use to 'embark' was to board a ship, in its transitive use it was to put something on board a ship, the 'bark' being the vessel. Equally unacceptable is the following sentence:

> The process is stripped away of inessentials.

'The process' has not been 'stripped away'. It is the inessentials that have been 'stripped away'. One might say 'He was stripped of his clothes' or 'His clothes were stripped away' but not 'He was stripped away of his clothes.' For all the freedoms allowed in this matter of grammar, it is dangerous to take liberties and here the trick has gone too far. Yet the trick is catching on. Another journalist writes of a passionate love affair: 'It's stripped away of the complicated stuff' when she means that the complicated stuff has been stripped away from it. Headline writers sometimes take too far the freedom granted to them in this respect, anarchically misplacing passive verbs.

> Newcastle Pair Torn Off a Strip by Angry Investors.

This headline illustrates the point. The Newcastle Pair were certainly not 'torn off a strip' by the investors. Why, we may ask, did the headline writer not write: 'Strip Torn off Newcastle Pair by Angry Investors'?

The extempore manufacture of intransitive verbs by the insertion of redundant prepositions is not restricted to verbs of speaking such as 'eulogize' and 'expound'.

> Making the most of what you have and minimizing on waste is the key when you're on a budget.

To 'minimize' is to reduce to the minimum. The intrusive 'on' is out of place.

> Munch on vegetable sticks or a handful of raisins or other dried fruit.

Again the intrusive 'on' is ugly as well as redundant. There is an old intransitive use of 'munch', just as there is an intransitive use of the verb to 'eat'. You can say 'He is eating' or 'He is munching', but you would not say 'He is eating on toast.' Very relevantly I have just heard on the radio a comparable misuse of the verb to 'segregate'. The dictionary definition of the verb is 'to set or be set apart from others'. But the Radio 4 speaker spoke of a plan to segregate something 'off', as though the verb were not a clear transitive one.

Perhaps we may usefully include here three further examples in which the freedom to juggle with generally intransitive verbs is exploited too far.

> Each paper motif must be completely adhered to the furniture surface.

The verb to 'adhere' is intransitive. 'Flattery adheres to power', Gibbon observed. We do not 'adhere' a postage stamp to an envelope. We 'stick' it to the envelope, and thereby the stamp 'adheres' to the envelope. And I read a reference to 'the shoe shops that proliferate Oxford Street'. To 'proliferate' is to grow or increase rapidly. A transitive use of the verb is possible in zoology, where it would mean to produce by proliferation. The notion that shoe shops might 'proliferate' a street is therefore absurd. Avoidance here of the natural intransitive usage ('shoe shops that proliferate in Oxford Street') has led to error. And here is a newish verb even more boldly mistreated:

> A girl aged 12 has been questioned by police over the death of the 16-month-old toddler she was babysitting.

No doubt the girl was 'babysitting', but she was not babysitting the toddler. To try to turn 'babysit' into a transitive verb that takes the cared-for baby as its object will not do.

## THE USE OF POSSESSIVES

We have seen how modern English has largely lost the inflexions which enabled the Anglo-Saxons to distinguish one case of a noun from another. There are only a few lingering relics of the old Anglo-Saxon inflexions with us. One is the surviving distinction between the singular noun and the plural noun. In most cases we add an 's' to our nouns to make the plural form. 'Book' becomes 'books', 'father' becomes 'fathers' and so on. The relics of other, 'irregular', inflectional changes from singular to plural are few. 'Man' becomes 'men', 'woman' becomes 'women' and 'child' becomes 'children'. These forms have survived, but not (for general purposes) 'brethren' as the plural of 'brother'. And of course there is a handful of nouns which are the same in the plural as the singular, notably 'sheep' and 'deer'.

Another relic of the old inflexions of the noun is the genitive case which is formed by the apostrophe 's'. We speak of the 'teacher's book' rather than of 'the book of the teacher', thus preserving the distinctive genitive case for the possessive. We have two uses of this possessive case in modern English. We may speak of the 'doctor's treatment of Mary' or of 'Mary's treatment by the doctor'. The doctor's 'treatment' is something that he does. Mary's 'treatment' is something that she receives. The one usage may loosely be called 'objective', the other 'subjective'.

There are certain nouns like 'treatment' which lend themselves either to objective or subjective use in the possessive case, for instance the nouns 'selection' and 'portrayal'. In such cases, generally speaking, the objective usage is the safer. We can be slightly happier with 'the local party's selection of John Smith as their candidate' than with 'John Smith's selection by the local party as their candidate'. It is better to speak of

'Shakespeare's portrayal' of Julius Caesar than of 'Julius Caesar's portrayal by Shakespeare'.

Nevertheless the latter usage is not uncommon. Increasingly the subjective possessive is being used where it would be better avoided. Perhaps the worst instances of poor usage in this respect occur when writers use the genitive case of an impersonal noun.

> The Bill's passage, by 33 votes to 21, came after an acrimonious debate.

Surely this should be 'The passage of the Bill' or, better still, 'The Bill was passed by 33 votes to 21 after an acrimonious debate.' The tendency of journalists to use such constructions as 'The passage of the Bill came' rather than 'The Bill was passed' is to be regretted.

> If the existing power struggle in Beijing survives the Asian depression, it will be one of history's more remarkable achievements.

The great achievements are not 'history's' achievements, they are men's or women's achievements ('one of the more remarkable achievements in history').

We turn to a press comment on the national temper:

> There are two reasons for the mood's sudden turn to the worse.

Once more, though 'the sudden change in mood' would be better, better still would be to use a verb instead of either of the nouns 'turn' or 'change' ('There are two reasons why the mood has suddenly changed').

Although the use of an apostrophe 's' with an impersonal noun can be very tasteless, the more common misuse of the subjective possessive occurs with pronouns. We speak of 'his conversion of the stable into a cottage', where he has effected the change, or of 'his conversion to Buddhism', where he has been affected by the change. Clearly there is no reason to question such usages of the pronouns in the appropriate contexts. 'My present' to you becomes 'your present' from me, the moment it is handed over. But 'my message' to you does not become 'your message' from me, once it is delivered. The difference may be a 'conventional' one, but all language is conventional. So the BBC newswriter was at fault to give us this account of an English mother's acquittal on a charge in a foreign country.

> She has already telephoned them [her children] with news of her verdict.

The court's 'acquittal' of the woman may be said to be 'her acquittal' by the court. But the court's verdict on her is in no sense 'her' verdict. No person in the dock can deliver a 'verdict'.

> The foster-father of Billie-Jo Jenkins has launched an appeal against his conviction for her murder.

The awkwardness of combining 'his conviction' with 'her murder' would not be removed by writing 'his murder of her'. It would be better to write: 'his conviction for murdering her'. The press seem to be fond of this usage:

> A Briton who doused his former girlfriend with petrol and set her on fire pleaded guilty yesterday to her attempted murder.

The addition of 'attempted' makes the usage even more illogical. We have got used to 'her attempted suicide', recognizing that the woman may indeed have 'attempted' the act. But 'his attempted' act against her can no more become 'her attempted' act than his crime can become her crime.

We have already seen that the noun 'selection' lends itself to either the objective or the subjective use. But extreme care should be exercised in opting for the latter.

> Almost all his potential rivals in the Republican leadership are even more conservative. Their selection would be an enormous risk for a party that enters the next House election in 2000 with a slender six-seat advantage.

The uncomfortable use of 'Their selection' should be replaced either by: 'Selecting them would be an enormous risk' or by: 'To select them would be an enormous risk'.

We have referred to other nouns which present the same problems as 'selection'.

> She must have been hurt by her portrayal as a fairly clueless mother.

An improvement on that would be: 'She must have been hurt at being portrayed as a fairly clueless mother.'

One may question whether the word 'purchase' fitly allows of the double usage in question. 'My purchase of a new suit' can scarcely be presented as 'the new suit's purchase by me'. Nevertheless we find this in a railway magazine:

> It has been undergoing restoration at the Gloucester Warwickshire Railway since its purchase by the group.

It would be better to change 'since its purchase' to 'since it was purchased'.

The word 'approval' also resists this usage. 'My approval of a new novel' cannot be paraphrased as 'the new novel's approval by me'. Yet I heard talk on the radio of the Northern Ireland Agreement and the speaker referred to 'its overwhelming approval by popular vote'. She should have spoken instead of how it had been 'overwhelmingly approved by popular vote'.

The HSBC Bank advertises what it calls its 'Choice points programme'. 'You can now spend your Choice points on just about anything you want', it says, and then declares 'We've kept your favourite offers.' But we readers know that they are not 'our' offers, they are the Bank's offers. 'Your' present may become 'my' present when I receive it, but 'your' offer of help does not become 'my' offer when I accept it.

> The Masters of the Devon and Somerset Staghounds have been out on Exmoor as normal putting casualty deer out of their misery despite their ban from hunting for five weeks.

'Whose ban?' we may ask. It sounds as though 'their ban' follows on 'their misery' as an additional burden on the deer. In any case it is not very felicitous to speak of 'banning' either man or beast 'from' doing anything. The simplest solution here would be to replace 'their ban from hunting' by 'the ban on hunting'.

The possibility of confusion arising from such careless use of the possessive pronoun is illustrated in the following:

> Computerized typesetting systems fascinated Kindersley and he worked with Cambridge scientific colleagues on their study.

According to general practice in English usage 'worked with scientific colleagues on their study' would suggest 'on the study they were involved in'. But the context indicates that here 'their study' means the study of the computerized typesetting systems. Better write 'worked with Cambridge scientific colleagues in studying them'.

Finally, there is a particular kind of false economy with words in use of the possessive forms.

> A pathologist is going out to report on the Nigerian Chief's death in gaol . . . and remove suspicions about its circumstances.

Our criticism here is about the use of 'its'. The 'circumstances of his death' ought not to be rendered 'his death's circumstances' or as here 'its circumstances'. As so often error would have been avoided and style improved if the noun 'circumstances' had been avoided: 'and remove suspicions about how it happened'.

## NOUNS USED AS ADJECTIVES

A practice has developed of using nouns as adjectives might be used, jamming them up against other nouns. We have long run nouns together in such useful combinations as 'family outing', 'dairy farmer' and 'university degrees'. And new compounds have continued to be established more recently on the pattern of 'jumbo jet' and 'word processor'. Here we look at the practice of sticking nouns together, sometimes seemingly with the intention to add useful compounds permanently to our vocabulary, like 'car registration number' or 'PIN number', and sometimes without any intention to establish what can properly be considered a 'compound'. Thus people talk about 'conflict resolution' and 'safety precautions' without mentally hyphenating the words. And the following usage is not uncommon:

> Nationwide Building Society will press the government to introduce new rules to protect societies against member attempts to force conversion.

Until fairly recently writers would have referred to 'members' attempts' or 'attempts by members'. But now writers jam nouns together in twos and in threes, economizing on both apostrophes and hyphens. Presumably the person who wrote 'member attempts' did not think that a new compound was being established on the pattern of 'gas-works' or even a stable relationship on the pattern of 'fruit salad'. Rather the word 'member' was picked up and treated as a pseudo-adjective. That has become a general practice. We read of a 'business strategy unit', and the three words remain separate in our minds. Since, generally speaking, such combinations are not hyphenated, they can scarcely be called 'compounds'.

Let us consider how the word 'customer' has been treated in this respect. We find that we have a 'customer reference number' on our electricity bill, and we notice that the partnership of nouns is a threesome. But whereas the 'customer reference number' is indeed the customer's own number, what is printed under the heading 'Customer Information' includes no facts about the customer at all, but only facts about the company. Some well-meaning businesses talk sympathetically about 'customer care' as though they were in league with the NHS. Indeed the Halifax no longer employs a clerk or an accountant to let you know what interest is now due to you. Instead you receive a communication from a 'Customer Care Manager'. At least one bank has supplied information to its members as what they call a 'customer convenience', words which surely ought to refer to toilet facilities.

Again we find firms talking about 'customer complaints', and the words do not refer to ailments, but to grumbles. A garage labels one of its doors a 'Customer Entrance'. Thus it seems that though a 'Theatre Entrance' would be an entrance to a theatre, a 'Customer Entrance' is neither the mouth nor any other human orifice. It may be argued that only at the dentist's or in a hospital operating theatre could the expression 'Customer Entrance' or 'Patient Entrance' be said to be ambiguous. I do not know whether there is a hospital which marks a 'Patient Waiting Room', though the usage might not be inappropriate. We have long used the expression 'Car Parking' and are well acquainted with what it means. Now we find notices advertising 'Customer Parking'. It may well be argued that no one is going to misinterpret this and treat the area as a human dump, but a current news item informs us that women shoppers are wanting superstores to provide crèches in which they can deposit their menfolk while they get on with the serious business of stocking up with foodstuffs, unimpeded by masculine attendance. Such a room would surely be more justifiably labelled 'Customer Parking'. And now I read that the Halifax is to open '50 Customer Marketing Areas' throughout the country. The marketing of wives was not unknown in nineteenth-century England, as we know from Thomas Hardy's *The Mayor of Casterbridge*. Whether customer marketing can escape the attentions of the law remains to be seen.

## THE PARENTHETICAL ADVERB

Controversy has recently drawn the attention of writers to certain freedoms taken in the use of adverbs. Consider the following two sentences.

> We decided to ask the Smiths to come to our party, and they gratefully accepted.

> We decided to ask the Smiths to come to our party and, surprisingly enough, they accepted.

In the first sentence the adverb 'gratefully' tells us how the Smiths responded to the invitation. It does so by its relationship with the verb 'accepted'. In the second sentence the adverb 'surprisingly' does not tell us in what manner the Smiths accepted. Presumably they themselves felt no surprise in agreeing. Rather 'surprisingly' covers the response of the speaker to the Smiths' acceptance. This is a valid construction. Yet in the journal of the *Queen's English Society* the Membership Secretary was taken to task for writing thus of the loss of members:

> Of these 34 have resigned, 28 have been 'lapsed' . . . nine have gone away and 16 – sadly – have died.

The critic protests: How does one know the state of mind of those who died, sad or not? The complaint is unsound. The adverb 'sadly' modifies the verb 'died' only from the point of view of the writer. It comments parenthetically on the clause which it interrupts, '16 have died'. It is the equivalent of 'sad to say'.

What are the limits to this use of adverbial parentheses?

> Thankfully, when baby is feverish and in pain, many new mums seem to know instinctively what's needed.

The word 'thankfully' is accepted as indicating the feeling of the writer. It is almost the equivalent of 'You will be glad to know that . . .'

> You can easily make sponge from a packet, but baking the real thing takes very little effort and, more importantly, it tastes better.

Here again, we are not being told that the mixture tastes 'importantly'. Rather, 'importantly' relates to the whole clause 'it tastes better' as a fact which the writer is attaching the importance to. 'More importantly' is the writer's parenthetical observation.

Let us turn to a common conversational usage in this respect:

> Our noisy neighbours have mercifully removed to London.

We can take it that the neighbours did not act mercifully in removing themselves. 'Mercifully' is the speaker's ironic comment on the event represented by the whole clause it interrupts.

It is perhaps in this context that we should consider the fairly recent development in usage which gives the word 'hopefully' a distinct kind of parenthetical status. Strict traditional usage requires one to use 'hopefully' in clear direct relationship to a verb ('We looked at the recent developments hopefully'). But recent practice has been to use it as a substitute for a parenthetical 'I hope' or 'we hope'. Thus, instead of saying 'Electricity shares will rise rapidly this year, I hope', someone will say 'Hopefully, electricity shares will rise rapidly this year.' Plainly the electricity shares are incapable of feeling hope. Thus the usage is condemned as barbaric by many grammarians. It is said that in the offices of the *Times Literary Supplement* there is a notice over one journalist's door, reading 'Abandon "hopefully" all ye who enter here.' Nevertheless, it looks as though the usage is here to stay. It has a certain usefulness. It is not markedly different in construction from the usage cited above of 'more importantly'.

## POLITICAL CORRECTNESS

What we call 'Political Correctness' has had its main effect on English in two areas of usage: the traditional vocabulary of gender and the vocabulary used in reference to human abnormalities.

### Gender

Feminists have called for abolition of the practice of using the words 'man', 'men' and 'mankind' to cover both sexes. Words such as 'person', 'people' and 'humanity' are employed instead. Where past usage has left us with male and female forms for certain roles and posts, feminists have sought standardization. In this respect the current situation is somewhat chaotic. The two words 'actor' and 'actress' survive. So do 'host' and 'hostess', 'waiter' and 'waitress', and even 'proprietor' and 'proprietress'. It would seem unlikely that we shall lose the differentiation represented by 'hero' and 'heroine'; and the words 'master' and 'mistress', in their various usages, seem indispensable. But a large number of feminine terms are being discarded. We do not now hear the words 'authoress', 'poetess', 'instructress' or 'sculptress'. Other feminine forms, such as 'creatrix' from 'creator', have also gone out of fashion. However, interesting survivals of that feminized form are still with us. There is the word 'executrix', still used officially and unofficially. The word 'dominatrix' appears in an article by Libby Purves in *The Times*. In the same paper, in a survey of television programmes, a photograph of Amelia Earhart, who flew the Atlantic in record time in 1932, is captioned 'Amelia Earhart, Aviatrix'. But the word 'doctor' never had 'doctrix' as a matching feminine form in English. The words once used were 'doctoress' or 'doctress', and they have long gone out of use. The favoured present practice is to insert the word 'woman' before the masculine term ('woman doctor') where needed.

Awkward linguistic problems can arise where the attempt is made to change the suffix 'man'. American influence has given us 'chair' for 'chairwoman', though there have been female protests in this country against the implicit dehumanization of the role. But we hear such compounds as 'chairperson' and 'spokesperson'. Traditionally we have distinguished between a 'postman' and a 'postwoman', a 'milkman' and a 'milkwoman'. The attempt to popularize 'person' in cases like these has not proved popular. And it would seem impracticable to eliminate the syllable 'man' in such words as 'craftsmanship', 'horsemanship' and 'one-upmanship'. Compounds which have 'man' as a prefix, such as 'manhole', 'manslaughter', 'manpower' and 'manhandle', also resist adaptation. It is likely that inconsistency and illogicality will be with us in this sphere for some time. For instance, the feminine form 'hostess' is still being used in the partying world, whereas there is talk in the sphere of surrogate motherhood of the 'host mother'. It is interesting that when foreign words are adopted, they do not necessarily come in for homogenization. We still distinguish a 'masseur' from a 'masseuse', but we seem to have lost the feminine 'chauffeuse', used early in the twentieth century. Compounds involving 'master' and 'mistress' were once common enough. 'Schoolmaster' and 'schoolmistress' survive. We used to speak of a 'postmaster' in charge of a post office and a 'postmistress' too; we even had both 'stationmaster' and 'stationmistress'.

There are still a few words in use which distinguish masculine from feminine by the addition of the suffix 'ette' for the feminine version. An 'usher' (a word perhaps chiefly used now of a man showing guests to their places at a church wedding service) is balanced by an 'usherette' (used of the woman who shows you to your seat in the cinema). We describe as 'drum majorettes' the young girls fitted out in uniform for their musical parades. In pre-war Oxbridge it was common to speak (if not to write) of 'undergraduates' and 'undergraduettes'. *Private Eye* has established the word 'hackette' for a female 'hack', a disparaging word for a cheap journalist. The French basis of these usages is obvious. The masculine French ending 'et' becomes 'ette' in the feminine. There are cases where we have taken one of a French pair without taking the other. The French 'coq' (English 'cock') produced the French word 'coquet' (for an amorously inclined gallant) as well as the word 'coquette' (for a flirtatious woman). We have adopted the latter but not the former.

On the whole the flavour of delicacy and femininity does hang around the ending 'ette'. Where the word 'toilet' is now used chiefly for a lavatory, the word 'toilette' is associated with refined feminine attention to personal appearance. Associations of refinement also resonate in the word 'etiquette', whose history is oddly interesting. Deriving from the same word as the word 'ticket', and meaning a soldier's billet for lodgings, then a label for admission, it somehow came to stand for the code of polite behaviour.

Strictly speaking, the ending 'ette' was a diminutive form too. Thus we have 'cigarette' as a small version of 'cigar'. We have also taken over 'maisonette', the diminutive of 'maison' without 'maison' itself. And now the small disk used in computers is called a 'diskette'.

The main linguistic problems arise with the use of pronouns. The singular pronoun 'everyone' has always taken a singular verb. 'Everyone goes home at the same time', we say. But when a possessive pronoun is introduced the official usage used to be masculine. 'Everyone must search his own heart' was the usage, and even 'Everyone must look after himself.' Now people had been unhappy with this particular usage well before the feminists attacked it. A headteacher of a mixed school, addressing his pupils, would generally say 'Every one must lock their own locker properly', using 'their' as a singular pronoun. This practice has now become established. But there are cases where awkwardness can be avoided by use of the plural 'all' instead of the singular 'every'.

> It combines the power every motorist needs with the refinement they expect.

This collision between the singular 'motorist' and the plural 'they' could be avoided by use of the plural throughout: 'It combines the power all motorists need with the refinement they expect.'

The reference to motorists reminds us that we perhaps ought not to leave this topic without mentioning the odd use of feminine pronouns in connection with ships and machines. The practice of treating ships as feminine has lingered on. It has been claimed that this practice has sometimes led to comic misunderstandings, as when a journalist is reported to have described the launching of a liner thus:

> Her Majesty smashed a bottle of champagne against the bows and then she slid gracefully down the slipway into the water.

Certainly in the early decades of the twentieth century no garage mechanic and no motorist with a serious interest in the new automobiles would have spoken of a car's performance or discussed problems in the engine except with feminine pronouns. 'She pinks when she gets down to thirty in top on a hill.' This was a spoken rather than a written idiom. It expressed a kind of knowing familiarity between man and machine.

The converse practice of using the neutral 'it' where human beings are involved is unsatisfactory.

> We feel that the smart employer should be concerned with the general health, morale and efficiency of its workforce.

An employer cannot become 'it'. Use of the plural would eliminate the problem: 'Smart employers should be concerned with the general health, morale and efficiency of their employees.' It is odd that the one context in which the use of 'it' for a human being was once acceptable was in reference to babies. 'Lay the baby on its tummy' surely still sounds unpatronizing, though in the case of older children we should find the neutral pronoun uncomfortable. That is presumably why some journalists try to solve the problem by a quota system. Cheek by jowl, we find such sentences as the following:

> Sometimes teasing can bring a child's morale so low that she sees no way out . . .

> But if the child feels that he's not only failed his tests but failed your expectations too, it's doubly hard to bounce back.

> Unless your child is one of those enviable creatures, a good eater, it's easy to become worried or obsessive about their food.

The question about the use of 'man' and 'men' to cover both sexes may be looked at in the light in which we speak of other living creatures. There has always been inconsistency here. The dictionary will define a 'mare' as a female horse and a 'vixen' as a female fox, but would not define a 'woman' as a female man, rather as a 'female human being'. 'Horse' seems to be used rather as 'man' was used. We speak of 'wild horses' and we do not think we are excluding mares. We speak of the 'swans' on the river, and we do not feel that we are excluding the pens. Contrariwise, we say that we are 'keeping hens' even when a cock is included. The feminine sex takes precedence also in reference to 'geese', where the masculine creature is a 'gander'.

It is not easy to discover what current etiquette requires of us now that there has been a reaction against the feminist pressures of a few decades ago. A recent letter to *The Times* runs thus:

> The use of the ugasp – ungrammatical gender-ambiguous singular pronoun – which pollutes our language in the cause of political correctness reaches new depths of absurdity in your report of September 5 on a case of unfair dismissal. You quote the employer as saying '. . . the applicant does not have to tell us they are pregnant'. A cherished ugasp of a similar type comes from a magistrate I heard addressing a defendant: 'You kicked your victim in the testicles and went on to break their nose.'

Certainly it would seem that pursuit of political correctness in this respect can lead to curious logical dilemmas. It would appear to require one to choose between the kind of statement above, using 'they' ('the applicant does not have to tell us they are pregnant') or such usages as: 'If an employee becomes pregnant, he/she will be allowed the usual period of absence.'

## Disability

The political correctness that requires ever more evasive euphemisms in reference to physical or mental abnormalities or deficiencies is difficult to talk about objectively because it directs our minds to tragic human problems. One has to accept that where terms carry a physically, mentally or morally pejorative connotation sheer politeness often requires a certain blanketing of the reality. It would be offensive to describe someone as 'grossly fat' or 'obese', when gentler terms such as 'overweight' are available. It may be, of course, that the overweight are a special case in that putting on weight is sometimes the result of over-eating rather than of an inescapable affliction. A well-rounded woman of my acquaintance, concerned about her weight, received from her GP the brutal verdict: 'There were no overweight people in Belsen.'

We are concerned here rather with afflictions which no one would think of as in any way brought upon themselves by the afflicted. What the King James Bible calls 'the blind, the halt and the lame' we now call 'the disabled' or 'the physically disadvantaged'. The once much-used word 'cripple' has become unacceptable. So too have terms such as 'mental deficiency' and 'mentally defective'. What once was a 'deficiency' is now an 'impairment'. Along with the word 'impaired' the word 'challenged' has been attached to various adverbs, as in 'visually challenged'. Some seemingly less serious inventions of this kind include 'vertically challenged' as an alternative to 'short' and 'follically challenged' as an alternative to 'bald' or 'balding'.

In the educational world care has been increasingly exercised to avoid terminology that might damage sensitive children or depress their parents. Where the use of words such as 'backward' and 'retarded' was common in the earlier half of the twentieth century to describe less mentally able pupils, contemporary teachers speak of children with 'learning difficulties'. A deaf, dyslexic, or mentally retarded child is classed as having 'special needs'. An inattentive child is described as suffering from an 'attention deficit syndrome'.

If we can disentangle our thinking from the emotive elements in this matter, we shall have to recognize that the now discredited words 'mental deficiency' and 'mental defective' were introduced as polite and humane words to replace terms such as 'dementia' and 'feeble-mindedness', which themselves were probably introduced to replace terms such as 'dotage' and 'insanity'. If we go far enough back, the words 'lunacy' and 'lunatic', 'idiocy' and 'idiot' were usable. Wordsworth, a very compassionate man, wrote a moving poem called *The Idiot Boy*. It is the touching story of young Johnny Foy, the darling son of Betty Foy, and the adventure that befalls them when she sends him at night on her pony to fetch the doctor for an ailing neighbour. Throughout the poem the words 'idiot boy' are repeated several times in reference to Betty Foy's devotion to her son, 'Him whom she loves, her idiot boy'. The two words together, 'idiot boy', are made to hold a great weight of sympathy and tenderness. They resonate with compassionate understanding of the boy's lot. Yet nowadays they could not be so used.

It would appear to be the case that attempting to blur the reality of what we are talking about generally works only temporarily. When 'disabled' has had a few decades of use, the direct connection apparent between the word and sometimes gross human deformities will initiate the kind of disgust with the word which recent generations have felt with the word 'cripple'. On the basis of historical experience there is reason to believe that the now respectable words 'impairment' and 'disability' will eventually go the way of 'deficiency'. For in the choice of euphemisms the passing ages run from one at first polite word to another as the full significance of the former sinks home. Today's polite word is tomorrow's impolite word.

We have to live in the real world, not in a philological hothouse. And for the moment the real world requires us to describe a blind or nearly blind person as 'visually impaired' and a person with abnormal mental limitations as someone with 'learning difficulties'. This book, however, is about the use of English. Its statements about usage cannot properly be measured according to the degree of compassion seemingly evidenced for those who suffer appalling afflictions. It is the relationship between word and reality that concerns us here. When a man who has brutally raped, strangled and then carved up a number of young women is described as a person 'with mental health problems', there is a peculiar discrepancy between word and fact which in other contexts would produce humour. What we call the 'discrepancy', that is to say the immense disproportion between the reality and the word defining it, is precisely what political correctness exists to establish. Verbally speaking, political correctness in these matters is the denial of literalness. Instead of trying to match act and experience with commensurate terminology, it determines to create a gap between the two. In this respect it moves in the opposite direction from rhetoric and poetry, which augment meaning by exaggeration and amplification, pressing it home in terminology that brings the maximum intensity and vividness to bear on facts and events defined. By contrast political correctness of this particular brand dilutes and disembodies everything it touches. Regular addiction to its terminology is a form of linguistic anorexia nervosa.

CHAPTER 13

# Workaday English

It remains to take a look at some questionable verbal habits now adopted in various spheres of commerce, in certain national institutions and in our cultural life, and to recommend simplifications.

## BUSINESS-SPEAK

The term 'business-speak' covers a wide field of usage. One would hesitate before attempting to write about 'science-speak' as though one could generalize about the linguistic characteristics of writers in psychology and physics, medicine and metallurgy *en bloc*. To enter into the linguistic world of any such speciality is a study in itself. Business-speak too is a house with many mansions. Quite apart from the distinguishing linguistic features that mark a given form of commerce, there are linguistic features appropriate to various specialisms such as management and marketing, and to sub-divisions of the former, say, such as those concerned with overall strategy and those concerned with human resources. The general public, however, comes across business-speak chiefly through publicity, whether in the form of advertisements in the press or direct mail. It is to this that we turn our attention.

### Publicity and Recruitment

We had something to say about the use of hyperbole in Chapter 9. At the present day a certain group of extravagant terms has been seized on by the business world and they are so over-used that their meaning is dissipated. Consider the following.

The company's growth has been meteoric and Worldcom has very quickly

> established itself as the most dynamic player in the market. Essential to achieving continued success is the recruitment of high quality people and two new fabulous opportunities have been created to play a key part in Worldcom's expansion.

The extravagance here is obvious. 'Meteoric', 'dynamic', 'fabulous' and even 'essential' are, or used to be, powerful words, and their use here devalues them. The sentences are unnecessarily wordy. 'Essential to achieving continued success is the recruitment of high quality people' conveys no more than 'We need to recruit good people' would. That firms intend to remain successful can be taken for granted. Declarations of this kind are now familiar, and we cannot help wondering whether a greater impact might be made by a simple statement, directly noting that the firm is a big one and a growing one, and is making two new appointments to crucial posts.

An even greater extravagance is shown in the following:

> At Ostagon you will be immersed in an innovative, energetic and driven culture, focused around your accelerated development and achievement of personal goals. The experience gained through this programme creates an awesome platform for your ultimate success.

Words such as 'innovative', 'driven', 'focused', 'achievement' and 'goals' are nowadays peppered over statements in the business world as exclamation marks were in the Victorian age. As for the 'awesome' platform, the words might be an appropriate description of the site of a public execution. But, since the platform is represented as a starting-point, one must assume that it is the kind of platform from which one catches the train rather than the kind from which one appears in public for whatever purpose.

The business pages of the press abound in this kind of sticky-toffee-pudding vocabulary.

> Our continued growth has been achieved through our unique ability to create business solutions that integrated expertise and experience across the full range of business needs – strategy, technology, processes and people.

'Continued', 'achieved', 'unique', 'create', 'business solutions', 'integrated expertise', 'strategy', 'processes' . . . The words tumble out of the business-speak thesaurus, and they have all been heard so many times before in this kind of context that they simply do not register at all. They are dead counters.

The epidemic is raging everywhere. Instead of finding a way to improve a business, you have to discover a 'high performance vehicle for adding real value' to it. Instead of having an eye for profit, you have to have 'a proactive response to the market's ongoing consolidation'. Instead of directing a firm's marketing, you have to 'take immediate responsibility for the creation and implementation of a sales development strategy'. Instead of watching carefully for new ways of improving sales, you have to be a 'catalyst for growth' whose 'focus will be to identify opportunities and convert these into a business reality'. Instead of looking for the right man for the job, the employers seek someone who will have the 'credibility to make an immediate and sustained impact'.

Efficient businessmen ought not to be able to endure this waste of verbiage. Its sheer excess simply does not go with the image of the slick and the streamlined which is supposed to characterize modern commerce. It is a vocabulary that belongs, not in the age of the Eurostar, but in the age of transatlantic liners whose rooms were burdened and littered with the unnecessary ornament of the age. It should have gone down with the *Titanic*.

## The Personal Touch

We have seen how the verbal excess is sometimes combined with a personal touch in advertisements for posts. The imaginary applicant is addressed in the second person, often with fulsome flattery. The appeals made to would-be employees in such advertisements can reach a pantomimic level of hyperbole. We turn to an advertisement for 'NT Server Product Managers (Hardware and Software)'.

> Standing up in front of a senior level audience, convincing them you're the most knowledgeable server guru alive, leveraging your technology and marketing skills to enthuse customers about the supremacy of our products – by doing these things you'll become the ultimate products champion, bringing confidence and a drive for results to all you do. A proven relationship builder and project manager, you'll probably be straining at the leash of a national remit and keen to upgrade to a truly pan-European environment.

This is the kind of excess which makes the layman gasp. We who would like to be regarded as plain-speaking, we who are quite prepared to talk about people doing their best to make their products popular, do we now need to learn the language of 'leveraging technology and marketing skills to enthuse customers about the supremacy of our products' and all in the cause of winning the ultimate products championship? What sort of people are they who talk like that? It is the same question that arises in our minds when we look at a mediaeval tapestry of knightly jousting or a picture of a gorgeous Elizabethan banquet. What on earth were these people really like behind all this fancery and flummery? And yet, in truth, there is something about this excess which one wants to call its 'innocence'. There seems to be a childish delight in having a go, in discovering and verbally dressing up in grandma's discarded finery that maturer heads have put away in the attic.

And if one tries to enter the mind of the would-be applicant for the post advertised above, the natural question arises: In what idiom shall I respond? To begin 'Dear Sir/Madam, With reference to your advertisement of such and such a date' would seem totally inappropriate to the grandeurs on offer. And to take the advertisement too literally would surely suggest a lack of respectful subservience: 'Dear Sir/Madam, Thank you for the tribute you paid me in the advertisement of such and such a date. I could not agree more and I can only applaud your insight.' The advertisement would surely seem to require adoption of an idiom that does justice to the character of the challenge and yet avoids tedious formalities: 'Now you're talking!' perhaps.

## The Worst Excesses

What it all amounts to is that verbosity now runs riot in the kind of publicity material we have been sampling. The first rule of the crudest business-speak appears to be: Never use one word where two will do, or two words where three will do. Do not talk about such things as 'management'. Far better to talk about 'management systems' or 'management issues', better still about 'management systems issues' and best of all about 'management systems issues strategy'. The question arises whether courses in business studies and management ought not to be classified under the 'Modern Languages' umbrella. At the extreme point business-speak seems to be making a lot of noise yet saying nothing at all. Consider the following from a letter to *Marketing Week* usefully preserved in the 'Pseuds Corner' of *Private Eye*.

> Surely marketing is and will always remain a transactional-based function responsible for the designated tangible and intangible interactions between internal and external customers.

However one struggles to translate this into decent English, the verbiage resists the attempt. 'Surely marketing is marketing' might perhaps say it all. Even to add 'and will always remain so' merely compounds the redundancy. To say 'Marketing is a matter of transactions between people' is to function as a dictionary. The pile-up of unnecessary and indeed redundant terms such as 'function', 'designated', 'tangible', 'intangible', 'internal' and 'external' adds nothing but noise. Suppose we try to describe driving a car in the same idiom. 'Surely driving is and will always remain a directional-based function responsible for the designated and co-ordinated operational interactions between internal combustion and external propulsion.'

An interesting feature of business-speak is the way it sometimes reaches out to involve linguistic currencies from other spheres of life in the effort to give an upmarket flavour to simple statements about buying and selling, advertising and marketing.

> Communicating a brand's core equity and being able to leverage a media brand's value as part of a more holistic and integrated sell is something I know advertisers are simply crying out for.

One may be a little sceptical about the notion that people in the business world are crying out for this kind of thing. The wording of the business world proper is evident in talk about being able to 'leverage a media brand's value'. What the writer appears to be getting at is that somehow a brand's worth should be exploited as part of a new kind of 'sell', indeed a more 'holistic' and 'integrated' sell. The words 'holistic' and 'integrated' carry overtones of what is comprehensively health-preserving and thoroughly purified of limitations and peripherals. To try to bring these resonances to bear upon an act of handing over a product in exchange for cash is to plumb the depths of bathos.

## Post Office

The world of business-speak, once perhaps a small domain, has now taken over in the former nationalized institutions and colonized the professions. This is the idiom of Post Office Counters:

> Delivering coherent strategies through effective change management, Post Office Counters is a commercially focused customer driven quality retail business.

Do the first seven words say anything at all that is worth communicating? And is it not self-evident that a business must be 'commercially focused' and 'customer driven'?

> With continuous customer service improvement seen as a key to ensuring continued long term success, our business strategy unit has identified a need for an energetic change management professional, to be based in Chesterfield, to support the delivery of the company's strategies within the individual business unit through the integration of new, with existing, initiatives and the management of the planning process within the unit.

What is the difference between seeing continuous customer service as a key to ensuring continued long-term success and believing that it pays in the long run to do your best for your customers? And, while we have long benefited from newspapers on our doormats and milk bottles on our doorsteps, why does every firm in the land now want to start 'delivering' strategies or flexibility, solutions or added value, bottom-line efficiency or integrated expertise? The Post Office, at least, has better material to deliver.

## Electricity Industry

We turn to the electricity industry to illustrate the language of company reports. This is how a major supplier of electricity explains that it is going to pay its employees as well as it can:

> National Power's remuneration policy takes account of the changing nature of the business in both the UK, where competition has increased significantly, and overseas. In order to compete and meet these challenges the

> Committee has established remuneration levels which will retain and motivate top quality executives but which are sufficiently incentivized to link remuneration to Company performance.

Before commenting on style, let us note an elementary error. One cannot speak of the nature of the business 'in both the UK. . . and overseas', because we do not use the expression 'in overseas'. The word 'in' is on the wrong side of 'both'. Correct the passage to 'both in the UK. . . and overseas'. What exactly do we learn from the two wordy sentences? We might try to put it succinctly. 'National Power's business is growing at home and abroad. It will pay top employees enough to keep, encourage and reward them in an increasingly competitive market.' The words and phrases happily sacrificed include 'remuneration policy', 'changing nature of the business', 'in order to compete and meet these challenges', and 'sufficiently incentivized'.

We may cite a further example of National Power's increasingly lavish output of verbiage.

> Activities in the UK have continued to focus on maximizing our operational and commercial performance.

Plainly this means that the firm has gone on trying to do its best.

## Banking

We turn to banking to explore the language of direct marketing used to make a personal appeal to the customer. A few years ago a much used word in advertising was 'choice'. It had become an approval noise to be voiced alongside political claims for 'freeing' the population from this or that programme pressed by the rival party. A bank seized on the word.

> Midland Choice . . . We are proud to introduce Midland Choice . . . A world of innovative ideas, exclusive offers and awards designed specifically for you. Midland rewards your loyalty . . . as a valued customer and cardholder. It provides us with a means to express our thanks in the most direct way possible for using our credit cards and enjoying the variety of benefits they provide – Midland Choice offers you a wealth of opportunities and special awards. You have only to look through this brochure to get an idea of the quality and range of existing benefits available.

The business-speak we have already encountered reappears here in such terms as 'innovative ideas', 'exclusive offers', 'valued customer' and 'wealth of opportunities'. These expressions derive from the Business-speak All-Purpose Guide to Recommended Terms. But that vocabulary is threaded through with a vocabulary more appropriate to the world of personal communications between friends. We might speak of seizing a 'means to express our thanks in the most direct way possible' if we were writing round to those friends who had sent us wedding presents or indeed sent letters of sympathy to us after a bereavement. That vocabulary is here used in the process of drawing attention to a catalogue of items that are purchased by the 'points' accumulated through lavish use of the bank's credit card. This merging of idioms prompts one to ask the question: Does it take anyone in? Are there customers who feel a warm glow as the bank talks about rewarding their loyalty? Indeed, are there customers who, as they hand over their card at the check-out, are not wondering 'Have I spent too much?', but 'Have I been loyal enough to the bank in being content with this modest trolley-full?' Does the departing customer have second thoughts: 'Ought I perhaps to have bought that extra bottle of claret? It might have earned me a special word of thanks from the bank manager. It would certainly have opened the way to a special award. I should have won increased freedom of choice to plunder that range of existing benefits.'

## National Health Service

The NHS is run by a bureaucracy and when the bureaucracy makes its announcements one expects to hear the voice of bureaucracy. Nor is one disappointed. Hear a comment made on BBC Radio 4 by a representative of one of the country regions. The question at issue was the need to avoid overspending. How could the trust economize?

> One of the areas identified was the potential closure of regional hospitals.

Here we have the words 'areas' and 'potential' introduced and a matter of identification touched on all in the process of translating into the language of bureaucracy the statement 'We may have to close some regional hospitals.'

We have come to expect this usage from managers. But, alas, the idiom is not restricted to managers. The caring professionals may not talk like that, but some of them are capable of writing like that. Here is a comment from the *Nursing Standard* on how a nurse valued what she had gained from taking a certain course.

> If she had acquired this earlier, she says, the transition to her desired goals could have been achieved more quickly.

Did the nurse really say 'The transition to my desired goals could have been achieved more quickly'? Did she not rather speak of having got more quickly to where she wanted to be?

The possibilities of using a lot of words to say nothing are explored in many directions in the same journal. Here we have one among a series of paragraphs presented as 'challenges for debate' on the importance of a balanced diet for patients in hospital.

> To measure how nutrition outcomes have been achieved and assessed. Debate assists in clarifying expected learning outcomes for nutrition components of a programme. Reflections on and the use of learning outcomes for the key characteristics of the board's framework will help to determine progress in meeting nutrition education outcomes and will also help to specify the professional and academic standards to be achieved in different programmes and modules at both pre- and post-registration levels.

We seem to drown in a sea of words designed only to fill space. We are in a mental world of 'components' and 'outcomes', of 'programmes' and 'key characteristics' in which no clear line of utterance emerges. What do we know at the end of the paragraph that we did not know at the beginning? By thinking about the use of learning outcomes we are going to make progress in meeting nutrition education outcomes. Is this what the National Health Service is all about?

## Dialects of Business-Speak

There are various dialects of business-speak, and some of them go in for brevity, for instance the idiom in use by professionals for publicity purposes within their own field of activity. It is designed to make a quick impact and not to waste words. In this idiom practitioner is speaking to practitioner, and much can be taken as understood. Thus it trims business-speak down:

> TRUEDATA is a proven 7 step data quality framework for dealing with UK domestic and international data within a scalable architecture.

This presents the product with a directness that suggests efficiency. 'Scalable architecture' may be a less than exact image but, like the rest of the sentence, it does not waste words. Nor does the following:

> Our vendor independent approach will allow us to support TRUEDATA with best of breed software as it becomes available and thus free IT resources from time consuming product assessment exercises.

The point to be made here is that business-speak has an in-business dialect which makes a no-nonsense approach that values brevity. And the message is phrased so as to achieve the kind of impact made by headlines and newspaper placards. This dialect extends further the freedoms of the business-speak that is directed at the outside world. Usages such as '7 step data quality framework' and 'best of breed software' illustrate the queer amalgam of influences from business jargon and from literature.

There is also a business-speak dialect far less formal, far chattier and more intimate than the public voice. It tends to be used within the management world rather than in communicating with the public outside. We perhaps feel some reluctance in exploring what is after all an area of intimacies into which outsiders are not expected to intrude.

> If you have any ideas/views; know of the key documents etc. other areas have please let me know. I believe that within the business we have excellent well thought through ideas, there are some key issues/challenges that need to be bottomed out and the task is to pull these threads together into a realistic focused strategy.

Here we have the intimate word-in-your-ear approach. Button-holing fellow workers does not call for the heavy hand of verbal solemnity. If we are to subject the passage to criticism/judgement/analysis, we must appreciate that it was not intended for the pages of the *Financial Times* etc., but for distribution among the office fraternity. If there are grammatical/logical errors/solecisms in it that need to be bottomed out/topped up, then we may overlook them. All the writer was anxious to do was to pull a lot of threads together into a realistic focused strategy.

## E-mail

E-mail is of course used outside the business world as well as within it. Academics converse across the Atlantic by e-mail about their studies in this or that abstruse field of research. In such communications appropriate idiomatic shorthands are used which to outsiders may make no sense at all. That is true too of the continuous on-line chat which lightens the daily burdens of the business world. And lovers are increasingly sending billets-doux by e-mail. Here is another sphere of usage into which outsiders can scarcely dare to intervene. We regard Jonathan Swift as a master of English prose. If a model of simplicity, directness and plainness in English prose is called for, then Swift is the writer to whom literati turn. But he was quite prepared to end a letter to his dearest Stella with such messages as:

> I'm angry alomost; but I won't tause see im a dood dallar in odle sings, iss and so im Dd too . . . Lele I can say lele it ung oomens iss I tan, well as oo.

Such mysterious idioms survive in the personal columns of the press on St Valentine's Day. The point to be made is that much e-mail is a kind of private correspondence. And according to the degree of intimacy between correspondents private languages are adopted. This applies to the business world too.

Leisurely pen-pushing is not the only parent of e-mail. It is equally the offspring of the telegram. And the telegram made the maximum demand for brevity: HOUSE BURNT DOWN STOP COME QUICKLY STOP PHONE INSURANCE STOP. The use of e-mail by the business world must be noted because it is another medium which demands brevity.

We have just dealt with communications within the sphere of a given set of business interests. Communication by e-mail is common within limited segments of that world. And, where communication is between people engaged in the same work and perhaps in many cases familiar with each other, the freedoms cited above are further extended. The in-house e-mail dialect of business-speak thus makes a fascinating field of study. As one might expect, the modern liberties taken with nouns and verbs are further extended:

> Please action as below if possible.
>
> What products are available to mailed customers?
>
> Confirm Wilkinson order processed/despatched.

Such terse messages as these three exemplify the point. (We now accept liberties taken with the verb to 'mail', though, if my recent dictionary is comprehensive and authoritative, one could only 'mail' customers by posting them in letter-boxes.)

When records are at issue in in-house e-mail, computerology inserts another vein into the verbal amalgam.

> This is currently not in scope of the programme and needs consideration (eg keep excluded? include in XYZL WN3456? delay until resource resolved?)

Outsiders are likely to have just as much difficulty with this as with the *Journal to Stella*. Yet there is no doubt that the bracketed questions save space by obviating the need to spell out the three options with grammatical clarity. Indeed brackets are used with some versatility in this dialect:

> What do you think is the (business as usual) route by which these things will be addressed?

But perhaps the most interesting feature of in-house e-mail is that, because personal contacts exist between correspondents there is a natural tendency to use conversational expressions which one would not find in externally directed business-speak.

> Please let me know how this is working once it has had time to bed down.
>
> We need another meeting to sweep up any other matters.
>
> Feed this to Robinson.

Usages such as 'bed down', 'sweep up' and 'feed' give the in-house e-mail dialect a vein of refreshing simplicity absent from so much business-speak.

## VERBIAGE IN THE ARTISTIC WORLD

### Visual Arts

The peddlers of verbiage in the arts are a special breed. They have an inestimable advantage over writers in the fields we have been looking at. They can rely on the assumption that if readers do not understand what they read, they will believe that this is due to their own ignorance and not to any failing on the part of the writer. Writers on the arts are protected from the judgements of common sense by a mystique. The mystique derives from the notion that all worthwhile new developments in the arts meet at first with popular opposition because they are not properly understood. It follows that the cognoscenti can brainwash the public into laying aside the judgements of common sense when face to face with new art. The notion that great art is generally unappreciated by the contemporary world cannot be supported by reference to history. But the artistic world keeps it alive, and it fills the laity with apprehension. If a new work does not make sense to them, then probably that is because they are old-fashioned ignoramuses.

We are not here concerned with the larger civilizational aspect of this attitude. We are concerned with the treatment of the English language which art critics can indulge in on the basis of that attitude. Mystification pays off when the truly great is likely to be the incomprehensible.

It is with these observations in mind that we should approach the field of aesthetic criticism. For it is a field rich in empty verbiage. We may have seemed to some readers to have been over-caustic in our treatment of the business world. Let it be clearly understood, therefore, that the misuse of language in the business world pales into insignificance compared with the misuse of language in the world of the arts. To begin with, business uses a vocabulary with limits. Business may reach out into the field of personal vocabulary or even, as we have seen, into the vocabulary of personal well-being, but these tend to be sporadic incursions into recognizable fields of discourse. Moreover, as we saw above, when a firm brought in the word 'guru' from a different field of discourse, it really meant 'guru'. The concept came in as well as the noise. The world of artistic appreciation criticism knows no such inhibitions. It is not just that in context after context any word will seemingly do, but that whatever meaning that haphazardly chosen word drags along with it from its normal contextual backgrounds can be happily ignored. Let us look at this sphere of the aesthetic at a modest level of discourse where a magazine article deals with restoring an old house.

> Drawing the line between ethics and personal preference has to be considered and controlled, but where an overall scheme of decoration of this type was carried out, the only way it can be interpreted satisfactorily is to return to its nearest state of originality.

The reference to ethics ('the philosophical study of the moral aspects of human conduct') illustrates the point made above about the tendency among aesthetic writers to make forays into alien verbal territory. What it means, if it means anything, to 'consider and control' a line drawn between ethics and personal preference scarcely seems to matter. The grammatical and logical collapse that follows ('where a scheme was carried out . . . the only way it can be interpreted satisfactorily is to return it to its nearest state of originality') is complete. How a scheme can be interpreted by being so treated is incomprehensible.

The point that needs to be made here is, not that the passage makes nonsense, but that the passage can nevertheless be found in print. And that point is worth making. Because, once we have appreciated that the world of aesthetic criticism, at a fairly low level of expertise, can play havoc with meaning and logic, we shall be better prepared to face the horrors of more 'highbrow' utterance. Let us look at an account of the massive sculpture known as the 'Angel of the North', an account for which we are indebted to the 'Pseuds Corner' of *Private Eye*.

> The body of the Angel is trapped. It exists between vulnerability and strength. It is a millennial work witnessing the transition between the industrial and the information ages. This is not a logo, symbol, or even a representation in the traditional sense. It is based on reality; a moment of lived time in which my body was registered in plaster, a moment when biological time was captured in geological time.

If the terms 'vulnerability' and 'strength' are properly understood, then the notion of being 'trapped' between them is untenable. If the millennium marks a transition between the ages of industry and information, that does not mean that a contemporary work of art will somehow 'witness' to that idea. To say something is 'based on reality' adds nothing to our understanding of it. As for 'lived' time, 'biological' time and 'geological' time, the terms reek of imprecision.

## Literature

The story of the development of literary criticism during the last hundred years or so is one of increasing specialism. Time was, in the Victorian age, when critics were content to comment on works of fiction on the understanding that, say, Tess in Hardy's *Tess of the D'Urbervilles* was a portrait of a human being such as you or I might meet, and the novelist's ability to render her lifelike was one of his major gifts as a writer. Literary criticism then began to interest itself in the relationship between the fictional content of a writer's books and the actual events of the author's life. In the early years of the twentieth century, therefore, literary studies of authors were often combinations of biographical material from the author's own life and commentary on related material in the fictional output. Various changing emphases on the aesthetic, the social, the psychological and the political aspects of fictional constructions emerged during the mid-century years. These attitudes were superseded in the last decades of the century by theorists who cut away the traditional assumption that literature expressed some kind of reality in exploring the life of humanity. Attention shifted to works of literature as constructs manufactured from words. The business of criticism was not to comment on the world as presented in art form but to examine the linguistic formulations from which works of literature were constructed.

It is necessary to give this brief account of developments in a now very technical field in order to explain how the stage has been reached at which what literary critics say on paper can make seeming nonsense; that is to say, how writers can conceal the true quality of their thinking behind a flow of contrivedly abstruse terminology. The following is a review of a critical work for which we are again indebted to *Private Eye*.

> The first part of her essay concludes with naming the spatialized polity of the (Derridean) sophist – the city of modernity – as necropolis. For, in denying temporality and the spoken word, and 'being' as the gift of an excessive beyond, eliciting an erotic gaze (sight which participates in that which is seen), in favour of spatialized writing and being as the 'given'

> commanded by a panoptic vision, modernity ironically embraces necrophilia where it should affirm only life.

It is not my intention here to try to elucidate this. Half an hour spent with a dictionary, checking up on the meaning of such words as 'spatialized', 'polity' and 'panoptic' will not get one far, for it is not the individual words that present a problem to the reader but the eccentric juxtapositioning of one with another: 'spatialized' along with 'polity', 'spatialized' along with 'writing', and 'excessive' along with 'beyond'.

Taking a glance at this specimen of recent literary criticism, we recognize that this area of study has become a closed world for specialists. But imaginative literature, unlike nuclear physics, is meant to be open to all comers. And if one asked seriously the questions 'Would Shakespeare understand this?' 'Would Dickens understand this?' they would have to be answered in the negative.

## Music

It is a common view that music is the most incorruptible of the arts. Yet it has suffered from the regrettable recent developments here explored, the bold exploitation of the public by a seemingly informed use of words that is specious and often nugatory. It is a brand of verbosity that covers near-meaninglessness. We have to distinguish this from wasting words to convey something easily said with far fewer words. What we are here concerned with is rather a matter of using words to say little or nothing at all while seeming to be profound. There is a flavour of bogusness about this kind of utterance which it would be unjust to impute to those whose often wasteful, but scarcely dishonest, manner of speaking and writing we illustrate elsewhere. Let us turn to a programme note about one of Beethoven's major works . . .

> It is what it is, says what it says, offers what it offers, with immediacy, confidence and transcendental pertinence.

Now clearly, once you've started on this 'says what it says' lark, you can really make a meal of it: 'urges what it urges, announces what it announces, bubbles up with what it bubbles up with' and so on. As for the list of qualities: 'immediacy', 'confidence' and 'pertinence' (whether 'transcendental' or not), there is no reason why one should not add several more abstractions, say 'vigour', 'astuteness', and 'determination'. And what makes 'pertinence' 'transcendent'? Why not 'eternal immediacy, infinite confidence and transparently transcendental pertinence'? If music critics are paid by the shovelful of words, we could easily add to the income.

If a writer is seriously engaged in describing a composition intelligibly, that writer is surely limited in the intensity of the nonsense he or she can produce. What is written may be awkward, ill-phrased, even highly ungrammatical, and yet what the writer is trying to say may make sense. Here is a sentence from a programme note on Rachmaninov's third symphony.

> An urgent triplet rhythm takes us into the development with wind meanderings leading to disparate pockets of themes (based on the first subject) eventually coming together in a tramping rhythm with trumpets pealing, alternating with the afore-mentioned xylophone/piccolo/bassoon passage.

It is not elegant prose. If a schoolboy handed it in, one would suggest a re-write. But it is not nonsense. Indeed, having swallowed our reservations about the idea of 'disparate pockets' eventually merging in a 'tramping rhythm', we may feel that the connection between the prose and the matter in hand is firm, and that the sequence of ideas rather clumsily assembled actually helps us to understand the work in question. In the present climate of aesthetic utterance, that is no mean achievement.

Unfortunately music critics do not restrict themselves to elucidation of musical form. Here we have a piece from the Programme Notes for the Huddersfield Contemporary Music Festival, again courtesy of *Private Eye*.

> To ask if the artist has a moral responsibility implies, paradoxically, that the artist is not divorced from the social reality despite there being no empirical evidence that art has a function beyond the aesthetic. But asking the question at all amounts to a confession that society – and art – is in a crisis, and emphasises the inability of the Marxist or any other readily available vision to direct the way to the creation of a value structure which suggests the possibility of hope in the final few years of the twentieth century. The search for meaningfulness is as old as time, but during this climacteric there has never been a greater need for affirmation.

The supporters of the Huddersfield Contemporary Music Festival may be generous people. They need to be. Presumably they purchased their programme notes in the belief that they would find guidance towards full appreciation of the new music. They would probably have been quite content to swallow a few verbal gob-stoppers about the adventures of 'disparate pockets', provided that they thereby got some signposts to the thematic content of the work under review. But what have they been sold instead? A forced question about the connection between morality and art leads to the assertion that 'there is no empirical evidence' to support such a connection. 'No empirical evidence?' Does not Defoe's *Robinson Crusoe* have a moral message? Does not Bunyan's *Pilgrim's Progress* have a moral message? What about Dickens's novels? And, in the sphere of music, what about Beethoven's *Fidelio* and Tchaikovsky's *Eugene Onegin?* These works ooze with moral overtones. As for the statement that 'Asking the question at all amounts to a confession that society – and art – is in crisis', it is totally mistaken. Asking the question as he does merely reveals that the writer is intellectually in deep trouble. The words that follow about directing the way to 'the creation of a value structure' which suggests the possibility of hope are so much empty froth. The 'possibility' of hope is always there. What is needed now is the possibility that careless critics of the arts will learn to use their native tongue.

## SPORTSPEAK

One cannot listen to the reports on the radio of football matches and cricket matches without wishing that the sports writers could be persuaded to give advice to the newswriters and to fellow journalists on how to produce lively prose. The same can be said of the reports on matches in the daily press. It is not that sports writers generally deserve the highest marks for economy of utterance, but they have a way of vivifying their prose with metaphor. Now it has to be accepted that there is often a touch of self-conscious irony in their recourse to grandiloquent image and vocabulary. Great commentators on cricket for long relied on the language of heroism on the battlefield. Their presentation of events might endow noble stands at the wicket with the heroism of Horatius on the bridge at Rome or give to the struggle on the field the flavour of epic encounters under the walls of Troy. This tradition seems to justify the grandiloquence still adopted. Here is a comment on the news that an English FA club had just signed a young Italian.

> It also sends a signal down through the English fabric of the game, descending through the Nationwide League into the semi-professional and even amateur roots. Whither the opportunity for our embryonic talents if we are importing the seed as well as the full-grown plant?

The progress of the signal down through the very 'fabric' of the game all but reminds one of how, in Macaulay's ballad, the approach of the Spanish Armada was signalled by beacons right up the kingdom from hill top to hill top until the red glare on Skiddaw aroused the burghers of Carlisle. The question 'Whither . . . ?' maintains the grandiloquent flavour. When, in a previous book on usage, I happened to observe that we had all but lost two very useful words in ceasing to say 'whence' instead of the clumsier 'where from' and 'whither' instead of the clumsier 'where to', a critic pounced on this as a sign of my unfittedness to address the contemporary world on the subject of usage. Who on earth would want to use either 'whence' or 'whither' nowadays? Apparently the sports commentator does. One may argue that the 'fabric' of the game through which the signal is transmitted sounds more like a block of flats than a living thing and that therefore the reference to 'roots' (instead of perhaps 'basement'?) and the quick change of metaphor to that of seed and plant is a little wayward. But the prose is alive. And the idiom is with us daily. I turn to this morning's *Times*.

> After all the subterfuge and the paranoia of the reign of Glen Hoddle, the sheer boldness of Kevin Keegan swept through the England camp like a river of hope yesterday. The caretaker English coach did not just flout convention by naming his team to play Poland a day early, he nailed it to a tree.

We are learning about the end of a 'reign'. As the news in the previous specimen seeped down through a fabric to its roots, so the newcomer's boldness sweeps here through a camp like a river. Now, if you have ever put up a tent in Wales or in the Yorkshire Dales, you will know that when a river sweeps through the camp it is not exactly a symbol of hope. But water is refreshing and it could be that the picture here is of a camp in the Sahara or in the desert of Arizona. The image of the new caretaker is of one who flouts convention. Indeed the picture of him, nailing to a tree – not convention (as the grammar suggests) – but the list of his chosen team, brings back associations of Martin Luther taking on the whole might of Rome. That the writer is not unconscious of the implicit similarity with mighty historical events becomes obvious in what follows.

> A small crowd gathered round the proud old oak outside the team hotel to peer at the 11 names he had written in black capital letters on a white sheet and felt the thrill of a visceral challenge pass through them. Keegan could not have made it much more stirring if he had been a medieval knight.

The pathetic convention is employed to make the old oak 'proud' of the privilege it has been granted. After all, we are in a world where black capital letters on white paper can send the thrill of a visceral challenge coursing through the veins of grown men. And now the cat is out of the bag. We are not picturing a humdrum contemporary in action, but a mediaeval knight. Later in the piece the knight himself speaks. He does so with a different idiom.

> I see the team playing on a wonderful pitch. I see us winning and I see people cheering when we come off. But that is me.

Here is someone who can make simple words, framed in simple rhetorical repetitions, touch the heart, like Martin Luther King's repetitive words 'I have a dream'. They are the words of a visionary, but a visionary with his feet on the ground.

## JOURNALESE AND MAGAZINE-SPEAK

This book has relied greatly on quotations from the daily press and from magazines. It may therefore seem to the reader to be superfluous to devote a special section to issues that have been with us throughout the book. But a glance at certain journalistic habits may not come amiss in this survey of the current scene.

## Verbal Ostentation

We have just looked at the kind of hyperbole found in sportspeak. Some readers may even feel that we have been too tender in our treatment of sports writers in this respect. After all, the touch of hyperbole and the taste for avoiding plain, direct utterance are not features peculiar to sportspeak. The same kind of ironic over-statement that the sports writers use may be found in many different contexts. Here is part of an account of a well-decorated home in a magazine on style.

> But the *coup de grâce* could be her bathroom, whose cupboards belie a mundane function. Instead they resemble one of those charming Victorian screens pasted with nostalgic snapshots . . .

A 'coup de grâce' is originally an expression from battle. Literally a 'stroke of mercy', it represents the final blow which puts an end to the opponent's life and suffering. Hence it is used of momentous acts which terminate a struggle, then, less seriously as here, of the final touch which comes as a climax to what has been done or said. Just as one senses the authorial smile behind this expression, so too it is there behind the consciously sophisticated way of saying that in appearance the cupboards belie their mundane function. Even advertisers rely on not being taken too seriously in their adventures with words.

> Shimmer the summer away with Pastel Lumière Eyeshadows from Bourjois – fabulously strong, long-lasting colours . . .

The notion of a woman 'shimmering' her summer away asks not to be conceptually analysed any more than the claim that the colours are 'fabulously' strong.

But when the hint of humour is lacking, such artificial verbal poses may fail to come off. In a journal directed at the field sports community a writer lets off steam about the threats from the Green movement. He has just come across a piece of scientific research which throws doubt on some of the claims of the environmentalists.

> We can but hope that this incident marks a new era when there will be further stirrings in the scientific thickets to apply correctives to the miasma of humbug with which we are at present enveloped.

The writer might argue that a simpler and more direct sentence would not have conveyed the sense of outrage which expressions such as 'miasma of humbug' reveal. Nevertheless, by being too indigestible, the image of correctives to a miasma that emerge somehow from stirrings in the thickets turns almost to parody. The result is that, where readers are meant to receive the image of a righteously wrathful opponent of non-sense, they receive instead an image of someone all but frothing at the mouth uncontrollably. In short, the thing becomes comic.

The kind of verbal finery we are exploring does require a certain degree of sophistication in the writer, for the vocabulary is rich in artifices. Because of this, it cannot afford to lapse grammatically. To hear a lout being noisily ungrammatical is not hair-raising. But to hear the smart, supposedly educated person on a platform being ungrammatical is embarrassing. So too the user of verbal finery cannot afford to trip up in elementary grammar. Yet it happens. Here we have a writer praising alfresco meals taken in various places, and he describes lunch at a club in St Tropez where a mist of water is sprayed from concealed piping.

> This cooled the air but was sufficiently well judged and fine enough so as not to militate against a post-prandial cigar.

We are in a sophisticated world where one can measure the degree of atmospheric interference that might mar enjoyment of a post-prandial cigar. How inappropriate, then, to commit a grammatical howler that might disgrace a schoolboy by saying 'sufficiently fine enough so as not to militate' instead of the correct 'fine enough not to militate'. One or the other, 'sufficiently' or 'enough', is redundant. And that 'so as' represents a lapse into illiteracy.

In this respect a kind of moral code comes into operation when one is picking holes in other people's writing. A modest writer slipping up with a difficult word or concept does not seem fair game, as does the sophisticated writer slipping up when showing off. So when a third leader in *The Times* comes a cropper, while dealing with a literary subject and ostentatiously dropping names of writers and works, conscience allows one to record it for posterity. The topic is the lighthearted question whether the dawn of a new century will turn today's avant-garde writers into yesterday's men. After attributing to Keats Browning's oft-quoted lines, 'Oh, to be in England / Now that April's there', the writer continues:

> But for the *Times Literary Supplement*, Eliot's *Prufrock* was 'of the very smallest

importance' and, in *The Waste Land*, he was rebuked for neglecting 'the limitations of his medium'.

Eliot was not rebuked in *The Waste Land*, but in a review of the poem. The mistake is the error we called 'verbal leapfrog'.

## Overstatement

We turn to a less sophisticated brand of verbal finery where hyperbole is used to express enthusiasm. Our conversation and our private letters abound in simple and 'innocent' forms of overstatement. How else can we express our grateful appreciation of our friend's cooking and hospitality? Words like 'wonderful', 'superb', and 'delightful' fall from our lips or are penned in our letters of thanks. When we have to pay tributes to people on occasions of celebration, we tend to use a ready vocabulary of praise. And when journalists have the duty to report achievements in competitive events, they tend to tap a familiar vein of overstatement.

> Once again Mrs Ronnie Wallace's Anchor Herd stallion, Icecream, won an impressive collection of silverware at the Exmoor Breed show, at Exford on the moor.

A few lines below this, we read:

> Also well laden with trophies was Vera Lipsombe, from Wootton Courtenay, near Minehead . . .

Talk of winning an impressive collection of silverware and of being laden with trophies is the product of three motives. The first motive is the wish to say something different from 'The horse came first'; the second motive is the wish to say something that takes up a little more space than 'The horse came first'; and the third motive is to say something that expresses more enthusiasm than 'The horse came first.' We see the same three motives in operation when we read how a certain competitor 'crowned a marvellous season' with a win, how another 'followed up earlier triumphs' with a victory, and how a third 'belied his age with a scintillating performance' to claim first prize. The sports writers we cited above used imagery to create a definable verbal ambience, but the over-used expressions here do not carry authentic feeling and drop into the mind as dead counters.

The trouble is that certain kinds of writing are the product of the necessity to pen sentences when the material available for utterance would be more appropriately put in note form. In reading reports of competitive events, one can often sense the struggling mind of the writer adopting this device and that in order to put in seemingly natural prose the ordered list of winners and losers.

## Experimentation

Adventurousness in the choice of words is tempting, but purposely pushing a verb into a new usage by a kind of colloquial inventiveness may come off or may fail to come off. Consider the use of the verb 'guarantee' in the following.

> The pursuit of ratings is now such an all-consuming matter that bagging a face that will guarantee the cover of the *TV Times* has become almost more important than signing the best actor for the part.

The usage is neither precise nor grammatical but there is a touch of verbal legerdemain about translating 'a face that is sure to appear on the cover of the *TV Times*' into 'a face that will guarantee the cover of the *TV Times*'. With this kind of experimentation one does of course run the risk of seeming illiterate rather than clever, as we see in this use of the verb to 'muster':

> The sheep gave me as filthy a look as a sheep can muster to display their displeasure at being kept waiting.

The verb to 'muster' has been primarily used of collecting together bodies of men for military or other duties. Thus the notion of assembling personnel is basic to the usage. The fact that failure to assemble enough people for a given purpose produced the usage 'Is that all you can muster?' should not be the basis for eliminating the basic meaning of the verb in its connection with gathering numbers together. In short the experiment does not come off and the writer should have been satisfied with: 'gave me as filthy a look as a sheep can give'.

Fanciful coinages manufactured by journalists with a sense of humour can brighten sober prose. Some decades ago the word 'couth' was used in print. It was intended to mean the converse of 'uncouth'. As 'uncouth' means 'lacking in good manners', so 'couth' was used to mean 'civilized and cultivated'. Whoever it was that first used 'couth' thus provided others with an entertaining word to drop in conversation. But etymologically the usage does not make sense. Although the current meaning of 'uncouth' is 'lacking in good manners', the word 'couth' once meant 'known'. We find the word in Chaucer. There is a point in his narrative poem *Troilus and Criseyde* at which an exchange of prisoners is planned between the Trojans in Troy and the besieging Greeks. The news of this plan spreads rapidly. 'This thing anon was couth in every street' Chaucer tells us. And we do not need to look as far back as that for use of 'couth', meaning 'known'. It still survives in Scotland.

That said, the joke was a good one and produced some imitations. 'They behaved perfectly, which gruntled me no end', I read in a magazine. Here again the joke depends on assuming that 'gruntle' must be the converse of 'disgruntle'. The reasoning is that if being 'disgruntled' is being displeased and put into a bad mood, then 'gruntled' must mean pleased and satisfied. But this is to ignore etymology and history. In fact the verb 'gruntle' is the frequentative form of 'grunt' (as 'prattle' is the frequentative form of 'prate') and is not therefore the opposite of 'disgruntle' (to put in a bad temper) but a near equivalent.

There are certain other words which exist in a seemingly negative form for which the converse positive form is not used. We speak of a clumsy, physically unprepossessing person as being 'ungainly', but the positive form 'gainly', meaning 'graceful', has long dropped out of use. We use the words 'scrutiny' and 'scrutinize' for close examination and we describe a taxingly unreadable personality as 'inscrutable', but the word 'scrutable' has also gone from common use. Used in journalism, the two words 'gainly' and 'scrutable' give a piquancy to the text.

No doubt the temptation to use or adapt archaic or rarely used words comically will always find takers.

> Your swash has never been buckled until you've experienced Errol Flynn in full doublet and hose as Robin of Locksley.

'Swashbuckling' is a colourful word, but to talk of buckling a swash is really topsy turvy. It would be nearer the point to talk of 'swashing the buckle', for the 'swash' was the clattering stroke of sword on metal. A 'swashbuckler' was one who made a noisy display by striking his own or his opponent's shield with his sword. It is safer philologically to make such jokes with purely imaginary words, as the writer of the following does.

> On behalf of her mates she keeps alert (surely this country's got enough lerts, perhaps she should be a loof instead?).

## Slang

Usages which exploit slang or crude colloquialisms may brighten journalism or cheapen it. Perhaps the following advertisement manages to do both.

> Let Direct Line guide you to a bright career as the glammest gran on the block.

We all know what 'glammest' must mean, though we may never have met it before. 'Glamorous' is not an adjective that can be turned into 'glamorousest'. Evading the usage 'most glamorous' in the interests of brevity and of sustaining a tone of informal chatter serves its purpose.

One may feel less indulgent towards the comparatively recent usage of the verb to 'forget' in a piece about the treatment of children.

> Forget shouting at them to clear up.

As a substitute for saying 'Don't do this' or 'Stop doing that', 'Forget doing it' has a certain colloquial freshness at first, but that kind of freshness soon palls, and one begins to sense that, after all, desisting from doing something is one thing and forgetting to do it is another and very different thing. But the usage is part of the 'Listen-to-me-being-informal' idiom which is to be heard all around us.

> Disclosing tablets can be a fun way of testing that all the plaque has been removed.

Too many liberties are taken here in the advice for looking after a child's teeth. Using 'fun' as an adjective and defining tablets as a 'way' are no doubt devices for keeping up a light-hearted tone, but the price paid in verbal 'finish' is too high. On the other hand one can see what is gained in briskness and conciseness by the following opening:

> Spring is the ideal time to dejunk your wardrobe.

The word 'dejunk' carries the suggestion of someone who means business and it doesn't convey the tone of a person from whom the polite might shrink, as does the following:

> I take real pleasure in slobbing around in T-shirts with holes in.

We are not, of course, expected to want to join her, and she makes sure of that. There is no verb to 'slob', but the noun 'slob' means someone unattractively coarse and crude. To suggest that you enjoy indulging in the coarse and the crude sounds too much like a challenge. One feels the need for a word to define the practice of verbal slumming.

> When you're done being all cultural, hit the clubs, blag your way into the impossibly trendy Met Bar . . .

One assumes that the writer was perfectly aware that 'when you're done' is a crudely illiterate version of 'when you've done'. This amusingly exaggerates the shift in mood from 'cultural' interests to something earthier. 'Hitting' clubs or other high spots is established slang. The slang verb to 'blag' officially means to rob but the effect on us ordinary readers of seeing it used to mean something else is to make us feel out of touch with the latest trends. We recognize that it must be 'hip' to say 'when you're done' instead of 'when you've done' and hipper still to speak of 'hitting' clubs. So we must assume that it is hippest of all to talk of 'blagging your way' into a bar. If we really appreciate that we are not just trendy, we are positively funky.

# Index

Words and phrases discussed in the text are indexed in *italics*; topics discussed are in roman type.

# THE PENGUIN A–Z THESAURUS

(previously published as THE PENGUIN DICTIONARY OF SYNONYMS AND ANTONYMS)

---

EDITED BY ROSALIND FERGUSSON,
MARKET HOUSE BOOKS LIMITED

PENGUIN BOOKS

PENGUIN BOOKS

Published by the Penguin Group
Penguin Books Ltd, 80 Strand, London WC2R 0RL, England
Penguin Putnam Inc., 375 Hudson Street, New York, New York 10014, USA
Penguin Books Australia Ltd, 250 Camberwell Road, Camberwell, Victoria 3124, Australia
Penguin Books Canada Ltd, 10 Alcorn Avenue, Toronto, Ontario, Canada M4V 3B2
Penguin Books India (P) Ltd, 11 Community Centre, Panchsheel Park, New Delhi – 110 017, India
Penguin Books (NZ) Ltd, Cnr Rosedale and Airborne Roads, Albany, Auckland, New Zealand
Penguin Books (South Africa) (Pty) Ltd, 24 Sturdee Avenue, Rosebank 2196, South Africa

Penguin Books Ltd, Registered Offices: 80 Strand, London WC2R 0RL, England

www.penguin.com

*The Nuttall Dictionary of English Synonyms and Antonyms*, a revised edition,
first published by Frederick Warne & Co. Ltd 1943
A fully revised and updated edition,
under the title *The New Nuttall Dictionary of English Synonyms and Antonyms*,
first published by Viking 1986
Published under the title *The Penguin Dictionary of Synonyms and Antonyms* in Penguin Books 1992
Reprinted under the present title 2001
14



Printed in England by Clays Ltd, St Ives plc

PENGUIN REFERENCE

# THE PENGUIN A–Z THESAURUS

Rosalind Fergusson was born in Liverpool in 1953 and obtained her degree in French from Exeter University. From here she took a teaching certificate and became an assistant teacher at a school in West Sussex. From 1978 to 1984 she worked for Market House Books where she trained as an assistant editor and lexicographer and rose to the position of Senior Editor. During this time she worked on a range of reference books. Since leaving Market House Books she has worked as a freelance editor.

Her other publications include *The Penguin Dictionary of Proverbs* (1983), *The Penguin Rhyming Dictionary* (1985), *Choose your Baby's Name* (1987), *The Hamlyn Dictionary of Quotations* (1989), *Chambers Dictionary of Foreign Words and Phrases* (1995), *Cassell Dictionary of English Idioms* (1999) and *The New Penguin Dictionary of Abbreviations* (2000). Rosalind Fergusson has also edited and co-edited a number of dictionaries and reference books, and has contributed to *The Bloomsbury Good Word Guide* (1988) and *Brewer's Dictionary of 20th-Century Phrase and Fable* (1991), among others.

Rosalind Fergusson is married and lives in Kent. Her leisure interests include walking, sailing and music.

# Preface

This classic work, formerly entitled *The Nuttall Dictionary of English Synonyms and Antonyms,* was last revised in 1943. It was reprinted twenty-eight times, indicating that it had found a substantial and continuing market. For this entirely new edition the dictionary has been updated and considerably enlarged, both in the selection of words covered and in the range of synonyms and antonyms offered. In the last half-century many words and senses have changed their meaning, and many new ones have appeared. This edition reflects these changes in the English language without altering the essential flavour of the book, although it has now been computerized and typeset using the latest technology.

The aim of this edition, as with earlier versions, is to collect together groups of words of similar meaning, enabling the user to avoid repetition in both writing and speaking and to find quickly and easily the most appropriate word for any occasion. English has a uniquely prolific vocabulary reflecting the multiplicity of its sources – the Anglo-Saxon of its early inhabitants, the enrichment provided by its Roman, Viking, and Norman invaders, the borrowings from all parts of the globe acquired by generations of seafarers, and the two-way trade in vocabulary from the Empire and Colonies. The result is a language more precise than any other in its ability to differentiate shades and nuances of meaning; for the users of such an affluent language a dictionary of synonyms becomes a near-necessity.

While it is probable that there are no true synonyms – that few words can really be interchanged in all contexts without any shift of connotation – on many occasions memories need to be nudged for the appropriate near-synonym to complete a sentence or paragraph without repetition. To provide this service, this dictionary consists of a single alphabetical list of headwords, each followed by a selection of synonyms grouped together according to the various senses of the word and the different shades of meaning within each sense. Clearly a book of this size cannot list all the words in the language, but what it does provide is a broad selection of the words in the general language. Concrete nouns with simple synonyms, such as **car**, **automobile**, and **radio**, **wireless**, have not been included. Our aim, like those of the original editors of the book, has been to cover the more interesting semantic areas of abstract nouns and adjectives, especially those with metaphorical senses.

In addition to the synonym lists, for many of the entries an antonym is given in small capital letters at the end of the entry. (Further antonyms may be obtained by seeking the antonyms of words listed as synonyms.)

Where the derived form of a word is not given as an independent headword, its synonyms may be formed from those given for its stem. For example, from the entry

**sad**, unhappy, sorrowful, downcast, dejected, depressed, despondent, etc.

both

**sadly**, unhappily, sorrowfully, dejectedly, despondently,

and

**sadness**, unhappiness, sorrow, dejection, depression, despondency, etc.

may be derived.

Part-of-speech labels are given where necessary to distinguish between the different senses of a headword or between headwords with identical spelling. They are abbreviated as follows:

*adj* adjective
*adv* adverb
*conj* conjunction
*interj* interjection
*n* noun
*prep* preposition
*v* verb
*vi* intransitive verb
*vt* transitive verb

The label (*inf*), as an abbreviation of the word 'informal', has been introduced to designate synonyms that may be unacceptable in formal usage.

Finally we would like to thank Commander F. Val. Jones, who, with his late wife, made many helpful suggestions for bringing this book up to date.

R.F.
1985

# A

**aback** backwards, rearwards, behind, aft.
**taken aback,** surprised, startled, dumbfounded, nonplussed, disconcerted.

**abandon** *v*, desert, leave, forsake, jilt, discard, get rid of, drop.
quit, vacate, evacuate, withdraw from.
give up, forgo, yield, surrender, cede, relinquish, renounce, abdicate, resign. RETAIN
*n*, unrestraint, dash, verve, impulsiveness, wantonness, lawlessness. RESTRAINT

**abandoned** deserted, forsaken, left, discarded, cast away, rejected, forlorn, derelict. KEPT
unrestrained, uninhibited, wanton, dissolute, shameless, impenitent, licentious, depraved, corrupt, sinful. VIRTUOUS

**abase** lower, reduce, depress, degrade, disgrace, dishonour, humiliate, humble, demean, demote, debase, belittle. EXALT

**abasement** degradation, lowering, disgrace, dishonour, ignominy, shame, humiliation, mortification. EXALTATION

**abash** confound, confuse, disconcert, discompose, discomfit, embarrass, shame, humble, humiliate, daunt, overawe, intimidate.

**abashment** confusion, discomposure, discomfiture, chagrin, embarrassment, shame, humiliation.

**abate** lessen, reduce, decrease, diminish, attenuate, alleviate, ease, moderate, assuage, soothe, calm, pacify, appease, quell, subside, let up, ebb, decline, wane, slacken, remit. INCREASE
deduct, subtract, discount.

**abatement** decrease, diminution, lessening, reduction, decline, easing, moderation, alleviation, relief. INCREASE
suppression, termination, control, restraint, limitation.
deduction, subtraction, discount, reduction, rebate.

**abbey** monastery, friary, priory, nunnery, convent, cloister, church, minster.

**abbreviate** condense, shorten, curtail, abridge, cut, reduce, contract, compress, paraphrase, summarize, précis. LENGTHEN

**abbreviation** shortening, abridgment, reduction, contraction, compression, condensation, summary, résumé, synopsis. EXTENSION

**abdicate** resign, renounce, give up, relinquish, cede, surrender, vacate, retire, quit.

**abdomen** belly, paunch, stomach, tummy (*inf*), gut, intestines.

**abdominal** intestinal, visceral, gastric, stomachic, ventral.

**abduct** kidnap, carry off, seize, remove, run off with, appropriate. RESTORE

**abduction** kidnapping, seizure, appropriation. RESTORATION

**aberrant** irregular, abnormal, eccentric, peculiar, untypical, anomalous, unusual, singular, odd. REGULAR
deviant, wandering, deviating, divergent, rambling.
erroneous, wrong, perverse, perverted, corrupt.

**aberration** deviation, divergence, irregularity, abnormality, peculiarity, anomaly. REGULARITY
delusion, vagary, mental disorder, hallucination.

**abet** aid, assist, help, succour, sustain, support, back, condone, favour, sanction, encourage, advocate, incite, urge, egg on. OPPOSE

**abettor** accomplice, accessory, henchman, partner in crime, assistant, helper, associate, confederate, instigator, adviser. OPPONENT

**abeyance** suspension, intermission, deferment, postponement, reservation, dormancy. REVIVAL
**in abeyance,** suspended, put aside, shelved, pending, hanging fire, on ice (*inf*).

**abhor** abominate, loathe, detest, execrate, shrink from, hate. ADORE

**abhorrence** abomination, loathing, execration, detestation, odium, repugnance, horror, aversion, antipathy, hate, hatred. LOVE

**abhorrent** loathsome, detestable, execrable, abominable, obnoxious, repugnant, odious, hateful, horrid. ADORABLE

**abide** *vt*, bear, tolerate, put up with, suffer, stand, brook, endure, sustain, accept, submit to.
*vi*, remain, last, endure, persist, continue, survive. PERISH
dwell, reside, live, lodge, sojourn, settle, rest, tarry, stay. DEPART
**abide by,** comply with, conform to, observe, obey, submit to, fulfil, carry out, keep to. BREAK

**abiding** lasting, permanent, durable, enduring, eternal, changeless, unchanging, steadfast. CHANGING

**ability** capacity, capability, competence, efficiency, proficiency, skill, aptitude, cleverness, talent, gift, knack, flair, potential, power, might, force. INABILITY

**abject** contemptible, despicable, base, vile, mean, low, ignoble, worthless, degraded, sordid, servile, grovelling, cringing, slavish. HONOURABLE
miserable, wretched, forlorn, dejected, pitiable, pathetic.

**abjectness** abjection, baseness, dishonour, degradation, vileness, meanness, worthlessness, servility.
destitution, forlornness, wretchedness, misery, humiliation.

**abjure** retract, recant, withdraw, disclaim, forswear, disavow. ACKNOWLEDGE
renounce, reject, repudiate, discard, disown, abandon, forsake, abstain from.

**able** capable, competent, fit, efficient, accomplished, qualified, adept, proficient, adroit, skilful, clever, talented, expert, masterly, powerful, strong. INCAPABLE

**ablution** washing, cleansing, bathing, purification.

**abnegate** deny, renounce, abstain from, abjure, forgo, reject.

**abnegation** denial, renunciation, abjuration, surrender, self-denial, abstinence.

**abnormal** irregular, unusual, uncommon, extraordinary, singular, eccentric, aberrant divergent, atypical, exceptional, monstrous, peculiar, strange, odd, curious, weird, queer. NORMAL

**abnormality** anomaly, irregularity, deformity, monstrosity, aberration, peculiarity, idiosyncrasy, strangeness, oddity. NORMALITY

**aboard** on board, afloat, on, in, inside, within.

**abode** dwelling, home, domicile, residence, habitation, lodging, house, seat, quarters.

**abolish** destroy, do away with, annihilate, nullify, annul, abrogate, eradicate, terminate, end, put an end to, suppress, revoke, cancel, erase, obliterate, eliminate. RETAIN

**abolition** destruction, annihilation, annulment, abrogation, eradication, end, suppression, cancellation, obliteration, elimination.

**abominable** detestable, loathsome, horrible, hateful, execrable, odious, obnoxious, foul, vile, repulsive, repugnant, hellish, damnable, accursed, terrible, unpleasant. LOVABLE

**abominate** abhor, detest, loathe, execrate, hate. ADORE

**abomination** abhorrence, loathing, detestation, aversion, hatred. LOVE
plague, torment, nuisance, annoyance, bugbear, curse, pest. BLESSING
evil, villainy, wickedness, corruption, pollution.

**aboriginal** original, first, earliest, primary, autochthonous, native, indigenous, primitive, primeval. ALIEN

**aborigine** native, indigene, aboriginal, autochthon.

**abort** miscarry, terminate, halt, stop, check, arrest, go wrong, fail. ACHIEVE

**abortion** miscarriage, termination of pregnancy, stillbirth, aborticide, feticide.
failure, disappointment, fiasco, mishap, misadventure, blunder. ACHIEVEMENT

**abortive** fruitless, vain, unavailing, ineffectual, futile, failed, failing. SUCCESSFUL
immature, incomplete, imperfect, rudimentary, stunted, untimely, premature.

**abound** teem, swarm, flow, overflow, be plentiful, proliferate, flourish, thrive.

**about** *prep*, concerning, relating to, regarding, touching, with respect to.
near, close to, around, nearby, nigh.
around, encircling, surrounding, on all sides, throughout, all over.
*adv*, approximately, roughly, more or less, circa, around, almost, nearly, well-nigh. PRECISELY

**about to,** on the point of, soon to, ready to, on the verge of.

**above** *prep*, over, on top of, higher than, exceeding, beyond, superior to. BELOW
*adv*, overhead, atop, aloft, higher, earlier, before, previously. BELOW

**aboveboard** frank, honest, truthful, open, candid, forthright, ingenuous, artless. DISHONEST

**abrasion** attrition, erosion, wearing down, rubbing, scraping, scouring.
scratch, graze, scrape.

**abrasive** *adj*, rough, scratching, grating, harsh.

irritating, annoying, biting, caustic, sharp. *n*, scourer, abradant, emery, pumice, sandpaper, grindstone, rasp, file.

**abreast** beside, alongside, side by side, aligned, level.
informed, knowledgeable, conversant, familiar, up to date, *au courant*.

**abridge** condense, shorten, compress, contract, cut, reduce, abbreviate, summarize, cut down, curtail, lessen, diminish. EXPAND

**abridgment** shortening, condensation, abbreviation, summary, précis, abstract, digest, synopsis, outline, résumé, compendium. EXPANSION

**abroad** overseas, in foreign parts, out of the country.
away, out, elsewhere, at large, apart, dispersed, far, widely, publicly. NEAR

**abrogate** repeal, revoke, countermand, annul, nullify, cancel, expunge, quash, overrule, invalidate, abolish, terminate. ENACT

**abrupt** sudden, unexpected, unanticipated, unforeseen, hasty, precipitate, rash.
steep, sheer, precipitous. GRADUAL
curt, brusque, short, unceremonious, gruff, blunt, impolite, rude. COURTEOUS
broken, jagged, rough, uneven, disconnected, jerky.

**abscess** sore, boil, ulcer, inflammation, festering.

**abscond** flee, fly, run away, run off, elope, decamp, bolt, escape, leave, withdraw, beat it (*inf*), clear off (*inf*), disappear, hide. APPEAR

**absence** nonattendance, nonappearance. PRESENCE
lack, want, need, deficiency, default, unavailability.

**absent** *adj*, away, off, missing, out, abroad, gone, lacking, wanting, nonexistent. PRESENT
inattentive, preoccupied, distracted, oblivious, unaware, dreaming, faraway. ATTENTIVE

**absent oneself,** *v*, stay away, play truant, leave, depart, withdraw, abscond.

**absent-minded** forgetful, distracted, preoccupied, absorbed, absent, faraway, oblivious, unthinking, unconscious.

**absolute** complete, entire, utter, total, unlimited, unrestricted, unconditional, unqualified, perfect, pure, unadulterated, unalloyed, unmixed. PARTIAL
despotic, autocratic, tyrannical, authoritative, dictatorial, supreme, arbitrary.
undoubted, real, genuine, actual, veritable, certain, unquestionable. DUBIOUS

**absolutely** completely, entirely, utterly, totally, wholly, perfectly, categorically. PARTIALLY
really, unquestionably, definitely, indeed, positively, certainly, indubitably. POSSIBLY

**absolution** remission, forgiveness, pardon, acquittal, discharge, dispensation, amnesty, liberation, deliverance. CONDEMNATION

**absolve** forgive, pardon, excuse, acquit, exonerate, clear, exculpate, release, discharge, liberate, free, remit. CONDEMN

**absorb** consume, assimilate, incorporate, imbibe, soak up, suck up, take in, swallow, engulf. EXUDE
engross, fascinate, enthral, engage, preoccupy, monopolize.

**absorbent** porous, permeable, pervious, spongy, blotting, receptive, assimilative. IMPERMEABLE

**absorbing** engrossing, fascinating, riveting, gripping, interesting. DULL

**abstain** refrain, forbear, desist, decline, refuse, forgo, renounce, give up, shun, avoid, withhold. INDULGE

**abstemious** abstinent, temperate, moderate, sober, teetotal, continent, self-denying, ascetic, sparing, frugal. GREEDY

**abstinence** teetotalism, sobriety, temperance, moderation, abstemiousness, continence, self-denial. SELF-INDULGENCE

**abstract** *adj*, theoretical, hypothetical, unreal, spiritual, vague, conceptual, imaginary, indefinite, abstruse, recondite, profound, philosophical. CONCRETE
*n*, abridgment, summary, synopsis, digest, outline, précis, résumé.
*v*, separate, detach, remove, isolate, dissociate, extract, take out. UNITE
abbreviate, condense, shorten, abridge, epitomize, summarize. EXPAND

**abstracted** preoccupied, inattentive, absent-minded, faraway, daydreaming, unaware, distracted. ATTENTIVE

**abstraction** inattention, preoccupation, reverie, absence, brown study, absorption. ATTENTION

concept, idea, notion, theory, hypothesis, generality.
separation, isolation, removal, withdrawal, disconnection. UNION

**abstruse** obscure, recondite, abstract, vague, esoteric, arcane, occult, mysterious, perplexing, incomprehensible, unfathomable, profound, remote, subtle. CLEAR

**absurd** ridiculous, preposterous, irrational, incongruous, unreasonable, foolish, silly, asinine, crazy, stupid, ludicrous, nonsensical, senseless, laughable, farcical. SENSIBLE

**abundance** plenty, plentifulness, copiousness, profusion, exuberance, luxuriance, ampleness, fullness, bounty, affluence, richness, wealth, flood, overflow, surfeit, glut, excess. SCARCITY

**abundant** plentiful, copious, profuse, luxuriant, ample, bountiful, lavish, rich, replete, overflowing, teeming. SCARCE

**abuse** *v*, misuse, misapply, misemploy, pervert, exploit, take advantage of.
maltreat, harm, injure, hurt, ill-treat, persecute.
insult, slander, revile, disparage, defame, calumniate, malign, vilify, reproach, upbraid. PRAISE
*n*, misuse, misapplication, exploitation, perversion.
maltreatment, ill-treatment, injury, damage, persecution.
slander, calumny, insults, defamation, invective, disparagement. PRAISE

**abusive** insulting, offensive, defamatory, slanderous, rude, derogatory, derisive. COMPLIMENTARY

**abut** adjoin, touch, meet, join, impinge, border on, end at.

**abyss** gulf, gorge, chasm, crevasse, ravine, abysm, bottomless pit, void.

**academic** scholarly, learned, erudite, highbrow, intellectual, scholastic, literary, collegiate.
abstract, theoretical, hypothetical, speculative, artificial, unreal, irrelevant, unimportant. REAL

**academy** school, college, university, institution, institute, seminary.

**accede** agree, concur, assent, acquiesce, accept, consent, grant, concede, comply. DISAGREE
attain, succeed, inherit, assume, ascend, enter upon.

**accelerate** hasten, quicken, speed up, hurry, expedite, urge on, spur, stimulate, advance. RETARD

**accent** *n*, stress, accentuation, emphasis, force, beat, rhythm, cadence, pitch, tone, intonation, modulation, pronunciation, inflection.
*v*, accentuate, emphasize, stress.

**accentuate** accent, stress, emphasize, underline, highlight, draw attention to.

**accept** take, receive, gain, acquire, obtain. REFUSE
agree to, accede to, assent to, admit, acknowledge, acquiesce, allow, affirm, avow. REPUDIATE
tolerate, put up with, bear, stand, suffer.

**acceptable** satisfactory, adequate, passable, tolerable, all right, not bad, so-so. UNACCEPTABLE
welcome, agreeable, gratifying, pleasant, pleasing, delightful. UNWELCOME

**acceptance** acknowledgment, receipt, accepting, taking, reception. REFUSAL
approval, approbation, favour, sanction, assent, agreement, ratification.

**accepted** approved, authorized, usual, customary, normal, standard, conventional, traditional, established. UNCONVENTIONAL

**access** admission, admittance, approach, entrance, door, entry, way, passage, path.
attack, onset, fit, paroxysm, spasm, seizure, outburst.

**accessible** approachable, reachable, getatable (*inf*), obtainable, available, to hand. INACCESSIBLE
affable, cordial, friendly, approachable, genial. UNFRIENDLY

**accession** succession, inheritance, attainment, arrival, inauguration, investiture, installation.
addition, augmentation, increase, enlargement, extension, expansion. DECREASE

**accessory** *n*, supplement, subsidiary, component, element, minor part, detail, appendage, addition, attachment. ESSENTIAL
accomplice, abettor, confederate, partner, helper, assistant.
*adj*, subsidiary, supplementary, auxiliary, subordinate, additional, extra, minor. CHIEF

**accident** mishap, misadventure, mischance, casualty, calamity, chance, fluke, fortuity, contingency.

**accidental** casual, fortuitous, chance, unintentional, unplanned, contingent, unforeseen, unexpected. PLANNED

**accidentally** by accident, by mistake, inadvertently, unintentionally, by chance.

**acclaim** *v*, cheer, hail, welcome, applaud, praise, extol. DENOUNCE
*n*, praise, applause, acclamation.

**acclamation** applause, cheers, shouting, acclaim, praise, tribute, homage. DENUNCIATION

**acclimatize** habituate, familiarize, inure, season.

**acclivity** ascent, upward slope, rising ground, elevation, incline, hill. DECLIVITY

**accommodate** adapt, adjust, fit, suit, settle, compose, reconcile, harmonize.
oblige, help, aid, serve, provide, supply, give. DISOBLIGE
lodge, house, put up, billet, receive, hold, contain.

**accommodating** obliging, conciliatory, adaptable, yielding, compliant, considerate, kind, friendly, unselfish, polite. UNFRIENDLY

**accommodation** lodgings, housing, quarters, digs (*inf*), service, advantage, provision, supply, convenience.
adjustment, adaptation, conformity, harmonization.

**accompaniment** appendage, adjunct, appurtenance, attachment, accessory, attendant.

**accompany** escort, go with, attend, wait on, conduct, chaperon, convoy, follow. DESERT

**accomplice** accessory, abettor, partner in crime, conspirator, collaborator, associate, confederate, helper. OPPONENT

**accomplish** complete, finish, achieve, effect, execute, perform, do, perfect, fulfil, consummate.

**accomplished** talented, skilled, expert, experienced, proficient, competent, able, qualified, educated, refined, polished, cultured, sophisticated. UNSKILLED
finished, consummated, done, completed. UNFINISHED

**accomplishment** achievement, exploit, feat, attainment, success, completion, perfection, consummation. FAILURE

**accord** *v*, grant, concede, yield, give, award, allow, vouchsafe. DENY
agree, consent, concur, correspond, tally, harmonize, be in unison, match. DIFFER
*n*, harmony, concord, agreement, unanimity. DISCORD

**accordance** accord, agreement, conformity, harmony, unison. DIFFERENCE

**accordant** agreeing, harmonious, consonant, suitable. DISCORDANT

**accordingly** correspondingly, agreeably, suitably, in accordance.
consequently, therefore, so, thus.

**accost** confront, approach, greet, address, hail, stop, buttonhole, waylay, assail. AVOID

**account** *v*, judge, esteem, deem, regard, consider, think, reckon.
**account for,** explain, elucidate, justify, be responsible for, answer for.
*n*, narrative, narration, tale, story, description, report, statement, explanation, exposition, record, chronicle.
reckoning, bill, invoice, statement, ledger, tally, score, calculation, count.
consideration, importance, note, consequence, repute, worth, profit, advantage. UNIMPORTANCE

**accountable** responsible, answerable, liable, amenable.

**accoutrements** equipment, paraphernalia, gear, trappings, dress, apparel, attire.

**accredit** attribute, credit, ascribe, assign.
endorse, guarantee, certify, attest, vouch for. REPUDIATE
authorize, appoint, sanction, commission, delegate, entrust.

**accretion** growth, increase, enlargement, accumulation, agglomeration. DISPERSION

**accrue** result, come, proceed, issue, accumulate, amass, increase. DIMINISH

**accumulate** *v*, gather, collect, assemble, heap, amass, hoard, store, increase, grow, accrue, multiply. DISPERSE

**accumulation** hoard, store, heap, pile, mass, accretion, build-up, collection, assembly, aggregation. DISPERSION

**accuracy** accurateness, exactness, exactitude, precision, correctness, veracity, truth. INACCURACY

**accurate** exact, precise, spot-on (*inf*), correct, unerring, true, veracious, careful, scrupulous, rigorous, nice. INACCURATE

**accursed** doomed, ill-fated, damned.

execrable, damnable, diabolical, obnoxious, despicable, wretched. BLESSED

**accusation** charge, allegation, indictment, impeachment, incrimination, arraignment. VINDICATION

**accuse** charge, indict, incriminate, impeach, arraign, summon, cite, inculpate, censure, blame, denounce, impute. EXCULPATE

**accuser** plaintiff, complainant, prosecutor, blamer, informer. DEFENDANT

**accustom** familiarize, acquaint, habituate, acclimatize, make used (to), inure, train, drill.

**accustomed** customary, usual, habitual, routine, regular. UNUSUAL

**ace** *n*, expert, adept, master, dab hand (*inf*), professional, pro (*inf*).
*adj*, excellent, first-rate, first-class, outstanding, superb. TERRIBLE

**acerbity** sourness, bitterness, acidity, acridity, pungency, sharpness, harshness, roughness, asperity, acrimony. SWEETNESS

**ache** *v*, hurt, pain, throb, be sore, be in pain, suffer, sorrow, grieve.
*n*, pain, soreness, hurt, discomfort, throb, pang, agony, suffering, anguish, distress, grief, sorrow.

**achieve** accomplish, complete, finish, conclude, consummate, perfect, do, perform, execute, carry out, realize, effect, get, acquire, reach, attain, obtain, win, earn, gain.

**achievement** accomplishment, completion, perfection, attainment, execution, realization, performance, exploit, feat, deed, act. FAILURE

**acid** sour, bitter, tart, sharp, pungent, acerbic, acidulous, vinegary. SWEET
biting, cutting, sarcastic, caustic, sharp, hurtful, trenchant, vitriolic. MILD

**acknowledge** recognize, admit, grant, own, concede, allow, confess, accept, acquiesce, declare, profess. DENY
answer, reply to, respond to, give thanks for.
greet, address, hail, recognize, notice. IGNORE

**acknowledgment** recognition, admission, acceptance, declaration, avowal. DENIAL
reply, answer, response, reaction, thanks.

**acme** top, summit, peak, pinnacle, apex, vertex, zenith, crown, climax, culmination. BASE

**acolyte** follower, admirer, attendant, assistant.

**acquaint** inform, tell, advise, let know, notify, apprise, teach, familiarize.

**acquaintance** friend, companion, colleague, associate.
familiarity, awareness, knowledge, understanding, experience. IGNORANCE

**acquainted** familiar, conversant, knowledgeable, aware, informed, privy. IGNORANT

**acquiesce** assent, agree, accede, concur, consent, conform, comply, submit, yield. OBJECT

**acquiescence** assent, agreement, consent, compliance, submission, yielding. OBJECTION

**acquire** obtain, get, procure, buy, purchase, pick up, gain, secure, achieve, attain, win, earn, appropriate. LOSE

**acquisition** possession, property, purchase, prize.
acquirement, achievement, attainment, gaining, procurement, appropriation, purchase. LOSS

**acquisitive** avid, grasping, greedy, avaricious, rapacious, covetous.

**acquit** free, release, liberate, pardon, forgive, excuse, absolve, exonerate, exculpate, clear, discharge. CONDEMN
repay, settle, discharge.

**acquittal** release, deliverance, liberation, exoneration, pardon, discharge.

**acrid** pungent, sharp, biting, caustic, acid, tart, harsh, cutting, acrimonious, sarcastic, sardonic. SWEET

**acrimonious** bitter, sour, tart, sharp, caustic, astringent, harsh, acrid, acerbic, trenchant, cutting, mordant, sarcastic, spiteful, virulent, malignant, petulant, peevish, testy, crabbed, snappish, cross, ill-tempered. AMICABLE

**acrimony** bitterness, sourness, acridity, astringency, harshness, severity, trenchancy, virulence, asperity, peevishness, churlishness, spleen. MILDNESS

**across** crosswise, transversely, athwart, astride, over, opposite. ALONG

**act** *v*, do, perform, carry out, execute, operate, work, function, behave.

pretend, assume, feign, counterfeit, simulate, play, represent, portray, pose, mimic, impersonate, enact, stage.
**act on,** follow, obey, carry out, comply with.
*n*, action, deed, feat, exploit, achievement, accomplishment, performance, execution, operation.
statute, law, ordinance, edict, decree, judgment, ruling, enactment, measure, bill.
**action** act, deed, feat, exploit, enterprise, undertaking.
movement, motion, gesture, gesticulation.
operation, exertion, exercise, performance, agency, movement.
activity, energy, force, effort, liveliness, vigour, vim. INACTION
battle, skirmish, encounter, fight, fighting, conflict, warfare, engagement.
lawsuit, case, litigation, prosecution.
**active** operative, efficient, potent, effective, functioning, working, running, in action. INACTIVE
busy, industrious, diligent, hard-working, occupied, on the go (*inf*). INDOLENT
agile, nimble, quick, alert, prompt, ready, energetic, lively, vigorous. SLUGGISH
**activity** bustle, movement, stir, action, animation, industry. IDLENESS
undertaking, venture, hobby, pastime, pursuit, enterprise, endeavour, act, deed, job, work.
**actor** actress, performer, player, Thespian, entertainer, star.
**actual** real, true, veritable, genuine, positive, absolute, certain, definite, factual, physical, substantial, present, existent. FALSE
**actually** really, truly, indeed, in fact, in truth, veritably.
**actuate** motivate, stimulate, prompt, inspire, instigate, urge, impel, drive, incite, encourage, spur. DETER
activate, trigger, switch on, set in motion, animate.
**acumen** keenness, shrewdness, insight, perspicacity, astuteness, perception, discernment, ingenuity, sagacity, wisdom, sharpness, acuteness. STUPIDITY
**acute** sharp, keen, quick, astute, shrewd, perspicacious, perceptive, discerning, penetrating, sagacious. OBTUSE
intense, sharp, cutting, stabbing, piercing, excruciating, violent, severe, distressing, poignant. DULL

**adage** saying, proverb, maxim, saw, aphorism, precept, dictum, byword, apophthegm.
**adamant** unyielding, inflexible, rigid, firm, unbending, intransigent, determined, resolute, stubborn, obdurate. FLEXIBLE
**adapt** adjust, accommodate, fit, conform, suit, match, harmonize, coordinate, prepare, alter, modify, familiarize, acclimatize.
**adaptable** adjustable, convertible, alterable, versatile, flexible, pliant, amenable, compliant, easy-going. INFLEXIBLE
**adaptation** adjustment, accommodation, conformity, modification, alteration, acclimatization, familiarization.
**add** join, attach, append, affix, annex, connect, adjoin, combine. REMOVE
add up, sum up, total, reckon, tot up. SUBTRACT
**add to,** increase, enlarge, augment, supplement, aggravate, intensify.
**addendum** addition, adjunct, appendage, appendix, supplement, codicil, postscript, tag.
**addict** *v*, accustom, habituate, devote, dedicate.
*n*, drug addict, dope fiend (*inf*), junkie (*inf*), pothead (*inf*).
enthusiast, devotee, fan, buff (*inf*).
**addicted** dependent, hooked (*inf*), devoted, dedicated, habituated, prone, inclined.
**addiction** dependence, craving, habit, obsession, enslavement.
**addition** adding, joining, attachment, increase, extension, augmentation, enlargement. DECREASE
addendum, adjunct, appendage, affix, extra, supplement, appurtenance, accessory, increment.
**in addition,** also, as well, too, besides, moreover, additionally.
**additional** supplementary, extra, added, further, more, new, fresh.
**address** *n*, domicile, abode, lodging, residence, home, location, whereabouts.
speech, discourse, talk, lecture, oration, presentation, harangue, sermon.
skill, dexterity, adroitness, expertness, ability, cleverness, ingenuity, tact, art. CLUMSINESS
*v*, greet, hail, accost, approach, speak to, talk to, invoke, entreat, appeal to, direct, apply. IGNORE

**adduce** cite, quote, mention, name, give, offer, present, advance, allege.

**adept** *adj*, proficient, skilled, expert, masterly, adroit, versed, practised, accomplished, experienced, able, clever, talented. INCOMPETENT
*n*, expert, master, dab hand (*inf*), genius, professional, specialist.

**adequacy** sufficiency, adequateness, completeness, capacity, acceptability, competence. INADEQUACY

**adequate** enough, sufficient, fit, suitable, satisfactory, acceptable, passable, fair. INADEQUATE

**adhere** stick, cohere, glue, fix, hold fast, cling, cleave, attach, unite. SEPARATE

**adhere to,** follow, observe, heed, keep, respect, comply with, abide by, be faithful to.

**adherent** *n*, disciple, follower, supporter, admirer, fan, partisan, ally. OPPONENT
*adj*, adhering, clinging, attached, sticking, adhesive.

**adhesion** adhesiveness, stickiness, sticking, cohesion, attachment.
adherence, devotion, attachment, constancy, fidelity, loyalty, allegiance.

**adhesive** *n*, glue, gum, paste, mucilage, cement, plaster.
*adj*, sticky, gummed, tacky, viscous, glutinous, tenacious, clinging.

**adieu** *interj*, goodbye, farewell, so long (*inf*). HELLO
*n*, farewell, valediction, parting, leave-taking. GREETING

**adjacent** adjoining, contiguous, touching, bordering, connecting, neighbouring, next-door, near, close. DISTANT

**adjoin** abut, touch, border on, be next to, join, attach, unite, combine, add, annex. SEPARATE

**adjourn** postpone, put off, defer, suspend, interrupt, delay, procrastinate, prorogue. COMPLETE

**adjournment** postponement, deferral, suspension, interruption, delay, procrastination. COMPLETION

**adjudge** pronounce, declare, decree, judge, adjudicate, decide, award, allot, assign.

**adjudicate** judge, arbitrate, determine, decide, settle, umpire, referee.

**adjudication** judgment, judging, arbitration, decision, verdict, ruling, sentence, award.

**adjunct** appendage, addition, attachment, addendum, appurtenance, accessory, supplement, auxiliary. ESSENTIAL

**adjure** charge, command, enjoin, invoke, appeal to, entreat, implore, beseech, beg, pray, supplicate.

**adjust** alter, adapt, modify, change, rectify, fix, regulate, trim, fit, suit, accommodate, harmonize, arrange, dispose, acclimatize, habituate, become accustomed.

**adjustment** alteration, adaptation, modification, change, regulation, arrangement, acclimatization, habituation.

**ad-lib** *v*, improvise, make up, extemporize.
*adj*, improvised, impromptu, extempore, unrehearsed, off-the-cuff (*inf*), spontaneous. PREPARED
*adv*, spontaneously, freely, extempore, off the cuff (*inf*).

**administer** manage, control, conduct, direct, govern, superintend, supervise, oversee, run.
distribute, dispense, supply, give, contribute, apply, mete out, perform, execute.

**administration** management, government, running, direction, supervision, control, ministry, executive.
distribution, dispensing, supply, application, execution.

**admirable** excellent, fine, superb, wonderful, laudable, praiseworthy, commendable. DESPICABLE

**admiration** esteem, regard, respect, reverence, awe, wonder, approval, liking, love. CONTEMPT

**admire** esteem, respect, value, revere, venerate, wonder at, adore, love, like, approve, appreciate, prize, extol, praise. DESPISE

**admirer** devotee, fan, aficionado, supporter, follower, disciple, adherent, worshipper.
suitor, beau, boyfriend, lover, sweetheart.

**admissible** allowable, acceptable, permissible, lawful, just, fair, right, proper, reasonable, justifiable. INADMISSIBLE

**admission** acknowledgment, confession, avowal, declaration, affirmation, allowance, concession. DENIAL
admittance, introduction, access, entrance, entry. EXCLUSION

**admit** acknowledge, confess, own, declare, avow, divulge, accept, allow, grant, concede. DENY
let in, give access to, allow to enter, receive, welcome. EXCLUDE

**admittance** entrance, admission, right of entry, access, passage, reception, welcome, introduction. EXCLUSION

**admonish** warn, caution, advise, counsel, instruct, urge, enjoin.
scold, rebuke, reprove, chide, upbraid, reprimand, tell off (*inf*), censure. COMMEND

**admonition** warning, caution, advice, counsel.
reprimand, rebuke, reproof, remonstrance, scolding. PRAISE

**ado** fuss, bustle, commotion, hubbub, flurry, stir, tumult, turmoil, excitement, to-do, bother, trouble. TRANQUILLITY

**adolescence** youth, teens, minority, pubescence, boyhood, girlhood, immaturity. MATURITY

**adolescent** *adj*, teenage, young, youthful, immature, juvenile, growing. MATURE
*n*, teenager, youth, youngster, minor, juvenile. ADULT

**adopt** foster, take in, affiliate, father, mother. ABANDON
assume, appropriate, choose, select, accept, take on, endorse, approve. REJECT

**adorable** delightful, divine, wonderful, lovely, captivating, charming, lovable. ABOMINABLE

**adoration** devotion, worship, veneration, reverence, homage, admiration, esteem, love, passion. ABOMINATION

**adore** love, dote on, worship, idolize, venerate, revere, esteem, admire. DESPISE

**adorn** decorate, ornament, embellish, deck, garnish, trim, gild, beautify, enhance, enrich. STRIP

**adornment** decoration, ornament, embellishment, trimming, frill, accessory.

**adrift** drifting, floating, afloat, unanchored, loose, astray, amiss. SECURE

**adroit** dexterous, skilful, adept, able, clever, ingenious, masterly, expert, handy, nimble. CLUMSY

**adulation** flattery, blandishment, cajolery, compliment, sycophancy, fawning, servility, obsequiousness. OBLOQUY

**adulatory** flattering, fawning, sycophantic, servile, obsequious.

**adult** *n*, grown-up, man, woman. CHILD
*adj*, mature, fully grown, fully developed, grown-up, of age. IMMATURE

**adulterate** debase, vitiate, alloy, water down, tamper with, contaminate, pollute. PURIFY

**adulterated** debased, vitiated, watered down, impure, contaminated. PURE

**adultery** infidelity, unfaithfulness, affair, unchastity. FIDELITY

**adumbrate** outline, sketch, delineate, silhouette.
foreshadow, presage, forecast, predict, denote, represent, indicate, hint, suggest.
darken, obscure, overshadow, bedim, eclipse, conceal, hide. REVEAL

**advance** *vt*, push forward, hasten, spur, propel, send onward.
promote, further, improve, strengthen, increase, augment, foster, support. RETARD
suggest, allege, put forward, proffer, propose, propound. WITHDRAW
lend, loan, pay, give.
*vi*, go on, go forward, progress, proceed, continue, improve, rise, thrive, flourish, prosper. RETREAT
*n*, advancement, rise, promotion, development, progress, headway, improvement, breakthrough, innovation. RETROGRESSION
loan, retainer, deposit, down payment.
proposal, offer, proposition, approach.
**in advance,** ahead, beforehand, earlier, previously.

**advanced** forward, ahead, avant-garde, progressive, precocious. RETARDED

**advantage** help, assistance, avail, convenience, benefit, gain, profit, boon, blessing. DISADVANTAGE
superiority, ascendancy, power, upper hand, edge.

**advantageous** beneficial, profitable, helpful, convenient, useful. PREJUDICIAL

**advent** arrival, coming, approach, visitation, appearance, onset. DEPARTURE

**adventitious** accidental, casual, fortuitous, unexpected, incidental, extrinsic, extraneous, superfluous.

**adventure** *n*, venture, undertaking, enterprise, exploit, incident, event, occurrence, risk, hazard, experiment, trial, speculation.
*v*, venture, risk, hazard, imperil, endanger.

**adventurous** daring, bold, enterprising, venturesome, brave, intrepid, fearless, foolhardy, rash, dangerous. TIMID

**adversary** opponent, antagonist, enemy, foe, rival, competitor. ALLY

**adverse** unfavourable, hostile, inimical, antagonistic, opposing, contrary, conflicting, harmful, injurious, unfortunate, unlucky. FAVOURABLE

**adversity** misfortune, ill-luck, affliction, trouble, woe, misery, hardship, suffering, distress, calamity, disaster, ruin, desolation. PROSPERITY

**advertise** announce, declare, proclaim, publicize, broadcast, promulgate, make known, promote, praise, plug (*inf*). CONCEAL

**advertisement** announcement, notice, placard, poster, bill, circular, commercial, advert, ad (*inf*), promotion, plug (*inf*).

**advice** counsel, admonition, caution, warning, guidance, instruction, recommendation, opinion, view.
information, notification, news, intelligence, word.

**advisable** prudent, sensible, judicious, wise, recommended, expedient, advantageous, proper, appropriate, fit. INADVISABLE

**advise** counsel, recommend, suggest, guide, persuade, urge, admonish, caution. DETER
inform, tell, notify, apprise, acquaint.

**adviser** counsellor, mentor, confidant, consultant, tutor, teacher, guide, aide, helper.

**advocacy** support, advancement, recommendation, backing, sponsorship, endorsement, defence. OPPOSITION

**advocate** *v*, support, recommend, advise, endorse, favour, countenance, maintain, uphold, defend, plead for, champion, promote. OPPOSE
*n*, supporter, backer, sponsor, champion, defender, promoter, upholder, apologist. OPPONENT
lawyer, counsel, barrister, attorney, solicitor.

**aegis** support, patronage, sponsorship, protection, auspices.

**aerial** high, lofty, empyrean, airy, gaseous, ethereal, light.

**aeronaut** pilot, aviator, airman, flyer, balloonist.

**aeronautics** aviation, flying, flight, ballooning, aerostatics.

**aeroplane** plane, aircraft, airliner, glider, jet.

**aesthetic** tasteful, beautiful, artistic, classic, cultured, refined. UGLY

**afar** far off, far away, yonder, away, abroad. NEARBY

**affable** amicable, friendly, congenial, cordial, complaisant, approachable, easygoing, open, sociable, amiable, mild, kind, kindly, good-natured, benign, benevolent, obliging, gracious, civil, urbane, suave, polite, courteous. HAUGHTY

**affair** matter, subject, question, business, concern, interest, duty.
incident, event, circumstance, episode, occurrence, happening.
liaison, intrigue, amour, relationship.

**affairs** business, concerns, finances, interests, activities.

**affect** influence, alter, modify, change, act on, relate to, concern, interest.
move, touch, impress, stir, upset, disturb.
feign, simulate, assume, adopt, fake, counterfeit.

**affectation** pretence, sham, display, artifice, insincerity, hypocrisy, affectedness, mannerism, airs. NATURALNESS

**affected** artificial, unnatural, studied, insincere, sham, put-on, feigned, mannered, pretentious. NATURAL
moved, touched, altered, changed. UNAFFECTED

**affection** love, devotion, caring, fondness, liking, inclination, partiality, tenderness, kindness, warmth, feeling, passion. DISLIKE

**affectionate** loving, devoted, attached, doting, caring, fond, tender, warm, friendly. COLD

**affiance** betroth, engage, bind, pledge, promise.

**affidavit** declaration, statement, deposition, testimony, evidence.

**affiliate** join, unite, combine, amalgamate, incorporate, annex, adopt. SEVER

**affiliation** amalgamation, annexation, incorporation, alliance, coalition, union, relationship, adoption. SEVERANCE

**affinity** attraction, liking, inclination, partiality, rapport, sympathy. ANTIPATHY relationship, kinship, connection, correspondence, correlation, analogy, resemblance, similarity, likeness.

**affirm** assert, declare, state, profess, aver, maintain, attest, ratify, confirm, vouch for, uphold, certify, endorse. DENY

**affirmation** assertion, declaration, statement, avowal, testimony, ratification, confirmation. DENIAL

**affirmative** asserting, confirming, declaratory, positive, agreeing, favourable. NEGATIVE

**affix** *v*, attach, join, fasten, stick, connect, subjoin, add, append, annex. DETACH
*n*, appendage, addition, prefix, suffix.

**afflict** trouble, distress, hurt, pain, grieve, torment, harass, vex, plague, persecute. CONSOLE

**affliction** trouble, distress, suffering, anguish, pain, torment, agony, grief, sorrow, misery, woe, trial, tribulation, adversity, misfortune, calamity, scourge, plague, disease. COMFORT

**afflictive** distressing, painful, grievous, sorrowful, wretched, miserable, harrowing, piteous, deplorable, tragic, dire.

**affluence** abundance, plenty, opulence, wealth, riches, fortune, prosperity. POVERTY

**affluent** wealthy, rich, opulent, prosperous, well-off, well-heeled (*inf*), loaded (*inf*), moneyed.
abundant, profuse, copious, plentiful, luxuriant, exuberant. SCARCE

**afford** spare, give, bestow, supply, provide, furnish, produce, yield, support. DENY

**affray** brawl, mêlée, fight, fray, scrap, scuffle, fracas, rumpus, disturbance, tumult, contest, conflict, quarrel, strife. ORDER

**affront** *v*, insult, abuse, outrage, slight, offend, annoy, vex, irritate, provoke, pique, anger. PACIFY
*n*, insult, offence, slight, outrage, indignity, wrong.

**afire** ablaze, alight, aflame, burning, blazing, on fire, ignited. EXTINGUISHED
aglow, aroused, passionate, fervent. INDIFFERENT

**afloat** floating, drifting, loose, abroad, at sea, flooded. AGROUND

**afoot** astir, about, abroad, in circulation, in motion, going on, up, in operation.

**aforesaid** aforementioned, above-mentioned, above-named, described above, preceding.

**afraid** frightened, scared, terrified, fearful, alarmed, anxious, uneasy, apprehensive, timid. BOLD

**afresh** again, anew, once more, newly.

**aft** astern, abaft, back, behind, rearward. FORWARD

**after** *prep*, following, behind, succeeding, below. BEFORE
*adv*, afterwards, later, subsequently, behind.

**aftermath** results, consequences, aftereffects, repercussions, issue, outcome, upshot, effect.

**afterthought** reflection, second thought, addition, appendix, postscript.

**afterwards** after, subsequently, later, thereafter. BEFORE

**again** anew, afresh, once more, another time.
besides, moreover, also, furthermore.

**against** hostile to, opposing, counter, resisting, versus, opposite to.
facing, abutting, touching, on, in contact with.

**agape** gaping, yawning, wide open.
open-mouthed, spellbound, dumbfounded, thunderstruck, astonished, amazed, stupefied, dazed, agog, eager.

**age** *n*, epoch, era, eon, period, span, time, duration, date, generation.
old age, maturity, senility, antiquity, seniority. YOUTH
*v*, grow old, mature, ripen, season, decline.

**aged** old, elderly, senescent, ancient, antiquated. YOUNG

**agency** organization, business, bureau, office, institution.
action, operation, influence, power, force, means, medium, instrumentality, intervention.

**agenda** list, schedule, programme, plan, calendar, timetable.

**agent** representative, deputy, substitute, middleman, go-between, envoy, factor, delegate, broker, salesman.
executor, doer, operator, performer.
instrument, cause, force, means, vehicle.

**agglomerate** gather, cluster, collect, accumulate, conglomerate, mass, amalgamate. DISPERSE

**agglomeration** mass, lump, heap, pile, accumulation, gathering, cluster, clump.

**agglutinate** adhere, fuse, unite, stick, glue, paste, cement, bond, weld, solder, attach, cling. DETACH

**agglutination** adhesion, bonding, attachment, union, conglomeration, mass, group.

**aggrandize** magnify, enlarge, amplify, augment, inflate, exaggerate, exalt, promote, elevate, advance, ennoble. DEBASE

**aggravate** worsen, make worse, exacerbate, increase, heighten, intensify, magnify, exaggerate. MITIGATE
irritate, annoy, provoke, exasperate, vex, nettle, irk, tease. SOOTHE

**aggravation** exacerbation, increase, heightening, intensification. MITIGATION
irritation, annoyance, exasperation, vexation.

**aggregate** *v*, collect, gather, accumulate, amass, heap, pile, agglomerate, cluster. DISPERSE
*adj*, total, collected, massed, composite, collective, corporate.
*n*, total, sum, amount, whole, totality, mass, lump, collection, assemblage, group, agglomeration. UNIT

**aggregation** collection, gathering, accumulation, cluster, clump, heap, pile, mass. DISTRIBUTION

**aggression** attack, onslaught, assault, invasion, encroachment, offence. RESISTANCE
aggressiveness, hostility, belligerence, pugnacity, militancy. PASSIVITY

**aggressive** attacking, pugnacious, belligerent, hostile, militant, quarrelsome. PEACEFUL
assertive, vigorous, bold, forceful, dynamic, energetic, enterprising, pushy (*inf*). PASSIVE

**aggressor** attacker, assailant, assaulter, invader, instigator, enemy, foe.

**aggrieve** trouble, distress, afflict, torment, grieve, hurt, injure, wound, annoy, aggravate, vex, wrong, abuse, maltreat. SOOTHE

**aghast** horrified, appalled, terrified, frightened, shocked, dismayed. RELIEVED
astounded, astonished, stunned, dumbfounded, thunderstruck, amazed, stupefied.

**agile** nimble, active, spry, sprightly, lively, brisk, quick, fleet, lithe, supple, prompt, ready, alert, smart. CLUMSY

**agility** nimbleness, sprightliness, activity, liveliness, briskness, quickness, litheness, suppleness, acumen, alertness. CLUMSINESS

**agitate** stir, disturb, shake up, churn, beat, toss.
excite, stir up, arouse, provoke, incite, disturb, trouble, ruffle, fluster, disconcert, perturb. CALM
discuss, debate, talk over, consider, examine, ventilate, moot. SETTLE

**agitated** nervous, jumpy, unsettled, fidgety, ruffled, uneasy, worked-up.

**agitation** excitement, arousal, trouble, disturbance, upheaval, commotion, disquiet, discomposure, upset, flurry, fluster. CALMNESS
discussion, debate, examination, consideration.

**agitator** demagogue, instigator, *agent provocateur*, revolutionary, firebrand, rabble-rouser, troublemaker.

**agnostic** sceptic, doubter, unbeliever, cynic, phenomenalist, freethinker, pagan, heathen. BELIEVER

**ago** past, gone by, earlier, before now, in the past.

**agog** eager, avid, keen, impatient, excited, expectant, on tenterhooks, curious. COOL

**agonize** *vi*, suffer, writhe, be in agony, worry, labour, struggle, strive.
*vt*, torture, torment, pain, afflict, distress, grieve. SOOTHE

**agony** torment, torture, pain, anguish, distress, misery, suffering, pangs. ECSTASY

**agree** concur, coincide, conform, settle, correspond, tally, match, suit, fit, harmonize, accord. DIFFER
assent, consent, acquiesce, accede, comply, concede, yield, grant, allow, permit, promise, engage. REFUSE

**agreeable** pleasant, pleasing, attractive, acceptable, gratifying, delightful, delicious, charming, amiable. OBNOXIOUS
suitable, consistent, appropriate, harmonious, in keeping, in accord.

**agreement** accord, concord, unison, unanimity, harmony, amity, correspondence, conformity, congruity, settlement. DISAGREEMENT contract, undertaking, obligation, bond, treaty, pact, compact, covenant, deal, transaction.

**agriculture** farming, husbandry, cultivation, tillage, agronomy, agronomics.

**aground** grounded, ashore, beached, stranded, high and dry. AFLOAT

**ahead** in front, leading, in advance, before, onwards, forwards. BEHIND

**aid** *v*, help, assist, abet, support, back, second, encourage, facilitate, serve, relieve, subsidize, succour. IMPEDE

*n*, help, assistance, support, backing, encouragement, service, relief, subsidy, benefit, alms. HINDRANCE

helper, aider, assistant, abettor, supporter, second, colleague, ally, associate, aide-de-camp. OPPONENT

**ail** *vt*, afflict, trouble, distress, pain, upset.

*vi*, be ill, suffer, be unwell, pine, ache.

**ailing** sick, ill, unwell, indisposed, poorly, off colour, under the weather (*inf*), suffering, diseased, infirm, weak, sickly. WELL

**ailment** illness, sickness, disorder, complaint, affliction, infirmity, malady.

**aim** *v*, point, direct, level.

intend, propose, mean, plan, design, aspire, strive.

*n*, intention, purpose, plan, design, end, target, objective, mark, goal.

direction, sighting, bearing.

**aimless** purposeless, pointless, useless, futile, random, chance, haphazard, wayward, wandering, stray. PURPOSEFUL

**air** *n*, atmosphere, sky, heavens, breeze, draught.

manner, aspect, look, appearance, demeanour, bearing, behaviour, mien, attitude, character, aura, impression.

tune, melody, strain, theme, song, lay.

*v*, ventilate, freshen, cool, fan, aerate.

display, exhibit, expose, publicize, show, reveal. CONCEAL

**aircraft** aeroplane, plane, airliner, jet, glider, helicopter, chopper (*inf*), balloon, airship, rocket.

**airiness** lightness, buoyancy, weightlessness, ethereality, incorporeality. HEAVINESS

liveliness, gaiety, vivacity, levity, sprightliness, jauntiness, blitheness. SULLENNESS

grace, gracefulness, suppleness, flexibility. AWKWARDNESS

**airing** ventilation, aeration, drying, freshening.

stroll, walk, outing, excursion, jaunt, drive, ride.

**airless** close, heavy, muggy, oppressive, sultry, stifling, stuffy. BREEZY

**airs** affectation, affectedness, pretension, superciliousness, haughtiness, pomposity.

**airtight** sealed, impermeable, unassailable, invulnerable, indisputable.

**airy** breezy, draughty, exposed, ventilated, open, spacious, uncluttered. AIRLESS

light, buoyant, insubstantial, weightless, ethereal, incorporeal, flimsy. HEAVY

lively, gay, sprightly, jaunty, vivacious, blithe. SULLEN

graceful, supple, lithe, nimble. AWKWARD

**aisle** passageway, gangway, corridor, passage, path, lane.

**ajar** unclosed, partly open, gaping, open. SHUT

**akin** related, kindred, cognate, consanguineous, homogeneous, analogous, allied, similar, like, corresponding. UNRELATED

**alacrity** quickness, promptness, readiness, willingness, eagerness, zeal, enthusiasm, alertness, agility, sprightliness, liveliness. RELUCTANCE

**alarm** *v*, frighten, scare, startle, terrify, dismay, daunt, intimidate, unnerve. REASSURE

*n*, fear, fright, terror, panic, dread, apprehension, trepidation, dismay, anxiety, consternation. REASSURANCE

siren, tocsin, alarm-bell, danger signal, alert.

**alarming** frightening, terrifying, ominous, daunting, intimidating, distressing, unnerving, disturbing, terrible, dreadful, appalling, shocking. REASSURING

**albeit** although, even though, notwithstanding that.

**album** book, folder, scrapbook, file, collection.

record, LP, disc.

**alchemy** magic, sorcery, witchcraft, thaumaturgy.

**alcohol** spirits, liquor, intoxicant, booze (*inf*), hard stuff (*inf*).

**alcoholic** *adj*, intoxicating, spirituous, inebriant.

*n*, drunk, drunkard, dipsomaniac, inebriate, boozer (*inf*), wino (*inf*).

**alcove** recess, niche, nook, cubbyhole, bay, bower, arbour, retreat.

**alert** *adj*, watchful, vigilant, attentive, observant, on guard, wide-awake, wary, circumspect, heedful, ready, prepared, prompt.
agile, nimble, active, lively, spry, brisk, smart. LETHARGIC
*n*, alarm, warning, signal, siren.
*v*, warn, signal, notify, inform, tell.

**alertness** vigilance, watchfulness, attention, wariness, caution, circumspection.
agility, liveliness, sprightliness, activity, briskness. LETHARGY

**alias** *adv*, also called, otherwise, formerly.
*n*, pseudonym, assumed name, pen name, *nom de plume*, stage name.

**alibi** defence, excuse, pretext, reason, explanation, justification.

**alien** *adj*, foreign, strange, unfamiliar, incongruous, outlandish, exotic, remote, estranged. NATIVE
opposed, hostile, repugnant, contrary, conflicting, differing. HARMONIOUS
*n*, foreigner, immigrant, stranger, outsider, newcomer. NATIVE

**alienate** estrange, separate, disaffect, set against, divert, turn away, break off, withdraw. CONCILIATE

**alienation** estrangement, separation, disaffection, withdrawal, breaking off, rupture, breach, division. CONCILIATION

**alight**[1] *v*, get off, disembark, dismount, descend, land, settle, perch, come to rest. ASCEND

**alight**[2] *adj*, lit, illuminated, bright, burning, on fire. EXTINGUISHED

**align** straighten, range, line up, even up, make parallel, adjust, regulate, arrange.
affiliate, associate, ally, join, sympathize.

**alike** *adj*, similar, resembling, like, allied, related, akin, analogous, corresponding, same, identical. UNLIKE
*adv*, the same, similarly, equally.

**aliment** food, nourishment, nutriment, sustenance, alimentation, subsistence, fare, provisions, bread, meat.

**alive** living, live, breathing, animate, existent, extant, active, operative, in force. DEAD
lively, brisk, sprightly, alert, quick, smart, prompt, animated, vivacious, spirited, cheerful. SLUGGISH

**all** *adj*, whole, entire, complete, total, every, each. SOME
*adv*, wholly, entirely, completely, totally, altogether, quite, fully. PARTLY
*n*, whole, total, aggregate, entirety, totality, everything, everybody. NOTHING

**allay** soothe, alleviate, ease, relieve, lessen, reduce, mitigate, moderate, mollify, abate, restrain, subdue, quiet, still, calm, appease, pacify, assuage, repress, quell, check. AGGRAVATE

**allegation** assertion, statement, declaration, affirmation, avowal, deposition, accusation, charge. DENIAL

**allege** assert, state, declare, maintain, affirm, profess, claim, plead, put forward, advance. DENY

**alleged** supposed, assumed, doubtful, unlikely, dubious, so-called.

**allegiance** loyalty, faithfulness, fidelity, constancy, devotion, obedience, duty, fealty, homage. DISLOYALTY

**allegorical** metaphorical, figurative, symbolic, representative, typical. LITERAL

**allegory** fable, parable, apologue, story, tale, myth, symbol, illustration, metaphor, analogy.

**allergy** sensitivity, hypersensitivity, susceptibility, antipathy, aversion, hostility.

**alleviate** allay, soothe, relieve, ease, palliate, assuage, mitigate, lessen, diminish, moderate, mollify, soften, quell, dull, deaden, abate. INTENSIFY

**alleviation** soothing, relief, easing, palliation, mitigation, dulling, deadening. INTENSIFICATION

**alley** alleyway, passage, path, footpath, way, walk, lane, back street.

**alliance** treaty, pact, compact, agreement, contract, union, league, confederacy, confederation, coalition, bloc, affiliation, partnership, cooperation, merger, association, combination, marriage. DISUNION
affinity, correspondence, relationship, similarity, connection.

**allied** united, joined, confederate, amalgamated, cooperating.
related, akin, cognate, alike, similar, analogous. UNRELATED

**allocate** assign, allot, apportion, designate, earmark, set aside, divide, distribute, share out.

**allocation** portion, share, quota, ration, allowance.

**allot** allocate, apportion, assign, designate, set aside, distribute, divide, deal, mete, dispense, grant, administer. WITHHOLD

**allotment** allocation, apportionment, portion, quota, share, allowance, dole.
plot, strip of land, patch, garden.

**allow** permit, let, authorize, approve, sanction, tolerate, suffer, bear, put up with, endure. FORBID
acknowledge, concede, grant, admit, confess, own. DENY
apportion, allot, allocate, assign, set aside, deduct, give, grant, let have, provide. WITHHOLD

**allow for,** consider, take into account, provide for, keep in mind.

**allowable** permissible, admissible, justifiable, warrantable, lawful, legitimate, proper, right, acceptable. INADMISSIBLE

**allowance** ration, share, allocation, grant, pension, subsidy, discount, rebate, concession.
authorization, approval, permission, leave, consent, sanction, licence, toleration. PROHIBITION

**alloy** *n*, compound, mixture, blend, amalgam, composite.
admixture, combination, adulteration, debasement.
*v*, mix, combine, blend, amalgamate, compound. SEPARATE
adulterate, debase, impair, diminish, depreciate. PURIFY

**all right** *adj*, acceptable, satisfactory, OK (*inf*), adequate, passable, fair. UNACCEPTABLE
well, healthy, sound, safe, unharmed, unhurt, unbroken.
*adv*, satisfactorily, well enough, acceptably, passably.

**allude** refer, touch upon, mention, suggest, hint, insinuate, imply.

**allure** *v*, tempt, entice, lure, seduce, bait, attract, beguile enchant, cajole, coax, inveigle, persuade. REPEL
*n*, attraction, appeal, charm, enchantment, lure, allurement, temptation, enticement.

**alluring** tempting, enticing, seductive, beguiling, captivating, fascinating, attractive, charming. REPULSIVE

**allusion** reference, mention, suggestion, hint, insinuation, innuendo, implication.

**allusive** suggestive, hinting, insinuating, referential, indicative, symbolic, figurative.

**ally** *v*, unite, unify, join, marry, combine, league, confederate, associate, collaborate. SEPARATE
*n*, confederate, associate, colleague, partner, friend, accomplice, abettor, assistant, helper, coadjutor. ENEMY

**almanac** calendar, register, yearbook, annual, ephemeris.

**almighty** all-powerful, omnipotent, supreme, absolute. IMPOTENT

**almost** nearly, well-nigh, virtually, practically, just about, all but, not quite.

**alms** charity, bounty, dole, gift, donation, handout, gratuity.

**aloft** above, overhead, high up, on high, skyward, up. BELOW

**alone** solitary, lone, single, only, sole, isolated, apart, detached, lonely, forsaken, deserted, unaccompanied, solo, unaided, single-handed. TOGETHER

**along** *prep*, beside, alongside, by, through. ACROSS
*adv*, lengthwise, longitudinally, beside, parallel with.
together, in company, simultaneously.
forward, onward, ahead.

**aloof** distant, detached, apart, remote, unapproachable, forbidding, cool, haughty, supercilious, standoffish, unfriendly, reserved, uninterested. FRIENDLY

**aloud** audibly, distinctly, clearly, out loud, loudly, noisily. SILENTLY

**already** by now, by this time, before, previously, yet.

**also** as well, too, in addition, besides, furthermore, moreover.

**altar** shrine, sanctuary, holy of holies, holy table.

**alter** change, modify, adjust, adapt, amend, revise, vary, transform, convert, turn. MAINTAIN

**alteration** change, modification, adjustment, amendment, adaptation, transformation, conversion, variation, difference. CONSERVATION

**altercation** quarrel, argument, dispute, wrangle, row, disagreement, difference, dissension, controversy, contention, strife. AGREEMENT

**alternate** *v*, rotate, interchange, take turns, reciprocate, substitute.

*adj*, alternating, every other, in rotation, successive, consecutive, reciprocal.

**alternative** *n*, choice, option, recourse, substitute.

*adj*, different, other, second.

**although** though, even though, even if, notwithstanding, despite the fact that, albeit.

**altitude** height, elevation, loftiness, tallness. DEPTH

**altogether** completely, entirely, wholly, fully, utterly, totally, quite, thoroughly, absolutely. PARTIALLY

in all, in sum, all told, *in toto*, with everything included.

collectively, all in all, on the whole, in general, all things considered.

**altruistic** unselfish, philanthropic, public-spirited, charitable, benevolent. SELFISH

**always** continually, incessantly, unceasingly, perpetually, forever, eternally, everlastingly, constantly, regularly, every time, without exception. NEVER

**amalgam** compound, alloy, composite, mixture, combination, blend.

**amalgamate** unite, join, fuse, combine, mix, mingle, blend, compound, alloy, incorporate, integrate, merge, consolidate. SEPARATE

**amalgamation** mixture, combination, compound, union, fusion, joining, incorporation, merger. SEPARATION

**amanuensis** secretary, copyist, scribe, transcriber, clerk.

**amass** gather, collect, accumulate, heap up, pile up, assemble, aggregate, agglomerate. SCATTER

**amateur** nonprofessional, layman, dilettante, dabbler, novice, learner.

beginner, tyro. EXPERT

**amateurish** unprofessional, inexpert, unskilled, incompetent, bungling, crude, inferior, second-rate. PROFESSIONAL

**amatory** amorous, passionate, sensual, erotic, romantic, tender.

**amaze** astonish, astound, stun, stupefy, flabbergast (*inf*), dumbfound, stagger, daze, nonplus, bewilder, confound.

**amazement** astonishment, incredulity, surprise, wonder, awe, stupefaction, bewilderment.

**amazing** astonishing, astounding, remarkable, striking, prodigious, extraordinary, stupendous, marvellous. ORDINARY

**ambassador** diplomat, envoy, emissary, plenipotentiary, legate, deputy, representative, consul, minister.

**ambience** atmosphere, surroundings, setting, milieu, mood, aura, feeling, vibrations (*inf*).

**ambient** surrounding, encircling, encompassing, enfolding.

**ambiguity** vagueness, obscurity, uncertainty, doubtfulness, equivocation, *double entendre*. LUCIDITY

**ambiguous** vague, obscure, unclear, uncertain, indefinite, indeterminate, cryptic, enigmatic, doubtful, dubious, equivocal. CLEAR

**ambition** aspiration, desire, yearning, dream, goal, objective, target, enterprise, drive, energy, eagerness, get-up-and-go (*inf*).

**ambitious** aspiring, desirous, intent, eager, avid, enterprising, go-ahead, pushy (*inf*), zealous, bold. LETHARGIC

challenging, exacting, arduous, strenuous, formidable. EASY

**ambivalence** uncertainty, irresolution, indecision, doubt, hesitation, wavering, conflict, contradiction, clash, opposition.

**ambivalent** uncertain, unsure, doubtful, hesitant, in two minds, conflicting, contradictory, opposing.

**amble** dawdle, saunter, stroll, meander, ramble, mosey (*inf*), walk. HURRY

**ambush** *n*, ambuscade, surprise attack, hiding-place, cover, concealment, retreat, trap, snare, pitfall.

*v*, ambuscade, lie in wait, lurk, surprise, waylay, trap, ensnare, lure.

**ameliorate** improve, better, amend, advance, promote, raise, elevate. DETERIORATE

**amelioration** improvement, betterment, amendment, advancement, promotion. DETERIORATION

**amenable** agreeable, persuadable, open to suggestion, flexible, pliant, susceptible, tractable, docile. OBSTINATE

liable, accountable, answerable, responsible.

**amend** alter, change, modify, revise, improve, ameliorate, correct, rectify, repair. MAR

**amendment** alteration, change, modification, reform, revision, correction, improvement, amelioration.
addition, appendage, attachment, addendum.

**amends** recompense, compensation, atonement, reparation, satisfaction, indemnity, redress, apology. INJURY
**make amends,** compensate, recompense, conciliate, atone, make good, repay, apologize.

**amenity** facility, convenience, service, advantage.
pleasantness, agreeableness, mildness, affability, amiability, graciousness, politeness, courtesy, suavity. AUSTERITY

**amiable** pleasant, agreeable, likeable, friendly, affable, amicable, hearty, genial, good-natured, kind, kindly, warm, benign, benevolent, outgoing, unreserved, sociable, attractive, charming, polite, cordial. DISAGREEABLE

**amicable** friendly, cordial, congenial, amiable, neighbourly, civil, sociable, harmonious, peaceable, polite. HOSTILE

**amid** amidst, among, amongst, between, surrounded by, with.

**amiss** *adj*, wrong, incorrect, inaccurate, erroneous, untoward, improper, faulty, false, untrue. RIGHT
*adv*, wrong, awry, astray, wrongly, incorrectly, erroneously, badly, improperly, falsely.

**amity** friendship, friendliness, amicableness, cordiality, accord, harmony, understanding, good will, peacefulness, comradeship, fellowship. HOSTILITY

**ammunition** munitions, armaments, shells, cartridges, bullets, rounds, powder, explosives, missiles, rockets.

**amnesty** pardon, forgiveness, absolution, acquittal, remission, reprieve, immunity, dispensation, clemency, indulgence. CONDEMNATION

**among** amongst, amid, amidst, surrounded by, between, with, out of.

**amorous** fond, affectionate, loving, tender, amatory, passionate, impassioned, ardent, lustful, erotic. COLD

**amorphous** shapeless, formless, unformed, unstructured, inchoate, irregular, vague, nebulous, confused, chaotic. ORDERED

**amount** *n*, quantity, number, measure, total, sum, aggregate, whole.
**amount to,** *v*, add up to, come to, total, reach, equal, correspond with, become, develop into.

**ample** sufficient, abundant, plentiful, copious, rich, lavish, unrestricted, liberal, large, great, broad, big, spacious, capacious, extensive. SCANTY

**amplification** expansion, enlargement, extension, augmentation, increase, dilation, broadening, development, fleshing out, addition, supplement, appendix. REDUCTION

**amplify** expand, enlarge, extend, augment, increase, magnify, boost, intensify, broaden, develop, flesh out, expatiate. REDUCE

**amplitude** ampleness, abundance, profusion, copiousness, magnitude, dimensions, size, bulk, mass, volume, capaciousness, bigness, largeness, width, breadth, extent, range, scope, sweep, compass.

**amputate** cut off, sever, lop, clip, prune, remove, separate, curtail, truncate.

**amuse** entertain, divert, interest, please, cheer, gladden, charm, delight, regale, enliven, gratify, tickle. BORE

**amusement** entertainment, diversion, pastime, hobby, game, sport, recreation, prank, lark, joke, fun, enjoyment, pleasure, delight, merriment, mirth, laughter.

**amusing** entertaining, diverting, funny, droll, comical, humorous, witty, pleasing, pleasant, delightful, interesting. BORING

**anaemic** bloodless, colourless, pale, pallid, wan, ashen, sickly, weak, feeble, languid.

**analogous** similar, like, alike, resembling, corresponding, homologous, equivalent, comparable. DIFFERENT

**analogy** similarity, likeness, resemblance, comparison, parallel, correspondence, agreement, equivalence. DIFFERENCE

**analyse** examine, investigate, interpret, explain, break down, separate, dissect, anatomize.

**analysis** examination, investigation, interpretation, breakdown, separation, dissection, partition, decomposition, resolution. SYNTHESIS

**analytic** analytical, inquiring, questioning, investigative, critical, detailed, logical, systematic, organized, interpretative, problem-solving, diagnostic.

**anarchic** lawless, riotous, disorderly, disorganized, confused, chaotic, rebellious, revolutionary. ORDERED

**anarchist** rebel, insurgent, revolutionary, rabble-rouser, agitator, terrorist, radical, nihilist.

**anarchy** lawlessness, disorder, confusion, chaos, riot, tumult, mayhem, revolution, rebellion, insurgence, misrule. ORDER

**anathema** curse, imprecation, malediction, excommunication, denunciation, ban, proscription. BLESSING
aversion, antipathy, enemy, bugbear, bane, *bête noire*.

**anatomize** dissect, vivisect, analyse, examine, scrutinize, study, investigate, probe, sift.

**anatomy** structure, skeleton, framework, composition.
analysis, dissection, examination, scrutiny.

**ancestor** forebear, forefather, progenitor, predecessor, parent, forerunner, precursor, prototype. DESCENDANT

**ancestral** inherited, hereditary, patrimonial.

**ancestry** ancestors, family, house, line, lineage, pedigree, race, stock, descent, parentage, extraction, genealogy, origin, heritage, background. POSTERITY

**anchor** *n*, security, stay, mainstay, defence, support.
*v*, fasten, secure, fix, make fast, attach. LOOSEN

**anchorage** mooring, wharf, quay, harbour, dock, port.
refuge, shelter, sanctuary.

**anchorite** anchoress, recluse, hermit, solitary.

**ancient** old, aged, hoary, olden, bygone, antique, antiquated, archaic, obsolete, outmoded, old-fashioned, primitive, primeval, primordial, prehistoric. MODERN

**ancillary** subsidiary, auxiliary, accessory, secondary, additional, supplementary, extra, contributory, helping, subordinate, subservient. ESSENTIAL

**and** plus, in addition, including, along with, also, furthermore.

**androgynous** hermaphrodite, hermaphroditic, bisexual, epicene, gynandrous.

**anecdote** story, tale, yarn, sketch, illustration, narrative, memoir, reminiscence, incident, occurrence.

**anew** afresh, again, newly, once more, over again.

**anfractuous** winding, sinuous, tortuous, devious, meandering, intricate, convoluted, circuitous. STRAIGHT

**angel** seraph, cherub, archangel, spirit, divine messenger, guardian angel. DEVIL
paragon, saint, darling, treasure, gem, beauty.

**angelic** seraphic, cherubic, divine, celestial, heavenly, ethereal.
adorable, delightful, entrancing, beautiful, lovely, pure, virtuous, saintly. DIABOLIC

**anger** *n*, rage, wrath, ire, fury, choler, exasperation, annoyance, irritation, vexation, displeasure, indignation, resentment, passion, temper, spleen. COMPOSURE
*v*, enrage, infuriate, incense, outrage, madden, exasperate, annoy, irritate, provoke, antagonize, rile, rouse, vex, nettle, irk, displease. APPEASE

**angle**[1] *n*, corner, bend, crook, hook, elbow, knee, nook, niche, recess.
viewpoint, position, standpoint, aspect, outlook, slant, approach, perspective.

**angle**[2] *v*, fish, hook, catch.
**angle for,** fish for, look for, invite, solicit, be after (*inf*), scheme, contrive.

**angry** furious, irate, mad (*inf*), enraged, infuriated, livid, fuming, wrathful, vexed, exasperated, riled, inflamed, annoyed, indignant, displeased, piqued, chafed, hot, passionate, cross, irritable, moody, bad-tempered, irascible, choleric. CALM

**anguish** *n*, agony, torture, torment, pain, pang, distress, suffering, woe, misery, heartache, grief. ECSTASY
*v*, afflict, distress, torture, torment, agonize, hurt, pain, wound. SOOTHE

**angular** bony, lean, rangy, scrawny, lanky, gaunt, awkward, ungainly, stiff, austere.

**animadversion** censure, rebuke, reproof, blame, condemnation, disapproval, stricture, aspersion, criticism, comment. PRAISE

**animal** *n*, creature, beast, brute, monster, barbarian.
*adj*, bestial, brutal, brutish, carnal, fleshly, bodily, physical, sensual. SPIRITUAL

**animate** *v*, enliven, vitalize, stimulate, invigorate, vivify, activate, quicken, encourage, waken, rouse, excite, goad, provoke, stir, inspire, incite, embolden. DEPRESS
*adj*, alive, living, breathing, moving. INANIMATE

**animated** lively, spirited, vigorous, dynamic, brisk, vivacious, gay, blithe, buoyant, elated, excited, ebullient, enthusiastic, zestful, fervent, aroused, passionate. DULL

**animation** liveliness, activity, spirit, vitality, energy, vigour, vivacity, zest, ardour, buoyancy, elation, ebullience, zeal, passion.

**animosity** hatred, hate, aversion, loathing, dislike, virulence, spleen, antipathy, hostility, enmity, malice, ill will, malignity, bitterness, acrimony, rancour, resentment, grudge, antagonism. LOVE

**animus** animosity, hate, antipathy, dislike, hostility, ill will, rancour, malice. LOVE
intention, aim, purpose, will, motive, spirit, inclination, disposition.

**annals** archives, records, chronicles, registers, rolls, journals, memoirs, memorials, history.

**annex** add, append, adjoin, attach, affix, fasten, join, subjoin, connect, unite. DETACH
appropriate, acquire, occupy, seize, take over.

**annexation** addition, appending, attachment, union, connection. SEPARATION
appropriation, conquest, seizure, takeover, confiscation.

**annexe** extension, wing, attachment, appendage, addition.

**annihilate** abolish, exterminate, wipe out, obliterate, efface, extinguish, blast, raze, destroy, kill, decimate, liquidate, nullify.
annul, extirpate, eradicate, uproot, root out. PRESERVE

**annihilation** abolition, extermination, obliteration, extinction, eradication, extirpation, destruction, decimation, liquidation. PRESERVATION

**annotate** comment on, commentate, interpret, explain, gloss, elucidate, illustrate.

**annotation** note, explanation, exegesis, footnote, gloss, illustration, comment, observation, remark, interpretation, commentary.

**announce** declare, proclaim, publish, make known, broadcast, publicize, advertise, promulgate, propound, report, divulge, intimate, reveal, disclose. CONCEAL
herald, signal, presage, portend.

**announcement** declaration, proclamation, bulletin, notice, statement, report, publication, revelation, disclosure, advertisement, promulgation, broadcast. SUPPRESSION

**annoy** vex, irritate, irk, nettle, exasperate, enrage, anger, infuriate, bother, trouble, disturb, harass, pester, hector, badger, tease, torment, provoke, rile, madden. SOOTHE

**annoyance** vexation, irritation, pique, exasperation, displeasure, anger.
nuisance, pest, bother, affliction, pain (*inf*), bore, bind (*inf*). PLEASURE

**annual** yearly, every year, once a year.

**annually** yearly, per annum, each year.

**annul** nullify, abolish, invalidate, render null and void, repeal, revoke, abrogate, cancel, countermand, overrule, quash, rescind, eliminate, annihilate, extinguish, obliterate. CONFIRM

**annular** circular, ring-shaped, round.

**annulment** nullification, invalidation, cancellation, repeal, revocation, abrogation, negation, abolition.

**anodyne** *adj*, pain-killing, analgesic, anaesthetic, narcotic, palliative, lenitive, sedative, assuasive.
*n*, pain-killer, analgesic, narcotic, opiate, palliative, sedative. STIMULANT

**anoint** rub, smear, spread, daub, embrocate, oil.
consecrate, sanctify, bless, anele.

**anomalous** abnormal, irregular, unusual, unnatural, incongruous, deviating, aberrant, eccentric, peculiar, exceptional, singular. NORMAL

**anomaly** irregularity, abnormality, incongruity, inconsistency, deviation, aberration, exception, eccentricity, peculiarity, quirk, oddity.

**anon** soon, shortly, presently, before long, forthwith.

**anonymous** nameless, unnamed, unidentified, incognito, unsigned, unacknowledged.

**answer** *v*, reply, respond, acknowledge, retort, rejoin.
satisfy, fulfil, suffice, serve, suit, measure up to, conform.
*n*, reply, response, acknowledgment, retort, riposte, rejoinder, solution, defence, plea. QUESTION

**answerable** liable, responsible, accountable, amenable.

**antagonism** hostility, animosity, enmity, opposition, contradiction, conflict, discord, disharmony, rivalry, competition, contention. AMITY

**antagonist** opponent, adversary, enemy, foe, rival, competitor, contender. ALLY

**antagonistic** opposed, opposing, opposite, adverse, hostile, unfriendly, inimical, conflicting, rival, dissonant, disharmonious. FRIENDLY

**antecedence** precedence, priority, anteriority.

**antecedent** *adj*, prior, preceding, previous, earlier, anterior, foregoing, precursory. FOLLOWING
*n*, precursor, forerunner, harbinger, herald.

**antedate** predate, precede, forego, forestall, anticipate.

**antediluvian** antiquated, antique, archaic, ancient, age-old, old-fashioned, out-of-date, obsolete, prehistoric, primeval, primordial. MODERN

**anterior** front, fore, forward. POSTERIOR
prior, preceding, earlier, previous, foregoing, former, introductory.

**anteroom** antechamber, hall, lobby, vestibule, foyer, waiting room.

**anthem** hymn, song, psalm, canticle, chorale, chant.

**anthology** collection, compilation, compendium, treasury, miscellany, selection, excerpts, extracts.

**anticipate** expect, foresee, forecast, await, prepare for, hope for, look forward to, reckon on.
forestall, intercept, prevent, antedate.

**anticipation** expectation, prospect, foresight, presentiment, premonition, forecast, foretaste, expectancy, hope, apprehension.

**antics** pranks, tricks, jokes, mischief, capers, larks, skylarking, frolics, tomfoolery, buffoonery.

**antidote** remedy, cure, corrective, restorative, neutralizer, antivenin, antitoxin, antibody. POISON

**antipathy** aversion, loathing, hatred, abhorrence, detestation, repugnance, disgust, dislike, hostility, animosity. SYMPATHY

**antiquated** archaic, ancient, antediluvian, antique, superannuated, aged, fossilized, bygone, obsolete, old-fashioned, out-of-date, outmoded, old hat (*inf*). MODERN

**antique** *adj*, old, ancient, early, primitive, antiquated, archaic, old-fashioned, outdated. MODERN
*n*, curio, *objet d'art*, rarity, heirloom, fossil, relic, antiquity.

**antiseptic** *adj*, aseptic, sterile, hygienic, germ-free, sanitary, clinical, clean, pure, uncontaminated. POLLUTED
*n*, disinfectant, germicide, bactericide.

**antisocial** unsociable, uncommunicative, withdrawn, reserved, unfriendly, misanthropic, asocial, hostile, antagonistic, disruptive. FRIENDLY

**antithesis** opposition, contrast, opposite, reverse, converse, contrary.

**anxiety** uneasiness, worry, concern, disquiet, misgiving, foreboding, apprehension, fear, dread, trouble, care, solicitude, distress. TRANQUILLITY

**anxious** worried, troubled, concerned, fretful, uneasy, on edge, nervous, apprehensive, fearful. CALM

**anyway** in any case, at any rate, nevertheless, however, anyhow.

**apace** quickly, rapidly, swiftly, fast, speedily, hastily, hurriedly, without delay. SLOWLY

**apart** separately, aside, away, aloof, alone.
asunder, in pieces. TOGETHER
**apart from,** besides, other than, excluding, not counting, save.

**apartment** room, chamber, quarters, accommodation, lodging, suite, flat.

**apathetic** indifferent, unconcerned, uninterested, impassive, unfeeling, unresponsive, unmoved, insensible, cold, cool, callous, soulless, dull, listless, languid, passive, lethargic, torpid, sluggish. ENTHUSIASTIC

**apathy** indifference, unconcern, impassivity, insensibility, coldness, unfeelingness, listlessness, passiveness, lethargy, torpor. ENTHUSIASM

**ape** *n*, anthropoid, monkey, gorilla, baboon, gibbon, chimpanzee, orang-utan.
mimic, imitator, copycat (*inf*).

*v*, imitate, mimic, copy, counterfeit, parody, echo, mirror.

**aperture** opening, hole, perforation, gap, chink, cleft, crack, rift, slit, slot, mouth, orifice, eye, eyelet, space, passage.

**apex** top, summit, pinnacle, peak, vertex, apogee, acme, zenith, culmination, height. BASE

**aphorism** proverb, maxim, dictum, axiom, adage, apophthegm, saying, saw, byword, precept.

**apiece** each, individually, separated, severally. COLLECTIVELY

**apish** foolish, stupid, silly, affected, foppish, imitative, mimicking.

**aplomb** poise, assurance, self-assurance, confidence, self-confidence, self-possession, composure, collectedness, sang-froid, equanimity. AGITATION

**apocalypse** revelation, disclosure, manifestation, unveiling.

**apocalyptic** revelatory, prophetic, oracular, predictive, ominous, warning, threatening.

**apocryphal** unauthentic, unsubstantiated, dubious, doubtful, questionable, spurious, legendary, fictitious, false, untrue. AUTHENTIC

**apologetic** sorry, regretful, remorseful, contrite, penitent, repentant. UNREPENTANT
defensive, vindicative, justificatory, exculpatory.

**apologist** supporter, defender, advocate, champion, vindicator. ADVERSARY

**apologize** beg pardon, say sorry, regret, be sorry.
defend, plead, support, maintain, vindicate, excuse.

**apologue** allegory, fable, parable, moral tale, story.

**apology** explanation, excuse, justification, defence, plea, vindication, confession, acknowledgment, expression of regret. ACCUSATION

**apophthegm** adage, saying, saw, proverb, aphorism, maxim, precept, dictum, axiom.

**apostasy** desertion, abandonment, dereliction, defection, backsliding, disloyalty, perfidy, treason, faithlessness. LOYALTY

**apostate** *n*, deserter, renegade, turncoat, backslider, defector, traitor. LOYALIST
*adj*, disloyal, perfidious, unfaithful, false, treacherous, traitorous, heretical, backsliding. LOYAL

**apostle** messenger, missionary, preacher, evangelist, crusader, pioneer, champion, advocate, supporter.

**apotheosis** deification, elevation, exaltation, glorification, idealization.

**appal** horrify, outrage, shock, harrow, dismay, daunt, unnerve, alarm, frighten, terrify, petrify, astound, stun. REASSURE

**appalling** dreadful, frightful, awful, dire, terrible, horrifying, horrific, shocking, ghastly, hideous. WONDERFUL

**apparatus** equipment, tools, utensils, device, instrument, appliance, contrivance, mechanism.

**apparel** clothes, clothing, attire, dress, garments, wear, garb, outfit, costume, robes, habit, trappings.

**apparent** obvious, evident, patent, plain, clear, conspicuous, manifest, visible, perceptible, discernible, distinct. HIDDEN
seeming, ostensible, external, outward, superficial. ACTUAL

**apparently** obviously, evidently, patently, clearly, unmistakeably, plainly, perceptibly.
seemingly, ostensibly, outwardly, on the face of it, allegedly. ACTUALLY

**apparition** ghost, spirit, spectre, phantom, spook (*inf*), vision, illusion, chimera, hallucination.
appearance, manifestation, presence, materialization.

**appeal** *n*, entreaty, plea, prayer, petition, request, suit, address.
attraction, allure, attractiveness, charm, fascination. UNATTRACTIVENESS
*v*, entreat, implore, beg, beseech, plead, petition, invoke, solicit, request, address.
attract, engage, interest, fascinate, captivate, charm, entice, tempt. REPEL

**appear** emerge, arrive, arise, dawn, loom up, come into view, be present, turn up (*inf*). DISAPPEAR
seem, look.

**appearance** emergence, arrival, advent, coming, presence, debut, manifestation, publication. DISAPPEARANCE
look, aspect, demeanour, manner, air, bearing, mien, expression, semblance, pretence, show.

**appease** pacify, calm, assuage, moderate, mitigate, lull, still, soothe, allay, tranquillize, alleviate, ease, lessen, abate, compose, placate, propitiate, conciliate, satisfy, quell. AGGRAVATE

**appellation** name, title, designation, cognomen, sobriquet, term, denomination.

**append** add, attach, affix, annex, join, fasten, hang, subjoin, tag on, tack on. DETACH

**appendage** attachment, adjunct, addition, appendix, supplement, addendum, accessory. ESSENTIAL

**appendant** attached, affixed, added, annexed, appended, supplementary, additional, attendant, associated, consequential. SEPARATE

**appendix** appendage, adjunct, annexation, addition, addendum, supplement, postscript, epilogue.

**appertain** belong, pertain, refer, relate, touch, concern, apply, be connected.

**appetite** desire, want, craving, longing, hunger, thirst, passion, relish, liking, affinity, inclination, propensity. INDIFFERENCE

**appetizing** tempting, inviting, appealing, savoury, delicious, mouthwatering, tasty. UNAPPETIZING

**applaud** clap, cheer, praise, laud, acclaim, extol, approve, commend, encourage, congratulate, compliment. DENOUNCE

**applause** clapping, ovation, cheers, praise, acclamation, acclaim, laudation, plaudit, accolade, eulogy, approbation, approval, commendation. DENUNCIATION

**appliance** device, machine, mechanism, contrivance, gadget, instrument, tool, implement, utensil, apparatus, piece of equipment.

application, use, exercise, practice.

**applicable** appropriate, apt, suitable, fitting, suited, proper, apposite, apropos, relevant, pertinent, adjustable, useful, convenient. INAPPROPRIATE

**applicant** candidate, aspirant, suitor, petitioner, claimant.

**application** request, petition, appeal, suit, claim, demand, inquiry.

relevance, pertinence, value, purpose, use, function.

assiduity, industry, diligence, perseverance, commitment, attention, dedication, effort, study. INDOLENCE

**apply** *vt*, use, utilize, employ, put to use, exercise, practise, execute, bring to bear, assign, administer. NEGLECT

devote, commit, dedicate, direct, address. DIVERT

*vi*, be relevant, be appropriate, pertain, appertain, fit, refer, relate.

request, appeal, solicit, claim, seek, inquire.

**appoint** assign, designate, nominate, name, elect, select, install. DISMISS

fix, arrange, settle, establish, ordain, prescribe, decree. CANCEL

furnish, equip, fit out, supply.

**appointment** arrangement, engagement, assignation, tryst, meeting, rendezvous, date, interview.

office, post, position, job, situation, place.

appointing, nomination, election, selection, designation, ordainment.

fixture, fitting, furnishing, appurtenance, accoutrement.

**apportion** allot, assign, allocate, divide, share, administer, dispense, distribute, deal out. RETAIN

**apportionment** allocation, allotment, division, sharing, distribution, dispensing.

**apposite** apt, appropriate, fitting, fit, suitable, proper, relevant, pertinent, applicable, germane, apropos. INAPPROPRIATE

**appraisal** appraisement, evaluation, valuation, estimate, assessment, judgment.

**appraise** evaluate, assess, inspect, survey, value, price, rate, estimate, judge.

**appreciable** noticeable, perceptible, detectable, discernible, marked, obvious, evident, substantial, considerable. IMPERCEPTIBLE

**appreciate** *vt*, value, prize, rate highly, esteem, respect, acknowledge, be grateful for. SCORN

recognize, perceive, comprehend, realize, be aware of.

*vi*, rise in value, increase, grow, multiply, gain, intensify. DEPRECIATE

**appreciation** value, esteem, respect, admiration, acknowledgment, gratitude, thanks. SCORN

recognition, perception, comprehension, awareness.

**apprehend** seize, catch, capture, arrest, take into custody, nick (*inf*), run in (*inf*). RELEASE

understand, comprehend, perceive, grasp, recognize, realize, appreciate, conceive, imagine.
dread, fear, anticipate.

**apprehension** fear, foreboding, dread, trepidation, anxiety, misgiving, disquiet, uneasiness, mistrust, suspicion. COMPOSURE
arrest, seizure, capture.
understanding, comprehension, grasp, perception, conception, concept, notion, view, belief. MISAPPREHENSION

**apprehensive** fearful, anxious, worried, troubled, uneasy, afraid, scared, suspicious, mistrustful. COMPOSED

**apprentice** novice, beginner, tyro, learner, student, pupil, probationer. MASTER

**apprise** acquaint, inform, tell, notify, make aware, advise, warn.

**approach** *v*, near, come near, draw near, advance, move towards, accost, address, broach, embark on. RECEDE
approximate, resemble, come close to.
*n*, advent, coming, nearing, advance, arrival.
access, passage, entrance, way, road, path. EXIT
method, procedure, technique, means, attitude, manner.

**approbation** approval, sanction, assent, consent, recognition, praise, commendation, acclaim, encouragement, support. CENSURE

**appropriate** *adj*, fitting, suitable, adapted, apt, proper, seemly, becoming, befitting, timely, apposite, pertinent, relevant, germane. INAPPROPRIATE
*v*, seize, take over, commandeer, annex, confiscate, impound.
assign, allot, apportion, earmark, set aside.

**appropriateness** suitability, fitness, aptness, propriety, timeliness, relevance, pertinence.

**appropriation** seizure, capture, arrogation, confiscation, impounding. RETURN
allocation, apportionment, allotment, assignment.

**approval** approbation, appreciation, recommendation, praise, commendation, acclaim, admiration, esteem. CENSURE
sanction, consent, assent, agreement, acquiescence, endorsement, encouragement, support. DISAPPROVAL

**approve** appreciate, praise, commend, admire, esteem, value, prize. DISAPPROVE
sanction, authorize, assent, consent, agree, endorse, bless, uphold, support, encourage, recommend. OPPOSE

**approximate** *adj*, rough, inexact, imprecise, loose, near, close. EXACT
*v*, approach, come near, resemble. DIFFER

**approximately** roughly, about, around, more or less, nearly, almost. PRECISELY

**approximation** estimate, guess, guesstimate (*inf*), conjecture, rough idea, approach, semblance.

**appurtenance** appendage, adjunct, accessory, attachment, addition, supplement, incidental, concomitant. ESSENTIAL

**appurtenances** equipment, paraphernalia, trappings, belongings.

**appurtenant** pertaining, connected, related, relevant, belonging, attached, supplementary, incidental.

**apropos** *adj*, appropriate, apt, timely, opportune, suitable, fit, proper. INOPPORTUNE
*adv*, appropriately, aptly, timely, opportunely, to the purpose.
**apropos of,** regarding, with reference to, in respect of.

**apt** appropriate, suitable, fitting, proper, opportune, timely, apropos, apposite, pertinent, relevant. INAPPROPRIATE
disposed, inclined, prone, liable, subject, given, likely.
quick, sharp, able, dexterous, clever, bright, intelligent, gifted, adroit, expert, adept. SLOW

**aptitude** ability, disposition, faculty, gift, talent, knack, flair, intelligence, cleverness, inclination, leaning, aptness, readiness, competence. INCOMPETENCE

**aptness** appropriateness, suitability, fitness, timeliness, appositeness, relevance, pertinence. UNSUITABILITY
aptitude, disposition, inclination, ability, faculty.

**aquiline** eagle-like, hooked, bent, curved, Roman. STRAIGHT

**arable** cultivable, tillable, farmable, ploughable, fertile, fruitful, productive.

**arbiter** judge, adjudicator, arbitrator, referee, umpire, controller, governor, ruler, sovereign, master, lord.

**arbitrament** decision, verdict, judgment, decree, award, sentence.

**arbitrary** capricious, whimsical, random, chance, subjective, discretionary, wilful, unreasonable. REASONED
despotic, dictatorial, autocratic, absolute, tyrannical, imperious, magisterial, domineering, overbearing.

**arbitrate** settle, decide, determine, judge, adjudicate, mediate, intervene, negotiate, conciliate.

**arbitration** judgment, adjudication, decision, settlement, mediation, intervention, negotiation, conciliation.

**arbitrator** judge, arbiter, adjudicator, mediator, negotiator, peacemaker, go-between.

**arbour** bower, retreat, recess, shelter, pergola.

**arc** bend, curve, bow, arch, crescent.

**arcade** colonnade, peristyle, portico, cloister, gallery, loggia, passageway, precinct.

**arcane** mysterious, abstruse, occult, esoteric, recondite, secret, hidden.

**arch**[1] *n*, curve, bend, arc, vault, span, archway, dome.

**arch**[2] *adj*, chief, main, principal, leading, first, greatest. MINOR
shrewd, knowing, cunning, artful, roguish, waggish, mischievous, playful.

**archaic** ancient, old, bygone, obsolete, outdated, obsolescent, old-fashioned, antiquated, superannuated. MODERN

**arched** curved, domed, vaulted, bowed, concave. STRAIGHT

**archetype** type, model, pattern, paradigm, original, prototype, precursor, example, paragon, ideal.

**architect** designer, planner, draughtsman, builder, constructor, maker, creator, author, contriver, instigator.

**architecture** design, planning, building, construction, structure, framework.

**archives** records, annals, chronicles, registers, rolls, documents, papers.

**arctic** northern, boreal, polar, hyperborean. ANTARCTIC
cold, freezing, glacial, icy, wintry, chilly, bleak. HOT

**ardent** intense, fervent, passionate, impassioned, burning, hot, fiery, keen, eager, avid, enthusiastic, spirited, zealous, vehement, fierce. COOL

**ardour** intensity, fervour, passion, feeling, warmth, heat, eagerness, enthusiasm, spirit, zeal, vehemence. APATHY

**arduous** difficult, hard, laborious, onerous, tiring, exhausting, toilsome, strenuous, rigorous, gruelling, formidable, harsh, severe, steep, uphill. EASY

**area** district, region, locality, zone, territory, realm, domain, sphere, field, expanse, surface, space, extent, scope, range.
part, section, portion, tract, sector. WHOLE
yard, enclosure, plot.

**arena** enclosure, amphitheatre, ring, stage, stadium, ground, field, track.

**argue** debate, discuss, moot, reason, maintain, contend, persuade, plead.
dispute, disagree, quarrel, wrangle, squabble, bicker, row. AGREE
denote, indicate, betoken, demonstrate, show, suggest, imply.

**argument** dispute, disagreement, quarrel, altercation, row, squabble, wrangle, conflict, clash. AGREEMENT
discussion, debate, polemic, controversy.
defence, case, evidence, reason, reasoning, grounds, proof.
summary, outline, abstract, gist, plot, theme, subject, topic.

**argumentative** contentious, quarrelsome, disputatious, contrary, belligerent, combative.

**arid** dry, parched, barren, sterile, dreary, dull, uninteresting, boring. FERTILE

**aridity** aridness, dryness, barrenness, sterility, dreariness, dullness. FERTILITY

**arise** originate, proceed, begin, spring, issue, flow, emerge, appear, emanate, result, ensue. END
rise, get up, stand up, ascend, go up, mount, soar. SINK

**aristocracy** nobility, gentry, peerage, ruling class, upper class, elite.

**aristocrat** noble, nobleman, patrician, gentleman, lady, lord, earl, peer. PLEBEIAN

**aristocratic** noble, titled, patrician, blue-blooded, genteel, highborn, elite, upper-class. LOWBORN
elegant, stylish, refined, sophisticated, well-bred, ladylike, dignified, haughty, snobbish, arrogant. VULGAR

**arm**[1] *n*, limb, appendage, branch, bough, offshoot, division, department.
inlet, channel, strait, sound, estuary, firth, cove.

power, authority, might, strength.

**arm**[2] *v*, equip, provide, supply, furnish, fit out, prepare, fortify, strengthen, guard, protect. DISARM

**armada** fleet, flotilla, squadron, navy.

**armament** arms, weapons, weaponry, munitions, materiel.

**armistice** truce, ceasefire, peace, reprieve, suspension, intermission.

**armoury** arsenal, magazine, ammunition dump, depot, depository, warehouse.

**arms** weapons, weaponry, munitions, armament, materiel, firearms, guns, ammunition.
shield, crest, escutcheon, insignia, blazonry, armorial bearings.

**army** military, soldiers, troops, armed forces.
multitude, host, crowd, throng, horde.

**aroma** odour, smell, scent, redolence, fragrance, perfume, bouquet, savour.

**aromatic** fragrant, scented, perfumed, balmy, redolent, sweet-smelling, spicy, pungent.

**around** *prep*, round, surrounding, encircling, about. AMID
roughly, approximately, about, circa.
*adj*, on all sides, everywhere, all over, throughout, about, here and there.
near, nearby, at hand, close by.

**arouse** awaken, stir, excite, stimulate, whet, spur, provoke, rouse.
agitate, animate, instigate, kindle, incite, inflame. PACIFY

**arraign** summon, accuse, charge, indict, impeach, incriminate, denounce. CONDONE

**arraignment** summons, accusation, charge, indictment, impeachment, incrimination, denunciation.

**arrange** order, dispose, array, assort, distribute, group, classify, class, marshal, organize, range, place, position. DISARRANGE
adjust, settle, agree to, fix, contrive, devise, prepare, plan, organize.
adapt, orchestrate, score.

**arrangement** order, disposition, array, grouping, classification, organization.
plan, preparation, provision, measure, schedule.
agreement, settlement, understanding, compact, contract.
adaptation, interpretation, version, orchestration, score.

**arrant** utter, downright, out-and-out, thorough, absolute, veritable, undisguised, blatant, rank, gross.
infamous, notorious, vile, atrocious, monstrous.

**array** *v*, dress, clothe, attire, adorn, deck, bedeck, equip, fit out, supply. STRIP
marshal, dispose, arrange, draw up, order, place, rank, line up. DISARRANGE
*n*, display, collection, parade, show, exhibition, arrangement, disposition, line-up, order, formation. DISARRAY
dress, attire, apparel, clothing, finery, regalia.

**arrears** arrearage, debt, liabilities, amount overdue, deficiency.
**in arrears,** overdue, behind, late, in debt, in the red.

**arrest** *v*, seize, capture, take prisoner, apprehend, take into custody, detain, nick (*inf*), run in (*inf*), bust (*inf*). RELEASE
check, restrain, hold, halt, stop, interrupt, inhibit, slow, delay, retard, hinder, obstruct. STIMULATE
attract, rivet, engage, occupy, absorb, engross, fascinate. BORE
*n*, seizure, capture, apprehension, detention. RELEASE
check, restraint, halt, stoppage, cessation, blockage, obstruction, delay, slowing, inhibition, suppression.

**arresting** striking, conspicuous, impressive, remarkable, noticeable, extraordinary.

**arrival** advent, coming, appearance, entrance. DEPARTURE
newcomer, visitor, caller, guest.

**arrive** come, land, turn up, appear, show up (*inf*). DEPART
occur, happen, befall.
succeed, make it (*inf*), thrive, prosper. FAIL
**arrive at,** reach, get to, attain, realize.

**arrogance** pride, haughtiness, loftiness, hauteur, self-importance, conceit, superciliousness, disdain, contemptuousness, pomposity, lordliness, insolence, self-assurance, self-assertion. HUMILITY

**arrogant** proud, haughty, self-important, conceited, disdainful, supercilious, contemptuous, overbearing, lordly, pompous, insolent, self-assured. MODEST

**arrogate** appropriate, assume, claim, usurp, commandeer, demand. WAIVE
assign, impute, attribute, ascribe.

**arrow** shaft, dart, bolt, missile.
pointer, marker, indicator.

**arsenal** armoury, magazine, store, depot, depository, warehouse.

**art** skill, dexterity, adroitness, aptitude, address, cleverness, ingenuity, facility, knack, flair, expertise, mastery. CLUMSINESS
artfulness, shrewdness, astuteness, slyness, cunning, guile, deceit, duplicity, artifice, craft, trickery. HONESTY

**artful** cunning, sly, wily, subtle, shrewd, astute, sharp, knowing, crafty, insidious, deceitful, tricky, clever, skilful, dexterous, adroit. ARTLESS

**article** item, thing, object, commodity, component, part, portion, section, piece, division.
essay, composition, paper, feature, treatise, story, column, report, review, commentary.

**articulate** *v*, pronounce, enunciate, utter, speak, say, voice, express.
join, unite, connect, link, hinge, joint. SEVER
*adj*, clear, distinct, coherent, intelligible, audible, eloquent, well-spoken, fluent. INARTICULATE

**articulation** pronunciation, enunciation, diction, delivery, presentation, elocution, expression, inflection.
connection, joint, linkage, hinge, coupling.

**artifice** trick, stratagem, wile, deception, fraud, subterfuge, machination, contrivance, device, manoeuvre, ruse, dodge.
cunning, artfulness, deceit, duplicity, trickery, guile, craft, craftiness, slyness. HONESTY
skill, art, cleverness, dexterity, finesse, invention, ingenuity, facility. INCOMPETENCE

**artificer** maker, creator, craftsman, artisan, designer, inventor, mechanic.

**artificial** unnatural, man-made, synthetic, manufactured, ersatz, simulated, imitation, mock, sham, phoney (*inf*), counterfeit, fake, spurious. GENUINE
affected, insincere, forced, contrived, assumed, feigned, pretended. SINCERE

**artillery** guns, gunnery, cannon, cannonry, ordnance, battery, enginery.

**artisan** craftsman, master, artificer, handicraftsman, skilled workman, technician, mechanic.

**artist** painter, sculptor, designer, master, adept, expert.

**artistic** tasteful, exquisite, beautiful, stylish, refined, aesthetic, sensitive, creative, imaginative, decorative, ornamental. TASTELESS

**artless** simple, unaffected, natural, unpretentious, guileless, honest, truthful, straightforward, sincere, open, frank, forthright, candid, plain, naive, unsophisticated, ingenuous, innocent. ARTFUL
awkward, clumsy, inexpert, inept, untaught, ignorant, rude, primitive. REFINED

**as** *conj*, while, when, just as.
like, in the manner that, in the same way that.
since, because, seeing that, considering that.
for example, for instance, such as, like.
*prep*, being, in the role of.

**ascend** go up, climb, scale, rise, mount, soar, slope upwards. DESCEND

**ascendancy** superiority, advantage, authority, upper hand, control, power, sway, influence, mastery, supremacy, dominion, command, sovereignty, rule, domination. SERVITUDE

**ascendant** *n*, ascendancy, superiority, dominance, dominion, supremacy, control, rule, command, power.
*adj*, rising, ascending, climbing, mounting. DESCENDING
dominant, prevailing, superior, powerful, commanding, ruling, authoritative, influential. SUBORDINATE

**ascent** ascension, ascending, rising, rise, climbing, climb, mounting, scaling. DESCENT
gradient, incline, slope, acclivity, rising ground, ramp, elevation, height, eminence.

**ascertain** discover, find out, determine, verify, make certain, confirm, settle, establish, resolve. SURMISE

**ascetic** *n*, abstainer, self-denier, recluse, hermit, anchorite, monk, nun.
*adj*, abstemious, abstinent, self-denying, continent, celibate, temperate, moderate, austere, puritanical, severe, rigorous, harsh, stern. LAX

**ascribe** attribute, assign, credit, charge, impute, put down, refer.

**ashamed** abashed, shamefaced, conscience-stricken, mortified, embarrassed, humiliated, sheepish, guilty, remorseful, sorry, chagrined, distressed, crestfallen, bashful, shy. PROUD

**ashen** ashy, pale, pallid, wan, livid, ghastly, colourless, pasty, grey. COLOURED

**ashore** on shore, to the shore, on land, aground, beached, stranded. AFLOAT

**aside** away, apart, aloof, separately, on one side, in reserve, out of the way.
beside, alongside, laterally.

**asinine** stupid, foolish, idiotic, absurd, senseless, doltish, thickheaded, brainless, obstinate, stubborn. CLEVER

**ask** inquire, question, quiz, interrogate. REPLY
request, seek, demand, expect, require, desire, crave, petition, sue, solicit, entreat, beg, implore, beseech, supplicate.
invite, bid, summon.

**askance** awry, obliquely, aslant, sideways, indirectly. STRAIGHT
suspiciously, mistrustfully, dubiously.

**askew** awry, crooked, aslant, oblique, askance, lopsided, off-centre. STRAIGHT

**asleep** sleeping, slumbering, dozing, napping, resting, dormant, inactive, numb, insensible. AWAKE

**aspect** look, appearance, bearing, demeanour, mien, attitude, air, expression.
outlook, prospect, direction, situation, position, viewpoint, view.
side, angle, slant, feature, facet, part, phase.

**asperity** harshness, roughness, ruggedness, sharpness, tartness, bitterness, acerbity, acrimony, sourness, moroseness, sullenness, churlishness, crabbedness, peevishness, irascibility, severity, virulence. MILDNESS

**asperse** slander, calumniate, defame, abuse, vilify, traduce, slur, besmirch, defile, smear, disparage, impugn. EULOGIZE

**aspersion** slander, calumny, defamation, abuse, vilification, disparagement, censure, obloquy, slur, smear. COMMENDATION

**asphyxiate** suffocate, smother, stifle, choke, strangle, throttle.

**aspirant** aspirer, seeker, hopeful, suitor, postulant, claimant, applicant, candidate, competitor.

**aspiration** longing, yearning, hope, desire, craving, dream, goal, ambition, aim, objective, eagerness, zeal, endeavour, enterprise. APATHY

**aspire** long, yearn, hope, desire, crave, seek, dream, aim, rise, mount, soar.

**ass** donkey, jackass, dolt, blockhead, simpleton, fool, idiot, nincompoop, dope (*inf*), dunce, halfwit, twit (*inf*).

**assail** attack, assault, beset, set upon, invade. RESIST
abuse, slander, calumniate, defame, vilify, malign, asperse, revile, impugn, vituperate, attack, berate, criticize, deride, ridicule. VINDICATE

**assailable** vulnerable, sensitive, unprotected, defenceless, lame, weak. UNASSAILABLE

**assailant** attacker, assaulter, assailer, aggressor, invader, antagonist, opponent. PROTECTOR

**assassin** killer, murderer, slayer, liquidator, gunman, hit man (*inf*), cut-throat, executioner.

**assassinate** kill, slay, murder, liquidate, eliminate (*inf*), dispatch, execute.

**assassination** murder, killing, dispatch, execution, liquidation, elimination.

**assault** *v*, attack, assail, set upon, invade, charge, beset, molest, rape. DEFEND
*n*, attack, onslaught, onset, charge, strike, invasion, aggression, offensive. DEFENCE

**assay** *v*, test, try, prove, analyse, examine, inspect, investigate, assess.
*n*, test, trial, analysis, examination, inspection, investigation, assessment.

**assemblage** assembly, gathering, meeting, rally, throng, crowd, group, conclave, congregation, body, collection, combination, union, aggregation, mass, cluster, accumulation. DISPERSION

**assemble** collect, gather, muster, congregate, convene, rally, come together, bring together, convoke, summon, call. DISPERSE
put together, join, connect, make, fabricate, manufacture, build, erect, construct. DISMANTLE

**assembly** gathering, meeting, rally, conference, congress, council, conclave, congregation,. assemblage, group, body, crowd, throng, collection.
construction, fabrication, manufacture.

**assent** *v*, agree, acquiesce, concur, accept, go along with, approve, consent, accord, grant. DISSENT *n*, agreement, acquiescence, concurrence, acceptance, approval, consent, compliance, accord. OPPOSITION

**assert** declare, affirm, aver, avow, asseverate, maintain, state, pronounce, predicate, allege, claim, emphasize, insist upon, uphold, support. DENY

**assertion** declaration, statement, pronouncement, affirmation, averment, asseveration, insistence. DENIAL

**assertive** positive, decided, confident, self-assured, emphatic, dogmatic, insistent, pushy (*inf*), strong-willed, demanding, forceful, aggressive, overbearing. HESITANT

**assess** estimate, gauge, value, rate, appraise, evaluate, compute, determine, fix, impose, levy, tax.

**assessment** evaluation, appraisal, review, estimation, estimate, valuation, rating, rate, charge, levy, tax, duty, toll.

**asset** advantage, benefit, boon, blessing, resource, help. DISADVANTAGE

**assets** property, goods, possessions, estate, capital, wealth, resources. LIABILITIES

**asseverate** declare, affirm, assert, state, pronounce, avow, maintain, attest, aver, predicate. DENY

**asseveration** declaration, affirmation, assertion, statement, pronouncement, attestation, averment. DENIAL

**assiduity** assiduousness, industry, diligence, application, devotion, constancy, sedulousness, effort, labour, exertion, pains, persistence, tirelessness, perseverance, care, attention. INDOLENCE

**assiduous** industrious, hard-working, diligent, sedulous, persistent, persevering, studious, painstaking, attentive, untiring, tireless, indefatigable, constant, steady. INDOLENT

**assign** appoint, designate, select, choose, delegate, charge, commission. DISMISS

allot, allocate, apportion, appropriate, set aside, fix, determine, specify, give, distribute, dispense.

attribute, ascribe, accredit, put down.

**assignation** meeting, rendezvous, appointment, tryst, date.

**assignment** task, mission, job, duty, obligation, post, appointment, commission.

allotment, allocation, apportionment, distribution, designation, appointment, specification, determination, attribution, ascription.

**assimilate** digest, absorb, incorporate, take in, learn. REJECT

adjust, adapt, acclimatize, accustom, naturalize, blend, mingle, merge, conform.

**assist** help, aid, abet, support, back, sustain, second, reinforce, promote, further, expedite, work with, cooperate, collaborate, relieve, succour. HINDER

**assistance** help, aid, service, support, backing, cooperation, collaboration, relief, succour. HINDRANCE

**assistant** helper, helpmate, aider, aide, right-hand man, ally, accomplice, abettor, partner, colleague, collaborator, auxiliary, accessory, second, supporter. OPPONENT

**associate** *v*, link, join, connect, relate, unite, combine, affiliate, ally. DISSOCIATE

consort, fraternize, team up, befriend, mix, keep company, go around.

*n*, colleague, co-worker, partner, confederate, ally, accomplice, fellow, mate, comrade, friend, companion, intimate. ENEMY

**association** society, union, company, partnership, corporation, confederation, alliance, consortium, syndicate, body, group, organization, club, fraternity, guild, lodge.

friendship, companionship, fraternization, intimacy.

connection, relation, relationship, correlation, bond, tie, linking, union. DISSOCIATION

**assort** *vt*, arrange, sort, group, classify, rank, distribute, dispose, array.

*vi*, match, suit, coordinate.

**assorted** mixed, varied, various, miscellaneous, heterogeneous, diverse, different, motley, sundry. HOMOGENEOUS

**assortment** mixture, variety, miscellany, medley, pot-pourri, hotchpotch, jumble, selection, collection, array.

class, type, sort, group, category, set, batch, lot.

arrangement, distribution, classification, sorting.

**assuage** mitigate, soothe, moderate, lessen, ease, alleviate, tranquillize, pacify, appease, calm, relieve, quell, abate, allay, mollify, soften. AGGRAVATE

**assuagement** mitigation, moderation, alleviation, pacification, appeasement, relief, easing, abatement. AGGRAVATION

**assume** suppose, presume, surmise, infer, postulate, believe, think, take for granted. KNOW
affect, feign, pretend, counterfeit, simulate.
take on, undertake, adopt, acquire, appropriate, seize, usurp, arrogate. DISCARD

**assumed** false, fictitious, bogus, phoney (*inf*), made-up, counterfeit, spurious, feigned, affected. GENUINE

**assuming** presumptuous, arrogant, imperious, overbearing, haughty, conceited, forward, brazen, bold, audacious. MODEST

**assumption** supposition, presumption, conjecture, guess, hypothesis, theory, postulate, surmise, inference. KNOWLEDGE
arrogance, presumption, conceit, self-importance, forwardness, boldness. MODESTY
assuming, taking, undertaking, acceptance, adoption, appropriation, seizure, usurpation.

**assurance** pledge, promise, vow, oath, guarantee, assertion, affirmation, declaration. EQUIVOCATION
certainty, conviction, confidence, courage, boldness, nerve, assuredness, sureness, self-confidence, poise, security, belief, persuasion. DOUBT
arrogance, presumption, conceit, effrontery, impertinence, impudence. MODESTY

**assure** promise, guarantee, warrant, aver, pledge, vow, attest, affirm, confirm, give one's word, clinch, make certain. EQUIVOCATE
convince, persuade, encourage, reassure, comfort, hearten, embolden.

**assured** indubitable, unquestionable, certain, sure, guaranteed, secure. DOUBTFUL
self-confident, self-possessed, self-assured, positive, complacent, assertive, pushy (*inf*), audacious, bold. TIMID

**astir** active, on the move, in motion, afoot, alert, stirring, roused, awake, up and about. IDLE

**astonish** amaze, astound, stagger, dumbfound, flabbergast (*inf*), stupefy, stun, daze, startle, confound. BORE

**astonished** amazed, astounded, flabbergasted (*inf*), dumbfounded, stunned, surprised, open-mouthed, bowled over (*inf*).

**astonishing** amazing, astounding, staggering, surprising, stunning, impressive, breathtaking. ORDINARY

**astonishment** amazement, stupefaction, surprise, awe, wonder, bewilderment, confusion.

**astound** amaze, astonish, stagger, dumbfound, flabbergast (*inf*), stupefy, stun, daze, startle, confound. BORE

**astral** starry, starlike, stellar, sidereal.

**astray** wrong, off course, straying, wandering, loose, adrift, amiss, abroad, missing, absent. SAFE

**astringent** harsh, severe, rigorous, strict, stringent, austere, acerbic, caustic, sharp. LAX
contractive, styptic, binding, constrictive.

**astute** shrewd, cunning, crafty, wily, artful, subtle, knowing, perceptive, intelligent, discerning, sharp, keen, penetrating, adroit, clever, ingenious. SLOW

**astuteness** shrewdness, perception, insight, intelligence, subtlety, artfulness, guile, craftiness, cunning, sharpness, keenness, acumen, cleverness. SLOWNESS

**asunder** apart, to bits, in pieces. TOGETHER

**asylum** sanctuary, refuge, haven, shelter, retreat, safety.
institution, home, hospital, mental hospital, mad house (*inf*), loony bin (*inf*).

**atheist** unbeliever, disbeliever, sceptic, doubter, freethinker, infidel, heathen, pagan. BELIEVER

**athlete** sportsman, sportswoman, competitor, contestant, runner, gymnast, player.

**athletic** strong, muscular, sinewy, robust, sturdy, powerful, lusty, stalwart, energetic, fit, able-bodied, active. WEAK

**athwart** *adv*, across, crosswise, transversely, awry, askew, aslant, obliquely. STRAIGHT
*prep*, across, over. ALONG
against, in opposition to, counter to, versus.

**atmosphere** air, climate, sky, heavens.
mood, tone, character, feeling, ambience, aura, environment, milieu, surroundings, setting.

**atom** molecule, particle, jot, iota, scrap, whit, bit, mite, shred, crumb, morsel, trace.

**atone** expiate, redeem, appease, recompense, make up, redress, do penance, make amends. OFFEND

**atonement** expiation, reparation, satisfaction, propitiation, amends, recompense, compensation, redress, penance. OFFENCE

**atrocious** monstrous, abominable, infamous, nefarious, outrageous, heinous, horrible, infernal, diabolical, cruel, brutal, inhuman, savage, vicious, ruthless, vile, wicked, villainous. NOBLE
appalling, terrible, awful, horrible, detestable, shocking, horrifying. EXCELLENT

**atrocity** outrage, brutality, monstrosity, enormity, horror, crime, act of cruelty.
atrociousness, barbarity, savagery, inhumanity, monstrousness, heinousness, vileness, wickedness, ruthlessness, fiendishness. NOBILITY

**atrophy** *n*, decline, wasting, degeneration, decay, diminution, emaciation, shrivelling, withering.
*v*, decline, wither, shrivel, waste away, decay, diminish, dwindle, dry up. FLOURISH

**attach** join, fasten, affix, connect, append, tie, bind, tack, hitch, fix, stick, adhere. DETACH
assign, attribute, ascribe, accredit, associate, impute.

**attached** fond, loving, affectionate, devoted, enamoured.
engaged, spoken for, married. UNATTACHED

**attachment** fastening, joint, connection, bond, clamp, coupling, link, tie.
appendage, adjunct, accessory, appurtenance, addition, extra, fitting, extension. ESSENTIAL
affection, fondness, love, tenderness, liking, partiality, regard, affinity, attraction, bond, fidelity, devotion. HATRED

**attack** *v*, assault, assail, storm, beset, raid, charge, invade, violate, set upon, lay into (*inf*). DEFEND
abuse, berate, vilify, calumniate, impugn, malign, censure, blame. PRAISE
*n*, assault, onslaught, onset, raid, charge, invasion, incursion, aggression, offensive. DEFENCE
bout, spasm, access, fit, paroxysm, seizure.

**attacker** assailant, aggressor, invader, intruder, raider. DEFENDER

**attain** achieve, realize, accomplish, fulfil, arrive at, get to, reach, grasp, secure, get, obtain, acquire, gain, win, earn. LOSE

**attainable** achievable, realizable, reachable, within reach, accessible, at hand, possible, likely, feasible, practicable. IMPOSSIBLE

**attainment** achievement, accomplishment, feat, exploit, qualification, talent, ability.
realization, success, fulfilment, achievement, acquisition. FAILURE

**attempt** *v*, try, endeavour, have a go, strive, seek, venture, undertake, tackle.
*n*, try, effort, endeavour, undertaking, venture, experiment, trial, go, stab (*inf*), crack (*inf*).

**attend** be present, go to, frequent, visit.
accompany, follow, escort, guard, serve, wait on, minister to, care for, tend, look after. DESERT
listen, heed, pay attention, observe, mark, note. IGNORE

**attendance** presence, attending, appearance. ABSENCE
audience, turnout, house, gate, number present.
service, aid, assistance, care, ministration. NEGLECT

**attendant** escort, companion, servant, maid, waiter, waitress, valet, footman, steward, aide, assistant, usher, guide.
consequence, result, accompaniment, concomitant.

**attention** heed, heedfulness, alertness, observation, awareness, regard, notice, thought, consideration, concentration, application, intentness, deliberation. INATTENTION
care, concern, ministration, treatment, service, respect, courtesy, civility, deference, politeness, compliment, address. NEGLECT

**attentive** heedful, alert, mindful, careful, observant, aware, intent, concentrating, diligent, sedulous. INATTENTIVE
considerate, thoughtful, kind, obliging, civil, gallant, chivalrous, polite, courteous. NEGLECTFUL

**attenuate** thin, extend, draw out, rarefy, diminish, reduce, lessen, weaken, dilute.

**attenuation** thinning, rarefaction, diminution, reduction, lessening, weakening, dilution.
thinness, slenderness, fineness, elongation.

**attest** affirm, adjure, aver, confirm, corroborate, verify, witness, testify, certify, ratify, endorse, vouch for. DENY show, exhibit, manifest, display, demonstrate, prove, bear out.

**attestation** testimony, evidence, witness, statement.
affirmation, confirmation, endorsement, ratification, averment. DENIAL

**attic**[1] *n*, loft, garret, mansard. BASEMENT

**attic**[2] *adj*, classic, classical, elegant, tasteful, refined, polished, pure, simple, delicate. VULGAR

**attire** *v*, dress, clothe, robe, array, apparel, rig out, equip. STRIP
*n*, dress, clothing, clothes, garments, wear, apparel, costume, outfit, garb, finery, vestments, robes.

**attitude** opinion, point of view, stance, position, outlook, view, perspective, approach, disposition, frame of mind.
pose, posture, position, stance, air, demeanour, bearing, manner.

**attorney** agent, deputy, substitute, proctor, factor, lawyer.

**attract** draw, pull, allure, entice, engage, win, charm, fascinate, captivate. REPEL

**attraction** draw, pull, magnetism, affinity, appeal, allure, lure, bait, enticement, temptation, inducement, fascination, charm, captivation, attractiveness. REPULSION

**attractive** appealing, pleasing, lovely, beautiful, pretty, fetching, prepossessing, winsome, charming, engaging, winning, seductive, tempting, inviting. UNATTRACTIVE

**attributable** ascribable, assignable, imputable, chargeable, traceable.

**attribute** *v*, ascribe, assign, credit, impute, charge, blame, put down.
*n*, quality, virtue, characteristic, trait, feature, property, peculiarity, quirk, idiosyncrasy, mark, note, sign, indication.

**attrition** abrasion, friction, wear, wearing down, rubbing, scraping, erosion. ACCRETION

**attune** harmonize, accord, coordinate, adjust, adapt, acclimatize. DISTURB

**auburn** reddish-brown, copper-coloured, chestnut, henna, russet, rust-coloured, Titian red, bronze, tawny.

**audacious** bold, daring, fearless, intrepid, dauntless, venturesome, courageous, brave, valiant, rash, foolhardy, reckless. TIMID
forward, shameless, brazen, impertinent, impudent, cheeky, insolent, arrogant, presumptuous, assuming. MODEST

**audacity** boldness, fearlessness, guts (*inf*), nerve, courage, valiance, bravery, rashness, recklessness, foolhardiness. TIMIDITY
forwardness, shamelessness, effrontery, impertinence, gall, cheek, nerve, impudence, insolence, arrogance, presumption. MODESTY

**audible** perceptible, discernible, distinct, clear, hearable. INAUDIBLE

**audience** assembly, congregation, crowd, turnout, house, onlookers, spectators, viewers, listeners, patrons, public.
interview, hearing, reception, meeting.

**audit** *v*, examine, inspect, scrutinize, check, verify.
*n*, examination, inspection, scrutiny, checking, verification.

**audition** hearing, test, trial.

**augment** increase, enlarge, magnify, amplify, swell, expand, add to, boost, strengthen, extend, raise, enhance. DECREASE

**augmentation** increase, enlargement, amplification, expansion, addition, extension, boost, rise. DECREASE

**augur** *v*, predict, foretell, prophesy, portend, presage, foreshadow, signify.
*n*, prophet, soothsayer, seer, oracle.

**augury** divination, soothsaying, prophecy, prediction.
omen, sign, portent, presage, prophecy, harbinger.

**august** dignified, majestic, imposing, lofty, grand, magnificent, noble, regal, venerable, exalted, solemn, stately. HUMBLE

**aura** air, atmosphere, ambience, feeling, mood, quality, aroma, scent, emanation, odour.

**auspice** augury, omen, portent, sign, presage.

**auspices** patronage, backing, sponsorship, favour, influence, protection, aegis, support, guidance.

**auspicious** favourable, happy, bright, rosy, promising, propitious, opportune, timely, encouraging, hopeful, successful, fortunate, lucky. INAUSPICIOUS

**austere** stern, severe, harsh, strict, firm, inflexible, unbending, rigid, stringent,

grim, solemn, grave, serious, cold, unfeeling. LENIENT
abstemious, ascetic, self-denying, self-disciplined, Spartan, abstinent, sober, puritanical, chaste, pure, simple, unadorned. LUXURIOUS

**austerity** severity, harshness, strictness, firmness, rigidity, solemnity, coldness. LENIENCY
abstemiousness, asceticism, self-denial, self-discipline, abstinence, economy, privation, hardship. LUXURY

**authentic** genuine, true, veritable, real, pure, legitimate, valid, reliable, dependable, trustworthy, accurate, faithful, bona fide, authoritative. SPURIOUS

**authenticate** verify, prove, substantiate, validate, certify, confirm, seal, endorse, guarantee, attest, vouch for. DISPROVE

**author** writer, novelist, storyteller, biographer, essayist, poet, playwright, dramatist, composer, lyricist.
creator, originator, parent, inventor, designer, architect, producer, perpetrator.

**authoritarian** *adj*, despotic, dictatorial, domineering, strict, severe, disciplinarian, absolute, imperious, autocratic. LENIENT
*n*, disciplinarian, despot, dictator, autocrat.

**authoritative** official, legitimate, approved, authentic, reliable, true, definitive, decisive, conclusive, certain, sure, positive, imperative, ruling.
dictatorial, imperious, dogmatic, peremptory, commanding, assertive, arrogant. SUBORDINATE

**authority** power, dominion, supremacy, ascendancy, sway, sovereignty, rule, control, command, influence, direction, government. SUBORDINATION
permission, sanction, authorization, right, justification, warrant, licence, permit. BAN
expert, master, scholar, connoisseur, specialist, professional. NOVICE
evidence, testimony, say-so (*inf*), avowal, declaration.

**authorize** empower, commission, accredit, enable, entitle, license, legalize, sanction, ratify, permit, allow, warrant. FORBID

**autocracy** dictatorship, despotism, absolutism, tyranny, totalitarianism. DEMOCRACY

**autocrat** dictator, despot, tyrant, absolute ruler.

**autocratic** dictatorial, despotic, absolute, unlimited, all-powerful, tyrannical, totalitarian, oppressive, domineering, overbearing, imperious. DEMOCRATIC

**automatic** mechanical, self-activating, automated, mechanized, push-button. MANUAL
involuntary, unconscious, instinctive, reflex, spontaneous, mechanical, uncontrolled. DELIBERATE

**autonomous** self-governing, self-ruling, self-reliant, independent, free, unfettered. DEPENDENT

**autonomy** self-government, home rule, self-rule, independence, freedom. DEPENDENCE

**autopsy** post mortem, necropsy, dissection.

**auxiliary** *adj*, supplementary, accessory, ancillary, subsidiary, additional, extra, secondary, reserve, supporting, assisting, helping. ESSENTIAL
*n*, assistant, accessory, subordinate, aide, helper, right-hand man, second, supporter, partner, ally, confederate, associate. OPPONENT

**avail** *v*, benefit, profit, advantage, help, serve, be of use. HINDER
**avail oneself of,** use, exploit, make use of, take advantage of. WASTE
*n*, use, service, efficacy, benefit, good, profit, advantage, help.

**available** obtainable, accessible, to hand, attainable, handy, ready, convenient, at one's disposal. UNAVAILABLE

**avalanche** landslide, deluge, flood, inundation.

**avant-garde** experimental, innovative, progressive, unconventional, way-out (*inf*), modernistic. OLD-FASHIONED

**avarice** greed, greediness, cupidity, rapacity, covetousness, acquisitiveness, miserliness, parsimony, close-fistedness, meanness. LIBERALITY

**avaricious** greedy, rapacious, grasping, covetous, acquisitive, miserly, niggardly, parsimonious, close-fisted, mean, stingy. LIBERAL

**avenge** revenge, vindicate, retaliate, requite, repay, get even (*inf*), punish. PARDON

**avenue** approach, access, entrance, entry, way, path, passage, alley, drive, road, route, street, boulevard.

**aver** assert, affirm, asseverate, avow, predicate, state, declare, pronounce, say, allege, maintain. DENY

**average** *n*, mean, medium, norm, standard, rule. EXTREME
*adj*, mean, medium, median, middling, mediocre, passable, fair, not bad, indifferent, moderate, tolerable, normal, typical, usual, ordinary, commonplace, run-of-the-mill. EXCEPTIONAL
*v*, equate, even out, balance out, proportion.

**averment** assertion, affirmation, asseveration, avowal, statement, declaration, pronouncement, allegation. DENIAL

**averse** unwilling, indisposed, disinclined, reluctant, loath, opposed, hostile, inimical, adverse. READY

**aversion** loathing, repugnance, abhorrence, detestation, disgust, horror, antipathy, hatred, dislike, distaste, revulsion, opposition, hostility, reluctance, indisposition, unwillingness. LOVE

**avert** turn away, divert, deflect. DIRECT
ward off, avoid, forestall, prevent, preclude, fend off. ENCOURAGE

**aviation** flight, flying, aeronautics.

**aviator** aviatrix, airman, airwoman, flier, pilot, aeronaut.

**avid** keen, eager, enthusiastic, fervent, passionate, ardent, zealous, fanatical. APATHETIC
greedy, rapacious, acquisitive, avaricious, grasping.

**avidity** keenness, eagerness, impatience, longing, enthusiasm, ardour, zeal. APATHY
greed, greediness, rapacity, avarice, acquisitiveness, cupidity.

**avocation** hobby, pastime, recreation, amusement, diversion.
calling, vocation, trade, occupation, job, business, profession, employment, work.

**avoid** evade, elude, dodge, shun, shirk, refrain from, eschew, escape, avert, circumvent, steer clear of, keep away from. CONFRONT

**avow** affirm, assert, asseverate, aver, state, declare, proclaim, admit, acknowledge, recognize, confess. DENY

**avowal** assertion, affirmation, proclamation, declaration, averment, admission, acknowledgment, confession, profession, oath, testimony, deposition. DENIAL

**await** wait for, abide, expect, anticipate, look forward to, be ready for, be in store.

**awake** *v*, wake up, rouse, awaken, arouse, excite, stimulate, kindle, provoke, stir up, activate. LULL
*adj*, astir, waking, aware, conscious, alert, attentive, vigilant, watchful, lively, active. ASLEEP

**awaken** arouse, excite, stimulate, spur, kindle, rouse, provoke, incite, stir up, activate, animate. LULL

**award** *v*, give, grant, bestow, present, endow, confer, assign, allot, appoint, apportion, adjudge, decree. WITHDRAW
*n*, prize, trophy, medal, decree, verdict, endowment, grant, gift, bestowal, conferment.

**aware** conscious, sensible, cognizant, enlightened, apprised, informed, knowledgeable, mindful, awake, alert, appreciative, acquainted, familiar, conversant. UNAWARE

**awareness** perception, understanding, recognition, enlightenment, knowledge, cognizance, consciousness, sensibility, acquaintance, familiarity. IGNORANCE

**away** *adj*, absent, out, not present, elsewhere, abroad, gone, distant, remote. PRESENT
*adv*, off, hence, abroad, apart, far, at a distance, aside. NEAR
continuously, incessantly, relentlessly, interminably.

**awe** *n*, admiration, wonder, respect, reverence, amazement, dread, fear, terror. CONTEMPT
*v*, impress, amaze, overwhelm, daunt, intimidate, cow, subdue, frighten, alarm, dismay. REASSURE

**awesome** awe-inspiring, impressive, breathtaking, overwhelming, majestic, magnificent, venerable, formidable, daunting, intimidating, frightening, dreadful, fearsome. CONTEMPTIBLE

**awful** dreadful, terrible, fearful, dire, abominable, appalling, ghastly, horrendous, frightful, nasty, unpleasant, bad. WONDERFUL

**awhile** briefly, for a moment, for a short time.

**awkward** ungainly, graceless, clumsy, maladroit, inept, bungling, unskilful,

hamfisted, gauche, lumbering, uncouth, coarse, rough, crude, unpolished, oafish. DEXTEROUS
unwieldy, unmanageable, cumbersome, difficult, troublesome, inconvenient, inopportune, untimely, embarrassing.
perverse, trying, vexatious, stubborn, unhelpful, bloody-minded (*inf*). OBLIGING
**awning** canopy, tarpaulin, tilt, baldachin.
**awry** *adv*, askew, askance, amiss, wrongly, obliquely, off-centre, to one side, crookedly.
*adj*, askew, askance, amiss, wrong, oblique, slanting, off-centre, crooked, distorted, skew-whiff (*inf*). STRAIGHT
**axe** *n*, chopper, hatchet, cleaver, pickaxe.
*v*, cut, chop, fell, hew.
cancel, terminate, dismiss, discharge, cut back.
**axiom** truism, postulate, maxim, adage, aphorism, apophthegm, precept, dictum.
**axiomatic** self-evident, absolute, certain, manifest, unquestioned, indubitable, assumed, understood.
**azure** blue, sky-blue, cerulean, ultramarine.

# B

**babble** *v*, prattle, gibber, blab, gossip, mutter, chatter, gabble, jabber, prate, mumble, murmur.
*n*, chatter, prattle, gabble, gibberish, drivel, nonsense, murmur, whisper.
**babbler** chatterbox, prattler, gabbler, gossip, blabbermouth.
**babe** baby, infant, nursling, suckling. ADULT
babe in arms, innocent, ingénue, novice, beginner.
**babel** hubbub, din, clamour, uproar, tumult, confusion, disorder, pandemonium, hullabaloo. QUIET
**baby** *n*, infant, babe, newborn, suckling, nursling, child, toddler, tot, youngest. ADULT
*adj*, tiny, miniature, minute, dwarf, small, little. GIANT
*v*, coddle, mollycoddle, pamper, pet, cosset, indulge, spoil.
**babyish** childish, infantile, puerile, immature, silly, foolish. ADULT
**bacchanalia** revelry, revel, orgy, saturnalia, carousal, debauch, spree, merrymaking, festival.
**bacchanalian** riotous, wild, drunken, orgiastic, debauched, licentious, unrestrained, merry, festive. SOBER
**back** *n*, rear, stern, reverse, posterior, end, hindquarters. FRONT
*v*, support, encourage, second, sustain, help, aid, assist, abet, finance, sponsor, subsidize, advocate, endorse, favour, countenance. OBSTRUCT
go back, move back, reverse, retreat, retire, recoil, withdraw. ADVANCE
**back out,** abandon, give up, withdraw, retreat, renege, chicken out (*inf*).
*adj*, rear, hind, hindmost, end, last. FRONT
earlier, former, past, bygone, previous, elapsed, overdue.
*adv*, backward, rearward, to the rear, behind. ONWARD
**backbite** malign, revile, defame, vilify, asperse, denigrate, run down, slander, calumniate, traduce, attack, abuse. PRAISE
**backbiting** defamation, denigration, aspersion, slander, calumny, malice, spitefulness, bitchiness (*inf*), vilification, mudslinging, gossip, scandalmongering. PRAISE
**backbone** spine, spinal column, vertebral column, vertebrae.
stamina, fortitude, mettle, courage, nerve, pluck, determination, resolution, firmness, character, moral fibre. WEAKNESS
**backer** patron, sponsor, benefactor, promotor, supporter, advocate, well-wisher. OPPONENT
**background** setting, context, environment, milieu, circumstances, breeding, upbringing, education, qualifications, experience, grounding, preparation.
**in the background,** unobtrusive, inconspicuous, behind the scenes, unnoticed, out of sight.
**backhanded** indirect, oblique, equivocal, ambiguous, double-edged, ironic, sarcastic.
**backing** support, aid, help, assistance, sponsorship, patronage, advocacy, endorsement, approval. OPPOSITION
**backslide** relapse, regress, revert, lapse, go wrong, go astray, sin, fall from grace.
**backslider** apostate, renegade, deserter, recreant, recidivist. ADHERENT

**backward** *adj*, slow, retarded, underdeveloped, dull, stupid, behind, tardy, late. ADVANCED
reluctant, hesitant, unwilling, averse, disinclined, loath, bashful, shy. FORWARD
*adv*, backwards, rearwards, behind, in reverse, retrogressively, back to front. FORWARDS

**bad** wicked, evil, villainous, immoral, depraved, corrupt, sinful, dishonest, criminal. VIRTUOUS
harmful, injurious, pernicious, detrimental, deleterious, unwholesome, noxious, vile. GOOD
inferior, poor, defective, imperfect, substandard, faulty, unsatisfactory.
rotten, mouldy, putrid, rancid, off, spoiled, tainted, contaminated.
naughty, mischievous, disobedient. WELL-BEHAVED
unpleasant, disagreeable, distressing, discouraging, unwelcome, unfortunate, adverse, serious, grave, severe, harsh. SPLENDID
sick, ill, unwell, miserable, wretched. WELL
**not bad,** fair, average, all right, passable, tolerable, so-so (*inf*), OK (*inf*).

**badge** emblem, device, insignia, sign, mark, token, stamp, brand.

**badger** harass, torment, plague, harry, persecute, worry, trouble, tease, bait, vex, annoy, try, hector, pester, nag.

**badinage** banter, raillery, teasing, chaff, repartee, persiflage.

**baffle** perplex, bewilder, confuse, confound, puzzle, mystify. ENLIGHTEN
frustrate, foil, balk, check, thwart, hinder, defeat. ABET

**bag** sack, pouch, container, receptacle, satchel, handbag, case, purse.

**baggage** luggage, suitcases, bags, belongings, effects, paraphernalia, things, gear, equipment.

**baggy** loose, ill-fitting, billowing, puffed out, bulging, slack, floppy, shapeless, lumpish. TIGHT

**bail** *n*, surety, security, bond, guarantee, warranty, pledge.
**bail out,** *v*, release, rescue, aid, assist, help, relieve.

**bait** *n*, lure, decoy, snare, enticement, allurement, temptation, inducement, incentive, bribe.
*v*, badger, tease, persecute, torment, harry, harass, hector, plague, worry, try, vex, annoy, bother.
lure, entice, tempt, seduce, beguile. REPEL

**bake** cook, braise, roast, scorch, sear, dry, parch, harden.

**balance** *v*, weigh, estimate, compare, consider, ponder.
poise, stabilize, adjust, level, square, match, equalize, counterbalance, offset, counteract, neutralize, compensate, make up for. UPSET
*n*, equilibrium, equipoise, evenness, symmetry, parity, equivalence.
equanimity, composure, self-possession, self-control, poise, aplomb, stability. AGITATION
remainder, rest, surplus, excess, residue, difference.

**balcony** terrace, veranda, loggia, gallery, upper circle.

**bald** hairless, bare, naked, uncovered, barren, bleak, plain, unadorned, simple, unvarnished, undisguised, outright, straightforward, blunt.

**balderdash** rubbish, nonsense, drivel, rot, trash, humbug, poppycock (*inf*), claptrap (*inf*), bombast, verbiage. WISDOM

**bale** bundle, package, pack, parcel, truss, bunch.

**baleful** harmful, injurious, ruinous, disastrous, pernicious, noxious, malevolent, menacing, ominous, sinister, evil. BENIGN

**balk** hesitate, shrink from, recoil, flinch, jib, stop, refuse, demur.
thwart, frustrate, baffle, hinder, confound, defeat, foil, check, prevent, disappoint. ABET

**ball**[1] sphere, globe, globule, drop.
bullet, pellet, shot, projectile.

**ball**[2] dance, hop (*inf*), party, soirée, social.

**ballast** weight, packing, filling, stabilizer, balance, counterweight, equilibrium, stability.

**ballot** poll, vote, election, referendum.

**balm** ointment, unguent, lotion, salve, cream, oil, liniment, embrocation. IRRITANT
comfort, consolation, solace, remedy, cure.

**balmy** mild, pleasant, clement, temperate, sweet, fragrant, scented, aromatic, soothing, mitigating, assuasive, sedative, healing. HARSH

**bamboozle** cheat, defraud, deceive, mislead, trick, hoax, dupe, hoodwink, con (*inf*), confuse, baffle, perplex, mystify.

**ban** *v*, prohibit, forbid, proscribe, interdict, outlaw, disallow, exclude, bar. PERMIT
*n*, prohibition, embargo, interdiction, proscription, taboo, proclamation, edict, decree. PERMISSION

**banal** trite, commonplace, everyday, clichéd, hackneyed, unoriginal, humdrum, ordinary, stereotyped. ORIGINAL

**banality** platitude, commonplace, cliché, truism, bromide (*inf*).

**band**[1] *n*, group, company, body, troop, gang, crew, party, society, association, club, horde, crowd. INDIVIDUAL
*v*, join, unite, combine, merge, affiliate, ally, confederate, gather, group. SEPARATE

**band**[2] *n*, strip, belt, girdle, ribbon, bandage, tie, cord, ligament, ligature, strap, bond, binding.

**bandage** *n*, ligature, dressing, compress, tourniquet, gauze, plaster, band, fillet.
*v*, dress, bind, swathe, wrap.

**bandit** brigand, outlaw, robber, thief, marauder, pirate, hijacker, gangster, desperado, highwayman, footpad.

**bandy** *v*, exchange, interchange, swap, trade, toss, throw, pass.
*adj*, bent, crooked, bowed, bow-legged. STRAIGHT

**bane** woe, misery, affliction, curse, plague, scourge, torment, pest, nuisance, blight, ruin, calamity, disaster, injury, harm. DELIGHT
poison, venom, toxin.

**bang** *n*, explosion, boom, shot, report, burst, thud, thump, crash, clap, peal, clash, clang.
blow, knock, stroke, hit, bump, thump, whack, slap.
*v*, knock, hit, bump, strike, bash (*inf*), thump, rap, hammer, pound.
boom, explode, crash, thump, clatter, echo, resound, ring, peal.
*adv*, precisely, directly, straight, headlong, smack (*inf*), suddenly, abruptly.

**banish** expel, eject, exile, deport, expatriate, outlaw, cast out, dismiss, repudiate, spurn, exclude, ostracize, abandon, dispel, get rid of. HARBOUR

**banishment** exile, deportation, expatriation, expulsion, repudiation, exclusion.

**bank**[1] *n*, shore, margin, border, edge, brink, side.
heap, pile, mound, knoll, ridge, embankment.

**bank**[2] *n*, depository, storehouse, hoard, store, stock, fund, reserve, savings, accumulation.

**bank on**, *v*, depend on, count on, rely on, trust, expect.

**bankrupt** insolvent, broke (*inf*), in debt, ruined, destitute, impoverished, depleted, lacking, deficient. AFFLUENT

**bankruptcy** insolvency, liquidation, ruin, failure, disaster, depletion, deficiency. AFFLUENCE

**banner** standard, flag, colours, ensign, streamer, pennant, banderole.

**banquet** feast, dinner, repast, revel, celebration, entertainment, regalement, treat, spread (*inf*).

**banter** *v*, chaff, tease, rib (*inf*), twit, ridicule, mock, jeer, deride, make fun of.
*n*, badinage, raillery, chaff, repartee, joking, mockery, ridicule, derision.

**bar** *n*, rod, rail, pole, shaft, crosspiece.
barrier, obstacle, barricade, hindrance, impediment, ban, prohibition, injunction, embargo, boycott. AID
counter, saloon, lounge, pub (*inf*), inn, tavern, hotel.
tribunal, bench, court.
*v*, prohibit, forbid, ban, hinder, obstruct, impede, stop, prevent, deter, restrain, exclude, ostracize. ALLOW

**barb** point, bristle, spine, quill, thorn, prickle.

**barbarian** *n*, savage, brute, ruffian, boor, ignoramus, philistine.
*adj*, primitive, savage, barbarous, uncivilized, unsophisticated, uncouth, boorish, vulgar. CIVILIZED

**barbaric** savage, brutal, cruel, inhuman, barbarous, uncivilized, wild, primitive, barbarian. HUMANE

**barbarity** cruelty, brutality, savagery, inhumanity, ruthlessness, viciousness. HUMANITY
barbarism, outrage, atrocity, enormity.
coarseness, vulgarity, crudity, rudeness. REFINEMENT

**barbarous** uncivilized, primitive, barbarian, uncouth, ignorant, uncultured, rough, rude, coarse, vulgar, crude. CIVILIZED brutal, savage, barbaric, cruel, inhuman, ferocious, vicious, ruthless. HUMANE

**bare** naked, nude, unclothed, undressed, stripped, denuded, uncovered, exposed, unprotected. CLOTHED

plain, simple, stark, bald, unadorned, unfurnished, empty, barren. ORNAMENTED

**barefaced** impudent, brazen, shameless, audacious, bold, undisguised, unconcealed, manifest, glaring, blatant, palpable, flagrant. CONCEALED

**barely** scarcely, only just, no more than, hardly, merely, just.

**bargain** *n*, agreement, arrangement, contract, compact, stipulation, deal, transaction, understanding, promise, pledge.

discount, reduction, giveaway, snip (*inf*), good buy.

*v*, haggle, barter, deal, trade, traffic.

agree, arrange, contract, pledge, promise.

**bargain for,** anticipate, expect, foresee, contemplate, imagine.

**bark** *v*, yelp, yap, bay, howl, snap, snarl, growl, shout, yell, bawl.

*n*, yelp, yap, howl, woof, snarl.

**barmy** crazy, idiotic, insane, daft, nuts (*inf*), silly, foolish, stupid. SENSIBLE

**barrage** bombardment, battery, volley, hail, deluge, torrent, plethora.

**barrel** cask, keg, vat, tank, vessel, container.

**barren** infertile, sterile, infecund, childless, unfruitful, unproductive, bare, arid, desolate, empty. FERTILE

futile, useless, fruitless, unprofitable, ineffectual, unavailing, vain. USEFUL

**barricade** *n*, barrier, obstruction, blockade, bulwark, obstacle, hindrance.

*v*, obstruct, block, blockade, bar, fortify, protect, defend, shut in.

**barrier** barricade, obstacle, obstruction, bar, blockade, fence, railing, wall, rampart, ditch, moat. GATE

hindrance, impediment, stumbling block, obstruction, obstacle, hurdle, limitation, restriction, restraint, difficulty. AID

**barrister** lawyer, counsel, solicitor, advocate.

**barrow** handcart, truck, wheelbarrow, handbarrow.

**barter** exchange, trade, swap, deal, traffic, haggle, bargain.

**base**[1] *n*, bottom, foot, foundation, support, stand, pedestal. TOP

basis, core, heart, essence, root, principal.

home, settlement, camp, headquarters, starting point.

*v*, establish, found, build, rest, hinge, depend.

station, locate, post.

**base**[2] *adj*, low, mean, despicable, vile, wicked, bad, evil, contemptible, abject, ignoble, dishonourable, disgraceful, shameful, depraved, immoral, worthless, wretched, miserable, pitiful, sorry, menial, lowly. NOBLE

false, fake, spurious, counterfeit, alloyed, impure, debased, cheap, inferior, poor. REFINED

**baseless** groundless, unfounded, unsubstantiated, unreasonable, unjustifiable. REASONABLE

**bashful** shy, timid, timorous, coy, diffident, modest, reserved, reticent, shrinking, sheepish, abashed, shamefaced. BOLD

**bashfulness** shyness, timidity, coyness, diffidence, modesty, reserve, reticence, constraint. BOLDNESS

**basic** fundamental, essential, intrinsic, inherent, underlying, primary, elementary. SUBSIDIARY

**basics** fundamentals, essentials, rudiments, brass tacks (*inf*), hard facts, practicalities, nitty-gritty (*inf*).

**basis** base, foundation, bottom, ground, cause, reason, principle, fundamental, essence, core, root.

**bask** revel, bathe, luxuriate, wallow, indulge oneself, enjoy, delight, savour, relish, lounge, lie, relax, laze.

**bass** deep, low, grave, sonorous, resonant. TREBLE

**bastard** *adj*, illegitimate, natural, baseborn. LEGITIMATE

abnormal, irregular, imperfect, inferior, impure, adulterated, counterfeit, fake, spurious.

*n*, illegitimate child, love child, natural child.

villain, rogue, scoundrel, wretch, cad, heel (*inf*), rotter (*inf*).

**bastion** citadel, fortress, stronghold, bulwark, support, prop, mainstay.

**bat** stick, club, mallet, racquet, cudgel.

**batch** set, lot, quantity, amount, group, bunch, collection, crowd, aggregation.

**bath** *n*, wash, washing, bathing, ablution, soak, scrub, shower, douche.

*v*, wash, bathe, scrub, soak, shower.

**bathe** wash, cleanse, rinse, immerse, soak, steep, wet, moisten, suffuse.
swim, float, paddle.

**bathos** anticlimax, comedown, triteness, superficiality, shallowness, sentimentality, mawkishness.

**baton** stick, wand, rod, staff, club, truncheon.

**batten** fatten, grow fat, flourish, thrive, prosper, gain.

**batter** beat, pound, pummel, thrash, lash, buffet, smite, hit, strike, assault, attack, hurt, injure, wear, bruise, deface, mar, shatter, smash, demolish, destroy.

**battle** *n*, fight, combat, engagement, skirmish, encounter, contest, action, war, hostilities. PEACE
conflict, campaign, struggle, strife, clash, dispute, debate.
*v*, fight, struggle, contest, combat, contend, strive, dispute, argue. AGREE

**bauble** trinket, trifle, toy, gewgaw, bagatelle, knick-knack, ornament.

**bawdy** obscene, blue, lewd, indecent, coarse, vulgar, rude, risqué, salacious, filthy, dirty, smutty. DECOROUS

**bawl** yell, shout, cry, vociferate, roar, bellow, howl. WHISPER
wail, lament, cry, weep, sob, blubber.

**bay**[1] *n*, cove, inlet, gulf, bight, sound, estuary.

**bay**[2] *n*, recess, alcove, niche, compartment.

**bay**[3] *v*, bark, yelp, howl, cry.

**bazaar** market, market-place, mart, exchange.
fête, fair, sale.

**be** exist, live, breathe.
occur, happen, take place, come about.
survive, persist, remain, stay, continue, endure, last.

**beach** shore, seashore, strand, sands, shingle, coast, seaside, littoral, margin, brink, rim.

**beached** aground, ashore, wrecked, grounded, stranded, marooned, high and dry, deserted, forsaken, abandoned.

**beacon** signal, flare, rocket, lighthouse, bonfire, warning, sign, mark, landmark, guidepost.

**bead** drop, droplet, globule, bubble, blob, spherule, pellet, ball.

**beads** necklace, necklet, pearls, choker, pendant, chaplet, rosary.

**beak** bill, mandible, nib, prow, bow, stem.

**beaker** cup, glass, mug, goblet, tankard.

**beam** *n*, plank, board, rafter, girder, support, joist.
ray, streak, shaft, flash, gleam, glint, glimmer.
*v*, shine, gleam, glitter, glisten, radiate, emit, transmit.
smile, grin. FROWN

**beaming** bright, brilliant, gleaming, shining, radiant, sunny, smiling, grinning, cheerful, joyful. DULL

**bear** carry, convey, transport, take, bring, move, waft. DROP
support, sustain, hold up, lift, shoulder, uphold.
endure, stand, tolerate, suffer, abide, brook, stomach, allow, permit, admit, submit to, put up with. RESIST
harbour, cherish, hold, maintain, keep, entertain. DISCARD
give birth to, bring forth, beget, engender, produce, generate, yield.

**bear on,** affect, concern, regard, relate to, pertain to.

**bear out,** confirm, substantiate, corroborate, prove, justify, vindicate.

**bearable** tolerable, supportable, endurable, admissible, passable. UNBEARABLE

**beard** *n*, whiskers, stubble, bristles.
*v*, confront, face, defy, oppose, brave.

**bearer** carrier, porter, messenger, agent, conveyor, courier, holder, incumbent, beneficiary, payee.

**bearing** behaviour, conduct, deportment, carriage, manner, attitude, posture, mien, demeanour, air, aspect.
relevance, connection, relation, pertinence.
direction, course, aim, position, location.

**bearish** surly, gruff, churlish, boorish, clumsy, rough, coarse, uncouth, rude. POLITE

**beast** brute, animal, creature, savage, monster, ogre, barbarian, swine.

**beastly** unpleasant, vile, nasty, mean, rotten, foul, loathsome, abominable, terrible, awful, disagreeable. SPLENDID
brutal, bestial, cruel, inhuman, savage, coarse, depraved. HUMANE

**beat** *v*, strike, hit, thrash, whip, flog, lash, cane, whack, batter, bash, pound, pummel,

hammer, knock, thump, cudgel, maul. CARESS
defeat, overcome, subdue, quell, vanquish, trounce, rout, conquer, outstrip, surpass, excel.
whisk, whip, blend, stir.
throb, pulsate, pound, thump, palpitate.
*n*, throb, pulsation, pulse, accent, rhythm.
blow, stroke, hit, lash, thump.
round, circuit, course, route, zone, area.
**beaten** defeated, conquered, subdued, baffled, thwarted. VICTORIOUS
trampled, trodden, worn, well-used. UNTRODDEN
**beatific** ecstatic, glorious, joyful, blissful, serene, heavenly, enchanting, rapturous. WOEFUL
**beating** defeat, conquest, rout, overthrow, downfall, ruin. SUCCESS
thrashing, spanking, flogging, whipping, caning, pasting (*inf*).
**beatitude** ecstasy, delight, joy, happiness, bliss, blissfulness, felicity, blessedness, saintliness, beatification.
**beau** admirer, suitor, escort, sweetheart, boyfriend, lover.
dandy, fop, ladies' man, popinjay.
**beautiful** attractive, lovely, fair, elegant, graceful, seemly, handsome, pretty, comely, good-looking, ravishing, stunning (*inf*). UGLY
**beautify** adorn, embellish, titivate, ornament, bedeck, array, enhance, garnish, gild, embroider, decorate. DISFIGURE
**beauty** comeliness, attractiveness, fairness, loveliness, prettiness, elegance, grace, glamour, charm. UGLINESS
belle, Venus, goddess, good-looker (*inf*).
advantage, benefit, attraction, boon, asset. DISADVANTAGE
**because** as, since, for, seeing that.
**because of,** owing to, on account of, thanks to, as a result of.
**beck** nod, signal, gesture, wave, summons.
**beckon** summon, invite, bid, signal, wave, gesticulate.
entice, lure, tempt, attract.
**becloud** dim, bedim, darken, obscure, befog, cloud, veil, confuse, obfuscate. ILLUMINATE
**become** grow, turn, get, develop into, change into, come to be.
suit, grace, enhance, embellish, befit.

**becoming** attractive, comely, pretty, pleasing, suitable, appropriate, fitting, seemly, in keeping. UNBECOMING
**bed** bunk, couch, divan, berth, cot, cradle, hammock.
bottom, base, foundation, layer, stratum, seam.
**bedaub** daub, smear, plaster, besmear, bespatter, splash, stain, smirch, deface, mar.
**bedding** bedclothes, covers, sheets, linen, blankets.
litter, straw, hay.
**bedeck** array, adorn, deck, festoon, ornament, embellish, decorate, garnish. STRIP
**bedevil** harass, torment, pester, plague, annoy, irritate, vex, confuse, muddle, confound.
**bedew** moisten, dampen, sprinkle, spray, wet.
**bedim** dim, darken, cloud, becloud, shadow, obscure, befog. ILLUMINATE
**bedlam** uproar, pandemonium, hubbub, clamour, chaos, confusion, commotion. QUIET
**bedraggled** untidy, unkempt, dishevelled, grimy, sodden, drenched, dripping. NEAT
**beetle** *v*, jut, project, overhang, protrude, stick out.
*adj*, overhanging, beetling, jutting, projecting, prominent.
**befall** *vi*, happen, occur, take place, supervene, chance, transpire, ensue.
*vt*, happen to, overtake, betide.
**befitting** suitable, appropriate, fitting, right, proper, seemly, becoming. UNSUITABLE
**befog** obscure, confuse, muddle, perplex, obfuscate, blur. CLARIFY
**befool** fool, dupe, trick, hoodwink, deceive, cheat, beguile, bamboozle, mislead, delude.
**before** *prep*, in front of, ahead of, prior to, earlier than. AFTER
*adv*, previously, formerly, beforehand, earlier, sooner, ahead, in advance. AFTERWARDS
**befriend** assist, help, aid, defend, protect, look after, stand by, support, encourage, patronize, favour, advocate. OPPOSE
**befuddle** confuse, muddle, perplex, bewilder, intoxicate, inebriate.

**beg** ask, request, entreat, beseech, pray, plead, supplicate, implore, crave, solicit, petition.
cadge, scrounge (*inf*), sponge off, solicit alms, seek charity.

**beget** father, sire, breed, generate, procreate, engender, create, produce, cause.

**beggar** *n*, pauper, down-and-out, mendicant, tramp, vagrant, cadger, scrounger (*inf*), sponger (*inf*), parasite.
*v*, impoverish, ruin, bankrupt. ASSIST
surpass, exceed, challenge, defy.

**beggarly** destitute, impoverished, poor, indigent, needy, wretched, miserable, pitiful, contemptible, abject, paltry, inadequate, meagre, mean, shabby, vile.

**begin** start, commence, arise, come into being, originate, inaugurate, institute, initiate, embark on, set about. END

**beginner** novice, learner, tyro, neophyte, recruit, initiate, pupil, apprentice, trainee, student, amateur. EXPERT

**beginning** start, commencement, opening, outset, dawn, birth, origin, source, creation, inception, initiation, inauguration. END

**begrime** soil, dirty, foul, sully, defile, tarnish, besmirch, blacken, bedaub, smear, spatter. CLEANSE

**begrudge** envy, grudge, resent.

**beguile** delude, deceive, cheat, trick, hoodwink, mislead, dupe, fool.
charm, delight, enchant, amuse, entertain, divert, cheer, solace.

**behalf** interest, benefit, advantage, good, part, side, sake.

**behave** act, function, operate, perform, work.
comport, conduct, bear, deport.
be good, toe the line, mind one's manners, obey. MISBEHAVE

**behaviour** conduct, deportment, comportment, demeanour.
manners, actions, habits, ways.

**behead** decapitate, decollate, guillotine, execute.

**behest** injunction, command, order, instruction, mandate, precept, demand, bidding, request, wish.

**behind** *prep*, after, following, later than, at the back of. BEFORE
supporting, on the side of, backing. AGAINST
*adv*, in the rear, following, after, afterwards, next. AHEAD
behindhand, late, in arrears, overdue, in debt.

**behold** *v*, see, look at, observe, eye, contemplate, view, regard, survey, watch, witness, discern, perceive. MISS
*interj*, look, see, mark, watch, observe.

**beholden** obliged, indebted, bound, obligated, grateful. UNGRATEFUL

**behove** befit, become, be fitting, be necessary, be incumbent upon.

**being** existence, actuality, reality, living, animation, presence. NONEXISTENCE
essence, substance, soul, spirit, nature.
creature, animal, thing, individual, body.

**belabour** beat, strike, hit, thrash, batter, pound, pummel.
attack, criticize, censure, berate, lay into. PRAISE

**belated** late, overdue, behindhand, tardy, delayed, postponed. PROMPT

**belch** burp (*inf*), eruct, eructate, hiccup.
emit, discharge, eject, spew, gush, disgorge, expel.

**beleaguer** besiege, surround, encompass, hem in, blockade, beset, assail. RELIEVE
harass, badger, plague, pester, bother, annoy, vex.

**belie** contradict, disprove, gainsay, deny, negate. CONFIRM
misrepresent, falsify, disguise, distort, gloss over.

**belief** faith, believing, conviction, confidence, assurance, trust, credence, view, opinion, notion, theory, feeling, impression. DISBELIEF
creed, doctrine, dogma, faith, ideology, religion.

**believe** be convinced, have faith, have confidence, trust, credit, accept, rely on, depend on. DOUBT
think, reckon, maintain, hold, opine, suppose, assume, imagine, gather, understand.

**belittle** disparage, decry, deprecate, depreciate, underestimate, undervalue, deride, scorn, sneer at, detract, diminish, minimize. EXTOL

**bellicose** aggressive, belligerent, pugnacious, warlike, militant, combative, contentious, quarrelsome. GENIAL

**belligerent** warlike, martial, militant, bellicose, hostile, antagonistic, aggressive, pugnacious, argumentative, quarrelsome. PEACEFUL

**bellow** roar, bawl, yell, cry, shout, blare, trumpet, howl, screech. WHISPER

**belly** abdomen, paunch, stomach, tummy (*inf*), gut.

**belong** be owned by, be the property of, be part of, be a member of, be associated with, relate to, go with, fit.

**belongings** possessions, property, effects, chattels, things (*inf*), stuff (*inf*), gear, paraphernalia.

**beloved** dear, dearest, darling, favourite, pet, cherished, treasured, precious, loved, adored, worshipped. HATED

**below** *prep*, under, underneath, beneath. ABOVE
less than, lower than, inferior to, subordinate to.
unbefitting, unworthy of, unbecoming.
*adv*, under, underneath, beneath, down, lower. ABOVE

**belt** band, girdle, sash, cummerbund, waistband.
zone, region, area, tract.

**bemire** soil, dirty, muddy, bedaub, begrime, spatter, smear, sully, defile. CLEANSE

**bemoan** lament, mourn, grieve over, bewail, deplore, regret, moan, wail. REJOICE

**bemuse** bewilder, baffle, confuse, muddle, perplex, puzzle, daze, stupefy, stun, overwhelm, amaze.

**bench** settle, form, pew, stall, seat.
workbench, trestle table, board, counter.
court, tribunal, judiciary, judge, magistrate.

**bend** *v*, curve, bow, crook, flex, deflect, deviate, diverge, veer, swerve, twist, contort, turn. STRAIGHTEN
stoop, crouch, squat, bow, incline, lean.
yield, submit, give way, bow, concede, agree. RESIST
mould, influence, dispose, sway, subdue, overwhelm.
*n*, curve, bow, arc, angle, turn, twist, zigzag, crook, hook.

**beneath** *prep*, below, under, underneath. ABOVE
unworthy of, unbefitting, undignified for.
lower than, inferior to, subordinate to, less than.
*adv*, below, under, underneath, down, lower. ABOVE

**benediction** blessing, grace, consecration, prayer, invocation, thanksgiving. CURSE

**benefaction** donation, contribution, gift, present, bequest, legacy, endowment, grant, alms, boon.
generosity, philanthropy, charity, beneficence, benevolence. AVARICE

**benefactor** patron, sponsor, donor, backer, supporter, helper, friend, well-wisher.

**benefice** living, office, sinecure, stipend, emolument.

**beneficence** generosity, liberality, bounty, charity, benevolence, kindness, unselfishness, altruism. AVARICE
gift, donation, benefaction, aid, relief.

**beneficent** generous, liberal, munificent, charitable, benevolent, benign, kind, helpful. HARD

**beneficial** helpful, useful, valuable, advantageous, profitable, favourable, good, wholesome, salutary, salubrious, healthy. UNWHOLESOME

**benefit** *n*, good, sake, interest, advantage, profit, gain, avail, use, service, help, aid, boon, blessing. LOSS
*v*, help, aid, avail, serve, profit, improve, promote, further, advantage. DAMAGE

**benevolence** kindness, compassion, goodwill, humanity, philanthropy, altruism, charity, beneficence, liberality. MALEVOLENCE

**benevolent** kind, kindly, benign, compassionate, humane, kind-hearted, good, unselfish, charitable, philanthropic, beneficent, bountiful, liberal. MALEVOLENT

**benighted** unenlightened, uncivilized, primitive, ignorant, backward. SOPHISTICATED

**benign** kind, kindly, benevolent, sympathetic, gentle, compassionate, genial, amiable, friendly, obliging, gracious. COLD
favourable, propitious, beneficial, advantageous, good, lucky. UNFAVOURABLE

**bent** *adj*, crooked, twisted, curved, bowed, arched, stooped, hunched. STRAIGHT
determined, set, resolved, decided, fixed, inclined, disposed.
*n*, inclination, tendency, disposition, leaning, aptitude, forte, flair, faculty, talent, predilection, partiality, liking, fondness, predisposition.

**benumb** deaden, numb, anaesthetize, blunt, stupefy, paralyse. STIMULATE
**bequeath** leave, will, bestow, endow, pass on, hand down, transmit, impart, grant, give.
**bequest** legacy, inheritance, endowment, settlement, trust, gift.
**berate** reprove, reprimand, chide, scold, rebuke, upbraid, castigate, tell off (*inf*), censure, vituperate, revile. COMMEND
**bereave** deprive, rob, dispossess, strip, divest, despoil. RESTORE
**bereavement** loss, deprivation, distress, affliction, misfortune, tribulation. CONSOLATION
**bereft** deprive, cut off, parted from, lacking, devoid, stripped, destitute.
**berserk** frenzied, insane, mad, enraged, violent, raging, rabid, wild, crazy, maniacal, uncontrollable. SUBDUED
**berth** bed, bunk, billet.
mooring, anchorage, harbour, dock, quay, wharf.
post, position, appointment, situation, job, employment.
*v*, dock, anchor, moor, land, tie up.
**beseech** implore, beg, entreat, pray, plead, supplicate, petition, adjure, crave, solicit, ask.
**beset** beleaguer, surround, encircle, encompass, assail, attack, harass, trouble, bother, badger, plague, perplex. RELIEVE
**beside** next to, alongside, adjacent to, near, close to.
compared with, next to, in contrast with.
**besides** *prep*, apart from, other than, except, excepting, in addition to, over and above.
*adv*, moreover, furthermore, in addition, as well, too, also.
**besiege** surround, encompass, hem in, blockade, lay siege to, beleaguer, beset, importune, harass, plague, hound. RELIEVE
**besmear** besmirch, smear, daub, bedaub, soil, dirty, spatter, begrime, defile, sully, stain, tarnish.
**besotted** infatuated, doting, smitten, intoxicated, befuddled, stupefied, foolish, confused, muddled.
**bespatter** splash, spatter, daub, bedaub, soil, dirty, begrime, besmear, besmirch, defile, sully.
**bespeak** order, engage, solicit, request, ask for.
denote, signify, indicate, betoken, suggest, imply, reveal, show, exhibit, display.
**besprinkle** sprinkle, scatter, strew, dust, dredge, bedew, moisten, spray, spatter.
**best** *adj*, finest, outstanding, excellent, first-rate, highest, supreme, leading, unsurpassed, perfect, superlative. WORST
*n*, choice, pick, flower, élite, cream, prime.
**bestial** brutish, beastly, brutal, savage, barbaric, inhuman, depraved, degraded, carnal, sensual, vile, sordid, low.
**bestir** stir, rouse, awaken, animate, get going (*inf*), activate, stimulate, exert, bustle, hasten, hurry. RESTRAIN
**bestow** confer, give, grant, accord, present, award, impart, bequeath, endow. WITHHOLD
**bestrew** strew, scatter, sprinkle, spread, sow, disseminate, broadcast. GATHER
**bestride** straddle, bridge, span, extend across, step over, dominate, tower over.
**bet** *v*, wager, stake, put money on, pledge, gamble, risk, speculate, hazard.
*n*, wager, gamble, ante, stake, pledge.
**betide** befall, chance, happen, occur, crop up, supervene, come to pass, ensue, transpire.
**betoken** denote, indicate, signify, represent, show, manifest, betray, proclaim, declare, bespeak, presage, augur, portend, bode. HIDE
**betray** inform on, double-cross, be disloyal, be treacherous, sell out (*inf*).
disclose, reveal, divulge, expose, tell, give away, let slip, show, exhibit, manifest, display. CONCEAL
conceive, mislead, delude, beguile, ensnare, trap, lure, seduce, lead astray, corrupt, undo.
abandon, desert, walk out on, forsake, jilt.
**betroth** engage, affiance, plight, pledge, promise.
**betrothal** engagement, marriage contract, plighting, troth, promise, pledge, vow.
**better** *adj*, superior, finer, surpassing, greater, preferable, more desirable. WORSE
improving, recovering, on the mend (*inf*), fitter, well, healthy. ILL
*v*, improve, ameliorate, advance, promote, further, amend, correct, rectify, reform. WORSEN
surpass, exceed, outstrip, beat, improve on.

**betterment** improvement, amelioration, edification. DETERIORATION

**between** mid, amidst, in the middle of, betwixt, among.

**bevel** angle, cant, chamfer, oblique, slant, slope, incline.

**beverage** drink, potable, potation, libation, draught.

**bevy** flock, swarm, flight, pack, troop, group, company, throng, bunch, collection, band, troupe, party.

**bewail** lament, mourn, bemoan, grieve for, deplore, regret, sorrow, wail, moan. REJOICE

**beware** take care, watch out, look out, be careful, mind, take heed, avoid, steer clear of, guard against.

**bewilder** confuse, puzzle, perplex, confound, muddle, distract, bemuse, baffle, mystify, daze, stupefy. ENLIGHTEN

**bewilderment** confusion, perplexity, puzzle, muddle, bafflement, mystification, stupefaction. ENLIGHTENMENT

**bewitch** enchant, spellbind, fascinate, captivate, entrance, hypnotize, charm, beguile, allure, enrapture, transport. REPEL

**beyond** above, over, past, further than, apart from, out of reach of, more than, over and above. WITHIN

**bias** *n*, tendency, inclination, proclivity, predisposition, bent, propensity, leaning, predilection, partiality, prejudice, favouritism, one-sidedness. IMPARTIALITY

*v*, influence, predispose, incline, sway, prejudice.

**bibulous** alcoholic, boozy (*inf*), intemperate. TEETOTAL

**bicker** quarrel, squabble, wrangle, row, fight, spar, argue, dispute, disagree. AGREE

**bid** *v*, offer, tender, proffer, propose, submit.

command, order, demand, require, direct, instruct, summon, enjoin, invite, request, ask. FORBID

say, wish, tell.

*n*. offer, tender, proposal, submission, price, amount, sum.

attempt, try, endeavour.

**bidding** order, command, behest, injunction, instruction, summons, invitation, request.

**big** large, great, huge, massive, enormous, immense, colossal, gigantic, vast, spacious, voluminous, burly, hulking, bulky, fat, gross. SMALL

important, significant, prominent, influential, notable, famous, principal, main. INSIGNIFICANT

generous, magnanimous, unselfish, altruistic, gracious, benevolent. MEAN

arrogant, boastful, pompous, conceited, inflated, pretentious. HUMBLE

**bigot** fanatic, zealot, dogmatist, sectarian, racialist, sexist, chauvinist.

**bigoted** intolerant, narrow-minded, illiberal, dogmatic, opinionated, obstinate, prejudiced, biased. TOLERANT

**bigotry** prejudice, one-sidedness, bias, discrimination, narrow-mindedness, intolerance, dogmatism, obstinacy. TOLERANCE

**bile** anger, spleen, ill humour, irritability, irascibility, peevishness, rancour, bitterness, resentment, indignation.

**bilious** queasy, sick, nauseated, liverish.

bad-tempered, irritable, peevish, cross, grumpy, testy, touchy. AFFABLE

**bilk** thwart, balk, frustrate, foil.

deceive, cheat, defraud, trick, bamboozle.

elude, dodge, escape.

**bill**[1] account, statement, invoice, reckoning, tally, score, charge, fee.

poster, notice, placard, advertisement, bulletin, circular, leaflet.

list, agenda, programme, schedule.

**bill**[2] beak, nib, mandible.

**billet** *n*, quarters, accommodation, lodgings, rooms, barracks.

*v*, quarter, accommodate, lodge, assign station.

**billow** *v*, roll, surge, swell, heave, puff out, balloon.

*n*, wave, breaker, roller, surge, swell, deluge, rush, outpouring.

**billowy** rolling, heaving, surging, swelling, rippling, undulating, swirling. SMOOTH

**bin** receptacle, container, box, can, case, crate.

**bind** *v*, tie, tie up, truss, secure, fasten, strap, lace, lash, wrap, bandage, encircle, gird. LOOSE

restrict, confine, restrain, hamper, encumber. LIBERATE

oblige, force, compel, constrain, obligate, require, prescribe.

*n*, nuisance, bore, predicament, quandary, dilemma.
**binding** *adj*, obligatory, compulsory, imperative, irrevocable.
*n*, cover, covering, fastening, band.
**biography** life, history, life story, memoir, profile, account.
**birth** childbirth, parturition, delivery, confinement.
nativity, genesis, origin, beginning, source, creation, emergence, appearance. DEATH
ancestry, descent, extraction, line, lineage, family, blood, race, stock, pedigree, parentage, background, breeding.
**bisect** halve, cut in two, divide, split, intersect, cross. UNITE
**bisexual** androgynous, hermaphrodite, hermaphroditic, epicene, gynandrous, AC /DC (*inf*).
**bishop** prelate, patriarch, suffragan, overseer.
**bishopric** diocese, see, episcopacy, episcopate.
**bit** morsel, crumb, scrap, sliver, fragment, piece, particle, jot, iota, atom, mite, whit, tittle, speck, grain, drop, trace, hint. LOT
**bite** *v*, chew, gnaw, champ, munch, crunch, nibble, nip, snap, tear, rend, pierce, wound.
smart, sting, tingle, burn, corrode, eat into.
grip, hold, grasp, clutch, clasp.
*n*, nip, sting, wound.
morsel, mouthful, taste, snack.
**biting** piercing, keen, nipping, sharp, piquant, pungent, penetrating, cold, freezing. MILD
stinging, caustic, cutting, incisive, mordant, trenchant, sarcastic, scathing. GENIAL
**bitter** acrid, pungent, biting, harsh, sharp, sour, acid, tart, vinegary. SWEET
acrimonious, resentful, embittered, sour, morose, hostile, sullen, crabbed.
intense, severe, harsh, fierce, virulent, piercing, biting, stinging, cruel. MILD
distressing, sore, painful, grievous, poignant, harrowing, heartbreaking. CHEERY
**bitterness** acridity, pungency, harshness, sharpness, sourness, tartness. SWEETNESS
acrimony, resentment, malice, rancour, spleen, pique, grudge, hostility, animosity, asperity.
intensity, severity, harshness, fierceness, cruelty, virulence. MILDNESS
**bizarre** strange, odd, weird, extraordinary, grotesque, peculiar, unusual, fantastic, outlandish, eccentric. NORMAL
**blab** divulge, reveal, let slip, tell, tattle, prate, prattle, gossip.
**black** dark, inky, sooty, swarthy, dusky, ebony, jet, pitchy. WHITE
murky, dingy, dark, sombre, gloomy, dismal, depressing, mournful, forbidding, ominous. BRIGHT
dirty, filthy, soiled, grubby, grimy. CLEAN
evil, villainous, heinous, nefarious, wicked, atrocious, horrible. GOOD
**blacken** soil, begrime, dirty, darken, cloud, obscure.
defame, slander, calumniate, besmear, besmirch, sully, defile, vilify, traduce, malign, denigrate. VINDICATE
**blackguard** scoundrel, rogue, rascal, villain, wretch, knave, bounder (*inf*). GENTLEMAN
**blacklist** exclude, ban, bar, black, boycott, reject, repudiate, proscribe, ostracize. ACCEPT
**blackmail** *n*, extortion, exaction, hush money (*inf*), bribe, ransom, protection (*inf*), tribute.
*v*, extort, exact, bribe, milk, squeeze, bleed (*inf*), coerce, compel, force.
**blamable** culpable, blameworthy, in the wrong, guilty, liable, answerable, responsible. BLAMELESS
**blame** *v*, censure, condemn, criticize, find fault with, disapprove, reproach, reprove, chide, rebuke. PRAISE
accuse, charge, hold responsible, ascribe, attribute. VINDICATE
*n*, censure, condemnation, disapproval, criticism, reproach, reproof. APPROVAL
accusation, charge, incrimination, responsibility, culpability, fault, guilt. VINDICATION
**blameless** inculpable, innocent, guiltless, in the clear, above suspicion, unimpeachable, irreproachable, unsullied, unblemished, spotless, immaculate, perfect, faultless, virtuous. BLAMEWORTHY
**blameworthy** reprehensible, inexcusable, indefensible, discreditable, shameful, blamable. BLAMELESS
**blanch** whiten, bleach, fade, pale, blench. COLOUR
**bland** mild, gentle, soft, soothing, benign, suave, affable, amiable, agreeable. HARSH

dull, boring, uninteresting, insipid, nondescript, unexciting. PIQUANT

**blandishments** flattery, blarney, compliments, cajolery, coaxing, wheedling, fawning, ingratiation.

**blank** *adj*, empty, void, unfilled, bleak, plain, unadorned, bare, unmarked, spotless. FILLED
expressionless, deadpan, poker-faced (*inf*), impassive, uninterested, indifferent, apathetic. ALERT
confused, confounded, at a loss, perplexed, disconcerted, dumbfounded, uncomprehending.
outright, absolute, utter, complete, unqualified, unmitigated. PARTIAL
*n*, void, emptiness, vacuum, space, gap.

**blanket** *n*, cover, rug, carpet, cloak, mantle, sheet, wrapping, envelope, coating, layer, film.
*v*, cover, overlie, envelop, coat, cloak, mask, conceal. UNCOVER

**blare** proclaim, broadcast, trumpet, blast, roar, bellow, resound, clamour, sound, blow, toot.

**blarney** flattery, blandishments, compliments, cajolery, soft soap (*inf*), fawning, adulation. BLUNTNESS

**blasé** satiated, surfeited, cloyed, jaded, hardened, bored, weary, apathetic, indifferent, offhand, nonchalant, unmoved. EXCITED

**blaspheme** swear, curse, execrate, damn, revile, abuse, profane, desecrate. WORSHIP

**blasphemous** impious, profane, sacrilegious, irreligious, irreverent, ungodly. REVERENT

**blasphemy** impiety, profanity, swearing, execration, sacrilege, irreverence. REVERENCE

**blast** *v*, explode, blow up, burst, shatter, demolish, destroy, annihilate, ruin.
blight, wither, shrivel, kill.
*n*, explosion, discharge, burst, eruption, boom, bang, roar, thunder.
blare, honk, toot, bellow, peal, clang.
gust, squall, flurry, gale, storm.
blight, pestilence, infestation, affliction.

**blatant** conspicuous, obvious, glaring, flagrant, brazen, bald, naked, sheer, outright. CONCEALED
clamorous, noisy, obstreperous, vociferous, loud, deafening. QUIET

**blaze** *v*, flame, burn, flare up, flash, shine, gleam.
*n*, flame, fire, inferno, conflagration.
glow, glimmer, flash, flare, glare, light, radiance, brilliance.
outburst, eruption, storm, blast, torrent, flare-up.

**blazon** proclaim, broadcast, publicize, blaze, herald, trumpet. SUPPRESS

**bleach** blanch, whiten, etiolate, fade, lighten. DARKEN

**bleak** bare, exposed, open, unsheltered, barren, desolate, windswept, cold, raw, chilly. SHELTERED
gloomy, dismal, dreary, cheerless, depressing, hopeless, discouraging. CHEERFUL

**bleary** blurred, hazy, dim, indistinct, watery, rheumy.

**bleed** *vt*, draw blood, drain, sap, exhaust, extract, milk, extort.
*vi*, lose blood, exude, ooze, trickle, flow, spurt, gush.

**blemish** *n*, defect, fault, imperfection, spot, mark, speck, stain, scratch, blotch.
*v*, flaw, impair, deface, mark, spot, stain, taint, sully, tarnish, spoil, mar.

**blench** shrink, recoil, flinch, shy, shudder, quail, cower, hesitate, falter, shirk, avoid, evade, shun. FACE

**blend** *v*, mix, mingle, intermingle, combine, amalgamate, fuse, coalesce, merge, unite. SEPARATE
harmonize, go with, suit, fit, complement. CLASH
*n*, mixture, combination, compound, amalgamation, synthesis.

**bless** praise, extol, glorify, magnify, hallow, sanctify, consecrate, dedicate, anoint. CURSE
bestow, endow, grant, give, favour.

**blessed** sacred, holy, hallowed, divine, revered, adored, beatified.
happy, blissful, joyful, contented. SAD
favoured, fortunate, lucky, endowed. WRETCHED

**blessing** benediction, grace, thanksgiving, invocation, prayer, praise, honour, glory. CURSE
approval, sanction, consent, favour, good wishes.
boon, advantage, benefit, godsend, bounty, gain, profit, favour, good fortune.

**blight** *n*, disease, infestation, pestilence, canker, fungus, scourge, plague, bane, curse, woe, affliction.
*v*, blast, wither, shrivel, destroy, crush, ruin, wreck, dash, frustrate, disappoint, damage, mar.

**blind** *adj*, sightless, unseeing, unsighted, eyeless. SEEING
ignorant, unaware, unconscious, uninformed, unenlightened, oblivious, neglectful, thoughtless, inconsiderate, heedless, inattentive. AWARE
injudicious, unreasoning, unthinking, rash, reckless, hasty, impetuous, careless, mindless. CAREFUL
closed, shut, blocked, without exit. OPEN
*n*, shade, screen, curtain, shutter, cover.
mask, cloak, camouflage, disguise, feint, façade, stratagem, ruse.

**blink** *v*, wink, nictitate, flutter, bat, squint, peer.
flicker, twinkle, glitter, gleam, sparkle.
**blink at,** ignore, disregard, overlook, turn a blind eye to, condone.
*n*, glance, glimpse, wink, flutter.
twinkle, gleam, flash, glimmer.

**bliss** blissfulness, ecstasy, happiness, joy, rapture, elation, felicity, gladness. MISERY

**blissful** happy, joyful, ecstatic, euphoric, elated. MISERABLE

**blister** pustule, vesicle, bleb, boil, carbuncle, abscess, ulcer, cyst, wen, sore, bubble, swelling.

**blithe** merry, gay, jolly, cheerful, carefree, joyful, happy, vivacious, lively, animated, buoyant, sprightly, jaunty. DEJECTED
heedless, indifferent, casual, nonchalant, thoughtless.

**blitz** attack, bombardment, onslaught, offensive.

**bloat** swell, puff up, inflate, balloon, distend, dilate, enlarge. SHRINK

**blob** drop, globule, bead, ball, bubble, pearl, lump, mass, spot, dab.

**block** *n*, lump, mass, chunk, piece, cake, bar, brick.
blockage, obstruction, hindrance, impediment, bottleneck, jam, stoppage, obstacle, barrier, blockade. PASSAGE
*v*, obstruct, impede, blockade, check, stop, halt, arrest, thwart, deter, clog, plug. CLEAR

**blockade** barrier, obstacle, impediment, restriction, closure, siege.
block, obstruct, close, besiege.

**blockhead** dunce, simpleton, dolt, idiot, fool, numbskull, nitwit, noodle, dope, half-wit, ignoramus.

**blond** blonde, light, fair, flaxen, fair-haired. BRUNETTE

**blood** gore, life fluid, plasma.
ancestry, descent, family, extraction, lineage, race, stock, kinship, kindred, relations.
feeling, temper, spirit, temperament, disposition.

**bloodcurdling** terrifying, horrifying, fearful, hair-raising, spine-chilling, appalling, frightening.

**bloodless** pale, wan, pallid, pasty, sickly, anaemic, ashen. RUDDY
listless, languid, sluggish, torpid, unfeeling, cold, indifferent.

**bloodshed** carnage, slaughter, butchery, murder, massacre.

**bloodthirsty** murderous, savage, ferocious, vicious, cruel, inhuman, brutal, barbaric, ruthless.

**bloody** gory, sanguinary, bleeding, bloodstained.
bloodthirsty, murderous, savage, ferocious, cruel.

**bloom** *n*, blossom, flower, inflorescence, bud, efflorescence, flowering.
freshness, beauty, radiance, flush, lustre, prime, heyday, health, vigour. DECADENCE
*v*, blossom, flower, bud, burgeon, blow, open. WITHER
flourish, prosper, thrive, grow, wax. FADE

**blossom** *n*, bloom, flower, bud, floret, flowers.
*v*, bloom, flower, burgeon, bud, blow. WITHER
develop, mature, bloom, thrive, flourish. DECLINE

**blot** *n*, spot, stain, smudge, mark, blotch.
blemish, taint, stain, flaw, blur, disgrace.
*v*, absorb, dry, soak up.
sully, spot, soil, mar, spoil, disfigure, tarnish, disgrace, dishonour. CLEAR
**blot out,** cancel, erase, expunge, obliterate, efface, destroy, eliminate, obscure, darken, shadow. PERPETUATE

**blotch** patch, spot, splodge, smudge, blot, mark, stain, blemish.

**blow**[1] *v*, breathe, exhale, expel, pant, puff.

waft, fan, drive, move, sweep, whirl, spread.
sound, blast, whistle, toot, play.
**blow out,** extinguish, snuff, douse, put out.
**blow up,** explode, go off, detonate, burst, shatter, bomb.
exaggerate, enlarge, distend, inflate, swell.
*n*, blast, gust, puff, breath.

**blow**[2] *n*, hit, stroke, knock, thump, buffet, slap, punch, rap, whack, bang.
shock, calamity, disaster, bombshell, disappointment, setback, misfortune, affliction.

**blubber** sob, cry, weep, wail, whine.

**bludgeon** *n*, cudgel, club, truncheon.
*v*, coerce, force, bully, hector, browbeat.

**blue** azure, sapphire, cobalt, turquoise, aquamarine, ultramarine, navy.
dejected, depressed, unhappy, sad, melancholy, gloomy, glum, downcast, downhearted, despondent. CHEERFUL
obscene, indecent, coarse, risqué, bawdy, smutty, dirty, near the knuckle (*inf*).

**blueprint** design, pattern, model, template, prototype, plan, sketch, draft.

**blues** depression, dejection, melancholy, despondency, doldrums, dumps (*inf*). ELATION

**bluff**[1] *v*, mislead, deceive, delude, pretend, sham, feign.
*n*, deceit, fraud, pretence, feint, show, bravado, bluster.

**bluff**[2] *adj*, hearty, genial, good-natured, open, blunt, frank. RESERVED
*n*, cliff, ridge, crag, scarp, headland, promontory, bank.

**blunder** *v*, stumble, flounder, err, bungle, botch, miss, misjudge, mistake. SUCCEED
*n*, error, mistake, oversight, slip, gaffe, faux pas, clanger (*inf*), indiscretion.

**blunt** *adj*, dull, unsharpened, rounded, worn, pointless. SHARP
bluff, unceremonious, plain, frank, open, candid, straightforward, tactless, outspoken, rude, impolite, abrupt, brusque, curt. TACTFUL
*v*, dull, deaden, numb, weaken, soften, alleviate. SHARPEN

**blur** *v*, dim, obscure, becloud, befog, make indistinct. CLARIFY
blot, stain, spot, smear, smudge, sully, tarnish, mar.
*n*, haze, fog, confusion, obscurity, indistinctness. CLARITY
blot, stain, spot, smear, smudge, blemish.

**blurred** hazy, fuzzy, blurry, indistinct, vague, unclear, out of focus. CLEAR

**blush** *v*, redden, flush, colour, go red, glow. BLANCH
*n*, flush, reddening, colour, rosiness, glow. PALLOR

**bluster** *v*, swagger, boast, vaunt, brag, roar, storm, bully, domineer, hector.
*n*, boasting, bravado, swaggering, bluff, boisterous, tumult, commotion. RETICENCE

**blustery** windy, gusty, squally, stormy, tempestuous, wild, blusterous, boisterous. QUIET

**board** *n*, plank, panel, slat, lath, timber.
food, meals, provisions, victuals.
committee, council, panel, directors.
*v*, get on, embark, mount, enter, go aboard. ALIGHT
lodge, house, put up, accommodate, feed.

**boast** *v*, brag, vaunt, crow, exaggerate, swagger, bluster, flaunt, show off, swank (*inf*).
*n*, brag, vaunt, bragging, bluster, gasconade, rodomontade. MODESTY
pride, treasure, gem, pride and joy.

**boastful** bragging, vaunting, vain, conceited, egotistical, cocky, swollen-headed, swanky (*inf*). MODEST

**boat** vessel, craft, yacht, dinghy, canoe, barge, ferry, ship.

**bob** bounce, jerk, nod, duck, quiver, waggle.
**bob up,** emerge, pop up, appear, materialize.

**bode** presage, portend, betoken, signify, augur, import, predict, foretell, foreshadow.

**bodily** *adj*, physical, corporeal, material, carnal, fleshly, sensual, actual, tangible. SPIRITUAL
*adv*, wholly, entirely, completely, altogether, collectively, en masse.

**body** trunk, torso, physique, build, figure.
corpse, cadaver, carcass, stiff (*inf*).
person, individual, being, creature, mortal.
crowd, throng, multitude, group, collection, party, company, band, association, corporation, confederation. INDIVIDUAL
substance, mass, whole, bulk, essence, majority. PART

density, solidity, firmness, substance, consistency.

**bog** swamp, marsh, quagmire, fen, morass, slough.

**boggle** start, take fright, shy, be alarmed, be surprised.
hesitate, falter, vacillate, waver, shrink from, demur.

**bogus** false, counterfeit, sham, fake, phoney (*inf*), spurious. GENUINE

**boil**[1] *v*, seethe, bubble, foam, froth, simmer, stew. COOL
fume, rage, storm, be angry.

**boil**[2] *n*, furuncle, carbuncle, tumour, ulcer, pustule, blister, gathering, sore.

**boisterous** lively, unruly, unrestrained, rowdy, noisy, loud, vociferous, obstreperous, clamorous, riotous, uproarious. QUIET
tumultuous, tempestuous, stormy, blustery, raging, turbulent. CALM

**bold** brave, fearless, valiant, lion-hearted, daring, dauntless, courageous, intrepid, heroic, audacious, adventurous. TIMID
insolent, rude, brazen, brash, shameless, impudent, pert, cheeky, forward, confident.
prominent, striking, conspicuous, eye-catching. FAINT

**boldness** bravery, valiance, courage, audacity, bravura. TIMIDITY
insolence, rudeness, shamelessness, impudence, cheek, forwardness. MODESTY
prominence, conspicuousness. FAINTNESS

**bolster** *v*, support, prop up, brace, hold up, maintain, reinforce, strengthen, boost, aid, help.
*n*, pillow, cushion, pad.

**bolt** *n*, bar, latch, catch, lock, fastening, rod, pin, peg.
arrow, dart, shaft, missile, projectile.
*vt*, fasten, secure, latch, lock, bar. UNBOLT
gulp, devour, wolf, gobble, cram, stuff.
*vi*, abscond, flee, escape, run away, fly, dash, rush. STAY

**bomb** *n*, explosive, torpedo, mine, shell, grenade.
*v*, shell, bombard, torpedo, strafe.

**bombard** attack, assail, barrage, pelt, harass, pester.

**bombast** pomposity, grandiloquence, magniloquence, rant, bluster, bravado, braggadocio, fustian.

**bombastic** pompous, grandiloquent, magniloquent, grandiose, fustian, pretentious, high-flown, turgid, flatulent, verbose, ranting, declamatory.

**bond** *n*, cord, band, ligament, ligature, tie, fastening, chain, fetter, manacle, shackle.
link, tie, connection, affinity, attachment, union.
contract, compact, agreement, obligation, pledge, guarantee, promise.
*v*, bind, fasten, fuse, connect. SEPARATE

**bondage** slavery, servitude, captivity, imprisonment, confinement, duress, subjugation. FREEDOM

**bonny** fair, pretty, comely, beautiful, handsome, sweet, lovely, fine. UGLY
chubby, plump, bouncing, round, healthy, buxom.
cheerful, blithe, merry, joyful, gay, jolly. MISERABLE

**bonus** award, reward, gift, bounty, premium, extra, dividend, honorarium, gratuity, commission, perquisite, perk (*inf*).

**booby** dunce, fool, simpleton, idiot, blockhead.

**book** *n*, volume, tome, tract, text, novel, manual, work, publication.
*v*, reserve, engage, charter, schedule, programme.
register, enter, record, log, put down.

**bookish** studious, learned, erudite, scholarly, intellectual, academic, pedantic. ILLITERATE

**boom** *v*, resound, reverberate, roar, thunder, bang, blast.
prosper, thrive, flourish, develop, increase, gain. DECLINE
*n*, roar, thunder, crash, blast, bang.
rise, increase, development, upsurge, boost. DECLINE

**boon** blessing, benefit, advantage, godsend, grant, favour, gift, present. DRAWBACK

**boor** lout, oaf, churl, bumpkin, rustic, clodhopper, peasant, barbarian, philistine.

**boorish** loutish, oafish, clumsy, awkward, rustic, uncouth, coarse, ill-bred, vulgar, uncivilized, churlish, gruff, rude. REFINED

**boost** *v*, promote, advertise, publicize, plug (*inf*), encourage, raise, lift, increase, expand, support, assist, further, improve, push.

*n*, encouragement, help, support, promotion, improvement, increase, rise, push, thrust.

**bootless** unavailing, useless, futile, vain, fruitless, ineffective, worthless, abortive. USEFUL

**booty** spoils, plunder, pillage, loot, haul (*inf*), swag (*inf*), takings.

**booze** drink, alcohol, liquor, beer, wine, spirits.

**border** *n*, boundary, frontier, limit, bound, edge, margin, fringe, rim, hem, skirt, verge, brink. CENTRE
*v*, adjoin, abut, impinge, touch, join, connect.

**border on,** verge on, approach, resemble, come close to.

**bore**[1] *v*, drill, mine, pierce, perforate, penetrate.
*n*, hole, tunnel, shaft, calibre.

**bore**[2] *v*, tire, weary, fatigue, jade, vex, annoy, bother. EXCITE
*n*, pest, nuisance, bother, drag (*inf*), pain (*inf*).

**boredom** weariness, dullness, tedium, monotony, ennui, apathy. EXCITEMENT

**boring** dull, tedious, monotonous, repetitious, routine, humdrum, flat, unvaried, tiresome, wearisome. EXCITING

**borough** town, township, municipality.

**borrow** take, cadge, scrounge, appropriate, adopt, usurp, pirate, steal, plagiarize, imitate. LEND

**bosh** nonsense, balderdash, rubbish, rot.

**bosom** chest, breast, bust.
heart, soul, mind, spirit, emotions, feelings.
centre, heart, core, depths, recesses, midst, protection, shelter.

**boss**[1] *n*, employer, supervisor, superintendent, overseer, manager, director, foreman, master, leader, chief, governor (*inf*). EMPLOYEE
*v*, employ, supervise, direct, manage, command, control.

**boss around,** bully, domineer, oppress, tyrannize.

**boss**[2] *n*, stud, knob, protuberance, umbo.

**bossy** domineering, overbearing, authoritarian, imperious, arrogant. MEEK

**botch** *v*, bungle, spoil, mar, muff, mismanage, mess up, screw up (*inf*), blunder. ACCOMPLISH
mend, patch, cobble.
*n*, mess, hash, miscarriage, failure, blunder, bungle. SUCCESS

**both** the two. NEITHER

**bother** *v*, trouble, annoy, irritate, vex, pester, harass, plague, worry, disturb, upset, perplex, perturb. COMFORT
*n*, trouble, annoyance, vexation, irritation, nuisance, inconvenience, upset, problem, difficulty, fuss, flurry.

**bottom** *n*, base, foot, floor, ground, bed, depths, foundation, basis. TOP
underside, underpart, underneath, sole. TOPSIDE
seat, rump, buttocks, rear, posterior, backside (*inf*), behind (*inf*), bum (*inf*), fundament.
origin, root, source, root, essence, core, heart.
*adj*, lowest, last, basic, fundamental. TOP

**bottomless** unfathomable, abysmal, deep, immeasurable, infinite, boundless, unlimited.

**bough** branch, limb, stem, stalk, shoot, twig. TRUNK

**bounce** *v*, rebound, recoil, spring, jump, leap, bound, bob.
*n*, springiness, elasticity, give, resilience.
spring, leap, jump, bound.
vitality, energy, liveliness, go (*inf*), pep. LETHARGY

**bound**[1] *adj*, tied, fastened, shackled, fettered. FREE
certain, sure, destined, fated. UNLIKELY
obliged, forced, compelled, constrained, required.

**bound**[2] *v*, spring, leap, jump, vault, bounce, skip, hop, prance, caper.
*n*, spring, leap, jump, vault, bounce, hop.

**bound**[3] *n*, limit, boundary, border, confine, margin.
*v*, limit, restrict, confine, border, enclose, surround, circumscribe, demarcate.

**boundary** border, perimeter, circumference, limit, confine, bound, barrier, pale, frontier, margin, edge, extremity, termination.

**boundless** unlimited, infinite, endless, immense, vast, immeasurable, untold. LIMITED

**bountiful** plentiful, abundant, ample, copious, profuse, lavish, luxuriant. MEAGRE
generous, liberal, bounteous, princely, beneficent, munificent, magnanimous, benevolent. MISERLY

**bounty** generosity, liberality, charity, beneficence, philanthropy, almsgiving. MEANNESS
largess, gift, present, donation, grant, award, bonus, premium, reward.
**bouquet** bunch, posy, nosegay, spray, corsage, garland, wreath.
**bourgeois** middle class, conservative, conventional, traditional, unimaginative, materialistic. ARISTOCRATIC
**bout** fight, contest, conflict, encounter, match.
spell, period, session, spree, turn, fit.
**bow**[1] *v*, salaam, kowtow, bob, curtsy, genuflect, kneel, nod.
incline, stoop, bend, curve, flex, arch, warp, droop. STRAIGHTEN
submit, yield, surrender, give in, accept, comply. RESIST
subdue, crush, conquer, vanquish, depress, weigh down.
*n*, salaam, bob, curtsy, genuflection, nod.
**bow**[2] *n*, prow, beak, stem.
**bowels** intestines, entrails, guts, viscera, innards (*inf*), insides (*inf*).
depths, interior, belly, core. SURFACE
**bower** arbour, alcove, recess, grotto, shelter, summerhouse.
**bowl** basin, receptacle, vessel, dish, plate, saucer.
**box**[1] *n*, carton, package, case, chest, trunk, casket, receptacle, container.
*v*, encase, pack, wrap, confine.
**box**[2] *v*, spar, fight.
cuff, buffet, strike, hit.
*n*, cuff, buffet, stroke, blow.
**boy** lad, youth, youngster, stripling. MAN
**boycott** ostracize, shun, refuse, spurn, reject, black, blacklist, blackball, ban, prohibit, proscribe, embargo, bar, exclude.
**boyfriend** beau, date, young man, lover, sweetheart, suitor, admirer.
**boyish** young, youthful, juvenile, childish, immature, puerile. ADULT
**brace** *v*, support, prop, steady, reinforce, strengthen, fortify, bind, fasten, tie, tighten.
*n*, support, prop, strut, spar, truss, bracket.
pair, couple.
**bracing** invigorating, stimulating, restorative, tonic, refreshing, exhilarating, crisp, brisk. RELAXING
**bracket** support, prop, corbel, console, shelf, brace.
group, category, division, class, status.
**brackish** salty, briny, saline.
**brag** *v*, boast, vaunt, crow, swagger, bluster, gasconade, flaunt, flourish.
*n*, boast, boasting, vaunt, bluster, gasconade. MODESTY
**braggart** brag, braggadocio, boaster, show-off, big mouth (*inf*), blusterer, swaggerer.
**braid** weave, interweave, plait, twine, intertwine, lace, interlace. UNRAVEL
**brainless** stupid, foolish, thoughtless, witless, senseless, idiotic. WISE
**brains** mind, sense, intellect, reason, intelligence, understanding, shrewdness, common sense. STUPIDITY
**brainy** clever, intelligent, smart, bright. STUPID
**brake** *n*, curb, rein, restraint, control, check.
*v*, slow down, decelerate, moderate, check, halt, stop. ACCELERATE
**branch** *n*, limb, bough, arm, shoot, ramification, spray.
offshoot, tributary, affluent, channel.
division, subdivision, section, department, wing, office.
*v*, ramify, diverge, fork. CONVERGE
**branch out,** expand, extend, develop, diversify.
**brand** *n*, kind, sort, type, grade, quality, make.
mark, stamp, emblem, label, trademark, symbol.
stigma, disgrace, infamy, blot, stain, taint. HONOUR
*v*, mark, label, stamp, burn.
stigmatize, denounce, disgrace, discredit.
**brandish** flourish, wield, swing, wave, shake, flaunt, exhibit, display.
**brash** rash, hasty, precipitate, reckless, foolhardy, impulsive, impetuous. CAUTIOUS
insolent, impudent, rude, audacious, bold, forward, brassy, brazen, cheeky, saucy. MODEST
**brass** audacity, cheek, gall, nerve (*inf*), boldness, effrontery, impertinence, impudence, assurance, presumption.
**brat** urchin, guttersnipe, child, kid (*inf*), youngster, rascal, whippersnapper.
**bravado** brag, braggadocio, boast, boasting, swagger, vaunting, bluster, bombast. MODESTY

**brave** *adj*, courageous, valiant, heroic, gallant, dauntless, daring, fearless, intrepid, bold, plucky. COWARDLY
*v*, confront, face, defy, challenge, dare.

**bravery** courage, valour, heroism, gallantry, daring, fearlessness, boldness, mettle, pluck, guts (*inf*). COWARDICE

**brawl** *v*, fight, wrangle, tussle, scuffle, wrestle, scrap (*inf*), dispute, argue, quarrel, bicker, squabble, row. AGREE
*n*, fight, wrangle, scrap (*inf*), punch-up (*inf*), fracas, fray, affray, broil, row, rumpus, uproar, tumult, quarrel, dispute, altercation.

**brawny** strong, powerful, muscular, sinewy, strapping, lusty, sturdy, robust, stalwart, athletic, herculean. WEAK

**bray** heehaw, neigh, whinny, call, roar, blare, hoot, bellow.

**brazen** bold, audacious, forward, brassy, brash, barefaced, shameless, immodest, impudent, insolent, saucy, pert, impertinent. MODEST

**breach** rupture, fracture, break, crack, fissure, rift, gap, opening, chasm.
violation, infringement, infraction, contravention, transgression, trespass. OBSERVANCE
separation, schism, alienation, estrangement, dissension, difference, variance, disagreement, quarrel. RECONCILIATION

**bread** nourishment, nutriment, sustenance, food, fare, provisions, aliment.
money, cash, funds, dough (*inf*).

**breadth** width, broadness, span, spread. LENGTH
magnitude, amplitude, vastness, expanse, extent, range, scope, size, measure, dimensions. NARROWNESS
latitude, liberality, freedom, openness, broad-mindedness.

**break** fracture, snap, crack, rend, sever, split, divide, separate, smash, shatter, shiver, splinter, disintegrate, demolish, destroy, wreck. MEND
violate, infringe, disobey, breach. OBEY
weaken, enervate, enfeeble, tame, cow, subdue, impair, cripple. STRENGTHEN
discontinue, break off, interrupt, halt, stop, suspend, pause, rest. CONTINUE
appear, emerge, erupt, dawn, burst forth.
reveal, disclose, divulge, let out, betray, tell, inform, impart.
**break down,** collapse, fall apart, fail, stop working, go to pieces, crack up (*inf*).
**break in,** train, accustom, habituate, condition, initiate, prepare.
interrupt, butt in, intrude, enter, invade, barge in.
**break out,** begin, start, commence, emerge, erupt.
**break through,** penetrate, pass, get past, succeed, achieve.
**break up,** divide, separate, dissolve, dismantle, split, part, disband, disperse, scatter, end, terminate. UNITE
*n*, fracture, crack, split, gap, breach, rupture, rift, opening, fissure.
pause, hiatus, interruption, recess, respite, suspension, intermission.
opportunity, advantage, chance, stroke of luck.

**breakdown** collapse, downfall, failure, ruin. RESTORATION
analysis, itemization, dissection, review, summary.

**breakthrough** advance, development, progress, step forward, discovery, invention.

**breakwater** mole, groyne, jetty, sea wall.

**breast** chest, front, thorax, bosom, bust, udder, teat, tit (*inf*), boob (*inf*).
heart, soul, emotions, feelings, conscience.

**breath** respiration, breathing, inhalation, exhalation, air, gasp, pant, wheeze.
odour, aroma, whiff, vapour.
pause, respite, rest, breather, break.
hint, suggestion, whisper, murmur, sigh, gust, puff, waft.
animation, life, vitality, existence.

**breathe** respire, inhale, exhale, gasp, wheeze, pant, puff, sigh.
exist, live, be alive.
say, utter, articulate, voice, whisper, murmur.
imbue, instil, infuse, impart.

**breathless** gasping, panting, winded, out of breath, exhausted, spent.
eager, agog, excited, open-mouthed, amazed, thunderstruck, anxious, on tenterhooks.

**breathtaking** awesome, awe-inspiring, impressive, magnificent, stunning (*inf*), exciting, thrilling. UNINSPIRING

**breed** *v*, bear, produce, bring forth, engender, beget, procreate, propagate, reproduce, generate.

rear, raise, bring up, nurture, foster, educate, train, teach, school, instruct, discipline.
create, produce, generate, originate, cause, bring about, arouse.
*n*, race, stock, strain, variety, kind, sort, type, species, pedigree, lineage, progeny, family, extraction.

**breeding** reproduction, propagation, procreation, bearing, begetting.
training, education, upbringing, development, background, ancestry, manners, bearing, conduct, refinement, culture, civility, politeness.

**breeze** light wind, zephyr, gust, flurry, waft, puff, breath of air, draught. HURRICANE

**breezy** windy, fresh, airy, blowy. CALM
carefree, casual, light-hearted, cheerful, blithe, buoyant, sprightly, lively, vivacious, jaunty.

**brevity** conciseness, terseness, succinctness, pithiness. PROLIXITY
briefness, shortness, transience, ephemerality.

**brew** ferment, infuse, boil, stew, steep, soak, prepare, make.
plot, hatch, contrive, devise, concoct, design, plan.

**bribe** *v*, suborn, corrupt, square, tempt, entice, lure, reward.
*n*, inducement, enticement, reward, backhander (*inf*), graft, hush money (*inf*).

**bridal** nuptial, conjugal, matrimonial, marital, connubial, wedding, marriage.

**bridge** *n*, span, arch, flyover, viaduct, overpass.
*v*, span, traverse, cross, connect, unite, join. DIVIDE

**bridle** *n*, curb, restraint, check, control, halter.
*v*, curb, restrain, check, control, govern, master. RELEASE
bristle, be indignant, raise one's hackles, get angry.

**brief** *adj*, short, fleeting, transitory, transient, ephemeral, momentary, temporary. LONG
concise, terse, succinct, pithy, laconic, curt, abrupt, brusque. LENGTHY
*n*, abstract, synopsis, outline, summary, epitome, digest.
*v*, instruct, inform, fill in (*inf*), enlighten, explain, prepare, advise.

**briefly** in brief, in short, in a nutshell, concisely.
momentarily, in passing, fleetingly, hurriedly.

**brigade** group, party, troop, squad, unit, team, crew, corps, company.

**brigand** bandit, robber, outlaw, ruffian, thug, desperado, gangster, marauder, plunderer.

**bright** luminous, shining, brilliant, radiant, gleaming, glittering, sparkling, flashing, glowing, glossy, lustrous, resplendent, glorious, dazzling, vivid, intense. DULL
intelligent, clever, smart, acute, keen, sharp, astute, quick-witted. STUPID
cheerful, happy, gay, merry, jolly, genial, lively, vivacious. MISERABLE
favourable, auspicious, promising, encouraging, rosy.
clear, transparent, translucent, lucid, limpid. MUDDY

**brighten** illuminate, lighten, clear, grow bright, shine, polish, enhance. DARKEN
enliven, cheer, gladden, hearten, encourage, perk up, buck up (*inf*). DISHEARTEN

**brilliance** brightness, radiance, brilliancy, lustre, sheen, glitter, sparkle, splendour, magnificence. DULLNESS
excellence, distinction, talent, genius, wisdom, cleverness. MEDIOCRITY

**brilliant** bright, radiant, shining, sparkling, glittering, lustrous, intense, vivid, dazzling, splendid, magnificent. DULL
excellent, outstanding, exceptional, distinguished, illustrious, eminent, famous, accomplished, expert, talented, gifted, intelligent, clever, bright, brainy. MEDIOCRE

**brim** rim, lip, edge, brink, margin, verge. CENTRE

**brindled** mottled, speckled, patched, spotted, dappled, streaked, tabby.

**brine** salt water, sea water, sea, saline solution, pickle.

**bring** bear, carry, convey, conduct, lead, usher, escort, accompany, take, fetch. REMOVE
cause, engender, produce, result in.
draw, pull, attract, prompt, force, compel.
**bring about,** cause, effect, occasion, accomplish, achieve, realize.
**bring in,** yield, fetch, return, produce, profit, earn.

**bring up,** raise, rear, nurture, train, educate, teach.
propose, put forward, raise, mention, introduce, broach.

**brink** border, edge, rim, margin, verge, threshold, bank, shore, boundary, limit. CENTRE

**brisk** lively, active, animated, vigorous, energetic, agile, nimble, spry, quick, alert. SLUGGISH
sharp, keen, crisp, fresh, invigorating, bracing. OPPRESSIVE

**bristle** *n*, hair, whisker, barb, spine, prickle.
*v*, stand up, rise, prickle.
be indignant, be angry, bridle, seethe, flare up.
swarm, teem, crawl, be alive, abound.

**brittle** fragile, frail, delicate, crisp, breakable, frangible, crumbly, friable. FLEXIBLE

**broach** introduce, suggest, mention, bring up, open, propose, advance.
open, tap, pierce, uncork, break into. SEAL

**broad** wide, ample, vast, large, extensive, spacious, roomy, capacious. NARROW
wide-ranging, full, comprehensive, sweeping, all-embracing, universal, general. LIMITED
vulgar, coarse, indecent, blue, gross.

**broadcast** *v*, transmit, relay, show, air, publish, proclaim, announce, advertise, disseminate, spread.
*n*, show, programme, transmission.

**broaden** widen, enlarge, amplify, expand, swell, develop, augment, increase. RESTRICT

**broad-minded** liberal, tolerant, indulgent, permissive, unbiased, dispassionate, open-minded, catholic. NARROW-MINDED

**broadside** attack, assault, bombardment, criticism, censure, abuse.

**brochure** leaflet, pamphlet, booklet, handbill, circular, advertisement.

**broil** *n*, quarrel, dispute, row, brawl, scuffle, wrangle, fray, fracas.
*v*, quarrel, dispute, brawl, wrangle.

**broke** penniless, insolvent, bankrupt, ruined, skint (*inf*). RICH

**broken** shattered, smashed, fractured, ruptured, torn, rent, separated, destroyed. MENDED
imperfect, defective, feeble, weakened, spent, exhausted, run-down, demoralized, beaten.
discontinuous, interrupted, disconnected, fragmentary, intermittent, spasmodic. CONTINUOUS
halting, imperfect, hesitant, disjointed, stammering. FLUENT

**brokenhearted** inconsolable, desolate, sorrowful, grief-stricken, miserable, wretched, heartbroken, crestfallen, disappointed. DELIGHTED

**broker** agent, middleman, intermediary, factor, dealer.

**brooch** pin, clasp.

**brood** *v*, ponder, muse, meditate, reflect, ruminate, dwell on.
*n*, litter, clutch, offspring, family, young, progeny, issue.

**brook**[1] *n*, stream, beck, rivulet, rill, burn.

**brook**[2] *v*, bear, endure, suffer, stand, abide, tolerate, put up with (*inf*), allow.

**brother** sibling, kinsman, comrade, mate, companion, friend, colleague, associate, partner. SISTER

**brotherhood** fraternity, society, association, club, league, union, guild.
brotherliness, comradeship, friendliness, fellowship, camaraderie.

**brotherly** fraternal, friendly, affectionate, kind, sympathetic, benevolent, philanthropic. UNKIND

**brow** forehead, temple, front, eyebrow, face, countenance, appearance.
brink, verge, edge, rim, crown, summit, peak, top.

**browbeat** bully, intimidate, cow, overbear, domineer, badger, hector.

**brown** chestnut, bronze, copper, rust, auburn, ginger, tan, tawny, chocolate, coffee, hazel, umber, brunette.
tanned, bronzed, sunburnt. PALE

**browse** scan, glance at, skim, dip into, leaf through, peruse, look around.
nibble, crop, feed, graze.

**bruise** *v*, contuse, injure, damage, batter, pound, crush, mark, discolour, blacken.
offend, injure, wound, hurt.
*n*, contusion, discoloration, mark, blemish, injury.

**brunt** shock, force, full force, impact, violence, stress, strain.

**brush**[1] *n*, broom, besom, hairbrush, paintbrush.
skirmish, clash, encounter, engagement, contest, fight, scrap (*inf*).
*v*, sweep, wipe, clean, dust, groom.

touch, graze, stroke, kiss, scrape.
**brush up,** relearn, revise, study, polish.
**brush**[2] *n*, scrub, thicket, undergrowth, bushes, copse.
**brush-off** rejection, snub, slight, rebuff, cold shoulder.
**brusque** curt, abrupt, short, gruff, bluff, blunt, rude, unceremonious. POLITE
**brutal** cruel, inhuman, pitiless, merciless, savage, ferocious, vicious, barbarous, ruthless, remorseless. HUMANE
harsh, severe, gruff, rude, uncivil, callous, heartless, unfeeling. GENTLE
coarse, crude, gross, vulgar, brutish, uncouth, carnal, sensual. REFINED
**brutality** cruelty, inhumanity, savagery, ferocity, harshness, severity, barbarism, atrocity, pitilessness, ruthlessness. HUMANITY
**brute** *n*, animal, beast, creature.
barbarian, savage, monster, ogre, devil, fiend, swine.
*adj*, physical, bodily, carnal, sensual, bestial, savage, brutish, coarse, rude, uncivilized.
instinctive, mindless, unthinking.
**bubble** *n*, blob, drop, bead, globule, blister, vesicle.
*v*, foam, froth, seethe, boil, fizz, effervesce.
gurgle, burble, babble, murmur.
**buccaneer** pirate, corsair, freebooter, privateer, sea-rover.
**buck** spring, jump, leap, prance, jerk, throw, unseat.
**buck up,** cheer up, encourage, brighten, hearten.
hasten, hurry, speed up, get a move on.
**buckle** *n*, clasp, clip, fastener, catch, hasp.
*v*, bow, bend, warp, distort, contort, twist, bulge, crumple, collapse, cave in.
fasten, secure, close, clasp.
**bud** *n*, shoot, germ, sprout, burgeon.
*v*, sprout, shoot, burgeon, germinate, grow, develop, burst forth. WITHER
**budge** move, stir, go, shift, push, dislodge, give way.
**budget** *n*, estimate, statement, cost, funds, resources, allocation, allowance.
*v*, plan, cost, estimate, allocate.
**buffer** bumper, shock absorber, cushion, fender, shield, guard.
**buffet**[1] *n*, cafeteria, snack bar, counter, bar, table, sideboard.
**buffet**[2] *v*, knock, bump, batter, pound, strike, hit, beat, box, thump, slap.
*n*, knock, bump, stroke, slap, cuff, hit, blow, thump.
**buffoon** jester, clown, harlequin, fool, comic, comedian, joker, wag.
**buffoonery** clowning, jesting, drollery, tomfoolery, silliness, nonsense. WISDOM
**bug** *n*, germ, virus, bacterium, infection, disease.
flaw, defect, error, fault, imperfection.
*v*, irritate, annoy, vex, bother, pester, harass, plague.
eavesdrop, tap, listen in.
**bugbear** bogey, hobgoblin, ogre, nightmare, bane, pet hate, *bête noire*, anathema.
**build** *v*, erect, put up, raise, construct, make, fabricate, assemble, put together, form. DEMOLISH
base, establish, found, originate, institute.
**build up,** develop, increase, expand, amplify, intensify, strengthen, reinforce.
*n*, physique, body, figure, form, shape.
**building** edifice, erection, construction, structure, house, pile.
**bulbous** rounded, swollen, bloated, bulging.
**bulge** *v*, swell, expand, dilate, distend, balloon, protrude, stick out.
*n*, swelling, lump, bump, protuberance, protrusion, projection. HOLLOW
**bulk** size, volume, mass, magnitude, dimensions, substance, largeness, immensity, bulkiness.
majority, preponderance, greater part, lion's share, body, mass, most. MINORITY
**bulky** large, big, massive, huge, enormous, colossal, unwieldy, cumbersome, unmanageable, awkward. SMALL
**bulletin** announcement, news flash, statement, report, communiqué, dispatch.
**bully** *n*, browbeater, ruffian, tough, hector, tormentor, persecutor, oppressor, intimidator.
*v*, browbeat, intimidate, overbear, domineer, hector, coerce, terrorize, torment, persecute, harass, tyrannize.
**bulwark** rampart, fortification, redoubt, bastion, outwork, buttress.
buffer, guard, security, support, mainstay.
**bump** *v*, knock, bang, strike, hit, collide, crash.
jostle, bounce, jolt, jar.

**bump into,** come across, meet, encounter, run into, chance upon.
*n*, blow, knock, bang, crash, collision, impact, shock, jar, jolt.
swelling, lump, protuberance.
**bumper** generous, abundant, plentiful, excellent, exceptional, large, jumbo (*inf*), whopping (*inf*), massive. MEAGRE
**bumpkin** rustic, peasant, yokel, clown, oaf, boor, lubber, clod.
**bumptious** conceited, vain, arrogant, self-assertive, pushy (*inf*), overbearing, cocky. MODEST
**bunch** cluster, clump, collection, assortment, group, bundle, sheaf, bouquet, tuft, batch, lot, heap, pile, mass.
**bundle** bunch, sheaf, collection, batch, parcel, package, pack, packet, bale, heap, pile, stack.
**bungle** botch, mismanage, mess up, spoil, mar, screw up (*inf*). ACCOMPLISH
**bungler** botcher, fumbler, incompetent, novice, dunce, duffer (*inf*), butterfingers (*inf*). ADEPT
**bungling** awkward, clumsy, maladroit, gauche, incompetent, inept, ham-fisted (*inf*). ADROIT
**bunker** container, bin, chest, tank.
obstacle, hazard.
**bunkum** nonsense, claptrap, balderdash, rubbish, twaddle, bunk (*inf*), rot (*inf*), poppycock (*inf*).
**buoy** *n*, float, marker, signal, beacon, guide.
*v*, cheer, hearten, encourage, sustain, support. DEPRESS
**buoyancy** lightness, weightlessness, floatability. HEAVINESS
cheerfulness, joy, high spirits, gaiety, liveliness, animation. DESPONDENCY
**buoyant** light, weightless, floating, floatable. HEAVY
cheerful, gay, bright, breezy, light-hearted, lively, vivacious, animated, carefree, blithe. DESPONDENT
**burden** *n*, load, weight, millstone, onus, responsibility, encumbrance, impediment, trouble, affliction, trial, worry, strain, sorrow.
cargo, freight, load, capacity, tonnage.
*v*, load, weigh down, saddle, oppress, overload, afflict, trouble, encumber, tax. RELIEVE
**bureau** desk, chest, dresser.
department, office, agency, branch, division.
**burglar** housebreaker, robber, thief, picklock, safe-cracker.
**burial** burying, interment, inhumation, entombment, funeral, obsequies. EXHUMATION
**burlesque** *n*, caricature, parody, satire, lampoon, travesty, take-off (*inf*).
*adj*, caricatural, parodic, ludicrous, comic, mocking, satirical, ironical, mock-heroic, hudibrastic.
**burly** sturdy, stout, stocky, thickset, well-built, strong, powerful, hefty, strapping. FRAIL
**burn** flame, blaze, flare, flicker, glow, smoulder.
ignite, light, set on fire, kindle, incinerate. EXTINGUISH
scorch, char, singe, sear, toast, parch, scald.
smart, sting, tingle.
**burning** flaming, blazing, fiery, hot, glowing, ardent, fervent, intense, passionate, vehement, earnest. COOL
urgent, pressing, crucial, vital, essential. UNIMPORTANT
**burnish** polish, shine, buff, furbish, glaze, brighten. DULL
**burrow** *n*, tunnel, hole, den, lair, retreat.
*v*, dig, excavate, scoop out, tunnel.
**bursar** treasurer, cashier.
**burst** *v*, explode, blow up, puncture, split, crack, rupture, break, bust (*inf*), shatter.
erupt, rush, gush, spout, surge.
*n*, explosion, blast, blasting, break, split, rupture, breach.
eruption, outburst, torrent, gush, outbreak, spate, fit.
**bury** inter, inhume, entomb, lay to rest. EXHUME
cover, conceal, hide, secrete.
sink, embed, submerge, engulf, immerse, engross.
**bush** shrub, hedge, thicket, undergrowth, brush, scrub.
**bushy** thick, shaggy, luxuriant, fuzzy, bristly.
**business** occupation, trade, craft, profession, employment, work, job, vocation, calling, pursuit, career. LEISURE
company, firm, organization, concern, partnership.
commerce, trade, dealings, industry, transaction.

affair, concern, problem, matter, issue, responsibility, duty, function.

**businesslike** efficient, orderly, methodical, systematic, thorough, assiduous, correct, professional.

**bust** chest, bosom, breast.

**bustle** *v*, hurry, rush, scamper, scurry, scuttle, stir, fuss, flutter.
*n*, fuss, flurry, activity, commotion, stir, ado, hurry, haste. CALM

**busy** occupied, engaged, employed, engrossed, involved. FREE
industrious, diligent, sedulous, assiduous, active, energetic, on the go (*inf*), bustling, astir. IDLE
nosy, inquisitive, fussy, officious, interfering, meddling.

**busybody** meddler, snooper, nosy parker (*inf*), eavesdropper, gossip, scandalmonger.

**but** *conj*, yet, still, on the contrary, however, nevertheless.
*prep*, except, save, barring, notwithstanding.
*adv*, only, merely, just, simply.

**butcher** *v*, slaughter, massacre, kill, slay, murder, assassinate, mutilate, destroy.
*n*, slaughterer, killer, murderer, assassin, destroyer.

**butchery** slaughter, massacre, carnage, blood bath, murder, bloodshed.

**butt**[1] *n*, stock, shaft, handle, end, stub.

**butt**[2] *n*, target, object, subject, victim, laughing stock.

**butt**[3] *v*, push, shove, ram, poke, prod, bump, knock.
**butt in,** interfere, meddle, intrude, interrupt, chip in (*inf*).

**butt**[4] *n*, cask, barrel.

**buttocks** rump, hindquarters, rear, posterior, seat, behind (*inf*), bottom, bum (*inf*).

**buttonhole** accost, waylay, catch, grab, detain, importune, bore.

**buttress** support, stay, prop, strut, brace, shore.

**buxom** plump, healthy, lusty, ample, full-bosomed, voluptuous, hearty, lively, jolly, attractive, comely, bonny. THIN

**buy** purchase, pay for, procure, obtain, acquire, get. SELL
bribe, corrupt, suborn.

**buzz** hum, murmur, drone, ring, purr, whisper, hiss.

**by** *prep*, through, via, over, past, along, beside, near, next to, at, on, before.
*adv*, near, aside, past, beyond.

**bygone** past, gone by, departed, former, erstwhile, previous, ancient, of old. FUTURE

**bypass** *v*, avoid, get round, circumvent, overlook, neglect, ignore.

**bystander** onlooker, spectator, observer, witness, watcher, viewer, passer-by.

**byword** slogan, motto, epithet, saying, proverb, maxim, adage, aphorism, precept.

# C

**cab** taxi, taxicab, minicab, hackney.

**cabal** clique, coterie, faction, junta, league, party, gang, coalition, confederacy.
plot, intrigue, conspiracy, scheme.

**cabaret** show, floor show, entertainment, nightclub, club, discotheque, disco (*inf*).

**cabbalistic** mystic, occult, secret, mysterious, cryptic, obscure, esoteric. PATENT

**cabin** shed, hut, cottage, shack, chalet, lodge, shanty, hovel.
room, apartment, compartment, berth.

**cabinet** dresser, commode, cupboard, chiffonier, chest, locker, case.
council, assembly, ministry, administration, committee.

**cable** line, wire, rope, cord.
cablegram, telegram, message.

**cache** hiding place, repository, store, hoard, stockpile, supply, reserve.

**cackle** cluck, crow, squawk, quack.
chuckle, giggle, snigger, titter, laugh.
chatter, gabble, jabber, prattle, prate, babble.

**cacophonous** discordant, dissonant, inharmonious, jarring, harsh, strident, grating, raucous, cacophonic. HARMONIOUS

**cacophony** discord, dissonance, stridency, jarring, jar, caterwauling. CONCORD

**cad** scoundrel, rogue, rascal, knave, rotter (*inf*), heel (*inf*), bounder (*inf*).

**cadaver** corpse, body, remains, stiff (*inf*).

**cadaverous** deathly, deathlike, ghastly, pallid, pale, ashen, wan, haggard, gaunt, emaciated. RUDDY

**cadence** intonation, tone, modulation, inflection, accent, rhythm, lilt, swing.

**cadre** nucleus, core, key group, framework, infrastructure.

**café** cafeteria, snack bar, bistro, restaurant, teashop, tearoom, coffee bar.

**cage** *n*, enclosure, pen, pound, box, aviary.
*v*, confine, fence in, coop up, impound, imprison, incarcerate, restrain, restrict. FREE

**cagey** cautious, guarded, wary, discreet, noncommittal, evasive. FRANK

**cajole** coax, wheedle, persuade, beguile, tempt, entice, lure, entrap, inveigle, flatter, blandish, dupe.

**cajolery** coaxing, wheedling, persuasion, beguilement, temptation, enticement, flattery, blandishments, blarny, soft soap (*inf*), sweet talk (*inf*).

**cake** *n*, lump, block, bar, slab, piece, mass.
pastry, bun, tart, patisserie, gâteau, biscuit.
*v*, solidify, congeal, harden, bake, encrust.

**calamitous** disastrous, catastrophic, dire, devastating, ruinous, ill-starred, ill-fated, unfortunate, unlucky, adverse, deplorable, dreadful, tragic, woeful. FORTUNATE

**calamity** disaster, catastrophe, misfortune, adversity, hardship, affliction, trouble, setback, reverse, blow, trial, tribulation, distress, woe. BLESSING

**calculate** compute, reckon, work out, count, enumerate, measure, gauge, estimate, value, assess, weigh, consider.

**calculated** aimed, adapted, designed, planned, intended, considered, intentional, deliberate, premeditated.

**calculating** crafty, scheming, devious, cunning, sly, shrewd, sharp, cautious, wary, politic, circumspect, far-sighted. DIRECT

**calculation** computation, reckoning, working out, estimation, forecast, valuation, assessment.
foresight, forethought, prudence, care, caution, discretion, circumspection, wariness, deliberation. RASHNESS

**calendar** almanac, chronology, list, schedule, register, agenda.

**calibre** gauge, diameter, bore.
capacity, ability, faculty, talent, gifts, endowment, distinction, merit, worth, quality.

**call** *v*, shout, cry, yell, exclaim, call out. WHISPER
name, dub, christen, entitle, designate, label, term, style, proclaim, announce.
summon, invite, bid, convene, convoke, muster, assemble. DISMISS
ring, ring up, telephone, phone.
rouse, arouse, waken, wake up, awaken.
**call for,** demand, require, necessitate, involve, entail.
fetch, pick up, collect.
**call off,** cancel, abandon, postpone.
**call on,** visit, look up, drop in on.
invoke, appeal to, call upon, request.
*n*, shout, cry, exclamation, yell, scream.
summons, signal, appeal, request, invitation, command, claim, demand.
need, cause, occasion, grounds, excuse, reason, justification.

**calling** vocation, mission, career, profession, occupation, métier, trade, craft, business, job, work, pursuit.

**callous** unfeeling, insensible, insensitive, hard, hardened, obdurate, cold, unsympathetic, indifferent, uncaring, apathetic, hard-hearted, heartless. TENDER

**callow** green, inexperienced, naive, ingenuous, jejune, immature, simple, unsophisticated, guileless. EXPERIENCED

**calm** *adj*, serene, tranquil, peaceful, still, smooth, quiet, mild. STORMY
placid, composed, self-possessed, collected, unruffled, unexcited, unmoved, cool, impassive, relaxed, sedate, imperturbable. AGITATED
*v*, pacify, placate, appease, mollify, still, quiet, hush, lull, allay, assuage, soothe, alleviate, compose, relax, sedate, tranquillize. AGITATE
*n*, calmness, peace, serenity, tranquillity, stillness, lull, smoothness, quiet, hush. STORM

**calmness** calm, peacefulness, serenity, tranquillity, quietness, stillness. DISTURBANCE
composure, self-possession, placidity, coolness, equanimity, poise, sang-froid. AGITATION

**calumniate** slander, libel, defame, vilify, malign, asperse, denigrate, blacken, traduce, detract, revile, abuse, insult. EULOGIZE

**calumnious** slanderous, libellous, defamatory, derogatory, aspersive, abusive, scurrilous, insulting, vituperative. COMPLIMENTARY

**calumny** slander, libel, misrepresentation, defamation, aspersion, slur, smear, denigration, vituperation, abuse, insult, vilification, obloquy, revilement. EULOGY
**camaraderie** comradeship, companionship, fellowship, brotherhood, brotherliness, friendliness, esprit de corps. ENMITY
**camber** curve, arch, curvature, convexity.
**camouflage** *n*, disguise, mask, cloak, screen, veil, blind, guise, front, covering, concealment, subterfuge, deception.
*v*, disguise, mask, screen, veil, cover, conceal, hide. EXPOSE
**camp**[1] *n*, encampment, cantonment, bivouac, tents, cabins, quarters.
faction, clique, party, group, set, sect.
*v*, encamp, pitch one's tent, settle, lodge.
**camp**[2] *adj*, effeminate, gay (*inf*), limp-wristed, mannered, affected, studied, extravagant, ostentatious, posing, posturing, theatrical.
**campaign** operation, exercise, expedition, crusade, drive, fight, battle, attack, offensive.
**can** *n*, container, receptacle, tin, jar.
*v*, tin, preserve.
**canaille** populace, masses, mob, rabble, proletariat, plebs, hoi polloi, riffraff, scum. NOBILITY
**canal** channel, waterway, watercourse.
duct, tube, pipe, passage.
**cancel** annul, nullify, revoke, repeal, rescind, countermand, abrogate, quash, call off. CONFIRM
obliterate, erase, delete, expunge, cross out, efface, eliminate, abolish, do away with. RETAIN
neutralize, counterbalance, compensate for, offset, make up for.
**cancellation** annulment, repeal, revocation, abrogation, deletion, obliteration, elimination, abolition. CONFIRMATION
**cancer** tumour, carcinoma, malignancy, growth, canker, blight, evil, scourge, corruption.
**candid** frank, open, straightforward, honest, truthful, sincere, plain, blunt, forthright, outspoken, unreserved, fair, unbiased, impartial, guileless, artless, naive, ingenuous. DEVIOUS
**candidate** aspirant, applicant, claimant, suitor, nominee, contestant, competitor, contender, entrant, runner.
**candle** taper, light, torch.
**candour** frankness, openness, straightforwardness, honesty, sincerity, plainness, bluntness, forthrightness, fairness, impartiality, artlessness, naiveté, ingenuousness. DEVIOUSNESS
**cane** *n*, stick, staff, rod.
*v*, beat, thrash, flog, whip, strike.
**canker** *n*, abscess, ulcer, infection, lesion, sore, chancre.
blight, bane, evil, corruption, rot, curse, scourge, pestilence.
*v*, infect, blight, corrupt, pollute, poison, envenom, rot, corrode, erode, eat away. PURIFY
**cannonade** bombardment, shelling, battery, barrage, assault, broadside, volley, salvo.
**canny** astute, shrewd, knowing, perspicacious, discerning, sharp, acute, subtle, sagacious, prudent, cautious, circumspect.
**canon** law, rule, decree, edict, precept, statute, formula, standard, principle, criterion.
catalogue, list, roll.
**canonical** authorized, accepted, approved, recognized, orthodox. UNORTHODOX
**canopy** awning, baldachin, shade, cover, tarpaulin, tester, tilt.
**cant**[1] hypocrisy, insincerity, lip service, false piety, sanctimoniousness, platitudes.
jargon, lingo, argot, slang, patter.
**cant**[2] inclination, slope, slant, tilt, angle, bevel.
**cantankerous** irascible, testy, crabby, bad-tempered, peevish, irritable, crotchety (*inf*), grumpy, ill-humoured, perverse, contrary, quarrelsome, argumentative. AFFABLE
**canteen** cafeteria, snack bar, restaurant, dining room.
bottle, flask, canister.
**canter** amble, trot, jog, lope, gallop.
**canticle** hymn, song, psalm, poem.
**canting** hypocritical, insincere, two-faced, sanctimonious.
**canvas** sailcloth, tarpaulin, ticking, drill, painting, tent.
**canvass** *v*, electioneer, solicit votes, campaign, poll, survey.
examine, sift, scrutinize, investigate, study, inspect.
debate, discuss, dispute, air.

*n*, inspection, scrutiny, examination, investigation, study, survey, poll.

**canyon** ravine, gulch, gully, gorge, chasm.

**cap** *n*, hat, headgear, beret, bonnet, covering, cover, lid.
top, peak, summit, apex, acme. FOOT
*v*, cover, top, surmount, crown, complete, perfect, surpass, exceed, excel, outdo.

**capability** ability, capacity, faculty, means, potential, power, proficiency, skill, aptitude. INCAPABILITY

**capable** able, competent, proficient, adequate, fitted, suited, qualified, adept, clever, skilful, gifted, intelligent, efficient, accomplished. INCOMPETENT

**capacious** spacious, roomy, ample, wide, broad, large, vast, immense, voluminous, extensive, comprehensive. NARROW

**capaciousness** spaciousness, roominess, ampleness, vastness, immensity. NARROWNESS

**capacitate** enable, empower, qualify, authorize, sanction. PREVENT

**capacity** volume, dimensions, size, magnitude, amplitude, scope, extent, range, compass.
ability, capability, competence, aptitude, faculty, power, strength, talent, gift, skill, genius, intelligence, cleverness, readiness, facility. INABILITY
position, office, post, function, role, sphere, province, duty, service.

**cape** headland, promontory, peninsula, point.

**caper** *v*, frolic, gambol, frisk, romp, hop, skip, jump, leap, bound, spring, dance, cavort, prance.
*n*, frolic, romp, hop, skip, jump, leap, bound, spring.
prank, practical joke, stunt, antic, escapade, sport, jest, lark (*inf*).

**capital** *adj*, principal, chief, main, leading, major, key, cardinal, first, primary, foremost, paramount, prime, important. MINOR
excellent, first-rate, splendid, fine, superb. POOR
*n*, assets, funds, cash, finance, investments, stock, principal, resources, means, wealth, property.

**capitalist** financier, investor, banker, tycoon.

**capitalize** take advantage of, profit by, turn to account, exploit, realize.

**capitulate** yield, surrender, submit, give in, relent. RESIST

**capitulation** yielding, surrender, submission, acquiescence. RESISTANCE

**caprice** whim, whimsy, vagary, notion, impulse, fancy, humour, crotchet, freak, quirk, oddity.

**capricious** fickle, inconstant, changeable, mercurial, whimsical, fanciful, freakish, impulsive, wayward, odd, queer, erratic, fitful, irresolute, uncertain. FIRM

**capsize** upturn, overturn, upset, keel over, turn turtle (*inf*), turn over, tip over.

**capsule** lozenge, tablet, pill.
case, sheath, covering, shell, pod, seed vessel, receptacle.

**captain** commander, leader, head, chief, chieftain, pilot, skipper, master, officer.

**caption** title, heading, legend, inscription, explanation, note, comment.

**captious** carping, cavilling, hypercritical, censorious, fault-finding, nit-picking (*inf*). APPRECIATIVE
cantankerous, touchy, irritable, testy, peevish, crabbed, waspish, acrimonious, cross. AFFABLE

**captivate** fascinate, charm, enchant, bewitch, enthral, entrance, enamour, delight, transport, attract, allure, seduce, win. REPEL

**captivating** fascinating, charming, enchanting, delightful, attractive, winning. REPULSIVE

**captive** prisoner, hostage, slave, convict, detainee.

**captivity** imprisonment, incarceration, confinement, custody, detention, internment, duress, bondage, slavery, servitude, thraldom. FREEDOM

**capture** *v*, catch, take, seize, collar (*inf*), arrest, apprehend, take prisoner. RELEASE
*n*, catching, seizure, arrest, apprehension. RELEASE

**car** automobile, vehicle, motorcar, cab, limousine, jalopy (*inf*), wheels (*inf*).

**carafe** flask, decanter, bottle, flagon, jug, pitcher.

**carcass** corpse, body, cadaver, remains, stiff (*inf*).
structure, framework, skeleton, hulk, shell.

**cardinal** principal, chief, main, capital, vital, essential, fundamental, central, key, primary, first, leading, foremost, paramount, important. SECONDARY

**care** *n*, concern, anxiety, trouble, worry, affliction, distress, sorrow, pressure, strain, burden, responsibility. INDIFFERENCE
attention, heed, caution, prudence, pains, carefulness, regard, consideration, watchfulness, vigilance, circumspection, forethought. CARELESSNESS
protection, keeping, custody, guardianship, charge, control, supervision.
*v*, worry, be concerned, mind, bother, give a damn (*inf*).
**care for,** tend, nurse, minister to, attend, mind, look after, protect. NEGLECT
like, enjoy, be fond of, fancy, want, desire.

**career** *n*, calling, vocation, occupation, profession, work, job, livelihood.
progress, path, course, passage.
*v*, rush, dash, hurtle, speed, race, tear, bolt.

**carefree** cheerful, light-hearted, buoyant, blithe, untroubled, happy-go-lucky, nonchalant, breezy. ANXIOUS

**careful** cautious, wary, prudent, circumspect, judicious, vigilant, watchful, heedful, mindful. INCAUTIOUS
attentive, thoughtful, conscientious, painstaking, meticulous, scrupulous, thorough, precise. CARELESS

**careless** negligent, remiss, heedless, unmindful, thoughtless, unthinking, forgetful, imprudent, rash, hasty, inattentive, unguarded. PRUDENT
neglectful, sloppy, slipshod, untidy, disorderly, slapdash, offhand, lackadaisical, nonchalant, unconcerned, casual, indifferent. CAREFUL

**carelessness** inattention, neglect, negligence, heedlessness, thoughtlessness, imprudence, rashness. CARE

**caress** *n*, pat, stroke, touch, fondling, hug, cuddle, embrace, kiss.
*v*, stroke, fondle, pet, pat, touch, hug, cuddle, embrace, kiss. PUNISH

**caretaker** janitor, curator, custodian, keeper, warden, porter.

**cargo** load, lading, burden, freight, consignment, shipment, goods, merchandise.

**caricature** cartoon, representation, lampoon, burlesque, parody, take-off (*inf*), send-up (*inf*), travesty, satire, distortion.

**carnage** butchery, slaughter, massacre, holocaust, blood bath, bloodshed, mass murder.

**carnal** sensual, fleshly, voluptuous, licentious, lascivious, prurient, salacious, lewd, lecherous, lustful, libidinous, wanton, impure, base. CHASTE
physical, human, corporeal, natural, unspiritual, worldly, earthly, temporal, secular, profane. SPIRITUAL

**carnality** sensuality, voluptuousness, lust, lechery, prurience, salaciousness, lewdness.
earthliness, worldliness, corporeality, secularity.

**carnival** festival, fair, gala, jamboree, celebration, festivity, revel, masquerade, merrymaking, revelry.

**carol** *n*, song, hymn, canticle, noel, chorus, ditty, lay.
*v*, sing, chant, troll, warble, chirp.

**carousal** revel, revelry, merrymaking, carouse, spree, bacchanalia, drinking bout, booze-up (*inf*), binge (*inf*), debauch, orgy, saturnalia.

**carouse** drink, booze (*inf*), make merry, revel, roister, wassail.

**carp** cavil, censure, hypercriticize, find fault, quibble, complain, nag, reproach. PRAISE

**carpenter** joiner, woodworker, cabinet-maker.

**carping** cavilling, hypercritical, critical, captious, fault-finding, censorious, hard to please, nit-picking (*inf*). APPRECIATIVE

**carriage** carrying, conveyance, transport, transportation, freight, delivery.
vehicle, conveyance, coach, cab, car.
bearing, demeanour, mien, air, posture, deportment, conduct, behaviour.

**carry** bear, take, transport, convey, transmit, transfer, move, bring, fetch.
support, sustain, uphold, hold up, bear, maintain, shoulder. DROP
impel, drive, urge, spur, propel, influence. DETER
extend, reach, spread.
win, secure, gain, accomplish, effect. LOSE
**carry on,** continue, go on, persist, persevere, keep going. STOP
conduct, run, administer, manage, operate.
**carry out,** perform, execute, effect, implement, discharge, fulfil, complete, accomplish, achieve, realize.

**cart** wagon, barrow, handcart, vehicle, carriage.

**carton** box, container, case, packet, pack, package.

**cartoon** caricature, lampoon, satire, sketch, line drawing, comic strip.

**cartridge** capsule, cylinder, case, magazine, cassette, container.

**carve** cut, chisel, sculpt, fashion, mould, form, whittle, incise, engrave, etch, hew, slice, divide.

**carving** sculpture, model, engraving, etching.

**cascade** waterfall, cataract, torrent, deluge, flood.

**case**[1] instance, occurrence, occasion, example, illustration, specimen.
situation, state, event, circumstance, condition, predicament, plight.
action, suit, lawsuit, dispute, cause, trial, process, proceedings, testimony, evidence, plea.

**case**[2] box, chest, trunk, crate, carton, package, container, receptacle.
covering, capsule, sheath, shell, pod, envelope, wrapper, jacket, holder, socket.

**cash** money, coin, specie, currency, ready money, banknotes, coins, change, payment.

**cashier**[1] *n*, teller, bank clerk, bursar, banker, treasurer, accountant.

**cashier**[2] *v*, dismiss, discharge, expel, drum out, reject, discard.

**casino** gaming house, gambling den, club.

**cask** barrel, vat, keg, vessel, container.

**casket** box, chest, coffer, case, receptacle.

**cast** *v*, throw, fling, pitch, sling, hurl, toss, chuck, launch, send, drive, thrust, impel. KEEP
radiate, diffuse, emit, spread, scatter, distribute, direct.
shed, drop, throw off, discard, reject. RETAIN
shape, mould, form, model.
compute, calculate, reckon, figure.
*n*, throw, toss, fling, thrust.
mould, shape, form, stamp, style, tone, look, air, manner, bearing, mien, demeanour.
tinge, shade, touch, trace, suggestion.
actors, players, performers, characters, dramatis personae, company, troupe.

**castaway** *n*, outcast, exile, wanderer, vagabond, discard, cast-off.
*adj*, shipwrecked, adrift, marooned, stranded, discarded, rejected.

**caste** class, order, rank, status, position, station, race, lineage.

**castigate** chastise, rebuke, reprimand, censure, berate, upbraid, correct, discipline, punish, whip, beat, cane, flog, thrash, lash. CARESS

**castigation** chastisement, rebuke, censure, upbraiding, correction, discipline, punishment, beating, flogging, caning, thrashing.

**castle** citadel, keep, fortress, stronghold, palace, mansion, chateau.

**castrate** geld, emasculate, neuter, spay, unman, weaken.
expurgate, censor, bowdlerize, purge.

**castration** gelding, emasculation, orchidectomy, oophorectomy.

**casual** accidental, chance, fortuitous, unexpected, unforeseen, unplanned, incidental, occasional, contingent, random, irregular. DELIBERATE
informal, unceremonious, offhand, nonchalant, easy-going, relaxed, blasé, indifferent, apathetic, unconcerned. FORMAL

**casualty** victim, sufferer, fatality, loss, injured person, dead person. SURVIVOR
accident, mishap, misfortune, disaster, calamity, catastrophe, blow. BLESSING

**casuistry** sophistry, sophism, quibbling, equivocation, subtlety, chicanery, speciousness.

**cataclysm** upheaval, convulsion, debacle, collapse, catastrophe, disaster, calamity, deluge, flood, inundation, avalanche.

**catacomb** crypt, tomb, vault, sepulchre, ossuary.

**catalogue** list, inventory, register, roll, record, file, index, directory, schedule.

**catapult** *n*, sling, ballista, trebuchet.
*v*, hurl, propel, shoot, launch, pitch, toss.

**cataract** cascade, waterfall, falls, rapids, deluge, downpour.

**catastrophe** disaster, calamity, cataclysm, blow, reverse, misfortune, affliction, adversity, distress, tragedy, mishap, trouble, trial, failure, fiasco, flop (*inf*). TRIUMPH culmination, climax, dénouement, debacle, end, conclusion, termination, finale, upshot, issue. BEGINNING

**catastrophic** disastrous, calamitous, dire, terrible, tragic, distressing.

**catcall** boo, hiss, whistle, raspberry, hoot, cry, jeer.

**catch** *v*, take, seize, snatch, grab, grasp, grip, clutch. DROP
capture, nab (*inf*), arrest, apprehend, snare, ensnare, trap, entrap, entangle, hook, net. RELEASE
captivate, charm, fascinate, enchant, bewitch. REPEL
reach, catch up, intercept, overtake, pass.
discover, find out, detect, surprise, expose, unmask.
contract, develop, succumb to, go down with.
hear, discern, perceive, grasp, take in, understand, catch on, twig (*inf*).
*n*, clasp, fastener, clip, hook, hasp, bolt, latch.
snag, drawback, stumbling block, hitch, trap, trick.
take, haul (*inf*), bag, trophy, prize.

**catching** infectious, contagious, communicable, transmittable.
captivating, winning, charming, fascinating, enchanting, bewitching, fetching, attractive, taking. REPULSIVE

**catchword** slogan, motto, byword, refrain, cliché.

**catechism** interrogation, questioning, examination, drill, instruction.

**catechize** interrogate, question, examine, drill.

**catechumen** pupil, learner, beginner, novice, initiate, neophyte, tyro, proselyte, convert. MASTER

**categorical** positive, emphatic, unqualified, unconditional, absolute, unreserved, downright, direct, explicit, plain, unequivocal, unambiguous. VAGUE

**category** class, classification, division, section, heading, grouping, group, grade, order, rank, sort, kind, type.

**cater** provide, furnish, supply, purvey.

**cater to,** indulge, humour, gratify, oblige, satisfy, pamper, coddle, spoil.

**caterwaul** yell, howl, scream, screech, shriek, bawl.

**catharsis** purification, cleansing, purging, purgation.

**cathartic** purgative, cleansing, purifying.

**catholic** general, universal, world-wide, global, comprehensive, all-inclusive, liberal, tolerant, broad-minded, unbiased. NARROW

**cattle** cows, bulls, livestock, stock, animals.

**cauldron** pot, kettle, boiler, copper, crock.

**causation** production, creation, origination, causality.

**cause** *n*, source, origin, root, spring, agent, creator, maker, producer. EFFECT
reason, basis, justification, grounds, occasion, motive, inducement, incentive, object, purpose, aim, end.
matter, topic, subject, principle, ideal, purpose, enterprise, undertaking, attempt.
lawsuit, action, case.
*v*, occasion, bring about, engender, generate, originate, create, produce, effect, precipitate, provoke, begin, give rise to, result in.
compel, induce, make, force, constrain.

**caustic** burning, corrosive, acid, keen, pungent, acrid, mordant, biting, sharp, cutting, trenchant, stinging, scathing, sarcastic, severe, acrimonious, bitter, virulent. MILD

**cauterize** burn, sear, scorch, singe.

**caution** *n*, carefulness, care, wariness, heedfulness, heed, vigilance, watchfulness, discretion, prudence. RASHNESS
admonition, warning, advice, counsel, injunction.
*v*, warn, forewarn, admonish, advise, urge, enjoin.

**cautious** careful, wary, heedful, vigilant, watchful, prudent, judicious, discreet, guarded. RASH

**cavalcade** procession, parade, march-past, array, spectacle, train, cortege.

**cavalier** *n*, knight, gentleman, gallant, escort, beau.
*adj*, arrogant, haughty, disdainful, supercilious, proud, insolent, curt, offhand. MEEK

**cave** cavern, grotto, den, hollow, cavity, pothole.

**cavern** cave, grotto, hollow, underground chamber.

**cavernous** hollow, sunken, deep-set, concave, yawning.

**cavil** *v*, carp, censure, hypercriticize, quibble, complain, object, find fault. PRAISE
*n*, objection, quibble, criticism, carping, censure, hypercriticism.

**cavilling** carping, captious, hypercritical, quibbling, fault-finding, nit-picking (*inf*). APPRECIATIVE

**cavity** hole, hollow, pit, crater, fissure, gap.

**cease** stop, end, finish, terminate, conclude, discontinue, halt, desist, refrain, leave off. BEGIN

**ceaseless** unceasing, continuous, constant, unremitting, nonstop, endless, unending, continual, perpetual, eternal, everlasting. FITFUL

**cede** yield, surrender, relinquish, abandon, abdicate, resign, transfer, hand over, convey, grant, allow, concede. RETAIN

**celebrate** honour, commemorate, observe, keep, glorify, extol, praise, applaud, toast, drink to, proclaim, rejoice, make merry. IGNORE

**celebrated** famous, distinguished, eminent, noted, acclaimed, illustrious, renowned, notable, well-known, popular. UNKNOWN

**celebration** festivity, festival, gala, carnival, party, revelry, merrymaking, carousal.
commemoration, observance, remembrance, anniversary, ceremony, rite, performance.

**celebrity** star, personality, lion, hero, heroine, personage, dignitary, VIP, bigwig (*inf*), big shot (*inf*), somebody. NOBODY
fame, distinction, renown, note, eminence, glory, honour, reputation, repute, prominence, popularity, stardom. IGNOMINY

**celerity** speed, swiftness, rapidity, quickness, haste, promptness, dispatch, velocity, pace. SLOWNESS

**celestial** heavenly, divine, angelic, seraphic, immortal, eternal, ethereal, empyrean, astral, spiritual, supernatural. EARTHLY

**celibacy** continence, abstinence, self-denial, chastity, virginity, purity, singleness, bachelorhood.

**celibate** *adj*, single, unmarried, continent, abstinent, chaste, virginal. MARRIED
*n*, bachelor, spinster, single person, virgin, monk, nun.

**cell** chamber, room, cubicle, compartment, stall, recess, cavity, cage, dungeon.

**cellar** basement, vault, storeroom, larder. ATTIC

**cellular** alveolated, honeycombed, open, porous.

**cement** *v*, unite, join, connect, attach, cleave, cohere, bind, stick, glue, gum, paste, bond. SEPARATE
*n*, mortar, plaster, adhesive, glue, gum, paste, sealant, bond.

**cemetery** graveyard, churchyard, necropolis, burial ground, God's acre.

**cenotaph** monument, memorial, shrine.

**censor** *v*, expurgate, cut, bowdlerize, purge, edit, delete.
*n*, inspector, examiner, reviewer, critic.

**censorious** critical, fault-finding, hypercritical, captious, carping, cavilling, disapproving, disparaging. APPRECIATIVE

**censurable** blamable, blameworthy, at fault, guilty, culpable, reprehensible. BLAMELESS

**censure** *v*, blame, condemn, denounce, criticize, reprove, rebuke, reproach, reprimand, chide, castigate, upbraid, disapprove. PRAISE
*n*, condemnation, denunciation, disapproval, disapprobation, blame, criticism, stricture, reproof, reproach. APPROVAL

**central** middle, median, mid, inner, interior. EXTREME
key, focal, chief, cardinal, main, essential, principal, fundamental, primary. PERIPHERAL

**centralize** concentrate, converge, congregate, collect, focus, consolidate, amalgamate, compact, unify. DECENTRALIZE

**centre** *n*, middle, midst, midpoint, focus, hub, pivot, core, heart, nucleus.
*v*, focus, converge, concentrate.

**century** centenary, hundred years, hundred, era, period, age.

**cereal** grain, corn, wheat, oats, barley, maize, rye, grass, crop, seed, meal.

**ceremonial** *adj*, formal, solemn, ritual, stately, imposing, dignified, majestic, official, functional, liturgical. CASUAL
*n*, ceremony, solemnity, ritual, rite, formality, etiquette.

**ceremonious** formal, precise, punctilious, exact, stiff, starchy (*inf*), courteous, civil, polite. UNCEREMONIOUS
stately, dignified, solemn. INFORMAL

**ceremony** rite, ritual, ceremonial, observance, service, sacrament, commemoration, parade, show.
formality, pomp, stateliness, protocol, etiquette, form, decorum. INFORMALITY

**certain** sure, positive, convinced, confident, assured. DOUBTFUL
unquestionable, indubitable, undoubted, indisputable, incontestable, incontrovertible, irrefutable, absolute, conclusive, positive, manifest, plain. UNCERTAIN
bound, destined, sure, inevitable. UNLIKELY
definite, decided, settled, determined, fixed, established.
infallible, unfailing, reliable, dependable, stable, constant. UNRELIABLE
particular, specific, special, precise, express, individual.

**certainly** undoubtedly, unquestionably, without doubt, positively, absolutely, plainly.
willingly, surely, of course, by all means, definitely.

**certainty** conviction, sureness, confidence, assurance, certitude, trust, faith. DOUBT
fact, reality, truth, actuality. POSSIBILITY
unquestionableness, indubitableness, irrefutability, incontestability, incontrovertibility, positiveness, plainness. UNCERTAINTY

**certificate** credential, testimonial, diploma, document, licence, warrant, authorization, voucher.

**certify** attest, testify, witness, avow, aver, corroborate, confirm, verify, validate, declare, guarantee, vouch for, endorse, prove, show. DENY

**certitude** certainty, confidence, assurance, conviction. DOUBT

**cessation** ceasing, ending, stop, termination, discontinuance, arrest, stoppage, halt, pause, stay, suspension, intermission, interval, abeyance, respite, remission, rest, let-up (*inf*). CONTINUANCE

**cession** surrender, yielding, capitulation, submission, abandonment, relinquishment, renunciation, transfer, conveyance, grant, concession. RETENTION

**chafe** rub, warm, wear, scrape, scratch, rasp, grate, inflame, irritate, vex, annoy, exasperate, anger, incense, gall, fume, rage, provoke, offend, fret, worry, trouble. SOOTHE

**chaff**[1] *n*, husks, hulls, remains, dregs, refuse, waste, rubbish.

**chaff**[2] *v*, tease, banter, rib (*inf*), mock, ridicule, taunt, jeer, scoff, deride.
*n*, banter, raillery, teasing, joking, badinage, persiflage.

**chaffer** haggle, bargain, negotiate.

**chagrin** *n*, irritation, vexation, annoyance, exasperation, anger, displeasure, mortification, embarrassment, discomfiture, disquiet, discomposure, humiliation. PLEASURE
*v*, irritate, vex, annoy, exasperate, anger, displease, mortify, embarrass, discomfit, humiliate. PLEASE

**chain** *n*, bond, restraint, fetter, shackle, manacle.
series, succession, progression, sequence, string, train.
*v*, restrain, confine, tether, fasten, tie, bind, shackle, fetter, enslave. LOOSE

**chair** *n*, seat, stool, bench, pew, throne.
professorship, professorate.
*v*, preside over, lead, direct, supervise, manage, control.

**chairman** chairwoman, chairperson, speaker, director, president, master of ceremonies, MC (*inf*), toastmaster.

**chalice** goblet, cup, bowl.

**challenge** *v*, dare, defy, invite, summon, brave, beard, confront, accost.
arouse, stimulate, test, tax.
question, dispute, dissent, oppose, protest. PASS
*n*, dare, defiance, ultimatum, confrontation, provocation, summons, invitation, test, trial.
question, protest, objection, dissension, disputation.

**chamber** room, hall, apartment, bedroom, cell, cubicle.
cavity, hollow, compartment, recess.
assembly, council, judicature, legislature.

**champ** chew, gnaw, bite, munch, crunch.

**champion** *n*, winner, title-holder, victor, conqueror, hero, defender, protector, upholder, guardian, patron, backer, supporter, advocate. RENEGADE
*v*, back, promote, support, defend, fight for, advocate, uphold. OPPOSE

**chance** *n*, luck, fortuity, fortune, providence, fate, destiny, accident, contingency. DESIGN
opportunity, opening, occasion, time.
possibility, likelihood, prospect, probability. CERTAINTY
risk, gamble, hazard, peril, jeopardy, uncertainty.
*v*, happen, occur, befall, come about, betide.
risk, hazard, venture, gamble, speculate, jeopardize.
*adj*, accidental, unintentional, fortuitous, unforeseen, incidental, casual, random. INTENTIONAL

**change** *v*, alter, vary, modify, transform, convert, transmute, shift, veer, alternate, fluctuate, vacillate. REMAIN
replace, substitute, exchange, swap, trade, barter, commute. RETAIN
*n*, alteration, variation, modification, transformation, conversion, metamorphosis, mutation, shift, difference. IMMUTABILITY
variety, innovation, novelty, revolution, alternation, fluctuation, vicissitude. CONSERVATION

**changeable** variable, inconstant, fickle, capricious, irregular, fluctuating, wavering, vacillating, unsteady, unstable, shifting, mobile, fitful, mercurial, volatile, unpredictable, unreliable. STEADFAST

**changeless** steadfast, constant, unchanging, immutable, unvarying, consistent, unalterable, permanent, fixed, regular, steady, reliable, abiding, perpetual, everlasting. CHANGEABLE

**channel** *n*, duct, conduit, passage, canal, strait, gutter, groove, furrow.
approach, way, avenue, route, course, path.
*v*, direct, guide, conduct, convey.
groove, flute, carve.

**chant** *n*, song, psalm, cantata, canticle, carol, plainsong, intonation, melody, tune, chorus, incantation.
*v*, sing, carol, intone, chorus, recite.

**chaos** disorder, confusion, anarchy, turmoil, tumult, havoc, pandemonium. ORDER

**chaotic** disordered, confused, disorganized, topsy-turvy, anarchic, lawless, riotous, tumultuous. ORDERED

**chap**[1] *v*, crack, split, open, redden, roughen.

**chap**[2] *n*, boy, man, fellow, bloke (*inf*), guy (*inf*), character, type, sort.

**chaperon** *n*, escort, companion, duenna, governess, attendant, protector, shepherd.
*v*, escort, accompany, watch over, protect, shepherd, attend.

**chapfallen** crestfallen, despondent, dejected, downcast, dispirited, disheartened, discouraged, sad, depressed, downhearted. HAPPY

**chaplet** wreath, garland, coronal, circlet.

**chapter** division, section, part, episode, phase, period, stage.

**char** burn, scorch, singe, sear, carbonize, cauterize.

**character** personality, temperament, disposition, nature, individuality, attributes, constitution, cast, complexion, quality.
reputation, repute, status, position, honour, integrity, uprightness, rectitude. DISREPUTE
person, individual, sort, type, fellow, eccentric, oddity, card (*inf*).
role, part, persona, portrayal, characterization.
symbol, letter, type, mark, device, emblem, sign, figure.

**characteristic** *adj*, distinctive, peculiar, special, individual, specific, representative, typical. GENERAL
peculiarity, idiosyncrasy, trait, feature, quality, attribute, property, mark.

**characterize** mark, distinguish, brand, stamp, identify, designate, indicate, represent, describe, portray.

**charade** travesty, pretence, pantomime, farce.

**charge** *v*, accuse, impeach, arraign, impute, indict, incriminate. CLEAR
attack, assault, assail, rush, storm. RETREAT
entrust, commit, load, burden, afflict. RELIEVE
demand, ask, levy, price.
command, enjoin, bid, direct, order, instruct, require.
fill, suffuse, permeate, imbue.
*n*, accusation, imputation, indictment, allegation. PLEA
attack, assault, onset, onslaught, sortie, raid. RETREAT
responsibility, duty, office, trust, commission, custody, care, safekeeping, ward.
burden, load, cargo, freight.

price, payment, fee, rate, levy, cost, outlay, expense.
command, order, injunction, direction, instruction, mandate.

**chargeable** liable, accountable, imputable, attributable, blamable, imposable, taxable, rateable.

**charger** war-horse, mount, steed, horse.

**charily** cautiously, carefully, warily, guardedly, circumspectly, heedfully. RECKLESSLY
sparingly, frugally, prudently, judiciously.

**charitable** kind, benevolent, beneficent, philanthropic, generous, liberal, bountiful. MEAN
lenient, considerate, compassionate, gracious, magnanimous, indulgent, tolerant, understanding, humane, forgiving. HARSH

**charity** alms, almsgiving, benefaction, relief, assistance, donation, contribution, gift.
kindness, benevolence, compassion, love, goodness, humanity, generosity, bounty. SELFISHNESS

**charlatan** quack, mountebank, cheat, swindler, con man (*inf*), impostor, pretender, fraud.

**charm** *v*, enchant, fascinate, captivate, bewitch, mesmerize, entrance, delight, please, win, allure, attract, transport, enrapture, enamour. REPEL
*n*, attractiveness, allure, appeal, desirability, fascination, magic, enchantment, spell, sorcery. REPULSION
amulet, talisman, trinket.

**charming** attractive, fetching, delightful, pleasing, lovely, appealing, engaging, alluring, enchanting, bewitching, fascinating, captivating. REPULSIVE

**chart** plan, diagram, graph, map, table.

**charter** *n*, licence, permit, franchise, concession, authority, privilege, right, prerogative, document, deed, bond.
*v*, lease, hire, rent, commission, sanction, authorize.

**chary** cautious, prudent, careful, circumspect, heedful, wary, guarded, slow, reluctant, shy. RECKLESS
sparing, frugal, thrifty, parsimonious, mean, niggardly.

**chase** *v*, pursue, follow, run after, hunt, track, hound, drive away, send packing, put to flight.
*n*, pursuit, hunt, hunting, race.

**chasm** abyss, gorge, crevasse, ravine, gulf, rift, cleft, fissure, cavity, crater, opening, gap, hiatus.

**chaste** pure, undefiled, unsullied, immaculate, vestal, virginal, virtuous, innocent, modest, decent, simple, unaffected. CORRUPT

**chasten** correct, discipline, chastise, castigate, repress, humble, subdue, tame, curb. PAMPER

**chastise** correct, discipline, punish, castigate, beat, flog, lash, whip, cane, spank, thrash, scourge, berate, upbraid, scold. REWARD

**chastisement** discipline, punishment, castigation, beating, flogging, caning, spanking, thrashing, censure, scolding. PRAISE

**chastity** purity, virtue, virginity, maidenhood, celibacy, continence, modesty, decency, innocence, simplicity. CORRUPTION

**chat** *v*, talk, natter, gossip, chatter, prattle, confabulate, converse.
*n*, conversation, talk, natter, gossip, confab (*inf*), tête-à-tête, chinwag (*inf*).

**chattels** goods, belongings, property, effects, furniture, movables.

**chatter** *v*, chat, natter, gossip, prattle, prate, tattle, babble, jabber, gab (*inf*).
*n*, prattle, talk, gossip, babbling, prating, chit-chat.

**chatterbox** chatterer, babbler, gossip, blabbermouth, prattler, windbag (*inf*).

**chatty** talkative, loquacious, garrulous, babbling, prating. RESERVED
gossipy, newsy, informal, friendly, familiar, colloquial. FORMAL

**cheap** inexpensive, low-priced, cut-price, reduced, reasonable, economical. EXPENSIVE
shoddy, inferior, second-rate, poor, indifferent, paltry, worthless, common, vulgar. SUPERIOR
mean, shabby, contemptible, despicable, low. NOBLE

**cheapen** debase, devalue, lower, depreciate, belittle, disparage, demean. APPRECIATE

**cheat** *v*, deceive, delude, beguile, hoodwink, bamboozle, dupe, fool, trick, hoax, defraud, swindle, con (*inf*), diddle (*inf*), rip off (*inf*), do (*inf*), double-cross.

*n*, swindler, con man (*inf*), fraud, impostor, liar, deceiver, rogue, trickster, sharper, cheater, charlatan.
deception, hoax, fraud, swindle, rip-off (*inf*), trick, imposture, artifice.

**check** *v*, examine, inspect, scrutinize, look over, test, verify, confirm, compare, investigate, enquire into, probe.
curb, restrain, control, bridle, repress, inhibit, hinder, impede, obstruct, retard, halt, stop, arrest, pause. ADVANCE
chide, rebuke, reprove, reprimand, scold. ENCOURAGE
*n*, examination, inspection, scrutiny, test, trial, comparison, verification, confirmation, investigation, probe.
criterion, norm, yardstick, standard, model.
curb, restraint, control, inhibition, hindrance, impediment, obstruction, barrier, bar, stoppage.

**checkmate** *n*, defeat, rout, conquest, victory.
stalemate, deadlock, halt, stoppage, arrest, check.
*v*, frustrate, foil, thwart, overcome, conquer, defeat, vanquish, beat.

**cheek** impertinence, impudence, effrontery, sauce (*inf*), insolence, disrespect, nerve, gall, audacity, temerity. RESPECT

**cheer** *v*, applaud, clap, acclaim, shout, yell, encourage, spur, urge. BOO
gladden, hearten, brighten, cheer up, comfort, console, solace, encourage, enliven, animate, inspirit, exhilarate, uplift. DEPRESS
*n*, cheerfulness, gladness, happiness, joy, gaiety, merriment, comfort, solace, hope, hopefulness, buoyancy, animation, liveliness. DEJECTION
shout, yell, cry, hurrah, applause, acclamation. BOO

**cheerfulness** happiness, joy, joyfulness, gaiety, merriment, cheer, buoyancy, blitheness, good spirits, hopefulness, enthusiasm. DEJECTION

**cheerless** dreary, dull, gloomy, dismal, dark, sombre, bleak, depressing, melancholy, mournful, doleful, dejected, depressed, despondent, miserable, sad, disconsolate, forlorn, desolate, morose, pessimistic. CHEERFUL

**cheery** cheering, cheerful, joyous, gay, merry, sprightly, blithe, lively, hearty, jovial, sunny, breezy, carefree. GLUM

**chequered** varied, diverse.
variegated, multicoloured, checked, tartan.

**cherish** treasure, prize, hold dear, love, cling to, harbour, entertain, nurture, nourish, nurse, cosset, foster, support, promote. ABANDON

**cherub** angel, child, baby, innocent, darling.

**chest** box, case, trunk, coffer, casket.
breast, bosom, bust, thorax.

**chew** masticate, munch, champ, grind, crunch, gnaw, bite, nibble.

**chew over,** ponder, ruminate, consider, deliberate, mull over, meditate.

**chic** fashionable, modish, trendy (*inf*), stylish, smart, elegant.

**chicanery** trickery, artifice, subterfuge, chicane, sophistry, deception, duplicity, wiles, stratagems, intrigue, underhandedness. HONESTY

**chide** rebuke, scold, reprimand, admonish, upbraid, tick off (*inf*), tell off (*inf*), reprove, reproach, berate, censure, criticize, blame. PRAISE

**chief** *n*, leader, head, chieftain, ruler, captain, commander, master, governor, principal, boss (*inf*), director, manager. SUBORDINATE
*adj*, principal, cardinal, capital, main, leading, first, foremost, primary, prime, supreme, paramount, grand, key, essential, vital, prevailing, predominant. MINOR

**chiefly** especially, above all, principally, mainly, mostly, predominantly, on the whole, primarily.

**chieftain** chief, head, leader, ruler, commander.

**child** baby, infant, toddler, youngster, youth, juvenile, boy, girl, offspring, progeny, issue, suckling, nursling, nipper (*inf*), brat, kid (*inf*). ADULT

**childbirth** confinement, accouchement, lying-in, labour, delivery, parturition.

**childhood** babyhood, infancy, youth, minority, boyhood, girlhood. ADULTHOOD

**childish** babyish, infantile, puerile, juvenile, immature, boyish, girlish, silly, foolish, trivial, trifling, simple, young, tender. MATURE

**childlike** innocent, artless, guileless, naive, ingenuous, credulous, gullible, trustful, trusting.

**chill** *adj*, chilly, cool, cold, bleak, frigid. WARM

*v*, cool, refrigerate, freeze. HEAT
depress, discourage, dishearten, dampen. ENCOURAGE
*n*, cold, coldness, chilliness, coolness, bleakness, frigidity, rawness, nip, bite. WARMTH
**chilly** chill, cool, cold, bleak, frosty, freezing, raw, wintry, nippy, fresh, crisp. WARM
unfriendly, cool, frigid, hostile, unwelcoming, unresponsive. FRIENDLY
**chime** toll, sound, strike, peal, ring, clang, dong, tinkle.
harmonize, accord, agree, blend, coordinate, complement. CLASH
**chimera** hallucination, fantasy, dream, delusion, fancy, illusion, phantom, spectre, nightmare, monster. REALITY
**chimerical** illusory, fanciful, imaginary, hallucinatory, visionary, unreal, wild, fantastic. REAL
**china** porcelain, ceramics, pottery, earthenware, crockery, tableware, service, dishes.
**chink**[1] *n*, crack, fissure, cleft, rift, cranny, crevice, gap, opening, aperture.
**chink**[2] *v*, jingle, ring, clink, tinkle, jangle.
*n*, clink, jingle, tinkle, ring.
**chip** *n*, piece, fragment, flake, sliver, splinter, shard, shaving, scrap, bit.
dent, scratch, nick, flaw, defect.
*v*, chisel, whittle, nick, scratch, gash, cut, hew.
**chip in,** contribute, donate, pay.
interrupt, interpose, break in.
**chirography** calligraphy, handwriting, hand, penmanship.
**chiromancy** palmistry, fortune-telling, prediction, divination.
**chirp** chirrup, cheep, twitter, tweet, warble, trill, pipe, peep.
**chisel** carve, sculpt, cut, hew, engrave, incise, chase, shape, model.
**chit** chitty, memo, memorandum, note, slip, voucher, receipt.
**chivalrous** knightly, heroic, courageous, valiant, brave, bold, intrepid, gallant, courtly, courteous, gentlemanly, generous, magnanimous, noble, high-minded. COWARDLY
**chivalry** knighthood, heroism, courage, valour, bravery, gallantry, courtesy, nobility.
**chock** block, wedge, stop.
**choice** *n*, option, alternative, selection, pick, variety, adoption, election, preference.
*adj*, select, hand-picked, elite, excellent, superior, prime, rare, uncommon, unusual, exquisite, dainty, exclusive, special, valuable, precious. INFERIOR
**choke** *v*, throttle, strangle, stifle, suffocate, smother, asphyxiate, block, obstruct, congest, clog, dam, suppress, overcome, overpower.
*vi*, gag, retch, gasp, cough.
**choler** anger, ire, wrath, fury, rage, indignation. MILDNESS
**choleric** irritable, bad-tempered, testy, irascible, touchy, petulant, angry, fiery, hot, passionate. PLACID
**choose** select, pick, elect, adopt, cull, single out, settle on, opt for, prefer, fancy, desire, wish, see fit. REJECT
**choosy** discriminating, selective, particular, fussy, faddy, finicky, exacting, fastidious.
**chop** cut, hew, fell, axe, lop, shear, hack, slice, dice, cube, mince, chop up.
**choppy** rough, ruffled, broken, uneven, squally, blustery, tempestuous, turbulent.
**chops** jaws, jowls, mouth, muzzle.
**chore** job, task, duty, burden, bother, drag (*inf*), fag (*inf*).
**chortle** chuckle, snigger, cackle, crow.
**chorus** choir, choristers, singers, ensemble.
refrain, burden, response. VERSE
song, carol, ballad, hymn, anthem, tune, melody.
accord, unison, harmony, concert, unity, concord. DISCORD
**christen** baptize, name, call, dub, designate, entitle, style, term.
**chronic** inveterate, habitual, confirmed, deep-seated, deep-rooted, ingrained, persistent, constant, incessant, permanent, incurable, recurring, perennial, lingering.
appalling, dreadful, awful, atrocious. EXCELLENT
**chronicle** *n*, journal, diary, log, record, register, history, annals, account, narrative, story, saga.
*v*, record, register, enter, set down, relate, tell, recount, narrate.
**chronicler** historian, historiographer, annalist, diarist, recorder, narrator, reporter.

**chronological** consecutive, sequential, in sequence, ordered, progressive, historical.

**chronometer** timepiece, watch, clock.

**chubby** plump, tubby, podgy, round, portly, rotund, flabby, fleshy, buxom. LEAN

**chuck** throw, toss, hurl, cast, pitch, sling, discard, reject, abandon, forsake, quit, give up.

**chuckle** giggle, titter, chortle, snigger, laugh, crow, cackle, grin, smile.

**chum** friend, companion, comrade, crony, pal (*inf*), mate (*inf*).

**chunk** lump, block, hunk, slab, wedge, mass, piece.

**church** chapel, cathedral, abbey, temple, meeting-house, mosque, synagogue, sanctuary.
denomination, faith, congregation, parish, clergy.

**churchyard** graveyard, cemetery, necropolis, burial ground.

**churl** boor, lout, oaf, rustic, peasant, bumpkin, clodhopper, yokel. GENTLEMAN
niggard, miser, skinflint, Scrooge.

**churlish** rude, impolite, uncivil, brusque, surly, waspish, crabbed, sullen, morose, rough, harsh, vulgar, uncouth, crass, boorish, oafish, loutish. POLITE
miserly, niggardly, mean, stingy, close-fisted, illiberal, inhospitable, unneighbourly. GENEROUS

**churlishness** rudeness, impoliteness, brusqueness, surliness, sullenness, roughness, uncouthness, boorishness. POLITENESS
meanness, miserliness, parsimony, illiberality, inhospitality. GENEROSITY

**churn** agitate, stir, beat, whip, foam, froth, convulse, toss, shake, disturb, upset.

**chute** channel, trough, groove, gutter, shaft, slide, slope, ramp.

**cicerone** guide, courier, escort, pilot.

**cigarette** smoke, cig (*inf*), ciggy (*inf*), fag (*inf*), coffin nail (*inf*), cancer stick (*inf*), joint, reefer.

**cincture** belt, girdle, band, border.

**cinder** ash, ember, coal, clinker, remnant.

**cinema** pictures, movies, flicks (*inf*), films, motion pictures, big screen (*inf*).

**cinereous** cineritious, ashy, ashen, greyish.

**cipher** code, cryptograph, symbol, character, figure, number, numeral, device, logo, monogram.
nil, zero, nought, nothing, nonentity, nobody.

**circle** ring, round, hoop, loop, disc, globe, sphere, orb, cycle, revolution, circumference, periphery.
coterie, club, clique, set, society, fraternity, group, company.
domain, province, realm, sphere, orbit, range, compass, field, area, region, circuit, bounds.

**circuit** revolution, round, lap, orbit, tour, course, journey, perambulation.
circle, boundary, circumference, ambit, limit, compass, district, region.

**circuitous** roundabout, indirect, devious, tortuous, winding, serpentine, meandering, rambling. DIRECT

**circular** *adj*, round, annular, ring-shaped, discoid, spherical, globular. SQUARE
*n*, notice, advertisement, handbill, broadsheet, leaflet, pamphlet, brochure.

**circulate** distribute, spread, propagate, publish, promulgate, broadcast, disseminate, diffuse, send round. RETAIN
rotate, revolve, gyrate, move round, pass round, flow, radiate. STAGNATE

**circulation** dissemination, spread, spreading, promulgation, propagation, diffusion, transmission. RETENTION
flow, movement, motion, circling, rotation. STAGNATION

**circumference** periphery, circuit, perimeter, outline, border, edge, rim, verge, fringe, boundary, limits, extremity. DIAMETER

**circumlocution** periphrasis, verbosity, long-windedness, prolixity, indirectness, euphemism, ambiguity. TERSENESS

**circumlocutory** periphrastic, verbose, long-winded, prolix, indirect, roundabout, euphemistic, ambiguous. TERSE

**circumscribe** surround, encircle, encompass, enclose, bound, limit, confine, restrict, hem in, restrain, define, demarcate, delineate, mark off.

**circumspect** cautious, wary, careful, vigilant, watchful, heedful, attentive, scrupulous, discreet, prudent, judicious, politic. RASH

**circumspection** caution, wariness, care, vigilance, prudence, discretion, attention. RASHNESS

**circumstance** incident, event, occurrence, happening, element, factor, detail, particular, point, item, condition.

**circumstances** situation, condition, position, state, state of affairs, means, resources, status, surroundings, background.

**circumstantial** inferential, conjectural, presumed, implied, indirect, hearsay, incidental, contingent. POSITIVE
detailed, elaborate, particular, specific, minute, precise. VAGUE

**circumvent** bypass, get round, evade, elude, avoid, steer clear of, sidestep. CONFRONT
outwit, beguile, dupe, cheat, deceive, trick, delude, bamboozle, hoodwink, mislead.
ensnare, entrap, encircle, surround, hem in, thwart, foil, checkmate.

**circumvention** evasion, avoidance, sidestepping, dodge.
deception, deceit, cheating, fraud, imposture, chicanery, trickery, duplicity. HONESTY

**cistern** tank, reservoir, well, vat, sink, tub.

**citadel** fortress, stronghold, castle, keep, tower, bastion.

**citation** quoting, quotation, passage, excerpt, extract, source, reference.
commendation, award, mention, honour.

**cite** quote, name, mention, allude to, refer to, adduce, enumerate.
summon, call, subpoena.

**citizen** townsman, inhabitant, dweller, resident, householder, ratepayer, voter, burgher, burgess, freeman, denizen, subject, native. OUTSIDER

**city** metropolis, municipality, town, conurbation.

**civic** municipal, community, communal, public, borough, civil. RURAL

**civil** civic, municipal, domestic, home, internal, political.
polite, courteous, well-mannered, respectful, civilized, refined, urbane, suave, gracious, complaisant, obliging, accommodating. CHURLISH

**civility** politeness, courtesy, urbanity, graciousness, complaisance. CHURLISHNESS

**civilization** refinement, sophistication, cultivation, culture, education, development, advancement, progress. BARBARISM
society, nation, people, customs, way of life.

**civilize** refine, sophisticate, cultivate, educate, enlighten, polish, improve.
humanize, domesticate, tame, school, teach. BARBARIZE

**clack** click, clatter, crack, rap.
chatter, jabber, gabble, prattle, babble, prate.

**claim** *v*, demand, call for, require, request, ask for, exact, requisition, commandeer, appropriate, usurp, take. WAIVE
assert, maintain, insist, allege, profess, declare.
*n*, demand, call, requirement, requisition, request, petition, application, privilege, right, title, pretension.
assertion, allegation, affirmation, profession, declaration.

**claimant** applicant, supplicant, petitioner, pretender, candidate.

**clairvoyant** *adj*, psychic, extrasensory, second-sighted, telepathic, prescient, prophetic, oracular.
*n*, fortune-teller, soothsayer, seer, prophet, prophetess, augur, diviner, oracle.

**clamber** climb, scramble, crawl, scale, shin.

**clammy** damp, moist, wet, sticky, viscous, slimy, sweaty, dank, close, humid. DRY

**clamorous** vociferous, noisy, loud, deafening, uproarious, riotous, boisterous, unruly, obstreperous. QUIET

**clamour** *n*, noise, din, racket, hullabaloo, uproar, outcry, shouting, vociferation, hubbub, commotion, fuss. QUIET
*v*, shout, cry, yell, vociferate, demand, insist.

**clamp** *n*, vice, brace, clasp, grip, bracket.
*v*, secure, fix, brace, grip, fasten, press, impose, inflict.

**clan** family, sept, tribe, race, house, group, set, band, company, clique, coterie, fraternity, brotherhood, sect, faction.

**clandestine** furtive, surreptitious, sly, secret, private, hidden, concealed, stealthy, underhand, cloak-and-dagger, underground, covert. OPEN

**clang** *v*, ring, resound, reverberate, toll, chime, clank, clash, jangle.

*n*, clank, clash, clangour, reverberation.

**clangour** clang, clash, reverberation, clamour, din, uproar, racket.

**clank** clash, clang, clink, chink, rattle, clatter.

**clannish** cliquish, exclusive, select, insular, sectarian, parochial, narrow.

**clap** *v*, applaud, cheer, acclaim. HISS
slap, slam, whack, bang, pat, strike, thrust.
*n*, applause, ovation, acclaim.
burst, peal, explosion, slap, bang, slam.

**claptrap** bombast, cant, rodomontade, humbug, nonsense, rubbish, bunk (*inf*), drivel (*inf*), flannel (*inf*), blarney, insincerity, hypocrisy.

**clarification** explanation, illumination, elucidation, simplification, interpretation, exposition. MYSTIFICATION

**clarify** explain, elucidate, elaborate, make clear, simplify, illuminate, enlighten, clear up, resolve, shed light on. OBSCURE
purify, refine, cleanse, filter, strain. POLLUTE

**clarity** clearness, limpidity, transparency, purity. MURKINESS
lucidity, precision, definition, distinctness, comprehensibility, intelligibility, obviousness, simplicity. OBSCURITY

**clash** *n*, collision, crash, conflict, disagreement, discord, opposition, brush, confrontation, fight, struggle, showdown. HARMONY
clang, clank, crash, clatter.
*v*, conflict, jar, collide, disagree, differ, quarrel, cross swords. AGREE
crash, bang, clang, clank, clatter, jangle.

**clasp** *v*, grasp, clutch, hold, grip, seize, press, squeeze, hug, embrace, enfold. RELEASE
fasten, join, connect, concatenate, link, unite. DETACH
*n*, fastener, hook, catch, hasp, button, buckle, clip, pin, brooch.
grasp, clutch, hold, grip, hug, embrace.

**class** *n*, set, collection, group, division, classification, category, section, grade, rank, order, degree, league, status, caste, kind, sort, type, genre, species, genus.
form, year, pupils, students, lesson, seminar.
*v*, classify, rank, grade, order, dispose, group, categorize, designate.

**classic** *adj*, first-rate, excellent, masterly, consummate, outstanding. INFERIOR
standard, model, archetypal, definitive, ideal, time-honoured, traditional, usual.
*n*, masterpiece, exemplar, paradigm, prototype, model, standard.

**classical** Greek, Attic, Grecian, Roman, Latin, Augustan.
pure, chaste, refined, polished, elegant, harmonious, symmetrical. VULGAR

**classification** arrangement, grouping, organization, codification, categorization, sorting. MUDDLE
category, group, class, division, set, collection.

**classify** arrange, sort, group, class, rank, rate, grade, categorize, pigeonhole, assort, dispose, distribute, tabulate, catalogue, file. MUDDLE

**clatter** rattle, crash, clash, clank, clang.

**clause** provision, proviso, article, stipulation, specification, condition, term, rider, addendum, codicil.
section, passage, paragraph, part, chapter, division, heading.

**claw** *n*, nail, talon, pincer.
*v*, scratch, tear, lacerate, rip, gouge, dig, scrape, scrabble.

**clean** *adj*, spotless, immaculate, unsullied, unsoiled, washed, laundered, scrubbed, dusted. DIRTY
pure, unadulterated, uncontaminated, unpolluted, sterile, antiseptic, hygienic, sanitary. CONTAMINATED
unblemished, flawless, faultless, perfect, whole, entire, complete. IMPERFECT
neat, tidy, elegant, graceful, simple, uncluttered. UNTIDY
innocent, chaste, virginal, decent, respectable, honourable, virtuous, moral. INDECENT
*v*, cleanse, purify, wash, launder, rinse, scrub, scour, dust, vacuum, sweep, mop, wipe. SOIL
*adv*, completely, utterly, altogether, entirely, fully, quite.

**cleanse** clean, wash, scrub, rinse, bathe, purify, clear, absolve. POLLUTE

**cleanser** soap, detergent, solvent, scourer, disinfectant, purifier.

**clear** *adj*, bright, light, sunny, cloudless, fine, luminous, undimmed. DULL
transparent, see-through, crystalline, glossy, unclouded, pellucid, limpid, translucent. CLOUDY

plain, distinct, coherent, intelligible, comprehensible, obvious, evident, conspicuous, visible, apparent, patent, manifest, palpable, unquestionable, indisputable, unmistakable, unequivocal, unambiguous, explicit, clear-cut. INDISTINCT
open, free, empty, unobstructed, unencumbered, unhindered, unimpeded, unhampered. BLOCKED
clean, pure, spotless, unsullied, immaculate, innocent, guiltless, unblemished, untarnished, faultless, flawless. TARNISHED
certain, sure, convinced, confident, positive. UNSURE
*v*, clean, cleanse, sweep, wipe, erase, tidy, refine, purify. POLLUTE
brighten, lighten, clear up, clarify. DARKEN
liberate, free, emancipate, release, discharge, let go, absolve, acquit, exonerate, vindicate, justify. CHARGE
evacuate, empty, disencumber, unload, rid, disentangle, extricate, free, loosen, unblock, remove. ENCUMBER
settle, square, pay off, discharge.
jump, leap, vault, pass over, miss. HIT
authorize, pass, sanction, permit, approve. BAR
**clear out,** leave, withdraw, depart, go away, beat it (*inf*), clear off (*inf*), decamp.
**clear up,** clarify, elucidate, explain, solve, resolve.

**clearance** permission, consent, sanction, authorization, green light, go-ahead.
headroom, leeway, margin, gap, allowance.

**cleave**[1] split, divide, separate, part, open, sunder, rend, crack, sever, hew, chop, slash. UNITE

**cleave**[2] cling, adhere, stick, cohere, hold, hold fast, remain faithful, be devoted, stand by. LEAVE

**cleft** *n*, rift, fissure, crevice, crack, chink, cranny, fracture, break, breach, chasm, hole, gap, opening.
*adj*, split, divided, separated, parted, rent, torn, cloven, branched, forked.

**clemency** mercy, leniency, forgiveness, indulgence, tolerance, compassion, tenderness, kindness, humanity, mildness, moderation. HARSHNESS

**clement** merciful, lenient, forgiving, forbearing, indulgent, tolerant, compassionate, tender, soft-hearted, kind, kind-hearted, benevolent. HARSH
mild, temperate, moderate, balmy, fair, fine.

**clench** close, shut, grit, tighten, grip, grasp, hold. RELAX

**clergyman** cleric, churchman, ecclesiastic, divine, minister, vicar, parson, pastor, rector, curate, priest, padre, chaplain, preacher, man of God. LAYMAN

**clerical** ecclesiastical, priestly, sacerdotal, pastoral, ministerial. LAY
secretarial, office, clerkly, book-keeping, white-collar.

**clerk** secretary, typist, office worker, junior, recorder, registrar, book-keeper, scribe, pen-pusher.

**clever** bright, intelligent, brainy (*inf*), quick-witted, smart, astute, sharp, knowledgeable, gifted, talented, able, adroit, apt, skilful, expert, dexterous, capable, ingenious, resourceful, shrewd, cunning, sly. STUPID

**cleverness** brightness, intelligence, brains, smartness, talent, flair, gift, ability, adroitness, skill, dexterity, ingenuity, resourcefulness, shrewdness, cunning. STUPIDITY

**cliché** platitude, commonplace, truism, banality, bromide, saw, maxim.

**click** snap, clack, crack, clink, tick, beat, clap.

**client** patron, regular, customer, buyer, consumer, user, patient, protégé, dependant.

**clientele** clients, patrons, regulars, customers, market, business, trade, following.

**cliff** crag, bluff, precipice, scar, escarpment, headland.

**climate** weather, clime, temperature, region, area, place, country.
feeling, mood, ambience, atmosphere, trend, tendency.

**climax** culmination, acme, peak, height, top, head, zenith, high spot (*inf*), crisis, turning point.

**climb** ascend, mount, scale, go up, shin, clamber, scramble, rise, soar. DESCEND

**clinch** *v*, secure, fasten, fix, rivet, bolt, clamp, hold, grip, clutch. LOOSE
settle, decide, conclude, complete, cap, close, sew up (*inf*).
*n*, hold, grip, clasp, clutch.

**cling** hold fast, cleave, stick, adhere, clasp, clutch, grip, hug, embrace, remain faithful, be devoted. SEPARATE

**clinical** cold, dispassionate, unemotional, detached, objective, impersonal, scientific, analytic. SUBJECTIVE

**clink** ring, jingle, chink, tinkle.

**clip**[1] *v*, trim, cut, snip, prune, pare, crop, shear, shorten, curtail, abridge. ELONGATE
strike, hit, smack, cuff, box, thump.
*n*, hit, blow, smack, cuff, box, thump.
speed, pace, rate, lick (*inf*).

**clip**[2] *v*, fasten, fix, pin, hold, attach. DETACH

**clipping** cutting, excerpt, extract, snippet, piece.

**clique** set, coterie, gang, clan, party, faction, group, fraternity, club.

**cloak** *v*, hide, conceal, cover, veil, screen, mask, disguise, camouflage. EXPOSE
*n*, cape, mantle, wrap, shawl.
cover, screen, mask, veil, blind, front, pretext.

**clock** timepiece, chronometer, timer, dial, speedometer, taximeter, mileometer.

**clod** lump, mass, sod, turf, earth.
fool, blockhead, dolt, dunce, clodpoll, clodpate.

**clodhopper** lout, oaf, clown, yokel, rustic, bumpkin, peasant.

**clog** *v*, block, obstruct, choke, congest, jam, hamper, hinder, impede, encumber, burden, load, restrain, shackle, fetter. FREE
*n*, obstruction, hindrance, impediment, burden, encumbrance, drag, restraint, handicap.

**cloister** colonnade, arcade, piazza, gallery, covered walk, corridor.
monastery, priory, abbey, convent, nunnery.

**cloistered** cloistral, secluded, sequestered, restricted, confined, sheltered, shielded, reclusive, solitary, monastic, withdrawn. SOCIABLE

**close** *v*, shut, seal, fasten, secure, lock, bar, stop, block, obstruct, clog, plug. OPEN
finish, end, cease, terminate, conclude, complete, wind up. BEGIN
join, come together, grapple, connect, unite, coalesce, merge, fuse. SEPARATE
**close in,** approach, draw near, encircle, surround, hem in.
*n*, end, finish, conclusion, cessation, termination, completion. BEGINNING
courtyard, quadrangle, enclosure, grounds, road, cul-de-sac.
*adj*, near, nearby, adjacent, adjoining, neighbouring, nigh, imminent, impending, at hand. DISTANT
dense, solid, compact, compressed, tight, packed, crowded.
stuffy, oppressive, stifling, confined, airless, heavy, muggy, humid, stale, stagnant. FRESH
mean, niggardly, miserly, tight-fisted, stingy, near, parsimonious, illiberal, ungenerous. GENEROUS
secret, hidden, concealed, private, secretive, reticent, reserved, taciturn, uncommunicative. OPEN
accurate, exact, precise, faithful, conscientious, true, strict, literal. IMPRECISE
dear, intimate, familiar, devoted, attached, inseparable, loving. DISTANT
intense, keen, fixed, concentrated, earnest, intent, assiduous, thorough, painstaking, dogged.

**closet** cupboard, cabinet, recess, room, chamber.

**closure** close, closing, stoppage, end, finish, conclusion. START
stopper, plug, cork, cap, lid, top.

**clot** *n*, lump, mass, concretion, thrombus, coagulation, clotting.
fool, buffoon, blockhead, dolt, ass, idiot, dope (*inf*), nincompoop.
*v*, coagulate, congeal, thicken, curdle.

**cloth** fabric, textile, material, stuff, rag.

**clothe** dress, attire, array, apparel, garb, robe, deck, fit out, rig out, cover, enwrap, drape, swathe, endow, invest. STRIP

**clothes** clothing, garments, attire, dress, apparel, vestments, habits, garb, wear, wardrobe, costume, outfit, get-up (*inf*), rig-out (*inf*), gear (*inf*), togs (*inf*).

**cloud** *n*, haze, mist, vapour, fog, nebulosity, obscurity, darkness, gloom, pall, shroud, blur, smudge.
mass, crowd, horde, throng, host, multitude, swarm, shower, flock.
*v*, dim, darken, obscure, shadow, overshadow, blur, veil, shroud, eclipse, conceal. CLEAR

**cloudy** overcast, dark, grey, gloomy, lowering, sunless, murky, muddy, dull, lustreless. BRIGHT
dim, obscure, confused, blurred, indistinct, vague, indefinite. CLEAR

**clown** buffoon, jester, fool, harlequin, pierrot, joker, comedian.

boor, lout, oaf, clodhoppper, yokel, peasant, bumpkin, dolt. GENTLEMAN

**clownish** foolish, awkward, clumsy, ungainly, coarse, rough, loutish, boorish, churlish. GENTEEL

**cloy** surfeit, sate, satiate, pall, glut, gorge, sicken, nauseate.

**club** *n*, society, association, organization, company, group, circle, clique, coterie, set, fraternity, brotherhood, guild, league, union.
cudgel, truncheon, bludgeon, stick, bat, staff, mace.
*v*, beat, cudgel, bludgeon, batter, cosh, bash, hammer, strike.
unite, combine, join, amalgamate, confederate, affiliate. SEPARATE

**clue** hint, guide, indication, tip, tip-off, lead, pointer, sign, key, inkling, suggestion, trace, suspicion.

**clump** *n*, bunch, cluster, group, collection, mass, bundle, gathering, assemblage.
*v*, clomp, stomp, stamp, thump, thud, tramp, plod, trudge, lumber.
cluster, gather, bunch, agglutinate, assemble. DISPERSE

**clumsy** awkward, maladroit, bungling, blundering, unskilful, inexpert, ham-fisted (*inf*), lumbering, ungainly, gauche, ungraceful, ponderous, heavy, unwieldy. ADROIT

**cluster** *n*, clump, bunch, knot, gathering, collection, group, accumulation, aggregation, agglomeration.
*v*, bunch, gather, collect, flock, throng, crowd, aggregate, agglomerate, accumulate. DISPERSE

**clutch** *v*, grasp, grip, hold, clasp, seize, snatch, grab.
*n*, grasp, grip, hold, clasp.

**clutches** power, control, keeping, custody, possession, hands, claws, talons.

**clutter** *v*, strew, scatter, litter, disorder, disarrange, mess.
clatter, rattle, bustle, chatter, gabble.
*n*, litter, mess, jumble, disorder, disarray, confusion, muddle, hotchpotch, rubbish, lumber.

**coach** *n*, bus, vehicle, car, carriage.
tutor, instructor, trainer, teacher, manager.
*v*, train, drill, exercise, instruct, teach, cram (*inf*).

**coagulate** clot, thicken, curdle, congeal, jell, harden, set.

**coalesce** unite, combine, incorporate, integrate, amalgamate, blend, mix, merge, fuse, consolidate. SEPARATE

**coalition** alliance, confederation, confederacy, affiliation, league, bloc, union, compact, amalgamation, merger, fusion, combination. SEPARATION

**coarse** rough, crude, impure, unrefined, unpolished, unfinished, uneven, scaly, bristly, thick. FINE
rude, vulgar, impolite, indecent, earthy, dirty, smutty, gross, indelicate, immodest, inelegant, lewd, ribald, bawdy. POLITE
uncivil, boorish, uncouth, crass, unsophisticated, brutish. REFINED

**coast** *n*, seaside, shore, beach, strand, seaboard.
*v*, sail, glide, cruise, drift, freewheel.

**coat** *n*, jacket, blazer, overcoat, fur, mackintosh, cape, mantle.
covering, coating, layer, film, sheet, blanket, cover.
hair, fur, pelt, hide, fleece, wool.
*v*, cover, spread, paint, apply.

**coating** coat, layer, film, blanket, covering, glaze, varnish, finish.

**coax** cajole, wheedle, persuade, induce, entice, lure, flatter, soft-soap (*inf*), urge, implore. COERCE

**cobble** mend, patch, botch, bungle.

**cock** *n*, rooster, cockerel, chanticleer, male bird. HEN
tap, valve, spigot, stopcock.
*v*, raise, prick, stick up, stand up, perk up.

**cockeyed** crooked, askew, awry, lopsided, aslant, skew-whiff (*inf*), crazy, absurd, insane, ludicrous, preposterous.

**cocksure** overconfident, arrogant, cocky, presumptuous, bumptious, pushy (*inf*). HUMBLE

**cocky** vain, conceited, egotistical, proud, swollen-headed, arrogant, cocksure. MODEST

**coddle** pamper, indulge, humour, cosset, mollycoddle, baby, spoil, pet. HARDEN

**code** system, canon, maxim, rule, regulation, guideline, ethics, morals, custom, convention, etiquette, manners.
cipher, cryptograph, secret writing.

**codicil** supplement, addendum, addition, rider, postscript, appendix.

**codify** systematize, organize, classify, catalogue, order, tabulate, collect, summarize, condense, digest.

**coerce** force, constrain, compel, press, drive, impel, bulldoze (*inf*), browbeat, bully, intimidate. COAX

**coercion** force, constraint, compulsion, pressure, duress, browbeating, bullying, intimidation. COAXING

**coeval** coetaneous, coexistent, contemporary, contemporaneous, simultaneous, synchronous, concurrent.

**coexistent** coetaneous, coeval, contemporary, contemporaneous, simultaneous, synchronous, concurrent.
compatible, cooperating, symbiotic.

**coffer** chest, trunk, case, box, casket, repository, treasury, safe, strongbox.

**coffin** casket, sarcophagus, box.

**cogency** force, strength, conviction, power, potency. WEAKNESS

**cogent** forceful, strong, convincing, persuasive, potent, powerful, weighty, influential, effective, compelling, irresistible, conclusive. WEAK

**cogitate** ponder, ruminate, meditate, muse, reflect, contemplate, consider, think, speculate, deliberate, mull over.

**cogitation** meditation, rumination, reflection, contemplation, consideration, thought, deliberation.

**cognate** related, akin, kindred, connected, allied, affiliated, analogous, alike, similar. UNRELATED

**cognition** perception, awareness, discernment, intuition, insight, reasoning, intelligence, comprehension, understanding, knowledge, cognizance.

**cognizance** knowledge, acquaintance, perception, cognition, recognition, acknowledgment, notice, apprehension. IGNORANCE

**cognizant** aware, informed, knowledgeable, conscious, acquainted, familiar, conversant. IGNORANT

**cognize** perceive, comprehend, recognize, know, notice, discern.

**cognomen** surname, title, name, nickname, sobriquet.

**cohere** stick, adhere, cling, cleave, join, unite, fuse, coalesce. PART
be consistent, be connected, follow, make sense, hang together, hold good, correspond, agree.

**coherence** consistency, connection, agreement, congruity, unity, harmony, logic, intelligibilty, comprehension. INCOHERENCE

**coherent** consistent, connected, congruous, logical, orderly, rational, articulate, intelligible, comprehensible. INCOHERENT

**cohesion** adhesion, adherence, union, fusion, coalescence, accretion, consolidation. DISINTEGRATION

**cohort** band, company, troop, legion, squadron, regiment.

**coil** *n*, spiral, helix, convolution, curl, loop.
*v*, wind, twine, twist, curl, loop, spiral, convolute, convolve, wreathe, entwine. UNCOIL

**coin** *v*, devise, invent, create, formulate, make up, originate, fabricate, make, mould, stamp, mint, forge, counterfeit.
*n*, money, specie, cash, change, silver, copper.

**coincide** agree, concur, correspond, tally, harmonize, match, square. CLASH
synchronize, be concurrent, coexist, happen together, occur simultaneously.

**coincidence** chance, accident, fluke, fortuity, stroke of luck. DESIGN
correspondence, harmony, concurrence, agreement. DIFFERENCE
synchronism, coexistence, simultaneity, concomitance.

**coincident** corresponding, agreeing, concurring, coinciding, harmonious, coordinate. DIFFERING
synchronous, simultaneous, concurrent, concomitant, contemporaneous, coexistent.

**coincidental** chance, fortuitous, casual, accidental, unplanned, unforeseen. PLANNED

**cold** *adj*, cool, chill, chilly, frigid, gelid, freezing, icy, frozen, frosty, arctic, polar, wintry, raw, bitter, biting, nippy. HOT
unfeeling, unsympathetic, unresponsive, impassive, indifferent, apathetic, unmoved, unconcerned, distant, stand offish, aloof, frigid, glacial, stony, lukewarm, unfriendly, inhospitable. WARM
*n*, coldness, chill, chilliness, frigidity, iciness, frost. HEAT

**cold-blooded** cruel, inhuman, barbarous, brutal, savage, vicious, ruthless, merciless, heartless, callous, unfeeling. HUMANE

**collaborate** cooperate, work together, join forces, team up. COMPETE

**collaborator** partner, associate, confederate, colleague, contributor, participant. RIVAL
traitor, turncoat, double-dealer, collaborationist, quisling. PATRIOT

**collapse** *v*, subside, cave in, give way, crumble, fall, break down, founder, fail, fold, faint. RECOVER
*n*, subsidence, breakdown, fall, downfall, failure, faint, exhaustion, prostration. RECOVERY

**collar** *n*, ruff, gorget, neckband, collarette, band, necklace.
*v*, grab, seize, catch, capture, apprehend, arrest. RELEASE

**collate** compare, analogize, check, verify, collect, gather, sort, collocate.

**collateral** *n*, security, surety, deposit, pledge, assurance, guarantee.
*adj*, parallel, indirect, related, subordinate, secondary, supporting.

**collation** comparison, verification, collocation, collection.
snack, bite, light meal.

**colleague** partner, associate, co-worker, teammate, workmate, helper, aider, assistant, auxiliary, ally, confederate, collaborator, cooperator, friend, companion, comrade. OPPONENT

**collect** gather, muster, assemble, amass, accumulate, aggregate, congregate, cluster, agglomerate, heap, pile, glean, hoard, save, stockpile. DISPERSE
fetch, pick up, call for.

**collection** gathering, muster, assembly, crowd, congregation, cluster, group, assortment, set, accumulation, heap, pile, hoard, store, anthology, compilation. DISPERSION
offering, offertory, alms, donation, contribution, whip-round (*inf*).

**college** school, polytechnic, university, academy, institution, department, faculty.
association, society, guild, league, body, company, corporation.

**collide** crash, smash, bump, encounter, clash, conflict.

**colligate** connect, link, tie, fasten, bind, join, unite, combine, relate.

**collision** crash, smash, impact, bump, encounter, accident, pile-up.
clash, conflict, opposition. ACCORD

**collocate** arrange, order, dispose, classify, tabulate, sort, place, group, put together, collate.

**collocation** grouping, order, arrangement, organization, sorting, placing, allocation.

**colloquial** conversational, idiomatic, vernacular, informal, casual, familiar, everyday. FORMAL

**colloquy** conversation, discourse, talk, dialogue, debate, discussion, conference.

**collude** connive, conspire, plot, intrigue, scheme, machinate, collaborate, abet.

**collusion** connivance, conspiracy, complicity, intrigue, cahoots (*inf*), plot, scheme.

**collusive** conniving, scheming, deceitful, fraudulent, dishonest. HONEST

**colony** settlement, community, group, district, quarter, province, dependency, dominion, territory.

**colossal** enormous, huge, gigantic, immense, massive, mammoth, vast, mountainous, herculean, titanic, prodigious, tremendous. TINY

**colour** *n*, tint, hue, shade, tinge, tincture, dye, paint, pigment, colorant, colouring, complexion, tone.
rosiness, ruddiness, flush, blush, glow, bloom. PALLOR
disguise, pretence, guise, semblance, front, façade, appearance, pretext, excuse.
*vt*, dye, stain, paint, tint, tinge.
distort, pervert, garble, falsify, disguise, varnish, exaggerate.
*vi*, blush, flush, redden, go crimson. BLANCH

**colourful** bright, vivid, rich, intense, brilliant, multicoloured, psychedelic, kaleidoscopic. COLOURLESS

**colourless** achromatic, hueless, uncoloured, blanched, bleached, washed out, anaemic, wan, ashen, pale, pallid, pasty, livid. COLOURFUL
dull, dreary, dry, insipid, vapid, monotonous, boring, uninteresting, characterless. EXCITING

**colours** banner, ensign, standard, flag.
nature, character, personality, identity, attitude, breed, strain, stamp.

**colt** foal, youngster, novice, beginner, junior.

**coltish** frisky, frolicsome, playful, lively, spirited, sportive, unruly. LETHARGIC

**column** pillar, post, shaft, support, upright, obelisk, monolith, caryatid.
list, file, row, line, string, procession, train.
article, feature, editorial, review.

**coma** stupor, unconsciousness, oblivion, torpor, lethargy, somnolence. CONSCIOUSNESS

**comatose** unconscious, insensible, drugged, stupefied, torpid, drowsy, sleepy, somnolent, sluggish, lethargic. LIVELY

**comb** *v*, disentangle, untangle, groom, curry, smooth, arrange, dress.
sift, search, rake, rummage, scour.

**combat** *v*, fight, oppose, resist, withstand, defy, battle, contest, contend, struggle, strive. SURRENDER
*n*, war, battle, action, fight, conflict, encounter, contest, engagement, skirmish, struggle, strife. PEACE

**combatant** fighter, soldier, adversary, opponent, enemy, contestant, competitor, champion. NEUTRAL

**combination** mixture, blend, compound, synthesis, amalgamation, composite.
fusion, conjunction, blending, coalescence, mixing, mingling. SEPARATION
association, union, combine, alliance, coalition, confederacy, league, consortium, cabal, conspiracy.

**combine** *v*, mix, blend, compound, synthesize, mingle, amalgamate, put together, incorporate, integrate, unite, join, fuse, bond, marry, link, connect, pool, merge. SEPARATE
*n*, association, alliance, coalition, league, confederacy.

**combustible** inflammable, flammable, ignitable, incendiary.

**combustion** burning, incineration, cremation, ignition.

**come** approach, advance, near, move towards, arrive, reach, turn up (*inf*), appear. DEPART
occur, happen, take place, befall, come about, transpire.
issue, originate, proceed, flow, emanate, result, ensue, arise, spring.

**come across,** find, discover, stumble upon, chance upon, meet, encounter, run into, bump into (*inf*).

**come at,** attack, assault, assail, charge, rush, fall upon, fly at. RESIST

**come by,** obtain, get, acquire, procure.

**come in,** enter, cross the threshold, penetrate, arrive, appear, show up (*inf*). LEAVE

**come round,** relent, submit, yield, bend, mellow, soften, acquiesce, concede, allow.

**come to,** recover, revive, regain consciousness, come round, stir. FAINT

**come up with,** advance, propose, put forward, suggest, submit, present, produce, provide, supply.

**comedian** comic, wit, humorist, joker, clown, jester.

**comedown** decline, humiliation, deflation, reverse, blow, disappointment, anticlimax.

**comedy** farce, satire, slapstick, sitcom, pantomime, burlesque, revue.
wit, drollery, humour, fun, joking, badinage, witticisms, buffoonery.

**comeliness** prettiness, beauty, fairness, attractiveness, loveliness, grace, elegance. UGLINESS

**comely** pretty, good-looking, attractive, beautiful, handsome, fair, lovely, winsome, elegant, graceful. UGLY

**comfort** *v*, console, solace, cheer, encourage, hearten, gladden, inspirit, enliven, reassure, relieve, ease, alleviate, soothe, assuage, calm, revive, refresh, strengthen, invigorate. TROUBLE
*n*, consolation, compensation, solace, cheer, encouragement, reassurance, relief, ease, alleviation, help, aid, succour. DISTRESS
well-being, ease, contentment, satisfaction, peace, snugness, cosiness, luxury, opulence, plenty. NEED

**comfortable** snug, cosy, comfy (*inf*), agreeable, pleasant, luxurious, ample, easy, relaxing, restful, convenient, commodious. UNCOMFORTABLE
relaxed, at ease, satisfied, contented, cheerful, serene, tranquil, well-off, prosperous, affluent. UNEASY

**comfortless** dismal, bleak, cheerless, dreary, cold, inhospitable. COMFORTING
disconsolate, forlorn, wretched, miserable, woebegone. CHEERFUL

**comic** *adj*, humorous, witty, droll, zany, amusing, funny, farcical, slapstick, comical. SERIOUS
*n*, comedian, humorist, wit, joker, clown, jester.

**comical** funny, amusing, entertaining, diverting, comic, droll, ludicrous, ridiculous, absurd, laughable, hilarious, side-splitting. SERIOUS

**coming** *adj*, approaching, near, at hand, imminent, impending, in store, forthcoming, future, next. PAST
*n*, arrival, advent, approach. DEPARTURE

**comity** civility, courtesy, politeness, urbanity, suavity, affability. INCIVILITY

**command** *v*, order, enjoin, bid, direct, charge, require, instruct, compel, demand. OBEY
govern, rule, control, lead, head, supervise, dominate.
*n*, order, injunction, bidding, behest, charge, direction, instruction, decree, commandment, edict, precept, demand, requirement, mandate. ENTREATY
government, rule, control, authority, mastery, power, sway, charge, leadership, dominion, domination. SUBORDINATION

**commandeer** seize, take, usurp, appropriate, requisition, expropriate, hijack, confiscate, sequester, impound. SURRENDER

**commander** captain, chief, leader, head, ruler, governor, boss, director, commanding officer.

**commanding** dominant, superior, advantageous, dominating, overlooking.
impressive, imposing, forceful, assertive, compelling, authoritative, imperious, peremptory. MEEK

**commemorate** celebrate, observe, keep, mark, honour, solemnize, immortalize, perpetuate, memorialize, remember, pay tribute to, salute. FORGET

**commemoration** celebration, observance, memorial service, ceremony, remembrance, tribute, memoralization, perpetuation.

**commemorative** memorial, celebratory, dedicatory, perpetuating, acknowledging, marking, in remembrance, in memory, in honour.

**commence** begin, start, embark on, open, inaugurate, institute, initiate, originate, instigate. END

**commencement** beginning, start, opening, outset, inauguration, institution, initiation, origin, dawn, birth. END

**commend** praise, extol, laud, applaud, acclaim, eulogize, speak highly of, compliment, approve, recommend, promote, endorse, advocate. CENSURE
entrust, commit, hand over, yield, give, deliver, consign, confide.

**commendable** laudable, praiseworthy, admirable, exemplary, noble, estimable, worthy, deserving, creditable. DEPLORABLE

**commendation** praise, compliment, tribute, approval, approbation, eulogy, panegyric, encomium, acclaim, applause, encouragement. CONDEMNATION

**commensurate** corresponding, proportionate, to scale, equal, coextensive, equivalent, comparable, appropriate, due, fit, in accord, compatible, adequate, sufficient.

**comment** *v*, remark, observe, say, point out, mention, note, annotate, explain, interpret, criticize, illustrate.
*n*, remark, observation, statement, note, annotation, explanation, commentary, exposition, criticism, illustration.

**commentary** narration, comments, remarks, notes, annotation, exposition, explanation, interpretation, analysis, critique, review, dissertation, essay, record, chronicle, journal.

**commentator** reporter, broadcaster, sportscaster, narrator, commenter, interpreter, annotator, critic.

**commerce** trade, business, traffic, barter, dealing, exchange, merchandising.
communication, intercourse, relations, dealings, interchange, communion.

**commercial** trading, mercantile, business, saleable, marketable, profit-making, mercenary.

**commingle** mingle, intermingle, mix, commix, intermix, blend, combine, amalgamate, join, unite. SEPARATE

**comminute** break, shatter, splinter, fragment, pulverize, triturate, grind.

**commiserate** sympathize, condole, pity, feel sorry for, feel for, grieve, console, comfort, solace.

**commiseration** sympathy, condolence, pity, compassion, fellow feeling, consolation, comfort, solace.

**commission** *n*, errand, duty, task, mission, assignment, appointment, job, function, employment, charge, mandate, authority, warrant, permit.
committee, board, delegation, deputation, council.
allowance, dividend, percentage, cut, share, rake-off (*inf*), fee, brokerage.

perpetration, committal, execution, performance.
*v*, authorize, empower, nominate, appoint, delegate, depute, assign, detail, engage, contract, order.

**commissioner** agent, deputy, delegate, representative, envoy, ambassador, official, officer.

**commit** do, perform, perpetrate, enact, execute, carry out.
entrust, consign, deliver, confide, hand over, charge, commend.
engage, align, pledge, obligate, bind, implicate, compromise.
confine, imprison, jail, intern, incarcerate. RELEASE

**commitment** pledge, engagement, promise, guarantee, vow, undertaking, obligation, duty, responsibility, liability.
dedication, involvement, loyalty, devotion.

**committal** consignment, delivery, entrustment, assignment, commission, delegation.
perpetration, commission, execution, performance.
imprisonment, confinement, custody, detention, incarceration.

**committee** board, council, panel, commission, jury, working party.

**commodious** spacious, ample, roomy, capacious, large, extensive, vast, expansive, comfortable, convenient. NARROW

**commodities** goods, wares, produce, merchandise, products, stock.

**common** universal, general, public, communal, joint, shared, mutual. PRIVATE
ordinary, everyday, usual, average, standard, customary, habitual, regular, plain, simple, workaday, run-of-the-mill, widespread, general, familiar, popular, conventional. RARE
trite, hackneyed, stale, commonplace, inferior, vulgar, cheap, low, coarse, undistinguished. REFINED

**commonplace** *adj*, ordinary, everyday, common, undistinguished, humdrum, trite, obvious, banal, hackneyed, stale, threadbare. DISTINCTIVE
*n*, cliché, platitude, truism, banality.

**common-sense** *adj*, common-sensical, sensible, sound, wise, practical, reasonable, realistic, prudent, judicious, level-headed, shrewd, astute, down-to-earth, matter-of-fact. FOOLISH
*n*, intelligence, good sense, mother wit, prudence, practicality, wisdom, discernment, gumption (*inf*), nous (*inf*). FOLLY

**commonwealth** empire, realm, state, nation, people, republic.

**commotion** turmoil, tumult, upheaval, disorder, disturbance, fuss, ado, furore, agitation, perturbation, bustle, uproar, hullabaloo, to-do, riot, rumpus, brouhaha. CALM

**communal** public, common, shared, collective, joint. PRIVATE

**commune**[1] *v*, communicate, converse, talk, confer, discourse, discuss, confide.

**commune**[2] *n*, community, collective, cooperative, kibbutz.

**communicable** transferable, transmittable, infectious, contagious, catching.

**communicate** impart, transmit, inform, tell, declare, announce, divulge, disclose, reveal, disseminate, spread, pass on, bestow, confer, convey. WITHHOLD
converse, talk, commune, correspond, ring up, call, be in contact, get in touch.
connect, adjoin.

**communication** announcement, declaration, disclosure, communiqué, dispatch, news, information, report, account, statement, bulletin, message.
conversation, discourse, intercourse, correspondence, contact, touch, link, connection.
dissemination, spreading, transmission, conveyance.

**communicative** open, unreserved, forthcoming, expansive, frank, candid, talkative, voluble, loquacious, chatty, sociable. RESERVED

**communion** intercourse, exchange, conversation, dialogue, rapport, sympathy, affinity, participation, intimacy, closeness, togetherness, harmony, accord, concord, agreement, unity. ESTRANGEMENT
Eucharist, Lord's Supper, Sacrament, Mass.

**communist** Marxist, Bolshevik, collectivist, socialist, leftist, radical, Red (*inf*). FASCIST

**community** society, general public, nation, state, people, populace, brotherhood, association, company, colony, village, township, district, neighbourhood, parish.
similarity, likeness, affinity, agreement.

**commute** exchange, barter, substitute, switch, replace, change, alter.
reduce, shorten, curtail, remit, mitigate, alleviate.

**compact**[1] *adj*, close, dense, thick, impenetrable, impermeable, solid, firm, compressed, condensed, packed, tight, small, neat, portable. LOOSE
short, terse, concise, brief, succinct, pithy, laconic. LENGTHY
*v*, compress, condense, pack, cram, stuff, consolidate, fuse, bind, join, unite. DIFFUSE

**compact**[2] *n*, contract, covenant, treaty, concordat, alliance, pact, entente, bond, agreement, arrangement, bargain, deal.

**companion** associate, comrade, colleague, partner, consort, fellow, counterpart, mate, accomplice, ally, friend, acquaintance. FOE
attendant, escort, chaperon, duenna, aide, assistant, squire.

**companionship** fellowship, friendship, amity, brotherhood, fraternity, comradeship, camaraderie, esprit de corps, rapport, conviviality, company, togetherness, society, association. LONELINESS

**company** business, firm, corporation, association, syndicate, partnership, concern, establishment, house.
assembly, assemblage, gathering, concourse, convention, meeting, collection, group, band, troop, troupe, body, party, ensemble, gang, set, circle, association, crowd, congregation.
companionship, fellowship, society, visitors, guests, callers, party.

**comparable** like, similar, akin, related, alike, resembling, corresponding, equivalent, commensurate, approximate, tantamount, as good as, equal, on a par. INCOMPARABLE

**comparative** relative, by comparison, qualified, approximate, near. ABSOLUTE

**compare** liken, equate, correlate, relate, parallel, match, juxtapose, contrast, collate, balance, weigh.
resemble, equal, correspond, be on a par, approximate, approach, compete, vie.

**comparison** likeness, resemblance, similarity, relation, correlation, comparability, likening, parallel, analogy, simile. CONTRAST
juxtaposition, collation, contrast, distinction.

**compartment** partition, division, section, part, space, area, department. WHOLE
locker, cubbyhole, pigeonhole, booth, cubicle, cell, alcove, niche.

**compass** *n*, range, scope, extent, reach, stretch, circumference, bound, boundary, limit, sphere, realm, zone, field, area, enclosure.
*v*, encircle, encompass, surround, circumscribe, environ, gird, enclose, hem in, besiege, beset.
attain, achieve, accomplish, realize, fulfil, effect, perform, execute, obtain, procure. FAIL

**compassion** sympathy, commiseration, pity, tenderness, kindliness, kindness, clemency, mercy, humanity, charity. CRUELTY

**compassionate** kind, kindly, tender, sympathetic, benign, understanding, humane, soft-hearted, indulgent, clement, lenient, merciful, charitable, benevolent, magnanimous. HARSH

**compatible** congruous, consistent, accordant, reconcilable, in keeping, consonant, harmonious, in harmony, agreeable, like-minded, at one. INCOMPATIBLE

**compatriot** fellow countryman, fellow citizen.

**compeer** peer, equal, mate, fellow, counterpart, companion, comrade. SUPERIOR

**compel** force, coerce, drive, impel, urge, make, oblige, constrain, require, exact, necessitate. COAX
subdue, overpower, crush, bow.

**compelling** enthralling, gripping, riveting, spellbinding, hypnotic. BORING
forceful, convincing, irrefutable, cogent, weighty, powerful. WEAK

**compendious** concise, succinct, brief, short, terse, abridged, condensed, compressed, compact, pithy, comprehensive, summary. EXTENDED

**compendium** synopsis, summary, digest, abstract, epitome, abridgment, condensation, résumé, précis, syllabus, prospectus. AMPLIFICATION

**compensate** recompense, reimburse, refund, repay, remunerate, reward, requite, indemnify, satisfy, atone, make amends, make good, make up for, redress. INJURE offset, balance, counterbalance, cancel out, neutralize, nullify.

**compensation** recompense, reimbursement, repayment, refund, remuneration, reward, indemnity, reparation, damages, satisfaction, atonement, amends. INJURY

**compete** contest, contend, vie, rival, emulate, challenge, oppose, struggle, strive, fight, participate. ALLY

**competence** ability, capability, capacity, adequacy, fitness, suitability, qualification, skill, expertise, proficiency, mastery. INCOMPETENCE

sufficiency, enough, subsistence, means, wherewithal, livelihood. POVERTY

**competent** able, capable, adequate, sufficient, fit, suitable, equal, qualified, expert, proficient, masterful, skilled, skilful, adept, knowledgeable. INCOMPETENT

**competition** contest, tournament, match, championship, race, game, quiz.

rivalry, emulation, one-upmanship (*inf*), contention, strife, conflict, opposition. ALLIANCE

**competitive** rival, competing, vying, combative, aggressive, cutthroat, striving, ambitious.

**competitor** rival, opponent, adversary, antagonist, opposition, competition, emulator, challenger, contestant, contender, entrant, candidate, aspirant. PARTNER

**compilation** collection, anthology, treasury, assortment, selection, compendium.

compiling, gathering, assembly, combination, accumulation.

**compile** collect, gather, garner, cull, amass, accumulate, assemble, put together, prepare, compose, organize, arrange.

**complacency** self-satisfaction, smugness, contentment, pleasure, satisfaction, gratification, ease, tranquillity. UNEASINESS

**complacent** self-satisfied, smug, contented, pleased, satisfied, serene, tranquil, at ease, placid, unconcerned. UNEASY

**complain** grumble, moan, groan, grouse, gripe (*inf*), bellyache (*inf*), beef (*inf*), bewail, bemoan, lament, deplore, murmur, carp, find fault, cavil. REJOICE

**complainant** accuser, claimant, plaintiff, petitioner. DEFENDANT

**complaint** grumble, grievance, grouse, plaint, lament, moan, quibble, cavil, criticism, accusation, charge, remonstrance, protest.

ailment, disorder, malady, affliction, indisposition, illness, sickness, disease. HEALTH

**complaisance** deference, compliance, obligingness, acquiescence, agreeableness, graciousness, urbanity, suavity, politeness, courtesy, civility. CHURLISHNESS

**complaisant** deferential, compliant, obliging, acquiescent, agreeable, accommodating, gracious, urbane, polite, civil, courteous. CHURLISH

**complement** *n*, quota, total, totality, aggregate, full number, capacity, entirety, whole. PART

counterpart, companion, match, coordinate, supplement, accessory, finishing touch.

*v*, complete, supplement, add to, make up, round off, crown, set off. CLASH

**complementary** completing, perfecting, consummating, corresponding, reciprocal, correlative, interdependent, matched. CONFLICTING

**complete** *adj*, entire, whole, total, full, integral, unabridged, undivided, unimpaired, perfect. INCOMPLETE

completed, finished, ended, concluded, fulfilled, accomplished, achieved, done. UNFINISHED

absolute, utter, thorough, downright, total, out-and-out, perfect, consummate. PARTIAL

*v*, finish, end, conclude, terminate, fulfil, realize, achieve, attain, accomplish, perform, do, execute, perfect, consummate, crown, cap. BEGIN

**completion** conclusion, end, finish, termination, close, fulfilment, realization, achievement, fruition, accomplishment, performance, execution, perfection, consummation. BEGINNING

**complex** manifold, multiple, composite, compound, mingled, mixed, elaborate, intricate, involved, knotty, tangled, complicated, tortuous, labyrinthine. SIMPLE

**complexion** colour, colouring, skin tone, pigmentation, cast, appearance, aspect, countenance, look, character, nature, angle, light.

**complexity** intricacy, complication, ramification, involvement, entanglement, network, labyrinth. SIMPLICITY

**compliance** acquiescence, yielding, concession, concurrence, consent, assent, agreement, complaisance, submission, docility, obedience, cooperation, conformity. RESISTANCE

**compliant** acquiescent, yielding, obliging, accommodating, complaisant, agreeable, submissive, docile, obedient, cooperative. OBSTINATE

**complicate** confuse, involve, entangle, muddle, confound. SIMPLIFY

**complicated** confused, involved, complex, intricate, elaborate, convoluted, tangled, knotty, perplexing, labyrinthine. SIMPLE

**complication** complexity, intricacy, confusion, tangle, entanglement, web, network. SIMPLICITY
difficulty, problem, drawback, snag, obstacle.

**complicity** collusion, conspiracy, connivance, collaboration, abetment.

**compliment** *v*, praise, speak highly of, commend, acclaim, laud, extol, flatter, congratulate, felicitate. INSULT
*n*, praise, commendation, eulogy, encomium, tribute, honour, flattery, admiration, congratulations. ABUSE

**complimentary** flattering, congratulatory, laudatory, eulogistic, commendation, appreciative, approving, adulatory. INSULTING
free, gratis, on the house.

**compliments** greetings, respects, regards, good wishes.

**comply** obey, conform, accede, abide by, observe, respect, defer, submit, yield, acquiesce, agree, consent, fulfil, discharge, perform, execute, meet, satisfy. REFUSE

**component** *n*, constituent, element, part, ingredient, unit, item, piece, factor. WHOLE
*adj*, constituent, integral, intrinsic.

**comport** agree, tally, correspond, harmonize, accord, match, suit, square, coincide. DIFFER
behave, conduct, act, demean, carry, bear, acquit.

**compose** form, make, put together, construct, build, comprise, constitute, make up, invent, create, contrive, devise, write, frame, produce.
adjust, arrange, organize, settle, resolve, regulate. DISORGANIZE
pacify, calm, soothe, assuage, appease, still, quiet, quell, control, collect. DISTURB

**composed** calm, tranquil, serene, sedate, cool, collected, self-possessed, unruffled, poised, imperturbable, placid, relaxed, at ease, untroubled. AGITATED

**composite** *adj*, compound, complex, intricate, manifold, multiple, mixed, combined, synthesized, hybrid. SIMPLE
*n*, compound, blend, mixture, synthesis, combination.

**composition** formation, make-up, structure, arrangement, organization, form, constitution.
making, creation, production, manufacture, fabrication, formulation.
work, essay, opus, piece, exercise.

**compost** fertilizer, manure, muck, dung, mulch.

**composure** calmness, tranquillity, serenity, coolness, self-possession, sang-froid, poise, aplomb, imperturbability, placidity, ease, equanimity. AGITATION

**compound** *v*, mix, blend, combine, mingle, intermingle, amalgamate, unite, synthesize, fuse. SEPARATE
intensify, augment, heighten, aggravate, exacerbate, complicate. LESSEN
arrange, settle, agree, compromise.
*n*, mixture, blend, combination, composite, synthesis, amalgam, alloy, medley, composition.
*adj*, composite, complex, complicated, intricate, multiple, combined. SIMPLE

**comprehend** understand, fathom, apprehend, grasp, see, perceive, conceive, discern, make out, assimilate, take in.
include, comprise, embrace, involve, contain. EXCLUDE

**comprehensible** understandable, intelligible, clear, coherent, explicit, plain, distinct, articulate. INCOMPREHENSIBLE

**comprehension** understanding, apprehension, grasp, perception, conception, discernment, awareness, sense, intelligence, intellect, knowledge, wisdom. INCOMPREHENSION
compass, scope, range, extent, reach, field, limits.

**comprehensive** wide, broad, large, extensive, sweeping, full, encyclopedic, inclusive, all-inclusive, all-embracing, exhaustive, thorough, universal, catholic. LIMITED

**compress** compact, concentrate, press, squeeze, squash, crush, cram, pack, constrict, contract, condense, abbreviate, shorten, summarize, abridge. EXPAND

**compression** contraction, constriction, pressure, squeezing, condensation, abbreviation, shortening. EXPANSION

**comprise** include, contain, embrace, comprehend, consist of. EXCLUDE
form, compose, constitute, make up.

**compromise** *v*, agree, concede, settle, compose, adjust, accommodate, meet halfway, give and take. DIFFER
imperil, endanger, jeopardize, hazard, expose, implicate, prejudice, discredit, weaken. PROTECT
*n*, agreement, settlement, concession, give-and-take, adjustment, accommodation, middle ground, happy medium, balance.

**compulsion** force, constraint, coercion, obligation, duress, pressure. COAXING
urge, drive, need, obsession, preoccupation.

**compulsive** compelling, urgent, driving, overwhelming, uncontrollable, obsessive, habitual, inveterate.

**compulsory** obligatory, binding, imperative, mandatory, necessary, requisite, unavoidable. VOLUNTARY

**compunction** remorse, regret, contrition, repentance, penitence, qualm, misgiving, hesitation, reluctance, sorrow, guilt, embarrassment. SATISFACTION

**compunctious** remorseful, regretful, sorry, apologetic, contrite, repentant, penitent, hesitant, reluctant, sorrowful, ashamed, embarrassed.

**computation** calculation, reckoning, estimation, valuation, measurement, adding up, counting, enumeration.

**compute** calculate, work out, reckon, figure, estimate, rate, total, add up, count, enumerate, measure. GUESS

**comrade** companion, associate, mate, fellow, compeer, colleague, partner, ally, friend, pal (*inf*). ENEMY

**con** *v*, swindle, defraud, deceive, dupe, cheat, hoodwink, mislead, rip off (*inf*).
*n*, swindle, fraud, deception, trick, hoax, rip-off (*inf*).

**concatenate** join, connect, link, unite, couple, string, chain. SEVER

**concatenation** chain, series, succession, sequence, continuity, connection, linking, link, nexus, coupling.

**concave** hollow, hollowed, sunken, depressed, cupped, scooped, excavated. CONVEX

**conceal** hide, secrete, disguise, dissemble, screen, cloak, mask, camouflage, veil, obscure, cover, bury, suppress. REVEAL

**concealment** hiding, disguise, camouflage, masking, screening, cover-up, blind, cover, hideaway, shelter, retreat, privacy. REVELATION

**concede** admit, acknowledge, grant, allow, recognize, accept, yield, surrender, cede, relinquish, hand over, deliver. DENY

**conceit** vanity, egotism, vainglory, pride, self-esteem, self-love, narcissism, boastfulness, swagger, arrogance, complacency. MODESTY
notion, fancy, idea, thought, belief, concept, whim.

**conceited** vain, egotistical, vainglorious, arrogant, proud, cocky, bigheaded (*inf*), boastful, smug, complacent, self-important, narcissistic. MODEST

**conceivable** possible, imaginable, thinkable, picturable, believable, credible. INCONCEIVABLE

**conceive** imagine, think, picture, envisage, fancy, suppose, comprehend, understand, perceive, apprehend, grasp, fathom, see.
devise, contrive, invent, think up, formulate, design, plan, project.

**concentrate** focus, converge, centre, centralize, localize, cluster, conglomerate, congregate, assemble, muster, amass, collect. DISPERSE
condense, reduce, distil, purify, intensify, thicken, compress, compact. DILUTE
meditate, ponder, ruminate, think, be engrossed, pay attention.

**concentration** attention, application, absorption, heed, deliberation, meditation. DISTRACTION
convergence, focus, centralization, intensification, consolidation, collection, gathering, conglomeration, cluster, aggregation, accumulation, mass. DISPERSAL

**concept** conception, idea, notion, thought, abstraction, impression, hypothesis, theory.

**conception** idea, notion, concept, thought, theory, design, plan.
impression, picture, image, perception, understanding, comprehension, inkling, clue.
fertilization, fecundation, impregnation, insemination.
beginning, origin, birth, inception, genesis, outset, inauguration, invention. TERMINATION

**concern** interest, affect, involve, relate to, touch, regard, bear on, apply to.
disturb, trouble, distress, worry, disquiet, perturb, bother.
*n*, affair, business, duty, responsibility, field, matter, interest, importance, consequence, bearing, relevance.
anxiety, worry, care, solicitude, sympathy, regard, heed, attention, distress, disquiet, sorrow, grief. INDIFFERENCE
company, firm, business, enterprise, establishment, corporation, house.

**concerning** about, touching, regarding, respecting, re, with reference to, relating to, apropos of. DISREGARDING

**concert** *n*, performance, entertainment, recital, symphony, concerto, festival, gig (*inf*).
agreement, accord, concord, harmony, unison, unanimity, concensus, cooperation. DISAGREEMENT
*v*, arrange, contrive, devise, design, concoct, plan, plot, scheme.

**concerted** combined, united, joint, mutual, cooperative, collaborative, prearranged, planned. INDIVIDUAL

**concession** yielding, surrender, admission, acknowledgment, assent, grant, licence, permit, right, privilege, boon, exemption, dispensation, indulgence, allowance, adjustment, compromise. REFUSAL

**conciliate** win, win over, placate, appease, propitiate, pacify, mollify, reconcile, reunite, mediate, negotiate. ALIENATE

**conciliation** appeasement, propitiation, placation, peace, pacification, reconciliation. ESTRANGEMENT

**conciliatory** placatory, pacifying, appeasing, propitiative, pacific, peaceable, disarming, winning, friendly.

**concise** brief, short, terse, to the point, compact, pithy, succinct, laconic, condensed, compressed, summary, compendious, epigrammatic. LENGTHY

**conclave** council, assembly, meeting, session, cabinet, synod, convention, conference.

**conclude** close, end, terminate, finish, complete, wind up (*inf*), wrap up (*inf*). BEGIN
settle, resolve, decide, determine, negotiate, effect, accomplish, pull off (*inf*), clinch (*inf*).
infer, deduce, construe, surmise, guess, assume, suppose, gather, reckon, judge, decide.

**conclusion** close, end, ending, termination, finish, completion, outcome, issue, result, upshot. BEGINNING
inference, deduction, surmise, guess, assumption, supposition, opinion, judgment, decision, resolution, verdict.

**conclusive** final, definitive, ultimate, definite, positive, decisive, convincing, clinching, indisputable, irrefutable, unanswerable. INCONCLUSIVE

**concoct** contrive, devise, invent, think up, cook up (*inf*), brew, hatch, plot, plan, prepare, project, design, make up, formulate.

**concoction** mixture, compound, blend, brew, potion.

**concomitant** attendant, accompanying, associative, connected, concurrent, synchronous, coincident, contemporaneous. INDEPENDENT

**concord** harmony, agreement, accord, concert, unanimity, consensus, concordance, amity, unity, peace, rapport, friendship, good will. DISCORD
treaty, compact, concordant, entente, convention, pact, agreement.

**concordant** harmonious, in agreement, consonant, agreeing, accordant, unanimous, at one. DISCORDANT

**concordat** covenant, agreement, bond, compact, treaty, pact, convention, settlement, bargain.

**concourse** assembly, assemblage, gathering, meeting, collection, crowd, throng, mob, multitude, horde, crush, cluster, convergence, confluence.

**concrete** *n*, cement, mortar.
*adj*, real, material, tangible, substantial, physical, actual, factual. ABSTRACT
specific, particular, precise, explicit, definite. VAGUE

firm, solid, solidified, consolidated, compressed, compact, petrified, calcified. FLUID

**concubine** mistress, paramour, courtesan, kept woman, odalisque.

**concupiscence** desire, passion, lust, lechery, lasciviousness, prurience, randiness (*inf*). CONTINENCE

**concur** agree, assent, acquiesce, accede, accord, harmonize, coincide, cooperate, combine, collaborate. DISSENT

**concurrence** agreement, assent, accord, harmony, unity, coincidence, simultaneity, cooperation, collaboration, alliance, combination. DISAGREEMENT

**concurrent** simultaneous, synchronous, contemporaneous, parallel, coincident, concomitant, attendant.
convergent, confluent, intersecting. DIVERGENT
agreeing, accordant, harmonious, consentient, in agreement, unanimous, at one. DISCORDANT

**concussion** collision, crash, impact, shock, clash, blow, jolt, jarring.
shaking, agitation.

**condemn** doom, damn, sentence, convict, find guilty. ACQUIT
censure, blame, disapprove, rebuke, upbraid, reproach, reprove, reprobate, denounce, proscribe, prohibit, ban, bar. PRAISE

**condemnation** conviction, sentence, judgment, doom, damnation. ACQUITTAL
censure, blame, disapproval, disapprobation, reproof, reproach, reprobation, denunciation, proscription, banning, prohibition. PRAISE

**condemnatory** accusatory, incriminating, damning, imputative, denunciatory, censorious, critical, disapproving, reproachful, defamatory, deprecatory. LAUDATORY

**condensation** contraction, compression, reduction, abridgment, abbreviation, curtailment, diminution, concentration, consolidation, crystallization, precipitation, distillation, liquefaction. AMPLIFICATION
digest, epitome, summary, abridgment, synopsis, précis, résumé, abstract.

**condense** contract, compress, reduce, compact, encapsulate, abridge, abbreviate, curtail, shorten, diminish, concentrate, consolidate, solidify, coagulate, thicken, boil down, precipitate, crystallize, liquefy. AMPLIFY

**condescend** deign, stoop, vouchsafe, see fit, unbend, descend, lower oneself, humble oneself, patronize, talk down.

**condescending** patronizing, disdainful, supercilious, pompous, lofty, haughty, arrogant, snobbish, toffee-nosed (*inf*). HUMBLE

**condescension** stooping, patronage, disdain, snobbery, airs, haughtiness, loftiness, superciliousness. HUMILITY
favour, grace, deference, graciousness, indulgence, civility, courtesy.

**condign** fitting, suitable, appropriate, just, fair, deserved, merited. UNDESERVED

**condiment** sauce, relish, seasoning, flavouring, dressing, spice.

**condition** *n*, state, situation, position, circumstances, case, plight, predicament.
stipulation, proviso, provision, term, clause, qualification, restriction, requirement, necessity.
estate, rank, station, standing, position, class, caste.
shape, order, fitness, fettle, health.
*v*, habituate, accustom, inure, adapt, prepare, equip, educate, train.

**conditional** provisional, qualified, restricted, dependent, relative, subject to, contingent. ABSOLUTE

**condole** commiserate, sympathize, feel for, console, grieve, lament. REJOICE

**condolence** commiseration, sympathy, pity, fellow feeling, compassion, consolation, comfort, solace.

**condonation** pardon, forgiveness, dispensation, amnesty, remission, excusing, ignoring, overlooking. PUNISHMENT

**condone** pardon, forgive, excuse, overlook, ignore, disregard, wink at, turn a blind eye to. PUNISH

**conduce** lead, tend, contribute, aid, help, advance, promote, forward. HINDER

**conducive** leading, tending, contributory, helpful, useful, instrumental, favourable, advantageous, productive.

**conduct** *n*, behaviour, bearing, manners, mien, demeanour, attitude, deportment, comportment, carriage, ways, actions, habits.
leadership, management, administration, control, handling, direction, guidance, running, operation, supervision.

*v*, lead, guide, direct, usher, steer, pilot, escort, accompany, bring, convey, transmit.
control, manage, run, direct, administer, handle, supervise, preside over.
act, behave, comport, acquit, bear, carry.

**conductor** leader, guide, director, official, maestro.
transmitter, carrier, bearer.

**conduit** duct, passage, pipe, tube, channel, canal.

**confabulate** converse, talk, chat, gossip, natter, chatter, prate, prattle.

**confection** making, manufacture, production, composition.
sweet, sweetmeat, candy, comfit, preserve, confectionery.

**confederacy** league, confederation, federation, coalition, union, alliance, bloc.

**confederate** *adj*, allied, combined, united, federal, confederated. OPPOSED
*n*, ally, associate, partner, colleague, abettor, accomplice, accessory. OPPONENT
*v*, ally, combine, unite, merge, amalgamate, federate. SEPARATE

**confederation** alliance, federation, confederacy, league, union, coalition.

**confer** *vt*, bestow, grant, award, present, accord, vouchsafe, give. WITHDRAW
*vi*, converse, talk, consult, parley, deliberate.

**conference** meeting, congress, convention, council, forum, symposium, seminar, discussion, talk, parley, consultation, debate.

**confess** acknowledge, admit, own, own up (*inf*), come clean (*inf*), grant, concede, recognize, aver, assert, affirm, avow, declare, profess, attest, confirm. DENY

**confession** acknowledgment, admission, declaration, avowal, disclosure, revelation, recognition. DENIAL

**confide** trust, depend, rely, have faith, believe. DISTRUST
disclose, reveal, divulge, tell, impart, confess, admit. CONCEAL
entrust, commit, commend, consign.

**confidence** trust, faith, reliance, dependence, belief, assurance, conviction. DOUBT
self-assurance, self-reliance, aplomb, poise, courage, nerve, boldness, audacity. TIMIDITY

**confident** sure, positive, certain, assured, convinced, satisfied. DOUBTFUL
self-assured, self-reliant, self-possessed, assured, bold, courageous, dauntless. TIMID

**confidential** private, secret, personal, intimate, privy, classified, restricted, hush-hush (*inf*). PUBLIC
trusty, trustworthy, reliable, dependable, faithful. UNRELIABLE

**confidentially** in confidence, between ourselves, off the record, sub rosa, in camera, behind closed doors, secretly, privately. PUBLICLY

**configuration** figure, form, shape, cast, outline, contour, formation, structure, arrangement.

**confine** *v*, restrict, limit, circumscribe, straiten, hem in, bound, bind, restrain, hold back, imprison, cage, incarcerate, immure, impound, pen, intern. RELEASE
*n*, limit, boundary, border, frontier, edge.

**confinement** imprisonment, incarceration, internment, detention, custody, duress, restraint, restriction. LIBERATION
childbirth, lying-in, *accouchement*, labour, parturition, delivery.

**confirm** verify, corroborate, substantiate, validate, bear out, prove, endorse, ratify, sanction, approve, affirm. REFUTE
strengthen, reinforce, fortify, fix, establish, settle, clinch, assure. ANNUL

**confirmation** verification, corroboration, substantiation, proof, evidence, ratification, endorsement, sanction, approval, affirmation. REFUTATION

**confirmed** habitual, chronic, inveterate, dyed-in-the-wool, hardened, seasoned, established, ingrained.

**confiscate** seize, sequester, sequestrate, dispossess, distrain, impound, appropriate, expropriate. RESTORE

**conflagration** fire, blaze, inferno, holocaust.

**conflict** *v*, clash collide, disagree, differ, be at variance, interfere, oppose, contest, contend, struggle, fight.
*n*, clash, collision, disagreement, difference, discord, dispute, variance, friction, opposition, antagonism, strife, struggle, battle, fight, combat, contest, contention, encounter, engagement. AGREEMENT

**confluence** conflux, convergence, junction, meeting, union, concurrence. DIVERGENCE
concourse, assembly, assemblage, crowd, throng, host, multitude, congregation.

**confluent** meeting, converging, merging, mingling, blending. DIVERGENT

**conform** comply, yield, submit, obey, follow, consent, adapt, adjust, reconcile. REBEL
agree, correspond, tally, match, accord, harmonize, suit, square, fit. DISAGREE

**conformity** compliance, yielding, submission, obedience, observance, allegiance, orthodoxy, conventionality. NONCONFORMITY
agreement, correspondence, likeness, resemblance, similarity, harmony, accord, congruity, compatibility. DISCORD

**confound** astound, amaze, surprise, stun, dumbfound, astonish, perplex, bewilder, nonplus, mystify, confuse, embarrass, disconcert.
defeat, annihilate, destroy, ruin, overwhelm, upset, quash, contradict, refute.

**confounded** miserable, wretched, accursed, damnable, blasted, abominable, execrable, detestable, odious. BLESSED

**confront** face, encounter, challenge, defy, brave, beard, tackle, face up to, accost, oppose, resist, stand up to. EVADE

**confrontation** encounter, conflict, contest, battle, crisis, showdown (*inf*).
defiance, opposition, challenge, resistance.

**confuse** bewilder, perplex, puzzle, mystify, baffle, bemuse, nonplus. ENLIGHTEN
muddle, mix up, mistake, confound, jumble, disorder, garble, disarrange, derange, mingle, intermingle, blend.
abash, mortify, shame, embarrass, disconcert, discomfit, discompose, fluster.

**confusion** bewilderment, perplexity, puzzlement, mystification, bafflement. ENLIGHTENMENT
muddle, mess, disorder, disarray, jumble, garble, chaos, anarchy, turmoil, tumult, commotion, upheaval. ORDER
abashment, mortification, shame, embarrassment, chagrin, discomfiture, discomposure.

**confute** refute, disprove, rebut, invalidate, belie, contradict, controvert, overthrow, overcome. PROVE

**congeal** coagulate, clot, curdle, thicken, set, jell, stiffen, harden, solidify, freeze.

**congenial** pleasant, agreeable, friendly, genial, affable, complaisant, kindly, sympathetic, kindred, compatible, suited, well-matched, congruous, consonant, favourable. DISAGREEABLE

**congenital** inherent, innate, inborn, inbred, connate, natural, ingrained, inveterate.

**congested** blocked, clogged, jammed, full, crowded, packed, crammed, stuffed, overflowing, teeming. CLEAR

**congestion** crowding, jam, bottleneck, blocking, clogging, packing, cramming, surfeit, repletion. CLEARANCE

**conglomerate** *v*, cluster, gather, amass, accumulate, aggregate, agglomerate. DISPERSE
*n*, conglomeration, mass, aggregate, agglomerate.
multinational, corporation, merger, cartel.

**conglomeration** cluster, mass, conglomerate, aggregate, aggregation, agglomeration, accumulation, assortment, medley, miscellany.

**congratulate** compliment, felicitate, acclaim, praise.

**congratulations** felicitations, compliments, best wishes, good wishes, well done, bravo.

**congregate** collect, gather, assemble, muster, convene, meet, rally, mass, throng, flock. DISPERSE

**congregation** gathering, assembly, assemblage, muster, meeting, host, crowd, throng.
parish, flock, parishioners, fellowship, brethren, laity.

**congress** meeting, conference, convention, assembly, council, conclave, convocation, legislature, parliament, senate.

**congruity** congruence, agreement, accord, concord, correspondence, consistency, harmony, compatibility, suitability, fitness, appropriateness. INCONGRUITY

**congruous** agreeing, accordant, concordant, corresponding, congruent, consonant, consistent, harmonious, compatible, suitable, fit, appropriate. INCONGRUOUS

**conjectural** hypothetical, theoretical, academic, speculative, supposed, putative, surmised, guessed, suspected. PROVEN

**conjecture** *v*, guess, surmise, suppose, suspect, assume, infer, imagine, fancy, theorize, hypothesize, postulate. PROVE
*n*, guess, surmise, supposition, assumption, inference, speculation, theory, hypothesis,

conclusion, judgment, belief, suspicion, fancy, divination. PROOF

**conjoin** join, connect, link, unite, tie, bind, fasten, hitch, combine, associate, league, merge, confederate. SEVER

**conjugal** connubial, matrimonial, married, wedded, marital, nuptial, bridal, hymeneal. CELIBATE

**conjunction** joining, connection, link, union, combination, association, junction, juxtaposition, concurrence, coincidence. SEPARATION

**conjuncture** juncture, stage, pass, point, turning point, crisis, crossroads, emergency, exigency, predicament, dilemma, quandary.

**conjuration** incantation, chant, invocation, spell, charm, magic, sorcery, enchantment.

**conjure** perform magic, juggle, do tricks. enchant, bewitch, charm, fascinate, cast a spell, invoke, call up, summon, rouse.

beseech, implore, appeal to, entreat, crave, adjure, beg, pray, supplicate. ORDER

**conjure up,** evoke, call to mind, bring to mind, recall, recollect.

**conjurer** magician, sorcerer, wizard, juggler, illusionist.

**connate** inborn, congenital, innate, natural, inherent.

akin, related, cognate, allied, similar, associated.

**connect** join, link, tie, fasten, bind, unite, couple, affix, adhere, combine, associate, relate, ally, adjoin, communicate. SEVER

**connected** joined, linked, bound, united, combined, associated, related, akin, allied, adjoining, adjacent. UNCONNECTED

coherent, intelligible, comprehensible, fluent, consecutive. DISCONNECTED

**connection** junction, union, link, tie, attachment, bond, alliance, association, relationship, liaison, correspondence, communication, intercourse, commerce.

contact, acquaintance, friend, associate, ally.

relative, relation, kin, kindred, family.

**connivance** conspiracy, intrigue, collusion, complicity, abetment, consent, approval, condonation.

**connive** conspire, intrigue, plot, scheme, collude.

**connive at,** overlook, disregard, blink at, wink at, turn a blind eye to, let pass, condone. OPPOSE

**connoisseur** expert, authority, specialist, savant, devotee, buff (*inf*), judge, arbiter, critic, epicure, gourmet, aesthete.

**connotation** implication, significance, meaning, nuance, undertone, suggestion, inference, association, allusion, reference.

**connote** imply, suggest, infer, hint at, signify, mean, betoken, indicate, involve, implicate.

**connubial** conjugal, matrimonial, married, wedded, marital, nuptial, bridal, hymeneal. CELIBATE

**conquer** defeat, vanquish, beat, surmount, overcome, overpower, master, subdue, crush, quell, suppress, subjugate, rout, checkmate, humble, humiliate. SURRENDER

triumph, prevail, succeed, win, gain, achieve, obtain, acquire, occupy, annex, seize. LOSE

**conqueror** victor, winner, champion, master, lord, conquistador, hero. VICTIM

**conquest** victory, triumph, success, mastery, defeat, vanquishment, overthrow, rout, subjugation, humiliation, invasion, occupation, annexation, coup. SURRENDER

seduction, enchantment, captivation, allurement, enticement, enthralment. REPULSION

catch, prize, trophy, booty, plunder, spoils.

**consanguinity** kinship, blood tie, family tie, common ancestry, relationship, affinity, association, connection.

**conscience** scruples, principles, morals, ethics, moral sense, integrity, honesty, conscientiousness.

**conscientious** diligent, painstaking, assiduous, scrupulous, meticulous, thorough, exact, precise, strict, faithful, careful. CARELESS

honest, upright, just, fair, incorruptible, scrupulous, principled, moral, high-minded, good, honourable. UNPRINCIPLED

**conscious** aware, awake, alert, cognizant, mindful, sensible, sentient, alive, knowing, percipient, thinking, reasoning, rational. UNCONSCIOUS

deliberate, intentional, planned, premeditated, calculated, wilful. UNINTENTIONAL

**consciousness** awareness, realization, recognition, cognizance, perception, apprehension, mindfulness, knowledge. IGNORANCE

**consecrate** sanctify, bless, anoint, hallow, dedicate, devote, assign, ordain, venerate, honour, exalt. DESECRATE

**consecutive** sequential, successive, serial, following, continuous, uninterrupted, orderly, logical. DISCONTINUOUS

**consensus** agreement, concurrence, unanimity, common consent, harmony, concord, accord, unity. DISSENSION

**consent** *v*, agree, concur, assent, accede, acquiesce, concede, submit, yield, comply, permit, allow, approve, grant. REFUSE
*n*, agreement, concurrence, assent, acquiescence, permission, sanction, approval, go-ahead (*inf*), green light (*inf*). REFUSAL
accord, harmony, unison, unanimity, consensus, agreement. DISSENSION

**consequence** result, outcome, issue, effect, end, event, upshot, aftermath, repercussion. CAUSE
importance, significance, moment, weight, note, concern, matter, value, influence, distinction, standing, repute, notability, eminence. INSIGNIFICANCE

**consequent** resultant, consequential, ensuing, following, subsequent, successive, sequential. PRECEDING

**consequential** important, significant, momentous, weighty, substantial, serious. INSIGNIFICANT
pompous, self-important, conceited, vain, proud, arrogant, bumptious, supercilious, pretentious. MODEST

**conservation** preservation, maintenance, upkeep, protection, custody, keeping, perpetuation, saving, economy. ABOLITION

**conservative** cautious, moderate, sober, middle-of-the-road, conventional, traditional, old-fashioned, hidebound, die-hard. right-wing, Tory, reactionary. LIBERAL

**conserve** preserve, maintain, keep, protect, save, spare, go easy on (*inf*). SQUANDER

**consider** contemplate, deliberate, reflect, ponder, meditate, ruminate, cogitate, muse, mull over, study, examine, weigh, chew over.
deem, think, believe, judge, regard, rate, estimate.
respect, have regard for, care for, heed, bear in mind, mark, remember, take into account. IGNORE

**considerable** large, great, substantial, sizable, marked, appreciable, ample, abundant, plentiful, much. TRIFLING
important, significant, noteworthy, remarkable, distinguished, renowned, influential, venerable. INSIGNIFICANT

**considerate** thoughtful, kind, charitable, unselfish, benevolent, compassionate, attentive, solicitous, obliging, mindful, tactful, discreet, patient, forbearing. INCONSIDERATE

**consideration** contemplation, meditation, deliberation, reflection, rumination, thought, attention, notice, regard, heed, study, examination, scrutiny. DISREGARD
thoughtfulness, kindness, unselfishness, benevolence, compassion, concern, solicitude, tact, discretion, patience, forbearance. THOUGHTLESSNESS
issue, factor, circumstance, concern, point.
payment, fee, recompense, reward, remuneration, perquisite, tip, gratuity.
esteem, estimation, respect, regard, admiration.

**consign** commit, entrust, hand over, deliver, transfer, convey, transmit, send, dispatch, ship.

**consignment** committal, commitment, handing over, delivery, transferral, conveyance, dispatch.
load, shipment, batch.

**consignor** sender, shipper, merchant, seller.

**consist** accord, harmonize, agree, be compatible, conform, be consistent. CLASH
**consist of,** comprise, be composed of, include, contain, incorporate, embody, involve, amount to.

**consistency** accordance, harmony, agreement, correspondence, consonance, correlation, compatibility, congruity. INCONSISTENCY
viscosity, firmness, thickness, density, coherence.

**consistent** accordant, harmonious, agreeing, corresponding, consonant, coherent, congruous, compatible. INCONSISTENT
regular, constant, persistent, unchanging, steady, dependable, faithful, loyal. ERRATIC

**consolation** comfort, solace, cheer, encouragement, ease, relief, help, support. DISTRESS

**console** comfort, solace, cheer, encourage, soothe, calm, relieve, support. UPSET

**consolidate** unite, join, conjoin, combine, fuse, amalgamate, coalesce, condense, compact, compress, congeal, harden, solidify. DISINTEGRATE
strengthen, fortify, reinforce, stabilize. WEAKEN

**consonance** congruity, consistency, agreement, harmony, unison, accord, concord, conformity, correspondence. DISCORD

**consonant** consistent, congruous, accordant, harmonious, in agreement, concordant, correspondent, compatible. DISCORDANT

**consort** *n*, companion, partner, mate, spouse, husband, wife, associate, fellow, friend, comrade.
*v*, associate, fraternize, keep company, mix, mingle, go around with.

**conspectus** outline, synopsis, summary, résumé, précis, abstract, digest, compendium, survey.

**conspicuous** obvious, evident, plain, clear, patent, manifest, visible, marked, prominent, outstanding, noticeable, discernible, perceptible, apparent. INCONSPICUOUS
blatant, flagrant, garish, loud, showy. SUBDUED
remarkable, striking, impressive, eminent, notable, distinguished, celebrated, famous, illustrious. INSIGNIFICANT

**conspiracy** intrigue, plot, scheme, cabal, league, collaboration, collusion, connivance, machination, treason, treachery.

**conspire** plot, plan, scheme, intrigue, machinate, collude, combine, concur, collaborate, cooperate.

**constancy** steadfastness, resolution, perseverance, tenacity, firmness, determination, decision, inflexibility, permanence, stability, regularity, uniformity, steadiness, faithfulness, fidelity, loyalty, devotion. FICKLENESS

**constant** regular, uniform, unchanging, invariable, fixed, permanent, stable, steady, firm. CHANGEABLE
perpetual, continuous, incessant, unending, interminable, nonstop, uninterrupted, unbroken, unrelenting, sustained, persistent. INTERMITTENT
faithful, loyal, steadfast, devoted, staunch, dependable, trusty, true. FICKLE

**constellation** galaxy, cluster, collection, group, assemblage, gathering.

**consternation** dismay, distress, alarm, shock, fear, terror, fright, anxiety, trepidation, panic, confusion, bewilderment, astonishment, amazement. RELIEF

**constituent** *adj*, component, integral, composing, constituting, elemental, basic, essential.
*n*, component, ingredient, element, part, unit, factor. WHOLE
voter, elector.

**constitute** compose, make up, comprise, form.
found, establish, set up, create. ABOLISH
appoint, nominate, depute, ordain, empower, commission, authorize.

**constitution** composition, structure, formation, organization, establishment, creation, foundation.
physique, build, make-up, health, disposition, temper, temperament, character, nature, spirit.
code, charter, rules, laws.

**constitutional** *adj*, inherent, innate, inborn, inbred, organic, congenital, natural, connate.
lawful, legitimate, legal, statutory, chartered, vested, authorized. UNCONSTITUTIONAL
*n*, stroll, walk, airing, promenade.

**constrain** compel, force, oblige, make, coerce, drive, impel, urge, press.
restrain, confine, curb, check, restrict, limit, hem in, cage. FREE

**constraint** compulsion, force, obligation, coercion, necessity, pressure.
restraint, confinement, restriction, repression, suppression, inhibition, limitation, check, hindrance, obstruction, deterrent. FREEDOM

**constrict** squeeze, tighten, contract, narrow, shrink, compress, cramp, pinch, choke, strangle, restrict, limit, inhibit, restrain. EXPAND

**constriction** tightness, narrowing, stricture, pressure, cramp, strangulation, restriction, knot, lump, blockage, impediment, restraint, constraint, inhibition, limitation. EXPANSION

**construct** build, erect, raise, put up, assemble, fabricate, make, form, fashion, shape, create, design, invent, frame, compose. DESTROY

**construction** building, erection, structure, edifice, assembly, fabrication, formation, creation, design, composition. DEMOLITION

interpretation, explanation, rendering, reading, analysis, inference.

**constructive** positive, useful, helpful, practical, productive, valuable. DESTRUCTIVE

**construe** interpret, translate, render, analyse, parse, expound, explain, read, take, deduce, infer.

**consult** ask, question, interrogate, canvass, confer, discuss, deliberate, refer to, turn to, seek advice from.

consider, regard, respect, take into account. IGNORE

**consultation** conference, deliberation, examination, consideration, council, parley, powwow, colloquy, dialogue, discussion, interview, hearing, meeting, session.

**consume** devour, eat, drink, swallow, bolt, put away (*inf*).

use, use up, exhaust, expend, drain, dissipate, waste, squander, lavish, fritter away, spend, deplete, absorb, devour, eat up, swallow up. CONSERVE

destroy, devastate, ravage, raze, gut, demolish, lay waste.

engross, absorb, preoccupy, obsess, monopolize, rivet, fascinate, enthral.

**consumer** buyer, purchaser, shopper, user, customer, client. PRODUCER

**consummate** *v*, accomplish, fulfil, achieve, compass, peform, execute, complete, finish, conclude, perfect, crown. ABORT

*adj*, accomplished, skilled, masterly, proficient, practised, polished, perfect, excellent, superb, supreme, utter, complete, absolute, total, unqualified, matchless.

**consummation** perfection, completion, finish, end, conclusion, culmination, fulfilment, achievement, realization. FRUSTRATION

**consumption** use, expenditure, depletion, reduction, dissipation, exhaustion, waste, destruction, decay. CONSERVATION

tuberculosis, emaciation, decline, wasting, atrophy.

**contact** *n*, communication, connection, touch, union, junction, contiguity, juxtaposition, association, conjunction. ISOLATION

acquaintance, connection.

*v*, call, ring, phone, write to, communicate with, get in touch with, approach, reach, get hold of

**contagion** infection, transmission, communication, spread, contamination, corruption, pollution, pestilence, plague.

**contagious** infectious, catching, communicable, transmissible, transferable, spreading, epidemic, pestilential.

**contain** hold, include, comprise, consist of, embody, embrace, comprehend, incorporate, accommodate, seat, admit, enclose.

restrain, curb, control, repress, hold back, suppress. RELEASE

**container** receptacle, holder, vessel, repository, box, case, tin, jar, pot, bowl.

**contaminate** pollute, adulterate, debase, infect, poison, corrupt, vitiate, deprave, soil, defile, sully, taint, tarnish. CLEANSE

**contamination** pollution, adulteration, infection, poisoning, contagion, corruption, vitiation, defilement, debasement, impurity, foulness. PURIFICATION

**contemn** scorn, despise, disdain, spurn, slight, deride, shun, hold in contempt. RESPECT

**contemplate** consider, deliberate, ponder, think about, reflect, muse, meditate, ruminate, mull over, study, examine.

behold, regard, observe, watch, eye, look at, stare at, gaze at, view, survey, scrutinize, inspect. IGNORE

intend, plan, mean, propose, envisage, have in mind.

**contemplation** reflection, meditation, rumination, consideration, deliberation, cogitation, thought, reverie.

observation, scrutiny, examination, inspection, viewing, surveying.

purpose, intention, plan, project, prospect, anticipation, expectation, ambition, aspiration.

**contemplative** thoughtful, meditative, reflective, ruminative, pensive, intent, rapt, lost in thought.

**contemporary** contemporaneous, coexistent, coexisting, coeval, coetaneous, concurrent, synchronous.
modern, up-to-date, fashionable, newfangled, latest, recent, current, present, present-day. ANCIENT

**contempt** scorn, derision, mockery, disdain, disregard, disrespect, condescension, superciliousness, contemptuousness. RESPECT

**contemptible** despicable, derisory, base, mean, abject, low, vile, paltry, worthless, disreputable, shabby, ignominious, detestable, wretched, miserable, pitiful. NOBLE

**contemputuous** scornful, disdainful, supercilious, haughty, condescending, arrogant, derisive, insulting, insolent, cynical, sneering. RESPECTFUL

**contend** struggle, strive, compete, vie, combat, fight, contest, grapple, wrestle, cope. SURRENDER
debate, dispute, argue, maintain, hold, aver, assert, affirm, claim, allege, declare. DISCLAIM

**content**[1] *v*, satisfy, gratify, appease, mollify, placate, humour, indulge, gladden, delight, please.
*adj*, contented, satisfied, at ease, comfortable, pleased, happy, glad, willing, agreeable. DISSATISFIED
*n*, contentment, satisfaction, gratification, ease, comfort, peace of mind. DISCONTENT

**content**[2] *n*, matter, substance, essence, gist, pith, meaning, significance, text, subject, matter, topics, ideas, themes.
capacity, volume, size, measure, dimensions, magnitude, scope.

**contented** content, satisfied, gratified, at ease, comfortable, complacent, placid, glad, happy, pleased. DISCONTENTED

**contention** struggle, strife, rivalry, competition, conflict, discord, dispute, debate, dissension, controversy, wrangle, quarrel, squabble, altercation. AGREEMENT
claim, assertion, affirmation, declaration, view, opinion, belief, argument, point.

**contentious** quarrelsome, argumentative, pugnacious, combative, disputatious, bickering, querulous, peevish, captious, perverse, petulant. OBLIGING
controversial, litigious, debatable, disputable.

**contentment** content, contentedness, satisfaction, gratification, ease, comfort, complacency, equanimity, happiness, pleasure. DISCONTENT

**contents** ingredients, constituents, filling, load, content, chapters, topics, subjects.

**contest** *n*, competition, match, tournament, game, race.
struggle, battle, fight, combat, conflict, discord, dispute, dissension, contention, quarrel, altercation. AGREEMENT
*v*, dispute, argue, litigate, oppose, challenge, question, contend.
fight, battle, contend, struggle, strive, vie, compete.

**contestant** competitor, contender, entrant, participant, player, aspirant, candidate.

**context** background, framework, connection, relation, meaning, substance.
conditions, circumstances, situation, state of affairs, facts.

**contiguity** contiguousness, juxtaposition, adjacency, nearness, proximity, contact, meeting.

**contiguous** meeting, touching, in contact, abutting, adjoining, conterminous, bordering, beside, next to, adjacent, juxtaposed, neighbouring, near. REMOTE

**continence** self-restraint, self-control, moderation, temperance, sobriety, restraint, abstinence, chastity, celibacy, asceticism, austerity, self-denial. LICENTIOUSNESS

**continent** self-restrained, self-controlled, moderate, temperate, sober, abstinent, abstemious, chaste, celibate, ascetic, austere. LICENTIOUS

**contingency** possibility, eventuality, event, occasion, occurrence, incident, happening, chance, fortuity, uncertainty, accident, casualty, emergency, situation, circumstance, case, juncture, factor, aspect, detail.

**contingent** *adj*, dependent, depending, subject to, conditional, provisional, possible, uncertain.
accidental, incidental, casual, chance, fortuitous, random, haphazard, unforeseen.
*n*, group, body, band, party, company, faction, deputation, detachment, section, batch, quota, portion.

**continual** recurrent, regular, repeated, frequent, persistent, perpetual, sustained, constant, nonstop, incessant, continuous, uninterrupted, unremitting. INTERMITTENT

**continually** constantly, incessantly, forever, always, all the time, repeatedly, persistently. OCCASIONALLY

**continuance** continuation, constancy, permanence, persistence, perseverance, duration, term, period.

**continuation** sequel, addition, supplement, postscript, epilogue, appendix, extension, protraction, prolongation.
resumption, perpetuation, maintenance, continuance. CESSATION

**continue** persist, carry on, go on, persevere, sustain, keep up, maintain, prolong, extend, draw out, protract, perpetuate. STOP
resume, recommence, carry on, proceed, advance. INTERRUPT
remain, last, endure, abide, stay, persist, survive. CEASE

**continuity** connection, interrelationship, cohesion, flow, progression, sequence, succession, continuousness. INTERRUPTION

**continuous** unbroken, uninterrupted, connected, prolonged, extended, constant, endless, unending, incessant, ceaseless, eternal, everlasting, nonstop, sustained, perpetual, continual. BROKEN

**contort** distort, deform, misshape, twist, warp, gnarl, convolute, writhe, squirm. STRAIGHTEN

**contortion** distortion, deformity, twist, warp, convolution, convulsion, grimace.

**contour** outline, silhouette, profile, relief, shape, form, figure, line, curve.

**contraband** *n*, smuggling, trafficking, bootlegging, gunrunning.
*adj*, smuggled, illegal, illicit, unlawful, banned, prohibited, black-market, hot (*inf*). LAWFUL

**contract** *v*, shrink, reduce, lessen, diminish, condense, compress, shorten, abbreviate, abridge, curtail, epitomize, narrow, constrict, squeeze, tighten, purse, shrivel, wrinkle. EXPAND
agree, stipulate, covenant, pledge, engage, enter into, undertake, commit oneself, bargain, negotiate, come to terms.
catch, get, acquire, develop, go down with (*inf*).
*n*, agreement, pact, compact, treaty, covenant, bond, pledge, bargain, deal (*inf*), settlement, stipulation, commitment, arrangement, understanding.

**contraction** shrinkage, reduction, diminution, lessening, compression, shortening, abbreviation, narrowing, constriction, tightening, shrivelling. EXPANSION

**contradict** deny, controvert, gainsay, dispute, oppose, challenge, refute, disprove, negate, confute, dissent, belie, contravene, be at variance. CONFIRM

**contradiction** denial, opposition, negation, refutation, confutation, dissension, contravention. AGREEMENT
inconsistency, incongruity, variance, conflict, clash. HARMONY

**contradictory** contrary, opposite, at variance, antagonistic, irreconcilable, repugnant, incompatible, inconsistent, paradoxical, antithetical, incongruous. AFFIRMATIVE

**contraption** contrivance, device, gadget, rig, gear, apparatus, mechanism, appliance.

**contrariety** opposition, contrast, disagreement, antagonism, repugnance, contradiction, inconsistency. HARMONY

**contrary** *adj*, opposed, opposite, counter, hostile, adverse, antagonistic, repugnant, inimical, contradictory, discordant, conflicting, at variance. LIKE
perverse, awkward, difficult, obstinate, stubborn, froward, intractable, refractory, self-willed, headstrong. OBLIGING
*n*, opposite, reverse, converse, antithesis.

**contrast** *v*, differentiate, distinguish, oppose, compare, differ, stand out, set off. LIKEN
*n*, difference, distinction, contrariety, opposition, polarity, dissimilarity, disparity, differentiation, comparison. SIMILARITY

**contravene** infringe, break, violate, disobey, transgress. KEEP
dispute, contradict, refute, oppose, cross, counteract, hinder, obstruct, impede, thwart, frustrate, nullify, annul, abrogate. ASSIST

**contravention** infringement, violation, transgression, trespass, disobedience.
contradiction, opposition, antagonism, obstruction, frustration, nullification, abrogation.

**contretemps** mishap, accident, mistake, blunder, gaffe, difficulty, predicament.

**contribute** supply, furnish, provide, give, donate, bestow, grant, afford, subscribe, chip in (*inf*). WITHHOLD
conduce, lead, tend, add, influence, help, advance, be instrumental in, have a hand in, be responsible for.

**contribution** donation, gift, offering, addition, grant, subscription.

**contributor** donor, giver, subscriber, backer, patron, supporter.
writer, freelance, reporter, correspondent, journalist.

**contributory** instrumental, accessory, conducive, helpful.

**contrite** penitent, repentant, sorry, regretful, remorseful, conscience-stricken, chastened, humble. UNREPENTANT

**contrition** penitence, repentance, sorrow, regret, remorse, self-reproach, compunction, shame, embarrassment, humiliation. IMPENITENCE

**contrivance** device, invention, contraption, gadget, machine, mechanism, apparatus, appliance, implement, tool.
scheme, plan, plot, ruse, stratagem, artifice, design, expedient.

**contrive** devise, invent, frame, design, create, concoct, fabricate, improvise, construct.
engineer, manoeuvre, arrange, manage, effect, bring about.
scheme, plot, brew, hatch, conspire, intrigue.

**contrived** artificial, forced, unnatural, elaborate, recherché. SPONTANEOUS

**control** *v*, rule, govern, reign over, command, direct, lead, conduct, supervise, manage, dominate, boss, discipline.
restrain, curb, check, subdue, master, bridle, hold back, contain, confine, limit, constrain, suppress.
regulate, monitor, verify.
*n*, management, mastery, direction, guidance, government, rule, authority, command, discipline, supervision, charge.
restraint, check, curb, restriction, constraint, limitation, regulation.
lever, switch, instrument, dial, knob, handle.

**controversial** contentious, disputed, debatable, controvertible, disputable, at issue, contended, questionable, polemic, dialectic. INDISPUTABLE

**controversy** dispute, debate, polemic, discussion, argument, wrangle, quarrel, altercation, disagreement, contention, dissension, strife. AGREEMENT

**controvert** deny, refute, oppose, counter, challenge, contest, dispute, contend, contradict. AFFIRM
debate, discuss, argue, wrangle.

**contumacious** stubborn, obstinate, perverse, contrary, froward, refractory, recalcitrant, rebellious, insubordinate, obdurate, intractable, headstrong, tenacious, wilful. DOCILE

**contumacy** stubbornness, obstinacy, perverseness, recalcitrance, rebelliousness, mutiny, disobedience, insubordination, resistance, contempt, intractability, obduracy, tenacity, wilfulness. DOCILITY

**contumelious** insulting, abusive, rude, humiliating, scornful, disdainful, contemptuous, supercilious, arrogant, overbearing. RESPECTFUL

**contumely** insult, affront, abuse, invective, obloquy, opprobrium, reproach, contempt, scorn, derision, disdain, arrogance, superciliousness, insolence, rudeness. RESPECT

**contuse** bruise, discolour, injure, knock, bump.

**contusion** bruise, discoloration, mark, injury, bump, lump, swelling.

**conundrum** riddle, puzzle, poser, brainteaser (*inf*), enigma, mystery, problem.

**convalesce** recover, recuperate, improve, mend, get well, get better. DETERIORATE

**convalescence** recovery, recuperation, improvement, restoration, cure, rehabilitation.

**convalescent** recovering, recuperating, improving, on the mend, getting better. DETERIORATING

**convene** gather, congregate, assemble, muster, meet, collect, rally, convoke, summon, call. DISBAND

**convenience** suitability, appropriateness, fitness, opportuneness, availability, accessibility, utility, usefulness, handiness. INCONVENIENCE
advantage, benefit, aid, help, assistance, service, use, facility, amenity, comfort, ease, accommodation. HINDRANCE

**convenient** suitable, fit, appropriate, timely, seasonable, opportune, adapted,

handy, useful, serviceable, helpful, beneficial, advantageous. INCONVENIENT
accessible, available, at hand, handy, nearby, within reach. INACCESSIBLE

**convent** nunnery, cloister, abbey, priory, religious community, school.

**convention** meeting, assembly, conference, congress, council, convocation.
agreement, contract, treaty, entente, concordat, compact, arrangement, pact.
custom, tradition, practice, protocol, etiquette, usage, formality.

**conventional** accepted, approved, proper, formal, orthodox, traditional, customary, standard, regular, normal, usual, habitual, ordinary, common. UNCONVENTIONAL

**converge** meet, join, unite, merge, blend, mingle, focus, concentrate, coincide, concur, come together, approach, tend. DIVERGE

**convergence** meeting, junction, merging, mingling, conflux, confluence, focus, concentration, coincidence, concurrence, approach. DIVERGENCE

**conversable** communicative, sociable, affable, open, out-going, expansive, unreserved, talkative, loquacious. RESERVED

**conversant** familiar, acquainted, *au fait*, versed, knowledgeable, experienced, skilled, proficient, practised. UNFAMILIAR

**conversation** talk, discussion, dialogue, communication, discourse, intercourse, colloquy, exchange, conference, parley, powwow, chat, gossip, confabulation, confab (*inf*), chinwag (*inf*), tête-à-tête.

**conversational** colloquial, informal, chatty, communicative, conversable, open, unreserved.

**converse**[1] *v*, talk, speak, chat, confabulate, discourse, commune.
*n*, conversation, talk, chat, dialogue, discourse.

**converse**[2] *n*, opposite, reverse, contrary, antithesis. SAME
*adj*, opposite, contrary, reversed, transposed.

**conversion** change, transformation, metamorphosis, transfiguration, alteration, modification, adaptation, remodelling, reconstruction. CONSERVATION
reformation, rebirth, regeneration, proselytization, proselytism.

**convert** change, transform, transfigure, transmute, alter, modify, adapt, revise, remodel, restyle, transpose, interchange.
proselytize, reform, convince, win over, regenerate, baptize.

**convex** bulging, rounded, gibbous, protuberant. CONCAVE

**convey** carry, take, transfer, transport, bear, conduct, bring, fetch.
transmit, send, communicate, impart, reveal, disclose, tell.

**conveyance** transport, transportation, carriage, movement, conveying, transfer, transference, transmission.
vehicle, transport, car, cab, carriage, van, lorry, bus, coach.

**convict** *v*, condemn, sentence, find guilty. ACQUIT
*n*, criminal, felon, culprit, malefactor, crook (*inf*), prisoner, jailbird, con (*inf*).

**conviction** sentence, condemnation, judgment, punishment.
assurance, confidence, certainty, certitude, persuasion, trust, belief, faith, opinion, view, principle, tenet. DOUBT

**convince** persuade, satisfy, assure, prove to, win over, bring round, sway.

**convincing** plausible, credible, probable, likely, cogent, persuasive, conclusive, powerful, impressive. UNCONVINCING

**convivial** sociable, jovial, festive, jolly, gay, merry, cheerful, hearty, genial, friendly. GLOOMY

**convocation** assembly, meeting, convention, congress, council, synod, congregation, concourse.

**convoke** call, summon, convene, muster, assemble, gather, collect. DISBAND

**convolution** coil, curl, twist, loop, spiral, helix, roll, fold, undulation.
intricacy, complexity, complication, involvement, entanglement, tortuousness.

**convoy** *n*, escort, guard, protection, attendance, entourage, fleet, company, line, file, train.
*v*, escort, accompany, attend, guard, protect, usher, pilot, lead, direct.

**convulse** disturb, agitate, shake, churn, heave, toss, discompose, derange. COMPOSE

**convulsion** spasm, paroxysm, contraction, cramp, seizure, stroke, fit, tremor.
agitation, disturbance, upheaval, commotion, turbulence, tumult, turmoil. CALM

**cook** *v*, boil, fry, roast, toast, poach, grill, stew, bake.
**cook up,** concoct, devise, invent, contrive, prepare, fabricate, improvise, plot, scheme.
*n*, chef, baker, pastry cook, confectioner.

**cool** *adj*, chilly, chill, cold, nippy, breezy, fresh, chilled. WARM
composed, calm, collected, unruffled, unperturbed, placid, quiet, serene, self-possessed, dispassionate. AGITATED
unfriendly, cold, frigid, chilly, lukewarm, uninviting, unresponsive, uncommunicative, reserved, aloof, distant, standoffish, indifferent, unconcerned, unenthusiastic. FRIENDLY
audacious, bold, presumptuous, impudent, shameless, brazen.
*v*, chill, refrigerate, freeze. WARM
moderate, temper, dampen, quench, calm, assuage, abate, lessen, quiet. EXCITE

**coop** *n*, cage, pen, enclosure, box.
*v*, cage, pen, imprison, confine. LIBERATE

**cooperate** help, aid, assist, abet, conspire, collaborate, combine, unite, join forces, work together, contribute, pitch in, participate, go along, play ball (*inf*). OPPOSE

**cooperation** help, assistance, collaboration, interaction, teamwork, combined effort, give and take, participation. OPPOSITION

**cooperative** helpful, obliging, accommodating. REBELLIOUS
collective, combined, joint, united, concerted. INDIVIDUAL

**coordinate** *v*, organize, systematize, categorize, arrange, integrate, harmonize, match, correspond, mesh, synchronize.
*adj*, equal, equivalent, tantamount, synonymous, correspondent, correlative.

**cope** manage, get by, survive, hold one's own.
contend, deal, grapple, struggle, handle, dispatch, take care of.

**copious** abundant, plentiful, plenteous, ample, profuse, exuberant, luxuriant, lavish, rich, overflowing, full, bountiful, unstinted. SCANTY

**copiousness** abundance, plenty, amplitude, exuberance, richness, fullness, bounty. SPARSENESS

**copse** coppice, thicket, grove, wood.

**copulation** mating, coupling, coition, coitus, sexual intercourse, sex, lovemaking, carnal knowledge.

**copulative** linking, joining, connecting, uniting.

**copy** *v*, duplicate, replicate, reproduce, photocopy, transcribe, plagiarize, crib (*inf*), counterfeit. ORIGINATE
imitate, mimic, ape, echo, mirror, simulate, follow.
*n*, duplicate, replica, reproduction, facsimile, transcription, photocopy, print, carbon, representation, counterfeit, forgery, likeness, imitation. ORIGINAL

**coquet** flirt, philander, dally, trifle, tease, ogle, make eyes at, vamp.

**coquetry** flirtation, philandering, dalliance, trifling, ogling, vamping.

**cord** line, string, twine, rope, braid.
bond, tie, link, connection.

**cordial** friendly, warm, courteous, affectionate, genial, amiable, affable, hearty, sincere, heartfelt, earnest, ardent, wholehearted. DISTANT

**cordiality** friendliness, warmth, affection, geniality, affability, heartiness, sincerity, wholeheartedness. HOSTILITY

**core** centre, heart, kernel, nucleus, essence, gist, nub. EXTERIOR

**corner** *n*, angle, bend, crook, knee, elbow, joint, junction.
niche, recess, nook, cranny, hole, retreat.
*v*, trap, bring to bay.
monopolize, hog (*inf*).

**corny** trite, banal, hackneyed, old-fashioned, mawkish, sentimental, feeble.

**corollary** inference, deduction, conclusion, consequence, result.

**corporal** bodily, fleshly, physical, carnal, corporeal. MENTAL

**corporation** association, company, partnership, corporate body, council.
paunch, spare tyre, potbelly.

**corporeal** physical, material, bodily, flesly, tangible, substantial. SPIRITUAL

**corps** body, company, band, crew, troupe, troop, regiment, squadron, unit, squad, platoon, division, detachment, contingent.

**corpse** body, cadaver, carcass, remains, stiff (*inf*).

**corpulence** fatness, stoutness, plumpness, tubbiness, rotundity, portliness, *embonpoint*, obesity, fleshiness. THINNESS

**corpulent** fat, stout, plump, tubby, rotund, portly, large, big, obese, overweight, bulky, burly, strapping. THIN

**correct** *adj*, accurate, true, right, faultless, unerring, exact, precise, strict, spot on (*inf*). INCORRECT
proper, fitting, seemly, accepted, appropriate, conventional. IMPROPER
*v*, rectify, redress, amend, emend, reform, adjust, put right, remedy, improve.
discipline, punish, chasten, castigate, admonish, reprove, reprimand, chide, scold, rebuke. INDULGE

**correction** rectification, amendment, modification, improvement, remedy, reparation.
discipline, punishment, castigation, chastisement, admonition, reproof, reprimand, scolding. INDULGENCE

**corrective** remedial, therapeutic, restorative, rectifying, improving. DETRIMENTAL
disciplinary, punitive, reformatory, penal.

**correctness** accuracy, truth, faultlessness, exactness, exactitude, precision, strictness, fidelity. INCORRECTNESS
propriety, correctitude, decorum, etiquette, civility, good manners, *bon ton*. IMPROPRIETY

**correlate** compare, contrast, equate, associate, correspond, connect, relate, tie in.

**correlation** correspondence, equivalence, interrelationship, reciprocity, mutuality, interdependence, connection. INDEPENDENCE

**correlative** corresponding, reciprocal, mutual, complementary, interrelated. INDEPENDENT

**correspond** agree, accord, harmonize, conform, tally, coincide, match, square, fit, correlate, reciprocate, complement. DIFFER
communicate, write, keep in touch.

**correspondence** agreement, accord, harmony, concurrence, conformity, coincidence, correlation, match, similarity, analogy, comparison, congruity. DIFFERENCE
letters, mail, post, communication, writing.

**correspondent** *n*, journalist, reporter, contributor.
writer, letter writer, pen friend, pen pal.
*adj*, corresponding, analogous, comparable, similar, reciprocal, parallel, equivalent, matching, accordant. DIFFERENT

**corridor** passage, passageway, hall, hallway, aisle, gallery, cloister.

**corrigible** tractable, submissive, yielding, compliant, amenable, docile. INTRACTABLE

**corroborate** confirm, support, ratify, substantiate, verify, validate, bear out, endorse, document, establish, uphold, sustain, back up. INVALIDATE

**corroboration** confirmation, ratification, substantiation, verification, validation, endorsement. INVALIDATION

**corrode** rust, oxidize, erode, eat away, wear away, consume, gnaw, impair, destroy, ruin, crumble, waste. RESTORE

**corrosion** rust, oxidation, erosion, attrition, wearing, deterioration, destruction, crumbling.

**corrosive** corroding, erosive, gnawing, wearing, acid, biting, caustic, mordant, acrid, trenchant, cutting, incisive.

**corrugate** wrinkle, pucker, crinkle, ruffle, rumple, crumple, crease, furrow, groove, ridge. SMOOTH

**corrupt** *adj*, dishonest, unscrupulous, unprincipled, bent (*inf*), bribable, venal, crooked, untrustworthy. HONEST
immoral, depraved, degenerate, abandoned, dissolute, profligate, wicked, evil. VIRTUOUS
rotten, putrid, contaminated, polluted, tainted, adulterated, impure, defiled, infected. PURE
*v*, deprave, debauch, pervert, bribe, suborn, square (*inf*), lure, entice, seduce. EDIFY
contaminate, defile, debase, vitiate, pollute, infect, putrefy, adulterate, doctor, taint, spoil. PURIFY

**corruption** dishonesty, unscrupulousness, bribery, venality, fraud, deception, deceit. HONESTY
immorality, depravity, vice, iniquity, turpitude, sin, degeneracy, decadence, dissolution, profligacy, evil, wickedness. VIRTUE
contamination, adulteration, pollution, debasement, vitiation, rot, decay, putrefaction. PURIFICATION

**corsair** pirate, privateer, buccaneer, freebooter, sea rover.

**corset** girdle, foundation, stays, corselet, bodice, belt.

**cortege** procession, cavalcade, train, suite, retinue.

**coruscate** sparkle, flash, gleam, scintillate, glitter, twinkle, glisten, glimmer, glint.

**coruscation** sparkle, flash, gleam, scintillation, glimmer, ray, beam, glint.

**cosmopolitan** universal, global, catholic, widely distributed.
broad-minded, urbane, sophisticated, worldly.

**cosmos** world, universe, nature, creation, macrocosm.
order, harmony.

**cosset** pamper, coddle, mollycoddle, baby, pet, caress, fondle, hug, cuddle. NEGLECT

**cost** *n*, price, charge, rate, expense, outlay, expenditure, payment, amount, figure, worth, value.
loss, penalty, sacrifice, damage, detriment, suffering, pain, injury, harm.
*v*, sell for, amount to, set back (*inf*).
necessitate, require.

**costly** dear, expensive, valuable, priceless, extortionate, excessive, exorbitant, steep (*inf*). INEXPENSIVE
sumptuous, lavish, splendid, fine, luxurious, rich, opulent, precious. POOR

**costume** uniform, livery, robes, dress, apparel, garb, habit, outfit, attire, clothes, clothing.

**cosy** snug, comfortable, comfy (*inf*), warm, sheltered, homely, intimate, easy, relaxed. UNCOMFORTABLE

**coterie** clique, set, gang, group, circle, clan, fraternity, club, society, association, company.

**cottage** lodge, cabin, chalet, hut, shack, shanty.

**couch** *n*, sofa, settee, divan, bed, chaise longue, chesterfield.
*v*, utter, express, phrase, word, frame.
lie down, recline, loll, lounge, repose.

**council** assembly, congress, committee, board, panel, cabinet, chamber, parliament, ministry, diet, synod, conclave, convention.

**counsel** *n*, advice, guidance, admonition, warning, caution, instruction, direction, recommendation, suggestion, opinion, consultation, deliberation, discussion.
advocate, lawyer, solicitor, barrister, attorney.
*v*, advise, guide, urge, exhort, instruct, warn, admonish, suggest, recommend, advocate. DISCOURAGE

**counsellor** adviser, mentor, confidant, guide, tutor, teacher.

**count** *v*, enumerate, number, calculate, reckon, add up, sum up, total, tally, compute, estimate.
include, take into account, number among.
consider, regard, deem, judge, esteem, hold, look upon.
matter, signify, rate, tell, weigh, carry weight.
**count on,** depend on, rely on, bank on, trust, take for granted.
*n*, enumeration, reckoning, calculation, computation, sum, total, tally, score.

**countenance** *n*, face, visage, features, physiognomy, expression, aspect, appearance, look, mien, air.
approval, support, sanction, favour, endorsement, backing, encouragement, aid, assistance. DISAPPROVAL
*v*, support, encourage, endorse, sanction, approve, back, aid, help, promote, champion. OPPOSE
tolerate, endure, brook, stand for (*inf*), put up with (*inf*), permit, allow. FORBID

**counter**[1] *adv*, against, versus, in opposition, at variance.
*adj*, contrary, opposite, opposed, opposing, conflicting, contrasting. LIKE
*v*, retaliate, parry, hit back, respond, answer, return, offset, dispute, contend.

**counter**[2] *n*, table, board, bar, stall.
disc, token, marker, piece, man.

**counteract** neutralize, annul, nullify, counterbalance, offset, negate, foil, frustrate, thwart, defeat, check, resist, oppose, contravene. ASSIST

**counteraction** opposition, resistance, contravention, check, frustration, negation, neutralization, annulment, nullification.

**counterbalance** balance, equilibrate, offset, compensate, counterpoise, countervail, make up for.

**counterfeit** *v*, forge, fake, sham, pretend, feign, simulate, copy, imitate, impersonate.
*adj*, forged, fake, sham, false, mock, spurious, feigned, simulated, imitation, ersatz, bogus, phoney (*inf*), fraudulent. GENUINE
*n*, forgery, fake, copy, reproduction, imitation, sham, fraud, phoney (*inf*).

**countermand** revoke, rescind, repeal, abrogate, annul, cancel, retract, withdraw. CONFIRM

**counterpart** fellow, match, double, twin, mate, partner, opposite number, equivalent, complement, supplement, correlative, copy, duplicate, likeness.

**counterpoise** *v*, counterbalance, balance, compensate, equalize, countervail, offset, neutralize.
*n*, counterweight, counterbalance, balance, equilibrium.

**countless** innumerable, incalculable, myriad, legion, numberless, untold, immeasurable, infinite, endless. FEW

**country** *n*, nation, people, state, kingdom, realm, commonwealth, homeland, fatherland, motherland.
region, territory, land, terrain, area, district.
countryside, farmland, provinces, rural areas, sticks (*inf*), backwoods, outback, bush, wilds. TOWN
*adj*, rural, rustic, pastoral, countrified, bucolic, provincial, Aracadian, agrarian, agricultural. URBAN
uncouth, unrefined, unpolished, unsophisticated, rough, rude. POLISHED

**countryman** rustic, provincial, yokel, bumpkin, peasant, farmer. TOWNSMAN
compatriot, fellow citizen, native, indigene. FOREIGNER

**countryside** country, farmland, rural areas, green belt, outdoors, scenery, panorama, view, landscape. TOWN

**coup** feat, exploit, master stroke, tour de force, accomplishment, deed, action, manoeuvre, stunt. FAILURE
coup d'état, rebellion, revolution, uprising, putsch, takeover, overthrow, seizure.

**couple** *n*, pair, brace, team, duo, twosome.
*v*, connect, join, conjoin, unite, yoke, bracket, link, pair, marry, wed, mate. SEPARATE

**coupon** voucher, certificate, slip, ticket, card.

**courage** bravery, valour, fearlessness, boldness, audacity, pluck, nerve, mettle, intrepidity, daring, grit, spunk (*inf*), guts (*inf*), bottle (*inf*), heroism, gallantry, fortitude, resolution. COWARDICE

**courageous** brave, valiant, valorous, fearless, dauntless, unafraid, bold, audacious, plucky, intrepid, daring, heroic, gallant, resolute, indomitable, lion-hearted. COWARDLY

**courier** messenger, bearer, carrier, runner, herald, envoy, emissary, representative, guide.

**course** *n*, progression, series, sequence, order, succession, continuity, progress, advance, march, flow, development.
duration, period, time, term, season, spell, lapse, passage.
route, path, road, track, way, channel, direction, line, trajectory, circuit, orbit, round, beat.
policy, procedure, programme, plan, regimen, mode, method, conduct, behaviour, deportment.
classes, lectures, lessons, studies, curriculum, programme, schedule.
**of course,** certainly, surely, by all means, obviously, naturally, undoubtedly, definitely. MAYBE
*v*, race, dash, rush, speed, bolt, charge, surge, gush, run, flow. DAWDLE
chase, pursue, hunt, follow.

**court** *n*, courtyard, yard, quadrangle, square, plaza, cloister.
retinue, train, entourage, cortege, attendants, royal household, palace, castle.
tribunal, bar, bench, assize, trial, session.
homage, deference, attention, addresses, respects, civilities, suit.
*v*, woo, make love to, date, take out, go out with, go steady (*inf*).
invite, solicit, seek, provoke, ask for, prompt, attract. AVOID
flatter, blandish, wheedle, cajole, curry favour with, fawn on, pander to, butter up (*inf*).

**courteous** polite, well-mannered, respectful, civil, gracious, gallant, courtly, ladylike, gentlemanly, urbane, debonair, ceremonious, complaisant, affable, obliging, attentive. IMPOLITE

**courtesan** prostitute, whore, harlot, paramour, kept woman, mistress, call girl, *fille de joie*.

**courtesy** politeness, respect, good manners, civility, graciousness, gallantry, courtliness, urbanity, refinement, polish, cordiality, affability. RUDENESS
consent, favour, indulgence, generosity, kindness, benevolence.

**courtly** refined, polished, well-bred, dignified, decorous, ceremonious, stately, gallant, chivalrous, gentlemanly, polite, well-mannered, respectful, gracious, affable. CHURLISH

**courtship** wooing, suit, romance, dating, engagement.

**courtyard** court, quadrangle, quad (*inf*), yard, enclosure, area, peristyle.

**cove** bay, bight, inlet, creek, firth, sound.

**covenant** agreement, contract, compact, pact, treaty, convention, concordat, promise, pledge, bond, commitment, bargain, deal, stipulation.

**cover** *v*, cloak, veil, mask, screen, shroud, conceal, hide, disguise, camouflage, secrete. UNCOVER
coat, spread, daub, plaster, overlay, blanket, mantle, carpet, clothe, envelop, invest, wrap. STRIP
protect, shield, shelter, guard, defend, watch over, fortify. EXPOSE
include, embrace, incorporate, embody, contain, comprise, comprehend, encompass, involve, deal with. EXCLUDE
replace, substitute, stand in, fill in, relieve, take over.
traverse, cross, pass through, travel over.
**cover up,** suppress, conceal, repress, hush up (*inf*), keep secret, whitewash (*inf*). REVEAL
*n*, covering, lid, top, wrapper, jacket, sheath, case, envelope, blanket, bedspread.
cloak, veil, mask, screen, shroud, disguise, camouflage, façade, front, cover-up, smokescreen.
defence, protection, shield, guard, shelter, refuge, camouflage, hiding place, undergrowth, woods.

**covering** cover, top, protection, shelter, wrapper, blanket, mantle, coating, layer, film.

**covert** *adj*, clandestine, secret, concealed, hidden, disguised, surreptitious, furtive, stealthy, underhand, sly, insidious. OPEN
*n*, undergrowth, thicket, bushes, shrubbery, woodland.
shelter, cover, protection, refuge, sanctuary, asylum, retreat, den, lair.

**covet** desire, long for, hanker after, crave, lust for, yearn for, aspire to, dream of, fancy, envy. DESPISE

**covetous** jealous, envious, desirous, acquisitive, grasping, avaricious, greedy, rapacious, eager, avid, craving.

**covetousness** desire, avarice, greed, rapacity, cupidity, avidity, yearning, craving.

**covey** brood, flock, group, party, set, company.

**cow** frighten, awe, overawe, daunt, unnerve, intimidate, browbeat, bully, oppress, subdue, break, discourage, dishearten, dismay. ENCOURAGE

**coward** craven, poltroon, dastard, baby, sissy, weakling, chicken (*inf*), scaredy-cat (*inf*), yellow-belly (*inf*). HERO

**cowardice** cowardliness, pusillanimity, timidity, timorousness, fear, faint-heartedness, cold feet (*inf*). BRAVERY

**cowardly** timid, timorous, fearful, scared, afraid, craven, pusillanimous, faint-hearted, lily-livered, spineless, yellow (*inf*), chicken (*inf*), dastardly. BRAVE

**cower** cringe, shrink, recoil, flinch, quail, tremble, crouch, stoop, fawn, grovel, skulk, slink. CONFRONT

**coxcomb** dandy, fop, prig, beau, popinjay, swell (*inf*), poser (*inf*).

**coy** shy, bashful, diffident, reserved, retiring, timid, shrinking, modest, demure, arch, coquettish, flirtatious. FORWARD

**cozen** cheat, trick, dupe, deceive, swindle, defraud, con (*inf*), take for a ride (*inf*), beguile, inveigle, hoodwink.

**crabbed** crabby, irritable, bad-tempered, testy, touchy, waspish, crusty, cantankerous, captious, perverse, peevish, petulant, surly, morose, sour, tart, acrid, acrimonious, harsh. GENIAL

**crabbedness** ill humour, bad temper, irritability, spleen, captiousness, peevishness, petulance, surliness, moroseness, sourness, acrimony. GENIALITY

**crack** *v*, break, split, cleave, burst, shatter, chip, splinter, shatter, craze, chap. MEND
snap, pop, clap, crash, crackle, burst, explode.
yield, succumb, break down, collapse, go to pieces, crack up (*inf*). RESIST
decipher, solve, unravel, work out, fathom, decode.
*n*, fissure, gap, rift, split, break, breach, crevice, cleft, chink, cranny, hole, aperture.
snap, pop, clap, crash, burst, explosion, report.
joke, quip, wisecrack, witticism, jibe, dig (*inf*).

**cracked** broken, chipped, split, crazed, damaged, imperfect, faulty.
crazy, mad, insane, crackers (*inf*), nuts (*inf*), round the bend (*inf*). SANE

**crackle** snap, crack, pop, crepitate.

**cradle** *n*, cot, bed, crib, bassinet.
source, origin, fountainhead, birthplace.
*v*, hold, rock, lull, nurse, nurture, foster, tend.

**craft** skill, ability, dexterity, aptitude, talent, knack, flair, cleverness, art, expertness, mastery. INCOMPETENCE
guile, cunning, artfulness, deceitfulness, wiliness, craftiness, subtlety, deceit, duplicity, trickery, artifice, wiles, stratagem, subterfuge. ARTLESSNESS
trade, vocation, calling, occupation, employment, business, work, pursuit, handicraft, art.
vessel, boat, ship, barque, plane, aircraft.

**craftsman** artisan, artificer, master, technician, skilled worker.

**crafty** cunning, sly, artful, guileful, wily, foxy, subtle, sharp, shrewd, astute, canny, calculating, designing, scheming, tricky, insidious, deceitful, fraudulent, crooked. ARTLESS

**craggy** rough, uneven, broken, rugged, jagged, rocky. SMOOTH

**cram** stuff, fill, press, ram, shove, force, pack, crowd, jam, choke, squeeze, crush, compress.
gorge, stuff, overeat, guzzle, glut, gormandize.
coach, study, revise, swot, mug up (*inf*).

**cramp**[1] *v*, hinder, obstruct, impede, encumber, hamper, check, restrain, restrict, confine, constrain, shackle, inhibit. LOOSE

**cramp**[2] *n*, spasm, contraction, convulsion, twinge, pang, stitch, crick, ache, pain.

**crank** *n*, lever, arm, shaft, handle.
eccentric, oddity, crackpot (*inf*), nut (*inf*), maniac, enthusiast, devotee, fanatic.
*v*, start, turn over, turn, rotate, spin.

**cranky** eccentric, odd, strange, peculiar, bizarre, queer. NORMAL

**cranny** chink, crevice, fissure, rift, cleft, crack, breach, gap, opening, interstice.

**crapulent** crapulous, drunk, inebriated, intoxicated, tipsy, tight (*inf*). SOBER

**crash** *v*, smash, shatter, shiver, splinter, dash, break, fracture. MEND
collide, bump, bang, hit, drive, wreck.
clatter, clash, clang, bang, boom, roar, thunder.
fall, topple, tumble, collapse, fold, crumble, fail. SOAR
rush, hurtle, precipitate, dash. AMBLE
*n*, bang, clatter, clash, clang, boom, thunder, racket, din, clangour.
collision, bump, accident, pile-up (*inf*), smash, wreck.
collapse, downfall, ruin, failure, bankruptcy.

**crass** stupid, dense, thick, asinine, obtuse, oafish, boorish, indelicate, insensitive, gross, coarse, unrefined.

**crate** case, box, container, chest, basket, hamper.

**crave** desire, long for, yearn for, hanker after, hunger for, thirst for, want, covet, fancy, need, require, cry out for. SPURN
beseech, entreat, implore, ask, beg, plead, pray, petition, solicit, supplicate.

**craven** *adj*, cowardly, pusillanimous, timorous, fearful, dastardly, base, faint-hearted, yellow (*inf*). BRAVE
*n*, coward, poltroon, dastard, yellow-belly (*inf*), chicken (*inf*). HERO

**craving** longing, yearning, hunger, thirst, desire, yen (*inf*), lust, hankering.

**crawl** creep, inch, steal, slink, worm, slither, move slowly. RACE
swarm, team, be overrun.
grovel, cringe, fawn, toady, abase oneself.

**craze** *n*, fashion, fad, vogue, rage, mania, passion, enthusiasm, obsession, infatuation.
*v*, madden, derange, unbalance, unhinge, drive crazy, enrage, inflame. CALM

**crazy** mad, deranged, demented, insane, lunatic, daft, nuts (*inf*), barmy (*inf*), round the bend (*inf*), potty (*inf*). SANE
silly, foolish, absurd, idiotic, inane, senseless, ludicrous, asinine, half-baked (*inf*), impractical, unwise, imprudent, reckless. SENSIBLE
strange, bizarre, fantastic, odd, peculiar. NORMAL
infatuated, enamoured, wild, passionate, ardent, enthusiastic, fanatical. INDIFFERENT

**creak** squeak, grate, rasp, scrape, grind, squeal, groan.

**crease** *v*, fold, ridge, wrinkle, crumple, pucker, corrugate, crinkle.
*n*, fold, wrinkle, ridge, furrow, line, groove, pucker, pleat, tuck.

**create** invent, originate, coin, concoct, devise, formulate, design, make, fashion, produce, generate, beget, spawn, hatch. DESTROY appoint, invest, install, constitute, establish, set up. ABOLISH

cause, occasion, bring about, start, lead to.

**creation** invention, conception, design, origination, start, beginning, generation, genesis, inception, foundation, production, making, formation, construction. DESTRUCTION

universe, cosmos, world, earth, nature, life.

**creative** inventive, artistic, imaginative, inspired, original, ingenious, clever, talented, skilled. UNIMAGINATIVE

**creator** maker, inventor, originator, author, architect, designer, founder, father, prime mover, God.

**creature** being, living thing, animal, beast, brute, person, human being, individual, mortal, body, soul, character.

wretch, cur, rascal, minion, lackey, parasite, hanger-on, dependant, puppet, tool, hireling.

**credence** belief, acceptance, credit, faith, trust, reliance, confidence, assurance. DISBELIEF

**credentials** certificate, diploma, licence, warrant, authorization, authority, docket, pass, passport, testimonial, letter of introduction, reference, deed, title.

**credible** believable, probable, likely, plausible, conceivable, imaginable, thinkable, tenable. INCREDIBLE

trustworthy, trusty, reliable, dependable, honest, truthful. UNRELIABLE

**credit** *n*, praise, commendation, recognition, acknowledgment, honour, merit, acclaim, glory, tribute. BLAME

belief, credence, faith, trust, confidence. DISBELIEF

reputation, standing, status, influence, regard, esteem, name, character.

reliability, credibility, trustworthiness, integrity, probity, honesty.

**on credit,** on account, by instalments, by hire-purchase, by deferred payment, on tick (*inf*), on the slate (*inf*).

*v*, ascribe, attribute, accredit, assign, impute.

believe, accept, trust, have faith in, buy (*inf*), swallow (*inf*). DISBELIEVE

**creditable** praiseworthy, admirable, estimable, meritorious, laudable, commendable, worthy, reputable, honourable, respectable. SHAMEFUL

**credulous** gullible, naive, green, trustful, trusting, unsuspicious, unsuspecting, deceivable, simple, soft. SUSPICIOUS

**creed** belief, faith, dogma, doctrine, tenet, principles, credo, canon, catechism, articles of faith.

**creek** inlet, bay, bight, cove, firth, sound, estuary.

stream, brook, rivulet, watercourse.

**creep** steal, sneak, tiptoe, slink, slither, wriggle, glide, worm, insinuate, crawl, inch, edge. RUSH

fawn, grovel, cringe, crawl, toady, kowtow, bootlick (*inf*).

**creepy** eerie, weird, ghoulish, macabre, ghostly, frightening, scary (*inf*), gruesome, nightmarish, sinister, ominous.

**crepitate** crackle, rattle, snap, crack.

**crest** top, apex, summit, pinnacle, peak, ridge, crown, head. FOOT

tuft, mane, comb, topknot, plume, tassel.

bearings, arms, device, badge, emblem, symbol, insignia, charge.

**crestfallen** dejected, discouraged, dispirited, disheartened, downcast, depressed, downhearted, despondent, sad, melancholy, disconsolate, gloomy. ELATED

**crevasse** chasm, abyss, ravine, gorge, fissure, cleft.

**crevice** chink, crack, slit, cranny, cleft, rift, fissure, gap, breach, split.

**crew** company, team, squad, corps, gang, party, band, group, troupe, crowd, horde, throng, mob, pack.

**crib** *n*, cot, cradle, bassinet, bed.

rack, manger, box, bin, stall, pen.

*v*, steal, pilfer, purloin, plagiarize, pirate, copy, cheat.

confine, pen, enclose, imprison, cage, coop up, shut in, restrict. FREE

**crick** cramp, spasm, twinge.

**crime** felony, misdemeanour, offence, violation, misdeed, trespass, transgression, atrocity, fault.

wrongdoing, misconduct, lawbreaking, vice, wrong, sin, iniquity, villainy, corruption, delinquency.

**criminal** *n*, felon, offender, lawbreaker, malefactor, wrongdoer, delinquent, recidivist, villain, crook (*inf*), transgressor, sinner, culprit, convict, jailbird (*inf*).

*adj*, illegal, unlawful, illicit, wrong, felonious, culpable, guilty, crooked (*inf*), cor-

rupt, iniquitous, wicked, nefarious, villainous, heinous. LAWFUL
deplorable, scandalous, senseless, preposterous, ridiculous.

**crimp** flute, curl, wave, ridge, corrugate, crinkle, pucker, press, crease.

**cringe** shrink, flinch, cower, recoil, duck, shy, quail, blench, wince, tremble.
fawn, grovel, crawl, creep, toady, truckle, kowtow, stoop, bend, bow, crouch.

**cringing** servile, obsequious, fawning, toadying, sycophantic, bootlicking (*inf*).

**crinkle** crimp, rumple, crumple, wrinkle, crease, pucker, furrow, fold, flute, corrugate, curl. SMOOTH
rustle, crackle, whisper, swish.

**cripple** lame, disable, maim, mutilate, hamstring, incapacitate, paralyse, injure, impair, damage, handicap, enfeeble, weaken, mar, ruin, spoil.

**crisis** emergency, exigency, dilemma, quandary, plight, strait, predicament, disaster, catastrophe.
turning point, crux, climax, height, juncture, pass.

**crisp** brittle, friable, crumbly, crunchy, dry, firm, fresh. PLIABLE
bracing, invigorating, fresh, brisk, stimulating, refreshing. SULTRY
terse, short, brusque, abrupt, brief, succinct, pithy, incisive. LENGTHY

**criterion** standard, norm, test, rule, measure, touchstone, benchmark, yardstick, canon, principle, guide, model, example.

**critic** judge, arbiter, reviewer, commentator, analyst, authority, expert, connoisseur, specialist.
censurer, censor, faultfinder, carper, attacker, knocker (*inf*), detractor, Momus.

**critical** faultfinding, carping, cavilling, censorious, captious, nit-picking (*inf*), disparaging, derogatory. FLATTERING
analytical, diagnostic, perceptive, discerning, penetrating, fastidious, accurate, precise, exact, scrupulous.
crucial, all-important, decisive, vital, essential, momentous, urgent, pressing, serious, grave. UNIMPORTANT
dangerous, perilous, risky, touch-and-go. SAFE

**criticism** judgment, evaluation, appraisal, assessment, analysis, examination, review, notice, commentary, critique.
censure, animadversion, condemnation, disapproval, objection, stricture, disparagement, brickbat, slating (*inf*), flak (*inf*). PRAISE

**criticize** censure, find fault, carp, cavil, disparage, disapprove, condemn, denounce, knock (*inf*), slate (*inf*), pan (*inf*). PRAISE
judge, appraise, evaluate, review, analyse, comment on.

**croak** grunt, squawk, groan, murmur, gasp.
complain, grumble, grouse, moan, mutter.

**crockery** pottery, earthenware, china, dishes, crocks, pots.

**crone** hag, witch, old woman, old bag (*inf*), old bat (*inf*).

**crony** friend, companion, chum, pal (*inf*), mate, associate, ally, sidekick (*inf*). ENEMY

**crook** *n*, bend, angle, hook, bow, curve, turn.
criminal, thief, robber, swindler, rogue, villain, cheat.
*v*, bend, curve, bow, flex, turn, twist. STRAIGHTEN

**crooked** bent, curved, bowed, hooked, twisted, winding, tortuous, zigzag, askew, lopsided, awry, oblique, distorted, deformed, misshapen, irregular, asymmetric. STRAIGHT
dishonest, fraudulent, criminal, illegal, unlawful, underhand, deceitful, dubious, shady (*inf*), unscrupulous, bent (*inf*), corrupt. HONEST

**crop** *n*, harvest, yield, produce, gathering.
assortment, collection, batch, lot, group.
*v*, cut, trim, clip, shear, mow, lop, pare, prune, shorten, curtail.

**cross** *n*, crucifix, rood, X.
burden, affliction, trial, trouble, woe, vexation, misfortune.
hybrid, mongrel, crossbreed, blend, combination, mixture.
*v*, traverse, pass over, go across, ford, span, bridge.
intersect, crisscross, interweave, entwine, lace.
interbreed, crossbreed, hybridize, mix, blend.
hinder, impede, obstruct, frustrate, foil, thwart, oppose, resist. HELP
**cross out,** delete, cancel, strike out, blue-pencil.
*adj*, angry, annoyed, vexed, ill-tempered, grumpy, irritable, testy, touchy, fractious,

peevish, petulant, crusty, snappy, waspish, cantankerous, short, shirty (*inf*). AFFABLE
transverse, crosswise, oblique, athwart.
contrary, adverse, unfavourable, opposing. FAVOURABLE

**cross-examine** interrogate, question, grill (*inf*), quiz, catechize, pump.

**cross-grained** stubborn, obdurate, perverse, headstrong, wilful, cantankerous, peevish, wayward, refractory, intractable, awkward, difficult. OBLIGING

**crotch** crutch, groin, angle, fork.

**crotchet** notion, whim, whimsy, caprice, fancy, fad, quirk, vagary.

**crotchety** cross, irritable, peevish, crusty, testy, touchy, grumpy, crabby, irascible, bad-tempered, cantankerous, contrary, awkward. AFFABLE
capricious, whimsical, fanciful, fitful, erratic, fickle.

**crouch** stoop, hunch, bend, bow, duck, squat, kneel.
cower, cringe, fawn, grovel, truckle.

**crow** brag, boast, vaunt, gloat, swagger, bluster, exult, triumph, rejoice.

**crowd** *n*, host, multitude, throng, mob, rabble, horde, pack, herd, swarm, assembly, concourse, congregation, company, group, bunch.
*v*, throng, swarm, flock, herd, congregate, gather, cluster, huddle. DISPERSE
press, pack, cram, squeeze, compress, congest, fill, stuff, shove, push, jostle.

**crown** *n*, diadem, coronet, coronal, circlet, tiara, chaplet, wreath, garland.
reward, award, prize, trophy, laurels, kudos, honour.
sovereign, monarch, ruler, king, queen, royalty, monarchy.
top, head, summit, brow, crest, apex, pinnacle, peak, acme, zenith, culmination. FOOT
*v*, adorn, honour, decorate, reward, invest, endow, install.
perfect, consummate, cap, top, surmount, complete, fulfil, round off, finish, conclude. BEGIN

**crucial** critical, decisive, central, pivotal, vital, all-important, momentous, essential, imperative, urgent, pressing. TRIVIAL

**crucify** torture, torment, persecute, rack, harrow.
overcome, subdue, mortify.
execute, put to death.

**crude** rude, vulgar, ribald, smutty, tasteless, gross, lewd, obscene, indecent, coarse, uncouth, crass, boorish.
raw, rough, unrefined, coarse, unfinished, unpolished, unprocessed, natural, primitive, rudimentary, sketchy, incomplete. REFINED

**crudeness** crudity, rawness, roughness, coarseness, vulgarity, rudeness, indecency, indelicacy, obscenity, ribaldry, impropriety. REFINEMENT

**cruel** savage, barbarous, brutal, ferocious, bloodthirsty, vicious, sadistic, merciless, pitiless, unrelenting, ruthless, harsh, severe, heartless, inhuman, unfeeling, unkind, callous, hard-hearted, cold-blooded, implacable. HUMANE

**cruelty** barbarity, brutality, savagery, ferocity, sadism, mercilessness, ruthlessness, harshness, severity, inhumanity, callousness. COMPASSION

**cruise** *n*, voyage, trip, sail.
*v*, sail, travel, journey, voyage, coast, drift, rove.

**crumb** scrap, morsel, bit, fragment, mite, shred, particle, speck, grain, sliver, bite, *soupçon*, atom, snippet.

**crumble** *vi*, disintegrate, fall apart, break up, fragment, decompose, perish. ENDURE
*vt*, crush, bruise, pulverize, pound, grind, triturate.

**crumple** rumple, wrinkle, crinkle, crease, corrugate, ruffle, crush, pucker, screw up. SMOOTH
collapse, fall, cave in, give way, break down, go to pieces, shrivel, shrink.

**crunch** munch, gnaw, chew, champ, grind, masticate.

**crusade** campaign, movement, cause, struggle, drive.

**crush** squeeze, squash, compress, pinch, break, smash, crumble, pound, pulverize, mash, grind, triturate, bruise, contuse, crumple, wrinkle, crease, demolish, raze, flatten.
overpower, subdue, overcome, overwhelm, suppress, quash, quell, put down, vanquish, conquer. RESIST
abash, humiliate, mortify, shame, chagrin, put down (*inf*).

**crust** covering, coating, layer, film, surface, skin, rind, shell, incrustation, scab.

**crusty** peevish, touchy, testy, crabbed, fractious, captious, bad-tempered, irritable, waspish, cantankerous, surly, curt, gruff, brusque, short. AFFABLE

**cry** *v*, sob, weep, wail, bawl, whine, whimper, snivel, blubber, lament, keen. LAUGH

call, shout, exclaim, vociferate, ejaculate, yell, shriek, scream, roar, bellow, holler (*inf*). WHISPER

proclaim, announce, broadcast, trumpet, blazon, noise, advertise, hawk.

**cry down,** disparage, belittle, denigrate, run down, decry.

*n*, sob, sobbing, weep, weeping, wail, bawl, blubber, lamentation, crying. LAUGH

call, shout, exclamation, ejaculation, yell, shriek, scream, roar, bellow, outcry. WHISPER

proclamation, announcement, slogan.

plea, entreaty, appeal, supplication, prayer, request.

**crypt** vault, tomb, catacomb, burial chamber, sepulchre.

**cryptic** secret, hidden, occult, esoteric, arcane, abstruse, obscure, vague, oracular, cabbalistic, enigmatic, mysterious, puzzling.

**cuddle** embrace, hug, clasp, fondle, caress, snuggle, nestle.

**cudgel** *n*, club, bludgeon, truncheon, cosh, stick, bastinado.

*v*, beat, batter, pound, baste, drub, club, bludgeon, thrash.

**cue** signal, sign, indication, nod, wink, hint, suggestion, intimation, reminder, prompt, catchword.

**cuff** *v*, strike, hit, box, slap, smack, buffet, punch, belt (*inf*).

*n*, blow, box, slap, smack, buffet, punch.

**cuisine** cookery, cooking, menu, food, fare.

**cull** pick, choose, select, single out, pluck, gather, collect, glean.

**culminate** end, finish, close, conclude, terminate, result, climax, come to a head. START

**culmination** climax, zenith, meridian, acme, height, peak, top, summit, pinnacle, crown, consummation, conclusion, completion, close, finishing touch, finale. BEGINNING

**culpable** blameworthy, blamable, censurable, wrong, reprehensible, at fault, guilty, sinful. INNOCENT

**culprit** offender, guilty party, wrongdoer, malefactor, criminal, felon, miscreant, delinquent, sinner.

**cult** sect, clique, faction, party, school, belief, faith, religion, denomination.

worship, homage, veneration, adoration, devotion, idolization.

craze, fashion, fad.

**cultivate** till, work, farm, plant, plough, fertilize.

promote, foster, nurture, further, support, encourage, help, aid. IMPEDE

improve, better, ameliorate, develop, refine, civilize, enrich, polish, train, educate. NEGLECT

**cultivation** agriculture, agronomy, farming, husbandry, tillage, gardening.

civilization, culture, refinement, polish, breeding, education, training, development, enlightenment, improvement. NEGLECT

promotion, support, encouragement, furtherance, patronage, advocacy, nurture, help, aid.

**cultural** edifying, enriching, instructive, educational, enlightening, civilizing, artistic, elevating.

**culture** refinement, sophistication, polish, cultivation, urbanity, gentility, breeding, education, enlightenment, edification. BARBARITY

civilization, society, customs, way of life, life style, mores.

agriculture, farming, cultivation, husbandry, agronomy.

**cultured** refined, sophisticated, civilized, polished, well-bred, genteel, urbane, educated, knowledgeable, erudite, scholarly, enlightened. BARBAROUS

**cumbersome** awkward, unwieldy, bulky, heavy, burdensome, oppressive, inconvenient, incommodious. LIGHT

**cumulative** increasing, snowballing, accumulative, collective, accruing, growing. DECREASING

**cunning** *adj*, artful, crafty, sly, wily, foxy, sharp, shrewd, astute, canny, arch, subtle, devious, calculating, designing, deceitful, dishonest, shifty. ARTLESS

ingenious, skilful, clever, deft, dexterous.

*n*, artfulness, craft, craftiness, slyness, wiliness, guile, sharpness, shrewdness, subtlety, trickery, deception. ARTLESSNESS ingenuity, skill, dexterity, cleverness, ability, art.

**cup** chalice, goblet, beaker, mug, trophy.

**cupboard** cabinet, locker, closet, sideboard, wardrobe.

**cupidity** avarice, greed, acquisitiveness, rapacity, covetousness, desire, lust, longing, hankering, thirst, hunger.

**cur** hound, dog, mongrel, mutt (*inf*).
scoundrel, blackguard, wretch, rotter (*inf*), cad, villain, rat (*inf*).

**curative** healing, restorative, therapeutic, medicinal, remedial, salutary, healthy. NOXIOUS

**curb** *v*, restrain, check, control, bridle, repress, muzzle, hold back, suppress, moderate, restrict. ENCOURAGE
*n*, restraint, check, control, bridle, rein, moderation, restriction, limitation.

**curdle** coagulate, congeal, thicken, curd, clot, go sour, turn.

**cure** *v*, heal, restore, remedy, make well, correct, ease, alleviate, relieve, treat. AGGRAVATE
preserve, dry, salt, smoke, pickle.
*n*, remedy, antidote, restorative, treatment, therapy, medicine, drug, panacea, corrective, healing, restoration, recovery.

**curiosity** inquisitiveness, nosiness (*inf*), snooping, prying, interest, questioning. INDIFFERENCE
oddity, rarity, novelty, curio, phenomenon, freak, spectacle, sight, marvel, wonder.

**curious** inquisitive, inquiring, questioning, interested, prying, snooping, meddlesome, nosy (*inf*). INDIFFERENT
odd, strange, queer, unusual, uncommon, extraordinary, peculiar, singular, bizarre, rare, exotic, unexpected. ORDINARY

**curl** *v*, twist, wind, coil, spiral, snake, twine, convolute, bend, curve, loop, wave, crimp, frizz. STRAIGHTEN
*n*, coil, spiral, whorl, curlicue, convolution, loop, kink, wave, ringlet, lock, tress.

**curmudgeon** miser, skinflint, churl, bear, crosspatch (*inf*), sourpuss (*inf*), grumbler, grouch (*inf*).

**currency** money, cash, notes, coins, legal tender.
circulation, transmission, acceptance, prevalence, popularity, vogue, fashion, publicity, exposure.

**current** *adj*, present, ongoing, prevailing, in progress, latest, up-to-date, contemporary, fashionable, popular. OBSOLETE
widespread, rife, circulating, general, common, prevalent.
*n*, flow, stream, tide, drift, trend, course, progression.

**curse** *n*, oath, expletive, swearword, blasphemy, profanity, obscenity.
execration, imprecation, anathema, malediction, malison, denunciation, excommunication, damnation, incantation, charm, spell, jinx, voodoo. BENEDICTION
scourge, bane, affliction, trouble, torment, plague, vexation, burden, misfortune, evil. BLESSING
*v*, swear, blaspheme, cuss (*inf*).
execrate, imprecate, anathematize, denounce, damn, blast, fulminate, excommunicate. BLESS
blight, destroy, plague, scourge, afflict, vex, torment.

**cursory** superficial, perfunctory, summary, hasty, rapid, hurried, brief, slight, passing, fleeting, careless, slapdash. THOROUGH

**curt** terse, short, brief, concise, succinct, laconic, blunt, brusque, abrupt, rude, unceremonious, gruff.

**curtail** shorten, cut short, abridge, abbreviate, cut, lop, reduce, decrease, diminish, lessen, contract. LENGTHEN

**curtailment** shortening, abridgment, abbreviation, reduction, cutting, docking, retrenchment, diminution, contraction. EXTENSION

**curtain** *n*, hanging, shade, screen, blind, drape, veil.
*v*, conceal, hide, shut off, screen, veil, shroud. EXPOSE

**curvature** curve, incurvation, flexure, bend, bending.

**curve** *v*, bend, turn, twist, wind, inflect, arch, hook, bow, curl, coil, spiral. STRAIGHTEN
*n*, bend, arc, arch, camber, vault, turn, hook, loop, crescent, curvature.

**cushion** *n*, pad, bolster, pillow, hassock, headrest, buffer.
*v*, protect, support, bolster, brace.
lessen, stifle, muffle, soften, deaden, suppress.

**cusp** point, tip, apex, angle.

**custodian** guardian, keeper, warden, warder, protector, curator, caretaker, watchman.

**custody** care, protection, keeping, safekeeping, charge, ward, tutelage, guardianship, trusteeship, supervision, watch, auspices, aegis.
arrest, confinement, imprisonment, detention, duress. RELEASE

**custom** convention, usage, habit, wont, routine, policy, rule, practice, use, formality, etiquette, fashion, way, manner, procedure, ritual.

**customary** usual, habitual, wonted, accustomed, regular, routine, conventional, traditional, normal, ordinary, common, popular, familiar. UNUSUAL

**customer** client, patron, buyer, purchaser, shopper, consumer. SELLER

**cut** *v*, sever, cut off, slice, chop, carve, divide, cut up, cleave, gash, slash, score, nick, lacerate, wound. JOIN
trim, shear, mow, lop, crop, dock, prune, fell, hew, cut down, pare, shave.
shorten, abridge, edit, abbreviate, curtail, reduce, retrench, cut back, cut down, lessen, lower, decrease. EXTEND
snub, ignore, cold-shoulder, avoid, spurn, slight, rebuff. ACKNOWLEDGE
**cut in,** interpose, interrupt, butt in, intervene.
**cut off,** intercept, interrupt, discontinue, stop, halt, suspend, disconnect.
**cut out,** delete, eliminate, exclude, remove, extract, excise.
**cut short,** break off, halt, suspend, interrupt, abort, terminate, end, stop.
*n*, incision, gash, wound, laceration, slash, nick.
reduction, cutback, decrease, lowering, fall.
share, percentage, slice, portion, piece.
style, shape, form, fashion, mode.

**cute** sweet, appealing, attractive, delightful, pretty, charming. REPULSIVE
clever, shrewd, astute, canny, sharp. DULL

**cutting** *adj*, keen, sharp, trenchant, piercing, biting, caustic, acid, mordant, incisive, acerbic, sardonic, sarcastic, cruel, bitter, hurtful, stinging. SOOTHING
*n*, clipping, excerpt, abstract, piece, slip, snippet.

**cycle** circle, revolution, rotation, round, series, succession.
period, era, aeon, age, epoch.

**cyclone** tornado, typhoon, whirlwind, hurricane, tempest, storm.

**cynical** pessimistic, misanthropic, sceptical, distrustful, suspicious, unbelieving, contemptuous, scornful, derisive, sardonic, sarcastic, ironic, mocking, sneering.

**cynosure** focus, focal point, centre, attraction, centre of attention, polestar, leading light, paragon, ideal.

**cyst** blister, sac, vesicle, bladder, bleb.

# D

**dab** *v*, pat, tap, touch, daub, spot, blot.
*n*, spot, drop, speck, touch, bit, trace.
pat, tap, stroke, blow, touch.
**dab hand,** expert, master, adept, ace (*inf*), dabster.

**dabble** dip, paddle, splash, spatter, sprinkle, moisten, wet.
potter, tinker, trifle, dally, toy with, play at, dip into.

**daft** silly, foolish, stupid, idiotic, simple, soft (*inf*), crazy, absurd, senseless, lunatic, insane, crackers (*inf*), potty (*inf*), nuts (*inf*). SENSIBLE

**dagger** dirk, stiletto, poniard, skean, knife, blade.

**dainty** delicate, fine, elegant, refined, exquisite, charming, pretty, beautiful, graceful, petite, neat, trim. CLUMSY
delicious, tasty, tender, choice, savoury, luscious, delectable, toothsome, palatable. LOATHSOME
scrupulous, fastidious, squeamish, particular, fussy, finicky, choosy.

**dale** valley, vale, dell, dingle, glen. HILL

**dalliance** dawdling, dilly-dallying, idling, loafing, delay, procrastination, pottering, trifling, dabbling. HASTE

**dally** dawdle, loiter, linger, dilly-dally, tarry, delay, waste time, hang around. HURRY
trifle, toy, play, sport, flirt, fool around, tease, caress, pet, fondle.

**damage** *n*, harm, injury, hurt, suffering, mischief, impairment, detriment, loss, destruction, ruin. REPARATION
*v*, harm, hurt, injure, impair, tamper with, mar, spoil, ruin, wreck, deface, mutilate. REPAIR

**damages** compensation, satisfaction, reparation, indemnity, costs, expenses, fine, penalty.

**dame** lady, noblewoman, peeress, baroness, matron, dowager.

**damn** *v*, condemn, denounce, censure, criticize, berate, vituperate, vilify, slate (*inf*). EXTOL
curse, swear, blaspheme, blast, cuss (*inf*), anathematize, imprecate. BLESS
doom, sentence, condemn, convict. ACQUIT
*n*, trifle, jot, whit, iota, hoot (*inf*), brass farthing.
**give a damn,** care, mind, be concerned.

**damnable** abominable, execrable, odious, detestable, accursed, despicable, horrible, atrocious. SPLENDID

**damnation** condemnation, denunciation, objurgation, excommunication, proscription, exile, ban, doom, anathema, curse. BLESSING

**damp** *adj*, moist, dewy, wet, dank, humid, muggy, clammy, soggy, sodden, misty, drizzly. DRY
*n*, dampness, moisture, humidity, fog, mist, vapour, dankness, dew. DRYNESS
*v*, moisten, dampen, wet, bedew, humidify. DRY
check, curb, restrain, moderate, abate, allay, temper, dull, deaden, blunt, cool, inhibit, stifle, muffle, discourage, dishearten, depress, deject. ENCOURAGE

**dampen** damp, wet, moisten, bedew, humidify. DRY
moderate, restrain, temper, dull, blunt, deaden, stifle, discourage, depress, damp. ENCOURAGE

**damper** obstacle, hindrance, impediment, hitch, check, restraint, discouragement, pall, cloud, wet blanket, kill-joy.

**dance** *v*, caper, skip, hop, jig, swing, rock, prance, frolic, gambol.
*n*, ball, social, hop (*inf*), disco (*inf*).

**dandle** caress, pet, fondle, rock, cradle, amuse.

**dandy** *n*, beau, fop, coxcomb, swell (*inf*), popinjay, ladies' man.
*adj*, fine, excellent, splendid, first-rate.

**danger** peril, risk, jeopardy, hazard, vulnerability, precariousness, threat, menace. SAFETY

**dangerous** perilous, risky, hazardous, unsafe, chancy, hairy (*inf*), vulnerable, insecure, precarious, ominous, threatening, menacing. SAFE

**dangle** hang, suspend, swing, droop, trail, sway, oscillate.
flaunt, brandish, wave, flourish.

**dank** damp, clammy, moist, dewy, humid, wet, chilly. DRY

**dapper** smart, spruce, neat, trim, natty, chic, elegant. SLOVENLY
nimble, spry, brisk, agile, lively, sprightly, active, quick. SLOW

**dappled** mottled, variegated, spotted, speckled, brindled, piebald, pied, brindled, dapple.

**dare** *v*, challenge, defy, provoke, goad, taunt, brave, confront.
risk, hazard, venture, endanger, gamble, stake, attempt, presume. QUAIL
*n*, challenge, provocation, ultimatum, gauntlet.

**daring** *adj*, bold, brave, adventurous, venturesome, intrepid, dauntless, fearless, courageous, plucky, rash, reckless, daredevil, foolhardy, death-defying. TIMOROUS
*n*, boldness, audacity, bravery, intrepidity, courage, valour, nerve, mettle, pluck, guts (*inf*), bottle (*inf*), temerity, rashness, recklessness. TIMOROUSNESS

**dark** *adj*, dim, unlit, sunless, shadowy, dingy, murky, cloudy, overcast, dusky, swarthy, black, ebony, sable, pitchy. LIGHT
sombre, drab, dismal, gloomy, cheerless, bleak, mournful, discouraging. BRIGHT
dour, sullen, morose, glowering, threatening, forbidding, ominous, menacing, sinister. CHEERFUL
ignorant, unenlightened, benighted, uneducated. ENLIGHTENED
secret, hidden, abstruse, recondite, cryptic, incomprehensible, unintelligible, obscure, mysterious, enigmatic, occult, arcane. PLAIN
infernal, hellish, satanic, nefarious, infamous, evil, wicked, vile, atrocious, horrible. GOOD
*n*, darkness, dimness, blackness, gloom, obscurity, murkiness, dusk, twilight, evening, night. LIGHT
ignorance, blindness, secrecy, concealment. ENLIGHTENMENT

**darken** dim, obscure, eclipse, shade, shadow, overshadow, cloud, blacken, make dark, go dark. LIGHTEN deject, depress, dishearten, discourage, oppress, sadden, make gloomy. BRIGHTEN

**darkness** *n*, dark, gloom, murkiness, murk, dimness, obscurity, shadows, dusk, night, blackness. BRIGHTNESS
ignorance, blindness, secrecy, concealment. ENLIGHTENMENT

**darling** *n*, dear, sweetheart, beloved, pet, love, favourite.
*adj*, dear, beloved, precious, cherished, adored, loved, treasured, pet, favourite.
charming, lovely, sweet, adorable, enchanting. REPULSIVE

**darn** mend, repair, stitch, sew, patch.

**dart** *vi*, shoot, dash, race, sprint, fly, run, scoot, tear, rush. AMBLE
*vt*, hurl, throw, fling, cast, pitch, sling, propel.

**dash** *v*, rush, run, race, dart, hurry, hasten, fly, bolt, sprint. AMBLE
hurl, throw, cast, fling, strike, crash, break, shatter, splinter.
frustrate, thwart, foil, ruin, destroy.
*n*, dart, rush, spurt, sprint, onset.
tinge, touch, trace, *soupçon*, hint, drop, bit, pinch, grain, smack, sprinkling.
élan, flair, style, flourish, panache, vigour, spirit.

**dashing** lively, spirited, impetuous, dynamic, gallant, valiant, plucky. LETHARGIC
showy, flamboyant, brilliant, dazzling, elegant, chic, stylish, dapper, jaunty.

**dastard** coward, craven, poltroon, cur, worm, mouse.

**dastardly** dastard, cowardly, craven, faint-hearted, timorous, pusillanimous, yellow (*inf*). BRAVE
base, mean, despicable, low, underhand. NOBLE

**data** facts, information, input, figures, statistics.

**date** *n*, age, period, era, epoch, time, day, month, year, century.
appointment, engagement, assignation, tryst, rendezvous.
escort, boyfriend, girlfriend, lover, steady (*inf*).
**out of date,** old-fashioned, outmoded, dated, passé, obsolete, antiquated, superannuated. MODERN
expired, invalid, lapsed. CURRENT
**up to date,** modern, fashionable, trendy (*inf*), up-to-the-minute, current, contemporary. DATED
*v*, take out, go out with, court.
obsolesce, become old-fashioned.

**dated** out of date, old-fashioned, outmoded, passé, old hat, antiquated, obsolescent. MODERN

**daub** *v*, smear, paint, plaster, cover, bedaub, spatter, smudge, soil, begrime, deface, sully, stain.
*n*, smear, smudge, spot, blot, smirch.

**daunt** intimidate, unnerve, dismay, alarm, scare, frighten, terrify, appal, cow, overawe.
discourage, dispirit, deter, put off, stop, check, thwart. ENCOURAGE

**dauntless** undaunted, bold, daring, brave, fearless, intrepid, valiant, doughty, indomitable, courageous, stout-hearted, heroic. COWARDLY

**dawdle** lag, loiter, dilly-dally (*inf*), dally, waste time, idle, trifle, potter. HURRY

**dawdler** laggard, loiterer, snail, slowcoach (*inf*), idler.

**dawn** *n*, daybreak, sunrise, sun-up, cockcrow, aurora, daylight, morning. SUNSET
beginning, start, outset, origin, birth, genesis, inception, advent, onset, emergence. END
*v*, break, gleam, grow light, brighten.
begin, start, appear, emerge, rise, open, originate. CLOSE

**day** daylight, daytime, sunshine. NIGHT
generation, age, period, epoch, era, lifetime, heyday, prime.

**daybreak** dawn, sunrise, sun-up, cockcrow, first light, morning. NIGHTFALL

**daydream** *n*, dream, reverie, woolgathering, fancy, pipe dream, fantasy, castle in the air.
*v*, dream, muse, fantasize, stargaze, imagine.

**daylight** sunshine, sunlight, day, daytime, light of day. NIGHT

**daze** *v*, stun, stupefy, shock, dumbfound, amaze, astonish, flabbergast (*inf*), bewilder, confuse, blind, dazzle.
*n*, stupor, trance, confusion, distraction, bewilderment.

**dazzle** *v*, blind, bedazzle, daze, stun, stagger, amaze, astonish, strike dumb, impress, overawe, bowl over (*inf*), fascinate. BORE *n*, brilliance, splendour, magnificence, sparkle, flash. DULLNESS

**dead** *adj*, lifeless, defunct, deceased, late, departed, gone, extinct, inanimate. ALIVE
numb, insensitive, unresponsive, unfeeling, cold, frigid, lukewarm, indifferent, apathetic, spiritless, torpid, dull.
inactive, inert, still, inoperative, not working.
complete, utter, downright, total, absolute, thorough.
*n*, midst, depth, darkness, coldness, stillness.
*adv*, completely, utterly, totally, absolutely, entirely.

**deaden** damp, dampen, muffle, blunt, subdue, weaken, moderate, diminish, lessen, abate, alleviate, dull, numb, anaesthetize, paralyse. INTENSIFY

**deadlock** stalemate, impasse, standstill, halt, cessation, tie, draw.

**deadly** mortal, fatal, lethal, malignant, pernicious, noxious, venomous, destructive, baleful, murderous, savage, sanguinary, implacable.
pale, ashen, deathly, deathlike, wan, ghostly, livid. RUDDY
boring, dull, tedious, monotonous, tiresome. ENTHRALLING

**deaf** unhearing, stone deaf, hard of hearing.
heedless, oblivious, insensitive, unmoved, indifferent. AWARE

**deafen** make deaf, din, drown out, muffle.

**deafening** ear-splitting, piercing, thunderous, resounding, intense. QUIET

**deal** *v*, distribute, dispense, mete, dole, bestow, give, divide, share, allot, apportion.
trade, traffic, bargain, negotiate, do business.
act, behave, conduct oneself.
**deal with,** handle, manage, cope with, see to, take care of, attend to, treat.
*n*, agreement, bargain, transaction, contract, pact, understanding.
quantity, amount, degree, extent.

**dealer** merchant, trader, tradesman, wholesaler, retailer, vendor, trafficker.

**dealings** business, commerce, trade, traffic.
action, behaviour, relations.

**dear** *adj*, beloved, darling, precious, cherished, treasured, prized, favourite. LOATHSOME
expensive, costly, pricey (*inf*). CHEAP
*n*, darling, beloved, treasure, love, precious.

**dearth** lack, deficiency, scarcity, shortage, insufficiency, want, need, famine, poverty, absence. ABUNDANCE

**death** decease, demise, expiration, dying, passing, departure, quietus, exit, end, cessation, dissolution. BIRTH
destruction, annihilation, extermination, extinction, eradication.

**deathless** immortal, undying, imperishable, everlasting, eternal, unceasing, timeless. MORTAL

**deathly** deathlike, ghastly, livid, pale, wan, gaunt, haggard, cadaverous.

**debacle** rout, defeat, overthrow, ruin, collapse, downfall, break-up, wreck, havoc, devastation, catastrophe.

**debar** bar, exclude, shut out, blackball, proscribe, prohibit, restrain, impede, hinder, obstruct, thwart, stop. ADMIT

**debase** degrade, lower, abase, reduce, humble, humiliate, shame, disgrace, dishonour, demean, devalue, depreciate, deteriorate. RAISE
adulterate, vitiate, contaminate, deprave, corrupt, taint, defile, pollute, sully, alloy, impair. PURIFY

**debasement** degradation, lowering, abasement, humiliation, disgrace, dishonour, depreciation, reduction, deterioration, adulteration, contamination, pollution, corruption, depravation.

**debatable** disputable, questionable, unsettled, undecided, moot, contestable, controversial, doubtful, dubious, uncertain. CERTAIN

**debate** *v*, discuss, dispute, argue, contend, question, moot, wrangle, controvert. AGREE
deliberate, consider, ponder, reflect, mull over. DECIDE
*n*, discussion, dispute, disputation, polemic, controversy, wrangle, altercation, contention, contest. AGREEMENT

**debauch** *v*, deprave, corrupt, debase, demoralize, pervert, vitiate, defile, deflower, violate, seduce, lead astray. PURIFY
*n*, spree, orgy, fling, revel, carousal, saturnalia, binge (*inf*), bout.

**debauched** depraved, corrupt, licentious, degenerate, dissolute, dissipated, immoral, abandoned, wanton. ASCETIC

**debauchery** depravity, dissipation, dissoluteness, lust, licentiousness, intemperance, incontinence, indulgence, excess, revelry, debauch. RESTRAINT

**debilitate** enfeeble, weaken, enervate, sap, exhaust, prostrate, incapacitate, undermine. STRENGTHEN

**debility** feebleness, weakness, enervation, prostration, exhaustion, infirmity, decrepitude, frailty, languor, lassitude, incapacity. STRENGTH

**debonair** affable, gracious, courteous, polite, suave, urbane, refined, elegant, dashing, jaunty, sprightly, buoyant, cheery, sunny, breezy, light-hearted, gay.

**debris** remains, ruins, wreckage, detritus, fragments, pieces, rubble, rubbish, litter.

**debt** liability, obligation, due, duty, debit, arrears, deficit, bill, account, score. ASSET

**in debt,** owing, liable, accountable, beholden, in arrears, in the red.

**debut** beginning, launch, premiere, coming out, introduction, presentation, entrance, first appearance.

**decadence** decay, decline, degeneration, deterioration, wane, fall, retrogression, debasement, corruption, dissipation, dissolution. RISE

**decadent** depraved, dissolute, dissipated, self-indulgent, immoral, corrupt, degenerate.
decaying, declining, waning, deteriorating. RISING

**decamp** abscond, bolt, fly, flee, run away, make off, escape, scarper (*inf*), do a bunk (*inf*).

**decapitate** behead, guillotine, execute.

**decay** *v*, decline, deteriorate, waste away, wither, crumble, atrophy, degenerate, wane, decrease, dwindle. FLOURISH
rot, decompose, spoil, perish, go bad, putrefy.
*n*, decline, deterioration, decadence, wasting, atrophy, degeneration, wane, collapse, downfall. GROWTH
rot, decomposition, spoilage, putrefaction, caries, gangrene, mould.

**decease** death, demise, dying, expiration, passing, departure, exit, release. BIRTH

**deceased** dead, lifeless, defunct, departed, gone, late, former. ALIVE

**deceit** fraud, deception, guile, duplicity, cheating, trickery, artifice, deceitfulness, dishonesty. HONESTY
trick, ruse, stratagem, wile, subterfuge, pretence, imposture, fraud, swindle, lie, falsehood.

**deceitful** dishonest, untruthful, mendacious, hollow, false, insincere, hypocritical, fraudulent, crooked, treacherous, wily, scheming, tricky, guileful, artful, deceptive. HONEST

**deceive** mislead, cheat, trick, fool, beguile, dupe, hoodwink, cozen, delude, hoax, swindle, con (*inf*), bamboozle (*inf*), double-cross (*inf*), take in (*inf*), take for a ride (*inf*).

**deceiver** cheat, fraud, impostor, swindler, sharper, con man (*inf*), hypocrite, liar, charlatan.

**decency** propriety, modesty, decorum, correctness, respectability, seemliness, etiquette. IMPROPRIETY

**decent** proper, seemly, fitting, appropriate, seemly, becoming, decorous, nice, polite, pure, modest, respectable. INDECENT
adequate, passable, fair, reasonable, not bad, acceptable, tolerable.
obliging, accommodating, kind, generous, thoughtful, courteous. UNKIND

**deception** deceit, fraud, cheating, guile, artifice, duplicity, hypocrisy, trickery, cunning, treachery, deceitfulness, dishonesty. HONESTY
trick, ruse, wile, fraud, imposture, swindle, hoax, lie, bluff, sham, illusion.

**deceptive** misleading, deceiving, unreliable, illusory, illusive, delusive, fallacious, ambiguous, fraudulent, false, fake, counterfeit, dishonest, deceitful. TRUE

**decide** determine, settle, adjudicate, judge, rule, decree, resolve, make up one's mind, choose, elect, conclude, terminate, end. WAVER

**decided** determined, resolute, unwavering, firm, decisive, unhesitating. IRRESOLUTE
certain, unquestionable, indisputable, unmistakable, unequivocal, positive, distinct, clear, definite, categorical. DUBIOUS

**decipher** solve, unravel, decode, translate, interpret, explain, construe, read, make out. ENCODE

**decision** resolution, conclusion, verdict, judgment, ruling, settlement, finding.
determination, resolution, resolve, firmness, decisiveness, purpose. INDECISION
**decisive** conclusive, deciding, definitive, absolute, categorical, final, emphatic, momentous, crucial, influential. INCONCLUSIVE
resolute, decided, determined, firm, unwavering. INDECISIVE
**deck** adorn, bedeck, array, clothe, dress, attire, decorate, trim, ornament, embellish. STRIP
**declaim** orate, harangue, perorate, hold forth, rant, proclaim, speak, enunciate, recite, spout.
**declaim against,** criticize, attack, denounce, decry, inveigh against, rail at.
**declamation** harangue, tirade, recitation, oration, speech, address, lecture, oratory, grandiloquence.
**declamatory** rhetorical, bombastic, grandiloquent, magniloquent, fustian, turgid, orotund, pompous, theatrical, stilted.
**declaration** statement, affirmation, avowal, assertion, asseveration, averment, acknowledgment, testimony, deposition, profession. DENIAL
proclamation, announcement, notice, publication, manifesto, pronouncement, notification.
**declare** state, affirm, avow, assert, attest, aver, say, maintain, claim, swear, testify, certify. DENY
proclaim, announce, broadcast, trumpet, pronounce, decree.
**declension** decline, fall, deterioration, decay, decadence, degeneracy. RISE
**declination** inclination, slope, descent, declivity, deviation, divergence, departure.
**decline** *v*, refuse, turn down, reject, forgo, deny. ACCEPT
decrease, diminish, lessen, dwindle, wane, ebb, sink, fall, fail, deteriorate, weaken, droop, languish, pine, degenerate, decay, waste away. FLOURISH
descend, sink, dip, slope, incline. ASCEND
*n*, decrease, diminution, lessening, recession, wane, deterioration, failing, weakening, degeneration, decay, senility, decrepitude.
declivity, slope, incline, descent. ASCENT
**declivity** descent, declination, downward slope, decline, incline, hill. ACCLIVITY
**decompose** rot, go bad, putrefy, decay, crumble, fall apart, break up.
disintegrate, dissolve, break down, analyse, dissect, atomize, distil, separate, resolve.
**decomposition** rotting, putrefaction, putrescence, decay, corruption.
disintegration, analysis, dissection, dissolution, separation, resolution. SYNTHESIS
**decorate** embellish, ornament, adorn, deck, bedeck, trim, beautify. MAR
paint, wallpaper, renovate, do up (*inf*).
cite, honour.
**decoration** embellishment, ornament, ornamentation, adornment, trimming, garnish, flourish, frill, bauble.
medal, ribbon, badge, order, award, citation.
**decorous** proper, seemly, decent, becoming, fitting, appropriate, suitable, correct, mannerly, dignified, sedate, refined, elegant, polite. UNSEEMLY
**decorum** propriety, correctness, seemliness, decency, etiquette, protocol, breeding, good manners, politeness, dignity, respectability. IMPROPRIETY
**decoy** *v*, lure, allure, entice, tempt, bait, inveigle, seduce, deceive, mislead, ensnare, entrap.
*n*, lure, enticement, bait, trap, pretence, fake.
**decrease** *v*, lessen, diminish, reduce, dwindle, decline, lower, wane, subside, ebb, fall, drop, abate, ease, cut down, curtail, shrink, contract. INCREASE
*n*, lessening, diminution, reduction, decline, lowering, decrement, ebb, recession, wane, fall, abatement, cutback, retrenchment, curtailment, shrinkage, contraction. INCREASE
**decree** *n*, edict, order, command, precept, law, enactment, statute, mandate, rule, regulation, injunction, dictum, ordinance.
*v*, order, command, adjudge, ordain, rule, enact, appoint, proclaim, pronounce, decide, determine.
**decrement** decrease, diminution, decline, reduction. INCREMENT
**decrepit** infirm, enfeebled, feeble, weak, frail, crippled, incapacitated, aged, doddering, tottering. YOUTHFUL
dilapidated, ramshackle, broken-down, run-down, rickety, worn-out, antiquated, superannuated.

**decrial** disparagement, condemnation, denunciation, depreciation, belittlement. APPRECIATION

**decry** disparage, belittle, deprecate, depreciate, underrate, undervalue, discredit, run down, abuse, criticize, condemn, denounce, rail against, defame, vilify. APPRECIATE

**dedicate** devote, pledge, commit, assign, give.
consecrate, sanctify, hallow, bless, set apart. DESECRATE
inscribe, address.

**dedication** devotion, commitment, wholeheartedness, allegiance, loyalty, fidelity.
consecration, sanctification, hallowing, ordination, blessing. DESECRATION
inscription, address.

**deduce** conclude, infer, gather, understand, derive, reason, presume, surmise. GUESS

**deduct** subtract, take away, dock, withdraw, remove, take off. ADD

**deduction** conclusion, inference, corollary, finding, reasoning, result, assumption. GUESS
subtraction, reduction, decrease, withdrawal, removal, allowance, discount. ADDITION

**deed** action, act, feat, exploit, achievement, accomplishment, performance, doing.
title, document, contract, indenture.

**deem** consider, judge, hold, regard, think, imagine, believe, estimate, account, suppose.

**deep** *adj*, profound, bottomless, unfathomable, immeasurable, broad, wide, extensive, cavernous, yawning. SHALLOW
abstruse, obscure, difficult, mysterious, arcane, recondite, esoteric, incomprehensible. PLAIN
learned, intellectual, astute, shrewd, knowing, discerning, intelligent, sagacious, wise.
engrossed, absorbed, preoccupied, rapt, immersed, involved.
grave, great, intense, extreme, profound.
dark, rich, intense, vivid, full. LIGHT
low, bass, sonorous, resonant, rumbling. HIGH
*n*, sea, ocean, main.
depth, bottom, vastness, midst, dead, still.

**deepen** dig, hollow, excavate, scoop out, dredge, mine, sink.
intensify, increase, amplify, augment, strengthen, enhance. LESSEN

**deface** disfigure, mar, spoil, deform, blemish, flaw, mutilate, vandalize, sully, tarnish. BEAUTIFY

**defacement** disfigurement, injury, damage, mutilation, vandalism, blemish, flaw. BEAUTIFICATION

**de facto** *adj*, real, actual, existing.
*adv*, in fact, in reality, in effect, actually, really.

**defalcation** misappropriation, embezzlement, deficit, shortage, deficiency, default.

**defamation** aspersion, calumny, abuse, slander, libel, traducement, obloquy, scandal, smear, backbiting, vilification, denigration, disparagement. PRAISE

**defamatory** calumnious, abusive, slanderous, libellous, injurious, scandalous, insulting, denigrating, maledictory, disparaging. COMPLIMENTARY

**defame** calumniate, asperse, slander, libel, traduce, denigrate, vilify, discredit, dishonour, malign, speak ill of, abuse, smear, besmirch, disparage, belittle. PRAISE

**default** *n*, failure, omission, neglect, lapse, oversight, want, lack, absence, deficiency, deficit, nonpayment.
*v*, fail, neglect, dodge, evade, cheat, bilk, welsh (*inf*).

**defaulter** offender, delinquent, nonpayer, embezzler, cheat.

**defeat** *v*, beat, conquer, vanquish, overcome, rout, worst, overpower, subdue, quell, crush, thrash. SURRENDER
thwart, foil, frustrate, discomfit, checkmate, balk, check, baffle, confound.
*n*, conquest, overthrow, beating, rout, vanquishment, subjugation, trouncing. VICTORY
frustration, reverse, setback, discomfiture, checkmate, failure, disappointment.

**defecate** excrete, egest, evacuate, move the bowels.
purge, cleanse, purify, clarify, refine. POLLUTE

**defecation** excretion, egestion, evacuation, bowel movement.
purification, cleansing, clarification, purge. POLLUTION

**defect** *n*, imperfection, flaw, blemish, spot, fault, error, failing, weakness, shortcoming, deficiency, omission, default, lack, want. PERFECTION
*v*, desert, abandon, forsake, change sides, apostatize, tergiversate, go over, rebel, mutiny.

**defection** desertion, abandonment, dereliction, backsliding, apostasy, disloyalty, mutiny, conversion.

**defective** faulty, imperfect, flawed, impaired, broken, out of order, not working, inadequate, incomplete, deficient, lacking, wanting, short. PERFECT

**defence** resistance, protection, guard, shelter, cover, shield, screen, fortification, bulwark, barricade. ATTACK
vindication, justification, excuse, plea, apology, argument. ACCUSATION

**defenceless** unprotected, unguarded, unarmed, exposed, vulnerable, wide open, weak, helpless. PROTECTED

**defend** resist, protect, guard, safeguard, shield, screen, shelter, preserve, fortify, arm. ATTACK
support, endorse, uphold, maintain, vindicate, justify, plead, argue for, champion, stick up for, represent. ACCUSE

**defendant** accused, offender, prisoner, respondent. PLAINTIFF

**defender** protector, guard, escort, bodyguard, keeper, guardian. ASSAILANT
champion, advocate, supporter, upholder, backer, vindicator. ACCUSER

**defensive** defending, protective, opposing, watchful, on the defensive, on guard. ATTACKING

**defer**[1] delay, postpone, put off, adjourn, shelve, prorogue, suspend, hold over, procrastinate, temporize. HASTEN

**defer**[2] comply, yield, submit, bow, accede, capitulate, give in. RESIST

**deference** compliance, submission, yielding, capitulation, acquiescence, complaisance, obedience, nonresistance. RESISTANCE
respect, regard, esteem, honour, reverence, homage, consideration, courtesy, politeness. DISRESPECT

**deferential** submissive, compliant, obeisant, obsequious, complaisant, obedient, respectful, considerate, courteous, polite. DEFIANT

**deferment** deferral, delay, postponement, suspension, adjournment, moratorium, abeyance, procrastination.

**defiance** resistance, opposition, confrontation, challenge, insubordination, disobedience, rebelliousness, contumacy, disregard, contempt. COMPLIANCE

**defiant** antagonistic, resistant, aggressive, belligerent, challenging, provocative, audacious, bold, daring, insolent, disobedient, insubordinate, recalcitrant, contumacious, stubborn, unyielding. COMPLIANT

**deficiency** lack, shortage, want, insufficiency, dearth, deficit, scarcity, inadequacy, absence. ABUNDANCE
weakness, failing, shortcoming, imperfection, defect, flaw. PERFECTION

**deficient** lacking, short, wanting, insufficient, inadequate, scarce, scant, scanty. ABUNDANT
defective, imperfect, incomplete, flawed, faulty, infirm, weak. PERFECT

**deficit** shortage, shortfall, deficiency, loss, arrears. SURPLUS

**defile** pollute, soil, dirty, befoul, contaminate, sully, taint, tarnish, corrupt, poison, vitiate, besmirch, disgrace, degrade, debase. PURIFY
profane, desecrate, molest, violate, rape, deflower, debauch.

**definable** specific, determinable, perceptible, describable, definite. INDEFINABLE

**define** describe, explain, interpret, spell out, specify, determine, designate, fix, lay down.
delineate, outline, demarcate, limit, bound, circumscribe.

**definite** certain, fixed, settled, positive, sure, decided, determined. POSSIBLE
clear, clear-cut, explicit, exact, precise, specific, marked, particular, plain, obvious, unambiguous. VAGUE

**definition** description, explanation, meaning, interpretation, exposition.
distinctness, clarity, sharpness, precision, contrast, focus. BLURREDNESS
demarcation, delineation, delimitation, determination, specification, fixing, settling.

**definitive** final, conclusive, decisive, ultimate, authoritative, exhaustive, complete, perfect, absolute, positive.

**deflate** collapse, let down, flatten, empty, shrink, contract, puncture. INFLATE chasten, humble, humiliate, mortify, squash, dash, discourage, dispirit. BOOST

**deflect** deviate, diverge, veer, swerve, bend, turn, twist, divert, sidetrack, shy, turn aside.

**deflection** deviation, divergence, declination, refraction, aberration, diversion, bend, turn, twist, swerve.

**deflower** rape, ravish, violate, despoil, defile, mar, molest, assault, debauch, corrupt, seduce.

**deform** distort, misshape, contort, twist, warp, malform, disfigure, deface, mar, injure, maim, cripple.

**deformity** malformation, abnormality, misshapenness, distortion, disfigurement, ugliness, monstrosity.

**defraud** cheat, swindle, fleece, rook (*inf*), cozen, dupe, deceive, beguile, trick, hoodwink, bamboozle (*inf*), rip off (*inf*), diddle (*inf*), do (*inf*), con (*inf*).

**defray** meet, pay, cover, clear, discharge, settle, liquidate.

**deft** adept, dexterous, adroit, skilful, clever, able, expert, proficient, handy, neat, agile, nimble, brisk. CLUMSY

**defunct** dead, gone, deceased, departed, extinct. LIVING
obsolete, expired, invalid, inoperative, not functioning.

**defy** flout, disregard, ignore, scorn, spurn, slight, disobey, challenge, brave, dare, confront, provoke, resist, oppose. OBEY
elude, frustrate, foil, baffle, withstand.

**degeneracy** dissoluteness, dissipation, depravity, decadence, corruption, immorality, debasement, degradation, meanness, lowness, inferiority, baseness. REFINEMENT
decline, deterioration, degeneration, decay, descent, decrease, retrogression. AMELIORATION

**degenerate** *v*, decline, deteriorate, decay, retrogress, sink, lapse, slip, fall. IMPROVE
*adj*, dissolute, debauched, depraved, corrupt, decadent, fallen, immoral, low, mean, base, debased, degraded, inferior. SUPERIOR

**degeneration** decline, deterioration, degeneracy, decay, descent, decrease, retrogression, depravation, debasement, degradation, dissolution. AMELIORATION

**degradation** disgrace, dishonour, humiliation, mortification, shame, ignominy, discredit, demotion. HONOUR
degeneration, abasement, decline, deterioration, decadence, debasement.

**degrade** disgrace, dishonour, lower, abase, humiliate, demean, cheapen, debase, corrupt, pervert, vitiate, deprave, defame, disparage, depreciate, deteriorate. EXALT
demote, downgrade, cashier, depose. PROMOTE

**degree** grade, rank, class, order, standing, status, station, position.
stage, step, rung, gradation, mark, notch, division, interval.
extent, measure, amount, intensity, range, scope, level, standard, rate.

**dehydrate** dry, parch, desiccate, exsiccate, drain, evaporate. MOISTEN

**deify** elevate, exalt, ennoble, glorify, idolize, apotheosize, immortalize, venerate, idolize, worship. DEBASE

**deign** condescend, stoop, lower oneself, see fit, consent. REFUSE

**deity** god, goddess, immortal, divine being, divinity, godhead. MORTAL

**deject** dishearten, dispirit, depress, cast down, sadden, demoralize, dismay, discourage. CHEER

**dejected** downcast, despondent, disconsolate, downhearted, dispirited, disheartened, crestfallen, depressed, sad, unhappy, miserable, doleful, woebegone, gloomy, glum, melancholy, blue. CHEERFUL

**dejection** despondency, downheartedness, depression, sadness, gloom, low spirits, melancholy, sorrow, blues, dumps (*inf*). CHEERFULNESS

**delay** *v*, defer, postpone, put off, suspend, shelve, hold over, procrastinate, temporize, stall. ADVANCE
obstruct, hinder, impede, hold back, slow down, retard, set back, detain, arrest, stop, halt. HASTEN
dawdle, linger, loiter, lag, dilly-dally (*inf*). HURRY
*n*, deferment, postponement, suspension, procrastination.
lull, interlude, pause, wait, break, breather, hiatus, interval. CONTINUATION
obstruction, hindrance, impediment, stoppage, setback, hold-up.

dawdling, lingering, loitering, dalliance, hesitation. HASTE

**delectable** delightful, delicious, choice, luscious, ambrosial, scrumptious (*inf*), tasty, dainty, appetizing, inviting, adorable, charming, agreeable, pleasant. REPULSIVE

**delectation** delight, enjoyment, pleasure, gratification, ecstasy, rapture, joy, amusement, entertainment, refreshment, relish.

**delegate** *n*, representative, envoy, ambassador, agent, deputy, commissioner.
*v*, depute, appoint, commission, authorize, empower, nominate, elect, ordain, charge, commit, entrust, assign, devolve, transfer.

**delegation** deputation, contingent, committee, embassy, legation, mission.
assignment, devolvement, authorization, commissioning, appointment, nomination.

**delete** cross out, strike out, obliterate, efface, cancel, expunge, remove, erase, cut out, edit, blue-pencil. INSERT

**deleterious** harmful, noxious, injurious, hurtful, pernicious, destructive, damaging, detrimental, unwholesome, bad, noisome. BENEFICIAL

**deliberate** *v*, consider, ponder, ruminate, reflect, think, cogitate, meditate, mull over, weigh, evaluate, debate. DECIDE
*adj*, intentional, premeditated, calculated, planned, designed, purposeful, conscious, meant, wilful, studied. ACCIDENTAL
cautious, careful, circumspect, thoughtful, methodical, unhurried, slow, leisurely, measured. HASTY

**deliberately** intentionally, on purpose, wilfully, knowingly. ACCIDENTALLY

**deliberation** consideration, rumination, reflection, thought, cogitation, meditation, study, scrutiny, speculation, discussion, debate, consultation.
care, caution, circumspection, wariness, prudence. RASHNESS

**delicacy** fineness, daintiness, fragility, flimsiness, slightness, slenderness, lightness, exquisiteness, subtlety. COARSENESS
tact, sensitivity, sensibility, scrupulousness, fastidiousness, discrimination, refinement, finesse, elegance, nicety, purity, precision, accuracy. INDELICACY
frailty, weakness, debility, infirmity. ROBUSTNESS
morsel, titbit, dainty, sweetmeat, luxury, treat.

**delicate** fine, dainty, exquisite, choice, elegant, graceful, flimsy, slender, slight, fragile, tender. ROBUST
weak, frail, infirm, ailing, sickly. HEALTHY
faint, muted, subdued, soft, subtle, pastel. GARISH
sensitive, tactful, diplomatic, scrupulous, fastidious, discriminating, refined, pure. INDELICATE
critical, precarious, difficult, ticklish, sensitive.

**delicious** tasty, appetizing, luscious, scrumptious (*inf*), ambrosial, toothsome, succulent, mouthwatering, savoury, palatable, delectable, dainty, choice. UNPALATABLE
delightful, exquisite, charming, agreeable, nice, pleasant, enjoyable. LOATHSOME

**delight** *v*, charm, enchant, ravish, thrill, transport, enrapture, please, gratify, cheer. DISAPPOINT
**delight in,** enjoy, love, like, relish, savour, revel in. DISLIKE
*n*, charm, enchantment, ecstasy, rapture, transport, elation, felicity, joy, delectation, pleasure, gratification, enjoyment. DISGUST

**delighted** enchanted, elated, overjoyed, ecstatic, thrilled, jubilant, joyous, pleased, happy. DISAPPOINTED

**delightful** charming, enchanting, ravishing, captivating, engaging, attractive, heavenly, lovely, delectable, agreeable, pleasant, enjoyable, gratifying. NASTY

**delineate** describe, depict, portray, picture, draw, sketch, outline, trace, design, chart, map out.

**delineation** description, representation, depiction, portrayal, portrait, picture, drawing, sketch, draft, outline, profile, diagram, chart, account, narration.

**delinquency** crime, offence, misdeed, misdemeanour, misconduct, wrongdoing, dereliction, negligence.

**delinquent** offender, wrongdoer, criminal, malefactor, miscreant, lawbreaker, culprit.

**delirious** raving, incoherent, demented, deranged, insane, mad, crazy, hysterical, frenzied, frantic, wild, ecstatic, carried away. SANE

**delirium** madness, insanity, derangement, raving, incoherence, hallucination, frenzy, passion, fever, hysteria, ecstasy. SANITY

**deliver** transfer, entrust, commit, hand over, consign, give, grant, surrender, relinquish, yield, cede. APPROPRIATE

send, transmit, convey, transport, bear, carry, bring.

release, liberate, set free, emancipate, acquit, discharge, free, rescue, save, redeem. CAPTURE

utter, speak, present, give, declare, announce, proclaim.

direct, deal, administer, inflict, throw, launch.

**deliverance** release, liberation, emancipation, rescue, salvation. CAPTURE

**delivery** conveyance, transmission, consignment, dispatch, shipment, transfer, surrender, handing over, distribution.

articulation, enunciation, elocution, intonation, diction, utterance, speech.

childbirth, parturition, confinement, labour, accouchement.

**delude** deceive, mislead, misguide, dupe, beguile, cheat, fool, trick, cozen, take in, hoodwink, bamboozle (*inf*), con (*inf*).

**deluge** *n*, flood, inundation, cataclysm, downpour, cloudburst, overflow, rush, torrent, spate, avalanche. DROUGHT

*v*, flood, inundate, soak, drench, overrun, overwhelm, swamp, engulf, drown, submerge.

**delusion** illusion, hallucination, fancy, mirage, vision, dream, misapprehension, misconception, error, mistake, fallacy, self-deception. REALITY

trick, artifice, ruse, deception, deceit, imposture, fraud, hoax.

**delusive** misleading, deceptive, fallacious, illusive, illusory, imaginary. REAL

**delve** dig, burrow, ferret out, unearth, probe, search, rummage, penetrate, investigate, look into.

**demand** *v*, request, ask for, solicit, claim, insist on, order, exact. WAIVE

require, need, necessitate, call for, involve. OBVIATE

ask, question, interrogate, inquire, query. REPLY

*n*, request, claim, order, requisition, command, direction, charge, bidding, behest.

requirement, need, want, necessity.

question, query, inquiry, interrogation. ANSWER

**demanding** challenging, trying, difficult, hard, tough, exacting, taxing, tiring. EASY

**demarcation** distinction, differentiation, division, separation, delimitation, definition, boundary, border, limit, bound, confine.

**demean** lower, humble, abase, descend, stoop, debase, degrade. EXALT

**demeanour** behaviour, conduct, bearing, manner, air, mien, carriage, deportment.

**demented** insane, deranged, unhinged, unbalanced, mad, crazy, idiotic, lunatic, daft (*inf*), barmy (*inf*), nuts (*inf*). SANE

**demerit** fault, misdeed, crime, offence, delinquency.

**demesne** estate, land, property, realm, domain.

**demise** *n*, death, decease, expiration, passing. BIRTH

collapse, downfall, failure, ruin, end, termination.

transfer, conveyance, transmission, alienation.

*v*, bequeath, leave, will, transfer, convey.

**democratic** egalitarian, republican, autonomous, self-governing, popular, representative. AUTOCRATIC

**demolish** destroy, raze, level, flatten, bulldoze, tear down, break down, dismantle, take down. BUILD

wreck, ruin, destroy, devastate, undo, crush, overturn, annihilate, obliterate.

**demolition** destruction, razing, bulldozing, devastation, ruin, wrecking. BUILDING

**demon** fiend, devil, goblin, imp, evil spirit. ANGEL

rogue, villain, scoundrel, knave, fiend, monster, ogre.

**demonic** demoniac, demoniacal, fiendish, diabolic, diabolical, devilish, satanic, hellish, infernal. ANGELIC

frenzied, frenetic, frantic, hectic, maniacal, rabid, feverish, delirious, crazed, demented, mad.

**demonstrate** show, display, exhibit, manifest, evince, indicate, prove, substantiate, establish. DISPROVE

explain, illustrate, describe, show how.

protest, march, rally, strike, picket.

**demonstration** display, exhibition, manifestation, showing, show, evidence, proof, substantiation, testimony, confirmation. CONCEALMENT

explanation, exposition, presentation, experiment, trial, illustration, example.
march, rally, parade, protest, sit-in.
**demonstrative** open, unreserved, expressive, communicative, loving, affectionate. RESERVED
illustrative, indicative, symptomatic, explanatory.
indisputable, convincing, conclusive, absolute, certain, sure. DEBATABLE
**demoralize** dishearten, dispirit, discourage, depress, deject, daunt, unnerve, weaken, enfeeble, crush, subdue. ENCOURAGE
corrupt, deprave, pervert, debase, debauch, vitiate. IMPROVE
**demote** downgrade, degrade, cashier, depose, relegate, humble. PROMOTE
**demulcent** soothing, lenitive, mild, calming, sedative, emollient, softening, mollifying. IRRITANT
**demur** *v*, object, protest, dispute, take exception, be reluctant, scruple, hesitate, balk, cavil. CONSENT
*n*, demurral, objection, dissent, hesitation, qualm, scruple.
**demure** modest, diffident, shy, reserved, unassuming, sedate, staid, sober, grave, discreet, decorous, prudish, strait-laced, prim. WANTON
**den** lair, hole, cavern, cave, haunt, shelter.
study, retreat, hideaway, sanctuary, cloister, snuggery.
**denial** contradiction, negation, refutation, disavowal, disclaimer, repudiation, retraction, renunciation, abjuration. CONFIRMATION
refusal, rejection, rebuff, veto, proscription prohibition. CONSENT
**denigrate** disparage, belittle, defame, run down, slander, besmirch, blacken, traduce, vilify, malign, speak ill of. PRAISE
**denizen** citizen, resident, occupant, inhabitant, dweller. ALIEN
**denominate** designate, name, style, entitle, dub, christen, call, term.
**denomination** sect, school, creed, faith, persuasion, religion.
class, group, kind, sort, type, category.
grade, unit, value.
designation, appellation, name, style, title.
**denote** indicate, betoken, signify, mean, imply, stand for, represent, designate, mark.
**denouement** climax, culmination, conclusion, finale, termination, resolution, solution, outcome, issue, result, upshot.
**denounce** condemn, decry, denunciate, deplore, arraign, attack, censure, revile, impugn, upbraid, rebuke, castigate. EXTOL
accuse, charge, impeach, vilify, defame, brand, stigmatize.
**dense** thick, compressed, compact, condensed, heavy, solid, thickset, close, close-knit, packed, crowded, impenetrable. THIN
stupid, obtuse, dull, slow, thick (*inf*), stolid, crass, blockish. CLEVER
**density** denseness, thickness, solidity, bulk, mass, closeness, compactness, impenetrability.
stupidity, obtuseness, dullness, slowness, stolidity, crassness. CLEVERNESS
**dent** *v*, indent, dint, press in, chip, notch, groove, hollow.
*n*, hollow, depression, dint, pit, concavity, hole, impression, indentation, notch, chip.
**denude** strip, divest, bare, expose, uncover, denudate. CLOTHE
**denunciation** condemnation, denouncement, fulmination, censure, animadversion, obloquy, reproof, castigation, vituperation, accusation, arraignment. EULOGY
**deny** contradict, dispute, gainsay, controvert, negate, refute, disprove, oppose, disagree. CONFIRM
refuse, withhold, reject, turn down, prohibit, forbid, veto, proscribe. ALLOW
disown, disavow, renounce, abjure, disclaim, recant, repudiate. AVOW
**depart** go, leave, start, set out, decamp, abscond, escape, go away, disappear, vanish, exit, quit, withdraw, retire. ARRIVE
deviate, diverge, digress, veer, swerve, differ, vary.
**department** branch, division, subdivision, section, office, bureau, unit.
sphere, realm, domain, province, line, station, function, responsibility.
**departure** exit, going, leaving, disappearance, withdrawal, retirement. ARRIVAL
deviation, divergence, digression, variation, difference, novelty, innovation.
**depend** rely, count, bank, trust, confide.
be dependent, hang, hinge, turn, rest, be contingent, be subject to.
**dependable** reliable, trusty, trustworthy, sure, steady, faithful, true. UNRELIABLE

**dependant** child, minor, relative, hanger-on, protégé, minion, retainer, henchman.

**dependence** reliance, trust, faith, confidence.
subordination, subjection, helplessness, weakness, attachment, addiction. INDEPENDENCE

**dependent** relying, reliant, counting, clinging, helpless, weak, defenceless, vulnerable, immature, subordinate, subject. INDEPENDENT
contingent, conditional, subject to, depending.

**depict** delineate, portray, sketch, draw, paint, outline, picture, illustrate, represent, describe, characterize, detail.

**deplete** empty, drain, evacuate, exhaust, use up, spend, consume, reduce, lessen, decrease. FILL

**depletion** emptying, evacuation, exhaustion, using up, consumption, reduction, decrease.

**deplorable** lamentable, grievous, regrettable, pitiable, wretched, miserable, pathetic, distressing, unfortunate, disastrous, calamitous. AUSPICIOUS
scandalous, disgraceful, shameful, reprehensible, opprobrious, despicable. COMMENDABLE

**deplore** lament, mourn, regret, bemoan, bewail, grieve for, sorrow over. WELCOME
condemn, denounce, censure, abhor, disapprove of. EXTOL

**deploy** dispose, arrange, position, station, spread out, distribute, use, utilize.

**deport** expel, banish, exile, expatriate, extradite, transport, remove.
conduct, behave, comport, bear, carry, acquit.

**deportment** carriage, bearing, posture, air, mien, demeanour, behaviour, conduct, comportment, manner.

**depose** dethrone, oust, displace, unseat, dismiss, cashier, demote, degrade. ENTHRONE
declare, testify, asseverate.

**deposit** *v*, lay, drop, place, put, set down, settle, precipitate.
save, store, hoard, bank, lodge, consign, entrust. WITHDRAW
*n*, sediment, precipitate, deposition, silt, alluvium, dregs, lees.
security, pledge, stake, warranty, retainer, down payment.

**depositary** trustee, guardian, steward, fiduciary.

**deposition** affidavit, statement, declaration, testimony, evidence.
dethronement, ousting, displacement, dismissal, demotion, removal. ENTHRONEMENT

**depository** depot, storehouse, warehouse, repository, safe.

**depot** storehouse, warehouse, depository, repository, magazine, arsenal.
bus station, terminus, garage.

**deprave** corrupt, vitiate, debauch, subvert, demoralize, pervert, lead astray, seduce, debase, degrade, degenerate. IMPROVE

**depraved** corrupt, immoral, debauched, demoralized, degenerate, dissolute, abandoned, licentious, profligate, perverted, warped, wicked, evil, vicious, sinful, shameless, wanton. VIRTUOUS

**depravity** corruption, immorality, debauchery, degeneracy, turpitude, depravation, demoralization, profligacy, perversion, vice, evil, iniquity, sin. VIRTUE

**deprecate** deplore, condemn, denounce, censure, inveigh against, frown on, disapprove of, object to, protest. COMMEND
belittle, disparage, depreciate. PRAISE

**depreciate** devalue, devaluate, deflate, reduce, lower, lose value, fall, decline. APPRECIATE
disparage, belittle, deprecate, malign, traduce, underrate, undervalue, underestimate, decry, deride, slight. PRAISE

**depreciation** devaluation, deflation, depression, decline, fall, drop, slump. APPRECIATION
disparagement, belittlement, deprecation, detraction, derogation, underestimation. PRAISE

**depredation** plunder, pillage, spoliation, rapine, robbery, theft, marauding, raid, inroad, devastation.

**depredator** robber, thief, plunderer, looter, pillager, marauder, raider, despoiler.

**depress** deject, sadden, dishearten, discourage, dispirit, cast down, damp, chill. CHEER
weaken, debilitate, enfeeble, exhaust, drain, sap. FORTIFY
depreciate, devalue, devaluate, cheapen, reduce, lower, diminish, downgrade. RAISE

**depressed** dejected, dispirited, blue, glum, low, despondent, downcast, morose, gloomy, pessimistic, miserable, sad, melancholy. ELATED
poor, needy, disadvantaged. deprived, distressed, run-down. AFFLUENT

**depression** dejection, gloom, despondency, melancholy, sadness, low spirits, despair, blues, dumps (*inf*). ELATION
indentation, concavity, hollow, pit, dent, dint, dimple, hole, cavity. MOUND
recession, slump, decline, hard times, stagnation, inactivity. BOOM

**deprivation** privation, need, want, hardship, distress, disadvantage, loss, bereavement.
dispossession, expropriation, removal, denial, deprival, withholding. ENDOWMENT

**deprive** strip, divest, dispossess, rob, bereave. ENDOW
deny, withhold, refuse, debar. PROVIDE

**depth** deepness, profoundness, profundity, extent, measure, drop. SHALLOWNESS
wisdom, sagacity, penetration, discernment, astuteness, shrewdness, perspicacity.
middle, midst, innermost part, deep, bowels, pit, abyss, chasm. SURFACE
intensity, vividness, strength, richness.

**depurate** cleanse, purify, clarify.

**deputation** delegation, embassy, legation, commission, committee.
appointment, designation, nomination, authorization, assignment.

**depute** appoint, nominate, designate, commission, delegate, deputize, authorize, empower, entrust, charge. DISMISS

**deputy** agent, representative, delegate, envoy, ambassador, commissioner, legate, surrogate, substitute, proxy, vicegerent, nuncio, lieutenant, assistant.

**deracinate** uproot, extirpate, eradicate, exterminate, stamp out.

**derange** disorder, disarrange, displace, disturb, upset, ruffle, discompose, disconcert, confuse. ORDER
unhinge, unbalance, madden, craze, drive mad.

**derangement** disorder, disarray, disarrangement, disturbance, upset, confusion.
madness, insanity, lunacy, dementia, unbalance, loss of reason, mania, delirium. SANITY

**derelict** *adj*, abandoned, forsaken, deserted, discarded, neglected, dilapidated, ruined.
remiss, negligent, neglectful, lax.
*n*, tramp, vagrant, down-and-out, outcast, wastrel, ne'er-do-well.

**dereliction** neglect, negligence, laxity, delinquency, default, omission, nonperformance, fault, failure. OBSERVANCE
abandonment, desertion, forsaking, relinquishment, abdication, renunciation, rejection.

**deride** mock, ridicule, scoff, jeer, laugh at, taunt, chaff, scorn, disdain, sneer at, contemn, lampoon, satirize, disparage, belittle, knock (*inf*), insult, abuse. RESPECT

**derision** mockery, ridicule, scoffing, jeer, taunt, raillery, scorn, contempt, disrespect, contumely, satire, lampoon, irony, abuse, insult. RESPECT

**derisive** scornful, contemptuous, disdainful, mocking, jeering, sarcastic, insulting. RESPECTFUL
derisory, contemptible, laughable, ridiculous, ludicrous.

**derivation** source, origin, etymology, root, spring, foundation, beginning, cause, rise, ancestry, descent, extraction.

**derivative** *adj*, derived, acquired, borrowed, unoriginal, secondary.
*n*, derivation, offshoot, by-product, spin-off.

**derive** draw, extract, get, obtain, gain, acquire, procure, receive, elicit, glean, collect, gather.
deduce, infer, trace, track.
originate, arise, spring, flow, proceed, come.

**derogate** disparage, run down, belittle, decry, depreciate, cheapen, lessen, diminish, devalue, defame, denigrate, malign, discredit, degrade, debase. EXTOL

**derogation** disparagement, detraction, belittlement, depreciation, defamation, denigration, discredit. PRAISE

**derogatory** disparaging, belittling, detracting, depreciative, defamatory, insulting, offensive, abusive, injurious, damaging, unfavourable, opprobrious. FLATTERING

**descant** *v*, discourse, dilate, expatiate, discuss, elaborate, enlarge, amplify.
*n*, melody, tune, counterpoint, variation.

discourse, dissertation, discussion, commentary.

**descend** go down, sink, fall, drop, plunge, slope downwards. ASCEND
dismount, alight, disembark, get off. EMBARK
originate, derive, issue, spring.
stoop, condescend, lower oneself, degenerate, deteriorate.

**descendants** offspring, issue, progeny, seed, posterity, family, children. ANCESTORS

**descent** fall, drop, plunge, dip, declination, declivity. ASCENT
ancestry, parentage, extraction, stock, heredity, genealogy, lineage, origin, derivation.
decline, deterioration, degeneration, decadence, degradation.
attack, assault, onslaught, incursion, raid, invasion, foray.

**describe** delineate, portray, depict, picture, illustrate, characterize, detail, explain, tell, narrate, relate, recount, define, specify.

**description** delineation, portrayal, depiction, explanation, account, narration, report, explanation, sketch, representation.
sort, kind, type, variety, breed, genre, ilk.

**descry** discern, make out, distinguish, espy, detect, perceive, discover, see, observe, notice. MISS

**desecrate** profane, defile, violate, pollute, pervert, abuse, misuse, blaspheme. CONSECRATE

**desecration** profanation, defilement, sacrilege, blasphemy, impiety, violation, outrage, abuse. CONSECRATION

**desert**[1] *n*, wilderness, wasteland, wilds, dust bowl.
*adj*, barren, infertile, arid, parched, uncultivated, desolate, bare, wild, uninhabited, waste. FERTILE

**desert**[2] *v*, abandon, leave, forsake, quit, jilt, strand, renounce, relinquish, defect, abscond, decamp.

**desert**[3] due, right, reward, recompense, retribution, come-uppance (*inf*).
worth, value, merit, virtue.

**deserted** abandoned, derelict, forsaken, empty, vacant, unoccupied, uninhabited, desolate, lonely, solitary, isolated, forlorn, bereft. POPULOUS

**deserter** runaway, truant, absconder, fugitive, defector, renegade, apostate, turncoat, traitor, rat (*inf*).

**desertion** abandonment, dereliction, defection, apostasy, flight, escape, relinquishment, renunciation.

**deserve** earn, win, merit, be worthy of, be entitled to, justify, warrant.

**deserved** merited, due, rightful, just, fair, fitting, suitable, appropriate, condign. UNDESERVED

**deserving** worthy, meritorious, estimable, commendable, laudable, good, righteous. UNDESERVING

**desiccate** dry, parch, exsiccate, dehydrate, drain, evaporate. MOISTEN

**desideratum** need, want, lack, essential, aspiration, goal, aim, objective, hope, dream.

**design** *v*, plan, plot, scheme, intend, purpose, mean, aim, devise, contrive.
sketch, outline, delineate, draft, draw, trace.
invent, originate, conceive, think up, create.
*n*, sketch, draft, drawing, plan, model, blueprint, prototype.
style, form, shape, configuration, arrangement, motif, pattern.
plan, plot, scheme, project, proposal, aim, intention, purpose, point, objective.

**designate** name, call, style, term, dub, christen, entitle.
indicate, denote, make, show, specify, particularize, pinpoint, earmark, define, describe.
appoint, assign, nominate, choose, depute, allot.

**designation** name, title, denomination, appellation, epithet, label.
indication, specification, particularization, description.
appointment, nomination, delegation, selection.

**designing** artful, crafty, wily, foxy, sly, scheming, tricky, cunning, Machiavellian, intriguing, astute, treacherous, insidious, crooked (*inf*), dishonest, deceitful. ARTLESS

**desirable** profitable, advantageous, beneficial, advisable, enviable, sought-after, eligible, popular, good, pleasing, attractive, captivating, seductive, sexy (*inf*). UNDESIRABLE

**desire** *v*, crave, long for, covet, hanker after, yearn for, fancy, wish for, want. ABHOR
ask, request, solicit, petition, entreat.
*n*, craving, longing, yearning, yen (*inf*), wish, want, aspiration, inclination, appetite. AVERSION
lust, passion, libido, lechery, lasciviousness.
request, solicitation, petition, entreaty.

**desirous** eager, avid, longing, yearning, craving, wishing, hopeful, anxious, impatient. APATHETIC

**desist** stop, cease, break off, discontinue, suspend, abstain, refrain from, forbear, give up. PERSIST

**desolate** *adj*, deserted, uninhabited, desert, wild, waste, barren, bare, bleak, dreary, empty, lonely, isolated. POPULOUS
forlorn, forsaken, abandoned, bereft, lonely, friendless, despondent, sad, cheerless, comfortless, wretched, miserable. CHEERFUL
*v*, destroy, devastate, lay waste, pillage, plunder, despoil, depopulate. CULTIVATE
depress, dishearten, deject, sadden, grieve, distress, dismay, daunt. CHEER

**desolation** destruction, devastation, ruin, ravage, pillage, depopulation. CULTIVATION
barrenness, bleakness, desolateness, wildness, dreariness, loneliness, isolation.
gloom, gloominess, despondency, dejection, despair, sadness, grief, anguish, sorrow, distress, misery, melancholy. JOY

**despair** *n*, hopelessness, desperation, despondency, gloom, dejection, distress, wretchedness, anguish, discouragement, resignation. HOPE
*v*, lose hope, lose heart, give up, despond.

**desperado** ruffian, thug, gangster, criminal, cutthroat, hoodlum, mugger, bandit, outlaw.

**desperate** rash, reckless, daring, audacious, impetuous, precipitate, madcap, foolhardy, dangerous, risky, frantic, wild. CAUTIOUS
grave, critical, urgent, dire, acute, extreme.
despairing, hopeless, despondent, forlorn, wretched, inconsolable, irretrievable, irredeemable. HOPEFUL

**desperation** recklessness, rashness, impetuosity, madness, frenzy, fury, rage. COOLNESS
despair, despondency, hopelessness, anxiety, anguish, distress, wretchedness. HOPE

**despicable** contemptible, low, mean, base, abject, ignominious, vile, sordid, disreputable, pitiful, wretched, worthless. ADMIRABLE

**despise** scorn, contemn, disdain, spurn, slight, disregard, flout, deride, dislike, detest, abhor. ADMIRE

**despite** in spite of, notwithstanding, even with, regardless of, against, in defiance of.

**despoil** pillage, plunder, loot, ravage, rifle, rob, deprive, strip, denude, divest, devastate, desolate, wreck, lay waste.

**despond** despair, lose hope, lose heart, give up, be depressed, mope, grieve. HOPE

**despondency** depression, dejection, gloom, melancholy, downheartedness, low spirits, discouragement, hopelessness, despair. CHEERFULNESS

**despondent** depressed, dejected, gloomy, miserable, doleful, downcast, downhearted, discouraged, glum, sad, melancholy, blue. CHEERFUL

**despot** tyrant, autocrat, dictator, oppressor. DEMOCRAT

**despotic** tyrannical, tyrannous, autocratic, dictatorial, oppressive, imperious, absolute, arbitrary, authoritarian. DEMOCRATIC

**despotism** tyranny, autocracy, dictatorship, absolutism, totalitarianism. DEMOCRACY

**dessert** sweet, pudding, afters (*inf*).

**destination** goal, objective, end, target, ambition, aim, purpose.
terminus, stop, station, harbour, haven, journey's end. START

**destine** ordain, design, intend, purpose, appoint, assign, allot, designate, earmark, consecrate, devote.

**destined** bound, heading, en route, directed.
fated, doomed, foreordained, predestined, certain, sure, unavoidable, inescapable, bound, meant, intended.

**destiny** lot, fate, fortune, doom, karma, kismet.

**destitute** impoverished, penurious, penniless, poverty-stricken, impecunious, indigent, poor, needy, down and out, distressed, ruined, hard up (*inf*). RICH
devoid, bereft, without, deficient, lacking, wanting, deprived.

**destitution** penury, pennilessness, beggary, indigence, poverty, need, privation, distress, dire straits. WEALTH

**destroy** demolish, raze, gut, ruin, wreck, devastate, overturn, crush, smash, shatter, annihilate, eradicate, extirpate, extinguish, wipe out, slay, kill. CREATE

**destruction** demolition, ruin, devastation, havoc, wreckage, crushing, shattering, annihilation, eradication, end, extinction, liquidation, massacre, slaughter. CREATION

**destructive** pernicious, noxious, baneful, harmful, damaging, hurtful, injurious, detrimental, deleterious, deadly, fatal, lethal, ruinous, devastating, catastrophic. BENEFICIAL
negative, adverse, contrary, unfavourable, hostile, disparaging, derogatory. CONSTRUCTIVE

**desuetude** disuse, obsolescence, discontinuance. USE

**desultory** random, haphazard, irregular, unmethodical, unsystematic, unconnected, spasmodic, fitful, discursive, rambling, roving, erratic, capricious. METHODICAL

**detach** separate, disconnect, uncouple, unfasten, disengage, disjoin, cut off, sever, divide, isolate, free. ATTACH

**detached** separate, unconnected, disconnected, discrete, free, isolated. ATTACHED
aloof, uninvolved, objective, impartial, disinterested, dispassionate, neutral. INVOLVED

**detachment** separation, disconnection, disunion, disengagement, division. CONNECTION
aloofness, indifference, unconcern, objectivity, impartiality, disinterestedness, neutrality. INVOLVEMENT
squad, unit, party, detail, force.

**detail** *n*, particular, item, component, element, factor, point, feature, aspect, circumstance.
detachment, squad, unit, party, group.
*v*, list, catalogue, enumerate, recount, narrate, describe, particularize, itemize, specify, delineate. SUMMARIZE
appoint, assign, delegate, commission, charge.

**detailed** comprehensive, exhaustive, thorough, minute, meticulous, precise, blow-by-blow, involved, elaborate, intricate. CURSORY

**detain** delay, hold up, retard, slow, hinder, impede, stay, keep back, stop, check, restrain, hold, confine, arrest. FREE

**detect** discover, perceive, discern, observe, notice, descry, sense, ascertain, expose, reveal, uncover, unmask, find, trace.

**detection** discovery, exposure, revelation, observation, perception.

**detective** investigator, private eye, sleuth (*inf*), policeman, copper (*inf*).

**detention** custody, confinement, imprisonment, incarceration, duress, restraint. RELEASE

**deter** discourage, put off, dissuade, warn, daunt, disincline, inhibit, restrain, prevent, stop, check, hinder, thwart. ENCOURAGE

**detergent** *adj*, cleansing, detersive, abstergent, depurative.
*n*, cleanser, cleaner, solvent, depurative, soap powder.

**deteriorate** decline, degenerate, worsen, depreciate, debase, degrade, impair, vitiate, decay, fall apart, go to pot (*inf*), go downhill (*inf*). IMPROVE

**deterioration** decline, degeneration, worsening, depreciation, debasement, degradation, vitiation, retrogression, slump, lapse, fall, erosion, decay. IMPROVEMENT

**determinate** fixed, definite, established, settled, positive, certain, absolute, conclusive, limited, precise, explicit. INDETERMINATE

**determination** resolution, resolve, resoluteness, firmness, constancy, conviction, single-mindedness, persistence, perseverance, drive, doggedness, tenacity, willpower. IRRESOLUTION
decision, conclusion, result, solution, settlement, verdict, judgment, purpose, resolve.

**determine** settle, decide, resolve, conclude, terminate, judge, arbitrate.
ascertain, detect, find out, discover, learn, establish, verify, fix.
decide, resolve, purpose, choose, elect, make up one's mind. WAVER
influence, affect, shape, condition, lead, incline, govern, control, dictate.

**determined** resolute, firm, single-minded, set, fixed, intent, dogged, persevering, persistent, tenacious, purposeful, strong-willed. IRRESOLUTE

**deterrent** impediment, hindrance, obstacle, discouragement, disincentive, restraint, curb, check. ENCOURAGEMENT

**detest** abhor, loathe, abominate, execrate, hate, despise. LOVE

**detestable** abhorrent, loathsome, abominable, execrable, hateful, odious, repugnant, repulsive, abnoxious, despicable, vile, accursed, disgusting, heinous. ADORABLE

**detestation** abhorrence, loathing, abomination, execration, odium, repugnance, hate, aversion, antipathy, disgust. LOVE

**dethrone** depose, uncrown, unseat, oust. ENTHRONE

**detonate** explode, set off, go off, blow up, blast.

**detour** diversion, deviation, bypass, roundabout way, circuitous route, indirect course.

**detract** diminish, lessen, reduce, devaluate, depreciate. ENHANCE
divert, avert, deflect, distract, sidetrack.

**detraction** disparagement, depreciation, belittlement, derogation, aspersion, denigration, defamation, vilification, abuse, calumny, slander, traducement. FLATTERY

**detriment** damage, harm, injury, hurt, loss, mischief, disadvantage, prejudice. BENEFIT

**detrimental** damaging, harmful, injurious, hurtful, deleterious, pernicious, prejudicial, disadvantageous, adverse, unfavourable. BENEFICIAL

**devastate** desolate, despoil, ravage, lay waste, destroy, demolish, raze, wreck, ruin, pillage, plunder, sack.
overwhelm, confound, disconcert, take aback, nonplus, floor.

**devastation** desolation, despoliation, destruction, demolition, havoc, ravages, ruin, waste, wreckage, pillage, plunder.

**develop** advance, grow, evolve, mature, ripen, progress, flourish, foster, cultivate. STUNT
elaborate, amplify, expand, enlarge, enhance, unfold, disclose. ABRIDGE
acquire, contract, begin, start, invent, create, generate, originate.

**development** growth, evolution, advance, advancement, progress, increase, maturation, maturity, unfolding, blossoming. RETROGRESSION
amplification, expansion, enlargement, elaboration. ABRIDGMENT
incident, occurrence, event, happening, circumstance, situation, change.

**deviate** veer, diverge, wander, stray, err, depart, digress, swerve, turn aside, deflect, differ, vary, change.

**deviation** divergence, aberration, departure, digression, deflection, shift, variation, difference, declination, disparity, discrepancy.

**device** contrivance, contraption (*inf*), gadget, tool, machine, instrument, implement, utensil, appliance.
ruse, wile, stratagem, artifice, plan, design, scheme, ploy, expedient, manoeuvre, shift.
emblem, symbol, design, motif, figure, motto, legend, crest, badge, logo.

**devil** demon, fiend, evil spirit, prince of darkness, Satan, Lucifer, Beelzebub, Old Nick. ANGEL
rogue, scoundrel, villain, demon, imp, beast, monster, ogre.

**devilish** diabolic, demonic, demoniacal, satanic, fiendish, hellish, infernal, evil, wicked, accursed, damnable, atrocious, execrable. ANGELIC

**devious** underhand, deceitful, surreptitious, sly, tricky, wily, scheming, calculating, evasive, shifty. STRAIGHTFORWARD
rambling, circuitous, roundabout, indirect, tortuous, crooked, meandering, wandering, deviating, erratic. DIRECT

**devise** invent, contrive, scheme, plan, project, design, concoct, create, think up, formulate, work out.

**devoid** destitute, bereft, barren, void, empty, lacking, wanting, deficient, without, free from. FULL

**devolve** delegate, depute, transfer, commission, fall upon, rest with.

**devote** dedicate, consecrate, give, pledge, assign, allot, reserve, commit, apply. WITHHOLD

**devoted** ardent, zealous, dedicated, committed, devout, faithful, loyal, true, fond, loving, affectionate. INDIFFERENT

**devotee** enthusiast, fanatic, fan, admirer, aficionado, addict, buff (*inf*), zealot, adherent, disciple, votary.

**devotion** dedication, commitment, consecration, loyalty, allegiance, fidelity, passion, zeal, ardour, enthusiasm, attachment, affection, love, fondness. APATHY

devoutness, piety, holiness, sanctity, godliness, saintliness. IMPIETY
prayer, worship, service, observance.

**devotional** devout, pious, holy, sacred, religious, spiritual. PROFANE

**devour** consume, eat, gorge, gobble, bolt, wolf, gulp, swallow.
destroy, consume, ravage, annihilate, waste, wipe out, engulf, overwhelm, absorb.

**devout** pious, godly, saintly, holy, religious, reverent, devotional. IMPIOUS
sincere, genuine, heartfelt, earnest, fervent, ardent, intense, profound. INSINCERE

**dexterity** skill, skilfulness, adroitness, handiness, cleverness, ability, aptitude, expertise, proficiency, mastery, finesse, deftness, knack, facility, art, address, agility, nimbleness. CLUMSINESS

**dexterous** deft, adroit, adept, skilled, skilful, apt, able, clever, expert, proficient, masterly, agile, nimble, handy. CLUMSY

**diabolic** devilish, demonic, demoniacal, satanic, fiendish, infernal, hellish, nefarious, evil, wicked, monstrous. ANGELIC

**diabolical** outrageous, appalling, atrocious, dreadful, shocking, excruciating, vile, damnable.

**diadem** crown, coronet, circlet, tiara, chaplet, wreath.

**diagnosis** analysis, investigation, examination, interpretation, conclusion, opinion, verdict.

**diagram** plan, chart, drawing, sketch, representation, outline, figure, graph.

**dialect** language, idiom, vernacular, patois, jargon, localism, provincialism, regionalism, accent, speech, tongue.

**dialectic** *adj*, dialectical, logical, rational, analytic, polemical, argumentative.
*n*, argumentation, disputation, polemics, logic, reasoning.

**dialogue** conversation, confabulation, colloquy, interlocution, discourse, converse, talk, chat, communication, discussion, conference.

**diametric** diametrical, opposite, opposed, contrary, counter, antithetical, antipodal.

**diaphanous** translucent, pellucid, gauzy, gossamer, silken, fine, delicate, sheer, transparent, clear. OPAQUE

**diary** chronicle, journal, log, record, appointment book.

**diatribe** tirade, philippic, invective, abuse, harangue, criticism, denunciation, vituperation. EULOGY

**dictate** *v*, say, speak, utter.
command, order, direct, enjoin, decree, bid, prescribe, impose.
*n*, command, order, decree, injunction, ordinance, bidding, behest, mandate, edict.
principle, rule, code, precept, law, dictum.

**dictator** tyrant, despot, autocrat, oppressor, ruler.

**dictatorial** tyrannnical, tyrannous, despotic, autocratic, absolute, arbitrary, imperious, oppressive, overbearing, domineering, authoritarian. DEMOCRATIC

**diction** speech, language, vocabulary, phraseology, usage, style, intonation, pronunciation, articulation, enunciation, elocution, delivery, eloquence, oratory, rhetoric.

**dictionary** lexicon, glossary, vocabulary, wordbook, encyclopedia.

**dictum** decree, pronouncement, edict, fiat.
saying, maxim, adage, proverb, saw, axiom, aphorism.

**didactic** instructive, informative, educational, preceptive, moralistic, edifying, homiletic.

**die** expire, decease, perish, depart, pass away, snuff it (*inf*), kick the bucket (*inf*). LIVE
dwindle, fade, ebb, subside, abate, die down, wane, decline, sink, wither, fail, peter out, disappear, vanish, end, stop. GROW

**diet**[1] *n*, food, fare, nourishment, nutriment, sustenance, subsistence, aliment, comestibles, provisions, victuals.
regimen, regime, dietary, fast, abstinence.
*v*, slim, lose weight, reduce, fast, abstain.

**diet**[2] *n*, parliament, congress, council, assembly, legislature.

**differ** vary, diverge, contrast, be different, contradict. COINCIDE
disagree, argue, contend, dispute, demur, clash, oppose, be at variance. AGREE

**difference** dissimilarity, unlikeness, contrast, disparity, discrepancy, divergence, deviation, variation, alteration, change. SIMILARITY
disagreement, argument, contention, wrangle, dispute, strife, discord, conflict,

variance, altercation, clash, quarrel, bickering, tiff. AGREEMENT
balance, remainder, residue, rest.

**different** dissimilar, unlike, contrasting, disparate, discrepant, divergent, deviating, at variance, altered, changed. SIMILAR
varied, various, diverse, miscellaneous, assorted, sundry.
unusual, unique, distinctive, out of the ordinary, new, novel. ORDINARY

**differentiate** distinguish, set apart, separate, tell apart, discriminate, tell the difference.

**difficult** hard, arduous, demanding, uphill, laborious, strenuous, wearisome, formidable. EASY
intricate, involved, complex, complicated, abstruse, obscure, baffling, perplexing, knotty, thorny, ticklish. SIMPLE
awkward, unaccommodating, unamenable, intractable, unmanageable, refractory, obstreperous, trying, demanding, fussy, finicky, rigid, unyielding. TRACTABLE

**difficulty** arduousness, laboriousness, strenuousness, strain, hardship, trouble, trial, tribulation. EASE
problem, perplexity, dilemma, quandary, predicament, plight, fix (*inf*), trouble, hot water, exigency, embarrassment.
obstacle, hurdle, hindrance, impediment, problem, complication, objection.

**diffidence** shyness, bashfulness, timidity, backwardness, hesitation, reluctance, sheepishness, modesty, self-effacement, constraint, reserve, insecurity. CONFIDENCE

**diffident** shy, bashful, timid, backward, hesitant, reluctant, sheepish, modest, shrinking, self-effacing, constrained, self-conscious, reserved, withdrawn, insecure. CONFIDENT

**diffuse** *v*, spread, scatter, disperse, disseminate, propagate, circulate, dispense, distribute. GATHER
*adj*, wordy, prolix, verbose, long-winded, rambling, discursive, circumlocutory, vague, loose. CONCISE
scattered, spread out, dispersed. CONCENTRATED

**diffusion** dispersion, scattering, spread, dissemination, radiation, propagation, circulation, distribution. AGGLOMERATION
verbosity, prolixity, wordiness, rambling, long-windedness, discursiveness, circumlocution. TERSENESS

**dig** *v*, excavate, scoop, gouge, burrow, tunnel, quarry, mine, till, work, turn over, break up, delve, probe.
poke, prod, jab, thrust, drive, force.
**dig up,** discover, find, expose, unearth, exhume.
*n*, poke, prod, jab, punch, thrust.
gibe, taunt, jeer, insult, quip, crack (*inf*).

**digest** *v*, assimilate, absorb, dissolve, break down.
take in, grasp, assimilate, master, comprehend, understand, ponder, meditate, reflect, consider, study.
systematize, codify, classify, order, methodize, tabulate.
abridge, condense, summarize, shorten. AMPLIFY
*n*, abridgment, summary, compendium, abstract, synopsis, résumé, précis, epitome.

**digit** figure, numeral, symbol.
finger, toe.

**dignified** stately, grand, majestic, august, noble, honourable, distinguished, lofty, imposing, solemn, grave, staid, formal, decorous. LOWLY

**dignify** ennoble, honour, exalt, elevate, raise, advance, promote, aggrandize, adorn, grace. DEGRADE

**dignitary** notable, personage, celebrity, public figure, VIP (*inf*), bigwig (*inf*).

**dignity** nobility, stateliness, majesty, grandeur, loftiness, eminence, elevation, greatness, importance, standing, rank, status, station, honour, respectability, solemnity, gravity, propriety, decorum, formality, pride, self-esteem. LOWLINESS

**digress** deviate, diverge, wander, stray, depart, drift, ramble, go off at a tangent.

**digression** deviation, divergence, departure, wandering, detour, apostrophe, aside, footnote.

**dilapidated** ramshackle, tumble-down, ruined, broken-down, shabby, battered, neglected, decayed, decaying, crumbling, decrepit, run-down. RESTORED

**dilapidation** ruin, decay, deterioration, disintegration, disrepair, downfall, collapse. RENOVATION

**dilate** expand, extend, stretch, enlarge, widen, broaden, spread, swell, distend, inflate, puff out. CONTRACT
develop, amplify, enlarge, expatiate, descant, dwell on. ABRIDGE

**dilation** dilatation, expansion, extension, enlargement, increase, widening, broadening, distension, inflation, amplification. CONTRACTION

**dilatory** dawdling, lagging, lingering, slow, sluggish, tardy, behindhand, procrastinating, delaying, backward. PROMPT

**dilemma** quandary, predicament, plight, fix (*inf*), spot (*inf*), difficulty, problem, perplexity, strait.

**dilettante** dabbler, amateur, nonprofessional.
aesthete, art lover, connoisseur.

**diligence** assiduity, assiduousness, application, industry, intentness, care, attention, heed, perseverance, persistence, tenacity, sedulousness. CARELESSNESS

**diligent** assiduous, industrious, hardworking, sedulous, painstaking, thorough, attentive, careful, intent, persistent, persevering, tireless, busy, active. LAZY

**dilly-dally** loiter, lag, dawdle, dally, linger, delay, potter, falter, hesitate, waver, vacillate. HURRY

**dilute** adulterate, attenuate, water down, cut, thin, weaken, reduce. CONCENTRATE

**dim** *adj*, dark, dusky, shadowy, tenebrous, gloomy, dingy, dull, grey, cloudy, overcast. BRIGHT
obscure, indistinct, vague, blurred, hazy, faint, ill-defined, confused. CLEAR
dense, obtuse, slow, thick, stupid, doltish. CLEVER
*v*, darken, dull, obscure, cloud, tarnish, lower, fade, pale, blur. BRIGHTEN

**dimension** measurement, measure, extent, size, capacity, volume, bulk, mass, magnitude, range, scope, importance, scale, proportion.

**diminish** lessen, decrease, reduce, lower, shrink, contract, shorten, retrench, curtail, abate, weaken, subside, decline, wane, dwindle. INCREASE
disparage, belittle, deprecate, depreciate, devalue, cheapen. APPRECIATE

**diminution** decrease, reduction, lessening, lowering, contraction, shortening, retrenchment, cutback, abatement, weakening, decline, ebb. INCREASE

**diminutive** tiny, minute, small, little, wee, pygmy, midget, dwarfish, miniature, mini, Lilliputian, undersized, puny. LARGE

**din** noise, clangour, clamour, uproar, racket, row, crash, clatter, commotion, hullabaloo, bedlam, pandemonium. SILENCE

**dine** eat, sup, feast, banquet, lunch.

**dingy** dull, dark, dim, dusky, sombre, gloomy, murky, obscure, drab, colourless, faded, shabby, seedy, dirty, grimy. BRIGHT

**dinner** supper, lunch, main meal, meal, repast, spread, feast, banquet.

**dint** dent, impression, indentation, pit, hollow, depression.
means, use, force, power, virtue.

**diocese** see, bishopric, episcopate, province, jurisdiction.

**dip** *v*, plunge, immerse, duck, submerge, souse, douse, dunk, bathe, dive.
descend, sink, lower, drop, decline, slope, incline, droop, sag, subside. RISE
*n*, plunge, ducking, bathe, swim.
incline, slope, hollow, depression, basin, decline, fall, slump.

**diplomacy** tact, discretion, subtlety, finesse, skill. TACTLESSNESS
statecraft, statesmanship, negotiation, politics.

**diplomat** ambassador, envoy, plenipotentiary, consul, politician, negotiator, mediator, conciliator, diplomatist.

**diplomatic** tactful, discreet, sensitive, judicious, prudent, politic, subtle. TACTLESS

**dire** direful, dreadful, terrible, frightful, fearful, shocking, appalling, awful, horrible, disastrous, calamitous, catastrophic. SPLENDID
desperate, urgent, pressing, imperative, critical, crucial.

**direct** *adj*, straight, unswerving, undeviating, uninterrupted, through, shortest. CIRCUITOUS
straightforward, honest, frank, candid, blunt, open, sincere, plain, unambiguous, explicit, categorical, absolute. EQUIVOCAL
immediate, first-hand, face-to-face, personal. INDIRECT
*v*, manage, control, run, govern, rule, regulate, administer, lead, superintend.
command, order, enjoin, bid, instruct.
guide, lead, conduct, show, usher. MISLEAD
aim, point, level, fix, focus, steer, destine, address.

**direction** way, course, route, path, line, bearing, orientation, trend, tendency, aim.

instruction, guidance, guideline, recommendation, injunction, order, command, directive.

management, control, administration, running, leadership, supervision, guidance, charge, rule.

**directly** immediately, straightaway, at once, without delay, instantly, quickly, promptly, forthwith, soon, in a moment, presently. LATER

**director** manager, executive, administrator, governor, head, chief, boss (*inf*), supervisor, controller.

**dirge** requiem, elegy, lament, threnody, coronach.

**dirt** filth, grime, muck, excrement, mud, dust, stain, smudge, pollution, impurity, dirtiness, foulness. CLEANNESS

earth, soil, clay.

**dirty** *adj*, filthy, grimy, soiled, mucky, grubby, unwashed, foul, polluted, cloudy, muddy, murky. CLEAN

obscene, salacious, indecent, blue, smutty, risqué, suggestive, pornographic.

mean, low, contemptible, abject, base, vile, nasty, despicable, shabby, sordid, squalid, ignominious, unscrupulous, unsporting, unfair, dishonest. HONOURABLE

*v*, soil, begrime, befoul, stain, smear, muddy, foul, pollute, sully, defile. CLEAN

**disability** handicap, infirmity, affliction, disorder, disablement, incapacity, inability, impotency, unfitness, incompetence, disqualification. FITNESS

**disable** cripple, lame, incapacitate, prostrate, handicap, paralyse, immobilize, hamstring, impair, damage, weaken, enfeeble. STRENGTHEN

**disabuse** undeceive, enlighten, correct, set right, disillusion. DECEIVE

**disadvantage** drawback, snag, flaw, hindrance, impediment, handicap, inconvenience, trouble, nuisance, privation, weakness. ADVANTAGE

detriment, harm, prejudice, disservice, injury, hurt, loss. BENEFIT

**disadvantageous** detrimental, prejudicial, deleterious, injurious, damaging, harmful, adverse, unfavourable, inconvenient, ill-timed, inopportune, troublesome. ADVANTAGEOUS

**disaffect** estrange, alienate, disunite, divide, antagonize, embitter. WIN

**disaffected** disloyal, unfaithful, estranged, alienated, antagonistic, hostile, dissatisfied, disgruntled, mutinous, rebellious. LOYAL

**disaffection** estrangement, alienation, breach, disagreement, disloyalty, hostility, animosity, bad blood, dissatisfaction, dislike, aversion. LOYALTY

**disagree** dissent, debate, dispute, contend, contest, object, differ, argue, wrangle, quarrel, bicker, fall out (*inf*), oppose. AGREE

conflict, clash, differ, vary, contradict, diverge, deviate, be at variance. CORRESPOND

**disagreeable** unpleasant, offensive, nasty, obnoxious, objectionable, repugnant, repulsive, disgusting, distasteful. PLEASANT

unfriendly, brusque, churlish, surly, ill-tempered, cross, rude, impolite, unpleasant. AGREEABLE

**disagreement** argument, dispute, wrangle, bickering, quarrel, tiff (*inf*), altercation, dissension, contention, strife, conflict, clash, discord, debate, controversy, misunderstanding. HARMONY

difference, variance, deviation, divergence, dissimilarity, disparity, discrepancy, incompatibility, discord, incongruity. SIMILARITY

**disallow** forbid, prohibit, ban, proscribe, bar, veto. SANCTION

reject, repudiate, disclaim, disavow, abjure, disown, rebuff, shun. ACCEPT

**disannul** annul, nullify, void, invalidate, quash, cancel, rescind, abrogate, repeal, abolish. CONFIRM

**disappear** vanish, fade, melt, dissolve, evaporate, perish, cease, die, ebb, recede, withdraw, go, depart, flee. APPEAR

**disappoint** fail, let down, dissatisfy, disillusion, disenchant, delude, deceive, vex, sadden. SATISFY

frustrate, foil, thwart, defeat, confound, baffle, balk, hamper, disconcert. GRATIFY

**disappointment** frustration, disenchantment, chagrin, regret, dissatisfaction, discontent, distress, discouragement. SATISFACTION

letdown, setback, failure, defeat, misfortune, blow.

**disapprobation** disapproval, displeasure, censure, blame, condemnation, reproof. APPROBATION

**disapproval** disapprobation, displeasure, dissatisfaction, censure, criticism, condemnation, reproof, objection, exception. APPROVAL

**disapprove** censure, condemn, frown on, discountenance, deplore, deprecate, object to, criticize, dislike. APPROVE
disallow, veto, turn down, refuse. SANCTION

**disarm** disable, unman, unarm, demilitarize, demobilize. ARM
win over, persuade, set at ease, appease, conciliate.

**disarrange** derange, disorder, confuse, disorganize, disturb, unsettle, discompose, untidy, mess up, tousle, jumble. ARRANGE

**disarray** disorder, disarrangement, confusion, muddle, jumble, disorganization, derangement, discomposure, untidiness, mess, chaos. ORDER

**disaster** calamity, catastrophe, tragedy, stroke, blow, misfortune, accident, mishap, reverse, adversity, ruin, trouble, affliction. BLESSING

**disastrous** calamitous, catastrophic, dire, ruinous, destructive, cataclysmic, devastating, terrible, dreadful, tragic, adverse, unfortunate, untoward, unlucky, ill-fated, hapless. AUSPICIOUS

**disavow** deny, repudiate, reject, disown, disclaim, retract, contradict, abjure. ACKNOWLEDGE

**disband** disperse, break up, dissolve, scatter, separate, part company, dismiss, demobilize. MUSTER

**disbelief** unbelief, incredulity, doubt, scepticism, distrust, mistrust, rejection. BELIEF

**disbelieve** discredit, reject, discount, mistrust, suspect, doubt. BELIEVE

**disburden** unburden, disencumber, unload, relieve, free, ease, discharge. ENCUMBER

**disburse** spend, pay out, expend, fork out (*inf*). SAVE

**disc** plate, circle, ring, counter.
record, recording, single, LP, album.

**discard** reject, abandon, cast aside, shed, throw away, get rid of, drop, dispose of, dispense with, jettison, scrap. RETAIN

**discern** perceive, descry, make out, see, observe, notice, espy, detect, discover, recognize. MISS
differentiate, distinguish, discriminate, judge.

**discernible** perceptible, noticeable, apparent, obvious, plain, visible, conspicuous, distinct, palpable, detectable, recognizable. IMPERCEPTIBLE

**discerning** discriminating, critical, judicious, wise, perceptive, perspicacious, clear-sighted, astute, shrewd, intelligent. DULL

**discernment** discrimination, perspicacity, perception, judgment, sagacity, astuteness, shrewdness, sharpness, insight, ingenuity, intelligence, clear-sightedness. DULLNESS

**discharge** *v*, release, free, liberate, loose, absolve, acquit, exonerate, clear. DETAIN
expel, eject, oust, dismiss, fire (*inf*), sack (*inf*). APPOINT
emit, exude, eject, excrete, disembogue, release, gush, ooze, leak, empty. ABSORB
fire, shoot, detonate, explode, set off.
unload, unburden, disburden, relieve, remove. LOAD
perform, execute, carry out, fulfil, accomplish, do. NEGLECT
*n*, liberation, release, acquittal, exoneration. DETENTION
dismissal, congé, sack (*inf*). RECRUITMENT
emission, secretion, suppuration, excretion, voidance, ejection. ABSORPTION
blast, volley, salvo, shot, report, explosion, detonation.
performance, execution, fulfilment, accomplishment. NEGLECT

**disciple** follower, adherent, partisan, votary, devotee, supporter, believer, student, scholar, pupil, convert, proselyte, apostle.

**discipline** *n*, training, routine, drill, exercise, instruction, schooling, practice.
regulation, control, order, rule, government, restraint, check. INDISCIPLINE
punishment, chastisement, castigation, correction. INDULGENCE
*v*, train, drill, break in, exercise, teach, instruct, school.
control, restrain, check, govern, regulate.
punish, castigate, chastise, correct, reprimand, reprove. INDULGE

**disclaim** deny, abjure, abnegate, renounce, disown, abandon, disavow, retract, repudiate. CONFESS

**disclaimer** denial, abjuration, repudiation, retraction, disavowal, contradiction, renunciation, disowning, rejection. CONFESSION

**disclose** divulge, let slip, confess, reveal, make known, tell, impart, communicate, broadcast. SUPPRESS
expose, lay bare, reveal, uncover, unveil, show, bring to light. CONCEAL

**disclosure** divulgence, revelation, confession, admission, announcement, broadcast, discovery, exposure. SUPPRESSION

**discolour** stain, tarnish, taint, tinge, mark, streak, bruise, fade, bleach, soil, mar.

**discomfit** embarrass, fluster, ruffle, abash, unsettle, perturb, discompose, disconcert, confuse, perplex, confound.
thwart, frustrate, foil, baffle. ASSIST

**discomfiture** embarrassment, abashment, chagrin, unease, discomposure, disconcertion, confusion. EASE
frustration, undoing, failure, disappointment.

**discomfort** uneasiness, disquiet, trouble, distress, affliction, malaise, pain, ache, irritation, annoyance, vexation, nuisance, inconvenience. EASE

**discommode** trouble, inconvenience, incommode, bother, disturb, annoy.

**discompose** disconcert, ruffle, discomfit, fluster, perturb, agitate, disquiet, fret, worry, vex, annoy, irritate, nettle, perplex, confuse, unsettle, disturb, upset. CALM

**discomposure** disconcertion, discomfiture, perturbation, agitation, disquiet, vexation, annoyance, irritation, perplexity, confusion, disturbance. EASE

**disconcert** discompose, ruffle, discomfit, fluster, unsettle, perturb, perplex, bewilder, nonplus, take aback, abash, worry, agitate, trouble, upset. REASSURE
frustrate, thwart, balk, baffle, confuse, defeat, undo. ASSIST

**disconnect** disengage, uncouple, separate, part, divide, sever, detach, cut off, unplug. CONNECT

**disconnected** confused, garbled, disjointed, rambling, illogical, unconnected, incoherent, unintelligible. COHERENT

**disconnection** separation, division, severance, discontinuity, interruption, cessation, detachment, disunion. UNION

**disconsolate** forlorn, unhappy, sad, desolate, dejected, heartbroken, inconsolable, woeful, wretched, miserable, melancholy. JOYFUL

**discontent** discontentment, dissatisfaction, displeasure, uneasiness, impatience, envy, fretfulness, vexation, restlessness. CONTENT

**discontented** discontent, dissatisfied, disgruntled, fed up, cheesed off (*inf*), fretful, exasperated, unhappy, miserable, displeased. CONTENTED

**discontinue** stop, terminate, end, cease, halt, suspend, interrupt, abandon, drop. CONTINUE

**discontinuous** broken, interrupted, intermittent, fitful, spasmodic, disjointed, disconnected. CONTINUOUS

**discord** dissonance, disharmony, cacophony, harshness, jarring, jangle. HARMONY
discordance, dissension, strife, contention, friction, conflict, dispute, disagreement, variance, difference, wrangling, disunity, breach, rupture. ACCORD

**discordant** dissonant, inharmonious, cacophonous, unmelodious, atonal, harsh, jarring, grating, strident. HARMONIOUS
conflicting, incompatible, incongruous, contrary, different, divergent, disagreeing, contradictory, at variance. CONCORDANT

**discount** *n*, reduction, rebate, allowance, concession, deduction, cut price. PREMIUM
*v*, disregard, ignore, overlook, pass over.
deduct, take off, reduce, lower, mark down.

**discountenance** embarrass, abash, chagrin, discompose, discomfit, disconcert, perturb, shame, humiliate.
disapprove, disfavour, discourage, frown on, condemn, object to, oppose, veto. COUNTENANCE

**discourage** damp, dampen, dishearten, dispirit, cow, daunt, intimidate, unnerve, dismay, deject, depress. INSPIRE
deter, dissuade, put off, check, curb, prevent, inhibit, hinder. ENCOURAGE
disapprove, disfavour, discountenance, frown on, oppose. SANCTION

**discourse** *n*, conversation, confabulation, talk, chat, discussion, dialogue, converse.
speech, sermon, homily, lecture, address, dissertation, essay, treatise.

*v*, converse, talk, speak, hold forth, expatiate, discuss, confer, confabulate, debate.

**discourteous** rude, bad-mannered, unmannerly, impolite, uncivil, ill-bred, disrespectful, curt, short, abrupt, brusque. COURTEOUS

**discourtesy** rudeness, bad manners, impoliteness, incivility, disrespect, insolence, curtness, brusqueness. COURTESY

**discover** find, come across, happen upon, unearth, dig up, ferret out, locate, bring to light, uncover, disclose, reveal. CONCEAL

ascertain, find out, learn, determine, see, discern, perceive, notice, descry, detect. MISS

**discovery** find, finding, location, uncovering, revelation, detection, ascertainment, perception, realization.

**discredit** *v*, disbelieve, doubt, question, dispute, challenge, distrust, mistrust. BELIEVE

dishonour, disgrace, degrade, defame, vilify, smear, denigrate, slur, slander, disparage. HONOUR

invalidate, refute, disprove. PROVE

*n*, disbelief, doubt, scepticism, distrust, mistrust. BELIEF

dishonour, disgrace, shame, ignominy, disrepute, obloquy, scandal, reproach, odium, opprobrium, ill-repute. CREDIT

**discreditable** dishonourable, disgraceful, shameful, ignoble, degrading, ignominious, scandalous, blameworthy, reprehensible, improper, unworthy. HONOURABLE

**discreet** tactful, politic, diplomatic, guarded, reserved, cautious, wary, careful, circumspect, prudent, sagacious, judicious, wise, thoughtful, considerate. INDISCREET

**discrepancy** difference, variation, variance, inconsistency, disagreement, conflict, disparity, incongruity, dissimilarity, divergence, contrariety, discordance. CORRESPONDENCE

**discrepant** different, at variance, inconsistent, conflicting, disagreeing, discordant, contrary, incongruous. CONSISTENT

**discrete** separate, distinct, individual, detached, disjunct, discontinuous.

**discretion** tact, diplomacy, prudence, judgment, wisdom, sagacity, judiciousness, caution, circumspection, wariness, care, consideration, thoughtfulness, discrimination, discernment. RASHNESS

liberty, freedom, will, wish, option, choice, liking, inclination, disposition.

**discretionary** discretional, optional, elective, arbitrary, voluntary, unrestricted, open. MANDATORY

**discriminate** distinguish, differentiate, discern, separate, isolate, segregate, single out, judge, assess.

**discriminating** discerning, selective, critical, particular, fastidious, sensitive, astute.

**discrimination** distinction, differentiation, prejudice, bigotry, intolerance, bias, favouritism, racism, sexism.

discernment, judgment, acumen, shrewdness, astuteness, perception, refinement, taste, subtlety, insight, penetration, wisdom, sagacity.

**discriminatory** discriminative, biased, prejudiced, one-sided, partisan, unjust, preferential, racist, sexist. UNBIASED

discriminating, discerning, perceptive, critical, analytical.

**discursive** rambling, wandering, roving, desultory, digressive, prolix, wordy, circuitous, roundabout, circumlocutory, long-winded, verbose, diffuse. TERSE

**discuss** debate, talk about, confer, argue, thrash out, consider, deliberate, examine, review, sift.

**discussion** debate, argument, conference, talk, conversation, consultation, consideration, deliberation, examination, review, analysis.

**disdain** *v*, scorn, spurn, contemn, despise, deride, belittle, slight, ignore, disregard. RESPECT

*n*, scorn, contempt, contumely, superciliousness, haughtiness, arrogance, indifference, derision, sneering, dislike. ADMIRATION

**disdainful** scornful, contemptuous, contumelious, supercilious, haughty, proud, arrogant, sneering, derisive, insolent. RESPECTFUL

**disease** sickness, illness, complaint, malady, ailment, affliction, disorder, ill health, indisposition, infirmity, infection, contagion. HEALTH

**diseased** infected, contaminated, sick, ill, sickly, ailing, unwell, unhealthy, unsound. HEALTHY

**disembark** land, go ashore, alight, get off, dismount. EMBARK

**disembarrass** relieve, ease, clear, rid, free, disburden, disencumber, extricate, disentangle.

**disembodied** spiritual, incorporeal, bodiless, immaterial, intangible, ghostly.

**disembowel** eviscerate, gut, draw.

**disenable** disable, incapacitate, cripple, enfeeble, disqualify, prevent, hinder, impede, hamstring. ENABLE

**disenchant** disillusion, disabuse, undeceive, bring down to earth, disappoint.

**disencumber** disburden, unburden, disembarrass, unload, discharge, unhamper, relieve, free. ENCUMBER

**disengage** release, free, liberate, loose, unloose, unfasten, untie, unfetter, extricate. ENGAGE
detach, sever, separate, disjoin, divide, undo, disunite, disconnect, uncouple. JOIN

**disengaged** free, loose, separate, detached, unattached, unoccupied, at leisure, not busy. ENGAGED

**disentangle** disembroil, extricate, release, free, loose, disengage, untangle, unsnarl, undo, unravel, unknot. ENTANGLE
resolve, work out, sort out, clarify, clear up. EMBROIL

**disenthral** liberate, free, release, emancipate, manumit, enfranchise, unfetter, loose. ENSLAVE

**disfavour** *n*, disapproval, disapprobation, displeasure, dislike, disrespect, disesteem, discredit, disgrace. APPROVAL
disservice, bad turn, affront, offence. FAVOUR
*v*, disapprove, dislike, disesteem. APPROVE

**disfigure** deface, mutilate, scar, distort, deform, spoil, mar, damage, blemish, disfeature. EMBELLISH

**disfigurement** defacement, mutilation, scar, deformity, blemish, defect, ugliness. EMBELLISHMENT

**disgorge** vomit, spew, belch, eject, expel, empty, discharge.
surrender, yield, relinquish, resign, cede, give up, renounce, hand over. RETAIN

**disgrace** *v*, dishonour, discredit, shame, degrade, debase, humiliate, sully, taint, stain, tarnish, slur, defame, disparage, depreciate, lower. HONOUR
*n*, shame, dishonour, discredit, humiliation, disesteem, obloquy, disfavour, disrepute, ignominy, infamy, odium, opprobrium, reproach, disparagement, depreciation, defamation, slur, scandal. ESTEEM

**disgraceful** shameful, scandalous, ignominious, discreditable, dishonourable, infamous, opprobrious, low, degrading, disreputable, reprehensible, bad, shocking, outrageous, unworthy. HONOURABLE

**disgruntled** discontented, malcontent, displeased, dissatisfied, sulky, peevish, put out, annoyed, irritated, grumpy, fed up (*inf*). CONTENTED

**disguise** *v*, conceal, hide, mask, veil, shroud, cloak, muffle, gloss over, dissemble, misrepresent, falsify, camouflage, screen, cover. REVEAL
*n*, camouflage, incognito, mask, costume, concealment, cover, screen, blind, façade, pretence, guise, semblance, front.

**disgust** *v*, sicken, nauseate, revolt, repel, offend, displease, shock, appal, scandalize, outrage. PLEASE
*n*, distaste, nausea, repulsion, repugnance, disrelish, loathing, abhorrence, dislike, displeasure, aversion, hatred, antipathy, abomination. RELISH

**disgusting** sickening, nauseating, revolting, repulsive, repugnant, obnoxious, nasty, foul, noisome, odious, abhorrent, loathsome, unpleasant, outrageous, shocking, scandalous. DELIGHTFUL

**dish** *n*, plate, saucer, platter, bowl, vessel, receptacle.
food, fare, recipe, serving, helping, course.
*v*, ruin, spoil, wreck.

**dish out,** distribute, dole out, mete out, inflict.

**dish up,** serve, present, ladle, spoon.

**dishearten** discourage, dispirit, damp, dampen, depress, cast down, sadden, deject, crush, dismay, daunt, disconcert. ENCOURAGE

**dishevelled** unkempt, uncombed, bedraggled, untidy, disarranged, disordered, tousled. TIDY

**dishonest** fraudulent, deceitful, lying, untruthful, mendacious, false, crooked (*inf*), perfidious, knavish, tricky, unscrupulous, treacherous, corrupt, unfair, unlawful, untrustworthy, faithless. HONEST

**dishonesty** fraudulence, cheating, deceit, mendacity, duplicity, falsity, perfidy, trickery, unscrupulousness, treachery, corruption, crime, chicanery, improbity, fraud, criminality, crookedness. HONESTY

**dishonour** *n*, disgrace, shame, disrepute, discredit, ignominy, infamy, scandal, obloquy, opprobrium, reproach, degradation, abasement, disesteem, disfavour. ESTEEM
*v*, disgrace, discredit, shame, degrade, debase, abase, lower, humiliate, defame, sully. HONOUR
deflower, rape, seduce, ravish, molest, violate, defile, pollute, debauch.

**dishonourable** discreditable, disgraceful, shameful, scandalous, infamous, ignominious, despicable, contemptible, low, base, disreputable, unscrupulous, shameless. HONOURABLE

**disillusion** disenchant, disabuse, undeceive, enlighten, bring down to earth, disappoint.

**disinclined** reluctant, unwilling, indisposed, averse, loath, opposed, antipathetic. WILLING

**disinfect** fumigate, sterilize, sanitize, decontaminate, purify, cleanse. CONTAMINATE

**disingenuous** insincere, deceitful, dishonest, lying, two-faced, false, insidious, artful, guileful, sly, shifty, crafty. INGENUOUS

**disinherit** dispossess, deprive, cut off, disown, repudiate, oust.

**disintegrate** crumble, break up, fall apart, separate, shatter, splinter, decompose, decay, rot.

**disinter** exhume, disentomb, dig up, unearth, bring to light, expose, uncover. BURY

**disinterested** impartial, unbiased, objective, dispassionate, neutral, impersonal, uninvolved, detached, equitable, fair, just, unselfish, honest, candid. BIASED

**disjoin** detach, separate, disconnect, disunite, sever, divide, split. JOIN

**disjointed** disconnected, unconnected, fitful, rambling, incoherent, desultory, loose, aimless, disordered, confused. COHERENT
dislocated, displaced, dismembered, disunited, divided, split.

**disjunction** separation, disconnection, severance, disunion, disjuncture, detachment, split. UNION

**dislike** *v*, hate, detest, loathe, abhor, disapprove, disfavour, disrelish, object to, mind, despise. LIKE
*n*, hate, hatred, detestation, loathing, abhorrence, aversion, antipathy, disgust, repugnance, hostility, disfavour, disapproval, disrelish, displeasure. LIKING

**dislocate** disjoint, displace, luxate, disarticulate, disengage, unhinge, disconnect, derange, disorder, disrupt, misplace.

**dislocation** luxation, displacement, disarticulation, disconnection, derangement, disorder, disarray, disorganization, disruption, disturbance.

**dislodge** remove, displace, uproot, extricate, oust, expel, eject, evict. PLACE

**disloyal** unfaithful, faithless, perfidious, treacherous, false, untrue, apostate, recreant, disaffected. LOYAL

**disloyalty** unfaithfulness, faithlessness, infidelity, perfidy, treachery, treason, falseness, inconstancy, apostasy, disaffection. LOYALTY

**dismal** gloomy, dreary, cheerless, sombre, dull, dark, drab, bleak, depressing, melancholy, lugubrious, doleful, sad, joyless, wretched, miserable, dolorous, funereal, forlorn, grim, gruesome. CHEERFUL

**dismantle** disassemble, take apart, demolish, raze, strip, divest. ASSEMBLE

**dismay** *n*, consternation, alarm, apprehension, dread, fear, terror, horror, panic, anxiety, trepidation, agitation, misgiving, disappointment, discouragement, chagrin. REASSURANCE
*v*, alarm, frighten, scare, perturb, upset, disconcert, daunt, intimidate, terrify, horrify, appal, discourage, dishearten, depress, sadden, disappoint, chagrin. REASSURE

**dismember** dissect, cut up, anatomize, disjoint, divide, sever, amputate, mutilate.

**dismiss** discharge, send away, banish, disband, disperse, demobilize, release, free, let go, remove, oust, cashier, lay off, sack (*inf*), fire (*inf*). RETAIN
discard, reject, dispel, banish, set aside, shelve, drop.

**dismissal** discharge, release, freedom, expulsion, removal, notice, sack (*inf*).

**dismount** descend, alight, get off, get down, disembark. MOUNT

**disobedience** insubordination, noncompliance, wilfulness, contumacy, recalcitrance, defiance, indiscipline, mutiny, infraction. OBEDIENCE

**disobedient** insubordinate, noncompliant, contrary, wayward, contumacious, refractory, defiant, undisciplined, naughty, unruly, wilful, mutinous, rebellious. OBEDIENT

**disobey** infringe, violate, contravene, transgress, break, disregard, ignore, defy, flout. OBEY

**disoblige** displease, annoy, bother, trouble, disturb, put out, inconvenience, discommode, offend, affront, slight, insult. OBLIGE

**disobliging** unaccommodating, uncooperative, awkward, unhelpful, unpleasant, disagreeable, rude, discourteous, offensive, unkind, unfriendly. OBLIGING

**disorder** *n*, disarray, confusion, muddle, jumble, mess, chaos, disarrangement, derangement, disorderliness, disorganization, turmoil, tumult, riot, commotion, disturbance. ORDER

ailment, complaint, malady, illness, disease, affliction, indisposition, sickness.

*v*, disarrange, derange, disorganize, disturb, upset, confuse, muddle, jumble, mess up, turn upside down, discompose, unsettle. ARRANGE

**disorderly** untidy, disordered, disorganized, disarranged, confused, chaotic, irregular, unsystematic. NEAT

unruly, unmanageable, lawless, riotous, boisterous, disruptive, obstreperous, rebellious, wild. ORDERLY

**disorganize** disarrange, derange, disorder, disrupt, disturb, upset, confuse, muddle, jumble. ORGANIZE

**disorientated** disoriented, confused, perplexed, bewildered, lost, all at sea, astray, unsettled, mixed up, unbalanced.

**disown** repudiate, disclaim, abandon, reject, cast off, renounce, deny, disavow, ignore, disinherit, cut off. ACKNOWLEDGE

**disparage** belittle, depreciate, underrate, undervalue, underestimate, decry, derogate, run down, deprecate, denigrate, vilify, defame, traduce, malign, discredit, degrade, debase, asperse, criticize. EXTOL

**disparagement** belittlement, depreciation, underestimation, derogation, deprecation, denigration, vilification, defamation, discredit, disdain, contempt, scorn, aspersion, slander. APPRECIATION

**disparate** distinct, different, contrasting, unlike, dissimilar, diverse. IDENTICAL

**disparity** difference, inequality, discrepancy, incongruity, disproportion, gap, contrast, dissimilarity, unlikeness. EQUALITY

**dispassionate** objective, impartial, unbiased, disinterested, neutral, detached, impersonal, candid, fair, just. BIASED

composed, calm, collected, cool, unruffled, imperturbable, serene, poised, impassive, placid, unexcited. EXCITABLE

**dispatch** *v*, send, post, mail, transmit, remit, consign, ship, forward, expedite, hasten, hurry, accelerate. RETAIN

conclude, finish, complete, discharge, perform, dispose of.

murder, kill, slay, assassinate, execute, put to death, slaughter.

*n*, promptness, alacrity, speed, rapidity, celerity, haste, swiftness, quickness. SLOWNESS

communication, message, report, bulletin, communiqué, missive, note, letter, story, account.

**dispel** disperse, scatter, dismiss, banish, expel, dissipate, dissolve, rout, drive away. COLLECT

**dispensable** expendable, disposable, unnecessary, nonessential, superfluous, needless, redundant. ESSENTIAL

**dispensation** distribution, apportionment, allotment, assignment, allocation, bestowal, endowment. WITHHOLDING

management, administration, direction, regulation, control, system, order, scheme, plan, arrangement.

exemption, immunity, indulgence, licence, permission, privilege, exception, relaxation, reprieve, remission.

**dispense** distribute, give out, apportion, share, allot, assign, allocate, dole out, mete out. WITHHOLD

administer, apply, implement, enforce, discharge, execute.

exempt, excuse, release, except, reprieve, let off (*inf*).

**dispense with,** dispose of, get rid of, do away with, abolish, cancel. RETAIN

do without, abstain, forgo, give up, renounce.

**disperse** scatter, dispel, dissipate, broadcast, spread, disseminate, diffuse, dissolve, separate, break up, disband, dismiss, rout, disappear, vanish. GATHER

**dispirit** dishearten, discourage, damp, dampen, depress, deject, cast down, deter, disincline. ENCOURAGE

**dispirited** downhearted, downcast, disheartened, discouraged, depressed, dejected, crestfallen, despondent, glum. BLITHE

**displace** move, shift, disturb, derange, transpose, relocate, dislodge, dislocate. FIX
remove, depose, dismiss, discharge, cashier, sack (*inf*), fire (*inf*), oust, supplant, replace. RETAIN
eject, evict, force out, exile, banish.

**display** *v*, show, exhibit, demonstrate, manifest, betray, evince, reveal, expose, present. DISGUISE
parade, flaunt, show off, flourish, vaunt. CONCEAL
unfold, unfurl, spread out, open out, extend, expand.
*n*, show, exhibition, demonstration, exposition, presentation, array, revelation, exposure.
parade, spectacle, pageant, pomp, ceremony, ostentation, splash (*inf*).

**displease** offend, annoy, vex, irritate, nettle, pique, anger, incense, provoke, exasperate, aggravate (*inf*), disgust, dissatisfy, upset, hurt. PLEASE

**displeasure** offence, annoyance, irritation, anger, exasperation, wrath, disgust, disfavour, disapproval, dislike, dissatisfaction, resentment.

**disport** *vt*, amuse, entertain, divert, cheer, beguile, delight. BORE
*vi*, frolic, gambol, caper, frisk, romp, play, sport. WORK

**disposal** arrangement, array, disposition, order, grouping, placing.
removal, clearance, scrapping, dumping, discarding, ejection.
conveyance, transfer, dispensation, bestowal, bequest, consignment, assignment.
control, command, discretion, direction, regulation, power, authority.

**dispose** arrange, group, place, set, put, array, order, marshal, range, rank, organize, regulate, settle, adjust. DERANGE
incline, lead, move, prompt, tempt, induce, predispose, bias, influence, adapt, condition.

**dispose of,** get rid of, discard, throw away, scrap, dump (*inf*), destroy. RETAIN
settle, determine, decide, deal with, end.
distribute, allocate, transfer, bestow, make over, sell.

**disposed** apt, liable, subject, likely, given, inclined, prone, ready.

**disposition** character, nature, temperament, constitution, temper, humour, spirit.
inclination, tendency, turn, leaning, proneness, predisposition, proclivity, propensity, readiness.
disposal, arrangement, distribution, grouping, order, placement.

**dispossess** deprive, divest, strip, take away, confiscate, expropriate.
evict, expel, eject, oust, turn out, drive out. HOUSE

**dispraise** *v*, censure, criticize, reproach, condemn, denounce, disparage, discredit, disapprove. PRAISE
*n*, censure, criticism, animadversion, condemnation, disparagement, obloquy, disapproval, disapprobation, disgrace.

**disproof** confutation, refutation, rebuttal, negation, denial, disproval, invalidation. PROOF

**disproportion** disparity, inequality, discrepancy, difference, imbalance, unevenness, asymmetry. EQUALITY

**disproportionate** unequal, uneven, unbalanced, out of proportion, top-heavy, incommensurate, excessive, extreme, inordinate. COMMENSURATE

**disprove** confute, refute, rebut, negate, invalidate, controvert, contradict, discredit, expose, overturn. PROVE

**disputable** debatable, arguable, moot, controversial, questionable, doubtful, dubious, uncertain. INDISPUTABLE

**disputant** debater, arguer, wrangler, contender, opponent, adversary, antagonist, litigant. ADVOCATE

**disputatious** argumentative, contentious, captious, polemical, controversial, quarrelsome, irascible, cantankerous, litigious. GENIAL

**dispute** *v*, argue, debate, discuss, quarrel, wrangle, squabble, brawl, bicker, altercate. AGREE
question, challenge, contest, controvert, contradict, deny, impugn, resist. UPHOLD
*n*, argument, debate, discussion, disputation, controversy, contest, conflict, strife, wrangle, quarrel, altercation, row, disagreement. AGREEMENT

**disqualify** incapacitate, disable, injure, invalidate.
preclude, debar, disenable, disentitle, prohibit, exclude, rule out, eliminate. QUALIFY

**disquiet** *n*, disquietude, anxiety, worry, concern, foreboding, uneasiness, restlessness, unrest, fear, alarm, distress, trouble, fretfulness, agitation, disturbance, discomposure. CALM
*v*, worry, concern, unsettle, fret, perturb, agitate, discompose, distress, upset, disturb, annoy, irritate, bother, harass. APPEASE

**disquisition** dissertation, essay, treatise, thesis, paper, discourse, discussion, exposé.

**disregard** *v*, ignore, overlook, neglect, pass over, discount, take no notice of, disobey. HEED
slight, snub, cold-shoulder (*inf*), contemn, disdain, disparage.
*n*, inattention, neglect, oversight, heedlessness, indifference, slight, disrespect, disdain, contempt.

**disrelish** *v*, dislike, disfavour, loathe, detest. LIKE
*n*, aversion, antipathy, dislike, distaste, repugnance, loathing. LIKING

**disrepair** dilapidation, decay, deterioration, collapse, ruination, decrepitude.

**disreputable** discreditable, shameful, disgraceful, opprobrious, ignominious, base, abject, dishonourable, despicable, contemptible, mean, low, notorious, infamous, shady, unscrupulous, unprincipled. RESPECTABLE
scruffy, shabby, bedraggled, dishevelled, disorderly, seedy, threadbare. SMART

**disrepute** discredit, disesteem, disgrace, dishonour, shame, infamy, ignominy, ill repute. ESTEEM

**disrespect** rudeness, discourtesy, impoliteness, incivility, irreverence, insolence, impertinence, disregard, neglect, contempt. RESPECT

**disrespectful** rude, discourteous, impolite, uncivil, bad-mannered, cheeky, insolent, impudent, impertinent, irreverent, contemptuous. POLITE

**disrobe** undress, unclothe, doff, shed, strip, divest, denude, bare, uncover. DRESS

**disrupt** disturb, upset, disorganize, disorder, unsettle, agitate, confuse, break up, interrupt, intrude, interfere with.

**disruption** disturbance, disorder, confusion, disarray, interruption, interference.
rupture, split, breach, cleft, rift, cleavage, separation, division.

**dissatisfaction** discontent, displeasure, dislike, unhappiness, uneasiness, disquiet, disappointment, dismay, distress, chagrin, annoyance, exasperation, frustration, disapproval, resentment. SATISFACTION

**dissatisfied** discontented, displeased, disgruntled, put out, unhappy, annoyed, frustrated, disappointed, unfulfilled, uneasy, restless. SATISFIED

**dissect** anatomize, cut up, dismember, analyse, scrutinize, examine, investigate, study, explore, sift, probe.

**dissemble** hide, conceal, cloak, mask, camouflage, dissimulate. REVEAL
pretend, feign, simulate, affect, sham, fake, counterfeit.

**disseminate** disperse, diffuse, spread, scatter, distribute, circulate, broadcast, promulgate, propagate, publish, proclaim, publicize, preach. SUPPRESS

**dissemination** dispersion, diffusion, spread, distribution, circulation, broadcasting, promulgation, propagation, publication. SUPPRESSION

**dissension** disagreement, discord, strife, conflict, quarrel, contention, dissent, dispute, variance, difference. AGREEMENT

**dissent** *v*, disagree, differ, dispute, object, protest, reject, refuse, abjure. ASSENT
*n*, disagreement, discord, dissidence, dissension, difference, opposition, disaffection, nonconformity.

**dissenter** dissident, nonconformist, objector, protestant, sectarian. CONFORMIST

**dissentient** dissenting, disagreeing, dissident, conflicting, opposing, objecting, unorthodox. COMPLIANT

**dissertation** discourse, treatise, essay, thesis, disquisition, exposition.

**disservice** disfavour, wrong, bad turn, ill turn, injury, harm, injustice, unkindness. FAVOUR

**dissever** sever, sunder, cleave, disunite, separate, disjoin, disjoint, part, dissociate. UNITE

**dissident** dissenter, protester, rebel, nonconformist.

**dissimilar** unlike, different, divergent, disparate, unrelated, heterogeneous, diverse, various. ALIKE

**dissimilarity** dissimilitude, difference, unlikeness, divergence, disparity, heterogeneity, diversity. SIMILARITY

**dissimulation** dissembling, concealment, disguise, feigning, sham, pretence, deception, deceit, hypocrisy, duplicity. HONESTY

**dissipate** spend, expend, consume, drain, deplete, burn up, waste, squander, fritter away, lavish, indulge oneself. HOARD
scatter, disperse, diffuse, dispel, disappear, vanish, evaporate, dissolve. COLLECT

**dissipated** debauched, dissolute, licentious, profligate, abandoned, intemperate, self-indulgent.

**dissipation** debauchery, profligacy, licentiousness, dissoluteness, abandonment, depravity, self-indulgence, intemperance.
expenditure, squandering, wastefulness, waste, extravagance, excess, lavishness, prodigality. FRUGALITY
dispersion, diffusion, dissemination, dissolution, evaporation, disappearance. ACCUMULATION

**dissociate** separate, disunite, sever, detach, break off, disconnect, disjoin, divorce, set apart, isolate. JOIN

**dissociation** separation, disunion, severance, detachment, division, disjunction, divorce, parting, isolation. UNION

**dissolute** dissipated, debauched, wanton, depraved, loose, profligate, abandoned, licentious, lewd, corrupt, degenerate, rakish, intemperate, unrestrained. AUSTERE

**dissolution** disintegration, decomposition, breaking up, separation, resolution, parting, division, dispersion. CONSOLIDATION
termination, end, conclusion, finish, discontinuation, divorce, dismissal, dispersal, destruction, overthrow, ruin, annihilation, extinction, death.
dissolving, liquefaction, solution, evaporation, disappearance.

**dissolve** liquefy, melt, thaw, deliquesce, fuse. SOLIDIFY
disintegrate, crumble, collapse, decompose, disperse, diffuse, dissipate, evaporate, fade, dwindle, vanish, disappear. ENDURE
terminate, end, wind up, discontinue, dismiss, break up, destroy, overthrow, ruin.
sever, disunite, separate, part, divorce, divide, break up. UNITE

**dissonance** discord, discordance, cacophony, harshness, stridency, jarring, jangle. HARMONY
disagreement, difference, discrepancy, inconsistency, incongruity, variance, disparity. ACCORD

**dissonant** discordant, inharmonious, unmelodious, cacophonous, harsh, strident, jarring, grating, raucous. HARMONIOUS
inconsistent, incongruous, discrepant, at variance, disagreeing, differing, divergent. CONGRUOUS

**dissuade** deter, discourage, disincline, put off, talk out of, advise against, expostulate, remonstrate. URGE

**distance** space, interval, gap, remove, separation, extent, range, span, reach, length, width, remoteness, farness.
reserve, coolness, aloofness, constraint, stiffness. CORDIALITY

**distant** far, remote, outlying, faraway, far-flung, removed, separate, apart. NEAR
reserved, cool, frigid, aloof, stiff, formal, haughty, standoffish, unfriendly, unapproachable. AFFABLE
faint, indistinct, obscure, slight. CLEAR

**distaste** dislike, disrelish, disgust, repugnance, aversion, loathing, revulsion, antipathy, displeasure. RELISH

**distasteful** unpleasant, disagreeable, undesirable, offensive, repugnant, disgusting, loathsome, hateful, abhorrent, repulsive, uninviting, unsavoury, unpalatable, nauseating. PLEASANT

**distend** dilate, enlarge, expand, swell, inflate, bloat, puff out, balloon, stretch, extend. CONTRACT

**distension** dilation, dilatation, enlargement, expansion, swelling, inflation, intumescence, extension. CONTRACTION

**distil** condense, vaporize, sublimate, evaporate, purify, refine, brew, extract, draw out, separate.
drip, drop, dribble, trickle.

**distinct** clear, sharp, clear-cut, well-defined, plain, obvious, apparent, evident, definite, unmistakable, marked, conspicuous, noticeable, palpable, patent, lucid, unambiguous. INDISTINCT
separate, detached, individual, discrete, unconnected, different, dissimilar, unlike.

**distinction** differentiation, discrimination, discernment, separation, difference, dissimilarity, contrast.

characteristic, peculiarity, individuality, feature, quality, mark.
fame, renown, repute, reputation, eminence, note, prominence, celebrity, honour, credit, importance, account, merit, worth, superiority, greatness, excellence. INSIGNIFICANCE

**distinctive** distinguishing, characteristic, individual, particular, unique, idiosyncratic, notable, remarkable, different, unusual.

**distinguish** differentiate, tell apart, discriminate, judge, separate, divide, categorize, classify, single out, characterize, mark, set apart.
discern, perceive, see, descry, make out, detect, recognize.
honour, ennoble, dignify, celebrate, immortalize, make famous.

**distinguished** eminent, illustrious, notable, renowned, famous, well-known, celebrated, noted. UNKNOWN
dignified, august, stately, majestic, lordly, aristocratic, noble.
marked, conspicuous, striking, outstanding, signal.

**distort** deform, twist, contort, buckle, warp, misshape, bend, turn, wrest. STRAIGHTEN
falsify, misrepresent, pervert, colour, slant, misinterpret, garble.

**distortion** deformation, deformity, contortion, crookedness, twist, bend, buckle.
falsification, misrepresentation, perversion, misinterpretation, colouring, slant, bias.

**distract** divert, deflect, sidetrack, turn aside, draw away. FOCUS
amuse, entertain, occupy, engage, engross, absorb. BORE
confuse, perplex, bewilder, confound, disturb, discompose, harass, torment, derange, madden, craze. COMPOSE

**distracted** confused, perplexed, bewildered, troubled, agitated, flustered, harassed, overwrought, distraught, frantic, mad, deranged, crazy, insane. COMPOSED

**distraction** confusion, bewilderment, perplexity, discomposure, agitation, turmoil, abstraction, aberration, derangement, frenzy, desperation, delirium, madness, mania, lunacy, insanity. COMPOSURE
amusement, entertainment, diversion, pastime, recreation.
interruption, disturbance, diversion, interference, disruption.

**distrait** absent-minded, forgetful, abstracted, preoccupied, distracted, inattentive, oblivious.

**distraught** agitated, anxious, upset, overwrought, distracted, worked up, beside oneself, frantic, hysterical, wild, mad. CALM

**distress** *v*, upset, grieve, sadden, afflict, pain, harrow, disturb, trouble, worry, bother, torment, agonize, vex, harass. PLEASE
*n*, grief, sorrow, heartache, anguish, suffering, affliction, pain, agony, trouble, worry, anxiety, desolation, torment. JOY
adversity, hardship, privation, poverty, destitution, misfortune, disaster, calamity, trial, straits. RELIEF

**distribute** dispense, dole out, mete out, allot, share, divide, apportion, allocate, administer, give, assign. WITHHOLD
deliver, hand out, issue, pass round, circulate, disseminate, spread, scatter, disperse, diffuse. COLLECT
classify, sort, order, arrange, class, group.

**distribution** dispensation, dole, sharing, division, apportionment, allotment, allocation, assignment, administration.
circulation, spread, dissemination, dispersal, diffusion, scattering.
classification, grouping, arrangement, organization, location, disposition, situation.

**district** region, quarter, area, section, locality, community, neighbourhood, sector, ward, borough, zone.

**distrust** *v*, doubt, mistrust, disbelieve, question, suspect, be wary of. BELIEVE
*n*, doubt, mistrust, disbelief, suspicion, wariness, misgiving, scepticism. TRUST

**distrustful** suspicious, mistrustful, doubtful, dubious, sceptical, cynical, disbelieving, chary, wary. TRUSTFUL

**disturb** disrupt, interrupt, rouse, inconvenience, put out, bother, pester, harass, trouble, annoy, vex.
disarrange, derange, upset, disorder, unsettle, muddle, confuse. ARRANGE
worry, concern, trouble, agitate, upset, distress, alarm, perturb, discompose, ruffle, shake. CALM

**disturbance** disruption, upheaval, interruption, distraction, intrusion, inconvenience, bother, nuisance.

commotion, disorder, turmoil, tumult, riot, brawl, fray, fracas, uproar, hubbub, noise, racket. PEACE
agitation, confusion, discomposure, perturbation, derangement, upset. CALM

**disunite** separate, part, disjoin, disconnect, sever, split, sunder, detach, disengage, dissociate. JOIN
estrange, alienate, set at odds, embroil. UNITE

**disuse** desuetude, nonuse, neglect, abandonment, discontinuance. USE

**ditch** *n*, trench, dyke, channel, furrow, moat, drain, gully.
*v*, discard, get rid of, scrap, jettison, abandon, dump (*inf*).

**dither** waver, vacillate, hesitate, falter, shillyshally (*inf*). DECIDE
shiver, tremble, shake, quiver, shudder.

**diurnal** daily, quotidian, circadian, daytime, day-to-day.

**dive** plunge, submerge, dip, duck, plummet, descend, fall, drop, swoop, pitch, lunge, dart, jump.

**diverge** divide, separate, split, fork, branch, divaricate, part, spread, radiate, open. CONVERGE
deviate, digress, wander, stray, swerve, depart, veer, drift.
differ, vary, conflict, disagree, be at variance. AGREE

**divergence** division, separation, forking, branching, divarication, ramification, spreading. CONVERGENCE
deviation, digression, divagation, departure, deflection, difference, variation, disagreement.

**divergent** diverging, separating, branching, radial, spreading. CONVERGENT
different, conflicting, diverse, variant, disagreeing, differing, separate. CONCORDANT

**divers** sundry, various, different, manifold, multifarious, some, several, numerous, many.

**diverse** different, varied, assorted, mixed, miscellaneous, separate, distinct, discrete, unlike, dissimilar, divergent, varying. SIMILAR

**diversify** vary, variegate, chequer, assort, change, alter, modify, branch out.

**diversion** detour, deviation, digression, departure, deflection, alteration, variation.
amusement, entertainment, distraction, sport, play, recreation, pastime, relaxation, fun, pleasure, enjoyment. WORK

**diversity** variety, assortment, medley, miscellany, multiplicity, difference, variation, divergence, dissimilarity, unlikeness. SIMILARITY

**divert** deflect, turn aside, avert, sidetrack, distract, switch, redirect, shift, change.
amuse, entertain, distract, interest, occupy, beguile, delight, regale. BORE

**divest** strip, deprive, dispossess, denude, unclothe, undress, disrobe, doff, shed, take off. CLOTHE

**divide** separate, split, part, sever, cleave, disunite, cut, bisect, disjoin, detach, disconnect, divert, branch, fork. JOIN
share, apportion, distribute, dispense, deal out, allot, allocate, parcel out. COLLECT
alienate, estrange, come between, disunite, split, set at odds. UNITE
categorize, classify, group, arrange, sort, dispose.

**dividend** share, portion, cut (*inf*), surplus, gain, bonus, extra.

**divination** prophecy, prediction, augury, divining, soothsaying, fortune-telling, clairvoyance.

**divine** *adj*, godlike, godly, supernatural, superhuman, spiritual, angelic, heavenly, celestial, transcendent, mystical. EARTHLY
holy, sacred, religious, consecrated, hallowed, sanctified. PROFANE
lofty, exalted, supreme, rapturous, ecstatic, blissful, beatific.
splendid, wonderful, excellent, gorgeous, beautiful, perfect. DRFADFUL
*v*, predict, foretell, prophesy, prognosticate, surmise, guess, conjecture, suspect, intuit, discern, perceive.

**diviner** prophet, seer, soothsayer, clairvoyant, fortune-teller, augur, oracle, astrologer.

**divinity** god, goddess, deity, spirit, angel, godhead, godhood, godliness, holiness.
theology, religion.

**division** section, part, segment, portion, group, class, category, branch, department, sector, compartment, partition, border, boundary.
separation, parting, partition, dividing, disunion, disconnection, detachment, severance, split. UNION

distribution, sharing, apportionment, allotment. COLLECTION

breach, rupture, split, feud, discord, variance, disagreement, disunion, estrangement. UNITY

**divorce** *v*, separate, divide, part, split up, split, disunite, sever, dissociate, detach. JOIN

*n*, dissolution, annulment, split, disunion, separation, break-up. MARRIAGE

**divulge** disclose, reveal, make known, communicate, tell, impart, leak, betray, let slip, confess, declare, proclaim, expose, uncover, publish, broadcast. CONCEAL

**dizzy** giddy, light-headed, reeling, vertiginous, shaky, unsteady, faint, woozy (*inf*).

confused, bewildered, bemused, dazed, befuddled. CLEAR-HEADED

foolish, silly, scatterbrained, fickle, flighty, capricious. RELIABLE

**do** *v*, perform, execute, carry out, fulfil, attain, accomplish, achieve, effect, complete, conclude, finish, end, work at, practice. NEGLECT

act, behave, comport oneself, conduct oneself.

suffice, serve, be adequate, satisfy, suit, answer.

prepare, make, fix, arrange, organize, see to, look after, produce, create, cause.

cheat, swindle, defraud, diddle (*inf*), con (*inf*), dupe, deceive, hoax.

manage, get along, proceed, fare, make out.

**do away with,** get rid of, dispose of, dispense with, discard, abolish, remove, eliminate, destroy, kill, murder.

**do in,** tire, exhaust, weary, fatigue, shatter (*inf*).

kill, murder, slay, slaughter, eliminate (*inf*), bump off (*inf*).

**do up,** tie, lace, fasten, wrap, pack, enclose.

renovate, restore, modernize, redecorate, refurbish, adorn, beautify.

**do without,** forgo, abstain from, give up, dispense with.

*n*, party, function, soirée, gathering, event, affair.

**do's and don'ts,** rules, regulations, customs, etiquette, code, policy.

**docile** tractable, manageable, amenable, compliant, submissive, yielding, ductile, pliant, obedient, biddable, meek, passive. OBSTINATE

**docility** tractability, manageability, amenability, compliance, submissiveness, obedience, meekness, passiveness. OBSTINACY

**dock**[1] *v*, clip, crop, cut off, shorten, curtail, reduce, diminish, decrease, lessen, deduct, subtract. INCREASE

**dock**[2] *n*, wharf, pier, quay, harbour.

*v*, moor, berth, anchor, tie up, land.

**doctor** *n*, physician, GP, locum, medic (*inf*), surgeon, specialist, consultant.

*v*, alter, tamper with, falsify, distort, fudge, adulterate, cut.

fix, repair, mend, patch up.

**doctrinaire** dogmatic, insistent, opinionated, overbearing, inflexible, intolerant. AMENABLE

theoretical, hypothetical, speculative, unrealistic, impractical. REALISTIC

**doctrine** dogma, creed, tenet, principle, precept, teaching, canon, belief, opinion, conviction.

**document** *n*, paper, certificate, instrument, record, charter, deed, credential.

*v*, support, back up, substantiate, corroborate, authenticate, validate.

**doddering** weak, feeble, shaky, infirm, unsteady, tottering, decrepit, aged, senile. ROBUST

**dodge** *v*, evade, elude, avoid, shirk, hedge, equivocate, parry, fend off, duck, dart, sidestep, swerve. FACE

*n*, artifice, trick, ruse, wile, stratagem, ploy, device.

**dodgy** risky, dangerous, delicate, dicey (*inf*), difficult, tricky, uncertain, unreliable. SAFE

**doer** performer, agent, operator, achiever, entrepreneur, go-getter (*inf*), dynamo (*inf*). IDLER

**doff** raise, lift, take off, remove, shed, cast off, disrobe, undress, strip, divest. DON

**dog** *n*, hound, cur, mongrel, whelp, pup, puppy, bitch, canine, mutt (*inf*), pooch (*inf*).

*v*, follow, pursue, trail, track, hound, plague, haunt, trouble.

**dogged** determined, resolute, intent, tenacious, firm, steadfast, persevering, persistent, unwavering, indefatigable, set, wilful, headstrong, stubborn, obstinate, inflexible, unyielding. APATHETIC

**dogma** doctrine, creed, principle, tenet, code, precept, teaching, belief, opinion, article of faith.

**dogmatic** assertive, opinionated, obdurate, emphatic, positive, insistent, doctrinaire, arbitrary, overbearing, imperious, authoritative, categorical, peremptory, dictatorial, arrogant, intolerant. AMENABLE

**doing** action, act, deed, exploit, achievement, accomplishment, work, handiwork, performance, event, concern, affair, dealing, transaction.

**dole** *n*, allowance, benefit, grant, subsidy, handout (*inf*), charity, alms, donation, gift. WAGE
share, portion, quota, allotment, allocation, apportionment, distribution, dispensation, division.
*v*, distribute, dispense, apportion, allot, assign, share, divide, deal, mete, administer. WITHHOLD

**doleful** gloomy, melancholy, sad, miserable, unhappy, sorrowful, woebegone, dejected, depressed, dismal, dreary, cheerless, lugubrious, mournful, wretched, dolorous, pitiful, pathetic. JOYFUL

**dolorous** painful, harrowing, grievous, distressing, doleful, melancholy, mournful, sad, miserable, woebegone, wretched. HAPPY

**dolt** fool, idiot, simpleton, blockhead, ass, dunce, dullard, ignoramus, clot (*inf*), dope (*inf*), nincompoop. GENIUS

**doltish** foolish, idiotic, simple, blockish, asinine, dull, halfwitted, brainless, dense, thick, dopey (*inf*), dumb (*inf*). CLEVER

**domain** dominion, kingdom, realm, empire, land, territory, demesne, estate, province, region.
area, field, sphere, department, concern, specialty, discipline, jurisdiction, authority.

**domestic** *adj*, home, family, household, domiciliary, private, home-loving. PUBLIC
domesticated, tame, pet, house-trained. WILD
internal, civil, native, indigenous, home-grown, home-made. FOREIGN
*n*, servant, maid, housekeeper, charwoman, help, menial, drudge.

**domesticate** tame, house-train, train, break in, habituate, familiarize, accustom, acclimatize, naturalize.

**domicile** abode, home, residence, dwelling, house, habitation, quarters, lodgings, address.

**dominant** commanding, controlling, ruling, governing, supreme, paramount, predominant, prevailing, prevalent, principal, chief, main, primary, leading, ascendant, assertive, authoritative. SUBORDINATE

**dominate** control, rule, govern, reign, command, direct, master, domineer, subdue, tyrannize, subjugate, crush, suppress, monopolize, prevail, predominate, override, overshadow, eclipse.
bestride, tower above, overlook, survey, loom over.

**domination** power, authority, dominion, ascendancy, supremacy, sway, rule, control, influence, mastery.
tyranny, despotism, oppression, subjugation, subjection, subordination. SUBMISSION

**domineer** tyrannize, oppress, overbear, dominate, browbeat, intimidate, bully, hector. SUBMIT

**domineering** overbearing, imperious, tyrannical, authoritarian, dictatorial, lordly, magisterial, high-handed, masterful, bossy (*inf*), haughty, arrogant. MEEK

**dominion** power, authority, domination, ascendancy, supremacy, sway, rule, control, mastery, command, jurisdiction.
domain, country, territory, province, realm, kingdom, empire.

**don** put on, get into, slip on, dress in, wear. DOFF

**donate** give, bestow, bequeath, grant, confer, present, contribute, subscribe. RECEIVE

**donation** gift, present, grant, bequest, contribution, offering, subscription, benefaction, alms, charity.

**done** finished, over, through, ended, completed, concluded, accomplished. UNFINISHED
cooked, ready.
exhausted, spent, drained, depleted.
conventional, acceptable, proper.
**done for,** ruined, wrecked, broken, destroyed, lost, foiled, dashed, beaten, defeated, undone, finished.
**done in,** tired out, exhausted, worn out, all in (*inf*), dead beat (*inf*), knackered (*inf*).

**donkey** ass, mule, jackass, dunce, fool, blockhead, dolt, simpleton, dullard, dope (*inf*), nincompoop. GENIUS

**donor** giver, donator, benefactor, contributor. RECIPIENT

**doom** *v*, destine, ordain, fate, damn, condemn, sentence, judge, decree.
*n*, fate, destiny, fortune, lot, ruin, destruction, death.
judgment, verdict, decision, sentence, condemnation.

**door** entrance, exit, doorway, opening, hatch, gate, portal.

**dope** *n*, drug, narcotic, opiate, barbiturate, sedative, stimulant.
dolt, nincompoop, blockhead, fool, idiot, simpleton, dunce. GENIUS
facts, information, details, news, gen (*inf*), info (*inf*).
*v*, sedate, drug, narcotize, anaesthetize, stupefy.

**dormant** sleeping, asleep, hibernating, resting, quiescent, latent, inactive, inert, sluggish, torpid. ACTIVE

**dose** draught, measure, portion, quantity, dosage, drench.

**dot** *n*, point, spot, speck, mark, fleck, jot, iota, atom.
**on the dot,** punctually, promptly, precisely, exactly, on time.
*v*, spot, speckle, fleck, stud, pepper, sprinkle, scatter.

**dotage** senility, caducity, old age, decrepitude, feebleness, imbecility, second childhood. YOUTH

**dote** idolize, adore, love, treasure, hold dear, indulge, pamper, spoil. LOATHE

**double** *adj*, twice, twofold, dual, duplex, coupled, paired, twin, doubled. SINGLE
deceitful, false, insincere, hypocritical, two-faced, dishonest. HONEST
*v*, duplicate, fold, repeat, multiply, enlarge, magnify, increase. HALVE
*n*, twin, duplicate, copy, counterpart, replica, clone, look-alike, Doppelgänger, dead ringer (*inf*), spitting image (*inf*).
**at the double,** quickly, briskly, posthaste, without delay, immediately. SLOWLY

**double-cross** cheat, hoodwink, trick, swindle, defraud, betray.

**doublet** jacket, jerkin, waistcoat.

**doubt** *vt*, suspect, question, query, mistrust, distrust, disbelieve, discredit. TRUST
*vi*, waver, vacillate, hesitate, demur, be uncertain, scruple, lack conviction. RESOLVE
*n*, suspicion, mistrust, distrust, misgiving, qualm, uncertainty, hesitation, vacillation, irresolution, indecision, dubiety, doubtfulness, disbelief, scepticism. TRUST

**doubtful** uncertain, unsure, undecided, irresolute, wavering, vacillating, distrustful, suspicious, sceptical. CERTAIN
dubious, questionable, debatable, unlikely, improbable, vague, obscure, ambiguous, equivocal, unsettled, problematic. DEFINITE

**doubtless** certainly, surely, indisputably, undoubtedly, assuredly, clearly, of course, without doubt. MAYBE
probably, most likely, apparently, seemingly, presumably.

**doughty** brave, bold, valiant, valourous, courageous, heroic, intrepid, fearless, dauntless, hardy, resolute, redoubtable, gallant. TIMOROUS

**dour** sullen, morose, sour, gloomy, grim, forbidding.
hard, inflexible, austere, rigorous, harsh, strict, severe, unyielding, obstinate.

**douse** souse, dip, plunge, duck, immerse, submerge, soak, drench.
extinguish, snuff, put out, blow out. LIGHT

**dowdy** shabby, untidy, slovenly, drab, dingy, frumpish, frowzy, old-fashioned. SMART

**dower** estate, property, legacy, inheritance, bequest, provision, settlement, dowry.
gift, talent, faculty, knack, endowment.

**down**[1] *adv*, downwards, low, below, beneath, under, to the ground. UP
*adj*, depressed, dejected, downcast, sad, miserable, unhappy, low, blue. CHEERFUL
**down and out,** destitute, impoverished, penniless, derelict. WEALTHY
*n*, descent, drop, fall, decline, reverse. RISE
*v*, prostrate, fell, knock down, floor, bring down, overthrow, subdue.
drink, swallow, gulp, put away.

**down**[2] *n*, feathers, fluff, fur, fuzz.

**downcast** dejected, downhearted, depressed, discouraged, disheartened, dispirited, crestfallen, unhappy, sad, miserable, despondent. HAPPY

**downfall** fall, ruin, destruction, collapse, debacle, overthrow, undoing. RISE

**downgrade** degrade, demote, humble, lower. UPGRADE
denigrate, disparage, belittle, depreciate, run down, decry. PRAISE

**downhearted** discouraged, disheartened, dispirited, despondent, depressed, dejected, downcast, crestfallen, sad, unhappy, miserable. CHEERFUL

**downpour** cloudburst, deluge, torrent, flood, inundation, pouring rain.

**downright** absolute, positive, utter, categorical, outright, complete, total, thorough, sheer, unqualified, clear, plain, unequivocal.
candid, frank, open, honest, blunt, straightforward, forthright, plain-spoken, sincere. EVASIVE

**downward** descending, declining, slipping, sliding, down. UPWARD

**dowry** dot, marriage portion, marriage settlement, gift, endowment.

**doze** *v*, drowse, nap, catnap, snooze (*inf*), sleep, slumber. WAKE
*n*, nap, catnap, forty winks (*inf*), snooze (*inf*), siesta.

**drab** dull, dingy, dreary, flat, colourless, grey, lacklustre, dark, gloomy, cheerless, dismal. BRIGHT

**draft** *v*, draw, sketch, outline, delineate, draw up, put together, prepare, frame, plan, compose, formulate, write.
*n*, sketch, outline, plan, rough, delineation, skeleton.
bill of exchange, cheque, money order.

**drag** *v*, draw, pull, haul, heave, lug, tug, tow, trail. PUSH
crawl, shuffle, creep, inch, plod, trudge, lag, linger, loiter, dawdle. HURRY
prolong, protract, spin out, draw out, lengthen, stretch out, extend.
*n*, bore, nuisance, bother, annoyance, pain (*inf*).

**draggle** bedraggle, begrime, drabble, soil, dirty, befoul, trail.
lag, dawdle, straggle, trail, dilly-dally (*inf*). HURRY

**dragoon** force, compel, coerce, drive, impel, constrain, bully, browbeat. COAX

**drain** *v*, empty, draw off, pump out, remove, evacuate, dry, strain, tap, bleed, milk. FILL
exhaust, sap, deplete, consume, expend.
drip, trickle, seep, leak, exude, discharge, flow out.
*n*, channel, culvert, duct, conduit, pipe, gutter, ditch, sewer, outlet.
depletion, exhaustion, strain, reduction, expenditure.

**drama** play, show, piece, work, dramatization.
acting, theatre, dramaturgy, stagecraft, histrionics, dramatics, theatrics, scene, spectacle, excitement, crisis.

**dramatic** theatrical, Thespian, histrionic, dramaturgic.
striking, vivid, effective, impressive, spectacular, breathtaking, powerful, exciting, sensational, melodramatic, sudden, startling. UNIMPRESSIVE

**drape** hang, cover, clothe, dress, adorn, deck, festoon, array, shroud, cloak, wrap. DIVEST
drop, hang, droop, dangle, suspend.

**drastic** extreme, radical, violent, forceful, powerful, strong, severe, intensive, desperate. MODERATE

**draught** breath, puff, air current, movement, flow, breeze.
drink, potion, dose, drench, quantity, cup.
pulling, drawing, haulage, traction.

**draw** *v*, pull, drag, haul, tow, tug, heave. PUSH
attract, allure, entice, invite, tempt, induce, persuade, influence, elicit, call forth, evoke. REPEL
sketch, delineate, map out, outline, trace, depict, portray, represent.
extract, pull out, take out.
inhale, breathe in, inspire, suck, drain, siphon, draw off.
move, go, come, proceed, advance, approach.
deduce, infer, conclude, derive, glean, get, take.
pick, choose, select, take.
**draw back,** recoil, shrink, retreat, withdraw, retract.
**draw out,** protract, extend, prolong, drag out, spin out, stretch, lengthen.
**draw up,** draft, compose, formulate, prepare.
halt, stop, pull up.
*n*, attraction, pull, lure, influence, magnetism, charisma.
tie, stalemate, dead heat.
raffle, lottery, sweepstake.

**drawback** disadvantage, snag, hitch, hindrance, impediment, obstacle, flaw, fault, imperfection, defect, difficulty, problem, detriment, shortcoming, deficiency. ADVANTAGE

**drawing** sketch, picture, delineation, outline, diagram, plan, illustration, cartoon, representation, portrait.

**drawl** drag, protract, draw out, prolong, lengthen, drone, twang. GABBLE
**dread** *v*, fear, quail, tremble, shudder, apprehend, anticipate.
*n*, fear, terror, horror, fright, alarm, apprehension, trepidation, misgiving, qualm. CONFIDENCE
*adj*, dreaded, dreadful, fearful, awful, terrible, alarming, frightful, dire.
**dreadful** awful, terrible, frightful, horrible, dire, appalling, shocking, alarming, ghastly, horrendous, monstrous, atrocious, distressing, tragic, formidable, tremendous, terrific. WONDERFUL
**dream** *n*, vision, illusion, delusion, hallucination, fantasy, trance, reverie, daydream, fancy, notion, nightmare. REALITY
ambition, goal, target, aspiration, hope, wish.
*v*, imagine, envisage, visualize, fancy, conceive, think, conjure up, fantasize, hallucinate, daydream.
**dream up,** invent, create, devise, concoct, think up, hatch.
**dreamer** visionary, idealist, utopian, daydreamer, romancer, fantast. REALIST
**dreary** dull, flat, drab, colourless, monotonous, boring, tedious, uninteresting, wearisome, routine, humdrum. EXCITING
gloomy, sombre, dark, cheerless, comfortless, bleak, dismal, uninviting, depressing, chilling. BRIGHT
**dregs** sediment, residue, lees, grounds, draff, dross, refuse, waste, deposit, scum, leavings, remains.
rabble, riffraff, *canaille*, good-for-nothings, scum.
**drench** soak, wet, saturate, steep, douse, souse, submerge, inundate, drown. DRY
**dress** *v*, clothe, garb, rig, fit, turn out, attire, robe, drape, cover, array, deck, adorn, decorate. STRIP
arrange, dispose, adjust, straighten, align, prepare, groom, comb. DISARRANGE
treat, bandage, plaster, strap up, attend to. NEGLECT
*n*, frock, gown, costume, suit, outfit.
clothes, clothing, attire, garb, apparel, garments, wardrobe, costume, guise, habit, vestments, gear (*inf*), togs (*inf*).
**dressing** sauce, relish, condiment, garnish.
bandage, plaster, compress, covering.
manure, fertilizer, compost, dung, muck.
**dribble** trickle, drip, drop, ooze, seep, run.
drool, slaver, slobber, drivel.
**driblet** scrap, bit, morsel, fragment, piece, dash, trace, drop.
**drift** *v*, wander, meander, stray, digress, float, coast, waft.
accumulate, pile up, amass, gather, drive, bank up.
*n*, trend, tendency, bearing, course, direction, flow, movement, current, rush, sweep, drive.
meaning, intention, purpose, aim, design, tenor, gist, implication, significance, import.
bank, mound, pile, heap, mass, accumulation.
**drill** *v*, teach, instruct, train, coach, rehearse, exercise, discipline, school.
bore, pierce, perforate, puncture, penetrate.
*n*, instruction, training, coaching, exercise, practice, repetition, discipline.
borer, bit, gimlet, rotary tool.
**drink** *vt*, imbibe, quaff, sup, swallow, gulp, swig (*inf*), sip, drain, absorb, take in, assimilate.
*vi*, tipple, tope, indulge, booze (*inf*), carouse, revel.
**drink to,** toast, pledge, salute, drink the health of.
*n*, potion, beverage, liquid, refreshment.
draught, sip, gulp, glass, cup.
alcohol, liquor, spirits, booze (*inf*).
**drip** *v*, drop, dribble, trickle, filter, percolate, seep, ooze, sprinkle.
*n*, drop, trickle, dribble.
weakling, milksop, weed (*inf*), wet (*inf*), bore.
**drive** *v*, propel, push, thrust, send, hurl, impel, herd, shepherd, pilot, steer, direct, guide, control, handle, operate, ride, motor.
force, oblige, constrain, urge, coerce, press, compel, dragoon, goad, spur, motivate. DETER
*n*, ride, jaunt, outing, excursion, journey, trip, run, spin (*inf*).
vigour, energy, effort, enterprise, initiative, ambition, get-up-and-go (*inf*). APATHY
campaign, crusade, effort, appeal, action.
**drivel** *v*, dribble, slaver, slobber, drool.
prate, babble, jabber, chatter, ramble, waffle (*inf*).

*n*, nonsense, gibberish, twaddle, balderdash, rubbish, rot (*inf*). SENSE
slaver, slobber, dribble, saliva.

**drizzle** *n*, mist, spray, light rain.
*v*, spit, spot, rain, sprinkle, spray.

**droll** comical, amusing, funny, humorous, clownish, ridiculous, ludicrous, laughable, farcical, zany, whimsical, quaint, odd. SERIOUS

**drollery** comedy, humour, fun, buffoonery, farce, wit, waggishness.

**drone**[1] *n*, parasite, leech, sponger (*inf*), shirker, idler, loafer, sluggard, lounger. WORKER

**drone**[2] *v* + *n*, hum, buzz, whirr, purr, murmur, thrum.

**drool** dribble, slaver, slobber, drivel, salivate.

**droop** sag, sink, drop, bow, bend, hang, wilt, fade, wither, languish, weaken, faint, flag, decline, slump. FLOURISH

**drop** *v*, fall, sink, droop, decline, lower, diminish, lessen, subside, descend, dive, plummet, plunge, tumble. RISE
drip, trickle, dribble.
abandon, desert, forsake, relinquish, give up, discontinue, cease, forbear, quit. CONTINUE
discharge, deposit, set down, unload, let off, leave.

**drop off,** fall asleep, drowse, doze, catnap, nod off, snooze (*inf*).
decline, decrease, lessen, dwindle, fall off.
*n*, bead, pearl, globule, drip, droplet, blob, driblet, spot, dash, trickle, trace, bit, sip, tot, draught, nip.
fall, decline, slump, fall-off, decrease, reduction, diminution, deterioration. RISE

**dross** scum, waste, dregs, lees, scoria, refuse, recrement.

**drought** aridity, dryness, parchedness, dehydration. DELUGE
shortage, deficiency, dearth, scarcity, lack, want. GLUT

**drove** herd, flock, pack, swarm, crowd, mob, horde, multitude, throng.

**drown** submerge, immerse, sink, go under, engulf, inundate, flood, deluge, swamp.
overwhelm, overpower, overcome, muffle, stifle, suppress, silence, obliterate, wipe out.

**drowse** be sleepy, be drowsy, doze, nap, sleep, slumber, snooze (*inf*). WAKE

**drowsy** sleepy, tired, dozy, somnolent, comatose, lethargic, sluggish, torpid, heavy, dull, dazed, dopey (*inf*), groggy (*inf*). ALERT
soporific, hypnotic, dreamy, soothing, restful.

**drub** beat, club, cudgel, pound, pummel, cane, flog, thrash, whack, hit, strike.
defeat, beat, trounce, rout, lick (*inf*), hammer (*inf*).

**drudge** *v*, toil, slave, labour, plod, work. IDLE
*n*, toiler, plodder, labourer, slave, factotum, dogsbody (*inf*), menial, hack. IDLER

**drudgery** toil, hard work, labour, chore, slog, fag (*inf*), grind (*inf*), slavery.

**drug** *n*, medicine, medication, medicament, remedy, cure, physic.
narcotic, opiate, barbiturate, amphetamine, sedative, stimulant, dope (*inf*).
*v*, sedate, stupefy, dope (*inf*), narcotize, anaesthetize, deaden, benumb, dull.

**drum** *n*, tambour, tabor, kettledrum, tympanum, tom-tom.
*v*, beat, tap, thrum, hammer.

**drum into,** instil, drive home, reiterate, harp on, din into.

**drum out,** cashier, discharge, expel, dismiss, oust.

**drum up,** obtain, round up, canvass, solicit, petition.

**drunk** *adj*, drunken, boozy (*inf*), inebriated, intoxicated, tipsy, tiddly (*inf*), merry (*inf*), tight (*inf*), plastered (*inf*), well-oiled (*inf*), blotto (*inf*). SOBER
*n*, drunkard, inebriate, alcoholic, dipsomaniac, boozer (*inf*), wino (*inf*).

**drunkard** drunk, drinker, inebriate, tippler, toper, sot, alcoholic, dipsomaniac, boozer (*inf*), wino (*inf*). TEETOTALLER

**drunkenness** inebriety, intoxication, intemperance, alcoholism, dipsomania. TEMPERANCE

**dry** *adj*, arid, parched, thirsty, dehydrated, desiccated, waterless, barren. WET
dull, flat, boring, tedious, tiresome, uninteresting, plain, dreary, vapid, insipid, jejune. INTERESTING
witty, droll, sharp, keen, cutting, ironic, sarcastic, satirical.
*v*, parch, dehydrate, exsiccate, desiccate, drain. SOAK
sponge, towel, wipe, blot, mop. WET

**dual** double, twofold, duplex, binary, twin, paired. SINGLE

**dub** name, christen, entitle, designate, denominate, nickname, style, call, term.

**dubious** doubtful, uncertain, hesitant, wavering, vacillating, undecided, unsettled, sceptical, suspicious. CERTAIN
questionable, debatable, ambiguous, equivocal, suspect, unreliable, untrustworthy, shady (*inf*), fishy (*inf*). TRUSTWORTHY

**duck** dip, dunk, immerse, plunge, dive, submerge, douse, souse.
bob, crouch, stoop, bow, bend. STRAIGHTEN
dodge, avoid, evade, shirk, parry, sidestep. FACE

**duct** conduit, pipe, tube, canal, channel, passage.

**ductile** malleable, plastic, flexible, pliant, extensible.
compliant, yielding, tractable, docile, amenable, accommodating, passive. OBDURATE

**dudgeon** anger, wrath, ire, indignation, resentment.
**in high dudgeon,** angry, irate, vexed, indignant, resentful.

**due** *adj*. owing, owed, payable, unpaid, outstanding, in arrears. PAID
rightful, fitting, proper, apposite, appropriate, apt, justified, merited, deserved, requisite, obligatory. UNDUE
adequate, sufficient, enough, ample. INSUFFICIENT
scheduled, expected, anticipated.
*n*, right, prerogative, just deserts, comeuppance (*inf*).

**duel** combat, contest, fight, affair of honour.

**dulcet** sweet, pleasant, agreeable, delightful, charming, melodious, harmonious, euphonious, mellifluous, soothing, soft. RAUCOUS

**dull** *adj*. gloomy, dark, drab, murky, grey, overcast, cloudy, opaque, faded, dim, dismal, cheerless. BRIGHT
blunt, dulled, muted, subdued, indistinct, muffled. SHARP
obtuse, stolid, stupid, slow, thick, dense, witless, unintelligent. CLEVER
boring, uninteresting, dry, dreary, vapid, jejune, plain, flat, humdrum, prosaic, insipid. INTERESTING
insensitive, numb, callous, dead, unfeeling, insensible, apathetic, listless, sluggish, lethargic, torpid, slow, heavy, inactive, inert. LIVELY
*v*, blunt, alleviate, assuage, mitigate, lessen, soften, moderate, reduce, ease. AGGRAVATE
benumb, deaden, paralyse, stupefy, sedate, drug.
depress, deject, dispirit, dishearten, discourage, dampen. CHEER
dim, fade, cloud, obscure, tarnish, stain. BRIGHTEN

**dullard** dunce, simpleton, ignoramus, dolt, blockhead, dope (*inf*). GENIUS

**duly** rightly, properly, fittingly, appropriately, accordingly. UNDULY

**dumb** silent, mute, speechless, voiceless, inarticulate, tongue-tied. ARTICULATE
stupid, foolish, unintelligent, dull, thick, dense, ignorant. INTELLIGENT

**dumbfound** astonish, astound, amaze, stun, stagger, take aback, bowl over (*inf*), flabbergast (*inf*), nonplus, confuse, bewilder.

**dummy** figure, model, mannequin.
sham, counterfeit, substitute, imitation, copy, duplicate, sample.
dolt, dullard, blockhead, fool, simpleton, dunce.

**dump** *v*, drop, deposit, throw down, discharge, unload, empty out, tip.
scrap, jettison, get rid of, dispose of. KEEP
*n*, tip, rubbish heap, junkyard.
hovel, pigsty, slum, hole (*inf*).

**dun** urge, press, importune, pester.

**dunce** ignoramus, dullard, simpleton, idiot, fool, blockhead, dolt, halfwit, dimwit (*inf*). GENIUS

**dung** muck, excrement, ordure, manure, fertilizer.

**dungeon** cell, cage, oubliette, prison, jail, donjon, keep.

**dupe** *v*, cheat, deceive, hoodwink, trick, fool, cozen, beguile, delude, outwit, overreach, bamboozle (*inf*), con (*inf*).
*n*, victim, fool, simpleton, sucker (*inf*), pushover (*inf*).

**duplicate** *v*, copy, replicate, clone, reproduce, photocopy, double, repeat, echo.
*adj*, identical, twin, matching, double, duplex, twofold.

*n*, copy, replica, facsimile, carbon, photocopy, transcript, reproduction, clone, twin, double, look-alike. ORIGINAL

**duplicity** deceit, deception, double-dealing, guile, trickery, fraud, artifice, chicanery, hypocrisy, dissimulation, dishonesty. HONESTY

**durable** lasting, enduring, abiding, persistent, resistant, long-lasting, strong, stout, sturdy, substantial, firm, stable, constant, reliable, permanent. PERISHABLE

**duration** continuance, term, spell, period, time, span, stretch, length, extent, course.

**duress** constraint, coercion, compulsion, pressure, force.
imprisonment, detention, confinement, incarceration, captivity, restraint. FREEDOM

**during** throughout, in, through, over.

**dusk** twilight, nightfall, sunset, evening, eventide, gloaming, gloom, shade, darkness, obscurity. DAWN

**dusky** swarthy, dark, dark-skinned. PALE
dark, dim, gloomy, shadowy, murky, cloudy, overcast, obscure, tenebrous. LIGHT

**dust** *n*, powder, particles, dirt, earth, soil.
*v*, sprinkle, dredge, sift, scatter, spread, powder.
clean, wipe, sweep, brush.

**dutiful** obedient, respectful, deferential, filial, conscientious, faithful, devoted, submissive, docile, compliant, obliging. DISOBEDIENT

**duty** obligation, responsibility, onus, trust, charge, role, part, function, task, business, mission, calling, office, assignment, commission, service.
respect, deference, obedience, allegiance, loyalty.
tax, impost, excise, customs, toll, tariff.

**dwarf** *n*, midget, pygmy, manikin, homunculus, runt. GIANT
*v*, dominate, overshadow, bestride, tower over, rise above, diminish.
stunt, retard, check.

**dwarfish** stunted, undersized, pygmy, miniature, small, little, tiny, diminutive, Lilliputian. GIGANTIC

**dwell** live, reside, inhabit, lodge, abide, sojourn, tarry, stay, remain, settle, stop. MOVE
expatiate, elaborate, harp, descant, linger.

**dwelling** abode, residence, house, home, lodgings, quarters, domicile, habitation.

**dwindle** diminish, decrease, lessen, shrink, wane, ebb, decline, fade, peter out, shrivel, wither, waste away. INCREASE

**dye** *n*, colour, colouring, pigment, tint, stain, tinge, hue, shade.
*v*, stain, tint, colour.

**dying** moribund, expiring, fading, sinking, going, at death's door, *in extremis*, last, final.

**dynamic** forceful, powerful, energetic, vigorous, lively, spirited, driving, go-ahead, electric. LETHARGIC

**dynasty** house, line, succession, empire, ascendancy, dominion, rule, sway, government, sovereignty.

# E

**each** *pron*, every one, one and all.
*adj*, every, individual, separate.
*adv*, apiece, per person, per capita, individually, singly, respectively.

**eager** desirous, longing, yearning, impatient, avid, ardent, earnest, fervent, keen, enthusiastic, anxious, agog, vehement, zealous. INDIFFERENT

**eagerness** longing, yearning, impatience, avidity, ardour, earnestness, fervour, keenness, enthusiasm, vehemence, zeal. INDIFFERENCE

**ear** heed, attention, notice, regard, consideration.
sensitivity, discrimination, taste, appreciation.

**early** *adj*, premature, forward, advanced, precocious, untimely. LATE
primitive, primordial, primeval, ancient, initial, first. LATEST
*adv*, in advance, beforehand, too soon, prematurely. LATE

**earn** gain, get, obtain, procure, acquire, achieve, win, deserve, merit. FORFEIT
make, yield, bring in, gross, net, take home (*inf*). PAY

**earnest**[1] *adj*, serious, intent, determined, resolute, fixed, passionate, fervent, ardent, eager, avid, keen, dedicated, committed. CASUAL
sincere, serious, solemn, heartfelt, profound, warm. FLIPPANT

*n*, seriousness, earnestness, sincerity, truth, reality, determination, resolution.

**earnest**[2] pledge, promise, assurance, security, deposit, guarantee.

**earnings** pay, wages, salary, remuneration, emolument, stipend, income, profits, receipts, proceeds, return. EXPENDITURE

**earth** land, ground, soil, dirt, clay, loam, turf, sod.
world, globe, planet, sphere, orb, mankind, people.

**earthly** terrestrial, tellurian, worldly, mundane, temporal, material, materialistic, physical, fleshly, carnal. SPIRITUAL

**earthy** coarse, crude, lusty, robust, uninhibited, ribald, bawdy, vulgar, rude, rough, down-to-earth, unsophisticated. REFINED

**ease** *v*, alleviate, allay, assuage, soothe, mitigate, relieve, comfort, moderate, abate, appease, calm, still, lessen, reduce, diminish, lighten, disburden. AGGRAVATE
facilitate, assist, aid, simplify, smooth, expedite, speed up, advance, forward. HINDER
*n*, comfort, relief, peace, tranquillity, quiet, rest, repose, relaxation, content, contentment, serenity, complacency. DISQUIET
facility, readiness, easiness, dexterity, proficiency. DIFFICULTY
freedom, liberty, unconstraint, affluence, opulence, wealth, prosperity, luxury. CONSTRAINT

**easily** with ease, readily, effortlessly, simply, without difficulty.
by far, far and away, indisputably, undoubtedly, clearly, plainly, obviously, without a doubt. POSSIBLY

**easy** simple, effortless, straightforward, uncomplicated, facile, light, smooth, child's play (*inf*), a piece of cake (*inf*). DIFFICULT
tranquil, quiet, serene, untroubled, contented, comfortable, relaxed, secure. UNEASY
tolerant, lenient, indulgent, permissive, light, mild, gentle, easy-going, relaxed, casual, unaffected, natural. STRICT
compliant, tractable, yielding, submissive, docile, amenable, biddable, gullible, trusting. INTRACTABLE
leisurely, unhurried, moderate, gentle, undemanding, comfortable. STRENUOUS

**easy-going** relaxed, calm, carefree, nonchalant, happy-go-lucky, casual, easy, tolerant, flexible, amenable. STRICT

**eat** consume, devour, eat up, scoff (*inf*), chew, munch, masticate, swallow, ingest.
feed, dine, lunch, breakfast, feast.
erode, corrode, wear away, eat away, rot, decay, destroy, use up, eat into.

**eatable** edible, comestible, esculent, wholesome, palatable. UNEATABLE

**eavesdrop** listen in, overhear, pry, snoop (*inf*), spy, tap (*inf*), bug (*inf*).

**ebb** *v*, recede, retreat, retire, withdraw, flow back, go out. FLOW
subside, abate, sink, decline, fall, flag, fade, wane, decrease, diminish, dwindle, peter out. GROW
*n*, regression, recession, reflux, abatement, decline, fall, drop, wane, decrease, diminution, dwindling, weakening, degeneration. INCREASE

**ebullience** exuberance, enthusiasm, excitement, vivacity, exhilaration, buoyancy, high spirits. LETHARGY
boiling, ebullition, fermentation, effervescence.

**ebullient** exuberant, enthusiastic, excited, irrepressible, vivacious, effusive, exhilarated, buoyant, elated. LETHARGIC
boiling, seething, bubbling, effervescent.

**ebullition** boiling, seething, ebullience, effervescence.
outburst, explosion, fit, paroxysm, outbreak, storm, rage.

**eccentric** *adj*, irregular, abnormal, aberrant, strange, odd, peculiar, singular, bizarre, weird, freakish, whimsical, unconventional, idiosyncratic, wayward, capricious. NORMAL
*n*, character, oddity, original, weirdo (*inf*), freak (*inf*), crank (*inf*).

**eccentricity** irregularity, abnormality, oddity, peculiarity, singularity, weirdness, whimsicality, unconventionality, idiosyncrasy, quirk, caprice. NORMALITY

**ecclesiastic** *n*, clergyman, cleric, churchman, divine, priest, parson, minister. LAYMAN
*adj*, ecclesiastical, clerical, religious, holy, spiritual, divine. SECULAR

**echo** *v*, resound, reverberate, ring, repeat, reflect.
copy, imitate, ape, mimic, mirror, parallel, resemble.
*n*, resonance, reverberation, repetition, reflection.

copy, imitation, reproduction, replica, parallel, counterpart, semblance, likeness, reminder, repercussion.

**éclat** splendour, brilliance, lustre, pomp, pageantry, show, display, ostentation, effect.

glory, fame, renown, celebrity, acclaim, acclamation, applause. OBLOQUY

**eclectic** complex, multifarious, diverse, varied, heterogeneous, comprehensive, all-embracing, catholic, broad, wide-ranging, general.

**eclipse** *v*, obscure, blot out, block, hide, veil, shadow, darken, dim, extinguish.

surpass, transcend, excel, outstrip, outdo, overshadow, outshine.

*n*, obscuration, occultation, shading, darkening, concealment, obliteration, extinction.

decline, fall, loss, overshadowing.

**economic** monetary, financial, fiscal, pecuniary, budgetary, commercial, industrial, mercantile.

profitable, viable, productive, remunerative. UNECONOMIC

cheap, inexpensive, low-priced, reasonable. DEAR

**economical** thrifty, prudent, careful, frugal, sparing, saving. EXTRAVAGANT

cost-effective, efficient, money-saving. WASTEFUL

**economize** save, conserve, husband, scrimp, cut back, retrench, tighten one's belt. SQUANDER

**economy** thrift, thriftiness, husbandry, saving, frugality, parsimony, retrenchment, cutback. EXTRAVAGANCE

**ecstasy** rapture, transport, bliss, joy, delight, seventh heaven, elation, euphoria, felicity, exhilaration, thrill, exaltation, fervour. MISERY

**ecstatic** overjoyed, enraptured, blissful, euphoric, delirious, elated, delighted, on cloud nine (*inf*), rapturous, fervent, enthusiastic. INDIFFERENT

**ecumenical** universal, worldwide, general, catholic.

**eddy** whirlpool, vortex, swirl.

**edge** *n*, border, rim, lip, margin, periphery, fringe, verge, brink, threshold, side, outline, boundary, limit. CENTRE

sharpness, keenness, intensity, acuteness, bite, sting, force, zest. DULLNESS

**on edge,** nervous, tense, keyed up, on tenterhooks, eager, impatient, edgy, irritable. CALM

*v*, trim, bind, border, fringe.

creep, inch, steal, sidle, worm. DASH

sharpen, whet, hone. BLUNT

**edging** border, fringe, frill.

**edgy** nervous, tense, on edge, anxious, ill at ease, irritable, touchy, testy, sensitive. PLACID

**edible** eatable, comestible, esculent, good, wholesome, palatable. INEDIBLE

**edict** decree, ordinance, pronouncement, proclamation, mandate, command, order, statute, law.

**edification** improvement, uplifting, elevation, enlightenment, instruction, education, schooling, guidance, information. CORRUPTION

**edifice** building, structure, erection, construction, pile.

**edify** improve, uplift, elevate, enlighten, instruct, teach, educate, school, guide, inform. CORRUPT

**edit** correct, emend, revise, rewrite, modify, adapt, annotate, polish, redact, check, censor, compile, prepare, compose, assemble.

**edition** copy, volume, impression, printing, version, issue, number.

**editor** reviser, redactor, annotator, compiler, reader, writer, journalist.

**educate** school, instruct, teach, train, coach, tutor, exercise, drill, edify, enlighten, civilize, cultivate, develop, nurture, rear, discipline.

**educated** scholarly, learned, erudite, intellectual, literate, lettered, well-read, knowledgeable, versed, schooled, cultivated, cultured, refined, enlightened, informed. IGNORANT

**education** schooling, instruction, teaching, tuition, training, edification, enlightenment, development, civilization, culture, learning, knowledge, scholarship, erudition. IGNORANCE

**educational** educative, informative, instructive, edifying, didactic, heuristic.

**educe** elicit, evoke, bring out, draw forth, extract, derive, develop, evolve.

**eerie** weird, uncanny, strange, mysterious, frightening, unearthly, ghostly, creepy (*inf*), spooky (*inf*).

**efface** erase, rub out, obliterate, wipe out, eradicate, cancel, expunge, remove, delete, cross out, blot out, annihilate, destroy. IMPRINT

**effect** *n*, result, consequence, outcome, upshot, issue, event, conclusion, aftermath. CAUSE

efficacy, efficiency, power, force, strength, weight, influence, impact, validity.

action, operation, implementation, execution, performance.

meaning, significance, import, sense, drift.

**in effect,** in fact, actually, in reality, really, essentially, effectively, virtually.

*v*, cause, bring about, create, produce, make, procure, actuate, effectuate, achieve, accomplish, secure, perform, execute. PREVENT

**effective** efficient, effectual, efficacious, productive, competent, adequate, capable, able, useful. INEFFECTIVE

operative, functioning, active, current, in force, in effect, actual. INOPERATIVE

striking, impressive, cogent, forceful, telling, convincing, powerful. UNIMPRESSIVE

**effects** goods, chattels, movables, belongings, property, possessions.

**effectual** effective, efficient, efficacious, productive, powerful, influential, telling, cogent, useful, operative, functional. INEFFECTUAL

legal, lawful, binding, in force, valid, authoritative.

**effectuate** effect, cause, bring about, create, produce, make, procure, actuate, achieve, accomplish, secure, perform, execute. THWART

**effeminate** unmanly, womanish, feminine, soft, sissy, camp. VIRILE

**effervesce** bubble, foam, froth, fizz, sparkle, ferment, boil.

**effervescent** bubbling, bubbly, foaming, frothy, fizzy, sparkling, carbonated. FLAT

ebullient, vivacious, lively, gay, exuberant, animated, buoyant, excited, exhilarated. LISTLESS

**effete** weak, feeble, drained, spent, exhausted, worn out, enfeebled, decrepit, decadent, degenerate, dissipated. VIGOROUS

barren, sterile, infertile, unprolific, fruitless, unproductive. FERTILE

**efficacious** effective, effectual, productive, efficient, able, competent, potent, powerful, active, vigorous, useful, adequate. USELESS

**efficacy** effectiveness, efficiency, effect, power, force, potency, success, productivity, competence, ability, usefulness. INEFFICACY

**efficiency** effectiveness, efficacy, competence, proficiency, skill, expertise, ability, capability, success, productivity, power. INEFFICIENCY

**efficient** effective, effectual, efficacious, competent, proficient, skilled, skilful, expert, adept, able, capable, powerful, productive, economic, businesslike, successful. INEFFICIENT

**effigy** image, representation, likeness, icon, idol, figure, statue, portrait.

**effloresce** flower, bloom, blossom, blow.

**effluence** efflux, effluent, outflow, effusion, discharge, emission, emanation, exhalation. INFLUX

**effluvium** exhalation, emanation, vapour, gas, fumes, miasma, odour, smell, stench, reek, stink, pong (*inf*).

**effort** attempt, try, endeavour, essay, go (*inf*).

exertion, struggle, strain, application, labour, toil, pains. IDLENESS

achievement, exploit, feat, accomplishment, creation, product.

**effortless** easy, simple, facile, smooth, painless, undemanding. DIFFICULT

**effrontery** audacity, temerity, boldness, impudence, nerve, cheek (*inf*), impertinence, insolence, sauciness, shamelessness, presumption, assurance, brass (*inf*), gall (*inf*). TIMIDITY

**effulgence** brilliance, brightness, radiance, dazzle, blaze, shine, splendour, lustre, sheen, sparkle, glow, incandescence. DULLNESS

**effulgent** brilliant, radiant, bright, shining, dazzling, fiery, splendid, resplendent, lustrous, sparkling, luminous, incandescent, fluorescent. DULL

**effuse** pour out, spill, disembogue, emanate, issue, gush, diffuse.

**effusion** effluence, outflow, emission, discharge, outpouring, gush, stream.

**effusive** gushing, unreserved, expansive, lavish, fulsome, demonstrative, exuberant, ebullient, enthusiastic, profuse, unrestrained. RESERVED

**egg on** urge, press, push, goad, spur, incite, encourage, provoke, stimulate. DETER

**egoism** selfishness, self-interest, self-centredness, egomania, egotism, self-regard, self-esteem, self-importance, vanity, conceit, self-love. ALTRUISM

**egoistic** selfish, self-centred, egocentric, self-seeking, egotistic, self-important. ALTRUISTIC

**egotism** conceit, vanity, narcissism, self-love, self-centredness, self-esteem, self-importance, egoism. MODESTY

**egotistic** conceited, vain, self-centred, self-important, egocentric, self-admiring, boastful, narcissistic, egoistic. MODEST

**egregious** blatant, flagrant, glaring, striking, gross, scandalous, shocking, outrageous, notorious, infamous, heinous, monstrous.

**egress** exit, way out, outlet, emergence, issue, departure, exodus. ENTRANCE

**ejaculate** exclaim, cry, blurt out, utter, say.
discharge, emit, eject, spurt, spout.

**ejaculation** exclamation, cry, shout, utterance.
discharge, emission, ejection, release, spurt.

**eject** expel, emit, discharge, throw out, spout, spew, disgorge.
evict, throw out, dismiss, cashier, banish, exile, oust, drive out, remove, discharge, expel. RETAIN

**ejection** expulsion, emission, discharge, throwing out, eviction, dismissal, exile, ouster, removal.

**eke out** supplement, add to, increase, extend, stretch out, economize on, scrimp, be frugal with.

**elaborate** *adj*, detailed, thorough, minute, studied, laboured, intricate, complex, complicated, ornate, decorated, fancy, fussy, showy. SIMPLE
*v*, devise, work out, develop, amplify, expand, flesh out, improve, refine, enhance, embellish, decorate.

**elapse** lapse, intervene, transpire, pass by, slip away, go by, roll on.

**elastic** flexible, pliable, supple, yielding, resilient, springy, rubbery, ductile, extensible, stretchy. RIGID
adaptable, flexible, adjustable, accommodating, yielding, compliant. INFLEXIBLE

**elasticity** flexibility, suppleness, resilience, springiness, plasticity, ductility, stretch, give (*inf*). RIGIDITY
adaptability, flexibility, adjustability, compliance. INFLEXIBILITY

**elated** exhilarated, animated, excited, euphoric, ecstatic, jubilant, exultant, blissful, overjoyed, delighted, joyful, happy, proud. DEJECTED

**elation** exhilaration, animation, excitement, high spirits, euphoria, ecstasy, bliss, rapture, jubilation, joy, delight, happiness, glee. DEJECTION

**elbow** *n*, angle, corner, bend, turn, joint, flexure.
*v*, jostle, push, shove, nudge, knock, shoulder, hustle.

**elder** *adj*, older, senior, earlier, former, superior. YOUNGER
*n*, senior, superior, patriarch, chief, presbyter.

**elect** *v*, choose, select, prefer, pick, appoint, designate, vote for, decide on, opt for. REJECT
*adj*, elite, choice, select, hand-picked, appointed, chosen, selected.

**election** vote, voting, ballot, poll, appointment, selection, choice, preference. REJECTION

**elector** voter, constituent, selector, chooser.

**electric** exciting, thrilling, stirring, rousing, stimulating, charged, dynamic.

**electrify** thrill, excite, shock, startle, amaze, astound, stir, rouse, animate, galvanize.

**elegance** beauty, grace, refinement, polish, dignity, distinction, grandeur, luxury, style, taste, propriety, politeness, gentility. COARSENESS

**elegant** smart, stylish, chic, fashionable, neat, refined, cultivated, tasteful, fine, beautiful, classical, exquisite, choice, luxurious, sumptuous, graceful, genteel, sophisticated, polite, courtly, debonair. COARSE

**elegiac** plaintive, mournful, sorrowful, sad, melancholy, dirgeful, threnodic. MERRY

**elegy** dirge, lament, threnody, coronach, requiem.

**element** component, constituent, member, unit, part, section, ingredient, factor, feature, detail, particular. WHOLE
trace, hint, suggestion.

medium, habitat, domain, sphere, milieu, environment.

**elementary** basic, fundamental, elemental, rudimentary, primary, simple, uncomplicated, straightforward, introductory, preliminary. ADVANCED

**elephantine** huge, immense, gigantic, colossal, mammoth, enormous, ponderous, heavy, clumsy, hulking. TINY

**elevate** lift, raise, hoist, erect, heighten, magnify, boost, intensify. LOWER
exalt, advance, promote, ennoble, dignify, aggrandize. DOWNGRADE
elate, exhilarate, cheer, boost, uplift, hearten, rouse, animate, inspirit. DEPRESS

**elevated** lofty, high, raised, exalted, sublime, noble, dignified, grand, high-flown. BASE

**elevation** height, altitude, eminence, hill, rise, acclivity. DEPTH
exaltation, grandeur, loftiness, nobility, dignity.
lifting, raising, promotion, advancement, preferment, aggrandizement. LOWERING

**elf** imp, sprite, puck, pixie, brownie, leprechaun, fairy, gnome, dwarf.

**elfin** elfish, impish, puckish, mischievous, playful, arch, sprightly, elf-like, dainty.

**elicit** evoke, educe, bring forth, draw out, extract, derive, cause, give rise to.

**eligible** qualified, fit, appropriate, suitable, acceptable, worthy, desirable. INELIGIBLE

**eliminate** remove, take out, get rid of, discard, reject, dismiss, expel, oust, eject, throw out, exclude, omit, leave out, drop, eradicate, exterminate, annihilate, stamp out. INCLUDE

**elimination** removal, rejection, expulsion, ejection, exclusion, omission, eradication, extermination, annihilation. INCLUSION

**elite** *n*, best, cream, flower, aristocracy, nobility, gentry, upper class, *crème de la crème*. RABBLE
*adj*, select, exclusive, choice, first-class, aristocratic, noble, upper-class.

**elliptical** oval, egg-shaped.
concise, terse, laconic, succinct, ambiguous, obscure, circumlocutory.

**elocution** delivery, diction, articulation, eloquence, speech, oratory, rhetoric, declamation, public speaking.

**elongate** lengthen, extend, stretch, prolong, draw out, protract. CONDENSE

**elope** abscond, run away, slip off, flee, decamp, disappear, leave.

**eloquence** oratory, rhetoric, delivery, fluency, expressiveness, forcefulness, cogency, way with words.

**eloquent** fluent, glib, articulate, expressive, persuasive, cogent, forceful, impressive. INARTICULATE

**else** other, different, besides, more, in addition.

**elucidate** explain, expound, clarify, clear up, illuminate, shed light on, spell out, illustrate, unfold. MYSTIFY

**elucidation** explanation, clarification, illumination, illustration, exposition, commentary, annotation, gloss, footnote. MYSTIFICATION

**elude** evade, avoid, escape, dodge, duck, shun, shirk. FACE
baffle, confound, puzzle, frustrate, thwart.

**elusive** elusory, intangible, fugitive, fleeting, transient, indefinable.
slippery, shifty, tricky, deceptive, fallacious, equivocal, evasive.

**Elysian** blissful, happy, heavenly, celestial, blessed, paradisiacal, delightful, enchanting, charming, glorious. ABOMINABLE

**emaciated** lean, thin, gaunt, haggard, pinched, attenuated, scrawny, skinny, skeletal, wizened, wasted. OBESE

**emaciation** leanness, thinness, gauntness, haggardness, attenuation, scrawniness, wasting, marasmus. OBESITY

**emanate** proceed, originate, arise, issue, spring, flow, emerge. CULMINATE
emit, send forth, give off, radiate, exhale. ABSORB

**emanation** proceeding, origination, arising, flowing, springing, emergence. CULMINATION
emission, discharge, effusion, effluent, radiation, exhalation.

**emancipate** liberate, free, enfranchise, release, loose, unshackle, unfetter, unchain, manumit, disenthral. ENSLAVE

**emancipation** liberation, freeing, enfranchisement, release, deliverance, unshackling, manumission, freedom, liberty. ENSLAVEMENT

**emasculate** castrate, geld, unman.

weaken, debilitate, soften, enervate. STRENGTHEN

**emasculation** castration, gelding.
weakening, debilitation, enervation.

**embalm** mummify, preserve.
cherish, enshrine, consecrate, immortalize, treasure, store, keep, conserve. FORGET
perfume, scent.

**embargo** restraint, restriction, prohibition, ban, proscription, bar, barrier, stoppage, check, impediment, hindrance. LICENCE

**embark** board, get on, go aboard. DISEMBARK

**embark on,** begin, start, commence, set about, undertake, launch, broach, plunge into. COMPLETE

**embarrass** abash, shame, disconcert, discomfit, fluster, chagrin, mortify, confuse, confound, perplex, nonplus. EXTRICATE
encumber, burden, impede, hamper, trouble, plague. ASSIST

**embarrassment** abashment, shame, humiliation, awkwardness, self-consciousness, disconcertion, chagrin, mortification, confusion. EASE
predicament, plight, difficulty, scrape (*inf*), pickle (*inf*).

**embed** fix, implant, root, sink, set, drive in, hammer in.

**embellish** adorn, deck, ornament, decorate, garnish, beautify, enhance, enrich, gild, varnish, embroider, colour, elaborate. DISFIGURE

**embellishment** adornment, ornament, ornamentation, decoration, enhancement, enrichment, embroidery, exaggeration, elaboration. DISFIGUREMENT

**embers** cinders, ashes, remains.

**embezzle** steal, purloin, pilfer, appropriate, misappropriate, peculate, defalcate, defraud, cheat.

**embezzlement** stealing, pilfering, theft, appropriation, misappropriation, peculation, defalcation, fraud.

**embitter** sour, poison, envenom, anger, madden, irritate, exasperate, aggravate, exacerbate, disillusion, disaffect.

**emblazon** blazon, colour, illuminate, decorate, ornament, embellish.
proclaim, herald, trumpet, glorify, extol, praise.

**emblem** symbol, token, representation, sign, mark, badge, device, figure, insignia, logo.

**embodiment** incarnation, incorporation, personification, reification, expression, representation, symbol, example.
fusion, amalgamation, combination, unification, consolidation, inclusion, comprehension.

**embody** incarnate, incorporate, personify, reify, express, represent, symbolize, typify, exemplify.
embrace, encompass, include, comprise, comprehend, contain, collect, combine, unite.

**embolden** encourage, inspirit, hearten, rouse, animate, stimulate, spur, impel, rally, invigorate, cheer, reassure. DISCOURAGE

**embowed** bowed, arched, vaulted, arcuate, curved, bent. STRAIGHT

**embrace** *v*, clasp, hug, enfold, cuddle, squeeze.
adopt, take up, seize, grasp, accept, welcome. REJECT
include, comprise, encompass, comprehend, embody, cover, contain, encircle, enclose. EXCLUDE
*n*, clasp, hug, cuddle, squeeze, hold.

**embroider** embellish, exaggerate, colour, varnish, elaborate, dress up, fabricate.

**embroil** involve, implicate, compromise, incriminate, entangle, enmesh, complicate, confuse, disorder, perplex, muddle, disturb, discompose, trouble. EXTRICATE

**embryo** germ, nucleus, seed, root, beginning, rudiment.

**embryonic** rudimentary, undeveloped, early, elementary, primary, inchoate, incipient, beginning, immature. MATURE

**emend** correct, amend, improve, polish, rewrite, edit, redact, revise.

**emendation** correction, amendment, improvement, revision, alteration, editing, redaction.

**emerge** appear, come out, materialize, rise, surface, come up, proceed, issue, arise, emanate, come forth. DISAPPEAR

**emergence** appearance, apparition, materialization, rise, coming, advent, issue, emanation, evolution, development. DISAPPEARANCE

**emergency** crisis, exigency, urgency, juncture, extremity, pinch, necessity, contingency, predicament, difficulty, strait, plight, quandary.

**emigrate** migrate, move, relocate, depart, leave, quit. IMMIGRATE

**emigration** migration, relocation, expatriation, exodus, departure. IMMIGRATION

**eminence** distinction, celebrity, fame, renown, prominence, mark, note, notability, dignity, prestige, reputation, repute, esteem, greatness, loftiness, superiority. OBSCURITY
hill, mound, height, elevation.

**eminent** distinguished, illustrious, celebrated, well-known, famous, renowned, prominent, noted, notable, noteworthy, conspicuous, esteemed, revered, venerable, important, great, grand, lofty, superior, outstanding. UNKNOWN

**emissary** agent, ambassador, envoy, delegate, messenger, courier, herald, scout, spy.

**emission** discharge, issue, ejection, ejaculation, emanation, exhalation, diffusion, radiation, utterance.

**emit** discharge, issue, eject, ejaculate, expel, send forth, cast out, emanate, exhale, give off, radiate, diffuse, utter, give vent to.

**emollient** *adj*, soothing, lenitive, assuasive, palliative, balsamic, softening, relaxing. ASTRINGENT
*n*, ointment, balm, liniment, embrocation, lotion, salve.

**emolument** remuneration, pay, earnings, salary, wages, fee, stipend, profit, gain, income, living, compensation, benefit.

**emotion** feeling, passion, sensation, sentiment, ardour, fervour. INDIFFERENCE

**emotional** sensitive, susceptible, feeling, warm, tender, sentimental. EMOTIONLESS
passionate, ardent, fervent, zealous, enthusiastic, excitable, temperamental, heated, impassioned, fiery, melodramatic, hysterical, overwrought. CALM
emotive, touching, moving, stirring, poignant, pathetic.

**emphasis** weight, significance, importance, force, power, strength, stress, accent, insistence, pre-eminence, priority, attention, prominence, clarity.

**emphasize** stress, accentuate, accent, underline, highlight, point up, mark, press home, insist on. UNDERSTATE

**emphatic** positive, forceful, insistent, earnest, certain, definite, absolute, categorical, unequivocal, decided, marked, pointed, stressed, accented, pronounced, strong, energetic, important, significant.

**empire** domain, dominion, realm, commonwealth, province.
supremacy, sovereignty, sway, dominion, control, command, authority, power, rule, government.

**empirical** experimental, experiential, observed, practical, pragmatic. THEORETICAL

**employ** engage, hire, enlist, enrol, take on, commission. DISMISS
use, make use of, utilize, exercise, apply, wield.
occupy, keep busy, engage, engross.

**employee** worker, hand, wage-earner, staff member. EMPLOYER

**employer** boss, director, proprietor, owner, company, firm, business. EMPLOYEE

**employment** occupation, situation, job, work, trade, craft, business, profession, vocation, post, appointment. UNEMPLOYMENT
use, utilization, exercise, application.

**emporium** store, shop, market, mart, bazaar, fair.

**empower** authorize, warrant, license, commission, entitle, sanction, permit, allow, enable, qualify. DISQUALIFY

**empty** *adj*, void, unfilled, hollow, vacant, unoccupied, deserted, uninhabited, devoid, destitute, bare, blank, clear. FULL
futile, useless, vain, aimless, meaningless, worthless, senseless, insignificant, trivial, idle, hollow, insincere, unsubstantial. MEANINGFUL
expressionless, vacuous, blank, vacant, silly, inane.
*v*, drain, exhaust, deplete, void, evacuate, vacate, clear, discharge, unload, pour out, disembogue. FILL

**empyreal** empyrean, aerial, ethereal, celestial, heavenly, sublime, unworldly. EARTHLY

**emulate** imitate, copy, follow, take after, rival, compete with, vie with, equal, match.

**emulation** imitation, competition, rivalry, envy.

**emulous** imitative, competitive, competing, emulating, aspiring.

**enable** capacitate, qualify, arm, equip, empower, authorize, sanction, permit, allow, facilitate, assist. PREVENT

**enact** decree, ordain, pronounce, rule, establish, legislate, ratify, sanction, authorize. ABROGATE
perform, act out, play, act, represent, portray.

**enactment** decree, ordinance, edict, proclamation, law, statute, rule, act, legislation, ratification.
performance, acting, representation, portrayal.

**enamour** charm, captivate, enchant, bewitch, fascinate, endear, infatuate. REPEL

**encamp** camp, pitch camp, bivouac, lodge, settle.

**encampment** camp, campsite, bivouac, base, lodgment, quarters.

**encase** box, crate, pack, enclose, wrap, sheathe.

**enchain** shackle, fetter, manacle, bind, hold, rivet. LOOSE

**enchant** captivate, charm, beguile, win, fascinate, delight, enamour. REPEL
bewitch, spellbind, entrance, enthral, hypnotize, mesmerize, cast a spell on.

**enchanting** delightful, charming, captivating, winning, alluring, attractive, winsome, lovely, beguiling, fascinating, appealing, endearing. REPULSIVE

**enchantment** spell, charm, incantation, magic, sorcery, witchcraft.
delight, charm, fascination, allurement, bliss, rapture, captivation, mesmerism. REPULSION

**encircle** encompass, surround, gird, circumscribe, ring, environ, hem in, enclose.

**enclose** surround, encircle, encompass, fence, encase, envelop, wrap, hem in, confine, cage, hold, contain, include, embrace. EXCLUDE

**enclosure** pound, compound, paddock, pen, yard, arena, ring, close, cloister.
fence, railings, palisade, hedge, wall, barricade.

**encomium** eulogy, panegyric, laudation, homage, tribute, praise, acclaim. VITUPERATION

**encompass** encircle, surround, circumscribe, gird, environ, ring, enclose.
include, embrace, cover, comprise, contain, comprehend, embody. EXCLUDE

**encounter** *v*, meet, happen upon, come across, bump into (*inf*), accost, confront, face, experience, undergo. AVOID
fight, contend, grapple, struggle, clash with, do battle with.
*n*, meeting, confrontation, brush.
clash, conflict, combat, engagement, skirmish, battle, fight, contest, action.

**encourage** hearten, cheer, rally, buoy up, reassure, comfort, inspirit, rouse, animate, stimulate, embolden, incite, persuade, urge, exhort, egg on, spur. DISCOURAGE
support, advocate, back, help, aid, abet, foster, promote, advance, further, boost.

**encroach** intrude, invade, trespass, infringe, impinge, trench, overstep, arrogate, usurp.

**encrust** plaster, coat, cover, face, overlay.

**encumber** hamper, hinder, impede, obstruct, clog, burden, load, weigh down, oppress, saddle, cramp, trammel. RELIEVE

**encumbrance** hindrance, impediment, obstacle, handicap, inconvenience, burden, load, millstone, drag.

**end** *v*, finish, conclude, terminate, close, complete, cease, stop, wind up, culminate. START
kill, destroy, exterminate, annihilate, eradicate, abolish.
*n*, finish, conclusion, termination, close, completion, cessation, stoppage, ending, finale, denouement, culmination. BEGINNING
extremity, tip, limit, bound, boundary, edge, border, terminus.
aim, object, purpose, intention, reason, design, goal, objective.
scrap, fragment, remnant, stub, butt.
death, demise, ruin, destruction, annihilation, extinction, extermination. BIRTH
result, consequence, event, outcome, issue, upshot.

**endanger** imperil, jeopardize, hazard, risk, expose, commit, compromise. PROTECT

**endear** attract, charm, win, captivate, attach, engage. ALIENATE

**endearing** attractive, charming, winning, adorable, lovable, sweet, winsome. REPULSIVE

**endearment** affection, fondness, love, attachment. HATRED loving word, sweet nothing, pet name, caress, hug, kiss.

**endeavour** *v*, try, attempt, strive, struggle, labour, essay, aspire, aim, do one's best, have a go (*inf*).

*n*, attempt, try, essay, go (*inf*), shot (*inf*), struggle, effort, venture, enterprise, undertaking, aim.

**endemic** local, indigenous, native, present, restricted, confined. UNIVERSAL

**endless** unending, boundless, unlimited, limitless, immeasurable, interminable, unceasing, ceaseless, incessant, constant, perpetual, continuous, uninterrupted, eternal, everlasting, infinite, immortal, undying. FINITE

**endorse** approve, sanction, ratify, confirm, authorize, support, back, second, advocate, champion, vouch for, sustain, uphold.

sign, countersign, superscribe.

**endow** bestow, bequeath, will, leave, give, present, supply, provide, furnish, grant, award, invest, endue. DIVEST

**endowment** bequest, legacy, grant, award, gift, benefaction, bounty, fund, provision, revenue, inheritance.

talent, gift, faculty, attribute, quality, property, aptitude, ability.

**endue** invest, endow, provide, supply, furnish. DIVEST

**endurance** fortitude, stamina, patience, resignation, stoicism, tolerance, perseverance, persistence, tenacity. WEAKNESS

permanence, durability, stability, immutability, duration, continuance. IMPERMANENCE

**endure** bear, stand, brook, tolerate, permit, allow, abide, stomach, swallow, put up with, suffer, undergo, experience, sustain, withstand.

last, persist, remain, continue, abide, prevail, survive. PERISH

**enemy** adversary, opponent, foe, rival, antagonist. ALLY

**energetic** vigorous, active, lively, dynamic, spirited, tireless, busy, strenuous, forceful, powerful, strong. LETHARGIC

**energize** invigorate, animate, enliven, stimulate, galvanize, activate. ENERVATE

**energy** vigour, activity, vitality, stamina, intensity, force, strength, power, drive, dynamism, animation, spirit, life, vivacity, zeal, ardour, fire. LETHARGY

**enervate** weaken, debilitate, enfeeble, unman, unnerve, sap, tire, exhaust, prostrate, disable, incapacitate, paralyse. INVIGORATE

**enfeeble** weaken, debilitate, enervate, devitalize, unman, unnerve, sap, tire, exhaust, wear out. STRENGTHEN

**enfold** envelop, wrap, swathe, shroud, enclose, encompass, embrace, clasp, hug.

**enforce** impose, apply, administer, implement, execute, carry out, force, compel, oblige, urge, constrain, require, insist on, exact. WAIVE

**enfranchise** emancipate, liberate, free, release, manumit, disenthral. ENSLAVE

**engage** hire, employ, take on, enlist, enrol, commission, appoint. DISMISS

engross, occupy, busy, absorb, involve, tie up.

attract, allure, draw, catch, win, captivate, charm. REPEL

pledge, promise, vow, undertake, agree, commit, bind, oblige.

participate, take part, embark on, take up, practise.

fight, battle, combat, attack, take on, encounter, meet. RETREAT

interlock, mesh, join, activate, apply. DISENGAGE

**engaged** betrothed, affianced, pledged, spoken for.

busy, occupied, in use, unavailable, tied up, involved, engrossed, absorbed. FREE

**engagement** betrothal, pledge, promise, vow, oath, assurance, contract, pact, covenant, bond, obligation, commitment.

appointment, meeting, rendezvous, date, assignation, arrangement, commitment.

employment, job, post, situation, work, business.

fight, battle, conflict, encounter, skirmish, action. RETREAT

**engaging** charming, delightful, enchanting, captivating, winning, appealing, attractive, pleasing, agreeable. REPULSIVE

**engender** produce, cause, occasion, bring about, create, generate, give rise to, provoke. SUPPRESS

beget, breed, procreate, propagate, sire, give birth to, spawn.

**engine** locomotive, motor, machine, mechanism, device, contrivance, implement, tool, instrument, agent, means.

**engineer** *n*, designer, architect, inventor, originator, planner, deviser.
*v*, plan, devise, contrive, manoeuvre, cause, bring about, direct, mastermind, orchestrate.

**engorge** devour, bolt, gulp, wolf, gobble, gorge, cram, stuff.

**engrave** inscribe, etch, cut, carve, chisel, chase.
imprint, impress, stamp, fix, lodge. ERASE

**engraving** print, impression, etching, woodcut, carving, inscription, plate, block.

**engross** absorb, immerse, occupy, engage, involve, preoccupy, grip, hold, fix, arrest, monopolize, corner. BORE

**engulf** consume, swallow up, overwhelm, swamp, flood, inundate, bury, immerse, submerge, plunge, absorb, engross.

**enhance** heighten, intensify, increase, swell, augment, raise, boost, improve, enrich, strengthen, reinforce. DEPRECIATE

**enigma** mystery, riddle, conundrum, puzzle. SOLUTION

**enigmatic** puzzling, perplexing, cryptic, mysterious, obscure, recondite, occult, esoteric, abstruse, incomprehensible, unfathomable, unintelligible, ambiguous, equivocal, inscrutable. PLAIN

**enjoin** order, command, direct, charge, instruct, require, bid, urge, advise, counsel, admonish, warn.
ban, prohibit, proscribe, disallow, forbid, interdict. PERMIT

**enjoy** like, love, relish, appreciate, take pleasure in, delight in, revel in. DETEST
possess, own, have, benefit from, experience, use. LOSE

**enjoy oneself,** have fun, have a good time, have a ball (*inf*).

**enjoyable** pleasant, agreeable, delightful, lovely, amusing, entertaining, delicious, delectable. ABOMINABLE

**enjoyment** delight, pleasure, gratification, amusement, entertainment, relish, joy, happiness, fun. DISPLEASURE
possession, ownership, use, benefit, advantage.

**enkindle** kindle, ignite, set fire to, light, fire. EXTINGUISH
arouse, stir, provoke, inflame, excite, stimulate. DAMP

**enlarge** expand, increase, augment, wax, swell, grow, amplify, magnify, extend, stretch, broaden, distend, dilate, inflate, heighten. DIMINISH
expatiate, descant, expound, develop, elaborate.

**enlargement** expansion, increase, augmentation, amplification, extension, magnification, dilation. CONTRACTION

**enlighten** instruct, edify, teach, educate, inform, apprise. CONFUSE

**enlightened** aware, informed, knowledgeable, educated, civilized, refined, sophisticated, broad-minded, liberal. IGNORANT

**enlightenment** understanding, awareness, insight, education, instruction, edification, information, learning, knowledge, wisdom, refinement, cultivation, broadmindedness. IGNORANCE

**enlist** engage, enrol, sign up, register, recruit, secure, obtain, draft, conscript, volunteer, join up.

**enliven** animate, invigorate, stimulate, inspirit, excite, rouse, fire. DAMP
brighten, cheer up, perk up, gladden, hearten.

**enmesh** entangle, snarl, catch, ensnare, trap, embroil, involve. EXTRICATE

**enmity** hostility, animosity, strife, discord, hate, antagonism, bad blood, rancour, ill will, bitterness, spite, malice, malignity. FRIENDSHIP

**ennoble** elevate, raise, aggrandize, magnify, exalt, glorify, dignify, honour. DEGRADE

**ennui** boredom, tedium, languor, lassitude, listlessness, lethargy. ENERGY

**enormity** atrocity, outrage, scandal, horror, monstrosity, abomination, outrageousness, wickedness, villainy, heinousness, depravity, disgrace.

**enormous** huge, gigantic, massive, immense, colossal, vast, elephantine, gargantuan, mammoth, tremendous, prodigious, stupendous. TINY

**enough** *adj*, sufficient, adequate, ample, abundant, plentiful. INSUFFICIENT
*n*, sufficiency, adequacy, plenty, abundance. INSUFFICIENCY
*adv*, sufficiently, adequately, tolerably, passably, reasonably, moderately, abundantly, amply. INSUFFICIENTLY

**enquire** ask, question, interrogate, query, examine, inquire, investigate, look into, probe, explore.

**enquiry** question, query, interrogation, inquest, inquiry, investigation, survey, study.

**enrage** incense, infuriate, madden, exasperate, anger, rouse, provoke, inflame, irritate, annoy. PACIFY

**enrapture** delight, enchant, entrance, fascinate, captivate, bewitch, charm, ravish, transport. REPEL

**enrich** endow, make rich, enhance, improve, ameliorate, refine, augment, supplement, develop, aggrandize, uplift. IMPOVERISH
adorn, deck, decorate, ornament, embellish, beautify. DISFIGURE

**enrol** matriculate, register, enlist, sign up, join up, recruit, admit.
record, chronicle, list, note.

**ensconce** nestle, snuggle up, curl up, settle, lodge, install.
hide, screen, cover, shield, protect, shelter. EXPOSE

**ensemble** *n*, whole, totality, entirety, aggregate, assemblage, sum. ELEMENT
outfit, costume, attire, getup (*inf*).
group, company, troupe, band, choir, cast.
*adv*, together, en masse, as a group, in concert, at the same time, all at once. INDIVIDUALLY

**enshrine** dedicate, consecrate, hallow, sanctify, revere, immortalize, cherish, treasure, preserve, embalm.

**ensign** banner, standard, flag, pennant, colours, insignia, badge, emblem, device.

**enslave** subjugate, subject, master, dominate, bind, enchain, fetter. LIBERATE

**ensnare** snare, trap, entrap, catch, net, enmesh, entangle, inveigle, allure. LOOSE

**ensue** follow, come next, succeed, proceed, result, arise, issue, happen, occur, turn up. PRECEDE

**ensure** guarantee, assure, make sure, secure, confirm, certify.
guard, safeguard, protect. IMPERIL

**entail** involve, necessitate, call for, demand, require, occasion, cause, result in, bring about, impose.

**entangle** enmesh, embroil, involve, implicate, ensnare, entrap, catch, tangle, snarl, knot, ravel, muddle, confuse, perplex, puzzle, bewilder. EXTRICATE

**entanglement** tangle, knot, muddle, confusion, perplexity, bewilderment, complication, intricacy, involvement, difficulty.

**enter** go into, come into, arrive, penetrate, pierce, invade, introduce, insert. LEAVE
record, note, register, log, take down, inscribe. EXPUNGE
join, enrol, enlist, embark on, set about, begin, start, commence, participate in, engage in.

**enterprise** undertaking, venture, project, plan, effort, endeavour, attempt.
initiative, resourcefulness, gumption (*inf*), drive, energy, push (*inf*), get-up-and-go (*inf*), courage, boldness, daring, adventurousness, readiness, enthusiasm, zeal. TIMIDITY
business, company, firm, establishment, concern.

**enterprising** venturesome, adventurous, bold, daring, eager, ready, energetic, vigorous, strenuous, zealous, enthusiastic, spirited, active, alert, resourceful, inventive. APATHETIC

**entertain** amuse, divert, occupy, interest, please, charm, regale, cheer. BORE
receive, welcome, accommodate, lodge, host, have company, throw a party (*inf*).
harbour, foster, nurture, cherish, hold, consider, contemplate, ponder. BANISH

**entertainment** amusement, diversion, recreation, pastime, sport, play, fun, pleasure, enjoyment.
show, performance, carnival, festival, gala, spectacle.

**enthral** captivate, charm, fascinate, spellbind, entrance, enchant, beguile, thrill, hypnotize, rivet, transport, enrapture. BORE

**enthrone** crown, install, ennoble, exalt, glorify, honour, elevate, aggrandize, idolize. DETHRONE

**enthusiasm** zeal, ardour, fervour, passion, frenzy, vehemence, keenness, eagerness, avidity, earnestness, excitement, warmth, devotion, fanaticism, mania, craze. APATHY

**enthusiast** zealot, devotee, admirer, supporter, fanatic, fan, aficionado, buff (*inf*), fiend (*inf*).

**enthusiastic** keen, eager, avid, earnest, ardent, fervent, fervid, warm, whole-hearted, devoted, vehement, zealous, passionate, spirited, lively, exuberant, ebullient, excited. INDIFFERENT

**entice** tempt, lure, allure, attract, draw, seduce, inveigle, cajole, wheedle, coax, persuade. DETER

**enticement** bait, lure, decoy, temptation, allurement, attraction, seduction, cajolery, persuasion. DETERRENT

**entire** complete, whole, total, full, unbroken, undivided, intact, perfect, pure, unalloyed, unimpaired, thorough, absolute, unmitigated, unqualified, exhaustive, comprehensive. PARTIAL

**entirely** completely, wholly, totally, fully, perfectly, absolutely, utterly, in every respect, without reservation. PARTIALLY

**entirety** completeness, wholeness, totality, fullness, unity, aggregate, ensemble, sum total, whole. PART

**entitle** qualify, authorize, empower, permit, allow, enable, license. DISQUALIFY
name, style, call, dub, christen, designate, denominate, term.

**entity** thing, object, body, creature, being, existence, essence, quiddity.

**entomb** bury, inter, inhume, sepulchre. EXHUME

**entourage** attendants, staff, retinue, suite, train, cortege, escort, followers, companions.
surroundings, environment, milieu, ambience.

**entrails** intestines, bowels, guts, viscera, offal, insides, innards (*inf*).

**entrance**[1] *n*, entry, admission, admittance, entrée, access, way in, ingress, door, gate, portal, opening, inlet, passage, lobby, vestibule, foyer. EXIT
appearance, arrival, introduction, debut, beginning, start, commencement, outset. DEPARTURE

**entrance**[2] *v*, enrapture, charm, enchant, captivate, ravish, transport, delight, fascinate, enthral, spellbind, hypnotize, mesmerize. REPEL

**entrant** newcomer, novice, beginner, tyro, neophyte, new member, initiate, convert.
competitor, contestant, entry, candidate, applicant, player, participant.

**entrap** trap, snare, ensnare, catch, net, entangle, enmesh, involve, implicate, embroil, inveigle, lure, trick, lead on. LOOSE

**entreat** beg, implore, plead, crave, supplicate, petition, beseech, enjoin, pray, importune, ask, request. COMMAND

**entreaty** appeal, plea, prayer, suit, petition, supplication, cry, request. ORDER

**entrench** establish, fix, dig in, embed, root, implant, lodge, settle. MOVE
encroach, trespass, infringe, impinge, intrude.

**entrust** commit, confide, consign, hand over, deliver, commend, assign, delegate.

**entry** entrance, admission, admittance, entrée, access, way in, ingress, avenue, passage, door, gate, opening, inlet. EXIT
appearance, arrival, introduction, debut. DEPARTURE
item, note, record, minute, statement, memorandum.

**entwine** twine, weave, interweave, lace, interlace, twist, braid, plait, knit, splice, wind. SEPARATE

**enumerate** list, name, cite, detail, specify, itemize, recount, relate, tell, number, count, reckon, tally, calculate.

**enumeration** list, catalogue, listing, naming, recapitulation, specification, itemization, narration, counting, reckoning, calculation.

**enunciate** articulate, pronounce, intone, vocalize, voice, utter, say, speak, express. STAMMER
state, assert, declare, proclaim, announce, promulgate, publish. SUPPRESS

**enunciation** articulation, pronunciation, delivery, presentation, intonation, modulation, inflection, voice, utterance, speech.
statement, assertion, declaration, proclamation, announcement.

**envelop** wrap, enwrap, enfold, sheathe, encase, cover, enshroud, hide, conceal, cloak, veil, surround, encompass, encircle, enclose. EXPOSE

**envelope** wrapper, wrapping, case, casing, sheath, cover, skin, shell, capsule, coating, covering.

**envenom** poison, contaminate, pollute, taint.
embitter, sour, exacerbate, anger, enrage, incense, madden, provoke, inflame, irritate. APPEASE

**enviable** desirable, covetable, favoured, privileged, lucky, fortunate. UNENVIABLE

**envious** covetous, desirous, jealous, grudging, begrudging, resentful, dissatisfied. CONTENT

**environ** encircle, surround, encompass, gird, ring, circumscribe, enclose, envelop, hem in.

**environment** surroundings, milieu, circumstances, conditions, element, medium, habitat, background, setting, atmosphere, ambience.

**environs** vicinity, neighbourhood, district, locality, surroundings, suburbs, outskirts.

**envisage** visualize, imagine, picture, contemplate, conceive, envision, foresee, anticipate.

**envoy** agent, representative, diplomat, ambassador, minister, plenipotentiary, legate, emissary, messenger, courier.

**envy** *v*, covet, desire, resent, grudge, begrudge, be jealous of.

*n*, enviousness, covetousness, desire, jealousy, resentment, grudge, malice, spite, discontent. CONTENTEDNESS

**ephemeral** transitory, transient, fleeting, passing, brief, short, short-lived, fugacious, evanescent, momentary, temporary. PERMANENT

**epic** *adj*, heroic, impressive, great, grand, legendary, historic.

*n*, saga, épopée, narrative, story, legend.

**epicure** epicurean, gourmet, gastronome, *bon vivant*, voluptuary, sensualist, hedonist, sybarite, gourmand, glutton.

**epidemic** *adj*, widespread, extensive, prevalent, rampant, rife, pandemic.

*n*, plague, outbreak, upsurge, increase, wave, rash.

**epigrammatic** laconic, terse, concise, succinct, pithy, sharp, pointed, pungent, piquant, witty. VERBOSE

**episode** incident, event, occurrence, happening, occasion, circumstance, affair, matter, adventure, experience.

instalment, chapter, section, part, scene.

**epistle** letter, missive, communication, message, note.

**epithet** name, title, appellation, designation, nickname, sobriquet, label, tag.

**epitome** personification, embodiment, archetype, exemplar, representation, quintessence.

summary, digest, abstract, compendium, précis, résumé, conspectus, synopsis, abridgment. AMPLIFICATION

**epitomize** typify, represent, exemplify, embody, personify, symbolize.

summarize, abridge, condense, abstract, shorten, abbreviate, contract, précis. AMPLIFY

**epoch** age, era, period, time, date.

**equable** placid, serene, calm, even-tempered, unruffled, collected, composed, imperturbable. EXCITABLE

even, uniform, unvarying, stable, constant, steady, regular, consistent. VARIABLE

**equal** *adj*, identical, the same, like, alike, equivalent, commensurate, proportionate, tantamount. DIFFERENT

even, unvarying, uniform, steady, regular, constant, level, balanced, matched, symmetrical. UNEQUAL

adequate, suitable, fit, competent, capable, able. UNSUITABLE

*n*, peer, compeer, fellow, partner, mate, match, twin, counterpart, equivalent.

*v*, match, parallel, correspond, balance, come up to, rival, amount to.

**equality** uniformity, evenness, equivalence, parity, par, symmetry, balance, sameness, identity, correspondence, justice, fairness, impartiality, egalitarianism. INEQUALITY

**equalize** level, even up, square, make equal, match, balance, regularize, equate.

**equanimity** composure, self-possession, calmness, serenity, tranquillity, placidity, imperturbability, coolness, sang-froid, aplomb. AGITATION

**equate** compare, liken, parallel, pair, offset, balance, correspond, equalize.

**equestrian** rider, jockey, horseman, horsewoman, equestrienne, knight, cavalryman, dragoon. PEDESTRIAN

**equilibrium** balance, equipoise, stability, parity, symmetry.

equanimity, composure, calmness, sang-froid, aplomb, self-possession, coolness, poise. AGITATION

**equip** supply, furnish, provide, fit out, rig, prepare, stock, arm, dress, array, accoutre. DIVEST

**equipage** carriage, coach.

accoutrements, paraphernalia, belongings, effects, baggage, outfit, gear, equipment, stores, munitions, materiel.

**equipment** apparatus, tackle, rig, tools, accoutrements, furniture, outfit, gear, kit, supplies, belongings, effects, baggage, paraphernalia.

**equipoise** balance, equilibrium, counterbalance, counterpoise.

**equitable** just, fair, even-handed, impartial, unbiased, disinterested, right, rightful, proper, reasonable. UNJUST

**equity** justice, fairness, impartiality, objectivity, rightfulness, reasonableness, rectitude, honesty, integrity. INJUSTICE

**equivalence** parity, equality, identity, sameness, correlation, correspondence, similarity, analogy, parallel. DIFFERENCE

**equivalent** *adj*, equal, equipollent, commensurate, tantamount, synonymous, the same, interchangeable, comparable, correspondent, similar, alike. DIFFERENT
*n*, same, equivalence, match, twin, counterpart, equal, parallel.

**equivocal** ambiguous, ambivalent, vague, obscure, uncertain, indefinite, oblique, evasive, misleading, dubious, questionable, doubtful, suspicious. CLEAR

**equivocate** prevaricate, fence, hedge, dodge, evade, shuffle, shift, quibble, fudge, tergiversate, beat about the bush (*inf*).

**equivocation** prevarication, evasion, hedging, ambiguity, vagueness, tergiversation, waffle (*inf*).

**era** epoch, age, period, time, date, day, cycle, generation.

**eradicate** annihilate, extirpate, destroy, exterminate, efface, obliterate, stamp out, uproot, deracinate, remove, abolish, extinguish, eliminate. RESTORE

**eradication** annihilation, extirpation, destruction, extermination, obliteration, deracination, abolition, extinction, elimination. RESTORATION

**erase** expunge, rub out, eradicate, obliterate, efface, remove, delete, cancel, blot out. ENGRAVE

**erasure** rubbing out, eradication, obliteration, effacement, removal, deletion. ENGRAVING

**erect** *v*, build, construct, put up, set up, found, establish, raise, lift up, stand up, rear, elevate. DEMOLISH
*adj*, upright, vertical, straight, raised, standing, firm, stiff, rigid. FLAT

**erection** building, construction, structure, edifice.
raising, elevation, fabrication, construction, assembly. DEMOLITION

**eremite** recluse, hermit, solitary, anchorite.

**ergo** therefore, hence, consequently, so, thus.

**eristic** polemic, polemical, controversial, disputative, disputatious, argumentative.

**erode** wear, eat away, corrode, abrade, grind down, consume, devour, destroy, deteriorate.

**erosion** wear, attrition, corrosion, abrasion, eating away, consumption, destruction, deterioration.

**erotic** aphrodisiac, seductive, titillating, sexy (*inf*), carnal, sensual, voluptuous, amatory.

**err** miscalculate, misjudge, be wrong, make a mistake, blunder, slip up (*inf*).
sin, transgress, do wrong, go astray, lapse, fall, wander, stray, deviate.

**errand** commission, mission, assignment, task, charge, message.

**errant** erring, wrong, incorrect, straying, deviant, aberrant. RIGHT
wandering, roving, roaming, rambling, travelling, itinerant.

**erratic** changeable, capricious, variable, irregular, inconsistent, unstable, unreliable, unpredictable, aberrant, eccentric, abnormal, desultory, wandering. STEADY

**erratum** error, mistake, misprint, typo (*inf*), omission, corrigendum, correction.

**erroneous** wrong, incorrect, mistaken, untrue, false, inexact, inaccurate, unfounded, unsound, faulty. RIGHT

**error** mistake, inaccuracy, slip, blunder, oversight, omission, miscalculation, misapprehension, fault, flaw, fallacy. ACCURACY
offence, transgression, trespass, sin, wrong, wrongdoing, misdeed, fault, crime.

**ersatz** artificial, imitation, simulated, synthetic, sham, bogus, counterfeit, spurious. GENUINE

**erudite** learned, scholarly, knowledgeable, well-read, educated, literate, cultured, refined. ILLITERATE

**erudition** learning, scholarship, knowledge, lore, education, culture, refinement. ILLITERACY

**erupt** eject, emit, discharge, gush, spout, burst forth, break out, burst open, explode, blow up.

**eruption** ejection, emission, discharge, outburst, outbreak, explosion.
rash, inflammation.

**escalate** increase, grow, intensify, heighten, step up, raise, rise, mount, expand, magnify. DIMINISH

**escapade** adventure, scrape (*inf*), prank, caper, stunt, trick, romp, lark (*inf*).

**escape** *v*, get away, break free, flee, fly, run away, bolt, decamp, abscond. STAY
avoid, evade, dodge, elude. FACE
leak, seep, drain, flow, issue, gush, spurt.
*n*, getaway, flight, decampment, departure, break-out, release.
avoidance, evasion, elusion.
leak, leakage, seepage, discharge, emission, outflow, gush, spurt.

**eschew** shun, avoid, steer clear of, abstain from, forgo, refrain from, elude, shrink from.

**escort** *n*, companion, partner, chaperon, attendant, guide, protector, bodyguard.
entourage, cortege, retinue, company, convoy, guard, protection.
*v*, accompany, attend, conduct, guide, lead, usher, chaperon, protect, guard.

**esculent** edible, eatable, wholesome. INEDIBLE

**escutcheon** shield, scutcheon, arms.

**esoteric** abstruse, recondite, inscrutable, occult, cryptic, obscure, hidden, arcane, private, secret. EXOTERIC

**especial** special, exceptional, unusual, outstanding, marked, notable, remarkable, distinguished, signal, principal, chief. ORDINARY
particular, singular, individual, specific, distinctive, unique, personal, peculiar.

**espousal** adoption, support, advocacy, promotion, maintenance, defence, championship. REJECTION

**espouse** adopt, embrace, take up, support, uphold, maintain, defend, champion, advocate, promote. REJECT

**espy** notice, perceive, catch sight of, see, descry, make out, discern, detect, spot, glimpse, observe. MISS

**essay** *n*, composition, dissertation, treatise, article, paper, commentary, piece.
attempt, try, endeavour, effort, bid, go, shot, trial, test, experiment.
*v*, attempt, endeavour, try, have a go, strive, aim, test, try out.

**essence** quintessence, quiddity, principle, nature, entity, being, substance, pith, core, heart, spirit, life, significance, meaning.
concentrate, extract, distillate.

**essential** *adj*, vital, indispensable, crucial, important, necessary, requisite. DISPENSABLE
basic, fundamental, inherent, intrinsic, principal, main.
*n*, necessity, requisite, must, fundamental, rudiment, vital part.

**establish** found, start, form, set up, institute, organize, create, base, plant, settle, install, entrench, lodge, secure, fix. UPROOT
prove, substantiate, demonstrate, validate, confirm, certify, verify, ratify, support, corroborate. REFUTE

**establishment** foundation, institution, organization, creation, formation, setting up, installation.
business, concern, firm, company, corporation, house, organization, institute, institution, system.
household, house, home, abode, domicile, residence.

**estate** land, demesne, manor, lands, property, assets, effects, belongings, possessions, holdings, wealth.
status, standing, position, station, condition, rank, class.

**esteem** *v*, respect, admire, think highly of, value, prize, treasure, cherish, love, like, hold dear, honour, revere, venerate. SCORN
deem, consider, regard, judge, think, believe, reckon, hold.
*n*, respect, admiration, estimation, regard, consideration, honour, reverence, veneration, love. CONTEMPT

**estimable** admirable, respected, esteemed, valued, honourable, worthy, meritorious, deserving, good, excellent. DESPICABLE

**estimate** *v*, reckon, gauge, guess, assess, evaluate, value, appraise, rate, rank, judge.
*n*, reckoning, rough calculation, educated guess, approximation, guesstimate (*inf*), assessment, evaluation, valuation, appraisal, judgment, opinion, estimation.

**estimation** judgment, opinion, belief, view, consideration, estimate, evaluation, assessment, reckoning.
esteem, respect, regard, honour, credit, admiration, reverence. CONTEMPT

**estrange** alienate, disaffect, antagonize, separate, divide, disunite, withdraw. RECONCILE

**estuary** inlet, mouth, firth, fiord, creek.

**etch** corrode, eat into, cut, engrave, carve, incise, impress, stamp, imprint.

**etching** print, impression, engraving, inscription.

**eternal** everlasting, enduring, abiding, immortal, undying, imperishable, unchanging, infinite, unending, endless, interminable, incessant, ceaseless, perpetual, continuous, perennial. TRANSIENT

**eternity** perpetuity, infinity, timelessness, evermore, forever, ages.
immortality, afterlife, hereafter, heaven.

**ethereal** light, airy, impalpable, delicate, fine, dainty, insubstantial, tenuous, subtle, rarefied, heavenly, celestial, empyreal, spiritual.

**ethical** moral, right, proper, just, fair, righteous, honest, upright, conscientious, honourable, decent, principled. UNETHICAL

**ethnic** racial, native, indigenous, national, traditional, cultural.

**etiolate** bleach, whiten, blanch, pale, fade, wash out, achromatize.

**etiquette** propriety, decorum, manners, politeness, protocol, form, convention, code, usage. IMPROPRIETY

**Eucharist** Communion, Lord's Supper, Mass.

**eulogize** praise, extol, laud, panegyrize, exalt, glorify, acclaim, commend. CENSURE

**eulogy** panegyric, encomium, praise, laudation, paean, accolade, plaudit, acclaim, commendation, exaltation, glorification. OBLOQUY

**euphonious** euphonic, melodious, harmonious, tuneful, dulcet, musical, mellifluous, mellow, clear, silvery. CACOPHONOUS

**euphony** harmony, melody, tunefulness, music, sweetness, smoothness, mellowness. HARSHNESS

**euphoria** elation, bliss, ecstasy, joy, rapture, jubilation, exhilaration, intoxication. DESPONDENCY

**evacuate** leave, depart, quit, withdraw, vacate, clear, abandon, desert, forsake. OCCUPY
empty, void, eject, expel, discharge, eliminate, excrete, defecate.

**evacuation** departure, exodus, withdrawal, retreat, emptying, clearance. OCCUPATION
ejection, expulsion, discharge, elimination, defecation, excretion.

**evade** avoid, circumvent, escape, get away from, dodge, elude, sidestep, shun, steer clear of. FACE
quibble, prevaricate, equivocate, fence, hedge.

**evaluate** appraise, assess, value, estimate, weigh, calculate, gauge, reckon, judge, rate.

**evanesce** fade, dissipate, disperse, evaporate, dissolve, melt, disappear, vanish. APPEAR

**evanescent** fading, vanishing, fleeting, passing, brief, ephemeral, transient, transitory. PERMANENT

**evaporate** vaporize, exhale, dry, dehydrate, desiccate. CONDENSE
disappear, vanish, dematerialize, fade, evanesce, dissolve, melt, dissipate, dispel. APPEAR

**evaporation** vaporization, exhalation, dehydration, desiccation. CONDENSATION
disappearance, dematerialization, evanescence, dissipation, dispersion. APPEARANCE

**evasion** avoidance, circumvention, escape, dodge, ruse, artifice, subterfuge, prevarication, equivocation, tergiversation, sophistry.

**evasive** prevaricating, equivocating, indirect, oblique, devious, misleading, deceptive, deceitful, tricky, slippery, elusive, cagey (*inf*). STRAIGHTFORWARD

**even** *adj*, level, smooth, flat, plane, uniform, regular, steady, constant, unvarying, equable, equal, parallel, abreast, symmetrical, balanced. UNEVEN
same, identical, equal, level, neck and neck, square, similar, like. UNEQUAL
calm, placid, serene, tranquil, even-tempered, composed, unruffled, imperturbable. AGITATED
balanced, even-handed, fair, just, equitable, impartial, unbiased. UNJUST
*adv*, notwithstanding, in spite of, although, even so, yet, still, nonetheless, all the more.
just, exactly, precisely, at the same time.
*v*, level, smooth, flatten, equalize, square, align, steady, balance.

**evening** dusk, twilight, nightfall, eventide, sunset. MORNING

**event** happening, occurrence, incident, affair, matter, occasion, episode, circumstance, fact.
consequence, result, outcome, upshot, issue, sequel. CAUSE
**in any event,** come what may, regardless, irrespective, at any rate, in any case, anyway.

**eventful** busy, full, lively, memorable, notable, remarkable, signal, momentous, significant, important, crucial, critical. UNEVENTFUL

**eventual** final, ultimate, resulting, consequent, prospective, future, inevitable.

**eventually** finally, ultimately, at last, in the end, in the long run, sooner or later.

**eventuate** result, issue, follow, ensue, happen, come about, end. BEGIN

**ever** always, continually, perpetually, constantly, relentlessly, at all times, forever, eternally, evermore, to the end of time. NEVER
at any time, on any occasion, by any chance, at all.

**everlasting** eternal, undying, imperishable, immortal, enduring, abiding, unchanging, infinite, endless, unending, perpetual, continuous, incessant, ceaseless, unremitting, interminable. PASSING

**evermore** always, ever, eternally, perpetually, forever.

**every** all, each. NO

**everyday** ordinary, common, commonplace, usual, habitual, routine, accustomed, customary, conventional, familiar, mundane, workaday, run-of-the-mill. UNUSUAL

**evict** expel, eject, turn out, kick out (*inf*), remove, oust, dispossess. HOUSE

**evidence** *n*, proof, verification, confirmation, substantiation, documentation, data, grounds, testimony, deposition, indication, sign, mark, demonstration.
*v*, evince, manifest, show, demonstrate, denote, indicate.

**evident** apparent, plain, clear, obvious, patent, manifest, visible, palpable, conspicuous, unmistakable, indisputable, incontrovertible.

**evil** *adj*, wrong, bad, sinful, wicked, iniquitous, base, vile, immoral, corrupt, villainous, vicious, malevolent, malignant, malicious, nefarious. GOOD
harmful, pernicious, injurious, baleful, baneful, noxious, deleterious, mischievous, hurtful, ruinous. BENEFICIAL
disastrous, calamitous, adverse, ill, unfortunate, unlucky, unpropitious, inauspicious. LUCKY
foul, vile, offensive, unpleasant, noxious, pestilential. PLEASANT
*n*, wrong, badness, sin, wickedness, iniquity, baseness, vice, immorality, depravity, corruption, malevolence, malignity, maleficence. GOODNESS
harm, ill, injury, hurt, mischief, affliction, suffering, pain, sorrow, misery, ruin, disaster, calamity.

**evince** evidence, show, display, exhibit, manifest, establish, indicate, demonstrate, betoken, reveal. CONCEAL

**eviscerate** disembowel, gut, draw.

**evoke** summon, call, elicit, educe, rouse, provoke, stimulate, stir, excite, awaken, rekindle, conjure up, call forth, invoke. STIFLE

**evolution** development, evolvement, unfolding, progression, growth, expansion, increase, ripening, maturation. RETROGRESSION

**evolve** develop, unfold, unroll, open, progress, grow, expand, increase, result, emerge. RETROGRESS

**exacerbate** aggravate, worsen, intensify, inflame, irritate, provoke, infuriate, exasperate, enrage, madden, embitter, envenom. SOOTHE

**exacerbation** aggravation, intensification, irritation, provocation, infuriation, exasperation. APPEASEMENT

**exact** *adj*, precise, accurate, correct, right, faultless, faithful, literal, strict, rigid, specific, explicit, definite. INEXACT
careful, meticulous, scrupulous, punctilious, particular, exacting, conscientious, painstaking, methodical, orderly, critical, rigorous, severe. LOOSE
*v*, extort, extract, wring, elicit, compel, impose, demand, require, call for, insist on, ask, request, claim.

**exacting** difficult, hard, demanding, taxing, critical, rigorous, severe, harsh, oppressive, tough, stern, imperious. EASY

**exaction** extortion, extraction, demand, imposition, requisition, tribute.

**exactitude** exactness, precision, accuracy, correctness, faultlessness, faithfulness, fidelity, carefulness, scrupulousness, strictness, rigour. INEXACTITUDE

**exactly** precisely, accurately, faithfully, literally, definitely, strictly, scrupulously.
just, quite, absolutely, indeed, truly, of course.

**exaggerate** magnify, inflate, overstate, overdo, stretch, embroider, embellish, amplify, emphasize, overemphasize, hyperbolize, overestimate. UNDERSTATE

**exaggeration** overstatement, hyperbole, magnification, inflation, embellishment, amplification, overestimation. UNDERSTATEMENT

**exalt** ennoble, elevate, raise, promote, advance, aggrandize, dignify, honour. DOWNGRADE
praise, extol, glorify, acclaim, applaud, commend. DISPARAGE
excite, stimulate, inspire, animate, exhilarate, thrill, elate. DAMP

**exaltation** ennoblement, elevation, promotion, advancement, aggrandizement, dignity, honour, grandeur, loftiness, eminence, prestige.
praise, laudation, extolment, glorification, acclaim, acclamation, tribute. DISPARAGEMENT
excitement, animation, elation, exhilaration, exultation, joy, rapture. DEPRESSION

**examination** inspection, scrutiny, inquiry, investigation, observation, study, survey, research, exploration, probe, analysis.
test, quiz, trial, interrogation.

**examine** inspect, investigate, scrutinize, study, analyse, explore, survey, research, look into, probe, sift, check out, observe. IGNORE
test, quiz, question, interrogate, cross-examine.

**example** sample, specimen, illustration, exemplification, instance, case, precedent, exemplar, model, pattern, standard, prototype, ideal, paragon.
warning, caution, lesson.

**exasperate** anger, incense, infuriate, enrage, vex, annoy, irritate, madden, irk, nettle, provoke, aggravate, exacerbate. APPEASE

**exasperation** anger, infuriation, fury, rage, vexation, annoyance, irritation, provocation, aggravation, exacerbation. APPEASEMENT

**excavate** dig, delve, burrow, tunnel, scoop, hollow, dig out, quarry, mine, dig up, unearth, disinter.

**excavation** hole, cavity, trench, trough, hollow, pit, mine, quarry, burrow, dugout, cutting, dig.

**exceed** surpass, outstrip, pass, outdo, beat, transcend, surmount, outshine, eclipse, excel, cap, top, go beyond, overstep.

**exceedingly** very, extremely, exceptionally, especially, greatly, vastly, tremendously, enormously, highly. SLIGHTLY

**excel** *vt*, surpass, outshine, eclipse, exceed, outstrip, outdo, outclass, beat, cap, top.
*vi*, shine, predominate, lead, be proficient, be talented, succeed.

**excellent** superior, first-rate, exceptional, outstanding, superlative, prime, capital, choice, select, first-class, supreme, matchless, sterling, fine, very good, admirable, estimable, worthy, eminent, great, splendid, wonderful, marvellous. INFERIOR

**except** *prep*, but, excepting, save, saving, other than, apart from, besides, excluding, barring. INCLUDING
*v*, omit, exclude, leave out, reject, bar, ban. INCLUDE

**exception** omission, exclusion, rejection, debarment. INCLUSION
anomaly, oddity, odd one out, freak, irregularity, peculiarity. RULE
**take exception,** object, demur, be offended, take offence.

**exceptional** anomalous, abnormal, aberrant, unusual, rare, uncommon, special, irregular, deviant, odd, strange, peculiar, extraordinary. NORMAL
outstanding, remarkable, excellent, prodigious, phenomenal, superior, above average. ORDINARY

**excerpt** *n*, extract, passage, section, citation, quotation, selection, pericope, fragment, piece.
*v*, extract, take, quote, cite, select, pick out.

**excess** *n*, surfeit, overabundance, glut, plethora, profusion, surplus, remainder, balance, superfluity. DEFICIENCY

overindulgence, immoderation, unrestraint, dissipation, debauchery, intemperance, extravagance. RESTRAINT
*adj*, extra, surplus, superfluous, spare, left-over. INSUFFICIENT

**excessive** immoderate, extreme, inordinate, undue, disproportionate, fulsome, unreasonable, needless, extravagant, exorbitant, too much, overmuch. MODERATE

**exchange** *v*, trade, barter, swap, change, interchange, commute, switch, substitute, reciprocate, bandy.
*n*, trade, barter, swap, change, interchange, commutation, switch, substitution, reciprocation.
market, fair, Bourse.

**excise**[1] *n*, duty, tax, impost, toll, customs.

**excise**[2] *v*, delete, expunge, cross out, cut out, remove.

**excitable** volatile, mercurial, nervous, highly-strung, emotional, passionate, sensitive, temperamental, quick-tempered, irascible, touchy. IMPERTURBABLE

**excite** rouse, arouse, awaken, stir up, animate, stimulate, kindle, evoke, raise, elicit, incite, provoke, spur, agitate, foment, disturb, inflame, inspire, galvanize, electrify, thrill, exhilarate. CALM

**excitement** animation, enthusiasm, passion, agitation, commotion, restlessness, fever, thrill, stimulation, exhilaration. CALMNESS
stimulus, provocation, incentive, motive, urge, impulse.

**exclaim** cry, shout, yell, vociferate, ejaculate, call, call out, declare.

**exclamation** cry, ejaculation, interjection, vociferation, call, shout, yell, clamour, outcry.

**exclude** ban, bar, debar, blackball, keep out, shut out, proscribe, prohibit, veto, disallow. ADMIT
omit, except, leave out, preclude, pass over, rule out, eliminate, reject, ignore. INCLUDE
expel, eject, throw out, oust, evict, remove.

**exclusion** omission, exception, elimination, rejection. INCLUSION
ban, bar, proscription, prohibition, veto, embargo. ADMISSION
expulsion, ejection, eviction, removal.

**exclusive** individual, sole, single, only, unique, unshared, undivided, total, full, complete. SHARED
limited, restricted, narrow, closed, cliquish, snobbish, select, choice, posh, elegant. COMMON
excluding, barring, excepting, omitting. INCLUSIVE

**excogitate** contrive, invent, devise, think up, coin, create, hatch, frame, conceive, imagine, contemplate, deliberate, ponder.

**excommunicate** exclude, remove, banish, expel, cast out, unchurch, anathematize, denounce, proscribe. ADMIT

**excoriate** skin, flay, strip, peel, scrape, abrade, gall, scarify.
denounce, condemn, censure, reprove, rebuke, reproach, upbraid, castigate, attack, scourge, vilify, defame. EXTOL

**excrement** excretion, excreta, faeces, stools, ordure, dung, droppings.

**excrescence** protuberance, lump, growth, swelling, tumour, protrusion, prominence, projection, outgrowth.

**excrete** discharge, eject, expel, eliminate, evacuate, void, defecate, urinate, egest, exude.

**excruciate** torment, torture, afflict, harrow, distress, agonize. SOOTHE

**excruciating** agonizing, painful, intense, severe, acute, unbearable, racking, harrowing, distressing. SOOTHING

**exculpate** exonerate, vindicate, clear, absolve, acquit, free, release, discharge, pardon. CHARGE

**excursion** trip, outing, jaunt, expedition, tour, ramble, drive, ride, journey.
digression, excursus, deviation, detour.

**excursive** discursive, digressive, rambling, wandering, roving, errant. DIRECT

**excuse** *v*, pardon, forgive, overlook, condone, tolerate, remit, absolve, exculpate, exonerate, acquit, clear, vindicate, justify, explain. CONDEMN
exempt, free, release, let off, spare, discharge, dismiss.
*n*, explanation, justification, defence, plea, apology, reason, grounds, pretext, pretence, feint, subterfuge, evasion, cop-out (*inf*).

**execrable** abominable, abhorrent, detestable, odious, hateful, horrible, vile, loathsome, obnoxious, repulsive, disgusting, damnable, accursed, bad, appalling, atrocious. DELIGHTFUL

**execrate** abominate, abhor, detest, loathe, hate, curse, damn, imprecate, revile, deplore, condemn, denounce. LOVE

**execute** perform, do, carry out, fulfil, complete, finish, accomplish, achieve, effect, enforce, enact, administer.
kill, put to death, behead, hang, electrocute, shoot.

**execution** performance, operation, discharge, fulfilment, completion, accomplishment, achievement, enforcement, implementation, administration.
killing, capital punishment, beheading, hanging, electrocution, shooting.
style, technique, manner, delivery, rendition, interpretation.

**executive** *n*, administration, management, government, leadership, administrator, manager, leader, director, official.
*adj*, administrative, managerial, directorial, governing, controlling.

**exegetic** explanatory, expository, explicative, interpretative.

**exemplary** model, admirable, estimable, commendable, praiseworthy, laudable, good, fine, excellent, worthy, honourable, perfect, ideal. DESPICABLE
admonitory, cautionary, warning.
typical, representative, illustrative.

**exemplify** illustrate, instance, show, demonstrate, exhibit, manifest, represent, embody.

**exempt** *v*, excuse, release, free, relieve, except, spare, let off, absolve, exonerate. COMPEL
*adj*, exempted, excused, released, free, spared, immune, not liable, excepted, privileged. LIABLE

**exemption** release, exception, exclusion, immunity, privilege, dispensation, freedom. LIABILITY

**exercise** *v*, use, utilize, employ, exert, bring to bear, apply, wield, practise.
drill, train, practise, limber up, work out, develop, discipline. RELAX
worry, trouble, disturb, afflict, annoy, vex.
*n*, effort, exertion, work, labour, workout, activity, drill, training, practice, task, lesson, discipline, development. REST
use, employment, exertion, application, practice, performance, operation, discharge.

**exert** use, utilize, employ, exercise, apply, bring to bear.

**exert oneself,** struggle, strive, toil, labour, make an effort, try hard, do one's best. IDLE

**exertion** effort, labour, toil, struggle, strain, endeavour, attempt. IDLENESS
use, employment, exercise, application.

**exhalation** breath, expiration, emission, emanation, evaporation, vapour, steam, mist, smoke, fume, effluvium.

**exhale** breathe out, respire, emit, expel, emanate, give off, evaporate, steam. ABSORB

**exhaust** consume, use up, drain, deplete, expend, spend, dissipate, squander, waste. REPLENISH
weary, tire out, fatigue, wear out, prostrate, weaken, debilitate, sap, drain. STRENGTHEN

**exhausted** weary, tired out, fatigued, worn out, drained, jaded, dead beat (*inf*), all in (*inf*), knackered (*inf*). REFRESHED
used up, spent, drained, depleted, empty, bare, gone, finished, at an end.

**exhaustive** comprehensive, all-embracing, wide-ranging, far-reaching, all-inclusive, full, thorough, extensive, in-depth. RESTRICTED

**exhibit** display, show, demonstrate, manifest, evince, evidence, indicate, betray, reveal, disclose, express, parade, flaunt, air, expose. CONCEAL

**exhibition** display, show, demonstration, manifestation, indication, expression, airing, presentation, exposition, fair, performance, spectacle.
scholarship, allowance, grant, bursary.

**exhilarate** elate, thrill, animate, enliven, invigorate, stimulate, inspirit, cheer, gladden, delight. DEPRESS

**exhilaration** elation, thrill, joy, glee, hilarity, mirth, gaiety, high spirits, exaltation, animation, excitement, gladness, cheerfulness, delight. DEPRESSION

**exhort** urge, enjoin, bid, persuade, prevail upon, induce, advise, counsel, entreat, beseech, encourage, incite, spur. DETER

**exhortation** urging, persuasion, advice, entreaty, encouragement, lecture, sermon, homily. DISCOURAGEMENT

**exhume** disinter, dig up, unearth, unbury, disentomb. INTER

**exigency** crisis, emergency, juncture, extremity, pinch, strait, pass, predicament, plight, quandary.

urgency, need, necessity, demand, requirement, pressure, constraint.

**exigent** urgent, pressing, critical, crucial, pivotal, imperative, importunate. UNIMPORTANT

demanding, taxing, exacting, arduous, difficult, hard, harsh, severe, rigorous. EASY

**exiguous** scanty, meagre, paltry, tiny, small, thin, slender, slight, bare, sparse. AMPLE

**exile** *v*, expel, banish, expatriate, deport, drive out, ostracize, proscribe, eject, oust. WELCOME

*n*, expulsion, banishment, expatriation, deportation, ostracism, proscription, ejection.

expatriate, refugee, émigré, outcast, displaced person.

**exist** be, live, breathe, subsist, survive, remain, endure, last, continue, abide, be present, prevail, occur, obtain.

**existence** being, life, breath, animation, subsistence, survival, continuance, duration, persistence, reality, actuality, presence. NONEXISTENCE

**exit** *n*, egress, way out, door, gate, outlet, vent. ENTRANCE

departure, going, withdrawal, retirement, exodus, demise, death. ARRIVAL

*v*, depart, leave, go, withdraw, retire, issue, go out. ENTER

**exodus** exit, departure, withdrawal, retreat, escape, flight, migration. ARRIVAL

**exonerate** absolve, acquit, clear, exculpate, vindicate, justify, excuse, pardon, discharge, free, release. CHARGE

exempt, relieve, release, spare, excuse, let off. COMPEL

**exorbitant** excessive, immoderate, unreasonable, inordinate, disproportionate, extreme, preposterous, outrageous, extortionate, prohibitive, extravagant. MODERATE

**exorcism** expulsion, casting out, deliverance, adjuration, incantation, invocation.

**exordium** preamble, introduction, preface, foreword, prologue, prelude, opening. EPILOGUE

**exoteric** public, open, communal, accessible, comprehensible, simple, plain, common, vulgar. ESOTERIC

external, outer, exterior, superficial. INNER

**exotic** foreign, alien, imported, extraneous, extrinsic. NATIVE

remarkable, striking, strange, unusual, extraordinary, outlandish, bizarre, glamorous, exciting, fascinating. ORDINARY

**expand** stretch, spread, enlarge, increase, amplify, magnify, swell, dilate, distend, inflate, open, unfold, prolong, extend, broaden, widen, grow, augment, multiply, develop, elaborate, flesh out. CONTRACT

**expanse** stretch, extent, area, space, spread, field, scope, range, breadth.

**expansion** enlargement, increase, amplification, dilation, inflation, spread, unfolding, extension, growth, augmentation, development, elaboration. CONTRACTION

**expansive** extensive, wide, broad, vast, comprehensive, far-reaching, wide-ranging, universal, global. NARROW

expanding, swelling, inflatable, extendable, elastic, stretchy, spreading.

talkative, loquacious, garrulous, outgoing, sociable, unreserved, communicative, affable, genial. RESERVED

**expatiate** enlarge, expand, elaborate, descant, dwell, dilate, amplify. SUMMARIZE

**expatriate** *v*, deport, exile, banish, expel, proscribe, ostracize.

*n*, exile, émigré, emigrant, displaced person.

**expatriation** exile, banishment, expulsion, deportation, emigration.

**expect** anticipate, await, look forward to, envisage, contemplate, foresee, hope, bargain for.

require, demand, insist on, call for, count on.

suppose, presume, surmise, believe, think, imagine, reckon.

**expectant** hopeful, awaiting, apprehensive, anxious, eager, ready, in suspense, on tenterhooks.

pregnant, expecting (*inf*), gravid, enceinte.

**expectation** anticipation, prospect, outlook, expectancy, contemplation, hope, apprehension, suspense, trust, reliance, assurance, belief, supposition, presumption, probability, likelihood, possibility.

**expediency** expedience, suitability, appropriateness, fitness, propriety, usefulness, desirability, advisability, wisdom, prudence, advantageousness, helpfulness, convenience, profit, gain, benefit, utility, practicality.

**expedient** *adj*, appropriate, suitable, fitting, seemly, proper, right, useful, desirable, advisable, wise, prudent, judicious, advantageous, helpful, worthwhile, valuable, profitable, convenient, practical. UNWISE
*n*, means, contrivance, device, shift, resource, resort, scheme, stratagem, makeshift, stopgap.

**expedite** accelerate, hasten, precipitate, speed, hurry, promote, advance, forward, assist, facilitate, dispatch. DELAY

**expedition** journey, voyage, trip, excursion, tour, safari, trek, exploration, mission, crusade, campaign, march.
haste, speed, dispatch, celerity, swiftness, alacrity, promptness. TARDINESS

**expeditious** prompt, instant, quick, rapid, speedy, fast, brisk, efficient, nimble. SLOW

**expel** eject, drive out, evict, exile, banish, expatriate, remove, oust, throw out, dismiss, proscribe, exclude. WELCOME
discharge, eject, void, evacuate, cast out, spew.

**expend** spend, disburse, pay out, fork out (*inf*). SAVE
consume, use up, exhaust, deplete, dissipate. CONSERVE

**expenditure** spending, disbursement, outlay, outgoings, expense, cost, charge, payment. INCOME

**expense** cost, charge, price, expenditure, disbursement, outlay, payment. RECEIPT
sacrifice, cost, loss, detriment.

**expensive** dear, costly, high-priced, steep (*inf*), exorbitant, extortionate, extravagant, rich, lavish, valuable. CHEAP

**experience** *v*, undergo, feel, suffer, go through, live through, endure, encounter, meet, face, try, know, perceive. MISS
*n*, incident, event, episode, adventure, encounter, ordeal, trial.
knowledge, familiarity, contact, involvement, participation, exposure, practice, understanding, observation. INEXPERIENCE

**experienced** practised, versed, familiar, knowledgeable, expert, proficient, skilled, trained, qualified, accomplished, able, competent, adept, professional, veteran. INEXPERIENCED

**experiment** *n*, trial, test, investigation, examination, research, experimentation, attempt, essay, venture.
*v*, try, test, investigate, examine, research, attempt, venture.

**experimental** empirical, tentative, speculative, exploratory, provisional, test, trial.

**expert** *n*, specialist, connoisseur, authority, professional, master, dab hand (*inf*), ace (*inf*), adept, past master, old hand. NOVICE
*adj*, proficient, adept, skilful, skilled, adroit, dexterous, practised, experienced, knowledgeable, versed, masterly.

**expiate** atone for, make amends for, redress, redeem, do penance for, pay for.

**expiation** atonement, amends, redress, reparation, satisfaction, redemption, penance.

**expiration** termination, end, finish, close, cessation, expiry, demise, decease, death. BEGINNING
exhalation, breathing out, respiration. INHALATION

**expire** end, finish, cease, close, terminate, stop, run out, lapse, die, perish. BEGIN
exhale, breathe out, respire. INHALE

**explain** interpret, expound, define, describe, explicate, clarify, make clear, elucidate, solve, unravel, unfold, illustrate, demonstrate. MYSTIFY
justify, account for, warrant, excuse.

**explanation** interpretation, exposition, definition, description, explication, clarification, elucidation, solution, theory, illustration, demonstration. MYSTIFICATION
justification, warrant, reason, motive, excuse, defence, account, meaning, key, answer.

**explanatory** explicative, descriptive, elucidative, illustrative, interpretative, expository, justificatory.

**expletive** *adj*, unnecessary, nonessential, superfluous, redundant. ESSENTIAL
*n*, oath, swearword, obscenity, curse, exclamation, ejaculation.

**explication** explanation, exposition, interpretation, illustration, clarification, elucidation, analysis, exegesis, commentary, formulation, development.

**explicit** plain, clear, distinct, unambiguous, precise, specific, express, definite, positive, categorical, absolute, full, detailed, straightforward, blunt, unreserved, open. IMPLIED

**explode** burst, blow up, blast, discharge, detonate, set off, go off.
discredit, invalidate, refute, repudiate, disprove, belie. CONFIRM

**exploit** *v*, use, utilize, capitalize on, profit from, take advantage of, misuse, abuse, manipulate.
*n*, feat, deed, act, achievement, accomplishment, adventure.

**exploration** examination, investigation, search, probe, research, study, analysis, inspection, scrutiny, survey, inquiry.

**explore** examine, investigate, probe, study, analyse, plumb, inspect, scrutinize, survey, inquire into, pry into.
travel, traverse, search, prospect, reconnoitre.

**explosion** blast, detonation, burst, discharge, bang, boom, crack, pop.
outburst, eruption, outbreak, increase.

**exponent** advocate, champion, defender, promoter, interpreter, expounder, expositor, presenter.
example, specimen, symbol, indication, representation, illustration.

**export** ship, send abroad, sell overseas. IMPORT

**expose** exhibit, display, show, reveal, disclose, divulge, air, make known, unmask, unveil, uncover, bare, unearth, bring to light, detect. HIDE
endanger, jeopardize, imperil, risk, hazard, venture. PROTECT

**exposition** explanation, interpretation, explication, description, account, commentary, critique, exegesis, presentation.
display, show, exhibition, demonstration, presentation, fair, market.

**expostulate** object, protest, argue, remonstrate, exhort, reason.

**expostulation** objection, protest, argument, remonstrance, exhortation.

**exposure** revelation, disclosure, exposé, unmasking, unveiling, airing, divulgence, publication, presentation, display, exhibition, baring. CONCEALMENT
jeopardy, peril, danger, risk, hazard, vulnerability. SAFETY

**expound** explain, elucidate, define, set forth, unfold, develop, describe, interpret.

**express** *v*, utter, say, voice, verbalize, articulate, phrase, communicate, put across, convey, state, declare, assert, announce. SUPPRESS
show, manifest, exhibit, evince, demonstrate, reveal, denote, depict, indicate, represent, symbolize, stand for.
*adj*, rapid, fast, quick, swift, direct, nonstop, high-speed. SLOW
explicit, specific, definite, precise, plain, clear, unambiguous, unmistakable, distinct, positive, categorical. VAGUE

**expression** look, countenance, face, air, aspect, mien, appearance.
utterance, verbalization, articulation, communication, statement, declaration, assertion, announcement. SUPPRESSION
phrase, locution, word, term, saying.
manifestation, exhibition, demonstration, indication, evidence, sign, symbol, token.
tone, feeling, modulation, intonation, delivery, execution.

**expressive** forceful, eloquent, meaningful, significant, pregnant, pointed, demonstrative, suggestive, indicative, telling, vivid, graphic, striking, strong, emphatic, moving, poignant, emotional.

**expulsion** ejection, eviction, exile, banishment, expatriation, dismissal, proscription, exclusion, discharge. WELCOME

**expunge** erase, delete, cross out, cancel, efface, blot out, obliterate, eradicate, extirpate, annihilate, wipe out, destroy, exterminate.

**expurgate** bowdlerize, censor, purge, clean up (*inf*), cut.

**exquisite** fine, delicate, dainty, beautiful, lovely, attractive, elegant. UGLY
choice, select, excellent, fine, rare, matchless, perfect, valuable, precious, splendid, outstanding, superb. ORDINARY
refined, cultivated, discriminating, selective, impeccable, fastidious, sensitive, appreciative. COARSE
intense, sharp, keen, acute. DULL

**extant** existing, existent, surviving, present, remaining, undestroyed.

**extemporaneous** extemporary, extempore, improvised, impromptu, ad-lib, spontaneous, unrehearsed, unprepared, off-the-cuff (*inf*). PREPARED

**extempore** extemporaneous, improvised, impromptu, ad lib, off the cuff (*inf*), spontaneously.

**extend** stretch, spread, reach, unfold, draw out, lengthen, prolong, elongate, protract, spin out, continue.

expand, enlarge, increase, amplify, widen, broaden, augment, add to. CONTRACT

offer, hold out, proffer, give, bestow, present, impart, confer. WITHHOLD

**extension** stretching, lengthening, prolongation, elongation, protraction, continuation, expansion, enlargement, increase, augmentation. CONTRACTION

delay, postponement, deferment.

addition, addendum, adjunct, supplement, appendix, appendage, annexe, wing, branch.

**extensive** broad, wide, large, huge, vast, spacious, capacious, widespread, universal, all-embracing, comprehensive, exhaustive, wide-ranging, long, lengthy, protracted. LIMITED

**extent** degree, amount, measure, quantity, size, magnitude, volume, length, breadth, width, height, depth, range, scope, limit, reach, compass, bounds.

**extenuate** mitigate, palliate, lessen, diminish, reduce, temper, moderate, qualify, play down, minimize, make light of, underestimate. EXAGGERATE

**exterior** *n*, outside, surface, face, shell, skin, covering, façade, appearance, aspect. INTERIOR

*adj*, outer, outside, external, outward, superficial, surface. INNER

**exterminate** annihilate, eradicate, extirpate, wipe out, destroy, kill, eliminate, abolish.

**extermination** annihilation, eradication, extirpation, destruction, extinction, elimination.

**external** outer, exterior, outside, outward, superficial, apparent, visible. INTERNAL

**extinct** dead, defunct, wiped out, vanished, gone, lost, finished, ended, obsolete, abolished, extinguished, quenched, inactive. LIVING

**extinction** annihilation, extermination, eradication, extirpation, destruction, abolition, death, dying out. SURVIVAL

**extinguish** quench, put out, snuff, douse, blow out, smother, stifle, suffocate, choke. LIGHT

annihilate, destroy, eradicate, extirpate, eliminate, kill, suppress, quash, erase, remove.

**extirpate** destroy, wipe out, annihilate, exterminate, eradicate, uproot, stamp out, abolish, extinguish. ESTABLISH

**extirpation** destruction, annihilation, extermination, eradication, abolition, extinction. ESTABLISHMENT

**extol** praise, laud, eulogize, panegyrize, exalt, glorify, acclaim, applaud, commend. DECRY

**extort** extract, wring, wrest, milk, squeeze, blackmail, bleed (*inf*), coerce, force, exact, elicit.

**extortionate** exorbitant, excessive, immoderate, unreasonable, outrageous, usurious, exacting, hard, severe, harsh, grasping, rapacious. MODERATE

**extra** *adj*, additional, supplementary, spare, reserve, accessory, ancillary, auxiliary, more, further, surplus, leftover, excess, superfluous.

*n*, addition, supplement, accessory, appurtenance, bonus.

*adv*, especially, exceptionally, particularly, unusually.

**extract** *v*, remove, pull out, draw out, take out, withdraw, exact, extort, wrest, uproot, tear out. INSERT

derive, draw, distil, squeeze out, get, obtain, elicit, educe, glean.

cite, quote, abstract, select.

*n*, excerpt, quotation, citation, abstract, passage, clipping, selection.

essence, concentrate, distillate, juice.

**extraction** removal, withdrawal, derivation, distillation, separation.

parentage, descent, ancestry, lineage, family, stock, blood, birth, origin.

**extradition** surrender, delivery, handing over.

**extraneous** extrinsic, external, alien, foreign, adventitious, incidental, additional, extra, nonessential, unnecessary, superfluous, redundant. INTRINSIC

irrelevant, immaterial, beside the point, unconnected, unrelated. RELEVANT

**extraordinary** strange, peculiar, singular, odd, curious, bizarre, weird, unusual, uncommon, rare, signal, remarkable, striking, outstanding, exceptional, surprising, amazing. ORDINARY

**extravagance** prodigality, lavishness, wastefulness, profligacy, overspending, recklessness, improvidence. ECONOMY
immoderation, unrestraint, excess, absurdity, wildness, folly, preposterousness, unreasonableness. MODERATION

**extravagant** prodigal, lavish, wasteful, profligate, spendthrift, reckless, improvident, thriftless. THRIFTY
immoderate, unrestrained, inordinate, excessive, exaggerated, outrageous, preposterous, wild, absurd, foolish. MODERATE
costly, dear, expensive, overpriced, exorbitant, extortionate. REASONABLE

**extreme** *adj*, great, intense, severe, acute, ultimate, maximum, greatest, highest, utmost, excessive, immoderate, unreasonable, utter, downright, out-and-out, exceptional, remarkable. REASONABLE
fanatical, radical, zealous, extremist. MODERATE
farthest, outermost, faraway, last, final, ultimate, endmost. NEAR
drastic, radical, uncompromising, rigid, severe, dire.
*n*, extremity, top, acme, apex, peak, height, depth, climax, end, termination, edge, limit, maximum, minimum. MEDIAN

**extremity** extreme, limit, boundary, border, edge, verge, brink, end, termination, height, depth, maximum, minimum.
emergency, crisis, exigency, plight, hardship, adversity.

**extricate** disentangle, disembarrass, disengage, clear, free, release, deliver, liberate, rescue, relieve, remove, withdraw, get out. INVOLVE

**extrinsic** extraneous, external, exterior, outside, foreign, alien, exotic, unrelated. INTRINSIC

**extrude** eject, force out, squeeze out, press out, expel, discharge.

**exuberance** liveliness, vivacity, ebullience, buoyancy, vitality, animation, vigour, enthusiasm. LETHARGY
abundance, profusion, plenty, copiousness, superabundance, richness, luxuriance, lavishness, prodigality. SCARCITY

**exuberant** lively, vivacious, ebullient, effervescent, buoyant, elated, animated, sparkling, enthusiastic. LETHARGIC
abundant, plentiful, copious, profuse, superabundant, rich, luxuriant, lavish, prodigal, extravagant. SCARCE

**exudation** sweating, sweat, perspiration, oozing, secretion, discharge, emanation. ABSORPTION

**exude** ooze, seep, leak, filter, trickle, drip, flow out, secrete, discharge, emanate, sweat, excrete. ABSORB

**exult** rejoice, triumph, jubilate, crow, gloat, be joyful, make merry, jump for joy. MOURN

**exultant** triumphant, jubilant, exulting, rejoicing, joyful, overjoyed, elated, delighted. MISERABLE

**eye** *n*, look, glimpse, glance, gaze.
appreciation, sensitivity, discernment, taste, discrimination.
viewpoint, opinion, judgment, mind.
watch, surveillance, observation, lookout.
*v*, look at, watch, observe, peruse, scrutinize, scan, survey, gaze at, stare at. IGNORE

# F

**fable** allegory, parable, apologue, tale, story, myth, legend.
untruth, lie, falsehood, fib, fiction, fabrication, invention, romance, tall story (*inf*). TRUTH

**fabric** cloth, material, stuff, textile, texture, weave.
structure, framework, organization, make-up, constitution, construction.

**fabricate** build, construct, make, manufacture, produce, form, frame, assemble, erect. DESTROY
devise, invent, coin, formulate, make up, concoct, fake, forge, counterfeit, falsify.

**fabrication** building, construction, manufacture, production, assembly, erection. DESTRUCTION
invention, formulation, concoction, fake, forgery, fable, lie, falsehood, fiction.

**fabulous** legendary, mythical, fantastic, unreal, imaginary, fictitious, invented, incredible, unbelievable, amazing, astounding, marvellous, superb, wonderful.

**façade** front, appearance, exterior, mask, disguise, veneer, show, pretence, semblance, illusion.

**face** *n*, countenance, visage, physiognomy, features, mug (*inf*), phiz (*inf*).
appearance, look, expression, aspect, air, façade, front, surface, exterior, veneer, pretence, semblance.

dignity, honour, repute, prestige, standing, image.

boldness, audacity, effrontery, brass, gall, impudence, cheek (*inf*). TIMIDITY

*v*, confront, brave, beard, defy, oppose, meet, encounter, come up against, deal with, face up to. AVOID

overlook, front on, be opposite.

cover, coat, veneer, encrust, dress, line, finish, level, smooth.

**facet** face, surface, side, aspect, angle, slant, element, detail.

**facetious** joking, jesting, jocular, witty, droll, waggish, frivolous, flippant, tongue-in-cheek, funny, humorous, amusing, comical. SERIOUS

**facile** easy, simple, effortless, smooth, fluent, skilful, adept, dexterous, adroit, proficient. AWKWARD

glib, slick, superficial, shallow.

complaisant, easy-going, affable, mild, compliant, docile, yielding. OBDURATE

**facilitate** assist, aid, help, forward, advance, expedite, speed up, ease, make easy, simplify. HINDER

**facility** ease, easiness, effortlessness, smoothness, fluency, readiness, skill, dexterity, proficiency, ability, knack, talent, aptitude. AWKWARDNESS

convenience, advantage, resource, amenity, aid, means.

**facsimile** copy, reproduction, replica, duplicate, carbon, photocopy, transcript. ORIGINAL

**fact** truth, actuality, reality, certainty. FICTION

event, happening, occurrence, incident, circumstance, deed, act.

element, detail, point, particular, item, factor.

**in fact,** actually, in reality, indeed, really, truly.

**faction** group, party, gang, band, clique, set, junta, confederacy, cabal, contingent, division, splinter group, camp.

discord, dissension, strife, conflict, disagreement, rebellion, sedition, upheaval, tumult, division. UNANIMITY

**factious** discordant, disagreeing, at variance, quarrelsome, disputatious, warring, rebellious, seditious, dissident, divisive, disruptive.

**factitious** artificial, false, unnatural, contrived, affected, simulated, insincere, sham, mock, fake. GENUINE

**factor** element, part, component, detail, item, facet, point, aspect, circumstance, cause.

agent, middleman, intermediary, deputy, proxy, representative.

**factory** plant, shop, works, mill, foundry.

**factual** authentic, genuine, true, real, actual, accurate, precise, correct, unbiased, objective, literal. FALSE

**faculty** ability, aptitude, facility, gift, knack, talent, skill, dexterity, proficiency, power, capacity, capability. INABILITY

department, school, discipline, profession.

right, licence, power, authority, prerogative, privilege.

**fad** fashion, vogue, trend, craze, rage, mania, whim, fancy.

**fade** pale, dim, bleach, blanch, blench, discolour, etiolate, wash out. DARKEN

diminish, decrease, dwindle, wane, ebb, fall, decline, fail, languish, wither, perish, dissolve, disperse, evanesce, vanish, disappear. GROW

**fag** *v*, fatigue, weary, tire out, exhaust, jade, wear out, prostrate. REFRESH

*n*, chore, drag (*inf*), bother, nuisance, inconvenience, bind (*inf*).

**fail** miscarry, fall through, go wrong, be unsuccessful, flop (*inf*), founder, fall short, miss, be in vain, come to nothing, fizzle out (*inf*), disappoint, let down. SUCCEED

omit, neglect, forget, desert, forsake, abandon.

decline, decay, wane, dwindle, fade, sink, weaken, flag, collapse, crumble, cease, die, disappear, go bankrupt, go under, fold (*inf*). FLOURISH

**failing** flaw, fault, defect, weakness, frailty, imperfection, deficiency, shortcoming, drawback, foible, failure. STRENGTH

**failure** miscarriage, abortion, lack of success, frustration, defeat, breakdown, collapse, fiasco, washout (*inf*), disappointment, flop (*inf*), dud (*inf*), loser, also-ran (*inf*). SUCCESS

omission, neglect, negligence, dereliction, delinquency, default, nonperformance.

decline, decay, failing, deterioration, collapse, bankruptcy, insolvency, ruin.

**faint** *adj*, weak, feeble, dim, pale, faded, indistinct, imperceptible, soft, low, muffled, slight, little, remote. STRONG
dizzy, giddy, light-headed, weak, drooping, languid, exhausted, weary.
*v*, collapse, pass out, lose consciousness, black out, swoon, keel over (*inf*), flake out (*inf*).
*n*, blackout, collapse, unconsciousness, swoon, syncope.

**faint-hearted** timid, diffident, timorous, cowardly, fearful, chicken (*inf*), yellow (*inf*). BRAVE

**fair**[1] *adj*, just, equitable, impartial, dispassionate, objective, square, legitimate, right, proper, above board, honest, trustworthy, honourable, upright. UNFAIR
blond, blonde, flaxen, light, pale. DARK
attractive, beautiful, handsome, pretty, lovely, bonny, comely, good-looking. UGLY
passable, average, reasonable, moderate, middling, mediocre, so-so (*inf*), all right, OK (*inf*), not bad, adequate, satisfactory. EXCELLENT
sunny, clear, bright, cloudless, fine, favourable. STORMY

**fair**[2] fête, bazaar, show, exhibition, market, gala, festival, carnival.

**fairy** elf, sprite, pixie, brownie, leprechaun, fay, peri.

**faith** belief, credence, conviction, confidence, assurance, trust, reliance, dependence. DOUBT
religion, creed, doctrine, dogma, belief, persuasion, denomination, sect.
faithfulness, fidelity, loyalty, allegiance, steadfastness, constancy, truthfulness, truth. FAITHLESSNESS

**faithful** loyal, true, devoted, steadfast, constant, staunch, trusty, trustworthy, reliable, dependable. UNFAITHFUL
accurate, exact, precise, close, strict, just, true, literal, factual. INACCURATE

**faithless** unfaithful, disloyal, untrue, perfidious, treacherous, untrustworthy, unreliable, fickle, inconstant, false, dishonest. FAITHFUL
unbelieving, doubting, sceptical, agnostic.

**fake** *v*, counterfeit, forge, fabricate, falsify, pretend, feign, affect, put on, sham, dissemble.
*n*, counterfeit, forgery, imitation, copy, sham, hoax, fraud, impostor, charlatan.
*adj*, counterfeit, forged, false, bogus, spurious, phoney (*inf*), artificial, ersatz, synthetic, pseudo. GENUINE

**fall** drop, descend, sink, go down, slope, incline, plunge, dive, plummet, fall down, trip, tumble, come a cropper (*inf*), topple, slide, decline, subside, abate, decrease, lessen, fall off, dwindle, ebb, slump, crash, collapse, fall in. RISE
yield, surrender, submit, capitulate, be defeated, be taken. TRIUMPH
be killed, be slain, perish, die. SURVIVE
happen, occur, befall, chance, come to pass, take place.
lapse, err, sin, transgress, go astray.

**fall apart,** crumble, disintegrate, break up, fall to pieces.

**fall on,** fall upon, attack, assail, descend on, set upon, lay into.

**fall out,** quarrel, argue, disagree, fight, wrangle.
*n*, drop, descent, slope, declivity, incline, plunge, dive, trip, tumble, decline, abatement, decrease, ebb, slump, collapse. RISE
surrender, capitulation, failure, defeat, overthrow, capture, downfall, ruin, destruction, death. TRIUMPH
lapse, sin, transgression.

**fallacious** wrong, erroneous, mistaken, incorrect, misleading, deceptive, delusive, illusory, false, untrue, fictitious, spurious, illogical, unsound, invalid, sophistic. TRUE

**fallacy** misconception, misapprehension, mistake, error, illusion, delusion, chimera, falsehood, untruth, deception, sophistry, casuistry. TRUTH

**fallible** imperfect, erring, weak, frail, mortal, human, unreliable. INFALLIBLE

**fallow** uncultivated, untilled, unsown, undeveloped, dormant, inactive, idle, inert, resting. CULTIVATED

**falls** waterfall, cascade, cataract, rapids.

**false** untrue, unsound, misleading, fallacious, fictitious, inaccurate, erroneous, wrong, incorrect, mistaken, untruthful, unreliable, mendacious, lying, deceitful, deceptive, delusive. TRUE
treacherous, perfidious, disloyal, faithless, unfaithful, hypocritical, two-faced, untrustworthy, dishonest, dishonourable. FAITHFUL
counterfeit, forged, fake, imitation, spurious, ersatz, artificial, synthetic, unreal, mock, feigned, sham, bogus. GENUINE

**falsehood** lie, fib, untruth, fabrication, fiction, falsity, mendacity, untruthfulness, deceit, deception. TRUTH

**falsify** misrepresent, belie, distort, pervert, doctor, alter, cook (*inf*), adulterate, counterfeit, forge, fake.

**falter** hesitate, waver, vacillate, be unsure. DECIDE
stammer, stutter, speak haltingly.
stumble, totter, dodder, tremble, shake.

**fame** renown, celebrity, stardom, name, reputation, repute, credit, honour, glory, acclaim, eminence, illustriousness. OBLIVION

**familiar** well-known, recognizable, common, household, domestic, everyday, ordinary, customary, routine, frequent. UNFAMILIAR
intimate, close, confidential, friendly, amicable, sociable, informal, unceremonious, easy, relaxed, unconstrained, open, free. FORMAL
forward, bold, presumptuous, impudent, disrespectful.
**familiar with,** conversant with, acquainted with, versed in, conscious of, aware of, no stranger to.

**familiarity** knowledge, acquaintance, grasp, understanding, experience, awareness. IGNORANCE
intimacy, closeness, friendliness, sociability, informality, openness, ease. FORMALITY
boldness, presumption, liberty, impudence, disrespect.

**familiarize** acquaint, accustom, habituate, inure, acclimatize, break in, train, instruct, school.

**family** relatives, relations, kin, children, offspring, progeny, household, ménage.
ancestry, lineage, parentage, extraction, blood, race, stock, pedigree, clan, tribe, house, dynasty.
group, class, subdivision, genus, species, kind, type, system.

**famine** starvation, hunger, want, lack, dearth, scarcity. PLENTY

**famished** starving, ravenous, hungry, empty, voracious. FULL

**famous** well-known, renowned, celebrated, famed, illustrious, eminent, distinguished, noted, great, acclaimed, legendary, memorable. UNKNOWN

**fan**[1] *v*, agitate, excite, arouse, stimulate, stir up, whip up, inflame, provoke. QUELL
ventilate, air-condition, blow, cool, refresh.
*n*, ventilator, air conditioner, blower.

**fan**[2] *n*, devotee, enthusiast, aficionado, addict, freak (*inf*), buff (*inf*), admirer, follower, supporter, fanatic.

**fanatic** zealot, bigot, extremist, radical, militant, visionary, enthusiast, devotee, fan. MODERATE

**fanatical** zealous, bigoted, immoderate, extreme, radical, visionary, enthusiastic, fervent, frenzied, wild, mad, obsessive. RESTRAINED

**fanciful** capricious, flighty, whimsical, wild, fantastic, fabulous, chimerical, imaginary, unreal, visionary, extravagant, impractical, romantic, imaginative, inventive. REALISTIC

**fancy** *v*, imagine, conceive, think, reckon, believe, suppose, conjecture, guess, picture, visualize, envisage.
want, desire, wish for, crave, long for, feel like, hanker after, like, be attracted to, prefer, favour.
*n*, caprice, whim, vagary, crotchet, notion, idea, conception, image, picture, impression, vision, dream, fantasy.
desire, urge, impulse, hankering, inclination, tendency, liking, predilection, fondness, partiality. AVERSION
*adj*, ornate, ornamental, decorative, ornamented, decorated, elaborate, showy, ostentatious. PLAIN
capricious, whimsical, fanciful, extravagant, fantastic. PRACTICAL

**fantastic** fanciful, imaginary, unreal, weird, odd, strange, grotesque, chimerical, bizarre, outlandish, ridiculous, absurd, wild, extravagant, capricious, whimsical, far-fetched, unrealistic, preposterous, incredible, mad, crazy, irrational. REALISTIC
wonderful, splendid, marvellous, excellent, first-rate, great, tremendous.

**fantasy** fancy, imagination, invention, image, dream, nightmare, illusion, hallucination, mirage, phantom, vision, daydream, reverie. REALITY

**far** *adj*, distant, remote, removed, faraway, far-flung. NEAR
*adv*, afar, a long way, miles.
greatly, considerably, much, very much, extremely, decidedly.

**farce** comedy, burlesque, slapstick, buffoonery, satire. TRAGEDY
mockery, travesty, sham, absurdity, nonsense, joke.

**farcical** ludicrous, ridiculous, absurd, preposterous, laughable.
comic, funny, humorous, amusing, droll. TRAGIC

**fare** *n*, charge, fee, price, cost.
food, diet, meals, menu, provisions, victuals, nourishment, sustenance.
*v*, manage, get along, do, make out.

**farewell** *interj*, goodbye, adieu, so long (*inf*).
*n*, departure, leave-taking, valediction, goodbye, parting.

**far-fetched** improbable, implausible, unlikely, unbelievable, incredible, fantastic, doubtful, dubious. PROBABLE

**farm** *n*, farmstead, grange, homestead, smallholding, croft, ranch, plantation.
*v*, till, cultivate, work.

**farming** agriculture, agronomy, husbandry.

**farrago** hotchpotch, miscellany, jumble, mixture, medley, potpourri, mishmash, salmagundi.

**farther** further, beyond, past, longer, more, in addition. NEARER

**farthest** furthest, longest, last, utmost, remotest, most distant, extreme. NEAREST

**fascinate** charm, captivate, beguile, enchant, delight, attract, allure, entrance, spellbind, hypnotize, mesmerize, rivet, transfix, engross, absorb. BORE

**fascination** charm, appeal, allure, attraction, draw, pull, magnetism, enchantment, entrancement, captivation, hypnotism, mesmerism. REPULSION

**fashion** *n*, vogue, mode, look, style, trend, craze, fad, custom, convention, usage.
form, mould, shape, style, cut, stamp, cast, model, design, pattern.
way, method, manner, sort, kind, type.
*v*, make, form, mould, shape, design, create, forge, construct.
adapt, accommodate, suit, fit, adjust, tailor.

**fashionable** stylish, modish, in vogue, à la mode, chic, elegant, smart, trendy (*inf*), all the rage, modern, up-to-date, current, in (*inf*), popular. UNFASHIONABLE

**fast** *adj*, rapid, swift, quick, speedy, accelerated, brisk, fleet. SLOW
secure, fixed, firm, immovable, tight, fastened, loyal, staunch, constant, steadfast, sound, lasting. LOOSE
dissolute, dissipated, rakish, loose, wild, reckless, immoral, promiscuous, extravagant, self-indulgent. RESTRAINED
*adv*, rapidly, swiftly, quickly, speedily, briskly, in haste. SLOWLY
securely, firmly, tightly, immovably. LOOSELY
deeply, soundly.
wildly, recklessly, extravagantly, loosely, promiscuously, wantonly.

**fasten** secure, fix, make fast, bind, tie, tether, attach, join, unite, connect, bolt, chain, strap, lace, buckle, button, hook, pin, latch, lock. UNFASTEN
aim, direct, focus, point, bend, fix.

**fastidious** critical, hard to please, particular, fussy, finicky, pernickety, meticulous, dainty, delicate, squeamish.

**fat** plump, obese, flabby, podgy, chubby, rotund, tubby, portly, corpulent, stout, overweight, large, big, broad, wide, thick, heavy, gross. THIN
fatty, greasy, oily.
profitable, lucrative, rich, fertile, fruitful, productive, abundant, plentiful, wealthy, affluent. POOR

**fatal** deadly, lethal, mortal, destructive, ruinous, calamitous, disastrous, incurable, terminal, malignant, harmful, pernicious, baleful, baneful. BENEFICIAL
critical, crucial, decisive, fateful, inevitable, destined, fated.

**fatality** death, disaster, catastrophe, casualty, mortality, accident, fate, destiny.

**fate** destiny, providence, chance, fortune, lot, portion, doom, kismet, predestination, destination, future, end, death, destruction, ruin.

**fated** destined, doomed, predestined, preordained, foreordained, sure, certain, inevitable, inescapable.

**fateful** crucial, critical, decisive, pivotal, momentous, portentous, important, significant.
disastrous, ruinous, fatal, deadly.

**father** *n*, parent, progenitor, sire, ancestor, forefather, predecessor. OFFSPRING
pater, dad (*inf*), daddy (*inf*), papa, pa (*inf*), old man (*inf*). MOTHER

creator, maker, author, inventor, architect, founder, prime mover.
*v*, sire, beget, procreate, generate, engender.
create, make, invent, originate, found.

**fatherly** paternal, kind, benevolent, benign, caring, tender, affectionate, sympathetic, understanding, protective, supportive, parental.

**fathom** measure, sound, gauge, plumb, probe, penetrate, understand, comprehend, grasp, see, get to the bottom of.

**fathomless** unfathomable, impenetrable, incomprehensible, immeasurable, bottomless, abysmal, deep, profound. SHALLOW

**fatigue** *v*, exhaust, weary, tire out, jade, fag, drain, weaken, debilitate, prostrate. REFRESH
*n*, exhaustion, weariness, tiredness, lassitude, lethargy, listlessness, debility, prostration. VIGOUR

**fatten** stuff, cram, feed, build up, bloat, make fat, get fat, swell, broaden, spread, put on weight. SLIM

**fatuity** fatuousness, foolishness, folly, silliness, absurdity, inanity, stupidity, idiocy, imbecility, madness, lunacy. SENSE

**fatuous** foolish, silly, absurd, inane, stupid, idiotic, senseless, asinine, witless, vacuous, moronic. SENSIBLE

**fault** flaw, blemish, defect, imperfection, failing, weakness, frailty, shortcoming. VIRTUE
offence, misdeed, crime, wrong, sin, transgression, misdemeanour, error, mistake, slip, lapse, omission.
culpability, responsibility, accountability, blameworthiness.
**at fault,** culpable, responsible, guilty, to blame, in the wrong.
**find fault,** complain, carp, cavil, quibble, criticize.

**faultless** perfect, flawless, model, exemplary, impeccable, unblemished, immaculate, spotless, pure, blameless, guiltless, innocent. IMPERFECT

**faulty** defective, imperfect, broken, damaged, impaired, not working, out of order, unsound, weak, incorrect, erroneous, wrong, fallacious, invalid, flawed. PERFECT

**favour** *n*, approval, approbation, countenance, sanction, backing, support, patronage, preference, partiality, bias, favouritism, good will, kindness, friendliness, graciousness. DISAPPROVAL
good turn, good deed, benefaction, boon, service, courtesy, kindness.
gift, present, souvenir, memento, keepsake, token, badge, rosette, decoration.
**in favour of,** for, pro, approving, supporting, backing, on the side of, for the sake of.
*v*, approve, countenance, sanction, back, support, patronize, befriend, champion, advocate, encourage, oblige, help, assist, facilitate, ease, advance. OPPOSE
prefer, side with, choose, select, like, fancy, be partial to, esteem, value, indulge, spoil, pamper.
resemble, take after, look like.

**favourable** encouraging, promising, propitious, auspicious, advantageous, beneficial, helpful, suitable, fit, opportune, timely. UNFAVOURABLE
approving, agreeable, amicable, well-disposed, kind, friendly, understanding, sympathetic, congenial, encouraging, enthusiastic. DISAPPROVING

**favourite** *n*, pet, darling, dearest, beloved, preference, choice, blue-eyed boy (*inf*), apple of one's eye.
*adj*, dearest, best-loved, preferred, chosen, pet.

**fawn** grovel, cringe, crawl, creep, kowtow, bow and scrape, toady, truckle, flatter, court.

**fawning** servile, obsequious, sycophantic, bootlicking (*inf*), grovelling, cringing, crawling, flattering. INDEPENDENT

**fealty** loyalty, allegiance, fidelity, faithfulness, devotion, homage.

**fear** *n*, terror, horror, panic, alarm, fright, cowardice, timidity, dread, apprehension, trepidation, misgiving, qualm. BOLDNESS
anxiety, worry, distress, concern, solicitude, uneasiness, foreboding. REASSURANCE
phobia, bogey, bugbear, *bête noire*, nightmare.
awe, reverence, veneration, respect. DISRESPECT
*v*, dread, be afraid of, be frightened of, shudder at, apprehend, anticipate, expect, worry, be anxious, feel concern.
revere, venerate, respect.

**fearful** terrified, afraid, frightened, scared, alarmed, uneasy, apprehensive, anxious, nervous, jumpy, timid, timorous, diffident. BOLD fearsome, dreadful, terrible, horrendous, awful, frightful, dire, grim, formidable, horrible, ghastly, hideous, shocking, appalling, atrocious. WONDERFUL

**fearless** bold, brave, courageous, dauntless, undaunted, intrepid, heroic, gallant, valiant, valorous, daring, unafraid. FEARFUL

**feasible** practicable, workable, viable, possible, likely, reasonable, practical, realistic, realizable, attainable. IMPOSSIBLE

**feast** *n*, banquet, spread (*inf*), dinner, barbecue, blowout (*inf*), slap-up meal (*inf*), repast, treat.
festival, celebration, holy day, saint's day, fête.
*v*, dine, banquet, eat one's fill, gorge, stuff, regale, treat, wine and dine, entertain.
delight, please, gladden, gratify, thrill.

**feat** deed, act, exploit, achievement, accomplishment, stroke, coup.

**feature** *n*, characteristic, peculiarity, trait, mark, hallmark, attribute, property, quality, aspect, facet.
highlight, speciality, main item, attraction, focal point.
article, story, item, piece, column, report.
*v*, highlight, emphasize, accentuate, play up, spotlight, give prominence to, promote, star.

**features** face, countenance, physiognomy, lineaments.

**feculence** scum, sediment, residue, dregs, lees, muck, filth, mud, dirt.

**fecund** fruitful, productive, fertile, rich, prolific, abundant. BARREN

**federation** confederation, confederacy, union, league, alliance, coalition, syndicate, combination, amalgamation.

**fee** payment, remuneration, reward, recompense, pay, hire, emolument, honorarium, allowance, charge, toll, bill, account.

**feeble** weak, frail, infirm, delicate, sickly, puny, debilitated, enervated, languid, drooping, failing, faint, slight, thin. STRONG
ineffectual, powerless, unavailing, inefficient, incompetent, inadequate, lame, flimsy, unconvincing. POWERFUL

**feed** *v*, nourish, sustain, satisfy, provide for, supply, cater for, provision. STARVE
eat, devour, dine, fare, subsist, graze.
*n*, fodder, forage, food.

**feel** touch, handle, finger, stroke, caress.
sense, experience, perceive, be aware of, know, undergo, suffer, enjoy.
fumble, grope, try, test.
seem, appear.

**feel for,** sympathize with, commiserate with, bleed for, be sorry for, grieve for.

**feeling** *n*, sense, sensation, impression, perception, consciousness, awareness, touch, contact, feel.
hunch, inkling, suspicion, idea, notion, premonition, presentiment, opinion, viewpoint, thought.
emotion, sentiment, sensibility, sensitivity, sympathy, compassion, affection, tenderness, passion, ardour, fervour. INSENSITIVITY
*adj*, sentient, sensible, sensitive, emotional, sympathetic, compassionate, tender, warm, passionate, ardent, fervent. UNFEELING

**feign** affect, put on, assume, pretend, act, sham, simulate, fake, counterfeit, forge, fabricate, copy, imitate, dissemble.

**feint** dodge, trick, stratagem, ruse, artifice, pretext, expedient, blind, bluff, sham, hoax, pretence, show.

**felicitate** congratulate, compliment.

**felicitous** apt, appropriate, well-chosen, suitable, pertinent, apposite, opportune, timely, propitious, seasonable, happy, fortunate, lucky, successful. INAPPROPRIATE

**felicity** happiness, joy, bliss, ecstasy, rapture, delight. MISERY
aptness, appropriateness, suitability, pertinence, propitiousness. INAPPROPRIATENESS

**fell** hew, cut down, knock down, prostrate, level, raze, demolish.

**fellow** man, boy, person, chap (*inf*), bloke (*inf*), guy (*inf*).
companion, comrade, friend, colleague, partner, associate, equal, peer, compeer, mate, counterpart, match, twin.

**fellowship** companionship, comradeship, camaraderie, friendship, amity, brotherhood, intimacy, familiarity, sociability, company, communion, intercourse. ENMITY
association, society, club, fraternity, guild, league.

**felon** criminal, offender, malefactor, wrongdoer, culprit, convict.

**felony** crime, offence, misdemeanour.

**feminine** womanly, girlish, ladylike, soft, gentle, tender, delicate, graceful. MASCULINE
effeminate, womanish, unmanly, sissy, weak, effete. MANLY

**fen** bog, marsh, swamp, morass, quagmire.

**fence** *n*, railing, paling, hedge, wall, barrier, barricade, defence, guard.
*v*, enclose, shut in, surround, encircle, circumscribe, bound, defend, protect, guard. EXPOSE
hedge, quibble, prevaricate, equivocate, fudge, evade, dodge, parry, shuffle, tergiversate.

**fend** **fend for,** provide for, support, look after, take care of.
**fend off,** ward off, avert, forestall, deflect, turn aside, parry, stave off, repulse, drive back.

**feral** ferine, wild, untamed, unbroken, uncultivated. DOMESTICATED
savage, fierce, ferocious, vicious, brutal, cruel. GENTLE

**ferment** *v*, foam, froth, bubble, effervesce, boil, seethe, brew, rise, leaven.
rouse, stir up, excite, inflame, agitate, foment, provoke. CALM
*n*, yeast, leaven, enzyme, bacteria.
excitement, commotion, tumult, uproar, turmoil, agitation, unrest, stew, heat, fever, frenzy. PEACE

**ferocious** fierce, savage, vicious, feral, bestial, cruel, brutal, barbarous, violent, inhuman, bloodthirsty, sanguinary, ruthless, merciless, pitiless, relentless, harsh, severe. GENTLE

**fertile** fecund, productive, fruitful, prolific, teeming, abundant, profuse, plentiful, rich, luxuriant. BARREN

**fertilize** fecundate, impregnate, inseminate, pollinate.
enrich, dress, feed, manure, marl, mulch, compost.

**fervent** fervid, ardent, passionate, eager, keen, earnest, zealous, animated, intense, vehement, burning, glowing, warm. APATHETIC

**fervour** ardour, passion, fervency, eagerness, keenness, earnestness, zeal, animation, intensity, vehemence. APATHY

**fester** *v*, suppurate, ulcerate, putrefy, rot, decay, corrupt.
rankle, irk, gall, rile, inflame, chafe, irritate.
*n*, abscess, ulcer, boil, pustule, gathering.

**festival** gala, carnival, celebration, commemoration, anniversary, jubilee, fair, fête, banquet, feast, saint's day, holiday.

**festive** festal, merry, jovial, jolly, convivial, hearty, joyful, joyous, mirthful, cheery, gay. MOURNFUL

**festivity** merriment, joviality, conviviality, joyfulness, mirth, gaiety, revelry, fun. MOURNING
festival, carnival, celebration, party, carousal.

**festoon** *v*, decorate, adorn, array, deck, wreathe, garland, drape, hang. STRIP
*n*, garland, wreath, chaplet.

**fetch** bring, carry, convey, deliver, get, obtain, retrieve, go for.
realize, yield, bring in, make, sell for.

**fetching** attractive, sweet, taking, fascinating, charming, enchanting, alluring. REPULSIVE

**fête** fair, bazaar, gala, festival, carnival, garden party.
holiday, feast day, saint's day, festival.

**fetid** foul, rank, malodorous, stinking, noisome, offensive, mephitic, rancid, corrupt, foul. FRAGRANT

**fetish** charm, talisman, amulet.
obsession, mania, fixation, compulsion.

**fetter** *v*, chain, shackle, manacle, tie, bind, trammel, encumber, hamper, restrain, restrict, confine. LOOSE
*n*, chain, shackle, manacle, bond, iron.

**feud** vendetta, hostility, antagonism, enmity, bad blood, discord, strife, conflict, dissension, contention, quarrel, row, argument, rupture, breach, faction. AGREEMENT

**fever** feverishness, pyrexia, high temperature.
agitation, excitement, heat, flush, passion, fervour, frenzy, ferment, turmoil. COMPOSURE

**few** rare, scarce, scanty, meagre, hardly any, not many, infrequent, sporadic. MANY

**fiasco** failure, disaster, catastrophe, mess, flop (*inf*), washout (*inf*), fizzle (*inf*). SUCCESS

**fiat** permission, sanction, authorization, warrant. BAN

order, command, decree, edict, proclamation, ordinance, law, dictum.

**fib** *n*, lie, untruth, falsehood, fabrication, story, whopper (*inf*). TRUTH
*v*, lie, misrepresent, falsify, prevaricate, equivocate.

**fibre** thread, strand, filament, fibril, staple, texture.
spirit, nature, constitution, disposition, strength, stamina, toughness.

**fickle** changeable, variable, capricious, mercurial, volatile, flighty, unpredictable, fitful, erratic, irresolute, vacillating, wavering, inconstant, unstable, unsteady, unreliable. CONSTANT

**fiction** story, tale, novel, fable, legend, fantasy, romance, invention, fabrication, fancy, imagination, lie, falsehood, untruth. FACT

**fictitious** false, untrue, invented, imaginary, fanciful, make-believe, mythical, unreal, bogus, spurious, counterfeit, artificial, feigned, assumed. TRUE

**fiddle** play, tinker, tamper, toy, trifle, mess around, idle, fidget.
swindle, cheat, falsify, cook (*inf*), manoeuvre, finagle (*inf*), wangle (*inf*).

**fiddling** trifling, trivial, small, insignificant, petty. IMPORTANT

**fidelity** faithfulness, loyalty, devotion, fealty, allegiance, staunchness, constancy, steadfastness, trustworthiness, dependability. INFIDELITY
closeness, faithfulness, exactness, accuracy, precision, correspondence, conformity, accordance.

**fidget** squirm, twitch, fiddle, twiddle, move about, jitter (*inf*), worry, fret.

**fidgety** restless, restive, impatient, nervous, fretful, uneasy, jumpy, jittery (*inf*). STILL

**field** meadow, pasture, green, common, ground, pitch.
domain, province, realm, sphere, department, discipline, speciality, territory, area, range, scope, extent, limits, bounds.

**fiend** demon, devil, evil spirit, monster, brute, beast, savage, ogre. ANGEL
addict, enthusiast, fan, devotee, maniac, fanatic.

**fiendish** demonic, devilish, diabolical, infernal, wicked, evil, malicious, malignant, malevolent, cruel, inhuman, savage, monstrous. ANGELIC

**fierce** savage, ferocious, vicious, dangerous, menacing, threatening, wild, feral, brutal, barbarous, bloodthirsty, sanguinary, cruel, ruthless. HARMLESS
violent, raging, furious, relentless, stormy, tempestuous, wild, intense, keen, powerful, strong, uncontrollable, passionate, ardent, fervent. GENTLE

**fiery** hot, burning, blazing, flaming, glowing, heated, ardent, fervent, vehement, passionate, excitable, temperamental, violent, fierce. COOL

**fight** *n*, battle, combat, strife, conflict, war, fighting, hostilities, action, engagement, encounter, bout, duel, scrap (*inf*), struggle, brawl, fray, fracas, riot, dispute, row, quarrel. PEACE
*v*, battle, combat, war, contend, strive, struggle, oppose, contest, resist, defy, attack, assault, grapple, wrestle, spar, box, brawl, dispute, argue, bicker, wrangle.

**figment** invention, fabrication, creation, illusion, fancy, notion, fiction, fable, story, falsehood. FACT

**figurative** metaphorical, emblematic, symbolic, allegorical, representative, typical, illustrative.

**figure** *n*, number, numeral, digit, cipher, symbol, character. LETTER
outline, shape, silhouette, form, configuration, body, build, physique, frame, structure.
diagram, drawing, picture, illustration, representation, effigy, image, design, pattern, device, motif, emblem.
personage, character, notable, celebrity, somebody, worthy. NOBODY
*v*, calculate, reckon, compute, work out, add up, count.
represent, symbolize, depict, portray, feature, appear.
decorate, adorn, ornament, embellish, mark, variegate.
imagine, picture, conceive.

**figure out,** understand, comprehend, grasp, see, fathom, work out, solve.

**filament** strand, thread, fibre, fibril, staple, hair, wire, string.

**filch** steal, pilfer, purloin, thieve, take, abstract, lift (*inf*), pinch (*inf*). RETURN

**file**[1] *v*, rasp, scrape, grind, abrade, rub down, smooth, polish, shape.

**file**[2] *n*, folder, portfolio, dossier, documents, information.

line, row, rank, queue, column, list, string, chain.
*v*, record, register, place, classify, arrange, pigeonhole.
march, troop, parade, pass.

**fill** stuff, cram, pack, fill up, satisfy, content, satiate, glut, sate, swell, inflate, fill out, stock, supply, furnish, replenish. EMPTY
pervade, suffuse, imbue, impregnate, infuse, overspread, cover.
plug, cork, bung, stop, close, block.
occupy, hold, discharge, execute, perform, carry out, do, fulfil.
**fill in,** complete, fill out, answer.
replace, substitute, stand in, deputize.
inform, apprise, acquaint, bring up to date.

**film** covering, coat, layer, sheet, skin, membrane, pellicle, veil, haze, blur, cloud, mist.
picture, motion picture, movie (*inf*), flick (*inf*), video.

**filter** *v*, strain, clarify, filtrate, purify, refine, screen, sift.
exude, ooze, transude, seep, leak, trickle, leach, percolate.
*n*, strainer, screen, sieve, riddle, net, mesh, gauze.

**filth** dirt, muck, grime, ordure, sewage, refuse, pollution, foulness, defilement, corruption, squalor, filthiness, uncleanness. CLEANNESS
obscenity, vulgarity, pornography, smut, grossness, indecency.

**filthy** dirty, mucky, grimy, grubby, unwashed, foul, unclean, polluted, defiled, corrupt, squalid. SPOTLESS
obscene, vulgar, pornographic, smutty, lewd, indecent, ribald, bawdy, blue.

**final** ultimate, last, terminal, concluding, closing, eventual. FIRST
conclusive, decisive, definitive, irrevocable.

**finale** end, conclusion, finish, close, termination, climax, culmination, finis. BEGINNING

**finality** conclusiveness, decisiveness, definitiveness, irrevocability, unavoidability, inevitability.

**finally** ultimately, eventually, at last, in the end, in the long run, lastly. INITIALLY
conclusively, decisively, irrevocably, definitely, absolutely, completely, once and for all.

**finance** *n*, banking, economics, commerce, investment, money, funds, accounts.
*v*, fund, pay for, back, support, subsidize, underwrite.

**finances** resources, assets, wealth, wherewithal, funds, money, cash, capital.

**financial** monetary, money, pecuniary, fiscal, economic.

**find** *v*, discover, come across, happen upon, uncover, unearth, locate, track down, ferret out, encounter, meet, notice, observe, descry, perceive, detect, realize, attain, obtain, acquire, get. LOSE
provide, supply, furnish, contribute.
**find out,** ascertain, learn, discover, determine, detect, expose, uncover, unmask.
*n*, discovery, finding, strike, catch, bargain.

**finding** verdict, judgment, decision, conclusion, award, sentence, decree, pronouncement.

**fine**[1] *adj*, excellent, choice, select, superior, outstanding, exceptional, first-rate, first-class, splendid, magnificent, ornate, showy, beautiful, lovely, exquisite, elegant, smart, stylish, tasteful. INFERIOR
thin, slender, attenuated, tenuous, slight, small, little, dainty, delicate, fragile, flimsy, sheer, light. COARSE
pure, clear, unadulterated, refined, subtle, keen, acute, sharp, precise, minute, nice.
sunny, cloudless, dry, bright, clear, fair, clement. CLOUDY
acceptable, satisfactory, all right, OK (*inf*).

**fine**[2] *n*, penalty, punishment, mulct, forfeit, damages.
*v*, penalize, punish, mulct.

**finery** trappings, trinkets, decorations, ornaments, splendour, frippery, Sunday best, glad rags (*inf*).

**finesse** subtlety, tact, diplomacy, delicacy, grace, polish, skill, adroitness, mastery, craft. CLUMSINESS
artifice, trick, ruse, wile, stratagem.

**finicky** fussy, particular, meticulous, fastidious, dainty, squeamish, choosy (*inf*), difficult, hard to please, critical.

**finish** *v*, complete, conclude, close, terminate, end, stop, cease, fulfil, achieve, accomplish, do discharge, execute, perform, settle, finalize, perfect, consummate, culminate, round off. START

consume, use up, drain, empty, dispatch, dispose of, get rid of, destroy, kill, ruin, defeat, overcome, finish off.
polish, varnish, face, dress, gild, veneer, glaze, coat.
*n*, completion, conclusion, close, termination, end, cessation, perfection, consummation, culmination. BEGINNING
surface, polish, varnish, lustre, shine, texture, veneer, appearance, coating.

**finished** complete, done, over, through, completed, ended, achieved, fulfilled. UNFINISHED
accomplished, masterly, proficient, expert, skilled, consummate, polished, refined, elegant, perfect, impeccable.
ruined, bankrupt, lost, gone, done for (*inf*), doomed, defeated.

**finite** limited, restricted, bounded, circumscribed, demarcated, terminable, measurable. INFINITE

**fire** *n*, burning, combustion, spark, flame, blaze, conflagration, inferno, holocaust.
ardour, fervour, heat, passion, enthusiasm, eagerness, spirit, élan, vigour, energy, force, intensity, animation, excitement, inspiration, life, vivacity. COLDNESS
light, radiance, lustre, splendour, glow, sparkle.
bombardment, barrage, salvo, volley, fusillade, cannonade, flak, shelling.
**on fire,** alight, ablaze, burning, blazing, in flames. EXTINGUISHED
*v*, discharge, shoot, detonate, explode, shell, hurl, launch.
ignite, kindle, light, set fire to, set on fire, set alight. EXTINGUISH
animate, rouse, stir, stimulate, inspire, invigorate, excite, arouse, inspirit, inflame. DAMP
dismiss, discharge, cashier, sack (*inf*). APPOINT

**firm**[1] *adj*, solid, hard, compact, dense, stiff, rigid, inflexible, unyielding, set, congealed, frozen. SOFT
secure, fixed, fast, immovable, rooted, anchored, steady, stable, constant, enduring, sturdy, strong. UNSTABLE
steadfast, staunch, unwavering, unshakable, dogged, tenacious, fixed, resolute, determined, obdurate, adamant, unyielding, inflexible, strict, unbending.

**firm**[2] *n*, company, business, concern, establishment, organization, corporation, house, partnership.

**firmament** sky, heavens, empyrean, vault, space, universe. EARTH

**first** *adj*, earliest, primeval, primordial, primitive, original, initial, introductory, primary, rudimentary, elementary, basic, fundamental. LAST
foremost, chief, leading, greatest, principal, head, highest, top, supreme. LOWEST
*adv*, beforehand, firstly, initially, to begin with, in the first place. LAST

**fish** angle, trawl, cast, net.
**fish for,** seek, solicit, invite, angle for, look for, search for.

**fishy** suspicious, suspect, dubious, doubtful, questionable, unlikely, improbable, odd, queer.

**fission** cleavage, splitting, parting, division, rupture.

**fissure** rift, cleft, crevice, cranny, chasm, crack, break, fracture, breach, rupture, split, gap, opening, interstice.

**fit**[1] *v*, adapt, adjust, accommodate, alter, modify, fashion, shape.
match, tally, correspond, conform, agree, suit, go, belong, dovetail, harmonize, meet.
equip, rig, furnish, supply, provide, arm, accoutre, prepare, clothe, dress. STRIP
*adj*, suitable, fitting, appropriate, well-suited, apt, right, correct, proper, seemly, becoming. INAPPROPRIATE
able, capable, competent, qualified, eligible, ready, prepared, adequate, worthy, deserving. INELIGIBLE
healthy, robust, sturdy, strong, hale, well. UNFIT

**fit**[2] *n*, convulsion, paroxysm, spasm, seizure, attack, bout, spell, outburst, outbreak.

**fitful** irregular, intermittent, spasmodic, erratic, variable, inconstant, unstable, fluctuating, broken, disturbed, desultory, impulsive. REGULAR

**fitness** suitability, appropriateness, aptness, propriety, seemliness. IMPROPRIETY
competence, qualifications, eligibility, readiness. INELIGIBILITY
health, vigour, strength, fine fettle, good shape, condition. UNFITNESS

**fix** *v*, secure, make fast, anchor, cement, root, plant, place, locate, install, position, fasten, attach, connect, join, tie, bind, stick, glue, rivet, nail, pin. MOVE settle, resolve, establish, decide, determine, limit, define, specify, arrange, appoint, name, set.

mend, repair, patch up, restore, regulate, correct. DAMAGE

direct, focus, level, rivet.

*n*, dilemma, predicament, quandary, plight, mess, spot (*inf*), pickle (*inf*).

**fixation** obsession, *idée fixe*, compulsion, mania, fetish, preoccupation, thing (*inf*).

**fixed** established, stable, firm, secure, fast, steady, constant, unchanging, immovable, rooted, set, intent, resolute, unwavering.

**fizz** sparkle, effervesce, bubble, froth, ferment, fizzle, hiss.

**flabbergasted** amazed, astounded, dumbfounded, astonished, stunned, staggered, bowled over, speechless, nonplussed.

**flabby** flaccid, limp, drooping, floppy, loose, slack, yielding, soft. FIRM

**flaccid** limp, drooping, floppy, flabby, soft, yielding. FIRM

**flag**[1] *n*, standard, ensign, colours, banner, pennant, streamer, bunting, jack.

**flag**[2] *v*, droop, languish, faint, fail, tire, weary, weaken, wilt, sag, drop, sink, decline, fall.

**flagellate** scourge, flog, lash, whip, beat, thrash, cane, birch, castigate, chastise.

**flagitious** monstrous, atrocious, outrageous, scandalous, shocking, heinous, villainous, wicked, notorious, infamous. HONOURABLE

**flagrant** blatant, glaring, bold, barefaced, arrant, conspicuous, open, ostentatious, outrageous, scandalous, shocking, atrocious, egregious. DISGUISED

**flair** talent, gift, knack, faculty, aptitude, disposition, skill, ability, genius.

style, dash, panache, elegance, discernment, taste.

**flake** *n*, scale, chip, sliver, shaving, wafer.

*v*, scale, peel, desquamate, exfoliate, chip.

**flake out,** faint, pass out, collapse, swoon.

**flamboyant** showy, ostentatious, gaudy, flashy, dazzling, brilliant, resplendent, florid, ornate, elaborate, fancy, extravagant. PLAIN

**flame** *v*, burn, blaze, flare, flash, glow, shine.

*n*, fire, blaze, spark, flash, light, glow.

ardour, fervour, passion, zeal, eagerness, keenness, warmth, heat, intensity. COLDNESS

sweetheart, lover, beau, boyfriend, girlfriend.

**flank** *n*, side, wing, loin, haunch, thigh, hip.

*v*, border, edge, fringe, skirt, limit, bound.

**flap** *v*, wave, swing, wag, flutter, shake, agitate, vibrate, beat, flail, thresh.

*n*, fold, tab, overlap, fly, skirt, cover.

commotion, fuss, panic, agitation, tizzy (*inf*), state (*inf*).

**flare** blaze, flash, gleam, sparkle, flicker, flutter, glare.

widen, broaden, splay, spread out, expand. TAPER

**flare up,** explode, blow one's top (*inf*), lose control, boil over, fly off the handle (*inf*).

**flash** *v*, flare, flame, glare, blaze, sparkle, scintillate, coruscate, gleam, glint, twinkle, glitter, shimmer, glisten.

dart, dash, streak, fly, race, bolt, speed. CRAWL

show, display, flaunt, flourish. CONCEAL

*n*, beam, ray, flare, blaze, burst, glint, gleam, spark, streak, patch.

instant, moment, second, trice, twinkling, split second.

display, show, showing, demonstration, manifestation.

**flashy** showy, ostentatious, gaudy, flamboyant, flash (*inf*), loud, garish, cheap, tawdry.

**flat**[1] *adj*, level, even, smooth, unbroken, plane, low, horizontal, prostrate, recumbent, supine.

vapid, uninteresting, dull, insipid, bland, boring, tedious, monotonous, prosaic, lifeless, spiritless. EXCITING

direct, downright, out-and-out, positive, absolute, categorical, final, unconditional.

punctured, burst, deflated, collapsed.

*n*, lowland, plain, marsh, swamp, shallow, shoal, sandbank.

**flat**[2] *n*, apartment, rooms, penthouse.

**flatten** level, smooth, even out, iron, press, roll, crush, squash, demolish, raze.

**flatter** praise, compliment, fawn, court, butter up, humour, adulate, blandish, cajole, wheedle, coax, soft-soap (*inf*). INSULT

**flattery** praise, compliments, fawning, sycophancy, servility, adulation, blandishments, blarney, cajolery, soft-soap (*inf*), flannel (*inf*). ABUSE

**flatulent** windy, gassy.
wordy, verbose, long-winded, bombastic, pompous, pretentious, inflated, turgid. TERSE

**flaunt** display, show off, parade, sport, flash, brandish, flourish, vaunt, boast. HIDE

**flavour** taste, savour, tang, smack, zest, piquancy, relish, seasoning, flavouring.
essence, spirit, tone, character, quality, aspect, suggestion, style, touch.

**flaw** defect, fault, blemish, imperfection, spot, mark, weakness, failing.
crack, rift, cleft, fissure, split, rent, break, fracture, breach.

**flawless** perfect, faultless, unblemished, whole, intact, sound, undamaged, spotless, impeccable. FLAWED

**flay** skin, excoriate, peel, strip.
attack, criticize, pan (*inf*), castigate, berate, pull to pieces (*inf*). PRAISE

**fleck** *v*, streak, speckle, spot, dot, dapple, variegate, mottle, mark.
*n*, streak, spot, dot, speck, mark.

**flee** fly, run away, abscond, make off, escape, bolt, decamp, scarper (*inf*), take off (*inf*), leave, depart. STAY

**fleece** shear, clip, strip.
swindle, defraud, cheat, diddle (*inf*), overcharge, rip off (*inf*), rob, plunder, rifle.

**fleet**[1] *adj*, rapid, swift, fast, quick, speedy, nimble, agile. SLOW

**fleet**[2] *n*, armada, flotilla, argosy, squadron, task force, navy.

**fleeting** ephemeral, transitory, transient, evanescent, passing, brief, short-lived, momentary, temporary. LASTING

**fleetness** rapidity, swiftness, quickness, speed, velocity, celerity, nimbleness, agility. SLOWNESS

**flesh** tissue, fat, meat, body, carnality, physicality.
mankind, humanity, mortality, human race, stock, family, kin, kindred, blood.

**fleshly** carnal, sensual, lustful, lascivious, lecherous, animal, physical, bodily, corporeal, material, earthly, worldly. SPIRITUAL

**fleshy** fat, plump, corpulent, stout, rotund, podgy, chubby, tubby, obese, overweight. THIN

**flexible** pliable, pliant, bendable, ductile, elastic, tensile, malleable, plastic, supple, lithe, yielding. RIGID
adaptable, adjustable, variable, compliant, docile, biddable, amenable, tractable, complaisant. INFLEXIBLE

**flexuous** winding, serpentine, sinuous, tortuous, twisting, turning, bending, curving. STRAIGHT

**flexure** bending, flexing, incurvation, curvature, bend, turn, fold.

**flick** flip, rap, tap, dab, touch, snap, click, fillip.

**flicker** *v*, flash, twinkle, glimmer, shimmer, blink, flutter, waver, fluctuate, vibrate, quiver, tremble.
*n*, flash, gleam, glimmer, spark, trace, vestige.

**flight** flying, soaring, gliding, aviation, aeronautics.
journey, trip, run, shuttle.
cloud, swarm, flock, squadron, unit, formation.
fleeing, escape, getaway, stampede, exodus, departure, retreat, rout, migration. RETURN

**flighty** frivolous, capricious, fickle, volatile, mercurial, inconstant, changeable, irresponsible, scatterbrained, giddy, wild, impulsive, thoughtless, unstable, erratic. CONSTANT

**flimsy** frail, fragile, delicate, thin, sheer, light, insubstantial, slight, superficial, trivial, frivolous, poor, inadequate, weak, feeble, unsubstantial, rickety, shaky. STRONG

**flinch** wince, shrink, cower, quail, blench, recoil, draw back, shy away, withdraw, retreat, dodge, shirk, flee.

**fling** *v*, hurl, toss, throw, shy, pitch, cast, sling, lob (*inf*), chuck (*inf*).
*n*, toss, throw, pitch.
spree, binge, debauch, fun.

**flip** flick, jerk, toss, pitch, throw, spin, turn, twist, rap, tap, snap, fillip.

**flip through,** skim, flick through, thumb through, browse, glance at. STUDY

**flippancy** frivolity, levity, irreverence, impudence, pertness, impertinence, sauce (*inf*), cheek (*inf*). RESPECT

**flippant** frivolous, offhand, irreverent, disrespectful, rude, impudent, pert, impertinent, cheeky, saucy. SERIOUS

**flirt** *v*, philander, coquet, tease, lead on, make advances, ogle, chat up (*inf*), dally, toy, trifle.
*n*, philanderer, playboy, coquette, vamp, tease.

**flit** fly, dart, skim, flash, speed, dash, hop, flutter, flicker

**float** sail, drift, waft, glide, slide, ride, swim, bob, hover, hang. SINK
launch, start, get going, establish, set up, promote.

**flock** *n*, herd, pack, flight, swarm, bevy, crowd, throng, mass, group, company, collection, gathering, assembly, congregation.
*v*, congregate, gather, collect, assemble, herd, swarm, throng, crowd, cluster. DISPERSE

**flog** whip, lash, beat, scourge, flagellate, thrash, castigate, chastise, cane.

**flood** *v*, inundate, deluge, submerge, drown, swamp, engulf, overwhelm, overflow, brim over, pour forth, gush, surge. DRAIN
*n*, inundation, deluge, overflow, outpouring, torrent, downpour, spate, freshet, flow, stream, abundance, profusion. DROUGHT

**floor** *n*, bottom, ground, level, storey, stage, flooring. CEILING
*v*, knock down, fell, overthrow, defeat, beat, confound, nonplus, disconcert, perplex, puzzle, baffle.

**flop** *v*, collapse, fall, slump, droop, sag, drop, hang, dangle.
fail, founder, fall flat. SUCCEED
*n*, failure, fiasco, disaster, washout (*inf*). SUCCESS

**florid** ruddy, rubicund, flushed, rosy. PALE
flowery, ornate, elaborate, fussy, flamboyant, showy, high-flown, euphuistic. PLAIN

**flounce** fling, toss, jerk, bounce, spring, stamp, storm.

**flounder** wallow, struggle, thrash, toss, stumble, blunder, grope, fumble.

**flourish** *v*, thrive, prosper, succeed, do well, get on, grow, increase, wax, boom, burgeon, blossom. DECLINE
brandish, wield, wave, swing, shake, flaunt, parade, vaunt, display.
*n*, show, display, ostentation, parade, wave, twirl, dash, fanfare.
ornament, decoration, embellishment, curlicue.

**flout** mock, jeer, scoff, deride, sneer, scorn, disdain, contemn, spurn, defy. RESPECT

**flow** *v*, run, pour, stream, course, roll, sweep, drift, glide, move, circulate, ooze, seep, surge, rush, gush, spurt, cascade, abound, teem. STOP
issue, proceed, arise, spring, emanate, result.
*n*, stream, course, drift, movement, circulation, progression, current, tide, surge, rush, outpouring, discharge, flood, deluge, abundance, plethora.

**flower** *n*, bloom, blossom.
prime, peak, height, cream, pick, best, finest, elite.
*v*, bloom, blossom, blow, effloresce, come out, open, unfold, develop, mature. WITHER

**flowery** florid, ornate, fancy, elaborate, high-flown, rhetorical, figurative, grandiloquent. PLAIN

**flowing** fluent, smooth, easy, graceful, unbroken, continuous. STILTED
rich, prolific, teeming, abounding. LACKING

**fluctuate** vacillate, waver, vary, change, alter, undulate, shift, veer, swing, oscillate. STABILIZE

**fluctuation** vacillation, wavering, instability, unsteadiness, inconstancy, change, variation, shift, undulation, oscillation. STABILITY

**fluency** smoothness, ease, facility, control, command, eloquence, articulateness, glibness, flow.

**fluent** smooth, flowing, fluid, easy, effortless, natural, articulate, eloquent, glib, ready, voluble. STILTED

**fluffy** furry, fuzzy, fleecy, woolly, downy, flossy, silky, soft, light.

**fluid** *n*, liquid, solution, gas, vapour. SOLID
*adj*, liquid, gaseous, molten, flowing, running, fluent.
changeable, shifting, mobile, flexible, protean.

**fluke** accident, chance, coincidence, stroke of luck, windfall, blessing, lucky break.

**flummery** nonsense, rubbish, trash, balderdash, humbug, poppycock, flattery, blandishments, adulation.

**flunky** footman, lackey, servant, valet, underling, menial, minion, drudge.
sycophant, toady, yes man, bootlicker (*inf*).

**flurry** *n*, bustle, stir, commotion, ado, excitement, agitation, to-do (*inf*), fuss, fluster, hurry, haste. CALM
squall, gust, outbreak, burst, spell.
*v*, fluster, agitate, ruffle, disconcert, perturb, confuse, bewilder, perplex, confound. COMPOSE

**flush**[1] *v*, blush, colour, redden, go red, glow, burn, suffuse. BLANCH
flood, drench, douse, cleanse, wash, clean out, rinse, drain, empty.
excite, elate, elevate, exhilarate, thrill, animate, stir, rouse, cheer, encourage. DAMP
*n*, blush, colour, redness, rosiness, bloom, glow, radiance. PALLOR
excitement, thrill, elation, exhilaration, animation.

**flush**[2] *adj*, even, level, flat, plane, smooth. UNEVEN
wealthy, rich, affluent, well-off. POOR
generous, liberal, prodigal, lavish, abundant. MEAN

**fluster** *v*, flurry, agitate, ruffle, disconcert, perturb, bother, disturb, upset, rattle (*inf*), excite, confuse, bustle, hurry. COMPOSE
agitation, flutter, flap (*inf*), bustle, flurry, turmoil, confusion. COMPOSURE

**fluted** grooved, furrowed, corrugated, channelled.

**flutter** *v*, flap, wave, vibrate, shake, quiver, tremble, ripple, waver, fluctuate, oscillate, flicker, bat, beat, palpitate.
*n*, vibration, quiver, shudder, tremble, tremor, palpitation.
fluster, flurry, stir, commotion, agitation, excitement, confusion, perturbation. COMPOSURE

**flux** flow, fluidity, motion, transition, change, alteration, mutation, fluctuation, instability. STAGNATION

**fly** *v*, mount, soar, wing, hover, flutter, flap, flit, glide, float, sail.
dash, dart, bolt, shoot, tear, rush, hurry, race, speed, career, hare (*inf*). AMBLE
escape, flee, abscond, decamp, run, take flight. REMAIN
pass, elapse, go by, slip away, glide, roll on.
pilot, aviate, control, manoeuvre.

**foam** *n*, froth, spume, spray, bubbles, suds, lather.
*v*, froth, lather, bubble, fizz, effervesce.

**focus** *n*, centre, core, heart, nucleus, focal point, centre of attention, cynosure.
*v*, aim, direct, fix, concentrate, centre, line up, converge, meet.

**fodder** feed, food, forage, silage, hay, provender, rations.

**foe** enemy, opponent, adversary, antagonist, rival, competitor. FRIEND

**fog** *n*, mist, haze, smog, peasouper (*inf*), gloom, murk, murkiness.
obscurity, vagueness, haziness, daze, stupor, confusion, perplexity, bewilderment.
*v*, cloud, obscure, veil, shroud, dim, darken, obfuscate, confuse, bewilder, perplex. CLARIFY

**foggy** misty, hazy, murky, cloudy, obscure, dim, vague, blurred, indistinct, confused, unclear. CLEAR

**foible** weakness, failing, infirmity, fault, defect, imperfection, quirk, peculiarity, idiosyncrasy. FORTE

**foil**[1] *v*, frustrate, thwart, baffle, balk, outwit, defeat, checkmate, counter, circumvent, hamper, impede. ASSIST

**foil**[2] *n*, contrast, antithesis, complement, background, setting.
leaf, lamina, sheet, film.

**foist** pass, palm, fob, unload, get rid of, impose, thrust, insert, interpolate.

**fold** *v*, bend, double, overlap, turn under, crease, pleat, tuck, gather. FLATTEN
enfold, envelop, wrap, enclose, clasp, embrace, entwine, intertwine.
collapse, fail, go under (*inf*), go bust (*inf*), close, shut down. PROSPER
*n*, crease, wrinkle, pleat, tuck, bend, turn, overlap, layer.

**folk** people, nation, race, tribe, clan, kin, kindred, family.

**follow** succeed, come next, go after, replace. PRECEDE
pursue, chase, run after, hound, hunt, track, stalk, trail.
ensue, result, arise, spring, issue, proceed.
obey, observe, note, heed, conform to, comply with. BREAK
attend, accompany, escort, go with. DESERT
copy, imitate, ape, emulate, adopt.
understand, comprehend, grasp, see, take in, keep up with.

**follower** disciple, adherent, partisan, convert, supporter, backer, pupil, student, attendant, companion, devotee, fan, admirer, hanger-on.

**following** *adj*, next, subsequent, successive, ensuing, consequent, resulting, coming, later. PRECEDING
*n*, entourage, train, suite, clientele, circle, public, supporters, admirers.

**folly** foolishness, stupidity, silliness, absurdity, nonsense, madness, craziness, idiocy, lunacy, rashness, recklessness, indiscretion, imprudence. WISDOM

**foment** encourage, stimulate, instigate, incite, provoke, stir up, arouse, brew, agitate, excite, goad, spur, promote, foster. QUELL

**fomentation** encouragement, stimulation, instigation, incitement, provocation, arousal, agitation, excitement.

**fond** loving, tender, warm, affectionate, amorous, adoring, devoted, doting, caring. COLD
foolish, absurd, empty, vain, optimistic, naive, credulous. SENSIBLE

**fond of,** partial to, attached to, keen on, enamoured of, having a liking for. AVERSE

**fondle** caress, stroke, pet, pat, cuddle.

**fondness** liking, predilection, partiality, penchant, fancy, weakness. AVERSION
love, affection, tenderness, devotion, care. COLDNESS

**food** nourishment, sustenance, nutriment, aliment, fare, diet, meals, board, foodstuffs, provisions, victuals, comestibles, eats (*inf*), grub (*inf*), commons, rations.
fodder, feed, provender, forage.

**fool** *n*, blockhead, dunce, dolt, ninny, nincompoop, simpleton, idiot, halfwit, ass, donkey, chump (*inf*), twit (*inf*), clot (*inf*), dope (*inf*).
clown, jester, buffoon, harlequin, pierrot.
*v*, deceive, dupe, trick, hoodwink, beguile, cheat, delude, mislead, hoax, cozen, take in, con (*inf*).
jest, joke, pretend, play, trifle, toy, meddle, fiddle, tamper.

**foolery** antics, capers, mischief, pranks, tricks, buffoonery, tomfoolery, horseplay.

**foolhardy** reckless, rash, incautious, irresponsible, daredevil, madcap, temerarious, bold, daring, adventurous, impetuous, precipitate, desperate. CAUTIOUS

**foolish** silly, unwise, injudicious, imprudent, ill-advised, absurd, ridiculous, fatuous, senseless, unreasonable, irrational, brainless, witless, stupid, unintelligent, simple, puerile, mad, crazy, idiotic, daft (*inf*). SENSIBLE

**foolishness** folly, stupidity, imprudence, senselessness, absurdity, inanity, madness, craziness, foolery, nonsense. SENSE

**foot** *n*, paw, hoof, trotter, pad.
bottom, base, foundation, pedestal, support. TOP
*v*, pay, settle, discharge, meet.

**footing** basis, foundation, establishment, settlement, groundwork, foothold.
standing, status, position, condition, rank, grade, relationship, terms.

**footstep** footprint, footmark, track, trace.
footfall, step, tread.

**fop** dandy, coxcomb, beau, popinjay, swell (*inf*).

**foppery** foppishness, dandyism, vanity, affectation.

**foppish** dandyish, dandified, vain, conceited, affected, spruce, dapper. SLOVENLY

**for** *prep*, towards, to, in order to. FROM
belonging to, appropriate to, concerning.
during, through, throughout.
in favour of, pro, with, in support of, on behalf of. AGAINST
because of, owing to, due to.
*conj*, since, as, because.

**forage** *n*, fodder, food, feed, provender.
*v*, search, hunt, seek, scour, scavenge, rummage, ransack, plunder, pillage, raid.

**foray** raid, incursion, inroad, invasion, sally, sortie, attack, assault. RETREAT

**forbear** refrain, abstain, desist, cease, stop, pause, hold back, withhold, restrain oneself, avoid, shun, eschew, decline. INDULGE

**forbearance** abstinence, restraint, self-control, moderation, temperance, patience, tolerance, leniency, clemency.

**forbid** prohibit, ban, interdict, proscribe, outlaw, taboo, veto, disallow. PERMIT
impede, hinder, inhibit, prevent, exclude, rule out. ALLOW

**forbidding** menacing, threatening, ominous, sinister, hostile, unfriendly, grim, daunting, off-putting (*inf*), repulsive, repellent, unpleasant. ATTRACTIVE

**force** *v*, compel, constrain, oblige, make, drive, impel, coerce, press, urge. COAX strain, wrench, break open, blast, push, thrust. EASE

*n*, compulsion, constraint, coercion, duress, pressure, violence.

power, might, strength, vigour, drive, energy, dynamism, potency, efficacy, cogency, impact, stress, emphasis, weight. WEAKNESS

army, host, legion, squadron, troop, regiment, unit, division, detachment, battalion.

**forced** compulsory, obligatory, mandatory, involuntary, enforced, compelled, constrained. VOLUNTARY

unnatural, strained, artificial, false, affected, mannered, laboured, stiff. NATURAL

**forcible** forceful, compelling, powerful, mighty, strong, potent, cogent, pithy, effective, weighty, impressive. WEAK

forced, compulsory, obligatory, violent, aggressive, coercive.

**fore** front, lead, head, top, bow, forefront, foreground. REAR

**forebear** ancestor, forefather, progenitor, predecessor, forerunner. DESCENDANT

**forebode** portend, augur, presage, foretell, predict, prophesy, foreshadow, betoken, indicate, promise, warn, forewarn.

**foreboding** premonition, presentiment, apprehension, misgiving, dread, fear, anxiety. REASSURANCE

omen, portent, token, augury, prediction, prophecy, warning.

**forecast** *v*, predict, augur, prophesy, divine, foresee, prognosticate, anticipate, speculate, estimate, calculate, plan, project.

*n*, prediction, augury, prophecy, divination, prognosis, anticipation, speculation, projection, outlook.

**foreclose** exclude, shut out, preclude, debar, block, hinder, prevent, stop.

**forefather** ancestor, forebear, progenitor, procreator, father. OFFSPRING

**foregoing** preceding, prior, previous, former, antecedent, anterior. FOLLOWING

**foregone** past, previous, former, earlier, bygone. FUTURE

predetermined, preordained, fixed, inevitable.

**foreign** alien, strange, unfamiliar, imported, exotic, outlandish, external, exterior, remote, distant. NATIVE

extrinsic, extraneous, irrelevant, unrelated. RELEVANT

**foreigner** alien, immigrant, stranger, outsider, newcomer. NATIVE

**foreknowledge** prescience, foresight, precognition, premonition, clairvoyance.

**foreland** cape, headland, promontory, spur, point.

**foreman** supervisor, overseer, superintendent, charge hand, manager, boss (*inf*).

**foremost** chief, leading, front, head, first, primary, principal, main, supreme, paramount, prime.

**forerunner** precursor, harbinger, herald, predecessor, ancestor, forebear, forefather. SUCCESSOR

omen, portent, sign, token, indication, forewarning, premonition.

**foresee** anticipate, expect, envisage, forecast, predict, prophesy, divine, foretell.

**foreshadow** augur, presage, predict, prophesy, prefigure, portend, forebode, betoken, indicate, signify.

**foresight** forethought, anticipation, provision, precaution, prudence, care, circumspection, far-sightedness. IMPROVIDENCE

**forest** wood, woodland, woods, grove, copse, plantation.

**forestall** anticipate, thwart, frustrate, intercept, ward off, fend off, parry, obviate, preclude, prevent, hinder.

**foretell** predict, prophesy, augur, divine, forecast, prognosticate, presage, foreshadow, forebode, prefigure, betoken.

**forethought** anticipation, foresight, provision, precaution, prudence, far-sightedness. IMPROVIDENCE

**forever** evermore, always, till the end of time, eternally, constantly, perpetually, incessantly, all the time. TEMPORARILY

**forewarn** warn, alert, put on guard, caution, admonish, advise.

**foreword** preface, introduction, preamble, prologue. EPILOGUE

**forfeit** *v*, lose, surrender, relinquish, give up, renounce. EARN

*n*, loss, penalty, fine, mulct, forfeiture. REWARD

**forge** *v*, make, shape, form, mould, work, hammer out, create, fabricate, devise, invent, frame, coin.

fake, counterfeit, falsify, copy, imitate.

*n*, smithy, foundry, furnace, hearth.

**forged** fake, counterfeit, false, fraudulent, imitation, sham, bogus, spurious. GENUINE

**forgery** fake, counterfeit, falsification, imitation, sham, fraud.

**forget** overlook, neglect, disregard, ignore, omit, pass over, let slip. REMEMBER

**forgetful** absent-minded, inattentive, negligent, neglectful, heedless, careless, oblivious, unmindful. MINDFUL

**forgive** pardon, absolve, excuse, acquit, exonerate, remit, condone, overlook, let off (*inf*). PUNISH

**forgiveness** pardon, absolution, acquittal, remission, clemency, mercy. PUNISHMENT

**forgo** surrender, relinquish, give up, yield, hand over, renounce, abandon, waive, do without, abstain from, shun.

**forgotten** unremembered, past, bygone, lost, irretrievable, neglected, overlooked. REMEMBERED

**fork** *v*, branch, bifurcate, divide, part, split, separate, diverge, divaricate. UNITE
*n*, bifurcation, divarication, separation, division, branch.

**forlorn** miserable, wretched, desolate, cheerless, comfortless, unhappy, woebegone, pathetic, pitiful, helpless, friendless, homeless, destitute, lost, abandoned, deserted, forsaken. HAPPY

**form** *n*, shape, configuration, figure, appearance, cast, mould, pattern, model, cut, structure, frame, outline, contour, build, body.
type, kind, sort, variety, style, design, description, nature, character, mode, manner, method, arrangement, system, order.
document, paper, blank.
convention, etiquette, protocol, formality, procedure, ritual, ceremony, practice, custom, conduct, behaviour.
condition, health, fitness, shape, fettle.
class, grade, group, stream, year.
bench, seat.
*v*, make, shape, mould, model, fashion, create, fabricate, build, construct, assemble, produce. DESTROY
frame, devise, invent, conceive, formulate, think up, design, plan, arrange, dispose, organize.
compose, make up, constitute, comprise.
take shape, materialize, crystallize, appear, develop. VANISH
contract, acquire, get, pick up. LOSE
train, educate, instruct, teach, school, discipline.

**formal** conventional, customary, regular, standard, approved, official, set, fixed, methodical, strict, precise, exact, correct, punctilious. UNCONVENTIONAL
ceremonious, stiff, starched, prim, solemn, dignified, ceremonial, stately, pompous, aloof, reserved. INFORMAL

**formality** convention, form, custom, usage, practice, procedure, ritual, ceremony, protocol, etiquette, decorum.

**format** design, layout, appearance, arrangement, organization, style, form, composition, plan.

**formation** forming, making, creation, generation, production, manufacture, construction, composition, constitution, establishment, development. DESTRUCTION
arrangement, grouping, pattern, design, layout, structure.

**former** previous, earlier, prior, preceding, foregoing, antecedent, past, bygone, foregone, anterior, one-time, erstwhile, late. FUTURE

**formerly** previously, heretofore, hitherto, once, at one time.

**formidable** alarming, terrifying, fearful, dreadful, frightful, menacing, threatening, horrible, awful, terrible, daunting, overwhelming, arduous, difficult. REASSURING
tremendous, colossal, terrific, great, strong, powerful, mighty, impressive, redoubtable, indomitable. CONTEMPTIBLE

**formless** amorphous, vague, indefinite, nebulous, shapeless, unformed, chaotic, disorganized.

**formula** rule, principle, prescription, recipe, procedure, method, ritual, formulary, equation.

**formulate** define, specify, detail, itemize, set down, articulate, express, state.
devise, invent, forge, coin, think up, conceive, plan, draw up.

**forsake** desert, leave, quit, abandon, cast off, give up, relinquish, forgo, surrender, yield, forswear, renounce. KEEP

**forswear** abjure, renounce, reject, forgo, relinquish, give up, forsake, abandon. RETAIN
disavow, retract, deny, recant, repudiate, disown. AFFIRM

**fort** fortress, stronghold, citadel, fastness, garrison, castle, defence, fortification.

**forte** strength, strong point, gift, talent, métier, speciality. FOIBLE

**forth** forward, onward, ahead, out, away, abroad.

**forthcoming** future, prospective, coming, approaching, expected, imminent, impending. PREVIOUS
communicative, open, sociable, expansive, chatty, talkative, responsive. RETICENT

**forthright** direct, straightforward, candid, frank, blunt, outspoken. EVASIVE

**forthwith** directly, immediately, at once, instantly, straightaway, without delay, right away. PRESENTLY

**fortification** defence, bastion, rampart, battlement, bulwark, fort, stronghold, citadel, fastness.

**fortify** strengthen, reinforce, stiffen, brace, buttress, support, protect, defend, garrison.
encourage, cheer, hearten, invigorate, revive, sustain.

**fortitude** endurance, patience, forbearance, hardihood, courage, bravery, backbone, strength, firmness, resolution, determination, perseverance. WEAKNESS

**fortuitous** accidental, unplanned, contingent, chance, unforeseen, casual, arbitrary, lucky, fortunate. PLANNED

**fortunate** lucky, happy, felicitous, fortuitous, blessed, favoured, prosperous, successful, auspicious, propitious, favourable, advantageous, opportune, timely. UNFORTUNATE

**fortune** wealth, riches, opulence, affluence, assets, possessions, property, estate. POVERTY
luck, chance, accident, contingency, fortuity, fate, destiny, lot, portion, doom, kismet, future, prospect, expectation.

**forward** *adj*, advanced, early, premature, precocious, progressive, onward. BACKWARD
front, leading, first, foremost, head, anterior, fore. BACK
bold, brazen, cheeky, pert, impertinent, impudent, presumptuous, assuming, familiar, fresh (*inf*), confident, cocky (*inf*). RESERVED
*adv*, forwards, on, onward, forth, ahead. BACKWARD
out, into view, into the open, to the fore, into prominence.
*v*, advance, further, promote, foster, support, aid, help, encourage, expedite, quicken, hasten, hurry, speed, accelerate, dispatch. HINDER
send, transmit, dispatch, mail, post, ship, send on.

**foster** promote, advance, further, encourage, stimulate, cultivate, support, maintain, cherish, nurture, nurse, harbour, sustain, nourish, raise, rear, bring up.

**foul** adj, dirty, filthy, soiled, unclean, impure, contaminated, polluted, tainted, sullied, offensive, disgusting, revolting, loathsome, putrid, fetid, stinking, rank, noisome. PURE
wicked, vile, ignoble, despicable, disgraceful, shameful, heinous, infamous, base, low, vulgar, coarse, gross, obscene, ribald, scurrilous, profane, blasphemous. NOBLE
unfair, dishonourable, dishonest, crooked, underhand, unsportsmanlike, unscrupulous. FAIR
rainy, wet, gloomy, murky, overcast, bad, stormy, rough, wild. FINE
*v*, soil, dirty, begrime, pollute, contaminate, taint, sully, defile.
block, clog, jam, choke, snarl, entangle. CLEAR

**found** establish, set up, institute, organize, originate, start, create, build, raise, erect. ABOLISH
base, ground, root, fix, set, rest, place.

**foundation** base, basis, footing, groundwork, bottom, substructure, root. SUPERSTRUCTURE
establishment, institution, organization, endowment, settlement.

**founder**[1] *v*, sink, go down, collapse, fail, abort, miscarry, fall through, break down, fall, trip, stumble, stagger.

**founder**[2] *n*, originator, creator, organizer, benefactor, architect, designer, builder, author, father.

**fountain** jet, spout, spray, fount, spring, well.
fountainhead, source, origin, cause, beginning.

**foxy** wily, artful, cunning, sly, crafty, subtle, shrewd, astute, tricky, guileful, scheming. ARTLESS

**fracas** quarrel, row, brawl, fight, disturbance, fray, uproar, commotion, rumpus.

**fraction** part, piece, fragment, bit, portion, section, segment, division. WHOLE

**fractious** irritable, peevish, testy, touchy, captious, cross, waspish, crabby, petulant, fretful. AFFABLE
unruly, refractory, recalcitrant, rebellious, awkward, contrary, perverse. DOCILE

**fracture** *v*, break, crack, split, rupture, tear. MEND
*n*, break, breach, crack, rift, division, split, fissure, cleft, rupture, rent.

**fragile** brittle, frangible, breakable, frail, delicate, dainty, flimsy, slight, weak, feeble. STRONG

**fragility** brittleness, frangibility, frailty, delicacy, flimsiness, weakness, feebleness. STRENGTH

**fragment** piece, portion, fraction, part, bit, morsel, scrap, remnant, chip, sliver. WHOLE

**fragmentary** broken, disconnected, disjointed, bitty, incomplete, partial, sketchy, unfinished, scattered, piecemeal.

**fragrance** perfume, scent, aroma, smell, odour, redolence, balm, bouquet. FETOR

**fragrant** perfumed, scented, ambrosial, balmy, aromatic, sweet-smelling, redolent, odoriferous. FETID

**frail** weak, feeble, infirm, fragile, delicate, slight, slender, thin, flimsy. STURDY

**frailty** weakness, feebleness, infirmity, fragility, delicacy, slenderness. STURDINESS
failing, faulty, defect, imperfection, foible, weakness, fallibility, susceptibility. STRENGTH

**frame** *v*, make, form, construct, build, fashion, model, forge, fabricate, devise, invent, concoct, compose, draw up, formulate, draft, sketch, outline, map out, plan.
enclose, surround, border, mount, encase.
*n*, structure, construction, framework, skeleton, shell, casing, support, substructure, form, shape, fabric, constitution, system.
mount, setting, border, case.
condition, state, mood, temper, humour, disposition.

**franchise** vote, suffrage, right, privilege, licence, authorization, exemption, immunity, freedom.

**frank** honest, straightforward, direct, forthright, candid, outspoken, unreserved, blunt, open, sincere, guileless, artless, ingenuous. DEVIOUS
indisguised, unconcealed, avowed, apparent, obvious, plain, clear, transparent. CONCEALED

**frantic** frenzied, wild, mad, delirious, hysterical, distraught, distracted, raging, furious, beside oneself, hectic, frenetic. CALM

**fraternity** brotherhood, fellowship, association, society, league, guild, union, circle, set, clan, company, companionship, camaraderie.

**fraternize** associate, league, unite, cooperate, sympathize, socialize, mix, mingle, go around, keep company, consort, hobnob.

**fraud** deception, deceit, trickery, cheating, fraudulence, imposture, duplicity, treachery. HONESTY
trick, artifice, swindle, hoax, wile, ruse, stratagem.
impostor, charlatan, quack, cheat, swindler, fake, phoney (*inf*).

**fraudulent** deceitful, tricky, crafty, wily, knavish, treacherous, dishonest, crooked, false, counterfeit, fake. HONEST

**fraught** filled, full, charged, loaded, laden, replete, abounding, attended, accompanied. DEVOID

**fray**[1] *n*, fight, battle, combat, conflict, quarrel, row, brawl, melee, riot, fracas. PEACE

**fray**[2] *v*, wear, unravel, shred, tatter, chafe, rub, fret.

**freak** monstrosity, monster, abnormality, anomaly, oddity, curiosity, mutant, teratism, malformation, deformity, abortion.
whim, caprice, fancy, notion, vagary, crotchet, quirk, humour.

**freakish** abnormal, aberrant, unnatural, bizarre, weird, strange, monstrous, malformed, grotesque. NORMAL
whimsical, capricious, fanciful, wayward, fitful, erratic, odd. CONSISTENT

**free** *adj*, independent, unconfined, loose, unattached, liberated, released, unfettered, unrestrained, unrestricted, unbridled, at large. CONFINED
gratis, gratuitous, on the house, complimentary, without charge, for nothing.
idle, at leisure, unoccupied, vacant, empty, available, spare. BUSY
clear, unobstructed, unimpeded, unhampered, open, permitted, allowed. BLOCKED

exempt, immune, not liable, devoid, without. LIABLE
informal, easy, relaxed, casual, unceremonious, familiar, uninhibited, natural, open, frank. CONSTRAINED
liberal, generous, prodigal, lavish, bountiful, extravagant, munificent. MEAN
voluntary, unforced, willing, spontaneous, unbidden. FORCED
*v*, liberate, release, loose, let go, set free, emancipate, manumit, unfetter, unchain, unbind, untie. BIND
deliver, rescue, relieve, rid, clear, extricate, disentangle, disengage, discharge, exempt, except. EMBROIL

**freebooter** pirate, buccaneer, bandit, brigand, robber, raider, marauder, highwayman.

**freedom** liberty, emancipation, independence, liberation, release, deliverance. CAPTIVITY
exemption, exception, immunity, privilege. LIABILITY
range, scope, play, latitude, leeway, licence, authority, carte blanche. RESTRICTION
informality, unconstraint, ease, familiarity, frankness, openness. CONSTRAINT

**freeze** solidify, congeal, harden, ice up, refrigerate, chill, benumb. MELT
stop, stand still, suspend, hold, fix, peg.

**freezing** icy, bitter, biting, raw, wintry, arctic, polar, glacial, frigid. HOT

**freight** transportation, conveyance, carriage, shipment, cargo, load, lading, burden, charge, consignment, goods, merchandise.

**frenetic** frantic, frenzied, wild, mad, demented, distraught. CALM

**frenzy** agitation, excitement, fury, rage, passion, madness, derangement, distraction, aberration, hysteria, delirium, fit, paroxysm, outburst. COMPOSURE

**frequent** *adj*, recurrent, repeated, incessant, continual, persistent, constant, many, numerous. RARE
common, everyday, familiar, customary, usual, habitual. UNUSUAL
*v*, visit, attend, patronize, haunt.

**frequently** often, repeatedly, again and again, over and over, many times, constantly, regularly, commonly, usually. SELDOM

**fresh** new, recent, latest, modern, up-to-date, novel, original, different, unfamiliar. OLD
additional, extra, more, further, renewed, other.
cool, refreshing, invigorating, bracing, brisk, crisp, clear, clean, pure, sweet. STALE
energetic, vigorous, lively, hearty, healthy, keen, alert, revived, refreshed, rested, strong, hardy, flourishing, blooming, glowing, fair. TIRED
inexperienced, green, raw, callow, youthful, artless, unsophisticated, untrained. EXPERIENCED
natural, unprocessed, uncured, raw, crude. PROCESSED
familiar, forward, presumptuous, bold, cheeky, saucy, impertinent, impudent, disrespectful.

**freshen** refresh, invigorate, revive, revitalize, enliven, renew, ventilate, air.

**fret** worry, brood, agonize, grieve, pine, distress, torment, irritate, annoy, vex, trouble, disturb, upset, bother, ruffle, harass, provoke, goad. SOOTHE
rub, chafe, wear, abrade, fray, erode, corrode, eat away.

**fretful** irritable, petulant, peevish, waspish, captious, testy, touchy, fractious, querulous, edgy, anxious, uneasy.

**friable** crumbly, powdery, brittle. TOUGH

**friction** attrition, abrasion, rubbing, grating, scraping, grinding.
discord, dissension, dispute, disagreement, conflict, strife, hostility, antagonism, animosity. AGREEMENT

**friend** companion, intimate, confidant, familiar, comrade, ally, associate, partner, crony, chum (*inf*), pal (*inf*), mate (*inf*), benefactor, patron, supporter. ENEMY

**friendly** amicable, kind, kindly, benevolent, neighbourly, brotherly, sisterly, cordial, amiable, genial, affable, sociable, outgoing, approachable, close, intimate, familiar, fond, affectionate, sympathetic, understanding. UNFRIENDLY
favourable, propitious, auspicious, advantageous, beneficial, helpful. HOSTILE

**friendship** amity, harmony, rapport, comradeship, companionship, friendliness, amicability, cordiality, kindness, benevolence, intimacy, familiarity, love, affection, fondness, attachment, regard. ENMITY

**fright** fear, alarm, scare, terror, shock, horror, panic, dismay, consternation, dread, trepidation, apprehension. REASSURANCE

**frighten** alarm, scare, terrify, shock, startle, horrify, dismay, daunt, intimidate, unnerve. REASSURE

**frightful** frightening, alarming, terrifying, fearsome, fearful, dreadful, terrible, awful, horrible, hideous, gruesome, ghastly, dire, distressing, horrifying, shocking, appalling, outrageous, monstrous. DELIGHTFUL

**frigid** cold, cool, icy, glacial, formal, stiff, rigid, prim, aloof, unapproachable, forbidding, unfriendly, unresponsive, unfeeling, passionless, passive, indifferent. WARM

**frigidity** coldness, coolness, formality, stiffness, aloofness, unapproachability, unfriendliness, impassivity, indifference, apathy. WARMTH

**frill** flounce, ruche, furbelow, ruff, ruffle, valance, purfle, border, trimming.
affectation, mannerism, ostentation, showiness, fuss, frippery.

**fringe** border, edging, trimming.
edge, periphery, outskirts, limits, border, margin, verge. CENTRE

**frisk** frolic, gambol, caper, skip, jump, leap, dance, play, sport, romp, cavort.

**frisky** frolicsome, sportive, playful, lively, full of beans (*inf*), coltish, high-spirited, gay, animated. SEDATE

**fritter** waste, squander, spend, dissipate, misspend, idle, dally. SAVE

**frivolity** frivolousness, levity, flippancy, light-heartedness, foolishness, silliness, puerility, childishness, triviality, superficiality. SERIOUSNESS

**frivolous** foolish, silly, puerile, childish, flippant, idle, light, trivial, petty, unimportant, paltry, superficial, shallow. SERIOUS

**frolic** *v*, gambol, caper, frisk, romp, cavort, play, sport.
*n*, gambol, caper, romp, game, sport, lark, antic, prank, fun, merriment, gaiety, jollity.

**frolicsome** playful, sportive, frisky, coltish, lively, merry, gay. SEDATE

**front** *n*, anterior, forepart, foreground, face, exterior, façade, frontage. BACK
fore, head, top, lead, vanguard, forefront, beginning. REAR
aspect, appearance, air, demeanour, bearing, mien, exterior, façade, mask, disguise, show.
**in front,** ahead, leading, first, before, in advance. BEHIND
*adj*, anterior, frontal, forward, foremost, leading, head, first. BACK
*v*, face, be opposite, look out on, overlook, confront, encounter.

**frontier** boundary, border, marches, limits, confines, bounds, edge.

**frosty** icy, glacial, freezing, frigid, cold, chilly, wintry. HOT
unenthusiastic, indifferent, cool, frigid, distant, aloof, unfriendly, unwelcoming. WARM

**froth** *n*, foam, spume, bubbles, effervescence, lather, suds, head, scum.
triviality, emptiness, idle talk, nonsense, humbug, flummery.
*v*, foam, lather, fizz, bubble, effervesce.

**frown** scowl, glower, glare, lower, pout, grimace. SMILE
**frown on,** disapprove of, dislike, disfavour, discountenance, take a dim view of. APPROVE

**frowzy** unkempt, untidy, slovenly, slatternly, shabby, sloppy, frumpish, dirty. NEAT
stale, musty, frowsty, fusty, ill-smelling.

**frozen** icy, frigid, arctic, glacial, chilled, frosted, numb. HOT

**frugal** thrifty, sparing, economical, careful, provident, temperate, abstemious, parsimonious, niggardly, meagre, scanty. EXTRAVAGANT

**frugality** thrift, economy, providence, temperance, parsimony, meagreness. EXTRAVAGANCE

**fruit** produce, crop, harvest, yield, product, result, consequence, issue, outcome, return, profit, reward, advantage.

**fruitful** productive, prolific, fecund, fertile, rich, teeming, plentiful, plenteous, abundant, profuse. BARREN
profitable, worthwhile, effective, successful, useful, productive, rewarding. FRUITLESS

**fruition** fulfilment, attainment, achievement, realization, completion, consummation, perfection, maturation, gratification, enjoyment. ABORTION

**fruitless** futile, vain, useless, bootless, ineffectual, unproductive, unprofitable, unsuccessful, abortive, idle, worthless, unavailing, barren, sterile. FRUITFUL

**frustrate** thwart, foil, dash, balk, confound, baffle, defeat, undo, circumvent, check, block, stymie, hinder, prevent, disappoint, discourage, upset, annoy, irritate. GRATIFY

**frustration** thwarting, balking, defeat, failure, circumvention, hindrance, prevention, disappointment, annoyance, irritation. GRATIFICATION

**fuddled** inebriated, intoxicated, drunk, tipsy, stupefied, muddled, confused. SOBER

**fuel** combustible, wood, coal, gas, oil, petrol.
food, nourishment, sustenance, incitement, provocation, encouragement.

**fugacious** fleeting, transitory, transient, fugitive, brief, short-lived, passing, ephemeral, evanescent. PERMANENT

**fugitive** *n*, runaway, escapee, deserter, refugee.
*adj*, fleeting, transitory, transient, fugacious, brief, short-lived, passing, ephemeral, evanescent. PERMANENT

**fulcrum** pivot, support, prop.

**fulfil** complete, accomplish, achieve, realize, perfect, consummate, effect, effectuate, perform, execute, discharge, do, carry out, satisfy, fill, meet, answer, obey, observe, keep.

**fulfilment** completion, accomplishment, achievement, realization, perfection, consummation, performance, execution, discharge, satisfaction, observance.

**fuliginous** sooty, smoky, dusky, dark.

**full** *adj*, filled, brimming, packed, replete, sated, gorged, satiated, saturated. EMPTY
complete, entire, whole, intact, integral, unabridged. PARTIAL
abundant, plentiful, plenteous, copious, ample, generous, capacious, voluminous, vast, extensive, large, broad, comprehensive, thorough, detailed, exhaustive. RESTRICTED
plump, rounded, curvaceous, buxom, puffy, baggy, loose.
occupied, taken, in use. VACANT
resonant, rich, deep, loud, clear, distinct. MUTED
*adv*, directly, straight, right, squarely, exactly, precisely.
completely, entirely, fully, wholly, quite, altogether. PARTLY

**fully** completely, entirely, wholly, totally, utterly, absolutely, altogether, quite, thoroughly, perfectly. PARTLY
sufficiently, adequately, enough, amply, abundantly. INADEQUATELY

**fulminate** denounce, condemn, decry, rail, inveigh, roar, thunder, rage, fume, censure, upbraid, berate, animadvert, remonstrate, protest. EXTOL
explode, detonate, blow up, burst.

**fulmination** denunciation, condemnation, censure, animadversion, tirade, diatribe, obloquy, philippic. EULOGY
explosion, detonation, blast.

**fulsome** excessive, extravagant, overdone, adulatory, fawning, sycophantic, insincere, sickening, nauseating. MEAGRE

**fumble** grope, feel, scrabble, search, flounder, stumble, bungle, botch, muff.

**fume** *v*, rage, storm, rant, rave, seethe, boil, chafe, fret.
smoke, emit, exhale, reek.
*n*, rage, storm, fury, passion, agitation, fret, stew (*inf*). CALM

**fumes** gas, vapour, smoke, effluvium, exhalation, pollution, reek.

**fumigate** smoke, disinfect, purify, cleanse, sterilize. INFECT

**fun** amusement, entertainment, diversion, recreation, sport, pleasure, enjoyment, merriment, jollity, joy, gaiety, cheer, mirth. MISERY
**make fun of,** mock, jeer, gibe, taunt, deride, scoff at, satirize, lampoon. RESPECT

**function** *n*, purpose, use, part, role, province, duty, charge, task, job, office, position, business, mission, occupation.
operation, performance, execution, exercise, activity.
ceremony, party, reception, gathering, affair, do (*inf*).
*v*, work, operate, act, behave, run, go, perform.

**fund** *n*, stock, supply, store, reserve, accumulation, hoard, reservoir, pool, kitty, treasury, capital, endowment, investment, savings, money, resources, funds, finance.
*v*, finance, pay for, subsidize, support, endow, capitalize.

**fundamental** *adj*, basic, primary, first, elementary, important, necessary, essential,

principal, key, vital, indispensable, cardinal, underlying, organic, constitutional, integral. SECONDARY
*n*, basic, rudiment, essential, principle, rule, foundation, basis, cornerstone.

**funeral** burial, interment, inhumation, cremation, obsequies, exequies.

**funereal** mournful, dirgeful, lugubrious, gloomy, dismal, sorrowful, woeful, sombre, dark, dreary, grave, solemn. JOYOUS

**funk** *n*, fear, panic, terror, fright, alarm, dread, trepidation, nervousness. COURAGE
*v*, flinch, recoil, quail, cower, take fright, chicken out (*inf*). FACE

**funny** amusing, comic, comical, humorous, droll, witty, facetious, entertaining, diverting, hilarious, hysterical (*inf*), farcical, laughable, ridiculous, ludicrous. SERIOUS
odd, strange, queer, weird, curious, peculiar, mysterious, suspicious, dubious. NORMAL

**fur** hair, coat, hide, skin, pelt.

**furbish** polish, rub, burnish, shine, brighten, clean up, renovate, restore. TARNISH

**furcate** furcated, forked, branched, divided, divaricate, bifurcate.

**furious** angry, enraged, fuming, incensed, irate, infuriated, wrathful, raging, mad, frantic, frenzied, wild, violent, agitated, turbulent, stormy, tempestuous, savage, fierce, intense, unrestrained. CALM

**furl** roll, wrap, fold, wind. UNFURL

**furnish** equip, rig, fit out, appoint, decorate, stock, supply, provide, give, grant, afford, bestow, endow, invest. DIVEST

**furniture** fixtures, appliances, fittings, movables, furnishings, appointments, effects, goods, belongings, possessions, apparatus, equipment.

**furore** outcry, uproar, commotion, stir, outburst, rage, fury, frenzy. APATHY
craze, mania, rage, enthusiasm, fad.

**furrow** *n*, trench, trough, channel, rut, hollow, groove, flute, wrinkle, crease, line, seam. RIDGE
*v*, wrinkle, crease, knit, pucker.

**further** *adj*, additional, more, extra, supplementary, new, fresh, other.
*adv*, furthermore, besides, moreover, in addition, what's more, also, yet.
farther, beyond, past, longer, more. NEARER
*v*, advance, promote, forward, assist, help, foster, encourage, support, expedite, hasten. HINDER

**furtherance** advancement, promotion, boost, assistance, help, aid, encouragement, support, backing. HINDRANCE

**furthermore** moreover, yet, in addition, besides, what's more, further, too, also, as well.

**furthest** farthest, utmost, extreme, ultimate, remotest, most distant. NEAREST

**furtive** secret, secretive, clandestine, hidden, covert, sly, stealthy, surreptitious, underhand. OPEN

**fury** rage, anger, wrath, ire, passion, temper, frenzy, madness, wildness, violence, force, intensity, fierceness, ferocity, severity, vehemence, tempestuousness, turbulence. CALM
shrew, vixen, termagant, virago, hellcat, spitfire.

**fuse** unite, join, combine, integrate, amalgamate, blend, intermix, commingle, intermingle, merge, coalesce. SEPARATE
melt, liquefy, smelt, weld, solder.

**fusion** union, amalgamation, coalescence, synthesis, blend, mixture, merger, amalgam, alloy.

**fuss** *n*, agitation, commotion, stir, to-do (*inf*), bustle, fluster, flurry, bother, ado, palaver, flap (*inf*), excitement. PEACE
complaint, objection, difficulty, trouble, argument, altercation, quarrel, dispute, row.
*v*, bustle, fret, worry, fidget, fume, gripe (*inf*), bother, pester.

**fussy** particular, finicky, faddy, pernickety, choosy (*inf*), difficult, hard to please, fastidious, dainty, discriminating, exacting. EASY-GOING
fidgety, restless, fretful, crotchety. PLACID
ornate, elaborate, busy, cluttered. SIMPLE

**fustian** *n*, bombast, rant, pomposity, grandiloquence, magniloquence, bluster.
*adj*, bombastic, pompous, high-flown, lofty, euphuistic. PLAIN

**fusty** musty, mouldy, mildewy, damp, frowsty, stale, rank, ill-smelling, stuffy. FRESH
old-fashioned, out-of-date, antiquated, archaic, passé. MODERN

**futile** useless, vain, fruitless, bootless, ineffectual, unavailing, idle, empty, profit-

less, worthless, abortive, unsuccessful, unproductive, pointless. FRUITFUL
trifling, trivial, minor, insignificant, unimportant. IMPORTANT
**futility** uselessness, vanity, fruitlessness, idleness, worthlessness, pointlessness. USEFULNESS
triviality, insignificance, unimportance. IMPORTANCE
**future** *adj*, forthcoming, coming, to come, prospective, expected, impending, approaching, eventual, ultimate, subsequent, later. PAST
*n*, prospect, outlook, expectation, offing, hereafter.
**fuzzy** fluffy, woolly, downy. SMOOTH
blurred, indistinct, unclear, out of focus, bleary, misty, vague, obscure, distorted. SHARP

# G

**gab** *v*, chatter, gossip, prattle, blabber, babble.
*n*, chat, talk, small talk, chitchat, gossip, chatter, babble.
**gabble** *v*, jabber, gibber, spout, gush, chatter, babble, blather, prattle.
*n*, drivel, gibberish, chatter, babble, blather, prattle, jabber.
**gadget** device, contraption (*inf*), contrivance, appliance, tool, implement.
**gag**[1] *v*, muzzle, muffle, stifle, stop up, silence, quiet, suppress, curb.
throttle, choke, retch, heave, gasp.
**gag**[2] *n*, joke, quip, witticism, crack (*inf*), trick, hoax.
**gage** pledge, security, bond, guarantee, surety, deposit, pawn, token, earnest.
challenge, dare, glove, gauntlet.
**gaiety** joy, joyousness, glee, cheerfulness, hilarity, mirth, jollity, joviality, merriment, liveliness, animation, vivacity, buoyancy, high spirits, elation, jubilation. SADNESS
festivity, merrymaking, revelry, celebration. MOURNING
colour, brightness, brilliance, sparkle, showiness. DRABNESS
**gain** *v*, acquire, procure, obtain, get, secure, win, earn, capture, glean, gather, reap. LOSE
profit, benefit, make, yield, produce, net, clear, realize, bring in.
attain, reach, arrive at, get to.
**gain on,** catch up with, get nearer, approach, overtake, draw away from, leave behind.
*n*, profit, advantage, benefit, earnings, winnings, revenue, income, proceeds, return, yield. LOSS
increase, growth, rise, advance, progress, headway, improvement. DECLINE
**gainful** profitable, lucrative, remunerative, paying, rewarding, productive, fruitful, worthwhile, beneficial, advantageous. UNPROFITABLE
**gainsay** deny, contradict, controvert, dispute, oppose. AFFIRM
**gait** walk, step, pace, stride, tread, bearing, carriage.
**gala** celebration, festival, carnival, fête, jamboree, pageant.
**galaxy** assemblage, gathering, assembly, collection, bevy, host.
**gale** wind, hurricane, cyclone, tornado, blast, squall, storm, tempest. BREEZE
**gall** *n*, rancour, bitterness, spite, malice, acrimony, venom, spleen. CHARITY
impudence, insolence, effrontery, impertinence, cheek (*inf*), nerve (*inf*).
irritation, exasperation, vexation, annoyance, aggravation. APPEASEMENT
*v*, irritate, exasperate, vex, annoy, aggravate, irk, nettle, peeve (*inf*), rile (*inf*), bother, provoke, harass, plague. APPEASE
**gallant** *adj*, brave, courageous, valiant, valorous, heroic, intrepid, bold, daring, fearless, dauntless, dashing, noble, honourable. COWARDLY
polite, courteous, chivalrous, gracious, magnanimous, gentlemanly, courtly, obliging, considerate. CHURLISH
stately, dignified, majestic, august, imposing, grand, splendid, magnificent, glorious.
*n*, beau, suitor, admirer, lover, boyfriend, escort.
dandy, beau, ladies' man, man about town.
**gallantry** courage, bravery, valour, heroism, boldness, fearlessness, mettle, spirit, pluck. COWARDICE
courtesy, politeness, chivalry, graciousness, magnanimity, courtliness, nobility. CHURLISHNESS
**gallery** corridor, passage, hallway, cloister, loggia, veranda, balcony, platform.
**gallivant** gad about, rove, roam, range, wander, ramble.

**gallop** lope, canter, race, dash, speed, rush, hurry, fly, bolt, career, shoot. AMBLE

**galvanize** electrify, excite, stimulate, fire, rouse, animate, invigorate, startle, shock, jolt. DAMP

**gamble** *v*, bet, wager, game, punt, back, stake, speculate, risk, hazard, venture.
*n*, bet, wager, flutter (*inf*), speculation, risk, hazard, venture, chance, lottery. CERTAINTY

**gambol** frolic, frisk, romp, caper, leap, jump, play, sport, skip, prance.

**game** *n*, pastime, recreation, diversion, amusement, distraction, entertainment, sport, play, fun, frolic. WORK
match, contest, competition, meeting, event, fixture.
quarry, prey.
scheme, plan, plot, design, stratagem, device.
*adj*, brave, courageous, valiant, plucky, spirited, bold, intrepid, dauntless, fearless. COWARDLY
ready, willing, eager, inclined, disposed, prepared. RELUCTANT

**gammon** *v*, deceive, trick, hoax, dupe, beguile, hoodwink.
*n*, deception, trick, hoax, humbug.

**gamut** compass, range, scale, scope, series, sweep.

**gang** band, group, pack, crowd, mob, horde, company, party, ring, circle, set, coterie, clique, team, squad, troop.

**gangway** path, passage, aisle.

**gap** break, breach, rift, cleft, crack, crevice, chink, cranny, hole, opening, space, blank, void, interstice, interval, pause, hiatus, interruption.

**gape** stare, gaze, gawk, gawp (*inf*), goggle.
open, yawn, crack, split. CLOSE

**garb** dress, attire, clothes, clothing, garments, wear, apparel, outfit, costume, habit, uniform, livery, robes.

**garbage** rubbish, refuse, waste, trash, junk, litter, debris, scraps, leftovers.

**garble** confuse, mix up, jumble, misquote, misrepresent, falsify, corrupt, pervert, distort, twist, slant, colour.

**gargantuan** enormous, huge, immense, colossal, tremendous, prodigious, massive, mammoth, gigantic, elephantine, great, big, large. MINUTE

**garish** gaudy, flashy, showy, flamboyant, glaring, loud, bold, meretricious, tawdry, tasteless, vulgar. SUBDUED

**garland** wreath, festoon, coronal, chaplet, crown, laurels, bays.

**garments** clothes, clothing, wear, attire, apparel, dress, costume, garb, array, habit, wardrobe, outfit, togs (*inf*), gear (*inf*).

**garner** gather, collect, accumulate, amass, hoard, save, husband, store, lay in, put by, reserve, deposit. WASTE

**garnish** *v*, decorate, adorn, ornament, deck, beautify, embellish, trim, grace. STRIP
*n*, decoration, adornment, ornament, embellishment, trimming, garniture.

**garniture** decorations, ornaments, garnish, trimmings, adornment, embellishment.

**garret** attic, loft, mansard. BASEMENT

**garrulity** loquacity, talkativeness, garrulousness, volubility, chatter, babble, verbosity, prolixity, wordiness. TACITURNITY

**garrulous** loquacious, talkative, garrulous, voluble, chatty, babbling, verbose, prolix, wordy. TACITURN

**gas** vapour, fume, exhalation, effluvium, wind.

**gash** *n*, cut, incision, slash, slit, score, tear, rent, laceration, wound.
*v*, cut, incise, slash, slit, score, lacerate, wound.

**gasp** pant, puff, blow, choke, wheeze, gulp.

**gate** entrance, exit, access, opening, portal, door, barrier.

**gather** collect, assemble, muster, convene, congregate, accumulate, amass, hoard, garner, cluster, flock. DISPERSE
pick, pluck, glean, reap, harvest, cull.
conclude, assume, deduce, infer, understand, learn.
increase, grow, swell, rise, expand, heighten, intensify. DECREASE
pucker, ruffle, shirr, pleat, tuck, fold, crease, wrinkle, contract, knit.

**gathering** assembly, muster, meeting, rally, party, group, company, congregation, conclave, convention, concourse, crowd, throng.
collection, accumulation, mass, heap, pile, cluster.
pustule, abscess, ulcer, boil, carbuncle, pimple.

**gaudy** bright, colourful, gay, garish, flashy, showy, flamboyant, glaring, loud, bold, meretricious, tawdry, tasteless, vulgar. MUTED

**gauge** *v*, measure, weigh, determine, calculate, evaluate, appraise, judge, estimate, assess, check.
*n*, measure, standard, norm, criterion, yardstick, bench mark, touchstone, guideline, test.

**gaunt** thin, lean, lank, spare, meagre, skinny, scrawny, emaciated, bony, angular, pinched, haggard. PLUMP
bleak, desolate, dreary, bare, barren, harsh, grim, forbidding.

**gawk** *n*, boor, lout, churl, clod, oaf, dolt.
*v*, gape, gawp, goggle, stare, gaze.

**gawky** awkward, ungainly, clumsy, lumbering, oafish, loutish, clownish. GRACEFUL

**gay** merry, jolly, jovial, cheerful, blithe, carefree, bright, gleeful, happy, joyful, joyous, lively, animated, vivacious, sprightly, festive, convivial. SAD
bright, colourful, vivid, brilliant, gaudy, garish, flashy, flamboyant. SOMBRE
homosexual, lesbian, queer (*inf*), bent (*inf*).

**gaze** stare, look, gape, gawk, contemplate, watch. GLANCE

**gazette** journal, periodical, newspaper, paper.

**gear** wheel, cog, gearing, mechanism, machinery.
equipment, apparatus, appurtenances, trappings, accessories, paraphernalia, tools, instruments, kit, outfit, rig, supplies, material, harness, tackle, belongings, effects, things (*inf*).
clothes, clothing, wear, dress, attire, apparel, garments, togs (*inf*).

**gelatinous** viscous, glutinous, gummy, sticky, mucilaginous.

**gelid** icy, frigid, glacial, freezing, frozen, arctic, polar. WARM

**gem** jewel, stone, precious stone, pearl, treasure, prize, flower.

**genealogy** descent, pedigree, family tree, stemma, ancestry, extraction, derivation, lineage, stock, stirps.

**general** *adj*, widespread, extensive, broad, universal, catholic, public, common, collective, comprehensive, total, blanket, across-the-board, sweeping, overall. SPECIFIC
usual, regular, normal, customary, habitual, common, ordinary, conventional. RARE
vague, loose, indefinite, unspecified, ill-defined, inexact, approximate, miscellaneous. PRECISE
*n*, commander, leader, chief, head.

**generally** usually, as a rule, by and large, ordinarily, in general, mostly, mainly, chiefly, principally, on the whole, largely.

**generate** produce, create, make, form, engender, breed, beget, propagate, cause, bring about, originate. DESTROY

**generation** production, creation, formation, propagation, procreation, breeding, reproduction, origination, genesis. DESTRUCTION
era, age, epoch, day, time, lifetime.
breed, race, offspring, progeny, children, age group.

**generic** collective, general, common, sweeping, blanket, all-inclusive, universal. SPECIFIC

**generosity** liberality, munificence, charity, bounty, largess, beneficence, benevolence, magnanimity, unselfishness, goodness, nobleness. MEANNESS

**generous** liberal, lavish, open-handed, munificent, charitable, bountiful, benevolent, beneficent, magnanimous, philanthropic, unselfish, kind, good, noble, honourable. MEAN
abundant, plentiful, copious, rich, full, ample. SCANTY

**genial** hearty, cordial, warm, friendly, amiable, affable, jolly, jovial, happy, cheerful, cheery, pleasant, agreeable, good-natured, easy-going, kindly, sunny. COLD

**genius** prodigy, virtuoso, maestro, master, expert, adept. DUNCE
gift, talent, aptitude, faculty, flair, knack, ability, skill, power, inclination, bent, brilliance, cleverness, intelligence, brains, intellect. STUPIDITY

**genre** category, class, school, style, type, sort, kind, brand, species, genus.

**genteel** polite, civil, courteous, respectable, well-bred, mannerly, proper, gentlemanly, ladylike, cultured, refined, polished, aristocratic, fashionable, elegant, stylish. BOORISH

**gentility** politeness, civility, courtesy, respectability, breeding, manners, propriety, decorum, refinement, polish, elegance, urbanity. BOORISHNESS aristocracy, nobility, gentry, upper class, elite.

**gentle** tender, kind, kindly, compassionate, considerate, benign, mild, moderate, soft, merciful, clement, indulgent, lenient, humane. ROUGH
gradual, easy, slow, light, soft, bland, moderate, temperate, calm, quiet, tranquil. HARSH
meek, tame, tractable, biddable, docile, placid. WILD

**gentlemanly** genteel, well-bred, courteous, polite, civil, mannerly, courtly, gallant, chivalrous, noble, honourable, suave, urbane, refined, cultivated. CHURLISH

**gentry** aristocracy, upper class, elite, nobility, gentility.

**genuine** real, authentic, sterling, pure, unadulterated, true, veritable, actual, bona fide, legitimate, honest, sincere, earnest, unaffected, frank, candid. FALSE

**genus** order, class, species, breed, kind, sort, type, group, set, category, genre.

**germ** microbe, bacterium, virus, microorganism, bug (*inf*).
seed, embryo, bud, root, source, origin, beginning, start. FRUIT

**germane** relevant, pertinent, connected, cognate, allied, related, akin, apposite, apropos, appropriate, fitting, suitable, apt. IRRELEVANT

**germinate** sprout, shoot, grow, develop, vegetate, bud. WITHER

**gesticulate** gesture, signal, motion, wave, beckon, nod.

**gesture** *n*, gesticulation, signal, sign, indication, demonstration, action, motion, movement, wave, flourish.
*v*, gesticulate, motion, signal, wave, beckon.

**get** obtain, acquire, procure, secure, gain, earn, win, receive, come by, reap, glean, achieve, attain, realize. LOSE
fetch, pick up, collect, bring, carry.
catch, seize, capture, take. RELEASE
become, grow, turn, go.
understand, grasp, see, take in, perceive, hear, follow, fathom, work out, comprehend. MISS
persuade, induce, talk into, coax, prevail upon, influence, sway.
arrive, reach, come. LEAVE
affect, move, stir; irritate, annoy, vex.

**get away,** escape, flee, get out, break free, decamp, leave, depart.

**get back,** recover, retrieve, recoup, regain. LOSE

**get by,** cope, manage, get along, fare, survive, subsist.

**get off,** alight, disembark, dismount, get down, descend, leave, depart. EMBARK

**get on,** board, mount, ascend, embark. DISEMBARK
succeed, prosper, progress, advance, cope, get along.

**get round,** circumvent, bypass, evade, cajole, wheedle, win over.

**get up,** rise, stand, mount, ascend, climb.

**gewgaw** trinket, bauble, gaud, trifle, bagatelle, toy, plaything.

**ghastly** dreadful, frightful, terrible, awful, shocking, appalling, hideous, horrible, loathsome, repulsive, fearful, frightening, horrendous, grim, gruesome. PLEASANT
pale, ashen, cadaverous, livid, spectral, pallid, wan, pasty. RUDDY

**ghost** spectre, phantom, spirit, soul, apparition, revenant, shade, spook (*inf*), ghoul.
glimmer, trace, shadow, suggestion, hint.

**ghostly** eerie, weird, uncanny, unearthly, supernatural, spooky (*inf*), haunted, spectral, illusory, phantom, ghostlike.

**giant** *n*, colossus, titan, behemoth, leviathan, monster. DWARF
*adj*, gigantic, colossal, huge, immense, enormous, mammoth, elephantine, gargantuan, large, big. TINY

**gibber** gabble, jabber, prattle, babble, chatter, blather.

**gibberish** drivel, nonsense, rubbish, twaddle, prattle, chatter, gabble, blather, balderdash, humbug, gobbledegook (*inf*), mumbo jumbo, claptrap. SENSE

**gibbous** rounded, hunched, humpbacked, bulging, protuberant, convex, gibbose. CONCAVE

**gibe** jeer, scoff, mock, sneer, deride, taunt, rag, ridicule, make fun of. COMPLIMENT

**giddy** dizzy, vertiginous, faint, light-headed, reeling, unsteady, woozy (*inf*).
flighty, fickle, capricious, volatile, inconstant, erratic, thoughtless, scatterbrained, frivolous, impulsive, wild, reckless. SENSIBLE

**gift** present, offering, benefaction, bounty, largess, donation, contribution, grant, allowance, endowment, bequest, legacy.
talent, faculty, aptitude, flair, knack, genius, skill, power, ability, turn, bent. INABILITY

**gifted** talented, skilled, accomplished, expert, masterly, able, capable, clever, intelligent. INEPT

**gigantic** huge, enormous, immense, colossal, giant, tremendous, vast, prodigious, gargantuan, titanic, elephantine, mammoth, great, big, large. MINUTE

**giggle** snigger, titter, laugh, cackle, chortle, chuckle.

**gild** adorn, decorate, embellish, beautify, enhance, enrich, brighten.

**gimmick** device, contrivance, gambit, manoeuvre, ploy, scheme, stratagem, trick.

**gin** trap, snare, noose, net, springe.

**gingerly** cautiously, warily, carefully, daintily, tenderly, gently, hesitantly, reluctantly, timidly, guardedly, suspiciously. BOLDLY

**gird** encircle, surround, ring, encompass, environ, hem in, enclose, confine.
girdle, belt, strap, bind.

**girdle** *n*, corset, foundation, stays, belt, sash, cummerbund, waistband.
*v*, gird, encircle, surround, ring, encompass.

**girl** maiden, lass, miss, young lady, wench, damsel, daughter, bird (*inf*). BOY

**girth** circumference, perimeter, size, bulk.

**gist** substance, essence, pith, core, kernel, point, idea, meaning, import.

**give** grant, bestow, present, award, confer, accord, administer, distribute, give out, donate, contribute, supply, provide, offer, proffer, commit, consign, entrust. WITHHOLD
yield, surrender, concede, give in, relinquish, give up, cede, hand over, sacrifice, devote. RETAIN
utter, emit, pronounce, announce, give out, publish, transmit, communicate, impart, convey, render.
produce, cause, occasion, make, do, perform.
collapse, give way, break, yield, bend, buckle, sag, sink, fall, recede, retire.
**give away,** betray, expose, divulge, reveal, disclose, let slip, leak.
**give off,** exhale, exude, emit, discharge, release.
**give up,** renounce, forgo, forswear, desist, stop, cease, abandon, surrender, yield, capitulate, submit, resign, despair. CONTINUE

**given** inclined, disposed, apt, wont, prone, addicted.
specified, stated, fixed, set, arranged, appointed.

**glacial** icy, frozen, freezing, frigid, gelid, arctic, polar, raw, bitter, wintry. HOT
cold, unfeeling, hostile, unfriendly. WARM

**glad** happy, pleased, contented, gratified, delighted, elated, overjoyed, ready, willing, cheerful, merry, gay, joyful, gleeful. SAD
pleasing, gratifying, cheering, encouraging, pleasant, joyous, delightful, gladsome. GLOOMY

**gladden** please, gratify, delight, elate, exhilarate, cheer, encourage, hearten, brighten, animate. GRIEVE

**gladness** pleasure, gratification, animation, cheer, cheerfulness, happiness, glee, joy, joyfulness, delight, elation, merriment, gaiety. SORROW

**glamorous** elegant, smart, attractive, beautiful, fascinating, captivating, appealing, alluring, exciting, thrilling, glossy, glittering. DULL

**glamour** fascination, enchantment, allure, attraction, appeal, charm, beauty, elegance, excitement, glitter, sparkle.

**glance** glimpse, peek, peep, scan, look. STARE
glint, gleam, flash, shine, glitter, sparkle.
ricochet, rebound, bounce, skim, graze, brush.

**glare** *v*, glower, scowl, frown, lower, look daggers. SMILE
dazzle, blind, blaze, flame, flare, beam, shine.
*n*, dazzle, blaze, brilliance, brightness, radiance, flare, beam. DULLNESS

**glaring** conspicuous, prominent, obvious, manifest, patent, overt, blatant, flagrant, egregious, open, undisguised. CONCEALED
garish, gaudy, flashy, showy, loud, bright, brilliant, dazzling, blazing, blinding. MUTED

**glassy** clear, crystalline, transparent, smooth, slippery, shiny, glossy.

expressionless, blank, vacant, glazed, dull, dazed, fixed.

**glaze** *v*, lacquer, varnish, gloss, enamel, polish, burnish, furbish.
*n*, lustre, patina, sheen, shine, gloss, coat, finish, polish, enamel, lacquer, varnish.

**gleam** glint, glimmer, glisten, flash, flare, glance, sparkle, glitter, twinkle, shimmer, shine, beam, glow.

**glean** gather, collect, pick up, cull, harvest, reap, garner, amass. SCATTER

**glee** merriment, hilarity, mirth, jollity, joviality, joy, joyfulness, delight, elation, exhilaration, gaiety, cheer, cheerfulness, liveliness, exuberance. SORROW

**gleeful** merry, jolly, joyful, joyous, elated, exhilarated, gay, cheerful, lively, exuberant, happy, pleased. SAD

**glen** valley, vale, dale, dell, dingle. MOUNTAIN

**glib** smooth, slick, fluent, easy, ready, voluble, talkative, suave, insincere. HESITANT

**glide** slide, slip, sail, float, skate, skim, drift, coast, roll, flow, fly, soar.

**glimmer** *v*, gleam, glitter, glisten, flicker, shimmer, sparkle, twinkle, glow, shine.
*n*, gleam, glitter, flicker, shimmer, sparkle, twinkle, glow.
trace, hint, suggestion, inkling, ray, gleam, flicker.

**glimpse** *n*, glance, peep, peek, look, sight, view. SCRUTINY
*v*, spot, descry, catch sight of, espy. SCRUTINIZE

**glisten** gleam, glint, glitter, shine, sparkle, flash, glance, shimmer, glimmer, twinkle, scintillate, coruscate.

**glitter** *v*, flash, sparkle, gleam, glint, glisten, shine, scintillate, twinkle, glimmer, shimmer.
*n*, flash, beam, sparkle, gleam, twinkle, shine, scintillation, brightness, radiance, brilliance, sheen, lustre. DULLNESS
glamour, splendour, pageantry, tinsel, gaudiness, show, showiness.

**gloaming** dusk, twilight, half-light, nightfall.

**gloat** exult, triumph, rejoice, revel, crow, boast, vaunt.

**global** world-wide, international, universal, wide-ranging, extensive, comprehensive, all-inclusive, exhaustive, thorough, encyclopedic, total, general. RESTRICTED

**globe** orb, sphere, ball, earth, world, planet.

**globular** globate, globulous, globose, globoid, round, spherical, spheroid.

**globule** drop, bead, pearl, spherule, ball, pellet.

**gloom** dark, darkness, shade, shadow, obscurity, dimness, murkiness, cloudiness, dusk twilight. BRIGHTNESS
melancholy, depression, dejection, despondency, despair, sadness, sorrow, misery, low spirits, blues. CHEERFULNESS

**gloomy** dark, shadowy, obscure, dim, murky, cloudy, dull, dismal, dreary. BRIGHT
depressing, cheerless, comfortless, saddening, disheartening, discouraging, dispiriting, sombre, dismal, sad. ENCOURAGING
depressed, despondent, dejected, crestfallen, melancholy, glum, saturnine, taciturn, downcast, dispirited, downhearted, sad, unhappy, miserable, morose, pessimistic. CHEERFUL

**glorify** exalt, aggrandize, elevate, ennoble, dignify, honour, venerate, adore, worship, praise, extol, acclaim, magnify, enhance, augment, adorn. DEFAME

**glorious** illustrious, renowned, celebrated, famous, noted, eminent, distinguished, noble, exalted, grand, supreme, triumphant. HUMBLE
splendid, magnificent, radiant, brilliant, resplendent, bright, dazzling, glittering. DULL
delightful, wonderful, marvellous, enjoyable, pleasurable, agreeable, pleasant. AWFUL

**glory** *n*, praise, exaltation, acclaim, kudos, credit, distinction, honour, fame, renown, celebrity, eminence, prestige. BLAME
magnificence, splendour, grandeur, majesty, dignity, nobility, pomp, stateliness, pageantry, parade, triumph, success. HUMILITY
brilliance, resplendence, brightness, radiance, effulgence, lustre, beauty. DULLNESS
worship, adoration, veneration, respect, homage, praise, thanksgiving.
*v*, triumph, exult, rejoice, revel, bask, boast, crow, gloat.

**gloss** *n*, lustre, sheen, polish, shine, brightness, glaze, varnish. DULLNESS
appearance, façade, front, veneer, show, semblance.

*v*, polish, burnish, shine, varnish, glaze, lacquer.
disguise, mask, hide, conceal, cover up, smooth over. EXPOSE

**glossary** gloss, index, vocabulary, dictionary, lexicon.

**glossy** smooth, sleek, shiny, lustrous, bright, glassy, polished. MATT

**glow** *v*, shine, radiate, glimmer, gleam, burn, redden, blush.
*n*, light, luminosity, incandescence, phosphorescence, shine, lustre, brightness, brilliance, radiance, effulgence, blaze, gleam. DARKNESS
warmth, passion, ardour, fervour, eagerness, enthusiasm, intensity, vehemence, excitement, thrill. APATHY

**glower** glare, scowl, frown, lower, look daggers. SMILE

**glue** *n*, gum, paste, adhesive, cement.
*v*, stick, paste, gum, fix, seal, adhere.

**glum** gloomy, despondent, dejected, downcast, low, crestfallen, pessimistic, morose, sullen, unsmiling, moody, grumpy, sour. CHEERFUL

**glut** *n*, surfeit, excess, surplus, superfluity, superabundance, plethora, repletion, saturation. DEARTH
*v*, cram, stuff, fill, sate, satiate, surfeit, cloy, flood, inundate, saturate, choke, clog.

**glutinous** sticky, gummy, gluey, adhesive, mucilaginous, viscous, viscid.

**glutton** gourmand, gormandizer, gobbler, pig (*inf*).

**gluttony** greed, greediness, voraciousness, voracity, gourmandism. TEMPERANCE

**gnarled** lumpy, nodular, knotty, knurled, twisted, contorted, bent, weather-beaten, rugged, wrinkled, rough, leathery.

**gnaw** bite, nibble, chew, munch, eat, erode, corrode, consume, fret, worry, trouble, bother.

**go** *v*, move, proceed, advance, pass, travel, journey, start, set out, leave, depart, withdraw, go away, vanish, disappear. STOP
work, operate, perform, function, run. FAIL
become, grow, get, turn.
extend, stretch, reach, run, spread.
fit, suit, match, harmonize, blend, correspond, belong. CLASH
result, turn out, eventuate, end up, develop, fare.
contribute, serve, avail, lead, conduce, tend, incline.
elapse, slip away, pass, go by, lapse, expire.
**go for,** attack, assail, assault, set about.
**go off,** explode, blow up, detonate.
leave, depart, go away.
rot, go bad, turn.
**go on,** continue, proceed, persist, last, endure, abide, remain, stay.
occur, happen, take place.
**go through,** undergo, endure, suffer, experience, brave, bear, tolerate, stand.
**let go,** release, free, liberate, drop. HOLD
*n*, try, attempt, essay, bid, stab, shot (*inf*), crack (*inf*), turn.
drive, energy, vigour, verve, dynamism, spirit, animation. LETHARGY

**goad** *v*, spur, prick, prod, provoke, incite, prompt, arouse, stimulate, impel, urge, drive, hound, plague, annoy, needle, harass. DETER
*n*, spur, incentive, stimulus, motivation, incitement, provocation. DETERRENT

**go-ahead** *n*, permission, consent, authorization, sanction, OK (*inf*), green light (*inf*). BAN
*adj*, ambitious, aspiring, enterprising, pushy (*inf*).

**goal** aim, objective, mark, target, intention, object, purpose, end, ambition, aspiration, destination.

**gobble** bolt, gulp, guzzle, wolf, devour, gorge, cram.

**go-between** intermediary, mediator, middleman, agent, broker, factor.

**god** deity, divinity, goddess, spirit, idol, image. DEVIL

**God** Godhead, Almighty, Father, Lord, Creator, Jehovah. SATAN

**godless** atheistic, agnostic, impious, ungodly, profane, irreligious, sinful, wicked, evil. GODLY

**godly** pious, devout, religious, holy, saintly, good, righteous, god-fearing. GODLESS

**goggle** stare, gape, gawp, gawk.

**golden** gold, yellow, flaxen, blond, fair, bright, shining, brilliant, splendid, resplendent, rich, precious, priceless, valuable.
happy, joyful, blissful, glorious, prosperous, successful, flourishing, halcyon, palmy.

favourable, propitious, excellent, auspicious, timely, opportune, promising, rosy, advantageous. UNFAVOURABLE

**good** *adj*, virtuous, righteous, moral, upright, honest, honourable, admirable, worthy, well-behaved, obedient. WICKED
acceptable, satisfactory, agreeable, pleasant, enjoyable, fine, excellent, first-rate, splendid. BAD
beneficial, advantageous, profitable, worthwhile, useful, helpful, wholesome, healthy, salutary, favourable, propitious, opportune, convenient.
proficient, competent, skilful, dexterous, adept, adroit, expert, accomplished, able, talented, gifted. INCOMPETENT
kind, kindly, benevolent, obliging, gracious, good-natured, humane, merciful, friendly, generous. UNKIND
suitable, appropriate, apt, fitting, proper, correct, right. UNSUITABLE
reliable, dependable, trustworthy, sound, secure. UNRELIABLE
sizable, considerable, goodly, substantial, large, ample, adequate, sufficient. SMALL
*n*, advantage, benefit, profit, gain, welfare, interest, behalf, use, avail. HARM
virtue, righteousness, goodness, rectitude, morality, worth, merit, excellence. EVIL

**goodbye** farewell, adieu, so long (*inf*), bye-bye (*inf*), cheerio (*inf*), see you later, *au revoir*, *ciao* (*inf*). HELLO

**good-looking** attractive, fair, comely, pretty, beautiful, handsome. UGLY

**goodly** sizable, considerable, substantial, large, ample, tidy (*inf*). SMALL
attractive, good-looking, fair, comely, beautiful, handsome, pleasing, pleasant, agreeable. UNATTRACTIVE

**goodness** virtue, righteousness, good, rectitude, uprightness, honesty, integrity, probity, morality, honour. EVIL
kindness, benevolence, kindliness, compassion, thoughtfulness, generosity, graciousness, friendliness, humanity, mercy. UNKINDNESS
excellence, superiority, worth, value, merit. INFERIORITY

**goods** belongings, possessions, effects, chattels, property, trappings, appurtenances, paraphernalia, gear.
merchandise, wares, stock, commodities.

**goodwill** benevolence, kindliness, goodness, graciousness, favour, friendliness, amity, willingness, acquiescence, heartiness, zeal. ENMITY

**gore**[1] *v*, pierce, stab, impale.

**gore**[2] *n*, blood, bloodshed, carnage, slaughter, butchery.

**gorge** *v*, stuff, cram, fill, gormandize, devour, bolt, wolf, guzzle, gobble, gulp, glut, sate, surfeit, overeat. FAST
*n*, ravine, canyon, defile, pass, gulch.

**gorgeous** magnificent, superb, fine, splendid, resplendent, sumptuous, rich, exquisite, beautiful, grand, glittering, dazzling, glorious, marvellous, wonderful, excellent, great. POOR

**gormandize** gorge, devour, guzzle, stuff, cram, bolt, wolf.

**gory** bloody, bloodstained, bloodthirsty, sanguinary, savage, fierce, murderous.

**gospel** truth, fact, certainty, verity. FALSEHOOD
doctrine, creed, credo, teaching, message, news, tidings.

**gossip** *n*, chat, talk, natter, chitchat, small talk, prattle, tittle-tattle, scandal, rumour, hearsay.
scandalmonger, gossipmonger, prattler, tattler, busybody, quidnunc, blabbermouth (*inf*).
*v*, chat, chatter, talk, natter, gab (*inf*), prattle, tattle, blab.

**gouge** scratch, claw, scoop, dig, chisel, cut, score, gash.

**gourmet** gastronome, epicure, connoisseur, *bon vivant*.

**govern** rule, reign, direct, manage, administer, control, guide, lead, conduct, supervise, oversee, command, regulate, restrain, check, curb, bridle, discipline, master, steer, pilot, influence, sway.

**governable** controllable, manageable, tractable, docile, submissive, obedient. WILD

**government** rule, dominion, direction, management, administration, control, guidance, conduct, supervision, command, leadership, authority, regulation, restraint, discipline.
ministry, cabinet, parliament, council, executive, state, regime.

**governor** ruler, president, director, manager, administrator, executive, head, chief, leader, commander, controller, supervisor, overseer, superintendent, boss (*inf*).

**grab** seize, snatch, pluck, take hold of, catch, nab (*inf*), grasp, grip, clutch, clasp.

**grace** *n*, elegance, poise, gracefulness, ease, beauty, loveliness, charm, refinement, polish, propriety, decorum. CLUMSINESS
favour, goodwill, kindness, benevolence, goodness, generosity, compassion, clemency, mercy, pardon, forgiveness. UNKINDNESS
blessing, benediction, thanksgiving, prayer.
*v*, adorn, embellish, decorate, ornament, enhance, honour, favour, distinguish, dignify. MAR

**graceful** elegant, supple, nimble, agile, easy, smooth, flowing, pleasing, charming, lovely, beautiful, fine. CLUMSY

**graceless** clumsy, awkward, ungainly, inelegant, uncouth, coarse, crude, boorish, unsophisticated, rude, shameless, unabashed. GRACEFUL

**gracious** kind, kindly, benevolent, benign, friendly, affable, obliging, courteous, civil, polite, amiable, cordial, compassionate, gentle, mild, merciful, indulgent, condescending, patronizing, charitable. CHURLISH

**grade** *n*, degree, stage, step, rung, level, position, rank, station, quality, rating, mark, score, brand, class, group, category, measure, size.
*v*, arrange, sort, group, classify, categorize, brand, rate, rank.

**gradient** slope, incline, hill, ramp, acclivity, declivity.

**gradual** slow, unhurried, moderate, gentle, regular, steady, even, continuous, progressive. SUDDEN

**graduate** grade, mark off, divide, calibrate, regulate, adjust, adapt.
arrange, sort, group, classify, grade, rank.

**graft** *v*, join, unite, splice, implant, insert, attach, affix, transplant. SEPARATE
*n*, scion, slip, sprout, shoot, transplant.

**grain** cereal, corn, seed, kernel, grist.
particle, speck, granule, crumb, morsel, piece, bit, iota, atom, jot, scrap, trace.
texture, pattern, weave, nap, fibre.

**grand** impressive, great, large, imposing, majestic, august, lofty, exalted, illustrious, distinguished, lordly, noble, regal, princely, dignified, stately, glorious, splendid, magnificent, fine, superb, sumptuous, luxurious, showy, pretentious, ostentatious. HUMBLE
excellent, wonderful, marvellous, very good, first-class, first-rate, super (*inf*). POOR
chief, principal, main, head, leading, supreme. MINOR

**grandeur** splendour, magnificence, glory, pomp, stateliness, majesty, nobility, dignity, greatness, importance, eminence, loftiness. HUMILITY

**grandiloquent** bombastic, pompous, magniloquent, orotund, fustian, high-flown, euphuistic, rhetorical, pretentious. SIMPLE

**grandiose** pretentious, ostentatious, showy, flamboyant, extravagant, pompous, bombastic. PLAIN
grand, impressive, imposing, lofty, majestic, ambitious. HUMBLE

**grant** *v*, give, bestow, award, present, confer, accord, allot. WITHHOLD
allow, permit, consent to, agree to, acknowledge, admit, concede, cede, yield.
*n*, award, gift, present, benefaction, bequest, endowment, concession, allowance, donation, contribution, subsidy.

**graphic** striking, telling, vivid, expressive, descriptive, illustrative, diagrammatic, pictorial, picturesque, detailed, clear, lucid, explicit. UNCLEAR

**grapple** grip, clasp, grasp, seize, grab, clutch, hold. RELEASE
struggle, wrestle, battle, contend, tackle, face, encounter.

**grasp** *v*, grip, clasp, hold, clutch, grapple, grab, seize, snatch. RELEASE
understand, comprehend, take in, realize, see, perceive, follow, get.
*n*, grip, clasp, hold, clutches, possession.
reach, compass, scope, range, capacity, power, control.
understanding, comprehension, realization, awareness, perception, knowledge.

**grasping** greedy, avaricious, covetous, acquisitive, rapacious, miserly, niggardly, parsimonious, mean, stingy. GENEROUS

**grate** shred, mince, comminute, triturate, grind, rasp, scrape, scratch, creak.
annoy, irritate, exasperate, vex, irk, nettle, jar, aggravate. SOOTHE

**grateful** thankful, appreciative, obliged, beholden, indebted. UNGRATEFUL pleasant, agreeable, gratifying, satisfying, acceptable, welcome, refreshing, relaxing.

**gratification** satisfaction, fulfilment, indulgence, contentment, pleasure, enjoyment, fun, joy, delight. FRUSTRATION

**gratify** satisfy, fulfil, indulge, humour, favour, please, gladden, delight. DISPLEASE

**gratifying** satisfying, fulfilling, rewarding, pleasing, pleasant, agreeable, enjoyable, pleasurable, delightful. UNPLEASANT

**grating** harsh, strident, raucous, rasping, hoarse, scraping, grinding, jarring, irritating, annoying, vexatious, irksome, unpleasant, disagreeable.

**gratitude** gratefulness, thankfulness, appreciation, obligation, indebtedness, thanks, acknowledgment, recognition. INGRATITUDE

**gratuitous** free, gratis, voluntary, spontaneous, complimentary.
groundless, baseless, unfounded, unwarranted, unjustified, uncalled-for, unnecessary, needless, superfluous.

**gratuity** tip, gift, present, reward, recompense, bonus, perquisite, donation, benefaction, largess, bounty.

**grave**[1] *adj*, serious, solemn, staid, sober, sedate, thoughtful, pensive, unsmiling, grim. FRIVOLOUS
important, weighty, momentous, vital, crucial, critical, dangerous, perilous, serious. TRIVIAL

**grave**[2] *n*, tomb, sepulchre, crypt, vault, mausoleum, burial place.

**graveyard** cemetery, churchyard, burial ground, necropolis, God's acre.

**gravitate** incline, lean, tend, move, be drawn.
descend, sink, drop, fall, precipitate, settle. RISE

**gravity** seriousness, solemnity, dignity, sobriety, sedateness, thoughtfulness, grimness. FRIVOLITY
importance, weight, moment, seriousness, severity, enormity, significance, consequence. TRIVIALITY

**graze**[1] scrape, scratch, skin, bark, abrade, rub, brush, shave, touch, skim, glance off.

**graze**[2] feed, browse, crop, pasture.

**greasy** oily, fatty, sebaceous, slimy, slippery, unctuous, smooth, slick, glib, fawning, ingratiating.

**great** big, large, huge, vast, immense, massive, enormous, colossal, tremendous, gigantic. SMALL
excessive, inordinate, decided, pronounced, extreme, considerable, prodigious, high, strong. SLIGHT
eminent, illustrious, distinguished, renowned, noted, famed, celebrated, prominent, outstanding, impressive, remarkable, noteworthy, grand, august, majestic, noble, exalted, superior, sublime, magnificent, glorious, fine, heroic, lofty. LOWLY
chief, main, principal, leading, major, important, significant, consequential, weighty, momentous, critical, serious. MINOR
absolute, utter, perfect, complete, thoroughgoing, out-and-out, arrant, flagrant, downright.
excellent, wonderful, marvellous, fine, first-rate, terrific (*inf*), fantastic (*inf*). AWFUL

**greatness** vastness, immensity, largeness, enormity, magnitude, bulk, mass, size. SMALLNESS
eminence, renown, fame, note, grandeur, majesty, nobility, dignity, magnificence, glory. LOWLINESS
importance, significance, gravity, seriousness. TRIVIALITY

**greed** greediness, gluttony, esurience, edacity, voracity, hunger, desire, craving, longing, covetousness, avarice, selfishness, rapacity, cupidity, avidity, eagerness. UNSELFISHNESS

**greedy** gluttonous, esurient, edacious, voracious, insatiable, ravenous, hungry, desirous, covetous, avaricious, selfish, rapacious, grasping, avid, eager. UNSELFISH

**green** *adj*, verdant, verdurous, grassy, leafy, emerald.
fresh, new, recent, raw, unripe, immature, unseasoned, young, vigorous, flourishing. DECAYING
inexperienced, callow, unsophisticated, naive, ingenuous, gullible, credulous, inexpert, unskilled, untrained. EXPERIENCED
envious, jealous, covetous, resentful.
*n*, lawn, sward, common, turf, verdure.

**greet** hail, salute, address, accost, welcome, receive, meet.

**greeting** salutation, address, hail, salute, welcome, reception. FAREWELL

**greetings** respects, compliments, regards, best wishes.

**gregarious** sociable, social, outgoing, friendly, affable, companionable, genial, cordial, convivial. RECLUSIVE

**grey** dull, drab, dismal, dreary, gloomy, sombre, dark, cloudy, overcast. BRIGHT
pale, colourless, neutral.
old, aged, elderly, hoary, venerable, ancient. YOUNG

**grief** sorrow, sadness, misery, woe, heartache, mourning, distress, anguish, affliction, agony, pain, suffering, trouble, trial, tribulation, regret, remorse. JOY

**grievance** injury, damage, wrong, injustice, complaint, grudge, resentment, indignation.

**grieve** *vi*, sorrow, lament, mourn, weep, bewail, bemoan. REJOICE
*vt*, sadden, afflict, distress, hurt, wound, pain, agonize. PLEASE

**grievous** painful, distressing, afflicting, intolerable, unbearable, sorrowful, mournful, damaging, injurious, hurtful, harmful, serious, severe, intense. MILD
heinous, outrageous, monstrous, egregious, flagrant, gross, atrocious, appalling, shocking, dreadful, shameful, deplorable, lamentable. COMMENDABLE

**grim** stern, severe, resolute, firm, relentless, harsh, formidable, dire, dreadful, frightful, terrible, horrible, hideous, ghastly, grisly, fierce, savage, cruel, merciless, menacing, forbidding, sinister. BENIGN

**grimace** *n*, frown, scowl, pout, sneer, smirk, wry face.
*v*, frown, scowl, pout, sneer, smirk, make a face.

**grime** *n*, dirt, filth, muck, smut, soot.
*v*, begrime, dirty, soil, befoul, sully, defile. CLEANSE

**grimy** dirty, filthy, mucky, begrimed, smutty, sooty, foul, unclean. CLEAN

**grin** smile, beam, smirk, leer.

**grind** pulverize, triturate, comminute, powder, crush, pound, mill, grate, rasp, scrape, abrade.
sharpen, whet, sand, file, smooth, polish.
oppress, tyrannize, persecute, plague, afflict, torment, trouble.

**grip** *v*, hold, clutch, clasp, grasp, seize. RELEASE
*n*, hold, clasp, purchase, clutches, possession, keeping, grasp, understanding, comprehension, control, mastery, command.

**gripe** *v*, complain, moan, grumble, grouse, carp, beef (*inf*).
hurt, pain, ache, cramp, pinch, twinge.
*n*, complaint, grievance, moan, grumble, beef (*inf*).
pain, ache, twinge, pang, cramp, colic.

**grisly** grim, gruesome, macabre, hideous, horrible, dreadful, frightful, awful, ghastly, appalling, shocking, sickening, repugnant. PLEASANT

**grit** gravel, sand, pebbles, dust, dirt.
courage, nerve, pluck, mettle, spirit, guts (*inf*), fortitude, tenacity, resolution, toughness, stamina. WEAKNESS

**groan** *v*, moan, sigh, cry, lament, complain, grumble, creak.
*n*, moan, sigh, cry, complaint, creak.

**groom** brush, curry, smooth, preen, tidy, arrange, smarten up, clean.
prepare, prime, train, coach, drill, school.

**groove** furrow, channel, rut, trench, hollow, indentation, cut, score. RIDGE

**grope** fumble, feel, search, fish, scrabble, grabble.

**gross** big, large, great, fat, obese, bulky, heavy, thick, dense. SLIGHT
coarse, vulgar, tasteless, crude, rude, indecent, ribald, earthy, indelicate, unsophisticated, unrefined, crass, boorish, dull, stupid. REFINED
flagrant, glaring, blatant, arrant, egregious, outrageous, plain, manifest, sheer, outright, rank, unmitigated, downright.
entire, total, whole, aggregate. NET

**grotesque** bizarre, strange, weird, odd, fantastic, whimsical, fanciful, absurd, ludicrous, freakish, outlandish, unnatural, deformed, misshapen, distorted, hideous, repugnant. NORMAL

**ground** *n*, earth, soil, clod, sod, turf, land, terrain, field, area, pitch.
*v*, base, found, establish, fix, set.
instruct, teach, train, coach, familiarize, acquaint.

**groundless** baseless, unfounded, unsupported, idle, empty, unjustified, unreasonable, unwarranted, gratuitous. JUSTIFIED

**grounds** estate, land, property, domain, territory, park, garden, yard.
basis, base, foundation, reason, motive, cause, call, excuse, justification, pretext, argument.
dregs, sediment, lees, deposit, grouts.

**groundwork** foundation, basis, footing, bottom, basics, fundamentals, preliminaries, preparation, background.

**group** *n*, cluster, clump, bunch, batch, set, class, category, party, company, body, gang, crowd, congregation, gathering, collection, assemblage. INDIVIDUAL
*v*, collect, assemble, gather, cluster, congregate. SEPARATE
sort, classify, organize, arrange, dispose. DISARRANGE

**grove** wood, copse, thicket, spinney, brake, covert.

**grovel** cower, cringe, fawn, toady, kowtow, bow and scrape, crawl, creep, sneak.

**grovelling** servile, obsequious, fawning, sycophantic, slavish, cringing, crawling, base, mean, low, abject.

**grow** increase, expand, enlarge, wax, swell, spread, extend, stretch, develop, multiply. SHRINK
originate, arise, spring up, germinate, sprout, shoot, bud, blossom, flower, thrive, flourish, prosper, advance, progress, improve. DECLINE
become, turn, go, get.
cultivate, produce, raise, nurture, breed, propagate, farm.

**growl** snarl, rumble, roar, murmur, complain, grumble.

**growth** increase, expansion, enlargement, extension, development, advance, advancement, progress, rise, improvement. DECLINE
germination, sprouting, vegetation, crop, produce, cultivation.
tumour, lump, excrescence, protuberance.

**grubby** dirty, soiled, grimy, filthy, messy, mucky, unwashed, scruffy, shabby, seedy, squalid, sordid. CLEAN

**grudge** *v*, begrudge, resent, envy, covet, mind, be reluctant.
*n*, resentment, envy, grievance, spite, malice, ill will, bitterness, rancour, hard feelings, animosity, hatred, enmity.

**gruelling** arduous, strenuous, hard, difficult, harsh, severe, exhausting, tiring, taxing, demanding, punishing. EASY

**gruesome** grim, grisly, macabre, ghastly, hideous, loathsome, repulsive, repugnant, horrible, terrible, awful, frightful, dreadful, abominable. ATTRACTIVE

**gruff** surly, churlish, curt, brusque, blunt, sour, grumpy, rough, rude, uncivil, ungracious, discourteous, impolite. AFFABLE
throaty, guttural, harsh, raucous, husky, hoarse.

**grumble** *v*, complain, moan, grouse, carp, gripe (*inf*), grouch (*inf*), beef (*inf*).
growl, rumble, roar, murmur, mutter.
*n*, complaint, grievance, protest, objection, moan, grouse, gripe (*inf*), beef (*inf*).

**grumpy** cantankerous, irascible, crabbed, crusty, testy, surly, crotchety (*inf*), cross, irritable, grouchy (*inf*), peevish, petulant, sulky, sullen.

**guarantee** *n*, warranty, guaranty, pledge, promise, bond, assurance, certainty, security, surety, collateral, earnest.
*v*, warrant, certify, pledge, promise, assure, ensure, secure, insure, protect.

**guard** *v*, protect, defend, watch over, mind, supervise, shield, screen, shelter, cover, patrol, police, save, preserve, safeguard. NEGLECT
*n*, protection, defence, shield, screen, bulwark, rampart, buffer, security, safeguard.
sentry, sentinel, watchman, warder, keeper, custodian, guardian, defender, protector, escort, convoy, patrol.
watchfulness, vigilance, wariness, caution, care, heed, attention.

**guarded** careful, cautious, circumspect, wary, suspicious, prudent, discreet, reticent, noncommittal, cagey (*inf*). RASH

**guardian** protector, defender, keeper, custodian, warden, warder.

**guess** *v*, conjecture, surmise, speculate, hypothesize, estimate, reckon, judge, think, believe, suspect, suppose, imagine, fancy. KNOW
solve, work out, fathom, penetrate.
*n*, conjecture, surmise, speculation, hypothesis, theory, estimate, reckoning, judgment, belief, opinion, supposition.

**guest** visitor, caller, company, lodger, boarder. HOST

**guidance** direction, instruction, clue, hint, advice, counsel, help, leadership, control, government, management.

**guide** *v*, lead, direct, pilot, steer, conduct, usher, escort, accompany, control, regulate, handle, manage, govern, rule, influence, teach, instruct, advise, counsel. FOLLOW

*n*, leader, director, pilot, usher, escort, courier, cicerone, conductor, controller, adviser, counsellor, mentor, teacher. FOLLOWER
clue, hint, key, pointer, sign, beacon, landmark, guidebook, handbook, manual, directory.
model, pattern, example, exemplar, ideal, standard, criterion.

**guild** fellowship, fraternity, brotherhood, union, society, association, organization, league, lodge, order.

**guile** deceit, deception, fraud, duplicity, artfulness, craft, craftiness, cunning, artifice, wiles, wiliness, trickery, treachery. HONESTY

**guileful** deceitful, artful, crafty, cunning, wily, foxy, tricky, treacherous, sly, shrewd, clever. HONEST

**guileless** artless, ingenuous, naive, innocent, unsophisticated, sincere, candid, frank, open, straightforward, honest. GUILEFUL

**guilt** guiltiness, culpability, criminality, sinfulness, wrongdoing, blame, responsibility. INNOCENCE
remorse, contrition, regret, self-reproach, self-accusation, guilty conscience. IMPENITENCE

**guiltless** innocent, blameless, unimpeachable, irreproachable, sinless, clear, pure, spotless, immaculate, unsullied, clean (*inf*). GUILTY

**guilty** culpable, criminal, at fault, blameworthy, reprehensible, responsible, wrong, sinful. INNOCENT
remorseful, contrite, regretful, sorry, conscience-stricken, sheepish, shamefaced. IMPENITENT

**guise** appearance, exterior, front, façade, semblance, pretence, show, behaviour, air, mien, demeanour, form, shape, fashion, manner, mode, dress, costume, disguise.

**gulf** chasm, abyss, rift, breach, separation, gap, opening.
bay, bight, inlet, sound.

**gullible** credulous, unsuspecting, trustful, trusting, naive, ingenuous, innocent, green, born yesterday, simple, foolish.

**gulp** *v*, swallow, quaff, swill, guzzle, gobble, bolt, devour, wolf.
*n*, swallow, draught, mouthful.

**gumption** common sense, initiative, enterprise, resourcefulness, sagacity, nous (*inf*), acumen, shrewdness, ability, cleverness, spirit, courage.

**gun** pistol, revolver, rifle, shotgun.

**gurgle** babble, burble, murmur, bubble, ripple, purl.

**gush** flow, pour, run, stream, spurt, spout, jet, rush, cascade, flood, burst. DRIP

**gushing** flowing, pouring, streaming, spouting, rushing. DRIPPING
gushy, effusive, fulsome, demonstrative, sentimental, mawkish.

**gust** blast, puff, flurry, squall, gale, storm, burst, outburst, fit, paroxysm.

**gusto** relish, zest, enjoyment, pleasure, zeal, enthusiasm, fervour.

**guts** intestines, bowels, viscera, entrails, insides, innards (*inf*).
courage, grit, mettle, spirit, pluck, nerve, boldness, audacity, daring, stamina, tenacity, willpower. WEAKNESS

**gutter** channel, conduit, duct, trough, trench, ditch, drain.

**guttural** hoarse, husky, gruff, throaty, thick, deep, low.

**guy** man, boy, lad, fellow, chap, bloke (*inf*).

**guzzle** gobble, bolt, wolf, devour, gorge, gulp, quaff, swill, knock back (*inf*).

**gyration** rotation, revolution, spinning, whirling, pirouette, twirl, spiral.

# H

**habiliments,** clothes, clothing, dress, garb, attire, array, apparel, habit, costume, robes, regalia, uniform, livery.

**habit** *n*, practice, custom, usage, wont, routine, manner, way, tendency, disposition, propensity, inclination, bent.
addiction, dependence, weakness, compulsion, obsession.
clothing, garb, attire, apparel, dress, habiliments, vestments.
*v*, clothe, dress, garb, attire, array. STRIP

**habitat** environment, element, natural home, surroundings, territory, haunt, stamping ground.

**habitation** dwelling, abode, domicile, home, residence, lodgings, quarters, accommodation.
occupation, occupancy, inhabitance, residence, tenancy.

**habitual** customary, usual, wonted, accustomed, regular, routine, traditional, common, ordinary, familiar. UNUSUAL
chronic, inveterate, hardened, confirmed, fixed, set, established, frequent, recurrent, persistent. OCCASIONAL

**habituate** accustom, familiarize, condition, acclimatize, make used to, harden, inure, break in, train.

**hack**[1] *v*, cut, chop, hew, gash, slash, mutilate, mangle.

**hack**[2] *n*, jade, nag, workhorse, drudge, hireling, mercenary, scribbler.

**hackneyed** banal, commonplace, trite, clichéd, stale, tired, threadbare, worn-out, overworked, unoriginal, stock, stereotyped. ORIGINAL

**hag** crone, harridan, virago, vixen, shrew, nag, scold, witch.

**haggard** gaunt, drawn, worn, weary, pale, wan, pinched, wasted, shrunken, wrinkled. FRESH

**haggle** bargain, chaffer, barter, negotiate, wrangle, quarrel, bicker, quibble. AGREE

**hail**[1] *v*, greet, salute, address, welcome, receive, acknowledge, accost, signal, flag down, call, acclaim, cheer, exalt, glorify. IGNORE

**hail**[2] *n*, shower, rain, storm, volley, barrage, bombardment.

**hair** locks, tresses, mop, shock, mane, coat, fur.

**hairy** hirsute, shaggy, furry, woolly, fluffy, bearded, unshaven. HAIRLESS
difficult, dangerous, risky, exciting, frightening, scary (*inf*).

**halcyon** peaceful, tranquil, serene, placid, calm, still, quiet, mild, gentle. STORMY
happy, carefree, palmy, golden, prosperous.

**hale** healthy, hearty, robust, strong, hardy, sound, well, fit, in fine fettle, vigorous, energetic, lusty. FRAIL

**half** *n*, bisection, equal part, fifty per cent. WHOLE
*adv*, halfway, partly, partially, barely, incompletely, nearly. COMPLETELY

**half-hearted** indifferent, uncaring, apathetic, lukewarm, cool, unenthusiastic, languid, listless, careless, perfunctory. ENTHUSIASTIC

**hall** vestibule, lobby, foyer, corridor, passage, chamber, auditorium, amphitheatre.

**hallow** sanctify, consecrate, bless, dedicate, devote, venerate, revere, exalt, glorify. DESECRATE

**hallowed** holy, sacred, sanctified, consecrated, blessed, revered, sacrosanct. PROFANE

**hallucination** delusion, illusion, dream, fantasy, mirage, vision, apparition, phantasm, figment of the imagination. REALITY

**halt**[1] *v*, stop, cease, break off, rest, stand still, stay, wait, hold back, arrest, check, curb, impede, block, end, terminate. PROCEED
*n*, stop, standstill, rest, pause, break, interruption, end, termination.

**halt**[2] *v*, hesitate, falter, waver, pause, stammer, stutter, stumble, hobble.

**halve** bisect, divide, split, cut in half.

**hammer** beat, pound, batter, strike, hit, drive, drum, forge, shape, fashion.

**hamper** hinder, impede, obstruct, encumber, embarrass, handicap, cramp, shackle, restrain, restrict, confine, check, curb, prevent, thwart. ASSIST

**hand** *n*, palm, fist, paw (*inf*), mitt (*inf*). FOOT
agency, intervention, part, share, participation.
help, aid, assistance.
labourer, worker, operative, employee, assistant, helper, crew member.
handwriting, script, penmanship, calligraphy, chirography.
ovation, clap, round of applause.
**at hand,** nearby, close, handy, within reach, accessible, to hand, on hand, available, ready.
*v*, give, present, deliver, pass, transmit.
**hand down,** bequeath, will, transfer, pass on.
**hand out,** distribute, dispense, give out, deal out, mete. WITHHOLD
**hand over,** deliver, transfer, surrender, yield. RETAIN

**handicap** *n*, hindrance, disadvantage, drawback, disability, impediment, obstacle, barrier, restriction, limitation. ADVANTAGE
*v*, hinder, hamper, impede, encumber, restrict, disable, hold back. ASSIST

**handicraft** craft, art, skill, handiwork, craftsmanship, workmanship.

**handiwork** work, labour, creation, production, craft, handicraft.

**handle** *v*, feel, touch, finger, maul, pick up, hold.
manipulate, manage, wield, use, operate, control, direct, administer, treat, deal with, cope with.
*n*, knob, grip, haft, stock, hilt, shaft.

**hands** clutches, possession, keeping, custody, care, grip, power, control.

**handsome** good-looking, attractive, personable, fair, comely, elegant, fine, stately. UGLY
liberal, generous, ample, plentiful, large, considerable, magnanimous, gracious, noble. STINGY

**handy** nearby, near, close, at hand, on hand, available, ready, accessible, to hand, within reach, convenient, useful, practical, helpful. INCONVENIENT
adroit, dexterous, skilful, deft, adept, expert, proficient, clever. CLUMSY

**hang** suspend, hang up, drape, dangle, swing, droop, sag, drop, fall, trail, hang down. STAND
hover, float, drift, waft, linger, remain. DISPERSE
depend, hinge, turn, rest.
gibbet, string up (*inf*), execute, lynch.

**hang on**, cling, cleave, stick, adhere, hold fast, grip, grasp, clutch.
persevere, carry on, continue, persist, hold out, endure, remain, hold on, wait.

**hanker** long, yearn, itch, hunger, thirst, crave, desire, want, covet, lust.

**hankering** longing, yearning, yen (*inf*), itch, hunger, thirst, craving, desire, lust. AVERSION

**haphazard** random, chance, arbitrary, accidental. DELIBERATE
careless, slipshod, slapdash, disorderly, disorganized, unmethodical, aimless, casual. ORDERLY

**hapless** unfortunate, unlucky, luckless, ill-fated, ill-starred, wretched, miserable, unhappy. LUCKY

**happen** occur, take place, come about, come to pass, befall, betide, chance, arise, crop up, transpire, materialize, result, ensue, turn out.

**happening** event, occurrence, incident, episode, case, circumstance, chance, accident, phenomenon.

**happiness** joy, delight, bliss, ecstasy, elation, glee, felicity, gladness, contentment, pleasure, gaiety, merriment, cheerfulness, high spirits. SADNESS

**happy** joyful, joyous, delighted, overjoyed, thrilled, pleased, contented, satisfied, glad, gleeful, ecstatic, elated, blissful, blithe, cheerful, gay, merry, jolly. SAD
fortunate, lucky, favourable, felicitous, prosperous, successful, auspicious, seasonable, opportune, timely, appropriate, apt, befitting. UNFORTUNATE

**harangue** *v*, address, lecture, hold forth, rant, declaim, spout (*inf*).
*n*, address, speech, talk, oration, lecture, spiel (*inf*), sermon, declamation, tirade, diatribe, philippic.

**harass** plague, torment, persecute, harry, pester, nag, hector, badger, bother, trouble, annoy, vex, provoke, bait, tease, tire, weary, fatigue, exhaust.

**harbinger** precursor, forerunner, herald, messenger, announcer, sign, indication, omen, portent.

**harbour** *n*, port, anchorage, haven, shelter, refuge, sanctuary, asylum.
*v*, protect, shelter, lodge, house, hide, conceal, shield. EXPOSE
cherish, foster, nurture, nurse, hold, maintain, entertain. EXPEL

**hard** *adj*, solid, dense, compact, firm, rigid, stiff, unyielding, resistant, impenetrable, strong, tough, stony, steely. SOFT
difficult, arduous, laborious, gruelling, strenuous, rigorous, taxing, tiring, exhausting, fatiguing. EASY
puzzling, perplexing, intricate, complicated, complex, involved, knotty, thorny. SIMPLE
harsh, severe, stern, strict, cruel, ruthless, pitiless, unrelenting, obdurate, hard-hearted, callous, unfeeling, unsympathetic, cold, unkind. TENDER
painful, distressing, unpleasant, disagreeable, bad, grievous, calamitous, disastrous. PLEASANT

**hard up**, poor, short, penniless, bankrupt, broke (*inf*), skint (*inf*). RICH
*adv*, diligently, industriously, assiduously, conscientiously, earnestly, intently, vigorously, energetically, strenuously, laboriously, steadily, persistently.
violently, forcibly, forcefully, sharply, heavily, severely, harshly, badly, painfully. SOFTLY

**harden** solidify, compact, set, stiffen, petrify, freeze, bake. SOFTEN

strengthen, toughen, fortify, buttress, brace, steel, temper, anneal. WEAKEN
inure, season, habituate, accustom, acclimatize, break in, train, discipline.

**hardened** inveterate, confirmed, habitual, chronic, impenitent, incorrigible, set, fixed.

**hard-headed** shrewd, astute, keen, sharp, wise, level-headed, sensible, realistic, practical, cool, unsentimental, tough.

**hard-hearted** cold, callous, stony, obdurate, unfeeling, insensible, unkind, cruel, pitiless, merciless, implacable. SOFT-HEARTED

**hardihood** courage, bravery, pluck, mettle, intrepidity, boldness, audacity, daring, fearlessness, strength, hardiness, fortitude, determination, resolution. COWARDICE
assurance, effrontery, temerity, rashness, recklessness, foolhardiness. CAUTION

**hardly** scarcely, barely, narrowly, only just.

**hardness** solidity, firmness, rigidity, stiffness, resistance, strength, toughness. SOFTNESS
difficulty, arduousness, strenuousness, rigour, complexity, intricacy. EASINESS
harshness, severity, strictness, cruelty, callousness, coldness, unkindness. TENDERNESS

**hardship** trouble, difficulty, trial, tribulation, affliction, suffering, misfortune, adversity, privation, want, need, austerity, burden, oppression. PROSPERITY

**hardy** strong, tough, rugged, firm, sturdy, robust, hale, hearty, lusty, vigorous, sound, fit, healthy. WEAK
courageous, brave, plucky, valiant, intrepid, daring, bold, audacious, determined, resolute. COWARDLY
rash, reckless, foolhardy, headstrong, impetuous. CAUTIOUS

**hark** listen, give ear, hearken, pay attention, hear. IGNORE

**hark back,** revert, go back, regress, recall, recollect, think back.

**harlot** prostitute, whore, hussy, trollop, strumpet, scrubber (*inf*), tart (*inf*).

**harm** *v*, hurt, injure, damage, impair, mar, spoil, maltreat, abuse, molest. BENEFIT
*n*, hurt, injury, damage, abuse, detriment, mischief, ill, evil, wrong, sin, iniquity, wickedness. GOOD

**harmful** hurtful, injurious, damaging, deleterious, detrimental, pernicious, mischievous, baleful, baneful, noxious, dangerous, evil. BENEFICIAL

**harmless** innocuous, safe, inoffensive, innocent, innoxious, gentle, mild. PERNICIOUS

**harmonious** harmonic, tuneful, melodious, euphonious, mellifluous, dulcet, musical. CACOPHONOUS
concordant, consonant, congruous, consistent, correspondent, compatible, agreeable, amicable, friendly, congenial, cordial. DISCORDANT

**harmonize** agree, accord, correspond, coincide, match, coordinate, blend, adapt, attune. DIFFER

**harmony** accord, concord, accordance, concordance, consonance, congruity, correspondence, coordination, agreement, consensus, unanimity, unity, amity, friendship, peace, understanding, goodwill, rapport. DISCORD

**harness** *n*, equipment, tack, bridle, yoke, gear, tackle.
*v*, control, rein, yoke, utilize, exploit, channel.

**harp** dwell, go on, repeat, reiterate, press, push, persist, insist.

**harrow** distress, disturb, alarm, perturb, torment, torture, rack, agonize, wound, vex, frighten, terrify, chill. SOOTHE

**harry** harass, plague, torment, worry, fret, trouble, vex, annoy, exasperate, bother, disturb. APPEASE
ravage, devastate, raid, plunder, pillage, sack, rob, despoil.

**harsh** rough, coarse, raucous, guttural, strident, grating, cacophonous, discordant, jarring, glaring, acrid, bitter, sharp, sour. MELLOW
severe, hard, austere, bleak, Spartan, grim, stern, cruel, unkind, pitiless, ruthless, unfeeling, brutal, tough, stringent. GENTLE

**harvest** *n*, crop, yield, produce, fruits, result, consequence, outcome, issue, product, effect.
*v*, gather, reap, pick, pluck, glean, garner, collect.

**hash** *n*, mess, jumble, muddle, mix-up, confusion, medley, mishmash, hotchpotch.
*v*, chop, dice, mince, mangle, mutilate.

**haste** speed, rapidity, swiftness, quickness, fleetness, celerity, velocity, dispatch,

expedition, promptitude, alacrity, briskness, urgency. DELAY
hurry, rush, bustle, hustle, hastiness, precipitance, recklessness, rashness, impetuosity, impulsiveness, heedlessness. CAUTION

**hasten** *vt*, quicken, hurry, speed, accelerate, precipitate, expedite, dispatch, urge, press. RETARD
*vi*, hurry, rush, dash, race, fly, speed, run, bolt. DAWDLE

**hasty** quick, fast, rapid, speedy, swift, fleet, brisk, prompt, urgent. SLOW
hurried, rushed, superficial, cursory, perfunctory, fleeting, brief, slight. THOROUGH
reckless, rash, impetuous, impulsive, precipitate, headlong, heedless, thoughtless, indiscreet. CAUTIOUS
irascible, touchy, testy, short-tempered, irritable, peevish, petulant, waspish, impatient, excitable, fiery. PLACID

**hatch** incubate, brood, bring forth, emerge.
contrive, devise, concoct, brew, conceive, think up, plot, plan, scheme.

**hate** *v*, detest, loathe, abhor, abominate, execrate, dislike. LOVE
*n*, hatred, detestation, loathing, abhorrence, odium, abomination, execration, aversion, dislike, antipathy, hostility, enmity. LOVE

**hateful** detestable, loathsome, abhorrent, abominable, odious, execrable, horrible, obnoxious, vile, foul, offensive, repulsive, repugnant, revolting. DELIGHTFUL

**hatred** hate, detestation, loathing, abhorrence, odium, abomination, execration, aversion, dislike, antipathy, hostility, enmity, animosity, ill will, revulsion, repugnance. LOVE

**haughtiness** arrogance, self-importance, hauteur, loftiness, superciliousness, snobbishness, airs, pride, conceit, contempt, disdain. HUMILITY

**haughty** arrogant, self-important, lofty, vain, conceited, proud, supercilious, disdainful, contemptuous, snobbish, snooty (*inf*), stuck-up (*inf*), hoity-toity (*inf*), high and mighty (*inf*), imperious, lordly, aloof. HUMBLE

**haul** *v*, drag, lug, draw, pull, tow, tug, heave. PUSH
carry, convey, transport, cart.
*n*, catch, yield, takings, spoils, booty.

**haunt** *v*, visit, frequent.
obsess, beset, plague, torment, prey on, recur, come back.
*n*, retreat, refuge, den, meeting place, stamping ground.

**hauteur** arrogance, haughtiness, pride, conceit, superciliousness, contempt, disdain, loftiness, airs, snobbishness. HUMILITY

**have** own, possess, hold, keep, retain. LACK
get, obtain, gain, acquire, procure, receive, take, accept. LOSE
feel, experience, undergo, suffer, enjoy.
be obliged, be forced, be compelled, must.
entertain, consider, tolerate, allow, permit. FORBID
cheat, swindle, deceive, dupe, take in (*inf*), fool, outwit.
bear, give birth to, bring forth, deliver, beget.

**haven** harbour, port, anchorage.
shelter, refuge, sanctuary, asylum, retreat.

**havoc** destruction, devastation, desolation, waste, wreck, ruin, ravage, despoliation.
confusion, disorder, chaos, mayhem.

**hawk** peddle, sell, vend, cry, bark (*inf*).

**hazard** *n*, danger, risk, peril, jeopardy, threat.
chance, accident, fluke, gamble.
*v*, risk, venture, dare, gamble, stake, chance, endanger, imperil, expose.
advance, submit, offer, proffer, volunteer. WITHDRAW

**hazardous** dangerous, risky, perilous, hairy (*inf*), unsafe, insecure, precarious. SAFE
uncertain, unpredictable, random, haphazard, chancy (*inf*). CERTAIN

**haze** mist, fog, cloud, vapour, film, obscurity, dimness, haziness.

**hazy** misty, foggy, cloudy, nebulous, filmy, blurry, dim, obscure. CLEAR
vague, indistinct, unclear, ill-defined, muddled, confused. DEFINITE

**head** *n*, skull, cranium, pate, nut (*inf*). FOOT
top, summit, apex, crown, crest, peak, tip, vertex, acme, zenith, height. BASE
mind, brain, intellect, intelligence, thought, understanding, genius, aptitude, flair.

leader, chieftain, chief, principal, master, captain, commander, director, manager, superintendent. SUBORDINATE

front, vanguard, beginning, start, origin, source. END

climax, culmination, crisis, turning point.

section, division, category, class, department, heading.

*v*, lead, command, direct, control, guide, govern, rule, run, manage. FOLLOW

steer, turn, aim, direct, point, go, make.

**head off,** intercept, divert, deflect, avert, parry, forestall, prevent.

*adj*, leading, first, chief, principal, main, supreme, highest, top, front.

**heading** title, rubric, caption, headline.

section, division, head, category, class.

**headland** cape, promontory, foreland, spur, point, cliff, bluff.

**headlong** *adv*, headfirst, hastily, precipitately, pell-mell, helter-skelter, wildly, impetuously, recklessly, rashly, heedlessly. CAUTIOUSLY

*adj*, hasty, rash, precipitate, reckless, rash, heedless, thoughtless, impetuous, impulsive, foolhardy, breakneck. CAUTIOUS

**headstrong** wilful, self-willed, obstinate, stubborn, mulish, intractable, pig-headed, perverse, contrary, refractory, unruly, ungovernable, wayward. TRACTABLE

rash, reckless, imprudent, foolhardy, heedless. PRUDENT

**headway** progress, advance, improvement, progression, movement, motion. RETROGRESSION

**heady** intoxicating, exciting, thrilling, exhilarating, stimulating.

rash, reckless, headlong, precipitate, hasty, impulsive, impetuous, heedless, thoughtless. CAUTIOUS

**heal** cure, restore, repair, mend, remedy, treat, make well, get well, recover.

reconcile, conciliate, patch up, settle, compose, appease, assuage, soothe, alleviate. AGGRAVATE

**healing** curative, restorative, analeptic, remedial, medicinal, therapeutic, lenitive, soothing, comforting, gentle, mild. HARMFUL

**health** fitness, well-being, soundness, robustness, healthiness, haleness, strength, vigour, condition, state, shape, form, tone, fettle. ILLNESS

**healthy** fit, well, sound, robust, hale, hearty, sturdy, strong, vigorous, lusty. ILL

salubrious, salutary, healthful, wholesome, hygienic, beneficial, bracing, invigorating. UNHEALTHY

**heap** *n*, pile, mound, stack, mass, lot, hoard, store, accumulation, collection, abundance, plenty, great deal, load (*inf*).

*v*, pile, stack, amass, accumulate, gather, collect, hoard, store. SCATTER

load, burden, shower, pour, supply, bestow, assign.

**hear** listen to, attend, hark, hearken, catch, perceive, heed, eavesdrop, overhear. IGNORE

learn, be informed, be told, find out, gather.

try, examine, investigate, judge.

**hearing** ear, audition, audience, interview, examination, investigation, inquiry, trial.

earshot, range, sound.

**hearsay** rumour, gossip, talk, report, buzz, tittle-tattle.

**heart** core, centre, middle, kernel, nucleus, marrow, pith, essence, crux. SURFACE

soul, spirit, nature, character, disposition, temperament, passion, emotion, feeling, sentiment, sympathy, pity, compassion, love, tenderness, affection, humanity.

courage, bravery, fortitude, nerve, pluck, mettle, spirit, boldness, resolution. COWARDICE

**heartache** distress, anguish, grief, sorrow, woe, pain, agony, torment, suffering, affliction, despair, desolation, heartbreak. JOY

**hearten** cheer, buoy up, buck up (*inf*), comfort, console, assure, reassure, encourage, embolden, inspirit, inspire, animate, rouse, stimulate, invigorate. DEPRESS

**heartfelt** sincere, profound, deep, hearty, cordial, warm, earnest, fervent, wholehearted. INSINCERE

**heartless** cruel, unkind, unfeeling, uncaring, hard-hearted, cold, callous, harsh, brutal, pitiless, merciless, savage, cold-blooded. KIND

**hearty** genial, cordial, jovial, amiable, affable, friendly, warm, unreserved, heartfelt, sincere, genuine, profound, earnest, wholehearted, enthusiastic. COOL

strong, hale, healthy, robust, sturdy, sound, vigorous, lusty, energetic. FEEBLE
nourishing, filling, substantial, ample, square, solid. MEAGRE
**heat** *n*, warmth, hotness, calefaction, high temperature, fever. COLD
passion, zeal, ardour, fervour, vehemence, intensity, violence, frenzy, rage, fury, excitement. COOLNESS
*v*, warm, cook, heat up, make hot. CHILL
excite, inflame, stir, rouse, stimulate, animate, impassion. COOL
**heathen** *n*, pagan, infidel, unbeliever, idolater, barbarian, philistine.
*adj*, pagan, idolatrous, godless, ungodly, barbarous, primitive, uncivilized. GODLY
**heave** haul, drag, pull, hoist, raise, lift.
throw, cast, fling, hurl, sling, pitch, toss.
surge, swell, rise, throb, billow, roll, pant, sigh.
retch, gag (*inf*), vomit, throw up (*inf*).
**heaven** paradise, hereafter, afterworld, Elysium, Valhalla, Zion, utopia. HELL
ecstasy, rapture, bliss, happiness, felicity, joy, delight. TORMENT
**heavenly** wonderful, delightful, lovely, beautiful, exquisite, sublime, glorious, blissful, rapturous. ABOMINABLE
holy, angelic, saintly, blessed, divine, celestial, extraterrestrial, supernatural, spiritual, unearthly. EARTHLY
**heavens** sky, ether, firmament, empyrean.
**heaviness** weight, heftiness, ponderousness, bulk, mass. LIGHTNESS
intensity, violence, severity, harshness, oppressiveness, laboriousness, difficulty.
sadness, sorrow, dejection, despondency, gloom, melancholy. CHEERFULNESS
seriousness, gravity, importance, profundity, complexity.
sluggishness, languor, listlessness, apathy, dullness, slowness, inactivity, inertia. ACTIVITY
**heavy** weighty, ponderous, hefty, bulky, massive, large, great, considerable, fat, stout. LIGHT
intense, violent, severe, hard, harsh, grievous, oppressive, burdensome, laborious, arduous, difficult. SLIGHT
sad, sorrowful, downcast, crestfallen, dejected, despondent, gloomy, melancholy. CHEERFUL
serious, grave, critical, important, profound, deep, complex. TRIVIAL
sluggish, torpid, languid, listless, apathetic, drowsy, sleepy, dull, slow, inactive, inert. ACTIVE
burdened, laden, loaded, encumbered, weighted.
overcast, cloudy, dull, gloomy, dark, leaden, lowering. BRIGHT
**heckle** interrupt, disrupt, barrack (*inf*), taunt, jeer, bait, badger, hector, harass.
**hectic** feverish, frenetic, frantic, frenzied, furious, excited, animated, heated, riotous, boisterous, wild, chaotic, unruly. CALM
**hector** *v*, bully, browbeat, intimidate, threaten, menace, torment, plague, harass, badger, harry, worry.
bluster, boast, brag, swagger, roister.
*n*, bully, braggart, blusterer, swaggerer.
**hedge** *n*, hedgerow, quickset, fence, barrier, guard, protection.
*v*, surround, enclose, fence, confine, restrict, obstruct, hinder, impede, block.
evade, dodge, equivocate, prevaricate, fudge.
protect, guard, shield, safeguard, cover. EXPOSE
**heed** *v*, mind, attend, pay attention to, listen to, take notice of, regard, note, mark, observe, obey, follow. IGNORE
*n*, attention, notice, regard, mind, thought, consideration, care, caution, heedfulness, watchfulness. DISREGARD
**heedful** mindful, attentive, regardful, thoughtful, prudent, careful, circumspect, cautious, chary, wary, watchful, observant. HEEDLESS
**heedless** unmindful, regardless, oblivious, thoughtless, unthinking, careless, inattentive, neglectful, negligent, rash, reckless. HEEDFUL
**heel**[1] *n*, remnant, remainder, stub, stump, butt, rump, crust.
scoundrel, blackguard, cad (*inf*), rotter (*inf*).
**heel**[2] *v*, lean, list, tilt, cant, incline.
**hegemony** supremacy, primacy, dominion, domination, ascendancy, rule, sway, command, mastery, control, leadership.
**height** altitude, elevation, loftiness, tallness, stature. DEPTH
top, summit, apex, peak, pinnacle, zenith, apogee, acme, climax, culmination, maximum, utmost, limit, extremity, extreme.
mountain, hill, eminence.

**heighten** increase, augment, amplify, intensify, aggravate, enhance, enrich, improve, strengthen. MODERATE
raise, elevate, uplift, exalt, ennoble. LOWER

**heinous** wicked, evil, nefarious, infamous, atrocious, scandalous, outrageous, monstrous, villainous, flagitious, abominable, odious, hateful, deplorable. ADMIRABLE

**heir** child, offspring, descendant, successor, inheritor, beneficiary, heiress.

**hell** underworld, perdition, inferno, Hades, Gehenna. HEAVEN
torment, anguish, agony, suffering, affliction, misery, nightmare. ECSTASY

**hellish** infernal, diabolical, fiendish, satanic, demonic, demoniacal, devilish, damnable, accursed, wicked, evil, nefarious, heinous, monstrous, cruel, savage, barbaric, inhuman. HEAVENLY

**helm** rudder, wheel, tiller.
control, command, direction, reins, saddle, driver's seat.

**help** *v*, assist, aid, lend a hand, abet, succour, back, support, encourage, promote, further, serve, avail, cooperate, collaborate. HINDER
relieve, alleviate, improve, ameliorate, ease, facilitate, remedy, restore. AGGRAVATE
avoid, refrain from, resist, withstand, stop, prevent, control.
*n*, assistance, aid, succour, backing, support, encouragement, service, avail, use, cooperation, collaboration. HINDRANCE
relief, remedy, cure, corrective, improvement. AGGRAVATION
helper, assistant, aider, abettor, mate.

**helper** assistant, aider, aide, auxiliary, help, supporter, backer, second, ally, colleague, partner, mate, helpmate, collaborator, adjutant. OPPONENT

**helpful** useful, serviceable, beneficial, advantageous, practical, constructive, profitable, valuable. USELESS
friendly, neighbourly, caring, sympathetic, kind, benevolent, supportive, obliging.

**helpless** impotent, powerless, incapable, incompetent, weak, feeble, infirm, unfit, dependent, defenceless, unprotected, vulnerable, abandoned, forsaken. STRONG

**hem** *n*, edge, border, margin, edging, trimming.
*v*, edge, border, bind, trim.

**hem in,** surround, encircle, environ, gird, enclose, confine, shut in.

**hence** therefore, thus, for this reason, ergo.
henceforth, henceforward, hereafter, from now on. HITHERTO

**henchman** attendant, servant, retainer, follower, supporter, aide, right-hand man, crony.

**herald** *n*, messenger, runner, announcer, crier, harbinger, forerunner, precursor, sign, indication, omen, portent.
*v*, announce, proclaim, trumpet, promulgate, broadcast, advertise, publish. SUPPRESS
precede, usher in, portend, presage, foretoken.

**herbage** grass, plants, vegetation, pasture, pasturage.

**herculean** laborious, arduous, strenuous, toilsome, heavy, hard, difficult, formidable, gruelling, demanding. EASY
strong, mighty, powerful, stalwart, robust, strapping, muscular, brawny, athletic. PUNY

**herd** *n*, drove, pack, flock, swarm, horde, crowd, throng, multitude, mob, rabble, populace.
*v*, gather, assemble, muster, flock, congregate, collect. DISPERSE
drive, lead, guide, shepherd.

**hereditary** inheritable, heritable, hereditable, genetic, transmissible. ACQUIRED
inherited, bequeathed, transmitted, handed down, ancestral, traditional.

**heresy** unorthodoxy, heterodoxy, nonconformism, dissent, schism, apostasy, iconoclasm. ORTHODOXY

**heretical** unorthodox, heterodox, nonconformist, schismatic, iconoclastic, idolatrous, heathen, pagan. ORTHODOX

**heritage** inheritance, patrimony, tradition, birthright, portion, legacy, bequest.

**hermetic** hermetical, sealed, airtight.

**hermit** solitary, recluse, anchorite, eremite.

**heroic** courageous, brave, valiant, valorous, intrepid, fearless, dauntless, bold, daring, gallant, noble. COWARDLY
legendary, classical, classic, epic, grand, grandiose, extravagant.

**heroism** courage, bravery, valour, fortitude, intrepidity, fearlessness, boldness, daring, gallantry, chivalry. COWARDICE

**hesitate** pause, wait, delay, hold back, waver, vacillate, doubt, be uncertain, demur, be reluctant, scruple, think twice, falter, stammer, stutter. PROCEED

**hesitation** pause, delay, hesitancy, wavering, vacillation, doubt, uncertainty, irresolution, indecision, qualm, scruple, reluctance, faltering. DECISION

**heterodox** unorthodox, heretical, schismatic, iconoclastic. ORTHODOX

**heterodoxy** unorthodoxy, heresy, schism, iconoclasm, dissent. ORTHODOXY

**heterogeneous** dissimilar, different, unlike, disparate, unrelated, varied, diverse, mixed, miscellaneous. HOMOGENEOUS

**hew** chop, hack, axe, lop, sever, cut down, fell.
carve, sculpt, shape, fashion, form.

**hiatus** gap, break, interruption, pause, interval, blank, void, space, opening, aperture, rift, cleft.

**hidden** concealed, latent, unseen, masked, veiled, covert, cryptic, secret, private, close, clandestine, dark, obscure, occult, abstruse, recondite, mystical. OPEN

**hide**[1] *v*, conceal, cloak, shroud, cover, screen, mask, veil, dissemble, disguise, camouflage, obscure, eclipse, suppress, bury, secrete, lie low. REVEAL

**hide**[2] skin, pelt, coat, leather.

**hideous** ugly, grotesque, unsightly, repulsive, revolting, ghastly, monstrous, gruesome, grisly, grim, horrible, horrid, frightful, dreadful, terrible, horrific, appalling, shocking, odious, abominable. BEAUTIFUL

**hieratic** hieratical, priestly, sacerdotal, clerical, ecclesiastical, holy.

**higgledy-piggledy** disorderly, jumbled, confused, muddled, topsy-turvy, haphazard, helter-skelter, pell-mell. ORDERLY

**high** tall, lofty, elevated, towering, soaring. LOW
great, intense, extreme, strong, violent, sharp, excessive, expensive, dear.
shrill, piercing, piping, high-pitched, treble. DEEP
eminent, prominent, important, exalted, distinguished, dignified, noble, august, influential, leading, chief, ruling. LOWLY
haughty, arrogant, proud, high and mighty (*inf*), lordly, overbearing, domineering, supercilious, disdainful, contemptuous.
happy, cheerful, elated, exhilarated, euphoric, intoxicated, stoned (*inf*). DEPRESSED

**highlight** *n*, climax, peak, best part, outstanding feature, high spot, focal point.
*v*, stress, emphasize, accent, accentuate, underline, point up, spotlight, feature.

**highly** greatly, extremely, very, immensely, vastly, tremendously, supremely, exceptionally, extraordinarily.
favourably, well, appreciatively, approvingly, warmly, respectfully. BADLY

**hike** *v*, walk, tramp, trek, ramble.
hitch, pull, lift, raise.
*n*, walk, tramp, trek, ramble.

**hilarious** funny, amusing, side-splitting, hysterical (*inf*), uproarious, noisy, boisterous, merry, jolly, jovial, mirthful, cheerful, gay, joyful, happy, elated, exhilarated. SERIOUS

**hilarity** merriment, jollity, mirth, laughter, gaiety, cheerfulness, joy, exhilaration, exuberance, high spirits, boisterousness. DESPONDENCY

**hill** mound, knoll, hillock, hummock, eminence, elevation, rise, incline, slope, acclivity. PLAIN

**hind** back, rear, posterior, hinder. FRONT

**hinder** impede, obstruct, block, hamper, thwart, frustrate, retard, delay, check, stop, arrest, prevent, oppose. HELP

**hindrance** impediment, encumbrance, handicap, obstacle, obstruction, block, barrier, hitch, snag, difficulty, delay, check, restriction, limitation. ASSISTANCE

**hinge** turn, hang, depend, rest, pivot, revolve around.

**hint** *n*, suggestion, intimation, implication, insinuation, innuendo, allusion, mention, inkling, clue, tip.
trace, suspicion, *soupçon*, dash, touch, whisper, taste.
*v*, suggest, intimate, imply, insinuate, allude, mention, tip off.

**hire** *v*, rent, charter, lease, let, engage, commission, appoint, employ, take on.
*n*, rental, rent, charge, fee, pay, payment, wages, cost, price.

**hireling** mercenary, tool, puppet, employee, servant, slave, menial.

**hirsute** hairy, shaggy, hispid, bristly, bearded, unshaven. SMOOTH

**hiss** *v*, sibilate, whistle, rasp, wheeze, whiz.

boo, hoot, catcall, jeer, mock, deride, decry, shout down. APPLAUD
*n*, sibilation, sibilance, whistle, hissing, buzz, whiz.
boo, hoot, catcall, raspberry, jeer, mockery, derision. APPLAUSE

**historic** famous, celebrated, noteworthy, memorable, remarkable, important, significant, consequential, momentous. INCONSEQUENTIAL

**historical** authentic, real, true, actual, factual, documented, chronicled. LEGENDARY

**history** chronicle, annals, record, account, story, narration, narrative, memoirs, biography.
antiquity, the past, olden days, yesteryear. FUTURE

**histrionic** theatrical, melodramatic, dramatic, affected, forced, insincere, unnatural, false, artificial.

**hit** *v*, strike, knock, beat, batter, smack, slap, whack, punch, thump, box, cuff, bash (*inf*), clout (*inf*).
bump, bang, crash into, smash into, collide with, clash with. MISS
reach, attain, achieve, arrive at, gain, touch.
**hit upon,** find, discover, come upon, light upon, chance upon, happen upon, think of, dream up.
*n*, stroke, blow, knock, smack, slap, thump, cuff, bump, crash, collision, clash, impact.
success, triumph, winner, sellout, sensation, smash (*inf*). FAILURE

**hitch** *v*, tie, fasten, attach, connect, unite, couple, tether, moor, harness. LOOSE
pull, tug, hike, jerk.
*n*, impediment, obstacle, hindrance, problem, difficulty, snag, catch, delay, hold-up.
jerk, tug, pull.

**hoard** *v*, gather, collect, amass, accumulate, garner, store, stockpile, save, husband, reserve, put by, lay up, stash away (*inf*). SQUANDER
*n*, collection, store, stockpile, reserve, fund, cache, accumulation, mass, heap, pile.

**hoarse** husky, raucous, throaty, croaky, guttural, gruff, harsh, rough, grating, rasping. MELLOW

**hoary** grey, silvery, frosty, white, grizzled, grey-haired, white-haired. DARK
venerable, aged, old, ancient.

**hoax** *n*, trick, practical joke, prank, deception, fraud, imposture, cheat, swindle.
*v*, trick, deceive, dupe, fool, hoodwink, bamboozle (*inf*), cheat, swindle.

**hobble** limp, stumble, totter, dodder, falter. RUN
fetter, shackle, tie, bind, fasten. UNFETTER

**hobby** pastime, recreation, amusement, diversion, leisure, activity, sideline. WORK

**hobnob** fraternize, socialize, mingle, mix, consort, keep company, go around.

**hog** *n*, pig, swine, porker, grunter.
glutton, gourmand.
*v*, monopolize, corner, keep for oneself. SHARE

**hoggish** piggish, swinish, selfish, greedy, grasping, rapacious, gluttonous, voracious, dirty, filthy, unclean, squalid, sordid.

**hoist** raise, lift, crane, winch, elevate, heave, erect, rear. LOWER

**hold** *v*, grip, grasp, clutch, clasp, seize, keep, retain, have, possess, own, occupy. DROP
support, sustain, bear, carry, take, contain, accommodate.
detain, arrest, imprison, confine, restrain, hold back, check, curb, stop. RELEASE
maintain, think, believe, consider, regard, judge, deem, reckon.
stick, adhere, cling, hold on, cleave, embrace, hug, cradle.
last, endure, abide, remain, stay, persist, continue, stand. PERISH
convene, call, conduct, run, preside over, engage in, carry on.
**hold forth,** speak, orate, preach, lecture, harangue, discourse, spout (*inf*).
**hold out,** offer, proffer, extend, present.
last, endure, stand firm, hang on, persevere.
**hold up,** delay, retard, slow down, hinder, impede. ADVANCE
support, sustain, brace, prop, buttress.
brandish, wave, flaunt, display, show, exhibit.
*n*, grip, grasp, clasp, embrace, foothold, purchase.
influence, control, power, sway, mastery, dominion, ascendancy.

**hole** aperture, opening, gap, break, breach, rift, cleft, fissure, split, tear, rent, puncture, perforation, fault, flaw.
cavity, hollow, depression, concavity, pit, cave, cavern, chamber, burrow, den, lair.
hovel, slum, dive (*inf*), dump (*inf*).

predicament, quandary, dilemma, plight, strait, fix (*inf*).

**holiday** leave, vacation, time off, break. festival, feast, saint's day, anniversary, celebration, gala, fête, carnival.

**holiness** devoutness, piety, religiousness, saintliness, godliness, sanctity, sacredness, divinity, purity, virtue. PROFANITY

**hollow** *adj*, empty, unfilled, vacant, concave, cavernous, sunken.
muffled, muted, low, deep, rumbling, reverberating, flat, dull.
meaningless, pointless, empty, vain, fruitless, unavailing, worthless, useless.
insincere, hypocritical, artificial, sham, false, deceitful. SINCERE
*n*, depression, dip, basin, bowl, cavity, pit, hole, crater, dent, dimple, indentation.
*v*, dig, excavate, scoop, gouge, pit, dent.

**holy** devout, pious, religious, saintly, godly, good, virtuous, righteous, pure, divine, spiritual, sacred, hallowed, consecrated, blessed. PROFANE

**homage** honour, respect, deference, worship, adoration, veneration, reverence, esteem, admiration. DISRESPECT
loyalty, allegiance, constancy, devotion, fidelity, fealty, duty, tribute.

**home** *n*, house, abode, dwelling, residence, domicile, habitation, habitat, territory, environment, element.
family, household, hearth, fireside, birthplace, native land.
*adj*, domestic, family, household, internal, interior, national, native. FOREIGN

**homely** simple, plain, unpretentious, ordinary, familiar, domestic, homelike, homy, comfortable, cosy, welcoming, informal. GRAND

**homicide** murder, manslaughter, killing, slaying, assassination.

**homily** sermon, discourse, lecture, harangue, address, speech.

**homogeneous** uniform, consistent, identical, alike, like, similar, akin. HETEROGENEOUS

**hone** sharpen, whet, grind, file, polish. BLUNT

**honest** trustworthy, trusty, reliable, upright, law-abiding, virtuous, honourable, conscientious, principled, truthful, veracious, sincere, candid, frank, straightforward, open, fair, just, equitable, lawful, legal, genuine, authentic, real, true. DISHONEST

**honesty** truthfulness, veracity, probity, integrity, honour, morality, rectitude, uprightness, sincerity, candour, frankness, fairness, justice, equity. DISHONESTY

**honorary** titular, nominal, ex officio, unofficial, unpaid.

**honour** *n*, distinction, eminence, fame, glory, repute, reputation, esteem, regard, dignity, prestige, standing, credit. DISGRACE
honesty, integrity, probity, rectitude, uprightness, morality, principles, justice, fairness, virtue, decency, sincerity. DISHONESTY
praise, acclaim, acclamation, tribute, homage, reverence, veneration, worship, adoration, respect, deference. CONTEMPT
privilege, pleasure, joy, pride, satisfaction.
virginity, chastity, purity, virtue.
*v*, respect, esteem, value, prize, admire, revere, reverence, venerate, worship, adore. DESPISE
glorify, dignify, exalt, ennoble, praise, acclaim, celebrate, commemorate. DISHONOUR
keep, observe, discharge, fulfil, accept, acknowledge, pay.

**honourable** honest, upright, moral, principled, right, proper, virtuous, trustworthy, respectable, reputable, creditable, true, just, fair. DISHONOURABLE
noble, distinguished, illustrious, noted, eminent, great, venerable, respected, esteemed. DESPISED

**hoodwink** dupe, deceive, delude, trick, hoax, fool, bamboozle (*inf*), cheat, swindle, cozen, con (*inf*).

**hook** *n*, hasp, clasp, catch, fastener.
snare, trap.
angle, crook, bend, curve, twist, loop.
*v*, catch, snare, ensnare, trap, entrap. RELEASE
fasten, clasp, join, link, connect. UNHOOK

**hooked** bent, curved, crooked, aquiline, hamate, uncinate, hooklike.
addicted, dependent, obsessed, enamoured.

**hoop** band, ring, circlet, wheel.

**hoot** *v*, screech, shriek, howl, yell, cry, shout, whoop, toot.
boo, catcall, hiss, decry, shout down, jeer, deride. CHEER
*n*, screech, shriek, call, cry, toot.

boo, catcall, hiss, jeer. CHEER
clown, card (*inf*), scream (*inf*), laugh (*inf*).

**hop** skip, caper, jump, leap, spring, bound, dance.

**hope** *n*, dream, ambition, aspiration, expectation, expectancy, anticipation, longing, yearning, desire, hopefulness, faith, trust, belief, confidence. DESPAIR
*v*, desire, long, yearn, wish, expect, anticipate, await, look forward to, count on, trust, believe.

**hopeful** optimistic, sanguine, expectant, confident, assured. DESPAIRING
promising, encouraging, favourable, auspicious, propitious, bright, rosy. DISCOURAGING

**hopeless** despairing, desperate, despondent, downcast, downhearted, disconsolate, dejected, forlorn. HOPEFUL
lost, irretrievable, irredeemable, irreparable, irremediable, incurable. PROMISING
impossible, impracticable, vain, futile, useless, worthless, pointless. WORTHWHILE
incompetent, inadequate, poor, inferior, no good. PROFICIENT

**horde** crowd, multitude, throng, mob, host, gang, pack, troop, band, company, swarm, flock, herd.

**horizontal** flat, level, plane, prone, supine. VERTICAL

**horrible** horrid, unpleasant, disagreeable, nasty, awful, dreadful, frightful, fearful, terrible, horrifying, horrific, horrendous, ghastly, grim, formidable, hideous, loathsome, abominable, revolting, disgusting, repulsive. WONDERFUL

**horrid** horrible, unpleasant, disagreeable, nasty, mean, unkind, beastly (*inf*). PLEASANT
frightening, alarming, terrifying, horrific, horrendous, ghastly, repulsive, hideous, dreadful, awful, frightful, terrible. WONDERFUL

**horrific** horrendous, horrifying, frightening, alarming, terrifying, shocking, appalling, dreadful, awful, frightful. REASSURING

**horrify** shock, appal, disgust, sicken, dismay, distress, outrage, alarm, frighten, scare, terrify, petrify. REASSURE

**horror** terror, fear, panic, fright, alarm, dread, dismay. REASSURANCE
loathing, hatred, detestation, abomination, abhorrence, repugnance, revulsion, disgust. LIKING

**horse** mount, steed, stallion, gelding, mare, filly, colt, foal, pony, cob, nag, jade.

**hospitable** welcoming, friendly, neighbourly, genial, amicable, cordial, convivial, sociable, warm, kind, benevolent, generous, liberal, amenable, receptive, approachable. INHOSPITABLE

**hospitality** welcome, hospitableness, kindness, geniality, cordiality, conviviality, sociability, warmth, kindness, benevolence, generosity, liberality. UNFRIENDLINESS

**host**[1] proprietor, landlord, landlady, innkeeper, hostess, entertainer, master of ceremonies, compere, presenter. GUEST

**host**[2] throng, multitude, horde, crowd, mob, drove, herd, swarm, pack.

**hostage** prisoner, captive, pawn, surety, security.

**hostile** opposed, anti (*inf*), contrary, antagonistic, adverse, unfavourable, inimical, unfriendly, inhospitable, aggressive, belligerent, bellicose, warlike. FRIENDLY

**hostilities** war, warfare, conflict, fighting. PEACE

**hostility** opposition, antagonism, enmity, unfriendliness, hatred, ill will, animosity, antipathy. FRIENDLINESS

**hot** warm, heated, fiery, burning, flaming, blazing, roasting, baking, scorching, scalding, blistering, sweltering, torrid, sultry. COLD
pungent, sharp, acrid, spicy, peppery, piquant. MILD
ardent, fervent, fervid, passionate, inflamed, irate, violent, intense, vehement, animated, excited, enthusiastic, eager, impetuous. APATHETIC
recent, latest, new, fresh.

**hotel** inn, motel, guest house, boarding house, pension, hostel.

**hound** chase, pursue, dog, hunt, harry, harass, persecute, provoke, goad, spur, drive, urge.

**house** *n*, dwelling, abode, residence, domicile, home, habitation, building, cottage, bungalow, villa, mansion.
household, family, pedigree, lineage, ancestry, race, tribe, clan, dynasty.
firm, business, company, partnership, concern, establishment, organization.

*v*, domicile, lodge, quarter, billet, accommodate, put up, contain, shelter, protect.
**household** *n*, family, ménage, house, home.
*adj*, domestic, family, home, ordinary, plain, common.
**hovel** hut, shack, shanty, cabin, shed. PALACE
**hover** hang, fly, float, drift, flutter, linger. waver, vacillate, fluctuate, oscillate, falter. DECIDE
**however** nevertheless, notwithstanding, but, still, yet, though.
**howl** bay, yowl, wail, hoot, bellow, roar, cry, shriek, yell.
**hubbub** noise, din, racket, uproar, tumult, commotion, hullabaloo, brouhaha, clamour, rumpus, riot, confusion, disorder. QUIET
**huddle** *v*, cluster, bunch, gather, crowd, throng, flock. DISPERSE
nestle, snuggle, curl up, crouch.
*n*, heap, mass, cluster, bunch, crowd, muddle, jumble, confusion, disorder.
**hue** colour, shade, tint, tinge, tone, cast, complexion.
**huff** temper, bad mood, pet, pique, rage, anger, passion, miff (*inf*).
**huffish** huffy, pettish, peevish, petulant, waspish, cross, irritable, touchy, testy, grumpy, angry, impatient, sullen, resentful. AFFABLE
**hug** embrace, enfold, clasp, squeeze, cuddle, hold, cling to, cherish.
**huge** enormous, tremendous, prodigious, vast, immense, colossal, gigantic, gargantuan, elephantine, mammoth, great, big, large, bulky. TINY
**hull** body, skeleton, frame, framework, casing, shell, husk, peel, rind, skin.
**hullabaloo** noise, din, racket, bedlam, outcry, uproar, hubbub, clamour, brouhaha, commotion, tumult, rumpus, disturbance, pandemonium. QUIET
**hum** drone, buzz, whirr, purr, murmur, thrum, vibrate.
**human** *adj*, anthropoid, manlike, mortal, physical, natural, vulnerable, fallible.
kind, humane, sensitive, compassionate, understanding. INHUMAN
*n*, person, individual, human being, mortal, man, woman, child. BEAST
**humane** kind, kindly, benevolent, benign, tender, compassionate, sympathetic, merciful, clement, mild, gentle, good, charitable, humanitarian. CRUEL
**humanity** mankind, humankind, human race, people, mortality, human nature. BESTIALITY
kindness, benevolence, tenderness, compassion, mercy, clemency, charity. INHUMANITY
**humanize** civilize, tame, educate, enlighten, cultivate, refine, soften, mellow. BRUTALIZE
**humble** *adj*, modest, unassuming, unpretentious, simple, plain, poor, mean, lowly, meek, submissive, docile, servile, obsequious, deferential, respectful, polite, courteous. HAUGHTY
*v*, lower, reduce, degrade, abase, demean, humiliate, abash, shame, mortify, chagrin, subdue, crush. EXALT
**humbug** trick, trickery, deception, deceit, hoax, fraud, imposture, pretence, sham, ruse, wile.
cheat, fraud, swindler, trickster, charlatan, quack, impostor.
nonsense, rubbish, flummery, bunkum, baloney (*inf*), bosh (*inf*).
**humdrum** monotonous, boring, tiresome, wearisome, dull, routine, uninteresting, prosaic, prosy, dry, dreary, mundane, commonplace, ordinary. INTERESTING
**humid** damp, moist, wet, dank, steamy, muggy, clammy, sticky, sultry. DRY
**humiliate** humble, shame, disgrace, abase, demean, degrade, lower, mortify, chagrin, embarrass, abash, crush, subdue. DIGNIFY
**humiliation** shame, disgrace, degradation, lowering, mortification, chagrin, embarrassment, abashment, indignity. DIGNITY
**humility** humbleness, modesty, diffidence, lowliness, meekness, submissiveness, servility. HAUTEUR
**hummock** knoll, hillock, hump, mound, ridge.
**humorous** funny, amusing, entertaining, comic, comical, droll, witty, waggish, facetious, farcical, laughable, ludicrous. SERIOUS
**humour** *n*, comedy, wit, drollery, facetiousness, amusement, fun, funniness, jocularity, pleasantry, jokes, farce. SERIOUSNESS

mood, temper, frame of mind, disposition, temperament, nature.
whim, caprice, fancy, vagary, crotchet, quirk, freak.
*v*, gratify, placate, indulge, pamper, cosset, spoil, accommodate.

**hump** *n*, protuberance, bulge, swelling, lump, bump, knob, mound, hunch.
*v*, arch, vault, hunch, curve. STRAIGHTEN
carry, lug, heave, hoist, shoulder.

**hunch** *n*, guess, intuition, feeling, notion, idea, premonition, suspicion.
*v*, crouch, stoop, hump, arch, bend. STRAIGHTEN

**hunger** *n*, hungriness, appetite, emptiness, famine, starvation.
longing, yearning, desire, craving, lust, thirst.
*v*, starve, long, yearn, desire, crave, hanker, lust, thirst.

**hungry** ravenous, starving, famished, hollow, empty, peckish (*inf*).
desirous, longing, yearning, craving, greedy, eager. CONTENTED

**hunk** chunk, lump, block, wedge, slab, piece, portion, slice.

**hunt** *v*, chase, pursue, hound, follow, stalk, trail, track.
seek, search, scour, look for, rummage, forage. FIND
*n*, chase, pursuit, hunting, stalking, tracking.
search, quest. DISCOVERY

**hurdle** barrier, obstacle, fence, wall, hedge.
impediment, hindrance, obstacle, barrier, snag, difficulty, stumbling block.

**hurl** throw, sling, fling, cast, pitch, chuck (*inf*), shy, launch, propel.

**hurricane** gale, storm, tempest, cyclone, typhoon, tornado. BREEZE

**hurried** quick, swift, hasty, cursory, superficial, perfunctory, brief, short, rushed, slapdash, careless. THOROUGH

**hurry** *v*, rush, hasten, race, dash, fly, scurry, bustle. DAWDLE
accelerate, quicken, speed up, hasten, precipitate, expedite, dispatch, drive, urge, goad, hustle. RETARD
*n*, rush, haste, bustle, hustle, flurry, speed, quickness, celerity, dispatch, expedition, promptitude, precipitation, urgency. LEISURE

**hurt** *v*, harm, injure, damage, impair, mar, wound, bruise, pain, afflict, grieve, distress, upset, offend, aggrieve. SOOTHE
ache, be sore, throb, sting.
*n*, pain, suffering, distress, affliction, wound, injury, harm, damage.
*adj*, injured, wounded, cut, bruised, upset, aggrieved, offended.

**hurtful** injurious, wounding, upsetting, distressing, unkind, cruel, spiteful, malicious, offensive, damaging, harmful, detrimental, deleterious, pernicious. HARMLESS

**hurtle** *vi*, rush, tear, fly, race, charge, plunge.
*vt*, fling, hurl, pitch, propel, impel.

**husband** *n*, married man, spouse, consort, bridegroom, old man (*inf*), lord and master, widower.
*v*, conserve, save, economize, store, hoard. WASTE

**husbandry** agriculture, agronomy, farming, tillage, cultivation.
frugality, thrift, economy, good housekeeping.

**hush** *v*, silence, quieten, shush, still, mute, muzzle.
soothe, calm, allay, appease, assuage.
**hush up,** suppress, smother, squash, keep dark, cover up.
*interj*, shush, quiet, silence, be quiet, shut up (*inf*).
*n*, quiet, silence, stillness, peace. NOISE

**husk** shell, hull, shuck, chaff, rind, covering, coating. KERNEL

**husky** hoarse, guttural, raucous, harsh, grating, rasping, croaky, throaty.
burly, brawny, muscular, strapping, sturdy, well-built, stocky. PUNY

**hustle** push, shove, jostle, elbow, bustle, hurry, hasten, rush, speed, force, impel.

**hut** shed, cabin, hovel, shanty, shack, shelter. PALACE

**hutch** cage, box, pen, coop, hut, shed.

**hybrid** cross, crossbreed, mongrel, mule, mixture, compound, composite, combination.

**hygienic** clean, sanitary, sterile, aseptic, disinfected, pure, healthy. UNHYGIENIC

**hypercritical** captious, carping, fussy, pernickety, finicky, overscrupulous, overcritical, pedantic.

**hypnotic** mesmeric, mesmerizing, fascinating, entrancing, spellbinding, soporific, somniferous, narcotic, opiate.

**hypochondria** hypochondriasis, valetudinarianism, depression, melancholy.

**hypochondriac** hypochondriacal, valetudinarian, depressed, melancholy.

**hypocrisy** insincerity, two-facedness, duplicity, deceit, deception, falseness, pretence, dissimulation, cant, sanctimoniousness, pharisaism. SINCERITY

**hypocrite** fraud, impostor, deceiver, charlatan, pretender, dissembler, whited sepulchre, pharisee.

**hypocritical** insincere, two-faced, duplicitous, deceitful, false, dissembling, hollow, canting, sanctimonious, pharisaic. SINCERE

**hypothesis** theory, postulate, premiss, assumption, supposition, conjecture, speculation. PROOF

**hypothetical** theoretical, academic, supposed, assumed, putative, conjectural, speculative. REAL

**hysterical** mad, crazed, raving, frenzied, wild, uncontrollable, berserk, frantic, distraught. CALM

hilarious, side-splitting, uproarious, very funny.

# I

**ice** freeze, frost, chill, glaze. HEAT

**icy** frozen, freezing, glacial, arctic, ice-cold, gelid, bitter, cold, chilly, frosty, glassy, slippery. HOT

frigid, cold, frosty, glacial, aloof, distant, stony, steely, unfeeling, unfriendly. WARM

**idea** thought, conception, concept, abstraction, fancy, notion, belief, opinion, viewpoint, doctrine, impression, perception, understanding, inkling, clue, hint, suspicion, guess, theory, hypothesis, suggestion, plan, scheme, design, aim, intention, purpose, object. FACT

**ideal** *n*, model, exemplar, paragon, nonpareil, paradigm, example, pattern, standard, prototype, archetype, epitome.

aim, objective, goal, target.

*adj*, perfect, exemplary, model, supreme, classic, consummate. IMPERFECT

fanciful, imaginary, illusory, unreal, abstract, mental, intellectual, theoretical, idealistic. REAL

**idealistic** perfectionist, utopian, visionary, optimistic, romantic, quixotic, unrealistic, impractical, impracticable. REALISTIC

**identical** same, selfsame, indistinguishable, duplicate, twin, matching, equal, corresponding, congruous, tantamount, equivalent, like, alike. DIFFERENT

**identification** recognition, naming, perception, differentiation, designation.

credential, papers, ID, identity card.

rapport, empathy, sympathy, fellow feeling, association, involvement.

**identify** recognize, name, label, perceive, make out, detect, pick out, single out, classify.

relate, associate, ally, sympathize, empathize.

**identity** individuality, particularity, singularity, uniqueness, self, personality, name.

sameness, oneness, unity, correspondence, equality, likeness. DIFFERENCE

**ideology** ideas, beliefs, creed, doctrine, teachings, dogma, tenets, philosophy, theory.

**idiocy** imbecility, foolishness, asininity, stupidity, fatuity, lunacy, insanity, absurdity, inanity. SENSE

**idiom** locution, expression, set phrase.

language, talk, parlance, vernacular, jargon, argot, usage, style.

**idiosyncrasy** characteristic, peculiarity, quirk, eccentricity, singularity, mannerism, affectation, trait, speciality.

**idiot** imbecile, moron, cretin, halfwit, simpleton, dunce, fool, nincompoop, ass, donkey, dolt, blockhead.

**idiotic** foolish, asinine, stupid, fatuous, senseless, imbecilic, moronic, witless, crazy, daft (*inf*), insane, absurd, inane. WISE

**idle** *adj*, inactive, unemployed, jobless, unoccupied, vacant, empty, unused. ACTIVE

lazy, indolent, slothful, sluggish, lethargic, inert, shiftless. BUSY

trivial, frivolous, superficial, unimportant, foolish, vain, futile, useless, abortive, unprofitable, fruitless, unavailing, bootless, ineffectual, unproductive. FRUITFUL

*v*, loaf, lounge, laze, loiter, dawdle, waste time, drift, coast, mark time, do nothing, vegetate. WORK

**idler** loafer, lounger, lazybones, sluggard, sloth, laggard, dawdler, layabout, good-for-nothing, malingerer, shirker.

**idol** image, effigy, icon, god, hero, favourite, pet, darling, beloved.

**idolize** worship, revere, reverence, venerate, admire, adore, love, exalt, glorify, lionize, deify. DESPISE

**idyllic** charming, picturesque, heavenly, blissful, ideal, Arcadian, pastoral, rustic.

**if** provided, supposing, granting, though, whether.

**ignite** kindle, light, set fire to, catch fire, burn, inflame, fire. EXTINGUISH

**ignoble** low, base, vile, abject, contemptible, despicable, dishonourable, ignominious, shameful, disgraceful, heinous, infamous, mean, wretched, humble, common, vulgar, inferior. NOBLE

**ignominious** disgraceful, shameful, contemptible, despicable, ignoble, dishonourable, unworthy, base, low, mean, shabby, disreputable. HONOURABLE

**ignominy** disgrace, shame, dishonour, infamy, disrepute, discredit, contempt, obloquy, opprobrium, odium, stigma, humiliation. CREDIT

**ignoramus** dunce, dullard, dolt, simpleton, donkey, ass, blockhead, fool. GENIUS

**ignorance** unawareness, unenlightenment, darkness, blindness, nescience, innocence, illiteracy, unintelligence, inexperience. KNOWLEDGE

**ignorant** unaware, unenlightened, uninformed, benighted, in the dark, unknowing, unwitting, blind, oblivious, innocent, inexperienced. AWARE
illiterate, unlettered, unread, untaught, uneducated, unlearned, unschooled, unscholarly, thick, dense, crass. LEARNED

**ignore** disregard, neglect, overlook, wink at, skip, pass over, cut, snub, cold-shoulder. ACKNOWLEDGE

**ill** *adj*, sick, unwell, poorly (*inf*), out of sorts (*inf*), ailing, indisposed, laid up (*inf*), diseased, infirm, unhealthy. WELL
bad, evil, wicked, vile, sinful, iniquitous, wrong, unfavourable, unpropitious, adverse, hostile, harmful, pernicious, damaging, injurious, unlucky, unfortunate. GOOD
unfriendly, unkind, malevolent, malicious, harsh, surly, cross, crabbed, irritable.
*adv*, badly, poorly, insufficiently, improperly, unfortunately, unluckily, adversely, unfavourably. WELL
*n*, evil, harm, mischief, hurt, injury, affliction, pain, suffering, misery, trouble, misfortune, disaster, calamity. GOOD
ailment, illness, malady, complaint, disorder, sickness, indisposition, disease.

**ill-advised** incautious, imprudent, foolish, injudicious, unwise, impolitic, ill-judged, foolhardy, hasty, rash, reckless, thoughtless, ill-considered, misguided. WISE

**ill-bred** ill-mannered, rude, impolite, discourteous, uncivil, unmannerly, vulgar, coarse, unrefined, unladylike, ungentlemanly. POLITE

**illegal** unlawful, illicit, illegitimate, criminal, unauthorized, unlicensed, unofficial, unconstitutional, banned, prohibited, forbidden, contraband, black-market, lawless. LEGAL

**illegible** unreadable, undecipherable, indecipherable, hieroglyphic, crabbed, scrawly, scribbly.

**illegitimate** natural, bastard, fatherless, baseborn. LEGITIMATE
illegal, unlawful, illicit, unauthorized, forbidden. LAWFUL

**ill-fated** ill-starred, star-crossed, doomed, unfortunate, unlucky, luckless, hapless. LUCKY

**illiberal** narrow-minded, intolerant, bigoted, prejudiced, hidebound, reactionary. BROAD-MINDED
miserly, mean, stingy, parsimonious, close-fisted, tight-fisted, niggardly, ungenerous. LIBERAL

**illicit** illegal, unlawful, illegitimate, criminal, unauthorized, unlicensed, unofficial, unconstitutional, prohibited, banned, contraband, black-market, improper, wrong, immoral. LAWFUL

**illimitable** limitless, unlimited, boundless, unbounded, infinite, endless, unending, eternal, vast, immense, immeasurable. LIMITED

**illiterate** ignorant, uneducated, untaught, unlearned, unlettered, uncultured, benighted. LITERATE

**ill-mannered** bad-mannered, unmannerly, ill-bred, rude, impolite, discourteous, uncivil, uncouth, churlish, boorish. POLITE

**illness** ailment, sickness, disease, disorder, malady, complaint, indisposition, affliction. FITNESS

**illogical** unreasonable, irrational, unsound, invalid, sophistic, faulty, fallacious, inconsistent, absurd, senseless. LOGICAL

**ill-treat** maltreat, abuse, misuse, ill-use, mishandle, harm, injure, batter, persecute.

**illuminate** light, light up, brighten. DARKEN

clarify, elucidate, explain, shed light on, enlighten, inform. MYSTIFY

adorn, decorate, ornament, embellish, illustrate.

**illusion** delusion, hallucination, mirage, vision, dream, fantasy, phantasm, chimera, mockery, deception, error, fallacy, misconception, misapprehension, notion, fancy. REALITY

**illusory** illusive, imaginary, unreal, fanciful, chimerical, deceptive, misleading, delusive, false, fallacious. REAL

**illustrate** exemplify, instance, clarify, explain, illuminate, demonstrate, show. OBSCURE

adorn, decorate, embellish, ornament, draw, sketch, depict.

**illustration** example, instance, case, sample, specimen, analogy, explanation, clarification, elucidation, demonstration.

picture, plate, figure, drawing, photograph, diagram.

**illustrative** typical, representative, exemplary, explanatory, descriptive, graphic, pictorial, diagrammatic.

**illustrious** famous, renowned, famed, celebrated, distinguished, noted, eminent, notable, great, brilliant, glorious, splendid. INFAMOUS

**ill will** hostility, enmity, antagonism, animosity, hate, hatred, dislike, spite, malice, rancour, venom, acrimony, bitterness, bad blood, grudge, resentment, envy. GOODWILL

**image** likeness, representation, effigy, icon, picture, portrait, statue, figure, reflection.

copy, duplicate, replica, facsimile, reproduction, twin, double, Doppelgänger, dead ringer (*inf*), match, counterpart, conception, concept, idea, impression, perception, vision, notion.

**imaginary** unreal, fanciful, fancied, illusory, illusive, fictitious, made-up, invented, legendary, mythical, hypothetical, supposed, abstract, ideal, visionary, chimerical, shadowy, unsubstantial. REAL

**imagination** creativity, inventiveness, imaginativeness, ingenuity, resourcefulness, enterprise, originality, vision, insight, perception.

conception, impression, idea, notion, fancy, unreality, dream, illusion, fantasy, chimera. REALITY

**imaginative** creative, inventive, ingenious, resourceful, enterprising, clever, original, visionary, dreamy, fanciful. UNIMAGINATIVE

**imagine** conceive, picture, visualize, envisage, conjure up, invent, dream up, devise, create.

think, believe, fancy, guess, suppose, assume, deduce, infer. KNOW

**imbecile** *n*, idiot, moron, fool, dolt, dullard, simpleton, halfwit.

*adj*, imbecilic, idiotic, moronic, feeble-minded, simple, witless, foolish, stupid, asinine, inane, fatuous. CLEVER

**imbecility** idiocy, feeble-mindedness, incompetence, foolishness, stupidity, asininity, inanity, fatuity. CLEVERNESS

**imbibe** drink, quaff, swallow, tipple, tope.

absorb, assimilate, take in, acquire, gain.

**imbue** instil, inspire, infuse, pervade, permeate, impregnate, penetrate, steep, soak, bathe, saturate, dye, stain, colour, tint. PURGE

**imitate** copy, mimic, ape, impersonate, follow, emulate, repeat, echo, mirror, reflect, mock, burlesque, parody, take off (*inf*), simulate, forge, fake, counterfeit, duplicate, reproduce.

**imitation** *n*, copy, mimicry, impersonation, impression, emulation, echo, reflection, resemblance, mockery, burlesque, parody, travesty, takeoff (*inf*), simulation, forgery, fake, counterfeit, reproduction, replica. ORIGINAL

*adj*, simulated, artificial, synthetic, man-made, ersatz, fake, spurious, counterfeit. GENUINE

**immaculate** spotless, pure, pristine, unsullied, undefiled, unpolluted, stainless, untarnished, perfect, impeccable, faultless, flawless, unblemished, sinless, virtuous, irreproachable, clean, neat, spick-and-span. IMPURE

**immanent** innate, inborn, congenital, inherent, intrinsic, internal, indwelling, ingrained, natural. EXTRINSIC

**immaterial** unimportant, insignificant, inconsequential, trivial, trifling, minor, irrelevant. IMPORTANT
incorporeal, spiritual, metaphysical, disembodied, bodiless, ethereal, supernatural, intangible, unsubstantial. PHYSICAL

**immature** undeveloped, unripe, green, young, premature, untimely, imperfect, unfinished, incomplete, unformed, rudimentary.
inexperienced, raw, callow, unsophisticated, jejune, youthful, puerile, childish, infantile. MATURE

**immaturity** unripeness, greenness, imperfection, incompleteness, crudity, rawness, youth, childishness, puerility, inexperience. MATURITY

**immeasurable** illimitable, limitless, unlimited, boundless, unbounded, infinite, endless, unfathomable, incalculable, vast, immense. LIMITED

**immediate** instant, instantaneous, prompt, direct, next, nearest, closest, near, close, adjacent, contiguous, proximate. DISTANT
present, current, latest, actual, existing. FUTURE

**immediately** instantly, at once, now, without delay, right away, straightaway, forthwith, promptly, directly. LATER

**immemorial** ancient, age-old, olden, archaic, of yore, fixed, permanent, traditional, time-honoured. MODERN

**immense** huge, enormous, colossal, gigantic, elephantine, massive, mammoth, great, tremendous, prodigious, stupendous, vast, extensive, immeasurable, boundless, unbounded, illimitable, limitless, unlimited. SMALL

**immerse** dip, plunge, duck, dunk, submerge, sink, douse, souse, bathe, baptize.
involve, engross, absorb, engage, occupy.

**imminent** impending, forthcoming, coming, approaching, at hand, near, close, menacing, threatening, looming, in the offing. PAST

**immobile** motionless, stationary, still, unmoving, static, immovable, fixed, rooted, stiff, rigid, stable. MOBILE

**immoderate** extreme, excessive, inordinate, unreasonable, unwarranted, undue, uncalled-for, exorbitant, intemperate, extravagant, unrestrained, unbridled, wanton. MODERATE

**immodest** indecent, indecorous, improper, impure, unchaste, obscene, rude, coarse, gross, lewd, bawdy. DECOROUS
bold, brazen, shameless, forward, impudent. BASHFUL

**immoral** corrupt, depraved, degenerate, dissolute, profligate, licentious, lewd, obscene, indecent, impure, sinful, wicked, bad, wrong, unprincipled, unscrupulous, unethical. VIRTUOUS

**immorality** corruption, depravity, degeneracy, profligacy, licentiousness, obscenity, indecency, sin, wickedness, vice, wrong, unscrupulousness. VIRTUE

**immortal** deathless, undying, imperishable, indestructible, eternal, everlasting, unfading, perennial, endless, ceaseless, lasting, enduring, abiding, perpetual, constant, permanent. PERISHABLE

**immortality** deathlessness, indestructibility, eternity, everlasting life, endlessness, ceaselessness, perpetuity, constancy, permanence. DEATH
fame, renown, celebrity, glory, greatness.

**immovable** fixed, riveted, fast, secure, firm, stiff, rigid, stable, immobile, stationary, unalterable, unchangeable, unchanging, steadfast, staunch, inflexible, unyielding, unshakable, impassive. FLEXIBLE

**immune** safe, protected, resistant, insusceptible, invulnerable, unaffected, exempt, free, not liable. SUSCEPTIBLE

**immunity** protection, resistance, exemption, exoneration, freedom, release, liberty, charter, privilege, right. LIABILITY

**immunize** inoculate, vaccinate, protect.

**immure** imprison, incarcerate, confine, enclose, shut in, cage.

**immutable** constant, invariable, unalterable, unchangeable, unchanging, changeless, fixed, constant, permanent, stable, enduring, abiding, ageless, perpetual. CHANGEABLE

**imp** sprite, demon, devil, scamp, rascal, urchin, brat. CHERUB

**impact** collision, crash, bump, knock, bang, blow, shock, force, contact.
impression, effect, influence, bearing, repercussions, consequences.

**impair** damage, injure, harm, mar, spoil, weaken, lessen, reduce, enfeeble, enervate, vitiate, diminish, deteriorate. IMPROVE

**impale** pierce, transfix, stick, spear, spit, run through.

**impalpable** imperceptible, intangible, insubstantial, tenuous, shadowy, indistinct, airy. PALPABLE

**impart** communicate, tell, relate, transmit, pass on, disclose, reveal, divulge, make known. SUPPRESS
bestow, confer, give, grant, assign, contribute. WITHHOLD

**impartial** unbiased, unprejudiced, disinterested, objective, detached, dispassionate, neutral, just, fair, equitable. BIASED

**impassable** impenetrable, impervious, impermeable, pathless, unnavigable, blocked, closed. PENETRABLE

**impassioned** passionate, fervent, fervid, ardent, warm, vehement, zealous, excited, animated, eager, glowing, fiery, forceful, intense. COOL

**impassive** impassible, emotionless, unemotional, unmoved, unfeeling, cool, aloof, reserved, inscrutable, imperturbable, unruffled, composed, serene, indifferent, dispassionate, passionless, apathetic. SUSCEPTIBLE

**impatient** restless, fretful, jumpy, nervous, anxious, uneasy, excitable, eager, agog, impetuous, reckless, hasty, precipitate, headlong, vehement, violent. PATIENT
irritable, testy, edgy, irascible, waspish, short-tempered, brusque, curt, abrupt, intolerant.

**impeach** indict, accuse, araign, charge, incriminate, denounce, censure, blame. VINDICATE
challenge, question, impugn, discredit, disparage, malign.

**impeccable** faultless, flawless, perfect, immaculate, spotless, unblemished, pure, irreproachable, exemplary, innocent. IMPERFECT

**impede** obstruct, hinder, block, clog, encumber, hamper, hold up, delay, retard, thwart, prevent, restrain, check, curb, stop. ASSIST

**impediment** obstruction, hindrance, block, obstacle, bar, barrier, encumbrance, defect, snag, difficulty, stumbling block. AID

**impel** urge, press, drive, force, compel, constrain, oblige, spur, goad, incite, stimulate, motivate, move, push, inspire, influence, induce, persuade. DETER

**impend** approach, be imminent, come, hover, gather, loom, threaten, menace. PASS

**impenetrable** thick, dense, impervious, impermeable, solid, sealed, hermetic, impassable, pathless. PENETRABLE
incomprehensible, unintelligible, unfathomable, dark, obscure, abstruse, recondite, inscrutable, enigmatic. INTELLIGIBLE

**impenitent** unrepentant, uncontrite, unabashed, hardened, obdurate, incorrigible, unreformed. PENITENT

**imperative** urgent, pressing, exigent, essential, vital, crucial, necessary, compulsory, obligatory, binding. UNIMPORTANT
authoritative, dictatorial, peremptory, imperious, lordly, magisterial, commanding.

**imperceptible** indiscernible, impalpable, inaudible, invisible, microscopic, tiny, minute, slight, gradual, fine, subtle, faint, shadowy. NOTICEABLE

**imperfect** faulty, defective, flawed, impaired, damaged, broken, incomplete, unfinished, partial, undeveloped, rudimentary, inexact, crude, deficient. PERFECT

**imperfection** fault, defect, flaw, blemish, stain, scratch, tear, crack.
frailty, infirmity, weakness, foible, failing, shortcoming, inadequacy, deficiency.

**imperial** regal, royal, majestic, sovereign, supreme, grand, imposing, stately, august, imperious, lordly, magisterial, lofty, noble, great, magnificent. LOWLY

**imperil** endanger, jeopardize, risk, hazard, expose. PROTECT

**imperious** despotic, tyrannical, dictatorial, autocratic, authoritative, domineering, overbearing, lordly, magisterial, commanding, high-handed, arrogant, haughty. HUMBLE

**imperishable** undying, unfading, indestructible, incorruptible, perennial, lasting, enduring, abiding, eternal, everlasting, immortal. PERISHABLE

**impersonal** objective, dispassionate, detached, remote, cold, stiff, formal, businesslike. PERSONAL

**impersonate** mimic, ape, imitate, copy, mock, parody, burlesque, take off (*inf*).

**impertinence** impudence, insolence, rudeness, effrontery, pertness, sauce (*inf*), cheek (*inf*), nerve (*inf*), gall (*inf*), boldness, audacity, forwardness, assurance. POLITENESS
irrelevance, inapplicability, inappropriateness, inappositeness. PERTINENCE

**impertinent** impudent, insolent, rude, impolite, disrespectful, pert, saucy, cheeky, bold, audacious, forward, presumptuous. POLITE
irrelevant, inapplicable, inappropriate, inapposite. PERTINENT

**imperturbable** composed, collected, self-possessed, calm, serene, placid, tranquil, cool, unruffled, unmoved, impassive, sedate. AGITATED

**impervious** impermeable, impenetrable, impassable, sealed, hermetic, resistant, proof, tight. PERMEABLE
invulnerable, unreceptive, immune, insensitive, thick-skinned, unaffected. RECEPTIVE

**impetuous** hasty, precipitate, headlong, rash, reckless, impulsive, spontaneous, thoughtless, heedless, spur-of-the-moment, passionate, eager, vehement, violent, fierce, furious. CAUTIOUS

**impetus** force, energy, momentum, push, spur, goad, stimulus, incentive, motivation, impulse.

**impiety** ungodliness, godlessness, unholiness, irreligion, profanity, blasphemy, sacrilege, irreverence, disrespect, sin, iniquity, wickedness, vice. PIETY

**impinge** encroach, infringe, trespass, intrude, invade.
strike, hit, dash, clash, collide.

**impious** ungodly, godless, unholy, irreligious, profane, blasphemous, sacrilegious, irreverent, disrespectful, sinful, iniquitous, wicked, unrighteous. PIOUS

**impish** mischievous, elfin, elfish, arch, roguish, puckish, devilish.

**implacable** unbending, inflexible, unyielding, unappeasable, intractable, firm, adamant, inexorable, relentless, unrelenting, pitiless, merciless, harsh, cruel. MERCIFUL

**implant** inculcate, instil, infix, infuse, imbue.
plant, embed, root, insert, graft, sow. ERADICATE

**implement** *n*, tool, utensil, appliance, instrument, device, contrivance, gadget.
*v*, execute, carry out, perform, effect, fulfil, realize.

**implicate** incriminate, inculpate, involve, embroil, entangle, associate, concern, affect, imply.

**implication** suggestion, insinuation, innuendo, inference, meaning, signification, connotation.
incrimination, inculpation, involvement, association.

**implicit** implied, tacit, understood, inferred, unspoken, unexpressed. EXPLICIT
absolute, unreserved, unconditional, unqualified, complete, total, utter, unquestioning, unhesitating. RESERVED

**implore** beg, beseech, entreat, supplicate, petition, solicit, conjure, plead, pray, crave, ask. DEMAND

**imply** suggest, insinuate, intimate, hint, infer, connote, signify, mean, betoken, indicate, import, involve, entail. DECLARE

**impolite** rude, uncivil, discourteous, impudent, impertinent, insolent, bad-mannered, unmannerly, unladylike, ungentlemanly, churlish, boorish. POLITE

**impolitic** unwise, injudicious, unsagacious, imprudent, indiscreet, inexpedient, ill-advised, misguided. WISE

**import** *v*, introduce, bring in. EXPORT
mean, signify, denote, betoken, connote, imply.
*n*, significance, importance, consequence, moment, weight. INSIGNIFICANCE
meaning, signification, purport, sense, gist, intention, implication, connotation.

**importance** significance, import, consequence, moment, weight, concern, value, worth. UNIMPORTANCE
status, standing, prestige, esteem, regard, eminence, distinction, influence, power.

**important** significant, consequential, momentous, weighty, material, critical, crucial, urgent, serious, grave, primary, essential, valuable, considerable. UNIMPORTANT
influential, powerful, prominent, eminent, prestigious, distinguished, esteemed, leading, notable.

**importunate** persistent, dogged, insistent, demanding, exigent, pressing, urgent, clamorous, solicitous, troublesome, annoying.

**importune** harass, badger, pester, plague, beset, dun, press, urge, beseech, entreat, beg, solicit.

**impose** inflict, lay, place, set, put, establish, levy, exact, charge, prescribe, dictate, enforce, require, enjoin. LIFT
encroach, trespass, intrude, obtrude, inconvenience, bother, put out, abuse, exploit, take advantage.

**imposing** impressive, grand, majestic, stately, august, dignified, commanding, striking, effective. INSIGNIFICANT

**imposition** burden, charge, task, duty, tax, levy.
infliction, enforcement, prescription, injunction.
encroachment, intrusion, liberty, presumption.
imposture, trick, fraud, deception, hoax.

**impossible** impracticable, unfeasible, unworkable, unattainable, unobtainable, unachievable, unthinkable, inconceivable, absurd, ludicrous, outrageous, preposterous, illogical, unreasonable, inadmissible, unacceptable, out of the question. POSSIBLE

**impost** tax, levy, toll, duty, customs, excise, rates. REVENUE

**impostor** fraud, charlatan, quack, cheat, humbug, trickster, rogue, fake, pretender, dissembler, hypocrite, deceiver, con man (*inf*).

**imposture** deception, fraud, pretence, humbug, imposition, artifice, trick, hoax, wile, ruse, cheat, swindle. HONESTY

**impotent** powerless, weak, feeble, frail, helpless, infirm, disabled, incapacitated, incapable, unable, ineffective, inefficient, incompetent, inept, inadequate. POWERFUL

**impound** imprison, confine, cage, pen. FREE
seize, confiscate, appropriate, expropriate, distrain.

**impoverish** beggar, ruin, bankrupt, pauperize.
exhaust, deplete, drain, sap, use up. ENRICH

**impoverished** penniless, penurious, impecunious, indigent, destitute, poverty-stricken, poor, needy, ruined, bankrupt, broke (*inf*), hard up (*inf*). WEALTHY
barren, sterile, empty, exhausted, depleted, spent. RICH

**impracticable** impossible, unfeasible, unworkable, unattainable, unachievable, out of the question. POSSIBLE
unsuitable, inconvenient, impractical, useless, unserviceable. SERVICEABLE

**impractical** unrealistic, idealistic, visionary, wild, impracticable, impossible, unworkable, unserviceable, inapplicable. PRACTICAL

**imprecate** curse, swear, anathematize, execrate, denounce, damn, blaspheme. BLESS

**imprecation** curse, malediction, anathema, execration, denunciation, slander, blasphemy, profanity. BLESSING

**impregnable** invincible, unassailable, invulnerable, indestructible, impenetrable, inviolable, strong, secure, unshakable, irrefutable. WEAK

**impregnate** saturate, soak, steep, fill, suffuse, infuse, imbue, permeate, pervade, penetrate.
fertilize, fecundate, inseminate, make pregnant.

**impress** influence, sway, move, affect, touch, stir, strike.
imprint, stamp, mark, print, engrave, emboss, indent.
stress, emphasize, instil, inculcate, fix.

**impression** effect, influence, impact, mark, stamp, imprint, indentation, brand, impress.
feeling, sensation, sense, idea, notion, fancy, belief, concept, awareness, perception, recollection, remembrance.
edition, printing, issue.
impersonation, imitation, parody, take off (*inf*).

**impressionable** susceptible, receptive, open, suggestible, gullible, sensitive, vulnerable.

**impressive** imposing, striking, commanding, awe-inspiring, moving, stirring, powerful. UNIMPRESSIVE

**imprint** *n*, mark, impression, print, stamp, indentation.
*v*, impress, stamp, print, engrave, etch.

**imprison** jail, incarcerate, confine, intern, immure, detain, lock up, put away. RELEASE

**imprisonment** incarceration, confinement, internment, durance, duress, detention, custody. FREEDOM

**improbable** unlikely, doubtful, dubious, questionable, implausible, far-fetched, incredible, unbelievable, uncertain. LIKELY

**improbity** dishonesty, fraud, falseness, crookedness (*inf*), wickedness, villainy, knavery, unscrupulousness. PROBITY

**impromptu** extempore, extemporary, improvised, unrehearsed, unprepared, spontaneous, unpremeditated, off the cuff, ad lib, offhand. PREPARED

**improper** unseemly, indecorous, unbecoming, impolite, indecent, risqué, obscene, offensive, indelicate. PROPER
unsuitable, inappropriate, unfit, inapt, uncalled-for, unwarranted, unseasonable, untimely, inapplicable, impractical. APPROPRIATE
irregular, abnormal, wrong, incorrect, erroneous, false. CORRECT

**improve** better, ameliorate, amend, mend, reform, correct, rectify, put right, restore, touch up, polish, enhance. IMPAIR
develop, increase, rise, augment, advance, further, rally, pick up, recover, recuperate. WORSEN

**improvement** amelioration, amendment, correction, rectification, restoration, enhancement, development, increase, rise, advancement, progress, betterment, change, alteration, addition, rally, recovery. DETERIORATION

**improvident** thriftless, unthrifty, extravagant, lavish, prodigal, wasteful, spendthrift, imprudent, incautious, careless, heedless, reckless, rash. PROVIDENT

**improvise** ad-lib, extemporize, play by ear (*inf*), invent, devise, contrive, throw together.

**imprudent** unwise, injudicious, incautious, rash, hasty, heedless, careless, thoughtless, indiscreet, impolitic, ill-advised, foolish. PRUDENT

**impudence** impertinence, insolence, rudeness, disrespect, effrontery, audacity, boldness, shamelessness, assurance, presumption, cheek (*inf*), sauce (*inf*), lip (*inf*), face (*inf*). POLITENESS

**impudent** impertinent, insolent, rude, disrespectful, impolite, audacious, bold, shameless, forward, presumptuous, pert, fresh (*inf*), cheeky, saucy. POLITE

**impugn** dispute, challenge, question, oppose, gainsay, contradict, deny, criticize, attack, assail. SUPPORT

**impulse** impetus, thrust, boost, surge, force, momentum, push, spur, stimulus, incitement, motive.
urge, desire, yen (*inf*), drive, whim, caprice, notion, feeling, instinct, passion, inclination.

**impulsive** impetuous, rash, hasty, precipitate, heedless, passionate, emotional, spontaneous, unplanned, unpremeditated, instinctive, natural. DELIBERATE

**impure** contaminated, polluted, adulterated, mixed, unrefined, sullied, tainted, defiled, soiled, unclean, dirty, foul. PURE
unchaste, depraved, corrupt, immoral, indecent, obscene, lewd, licentious, coarse, gross. CHASTE

**imputation** ascription, attribution, accusation, charge, blame, censure, reproach, defamation, aspersion, slander, calumny.

**impute** ascribe, attribute, accredit, assign, charge, blame, put down.

**in** *prep*, within, inside, among, during, while, into.
*adj*, fashionable, modish, stylish, chic, all the rage (*inf*). OUT

**inability** incapacity, incapability, impotence, powerlessness, incompetence, ineptitude, disability. ABILITY

**inaccurate** inexact, imprecise, incorrect, wrong, erroneous, mistaken, faulty, unsound. ACCURATE

**inactive** inert, immobile, still, idle, dormant, quiescent, inoperative, unoccupied, unemployed, in abeyance. ACTIVE
indolent, slothful, lazy, lethargic, sluggish, torpid, slow, dull, passive. BUSY

**inadequate** insufficient, deficient, lacking, scanty, meagre, skimpy, sparse, short, incomplete, imperfect, defective, faulty, unsatisfactory. ADEQUATE
incompetent, incapable, inapt, inept, unfit, unequal, unqualified. COMPETENT

**inadvertence** oversight, blunder, error, mistake, slip, omission, negligence, neglect, heedlessness, inattention, carelessness, thoughtlessness. ATTENTION

**inadvertent** careless, thoughtless, unthinking, heedless, inattentive, unmindful, negligent. CAREFUL
chance, accidental, unintentional, unpremeditated, involuntary, unwitting. DELIBERATE

**inane** fatuous, foolish, silly, senseless, stupid, idiotic, asinine, absurd, unintelligent, puerile, frivolous, empty, vacuous, vain, worthless. SENSIBLE

**inanimate** lifeless, dead, inorganic, mineral. LIVING
inert, inactive, immobile, dormant, quiescent, sluggish, dull, vapid, soulless, spiritless. ACTIVE

**inapplicable** irrelevant, inapposite, impertinent, unsuitable, inappropriate, inapt, unfit. APPLICABLE

**inapposite** inappropriate, unsuitable, unfit, inapt, inapplicable, irrelevant, impertinent. APPOSITE

**inappreciable** imperceptible, microscopic, infinitesimal, minuscule, minute, slight, insignificant, negligible. APPRECIABLE

**inappropriate** unsuitable, unfit, ill-suited, unfitting, inapt, inapposite, incongruous, out of place, unseemly, unbecoming, improper, inapplicable, untimely, infelicitous, irrelevant. APPROPRIATE

**inapt** inappropriate, unsuitable, unfit, inapposite, infelicitous. SUITABLE
inept, incompetent, incapable, maladroit, clumsy, awkward, dull, slow. CLEVER

**inattention** inattentiveness, absent-mindedness, daydreaming, woolgathering, forgetfulness, oversight, inadvertence, negligence, neglect, carelessness, thoughtlessness, heedlessness, disregard, unconcern, indifference. CARE

**inaudible** imperceptible, silent, noiseless, quiet, muted, low, faint, indistinct, muffled, stifled. AUDIBLE

**inaugurate** commence, begin, start, initiate, institute, originate, launch, open, introduce. TERMINATE
induct, invest, install, ordain.

**inauguration** commencement, beginning, start, initiation, institution, origination, launch, opening, introduction. TERMINATION
induction, investiture, installation, ordination.

**inauspicious** unpromising, discouraging, unpropitious, ominous, black, dark, ill-omened, unfavourable, unlucky, unfortunate, untoward. AUSPICIOUS

**inborn** innate, congenital, inbred, inherent, natural, instinctive, inherited, hereditary. ACQUIRED

**incalculable** countless, innumerable, numberless, untold, inestimable, immeasurable, unfathomable, vast, immense, boundless, infinite.

**incandescent** glowing, phosphorescent, luminous, radiant, bright, brilliant, shining. DULL

**incantation** spell, charm, chant, invocation, conjuration, magic, sorcery, witchcraft.

**incapable** unable, powerless, impotent, helpless, weak, feeble, inadequate, unequal, incompetent, inept, unfit, unqualified. CAPABLE

**incapacitate** disable, cripple, immobilize, paralyse, debilitate, enervate, weaken, enfeeble, disenable, disqualify, scupper (*inf*). ENABLE

**incarcerate** imprison, jail, immure, cage, confine, intern, impound, lock up, put away. RELEASE

**incarnation** embodiment, archetype, personification, manifestation, avatar.

**incautious** imprudent, unwise, injudicious, impolitic, unwary, careless, thoughtless, unthinking, heedless, hasty, headlong, precipitate, rash, reckless, negligent, improvident, indiscreet. CAUTIOUS

**incendiary** *adj*, inflammatory, seditious, subversive, provocative, rabble-rousing.
combustible, flammable.
*n*, arsonist, pyromaniac, fire raiser.
agitator, rabble-rouser, firebrand, insurgent, rebel, revolutionary, troublemaker.

**incense**[1] *v*, enrage, infuriate, madden, anger, provoke, rouse, inflame, irk, irritate, annoy, exasperate. PACIFY

**incense**[2] *n*, perfume, fragrance, balm, scent, aroma.

**incentive** inducement, enticement, bait, lure, incitement, stimulus, spur, impulse, motivation, persuasion, encouragement, motive, cause. DETERRENT

**inception** beginning, start, commencement, inauguration, initiation, outset, birth, dawn. END

**incessant** unceasing, ceaseless, continual, continuous, unremitting, uninterrupted, perpetual, constant, persistent, relentless, eternal, everlasting, unending, endless, interminable. INTERMITTENT

**inchoate** incipient, inceptive, beginning, commencing, initial, elementary, rudimentary, embryonic, undeveloped, immature. FINISHED

**incident** occurrence, event, happening, occasion, circumstance, episode, scene, affair, matter.
disturbance, commotion, encounter, confrontation, clash, skirmish.

**incidental** chance, accidental, casual, fortuitous, random.
minor, unimportant, subsidiary, secondary, nonessential, occasional. ESSENTIAL
concomitant, related, attendant, accompanying, contingent.

**incipient** inchoate, inceptive, beginning, commencing, starting, initial, nascent, rudimentary, embryonic. COMPLETE

**incision** cut, gash, slit, slash, notch.

**incisive** sharp, keen, acute, piercing, penetrating, cutting, trenchant, mordant, biting, acid, caustic, sarcastic, satirical, sardonic. MILD

**incite** rouse, stir up, stimulate, animate, provoke, foment, prompt, goad, spur, urge, encourage, impel, excite, inflame. DETER

**incitement** stimulation, provocation, fomentation, agitation, encouragement, spur, goad, impulse, stimulus, motivation, incentive, inducement.

**incivility** impoliteness, rudeness, discourtesy, discourteousness, disrespect, unmannerliness, ill-breeding. CIVILITY

**inclement** stormy, tempestuous, windy, rainy, foul, bad, rough, intemperate, harsh, severe. MILD
cruel, unmerciful, merciless, pitiless, hardhearted, unfeeling, harsh, severe, rigorous, tyrannical. KIND

**inclination** tendency, leaning, bent, proclivity, propensity, disposition, predisposition, penchant, partiality, predilection, bias, preference, liking, fondness, taste, desire, wish. AVERSION
slope, slant, incline, gradient, angle, pitch.
bend, bow, nod.

**incline** *v*, slope, slant, lean, tilt, cant, bend, bow, lower.
tend, be disposed, predispose, sway, influence, bias, prejudice.
*n*, inclination, slope, slant, gradient, acclivity, declivity.

**inclined** disposed, prone, apt, likely, liable, given, willing. UNLIKELY

**include** contain, comprise, embrace, encompass, embody, incorporate, cover, involve. EXCLUDE
count, number, add, insert, subsume, group, categorize. OMIT

**incognito** disguised, in disguise, concealed, unrecognized, undercover, in secret.

**incoherent** disjointed, unconnected, rambling, discursive, confused, disordered, muddled, wild, loose, inconsistent, illogical, unintelligible, inarticulate. COHERENT

**income** revenue, receipts, takings, proceeds, yield, return, gains, profits, earnings, pay, wages, salary. EXPENDITURE

**incommensurate** unequal, disproportionate, insufficient, inadequate. COMMENSURATE

**incommode** inconvenience, bother, disturb, trouble, put out, hinder, upset, annoy. ASSIST

**incommodious** inconvenient, awkward, cramped, restricted, confined, narrow. COMMODIOUS

**incomparable** matchless, peerless, unequalled, unrivalled, unparalleled, transcendent, supreme, beyond compare, unique, inimitable. ORDINARY

**incompatible** conflicting, discordant, contrary, antagonistic, antipathetic, irreconcilable, unsuited, mismatched, incongruous, inconsistent, contradictory. COMPATIBLE

**incompetent** incapable, unfit, unable, inadequate, inefficient, unequal, useless, inept, bungling, inexpert, unskilful. COMPETENT

**incomplete** unfinished, imperfect, partial, deficient, lacking, wanting, short, abridged, undeveloped. COMPLETE

**incomprehensible** unintelligible, incoherent, unfathomable, impenetrable, obscure, enigmatic, mysterious, inexplicable, puzzling, inconceivable, unthinkable. PLAIN

**inconceivable** unthinkable, unimaginable, incomprehensible, impossible, incredible, unbelievable, unheard-of, preposterous, absurd. POSSIBLE

**inconclusive** indecisive, undecided, unsettled, uncertain, open, indeterminate, unconvincing. CONCLUSIVE

**incongruous** incompatible, inappropriate, inapt, unsuitable, improper, discrepant, discordant, conflicting, contradictory, inconsistent, out of place, absurd. CONGRUOUS

**inconsequential** insignificant, unimportant, negligible, paltry, trifling, trivial, petty, minor. IMPORTANT
inconsequent, disconnected, inconsistent, incongruous, illogical, irrelevant, immaterial.

**inconsiderable** small, slight, minor, inconsequential, negligible, insignificant, unimportant, immaterial, trivial, trifling, petty. CONSIDERABLE

**inconsiderate** thoughtless, unkind, uncharitable, unthinking, heedless, tactless, insensitive, rude, selfish. CONSIDERATE

**inconsistent** contradictory, conflicting, irreconcilable, incompatible, incongruous, discrepant, discordant, at odds, out of keeping. CONSISTENT
inconstant, irregular, changeable, variable, unsteady, unstable, erratic, fickle, capricious. CONSTANT

**inconsolable** disconsolate, comfortless, forlorn, desolate, heartbroken, brokenhearted, despairing, hopeless. CHEERFUL

**inconstant** variable, changeable, mutable, vacillating, wavering, uncertain, unsteady, unstable, unsettled, inconsistent, erratic, mercurial, volatile, fickle, capricious, unreliable. STEADY

**incontestable** indisputable, incontrovertible, unquestionable, indubitable, undeniable, irrefutable, unassailable, certain, sure. DUBIOUS

**incontinent** unrestrained, uncontrolled, unchecked, unbridled, ungovernable, uncontrollable. CONTROLLED
dissolute, debauched, licentious, lascivious, lecherous, lewd, lustful, wanton, profligate, promiscuous, unchaste, impure. CHASTE

**incontrovertible** indisputable, incontestable, undeniable, irrefutable, unquestionable, indubitable, certain, sure, positive. DUBIOUS

**inconvenience** *n*, trouble, bother, nuisance, annoyance, vexation, disturbance, disruption, difficulty, drawback, disadvantage, hindrance. HELP
awkwardness, unwieldiness, cumbersomeness, untimeliness, inopportuneness. CONVENIENCE
*v*, trouble, bother, put out, upset, disturb, disrupt, hinder. ASSIST

**inconvenient** awkward, troublesome, bothersome, annoying, inopportune, untimely, unseasonable, inappropriate, unsuitable, disadvantageous, difficult. CONVENIENT
unwieldy, cumbersome, awkward, incommodious.

**incorporate** include, comprise, embody, integrate, merge, blend, amalgamate, combine, unite, consolidate, assimilate. SEVER

**incorporeal** disembodied, bodiless, immaterial, insubstantial, metaphysical, spiritual. MATERIAL

**incorrect** wrong, erroneous, false, untrue, inexact, inaccurate, mistaken, faulty, unsound, flawed, fallacious. CORRECT
improper, unbecoming, unseemly, inappropriate, unsuitable. PROPER

**incorrigible** hardened, inveterate, incurable, irremediable, irredeemable, lost, hopeless, obdurate, intractable. REFORMABLE

**incorruptible** honest, upright, honourable, just, high-minded, unbribable, above suspicion. DISHONEST
imperishable, immortal, deathless, undying, everlasting, eternal, abiding, lasting, indestructible. PERISHABLE

**increase** *v*, enlarge, expand, swell, grow, spread, extend, prolong, lengthen, accrue, augment, add to, raise, rise, mount, escalate, intensify, heighten, enhance, amplify, boost, magnify, multiply, proliferate. DECREASE
*n*, enlargement, expansion, growth, extension, augmentation, addition, increment, rise, escalation, intensification, boost, upsurge. REDUCTION

**incredible** unbelievable, beyond belief, inconceivable, unthinkable, preposterous, absurd, improbable, unlikely, impossible. CREDIBLE
marvellous, wonderful, astonishing, amazing, fantastic, fabulous, great, tremendous, prodigious.

**incredulity** disbelief, unbelief, scepticism, distrust, mistrust, doubt, incredulousness. BELIEF

**incredulous** disbelieving, unbelieving, sceptical, distrustful, mistrustful, doubtful, dubious, suspicious. CREDULOUS

**increment** increase, addition, augmentation, rise, growth, enlargement, gain, accrual. DECREASE

**incriminate** accuse, charge, indict, arraign, impeach, blame, implicate, involve, inculpate. VINDICATE

**inculcate** instil, infuse, ingrain, implant, impress, drum, drill, indoctrinate.

**inculpable** innocent, guiltless, blameless, irreproachable, unimpeachable, above suspicion. GUILTY

**inculpate** incriminate, accuse, charge, blame, indict, arraign, impeach, involve, implicate. ACQUIT

**incumbent** binding, obligatory, necessary, mandatory, compulsory. OPTIONAL
resting, reclining, lying, leaning.

**incur** bring, draw, earn, gain, contract, meet with, provoke. AVOID

**incurable** irremediable, hopeless, terminal, inoperable. CURABLE
incorrigible, inveterate, hardened, dyed-in-the-wool.

**incursion** raid, invasion, attack, foray, sally, inroad, encroachment, infiltration, penetration. RETREAT

**indebted** obliged, obligated, owing, beholden, grateful, thankful.

**indecent** obscene, vulgar, coarse, gross, offensive, lewd, salacious, crude, foul, dirty, filthy, impure, unchaste, immodest, indelicate, improper, indecorous, unseemly, tasteless, outrageous, shocking. DECENT

**indecipherable** undecipherable, illegible, unreadable, unintelligible, crabbed, hieroglyphic. LEGIBLE

**indecision** indecisiveness, irresolution, hesitation, hesitancy, vacillation, wavering, uncertainly, doubt. RESOLUTION

**indecisive** irresolute, hesitant, wavering, vacillating, undecided, unresolved, uncertain, in two minds, open, inconclusive, unsettled. DECISIVE

**indecorous** improper, unseemly, unbecoming, ill-bred, uncouth, rude, vulgar, indecent, immodest. DECOROUS

**indeed** really, truly, in truth, in fact, certainly, positively, absolutely, actually, strictly, exactly.

**indefatigable** tireless, untiring, unwearied, unwearying, unflagging, indomitable, diligent, assiduous, sedulous, dogged, persistent, persevering, relentless, unremitting. INDOLENT

**indefensible** inexcusable, unjustifiable, unwarrantable, insupportable, unpardonable, unforgivable. JUSTIFIABLE
untenable, weak, flawed, unsound, faulty, wrong. TENABLE

**indefinite** undefined, undetermined, unlimited, indeterminate, indistinct, unclear, vague, loose, general, obscure, confused, unsettled, indecisive, uncertain, unknown, inexact, imprecise, ambiguous, equivocal, evasive. DEFINITE

**indelible** ineffaceable, ineradicable, indestructible, lasting, permanent, ingrained, fixed. ERASABLE

**indelicate** indecent, coarse, crude, rude, vulgar, gross, obscene, offensive, tasteless, improper, indecorous, unseemly, unbecoming, immodest.

**indemnify** secure, guarantee, endorse, underwrite, insure.
compensate, reimburse, repay, pay, remunerate, satisfy, requite.

**indemnity** insurance, protection, security, guarantee.
compensation, reimbursement, remuneration, reparation, restitution, satisfaction.
exemption, immunity, impunity, privilege.

**indentation** notch, nick, cut, dent, hollow, dimple, depression.

**independence** autonomy, freedom, liberty, self-rule, self-government, self-reliance, self-sufficiency. DEPENDENCE

**independent** autonomous, free, sovereign, self-governing, self-reliant, bold, self-confident, unaided, self-sufficient, self-supporting, separate, unconnected, unrestricted, unrestrained. DEPENDENT

**indescribable** inexpressible, ineffable, unutterable, beyond words. COMMONPLACE

**indestructible** durable, unbreakable, imperishable, incorruptible, indelible, permanent, lasting, abiding, enduring, everlasting. PERISHABLE

**indeterminate** indefinite, vague, undefined, undetermined, unsettled, unfixed, uncertain, unknown, inexact, imprecise, obscure, confused. DEFINITE

**index** catalogue, list, directory, file.
sign, indication, mark, token, clue, guide, pointer, needle, hand, forefinger.

**indicate** denote, betoken, show, mark, signify, mean, suggest, imply, evince, mani-

fest, exhibit, display, reveal, express, register, betray. CONCEAL
designate, point out, show.

**indication** sign, mark, token, symbol, signal, symptom, warning, omen, suggestion, hint, clue, evidence, manifestation.

**indict** charge, accuse, arraign, impeach, incriminate, inculpate, prosecute, summon. ACQUIT

**indictment** charge, accusation, allegation, arraignment, impeachment, incrimination, prosecution, summons. ACQUITTAL

**indifference** apathy, unconcern, lack of interest, disregard, negligence, inattention, coolness, aloofness, detachment, disinterest, neutrality, impartiality, objectivity, dispassion, insensibility, insensitivity. CONCERN
unimportance, insignificance, triviality, irrelevance. IMPORTANCE

**indifferent** apathetic, unconcerned, uninterested, heedless, regardless, nonchalant, uncaring, cool, aloof, detached, impassive, insensitive, unmoved. CONCERNED
impartial, disinterested, neutral, objective, dispassionate, unbiased, unprejudiced. BIASED
mediocre, fair, passable, average, middling, so-so (*inf*), moderate, ordinary. EXCELLENT
unimportant, insignificant, irrelevant, immaterial, inconsequential. IMPORTANT

**indigenous** native, aboriginal, autochthonous, home-grown. EXOTIC
inherent, innate, connate, congenital, inborn. ACQUIRED

**indigent** poor, needy, necessitous, destitute, penniless, impecunious, impoverished, poverty-stricken, penurious. RICH

**indignant** irate, angry, incensed, wrathful, furious, mad (*inf*), exasperated, annoyed, riled, irked, peeved (*inf*). CALM

**indignation** anger, ire, wrath, rage, fury, exasperation, annoyance, vexation, pique, umbrage, resentment. COMPOSURE

**indignity** slight, snub, insult, affront, outrage, abuse, obloquy, aspersion, reproach, disrespect, humiliation. RESPECT

**indirect** roundabout, circuitous, tortuous, meandering, oblique, circumlocutory, devious, evasive. STRAIGHT
secondary, ancillary, incidental, contingent, collateral. PRIMARY

**indiscernible** imperceptible, indistinguishable, invisible, slight, subtle, inconsiderable. VISIBLE

**indiscreet** unwise, injudicious, imprudent, incautious, heedless, rash, reckless, hasty, precipitate, unthinking, inconsiderate, tactless, undiplomatic. CAUTIOUS

**indiscretion** folly, imprudence, heedlessness, rashness, recklessness, tactlessness. CAUTION
gaffe, faux pas, blunder, slip, error, mistake.

**indiscriminate** random, haphazard, unsystematic, unmethodical, unselective, promiscuous, broad, wide, wholesale, general, desultory, confused, jumbled, mixed, assorted, miscellaneous, motley.

**indispensable** essential, vital, necessary, needed, required, requisite, key, crucial, basic, fundamental. NONESSENTIAL

**indisposed** unwell, ill, sick, ailing, poorly (*inf*), out of sorts (*inf*). WELL
disinclined, unwilling, reluctant, hesitant, loath, averse. EAGER

**indisputable** undeniable, irrefutable, unquestionable, indubitable, incontrovertible, incontestable, unassailable, certain, sure, positive, absolute. DUBIOUS

**indissoluble** indestructible, imperishable, incorruptible, indivisible, inseparable, permanent, lasting, abiding, enduring, fixed, binding. PERISHABLE

**indistinct** dim, faint, hazy, blurred, shadowy, weak, muffled, vague, indefinite, obscure, confused, doubtful, unclear, ambiguous, indistinguishable, imperceptible, indiscernible. DISTINCT

**indistinguishable** identical, twin, same, alike, like, similar. DIFFERENT
indiscernible, imperceptible, indistinct, indefinite, obscure, invisible. CONSPICUOUS

**indite** write, pen, compose, formulate, word, draft, frame.

**individual** *adj*, separate, distinct, particular, peculiar, characteristic, distinctive, singular, personal, own, exclusive, unique, special, single, solitary, sole. GENERAL
*n*, person, being, creature, mortal, human, personage, soul, body, head, character. GROUP

**indocile** intractable, ungovernable, uncontrollable, unruly, unmanageable, stubborn, obstinate, headstrong, wilful, perverse, recalcitrant, refractory, contumacious. DOCILE

**indoctrinate** inculcate, instil, infuse, imbue, brainwash, drill, school, instruct, teach, ground, initiate.

**indolent** idle, lazy, slothful, sluggish, lethargic, apathetic, listless, slow, inert, inactive. DILIGENT

**indomitable** invincible, unconquerable, unbeatable, unyielding, irrepressible, indefatigable, staunch, steadfast, unwavering. FEEBLE

**indubitable** unquestionable, undoubted, indisputable, undeniable, irrefutable, incontrovertible, incontestable, certain, sure. DUBIOUS

**induce** persuade, influence, move, encourage, urge, prevail upon, convince, impel, incite, prompt, spur, actuate, coax, entice. DETER
cause, bring about, effect, produce, lead to, generate. PREVENT

**inducement** incentive, motive, incitement, stimulus, impulse, spur, enticement, lure, attraction, bait, influence, encouragement, persuasion. DETERRENT

**induct** install, invest, inaugurate, initiate, introduce. OUST

**indulge** gratify, satisfy, yield to, cater to, humour, pander to, pamper, cosset, coddle, pet, spoil. DENY
luxuriate, revel, wallow, regale, treat.

**indulgence** dissipation, intemperance, self-indulgence, luxury, treat, extravagance, immoderation, excess. TEMPERANCE
gratification, satisfaction, fulfilment, humouring, pampering, spoiling. DENIAL
favour, privilege, kindness, leniency, tolerance, clemency, forbearance. SEVERITY

**indulgent** lenient, permissive, tolerant, liberal, forbearing, clement, mild, gentle, kind, tender, fond, obliging, compliant. STRICT

**indurate** harden, toughen, strengthen, temper, inure, accustom, season, habituate. SOFTEN

**industrious** diligent, assiduous, sedulous, hard-working, busy, active, energetic, laborious, tireless, persistent, persevering, conscientious. LAZY

**industry** manufacture, production, trade, commerce, business.
diligence, assiduity, sedulity, work, toil, labour, effort, activity, persistence, perseverance, application. IDLENESS

**inebriated** drunk, intoxicated, inebriate, tight (*inf*), plastered (*inf*), well-oiled (*inf*), blotto (*inf*). SOBER

**inebriation** inebriety, drunkenness, intoxication, insobriety, intemperance, crapulence, alcoholism, dipsomania. SOBRIETY

**ineffable** unutterable, unspeakable, inexpressible, indescribable, indefinable, beyond words. COMMONPLACE

**ineffectual** ineffective, inefficacious, unavailing, useless, futile, bootless, fruitless, unproductive, vain, idle, abortive, impotent, powerless, weak, effete, feeble, inefficient, incompetent, inadequate. EFFECTUAL

**inefficacious** ineffectual, ineffective, unavailing, useless, futile, bootless, fruitless, unproductive, barren, abortive, unsuccessful. EFFICACIOUS

**inefficient** incompetent, inept, incapable, ineffectual, weak, wasteful, careless. EFFICIENT

**inelegant** unrefined, unpolished, coarse, crude, rough, rude, uncouth, uncourtly, ungainly, clumsy, awkward, graceless. ELEGANT

**ineligible** unqualified, disqualified, unsuitable, unacceptable, undesirable, objectionable. ELIGIBLE

**inept** incompetent, inefficient, ineffectual, unskilful, inexpert, clumsy, awkward, bungling. COMPETENT
inapt, inappropriate, unsuitable, unseemly, unfit, improper, out of place, absurd, foolish, nonsensical, pointless, meaningless. APT

**inequality** disparity, imbalance, disproportion, unevenness, irregularity, difference, diversity, unfairness, injustice, inequity, prejudice, bias, discrimination. EQUALITY

**inequitable** unfair, unjust, biased, prejudiced, partial, partisan, discriminatory. EQUITABLE

**inert** immobile, static, motionless, still, inactive, inanimate, idle, indolent, lazy, slothful, sluggish, lethargic, torpid, slow, dull. ACTIVE

**inertia** immobility, stillness, inactivity, idleness, indolence, laziness, sloth, apathy, lethargy, torpor, dullness. ACTIVITY

**inestimable** invaluable, priceless, precious, incalculable, immeasurable.

**inevitable** unavoidable, inescapable, ineluctable, certain, sure, destined, ordained. AVOIDABLE

**inexact** inaccurate, incorrect, wrong, erroneous, imprecise, indefinite, loose. EXACT

**inexcusable** indefensible, unjustifiable, unwarrantable, unpardonable, unforgivable. EXCUSABLE

**inexhaustible** unlimited, limitless, boundless, infinite, endless. LIMITED tireless, unwearying, indefatigable, unflagging, unfailing. INDOLENT

**inexorable** inflexible, unbending, unyielding, immovable, adamant, cruel, harsh, severe, pitiless, merciless, relentless, unrelenting, implacable, remorseless. INDULGENT

**inexpedient** imprudent, injudicious, unwise, impolitic, ill-advised, inadvisable, misguided, indiscreet, inappropriate, unsuitable, disadvantageous. JUDICIOUS

**inexpensive** cheap, reasonable, low-priced, economical, low-cost. EXPENSIVE

**inexperienced** green, raw, callow, fresh, new, untrained, unschooled, unpractised, unskilled, inexpert, unversed, ignorant, unfamiliar, unaccustomed. EXPERIENCED

**inexpiable** unpardonable, unforgivable, inexcusable, unjustifiable, irremissible. PARDONABLE

**inexplicable** unexplainable, unaccountable, insoluble, unfathomable, incomprehensible, enigmatic, mysterious, strange, puzzling, baffling. EXPLICABLE

**inexpressible** unutterable, ineffable, indescribable, incommunicable, unspeakable, beyond words. COMMONPLACE

**inextricable** involved, intricate, complicated, entangled, knotty, insoluble. EXTRICABLE

**infallible** sure, certain, dependable, reliable, foolproof, unfailing, unerring, faultless, perfect. FALLIBLE

**infamous** notorious, ignominious, disreputable, dishonourable, shameful, disgraceful, shocking, scandalous, outrageous, nefarious, egregious, heinous, vile, base, wicked, monstrous, atrocious, loathsome, detestable, abominable. ILLUSTRIOUS

**infamy** notoriety, ignominy, shame, disgrace, disrepute, obloquy, opprobrium, discredit, dishonour, scandal, wickedness, villainy, baseness. HONOUR

**infant** baby, babe, suckling, toddler, tot, child, minor. ADULT

**infantile** babyish, childish, puerile, immature, young, newborn. MATURE

**infatuated** enamoured, besotted, smitten (*inf*), crazy about (*inf*), captivated, fascinated, bewitched, beguiled, obsessed, possessed.

**infatuation** obsession, fixation, passion, crush (*inf*), madness, folly, captivation, beguilement.

**infect** contaminate, pollute, taint, blight, corrupt, defile, vitiate, poison. STERILIZE

**infection** contamination, pollution, taint, corruption, defilement, contagion, germ, virus, poison. ASEPSIS

**infectious** contagious, catching, spreading, communicable, transmittable, infective, virulent, pestilent.

**infelicitous** unfortunate, unlucky, inauspicious, unfavourable, unhappy, wretched, miserable. FELICITOUS inapt, inappropriate, unsuitable, unfitting, unfit, incongruous. APPROPRIATE

**infer** conclude, deduce, derive, gather, presume, surmise, guess.

**inference** conclusion, deduction, corollary, presumption, assumption, surmise, guess, conjecture.

**inferior** lower, lesser, subordinate, minor, junior, secondary, subsidiary, insignificant, unimportant, lowly, menial, subservient. SUPERIOR mediocre, poor, bad, shoddy, second-rate, second-class, indifferent, imperfect, substandard. EXCELLENT

**infernal** demoniacal, demonic, devilish, diabolical, satanic, fiendish, hellish, damnable, accursed, confounded (*inf*), abominable, execrable. HEAVENLY

**infertile** sterile, barren, infecund, unfruitful, unproductive. FERTILE

**infest** overrun, swarm, throng, crawl, pervade, penetrate, invade, beset, plague.

**infidelity** unfaithfulness, adultery, faithlessness, disloyalty, treachery, perfidy. FAITHFULNESS disbelief, unbelief, scepticism, irreligion. BELIEF

**infiltrate** permeate, pervade, percolate, penetrate, insinuate oneself.

**infinite** limitless, unlimited, boundless, unbounded, endless, eternal, everlasting, interminable, immeasurable, unfathomable, bottomless, inexhaustible, inestimable, incalculable, vast, immense, all-embracing, total, absolute. LIMITED

**infinitesimal** microscopic, minuscule, minute, tiny, small, little, negligible, insignificant, inappreciable, imperceptible. VAST

**infirm** weak, feeble, frail, decrepit, debilitated, enfeebled, doddering, shaky, unsteady, unstable, unsound, insecure. STRONG

indecisive, irresolute, faltering, wavering, vacillating. RESOLUTE

**infirmity** weakness, feebleness, frailty, decrepitude, debility, ill health, disorder, ailment, disability, defect, failing. STRENGTH

**infix** implant, engraft, fix, fasten, set, place, ingrain, impress, instil, infuse, inculcate. EXTIRPATE

**inflame** arouse, excite, impassion, fire, kindle, stimulate, animate, incite, provoke, rouse, madden, enrage, incense, infuriate, anger, exasperate. PACIFY

aggravate, exacerbate, fan, increase, intensify. MITIGATE

**inflammable** flammable, combustible, ignitable, incendiary. NONFLAMMABLE

excitable, temperamental, volatile, fiery. PLACID

**inflammation** heat, burning, redness, rash, swelling, pain, soreness, tenderness.

**inflate** expand, swell, blow up, puff up, bloat, dilate, distend, increase, enlarge, amplify. DEFLATE

**inflated** swollen, bloated, distended, conceited, pompous, bombastic, high-flown, turgid, flatulent, tumid, grandiloquent, magniloquent.

**inflect** curve, bend, bow, crook, arch. STRAIGHTEN

modulate, intonate, intone, conjugate, decline.

**inflection** modulation, intonation, accent, stress, conjugation, declension, affix.

angle, bend, curve, arc, arch, flexure, curvature.

**inflexible** rigid, stiff, hard, firm, unbending, unyielding, stubborn, obstinate, intractable, obdurate, adamant, implacable, immovable, fixed, hard and fast, unchangeable, unalterable, inexorable, resolute, persevering, dogged, steadfast. FLEXIBLE

**inflict** impose, apply, administer, mete out, deal out, wreak, visit. SPARE

**influence** *n*, power, sway, hold, control, authority, effect, weight, pressure, guidance, direction, rule, mastery, spell, magnetism.

connections, good offices, prestige, importance, pull (*inf*), clout (*inf*).

*v*, affect, modify, move, persuade, induce, impress, control, guide, direct, lead, sway, incline, dispose, prompt, impel, incite, instigate.

**influential** powerful, potent, forceful, forcible, effective, cogent, persuasive, moving, controlling, guiding, authoritative, weighty, important, significant. INSIGNIFICANT

**inform** tell, apprise, advise, let know, notify, communicate, acquaint, enlighten, instruct.

betray, denounce, grass (*inf*), squeal (*inf*), tell on (*inf*), rat (*inf*).

**informal** casual, inceremonious, easy, relaxed, natural, simple, unofficial, familiar, colloquial, irregular, unconventional. FORMAL

**information** knowledge, intelligence, facts, data, gen (*inf*), news, word, message, report, notice, advice, instruction, lowdown (*inf*).

**informer** betrayer, stool pigeon, grass (*inf*), nark (*inf*), sneak.

informant, adviser, reporter, announcer, source.

**infraction** violation, breach, infringement, contravention, transgression, trespass. OBSERVANCE

**infrequent** rare, unusual, uncommon, occasional, sporadic, few, scarce. FREQUENT

**infringe** violate, break, disobey, contravene, infract, transgress. OBSERVE

encroach, trespass, intrude, impinge.

**infringement** violation, breach, contravention, infraction, transgression, trespass. OBSERVANCE

**infuriate** enrage, incense, madden, anger, provoke, exasperate, vex, irritate, rile. PACIFY

**infuriated** furious, enraged, raging, incensed, fuming, mad (*inf*), wrathful, irate, angry, indignant, exasperated. CALM

**infuse** instil, inculcate, engraft, implant, infix, ingrain, inspire, introduce, imbue, pervade, permeate, saturate, steep, soak, macerate, brew.

**infusion** instillation, inculcation, inspiration, introduction, saturation, soaking, maceration, brew.

**ingenious** clever, skilful, adroit, dexterous, talented, gifted, masterly, inventive, resourceful, creative, original, shrewd, subtle, crafty. STUPID

**ingenuity** ingeniousness, cleverness, skill, dexterity, talent, flair, inventiveness, resourcefulness, creativity, imagination, shrewdness. STUPIDITY

**ingenuous** artless, naive, unsophisticated, simple, innocent, guileless, open, sincere, honest, frank, candid, straightforward.

**ingenuousness** artlessness, naivety, simplicity, innocence, guilelessness, openness, sincerity, honesty, frankness, candour. ARTFULNESS

**inglorious** disgraceful, shameful, dishonourable, ignominious, infamous, ignoble, despicable, base, low, disreputable, discreditable, humiliating. GLORIOUS
unknown, obscure, unrenowned, humble, lowly. FAMOUS

**ingrain** instil, impress, implant, engraft, imprint, fix, imbue, infuse, impregnate. ERADICATE

**ingrained** fixed, rooted, deep-seated, inveterate, built-in, inherent, intrinsic, inbred, innate, fundamental.

**ingratiate** flatter, blandish, fawn, crawl, grovel, toady, curry favour, suck up to (*inf*).

**ingredient** constituent, component, part, element. WHOLE

**ingress** entrance, entry, way in, admission, admittance, access, entrée. EGRESS

**inhabit** occupy, live, dwell, reside, abide, populate, people, tenant. VACATE

**inhabitant** native, aborigine, indigene, citizen, denizen, resident, occupant, occupier, dweller, tenant. VISITOR

**inhale** breathe in, respire, inspire, sniff, gulp, gasp, puff, take in, suck in. EXHALE

**inharmonious** discordant, cacophonous, unharmonious, unmusical, atonal, clashing, jarring, grating, harsh, strident. HARMONIOUS

**inherent** intrinsic, built-in, inborn, innate, immanent, ingrained, natural, native, congenital, hereditary, basic, fundamental. EXTRANEOUS

**inherit** receive, get, acquire, come into, be left, succeed to, accede to, take over. BEQUEATH

**inheritance** heritage, legacy, bequest, patrimony, birthright.

**inhibit** restrain, suppress, repress, constrain, curb, hold back, hinder, impede, prevent, stop, arrest, check, discourage, prohibit, forbid, ban, bar. ENCOURAGE

**inhibition** restraint, repression, constraint, reserve, reticence, hang-up (*inf*), hindrance, impediment, arrest, check, prohibition, ban, embargo.

**inhospitable** unfriendly, cool, unwelcoming, unsociable, hostile, uncongenial, ungracious, unkind, ungenerous. FRIENDLY
barren, desolate, bleak, uninviting, forbidding, unfavourable, uninhabitable, wild. HOSPITABLE

**inhuman** inhumane, unkind, cruel, brutal, heartless, unfeeling, hard-hearted, callous, pitiless, merciless, ruthless, implacable, remorseless, savage, barbarous, barbaric, cold-blooded. HUMANE

**inhume** inter, bury, entomb, sepulchre. EXHUME

**inimical** hostile, antagonistic, adverse, unfavourable, opposed, contrary, unfriendly, harmful, pernicious, destructive. FAVOURABLE

**inimitable** unique, peerless, unmatched, matchless, unparalleled, incomparable, consummate, unequalled, unrivalled, unexampled. COMMONPLACE

**iniquity** sin, vice, wickedness, evil, wrong, crime, offence, misdeed, wrongdoing, sinfulness, unrighteousness, injustice, unfairness, inequity. RIGHTEOUSNESS

**initial** first, primary, opening, beginning, commencing, early, original, introductory, inaugural, incipient, inceptive, inchoate. FINAL

**initiate** begin, start, commence, open, originate, inaugurate, institute, found, set up, launch, pioneer. CLOSE
introduce, teach, instruct, coach, train, prime, ground, break in, indoctrinate, in-

culcate, induct, instate, invest, enrol, admit.

**initiative** lead, first move, beginning, commencement.
enterprise, drive, ambition, dynamism, get-up-and-go (*inf*), resourcefulness, inventiveness. APATHY

**inject** introduce, insert, vaccinate, inoculate, infuse, interject.

**injection** introduction, insertion, vaccination, inoculation, jab (*inf*), shot (*inf*), dose.

**injudicious** imprudent, unwise, ill-judged, ill-advised, impolitic, inexpedient, indiscreet, rash, hasty, foolish. JUDICIOUS

**injunction** instruction, order, command, mandate, ruling, precept, behest, exhortation, admonition.

**injure** hurt, wound, damage, harm, impair, abuse, maltreat, mar, spoil, deface, disfigure, disable, weaken, wrong, offend. BENEFIT

**injurious** hurtful, damaging, harmful, pernicious, deleterious, detrimental, bad, noxious, baneful, mischievous, disadvantageous, unfavourable, adverse, ruinous, destructive, abusive, offensive, slanderous, libellous. BENEFICIAL

**injury** hurt, wound, harm, damage, impairment, ill, evil, wrong, mischief, detriment, loss, prejudice, injustice, grievance, abuse, offence. REPARATION

**injustice** unfairness, inequity, inequality, discrimination, prejudice, bias, favouritism, partiality, iniquity, wrong, grievance, injury. JUSTICE

**inkling** intimation, suggestion, hint, clue, whisper, suspicion, idea, notion, glimmering.

**inland** internal, interior, upcountry, home, domestic. FOREIGN

**inlet** bay, bight, cove, creek, arm, firth, opening, entrance, passage.

**inmate** prisoner, convict, patient, resident, inhabitant.

**inn** pub, public house, tavern, hotel.

**innate** inborn, inbred, connate, congenital, native, natural, instinctive, inherent, intrinsic, immanent, ingrained. ACQUIRED

**inner** interior, internal, inward, inside, innermost, central, private, intimate, secret, hidden. OUTER

**innermost** inmost, deepest, central, private, intimate, secret, basic, fundamental, essential. OUTERMOST

**innocent** guiltless, blameless, inculpable, clear, not guilty, above suspicion, irreproachable. GUILTY
pure, chaste, virginal, sinless, virtuous, upright, unsullied, spotless, immaculate, clean, faultless, impeccable. IMPURE
harmless, innocuous, innoxious, inoffensive, safe. INJURIOUS
naive, unsophisticated, artless, ingenuous, simple, guileless, credulous.

**innocuous** harmless, innoxious, innocent, inoffensive, safe. HARMFUL

**innovation** novelty, change, alteration, modernism. CONSERVATISM

**innoxious** harmless, innocuous, innocent, inoffensive, safe. NOXIOUS

**innuendo** insinuation, allusion, implication, suggestion, hint, intimation, whisper.

**innumerable** countless, untold, many, numerous, myriad, incalculable, numberless. FEW

**inoculate** vaccinate, immunize, protect, inject, imbue.

**inoffensive** unobjectionable, innocent, harmless, innocuous, innoxious, mild, quiet. OFFENSIVE

**inoperative** ineffectual, ineffective, inefficacious, inefficient, useless, worthless, broken, out of order, unserviceable, invalid, null and void. OPERATIVE

**inopportune** untimely, unseasonable, ill-timed, inconvenient, unsuitable, inappropriate, inauspicious, unfavourable. TIMELY

**inordinate** excessive, immoderate, extreme, exorbitant, disproportionate, unwarranted, undue, uncalled-for, unreasonable, extravagant, intemperate, unrestrained. MODERATE

**inorganic** inanimate, mineral, chemical, artificial, man-made. ORGANIC

**inquietude** uneasiness, anxiety, nervousness, restlessness, disquiet, disquietude, discomposure. EASE

**inquire** investigate, look into, inspect, study, examine, probe, explore, enquire, ask, question, interrogate.

**inquiry** investigation, inquest, inquisition, hearing, study, examination, scrutiny, survey, research, probe, exploration, interrogation, enquiry, question, query.

**inquisitive** inquiring, questioning, curious, nosy (*inf*), prying, intrusive, meddlesome. UNINTERESTED

**inroad** incursion, raid, foray, irruption, invasion, intrusion, encroachment. RETREAT

**insalubrious** unhealthy, unwholesome, noxious, insanitary, unhygienic, dirty, unclean. SALUBRIOUS

**insane** mad, crazy (*inf*), deranged, demented, lunatic (*inf*), unbalanced, *non compos mentis*, mentally ill, nuts (*inf*), bonkers (*inf*), barmy (*inf*), crackers (*inf*). SANE
foolish, stupid, senseless, idiotic, irresponsible, irrational, absurd. SENSIBLE

**insanity** madness, craziness (*inf*), derangement, dementia, mental disorder, mental illness, aberration. SANITY
folly, foolishness, stupidity, idiocy, lunacy, irresponsibility, absurdity. SENSE

**insatiable** rapacious, voracious, ravenous, greedy, gluttonous, omnivorous, unappeasable, unquenchable, insatiate.

**inscribe** engrave, carve, cut, etch, impress, imprint, write, pen. ERASE
enter, record, register, enrol, enlist. DELETE
sign, autograph, dedicate, address.

**inscription** engraving, legend, words, lettering, epitaph, dedication, autograph.

**inscrutable** mysterious, inexplicable, unfathomable, incomprehensible, hidden, impenetrable, enigmatic, deadpan, pokerfaced, sphinxlike. OBVIOUS

**insecure** uncertain, unsure, hesitant, anxious, nervous, afraid. CONFIDENT
unsafe, risky, perilous, dangerous, hazardous, exposed, vulnerable, unprotected, defenceless. SAFE
unstable, unsteady, shaky, wobbly, loose, infirm, unsound, weak, frail. STABLE

**insensate** insensible, insentient, numb, anaesthetized, unfeeling, unconscious, inanimate, lifeless, dead. SENTIENT
insensitive, unfeeling, hard, callous, thick-skinned, impassive, indifferent, apathetic, blind, unperceiving. SENSITIVE
senseless, foolish, stupid, witless, brainless. SENSIBLE

**insensible** insensate, insentient, numb, unfeeling, unconscious. SENTIENT
indifferent, impervious, oblivious, unaware, unaffected, unmoved, blind, deaf, callous, hard. SUSCEPTIBLE

**insensitive** unfeeling, insensate, insensible, hard, callous, uncaring, indifferent, unsympathetic. CARING
immune, proof, unsusceptible, unaffected. SENSITIVE

**inseparable** indissoluble, indivisible, devoted, close.

**insert** introduce, put in, enter, interpolate, intercalate, inject, interject, inset, infix, imbue, infuse. EXTRACT

**inside** *n*, interior, contents. SURFACE
*adj*, interior, inner, internal, innermost, inward. EXTERNAL
*adv*, indoors, within. OUTSIDE

**insidious** stealthy, subtle, slick, crafty, artful, sly, wily, cunning, guileful, tricky, deceitful, deceptive, treacherous. STRAIGHTFORWARD

**insight** penetration, perception, intuition, perspicacity, acumen, discernment, shrewdness, awareness, realization, understanding, comprehension, knowledge, vision.

**insignificant** unimportant, trivial, trifling, nugatory, immaterial, irrelevant, negligible, minor, paltry, petty, meaningless, of no account. SIGNIFICANT

**insincere** hypocritical, dissembling, two-faced, deceitful, dishonest, untruthful, false, untrue, hollow, empty, faithless, perfidious, disingenuous, evasive, shifty. SINCERE

**insinuate** intimate, hint, suggest, imply, allude, refer. STATE
introduce, infuse, instil, infiltrate, ingratiate, fawn, curry favour, worm.

**insinuation** intimation, hint, suggestion, implication, innuendo, allusion. STATEMENT
introduction, infusion, instillation, infiltration, ingratiation.

**insipid** bland, tasteless, watery, colourless, anaemic, vapid, dull, boring, uninteresting, tedious, flat, lifeless, spiritless, jejune, banal, trite, prosaic, stale, tame, characterless, wishy-washy (*inf*).

**insist** demand, require, command, urge, stand firm, stress, emphasize. WAIVE
maintain, assert, aver, vow, contend, claim. DENY

**insistent** demanding, persistent, tenacious, repeated, incessant, urgent, pressing, forceful, emphatic, dogmatic.

**insobriety** drunkenness, intoxication, inebriety, intemperance, crapulence. SOBRIETY

**insolence** impudence, impertinence, rudeness, sauce (*inf*), cheek (*inf*), pertness, boldness, audacity, effrontery, disrespect, contumely, arrogance. DEFERENCE

**insolent** impudent, impertinent, rude, saucy, cheeky, pert, fresh (*inf*), bold, disrespectful, offensive, insulting, presumptuous, arrogant, contemptuous. DEFERENTIAL

**insolvent** bankrupt, ruined, beggared, bust (*inf*), penniless, broke (*inf*). RICH

**inspect** examine, scrutinize, scan, peruse, study, check, vet, investigate, view, review, survey, observe.

**inspection** examination, scrutiny, perusal, checkup, once-over (*inf*), investigation, review, survey.

**inspector** examiner, scrutineer, censor, checker, investigator, observer.

**inspiration** stimulation, arousal, awakening, exaltation, exhilaration, elevation, passion, enthusiasm, genius, creativity.
stimulus, incentive, spur, influence, encouragement, muse, afflatus, revelation, enlightenment, idea.

**inspire** inspirit, enliven, animate, invigorate, stimulate, arouse, excite, stir, exalt, exhilarate, elevate, cheer, hearten, encourage, imbue, infuse, instil, prompt, spark off, inflame.

**inspirit** enliven, animate, invigorate, inspire, stimulate, arouse, excite, stir, rouse, fire, cheer, hearten. DEPRESS

**install** place, put in, fix, lodge, ensconce, settle, position, establish, set up.
invest, induct, instate, introduce, inaugurate, initiate. OUST

**installation** placing, establishment, fitting, fixture, machinery, equipment.
investiture, induction, instatement, introduction, inauguration, initiation. EJECTION

**instalment** portion, part, section, episode, chapter, payment.

**instance** *n*, example, case, illustration, precedent, occasion, time, situation, place, stage, step.
request, demand, entreaty, solicitation, suggestion, prompting, instigation.
*v*, cite, quote, adduce, mention, specify.

**instant** *n*, moment, second, minute, twinkling, trice, flash, jiffy (*inf*).
*adj*, immediate, instantaneous, quick, prompt, direct. SLOW
urgent, pressing, imperative, importunate, exigent, critical.

**instantaneous** instant, immediate, quick, prompt, direct, on-the-spot, sudden, abrupt. SLOW

**instantly** immediately, at once, now, without delay, forthwith, directly, straightaway, instantaneously. LATER

**instead** in lieu, preferably, rather, in place of, as an alternative.

**instigate** incite, provoke, spur, goad, actuate, start, initiate, bring about, prompt, urge, impel, encourage, influence, persuade, foment, rouse, stir up. SUPPRESS

**instigation** incitement, provocation, actuation, initiation, prompting, urging, impulse, encouragement, influence, persuasion, fomentation, agitation. SUPPRESSION

**instil** infuse, imbue, implant, engraft, inculcate, impress, infix, introduce. ERADICATE

**instinct** intuition, feeling, sixth sense, prompting, impulse, inclination, tendency, proclivity, predisposition. REASON
aptitude, knack, flair, talent, gift, faculty.

**instinctive** intuitive, automatic, spontaneous, impulsive, involuntary, reflex, unpremeditated, natural, inborn, innate. RATIONAL

**institute** *v*, found, establish, set up, organize, start, begin, commence, originate, initiate, inaugurate, introduce, launch, pioneer, enact, appoint, install, induct. TERMINATE
*n*, institution, school, college, academy, seminary, conservatory, society, association, organization, foundation.

**institution** introduction, initiation, inauguration, origination, launch, appointment, installation, induction. TERMINATION
institute, school, college, hospital, asylum, establishment, organization, foundation, society, association, business, company.
custom, tradition, usage, convention, rule, law, principle, practice.

**instruct** tell, order, command, direct, bid, enjoin.
teach, educate, school, edify, enlighten, train, coach, drill, indoctrinate.

inform, notify, apprise, acquaint, brief.

**instruction** order, command, mandate, direction, ruling, directive, briefing, recommendation, advice, guideline, rule.

teaching, education, tuition, training, coaching, guidance, enlightenment, indoctrination.

**instructor** teacher, coach, trainer, tutor, pedagogue, schoolmaster, schoolmistress, adviser, guide, demonstrator. PUPIL

**instrument** implement, tool, utensil, device, contrivance, gadget, appliance, mechanism.

agency, means, vehicle, medium, agent, factor, pawn, puppet.

document, paper, contract, charter.

**instrumental** helpful, serviceable, useful, contributory, conducive, important, significant, influential, active, involved.

**instrumentality** helpfulness, usefulness, service, utility, importance, influence, action, help.

intervention, mediation, medium, agency, means, vehicle, instrument.

**insubordinate** recalcitrant, refractory, disobedient, contumacious, defiant, rebellious, mutinous, seditious, intractable, ungovernable, unruly, disorderly, riotous, turbulent. DOCILE

**insubordination** recalcitrance, disobedience, defiance, rebellion, mutiny, sedition, revolt, insurrection, disorder, riot, unruliness. COMPLIANCE

**insufferable** unbearable, intolerable, unendurable, insupportable, too much, impossible, outrageous, detestable, dreadful. TOLERABLE

**insufficient** deficient, lacking, wanting, short, scanty, scarce, inadequate, incapable, incompetent. SUFFICIENT

**insular** narrow-minded, illiberal, parochial, provincial, petty, limited, restricted, circumscribed, isolated, detached, remote, aloof.

**insulate** isolate, separate, detach, cut off, sever, part.

protect, shield, cover, wrap, pad, cushion.

**insult** *v*, abuse, affront, offend, outrage, hurt, injure, snub, slight, slander, call names, mock, humiliate. FLATTER

*n*, abuse, affront, offence, outrage, rudeness, disrespect, insolence, snub, slight, slander, aspersion, contumely, contempt, scorn, humiliation, indignity. RESPECT

**insuperable** insurmountable, impassable, unconquerable, invincible, overpowering, overwhelming.

**insurance** assurance, protection, cover, security, indemnity, guarantee, warranty, provision, safeguard, providence. JEOPARDY

**insure** protect, cover, indemnify, underwrite, guarantee, warrant, assure, safeguard. IMPERIL

**insurgent** *n*, rebel, revolutionary, insurrectionist, rioter, mutineer.

*adj*, rebellious, revolutionary, insurrectionary, riotous, mutinous, seditious, insubordinate, disobedient. OBEDIENT

**insurmountable** insuperable, impassable, unconquerable, invincible, overpowering, overwhelming.

**insurrection** rebellion, revolt, revolution, coup, uprising, mutiny, sedition, insurgency, insubordination, riot. SUBJUGATION

**insusceptible** insensible, insensitive, indifferent, unmoved, unresponsive, immune, unimpressible. SUSCEPTIBLE

**intact** whole, entire, complete, integral, perfect, unbroken, sound, unhurt, uninjured, unharmed, undamaged, unimpaired, unscathed, untouched, inviolate. BROKEN

**intangible** impalpable, insubstantial, airy, vague, indefinite, shadowy, evanescent, incoporeal, unreal, imperceptible. TANGIBLE

**integral** intact, whole, entire, complete, individed, total. PARTIAL

intrinsic, inherent, essential, indispensable, basic, fundamental, component, constituent. NONESSENTIAL

**integrate** incorporate, combine, amalgamate, mix, mingle, blend, merge, unite, join. SEGREGATE

**integrity** honesty, uprightness, rectitude, probity, honour, principle, morality, virtue, goodness, purity. DISHONESTY

unity, wholeness, completeness, soundness.

**intellect** mind, intelligence, brains, sense, reason, understanding, judgment.

**intellectual** *adj*, mental, cerebral, learned, erudite, academic, scholarly, highbrow, intelligent, thoughtful, rational.

*n*, scholar, academic, thinker, genius, egghead (*inf*). DUNCE

**intelligence** intellect, mind, brains, aptitude, cleverness, understanding, comprehension, perception, discernment, acumen, quickness, alertness, brightness, sharpness, reason, sense, nous (*inf*). STUPIDITY
information, knowledge, facts, data, news, word, report, notification.

**intelligent** clever, brainy (*inf*), smart, bright, quick, sharp, alert, astute, perceptive, discerning, perspicacious, knowledgeable, wise, sensible, rational. STUPID

**intelligible** comprehensible, understandable, clear, plain, distinct, explicit. UNINTELLIGIBLE

**intemperate** excessive, immoderate, inordinate, extreme, wild, uncontrolled, unrestrained, unbridled, extravagant, self-indulgent, profligate, incontinent. MODERATE
drunken, intoxicated, bibulous, crapulent, alcoholic. TEMPERATE

**intend** mean, propose, have in mind, contemplate, plan, design, purpose, aim, destine, resolve, determine.

**intense** great, extreme, concentrated, strong, powerful, forceful, acute, fierce, harsh, deep, profound, intensive, vigorous, energetic. MILD
earnest, eager, ardent, fervent, vehement, zealous, passionate. APATHETIC

**intensify** heighten, enhance, deepen, strengthen, reinforce, sharpen, concentrate, magnify, increase, boost, escalate, raise, aggravate, exaggerate. MODERATE

**intensity** greatness, extremity, concentration, depth, strength, power, force, vigour, energy, ardour, fervour, vehemence, passion. MILDNESS

**intent** *adj*, set, determined, resolute, bent, fixed, steadfast, concentrated, intense, eager, earnest, absorbed, engrossed, rapt, alert, attentive. INDIFFERENT
*n*, intention, aim, goal, object, end, purpose, design, plan.

**intention** aim, goal, object, objective, target, end, intention, plan, design, purpose, meaning.

**intentional** intended, premeditated, planned, deliberate, calculated, wilful, voluntary, studied, purposeful. ACCIDENTAL

**inter** bury, inhume, entomb, sepulchre. EXHUME

**intercede** mediate, arbitrate, intervene, interpose, step in, plead, advocate.

**intercept** interrupt, stop, check, arrest, obstruct, block, deflect, head off, cut off, catch, seize.

**intercession** mediation, arbitration, intervention, advocacy, plea, prayer, entreaty, petition, supplication.

**interchange** *v*, exchange, alternate, switch, swap, trade, barter, replace, substitute, change places, reciprocate.
*n*, exchange, alternation, swap, trade, reciprocation, give and take.

**intercourse** communication, dealings, commerce, trade, traffic, communion, liaison, contact.
copulation, coitus, sexual intercourse, sex (*inf*), carnal knowledge.

**interdict** *v*, prohibit, ban, forbid, disallow, veto, bar, proscribe. ALLOW
*n*, interdiction, prohibition, ban, veto, taboo, proscription.

**interest** *n*, curiosity, attention, notice, regard, concern, care, importance, consequence, moment, weight. INDIFFERENCE
hobby, pastime, diversion, activity, pursuit.
benefit, advantage, good, profit, gain, avail, use, worth, behalf, sake.
share, stake, portion, part, right, claim, involvement, business, affair, concern, matter.
premium, dividend, percentage. PRINCIPAL
*v*, engage, absorb, captivate, fascinate, intrigue, attract, amuse, move, excite, arouse. BORE
affect, concern, touch, involve.

**interested** curious, inquisitive, intrigued, attracted, drawn, attentive, held, engaged, absorbed, fascinated. UNINTERESTED
concerned, involved, prejudiced, biased, partial. DISINTERESTED

**interesting** intriguing, engaging, absorbing, fascinating, amusing, entertaining, stimulating, exciting, gripping, appealing, attractive, pleasing. BORING

**interfere** interpose, intervene, meddle, tamper, intrude, butt in.
hinder, impede, hamper, obstruct, restrain, cramp, thwart, clash, conflict, oppose.

**interim** *n*, interval, meantime, meanwhile.
*adj*, temporary, provisional, makeshift.

**interior** *adj*, internal, inner, inside, inward. EXTERIOR

inland, upcountry, home, domestic.
*n*, inside, contents, heart, core, centre. SURFACE

**interject** interpose, interpolate, intercalate, insert, put in, throw in.

**interjection** exclamation, ejaculation, cry, remark, interpolation, intercalation.

**interlace** interweave, twine, intertwine, plait, braid, interlock, twist, cross, reticulate. UNRAVEL

**interlock** join, lock, interconnect, interlink.

**interlocution** conversation, dialogue, colloquy, discussion, discourse, confabulation.

**interloper** meddler, interferer, intruder, trespasser, gate-crasher.

**intermediate** intervening, intermediary, mean, middle, halfway, in-between, transitional.

**interminable** endless, unending, never-ending, incessant, ceaseless, perpetual, eternal, everlasting, infinite, boundless, limitless, unlimited, illimitable, long, protracted, long-winded, monotonous, boring. BRIEF

**intermingle** intermix, mingle, mix, commingle, commix, blend, merge, combine, amalgamate. SEPARATE

**intermission** interlude, interval, entr'acte, break, pause, stop, rest, respite, lull, recess, suspension, interruption. CONTINUANCE

**intermittent** spasmodic, fitful, sporadic, periodic, recurrent, occasional, broken, discontinuous, interrupted. CONTINUOUS

**internal** inner, interior, inside, inward. EXTERNAL
domestic, home, civil, in-house.

**international** global, worldwide, universal, cosmopolitan. NATIONAL

**internecine** destructive, ruinous, deadly, mortal, bloody, sanguinary.
internal, civil, domestic.

**interpolate** insert, introduce, interpose, interject, intercalate, add. DELETE

**interpose** intervene, intercede, come between, mediate, interfere, meddle, introduce, insert, interpolate, intercalate, interject.

**interpret** explain, expound, elucidate, clarify, define, construe, understand, read, solve, decode, decipher, unravel, render, translate. MYSTIFY

**interpretation** explanation, exposition, elucidation, clarification, construction, reading, analysis, exegesis, rendition, version, translation.

**interrogate** question, catechize, quiz, grill (*inf*), pump, cross-examine, examine, ask, enquire.

**interrupt** discontinue, suspend, stop, break off, disjoin, sever, cut. CONTINUE
intrude, break in, butt in, interpose, interfere, disturb, hinder, obstruct.

**interruption** disturbance, disruption, intrusion, break, pause, stoppage, cessation, suspension, discontinuance, hindrance, obstacle. CONTINUANCE

**intersect** divide, cut, cross, meet.

**intersperse** scatter, sprinkle, pepper, dot, interlard, intermix.

**interstice** gap, opening, chink, cranny, crevice, cleft, fissure, crack, space, interval.

**intertwine** twine, entwine, twist, intertwist, interweave, interlace, interwind, reticulate. UNRAVEL

**interval** space, gap, interstice, interspace, opening, distance.
interim, meantime, spell, period, interlude, intermission, break, pause, rest, hiatus.

**intervene** interpose, step in, intercede, mediate, arbitrate, intrude, interfere.
happen, occur, take place, befall, ensue.

**interview** *n*, meeting, dialogue, discussion, conference, consultation, audience.
*v*, examine, question, interrogate.

**interweave** inweave, interlace, intertwine, entwine, braid, mesh, blend, mix, intermingle. UNRAVEL

**intestines** bowels, guts, entrails, viscera, innards (*inf*), insides (*inf*).

**intimate**[1] *adj*, close, dear, bosom, familiar, confidential, personal, private, secret, warm, cosy, friendly.
deep, profound, thorough, exhaustive, detailed, personal, first-hand, direct. SUPERFICIAL
*n*, friend, confidant, familiar, crony.

**intimate**[2] *v*, suggest, imply, insinuate, hint, allude, indicate, communicate, make known. CONCEAL

**intimation** suggestion, implication, insinuation, innuendo, hint, allusion, inkling, indication, communication, notice.

**intimidate** frighten, scare, alarm, appal, daunt, cow, overawe, dismay, dishearten, dispirit, discourage, deter, bully, browbeat, coerce, threaten, terrorize. ENCOURAGE

**intolerable** unbearable, insufferable, unendurable, too much, insupportable. BEARABLE

**intolerant** narrow-minded, illiberal, bigoted, biased, prejudiced, chauvinistic, dogmatic, self-opinionated, small-minded, insular. TOLERANT

**intonation** modulation, tone, pitch, accentuation, cadence, inflection.

**intoxicate** inebriate, make drunk, addle, fuddle, stupefy, exhilarate, elate, excite, stimulate, invigorate.

**intoxication** drunkenness, inebriation, inebriety, insobriety, crapulence. SOBRIETY

euphoria, exhilaration, elation, excitement, delirium.

**intractable** stubborn, obstinate, obdurate, headstrong, wilful, intransigent, perverse, contrary, indocile, refractory, contumacious, insubordinate, unmanageable, ungovernable, unruly, wayward, difficult. TRACTABLE

**intransigent** uncompromising, unbending, unyielding, intractable, stubborn, obstinate, obdurate, tough, rigid, immovable. AMENABLE

**intrepid** fearless, dauntless, unafraid, daring, brave, courageous, valiant, valorous, bold, heroic, lion-hearted, doughty, stalwart, indomitable, plucky, spirited. COWARDLY

**intricate** involved, complicated, complex, obscure, difficult, puzzling, perplexing, tortuous, labyrinthine, entangled, knotty, convoluted, ornate, fancy. SIMPLE

**intrigue** *v*, attract, interest, fascinate, charm, tantalize, arouse, stir, puzzle, baffle. BORE

conspire, plot, scheme, connive, machinate.

*n*, conspiracy, plot, scheme, machination, cabal, ruse, wile, stratagem.

affair, liaison, amour, romance.

**intrinsic** inherent, essential, basic, fundamental, built-in, inborn, inate, immanent, natural, native, real, true, genuine. EXTRINSIC

**introduce** present, acquaint, familiarize, bring together, begin, start, commence, initiate, inaugurate, launch, establish, found, bring in, announce, herald, usher in. END

propose, suggest, submit, offer, advance, put forward, broach, bring up. WITHDRAW

insert, inject, interpose, interpolate, interject. REMOVE

**introduction** presentation, announcement, debut, induction, initiation, inauguration, launch, opening, beginning, establishment.

preface, foreword, preamble, prologue, preliminary, prelude, overture. EPILOGUE

**intrude** obtrude, push in, butt in, break in, interrupt, interpose, interfere, meddle, trespass, encroach, infringe. WITHDRAW

**intruder** interloper, trespasser, invader, raider, burglar, prowler, snooper (*inf*), meddler, gate-crasher (*inf*).

**intrusion** encroachment, infringement, invasion, trespass, violation, interruption, obtrusion, meddling, interference, interposition.

**intuition** insight, instinct, clairvoyance, divination, sixth sense, presentiment, hunch, perception, discernment, knowledge, understanding. REASON

**intumescence** swelling, tumefaction, turgescence, tumidity, distension.

**inundate** flood, deluge, swamp, submerge, drown, engulf, overwhelm, overflow. DRAIN

**inure** harden, toughen, indurate, temper, accustom, make used to, habituate, familiarize, acclimatize.

**invade** attack, assault, raid, storm, enter, penetrate, occupy, overrun, infest, pervade. EVACUATE

intrude, encroach, infringe, trespass, violate.

**invalid**[1] *n*, patient, convalescent, valetudinarian.

*adj*, ill, sick, weak, feeble, frail, infirm, bedridden, valetudinarian, disabled, handicapped. HALE

**invalid**[2] *adj*, null, void, inoperative, unsound, fallacious, untrue, illogical, irrational, baseless, unfounded. VALID

**invalidate** annul, nullify, abrogate, repeal, rescind, quash, cancel, overthrow, refute, undermine, weaken. VALIDATE

**invaluable** priceless, inestimable, precious, valuable, indispensable. WORTHLESS

**invariable** changeless, unchanging, unchangeable, immutable, unalterable, unvarying, constant, fixed, set, uniform, regular, consistent, unfailing. VARIABLE

**invariably** always, without exception, every time, inevitably, habitually, regularly, perpetually. SOMETIMES

**invasion** attack, assault, raid, foray, irruption, inroad, incursion, aggression, offensive. RETREAT
intrusion, encroachment, infringement, trespass, violation, breach, infraction.

**invective** vituperation, revilement, censure, condemnation, denunciation, reproach, abuse, obloquy, diatribe, philippic, tirade, castigation, contumely, sarcasm. EULOGY

**inveigh** rail, vituperate, revile, denounce, condemn, censure, blame, abuse, reproach, berate, expostulate, protest. PRAISE

**inveigle** entrap, ensnare, entice, lure, tempt, beguile, coax, cajole, persuade, bamboozle (*inf*).

**invent** originate, create, discover, design, think up, conceive, imagine, devise, contrive, concoct, coin, formulate, fabricate, make up, cook up (*inf*).

**invention** origination, formulation, creation, discovery, design, device, contrivance, gadget, concoction.
inventiveness, originality, resourcefulness, creativity, imagination, inspiration, genius.
fabrication, lie, fib (*inf*), untruth, falsehood, fiction, story, fantasy, romance. TRUTH

**inventory** list, catalogue, register, roll, record, account, schedule, enumeration.

**inverse** opposite, contrary, converse, counter, reversed, transposed, inverted.

**inversion** reversal, transposition, opposite, contrary, antithesis, reverse, converse.

**invert** reverse, transpose, turn upside down, overturn, capsize, introvert, turn inside out.

**invest** spend, lay out, put in, advance, fund, supply, provide, endow, give, devote. WITHDRAW
install, induct, instate, inaugurate, enthrone.
clothe, dress, robe, deck, array, adorn, cover. STRIP

**investigate** explore, examine, probe, sift, scrutinize, study, inspect, inquire into, look into, check out. IGNORE

**investigation** exploration, search, examination, probe, scrutiny, study, review, analysis, inspection, inquiry, inquest, inquisition.

**investiture** installation, induction, instatement, inauguration, enthronement, coronation, ordination.

**investment** asset, venture, speculation, stake, contribution.

**inveterate** ingrained, deep-seated, deep-rooted, entrenched, set, established, hardened, chronic, habitual, confirmed, incurable, dyed-in-the-wool.

**invidious** unpopular, undesirable, objectionable, offensive, hateful, odious, unfair, malignant.

**invigorate** enliven, animate, stimulate, quicken, brace, refresh, energize, fortify, strengthen, revitalize, pep up, exhilarate. ENERVATE

**invincible** unconquerable, indomitable, unbeatable, invulnerable, unassailable, impregnable, insuperable, insurmountable, indestructible. VULNERABLE

**inviolate** intact, whole, undamaged, unimpaired, unharmed, uninjured, unhurt, unsullied, undefiled, pure, virginal, untouched, stainless, unpolluted. DEFILED
inviolable, sacred, sacrosanct, hallowed, holy.

**invisible** unseen, hidden, concealed, out of sight, imperceptible, indiscernible, unapparent, inconspicuous. VISIBLE

**invitation** summons, call, invite (*inf*), request, bidding, solicitation, challenge, dare, proposition, offer.
attraction, allurement, lure, enticement, temptation, come-on (*inf*). REPULSION

**invite** summon, call, ask, request, bid, solicit, beg.
attract, welcome, provoke, bring on, encourage, court, tempt, entice, allure. REPULSE

**inviting** attractive, pleasing, welcoming, tempting, alluring, seductive, appealing, engaging, fascinating, captivating, irresistible. REPULSIVE

**invocation** prayer, supplication, entreaty, solicitation, petition, appeal.

**invoice** bill, statement, list, schedule, record.

**invoke** adjure, call on, appeal to, implore, entreat, supplicate, beg, beseech, pray.
summon, call forth, conjure up, raise.

**involuntary** automatic, mechanical, reflex, spontaneous, instinctive, unintentional, unconscious, unthinking, blind, uncontrolled. VOLUNTARY
compulsory, obligatory, forced, reluctant, unwilling. WILLING

**involve** entail, require, imply, signify, mean, include, contain, comprise, embrace, cover. EXCLUDE
implicate, incriminate, inculpate, embroil, entangle, complicate, confuse, mix up. EXTRICATE
absorb, engross, preoccupy, engage, commit, concern, affect.

**involvement** connection, association, participation, concern, interest, responsibility, commitment, implication.
complexity, intricacy, complication, convolution, entanglement, imbroglio, confusion.

**invulnerable** safe, secure, unassailable, invincible, indestructible, insusceptible. VULNERABLE

**inward** inner, internal, interior, inside, innermost, private, personal, confidential, secret, mental, spiritual. OUTWARD
ingoing, incoming. OUTGOING

**inweave** weave, interweave, interlace, intertwine, entwine, mesh, reticulate. UNRAVEL

**iota** atom, jot, tittle, whit, bit, scrap, mite, grain, trace, glimmer, shadow, touch, hint.

**irascible** irritable, touchy, testy, short-tempered, cross, waspish, snappish, peppery, cantankerous, crabbed, peevish, petulant. AFFABLE

**irate** angry, furious, incensed, enraged, fuming, ireful, wrathful, indignant, annoyed, exasperated, riled, piqued. CALM

**ire** anger, rage, fury, choler, wrath, indignation, exasperation, annoyance, irritation. COMPOSURE

**iridescent** shimmering, pearly, nacreous, opalescent, opaline, multicoloured, polychromatic, prismatic, rainbow-like. DULL

**irk** irritate, annoy, vex, nettle, rile, peeve (*inf*), aggravate. PLEASE

**irksome** tiresome, wearisome, annoying, irritating, aggravating, vexatious, troublesome, bothersome, tedious, boring, monotonous. PLEASANT

**ironic** ironical, sarcastic, sardonic, satirical, mocking, derisive, contemptuous.
paradoxical, incongruous, coincidental.

**irony** sarcasm, satire, ridicule, derision, mockery.
paradox, incongruity, contrariety.

**irradiate** brighten, illuminate, illumine, light up, enlighten. DARKEN

**irrational** illogical, unreasonable, absurd, preposterous, ridiculous, ludicrous, nonsensical, meaningless, foolish, crazy, stupid, senseless, idiotic, insane, demented, raving, brainless, unwise, injudicious. RATIONAL

**irreclaimable** irrecoverable, irretrievable, lost, irredeemable, incurable, irremediable, irreparable, hopeless, incorrigible.

**irreconcilable** incompatible, conflicting, opposed, at variance, incongruous. COMPATIBLE
implacable, inexorable, uncompromising, intransigent, inflexible. APPEASABLE

**irrecoverable** irretrievable, lost, irreclaimable, irredeemable. RECOVERABLE

**irrefutable** incontrovertible, undeniable, incontestable, indisputable, unquestionable, irrefragable, unassailable, invincible, conclusive, sure, certain. QUESTIONABLE

**irregular** uneven, rough, bumpy, crooked, unsymmetrical, asymmetric, unequal. LEVEL
fitful, spasmodic, changeable, variable, unsettled, erratic, inconstant, capricious, desultory, unmethodical, unsystematic, disorderly, random, haphazard. REGULAR
unusual, uncommon, exceptional, anomalous, aberrant, abnormal, eccentric, unconventional, unorthodox, odd, peculiar. NORMAL

**irrelevant** inapplicable, impertinent, immaterial, inapposite, inappropriate, inapt, beside the point, unrelated, unconnected, foreign, extraneous. RELEVANT

**irreligious** impious, ungodly, godless, pagan, heathen, unbelieving, agnostic, atheistic, irreverent, sacrilegious, profane. RELIGIOUS

**irremediable** incurable, irreparable, hopeless, remediless, irrecoverable. REMEDIABLE

**irreparable** irreclaimable, irrecoverable, irreversible, beyond repair, irremediable, uncurable. REPARABLE

**irrepressible** uncontrollable, unrestrainable, insuppressible, ebullient, buoyant. REPRESSIBLE

**irreproachable** blameless, faultless, impeccable, immaculate, spotless, perfect, pure, innocent, guiltless, inculpable, beyond reproach. REPROACHABLE

**irresistible** overwhelming, overpowering, compelling, powerful, imperative, indomitable, invincible, irrepressible, unsuppressible, unavoidable, inescapable, ineluctable. RESISTIBLE
tempting, seductive, alluring, fascinating, enchanting, charming. REPULSIVE

**irresolute** undecided, unresolved, undetermined, uncertain, in two minds, hesitant, vacillating, wavering, faltering, unstable, inconstant, weak, feeble, half-hearted. RESOLUTE

**irrespective** regardless, despite, in spite of, notwithstanding, apart from, independent.

**irresponsible** unreliable, untrustworthy, thoughtless, careless, reckless, rash, devil-may-care. RESPONSIBLE

**irretrievable** irrecoverable, irreclaimable, lost, irredeemable. RETRIEVABLE

**irreverent** disrespectful, discourteous, impolite, impudent, impertinent, cheeky (*inf*), impious, irreligious, sacrilegious, profane. REVERENT

**irreversible** unalterable, unchangeable, irrevocable, incurable, irremediable, irreparable. REVERSIBLE

**irrevocable** irreversible, unalterable, unchangeable, immutable, irreclaimable, irrecoverable. REVOCABLE

**irrigate** water, wet, moisten, soak, flood, wash, bathe. DRAIN

**irritable** touchy, testy, irascible, waspish, snappish, peppery, peevish, petulant, captious, hasty, fiery, short-tempered, quick-tempered, excitable, prickly, cross, crabbed, crusty, grumpy, cantankerous, ill-humoured, bad-tempered. AFFABLE

**irritate** annoy, vex, nettle, needle, rattle, chafe, fret, pique, aggravate, exasperate, anger, enrage, incense, infuriate, provoke, bother, pester, harass.
rub, chafe, inflame, exacerbate. SOOTHE

**irruption** invasion, incursion, inroad, raid, foray, sally. RETREAT

**isolate** separate, set apart, segregate, quarantine, insulate, cut off, detach, sever, disconnect, dissociate. UNITE

**isolated** solitary, alone, lonely, remote, detached, separate, single, unique.

**isolation** separation, segregation, quarantine, insulation, detachment, disconnection, dissociation, solitude, seclusion, exile, loneliness.

**issue** *n*, issuance, supply, delivery, distribution, circulation, dissemination, promulgation, publication. SUPPRESSION
edition, impression, copy, number.
outflow, outlet, egress, exit. INFLUX
offspring, progeny, children, descendants, posterity.
topic, subject, point, question, problem, matter, affair, concern.
result, consequence, outcome, upshot, effect, end, conclusion.
*v*, emerge, appear, come forth, emit, discharge, flow, proceed, spring, arise, originate, emanate.
deliver, supply, give out, distribute, send out, circulate, disseminate, promulgate, publish, announce, broadcast, put out, release. WITHHOLD

**itch** *v*, tingle, prickle, tickle, crawl.
yearn, long, crave, hunger, thirst, hanker, lust.
*n*, itchiness, irritation, tingling, prickling.
yearning, longing, craving, hunger, thirst, hankering, yen (*inf*).

**item** article, thing, point, aspect, particular, detail, entry, note.

**iterate** repeat, reiterate, restate, recapitulate.

**itinerant** wandering, roving, roaming, strolling, travelling, peripatetic, nomadic, unsettled, vagrant.

**itinerary** route, schedule, programme, circuit, course, guide, guidebook.

# J

**jab** poke, prod, thrust, stab, dig, nudge.

**jabber** chatter, prattle, prate, gibber, babble, gabble, rabbit (*inf*).

**jacket** coat, covering, casing, case, sheath, wrapping, wrapper, skin.

**jade** *n*, hack, nag, shrew, harridan, hag, crone, hussy, trollop.
*v*, exhaust, weary, tire, fatigue, wear out, fag (*inf*). REFRESH

**jagged** notched, serrated, indented, uneven, rough, ragged, ridged.

**jail** *n*, gaol, prison, lockup, nick (*inf*), jug (*inf*), clink (*inf*), cooler (*inf*), inside (*inf*).

*v*, imprison, incarcerate, lock up, confine, intern, detain. RELEASE

**jam**[1] *v*, wedge, cram, pack, crowd, press, squeeze, stuff, ram, force.

block, obstruct, congest, clog, stick, stall, stop.

*n*, crowd, press, crush, congestion, pack, mob, throng.

predicament, plight, trouble, dilemma, quandary, fix (*inf*), pickle (*inf*).

**jam**[2] *n*, preserve, conserve.

**jangle** *v*, clash, jar, clang, clank, rattle.

*n*, clash, clang, clank, rattle, clangour, din, racket, cacophony, dissonance, discord.

**jar**[1] *n*, pot, vessel, container, receptacle, vase, jug, crock.

**jar**[2] *v*, jolt, jerk, jog, rattle, vibrate, shake, agitate, disturb.

clash, jangle, grate, rasp, disagree, quarrel. AGREE

*n*, jolt, jerk, shock, vibration, agitation.

clash, disagreement, discord, jangle, cacophony, grating, rasping. HARMONY

**jargon** vocabulary, phraseology, language, usage, idiom, parlance, cant, argot, lingo (*inf*).

nonsense, gibberish, drivel, balderdash, mumbo jumbo.

**jaunt** excursion, outing, trip, ramble, stroll, airing, spin (*inf*).

**jaunty** brisk, sprightly, lively, breezy, airy, buoyant, blithe, gay, spruce, trim, smart, dapper.

**jealous** envious, covetous, grudging, resentful, green. CONTENT

suspicious, distrustful, mistrustful, anxious, watchful, attentive, possessive.

**jeer** *v*, scoff, mock, deride, taunt, gibe, ridicule, sneer, scorn, contemn, heckle, boo, hiss. ACCLAIM

*n*, mockery, derision, ridicule, gibe, taunt, sneer, catcall, boo, hiss. ACCLAMATION

**jejune** naive, unsophisticated, inexperienced, simple, childish, puerile, juvenile.

insipid, tasteless, dull, vapid, dry, tame, uninteresting, banal. EXCITING

meagre, scanty, insubstantial, barren, sterile. RICH

**jeopardize** risk, venture, gamble, hazard, endanger, imperil. PROTECT

**jerk** jolt, jar, bump, pull, tug, yank, twitch, tweak, lurch, start.

**jest** *n*, joke, quip, crack (*inf*), banter, raillery, prank, jape, fun, sport, play.

*v*, joke, quip, tease, banter, chaff, gibe, jeer, mock, scoff.

**jester** clown, harlequin, fool, buffoon, joker.

**jet** gush, stream, spurt, squirt, spout, spring, spray.

**jetty** breakwater, groyne, mole, pier, dock, wharf, quay.

**jewel** gem, gemstone, precious stone, rock (*inf*), trinket, ornament, bauble, pearl, diamond, treasure.

**jilt** abandon, forsake, desert, leave, throw over, discard, reject, drop, ditch (*inf*).

**jingle** ring, tinkle, chime, clink, chink, rattle.

**jinx** *n*, curse, voodoo, black magic, evil eye, hex.

*v*, curse, bewitch, hex.

**job** work, employment, position, situation, post, occupation, profession, business, calling, vocation, trade, craft, métier.

task, chore, duty, responsibility, charge, office, role, function, concern, affair, venture, undertaking.

**jockey** *n*, rider, horseman, horsewoman, equestrian.

*v*, manoeuvre, manipulate, engineer, negotiate, cajole, wheedle, finagle (*inf*).

trick, cheat, deceive, delude, bamboozle, hoodwink, dupe.

**jocose** jocund, merry, jovial, jolly, blithe, cheerful, jocular, jesting, joking, playful, sportive, witty, droll, funny, humorous, comical. MELANCHOLY

**jocular** jesting, joking, waggish, facetious, witty, droll, comical, funny, humorous, jocose, merry, playful. SERIOUS

**jog** jolt, jar, nudge, prod, shake, jerk, jostle, joggle, jiggle, bounce.

prompt, arouse, stir, stimulate, remind.

trot, run, plod, trudge.

**join** unite, connect, link, conjoin, adjoin, meet, attach, fasten, couple, tie, splice, combine, amalgamate, ally, affiliate, add, append, enrol, enlist, sign up, join up, contribute, participate, join in. SEPARATE

**joint** *n*, junction, connection, union, join, link, knot, seam, hinge, articulation.

*adj*, common, communal, shared, mutual, combined, collective, concerted, united, joined. INDIVIDUAL

**joke** *n*, jest, quip, witticism, pun, crack (*inf*), gag (*inf*), anecdote, jape, lark, prank, trick.

*v*, jest, quip, banter, chaff, tease, kid (*inf*).

**joker** comedian, comic, wag, wit, humorist, clown, prankster.

**jollity** merriment, fun, mirth, hilarity, gaiety, joviality, jocundity, jocosity, jocularity. MELANCHOLY

**jolly** jovial, jocund, jocose, mirthful, merry, happy, joyful, joyous, cheerful, cheery, blithe, gay, playful, sportive, frolicsome, lively, genial, convivial, festive, spirited. SOMBRE

**jolt** jar, jerk, jog, jostle, push, shove, bump, knock, shake, shock, start, lurch.

**jostle** push, shove, hustle, elbow, crowd, jolt, jog, bump, shake.

**jot** *n*, iota, atom, whit, tittle, bit, scrap, grain, mite.
*v*, write, note, record, list, scribble.

**journal** newspaper, paper, periodical, magazine, review, gazette, chronicle, record, diary, log, daybook.

**journalist** reporter, newspaperman, hack (*inf*), newspaperwoman, pressman, correspondent, columnist, editor, broadcaster, commentator.

**journey** *n*, voyage, trip, travel, passage, expedition, trek, safari, excursion, jaunt, outing, tour, drive, ride, flight, sail.
*v*, travel, voyage, go, proceed, roam, rove, trek, tour.

**jovial** jolly, genial, convivial, jocose, jocund, jocular, blithe, cheerful, cheery, merry, gay, mirthful, hearty, cordial.

**joy** happiness, pleasure, gladness, glee, delight, rapture, ecstasy, bliss, felicity, elation, joyfulness, joyousness, gaiety, cheerfulness. SORROW

**joyful** happy, pleased, glad, gleeful, jubilant, delighted, elated, joyous, gay, merry, jolly, jocose, jocund, cheerful, blithe, buoyant. SAD

**jubilant** joyful, joyous, ecstatic, overjoyed, thrilled, elated, triumphant, exultant, rejoicing. MOURNFUL

**jubilation** triumph, exultation, joy, ecstasy, elation, celebration, festivity. MOURNING

**judge** *v*, adjudicate, referee, umpire, arbitrate, try, find, sentence, condemn, decree, rule.
determine, ascertain, decide, conclude, appraise, evaluate, assess, estimate, reckon, deem, consider, think, believe.
*n*, justice, magistrate, adjudicator, referee, umpire, arbiter.
connoisseur, authority, expert, critic, reviewer.

**judgment** verdict, sentence, decree, ruling, award, finding, decision, adjudication, arbitration. PLEADING
discernment, perspicacity, discrimination, taste, perception, insight, penetration, understanding, wisdom, sagacity, prudence, discretion, sense, acumen, intelligence.
assessment, evaluation, appraisal, view, opinion, belief, estimation.

**judicious** wise, prudent, sagacious, politic, provident, discreet, careful, cautious, circumspect, sober, sensible, rational, sound, shrewd, astute, clever, intelligent, informed. INJUDICIOUS

**jug** pitcher, ewer, urn, carafe, flagon, vessel, container.

**juggle** manipulate, alter, change, falsify, tamper with, rig, fix (*inf*).

**juice** liquid, fluid, extract, secretion, sap.

**juicy** succulent, lush, moist, wet, dripping. DRY
racy, risqué, spicy, sensational, vivid, colourful, exciting, provocative.

**jumble** *v*, disorder, disarrange, disorganize, mix, muddle, confuse. ARRANGE
*n*, disorder, disarray, muddle, confusion, chaos, mess, mixture, medley, hotchpotch. ORDER

**jump** *v*, leap, spring, bound, vault, clear, skip, hop, caper, gambol, frolic.
start, jerk, flinch, recoil.
miss, omit, skip, leave out. INCLUDE
*n*, leap, spring, bound, vault, skip, hop.
hurdle, fence, obstacle.
start, jerk, jolt, lurch.
rise, increase, boost, escalation, upsurge. DROP

**jumpy** nervous, anxious, fretful, agitated, jittery, fidgety, restless, on edge, tense, apprehensive. CALM

**junction** joint, connection, seam, union, alliance, link, intersection, combination. DIVISION

**juncture** point, stage, time, moment, crux, crisis, emergency, exigency.

**junior** younger, minor, lesser, lower, inferior, subordinate. SENIOR

**junk** rubbish, refuse, trash, garbage, scrap, waste, litter.

**jurisdiction** judicature, power, authority, control, sway, rule, dominion, domain, province, sphere, field, area.

**just** *adj*, fair, equitable, impartial, unbiased, objective, right, lawful, honest, conscientious, good, sound, valid. UNJUST
deserved, merited, rightful, proper, reasonable, due, fitting, appropriate, suitable, condign. UNMERITED
true, exact, precise, accurate, correct. INACCURATE
*adv*, exactly, precisely, absolutely, perfectly.
barely, hardly, scarcely, only, merely, simply.

**justice** fairness, equity, justness, impartiality, objectivity, honesty, integrity, right, propriety, legality, legitimacy, lawfulness. INJUSTICE
judge, magistrate. DEFENDANT

**justifiable** warrantable, defensible, reasonable, acceptable, right, proper, fit, lawful, legitimate, vindicable, excusable. UNJUSTIFIABLE

**justification** defence, plea, apology, explanation, reason, grounds, excuse, vindication, exculpation, exoneration. CONDEMNATION

**justify** vindicate, exculpate, exonerate, acquit, warrant, substantiate, support, uphold, maintain, defend, excuse, explain. CONDEMN

**jut** project, protrude, stick out, overhang.

**juvenile** *adj*, young, youthful, boyish, girlish, adolescent, immature, inexperienced, puerile, infantile, childish. ADULT
*n*, child, minor, youth, adolescent, boy, girl. ADULT

**juxtaposition** contiguity, contact, adjacency, proximity, nearness, closeness.

# K

**keel over** overturn, capsize, upset, turn turtle.
faint, collapse, pass out, black out (*inf*).

**keen** eager, avid, enthusiastic, ardent, fervent, fervid, zealous, earnest, diligent, ambitious. APATHETIC
sharp, acute, penetrating, piercing, cutting, incisive, pointed, biting, caustic, trenchant, mordant, tart, acid, pungent. DULL
shrewd, astute, quick, clever, perceptive, discerning, sensitive. STUPID
intense, strong, deep, profound. MILD

**keen on,** fond of, devoted to.

**keep** *v*, retain, hold, preserve, conserve, maintain, support, protect, defend, guard, possess, control. DISCARD
continue, carry on, persist, keep on, keep up, remain, last, endure. CEASE
store, amass, accumulate, put, place, deposit, save. USE
detain, delay, retard, hold back, restrain, check, curb, prevent, hinder, keep back, withhold.
tend, look after, sustain, support, maintain, subsidize, provide for, board. NEGLECT
observe, obey, comply with, fulfil, respect, honour, celebrate, commemorate, solemnize. BREAK
*n*, board, subsistence, maintenance, support, living, livelihood.
dungeon, stronghold, castle, fort.

**keeper** custodian, curator, guard, warden, jailer, guardian, steward, proprietor.

**keeping** custody, charge, care, aegis, auspices, hands, possession, protection, guardianship.
conformity, agreement, harmony, accord, correspondence, consistency, congruity, compliance, observance.

**ken** knowledge, acquaintance, cognizance, awareness, perception, comprehension, view, sight, vision, range, field.

**kernel** seed, grain, core, nucleus, heart, centre, substance, essence. SHELL

**key** solution, answer, explanation, guide, clue, means.
style, mood, tone, scale, tonic.

**kick** *v*, boot, punt, strike, hit, drive.
recoil, kick back, resist, oppose, object, protest.
give up, abandon, stop.

**kick out,** eject, expel, oust, throw out, dismiss, discharge, get rid of.
*n*, boot, punt, blow.
zest, vitality, energy, sparkle, excitement, thrill, pleasure, enjoyment, fun.

**kid** *n*, child, youngster, baby, son, daughter, boy, girl, youth. ADULT
*v*, tease, rib (*inf*), joke, jest, trick, dupe, deceive, delude.

**kidnap** abduct, carry off, seize, capture, hijack, hold to ransom. FREE

**kill** slaughter, slay, murder, assassinate, execute, do in (*inf*), bump off (*inf*), dispatch, destroy, annihilate, exterminate, liquidate, butcher, massacre.
deaden, stifle, quash, negate, neutralize, cancel, delete, obliterate, stop.

**killing** *n*, slaughter, butchery, massacre, carnage, murder, manslaughter, homicide, assassination, execution.
coup, success, gain, profit, stroke of luck, windfall.
*adj*, deadly, fatal, lethal, mortal, murderous, homicidal. HARMLESS
tiring, exhausting, taxing, punishing, hard, arduous.
hilarious, side-splitting, uproarious, funny, comical.

**kin** *n*, kindred, relations, relatives, family, kinsfolk, people.
kinship, consanguinity, relationship, connection, blood, extraction, descent.
*adj*, consanguineous, related, kindred, akin, allied, cognate. UNRELATED

**kind**[1] *adj*, benign, benevolent, beneficent, kindly, charitable, philanthropic, generous, bounteous, gracious, humane, gentle, tender, kind-hearted, warm, affectionate, compassionate, sympathetic, understanding, indulgent, lenient, clement, mild, good, friendly, amiable, obliging, considerate, thoughtful. UNKIND

**kind**[2] *n*, sort, type, class, group, genre, set, variety, species, genus, breed, race, family, ilk, style, nature, character, manner, make, brand.

**kindle** ignite, light, set on fire. EXTINGUISH
fire, inflame, arouse, stimulate, excite, rouse, provoke, incite, foment, agitate, stir. QUELL

**kindly** *adj*, kind, warm, sympathetic, compassionate, benign, benevolent, genial, cordial. CRUEL
*adv*, gently, mildly, well, tenderly, warmly, graciously, considerately, thoughtfully, sympathetically. UNKINDLY

**kindness** benevolence, kindliness, charity, philanthropy, generosity, graciousness, humanity, tenderness, warmth, affection, compassion, clemency, mildness, goodness, friendliness, consideration, thoughtfulness. UNKINDNESS
favour, service, good turn, aid, assistance, help. DISSERVICE

**kindred** *n*, kinship, consanguinity, relationship, blood.
kin, kinsfolk, relations, relatives, family, connections.
*adj*, related, akin, allied, cognate, similar, like, matching, corresponding. UNRELATED

**king** monarch, ruler, sovereign, prince, overlord, chief. SUBJECT

**kingdom** monarchy, sovereignty, principality, empire, realm, dominion, country, nation, state, land, territory, province, domain.

**kingly** royal, regal, sovereign, princely, imperial, majestic, stately, imposing, grand, august, noble, splendid. LOWLY

**kink** *n*, curl, twist, bend, coil, crimp, wrinkle, knot.
crick, twinge, spasm.
flaw, fault, quirk, whim, vagary, crotchet, fetish.
*v*, curl, twist, bend, coil, frizz. STRAIGHTEN

**kiosk** booth, stall, stand.

**kiss** *v*, greet, embrace, osculate, buss, peck (*inf*), neck (*inf*).
touch, brush, graze, glance.
*n*, osculation, peck (*inf*), smack.

**kit** *n*, set, parts, tools, implements, equipment, apparatus, outfit, gear, tackle, supplies, provisions.
*v*, **kit out**, equip, supply, provide, fit, arm.

**knack** flair, faculty, aptitude, ability, skill, talent, gift, forte, genius, trick, dexterity, adroitness, expertise. INABILITY

**knavery** deceit, deception, dishonesty, trickery, fraud, duplicity, chicanery, villainy, roguery, rascality. HONESTY

**knavish** rascally, roguish, villainous, dishonest, fraudulent, deceitful, tricky, unscrupulous, unprincipled. HONEST

**knell** toll, ring, chime, peal, sound.

**knickers** pants, panties, drawers, briefs, smalls (*inf*), undies (*inf*).

**knit** join, unite, connect, bind, tie, interlace, interweave, intertwine, heal, mend. SEPARATE
furrow, wrinkle, crease.

**knob** lump, boss, protuberance, projection, bump, swelling, knot, handle.

**knock** *v*, hit, strike, tap, rap, bump, buffet, thump, pound, hammer, beat, smack, slap.

carp, cavil, find fault, criticize, run down, belittle, deprecate, pan (*inf*), slam (*inf*). PRAISE

**knock down,** fell, floor, level, raze, demolish, destroy. RAISE

*n*, blow, hit, tap, rap, bump, thump, smack, slap.

**knoll** hill, hillock, hummock, mound.

**knot** *v*, tie, secure, bind, twist, knit, entangle, ravel. UNTIE

*n*, tie, bond, connection, fastening, loop, bow.

bunch, clump, cluster, group, company, set, circle, crowd, mob.

protuberance, node, swelling.

problem, difficulty, complication, complexity, intricacy, tangle.

**knotty** gnarled, nodular, lumpy, rough. SMOOTH

complicated, complex, intricate, difficult, thorny, puzzling, perplexing. SIMPLE

**know** understand, comprehend, perceive, apprehend, realize, see, be aware, experience, undergo.

recognize, identify, be familiar with, be acquainted with, fraternize with.

differentiate, distinguish, discriminate, discern, tell.

**knowing** shrewd, astute, sagacious, sharp, smart, clever, subtle, cunning, perceptive, discerning, aware. ARTLESS

meaningful, significant, eloquent, expressive.

deliberate, intentional, wilful, conscious. UNCONSCIOUS

**knowledge** erudition, learning, scholarship, education, instruction, enlightenment, information, facts, data.

acquaintance, familiarity, cognizance, ken, experience, awareness, consciousness, realization. IGNORANCE

understanding, comprehension, perception, apprehension, cognition, grasp, recognition, judgment, discernment, wisdom.

**kowtow** bow, kneel, grovel, fawn, cringe, truckle, toady, curry favour, suck up (*inf*).

**kudos** glory, prestige, fame, renown, acclaim, praise, credit. DISGRACE

# L

**label** *n*, tag, ticket, sticker, marker, mark, brand, epithet, name, description.

*v*, mark, stamp, tag, brand, call, name, describe, classify.

**laborious** hard, arduous, strenuous, tiring, fatiguing, wearisome, toilsome, burdensome, difficult, tough, uphill. EASY

diligent, industrious, assiduous, sedulous, painstaking, thorough, tireless, indefatigable, persevering. INDOLENT

**labour** *n*, work, toil, drudgery, industry, effort, exertion, pains. IDLENESS

workers, labourers, employees, work-force. MANAGEMENT

job, task, chore.

childbirth, parturition, delivery, confinement, travail.

*v*, work, toil, drudge, slave, struggle, strive. REST

**labyrinthine** labyrinthian, mazelike, mazy, circuitous, tortuous, involved, intricate, complex, complicated, convoluted, tangled, knotty, confused, confusing, perplexing, puzzling. SIMPLE

**lace** *n*, netting, web, filigree, openwork, tatting.

string, cord, thong, tie.

*v*, tie, fasten, bind, thread, interlace, interweave, intertwine. UNRAVEL

mix, fortify, spike (*inf*).

**lacerate** tear, rip, rend, claw, gash, slash, cut, wound, mangle, mutilate, hurt, pain, harrow. MEND

**lack** *n*, need, want, shortage, deficiency, insufficiency, dearth, scarcity, absence. ABUNDANCE

*v*, need, want, require, be short of, be without. HAVE

**lackey** sycophant, toady, fawner, yes man, parasite, hanger-on, minion, pawn, tool, puppet.

servant, valet, attendant, flunky, underling, menial. MASTER

**laconic** terse, succinct, concise, brief, short, pithy, curt. VERBOSE

**lad** boy, youngster, youth, stripling, young man, fellow, chap (*inf*). LASS

**laden** loaded, burdened, encumbered, weighed down, full, fraught, charged.

**lading** cargo, freight, load, burden, charge.

**ladylike** refined, genteel, elegant, courtly, proper, decorous, well-bred, mannerly, polite. UNSEEMLY

**lag** dawdle, saunter, loiter, linger, dally, idle, fall behind, trail, straggle, hang back, tarry, delay. HURRY

**laggard** dawdler, loiterer, idler, loafer, straggler, sluggard, slowcoach (*inf*).

**lair** den, hole, cave, burrow, nest, hideaway, retreat.

**lambent** flickering, twinkling, dancing, fluttering, licking, glowing, shimmering, sparkling, brilliant.

**lame** crippled, disabled, handicapped, hobbling, limping.
weak, feeble, flimsy, unconvincing, inadequate, unsatisfactory, poor, ineffectual. STRONG

**lament** *v*, mourn, bewail, bemoan, sorrow, grieve, repine, cry, weep, wail, moan, regret, rue, deplore. REJOICE
*n*, lamentation, complaint, moan, wail.
dirge, requiem, elegy, threnody, coronach.

**lamentable** deplorable, regrettable, unfortunate, pitiful, miserable, wretched, sorry, poor, mean, sad, sorrowful, tragic, grievous, distressing.

**lamentation** lament, mourning, sorrow, grief, weeping, wailing, ululation. REJOICING

**lampoon** *n*, satire, parody, burlesque, skit, caricature.
*v*, satirize, ridicule, mock, parody, burlesque, send up (*inf*).

**land** *n*, earth, ground, terra firma, soil, dirt, sod.
estate, property, demesne, realty, grounds, acres.
country, nation, state, province, region, area, territory, realm, empire.
*v*, alight, disembark, dock, touch down, arrive, settle, come down.

**landscape** scene, panorama, view, prospect, vista.

**language** speech, tongue, dialect, idiom, parlance, vernacular, slang, lingo (*inf*), jargon, vocabulary, terminology, phraseology, wording, style, expression, diction, talk, conversation, communication.

**languid** weak, feeble, faint, drooping, flagging, languishing, tired, weary, exhausted. STRONG
listless, lethargic, languorous, sluggish, torpid, heavy, inactive, inert, lazy, slothful, apathetic, spiritless, unenthusiastic, uninterested, indifferent. SPIRITED

**languish** droop, flag, fail, fade, wither, decline, weaken, faint. FLOURISH
pine, long, yearn, hanker, desire, want.

**languor** weakness, feebleness, debility, enervation, tiredness, weariness, exhaustion, fatigue. ENERGY
listlessness, lassitude, lethargy, apathy, sluggishness, torpor, heaviness, laziness, sloth, sleepiness, drowsiness. ENTHUSIASM
stillness, tranquillity, calm, lull, silence.

**lank** limp, lifeless, dull, straight, long.
gangling, lanky, tall, thin, slim, slender, skinny, scrawny, bony, gaunt, angular. DUMPY

**lap** *n*, circuit, round, tour, loop, circle, orbit, stage, part.
*v*, fold, wrap, envelop, cover, overlap.

**lapse** *n*, drop, fall, decline, deterioration. IMPROVEMENT
slip, error, mistake, fault, failing, oversight, omission, negligence.
break, gap, interval, lull, pause. CONTINUATION
*v*, drop, fall, sink, decline, slip, slide, drift.
expire, terminate, discontinue, end, stop. CONTINUE

**larceny** theft, stealing, robbery, burglary.

**large** *adj*, big, great, massive, immense, enormous, huge, vast, considerable, substantial, extensive, broad, wide, full, ample, abundant, copious, generous, bulky, heavy, stout. SMALL
*n*, **at large,** free, loose, at liberty, unconfined, on the run. CAPTIVE

**largely** chiefly, mainly, principally, in general, as a whole, by and large, mostly, greatly, considerably. PARTLY

**largess** generosity, liberality, bounty, charity, beneficence, philanthropy. MEANNESS
gift, present, donation, benefaction, bequest, endowment.

**lascivious** lecherous, lustful, lewd, libidinous, concupiscent, prurient, salacious, licentious, unchaste, incontinent, randy (*inf*), voluptuous, sensual. CHASTE
obscene, indecent, dirty, pornographic, blue, ribald, bawdy, crude.

**lash**[1] *n*, whip, scourge, stroke, blow, stripe.
*v*, whip, flog, beat, scourge, flagellate, cane, birch. CARESS
hit, beat, pound, hammer, buffet, dash, strike.

attack, criticize, satirize, ridicule, castigate, scold, berate, censure. PRAISE

**lash²** *v*, tie, bind, fasten, secure, join, attach. UNTIE

**lass** girl, miss, young woman, bird (*inf*), maiden, damsel.

**lassitude** languor, lethargy, listlessness, apathy, tiredness, weariness, heaviness, sluggishness, torpor, drowsiness. VIGOUR

**last¹** *adj*, ultimate, final, closing, concluding, terminal, utmost, extreme, hindmost, rearmost, latest, most recent. FIRST
*n*, end, finish, termination, conclusion, close. BEGINNING
**at last,** finally, eventually, in the end, at length.

**last²** *v*, continue, persist, remain, stay, abide, endure, survive, hold out, wear, keep. PERISH

**lasting** abiding, enduring, continuing, persisting, permanent, eternal, everlasting, constant, durable, strong. TRANSIENT

**late** delayed, tardy, belated, overdue, unpunctual, behind, slow. EARLY
recent, up-to-the-minute, current, latest, fresh, new, advanced.
dead, deceased, former, previous, past, old.

**lately** recently, latterly, of late.

**latent** potential, dormant, quiescent, unrealized, undeveloped, hidden, concealed, veiled, unseen, invisible, secret, tacit, implicit. CONSPICUOUS

**lateral** side, sideways, sideward, indirect, oblique.

**lather** *n*, suds, foam, froth, bubbles.
fuss, fluster, state (*inf*), flap (*inf*).
*v*, foam, froth.

**latitude** freedom, liberty, laxity, indulgence, licence, leeway, scope, range, room, space, extent, compass. RESTRICTION

**latter** later, last, closing, second, last-mentioned, latest, recent, modern. FORMER

**latterly** recently, lately, of late. FORMERLY

**laud** praise, extol, glorify, honour, acclaim. DECRY

**laudable** praiseworthy, commendable, meritorious, admirable, estimable, creditable, worthy. BLAMEWORTHY

**laugh** *v*, giggle, chuckle, snigger, titter, chortle, guffaw, roar with laughter. CRY
**laugh at,** mock, deride, jeer, scoff, make fun of.
*n*, giggle, chuckle, chortle, guffaw. SOB

**laughable** ludicrous, ridiculous, absurd, preposterous, derisory. REASONABLE
funny, comical, amusing, droll, humorous, farcical, risible. SERIOUS

**laughter** laughing, giggling, chuckling, tittering, chortling. CRYING
fun, amusement, glee, mirth, merriment, hilarity. GLOOM

**launch** propel, send off, dispatch, move, set in motion, set afloat, fire, hurl, cast, throw.
begin, start, commence, initiate, inaugurate, establish, found. TERMINATE

**lavatory** toilet, WC, loo (*inf*), bathroom, cloakroom, Ladies, Gents, public convenience, bog (*inf*).

**lavish** *adj*, abundant, plentiful, profuse, copious, lush, luxuriant, sumptuous, effusive, fulsome. SCANT
extravagant, prodigal, wasteful, improvident, thriftless, immoderate, intemperate, excessive. THRIFTY
generous, liberal, unstinting, open-handed, bountiful. MEAN
*v*, shower, pour, heap, waste, squander, dissipate.

**law** statute, rule, regulation, decree, edict, enactment, ordinance, order, command, act, code, charter, constitution.
principle, formula, canon, standard, criterion.
jurisprudence, legislation, litigation, police.

**lawful** legal, licit, legitimate, constitutional, rightful, right, proper, just, valid, permissible, allowable. UNLAWFUL

**lawless** rebellious, mutinous, seditious, insurgent, insubordinate, unruly, disorderly, riotous, chaotic, anarchic, wild, unbridled, unrestrained. LAW-ABIDING

**lawsuit** litigation, suit, action, case, proceedings, cause, dispute, prosecution, trial.

**lawyer** solicitor, barrister, counsel, advocate, attorney.

**lax** loose, slack, negligent, neglectful, remiss, permissive, lenient, tolerant, indulgent, easy-going. STRICT
imprecise, inexact, inaccurate, broad, general, vague. EXACT

**laxative** purgative, cathartic, aperient.

**laxity** laxness, looseness, slackness, negligence, neglect, freedom, latitude, permissiveness, indulgence, licence. STRICTNESS imprecision, inexactitude, inaccuracy, vagueness, generality. PRECISION

**lay**[1] *v*, put, place, set down, deposit, establish, spread, rest. REMOVE
arrange, dispose, position, locate, set out, lay out, prepare, devise, work out, plan, plot.
present, put forward, submit, lodge. WITHDRAW
attribute, ascribe, assign, impute, charge.
bet, wager, gamble, stake, risk, hazard.
suppress, allay, quiet. still, appease, pacify. AROUSE
**lay off,** discharge, dismiss, let go, make redundant, sack (*inf*), fire (*inf*).

**lay**[2] *adj*, laic, laical, secular, nonclerical, amateur, nonprofessional.

**layer** stratum, seam, bed, thickness, tier, cover, covering, coat, coating, film, blanket.

**laze** loaf, idle, lounge, kill time, waste time, fritter away. WORK

**lazy** slothful, idle, indolent, slack, inactive, inert, sluggish, torpid, slow, languid. INDUSTRIOUS

**lead** *v*, guide, conduct, precede, escort, convoy, marshal, usher, pilot, steer. FOLLOW
head, rule, govern, command, direct.
influence, induce, persuade, incline, dispose.
surpass, excel, outstrip, transcend.
pass, spend, live, have.
**lead on,** entice, lure, tempt, seduce, deceive, delude.
**lead to,** cause, produce, result in, bring on, contribute to, tend to, serve to.
*n*, priority, first place, precedence, supremacy, front, vanguard, advantage, initiative.
leadership, direction, guidance, example, model.
clue, hint, tip, guide, indication, pointer.

**leader** head, chief, ruler, director, commander, captain, principal, superior, boss (*inf*), guide, pioneer. FOLLOWER

**leading** principal, main, chief, primary, first, foremost, supreme, best, greatest, highest, ruling, governing, commanding. MINOR

**league** *n*, association, confederation, confederacy, union, guild, alliance, coalition, combination, fellowship, partnership, consortium.
class, category, group.
*v*, associate, confederate, unite, ally, combine, collaborate. PART

**leak** *v*, seep, ooze, drip, trickle, escape.
disclose, divulge, reveal, expose, give away, let slip. CONCEAL
*n*, crack, split, chink, hole, opening, puncture.
leakage, seepage, drip, escape.

**lean**[1] *v*, rest, recline, repose.
bend, slant, slope, tilt, list, incline, tend.
depend, rely, count, trust, have faith.

**lean**[2] *adj*, thin, spare, slender, slim, lank, skinny, scrawny, bony, angular, gaunt, emaciated. FAT
meagre, scanty, sparse, poor, barren, unproductive. RICH

**leaning** tendency, inclination, propensity, disposition, bent, bias, prejudice, partiality, liking, proclivity.

**leap** *v*, jump, bound, spring, vault, clear, hop, skip, caper, gambol, frisk, frolic.
surge, rocket, soar, rise, increase, escalate. DROP
*n*, jump, bound, spring, vault, hop, skip, caper, frolic.
upsurge, rise, increase, escalation. DROP

**learn** master, grasp, comprehend, pick up, acquire, glean, gather.
memorize, commit to memory. FORGET
discover, find out, hear, ascertain, detect, determine.

**learned** scholarly, erudite, versed, lettered, literate, well-read, well-informed, academic, intellectual. IGNORANT

**learner** novice, beginner, tyro, neophyte, apprentice, trainee, pupil, student. EXPERT

**learning** scholarship, erudition, letters, education, schooling, instruction, knowledge, information, lore, study, research. IGNORANCE

**lease** let, rent, hire, charter.

**least** smallest, lowest, slightest, fewest, minimum, poorest, meanest. MOST

**leave**[1] *v*, depart, go, set out, quit, retire, withdraw, disappear. ARRIVE
abandon, desert, forsake, renounce, relinquish, give up, vacate, evacuate. KEEP
bequeath, will, devise, consign, commit, entrust.
**leave off,** stop, cease, discontinue, desist, refrain. CONTINUE
**leave out,** omit, exclude, overlook, ignore, disregard, reject. INCLUDE

**leave**[2] *n*, permission, allowance, sanction, consent, liberty, freedom, licence. PROHIBITION
holiday, vacation, time off.
farewell, adieu, goodbye, parting, leave-taking, departure, retirement, withdrawal. GREETING

**leavings** scraps, leftovers, remnants, remains, residue, dregs, waste, refuse.

**lecherous** lustful, lewd, lascivious, libidinous, concupiscent, prurient, salacious, licentious, unchaste, wanton, incontinent, randy (*inf*). CHASTE

**lecture** *n*, discourse, address, speech, talk, harangue, sermon, homily.
reprimand, rebuke, reproof, scolding, lesson, telling-off (*inf*), dressing-down (*inf*).
*v*, discourse, speak, talk, hold forth.
reprimand, rebuke, reprove, scold, chide, berate, upbraid, tell off (*inf*).

**ledge** shelf, mantelpiece, sill, step, ridge.

**lees** dregs, residue, grounds, sediment, deposit, precipitate.

**legacy** bequest, gift, devise, inheritance, heritage, patrimony.

**legal** legitimate, licit, lawful, constitutional, permissible, allowable, proper, rightful, valid. ILLEGAL

**legalize** legitimize, legitimatize, warrant, authorize, sanction, license, permit, allow. VETO

**legate** envoy, ambassador, emissary, plenipotentiary, delegate, deputy.

**legend** myth, tale, story, fable, fiction. HISTORY
inscription, device, motto, caption.

**legendary** mythical, fictitious, fabled, storied, fabulous, fanciful, make-believe. HISTORICAL
famous, renowned, celebrated, illustrious, great. UNKNOWN

**legible** readable, decipherable, clear, plain, neat, tidy. ILLEGIBLE

**legion** army, brigade, troop, division, unit.
host, multitude, throng, horde, mass, myriad.

**legislation** lawmaking, codification, enactment.
law, statute, ruling, act.

**legitimate** legal, lawful, licit, constitutional, authorized, proper, rightful, permissible, allowable. ILLEGAL
reasonable, logical, sound, valid, correct. INVALID

**leisure** rest, relaxation, ease, convenience, recreation, freedom, liberty, spare time, time off, holiday, vacation, break, respite, peace, quiet. WORK

**leisurely** unhurried, slow, relaxed, comfortable, easy, gentle. HASTY

**lend** loan, advance. BORROW
give, grant, bestow, provide, furnish, contribute, impart.

**length** extent, reach, span, stretch, distance, duration. BREADTH
piece, portion, section, measure.
**at length,** in detail, in depth, in full, fully, thoroughly, interminably, for ages. BRIEFLY
eventually, finally, at last, in the end.

**lengthen** stretch, extend, elongate, prolong, protract, draw out, continue, increase. SHORTEN

**lengthy** long, extended, prolonged, protracted, interminable, long-winded, verbose, wordy, prolix. SHORT

**lenient** tolerant, indulgent, clement, merciful, mild, gentle, moderate, soft, tender, compassionate. STRICT

**lenitive** soothing, palliative, mitigative, emollient, balmy, alleviating, easing. IRRITANT

**less** smaller, slighter, fewer, lower, inferior, lesser, minor, secondary. MORE

**lessen** reduce, diminish, decrease, lower, abate, ease, decline, dwindle, shorten, curtail, abridge, contract, shrink. INCREASE

**lesser** lower, inferior, minor, secondary, less, smaller, slighter. GREATER

**lesson** class, period, lecture, tutorial, seminar, teaching, instruction.
assignment, task, exercise, drill, practice, homework.
example, model, deterrent, punishment, warning, correction, reprimand, rebuke, reproof, scolding, admonition.

**let**[1] *v*, permit, allow, grant, sanction, authorize, enable.
lease, rent, hire, charter.
**let down,** disappoint, disenchant, disillusion, fail, leave in the lurch.
**let off,** excuse, exempt, pardon, forgive, absolve, exonerate, acquit.
**let up,** abate, subside, ease, lessen, diminish, moderate.

**let²** *n*, hindrance, obstruction, impediment, obstacle, restriction, constraint.

**lethal** fatal, deadly, mortal, murderous, destructive, dangerous, noxious, poisonous. SAFE

**lethargic** sluggish, torpid, dull, slow, heavy, sleepy, drowsy, stupefied, inactive, inert, idle, lazy, apathetic. ENERGETIC

**lethargy** sluggishness, torpor, dullness, slowness, heaviness, sleepiness, drowsiness, stupor, inactivity, inertia, idleness, laziness, apathy. VITALITY

**letter** note, line, message, communication, missive, epistle, reply, answer, acknowledgment.
charter, symbol.

**lettered** learned, scholarly, erudite, educated, well-read, cultured, cultivated, literate. IGNORANT

**level** *adj*, horizontal, plane, flat, even, smooth, uniform. UNEVEN
equal, even, balanced, on a par, neck and neck. UNEQUAL
*v*, flatten, smooth, plane.
demolish, raze, destroy, devastate, pull down, knock down, bulldoze. BUILD
direct, aim, point, focus, train.
*n*, height, altitude, elevation.
position, rank, status, degree, grade, stage, floor, layer.

**lever** *n*, bar, crowbar, jemmy, handle.
*v*, force, prise, jemmy.

**levity** frivolity, flippancy, facetiousness, light-heartedness, triviality, silliness, giddiness, flightiness, fickleness, inconstancy. SERIOUSNESS

**levy** *v*, impose, exact, charge, tax, raise, collect, gather, muster.
*n*, imposition, exaction, charge, fee, tax, duty, toll, tariff, collection, gathering.

**lewd** obscene, pornographic, blue, coarse, vulgar, dirty, smutty, bawdy, ribald, indecent, salacious, lascivious, lecherous, lustful, libidinous. DECOROUS

**lexicon** dictionary, wordbook, glossary, vocabulary, thesaurus.

**liabilities** debts, obligations, responsibilities, duties. ASSETS

**liable** responsible, answerable, accountable, amenable.
subject, susceptible, exposed, open, vulnerable. INSUSCEPTIBLE
likely, probable, apt, inclined, disposed. UNLIKELY

**liaison** communication, contact, connection, link, bond, tie, alliance, relationship.
affair, romance, amour, intrigue.

**libel** *n*, defamation, calumny, slander, aspersion, slur, obloquy, denigration, vilification. EULOGY
*v*, defame, calumniate, slander, traduce, denigrate, vilify, malign. PRAISE

**liberal** progressive, reformist, enlightened, broad-minded, permissive, tolerant, indulgent, open-minded, unbiased, unbigoted, catholic. NARROW-MINDED
generous, charitable, bounteous, munificent, unstinting, unselfish, philanthropic, kind, princely, handsome, ample, abundant, lavish, profuse, plentiful, bountiful. MEAN

**liberality** broad-mindedness, permissiveness, tolerance, indulgence, latitude, open-mindedness, catholicity. NARROW-MINDEDNESS
generosity, charity, bounty, munificence, unselfishness, philanthropy, kindness, abundance, profusion, plenty. MEANNESS

**liberate** free, loose, emancipate, manumit, disenthral, release, discharge, deliver, rescue. CONFINE

**libertine** *n*, profligate, debauchee, lecher, rake, roué, playboy, womanizer, philanderer. ASCETIC
*adj*, dissolute, profligate, debauched, depraved, corrupt, loose, wanton, abandoned, rakish, licentious, immoral. CHASTE

**liberty** freedom, independence, autonomy, liberation, emancipation, release. SERVITUDE
privilege, right, exemption, immunity, authorization, permission, leave, licence, latitude, carte blanche.
familiarity, impertinence, impudence, disrespect, presumptuousness, forwardness. RESPECT

**libidinous** lecherous, lustful, lascivious, randy (*inf*), concupiscent, incontinent, carnal, sensual, prurient, salacious, unchaste. CHASTE

**licence** certificate, permit, warrant, authority, authorization, permission, leave, charter, right, privilege, exemption, immunity, liberty, freedom, latitude, carte blanche. PROHIBITION
abandon, immoderation, unrestraint, anarchy, disorder, laxity, indulgence, licen-

tiousness, dissipation, debauchery. RESTRAINT

**license** allow, permit, authorize, warrant, sanction, empower, commission, certify, charter. PROHIBIT

**licentious** dissolute, debauched, profligate, abandoned, loose, wanton, promiscuous, unchaste, immoral, libidinous, lecherous, lustful, lascivious, lewd. CHASTE

**lick** tongue, touch, brush, taste, lap, flicker, dart.
defeat, beat, conquer, vanquish, trounce.
flog, thrash, beat, spank.

**lid** top, cap, cover.

**lie**[1] *v*, fib, fabricate, invent, equivocate, prevaricate, falsify, misrepresent.
*n*, untruth, falsehood, fib, fiction, invention, fabrication, equivocation, prevarication, mendacity. TRUTH

**lie**[2] *v*, rest, repose, recline, be prostrate, sprawl, stretch, extend.
be, be situated, be found, remain, exist, consist.

**liege** lord, master, chief, leader, sovereign, superior. VASSAL

**lieu** place, stead.

**life** being, existence, viability, animation. DEATH
lifetime, duration, span, days.
biography, autobiography, memoir, memoirs, history.
energy, vitality, vigour, verve, sparkle, animation, liveliness, vivacity, spirit, enthusiasm. LETHARGY

**lifeless** dead, deceased, defunct, cold, inanimate, inorganic. LIVING
lethargic, sluggish, torpid, spiritless, listless, inactive, inert, dull, flat, insipid. LIVELY

**lift** *vt*, raise, elevate, hoist, jack, pick up, pull up. DROP
uplift, exalt, boost, enhance, improve, advance, promote. LOWER
revoke, rescind, cancel, stop, terminate, remove. IMPOSE
*vi*, rise, mount, ascend, disperse, dissipate. FALL

**ligature** bond, tie, link, connection, ligament, band.

**light**[1] *n*, illumination, brightness, brilliance, radiance, luminosity, ray, beam, glow, flash. DARKNESS
lamp, lantern, bulb, candle, torch.
daylight, sunshine, dawn, daybreak. NIGHT
enlightenment, elucidation, explanation, understanding, comprehension, insight, knowledge. MYSTIFICATION
*adj*, bright, clear, illuminated, luminous, well-lit. DARK
pale, pastel, whitish, faded, bleached, fair, blond.
*v*, ignite, kindle, fire, inflame. EXTINGUISH
illuminate, brighten, lighten, light up. DARKEN

**light**[2] *adj*, weightless, insubstantial, feathery, flimsy, delicate, airy, buoyant, easy, simple, effortless. HEAVY
trivial, trifling, slight, small, inconsiderable, insignificant, superficial. WEIGHTY
amusing, entertaining, humorous, funny, frivolous. SERIOUS
agile, nimble, sprightly, lithe, supple, deft, dexterous. CLUMSY
cheerful, blithe, gay, merry, jolly, happy, joyful, carefree, fickle, capricious, mercurial, volatile, flighty.
*v*, land, settle, alight.

**light on,** come across, find, discover, happen upon.

**lighten**[1] illuminate, brighten, light, light up, shine, flash. DARKEN
bleach, whiten, pale, fade.

**lighten**[2] disburden, disencumber, unload, ease, lessen, reduce, relieve, alleviate. ENCUMBER
cheer, brighten, hearten, encourage, gladden, perk up, uplift. DEPRESS

**light-headed** dizzy, giddy, faint, vertiginous, woozy (*inf*).
flighty, fickle, capricious, silly, foolish, scatterbrained, frivolous, superficial, trifling. SOBER

**light-hearted** cheerful, blithe, bright, gay, merry, jolly, happy, joyful, carefree, happy-go-lucky. SERIOUS

**like**[1] *adj*, similar, alike, resembling, same, identical, allied, akin, related, cognate, corresponding, parallel, analogous, equivalent. DIFFERENT
*n*, equal, peer, match, counterpart.

**like**[2] *v*, enjoy, delight in, relish, appreciate, be partial to, be fond of, love, admire, esteem, prize, fancy, take to, care for, approve. DISLIKE
prefer, choose, select, wish, want, desire, care.

*n*, liking, preference, partiality, predilection. DISLIKE

**likely** probable, possible, liable, apt, inclined, disposed, prone. IMPROBABLE
plausible, credible, believable, reasonable, conceivable, imaginable. IMPLAUSIBLE
promising, hopeful, appropriate, suitable, acceptable, pleasing, agreeable. UNSUITABLE

**likeness** similarity, resemblance, similitude, sameness, corresponding. DISSIMILARITY
image, representation, portrait, effigy, copy, replica, facsimile, reproduction, counterpart.
semblance, guise, appearance, form.

**likewise** moreover, furthermore, also, too, in addition, besides.
similarly, the same. OTHERWISE

**liking** fondness, love, affection, attraction, affinity, partiality, preference, predilection, taste, appreciation, fancy, inclination, tendency. AVERSION

**Lilliputian** tiny, diminutive, miniature, petite, small, little, short, dwarfish, pygmy, undersized. COLOSSAL

**limber** *adj*, lithe, lissom, supple, pliant, flexible, elastic. STIFF
*v*, **limber up,** warm up. loosen up, exercise, prepare, get ready.

**limit** *n*, boundary, frontier, confine, precinct, border, edge, extent, bound, end, termination, extreme, utmost.
restriction, restraint, check, curb, limitation, maximum, ceiling.
*v*, restrict, confine, curb, check, restrain, bound, circumscribe, delimit, demarcate.

**limitless** unlimited, illimitable, boundless, unbounded, infinite, endless, unending, vast, immense, incalculable, immeasurable. LIMITED

**limp**[1] *v*, hobble, falter, stumble, stagger, shuffle.
*n*, hobble, lameness.

**limp**[2] flaccid, flabby, soft, flexible, pliant, slack, loose, relaxed. STIFF

**limpid** clear, transparent, translucent, pellucid, crystalline. OPAQUE
plain, lucid, clear, intelligible, comprehensible. INCOMPREHENSIBLE
calm, peaceful, serene, tranquil, still, quiet. AGITATED

**line** *n*, row, rank, file, queue, column, series, sequence.
stroke, mark, streak, stripe, band, strip, bar, rule, dash.
string, rope, cord, thread, wire, cable.
crease, wrinkle, furrow.
limit, boundary, border, edge, frontier.
course, path, track, direction, route, way, method, policy.
occupation, business, profession, trade, field, area, activity, interest.
ancestry, descent, extraction, lineage, family, house, race.
*v*, mark, rule, score, streak, draw, trace, crease, wrinkle.
**line up,** align, range, straighten, arrange, array, order, queue up, fall in.

**lineage** ancestry, descent, extraction, birth, family, house, line, race, stock, pedigree, genealogy, offspring, progeny, succession.

**linger** loiter, tarry, wait, remain, stay, persist, endure, hang around, lag, dawdle, dally, saunter, delay, procrastinate.

**link** *v*, connect, join, couple, tie, fasten, unite, associate, relate. SEPARATE
*n*, connection, joint, coupling, tie, bond, association, relationship.
part, piece, member, element, division.

**lion-hearted** brave, courageous, bold, fearless, intrepid, daring, heroic, valiant, valorous, dauntless. COWARDLY

**lip** edge, brim, rim, brink, border, margin.
impudence, impertinence, insolence, cheek (*inf*), sauce (*inf*), rudeness, backchat (*inf*). POLITENESS

**liquefy** liquidize, liquesce, melt, thaw, fuse, condense, dissolve, deliquesce. SOLIDIFY

**liquid** *n*, liquor, fluid, juice. SOLID
*adj*, fluid, flowing, running, runny, watery, wet, liquefied, molten.
fluent, smooth, dulcet, sweet, pure, clear.

**liquidate** pay, settle, discharge, clear, sell, cash, realize.
terminate, dissolve, break up, abolish, annihilate, exterminate, kill.

**list** *n*, catalogue, inventory, roll, register, schedule, enumeration, series, file, index, directory.
*v*, enumerate, catalogue, file, index, tabulate, record, register, enter, write down.

**listen** hark, pay attention, concentrate, attend, hear, give ear, heed, mind, eavesdrop, overhear. IGNORE

**listless** lethargic, languid, sluggish, torpid, enervated, weary, spiritless, inactive, inert, apathetic, indifferent. ENERGETIC

**literal** verbatim, word-for-word, strict, close, exact, precise, accurate, faithful, true, actual, genuine. LOOSE

**literary** scholarly, erudite, learned, lettered, literate, well-read. ILLITERATE

**literature** letters, writings, literary works, books, publications, lore, information.

**lithe** lissom, limber, supple, pliant, pliable, flexible, elastic, agile, nimble, graceful.

**litigation** lawsuit, action, case, proceedings, dispute, contest.

**litigious** quarrelsome, argumentative, disputatious, contentious, belligerent, pugnacious, combative. GENIAL

**litter** *n*, rubbish, refuse, waste, debris, clutter, mess, disorder, jumble, confusion. TIDINESS
brood, young, progeny, offspring.
bedding, straw, hay.
*v*, strew, scatter, clutter, mess up, disarrange, disorder. TIDY

**little** *adj*, small, short, wee, tiny, minute, petite, diminutive, Lilliputian, dwarfish, pygmy, young, baby. BIG
brief, short, fleeting, passing, limited. LENGTHY
trivial, trifling, paltry, inconsiderable, slight, insignificant. CONSIDERABLE
insufficient, meagre, scant, skimpy. AMPLE
*adv*, barely, hardly, not much. MUCH
rarely, seldom, not often. OFTEN
*n*, bit, dash, pinch, drop, trace, spot, touch, trifle. LOT

**live**[1] *vi*, be, exist, be alive, breathe, subsist, survive, remain, endure, persist, continue, last. DIE
reside, dwell, occupy, inhabit, lodge, abide.
*vt*, pass, spend, lead.

**live**[2] *adj*, alive, living, breathing, animate, existent. DEAD
controversial, topical, current, active, connected, loaded, burning, unrecorded.
lively, brisk, energetic, vigorous, dynamic, spirited, alert.

**livelihood** occupation, job, employment, work, living, maintenance, support, subsistence, sustenance.

**lively** vivacious, animated, spirited, active, brisk, nimble, spry, agile, frisky, energetic, vigorous, dynamic, alert, keen, eager, quick, busy, bustling, astir, stimulating, exciting, buoyant, gay, vivid. DULL

**livery** uniform, costume, dress, attire, regalia.

**livid** greyish, leaden, ashen, pale, pallid, wan.
discoloured, bruised, purple, black-and-blue.
angry, furious, enraged, incensed, fuming. CALM

**living** *adj*, alive, live, breathing, animate, existent, extant, current, active, operative. DEAD
*n*, livelihood, maintenance, support, subsistence, sustenance, income, work, job, occupation.
being, existence, animation, life. DEATH

**load** *n*, burden, onus, encumbrance, weight, charge, cargo, freight, lading, shipment, consignment, worry, trouble, affliction, oppression.
*v*, burden, encumber, oppress, weigh down, weight, charge, fill, pack, lade, freight, heap, pile. UNLOAD

**loaf** lounge, idle, laze, loll, loiter, waste time, fritter away.

**loafer** idler, sluggard, lounger, shirker, layabout, good-for-nothing, ne'er-do-well, drone. WORKER

**loan** *n*, advance, credit, usury.
*v*, lead, advance. BORROW

**loath** loth, unwilling, reluctant, disinclined, indisposed, averse. EAGER

**loathe** detest, abhor, abominate, execrate, hate, dislike. ADORE

**loathing** detestation, abhorrence, abomination, execration, odium, hate, hatred, dislike, aversion, antipathy, repugnance, revulsion, disgust. LOVE

**loathsome** detestable, abhorrent, abominable, execrable, odious, hateful, repugnant, repulsive, disgusting, revolting, obnoxious, vile, nasty, offensive. DELIGHTFUL

**lobby** *n*, vestibule, foyer, hall, hallway, corridor, passage.
*v*, urge, press, influence, persuade.

**local** regional, provincial, parochial, neighbourhood, community, home, native, nearby, limited, restricted. GENERAL

**locality** neighbourhood, vicinity, district, area, region, location, place, spot, site, locale.

**locate** find, discover, unearth, come across, ferret out, track down, detect, pinpoint.
situate, place, put, set, fix, establish, settle. REMOVE

**location** position, situation, whereabouts, place, spot, site, locality, locale.

**lock**[1] *v*, fasten, secure, bolt, latch. UNLOCK
join, unite, link, engage, interlock, entangle.
clasp, embrace, hug, hold, clutch, grapple.
**lock up,** jail, imprison, incarcerate, confine. RELEASE
*n*, fastening, bolt, latch, hasp, padlock.

**lock**[2] *n*, tress, curl, ringlet, bunch, tuft, wisp, strand.

**locomotion** movement, motion, moving, progress, travel.

**lodge** *v*, live, reside, dwell, stay, sojourn, room, board, put up, accommodate, house, billet, quarter, take in, shelter, harbour, entertain.
fix, implant, embed, stick, put, place, deposit, lay, set. REMOVE
*n*, cottage, hut, cabin, chalet, retreat, den, lair.

**lodger** boarder, paying guest, tenant. LANDLORD

**lodgings** accommodation, digs (*inf*), rooms, quarters, abode, residence, dwelling, habitation.

**lofty** high, tall, towering, elevated, exalted, stately, imposing, majestic, august, dignified, noble, grand, eminent, illustrious. LOWLY
arrogant, proud, haughty, high-and-mighty (*inf*), lordly, overbearing, supercilious, disdainful, condescending. HUMBLE

**logic** reasoning, argumentation, deduction, dialectics, rationale, reason, sense, coherence.

**logical** reasonable, rational, sound, valid, clear, coherent, consistent, sensible, wise, judicious. ILLOGICAL

**loiter** loaf, idle, stand around, tarry, linger, dally, dilly-dally (*inf*), dawdle, saunter, lag. HURRY

**loll** lounge, sprawl, slouch, slump, flop, lie, rest, recline, repose, lean.
hang, dangle, droop, sag, flop.

**lone** single, isolated, separate, sole, only, solitary, unaccompanied, alone, lonely, lonesome.

**lonely** lonesome, friendless, abandoned, forsaken, forlorn, bereft, solitary, unaccompanied, by oneself, isolated, withdrawn, sequestered, reclusive, outcast.
remote, secluded, isolated, out-of-the-way, deserted, uninhabited, unfrequented.

**long**[1] *adj*, lengthy, extensive, extended, stretched, elongated, protracted, prolonged, long-winded, sustained, interminable. SHORT

**long**[2] *v*, yearn, desire, wish, crave, hunger, thirst, pine, hanker.

**longing** yearning, desire, wish, craving, hunger, thirst, hankering, yen (*inf*), aspiration.

**long-winded** long, lengthy, overlong, long-drawn-out, interminable, wordy, verbose, prolix, diffuse, discursive. TERSE

**look** *v*, watch, observe, contemplate, survey, view, regard, see, notice, scrutinize, study, examine, scan, gaze, stare, peer, glance, glimpse, peep. IGNORE
seem, appear.
search, hunt, seek. FIND
**look after,** mind, take care of, attend to, tend, nurse, supervise, protect, guard. NEGLECT
**look down on,** despise, scorn, disdain, contemn, misprize, disparage. RESPECT
**look into,** investigate, probe, explore, examine, study, research, inquire, check out.
**look up to,** admire, esteem, respect, revere. DESPISE
*n*, gaze, stare, glance, glimpse, view, sight, observation, examination, inspection, scrutiny.
appearance, aspect, air, demeanour, manner, expression, guise, semblance.

**loom** appear, bulk, hover, impend, be imminent, threaten, menace. RECEDE
overhang, tower, rise, soar, overshadow, dominate.

**loop** *n*, circle, ring, hoop, noose, bend, curve, curl, coil, twist.
*v*, encircle, ring, roll, turn, bend, curve, curl, coil, twist.

**loose** *adj*, slack, lax, relaxed, baggy, sloppy, hanging, drooping. TIGHT
free, unconfined, untied, unfastened, undone, detached, floating, movable, wobbly. SECURE
vague, indefinite, broad, imprecise, inexact, random. PRECISE

dissolute, debauched, immoral, unchaste, wanton, promiscuous, libertine, licentious. CHASTE

*v*, free, set free, release, let go, liberate, unfasten, undo, untie, unleash, detach, disengage. SECURE

**loosen** slacken, ease, relax, unbind, untie, undo, loose, free, release, liberate. TIGHTEN

**loot** *n*, spoils, booty, plunder.

*v*, pillage, plunder, despoil, ravage, sack, ransack, rifle, raid, rob, steal.

**lop** cut, chop, cut off, sever, detach, crop, dock, prune, truncate, shorten, curtail.

**loquacious** talkative, voluble, garrulous, babbling, chatty, gossipy. TACITURN

**lord** peer, nobleman, earl, baron. COMMONER

master, ruler, governor, monarch, sovereign, king, prince, commander, leader, chief, superior.

**lordly** haughty, arrogant, proud, overbearing, domineering, imperious, lofty, condescending, patronizing, supercilious, snooty (*inf*). HUMBLE

noble, dignified, lofty, exalted, regal, kingly, princely, majestic, imperial, grand, stately. LOWLY

**lore** knowledge, wisdom, learning, erudition, scholarship, traditions, beliefs, sayings.

**lose** mislay, misplace, drop, forget, miss, forfeit, fail, be defeated. GAIN

waste, squander, dissipate, expend, use up, exhaust. KEEP

elude, dodge, escape, evade, outrun, outstrip, leave behind.

**loss** deprivation, disadvantage, detriment, harm, damage, destruction, ruin, death, bereavement, sacrifice, forfeiture, failure, defeat. GAIN

waste, depletion, deficit, deficiency, shrinkage.

**at a loss,** bewildered, confused, perplexed, baffled, puzzled, helpless, lost.

**lost** missing, mislaid, misplaced, disappeared, vanished, gone, forgotten, irretrievable, irrecoverable, irreclaimable. FOUND

wasted, squandered, misused, misspent, forfeited, wrecked, ruined, destroyed, dead.

bewildered, perplexed, confused, baffled, puzzled, astray, adrift.

depraved, corrupt, abandoned, fallen, loose, wanton, unchaste, hardened, incorrigible, damned. VIRTUOUS

abstracted, absorbed, preoccupied, engrossed, rapt, absent.

**lot** collection, assortment, batch, set, group, band.

fate, destiny, fortune, luck, chance, hazard, doom, plight.

share, portion, part, allowance, ration.

heap, pile, stack, mass, great deal, abundance, plenty, lots.

**lotion** ointment, cream, balm, salve, embrocation, liniment.

**loud** noisy, deafening, ear-splitting, booming, thundering, blaring, resounding, sonorous, stentorian, piercing, strident, clamorous, vociferous, rowdy, boisterous. QUIET

garish, glaring, gaudy, lurid, flashy, showy, ostentatious, tasteless, vulgar. SUBDUED

**lounge** *v*, rest, relax, recline, repose, loll, lie, loaf, idle, laze. WORK

*n*, saloon, waiting room, living room, sitting room.

**lout** boor, churl, oaf, dolt, lubber, bumpkin, brute.

**lovable** adorable, endearing, winning, charming, sweet, attractive, likable. DETESTABLE

**love** *v*, adore, cherish, hold dear, treasure, be fond of, care for, desire, like, worship, idolize. HATE

*n*, affection, attachment, fondness, tenderness, warmth, devotion, adoration, passion, infatuation, ardour, rapture, liking, delight, enjoyment, partiality, inclination, weakness, taste. HATRED

**lovely** beautiful, attractive, pretty, comely, handsome, graceful, sweet, charming, enchanting, adorable, exquisite, delightful, pleasing, agreeable, enjoyable, pleasant, nice. HORRIBLE

**lover** boyfriend, fiancé, paramour, philanderer, mistress, girlfriend, fiancée.

**low**[1] *adj*, short, small, squat, stunted, shallow, flat, depressed, sunken, deep. HIGH

insufficient, inadequate, paltry, meagre, poor, inferior.

coarse, vulgar, rude, base, mean, vile, abject, contemptible, despicable, nasty, malicious, ignoble, unworthy. HONOURABLE

cheap, inexpensive, modest, moderate, reasonable. EXORBITANT
subdued, muted, soft, gentle, quiet, hushed. LOUD
depressed, dejected, blue, melancholy, gloomy, glum, miserable, sad, despondent, downcast. HAPPY

**low²** *v*, moo, bellow.

**lower¹** *v*, drop, fall, sink, descend, depress, let down. RAISE
reduce, cut, decrease, diminish, lessen, soften, moderate, abate, subside, dwindle, decline. INCREASE
abase, degrade, humble, humiliate, demean, belittle, debase, devalue.
*adj*, inferior, lesser, subordinate, minor, junior. SUPERIOR

**lower²** *v*, lour, darken, threaten, menace, loom, impend. BRIGHTEN
frown, scowl, glower, glare. SMILE

**lowering** dark, black, grey, overcast, cloudy, murky, threatening, menacing, ominous. BRIGHT

**lowly** humble, lowborn, plebeian, poor, simple, plain, unpretentious, modest, unassuming, meek, docile, submissive. LOFTY

**loyal** true, faithful, constant, devoted, patriotic, staunch, trusty, dependable, reliable, trustworthy. PERFIDIOUS

**loyalty** allegiance, faithfulness, fidelity, constancy, devotion, patriotism, staunchness, dependability, reliability. INFIDELITY

**lubberly** awkward, clumsy, maladroit, bungling, ungainly, gawky, clownish, oafish, loutish, churlish, boorish, uncouth.

**lubricate** oil, grease, smooth.

**lucent** bright, brilliant, effulgent, shining, luminous, radiant, translucent. DARK

**lucid** clear, plain, intelligible, comprehensible, distinct, explicit, obvious, sane, rational, sound. UNINTELLIGIBLE
bright, shining, radiant, clear, transparent, translucent, pellucid, crystalline, limpid, pure. OPAQUE

**luck** chance, fortune, hazard, accident, fortuity, destiny, fate, lot. DESIGN
success, prosperity, fluke, godsend, blessing, windfall. MISFORTUNE

**luckless** unlucky, unfortunate, hapless, unhappy, unsuccessful, ill-fated, ill-starred, disastrous, calamitous, doomed, fated. LUCKY

**lucky** fortunate, fortuitous, happy, blessed, charmed, successful, prosperous, favourable, propitious, auspicious, timely, opportune. UNLUCKY

**lucrative** paying, well-paid, remunerative, gainful, profitable, rewarding, productive, fruitful, advantageous. UNPROFITABLE

**lucre** wealth, riches, money, profit, gain.

**lucubration** study, brainwork, cogitation, meditation.
dissertation, thesis, treatise, work.

**ludicrous** absurd, ridiculous, preposterous, comical, farcical, laughable, droll, funny, crazy, nonsensical, illogical, incongruous, outlandish.

**lug** pull, drag, heave, tug, tow, haul, carry.

**luggage** baggage, suitcases, bags, things, belongings, effects, paraphernalia, impedimenta.

**lugubrious** mournful, sombre, gloomy, dismal, dreary, melancholy, sad, sorrowful, doleful, miserable, depressing. CHEERFUL

**lukewarm** tepid, warm. COLD
indifferent, uninterested, apathetic, unresponsive, cool, unenthusiastic, half-hearted. ENTHUSIASTIC

**lull** *v*, soothe, assuage, allay, calm, still, quiet, hush, quell, appease, pacify. DISTURB
abate, subside, diminish, wane, decrease, lessen, cease. INCREASE
*n*, calm, peace, quiet, hush, stillness, tranquillity, pause, break, respite.

**lumber** jumble, rubbish, trash, clutter, junk, refuse.

**lumbering** awkward, clumsy, lumpish, lubberly, ungainly, oafish, heavy, ponderous, unwieldy. DAINTY

**luminous** glowing, luminescent, phosphorescent, fluorescent, incandescent, bright, shining, brilliant, radiant, effulgent, resplendent, lit, illuminated. DARK
lucid, clear, plain, intelligible, comprehensible, explicit, obvious. UNINTELLIGIBLE

**lump** *n*, mass, clump, cluster, bunch, ball, piece, chunk.
bump, boss, swelling, growth, tumour, protuberance, bulge.
*v*, collect, gather, cluster, mass, conglomerate, aggregate, accumulate, combine, unite, group.

**lumpish** clumsy, awkward, dull, stupid, bovine, heavy, oafish, loutish.

**lunacy** madness, insanity, derangement, dementia, mania, craziness, aberration, idiocy, stupidity, foolishness, folly, absurdity. SANITY

**lunatic** *adj*, mad, insane, deranged, demented, crazy, idiotic, stupid, foolish, senseless, absurd. SANE
*n*, madman, maniac, psychopath, nutter (*inf*), loony (*inf*).

**lunge** thrust, pass, stab, jab, plunge, pounce.

**lurch** pitch, roll, toss, rock, sway, stagger.

**lure** *v*, tempt, entice, attract, draw, allure, decoy, seduce, inveigle. REPEL
*n*, temptation, enticement, attraction, allurement, bait, decoy. REPULSION

**lurid** vivid, graphic, exaggerated, melodramatic, sensational, grisly, gruesome, shocking, appalling, violent, intense, dazzling, glaring.

**lurk** skulk, prowl, sneak, slink, hide, lie in wait. EMERGE

**luscious** delicious, delectable, appetizing, tasty, mouthwatering, succulent, juicy, ambrosial, fragrant, aromatic, delightful, pleasurable, attractive, gorgeous. REVOLTING

**lush** succulent, juicy, moist, watery, fresh, tender, fleshy. DRY
luxuriant, dense, prolific, rank, abundant, flourishing, green, verdant. SPARSE

**lust** *n*, libido, sensuality, carnality, lechery, lasciviousness, lewdness, concupiscence, prurience. FRIGIDITY
desire, longing, craving, appetite, greed, passion. INDIFFERENCE
*v*, desire, covet, long, yearn, crave, hunger, thirst.

**lustful** libidinous, lecherous, lascivious, lewd, salacious, licentious, carnal, sensual, concupiscent, prurient, randy (*inf*). CHASTE

**lustre** sheen, gloss, shine, glow, brightness, brilliance, radiance, effulgence, dazzle, resplendence, splendour, sparkle, glitter. DULLNESS
glory, honour, distinction, fame, renown, illustriousness.

**lusty** strong, robust, sturdy, hardy, healthy, hale, vigorous, energetic, stout, stalwart, rugged, strapping. WEAK

**luxuriant** lush, dense, profuse, abundant, plentiful, plenteous, exuberant, rank, prolific, copious, rich, fertile, productive. SPARSE
elaborate, ornate, fancy, flowery, rococo, baroque, flamboyant. SIMPLE

**luxuriate** bask, revel, wallow, indulge, enjoy, delight, relish.
flourish, thrive, prosper, mushroom, boom, burgeon. WITHER

**luxurious** sumptuous, opulent, rich, expensive, extravagant, lavish, grand, splendid, magnificent, plush (*inf*), comfortable. AUSTERE
voluptuous, sensual, self-indulgent, epicurean, sybaritic. ASCETIC

**luxury** opulence, sumptuousness, richness, affluence, grandeur, splendour, magnificence, comfort, pleasure, delight, enjoyment, gratification, self-indulgence, voluptuousness, indulgence, extravagance, treat. AUSTERITY

**lying** *n*, deceit, fibbing, falsity, untruthfulness, mendacity, dishonesty, duplicity. HONESTY
*adj*, deceitful, untruthful, mendacious, false, dishonest. TRUTHFUL

# M

**macabre** gruesome, grim, grisly, morbid, horrible, frightful, ghastly, eerie, ghostly, frightening.

**macerate** soak, steep, soften, pulp, mash.

**machiavellian** crafty, artful, cunning, sly, wily, tricky, devious, shrewd, astute, deceitful, unscrupulous, opportunist, scheming, designing, intriguing.

**machinate** plot, plan, scheme, devise, contrive, design, intrigue, conspire.

**machination** plot, plan, scheme, design, intrigue, conspiracy, trick, ruse, stratagem.

**machine** instrument, tool, device, contrivance, mechanism, engine, apparatus, appliance.
agency, organization, structure, system, machinery.

**mad** insane, deranged, demented, unbalanced, unhinged, crazy, lunatic, daft (*inf*), bonkers (*inf*), nuts (*inf*), barmy (*inf*), crackers (*inf*), mental (*inf*). SANE

absurd, ridiculous, foolish, silly, idiotic, senseless, irrational, foolhardy, reckless, unwise. SENSIBLE
frenzied, frenetic, frantic, hysterical, delirious, excited, wild, riotous. CALM
angry, enraged, furious, incensed, infuriated, raging, fuming, irate, wrathful, exasperated, irritated, annoyed. PLEASED
ardent, fanatical, enthusiastic, avid, impassioned, infatuated. INDIFFERENT

**madden** anger, enrage, incense, infuriate, exasperate, irritate, annoy, vex, inflame, provoke, craze, unhinge, derange. PACIFY

**madness** insanity, derangement, dementia, mania, aberration, lunacy, craziness, frenzy, hysteria, delirium. SANITY
absurdity, foolishness, folly, stupidity, idiocy, foolhardiness, recklessness. SENSE
anger, rage, fury, ire, wrath, exasperation. COMPOSURE

**magazine** journal, periodical, review, publication, paper, pamphlet, brochure.
arsenal, storehouse, warehouse, depot.

**magic** *n*, sorcery, witchcraft, necromancy, theurgy, enchantment, spell.
conjuring, prestidigitation, legerdemain, sleight of hand, illusion.
charm, fascination, power.
*adj*, magical, miraculous, mystical, occult, supernatural, enchanting, charming, fascinating, bewitching, spellbinding.

**magician** conjurer, illusionist, wizard, warlock, sorcerer, witch, sorceress, enchantress, miracle-worker.

**magisterial** authoritative, commanding, imperative, peremptory, dictatorial, despotic, domineering, overbearing, imperious, lordly, lofty, haughty, arrogant. HUMBLE

**magnanimity** generosity, tolerance, forbearance, kindness, benevolence, charity, bounty, munificence. MEANNESS

**magnanimous** generous, liberal, openhanded, unselfish, philanthropic, charitable, kind, benevolent, clement, tolerant, forbearing, big, big-hearted, noble, high-minded. MEAN

**magnate** tycoon, industrialist, entrepreneur, baron, mogul, personage, VIP, big shot (*inf*). NOBODY

**magnetic** hypnotic, fascinating, enchanting, entrancing, attractive, alluring, seductive, irresistible, compelling, charismatic.

**magnificent** splendid, imposing, impressive, noble, august, grand, stately, majestic, regal, superb, glorious, sublime, excellent, fine, exquisite, gorgeous, sumptuous, rich, lavish, luxurious. POOR

**magnify** enlarge, increase, amplify, expand, inflate, blow up (*inf*), aggrandize, exaggerate, overstate, overemphasize, deepen, heighten, intensify, exacerbate. REDUCE

**magniloquent** bombastic, pompous, turgid, tumid, inflated, grandiloquent, high-flown, lofty, declamatory, rhetorical. SIMPLE

**magnitude** importance, significance, consequence, greatness, immensity, weight, moment, note. INSIGNIFICANCE
size, extent, measure, dimensions, proportion, volume, mass, amplitude, expanse.

**maid** servant, domestic, housemaid.

**maiden** *n*, girl, lass, miss, damsel, virgin. LAD
*adj*, first, initial, inaugural, fresh, new.

**maidenly** modest, decorous, demure, pure, chaste, virginal, gentle, girlish.

**mail** *n*, post, correspondence, letters, parcels.
*v*, post, send, dispatch, forward.

**maim** disable, incapacitate, cripple, lame, mutilate, injure, hurt, harm, mar, impair.

**main** *adj*, chief, principal, leading, first, foremost, primary, cardinal, capital, supreme, paramount, essential, vital, indispensable, necessary, critical, crucial. MINOR
sheer, pure, downright, utter, absolute, direct, brute.
*n*, pipe, conduit, duct, channel, line, cable.
bulk, mass, majority, preponderance, body. PART
strength, might, power, force.

**mainly** chiefly, principally, primarily, mostly, in the main, on the whole, largely, essentially, generally, usually, above all. PARTLY

**maintain** keep, retain, conserve, preserve, sustain, support, keep up, continue, perpetuate, look after, care for. ABANDON
state, assert, aver, affirm, asseverate, declare, allege, contend, claim, hold. DENY
defend, uphold, champion, advocate, back, justify, vindicate. ATTACK

**maintenance** conservation, preservation, upkeep, repairs, care, support, subsistence, living, livelihood, keep, allowance, alimony. NEGLECT
perpetuation, continuance, continuation, prolongation.

**majestic** grand, august, dignified, noble, regal, royal, kingly, princely, imperial, lofty, exalted, stately, pompous, magnificent, splendid, impressive, imposing. LOWLY

**majesty** grandeur, dignity, nobility, loftiness, stateliness, pomp, magnificence, splendour. HUMILITY

**major** larger, greater, chief, main, leading, supreme, important, significant. MINOR

**majority** bulk, mass, preponderance, body, greater part, greater number, more, most. MINORITY
adulthood, maturity, manhood, womanhood.

**make** create, fabricate, manufacture, produce, build, construct, fashion, form, shape, invent, originate, devise, contrive. DESTROY
cause, effect, bring about, occasion, generate, produce, render, do, perform, execute, accomplish. UNDO
force, oblige, require, compel, constrain, coerce, drive, urge, impel, induce. PREVENT
constitute, compose, comprise, form, amount to, add up to.
appoint, elect, nominate, assign, invest, install.
earn, clear, net, gross, gain, get, obtain, acquire. SPEND
**make believe,** pretend, imagine, fantasize, dream.
**make do,** cope, manage, get by, survive.
**make for,** head for, aim for, be bound for.
**make out,** discern, perceive, descry, espy, detect, recognize, see, understand, comprehend, ascertain, distinguish.
draw up, write out, fill in, complete.
**make up,** invent, fabricate, concoct, hatch, coin, formulate, create, originate, compose, write.
recompense, requite, make amends, make good, compensate, offset.
*n*, brand, type, sort, kind, shape, form, build, construction, composition.

**maker** creator, manufacturer, producer, builder, constructor.

**makeshift** temporary, provisional, improvised, rough-and-ready, emergency.

**maladministration** mismanagement, misgovernment, misrule, corruption, malpractice, inefficiency, incompetence, bungling.

**maladroit** clumsy, awkward, bungling, ham-fisted, inapt, inept, inexpert, unskilful, incompetent. DEXTEROUS

**malady** illness, sickness, ailment, complaint, disorder, disease, indisposition, affliction. FITNESS

**malcontent** *adj*, discontented, disgruntled, dissatisfied, displeased, uneasy, restive, factious, rebellious. CONTENTED
*n*, grumbler, complainer, fault-finder, agitator, troublemaker, rebel.

**malediction** curse, anathema, imprecation, execration, damnation, denunciation, condemnation, slander, calumny. BLESSING

**malefactor** criminal, felon, lawbreaker, wrongdoer, sinner, offender, miscreant, culprit.

**maleficent** harmful, hurtful, injurious, baleful, pernicious, noxious, deleterious, detrimental, malignant. HARMLESS

**malevolent** malicious, malignant, malign, ill-disposed, spiteful, vindictive, revengeful, bitter, rancorous, resentful. BENEVOLENT

**malice** malevolence, malignity, maliciousness, enmity, hostility, animosity, hate, ill will, spite, vindictiveness, bitterness, rancour, resentment, grudge, spleen, venom. LOVE

**malicious** malevolent, malignant, malign, ill-disposed, spiteful, vindictive, bitter, rancorous, maleficent, injurious, mischievous, pernicious, vicious. KIND

**malign** *v*, defame, slander, calumniate, traduce, vilify, denigrate, blacken, revile, disparage, derogate, run down. PRAISE
*adj*, malignant, malevolent, evil, bad, harmful, injurious, pernicious. GOOD

**malignant** malevolent, malign, malicious, spiteful, venomous, vindictive, bitter, rancorous, hostile, baleful, injurious, pernicious, harmful, destructive.
deadly, fatal, incurable, irremediable, uncontrollable, virulent. BENIGN

**malpractice** malversation, misconduct, misbehaviour, negligence, dereliction, mismanagement, misdeed, offence, transgression.

**maltreat** mistreat, ill-treat, abuse, injure, hurt, harm.

**mammon** riches, wealth, opulence, affluence, money, lucre, possessions, property.

**mammoth** huge, enormous, colossal, elephantine, gigantic, gargantuan, vast, immense, massive, titanic. TINY

**man** male, gentleman, fellow, chap (*inf*), bloke (*inf*), guy (*inf*). WOMAN
person, human being, adult, individual, body, soul. BEAST
mankind, humanity, human race.
employee, worker, hand, soldier, servant, attendant, follower, subject, dependant. MASTER

**manacle** *v*, handcuff, shackle, fetter, chain, bind, restrain, confine, curb, check. FREE
*n*, handcuff, shackle, fetter, iron, chain, bond.

**manage** administer, direct, command, rule, govern, run, conduct, supervise, superintend. MISMANAGE
contrive, succeed, engineer, manoeuvre, bring about, effect. FAIL
cope, fare, get by, make do, survive.
control, influence, guide, steer, pilot, manipulate, operate, handle, wield.

**manageable** tractable, governable, amenable, docile, compliant, submissive, controllable, handy, convenient, easy. UNMANAGEABLE

**management** administration, executive, board, directorate, directors, employers, managers. LABOUR
direction, administration, control, regulation, rule, government, command, supervision, conduct, running, handling, operation, care, charge. MISMANAGEMENT

**manager** director, administrator, executive, controller, overseer, supervisor, superintendent, governor, boss (*inf*), gaffer (*inf*).

**mandate** command, order, precept, edict, decree, injunction, charge, commission, authorization, authority, warrant, sanction.

**mandatory** obligatory, binding, compulsory, necessary, requisite, essential. OPTIONAL

**mangle** mutilate, disfigure, mar, spoil, maim, cripple, cut, lacerate, tear, crush, ruin, destroy.

**manhood** adulthood, maturity. BOYHOOD
virility, masculinity, manliness, strength, fortitude, hardihood, stamina, bravery, courage, valour, determination, resolution. WOMANHOOD

**mania** madness, insanity, derangement, dementia, aberration, lunacy, craziness, frenzy, delirium. SANITY
passion, obsession, fixation, craze, rage, urge, desire, craving. PHOBIA

**maniac** madman, lunatic, psychopath, nutter (*inf*), loony (*inf*).
enthusiast, fanatic, fiend (*inf*), freak (*inf*).

**maniacal** manic, mad, insane, deranged, unbalanced, lunatic, crazy, demented, crazed, frenzied, hysterical, delirious, wild, raving. SANE

**manifest** *v*, exhibit, show, display, prove, demonstrate, evince, reveal, expose, declare, make known. HIDE
*adj*, obvious, evident, plain, clear, visible, apparent, conspicuous, noticeable, glaring, unmistakable, patent, palpable, open, overt. QUESTIONABLE

**manifestation** display, demonstration, show, exhibition, revelation, exposure, proof, declaration, expression, sign, indication. CONCEALMENT

**manifesto** statement, declaration, pronouncement, proclamation.

**manifold** numerous, many, multiple, varied, diverse, assorted, multifarious. FEW

**manipulate** handle, wield, use, operate, work, manage, control, influence, direct, guide, engineer, exploit.

**mankind** man, humanity, human race.

**manly** virile, masculine, strong, mighty, hardy, robust, brave, courageous, valiant, bold, intrepid, resolute, firm, gallant, chivalrous. WOMANLY

**manner** way, method, means, style, fashion, mode, wont, custom, habit, practice, procedure, routine.
behaviour, conduct, bearing, carriage, deportment, demeanour, mien, air, aspect, appearance, guise, look.
kind, sort, type, variety, make, brand.

**mannerism** idiosyncrasy, peculiarity, quirk, trait, habit, gesture.

**mannerly** polite, courteous, well-mannered, civil, respectful, deferential, well-behaved, well-bred, refined, genteel, gentlemanly, ladylike. RUDE

**manners** behaviour, conduct, comportment, bearing, demeanour, etiquette, decorum, protocol, politeness, courtesy, breeding.

**manoeuvre** *v*, contrive, engineer, wangle (*inf*), plot, plan, scheme, intrigue, manage, manipulate, handle, steer, pilot, move, deploy.
*n*, move, movement, action, operation, plot, plan, scheme, intrigue, ruse, artifice, stratagem, tactic.

**mansion** palace, castle, villa, hall, manor house, stately home, country seat. HOVEL

**mantle** cloak, cover, blanket, shroud, veil, screen.

**manual** *n*, handbook, guide, guidebook, vade mecum.
*adj*, physical, human, hand-operated. AUTOMATIC

**manufacture** *v*, make, produce, fabricate, build, construct, assemble, turn out, mass-produce, process.
invent, make up, concoct, fabricate, think up.
*n*, making, production, fabrication, construction, assembly.

**manumission** liberation, emancipation, enfranchisement, release, deliverance. SERVITUDE

**manumit** liberate, free, set free, emancipate, enfranchise, release, deliver. ENSLAVE

**manure** fertilizer, compost, dressing, muck, dung, ordure.

**many** *adj*, numerous, manifold, myriad, countless, innumerable, umpteen (*inf*), abundant, copious, several, divers, sundry. FEW
*n*, plenty, a lot, hundreds, lots (*inf*), heaps (*inf*).

**map** *n*, chart, plan, diagram, graph.
*v*, plot, plan, map out, chart, delineate.

**mar** spoil, damage, impair, taint, sully, blight, disfigure, deface, mutilate, injure, hurt, harm, ruin. IMPROVE

**marauder** robber, bandit, brigand, raider, plunderer, pillager, looter, freebooter, pirate, corsair, buccaneer.

**march** *v*, walk, stride, step, pace, parade, file, tramp, tread, advance, proceed. HALT
*n*, parade, procession, file, column, demonstration.
trek, tramp, walk, hike.
step, pace, stride.
advance, progression, progress, development. RETROGRESSION

**margin** border, edge, periphery, rim, lip, brim, brink, verge, bound, limit, boundary.
allowance, extra, surplus, leeway, latitude, freedom, scope, space, room.

**marginal** borderline, peripheral, minimal, slight, negligible.

**marine** sea, maritime, oceanic, pelagic, nautical, naval, seafaring, ocean-going. LAND

**mariner** sailor, seaman, seafarer, bluejacket, tar (*inf*), matelot (*inf*).

**marital** conjugal, connubial, matrimonial, nuptial, wedded, married. CELIBATE

**maritime** marine, seafaring, nautical, naval, sea, oceanic, coastal, littoral. LAND

**mark** *n*, spot, stain, blemish, bruise, dent, impression, scar, line, scratch.
sign, symbol, indication, brand, stamp, badge, emblem, token, proof, characteristic, feature.
target, objective, goal, aim, purpose.
trace, track, trail, footprint, footmark.
distinction, eminence, fame, renown, note, importance, consequence, influence.
*v*, stain, blemish, bruise, dent, scar, scratch.
brand, stamp, label, identify, characterize, distinguish, designate, indicate.
note, heed, mind, pay attention, regard, observe, notice.
correct, assess, grade. IGNORE

**marked** noticeable, obvious, evident, conspicuous, pronounced, prominent, striking, outstanding, remarkable.

**market** *n*, mart, bazaar, fair, exchange.
trade, commerce, demand, call.
*v*, sell, retail, deal, trade.

**maroon** abandon, desert, forsake, leave, strand, isolate, cut off.

**marriage** wedlock, matrimony, match, wedding, nuptials. DIVORCE
alliance, union, merger, amalgamation, association. SEPARATION

**marrow** essence, substance, pith, core, kernel, heart, soul, spirit.

**marry** wed, espouse, get hitched (*inf*), get spliced (*inf*), join, unite, link, connect, ally, associate. SEPARATE

**marsh** bog, swamp, fen, quagmire, morass, slough.

**marshal** arrange, dispose, array, order, rank, line up, organize, assemble, gather. DISARRANGE lead, guide, conduct, usher, escort, shepherd.

**martial** warlike, bellicose, belligerent, military, soldierly, brave, courageous. PACIFIC

**marvel** *v*, wonder, gape, goggle, be amazed.
*n*, wonder, prodigy, miracle, phenomenon.

**marvellous** wonderful, splendid, magnificent, excellent, superb, smashing (*inf*), super (*inf*), fantastic (*inf*), terrific (*inf*). DREADFUL
wondrous, miraculous, astonishing, amazing, remarkable, extraordinary, stupendous, prodigious, incredible, unbelievable. ORDINARY

**masculine** male, manlike, manly, virile, mannish. FEMININE
strong, mighty, robust, hardy, brave, bold, gallant.

**mash** crush, pulp, beat, pound, bruise.

**mask** *n*, disguise, camouflage, front, façade, blind, screen, cover, veil, shield, protection.
*v*, cover, disguise, camouflage, hide, conceal, screen, veil, shield, protect. EXPOSE

**masquerade** *n*, masque, masked ball, fancy dress party, revel.
disguise, costume, mask, cloak, guise, pretence, subterfuge, dissimulation, imposture, deception.
*v*, disguise, impersonate, pose, pretend, dissimulate, dissemble.

**mass** *n*, lump, chunk, block, heap, pile, stack, load, lot, bunch, collection, group, crowd, throng, mob, host, number, quantity.
size, bulk, dimension, magnitude, body, majority, whole, aggregate, total, sum.
*adj*, large-scale, widespread, general, popular. LIMITED
*v*, collect, gather, assemble, muster, swarm, throng, cluster, amass, accumulate. DISPERSE

**massacre** *n*, slaughter, butchery, carnage, murder, killing, extermination, genocide.
*v*, slaughter, butcher, mow down, kill, slay, murder, exterminate, wipe out.

**massage** rub, knead, manipulate.

**massive** huge, enormous, colossal, immense, gigantic, big, large, imposing, bulky, solid, substantial, heavy, weighty, ponderous. TINY

**master** *n*, lord, ruler, governor, director, manager, controller, chief, head, leader, commander, owner, proprietor, holder, keeper, employer, boss (*inf*). SERVANT
expert, ace (*inf*), dab hand (*inf*), genius, maestro, virtuoso, adept, pro (*inf*). NOVICE
teacher, instructor, tutor, pedagogue, guide. PUPIL
*adj*, chief, principal, main, major, great, leading, controlling. MINOR
expert, masterly, adept, proficient, skilled, skilful. INEPT
*v*, conquer, vanquish, defeat, beat, overpower, overcome, crush, quell, subdue, subjugate. YIELD
rule, govern, dominate, control, command.
learn, grasp, acquire, become proficient.

**masterly** expert, ace (*inf*), skilful, skilled, adept, proficient, first-rate, excellent, supreme, consummate, polished, finished. INEPT

**masterpiece** masterwork, *chef-d'oeuvre*, magnum opus, classic.

**mastery** command, control, domination, upper hand, supremacy, ascendancy, sway, rule, dominion, power, conquest, victory. SERVITUDE
knowledge, command, grasp, understanding, acquisition.
skill, ability, proficiency, expertise, prowess, dexterity, virtuosity. INCOMPETENCE

**masticate** chew, munch, champ, eat.

**mat** *n*, rug, pad, cover, mesh.
*v*, tangle, ravel, interweave, interlace, intertwine, twist. UNRAVEL

**match** *n*, competition, contest, trial, bout, game.
equal, peer, fellow, mate, twin, counterpart, equivalent, rival, competitor.
marriage, alliance, union, partnership.
*v*, fit, adapt, suit, accord, agree, correspond, tally, harmonize, coordinate, blend, go with. CLASH
join, unite, marry, mate, couple, pair. SEPARATE
equal, compare, resemble, rival, compete, vie, pit, oppose.

**matchless** peerless, unrivalled, unmatched, unequalled, unparalleled, incomparable, inimitable, unique, ideal, superlative, consummate, perfect. ORDINARY

**mate** *n*, partner, spouse, friend, companion, comrade, compeer, colleague, associate, assistant, helper.
match, counterpart, fellow, twin.

*v*, pair, couple, copulate, breed.
join, match, marry, wed. SEPARATE

**material** *n*, substance, matter, stuff, fabric, cloth.
information, facts, data, notes, papers.
*adj*, physical, corporeal, bodily, worldly, earthly, concrete, substantial, tangible, palpable. SPIRITUAL
relevant, important, significant, essential, vital, momentous, weighty, grave, serious. IMMATERIAL

**materially** considerably, greatly, much, significantly, substantially, essentially.

**maternal** motherly, protective, caring.

**mathematical** exact, precise, accurate, strict, rigid.
arithmetic, geometric, algebraic.

**matrimonial** marital, nuptial, connubial, conjugal, married, wedded.

**matrimony** marriage, wedlock, wedding, nuptials.

**matronly** maternal, motherly, middle-aged, staid, sober, sedate, dignified, portly, plump.

**matter** *v*, signify, count, be important, carry weight, make a difference.
*n*, substance, material, stuff, body.
subject, topic, question, issue, business, affair, concern, thing, circumstance, event.
trouble, problem, difficulty, distress, worry.
importance, significance, consequence, note, moment, weight.
discharge, secretion, pus.

**mature** *adj*, ripe, mellow, seasoned, full-grown, grown-up, adult, of age, complete, perfect, fully developed, ready, prepared. IMMATURE
*v*, ripen, mellow, season, age, develop, grow up.

**maudlin** sentimental, emotional, mawkish, soppy (*inf*), tearful, weepy (*inf*).

**maul** paw, manhandle, batter, beat, claw, lacerate, ill-treat, abuse, injure, hurt, harm, damage.

**mawkish** maudlin, sentimental, emotional, soppy (*inf*), weak, feeble.
nauseating, sickly, foul, insipid, tasteless, stale, flat, vapid.

**maxim** saying, proverb, adage, aphorism, axiom, dictum, saw.

**maximum** *n*, height, peak, top, climax, limit, ceiling, extreme, utmost. MINIMUM
*adj*, maximal, greatest, highest, most, utmost, supreme. MINIMAL

**maybe** perhaps, possibly, perchance, peradventure. DEFINITELY

**maze** labyrinth, network, tangle, web, confusion, perplexity, bewilderment, complexity, intricacy.

**meadow** field, grassland, pasture, lea.

**meagre** scanty, scant, sparse, skimpy, short, deficient, inadequate, insufficient, poor, paltry, small, little, slight. AMPLE
thin, lean, skinny, scrawny, bony, emaciated. FAT
barren, sterile, infertile, unproductive, unfruitful. RICH

**meal** repast, feast, banquet, snack, breakfast, lunch, tea, dinner, supper. FAST

**mean**[1] *v*, signify, denote, betoken, represent, symbolize, stand for, indicate, portend, presage, imply, suggest, connote, purport.
intend, aim, purpose, contemplate, have in mind, propose, plan.
destine, design, make, predestine, preordain.
cause, bring about, produce, result in, involve, entail.

**mean**[2] *adj*, miserly, niggardly, stingy, parsimonious, close, tight-fisted, tight, selfish, ungenerous. GENEROUS
unkind, nasty, unpleasant, malicious, callous, cruel, base, low, despicable, contemptible, abject, shabby, shameful, disgraceful, dishonourable, ignoble, petty, small-minded. HONOURABLE
poor, lowly, humble, miserable, wretched, shabby, seedy, squalid, vulgar, common, ordinary, inferior, second-rate. MAGNIFICENT

**mean**[3] *n*, average, norm, median, midpoint, middle, compromise, happy medium. EXTREME
*adj*, medium, average, normal, middle, intermediate.

**meander** wind, zigzag, snake, twist, turn, bend.
wander, ramble, drift, stray.

**meaning** significance, signification, sense, import, purport, connotation, implication, gist, drift, interpretation, explanation.
aim, intention, idea, object, end, purpose, plan, design.
value, worth, point, use, effect.

**means** method, way, mode, medium, vehicle, instrument, agency, course, channel, resource, measure, expedient. END
resources, funds, income, revenue, property, estate, money, riches, wealth, substance. POVERTY
**by all means,** certainly, of course, definitely, absolutely.

**measure** *v*, weigh, sound, quantify, gauge, assess, rate, value, evaluate, appraise, estimate, calculate, compute, determine.
*n*, size, magnitude, quantity, amount, extent, degree, scope, range.
rule, meter, gauge, scale, standard, norm, criterion, yardstick, touchstone.
portion, share, ration, division, piece, part. WHOLE
limit, bounds, control, limitation.
step, action, course, procedure.

**measured** slow, leisurely, unhurried, deliberate, planned, studied, calculated, steady, regular, even, uniform, regulated, precise, exact.

**measureless** immeasurable, incalculable, limitless, unlimited, illimitable, boundless, unbounded, infinite, endless, interminable, vast, immense. FINITE

**measurement** dimension, size, extent, amount, height, depth, length, breadth, area, volume, capacity, weight.
mensuration, metage, assessment, evaluation, estimation, calculation.

**mechanical** automatic, involuntary, instinctive, unconscious, unthinking, habitual, routine, cold, unfeeling, emotionless, spiritless, lifeless.

**mechanism** machine, motor, engine, appliance, device, contrivance, instrument, tool, workings, machinery.
means, agency, system, procedure, process, method, technique.

**meddle** interfere, intermeddle, pry, snoop (*inf*), interpose, intervene, intrude, butt in.

**meddlesome** meddling, intrusive, interfering, officious, obtrusive, prying, inquisitive, nosy (*inf*).

**medial** middle, central, intermediate, median. EXTREME
average, mean, ordinary.

**mediate** arbitrate, referee, umpire, intercede, intervene, interpose, reconcile, conciliate.

**mediation** arbitration, good offices, intercession, intervention, reconciliation, conciliation.

**medicinal** therapeutic, healing, curative, remedial, restorative, medical.

**medicine** medicament, medication, remedy, cure, drug.

**mediocre** average, middling, passable, tolerable, so-so (*inf*), ordinary, commonplace, run-of-the-mill, indifferent, undistinguished, inferior, second-rate. EXCELLENT

**meditate** ruminate, contemplate, reflect, ponder, muse, brood, cogitate, deliberate, consider, think.
plan, scheme, intend, purpose, devise, contrive, design.

**meditation** rumination, contemplation, reflection, cogitation, deliberation, thought, cerebration, concentration, brown study.

**medium** *adj*, average, mean, medial, median, middle, intermediate, middling, mediocre. EXTREME
*n*, average, mean, midpoint, middle.
means, vehicle, agency, instrumentality, avenue, channel, way.
element, environment, milieu, surroundings, conditions.

**medley** mixture, assortment, miscellany, hotchpotch, pot-pourri, jumble, confusion.

**meek** patient, long-suffering, forbearing, mild, gentle, modest, unassuming, humble, lowly, deferential, compliant, submissive, yielding, docile, acquiescent, resigned, spiritless, tame.

**meet** encounter, come across, happen upon, run into, bump into, face, confront. MISS
join, converge, come together, touch, cross, intersect. DIVERGE
fulfil, satisfy, answer, match, measure up, discharge, carry out, handle, cope with, settle.
gather, collect, assemble, congregate, convene, muster. DISPERSE

**meeting** encounter, confrontation, rendezvous, tryst, assignation, introduction, presentation. PARTING
gathering, assembly, congregation, convention, conference, concourse, rally, reunion, get-together (*inf*), session, meet.
convergence, confluence, junction, intersection, crossing. DIVERGENCE

**melancholy** *n*, gloominess, gloom, depression, dejection, despondency, low spirits, blues, sadness, sorrow, unhappiness, misery. ELATION
*adj*, gloomy, glum, depressed, dejected, downcast, downhearted, dispirited, disconsolate, despondent, low-spirited, blue, doleful, dismal, mournful, sad, sorrowful, unhappy, miserable, woebegone. ELATED

**melee** fight, brawl, scuffle, fray, fracas, free-for-all.

**mellifluous** mellifluent, mellow, smooth, flowing, euphonious, melodious, harmonious, soft, sweet, honeyed, dulcet, silvery. HARSH

**mellow** ripe, mature, soft, tender, sweet, full-flavoured, rich, full, resonant, mellifluous, melodious, smooth.
genial, affable, amiable, jovial, cheerful.
*v*, age, develop, improve, mature, season, ripen, soften.

**melodious** tuneful, melodic, musical, concordant, harmonious, euphonious, sweet, dulcet, silvery. DISCORDANT

**melodramatic** histrionic, theatrical, stagy, exaggerated, overdramatic, hammy (*inf*), sensational, extravagant.

**melody** tune, music, theme, strain, air, song.
melodiousness, tunefulness, harmony, euphony. DISCORD

**melt** liquefy, thaw, fuse, dissolve, deliquesce, soften. FREEZE
fade, disappear, vanish, evanesce, disperse, dissipate.

**member** adherent, associate, fellow, subscriber.
part, component, constituent, element, limb, organ, appendage.

**memento** keepsake, souvenir, relic, reminder, memorial, remembrance.

**memoir** biography, life, history, record, account, essay, monograph.

**memoirs** reminiscences, recollections, experiences, autobiography, journal, diary.

**memorable** unforgettable, remarkable, striking, extraordinary, noteworthy, historic, important, significant, momentous, great, famous, illustrious, celebrated. INSIGNIFICANT

**memorandum** memo, note, message, record, statement, minute, reminder.

**memorial** remembrance, memento, monument, statue, plaque, inscription, commemoration.

**memorize** learn, learn by heart, commit to memory, remember. FORGET

**memory** recall, retention, recollection, remembrance, reminiscence, retrospection. FORGETFULNESS
commemoration, honour, glory, fame, renown, regard, repute. OBLIVION

**menace** *v*, threaten, alarm, scare, frighten, intimidate, terrorize, lower, impend, loom. REASSURE
*n*, threat, intimidation, warning. REASSURANCE
danger, peril, hazard, risk, jeopardy.
nuisance, pest, annoyance, vexation, pain (*inf*).

**mend** repair, fix, darn, patch, restore, renovate, remedy, cure, heal. DAMAGE
amend, emend, correct, rectify, reform, improve, ameliorate. DETERIORATE
recover, get better, recuperate, convalesce.

**mendacious** lying, untruthful, deceitful, dishonest, insincere, false, untrue, fraudulent. HONEST

**mendacity** lying, untruthfulness, deceit, dishonesty, insincerity, falsity, duplicity, deception, fraudulence. HONESTY
lie, fib, untruth, falsehood. TRUTH

**menial** *adj*, humble, lowly, low, base, mean, ignoble, degrading, demeaning, servile, obsequious, fawning, grovelling, sycophantic, subservient.
*n*, servant, domestic, attendant, lackey, flunky, slave, drudge, skivvy (*inf*). MASTER

**mensuration** measurement, measuring, survey, surveying, calculation, computation.

**mental** intellectual, cerebral, psychological, abstract. PHYSICAL
deranged, unbalanced, mentally ill, insane, mad. SANE

**mention** *v*, name, cite, quote, refer to, speak of, touch on, bring up, broach, point out, say, utter, declare, tell, communicate, disclose, divulge, make known, acknowledge. OMIT
*n*, reference, allusion, remark, observation, declaration, announcement, tribute, citation, acknowledgment, recognition.

**mentor** advisor, counsellor, guide, confidant, guru, master, teacher, instructor, tutor.

**mephitic** foul, putrid, rank, stinking, malodorous, fetid, noisome, noxious, poisonous, pestilential, miasmatic, unwholesome. SALUBRIOUS

**mercantile** commercial, trading, marketable, saleable.

**mercenary** greedy, avaricious, covetous, grasping, acquisitive, selfish, sordid. LIBERAL
hired, paid, bought, venal. VOLUNTARY

**merchandise** goods, ware, commodities, stock, produce.

**merchant** trader, dealer, broker, tradesman, shopkeeper, retailer, wholesaler, seller, vendor, salesman.

**merciful** compassionate, forgiving, forbearing, clement, lenient, kind, benignant, mild, humane, tender-hearted, sympathetic, gracious, magnanimous, generous. MERCILESS

**merciless** pitiless, unforgiving, unmerciful, cruel, unkind, harsh, hard, callous, heartless, unfeeling, ruthless, implacable, relentless, unrelenting, inhuman, savage, barbarous. MERCIFUL

**mercurial** lively, vivacious, active, energetic, spirited, volatile, capricious, fickle, changeable, variable, inconstant, impulsive.

**mercy** clemency, leniency, pardon, grace, forgiveness, forbearance, pity, compassion, kindness, tenderness, mildness, magnanimity, benevolence. CRUELTY

**mere** bare, sheer, simple, plain, pure, unadulterated, unmitigated, utter, absolute, entire, complete.

**merely** only, just, simply, solely, purely, utterly, entirely.

**meretricious** showy, flashy, gaudy, garish, tawdry, cheap.
sham, bogus, false, insincere, spurious, counterfeit. GENUINE

**merge** join, unite, meet, converge, combine, amalgamate, blend, mingle, mix, fuse. SEPARATE

**merger** amalgamation, combination, incorporation, coalition, union. SEPARATION

**meridian** zenith, peak, apex, summit, pinnacle, acme, height, climax, culmination. NADIR

**merit** *v*, deserve, be worthy of, earn, incur, be entitled to, have a right to.
*n*, worth, worthiness, excellence, quality, value, good, virtue, asset, credit, desert, due. FAULT

**meritorious** worthy, deserving, creditable, praiseworthy, commendable, admirable, excellent, good, honourable, virtuous. DESPICABLE

**merriment** mirth, hilarity, laughter, levity, jollity, gaiety, glee, joy, cheer, fun, pleasure, sport, revelry, merrymaking, festivity, conviviality. GLOOM

**merry** jolly, jovial, jocund, mirthful, hilarious, cheerful, blithe, happy, joyful, gleeful, gay, festive, convivial. GLOOMY
tipsy, tiddly (*inf*), squiffy (*inf*). SOBER

**mesh** *n*, net, netting, network, web, snare, trap, tangle, entanglement.
*v*, catch, net, snare, trap, entangle. FREE
engage, interlock, coordinate.

**mesmerize** hypnotize, fascinate, captivate, enthral, entrance, spellbind.

**mess** *n*, untidiness, dirtiness, disorder, disarray, clutter, litter, jumble, muddle, confusion, perplexity. ORDER
difficulty, trouble, plight, predicament, quandary, dilemma, fix (*inf*), pickle (*inf*).
*v*, untidy, dirty, disorder, disarrange, mess up, botch, bungle, muddle, confuse. CLEAR

**message** communication, intimation, missive, dispatch, bulletin, note, letter, memorandum, word, news.

**messenger** courier, runner, bearer, carrier, envoy, emissary, go-between, harbinger, herald.

**messy** untidy, unkempt, slovenly, sloppy, dirty, grubby, disordered, cluttered, muddled, confused. NEAT

**metamorphosis** change, alteration, modification, transformation, transfiguration, mutation, transmutation, conversion, regeneration.

**metaphor** allegory, image, symbol, figure of speech, analogy.

**metaphysical** abstract, theoretical, intangible, immaterial, supernatural, spiritual, intellectual, philosophical, ideal, speculative, abstruse, esoteric. MATERIAL

**mete** distribute, dispense, deal, administer, allot, assign, allocate, apportion. WITHHOLD

**method** way, manner, mode, procedure, process, means, approach, style, technique, system, routine, course.

order, orderliness, organization, planning, structure, regularity. DISORDER

**methodical** systematic, organized, orderly, neat, tidy, businesslike, efficient, structured, planned, exact, precise, meticulous. DISORGANIZED

**meticulous** precise, exact, scrupulous, punctilious, fastidious, particular, fussy, finicky, painstaking, thorough. SLAPDASH

**metropolis** capital, city.

**mettle** character, temperament, disposition, nature, make-up, temper, humour.
spirit, vigour, energy, animation, ardour, fervour, fire, pluck, nerve, grit, courage, bravery, valour, boldness, fortitude, resolution.

**miasmatic** miasmal, miasmic, mephitic, foul, putrid, rank, fetid, stinking, malodorous, noisome, noxious, poisonous, unwholesome. SALUBRIOUS

**microscopic** minute, tiny, minuscule, infinitesimal, imperceptible, negligible. HUGE

**middle** *n*, centre, midpoint, mean, midst, heart, core. EDGE
*adj*, central, halfway, intermediate, medium, mean, medial. EXTREME

**middling** mediocre, fair, average, medium, moderate, passable, tolerable, so-so (*inf*), OK (*inf*).

**midst** middle, centre, heart, thick. EDGE

**mien** bearing, carriage, deportment, manner, demeanour, air, appearance, look, aspect, aura.

**might** power, force, strength, vigour, energy, potency, ability, capability. WEAKNESS

**mighty** powerful, forceful, strong, robust, hardy, sturdy, stalwart, strapping, lusty, hearty, vigorous. WEAK
huge, enormous, gigantic, colossal, massive, immense. TINY

**migrate** move, relocate, resettle, emigrate, immigrate, travel, journey, wander, roam. REMAIN

**migratory** migrant, wandering, roving, nomadic, itinerant, peripatetic, travelling, displaced, unsettled.

**mild** bland, gentle, tender, soft, moderate, meek, docile, kind, compassionate, merciful, clement, lenient, amiable, genial, pacific, calm, placid, serene, equable, mellow, temperate, balmy, pleasant, soothing. HARSH

**mildew** mould, fungus, blight, rust, blast, smut, must, mustiness.

**militant** *adj*, aggressive, belligerent, bellicose, combative, warring, fighting, contending. PACIFIC
*n*, activist, combatant, fighter, warrior.

**military** soldierly, armed, martial, warlike. CIVIL

**militate** oppose, counter, conflict with, go against, contend, war.

**mill** *n*, factory, plant, works.
grinder, crusher, roller.
*v*, grind, pulverize, powder, comminute, triturate, crush, pound.

**mimic** *v*, imitate, ape, copy, impersonate, take off (*inf*), mock, simulate, mirror, echo. resemble.
*n*, mimicker, imitator, copycat (*inf*), impersonator, impressionist.
*adj*, imitative, mimetic, simulated, mock, sham. GENUINE

**minatory** minatorial, minacious, threatening, menacing.

**mince** chop, hash, dice, grind, crumble.
pose, attitudinize, put on airs.

**mind** *n*, intellect, brain, intelligence, mentality, sense, wits, reason, understanding, soul, spirit, attention, thoughts, imagination, head, sanity, rationality.
memory, recollection, remembrance.
opinion, view, attitude, feeling, sentiment, thought, belief, idea, judgment.
inclination, disposition, tendency, desire, wish, urge, notion, fancy, will, purpose, intention.
*v*, care, object, take offence, disapprove, dislike.
regard, heed, pay attention, attend, mark, note, obey, watch, observe, be careful. IGNORE
look after, tend, take care of, watch over. NEGLECT

**mindful** aware, conscious, alert, attentive, regardful, heedful, thoughtful, careful, wary, chary.

**mindless** thoughtless, unthinking, heedless, foolish, witless, senseless, stupid, careless, negligent, inattentive, oblivious. MINDFUL

**mine** *n*, pit, colliery, shaft, excavation, vein, seam, deposit.
source, supply, fund, reserve, treasury, wealth, abundance.

*v*, dig, bore, excavate, tunnel, quarry, extract.
undermine, sap, weaken. PROP

**mingle** mix, commingle, intermingle, intermix, merge, blend, combine, amalgamate, join, unite. SEPARATE
associate, fraternize, consort, hobnob, socialize, circulate.

**miniature** tiny, small, little, wee, minute, diminutive, mini, pygmy, dwarf, midget, baby, toy. LARGE

**minimum** *n*, least, lowest, bottom, nadir. MAXIMUM
*adj*, minimal, least, lowest, smallest, slightest. MAXIMAL

**minion** favourite, darling, pet, follower, dependant, parasite, hanger-on, underling, subordinate, flunky, lackey, bootlicker (*inf*), sycophant, toady, yes man. MASTER

**minister** *n*, clergyman, cleric, churchman, ecclesiastic, vicar, parson, rector, pastor, curate, preacher. LAYMAN
official, dignitary, administrator, executive, ambassador, diplomat, plenipotentiary, envoy, agent, servant.
*v*, attend, wait on, serve, take care of, tend, oblige, accommodate, help, aid, assist.

**ministration** help, aid, assistance, support, service, relief, care.

**ministry** church, clergy, priesthood, holy orders, religion.
government, cabinet, administration, department, office.

**minor** lesser, smaller, secondary, subsidiary, subordinate, inferior, junior, slight, trivial, petty, insignificant, unimportant, inconsiderable, small. MAJOR

**minstrel** musician, singer, troubadour, bard, performer, entertainer.

**mint** *v*, coin, stamp, strike, punch.
make, product, forge, create, fabricate, invent, coin, formulate, think up, devise.
*adj*, perfect, excellent, brand-new, unused.

**minus** less, lacking, without. PLUS

**minute**[1] *n*, moment, second, instant, flash, twinkling, trice, jiffy (*inf*).
note, memorandum, memo (*inf*), record, transcript.

**minute**[2] *adj*, tiny, minuscule, microscopic, infinitesimal, diminutive, small, little, wee, fine. HUGE
detailed, exact, precise, meticulous, painstaking, scrupulous, punctilious. CURSORY

**miracle** wonder, marvel, prodigy, phenomenon.

**miraculous** wonderful, marvellous, extraordinary, phenomenal, amazing, astonishing, incredible, unbelievable, inexplicable, supernatural, preternatural, superhuman, divine. ORDINARY

**mire** marsh, bog, swamp, quagmire, morass, fen, mud, dirt.

**mirror** *n*, glass, looking-glass, reflector.
reflection, copy, replica, representation, likeness, paragon, exemplar, model, pattern.
*v*, reflect, echo, imitate, copy, represent, depict.

**mirth** merriment, gaiety, glee, joy, happiness, cheerfulness, jollity, levity, hilarity, laughter, amusement, fun, sport, pleasure, revelry, festivity, merrymaking. MELANCHOLY

**mirthful** merry, gay, joyful, happy, blithe, cheerful, jolly, jovial, jocund, lighthearted, playful, sportive, festive, lively, vivacious. GLOOMY

**misadventure** misfortune, mischance, mishap, bad luck, accident, calamity, disaster, reverse, setback.

**misanthropy** cynicism, egoism, selfishness, malevolence, inhumanity. PHILANTHROPY

**misapprehend** misunderstand, misconceive, misconstrue, misinterpret, misread, mistake.

**misappropriate** steal, embezzle, peculate, defalcate, misuse, misspend.

**misbehaviour** misconduct, naughtiness, indiscipline, insubordination, disobedience, impropriety, rudeness, misdemeanour, delinquency.

**miscalculate** miscount, misjudge, overestimate, underestimate, err, go wrong, slip up, make a mistake.

**miscarriage** abortion, failure, defeat, frustration, mismanagement, misfortune, misadventure, mishap, mischance. SUCCESS

**miscarry** abort, fail, go wrong, misfire, fall through. SUCCEED

**miscellaneous** mixed, varied, various, diverse, sundry, assorted, heterogeneous, motley, multiform, multifarious.

**miscellany** mixture, variety, diversity, assortment, medley, hotchpotch, pot-pourri, jumble, collection, anthology.

**mischance** misadventure, mishap, bad luck, ill luck, misfortune, accident, calamity, disaster.

**mischief** naughtiness, misconduct, misbehaviour, roguery, rascality, impishness, devilment.
trouble, ill, harm, hurt, injury, damage, annoyance, nuisance. GOOD

**mischievous** naughty, roguish, rascally, impish, puckish, arch, playful, teasing, annoying, exasperating. GOOD
harmful, hurtful, injurious, damaging, detrimental, pernicious, bad, evil, wicked. BENEFICIAL

**misconceive** misunderstand, misapprehend, misinterpret, misconstrue, misread, mistake, misjudge, miscalculate.

**misconduct** misbehaviour, wrongdoing, delinquency, misdemeanour, misdeed, transgression, malpractice, negligence, impropriety, mismanagement.

**misconstrue** misinterpret, misread, misunderstand, misapprehend, misconceive, mistake, misjudge.

**miscreant** wrongdoer, malefactor, criminal, villain, rogue, rascal, scoundrel, blackguard, reprobate, sinner.

**misdeed** misdemeanour, felony, crime, offence, wrong, fault, sin, transgression, trespass, misdoing.

**misdemeanour** misdeed, offence, violation, infringement, peccadillo, transgression, trespass, misconduct, misbehaviour.

**miser** niggard, skinflint, churl, curmudgeon, Scrooge, hoarder, penny-pincher (*inf*), cheapskate (*inf*). SPENDTHRIFT

**miserable** unhappy, sad, sorrowful, forlorn, wretched, woebegone, doleful, depressed, dejected, downcast, despondent, gloomy, melancholy, distressed, disconsolate, heartbroken. HAPPY
contemptible, despicable, base, mean, low, abject, sordid, squalid, wretched, sorry, pathetic, pitiful, pitiable. NOBLE
poor, penniless, impoverished, poverty-stricken, destitute, indigent, needy. RICH

**miserly** niggardly, mean, stingy, close, tight, tight-fisted, parsimonious, penurious, avaricious, covetous, selfish, ungenerous, penny-pinching (*inf*), cheeseparing. GENEROUS

**misery** unhappiness, sadness, sorrow, woe, grief, wretchedness, depression, dejection, despondency, gloom, melancholy, distress, affliction, hardship, suffering, anguish, torment, despair, desolation. JOY
poverty, need, want, privation, indigence, destitution. AFFLUENCE

**misfortune** mischance, bad luck, ill luck, mishap, misadventure, accident, tragedy, calamity, disaster, adversity, affliction, hardship, trouble, trial, tribulation, blow, reverse, setback.

**misgiving** doubt, hesitation, uncertainty, suspicion, mistrust, distrust, qualm, scruple, reservation, anxiety, apprehension. ASSURANCE

**misguided** misled, misinformed, deluded, imprudent, ill-advised, injudicious, foolish, erroneous, mistaken, wrong.

**mishap** accident, misfortune, misadventure, mischance, bad luck, ill luck, calamity, disaster, contretemps.

**misinterpret** misconstrue, misread, misconceive, misunderstand, misapprehend, mistake, misjudge, misrepresent, distort, garble.

**misjudge** miscalculate, underestimate, underrate, overestimate, overrate, misinterpret, misconstrue, misunderstand.

**mislay** lose, misplace. FIND

**mislead** misguide, misdirect, misinform, deceive, delude, fool, trick, hoodwink, lead astray.

**mismanage** mishandle, botch, bungle, mess up, maladminister, misgovern, misdirect, misconduct.

**misprint** mistake, error, erratum, corrigendum, literal, typo (*inf*).

**misprize** underrate, undervalue, underestimate, despise, scorn, disparage, belittle, slight. VALUE

**misrepresent** falsify, distort, twist, pervert, garble, misinterpret, misstate, belie.

**misrule** maladministration, misgovernment, mismanagement, anarchy, lawlessness, chaos, disorder, confusion, tumult, turmoil. ORDER

**miss**[1] *v*, fail, miscarry, lose, omit, overlook, skip, escape, avoid, dodge.
want, need, long for, yearn for, desiderate. HAVE
*n*, failure, miscarriage, mistake, error, slip, blunder, oversight, omission, loss.

**miss**[2] *n*, girl, lass, young lady, damsel, maiden.

**misshapen** deformed, malformed, unshapely, twisted, warped, distorted, crooked, grotesque, ugly. SHAPELY

**missile** projectile, shot, arrow, rocket, weapon.

**missing** absent, lost, mislaid, lacking, wanting, gone. FOUND

**mission** duty, task, job, office, business, assignment, commission, charge, trust, errand, quest, goal, objective, aim, purpose, work, vocation, calling.
embassy, commission, delegation, deputation, legation, ministry.

**missive** letter, epistle, dispatch, communication, message.

**misspend** misuse, misapply, squander, waste, dissipate, throw away.

**misstate** misquote, misreport, misrepresent, falsify, distort, pervert, garble.

**mist** haze, fog, cloud, vapour, steam, condensation, film, drizzle, spray.

**mistake** *n*, error, slip, inaccuracy, fault, oversight, blunder, howler (*inf*), miscalculation, misunderstanding, misapprehension, misconception, gaffe, faux pas.
*v*, misinterpret, misconstrue, misconceive, misunderstand, misapprehend, misjudge, confuse, mix up, get wrong.
err, be wrong, miscalculate, slip up (*inf*).

**mistaken** wrong, erroneous, incorrect, inaccurate, inexact, imprecise, false, untrue, fallacious, unsound, faulty, misguided, misled, misinformed. CORRECT

**mistreat** maltreat, ill-treat, misuse, ill-use, abuse, molest, harm, injure, manhandle, batter.

**mistress** paramour, courtesan, concubine, kept woman, lover, girlfriend, inamorata.
head, proprietor, owner, teacher, governess.

**mistrust** *v*, distrust, doubt, suspect, disbelieve, be wary of, fear. TRUST
*n*, distrust, doubt, scepticism, suspicion, wariness, qualm, misgiving. CONFIDENCE

**misty** hazy, foggy, cloudy, murky, bleary, fuzzy, blurred, obscure, dim, vague, indistinct. CLEAR

**misunderstand** misapprehend, misinterpret, misconstrue, misconceive, mistake, misjudge, misread, mishear. UNDERSTAND

**misunderstanding** mistake, error, misapprehension, misinterpretation, misconstruction, misconception, misjudgment. UNDERSTANDING
disagreement, discord, dissension, clash, conflict, variance, difference, quarrel, argument. AGREEMENT

**misuse** *v*, misemploy, misapply, squander, waste, profane, pervert, abuse, mistreat, maltreat, ill-treat, ill-use, exploit.
*n*, misemployment, misapplication, waste, abuse, maltreatment, ill-use, exploitation.

**mitigate** moderate, lessen, reduce, diminish, abate, alleviate, allay, assuage, ease, relieve, soften, lighten, calm, appease, mollify, pacify, dull, blunt, subdue. AGGRAVATE

**mix** combine, blend, mingle, commingle, intermingle, intermix, compound, alloy, amalgamate, join, cross. SEPARATE
associate, fraternize, consort, hobnob, socialize, mingle.

**mix up,** confuse, muddle, confound, mistake, jumble, garble, scramble, bewilder, puzzle, entangle, involve.

**mixture** mix, combination, blend, compound, alloy, amalgamation, union, cross, hybrid, medley, miscellany, pot-pourri, hotchpotch, jumble, assortment, variety.

**moan** *v*, complain, grumble, lament, bewail, bemoan, mourn, grieve, sorrow, deplore, groan, sigh. REJOICE
*n*, complaint, grumble, lament, wail, cry, sob, groan, sigh.

**mob** crowd, throng, multitude, mass, horde, host, herd, pack, flock, swarm, gang. INDIVIDUAL
rabble, populace, hoi polloi, masses, commonalty.

**mobile** movable, portable, travelling, itinerant, peripatetic, moving, motile, changeable, variable, animated. IMMOBILE

**mock** ridicule, jeer, scoff, laugh at, make fun of, tease, taunt, deceive, delude, deride, sneer, scorn, flout, defy. RESPECT
mimic, ape, simulate, counterfeit, imitate, impersonate, take off (*inf*), lampoon, parody, burlesque, satirize.
*adj*, counterfeit, fake, bogus, spurious, false, sham, imitation, simulated, artificial, feigned, pretended. GENUINE

**mockery** ridicule, jeering, scoffing, gibe, taunt, derision, scorn, contempt. RESPECT
imitation, travesty, lampoon, parody, burlesque, send-up (*inf*), sham, pretence.

**mode** manner, way, method, approach, technique, style, fashion, form, custom, practice.

**model** *n*, example, pattern, template, mould, standard, norm, type, archetype, prototype, original, exemplar, paragon, epitome, ideal.
copy, replica, facsimile, representation, imitation, miniature.
dummy, mannequin, sitter, poser, subject.
design, style, version, mark.
*v*, make, mould, shape, form, fashion, sculpt, carve, cast, plan, design.
wear, show, display, sit, pose.

**moderate** *adj*, reasonable, restrained, controlled, temperate, equable, mild, gentle, steady, calm, middle-of-the-road. EXTREME
average, medium, modest, mediocre, middling, fair, passable, so-so (*inf*).
*v*, temper, control, regulate, lessen, reduce, diminish, mitigate, soften, abate, allay, assuage, appease, pacify, calm, subdue, repress, restrain. AGGRAVATE
arbitrate, judge, umpire, referee, preside, chair.

**moderation** temperance, restraint, control, regulation, reduction, diminution, mitigation, calm, composure, equanimity, fairness, justice. IMMODERATION

**modern** contemporary, current, present, new, novel, fresh, recent, latest, up-to-date, up-to-the-minute, stylish, fashionable. OUT-OF-DATE

**modest** humble, unassuming, unpretentious, self-effacing, retiring, quiet, shy, bashful, reticent, reserved, coy, diffident, meek, demure, discreet, decent, decorous. IMMODEST
moderate, medium, limited, fair, middling, ordinary, simple. EXCESSIVE

**modicum** bit, iota, atom, grain, pinch, drop, scrap, shred, ounce. LOT

**modification** change, alteration, variation, mutation, adjustment, modulation, revision, limitation, restriction, qualification.

**modify** change, alter, vary, adjust, adapt, remodel, revise, transform, convert.
moderate, temper, lower, lessen, limit, restrict, qualify.

**modulate** change, modify, adjust, regulate, vary, inflect, attune, tune, harmonize.

**moiety** half, fifty per cent, part, piece, fragment, portion, share. WHOLE

**moist** damp, clammy, dank, humid, muggy, dewy, wet. DRY

**moisture** liquid, water, damp, dampness, wetness, humidity, vapour, condensation, dew. DRYNESS

**mole** breakwater, groyne, pier, jetty, sea wall, embankment, dyke.

**molest** disturb, bother, pester, plague, harass, badger, harry, worry, annoy, vex, irritate, torment, tease.
accost, assault, attack, mistreat, maltreat, ill-use, abuse, hurt, injure.

**mollify** soothe, calm, pacify, appease, placate, compose, tranquillize, still, quiet. PROVOKE
abate, lessen, reduce, mitigate, moderate, temper, allay, assuage, alleviate, ease, soften. AGGRAVATE

**mollycoddle** pamper, cosset, coddle, spoil, ruin, indulge, pet, baby. DISCIPLINE

**moment** second, minute, instant, twinkling, flash, trice, jiffy (*inf*). AGE
point, juncture, stage, time, hour.
importance, significance, consequence, import, weight, gravity, worth, value, note, concern. INSIGNIFICANCE

**momentary** brief, short, temporary, transitory, transient, fleeting, passing, ephemeral, short-lived. LENGTHY

**momentous** important, significant, consequential, weighty, grave, serious, crucial, critical, vital, major, historic. TRIVIAL

**momentum** impetus, impulse, force, thrust, drive, push, power, strength.

**monarch** ruler, sovereign, crowned head, king, queen, emperor, empress. SUBJECT

**monarchal** monarchical, royal, regal, kingly, queenly.

**monastery** friary, abbey, priory, cloister, religious community.

**monastic** reclusive, solitary, sequestered, cloistered, ascetic, celibate, conventual, monkish, coenobitic, eremitic. SECULAR

**monetary** financial, pecuniary, fiscal.

**money** currency, legal tender, cash, coin, specie, bread (*inf*), dough (*inf*), lucre, wealth, riches, funds, capital, wherewithal, means.

**moneyed** rich, wealthy, affluent, prosperous, well-off, flush (*inf*), loaded (*inf*). POOR

**monitor** *n*, supervisor, overseer, prefect, guide.
*v*, check, observe, watch, supervise, oversee, record.

**monomania** fixation, obsession, *idée fixe*, bee in one's bonnet.

**monopolize** appropriate, take over, control, dominate, corner, hog (*inf*), engross, absorb.

**monopoly** control, domination, exclusiveness, corner, trust, cartel. COMPETITION

**monotonous** boring, tedious, dull, uninteresting, humdrum, repetitive, unvaried, unchanging, uniform, tiresome, wearisome. INTERESTING

**monotony** tedium, dullness, routine, sameness, uniformity.

**monster** freak, mutant, teratism, monstrosity, abortion.
brute, beast, fiend, demon, devil, ogre, villain, savage, barbarian.
giant, colossus, titan, behemoth. MIDGET

**monstrous** hideous, grotesque, horrible, horrendous, dreadful, awful, frightful, terrible, shocking, scandalous, outrageous, atrocious, heinous, fiendish, diabolical, infamous, villainous, odious, loathsome. WONDERFUL
abnormal, unnatural, freakish, deformed, misshapen. NORMAL
huge, colossal, gigantic, enormous, massive, immense, prodigious, gargantuan, titanic. TINY

**monument** memorial, cenotaph, shrine, tombstone, pillar, obelisk, statue, commemoration, remembrance, reminder, memento.

**monumental** enormous, colossal, immense, massive, significant, important, historic, classic, memorable, lasting, awe-inspiring, impressive, striking, majestic, grand. TRIVIAL

**mood** temper, humour, disposition, frame of mind, feeling, vein, spirit.

**moody** sullen, sulky, glum, gloomy, morose, melancholy, broody, peevish, petulant, fretful, irritable, irascible, crabbed, testy, touchy, temperamental, huffish, hurt, offended, cross, angry. EQUABLE
capricious, fickle, changeable, mercurial, volatile, impulsive, fitful, erratic.

**moor**[1] *n*, heath, moorland, fell, wasteland, common.

**moor**[2] *v*, fasten, secure, tie up, berth, anchor. UNTIE

**moot** *adj*, debatable, disputable, arguable, controversial, at issue, open, unresolved, unsettled, doubtful, questionable. INDISPUTABLE
*v*, broach, put forward, propose, introduce, bring up, discuss, debate, ventilate.

**mop** *v*, swab, wash, clean, wipe, sponge, soak up.
*n*, shock, mane, tangle.

**mope** brood, fret, sulk, pout, be gloomy, be dejected, grieve, pine, languish, moon.

**moral** *adj*, ethical, good, virtuous, pure, right, proper, just, fair, honest, upright, honourable, noble, high-minded, principled. IMMORAL
*n*, lesson, message, maxim, adage, proverb, saying, aphorism, saw.

**morale** confidence, spirit, heart, mood, humour, will.

**morals** morality, integrity, ethics, principles, scruples, ideals, standards, mores, customs, habits, manners, behaviour, conduct.

**morass** swamp, marsh, bog, fen, quagmire, slough.

**morbid** unhealthy, unwholesome, sick, ghoulish, macabre, gruesome, grisly, grim, sombre, melancholy, morose, gloomy, pessimistic.
pathological, diseased, infected, unsound, unhealthy, sick, sickly. HEALTHY

**mordant** mordacious, caustic, biting, cutting, trenchant, incisive, sarcastic, stinging, sharp, acid, acerbic, bitter, pungent. SOOTHING

**more** *adj*, further, additional, added, extra, fresh, new, other. FEWER
*adv*, further, longer, again, besides, in addition. LESS

**moreover** furthermore, further, besides, in addition, too, as well, also.

**morning** daybreak, sunrise, dawn, morn, forenoon.

**moron** idiot, imbecile, cretin, halfwit, simpleton, fool, ass, donkey, dolt, nincompoop, blockhead, dunce, ignoramus, dope (*inf*). GENIUS

**morose** gloomy, glum, melancholy, depressed, moody, sullen, sulky, sour, surly, crabbed, gruff, crusty, crotchety, ill-tempered. GENIAL

**morsel** bit, piece, fragment, crumb, scrap, grain, bite, mouthful, titbit, nibble, taste.

**mortal** *adj*, worldly, earthly, human, physical, corporeal, temporal, ephemeral. IMMORTAL
deadly, fatal, lethal, destructive, murderous, killing.
great, extreme, intense, terrible, awful, dire, severe, grave.
*n*, human being, man, person, individual, earthling. GOD

**mortality** humanity, temporality, ephemerality, death, fatality, destruction. IMMORTALITY

**mortification** humiliation, shame, chagrin, embarrassment, discomfiture, discomposure, abashment, confusion, annoyance, vexation, dissatisfaction, displeasure. DELIGHT

**mortify** humiliate, humble, abase, shame, chagrin, embarrass, discomfit, discompose, abash, confound, chasten, crush, annoy, vex, displease. PLEASE
discipline, control, subdue, subjugate. INDULGE
fester, putrefy, gangrene, necrose, rot, corrupt.

**mortuary** morgue, funeral parlour, chapel of rest.

**most** *adj*, greatest, utmost, extreme, nearly all. FEWEST
*n*, majority, greater part, greater number, nearly all, utmost. LEAST

**mostly** mainly, chiefly, principally, on the whole, largely, generally, usually, as a rule.

**mother** *n*, parent, mater, mum (*inf*), mummy (*inf*), mama, ma (*inf*). FATHER
*v*, bear, give birth to, nurture, rear, nurse, care for, protect, pamper, indulge.

**motherly** maternal, kind, loving, tender, affectionate, caring, protective, gentle, warm, parental.

**motion** *n*, movement, action, activity, mobility, locomotion, travel, passage, flow, drift. REST
gesture, gesticulation, signal, sign.
proposal, proposition, suggestion, recommendation.
*v*, signal, gesticulate, gesture, wave, beckon, nod.

**motionless** stationary, immobile, still, unmoving, paralysed, transfixed, fixed, immovable, static, inanimate, inert. MOVING

**motivate** incite, prompt, move, lead, spur, impel, drive, stimulate, provoke, persuade, induce, cause, instigate, actuate. DETER

**motive** reason, cause, ground, object, purpose, intention, stimulus, spur, incentive, inducement, motivation, drive, impulse, inspiration.

**motley** mixed, varied, assorted, miscellaneous, diverse, heterogeneous, dissimilar. UNIFORM
multicoloured, polychromatic, chequered, variegated.

**mottled** speckled, dappled, piebald, brindled, tabby, streaked, flecked, spotted, blotchy, motley, chequered, variegated.

**motto** slogan, watchword, legend, inscription, saying, maxim, proverb, adage, aphorism, saw.

**mould**[1] *n*, die, matrix, pattern, cast, form, shape, style, fashion, design, frame, structure, format, build, brand, make, stamp, type, sort, kind, nature, character.
*v*, shape, form, model, fashion, cast, forge, stamp, make, influence, affect.

**mould**[2] *n*, mildew, fungus, blight, mustiness, mouldiness.

**moulder** rot, decay, decompose, crumble, disintegrate, perish.

**mouldy** mildewed, blighted, musty, fusty, stale, rotting, decaying, rotten, bad. FRESH

**mound** hill, hillock, knoll, hummock, heap, pile, stack, bank, rampart, bulwark, earthwork, barrow, tumulus.

**mount** *v*, climb, ascend, go up, rise, soar, scale, board, get on. DESCEND
increase, grow, multiply, accummulate, escalate, intensify, swell. DECREASE
prepare, set up, exhibit, display, produce, stage.
*n*, mounting, backing, setting, frame, stand, base, support.
horse, steed, charger.

**mountebank** charlatan, quack, impostor, pretender, fraud, fake, cheat, con man (*inf*).

**mourn** lament, grieve, sorrow, bewail, bemoan, deplore, regret, miss, weep, wail. REJOICE

**mournful** sad, sorrowful, unhappy, woeful, distressing, tragic, grievous, lamentable, deplorable, piteous, plaintive, depressing, sombre, lugubrious, funereal, gloomy, melancholy, depressed, downcast, doleful, disconsolate, heartbroken. JOYFUL

**mourning** grief, sorrow, woe, lamentation, bereavement.

**mouth** jaws, lips, gob (*inf*), trap (*inf*).
orifice, opening, aperture, entrance, inlet.
impudence, insolence, cheek (*inf*), sauce (*inf*), lip (*inf*).

**movable** mobile, portable, transportable, transferable, changeable. FIXED

**movables** furniture, goods, chattels, belongings, possessions, effects, property. IMMOVABLES

**move** *v*, stir, budge, shift, go, advance, progress, proceed, carry, transport, change, transfer.
relocate, remove, migrate, leave, quit. STAY
push, shove, propel, drive, impel.
prompt, stimulate, urge, impel, induce, persuade, incite, provoke, actuate, instigate, motivate, inspire, cause, lead. DETER
touch, affect, impress, influence, stir, excite.
propose, suggest, recommend, advocate.
*n*, movement, motion, action, step, manoeuvre, stratagem.
relocation, removal, migration.

**movement** motion, move, action, gesture, activity, stir, shift, change, advance, progress, course, drift, trend.
campaign, crusade, drive, faction, party, group, organization.
rhythm, beat, tempo, lilt, swing, pace, metre.
part, passage, section, division.
works, workings, mechanism, machinery.

**moving** touching, affecting, emotive, poignant, pathetic, stirring, inspiring, impressive, stimulating.
mobile, movable, active, running, in motion. STILL

**mow** cut, trim, clip, shear, prune, crop.
**mow down,** slaughter, massacre, butcher.

**much** *adj*, abundant, plentiful, plenteous, ample, considerable, great, a lot of. LITTLE
*adv*, greatly, considerably, a lot, a great deal, often, frequently.
nearly, almost, practically.
*n*, plenty, a lot, lots (*inf*), loads (*inf*), heaps (*inf*).

**mucilaginous** sticky, gummy, viscous, glutinous, mucous, slimy, viscid, gelatinous.

**muck** dung, ordure, manure, sewage, sludge, dirt, filth, mud, mire.

**mucky** dirty, filthy, grimy, grubby, soiled, muddy. CLEAN

**mud** clay, dirt, muck, mire, sludge.

**muddle** *v*, confuse, mix up, jumble, scramble, disorder, disarrange, mess up.
perplex, bewilder, confuse, confound, befuddle, stupefy.
*n*, confusion, mix-up, jumble, disorder, disarray, mess, chaos. ORDER
perplexity, bewilderment, confusion, stupefaction, daze, disorientation.

**muddy** mucky, miry, boggy, swampy, marshy, dirty, grimy. CLEAN
cloudy, turbid, murky, dingy, dull, opaque, obscure, vague, unclear. CLEAR

**muffle** envelop, wrap, swathe, cover, cloak, conceal, mask, disguise. EXPOSE
deaden, damp, mute, stifle, gag, muzzle, silence, suppress.

**muffled** muted, subdued, stifled, suppressed, soft, faint, dull. LOUD

**muggy** humid, clammy, sticky, damp, dank, moist, sultry, oppressive, close. FRESH

**mulct** *v*, cheat, defraud, swindle.
fine, penalize, punish.
*n*, fine, penalty, damages, forfeiture.

**mulish** stubborn, obstinate, headstrong, wilful, obdurate, intransigent, inflexible, perverse, contrary, intractable, refractory, recalcitrant. AMENABLE

**multifarious** manifold, many, numerous, multitudinous, multiple, multiform, varied, diverse, miscellaneous, sundry, motley, variegated, diversified.

**multiply** increase, augment, grow, build up, intensify, expand, extend, spread, breed, reproduce, propagate, proliferate. DECREASE

**multitude** crowd, throng, horde, flock, swarm, mob, assembly, congregation, army, legion, host, mass, myriad, lot. FEW

**mum** quiet, silent, dumb, mute, speechless, uncommunicative, taciturn. TALKATIVE

**mumble** mutter, murmur. EXCLAIM

**munch** chew, masticate, champ, crunch.

**mundane** banal, ordinary, everyday, commonplace, trite, humdrum, routine. UNUSUAL
worldly, earthly, terrestrial, temporal, secular, physical, material. SPIRITUAL

**municipal** civil, civic, urban, town, city, borough, local, public, community.

**munificent** generous, bountiful, bounteous, open-handed, liberal, unstinting, lavish, princely, beneficent, magnanimous, charitable, philanthropic. MEAN

**munitions** ammunition, weapons, arms, materiel, stores, supplies, equipment, gear.

**murder** *v*, kill, slay, assassinate, dispatch, bump off (*inf*), do in (*inf*), slaughter, butcher, massacre, destroy.
*n*, homicide, manslaughter, killing, assassination, slaughter, butchery, massacre, destruction.

**murderer** killer, slayer, assassin, slaughterer, butcher.

**murderous** homicidal, savage, barbarous, cruel, brutal, ferocious, bloodthirsty, sanguinary, deadly, lethal.
difficult, arduous, rigorous, strenuous, exhausting, dangerous, perilous. EASY

**murky** dark, gloomy, dismal, dusky, dull, dim, cloudy, overcast, grey, misty, foggy, obscure. CLEAR

**murmur** *v*, mutter, mumble, whisper, babble, rumble, hum.
complain, grumble, grouse, carp.
*n*, mutter, mumble, whisper, undertone, babble, rumble, hum, drone.
complaint, grumble, grouse.

**muscular** brawny, sinewy, beefy (*inf*), husky (*inf*), strapping, stalwart, burly, lusty, strong, robust, vigorous, energetic, athletic. PUNY

**muse** ruminate, reflect, ponder, contemplate, meditate, brood, mull over, cogitate, consider, deliberate, think over.

**mushroom** increase, grow, expand, boom, spring up, burgeon, flourish, prosper, thrive. DECLINE

**music** tune, melody, harmony, composition, opus, score.

**musical** tuneful, melodious, melodic, harmonious, euphonious, mellifluous, dulcet, lyrical. DISCORDANT

**musician** player, instrumantalist, composer, singer, performer, artiste, minstrel.

**muster** *v*, convene, convoke, assemble, congregate, rally, meet, collect, gather, summon, marshal, round up. DISPERSE
*n*, meeting, rally, assembly, congregation, gathering, collection, convention, convocation.

**musty** mouldy, mildewy, stale, fusty, frowsty, rank, ill-smelling, stuffy, old, ancient. FRESH

**mutable** changeable, variable, alterable, changing, inconstant, unstable, unsteady, uncertain, irresolute, unsettled, vacillating, fluctuating, wavering, fickle, capricious. CONSTANT

**mutation** change, alteration, modification, variation, transformation, metamorphosis.

**mute** *adj*, silent, dumb, voiceless, speechless, mum, taciturn, uncommunicative, still, quiet, unexpressed, unspoken. LOUD
*v*, soften, lower, subdue, damp, deaden, muffle, stifle.

**mutilate** maim, cripple, disable, disfigure, deface, mar, damage, injure, mangle, butcher, dismember, amputate. MEND

**mutinous** rebellious, seditious, insurgent, revolutionary, riotous, unruly, turbulent, insubordinate, disobedient, refractory, contumacious, ungovernable. OBEDIENT

**mutiny** *n*, rebellion, sedition, insurrection, revolution, revolt, uprising, riot, insubordination, defiance, disobedience. OBEDIENCE
*v*, rebel, revolt, rise up, resist, disobey. OBEY

**mutter** mumble, murmur, complain, grumble. EXCLAIM

**mutual** reciprocal, interchangeable, interactive, joint, shared, common, communal.

**myopic** short-sighted, near-sighted. LONG-SIGHTED

**myriad** *adj*, innumerable, countless, untold, incalculable, many, numerous. FEW
*n*, host, mass, multitude, thousands, millions.

**mysterious** unexplainable, inexplicable, enigmatic, cryptic, puzzling, baffling, incomprehensible, unfathomable, strange, curious, weird, uncanny, dark, obscure, hidden, veiled, secret, secretive, inscrutable. PLAIN

**mystery** enigma, riddle, conundrum, puzzle, question, secret.

**mystical** occult, esoteric, cabalistic, abstruse, arcane, metaphysical, supernatural, transcendental, mysterious, enigmatic, cryptic.

**mystify** puzzle, baffle, perplex, nonplus, bewilder, confuse, confound, stump. ENLIGHTEN

**myth** legend, saga, tale, story, fable, parable, allegory, tradition. HISTORY
lie, fib, falsehood, untruth, fabrication, fiction, fantasy, illusion. FACT

**mythical** mythological, legendary, fabled, storied, traditional, fabulous, fantastic. HISTORICAL
fictitious, make-believe, made-up, invented, fanciful, imaginary, unreal, false, untrue. REAL

# N

**nab** seize, grab, snatch, catch, capture, arrest. RELEASE

**nag** *v*, scold, berate, henpeck, carp, cavil, pester, plague, badger, hector, harass, vex, irritate, annoy, worry, bother, torment.
*n*, shrew, termagant, virago, scold.

**naive** ingenuous, artless, guileless, unsophisticated, simple, innocent, trusting, credulous, gullible, open, frank, candid. ARTFUL

**naked** nude, unclothed, undressed, uncovered, exposed, bare, stripped, denuded, starkers (*inf*), in the altogether (*inf*). CLOTHED
unvarnished, unadorned, undisguised, open, stark, obvious, evident, manifest, plain, simple. CONCEALED

**name** *n*, title, appellation, denomination, designation, term, label, epithet, cognomen, nickname, sobriquet, handle (*inf*), moniker (*inf*).
reputation, character, credit, esteem, honour, distinction, note, fame, renown, eminence, celebrity.
*v*, call, baptize, christen, dub, style, term, label, entitle, denominate.
designate, nominate, appoint, select, choose, specify, mention, cite.

**nap** doze, slumber, drowse, snooze (*inf*), sleep, rest.

**narcotic** *n*, drug, opiate, sedative, tranquillizer, anodyne, analgesic, painkiller, anaesthetic. STIMULANT
*adj*, soporific, hypnotic, sedative, calming, numbing, analgesic.

**narrate** tell, relate, recount, rehearse, report, chronicle, detail, describe.

**narration** narrative, account, story, tale, report, chronicle, history, recital, description, relation.

**narrow** *adj*, thin, slender, attenuated, fine. WIDE
tight, cramped, pinched, constricted, confined, restricted, limited, straitened, close, meagre, scanty. BROAD
*v*, taper, attenuate, constrict, confine, restrict, limit, straiten, tighten. BROADEN

**narrow-minded** biased, prejudiced, bigoted, illiberal, intolerant, insular, parochial, provincial, limited. BROAD-MINDED

**nascent** beginning, incipient, budding, developing, young, embryonic. MATURE

**nasty** unpleasant, disagreeable, offensive, repulsive, revolting, disgusting, nauseating, odious, loathsome, objectionable, obnoxious, horrible, vile, foul, polluted, dirty, filthy, indecent, obscene. PLEASANT
spiteful, malicious, mean, vicious, malevolent, ill-tempered, ill-natured, wicked, evil, villainous. BENEVOLENT

**nation** people, race, country, land, realm, empire, commonwealth, state, population, society, community.

**national** civil, state, nationwide, general, domestic, internal. LOCAL

**native** *n*, inhabitant, resident, dweller, citizen, national, aborigine, autochthon, indigene. FOREIGNER
*adj*, inborn, inbred, innate, connate, congenital, hereditary, natural, inherent, immanent, intrinsic. ACQUIRED
local, vernacular, domestic, home, mother, indigenous, aboriginal, autochthonous, original. FOREIGN

**natural** normal, typical, regular, usual, ordinary, common, logical, reasonable. ABNORMAL
inborn, inbred, innate, congenital, inherent, intrinsic, native, indigenous, basic, fundamental, instinctive, intuitive. ACQUIRED
artless, guileless, ingenuous, naive, unsophisticated, simple, frank, open, candid,

sincere, unaffected, spontaneous, impulsive. ARTFUL
genuine, real, authentic, pure, unmixed, raw, unrefined. ARTIFICIAL

**naturalize** habituate, familiarize, domesticate, accustom, acclimatize, adapt, adopt, introduce.

**nature** essence, character, identity, constitution, make-up, quality.
disposition, temper, humour, mood, temperament, character, personality.
kind, sort, type, class, category, style, brand, variety.
creation, earth, world, universe, cosmos.

**naughty** bad, wicked, mischievous, disobedient, defiant, wayward, unruly, impish, roguish, vexatious, exasperating. GOOD
bawdy, ribald, risqué, titillating, smutty, vulgar, rude, improper, indecent.

**nausea** biliousness, queasiness, sickness, vomiting.
disgust, revulsion, repugnance, loathing, aversion, dislike. RELISH

**nauseate** sicken, disgust, revolt, repel, offend, appal.

**nauseous** nauseating, sickening, disgusting, revolting, repulsive, loathsome, offensive, distasteful. PLEASANT

**nautical** naval, marine, maritime, seafaring, seagoing, sailing.

**navigate** direct, guide, pilot, steer, drive, plot, plan, cross, sail, cruise, voyage.

**navy** fleet, flotilla, armada, marine.

**near** *adj*, close, nearby, neighbouring, adjacent, adjoining, contiguous. FAR
imminent, impending, forthcoming, approaching, next. DISTANT
dear, intimate, familiar, close, related, akin. REMOTE
mean, niggardly, parsimonious, stingy, miserly, tight-fisted, close-fisted, ungenerous. GENEROUS
*adv*, close, close by, nigh, nearby.
*v*, approach, draw near, border on, come close.

**nearly** almost, practically, all but, virtually, well-nigh, just about, approximately, roughly, more or less.

**neat** tidy, orderly, trim, smart, spruce, clean, spick-and-span, fastidious, methodical. UNTIDY
clever, dexterous, adroit, deft, adept, apt, skilful, expert. CLUMSY
pure, unadulterated, unmixed, undiluted, straight.

**neaten** tidy, straighten, spruce up, clean, groom, arrange, order. DISARRANGE

**nebulous** vague, indeterminate, obscure, indistinct, hazy, misty, cloudy, shapeless, amorphous. CLEAR

**necessary** needed, required, needful, requisite, essential, vital, indispensable, imperative, compulsory, obligatory, unavoidable, inescapable, inevitable, certain. UNNECESSARY

**necessitate** cause, require, entail, demand, call for, oblige, force, compel, impel, constrain, coerce.

**necessitous** needy, poor, impoverished, poverty-stricken, indigent, impecunious, penurious, penniless, destitute, distressed. RICH

**necessity** essential, fundamental, requisite, prerequisite, need, want, requirement, demand, exigency, indispensability, needfulness, compulsion, obligation, inevitability.
poverty, indigence, penury, destitution, need. WEALTH

**necromancy** magic, black magic, sorcery, witchcraft, wizardry, voodoo, divination.

**need** *v*, lack, miss, want, require, demand, call for, necessitate. HAVE
*n*, necessity, lack, want, desideratum, requirement, demand, requisite, obligation, exigency, urgency, emergency.
poverty, indigence, penury, destitution, distress, extremity, privation. WEALTH

**needful** needed, necessary, required, requisite, essential, vital, indispensable. UNNECESSARY

**needless** unnecessary, gratuitous, redundant, superfluous, unwanted, uncalled-for, excessive, dispensable, nonessential, expendable, useless. NEEDFUL

**needy** poor, necessitous, indigent, impecunious, impoverished, poverty-stricken, penniless, destitute, deprived, underprivileged. WEALTHY

**nefarious** wicked, evil, bad, sinful, iniquitous, heinous, flagitious, villainous, infa mous, vile, odious, abominable, execrable horrible, dreadful, atrocious, outrageous scandalous, monstrous. ADMIRABLE

**negate** nullify, annul, cancel, invalidate, revoke, repeal, rescind, abrogate, countermand.

deny, contradict, gainsay, refute, disprove, oppose. AFFIRM

**negation** opposite, reverse, contrary, antithesis.

denial, contradiction, disavowal, disclaimer, retraction, repudiation, refusal, rejection, renunciation.

nothing, nullity, nonentity, void, vacuity.

**negative** *adj*, denying, contradictory, opposing, contrary, nullifying, invalidating. POSITIVE

pessimistic, cynical, unhelpful, uncooperative, contrary, antagonistic.

*n*, contradiction, denial, negation, refusal, no.

**neglect** *v*, disregard, ignore, overlook, pass over, omit, miss, skip, forget, shirk, skimp, spurn, slight, abandon, leave alone.

*n*, negligence, disregard, oversight, omission, remissness, forgetfulness, default, dereliction, carelessness, inattention, laxity. ATTENTION

**neglectful** negligent, remiss, careless, heedless, regardless, disregardful, inattentive, unmindful, thoughtless, forgetful. ATTENTIVE

**negligence** neglect, disregard, oversight, omission, dereliction, default, remissness, forgetfulness, inattention, carelessness, heedlessness, thoughtlessness, indifference, laxity, slackness. ATTENTION

**negligent** neglectful, remiss, careless, heedless, inattentive, unmindful, forgetful, slack, lax, indifferent, offhand, nonchalant. ATTENTIVE

**negligible** unimportant, insignificant, inconsequential, trifling, trivial, minor, small, imperceptible. IMPORTANT

**negotiate** bargain, deal, debate, discuss, arrange, work out, mediate, arbitrate, conciliate, settle, compromise, transact, manage, get through, clear, pass.

**neighbourhood** vicinity, environs, surroundings, district, quarter, locality, community.

nearness, proximity, propinquity, region.

**neighbouring** adjoining, adjacent, contiguous, connecting, proximate, near, close, nearby, nigh. DISTANT

**neighbourly** sociable, friendly, amiable, cordial, hospitable, kind, generous, obliging, attentive, helpful, civil. UNFRIENDLY

**neophyte** convert, proselyte, novice, beginner, tyro, learner, student, pupil, apprentice, trainee. MASTER

**nerve** *n*, courage, bravery, valour, mettle, pluck, guts (*inf*), fortitude, endurance, will, firmness, determination, resolution, steadfastness, power, might, strength, vigour. WEAKNESS

audacity, boldness, effrontery, impudence, impertinence, insolence, gall, cheek (*inf*). TIMIDITY

*v*, steel, brace, strengthen, fortify, embolden, invigorate, hearten, encourage. WEAKEN

**nervous** excitable, highly strung, tense, agitated, shaky, anxious, worried, apprehensive, fearful, fidgety, jumpy, jittery (*inf*), nervy (*inf*), edgy, on edge, uneasy, hesitant, timid. CALM

**nestle** snuggle, cuddle, huddle, settle, lodge, shelter.

**net** *n*, mesh, web, netting, network, reticulum, lace.

*v*, catch, capture, bag, trap, ensnare, enmesh. RELEASE

**nether** lower, under, bottom, inferior. UPPER

**nettle** vex, annoy, irritate, irk, pique, chafe, provoke, ruffle, exasperate, bother, harass, incense, enrage. SOOTHE

**network** system, organization, complex, maze, labyrinth, grid, mesh, net, web.

**neutral** impartial, nonpartisan, unbiased, unprejudiced, disinterested, indifferent, dispassionate, objective, aloof, uninvolved, uncommitted, nonaligned. PARTISAN

bland, dull, drab, colourless, achromatic, indeterminate, indistinguishable.

**neutralize** counteract, counterbalance, offset, compensate for, cancel, negate, nullify, annul, undo. INTENSIFY

**nevertheless** nonetheless, notwithstanding, however, yet, but, still.

**new** recent, latest, modern, contemporary, current, novel, original, newfangled, unknown, unfamiliar, fresh, unused, other, additional, renewed, improved, changed. OLD

**news** report, account, information, intelligence, word, advice, tidings, dispatch, communiqué, bulletin.

**next** following, succeeding, subsequent, later, consequent. LAST
neighbouring, adjacent, adjoining, nearest, closest.

**nibble** *v*, bite, gnaw, peck at, eat.
*n*, bite, morsel, titbit, taste.

**nice** pleasant, agreeable, enjoyable, delightful, charming, attractive, pleasing, likable, friendly, kind, good, polite. NASTY
fine, subtle, delicate, fastidious, particular, discriminating, exact, precise, accurate, strict, scrupulous, minute.

**nicety** delicacy, subtlety, refinement, distinction, nuance.
precision, accuracy, exactitude, fastidiousness, scrupulousness.

**niche** recess, alcove, nook, cranny, corner.

**nick** *n*, notch, indentation, cut, chip, scratch, dent, groove.
*v*, notch, cut, chip, scratch, dent.

**niggardly** mean, miserly, stingy, parsimonious, close-fisted, tight, tight-fisted, ungenerous, frugal, sparing. GENEROUS
meagre, scanty, paltry, inadequate, insufficient. AMPLE

**nigh** *adj*, near, close, nearby, proximate, adjacent, next, imminent, impending. DISTANT
*adv*, nearly, almost, practically, about, approximately.

**night** dark, darkness, night-time. DAY

**nightfall** sunset, dusk, twilight, evening. DAYBREAK

**nil** nothing, nought, zero, love.

**nimble** agile, sprightly, spry, active, lively, smart, quick, brisk, prompt, ready, alert, deft, dexterous. CLUMSY

**nip**[1] *v*, bite, pinch, squeeze, compress, tweak, snip, clip, catch, grip.

**nip**[2] *n*, dram, draught, drop, sip, swig (*inf*), shot (*inf*).

**nipple** teat, tit, mamilla, papilla, dug, pap.

**nobility** gentry, aristocracy, upper class, peerage, lords, nobles. COMMONALTY
nobleness, dignity, exaltation, eminence, loftiness, greatness, distinction, grandeur, magnificence, honour, virtue, goodness, integrity. LOWLINESS

**noble** *n*, nobleman, noblewoman, aristocrat, patrician, peer, peeress, lord, lady. COMMONER
*adj*, aristocratic, patrician, highborn, blueblooded, titled. LOWBORN
magnanimous, generous, worthy, honourable, virtuous, good, great, dignified, distinguished, eminent, lofty, elevated, lordly, stately, grand, magnificent, superior, fine, excellent. BASE

**nobody** no-one, nonentity, nothing, cipher. SOMEBODY

**nocturnal** night, nightly, crepuscular. DIURNAL

**nod** bow, indicate, acknowledge, agree, assent.
drowse, nap, doze, sleep. WAKE

**node** protuberance, nodule, knob, knot, swelling, lump, bump.

**noise** sound, din, row, racket, clamour, outcry, uproar, hubbub, tumult, commotion, pandemonium, talk, cry. SILENCE

**noiseless** silent, inaudible, quiet, still, mute. LOUD

**noisome** offensive, foul, fetid, putrid, malodorous, mephitic, noxious, poisonous, pestilential, unhealthy, unwholesome, harmful, pernicious, deleterious, detrimental, mischievous, injurious, hurtful. WHOLESOME

**noisy** loud, clamorous, boisterous, obstreperous, riotous, uproarious, turbulent, tumultuous, vociferous, cacophonous, strident, blaring, deafening, ear-splitting. QUIET

**nomadic** wandering, roving, vagrant, travelling, itinerant, peripatetic, migrant, migratory.

**nominal** titular, formal, theoretical, so-called, supposed, would-be, self-styled. ACTUAL
token, minimal, small, inconsiderable. EXCESSIVE

**nominate** propose, suggest, present, name, choose, select, elect, appoint, assign, designate.

**nonchalant** unconcerned, dispassionate, indifferent, apathetic, careless, blasé, insouciant, carefree, cool, calm, easy, casual, offhand. CONCERNED

**nondescript** unclassifiable, indefinite, indeterminate, unremarkable, unexceptional, characterless, dull, bland, ordinary, commonplace. DISTINCTIVE

**nonentity** nothing, nobody, cipher. SOMEBODY

**nonesuch** paragon, nonpareil, ideal, exemplar, model, pattern.

**nonpareil** *adj*, peerless, matchless, unmatched, unequalled, unparalleled, incomparable, unique, unrivalled, supreme. ORDINARY

*n*, paragon, nonesuch, ideal, exemplar.

**nonplus** confound, perplex, bewilder, confuse, puzzle, baffle, mystify, stump, disconcert, take aback, dumbfound, astonish, astound. ENLIGHTEN

**nonsense** rubbish, trash, rot, balderdash, humbug, twaddle, drivel, bosh, gibberish, senselessness, absurdity, silliness, stupidity, foolishness, folly, fatuity. SENSE

**nonsensical** senseless, meaningless, ridiculous, ludicrous, absurd, crazy, silly, foolish. SENSIBLE

**nook** corner, recess, niche, alcove, cranny, cubbyhole, retreat.

**norm** average, mean, rule, standard, measure, criterion, yardstick, type, model.

**normal** usual, common, general, ordinary, conventional, customary, habitual, routine, regular, standard, typical, natural, rational, sane, well-adjusted. ABNORMAL

**nosegay** posy, bouquet, bunch, spray, corsage.

**nostalgia** yearning, longing, reminiscence, remembrance, wistfulness, regret, homesickness.

**nosy** inquisitive, curious, prying, meddlesome, interfering.

**notable** *adj*, remarkable, noteworthy, signal, noticeable, conspicuous, marked, striking, memorable, unusual, distinctive, noted, distinguished, celebrated, eminent, famous. INSIGNIFICANT

*n*, personage, celebrity, VIP, dignitary, somebody. NOBODY

**notch** *n*, cut, nick, incision, identation, groove, score.

*v*, cut, nick, indent, serrate.

**note** *n*, memorandum, memo, record, minute, jotting, annotation, comment, remark, message, letter, communication.

fame, renown, celebrity, distinction, prestige, eminence, regard, esteem, significance, importance, consequence. INSIGNIFICANCE

heed, attention, regard, notice, observation.

*v*, notice, perceive, remark, observe, heed, mark, register, record, jot down. IGNORE

**noted** famous, renowned, celebrated, well-known, illustrious, distinguished, eminent, notable. UNKNOWN

**noteworthy** remarkable, notable, signal, outstanding, memorable, exceptional, unusual, extraordinary, important, significant. ORDINARY

**nothing** nought, nil, zero, cipher, nonentity, nobody, void, nothingness, nihility, nullity, nonexistence. SOMETHING

**notice** *n*, attention, observation, note, heed, regard, consideration, respect.

information, notification, advice, warning, announcement, declaration, intimation, news.

poster, placard, sign, bill, advertisement.

review, criticism, comment.

*v*, note, perceive, remark, observe, see, detect, mark, heed. MISS

**noticeable** perceptible, appreciable, conspicuous, distinct, clear, plain, evident, obvious, manifest, visible, apparent. INCONSPICUOUS

**notification** announcement, declaration, notice, warning, advice, intimation, information, intelligence, statement, message, communication.

**notify** inform, tell, advise, warn, acquaint, apprise, announce, declare, disclose, reveal. SUPPRESS

**notion** idea, impression, concept, sentiment, thought, opinion, view, belief, theory, conception, apprehension, understanding.

whim, caprice, fancy, inclination.

**notoriety** infamy, disrepute, obloquy, opprobrium, disgrace, dishonour. ILLUSTRIOUSNESS

**notorious** infamous, disreputable, ignominious, dishonourable, disgraceful, scandalous. ILLUSTRIOUS

**notwithstanding** despite, although, though, nevertheless, however, yet.

**nought** zero, nil, nothing, naught, nothingness.

**nourish** feed, sustain, nurture, nurse, tend, maintain, support, harbour, cherish, foster, encourage, promote. STARVE

**nourishing** nutritive, nutritious, alimentary, alimentative, healthy, wholesome, beneficial. UNHEALTHY

**nourishment** nutrition, nutriment, food, sustenance, aliment, alimentation.

**novel** *adj*, new, fresh, original, innovative, different, uncommon, unusual, unfamiliar, strange. STALE
*n*, story, tale, narrative, romance, fiction, book.

**novelty** newness, freshness, originality, innovation, difference, unfamiliarity. STALENESS
trifle, bagatelle, trinket, knick-knack, toy, gadget.

**novice** beginner, tyro, neophyte, learner, pupil, student, apprentice, probationer, trainee, amateur. MASTER

**now** immediately, at once, straightaway, right away. LATER
nowadays, today, at the moment, at present. THEN

**noxious** poisonous, toxic, pernicious, harmful, hurtful, injurious, baleful, deleterious, detrimental, deadly, destructive, noisome, unwholesome, unhealthy, pestilential, foul. BENEFICIAL

**nuance** shade, gradation, distinction, subtlety, refinement, trace, touch, hint, suggestion.

**nucleus** centre, focus, core, kernel, heart, nub, essence.

**nude** naked, bare, unclothed, undressed, uncovered, exposed, starkers (*inf*), in the altogether (*inf*), *au naturel*. CLOTHED

**nudge** push, shove, poke, prod, dig, elbow, jog.

**nugatory** worthless, trifling, frivolous, insignificant, ineffective, futile, useless, vain, bootless, unavailing. VALUABLE

**nuisance** annoyance, vexation, bother, pest, pain (*inf*), bore, trouble, inconvenience. PLEASURE

**null** void, invalid, worthless, nugatory, useless, futile, ineffectual, characterless, nonexistent. VALID

**nullify** annul, abrogate, revoke, rescind, repeal, quash, invalidate, cancel, negate, abolish.

**numb** dead, deadened, benumbed, insensible, insensate, frozen, paralysed, immobile, unfeeling, insensitive. SENSITIVE

**number** *n*, figure, numeral, digit, integer.
sum, total, aggregate, collection, amount, quantity, crowd, multitude, host, throng, many.
copy, issue, edition.
*v*, count, enumerate, calculate, compute, reckon, total, add, include.

**numberless** countless, innumerable, infinite, incalculable, untold, many, myriad, multitudinous. FEW

**numeral** number, figure, digit, integer, character, symbol.

**numerous** many, manifold, several, multiple, abundant, plentiful, innumerable, numberless. FEW

**nuptial** conjugal, connubial, matrimonial, marital, bridal, wedding.

**nurse** tend, look after, care for, minister to, treat. NEGLECT
suckle, feed, nurture, rear.
harbour, preserve, keep, cherish, foster, encourage, promote. BANISH

**nurture** nourish, feed, sustain, support, nurse, tend, rear, bring up, raise, train, discipline, educate, school, instruct, cultivate, develop, foster.

**nutriment** nutrition, nourishment, food, aliment, alimentation, sustenance, subsistence.

**nutritious** nutritive, nourishing, alimentary, alimentative, wholesome, healthy, benficial. UNHEALTHY

**nymph** sylph, dryad, naiad, oread, damsel, maiden, girl, lass.

# O

**oaf** dolt, dunce, dullard, blockhead, idiot, fool, wally (*inf*), simpleton, lout, clod.

**oath** vow, pledge, promise, word, statement, asseveration, affirmation.
curse, imprecation, malediction, expletive, swearword, obscenity, profanity.

**obdurate** hard, hard-hearted, cold, callous, unfeeling, insensitive, relentless, unrelenting, harsh, inflexible, unyielding, adamant, firm, stubborn, obstinate, mulish, pig-headed, headstrong, wilful, unshakable, immovable. AMENABLE

**obedient** compliant, acquiescent, yielding, submissive, deferential, respectful, dutiful, law-abiding, docile, biddable, tractable, subservient. DISOBEDIENT

**obeisance** homage, deference, respect, reverence, worship, salutation, bow, curtsy, genuflection, salaam. DISRESPECT

**obese** fat, stout, overweight, corpulent, rotund, portly, plump, tubby, podgy, fleshy. THIN

**obey** comply, observe, keep, heed, mind, follow, abide by, conform, submit, yield, discharge, fulfil, carry out, perform. DISOBEY

**obfuscate** obscure, darken, cloud, befog, confuse, bewilder, muddle, perplex. CLEAR

**object** *n*, thing, article, entity, body. CONCEPT

aim, purpose, objective, goal, end, motive, intent, intention, design, mark, butt, target.

*v*, protest, disapprove, demur, mind, take exception, expostulate, oppose. AGREE

**objection** protest, disapproval, demur, opposition, dissent, scruple, qualm, complaint, grievance, exception, remonstrance, expostulation. ASSENT

**objectionable** unpleasant, disagreeable, offensive, repulsive, repugnant, obnoxious, abominable, loathsome, detestable, odious, vile, insufferable, intolerable, unacceptable. AGREEABLE

**objective** *adj*, impartial, unbiased, unprejudiced, neutral, detached, disinterested, fair, just, dispassionate. SUBJECTIVE

*n*, aim, purpose, goal, end, target, object, intention, design, ambition, aspiration.

**objurgate** scold, chide, rebuke, reprove, reprimand, upbraid, berate. PRAISE

**oblation** offering, sacrifice, gift, present, donation, contribution.

**obligation** duty, responsibility, charge, onus, liability, accountability, necessity, requirement, compulsion, contract, bond, agreement, commitment, debt.

**obligatory** compulsory, mandatory, binding, required, necessary, essential, imperative. OPTIONAL

**oblige** obligate, compel, constrain, force, bind, necessitate, require, coerce, make. RELEASE

accommodate, favour, serve, help, please, gratify.

**obliged** beholden, indebted, grateful, thankful, appreciative.

**obliging** accommodating, amenable, willing, agreeable, kind, friendly, cooperative, helpful, civil, gracious. UNOBLIGING

**oblique** slanting, aslant, sloping, inclined, tilted. VERTICAL

indirect, evasive, devious, circuitous, roundabout, backhanded, furtive, sidelong. DIRECT

**obliterate** eradicate, destroy, annihilate, wipe out, expunge, erase, cancel, delete, efface, blot out. RESTORE

**oblivion** darkness, obscurity, extinction, abeyance, neglect, forgetfulness, obliviousness, blankness, unconsciousness. AWARENESS

**oblivious** unaware, unconscious, insensible, unmindful, blind, deaf, heedless, careless, forgetful, absent-minded. AWARE

**obloquy** censure, criticism, denunciation, invective, abuse, aspersion, defamation, vilification, slander, calumny, reproach, reproof, blame, opprobrium, dishonour, shame, disgrace, infamy, ignominy. PRAISE

**obnoxious** objectionable, unpleasant, disagreeable, nasty, offensive, repulsive, repugnant, odious, vile, horrid, hateful, loathsome, detestable, intolerable, insufferable. DELIGHTFUL

**obscene** indecent, immoral, improper, offensive, disgusting, foul, dirty, filthy, smutty, blue, pornographic, salacious, lewd, bawdy, ribald, coarse, vulgar, rude, gross, outrageous, shocking, shameless, immodest, impure, unchaste. DECENT

**obscure** *adj*, unclear, indistinct, vague, indefinite, uncertain, doubtful, abstruse, arcane, recondite, hidden, concealed, cryptic, enigmatic, mysterious, impenetrable, unfathomable, incomprehensible, intricate, involved. CLEAR

faint, dim, hazy, blurred, dark, gloomy, murky, cloudy, shadowy. BRIGHT

unknown, inconspicuous, insignificant, undistinguished, inglorious, unheard-of, unsung, nameless, minor, humble. FAMOUS

*v*, obfuscate, cloud, befog, hide, conceal, cover, mask, screen, veil, shroud, eclipse, darken, dim, shade, shadow.

**obsequious** servile, flattering, fawning, sycophantic, ingratiating, grovelling, cringing, slavish, subservient, submissive. INDEPENDENT

**observance** adherence, compliance, discharge, fulfilment, performance, execution, attention, heed, regard, respect. DISREGARD rite, ritual, ceremony, service, celebration, custom, practice, convention, fashion, form, usage, tradition.

**observant** attentive, alert, vigilant, watchful, heedful, mindful, aware, perceptive. UNOBSERVANT

**observation** notice, attention, examination, scrutiny, inspection, surveillance, study, consideration, cognition. INATTENTION

comment, remark, statement, finding, discovery, note, annotation, reflection, thought, opinion.

**observe** watch, study, monitor, contemplate, regard, look at, view, espy, witness, see, perceive, notice, descry, discern, detect, discover, note, mark. MISS

remark, comment, say, utter, state, declare, mention, reflect.

keep, honour, heed, mind, follow, abide by, comply with, fulfil, perform, discharge, execute, respect, celebrate, commemorate. IGNORE

**observer** watcher, viewer, spectator, onlooker, witness, bystander, beholder.

**obsess** preoccupy, dominate, rule, monopolize, possess, grip, bedevil, plague, haunt.

**obsession** preoccupation, fixation, *idée fixe*, passion, mania, compulsion, fetish, complex, phobia.

**obsolete** discontinued, disused,outmoded, antiquated, dated, superannuated, passé, old-fashioned, archaic, old, ancient. MODERN

**obstacle** barrier, hurdle, obstruction, impediment, hindrance, check, snag, difficulty, stumbling block. ASSISTANCE

**obstinate** stubborn, mulish, pig-headed, opinionated, headstrong, wilful, self-willed, dogged, persistent, firm, adamant, immovable, unshakable, obdurate, inflexible, unyielding, contrary, perverse, refractory, contumacious. AMENABLE

**obstreperous** boisterous, rowdy, uproarious, clamorous, noisy, loud, unruly, disorderly, wild, tumultuous, turbulent, unmanageable, out of hand. QUIET

**obstruct** block, clog, choke, bar, barricade, hinder, impede, hamper, prevent, stop, arrest, check, curb, retard, inhibit, frustrate, thwart, interrupt, interfere. ASSIST

**obstruction** blockage, obstacle, barricade, blockade, barrier, bar, hindrance, impediment, block, stop, check, snag, difficulty. CLEARANCE

**obtain** get, acquire, procure, come by, secure, gain, win, earn, attain, achieve. LOSE

prevail, exist, stand, be in force.

**obtrude** push, thrust, impose, intrude, interfere. WITHDRAW

**obtrusive** conspicuous, obvious, noticeable, prominent, protruding, protuberant. UNOBTRUSIVE

intrusive, interfering, officious, importunate, forward, pushy (*inf*). RETIRING

**obtuse** slow, dull, stupid, thick, dense, stolid, insensitive, thick-skinned. SHARP

blunt, rounded. POINTED

**obviate** preclude, forestall, avert, prevent, counter, get rid of, do away with. NECESSITATE

**obvious** evident, manifest, patent, clear, plain, distinct, apparent, visible, palpable, overt, unconcealed, conspicuous, pronounced, unmistakable. HIDDEN

**occasion** *n*, time, occurrence, incident, event, opportunity, chance, opening.

affair, function, party, celebration.

reason, cause, motive, ground, excuse, justification.

*v*, cause, bring about, prompt, elicit, provoke, generate, produce, create, originate. PREVENT

**occasional** periodic, intermittent, sporadic, irregular, infrequent, rare, casual, incidental. CONSTANT

**occasionally** sometimes, periodically, intermittently, rarely, seldom, now and then, every so often, from time to time. OFTEN

**occult** mystical, supernatural, magical, abstruse, arcane, esoteric, recondite, mysterious, obscure, hidden, concealed, secret.

**occupant** holder, owner, occupier, tenant, resident, inhabitant, inmate, incumbent.

**occupation** job, profession, work, employment, craft, trade, business, vocation, calling, career, activity, pursuit.

occupancy, tenure, possession, holding, tenancy, residence. EVICTION

conquest, defeat, seizure, invasion, control, rule.

**occupy** fill, take up, use, hold, keep, own, possess, inhabit, live in, seize, capture, invade. VACATE
absorb, engross, preoccupy, engage, employ, busy, tie up, monopolize, entertain, amuse.

**occur** happen, take place, come about, chance, befall, betide, transpire, supervene, arise, result, appear, materialize, be present, exist.

**occurrence** happening, event, incident, episode, occasion, instance, affair, proceeding.

**ocean** sea, main, deep, briny (*inf*).

**odd** unusual, uncommon, strange, peculiar, curious, queer, eccentric, unconventional, weird, bizarre, singular, rare, extraordinary, unique. ORDINARY
occasional, incidental, casual, random, irregular, diverse. REGULAR
unmatched, single, sole, solitary, lone, spare, surplus, leftover, uneven.

**odds** probability, likelihood, chances.
advantage, lead, edge, superiority.
difference, disparity, inequality, distinction.

**odious** obnoxious, objectionable, offensive, repugnant, repulsive, disgusting, detestable, loathsome, abominable, execrable, hateful, horrid, nasty, unpleasant, vile. PLEASANT

**odium** dislike, disfavour, hate, hatred, antipathy, loathing, detestation, abhorrence, repugnance, obloquy, opprobrium, censure, shame, dishonour. LIKING

**odour** smell, scent, redolence, aroma, fragrance, perfume, stench.
air, aura, spirit, quality, emanation, flavour.

**off** *adv*, away, out, aside, apart. ON
*prep*, from, away from.
*adj*, cancelled, postponed, finished, gone, absent, free, poor, substandard, bad, rotten, mouldy, sour, rancid.

**offence** violation, infringement, crime, misdemeanour, wrong, fault, sin, trespass, transgression, misdeed, peccadillo. RIGHT
affront, insult, snub, slight, injury, hurt, outrage, indignity.
resentment, umbrage, pique, huff, indignation, displeasure, annoyance, anger.
attack, assault, offensive. DEFENCE

**offend** hurt, wound, injure, wrong, insult, affront, snub, slight, humiliate, outrage, upset, displease, annoy, vex, irritate, anger. PLEASE
disgust, repel, sicken, nauseate.
sin, transgress, trespass, err, go astray.

**offender** culprit, criminal, lawbreaker, miscreant, malefactor, wrongdoer, sinner, transgressor.

**offensive** *adj*, unpleasant, disagreeable, nasty, obnoxious, objectionable, repugnant, disgusting, revolting, vile, odious, loathsome, detestable, abominable, execrable. PLEASANT
insulting, abusive, rude, disrespectful, insolent, impertinent, irritating, annoying. POLITE
aggressive, attacking, invading. DEFENSIVE
*n*, attack, assault, aggression, onset, onslaught, invasion, incursion. DEFENCE

**offer** *v*, present, hold out, proffer, tender, bid, propose, put forward, submit, advance, extend, give, provide, furnish, volunteer. WITHDRAW
*n*, bid, tender, proposal, proposition, suggestion, advance, overture.

**offering** present, gift, donation, contribution, oblation, sacrifice.

**offhand** impromptu, extempore, ad lib, off the cuff (*inf*).
casual, informal, unceremonious, abrupt, curt, brusque, cavalier, careless, nonchalant.

**office** post, position, situation, appointment, commission, role, capacity, function, duty, responsibility, trust, charge, work, employment, service, place, station.

**official** *adj*, authoritative, formal, ceremonial, authorized, legitimate, sanctioned, licensed, proper, authentic, bona fide. UNOFFICIAL
*n*, officer, office bearer, functionary, bureaucrat, executive, agent, representative.

**officiate** preside, chair, conduct, run, direct, manage, oversee, supervise.

**officious** obtrusive, importunate, interfering, meddlesome, intrusive, pragmatic, forward, pushy (*inf*), overzealous.

**offset** *v*, counterbalance, countervail, compensate for, cancel out, counteract, neutralize.
*n*, counterbalance, counterpoise, compensation, equalizer.

**offshoot** branch, outgrowth, development, derivative, by-product, spin-off.

**offspring** child, children, young, progeny, issue, descendant, descendants, seed, posterity. PARENT

**often** frequently, repeatedly, oft, generally, time after time, again and again. OCCASIONALLY

**ogre** giant, monster, brute, fiend, demon, devil, bogeyman.

**oily** greasy, fatty, oleaginous.
smooth, unctuous, glib, flattering, servile, obsequious.

**ointment** balm, salve, lotion, liniment, embrocation, cream, unguent.

**OK** okay, satisfactory, acceptable, passable, tolerable, fair, all right, so-so (*inf*), good, fine, correct, approved, permitted. UNACCEPTABLE

**old** ancient, antique, early, primitive, original, archaic, antiquated, outmoded, outdated, obsolete, worn out, dilapidated, decrepit. NEW
aged, elderly, grey, hoary, senile. YOUNG
former, erstwhile, quondam, previous, one-time. CURRENT

**old-fashioned** outmoded, outdated, out-of-date, dated, unfashionable, passé, obsolete, antiquated, superannuated, old hat. MODERN

**omen** portent, sign, indication, foretoken, warning, premonition, presage, augury, prediction, prognostic, forecast.

**ominous** portentous, foreboding, unpropitious, inauspicious, threatening, menacing, premonitory.

**omission** exclusion, exception, gap, oversight, neglect, disregard, default, failure.

**omit** exclude, leave out, drop, miss, skip, pass over, overlook, ignore, disregard, neglect, forget, fail. INCLUDE

**omnipotent** almighty, all-powerful, supreme, sovereign. FEEBLE

**omniscient** all-knowing, all-wise, all-seeing. IGNORANT

**on** *prep*, upon, by. OFF
*adv*, onward, forward, ahead. BACK
continually, unceasingly.

**once** formerly, previously, at one time, long ago. NOW
**at once,** immediately, instantly, straightaway, right away, directly, forthwith, now. LATER
together, simultaneously, at the same time.

**one** single, individual, lone, sole, only, unique. MANY

**onerous** burdensome, oppressive, heavy, laborious, arduous, toilsome, difficult, hard, taxing. LIGHT

**one-sided** unfair, unjust, inequitable, partial, partisan, biased, prejudiced. IMPARTIAL

**onlooker** bystander, observer, spectator, watcher, viewer, witness.

**only** *adj*, sole, solitary, lone, single, individual, exclusive, unique.
*adv*, just, merely, simply, purely, at most, alone.

**onset** beginning, start, inception, commencement, outbreak. END
onslaught, onrush, attack, assault, charge. RETREAT

**onus** burden, load, responsibility, obligation.

**onward** onwards, forward, ahead, on. BACKWARD

**ooze** seep, exude, percolate, filter, leak, escape, drip, drop, secrete, discharge, emit.

**opalescent** opaline, iridescent, pearly, nacreous, prismatic.

**opaque** cloudy, hazy, murky, turbid, dull, lustreless. TRANSPARENT
obscure, unclear, unfathomable, unintelligible. CLEAR
thick, dense, unintelligent, stupid, obtuse. CLEVER

**open** *adj*, unclosed, gaping, ajar, unlocked, unfastened, unsealed, unfolded, extended. CLOSED
clear, unobstructed, free, unrestricted, public, accessible, available, vacant, bare, exposed, uncovered, wide, extensive. RESTRICTED
overt, plain, obvious, evident, manifest, undisguised, unconcealed, apparent, visible. HIDDEN
undecided, unsettled, unresolved, debatable, moot. SETTLED
frank, candid, unreserved, honest, sincere, artless, ingenuous, natural. SECRETIVE
liable, prone, susceptible, vulnerable, exposed, unprotected, undefended. SAFE
*v*, unfasten, unlock, undo, unwrap, uncover, expose, unblock, clear. CLOSE
spread, expand, extend, unfold, unfurl, split, part, separate.
begin, start, launch, inaugurate, commence. END
disclose, reveal, show, exhibit. HIDE

**opening** *n*, gap, breach, aperture, orifice, hole, cleft, split, rift, crack, fissure, crevice, chasm.
beginning, start, launch, inauguration, initiation, commencement, inception, dawn. CLOSE
opportunity, chance, occasion, break (*inf*), vacancy, place.
*adj*, beginning, starting, commencing, first, initial, introductory, inaugural. CLOSING

**open-minded** receptive, tolerant, catholic, broad-minded, liberal, fair, just, reasonable, unbiased, unprejudiced, impartial, dispassionate. BIGOTED

**operate** function, work, act, perform, go, run, manage, use, handle, manipulate, manoeuvre.

**operation** performance, working, action, motion, handling, manipulation.
procedure, process, exercise, manoeuvre, affair, business, undertaking, venture.

**operative** *adj*, operational, in operation, functioning, working, active, in force, effective. INOPERATIVE
influential, important, significant, key, crucial, relevant.
*n*, worker, hand, employee, labourer, artisan, mechanic, operator.

**opiate** narcotic, sedative, tranquillizer, soporific, anodyne. STIMULANT

**opine** believe, think, feel, consider, reckon, judge, deem, suppose, conclude, say, declare.

**opinion** belief, judgment, view, point of view, idea, notion, fancy, thought, impression, feeling, sentiment, theory, conjecture, estimation, assessment. KNOWLEDGE

**opinionated** opinionative, dogmatic, dictatorial, doctrinaire, overconfident, cocksure, arrogant, overbearing, pig-headed, obdurate, prejudiced, biased, bigoted. MEEK

**opponent** adversary, antagonist, foe, enemy, rival, competitor, contestant, opposer. ALLY

**opportune** timely, seasonable, convenient, appropriate, apt, suitable, fitting, fit, favourable, auspicious, propitious, lucky, fortunate. INOPPORTUNE

**opportunity** chance, occasion, time, moment, opening, break (*inf*).

**oppose** resist, withstand, counter, fight, contest, combat, attack, face, confront, defy, hinder, obstruct, block, bar, check, prevent, thwart. AID
contrast, compare, match, counterbalance, offset.

**opposite** *adj*, facing, corresponding.
opposed, opposing, conflicting, antagonistic, hostile, inimical, contrary, reverse, contrasting, different, antithetical, contradictory, incompatible, irreconcilable. SAME
*n*, converse, inverse, reverse, contrary, antithesis.

**opposition** antagonism, hostility, defiance, resistance, counteraction, obstruction, hindrance, prevention, disapproval, conflict, confrontation, competition. AGREEMENT

**oppress** burden, encumber, trouble, afflict, torment, sadden, depress. RELIEVE
subjugate, subdue, crush, suppress, overwhelm, overpower, tyrannize, persecute. FREE

**oppression** tyranny, despotism, subjection, persecution, cruelty, severity, harshness, injustice, suffering, misery, hardship. LIBERTY

**oppressive** tyrannical, despotic, overbearing, harsh, severe, cruel, unjust. MILD
burdensome, onerous, heavy, overwhelming, overpowering, close, sultry, stuffy, stifling, uncomfortable.

**opprobrious** shameful, disgraceful, dishonourable, infamous, ignominious, reprehensible, despicable, contemptible, odious, disreputable. HONOURABLE
scornful, contemptuous, reproachful, derogatory, defamatory, vituperative, slanderous, calumniatory, unfavourable, offensive, insulting. LAUDATORY

**oppugn** dispute, contest, question, oppose, resist, attack, assail.

**opt** choose, select, decide, elect, prefer.

**optimistic** hopeful, confident, assured, sanguine, cheerful, positive, idealistic, utopian. PESSIMISTIC

**option** choice, alternative, selection, election, preference, wish, will, discretion.

**optional** voluntary, unforced, discretionary, elective. COMPULSORY

**opulent** rich, wealthy, affluent, moneyed, prosperous, well-off. POOR
sumptuous, luxurious, lavish, exuberant, luxuriant, abundant, profuse, copious, plentiful. MEAGRE

**oracular** prophetic, sibylline, vatic, fatidic, mantic, augural, divinatory, prognostic, predictive, portentous, ominous, foreboding.
wise, sage, venerable, grave, authoritative, positive, dogmatic.
allegorical, figurative, obscure, arcane, mysterious, cryptic, ambiguous.

**oral** verbal, spoken, vocal, unwritten. WRITTEN

**oration** speech, discourse, declamation, harangue, address, lecture.

**orb** ball, sphere, globe, round.

**orbit** *n*, revolution, cycle, circle, circuit, path, course, trajectory.
range, scope, field, compass, sphere, domain.
*v*, revolve, circle.

**ordain** consecrate, anoint, frock, induct, invest, call, appoint. UNFROCK
destine, predestine, fate, doom, foreordain.
order, command, decree, rule, enact, establish, bid, enjoin, prescribe.

**ordeal** trial, test, tribulation, trouble, affliction, suffering, hardship, nightmare.

**order** *n*, arrangement, disposition, sequence, progression, grouping, classification, structure, organization, system, method, plan, neatness, tidiness, orderliness. DISORDER
command, injunction, instruction, direction, decree, mandate, edict, ordinance, regulation, rule, law, precept.
peace, quiet, calm, tranquillity, discipline, law and order. ANARCHY
association, society, fraternity, community, lodge, league, guild, sect, denomination.
kind, sort, type, class, species, genus, family, rank, degree.
requisition, request, commission, booking, reservation.
**out of order,** broken, inoperative, not working, kaput (*inf*), on the blink (*inf*).
wrong, unseemly, indecorous, improper, not done.
*v*, command, instruct, direct, bid, enjoin, decree, ordain, prescribe, demand, require. BESEECH
request, book, reserve, apply for, send for. RECEIVE
arrange, dispose, organize, marshal, classify, group, sort, neaten, tidy. DISARRANGE

**orderly** neat, tidy, shipshape, systematic, methodical, regular, well-organized. UNTIDY
well-behaved, disciplined, law-abiding, peaceable, quiet, restrained. DISORDERLY

**ordinance** decree, edict, order, command, precept, rule, regulation, law, statute.
ceremony, rite, ritual, sacrament, observance.

**ordinarily** usually, generally, as a rule, normally, customarily, habitually, commonly.

**ordinary** common, commonplace, everyday, familiar, unexceptional, run-of-the-mill, plain, simple, conventional, normal, standard, typical, usual, customary, habitual, wonted, accustomed, regular, routine, humdrum, average, medium, mediocre, indifferent. UNUSUAL

**organic** natural, biological, living, animate. INORGANIC
basic, fundamental, structural, integral, constitutional, inherent, intrinsic. EXTRANEOUS
systematic, methodical, organized, ordered, structured. UNSYSTEMATIC

**organization** arrangement, order, classification, system, structure, construction, method, plan, design, constitution, composition.
association, institution, company, group, league, guild, consortium, confederation, union, syndicate.

**organize** coordinate, marshal, order, systematize, arrange, dispose, classify, sort, shape, form, constitute, establish, set up. DISRUPT

**orgy** debauch, revel, carousal, bacchanalia, spree, binge (*inf*).

**orientate** orient, direct, position, align, adjust, adapt, familiarize, acclimatize, get one's bearings. DISORIENTATE

**orifice** opening, aperture, hole, mouth, vent.

**origin** source, root, fount, spring, cause, derivation, provenance, base, foundation. RESULT
beginning, start, commencement, genesis, dawn, inception, outset. END
ancestry, extraction, lineage, family, stock, pedigree, birth, descent.

**original** *adj*, first, initial, primary, earliest, primordial, primeval, primitive, aboriginal, autochthonous. LATEST
fresh, new, novel, innovative, creative, inventive, imaginative, unconventional, different. HACKNEYED
*n*, master, prototype, archetype, model, pattern, standard. COPY

**originate** *vt*, begin, start, initiate, inaugurate, commence, create, invent, formulate, conceive, launch, introduce, found, institute. ABOLISH
*vi*, rise, spring, issue, proceed, flow, emanate, come, derive, stem. END

**ornament** *n*, adornment, decoration, embellishment, garnish, trimming, frill, accessory, bauble, trinket, knick-knack, gewgaw.
*v*, adorn, decorate, embellish, garnish, trim, deck, festoon, beautify, prettify. STRIP

**ornate** elaborate, fancy, baroque, rococo, florid, flowery, ornamented, adorned, decorated, embellished, elegant, beautiful. PLAIN

**orotund** resonant, sonorous, rich, full, ringing, booming. SOFT
pompous, bombastic, grandiloquent, magniloquent, turgid, inflated. SIMPLE

**orthodox** conventional, conformist, accepted, approved, official, usual, customary, traditional, sound, correct, true. UNORTHODOX

**oscillate** swing, sway, vibrate, vacillate, fluctuate, vary, waver, hesitate, falter.

**ostensible** outward, superficial, pretended, alleged, supposed, professed, avowed, apparent, seeming, manifest. REAL

**ostentation** display, show, parade, pageantry, pomp, flourish, flamboyance, affectation, pretentiousness, window dressing. RESERVE

**ostentatious** showy, flashy, flamboyant, loud, vulgar, affected, mannered, pretentious, pompous, vain, boastful. SUBDUED

**ostracize** exclude, banish, exile, excommunicate, blacklist, blackball, reject, shun, cold-shoulder (*inf*), ignore, send to Coventry. ACCEPT

**other** different, unlike, dissimilar, separate, distinct, diverse. SAME
further, more, extra, additional, supplementary, spare, alternative.

**oust** eject, expel, throw out, evict, dispossess, dislodge, depose, unseat. INSTALL

**out** away, absent, abroad, elsewhere, outside. IN
unfashionable, passé, antiquated, dated, old-fashioned.
exposed, revealed, disclosed, published, broadcast.
extinguished, dead, finished, exhausted.
impossible, unacceptable, not allowed.
wrong, incorrect, inaccurate, erroneous.

**outbreak** outburst, eruption, explosion, flare-up, burst, fit, rush, surge, epidemic.

**outburst** outbreak, eruption, explosion, flare-up, tantrum, fit, spasm, attack, outpouring, burst.

**outcast** castaway, pariah, exile, expatriate, refugee, wanderer, vagabond.

**outcome** consequence, result, issue, upshot, sequel, aftermath. CAUSE

**outcry** protest, complaint, uproar, clamour, hullaballoo, hue and cry, vociferation, exclamation, shout, yell.

**outdo** surpass, exceed, beat, top, excel, transcend, outshine, eclipse, outclass, outstrip, outdistance, outrun, outwit.

**outer** external, exterior, outward, outside, peripheral, superficial. INNER

**outfit** clothes, garb, ensemble, costume, get-up (*inf*), rigout (*inf*), kit, set, gear, equipment.

**outing** excursion, trip, jaunt, airing.

**outlandish** unconventional, bizarre, eccentric, weird, odd, strange, unfamiliar, exotic, foreign, alien, freakish, grotesque. CONVENTIONAL

**outlaw** bandit, brigand, robber, marauder, pirate, freebooter, fugitive, criminal, outcast, pariah.

**outlay** expenditure, disbursement, cost, expense, spending, outgoings. INCOME

**outlet** vent, release, escape, exit, egress, way out, opening, channel.
market, mart, store, shop.

**outline** *n*, draft, sketch, plan, skeleton, framework, drawing, tracing, delineation, contour, silhouette, shape, form.
summary, synopsis, résumé, précis, recapitulation, thumbnail, sketch.
*v*, draft, sketch, delineate, summarize, recapitulate.

**outlook** attitude, viewpoint, perspective, frame of mind, slant, angle.
prospect, expectation, future.
view, vista, panorama, scene.

**outlying** distant, remote, outer, peripheral. INNER

**outrage** *n*, atrocity, enormity, wrong, injury, harm, violation, desecration, abuse, offence, affront, insult, indignity.
anger, rage, fury, wrath, indignation, shock.
*v*, anger, enrage, infuriate, madden, offend, insult, disgust, shock, horrify.
abuse, injure, violate, desecrate.

**outrageous** shocking, scandalous, atrocious, abominable, unspeakable, vile, horrible, monstrous, heinous, disgraceful, offensive, intolerable, insufferable.
immoderate, excessive, extravagant, unreasonable, preposterous. REASONABLE

**outright** *adj*, total, complete, utter, absolute, sheer, perfect, consummate, unconditional, downright, unmitigated, unqualified, direct, straightforward.
*adv*, totally, completely, utterly, absolutely, openly, unreservedly, directly, instantly, immediately, at once.

**outrun** outstrip, outpace, outdistance, pass, overtake, behind, escape, beat, surpass, excel, outdo.

**outset** start, beginning, commencement, inception, opening, inauguration. END

**outshine** eclipse, overshadow, surpass, excel, transcend, outclass, outrival, outdo, outstrip.

**outside** *n*, exterior, surface, edge, border, appearance, façade.
*adj*, exterior, external, outer, outward, superficial, peripheral, extraneous. INSIDE
distant, remote, unlikely, slim, marginal.

**outsider** stranger, alien, foreigner, newcomer, intruder, interloper, visitor, nonmember, gate-crasher (*inf*).

**outskirts** suburbs, environs, precincts, periphery, edge, border, boundary. CENTRE

**outspoken** candid, frank, blunt, explicit, open, free, unreserved, direct, straightforward, forthright. RESERVED

**outspread** outstretched, open, unfolded, unfurled, extended, expanded, spread out. CLOSED

**outstanding** excellent, superb, superior, exceptional, great, distinguished, eminent, notable, striking, impressive, prominent, salient, signal, noticeable, conspicuous, memorable. INSIGNIFICANT
owing, due, unpaid, unsettled, remaining. PAID

**outstretch** outspread, extend, stretch out, expand, spread out, open, unfold, unfurl. CLOSE

**outstrip** outrun, outpace, outdistance, outdo, surpass, exceed, excel, beat, outclass, outshine, eclipse.

**outward** outer, external, exterior, outside, superficial, apparent, visible, ostensible. INWARD

**outweigh** override, overcome, prevail over, outbalance, overbalance, preponderate, surpass, exceed.

**outwit** cheat, defraud, trick, dupe, deceive, outjockey, outfox, outsmart (*inf*), get the better of, outthink, overreach, circumvent.

**ovation** applause, plaudits, clapping, cheering, acclaim, acclamation, laudation, praise.

**over** *prep*, above, on, upon, on top of, higher than. UNDER
across, through, during.
exceeding, in excess of, more than, greater than.
*adv*, above, overhead, out, beyond, across, through.
extra, surplus, remaining, left over, in excess, in addition. SHORT
*adj*, finished, ended, concluded, completed, done, gone, past.

**overall** general, universal, global, comprehensive, all-embracing, inclusive, complete, total, sweeping.

**overawe** intimidate, cow, daunt, abash, frighten, scare, domineer, browbeat. REASSURE

**overbearing** domineering, imperious, lordly, high-handed, haughty, arrogant, autocratic, dictatorial, tyrannical, oppressive. HUMBLE

**overcast** cloudy, grey, dull, gloomy, dreary, dismal, sombre, murky, dark, lowering, leaden. CLEAR

**overcharge** surcharge, cheat, shortchange, rook (*inf*), rip off (*inf*), do (*inf*), diddle (*inf*). UNDERCHARGE
overload, overburden, strain, overtax.

**overcome** conquer, vanquish, defeat, beat, best, worst, overpower, overwhelm, crush, quell, subdue, master, surmount, triumph over, rise above. SUBMIT

**overdo** exaggerate, go overboard (*inf*), overact, overplay, overstate, overindulge, overwork, overtax, overcook.

**overdue** late, tardy, behind, behindhand, delayed, belated, owing, in arrears, due, payable. PUNCTUAL

**overestimate** overrate, overvalue, overpraise, exaggerate. UNDERESTIMATE

**overflow** overrun, overspill, run over, spill over, surge, pour forth, flood, inundate, deluge, swamp, overspread, cover, abound, teem. SUBSIDE

**overhaul** inspect, examine, check, service, repair.
catch up, overtake, pass, outstrip.

**overjoyed** delighted, ecstatic, elated, jubilant, thrilled, over the moon (*inf*). UPSET

**overload** overcharge, overburden, strain, overtax, oppress, burden, encumber. RELIEVE

**overlook** miss, neglect, omit, leave out, skip, pass over, disregard, ignore, forget. NOTE
forgive, pardon, excuse, condone, blink at, wink at. PUNISH

**overpower** overwhelm, overcome, conquer, vanquish, defeat, beat, master, surmount, crush, quell, subdue, best, worst. SUBMIT

**overpowering** overwhelming, strong, powerful, forceful, weighty, irresistible, uncontrollable. WEAK

**overrate** overestimate, overvalue, overpraise, exaggerate. UNDERRATE

**overreach** outwit, outsmart (*inf*), cheat, defraud, swindle, trick, dupe, deceive, circumvent.

**override** disregard, ignore, supersede, outweigh, prevail over, quash, annul, reverse, cancel, overrule.

**overrule** disallow, reject, override, supersede, annul, rescind, abrogate, countermand, revoke, repeal, cancel, nullify.
rule, govern, dominate, prevail over, influence, sway, control, direct.

**overrun** attack, invade, overwhelm, ravage, devastate, infest, inundate, swarm, spread, overflow.
exceed, go beyond, overshoot, overreach.

**overseer** supervisor, superintendent, manager, foreman, boss (*inf*).

**overshadow** eclipse, outshine, surpass, excel, dwarf, dominate, tower over, rise above.
cloud, darken, dim, obscure, veil, spoil, blight.

**oversight** omission, fault, lapse, slip, blunder, mistake, error, neglect, inattention. ATTENTION
supervision, surveillance, administration, management, direction, control, care, custody.

**overt** plain, clear, manifest, patent, apparent, visible, open, public, unconcealed, undisguised, blatant, deliberate. SECRET

**overtake** pass, leave behind, outrun, outstrip, catch up, overhaul.

**overthrow** *v*, oust, depose, unseat, dethrone, conquer, vanquish, defeat, beat, overcome, overpower, subvert, overturn, upset, bring down, demolish, raze, ruin, destroy, abolish. RESTORE
*n*, deposition, dethronement, defeat, fall, subversion, demolition, downfall, ruin, destruction, abolition. RESTORATION

**overture** advance, approach, offer, proposal, proposition, invitation. REJECTION
introduction, prelude, opening, preface, prologue. FINALE

**overturn** upset, capsize, keel over, tip over, upend, invert, topple, spill.
overthrow, subvert, bring down, destroy, abolish, reverse.

**overweening** arrogant, haughty, supercilious, proud, vain, lordly, high and mighty (*inf*), pompous, opinionated, cocky, cocksure. MEEK
excessive, immoderate, extravagant, exaggerated.

**overweight** obese, fat, plump, stout, portly, heavy, outsize, flabby, fleshy. SKINNY

**overwhelm** overcome, devastate, stagger, bowl over (*inf*), engulf, submerge, inundate, flood, deluge, swamp, bury.
overpower, overthrow, conquer, vanquish, defeat, master, crush. SUBMIT

**overwrought** agitated, frantic, tense, on edge, keyed up, worked up (*inf*), excited, overexcited. CALM
elaborate, fancy, ornate, flowery, overdone, overworked. PLAIN

**owing** due, unpaid, payable, owed, outstanding, unsettled, overdue, in arrears. PAID

**own** *adj*, personal, private, individual, particular.

**on one's own,** alone, by oneself, singly, independently, unaided.
*v*, possess, have, hold, keep.
recognize, grant, concede, avow, acknowledge, admit, confess, own up. DENY

**owner** possessor, holder, proprietor, proprietress, master, mistress.

# P

**pace** *n*, step, stride, gait, walk.
speed, velocity, rate, tempo, progress, rapidity, swiftness.
*v*, walk, stride, step, measure.

**pacific** conciliatory, placatory, peacemaking, irenic, peaceable, peace-loving, mild, gentle, nonviolent. BELLIGERENT
peaceful, calm, serene, tranquil, quiet, still. TURBULENT

**pacify** appease, conciliate, propitiate, placate, mollify, calm, compose, lull, quiet, soothe, tranquillize, allay, assuage, moderate, mitigate, quell, subdue. AGGRAVATE

**pack** *n*, bundle, package, parcel, packet, load, burden.
herd, flock, crowd, throng, mob, group, band, gang, company, lot, set, collection, assortment.
*v*, cram, stuff, jam, wedge, press, ram, compact, compress, fill, crowd.
load, stow, store.

**package** *n*, bundle, pack, parcel, packet, box, carton, wrapper, wrapping.
*v*, pack, box, wrap.

**packet** pack, package, parcel, box, carton, container, receptacle.

**pact** agreement, compact, covenant, concordat, bond, contract, treaty, entente, league, alliance, bargain, deal, arrangement.

**pad** *n*, cushion, bolster, wad, buffer, stuffing, padding, filling, wadding.
block, tablet, jotter, notepad.
*v*, cushion, stuff, fill, pack.

**pagan** *n*, heathen, unbeliever, infidel, idolater, atheist, agnostic. BELIEVER
*adj*, heathen, idolatrous, irreligious, godless, atheistic, agnostic.

**page**[1] *n*, leaf, sheet, folio, side.
episode, chapter, period, era, point, stage.

**page**[2] *n*, pageboy, bellboy, servant, attendant.
*v*, call, summon, send for, announce.

**pageant** parade, procession, tableau, spectacle, show, display, exhibition, extravaganza.

**pageantry** pomp, ceremony, state, magnificence, splendour, glamour, grandeur, show, display, showiness, ostentation.

**pain** *n*, hurt, discomfort, suffering, agony, ache, throb, pang, twinge, soreness, tenderness. RELIEF
distress, anguish, trouble, affliction, torment, torture, misery, sorrow, grief, woe. JOY
*v*, hurt, ache, throb, sting, smart, chafe, injure, wound. EASE
distress, trouble, afflict, torment, torture, agonize, grieve, sorrow, vex, annoy. COMFORT

**painful** sore, tender, hurting, aching, throbbing, stinging, smarting, agonizing, excruciating.
distressing, harrowing, unpleasant, disagreeable, grievous, unhappy. PLEASANT
hard, difficult, arduous, laborious, toilsome, troublesome, vexatious. EASY

**painstaking** careful, scrupulous, punctilious, meticulous, conscientious, diligent, assiduous, sedulous, thorough. CARELESS

**paint** *n*, colour, colouring, pigment, stain, dye, tint.
*v*, colour, tint, coat, cover, decorate.
portray, depict, picture, represent, delineate, draw, sketch.

**pair** *n*, couple, brace, twosome, duo, doublet.
*v*, match, couple, mate, twin, partner, join, yoke, marry, wed. SEPARATE

**palatable** tasty, toothsome, savoury, delicious, appetizing, mouthwatering, luscious, delectable.
pleasant, agreeable, acceptable, satisfactory. UNPLEASANT

**palatial** grand, stately, majestic, imposing, splendid, magnificent, sumptuous, luxurious, opulent. MEAN

**palaver** rigmarole, procedure, business, affair, fuss, carry-on (*inf*).
chatter, babble, prattle, blather.
conference, colloquy, discussion, confabulation, conversation.

**pale** *adj*, colourless, whitish, wan, pallid, pasty, ashen, sallow, white, bleached, faded, light. DARK
dim, faint, feeble, weak.

*v*, blanch, whiten, fade, dim, lessen, diminish.

**pall[1]** *n*, shroud, mantle, shadow, damper, gloom, melancholy.

**pall[2]** *v*, cloy, satiate, glut, surfeit, bore, tire.

**palliate** alleviate, mitigate, allay, assuage, soothe, ease, relieve, abate, soften. AGGRAVATE
extenuate, excuse, minimize, lessen, diminish, varnish, gloss over, whitewash (*inf*), conceal, cover up. EXPOSE

**palliative** analgesic, anodyne, sedative, lenitive, demulcent.

**pallid** pale, wan, ashen, pasty, sallow, white, whitish, colourless, vapid, insipid.

**pallor** paleness, pallidness, pallidity, wanness, whiteness. RUDDINESS

**palmy** prosperous, thriving, flourishing, halcyon, golden, glorious, triumphant, happy, fortunate. UNFORTUNATE

**palpable** obvious, evident, manifest, patent, clear, plain, overt, blatant, perceptible, visible, apparent, conspicuous, unmistakable.
tangible, real, concrete, solid, substantial, material, corporeal. IMPALPABLE

**palpitate** pulsate, beat, throb, pound, flutter, tremble, quiver, vibrate.

**palter** equivocate, fudge, hedge, shuffle, quibble, prevaricate, tergiversate.
haggle, bargain, chaffer.

**paltry** trivial, trifling, minor, petty, small, little, slight, insignificant, inconsiderable, meagre, derisory, worthless, wretched, miserable, poor, contemptible, despicable, abject, mean, base, low. CONSIDERABLE

**pamper** indulge, humour, spoil, ruin, coddle, mollycoddle, cosset, baby, pet. DISCIPLINE

**pamphlet** booklet, leaflet, brochure, circular, hand-out, tract, treatise.

**panacea** cure-all, elixir, nostrum, universal, remedy.

**pandemonium** chaos, confusion, disorder, tumult, turmoil, riot, uproar, commotion, hullaballoo. PEACE

**pander to** gratify, satisfy, indulge, humour, please, cater to.

**panegyric** eulogy, encomium, praise, commendation, paean, accolade, tribute. TIRADE

**panegyrize** eulogize, praise, commend, extol, laud, glorify, acclaim. DECRY

**panel** sheet, board, section.
board, council, committee, jury.

**pang** pain, stab, prick, twinge, spasm.

**panic** *n*, terror, alarm, fright, fear, consternation, dismay, confusion, turmoil. COMPOSURE
*v*, be alarmed, overreact, go to pieces (*inf*).
terrify, alarm, frighten, scare.

**pant** puff, blow, gasp, wheeze, pulsate, throb, heave.

**paper** newspaper, journal, gazette, daily, rag (*inf*).
document, certificate, credential, instrument, deed.
article, report, monograph, treatise, essay, composition, dissertation, thesis.

**par** level, standard, norm, average, mean.
parity, equality, balance, equilibrium.
**above par,** excellent, first-rate, superior, exceptional, outstanding. INFERIOR
**below par,** substandard, inferior, second-rate, poor. EXCELLENT
**on a par,** equal, the same, well-matched. UNEQUAL
**up to par,** acceptable, satisfactory, passable, adequate. UNACCEPTABLE

**parable** fable, allegory, tale, story, lesson.

**parabolic** allegorical, figurative, symbolic, metaphorical.

**parade** *n*, procession, train, column, file, review, march, cavalcade, pageant, array.
show, display, exhibition, spectacle, ostentation, pomp. MODESTY
*v*, march, file, process.
flaunt, vaunt, show off, display, exhibit, air, swagger, strut. HIDE

**paradise** heaven, Elysium, Eden, utopia, bliss. PURGATORY

**paradox** contradiction, incongruity, inconsistency, absurdity, puzzle, riddle, enigma, mystery. TRUISM

**paragon** model, pattern, paradigm, ideal, exemplar, archetype, prototype, nonesuch, nonpareil, standard, norm, criterion.

**paragraph** section, subdivision, clause, passage.

**parallel** *adj*, equidistant, aligned, even, equal, corresponding, similar, like, analogous, equivalent. DIVERGENT
*n*, counterpart, equivalent, match, twin. CONVERSE

analogy, correspondence, similarity, likeness, resemblance, comparison. DIFFERENCE
*v*, equal, match, correspond, resemble, compare. DIFFER

**paralyse** deaden, numb, anaesthetize, freeze, transfix, immobilize, incapacitate, disable, cripple.

**paramount** pre-eminent, supreme, chief, cardinal, principal, leading, dominant, prime, primary, first, foremost. MINOR

**parapet** wall, railing, breastwork, battlement.

**paraphernalia** belongings, effects, things, stuff, baggage, impedimenta, gear, equipment, tackle, accoutrements, appurtenances, trappings.

**paraphrase** *n*, explanation, interpretation, translation, rewording, restatement, rehash.
*v*, reword, restate, explain, interpret.

**parasite** hanger-on, leech, sponger (*inf*), scrounger (*inf*), sycophant, toady.

**parcel** *n*, package, bundle, pack, packet, lot, batch, bunch, group, collection.
piece, part, portion, plot, tract, patch.
*v*, package, wrap, pack. UNDO
divide, share, apportion, allot, mete, dole, deal, distribute. WITHHOLD

**parched** dry, arid, waterless, scorched, roasted, withered, shrivelled, dehydrated, thirsty. FLOODED

**pardon** *v*, forgive, excuse, condone, overlook, remit, absolve, acquit, clear, exonerate, discharge, release. PUNISH
*n*, forgiveness, excuse, clemency, mercy, grace, amnesty, remission, absolution, acquittal, exoneration, discharge, release. PUNISHMENT

**pare** peel, skin, shave, clip, trim, cut, crop, prune, dock, reduce, decrease, diminish, lessen.

**parentage** ancestry, lineage, descent, extraction, birth, origin, family, race, stock, pedigree.

**pariah** outcast, leper, untouchable, exile, outlaw.

**parity** equality, par, equivalence, parallelism, evenness, uniformity, identity, sameness, correspondence, analogy. DISPARITY

**parlance** idiom, vernacular, tongue, language, jargon, lingo (*inf*), speech, talk.

**parley** *v*, talk, discuss, negotiate, confer, converse, confabulate.
*n*, talk, discussion, meeting, conference, colloquy, dialogue, conversation, confabulation.

**parliament** legislature, assembly, council, congress, senate, diet.

**parochial** provincial, insular, small-minded, narrow-minded, restricted, limited, illiberal, petty.

**parody** *n*, burlesque, lampoon, caricature, satire, spoof, skit, send-up (*inf*), mockery, travesty, imitation, mimicry.
*v*, burlesque, lampoon, caricature, satirize, take off (*inf*), mock, imitate.

**paroxysm** fit, seizure, attack, spasm, convulsion, outburst, eruption.

**parry** deflect, ward off, fend off, stave off, repulse, avert, avoid, evade, dodge, sidestep, circumvent.

**parsimonious** mean, stingy, miserly, niggardly, close-fisted, tight-fisted, ungenerous, grasping, frugal, sparing. GENEROUS

**parson** clergyman, cleric, churchman, ecclesiastic, priest, minister, rector, vicar, pastor, preacher. LAYMAN

**part** *n*, piece, portion, share, section, division, segment, fraction, fragment, bit, scrap, ingredient, constituent, element, component, branch, member. WHOLE
character, role, function, office, duty, responsibility, participation, interest, concern, behalf, side, party, faction.
**in part,** partly, partially, to some extent, somewhat, moderately. ENTIRELY
*v*, divide, separate, split, break, sever, disunite, disjoin, disconnect, detach. JOIN
go, depart, quit, leave, withdraw, retire.
**part with,** relinquish, give up, renounce, abandon, surrender, yield. RETAIN

**partial** incomplete, fragmentary, unfinished, imperfect, restricted, limited. TOTAL
biased, prejudiced, partisan, one-sided, unfair, unjust, discriminatory. IMPARTIAL
**be partial to,** like, be fond of, care for. DISLIKE

**participate** share, partake, take part, join in, be involved, help, contribute.

**particle** grain, speck, atom, iota, whit, jot, tittle, bit, scrap, shred, crumb.

**particular** *adj*, special, specific, exact, distinct, separate, peculiar, individual. GENERAL

notable, remarkable, marked, especial, exceptional, unusual, uncommon. ORDINARY
fussy, finicky, fastidious, dainty, choosy (*inf*), discriminating, critical, difficult, exacting, careful, meticulous, painstaking, thorough, detailed, minute, strict.
*n*, particularity, detail, point, feature, item.
**in particular,** particularly, especially, specifically, exactly. GENERALLY

**particularize** specify, spell out, detail, itemize, enumerate. GENERALIZE

**parting** *n*, farewell, goodbye, valediction, leave-taking, departure, going.
division, separation, partition, cleavage, rift, split, break, rupture, severance, disunion. UNION
*adj*, farewell, valedictory, departing, final, last. OPENING

**partisan** *n*, adherent, follower, disciple, votary, champion, supporter, enthusiast, devotee.
*adj*, biased, prejudiced, partial, one-sided, factional, sectarian. NEUTRAL

**partition** *n*, division, separation, parting, severance. UNION
screen, barrier, wall, divider, separator.
share, portion, allotment, allocation, distribution.
*v*, divide, separate, split, apportion, share.

**partner** companion, comrade, ally, colleague, associate, copartner, confederate, collaborator, accomplice, helper, mate, consort, spouse. RIVAL

**partnership** association, collaboration, cooperation, sharing, participation, companionship, fellowship, union, alliance, corporation, company, firm, house.

**parts** region, area, district, locality, neighbourhood, vicinity.
ability, calibre, talents, gifts, attributes, faculties, intelligence, intellect, accomplishments.

**parturition** childbirth, confinement, *accouchement*, labour, delivery.

**party** social, soirée, celebration, gathering, get-together (*inf*), reception, at-home.
group, band, gang, team, crew, squad, troop, body, company.
side, faction, coterie, set, clique, circle, ring, league, alliance, association.
person, individual, participant, litigant, plaintiff, defendant.

**pass** *v*, go, move, proceed, flow, run, go by, elapse, go past, overtake. STOP
surpass, exceed, transcend, go beyond, outdo, outstrip.
succeed, get through, qualify, come up to scratch (*inf*), do. FAIL
spend, fill, occupy, employ, while away.
spread, circulate, transfer, exchange, convey, transmit, hand, give. WITHHOLD
enact, legislate, sanction, approve, ratify, accept, adopt, ordain, decree. REJECT
ignore, disregard, pass over, overlook, pass by, skip, miss, omit, neglect. NOTE
depart, leave, go, end, cease, die, pass on, pass away, fade, vanish, disappear. REMAIN
discharge, eliminate, void, evacuate, excrete.
**pass out,** faint, collapse, swoon, black out, flake out (*inf*), keel over (*inf*).
*n*, passage, way, gap, col, defile, gorge, ravine, canyon.
passport, visa, ticket, licence, warrant, permit, authorization, permission.
advance, overture, move, thrust, lunge, throw, kick, transfer.
plight, predicament, situation, condition, state of affairs.

**passable** fair, middling, all right, OK (*inf*), so-so (*inf*), acceptable, adequate, tolerable, admissible, allowable, ordinary, unexceptional. EXCELLENT
clear, unobstructed, open, traversable, navigable. IMPASSABLE

**passage** route, course, path, road, way, pass, thoroughfare, channel, avenue, access, opening, entrance, exit.
passageway, corridor, hall, hallway, lobby, vestibule, aisle, alley, alleyway.
section, piece, excerpt, extract, paragraph, verse, quotation, text.
journey, voyage, trip, crossing.
transition, passing, flow, movement, progression, motion, progress, transit. HALT
enactment, legislation, sanction, approval, ratification. REJECTION

**passenger** fare, rider, traveller, voyager, tourist.

**passing** transitory, transient, fleeting, momentary, ephemeral, brief, short, hasty, cursory, superficial, slight, casual.

**passion** emotion, feeling, ardour, fervour, zeal, enthusiasm, eagerness, excitement, animation, warmth, fire, intensity, vehemence, spirit, rapture. APATHY

desire, craving, lust, love, affection, fondness, adoration, infatuation, mania, obsession. LOATHING
rage, fury, anger, wrath, storm, outburst. COMPOSURE

**passionate** vehement, impassioned, ardent, fervent, warm, heartfelt, zealous, enthusiastic, eager, excited, animated, fierce, intense, strong, impulsive, impetuous. APATHETIC
loving, amorous, lustful, erotic, sensual, sexy (*inf*). FRIGID
hot, fiery, excitable, temperamental, stormy, violent, furious, irate, enraged, incensed. CALM

**passive** submissive, unresisting, docile, acquiescent, compliant, patient, resigned, indifferent, uninvolved, inert, still, inactive, lifeless. ACTIVE

**past** *adj*, over, finished, ended, done, gone, spent, elapsed, forgotten. AHEAD
ancient, old, bygone, obsolete, previous, former, prior, preceding, recent, late. FUTURE
*n*, history, antiquity, long ago, olden days, yesteryear, yesterday. PRESENT
life, background, experience, youth, memories.
*adv*, by, on, over, across, ago.
*prep*, beyond, over, above, after.

**paste** *n*, adhesive, glue, gum, mucilage.
*v*, stick, glue, gum, fix.

**pastime** hobby, recreation, activity, sport, game, entertainment, diversion, amusement. WORK

**pastor** clergyman, cleric, churchman, ecclesiastic, priest, minister, rector, parson, vicar, preacher. LAYMAN

**pastoral** rural, rustic, country, bucolic, idyllic.
clerical, ecclesiastical, ministerial.

**pasture** pasturage, grazing, grassland, meadow, herbage, grass.

**pat** tap, dab, hit, slap, rap, stroke, caress.

**patch** *n*, piece, scrap, area, tract, plot.
*v*, mend, repair, fix, reinforce, cover.

**patent** *adj*, obvious, plain, clear, manifest, evident, apparent, open, unconcealed, undisguised, unmistakable, conspicuous, blatant, glaring. HIDDEN
*n*, copyright, right, privilege, licence, grant, invention.

**paternal** fatherly, protective, solicitous, benevolent.

**path** track, trail, pathway, footpath, walk, way, road, passage, route, course, avenue.

**pathetic** moving, touching, affecting, poignant, plaintive, piteous, pitiable, sad, distressing, tender, emotional.
paltry, meagre, inadequate, pitiful, lamentable, feeble, contemptible, worthless, useless.

**patience** tolerance, forbearance, restraint, leniency, calmness, composure, equanimity, imperturbability, self-control, self-possession.
endurance, sufferance, stoicism, resignation, submission, perseverance, persistence, constancy, fortitude. IMPATIENCE

**patient** *adj*, tolerant, forbearing, clement, forgiving, lenient, indulgent, calm, composed, imperturbable, self-possessed.
enduring, long-suffering, uncomplaining, stoical, philosophical, resigned, submissive, passive, persevering, persistent. IMPATIENT
*n*, invalid, sufferer, case, inmate.

**patrician** *n*, aristocrat, noble, peer. COMMONER
*adj*, aristocratic, noble, highborn, blueblooded. PLEBEIAN

**patrimony** heritage, birthright, inheritance, legacy, bequest.

**patrol** *v*, guard, protect, police, keep watch, inspect.
*n*, guard, garrison, sentry, sentinel, watch, watchman.
protection, vigilance, round, beat.

**patron** sponsor, promoter, backer, supporter, advocate, benefactor, guardian, protector, defender, helper, friend.
customer, client, regular, habitué, buyer, shopper.

**patronize** frequent, buy from, deal with, sponsor, promote, back, support, help, befriend.
condescend, stoop, talk down to, look down on, contemn, disdain. RESPECT

**pattern** design, style, motif, figure, decoration, ornamentation.
method, system, plan, arrangement, order.
model, exemplar, paragon, standard, norm, original, archetype, prototype, mould, stencil, template, diagram, blueprint, sample, specimen. COPY

**paucity** dearth, lack, scarcity, scantiness, sparseness, fewness, shortage, deficiency, inadequacy, insuffiency. ABUNDANCE

**pauper** beggar, mendicant, indigent, down-and-out, poor person, bankrupt, insolvent.

**pause** *v*, stop, halt, cease, desist, break, rest, interrupt, discontinue, wait, delay, hesitate. PROCEED

*n*, stop, halt, cessation, suspension, break, rest, interval, intermission, interruption, wait, delay, hesitation. CONTINUANCE

**pave** flag, cobble, tile, floor, concrete, asphalt, tar, macadamize, surface, cover.

prepare, smooth, facilitate. IMPEDE

**pawn**[1] *v*, deposit, pledge, hock (*inf*), stake, wager. REDEEM

*n*, deposit, pledge, security, surety, gage, earnest, assurance, guarantee.

**pawn**[2] *n*, instrument, tool, puppet, cat's-paw.

**pay** *v*, remunerate, reward, recompense, requite, repay, pay back, refund, reimburse, compensate, remit, defray, settle, clear, discharge, pay off, liquidate, meet, satisfy, honour. OWE

spend, disburse, pay out, fork out (*inf*), cough up (*inf*).

yield, return, profit, benefit, be advantageous, be profitable, be lucrative.

give, offer, proffer, afford, bestow, render. WITHHOLD

suffer, answer, atone, make amends.

*n*, salary, wages, remuneration, earnings, payment, hire, fee, stipend, emolument, reward, compensation.

**payment** settlement, discharge, liquidation, defrayal, remittance, advance, premium, deposit, instalment, expenditure, outlay.

recompense, compensation, reward, remuneration, fee, pay, wage.

**peace** concord, harmony, amity, pacification, conciliation, truce, armistice. WAR

calm, calmness, tranquillity, serenity, rest, repose, quiet, silence, hush, stillness, peacefulness. DISTURBANCE

**peaceable** pacific, peace-loving, nonviolent, mild, gentle, amicable, friendly, peaceful, peacemaking, irenic, conciliatory, placatory. WARLIKE

**peaceful** calm, tranquil, serene, quiet, still, restful, placid, unruffled. AGITATED

peaceable, nonviolent, peace-loving, peacemaking, irenic, pacific. BELLIGERENT

**peak** top, summit, pinnacle, apex, point, tip, crest, crown, acme, apogee, zenith, climax, culmination, maximum. BASE

**peal** *v*, ring, chime, toll, tintinnabulate, sound, resound, resonate, reverberate, roar, thunder.

*n*, carillon, chime, toll, tintinnabulation, ringing, sound, reverberation, clap, rumble, roar, burst.

**peasant** countryman, rustic, provincial, bumpkin, yokel, boor, churl. CITIZEN

**peccant** sinful, bad, wicked, corrupt, criminal, culpable, guilty, wrong, faulty, morbid, unhealthy. RIGHTEOUS

**peck** tap, rap, hit, strike, kiss, bite, nibble, pick.

**peculate** embezzle, defalcate, appropriate, misappropriate, steal, purloin, defraud, swindle.

**peculiar** strange, odd, queer, curious, weird, bizarre, unusual, uncommon, rare, singular, exceptional, extraordinary. ORDINARY

distinct, special, specific, particular, characteristic, distinctive, unique, individual, personal. GENERAL

**peculiarity** idiosyncrasy, quirk, mannerism, eccentricity, oddity, curiosity, singularity, individuality, particularity, characteristic, trait, feature, mark.

**pecuniary** monetary, financial.

**pedagogue** teacher, educator, tutor, instructor, schoolmaster, schoolmistress. PUPIL

**pedantic** precise, exact, punctilious, fussy, finicky, particular, hairsplitting, nitpicking (*inf*), formal, puristic, bookish, academic, erudite, pompous, dogmatic.

**peddle** hawk, vend, sell, push (*inf*). BUY

**pedigree** *n*, descent, line, lineage, ancestry, parentage, family, extraction, race, stirps, stock, breed, genealogy, background, derivation.

*adj*, pedigreed, purebred, thoroughbred. HYBRID

**pedlar** hawker, vendor, seller, salesman, dealer, peddler, pusher (*inf*). BUYER

**peel** *v*, pare, skin, decorticate, scale, flake, desquamate, strip, excoriate. COVER

*n*, peeling, skin, rind.

**peep**[1] peek, glimpse, glance, spy, peer, squint, look.

**peep**[2] squeak, chirp, tweet, twitter.

**peer**[1] *n*, noble, nobleman, aristocrat, lord, duke, marquess, earl, viscount, baron. COMMONER
equal, compeer, match, like, mate, fellow.

**peer**[2] *v*, squint, gaze, scrutinize, peep, peek.

**peerless** matchless, unmatched, unequalled, unparalleled, unrivalled, unsurpassed, second to none, nonpareil, superlative, excellent, unique, incomparable. ORDINARY

**peevish** irritable, fretful, fractious, crotchety, cross, touchy, testy, waspish, snappish, petulant, crabbed, cantankerous, grumpy, sullen, sulky, moody, surly, churlish, captious, querulous, sour, acrimonious. GENIAL

**pelf** lucre, money, wealth, riches, mammon.

**pellucid** transparent, translucent, clear, limpid, crystalline. OPAQUE
lucid, coherent, comprehensible, intelligible, clear, plain. UNINTELLIGIBLE

**pelt**[1] *v*, bombard, pepper, shower, assail, belabour, batter, beat, strike, throw, hurl, cast, sling.
dash, race, rush, hurry, speed, tear. AMBLE
pour, teem, rain hard. DRIZZLE

**pelt**[2] *n*, skin, hide, fell, fur, coat.

**pen**[1] *n*, ballpoint, felt-tip, fountain pen, quill.
*v*, write, jot down, draft, compose.

**pen**[2] *n*, enclosure, pound, fold, sty, cage, coop.
*v*, enclose, confine, coop up, fence in, cage. FREE

**penal** punitive, disciplinary, corrective, retributive.

**penalize** punish, discipline, correct, handicap, disadvantage. REWARD

**penalty** punishment, retribution, forfeiture, forfeit, fine, mulct, handicap, disadvantage. REWARD

**penance** punishment, penalty, atonement, reparation, contrition, mortification, humilation.

**penchant** inclination, tendency, proclivity, propensity, leaning, bent, liking, predilection, partiality, fondness, taste. AVERSION

**pendent** hanging, suspended, dangling, swinging, pendulous, overhanging, projecting, jutting out, beetling. ERECT

**pending** *prep*, until, awaiting, during.
*adj*, unsettled, undecided, in abeyance, hanging fire, imminent, impending.

**penetrable** pervious, permeable, porous, accessible, passable, comprehensible, fathomable, vulnerable. IMPENETRABLE

**penetrate** pierce, pass through, enter, bore, perforate, prick.
permeate, pervade, percolate, impregnate, infiltrate, invade.
understand, comprehend, grasp, fathom, perceive, see, decipher, unravel, sink in, register (*inf*).

**penetrating** piercing, shrill, sharp, acute, keen, perceptive, discerning, discriminating, intelligent, clever, shrewd, astute, incisive, biting. DULL

**penitence** contrition, repentance, regret, remorse, compunction, sorrow, shame. IMPENITENCE

**penitent** contrite, repentant, regretful, remorseful, sorrowful, abject, sorry, apologetic. IMPENITENT

**penniless** poor, impecunious, penurious, broke (*inf*), skint (*inf*), bankrupt, indigent, destitute, needy, necessitous, impoverished, poverty-stricken. RICH

**pennon** pennant, streamer, banner, banderole, jack, flag, ensign, standard, colours.

**pension** annuity, allowance, grant.

**pensive** thoughtful, reflective, musing, meditative, ruminative, dreamy, wistful, brooding, melancholy, mournful, sad, sober, solemn, serious, grave. CAREFREE

**pent-up** repressed, suppressed, held back, restrained, bridled, confined, bottled up. RELEASED

**penurious** niggardly, miserly, mean, stingy, cheeseparing, penny-pinching (*inf*), parsimonious, tight-fisted, close-fisted. GENEROUS
poor, penniless, impecunious, impoverished, poverty-stricken, destitute, indigent. RICH
scanty, meagre, inadequate, deficient, poor, paltry. ABUNDANT

**penury** poverty, destitution, indigence, need, want, beggary, pauperism. AFFLUENCE
death, scarcity, deficiency, shortage, lack, paucity. ABUNDANCE

**people** *n*, persons, humans, human beings, men, women, children, mankind, humanity.
nation, race, tribe, community, society, population, inhabitants, public, folk.
populace, crowd, mob, general public, masses, commonalty, rabble, hoi polloi. NOBILITY
*v*, populate, inhabit, settle, colonize.

**peppery** hot, spicy, pungent, piquant, sharp, incisive, biting, caustic, trenchant. MILD
irritable, irascible, quick-tempered, hot-tempered, fiery, choleric, testy, touchy, snappish, waspish. AFFABLE

**per** each, every, a, by, through.

**perceive** sense, feel, be aware of, see, observe, notice, discern, make out, distinguish, recognize.
understand, comprehend, grasp, fathom, realize, learn, know, conclude, deduce.

**perceptible** perceivable, discernible, appreciable, recognizable, apparent, visible, noticeable, distinct, evident, obvious, palpable. IMPERCEPTIBLE

**perception** understanding, comprehension, apprehension, awareness, recognition, discernment, knowledge, percipience, sense, feeling, intuition, insight, idea, notion, conception. IGNORANCE

**perceptive** percipient, perspicacious, discerning, aware, observant, alert, sensitive, intuitive, sharp, penetrating, astute, shrewd. SLOW

**perch** *n*, pole, bar, branch, roost.
*v*, alight, land, settle, rest, sit, roost.

**percolate** strain, filter, drip, seep, ooze, exude, permeate, penetrate.

**percussion** impact, crash, collision, knock, bump, shock, concussion.

**perdition** damnation, destruction, ruin, downfall, hell. SALVATION

**peregrination** journey, voyage, trip, expedition, travel, globetrotting, wandering, roaming.

**peremptory** commanding, imperative, obligatory, mandatory, binding, absolute, categorical, decisive, final, arbitrary, imperious, dictatorial, dogmatic, assertive, positive.

**perennial** lasting, enduring, permanent, constant, incessant, continual, perpetual, everlasting, eternal, immortal, undying, imperishable, endless, ceaseless. EPHEMERAL

**perfect** *adj*, pure, unblemished, flawless, immaculate, spotless, faultless, impeccable, blameless, exemplary, ideal, excellent, superb. IMPERFECT
complete, finished, consummate, entire, full, whole, total, utter, absolute, sheer. INCOMPLETE
accurate, precise, exact, correct, right, true. INACCURATE
accomplished, practised, polished, expert, masterly, skilled, skilful.
*v*, finish, complete, consummate, realize, achieve, accomplish. COMMENCE
polish, elaborate, improve, ameliorate, rectify. SPOIL

**perfection** completion, consummation, realization, achievement, accomplishment.
perfectness, purity, spotlessness, flawlessness, faultlessness, excellence. IMPERFECTION
ideal, paragon, quintessence.

**perfectly** completely, totally, entirely, fully, altogether, quite, thoroughly, utterly, absolutely. PARTLY
flawlessly, faultlessly, superbly, admirably, ideally, exactly, precisely. BADLY

**perfidious** treacherous, traitorous, false, faithless, unfaithful, disloyal, dishonest, deceitful, untrustworthy, two-faced, double-dealing. LOYAL

**perforate** puncture, pierce, penetrate, punch, bore, drill, prick.

**perforce** necessarily, by necessity, unavoidably, inevitably.

**perform** do, carry out, discharge, execute, transact, effect, achieve, accomplish, complete, fulfil, comply with, observe, act, function, work. FAIL
play, act, stage, put on, enact, represent.

**performance** show, entertainment, production, presentation, appearance, gig (*inf*), play, exhibition.
accomplishment, achievement, completion, execution, discharge, act, deed, exploit, feat, action, operation, conduct, behaviour.

**performer** entertainer, player, actor, actress, artiste.

**perfume** scent, fragrance, essence, cologne, aroma, bouquet, balminess, redolence, odour, smell. STENCH

**perfunctory** cursory, superficial, sketchy, hasty, careless, slipshod, mechanical, routine, indifferent, offhand, negligent, headless, thoughtless. THOROUGH

**perhaps** maybe, possibly, perchance, peradventure. DEFINITELY

**peril** danger, jeopardy, risk, hazard, menace, vulnerability, exposure, insecurity, uncertainty. SAFETY

**perilous** dangerous, unsafe, risky, hazardous, vulnerable, exposed, precarious, insecure. SAFE

**perimeter** circumference, boundary, border, edge, margin, periphery. CENTRE

**period** time, age, era, epoch, term, spell, stretch, interval, season, generation, days, years, course, cycle.

**periodic** intermittent, recurrent, cyclic, regular, occasional, infrequent, sporadic, spasmodic. CONTINUOUS

**periodical** magazine, review, journal, paper, weekly, monthly.

**peripatetic** itinerant, wandering, roaming, travelling, mobile, nomadic, migratory.

**periphery** boundary, circumference, perimeter, ambit, edge, margin, fringe, border, outside, surface. CENTRE

**periphrastic** circumlocutory, verbose, wordy, prolix, circuitous, roundabout. DIRECT

**perish** die, expire, decease, pass away, be killed, rot, decay, waste, wither, fade, fail, decline, vanish, disappear. LAST

**perishable** destructible, frail, fragile, temporary, impermanent, transitory, fleeting. IMPERISHABLE

**perk up** cheer up, liven up, buck up (*inf*), brighten, take heart, rally, recover, recuperate, revive.

**perky** jaunty, sprightly, lively, vivacious, bouncy, animated, spirited, sparkling. LETHARGIC

**permanent** lasting, enduring, abiding, durable, indestructible, imperishable, eternal, everlasting, perpetual, constant, fixed, stable, changeless, unchanging, immutable, invariable. TEMPORARY

**permeable** pervious, porous, penetrable. IMPERMEABLE

**permeate** penetrate, infiltrate, pervade, percolate, impregnate, suffuse, imbue, saturate, fill.

**permissible** allowable, allowed, permitted, lawful, legal, licit, legitimate, right, proper, acceptable, admissible, all right, OK (*inf*). PROHIBITED

**permission** authorization, sanction, approval, warrant, licence, freedom, liberty, leave, consent, assent, allowance, tolerance, toleration, dispensation, go-ahead. PROHIBITION

**permit** *v*, allow, let, sanction, authorize, warrant, license, enable, empower, consent, assent, grant, tolerate, countenance. FORBID

*n*, permission, authorization, licence, warrant, pass, passport.

**permutation** alteration, transformation, change, shift, transposition, rearrangement.

**pernicious** deadly, fatal, lethal, mortal, ruinous, destructive, injurious, hurtful, harmful, damaging, deleterious, detrimental, noxious, noisome. BENEFICIAL

**perorate** discourse, expatiate, harangue, speechify, summarize, sum up, recapitulate, recap (*inf*).

**perpendicular** upright, vertical, straight, plumb, erect, standing, on end. OBLIQUE

**perpetrate** commit, do, execute, perform, carry out, effect, bring about.

**perpetual** continual, incessant, endless, unending, ceaseless, unceasing, constant, continuous, uninterrupted, interminable, never-ending, eternal, everlasting, permanent, perennial, lasting, enduring. TEMPORARY

**perpetuate** continue, keep up, maintain, sustain, preserve, keep alive, immortalize, eternalize. END

**perplex** puzzle, baffle, mystify, nonplus, flummox, bewilder, confuse, confound, muddle. ENLIGHTEN

complicate, involve, embroil, entangle, jumble, mix up. SIMPLIFY

**perplexity** bewilderment, confusion, puzzlement, bafflement, mystification, incomprehension, stupefaction. ENLIGHTENMENT

complication, involvement, entanglement, complexity, intricacy. SIMPLICATION

puzzle, mystery, enigma, quandary, dilemma, difficulty, muddle.

**persecute** harass, hound, torment, torture, martyr, molest, maltreat, ill-treat, victimize, oppress, plague, pester, badger, bother, worry, vex, annoy.

**perseverance** persistence, tenacity, dedication, diligence, sedulity, zeal, steadfastness, constancy, determination, resolution, doggedness, stamina, endurance, indefatigability.

**persevere** persist, continue, carry on, stand firm, hold fast, pursue, maintain. WAVER

**persiflage** banter, badinage, wit, repartee, frivolity, pleasantry, teasing, raillery.

**persist** continue, carry on, persevere, stand firm, insist. DESIST
last, endure, abide, remain, survive, continue, carry on. STOP

**persistent** persevering, tenacious, diligent, assiduous, determined, resolute, dogged, unflagging, indefatigable, stubborn, obstinate, obdurate, unshakable, immovable, fixed. WAVERING
constant, steady, incessant, interminable, continual, perpetual, unrelenting. INTERMITTENT

**person** individual, body, soul, human, human being, man, woman, child, someone, somebody.

**personal** private, intimate, secret, confidential, individual, own, particular, exclusive, special. COMMUNAL

**personality** character, nature, disposition, temperament, individuality, identity.
charisma, magnetism, attraction, charm.
personage, notable, VIP, public figure, celebrity, star, famous person, household name.

**personate** portray, play, act, represent, impersonate, imitate.

**personify** embody, incarnate, exemplify, epitomize, represent, symbolize, typify.

**perspective** viewpoint, outlook, angle, aspect, proportion, objectivity, view, vista, prospect, scene, panorama.

**perspicacious** perceptive, percipient, astute, shrewd, sharp, keen, acute, penetrating, discerning, sagacious, wise, intelligent, clever. DULL

**perspicacity** perception, percipience, astuteness, shrewdness, sharpness, keenness, penetration, discernment, insight, acumen, sagacity, wisdom. DULLNESS

**perspicuity** lucidity, clarity, clearness, plainness, intelligibility, comprehensibility. OBSCURITY

**perspicuous** lucid, clear, plain, distinct, intelligible, comprehensible, explicit, unambiguous, obvious, apparent. OBSCURE

**perspiration** sweat, sweating, diaphoresis, exudation, secretion, moisture, wetness.

**persuade** induce, urge, impel, influence, sway, prevail upon, incline, dispose, move, prompt, entice, coax, advise, counsel, convince, convert. DETER

**persuasion** inducement, enticement, temptation, cajolery, exhortation, advice. DISSUASION
power, potency, force, cogency, influence.
belief, faith, creed, credo, sect, cult, denomination, school.

**persuasive** convincing, cogent, telling, effective, forceful, influential, impressive, plausible, sound, valid, compelling, winning. UNCONVINCING

**pert** impudent, impertinent, insolent, rude, cheeky, saucy, bold, forward. BASHFUL
jaunty, perky, lively, sprightly, smart, dapper.

**pertain** appertain, relate, refer, regard, concern, belong.

**pertinacious** tenacious, dogged, persistent, persevering, determined, resolute, steadfast, constant, firm, unshakable, stubborn, obstinate, mulish, pig-headed, inflexible, unyielding, headstrong, wilful. IRRESOLUTE

**pertinent** relevant, germane, apposite, apropos, apt, appropriate, fit, fitting, suitable, proper, seemly. IRRELEVANT

**perturb** trouble, disturb, upset, worry, disquiet, alarm, agitate, discompose, ruffle, fluster, unsettle, disconcert, vex, confuse, muddle, disorder, disarrange. COMPOSE

**peruse** study, scrutinize, examine, inspect, read, browse, scan, survey.

**pervade** permeate, spread, diffuse, fill, saturate, impregnate, penetrate, percolate, imbue, suffuse.

**perverse** contrary, contumacious, refractory, wayward, headstrong, wilful, stubborn, obstinate, mulish, obdurate, intransigent, awkward, difficult, troublesome, deviant, abnormal. DOCILE
cantankerous, cross, peevish, petulant, ill-tempered, irascible, crabbed, surly. AFFABLE

**perversion** aberration, deviation, abnormality, irregularity, corruption, depravity, misuse, prostitution, debasement, vitiation, distortion, misinterpretation, misrepresentation, falsification.

**pervert** misuse, abuse, corrupt, deprave, subvert, lead astray, debase, vitiate, distort, twist, warp, misinterpret, misrepresent, falsify.

**pervious** permeable, porous, penetrable, passable, accessible, receptive. IMPERVIOUS

**pessimistic** cynical, gloomy, glum, depressed, despondent, hopeless, despairing, negative. OPTIMISTIC

**pest** nuisance, bother, annoyance, vexation, pain (*inf*), curse, bane, scourge, blight, plague, pestilence. BLESSING

**pester** plague, torment, trouble, worry, bother, disturb, harass, hound, badger, nag, annoy, irritate, vex, irk.

**pestilence** epidemic, plague, disease, scourge, curse, bane, blight.

**pestilent** annoying, irritating, vexatious, irksome, troublesome.
pernicious, dangerous, destructive, ruinous, deadly, fatal, deleterious, detrimental, harmful, injurious, noxious, corrupting. BENEFICIAL
pestiferous, pestilential, infectious, contagious, diseased, infected, contaminated, unhealthy, insalubrious, poisonous, venomous. PURE

**pet** *n*, favourite, darling, apple of one's eye, blue-eyed boy (*inf*).
*adj*, tame, domestic, house-trained. WILD
favourite, dearest, beloved, cherished, prized, treasured.
*v*, pamper, cosset, coddle, mollycoddle, indulge, spoil. DISCIPLINE
fondle, stroke, caress, pat, cuddle.

**petition** *n*, request, appeal, entreaty, plea, supplication, invocation, solicitation, application, suit.
*v*, ask, request, appeal, beg, beseech, plead, entreat, supplicate, solicit, apply, sue.

**petrify** calcify, fossilize, harden, solidify, turn to stone.
stupefy, stun, daze, paralyse, dumbfound, stagger, astonish, astound, amaze, appal, horrify, terrify. REASSURE

**pettish** peevish, petulant, touchy, testy, waspish, cross, irritable, querulous, fractious, fretful. GENIAL

**petty** trivial, minor, unimportant, insignificant, trifling, paltry, slight, small, little, inconsiderable. IMPORTANT
small-minded, narrow-minded, mean, stingy, niggardly, grudging. GENEROUS

**petulant** peevish, pettish, cross, grumpy, touchy, testy, irascible, irritable, waspish, snappish, fretful, querulous, impatient, sullen, moody. GENIAL

**phantasm** phantom, apparition, spectre, ghost, illusion, hallucination, chimera, figment, dream, vision.

**phantom** *n*, ghost, spectre, apparition, spirit, spook (*inf*), phantasm, chimera, illusion, hallucination, vision.
*adj*, phantasmal, phantasmagoric, unreal, illusory, spectral, ghostly. REAL

**pharisaic** pharisaical, sanctimonious, self-righteous, goody-goody, holier-than-thou, hypocritical, insincere.

**phase** period, stage, aspect, appearance, side, angle, state, condition.

**phenomenal** marvellous, wonderful, extraordinary, prodigious, remarkable, exceptional, outstanding, fantastic, miraculous. ORDINARY

**phenomenon** marvel, wonder, prodigy, miracle, sensation, spectacle.
fact, circumstance, occurrence, event, happening, incident.

**philander** flirt, coquet, dally, trifle, womanize (*inf*).

**philanthropic** charitable, benevolent, beneficent, munificent, liberal, generous, altruistic, humanitarian, kind, humane, benign, benignant, public-spirited. SELFISH

**philistine** *n*, boor, lout, barbarian, yahoo, lowbrow, bourgeois, vulgarian. AESTHETE
*adj*, uncultured, unrefined, uncultivated, uneducated, boorish, loutish, lowbrow, bourgeois. CULTURED

**philosopher** thinker, theorist, metaphysician, logician, sage.

**philosophical** wise, learned, erudite, thinking, logical, rational, theoretical, metaphysical.
calm, composed, cool, unruffled, tranquil, serene, stoical, resigned, imperturbable. AGITATED

**philosophy** logic, reasoning, metaphysics, knowledge, wisdom, thought, thinking.
viewpoint, attitude, ideology, beliefs, values.

calmness, composure, equanimity, self-possession, serenity, stoicism, resignation. AGITATION

**phlegmatic** sluggish, lethargic, apathetic, indifferent, uninterested, stolid, unemotional, impassive, unfeeling, cold, dull, placid, imperturable, philosophical. EMOTIONAL

**phobia** fear, terror, horror, dread, dislike, aversion, hatred, loathing. MANIA

**phosphorescent** luminous, radiant, fluorescent, bright.

**photograph** *n*, picture, photo (*inf*), snapshot, shot, snap (*inf*), print, slide, transparency.
*v*, shoot, film, take, snap (*inf*).

**phrase** *n*, expression, locution, idiom, saying, utterance, clause.
*v*, express, put, word, style, couch, frame, say, utter, voice, deliver.

**phraseology** phrasing, wording, syntax, style, diction, language, parlance, idiom.

**physical** bodily, corporeal, corporal, carnal, fleshly, earthly, mortal, natural, material, substantial, tangible, concrete, real, visible, external. SPIRITUAL

**physician** doctor, medical practitioner, GP, specialist, consultant.

**physiognomy** features, lineaments, face, countenance, visage, look, aspect, appearance.

**physique** build, frame, figure, body, shape, form, constitution, make-up.

**pick** *v*, choose, select, single out, decide on, opt for. REJECT
pluck, cull, glean, harvest, gather, collect. LEAVE
open, crack, jemmy, force, rob, steal.
**pick out,** choose, select, single out.
distinguish, discriminate, tell apart, discern, perceive, make out.
**pick up,** lift, raise, grasp, gather. DROP
improve, get better, mend, recover, gain, advance.
*n*, choice, selection, option, preference.
best, cream, flower, prize, elite. REJECT

**pickle** *v*, marinade, preserve, cure.
*n*, plight, predicament, quandary, dilemma, fix (*inf*), jam (*inf*).

**pictorial** graphic, illustrative, vivid, expressive, illustrated.

**picture** *n*, image, representation, likeness, portrait, sketch, drawing, painting, etching, engraving, photograph, print, illustration.
description, portrayal, depiction, account.
epitome, archetype, embodiment, personification.
*v*, imagine, visualize, conceive of, envisage.
depict, portray, draw, paint, photograph, illustrate, show, represent, describe.

**picturesque** scenic, quaint, attractive, beautiful, charming, delightful, colourful, vivid, graphic, pictorial, artistic, aesthetic. UGLY

**piece** *n*, part, section, division, bit, fragment, portion, share, slice, chunk, length, quantity, scrap, morsel, shred, element, component. WHOLE
example, specimen, case, instance.
composition, creation, production, work.
*v*, join, unite, connect, fit, assemble, fix, mend, repair, patch. SEPARATE

**pied** piebald, mottled, dappled, speckled, brindled, spotted, flecked, motley, variegated, multicoloured. PLAIN

**pierce** penetrate, enter, puncture, perforate, stab, prick, bore, drill.
touch, move, affect, strike, stir, rouse, excite, thrill.

**piercing** shrill, high-pitched, ear-splitting, loud, sharp, penetrating, probing, searching, keen, biting, bitter, fierce, acute, stabbing, excruciating. DULL

**piety** piousness, devoutness, godliness, saintliness, holiness, sanctity, devotion, reverence, faith, religion. IMPIETY

**pigeonhole** *n*, compartment, section, place, slot (*inf*), cubbyhole, niche, category, class.
*v*, classify, categorize, label, catalogue, sort.
shelve, postpone, defer, put off.

**piggish** hoggish, swinish, dirty, filthy, boorish, rude, greedy, gluttonous, mean, selfish, obstinate, stubborn, pig-headed.

**pigment** colour, colouring, tint, dye, paint, stain, colorant.

**pile** *n*, heap, mound, stack, mass, store, hoard, accumulation, collection.
lot, great deal, load, quantity. FEW
building, edifice, structure.
*v*, heap, stack, amass, store, hoard, accumulate, collect, gather. SCATTER

**pilfer** steal, purloin, filch, pinch (*inf*), nick (*inf*), thieve, rob, peculate, embezzle. RETURN

**pilgrim** crusader, palmer, devotee, wanderer, traveller, wayfarer.

**pilgrimage** expedition, excursion, tour, journey, trip, voyage, peregrination, crusade, mission.

**pill** tablet, capsule, pellet, bolus.

**pillage** *v*, ransack, rifle, rob, plunder, loot, maraud, raid, sack, despoil, ravage.
*n*, plunder, looting, marauding, depredation, spoliation, devastation, spoils, loot, booty.

**pillar** column, shaft, post, pier, upright, prop, support, mainstay.

**pilot** *n*, aviator, airman, aeronaut, flier, helmsman, steersman, navigator, guide, leader, director, conductor.
*v*, fly, steer, control, drive, navigate, guide, direct, lead, conduct, shepherd, usher.

**pimple** spot, pustule, boil, eruption.

**pin** *n*, peg, bolt, nail, tack, clip, brooch.
*v*, fasten, secure, fix, attach, hold.
**pin down,** constrain, force, press, confine, restrain, bind, tie, hold, immobilize. RELEASE
pinpoint, locate, identify, specify, determine.

**pinch** *v*, squeeze, press, crush, compress, grip, grasp, tweak, nip, hurt, constrict, cramp.
steal, filch, pilfer, purloin, nick (*inf*). RETURN
*n*, squeeze, nip.
bit, dash, trace, *soupçon*.
emergency, exigency, urgency, crisis, stress, pressure, difficulty, predicament.

**pine** long, yearn, thirst, hunger, hanker, crave, wish, desire. HAVE
languish, droop, flag, wilt, wither, decline, fade, fail, waste. REVIVE

**pinguid** fat, fatty, greasy, oily, oleaginous. DRY

**pinion** bind, tie, chain, shackle, fetter, confine, restrain.

**pinnacle** peak, summit, top, height, crown, apex, apogee, acme, zenith, meridian, climax, culmination. BASE

**pioneer** *n*, settler, colonist, explorer, trailblazer, leader, innovator.
*v*, launch, introduce, initiate, originate, inaugurate, institute, found, establish, lead.

**pious** devout, godly, saintly, holy, religious, reverent, good, righteous, sanctimonious, self-righteous, goody-goody, holier-than-thou. IMPIOUS

**pipe** *n*, tube, duct, conduit, passage, line.
*v*, squeak, tweet, chirp, peep, whistle, warble.

**piquant** pungent, sharp, tart, tangy, spicy, hot, peppery. BLAND
interesting, stimulating, intriguing, titillating, racy, lively, spirited, sparkling, scintillating. DULL

**pique** *v*, wound, hurt, sting, offend, affront, upset, put out, annoy, irritate, irk, vex. PLEASE
excite, arouse, stimulate, provoke, stir, rouse.
*n*, offence, umbrage, resentment, indignation, annoyance, irritation, vexation, displeasure. PLEASURE

**pirate** *n*, corsair, buccaneer, rover, freebooter, robber, plunderer, marauder.
*v*, plagiarize, copy, crib (*inf*), lift (*inf*), steal, appropriate.

**pit** *n*, hole, cavity, crater, mine, excavation, ditch, trench, shaft, well, abyss, chasm, hollow, depression, dent, indentation, pockmark, scar.
*v*, match, oppose, set against.
dent, indent, pockmark, scar, nick, notch.

**pitch** *v*, hurl, fling, throw, cast, toss, sling, heave. CATCH
erect, raise, set up, establish, fix, settle, locate, place. STRIKE
roll, reel, lurch, wallow, plunge, dive, fall, drop.
*n*, degree, height, depth, level, point, extent, range.
slope, gradient, incline, angle, tilt, slant, inclination.
tone, timbre, modulation.
throw, toss, plunge, roll.
field, ground, area, station.

**pitcher** jug, ewer, urn, vessel, container.

**piteous** pitiable, pitiful, pathetic, plaintive, mournful, sad, sorrowful, doleful, sorry, wretched, lamentable, deplorable, poignant, moving, touching, affecting, distressing, heart-rending.

**pitfall** trap, snare, catch, hazard, danger, snag, drawback.

**pith** essence, quintessence, substance, gist, crux, nub, core, heart, kernel, marrow.
importance, significance, consequence, moment, weight, force, power, strength, vigour.

**pithy** terse, succinct, concise, compact, brief, short, laconic, pointed, cogent, forceful, meaningful, weighty. VERBOSE

**pitiable** pitiful, pathetic, poor, sorry, wretched, miserable, piteous, lamentable, deplorable, distressing. ENVIABLE

**pitiful** pathetic, pitiable, sorry, wretched, miserable, piteous, poignant, heart-rending, distressing, poor, lamentable.
deplorable, contemptible, despicable, mean, meagre, worthless. ADMIRABLE

**pitiless** merciless, unmerciful, unsparing, harsh, hard-hearted, callous, cold, unfeeling, unsympathetic, heartless, unkind, inhuman, cruel, ruthless, relentless, unrelenting, implacable, inexorable. COMPASSIONATE

**pittance** allowance, ration, modicum, trifle, peanuts (*inf*), chicken feed (*inf*).

**pity** *n*, compassion, tenderness, mercy, clemency, grace, charity, humanity, kindness, sympathy, commiseration, condolence. CRUELTY
shame, regret, misfortune, bad luck.
**take pity on,** forgive, pardon, have mercy on, spare, relent, melt.
*v*, commiserate with, sympathize with, feel for, feel sorry for.

**pivot** *n*, fulcrum, axis, axle, spindle, pin, hinge, hub, centre, focal point.
*v*, revolve, rotate, spin, turn, hinge.

**placable** appeasable, reconcilable, mild, forgiving, merciful, magnanimous. IMPLACABLE

**placard** notice, advertisement, poster, bill, sign, billboard.

**placate** pacify, appease, mollify, conciliate, soothe, calm, reconcile, win over. INCENSE

**place** *n*, spot, location, scene, site, position, situation, point, whereabouts.
area, region, district, locality, town, city, village.
status, rank, standing, station, state, condition.
post, appointment, job, employment.
duty, responsibility, role, function, right, prerogative, affair, concern.
space, room, stead, lieu.
house, flat, home, abode, dwelling, residence, domicile, accommodation, quarters, lodgings.
**take place,** happen, occur, come about, come to pass, befall, betide, transpire.
*v*, put, lay, set, deposit, position, locate, situate, install, appoint. REMOVE
arrange, dispose, order, group, classify, sort. DISARRANGE
identify, recognize, know.

**placid** calm, serene, peaceful, tranquil, quiet, undisturbed, unmoved, unruffled, unperturbed, composed, collected, equable, imperturbable.

**plagiarize** pirate, borrow, crib (*inf*), lift (*inf*), steal, appropriate, copy, forge.

**plague** *n*, epidemic, pestilence, disease, contagion.
curse, scourge, affliction, torment, trouble, trial.
pest, nuisance, annoyance, vexation, bother, pain (*inf*), problem, trouble. BLESSING
*v*, torment, torture, distress, trouble, afflict, harass, badger, hound, pester, annoy, irritate, vex, irk, bother, worry.

**plain** *adj*, clear, distinct, apparent, visible, patent, obvious, evident, manifest, open, blatant, palpable, unmistakable, intelligible, understandable, comprehensible, lucid. OBSCURE
simple, unadorned, pure, basic, Spartan, austere, unpretentious, ordinary, everyday, homely. FANCY
unattractive, ugly. ATTRACTIVE
frank, candid, open, blunt, direct, straightforward, forthright, plain-spoken, honest, sincere, guileless, artless, ingenuous. DEVIOUS
flat, level, even, smooth, plane. UNEVEN
*n*, plateau, tableland, lowland, grassland, prairie.

**plaintiff** accuser, prosecutor, suitor, petitioner. DEFENDANT

**plaintive** mournful, doleful, sad, melancholy, sorrowful, woeful, piteous, heart-rending. JOYOUS

**plait** *v*, braid, weave, interweave, interlace, twist, twine, intertwine. UNRAVEL
*n*, braid, pigtail.

**plan** *n*, scheme, design, arrangement, programme, project, idea, proposal, proposition, plot, device, method, procedure, system, strategy.
diagram, chart, map, blueprint, drawing, sketch, draft.
*v*, scheme, plot, devise, design, formulate, work out, arrange, organize, prepare, outline, draft.

intend, purpose, mean, aim, envisage, contemplate.

**plane** *adj*, flat, level, even, smooth, regular, uniform, plain. UNEVEN
*n*, level, stratum, position, status, degree.
aeroplane, aircraft.

**plant** *n*, flower, herb, vegetable, weed, shrub, bush, tree.
factory, mill, works, machinery, equipment, apparatus.
*v*, sow, seed. UPROOT
set, place, insert, fix, establish, settle, lodge, root, implant, embed. REMOVE

**plaster** *n*, mortar, cement, stucco, gypsum.
dressing, bandage.
*v*, daub, smear, spread, cover, coat.

**plastic** soft, ductile, mouldable, malleable, pliable, pliant, supple, flexible, yielding, tractable, receptive, impressionable.

**plate** *n*, dish, platter.
sheet, pane, panel, slab, layer, coating.
illustration, print.
*v*, coat, cover, face, overlay, laminate, veneer, anodize, gild, silver.

**platform** stage, dais, podium, rostrum.
plan, programme, policy, principles.

**platitude** truism, commonplace, cliché, bromide (*inf*).
banality, triteness, insipidity, vapidity, flatness, dullness.

**plaudits** applause, ovation, acclaim, acclamation, praise, commendation, approval, approbation. DENUNCIATION

**plausible** reasonable, likely, probable, possible, conceivable, credible, believable. IMPLAUSIBLE
specious, smooth, glib.

**play** *v*, sport, revel, amuse oneself, have fun, romp, frolic, caper, gambol, clown, fool, toy, trifle, fiddle. WORK
contend, compete, participate, take part, challenge, oppose, take on.
perform, act, portray, represent, impersonate.
execute, discharge, fulfil, do, perform, carry out. NEGLECT
bet, wager, gamble, speculate, risk.
**play down,** minimize, make light of, underrate, underestimate, belittle, disparage. EMPHASIZE
**play on,** exploit, capitalize on, take advantage of, abuse, impose on.
**play up,** emphasize, stress, accentuate, highlight, underline, point up.
misbehave, irritate, bother, trouble, malfunction.
*n*, drama, piece, show, performance, comedy, tragedy, farce, melodrama.
recreation, amusement, entertainment, diversion, pastime, game, sport, fun, jest. WORK
action, movement, motion, function, operation, latitude, leeway, scope, range, sweep, swing, margin, room.

**player** competitor, contestant, contender, participant, sportsman, sportswoman.
performer, entertainer, artiste, actor, actress, musician, instrumentalist.

**playful** sportive, frolicsome, frisky, coltish, high spirited, gay, merry, cheerful, jolly, impish, mischievous, arch, waggish, humorous, joking, jesting. SERIOUS

**plea** request, entreaty, appeal, petition, suit, prayer, supplication.
excuse, pretext, apology, extenuation, vindication, justification, defence, claim, allegation. ACCUSATION

**plead** appeal, entreat, beg, beseech, implore, supplicate, petition, ask, request.
argue, reason, declare, assert, allege, maintain, put forward, present.

**pleasant** agreeable, pleasing, delightful, enjoyable, pleasurable, gratifying, nice, lovely, fine, acceptable, satisfactory, fair, charming, amiable, likable, affable, friendly, courteous. UNPLEASANT

**pleasantry** banter, badinage, persiflage, witticism, joke, jest.

**please** gratify, humour, delight, gladden, cheer, content, satisfy, amuse, entertain, charm. OFFEND
like, wish, want, desire, choose, prefer, will, see fit.

**pleased** glad, happy, contented, satisfied, delighted, thrilled, overjoyed, elated. UPSET

**pleasing** agreeable, pleasant, delightful, pleasurable, gratifying, nice, lovely, attractive, charming, likable, winning. OBNOXIOUS

**pleasure** gratification, contentment, satisfaction, enjoyment, delectation, delight, happiness, gladness, joy, comfort, amusement, recreation, fun. PAIN
choice, preference, wish, desire, will.

**plebian** *adj*, common, vulgar, coarse, unrefined, base, low, mean, ignoble, working-class, proletarian. ARISTOCRATIC
*n*, commoner, proletarian, peasant, pleb (*inf*). ARISTOCRAT
**pledge** *n*, promise, vow, oath, agreement, undertaking, assurance, word.
surety, security, collateral, deposit, earnest, gage, pawn, bond, guarantee, warranty.
*v*, promise, plight, vow, swear, engage, bind, guarantee, vouch.
toast, drink to.
**plenary** full, complete, entire, whole, thorough, absolute, unqualified, unconditional, unrestricted, unlimited. RESTRICTED
**plenipotentiary** ambassador, envoy, emissary, legate.
**plenitude** abundance, plenty, profusion, copiousness, fullness, repletion, completeness. SCANTNESS
**plentiful** plenteous, abundant, bountiful, copious, ample, profuse, lavish, generous, full, replete, bumper, prolific, fruitful. SCANTY
**plenty** plenitude, abundance, bounty, profusion, wealth, fund, mine, mass, great deal, lot, enough, sufficiency, excess, superfluity, plethora, glut, copiousness, plentifulness, amplitude, fullness, exuberance, fruitfulness, prosperity, affluence. LACK
**pleonastic** superfluous, redundant, tautological, repetitious, circumlocutory, periphrastic, verbose, wordy, prolix, diffuse, circuitous, roundabout. CONCISE
**plethora** superfluity, excess, surplus, surfeit, glut, overabundance, superabundance. SCARCITY
**pliant** pliable, flexible, bendy, supple, lithe, ductile, malleable, plastic, mouldable. STIFF
adaptable, amenable, yielding, tractable, compliant, docile, impressionable, susceptible, receptive. INTRACTABLE
**plight**[1] *n*, predicament, quandary, dilemma, fix (*inf*), jam (*inf*), difficulty, trouble, state, condition, position, situation.
**plight**[2] *v*, pledge, promise, vow, swear, engage, guarantee.
**plod** trudge, stump, tramp, lumber, drudge, toil, labour, slog, persevere, soldier on.
**plot**[1] *n*, plan, scheme, conspiracy, intrigue, cabal, machination, strategem.
story, narrative, theme, thread, action, scenario.
*v*, plan, scheme, conspire, intrigue, cabal, machinate, hatch, brew, concoct, frame, contrive, devise.
**plot**[2] *n*, patch, allotment, parcel, tract, area.
**ploy** manoeuvre, tactic, stratagem, gambit, ruse, wile, dodge, game, trick.
**pluck** *v*, pull out, draw, pick, gather, collect, tug, tweak, jerk, yank, snatch.
strum, thrum, plunk, twang.
*n*, courage, bravery, valour, mettle, spirit, nerve, grit, guts (*inf*), boldness, daring, heroism, fortitude, determination, resolution. COWARDICE
**plucky** courageous, brave, valiant, valorous, mettlesome, spirited, game (*inf*), bold, daring, heroic, intrepid, fearless, undaunted. COWARDLY
**plug** *n*, bung, stopper, cork.
publicity, promotion, mention, advertisement, puff, hype (*inf*).
*v*, stop, block, clog, choke, obstruct, bung, cork, seal. OPEN
publicize, promote, mention, advertise.
**plumb** *adv*, vertically, perpendicularly, straight, exactly, precisely. OBLIQUELY
*v*, sound, fathom, gauge, measure, probe, penetrate, explore, investigate.
**plump** fat, obese, stout, portly, rotund, fleshy, chubby, podgy, tubby, full, ample. THIN
**plunder** *v*, rob, steal, loot, pillage, rifle, ransack, sack, despoil, ravage, devastate, raid, maraud.
*n*, booty, spoils, loot, pillage, rapine, sack.
**plunge** *v*, dive, plummet, drop, fall, sink, descend, go down, swoop, pitch, jump. SOAR
immerse, submerge, dip, duck. EMERGE
dash, rush, race, tear, hurry, hasten, precipitate. AMBLE
*n*, dive, jump, drop, fall, dip.
**plus** *prep*, and, with, added to. MINUS
*n*, bonus, extra, perk (*inf*), benefit, advantage, gain, surplus.
**ply**[1] *v*, practise, exercise, carry on, pursue, follow, work at.
manipulate, wield, apply, utilize, use, employ.
provide, supply, shower, bombard, assail, beset, importune, press, urge.
**ply**[2] *n*, layer, thickness, fold, sheet, strand.

**poach** trespass, encroach, infringe, steal, appropriate, plunder.

**pocket** *n*, bag, pouch, receptacle, compartment, cavity, hollow.
*adj*, small, miniature, abridged, compact, portable.
*v*, take, appropriate, steal, purloin, filch, pilfer. RETURN

**poem** verse, rhyme, ode, sonnet, lyric, ballad.

**poetic** lyric, lyrical, metrical, rhythmical, rhyming. PROSAIC

**poetry** poems, verse, metre, rhyme. PROSE

**poignant** moving, touching, distressing, heart-rending, painful, agonizing, pathetic, piteous, plaintive, sad.
piercing, cutting, biting, caustic, sharp, keen, acute, intense, pungent, piquant. DULL

**point** *n*, dot, mark, speck.
spot, place, site, location, position, stage, phase, period, time, moment, instant, juncture, degree, extent.
tip, end, apex, spike, prong, nib.
cape, headland, foreland, promontory.
verge, brink.
aim, purpose, end, object, objective, goal, intent, intention, reason, motive.
gist, crux, heart, core, essence, substance, question, matter, subject, meaning, import, drift.
detail, item, feature, aspect, attribute, property, part, element.
*v*, direct, aim, level, train.
show, indicate, point to, point at, designate, specify, point out, denote, signify.
sharpen, whet, taper. BLUNT

**pointed** sharp, incisive, cutting, biting, trenchant, keen, acute, penetrating, cogent, telling. BLUNT
barbed, peaked, cuspidate, tapering.

**pointer** guide, indicator, needle, arrow.
tip, hint, advice, warning, recommendation, suggestion.

**pointless** meaningless, irrelevant, absurd, senseless, aimless, vain, futile, useless, fruitless, unproductive, unavailing, ineffectual, worthless. WORTHWHILE

**poise** *n*, composure, self-possession, aplomb, assurance, confidence, coolness, sang-froid, calmness, equanimity, dignity, grace.
balance, equilibrium, steadiness, stability. INSTABILITY
*v*, balance, hover, hang, hold.

**poison** *n*, venom, toxin, bane, contagion, contamination, corruption, blight, canker, virus.
*v*, envenom, infect, pollute, contaminate, taint, corrupt, vitiate, subvert. CLEANSE

**poisonous** venomous, toxic, deadly, fatal, lethal, mortal, virulent, infectious, contagious, pestiferous, pestilent, noxious, pernicious. HARMLESS

**poke** prod, jab, punch, dig, nudge, elbow, shove, push, thrust, stick, stab.

**polar** Arctic, Antarctic, frozen, extreme. TROPICAL
pivotal, central, guiding, leading.
opposite, contradictory, diametrically opposed, antagonistic, antipodal, antithetical.

**pole** shaft, post, rod, stick, staff, mast.

**polemic** *adj*, polemical, controversial, disputatious, contentious, argumentative.
*n*, controversy, debate, dispute, argument.

**policy** plan, programme, strategy, tactic, course, line, approach, system, procedure, action, code, protocol, rules, guidelines.
wisdom, sagacity, prudence, shrewdness. FOLLY

**polish** *v*, burnish, furbish, buff, wax, smooth, rub, clean, shine, brighten. TARNISH
refine, finish, perfect, improve.
*n*, shine, lustre, sheen, gloss, smoothness, finish, brilliance, brightness. DULLNESS
wax, varnish.
refinement, cultivation, sophistication, elegance, grace, style. COARSENESS

**polished** shiny, glossy, lustrous, smooth, glassy, bright, brilliant. DULL
refined, cultivated, sophisticated, elegant, courtly, genteel. COARSE
accomplished, masterly, expert, skilful, perfect, impeccable, excellent, outstanding. INCOMPETENT

**polite** courteous, civil, respectful, deferential, mannerly, charming, obliging, well-bred, courtly, genteel, refined, cultivated, polished, civilized, urbane, elegant. RUDE

**politic** artful, ingenious, shrewd, astute, crafty, cunning, wily, sly, subtle. ARTLESS
wise, sagacious, judicious, prudent, discreet, diplomatic, wary, cautious, advisable, expedient. RASH

**political** civil, civic, public, state, governmental, administrative.

**poll** vote, voting, ballot, survey, census, count, enumeration.

**pollute** contaminate, taint, corrupt, deprave, defile, desecrate, vitiate, adulterate, poison, infect, dirty, soil, foul, mar, spoil. PURIFY

**poltroon** coward, craven, dastard, chicken (*inf*), yellow-belly (*inf*). HERO

**pomp** show, display, state, ceremony, pageantry, parade, flourish, grandeur, splendour, magnificence, ostentation, pomposity. SIMPLICITY

**pompous** pretentious, self-important, vainglorious, arrogant, lofty, pontifical, imperious, magisterial, supercilious, affected, ostentatious, showy, bombastic, inflated, turgid, orotund, grandiloquent, magniloquent. HUMBLE

**ponder** think, consider, deliberate, meditate, ruminate, cogitate, muse, wonder, reflect, study, examine, weigh.

**ponderous** huge, massive, bulky, hefty, heavy, weighty, cumbersome, unwieldy, awkward, clumsy. LIGHT
dull, tedious, dreary, dry, laboured, stilted, pedestrian, pedantic.

**pool**[1] *n*, pond, lake, tarn, puddle.

**pool**[2] *n*, fund, reserve, kitty, bank.
syndicate, combine, consortium, trust, cartel, collective.
*v*, combine, merge, amalgamate, league. DISTRIBUTE

**poor** needy, necessitous, penniless, penurious, impecunious, impoverished, poverty-stricken, indigent, destitute, hard-up (*inf*), broke (*inf*), skint (*inf*). RICH
meagre, scanty, deficient, inadequate, insufficient, lacking, short, scant, slight. AMPLE
inferior, second-rate, substandard, shoddy, unsatisfactory, weak, feeble, mediocre, bad, worthless, useless. GOOD
barren, infertile, sterile, unproductive, unfruitful, depleted, impoverished. FERTILE
luckless, unlucky, unfortunate, hapless, wretched, miserable, sorry, pitiable. FORTUNATE

**pop** *v*, burst, explode, go off, bang, snap, crack.
put, insert, slip, tuck, push, stick.
*n*, burst, explosion, report, bang, snap, crack.

**populace** inhabitants, population, people, crowd, mob, rabble, hoi polloi, masses, commonalty, general public.

**popular** favoured, favourite, liked, well-liked, accepted, approved, admired, in demand, sought-after, famous, renowned, celebrated, acclaimed. UNPOPULAR
common, familiar, public, general, universal, prevailing, prevalent, current. EXCLUSIVE

**populate** inhabit, people, colonize, settle.

**population** inhabitants, residents, natives, populace, people, folk, society.

**populous** crowded, packed, teeming, swarming. DESERTED

**pore**[1] *v*, study, examine, scrutinize, peruse, brood, dwell, ponder, meditate.

**pore**[2] *n*, opening, orifice, aperture, hole, outlet, stoma.

**porous** permeable, pervious, penetrable, absorbent, spongy. IMPERMEABLE

**port** harbour, haven, anchorage, roadstead.

**portable** light, compact, handy, convenient, manageable, movable, transportable. PONDEROUS

**portend** forebode, foretoken, foretell, predict, prognosticate, foreshadow, augur, presage, indicate, betoken, herald, warn, forewarn.

**portent** omen, sign, indication, token, harbinger, augury, prognostication, prophecy, prediction, presage, premonition, foreboding, warning.
phenomenon, marvel, wonder, prodigy, miracle.

**portentous** ominous, minatory, threatening, menacing, inauspicious, unpropitious, momentous, weighty, consequential, significant, crucial, pivotal. INSIGNIFICANT
phenomenal, prodigious, miraculous, remarkable, extraordinary, amazing, astounding. ORDINARY

**portion** *n*, share, lot, allotment, allocation, quota, ration.
part, section, segment, division, fraction, piece, fragment, bit, scrap, morsel. WHOLE
helping, serving.
*v*, apportion, allot, allocate, share, divide, distribute, deal out.

**portly** stout, corpulent, rotund, fat, plump, obese, burly, well-built, large, heavy. SLIM

**portrait** picture, image, likeness, representation, painting, drawing, photograph.

**portray** depict, picture, represent, draw, paint, delineate, describe, characterize.

**pose** *v*, model, sit, arrange, dispose, position, stand.
feign, pretend, impersonate, masquerade, act, posture, attitudinize, put on airs, affect, assume.
ask, put, advance, present, assert, state.
*n*, posture, attitude, position, stance.
pretence, masquerade, act, airs, affectation.

**poser** riddle, enigma, mystery, puzzle, conundrum, brain-teaser (*inf*).

**posh** smart, elegant, stylish, fashionable, exclusive, classy (*inf*), rich, luxurious, ritzy (*inf*), upper-class, genteel. VULGAR

**position** *n*, place, situation, location, bearings, spot, point, locality, site, station, post.
arrangement, disposition, pose, attitude, posture, stance.
condition, state, circumstances, situation, plight, predicament.
job, post, situation, appointment, place, office, role, duty.
status, standing, station, rank, class.
viewpoint, attitude, stand, angle, outlook, view, feeling, opinion, belief.
*v*, place, pose, arrange, dispose, put, locate.

**positive** certain, sure, assured, confident, convinced. UNCERTAIN
clear, direct, precise, explicit, express, definite, categorical, unequivocal, indisputable, incontrovertible, unmistakable, conclusive, decisive, emphatic, firm, assertive, dogmatic, affirmative. VAGUE
real, actual, substantial, true, genuine, veritable, absolute. NEGATIVE
constructive, practical, helpful, useful, beneficial, optimistic, hopeful. ADVERSE
utter, complete, perfect, absolute, downright, out-and-out, unqualified.

**possess** own, have, hold, enjoy, acquire, take, occupy, control, influence, dominate, consume, obsess. LOSE

**possession** ownership, tenure, occupancy, title, custody, control.

**possessions** belongings, property, effects, things, wealth, assets, estate.

**possible** conceivable, imaginable, credible, likely, probable, potential, hopeful, feasible, practicable. IMPOSSIBLE

**possibly** perhaps, maybe, perchance, peradventure. CERTAINLY

**post**[1] *n*, pole, shaft, stake, picket, prop, support, upright, pillar, column.
*v*, affix, put up, announce, made known, publish, advertise.

**post**[2] *n*, position, situation, job, employment, assignment, appointment, place, station.
*v*, assign, appoint, station, place, position, locate, situate.

**post**[3] *n*, mail, correspondence, letters, parcels, collection, delivery.
*v*, mail, send, dispatch, forward.
enter, record, inform, notify.

**poster** placard, bill, notice, advertisement, sticker.

**posterior** rear, back, hind, hinder. FRONT
after, later, following, succeeding, ensuing, subsequent. ANTERIOR

**posterity** descendants, heirs, progeny, offspring, issue, children, family, future generations. ANCESTRY

**postpone** delay, defer, shelve, table, suspend, adjourn, procrastinate, put off. ADVANCE

**postscript** PS, afterthought, appendix, supplement, addition. PREFACE

**postulate** *v*, assume, suppose, presuppose, take for granted, posit. PROVE
claim, demand, ask, beg, solicit.
*n*, assumption, supposition, theory, hypothesis, axiom, principle, condition, prerequisite.

**posture** position, attitude, pose, stance, bearing, carriage, deportment.
disposition, frame of mind, attitude, point of view, feeling, opinion.
condition, state, situation, position.

**posy** bouquet, nosegay, bunch, spray, corsage.

**pot** container, receptacle, vessel, pan, casserole, bowl, jar, glass, mug, tankard, jug.

**potent** powerful, mighty, strong, forceful, influential, cogent, persuasive, convincing, effective, efficacious, effectual, authoritative, commanding. WEAK

**potentate** ruler, sovereign, monarch, emperor, mogul.

**potential** *adj*, possible, likely, future, prospective, budding, undeveloped, latent, dormant, hidden. ACTUAL *n*, capacity, capability, ability, potentiality, possibility, promise.

**pother** commotion, turmoil, tumult, uproar, hullabaloo, pandemonium, confusion, fuss, to-do. QUIET

**potion** drink, beverage, draught, dose, brew, concoction.

**pottery** ceramics, earthenware, crockery, china.

**pouch** bag, sack, purse, satchel, pocket, sac.

**pounce** swoop, descend, spring, jump, surprise, ambush.

**pound** strike, beat, batter, pummel, hammer, thump. CARESS
pulverize, comminute, levigate, triturate, powder, crush, bruise, mash.
throb, pulsate, palpitate, beat.

**pour** flow, stream, run, rush, gush, spout, emit, discharge, issue, emerge.
decant, serve.
rain, teem, pelt. DRIZZLE

**pout** frown, scowl, glower, grimace, sulk, mope, brood. SMILE

**poverty** want, need, impoverishment, indigence, destitution, beggary, pauperism, pennilessness, penury, impecuniousness, privation, distress, hardship. WEALTH
scarcity, dearth, paucity, lack, shortage, deficiency, insufficiency. PLENTY

**powder** *n*, dust, pounce, talc, grains, particles.
*v*, pulverize, comminute, levigate, triturate, pound, crush, grind.
dust, dredge, sprinkle, scatter, cover, coat.

**power** ability, capability, capacity, potential, aptitude, faculty, competence. INABILITY
potency, might, strength, force, intensity, energy, vigour. WEAKNESS
command, rule, sovereignty, mastery, control, dominion, domination, sway, authority, influence, ascendancy, supremacy. SUBJECTION
right, perogative, privilege, authority, warrant, licence.

**powerful** potent, strong, mighty, forceful, intense, energetic, vigorous, robust, sturdy. WEAK
effective, efficacious, telling, cogent, persuasive, convincing, influential, weighty, effectual, authoritative, commanding, supreme. INEFFECTIVE

**powerless** impotent, ineffectual, ineffective, weak, feeble, helpless, incapable, defenceless, vulnerable. POWERFUL

**practicable** possible, feasible, attainable, achievable, workable, viable. IMPRACTICABLE

**practical** actual, applied, pragmatic, useful, utilitarian, practicable, workable, efficient, businesslike, realistic, sensible, down-to-earth, ordinary, everyday. IMPRACTICAL
skilled, proficient, competent, qualified, trained, practised, experienced. INEXPERIENCED

**practically** virtually, in effect, almost, nearly, well-nigh, basically, fundamentally.

**practice** custom, habit, wont, use, usage, convention, tradition, way, method, system, procedure.
exercise, drill, training, study, repetition, rehearsal.
application, action, effect, operation, performance. THEORY

**practise** do, perform, carry out, apply, observe, follow, pursue, work at.
exercise, drill, train, study, repeat, rehearse, go over, run through.

**practised** expert, proficient, accomplished, skilled, versed, experienced, trained, qualified. INEXPERIENCED

**pragmatic** practical, practicable, realistic, sensible, down-to-earth, businesslike.
meddlesome, interfering, intrusive, officious, dogmatic, opinionated.

**praise** *v*, commend, extol, laud, eulogize, panegyrize, applaud, cheer, acclaim, congratulate, compliment, flatter, admire, approve, exalt, glorify, honour, worship. CENSURE
*n*, commendation, laudation, eulogy, panegyric, encomium, accolade, applause, plaudits, acclaim, acclamation, congratulation, compliment, flattery, admiration, approval, approbation, tribute, homage, glory, honour, worship. CRITICISM

**praiseworthy** commendable, laudable, meritorious, admirable, estimable, worthy, creditable, fine, excellent. REPREHENSIBLE

**prance** leap, spring, gambol, frolic, caper, romp, frisk, cavort, swagger, strut.

**prank** trick, practical joke, caper, lark (*inf*), mischief, antics, escapade.

**prattle** prate, babble, chatter, jabber, blather, gab (*inf*), witter (*inf*).

**pray** beg, beseech, entreat, implore, adjure, petition, supplicate, ask, request, crave, plead, invoke, call on, urge, importune.

**prayer** communion, devotion, litany, invocation, supplication, entreaty, adjuration, petition, appeal, plea, request.

**preach** evangelize, sermonize, proclaim, declare, promulgate, spread, disseminate, teach, exhort, urge, advocate, orate, lecture, harangue.

**preacher** evangelist, missionary, clergyman, churchman, minister, parson. LAYMAN

**preamble** exordium, introduction, preface, prolegomenon, prologue, proem, foreword, prelude. EPILOGUE

**precarious** uncertain, unsure, doubtful, dubious, shakey, unsteady, unstable, insecure, unsafe, dangerous, perilous, risky, hazardous, hairy (*inf*), dicey (*inf*). SAFE

**precaution** safeguard, protection, insurance, provision, anticipation, foresight, forethought, prudence, circumspection, caution, care.

**precede** antecede, go before, lead, head, herald, usher in, introduce, preface, come first, antedate, predate. FOLLOW

**precedence** antecedence, precession, lead, priority, preference, seniority, superiority, supremacy, pre-eminence. SUBORDINATION

**precedent** antecedent, instance, example, lead, model, pattern, standard, criterion, authority.

**preceding** precedent, antecedent, prevenient, anterior, previous, foregoing, earlier, prior, former, aforesaid, above-mentioned. SUBSEQUENT

**precept** rule, principle, canon, motto, maxim, adage, axiom, guideline, instruction, direction, order, command, injunction, mandate, edict, decree, ordinance, regulation, law.

**precincts** region, area, environs, purlieus, district, neighbourhood, limits, bounds, ambit, confines.

**precious** dear, cherished, beloved, prized, treasured, favourite, valued, esteemed.
valuable, expensive, costly, dear, priceless, invaluable, inestimable. WORTHLESS
affected, pretentious, flowery, artificial, overrefined, overnice, twee (*inf*). NATURAL

**precipitate** *v*, hasten, hurry, accelerate, quicken, speed, advance, further, bring on, trigger, expedite, dispatch. RETARD
throw, hurl, fling, cast, propel, launch.
*adj*, rapid, swift, headlong, hurried, hasty, rash, reckless, heedless, thoughtless, careless, abrupt, sudden, impetuous, impulsive. CAUTIOUS

**precipitous** steep, sheer, perpendicular, abrupt. GRADUAL
hasty, rash, reckless, precipitate. CAUTIOUS

**precise** exact, explicit, distinct, clear, unambiguous, definite, express, specific, accurate, correct, strict, literal, nice, particular, finicky, meticulous, scrupulous, punctilious, rigid, severe, inflexible, formal. VAGUE

**precision** exactitude, exactness, accuracy, correctness, fidelity, strictness, nicety, meticulousness, scrupulousness. VAGUENESS

**preclude** debar, exclude, rule out, prohibit, obviate, prevent, hinder, stop, check, inhibit, restrain. ENCOURAGE

**precocious** forward, advanced, bright, clever, smart, quick, premature, early. BACKWARD

**preconception** prejudgment, predetermination, preconceived idea, presumption, presupposition, bias, prejudice.

**precursor** harbinger, herald, usher, messenger, pioneer, forerunner, antecedent, predecessor, ancestor. FOLLOWER

**precursory** antecedent, precedent, previous, prior, preparatory, preliminary, introductory, prefatory. FINAL

**predatory** predacious, raptorial, rapacious, voracious, ravenous, greedy, ravaging, plundering, pillaging, marauding.

**predecessor** forerunner, precursor, antecedent, ancestor, forefather, forebear. SUCCESSOR

**predestination** predetermination, preordination, foreordination, foreordainment, fate, destiny, lot, doom.

**predetermined** predestined, preordained, foreordained, fated, destined, doomed.
prearranged, set, fixed, foregone, cut and dried (*inf*). OPEN

**predicament** plight, quandary, dilemma, fix (*inf*), jam (*inf*), pickle (*inf*), scrape (*inf*), spot (*inf*), hole (*inf*), difficulty, mess, state, situation, extremity, emergency.

**predicate** assert, aver, asseverate, affirm, maintain, proclaim, declare, state, contend, argue. DENY

**predict** prophesy, prognosticate, foretell, augur, divine, foresee, forecast, foreshadow, presage, portend, forebode.

**prediction** prophesy, prognostication, augury, divination, forecast.

**predilection** inclination, leaning, tendency, bent, predisposition, proclivity, propensity, bias, preference, partiality, liking, fondness, weakness, taste, fancy. AVERSION

**predispose** bias, prejudice, sway, influence, affect, incline, dispose, prepare, prime.

**predisposition** inclination, tendency, predilection, proclivity, propensity, bias, preference, proneness, susceptibility, vulnerability, likelihood.

**predominant** ruling, sovereign, pre-eminent, dominant, ascendant, controlling, prevailing, prevalent, principal, chief, supreme, paramount. MINOR

**predominate** prevail, preponderate, outweigh, override, dominate, rule.

**pre-eminent** supreme, transcendent, paramount, outstanding, peerless, matchless, unequalled, unrivalled, unsurpassed, incomparable, superior, distinguished, predominant, prevailing, main, chief. INFERIOR

**preen** groom, dress, primp, prink, spruce up, titivate.

**preface** *n*, introduction, foreword, prelude, prologue, proem, preamble, exordium. EPILOGUE

*v*, introduce, open, begin, prefix, precede. CLOSE

**prefatory** introductory, opening, preliminary, preparatory, precursory, antecedent, prelusive, prelusory, proemial. FINAL

**prefer** favour, like better, choose, select, opt for, elect, pick, single out, adopt, fancy, desire. REJECT

advance, promote, elevate, raise. DOWNGRADE

lodge, file, place, put forward. WITHDRAW

**preferable** better, superior, more desirable, favoured, chosen.

**preference** choice, selection, pick, option, favourite, desire, fancy, liking, partiality, bias, prejudice, favouritism, advantage, priority, precedence.

**preferment** advancement, promotion, elevation, rise. DEMOTION

**pregnable** assailable, open to attack, vulnerable, exposed, defenceless, unprotected. FORTIFIED

**pregnant** gravid, enceinte, with child, expectant, expecting (*inf*), in the club (*inf*), in the family way (*inf*).

meaningful, significant, loaded, charged, eloquent, expressive, suggestive.

inventive, imaginative, creative, original.

fraught, full, replete, teeming, prolific, fruitful, fertile, fecund. BARREN

**prejudice** *v*, bias, warp, predispose, sway, influence, dispose, incline, jaundice.

harm, damage, impair, hurt, injure, mar, hinder. AID

*n*, bias, predisposition, prepossession, prejudgment, preconception, partiality, favouritism, discrimination, bigotry, intolerance, unfairness, injustice. IMPARTIALITY

harm, damage, impairment, hurt, injury, mischief, detriment, disadvantage. BENEFIT

**prejudiced** biased, warped, predisposed, jaundiced, bigoted, intolerant, partial, one-sided, partisan, unfair, unjust, discriminatory. IMPARTIAL

**prejudicial** harmful, damaging, hurtful, injurious, mischievous, pernicious, detrimental, deleterious, disadvantageous. BENEFICIAL

**prelate** cardinal, archbishop, metropolitan, primate, pontiff, pope, bishop.

**preliminary** *adj*, introductory, opening, initial, preparatory, prefatory, proemial, prelusive, precursory, antecedent, prior. FINAL

*n*, preparation, groundwork, foundation, introduction, opening, beginning, preface, preamble, prelude.

**prelude** introduction, overture, preliminary, opening, beginning, start, preamble, exordium, preface, proem, prologue. FINALE

**premature** early, untimely, unseasonable, hasty, precipitate, advanced, forward, immature, unripe, green, undeveloped, incomplete, embryonic. LATE

**premeditate** plot, plan, scheme, calculate, intend, prearrange, precontrive, predesign, preplan. IMPROVISE

**premise** *v*, postulate, posit, predicate, assert, state, preface, introduce. CONCLUDE
*n*, premiss, postulate, proposition, hypothesis, assumption, presupposition, assertion, argument, basis, ground.

**premises** property, building, establishment, grounds.

**premium** bonus, extra, tip, commission, perk (*inf*), prize, reward, bounty, recompense, remuneration, fee, incentive, discount.
value, regard, esteem, appreciation.

**premonition** foreboding, presentiment, feeling, hunch, intuition, apprehension, misgiving, presage, portent, omen, forewarning.

**preoccupied** engrossed, absorbed, immersed, lost, rapt, abstracted, oblivious, unaware, distracted, inattentive, absent-minded, pensive. ATTENTIVE

**preordain** foreordain, predestine, predetermine, fate, doom.

**preparation** groundwork, foundation, background, experience, provision, measure, plan, arrangement.
readiness, preparedness, precaution, anticipation, expectation.
mixture, compound, concoction, medicine.

**preparatory** preliminary, introductory, opening, prefatory, basic, elementary, primary, precursory, prior. FINAL

**prepare** get ready, prime, arrange, order, adjust, adapt, fit, equip, provide, supply, plan, anticipate, practice, warm up, brief, train, make, produce, compose, draw up, concoct, put together, assemble. DESTROY

**preponderant** predominant, prevailing, prevalent, dominant, ascendant, supreme, paramount, chief, leading, major, greater. INSIGNIFICANT

**preponderate** predominate, prevail, outweigh, outnumber.

**prepossessing** attractive, fetching, good-looking, charming, engaging, taking, winning, appealing, pleasing, delightful, likable, fascinating, captivating, alluring, inviting, enchanting. REPULSIVE

**prepossession** preoccupation, absorption, abstraction, inattention. ATTENTION
bias, prejudice, predisposition, partiality, predilection, liking. INDIFFERENCE

**preposterous** ridiculous, ludicrous, absurd, foolish, laughable, farcical, crazy, irrational, illogical, unreasonable, senseless, nonsensical, outrageous, excessive, extravagant, incredible, impossible. REASONABLE

**prerogative** privilege, right, liberty, choice, authority, due, claim, advantage, exemption, immunity.

**presage** *v*, predict, forecast, prophesy, prognosticate, foretell, augur, portend, forebode, foresee, feel, sense.
*n*, omen, portent, sign, warning, prediction, forecast, prophecy, prognostication, augury, foreboding, presentiment, premonition, feeling, intuition.

**prescience** foreknowledge, precognition, clairvoyance, second sight, foresight, prevision.

**prescribe** direct, bid, enjoin, order, command, rule, ordain, decree, dictate, impose, lay down, urge, recommend. PROHIBIT

**prescription** direction, instruction, formula, recipe, medicine, drug, remedy.
directive, injunction, order, command, decree, ordinance, edict, mandate, ruling, prescript, rule, law.

**presence** attendance, company, being, existence, residence, habitation. ABSENCE
nearness, closeness, proximity, vicinity, neighbourhood.
air, appearance, demeanour, carriage, bearing, poise, personality.

**present**[1] *adj*, existing, existent, current, present-day, immediate.
here, in attendance, to hand, at hand, near, nearby. ABSENT
*n*, now, today, this day and age. FUTURE

**present**[2] *v*, introduce, show, display, exhibit, demonstrate, stage, put on.
give, donate, bestow, award, confer, grant, hand over, offer, proffer, hold out. WITHHOLD
*n*, gift, benefaction, donation, offering, tip, gratuity, largess.

**presentation** award, grant, conferral, bestowal, gift, present, donation, offering.
introduction, debut, launch, demonstration, exhibition, display, show, performance, representation, appearance, delivery.

**presentiment** premonition, foreboding, intuition, hunch, anticipation, apprehension, foreknowledge, prescience.

**presently** soon, shortly, in a minute, in a while, by and by, later.

**preservation** protection, defence, conservation, keeping, maintenance, support, prepetuation, continuation, safeguarding, safekeeping, storage. DESTRUCTION

**preserve** *v*, protect, defend, guard, safeguard, care for, save, conserve, keep, maintain, uphold, perpetuate, continue. DESTROY
store, can, bottle, cure, pickle, dry, freeze.
*n*, jam, jelly, marmalade, conserve, confection, sweetmeat.
domain, sphere, realm, field, area.

**preside** officiate, chair, lead, direct, control, manage, supervise, head, govern.

**president** chief, head, leader, director, executive, principal, chairman.

**press** *v*, push, squeeze, compress, crush, pinch, force, drive, cram, stuff, crowd, throng, mill.
iron, smooth, flatten, calender, mangle. CRUMPLE
hug, embrace, clasp.
urge, beg, plead, petition, importune, harass, worry, plague, torment, besiege, demand, constrain, compel.
hurry, hasten, rush, move, advance.
*n*, journalism, fourth estate, newspapers, journalists, reporters, photographers.
crowd, throng, multitude, mob, crush.
hurry, bustle, urgency, pressure, stress.

**pressing** urgent, exigent, crucial, vital, imperative, demanding, importunate, important, serious. TRIVIAL

**pressure** force, weight, compression, crushing, squeezing.
constraint, compulsion, coercion, obligation, insistence, urgency, power, influence.
stress, strain, tension, burden, load, harassment, oppression. RELAXATION

**prestige** authority, influence, eminence, distinction, stature, status, reputation, fame, renown, celebrity.

**presume** assume, take for granted, suppose, surmise, guess, conjecture, believe, think, conclude, infer, take it. KNOW
venture, dare, make so bold.

**presumption** assumption, supposition, surmise, guess, conjecture, belief, opinion, hypothesis, inference. KNOWLEDGE
boldness, audacity, temerity, effrontery, impertinence, cheek (*inf*), nerve (*inf*), gall (*inf*), forwardness, assurance, arrogance. MODESTY

**presumptive** probable, likely, believable, credible, plausible, reasonable, assumed, supposed, believed, inferred.

**presumptuous** bold, audacious, impertinent, impudent, disrespectful, fresh (*inf*), forward, brazen, pushy (*inf*), arrogant, overconfident, cocksure, assured. MODEST

**presuppose** assume, take for granted, suppose, presume, postulate, posit, imply.

**pretence** simulation, fabrication, make-believe, invention, semblance, appearance, guise, masquerade, mask, cloak, veneer, façade, show, affectation, pretension, sham, deception, deceit, falsehood, pretext, excuse. TRUTH

**pretend** imagine, make believe, fabricate, invent, simulate, sham, counterfeit, fake, feign, dissemble, affect, put on, assume, claim, allege, purport, profess.

**pretentious** ostentatious, showy, flamboyant, theatrical, affected, mannered, vain, conceited, arrogant, puffed-up, pompous, bombastic, inflated, high-flown. UNPRETENTIOUS

**preternatural** unnatural, anomalous, abnormal, irregular, unusual, exceptional, extraordinary, strange, weird, mysterious, inexplicable, unearthly, supernatural. NORMAL

**pretext** excuse, reason, claim, allegation, pretence, guise, semblance, appearance, show, cloak, mask, cover.

**pretty** attractive, good-looking, beautiful, fair, comely, appealing, cute, pleasing, charming, lovely, nice, dainty, delicate, neat, trim. UGLY

**prevail** predominate, preponderate, reign, rule, hold sway, persist, obtain.
succeed, win, triumph, be victorious, overcome. LOSE

**prevail upon,** persuade, induce, influence, sway, convince, win over.

**prevailing** prevalent, widespread, universal, general, common, usual, accepted, established, current, popular, fashionable. RARE
predominant, preponderant, dominant, ruling, chief, main, principal, superior, powerful. SUBORDINATE

**prevaricate** equivocate, tergiversate, evade, dodge, hedge, shift, shuffle, quibble, cavil, lie, deceive.

**prevent** stop, check, preclude, hinder, impede, obstruct, hamper, deter, restrain, inhibit, thwart, frustrate, foil, forestall, anticipate, avert, avoid, ward off. AID

**prevention** stoppage, check, preclusion, hindrance, impediment, obstruction, obstacle, deterrence, determent, inhibition, avoidance. ASSISTANCE

**preventive** preventative, prophylactic, deterrent, protective, counteractive.

**previous** prior, preceding, antecedent, anterior, earlier, former, erstwhile, foregoing. LATER

**prey** *n*, quarry, game, victim, target.
*v*, hunt, seize, devour, feed on.
victimize, intimidate, bully, terrorize, exploit, take advantage of.
oppress, weigh, burden, trouble, worry.

**price** *n*, cost, expense, fee, rate, charge, value, worth, amount, figure, expenditure, outlay, valuation, assessment, estimate, quotation, bounty, reward.
penalty, loss, sacrifice, consequence, cost.
*v*, value, assess, appraise, evaluate.

**priceless** invaluable, inestimable, beyond price, precious, treasured, dear, expensive, unique, irreplaceable. CHEAP

**prick** *v*, pierce, puncture, perforate, punch, stab, lance, cut, wound, pain, hurt, move, touch, affect.
**prick up,** raise, erect, rise, stand up.
*n*, puncture, perforation, hole, pinhole, cut, wound, pain, pang, twinge.

**prickle** *v*, sting, smart, tingle, itch, prick.
*n*, point, barb, thorn, needle, spine.

**pride** vanity, conceit, egotism, self-love, boastfulness, self-praise, smugness, complacency, arrogance, hauteur, loftiness, self-importance, presumption, pretension. MODESTY
dignity, self-respect, self-esteem, *amour-propre*. SHAME
treasure, jewel, prize, boast, cream, pick.
pleasure, delight, satisfaction, gratification.

**priest** ecclesiastic, divine, churchman, clergyman, cleric, minister, vicar, parson, rector, pastor. LAYMAN

**priggish** prim, strait-laced, prudish, puritanical, smug, self-righteous, sanctimonious, goody-goody (*inf*), stuffy, starchy (*inf*).

**prim** formal, proper, demure, stiff, staid, starchy (*inf*), strait-laced, priggish, prudish, puritanical, fussy, fastidious, precise. EASY-GOING

**primary** first, initial, primal, earliest, original, primeval, primordial, primitive, aboriginal. LAST
prime, principal, chief, main, leading. MINOR
basic, fundamental, elementary, rudimentary, introductory, preparatory. SECONDARY

**prime** *adj*, first, primary, original, fundamental, basic, principal, chief, main.
first-rate, excellent, superior, choice, select, supreme, best, top. INFERIOR
*n*, zenith, peak, height, flower, bloom, heyday, maturity. DECLINE
*v*, prepare, make ready, break in, train, brief, inform, notify, tell.

**primeval** primordial, original, aboriginal, primitive, primal, primary, first, pristine, early, ancient, prehistoric. MODERN

**primitive** primeval, primordial, pristine, early, first, primary, original, ancient, archaic. MODERN
crude, rough, rudimentary, simple, uncivilized, savage, unsophisticated, naive. SOPHISTICATED

**primordial** primeval, original, primitive, primal, primary, first, earliest, pristine. MODERN
basic, fundamental, radical, elementary.

**prince** monarch, sovereign, ruler, potentate, lord. SUBJECT

**princely** generous, liberal, bounteous, munificent, magnanimous, gracious, lavish, rich, ample, bountiful. MEAN
noble, royal, regal, majestic, stately, august, imposing, grand, lofty, dignified. LOWLY

**principal** *adj*, chief, main, leading, first, foremost, primary, prime, paramount, cardinal, major, key, essential. MINOR
*n*, head, chief, leader, ruler, master, boss (*inf*), director, headmaster, headmistress. SUBORDINATE
capital, assets.

**principle** rule, law, standard, criterion, formula, precept, dictum, tenet, axiom, maxim, truth, doctrine, belief, credo, code. PRACTICE
morals, ethics, conscience, scruples, probity, integrity, virtue, goodness, honesty, uprightness, rectitude. UNSCRUPULOUSNESS

**print** *v*, reproduce, copy, stamp, impress, imprint, engrave, publish, issue.
*n*, impression, imprint, mark, indentation.
type, lettering, typescript, newsprint, publication.
reproduction, copy, duplicate, picture, photograph, engraving.

**prior** preceding, antecedent, earlier, anterior, previous, former, foregoing. SUBSEQUENT

**priority** precedence, antecedence, preference, prerogative, superiority, supremacy, seniority, rank.

**prison** jail, lockup, nick (*inf*), jug (*inf*), clink (*inf*), cooler (*inf*), inside (*inf*), confinement, captivity.

**pristine** original, earliest, first, primary, primal, primeval, primordial. LATER
pure, immaculate, spotless, unspoiled, untouched, new, virgin, undefiled, uncorrupted. DEFILED

**privacy** seclusion, retirement, retreat, solitude, isolation, secrecy, concealment. PUBLICITY

**private** secret, confidential, hush-hush (*inf*), unofficial, off the record, concealed, hidden, clandestine. PUBLIC
personal, intimate, individual, own, particular, special, exclusive. COMMUNAL
secluded, retired, solitary, isolated, independent.
**in private,** privately, secretly, confidentially, in camera, behind closed doors. PUBLICLY

**privation** want, need, lack, loss, hardship, distress, poverty, penury, indigence, destitution, beggary, pauperism. WEALTH

**privilege** right, prerogative, due, entitlement, benefit, advantage, liberty, freedom, immunity, exemption, concession, favour, indulgence.

**privy** *adj*, informed, aware, cognizant, in on.
private, personal, secret, confidential. PUBLIC
*n*, lavatory, toilet, latrine, bog (*inf*).

**prize**[1] *n*, reward, recompense, premium, award, trophy, honour, accolade, jackpot, windfall, winnings, spoils, loot, booty. PENALTY

**prize**[2] *v*, value, esteem, appreciate, treasure, cherish, hold dear. UNDERRATE

**probable** likely, odds-on, presumable, apparent, ostensible, credible, believable, plausible, reasonable. UNLIKELY

**probably** likely, doubtless, in all probability, possibly, maybe, perhaps.

**probation** test, trial, apprenticeship, novitiate.

**probe** *v*, search, investigate, look into, scrutinize, examine, sift, explore, sound, question, inquire.
*n*, investigation, inquiry, scrutiny, examination, study, search, exploration.

**probity** integrity, uprightness, rectitude, honesty, truthfulness, honour, worth, virtue, goodness, morality, principle, justice, equity. DISHONESTY

**problem** difficulty, trouble, predicament, quandary, dilemma, complication.
question, poser, riddle, enigma, puzzle, conundrum. SOLUTION

**problematic** dubious, doubtful, questionable, debatable, moot, uncertain, unsettled, puzzling, enigmatic. CERTAIN

**procedure** process, method, system, course, plan of action, policy, approach, custom, practice, rule, formula, routine, rigmarole, operation, performance.

**proceed** advance, progress, go ahead, move on, go on, continue, carry on. RETREAT
arise, originate, spring, stem, emanate, issue, flow, derive, come, result, ensue.

**proceeding** act, deed, action, process, step, measure, undertaking, move.

**proceedings** affairs, matters, concerns, dealings, transactions, doings, goings-on (*inf*), minutes, record.

**proceeds** profit, gain, receipts, returns, income, earnings, yield, result. EXPENSES

**process** *n*, procedure, method, system, course, routine, practice, operation, performance.
step, move, action, stage, advance, progression, development.
*v*, handle, deal with, treat, prepare.

**procession** parade, march, train, cavalcade, file, column, string, series, sequence, succession, course, cycle.

**proclaim** declare, announce, promulgate, advertise, publish, broadcast, herald, blazon, cry, trumpet. SUPPRESS

**proclamation** declaration, announcement, notice, statement, manifesto, pronouncement, edict, decree.

**proclivity** bent, leaning, inclination, tendency, propensity, proneness, disposition, penchant, predilection, liking, fondness, partiality, bias. AVERSION

**procrastinate** defer, put off, postpone, adjourn, delay, stall, temporize, prolong, retard. EXPEDITE

**procreate** beget, engender, propagate, breed, sire, generate, produce.

**procure** obtain, get, acquire, secure, gain, come by, pick up, buy, win, effect, contrive, manage. LOSE

**prod** poke, jab, dig, nudge, push, shove, goad, spur.

**prodigal** extravagant, wasteful, spendthrift, thriftless, improvident, reckless, generous, lavish. ECONOMICAL

**prodigious** huge, immense, massive, enormous, colossal, gigantic, vast, tremendous, stupendous. SMALL
wonderful, marvellous, phenomenal, extraordinary, amazing, astounding, astonishing, staggering, striking, remarkable. ORDINARY

**prodigy** genius, wonder child, wunderkind, whiz kid (*inf*). DUNCE
marvel, wonder, phenomenon, miracle.
freak, monster, mutation, curiosity.

**produce** *v*, make, create, invent, formulate, compose, construct, fabricate, manufacture, generate, engender, occasion, cause, bring about. DESTROY
bear, bring forth, beget, yield, give, render, afford, furnish, supply, provide. WITHHOLD
show, exhibit, present, bring out, stage, direct.
*n*, product, yield, crop, harvest, fruit, vegetables.

**product** yield, fruit, result, consequence, effect, outcome, issue. CAUSE
commodity, merchandise, goods, produce, work, creation.

**production** making, creation, fabrication, manufacture, construction, assembly, preparation. DESTRUCTION
output, work, presentation, show, direction.

**productive** fertile, rich, fruitful, profitable, worthwhile, valuable, constructive, creative, inventive. UNPRODUCTIVE

**profane** *adj*, blasphemous, sacrilegious, irreverent, irreligious, impious, ungodly, godless, wicked, heathen, pagan. REVERENT
secular, lay, unconsecrated, unhallowed, unholy, unsanctified, worldly, temporal. SACRED
*v*, desecrate, violate, abuse, defile, corrupt, pollute, vitiate. HALLOW

**profanity** blasphemy, sacrilege, irreverence, irreligion, impiety, ungodliness, curse, malediction, imprecation, obscenity. REVERENCE

**profess** claim, allege, pretend, feign, assert, aver, proclaim, declare, affirm, avow, acknowledge, own, confess, admit. REPUDIATE

**profession** calling, vocation, career, métier, occupation, business, line, sphere, office, position.
declaration, assertion, affirmation, avowal, acknowledgment, confession. REPUDIATION

**professional** *adj*, skilled, proficient, expert, masterly, experienced, trained, qualified, paid. AMATEUR
*n*, expert, master, pro (*inf*), dab hand (*inf*), specialist, authority.

**proffer** offer, tender, extend, hold out, present, propose, suggest, volunteer. WITHHOLD

**proficient** skilled, skilful, expert, masterly, adept, polished, practised, experienced, capable, able, competent, trained, qualified, accomplished, talented, good. INCOMPETENT

**profile** side view, outline, silhouette, shape, form, contour, sketch, study, analysis.

**profit** *n*, gain, return, yield, proceeds, earnings, income, revenue, surplus. LOSS
advantage, benefit, good, avail, use, value, advancement, improvement.
*v*, gain, benefit, help, aid, serve, avail, improve, advance, exploit, take advantage of, use. LOSE

**profitable** lucrative, paying, remunerative, gainful, cost-effective, productive, fruitful, rewarding, worthwhile, valuable, useful, beneficial, advantageous. UNPROFITABLE

**profitless** unprofitable, worthless, unproductive, fruitless, unavailing, vain, useless, futile, bootless. PROFITABLE

**profligate** *adj*, dissolute, dissipated, debauched, abandoned, loose, wanton, im-

moral, degenerate, depraved, corrupt, unprincipled, shameless. VIRTUOUS
extravagant, prodigal, wasteful, spendthrift, thriftless, improvident. THRIFTY
*n*, rake, roué, libertine, debauchee, degenerate, reprobate, wastrel, spendthrift.

**profound** deep, bottomless, fathomless, abysmal, cavernous. SHALLOW
sagacious, wise, learned, erudite, intellectual, knowledgeable, thoughtful, philosophical, penetrating, abstruse, recondite, esoteric. SUPERFICIAL
intense, keen, acute, extreme, complete, utter, absolute, thorough. MILD

**profuse** copious, ample, plentiful, abundant, exuberant, bountiful, generous, liberal, lavish, extravagant, prodigal. SCANTY

**profusion** plenty, plenitude, abundance, bounty, exuberance, excess, surplus, surfeit, glut, plethora, lavishness, extravagance, prodigality. LACK

**progeny** descendants, issue, posterity, offspring, young, children, family. ANCESTRY

**prognostic** *adj*, predictive, prophetic, diagnostic.
*n*, sign, symptom, indication, warning, omen, portent, token, presage, foreboding, prediction, forecast, prophecy, prognostication, augury.

**prognosticate** foretell, prophesy, predict, forecast, presage, augur, betoken, portend, foreshadow.

**programme** list, schedule, agenda, syllabus, curriculum, plan, scheme.
show, production, performance, broadcast.

**progress** *n*, advance, advancement, movement, progression, growth, development, improvement, amelioration, furtherance, promotion, headway, breakthrough. RETROGRESSION
*v*, advance, proceed, continue, go forward, move on, make headway, gain ground, travel, grow, develop, improve, ameliorate. RETROGRESS

**prohibit** forbid, disallow, ban, interdict, proscribe, veto, debar, stop, prevent, rule out, hinder, impede, obstruct. PERMIT

**prohibitive** restrictive, preventive, repressive, proscriptive, prohibitory, forbidding. PERMISSIVE
exorbitant, extortionate, excessive, steep (*inf*).

**project** *n*, proposal, plan, scheme, design, purpose, idea, undertaking, venture, task, assignment, activity, work. ACHIEVEMENT
*v*, propose, intend, plan, scheme, devise, contrive, design, calculate, estimate, extrapolate, predict.
cast, throw, hurl, fling, propel, shoot, eject, launch, discharge. RETAIN
jut, protrude, stick out, overhang, beetle, bulge, extend.

**projection** protrusion, protuberance, bulge, overhang, prominence, extension, ledge.
scheme, plan, programme, proposal, estimate, prediction, blueprint, diagram, representation.

**proletariat** working class, commonalty, masses, rabble, hoi polloi, common people. ARISTOCRACY

**proliferate** increase, expand, spread, reproduce, breed, multiply, escalate, burgeon, mushroom, snowball.

**prolific** productive, fertile, fruitful, copious, profuse, abundant, teeming, rich. UNPRODUCTIVE

**prolix** verbose, wordy, long-winded, rambling, discursive, lengthy, protracted, long-drawn-out, tedious, boring, prosaic. TERSE

**prologue** introduction, preface, foreword, preamble, exordium, prolegomenon, proem, prelude. EPILOGUE

**prolong** extend, lengthen, protract, draw out, spin out, stretch, elongate, continue, sustain, keep up. CURTAIL

**prominent** conspicuous, noticeable, marked, pronounced, striking, unmistakable, obvious, evident. INCONSPICUOUS
eminent, distinguished, notable, noted, famous, celebrated, well-known, important, leading. MINOR
projecting, jutting, protruding, protuberant.

**promiscuous** loose, wanton, abandoned, licentious, libertine, profligate, dissolute, immoral, debauched. VIRTUOUS
indiscriminate, unselective, careless, heedless, casual, indifferent, diverse, miscellaneous, mixed, mingled, disorderly, confused. SELECTIVE

**promise** *v*, pledge, vow, swear, give one's word, engage, contract, covenant, assure, guarantee.

augur, betoken, suggest, indicate, look like, give hope of.

*n*, pledge, vow, oath, word, assurance, guarantee, engagement, contract, covenant, bond, agreement.

potential, capacity, ability, capability.

**promising** hopeful, likely, encouraging, reassuring, optimistic, bright, rosy, favourable, auspicious. HOPELESS

**promontory** headland, foreland, cape, point.

**promote** further, advance, forward, help, assist, aid, support, back, boost, encourage, foster, cultivate. HINDER

upgrade, raise, elevate, prefer, exalt, aggrandize, move up, kick upstairs (*inf*). DEMOTE

advertise, publicize, push, plug (*inf*), hype (*inf*), advocate, champion, endorse, sponsor.

**promotion** advancement, preferment, rise, elevation, aggrandizement, exaltation. DEMOTION

support, backing, encouragement, furtherance, publicity, advertising. HINDRANCE

**prompt** *adj*, immediate, instant, direct, quick, swift, rapid, fast, punctual, timely, ready, eager, alert, sharp, brisk, smart. SLOW

*v*, urge, encourage, induce, impel, move, goad, spur, incite, stimulate, motivate, inspire. DETER

remind, cue, assist, help, hint, suggest.

**promulgate** proclaim, declare, announce, decree, advertise, broadcast, disseminate, publish, circulate, cry, trumpet, blazon, divulge, make known. SUPPRESS

**prone** apt, inclined, disposed, liable, given, subject, likely, susceptible. UNLIKELY

prostrate, procumbent, face down, recumbent, supine, flat, horizontal. UPRIGHT

**pronounce** utter, articulate, enunciate, voice, say.

proclaim, declare, announce, decree, affirm, assert. SUPPRESS

**pronounced** marked, distinct, definite, clear, plain, noticeable, conspicuous, striking, unmistakable. VAGUE

**proof** *n*, evidence, confirmation, substantiation, corroboration, testimony, demonstration. CONJECTURE

trial, test, assay, examination, inspection.

print, impression, galley.

*adj*, resistant, repellant, impervious, impenetrable, strong.

**prop** *v*, support, hold up, shore up, brace, bolster, uphold, sustain, maintain.

lean, rest, stand, place.

*n*, support, brace, buttress, bolster, stay, pillar, upright, shore, mainstay.

**propaganda** publicity, promotion, advertising, advertisement, information, indoctrination, brainwashing.

**propagate** reproduce, breed, procreate, beget, generate, engender, produce, increase, multiply, proliferate. DESTROY

disseminate, spread, diffuse, promulgate, circulate, publish, advertise, broadcast, publicize, promote. SUPPRESS

**propel** drive, impel, urge, push, thrust, force, move, launch, project, shoot, throw. STOP

**propensity** tendency, disposition, inclination, proneness, proclivity, bent, leaning, aptness, liability, susceptibility, penchant, predisposition.

**proper** correct, right, accurate, exact, precise, accepted, usual, customary, conventional, just, real, actual. WRONG

appropriate, apt, suitable, fit, fitting, seemly, becoming, decorous, decent, polite, respectable, genteel, refined. IMPROPER

personal, own, individual, characteristic, peculiar, special. COMMON

**property** possessions, effects, belongings, goods, chattels, assets, capital, wealth, fortune, estate, land, building.

attribute, quality, mark, characteristic, feature, trait, peculiarity, idiosyncrasy.

**prophecy** prediction, forecast, prognostication, augury, divination, clairvoyance, second sight.

**prophesy** predict, foresee, foretell, divine, prognosticate, forecast, augur, presage.

**prophet** soothsayer, diviner, clairvoyant, seer, fortune-teller, augur, oracle, forecaster.

**prophetic** predictive, prognostic, oracular, augural, divinatory, sibylline, mantic, portentous, ominous.

**propinquity** nearness, closeness, proximity, vicinity, neighbourhood, contiguity, adjacency. DISTANCE

affinity, kinship, kindred, consanguinity, relationship.

**propitiate** pacify, placate, appease, conciliate, reconcile. OFFEND

**propitious** auspicious, favourable, advantageous, promising, encouraging, timely, opportune, lucky, fortunate, happy. UNFAVOURABLE
well-disposed, benign, benevolent, gracious, kind, friendly. HOSTILE

**proportion** *n*, ratio, relationship, distribution, balance, symmetry, uniformity, harmony, agreement, correspondence, congruity, conformity. DISPROPORTION
share, portion, division, lot, quota, ration, part, fraction, percentage. WHOLE
dimension, measurement, size, magnitude, extent, capacity.
*v*, adjust, arrange, regulate, balance, harmonize, fit.

**proportional** proportionate, balanced, symmetrical, corresponding, consistent, commensurate, equivalent. DISPROPORTIONATE

**proposal** proposition, suggestion, recommendation, offer, proffer, tender, bid, overture, plan, scheme, project, idea.

**propose** suggest, recommend, move, advance, put forward, submit, present, offer, proffer, tender, nominate, name. WITHDRAW
plan, intend, purpose, design, mean, have in mind.

**propound** suggest, propose, put forward, advance, submit, advocate, postulate, state, declare.

**proprietor** owner, possessor, holder, landowner, freeholder, master, mistress, landlord, landlady.

**propriety** correctness, seemliness, fitness, appropriateness, decorum, decency, etiquette, protocol, good manners, politeness, breeding, refinement, modesty, delicacy. IMPROPRIETY

**prorogue** adjourn, postpone, defer, suspend, discontinue. RECONVENE

**prosaic** prosy, dry, unimaginative, flat, tame, commonplace, ordinary, bland, uninteresting, uninspiring, vapid, dull, tedious, boring, monotonous, pedestrian, trite, hackneyed, banal, humdrum. IMAGINATIVE

**proscribe** condemn, denounce, censure, interdict, prohibit, forbid, ban, outlaw, exile, banish, expel, deport, excommunicate, exclude, reject, blackball, ostracize.

**prosecute** sue, take to court, summon, prefer charges, arraign, indict, accuse, try. DEFEND
practise, carry on, conduct, perform, pursue, follow, continue, persist. ABANDON

**proselyte** convert, catechumen, neophyte, novice, disciple.

**prospect** *n*, chance, possibility, likelihood, probability.
outlook, future, expectation, hope, anticipation, contemplation, calculation, plan.
view, vista, scene, landscape, panorama, spectacle, vision, outlook, perspective.
*v*, explore, survey, search, seek.

**prospective** future, coming, approaching, expected, anticipated, planned, intended, imminent, impending, likely, probable, possible, potential, eventual.

**prospectus** syllabus, outline, programme, plan, scheme, announcement, notice, catalogue, brochure.

**prosper** thrive, flourish, succeed, make good, advance, progress. FAIL

**prosperous** thriving, flourishing, successful, booming, lucky, fortunate, favourable, auspicious, promising, rich, wealthy, affluent, well-off. UNSUCCESSFUL

**prostitute** *n*, whore, harlot, fallen woman, strumpet, trollop, courtesan, call girl, streetwalker, tart (*inf*), hooker (*inf*).
*v*, devalue, cheapen, debase, degrade, demean, abuse, misuse, misapply.

**prostrate** *v*, bow, kneel, kowtow, grovel, submit.
overcome, overthrow, overpower, overwhelm, disarm, paralyse, crush, flatten, exhaust, weary, tire, fatigue. RESTORE
*adj*, flat, horizontal, prone, procumbent, recumbent, supine, grovelling, abject. ERECT
overcome, overwhelmed, disarmed, paralysed, helpless, defenceless, impotent. POWERFUL
exhausted, jaded, weary, tired, disconsolate, heartbroken.

**prosy** prosaic, unimaginative, uninspiring, pedestrian, commonplace, dull, tedious, boring, wearisome, tiresome, long-winded, wordy, prolix. LIVELY

**protagonist** hero, heroine, principal, lead, central character.
supporter, advocate, champion, defender, leader, prime mover.

**protean** variable, changeable, mutable, inconstant, mercurial, volatile, polymorphous, many-sided, versatile. CONSTANT

**protect** defend, guard, safeguard, secure, screen, cover, shield, shelter, harbour, save, preserve, keep, look after, care for, mind, foster. EXPOSE

**protection** defence, guard, safeguard, precaution, security, safety, shield, cover, shelter, refuge, preservation, safekeeping, care, custody, aegis, patronage, support, aid. EXPOSURE

**protective** defensive, protecting, guarding, shielding, covering, preventive, watchful, vigilant, possessive, jealous.

**protest** *v*, object, complain, oppose, take exception, demur, expostulate, remonstrate, demonstrate, disapprove. AGREE
maintain, contend, argue, assert, avow, aver, asseverate, attest, affirm, declare. DENY
*n*, objection, complaint, opposition, demurral, protestation, expostulation, remonstrance, outcry, demonstration. AGREEMENT

**protocol** etiquette, customs, conventions, formalities, manners, decorum.

**prototype** original, model, pattern, precedent, example, type, archetype, standard, norm, exemplar, ideal. COPY

**protract** prolong, draw out, spin out, extend, lengthen, elongate, stretch, continue, sustain. CURTAIL

**protrude** project, stick out, jut, extend, bulge, thrust out.

**protuberance** bulge, swelling, lump, bump, knob, excrescence, protrusion, projection. CAVITY

**proud** satisfied, content, pleased, glad, self-satisfied, smug, complacent, vain, conceited, egotistic, self-important, boastful, big-headed (*inf*), arrogant, haughty, imperious, lordly, overbearing, presumptuous, supercilious, stuck-up (*inf*). MODEST
self-respecting, dignified, high-minded, honourable, noble, majestic, stately, grand, magnificent, splendid, glorious, great, exalted, eminent, distinguished, illustrious. HUMBLE

**prove** demonstrate, show, manifest, evidence, evince, verify, confirm, corroborate, substantiate, uphold, sustain, establish. REFUTE
test, try, assay, examine, analyse, check.

**proverb** saying, maxim, aphorism, adage, apophthegm, saw, dictum, byword.

**proverbial** acknowledged, accepted, famous, well-known, notorious, legendary, traditional, axiomatic, self-evident.

**provide** supply, furnish, equip, stock, contribute, give, afford, yield, produce, present.
prepare, get ready, take precautions, anticipate, allow, plan, cater, arrange.
stipulate, specify, lay down, state, determine.

**provide for,** maintain, support, sustain, keep, look after, take care of. NEGLECT

**provided** providing, given, on condition that, subject to, if.

**providence** fate, destiny, fortune, divine intervention.
prudence, discretion, foresight, care, caution, economy, thrift.

**provident** judicious, far-sighted, prudent, sagacious, careful, cautious, wary, vigilant, economical, thrifty. RECKLESS

**province** territory, district, region, division, zone, realm, domain, colony, dependency, county, department. CAPITAL
field, discipline, line, sphere, orbit, role, function, duty, responsibility, business.

**provision** preparation, precaution, measure, step, arrangement, plan.
providing, supply, furnishing, equipment, catering.
proviso, condition, stipulation, specification, clause, term, reservation, qualification.

**provisional** temporary, interim, makeshift, conditional, contingent, provisory. ABSOLUTE

**provisions** food, sustenance, provender, victuals, comestibles, eatables, groceries, rations, stores, supplies.

**provocation** incitement, encouragement, instigation, agitation, motive, cause, insult, affront, offence, annoyance, irritation. APPEASEMENT

**provocative** provoking, inciting, stimulating, offensive, insulting, annoying, irritating, vexatious, exasperating. PACIFIC
alluring, tempting, inviting, tantalizing, seductive, sexy (*inf*). REPULSIVE

**provoke** anger, enrage, infuriate, incense, madden, exasperate, vex, irk, rile, annoy, irritate, insult, offend. APPEASE incite, encourage, foment, agitate, goad, spur, stimulate, stir, rouse, move, inspire, motivate, instigate, cause, occasion, bring about, elicit, evoke, prompt, promote, produce. DETER

**prowess** skill, ability, expertise, mastery, genius, talent, dexterity, adroitness, proficiency. INCOMPETENCE

strength, might, bravery, valour, courage, fearlessness. COWARDICE

**prowl** roam, rove, wander, range, steal, sneak, slink, skulk, lurk, scavenge, forage, hunt, stalk.

**proximity** nearness, closeness, propinquity, vicinity, neighbourhood, contiguity, adjacency. DISTANCE

**proxy** substitute, agent, representative, delegate, deputy, surrogate.

**prudent** judicious, sagacious, discreet, circumspect, sensible, wise, shrewd, careful, cautious, wary, vigilant, canny, politic, thoughtful, considerate, practical, provident, economical, thrifty, frugal. RASH

**prudish** prim, demure, modest, straitlaced, starchy (*inf*), proper, priggish, stuffy, puritanical, strict, narrow-minded, squeamish. BROAD-MINDED

**prune** trim, clip, snip, lop, dock, cut, shorten, reduce.

**prurient** lustful, lecherous, lewd, salacious, libidinous, concupiscent, erotic, obscene, pornographic, dirty. CHASTE

**pry** meddle, interfere, question, inquire, nose, snoop (*inf*), spy, peep, peer.

**prying** meddlesome, interfering, inquisitive, curious, nosy, snoopy (*inf*).

**pseudonym** alias, assumed name, pen name, nom de plume, stage name.

**psychic** clairvoyant, telepathic, extrasensory, supernatural, mystic, occult, spiritual, psychological, mental. NATURAL

**psychological** mental, cerebral, intellectual. PHYSICAL

emotional, irrational, subjective, imaginary.

**public** *adj*, open, unrestricted, communal, common, general, national, universal, civic, civil, popular. PRIVATE

known, acknowledged, published, overt, plain, exposed, unconcealed, obvious, patent. SECRET

*n*, population, people, community, society, populace, commonalty, hoi polloi, masses.

clientele, customers, followers, supporters, fans, admirers, audience.

**publication** publishing, issuance, appearance, announcement, proclamation, advertisement, broadcast, promulgation, dissemination, revelation, disclosure. SUPPRESSION

edition, issue, book, magazine, periodical, newspaper, pamphlet, booklet, leaflet, brochure.

**publicity** promotion, advertising, advertisement, puff, plug (*inf*), hype (*inf*), attention, spotlight. OBSCURITY

**publish** issue, bring out, distribute, circulate, disseminate, promulgate, announce, proclaim, advertise, publicize, trumpet, blazon, disclose, reveal, divulge, expose, tell, impart. SUPPRESS

**pucker** wrinkle, crinkle, crease, corrugate, furrow, purse, knit, tighten, contract, gather, ruck. SMOOTH

**puerile** childish, infantile, immature, silly, foolish, irresponsible, petty, trivial, frivolous. ADULT

**puff** *n*, gust, blast, whiff, breath, flurry.

praise, commendation, advertisement, publicity, plug (*inf*).

*v*, blow, pant, gasp, breathe, exhale.

smoke, draw, pull, drag (*inf*), inhale.

swell, inflate, bloat, distend, puff up. DEFLATE

praise, flatter, advertise, promote, push, plug (*inf*), hype (*inf*). DISPARAGE

**pugnacious** belligerent, bellicose, combative, aggressive, quarrelsome, argumentative, contentious, disputatious. PEACEABLE

**pull** *v*, draw, drag, haul, tow, trail, tug, yank. PUSH

pluck, pick, extract, remove, detach, rip, tear, wrench, sprain, stretch.

attract, draw, pull in, entice, lure. REPEL

**pull off,** succeed, accomplish, achieve. FAIL

**pull out,** leave, depart, quit, withdraw, retreat. ARRIVE

**pull through,** recover, get over, survive, weather.

*n*, drag, tow, tug, yank, jerk. PUSH

effort, exertion, force, power, magnetism, attraction, lure, appeal, influence, weight.

**pulpy** fleshy, succulent, soft, squashy, mushy. HARD

**pulsate** beat, throb, pulse, pound, palpitate, vibrate, quiver.

**pulse** *n*, beat, throb, rhythm, pulsation, vibration.
*v*, beat, throb, pulsate.

**pulverize** powder, pound, crush, grind, comminute, triturate, levigate.
destroy, annihilate, demolish, wreck, smash.

**pummel** batter, beat, thump, pound, hammer, punch, belabour, thrash.

**pump** drive, force, push, draw.
interrogate, question, quiz, cross-examine, grill (*inf*).
**pump up,** inflate, blow up. DEFLATE

**pun** play on words, double entendre, witticism, quip.

**punch**[1] *v*, strike, hit, box, thump, pummel, beat, bash (*inf*), clout (*inf*).
*n*, blow, hit, knock, thump, bash (*inf*) clout (*inf*).

**punch**[2] *v*, pierce, puncture, perforate, bore, drill.

**punctilious** strict, exact, precise, correct, proper, formal, meticulous, scrupulous, conscientious, careful, particular, fussy, nice, minute. LAX

**punctual** prompt, on time, timely, seasonable, punctilious, exact, precise, regular. LATE

**puncture** *v*, pierce, prick, perforate, punch, bore, deflate.
*n*, hole, perforation, opening, leak, flat tyre.

**pungent** acrid, bitter, biting, sour, tart, acid, burning, stinging, hot, piquant, strong, harsh, sharp, keen, pointed, cutting, incisive, caustic, trenchant, mordant, piercing, penetrating. MILD

**punish** discipline, correct, chastise, chasten, reprove, scold, castigate, spank, beat, flog, scourge, penalize, sentence. REWARD

**punitive** penal, disciplinary, corrective, retaliatory, revengeful, punishing, harsh.

**puny** weak, feeble, frail, delicate, stunted, undersized, dwarfish, pygmy, small, tiny, trivial, petty, paltry, insignificant. STURDY

**pupil** student, scholar, schoolboy, schoolgirl, learner, beginner, novice, neophyte, tyro, apprentice, trainee, disciple, follower. MASTER

**puppet** marionette, dummy, doll.
pawn, cat's-paw, tool, instrument, figurehead.

**purchase** *v*, buy, procure, acquire, obtain, get, pay for, invest in. SELL
*n*, acquisition, buy, investment, possession.
grasp, grip, hold, foothold, leverage, advantage.

**pure** unmixed, unadulterated, neat, undiluted, real, genuine, natural, simple, perfect, flawless. IMPURE
clear, clean, unpolluted, uncontaminated, spotless, immaculate, sterilized, disinfected. POLLUTED
chaste, virginal, undefiled, uncorrupted, unsullied, impeccable, virtuous, innocent, honest, upright. CORRUPT
sheer, downright, utter, mere, thorough, absolute. PARTIAL

**purely** only, solely, exclusively, merely, simply, completely, totally, entirely, wholly, utterly, absolutely.

**purgative** laxative, cathartic, aperient, evacuant.

**purge** *v*, cleanse, purify, deterge, clean out, wash, clear, absolve, rid, free, expel, eject, oust, remove, eradicate, eliminate.
*n*, enema, purgative, laxative, cathartic, aperient, evacuant.
purgation, purification, ejection, expulsion, removal, eradication, elimination.

**purify** cleanse, purge, clean, wash, disinfect, sanitize, clarify, refine, distil, filter. BEFOUL

**puritanical** puritan, prim, strait-laced, strict, austere, ascetic, severe, rigid, stiff, prudish, narrow-minded. IMMORAL

**purity** pureness, clearness, clarity, cleanness, spotlessness, flawlessness, perfection, simplicity. IMPURITY
chastity, virginity, virtue, innocence, honesty, integrity, honour, piety. CORRUPTION

**purlieus** outskirts, periphery, borders, limits, suburbs, precincts, environs, vicinity, neighbourhood.

**purloin** steal, pilfer, filch, thieve, rob, nick (*inf*), embezzle, appropriate. RESTORE

**purport** *v*, claim, profess, pretend, allege, maintain, assert, declare.
mean, signify, denote, betoken, imply, suggest.
*n*, meaning, significance, signification, import, implication, drift, gist.
purpose, intention, object, aim, design, plan.

**purpose** *n*, reason, point, idea, design, function, use.
aim, intention, intent, object, objective, end, goal, aspiration, hope, plan, design.
resolution, resolve, determination, will, drive, persistence, tenacity. INDECISION
avail, effect, good, use, advantage, benefit, gain, profit.
**on purpose,** purposely, deliberately, intentionally, wilfully, wittingly, knowingly, by design. ACCIDENTALLY
*v*, mean, intend, plan, design, propose, aim, aspire, resolve, determine.
**purposeful** determined, decided, resolved, resolute, firm, set, fixed, persistent, dogged, tenacious. INDECISIVE
**pursue** follow, chase, go after, hunt, trail, track, hound, dog, harass, harry, attend, accompany.
practise, engage in, conduct, prosecute, ply, work at, perform, see through, persist in, continue, carry on, proceed, maintain, hold to. ABANDON
seek, desire, aspire to, aim for, strive for.
**pursuit** chase, hunt, search, quest.
occupation, business, profession, vocation, hobby, pastime, activity, recreation.
**purvey** sell, provide, supply, furnish, cater, provision, retail.
**purview** scope, field, range, compass, sphere, orbit, province, limit, extent, reach.
**push** *v*, shove, thrust, drive, propel, move, force, press, squeeze, ram, crowd, jostle, elbow. PULL
urge, encourage, egg on, impel, spur, prompt, persuade, coerce, expedite, advocate, promote, advertise, publicize. DETER
*n*, shove, thrust, propulsion, nudge, prod.
effort, endeavour, attack, charge, drive, force, ambition, enterprise, energy, vigour, spirit, gumption (*inf*).
**pushy** pushing, ambitious, enterprising, go-ahead, dynamic, forceful, assertive, self-assertive, presumptuous, bumptious, aggressive, officious, intrusive. MEEK
**pusillanimous** timid, timorous, fearful, cowardly, faint-hearted, lily-livered, spineless, weak, feeble. BRAVE
**pustule** abscess, ulcer, fester, gathering, blister, pimple, boil.
**put** place, set, lay, deposit, situate, locate, position, stand, plant, fix. REMOVE
impose, inflict, levy, exact, enjoin, subject, condemn, commit.
say, express, utter, word, phrase, state, declare, advance, put forward, propose, present, offer, tender. WITHDRAW
assign, attribute, attach, impute, put down.
**put across,** communicate, convey, make clear, explain, spell out.
**put away,** replace, put back, tidy up.
save, keep, put aside, put by, store, lay in, lay up. USE
consume, devour, eat, drink, swallow, bolt, wolf, gobble.
lock up, confine, commit. RELEASE
**put down,** enter, inscribe, log, record, jot down.
suppress, repress, quash, quell, crush.
kill, destroy, put to sleep.
disparage, belittle, criticize, knock (*inf*), humiliate, mortify, shame. PRAISE
**put off,** postpone, defer, delay, shelve, adjourn. ADVANCE
repel, disgust, disconcert, unsettle, discourage. ENCOURAGE
**put on,** don, change into, wear, dress, clothe.
feign, fake, simulate, pretend, assume, affect.
present, produce, mount, stage, perform, do.
**put out,** extinguish, douse, quench, snuff out, blow out. LIGHT
annoy, irritate, vex, irk, confuse, disturb, bother, inconvenience, upset, trouble.
**put up,** erect, built, construct, raise. DEMOLISH
accommodate, house, lodge, board.
**put up with,** tolerate, suffer, bear, endure, stand, abide, take, swallow, stomach, brook.
**putative** accepted, recognized, imputed, alleged, reputed, supposed, assumed, presumed. PROVEN
**putrefy** rot, decompose, decay, go bad, spoil, corrupt, taint. PRESERVE
**putrid** rotten, decomposed, decayed, bad, off, rancid, fetid, rank, mephitic, foul, offensive, corrupt, tainted. FRESH
**puzzle** *v*, perplex, baffle, mystify, confuse, confound, nonplus, bewilder, stump. ENLIGHTEN
ponder, study, reflect, meditate, brood, muse, wonder, think.
**puzzle out,** solve, resolve, work out, figure out, decipher, crack, unravel, clear up.

*n*, riddle, conundrum, enigma, mystery, poser, question, problem, dilemma. SOLUTION
perplexity, bafflement, confusion, bewilderment. ENLIGHTENMENT

**pygmy** *n*, dwarf, midget, manikin, homunculus. GIANT
*adj*, miniature, diminutive, dwarfish, midget, undersized, stunted, small, little, tiny, Lilliputian. GIGANTIC

# Q

**quack** mountebank, impostor, fraud, charlatan, fake, pretender, humbug.

**quaff** drink, imbibe, gulp, swallow, swig (*inf*).

**quagmire** swamp, bog, marsh, fen, morass, slough.

**quail** shrink, recoil, blench, flinch, cower, falter, tremble, shake, quake.

**quaint** picturesque, old-world, old-fashioned, antiquated. MODERN
strange, unusual, uncommon, extraordinary, curious, odd, peculiar, bizarre, eccentric, singular, unique, fantastic, fanciful, whimsical. ORDINARY

**quake** tremble, shake, quiver, vibrate, shudder, shiver, quail, waver, falter, wobble, totter, rock, throb, pulsate.

**qualification** suitability, fitness, eligibility, competence, proficiency, experience, skill, ability, capability, capacity, aptitude, attribute, quality, accomplishment, achievement, attainment. DISQUALIFICATION
restriction, limitation, modification, condition, proviso, stipulation, requirement, criterion.

**qualify** fit, equip, endow, prepare, train, capacitate, empower, permit, certify, license. DISQUALIFY
restrict, limit, regulate, restrain, moderate, mitigate, temper, reduce, diminish, lessen, abate, soften, assuage, modify, alter, change, adapt.

**quality** characteristic, property, attribute, feature, trait, peculiarity, idiosyncrasy, condition, character, nature, kind, sort.
grade, rank, status, value, worth, distinction, excellence, superiority.

**qualm** scruple, compunction, remorse, contrition, regret, doubt, hesitation, misgiving, uneasiness, apprehension, trepidation, anxiety. EASE
pang, twinge, spasm, attack, nausea, sickness, queasiness.

**quandary** dilemma, predicament, difficulty, trouble, plight, puzzle, perplexity, doubt, uncertainty.

**quantity** amount, number, extent, measure, size, magnitude, volume, capacity, weight, mass, sum, total, lot, portion.

**quarrel** *v*, argue, disagree, dispute, squabble, altercate, wrangle, bicker, differ, contend, clash, row, fight, brawl. AGREE
*n*, argument, disagreement, dispute, tiff, squabble, altercation, wrangle, dissension, difference of opinion, contention, clash, row, fight, brawl, feud, vendetta. AGREEMENT

**quarrelsome** argumentative, contentious, disputatious, pugnacious, combative, belligerent, quick-tempered, choleric, irritable, irascible, peevish, petulant, touchy, testy, cross. GENIAL

**quarry**[1] *n*, pit, mine, excavation.
*v*, mine, extract.

**quarry**[2] *n*, game, prey, victim, object.

**quarter** *n*, fourth, three months.
district, region, neighbourhood, locality, place, part, area, zone, province, territory, point, direction.
mercy, clemency, forgiveness, compassion, pity, leniency.
*v*, accommodate, house, put up, lodge, board, billet, station, post.

**quarters** lodgings, digs (*inf*), accommodation, housing, residence, domicile, abode, dwelling, habitation, billet, station, post.

**quash** suppress, subdue, squash, crush, put down, quell, repress, overthrow.
annul, nullify, invalidate, cancel, repeal, revoke, rescind, abolish, overrule.

**quaver** tremble, shake, quake, quiver, vibrate, flicker, flutter, waver, twitter, trill, warble.

**quay** wharf, landing stage, dock.

**queasy** bilious, nauseous, sick, ill, squeamish, uncomfortable, uneasy.

**queer** odd, curious, strange, unusual, uncommon, weird, bizarre, extraordinary, peculiar, singular, irregular, abnormal, funny. ORDINARY
dubious, questionable, suspicious, shady (*inf*), fishy (*inf*).

dizzy, giddy, faint, queasy.
homosexual, lesbian, gay (*inf*), bent (*inf*).

**quell** suppress, subdue, put down, quash, crush, squelch, squash, stamp out, extinguish, conquer, overcome.
allay, assuage, mitigate, alleviate, moderate, soothe, mollify, dull, deaden, blunt, calm, pacify, quiet. AGGRAVATE

**quench** slake, satisfy, sate, satiate, allay, appease.
extinguish, douse, put out, snuff out. LIGHT
quell, quash, suppress, subdue, crush, put down.

**querulous** peevish, petulant, whining, grumbling, complaining, discontented, fretful, irritable, fractious, captious, cross, irascible, testy, touchy. CONTENTED

**query** *n*, question, enquiry, problem, issue, doubt, scepticism, reservation, objection. ANSWER
*v*, question, dispute, challenge, doubt, disbelieve, mistrust, distrust, suspect, ask, enquire. ACCEPT

**quest** search, pursuit, expedition, journey, crusade, mission, goal, objective, aim, target.

**question** *n*, query, enquiry, interrogation, examination, investigation. REPLY
problem, difficulty, doubt, uncertainty, issue, subject, point, matter.
*v*, interrogate, examine, quiz, catechize, grill (*inf*), pump (*inf*), ask, enquire. ANSWER
query, challenge, dispute, doubt, disbelieve, mistrust, distrust, suspect. ACCEPT

**questionable** debatable, dubious, doubtful, uncertain, moot, problematical, controversial, disputable, controvertible, equivocal, suspicious.

**queue** line, file, train, string, chain, series, succession.

**quibble** *v*, equivocate, prevaricate, palter, hedge, shift, shuffle, evade, cavil, carp, split hairs.
*n*, equivocation, prevarication, evasion, criticism, objection, protest.

**quick** fast, swift, rapid, speedy, fleet, express, expeditious, prompt, ready, sudden, hasty, hurried, cursory, perfunctory, brisk, brief, fleeting. SLOW
nimble, agile, spry, sprightly, alert, active, lively, vivacious, animated, spirited. SLUGGISH
sharp, keen, acute, quick-witted, shrewd, astute, smart, clever, intelligent, adroit, deft, dexterous, skilful. DULL
touchy, testy, quick-tempered, irascible, irritable, impatient, excitable, temperamental, waspish, peppery, petulant, choleric. AFFABLE

**quicken** accelerate, speed up, expedite, precipitate, hasten, hurry. RETARD
stimulate, rouse, kindle, inspire, whet, excite, animate, revive, vivify, resuscitate, refresh, energize, enliven, vitalize, invigorate. DEADEN

**quickly** fast, swiftly, rapidly, speedily, hastily, posthaste, apace, promptly, immediately, instantly, forthwith, soon. SLOWLY

**quiescent** still, motionless, inactive, dormant, quiet, calm, tranquil, serene, placid, unruffled, peaceful, restful. ACTIVE

**quiet** *adj*, silent, noiseless, inaudible, hushed, low, soft. LOUD
calm, quiescent, serene, tranquil, placid, unruffled, peaceful, restful, untroubled, undisturbed, smooth, still, motionless, mild, gentle, docile, subdued, sober.
private, secret, isolated, secluded, unfrequented. PUBLIC
*n*, quietness, silence, hush, peace, quiescence, calm, calmness, tranquillity, serenity, rest, repose, ease. DISTURBANCE

**quieten** quiet, silence, hush, mute, still, calm, lull, tranquillize, soothe, pacify, appease, allay, assuage, mitigate, soften, mollify, dull, blunt, quell, subdue. DISTURB

**quilt** bedspread, counterpane, eiderdown, duvet.

**quintessence** quiddity, essence, extract, pith, marrow, heart, core, kernel, spirit, embodiment, personification.

**quip** joke, jest, gag (*inf*), gibe, wisecrack (*inf*), witticism, bon mot, sally, riposte, retort, repartee, pleasantry, badinage.

**quirk** mannerism, habit, idiosyncrasy, characteristic, trait, peculiarity, oddity, eccentricity, whim, caprice, vagary, foible.

**quit** stop, desist, discontinue, cease, abandon, give up, resign, abdicate, relinquish, surrender, renounce.
leave, depart, go, decamp, retire, withdraw. ENTER

**quite** completely, totally, entirely, wholly, fully, altogether, utterly, absolutely, positively, perfectly, thoroughly. PARTLY

fairly, moderately, pretty (*inf*), rather, somewhat. VERY
really, truly, indeed.

**quiver** tremble, shake, quake, quaver, vibrate, shiver, shudder.

**quixotic** impractical, impracticable, unrealistic, idealistic, utopian, fanciful, visionary, romantic, fantastic, imaginary, wild, mad. PRACTICAL

**quiz** *n*, test, examination, investigation, interrogation, questioning.
*v*, interrogate, question, examine, catechize, grill (*inf*), pump (*inf*).

**quondam** former, one-time, past, previous, late, earlier. PRESENT

**quota** share, portion, allotment, allocation, allowance, ration, part, proportion.

**quotation** extract, excerpt, passage, line, reference, citation, quote (*inf*).
estimate, tender, cost, price, rate, charge.

**quote** cite, adduce, instance, repeat, recite, extract, excerpt, refer to, mention.

# R

**rabble** mob, crowd, horde, herd, masses, commonalty, populace, proletariat, hoi polloi, riffraff, *canaille*. ARISTOCRACY

**rabid** mad, wild, raging, raving, frantic, frenetic, frenzied, berserk, furious, violent, maniacal, fanatical, extreme, fervent, zealous. RATIONAL

**race**[1] *n*, contest, competition, chase, pursuit, dash, sprint, marathon, steeplechase.
flow, rush, stream, course, channel.
*v*, run, dash, sprint, tear, fly, career, speed, hurry, rush. AMBLE
compete, contend.

**race**[2] *n*, people, nation, tribe, clan, breed, family, line, descent, extraction, blood, stock, ancestry, lineage, house.

**racial** ethnic, ethnological, tribal, national.

**rack** *n*, frame, framework, stand, holder.
torture, torment, pain, agony, anguish, suffering, affliction.
*v*, torture, torment, excruciate, agonize, pain, afflict, distress, plague, harass. SOOTHE

**racket** din, noise, uproar, clamour, hubbub, hullabaloo, commotion, pandemonium, tumult, turmoil, disturbance, row. QUIET
scheme, confidence trick, fraud, swindle, business, line.

**racy** lively, spirited, animated, buoyant, interesting, entertaining, exciting, stimulating, piquant, pungent, sharp, spicy, distinctive, strong. DULL
risqué, suggestive, bawdy, ribald, blue, smutty, immodest, indecent.

**radiant** bright, shining, brilliant, resplendent, beaming, dazzling, effulgent, sparkling, glittering, gleaming, shiny, lustrous, glowing, luminous, lambent, glorious, splendid. DARK
happy, joyful, delighted, elated, ecstatic, overjoyed, beaming, glowing, sparkling. MISERABLE

**radiate** emit, emanate, diffuse, shed, disseminate, scatter, spread, diverge, branch out.
shine, beam, glow, glitter, sparkle.

**radical** *adj*, basic, fundamental, constitutional, essential, inherent, intrinsic, natural, organic, ingrained, deep-seated. SUPERFICIAL
complete, total, thorough, sweeping, drastic, severe, extreme, excessive, fanatical, revolutionary.
*n*, extremist, fanatic, militant, revolutionary, rebel. MODERATE

**radio** wireless, transistor, receiver, transmitter.

**raffle** lottery, draw, sweepstake.

**rage** *n*, anger, fury, wrath, ire, passion, mania, madness, frenzy, violence, vehemence. CALMNESS
craze, fad, fashion, mode, vogue, style.
*v*, rant, rave, seethe, fume, storm, rampage.

**ragged** tattered, torn, frayed, worn, threadbare, shabby, unkempt. SMART
rough, uneven, jagged, rugged, notched, serrated. SMOOTH

**raging** angry, furious, incensed, infuriated, enraged, fuming, ranting, raving, rabid, mad, wild, violent. CALM

**raid** *n*, attack, assault, incursion, invasion, irruption, inroad, foray, sally, seizure, pillage.
*v*, attack, assault, invade, descend on, plunder, pillage, sack, rifle.

**rail**[1] *n*, bar, balustrade, fence, barrier, railing.

**rail**[2] *v*, complain, criticize, denounce, fulminate, inveigh, attack, censure, upbraid, vituperate, revile, abuse.

**railing** fence, barrier, paling, palisade, rail, balustrade.

**raillery** banter, badinage, pleasantry, persiflage, joking, jesting, teasing, satire, ridicule, mockery.

**rain** *n*, precipitation, rainfall, drizzle, shower, downpour, cloudburst.
*v*, drizzle, spit, fall, shower, pour, teem.

**raise** lift, elevate, uplift, hoist, heave, jack up, erect, put up, build, construct. LOWER
increase, augment, heighten, intensify, amplify, magnify, strengthen, boost, escalate. DECREASE
promote, prefer, upgrade, advance, exalt, aggrandize. DEMOTE
arouse, awaken, stir, rouse, excite, provoke, stimulate, activate, cause, occasion, produce.
rear, bring up, breed, cultivate, grow, develop.
broach, introduce, present, put forward.
collect, gather, assemble, muster, levy, obtain, get.

**rake[1]** *v*, scrape, scratch, collect, gather, remove, comb, scour, hunt, search.

**rake[2]** *n*, debauchee, libertine, roué, profligate, playboy, womanizer (*inf*).

**rally** *v*, muster, assemble, unite, gather, collect, reassemble, regroup, mobilize, round up, meet, convene. DISPERSE
recover, recuperate, perk up, revive, improve, get better, mend, pull through. DETERIORATE
*n*, gathering, meeting, assembly, convention.
recovery, recuperation, renewal, revival, improvement, comeback (*inf*).

**ram** force, drive, cram, stuff, pack, crowd, hammer, pound, hit, strike, collide, crash, bump, butt.

**ramble** *v*, walk, hike, stroll, amble, saunter, wander, roam, rove, range, meander, stray.
digress, expatiate, maunder, babble, chatter, witter (*inf*), rabbit (*inf*).
*n*, walk, hike, stroll, amble, trip, excursion.

**ramification** branching, forking, divergence, divarication, branch, offshoot, development, consequence, result, sequel, complication.

**ramp** slope, incline, gradient, acclivity, declivity.

**rampage** *v*, rage, storm, go berserk, run riot, rush, tear.
*n*, rage, fury, frenzy, violence.
**on the rampage,** violent, destructive, amok, berserk, out of control, wild.

**rampant** unrestrained, uncontrolled, unchecked, unbridled, wild, raging, violent, riotous, uncontrollable, ungovernable, excessive, wanton, rife, rank, profuse, exuberant, luxuriant. CONTROLLED
erect, upright, standing, rearing. COUCHANT

**rampart** bulwark, fortification, defence, guard, security, embankment, earthwork, breastwork, parapet, barricade, fence, wall.

**ramshackle** tumbledown, dilapidated, derelict, rickety, shaky, decrepit. STURDY

**rancid** sour, off, stale, musty, rank, fetid, foul, offensive, bad, rotten, putrid. FRESH

**rancour** malice, spite, venom, ill will, malignity, malevolence, animosity, antipathy, enmity, hostility, hatred, hate, resentment, grudge, spleen, bitterness. BENEVOLENCE

**random** haphazard, casual, hit or miss, arbitrary, chance, fortuitous, unsystematic, unplanned, indiscriminate, irregular, aimless, stray, accidental, incidental. DELIBERATE

**range** *n*, scope, reach, extent, sweep, compass, limit, distance, span, gamut, area, field.
line, row, rank, tier, file, string, chain, series.
sort, kind, variety, assortment, class, order.
*v*, align, line up, order, dispose, array, arrange, classify, categorize, group, bracket.
extend, stretch, reach, run, vary, fluctuate.
roam, rove, wander, stray, stroll, ramble, traverse, travel.

**rank[1]** *n*, position, standing, station, status, class, grade, echelon, level, stratum, order, degree, division, group, dignity, nobility.
line, row, range, tier, file, column, string, series.
*v*, align, line up, arrange, range, class, group, classify, sort, grade, position.

**rank[2]** *adj*, exuberant, luxuriant, lush, dense, profuse, abundant, prolific, rampant. SCANTY
foul, offensive, fetid, malodorous, stinking, smelly, rancid, putrid, rotten, stale, disgusting, revolting. FRESH
complete, utter, sheer, absolute, downright, thorough, unmitigated, blatant, glaring.

**rankle** fester, annoy, irritate, chafe, vex, irk, rile, gall.

**ransack** search, scour, comb, rake, rummage, rifle, sack, loot, strip, raid, plunder, pillage, rob.

**ransom** *n*, release, deliverance, rescue, redemption.
price, payment.
*v*, redeem, rescue, deliver, release, free, liberate.

**rant** *v*, declaim, hold forth, shout, bluster, rave, vociferate.
*n*, bombast, rhetoric, bluster, vociferation, declamation, tirade, diatribe.

**rap** *v*, tap, knock, hit, strike, crack.
*n*, tap, knock, blow, hit, stroke.
blame, responsibility, punishment, sentence.

**rapacious** greedy, grasping, avaricious, ravenous, voracious, insatiable, predatory, predacious, marauding, plundering.

**rape** *v*, ravish, violate, deflower, defile, molest, abuse, assault, seduce.
plunder, pillage, despoil, spoliate, loot, sack.
*n*, ravishment, violation, molestation, assault.
plunder, pillage, rapine, spoliation.

**rapid** fast, quick, swift, speedy, fleet, express, expeditious, hurried, hasty, precipitate, brisk, prompt. SLOW

**rapidity** rapidness, speed, velocity, celerity, quickness, swiftness, fleetness, haste, hurry, rush, dispatch, expedition, briskness, promptness, alacrity. SLOWNESS

**rapine** plunder, pillage, spoliation, depredation, rape, robbery, theft, looting, marauding, raid, seizure.

**rapport** sympathy, empathy, understanding, harmony, affinity, bond, link, tie, relationship.

**rapt** absorbed, engrossed, preoccupied, lost, enthralled, entranced, fascinated, spellbound, transported, enchanted, delighted, charmed, thrilled, rapturous, ecstatic. BORED

**rapture** ecstasy, bliss, transport, ravishment, euphoria, elation, joy, happiness, delight, delectation, felicity, beatitude. SORROW

**rapturous** ecstatic, blissful, transported, ravished, euphoric, elated, thrilled, enthusiastic, delighted, overjoyed, joyful, happy. SAD

**rare** uncommon, unusual, unfamiliar, singular, exceptional, infrequent, scarce, sparse, scant, few. COMMON
excellent, fine, choice, superior, outstanding, incomparable, peerless, priceless, invaluable, precious. INFERIOR

**rarely** seldom, infrequently, hardly ever, once in a blue moon. OFTEN

**rascal** scoundrel, rogue, rapscallion, scamp, knave, blackguard, villain, reprobate, miscreant, wretch, imp, devil.

**rash**[1] *adj*, hasty, precipitate, reckless, thoughtless, heedless, careless, incautious, indiscreet, unwary, impetuous, impulsive, foolhardy, madcap, headlong, audacious. CAUTIOUS

**rash**[2] *n*, eruption, outbreak, epidemic, spate, flood, series, succession.

**rasp** *v*, scrape, scratch, rub, abrade, grate, grind, file, sand.
*n*, scraping, scratching, grating, grinding.
file, grater.

**rate**[1] *n*, speed, velocity, pace, tempo.
charge, price, cost, fee, tax, duty.
ratio, proportion, grade, class, degree, value, worth, rank.
*v*, value, evaluate, appraise, assess, estimate, reckon, esteem, regard, deem, consider, rank, grade, class, classify.

**rate**[2] *v*, scold, chide, upbraid, rebuke, reprove, reprimand, berate, chastise, castigate, censure. PRAISE

**rather** somewhat, fairly, moderately, relatively, slightly, quite. VERY
sooner, preferably, instead.

**ratify** authorize, sanction, warrant, approve, consent, endorse, confirm, corroborate, substantiate, establish, settle, seal, bind. REPUDIATE

**ratio** proportion, rate, percentage, fraction, relationship, correspondence.

**ration** *n*, quota, allowance, share, portion, allotment, part, measure, helping.
*v*, distribute, dole, divide, apportion, allot, allocate. WITHHOLD
restrict, control, conserve, save. SQUANDER

**rational** reasonable, logical, sensible, practical, realistic, right, proper, wise, intelligent, sagacious, judicious, prudent, discreet, sane, sound, lucid, normal, *compos mentis*, reasoning, thinking. IRRATIONAL

**rattle** clatter, knock, bang, jangle, tinkle, shake, jiggle, bounce, bump.
disconcert, confuse, fluster, disturb, perturb, upset, frighten. REASSURE
**raucous** hoarse, harsh, grating, rasping, rough, noisy, strident. SOFT
**ravage** *v*, spoil, mar, ruin, wreck, destroy, demolish, devastate, desolate, pillage, plunder, loot, sack. PRESERVE
*n*, damage, ruin, havoc, destruction, demolition, devastation, plunder, pillage, rape, rapine.
**rave** rage, storm, roar, rant, ramble, babble.
praise, extol, gush, enthuse.
**ravel** tangle, entangle, involve, complicate, interweave, intertwine. DISENTANGLE
disentangle, unravel, undo, resolve, elucidate, explain. ENTANGLE
**ravenous** starving, famished, hungry, greedy, gluttonous, rapacious, voracious, insatiable. SATED
**ravine** gorge, canyon, chasm, abyss, gully, defile, pass.
**raving** mad, crazy, insane, frantic, frenzied, delirious, hysterical, raging, rabid, wild, furious. COMPOSED
**ravish** charm, delight, transport, enrapture, captivate, enchant, fascinate. REPEL
rape, violate, deflower, molest, assault, abuse.
**ravishing** charming, delightful, lovely, beautiful, enchanting, bewitching, entrancing, captivating, fascinating, dazzling. REPULSIVE
**raw** uncooked, fresh. COOKED
natural, unprocessed, untreated, crude, unrefined, unfinished. PROCESSED
green, immature, callow, inexperienced, naive, unsophisticated, untried, new, unskilled, untrained, unpractised, ignorant. EXPERIENCED
tender, sore, painful, sensitive, scratched, grazed, open, exposed. HEALED
cold, chilly, wet, damp, bleak, bitter, biting, piercing. TORRID
**ray** beam, shaft, flash, gleam, glint, glimmer, flicker, spark, hint, trace.
**raze** demolish, destroy, level, flatten, bulldoze, pull down, knock down. BUILD
erase, efface, obliterate, expunge, delete, strike out, extirpate, annihilate.
**reach** *v*, stretch, extend, touch, grasp.
get to, arrive at, come to, attain.
contact, get hold of, communicate with, get through to.
*n*, extent, distance, sweep, range, scope, compass, stretch, extension, grasp, hold, control, influence.
**react** act, behave, function, operate, respond, reply, answer, retaliate, reciprocate, counteract, counterbalance, recoil, rebound.
**read** peruse, study, decipher, interpret, understand, comprehend.
recite, deliver, present, declaim.
indicate, show, record, register.
**readable** legible, decipherable, clear, intelligible, comprehensible. ILLEGIBLE
interesting, entertaining, pleasant, enjoyable, absorbing, gripping. TEDIOUS
**readily** promptly, quickly, at once, right away, easily, effortlessly, willingly, gladly, cheerfully, eagerly. RELUCTANTLY
**reading** perusal, study, interpretation, version, understanding, comprehension.
rendering, rendition, recital, recitation, lecture, lesson, sermon.
knowledge, learning, erudition, scholarship.
**ready** prepared, set, primed, fit, arranged, organized, done, completed.
willing, game (*inf*), eager, keen, happy, cheerful, inclined, disposed. RELUCTANT
prompt, quick, swift, speedy, sharp, acute, nimble, agile, deft, adroit, dexterous, skilful, clever, astute. SLOW
handy, convenient, accessible, available, near, at hand. INACCESSIBLE
**real** true, actual, genuine, authentic, veritable, legitimate, positive, factual, existent, substantial, tangible, natural, sincere, heartfelt, honest. FALSE
**realistic** practical, pragmatic, down-to-earth, matter-of-fact, sensible, rational, businesslike, hard-headed. IDEALISTIC
natural, lifelike, true-to-life, faithful, graphic, real, authentic, genuine, truthful. UNREALISTIC
**reality** actuality, truth, verity, fact, realism, existence, corporeality. IMAGINATION
**realize** understand, comprehend, be aware of, take in, grasp, perceive, recognize, appreciate. MISUNDERSTAND
accomplish, achieve, fulfil, carry out, actualize, effect, bring off, make happen.

make, produce, sell for, bring in, get, obtain, acquire, gain.

**really** actually, in reality, in fact, indeed, truly, verily, genuinely, certainly, assuredly, positively, absolutely, unquestionably, undoubtedly.

**realm** kingdom, empire, principality, domain, dominion, province, department, branch, field, area, region, territory.

**reap** cut, crop, harvest, glean, gather, get, obtain, acquire, gain, win. SOW

**rear**[1] *n*, back, end, stern, tail, rump, buttocks, posterior. FRONT

*adj*, back, hind.

**rear**[2] *v*, raise, bring up, nurse, nurture, foster, train, instruct, educate, breed, cultivate, grow.

erect, build, construct, put up. DEMOLISH

raise, elevate, lift, hoist. LOWER

rise, tower, loom, soar.

**reason** *n*, mind, intellect, intelligence, understanding, sense, rationality, judgment, wisdom, sanity, reasoning, logic. FOLLY

motive, cause, ground, basis, aim, object, intention, purpose, excuse, justification, defence, explanation.

*v*, think, ponder, ratiocinate, analyse, conclude, deduce, infer, work out, solve.

argue, debate, discuss, talk over, prevail upon, urge, persuade, dissuade.

**reasonable** rational, sensible, logical, practical, sane, sober, wise, intelligent, judicious, sagacious, advisable, well-advised, justifiable, arguable, credible, plausible. MAD

equitable, fair, just, right, proper, moderate, within reason, tolerable, acceptable, modest, inexpensive, cheap, low-priced. UNREASONABLE

**reassure** comfort, encourage, hearten, cheer, buoy up, embolden, inspirit. PERTURB

**rebate** refund, discount, reduction, deduction, allowance. SURCHARGE

**rebel** *v*, revolt, rise up, mutiny, resist, defy, dissent. CONFORM

*n*, revolutionary, insurgent, mutineer, traitor, dissenter, nonconformist.

**rebellion** revolt, revolution, insurgence, insurrection, uprising, mutiny, sedition, resistance, defiance, insubordination, dissent.

**rebellious** revolutionary, rebel, insurgent, insurrectionary, seditious, mutinous, unruly, contumacious, defiant, insubordinate, disobedient, intractable, refractory, recalcitrant. SUBMISSIVE

**rebound** *v*, bounce, ricochet, recoil, spring back, return, resound, reverberate, boomerang, backfire.

*n*, bounce, ricochet, recoil, return, reaction, repercussion.

**rebuff** *v*, snub, reject, repel, check, resist, spurn, refuse, turn down, slight, cut. ACCEPT

*n*, snub, rejection, check, refusal, slight, cut, cold shoulder, brushoff (*inf*). ACCEPTANCE

**rebuke** *v*, scold, chide, upbraid, berate, castigate, reprove, reprehend, reproach, reprimand, admonish, tell off (*inf*), censure, blame. COMMEND

*n*, scolding, dressing-down (*inf*), castigation, reproof, reproach, reprimand, admonition, telling-off (*inf*), censure, blame. PRAISE

**rebut** refute, disprove, negate, invalidate, confute, contradict, defeat, overturn. SUPPORT

**recalcitrant** refractory, contumacious, disobedient, insubordinate, intractable, ungovernable, unmanageable, uncontrollable, wilful, wayward, perverse, stubborn. AMENABLE

**recall** *v*, remember, recollect, reminisce, look back, think back, call to mind, evoke, commemorate. FORGET

summon, call back, revoke, retract, withdraw, take back, repeal, rescind, overrule, annul, nullify, cancel, recant, abjure.

*n*, memory, remembrance, recollection, reminiscence.

revocation, retraction, withdrawal, repeal, annulment, cancellation.

**recant** withdraw, retract, revoke, recall, deny, disavow, disclaim, disown, repudiate, abjure, take back, unsay. MAINTAIN

**recapitulate** restate, repeat, reiterate, review, go over, summarize, sum up, recap (*inf*).

**recede** retreat, withdraw, retire, go back, return, retrogress, retrocede, ebb, subside, abate, lessen, diminish, dwindle, wane. ADVANCE

**receipt** acknowledgment, quittance, voucher, ticket, stub, counterfoil, reception, acceptance.
**receive** take, accept, get, obtain, acquire, derive. GIVE
suffer, undergo, experience, bear, endure, sustain.
admit, greet, welcome, entertain.
**recent** modern, late, latter, new, novel, fresh, current, up-to-date, contemporary. OLD
**receptacle** container, vessel, holder, repository.
**reception** acceptance, admission, receipt, response, greeting, welcome, entertainment, party, function.
**recess** alcove, niche, nook, corner, bay, hollow, indentation, cavity. PROJECTION
break, interval, rest, respite, holiday, vacation.
**recipe** directions, instructions, formula, prescription, method, process, procedure, technique.
**recipient** receiver, beneficiary. DONOR
**reciprocal** mutual, exchanged, reciprocative, reciprocatory, interchangeable, alternate, complementary, corresponding. ONE-SIDED
**reciprocate** return, give back, requite, exchange, swap, interchange, alternate, correspond, equal.
**recital** solo, concert, performance, show.
recitation, reading, rehearsal, repetition, account, narration, narrative, description, relation, recapitulation, chronicle, history, tale, story.
**recite** repeat, rehearse, declaim, deliver, relate, tell, narrate, recount, detail, enumerate, itemize, list.
**reckless** rash, heedless, thoughtless, careless, imprudent, injudicious, unwise, foolish, hasty, impetuous, impulsive, foolhardy, madcap, daredevil, headlong, wild, irresponsible. CAUTIOUS
**reckon** calculate, compute, add up, total, count, enumerate, number, figure.
consider, regard, deem, judge, esteem, rate, estimate, value.
think, believe, imagine, fancy, suppose, assume, presume, guess.
rely, depend, count, bank.
**reckon with,** anticipate, expect, foresee, bargain for, take into account, bear in mind.
cope with, deal with, handle, face.
**reckoning** calculation, computation, addition, count, estimate.
settlement, account, bill, charge.
**reclaim** recover, regain, redeem, rescue, save, salvage, recycle, convert, reform, restore, regenerate.
**recline** lean, lie, rest, repose, loll, lounge, sprawl. STAND
**recluse** hermit, solitary, anchorite, anchoress, eremite, ascetic, monk, nun.
**recognize** identify, know, place, remember, recall, recollect.
acknowledge, admit, own, grant, concede, confess, accept, respect, see, perceive, realize, understand. DENY
honour, salute, greet, appreciate. IGNORE
**recoil** rebound, spring back, kick, react.
shy, draw back, shrink, flinch, quail, falter.
**recollect** remember, recall, reminisce, call to mind. FORGET
**recommend** advise, counsel, suggest, prescribe, urge, advocate. DISCOURAGE
praise, commend, promote, approve, endorse, vouch for. DISAPPROVE
**recompense** *v*, pay, reward, remunerate, repay, reimburse, indemnify, compensate, redress, requite, make amends.
*n*, compensation, indemnity, amends, redress, reparation, remuneration, reward, payment, repayment, reimbursement.
**reconcile** reunite, conciliate, propitiate, appease, pacify, placate, settle, resolve, adjust, harmonize, mend, patch up. ALIENATE
accept, resign, submit, yield. OPPOSE
**recondite** abstruse, esoteric, profound, deep, mystical, hidden, concealed, secret, cryptic, occult, arcane, mysterious, dark, obscure, difficult. PATENT
**reconnoitre** survey, spy out, scout, explore, inspect, examine, view, scan.
**reconstruct** rebuild, reassemble, remake, remodel, restore, renovate, regenerate, recreate. DESTROY
**record** *n*, journal, diary, chronicle, memoir, annals, archives, log, register, document, minute, memorandum, note, account, report.
evidence, testimony, reputation, performance, history, career.
recording, disc, album, LP, single.
*v*, enter, note, write down, register, log, minute, document, chronicle, tape.

**recount** narrate, relate, tell, report, recite, repeat, rehearse, detail, specify, enumerate, list, describe, depict.

**recourse** resort, refuge, resource, remedy, appeal.

**recover** *vt*, regain, recoup, get back, retrieve, reclaim, repossess, recapture, redeem, rescue, save, salvage. LOSE
*vi*, get better, get well, pull through, improve, mend, heal, rally, revive, recuperate, convalesce. DETERIORATE

**recovery** recuperation, convalescence, rally, revival, improvement, amelioration, cure, healing. RELAPSE
retrieval, reclamation, repossession, recapture, redemption, restoration. LOSS

**recreation** relaxation, refreshment, hobby, pastime, amusement, diversion, distraction, entertainment, pleasure, enjoyment, fun, play, sport, exercise. WORK

**recrimination** countercharge, retaliation, retort, accusation.

**recruit** *v*, enlist, draft, call up, mobilize, muster, round up, enrol, sign up, engage, take on. DISMISS
renew, replenish, reinforce, strengthen, supply, furnish.
*n*, novice, rookie (*inf*), beginner, tyro, neophyte, initiate, learner, trainee, apprentice, helper, supporter. VETERAN

**rectify** correct, put right, redress, reform, remedy, fix, mend, repair, improve, ameliorate, amend, emend, adjust, straighten, regulate.

**rectitude** uprightness, righteousness, virtue, goodness, integrity, probity, morality, honour, justice, equity, correctness, accuracy, precision, exactitude. CORRUPTION

**rector** cleric, clergyman, churchman, ecclesiastic, parson, vicar, minister, pastor. LAYMAN

**recumbent** lying, reclining, leaning, resting, prostrate, flat, horizontal, supine, prone. ERECT

**recuperate** recover, convalesce, improve, get better, get well, mend, heal. DECLINE

**recur** repeat, happen again, return, come back, reappear, persist, come and go.

**recurrent** recurring, repeated, frequent, regular, periodic, cyclical, intermittent, persistent. SOLITARY

**red** crimson, carmine, scarlet, ruby, cherry, vermilion, .maroon, coral, auburn, chestnut.
rosy, ruddy, florid, glowing, blooming, blushing, flushed. PALLID

**redeem** recover, regain, reclaim, repossess, buy back, ransom, rescue, save, deliver, free, liberate, emancipate. SURRENDER
exchange, cash, trade in.
discharge, fulfil, perform, carry out, meet, satisfy.
reinstate, rehabilitate, absolve, expiate, make amends for, atone for, redress, offset, compensate.

**redemption** recovery, reclamation, repossession, ransom, salvation, deliverance.
rehabilitation, absolution, expiation, atonement, reparation, compensation.

**redolent** fragrant, scented, perfumed, aromatic, odoriferous, sweet-smelling. MALODOROUS
reminiscent, remindful, suggestive, evocative.

**redouble** intensify, increase, augment, multiply. REDUCE

**redoubtable** formidable, awe-inspiring, fearsome, terrible, dreadful, awful. DERISIBLE

**redound** conduce, contribute, lead, tend, result, recoil, rebound.

**redress** *v*, rectify, put right, correct, remedy, compensate for, make amends for, repair, fix, amend, improve, adjust, regulate.
*n*, rectification, correction, remedy, cure, compensation, recompense, amends, atonement, reparation. WRONG

**reduce** lessen, diminish, decrease, shrink, contract, shorten, cut, abridge, curtail, abate, attenuate, moderate, lower, weaken, impair. INCREASE
degrade, debase, demote, downgrade, ruin, impoverish, humble, humiliate. EXALT
subdue, quell, crush, conquer, vanquish, overcome, overpower, overwhelm, master, subjugate.
discount, mark down, cut, slash. RAISE

**redundant** superfluous, unnecessary, *de trop*, surplus, extra, excessive. ESSENTIAL
verbose, wordy, prolix, diffuse, repetitious, tautological. TERSE

**re-echo** resound, resonate, reverberate, echo, repeat.

**reek** *v*, smell, stink.
steam, smoke, fumigate.
*n*, smell, odour, stink, stench, fetor, effluvium, pong (*inf*). PERFUME

**reel**[1] *n*, bobbin, spool.

**reel**[2] *v*, stagger, totter, falter, stumble, lurch, pitch, rock, sway, spin, whirl.

**refer** mention, allude, speak of, bring up, quote, cite, advert, touch on.
direct, point, guide, send, hand over, deliver, consign, commit.
relate, pertain, apply, concern, mean, indicate, signify, suggest.
consult, turn, apply, appeal, have recourse.
assign, attribute, ascribe, put down, impute, credit.

**referee** umpire, arbiter, judge, adjudicator, arbitrator.

**reference** mention, allusion, quotation, citation, note, remark, hint, intimation, suggestion, insinuation.
regard, respect, consideration, concern, bearing, connection, relation, relevance.
testimonial, character, recommendation, endorsement.

**refine** purify, rarefy, clarify, cleanse, filter, sift, process. POLLUTE
polish, cultivate, civilize, elevate, improve, ameliorate, hone, perfect. BARBARIZE

**refined** cultivated, cultured, civilized, polished, genteel, courtly, polite, well-bred, gentlemanly, ladylike, elegant, sophisticated. COARSE
pure, purified, clear, clarified, clean, distilled, processed. CRUDE

**reflect** mirror, throw back, return, give back, echo, imitate, copy, reproduce.
show, exhibit, demonstrate, manifest, indicate, betray. CONCEAL
meditate, contemplate, cogitate, ruminate, ponder, muse, think, deliberate, consider, wonder.

**reflection** image, echo, shadow, likeness.
thought, idea, opinion, view, impression, feeling, meditation, contemplation, cogitation, rumination, deliberation, consideration.
censure, blame, criticism, reproach, aspersion, slur.

**reflex** automatic, mechanical, involuntary, spontaneous, immediate. VOLUNTARY

**reform** *v*, improve, better, ameliorate, mend, repair, amend, emend, correct, rectify, change, revolutionize, remodel, rebuild, restore, renovate, rehabilitate, reclaim. DETERIORATE
*n*, reformation, improvement, amelioration, amendment, correction, rectification, change, progress, renovation, rehabilitation, reclamation. CORRUPTION

**refractory** recalcitrant, contumacious, obstinate, stubborn, intractable, perverse, wilful, wayward, unruly, unmanageable, ungovernable, uncontrollable. DOCILE

**refrain**[1] *v*, abstain, forbear, desist, stop, give up, renounce, forgo, do without. INDULGE

**refrain**[2] *n*, chorus, burden, melody, tune. VERSE

**refresh** freshen, cool, revive, reanimate, invigorate, revitalize, brace, fortify, rejuvenate, exhilarate, cheer, enliven, stimulate, regenerate, renew, restore, repair, renovate. WEARY

**refreshment** food, drink, sustenance, snack.
revival, reanimation, invigoration, revitalization, rejuvenation, regeneration, renewal, restoration. FATIGUE

**refrigerate** cool, chill, freeze. HEAT

**refuge** shelter, protection, safety, security, sanctuary, asylum, haven, harbour, retreat, hide-out, resort, recourse. EXPOSURE

**refulgent** radiant, brilliant, bright, shining, effulgent, resplendent, lambent, lustrous. DULL

**refund** *v*, repay, pay back, return, give back, restore, reimburse, recompense, make good. WITHHOLD
*n*, repayment, reimbursement, rebate.

**refuse**[1] *v*, decline, turn down, reject, spurn, repudiate, deny, withhold, rebuff, repel. ACCEPT

**refuse**[2] *n*, rubbish, waste, garbage, trash, junk, litter, dregs, dross, scraps, leftovers.

**refute** disprove, rebut, negate, confute, deny, discredit. CONFIRM

**regain** recover, get back, retrieve, recoup, recapture, repossess. LOSE

**regal** royal, kingly, queenly, princely, imperial, sovereign, majestic, stately, august, noble, magnificent, grand. LOWLY

**regale** entertain, amuse, delight, feast, banquet, fête, treat.

**regalia** emblems, insignia, robes, finery.

**regard** *v*, watch, observe, notice, remark, note, mark, heed, look at, eye. IGNORE
consider, deem, rate, judge, think, believe, see, view, look upon, esteem, value, honour, respect.
concern, relate to, pertain to, refer to, apply to.

*n*, notice, attention, heed, thought, consideration, care, concern. NEGLECT

esteem, respect, estimation, admiration, honour, deference, liking, fondness, affection, love. CONTEMPT

reference, relation, respect, concern, bearing, connection.

look, gaze, stare, observation.

**regardful** mindful, heedful, attentive, careful, thoughtful, considerate, watchful, vigilant, observant, aware. HEEDLESS

**regarding** about, re, concerning, respecting, as regards, with reference to, apropos of.

**regardless** *adj*, heedless, mindless, unmindful, inattentive, reckless, careless, neglectful, negligent, disregarding, thoughtless, inconsiderate, indifferent, unconcerned. MINDFUL

*adv*, anyway, notwithstanding, in any case, nevertheless.

**regenerate** renew, restore, renovate, revive, invigorate, rejuvenate, uplift, reform, convert, change, reconstruct, remodel.

**regime** government, administration, system, reign, rule, direction, management.

**region** area, zone, territory, district, quarter, province, department, place, spot, country, land, tract, part, section, division, realm, domain, sphere, orbit, field, range, scope, vicinity, neighbourhood, locality.

**register** *v*, record, enter, write down, inscribe, note, list, catalogue, chronicle, minute.

enrol, enlist, sign up, sign on.

show, indicate, read, express, display, manifest, exhibit, reveal.

*n*, record, roll, list, catalogue, journal, diary, log, schedule, minutes, annals, archives, chronicle.

**regnant** reigning, ruling, ascendant, predominant, prevalent, prevailing.

**regress** *v*, return, go back, retreat, ebb, recede, retrocede, retrogress, revert, relapse, backslide, degenerate, decline, retrograde. PROGRESS

*n*, regression, return, reversion, relapse, retrogression, retreat, retrocession, recession. PROGRESSION

**regret** *v*, deplore, bemoan, bewail, lament, rue, repent, repine, mourn, grieve, miss.

*n*, sorrow, grief, remorse, repentance, penitence, contrition, compunction, lamentation, disappointment. SATISFACTION

**regular** normal, usual, customary, habitual, routine, typical, standard, familiar, conventional, ordinary, commonplace, everyday, formal, official, orthodox, correct, traditional. ABNORMAL

steady, rhythmic, constant, unchanging, unvarying, fixed, set, established, periodic, recurrent, orderly, methodical, systematic, uniform, even, level, symmetrical. IRREGULAR

**regulate** adjust, control, rule, govern, direct, manage, run, administer, handle, guide, arrange, organize, establish, fix, set, systematize, methodize, order.

**regulation** *n*, adjustment, control, government, direction, management, administration.

rule, law, statute, ordinance, edict, decree, order, commandment, directive, direction.

*adj*, formal, official, standard, regular, usual, normal. UNORTHODOX

**regurgitate** vomit, throw up (*inf*), disgorge, bring back.

**rehabilitate** reform, improve, adapt, adjust, reintegrate, redeem, save.

restore, reinstate, reclaim, renovate, renew, revive, repair, mend, reconstruct.

**rehearse** practise, drill, exercise, train, prepare, run through, repeat, recite.

recount, relate, review, recapitulate, detail, list, enumerate, narrate, describe, depict.

**reign** *v*, rule, govern, command, hold sway, predominate, prevail. SUBMIT

*n*, rule, government, regime, command, control, sway, power, sovereignty, empire, dominion.

**reimburse** repay, pay back, refund, recompense, compensate, indemnify.

**rein** *n*, bridle, harness, curb, check, restraint, control.

*v*, restrain, check, curb, bridle, hold back, control, guide. INDULGE

**reinforce** strengthen, fortify, support, brace, buttress, harden, stiffen, augment, supplement, increase, redouble. WEAKEN

**reinstate** restore, replace, return, rehabilitate. REMOVE

**reiterate** repeat, iterate, restate, recapitulate.

**reject** refuse, turn down, decline, deny, disallow, spurn, rebuff, repel, cast aside, discard, throw away, scrap, renounce, repudiate, jilt, eliminate, exclude, eject, expel. ACCEPT

**rejoice** exult, triumph, glory, revel, celebrate, make merry, delight, joy. MOURN

**rejoinder** reply, answer, response, riposte, retort.

**relapse** *v*, revert, slip back, lapse, backslide, regress, retrogress, degenerate, deteriorate, decline, weaken. IMPROVE
*n*, reversion, lapse, regression, retrogression, deterioration, setback. IMPROVEMENT

**relate** narrate, tell, recount, recite, rehearse, describe, detail, report, communicate, impart, mention. SUPPRESS
connect, link, associate, ally, couple.
refer, apply, regard, respect, concern, pertain.

**relation** relationship, connection, link, bond, association, affiliation, affinity, interdependence, similarity, propinquity.
relative, kinsman, kinswoman, kin, kindred, kinship, consanguinity.
reference, respect, regard, concern, bearing, relevance, pertinence.
account, narrative, narration, report, story, tale, recital, description.

**relative** *n*, relation, kinsman, kinswoman, kin, family.
*adj*, comparative, proportionate, respective, corresponding, analogous, comparable, connected, related, allied, associated, contingent, dependent. ABSOLUTE
relevant, pertinent, germane, apropos, applicable, appropriate.

**relax** loosen, slacken, ease, let up, moderate, reduce, lessen, lower, diminish, abate, weaken. TIGHTEN
rest, unwind, laze, take it easy (*inf*), calm, tranquillize, unbend.

**relaxation** rest, leisure, recreation, amusement, diversion, entertainment, hobby, pastime, fun, pleasure. WORK
loosening, slackening, easing, moderation, reduction, diminution.

**relay** *n*, relief, shift.
broadcast, transmission, communication.
*v*, broadcast, transmit, communicate, spread, pass on.

**release** *v*, free, set free, loose, turn loose, let out, let go, drop, liberate, emancipate, unshackle, untie, clear, acquit, discharge, let off, exempt. HOLD
publish, issue, circulate, disseminate, announce, make known. SUPPRESS
*n*, freedom, liberation, emancipation, acquittal, discharge, exemption. IMPRISONMENT
publication, issue, circulation, dissemination, announcement, proclamation.

**relegate** demote, downgrade. PROMOTE
assign, delegate, consign, transfer, entrust.
banish, exile, deport, expatriate, oust, eject. REINSTATE

**relent** unbend, yield, give way, soften, relax, slacken. HARDEN

**relentless** unrelenting, unyielding, implacable, inexorable, remorseless, ruthless, hard, harsh, cruel, merciless, pitiless, unremitting, unflagging, persistent. MILD

**relevant** pertinent, germane, apropos, applicable, to the point, apposite, appropriate, apt, proper, related. IRRELEVANT

**reliable** trustworthy, dependable, trusty, unfailing, sure, certain, sound, stable, honest, truthful, true, faithful. UNRELIABLE

**reliance** trust, dependence, confidence, faith, belief.

**relic** keepsake, memento, souvenir, token, trace, vestige, remnant, fragment.

**relief** comfort, solace, consolation, reassurance, ease, alleviation, mitigation, palliation, assuagement, remedy, cure. AGGRAVATION
help, aid, assistance, support, rescue, deliverance.
lull, remission, break, respite.

**relieve** ease, alleviate, mitigate, palliate, assuage, allay, soothe, diminish, lessen, comfort, solace, console, reassure. AGGRAVATE
help, aid, assist, support, free, deliver, release, replace, take over from, stand in for.
break, interrupt, vary, relax.

**religious** pious, godly, devout, reverent, good, pure, righteous, saintly, holy, sacred, divine, spiritual, theological. PROFANE
strict, rigid, rigorous, exact, scrupulous, conscientious, faithful. LAX

**relinquish** abandon, give up, surrender, renounce, abdicate, resign, quit, leave, desert, forsake, repudiate, yield, waive, forgo, drop, let go, release. RETAIN

**relish** *v*, enjoy, delight in, savour, appreciate, look forward to. LOATH

*n*, enjoyment, pleasure, delight, gusto, zest, liking, appreciation, fondness, fancy, partiality, predilection. AVERSION
taste, flavour, savour, tang, appetizer, sauce, condiment, seasoning. INSIPIDITY

**reluctant** loath, loth, unwilling, disinclined, indisposed, averse, hesitant. EAGER

**rely** depend, count, bank, lean, trust, swear by, have confidence in, be sure of. DISTRUST

**remain** stay, continue, abide, last, endure, persist, survive, be left, linger, tarry, wait, rest. GO

**remainder** rest, remains, remnant, residue, balance, surplus, excess.

**remains** relics, remnants, remainder, residue, dregs, fragments, scraps, leavings, leftovers, oddments, odds and ends.

**remark** *v*, comment, observe, mention, say, state, declare.
notice, note, see, perceive, observe, regard, heed, mark. MISS
*n*, comment, observation, mention, utterance, statement, declaration, opinion, thought, attention, heed, regard, notice.

**remarkable** notable, noteworthy, outstanding, striking, noticeable, conspicuous, extraordinary, unusual, uncommon, exceptional, rare, singular, peculiar, strange, surprising, wonderful. ORDINARY

**remedy** *n*, cure, antidote, restorative, specific, treatment, medicine, therapy, panacea, solution.
*v*, cure, heal, restore, treat, relieve, ease, alleviate, palliate, mitigate, assuage.
rectify, correct, redress, put right, fix, repair, improve, solve. AGGRAVATE

**remember** recall, recollect, call to mind, recognize, reminisce, commemorate, memorize. FORGET

**remembrance** memory, recollection, reminiscence, retrospect, thought, regard.
souvenir, memento, keepsake, token, reminder, commemoration, memorial.

**remind** prompt, jog the memory, bring back, call up, put in mind.

**reminiscence** memory, recollection, remembrance, reflection, retrospection, memoir, anecdote.

**reminiscent** evocative, suggestive, remindful, redolent, nostalgic.

**remiss** negligent, neglectful, careless, inattentive, heedless, thoughtless, unmindful, forgetful, derelict, delinquent, dilatory, slack, lax, slow, tardy, indolent, slothful. DILIGENT

**remission** forgiveness, pardon, amnesty, reprieve, release, discharge, acquittal, exoneration, absolution. PUNISHMENT
diminution, reduction, lessening, abatement, ebb, decrease, moderation, relaxation, respite, let-up (*inf*). INCREASE

**remit** send, dispatch, mail, post, forward, pay.
halt, stop, desist, forbear, reprieve, release, cancel.
relax, slacken, mitigate, alleviate, moderate, weaken, abate, ebb, decrease, diminish, lessen, reduce. INCREASE
postpone, defer, put off, delay.

**remnant** remainder, rest, remains, residue, scrap, fragment, bit, piece, trace, vestige.

**remonstrate** protest, object, expostulate, argue, dissent, take issue. ACQUIESCE

**remorse** regret, sorrow, grief, contrition, penitence, repentance, guilt, shame, compunction. SATISFACTION

**remorseful** sorry, apologetic, regretful, contrite, penitent, repentant, guilty, ashamed, sorrowful, sad. IMPENITENT

**remorseless** relentless, unrelenting, inexorable, implacable, merciless, pitiless, cruel, hard, harsh, callous, ruthless. MERCIFUL

**remote** distant, far, removed, sequestered, secluded, isolated, lonely, inaccessible, out-of-the-way. NEAR
foreign, alien, extraneous, extrinsic, irrelevant, unconnected, unrelated.
slight, slender, slim, faint, inconsiderable, negligible, unlikely. CONSIDERABLE
detached, stand-offish, distant, aloof, indifferent, cool, frigid. FRIENDLY

**remove** take off, detach, doff, shed, take away, withdraw, abstract, dislodge, displace, move, transport, transfer, eliminate, eradicate, abolish, obliterate, efface, expunge, erase, delete, oust, depose, dismiss, discharge, expel, eject. REPLACE

**remunerate** pay, reward, recompense, reimburse, indemnify, repay, requite, redress.

**remuneration** payment, reward, recompense, reimbursement, pay, wages, salary, emolument, stipend, fee.

**remunerative** profitable, gainful, lucrative, rewarding, paying, advantageous, worthwhile. UNPROFITABLE

**renaissance** renascence, rebirth, revival, renewal, reappearance, resurgence, reemergence, awakening.

**rend** tear, rip, cleave, sever, sunder, rive, split, divide, rupture, fracture, break, crack. MEND
pierce, stab, lacerate, wound, pain, afflict, distress, harrow.

**render** give, supply, provide, furnish, present, submit, offer, tender, deliver, yield. WITHHOLD
show, exhibit, manifest, display, represent, depict, portray, do.
make, cause to be.
translate, transcribe, construe, interpret, explain.

**rendition** rendering, performance, execution, presentation, delivery, arrangement, version, interpretation, construction, transcription, translation.

**renegade** traitor, apostate, backslider, recreant, turncoat, defector, deserter, rat (*inf*), mutineer, outlaw, rebel.

**renew** recommence, resume, repeat, reiterate, revive, restore, replenish, restock, refresh, regenerate, rejuvenate, reinvigorate, revitalize, repair, renovate, refurbish, refit, recondition.

**renounce** give up, forgo, forswear, eschew, abandon, forsake, desert, abdicate, resign, relinquish, let go, yield, surrender, cede. RETAIN
disown, disinherit, repudiate, reject, decline, turn down, deny, disclaim, disavow, recant. ACKNOWLEDGE

**renovate** restore, renew, repair, do up (*inf*), recondition, refurbish, refit, rehabilitate, revive, refresh.

**renown** fame, celebrity, illustriousness, note, eminence, repute, distinction, honour, glory, acclaim. NOTORIETY

**rent**[1] *v*, lease, let, hire, charter.
*n*, rental, hire, lease, payment, tariff.

**rent**[2] *n*, tear, rip, slit, gash, opening, gap, crevice, cleft, fissure, crack, split, rift, break, rupture, breach, division, schism.

**repair**[1] *v*, mend, fix, patch up, restore, renovate, renew, correct, rectify, put right, adjust, redress, make good. DAMAGE
*n*, mend, patch, restoration, renovation, correction, adjustment, overhaul, service.

**repair**[2] *v*, go, betake oneself, leave for, head for, resort, have recourse.

**reparation** amends, atonement, redress, requital, satisfaction, recompense, compensation, indemnity, damages, repair, restoration. INJURY

**repartee** banter, badinage, raillery, persiflage, pleasantry, riposte, rejoinder, quip, witticism.

**repast** meal, feast, banquet, food.

**repay** refund, return, pay back, reimburse, requite, recompense, reward, square.
reciprocate, retaliate, revenge, avenge.

**repeal** *v*, rescind, revoke, abrogate, annul, nullify, abolish, invalidate, countermand, overrule, reverse, cancel. ENACT
*n*, revocation, abrogation, annulment, abolition, reversal, cancellation.

**repeat** reiterate, iterate, restate, recapitulate, rehearse, recite, quote, recount, retell, redo, rerun, reproduce, duplicate, echo, renew.

**repel** repulse, drive back, ward off, check, resist, parry, reject, spurn, rebuff. WELCOME
disgust, nauseate, sicken, revolt, put off, offend. ATTRACT

**repent** regret, rue, lament, deplore, be penitent, be contrite, feel remorse.

**repentance** penitence, contrition, regret, remorse, compunction, sorrow, grief, guilt, shame. SATISFACTION

**repentant** penitent, contrite, regretful, remorseful, sorry, apologetic. UNREPENTANT

**repercussion** result, consequence, aftermath, backlash, recoil, rebound, echo, reverberation.

**repetition** repeat, reiteration, iteration, tautology, redundancy, restatement, recapitulation, rehearsal, recital, reproduction, duplication, echo, renewal, return, recurrence. ORIGINALITY

**repine** grumble, complain, moan, lament, fret, mope, brood, sulk. REJOICE

**replace** supersede, take the place of, succeed, follow, supplant, take over, substitute.
return, put back, restore, reinstate. REMOVE

**replenish** refill, restock, recharge, reload, renew, stock, supply, furnish, provide, fill. EXHAUST

**replete** full, filled, well-stocked, packed, stuffed, bursting, overflowing, abounding, gorged, sated, satiated. EMPTY

**replica** copy, duplicate, reproduction, facsimile, model, imitation. ORIGINAL

**reply** *v*, answer, respond, acknowledge, rejoin, retort, riposte, return, echo. ASK
*n*, answer, response, acknowledgment, reaction, rejoinder, retort, riposte, echo. QUESTION

**report** *n*, account, statement, description, narrative, narration, relation, recital, article, story, review, write-up, paper, study, record, minute, announcement, declaration, news, tidings, word, communication, message, communiqué, dispatch, bulletin, rumour, hearsay.
reputation, repute, fame, renown, esteem, regard, character, performance.
bang, crack, boom, shot, blast, explosion, detonation, discharge, noise, sound, reverberation.
*v*, tell, relate, recount, narrate, describe, relay, communicate, announce, broadcast, state, declare, record, write up. SUPPRESS

**reporter** journalist, correspondent, columnist, newsman, newswoman, newscaster.

**repose**[1] *n*, rest, ease, relaxation, sleep, slumber, peace, quiet, tranquillity, stillness, inactivity, inertia. ACTIVITY
composure, calmness, poise, aplomb, self-possession, equanimity. AGITATION
*v*, rest, relax, lie, recline, sleep. WORK

**repose**[2] *v*, place, put, lodge, deposit, store.

**reprehend** blame, censure, criticize, find fault with, reprove, rebuke, reprimand, reproach, chide, berate, upbraid, scold, admonish. PRAISE

**reprehensible** blameworthy, censurable, culpable, disgraceful, shameful, opprobrious, ignoble, objectionable. COMMENDABLE

**represent** symbolize, stand for, epitomize, exemplify, typify, personify, embody, express, illustrate, depict, describe, reproduce, show.
act for, stand for, speak for, substitute for.
portray, impersonate, mimic, pose as, pretend to be, act, perform, produce, stage.

**representative** *n*, agent, deputy, delegate, spokesman, spokeswoman, proxy, substitute, stand-in.
salesman, commercial traveller, agent, rep.
*adj*, typical, characteristic, illustrative, symbolic, emblematic.

**repress** suppress, restrain, control, check, curb, hold back, bottle up, inhibit, stifle, smother, muffle, quash, quell, subdue, crush, overcome, overpower, master, subjugate. RELEASE

**reprieve** *v*, pardon, remit, postpone, relieve, allay, alleviate, mitigate, palliate.
*n*, remission, stay of execution, pardon, amnesty, respite, relief, alleviation, mitigation.

**reprimand** *v*, admonish, reprehend, scold, tell off (*inf*), rebuke, reprove, reproach, chide, upbraid, berate, castigate, censure, criticize. COMMEND
*n*, rebuke, reproof, reproach, admonition, reprehension, telling-off (*inf*), dressing-down (*inf*), castigation, censure. PRAISE

**reprisal** retaliation, retribution, revenge, vengeance.

**reproach** *v*, blame, censure, criticize, find fault with, rebuke, reprove, reprehend, reprimand, scold, chide, upbraid, admonish. APPROVE
*n*, blame, censure, criticism, disapproval, rebuke, reproof, reprimand, admonition. APPROVAL
shame, disgrace, dishonour, discredit, ignominy, odium, opprobrium, obloquy, slur, stigma. HONOUR

**reprobate** *adj*, corrupt, depraved, degenerate, immoral, abandoned, shameless, profligate, irredeemable, hardened, wicked, evil, vile, base. VIRTUOUS
*n*, villain, miscreant, wretch, rogue, scoundrel, rascal, sinner, wrongdoer. PARAGON
*v*, condemn, denounce, criticize, disapprove, censure, blame, reproach, reprehend. APPROVE

**reproduce** duplicate, replicate, copy, imitate, emulate, parallel, mirror, echo, repeat, represent, re-create.
propagate, multiply, breed, procreate, produce, generate.

**reproduction** propagation, breeding, procreation, generation.
duplicate, copy, replica, facsimile, print.

**reproof** reproval, reproach, rebuke, reprimand, reprehension, admonition, censure, blame. PRAISE

**reprove** rebuke, scold, tell off (*inf*), reproach, reprehend, reprimand, admonish, chide, upbraid, berate, blame, censure, condemn. PRAISE

**repudiate** reject, renounce, disavow, abjure, disclaim, forswear, retract, deny, disown, abandon, cast off, discard. ACKNOWLEDGE

**repugnant** repellent, repulsive, revolting, disgusting, offensive, objectionable, distasteful, obnoxious, odious, loathsome, abhorrent.
hostile, inimical, adverse, antagonistic, contrary, opposed, conflicting, incompatible.

**repulse** repel, drive back, ward off, check, reject, rebuff, spurn, turn down. WELCOME

**repulsive** repellent, repugnant, revolting, disgusting, nauseating, sickening, offensive, objectionable, obnoxious, odious, loathsome, abhorrent, detestable, hateful, hideous, ugly, foul, horrid. DELIGHTFUL

**reputation** repute, name, character, standing, status, respect, esteem, estimation, regard, fame, renown, celebrity, distinction, honour.

**reputed** supposed, putative, apparent, ostensible, seeming, alleged, believed, considered, reckoned, deemed, held.

**request** *v*, ask, beg, beseech, supplicate, entreat, appeal, petition, solicit, demand.
*n*, entreaty, supplication, appeal, petition, prayer, desire, demand, requisition.

**require** need, lack, want, desire, necessitate, involve, call for, demand.
ask, request, bid, enjoin, instruct, direct, order, command, oblige, compel.

**requisite** *adj*, required, needed, necessary, needful, essential, indispensable, vital, imperative, obligatory, compulsory, mandatory. NONESSENTIAL
*n*, requirement, need, necessity, must, essential, condition, prerequisite, stipulation, provision.

**requite** repay, reciprocate, return, reimburse, recompense, redress, make good, reward, retaliate, avenge.

**rescind** repeal, revoke, abrogate, reverse, annul, nullify, quash, invalidate, countermand, cancel. CONFIRM

**rescue** *v*, save, deliver, redeem, ransom, free, liberate, release, extricate, recover, salvage. ENDANGER
*n*, salvation, deliverance, redemption, ransom, liberation, release, recovery, salvage.

**research** *n*, investigation, inquiry, study, analysis, examination, scrutiny, groundwork, documentation.
*v*, investigate, look into, study, analyse, examine, scrutinize, experiment.

**resemblance** likeness, similarity, semblance, similitude, analogy, parity, correspondence, comparison, closeness, affinity. DISSIMILARITY

**resemble** look like, take after, favour, mirror, echo, duplicate, match, parallel.

**resent** begrudge, take offence, take umbrage, object to, dislike.

**resentful** bitter, embittered, indignant, angry, irate, wrathful, miffed (*inf*), peeved (*inf*), grudging, jealous, envious, aggrieved, wounded. CONTENTED

**resentment** bitterness, ill will, animosity, hatred, indignation, offence, umbrage, pique, anger, rage, ire, wrath, displeasure, grudge, jealousy, envy. SATISFACTION

**reservation** qualification, condition, proviso, qualm, scruple, demur.
reserve, preserve, sanctuary, territory, area, plot.

**reserve** *v*, withhold, hold, keep, keep back, save, conserve, husband, retain, set aside, put by. USE
book, engage, secure, retain.
*n*, stock, supply, store, stockpile, fund, reservoir.
park, sanctuary, reservation, tract.
reticence, taciturnity, shyness, restraint, modesty, formality, aloofness, detachment, coolness. FRANKNESS
*adj*, substitute, auxiliary, spare, extra.

**reserved** booked, engaged, taken, retained, held, kept, set aside. FREE
reticent, taciturn, shy, retiring, unsociable, uncommunicative, aloof, distant, standoffish, formal, restrained, prim, modest, demure, constrained, cool. FRANK

**reservoir** lake, tank, basin, receptacle, container.
stock, supply, reserve, store, fund, pool.

**reside** live, dwell, abide, sojourn, stay, lodge, inhabit, settle.
lie, rest, exist, abide, dwell, inhere.

**residence** house, home, abode, dwelling, habitation, quarters, lodging, accommodation.
mansion, palace, villa, castle, hall, manor.
sojourn, stay, occupancy, inhabitancy.

**resident** inhabitant, citizen, denizen, occupier, householder, inmate, lodger, tenant. VISITOR

**residue** residuum, remainder, remains, rest, balance, surplus, excess, remnant, leavings, leftovers, dregs.

**resign** abdicate, give up, renounce, relinquish, hand over, surrender, yield, leave, quit. RETAIN

**resignation** abdication, renunciation, relinquishment, surrender, departure, retirement, notice.
acquiescence, submission, compliance, nonresistance, passivity, acceptance, endurance, patience, forbearance. REBELLION

**resilient** springy, bouncy, elastic, rubbery, flexible, pliable, supple, buoyant, irrepressible.

**resist** withstand, repel, repulse, rebuff, stand firm, hold out, oppose, counteract, face, confront, fight, battle, contend with, check, curb, stop, block, hinder, thwart. YIELD
refrain from, abstain from, refuse, desist.

**resolute** steadfast, firm, set, intent, determined, resolved, decided, staunch, unwavering, unflinching, unyielding, obdurate, dogged, constant, steady, relentless, persistent, persevering, undaunted, unshaken. IRRESOLUTE

**resolution** firmness, determination, resolve, resoluteness, steadfastness, constancy, perseverance, tenacity, zeal, earnestness. IRRESOLUTION
decision, resolve, objective, intention, aim, purpose, verdict, judgment, declaration, statement.

**resolve** *v*, determine, decide, fix, settle, intend, purpose. WAVER
solve, explain, answer, fathom, clear up.
dispel, unravel, disentangle. EMBROIL
separate, dissect, anatomize, analyse, break down, reduce, dissolve.
*n*, decision, resolution, intention, purpose.
firmness, determination, resoluteness, resolution, steadfastness, constancy, persistence, doggedness, perseverance, tenacity, fortitude, willpower. IRRESOLUTION

**resonant** resounding, reverberant, ringing, booming, loud, sonorous, full, rich. QUIET

**resort** *v*, turn, have recourse, use, employ, utilize, exercise.
go, repair, frequent, haunt.
*n*, retreat, refuge, haunt, rendezvous, spot, place, holiday centre, spa.
recourse, expedient, alternative, possibility, chance, hope.

**resound** resonate, reverberate, ring, echo, re-echo.

**resource** ingenuity, enterprise, ability, inventiveness, resourcefulness, initiative.
device, expedient, resort, recourse.
source, store, hoard, stockpile.

**resources** wealth, capital, money, funds, assets, property, supplies, reserves, means.

**respect** *v*, honour, esteem, admire, revere, venerate, think highly of, look up to, appreciate, prize, value. DESPISE
notice, heed, observe, comply with, abide by, adhere to, obey, defer to, be polite to, regard, consider.
*n*, honour, esteem, admiration, reverence, veneration, appreciation, deference, regard, consideration, politeness, courtesy. DISRESPECT
reference, connection, relation, regard, point, detail, particular, feature.

**respectable** worthy, estimable, laudable, commendable, praiseworthy, admirable, honourable, venerable, reputable, honest, upright, proper, decent. DISREPUTABLE
acceptable, passable, tolerable, fair, goodly, considerable.

**respectful** courteous, polite, mannerly, civil, gracious, deferential, considerate, thoughtful, dutiful, obedient, submissive, humble. DISRESPECTFUL

**respective** individual, separate, several, specific, particular, own, corresponding.

**respite** pause, lull, rest, break, interval, breather (*inf*), recess, adjournment, postponement, delay, reprieve, remission.

**resplendent** splendid, glorious, bright, brilliant, radiant, shining, dazzling, effulgent, glittering, sparkling. DULL

**respond** reply, answer, rejoin, retort, react, acknowledge, reciprocate, return.

**response** reply, answer, rejoinder, retort, riposte, reaction, feedback, acknowledgment.

**responsibility** duty, obligation, onus, burden, charge, care, trust.
accountability, liability, culpability, guilt, fault, blame.

**responsible** accountable, answerable, liable, bound, culpable, guilty.

dependable, reliable, trustworthy, honest, upright, stable, sound, sensible, rational. IRRESPONSIBLE

**responsive** sensitive, reactive, susceptible, impressionable, sympathetic, receptive. INSENSITIVE

**rest**[1] *n*, relaxation, ease, leisure, inactivity, repose, sleep, slumber, nap, stillness, quiet, calm, tranquillity, motionlessness, inertia, standstill. TUMULT

pause, respite, break, breather (*inf*), recess, holiday, vacation, intermission, halt, cessation. CONTINUATION

support, prop, brace, stand.

*v*, relax, take it easy (*inf*), laze, lounge, sleep, slumber, repose, recline. WORK

stop, cease, desist, halt, pause, stay. CONTINUE

support, prop, stand, lean, lay, lie, hinge, hang, depend, rely.

**rest**[2] *n*, remainder, remains, residue, balance, surplus, excess, remnants, leftovers, others.

**restful** relaxing, soothing, calm, tranquil, serene, quiet, still, peaceful. TUMULTUOUS

**restitution** restoration, return, reparation, amends, redress, requital, satisfaction, compensation, indemnity, indemnification, recompense, remuneration, repayment, refund, reimbursement. INJURY

**restive** restless, uneasy, nervous, fretful, impatient, fidgety, refractory, recalcitrant, stubborn, obstinate, wilful, unruly. DOCILE

**restless** moving, active, unsettled, unstable, changeable, inconstant, wandering, roving, nomadic, migrant. STILL

uneasy, restive, unquiet, fidgety, jumpy, edgy, fretful, nervous, anxious, agitated, disturbed, sleepless, wakeful. RESTFUL

**restoration** renovation, repair, reconstruction, rehabilitation, renewal, revival, refreshment, rejuvenation. DECLINE

return, restitution, replacement, reinstatement, recovery, compensation. REMOVAL

**restore** return, give back, replace, put back, bring back, reintroduce, reinstate, re-establish. REMOVE

renovate, repair, fix, mend, recondition, reconstruct.

renew, revive, refresh, reinvigorate, strengthen, cure.

**restrain** hold back, constrain, curb, check, bridle, inhibit, contain, repress, suppress, subdue, moderate, control, restrict, limit, confine, imprison. RELEASE

**restraint** control, self-control, self-restraint, inhibition, reserve, moderation, repression, suppression, constraint, check, curb, restriction.

**restrict** limit, bound, demarcate, cramp, constrict, hamper, impede, confine, circumscribe, restrain, regulate.

**restriction** limitation, condition, stipulation, qualification, regulation, control, check, curb, confinement, demarcation. FREEDOM

**result** *n*, consequence, outcome, issue, effect, upshot, end, conclusion, sequel, aftermath, product, fruit, development, score. CAUSE

*v*, ensue, follow, eventuate, issue, proceed, arise, spring, happen, end, culminate. BEGIN

**resume** renew, recommence, restart, continue, proceed, carry on, go on. STOP

**résumé** summary, précis, abstract, synopsis, epitome, digest, compendium. AMPLIFICATION

**resurrection** resuscitation, revival, reappearance, comeback (*inf*), regeneration, rebirth, renaissance, resurgence, restoration, return. EXTINCTION

**resuscitate** revive, revivify, restore, bring round, reanimate, quicken, resurrect.

**retain** keep, hold, reserve, save, preserve, maintain, detain, hold back. RELINQUISH

remember, recall, recollect, memorize. FORGET

engage, employ, hire, pay.

**retainer** servant, domestic, attendant, valet, lackey, dependant.

fee, payment, deposit, advance.

**retaliate** return, repay, strike back, revenge, avenge, requite. FORGIVE

**retard** delay, slow down, hold back, detain, check, restrain, hinder, impede, hamper, handicap, arrest, halt. ACCELERATE

**reticent** reserved, taciturn, quiet, uncommunicative, tight-lipped, mum. GARRULOUS

**retinue** suite, train, entourage, attendants, escort, bodyguard.

**retire** withdraw, go away, leave, depart, retreat, recede, ebb, resign, go to bed.

**retiring** shy, reserved, diffident, bashful, timid, coy, modest, demure, meek, humble, unassuming, self-effacing. FORWARD

**retort** *v*, answer, reply, respond, riposte, rejoin.
*n*, answer, reply, response, riposte, rejoinder.

**retract** disavow, recant, withdraw, take back, unsay, deny, abjure, disclaim, repudiate, disown, revoke, cancel, recall, reverse, go back on, renege. CONFIRM
draw back, pull in, sheathe.

**retreat** *v*, retire, withdraw, depart, leave, fall back, recoil, turn tail, flee, recede, ebb. ADVANCE
*n*, retirement, withdrawal, departure, flight.
refuge, haven, asylum, sanctuary, shelter, privacy, seclusion.

**retrench** curtail, reduce, decrease, lessen, diminish, cut, shorten, abridge, abbreviate, crop, clip, trim, prune, limit, restrict, economize, cut back.

**retribution** punishment, just deserts, revenge, vengeance, retaliation, reprisal, requital, redress, satisfaction, recompense. PARDON

**retrieve** recover, regain, get back, recoup, recapture, salvage, rescue, save, redeem, restore, bring back, fetch. LOSE

**retrocede** recede, go back, retire, withdraw, retreat, retrograde, retrogress. ADVANCE

**retrograde** *adj*, backward, inverse, retreating, retrogressive, declining, waning, degenerate. FORWARD
*v*, recede, retrocede, retrogress, regress, revert, decline, deteriorate. ADVANCE

**retrogress** decline, deteriorate, worsen, degenerate, regress, revert, retrograde, recede, retrocede. PROGRESS

**retrospect** review, reminiscence, remembrance, recollection, hindsight, afterthought. SPECULATION

**return** *v*, go back, revert, retreat, come back, recur, reappear, recoil, rebound. DEPART
restore, replace, put back, give back, reinstate, re-establish. REMOVE
reciprocate, requite, refund, repay.
retort, rejoin, riposte, answer, reply, respond, come back.
*n*, reversion, retreat, recurrence, reappearance, recoil, rebound.
restoration, replacement, restitution, reinstatement, reciprocation, requital, reparation, recompense.
profit, gain, income, revenue, yield, interest, benefit, advantage. LOSS
retort, rejoinder, riposte, answer, reply, response, comeback (*inf*).

**reveal** disclose, divulge, expose, uncover, unfold, bare, unmask, unveil, show, exhibit, display, bring to light, make known, tell, impart, communicate, broadcast, betray, leak, give away. CONCEAL

**revel** *v*, wallow, bask, luxuriate, indulge, relish, savour, rejoice, delight.
carouse, make merry, celebrate, roister. MOURN
*n*, carousal, spree, debauch, orgy, party, celebration, gala, festival, carnival, revelry, festivity.

**revelation** disclosure, exposure, exposition, manifestation, unmasking, discovery, broadcast, publication, announcement, proclamation, betrayal, leak. CONCEALMENT

**revelry** merriment, jollification, merrymaking, carousal, revel, debauch, orgy, saturnalia. MOURNING

**revenge** *n*, vengeance, retribution, reprisal, retaliation, requital, satisfaction. FORGIVENESS
*v*, avenge, requite, retaliate, return, repay. FORGIVE

**revengeful** vengeful, vindictive, malevolent, spiteful, malicious, malignant, bitter, resentful, unforgiving, merciless, pitiless, implacable, cruel, harsh. MERCIFUL

**revenue** income, receipts, return, yield, profit, gain, proceeds, takings. EXPENDITURE

**reverberate** echo, re-echo, resound, resonate, ring, rebound, recoil.

**revere** reverence, venerate, worship, adore, admire, respect, think highly of, look up to. DESPISE

**reverence** veneration, worship, honour, adoration, devotion, homage, respect, deference, awe. CONTEMPT

**reverent** reverential, solemn, respectful, deferential, humble, submissive. DISRESPECTFUL

**reverie** dream, fantasy, daydream, trance, abstraction, woolgathering, daydreaming, preoccupation, brown study. ATTENTION

**reverse** *v*, invert, transpose, turn round, upend, upset, overturn. RIGHT
change, alter, negate, invalidate, cancel, quash, overrule, countermand, revoke, annul, rescind, repeal, undo, overthrow.
retreat, backtrack, back up, go backwards. ADVANCE
*n*, opposite, contrary, converse, antithesis.
back, rear, other side.
setback, reversal, check, defeat, misfortune, mishap, misadventure, mischance, adversity, hardship, trial, affliction. SUCCESS
*adj*, opposite, contrary, converse, inverse, backward, upside-down.

**revert** return, go back, relapse, backslide, regress, recur, come back.

**review** *v*, reconsider, re-examine, reassess, recall, recollect, remember, look back on.
inspect, examine, survey, study, revise, edit, assess, evaluate, criticize, discuss.
*n*, notice, criticism, critique, commentary, assessment, evaluation.
magazine, periodical, journal, newspaper.
inspection, examination, survey, report, re-examination, reconsideration, revision, study, analysis.
parade, procession, display, inspection.

**revile** abuse, vituperate, upbraid, reproach, vilify, asperse, traduce, malign, denigrate, defame, slander, calumniate. EXTOL

**revise** change, alter, amend, correct, review, reconsider, rework, rewrite, edit, update.
study, swot (*inf*), reread, go over, learn, memorize.

**revive** renew, restore, refresh, resuscitate, revivify, reanimate, reinvigorate, revitalize, rejuvenate, regenerate, rekindle, cheer, hearten, animate, invigorate, quicken, rouse, awaken, rally, recover.

**revoke** retract, withdraw, recant, take back, disavow, repudiate, rescind, renege, repeal, abrogate, annul, nullify, abolish, cancel, quash, reverse, countermand. CONFIRM

**revolt** *n*, rebellion, rising, uprising, insurrection, insurgence, mutiny, revolution. LOYALTY
*v*, rebel, rise up, mutiny. SUBMIT
disgust, repel, nauseate, sicken, offend, appal. ATTRACT

**revolting** repulsive, repellent, repugnant, offensive, obnoxious, disgusting, nauseating, sickening, foul, horrid, loathsome, abominable, shocking, appalling, nasty, horrible, hideous, obscene. ATTRACTIVE

**revolution** revolt, rebellion, rising, uprising, insurrection, insurgence, mutiny, sedition, putsch, coup de'état.
change, alteration, transformation, metamorphosis, innovation, upheaval. CONSERVATISM
rotation, turn, whirl, spin, circle, cycle, round, lap.

**revolve** rotate, turn, wheel, whirl, spin, gyrate, circle, orbit.

**revulsion** repugnance, repulsion, disgust, nausea, loathing, abomination, abhorrence, detestation, aversion, distaste, shrinking, recoil. ATTRACTION

**reward** *n*, payment, recompense, return, requital, compensation, remuneration, pay, prize, award, honour, premium, bonus, tip, gratuity. PUNISHMENT
punishment, retribution, just deserts, comeuppance (*inf*).
*v*, pay, recompense, repay, requite, compensate, remunerate. PUNISH

**rhetorical** oratorical, declamatory, eloquent, silver-tongued, flowery, florid, ornate, flamboyant, bombastic, orotund, pretentious, pompous, magniloquent, grandiloquent. SIMPLE

**rhyme** poetry, verse, poem, ode, limerick, jingle.

**rhythm** beat, pulse, tempo, cadence, measure, metre, accent, lilt, swing.

**ribald** bawdy, risqué, racy, naughty, smutty, dirty, rude, vulgar, obscene, indecent, lewd, licentious, gross, coarse. PURE

**rich** wealthy, affluent, opulent, moneyed, prosperous, well-off, flush (*inf*), loaded (*inf*). POOR
fertile, fecund, fruitful, productive, prolific, ample, abundant, plentiful, plenteous, copious, replete, full, well-stocked, abounding, profuse, exuberant. BARREN
valuable, precious, expensive, costly, dear, sumptuous, luxurious, splendid, gorgeous, fine, exquisite. CHEAP
juicy, succulent, luscious, delicious, spicy, piquant, creamy, heavy. TASTELESS
bright, vivid, intense, deep, sonorous, resonant, mellifluous, dulcet. SOFT

**riches** wealth, affluence, opulence, money, fortune, treasure, assets, funds, means, resources. POVERTY

**rickety** shaky, unstable, unsteady, tottering, infirm, frail, feeble, weak, decrepit, ramshackle, dilapidated, broken-down. STURDY

**rid** clear, free, relieve, disencumber, deliver, release.

**get rid of,** discard, throw away, dispose of, eject, eliminate, dispense with. RETAIN

**riddle** puzzle, conundrum, enigma, mystery, problem, poser, brain-teaser (*inf*). SOLUTION

**ride** *v*, travel, journey, move, go, sit on, control, handle, manage, propel.

*n*, journey, trip, excursion, jaunt, outing, drive, spin (*inf*), lift. WALK

**ridge** ledge, crest, summit, peak, chain, range, fold, corrugation, spine, chine.

**ridicule** *n*, mockery, derision, scorn, satire, sarcasm, irony, raillery, banter, taunt, jeer. RESPECT

*v*, mock, deride, burlesque, lampoon, parody, caricature, satirize, laugh at, make fun of, scoff, taunt, jeer. ADMIRE

**ridiculous** absurd, ludicrous, laughable, risible, comical, farcical, preposterous, outrageous, fantastic, unbelievable, nonsensical, foolish, contemptible, derisory. SERIOUS

**rife** prevalent, prevailing, current, rampant, widespread, general, universal, plentiful, abundant. RARE

**rifle** ransack, loot, sack, strip, rob, steal, plunder, pillage.

**rift** split, cleft, fissure, crevice, chink, crack, breach, gap, opening, space.

difference, disagreement, quarrel, schism, separation, division, alienation, estrangement. RECONCILIATION

**rig** *v*, equip, supply, furnish, fit, outfit, kit out, accoutre, deck, array, clothe, dress, rig out, turn out.

manipulate, falsify, fake, trump up, doctor, tamper with, fix, engineer, manoeuvre.

*n*, gear, equipment, outfit, accoutrements, apparatus, tackle, rigging, kit.

**right** *adj*, just, fair, equitable, lawful, good, virtuous, righteous, upright, moral, ethical, honourable, honest. WRONG

true, factual, actual, real, correct, accurate, precise, exact. INCORRECT

proper, seemly, becoming, fit, fitting, apt, appropriate, suitable, advantageous, convenient, opportune, desirable, favourable. INAPPROPRIATE

healthy, well, sound, normal, sane.

*adv*, properly, suitable, justly, fairly, well, correctly, accurately, precisely, exactly, straight, directly, immediately, promptly.

*n*, claim, title, privilege, prerogative, authority, power, due.

justice, fairness, equity, legality, lawfulness, goodness, virtue, rectitude, uprightness, honesty, truth, integrity, honour, morality, propriety. WRONG

*v*, straighten, adjust, rectify, correct, redress, fix, put right.

**righteous** good, virtuous, moral, upright, honest, honourable, holy, saintly, pure, innocent, just, fair, equitable. WICKED

**rightful** legal, lawful, licit, legitimate, proper, right, true, real, genuine, valid, just, fair. WRONGFUL

**rigid** stiff, inflexible, unbending, unyielding, unswerving, fixed, set, firm, strict, stern, severe, harsh, austere, tough, rigorous, stringent, exact, precise. FLEXIBLE

**rigorous** strict, stern, severe, harsh, austere, tough, stringent, firm, rigid, inflexible, demanding, exacting, meticulous, painstaking, conscientious, thorough, scrupulous, punctilious, exact, precise. LAX

**rigour** strictness, sternness, severity, harshness, austerity, hardship, privation, suffering, accuracy, precision, exactitude, meticulousness, conscientiousness, scrupulousness. LAXITY

**rile** annoy, irritate, vex, irk, nettle, exasperate, anger, incense. PACIFY

**rim** edge, border, lip, brim, brink, verge, margin. CENTRE

**rind** skin, peel, husk, shell, crust.

**ring**[1] *n*, band, circle, round, loop, hoop.

gang, mob, syndicate, combine, cartel, trust, clique, coterie, league, association.

*v*, encircle, surround, gird, girdle, circle, encompass, enclose.

**ring**[2] *v*, resound, resonate, reverberate, peal, chime, toll, tinkle, clang.

phone, telephone, call, summon.

**rinse** wash, clean, bathe, dip, flush, wet. DRY

**riot** *n*, uproar, commotion, tumult, turbulence, disturbance, rumpus, brawl, fray,

fracas, anarchy, lawlessness, disorder, confusion. ORDER
revelry, carousal, merrymaking, jollification, boisterousness, high jinks. SOBRIETY
display, show, splash, flourish.
*v*, rampage, run riot, fight, brawl, rebel, revolt.
revel, carouse, make merry, roister.

**rip** tear, rend, split, burst, lacerate, slash. MEND

**ripe** mature, seasoned, mellow, fully developed, fully grown, advanced, ready, prepared, set, fit, full, perfect, finished, complete. UNRIPE

**ripple** *v*, wave, undulate, lap, splash, babble, gurgle, ruffle, wrinkle.
*n*, wave, undulation, splash, gurgle.

**rise** *v*, arise, get up, stand up.
ascend, mount, climb, soar, go up, increase, grow, swell, intensify. FALL
advance, progress, improve, prosper, thrive, get on.
appear, emerge, spring, flow, stem, originate, occur, happen, eventuate.
rebel, revolt, mutiny, resist. SUBMIT
*n*, ascent, climb, slope, incline, elevation, increase, growth, advance, progress, improvement, upturn, upsurge, rising, uprising. FALL
appearance, emergence, origin, source, beginning, commencement.

**risible** ridiculous, ludicrous, absurd, laughable, farcical, comical, funny, amusing, humorous, droll. SERIOUS

**risk** *n*, hazard, peril, danger, jeopardy, chance, uncertainty, gamble, speculation. SAFETY
*v*, chance, venture, dare, gamble, hazard, imperil, endanger, jeopardize.

**risky** hazardous, perilous, dangerous, unsafe, precarious, dicey (*inf*). SAFE

**ritual** *n*, rite, ceremony, ceremonial, service, sacrament, observance, custom, practice, form, convention, usage, formality, habit, routine.
*adj*, ceremonial, ceremonious, formal, customary, conventional, routine.

**rival** *n*, competitor, opponent, antagonist, adversary, contender, contestant, challenger, emulator. ALLY
*adj*, competitive, competing, emulous, opposing, conflicting.
*v*, compete, vie, contend, oppose, challenge, emulate, equal, match.

**road** thoroughfare, street, highway, motorway, avenue, lane, route, path, way, course.

**roam** rove, range, wander, stray, drift, meander, ramble, stroll, saunter, prowl.

**roar** bellow, yell, shout, cry, howl, growl, rumble, thunder, guffaw. MURMUR

**rob** burgle, hold up, mug (*inf*), plunder, pillage, raid, rifle, ransack, strip, fleece, swindle, defraud, deprive. ENDOW

**robber** burglar, thief, bandit, brigand, pirate, highwayman, plunderer, marauder, raider, swindler.

**robbery** burglary, hold-up, theft, larceny, embezzlement, piracy, plunder, pillage, rapine, spoliation, swindle, fraud, rip-off (*inf*).

**robe** *n*, gown, vestment, habit, dress.
*v*, clothe, dress, garb, attire, drape, invest. STRIP

**robust** strong, hardy, hale, hearty, vigorous, lusty, sound, firm, stout, sturdy, powerful, stalwart, rugged, sinewy, muscular, brawny, strapping, athletic, boisterous, rough. DELICATE

**rock**[1] *n*, stone, boulder, crag, reef.
foundation, cornerstone, anchor, mainstay, support, protection.

**rock**[2] *v*, sway, reel, roll, pitch, swing, wobble, totter, stagger.

**rod** stick, wand, baton, staff, cane, switch, birch, bar, shaft, pole, dowel.

**rogue** rascal, scoundrel, scamp, blackguard, knave, villain, reprobate, charlatan, fraud, swindler, cheat, con man (*inf*), crook (*inf*). GENTLEMAN

**roguish** rascally, knavish, villainous, unscrupulous, unprincipled, dishonest, deceitful, crooked. HONEST
mischievous, impish, puckish, waggish, arch, sportive, playful, frolicsome.

**roister** revel, carouse, make merry, paint the town red (*inf*). MOURN
bluster, swagger, boast, brag.

**role** part, character, portrayal, impersonation.
function, purpose, use, job, task, position, capacity.

**roll** *v*, revolve, rotate, turn, whirl, twirl, spin, gyrate, wheel, swing, rock, sway, reel, pitch, toss, lurch, wallow.
flow, run, go, move, pass, elapse, undulate, trundle.

wrap, enfold, envelop, swathe, wind, twist, curl, coil, furl, entwine.
flatten, level, smooth, press.
rumble, thunder, roar, boom, resound, reverberate.
*n*, revolution, rotation, turn, twirl, spin, gyration, twist, coil, curl, undulation, wave.
cylinder, roller, reel, spool, bobbin, ball, scroll.
register, roster, list, inventory, catalogue, schedule, record, chronicle, index, directory.
rumble, thunder, roar, boom, resonance, reverberation.
bun, bread, cake, pastry.

**rollicking** boisterous, spirited, hearty, lively, playful, frisky, sportive, frolicsome, jolly, merry, gay, carefree. STAID

**romance** love, passion, affair, liaison, intrigue, amour.
story, tale, novel, fiction, love story, fairy tale, legend, fantasy, invention, fabrication, exaggeration, falsehood, lie. FACT

**romantic** sentimental, tender, loving, fond, passionate, amorous. COLD
unrealistic, idealistic, visionary, quixotic, fanciful, fantastic, imaginary, fictitious, wild, extravagant, impractical. REALISTIC

**romp** frolic, caper, frisk, gambol, sport, rollick, revel, carouse, make merry.

**roof** cover, top, ceiling, canopy, shelter. FLOOR

**rook** swindle, defraud, cheat, mulct, diddle (*inf*), rip off (*inf*).

**room** chamber, apartment.
space, expanse, extent, scope, range, compass, latitude, leeway, margin, play, capacity. RESTRICTION

**roomy** spacious, capacious, commodious, ample, large, broad, wide, extensive. NARROW

**root**[1] *n*, radix, radicle, rhizome, tuber.
base, foundation, source, origin, derivation, cause, motive, ground, bottom, germ, seed, crux, essence.
*v*, fix, plant, implant, embed, establish, set. UPROOT

**root**[2] *v*, dig, delve, burrow, rummage, ferret, hunt, search, poke, pry, nose.

**rooted** fixed, set, firm, rigid, ingrained, deep-seated, inveterate, confirmed, radical, fundamental. SUPERFICIAL

**rope** *n*, cable, cord, line, string.
*v*, tie, bind, fasten, secure, moor, tether. LOOSE

**roster** rota, list, roll, register, catalogue, table, schedule, agenda.

**rostrum** platform, dais, stage, stand, pulpit, lectern.

**rosy** pink, roseate, red, reddish, rubicund, ruddy, blushing, flushed, blooming, glowing. PALE
optimistic, hopeful, bright, cheerful, encouraging, promising, auspicious, favourable. HOPELESS

**rot** *v*, decay, decompose, putrefy, go bad, spoil, moulder, crumble, disintegrate, perish, corrode, corrupt, taint. PRESERVE
*n*, decay, decomposition, putrefaction, mould, mildew, blight.
nonsense, rubbish, twaddle, balderdash. SENSE

**rotate** revolve, turn, twirl, whirl, spin, wheel, pivot, swivel, gyrate, reel.
alternate, take turns, interchange, switch.

**rotation** revolution, turn, spin, gyration, cycle, alternation, sequence, succession.

**rotten** rotting, decayed, decaying, decomposed, decomposing, putrid, putrescent, bad, mouldy, rancid, rank, fetid, foul, tainted, spoiled. FRESH
despicable, contemptible, mean, low, base, vile, nasty, unpleasant, wicked, immoral, corrupt, degenerate.

**rotund** round, rounded, spherical, bulbous, globular. ANGULAR
plump, corpulent, portly, stout, podgy, tubby, fat, obese. SLIM
full, rich, sonorous, resonant, orotund, magniloquent.

**rough** uneven, irregular, bumpy, rugged, jagged, coarse, unkempt, bristly, unshaven, shaggy, hairy, bushy. SMOOTH
stormy, tempestuous, choppy, agitated, turbulent, wild, violent, boisterous. CALM
rude, impolite, discourteous, uncivil, unmannerly, churlish, uncouth, coarse, vulgar, unrefined, uncultured. REFINED
hard, harsh, sharp, severe, cruel, brutal, drastic, extreme, tough, austere. GENTLE
crude, unfinished, incomplete, shapeless, preliminary, rudimentary, cursory, sketchy, vague, approximate. FINISHED

**round** *adj*, circular, annular, curved, rounded, rotund, spherical, globular, cylindrical. ANGULAR

complete, entire, whole, full, ample.
candid, frank, blunt, plain, direct, straightforward. EVASIVE
rough, approximate. EXACT
*n*, circle, disc, ring, band, sphere, ball, orb, globe.
cycle, series, succession, sequence. bout, period, session, turn.
circuit, lap, compass, ambit, beat, course, route, routine, tour.
*prep*, around, about, surrounding, encircling.
*adv*, around, near, nearby, throughout.
*v*, curve, bow, turn, circle, encircle, surround.
**round off,** complete, finish, conclude, close, crown, cap. BEGIN
**round up,** gather, collect, assemble, marshal, muster, herd. DISPERSE

**roundabout** tortuous, circuitous, indirect, circumlocutory, periphrastic, long-winded. DIRECT

**rouse** wake, awaken, rise, get up, arouse, call, stimulate, whet, animate, stir, move, provoke, incite, foment, excite, agitate, enkindle, inflame, startle, disturb. SOOTHE

**rout** *n*, defeat, beating, overthrow, debacle, flight, retreat. VICTORY
*v*, defeat, vanquish, conquer, beat, overthrow, overpower, crush, thrash, disperse, scatter.

**route** way, road, path, course, itinerary, circuit, round, beat.

**routine** *n*, system, method, pattern, order, convention, custom, practice, habit, wont, procedure, course, way.
*adj*, customary, habitual, regular, usual, ordinary, everyday, humdrum, boring. UNUSUAL

**rove** wander, roam, range, stray, drift, meander, ramble, stroll, gallivant, travel. SETTLE

**rover** wanderer, roamer, drifter, rambler, nomad, gypsy, itinerant, vagrant, gadabout (*inf*), traveller.

**row**[1] *n*, line, rank, tier, file, column, queue, string, series, sequence, succession.

**row**[2] *n*, quarrel, dispute, argument, tiff, fight, brawl. HARMONY
noise, din, disturbance, commotion, fuss, tumult, turmoil, uproar. QUIET
*v*, quarrel, argue, squabble, wrangle, fight, brawl. AGREE

**rowdy** noisy, loud, boisterous, rough, unruly, disorderly. QUIET

**royal** regal, kingly, queenly, princely, imperial, sovereign, majestic, august, noble, stately, grand, magnificent. LOWLY

**rub** *v*, chafe, abrade, scour, scrape, grate, polish, smooth, wipe, clean, brush, graze, stroke, caress, knead, massage, apply, smear.
**rub out,** erase, efface, wipe out, obliterate, expunge, delete, cancel.
*n*, friction, polish, wipe, stroke, caress, massage.
difficulty, problem, obstacle, impediment, hindrance, hitch, snag.

**rubbish** waste, refuse, garbage, litter, trash, junk, debris, dross.
nonsense, rot, twaddle, balderdash, humbug, bunkum, codswallop (*inf*), bosh (*inf*), drivel, claptrap. SENSE

**rubicund** red, reddish, ruddy, florid, rosy, roseate, flushed, blushing. PALE

**ruddy** red, reddish, rubicund, florid, glowing, blooming, flushed, blushing, pink, rosy, roseate, sanguine. PALE

**rude** impolite, discourteous, uncivil, unmannerly, disrespectful, insolent, impudent, impertinent, cheeky, saucy, curt, abrupt, brusque, sharp, insulting, abusive, offensive, obscene, indecent. POLITE
coarse, vulgar, boorish, barbarous, uncouth, unrefined, uncultured, unpolished, uncivilized, untutored, uneducated, ignorant, rough, crude. REFINED

**rudimentary** rudimental, basic, fundamental, elementary, primary, initial, undeveloped, embryonic. ADVANCED

**rudiments** basics, fundamentals, essentials, principles, elements, foundation, beginning, commencement.

**rue** regret, repent, lament, deplore, bewail, bemoan, mourn, grieve, sorrow.

**ruffian** thug, tough, hooligan, rowdy, bully, brute, villain, scoundrel, rogue, rascal, wretch. GENTLEMAN

**ruffle** rumple, derange, disarrange, disorder, mess up, tousle, dishevel, crease, wrinkle. SMOOTH
agitate, disturb, upset, rattle (*inf*), unsettle, disconcert, fluster, perturb, annoy, irritate, vex, nettle, trouble. COMPOSE

**rug** carpet, mat, blanket.

**rugged** rough, uneven, irregular, bumpy, rocky, craggy, jagged, ragged, lined, wrin-

kled, gnarled, leathery, weather-beaten. SMOOTH
harsh, severe, stern, austere, difficult, hard, tough, strong, hardy, robust, rude, uncouth, churlish, blunt.

**ruin** *v*, destroy, devastate, desolate, lay waste, demolish, raze, wreck, shatter, break, smash, crush, defeat, overthrow, overturn. RESTORE
bankrupt, impoverish, pauperize.
spoil, mar, damage, mess up, botch. FIX
*n*, destruction, devastation, desolation, havoc, ruination, wreck, disrepair, dilapidation, decay, deterioration, disintegration, defeat, overthrow. RESTORATION
fall, downfall, collapse, failure, undoing, bankruptcy, insolvency, impoverishment, destitution. PROSPERITY

**ruinous** destructive, devastating, disastrous, calamitous, catastrophic, pernicious, deleterious, baneful, mischievous, injurious, baleful, noxious. BENEFICIAL

**rule** *n*, regulation, statute, ordinance, law, principle, precept, tenet, maxim, order, directive, direction, guide, guideline, standard, criterion, canon. EXCEPTION
government, direction, reign, regime, dominion, domination, control, command, authority, sway, mastery, supremacy.
habit, routine, wont, custom, practice.
**as a rule,** generally, usually, ordinarily, normally, mainly, on the whole. RARELY
*v*, reign, govern, direct, manage, administer, lead, command, control, regulate. SUBMIT
prevail, predominate, preponderate, thrive.
decree, judge, decide, settle.

**ruler** monarch, sovereign, king, queen, emperor, empress, potentate, lord, chief, leader, commander, governor. SUBJECT
measure, rule.

**ruling** *adj*, reigning, governing, controlling, chief, principal, main, dominant, predominant, prevailing, prevalent, current. SUBORDINATE
*n*, decree, judgment, decision, finding, verdict.

**rumble** thunder, roll, roar, growl, resound, reverberate.

**ruminate** meditate, cogitate, muse, ponder, think, reflect, consider, brood, mull over.

**rummage** search, hunt, ransack, explore, root, forage.

**rumour** *n*, gossip, hearsay, talk, word, report, story, information, news, tidings. TRUTH
*v*, circulate, publish, tell, report, gossip.

**rumple** ruffle, tousle, dishevel, wrinkle, crease, crumple, pucker. SMOOTH

**rumpus** commotion, uproar, disturbance, noise, row, brouhaha, tumult. PEACE

**run** *v*, sprint, race, dash, dart, tear, bolt, career, hare (*inf*), speed, hasten, hurry, rush, scamper, gallop, lope, jog. SAUNTER
go, proceed, move, pass, roll, glide, work, function, operate, perform. STOP
flow, stream, spill, pour, gush, leak, melt, dissolve.
spread, stretch, extend, reach, continue, last.
manage, direct, govern, control, command, lead, head, supervise.
drive, propel, convey, transport, ship, smuggle.
compete, contend, challenge, stand.
**run away,** run off, flee, abscond, escape, take flight, decamp, elope. RETURN
**run down,** hit, strike, knock down, run over.
reduce, decrease, decline, weaken, debilitate, tire, weary, exhaust.
criticize, knock (*inf*), disparage, belittle, denigrate, defame, vilify. PRAISE
find, locate, discover, track, hunt, catch, capture, seize.
**run out,** finish, terminate, end, expire, exhaust, consume, use up.
*n*, sprint, race, dash, rush, gallop, jog. WALK
trip, journey, excursion, outing, jaunt, ride, drive, spin (*inf*).
series, sequence, succession, string, chain, stream, course, spell, period.

**rupture** *v*, break, burst, crack, split, fracture, tear, cleave, separate, divide. MEND
*n*, break, burst, crack, split, breach, rift, cleft, tear.
quarrel, altercation, dispute, disagreement, feud, schism, division, hostility, estrangement. RECONCILIATION

**rural** country, rustic, bucolic, pastoral, agricultural, agrarian. URBAN

**ruse** wile, trick, artifice, stratagem, contrivance, device, subterfuge, deceit, deception, manoeuvre, ploy.

**rush** *v*, hurry, hasten, race, run, dash, speed, press, hustle, accelerate, quicken, dispatch, expedite. DAWDLE
charge, attack, assault, storm.

*n*, hurry, haste, run, dash, scramble, stampede, speed, quickness, dispatch, expedition.
charge, attack, assault, onslaught.

**rust** *n*, corrosion, oxidation, mould, mildew, blight.
*v*, corrode, oxidize, deteriorate, decline.

**rustic** *adj*, rural, country, countrified, provincial, pastoral, bucolic, sylvan, Arcadian. URBAN
simple, plain, homely, unsophisticated, artless, coarse, rough, uncouth, churlish, awkward, loutish. SOPHISTICATED
*n*, peasant, countryman, bumpkin, yokel.

**rustle** *v*, whisper, swish, susurrate, crinkle, crackle, crepitate.
*n*, rustling, whisper, susurration, crackle, crepitation.

**rut** groove, furrow, track, groove, hollow, indentation.
routine, habit, pattern, system.

**ruthless** pitiless, unpitying, merciless, unmerciful, hard, harsh, severe, cruel, brutal, savage, heartless, unfeeling, callous, hard-hearted, relentless, unrelenting, implacable, inexorable. COMPASSIONATE

# S

**sable** black, jet, raven, ebony, dark, dusky, sombre. WHITE

**sabotage** *n*, destruction, damage, subversion, treachery, treason.
*v*, destroy, damage, disable, wreck, undermine, subvert.

**sack**[1] *n*, bag, pouch.
dismissal, discharge, boot (*inf*).
*v*, dismiss, discharge, fire (*inf*). APPOINT

**sack**[2] *v*, plunder, pillage, despoil, ravage, maraud, ransack, loot, rifle, devastate, lay waste.
*n*, plunder, pillage, despoliation, rape, rapine, looting, devastation.

**sacred** holy, consecrated, hallowed, sanctified, blessed, divine, venerable, sacrosanct, inviolable, untouchable. PROFANE

**sacrifice** *n*, offering, oblation, immolation, slaughter, surrender, renunciation, loss, destruction. GAIN
*v*, offer, immolate, surrender, give up, forgo, let go, lose, destroy.

**sacrilege** desecration, profanation, violation, profanity, blasphemy, impiety, irreverence, disrespect, mockery. REVERENCE

**sad** unhappy, sorrowful, downcast, dejected, depressed, despondent, low, blue, melancholy, glum, gloomy, mournful, miserable, woebegone, heartbroken, disconsolate. HAPPY
distressing, depressing, heartbreaking, tragic, regrettable, grievous, lamentable, deplorable, unfortunate, sorry, pitiful, poignant, pathetic, wretched, cheerless, dismal, sombre, grave. JOYFUL

**sadden** upset, distress, grieve, deject, depress, dispirit, dishearten. CHEER

**saddle** burden, encumber, load, charge, tax, lumber (*inf*). RELIEVE

**safe** secure, protected, guarded, invulnerable, impregnable, sound, intact, unhurt, unharmed, undamaged, unscathed. EXPOSED
sure, certain, dependable, reliable, trustworthy, cautious, circumspect, conservative. RISKY
harmless, innocuous, tame, nonpoisonous. DANGEROUS

**safeguard** *v*, protect, guard, defend, shield, look after, watch over. IMPERIL
*n*, protection, guard, defence, shield, security, precaution, escort, convoy, bodyguard.

**sag** droop, dip, sink, drop, fall, slump, flag, weaken, decline. RISE

**sagacious** wise, sage, judicious, shrewd, astute, sharp, acute, discerning, penetrating, percipient, perspicacious, clever, intelligent, apt, quick-witted, far-sighted, knowing. STUPID

**sage** *n*, philosopher, savant, wise man, guru, master, expert, authority. FOOL
*adj*, wise, sagacious, sapient, judicious, sensible, learned. FOOLISH

**sail** *v*, embark, set sail, travel, journey, boat, yacht, cruise, drift, float, glide, pilot, steer, captain, navigate.
*n*, cruise, trip, journey, voyage, crossing.

**sailor** mariner, seaman, seafarer, bluejacket, salt, tar (*inf*), matelot (*inf*).

**saintly** godly, holy, pious, devout, reverent, religious, spiritual, righteous, virtuous, angelic, blessed. GODLESS

**sake** account, interest, behalf, welfare, benefit, good, regard, respect, consideration.
purpose, end, reason, motive, end, cause.

**salacious** lecherous, lascivious, licentious, lewd, lustful, libidinous, concupiscent, prurient, bawdy, ribald, smutty, dirty, obscene, pornographic. PURE

**salary** pay, wage, remuneration, earnings, emolument, stipend.

**sale** selling, vendition, trade, traffic, auction, market, demand, outlet, deal, transaction, bargain, reduction, discount, clearance. PURCHASE

**salient** prominent, striking, conspicuous, outstanding, noticeable, remarkable, marked, pronounced, projecting, jutting, protruding. INCONSPICUOUS

**sallow** yellow, yellowish, pale, pallid, wan, anaemic, pasty. RUDDY

**sally** *n*, sortie, charge, foray, offensive, raid, onslaught, rush, outburst.
excursion, trip, jaunt, outing.
retort, riposte, repartee, joke, jest, quip, crack (*inf*), witticism, bon mot.
*v*, rush, surge, charge, storm, issue, erupt.

**salt** *n*, flavour, savour, taste, relish, seasoning, spice, pungency, piquancy, bite, punch, zest, liveliness, wit.
sailor, seaman, seafarer, mariner.
*adj*, salty, saline, salted, briny, brackish. SWEET
*v*, preserve, cure, season, flavour.

**salubrious** wholesome, healthy, healthful, salutary. UNHEALTHY

**salutary** beneficial, advantageous, useful, helpful, valuable, profitable, good, wholesome, salubrious. HARMFUL

**salute** *v*, greet, hail, address, accost, welcome, receive, acknowledge, recognize, honour. IGNORE
*n*, greeting, salutation, address, welcome, homage, tribute.

**salvage** save, rescue, redeem, reclaim, recover, retrieve, restore. DESTROY

**salvation** saving, rescue, deliverance, redemption, restoration, preservation. DESTRUCTION

**salve** *n*, balm, lotion, cream, ointment, liniment, embrocation.
remedy, cure, antidote.
*v*, remedy, heal, soothe, alleviate, mitigate, palliate, ease, comfort. AGGRAVATE

**salvo** fusillade, broadside, volley, outburst.

**same** identical, selfsame, twin, duplicate, corresponding, equivalent, similar, like, alike, changeless, unvarying, consistent. DIFFERENT
**all the same,** . nonetheless, nevertheless, anyway, still, yet.
immaterial, unimportant, of no consequence.

**sample** *n*, specimen, example, instance, illustration, model, pattern, cross section, sampling.
*v*, try, test, inspect, taste.

**sanctify** hallow, consecrate, bless, anoint, purify, cleanse. PROFANE

**sanctimonious** self-righteous, self-satisfied, smug, holier-than-thou, goody-goody (*inf*), pharisaical, pietistic, hypocritical, unctuous.

**sanction** *n*, permission, consent, allowance, authorization, warrant, approval, endorsement, support, ratification. PROHIBITION
ban, embargo, boycott, penalty.
*v*, permit, allow, authorize, warrant, approve, countenance, endorse, support, ratify. PROHIBIT

**sanctity** holiness, saintliness, godliness, sanctitude, sacredness, inviolability, piety, righteousness, goodness, purity. PROFANITY

**sanctuary** shrine, sanctum, church, temple.
refuge, asylum, haven, retreat, shelter, reserve.

**sane** rational, normal, *compos mentis*, lucid, sound, sober, sensible, intelligent, reasonable, judicious. INSANE

**sang-froid** composure, calmness, coolness, self-possession, poise, aplomb, imperturbability. AGITATION

**sanguinary** bloody, gory, bloodthirsty, murderous, brutal, cruel, savage, ruthless.

**sanguine** hopeful, optimistic, assured, confident, cheerful, buoyant, lively, spirited, animated. PESSIMISTIC
ruddy, rubicund, reddish, red, florid. PALE

**sanitary** hygienic, clean, germ-free, salubrious, healthy, wholesome. INSANITARY

**sanity** saneness, reason, sense, normality, rationality, lucidity, wisdom, sagacity, judiciousness, common sense. INSANITY

**sap**[1] *n*, juice, lifeblood.
fool, dupe, idiot, simpleton, jerk (*inf*), sucker (*inf*).

**sap**[2] *v*, undermine, weaken, deplete, drain, enervate, exhaust. STRENGTHEN

**sapient** wise, sagacious, sage, discerning, perspicacious, discriminating, judicious, knowing, intelligent, clever, shrewd, astute, sharp, keen, acute. STUPID

**sarcasm** irony, satire, cynicism, ridicule, mockery, scorn, derision, contempt.

**sarcastic** ironical, sardonic, satirical, cynical, mocking, scornful, derisive, contemptuous, sneering, taunting, mordant, caustic, cutting, trenchant, bitter, acrimonious.

**sardonic** sarcastic, ironical, cynical, scornful, mocking, derisive, contemptuous, bitter, malicious, malignant, malevolent. PLEASANT

**satanic** devilish, diabolic, fiendish, demonic, demoniacal, hellish, infernal, wicked, evil, malevolent, black. ANGELIC

**sate** satisfy, fill, slake, satiate, surfeit, cloy, glut, overfill, stuff, gorge. STARVE

**satellite** moon, sputnik.
follower, disciple, minion, subordinate, attendant, dependant, retainer, vassal, parasite, hanger-on, sycophant. LEADER

**satiate** surfeit, cloy, glut, overfill, stuff, gorge, sate, satisfy, fill, slake. STARVE

**satire** irony, ridicule, sarcasm, lampoon, burlesque, parody, caricature, travesty, skit, spoof (*inf*), send-up (*inf*), take-off (*inf*).

**satirical** ironical, sarcastic, sardonic, burlesque, trenchant, biting, cutting, mordant, caustic, incisive, mocking, derisive.

**satirize** mock, deride, ridicule, lampoon, burlesque, parody, send up (*inf*), take off (*inf*), attack.

**satisfaction** gratification, fulfilment, contentment, content, pleasure, happiness, enjoyment, comfort, ease. DISSATISFACTION
reparation, compensation, indemnification, recompense, amends, atonement, redress, settlement, payment. INJURY

**satisfactory** adequate, sufficient, suitable, passable, acceptable, all right, fair, good. UNSATISFACTORY

**satisfy** gratify, indulge, content, please, appease, pacify, fill, sate, satiate. DISSATISFY
meet, fulfil, discharge, settle, answer, match, suffice, serve.
convince, persuade, assure, reassure.
atone, requite, compensate, recompense.

**saturate** soak, drench, waterlog, steep, sate, satiate, imbue, pervade, infuse, impregnate. DRAIN

**saturnine** gloomy, morose, dismal, glum, sombre, grave, phlegmatic, dour, taciturn, uncommunicative. JOVIAL

**sauce** condiment, relish, dressing, ketchup, seasoning.
impertinence, impudence, insolence, rudeness, cheek (*inf*), brass (*inf*), nerve (*inf*), lip (*inf*). RESPECT

**saucy** impertinent, pert, impudent, insolent, rude, disrespectful, bold, presumptuous, forward, fresh (*inf*), cheeky (*inf*), flippant. RESPECTFUL

**saunter** stroll, amble, ramble, wander, loiter, dawdle, dally, linger. HASTEN

**savage** *adj*, fierce, ferocious, vicious, cruel, brutal, brutish, inhuman, barbaric, barbarous, murderous, bloodthirsty, sadistic, diabolical, merciless, pitiless, ruthless, relentless, harsh. GENTLE
wild, untamed, undomesticated, feral, uncivilized, barbarian, primitive, rough, rude. CIVILIZED
*n*, barbarian, primitive, native, aborigine, beast, brute, boor, yahoo.

**savant** sage, philosopher, scholar, intellectual, master, expert, authority. FOOL

**save** rescue, free, liberate, deliver, redeem, salvage. ABANDON
keep, reserve, hoard, store, husband, economize, set aside, put by. SQUANDER
preserve, conserve, protect, guard, safeguard, shield. EXPOSE
spare, prevent, obviate, preclude, rule out.

**saviour** redeemer, deliverer, liberator, rescuer, protector, defender, guardian.

**savour** *n*, flavour, taste, relish, tang, piquancy, smack, smell, odour, scent, aroma, bouquet.
*v*, relish, enjoy, appreciate, revel, bask, wallow, luxuriate.

**savoury** tasty, delicious, delectable, appetizing, luscious, ambrosial, palatable, toothsome, piquant, pungent, spicy, tangy. INSIPID

**saw[1]** *n*, saying, adage, dictum, proverb, axiom, maxim, aphorism, apophthegm.

**saw[2]** *v*, cut, divide, sever, cleave, hack.

**say** *v*, utter, speak, pronounce, articulate, voice, answer, reply, remark, mention, state, declare, affirm, assert, tell, reveal, disclose, recite, deliver. SUPPRESS

allege, claim, report, rumour.
assume, suppose, conjecture, speculate, estimate.
*n*, utterance, expression, statement, declaration, assertion, speech.
turn, chance, vote, influence, weight.

**saying** saw, adage, dictum, proverb, axiom, maxim, aphorism, apophthegm.

**scaffold** scaffolding, frame, framework, platform, stage, gallows, gibbet.

**scale**[1] *n*, flake, squama, plate, layer, lamina.

**scale**[2] *n*, gradation, graduation, series, sequence, progression, hierarchy, ladder, spectrum, gamut, range, scope, extent, degree.
ration, proportion, measure.
*v*, climb, mount, ascend, escalade. DESCEND

**scamp** scallywag, rascal, rogue, scapegrace, imp, devil, knave, blackguard, villain, wretch.

**scamper** scurry, scoot, scuttle, run, speed, hasten, hurry, dash, dart, fly. AMBLE

**scan** examine, scrutinize, study, investigate, search.
skim, browse, look over, glance through.

**scandal** crime, sin, offence, outrage, disgrace, shame, dishonour, disrepute, reproach, infamy, ignominy, opprobrium, condemnation, censure, discredit. HONOUR
gossip, talk, backbiting, slander, calumny, aspersion, abuse.

**scandalize** horrify, appal, shock, outrage, offend, affront, repel, disgust.

**scandalous** shocking, outrageous, disgraceful, shameful, dishonourable, infamous, ignominious, opprobrious, atrocious, discreditable, disreputable, improper, unseemly. CREDITABLE
slanderous, libellous, scurrilous, defamatory.

**scanty** meagre, skimpy, exiguous, scant, limited, insufficient, inadequate, short, little, small, narrow, thin, sparse, poor, paltry. AMPLE

**scar** cicatrix, mark, disfigurement, blemish, wound, injury, trauma.

**scarce** rare, infrequent, uncommon, few, sparse, scanty, insufficient, deficient, short. PLENTIFUL

**scarcely** barely, hardly, only just.

**scarcity** dearth, paucity, lack, want, shortage, insufficiency, deficiency, rarity, infrequency. ABUNDANCE

**scare** *v*, frighten, affright, alarm, startle, shock, daunt, terrify, horrify, appal, dismay, intimidate. REASSURE
*n*, fright, alarm, start, shock, terror, panic. REASSURANCE

**scathing** caustic, mordant, biting, cutting, incisive, trenchant, critical, sarcastic, scornful, withering. PLEASANT

**scatter** sprinkle, strew, broadcast, disseminate, spread, diffuse. GATHER
disperse, dispel, dissipate, disband, separate. COLLECT

**scene** place, spot, locality, site, location, setting, background, milieu.
incident, episode, event, chapter.
view, vista, prospect, landscape, panorama, scenery.
display, show, exhibition, spectacle, sight, representation, tableau, pageant.
fuss, commotion, outburst, tantrum.

**scenery** landscape, panorama, view, vista, scene, setting.
set, backdrop, flats.

**scent** *n*, smell, odour, aroma, redolence, perfume, fragrance.
trail, track, spoor.
*v*, sniff, smell, detect, discern, recognize.
perfume, aromatize.

**sceptical** doubting, doubtful, dubious, questioning, suspicious, distrustful, mistrustful, unbelieving, incredulous, unconvinced, cynical. CREDULOUS

**scepticism** doubt, suspicion, distrust, mistrust, disbelief, incredulity, cynicism, Pyrrhonism, unbelief, agnosticism. FAITH

**schedule** plan, programme, agenda, calendar, timetable, itinerary, list, inventory, catalogue, record, register.

**scheme** *n*, plan, system, programme, schedule, project, design, proposal, idea, outline, diagram, arrangement, strategy, device, contrivance, wile, ruse, stratagem, ploy, plot, intrigue, conspiracy.
*v*, plan, project, devise, contrive, formulate, frame, design, imagine, plot, intrigue, machinate, conspire.

**schism** disunion, separation, division, split, breach, rift, rupture, faction. UNITY

**scholar** schoolboy, schoolgirl, student, pupil, learner. TEACHER savant, intellectual, academic, egghead (*inf*). DUNCE

**scholarship** erudition, learning, letters, schooling, education, knowledge, lore, accomplishments, attainments, achievements. IGNORANCE
grant, bursary, fellowship, exhibition.

**school** *n*, college, academy, seminary, institute, institution, faculty, department.
denomination, sect, faction, persuasion, creed, class, set, group, followers, disciples, pupils, adherents, devotees, admirers.
*v*, teach, educate, instruct, tutor, coach, train, discipline, drill, prepare, prime.

**scientific** natural, physical, technical, logical, systematic, methodical, mathematical, accurate, exact, precise. UNSCIENTIFIC

**scintilla** spark, glimmer, trace, hint, *soupçon*, iota, atom, jot, tittle, speck, particle.

**scintillate** sparkle, twinkle, gleam, coruscate, glitter, glint, glisten, flash.

**scintillating** lively, stimulating, spirited, animated, sparkling, brilliant, dazzling, exciting. DULL

**scion** descendant, heir, successor, offspring, child, issue, progeny.
offshoot, shoot, twig, branch, cutting, graft. STOCK

**scoff**[1] mock, jeer, sneer, gibe, make fun of, laugh at, ridicule, deride, taunt, scorn, flout. RESPECT

**scoff**[2] devour, wolf, bolt, guzzle, gobble, cram, stuff, gorge.

**scold** upbraid, berate, reprimand, reprehend, rebuke, reprove, reproach, chide, castigate, tell off (*inf*), blame, censure, nag. PRAISE

**scoop** *n*, ladle, spoon, shovel.
exclusive, sensation, inside story.
*v*, dig, excavate, hollow, gouge, ladle, shovel, gather, pick up, remove.

**scope** opportunity, freedom, liberty, latitude, space, room, range, extent, reach, span, area, sphere.

**scorch** burn, singe, char, toast, blister, scald, roast, bake, parch, sear, wither.

**score** *n*, record, tally, reckoning, sum, total, account, bill, points, result, mark.
twenty, lot, mass, crowd, legion, hundred, thousand, million.
reason, cause, basis, grounds, account.
grievance, grudge, wrong, injury, debt, obligation.
*v*, gain, achieve, win, earn, get, make, tally, count, record, register.
cut, gouge, nick, mark, scratch, scrape.

**scorn** *n*, contempt, disdain, contumely, scornfulness, derision, mockery, ridicule. RESPECT
*v*, disdain, contemn, reject, spurn, look down on, despise, slight, disregard, deride, mock, scoff at, sneer at.

**scornful** contemptuous, disdainful, supercilious, haughty, contumelious, sneering, derisive, mocking, sarcastic, sardonic. RESPECTFUL

**scoundrel** rogue, rascal, villain, miscreant, scapegrace, knave, blackguard, wretch, reprobate, ne'er-do-well. GENTLEMAN

**scour**[1] rub, abrade, scrub, clean, wash, polish, burnish, buff, cleanse, purge, clear, flush. SOIL

**scour**[2] search, hunt, ransack, comb, rake, range.

**scourge** *n*, whip, lash, strap, thong, switch, rod.
punishment, penalty, torment, torture, plague, affliction, bane, curse, misfortune, hardship, visitation. BLESSING
*v*, whip, lash, beat, flog, punish, chastise, castigate, correct. INDULGE

**scout** *n*, spy, lookout, outrider, vanguard.
*v*, reconnoitre, inspect, investigate, check out, spy, watch, observe, search, hunt, seek.

**scowl** *v*, frown, glower, glare, lower. SMILE
*n*, frown, glower, grimace, dirty look.

**scraggy** scrawny, lean, thin, skinny, bony, angular, gaunt, spare, lanky. FAT

**scramble** *v*, clamber, climb, struggle, strive, contend, compete, vie, contest, hasten, hurry, rush, bustle, scurry, scamper. DAWDLE
mix, blend, combine, jumble, disorder, confuse.
*n*, struggle, competition, race, rush, muddle, confusion.

**scrap**[1] *n*, piece, bit, fragment, part, morsel, crumb, iota, mite, atom, particle, trace. MASS
waste, leftovers, remains, remnants.
*v*, discard, throw away, reject, abandon, drop, get rid of. KEEP

**scrap**[2] *n*, fight, scuffle, brawl, row, quarrel, argument.

**scrape** *v*, grate, grind, rasp, file, rub, abrade, scrub, scour, scratch, graze, bark, scuff.
*n*, predicament, plight, dilemma, quandary, difficulty, fix (*inf*), trouble, pickle (*inf*).

**scratch** *v*, scrape, claw, cut, mark, score, scuff, graze, bark, rub, chafe.
erase, delete, cross out, expunge, obliterate, eliminate.
*n*, scrape, scuff, mark, scar, cut, laceration, graze, abrasion.
**up to scratch,** satisfactory, adequate, acceptable, capable. UNACCEPTABLE

**scream** screech, shriek, cry, yell, shout, bawl, wail, squeal, howl, squall. WHISPER

**screen** *n*, partition, divider, curtain, net, shade, blind, cover, shelter, protection, guard, shield, veil, cloak, shroud.
*v*, shelter, cover, protect, guard, shield, defend, hide, conceal, shroud, cloak, veil, mask. EXPOSE
sieve, sift, sort, pick, select, evaluate, examine, vet.

**screw** twist, turn, distort, contort, wrench, wrest, squeeze, press, force, coerce.

**scribble** scrawl, scratch, jot, write, doodle.

**scribe** copyist, amanuensis, secretary, clerk, pen-pusher, writer.

**scrimmage** scuffle, brawl, affray, melee, riot, rumpus, row, fight, struggle, scramble.

**scrimp** stint, pinch, restrict, limit, straiten, reduce, economize, skimp. LAVISH

**script** handwriting, penmanship, calligraphy, writing, hand.
manuscript, text, lines, libretto.

**scrounge** forage, hunt, beg, cadge, sponge (*inf*).

**scrub** rub, scour, wash, clean, cleanse. SOIL
cancel, drop, give up, scrap.

**scrubby** insignificant, puny, diminutive, small, dwarfish, stunted, undersized, underdeveloped. IMMENSE

**scruffy** untidy, messy, unkempt, disreputable, shabby, ragged, slovenly, seedy. SMART

**scrunch** crumple, crush, squash, crunch.

**scruple** *n*, qualm, misgiving, conscience, compunction, doubt, hesitation, uneasiness, reluctance. ASSURANCE
*v*, hesitate, falter, waver, think twice about, demur, doubt, be loath.

**scrupulous** punctilious, strict, exact, precise, meticulous, painstaking, fastidious, minute, nice, careful, cautious, conscientious, moral, ethical, principled. LAX

**scrutinize** examine, study, peruse, pore over, scan, probe, search, investigate, inspect, analyse, sift. IGNORE

**scrutiny** examination, study, perusal, probe, search, investigation, inquiry, inspection, analysis.

**scud** run, race, speed, fly, sail, skim.

**scuffle** *v*, fight, struggle, contend, grapple, tussle, brawl.
*n*, fight, struggle, tussle, brawl, riot, fray, melee, rumpus. PEACE

**scum** froth, dregs, deposit, residue, dross.

**scurrilous** abusive, offensive, insulting, vituperative, defamatory, gross, foul, coarse, vulgar, rude, obscene, dirty, indecent, ribald. COMPLIMENTARY

**scurry** scamper, scuttle, scoot, dash, dart, run, race, hurry, hasten, fly. AMBLE

**scurvy** low, base, mean, despicable, contemptible, abject, vile, rotten, shabby, worthless, dishonourable. HONOURABLE

**scuttle** scamper, scurry, scoot, dash, dart, run, race, hurry, hasten, fly. AMBLE

**sea** ocean, main, deep, briny (*inf*), swell, surge, wave, billow. LAND
**at sea,** adrift, astray, lost, disorientated, bewildered, baffled, perplexed, confused.

**seal** *v*, fasten, secure, close, shut, plug, cork, stop. OPEN
stamp, validate, sanction, endorse, confirm, settle, clinch.
*n*, stamp, cachet, insignia, pledge, assurance, confirmation.

**seam** joint, suture, line, furrow, ridge, wrinkle, scar.
stratum, vein, layer, lode.

**seaman** sailor, mariner, seaman, seafarer, bluejacket, tar (*inf*), matelot (*inf*).

**seamy** unpleasant, unattractive, disagreeable, nasty, repulsive, sordid, dark, low, rough. PLEASANT

**sear** burn, scorch, cauterize, brand, wither, dry, parch, desiccate.

**search** *v*, seek, look, hunt, rummage, sift, comb, examine, scrutinize, scour, probe, explore, inspect, check, frisk (*inf*).

*n*, hunt, pursuit, quest, examination, scrutiny, exploration, probe, inspection, investigation, inquiry. DISCOVERY

**searching** penetrating, piercing, keen, sharp, intent, thorough, close, inquiring, probing.

**season** *n*, time, period, spell, interval, term, quarter.
*v*, flavour, spice, enliven.
mature, prepare, harden, toughen, anneal, inure, habituate, accustom, acclimatize, train.
temper, moderate, qualify, mitigate.

**seasonable** opportune, timely, well-timed, suitable, appropriate, fit, convenient, auspicious, welcome. UNTIMELY

**seasoning** flavouring, spice, salt, pepper, relish, condiment, sauce, dressing.

**seat** *n*, chair, bench, stool, sofa, pew, stall.
situation, site, location, place, centre, cradle, base, foundation.
residence, abode, house, mansion.
*v*, accommodate, hold, contain, take.
install, establish, fix, settle, deposit, place, set, put, sit.

**secede** withdraw, retire, leave, pull out, break with, apostatize. AFFILIATE

**secluded** isolated, remote, solitary, sequestered, cloistered, withdrawn, retired, sheltered, private, hidden, screened. PUBLIC

**second**[1] *adj*, next, following, subsequent, alternate, other, further, extra, additional. FIRST
secondary, subordinate, inferior, minor. PRINCIPAL
*n*, attendant, assistant, helper, supporter, backer. OPPONENT
*v*, back, support, help, aid, assist, further, forward, advance, promote, encourage, endorse. OPPOSE

**second**[2] *n*, instant, moment, trice, twinkling, flash, jiffy (*inf*).

**secondary** subordinate, subsidiary, ancillary, auxiliary, extra, inferior, minor, lesser, lower, unimportant. PRIMARY

**secret** *adj*, hidden, concealed, disguised, camouflaged, unseen, covert, surreptitious, clandestine, undercover, stealthy, sly, underhand, secretive, reticent. OPEN
private, confidential, intimate, unknown, secluded, retired, isolated, out-of-the-way. PUBLIC
mysterious, cryptic, occult, arcane, esoteric, recondite, abstruse.
*n*, confidence, mystery, enigma, code, formula, recipe.

**secretary** clerk, typist, scribe, amanuensis, assistant, aide.

**secrete**[1] discharge, emit, exude, emanate, give off. ABSORB

**secrete**[2] hide, conceal, veil, screen, camouflage, disguise, stow, stash (*inf*). EXPOSE

**sect** faction, schism, group, party, school, denomination.

**sectarian** factional, denominational, partisan, bigoted, intolerant, insular, narrow-minded, narrow, limited, doctrinaire, fanatical. BROAD-MINDED

**section** part, segment, division, subdivision, piece, portion, slice, fragment, fraction. WHOLE

**secular** lay, profane, temporal, worldly, state, civil. RELIGIOUS

**secure** *adj*, safe, protected, defended, fortified, sheltered, immune, invulnerable, impregnable. VULNERABLE
firm, stable, steady, sound, fast, tight, dependable, reliable, fixed, settled, sure, certain, confident, assured. INSECURE
*v*, obtain, get, procure, acquire. LOSE
tie, fix, attach, fasten, lock, bind, fortify, defend, guard, protect. RELEASE
guarantee, assure, ensure, insure.

**security** safety, protection, precaution, safeguard, immunity, asylum, shelter, refuge, sanctuary. DANGER
confidence, assurance, conviction, certainty, sureness, reliance. INSECURITY
guarantee, warranty, surety, pledge, assurance, insurance.

**sedate** calm, composed, serene, tranquil, placid, cool, quiet, demure, staid, dignified, proper, decorous, sober, grave.

**sedative** *n*, tranquillizer, narcotic, opiate, anodyne. STIMULANT
*adj*, calming, soothing, assuasive, lenitive, anodyne, soporific.

**sedentary** seated, sitting, inactive, motionless, idle. ACTIVE

**sediment** precipitate, dregs, lees, grounds, deposit, residue, residuum, dross, scum.

**sedition** insurrection, rebellion, mutiny, subversion, incitement, agitation, treason. LOYALTY

**seditious** seditionary, rebellious, mutinous, insurgent, insurrectionary, revolutionary, refractory, insubordinate, subversive. OBEDIENT

**seduce** tempt, lure, lead astray, inveigle, ensnare, entice, beguile, attract, allure, corrupt, deprave, debauch, deflower. REPEL

**seductive** tempting, alluring, inviting, appealing, attractive, exciting, provocative, sexy (*inf*). REPULSIVE

**sedulous** assiduous, diligent, conscientious, scrupulous, painstaking, industrious, laborious, persevering, persistent, constant, unremitting, tireless, unflagging, energetic, active, busy. IDLE

**see**[1] *v*, perceive, discern, look at, behold, notice, observe, regard, watch, view, witness, note, mark, spot, make out, descry, espy, examine, inspect. MISS
comprehend, understand, grasp, know, feel, appreciate, realize, recognize.
ascertain, determine, learn, find out, discover.
envisage, visualize, imagine, conceive, foresee, anticipate.
consider, deliberate, think, reflect, ponder. DECIDE
meet, encounter, receive, speak to, escort, accompany, usher, lead.
**see to,** arrange, organize, see about, attend to, take care of, look after.

**see**[2] *n*, diocese, bishopric, episcopate.

**seed** germ, embryo, ovule, spore, grain.
source, origin, beginning, start, cause.

**seedy** shabby, scruffy, unkempt, rundown, squalid. SMART
ill, unwell, ailing, poorly (*inf*), sickly. WELL

**seek** hunt, look for, search for, pursue, follow. FIND
try, attempt, endeavour, aim, aspire. FAIL
want, desire, ask, beg, entreat, solicit.

**seem** look, appear, sound, pretend. BE

**seemingly** apparently, ostensibly, outwardly, on the face of it. ACTUALLY

**seemly** proper, decent, fit, fitting, suitable, appropriate, becoming, decorous. UNSEEMLY

**seep** ooze, trickle, leak, percolate, leach, bleed.

**seer** prophet, soothsayer, augur, clairvoyant.

**seethe** boil, foam, froth, ferment.
rage, fume, smoulder, simmer, be furious.

**segment** section, portion, part, division, piece, fragment, slice, wedge. WHOLE

**segregate** separate, dissociate, isolate, set apart. UNITE

**seize** grab, snatch, take, grasp, grip, clasp, clutch. DROP
capture, apprehend, arrest, confiscate, impound, sequestrate, usurp, commandeer, appropriate. RELEASE

**seizure** capture, apprehension, confiscation, sequestration. RELEASE
convulsion, fit, spasm, paroxysm, attack.

**seldom** rarely, infrequently, hardly ever, occasionally. OFTEN

**select** *v*, pick, choose, single out, opt for, prefer.
*adj*, selected, picked, preferred, choice, prime, excellent, first-class, chosen, elect, elite, exclusive. INFERIOR

**selection** pick, choice, option, preference.
collection, assortment, variety, range.

**self-centred** egotistic, egoistic, egocentric, narcissistic, selfish.

**self-conscious** shy, bashful, coy, diffident, embarrassed, sheepish, awkward, uncomfortable.

**selfish** self-centred, egotistic, egoistic, self-seeking, greedy, miserly, mean, ungenerous, mercenary. ALTRUISTIC

**self-possessed** cool, collected, composed, unruffled, poised, self-assured, imperturbable. NERVOUS

**self-righteous** sanctimonious, holier-than-thou, goody-goody (*inf*), pietistic, pharisaic, smug, complacent.

**sell** vend, exchange, barter, trade, traffic in, deal in, hawk, peddle, retail, market. BUY

**semblance** appearance, look, aspect, air, demeanour, mien, guise, pretence, show, façade, likeness, similarity, resemblance.

**seminary** academy, college, institute, school.

**send** forward, dispatch, remit, consign, transmit, convey, mail, post. RETAIN
hurl, propel, fling, cast, shoot.
emit, discharge, exude, give off.
**send for,** summon, call for, order.

**senile** aged, old, doting, gaga (*inf*), failing, doddering, decrepit. YOUNG

**senior** older, elder, superior, higher, major. JUNIOR

**sensation** feeling, sense, impression, awareness, perception.
excitement, thrill, stir, commotion, fuss, ado, agitation. APATHY

**sensational** exciting, thrilling, electrifying, hair-raising, shocking, scandalous, melodramatic, lurid, amazing, astounding, breathtaking, staggering, marvellous, superb, impressive, spectacular.

**sense** *n*, feeling, sensation, impression, sentiment, awareness, consciousness, perception, sensibility, faculty.
understanding, mind, intellect, brains, intelligence, discernment, discrimination, judgment, common sense, wisdom, sagacity, reason, sanity. FOLLY
meaning, gist, substance, import, significance, signification, connotation, implication.
*v*, feel, perceive, discern, apprehend, understand, appreciate.

**senseless** foolish, stupid, silly, asinine, crazy, mad, brainless, mindless, ridiculous, nonsensical, absurd, irrational, meaningless, pointless. SENSIBLE
unconscious, insensible, numb, deadened, insensate, unfeeling. SENSITIVE

**sensible** wise, sagacious, judicious, prudent, discreet, politic, sound, sane, rational, reasonable, practical, realistic, shrewd, intelligent. STUPID
aware, conscious, cognizant, mindful, observant. UNCONSCIOUS
tangible, palpable, appreciable, perceptible, visible. IMPERCEPTIBLE

**sensitive** susceptible, impressionable, receptive, responsive, conscious, sentient, delicate, fine, keen, tender, irritable, touchy. INSENSITIVE

**sensual** carnal, fleshly, voluptuous, bodily, physical, sexual, erotic, lascivious, libidinous, lecherous, licentious, lewd, salacious. SPIRITUAL

**sensuous** sensory, sumptuous, luxurious, rich, aesthetic, sybaritic.

**sentence** *n*, condemnation, judgment, ruling, decree, verdict, decision.
*v*, condemn, doom, penalize, pass judgment. ACQUIT

**sententious** terse, pithy, succinct, concise, pointed, laconic, aphoristic, axiomatic, pompous, moralistic.

**sentiment** feeling, emotion, sensibility, sentimentality. REASON
attitude, view, opinion, thought, idea, notion.

**sentimental** emotional, tender, romantic, maudlin, mawkish, sloppy (*inf*), nostalgic, corny (*inf*). REALISTIC

**sentinel** sentry, guard, picket, patrol, watch, lookout, watchman, guardian.

**separate** *v*, divide, part, split, sunder, cleave, sever, disjoin, disconnect, disunite, break up, come between, estrange, divorce, diverge, bifurcate. JOIN
sort, segregate, isolate, keep apart. MIX
*adj*, independent, individual, different, disparate, discrete, detached, unconnected, distinct, apart, isolated, unattached, divided, separated, divorced. CONNECTED

**separation** division, partition, break, split, severance, cleavage, disjunction, dissociation, disconnection, estrangement, divorce, isolation, segregation.

**sepulchral** funereal, lugubrious, mournful, woeful, sombre, grave, sad, melancholy, dismal, gloomy, hollow, deep. CHEERFUL

**sequel** development, continuation, follow-up, result, consequence, outcome, upshot, issue, end, aftermath. BEGINNING

**sequence** order, arrangement, series, progression, chain, succession, continuity. DISORDER

**sequestered** withdrawn, retired, cloistered, reclusive, solitary, isolated, remote, secluded. PUBLIC

**seraphic** angelic, cherubic, holy, divine, heavenly, celestial, pure, sublime, beatific, blissful. DIABOLIC

**serene** tranquil, calm, peaceful, quiet, placid, cool, composed, unruffled, undisturbed, imperturbable. AGITATED
clear, cloudless, bright, fair. MURKY

**series** sequence, succession, run, concatenation, chain, string, progression, set.

**serious** grave, solemn, thoughtful, pensive, sober, sedate, stern, unsmiling. JOCOSE
earnest, resolute, sincere, genuine.
weighty, momentous, important, significant, vital, crucial, critical, dangerous. TRIVIAL

**sermon** address, discourse, homily, exhortation, lecture, harangue.

**serpentine** snaky, sinuous, winding, meandering, twisting, tortuous, crooked, coiled, spiral. STRAIGHT

**serrated** serrate, serrulate, notched, jagged, sawlike, toothed. SMOOTH

**serried** close, compact, dense, massed.

**servant** domestic, maid, valet, retainer, attendant, assistant, helper, hireling, menial, lackey, drudge, slave. EMPLOYER

**serve** attend, wait on, minister to, oblige, help, aid, assist, benefit, work for, obey. COMMAND
function, perform, act, do, suffice, suit, answer, satisfy, fulfil.
present, distribute, dish up, provide, supply.

**service** help, aid, assistance, benefit, advantage, use, avail. USELESSNESS
maintenance, overhaul.
work, employment, duty, function, business, department, bureau.
ceremony, rite, ritual, sacrament, observance, worship.

**servile** obsequious, slavish, menial, submissive, cringing, grovelling, fawning, sycophantic, abject, humble, mean, base. INDEPENDENT

**servitude** bondage, slavery, serfdom, vassalage, captivity, enslavement, thrall, subjection, subjugation. COMMAND

**session** meeting, sitting, gathering, assembly, period, term.

**set**[1] *v*, place, put, position, locate, situate, plant, deposit, rest, stick, lodge, fix, establish, arrange, prepare, lay, apply. MOVE
determine, fix, establish, appoint, name, designate, settle, decide, resolve, decree, ordain. CHANGE
adjust, regulate, synchronize, coordinate, direct, aim.
solidify, harden, stiffen, congeal, jell, thicken, cake, crystallize. MELT
sink, go down, dip, drop, decline, disappear. RISE
**set about,** start, begin, tackle, undertake, get down to (*inf*). FINISH
**set back,** retard, delay, hold up, hinder, impede. ADVANCE
**set off,** set out, set forth, start out, begin, embark, leave, depart, go. ARRIVE
detonate, explode, light, ignite.
**set up,** build, erect, construct, raise, establish, found, inaugurate, institute, arrange, prepare. ABOLISH
*n*, bearing, carriage, posture, hang, tendency, drift.
scene, scenery, setting, *mise en scène*.
*adj*, fixed, established, prescribed, ordained, appointed, agreed, decided, settled, regular, usual. VARIABLE
rigid, firm, entrenched, hardened, inflexible, immovable, stubborn, determined, resolute, intent. FLEXIBLE

**set**[2] *n*, collection, assortment, group, series, batch, outfit, kit.
band, gang, crowd, company, party, faction, sect, circle, clique, coterie.

**setting** scene, set, scenery, background, surroundings, location, framework, mounting.

**settle** arrange, order, regulate, adjust, clear up, resolve, reconcile, conclude.
appoint, set, fix, establish, determine, agree on, decide, choose.
land, alight, perch, lodge, repose, rest.
dwell, live, reside, inhabit, populate, colonize. MIGRATE
pay, discharge, liquidate, clear. OWE
sink, drop, fall, descend, subside, abate. RISE

**settlement** arrangement, regulation, adjustment, reconciliation, resolution, conclusion, decision, agreement.
payment, discharge, liquidation, defrayal.
colonization, colony, community, encampment.

**sever** part, divide, separate, cut, split, cleave, sunder, disjoin, disunite, dissociate, break off, dissolve. JOIN

**several** some, a few, sundry, various, assorted, different, separate, distinct, own, individual, particular, respective.

**severe** strict, harsh, rigid, inflexible, relentless, unrelenting, inexorable, cruel, tough, hard, difficult, rigorous, exacting, stern, dour, grim, serious, grave, sober. MILD
plain, simple, unadorned, restrained, austere, ascetic, Spartan.
violent, fierce, intense, extreme, bitter, acute, critical, dangerous.

**shabby** ragged, tattered, worn, threadbare, faded, scruffy, dilapidated, rundown, seedy. SMART
mean, base, low, despicable, contemptible, ignoble, dishonourable, rotten. HONOURABLE

**shackle** *v*, bind, tie, chain, fetter, trammel, manacle. LOOSE
restrict, restrain, impede, hinder, hamper, obstruct. FREE

*n*, bond, chain, fetter, manacle, handcuff, iron.

**shade** *n*, shadow, darkness, dusk, gloom, obscurity. LIGHT
screen, shutter, blind, veil, cover, shelter, shield, protection.
degree, nuance, hint, trace, suspicion, suggestion, dash, touch.
colour, hue, tint, tinge.
*v*, shadow, eclipse, darken, dim, obscure, cloud.
screen, veil, cover, hide, shield, protect. EXPOSE

**shadow** *n*, shade, darkness, dusk, gloom, cloud, shelter, protection. BRIGHTNESS
image, adumbration, silhouette, phantom, spectre.
trace, vestige, hint, suggestion.
*v*, shade, eclipse, darken, screen, shield. EXPOSE
follow, trail, track, stalk, dog, hound.

**shadowy** shady, shaded, dark, murky, gloomy, tenebrous, dim, obscure, indistinct, vague. BRIGHT
imaginary, illusory, unreal, unsubstantial, impalpable, ghostly, spectral. REAL

**shady** shaded, shadowy, umbrageous, dark. LIGHT
dubious, questionable, suspicious, shifty, dishonest, crooked. HONEST

**shaft** pole, rod, bar, shank, handle.
ray, nbeam, streak.

**shaggy** hairy, hirsute, unkempt, dishevelled, rough, coarse. SMOOTH

**shake** *v*, vibrate, tremble, quiver, quake, shudder, shiver, waver, vacillate, oscillate, swing, rock, sway, totter, wobble, convulse, churn, rattle, jar, jolt, bump.
brandish, wave, flourish.
stir, agitate, disturb, upset, unsettle, unnerve, frighten, shock, weaken, impair, undermine.
*n*, vibration, tremor, shudder, shiver, oscillation, convulsion, rattle, jolt, wave, agitation.

**shaky** shaking, trembling, tremulous, shivery, wobbly, rickety, unstable, unsteady, tottering, doddering, weak. FIRM
unsound, unsupported, unreliable, dubious, questionable, uncertain. SOUND

**shallow** superficial, empty, meaningless, slight, trivial, trifling, petty, unimportant, frivolous, silly, foolish. DEEP

**sham** *n*, counterfeit, forgery, fake, imitation, pretence, feint, imposture, impostor, fraud.
*adj*, false, counterfeit, forged, fake, phoney (*inf*), bogus, spurious, mock, ersatz, artificial, simulated, pretended, feigned. GENUINE
*v*, pretend, feign, simulate, assume, affect, put on, fake, counterfeit.

**shame** *n*, mortification, humiliation, embarrassment, abashment, chagrin, guilt, remorse. PRIDE
disgrace, dishonour, scandal, ignominy, infamy, opprobrium, discredit, disrepute, obloquy, reproach. HONOUR
*v*, mortify, humiliate, humble, embarrass, abash, confound, disgrace, dishonour, reproach.

**shameful** disgraceful, dishonourable, scandalous, ignominious, infamous, opprobrious, discreditable, disreputable, despicable, contemptible, heinous, atrocious, outrageous, nefarious, vile, low, base. HONOURABLE

**shameless** brazen, bold, audacious, brash, barefaced, impudent, insolent, unabashed, unashamed, immodest, indecent, hardened, unprincipled, corrupt, depraved, abandoned, wanton. ASHAMED

**shanty** shack, hut, cabin, shed, hovel.

**shape** *n*, form, figure, outline, silhouette, cut, model, pattern, mould, cast, structure, build.
guise, appearance, aspect, likeness, semblance, phantom, apparition.
condition, state, fettle, health.
*v*, mould, model, form , fashion, make, produce, create, devise, adapt, modify.

**shapeless** amorphous, nebulous, unstructured, formless, misshapen, asymmetrical.

**shapely** neat, trim, attractive, comely, elegant, curvaceous. UGLY

**share** *n*, portion, part, division, lot, ration, quota, allocation, allotment, allowance, contribution. WHOLE
*v*, apportion, allocate, allot, divide, split, ration, parcel out, participate, partake.

**sharp** keen, acute, pointed, edged, thin, fine, cutting, jagged, serrated. BLUNT
sudden, abrupt, extreme, violent, fierce, intense, severe, acute, piercing, excruciating, stabbing. GENTLE

biting, cutting, caustic, trenchant, bitter, acrimonious, scathing, harsh, shrill, tart, acrid, piquant, pungent. MILD
clever, intelligent, shrewd, astute, sharp-witted, quick-witted, perspicacious, discerning, penetrating, knowing, smart, alert, bright, subtle, crafty, cunning, artful, sly. STUPID

**sharpen** hone, grind, strop, whet, edge, point. BLUNT

**shatter** break, smash, splinter, shiver, split, crack, burst, crush. MEND
demolish, wreck, ruin, destroy, devastate. RESTORE

**shave** shear, cut, pare, trim, clip, crop, plane, scrape, graze, brush, touch, skim.

**shear** fleece, poll, clip, trim, cut, shave.

**shed**[1] *n*, outhouse, lean-to, hut, shack, shelter.

**shed**[2] *v*, spill, pour forth, drop, emit, radiate, diffuse, scatter, spread, cast, slough, moult, discard. RETAIN

**sheen** lustre, gloss, polish, burnish, shine, gleam, brightness, brilliance. DULLNESS

**sheepish** abashed, ashamed, shamefaced, embarrassed, bashful, timid, diffident, self-conscious.

**sheer** steep, precipitous, abrupt, perpendicular, vertical. GENTLE
utter, complete, out-and-out, downright, absolute, unqualified, unmitigated, unadulterated, pure, simple. PARTIAL
thin, fine, transparent, diaphanous, gossamer. THICK

**sheet** layer, covering, coating, blanket, veneer, film, panel, plate, pane, slab, piece, leaf, expanse, stretch.

**shell** *n*, case, casing, capsule, cartridge, carapace, husk, pod.
skeleton, framework, frame, structure.
*v*, bomb, bombard, strafe, barrage, blitz.

**shelter** *n*, refuge, haven, harbour, sanctuary, asylum, retreat, covert, cover, protection, safety, security, defence, guard, screen, shield.
*v*, cover, protect, defend, guard, shield, screen, hide, harbour. EXPOSE

**shelve** postpone, defer, put aside, put off, pigeonhole, mothball.

**shield** *n*, buckler, escutcheon, aegis, protection, defence, guard, safeguard, cover, shelter, screen, rampart, bulwark.
*v*, protect, guard, defend, shelter, screen, cover, hide. EXPOSE

**shift** *v*, move, budge, change, alter, vary, fluctuate, relocate, transfer, switch, exchange, remove. FIX
manage, fend, get by, get along, contrive, devise.
*n*, move, swerve, change, alteration, transfer, switch.
device, contrivance, expedient, resort, resource, scheme, stratagem, artifice, trick, wile, ruse, dodge, subterfuge.

**shifty** crafty, artful, wily, tricky, slippery, evasive, furtive, underhand, dishonest, crooked, deceitful. HONEST

**shimmer** *v*, glimmer, glisten, gleam, flash, shine, twinkle, scintillate, phosphoresce.
*n*, glow, phosphorescence, incandescence, iridescence, lustre, shine, glimmer, glistening, gleam, flash. DULLNESS

**shine** *v*, gleam, beam, flash, glow, radiate, glisten, glimmer, sparkle, twinkle, glitter, shimmer.
polish, burnish, buff, rub.
excel, stand out.
*v*, lustre, sheen, gloss, polish, brightness, radiance, brilliance, effulgence, splendour, resplendence. DULLNESS

**shiny** bright, shining, radiant, gleaming, glossy, lustrous, polished. DULL

**ship** vessel, craft, liner, steamer, boat.

**shipshape** neat, tidy, orderly, trim. UNTIDY

**shirk** *v*, evade, avoid, dodge, sidestep, get out of, malinger, neglect. DISCHARGE
*n*, shirker, idler, slacker, dodger, malingerer.

**shiver**[1] *v*, shudder, tremble, shake, quiver, quake, palpitate, vibrate.
*n*, shudder, tremor, quiver, vibration.

**shiver**[2] *v*, shatter, splinter, smash, break, fragment. MEND

**shock** *v*, horrify, appal, revolt, disgust, offend, scandalize, outrage, disturb, stagger, stupefy, astound, stun, shake, jar, jolt. DELIGHT
*n*, blow, jolt, impact, collision, upset, disturbance, bombshell, horror, astonishment, stupefaction, trauma.

**shocking** horrifying, appalling, outrageous, scandalous, disgraceful, shameful, disgusting, sickening, offensive, revolting, repulsive, terrible, abominable, dreadful, ghastly, monstrous, atrocious, loathsome, detestable, foul. DELIGHTFUL

**shoe** footwear, sandal, boot, clog, plimsoll, slipper.

**shoot** *v*, fire, discharge, propel, project, launch, fling, hurl.
hit, wound, kill, bag, snipe. MISS
dart, dash, tear, rush, race, speed, scoot, fly, spring. AMBLE
germinate, sprout, bud, burgeon.
*n*, sprout, bud, burgeon, offshoot, scion, branch, twig.

**shop** store, supermarket, boutique.

**shore**[1] *n*, beach, strand, seaside, coast, land.

**shore**[2] *n*, support, prop, brace, buttress, strut, stay.
*v*, support, prop, hold up, strengthen, reinforce, underpin. UNDERMINE

**short** little, small, diminutive, petite, squat. TALL
brief, concise, succinct, terse, laconic, pithy, sententious, condensed, abridged, abbreviated, curtailed. LENGTHY
fleeting, momentary, transient, transitory, ephemeral, temporary, short-lived, brief. LONG
scant, scanty, deficient, insufficient, inadequate, lacking, wanting, meagre, sparse, limited. AMPLE
abrupt, curt, sharp, blunt, brusque, gruff, impolite, discourteous, rude, short-tempered, irascible. AFFABLE

**shortage** dearth, paucity, lack, want, need, scarcity, deficiency, deficit, insufficiency, inadequacy. GLUT

**shorten** cut, curtail, reduce, lessen, dock, trim, abbreviate, abridge. LENGTHEN

**shortly** soon, presently, before long. LATER
briefly, succinctly, concisely, tersely, abruptly, curtly, sharply.

**shot** report, discharge.
ball, pellet, bullet, slug, projectile, missile.
try, attempt, go, crack (*inf*), effort, endeavour.

**shout** *v*, cry, call, vociferate, exclaim, yell, bellow, roar, scream, holler (*inf*). WHISPER
*n*, cry, vociferation, exclamation, yell, roar, scream.

**shove** push, thrust, move, propel, drive, jostle, elbow, press, crowd. PULL

**show** *v*, display, exhibit, present, demonstrate, manifest, indicate, register, reveal, expose, evince, evidence, prove, explain, elucidate, point out, teach, instruct. CONCEAL
usher, escort, accompany, guide, lead, direct.
appear, be visible, stand out.
**show off**, parade, flaunt, swagger, boast.
**show up**, reveal, give away, expose, highlight.
outshine, upstage, shame, embarrass.
appear, turn up, arrive, come. LEAVE
*n*, display, exhibition, exposition, presentation, production, demonstration, parade, pageant, spectacle.
affectation, ostentation, pretence, illusion, appearance, semblance, indication, evidence.

**shower** *n*, cloudburst, torrent, flood, deluge, barrage, volley.
*v*, spray, sprinkle, pour, inundate, deluge, lavish.

**showy** flamboyant, flashy, gaudy, garish, loud, ostentatious, pretentious. SUBDUED

**shred** scrap, bit, fragment, piece, sliver, strip, rag, tatter, atom, iota, grain, particle, jot, whit. WHOLE

**shrew** nag, scold, termagant, virago, harridan, fury, vixen, spitfire. ANGEL

**shrewd** astute, sharp, keen, acute, smart, clever, intelligent, wise, sagacious, discriminating, discerning, knowing, artful, crafty, cunning, sly, wily. STUPID

**shriek** screech, scream, squeal, yell, cry, shout.

**shrill** sharp, acute, piercing, ear-splitting, high, high-pitched. LOW

**shrink** contract, shorten, narrow, shrivel, wither, decrease, reduce, diminish, dwindle. EXPAND
recoil, draw back, shy away, flinch, wince, quail, withdraw, retire. VENTURE

**shrivel** wither, wilt, wrinkle, shrink, contract, dry up, desiccate. SWELL

**shroud** *n*, cerecloth, cerement, winding sheet.
mantle, cloud, pall, veil, cover, covering.
*v*, wrap, swathe, envelop, cover, hide, conceal, mask, veil, screen, cloak. EXPOSE

**shudder** *v*, shiver, shake, tremble, quiver, quake.
*n*, shiver, tremor, quiver, spasm, convulsion.

**shuffle** shamble, falter, hobble, drag, scrape.

mix, intermix, jumble, muddle, confuse, disarrange, disorder, shift. SORT
equivocate, hedge, evade, dodge, quibble, cavil, prevaricate.
**shun** avoid, eschew, spurn, steer clear of, evade, elude, shirk, shrink from. COURT
**shut** *v*, close, lock, seal, fasten. OPEN
**shut in,** confine, imprison, enclose. RELEASE
**shut out,** exclude, bar, debar, ostracize. ADMIT
**shut up,** coop up, box in, cage, imprison, incarcerate, intern. RELEASE
silence, hush, be quiet, keep mum.
*adj*, closed, locked, sealed, fastened. OPEN
**shy** bashful, retiring, reserved, reticent, backward, diffident, coy, modest, self-conscious, timid, nervous, wary, chary, cautious, distrustful, suspicious. BOLD
**sibyl** prophetess, oracle, fortune-teller, witch, sorceress.
**sick** ill, unwell, ailing, poorly (*inf*), indisposed, laid up (*inf*), weak, sickly, queasy, nauseated. WELL
tired, weary, jaded, satiated, fed up.
morbid, sadistic, ghoulish, macabre, black.
**sicken** nauseate, disgust, revolt, repel, tire, weary. PLEASE
**sickly** unhealthy, delicate, infirm, weak, feeble, faint, languid, pale, wan, peaky, ailing. HEALTHY
**sickness** illness, ailment, disorder, complaint, malady, affliction, indisposition, disease, nausea, vomiting. HEALTH
**side** *n*, edge, border, margin, verge, flank, face, facet, surface. CENTRE
aspect, angle, view, viewpoint, standpoint.
team, party, faction, sect, camp, interest, cause.
*adj*, lateral, oblique, indirect.
subordinate, secondary, incidental, minor, unimportant. MAIN
*v*, support, join, ally, associate. OPPOSE
**sieve** *n*, colander, strainer, sifter, riddle.
*v*, sift, strain, filter, riddle, bolt, screen.
**sift** sieve, filter, riddle, bolt, screen, separate, sort, analyse, examine, scrutinize, investigate, probe.
**sigh** breathe, exhale, moan, lament, mourn, grieve, long, pine.
**sight** *n*, vision, eyesight, eyes, seeing. BLINDNESS
view, eyeshot, ken, perception, glimpse, look.
spectacle, scene, show, display, eyesore.
*v*, see, view, glimpse, catch sight of, perceive, observe. MISS
**sign** *n*, symbol, representation, token, indication, symptom, mark, emblem, device, password, countersign, signal, gesture, proof, evidence, trace, vestige, hint, suggestion, omen, portent, presage, warning, notice, placard.
*v*, initial, autograph, write, endorse, subscribe.
signal, gesture, gesticulate, beckon, wave.
**sign on,** sign up, enlist, enrol, register, join. LEAVE
recruit, hire, employ, engage, appoint, take on. DISMISS
**signal** *n*, sign, beacon, flag, siren, gesture, cue, token, indication.
*adj*, conspicuous, noteworthy, remarkable, notable, memorable, significant, striking, exceptional. ORDINARY
*v*, communicate, gesture, gesticulate, beckon, wave, sign.
**significant** important, consequential, weighty, momentous, crucial, vital, critical. TRIVIAL
meaningful, suggestive, indicative, expressive, telling. MEANINGLESS
**signify** *vt*, mean, denote, indicate, show, symbolize, represent, betoken, augur, portend, imply, suggest, impart, convey, utter, express, tell, proclaim, declare.
*vi*, matter, count, be significant, carry weight.
**silence** *n*, quiet, hush, peace, stillness, calm. NOISE
muteness, dumbness, speechlessness, taciturnity, reticence. GARRULITY
*v*, quieten, hush, still, suppress, quell, subdue, muffle, gag, stifle, smother.
**silent** quiet, still, soundless, noiseless, inaudible, hushed, calm, peaceful.
dumb, mute, speechless, voiceless, mum, taciturn, reticent, uncommunicative. TALKATIVE
tacit, unspoken, understood, implicit, implied.
**silly** absurd, foolish, senseless, nonsensical, ridiculous, fatuous, asinine, childish, puerile, frivolous, simple, stupid, unintelligent, brainless, witless, mad, insane, unwise, imprudent, foolhardy, indiscreet. SENSIBLE
**silt** deposit, sediment, alluvium, ooze, sludge.

**silvery** silver, white, bright, clear, dulcet, sweet.

**similar** like, alike, resembling, akin, allied, corresponding, analogous, uniform. DIFFERENT

**similarity** similitude, likeness, resemblance, correspondence, congruity, analogy, uniformity. DIFFERENCE

**simmer** boil, seethe, bubble, stew, fume, rage.

**simmer down,** calm down, control oneself, cool off.

**simper** smile, smirk, grimace, giggle, snigger, titter.

**simple** easy, effortless, clear, lucid, understandable, uncomplicated, uninvolved, straightforward, elementary, pure, single, natural, plain, unadorned, bare, unpretentious, homely, humble, lowly. COMPLEX
artless, guileless, ingenuous, naive, innocent, green, frank, candid, open, direct, sincere, credulous, silly, foolish, stupid, unintelligent, witless, feeble-minded, retarded. CLEVER

**simply** merely, only, just, purely, solely, absolutely, utterly, totally, altogether, really.

**simulate** pretend, feign, sham, counterfeit, reproduce, imitate, copy, assume, affect.

**simultaneous** concurrent, concomitant, coincident, synchronous, contemporaneous. SEPARATE

**sin** *n*, trespass, transgression, offence, crime, misdeed, wrong, iniquity, evil, wickedness, vice, guilt. VIRTUE
*v*, transgress, err, offend, lapse, go astray.

**since** as, because, seeing that.

**sincere** honest, truthful, guileless, artless, frank, candid, open, straightforward, direct, forthright, plain, unaffected, natural, genuine, true, heartfelt, wholehearted, earnest. INSINCERE

**sinewy** strong, powerful, muscular, brawny, strapping, robust, sturdy, stalwart, vigorous, lusty. PUNY

**sinful** bad, wicked, evil, wrong, iniquitous, criminal, guilty, immoral, corrupt, unholy, ungodly, irreligious. VIRTUOUS

**sing** trill, warble, carol, croon, pipe, chirp, chant.

**singe** burn, scorch, char, sear.

**single** *adj*, sole, only, one, lone, solitary, isolated, separate, distinct, individual, particular, singular, unique. NUMEROUS
unmarried, unwed, unattached. MARRIED

**single out,** *v*, choose, select, pick, prefer, separate, set apart, cull. REJECT

**singular** remarkable, outstanding, exceptional, unparalleled, noteworthy, notable, eminent, conspicuous, rare, unique, extraordinary, odd, curious, peculiar, queer, strange, eccentric, unusual, uncommon, particular, individual, single, sole. ORDINARY

**sinister** ominous, portentous, inauspicious, menacing, threatening, evil, wicked, bad, malign, malevolent, maleficent, baleful, injurious, treacherous.

**sink** fall, drop, descend, sag, droop, subside, ebb, recede, dip, plunge, submerge, immerse, abate, decrease, diminish, decline, fail, weaken, lapse. RISE
bore, drill, dig, excavate.

**sink in,** penetrate, register (*inf*), be understood.

**sinless** innocent, guiltless, faultless, perfect, spotless, pure, immaculate, undefiled, unsullied, virtuous. SINFUL

**sinner** transgressor, offender, wrongdoer, evildoer, delinquent, criminal. SAINT

**sinuous** serpentine, winding, tortuous, flexuous, crooked, curved, anfractuous, convoluted, intricate, devious, supple, lithe. STRAIGHT

**sip** *v*, taste, sup, drink.
*n*, taste, drink, swallow, drop.

**sit** be seated, rest, squat, perch, settle, seat. STAND
meet, assemble, convene, preside, officiate.

**site** location, place, position, situation, spot, plot, ground.

**situation** position, place, location, site, spot, locality, locale, setting, scene.
state, circumstances, condition, case, plight, predicament.
post, job, employment, place, position, status, rank.

**size** dimensions, measurements, proportions, magnitude, bulk, mass, volume, greatness, bigness, extent, amount, range, scope.

**skeleton** bones, structure, framework, frame, shell, outline, sketch, draft.

**sketch** *n*, drawing, delineation, draft, outline, skeleton, plan, design.

*v*, draw, delineate, represent, depict, portray, draft, outline.

**sketchy** rough, crude, unfinished, incomplete, imperfect, slight, superficial, cursory, skimpy, inadequate, vague. THOROUGH

**skilful** skilled, adept, proficient, expert, masterly, adroit, dexterous, gifted, clever, apt, able, competent, versed, experienced, practised, accomplished. CLUMSY

**skill** skilfulness, proficiency, expertise, mastery, dexterity, facility, adroitness, gift, talent, faculty, ability, cleverness, aptitude, art, technique, knack, address, finesse. INEPTITUDE

**skim** glide, coast, fly, skate, graze, touch, brush. PENETRATE

glance, scan, flip through. PORE

**skin** *n*, epidermis, cuticle, integument, hide, pelt, covering, coating, peel, rind, shell, outside.

*v*, peel, pare, flay, excoriate, graze, bark.

**skinny** thin, lean, lank, scrawny, scraggy, gaunt, emaciated. PLUMP

**skip** hop, spring, jump, leap, bound, caper, frisk, gambol, prance, dance, bounce.

omit, exclude, leave out, miss out, pass over, neglect.

**skirmish** battle, fight, conflict, tussle, scrap (*inf*), fray, combat, brush, encounter, engagement.

**skirt** edge, border, flank, circle, avoid, evade.

**skit** burlesque, parody, take-off (*inf*), send-up (*inf*), spoof (*inf*), sketch, satire.

**skittish** nervous, jumpy, excitable, highly strung, restive, fidgety, lively, playful, fickle, capricious. STEADY

**skulk** lurk, lie in wait, prowl, slink, sneak, steal, creep.

**sky** heaven, heavens, firmament, empyrean, ether, azure, upper atmosphere, outer space. EARTH

**slab** block, piece, chunk, lump, hunk, slice.

**slack** *adj*, loose, lax, limp, relaxed. TAUT

negligent, remiss, careless, lazy, indolent, idle, dilatory, sluggish, slow, inactive, quiet. BUSY

*v*, shirk, skive (*inf*), dodge, evade, neglect, idle.

**slacken** loosen, relax, ease, lessen, moderate, abate, reduce, diminish, let up. TIGHTEN

**slake** quench, satisfy, sate, satiate, allay, assuage.

**slam** bang, crash, smash, dash, hurl, fling, close, shut.

**slander** *n*, defamation, detraction, obloquy, scandal, calumny, libel, abuse, aspersion, slur, smear. EULOGY

*v*, defame, vilify, malign, disparage, decry, calumniate, libel, traduce, asperse, smear, abuse, backbite. PRAISE

**slant** *v*, slope, incline, lean, tilt, list, shelve.

angle, bias, twist, distort, colour.

*n*, slope, incline, ramp, gradient, pitch, angle.

viewpoint, approach, attitude, angle, bias, prejudice.

**slanting** oblique, aslant, sloping, slanted, inclined, tilted, diagonal. PERPENDICULAR

**slap** *v*, hit, strike, smack, spank, whack, cuff, clip (*inf*).

*n*, blow, hit, smack, whack, cuff.

**slash** cut, gash, score, slit, rip, lacerate. MEND

reduce, cut, drop, lower. RAISE

**slaughter** *n*, killing, slaying, butchery, murder, bloodshed, carnage, massacre, extermination.

*v*, kill, slay, butcher, massacre, murder, assassinate, exterminate, destroy.

**slave** *n*, bondservant, serf, helot, vassal, drudge, skivvy. MASTER

*v*, toil, labour, work, drudge.

**slavery** bondage, thraldom, serfdom, vassalage, servitude, enslavement, captivity. FREEDOM

toil, labour, drudgery.

**slavish** servile, obsequious, submissive, abject, sycophantic, fawning, grovelling, cringing, base, mean, low, menial. INDEPENDENT

**slay** kill, murder, assassinate, execute, dispatch, slaughter, butcher, massacre, exterminate, destroy. SAVE

**sleek** smooth, shiny, glossy, lustrous, silky, well-groomed. ROUGH

**sleep** *v*, slumber, doze, drowse, nap, snooze (*inf*), nod off (*inf*), drop off (*inf*), rest, repose, hibernate. WAKE

*n*, slumber, nap, catnap, siesta, snooze (*inf*), forty winks (*inf*), rest, repose, dormancy, hibernation. WAKEFULNESS

**sleepless** insomniac, wakeful, restless, disturbed, watchful, vigilant, alert, awake.

**sleepy** drowsy, somnolent, tired, weary, lazy, sluggish, torpid, lethargic, dormant, inactive. ALERT
soporific, sleep-inducing, hypnotic.

**slender** slim, thin, lean, spare, willowy, svelte, slight, narrow, frail, flimsy, fine, weak, feeble, faint, small, inconsiderable, trivial, meagre, scanty, inadequate, insufficient. AMPLE

**slice** *n*, piece, slab, wedge, sliver, portion, share.
*v*, cut, carve, split, divide.

**slide** slip, glide, skate, skim, slither, skid.
**let slide,** neglect, forget, ignore, let ride.

**slight** *adj*, small, little, inconsiderable, slim, slender, light, minor, petty, insignificant, unimportant, trivial, trifling, paltry, superficial, flimsy, frail, feeble, weak, faint. CONSIDERABLE
*v*, snub, cut (*inf*), ignore, disregard, cold-shoulder (*inf*), rebuff, insult, affront, scorn, disdain, disparage. ACKNOWLEDGE
*n*, snub, rebuff, cold shoulder (*inf*), disregard, indifference, neglect, scorn, contempt, insult, affront, disrespect, disparagement. RESPECT

**slim** slender, thin, lean, spare, willowy, svelte, slight, small, inconsiderable, poor. FAT

**slime** mud, mire, ooze, sludge, muck, mucus.

**slimy** muddy, miry, oozy, mucous, mucilaginous, viscous, glutinous.

**sling** throw, fling, hurl, toss, cast, chuck (*inf*).
suspend, hang, dangle, swing.

**slink** sneak, steal, creep, prowl, skulk.

**slip**[1] *v*, slide, glide, slither, skid, trip, fall.
err, blunder, slip up, go wrong.
sneak, steal, creep, slink.
**let slip,** disclose, reveal, divulge, blurt out, leak, give away.
*n*, error, mistake, blunder, boob (*inf*), oversight, omission, indiscretion, fault.

**slip**[2] *n*, scion, cutting, offshoot, sprout, twig.
strip, sliver, note, chit.

**slippery** smooth, glassy, icy, greasy, lubricated, perilous, unsafe.
treacherous, perfidious, faithless, unreliable, untrustworthy, shifty, tricky, crafty, cunning, dishonest. TRUSTWORTHY

**slipshod** negligent, careless, slapdash, disorderly, untidy, messy, slovenly, slatternly. CAREFUL

**slit** *v*, cut, slash, gash, split, rip, tear. MEND
*n*, cut, incision, slash, gash, split, opening, rip, tear. SEAM

**slope** *v*, incline, slant, lean, tilt, list, shelve.
*n*, incline, inclination, ramp, gradient, pitch, cant, slant, tilt, acclivity, declivity. LEVEL

**sloping** oblique, slanting, slanted, inclined.

**sloppy** wet, watery, slushy, muddy. DRY
careless, loose, slapdash, slipshod, messy, untidy.
sentimental, emotional, mawkish, maudlin, mushy (*inf*), soppy (*inf*).

**slot** opening, aperture, hole, slit, crack, groove.

**sloth** slothfulness, laziness, indolence, idleness, inertia, inactivity, torpor, sluggishness. INDUSTRY

**slothful** lazy, indolent, idle, sluggardly, inert, inactive, torpid, sluggish. INDUSTRIOUS

**slouch** stoop, droop, slump, shuffle, shamble, lumber.

**slough** bog, morass, swamp, quagmire.

**slovenly** slatternly, sluttish, untidy, unkempt, sloppy (*inf*), careless, slipshod, slapdash, disorderly, negligent, loose.

**slow** *adj*, leisurely, unhurried, easy, gradual, deliberate, measured, sluggish, lazy, dawdling, plodding, crawling, creeping, slack, inactive, protracted, lingering. FAST
late, behindhand, tardy, backward, dilatory. PROMPT
unintelligent, stupid, thick, dense, dull, obtuse, blockish, bovine. SMART
tedious, boring, uninteresting, dull, tiresome, wearisome. LIVELY
reluctant, hesitant, unwilling, loath, disinclined.
*v*, brake, decelerate, delay, retard, hold up, hold back, check. SPEED

**sluggish** slow, torpid, inert, inactive, heavy, dull, lethargic, lazy, slothful, indolent, idle, sleepy, drowsy. QUICK

**slumber** sleep, rest, repose, doze, drowse, nap, snooze (*inf*).

**slump** *v*, sink, fall, drop, plunge, decrease, decline, collapse, sag, droop, bend, slouch. RISE
*n*, recession, depression, decline, fall, collapse, failure. BOOM

**slur** slight, insult, aspersion, innuendo, insinuation, slander, calumny, stigma, brand, smear, stain, disgrace.

**slut** slattern, sloven, trollop, frump.

**sly** artful, cunning, crafty, wily, foxy, subtle, shrewd, astute, sharp, knowing, guileful, scheming, insidious, devious, underhand, furtive, clandestine, stealthy, roguish, impish, arch, mischievous. ARTLESS

**smack**[1] *n*, flavour, taste, savour, tang, smell, aroma, trace, hint, tinge, touch, dash.
*v*, **smack of**, resemble, be like, suggest, smell of.

**smack**[2] *v*, slap, hit, strike, cuff, box, spank, pat.
*n*, blow, hit, slap, pat.

**small** little, tiny, short, slight, diminutive, miniature, minute, microscopic. BIG
insignificant, unimportant, minor, trifling, trivial, paltry, petty, mean, small-minded, narrow-minded.
limited, meagre, scanty, insufficient, inadequate. AMPLE
humble, modest, unpretentious, simple, low, base. GRAND

**smart** *adj*, spruce, trim, neat, dapper, elegant, fashionable, chic, stylish, modish. UNTIDY
bright, clever, intelligent, witty, shrewd, astute, sharp, acute, quick-witted, ready, prompt, alert, apt, adept, active, agile, quick, lively, spirited, brisk. SLOW
keen, sharp, poignant, stinging, painful, severe. DULL
*v*, sting, prick, burn, tingle, throb, pain, hurt.
*n*, sting, prick, pain, pang.

**smash** *v*, break, shatter, splinter, shiver, dash, crash, pulverize, crush, demolish, destroy, wreck, ruin, defeat.
*n*, crash, collision, wreck, ruin, destruction, defeat, collapse, failure.

**smear** *v*, besmear, daub, bedaub, rub, spread, plaster, coat, cover, soil, dirty, smudge. SCOUR
slander, libel, calumniate, slur, vilify, sully, tarnish, blacken.
*n*, smudge, patch, spot, smear, blot.
slander, libel, calumny, defamation, slur, aspersion.

**smell** *v*, sniff, inhale, scent, detect.
stink, reek, pong (*inf*).
*n*, odour, scent, aroma, perfume, fragrance, redolence, bouquet, whiff, stink, stench, fetor.

**smile** grin, beam, smirk, simper. FROWN

**smirk** simper, grimace, grin, smile.

**smoke** *n*, fumes, gas, vapour, mist, fog, smog.
*v*, fume, smoulder, exhale, puff, draw, inhale, fumigate, cure.

**smooth** *adj*, level, even, flush, plane, horizontal, flat, uniform, regular. UNEVEN
glossy, shiny, polished, silky, sleek, glassy, calm, still, peaceful, unruffled, mild, bland. ROUGH
flowing, fluent, easy, facile, glib, slick, oily, unctuous, suave, urbane.
*v*, level, plane, flatten, iron, press.
polish, lubricate, ease, facilitate, calm, soothe, appease, pacify, assuage, allay, mitigate, alleviate.

**smother** suffocate, stifle, asphyxiate, choke, strangle, extinguish, snuff out. REVIVE
suppress, repress, hold back, conceal, hide, muffle, stifle.
envelop, cover, shroud, surround, heap, shower.

**smoulder** burn, smoke, fume, simmer, seethe, boil.

**smudge** *v*, smear, blur, soil, dirty, smirch, stain.
*n*, smear, blur, blot, spot, blotch, smut, streak.

**smug** complacent, self-satisfied, content, conceited, proud, self-righteous.

**smut** smudge, smear, spot, stain, streak, soot, dirt.

**smutty** dirty, filthy, obscene, indecent, risqué, racy, ribald, bawdy, vulgar, crude, coarse, earthy, blue, pornographic. CLEAN

**snag** drawback, disadvantage, difficulty, problem, catch, hitch, hindrance, impediment, obstacle, stumbling block. ADVANTAGE

**snap** *v*, break, crack, pop, come apart.
bite, nip, growl, bark, flash, sparkle.
**snap up**, grab, seize, take, nab (*inf*).
*n*, crack, pop, click, bite, nip, grab.
catch, clasp, fastener.

snapshot, photograph, photo (*inf*).

**snappy** snappish, waspish, testy, touchy, irritable, irascible, peevish, petulant, peppery, grumpy, crabbed, crusty, cross, ill-tempered. AFFABLE
brisk, quick, sharp, abrupt, brusque, curt.
smart, fashionable, chic, stylish, elegant. SHABBY

**snare** *n*, trap, gin, springe, noose, net.
*v*, catch, net, trap, entrap, ensnare. FREE

**snarl**[1] growl, bark, snap, threaten, grumble. PURR

**snarl**[2] tangle, entangle, ravel, confuse, complicate, embroil. DISENTANGLE

**snatch** *v*, grab, seize, grasp, clutch, clasp, grip, pluck, pull, take, wrest, rescue, save. RELEASE
*n*, bit, fragment, scrap, snippet, spell.

**sneak** steal, creep, slip, sidle, slink, skulk, prowl, lurk.
inform, grass (*inf*), tell tales.

**sneer** *v*, jeer, scoff, gibe, mock, scorn, deride, disdain. ADMIRE
*n*, jeer, gibe, taunt, mockery, scorn, derision, contempt, disdain. RESPECT

**sniff** inhale, breathe in, snuff, snuffle, smell.

**snigger** laugh, titter, giggle, chuckle, smirk, sneer.

**snip** *v*, cut, clip, trim, crop, nick, slit.
*n*, cut, nick, bit, piece, scrap, shred, fragment, snippet, cutting, clipping, bargain.

**snivel** cry, weep, sob, blubber, whine, whimper, sniffle, snuffle. LAUGH

**snobbish** condescending, patronizing, stuck-up (*inf*), snooty (*inf*), arrogant, supercilious, high and mighty. HUMBLE

**snub** *v*, slight, cut (*inf*), cold-shoulder (*inf*), rebuff, ignore, insult, humiliate, mortify.
*n*, slight, rebuff, insult, affront, humiliation, mortification. FLATTERY

**snug** cosy, comfortable, comfy (*inf*), intimate, homely, warm, sheltered, protected, safe, secure. EXPOSED
small, compact, trim, neat, tight, close-fitting.

**snuggle** nestle, cuddle, nuzzle, curl up.

**so** thus, therefore, hence.
also, too, likewise, similarly.
very, extremely.

**soak** wet, drench, saturate, steep, immerse, damp, moisten, permeate, infuse, penetrate, absorb. DRY

**soar** rise, mount, ascend, climb, tower, fly. SINK

**sob** cry, weep, blubber, bawl. LAUGH

**sober** temperate, moderate, teetotal, abstemious, abstinent. DRUNK
rational, reasonable, level-headed, calm, composed, cool, staid, sedate, solemn, serious, grave, sombre, dark, drab, subdued, plain, quiet, cold, realistic, practical, sound.

**sobriety** temperance, moderation, self-restraint, abstinence, soberness, teetotalism. DRUNKENNESS
calmness, composure, staidness, solemnity, seriousness, gravity.

**sociable** friendly, genial, cordial, neighbourly, amiable, affable, communicative, companionable, gregarious, outgoing, social. UNSOCIABLE

**social** communal, community, group, collective, common, public, civil, civic. PERSONAL
sociable, friendly, genial, amiable, affable, companionable, gregarious, convivial. ASOCIAL

**society** association, organization, club, circle, group, league, guild, union, fraternity, fellowship, body, community.
company, companionship, fellowship, camaraderie. PRIVACY
humanity, mankind, community, public, people, civilization.
elite, upper classes, high society, gentry, aristocracy, nobility. COMMONALTY

**sodden** soaked, saturated, drenched, waterlogged, sopping, dripping, wet, soggy, flooded, boggy, marshy. DRY

**soft** spongy, squashy, mushy, pulpy, yielding, elastic, pliable, malleable, flexible, plastic. HARD
silky, smooth, velvety, furry. COARSE
quiet, low, faint, dim, muted, subdued, light, pale, delicate, bland, mellow, sweet, dulcet, gentle, mild, moderate, temperate. HARSH
tender, kind, compassionate, soft-hearted, sympathetic, sensitive, sentimental, lenient, clement, indulgent, permissive, lax. SEVERE

**soften** melt, mellow, moderate, temper, cushion, lighten, ease, relax, lessen, diminish, weaken, abate, mitigate, allay, assuage, soothe, calm, pacify, appease, subdue, mute, muffle, lower.

**soil**[1] *v*, dirty, begrime, besmirch, stain, spot, sully, foul, defile, taint, pollute, tarnish, smear. CLEAN

**soil**[2] *n*, earth, ground, dirt, dust, clay, loam.

**sojourn** *v*, stay, stop, tarry, rest, abide, dwell, lodge, reside. TRAVEL
*n*, stay, visit, rest, holiday.

**solace** *n*, consolation, comfort, relief, cheer. DISTRESS
*v*, console, comfort, cheer, relieve, alleviate. AFFLICT

**sole** only, single, one, lone, solitary, unique, exclusive, individual. NUMEROUS

**solecism** mistake, error, slip, blunder, gaffe, faux pas, impropriety, indiscretion, incongruity, absurdity.

**solemn** serious, earnest, sincere, grave, sober, staid, sedate, sombre, glum, gloomy. FRIVOLOUS
grand, stately, august, imposing, majestic, impressive, dignified, formal, ceremonial, ceremonious, ritual. INFORMAL
sacred, holy, religious, devotional. PROFANE

**solemnize** observe, keep, celebrate, commemorate, honour.

**solicit** ask, request, seek, crave, beg, beseech, implore, entreat, pray, petition, canvass, urge, importune, accost.

**solicitous** concerned, anxious, worried, uneasy, apprehensive, troubled, disturbed, earnest, eager, zealous, careful, thoughtful, attentive. INDIFFERENT

**solid** hard, dense, compact, firm, solidified, frozen, congealed, set, substantial, strong, sound, stable.
reliable, dependable, trustworthy, sure, sensible, level-headed, reasonable, logical.
genuine, real, pure, unalloyed, complete, whole, united, undivided.

**solidarity** unity, concordance, accord, union, fellowship, camaraderie, unanimity, stability. DISSENT

**solidify** harden, set, congeal, coagulate, jell, consolidate, unite. MELT

**solitary** alone, lone, sole, single, one, only, lonely, companionless, separate, reclusive, unsociable.
unfrequented, secluded, private, isolated, lonely, remote, out-of-the-way, cut off, desolate, deserted.

**solitude** loneliness, isolation, remoteness, seclusion, privacy, retirement. SOCIETY

**solution** answer, explanation, key, elucidation, clarification, resolution. PROBLEM
mixture, compound, blend, emulsion, suspension.

**solve** answer, work out, resolve, crack, unravel, disentangle, fathom, explain, interpret, clear up, elucidate, unfold. COMPLICATE

**sombre** dark, shadowy, dim, dull, drab, dreary, dismal, gloomy, melancholy, doleful, sad, mournful, lugubrious, funereal, sober, grave. BRIGHT

**somebody** someone, personage, notable, dignitary, VIP, celebrity, star, luminary, bigwig (*inf*), household name, public figure. NOBODY

**sometimes** occasionally, at times, now and then, from time to time, every so often. NEVER

**somnolent** drowsy, sleepy, dozy, slumberous, soporific. ALERT

**song** carol, hymn, psalm, anthem, ballad, lay, ditty, air, tune, melody, lyric, ode, sonnet.

**sonorous** resonant, resounding, loud, deep, rich, full, rounded, ringing, orotund, grandiloquent. SOFT

**soon** shortly, before long, anon, presently, in a minute, promptly, quickly. LATER

**soothe** calm, compose, still, quieten, pacify, tranquillize, ease, relieve, comfort, moderate, temper, mitigate, assuage, allay, alleviate, palliate, appease, soften, mollify. IRRITATE

**soothsayer** prophet, seer, augur, diviner, sibyl.

**sophisticated** refined, cultured, educated, worldly-wise, cosmopolitan, urbane, elegant, jet-set, seasoned, blasé. UNCOUTH
complex, complicated, intricate, advanced. PRIMITIVE

**sophistry** sophism, casuistry, fallacy, paralogism, quibble. TRUTH

**soporific** soporiferous, somniferous, somnific, sleep-inducing, sedative, narcotic, hypnotic, somnolent, sleepy. STIMULANT

**sorcery** magic, black magic, witchcraft, wizardry, necromancy, spell, charm, enchantment. EXORCISM

**sordid** dirty, filthy, foul, unclean, squalid, seedy, seamy, poor, wretched, shabby, mean, ignoble, base, low, vile, shameful, disgraceful. RESPECTABLE
greedy, avaricious, grasping, selfish, miserly, niggardly, parsimonious, ungenerous, mercenary, venal. GENEROUS

**sore** *adj*, tender, painful, raw, sensitive, inflamed, irritated, hurting, injured.
annoying, irritating, vexing, irksome, distressing, harrowing, grievous, afflictive, troublesome, sharp, acute, severe, dire.
annoyed, vexed, irked, irritated, aggrieved, hurt, upset, distressed. PLEASED
*n*, wound, injury, inflammation, ulcer, abscess, boil, gathering.

**sorrow** *n*, sadness, grief, woe, heartache, misery, anguish, mourning, unhappiness, distress, affliction, trouble, worry, regret. JOY
*v*, mourn, grieve, weep, lament, bemoan, bewail, despair. REJOICE

**sorrowful** sad, unhappy, depressed, dejected, miserable, woebegone, melancholy, disconsolate, heartbroken, mournful, doleful, weeping, tearful, sorry. JOYFUL

**sorry** apologetic, penitent, repentant, contrite, remorseful, regretful, compunctious, sheepish, shamefaced. IMPENITENT
sad, distressed, sorrowful, unhappy, moved, sympathetic. GLAD
wretched, miserable, pitiful, pitiable, piteous, pathetic, abject, poor, mean, shabby, paltry. SPLENDID

**sort** *n*, kind, class, category, order, group, genus, species, variety, type, character, nature, description, denomination, make, brand, style, breed, race, family.
*v*, arrange, order, categorize, classify, class, group, separate, divide, sort out, select, assort, organize, systematize, catalogue, file. MUDDLE

**soul** spirit, mind, reason, intellect, life, heart, essence, embodiment.
person, being, individual, man, woman, body, mortal, creature.
energy, vitality, animation, ardour, fervour, feeling, emotion.

**sound**[1] *n*, noise, report, din, racket, voice, utterance, tone, resonance. SILENCE
earshot, hearing, range.
*v*, utter, voice, pronounce, articulate, declare, announce.
resound, echo, reverberate, resonate, ring.
seem, appear.

**sound**[2] *adj*, fit, healthy, hale, hearty, vigorous, robust, sturdy, firm, solid, strong, whole, intact, undamaged, unimpaired, uninjured, unhurt, unbroken, perfect. FAULTY
sensible, reasonable, logical, rational, valid, good, reliable, dependable, correct, right, proper, fair, wise, sane, responsible, level-headed, stable, secure, safe. UNRELIABLE

**sound**[3] *v*, fathom, measure, plumb, probe, test, examine.

**sound**[4] *n*, channel, strait, passage, inlet.

**soundless** noiseless, quiet, silent, still, inaudible, muffled. NOISY

**sour** *adj*, tart, acid, acerbic, bitter, sharp, pungent, bad, rancid, unpleasant, offensive. SWEET
acrimonious, embittered, surly, ill-tempered, cross, snappy, testy, touchy, peevish, petulant, waspish, crabbed, sullen, morose, nasty, disagreeable. GENIAL
*v*, embitter, envenom, disenchant, disillusion.
ferment, turn, curdle, go off.

**source** origin, beginning, commencement, derivation, rise, spring, fountainhead, cause. ISSUE

**souse** plunge, immerse, submerge, dip, duck, drench, soak, steep, pickle, marinate.

**souvenir** keepsake, memento, reminder, token, relic.

**sovereign** *n*, ruler, monarch, king, queen, emperor, empress, tsar, autocrat, potentate, lord. SUBJECT
*adj*, royal, regal, majestic, kingly, queenly, imperial, ruling, supreme, predominant, chief, principal, excellent, efficacious.

**sow** plant, scatter, strew, broadcast, disseminate, propagate. REAP

**space** room, area, expanse, extension, capacity, volume, scope, range, margin, latitude, seat, place, accommodation.
gap, blank, break, pause, hiatus, lacuna, interval, period, time, distance, span.
universe, cosmos, sky, infinity. EARTH

**spacious** capacious, ample, roomy, commodious, big, large, vast, huge, broad, wide, extensive. SMALL

**span** *n*, extent, stretch, reach, spread, distance, space, interval, period, spell, duration.
*v*, bridge, cross, traverse, extend across, reach across.

**spank** smack, slap, beat, thrash.

**spare** *v*, save, rescue, pardon, release, relieve, protect, withhold, forbear. PUNISH
afford, give, part with, relinquish, manage without. KEEP
*adj*, extra, additional, superfluous, surplus, over, unwanted, free, unoccupied, reserve, emergency.
thin, lean, gaunt, skinny, meagre, scanty, frugal, sparing. AMPLE

**sparing** economical, thrifty, frugal, saving, careful, chary, mean, parsimonious. LAVISH

**spark** *n*, flash, sparkle, gleam, flicker, scintilla, trace, hint, atom, jot.
*v*, excite, stimulate, kindle, animate, inspire, activate, stir, start.

**sparkle** *v*, glitter, glisten, twinkle, shine, gleam, beam, flash, coruscate, shimmer, scintillate.
fizz, effervesce, bubble.
*n*, twinkle, spark, glint, gleam, flash, shine, brilliance, radiance. DULLNESS
liveliness, vivacity, spirit, élan, gaiety, animation, ebullience, effervescence.

**sparse** scattered, scanty, meagre, thin, few, scarce. DENSE

**Spartan** austere, harsh, strict, severe, rigorous, disciplined, ascetic, abstemious. INDULGENT
brave, courageous, heroic, valiant, bold, hardy, fearless, intrepid. COWARDLY

**spasm** convulsion, paroxysm, fit, attack, seizure, cramp, contraction, twitch, outburst, eruption.

**spasmodic** fitful, irregular, sporadic, intermittent, jerky, convulsive. REGULAR

**spatter** splash, scatter, strew, sprinkle, spray, bespatter, spot, daub.

**speak** talk, converse, say, utter, express, voice, articulate, enunciate, pronounce, state, tell, communicate.
discourse, address, lecture, orate, hold forth, harangue.

**special** especial, specific, definite, express, particular, certain, distinct, distinctive, individual, peculiar, unique, different, uncommon, unusual, exceptional, extraordinary, memorable, momentous, important, significant, distinguished, noteworthy. ORDINARY

**specialist** expert, connoisseur, authority, master, professional, consultant.

**species** group, sort, class, kind, type, variety, category, genus, description.

**specific** particular, definite, express, explicit, exact, precise, clear, distinct, special, especial, characteristic, peculiar. GENERAL

**specification** particular, item, detail, condition, stipulation, qualification, requirement, description.

**specify** state, name, mention, itemize, enumerate, designate, indicate, detail, spell out, stipulate, particularize, describe, define.

**specimen** sample, example, exemplar, illustration, case, instance, pattern, model, type.

**specious** misleading, deceptive, fallacious, sophistic, casuistic, plausible.

**speck** spot, dot, mark, stain, blemish, flaw, fleck, speckle, bit, jot, iota, atom, whit, mite, grain, particle.

**spectacle** sight, show, display, exhibition, scene, phenomenon, curiosity, marvel, wonder, vision, picture, parade, pageant, extravaganza, performance.

**spectacular** impressive, striking, breathtaking, staggering, grand, magnificent, remarkable, sensational, dramatic. ORDINARY

**spectator** onlooker, bystander, watcher, viewer, observer, witness.

**spectre** ghost, apparition, phantom, spook (*inf*), spirit, wraith, image, vision.

**speculate** conjecture, guess, surmise, suppose, theorize, hypothesize, consider, think, meditate, cogitate, reflect, deliberate, contemplate, ponder, muse, ruminate. KNOW

**speculation** conjecture, guess, surmise, supposition, theory, hypothesis, opinion, view, thought, deliberation, contemplation, rumination. REALITY

**speech** talk, address, oration, lecture, discourse, harangue, conversation, dialogue, communication, language, tongue, dialect, idiom, diction, articulation, enunciation, utterance.

**speechless** mute, dumb, silent, voiceless, inarticulate, tongue-tied, wordless, dumbfounded, amazed, astounded, shocked, thunderstruck. TALKATIVE

**speed** *n*, velocity, celerity, rapidity, swiftness, quickness, haste, hurry, acceleration, pace, rate. SLOWNESS *v*, hasten, hurry, rush, race, tear, accelerate, quicken, expedite, advance, further, boost, aid, assist. DELAY

**speedy** hasty, hurried, precipitate, expeditious, fast, quick, rapid, swift, prompt, early. SLOW

**spell**[1] charm, incantation, enchantment, bewitchment, fascination, allure, magic, sorcery.

**spell**[2] period, time, stretch, interval, term, stint, bout, turn.

**spend** disburse, pay out, expend, fork out (*inf*), squander, dissipate, waste, fritter away, use up, consume. SAVE

employ, use, apply, devote, pass, occupy, while away.

**spendthrift** *n*, wastrel, prodigal, profligate, squanderer, spender. MISER

*adj*, extravagant, prodigal, improvident, thriftless. THRIFTY

**spent** exhausted, worn out, weary, tired, fagged out (*inf*), dead beat (*inf*), all in (*inf*), drained, consumed, used up.

**sphere** ball, globe, orb, round. CUBE

field, domain, realm, province, department, territory, beat, range, order, rank, class, station.

**spice** flavour, savour, relish, tang, zest, piquancy, seasoning, flavouring.

**spicy** piquant, pungent, aromatic, fragrant, tangy, hot, seasoned, savoury. INSIPID

racy, bawdy, ribald, indelicate, risqué, scandalous, sensational.

**spike** point, prong, nail, pin.

**spill** upset, overturn, overflow, run over, pour out, disgorge, shed, scatter.

**spin** *v*, rotate, revolve, turn, twirl, whirl, wheel, pirouette, gyrate, reel.

tell, recount, relate, narrate, unfold, develop, invent.

**spin out,** protract, prolong, lengthen, extend, drag out, draw out, amplify, pad out. ABRIDGE

*n*, ride, drive, jaunt, outing, whirl.

**spine** backbone, vertebrae, vertebral column, spinal column.

point, spike, barb, quill, needle, ridge.

**spineless** weak, feeble, weak-willed, irresolute, timid, pusillanimous, cowardly, faint-hearted, lily-livered. BOLD

**spinney** copse, coppice, thicket, grove, wood.

**spiral** *n*, helix, coil, corkscrew, whorl.

*adj*, helical, coiled, winding, twisting. STRAIGHT

**spirit** soul, life, breath, mind, will. BODY

mood, humour, temper, feeling, temperament, disposition, outlook, attitude.

liveliness, vivacity, animation, enthusiasm, zeal, ardour, fervour, vigour, energy, enterprise, dash, zest, valour, courage, mettle. APATHY

essence, quintessence, substance, character, nature, sense, drift, gist, tenor, significance, meaning, purport, intent.

ghost, apparition, spectre, phantom, fairy, sprite, imp, goblin, angel, demon.

**spirited** lively, vivacious, animated, active, energetic, vigorous, enthusiastic, ardent, fervent, courageous, brave, mettlesome. APATHETIC

**spiritless** listless, languid, torpid, sluggish, lethargic, lifeless, apathetic, melancholic, depressed, dejected, dispirited. SPIRITED

**spiritual** incorporeal, immaterial, intangible, ethereal, ghostly, supernatural. PHYSICAL

holy, sacred, religious, pious, devout, pure. PROFANE

**spite** *n*, malice, maliciousness, malevolence, malignity, venom, ill will, animosity, resentment, grudge, hate, gall, spleen, rancour, pique. BENEVOLENCE

**in spite of,** despite, notwithstanding, regardless of, in defiance of.

*v*, annoy, vex, offend, pique, nettle, provoke, hurt, injure. PLEASE

**spiteful** malicious, malevolent, malign, malignant, vindictive, rancorous, venomous, cruel. BENEVOLENT

**splash** *v*, spatter, bespatter, sprinkle, spray, shower, strew, dash, buffet, wash.

*n*, spot, splodge, daub, patch, dash, touch.

ostentation, display, spectacle, sensation.

**spleen** spite, spitefulness, malice, maliciousness, bitterness, acrimony, venom, gall, bile, pique, peevishness, petulance, ill will, irascibility, anger, wrath. BENEVOLENCE

**splendid** brilliant, resplendent, magnificent, fine, grand, stately, gorgeous, sumptuous, luxurious, showy, glorious, illustrious, superb, supreme, outstanding, admirable, excellent, first-class, marvellous, wonderful, super (*inf*). POOR

**splendour** brilliance, resplendence, magnificence, grandeur, pomp, display, parade, show, stateliness, majesty, glory.

**splenetic** spiteful, malicious, peevish, petulant, irritable, choleric, testy, touchy, surly, crabbed, crusty, churlish. GENIAL

**splice** join, unite, connect, bind, braid, plait, knit, interweave, intertwine, interlace. SEVER

**splinter** *v*, shatter, shiver, split, break up.
*n*, piece, fragment, sliver, shard, chip.

**split** *v*, separate, divide, part, break, sever, cleave, cut, crack, rupture, burst, rip, tear, branch, fork, disband, divorce, split up. UNITE
share, divide, apportion, partition, parcel out.
*n*, crack, fissure, rip, tear, rift, rupture, break, breach, separation, division, partition, schism, disunion. UNION

**spoil** mar, harm, damage, injure, hurt, impair, disfigure, deface, blemish, ruin, wreck, destroy. IMPROVE
indulge, pamper, coddle, cosset, baby.
decay, go bad, go off, turn, addle, rot, putrefy.

**spoils** booty, loot, plunder, pillage, pickings, prize.

**sponge** wipe, mop, rub, clean, rub out, efface, expunge.
cadge, scrounge (*inf*), live off.

**spongy** porous, absorbent, soft, light, springy.

**sponsor** *n*, patron, backer, supporter, promoter, guarantor, godparent.
*v*, back, support, finance, subsidize, promote, guarantee.

**spontaneous** instinctive, natural, impulsive, impetuous, free, voluntary, willing, unforced, unprompted, gratuitous, unpremeditated, unplanned, extempore, impromptu. STUDIED

**sporadic** irregular, random, occasional, intermittent, fitful, spasmodic, infrequent, scattered, dispersed, isolated, separate. CONTINUOUS

**sport** *n*, game, exercise, play, recreation, amusement, diversion, entertainment, pastime, fun. WORK
jest, joke, mirth, fun, banter, badinage, raillery, mockery, ridicule.
*v*, frolic, gambol, frisk, romp, caper, play, disport, amuse oneself.
wear, display, show off.

**sportive** playful, gamesome, frolicsome, frisky, coltish, skittish, lively, sprightly, gay, merry. SEDATE

**spot** *n*, mark, dot, speckle, speck, stain, blot, blemish, flaw, patch, blotch, pimple.
place, site, locality, location, scene, area.
*v*, discern, make out, espy, descry, see, recognize, identify. MISS
mark, dot, speckle, stain, blot, taint, tarnish, soil, sully, dirty. CLEAN

**spotless** unspotted, immaculate, clean, pure, unsullied, unblemished, stainless, untarnished, perfect, flawless. IMPURE

**spouse** husband, wife, consort, companion, partner, mate, better half (*inf*).

**spout** gush, spurt, squirt, jet, spray, surge, stream, flow, pour, discharge.
orate, declaim, hold forth, speechify.

**sprain** wrench, twist, strain, rick.

**sprawl** loll, lounge, slouch, slump, spread, straggle.

**spray**[1] *n*, mist, drizzle, spindrift, foam, spume.
sprinkler, atomizer, aerosol.
*v*, sprinkle, spatter, splash, shower, scatter, atomize.

**spray**[2] *n*, sprig, shoot, bough, branch, posy, nosegay, corsage.

**spread** *v*, stretch, extend, widen, expand, dilate, swell, escalate, unfold, unfurl, unroll, open, sprawl. FOLD
disseminate, distribute, circulate, broadcast, promulgate, propagate, publicize, advertise, scatter, strew, sow, disperse, shed, radiate, diffuse. SUPPRESS
apply, daub, smear, plaster, cover, lay.
*n*, extent, expanse, stretch, reach, compass, range.
dissemination, dispersion, diffusion, radiation, transmission, escalation, development, increase, growth, expansion.
feast, banquet, repast, meal.

**spree** fling, revel, binge (*inf*), bender (*inf*), orgy, debauch, romp, lark (*inf*).

**sprightly** spry, agile, nimble, brisk, active, jaunty, airy, lively, animated, vivacious, gay, bouyant, jocose, jolly, blithe, cheerful, playful, frolicsome. LIFELESS

**spring** *v*, jump, leap, bound, vault, hop, skip, rebound, recoil.
start, begin, commence, rise, arise, issue, emanate, flow, emerge, proceed, originate, derive, stem. END

**spring up,** appear, develop, sprout, burgeon, shoot up. DISAPPEAR
*n*, jump, leap, bound, vault, hop, skip.
elasticity, resilience, springiness, bounce, give (*inf*).
well, fountainhead, wellspring, fount, source, origin, root, cause.

**sprinkle** scatter, strew, spray, shower, dust, dredge.

**sprite** elf, brownie, fairy, pixie, goblin, leprechaun, nymph, dryad.

**sprout** bud, burgeon, germinate, shoot, spring, grow, develop. WITHER

**spruce** smart, trim, natty (*inf*), dapper, neat, tidy. UNTIDY

**spry** brisk, nimble, agile, active, lively, sprightly, quick, alert. SLUGGISH

**spur** *n*, goad, prick, stimulus, motive, incentive, inducement, incitement, encouragement. DETERRENT
*v*, goad, prick, prod, prompt, push, press, drive, impel, stimulate, animate, incite, provoke, urge, encourage. DETER

**spurious** false, unreal, counterfeit, fake, phoney (*inf*), bogus, mock, sham, simulated, feigned, pretended, artificial, specious. GENUINE

**spurn** reject, rebuff, snub, disregard, scorn, despise, contemn, disdain. RESPECT

**spurt** gush, spout, squirt, jet, burst, surge.

**spy** *n*, agent, secret agent, double agent, informer, detective, scout.
*v*, watch, observe, see, espy, descry, discern, make out, spot, detect, notice. MISS

**squabble** *v*, quarrel, row, altercate, contend, bicker, wrangle, argue, dispute, fight, brawl. AGREE
*n*, quarrel, row, altercation, contention, disagreement, argument, dispute, wrangle, fight, tiff. AGREEMENT

**squad** band, gang, crew, team, company, troop, unit, group.

**squalid** foul, filthy, unclean, dirty, repulsive, nasty, sordid, seedy, run-down, decayed. CLEAN

**squall** *n*, gust, blast, gale, hurricane, storm, tempest.
*v*, cry, bawl, yell, shriek, scream, howl.

**squander** waste, dissipate, spend, blow (*inf*), fritter away, throw away, lavish, splurge, misuse, misspend. SAVE

**square** *n*, quadrate, rectangle, quadrilateral, cube. CIRCLE
place, plaza, piazza, quadrangle.
*adj*, rectangular, quadrilateral, right-angled, perpendicular, straight, true, level, even, equal, balanced. UNEVEN
fair, just, honest, straightforward. DISHONEST
conservative, conventional, strait-laced, old-fashioned. AVANT-GARDE
*v*, straighten, set, regulate, adjust, align, tailor, fit, adapt, accord, suit, accommodate, balance, harmonize, conform, reconcile.
settle, pay, discharge, liquidate, satisfy.

**squash** crush, squeeze, press, mash, pulp, compress, flatten.
suppress, quash, quell, silence, humiliate.

**squat** *v*, crouch, sit, cower. STAND
*adj*, short, squab, dumpy, stubby, stout, stocky, thickset, broad, tubby, fat. LANKY

**squeak** creak, whine, squeal, yelp, peep, pipe.

**squeal** cry, wail, yell, squall, squeak, yelp, shriek, scream.

**squeamish** queasy, qualmish, delicate, dainty, finicky, particular, fastidious, prudish.

**squeeze** press, compress, squash, crush, wring, pinch, constrict, grip, clasp, hug, embrace, crowd, jam, pack, cram, stuff, force.

**squirm** writhe, wriggle, twist, turn, shift, move.

**squirt** spout, spurt, gush, jet, eject, discharge.

**stab** *v*, pierce, stick, knife, spear, gore, transfix, cut, wound, hurt, injure, jab, thrust.
*n*, wound, injury, cut, gash, jab, thrust, pang, twinge, pain, ache.
try, attempt, effort, go (*inf*), shot (*inf*).

**stable** firm, steady, fast, fixed, established, sound, sturdy, solid, secure, constant, durable, lasting, abiding, permanent, unchanging, immutable, invariable, unalterable, perpetual, steadfast, sure, reliable. UNSTABLE

**stack** *n*, pile, heap, mass, load, hoard, store, mound, mountain.
*v*, pile, heap, amass, accumulate, hoard, load.

**staff** employees, personnel, workers, work force, teachers, officers, team, crew.
stick, cane, rod, pole, stave, club, crook, mace, baton, wand, prop, support.

**stage** *n*, point, juncture, period, phase, leg, step, level.

platform, dais, rostrum, podium, theatre, boards, scene, setting.
*v*, produce, present, put on, mount, perform, organize.

**stagger** totter, wobble, reel, sway, lurch, falter, hesitate, waver, vacillate.
astound, astonish, amaze, flabbergast (*inf*), bowl over (*inf*), dumbfound, stupefy, nonplus, confound, bewilder, stun, shock.
alternate, zigzag.

**stagnant** still, quiet, motionless, static, inert, standing, brackish, foul, stale, dull, sluggish. FLOWING

**staid** sedate, sober, serious, grave, solemn, quiet, settled, steady, demure, prim. FRIVOLOUS

**stain** *v*, mark, spot, dye, colour, discolour, soil, dirty, sully, blot, blemish, tarnish, blacken, taint, contaminate, defile, disgrace.
*n*, mark, spot, dye, tint, discoloration, blot, blemish, taint, stigma, slur, shame, disgrace.

**stake**[1] *n*, pale, picket, palisade, stick, post, pole.
*v*, tether, tie, fasten, secure, prop, support.
**stake out,** demarcate, mark out, outline, define, delimit, claim.

**stake**[2] *n*, bet, wager, ante, pledge, venture, risk, hazard, chance.
interest, concern, share, involvement, investment.
*v*, bet, wager, gamble, hazard, risk, venture, imperil, jeopardize.

**stale** old, musty, fusty, hard, dry, flat, insipid, tasteless, mouldy. FRESH
trite, banal, hackneyed, commonplace, unoriginal, dull.

**stalk** hunt, track, trail, shadow, follow, pursue, chase.
strut, stride, pace, march, flounce. SLINK

**stall** *n*, stand, booth, compartment, cubicle, pen, stable.
*v*, stop, halt, stick, get stuck.
delay, hedge, equivocate, prevaricate, play for time.

**stalwart** sturdy, stout, rugged, athletic, robust, lusty, hardy, strong, brave, valiant, intrepid, courageous, bold, daring, staunch, steadfast, firm, resolute. WEAK

**stamina** strength, vitality, energy, vigour, fortitude, endurance, resistance, resilience, power, force. WEAKNESS

**stammer** stutter, falter, hesitate, pause, stumble.

**stamp** *v*, tread, step, tramp, stomp (*inf*), trample, crush, beat, pound.
mark, brand, label, characterize, impress, imprint, print, engrave.
**stamp out,** quell, suppress, crush, put down, eliminate, eradicate, extirpate, extinguish.
*n*, mark, brand, print, impression, hallmark, seal, die, mould, cast, sort, kind, type, variety, character, description.

**stampede** rush, charge, flight, rout.

**stand** *v*, rise, get up, place, put, set.
stop, halt, pause, rest, stay, abide, remain, hold, continue, persist.
bear, tolerate, endure, suffer, abide, brook, withstand, resist.
**stand by,** defend, uphold, support, stick up for (*inf*). ABANDON
**stand for,** represent, symbolize, exemplify, betoken, denote, mean.
permit, allow, countenance, tolerate, brook, put up with (*inf*). OPPOSE
**stand out,** be prominent, be conspicuous, project, stick out.
*n*, stance, standpoint, position, attitude, opinion, point of view.
stop, halt, standstill, rest, stay. MOTION
station, post, place, platform, stall, rack, frame, support.
opposition, resistance, defiance. SUBMISSION

**standard** *n*, model, pattern, example, type, gauge, measure, criterion, yardstick, scale, rule, principle, norm, average.
flag, banner, ensign, pennant, pennon, colours.
*adj*, typical, regular, normal, usual, customary, orthodox, official, approved, accepted, recognized, classic, basic, universal. IRREGULAR

**standing** *n*, rank, status, position, station, reputation, repute, credit, estimation.
*adj*, upright, vertical, perpendicular, erect. HORIZONTAL
fixed, set, lasting, permanent, regular, static.

**staple** principal, chief, main, primary, basic, fundamental, essential, vital. MINOR

**starchy** stiff, formal, prim, conventional, precise, punctilious. LIBERAL

**stare** gaze, gape, goggle, gawk, look, watch. IGNORE

**stark** *adj*, absolute, sheer, arrant, downright, utter, unmitigated, pure, mere, outright, flagrant, blunt, bald.
bare, barren, bleak, grim, dreary, harsh, severe, austere, plain, simple.
*adv*, absolutely, utterly, quite, altogether, totally, entirely, completely, wholly, fully. PARTIALLY

**start** *v*, begin, commence, depart, set off, appear, arise, issue, originate, inaugurate, found, establish, institute, initiate, pioneer, open, launch, instigate, set in motion. FINISH
jump, flinch, wince, twitch, jerk, shy, recoil.
*n*, beginning, commencement, outset, dawn, birth, inception, origin, source, foundation, initiation. END
lead, advantage, head start, chance, opportunity, break (*inf*), opening.
jump, twitch, jerk, surprise.

**startle** surprise, take aback, alarm, scare, frighten, shock, amaze, astound, astonish. COMPOSE

**starve** die, perish, fast, hunger, be famished, be ravenous. GORGE

**state** *n*, condition, situation, circumstances, shape, form, phase, plight, predicament, case, status, rank.
pomp, ceremony, grandeur, magnificence, splendour, glory, majesty, dignity.
nation, country, republic, commonwealth, realm, kingdom, body politic, government.
*v*, say, utter, express, articulate, declare, assert, asseverate, aver, affirm, avow, maintain, profess, announce, proclaim. SUPPRESS

**stately** pompous, grand, magnificent, splendid, august, dignified, imposing, lofty, majestic, regal, royal, noble. LOWLY

**statement** declaration, announcement, proclamation, utterance, assertion, asseveration, averment, avowal, testimony, account, report, record.

**station** *n*, depot, terminus, headquarters, base, post, location, place, position, situation.
status, standing, rank, class, condition, degree.
*v*, post, assign, place, locate, fix, establish. MOVE

**stationary** static, immobile, immovable, fixed, motionless, still, inert. MOBILE

**stature** height, tallness, size, eminence, prominence, prestige, rank, standing.

**status** standing, station, position, condition, rank, degree, grade, prestige.

**statute** decree, edict, act, enactment, law, ordinance, rule, regulation.

**staunch** loyal, faithful, constant, true, reliable, dependable, steady, steadfast, firm, unwavering, stout, resolute. WAVERING

**stave off** avert, evade, dodge, ward off, fend off, avoid, parry, deflect, keep at bay.

**stay**[1] *v*, remain, keep, continue, abide, endure, persist, last.
stop, halt, pause, wait, delay, tarry, linger, loiter, rest, settle, live, reside, lodge, sojourn. MOVE
check, curb, prevent, obstruct, hinder, impede, adjourn, suspend, put off, defer. HASTEN
*n*, sojourn, visit, holiday, rest, stop, halt, pause, wait, delay, reprieve.

**stay**[2] *n*, prop, support, brace, buttress.

**steadfast** steady, fixed, intent, firm, unwavering, resolute, constant, loyal, faithful, staunch, dependable, stable. WAVERING

**steady** stable, firm, safe, sound, solid, balanced, fixed, steadfast, reliable, sensible, rational, calm, imperturbable. UNSTEADY
even, regular, rhythmic, uniform, unvarying, continuous, continual, perpetual, ceaseless, unremitting, constant, habitual. IRREGULAR

**steal** take, pilfer, purloin, filch, thieve, rob, shoplift, nick (*inf*), pinch (*inf*), embezzle, peculate, appropriate, plagiarize, poach. RETURN
creep, tiptoe, slip, slink, sneak.

**stealthy** furtive, sly, sneaky, underhand, clandestine, surreptitious, covert, secret. OPEN

**steam** vapour, mist, fog, condensation, smoke, fume, exhalation.

**steel** brace, fortify, toughen, harden. RELAX

**steep**[1] *adj*, sheer, abrupt, precipitous, sudden. GRADUAL
unreasonable, extreme, excessive, exorbitant. MODERATE

**steep**[2] *v*, soak, marinate, souse, drench, immerse, submerge, saturate, imbue, impregnate, infuse, pervade, permeate. DRY

**steer** pilot, guide, direct, control, conduct, lead.
**steer clear of,** shun, eschew, avoid, evade.
**stem**[1] *n*, stalk, trunk, peduncle, shaft, stock.
*v*, arise, come, issue, emanate, originate, derive.
**stem**[2] *v*, stop, stay, check, curb, hold back, restrain, dam, stanch.
**stench** stink, fetor, mephitis, effluvium, reek, pong (*inf*). PERFUME
**stentorian** loud, thundering, booming, deafening, powerful, sonorous. SOFT
**step** *n*, pace, stride, footstep, footfall, footprint, track, gait, walk.
proceeding, measure, move, action, act, deed, phase, stage.
stair, rung, rank, degree, grade, level.
*v*, move, walk, stride, pace, tread.
**step up,** increase, raise, augment, boost, accelerate, intensify. REDUCE
**sterile** barren, infertile, infecund, unprolific, unfruitful, fruitless, unproductive, abortive, empty, bare. FRUITFUL
sterilized, disinfected, germ-free, aseptic.
**sterling** genuine, true, real, sound, solid, pure, excellent, first-class. SPECIOUS
**stern** strict, severe, harsh, hard, rigid, firm, adamant, inflexible, unyielding, uncompromising, relentless, inexorable, grim, forbidding, dour, austere. LENIENT
**stew** simmer, boil, seethe.
**stick**[1] *n*, rod, staff, wand, baton, pole, cane, twig, switch, birch, club.
**stick**[2] *v*, stab, pierce, puncture, penetrate, spear, transfix, impale, gore, jab, thrust.
fasten, attach, join, fix, set, glue, paste.
cement, weld, adhere, cling, cleave, hold. SEPARATE
put, place, lay, plant, drop, deposit.
stay, remain, persist, abide.
**stick out,** protrude, project, jut out, poke out, extend, bulge.
**stick up for,** support, champion, defend, stand up for. OPPOSE
**sticky** adhesive, gummy, gluey, glutinous, viscid, viscous, tacky. DRY
muggy, close, humid, sultry. FRESH
difficult, awkward, tricky, delicate, unpleasant.
**stiff** rigid, inflexible, unbending, unyielding, firm, hard, solid, thick, tight, taut, tense. LIMP
harsh, severe, stringent, unsparing, pitiless, merciless, cruel, oppressive, excessive, extreme. LENIENT
difficult, hard, arduous, laborious, strenuous, fatiguing, exacting, rigorous, tough, trying. EASY
formal, starchy (*inf*), strait-laced, prim, priggish, strict, precise, punctilious, ceremonious, pompous, chilly, cold, aloof, standoffish, constrained, unrelaxed, awkward, clumsy, graceless, inelegant.
strong, potent, powerful, vigorous, fresh, brisk, keen. LIGHT
**stifle** suffocate, asphyxiate, choke, smother, strangle, restrain, check, curb, suppress, repress, silence, hush, quell, extinguish.
**stigma** mark, spot, blot, stain, blemish, brand, slur, defamation, shame, disgrace, dishonour.
**still** *adj*, motionless, immobile, inert, stationary, static, stagnant, calm, tranquil, serene, sedate, placid, peaceful, pacific, unruffled, undisturbed, smooth, quiet, silent, noiseless. AGITATED
*n*, stillness, silence, quiet, hush, calm, tranquillity, peace, peacefulness. NOISE
*v*, hush, quieten, silence, lull, calm, tranquillize, appease, pacify, compose, soothe, allay, assuage, alleviate, settle, subdue, check, stop. AGITATE
*adv*, yet, even, however, nevertheless, notwithstanding, but.
**stilted** bombastic, pompous, turgid, inflated, high-flown, grandiloquent, formal, stiff, wooden, laboured, forced. SIMPLE
**stimulate** arouse, rouse, excite, foment, fire, kindle, inflame, goad, spur, prick, prompt, urge, incite, instigate, provoke, motivate, animate, invigorate, inspirit, encourage, impel. DETER
**stimulus** incentive, fillip, provocation, motive, spur, goad, impulse, urge, incitement, inducement, encouragement. DETERRENT
**sting** prick, bite, burn, smart, tingle, pain, hurt, injure, wound, afflict, distress. SOOTHE
**stingy** mean, parsimonious, niggardly, miserly, penurious, tight-fisted, close-fisted, ungenerous. GENEROUS
meagre, scanty, small, measly (*inf*), insufficient, inadequate. AMPLE
**stink** *n*, stench, fetor, mephitis, effluvium, reek, pong (*inf*). PERFUME

*v*, reek, smell, pong (*inf*).

**stint** *v*, limit, restrict, confine, restrain, scrimp, economize, save, skimp, begrudge. LAVISH
*n*, period, spell, shift, turn, share, ration, quota, part, duty, assignment, task, work.

**stipend** pay, salary, wages, remuneration, emolument, allowance, honorarium.

**stipulate** specify, insist, require, demand, agree, contract, guarantee, promise, pledge, engage.

**stipulation** condition, specification, prerequisite, requirement, demand, provision, proviso, qualification, clause, term, obligation, agreement, contract.

**stir** *v*, move, budge, exert oneself, shift, go. STAY
mix, blend, beat, whip, disturb, agitate, rustle, shake.
rouse, awaken, arouse, stimulate, provoke, spur, goad, incite, instigate, prompt, excite, thrill, animate, galvanize, inspire, inflame, affect, touch, move.
*n*, excitement, commotion, disorder, confusion, ado, to-do, fuss, bother, uproar, tumult, activity, movement, hustle, bustle, flurry, agitation. TRANQUILLITY

**stirring** rousing, stimulating, moving, exciting, thrilling, exhilarating, impassioned, dramatic, animated, spirited, lively, active, busy. DULL

**stock** *n*, store, supply, hoard, reserve, reservoir, fund, accumulation, collection, assortment, range, variety, goods, wares, commodities, capital.
cattle, sheep, horses, pigs, animals, livestock.
trunk, stalk, stem, shaft, butt, handle.
type, species, breed, race, family, house, lineage, descent, pedigree, ancestry, parentage, extraction.
*adj*, standard, staple, basic, usual, normal, customary, traditional, commonplace, hackneyed, trite, state. NOVEL
*v*, keep, deal in, sell, supply, provision, equip, store, amass, accumulate, hoard, save, reserve.

**stoical** philosophical, patient, long-suffering, resigned, indifferent, apathetic, impassive, dispassionate, cool, calm, imperturbable, phlegmatic. EXCITABLE

**stolid** dull, obtuse, bovine, stupid, slow, indifferent, apathetic, impassive, phlegmatic.

**stomach** *n*, abdomen, belly, tummy (*inf*), gut, paunch.
appetite, hunger, relish, liking, desire, inclination, leaning, proclivity. AVERSION
*v*, tolerate, bear, endure, suffer, abide, stand, put up with (*inf*), swallow.

**stone** pebble, rock, boulder, cobble, gem, jewel, seed, pip.

**stony** hard, flinty, impenetrable, adamant, unfeeling, callous, cold, pitiless, merciless, cruel, rigid, inflexible, obdurate, expressionless, blank.

**stoop** bend, lean, incline, bow, hunch, crouch, squat, kneel, slouch, droop, duck.
condescend, deign, submit, yield, acquiesce, descend, lower oneself.

**stop** *v*, halt, pause, cease, discontinue, quit, desist, finish, complete, conclude, end, terminate, arrest, check, curb, restrain, repress, suppress, stall, delay, hinder, hamper, impede, thwart, prevent, obstruct, block, stem, close, plug, seal.
visit, sojourn, stay, remain, rest, tarry, wait, linger. DEPART
*n*, halt, standstill, pause, break, interruption, intermission, cessation, end, finish, conclusion, termination, arrest, stoppage. CONTINUATION
visit, sojourn, stay, rest.
impediment, block, obstacle, hindrance, bar, plug, stopper.

**store** *v*, amass, accumulate, stockpile, garner, save, reserve, put aside, hoard, keep, preserve, husband. CONSUME
*n*, stock, stockpile, supply, fund, hoard, reserve, accumulation, mass, abundance, plenty.
warehouse, storehouse, depot, depository, repository.
shop, market, mart, emporium.

**storm** *n*, tempest, squall, gale, hurricane, tornado, blizzard. CALM
assault, attack, onslaught, onset, rush, raid, blitz.
disturbance, outbreak, disorder, commotion, tumult, turmoil, furore, riot, outburst, tantrum. PEACE
*v*, rage, roar, thunder, rant, rave, fume.
assail, assault, attack, raid, charge, rush.

**stormy** tempestuous, wild, violent, rough, turbulent, squally, windy, gusty, blustery, raging, furious. STILL

**story** tale, romance, novel, narrative, narration, account, recital, history, legend, myth, fable, anecdote, yarn (*inf*), fiction, lie, fib, falsehood. FACT

**stout** fat, obese, overweight, corpulent, portly, rotund, plump, heavy, large, big. THIN
sturdy, strong, substantial, robust, lusty, brawny, strapping, athletic, rugged, tough, hardy, brave, courageous, valiant, bold, fearless, intrepid, stout-hearted, resolute, firm, staunch, stalwart. WEAK

**stow** pack, stuff, cram, load, store, hoard, hide, secrete.

**straggle** stray, digress, deviate, ramble, wander, roam, rove, range, drift, lag, trail.

**straight** *adj*, direct, undeviating, unswerving, level, even, horizontal, vertical, upright, erect, right, true. CROOKED
honest, honourable, upright, respectable, just, fair, reliable, trustworthy, straightforward. DISHONEST
neat, tidy, orderly, shipshape. UNTIDY
*adv*, directly, immediately, instantly, frankly, candidly, honestly.

**straightaway** immediately, instantly, at once, right away, forthwith, directly, now. LATER

**straightforward** frank, candid, forthright, plain, open, sincere, genuine, honest, truthful, direct, straight. DECEITFUL
simple, easy, uncomplicated. COMPLICATED

**strain**[1] *v*, tighten, stretch, extend, pull, wrench, sprain, injure, exert, tax, force, drive, overexert, overtax, exhaust, fatigue, tire, weaken, strive, struggle, labour, overwork. RELAX
filter, percolate, screen, sieve, sift, purify.
*n*, stretch, pull, wrench, sprain, injury, effort, struggle, force, exertion, fatigue, tension, stress, pressure. RELAXATION
tune, melody, air, theme, song, lay.

**strain**[2] *n*, family, race, stock, ancestry, descent, lineage, extraction, pedigree, breed.
trace, streak, vein, tendency.

**strait** channel, sound, narrows.
dilemma, quandary, predicament, plight, difficulty, problem, trouble, distress, hardship.

**straitened** distressed, embarrassed, pinched, reduced, limited, restricted, impoverished, destitute.

**strand**[1] *v*, maroon, cast away, shipwreck, beach, ground, run aground, abandon, desert, leave. RESCUE
*n*, shore, coast, beach.

**strand**[2] thread, fibre, filament, string, hair.

**strange** odd, peculiar, curious, queer, uncommon, unusual, rare, singular, exceptional, remarkable, extraordinary, irregular, abnormal, weird, bizarre, eccentric, unaccountable, inexplicable. NORMAL
unfamiliar, unknown, untried, exotic, foreign, alien, new, novel, unaccustomed, inexperienced. FAMILIAR

**stranger** alien, foreigner, visitor, guest, newcomer, outsider. ACQUAINTANCE

**strangle** throttle, choke, suffocate, smother, asphyxiate, stifle, gag, repress, suppress.

**strap** *n*, belt, thong, strip, band.
*v*, tie, bind, truss, lash, fasten, secure. LOOSE
beat, flog, whip, lash, scourge, belt.

**stratagem** ruse, artifice, trick, wile, scheme, plot, plan, ploy, gambit, manoeuvre, machination, device.

**strategy** tactics, approach, policy, plan, programme, scheme.

**stratum** layer, bed, seam, vein.
level, grade, degree, rank, station, class.

**stray** *v*, wander, roam, rove, ramble, range, drift, straggle, meander, digress, deviate, swerve, go astray, err.
*adj*, lost, abandoned, homeless, vagrant, wandering.
scattered, random, accidental, chance, isolated.

**streak** strip, stripe, line, band, bar, stroke.
strain, vein, trace, element.

**stream** *n*, brook, beck, burn, river, freshet, rivulet, rill, run, tributary, current, race, drift, course, flow, tide, rush, gush, torrent, outpouring.
*v*, flow, issue, pour, cascade, run, course, rush, gush, spout. HALT

**streamer** pennon, pennant, flag, ensign, standard, banner, ribbon.

**street** thoroughfare, road, avenue, boulevard.

**strength** power, might, force, vigour, energy, sinew, muscle, brawn, hardiness, robustness, sturdiness, toughness, durability, fortitude, backbone. WEAKNESS
intensity, vehemence, potency, efficacy, cogency, validity, soundness.

**strengthen** fortify, reinforce, invigorate, energize, hearten, encourage, nerve, steel, brace, harden, toughen. WEAKEN
support, back up, confirm, substantiate, intensify, heighten.

**strenuous** energetic, vigorous, active, forceful, ardent, zealous, persistent, tireless, determined, resolute. FEEBLE
arduous, hard, difficult, laborious, toilsome, tough, tiring, taxing.

**stress** *n*, emphasis, accent, accentuation, weight, importance, significance, urgency.
strain, tension, force, pressure, worry, anxiety. RELAXATION
*v*, emphasize, accentuate, accent, underline, point up, harp on, dwell on, repeat.

**stretch** *v*, extend, lengthen, elongate, pull, draw out, expand, distend, tighten, strain, reach, spread, cover. CONTRACT
*n*, extent, reach, range, scope, compass.
expanse, area, space, spell, period, time.

**strew** scatter, spread, diffuse, disperse, sow, sprinkle, broadcast. GATHER

**stricken** afflicted, smitten, hit, struck, wounded, laid low.

**strict** rigorous, stringent, harsh, rigid, inflexible, stern, severe, austere. LENIENT
exact, precise, accurate, faithful, close, careful, particular, punctilious, scrupulous. LOOSE
complete, total, utter, absolute.

**stricture** censure, blame, criticism, animadversion. PRAISE

**stride** pace, step, walk, march.

**strident** harsh, grating, raucous, jarring, discordant, loud, clamorous, vociferous. SOFT

**strife** conflict, discord, dissension, friction, animosity, disagreement, contention, quarrel, row, dispute, brawl, battle, fight, struggle, contest, rivalry. PEACE

**strike** hit, tap, knock, buffet, cuff, box, punch, slap, smack, beat, pound, thump. CARESS
collide, crash, hit, bump, touch.
attack, assail, assault, set upon, afflict.
impress, affect, dawn on, occur to, reach.
walk out, down tools, mutiny, revolt.
**strike out,** delete, cross out, erase, efface, cancel.

**striking** impressive, stunning (*inf*), wonderful, extraordinary, noticeable, conspicuous. COMMONPLACE

**string** *n*, cord, twine, rope, thread.
series, chain, row, line, file, queue, procession.
*v*, hang, suspend, festoon, loop, join, link.
**string along,** deceive, fool, dupe, bluff.
**string out,** stretch, extend, lengthen, space out, spread out, straggle.

**stringent** strict, severe, harsh, rigorous, exacting, demanding, tough, tight, rigid, inflexible. LAX

**strip**[1] *v*, peel, skin, remove, deprive, divest, denude, bare, uncover, undress, disrobe, unclothe. COVER
rob, plunder, despoil, pillage, sack, loot, ransack, gut.

**strip**[2] *n*, band, stripe, belt, ribbon, fillet, piece, shred.

**stripe** band, bar, line, streak, strip.

**stripling** youth, youngster, lad, boy.

**strive** struggle, labour, toil, strain, try, attempt, exert, endeavour, aim, aspire, compete, contend, fight.

**stroke** *n*, blow, hit, knock, tap, rap, slap, cuff, thump.
feat, accomplishment, achievement, action.
apoplexy, paralysis, attack, fit, seizure, collapse.
*v*, caress, rub, pat, fondle, pet.

**stroll** *v*, walk, amble, saunter, ramble, wander. RUN
*n*, walk, constitutional, promenade, amble, saunter, airing, excursion, ramble.

**strong** powerful, mighty, muscular, sinewy, brawny, athletic, strapping, rugged, stalwart, lusty, hale, hearty, healthy, robust, hardy, tough, stout, sound, solid, sturdy, durable, substantial, firm, resolute. WEAK
intense, deep, bright, vivid, concentrated, potent, fierce, violent, vehement, vigorous, fervent, zealous, eager, keen, sharp, hot, spicy, piquant, pungent.
weighty, effective, forceful, cogent, convincing, persuasive.

**stronghold** fortress, fort, citadel, bastion, bulwark, keep.

**structure** building, edifice, erection, construction, fabric, form, formation, framework, arrangement, organization, composition, make-up.

**struggle** *v*, strive, fight, battle, contend, wrestle, compete, labour, endeavour, try, work. YIELD

*n*, fight, battle, skirmish, clash, conflict, strife, contention, contest. PEACE
effort, exertion, strain, trouble, labour, toil, work, endeavour.

**strut** swagger, prance, parade, stalk, flounce.

**stub** butt, end, tail, stump, counterfoil.

**stubborn** obstinate, mulish, pig-headed, headstrong, wilful, perverse, contrary, refractory, recalcitrant, contumacious, ungovernable, unmanageable, inflexible, unbending, unyielding, intractable, persistent, dogged, obdurate. AMENABLE

**stubby** short, squat, stumpy, dumpy, stocky, thickset. LONG
rough, stubbly, bristly. SMOOTH

**stuck** fixed, fast, lodged, jammed, embedded. FREE
baffled, mystified, stumped, nonplussed, puzzled, perplexed.

**student** pupil, scholar, learner, apprentice, trainee, undergraduate. MASTER

**studied** deliberate, wilful, premeditated, calculated, contrived, forced, planned, intentional, considered. SPONTANEOUS

**studious** scholarly, academic, intellectual, bookish, diligent, industrious, sedulous, assiduous, careful, attentive, thoughtful, reflective, serious, earnest. LAZY

**study** *v*, learn, swot (*inf*), work, read, peruse, pore over, scan, scrutinize, examine, investigate, research, consider, weigh, ponder, meditate, muse, reflect, cogitate, ruminate. IGNORE
*n*, learning, reading, work, application, thought, reflection, contemplation, meditation, attention, consideration, research, investigation, analysis, examination, scrutiny, inquiry, survey.

**stuff** *v*, fill, pack, cram, crowd, jam, press, squeeze, force, thrust, shove, ram.
*n*, cloth, fabric, material, matter, substance, essence.
belongings, effects, things, gear, paraphernalia, trappings, goods, chattels, possessions.
rubbish, nonsense, humbug, bunkum, balderdash, rot.

**stuffing** padding, packing, wadding, filling.
forcemeat, dressing.

**stuffy** close, airless, sultry, oppressive, musty, fusty, stale. FRESH
dull, uninteresting, stodgy, old-fashioned, square (*inf*), strait-laced, staid, prim, priggish, conservative, pompous.

**stumble** trip, fall, lurch, stagger, flounder, blunder, err, falter.

**stumble upon,** happen upon, chance upon, come across, find, discover. MISS

**stump** *n*, trunk, remnant, stub, butt, end.
*v*, baffle, mystify, nonplus, puzzle, perplex, confuse, confound. ENLIGHTEN
stamp, stomp (*inf*), trudge, plot, lumber, clump, clomp.

**stun** stupefy, daze, knock out, shock, amaze, astound, astonish, overwhelm, flabbergast (*inf*), bowl over (*inf*), stagger, dumbfound.

**stunt** feat, exploit, trick, act, deed.

**stunted** undersized, dwarfish, pygmy, diminutive, short, small, little, tiny. GIANT

**stupefy** benumb, stun, daze, bemuse, shock, amaze, astound, astonish, stagger, dumbfound, confound, confuse.

**stupendous** astounding, astonishing, amazing, staggering, wonderful, marvellous, extraordinary, phenomenal, fantastic, fabulous, tremendous, immense, vast, colossal, prodigious, massive, enormous, huge, gigantic. ORDINARY

**stupid** unintelligent, dull, slow, thick, dense, brainless, witless, dim-witted, simple, feeble-minded, foolish, silly, idiotic, asinine, inane, absurd, ridiculous, ludicrous, senseless, pointless, imprudent, unwise, rash, irresponsible. INTELLIGENT
stupefied, stunned, dazed, groggy, sluggish, torpid.

**stupor** coma, unconsciousness, daze, trance, numbness, stupefaction, torpor, lethargy, sluggishness.

**sturdy** strong, powerful, brawny, muscular, strapping, stalwart, robust, hardy, lusty, hale, hearty, healthy, vigorous, sound, solid, stout, tough, substantial, durable, firm, staunch. WEAK

**stutter** stammer, hesitate, pause, falter, stumble.

**style** *n*, manner, mode, method, way, approach, fashion, design, cut, shape, form, kind, type, sort, tone, tenor.
vogue, mode, fashion, trend, chic, elegance, smartness, taste, refinement, culture, sophistication, urbanity.
*v*, design, fashion, cut, shape, tailor, adapt.

name, call, designate, denominate, dub, label.

**stylish** fashionable, modish, chic, smart, elegant, classy (*inf*), suave, urbane, sophisticated. DOWDY

**suave** urbane, sophisticated, smooth, polite, courteous, civil, agreeable, pleasant, charming, gracious, affable. RUDE

**subconscious** inner, innermost, deep, hidden, latent, repressed, suppressed, unconscious, subliminal.

**subdue** conquer, vanquish, subjugate, rout, crush, defeat, overwhelm, overpower, overcome, master, control, discipline, humble, quell, check, curb, restrain, suppress, repress, reduce, moderate, soften, tone down, mute.

**subject** *n*, topic, theme, substance, point, object, matter, affair, issue, question.

patient, client, case, victim, guinea pig (*inf*), dependant, subordinate, citizen.

*adj*, subordinate, dependent, subservient, inferior, subjugated, obedient. RULING

exposed, vulnerable, open, susceptible, liable, prone. IMMUNE

conditional, dependent, depending, contingent.

*v*, expose, lay open, put through, treat, submit.

subdue, subjugate, quell, conquer, vanquish, crush, master, subordinate.

**subjection** subjugation, mastery, conquest, defeat, enslavement, servitude, subordination, dependence. INDEPENDENCE

**subjective** internal, mental, nonobjective, personal, biased, prejudiced, idiosyncratic. OBJECTIVE

**subjugate** conquer, vanquish, rout, defeat, overwhelm, overpower, overcome, master, crush, quell, subdue, humble, tame, discipline, subject, enslave, oppress. LIBERATE

**sublimate** refine, purify, exalt, uplift, heighten, elevate. DEGRADE

divert, redirect, transfer, channel.

**sublime** exalted, noble, dignified, eminent, lofty, elevated, glorious, superb, magnificent, grand, august, stately, majestic, imposing. RIDICULOUS

**submerge** submerse, immerse, plunge, dive, dip, duck, sink, drown, inundate, flood, deluge, engulf, overwhelm. SURFACE

**submissive** docile, tractable, yielding, compliant, acquiescent, amenable, accommodating, obliging, obedient, deferential, humble, meek, patient, resigned, passive, subservient, servile, obsequious. OBSTINATE

**submit** yield, surrender, capitulate, succumb, acquiesce, resign oneself, bow, bend, stoop, defer, obey, comply, conform. RESIST

refer, present, hand in, tender, offer, proffer, propose, advance, put forward, suggest. WITHDRAW

**subordinate** *adj*, inferior, lesser, lower, minor, junior, subaltern, subservient, dependent, subject, secondary, subsidiary, ancillary, auxiliary. CHIEF

*n*, inferior, junior, subaltern, hireling, assistant, dependant, subject. SUPERIOR

**subscribe** pledge, promise, pay, contribute, donate, chip in (*inf*).

endorse, support, assent, consent, agree, approve, countenance.

**subsequent** succeeding, following, ensuing, future, successive, consequent, later, next. PREVIOUS

**subservient** obsequious, servile, submissive, deferential, slavish, sycophantic, subordinate, inferior, dependent, subject. INDEPENDENT

instrumental, useful, helpful, ancillary, subsidiary, auxiliary.

**subside** abate, let up, moderate, lessen, diminish, lull, quieten, wane, ebb, dwindle, peter out. INCREASE

sink, descend, decline, lower, settle, fall, drop, cave in, collapse. RISE

**subsidence** sinking, descent, settling, fall, diminution, abatement.

**subsidiary** auxiliary, supplementary, ancillary, accessory, aiding, assistant, helpful, instrumental, subservient, inferior, lesser, subordinate. PRIMARY

**subsidy** aid, grant, allowance, contribution, assistance, help, support.

**subsist** exist, be, live, survive, last, continue, endure, remain, maintain, keep going, cope, make ends meet. DIE

**subsistence** food, nourishment, sustenance, upkeep, maintenance, keep, support, living, existence, being.

**substance** matter, material, stuff, fabric, body, element, solidity, reality, actuality, substantiality.

essence, gist, meaning, significance, sense, drift, import, point, subject, theme.
wealth, means, resources, property, estate.
**substantial** large, big, considerable, sizable, important, significant. SMALL
firm, strong, solid, stout, sound, durable. FLIMSY
real, actual, material, corporeal, genuine, true, valid, positive. IMAGINARY
wealthy, rich, prosperous, well-to-do, powerful, influential. POOR
**substantiate** prove, establish, confirm, verify, validate, authenticate, corroborate, bear out. REFUTE
**substitute** *v*, replace, exchange, change, interchange, commute, swap (*inf*), deputize, stand in, cover, relieve.
*n*, replacement, relief, surrogate, agent, deputy, proxy, understudy, stand-in, equivalent.
**subterfuge** artifice, stratagem, wile, ruse, trick, device, dodge, evasion, shift, manoeuvre, deception, excuse, pretext.
**subtle** faint, delicate, nice, refined, slight, implied, indirect. OBVIOUS
astute, shrewd, keen, acute, penetrating, discerning, discriminating, deep. STUPID
sly, cunning, crafty, wily, artful, designing, Machiavellian, clever, smart. ARTLESS
**subtract** deduct, take away, remove, withdraw. ADD
**suburbs** outskirts, environs, precincts, purlieus, neighbourhood, suburbia, edge, periphery. CENTRE
**subversive** *adj*, revolutionary, insurrectionary, seditious, disruptive, riotous, destructive.
*n*, rebel, revolutionary, insurrectionary, saboteur, traitor, seditionary.
**subvert** overthrow, overturn, upset, disrupt, demolish, destroy, undermine. CONSERVE
corrupt, deprave, pervert, vitiate, contaminate, poison.
**succeed** thrive, prosper, flourish, make good, triumph, prevail, work. FAIL
follow, ensue, supervene, come next, inherit, accede, replace, take over. PRECEDE
**success** prosperity, luck, fortune, triumph, victory, achievement, attainment, accomplishment, fame, celebrity, hit (*inf*). FAILURE
**successful** prosperous, thriving, flourishing, lucky, fortunate, triumphant, victorious, famous, wealthy, profitable, rewarding, paying, lucrative, favourable. UNSUCCESSFUL
**succession** chain, run, course, train, series, procession, cycle, concatenation, sequence, progression, order, consecution, continuity.
accession, inheritance, promotion.
descendants, posterity, lineage, descent.
**succinct** brief, short, concise, terse, pithy, laconic, curt, compact, condensed, compendious, summary. PROLIX
**succour** *n*, help, aid, assistance, support, relief, comfort.
*v*, help, aid, assist, support, relieve, comfort, nurse, minister to.
**succulent** juicy, sappy, fleshy, moist, luscious, lush, rich. DRY
**succumb** surrender, yield, give way, give in, submit, capitulate, die. RESIST
**such** like, similar, so, so much.
**suck** absorb, draw in, take in, extract.
**suck up to,** fawn on, truckle, toady, curry favour, flatter.
**sudden** abrupt, hasty, quick, rapid, swift, unexpected, unanticipated, unforeseen, brief, momentary. GRADUAL
**sue** prosecute, summon, take to court, prefer charges, indict, charge. DEFEND
solicit, petition, appeal, beg, plead, implore, entreat, beseech.
**suffer** undergo, experience, feel, endure, go through, sustain, bear, tolerate, brook, stand, put up with (*inf*), support.
ache, hurt, be in pain, grieve.
**suffering** pain, agony, affliction, torment, torture, discomfort, distress, anguish, misery, grief, ordeal. EASE
**sufficient** enough, adequate, ample, abundant, plentiful, satisfactory. DEFICIENT
**suffocate** asphyxiate, smother, stifle, choke, strangle.
**suffrage** franchise, ballot, vote, voice.
**suffuse** cover, overspread, colour, bathe, imbue, permeate, transfuse, infuse, steep. DRAIN
**suggest** propose, submit, put forward, advance, advise, recommend.
hint, intimate, imply, insinuate, evoke.
**suggestion** proposal, proposition, plan, idea, advice, recommendation.
implication, insinuation, intimation, indication, hint, trace, touch, suspicion.

**suggestive** evocative, reminiscent, redolent, indicative.
ribald, bawdy, dirty, smutty, obscene, indecent, risqué, racy, crude, vulgar.

**suit** *v*, befit, become, conform, harmonize, match, fit, correspond, accord, agree, satisfy, gratify, please.
adapt, fashion, proportion, adjust, accommodate, fit.
*n*, outfit, ensemble, costume, clothing.
lawsuit, case, action, trial, cause, proceeding, litigation.
petition, appeal, plea, prayer, request, entreaty, solicitation, addresses, courtship.

**suitable** appropriate, apt, apposite, fit, fitting, right, proper, seemly, becoming, relevant, pertinent, convenient, opportune, acceptable, agreeable. UNSUITABLE

**suite** set, series, collection, apartment.
retinue, train, entourage, attendants, followers, escort, bodyguard.

**suitor** beau, gallant, admirer, lover, wooer.

**sulk** pout, mope, brood, be put out.

**sullen** sulky, morose, scowling, glowering, cross, peevish, petulant, moody, surly, sour, bitter, resentful, put out, gloomy, sombre. CHEERFUL

**sully** soil, dirty, spot, stain, blemish, pollute, contaminate, taint, tarnish, defile, disgrace, dishonour, defame. CLEAN

**sultry** close, oppressive, muggy, humid, hot, sticky, stuffy, stifling. COOL

**sum** *n*, total, aggregate, tally, score, amount, quantity, whole, entirety, totality. PART
*v*, add, add up, total, tot up, count, tally, reckon, calculate.
**sum up,** summarize, epitomize, recapitulate, review.

**summarize** sum up, epitomize, encapsulate, outline, recapitulate, review, condense, abridge. AMPLIFY

**summary** *n*, abstract, synopsis, précis, compendium, conspectus, digest, epitome, outline, résumé, recapitulation, review. AMPLIFICATION
*adj*, quick, rapid, hasty, cursory, short, brief, concise, succinct, pithy, terse, curt, laconic, condensed, compendious, compact. LENGTHY

**summit** top, crown, cap, peak, pinnacle, apex, vertex, apogee, height, zenith, acme, culmination. BASE

**summon** call, invite, bid, send for, convoke, convene, muster, assemble. DISMISS

**sumptuous** costly, expensive, dear, extravagant, lavish, luxurious, rich, opulent, magnificent, splendid, gorgeous, grand, superb, plush (*inf*), de luxe. POOR

**sundry** various, diverse, assorted, miscellaneous, different, several.

**sunless** dark, black, grey, cloudy, murky, gloomy, dismal, bleak, sombre, dreary, depressing, cheerless. SUNNY

**sunny** bright, sunshiny, sunlit, shining, radiant, clear, cloudless, fine, summery. DULL
cheerful, cheery, blithe, jolly, genial, happy, joyful, buoyant, optimistic. GLOOMY

**super** wonderful, marvellous, excellent, outstanding, glorious, magnificent, splendid, superb, sensational, smashing (*inf*). AWFUL

**superannuated** old, aged, senile, decrepit, antiquated, passé, obsolete, retired, pensioned off.

**superb** excellent, first-rate, matchless, peerless, outstanding, superior, marvellous, wonderful, magnificent, splendid, glorious, gorgeous, sumptuous, fine, exquisite, grand. POOR

**supercilious** arrogant, haughty, insolent, contemptuous, scornful, disdainful, lofty, lordly, proud, vain, domineering, overbearing, patronizing, condescending. HUMBLE

**superficial** surface, exterior, external, outer, shallow, slight, trivial, frivolous, empty. DEEP
apparent, seeming, ostensible, outward. ACTUAL
hasty, cursory, slapdash, perfunctory. THOROUGH

**superfluity** superabundance, surfeit, surplus, excess, glut, plethora. LACK

**superfluous** superabundant, supererogatory, redundant, excessive, extra, surplus, unnecessary, needless. DEFICIENT

**superhuman** supernatural, preternatural, paranormal, divine, herculean, prodigious, phenomenal, miraculous. NATURAL

**superintend** supervise, manage, run, administer, oversee, direct, control.

**superintendent** supervisor, overseer, inspector, director, manager, administrator, chief, boss (*inf*).

**superior** *adj*, better, higher, greater, excellent, first-rate, exceptional, outstanding, superlative, supreme, matchless, peerless, choice, fine. INFERIOR
*n*, chief, boss (*inf*), manager, director, supervisor, senior. JUNIOR

**superlative** supreme, transcendent, superior, peerless, matchless, incomparable, unrivalled, excellent, first-class, first-rate, outstanding. POOR

**supernatural** preternatural, unnatural, abnormal, paranormal, unearthly, spiritual, mystical, occult, mysterious, miraculous. NORMAL

**supernumerary** extra, superfluous, redundant, surplus, excess, spare, odd.

**supersede** supplant, displace, oust, usurp, replace, succeed, discard, set aside, override, overrule.

**supervene** ensue, follow, succeed, occur, happen, transpire.

**supervise** oversee, superintend, administer, direct, manage, run, handle, control, watch over.

**supervision** direction, management, oversight, superintendence, control, guidance, surveillance, care, charge.

**supine** recumbent, prostrate, prone, flat, horizontal. UPRIGHT
lethargic, apathetic, indifferent, sluggish, torpid, languid, listless, lifeless, inactive, inert, lazy, idle, indolent, otiose, slothful. ENERGETIC

**supple** pliable, pliant, flexible, elastic, plastic, yielding, lithe, lissom, limber. STIFF

**supplement** *n*, addition, addendum, appendix, postscript, extension, complement.
*v*, add, augment, extend, top up, complement. REDUCE

**supplementary** additional, complementary, extra, ancillary, auxiliary, secondary, subsidiary.

**suppliant** *adj*, supplicant, supplicating, petitioning, entreating, beseeching, praying, imploring, asking, begging.
*n*, supplicant, petitioner, suitor, applicant.

**supplicate** petition, solicit, beg, plead, crave, beseech, ask, pray, implore, entreat, importune. DEMAND

**supplication** petition, solicitation, invocation, prayer, plea, entreaty, appeal, request.

**supply** *v*, provide, furnish, equip, stock, replenish, give, contribute, afford, yield, grant, bestow, satisfy. WITHHOLD
*n*, provision, stock, store, hoard, reserve, quantity, fund.

**support** *v*, bear, carry, hold up, uphold, sustain, maintain, prop, brace, buttress, bolster. DROP
back, second, further, forward, encourage, abet, help, assist, aid, promote, advocate, champion, defend, finance, subsidize, fund, foster, nurture. OPPOSE
endorse, verify, confirm, corroborate, substantiate. REFUTE
tolerate, put up with (*inf*), stomach, brook, bear, endure.
*n*, prop, brace, stay, base, foundation, stanchion, upright.
sustenance, subsistence, maintenance, keep, upkeep.
backing, encouragement, furtherance, help, assistance, aid, patronage, sponsorship, protection, friendship. OPPOSITION

**supporter** backer, patron, sponsor, advocate, champion, adherent, follower, admirer, fan, well-wisher, ally, colleague. OPPONENT

**suppose** presume, assume, presuppose, postulate, surmise, conjecture, guess, suspect, imagine, fancy, believe, opine, think, conclude, judge, imply. KNOW

**supposed** hypothetical, assumed, accepted, so-called, alleged.

**supposition** assumption, presumption, presupposition, postulate, hypothesis, theory, surmise, conjecture, guess, speculation, idea, notion. KNOWLEDGE

**suppress** restrain, curb, check, repress, smother, stifle, silence, conceal, withhold, censor, quash, quell, crush, overpower, conquer, stamp out, extinguish.

**supremacy** ascendancy, superiority, preeminence, primacy, sovereignty, rule, mastery, dominion, power, authority. SUBJECTION

**supreme** highest, greatest, utmost, extreme, best, superlative, top, paramount, pre-eminent, first, foremost, leading, principal, chief, main, sovereign, predominant. LOWEST

**sure** certain, positive, definite, convinced, persuaded, satisfied, confident, assured, decided. DOUBTFUL

reliable, dependable, trustworthy, trusty, guaranteed, unfailing, infallible, foolproof, unquestionable, indisputable, steady, firm, stable, secure, safe. PRECARIOUS
bound, destined, inevitable, unavoidable, inescapable.

**surety** security, guarantee, warranty, indemnity, insurance, pledge, bond, bail, deposit, hostage, guarantor, sponsor.

**surface** exterior, outside, façade, veneer, appearance, covering, coating, top. INTERIOR

**surfeit** *n*, excess, surplus, glut, superabundance, superfluity, plethora, satiety. DEFICIENCY
*v*, sate, satiate, glut, cloy, gorge, overfeed, stuff, cram. STARVE

**surge** *n*, rush, gush, flow, outpouring, rise, increase, swell, billow, wave.
*v*, rush, gush, rise, swell, billow, roll, heave, undulate.

**surly** sullen, sulky, cross, irritable, testy, touchy, irascible, crabbed, crusty, ill-tempered, gruff, brusque, curt, churlish, uncivil, rude. AFFABLE

**surmise** *v*, infer, guess, conjecture, suppose, imagine, suspect, presume, assume, conclude, deduce, opine. KNOW
*n*, inference, assumption, presumption, supposition, guess, conjecture, hypothesis, idea, thought. KNOWLEDGE

**surmount** overcome, conquer, vanquish, triumph over, scale, climb, ascend, top. SUCCUMB

**surpass** exceed, pass, transcend, excel, outstrip, outdo, beat, overshadow, eclipse.

**surplus** *n*, excess, surfeit, superabundance, plethora, residue, remainder, rest, balance. DEFICIT
*adj*, extra, spare, excess, superfluous, remaining.

**surprise** *v*, amaze, astound, astonish, stun, stagger, flabbergast (*inf*), bowl over (*inf*), startle, catch.
*n*, amazement, astonishment, wonder, shock, start, bolt from the blue.

**surprising** amazing, astounding, astonishing, staggering, startling, unexpected, incredible, extraordinary, remarkable. ORDINARY

**surrender** *v*, relinquish, part with, yield, hand over, give up, renounce, forgo, resign, abdicate, cede, capitulate, submit, give in, succumb. HOLD
*n*, capitulation, submission, yielding, relinquishment, renunciation, abdication, resignation.

**surreptitious** clandestine, stealthy, covert, underhand, furtive, sly, secret, hidden, unauthorized. OPEN

**surrogate** substitute, stand-in, proxy, deputy, agent, representative.

**surround** encircle, circle, encompass, environ, enclose, gird, girdle, hem in, fence in, besiege.

**surroundings** environment, milieu, setting, background, environs, neighbourhood.

**surveillance** supervision, watch, observation, inspection, scrutiny, care, control, superintendence, direction. FREEDOM

**survey** *v*, view, scan, scrutinize, observe, contemplate, review, study, examine, inspect, reconnoitre. IGNORE
assess, appraise, take stock of, size up, estimate, calculate, measure, plot.
*n*, review, study, examination, inspection, scrutiny, investigation, inquiry, assessment.

**survive** outlive, outlast, live, persist, last, continue, abide, remain, endure, subsist. DIE

**susceptible** vulnerable, subject, given, liable, disposed, inclined, prone, open, receptive, sensitive, impressionable.

**suspect** *v*, doubt, mistrust, distrust, disbelieve. BELIEVE
surmise, guess, conjecture, think, believe, imagine, fancy, suppose, assume, presume. KNOW
*adj*, suspicious, questionable, doubtful, dubious.

**suspend** hang, dangle, swing.
postpone, defer, delay, put off, withhold, shelve, adjourn, stop, stay, interrupt, discontinue, arrest, debar, expel. CONTINUE

**suspense** uncertainty, doubt, indecision, irresolution, hesitation, vacillation, insecurity, anxiety, expectation, anticipation, excitement.

**suspicion** doubt, distrust, mistrust, scepticism, misgiving, wariness. TRUST
surmise, guess, conjecture, supposition, thought, idea.
trace, hint, touch, suggestion, *soupçon*.

**suspicious** distrustful, mistrustful, sceptical, unbelieving, wary, apprehensive. TRUSTFUL doubtful, dubious, questionable, suspect, shady (*inf*), strange, queer.

**sustain** support, uphold, hold up, carry, bear. DROP
suffer, undergo, experience, endure, withstand.
maintain, keep up, continue, prolong, nurture, nourish, feed, strengthen, foster, help, aid, assist, relieve, comfort.
uphold, endorse, verify, validate, justify, confirm, establish, ratify, sanction, approve. OVERRULE

**sustenance** nourishment, nutrition, nutriment, food, subsistence, maintenance, livelihood, upkeep, keep, support. STARVATION

**swagger** strut, prance, parade, show off (*inf*), vaunt, boast, brag, bluster.

**swallow** gulp, down (*inf*), eat, drink, consume, devour, absorb, assimilate, engulf, overwhelm. VOMIT
believe, fall for, buy (*inf*), accept, take, tolerate, suffer, endure.

**swamp** *n*, marsh, bog, morass, fen, slough, quagmire.
*v*, flood, inundate, deluge, drench, soak, saturate, overwhelm, engulf, swallow up, submerge, immerse, sink.

**swap** exchange, barter, trade, switch, interchange.

**swarm** *n*, throng, crowd, multitude, mob, horde, host, herd, drove, flock, bevy, shoal, mass, concourse.
*v*, throng, crowd, cluster, flock, mass, teem, abound, crawl, overrun, infest. SCATTER

**swarthy** dark, dusky, dark-skinned, dark-complexioned, black, brown. PALE

**swathe** swaddle, bandage, bind, wrap, enwrap, envelop, fold, enfold, drape, clothe. UNWRAP

**sway** *v*, swing, rock, oscillate, wave, totter, reel, lean, incline, fluctuate, vacillate.
influence, move, persuade, win over, control, guide, direct, govern.
*n*, influence, control, command, power, authority, dominion, rule, sovereignty, ascendancy. SUBJECTION

**swear** affirm, avow, aver, asseverate, assert, declare, vow, promise, testify, depose. DENY
blaspheme, curse.

**sweat** *v*, perspire, exude, secrete.
*n*, perspiration, diaphoresis, sweating, exudation, secretion.

**sweep** *v*, brush, clean, clear.
*n*, arc, curve, bend, stroke, swing, compass, scope, range, stretch, extent, reach, span, spread.

**sweeping** comprehensive, wide-ranging, all-inclusive, all-embracing, broad, wide, extensive, global, universal, general, blanket, indiscriminate, wholesale. SPECIFIC

**sweet** sugary, sweetened, honeyed, saccharine, syrupy, tasty, toothsome, luscious, delicious. SOUR
fragrant, aromatic, balmy, redolent, perfumed, scented, sweet-smelling, fresh, clean, pure, wholesome. FOUL
dulcet, mellifluous, melodious, musical, tuneful, harmonious, euphonious, mellow, soft, silvery. DISCORDANT
attractive, appealing, charming, pleasant, agreeable, amiable, lovable, kind, gentle, dear, beloved, precious. NASTY

**swell** expand, dilate, spread, extend, inflate, distend, bloat, puff up, bulge, billow, balloon, enlarge, increase, augment, amplify, intensify. SHRINK

**swelling** bulge, bump, lump, protuberance, tumefaction, tumescence, distension, inflation, dilation, enlargement.

**swerve** turn, veer, stray, drift, wander, deviate, diverge, deflect.

**swift** fast, rapid, quick, speedy, fleet, expeditious, brisk, nimble, prompt, sudden, hurried, hasty. SLOW

**swimmingly** easily, effortlessly, smoothly, successfully.

**swindle** *v*, defraud, cheat, fleece, rook (*inf*), deceive, trick, overcharge, diddle (*inf*), do (*inf*), con (*inf*).
*n*, fraud, trickery, deception, sharp practice, racket (*inf*), con trick (*inf*), rip-off (*inf*). HONESTY

**swindler** fraud, con man (*inf*), crook (*inf*), trickster, cheat, sharper, impostor, charlatan, mountebank, rogue, scoundrel.

**swing** *v*, sway, oscillate, rock, vacillate, waver, wave, hang, dangle, veer, turn, whirl, spin, pivot, wheel, rotate.
*n*, oscillation, vacillation, fluctuation, sway, rock, sweep, rhythm.

**swirl** whirl, eddy, turn, gyrate, twist, spin.

**switch** *n*, rod, stick, birch, cane, twig.
change, shift, about-turn, reversal, exchange, swap (*inf*).
*v*, change, shift, turn, interchange, exchange, swap (*inf*), substitute, replace.

**swivel** turn, spin, pivot, rotate, revolve.

**swoop** *v*, descend, dive, plunge, sweep, rush, pounce, seize, snatch.
*n*, descent, dive, plunge, rush, pounce, snatch.

**sybarite** sensualist, voluptuary, epicure, hedonist. ASCETIC

**sycophant** flatterer, fawner, toady, truckler, yes man, lickspittle, bootlicker (*inf*), cringer, groveller, parasite, hanger-on.

**sycophantic** flattering, fawning, ingratiating, servile, obsequious, slavish, grovelling, cringing. INDEPENDENT

**syllabus** summary, synopsis, abstract, digest, conspectus, résumé, précis, outline, prospectus, curriculum.

**symbol** token, emblem, sign, representation, character, figure, letter, badge, logo.

**symbolic** representative, emblematic, typical, allegorical, figurative, metaphorical.

**symbolize** represent, stand for, signify, mean, denote, betoken, exemplify, typify, embody, personify.

**symmetry** balance, proportion, harmony, congruity, regularity, evenness, similarity, correspondence. ASYMMETRY

**sympathetic** compassionate, caring, concerned, supportive, affectionate, kind, warm, tender, considerate, understanding. UNSYMPATHETIC

**sympathize** pity, feel for, commiserate, condole, console, comfort, understand.
side with, back, support, agree.

**sympathy** compassion, concern, pity, commiseration, condolence, tenderness, thoughtfulness, understanding, empathy. INDIFFERENCE
agreement, accord, harmony, rapport, affinity. ANTIPATHY

**symptom** sign, indication, mark, symbol, token, warning, characteristic, manifestation, syndrome.

**synchronous** simultaneous, coincident, concurrent, contemporaneous.

**syndicate** trust, cartel, combine, alliance, federation, union.

**synonymous** equivalent, equal, tantamount, similar, identical, interchangeable. OPPOSITE

**synopsis** outline, précis, résumé, abstract, digest, epitome, condensation, abridgment, conspectus, compendium, summary.

**synthesis** combination, amalgamation, union, fusion, amalgam, compound, composite, blend. ANALYSIS

**synthetic** artificial, man-made, imitation, mock, ersatz, fake. GENUINE

**system** method, procedure, technique, approach, way, practice, plan, scheme, order, structure, arrangement, organization. CHAOS

**systematic** methodical, businesslike, regular, orderly, organized, planned. UNSYSTEMATIC

# T

**table** board, slab, counter, stand, bench, desk.
diagram, chart, graph, plan, index, tabulation, inventory, list, catalogue, register, schedule.

**tableau** representation, picture, scene, spectacle, pageant.

**taboo** prohibited, banned, forbidden, not allowed. PERMITTED

**tacit** implied, implicit, understood, inferred, unstated, unexpressed, unspoken, silent. AVOWED

**taciturn** silent, quiet, reserved, reticent, uncommunicative, tight-lipped, mum, mute. TALKATIVE

**tack** *n*, nail, pin, stitch.
direction, bearing, course, way, path, approach, method, procedure, line.
*v*, nail, pin, fasten, fix, attach, affix, append, annex, add.
stitch, baste.

**tackle** *n*, gear, equipment, rig, outfit, apparatus, trappings, impedimenta, paraphernalia, tools, implements.
*v*, undertake, attempt, try, begin, set about, embark on, turn one's hand to, deal with, take on, face, confront.
challenge, intercept, obstruct, stop, seize, grab, throw, bring down.

**tact** diplomacy, discretion, sensitivity, perception, discernment, finesse, savoir-faire, skill, dexterity, adroitness, judgment, sense. TACTLESSNESS

**tactful** diplomatic, discreet, prudent, politic, judicious, sensitive, perceptive, skilful, thoughtful, considerate, careful. TACTLESS

**tactics** strategy, plan, scheme, method, approach, policy, campaign, manoeuvres.

**tactless** undiplomatic, indiscreet, impolitic, imprudent, gauche, maladroit, clumsy, inept, thoughtless, inconsiderate, rude, impolite. TACTFUL

**tag** *n*, label, sticker, ticket, flap, tab.
*v*, label, mark, name, call, identify.
add, append, affix, attach, tack, trail, shadow, follow.

**tail** end, tip, extremity, conclusion, rear, rump. HEAD

**taint** *v*, contaminate, infect, poison, pollute, defile, befoul, begrime, dirty, soil, sully, tarnish, stain, besmirch, smear, spoil, ruin, blemish, blacken, vitiate, corrupt, brand, stigmatize, shame, disgrace. PURIFY
*n*, spot, stain, blot, blemish, flaw, defect, fault, stigma, shame, disgrace, infection, contamination, contagion, pollution.

**take** get, obtain, acquire, secure, gain, win, capture, catch, seize, grasp, clasp, grip, receive, accept, adopt, assume, have, hold, accommodate, pick, select, choose. LEAVE
subtract, deduct, take away, remove, carry off, appropriate, steal, purloin, pinch (*inf*), nick (*inf*). REPLACE
stand, put up with (*inf*), tolerate, brook, abide, bear, suffer, endure.
carry, bear, convey, transport, bring, escort, accompany, lead, conduct, guide, usher.
require, need, call for, demand.
attract, charm, captivate, fascinate, enchant, delight. REPEL
**take after,** resemble, favour (*inf*), be like, copy.
**take back,** retract, recant, unsay, disavow, withdraw.
regain, repossess, reclaim, recapture.
**take in,** understand, comprehend, grasp, absorb, assimilate.
include, embrace, encompass, cover, comprise, contain. EXCLUDE
accommodate, lodge, admit, let in.
deceive, trick, cheat, defraud, swindle, dupe, hoodwink.
**take on,** employ, hire, engage, retain, enlist. DISMISS
undertake, adopt, assume, tackle, face, challenge, contend with, compete with, oppose.
**take up,** occupy, cover, fill, use up, consume.
start, begin, continue, go on, resume, recommence. STOP

**tale** story, narration, account, narrative, novel, romance, fable, myth, legend, anecdote, yarn (*inf*), fiction, lie, fib, rumour.

**talent** gift, endowment, faculty, flair, knack, turn, bent, forte, genius, aptitude, ability, capacity, skill. INABILITY

**talk** *v*, speak, articulate, utter, express, say, communicate, converse, confer, parley, discuss, confabulate, gossip, chat, chatter, prattle, prate, natter.
*n*, speech, lecture, oration, address, discourse, harangue.
conversation, dialogue, confabulation, discussion, conference, chat, chatter, prattle, gossip, rumour, scandal.

**talkative** garrulous, loquacious, voluble, chatty, verbose, wordy, prolix. TACITURN

**tall** high, lofty, towering, elevated, big, giant. SHORT

**tally** *v*, agree, correspond, accord, coincide, match, harmonize, suit, fit, square. CLASH
*n*, score, total, count, record.
ticket, label, stub, counterfoil, mark, notch.

**tame** *adj*, domesticated, broken, fearless, unafraid, gentle, docile, tractable, submissive, subdued, meek, obedient. WILD
dull, flat, uninteresting, boring, tedious, insipid, vapid. EXCITING
*v*, domesticate, break, train, discipline, master, curb, subdue, moderate, soften, temper.

**tamper** meddle, interfere, mess about, fool around (*inf*), tinker, fiddle (*inf*), rig, corrupt.

**tang** flavour, taste, savour, relish, piquancy, pungency, odour, smell, smack, hint, trace, touch.

**tangible** palpable, tactile, perceptible, material, substantial, physical, corporeal, real, actual, positive, solid, concrete, evident, plain. INTANGIBLE

**tangle** *v*, entangle, ravel, snarl, mat, knot, twist, intertwine, interlace, interweave, confuse, complicate, involve, embroil, enmesh, ensnare, entrap. UNTANGLE
*n*, knot, snarl, mass, mess, jumble, muddle, confusion, complication, mix-up.

**tantalize** torment, torture, disappoint, frustrate, tease, taunt, titillate, provoke, tempt, entice. SATISFY

**tantamount** equivalent, equal, synonymous, commensurate, the same.

**tantrum** outburst, temper, rage, fit, paddy (*inf*).

**tap** *v*, rap, pat, touch, knock, hit, strike.
*n*, rap, pat, touch, knock, blow.

**taper** narrow, thin, diminish, decrease, dwindle, fade, lessen, die away.

**tardy** late, belated, overdue, delayed, retarded, slow, leisurely, sluggish, dilatory. PROMPT

**target** mark, objective, object, aim, goal, butt, victim.

**tariff** tax, impost, levy, duty, excise, toll, rate, charge, schedule, price list.

**tarnish** discolour, rust, dull, dim, stain, sully, soil, taint, blemish, spot, blot, besmirch, blacken. POLISH

**tarry** linger, loiter, dally, dawdle, delay, remain, stay, sojourn, abide, stop, rest, wait. MOVE

**tart** sour, acid, sharp, bitter, pungent, piquant. SWEET
biting, cutting, caustic, mordant, trenchant, incisive, acrimonious, sharp, barbed, curt, waspish, testy. MILD

**task** job, chore, duty, assignment, exercise, mission, undertaking, work, labour, toil, drudgery. LEISURE

**taste** *v*, smack, savour, relish, try, sample, sip, nibble.
experience, undergo, encounter, meet, know, feel.
*n*, flavour, savour, relish, tang, smack.
bit, morsel, mouthful, sample, bite, sip.
liking, fondness, predilection, penchant, appetite, longing, relish. AVERSION
perception, discernment, discrimination, judgment, appreciation, culture, cultivation, refinement, polish, elegance, style, delicacy, propriety.

**tasteful** refined, polished, cultured, cultivated, elegant, stylish, artistic, aesthetic, harmonious, restrained. TAWDRY

**tasteless** insipid, vapid, flavourless, bland, flat, stale, weak, watery, dull, tame, uninteresting, boring. TASTY
vulgar, coarse, crude, gross, tawdry, gaudy, flashy, showy, unrefined, inelegant, improper, indelicate. TASTEFUL

**tasty** savoury, sapid, palatable, toothsome, appetizing, delicious, delectable, luscious, scrumptious (*inf*). INSIPID

**tattle** *v*, gossip, tittle-tattle, gab (*inf*), chatter, prattle, prate, natter, blab, tell tales.
*n*, gossip, tittle-tattle, idle talk, chitchat, chatter, prattle.

**taunt** *v*, tease, torment, twit, mock, make fun of, jeer, sneer, ridicule, deride, insult, reproach, upbraid. RESPECT
*n*, gibe, jeer, sneer, insult, ridicule, derision, mockery.

**taut** tight, tense, stretched, strained. SLACK

**tautology** repetition, iteration, reiteration, verbosity, redundancy, pleonasm. CONCISENESS

**tawdry** flashy, showy, meretricious, loud, gaudy, garish, brummagem, cheap, vulgar. TASTEFUL

**tax** *n*, impost, levy, duty, excise, customs, toll, rate, charge, tariff, tribute.
*v*, assess, rate, charge, impose, exact, demand.
load, burden, encumber, strain, task, overload, overburden, wear out, exhaust, weary, tire. RELIEVE

**teach** educate, school, instruct, tutor, coach, train, ground, drill, discipline, tell, inform, enlighten, edify, explain, show, demonstrate, advise, guide, direct, warn.

**teacher** instructor, tutor, coach, trainer, educator, pedagogue, schoolmaster, schoolmistress, lecturer, professor.

**team** group, band, gang, crew, squad, side.

**tear** *v*, rip, rend, rive, split, divide, pull apart, rupture, shred, lacerate. MEND
race, speed, sprint, run, fly, shoot, dash, dart. AMBLE
*n*, rip, rent, split, rupture, laceration.

**tearful** weeping, crying, sobbing, in tears, lachrymose, weepy (*inf*), maudlin, sad, sorrowful, distressing, pathetic, pitiful, poignant. HAPPY

**tease** torment, plague, harass, pester, bother, worry, annoy, irritate, vex, provoke, tantalize, taunt, twit, rag (*inf*), rib (*inf*), mock, make fun of. PACIFY

**technique** manner, style, method, way, approach, system, procedure, line, course.
skill, art, facility, knack, know-how (*inf*), proficiency, expertise.

**tedious** boring, monotonous, dull, tiresome, wearisome, long-drawn-out, prosaic, banal, uninteresting, dreary, humdrum, routine, flat, vapid. INTERESTING

**teeming** swarming, bristling, crawling, alive, full, overflowing, prolific, abundant. EMPTY

**teeter** sway, rock, stagger, totter, wobble, waver, seesaw.

**telephone** *n*, phone, blower (*inf*).
*v*, phone, call, ring, buzz (*inf*), dial.

**tell** relate, narrate, report, recount, recite, rehearse, describe.
notify, let know, inform, impart, communicate, make known, disclose, reveal, divulge, publish, confess, blab, utter, declare. SUPPRESS
command, order, instruct, direct, require, bid.
distinguish, differentiate, discriminate, discern, make out, discover.
count, enumerate, reckon, compute, calculate, tally.

**tell off,** reprimand, tick off (*inf*), scold, chide, berate, upbraid, reprove, rebuke, reproach, censure.

**telling** striking, forceful, effective, cogent, influential, powerful, potent. WEAK

**temerity** rashness, recklessness, foolhardiness, heedlessness, boldness, audacity, nerve (*inf*), gall (*inf*), impudence, effrontery. TIMIDITY

**temper** *n*, mood, humour, frame of mind, disposition, temperament, constitution, nature, character, tone.
tantrum, paddy (*inf*), rage, fury, anger, passion, pique, irritation, annoyance, irritability, peevishness, petulance. CALMNESS
calmness, composure, cool (*inf*), self-control, equanimity. RAGE
*v*, moderate, mitigate, abate, lessen, palliate, allay, assuage, mollify, soften, tone down, modify, qualify. INTENSIFY
toughen, harden, anneal.

**temperament** character, nature, disposition, temper, mood, humour, frame of mind, spirit, constitution.

**temperamental** excitable, volatile, mercurial, capricious, highly-strung, sensitive, moody, irritable, touchy, impatient. PLACID
erratic, unpredictable, unreliable, inconsistent. RELIABLE

**temperate** mild, fair, clement, balmy, cool, calm.
moderate, self-controlled, self-restrained, calm, composed, sensible, reasonable, abstinent, abstemious, continent, sober, teetotal. INTEMPERATE

**tempest** storm, squall, hurricane, tornado, typhoon, cyclone. CALM
commotion, furore, upheaval, tumult, turmoil, disturbance. PEACE

**tempestuous** stormy, squally, windy, blustery, turbulent, violent, wild, intense, impassioned, furious, boisterous. CALM

**temporal** secular, lay, profane, mundane, earthly, worldly, terrestrial, mortal, carnal, material. SPIRITUAL
passing, transient, transitory, fleeting, ephemeral, evanescent, momentary, temporary, impermanent. PERMANENT

**temporary** impermanent, passing, transient, transitory, fleeting, ephemeral, evanescent, brief, short, short-lived, momentary. LASTING
provisional, makeshift, stopgap. PERMANENT

**temporize** delay, procrastinate, fence, hedge, equivocate, tergiversate, play for time, stall.

**tempt** allure, lure, entice, seduce, tantalize, invite, court, bait, provoke, inveigle, persuade, coax, attract, draw. REPEL

**tempting** attractive, alluring, inviting, appealing, seductive, appetizing. REPULSIVE

**tenable** sound, rational, reasonable, plausible, believable, maintainable, defensible. UNTENABLE

**tenacious** stubborn, obstinate, dogged, persistent, pertinacious, determined, resolute, steadfast, set, firm, adamant.
retentive, cohesive, tough, strong, forceful, adhesive, clinging.

**tenant** lodger, renter, lessee, leaseholder, holder, occupant, occupier, resident. LANDLORD

**tend**[1] incline, gravitate, lean, trend, be inclined, be disposed, head, aim, point, bear, lead, influence, contribute, conduce. DIVERGE

**tend**[2] care for, attend to, minister to, wait on, serve, watch over, protect, guard, take care of, nurse, nurture. NEGLECT

**tendency** leaning, bent, turn, inclination, disposition, propensity, proclivity, penchant, partiality, predilection, bias, proneness, susceptibility, gravitation, bearing, drift, trend. AVERSION

**tender¹** *adj*, soft, delicate, fragile, feeble, weak. TOUGH
gentle, kind, humane, merciful, compassionate, sympathetic, caring, thoughtful, tender-hearted, soft-hearted, sensitive, warm, affectionate, loving, fond, emotional. HARSH
callow, immature, inexperienced, raw, green, young, youthful, impressionable, vulnerable.
sore, painful, sensitive, inflamed.

**tender²** *v*, proffer, offer, present, extend, propose, suggest, volunteer, submit. WITHHOLD
*n*, offer, proposal, suggestion, bid.
currency, money.

**tenebrous** dark, gloomy, sombre, shady, shadowy, unlit, murky, obscure, dusky. LIGHT

**tenet** dogma, doctrine, principle, precept, maxim, canon, creed, belief, conviction, opinion, view.

**tenor** meaning, purport, intent, sense, gist, aim, direction, drift, trend, course.

**tense** *adj*, tight, taut, rigid, stiff, stretched, strained, nervous, keyed up, wound up (*inf*), worked up, jumpy, edgy, stressful, nerve-racking. SLACK
*v*, brace, tighten, strain, stretch. RELAX

**tension** tightness, tautness, rigidity, stiffness, stretch, strain, stress, pressure, nervousness, anxiety, agitation, excitement, suspense, apprehension. RELAXATION

**tentative** experimental, exploratory, probative, probatory, trial, speculative, provisional, hesitant, unsure, uncertain, faltering. SURE

**tenuous** flimsy, insubstantial, insignificant, slight, slender, slim, thin, attenuated, fine, delicate. SUBSTANTIAL

**tenure** holding, possession, occupancy, occupation, residence, tenancy, incumbency, term.

**tepid** lukewarm, warm, cool, half-hearted, apathetic.

**tergiversate** apostatize, change sides, desert, defect, renege.
vacillate, shift, fence, hedge, equivocate, prevaricate.

**term** *n*, name, title, denomination, designation, word, phrase, expression.
time, period, spell, space, span, interval, duration, stretch, season, session.
*v*, call, name, designate, denominate, style, dub, christen, entitle.

**termagant** shrew, scold, virago, harridan, vixen.

**terminal** *adj*, bounding, limiting, closing, concluding, final, ultimate, fatal, lethal, deadly, mortal, incurable.
*n*, end, termination, terminus, boundary, bound, limit, extremity.

**terminate** end, conclude, complete, finish, close, stop, cease, discontinue, abort, expire, lapse. BEGIN

**termination** end, conclusion, completion, close, finish, ending, issue, result, consequence. BEGINNING

**terminus** end, extremity, terminal, depot, station, limit, boundary, goal, target.

**terms** conditions, provisions, stipulations, qualifications.
price, charges, rates, fees.
language, terminology, phraseology.
footing, standing, relations, relationship.

**terrestrial** earthly, tellurian, terrene, sublunary, worldly, mundane, temporal. CELESTIAL

**terrible** extreme, severe, awful, dreadful, dire, frightful, fearful, terrifying, horrifying, shocking, horrible, horrendous, hideous, gruesome, abominable, detestable, loathsome, vile, repulsive. WONDERFUL

**terrific** extreme, intense, tremendous, great, excellent, superb, marvellous, wonderful, smashing (*inf*), super (*inf*). ORDINARY

**terrify** frighten, scare, shock, horrify, appal, alarm, dismay, petrify, terrorize. REASSURE

**territory** district, zone, area, region, realm, domain, province, state, land.

**terror** fear, fright, horror, dread, awe, panic, alarm, consternation, dismay. REASSURANCE

**terrorize** intimidate, threaten, menace, bully, terrify.

**terse** concise, succinct, compact, pithy, sententious, laconic, brief, short, curt, abrupt, brusque. PROLIX

**test** *v*, try, assay, prove, check, examine, analyse, assess, evaluate.
*n*, trial, experiment, attempt, essay, analysis, examination, exam, quiz, assessment, evaluation, proof, ordeal.

**testify** swear, state, depose, certify, witness, evidence, attest, assert, declare, affirm, avow. DENY

**testimonial** recommendation, reference, credential, endorsement.

**testimony** evidence, statement, deposition, affidavit, witness, declaration, asseveration, affirmation, avowal, proof, confirmation, corroboration, verification.

**testy** irritable, touchy, tetchy, irascible, petulant, peevish, waspish, peppery, grumpy, cantankerous, crabbed, splenctic, cross, crusty, quick-tempered, captious. GENIAL

**tether** *n*, rope, chain, lead, leash.
*v*, tie, fasten, secure, chain. LOOSE

**text** words, wording, contents, matter, subject, theme, topic, passage, book.

**texture** surface, feel, grain, weave, fabric, structure, composition, constitution.

**thankful** grateful, appreciative, obliged, indebted, beholden. UNGRATEFUL

**thankless** unthankful, ungrateful, unappreciative. GRATEFUL
unappreciated, unrewarding, unprofitable, vain, useless. REWARDING

**thanks** gratitude, gratefulness, thankfulness, appreciation, acknowledgment, recognition, credit, thanksgiving. INGRATITUDE

**thanks to,** because of, owing to, due to, through.

**thaw** melt, liquefy, dissolve, soften, defrost, unfreeze. FREEZE

**theatre** playhouse, auditorium, hall, arena, stage, drama.

**theatrical** dramatic, Thespian, histrionic, hammy (*inf*), stagy, melodramatic, overdone, affected, artificial.

**theft** thievery, stealing, pilfering, robbery, burglary, larceny, embezzlement, peculation, shoplifting, fraud.

**theme** subject, topic, matter, argument, text, idea, thesis.
motif, leitmotiv, melody, tune.

**theoretical** hypothetical, conjectural, speculative, abstract, impractical, academic, ideal. PRACTICAL

**theory** hypothesis, conjecture, speculation, thesis, postulate, presumption, assumption, supposition, idea, philosophy. PRACTICE

**therapeutic** curative, healing, remedial, corrective, restorative, beneficial, salutary, good.

**therefore** consequently, hence, whence, thence, then, so, thus, ergo, accordingly. BECAUSE

**thesaurus** dictionary, lexicon, wordbook, encyclopedia, treasury, repository.

**thesis** dissertation, essay, treatise, disquisition, monograph, paper.
theory, hypothesis, idea, postulate, supposition, proposition, subject, theme, topic.

**thews** strength, brawn, muscles, sinews.

**thick** broad, wide, fat, deep, solid, dense, close, crowded, heavy, impenetrable, condensed, compact, viscous. THIN
abundant, plentiful, numerous, full, packed, bristling, teeming, crawling, swarming. SPARSE
stupid, unintelligent, slow, dull, stolid, obtuse, brainless, dim-witted (*inf*). CLEVER
throaty, guttural, hoarse, husky, indistinct, inarticulate. CLEAR
friendly, close, familiar, intimate, matey (*inf*), pally (*inf*), chummy (*inf*). DISTANT

**thicken** condense, congeal, jell, set, solidify, harden, coagulate, clot, deepen, intensify. THIN

**thicket** coppice, copse, spinney, grove, wood. CLEARING

**thief** robber, burglar, housebreaker, shoplifter, pickpocket, swindler, embezzler, crook (*inf*).

**thieve** steal, rob, purloin, pilfer, filch, nick (*inf*), pinch (*inf*), peculate, embezzle, cheat, swindle.

**thievery** theft, stealing, robbery, burglary, larceny, shoplifting, peculation, embezzlement.

**thin** *adj*, narrow, fine, attenuated, slim, slender, lean, spare, skinny, scraggy, scrawny, lank, lanky, underweight, emaciated, gaunt, bony. FAT
sparse, scattered, scarce, scanty, deficient, poor, meagre. ABUNDANT
delicate, fine, gossamer, light, sheer, diaphanous, transparent, flimsy, weak, watery, diluted. THICK
*v*, attenuate, rarefy, weaken, dilute, water down, prune, trim, reduce. THICKEN

**thing** object, article, something, being, entity, body, substance, gadget, device, contrivance, item, point, factor, detail, particular, feature, aspect, deed, act, incident, occurrence, phenomenon.

**think** believe, consider, conceive, imagine, fancy, judge, deem, regard, reckon, suppose, presume, surmise, hold, maintain, feel, conclude, deduce, visualize, envisage, expect.

ponder, meditate, deliberate, reason, reflect, muse, mull over, cerebrate, cogitate, ruminate, weigh up, think over, contemplate, consider.

**think up,** devise, contrive, invent, create, dream up.

**thinking** *n*, reasoning, thought, judgment, opinion, view, meditation, rumination, contemplation, deliberation.

*adj*, rational, reasoning, sensible, logical, intelligent, philosophical, reflective, contemplative, thoughtful.

**thirst** *n*, thirstiness, dryness, dehydration, drought.

craving, desire, lust, hunger, appetite, yearning, longing, hankering, yen (*inf*).

*v*, crave, desire, hunger, yearn, long, hanker.

**thirsty** dry, dehydrated, parched, arid.

eager, avid, desirous, longing, yearning, greedy, hungry. SATISFIED

**thorn** prickle, spine, barb, point, spike.

nuisance, bother, vexation, irritation, annoyance, trouble, plague, scourge, curse.

**thorny** prickly, spiny, spinous, barbed, spiky, pointed, sharp. SMOOTH

difficult, hard, tough, trying, troublesome, vexatious, awkward, delicate.

**thorough** meticulous, painstaking, scrupulous, careful, exhaustive, in-depth, comprehensive, all-embracing. SUPERFICIAL

complete, total, entire, perfect, downright, out-and-out, unmitigated, unqualified, absolute, utter, thoroughgoing.

**though** *conj*, although, albeit, notwithstanding, despite the fact that, allowing, admitting, granting.

*adv*, nevertheless, still, yet, however.

**thought** idea, concept, conception, fancy, notion, view, opinion, belief, sentiment, judgment, assessment, conclusion.

thinking, brainwork, cerebration, concentration, reflection, cogitation, meditation, contemplation, speculation, consideration, deliberation, rumination.

thoughtfulness, care, concern, regard, attention, kindness, compassion. THOUGHTLESSNESS

hope, anticipation, dream, aspiration, plan, design, aim, intention, purpose.

**thoughtful** considerate, kind, regardful, concerned, solicitous, mindful, heedful, attentive, careful, cautious, wary, prudent, discreet. THOUGHTLESS

pensive, thinking, absorbed, lost in thought, reflective, ruminative, contemplative, meditative, quiet, serious.

**thoughtless** inconsiderate, unkind, insensitive, tactless, undiplomatic, indiscreet, unthinking, unmindful, heedless, careless, regardless, inattentive, negligent, neglectful, remiss, rash, reckless, imprudent, improvident. CAREFUL

**thraldom** thrall, servitude, slavery, enslavement, subjection, subjugation, bondage, captivity. FREEDOM

**thrash** beat, whip, flog, lash, cane, smack, spank, thresh, flail, defeat, trounce, conquer, overwhelm.

**thread** line, string, cord, yarn, cotton, fibre, filament, strand.

theme, motif, plot, story line, train of thought, drift, course.

**threadbare** worn, worn out, ragged, frayed, tatty, shabby, old, thin, poor. NEW

trite, hackneyed, commonplace, conventional, stale, stock.

**threat** intimidation, commination, warning, caution, menace, danger, peril, hazard, risk, omen, portent.

**threaten** intimidate, cow, warn, caution, menace, endanger, imperil, impend, loom, portend, forebode. REASSURE

**threshold** sill, doorstep, doorway, door, entrance.

start, beginning, outset, brink, verge, dawn. END

**thrift** economy, frugality, thriftiness, saving, parsimony. EXTRAVAGANCE

**thriftless** extravagant, lavish, prodigal, wasteful, spendthrift, improvident, unthrifty, imprudent. THRIFTY

**thrifty** economical, frugal, saving, sparing, parsimonious, provident, prudent, careful. THRIFTLESS

**thrill** *n*, excitement, stimulation, titillation, sensation, tingle, tremor, kick (*inf*).

*v*, excite, stimulate, galvanize, electrify, touch, move, stir, rouse, titillate, agitate. BORE

**thrilling** exciting, gripping, hair-raising, electrifying, stirring, rousing, stimulating, moving. BORING

**thrive** prosper, succeed, do well, make good, advance, get on, flourish, boom, grow, wax, bloom, blossom. FAIL

**thriving** prosperous, successful, flourishing, booming, growing, blooming, wealthy, rich.

**throb** *v*, beat, pulsate, pulse, palpitate, pound.
*n*, beat, pulsation, palpitation, throbbing.

**throes** pangs, pain, agony, anguish, suffering.

**throng** *n*, crowd, multitude, mob, horde, host, mass, swarm.
*v*, crowd, flock, swarm, herd, pack, cram, press.

**throttle** strangle, choke, suffocate, asphyxiate, smother, stifle.

**through** past, by, between, across, during, throughout.
finished, done.
via, by way of, by means of, because of.

**throw** *v*, cast, fling, toss, hurl, sling, pitch, lob (*inf*), chuck (*inf*), launch, propel, project, deliver. CATCH
floor, fell, bring down, prostrate, overturn, upset.

**throw away,** discard, reject, get rid of, scrap, dispose of, waste. KEEP

**throw out,** expel, eject, evict, dismiss, discard, get rid of. ADMIT
disconcert, confuse, bewilder, mislead, deceive, upset.
*n*, cast, fling, toss, sling, pitch. CATCH

**thrust** *v*, drive, propel, impel, urge, push, shove, force, press, ram, poke, stick, stab, jab, lunge. WITHDRAW
*n*, drive, push, shove, force, impetus, momentum, lunge, stab, poke, prod, attack, assault.

**thud** thump, knock, smack, crash, clonk, clunk.

**thug** ruffian, hooligan, tough, gangster, robber, murderer.

**thump** *v*, hit, strike, smack, whack, beat, batter, pummel, pound, thud.
*n*, blow, rap, knock, thud.

**thunder** *v*, resound, reverberate, rumble, roll, boom, crash, crack, blast, detonate, roar, bellow.
*n*, reverberation, rumble, roll, boom, roar, crash, peal.

**thus** so, in this way, like this.
therefore, consequently, hence, ergo, then.

**thwart** frustrate, balk, foil, check, stop, cross, oppose, contravene, defeat, hinder, impede, obstruct, prevent. AID

**tick** *v*, click, tap.
mark, check.

**tick off,** tell off, scold, reprimand, reprove, rebuke, chide, berate, upbraid. PRAISE
*n*, ticktock, click, tap.
moment, instant, minute, second, flash, trice, jiffy (*inf*).

**ticket** pass, certificate, token, coupon, voucher, card, slip, label, tag.

**tickle** titillate, gratify, please, delight, amuse, entertain, divert, thrill, excite.

**ticklish** sensitive, touchy, delicate, awkward, difficult, complex, thorny, risky, unstable, unsteady, uncertain.

**tide** ebb, flow, stream, current, drift, direction, movement, course.

**tidings** news, word, advice, information, message, report.

**tidy** *adj*, neat, orderly, trim, spruce, shipshape, spick-and-span, organized, systematic, methodical. UNTIDY
considerable, sizable, goodly, large, big, substantial, ample. SMALL
*v*, neaten, straighten, spruce up, clean, groom, arrange, order. DISORDER

**tie** *v*, bind, truss, knot, fasten, join, connect, unite, link, attach, secure, tether, moor, lash. UNTIE
restrict, confine, limit, curb, restrain, tie up, hinder, hamper. FREE
*n*, bond, link, connection, liaison, relationship, obligation, duty, responsibility, restriction, restraint.
knot, bow, string, rope, fastening.
draw, dead heat.

**tier** row, rank, line, band, layer, stratum, level, storey.

**tiff** quarrel, row, dispute, squabble, disagreement, argument. HARMONY
bad mood, ill humour, huff, pet, tantrum, temper.

**tight** taut, stretched, tense, stiff, rigid, firm, stable, fixed, fast, secure, snug, close, compact, cramped. LOOSE

mean, miserly, stingy, niggardly, tight-fisted, close-fisted. GENEROUS
sealed, hermetic, proof, impervious.
drunk, inebriated, intoxicated, tipsy, tiddly (*inf*). SOBER

**till** farm, cultivate, work, dig, plough.

**tilt** *v*, slope, slant, incline, lean, tip, list, cant. STRAIGHTEN
*n*, slope, slant, inclination, angle.
joust, tournament, contest, encounter.

**timbre** tone, tonality, tone colour, tone quality, ring, resonance.

**time** *n*, duration, period, span, spell, stretch, while, term, interval, season, era, epoch, age, date, hour, juncture, point, occasion.
tempo, beat, rhythm, metre, measure.
*v*, count, measure, clock, regulate, control, adjust, set, schedule.

**timely** opportune, seasonable, well-timed, propitious, auspicious, favourable, convenient. INOPPORTUNE

**timid** timorous, shy, bashful, coy, diffident, retiring, shrinking, fearful, afraid, pusillanimous, cowardly. BOLD

**tinge** *n*, tincture, stain, dye, tint, colour, hue, shade, touch, trace, hint, suggestion, *soupçon*, dash, smack.
*v*, tincture, dye, stain, tint, colour.

**tingle** *v*, prickle, sting, smart, itch, tickle, shiver.
*n*, itch, shiver, quiver, thrill.

**tinkle** jingle, ring, peal, chime.

**tint** *n*, colour, hue, shade, tone, tinge, tincture, dye, stain.
*v*, colour, stain, dye, tinge, tincture, affect, influence.

**tiny** minute, minuscule, infinitesimal, microscopic, miniature, diminutive, small, little, wee, dwarfish, pygmy, Lilliputian. ENORMOUS

**tip**[1] *n*, point, end, extremity, head, top, apex, summit, peak, pinnacle. BASE

**tip**[2] *v*, tilt, incline, lean, list, cant, upset, overturn, topple.

**tip**[3] *n*, gratuity, baksheesh, gift, perquisite, reward.
hint, suggestion, clue, tip-off (*inf*), warning.

**tip off,** *v*, warn, forewarn, caution, advise, tell, inform.

**tipsy** drunk, intoxicated, inebriated, tight (*inf*), tiddly (*inf*), merry (*inf*). SOBER

**tirade** diatribe, philippic, invective, denunciation, harangue, abuse. EULOGY

**tire** weary, fatigue, exhaust, drain, wear out, jade, fag (*inf*). REFRESH
bore, annoy, irritate, exasperate.
flag, droop, weaken, fail.

**tired** weary, fatigued, exhausted, drained, worn out, jaded, fagged (*inf*), dead beat (*inf*), knackered (*inf*), all in (*inf*), sleepy, drowsy. REFRESHED
bored, sick, fed up (*inf*).

**tiresome** wearisome, boring, tedious, monotonous, dull, annoying, irritating, irksome, vexatious, exasperating, trying, troublesome. PLEASANT

**tissue** fabric, paper, mesh, net, network, web, combination, collection, set, mass, accumulation, conglomeration.

**titanic** huge, gigantic, colossal, enormous, massive, immense, vast, herculean, elephantine, monstrous, stupendous. SMALL

**titillate** tickle, excite, thrill, arouse, stimulate, please.

**title** name, heading, caption, inscription, label, designation, denomination, appellation, epithet, nickname, sobriquet.
claim, right, due, privilege, prerogative, ownership, possession.

**titter** snigger, chuckle, chortle (*inf*), giggle, laugh. WEEP

**together** collectively, jointly, side by side, closely, in unison, en masse, all at once, simultaneously, concurrently, contemporaneously, mutually, reciprocally. SEPARATELY

**toil** *v*, work, labour, travail, slog, drudge, slave. RELAX
*n*, hard work, labour, travail, drudgery, slavery, effort, exertion, industry. REST

**toilet** lavatory, latrine, urinal, bathroom, washroom, powder room, cloakroom, water closet, WC, privy, public convenience, ladies, gents, loo (*inf*), bog (*inf*).

**toilsome** laborious, arduous, hard, difficult, tough, strenuous, taxing, tiring, fatiguing, exhausting, tiresome, wearisome. EASY

**token** *n*, symbol, sign, representation, emblem, mark, indication, evidence, proof, expression, manifestation, reminder, remembrance, memorial, keepsake, souvenir, memento.

*adj*, nominal, minimal, superficial, perfunctory, symbolic.

**tolerable** bearable, endurable, sufferable, supportable, acceptable, allowable, permissible. INTOLERABLE
passable, fair, indifferent, middling, mediocre, average, so-so (*inf*), not bad (*inf*). EXCEPTIONAL

**tolerant** broad-minded, open-minded, liberal, catholic, unprejudiced, unbigoted, patient, forbearing, long-suffering, benevolent, magnanimous, indulgent, lenient, permissive, easy-going. INTOLERANT

**tolerate** bear, suffer, endure, brook, abide, stand, put up with (*inf*), stomach, swallow, permit, allow, admit, countenance, sanction, indulge, condone.

**toll**[1] *v*, ring, knell, peal, chime, sound, strike.

**toll**[2] *n*, levy, tax, impost, duty, tariff, rate, charge.

**tomb** vault, crypt, sepulchre, grave.

**tome** volume, book.

**tomfoolery** antics, shenanigans (*inf*), horseplay, skylarking (*inf*), clowning, buffoonery, foolishness, folly, silliness, stupidity, nonsense.

**tone** *n*, sound, noise, note, pitch, tonality, timbre, intonation, inflection, modulation, cadence, accent, stress, emphasis.
colour, cast, tinge, tint, shade, hue.
tenor, quality, spirit, mood, temper, vein, style, manner, approach, drift, air.
*v*, harmonize, blend, fit, adapt.

**tone down,** moderate, temper, subdue, soften, dampen. ENHANCE

**tonic** *n*, stimulant, refresher, pick-me-up (*inf*), boost, shot in the arm (*inf*), restorative, analeptic.
*adj*, stimulating, invigorating, bracing, restorative.

**too** also, as well, in addition, besides, moreover, furthermore.
excessively, inordinately, immoderately, unduly, overly, extremely.

**tool** implement, instrument, gadget, device, contrivance, utensil, apparatus, appliance, machine.
vehicle, means, medium, agent, pawn, cat's-paw, puppet, hireling.

**toothsome** tasty, palatable, savoury, appetizing, delicious, luscious, scrumptious (*inf*), delectable, agreeable, attractive. NASTY

**top** *n*, summit, apex, vertex, apogee, peak, pinnacle, crown, acme, zenith, height, head, lead. BOTTOM
cap, lid, cover.
*adj*, highest, topmost, uppermost, upper, best, greatest, supreme, ruling, principal, chief, main, leading, first, foremost. LOWEST
*v*, cap, crown, tip, cover.
exceed, transcend, surpass, excel, eclipse, outshine, outdo, outstrip, beat, better, best.

**topic** subject, theme, matter, issue, question, point.

**topical** current, up-to-date, popular, familiar, local, regional.

**topple** totter, fall, tumble, fall over, collapse, tip over, knock down, upset, overturn, overthrow.

**torment** *v*, torture, agonize, rack, excruciate, pain, persecute, distress, harrow, afflict, plague, pester, bother, harass, harry, badger, annoy, vex, irritate, exasperate, provoke, tease, worry. SOOTHE
*n*, torture, agony, pain, suffering, anguish, distress, misery, affliction, plague, scourge, vexation, irritation, nuisance, pest. RELIEF

**tornado** cyclone, hurricane, typhoon, whirlwind, gale, squall, storm, tempest. CALM

**torpid** sluggish, slow, lethargic, languid, dull, listless, apathetic, lazy, indolent, dormant, inactive, inert, lifeless, inanimate. ACTIVE

**torpor** torpidity, torpidness, sluggishness, lethargy, listlessness, apathy, inactivity, inertia. ACTIVITY

**torrent** flood, deluge, cascade, downpour, stream, flow, rush, gush, outburst. TRICKLE

**torrid** hot, scorching, blistering, roasting, burning, fiery, tropical, sultry, parched, arid, dry. ARCTIC
passionate, ardent, fervent, erotic, lustful, steamy (*inf*).

**tortuous** sinuous, serpentine, twisting, winding, zigzag, meandering, curved, bent, crooked, twisted, mazy, labyrinthine, involved, complicated, indirect, circuitous, roundabout, devious. STRAIGHT

**torture** *v*, agonize, rack, excruciate, crucify, martyr, persecute, torment, pain, distress. SOOTHE
*n*, torment, persecution, martyrdom, agony, suffering, pain, anguish. EASE

**toss** *v*, throw, pitch, fling, chuck (*inf*), cast, hurl, sling, propel, project, flip.
roll, rock, shake, jolt, agitate, disturb, wriggle, writhe, turn.
*n*, throw, fling, cast, pitch, shake, movement.

**total** *n*, sum, all, totality, entirety, whole, aggregate, mass, amount. PART
*adj*, entire, whole, integral, complete, full, aggregate, absolute, utter, sheer, thorough, out-and-out, downright, unqualified, unmitigated. PARTIAL
*v*, amount to, come to, sum up, add up, tot up.

**totter** stagger, reel, sway, rock, teeter, wobble, waver, falter, tremble, shake.

**touch** *v*, feel, finger, handle, palpate, fondle, caress, stroke, pat, tap, hit, strike, meet, adjoin, brush, graze.
affect, influence, impress, inspire, move, stir, soften, melt, upset, disturb.
reach, arrive at, attain, match, equal, rival.
concern, regard, relate to, pertain to.
**touch on,** deal with, cover, refer to, mention.
**touch up,** enhance, improve, perfect, brush up, polish up, patch up, repair, retouch, renovate.
*n*, feel, feeling, contact, stroke, caress, pat, tap.
trace, hint, suggestion, suspicion, *soupçon*, dash, smack, tinge, tincture.
skill, knack, flair, talent, ability, art, facility, technique, approach, style, manner.

**touching** *adj*, moving, affecting, stirring, tender, poignant, pathetic, pitiable, pitiful, sad.
*prep*, regarding, respecting, apropos, with reference to, concerning, about, relating to.

**touchstone** standard, criterion, norm, measure, gauge, yardstick, test, proof.

**touchy** testy, irritable, irascible, petulant, peevish, waspish, peppery, grumpy, cantankerous, splenetic, choleric, cross, crusty, crabbed, fractious, captious, sensitive, thin-skinned. GENIAL

**tough** strong, durable, resilient, resistant, firm, solid, hard, rigid, stiff, inflexible, leathery, chewy, fibrous, stringy. TENDER
hardy, sturdy, rugged, stalwart, robust, strapping, brawny, muscular, rough, vicious. WEAK
obstinate, stubborn, obdurate, unyielding, stern, unfeeling, callous, hard-boiled (*inf*).
difficult, hard, arduous, laborious, exacting, thorny, knotty, baffling, puzzling, perplexing. SIMPLE

**tour** *n*, voyage, journey, excursion, trip, expedition, outing, jaunt, circuit, round, course.
*v*, travel, journey, voyage, visit, sightsee (*inf*).

**tournament** competition, contest, match, meeting.

**tousle** ruffle, rumple, dishevel, mess up, disarrange, disarray, disorder. GROOM

**tow** pull, draw, drag, haul, tug, lug, trail. PUSH

**towards** to, for, in the direction of.
nearly, almost, about, just before.
respecting, regarding, concerning, touching.

**tower** *n*, steeple, turret, spire, minaret, belfry, column, pillar.
citadel, fortress, castle, stronghold, refuge, keep.
*v*, rise, ascend, soar, mount, surpass, transcend, exceed, top, dominate, overlook. SINK

**town** borough, municipality, settlement, village, city, metropolis.

**toxic** poisonous, pestilent, pernicious, noxious, harmful, deadly, lethal. HARMLESS

**toy** *n*, plaything, game, trifle, trinket, bauble, knickknack.
*v*, play, sport, trifle, tinker, fiddle, dally, flirt.

**trace** *n*, mark, token, sign, indication, vestige, remains, evidence, clue, hint, suggestion, touch, tinge, dash, bit, jot, iota.
track, trail, spoor, footprint, footmark, footstep.
*v*, follow, pursue, trail, track, stalk, hunt, find, discover, ascertain, detect.
sketch, draw, outline, delineate, copy, depict, map, chart.

**track** *n*, trail, trace, scent, spoor, footprint, footstep, footmark, wake, path, line, route, course, way, road, rail.
*v*, trace, trail, follow, pursue, hunt, chase. CATCH
**track down,** find, discover, ferret out, sniff out, run to earth. MISS

**tract**[1] area, region, stretch, expanse, strip, patch, plot, lot, zone, district, territory.

**tract**[2] treatise, dissertation, disquisition, essay, sermon, homily, discourse, pamphlet, booklet, leaflet, brochure.

**tractable** amenable, complaisant, willing, yielding, submissive, docile, manageable, governable, malleable, pliable, pliant, ductile. INTRACTABLE

**trade** *n*, business, commerce, traffic, barter, exchange, transaction, deal.
occupation, profession, calling, vocation, job, employment, craft, métier.
*v*, deal, transact, buy and sell, traffic, bargain, barter, exchange, swap.

**tradition** custom, practice, way, habit, convention, usage, folklore, unwritten law.

**traditional** oral, unwritten, old, accustomed, customary, habitual, usual, regular, conventional.

**traduce** calumniate, slander, libel, misrepresent, defame, malign, vilify, asperse, denigrate, revile, vituperate, decry, denounce, disparage, depreciate. EULOGIZE

**traffic** vehicles, transport, transportation, freight.
trade, commerce, business, dealings, barter, exchange.

**tragedy** disaster, catastrophe, calamity, adversity, misfortune.

**tragic** disastrous, catastrophic, calamitous, dreadful, terrible, awful, dire, shocking, appalling, unfortunate, ill-fated, lamentable, deplorable, pathetic, pitiful, sad, sorrowful, unhappy, miserable. COMIC

**trail** *v*, drag, draw, pull, haul, tow, dangle, hang, droop, lag, linger, fall behind, straggle.
track, trace, follow, pursue, stalk, hunt. CATCH
*n*, track, trace, scent, spoor, footprint, footstep, footmark, path, way, road, wake, tail, stream, train.

**train** *v*, teach, instruct, school, educate, coach, drill, exercise, discipline, ground, prepare, rear, guide.
direct, aim, point, focus, level.
*n*, line, file, column, convoy, procession, chain, series, succession, sequence, order, progression, course.
retinue, suite, entourage, cortege, attendance, staff, following, followers.

**trait** characteristic, attribute, feature, quality, idiosyncrasy, peculiarity, quirk, mark.

**traitor** betrayer, Judas, quisling, informer, renegade, apostate, turncoat, defector, deserter, rebel. LOYALIST

**trammel** *n*, restraint, check, curb, obstacle, hindrance, impediment, fetter, bond. FREEDOM
*v*, restrict, restrain, hinder, impede, block, obstruct, fetter, chain, ensnare, entrap, enmesh, net, catch. RELEASE

**tramp** *v*, trudge, plod, stump, stomp (*inf*), stamp, trample, march, walk, hike, traipse (*inf*), trek, rove, range, ramble, wander.
*n*, vagrant, vagabond, drifter, down-and-out.
walk, ramble, hike, trek, march, footfall, tread, stamp.

**trample** crush, squash, stamp, tread, tramp.
encroach, infringe, violate, defy.

**trance** daze, stupor, dream, abstraction, coma, rapture, ecstasy.

**tranquil** peaceful, calm, still, quiet, smooth, undisturbed, serene, placid, composed, unruffled, unmoved, unperturbed, untroubled, sedate. AGITATED

**tranquillize** calm, compose, soothe, allay, still, hush, smooth, settle, relax, sedate. EXCITE

**transact** conduct, carry on, do, perform, execute, dispatch, negotiate, manage.

**transaction** deal, bargain, negotiation, settlement, business, performance, execution, action, proceeding, matter, affair.

**transcend** surpass, exceed, rise above, go beyond, excel, outrival, outvie, outstrip, outdo, eclipse, outshine.

**transcendent** surpassing, exceeding, matchless, peerless, unrivalled, unparalleled, unequalled, incomparable, supreme, consummate. ORDINARY
transcendental, supernatural, mystical, abstract, metaphysical.

**transcribe** copy, write out, translate, transliterate.

**transcript** transcription, copy, reproduction, duplicate, translation, transliteration.

**transfer** *v*, move, remove, transport, convey, carry, transmit, change, shift, relocate, transplant, hand over, pass on.
*n*, transference, move, transmission, change, shift, relocation.

**transfigure** transform, change, transmute, metamorphose, exalt, glorify, idealize, apotheosize.

**transfix** rivet, stun, captivate, fascinate, hypnotize, mesmerize.
pierce, impale, perforate, penetrate, spear, skewer.

**transform** change, convert, translate, transmogrify, transmute, metamorphose, transfigure, alter, modify, revolutionize.

**transgress** break, disobey, violate, infringe, contravene, exceed, overstep, go beyond, trespass, sin, err, go astray, offend. OBEY

**transgression** offence, crime, sin, wrong, fault, error, misdeed, misdemeanour, trespass, contravention, breach, infringement, infraction, violation.

**transgressor** sinner, wrongdoer, malefactor, culprit, offender, delinquent, criminal, felon.

**transient** transitory, temporary, impermanent, brief, short, ephemeral, evanescent, passing, fleeting, momentary, short-lived, fugitive, fugacious. PERMANENT

**transit** passage, crossing, movement, motion, change, transition, transport, transportation, conveyance, carriage, shipment.

**transition** change, conversion, transformation, alteration, passage, passing, movement, shift.

**transitory** transient, temporary, impermanent, brief, short, ephemeral, evanescent, passing, fleeting, momentary, short-lived, fugitive, fugacious. PERMANENT

**translate** render, interpret, transliterate, transcribe, decode, decipher, explain, elucidate.
transform, transmute, convert, change, transfer, transport.

**translucent** pellucid, diaphanous, limpid, transparent, clear. OPAQUE

**transmission** transmittal, transmittance, conveyance, transport, sending, transfer, transference, communication. RECEPTION
broadcast, programme.

**transmit** transfer, transport, carry, take, convey, send, forward, remit, communicate, pass on, hand down, spread, diffuse, disseminate, broadcast. RECEIVE

**transmute** change, transform, convert, alter, metamorphose, transfigure.

**transparent** clear, limpid, pellucid, lucid, crystalline, diaphanous, sheer, see-through, translucent. OPAQUE
obvious, patent, evident, apparent, clear, plain, distinct, manifest. UNCLEAR

**transpire** happen, occur, take place, come about, become known, come to light.

**transplant** move, remove, transfer, relocate, shift, displace.

**transport** *v*, convey, carry, bear, ship, take, transfer, shift, move.
banish, deport, exile, expatriate.
entrance, enrapture, enchant, captivate, delight, ravish. REPEL
*n*, transportation, conveyance, carriage, shipment, transit.
ecstasy, rapture, happiness, joy, delight, bliss, euphoria, enchantment. ANGUISH

**transpose** interchange, exchange, switch, swap (*inf*), change, move, shift, transfer.

**transude** ooze, seep, exude, percolate, filter, strain.

**transverse** crossways, crosswise, athwart, oblique, diagonal. PARALLEL

**trap** *n*, snare, gin, springe, net, pitfall, ambush, trick, ruse, wile, artifice, stratagem.
*v*, catch, net, snare, ensnare, entrap, trick, take in, dupe, deceive.

**trappings** appurtenances, accoutrements, gear, equipment, adornments, ornaments, finery, fixtures, fittings, paraphernalia.

**trash** rubbish, refuse, garbage, waste, litter.
nonsense, balderdash, rubbish, rot. SENSE

**trauma** shock, blow, upset, disturbance, ordeal, suffering, anguish, pain, injury, wound.

**travel** *v*, journey, voyage, tour, cross, traverse, trek, roam, rove, ramble, wander, go, move, proceed. SETTLE
*n*, journey, voyage, tour, trip, excursion, expedition, movement, passage.

**traveller** voyager, wayfarer, passenger, tourist, explorer, nomad, wanderer, salesman, representative.

**traverse** cross, cover, pass over, travel over, range, roam, wander, bridge, span.
obstruct, impede, thwart, frustrate, oppose, contravene. ASSIST

**travesty** parody, caricature, lampoon, burlesque, mockery, ridicule, distortion, perversion.

**treacherous** traitorous, perfidious, disloyal, faithless, unfaithful, false, untrue, deceitful, dishonest, untrustworthy, unreliable, treasonable. LOYAL dangerous, perilous, risky, hazardous, unsafe, precarious, deceptive. SAFE

**treachery** betrayal, perfidy, perfidiousness, treason, disloyalty, faithlessness, unfaithfulness, infidelity. LOYALTY

**tread** *v*, walk, step, pace, stride, march, tramp, trudge, plod, stump, stamp, trample, crush, squash.
*n*, step, pace, footfall, walk.

**treason** treachery, betrayal, disloyalty, sedition, subversion, mutiny, insurrection. ALLEGIANCE

**treasure** *n*, riches, wealth, fortune, cash, money, gold, silver, bullion, jewels, gems, valuables. RUBBISH
*v*, prize, value, hold dear, esteem, cherish, love, revere, worship. SCORN
hoard, store, save, accumulate.

**treat** *n*, party, entertainment, feast, banquet, gift, surprise, delight, pleasure, fun.
*v*, handle, deal with, regard, use, manage, negotiate, attend, minister to, nurse, doctor, medicate, heal. NEGLECT
entertain, regale, feast, wine and dine, pay for, stand (*inf*).

**treatise** discourse, disquisition, dissertation, essay, tract, thesis, paper, monograph, article, pamphlet.

**treatment** handling, use, usage, manipulation, dealing, management, care, nursing, medication, therapy, cure, remedy.

**treaty** agreement, compact, convenant, bargain, contract, pact, bond, convention, concordat, entente, alliance.

**trek** *n*, journey, voyage, expedition, odyssey, march, hike.
*v*, travel, journey, tramp, trudge, march, hike.

**tremble** *v*, shake, quiver, quaver, quake, shiver, shudder, vibrate, oscillate, rock, wobble.
*n*, tremor, shake, quiver, quake, shiver, shudder, vibration, oscillation.

**tremendous** huge, great, vast, immense, massive, enormous, colossal, gigantic, prodigious, monstrous, formidable, awful, terrible, dreadful. SMALL
wonderful, marvellous, remarkable, extraordinary, fantastic (*inf*), fabulous (*inf*), terrific (*inf*), super (*inf*). ORDINARY

**tremor** shudder, shiver, quiver, tremble, vibration, oscillation, agitation, palpitation.

**tremulous** trembling, quavering, quaking, quivering, shivering, shuddering, fearful, frightened, scared, afraid, anxious, nervous, jumpy, jittery (*inf*). STEADY

**trench** furrow, ditch, cut, channel, gutter, trough, earthwork, fosse.

**trenchant** keen, acute, sharp, pointed, incisive, cutting, caustic, biting, mordant, acid, tart, bitter, sarcastic, severe. MILD
effective, effectual, vigorous, energetic, powerful, potent, forceful, strong. INEFFECTUAL

**trend** *n*, tendency, course, drift, inclination, bearing, direction.
fashion, vogue, mode, style, craze, rage.
*v*, tend, lean, incline, drift, veer, turn.

**trepidation** fear, terror, fright, alarm, perturbation, consternation, dread, apprehension, anxiety, nervousness, agitation, trembling, shaking, quaking, tremor. COMPOSURE

**trespass** *v*, intrude, invade, encroach, infringe, poach.
*n*, intrusion, invasion, encroachment, infringement, poaching.
sin, offence, transgression, infraction, crime, misdemeanour, misdeed, error.

**trespasser** intruder, invader, interloper, gate-crasher (*inf*), poacher.

**trial** *n*, test, experiment, assay, analysis, examination, proof, probation, audition.
hearing, inquiry, tribunal, litigation.
try, attempt, effort, endeavour, go (*inf*), shot (*inf*).
hardship, adversity, trouble, tribulation, pain, distress, suffering, grief, affliction, ordeal, nuisance, pest, annoyance, vexation. RELIEF
*adj*, experimental, tentative, exploratory, pilot, provisional.

**tribe** clan, family, sept, race, stock, class, division, group, people.

**tribulation** trial, hardship, adversity, trouble, pain, distress, suffering, affliction, grief, misery, sorrow, woe, misfortune, bad luck, blow, burden. JOY

**tribunal** court, bar, bench, judicature, trial, hearing, assizes, session.

**tribute** acclaim, acclamation, recognition, acknowledgment, honour, homage, praise, commendation, eulogy, panegyric, testimonial. CENSURE gift, offering, donation, contribution, impost, duty, tax, levy, toll, charge, customs, excise.

**trice** moment, second, minute, instant, twinkling, flash, jiffy (*inf*). AGE

**trick** *n*, wile, stratagem, artifice, ruse, finesse, deceit, deception, feint, dodge, contrivance, device, subterfuge, hoax, fraud, imposture, swindle.
caper, prank, practical joke, jest, sleight of hand, legerdemain, knack, technique, art, craft.
trait, characteristic, idiosyncrasy, quirk, mannerism, habit.
*v*, dupe, cheat, defraud, deceive, delude, fool, hoodwink, bamboozle (*inf*), take in (*inf*), overreach, swindle, con (*inf*).

**trickle** drip, drop, dribble, ooze, seep, exude, percolate. GUSH

**tricky** difficult, problematic, complicated, knotty, delicate, ticklish. SIMPLE
crafty, cunning, artful, sly, wily, foxy, subtle, clever, deceitful, dishonest. ARTLESS

**trifle** *n*, toy, plaything, bauble, trinket, knickknack, bagatelle, triviality, nothing.
bit, drop, dash, pinch, touch, trace, jot, tittle, iota, particle.
*v*, toy, play, dally, tinker, fiddle, fritter, waste.

**trifling** trivial, unimportant, insignificant, inconsequential, inconsiderable, small, paltry, petty, worthless, valueless, frivolous, idle, silly. IMPORTANT

**trim** *adj*, neat, spruce, tidy, orderly, shipshape, smart, dapper, compact, slim, slender, sleek, fit. DISORDERLY
*v*, clip, prune, cut, crop, shave, shear, dock, lop, shorten, curtail, neaten, shape.
decorate, adorn, ornament, embellish, garnish, festoon, deck, beautify. STRIP
adjust, modify, amend, balance, arrange, order.
*n*, order, condition, state, shape, fitness, fettle.
trimming, decoration, adornment, ornament, embellishment, garnish, frill, fringe, edging, border.

**trinket** jewel, bijou, bauble, trifle, bagatelle, gewgaw, knickknack, ornament.

**trip** *n*, journey, excursion, tour, jaunt, outing, expedition, voyage.
stumble, fall, blunder, mistake, error, slip, lapse.
*v*, stumble, fall, tumble, slip, err, blunder, bungle.
hop, skip, dance, gambol, bound, spring.

**trite** hackneyed, corny (*inf*), stale, tired, thin, threadbare, old, unoriginal, stock, stereotyped, commonplace, ordinary, dull, banal. ORIGINAL

**triturate** pound, pulverize, comminute, levigate, bray, grind, crush, bruise.

**triumph** *n*, victory, win, conquest, mastery, coup, feat, accomplishment, achievement, attainment, success. FAILURE
jubilation, exultation, joy, pride. REGRET
*v*, win, prevail, conquer, vanquish, succeed. LOSE
rejoice, jubilate, exult, glory, celebrate, revel, gloat, swagger. LAMENT

**triumphant** winning, conquering, victorious, successful, unbeaten, undefeated, exultant, jubilant, proud, boastful. BEATEN

**trivial** trifling, unimportant, insignificant, inconsequential, negligible, inconsiderable, small, minor, immaterial, paltry, petty, frivolous, trite. IMPORTANT

**trollop** slut, slattern, sloven, whore, prostitute, tart (*inf*).

**troop** *n*, group, band, company, crew, team, squad, gang, crowd, throng, multitude, horde, herd, flock, pack.
*v*, flock, gather, collect, muster, throng, crowd, swarm, march, parade. DISPERSE

**trophy** prize, award, cup, medal, laurels, bays, spoils, booty, souvenir, memento.

**trot** canter, lope, run, jog.

**trouble** *n*, worry, concern, anxiety, agitation, distress, suffering, pain, grief, anguish, adversity, misfortune, trial, tribulation, affliction, burden, difficulty, problem, nuisance, pest, bother, inconvenience, vexation, irritation, annoyance. RELIEF
unrest, disturbance, disorder, commotion, tumult, strife, anarchy, mischief. ORDER
effort, exertion, pains, care, attention.
ailment, illness, disorder, complaint.
*v*, worry, agitate, alarm, concern, upset, distress, disturb, perturb, confuse, perplex, bother, inconvenience, pester, harass, plague, torment, vex, annoy, irk, irritate, grieve, afflict. SOOTHE

**troublesome** annoying, irksome, vexatious, bothersome, worrying, nagging, burdensome, oppressive, difficult, hard, laborious, arduous. EASY

**trough** ditch, trench, channel, gutter, furrow, groove, depression.

**trousers** pants, slacks, jeans, flannels.

**truant** *n*, absentee, dodger, shirker, malingerer, deserter, skiver (*inf*).
*adj*, absent, missing, AWOL, skiving (*inf*). PRESENT

**truce** armistice, cease-fire, peace, rest, break, intermission, lull, respite, treaty, pact. WAR

**truck**[1] *n*, lorry, van, wagon.

**truck**[2] *n*, dealings, business, commerce, trade, traffic, barter, exchange.
*v*, exchange, barter, swap, trade, traffic, deal, bargain, negotiate.

**truckle** yield, submit, give in, knuckle under, cower, cringe, grovel, crawl, kowtow, bow and scrape, fawn, toady. RESIST

**truculent** aggressive, hostile, belligerent, bellicose, pugnacious, combative, fierce, ferocious, cruel, brutal, savage, grim. GENTLE

**trudge** plod, tramp, stump, lumber, traipse (*inf*), march, walk.

**true** actual, real, factual, veritable, genuine, authentic, valid, veracious, truthful, honest, sincere, legitimate, rightful, proper, correct, accurate, precise, exact. FALSE
faithful, loyal, staunch, steadfast, trusty, trustworthy, reliable, dependable. FAITHLESS

**truism** platitude, commonplace, cliché, bromide, axiom, truth. PARADOX

**truly** really, indeed, in fact, actually, assuredly, positively, undoubtedly, genuinely, sincerely, exactly, precisely, rightly, legitimately.

**trumpery** *n*, rubbish, trash, nonsense, balderdash, rot, humbug, trinket, bauble.
*adj*, rubbishy, trashy, worthless, tawdry, flashy, showy, cheap, meretricious, trivial, trifling. VALUABLE

**trumpet** *n*, bugle, horn, clarion.
*v*, proclaim, announce, promulgate, advertise. SUPPRESS

**truncate** shorten, cut, lop, crop, dock, abbreviate.

**truncheon** club, cudgel, baton, staff.

**trunk** stem, stalk, bole.
body, torso.
chest, coffer, box, crate.

**truss** *v*, tie, bind, fasten, secure. LOOSE
*n*, support, prop, brace, buttress, strut.
bundle, package, packet.

**trust** *n*, faith, belief, conviction, certitude, confidence, assurance, reliance, dependence, hope, expectation, credit.
duty, responsibility, charge, custody, care, protection, safekeeping.
*v*, believe, have faith in, have confidence in, rely on, depend on, hope, expect. DOUBT
commit, entrust, consign, turn over, assign, delegate.

**trustworthy** trusty, dependable, reliable, loyal, faithful, true, constant, staunch, steadfast, firm, honest, truthful, honourable, upright. UNRELIABLE

**truth** verity, reality, actuality, fact, authenticity, genuineness, validity, accuracy, precision, exactness. FALSENESS
veracity, truthfulness, honesty, integrity, sincerity, candour, frankness. DECEIT
truism, platitude, axiom, maxim, principle, law.

**truthful** honest, veracious, sincere, frank, candid, straightforward, open, trustworthy, reliable. DECEITFUL
accurate, exact, precise, correct, faithful, literal, realistic, factual, true. FALSE

**try** *v*, attempt, endeavour, essay, undertake, seek, aim, strive, struggle, have a go, make an effort.
test, assay, experiment with, prove, examine, assess, analyse, sample.
tire, weary, strain, tax, bother, pester, annoy, irritate, vex, irk.
*n*, attempt, endeavour, effort, go (*inf*), shot (*inf*), crack (*inf*), stab (*inf*), trial, test, experiment, sample.

**trying** hard, difficult, arduous, tough, taxing, tiring, troublesome, bothersome, irksome, annoying, exasperating, infuriating. EASY

**tube** pipe, hose, line, passage, channel, conduit, duct.

**tuck** fold, pleat, gather, pucker, insert, put, push, thrust.

**tuft** bunch, clump, cluster, knot.

**tug** pull, jerk, wrench, yank, heave, haul, drag, draw, tow, lug. PUSH

**tuition** instruction, teaching, schooling, education, training, coaching.

**tumble** fall, slip, trip, stumble, sprawl, pitch, toss, roll, drop, plunge, topple, collapse.

**tumble-down** ramshackle, dilapidated, ruined, broken-down, crumbling, decrepit, rickety, shaky.

**tumefy** swell, puff up, distend, bloat, inflate.

**tumid** swollen, puffy, distended, bloated, inflated, enlarged, turgid, tumescent, bulging, protuberant. SHRUNKEN
pompous, bombastic, orotund, fustian, magniloquent, grandiloquent, rhetorical, flowery.

**tumour** swelling, lump, growth, neoplasm, sarcoma.

**tumult** commotion, uproar, turmoil, turbulence, disorder, ferment, hubbub, ado, racket, din, noise, clamour, confusion, pandemonium, riot, brawl, disturbance, agitation. PEACE

**tumultuous** uproarious, turbulent, stormy, tempestuous, wild, disorderly, boisterous, obstreperous, noisy, clamorous, riotous, excited, restless, agitated. QUIET

**tune** melody, air, song, strain, harmony, euphony. DISCORD

**tuneful** melodious, melodic, harmonious, euphonious, musical, sweet, dulcet, mellifluous. DISCORDANT

**turbid** muddy, cloudy, murky, opaque, foul, impure, thick, dense, foggy, hazy, muddled, confused. CLEAR

**turbulent** agitated, disturbed, restless, confused, disordered, choppy, rough, stormy, tempestuous, tumultuous, violent, wild, unruly, disorderly, boisterous, obstreperous, noisy, clamorous, uproarious, riotous. CALM

**turf** grass, sod, sward, green.

**turgid** swollen, puffy, distended, bloated, inflated, enlarged, tumid, tumescent, bulging, protuberant. SHRUNKEN
pompous, bombastic, orotund, fustian, magniloquent, grandiloquent, rhetorical, flowery.

**turmoil** tumult, turbulence, uproar, commotion, noise, din, racket, clamour, hubbub, stir, unrest, agitation, disturbance, disorder, confusion, fuss, ado, trouble. PEACE

**turn** *v*, rotate, revolve, spin, roll, twirl, wheel, whirl, pivot, gyrate, circle, go round.
change, move, shift, diverge, veer, swerve, bend, curve, twist, reverse, invert.
alter, modify, change, convert, transform, metamorphose, adjust, adapt, fit, suit, shape, form, apply, use, direct.
curdle, sour, go off, go bad, spoil.
become, go, grow, get.
hinge, hang, rest, depend.

**turn down,** lower, reduce, lessen, diminish, decrease. RAISE
reject, refuse, decline, spurn, repudiate. ACCEPT

**turn out,** expel, evict, dismiss, discharge, fire (*inf*), sack (*inf*). ADMIT
make, manufacture, fabricate, produce.
switch off, turn off, put out, unplug.
result, ensue, become, end up. BEGIN

**turn up,** arrive, appear, show up (*inf*), come.
raise, increase, amplify, intensify. LOWER

*n*, rotation, revolution, circle, cycle, round, gyration, spin, twirl, bend, curve, twist, turning, reversal, inversion.
change, alteration, variation, vicissitude, deviation, divergence, shift, adjustment.
shift, stint, spell, period, go (*inf*), shot (*inf*), chance, opportunity.
shape, form, style, manner, mode, fashion, mould, cast.
deed, act, action, service.
inclination, tendency, bent, aptitude, flair, gift, talent, knack, genius, faculty. DISINCLINATION
stroll, walk, drive, ride, airing, jaunt.

**turpitude** baseness, vileness, wickedness, evil, corruption, depravity, sin, iniquity, crime, vice. NOBILITY

**tussle** fight, wrestle, scuffle, struggle, brawl, scrap (*inf*).

**tutelage** guardianship, charge, care, protection, supervision, guidance, instruction, tuition, schooling, education.

**tutor** *n*, teacher, instructor, coach, preceptor, schoolmaster, schoolmistress, professor. PUPIL
*v*, teach, instruct, coach, train, educate, school, discipline, drill.

**twaddle** nonsense, rubbish, rot, drivel, balderdash, humbug, babble, prattle, chatter, gibberish. SENSE

**tweak** pinch, squeeze, twist, twitch, pull, jerk.

**twiddle** fiddle, play, toy, twirl, twist, turn.

**twig** stick, branch, shoot, offshoot, spray, sprig. LOG

**twin** *n*, double, duplicate, match, mate, counterpart.
*adj*, similar, like, corresponding, parallel, double, duplicate, paired, matching. SINGLE

**twine** *n*, string, rope, cord, yarn, thread, cotton.
*v*, twist, wind, turn, meander, wreathe, coil.
interlace, interweave, entwine, knit, splice, braid, plait. UNRAVEL

**twinge** pang, spasm, twitch, tic, throb, pain, stab, prick.

**twinkle** *v*, sparkle, shine, glisten, glitter, glint, gleam, flash, coruscate, scintillate, flicker, blink, wink.
*n*, sparkle, shine, glint, gleam, flash, coruscation, blink, wink.
twinkling, instant, moment, second, trice, jiffy (*inf*).

**twirl** revolve, rotate, spin, wheel, whirl, pirouette, pivot, turn, twist, twiddle.

**twist** *v*, coil, curl, wind, turn, twirl, spin, twine, entwine, weave.
sprain, wrench, rick, contort, distort, warp, pervert, garble, falsify, misrepresent, misinterpret.
*n*, coil, curl, roll, spin, turn, bend, curve, meander, zigzag.
sprain, wrench, distortion, perversion.

**twit**[1] *v*, tease, taunt, chaff, mock, reproach, upbraid, rebuke, censure. PRAISE

**twit**[2] *n*, idiot, fool, simpleton, halfwit, nincompoop, ass.

**twitch** *v*, jerk, jump, snatch, pull, tug, yank.
*n*, spasm, tic, tremor, twinge, jerk, pull.

**twitter** chirp, chirrup, cheep, tweet, warble, trill, whistle, chatter, prattle.

**tycoon** magnate, industrialist, mogul, baron, big cheese (*inf*).

**type** kind, sort, stamp, class, order, genre, form, species, variety.
specimen, sample, example, exemplar, model, pattern, standard, archetype, prototype, epitome, paradigm.
print, face, font, fount, characters, letters.

**typical** representative, illustrative, classic, exemplary, characteristic, indicative, symbolic, emblematic, normal, regular, standard, stock, usual, conventional. ABNORMAL

**typify** represent, exemplify, epitomize, embody, personify, illustrate, characterize, symbolize, denote, indicate.

**tyrannical** tyrannous, autocratic, despotic, dictatorial, arbitrary, absolute, domineering, overbearing, authoritarian, imperious, oppressive, harsh, severe, cruel, brutal, savage, inhuman. DEMOCRATIC

**tyranny** autocracy, absolutism, totalitarianism, despotism, dictatorship, oppression, harshness, severity, cruelty, inhumanity. DEMOCRACY

**tyrant** autocrat, despot, dictator, oppressor, martinet, slave-driver.

**tyro** novice, neophyte, beginner, learner, student, pupil, apprentice. MASTER

# U

**ugly** unsightly, plain, unattractive, unlovely, ill-favoured, hideous. BEAUTIFUL
unpleasant, disagreeable, nasty, revolting, repulsive, loathsome, vile, horrible, ominous, menacing, threatening, spiteful, bad-tempered. PLEASANT

**ulcer** sore, fester, gathering, abscess, boil, pustule.

**ulterior** hidden, concealed, secret, undisclosed, unrevealed. AVOWED

**ultimate** final, last, terminal, endmost, furthest, extreme, conclusive, decisive, eventual. FIRST
utmost, extreme, maximum, most, supreme, greatest, highest, top. LOWEST
basic, fundamental, elementary, primary.

**ultra** extreme, radical, immoderate, inordinate, excessive, fanatical. MODERATE

**umbrage** offence, resentment, grudge, indignation, huff, pique, annoyance, irritation, displeasure.

**umpire** *n*, referee, arbiter, adjudicator, judge, moderator, arbitrator.
*v*, referee, arbitrate, adjudicate, judge.

**unabashed** undaunted, undismayed, unblushing, brazen, bold, confident. ABASHED

**unable** incapable, powerless, impotent, incompetent, unfit, not able, not up to. ABLE

**unacceptable** unwelcome, undesirable, unpopular, disagreeable, objectionable, inadmissible. ACCEPTABLE

**unaccompanied** solitary, alone, lone, solo, unattended, unescorted. ACCOMPANIED

**unaccountable** inexplicable, unexplainable, incomprehensible, unfathomable, mysterious, odd, peculiar, strange, extraordinary, remarkable. UNDERSTANDABLE

**unaccustomed** unfamiliar, unexpected, strange, remarkable, unusual, uncommon, unused, inexperienced. FAMILIAR

**unadorned** plain, simple, stark, unvarnished, unembellished, unornamented, undecorated. ORNATE

**unadulterated** pure, unmixed, real, genuine, undiluted. MIXED

**unaffected**[1] artless, ingenuous, naive, unsophisticated, simple, plain, natural, unpretentious, sincere, honest, genuine, open. ARTIFICIAL

**unaffected**[2] unchanged, unaltered, untouched, unmoved, unfeeling, aloof. CHANGED

**unaided** unassisted, single-handed, alone. ASSISTED

**unanimity** agreement, accord, concord, unison, concert, harmony, unity, consensus. DISSENT

**unanimous** agreed, agreeing, accordant, concordant, concerted, united, solid, harmonious. DISAGREEING

**unanswerable** irrefutable, incontestable, undeniable, unarguable, incontrovertible, indisputable, conclusive, absolute. WEAK

**unappetizing** unappealing, unattractive, unpleasant, unsavoury, unpalatable, tasteless, insipid, vapid. APPETIZING

**unapproachable** aloof, standoffish, reserved, withdrawn, cool, frigid, unsociable, unfriendly. FRIENDLY
remote, distant, inaccessible, out-of-the-way. ACCESSIBLE

**unarmed** defenceless, vulnerable, unprotected, unguarded, exposed, open, helpless, weak. PROTECTED

**unassailable** impregnable, invulnerable, strong, secure. VULNERABLE
undeniable, indisputable, incontestable, irrefutable, incontrovertible, absolute, certain, sure. WEAK

**unassuming** modest, self-effacing, humble, retiring, reserved, diffident, unpretentious, unaffected, unobtrusive, unassertive. OSTENTATIOUS

**unattached** free, loose, detached, separate, at liberty, independent, autonomous, uncommitted, single, unmarried. ATTACHED

**unattended** alone, unaccompanied, unescorted, solitary, untended, unwatched, ignored, disregarded, neglected, abandoned. ATTENDED

**unattractive** unprepossessing, unappealing, uninviting, unappetizing, undesirable, plain, ugly, unlovely. ATTRACTIVE

**unauthorized** illegal, unlawful, illicit, unlicensed, unapproved, unofficial, unwarranted, forbidden. AUTHORIZED

**unavailing** vain, futile, useless, ineffectual, ineffective, bootless, fruitless, abortive, unproductive. SUCCESSFUL

**unavoidable** inevitable, necessary, inescapable, ineluctable, inexorable, irresistible, compulsory, obligatory, fated, destined, certain, sure. AVOIDABLE

**unaware** ignorant, unknowing, unacquainted, incognizant, unenlightened, uninformed, unconscious, oblivious, unmindful, heedless, unsuspecting, unprepared. AWARE

**unawares** suddenly, unexpectedly, abruptly, by surprise, off guard.
accidentally, unintentionally, by mistake, inadvertently, unwittingly, unknowingly. DELIBERATELY

**unbalanced** asymmetrical, lopsided, uneven, unequal, disproportionate, unstable. EVEN
unsound, irrational, deranged, insane, mad, crazy, lunatic, demented, unhinged, touched. SANE
biased, prejudiced, partisan, bigoted, unfair, unjust, one-sided, partial. UNBIASED

**unbearable** insufferable, insupportable, intolerable, unendurable, too much (*inf*). BEARABLE

**unbecoming** unseemly, indecorous, improper, indelicate, inappropriate, unsuitable, unfit, unbefitting, unattractive, unflattering. BECOMING

**unbelief** disbelief, incredulity, doubt, scepticism, distrust, mistrust, infidelity, atheism. BELIEF

**unbending** inflexible, unyielding, stiff, rigid, formal, severe, firm, resolute, intractable, stubborn. FLEXIBLE

**unbiased** fair, impartial, unprejudiced, unbigoted, disinterested, dispassionate, objective, neutral, just, equitable. BIASED

**unbidden** spontaneous, voluntary, willing, free, unforced. FORCED
uninvited, unasked, unwelcome, unwanted, unsolicited. WELCOME

**unbind** loose, free, release, let go, untie, unfetter, unchain, unshackle, unfasten, undo. BIND

**unblemished** perfect, flawless, faultless, immaculate, spotless, clean, pure, unsullied, untarnished, stainless. FLAWED

**unblinking** fearless, unafraid, unflinching, steady, unfaltering, unwavering, cool, calm, unemotional.

**unblushing** shameless, immodest, bold, brazen, unabashed, unashamed. ASHAMED

**unbosom** reveal, disclose, divulge, lay bare, unburden, admit, confess, confide. SUPPRESS

**unbounded** boundless, unlimited, limitless, illimitable, vast, immense, immeasurable, infinite, interminable, endless, unrestricted, unconfined, unrestrained, uncontrolled, unchecked, unbridled, immoderate. LIMITED

**unbridled** unrestrained, uncontrolled, unchecked, uninhibited, wild, unruly, rampant, immoderate, intemperate, wanton. RESTRAINED

**unbroken** whole, complete, sound, intact, integral, entire. BROKEN

uninterrupted, continuous, endless, ceaseless, incessant, constant.

**uncalled-for** unnecessary, needless, unjustified, unwarranted, gratuitous, undeserved, unfair, unjust, unsolicited, unwelcome, unwanted.

**uncanny** weird, strange, mysterious, odd, queer, eerie, ghostly, unnatural, extraordinary, remarkable, astonishing, amazing, exceptional, incredible. ORDINARY

**unceasing** incessant, ceaseless, endless, unending, constant, nonstop, unremitting, perpetual, eternal, everlasting, uninterrupted, continuous. INTERMITTENT

**unceremonious** informal, casual, natural, simple, abrupt, curt, brusque, blunt, gruff, rough, churlish, rude. FORMAL

**uncertain** doubtful, dubious, ambiguous, questionable, ambivalent, unsure, irresolute, undecided, unresolved, unsettled, undetermined, indefinite, unconfirmed, speculative, conjectural, indistinct, unclear, vague, chancy, risky, precarious, unreliable, unpredictable, capricious, changeable, variable, erratic, fitful, inconstant. SURE

**unchangeable** unalterable, invariable, immutable, changeless, fixed, permanent, stable, steady. CHANGEABLE

**unchanging** lasting, abiding, enduring, eternal, perpetual, constant, changeless, unvarying. TRANSITORY

**uncharitable** unkind, unfeeling, insensitive, unchristian, mean, selfish, cruel, harsh. CHARITABLE

**unchaste** impure, loose, wanton, depraved, indecent, immoral, dissolute, lewd, lascivious. CHASTE

**uncivil** rude, discourteous, impolite, unmannerly, ill-mannered, ill-bred, impudent, disrespectful, bearish, churlish. CIVIL

**uncivilized** uncouth, coarse, vulgar, unrefined, uncultured, uncultivated, uneducated, primitive, barbarian, barbarous, barbaric, savage. CIVILIZED

**unclean** dirty, filthy, soiled, foul, sullied, defiled, contaminated, impure. PURE

**uncomfortable** uneasy, ill-at-ease, disturbed, troubled, distressed, upset, restless, anxious, nervous, awkward, embarrassed. RELAXED

disagreeable, unpleasant, hard, rough, cramped, painful, irritating, troublesome. COMFORTABLE

**uncommon** rare, unusual, unfamiliar, scarce, infrequent, unique, singular, strange, odd, curious, queer, extraordinary, remarkable, exceptional, noteworthy, outstanding. ORDINARY

**uncommunicative** reserved, taciturn, reticent, shy, quiet, tight-lipped, unsociable, withdrawn, secretive, unforthcoming. TALKATIVE

**uncompromising** inflexible, unyielding, unbending, rigid, firm, obstinate, stubborn, obdurate, inexorable, implacable, determined, dogged. PLIANT

**unconcerned** indifferent, uninterested, apathetic, uninvolved, remote, aloof, dispassionate, detached, nonchalant, carefree, blithe, oblivious, untroubled, unworried, uncaring, unsympathetic, unmoved, unaffected. CONCERNED

**unconditional** total, complete, full, utter, downright, out-and-out, absolute, categorical, positive, unqualified, unreserved, unrestricted, unlimited. UNCONDITIONAL

**uncongenial** disagreeable, unpleasant, discordant, antagonistic, antipathetic, unsympathetic, uninviting. CONGENIAL

**unconnected** separate, detached, independent, unrelated, disconnected, disjointed, incoherent, illogical. CONNECTED

**unconquerable** invincible, indomitable, insuperable, insurmountable, overpowering, overwhelming, unbeatable, undefeatable. WEAK

**unconscionable** unscrupulous, unprincipled, amoral, unethical. PRINCIPLED
excessive, immoderate, unreasonable, inordinate, extreme, outrageous, preposterous. REASONABLE

**unconscious** insensible, senseless, out, asleep, comatose. CONSCIOUS
unaware, oblivious, blind, deaf, insensitive, unmindful, ignorant, unknowing. AWARE
automatic, involuntary, reflex, instinctive, subliminal, subconscious, unwitting, unthinking, inadvertent, accidental.

**uncontrollable** ungovernable, unmanageable, wild, unruly, intractable, irrepressible, mad, carried away, frantic, violent. CONTROLLABLE

**unconventional** unorthodox, unusual, uncommon, unfamiliar, irregular, abnormal, atypical, original, eccentric, offbeat, bizarre, odd, peculiar, informal. CONVENTIONAL

**unconvincing** weak, feeble, flimsy, thin, dubious, questionable, inconclusive, improbable, unlikely. CONVINCING

**uncouth** clumsy, awkward, ungainly, inelegant, graceless, crude, vulgar, coarse, rude, rough, rugged, churlish, impolite, discourteous, ill-bred, ill-mannered, uncivilized, uncultivated, unrefined, unpolished. REFINED

**uncover** bare, expose, unveil, unmask, unwrap, open, strip, show, discover, reveal, disclose, divulge. COVER

**unction** unguent, oil, lotion, ointment, salve, balm.
passion, feeling, fervour, ardour, enthusiasm, zest, spirit, verve, power, force.

**unctuous** smooth, suave, glib, sycophantic, fawning, ingratiating, flattering, insincere. SINCERE
oily, greasy, slippery.

**undaunted** undismayed, undeterred, unflinching, unfaltering, steadfast, resolute, intrepid, bold, brave, courageous, dauntless, fearless. AFRAID

**undeceive** enlighten, disabuse, disillusion, disenchant, correct, set straight. DECEIVE

**undecided** uncertain, unsure, doubtful, dubious, ambivalent, irresolute, indecisive, hesitant, wavering, torn. SURE
unsettled, unresolved, pending, up in the air, open, moot, undetermined, indefinite. SETTLED

**undefiled** pure, chaste, clean, immaculate, spotless, unspotted, stainless, untarnished, unblemished, unsullied, unpolluted, uncontaminated. DEFILED

**undemonstrative** reserved, unresponsive, uncommunicative, reticent, aloof, distant, unemotional, unexcitable, sedate, formal. DEMONSTRATIVE

**undeniable** unquestionable, indisputable, incontrovertible, irrefutable, incontestable, indubitable, definite, positive, certain, sure, proven, obvious, evident. QUESTIONABLE

**under** beneath, below, down, underneath, lower, inferior, subordinate, secondary, subservient. ABOVE

**undercover** secret, hidden, concealed, private, confidential, covert, surreptitious, clandestine, underground. PUBLIC

**underestimate** underrate, undervalue, misprize, miscalculate, misjudge, disparage, belittle, minimize. OVERESTIMATE

**undergo** suffer, endure, sustain, bear, experience, go through.

**underhand** underhanded, clandestine, surreptitious, furtive, stealthy, covert, undercover, secret, sly, crafty, unscrupulous, dishonest. OPEN

**underline** underscore, italicize, stress, emphasize, accent, accentuate, point up, highlight.

**underling** menial, lackey, flunky, servant, hireling, minion, subordinate, inferior. MASTER

**undermine** sap, subvert, sabotage, weaken, impair, ruin. STRENGTHEN
tunnel, burrow, dig, excavate, mine.

**underneath** *prep*, under, beneath, below. ABOVE
*n*, bottom, underside. TOP

**underprivileged** deprived, disadvantaged, poor, needy, impoverished, destitute. WEALTHY

**underrate** underestimate, undervalue, misprize, belittle, disparage. OVERRATE

**understand** comprehend, apprehend, perceive, discern, make out, fathom, follow, grasp, catch on (*inf*), recognize, see,

gather, hear, learn, take in, assimilate, appreciate, realize, believe, suppose, assume, presume.
sympathize, pity, commiserate, tolerate.

**understanding** *n*, intelligence, intellect, mind, brains, reason, sense, knowledge, comprehension, awareness, interpretation, view, opinion, judgment, insight, perception, discernment. IGNORANCE
agreement, bargain, pact, arrangement.
*adj*, compassionate, tender, kind, considerate, sympathetic, patient, tolerant, forgiving. INTOLERANT

**undertake** attempt, try, endeavour, essay, tackle, take on, venture, embark on, begin, start, commence, set about. ACHIEVE
promise, pledge, agree, vow, swear, guarantee, engage, contract.

**undertaking** venture, project, enterprise, affair, business, task, effort, endeavour.
promise, pledge, assurance, guarantee, word, vow.

**undertone** murmur, whisper, low voice. SHOUT
undercurrent, suggestion, connotation, nuance, trace, touch, tinge, flavour.

**undervalue** underestimate, underrate, misprize, disparage, depreciate, belittle, minimize. OVERESTIMATE

**underwear** underclothes, underclothing, undergarments, lingerie, undies (*inf*), smalls (*inf*).

**underwrite** endorse, sign, countersign, subscribe, approve, sanction, guarantee, back, support, sponsor, fund, finance.

**undesigned** unintentional, accidental, inadvertent, unpremeditated. INTENTIONAL

**undesirable** unpleasant, disagreeable, unattractive, uninviting, objectionable, obnoxious, unwelcome, unwanted, unacceptable, unsuitable, inappropriate. DESIRABLE

**undeveloped** immature, embryonic, latent, potential, primordial, rudimentary. MATURE

**undignified** unseemly, unbecoming, indecorous, improper, inelegant, infra dig (*inf*), inappropriate, unsuitable. DIGNIFIED

**undisciplined** wild, unruly, unrestrained, uncontrolled, wayward, erratic, untrained, unschooled. DISCIPLINED

**undisguised** open, overt, evident, manifest, plain, unconcealed, genuine, sincere. VEILED

**undisputed** undoubted, unquestioned, unchallenged, uncontested, recognized, acknowledged, accepted, certain, sure, indisputable, unquestionable, incontrovertible, undeniable. DEBATABLE

**undistinguished** ordinary, commonplace, everyday, run-of-the-mill, unexceptional, indifferent, mediocre, so-so (*inf*). EXCEPTIONAL

**undisturbed** tranquil, serene, placid, calm, composed, collected, unruffled, unperturbed, untroubled. AGITATED

**undivided** full, complete, entire, whole, intact, unbroken, solid, united. DIVIDED

**undo** untie, unfasten, release, loose, disengage, disentangle, open, unwrap. FASTEN
nullify, annul, reverse, invalidate, neutralize, counteract.
ruin, destroy, wreck, shatter, defeat, crush.

**undoubted** certain, sure, obvious, evident, undisputed, unquestioned, indisputable, unquestionable, indubitable, undeniable, accepted, acknowledged. DOUBTFUL

**undress** *v*, disrobe, unclothe, divest, strip. DRESS
*n*, nakedness, nudity, dishabille, informality.

**undue** excessive, immoderate, inordinate, extreme, disproportionate, unnecessary, uncalled-for, unwarranted, unjustified, undeserved, improper. MODERATE

**undulate** roll, ripple, heave, surge, swell, billow, wave.

**unduly** excessively, immoderately, inordinately, disproportionately, overmuch, overly. MODERATELY

**undying** immortal, deathless, eternal, everlasting, unending, endless, imperishable, indestructible, permanent, lasting. TRANSIENT

**unearth** excavate, dig up, exhume, disinter, find, discover, uncover, expose, reveal, disclose. BURY

**unearthly** weird, strange, eerie, uncanny, ghostly, spectral, spooky (*inf*), supernatural, preternatural, extraterrestrial.
unreasonable, ungodly, outrageous, ridiculous, abnormal, unheard-of. REASONABLE

**uneasy** uncomfortable, ill-at-ease, disturbed, perturbed, restless, restive, edgy, nervous, anxious, apprehensive, upset, agitated, worried, troubled. RELAXED

**uneducated** ignorant, illiterate, untaught, untutored, unschooled, uncultured, uncultivated, unenlightened, unread. EDUCATED

**unemployed** jobless, workless, out of work, on the dole (*inf*), laid off, redundant, idle, unoccupied. EMPLOYED

**unending** endless, interminable, never-ending, perpetual, ceaseless, unceasing, incessant, nonstop, continual, constant, eternal, everlasting. BRIEF

**unequal** uneven, unbalanced, asymmetrical, disproportionate, different, disparate, unlike, dissimilar. EQUAL
inadequate, insufficient, not up to, found wanting, incapable, unable. ADEQUATE

**unequalled** peerless, matchless, unmatched, unparalleled, unrivalled, unsurpassed, inimitable, incomparable, transcendent, supreme, paramount. INFERIOR

**unequivocal** clear, plain, obvious, evident, manifest, explicit, unambiguous, unmistakable, unquestionable, undeniable, indisputable, indubitable, sure, certain, absolute, categorical. AMBIGUOUS

**unerring** sure, certain, exact, accurate, precise, true, perfect, unfailing, infallible. FAULTY

**uneven** rough, rugged, lumpy, bumpy, hilly, undulating. FLAT
unequal, odd, different, disparate, unbalanced, asymmetrical, unfair, one-sided. EQUAL
irregular, variable, fitful, spasmodic, jerky, intermittent. REGULAR

**uneventful** ordinary, commonplace, dull, boring, monotonous, tedious, routine, humdrum, unexciting, uninteresting, exceptional, normal. EVENTFUL

**unexpected** unanticipated, unforeseen, sudden, abrupt, startling, surprising, unpredictable, fortuitous. EXPECTED

**unfailing** certain, sure, reliable, dependable, constant, staunch, steadfast, unflagging, inexhaustible, limitless, infallible, unerring. UNRELIABLE

**unfair** unjust, inequitable, uneven, one-sided, biased, prejudiced, partial, partisan. FAIR
wrongful, undue, unwarranted, unreasonable, dishonest, dishonourable, foul, unsporting.

**unfaithful** faithless, disloyal, false, perfidious, traitorous, treacherous, unreliable, untrustworthy, fickle, deceitful, adulterous, two-timing (*inf*). FAITHFUL
inaccurate, inexact, imprecise, incorrect, wrong, erroneous, faulty, imperfect. ACCURATE

**unfaltering** unflagging, untiring, tireless, indefatigable, unswerving, unwavering, steady, constant, staunch, steadfast, resolute, firm, determined, resolved. WAVERING

**unfamiliar** unusual, uncommon, unaccustomed, strange, odd, new, novel. FAMILIAR
unacquainted, unversed, unskilled, inexperienced. VERSED

**unfashionable** out-of-date, old-fashioned, dated, outmoded, obsolete, old hat (*inf*), passé, antiquated. FASHIONABLE

**unfasten** undo, detach, open, let go, untie, unlock, unbutton, unzip. FASTEN

**unfathomable** deep, bottomless, unplumbed, immeasurable. SHALLOW
incomprehensible, impenetrable, inscrutable, deep, profound, abstruse, mysterious, inexplicable.

**unfavourable** adverse, contrary, hostile, inimical, inauspicious, unpropitious, unpromising, discouraging, bad, threatening, ominous, untimely, unseasonable, unfortunate, unlucky, disadvantageous, detrimental. FAVOURABLE

**unfeeling** cold, callous, hard-hearted, unsympathetic, insensitive, uncaring, harsh, cruel, pitiless, inhuman. COMPASSIONATE
numb, dead, insensible, insensate.

**unfeigned** genuine, real, sincere, honest, heartfelt, pure, natural, unaffected. FEIGNED

**unfetter** unshackle, unchain, unbind, untie, loose, free, liberate, release. FETTER

**unfinished** incomplete, imperfect, lacking, wanting, deficient, sketchy, rough, raw, crude, unaccomplished, undone. FINISHED

**unfit** unsuitable, inappropriate, inadequate, unqualified, ineligible, ill-equipped, unprepared, incompetent, incapable, ineffectual, inept, useless, no good.

weak, feeble, frail, delicate, unhealthy, out of condition. FIT

**unflagging** indefatigable, tireless, untiring, unfailing, unwavering, unfaltering, unremitting, constant, persistent, steady.

**unfledged** undeveloped, immature, raw, green, callow, inexperienced. EXPERIENCED

**unflinching** unfaltering, unwavering, unshrinking, firm, resolute, brave, dauntless, undaunted, fearless, bold.

**unfold** open, unfurl, unroll, undo, spread out, extend, display, show, reveal, disclose, explain, unravel, expand, develop.

**unforeseen** unexpected, unanticipated, sudden, abrupt, surprising, startling. EXPECTED

**unforgivable** inexcusable, unpardonable, unjustifiable, unwarrantable, indefensible, reprehensible, deplorable, disgraceful. FORGIVABLE

**unfortunate** unlucky, luckless, hapless, cursed, unsuccessful, poor, wretched, unhappy, ill-fated, ill-starred, adverse, unfavourable, disastrous, calamitous, tragic, regrettable, lamentable, deplorable. FORTUNATE

**unfounded** baseless, groundless, idle, vain, unproven, unsubstantiated.

**unfrequented** deserted, uninhabited, remote, isolated, solitary, lonely.

**unfriendly** hostile, antagonistic, unsociable, inhospitable, unneighbourly, uncongenial, aloof, distant, cold, surly, inimical, unfavourable. FRIENDLY

**unfruitful** fruitless, barren, sterile, infertile, infecund, unproductive, unprofitable, unrewarding. FRUITFUL

**unfurl** open, unroll, unfold, spread out. FURL

**ungainly** awkward, clumsy, ungraceful, inelegant, lumbering, gangling, uncouth, unwieldy. GRACEFUL

**ungenerous** mean, stingy, parsimonious, penurious, tight-fisted, niggardly, penny-pinching (*inf*), cheeseparing, selfish. GENEROUS

**ungodly** impious, irreverent, irreligious, godless, profane, sacrilegious, wicked, sinful, corrupt, depraved, immoral, evil. PIOUS

**ungovernable** refractory, recalcitrant, intractable, unruly, wild, uncontrollable, unmanageable. MILD

**ungracious** discourteous, impolite, uncivil, rude, unmannerly, ill-bred, churlish, rough. GRACIOUS

**ungrateful** thankless, unthankful, unappreciative. GRATEFUL

**unguarded** unprotected, undefended, defenceless, vulnerable. PROTECTED
careless, incautious, unmindful, heedless, unthinking, thoughtless, indiscreet, imprudent, foolhardy, unwary. CAUTIOUS
artless, guileless, ingenuous, open, frank, candid. ARTFUL

**unhandy** clumsy, awkward, maladroit, bungling, unskilful, inexpert, incompetent. DEXTEROUS
unwieldy, unmanageable, awkward, inconvenient. HANDY

**unhappy** miserable, sad, depressed, dejected, despondent, disconsolate, downcast, crestfallen, glum, sorrowful, mournful, melancholy. HAPPY
wretched, unfortunate, unlucky, luckless, hapless, ill-fated, ill-starred. FORTUNATE

**unharmed** safe, sound, unhurt, uninjured, unscathed, undamaged, whole, intact. HURT

**unhealthy** sick, ill, unwell, ailing, poorly (*inf*), diseased, invalid, sickly, delicate, frail, feeble, weak, infirm. HEALTHY
morbid, unwholesome, insalubrious, noxious, unhygienic, insanitary, detrimental, deleterious. SALUBRIOUS

**unheard-of** unknown, unfamiliar, obscure, unsung. FAMOUS
unprecedented, new, novel, unusual, unique. CONVENTIONAL

**unheeded** ignored, disregarded, overlooked, neglected, unobserved, unnoticed. HEEDED

**unhesitating** unwavering, unfaltering, unswerving, unquestioning, unreserved, wholehearted, ready, prompt, immediate, instant. WAVERING

**unhinge** derange, unbalance, craze, madden, confuse, discompose, unsettle, disorder.

**unholy** impious, irreligious, ungodly, irreverent, profane, wicked, sinful, evil. DEVOUT
outrageous, shocking, appalling, dreadful, awful.

**unhurried** slow, leisurely, easy, easy-going.

**unidentified** anonymous, unrevealed, unnamed, nameless, unknown, unfamiliar, strange, mysterious. KNOWN

**uniform** *n*. outfit, costume, dress, livery. *adj*. regular, even, equable, unvarying, unchanging, constant, consistent, steady, same, identical, similar, alike. IRREGULAR

**unify** unite, join, merge, amalgamate, confederate, combine. SEPARATE

**unimaginative** dull, uninspired, unoriginal, ordinary, everyday, commonplace, trite, pedestrian, prosaic, unromantic. IMAGINATIVE

**unimpaired** undamaged, unharmed, uninjured, unhurt, unscathed, sound. IMPAIRED

**unimpassioned** cool, calm, composed, controlled, impassive, sedate, unemotional, dispassionate, rational, moderate. IMPASSIONED

**unimpeachable** blameless, irreproachable, faultless, impeccable, perfect, above reproach, unquestionable, unexceptionable. BLAMEWORTHY

**unimportant** insignificant, inconsequential, inconsiderable, slight, little, trivial, trifling, petty, minor, immaterial, nugatory. IMPORTANT

**uninhabited** deserted, abandoned, empty, vacant, unoccupied, unpopulated, unsettled, unfrequented. INHABITED

**uninhibited** free, unconstrained, unreserved, informal, casual, relaxed, open, frank, candid, uncontrolled, unrestrained, unbridled. INHIBITED

**unintelligent** stupid, foolish, dull, slow, brainless, dim-witted (*inf*), gormless (*inf*), thick, dense, obtuse, unthinking. INTELLIGENT

**unintelligible** incomprehensible, indecipherable, incoherent, inarticulate, meaningless, unfathomable. CLEAR

**unintentional** accidental, inadvertent, undesigned, unpremeditated, involuntary, unconscious, unwitting, fortuitous. INTENTIONAL

**uninteresting** boring, dull, unexciting, wearisome, tiresome, tedious, monotonous, uneventful, flat, stale, dreary. EXCITING

**uninterrupted** continuous, continual, unbroken, ceaseless, incessant, constant, perpetual, unending, nonstop. BROKEN

**uninviting** unappealing, undesirable, unattractive, repulsive, unpleasant, disagreeable, unappetizing, unwelcoming. INVITING

**union** conjunction, fusion, amalgamation, combination, blend, junction, connection. SEPARATION
league, alliance, coalition, association, confederacy, federation, society, guild.
unity, agreement, accord, concord, concert, harmony, unison, unanimity. DISCORD
marriage, matrimony, wedlock, copulation, coitus, intercourse.

**unique** single, sole, only, solitary, lone.
matchless, peerless, unequalled, unparalleled, incomparable, inimitable, unexampled, unrivalled, exceptional, peculiar, singular, rare. COMMON

**unison** agreement, harmony, accord, concord, unity, unanimity. DISCORD

**unit** whole, entity, group, system.
part, component, element, constituent, item, piece, section, module, measure, quantity.

**unite** join, unify, fuse, bind, connect, link, combine, amalgamate, marry, wed, ally, associate, league, band, cooperate, join forces. SEPARATE

**unity** oneness, singleness, wholeness, union.
agreement, harmony, accord, concord, unison, unanimity. DISCORD

**universal** general, comprehensive, all-embracing, all-inclusive, widespread, worldwide, ecumenical, catholic, total, whole, entire, unlimited. NARROW

**unjust** unfair, inequitable, biased, prejudiced, partial, one-sided, wrongful, undue, unmerited, undeserved. JUST

**unjustifiable** indefensible, unwarrantable, inexcusable, unforgivable, unpardonable, wrong. JUSTIFIABLE

**unkempt** dishevelled, tousled, uncombed, messy, untidy, disordered, disarranged, ungroomed, slovenly, slatternly, sluttish, scruffy. NEAT

**unkind** cruel, nasty, uncharitable, unfriendly, mean, spiteful, unfeeling, unsympathetic, thoughtless, inconsiderate, insensitive, callous, harsh, inhuman. KIND

**unknown** unfamiliar, strange, new, novel, unexplored, undiscovered, unheard-of, obscure, anonymous, nameless, unnamed, unidentified, unrevealed, secret, hidden, mysterious. KNOWN

**unlawful** illegal, illicit, illegitimate, unauthorized, criminal, banned, prohibited, forbidden. LAWFUL

**unlike** different, dissimilar, diverse, divergent, disparate, distinct, incompatible, unequal. SIMILAR

**unlikely** improbable, doubtful, dubious, implausible, incredible, unbelievable, remote, faint, slight, questionable, unpromising. LIKELY

**unlimited** infinite, limitless, illimitable, boundless, unbounded, immense, vast, great, immeasurable, incalculable, countless, endless, unrestricted, unfettered, absolute, full, unconditional, unqualified. LIMITED

**unload** disburden, unburden, unlade, empty, unpack, discharge, relieve, disencumber. LOAD

**unlock** open, unlatch, unbolt, unfasten, undo, free, release. LOCK

**unlucky** unfortunate, luckless, hapless, cursed, doomed, ill-fated, ill-starred, poor, wretched, unfavourable, adverse, inauspicious, ominous. LUCKY

**unman** demoralize, dishearten, discourage, dispirit, weaken, enfeeble, enervate, unnerve, daunt, intimidate.

**unmanageable** uncontrollable, ungovernable, difficult, unruly, refractory, recalcitrant, intractable, wild. DOCILE
unwieldy, inconvenient, unhandy, awkward, cumbersome, bulky. HANDY

**unmanly** effeminate, womanish, sissy, weak, feeble, cowardly, timid, timorous. MANLY

**unmannerly** rude, impolite, discourteous, uncivil, ungracious, bad-mannered, ill-bred, uncouth, boorish, churlish. POLITE

**unmask** expose, uncover, unveil, uncloak, show up, disclose, reveal. MASK

**unmatched** matchless, peerless, unequalled, unparalleled, unrivalled, unsurpassed, incomparable, supreme, consummate. INFERIOR

**unmentionable** unspeakable, unutterable, disgraceful, shameful, scandalous, shocking, indecent, immodest.

**unmerciful** merciless, pitiless, unpitying, cruel, harsh, hard, heartless, relentless, unrelenting, inexorable, implacable, ruthless, remorseless, unsparing, inhuman. MERCIFUL

**unmethodical** immethodical, unsystematic, disorganized, unorganized, disorderly, desultory, haphazard, irregular. METHODICAL

**unmindful** oblivious, unaware, unconscious, careless, negligent, neglectful, remiss, inattentive, heedless, mindless, unthinking. MINDFUL

**unmistakable** clear, distinct, plain, patent, obvious, evident, manifest, conspicuous, glaring, certain, sure, positive, unquestionable, indisputable. DOUBTFUL

**unmitigated** absolute, categorical, unqualified, thorough, utter, perfect, complete, total, downright, out-and-out. PARTIAL
undiminished, unmodified, intense, harsh, oppressive, relentless.

**unmoved** impassive, unfeeling, indifferent, uncaring, untouched, unaffected, cold, cool. MOVED
unshaken, unwavering, steadfast, firm, resolute, determined. SHAKEN

**unnatural** abnormal, aberrant, anomalous, irregular, unusual, odd, strange, uncanny, bizarre, extraordinary. NORMAL
cruel, inhuman, brutal, heartless, unfeeling, callous. HUMANE
artificial, forced, affected, mannered, stilted, stiff, assumed, feigned, insincere, self-conscious. SINCERE

**unnecessary** needless, unneeded, uncalled-for, nonessential, inessential, expendable, useless, superfluous, redundant. NECESSARY

**unnerve** daunt, dismay, intimidate, unman, discourage, dishearten, dispirit, demoralize, disconcert, fluster, rattle (*inf*), shake.

**unnoticed** unseen, unobserved, unheeded, ignored, disregarded, overlooked.

**unobtrusive** unpretentious, unassuming, restrained, low-key, inconspicuous, unostentatious, humble, modest, simple, quiet, reserved, retiring, meek, self-effacing. PRETENTIOUS

**unoccupied** empty, vacant, deserted, uninhabited, untenanted. OCCUPIED
idle, inactive, at leisure, unemployed. BUSY

**unorthodox** heterodox, heretical, unconventional, unusual, abnormal, irregular. ORTHODOX

**unpaid** due, overdue, outstanding, unsettled, owing, payable. PAID

**unpalatable** unpleasant, disagreeable, distasteful, unsavoury, unappetizing, inedible, uneatable, nasty, disgusting, offensive, repulsive. PALATABLE

**unparalleled** peerless, matchless, unmatched, unequalled, unrivalled, incomparable, inimitable, unprecedented, unexampled, unique, singular, supreme, consummate. ORDINARY

**unpardonable** unforgivable, inexcusable, unjustifiable, indefensible, reprehensible, deplorable, disgraceful, shameful. PARDONABLE

**unperturbed** calm, composed, serene, tranquil, unruffled, untroubled, placid, cool, poised, self-possessed, imperturbable. AGITATED

**unpleasant** disagreeable, obnoxious, offensive, nasty, repulsive, unattractive, objectionable, detestable, annoying, irksome, troublesome. PLEASANT

**unpolished** rough, coarse, rude, crude, unfinished, unrefined, uncultured, uncultivated, uncivilized, unsophisticated. POLISHED

**unpopular** disliked, unloved, unwelcome, rejected, undesirable, objectionable. POPULAR

**unprecedented** new, novel, unheard-of, unexampled, unparalleled, unequalled, original, unconventional.

**unpredictable** unforeseeable, doubtful, questionable, uncertain, unsure, erratic, capricious, fickle, changeable, unreliable, undependable, chance, accidental. PREDICTABLE

**unprejudiced** unbiased, impartial, disinterested, objective, detached, fair, just, neutral, indifferent. PREJUDICED

**unpremeditated** spontaneous, impulsive, spur-of-the-moment, impromptu, extempore, unprepared, unplanned. DELIBERATE

**unprepossessing** unattractive, unlovely, plain, ugly. ATTRACTIVE

**unpretentious** modest, humble, simple, plain, unaffected, unassuming, unostentatious, unobtrusive. PRETENTIOUS

**unprincipled** unscrupulous, dishonest, deceitful, crooked, unethical, amoral, immoral, unprofessional, dishonourable, corrupt. HONEST

**unproductive** fruitless, unfruitful, unprolific, sterile, barren, abortive, useless, futile, vain, unavailing, ineffective, unprofitable, worthless, unsuccessful. PRODUCTIVE

**unprofitable** unremunerative, unrewarding, worthless, valueless, unproductive, fruitless, bootless, useless, vain, unavailing. PROFITABLE

**unpromising** unpropitious, unfavourable, inauspicious, gloomy, ominous, discouraging, adverse, doubtful. PROMISING

**unprotected** unguarded, unarmed, undefended, defenceless, vulnerable, open, exposed, unsheltered. PROTECTED

**unqualified** incompetent, unfit, unsuited, ineligible, incapable. QUALIFIED

unmitigated, unconditional, categorical, unreserved, absolute, utter, complete, thorough, downright, out-and-out, perfect, consummate. PARTIAL

**unquestionable** indisputable, indubitable, irrefutable, undeniable, uncontestable, incontrovertible, certain, sure, clear, plain, evident, obvious, patent, manifest, conclusive, definite. QUESTIONABLE

**unravel** untangle, disentangle, undo, untwist, unwind, separate, solve, work out, clear up, explain, decipher, interpret. ENTANGLE

**unreal** imaginary, fanciful, illusory, visionary, intangible, nonexistent, fictitious, make-believe, false, artificial. REAL

**unreasonable** excessive, immoderate, extravagant, exorbitant, undue, unfair, unjust, uncalled-for. REASONABLE

irrational, illogical, senseless, foolish, silly, stupid, mad, crazy, absurd, preposterous. SENSIBLE

**unrelenting** relentless, implacable, inexorable, merciless, pitiless, cruel, ruthless, remorseless, unsparing. MERCIFUL

continuous, continual, constant, unbroken, unremitting, unabating, perpetual, incessant, ceaseless, endless. INTERMITTENT

**unreliable** undependable, untrustworthy, irresponsible, uncertain, fickle, changeable, capricious, erratic. RELIABLE

**unremitting** incessant, ceaseless, unceasing, perpetual, constant, continual, continuous, unrelenting, relentless, assiduous, diligent. INTERMITTENT

**unrepentant** impenitent, unregenerate, unreformed, incorrigible, inveterate, hardened. REPENTANT

**unreserved** unqualified, unrestricted, unlimited, unconditional, total, entire, full, wholehearted, open, frank, outspoken, uninhibited. RESERVED

**unrest** disquiet, uneasiness, restlessness, worry, anxiety, distress, agitation, turmoil, rebellion, strife, discord, discontent, dissatisfaction. PEACE

**unrestrained** unchecked, unhindered, unbridled, uncontrolled, unrestricted, unlimited, free, natural, uninhibited, unrepressed, wild, immoderate. RESTRAINED

**unrestricted** unlimited, limitless, unbounded, boundless, free, open, unhindered, unobstructed, unrestrained. RESTRICTED

**unrighteous** wicked, sinful, iniquitous, evil, bad, heinous, nefarious. GOOD
unfair, unjust, inequitable, wrongful. FAIR

**unripe** green, raw, immature, undeveloped, unready. RIPE

**unrivalled** matchless, unmatched, peerless, nonpareil, unequalled, unparalleled, incomparable, inimitable, unsurpassed, supreme. INFERIOR

**unroll** open, unfold, unfurl, unwind. ROLL

**unruffled** calm, composed, cool, collected, poised, self-possessed, unmoved, unperturbed, imperturbable, placid, serene, tranquil, peaceful, flat, smooth. AGITATED

**unruly** ungovernable, unmanageable, intractable, uncontrollable, refractory, recalcitrant, disobedient, insubordinate, mutinous, riotous, rebellious, restive, wild, disorderly, turbulent, lawless. ORDERLY

**unsafe** dangerous, hazardous, perilous, treacherous, risky, uncertain, precarious, insecure, unsound. SAFE

**unsatisfactory** inadequate, insufficient, deficient, poor, inferior, mediocre, unacceptable, unsuitable, not good enough. EXCELLENT

**unsavoury** insipid, vapid, tasteless, flat, unpalatable, unappetizing, nauseating, distasteful, unpleasant, disagreeable, objectionable, offensive, sordid, seamy, repulsive, revolting, nasty, obnoxious.

**unscathed** unharmed, unhurt, uninjured, undamaged, unimpaired, safe, sound, whole. HURT

**unscrupulous** unprincipled, unethical, amoral, unconscionable, shameless, corrupt, dishonest, dishonourable. HONEST

**unseasonable** untimely, ill-timed, inopportune, inappropriate, unsuitable. SEASONABLE

**unseat** unsaddle, unhorse, throw, depose, oust, dethrone, remove, dismiss, overthrow.

**unseemly** unbecoming, improper, indecorous, indecent, unbefitting, inappropriate. PROPER

**unselfish** charitable, selfless, altruistic, magnanimous, generous, liberal. SELFISH

**unsettle** upset, perturb, trouble, disturb, bother, fluster, rattle (*inf*), ruffle, agitate, disconcert, confuse, throw (*inf*).

**unsettled** disorderly, disorganized, unstable, shaky, unsteady, insecure, inconstant, changeable, variable, unpredictable. SETTLED
uneasy, tense, anxious, restless, flustered, ruffled, agitated, shaken, confused. CALM
unresolved, undecided, moot, debatable, open, pending, payable, owing, outstanding, due.

**unsheltered** unshielded, unprotected, open, exposed. SHELTERED

**unshrinking** unflinching, unfaltering, unwavering, firm, resolute, dauntless, undaunted, unblenching.

**unsightly** ugly, hideous, repulsive, unpleasant, disagreeable, unattractive, unprepossessing. BEAUTIFUL

**unskilful** clumsy, awkward, maladroit, unhandy, inexpert, inept, bungling, incompetent. SKILFUL

**unskilled** inexperienced, untrained, unqualified, inexpert, unprofessional, amateurish. SKILLED

**unsociable** unfriendly, uncongenial, unneighbourly, hostile, uncommunicative, reticent, retiring, withdrawn, aloof, distant. SOCIABLE

**unsolicited** unsought, unrequested, uncalled-for, uninvited, unwanted, unwelcome, voluntary, free. REQUESTED

**unsophisticated** innocent, childlike, naive, unworldly, inexperienced, guileless, artless, ingenuous, natural, simple, plain, unaffected, unrefined, unpolished, unadulterated, pure, genuine. SOPHISTICATED

**unsound** weak, feeble, infirm, unhealthy, unwell, diseased, deranged, unhinged, impaired, imperfect, defective, rotten, decayed. SOUND

fallacious, faulty, flawed, illogical, false, erroneous, wrong, invalid. VALID

unstable, shaky, rickety, unsteady, flimsy, unsafe. STABLE

**unsparing** profuse, lavish, abundant, bountiful, liberal, generous, unstinting, ungrudging. MEAN

merciless, unmerciful, pitiless, unpitying, relentless, unrelenting, inexorable, implacable, ruthless, cruel, harsh, severe, stern, unforgiving. MERCIFUL

**unspeakable** unutterable, ineffable, inexpressible, indescribable, unimaginable, unbelievable.

loathsome, odious, abominable, horrible, awful, unmentionable.

**unspoiled** unspoilt, perfect, unharmed, undamaged, preserved, unchanged, untouched, unaffected, natural, pure, simple, innocent.

**unspoken** tacit, understood, assumed, implied, implicit, unstated, unexpressed, unsaid, unuttered, silent, mute, wordless, voiceless. STATED

**unstable** unsteady, insecure, unsettled, shaky, wobbly, rickety, precarious, risky. STEADY

unpredictable, changeable, variable, inconstant, fickle, capricious, wavering, vacillating, fluctuating, erratic, irregular. STABLE

**unsteady** unstable, unsafe, insecure, precarious, wobbly, shaky, rickety, tottering, staggering. STABLE

irregular, erratic, wavering, vacillating, fluctuating, changeable, variable. STEADY

**unstinted** generous, liberal, lavish, profuse, ample, abundant, plentiful, bountiful. MEAGRE

**unstudied** natural, unaffected, unpremeditated, spontaneous, impromptu, casual.

**unsubstantial** insubstantial, fanciful, imaginary, unreal, visionary, illusory, airy, light, slight, thin, frail, fragile, flimsy, weak, tenuous, unsound. SOLID

**unsuccessful** futile, vain, unavailing, bootless, useless, ineffectual, worthless, fruitless, unproductive, abortive. FRUITFUL

unfortunate, unlucky, luckless, hapless, ill-fated, ill-starred, foiled, frustrated, defeated, losing. SUCCESSFUL

**unsuitable** inappropriate, inapt, unfitting, unfit, unsuited, incompatible, incongruous, out of place, out of keeping, impractical, unseemly, unbecoming, improper. SUITABLE

**unsullied** clean, pure, spotless, unspotted, immaculate, unsoiled, unblemished, stainless, unstained, untainted, untarnished, untouched, undefiled, unpolluted, uncontaminated. SULLIED

**unsung** unacclaimed, uncelebrated, unacknowledged, unrecognized, unrenowned, anonymous, unnamed, unknown. FAMOUS

**unsure** uncertain, doubtful, dubious, sceptical, suspicious, undecided, irresolute, hesitant, insecure. SURE

**unsurpassed** unexcelled, supreme, paramount, transcendent, unrivalled, unparalleled, unequalled, unmatched, matchless, peerless, nonpareil, incomparable. INFERIOR

**unsuspecting** unsuspicious, trusting, trustful, credulous, gullible, naive, ingenuous, unwary, off guard. SUSPICIOUS

**unswerving** straight, direct, undeviating, constant, steadfast, unfaltering, unwavering, untiring, unflagging.

**unsympathetic** unmoved, unconcerned, uncaring, unfeeling, unpitying, insensitive, callous, heartless, cold, cruel, unkind, inconsiderate. SYMPATHETIC

**unsystematic** unmethodical, unorganized, disorganized, disorderly, confused, muddled, random, haphazard, irregular. SYSTEMATIC

**untarnished** bright, shining, polished, clean, spotless, immaculate, pure, unstained, stainless, unblemished, untainted, unsullied. TARNISHED

**untaught** uneducated, unschooled, ignorant, illiterate, unlearned. EDUCATED

**untenable** indefensible, unsound, weak, flawed, faulty, fallacious, groundless, unreasonable, illogical. SOUND

**unthinkable** unimaginable, inconceivable, incredible, unbelievable, impossible, out of the question, unlikely, improbable, preposterous, absurd. CONCEIVABLE

**unthinking** thoughtless, inconsiderate, tactless, rude, senseless, witless, mindless, unmindful, heedless, regardless, neglectful, negligent, rash, careless, impulsive, automatic, mechanical, instinctive. THOUGHTFUL

**untidy** disorderly, messy, sloppy (*inf*), slovenly, unkempt, scruffy, bedraggled, littered, muddled, jumbled, chaotic. TIDY

**untie** undo, unfasten, unknot, unlace, release, loose, free, let go. TIE

**untimely** premature, early, unseasonable, ill-timed, inopportune, inconvenient, inappropriate, unsuitable. TIMELY

**untiring** tireless, indefatigable, unflagging, unwearying, unfaltering, unwavering, unremitting, determined, steady, constant, persistent, dogged. WAVERING

**untold** unspeakable, unutterable, indescribable, inexpressible, unimaginable, unthinkable.
countless, innumerable, numberless, myriad, incalculable, immeasurable.
secret, private, hidden, unknown, undisclosed, unrevealed.

**untouched** unused, new, pristine, intact, whole, undamaged, unharmed, unhurt, uninjured, unscathed. DAMAGED
unmoved, unaffected, dry-eyed, indifferent, apathetic, unconcerned. MOVED

**untoward** adverse, unfavourable, contrary, bad, inopportune, untimely, unseasonable, inauspicious, unfortunate, unlucky.
unseemly, unbecoming, indecorous, improper, unsuitable, inappropriate.

**untroubled** calm, composed, collected, cool, poised, self-possessed, unruffled, unperturbed, placid, tranquil, serene, peaceful. AGITATED

**untrue** false, untruthful, wrong, mistaken, erroneous, fallacious, incorrect, inaccurate, inexact, imprecise. CORRECT
unfaithful, faithless, disloyal, traitorous, perfidious, treacherous, false, untrustworthy. FAITHFUL

**untrustworthy** unreliable, undependable, dishonest, deceitful, false, untrue, disloyal, faithless, unfaithful, treacherous. TRUSTWORTHY

**untruth** falsehood, lie, fib, fabrication, fiction, story, tale. TRUTH
lying, mendacity, untruthfulness, falsity, deceit, deceitfulness. TRUTHFULNESS

**untruthful** lying, mendacious, deceitful, dishonest, insincere, hypocritical, false, untrue. TRUTHFUL

**unused** new, pristine, untouched, intact, leftover, surplus. USED
unaccustomed, unfamiliar, inexperienced. ACCUSTOMED

**unusual** uncommon, extraordinary, remarkable, odd, strange, queer, peculiar, curious, rare, singular, unfamiliar, unexpected, unwanted, unconventional. USUAL

**unutterable** ineffable, unspeakable, indescribable, inexpressible, beyond words.

**unvarnished** plain, simple, bare, naked, unembellished, unadorned, pure, direct, honest, frank.

**unvarying** unchanging, changeless, constant, steady, invariable, unchangeable. CHANGING

**unveil** reveal, expose, uncover, lay bare, disclose, divulge. VEIL

**unwanted** unsolicited, unsought, unasked, uninvited, unwelcome, undesirable, uncalled-for, unneeded, superfluous, rejected. WANTED

**unwarranted** unwarrantable, unjustified, uncalled-for, gratuitous, unjust, unfair, undeserved, unmerited, wrong, unjustifiable, indefensible, inexcusable. JUSTIFIED

**unwary** incautious, careless, heedless, thoughtless, unthinking, hasty, rash, reckless, indiscreet, imprudent, unwise, unguarded, unwatchful. WARY

**unwavering** unfaltering, unswerving, staunch, steadfast, constant, steady, unflagging, untiring, resolute, resolved, determined, firm. WAVERING

**unwelcome** unwanted, rejected, uninvited, unacceptable, unpopular, undesirable, unpleasant, disagreeable. WELCOME

**unwell** ill, sick, ailing, indisposed, poorly (*inf*), under the weather (*inf*), off colour, out of sorts. WELL

**unwieldy** bulky, large, heavy, weighty, ponderous, cumbersome, ungainly, clumsy, awkward, unmanageable, unhandy, inconvenient. HANDY

**unwilling** reluctant, averse, loath, indisposed, disinclined, opposed. WILLING

**unwind** unroll, uncoil, untwist, unravel, undo, slacken, loosen.
relax, calm down, slow down, take it easy (*inf*).

**unwise** injudicious, indiscreet, imprudent, incautious, impolitic, ill-advised, foolhardy, rash, reckless, irresponsible, foolish, senseless, silly, stupid. WISE

**unwitting** unknowing, unaware, ignorant, oblivious, unconscious, unsuspecting, accidental, inadvertent, unintentional, involuntary. CONSCIOUS

**unwonted** unusual, uncommon, uncustomary, unfamiliar, rare, exceptional, atypical, unheard-of, extraordinary, peculiar. USUAL

**unworthy** unseemly, unbecoming, unsuitable, inappropriate, unfitting, unbefitting, out of character, out of place, undeserving, ineligible. WORTHY
dishonourable, ignoble, discreditable, shameful, contemptible, base, worthless, paltry.

**unwrap** undo, open, uncover. WRAP

**unyielding** inflexible, unbending, stiff, rigid, firm, hard, adamant, steady, staunch, steadfast, resolute, determined, obstinate, stubborn, obdurate, intractable. FLEXIBLE

**upbraid** scold, chide, reprimand, reprove, reproach, rebuke, castigate, tell off (*inf*), berate, condemn, censure, blame. PRAISE

**upheaval** cataclysm, disruption, disturbance, disorder.

**uphill** hard, difficult, strenuous, toilsome, arduous, laborious, gruelling, punishing. EASY
rising, ascending, climbing, mounting. DOWNHILL

**uphold** sustain, maintain, support, back, endorse, aid, advocate, promote, champion, defend. OPPOSE

**upkeep** maintenance, conservation, preservation, subsistence, sustenance, expenses, costs.

**uplift** raise, elevate, lift up, hoist, heave. LOWER
improve, ameliorate, better, enhance, enrich, edify, advance, exalt, ennoble.

**upper** higher, top, superior, greater. LOWER

**upright** vertical, perpendicular, straight, erect. HORIZONTAL
just, fair, honest, honourable, ethical, principled, righteous, virtuous, good, decent. DISHONEST

**uprising** rebellion, revolt, revolution, insurrection, mutiny, riot.

**uproar** turmoil, tumult, clamour, brouhaha, hubbub, din, commotion, disturbance, disorder, riot, pandemonium, rumpus. PEACE

**uproarious** turbulent, tumultuous, riotous, disorderly, wild, noisy, clamorous, boisterous. QUIET
hilarious, hysterical, side-splitting, very funny.

**uproot** pull up, root out, extirpate, deracinate, displace, remove, eradicate, destroy, eliminate, wipe out.

**upset** *v*, overturn, knock over, tip over, capsize, topple, spill.
sadden, grieve, distress, dismay, worry, trouble, bother, disturb, perturb, discompose, agitate, ruffle, fluster, confuse, mix up, spoil, mess up.
*adj*, overturned, capsized, upside down, topsy-turvy, disordered, confused.
sad, distressed, worried, troubled, disturbed, perturbed, agitated, ruffled. CALM

**upshot** result, consequence, outcome, issue, effect, end, conclusion. BEGINNING

**up-to-date** modern, fashionable, stylish, trendy (*inf*), current, latest, new, up-to-the-minute. OLD

**urban** civic, municipal, metropolitan, town, city.

**urbane** elegant, refined, polished, suave, debonair, courteous, polite, civil, civilized, sophisticated. UNCOUTH

**urge** *v*, push, drive, force, propel, impel, press, constrain, incite, provoke, goad, spur, encourage, induce, persuade. DETER
plead, implore, beseech, supplicate, beg, entreat, exhort, advise, advocate, recommend.
*n*, desire, wish, itch, yearning, drive, impulse.

**urgent** pressing, instant, important, serious, grave, imperative, crucial, critical. UNIMPORTANT
insistent, importunate, earnest, persistent.

**usage** custom, practice, habit, tradition, convention, form, method, procedure, routine, rule, wont, fashion, mode.
use, employment, treatment, handling, management, operation, running, control.

**use** *v*, employ, utilize, apply, make use of, practise, exercise, operate, wield, handle, treat, manipulate. exploit, abuse, misuse.
consume, spend, expend, use up, exhaust, drain, waste, squander. SAVE

**used to,** accustomed to, familiar with, inured to, hardened to.

*n*, employment, utilization, application, practice, exercise, operation, treatment, usage, wear and tear.
utility, usefulness, advantage, benefit, profit, good, help, avail, service. FUTILITY
need, call, cause, occasion, purpose, reason, point.
custom, practice, habit, usage.

**useful** helpful, serviceable, advantageous, beneficial, valuable, profitable, worthwhile, effective, practical, handy. USELESS

**useless** futile, vain, idle, bootless, unavailing, ineffective, fruitless, abortive, unproductive, worthless, impractical, no good. USEFUL

**usher** *n*, guide, escort, usherette, doorkeeper.
*v*, guide, escort, pilot, steer, lead, direct, conduct, show.

**usual** customary, accustomed, habitual, wonted, routine, normal, stock, standard, typical, conventional, general, familiar, common, everyday, ordinary. UNUSUAL

**usurp** seize, take over, commandeer, appropriate, arrogate, assume, infringe, encroach.

**utensil** implement, instrument, tool, device, contrivance, apparatus, gadget.

**utility** usefulness, serviceability, use, advantage, benefit, profit, service, avail. FUTILITY

**utilize** use, employ, make use of, avail oneself of.

**utmost** uttermost, most, maximum, greatest, supreme, paramount, highest, top, extreme, farthest, last, final. MINIMUM

**utter**[1] *v*, say, speak, express, pronounce, articulate, voice, verbalize, enunciate, declare, proclaim, announce, promulgate. SUPPRESS

**utter**[2] *adj*, complete, total, thorough, absolute, downright, out-and-out, sheer, arrant, unqualified, unmitigated. PARTIAL

# V

**vacancy** opportunity, job, position, room.
emptiness, void, gap, space, blankness, inanity.

**vacant** empty, void, unfilled, unoccupied, free, not in use. OCCUPIED
blank, expressionless, vacuous, inane, thoughtless, unthinking.

**vacate** evacuate, abandon, desert, quit, leave, depart.

**vacation** holiday, recess, rest, break, intermission. TERM

**vaccinate** inoculate, immunize, protect.

**vacillate** fluctuate, oscillate, waver, falter, hesitate, dither, be indecisive, sway, rock.

**vacillating** indecisive, irresolute, uncertain, wavering, hesitant, fickle. FIRM

**vacuous** empty, vacant, void, unfilled. FULL
blank, expressionless, inane, stupid, unintelligent, mindless. INTELLIGENT

**vacuum** void, emptiness, vacuity.

**vagabond** vagrant, tramp, nomad, itinerant, wayfarer, wanderer, rogue, rascal.

**vagary** whim, fancy, humour, crotchet, caprice, notion.

**vagrant** *n*, tramp, vagabond, down-and-out, beggar, nomad, itinerant.
*adj*, nomadic, itinerant, peripatetic, wandering, roaming, roving, homeless, down and out. SETTLED

**vague** indistinct, indeterminate, unclear, obscure, nebulous, hazy, blurred, dim, faint, imprecise, ambiguous, loose, indefinite, uncertain. CLEAR

**vain** conceited, boastful, proud, arrogant, inflated, stuck-up (*inf*), overweening, cocky, egotistical, big-headed (*inf*). MODEST
worthless, trivial, unimportant, idle, hollow, empty, futile, useless, bootless, unavailing, ineffective, ineffectual, fruitless, abortive. WORTHWHILE

**valediction** farewell, goodbye, adieu. GREETING

**valiant** valorous, brave, courageous, heroic, intrepid, fearless, dauntless, undaunted, bold, daring, gallant, plucky, doughty, indomitable. COWARDLY

**valid** sound, good, well-founded, logical, cogent, convincing, powerful, efficacious, conclusive, just. WEAK
official, legal, lawful, legitimate, genuine, authentic, real, true, binding, effective. INVALID

**valley** dale, dell, vale, glen, hollow, depression. HILL

**valour** bravery, courage, heroism, intrepidity, fearlessness, dauntlessness, boldness, daring, gallantry, pluck, spirit, mettle. COWARDICE

**valuable** precious, costly, expensive, priceless, rare, prized, valued, cherished, dear, estimable, worthy, worthwhile, useful, important, beneficial. WORTHLESS

**value** *n*, worth, merit, importance, significance, use, usefulness, advantage, benefit, profit, gain.
cost, price, valuation, assessment.
*v*, prize, esteem, appreciate, respect, cherish, hold dear, treasure. SCORN
evaluate, assess, appraise, estimate, rate, price.

**vandalism** destruction, ruin, damage, mutilation.

**vanish** disappear, fade, evanesce, dissolve, melt, evaporate, go away. APPEAR

**vanity** conceit, egotism, self-love, narcissism, pride, arrogance, boastfulness, bigheadedness. MODESTY
worthlessness, emptiness, hollowness, uselessness, futility, pointlessness, frivolity, triviality, unreality.

**vanquish** defeat, conquer, subjugate, subdue, rout, overwhelm, overcome, overpower, overthrow, crush, quell, beat, master. SURRENDER

**vapid** insipid, flat, flavourless, tasteless, bland, tame, dull, boring, uninteresting. PIQUANT

**vapour** steam, smoke, fog, mist, haze, breath, exhalation.

**variable** changeable, mutable, protean, chameleonic, vacillating, wavering, fluctuating, capricious, mercurial, fickle, inconstant, unsteady, unstable, shifting. CONSTANT

**variance** discrepancy, disparity, divergence, difference, disagreement, discord, conflict, strife, dissent, dissension. AGREEMENT

**variation** diversity, variety, difference, departure, deviation, change, alteration, modification, variant, innovation, novelty.

**variegated** mottled, speckled, dappled, pied, motley, streaked, varicoloured, multicoloured. PLAIN

**variety** difference, dissimilarity, discrepancy, disparity, variation, change, diversity, multiplicity. UNIFORMITY
miscellany, assortment, mixture, medley, collection, range.
class, kind, type, sort, order, group, species, brand.

**various** different, diverse, assorted, miscellaneous, mixed, motley, varied, sundry, many, numerous, several, manifold. IDENTICAL

**varnish** glaze, lacquer, polish, gild, adorn, embellish, ornament, decorate.

**vary** change, alter, modify, diversify, transform, permutate, alternate, fluctuate, swerve, deviate, diverge, depart, differ, disagree.

**vast** immense, broad, wide, extensive, expansive, massive, huge, enormous, great, tremendous, colossal, gigantic, boundless, unbounded, limitless, illimitable, immeasurable, measureless. TINY

**vault**[1] *n*, arch, span, cellar, strongroom, tomb, crypt, mausoleum.

**vault**[2] *v*, leap, spring, jump, bound, hurdle, clear.

**vaunt** boast, brag, crow, trumpet, parade, show off. BELITTLE

**veer** change, swing, shift, turn, sheer, swerve, deviate, diverge.

**vegetate** sprout, grow, shoot, burgeon, germinate, swell. WITHER
idle, do nothing, waste time, stagnate. WORK

**vehement** ardent, fervent, impassioned, passionate, earnest, enthusiastic, intense, forceful, furious, violent, burning, fierce, strong, powerful. SUBDUED

**vehicle** conveyance, transport.
means, agency, instrument, medium, organ, channel.

**veil** *n*, cover, screen, cloak, mantle, shroud, mask, disguise, blind.
*v*, cover, screen, cloak, muffle, dim, obscure, conceal, hide, mask, disguise. EXPOSE

**vein** streak, stripe, line, lode, seam, stratum.
strain, tendency, bent, character, mood, humour.

**velocity** speed, rate, swiftness, rapidity, quickness, celerity. SLOWNESS

**velvety** velvet, velutinous, smooth, soft. COARSE

**venal** corrupt, corruptible, bribable, mercenary, grasping, rapacious, sordid. INCORRUPTIBLE

**vendetta** feud, quarrel, enmity, bad blood.

**veneer** coat, layer, covering, facing, front, façade, show, appearance.

**venerate** revere, reverence, honour, esteem, adore, worship. DESPISE

**vengeance** revenge, retribution, requital, retaliation, reprisal. FORGIVENESS

**vengeful** revengeful, vindictive, spiteful, unforgiving, avenging, retaliatory. FORGIVING

**venial** excusable, pardonable, forgivable, allowable, slight, minor, insignificant, trivial. UNFORGIVABLE

**venom** poison, toxin.
rancour, spite, spitefulness, ill will, bitterness, acrimony, malice, malignity, malevolence, hate, gall, spleen, grudge. BENEVOLENCE

**venomous** poisonous, toxic, virulent, envenomed, noxious, harmful. HARMLESS
spiteful, malicious, hostile, malevolent, malignant, rancorous. BENEVOLENT

**vent** *n*, hole, aperture, opening, outlet, spiracle, orifice, passage, duct.
*v*, air, express, utter, emit, discharge, release.

**ventilate** air, aerate, oxygenate, fan, air-condition, cool, freshen, purify.
discuss, talk about, go over, review, examine, scrutinize, broadcast, make known.

**venture** *v*, risk, hazard, endanger, imperil, jeopardize, speculate, stake, wager, chance, dare, presume, advance, put forward.
*n*, undertaking, enterprise, project, adventure, chance, gamble, speculation, risk, hazard.

**venturesome** daring, bold, adventurous, enterprising, brave, courageous, doughty, dauntless, fearless, intrepid, plucky, spirited, reckless, foolhardy. COWARDLY

**veracious** truthful, honest, frank, candid, trustworthy, reliable, true, factual, accurate, precise.

**verbal** spoken, oral, unwritten, verbatim, literal. WRITTEN

**verbiage** verbosity, prolixity, wordiness, long-windedness, loquacity, circumlocution, periphrasis, pleonasm, tautology, repetition, redundancy. TERSENESS

**verbose** prolix, wordy, long-winded, loquacious, garrulous, talkative, circumlocutory, roundabout, periphrastic, tautological. TERSE

**verdant** green, grassy, leafy, fresh.

**verdict** decision, judgment, conclusion, finding, opinion, sentence.

**verge** *n*, edge, border, margin, lip, rim, brim, brink, limit, boundary, threshold.
*v*, approach, border, incline, tend, bear, lean.

**verify** confirm, substantiate, corroborate, bear out, prove, establish, attest, affirm, authenticate, validate. REFUTE

**verisimilitude** probability, likelihood, credibility, plausibility, realism, authenticity. IMPROBABILITY

**veritable** real, actual, genuine, authentic, positive, absolute.

**verity** truth, reality, actuality, fact. FALSITY

**vernacular** *adj*, native, indigenous, local, informal, colloquial, popular, common, vulgar. FOREIGN
*n*, native language, mother tongue, dialect, patois, jargon, slang.

**versatile** adaptable, all-round, multifaceted, many-sided, flexible, all-purpose, variable, changeable, inconstant, fickle.

**verse** stanza, poem, poetry, metre.

**versed** skilled, proficient, accomplished, practised, experienced, acquainted, familiar, conversant, knowledgeable. INEXPERIENCED

**version** rendering, interpretation, account, translation, reading.
type, model, form, variant.

**vertex** apex, apogee, peak, summit, point, tip, top, crown, acme, zenith, pinnacle, height. BASE

**vertical** upright, perpendicular, erect. HORIZONTAL

**vertigo** giddiness, dizziness, lightheadedness.

**verve** vigour, energy, force, enthusiasm, spirit, life, dash, élan, vivacity, liveliness, animation, vitality, gusto. APATHY

**very** *adv*, extremely, exceedingly, terribly (*inf*), awfully (*inf*), remarkably, exceptionally, highly, greatly, really, truly. SLIGHTLY
*adj*, actual, real, true, genuine, perfect, exact, same, identical.

**vessel** boat, ship, craft.
container, receptacle, pot.

**vest** endow, bestow, confer, invest.
clothe, dress, robe, garb. STRIP

**vestal** virginal, chaste, pure, virtuous.

**vestibule** lobby, foyer, anteroom, antechamber, hall, porch.

**vestige** trace, mark, sign, indication, relics, remains, hint, touch, suggestion, suspicion.

**vestment** robe, habit, garment, clothes, clothing, apparel.

**veteran** *n*, old hand, past master, master, expert. NOVICE
*adj*, experienced, expert, proficient, seasoned, old.

**veto** *n*, prohibition, interdiction, ban, embargo, refusal, rejection. APPROVAL
*v*, reject, turn down, prohibit, forbid, disallow, ban. CONSENT

**vex** annoy, irritate, provoke, pique, nettle, chafe, exasperate, infuriate, irk, anger, bother, pester, harass, bug (*inf*), torment, tease, plague, trouble, worry, fret. SOOTHE

**vexation** annoyance, irritation, exasperation, anger, bother, nuisance, problem, trouble.

**vexatious** annoying, irritating, exasperating, infuriating, irksome, bothersome, troublesome, worrying.

**vexed** annoyed, irritated, nettled, peeved (*inf*), angry, irate, bothered, harassed, agitated, disturbed, troubled, worried.
contested, disputed, moot, controversial.

**vibrate** oscillate, swing, sway, wave, undulate, vacillate, fluctuate, shake, tremble, quiver, shiver, palpitate, pulse, pulsate, throb, resonate, reverberate.

**vicarious** indirect, second-hand, sympathetic, empathetic, surrogate, substitutive, delegated, deputed. PERSONAL

**vice** sin, wickedness, wrong, iniquity, evil, immorality, corruption, depravity.
fault, flaw, imperfection, defect, failing, shortcoming, weakness, foible. VIRTUE

**vicinity** neighbourhood, area, district, locality, precincts, environs, proximity, propinquity. DISTANCE

**vicious** savage, ferocious, fierce, violent, cruel, barbarous, harsh, severe, wicked, evil, bad, sinful, immoral, corrupt, depraved, mean, spiteful, malicious, bitter, rancorous, venomous. KIND

**vicissitude** variation, change, mutation, shift, alternation, fluctuation. STABILITY

**victim** sufferer, casualty, prey, scapegoat, sacrifice, martyr, dupe, sucker (*inf*), fall guy (*inf*), butt, target.

**victimize** persecute, discriminate against, pick on, exploit, use, deceive, fool, dupe, swindle, cheat, defraud.

**victor** winner, champion, conqueror, hero. LOSER

**victorious** winning, conquering, triumphant, successful. LOSING

**victory** win, conquest, triumph, success, superiority, mastery. DEFEAT

**victuals** food, provisions, rations, viands, eatables, edibles, grub (*inf*).

**vie** strive, struggle, compete, contend, contest.

**view** *n*, sight, vision, scene, vista, prospect, aspect, outlook, panorama, landscape.
survey, examination, inspection, scrutiny, study, observation.
opinion, judgment, belief, impression, idea, notion, estimation, sentiment, feeling.
aim, intention, purpose, design, object, end.
*v*, watch, observe, see, behold, look at, regard, survey, scan, examine, inspect, scrutinize, eye. IGNORE
consider, contemplate, think about, regard, deem, judge.

**viewpoint** attitude, angle, position, standpoint, stance, point of view.

**vigilant** watchful, observant, attentive, awake, alert, sleepless, unsleeping, wary, cautious, careful, circumspect. CARELESS

**vigorous** energetic, strenuous, active, dynamic, brisk, lively, strong, robust, lusty, hardy, hale, hearty, sound, sturdy, powerful, forceful. WEAK

**vigour** energy, vitality, activity, liveliness, strength, power, force, might, stamina, health, robustness, sturdiness, spirit, verve, vehemence, intensity. WEAKNESS

**vile** base, low, mean, bad, wicked, evil, sinful, immoral, depraved, corrupt, ignoble, villainous, heinous, nefarious, contemptible, despicable, odious, loathsome, wretched, miserable, abject, menial, degrading, humiliating, worthless, paltry, foul, disgusting, repulsive, revolting, nasty, offensive, obnoxious, objectionable, unpleasant, disagreeable. GOOD

**vilify** vituperate, defame, denigrate, revile, malign, slander, libel, calumniate, traduce, asperse, slur, disparage, decry. PRAISE

**villain** scoundrel, blackguard, reprobate, wretch, rogue, rascal, miscreant, evildoer, baddy (*inf*). HERO

**villainous** wicked, evil, sinful, bad, vile, base, mean, ignoble, nefarious, heinous, infamous, notorious, criminal, depraved. GOOD

**vindicate** clear, acquit, exculpate, exonerate, absolve, justify, defend, support, uphold, maintain, assert, advocate.

**vindictive** vengeful, revengeful, spiteful, malicious, rancorous, venomous, malevolent, malignant, unforgiving, implacable. FORGIVING

**violate** break, contravene, transgress, infringe, disobey, disregard. OBSERVE
rape, ravish, debauch, molest, defile, outrage, profane, desecrate, invade, disturb. RESPECT

**violent** strong, powerful, forceful, mighty, savage, brutal, cruel, bloodthirsty, wild, uncontrollable, boisterous, turbulent, stormy, tempestuous, raging, furious, fierce, vehement, ardent, fervent, impassioned, passionate, fiery, hot, harsh, severe, acute, sharp, extreme, intense. GENTLE

**virago** termagant, shrew, harridan, battle-axe (*inf*), fury, vixen, scold, nag. ANGEL

**virgin** *n*, maid, maiden, vestal, virgo intacta.
*adj*, virginal, vestal, chaste, pure, untouched, undefiled, unsullied, immaculate, spotless, celibate.

**virile** manly, masculine, potent, powerful, strong, lusty, robust, hardy, vigorous, forceful. EFFEMINATE

**virtual** practical, essential, effective, potential, implied, implicit. ACTUAL

**virtually** practically, as good as, in essence, in effect, almost, nearly. ACTUALLY

**virtue** goodness, righteousness, morality, rectitude, uprightness, probity, integrity, excellence, quality, credit, merit, worth, worthiness, chastity, purity, virginity, honour. VICE

**virtuoso** master, expert, maestro, genius, connoisseur.

**virtuous** good, righteous, moral, ethical, upright, excellent, exemplary, blameless, worthy, pure, chaste, virginal. WICKED

**virulent** poisonous, venomous, toxic, infective, deadly, lethal, noxious, pernicious. HARMLESS
bitter, acrimonious, hostile, resentful, spiteful, malicious, malevolent, malignant, rancorous, vicious. MILD

**visage** face, countenance, physiognomy, aspect, appearance.

**viscera** intestines, bowels, entrails, guts, innards (*inf*), insides (*inf*).

**viscous** viscid, thick, sticky, adhesive, gluey, mucilaginous, glutinous, syrupy, gelatinous, gooey (*inf*).

**visible** perceptible, discernible, apparent, evident, noticeable, observable, manifest, clear, plain, obvious, patent, conspicuous, distinct. INVISIBLE

**vision** sight, eyesight, seeing, view, perception, insight, discernment, penetration. BLINDNESS
apparition, spectre, phantom, ghost, mirage, hallucination, illusion, figment of the imagination, chimera, dream, conception, image.

**visionary** *adj*, romantic, idealistic, quixotic, utopian, impractical, impracticable, unreal, imaginary, illusory, fanciful, chimerical. REAL
*n*, romantic, idealist, dreamer, daydreamer, seer, prophet. CYNIC

**visit** *v*, call on, look up, stop by, drop in (*inf*), stay with, inspect, examine.
assail, attack, afflict, inflict, wreak.
*n*, call, stay, stop, sojourn, inspection, examination, visitation.

**visitor** caller, guest, company, visitant.

**vista** view, scene, prospect, outlook, panorama.

**visualize** picture, conjure up, envisage, imagine, conceive.

**vital** critical, crucial, key, important, essential, requisite, necessary, indispensable, imperative, urgent. UNIMPORTANT
living, alive, animate, life-giving, invigorative, lively, vivacious, animated, spirited, vigorous, forceful, dynamic. DEAD

**vitality** vigour, energy, life, animation, strength, power, stamina, spirit, liveliness, vivacity. WEAKNESS

**vitiate** impair, harm, mar, spoil, blight, debase, corrupt, deprave, pervert, defile, pollute, contaminate, adulterate, deteriorate. IMPROVE

**vituperate** censure, reproach, reprove, slate (*inf*), condemn, denounce, revile, rail against, berate, upbraid, vilify, denigrate, slander, abuse. PRAISE

**vivacious** lively, animated, spirited, sprightly, gay, merry, cheerful, jolly, sportive, bubbly, ebullient, effervescent. TORPID

**vivacity** liveliness, animation, high spirits, gaiety, energy, vigour, ebullience, effervescence. TORPOR

**vivid** bright, intense, brilliant, dazzling, colourful. DULL
graphic, striking, telling, dramatic, realistic, true to life, lifelike, clear, distinct, memorable.

**vivify** animate, vitalize, quicken, invigorate, stimulate, enliven.

**vocabulary** words, language, lexicon, glossary, dictionary, wordbook.

**vocal** oral, spoken, uttered, voiced.
noisy, vociferous, outspoken, articulate, eloquent. SILENT

**vocation** calling, career, profession, occupation, métier, trade, business, job, employment, pursuit.

**vociferate** shout, yell, bellow, bawl, scream, cry, roar, clamour. WHISPER

**vociferous** noisy, loud, clamorous, uproarious, loud-mouthed (*inf*), obstreperous. QUIET

**vogue** fashion, mode, style, trend, rage, craze, custom, practice, usage, use, favour, popularity, prevalence, currency.

**voice** *n*, speech, language, sound, tone, accent, articulation, expression, utterance. SILENCE
vote, say, preference, choice, option, wish, view, opinion.
*v*, express, state, utter, say, declare, proclaim, air, ventilate. SUPPRESS

**void** *adj*, empty, unfilled, vacant, unoccupied, blank, clear, free. FULL
devoid, destitute, lacking, wanting, without.
invalid, null, ineffectual, inoperative, worthless, useless, vain, nugatory. VALID
*n*, emptiness, vacuity, vacuum, space, blank, gap, hole, opening.

**volatile** changeable, variable, fickle, inconstant, capricious, whimsical, flighty, mercurial, unstable, unsteady, giddy, frivolous. STABLE

**volition** will, free will, discretion, determination, purpose, resolution, decision, choice, option, preference, wish. COMPULSION

**volley** barrage, bombardment, fusillade, salvo, report, discharge, explosion, blast, shower, storm, emission.

**voluble** fluent, glib, talkative, loquacious, garrulous. TACITURN

**volume** bulk, capacity, size, dimensions, mass, total, quantity, amount.
tome, book.

**voluminous** spacious, roomy, capacious, big, large, vast, ample, copious. SMALL

**voluntary** free, gratuitous, unasked, unsolicited, unconstrained, unforced, spontaneous, willing, intentional, deliberate, optional, unpaid. COMPULSORY

**volunteer** offer, proffer, tender, present, give, propose, put forward, step forward. WITHHOLD

**voluptuous** sensual, carnal, fleshly, licentious, hedonistic, self-indulgent, sybaritic, voluptuary. ASCETIC
seductive, provocative, erotic, sexy (*inf*), buxom, well-endowed, shapely, curvaceous (*inf*).

**vomit** disgorge, spew, puke (*inf*), bring up, throw up (*inf*), be sick, heave, retch, eject.

**voracious** greedy, ravenous, gluttonous, omnivorous, insatiable, rapacious, avid, hungry.

**vortex** whirlpool, maelstrom, eddy.

**votary** devotee, adherent, disciple, follower, zealot, fanatic, enthusiast, aficionado.

**vote** *n*, ballot, poll, election, referendum, suffrage, franchise, voice, say.
*v*, ballot, elect, appoint, opt.

**vouch** guarantee, assure, asseverate, attest, affirm, assert, certify, confirm, uphold, support, answer for. REPUDIATE

**voucher** receipt, chit, slip, note, document, paper, coupon, token.

**vouchsafe** grant, give, confer, accord, deign, condescend, yield, concede. REFUSE

**vow** *n*, promise, pledge, word, oath.
*v*, promise, pledge, swear, dedicate, devote, consecrate.

**voyage** journey, trip, expedition, cruise, passage, crossing.

**vulgar** coarse, rough, crude, rude, boorish, uncouth, unmannerly, ill-bred, unrefined, uncultivated, indecorous, indecent, obscene, dirty, tasteless, common, low, base. REFINED
ordinary, general, popular, colloquial, vernacular.

**vulnerable** unprotected, assailable, defenceless, exposed, weak, tender, sensitive, susceptible. TOUGH

# W

**wad** lump, mass, ball, hunk, chunk, block, roll, bundle.

**waft** drift, float, blow, puff, carry, bear, convey, transport.

**wag**[1] *v*, wave, swing, wiggle, waggle, flutter, nod, shake, quiver.

**wag**[2] *n*, humorist, comic, comedian, wit, joker, jester.

**wage** *n*, pay, emolument, salary, earnings, remuneration, compensation, hire, fee, stipend, payment, recompense, reward.
*v*, engage in, carry on, undertake, conduct, practise.

**wager** *n*, bet, gamble, stake, pledge, venture.
*v*, bet, gamble, stake, risk, hazard, speculate.

**waggish** impish, puckish, roguish, mischievous, arch, playful, sportive, witty, droll, humorous, comical, funny, jocular, merry. SERIOUS

**wail** *v*, cry, moan, lament, bewail, bemoan, mourn, weep, keen, ululate, howl. REJOICE
*n*, cry, moan, lament, lamentation, ululation, howl.

**wait** *v*, stay, remain, abide, rest, linger, tarry, pause, hesitate. PROCEED
**wait for,** await, expect, anticipate, look forward to, be ready for, be in store for.
**wait on,** serve, attend, minister to.
*n*, delay, stop, halt, pause, rest.

**waiter** attendant, servant, steward, stewardess, maid, waitress.

**waive** renounce, relinquish, give up, abandon, surrender, yield, forgo, dispense with, defer, postpone. ASSERT

**wake**[1] *v*, waken, come to, awake, awaken, rouse, arouse, stir, animate, stimulate, activate, enliven, kindle, fire, excite, quicken.
*n*, vigil, watch.

**wake**[2] *n*, trail, track, path, wash.

**wakeful** awake, sleepless, restless, insomniac. ASLEEP
alert, watchful, vigilant, wary, attentive, observant. UNWARY

**waken** wake, come to, awake, awaken, rouse, arouse, stir, animate, stimulate, activate, kindle, excite.

**walk** *v*, step, stride, pace, march, perambulate, saunter, amble, stroll, ramble, hike, tramp, trudge, go, move, advance, proceed. RUN
*n*, stroll, amble, saunter, promenade, ramble, hike, tramp, march, perambulation, constitutional. RIDE
step, pace, gait, carriage.
path, footpath, pathway, pavement, esplanade, promenade.
field, sphere, province, course, trade, profession, career, vocation.

**wall** divider, partition, screen, fence, enclosure, embankment, rampart, bulwark, barricade, barrier, block, obstacle, obstruction.

**wallow** roll, splash, welter, flounder, stagger, lurch.
bask, luxuriate, revel, delight, relish, savour.

**wan** pale, pallid, ashen, colourless, sallow, pasty, white, bloodless, ghastly, sickly, haggard, gaunt, tired, weary, worn, weak, faint, dim. RUDDY

**wand** stick, twig, rod, baton, staff, mace.

**wander** stray, roam, rove, meander, straggle, range, drift, ramble, stroll. SETTLE
deviate, swerve, veer, go astray, digress, rave, ramble.

**wandering** roaming, roving, itinerant, peripatetic, migratory, nomadic, vagrant, vagabond, wayfaring, travelling. SETTLED

**wane** *v*, diminish, decline, decrease, ebb, subside, abate, fade, peter out, dwindle, weaken, droop, sink. WAX
*n*, diminution, decline, decrease, ebb, subsidence, abatement, drop, fall.

**wangle** fix, arrange, manoeuvre, finagle (*inf*), bring off, pull off.

**want** *v*, need, require, demand, call for, lack, miss, wish, desire, long, yearn, hanker after, covet, crave, hunger, thirst. POSSESS
*n*, need, necessity, requirement, demand, wish, desire, longing, yearning, craving, appetite. POSSESSION
lack, absence, dearth, default, deficiency, inadequacy, insufficiency, shortage, paucity, scarcity. ABUNDANCE
poverty, privation, indigence, penury, destitution, neediness. WEALTH

**wanting** missing, absent, lacking, short, deficient, imperfect, defective, inferior.

**wanton** *adj*, lewd, lecherous, libidinous, prurient, licentious, loose, abandoned, dissolute, dissipated, promiscuous, impure, unchaste. CHASTE
needless, unnecessary, motiveless, groundless, unjustifiable, gratuitous, uncalled-for, wilful, deliberate, arbitrary, cruel, vicious, malicious, malevolent.
playful, sportive, capricious, irresponsible, careless, unrestrained, wild, lavish, extravagant, luxuriant.
*n*, whore, prostitute, loose woman, hussy, profligate, libertine, rake, roué.
*v*, dissipate, debauch, sleep around (*inf*).
waste, squander, misspend, fritter away. SAVE

**war** *n*, warfare, hostilities, fighting, combat, conflict, strife, contention, battle. PEACE
*v*, wage war, fight, battle, contend, combat.

**warble** trill, sing, chirp, pipe.

**ward** *n*, district, precinct, division, zone, quarter, area.
room, apartment.
minor, dependant, charge, protégé. GUARDIAN
guardianship, custody, charge, care, protection, safekeeping.

**ward off,** *v*, avert, deflect, parry, fend off, stave off, repel.

**warden** guardian, keeper, custodian, protector, guard, warder, curator, steward, janitor, caretaker.

**warehouse** depot, depository, store, storehouse, storeroom, stockroom.

**wares** goods, commodities, merchandise, produce, stock.

**warfare** war, hostilities, fighting, combat, strife, conflict, contention, battle. PEACE

**warlike** belligerent, bellicose, pugnacious, combative, hostile, militant, aggressive, martial, military. PACIFIC

**warm** *adj*, tepid, lukewarm, heated, hot, thermal. COOL
ardent, fervent, vehement, passionate, emotional, earnest, heartfelt, enthusiastic, animated, lively, energetic, vigorous. APATHETIC
friendly, affable, cordial, genial, hearty, amiable, affectionate, tender, kindly, warm-hearted, sympathetic. COLD
*v*, heat, reheat, animate, rouse, stir, awaken. COOL

**warmth** heat, warmness. COOLNESS
ardour, fervour, vehemence, passion, zeal, enthusiasm. APATHY
friendliness, cordiality, affection, tenderness. COLDNESS

**warn** caution, alert, forewarn, give notice, admonish, advise, notify, inform, apprise, tip off.

**warning** caution, admonition, advice, alert, alarm, notice, notification, tip, tip-off, threat, omen, portent, premonition, augury.

**warp** twist, bend, turn, contort, misshape, deform, distort, pervert, bias. STRAIGHTEN

**warrant** *n*, authorization, authority, permission, permit, sanction, licence, carte blanche, commission, warranty, guarantee.
*v*, guarantee, pledge, assure, declare, affirm, vouch for, endorse, support, uphold. REPUDIATE
authorize, entitle, empower, commission, license, sanction, approve, permit, allow, justify, excuse, require, call for.

**warrantable** permissible, allowable, lawful, acceptable, justifiable, defensible, reasonable, right. UNJUSTIFIABLE

**wary** cautious, careful, chary, circumspect, prudent, heedful, guarded, suspicious, distrustful, watchful, vigilant, attentive, alert. RASH

**wash** *v*, clean, cleanse, bath, bathe, launder, shampoo, scrub, rinse. SOIL
*n*, washing, bath, bathe, ablution, cleaning, cleansing, scrub, rinse.

**washy** watery, weak, thin, insipid, wishy-washy (*inf*).

**waspish** irritable, irascible, cross, cantankerous, peppery, crabbed, peevish, petulant, touchy, testy. GENIAL

**waste** *v*, squander, fritter away, misspend, dissipate, lose, use up, consume, throw away, blow (*inf*), lavish. SAVE
erode, wear, gnaw, eat away, dwindle, decrease, diminish, decline, decay, wither, shrivel, wilt, emaciate, weaken, wane, fade. FLOURISH
*n*, dissipation, prodigality, misuse, squandering, consumption, loss, extravagance, wastefulness. ECONOMY
destruction, devastation, ruin, desolation, havoc, ravage.
rubbish, refuse, trash, garbage, leftovers, scraps, litter, dross, dregs, debris.
wasteland, desert, wilderness, wild.
*adj*, useless, worthless, superfluous, leftover, unused, unwanted.
desolate, desert, wild, barren, bare, uninhabited, deserted, empty, dreary, bleak. CULTIVATED

**wasteful** extravagant, prodigal, lavish, spendthrift, thriftless, improvident, uneconomical. ECONOMICAL

**watch** *v*, observe, view, see, regard, look at, look on, contemplate, notice, note, mark. IGNORE
guard, protect, watch over, keep, mind, tend, look after, take care of. NEGLECT
be careful, pay attention, watch out, look out.
*n*, timepiece, chronometer, wristwatch, clock.
vigil, lookout, vigilance, watchfulness, attention, alertness, surveillance, observation.

**watchful** vigilant, alert, attentive, observant, guarded, cautious, chary, wary, heedful, careful, circumspect. HEEDLESS

**watchword** password, countersign, catchword, catch phrase, slogan, motto, byword.

**water** damp, moisten, wet, sprinkle, spray, hose, irrigate, flood. PARCH
**water down,** dilute, weaken, thin, adulterate.

**waterfall** cascade, cataract, fall, chute.

**watery** liquid, fluid, aqueous, wet, damp, moist. DRY
thin, runny, weak, diluted, adulterated, insipid, tasteless, washy, wishy-washy (*inf*).

**wave** *v*, flourish, brandish, shake, flap, flutter, wag, sway, rock, swing, oscillate, undulate, ripple.
beckon, gesture, gesticulate, signal.
*n*, undulation, ripple, roller, breaker, billow, swell, surge, rush, stream, drift, trend, current.

**waver** oscillate, vacillate, fluctuate, falter, hesitate, shillyshally (*inf*), dither, sway, wobble, flicker, quiver. DECIDE

**wax** grow, increase, develop, enlarge, expand, swell, rise. WANE

**way** method, manner, fashion, mode, means, procedure, system, technique, approach.
direction, route, course, path, road, track, lane, avenue, channel, passage, journey, advance.
custom, practice, wont, usage, habit, trait, idiosyncrasy, characteristic.
**by the way,** incidentally, in passing, en passant, by the bye.
**give way,** collapse, cave in, yield, acquiesce, accede, surrender.
**under way,** moving, going, in progress, begun.

**wayward** wilful, perverse, contrary, refractory, recalcitrant, contumacious, headstrong, stubborn, obstinate, unruly, intractable, ungovernable, unmanageable, capricious, fickle, flighty, inconstant. DOCILE

**weak** feeble, frail, fragile, delicate, flimsy, puny, enervated, sickly, unhealthy, debilitated, infirm, vulnerable. STRONG
powerless, impotent, ineffectual, lacking, wanting, poor, lame, unconvincing, inconclusive, timorous, spineless, irresolute, indecisive. POWERFUL
faint, low, muffled, imperceptible, dim, pale, dull, soft, slight, small.
watery, diluted, thin, runny, insipid, tasteless.

**weaken** enervate, debilitate, enfeeble, exhaust, sap, undermine, impair, dilute, adulterate, diminish, lessen, reduce, lower, droop, languish, flag, tire. STRENGTHEN

**weakness** feebleness, frailty, debility, infirmity, impotence, powerlessness, vulnerability. STRENGTH
fault, flaw, Achilles heel, deficiency, shortcoming, failing, foible.
liking, fondness, soft spot, partiality, predilection, inclination, penchant. AVERSION

**wealth** money, cash, capital, riches, assets, resources, means, fortune, affluence, opulence, prosperity, richness. POVERTY
abundance, plenty, profusion, bounty, plenitude, copiousness. SCARCITY

**wealthy** rich, prosperous, affluent, well-off, well-to-do, moneyed, loaded (*inf*). POOR

**wear** *v*, carry, bear, put on, don, have on, sport, show, display.
erode, waste, consume, eat away, corrode, abrade, rub, fray, impair, deteriorate. REINFORCE
last, endure.
tire, weary, fatigue, irritate, annoy, bore, tax, weaken, enervate, sap, exhaust, wear out. INVIGORATE
*n*, use, employment, utility, service.
clothes, clothing, attire, dress, garb, garments.
erosion, corrosion, abrasion, friction, wear and tear, deterioration.

**wearisome** tiring, fatiguing, wearing, exhausting, boring, tedious, monotonous, dull, flat, humdrum, routine, uninteresting. EXCITING

**weary** *adj*, tired, fatigued, worn out, exhausted, spent, jaded, fagged (*inf*), all in (*inf*), dead beat (*inf*), knackered (*inf*), bored, fed up. REFRESHED
wearisome, tiresome, boring, tedious, arduous, laborious, tiring.
*v*, tire, fatigue, exhaust, wear out, sap, drain, jade, bore, irk, vex. REFRESH

**weather** *n*, climate, conditions, temperature.
*v*, endure, withstand, resist, bear up, survive, pull through, surmount, rise above. SUCCUMB

**weave** interlace, lace, intertwine, twine, interweave, braid, plait, knit, join. UNRAVEL
make, create, build, construct, fabricate, spin. DESTROY

**web** cobweb, mesh, net, network, lattice.

**wed** marry, espouse, get hitched (*inf*), join, unite, fuse, blend, combine, ally. DIVORCE

**wedding** marriage, nuptials, matrimony, wedlock. DIVORCE

**wedge** *n*, lump, chunk, block, chock.
*v*, cram, pack, squeeze, stuff, block, jam, lodge.

**weep** cry, sob, wail, keen, moan, mourn, lament, grieve. REJOICE

**weigh** measure, balance, consider, contemplate, mull over, ponder, deliberate, reflect upon, examine, think about.
tell, count, carry weight, have influence.
load, weight, weigh down, encumber, burden, oppress. RELIEVE

**weight** *n*, heaviness, gravity, pressure, mass, load, burden.
importance, consequence, significance, moment, substance, power, influence, effect, impact.
*v*, load, weigh down, burden, oppress, bias.

**weighty** heavy, hefty (*inf*), ponderous, massive, burdensome, onerous. LIGHT
important, significant, consequential, momentous, grave, serious, crucial, critical. TRIVIAL

**weird** uncanny, eerie, supernatural, preternatural, unnatural, unearthly, ghostly, spooky (*inf*), mysterious, strange, bizarre, odd, queer, peculiar. ORDINARY

**welcome** *adj*, agreeable, pleasant, pleasing, desirable, acceptable, refreshing. UNWELCOME
*n*, greeting, salutation, reception, acceptance, hospitality.
*v*, greet, salute, hail, receive, meet.

**welfare** well-being, prosperity, health, happiness, comfort, advantage, benefit, good, interest.

**well**[1] *n*, spring, fountainhead, fount, wellspring, source, mine.
*v*, flow, gush, run, stream, ooze, spring, surge, pour, spout, jet.

**well**[2] *adv*, satisfactorily, adequately, sufficiently, considerably, highly, thoroughly, fully, completely, personally, intimately, properly, rightly, correctly, accurately, carefully, closely, skilfully, excellently, splendidly, smoothly, nicely, comfortably. BADLY
*adj*, healthy, fit, sound, hale, hearty, robust. ILL
satisfactory, good, fine, thriving, flourishing, lucky, fortunate, advisable. BAD

**well-bred** well-mannered, mannerly, civil, polite, courteous, gentlemanly, ladylike, refined, cultivated, polished, genteel. ILL-BRED

**well-known** famous, celebrated, renowned, illustrious, eminent, notable, popular, familiar. UNKNOWN

**welter** *v*, wallow, flounder, writhe, tumble, toss, roll, billow, swell, surge, heave.
*n*, jumble, muddle, hotchpotch, mess.

**wend** go, move, proceed, travel.

**wet** *adj*, damp, moist, soaked, drenched, saturated, dripping, sopping, sodden, sog-

gy, dank, humid, clammy, misty, showery, rainy, pouring. DRY
weak, feeble, spineless, timorous, soft, namby-pamby.
*n*, wetness, moisture, damp, dampness, water, rain.
*v*, damp, dampen, moisten, soak, drench, saturate, spray, sprinkle, irrigate. DRY

**wharf** dock, quay, pier, jetty.

**wheedle** cajole, coax, inveigle, charm, persuade, entice, entreat, implore, flatter, butter up, humour, court.

**wheel** *n*, disc, round, circle, ring, hoop, caster.
turn, revolution, rotation, roll, twirl, whirl, spin.
*v*, turn, spin, rotate, revolve, pivot, swivel, twirl, whirl, roll, swing.

**whereabouts** location, place, position, situation.

**wherewithal** means, resources, supplies, funds, cash, money.

**whet** sharpen, hone, edge, strop, file, grind. BLUNT
stimulate, arouse, rouse, stir, awaken, kindle, excite, provoke, incite, increase.

**whiff** *n*, breath, puff, gust, blast, trace, hint, smell, odour.
*v*, waft, blow, puff, breathe, inhale, sniff, smell.

**whim** fancy, crotchet, caprice, notion, idea, impulse, whimsy, humour, quirk, vagary, freak.

**whimper** cry, snivel, sob, weep, blubber, whine, moan. LAUGH

**whimsical** fanciful, capricious, impulsive, playful, freakish, eccentric, weird, odd, curious, quaint, funny, droll.

**whine** *v*, cry, sob, whimper, whinge (*inf*), wail, moan, complain, grumble, grouse, gripe (*inf*).
*n*, cry, whimper, wail, moan, complaint, grumble.

**whip** *v*, beat, lash, flog, scourge, flagellate, birch, cane, spank, thrash, punish, castigate, discipline, chastise. CARESS
pull, jerk, whisk, snatch, flash, show.
drive, push, spur, provoke, urge, encourage.
*n*, lash, scourge, cat-o'-nine-tails, birch, cane, crop.

**whirl** *v*, spin, twirl, pivot, pirouette, gyrate, reel, rotate, revolve, turn, wheel.
*n*, spin, twirl, pirouette, gyration, rotation, revolution, turn.
attempt, try, go, shot (*inf*), crack (*inf*), stab.

**whisk** beat, whip, snatch, seize, flap, flick, brush, sweep.
dart, dash, tear, fly, race, rush, hurry, speed. AMBLE

**whisper** *v*, murmur, mutter, mumble, breathe, sigh, hiss, rustle. SHOUT
hint, intimate, insinuate, reveal, disclose, divulge.
*n*, undertone, murmur, sigh, hiss, rustle.

**whit** iota, jot, tittle, particle, bit, scrap, grain, speck, mite, atom, trace, scintilla.

**white** pale, pallid, wan, ashen, pasty. RUDDY
light, snowy, silvery, hoary, grey. DARK
pure, clean, spotless, immaculate, unsullied, stainless. FOUL

**whiten** bleach, blanch, etiolate, fade, blench, pale. COLOUR

**whittle** cut, carve, shave, pare, trim, reduce.

**whole** *adj*, entire, complete, total, full, integral, undivided. PARTIAL
perfect, flawless, intact, sound, unbroken, in one piece, unimpaired, undamaged, unharmed, unscathed, fit, well, healthy, recovered.
*n*, aggregate, total, sum total, all, entirety, totality, ensemble, unit. PART

**wholehearted** hearty, unreserved, heartfelt, sincere, genuine, real, earnest, enthusiastic, dedicated, devoted. HALF-HEARTED

**wholesome** healthy, sanitary, hygienic, salubrious, salutary, beneficial, good, nourishing, nutritious, bracing, invigorating. DELETERIOUS

**wholly** entirely, purely, completely, totally, fully, perfectly, altogether, thoroughly, utterly, absolutely, exclusively. PARTLY

**whore** prostitute, harlot, fallen woman, strumpet, trollop, courtesan, call girl, streetwalker, tart (*inf*), hooker (*inf*).

**wicked** evil, bad, wrong, sinful, iniquitous, vile, villainous, heinous, nefarious, flagitious, atrocious, abominable, criminal, unprincipled, godless, profane, immoral, abandoned, depraved, corrupt. VIRTUOUS
naughty, mischievous, impish, roguish. GOOD

**wide** broad, extensive, large, thick, roomy, spacious, capacious, ample, full, vast, immense, comprehensive, catholic, encyclopedic, inclusive, general. NARROW

**widen** broaden, extend, expand, spread, stretch, enlarge, open. NARROW

**widespread** rife, prevalent, extensive, general, universal, sweeping, far-reaching, wide-ranging. RESTRICTED

**width** breadth, thickness, diameter, span, reach, scope, range, compass, extent, measure.

**wield** handle, manipulate, brandish, flourish, control, manage, hold, have, use, exercise, employ, exert.

**wild** untamed, undomesticated, feral, ferine, savage, ferocious, fierce, barbarous, primitive, uncivilized, natural, uncultivated, desolate, waste, desert, uninhabited. TAME

violent, furious, stormy, tempestuous, turbulent, riotous, boisterous, rowdy, rough, lawless, unruly, undisciplined, intractable, unmanageable, unbridled, unrestrained. RESTRAINED

rash, reckless, madcap, foolhardy, imprudent, foolish, outrageous, preposterous, extravagant, impracticable. SENSIBLE

disorderly, untidy, messy, dishevelled, tousled, unkempt. TIDY

**wile** stratagem, artifice, device, contrivance, subterfuge, trick, ruse, manoeuvre.

cunning, artfulness, slyness, craft, guile, trickery, chicanery, deceit, fraud. ARTLESSNESS

**wilful** headstrong, obstinate, stubborn, mulish, pig-headed, obdurate, adamant, intransigent, unyielding, perverse, contrary, wayward, self-willed. DOCILE

intentional, deliberate, premeditated, voluntary. ACCIDENTAL

**will** *n*, volition, option, choice, discretion, decision.

wish, desire, fancy, inclination, preference, pleasure.

purpose, determination, resolution, resolve, firmness, willpower.

*v*, ordain, decree, order, command, cause, determine, decide, choose, see fit, want, wish, desire.

leave, bequeath, pass on, hand down.

**willing** disposed, inclined, ready, game (*inf*), desirous, nothing loath, eager, enthusiastic, happy, pleased, agreeable, compliant, consenting, amenable. RELUCTANT

**willingly** freely, voluntarily, happily, gladly, cheerfully, readily, eagerly. RELUCTANTLY

**wilt** wither, shrivel, droop, sag, weaken, languish, fade, flag, dwindle, ebb, diminish, fail. THRIVE

**wily** artful, crafty, cunning, sly, foxy, subtle, shrewd, astute, tricky, shifty, scheming, designing, underhand, deceitful. ARTLESS

**win** *v*, triumph, succeed, conquer, vanquish, prevail, overcome, come first. LOSE

achieve, attain, accomplish, gain, get, obtain, acquire, procure, secure, earn, take, catch, net.

**win over,** persuade, convince, sway, influence, convert, carry, bring round, prevail upon.

*n*, victory, triumph, success, conquest. DEFEAT

**wince** flinch, start, blench, quail, shrink, recoil, draw back, cringe.

**wind[1]** *n*, air, draught, breeze, zephyr, puff, breath, blast, gust, gale, hurricane, typhoon, tornado, cyclone.

babble, idle talk, hot air, humbug.

gas, flatus, flatulence.

hint, suggestion, intimation, inkling, report, rumour.

**wind[2]** *v*, coil, curl, wreathe, twine, twist, turn, loop, bend, curve, zigzag, meander, snake.

**winding** twisting, turning, sinuous, serpentine, tortuous, circuitous, indirect, roundabout, meandering, flexuous, spiral, crooked. STRAIGHT

**windy** breezy, blowy, blustery, gusty, stormy, squally. STILL

verbose, wordy, prolix, loquacious, bombastic, empty.

**wing** arm, branch, group, set, faction, side, extension, annexe.

**wink** blink, flutter, twinkle, sparkle, flash, gleam.

**wink at,** ignore, disregard, overlook, tolerate, condone, connive at.

**winner** victor, champion, conqueror, hero. LOSER

**winnow** sift, screen, separate, sort out, select, cull.

**winsome** winning, engaging, charming, pleasing, delightful, agreeable, sweet, pretty, attractive, fetching (*inf*), alluring, captivating, fascinating, enchanting. REPULSIVE

**wintry** brumal, hibernal, cold, freezing, icy, frosty, bleak, desolate, cheerless, dismal. SUMMERY

**wipe** rub, clean, mop, sponge, dust, brush, dry.

**wipe out,** destroy, obliterate, erase, eradicate, exterminate, annihilate.

**wisdom** sagacity, sapience, discernment, penetration, sense, reason, judgment, judiciousness, perspicacity, acumen, understanding, intelligence, prudence, foresight, knowledge, learning, erudition, enlightenment. FOLLY

**wise** sage, sagacious, sapient, perceptive, discerning, judicious, prudent, politic, reasonable, rational, sensible, intelligent, smart, shrewd, astute, erudite, knowledgeable, learned, informed, aware. FOOLISH

**wish** *v*, desire, want, long, yearn, hanker after, covet, crave, hunger, thirst, prefer.
bid, ask, order, command.
*n*, desire, want, longing, yearning, hope, aspiration, hankering, craving, liking, preference.
bidding, request, command, order, will.

**wishful** desirous, longing, wishing, hopeful, optimistic, expectant.

**wistful** pensive, thoughtful, reflective, meditative, musing, dreaming, longing, yearning, melancholy, sad.

**wit** humour, drollery, facetiousness, wittiness, repartee, badinage, banter, raillery.
humorist, comic, comedian, wag.
intelligence, brains, understanding, wisdom, discernment, acumen, insight, perception, sense, common sense, cleverness, ingenuity. STUPIDITY

**witch** sorceress, enchantress, necromancer, magician, soothsayer.

**witchcraft** witchery, sorcery, magic, necromancy, wizardry, voodoo, occultism, incantation, spell, charm, enchantment.

**with** using, accompanying, among, having, possessing, concerning, regarding. WITHOUT

**withdraw** retract, recoil, draw back, remove, pull out, take back, recall, recant, disavow, unsay, disclaim, revoke, rescind. PRESENT
retire, retreat, pull out, secede, drop out, leave, depart, go. REMAIN

**withdrawn** shy, reserved, retiring, introverted, aloof, distant, quiet, taciturn, uncommunicative. EXTROVERT

**wither** shrivel, shrink, droop, wilt, fade, languish, waste, decay, dry, blast, blight. FLOURISH

**withering** scornful, humiliating, mortifying, devastating.

**withhold** retain, keep, keep back, hold back, restrain, check, suppress, repress, hide, conceal, reserve, refrain. GIVE

**without** lacking, short of, free from, excluding. WITH

**withstand** oppose, resist, stand up to, defy, confront, face, brave, weather, take, bear, endure, tolerate. YIELD

**witness** *n*, eyewitness, onlooker, spectator, viewer, observer, bystander.
testifier, deponent, attestant.
testimony, attestation, deposition, statement, evidence, proof.
*v*, see, observe, view, watch, look on, mark, note, notice, attend. MISS
testify, bear witness, give evidence, depose, confirm, corroborate, attest, endorse.

**witty** humorous, droll, funny, amusing, waggish, jocular, clever, original. DULL

**wizard** sorcerer, warlock, necromancer, magician, enchanter, conjurer.
expert, adept, ace (*inf*), master, virtuoso, genius.

**wizened** shrivelled, shrunken, dried up, withered, wrinkled.

**wobble** shake, tremble, quake, quiver, rock, totter, teeter, sway.

**woe** grief, misery, sorrow, sadness, unhappiness, heartache, depression, melancholy, anguish, distress, suffering, affliction, adversity, misfortune, trial, tribulation, disaster, calamity. JOY

**woeful** woebegone, sad, unhappy, sorrowful, miserable, wretched, depressed, dejected, disconsolate, despondent, tragic, grievous, disastrous, calamitous, piteous, pitiable, pitiful, pathetic, deplorable, lamentable. JOYFUL

**woman** female, lady, girl, lass, miss, bird (*inf*). MAN
maid, domestic, housekeeper, charwoman, lady-in-waiting.

**womanly** feminine, gentle, tender, motherly, ladylike, womanish.

**wonder** *n*, awe, wonderment, admiration, amazement, astonishment, surprise, bewilderment, curiosity. INDIFFERENCE
marvel, phenomenon, miracle, prodigy, curiosity, rarity, sight, spectacle.

*v*, meditate, ponder, muse, think, speculate, conjecture, question, query, puzzle, ask oneself.
marvel, gape, stare.

**wonderful** marvellous, extraordinary, remarkable, prodigious, phenomenal, amazing, astonishing, astounding, surprising, wondrous, awe-inspiring, incredible, miraculous, fantastic, super (*inf*), splendid, magnificent, superb, excellent, great (*inf*), smashing (*inf*). ORDINARY

**wont** habit, routine, practice, custom, use.

**wonted** habitual, customary, familiar, usual, regular, accustomed. UNUSUAL

**woo** court, make love to, chase, pursue, importune.

**wood** forest, woodland, thicket, copse, coppice, grove. CLEARING

**word** *n*, term, name, expression, utterance.
chat, talk, discussion, conversation.
news, tidings, communication, report, notice, message, information, intelligence.
promise, pledge, assurance, guarantee, oath, vow.
command, order, instruction, signal.
*v*, phrase, put, express, utter, say.

**wordy** verbose, prolix, garrulous, loquacious, windy, long-winded, rambling, discursive. TERSE

**work** *n*, toil, labour, effort, exertion, drudgery, industry. IDLENESS
task, job, chore, duty, assignment, commission.
occupation, employment, job, business, profession, vocation, calling, career, trade, craft.
product, creation, opus, composition, production, achievement.
*v*, toil, labour, drudge, slave, exert oneself, be busy. REST
be employed, have a job, earn a living, ply one's trade, do business.
operate, function, go, run, perform, act. FAIL
handle, manipulate, wield, ply, use, manage, control, operate.
accomplish, achieve, effect, cause, bring about, produce.

**work out,** solve, resolve, clear up, figure out, calculate.
plan, arrange, devise, contrive, formulate, elaborate.

**work up,** rouse, excite, stir, move, stimulate, animate, arouse, foment.

**worker** employee, workman, labourer, hand, tradesman, operative, artisan, craftsman.

**works** factory, mill, plant, workshop.
machinery, mechanism, movement, action, workings, parts.

**world** earth, globe, planet, star, universe, cosmos, creation.
mankind, humankind, humanity, human race, everybody, everyone.
sphere, realm, kingdom, domain, province, field.

**worldly** temporal, earthly, terrestrial, mundane, physical, material, secular, profane. SPIRITUAL
materialistic, greedy, avaricious, covetous.
cosmopolitan, urbane, sophisticated, worldly-wise. UNSOPHISTICATED

**worried** anxious, troubled, concerned, disturbed, uneasy, ill at ease, tense, on edge, nervous, apprehensive, fearful, afraid. CALM

**worry** *vi*, fret, be anxious, agonize, brood.
*vt*, disturb, bother, trouble, harass, plague, torment, tease, pester, badger, vex, irritate, annoy, distress, upset. REASSURE
*n*, anxiety, uneasiness, concern, trouble, problem, care, nervousness, apprehension, fear, annoyance, vexation, irritation, bother, pest, plague, torment. DELIGHT

**worsen** deteriorate, degenerate, decline, get worse, aggravate, exacerbate. IMPROVE

**worship** *v*, venerate, revere, reverence, honour, esteem, adore, idolize, deify, adulate, praise, exalt, glorify. SCORN
*n*, veneration, reverence, homage, adoration, honour, esteem, adulation, praise, glorification, exaltation. CONTEMPT

**worst** defeat, beat, conquer, vanquish, best, crush, overcome, overpower, overwhelm, rout.

**worth** worthiness, merit, quality, virtue, usefulness, utility, advantage, good, help, avail, cost, price, value, estimation.

**worthless** valueless, nugatory, trivial, insignificant, paltry, trashy, useless, unavailing, vain, futile, vile, base, abject, contemptible, despicable. WORTHY

**worthy** deserving, meritorious, laudable, praiseworthy, estimable, admirable, worthwhile, valuable, good, decent, honest, upright, noble, excellent, exemplary, reputable. UNWORTHY

**wound** *n*, injury, hurt, harm, damage, cut, gash, laceration, lesion, trauma, shock.
*v*, injure, hurt, harm, damage, cut, gash, lacerate, pierce, grieve, offend. HEAL

**wrangle** *v*, argue, quarrel, bicker, squabble, row, brawl, differ, disagree. AGREE
*n*, argument, quarrel, squabble, tiff, row, brawl, dispute, controversy. AGREEMENT

**wrap** envelop, enfold, encase, sheathe, enclose, cover, shroud, cloak, muffle, swathe, wind, fold, parcel, package. UNWRAP

**wrath** anger, ire, rage, fury, passion, indignation, resentment, exasperation. COMPOSURE

**wrathful** angry, irate, incensed, enraged, raging, furious, passionate, indignant, displeased, exasperated. PLEASED

**wreak** inflict, execute, carry out, cause, bring about, vent, indulge, gratify.

**wreath** garland, festoon, chaplet, coronal.

**wreathe** festoon, adorn, twist, wind, coil, twine, encircle, surround, envelop, enfold.

**wreck** *v*, ruin, destroy, demolish, devastate, smash, shatter, spoil, upset. BUILD
*n*, ruin, mess, destruction, devastation, desolation, demolition, wreckage, debris, remains, fragments.

**wrench** strain, sprain, rick, twist, jerk, pull, tug, force.

**wrest** seize, take, pull, twist, wrench, force.

**wrestle** fight, grapple, scuffle, tussle, battle, strive, struggle, contend.

**wretch** rogue, scoundrel, rascal, blackguard, ruffian, villain, miscreant, rotter (*inf*), vagabond, outcast, beggar, unfortunate.

**wretched** miserable, poor, sorry, pitiable, pitiful, pathetic, unfortunate, hapless, forlorn, woebegone, sad, unhappy, abject, contemptible, despicable, base, vile, worthless. FINE

**wriggle** squirm, writhe, twist, wiggle, worm, snake, slink, crawl.

**wring** squeeze, extract, twist, wrench, wrest, force, extort.

**wrinkle** *v*, crease, fold, crumple, crinkle, pucker, gather, furrow, corrugate. SMOOTH
*n*, crease, fold, crumple, pucker, line, ridge, furrow, corrugation.

**write** pen, inscribe, scribble, scrawl, record, jot down, draft, compose.

**writhe** wriggle, squirm, twist, turn, contort, distort.

**writing** handwriting, penmanship, script, calligraphy, scribble, scrawl.
book, publication, opus, work, composition, letter.

**wrong** *adj*, incorrect, inaccurate, imprecise, inexact, erroneous, mistaken, false, untrue. CORRECT
bad, sinful, iniquitous, immoral, wicked, evil, wrongful, unlawful, illegal, illicit, criminal, crooked, dishonest, dishonourable. GOOD
inappropriate, unsuitable, inapt, improper, unseemly, indecorous. RIGHT
*adv*, amiss, awry, astray, badly, wrongly, incorrectly. PROPERLY
*n*, sin, misdeed, trespass, transgression, offence, crime, error, mistake, wickedness, iniquity, unfairness, injustice. RIGHT
*v*, abuse, mistreat, maltreat, ill-treat, oppress, exploit, cheat, hurt, injure, malign.

**wrongful** unjust, unfair, improper, illegal, unlawful, criminal, immoral, wrong. RIGHTFUL

**wrought-up** worked up, excited, aroused, inflamed, animated, keyed up, overwrought, agitated. CALM

**wry** awry, askew, crooked, lopsided, twisted, distorted, contorted, deformed. STRAIGHT
droll, witty, dry, ironic. SERIOUS

# X

**Xmas** Christmas, Noel, Yule, Yuletide.

**x-ray** radiograph, shadowgraph, roentgenograph, roentgenogram.

# Y

**yank** pull, jerk, tug, snatch.

**yap** yelp, bark, yammer (*inf*), chatter, jabber.

**yard** quadrangle, courtyard, enclosure, compound.

**yardstick** measure, gauge, standard, criterion, touchstone, benchmark.

**yarn** tale, story, anecdote.
thread, fibre.

**yearn** desire, long, pine, hanker after, covet, crave, hunger, thirst, lust.

**yell** shout, scream, cry, shriek, bellow, roar, howl, bawl. WHISPER

**yelp** yap, bark, cry, yell.

**yet** still, but, nevertheless, however.
so far, until now, up to now, as yet.
moreover, besides, as well, in addition.

**yield** *v*, produce, bear, give, supply, furnish, afford, bring in, earn.
surrender, part with, relinquish, forgo, renounce, resign, cede, give up, quit, abandon, submit, capitulate, succumb, give in, acquiesce, comply, concede, agree, consent, allow. RESIST
*n*, crop, produce, harvest, return.

**yielding** submissive, docile, tractable, obedient, manageable, compliant, amenable, obliging, complaisant, accommodating. STUBBORN
flexible, pliant, pliable, supple, soft, elastic. RIGID

**yoke** *n*, collar, harness, link, tie, bond, coupling.
oppression, servitude, slavery, bondage. FREEDOM
*v*, couple, link, unite, join, connect, fasten, hitch, harness. RELEASE

**yokel** rustic, peasant, bumpkin, clodhopper (*inf*), boor.

**young** youthful, adolescent, juvenile, childish, immature, green, callow, inexperienced, fresh, new, early, recent. OLD

**youngster** child, kid (*inf*), boy, girl, youth, teenager. ADULT

**youth** childhood, early life, adolescence, immaturity. AGE
adolescent, teenager, youngster, boy, lad, stripling. MAN

**youthful** young, boyish, girlish, childish, immature, fresh, vigorous, active. OLD

# Z

**zany** comical, funny, clownish, crazy, loony (*inf*). SERIOUS

**zeal** fervour, ardour, passion, fire, warmth, enthusiasm, eagerness, keenness, earnestness, intensity, vigour, energy, vehemence, devotion, fanaticism. APATHY

**zealot** fanatic, enthusiast, partisan, bigot, extremist.

**zealous** fervent, ardent, passionate, enthusiastic, eager, keen, earnest, intense, vehement, devoted, fanatical. APATHETIC

**zenith** height, peak, summit, pinnacle, apex, vertex, top, acme, climax, culmination. NADIR

**zero** nought, nothing, nil, cipher, bottom, nadir.

**zest** relish, spice, tang, savour, flavour, taste, pungency, piquancy. INSIPIDITY
gusto, relish, appetite, enjoyment, keenness, enthusiasm.

**zigzag** crooked, tortuous, serpentine, meandering, twisting, winding. STRAIGHT

**zone** area, region, district, section, sector, territory, domain, sphere.

**zoom** shoot, fly, speed, race, rush, tear, buzz, whizz.

JMA DODD

PENGUIN REFERENCE

# THE PENGUIN DICTIONARY OF ENGLISH IDIOMS

Daphne Gulland was born in 1953. She was educated at Fidelis Grammar School in London. In 1975 she graduated with Honours in English and German at Bedford College, University of London. For many years she has been engaged in research into the origins of the most common idioms in the language, breaking new ground with her system of categorization for *The Penguin Dictionary of English Idioms*. She is married with four children. Her hobbies are gardening, walking, reading and history.

David Hinds-Howell was born in 1916. He was educated at Marlborough College, and obtained a Master of Arts degree in philosophy, politics and economics at Oxford University in 1938. After practising as a barrister, he had a long and distinguished career as director of the Hillcrest School of English (1952–1981) and as a teacher of English at advanced and intermediate level. He died in 1995.

THE PENGUIN DICTIONARY OF

# ENGLISH IDIOMS

---

DAPHNE M. GULLAND
AND DAVID HINDS-HOWELL

PENGUIN BOOKS

PENGUIN BOOKS

Published by the Penguin Group
Penguin Books Ltd, 80 Strand, London WC2R 0RL, England
Penguin Putnam Inc., 375 Hudson Street, New York, New York 10014, USA
Penguin Books Australia Ltd, 250 Camberwell Road, Camberwell, Victoria 3124, Australia
Penguin Books Canada Ltd, 10 Alcorn Avenue, Toronto, Ontario, Canada M4V 3B2
Penguin Books India (P) Ltd, 11 Community Centre, Panchsheel Park, New Delhi – 110 017, India
Penguin Books (NZ) Ltd, Cnr Rosedale and Airborne Roads, Albany, Auckland, New Zealand
Penguin Books (South Africa) (Pty) Ltd, 24 Sturdee Avenue, Rosebank 2196, South Africa

Penguin Books Ltd, Registered Offices: 80 Strand, London WC2R 0RL, England

www.penguin.com

First published 1986
Reprinted with revisions and an additional category 1994
29



Translated into Greek by Agricultural Cooperative
Publications, Athens, Greece

Printed in England by Clays Ltd, St Ives plc
Typeset in Linotron Times

# PREFACE

*The Penguin Dictionary of English Idioms* will be of absorbing interest to foreign and native speakers of English alike. Its aims are twofold: to provide a wide selection of the most commonly used idiomatic phrases in the English language; and, with the help of copious examples taken from real life, to offer guidance on the most effective way to use them.

The English language is rich in idioms, and although it is possible to converse correctly in non-idiomatic English, a student with only a superficial knowledge of English idioms will find himself at a serious disadvantage in his reading, and even more so when he takes part in discussions and debates. Finding idioms in a general dictionary is a slow and laborious task, so it is hoped that this dictionary of idioms will provide assistance in a practical and interesting way.

What then is an idiom? We would define an idiom as a combination of words with a special meaning that cannot be inferred from its separate parts. The examples that follow will help to make the matter clear:

1. 'John couldn't say boo to a goose!' On the face of it, this is a very strange thing to say. Of course it is quite possible to say boo to a goose, but who would want to do such a thing? However, the statement has an idiomatic meaning, namely that John is so timid that he wouldn't dare to make even the mildest protest, however badly he was treated. Clearly, it is impossible to deduce this meaning from the separate words in the sentence above. In other words, the meaning of the whole is different from the parts. The sentence then has two meanings – a literal meaning which means very little, and a metaphorical one which is the idiom.
2. 'Shall we go Dutch?' Unlike the first example, this one has no literal meaning at all, only an idiomatic one: 'I suggest that you pay for your meal, and I'll pay for mine?' Again, it is impossible to infer the meaning of the idiom from the separate words in the question.

Every idiom belongs either to the first group or to the second as described above.

Traditionally, dictionaries of idioms present idiomatic expressions in alphabetical order; but we believe that the aims we have set ourselves can be achieved more efficiently by categorizing idioms, i.e. by grouping them round a limited number of key-words and putting them in the appropriate categories. For example, the first category, Colours (see the list of Categories on page 9), contains 14 different colours: red, blue, green, yellow, white, white and black, black, brown, grey, purple, scarlet, pink, golden and silver. Each of these colours (key-words) is used to form an idiom or idioms. The key-word 'red', for instance, is included in 13 idioms, as in 'to paint the town red', 'a red rag to a bull', 'to see red', and so on. All the 'red' idioms make up a group. 'Colours' itself, the name of the category, makes up a group of 17 idioms, as in 'to see someone in his true colours', 'with flying colours', and so on. The total number of groups make up the complete category with altogether 130 idioms. The same principle applies to the remaining 33 categories.

Categorizing idioms in this way has a number of important advantages over the alphabetical system. First, idioms that include the same key-word will be concentrated in greater numbers than is possible with the alphabetical system. For instance, there are 37 idioms in the 'dog' group, 88 idioms in the 'hand' and 47 in the 'heart' groups. By concentrating idioms in such large numbers, the reader is in a position to make a systematic study of all the idioms in a given group, and to compare and distinguish them in a way that would not be possible were they scattered over a whole dictionary. Secondly, categorizing makes it possible to introduce idioms in a coherent, logical order instead of the arbitrary, inconsequential order of the alphabet; and this makes for more interesting reading for students who like to browse through a dictionary. Finally, the use of categories will enable students to complete their study of a selected category with the minimum of effort, since all the items in which they are interested have already been assembled for them. The student is, of course, free to start wherever he wishes. As he proceeds through this *Dictionary*, category by category, he will find his knowledge of idioms growing until finally he has acquired a mastery of the subject.

## HOW TO USE THE INDEX

We have provided an Index of idioms at the back of the *Dictionary*. The order of the idioms in the Index is strictly alphabetical. When you look an idiom up in the Index, look for it first under the noun, if there is one. If there are two or more nouns, look for the idiom under the first noun. If there are no nouns, then look for it under the first verb; if there is no verb, then under the first adjective.

Please note that if the idiom has two nouns standing next to each other, it will be indexed under both nouns, even if the first noun is a possessive, e.g. 'the lion's share' will be indexed under both 'lion's', and 'share'. Also note that idioms are not indexed under pronouns, e.g. 'one', 'someone', 'anyone', 'oneself', 'himself', etc., or the verb 'to be'.

Every idiom has a reference consisting of two numbers divided by a stroke, e.g. **000/0**. The first number of the pair, **000**, refers to the page on which the idiom you are looking for appears; the second number, **0**, refers to the actual idiom: 'to be too big for one's boots'. Here are some more idioms for you to look up, followed by the correct answers which you can check for yourself:

1. 'to sail against the wind'. There is one noun in this idiom, namely 'wind', so it will appear under 'wind' with the reference number **180/6**.
2. 'to pull the rug from under one's feet'. There are two nouns in this idiom, so it will be indexed under the first noun of the two, 'rug', with the reference number **152/5**.
3. 'to read the riot act'. In this idiom there are two nouns, 'riot' and 'act', that stand next to each other. The idiom can therefore be found in the Index under either of them. The reference number for this idiom is **231/14**.
4. 'at arm's length'. There are two nouns in this phrase, one next to the other, so this idiom can be found in the Index under 'arm's' (a possessive) or 'length', with the reference number **91/13**.
5. 'to do someone proud'. There is no noun here, but there is the verb 'to do', so this idiom will appear under 'do' in the Index with the reference number **119/10**.
6. 'fair, fat and forty'. As this phrase contains no noun or verb, it will appear under an adjective. There are, however, three adjectives, so, according to our rule, the phrase will appear under the first adjective, 'fair', with the reference number **219/16**.
7. 'Nobody's poodle'. 'Nobody' is a pronoun (which we have excluded) so the idiom will appear under 'poodle' which has the reference number **54/13**.

A number of variations on the idioms are listed in the Index; these appear immediately under the appropriate entry in the text.

When an idiom bears a close relation to one in a different category, it is given a cross-reference at the end of the note and the reader can follow this up, if he wishes, for further information. Apart from this, no cross-references are used and, once the reader has obtained the reference number of the idiom he is looking for from the Index, he can be sure of finding the idiom required without being referred to other parts of the *Dictionary*.

A number of proverbs have been included when the content of the proverb is idiomatic, as for example: 'Charity begins at home', and 'Don't look a gift-horse in the mouth'.

We hope that our readers will find as much interest in learning and using these idioms as we have had in collecting them.

Daphne Gulland
David Hinds-Howell
1986

# CATEGORIES

# 1. COLOURS

## COLOURS

1. to see someone in his **true colours** – to understand someone's true character, often for the first time. 'As soon as he made a fuss about returning her money, I saw him in his true colours.'

   to **show oneself in one's true colours** – to reveal one's true nature. 'When he lost his temper, he showed himself in his true colours.'

2. to **give/lend colour to** – to make (an account, story, explanation, etc.) more credible or more plausible. 'The broken window on the ground floor lent colour to Mrs Brown's story that her house had been burgled.'

3. with **flying colours** – with great success, with distinction. 'We were all expecting him to fail, but he passed with flying colours.'

4. to sail under **false colours** – to assume a false identity in order to conceal one's true purpose.

5. to paint in **bright/dark colours** – to describe something in a flattering or unflattering way. 'My brother wanted us all to emigrate to America and painted his life there in the brightest colours.'

6. to **win one's colours** – to win recognition for one's achievements. 'The young Minister won his colours with a brilliant defence of the government's policy.' Literally, to win a place in one's school or college team, which entitles one to wear the school or college colours. cf. 'to **win one's spurs' 252/7.**

7. to **nail (one's) colours to the mast** – to make absolutely clear what one's views are in a very forthright manner. 'Now he has nailed his colours to the mast, he cannot change his mind.'

8. (to join) **the colours** (slightly old-fashioned) – to join the army.

   to be **called to the colours** – to be conscripted into the army.

9. to look through **rose-coloured/tinted spectacles** – to see things in a flattering or over-optimistic light. 'Anne always enjoys her visits because she sees everything through rose-coloured spectacles, but she would feel differently if she had to live there.'

10. to be **colourless** – to lack personality, to be uninteresting or nondescript. 'We talked for over half an hour together, but nothing that he said stands out in my memory. I'm afraid he's a dull, colourless man.'

11. To be **off colour** – to be not quite at one's best, to feel queasy or slightly ill. 'She's a little off colour today; she was up very late last night and may have had a little too much to drink!'

12. **under colour of** – in the guise of, under the pretext of. 'Under colour of consulting the kidney specialist, the newspaper man wormed a lot of information out of him for the television programme.'

13. **local colour** – background information about a place or event.

14. to **have one's views coloured by** – to have one's ideas and opinions changed by external influences. 'Like everyone else, his views were coloured by his background and upbringing.'

15. to see the **colour of** (someone's) **money** – to take some money in advance before parting with one's goods or services.

16. **colour bar** – discrimination against black and coloured people in favour of the whites, legally, socially or economically.

17. a **highly coloured** report – a report that is exaggerated or biased.

## RED

1. to catch someone **red-handed** – to catch someone in the act of committing a crime, usually a theft. 'Caught you red-handed! I saw you take the money out of the box.' The reference is to the blood still on the hands of the criminal after stabbing his victim to death. The phrase is used now for less serious crimes.
2. to **paint the town red** (of American origin) – to celebrate by running wild, drinking and making a commotion. 'Richard has passed his exam. We are going to paint the town red tonight, so don't be surprised if we come home very late.'
3. a **red rag to a bull** – a source of violent anger to someone. 'Mention of animal experiments was like a red rag to a bull to the anti-vivisectionist.' The phrase originated in the belief that any red-coloured object will infuriate a bull.

   **like a red rag to** someone – has the same meaning. 'Property developers were like a red rag to the Prime Minister.'
4. **'Reds under the bed'** – the reds are everywhere. An ironic allusion to the obsession some people have that there are reds (communists) everywhere, plotting violent revolution.
5. **red in tooth and claw** – a violent revolutionary who shows no mercy and makes no compromises. Originally used as a description of Nature: Alfred Lord Tennyson, *In Memoriam*, Part LVI, Stanza 4: 'Nature, red in tooth and claw'.
6. to **see red** – to react with uncontrollable rage against an object of one's hatred. The object is usually a stereotype, for example civil servants, businessmen, Jews, blacks. 'The sight of demonstrators marching past his house made Stephen see red.' The idiom originated in the idea that red symbolizes both violent revolution and the colour of blood; however, it has shed its political motivation and is associated now with any person or thing that excites strong disapproval.
7. **red tape** – bureaucratic delay, excessive attention to rules and regulations, often resulting in injustice to the ordinary citizen. The 'red tape' is the red ribbon with which the civil servant ties his papers together.
8. a **red-letter day** – a day of special importance, for example a wedding, the celebration of a victory or the receiving of a great honour. The phrase originates in the custom of recording saints' days and holidays on calendars in red ink.
9. The **red-light** district – that part of the town which is given over to brothels and prostitution. The red light over the front door advertises the presence of prostitutes in the house.
10. to **see the red light** – to recognize approaching danger, the red light being a danger signal. 'When the doctor warned his patient that further drinking would damage his liver, the man saw the red light.' The phrase usually implies that the warning was heeded.
11. to be shown the **red card** – to be dismissed from one's job. 'The accountant was shown the red card for defrauding the company.' The phrase derives from football: a footballer is shown the red card by the referee for committing an offence after he has been warned and may be barred from playing for his side in future matches. cf. 'to be shown the **yellow card' 18/11**.
12. to be **in the red** – to have an overdraft, to be in debt. 'Oh, dear, I am overdrawn again. I hate being in the red.' The idiom originated in the banks' custom of showing the amount overdrawn in red type. Overdrafts are

shown in black today. cf. 'to be **in the black' 21/1**.

1. a **redneck** (American colloquialism) – a coarse, insensitive person.

## BLUE

2. to **blue one's money** – spend money wildly. 'Peter has blued all the money you gave him on gambling and drink.'
3. to **look/feel blue** – to look/feel depressed or discontented. 'Now my girlfriend has left me, things are looking blue.' Blue is associated with gloom and depression in such expressions as having the blues, feeling blue, a fit of the blues.
4. in a **blue funk** – in a state of cowardly fear. 'John is in a blue funk about fighting Jackson in the boxing tournament tomorrow.' The word 'funk' is a slang word first used by an Oxford undergraduate in the eighteenth century. The word probably comes from Flemish 'fonck', meaning agitation, alarm.
5. **once in a blue moon** – extremely rarely, only once in a life-time. 'What does it matter what your uncle thinks of you? He only visits you once in a blue moon.'
6. to appear **out of the blue** – to arrive unexpectedly, usually after a long absence. 'My brother suddenly appeared out of the blue yesterday. We hadn't seen him for years and had given him up for dead.'

   a **bolt from the blue** – some unexpected bad news. 'We had no idea that their marriage was breaking up. The news came like a bolt from the blue.' A bolt was originally an arrow from a cross-bow, and is probably derived from Latin 'catapulta'. 'Out of the blue' meant out of a blue sky; hence, a blow struck without warning.
7. to **make the air turn blue** – to give vent to one's rage by swearing violently. 'When the engineer heard that his plans had been rejected, he fairly made the air turn blue.'
8. to shout/scream **blue murder** – to protest most violently at an injustice. 'If you take away the baby's toy, he'll shout blue murder.'
9. to talk, argue, complain, protest, etc., until you are **blue in the face** – to make a huge but vain effort to win a person's agreement. 'You can argue with Harry until you are blue in the face, but you will never get him to change his mind.' 'Until you are blue in the face' means 'for ever'. cf. **'until the cows come home' 58/4**.
10. **blue riband/ribbon** – the blue riband was an accolade awarded to the ship that made the fastest crossing of the Atlantic. Riband and ribbon are etymologically the same word.
11. a **blue-stocking** – a woman who is more interested in learning and an academic career than in marriage and bringing up children. 'I don't want to go out with that blue stocking. She is only interested in books!' The phrase has a derogatory meaning and dates back to the 1750s, when Mrs Montagu gave parties for literary reading and discussions instead of card-playing. These parties were also attended by men, who wore blue worsted stockings instead of black silk ones.
12. **blue blood / blue-blooded** – of the nobility or aristocracy. The phrase is of Spanish origin.
13. **men/boys in blue** – the police, from the colour of their uniform.
14. **a blue-eyed boy** – a boy/young man who has been singled out for special favours by someone in authority. Derogatory, since it implies that he has won favour by flattery and talebearing. 'Roger is Smith's blue-eyed boy; he can do no wrong.'

1. a **true blue** – one whose loyalty can always be counted on.

   a **true blue Conservative** – a person who holds strong Conservative convictions.

2. to **be a blue / get one's blue** – to represent Oxford or Cambridge University at games or sports. Dark blue stands for Oxford, and light blue for Cambridge.

3. to **blue pencil** – to censor. 'Most of my report on the treatment of the political prisoners was blue pencilled by the authorities.'

4. a **blue film** – a pornographic film, so called after the brothels of pre-revolutionary China which were painted blue outside to advertise the presence of prostitutes within.

## GREEN

5. to **be green** – to be inexperienced or untried, from which comes the phrase 'to **be as green as grass'** – to be naïve, totally inexperienced in the ways of the world. 'You cannot expect Mary to do business with such people. She is only eighteen and as green as grass.'

6. to be **green with envy** – to feel extremely envious. 'If you buy that car, you'll make your friends green with envy.' At one time, a greenish complexion was believed to indicate jealousy. Shakespeare expresses the same idea in *Othello*: 'Beware of jealousy, it is a green-eyed monster' (III, iii, 165).

7. to have **green fingers** – to be blessed with luck in the growing of plants and flowers. 'She has green fingers! Everything she plants turns out well.'

8. a **green old age** (literary) – an old age in which a person's mental and physical powers are still strong and vigorous. 'I hope she will live to a green old age.' cf. **'a ripe old age' 38/9**.

9. to **give the green light to** – to give permission to go ahead; to encourage or approve an enterprise. 'The boss has given us the green light. We can make a start on the project straight away.'

## YELLOW

10. to **be yellow** – to be cowardly. Yellow is the traditional symbol of cowardice. 'You don't want to fight, do you? You are yellow.' cf. 'to be **yellow-livered' 114/5**.

    to **show a yellow streak** – to show cowardice.

11. to be shown the **yellow card** – to receive a warning that disciplinary action will be taken if an offence is repeated. 'I was shown the yellow card by the manager for coming in late to work.' The phrase derives from football: a player is shown the yellow card by a referee for committing an offence. cf. 'to be shown the **red card' 16/11**.

## WHITE

12. **whiter than white** – too pure to be true, hypocritical.

    a **whited sepulchre** – innocent and pure in appearance, but dirty and corrupt within. An allusion by Jesus Christ to the hypocrisy of the Pharisees (Matthew XXIII, 27). Jesus meant that one should judge someone by his inner self, not by his outward appearance. (Tombs in biblical times were whitened to make them conspicuous.)

13. **lily white** – of great purity and delicacy.

14. a **white wedding** – a wedding in church, so called because the bride is dressed in white, the symbol of chastity.

15. to **white-wash** – to exonerate someone

by ignoring the evidence against him. 'It's no good complaining to the Post Office about the telephone engineer. They will only white-wash him.'

1. to **bleed** someone **white** – to extort all of someone's money, to overcharge grossly for a service. 'Why do you let Thompson blackmail you like this? He has bled you white!'
2. a **white lie** – a harmless or well-intentioned lie. This is generally not considered morally wrong because the motive is to spare the feelings of the person lied to. 'It is better to tell a white lie than to lose a friend.'
3. as **white as a sheet** – in a state of very great fear. 'Have you seen a ghost? Your face is as white as a sheet.'
4. **white heat** – the most intense energy, dynamic expansion. 'The white heat of the technological revolution' (the slogan of the Labour Party in the General Election of 1964).
5. to show the **white feather** – to act in a cowardly way. In the Great War of 1914–18, young women used to seek out men who were dressed in civilian clothes and place a white feather in their coats in order to humiliate them for not having enlisted.
6. to **hang out / show the white flag** – when approaching the enemy, you show the white flag to indicate (1) that you have come to negotiate a peace and your mission is a peaceful one (it is an unwritten law that the enemy will not fire at you) or (2) that you wish to surrender and have no desire to continue resistance.
7. 'Hold your fire until you see **the whites of their eyes**' – wait until the last possible moment before firing on the enemy. Fire is at its most effective when delivered at maximum proximity to the enemy.
8. **white slave traffic** – the selling of girls into prostitution. This is often effected by luring them abroad with promises of employment in night clubs and cabarets, and then cancelling their contracts or withholding their wages.
9. a **white elephant** – a very big and useless possession which costs a lot of money to maintain and may prove to be a source of financial ruin. 'You have bought yourself a white elephant: this house is far too isolated. No one will stay here and the upkeep will ruin you.' A king of Siam is said to have given white elephants to his enemies in order to ruin them.
10. **white horses** – white waves, so called because they appear to be galloping forward on to the shore like horses.
11. a **white Christmas** – a Christmas when snow has fallen and the countryside is white.
12. a **white-collar worker** – the professional or office worker who wears a shirt with a white collar, as opposed to the manual or factory worker who wears overalls.
13. **white man's burden** – a phrase from Rudyard Kipling. He meant that the white colonialist has the duty and responsibility to educate and protect the primitive peoples. Not unnaturally, the phrase has aroused much resentment among coloured people.
14. **white trash** – white people living in the Southern States of America after the Civil War who were as destitute as the blacks, and were treated with the same contempt.

## WHITE AND BLACK

15. **white or black?** – with milk or without (in coffee).
16. **in black and white** – reduced to writing. Unless this has been done, some agreements are unenforceable in law. 'If you come to any agreement

with him, be sure to get it in black and white; you can't trust him.'

1. to **see** (everything) **in black and white** – to characterize everything and everyone as either very good or very bad, without any intermediate qualities.
2. to **swear black is white** – to perjure oneself or swear any falsehood, no matter how glaring.
3. **two blacks don't make a white** – two wrongs don't make a right. 'Just because Haines has cheated you, that's no reason why you should cheat his daughter; two blacks don't make a white.'

BLACK

4. **black and blue** – very badly bruised. 'The muggers beat the old woman black and blue.'
5. things are **looking black** – the prospects are very bad.
6. **black looks** – angry or revengeful looks. 'I got some black looks from the shopkeeper when I cancelled my order.'
7. to look **on the black side** – to see everything in a pessimistic light, to have gloomy forebodings.
   to be in a **black mood** – to be very depressed. 'George has been in a black mood ever since he lost his job.'
8. to **blacken** someone's **character** – to make someone appear worse than he really is by exaggerating his faults. 'Since you have blackened Miles' character, I shall give him the opportunity of defending himself.'
9. to be on the **black list** – to be on a list of persons under suspicion, who have committed crimes, or incurred the disapproval of the authorities. cf. **'to blackball' 21/7**.
10. **black art** – Satanic or devilish practices.
11. **black mass** – a travesty of the Christian Mass celebrated by practitioners of black magic and members of a Satanic cult.
12. the **black sheep (of the family)** – a member of the family who has disgraced himself, one whose name is generally not mentioned in the family circle.
13. the **Black Country** – the industrial Midlands of England, formerly discoloured by soot from its many open chimneys.
14. a **blackleg** – someone who continues to work during a strike in defiance of his union's instructions; hence **blackleg labour**, workers who refuse to come out when a strike has been called and who cross the picket lines to get to their work.
15. a **black eye** – an eye that is bruised and swollen as the result of a blow or a collision.
16. a **black-out** – (1) a sudden loss of consciousness. 'The accused told the judge that he couldn't remember what happened next because at that moment he had a black-out.' (2) concealing all source of light (in wartime) (3) total loss of electric power in a district.
17. a **black comedy** – a story or play in which the theme is sad or tragic, but the treatment is comic.
18. a **black economy** – that part of a country's economy which is carried on without the knowledge of the authorities for the purpose of avoiding tax. 'Despite the efforts of the government, the black economy continues to grow.'
19. to **black** (goods) – to refuse to handle goods coming from a source which has incurred the disapproval of the trade union responsible for their carriage. Such goods are said to be 'blacked'.
20. the **black market** – illegal buying and

selling of products that have been rationed by the government.

1. to be **in the black** – to be in credit. 'After making losses for the last six years, we are at last in the black.' cf. **'in the red' 16/12**.
2. to be **in** someone's **black books** – to have incurred the strong disapproval or enmity of someone. 'The boy was in the teacher's black books for having been disobedient.'
3. the **blackboard jungle** – lawlessness and violence in the classroom, with the pupils threatening and defying the teacher. (The term has been imported from America.)
4. as **black as thunder** – in a rage or fury. 'When I stood up to him, his face went as black as thunder.'
5. **black ice** – a layer of ice on the road which is invisible and therefore very dangerous.
6. **Black Power** – a militant organization of black people that uses force in furtherance of its struggle against the white establishment.
7. **to blackball** – to vote against a person's election to an organization when admission has to be by unanimous vote of its members. A white ball is dropped into the ballot box to signify a member's acceptance of the candidate, and a black ball, his rejection. cf. 'to be on the **black list' 20/9**.

BROWN

8. to be as **brown as a berry** – to be pleasantly tanned by the sun. 'The children are as brown as berries after three weeks at the seaside.'
9. to be **browned off** – to be bored, disgruntled. 'I am browned off with this place – there's nothing to do.'
10. to be in a **brown study** – to be in a reverie, a dreamy, distracted state of mind, unaware of one's surroundings.

GREY

11. **a grey-beard** – an old man. Often used in a derogatory sense. 'I don't want to spend my holiday with a lot of grey-beards!'
12. to **grow grey** (in the service) – to remain in one occupation (usually the army, navy or a government department) for most of one's working life.
13. **grey matter** (colloquial) – the brain. 'Alan hasn't got much in the way of grey matter, but intelligence isn't everything.' The phrase comes from the fact that the active part of the brain is coloured grey.
14. a **grey area** – an indeterminate area between two branches of learning, not covered by either, a kind of intellectual no man's land. 'Philosophy is the grey area between science and religion.'

PURPLE

15. Purple symbolized the monarchy and high rank in ancient Greece, the Roman Emperors, Consuls, Magistrates and Generals being dressed in purple robes. Hence there are a number of idioms derived from purple: (1) to be **born in/to the purple** – to be born the child of a king. (2) to **marry into the purple** – to marry a king or prince. (3) to be **raised to the purple** – to be created a cardinal in the Roman Catholic Church.
16. **purple passages/patches/prose** – passages in a book written in a florid, ornate style, contrasting with the style of the rest of the work, such as is to be found in the writings of Gibbon, Macaulay, Pater, Burke and sometimes Churchill.

SCARLET

17. a **scarlet woman** – a woman notorious for her many seductions of men; a

whore. The scarlet woman was seen by St John in a vision (Revelation XVII, 3–4).

## PINK

1. to be **tickled pink** – to be very much amused, to relish a comical situation. 'He was tickled pink at the idea of taking a month's holiday at the expense of his company.'
2. the **pink of perfection** – sheer perfection, perfect to the smallest detail. 'Her skating was marvellous – graceful, elegant and stylish – the pink of perfection!'
3. in the **pink of condition / in the pink** – at peak fitness, often used in reference to athletes, racehorses or greyhounds.
4. a **pink socialist** – one who is less extreme than a full-blooded socialist. Sometimes used in contrast to a 'conviction socialist', and has largely been replaced by Labour Moderate.
5. **pink elephants** – frightening hallucinations experienced during withdrawal from alcohol, when the patient is suffering an attack of delirium tremens (D.T.s) and thinks that he sees pink elephants or other impossible objects in the room.
6. to **pink** – a swordsman was 'pinked' when he was pricked just deep enough to draw blood. The pinking was often regarded as an initiation ceremony.

## GOLDEN (see also GOLD in Chapter 31)

7. a **golden opportunity** – a wonderful opportunity that may never recur.
8. the **golden rule** – a wise rule, the best rule. 'Never to let yourself be rushed into a decision you may afterwards regret is a golden rule.' The Golden Rule is found in Leviticus XIX, 34: 'do unto others as you would like them to do to you'.
9. a **golden handshake** – a lump-sum of money paid to a retiring director or manager, or to a redundant worker.
10. **golden opinions** – the highest praise. 'Peter's first book won golden opinions from the critics.'
11. a **golden boy** – a young man idolized for an outstanding skill, usually in sport, or for his good looks. 'Boris Becker, the youngest player ever to have won the men's singles at Wimbledon, was the golden boy of tennis in 1985.'
12. The **Golden Age** – (1) the first of the four ages when men were happy and innocent, the other three being the Silver, Bronze and Iron; (2) the finest period in a country's history and literature. 'The seventeenth century was the Golden Age of France.'
13. the **golden mean** – moderation in all things, a principle advocated by the Epicureans, a philosophic sect in Ancient Greece.
14. to worship the **golden calf** – to worship money, to subordinate everything else to mercenary considerations. The reference is to the wrath of God at the worship by the children of Israel of false idols (Exodus XXXII).
15. a **Golden Jubilee** – celebration of the fiftieth anniversary of an important event, such as the 50 years of Queen Victoria's reign in 1887.

    **Golden wedding** – the fiftieth anniversary of the wedding day.

## SILVER

16. a **Silver Jubilee** – celebration of the twenty-fifth anniversary of an important event, such as the twenty-fifth year after the accession of George V, in 1935.

**Silver wedding** – the twenty-fifth anniversary of the wedding day.

1. the **silver screen** – the cinema. 'Valentino was one of the earliest stars of the silver screen.'

2. a **silver / silvery tongue** – eloquence, persuasiveness and charm.

3. **born with a silver spoon in one's mouth** – born into a wealthy family, with all the advantages that that can give a child. 'I have to work for my living; I wasn't born like you with a silver spoon in my mouth.' The reference is to the custom of the godparents giving the child a silver spoon at the christening.

# 2. ELEMENTS

## ELEMENT

1. **in one's element** – in the conditions best suited to a person's tastes or abilities, enjoying oneself enormously. 'The sergeant-major is in his element drilling the young recruits.'
2. to **brave the elements** – to defy very bad weather. Used facetiously to mean simply going out in the rain. 'Well, I suppose I had better brave the elements or I shall miss my train.'

## AIR

3. to vanish/disappear **into thin air** – to disappear completely without leaving any trace. 'We used to see a lot of our next-door neighbours, then one day, without any warning, they vanished into thin air.'
   **out of thin air** – out of nothing at all. 'Where do you imagine I can find £500 – out of thin air? I'm not a magician!'
4. you could **cut the air/atmosphere with a knife** – to sense at once a state of nervous tension, resentment or suppressed anger. 'When I went into the dining-room, there was an uncomfortable silence; you could have cut the air with a knife.'
5. to **air one's views** – to express one's opinions very freely, often in inappropriate situations. 'When we visit Aunt Mary, I hope you won't air your views the way you did last time. You will only annoy her if you do.'
6. to **put on airs / give oneself airs** – to behave as if one were socially superior to other people. 'She had better not give herself airs when she comes to live with us. My wife won't like it.' cf. **'airs and graces' 25/3**.
7. **airy-fairy** – lofty and impractical. 'Jean wouldn't have these airy-fairy ideas if she had to work for a living.'
8. **a fresh-air fiend** – a fanatical believer in the importance of fresh air to one's health. 'My father was a terrible fresh-air fiend. Whenever he came into a room, he would throw all the windows wide open.'
9. **hot air** – bombastic nonsense. 'Don't take any notice of Hammond's letters; they are nothing but hot air.'
10. to **clear the air** – to remove any previous misunderstanding by open and frank discussion. 'I'm so glad we've had this talk, Irene; it has really cleared the air.'
11. to **give public airing** to something – to raise a question publicly so that the facts may be fully disclosed and debated.
12. **on/off the air** – to broadcast / to cease broadcasting. 'The first time I went on the air, I thought I would be terribly nervous, but when the time came I was perfectly all right.'
13. **castles in the air** – dreams or hopes that will never be realized. 'I am afraid that all Tom's schemes will come to nothing; they are just castles in the air.' cf. **'castles in Spain' 186/8** and **'pie in the sky' 160/15**, which mean the same.
14. to **walk/dance on air** – to be in a state of exaltation. 'Since Simon and Lilian have got engaged, they have been walking on air.'
15. to **go up in the air** – to become furiously angry. 'My parents went up in the air when I told them that I wanted to move out into a flat.' cf. 'to **fly off the handle' 156/8**.
16. **in the air** – of plans, undecided, uncertain. 'We haven't made up our minds

yet where we are going to live; our plans are still in the air.'

1. something **in the air** – rumours that something important is going to happen. 'The clerks were whispering together in the office today; something is in the air.'
2. **as free as (the) air** – without any burden or obligation. 'Now that I have passed my exams, I feel as free as the air and can do whatever I like.'
3. **airs and graces** – affected manners which are intended to impress other people. 'I have never met your sister before; does she always give herself such airs and graces?' cf. 'to **put on airs' 24/6**.

WATER

4. to **water down** – to soften (the language or tone), to dilute. 'You'll have to water down your article if you want me to publish it. At present the wording is far too strong.' Alcoholic drinks can be watered down by the addition of water.
5. to be **on the (water) wagon** (colloquial) – to abstain from alcohol, usually on doctor's orders. 'Thank you very much, but I'm on the water wagon; I'll have an orangeade.'
6. a **watershed** – a decisive turning-point. 'The general elections in 1979 and 1983 were a watershed in Britain's post-war history.' The watershed is the line which separates waters flowing into different river basins or seas.
7. **water-tight** – irrefutable. The analogy is with water-tight clothing or water-tight shoes which protect the wearer from the water, just as a water-tight alibi protects the accused from conviction or a water-tight case admits of no doubt.
8. to pour **oil on troubled waters** – to resolve a quarrel by the exercise of tact and diplomacy. 'Mandy and Ned do nothing but quarrel. What a pity Uncle Tom isn't here to pour oil on troubled waters.'
9. to **pour cold water** (on a scheme or idea) – to find fault with, disparage. 'I wish Father weren't so negative; he pours cold water on all my ideas.' cf. 'to **put a damper on' 123/4**.
10. **dull as ditchwater** – uninteresting, boring. 'The play we saw last night was as dull as ditchwater.'
11. to **hold water** – to be valid, tenable; used with reference to theories, arguments or explanations; in fact anything that is open to debate. 'At first the prisoner's explanation seemed reasonable enough, but under cross-examination it didn't hold water.'
12. to **pass water** – to urinate.
13. to **tread water** – to be inactive or static. 'You've done nothing but tread water for the last six months. Isn't it time you took a job?' Literally, to keep one's head above water in swimming by moving one's hands and feet up and down. cf. **'mark time' 33/13**.
14. in **hot water** – in serious trouble. 'Jack has had to change his address. He's in hot water with the police again!'
15. **in deep water** – in difficulties. 'We are in deep water; we may have to sell the house to pay our debts.'
16. to **make a hole in the water** – to commit suicide by drowning.
17. of the **first water** – of the finest quality. 'Rubinstein was a musician of the first water, absolutely superb.' The phrase is derived from the custom of valuing diamonds according to their 'waters'. The 'water' is the colour or lustre of the diamond.
18. to **turn on the waterworks** – to weep.

'Susan can turn on the waterworks whenever she wants to.'

## FIRE

1. a **fire-eater** – someone who is eager for a fight, who quarrels on the slightest pretext. 'What a fire-eater you are, Joe; you aren't happy unless you are fighting with someone, are you?' The reference is to the 'fire-eaters' at the circus.
2. to go **through fire and water** – to undergo any danger, for another's sake. 'You know I would go through fire and water, Elizabeth, to be with you.'
3. **'Fire away!'** – 'Say whatever you want to.' 'I am ready to listen to you now. Fire away!'
4. to **fire off questions** – to ask questions very fast, one after the other. 'They were firing off questions at me from all sides.'
5. to **hang fire** (of plans, arrangements) – to be delayed, to make no progress. 'Our plans to emigrate are hanging fire, but we are determined to go just the same.' The allusion is to a gun which is slow in detonating.
6. to **add fuel to the fire** – to aggravate someone's rage, to make someone still angrier. 'Philip added fuel to the fire by telling Jane that it was her own fault he had missed his date with her.' cf. 'to **fan the flames' 26/14**.
7. to **catch fire** – to arouse interest, excitement. 'Roger's play was well written and very realistic, but somehow it failed to catch fire.'
8. to have many/several/other **irons in the fire** – to have more than one interest at the same time. 'Don't worry if we have to close the shop; I have other irons in the fire.'
9. to **play with fire** – to take a needless risk, often by meddling in other people's affairs. 'I wouldn't advise Kate what to do when she and her husband quarrel; you'll be playing with fire if you do.'
10. to **pull the chestnuts out of the fire** – to get someone out of a predicament, often at some risk to oneself. 'I don't see why I should pull the chestnuts out of the fire for Andrew. He has only got himself to blame for the difficulty he is in.'
11. to **spread like wild fire** – to circulate very rapidly; said of scandal, gossip and news (particularly bad news). 'The news of the Minister's offer to resign spread like wild fire, although he hadn't discussed it with his staff.'
12. to threaten / call down **fire and brimstone** – to threaten dire penalties; generally in a humorous sense. 'Peter is threatening us with fire and brimstone if we don't pay him back the £10 he lent us by the end of the week.' Fire and brimstone is a biblical phrase, meaning the punishment in hell that awaits the sinner on his death.

## FLAME

13. **an old flame** – a former girl/boyfriend. 'Was that an old flame you were speaking to on the telephone? You seemed very pleased to hear her voice!'
14. to **fan the flames** – to worsen existing ill-feeling by one's words or actions. 'The thieves seem to have taken most of Marion's jewellery, but you are only fanning the flames by exaggerating its value.' cf. 'to **add fuel to the fire' 26/6**.

## EARTH

15. **down-to-earth** – practical, sensible; concerned with facts, not theories. 'I am surprised that a down-to-earth

character like Jim should suddenly start taking an interest in astrology.'

1. to **come down to earth** – to abandon one's dreams and take a realistic view of life. 'One of these days, Alan will have to come down to earth; no amount of theorizing will pay the bills.'

   to **bring** someone **down to earth** – to force someone to abandon his dreams and take a realistic view of life.

2. who/what/why/how, etc., **on earth** – whoever/whatever/whyever/however, etc. 'What on earth have you done to your face? Have you been in a fight?' The addition of 'on earth' to the interrogative is an emphatic way of asking a question and may express surprise or annoyance.

3. to **go to earth/ground** – to seek refuge in a hiding place. 'The film star eventually went to earth in a small, out-of-the-way cottage in Rottingdean.'

   to **run** someone **to earth/ground** – to discover someone in his hiding place after a lengthy search.

   These two phrases have been taken from hunting when the quarry 'goes to earth' or 'is run to earth'.

4. to **pay the earth** for – to pay a very large sum of money for something. 'You must have paid the earth for that mink coat!'

5. **no earthly reason** – no reason at all. 'There's no earthly reason why you should always follow your brother's advice.' This phrase is often used to express mild irritation.

6. not to have an **earthly chance** / an **earthly** – to have no chance of success at all. 'Swimming the Channel? In weather like this, she won't have an earthly chance of breaking the record.'

7. **like nothing on earth** (colloquial) – ghastly, awful. The phrase can be used with the verbs: look, feel, sound, taste and smell. 'You look like nothing on earth in that ridiculous outfit.'

8. to **move heaven and earth** – to do everything humanly possible to achieve one's aim. 'We have moved heaven and earth to get the squatters out of our house, but so far without success.'

## MUD

9. a **stick-in-the-mud** – someone without initiative who never takes a chance. 'My husband has been working as a clerk in that firm for the last twenty years. He has no ambition – he's a real stick-in-the-mud.'

# 3. WEATHER

## WEATHER

1. a **fair-weather friend** – a friend only for as long as things are going well.
2. to be/feel **under the weather** – to feel unwell, depressed or out of sorts. 'I'm afraid John was out celebrating last night and didn't get home till late, so he's feeling a bit under the weather this morning.'
3. to **make heavy weather** of something – to take excessive pains over a relatively simple task, to exaggerate its difficulties. 'He made terribly heavy weather of mending the puncture; it only took a few minutes when he finally did it.'
4. to **weather the storm** – to overcome a crisis, often financial. 'If we cut out all unnecessary expenses, we shall have a reasonable chance of weathering the storm.'
5. to **keep a weather eye open** – originally a seaman's phrase, meaning to be watchful – now used generally, as well as on board ship.
6. to **change like a weather-cock** – to be for ever changing one's mind, to be easily influenced. The weather-cock moves round according to the prevailing wind, and like the wind is always changing direction.

## RAIN

7. to be/feel **as right as rain** – to be perfectly well again. The phrase implies that the speaker has been ill, or met with some accident, from which he has completely recovered. Often used with the object of reassuring the inquirer. 'Ann has got over her 'flu. She's as right as rain now!'
8. to **rain cats and dogs** – to pour with rain. The raindrops are compared with cats and dogs fighting one another.

   **to rain in buckets** has the same meaning: it rains so hard that the raindrops feel as though water were being poured out of buckets.
9. a **rainy day** – bad times when it will be difficult to make a living. 'Here's £50 for a rainy day. If things go wrong, it may come in handy.'

   to **put something by for a rainy day** – to save money against the day one is too old or ill to work, or has lost one's job.
10. **come rain or shine** – whatever happens. 'Come rain or shine, Caroline always visits her husband in hospital after her work.'
11. a **drop in the ocean** – only a tiny fraction of what is needed. 'We need £70,000 to clear our debts. I'm afraid the £5,000 Ted has offered us is only a drop in the ocean.' In this phrase, the 'drop' is a raindrop.

## SNOW

12. **pure as the driven snow** – absolutely pure in one's moral character and behaviour. 'How Mary has changed! When she was a teenager, she was as pure as the driven snow.'
13. to be **snowed under** – to be overwhelmed. 'Since we issued our latest prospectus, we have been snowed under with inquiries.'

## ICE

14. to **cut no ice** – to make no impression at all, to fail to produce the desired effect. 'Peter's success at school and college cut no ice with the selection committee. They were not impressed with academic attainments but wanted a man with practical

experience.' The idiom comes from the cutting of the ice with the edge of the skate.

1. to **skate on thin ice** – to introduce a subject about which someone is especially sensitive. 'You were skating on thin ice, weren't you, when you praised his brother's book. Didn't you know they have nothing to do with each other!'
2. to **break the ice** – to overcome someone's shyness or reserve, usually in a social setting. 'I didn't know how to break the ice with him. We were both shy and had nothing in common.'
3. to **put on ice** – to defer a project for the time being while preserving it for future use. 'I'm sorry, Alan, but we've had to put your plan on ice. We'll have another look at it in six months' time.'
4. the **tip of the iceberg** – evidence that a great deal more exists but remains hidden. 'The police have uncovered a bad case of corruption, but they believe it is only the tip of the iceberg.' Only a small part of the iceberg is visible, nine-tenths or so remaining hidden from view below the surface of the water.

## CHILL

5. to **cast a chill on/over** – to depress or sadden. 'The news of her daughter's illness cast a chill over the party, and we all sat about in gloomy silence.'

## SHIVERS

6. to **give one the shivers** – to embarrass. 'He is so uneducated; it gives me the shivers to see him showing off in front of the guests.'

## FLOOD

7. **before the Flood** – a facetious comment on anything that is old-fashioned or out of date. 'Karen's room badly needs redecorating; the wallpaper looks as if it had been put up before the Flood.' 'Before the Flood' refers to before Noah and the Great Flood.

## FOG

8. to be (all) **in a fog** – to be confused, nonplussed. 'When I saw Jack this morning, he was all in a fog about what to do next.'
9. to have not **the foggiest (idea)** – to have not the least idea. This is sometimes abbreviated in colloquial language to **'not the foggiest'**. 'I haven't the foggiest idea what you are talking about.' 'I haven't the foggiest either; I was only practising my French.'

## RAY

10. a **ray of hope** – some grounds for hope. The negative form is often used – **not a ray of hope** – not the slightest hope. 'I am so sorry but the doctor didn't offer a ray of hope; it's very sad.'

## CLOUD

11. **Every cloud has a silver lining** (proverb) – however unfortunate one's circumstances, there is always some consolation to be found. 'William has lost his job, which is a great blow to him, but his redundancy payment is very substantial. Every cloud has a silver lining.'
12. to **cast a cloud** over – to sadden, to fill with gloom, to mar one's pleasure. 'The news of her father's illness cast a cloud over Mary's honeymoon.'
13. to be **under a cloud** – to be the object of someone's suspicion. 'Gerald has

been under a cloud at the office ever since the petty cash went missing.'

1. **on Cloud Nine** (American colloquialism) – very happy, joyful. 'Since her engagement to Peter, Joan has been on Cloud Nine.' Cloud Nine was originally Cloud Seven, which was probably derived from 'the seventh heaven'. cf. 'in the **seventh heaven**' **218/11**.

2. to **be** / to **have one's head in the clouds** – to be out of touch with reality. 'It's no good asking him what to do. He has his head in the clouds.'

3. to have **a cloud lifted** from over one – to be cleared of suspicion, to end a period of depression, to be restored to favour. 'Now that the cloud over Richard has been lifted, he will be much happier at the office.'

4. **wait till the clouds roll by** – wait until the difficulties have eased. 'I am sure our difficulties are only temporary. We must wait until the clouds roll by.'

5. to **live in Cloud-cuckoo-land** – to live in one's imagination in a world that bears no relation to reality. 'If you think Judy's scheme would ever work, then the two of you must be living in Cloud-cuckoo-land!' From Aristophanes' comedy, *The Birds*, written in fifth-century BC. Athens, which depicts the building of an imaginary city in the air by the birds.

6. a **cloud no bigger than a man's hand** – a distant, insignificant threat, but one that may become dangerous in the course of time.

## SQUALLS

7. **look out for squalls** – be on your guard against trouble. A nautical phrase, meaning a sudden gust of wind that may capsize your boat if you are not careful.

## WIND

8. a **fair wind** – favourable conditions (for a project or enterprise).

   to **wish** something or someone **a fair wind** – to wish something or someone success. 'Neil Kinnock, leader of the Labour Party, wished the new legislation against football hooliganism a fair wind.'

9. to **whistle in the wind** – to talk to someone without obtaining a sensible reply. 'You might just as well whistle in the wind as talk to Larry.'

10. **the wind of change** – a new outlook, a fresh point of view. The phrase was first used by Harold Macmillan in reference to political developments in Africa.

11. to know **which way the wind is blowing** – to foresee the general drift of events, to know in advance what is likely to happen, to make a correct prediction. A variant is **'wait and see which way the wind blows'** – to await developments before making up one's mind. 'I shall wait and see which way the wind is blowing before committing myself.' Much used in political comment.

12. to sail **close to the wind** – to verge on the improper or the illegal, to stop just short of breaking the social code. 'The comedian sailed close to the wind. Some ladies in the audience were looking distinctly uneasy.'

13. to **take the wind out of** someone's **sails** – to embarrass someone by forestalling him, anticipating his actions. 'Counsel for the accused was about to address the jury when he had the wind taken out of his sails by his client, who blurted out that he was guilty.' Literally, the phrase means to take the wind out of another ship's sails by sailing close to it on its windward side. cf. 'to **cut the ground from under one's feet**' **104/13**, 'to **pull the rug from under one's feet**' **152/5**.

1. to **sow the wind and reap the whirlwind** (proverb) – to suffer catastrophic consequences for one's wrong-doing. 'The French aristocracy were punished a hundredfold for their callous neglect of the poor; they sowed the wind and reaped the whirlwind.' (From the Bible: Hosea VII, 7.)
2. to get one's **second wind** – to regain one's energy, to acquire fresh strength. 'After a bad start, Paul got his second wind and tried again.'
3. **in the teeth of the wind** – literally, moving against the wind, despite the wind, and hence figuratively against any opposition. The wind can be a strong hindrance to the progress of a sailing ship.
4. **in the wind's eye** – directly facing the wind.
5. to **get to windward of** – to attack from a favourable angle.
6. to **put the wind up** someone – to alarm or frighten someone. 'You put the wind up me, telephoning at three in the morning. I thought that something terrible had happened.'

   to **get the wind up** – to become alarmed or frightened. 'We all got the wind up when the bride didn't arrive at the church. We thought she must have changed her mind, but she was only late.'
7. to **throw caution to the winds** – to take bold action without considering one's own safety.
8. to **get wind of** – to receive early warning of imminent events, often from a confidential source. 'We got wind of his resignation a week before it was announced in the newspapers.' This is on the analogy of an animal that scents danger in the wind.
9. **there is something in the wind** – something is about to happen; one suspects that something important is going to happen without knowing what. 'The clerks in the office have been exchanging knowing glances for the last week, and there's been a lot of whispering going on. Something is in the wind.'

   **What's in the wind?** – What's up? What's going on? The same idiom as above in the interrogative form.
10. to **raise the wind** – to obtain the necessary finance.
11. a **windfall** – an unexpected stroke of good luck, for example a legacy from a distant relative. The literal meaning is fruit blown from the tree to the ground which can be eaten without being picked.
12. a **windbag** – someone who is talkative but incapable of action.
13. **long-winded** – verbose, using several words when one would have done. Here are some examples taken from a memorandum of the British Tourist Authority on the teaching of English, BLE/1980: 'an integrated programme of studies' *instead of* 'a curriculum'; 'suitably graded groups for teaching purposes' – *instead of* 'classes'; 'teachers with appropriate training and relevant experience' *instead of* 'qualified teachers'; 'transfer of students between one group and another' *instead of* 'promotion'.
14. to **tilt at windmills** – to fight imaginary enemies, hence to squander one's energy uselessly. 'Why do you always attack the landlords, Jack? There are hardly any private landlords left in London. You are tilting at windmills.' From Cervantes' *Don Quixote* (1605.) in which an elderly knight attacked windmills, in the mistaken belief that they were giants who had imprisoned innocent girls.

## STORM

15. **the calm before the storm** – a period of quiet before an upheaval or crisis.

1. to **take by storm** – to exert an irresistible fascination over something (a woman, city, country, etc.). 'Caruso took all America by storm.'
2. to **ride the storm** – to confront a crisis resolutely. 'I refuse to resign; I shall ride the storm, no matter how long it lasts.'
3. to **bow before the storm** – to submit to public indignation and protest. 'There was such an outcry when the Government put forward its proposals that it was forced to bow before the storm and withdraw them.'
4. a **storm in a tea-cup** – a violent agitation over a trifle. 'Father was furious with Geoff for doing the *Times* crossword puzzle before he came down to breakfast, but they were soon friends again. It was all a storm in a tea-cup.'

## THUNDER

5. to **steal** someone's **thunder** – to divert attention from the person expecting it to oneself by adopting his methods. This happens when a minor actor overshadows the leading player, and receives the applause the other was expecting. 'Although Philip had only a minor role, he completely overshadowed the leading player and stole all his thunder.'
6. **blood and thunder** – violent, melodramatic. Almost always applied to plays and stories. 'There were at least six murders in that blood-and-thunder story.'

## LIGHTNING

7. **like (greased) lightning / like a streak of lightning** – with the speed of lightning; so fast that you barely have time to see it. 'I've never seen anyone move so fast. He ran like lightning across the field.'
8. a **lightning strike** – a strike that is called without warning.

# 4. TIME

## TIME

1. **high time** – the time has come when delay is no longer possible. 'It's high time you got ready or you will miss your train.'
2. to have a **rough time** – to be treated severely, to have a run of bad luck.
3. to have **the time of one's life** – to have a wonderfully happy time. 'James was dreading his military service but now he is in the army, he is having the time of his life.'
4. a **good-time girl** – a girl who lives for pleasure, a loose woman.
5. to be **born before/ahead of one's time** – to be born before people are in a position to appreciate one's true worth. Many important scientists and artists have died in obscurity.
6. **for the sake of old times / for old times' sake** – to honour past friendships, to do someone a favour. 'I've only got the afternoon between flights, but I had to see you for old times' sake.'
7. **time out of mind** – time immemorial, beyond human memory. 'Some are born to rule, and others are born to serve; so it has always been, time out of mind.'
8. **more times than I've had hot dinners** – more times than I can remember. 'I've shown tourists round the Houses of Parliament more times than I've had hot dinners.'
9. **behind the times** – out of date in one's ideas. 'Why, Grandfather, you haven't got a colour TV set. You *are* behind the times!'
10. to **take one's time** – to do something at one's own pace without hurrying. 'Our builder is taking his time, isn't he? He's been three days on that job already.'
11. to **fritter away** one's time, energy, money – to divide one's attention among a number of activities so that time, energy and money are wasted. 'If you hadn't frittered your time away on so many useless projects, you would have qualified by now.'
12. to **bide one's time** – to wait for the right moment to take one's revenge, or carry out a plan.
13. to **mark time** – to delay taking action until everyone else is ready; from the military command 'Mark time!' – to stamp the feet on the same spot without advancing. cf. 'to **tread water**' **25/13**.
14. to have a **rare time** (colloquial) – to have exceptional fun.
15. **time(s) without number** – many, many times. Often used to express impatience or annoyance. 'I have warned you time without number not to accept lifts from strangers.' Literally, so many times that they can no longer be counted.
16. **time is of the essence** – time is the most important consideration. A condition is sometimes made in a contract that time shall be of the essence, meaning that the work must be completed by a definite date, otherwise the contract is cancelled.
17. to be **pushed/pressed for time** – to have little or no time to spare, to be in a hurry.
18. **time is running out** – there is little time left. 'We have only three shopping days left till Christmas. Time is running out.' Time is here compared with sand running through an hour-glass.
19. to **live on borrowed time** – to regard each year exceeding the normal life-span as not one's own but for temporary use only.
20. **(dead) on time** – absolutely punctual.
21. **in the nick of time** – at the very last

moment, with no time to spare. 'I caught my aeroplane in the nick of time.'

1. **near her time** – approaching the moment when her baby will be born.
2. to **make up for lost time** – to work extra hard to compensate for time wasted.
3. to take **time off** – to absent oneself from work, often for a particular reason. 'I took time off this morning to visit my sister in hospital. I'll make it up this evening.'
4. to have **time on one's hands** – to have nothing to do, to be idle. 'Why don't you ask Tony round for a game? During the holidays he will have time on his hands.'
5. **How time drags!** – How slowly the time passes! What a boring time we are having!
6. to **kill (the) time** – to do anything, however trivial, to pass the time and so avoid being bored. 'We had an hour's wait, so we played cards to kill the time.'
7. to **serve one's time** – to work for the prescribed number of years in a service (army, navy, civil service, etc.).
8. to **do time** – to serve a prison sentence.
9. a **race against time** – a rush to get a task finished within a given time.
10. a **time-server** – someone who adopts the principles of his or her superiors in order to gain advancement.
11. a **time-lag** – the interval between a cause and its effect. For example, there is always a time-lag between the printing of money by the government and the resulting rise in prices.
12. **time-consuming** – requiring a great deal of time. 'It was time-consuming work, going through all the Jessops in the telephone directory, but we tracked him down in the end.'
13. a **question/matter of time** – sooner or later. 'It's only a question (or matter) of time before you are caught!'
14. **in the fullness of time** – at the proper time, in the end. 'In the fullness of time, your contribution to physics will be recognized; have patience and do not despair.'
15. to **have no time for** – to disapprove strongly of. 'I have no time for people who preach equality and then take their holidays in the Bahamas.'
16. to **make time** – to spare time, even when one is busy, for an additional duty. 'I know you have a lot to do, but you must make time for Henry. He's an old friend of yours.'
17. to **play for time** – to try to delay some undesirable action in the hope that conditions will meanwhile improve. 'They want their money at once, but if your uncle is coming back on Tuesday, I can play for time until then.'
18. to **march/move/keep up with the times** – to keep one's attitude and methods up to date. 'If we don't march with the times, our customers will go elsewhere.'

## YEAR, YEARS

19. **year in, year out** – repeatedly over a long period of time. The phrase is often used of fixed habits. 'Year in, year out, Mr Masters would make his way to his local pub on the stroke of one.'
20. the **man of the year** – the most talked-of man of the year, in a good sense, cf. 'the **man of the day**' **36/10**.
21. to be **light years away** from someone – to have nothing in common with someone, to hold views that cannot be reconciled with the other person's. The analogy is with the time light takes to travel, implying a vast distance.

1. the **lost years** – wasted years that can never be made up.
2. **years of discretion** – the age at which a boy or girl is old enough to make moral judgements.

## SEASON

3. **in season** – at the right time, at an opportune time. 'Why can't we have peaches? They are in season, aren't they?'

   **out of season** – at the wrong time, during the close season when game may not be shot.
4. a **word in season** – a timely piece of advice.
5. the **silly season** – the time of the year when Parliament is in recess, and newspapers, having little news to report, start idle theoretical discussions in their columns.

## THE SEASONS: SPRING, SUMMER, AUTUMN AND WINTER

6. to **spring clean** – to clean and redecorate one's house, when the winter is over.
7. an **Indian summer** – a period of great happiness that comes late in a person's life. Literally, a late summer, a spell of warm sunshine in October. (Late summers are common in the West of the USA, which was mostly settled by Red Indians when this phrase was first used.)
8. the **autumn of one's life** – well into middle age, with the best years behind one.
9. England's **Winter of Discontent** – the winter of 1979 when strikes broke out all over England, resulting in much hardship and suffering, especially in hospitals and schools. The reference is to Shakespeare's *King Richard III*, I, i, 1: 'Now is the winter of our discontent.'

## MONTHS: APRIL, MAY

10. to make an **April fool** of someone – to play a joke on someone on the morning of 1 April.
11. a **may-day warning** – an international call for help, a signal transmitted by ships and aeroplanes warning of impending danger. 'May-day' has nothing to do with the month of May but is a corruption of the French international signal, 'M'aider', meaning 'Help me'.

## DAYS OF THE WEEK: MONDAY, FRIDAY AND SUNDAY

12. that **Monday morning feeling** – a feeling of depression when people have to return to work after the weekend holiday.
13. **Black Monday** – the first day of the school term when lessons are resumed.
14. **Man Friday** – a faithful servant and companion. From Defoe's *Robinson Crusoe*.

    **Girl Friday** – a personal assistant in an office, the phrase having been coined from Man Friday (see above).
15. not in a **month of Sundays** – not for a long time, far longer than is necessary; usually said in an exasperated or impatient tone. 'That won't be ready in a month of Sundays.'
16. one's **Sunday best** – one's best clothes.

## DAY

17. **day in, day out** – day after day without any interruption.
18. **one of these (fine) days** – before long.

The phrase is used in predicting some (unpleasant) event. 'One of these fine days you'll get run over if you don't take care.'

1. an **off-day** – a day when one works badly. 'Pauline must have had an off-day; her typing is full of mistakes.'
2. it's **not my day** – everything is going wrong for me today.
   just **one of those days** – a day when everything goes wrong; said in a tone of resignation.
3. **not to have all day** – not to have any more time to spare for somebody. 'I do wish you'd tell me exactly what you want – I haven't got all day.' Used to express the speaker's impatience or exasperation (impolite).
4. **late in the day** – too late. The expression is often used as a reproach: 'It's a bit late in the day for you to cancel the booking; I've made all the arrangements.'
5. to **call it a day** – (1) to stop working, often said when the workers feel they have done enough for one day. (2) It can also mean that it would be better to put an end to an arrangement. 'I suggested to my partner that, since we didn't agree, we should call it a day.'
6. it's **early days** yet – it's too early to judge. 'Wait until you have got used to the work before you make up your mind. You've only been there a few days. It's early days yet.'
7. **'That will be the day!'** – used ironically to indicate a desirable event that will never occur. 'When Peter finishes his book, did you say? That'll be the day!'
8. to **make** someone's **day** – to delight someone, often in an unexpected way. 'Receiving a call from her daughter in Australia made Pamela's day.'
9. at the **end of the day** – ultimately, when the battle or campaign is over. 'At the end of the day, I am sure our policies will have been justified.'
10. to be the **man of the day** – to be the outstanding man of his time. cf. **'man of the year' 34/20**.
    the **man of his day** – the outstanding man of his time.
11. to **carry/win the day** – to triumph over one's adversary, to win the struggle.
12. a **field day** – a highly successful occasion when full advantage is taken of every opportunity, especially an opportunity to ridicule or punish an opponent. 'When Jennifer took over her father's firm, she had a field day dismissing her old colleagues on the office staff.' 'Your new book is full of mistakes; the critics will have a field day!' Originally a military term for allocating a special day to army exercises.
13. to have **had one's day** – to be past one's best.
14. a **hey-day** – the best days, the prime. 'The early nineteenth century was the hey-day of English romantic poetry.' 'hey' may be a corruption of 'high'. cf. 'in the **halcyon days' 70/4**, which has the same meaning.
15. **open as the day** – transparently honest, without subterfuge.
16. a **day's grace** – grace days are those allowed by law or by the creditor for the payment of a debt. Hence, an extra period of time allowed before being called to account. 'grace' in this idiomatic sense may apply to a number of days or months, or even to a year.
17. to **fall on evil days** – to live in poverty after having enjoyed better times.
18. in the **cold light of day** – in a mood of sober realism, as opposed to one of uncritical enthusiasm (frequently used with reference to ideas and plans that have been put forward). 'We discussed my idea at dinner and my

boss became terribly excited about it. However, in the cold light of day, he saw many objections to it.'

1. a **black day** – a day that has disastrous consequences. 'It was a black day for us when Harris joined the firm. He has done nothing but make trouble for us ever since.'
2. the **order of the day** – (1) the day's routine or programme. 'Swimming is the order of the day.' (2) It can also mean the way things are: 'Open prisons are the order of the day.'
3. **all in the day's work** – all part of one's normal duties. '"I am so grateful to you for giving my little girl first aid." "That's quite all right; it's all in the day's work."'
4. to **name the day** – to fix the date for the wedding.
5. **early-closing day** – one afternoon in the week, usually Wednesday or Thursday, when the shops are closed.
6. the **daily grind** – the monotonous routine of everyday life.
7. the **day of reckoning** – the time when one is obliged to answer for one's misdeeds. 'There will be a day of reckoning for what you have done to me!' The phrase comes from the biblical Day of Judgement.

DAYLIGHT

8. to **see daylight** – to gain an insight into a problem. 'After months of work, we are beginning to see daylight.'
9. **daylight robbery** – a shameless swindle. 'Charging you £200 for that simple repair was daylight robbery.'
10. to **frighten/scare the living daylights** out of someone – to terrify someone almost to death, by threats and intimidation.
11. to **beat the living daylights** out of someone – to give someone a severe beating.

YESTERDAY

12. not **born yesterday** – old or wise enough not to be easily taken in. 'You won't fool me with that trick. I wasn't born yesterday.'

NIGHT

13. to **burn the midnight oil** – to work late into the night.
14. a **fly-by-night** operator – someone who sets up business for only a short time in order to make a big profit, and then moves on.

HOUR

15. in the **small hours** of the morning – in the early hours of the morning.
16. at **all hours** – at an unusual time, often used in a censorious manner. 'The neighbours have parties at all hours.'
17. a **good hour** – at the very least one hour, probably more.
18. a **solid hour** – a full hour, often used when the time passes slowly. 'We waited for you a solid hour.'
19. to **improve the shining hour** – to make oneself useful. Used humorously: 'You can improve the shining hour by cleaning the car, Tom.'
20. the **question of the hour** – currently the most debated question.
21. in one's **hour of need** – at a time when help is most urgently required. 'Yes, £100 will be most useful. Thank you for helping me in my hour of need.'
22. the **rush hour** – the time of day when people travelling to and from their work are crowding the buses and trains.

MOMENT

23. **on the spur of the moment** – on a sudden impulse, without premeditation.

1. **in the heat of the moment** – at a moment when one's anger has been aroused. 'In the heat of the moment I suppose I might attack an armed burglar, but never in cold blood.'
2. the **man of the moment** – one who enjoys public acclaim, but only for a short time.
3. in an **unguarded moment** – in an indiscreet moment. 'In an unguarded moment Alison told me she had been convicted of shop-lifting many years ago.'
4. to **have its moments** – to be good, exciting, interesting, but only occasionally. 'The cruise was disappointing although it had its moments. I shall always remember our day in Madeira.'
5. The **moment of truth** – the moment of crisis when one learns the truth about oneself. 'I have often wondered how I would react if I saw a girl in the street being attacked by a gang of hooligans. For me, that would be the moment of truth.'
6. the **psychological moment** – the most propitious time, the best time to seize an opportunity. 'He was on the point of proposing to Karen when the telephone rang. The psychological moment had passed.'

## AGE

7. to **come of age** – to attain the legal age of manhood/womanhood.
8. the **age of consent** – the age when a girl may lawfully consent to have sexual intercourse. The age of consent in Britain is sixteen. Below that age, her consent, even if freely given, is deemed by law to be unreal, and the man is guilty of the crime of rape.
9. at a **ripe old age** – very old. 'He lived to a ripe old age.' cf. **'a green old age' 18/8**.
10. to take/be **an age** – to take a long time over something, to keep someone waiting. 'What an age you've been, Simon!'
11. **it's ages since . . .** – it's a very long time since . . . 'It's ages since we met.'
12. to **be one's age** – to behave like a grown-up person. 'For heaven's sake, be your age, Martin! You are eighteen, not eight!'
13. to **show one's age** – to betray one's age by trying to look younger than one really is. 'She showed her age when she dressed like a teenager.'

## DATE

14. to **date** something – (1) to establish the date an object was made, implying that it is the product of an earlier age. (2) Also used in reference to elderly people. 'His manners and speech date him.'
15. to **have a date** – to arrange a meeting with a member of the opposite sex. 'I've just made a date with Philip. We are going to the theatre tomorrow evening.'

## CLOCK

16. to work **round the clock** – to work without ceasing at a task until it is finished. 'For that money I'm prepared to work all round the clock.'
17. a **clock-watcher** – someone who has lost interest in his work and does the absolute minimum required. 'Alan was an enthusiastic teacher when he started here, but now he is a clock-watcher – just like the rest of the staff.'
18. to **put the clock back** – to recapture an earlier period of time. 'You can't order young people about any more. Times have changed, and it is useless trying to put the clock back.'

1. to go **like clockwork** – to go exactly according to plan. 'We got the group to Edinburgh without the least difficulty. Everyone co-operated, and it all went like clockwork.'

## BY-GONES

2. **let by-gones be by-gones** – let's forgive and forget.

# 5. LIFE AND DEATH

## LIFE

1. a **walk of life** – an occupation or profession. 'I have travelled all over the world and have met people from every walk of life.'
2. **for the life of me** – even if my life depended on it. 'I can't for the life of me see why you should take your holiday in Yorkshire just because you were born there.' The phrase is used negatively, generally with 'can't' or 'couldn't'.
3. **as large as life** – in person. 'I had just posted a letter to James in Cologne – when suddenly there he was, as large as life, standing right in front of me!'
4. a **fact of life** – a truth which must be accepted, no matter how unfair or unreasonable it may seem. 'I'm sorry that you find the rule unreasonable, but there is nothing I can do about it; it is a fact of life.'
5. **not on your life!** – in no circumstances, certainly not. An emphatic way of refusing a request. '"If you are going to the theatre this evening, would you mind very much taking my aunt along?" "Not on your life!"'
6. **you (can) bet your life** – you can be absolutely certain. This phrase is often used ironically of people who are expected to act in a particular way, judging by what one knows of their past behaviour. 'You can bet your life that, if Edward comes, Mary will come too. She won't let him out of her sight for a second.'
7. **for dear life** – as if one's life were in danger. 'When the two burglars saw Patrick come into the hall, they ran for dear life out of the house and down the garden.'
8. **within an inch of one's life** – very near to losing one's life. Often used as a hyperbole. 'If I catch you stealing again, I will thrash you to within an inch of your life.'
9. **to the life** – an exact likeness, a living likeness. 'The portrait has been very well done; it's you to the life.'
10. to **come to life** – (1) to regain consciousness after a faint; (2) to gain in vigour and excitement. 'The first act of the play was rather dull, but in the second act it really came to life.'
11. a new **lease of life** – an opportunity to enjoy a happier/longer life. 'Robin's change of job has given him a new lease of life. He is his own master now, and looks ten years younger.'
12. to bear/lead a **charmed life** – to escape unscathed from many dangers as if one were protected by a magic power. 'Henry's companions were all injured but he returned without a scratch; he must lead a charmed life.'
13. the **life and soul** of the party – the person who brings the most sparkle and excitement to a party –'Miss Sims is so quiet and demure in the office that you'd never think she was the life and soul of the party last night.'
14. the **high life** – a luxurious, pleasure-loving way of life. 'Donald will find Bromley rather quiet after the high life he has been living in Bermuda.'
15. the **low life** – the life led by riff-raff, vagabonds, tramps and petty criminals.
16. to **see life** – to broaden one's experience by mixing with men and women of all types, including the immoral and dissolute. 'Tom should see life before he marries and settles down.'
17. to lead a **double life** – to lead the life of two distinct and separate people. The classic example is R. L. Stevenson's *Dr Jekyll and Mr Hyde* in which the

same man is depicted as a respectable scientist by day and a monster by night.

1. There's **life in the old dog yet** – I may not be as young as I was, but I am still full of energy. Often said by elderly people to counter suggestions that their powers are failing.
2. I can't do it to **save my life** – it wouldn't be possible, even if my life depended on it. 'I can't play tennis to save my life, but I enjoy watching it.'

## LIVE

3. to **live beyond one's means** – to live in a style one cannot afford. 'No wonder the Howards have gone bankrupt; they have been living beyond their means for years.'
4. you **live and learn** – a comment on a new and unexpected fact. 'Who would have thought that Mr Saunders of all people would be arrested for shop-lifting? You live and learn.'
5. to **live up to** – to match someone else's standards. 'I don't want to go to the same school as my brother; I could never live up to him.'
6. to **live up to** one's **reputation** – to behave in a manner that may be expected by one's friends and acquaintances. 'The headmaster is certainly living up to his reputation. He is a real disciplinarian.'
7. to **live on** one's **reputation/name** – to rely on one's past achievements to earn a living. 'It's easy enough to live on one's reputation; the real problem is to win a reputation in the first place.'
8. to **live** something **down** – to repair damage to one's reputation by improving one's behaviour or skill in one's calling. 'The operation was a disaster; I shall never live it down.'
9. to **live a lie** – to be a hypocrite, to mislead people as to one's true nature. 'Mr Holmes had lived a lie for the past five years: by day, he worked as a parson in the parish of St Giles; by night, he frequented the night-clubs in the West End.'
10. **how the other half lives** – how people in a different class from oneself live. 'You should get around and see how the other half lives.'
11. to **live rough** – to live in uncomfortable conditions. 'However long you live rough, you never really get used to the hardship.'
12. to **live with** something – to put up with something unpleasant that one cannot rid oneself of, especially ailments. 'The doctor tells me that it is only a minor inconvenience which I must learn to live with.'
13. **Live and let live** (saying) – to be tolerant and not interfere in other people's lives. 'What does it matter to you who your brother spends his free time with? I believe in live and let live.'
14. to **live in sin** (old-fashioned) – to have a sexual relationship with a person to whom one is not married. 'When are Steven and Pamela going to get married, or are they going to live in sin for ever?'
15. **plain living and high thinking** – moral philosophy and tasteless food. 'After a week's plain living and high thinking at my cousin's, I'm in the mood for a good pub-crawl.'
16. to **live it up** – to spend money recklessly on one's own pleasure. 'I should have thought the Wallaces had better things to spend their money on than living it up in Paris.'
17. **alive and kicking** – very much alive. 'You needn't worry about Robert. He was alive and kicking when I saw him this afternoon.' The phrase derives from the kicking of the baby in the womb.
18. a **live wire** – a person with enormous

energy and initiative who is never inactive. 'If you want to raise money for the orphanage, you should put Bill in charge of the fund-raising; he is a real live wire.' Literally, a live wire is the wire that is charged with electricity.

## DEATH

1. **sick to death** – exasperated beyond endurance. 'I am sick to death of his stories. He tells me the same ones every time I meet him.'
2. to be **tickled to death** – to be extremely amused. 'We were tickled to death when we heard Roger had come top in the exams after his terrible school report.'
3. to **bleed to death** (not of a person) – to collapse, in consequence of mounting costs, debts, etc. 'If we don't get fresh orders soon, we shall bleed to death. There is no money to pay the bills.'
4. to hold/hang on **like grim death** – to hold very tightly, as if one's life depended on it. 'The old man was hanging on to his briefcase like grim death. I wonder what he had in it.'
5. to **work** oneself **to death** – to exhaust oneself from overwork. 'We have worked ourselves to death and all for a pittance!' cf. 'to **break one's back**' **101/5**.
6. to **work** something **to death** – to overwork something so much that it can no longer produce useful results, such as when an idea loses its force through constant repetition. 'You've been saying the same thing in your publicity for twenty years. You have worked our idea to death; it's time you thought of something new.'
7. to **catch one's death (of cold)** (colloquial) – to catch a very bad cold. 'You'll catch your death if you go out into the cold night air after that hot bath.' Often used as a warning.
8. the **kiss of death** – an act of betrayal that effectively destroys a project, relationship or life. 'On the pretext of showing concern for her husband's well-being, Mrs Andrews gave him the kiss of death by telephone. Having established his presence at home, she sent two hired assassins to murder him.' The allusion is to the betrayal of Christ by Judas Iscariot by means of a kiss.
9. to be **in at the death/kill** – to be present at the climax, at the final phase. 'Everyone is expecting the chairman to resign this afternoon. Do you want to be in at the death?' The phrase is taken from hunting when the fox is caught by the hounds and killed.

## DIE

10. to **die hard** – to resist change, especially changes in tradition, customs and ideas. 'The dogma dies hard that a student should master the grammar of a foreign language before starting to speak it.'
11. to **die in the last ditch** – to resist (something) to the very end, to fight to the death. 'If the government tries to demolish the Health Service, that is the last ditch in which many of us will die' (*Observer*, 8 January 1983).

## DEAD

12. to **cut** someone **dead** – to refuse to return someone's greeting, to ignore someone with intentional rudeness. 'Mrs Hammond must be very angry with you to have cut you dead; she is normally so polite.'
13. to make **a dead set** at – (1) to make a vigorous attack on a person (usually verbal). (2) to make a strong bid for a person's affection. 'From the moment I entered the ballroom, Susan made a dead set at me; she ruined my evening.'
14. a **dead loss** – completely unproduc-

tive, useless. 'That course Pietro went on was a dead loss; after three months, he still couldn't speak a word of English.'

1. a **dead letter** – a law (or rule) which has not been repealed but is no longer enforced. 'The punishment for high treason under the Treason Act is death, but it has become a dead letter.'
2. **dead wood** – superfluous material. 'If you cut out all the dead wood, we might consider your book for publication.'
3. **dead-beat** – completely exhausted. 'After a day's shopping in London, I am always dead-beat.' cf. 'to **be whacked' 224/9**.
4. the **dead spit / spit and image of** – exactly alike. 'The twins are the dead spit of each other. How do you tell them apart?'
5. in the **dead hours** of the night/in the **dead of night** – in the middle of the night. 'We'll leave in the dead of night when everyone is asleep; no one will hear us.'
6. to refuse to **be seen dead in** / I wouldn't **be seen dead in** (colloquial) – to have a violent dislike of particular clothes. 'Just look at the price they are asking for that horrible dress in the window. I wouldn't be seen dead in that rag!'
7. **over my dead body** – against my strong opposition. 'If that man wants to marry Joanne, it will be over my dead body.'
8. **dead and buried** – an old quarrel or dispute that was disposed of and forgotten long ago. 'I thought that quarrel you had with Jack over the house was dead and buried.'

## SPIRIT

9. to be **with** someone **in spirit** – to be thinking of someone with sympathy, anxiety, etc., without being with him/her in person. 'I wish you every success, Tina; I shall be with you in spirit.'
10. the **moving spirit** – the originator of an idea or project. 'I would like to know who the moving spirit is behind this idea. How stupid of him to put us on shift-work when business is so slack!'
11. to take something **in the right spirit** – to accept advice or criticism without bitterness or resentment. 'We have completed our report on the efficiency of your office staff and are sorry that they have not taken our advice in the right spirit.'
12. to **spirit away** – to remove quickly and secretly. 'I wonder what has happened to the vase Aunt Sheila gave us for Christmas. One of the children must have spirited it away!' The original meaning was to abduct or kidnap, when young Africans were 'spirited away' to the plantations in the West Indies.

## HEAVEN

13. **heaven on earth** – perfect conditions in which to live or work. The phrase is often used to draw a comparison. 'Having laboured for three years on his first novel in a Glasgow slum, it seemed like heaven on earth to the young writer to work on his second in Nice.'
14. **in heaven's name!** – an interjection used to express impatience or annoyance. 'What have you done with the plane tickets; in heaven's name, you haven't lost them, have you?'
15. **manna from heaven** – something that arrives unexpectedly to help someone out of his difficulties. 'The spare can of petrol the farmer produced when he found Paul stranded on the moor with his motor-bike, was like manna from heaven to him.' Manna was the

name given by the Israelites to the miraculous food they found on their journey out of Egypt (Exodus XVI. 15).

1. to **stink/smell to high heaven** – to be a public outrage, a scandal. 'The behaviour of these officials stinks to high heaven; there should be a public inquiry.'

GOD

2. a **(little) tin god** – a self-important, dictatorial person. 'Now Sanders has been made manager, he's behaving like a little tin god.'
3. to **put the fear of God into** – to terrify. 'When Ralph takes me out in his racing car, he puts the fear of God into me.'
4. to **tempt God/providence** – to provoke God/providence by taking a needless risk, or by taking the same risk again, especially after a lucky escape. 'To go climbing again today after your lucky escape yesterday would be to tempt providence.' The phrase is almost always used with 'providence'.
5. **There, but for the grace of God, go I** – I have been just as blameworthy but, thanks to good luck, have escaped the consequences. Shakespeare expresses the same idea in *Hamlet*, II, ii, 561: 'Use every man after his desert, and who would 'scape whipping?'
6. to think that one is **God's gift** to – to overestimate one's intelligence, skill or attractiveness. 'Just because Joe is moderately good-looking, he thinks he is God's gift to women!' cf. 'to **fancy oneself' 121/2**.
7. **an act of God** – (1) a legal term for a catastrophe of nature that no one could reasonably have foreseen. (2) In ordinary parlance, what seems like an act of divine mercy. 'It was an act of God that everyone escaped from the aeroplane unhurt.'

ANGEL, ANGELS

8. enough to **make the angels weep** – so foolish that even an angel would despair. 'The way you have treated Helen is enough to make the angels weep.' The allusion is to Shakespeare's *Measure for Measure*, II, ii, 117: 'But man, proud man, / Drest in a little brief authority . . . / His glassy essence, like an angry ape, / Plays such fantastic tricks before high heaven / As make the angels weep.'
9. **like an angel** – with the utmost innocence and purity. 'Thomas sings like an angel in the school choir, but you should see him on the football field!'
10. to be **on the side of the angels** – to be on the right side in the struggle between good and evil; to have the right principles or opinions, from the speaker's point of view. 'We shouldn't be critical of George; with all his faults, he is on the side of the angels.' The phrase has been taken from Disraeli's speech (made at Oxford, 1864): 'Is man an ape or an angel? I, my Lord, I am on the side of the angels.'
11. a **guardian angel** – one who protects another's interests from the purest and most unselfish of motives. 'Margaret has done so much for us without expecting anything in return; she has been a true guardian angel.'

HELL

12. **all hell broke loose** – there was a state of uproar and disorder. 'If you tell the men that they won't be getting the increase in wages you promised them, all hell will break loose.' The derivation is from Milton's *Paradise Lost*, Book IV, 918: 'All hell broke loose.'
13. **come hell or high water** – whatever the obstacles. 'Come hell or high water, I am determined to succeed.'

1. **for the hell of it** – for no particular reason except to give oneself pleasure. 'Asked why he had beaten up a complete stranger, the young man replied that he had done it for the hell of it.'
2. who/what/how (etc.) **the hell** (slang) – an emphatic exclamation expressing anger. 'Who the hell do you think you are, talking to me like that!'
3. **hell for leather** – at a mad speed, recklessly fast. 'Jack was driving his motor-bike hell for leather down the country lane.
4. to **play (merry) hell with** – to aggravate or cause harm. 'This constant damp weather plays hell with my rheumatism.'
5. to **give** someone **hell** – (1) to make someone's life very unpleasant. 'I love my father dearly, but really, he does give me hell sometimes.' (2) to berate someone. 'The manager gave his team hell at half-time when they were losing 3–0.'
6. **to hell with** – to be not in the least concerned with. 'To hell with all your complaints; I shall play the piano all day long if I want to.'
7. **go to hell!** (colloquial and rude) – go away and leave me in peace. Often said in reply to offensive comments or threats.
8. **hellbent on** – absolutely determined, regardless of the consequences. 'I don't know what's the matter with Roger; he seems hellbent on killing himself with those stunts of his!'

## DEVIL

9. **the devil's own job** – an immensely difficult task. 'Disentangling all this barbed wire is the devil's own job.'
10. **give the devil his due** – however bad a person may be, give him credit for any good quality he may have. 'Sergeant-Major Andrews used to bully the young recruits without mercy, but, to give the devil his due, he always treated me fairly.'
11. to have the **luck of the devil** – to have a great deal more luck than one deserves. 'Brian always invests his money in rubbish, but instead of going down, his shares always go up; he has the luck of the devil.'
12. to **talk/speak of the devil** – to be talking about someone when he suddenly appears. 'It's bad manners of Dennis always to keep us waiting. Shall we go? Oh, talk of the devil, there he is!'
13. **the very devil** – an appalling nuisance. 'Little Martin is so sweet most of the time but, when he gets cross, he can be the very devil.'
14. **Better the devil you know than the devil you don't** (proverb) – an evil never experienced may be worse than an evil one is already familiar with. 'I can't say I like Dr Knox, but if I change him for another doctor, I may be worse off than I was before. Better the devil you know than the devil you don't.'
15. **The devil looks after his own** (proverb) – a bad character never prevented a person from succeeding. 'That man has been in and out of prison and – would you believe it! – he has just won the football pools! The devil looks after his own.'

# 6. TREES AND FLOWERS

## FLOWERS

1. **flower power** – a social movement of the 1960s, begun in the USA, which believed that love could overcome enmity and hate. Flower power rejects the laws and morality of contemporary society. 'Mr Tebbit, the Trade and Industry Secretary, blamed the end of National Service and the emergence of flower power . . . for the violence in our society' (*Daily Mail*, 25 July 1985).

   **flower people** – advocates of flower power.

2. the **flower of her youth** – the best of her young men and women. 'England lost the flower of her youth in Flanders in the Great War [1914–18].'

3. as welcome as **flowers in May** – to be welcomed with much joy and happiness.

4. **'Say it with flowers!'** – women often prefer the gift of flowers to protestations of love.

## ROSE

5. the **English rose** – the delicate beauty of a young English girl.

6. **roses in her cheeks** – the tender, delicate pink colour in her cheeks. '"We'll get the roses back into her cheeks, Monica," the doctor told her.'

7. it was **roses, roses all the way** – a wonderful success in which everybody co-operated without any difficulty or unpleasantness.

8. a path **strewn with roses** – a career free from obstacles.

9. to **gather life's roses** – to savour the pleasures of life.

10. **'Gather ye rosebuds while ye may!'** – take your pleasures while there is still time. The reference is to Robert Herrick's poem 'To the Virgins to make much of Time'.

11. a **bed of roses** – a pleasant, enjoyable situation without any drawbacks or irritations. 'His job is a bed of roses compared with mine: short hours, a good salary and interesting work.'

12. It isn't a **bed of roses** – it isn't an easy life, the conditions are hard and disagreeable.

    It's not **all roses** – there are difficulties to be overcome, as well as pleasures to be enjoyed.

13. the **white rose** – a symbol of innocence and purity.

## OTHER FLOWERS

14. the **primrose path** – the path of self-indulgence that ends in ruin. From Shakespeare's two references: 'the primrose path of dalliance' (*Hamlet*, I, iii, 47), and 'primrose way to the everlasting bonfire' (*Macbeth*, II, iii, 22).

15. **lilies and roses** – a clear, fresh, beautiful complexion.

16. **lily-livered** – cowardly. cf. **'yellow-livered' 114/5**.

17. to **paint/gild the lily** – to flatter.

18. a **shrinking violet** (facetious) – a shy, self-effacing person. 'Adrian expressed his views very freely at the meeting last night; he is not such a shrinking violet as we imagined.'

19. a **wallflower** – a girl who has not been invited to dance, but sits with her back to the wall in the ballroom without a partner.

20. to **lay up in lavender** – to treat something as very precious, carefully preserved for a future occasion.

21. **as fresh as a daisy** – full of energy.

22. the **lotus-eaters** – people who neglect

their friends and families in order to enjoy a life of luxury and idleness. The phrase is taken from Homer's *Odyssey*.

1. an **open sesame** – a means of gaining immediate access to influence and patronage. The word comes from the Greek, sesame, a tropical and subtropical plant that is grown in the East Indies.
2. to **grasp/seize the nettle** – to take drastic action to overcome an unpleasant difficulty. 'It's time you grasped the nettle and told your friend that you can no longer support him.'
3. **'The ivy can grow no higher than its host'** – a remark made by the French philosopher Descartes about critics: No matter how brilliant and learned a critic may be, he can never surpass the writer on whom he is dependent.

## THE GARDEN

4. to lead someone **up the garden path** – to deceive, mislead someone. 'We never realized we were being led up the garden path until it was too late.'
5. **Everything in the garden is lovely** – everything is splendid, and there is nothing to worry about. (Often used to express the contrast between appearance and reality.) 'The food was perfect and the management were so friendly; everything in the garden was lovely until the waiter handed us the bill.'
6. in the **bloom of youth** / in her **first bloom** – in the full beauty of youth.
   **past her bloom** – past her best, when the beauty of her youth is beginning to fade.
7. to **blossom out** into – to develop very well. 'When Lloyd George became Prime Minister in 1916, he blossomed out into a statesman.'
8. the **pick of the bunch** – the best, the outstanding one in a group.
9. to **nip in the bud** – to frustrate a plan, plot, etc., before it has time to gather strength; to destroy at an early stage.
10. a **budding** writer/politician/artist – one who is just beginning to make a name for himself.

## THORN

11. a **thorn in the flesh/side** – a constant irritant, a source of continuous annoyance. 'The boy was a thorn in his father's flesh for many years, always contradicting him and criticizing his way of life.'
12. to **sit on thorns** – to be in a painful or embarrassing situation; to be in constant fear of being found out. 'For many years he was sitting on thorns; he had never qualified as a doctor, although he cured many of his patients.'
    a **bed of thorns** – an extremely painful or embarrassing situation.
13. a **crown of thorns** – a legacy of trouble, a source of great tribulation. The phrase suggests that the troubles are pushed on to an innocent and unwilling victim. '"I have inherited a crown of thorns," the young king said sadly.' Taken from Matthew XXVII, 29.

## THE FARM

14. to **reap a rich harvest** – to gain a splendid reward for one's efforts.
15. a **corny joke** – a hackneyed joke. cf. **'an old chestnut' 50/5**.
16. to **sow one's wild oats** – to experience youthful pleasures and excesses before settling down. 'What, twenty-two and still living at home! It's time he went abroad and sowed his wild oats.'

## HAY

1. to **hit the hay** – to go to bed. 'I think I'll hit the hay now. I have to be up early in the morning.'
2. to **make hay from** – to take advantage of an opponent's mistakes. 'The Republicans may be able to make almost as much hay from the misdeeds of a few Democrats as the Democrats did from the fall of President Nixon' (from *NOW!* magazine). The origin is from the proverb: to make hay while the sun shines.
3. to **make hay of** something, to **make hay with** – to throw into disorder, to confuse, to make a mess of.
4. to **go haywire** – to go crazy, to lose control of oneself. 'When his cat was run over, Michael went completely haywire and wrecked the motorist's car.'
5. **like looking for a needle in a haystack** – to look for something that is impossible to find. 'Robert's office is in such a mess; finding your letter will be like looking for a needle in a haystack.'

## STRAW

6. a **man of straw** – a worthless man, one without means or character.
7. a **straw poll / straw vote** – an impromptu, unofficial vote taken to test the direction in which public opinion is moving.
8. a **straw bid** – a worthless bid, one made without any financial backing.
9. to **draw straws** – to draw lots by picking straws of different sizes.
10. to **clutch at a straw** – to employ any means, however useless, to save oneself.

    **A drowning man will clutch at a straw** (proverb) – a desperate man will resort to any expedient, no matter how impractical or hopeless.
11. **not worth a straw** – worthless. cf. **'not worth a fig' 165/5**.
12. **not to care / give a straw** – a straw stands for something worthless; the expression **'not to give a straw for'**, or **'not to care two straws'**, means to place no value upon a person or object. 'I don't give a straw for his opinion.'
13. the **last straw** – beyond the limit; the breaking point. From the proverb: 'It's the last straw that breaks the camel's back.'
14. a **straw in the wind** – a slight indication of future developments. 'It may only be a straw in the wind, but she left half an hour after the dinner party last night. I don't think she is so keen on doing business with us as she was.'

## CUD AND SEED

15. to **chew the cud** – to ponder, consider a problem from every angle, think over carefully and deliberately.
16. to **run/go to seed** – to deteriorate in one's habits and appearance, to become shabby. 'When I called on him this morning, he was unshaven and wearing an old, stained dressing-gown. I am afraid he has run to seed.' The reference is to plants which, instead of developing new shoots, only produce seeds and lose their beauty.
17. to **sow the seeds** of doubt, etc. – to insinuate doubt, often with the idea of starting something without being noticed. 'He set to work sowing the seeds of doubt in their minds by hints and innuendoes.'
18. **seeded** players / **seeds** – players ranked by the organizers of a tournament in order of merit, and drawn so as not to meet one another until the closing rounds.

    an **unseeded** player – one not so ranked who may win, contrary to the opinion of the organizers; an 'outsider'.

1. to **eat the seedcorn** – to spend one's capital, and so destroy the source of one's income. 'Mr Callaghan warned that if we sold our assets in the North Sea, we would be eating the seedcorn.'

## CLOVER

2. to be **in clover** – to be in a comfortable situation, enjoying the best things in life without having to make an effort. From cattle feeding in a field of clover.

## GRASS, REEDS AND WEEDS

3. to put someone **out to grass** – to retire someone compulsorily on grounds of age. The phrase derives from putting horses that are too old to work out to pasture.
   to **go to grass** – to retire on grounds of age.
4. to **hear the grass grow** – to have very acute hearing.
5. **Keep off the grass!** – don't intrude on someone else's sphere of activity.
6. **grass roots** – the ordinary folk, those with their origins in the soil. In politics, the grass roots of a party are the ordinary membership, as opposed to the leadership.
7. not to **let the grass grow under one's feet** – to waste no time in getting a task done, to set to work quickly, without waiting for other people's agreement.
8. the **turf** – the world of horse-racing.
9. to **turf out** – to oust a person from a position, physically eject.
10. a **broken reed** – a weak, untrustworthy person; someone on whom it would be folly to rely. 'If you ever found yourself in serious trouble, Alex would abandon you without the least hesitation. He is a broken reed.'
11. a **reed shaken by the wind** – someone whose opinions are swayed by the latest fashion.
12. to **grow/spread like weeds** – to proliferate very fast. 'There is a crazy demand for his products. His business will grow like weeds.'
13. to **weed out** – to eliminate the undesirable.

## ROOTS

14. to **take root** – to grow, become established. 'The ideas of Karl Marx have never taken root in the United States or Germany.'
    to **have its roots in** – to stem from, to be caused by. 'All crime has its roots in the loveless childhood of the criminal.'
15. to **grow/put down roots** – to develop interests and friendships. 'We have grown too many roots here to emigrate.'
16. to be/stand **rooted to the ground/spot** – to be transfixed or rendered immobile through fear, astonishment or shock.
17. a **deep-rooted** habit – a long-established or chronic habit. 'It won't be easy to rid him quickly of such a deep-rooted habit.'
18. **root and branch** – in its entirety, without any exceptions being made. 'The old customs in China have been destroyed root and branch by the new regime.'

## TREES

19. a **family tree** – a genealogical record in the form of a diagram. 'My family tree goes back to the Normans.'
20. **the tree is known by its fruit** – you can judge someone best by his actions; deeds are more eloquent than

words. The origin is from the Bible (Matthew XII, 33).

1. **up a tree / gum tree** – in great difficulty; unable to make any further progress.
2. **at the top of the tree** – at the top of one's profession.
3. to **bark up the wrong tree** – to accuse or blame the wrong person. 'Alison couldn't have stolen your watch. She was out all day. You are barking up the wrong tree.'
4. a **heart of oak** – someone loyal and brave on whom one can rely. 'You can always count on William in a crisis. He has a heart of oak and will stand by you, whatever the consequences.'
5. an **old chestnut** – an old hackneyed joke, one that has been over-used. 'His speech was full of old chestnuts. People in the audience groaned at each one.' cf. 'a **corny joke**' **47/15**.
6. to **give the palm to** – to acknowledge as champion.
7. to **bear/carry the palm** – to signal one's triumph.
8. to **carry off the palm** – to win the victor's crown.
9. to **yield the palm** – to admit defeat, to acknowledge the victory of one's opponent.
10. **palmy** days – the days of one's triumphs, past glories.
11. to **look to one's laurels** – to be aware of a new challenge to one's supremacy.
12. to **rest on one's laurels** – to be content with past achievements without making any further effort.

## BUSH AND HEDGE

13. to **beat about the bush** – to broach a subject indirectly, to delay coming to the point. 'Stop beating about the bush and tell me what you want.' A shooting idiom: the 'beaters' beat about the undergrowth in order to put the birds up.
14. to **take to the bush** – to withdraw oneself to the wild country, away from civilization. The 'bush' is an Australian term, meaning wild woodland which was originally inhabited by the Aborigines.
15. **bush-telegraph** – the rapid unofficial communication of news or gossip. 'Europe's bush-telegraph spread the news of the abdication crisis long before the British public got to hear of it.' Originally, the spreading of information by the beating of drums, etc.
16. to **hide one's light under a bushel** – to be modest about one's achievements or virtues. The reference is to Christ's parable: 'Neither do men light a candle and put it under a bushel, but in a candlestick' (Matthew V, 15).
17. to **hedge one's bets** – to reduce one's potential betting losses by betting on more than one result.

## WOOD

18. **not to see the wood for the trees** – not to be able to make out the essential because of all the detail. 'You have put in so much unnecessary detail that one loses track of the story; one can't see the wood for the trees.'
19. to be **out of the wood** – to be out of trouble or danger. Often used negatively. 'Business is looking up, but there's still a lot of money to repay; we aren't out of the wood yet.'
20. to **touch wood** – a superstitious belief that after congratulating oneself on one's good fortune, one should touch wood in order to avoid supernatural retribution.
21. **against the grain** – against one's instincts, against one's inclinations. 'It

goes against the grain to rebuke a man old enough to be my grandfather.' Wood can be cut more easily if it is cut in the direction of the grain than across the grain.

## LOG AND BRANCH

1. to **sleep like a log** – to sleep soundly, without stirring. From the idea of someone in a deep sleep lying absolutely still 'like a log'.
2. **as easy as falling off a log** – something that needs no skill or effort to accomplish. cf. **'as easy as shelling peas' 165/16.**
3. to hold out **the olive branch** – to make a peace offering. 'I thought it was time we held out the olive branch to Angela, so I invited her to dinner tomorrow. This quarrel has gone on long enough.'

## STICK

4. a **dry old stick** – a dull, boring man, with very little to say for himself.
5. the policy of the **big stick** – the threat of force. From Theodore Roosevelt's speech on the need for America 'to speak softly and carry a big stick'.
6. to get hold of the **wrong end of the stick** – to misunderstand an explanation. The phrase is often used in reply to an unjust suspicion or accusation. 'You've got the wrong end of the stick; it was your friend, not I, who went through your things.'
7. to be caught **in a cleft stick** – to be forced to choose between two disastrous courses of action. 'Yvonne had promised to pay Susan's fine but then found she hadn't enough money. She would either have to let her friend down or sell her engagement ring; she was caught in a cleft stick.'
8. to **get the dirty/rough end of the stick** – to be treated unfairly, to bear all the blame.
9. to be **as cross as two sticks** – to be in a bad temper.
10. a few **sticks of furniture** – only a few pieces of furniture. 'Everything in the house had been taken except for a few sticks of furniture.'

## LEAF

11. to **turn over a new leaf** – to repent one's way of life and make a fresh start; to reform. 'Each time he comes out of prison, Jack promises to turn over a new leaf – but he never does.'
12. to **take a leaf out of** someone's **book** – to follow someone's example. 'I am going to take a leaf out of your book and go into business.' Originally the phrase meant to plagiarize by taking a leaf, i.e. a page, out of someone else's book and making a copy of it.
13. to **leaf through** a book – to turn over the pages of a book without reading it thoroughly, in order to get a general idea of what it is about.
14. to **shake like a leaf** – to tremble with fear.
15. to **read the tea-leaves** – to foretell someone's future by examining the tea-leaves at the bottom of the cup. This refers to an old superstition that the tea-leaves have a hidden meaning for the drinker.

# 7. ANIMALS

## ANIMAL

1. to **behave like an animal / worse than an animal** – a term of abuse for men of great villainy and cruelty, since animals are not credited with a moral sense. 'They have behaved like animals; not even the youngest children were spared.' A common variation of this phrase is **lower than the animals**.
2. a **political animal** – someone with a special talent for politics. 'The ancient Greek was a political animal.'
3. **animal spirits** – the exuberance and cheerfulness of youth that characterize a healthy body. 'He didn't mean any harm; it was only animal spirits.'
4. **animal passions** – what used to be called man's 'lowest instincts'. Often used in reference to lust and lechery.
5. a **rare animal** – an unusual person who may combine two contradictory features or interests. 'He was that rare animal, a scientist turned artist.' cf. **'a rare bird' 65/5.**

## CREATURE

6. **creature comforts** – those luxuries which make life pleasant and enjoyable, especially on a material level.

## BEAST

7. it's **the nature of the beast** – it's inherent in the character of the man, which will never change.
8. a **beast of burden** – someone on whom an excessive amount of work is imposed. 'I've become just a beast of burden instead of a wife to him.' The allusion is to beasts of burden like donkeys and camels which are used for carrying provisions.
9. **Beauty and the Beast** – a beautiful woman accompanied by a repulsively ugly man. A humorous phrase derived from the old fairy tale of 'Beauty and the Beast'.

## PET

10. **pet name** – a special name expressing affection, such as 'Honey', 'Angel', 'Bunny', 'Kitten'.
11. to be **in a pet** – to be in a temper or ill-humour, when the cause of the annoyance is quite trifling. 'When we called on him, he was in a pet because his daughter was late with his breakfast.'

## DOG

12. **Every dog has his day** (proverb) – everyone, however humble or unprepossessing, has his moment of glory. We all have our ups and downs; but no life, however bad, is entirely unsuccessful.
13. a **dog in the manger** – one who denies to others the pleasures he can't enjoy himself. From Aesop's Fables, in which the dog prevented the cows from eating the hay in the manger by lying in it and snarling at them, while not wanting the hay himself.
14. to lead a **dog's life** – to lead a thoroughly miserable existence.
15. to treat someone **worse than a dog** – to treat viciously. 'He is a cruel, callous bully; he treats her worse than a dog.'
16. **you can't teach an old dog new tricks** – it is difficult for the elderly to adapt themselves to new conditions, or to start learning again late in life. 'The young girls in the office soon learned how to use the telex, but I just can't

understand it. You can't teach an old dog new tricks.'

1. a **dog's dinner** (slang) – a horrible mess.
2. a **hang-dog air** – a shame-faced, woebegone look.
3. **give a dog a bad name and hang him** – once someone has acquired a bad reputation, it is almost impossible for him to shake it off, and even his most innocent actions will be misunderstood. 'He had a reputation for stealing, so when he handed in a £10 note at the office, he was suspected of having come by the money dishonestly. Give a dog a bad name . . .'
4. to **help a lame dog over a stile** – to help a struggling person. 'He lent me £1,000 to start up my business. It was good of him to help a lame dog over a stile.'
5. **any stick will serve to beat a dog with** – it is easy to find fault with a person if you want to; any excuse will serve your purpose.
6. not to have a **dog's chance** – to have no chance at all. 'He is so much heavier than you, you haven't a dog's chance against him, however cleverly you box.'
7. **love me, love my dog** – if you want to love me, you must put up with my faults, my friends and my relations.
8. **dog doesn't eat dog** – men of the same profession, school, etc., never make trouble for one another. 'It would be useless for you to appeal to the Law Society about your lawyer's behaviour. Dog doesn't eat dog!'
9. to be **top dog** – to dominate, to make oneself the master. By contrast, the **under-dog** – the loser in a fight, the inferior in strength. 'She always sympathizes with the under-dog, right or wrong.'
10. a **dog-fight** – (1) a fight between two people. (2) a battle between two aeroplanes. 'I don't want a dog-fight between the two of you, so behave!'
11. to be **in the dog-house** – to be in disgrace, usually with one's spouse. 'His wife isn't speaking to him. He has been in the dog-house since he came home from a party at four in the morning.'
12. a **dog's-body** – one who does the routine or mechanical work. 'When I was at Bader's, I was only a dog's-body; none of the work I did required any skill.'
13. **dog-eared** – said of the pages of a book which have been turned down or have curled at the corners through excessive use.
14. a **dull dog** – someone who has nothing to say for himself, whose conversation is always uninspired and boring.
15. a **dirty dog** – an evil character; but the phrase is often used humorously for a sly fellow who gets what he wants by dubious methods.
16. a **sly dog** – one who keeps his pleasures to himself, a man who is discreet about his vices.
17. a **gay dog** – a man who enjoys the company of women. 'Gay' has a pejorative meaning and is used today by some people as a synonym for homosexual. 'Gay' can, however, still be used in its original sense as it is here.
18. a **lucky dog** – one who enjoys undeserved luck. 'He isn't in the least good-looking or impressive, but all the girls fall for him – the lucky dog!'
19. to take a **hair of the dog that bit you** – to take more of the alcohol in which one has been over-indulging in order to cure a hangover. It was thought at one time that the hair of the dog that bit one was a cure for rabies.
20. the **tail wagging the dog** – the transfer of power from the leaders of a group to its least valued members. 'Instead

of the doctors giving the porters orders, we were telling the doctors what to do! It was a case of the tail wagging the dog.'

1. to be a **lap-dog** – to be pampered and over-protected. 'She never lets her son play with other children. She has turned him into a lap-dog.'
2. **dog-Latin** – inferior or degenerate Latin used by clerics, lawyers and doctors with an imperfect knowledge of the language. cf. **'pidgin English' 188/11**.
3. **dog-days** – the hottest weather. The phrase is a translation from the Latin 'caniculares dies' meaning the hottest days of the summer (in July and August). According to Roman theory, the hottest weeks of the year were determined by the rising of the dog-star Sirius which they believed contributed to the heat of the sun.
4. **don't keep a dog and bark yourself** – don't do your servants' work for them. There is no point in having servants, if you do their work.
5. to **call off the dogs** – to abandon an investigation when inquiries are leading nowhere. Huntsmen call off their dogs when they follow a wrong scent.
6. **sick as a dog** – horribly sick.
7. **dog-tired** – exhausted after a hard day's work. 'I was dog-tired after working the whole day in the garden.'
8. to **let sleeping dogs lie** – to leave well alone and refrain from stirring up trouble. 'You must have known that mentioning his ex-wife would upset him. You should have let sleeping dogs lie!'
9. **his bark is worse than his bite** – (1) bullies generally prefer bluster to fighting. (2) a person is not so unkind or fierce as he pretends to be.
10. the **dogs of war** – a term of abuse for war-makers, mercenaries and war profiteers. Its original meaning was the horrors of war, e.g. famine, killing and atrocities. Origin: *Julius Caesar*, III, i.
11. to **die like a dog** – to die without honour or dignity, to die in shameful circumstances.
12. to **go to the dogs** – to ruin oneself by licentious or degenerate living.

## POODLE

13. **nobody's poodle** – someone with a mind of his own, one who is not easily led or persuaded to act against his better judgement. A poodle is commonly regarded as a foppish breed of dog, due perhaps to its mincing gait. Always used negatively.

## PUP

14. to **sell** someone **a pup** – to swindle, to sell something under a false description. 'When we arrived at the hotel, we found we were paying twice as much as the other guests. The travel agent had sold us a pup.'
15. a **puppy / young puppy** – an arrogant or conceited young man. A cocksure young man who corrects his elders.
16. **puppy-fat** – plumpness that the boy or girl will shed on reaching maturity. 'She's a little on the tubby side, but it's only puppy-fat.'
17. **puppy love** – the love of a very young, immature person. cf. **'calf-love' 58/9**.

## CAT

18. to **lead a cat and dog life** – used to describe a husband and wife who quarrel furiously with each other most of the time.
19. to **play cat and mouse** – to alternate harshness and leniency in one's treatment of a helpless victim, in the manner of a cat playing with a mouse.

When human beings indulge in this game, there is a strong element of sadism in the character of the dominant party.

1. to **put/set the cat among the pigeons** – to provoke quarrelling and dissension. 'You shouldn't have criticized the vicar in the local newspaper; now you've really put the cat among the pigeons!'
2. to **be catty** – to make spiteful remarks. 'I thought it was catty of her to ask at dinner whether Jim was doing better at school. She knows how sensitive we are about the trouble he has been in.'
3. a **cat-call** – a whistle indicating one's disapproval. 'There were so many cat-calls from the gallery that the management were obliged to ring down the curtain.'
4. a **cat burglar** – someone who burgles houses by climbing up the drainpipe and entering by the window.
5. to **let the cat out of the bag** – to blurt out a secret. 'You let the cat out of the bag when you said you were pregnant.'
6. **like a cat on hot bricks** – extremely awkward and uneasy. 'He dropped in by accident at an ante-natal clinic and was like a cat on hot bricks while the exercises were in progress.'
7. a **cat-o'nine-tails** – a whip used for flogging delinquent soldiers, sailors and civilians for crimes of violence up to 1948 in the UK. The instrument consisted of nine thongs of leather which resembled cats' tails.
8. **no room to swing a cat** – a very small, cramped space. The original phrase was probably 'not room to swing a cat-o'nine-tails', and dates from the time when sailors were flogged on board ship. The floggings took place on the deck because the cabins were too small to swing a cat in.
9. **not a cat in hell's chance** – no chance at all. 'You haven't a cat in hell's chance of getting that job. There are half-a-dozen other men after it who are better qualified than you.'
10. **curiosity killed the cat** – excessive curiosity can lead one into trouble. A common rebuke by mothers to their offspring.
11. **there's more than one way to kill/skin a cat** – there is more than one method for achieving an object. If the more conventional method fails, one should try other methods.
12. to **see which way the cat jumps** – to remain uncommitted until it becomes clear which way public opinion is moving before coming to a decision.
13. to **bell the cat** – to attack a common enemy at great personal risk to oneself for the sake of others. The phrase is taken from Piers Plowman's fable of the mice who wanted to hang a bell around the neck of a cat.
14. **'Has the cat got your tongue?'** – 'Have you lost your power of speech?' A question often put jokingly to children who are shy.
15. to **be made a cat's paw of** – to serve as a tool for someone else. From Aesop's fable of the monkey which made use of the paw of his friend, the cat, for pulling hot chestnuts out of a fire.
16. **a cat may look at a king** – spoken by an inferior, meaning 'I have as much right to look at you as you have to look at me. We are both equal'. The remark can also be understood as a snub to the snobbish, viz.: 'However grand you may think you are, you can't stop me looking at you.'
17. to **grin like a Cheshire cat** – to grin widely, from ear to ear. From Lewis Carroll's *Alice in Wonderland*. Nobody knows where Carroll got the idea from.
18. **like the cat that swallowed the cream** –

looking very elated, very pleased with oneself.

1. **the cat's whiskers / the cat's pyjamas** – an American colloquialism for the very best. 'Now that he has beaten the champion, Paul thinks he is the cat's whiskers.'
2. a **wild-cat strike** – an unofficial strike, called without the approval of the trade union, by a number of individuals acting on their own initiative.
3. to **be a copy-cat** – to imitate someone else's behaviour. The expression 'Copy-cat!' is much used by schoolchildren.

## KITTEN

4. **as weak as a kitten** – feeble, very weak. 'After her operation, she felt as weak as a kitten.'

## PUSSY

5. to **pussy-foot** – to aim soft blows at your opponent which are not intended to hurt him. The blows may be verbal as well as physical. 'Say what you really think about Mark and stop pussy-footing!' The allusion is to the soft paws of the cat.

## HORSE

6. a **dark horse** – a person of unknown abilities or one who has kept his abilities to himself and may spring a surprise. This is a racing metaphor indicating an unknown horse which could win the race unexpectedly.
7. a **stalking horse** – a pretext to conceal one's real designs. 'Democracy has been used as a stalking horse for caucus rule.' Hunters would stalk game by hiding themselves behind their horses as they advanced on their prey.
8. an **old war horse** – a veteran of many battles who likes to reminisce over them.

   to **sniff the air like an old war horse** – to anticipate a battle, to sense a war atmosphere.
9. to **back the wrong horse** – to put your reliance on a person who then lets you down. 'If you think Walsh will ever repay you, you are mistaken; I'm afraid you've put your money on the wrong horse.'
10. to **eat like a horse** – to overeat, to eat without restraint.
11. to **work like a horse** – to do a huge quantity of work. 'It's time you had a rest; you've been working like a horse all the afternoon.'
12. a **willing horse** – one who is eager to work and do other people's as well.
13. a **horse-laugh** – a loud guffaw usually expressing derision or incredulity. 'When I told him the government had promised to reduce taxes next year, he gave a horse-laugh and said he had heard that one before.'
14. **horseplay** (school slang) – rough but good-natured games.
15. **horse sense** – rough, earthy common sense.
16. **horse-trading** – hard, shrewd bargaining with no sentiment on either side. 'After a lot of horse-trading we have at last agreed a price for the house.'
17. to **flog a dead horse** – to repeat the same outdated argument over and over again. 'Whatever you think, capital punishment will never come back. Why do you flog a dead horse?'
18. to **ride a hobby horse (to death)** – to introduce one's favourite subject into a conversation at every opportunity.
19. a **horse of another colour** – a completely different matter. '"I don't want the money for myself but for my

brother." "For your brother! That's a horse of another colour."'

1. to be/climb **on one's high horse** – to assume an attitude of moral superiority. Note also the phrase, **'Don't get on your high horse with me,'** meaning, 'Don't set yourself up as my moral superior.'
2. straight from the **horse's mouth** – information received from someone with actual experience whose testimony cannot be questioned. 'I've had it straight from the horse's mouth; he was there when the man was killed.'
3. **Never look a gift horse in the mouth** (proverb) – never find fault with a gift. This phrase is found in almost every language. One looks a horse in the mouth in order to tell its age from the teeth.
4. to **lock the stable door after the horse has bolted** – to take precautions after the event has occurred, instead of before.
5. to **put the cart before the horse** – to mistake the effect for the cause. 'To say that Alex can't take exercise because of his poor health is to put the cart before the horse. Alex is in poor health because he doesn't take any exercise.'
6. to **drive a coach and horses through** a law, rule or regulation – to find a very big loophole in it.
7. **if wishes were horses, beggars would ride** – a wish that cannot possibly be fulfilled. Most wishes are impractical, otherwise the strangest results would arise.
8. to **swap horses in midstream / halfway across the stream** – to make a critical change of plan after a contest has begun. Often used negatively to indicate that a mistake was made. 'It's always a mistake to swap horses halfway across the stream.'
9. **wild horses would not drag it out of me** – I won't give away the secret in any circumstances.
10. to **frighten the horses** – to be indiscreet, to shock public opinion. '. . . capital punishment was not so much as mentioned in the Conservative Manifesto (on the grounds presumably of not unnecessarily frightening the horses)' (*Observer*, 22 May 1983).
11. **hold your horses!** – wait a moment, don't do anything rash. 'Hold your horses! I only broke the window; I didn't burn the hole in the carpet.'
12. **'Horses for courses'** – different jobs require different skills. 'An employer will only offer you a job if you have the particular skill he is looking for. It's horses for courses so far as he is concerned.'

## MARE, ASS, MULE AND DONKEY

13. to find a **mare's nest** – to make a discovery that turns out to be worthless.
14. to **make an ass of oneself** – to behave in a ridiculous manner. The ass has always been a symbol of stupidity.
15. **as stubborn as a mule** – one who is unwilling to yield or make any concessions in a dispute.

    **as obstinate as a donkey** – unwilling to listen to reason or change one's mind. A donkey is proverbial for both its obstinacy and stupidity.
16. to **talk the hind leg off a donkey** – to talk endlessly.
17. **donkey-work** – the hard, boring part of a job; that which requires little or no intelligence. 'It was Joan's idea. I only did the donkey-work.'
18. **like a carrot to a donkey** – a strong inducement or incentive. 'They offered the men a carrot in the shape of a ten per cent rise in wages, and double overtime.'

1. **not for donkey's years** (colloquial) – not for a very long time. 'Wherever have you been all this time? I haven't seen you for donkey's years!' The phrase may have come from a play on the words 'ears' and 'years', which are pronounced the same in some parts of the country.

## COW, BULL AND CALF

2. the **sacred cow** – a derogatory term for any institution or custom generally regarded as sacrosanct which, in the opinion of its critics, is useless and should be abolished, such as Parliamentary Sovereignty and the Mixed Economy. The phrase originates in the Hindu belief that cows are sacred and should not be slaughtered, even in times of famine.
3. a **milch cow** – a universal provider, one from whom it is easy to obtain money. 'The boys are old enough to get a job. You are becoming the milch cow of the family.' 'Milch' means 'milk giving' and derives from Anglo-Saxon 'milch' (milk). It is still used in the phrases 'milch cow' and 'milch ewe'.
4. **till the cows come home** – for ever. 'You can argue about that till the cows come home. You won't ever agree.' cf. '. . . **until you are blue in the face' 17/9**.
5. to **take the bull by the horns** – to grapple fearlessly with a problem. 'The young man took the bull by the horns and asked his boss for a rise.'
6. to **score/hit a bull's eye** – to achieve one's exact aim, to make a spectacular success. 'John hit the bull's eye with his invention, and now he is a very rich man.'
7. **like a bull in a china shop** – very clumsy and destructive. This phrase is often used when tact and diplomacy are notably absent. 'In the short time Jack was with us, he upset every member of my family. He was like a bull in a china shop.'
8. to **kill the fatted calf** – to treat a person with special hospitality, usually after a long absence from home. 'We are all longing to see you, Peter. Father is going to kill the fatted calf for you.' The allusion is to 'The Prodigal Son' (Luke XV, 30).
9. **calf-love** – the first adolescent love-affair. cf. **'puppy-love' 54/17**.

## SHEEP AND LAMB

10. to **look sheepish** – to look embarrassed, guilty. 'Henry looked sheepish when the doctor told him to take off his clothes.'
11. to **cast/make sheep's eyes** at someone – to look furtively but amorously at someone. 'I saw you casting sheep's eyes at that girl. It was very embarrassing.'
12. **like a flock of sheep** – with mindless obedience. 'As soon as the trade-union leader set off towards the police cordon, the rest of the strikers followed like a flock of sheep.'
13. to **count sheep** – the monotony of counting sheep in one's imagination is a powerful inducement to falling asleep.
14. a **wolf in sheep's clothing** – someone who looks respectable and harmless but whose behaviour is quite the opposite.
15. **as well be hanged for a sheep as a lamb** (proverb) – if you are going to be punished for a small crime, you will have little to lose by committing a serious one.
16. to **separate the sheep from the goats** – to separate the good from the bad, the virtuous from the wicked. The allusion is to the Day of Judgement (Matthew XXV, 32), when the good

are rewarded with a place in heaven and the wicked are sent to hell. Nowadays, the distinction is more often drawn between efficient businesses and those that are inefficient or untrustworthy.

1. **like a lamb / as meek as a lamb** – meekly, without resistance. 'It must have been a terrible shock to Harry when I told him he would have to give up his room, but he took it like a lamb.'

   to go **like a lamb to the slaughter(house)** – to await one's destruction with complete docility.

## GOAT

2. to **get one's goat** – to annoy, exasperate. 'It gets my goat the way he lays down the law on every subject under the sun.'
3. to be a **scapegoat** – to be punished for the sins or crimes of others. 'He was made the scapegoat because he had been in trouble before.' From the sacrificial goat that was allowed to escape from the Hebrew temple after the high priest had transferred his sins and those of his people to it. The word would appear to be a contradiction in terms because, in modern speech, the 'scapegoat' does not escape but is wrongly punished in the place of the guilty party.
4. to **show the cloven hoof** – to betray one's evil intentions. The devil is depicted in art and legend as having the cloven hoof of the goat which he can never conceal, thus betraying his evil motives.

## PIG AND GUINEA-PIG

5. to look/stare **like a stuck pig** – to be petrified with amazement or fear, to stand with mouth and eyes wide open.
6. **pig-headed** – stubborn, unwilling to listen to advice or change one's mind. cf. 'to **be stiff-necked' 126/14**.
7. a **male chauvinist pig** – a term of abuse coined by the Women's Lib movement for any man who is domineering or aggressive in his attitude to women. 'Chauvinist' derives from Nicolas Chauvin, a French soldier, well known for his exaggerated nationalistic views; 'pig' stands for male greed and insensitivity.
8. to **eat like a pig** – to eat a huge quantity of food noisily and greedily.
9. to **pig it** – to live in squalor.
10. **pigs in clover** – people with more money than manners.
11. a **pig in a poke / to buy a pig in a poke** – something unsatisfactory, bought unseen by the buyer. 'What a pity you didn't get a surveyor to look over the house before you signed the contract. I am afraid you have bought a pig in a poke!' The word 'poke' originally meant 'bag'. Thus an animal in a bag that was taken to market and sold as a pig in a poke might, when the purchaser had time to inspect the bag, turn out to be a cat.
12. a **guinea-pig** – someone who allows himself to be used as a subject for experiments in hospitals and laboratories. (The animal of the same name is in great demand for experimental work on account of its docile nature.)

## SOW, SWINE AND HOG

13. **you cannot make a silk purse out of a sow's ear** – it is not possible to make something fine out of inferior material. 'I am afraid you'll never get that lad into the university, however much time you spend on him. You can't make a silk purse out of a sow's ear.' James Howell (1594–1666) wrote of the impossibility of making a 'satin purse out of a sow's ear'.

1. to **cast pearls before swine** – to waste gifts on those who are too uncultured to appreciate them.
2. a **road-hog** – a motorist who monopolizes the road by driving very slowly in the middle, or who drives too fast without any consideration for other road-users.
3. to **hog** (conversation, food, wine, attention, publicity, etc.) – to monopolize, to take more than one's fair share.
4. to **go the whole hog** – to go through with something to the very end. 'I wanted to perfect my knowledge of French so I went the whole hog and spent all my savings on a six months' stay with a family in Paris.' 'Hog' was originally slang for 'shilling'; so to go the whole hog meant to spend the whole shilling at once.

## RAT AND LEMMING

5. a **rat** – someone who will betray his cause to further his own interests. A traitor may be motivated by principle, but a rat is only interested in his own advantage.
6. the **rat race** – the frenzied scramble for success in one's job. 'I wish I could opt out of the rat race and just enjoy myself, but I can't afford to.'
7. to **smell a rat** – to suspect that something is not quite right, to have grounds for suspicion. 'I smelt a rat when he kept on postponing the wedding, even though his explanations seemed reasonable enough.'
8. **like a lemming / lemming-like** – self-destructive, suicidal. 'Unity, yes, but not the unity of lemmings!' (Gavin Laird on 'Weekend World', ITV, 9 December 1984). Lemmings are small rats which migrate across Norway to the sea, where they drown in huge numbers.

## RABBIT AND HARE

9. to **produce/pull the rabbit out of the hat** – to produce what seems an impossible result with no effort, as if by magic. 'When I told him I had no fancy dress for the party, he produced the costume of a toreador for me just like a rabbit out of a hat.'
10. to **breed like rabbits** – to breed very fast, to multiply at great speed.
11. **as mad as a March Hare** – insane. The March Hare was one of the characters in Lewis Carroll's *Alice in Wonderland*, who vied with the Mad Hatter in making crazy remarks. The month of March is the rutting season when hares go mad.
12. **hare and hounds** – a paper-chase, a trail of paper scattered along the ground by the 'hares' for the 'hounds' to follow.
13. to **run with the hare and hunt with the hounds** – to support both sides in a dispute at the same time.
14. **first catch your hare, then cook him** – make no plans until you have the means to carry them out.
15. to **start a hare, a conversational hare** – to divert a discussion by bringing in an irrelevant topic. 'She was not interested . . . in the dividing line between Journalism and Literature which was started as a conversational hare' (*Howards End* by E. M. Forster). cf. 'to **draw a red herring across the path' 73/2**.

## FOX

16. a **sly fox / an old fox** – someone who is very experienced and has acquired much guile. 'You won't take in an old fox like me with such a story.'
17. **as cunning as a fox** – very cunning indeed, as cunning as a fox is reputed to be.

1. to **be foxed** – to be outwitted, baffled or deceived. 'I was completely foxed by the crossword puzzle.'
2. to **shoot someone else's fox** – to demolish or destroy someone else's enemy. 'I was on the point of ordering Stanley's arrest when Scotland Yard did it for me; they shot my fox!'

## WOLF

3. to **wolf (food) down** – to swallow one's food without chewing, in the manner of a ravenously hungry wolf.
4. a **lone wolf** – someone who likes to be independent and live alone without having to co-operate with other people. 'Tony will never join your association, however much he sympathizes with your aims. He is too much of a lone wolf.'
5. to **keep the wolf from the door** – to have sufficient funds to pay one's bills and keep the bailiffs out. 'Here's £100. That should be enough to keep the wolf from the door!' The original meaning was to have enough money not to starve.
6. to **cry 'Wolf'** – to sound a false alarm so many times that, when at last you sound a genuine alarm, no one will come to your help. This phrase is taken from 'The Shepherd Boy who cried Wolf' in Aesop's Fables.
7. to **throw to the wolves** – to sacrifice a friend or dependant to appease one's enemies. 'He won't hesitate to throw you to the wolves to protect himself.'
8. a **wolf-whistle** – the whistle of a man at the sight of an attractive girl or woman in the street, made for the purpose of catching her attention.

## STAG

9. a **stag party** – a social gathering for men only.

## BEAVER, BADGER, FERRET AND WEASEL

10. to **beaver away** – to work hard at a task. 'He has been beavering away at his job for the last three months.' The beaver is renowned for its energy and perseverance.
11. to **badger** someone – to make persistent demands on someone. 'Whenever he sees me, he badgers me to join his club; he won't give me any peace until I do.'
12. to **ferret out** – to find out something after a very diligent search.
13. **weasel words** – words which weaken the force of the words that immediately precede them. They suck the life out of the words, just as a weasel sucks the egg out of its shell. 'We must expand our exports and at the same time protect our home industries' – the first half of the sentence is contradicted by the weasel words in the second half; if we stop countries exporting to us, they will not have enough foreign exchange to import our goods.

## OPOSSUM

14. to **play possum** – to avoid trouble by lying low, feigning illness or pretending to be unaware of the facts. The allusion is to the habit of the opossum which feigns death when it is attacked.

## HEDGEHOG AND MOLE

15. **as prickly as a hedgehog** – someone who takes offence very easily.
16. a **mole** – a traitor who undermines from the inside the organization in which he is employed.
17. to **make a mountain out of a molehill** – to exaggerate a difficulty. 'Aren't you

making a mountain out of a molehill? There's no need to cancel our holiday just because the airlines are grounded. We can go by boat-train instead.'

BAT

1. **as blind as a bat** – completely blind. 'You must have been as blind as a bat not to have seen me; I was sitting at the next table!'
2. **bats in the belfry** – slightly mad.

FROG

3. to **frogmarch** – to carry an obstinate or unruly person face downwards by holding the arms and legs. 'When I asked Crouch for my money, his servants practically frogmarched me out of his house!'
4. to have **a frog in the throat** – to have an obstruction in the throat which causes hoarseness or loss of voice.

SNAKE

5. a **snake in the grass** – a hidden, treacherous enemy. 'Your friend has been telling your boss tales about you. She's a real snake in the grass!'
6. to cherish **a snake in one's bosom** – to have one's kindness repaid with spite or ingratitude.
7. to **scotch the snake** – to spoil a plan.
8. **Snakes and Ladders** – the ups and downs in life. From the name of a children's game of chance played on a board that contains rewards and penalties.

TURTLE

9. to **turn turtle** – to turn round and run away in the face of danger. The allusion is to the turtle which turns upside down in the water. When the phrase is applied to a boat, it means that the boat capsizes and sinks.
10. to **come out of one's shell** – to overcome one's natural reserve and speak freely. 'Mark was always so shy but, since he has made friends with Nancy, he has come right out of his shell.'

WHALE

11. to have a **whale of a time** – to have a splendid time. The whale stands for something very big, and also something fine or splendid.

    a **whale of a job** – a wonderful job; a **whale of a task** – a huge task.

DRAGON

12. a **dragon** – a formidable, aggressive woman who makes a lot of trouble. 'She's a real dragon. You had better keep away from her.'
13. to **chase the dragon** – to take heroin. 'Two boys crouch in a corner, chasing the dragon. Their shirts are pulled over their heads so they can more easily breathe the smoke from the brown heroin which they bought for £5' (*The Mail on Sunday*, 4 August 1985). In myth and fable, dragons are sometimes represented as breathing out fire and smoke.

CROCODILE

14. a **crocodile** – schoolchildren walking in a procession two by two, usually with a teacher at the back.
15. to **shed crocodile tears** – to shed false, insincere tears. 'Take no notice of her crocodile tears. She's not in the least concerned about your injury.' The crocodile was believed by many

people to shed tears of remorse as it devoured its victim. In fact, the crocodile is getting rid of surplus salt from its nasal glands.

## RHINOCEROS AND ELEPHANT

1. to have a **skin like a rhinoceros** – to be insensitive to insults.
2. a **rogue elephant** – someone who flouts authority in order to vent his spite on everyone and everything. 'Your son is making enemies of all our customers; he's a real rogue elephant!' A rogue elephant is a vicious elephant that deserts the herd and runs amok, causing great damage.
3. an **elephant's memory** – a long memory, especially for an ill-turn or an insult. Elephants are proverbial for their long memories.

## CAMEL

4. to **swallow a camel and strain at a gnat** – to tolerate a great wrong while protesting at a minor lapse.

## KANGAROO

5. to **kangaroo** – to convict and punish unjustly without giving the accused a fair hearing.
6. **a kangaroo court** – a court without any legal authority which tries and punishes people who have endangered the interests of some group or association. The term was originally employed for the illegal trials that were held in jails for offences against the prison community. Today, the same term is used for trade unions when they try members for breaches of union rules and regulations.

## MONKEY AND APE

7. to **monkey with** – to interfere, usually with harmful results. 'Dennis has been monkeying with the grandfather clock. Now it won't chime.'
8. **monkey tricks** – spiteful, malicious behaviour.
9. to **make a monkey of** someone – to make someone look ridiculous. 'I don't like being made a monkey of in front of my friends; don't play your jokes on me again when we have guests.'
10. to **get one's monkey up** (slang) – to annoy or irritate someone very much. 'Whenever I turn on my radio, my neighbour knocks on the wall; he really gets my monkey up.'
11. **as clever as a cartload of monkeys** – very artful and sly.
12. **monkey business** – underhanded business, business that is not quite honest or straightforward. 'Paul has been getting up to some of his monkey business again. He needs watching.'
13. to **ape** one's superiors – to imitate people in a higher position than oneself.

## LYNX AND LEOPARD

14. to be **lynx-eyed** – to have very sharp eyesight.
15. **the leopard can never change its spots** – one can never change one's character; thus a man with an evil past never changes his ways.

## LION

16. **as brave as a lion** – very brave, the lion being a symbol of courage.
17. a **lion-hunter** – hosts or hostesses who seek out celebrities with whom to impress their guests.

1. to **lionize** someone – to make a celebrity of someone by lavishing praise and hospitality on him or her.
2. **the British Lion** – the symbol of Great Britain.
   to **twist the lion's tail** – to humiliate or provoke Great Britain.
3. **the lion's share** – much more than one's fair share, almost everything. 'He took the lion's share, and by the time he had finished there was nothing left for the rest of us except for a few crumbs.' Taken from Aesop's Fables.
4. the **lion's den** – a place of great danger.
5. to **beard the lion in his den** – to challenge a formidable enemy on his own ground.
6. to **put one's head in the lion's mouth** – to put oneself needlessly at the mercy of an enemy.

TIGER

7. he's **a tiger** – an expert, a person of dynamic energy.
   to **fight like a tiger** – to fight with savage, relentless ferocity.
8. **paper tiger** – a sham, a cowardly adversary who is unable to offer any real resistance. The phrase was coined by the Chinese leader Mao-Tse-tung at the height of the Vietnamese Civil War in reference to the capitalist countries who, the Chinese claimed, were too cowardly to defend their interests, although they made a lot of threats against their enemies.
9. to **ride a tiger** – to find that the person you are trying to make use of is your master and is in control of you.
10. to have **a tiger by the tail** – to get involved in unexpected trouble or danger, to find that the person you are hunting is much more formidable than you had supposed. 'You can't shake a tiger by the tail and not expect to get bitten' (from *NOW!* Magazine).

BEAR

11. **like a bear with a sore head** – in a specially bad mood or temper. 'Father is like a bear with a sore head this morning. I wonder what has upset him.' Bears are notoriously bad-tempered; hence the phrase.
12. **bears** and **bulls** on the Stock Exchange – a bull expects a share to rise, and a bear expects it to fall in price. So you can be **'bullish of a share'** and expect its price to rise, or **'bearish of a share'** and expect it to fall.
13. a **bear garden** – a place that is full of noise and contention. The name originated in the bear gardens of Tudor times when bears were baited and attacked by dogs. These 'bear gardens' were well known for the rowdy behaviour of the spectators.

# 8. BIRDS

## BIRD, BIRDS

1. **bird** (cockney) – girlfriend. D. H. Lawrence is known to have used the phrase.
2. an **old bird** – someone who is too experienced and shrewd to be taken in. 'You won't get an old bird like him to believe that tale!' From the proverb: You can't catch an old bird with chaff.
3. an **early bird** – someone who rises early. 'My husband was always an early bird.' From the proverb: It's the early bird that catches the worm.
4. an **odd bird** – an eccentric person.
5. a **rare bird** – an exceptional person who combines two contradictory interests. 'He was that rare bird – a poet and a chemist.' cf. **'a rare animal' 52/5**.
6. a **bird of passage** – someone who never stays long in the same place but is always on the move, a wanderer, like a swallow which migrates according to season.
7. a **jail-bird** – someone who spends his life in and out of prison.
8. to **get the bird** – to suffer a severe rebuff, to be greeted with abuse. 'He offered to give a talk on his travels in India, but he got the bird!'

   to **give** someone **the bird** – to hiss or boo at a person in order to express one's disapproval.
9. the **bird has flown** – the person you want has disappeared. 'The birds have flown' was said by Charles I when he and his henchmen arrived at the House of Commons too late to arrest his political enemies.
10. **free as a bird** – free to come and go as one pleases.
11. **a little bird told me** – someone whose name the speaker prefers not to reveal. Often used when speaking to an inquisitive child, in reference to some gossipy information.
12. a **bird's-eye view** – a general view.
13. a **bird of ill-omen** – someone who brings bad luck, like Jonah (in the Bible), or a messenger who is always bringing bad news. From a bird whose presence signifies misfortune, like the albatross or crow.
14. **A bird in the hand is worth two in the bush** (proverb) – a smaller advantage which can be taken now is better than a greater one at some uncertain time in the future.
15. to **kill two birds with one stone** – to achieve two results with the same means. 'We can kill two birds with one stone by combining our honeymoon with our business trip.'
16. to be **able to charm the birds off a tree** – to have so much charm that one can achieve almost anything with it. 'Richard could charm a bird off a tree if he put his mind to it.'

    to be **unable to charm birds off a tree** – to be lacking in charm.
17. **birds of a feather** – you can judge the character of a person by the company he keeps. The phrase is derogatory and derives from the proverb: Birds of a feather flock together.

## FEATHER AND WING

18. **in fine feather** – in splendid condition, lively and cheerful. 'Alan was in fine feather. He has quite recovered from his depression.'
19. **'You could have knocked me down with a feather!'** – I was so overcome with surprise that even an object as light as a feather would have been enough to knock me down.
20. to **smooth** someone's **ruffled feathers**

– to soothe someone's injured pride. 'The Vicar was very upset at the way you spoke to him this morning. You had better do something to smooth his ruffled feathers.'

1. to **make the feathers/fur fly** – to start an angry controversy which leads to quarrelling and fighting. 'Your scheme to convert the local church into a community centre has made the feathers fly.'
2. to **make** someone's **hackles rise** – to make someone very angry, to infuriate him. 'It makes my hackles rise when Len's father takes the credit for getting him into university and ignores the help we gave his son.' The hackles are the long feathers on the neck of the domestic cock which rise when it is angry and preparing for a fight.
3. to **take** someone **under one's wing** – to give a person one's help and protection. 'Since Lady Montague has taken Tim under her wing, the teachers at his school haven't given him any more trouble.'
4. to **clip** someone's **wings** – to tame someone, to curtail his powers. 'Every time I ring my doctor for an appointment, I am cross-examined by his receptionist. It's time her wings were clipped.'

## NEST

5. to **feather one's nest** – to make wrongful use of one's position, in order to make or save money for oneself. 'He is not going to feather his nest at our expense!'
6. to **foul one's nest** – to speak ill of one's own family to strangers. 'You shouldn't have fouled your nest like that at Susan's wedding. Your family will never forgive you.' The phrase comes from the proverb: It's an ill bird that fouls its own nest.
7. a **nest-egg** – a small amount of money that is kept in reserve, in case of need.

   to **break into one's nest-egg** – to spend money that has been saved up. 'Prices have gone up so fast in recent years that many people have been obliged to break into their nest-eggs.'
8. to **rule the roost** – to dominate or govern a group. 'In the early part of the century, it was the eldest son, not the widow, who ruled the roost.' The roost is the resting place of the hens where they perch at night.
9. to **come home to roost** – to recoil on the person responsible for a folly or wrong. 'There is always a price to pay for our follies; sooner or later they come home to roost.'

## ROBIN, LARK AND SWALLOW

10. a **round robin** – a letter of protest with the signatures in circular form in order to conceal the identity of the ring-leader.
11. **'Who killed Cock Robin?'** – the first line of a nursery rhyme which in modern parlance means 'Who is responsible for the fall of a prominent figure?', a question often posed by political commentators when a Minister is replaced.
12. to **have a lark / lark about** – to play jokes or indulge in horseplay with other children. 'I told the children to stop larking about and go to sleep.'
13. to be **up with the lark** – to be up early in the morning.
14. to be **as happy as a lark** – to be very happy, carefree, jolly. 'Steven is as happy as a lark, playing with his new model railway.'
15. **One swallow doesn't make a summer** (proverb) – one favourable occurrence doesn't prove that the others will be as good. 'That's an encouraging

order you've just had, but it doesn't prove that our business will succeed. One swallow doesn't make a summer.'

## JAY, MAGPIE AND CUCKOO

1. a **jay-walker** – a pedestrian who crosses the road without looking.
2. to **chatter like a magpie** – to chatter incessantly, without interruption; often used in reference to children.
3. a **cuckoo in the nest** – an unwelcome intruder. 'Hicks has been a cuckoo in the nest ever since he joined the association. Why join if he doesn't agree with our aims?'

## CROW

4. to **crow / crow over** – to gloat, to rejoice at the defeat of an opponent. 'I don't like the way Rolf crows over his opponents when he wins. It is very unsporting of him.'
5. **as the crow flies** – as an imaginary bird would fly; the distance as measured by a straight line from one point to another.
6. **crow's feet** – the little lines or wrinkles which appear under a person's eyes in middle age.
7. a **scarecrow** – the name given to a woman who wears shabby, torn or dowdy clothes. 'I can't possibly wear this at the ball; I shall look a proper scarecrow in it.' Literally, some old tattered clothes put on a stick in a field to frighten the crows away.

## PIGEON AND DOVE

8. to **pigeon-hole** – to delay action on a request or complaint indefinitely. A pigeon-hole is one compartment among many reserved for the filing of documents.
9. to **pluck a pigeon** – to swindle a credulous victim.
10. the **dove of peace** – the dove has been a symbol of peace from time immemorial. It was a dove which brought a message from God to Noah in his ark at the height of the flood.
11. to be **as gentle as a dove** – to behave in a peace-loving, tender manner.
12. **'Don't get lovey-dovey with me!'** – 'Don't get amorous with me, don't get the wrong ideas about me.'
13. to **flutter the dovecotes** – to cause a lot of excitement in a peaceful community. 'If you return to the village after all the publicity you've had, you will flutter the dovecotes all right!'

## HEN

14. a **hen party** – a party to which only women or girls are invited.
15. a **hen-pecked husband** – a man who is domineered over by his nagging wife.
16. **like a hen with one chicken** – overprotective of one's only child.

## COCK

17. to be **all cock-a-hoop** – to be exultant, triumphant. 'Hudson was all cock-a-hoop at the news. He had never expected to get a first-class degree.' The origin is unknown.
18. to **live like fighting cocks** – to be nourished on the best food, like a fighting cock.
19. **this beats cock-fighting** – more exciting, more thrilling than cock-fighting.
20. **that cock won't fight** – that plan won't do; it is impracticable. The phrase is also used when one party to a dispute disappoints his supporters by refusing to fight. 'I was looking forward to taking Peter's headmaster to court, but then Peter refused to testify against him; when the cock won't

fight, there is nothing you can do.' The reference is to cock-fighting.

1. to be **cock of the walk** – to be the champion or victor in one's own particular field, to dominate all one's rivals.
2. a **cock and bull story** – a wildly improbable story, often invented to glorify the speaker or to excuse some wrongful action. 'Harry told me a cock and bull story about a man robbing him of the money he owed me while he was on his way to my house.'
3. to **cock a snook at** – to make a long nose at, by putting one's thumb at the end of the nose and spreading out the fingers as a gesture of contempt. cf. 'to **make a long nose' 84/9**.
4. a **cock sparrow** – a bold, aggressive little fellow, always spoiling for a fight.
5. a **cock-eyed scheme** – a wild, foolish scheme, one that is bound to fail.
   **That's cock-eyed** – that's all wrong.
6. to **take a cockshot at** – to throw something at an object without taking much care; to make a wild throw at it.
7. at **cock-crow** – at sunrise.

## CHICKEN

8. to be **chicken/chicken-hearted** – to be cowardly, easily frightened, to be afraid of a fight.
9. to **chicken out** – to wriggle out of an obligation through cowardice.
10. **she's no chicken** – she's no longer young. 'No chicken' is often used in reference to a woman who is no longer as young as she would like to appear, and whose behaviour does not become a woman of her age.
11. **as tender as a chicken** – very soft, delicate.
12. **Don't count your chickens** – don't rely on your gains until you have them in your possession. 'Don't count your chickens. Your uncle may not leave you any money at all.' From the proverb: Don't count your chickens before they are hatched; from Aesop's Fables.
13. **that's like asking which came first, the chicken or the egg** – there are some questions to which there is no rational answer.
14. **chicken feed** (slang) – a poor, meagre reward for work done.
15. the **pecking order** – the order of seniority in an organized group of people. 'I am pretty low down in the pecking order, so I don't enjoy my job much.' The phrase is taken from the social order of domestic chickens which ranks chickens according to their strength. Each bird is pecked by the one immediately above it in rank, but pecks the one immediately below it.

## DUCK

16. a **sitting duck** – someone who is vulnerable to attack from his enemies. From the idea that it is easy to shoot a duck which is sitting still. cf. **'a sitting target' 205/8**.
17. a **lame duck** – a person who is incompetent and in need of financial assistance. Also a company or industry that is running at a loss and needs public money to survive. Second-term American presidents who have lost their power of patronage, and consequently their influence in the legislature, are known as 'lame ducks'.
18. a **dead duck** – a cause or campaign that no longer has relevance to modern life.
19. **like a dying duck in a thunderstorm** – all forlorn, bedraggled and miserable. 'You do sound sorry for yourself – like a dying duck in a thunderstorm.'
20. an **ugly duckling** – a plain, unprepossessing child who grows into a

beautiful woman. The phrase comes from Hans Andersen's fairy tale *The Ugly Duckling* in which an ugly duckling, after much ridicule, grows into a beautiful swan.

1. **(like) water off a duck's back** – without making the slightest impression. 'She scolded her son again and again for his dishonesty, but her words were water off a duck's back.'
2. to **take to** something **like a duck to water** – to adapt oneself to a new situation without any conscious effort or difficulty. 'Although he had never worked in an office before, he took to the routine like a duck to water.'
3. to **play ducks and drakes** with one's money – to take unjustifiable risks with one's money, to throw it away. The game of ducks and drakes consists in throwing a flat stone along the surface of the water and counting the number of times it bounces on the water.
4. a **duck's egg** (slang) – scoring nought at cricket.

   **a pair of ducks** – no score in either innings. The term is sometimes used in other connections. The American equivalent for no score is 'a goose's egg'.

   to **break one's duck** – to score a run in cricket, and so avoid making a 'duck' or 'duck's egg'.

## GOOSE

5. to be unable to **say boo to a goose** – to be so timid that one cannot make even the mildest protest, however badly one is treated. 'If you were to move your family into his house, he wouldn't try to stop you. He can't say boo to a goose!'
6. to **cook** someone's **goose** – to destroy one's opponent's chances by some dramatic coup. 'That's cooked his goose once and for all. He'll never survive the scandal.'
7. a **wild goose chase** – to go on a profitless journey, to take part in a useless search. Most wild goose chases are unsuccessful because wild geese fly very high and fast and are therefore difficult to shoot.
8. the **goose-step** – a kind of military step with the legs pushed aggressively forward.
9. **goose flesh/skin/pimples** – a rough condition of the skin resembling the skin of a plucked goose, which comes about as the result of cold or fear.
10. to **kill the goose that lays the golden egg** – to destroy the source of one's wealth. 'I know you don't like the way your father paints, but if you discourage him too much, you will be killing the goose that lays the golden egg.' From Aesop's Fables.
11. **What is sauce for the goose is sauce for the gander** (adage) – what is right for one person is also right for all. The same rules should be applied to everybody without exception or favouritism. 'If Roger is allowed the day off, why shouldn't I be? What is sauce for the goose is sauce for the gander.'
12. **all your geese are swans** – you overestimate the value of your possessions or ideas, just because they are yours.
13. **all your swans are geese** – all your hopes have been disappointed.

## TURKEY

14. to **talk turkey** – to talk bluntly, usually about business.
15. that's **cold turkey** – (1) the plain truth. (2) withdrawal from drug-taking.

## SWAN, STORMY PETREL, COOT AND ALBATROSS

16. **swan-song** – the last achievement of a writer, painter, musician, and so on.

According to legend, the swan only sings when it is about to die.

1. a **stormy petrel** – a turbulent, restless character who stirs up trouble wherever he goes. A stormy petrel is a small sea-bird whose appearance on the surface of the sea foretells a storm. The word 'petrel' is derived from St Peter, the apostle who walked on the water.
2. **as bald as a coot** – completely bald; so called because the coot has a featherless pate on its forehead which resembles the head of a bald man.
3. to have **an albatross round one's neck** – to suffer from some crippling disadvantage. 'We would have made real progress if it hadn't been for this albatross round our necks' (Premier James Callaghan on TV, 1977, referring to the danger of a run on the pound and its devaluation). The albatross has always been regarded as a bird of ill omen.

## KINGFISHER

4. **halcyon days** – times of undisturbed happiness and peace. 'Those were the halcyon days of Athens [fifth century BC] when she produced her finest poetry and drama, architecture and sculpture.' The halcyon is Greek for kingfisher, being a compound of Greek 'sea' and 'conceiving'. Thus the halcyon days were the calm days, when the kingfishers were able to breed in peace, undisturbed by wind and storm. cf. **'a hey-day' 36/14**.

## PARROT

5. **parrot-fashion / parrot-like / parrot-wise** – learnt by heart without regard to the meaning.
6. **as sick as a parrot** – a cliché often used by football managers, meaning very disappointed.

## PEACOCK, PHOENIX AND DODO

7. **as proud as a peacock** – conceited and vain. The comparison is based on the outstandingly beautiful plumage of the peacock's tail, which opens out like a fan to attract the hen.
8. to rise **like a phoenix from the ashes** – a force which has apparently been destroyed, but which emerges once again to triumph over its enemies. According to legend, the phoenix was an eastern bird which set fire to itself and then rose again from the ashes. It is also a symbol of the Resurrection.
9. **as dead as a dodo** – finished, dead, extinct. 'I thought that jazz was as dead as the dodo, but now it seems to have made a comeback.' The dodo was a large bird which died out at the end of the seventeenth century.

## OWL

10. **as wise as an owl / a wise old owl** – owls have a solemn look, and solemnity is often associated with wisdom; hence the phrase.
11. a **solemn owl** *(derogatory)* – an excessively solemn person who is lacking in humour.
12. a **night owl** – someone who does not go to bed until the early hours of the morning. 'Since Philip has started work on his book he has become a regular night-owl.'

## HAWK AND EAGLE

13. **'hawks and doves'** – in British politics, the 'hawks' are the hardliners of the Conservative right wing, and the 'doves' those on the left wing who favour conciliation and compromise with the other parties. There are also 'hawks' and 'doves' on both wings of the Republican and Democratic

parties in the USA, where the meaning is much the same.

1. an **eagle eye** – a very sharp gaze which takes in the smallest detail; a look from which it is impossible to escape.

## VULTURE

2. **like a vulture** – a grabbing, mercenary person. The vulture is a scavenger that feeds on the corpses of rotting animals. Consequently, the word is often used to describe the relations who gather round the rich man's death-bed.

## OSTRICH

3. **like an ostrich (with its head in the sand)** – someone who wilfully conceals the truth from himself, who refuses to face reality. Ostriches are generally believed to hide their heads in the sand in the mistaken belief that, if they cannot see the danger, the danger no longer exists. Hence all the phrases connected with ostrich, such as **'ostrich policy'**, **'ostrich belief'**, **'ostrich-like'**, which imply a refusal to face reality. cf. **'to bury one's head in the sand' 78/4**.

# 9. FISH

## FISH

1. a **big fish** – a very important person.
   **only a small fish** – only an unimportant person.
2. a **big fish in a small pond** – someone whose authority and influence is limited to a small area. 'I'd rather run my own shop in the village, where I'm a big fish in a small pond, than work in a large store, where I'd only be one in two hundred.'
3. a **queer fish** – an odd character.
4. a **cold fish** – a cold, unfeeling person.
5. to **land a fish** – to score a big success like, for example, winning an important contract.
6. to be **like a fish out of water** – to find oneself in an unfamiliar situation, to be ill-adapted to new conditions. 'When he was transferred from the Air Force to the Army, he felt like a fish out of water; the work was so different.'
7. a **pretty kettle of fish** – an awkward predicament with no easy solution. When Queen Mary learned that her son, King Edward VIII, was faced with the choice of giving up Mrs Simpson or of abdicating, she exclaimed: 'This is a pretty kettle of fish!'
8. to **drink like a fish** – to be a hard drinker, a habitual, excessive drinker.
9. to **cry stinking fish** – to disparage one's own wares. 'You shouldn't criticize your father's price rises in front of our customers. You'll lose us business, if you cry stinking fish.'
10. **neither fish, flesh, fowl nor good red herring** – to be neither one thing nor the other, with the result that it doesn't satisfy anyone. 'This is neither a game of chance nor skill. It is neither fish, flesh, fowl nor good red herring.'
11. to **have other fish to fry** – to have other more important things to engage one's attention. 'I tried to interest him in our venture, but he seemed preoccupied with something else. No doubt he has other fish to fry.'
12. **there are as good fish in the sea as ever came out of it** – often said with the object of consoling a person crossed in love. 'There are many other people, besides your boy-friend, who would suit you just as well, so there is no need for you to despair. There are as good fish in the sea as ever came out of it.'
13. to **feed the fishes** (colloquial) – (1) to be seasick. (2) to be drowned.
14. to **fish in troubled/muddy water** – to meddle in matters which may cause one a lot of trouble, to try to make capital out of somebody else's misfortune.
15. to **fish for compliments** – to invite compliments by making disparaging remarks about oneself in the hope that they will be contradicted. '"I'm not nearly as pretty as Isabel." "What are you saying! You are a hundred times prettier! You really are fishing for compliments!"'
16. to **fish for information** – to seek information by asking leading questions. The phrase suggests that the interrogator is relying on the witness to supply the missing evidence. 'The reporters were here all morning fishing for information about your intention to divorce Helen.'
    to **go on a fishing expedition** – this is similar but more explicit. It means to visit someone and interrogate him in the hope that he will incriminate himself.

## MACKEREL

1. to throw **a sprat to catch a mackerel** – to invest a small sum in the hope of making a big profit.

## HERRING

2. to draw **a red herring** across the path – to introduce an irrelevant issue into a discussion. The 'red herring' may either be introduced intentionally, in order to confuse one's opponent, or accidentally. cf. 'to **start a hare' 60/15**.

## EEL

3. **as slippery as an eel** – difficult to pin down, difficult to catch. 'I couldn't get anything in writing out of him; he is as slippery as an eel.'

## SARDINES

4. to be packed **like sardines** – to be squashed together among a lot of people. 'We were packed like sardines on the train. I could hardly move my arms.'

## FRY

5. **small fry** – unimportant people. 'He was too snobbish to greet the small fry.'

## CAVIARE

6. **caviare to the general** – something special that is wasted on the uncultivated. The reference is from Shakespeare's *Hamlet*, II, ii, 465: 'The play, I remember, pleased not the million; 'twas caviare to the general'.

## OYSTER

7. **as close as an oyster** – secretive, reluctant to give information.
8. **the world is mine oyster** – to have abundant opportunities, unlimited scope. 'Why, then the world is mine oyster, Which I with sword will open' (Shakespeare, *The Merry Wives of Windsor*, II, ii).

## WHELK

9. not to be able even to **run a whelk-stall** – to be hopelessly incompetent. 'Don't give me advice on how to run my business; you couldn't even run a whelk-stall!' A whelk is a small shellfish which is sold as a cheap food, especially at the seaside.

## CRAB

10. to **catch a crab** – when rowing, to dip the oar too deep into the water or to miss the water altogether. In either case, the effect is to stop the boat.

## SHARK

11. a **shark** – a swindler, a money-grabber, one who charges an extortionate price for his services. The verb 'shark' is derived from the North French 'cherquier' (English – search, but has the added meaning of searching greedily. See *Hamlet*, I, i, 98 – shark up, meaning to snap up. The name has been given to the fish in the same sense.

# 10. INSECTS

## WORM

1. a **worm** (derogatory) – someone lacking in moral fibre, despicable. 'What a worm!'
2. **the worm of conscience** – the nagging voice of conscience.
3. a **worm's eye view** – viewed from underneath.
4. **even a worm will turn** – there is a limit to the extent that even the weakest person can be bullied. The day will come when he will stand up for himself.
5. to **worm out information** – to extract information in a cunning underhand way.
6. to **worm oneself into** another's **favour** or **confidence** – to ingratiate oneself by devious means with another person.

## SPIDER

7. **'Come into my parlour, said the spider to the fly'** – an ironic comment on an invitation that, in the opinion of the speaker, could lead a person into a dangerous trap.
8. to **blow the cobwebs away** – to clear one's mind of out-of-date notions. 'Beethoven was a great innovator in his day who blew away the cobwebs in the world of music.'

## FLY, BUTTERFLY AND MOTH

9. a **fly in the ointment** – a small blemish that spoils one's pleasure. 'I would like to go to Spain next summer. The only fly in the ointment is we shall have to take our aunt with us.'
10. he **couldn't hurt a fly** – a gentle person who would never hurt anyone.
11. there are **no flies on him** – he is too sharp to be deceived or swindled.
12. to **break a butterfly on a wheel** – to use superfluous strength in order to secure a result.
13. to have **butterflies in one's stomach/tummy** – to have an attack of nerves before an important event.
14. **like a moth (that flies) round a light** – like someone who is unable to resist temptation.
15. **moth-eaten ideas** – out-of-date ideas. 'He has such moth-eaten ideas that he would be more at home in the Victorian age.'

## BEE, DRONE AND WASP

16. to be **as busy as a bee** – to work non-stop.
17. to **make a bee-line for** – to make one's way directly towards. 'Whenever I visit Mr Smith, his sister makes a bee-line for me.'
18. to **drone on** – to talk monotonously and at length on a subject.
19. to **bring a hornets' nest about one's ears / to put one's foot in a wasps' nest** – to bring down an avalanche of retribution on one's head by interference and criticism. 'When the government announced its intention of cutting out the waste in the National Health Service, it put its foot in a wasps' nest.'
20. a **wasp waist** – an exaggeratedly small waist. 'That tailor has given you a wasp waist. You'll have to have the jacket let out.'

## BUG

21. a **big bug** – a very important person, often self-important.
22. a **fire-bug** – a compulsive fire-raiser.

1. a **litter bug** – someone who drops litter in the street and doesn't make use of a litter bin.

2. to have a room **bugged** – to install an electronic device in a room for taping conversation.

## FLEA, NIT AND LEECH

3. a **(mere) flea bite** – a comparatively small sum of money. 'He was fined £500, but that was only a flea bite for a man of his wealth.'

4. to send someone away **with a flea in his ear** – to snub or rebuke a person. 'When he asked me for a loan, I sent him away with a flea in his ear. He must have felt very humiliated.'

5. **nit-picking** (derogatory) – making small, pettifogging criticisms. 'The critics were all mean, nit-picking people, totally devoid of any artistic sense.' The nit is the egg of a louse, and therefore barely visible.

6. to **stick/cling like a leech** – to act like a parasite whom it is difficult to shake off. 'Whenever we invite Cousin Harry, we can never get rid of him. He sticks like a leech.'

## SNAIL

7. **at a snail's pace** – very slowly indeed, unreasonably slowly. 'I'm sorry I'm so late. My train went at a snail's pace all the way.' Often used to express annoyance at someone's excessive slowness.

8. to **draw/pull in one's horns** – (1) to reduce one's spending. 'With the cut in my salary, I've been obliged to draw in my horns, so we won't be taking a holiday this year.' (2) to retract a statement, or withdraw from a position in a debate or controversy. From the snail which retracts its horns when it feels itself threatened.

## LIMPET AND CRICKET

9. to **cling like a limpet** – to cling tenaciously. 'I met Tom on the bus yesterday. He clung like a limpet to me the whole afternoon.'

10. **as merry as a cricket** – cheerful, happy. So called because the chirp of a cricket has a merry sound.

## LOCUST

11. to **swarm like locusts** – to appear in very great numbers. 'His poor relations swarmed like locusts around the rich man.'

# 11. BODY

## HEAD

1. to **head for** – (1) to go towards. (2) to ask for trouble, danger or disaster, etc. 'I warned you the company was heading for disaster.'
2. a **head start** – an advantage over one's competitors. 'You have a head start over your competitors; your business has been established longer than theirs.'
3. to **come to a head** – (of ill-feeling, disagreements, etc.) to reach a crisis.

   to **bring to a head** – to bring about a crisis. 'The Minister brought matters to a head by resigning from the government.' The reference is to the 'head' which forms on a boil when it is about to burst.
4. **over one's head** – (1) intellectually too difficult to grasp. 'They talked advanced mathematics together. It was completely over my head.' (2) to appeal against the decision of one's immediate superior to someone higher up in the hierarchy. 'The sergeant-major went over the head of his Company Commander and complained direct to the Commandant.'
5. **on one's head** – (1) to deserve blame if anything goes wrong. 'On your head be it if any of the patients suffer.' (2) to do something without the slightest difficulty or effort. 'I could have answered all the history questions on my head' (literally, with my feet in the air, upside-down).
6. to **be off one's head** – to be mad. 'He must have been off his head to try to climb the mountain without a guide!'

   to **go off one's head** – to go mad, to act like a madman. 'When Philip's marriage ended, he went completely off his head.' The idiom may express only a temporary lapse. 'Have you gone off your head? You paid him all that money in advance! You'll never see him again!'
7. **King Charles' head** – a synonym for any quaint or fanciful obsession. The phrase comes from Charles Dickens's novel *David Copperfield*, in which a half-crazy character, Mr Dick, constantly refers in his conversation to King Charles's head. (Charles I was beheaded by Parliament in 1649 after the Great Rebellion, 1642–6.)
8. to **have a head for** – to have a gift or aptitude for. Often used in connection with figures, accounts and business. 'With your head for figures, you should go in for accountancy.'

   to **have a head for heights** – to feel comfortable at great heights. Often used in the negative form. 'I could never be a mountaineer; I have no head for heights.'
9. to **hold one's head high** – to be free from any taint of guilt. 'Now you have been acquitted on all the charges, you can hold your head high.'
10. to **turn someone's head** – to give someone a high opinion of himself, to give him a false idea of his own importance. 'Jack's election to the presidency of our union has turned his head. He has started talking about himself in the third person as if he were royalty!'
11. to **keep one's head / to keep a level head** – to remain calm and sensible.

    to **lose one's head** – to lose one's power of reasoning, to get into a panic. 'When the boat sprang a leak, Susan completely lost her head and began to scream hysterically.'
12. to **keep one's head down** – to avoid drawing attention to oneself. 'All this bad publicity is not doing you any good. You had better keep your head down for the next six months.'

1. to **fling oneself at** someone's **head / at** someone – to pursue someone in a spirit of infatuation. 'The moment she saw the pop star, she flung herself at his head.'
2. to **snap off / bite off** someone's **head** – to speak sharply to someone, to snub or correct curtly. 'You needn't snap my head off. How was I to know?'
3. to **let** someone **have his head / give** someone **his head** – to let someone use his own initiative, his own judgement. Compare 'to **give the horse its head**' – to allow the horse freedom to decide the speed it will gallop at.
4. to **count heads / head-counting** – to accept the view of the majority. 'You are the only person on the committee who understands the subject, so what is the point of counting heads? You must decide.'
5. to **put their heads together** – to enlist someone else's advice in solving a problem, to discuss a problem with someone. From the proverb, 'Two heads are better than one'.
6. to **knock their heads together** – to take drastic action to end a quarrel. 'I wish Ralph and Mike wouldn't quarrel in front of the reporters. Someone should knock their heads together.'
7. to **take it into one's head** – to have a sudden idea, often with the implication that the idea is a mistaken one.
8. to **get into one's head** – to learn, comprehend. 'I can't get this Latin grammar into my head.'
9. to **put ideas into someone's head** – to have a bad influence on someone, to indoctrinate. 'Mark has beem putting ideas into Roger's head, and now he wants a bigger room and more food.'
10. to **put out of one's head** – to dismiss from one's mind some idea, hope or project.
11. to **make headway** against – to make progress, despite strong opposition; to prevail over. 'He made headway against the prejudices of the villagers.'
12. to **knock on the head** – to ruin a plan. 'Jane has broken her leg; that has knocked our skiing holiday on the head.'
13. to **scratch one's head** – to be puzzled, bewildered. 'I've been scratching my head over this game for the last half-hour, but I don't see how I can win; I give up!'
14. **soft in the head** – foolish, dense, mentally retarded; sometimes used as a reproach for some foolish action. 'Tim must be soft in the head to have believed that story.'
15. to be **bone-headed from the neck up** (slang) – to be completely stupid. From the idea of the bone replacing the brain.
16. **hot-headed** – easily aroused to anger. 'I don't know whether they will be happy together; she is mild and gentle, and her husband is quarrelsome and hot-headed, just the opposite of her.'
17. to be **at loggerheads** – to be in constant dispute with. 'He has been at loggerheads with his legal advisers throughout the proceedings.'
18. to **go to one's head** – to be made vain or conceited by success. 'John was much applauded for his speech last night. I only hope his success will not go to his head.'
19. to **have a swelled head** – to be conceited, to have a high opinion of oneself. 'Winning first prize in the song contest has given Jane a swelled head. Now she shows off terribly.'
20. to **go bald-headed at** – to attack with great energy, in total disregard of the consequences. 'Michael went for his enemy bald-headed, although he was unarmed and outmatched by his opponent.'
21. to **rear/raise its ugly head** – to become

a menace. 'The unemployment problem has raised its ugly head once more.'

1. **heads will roll** – those responsible for the blunder will be dismissed. In bygone times, guilty men in high places were sometimes executed. Today, they are removed from office, or transferred to positions of less importance, but the old phraseology has survived.
2. to have something **hanging over one's head** – to have an ordeal in front of one. 'This court case has been hanging over my head for the last six months. I shall be glad when it's over.'
3. to **need one's head examined** – to do something so stupid as to be almost insane. 'You drove at ninety miles an hour on that road! You should have your head examined!'
4. to **bury one's head in the sand** – wilfully to close one's eyes to danger. 'I warned him the company would crash if we didn't economize, but he didn't want to listen to me. For the last three years he has buried his head in the sand.' cf. **'like an ostrich' 71/3**.
5. to **put one's head on the chopping-block** – to take some action which effectively ends one's career. 'For you to vote against the Chairman after all he has done for you would be to put your head on the chopping-block.'
6. to **keep one's head above water** – to earn only just enough money to be able to live or to pay one's debts. 'I'm afraid Philip's business isn't doing at all well; he is barely keeping his head above water.'
7. a **head-on collision** – a violent disagreement with someone whose opinions are completely opposed to one's own.
8. to be **head over heels in love** with – to be madly in love with. Sometimes abbreviated to 'to **be head over heels**'.

   to **fall head over heels in love** – to fall in love very suddenly, very violently. Sometimes abbreviated to 'to **fall head over heels'**.
9. not to know whether one is **on one's head or one's heels** – to be in a state of total confusion. 'After severely reprimanding me for my work, my boss offered me promotion at twice the salary. I didn't know whether I was on my head or my heels.'
10. to **stand logic on its head** – to argue illogically. 'To say that Brian isn't clever enough to benefit from a university education is to stand logic on its head. If Brian weren't clever enough, he wouldn't have passed the entrance examination.'
11. to be **head and shoulders better than** – to be altogether superior to.
12. to **have a head on one's shoulders** – to possess good judgement.

    to have an **old head on young shoulders** – possessing greater wisdom than might be expected of a young person. 'If you are a young man confronted with a difficult problem, you need an old head on young shoulders.'
13. to **put one's head in a noose** – to invite disaster.
14. **Heads or tails?** – the call made when tossing a coin to decide the order of play, especially in a game. 'Heads' refers to the sovereign's head on one side of the coin, and 'tails' the reverse side.
15. **heads I win, tails you lose** – an unequal contest which only one person can possibly win. 'It's not fair. Whatever I decide to do, you will win the lot. It's heads you win, and tails I lose.'
16. to **make neither head nor tail of** something – to be completely baffled.
17. to **hit the headlines** – to achieve notoriety, to be the most important item of news on the front page of the national newspapers. 'What a scandal! If you publish that story, it will hit the headiines.'

## HAIR

1. to **have one's hair stand on end** – to be terrified. 'When he saw the ghost, his hair stood on end.'
2. a **hairy story** – an uncouth story.
3. a **hair-raising story** – a horror story, one that shocks you.
4. **don't lose your hair over it / keep your hair on** – keep calm, don't get too excited over it. cf. 'to **keep one's shirt on' 170/5**.
5. **without turning a hair** – without showing any emotion or surprise. 'When she was told her father was dying, she never turned a hair.'
6. to **tear one's hair (out)** – to be desperate, unbearably frustrated. 'He has been tearing his hair over the accounts.'
7. to **let one's hair down** – to speak one's mind, to give vent to one's feelings. 'When I'm with Peter, I can really let my hair down.'
8. enough to **make one's hair curl** – to shock very severely. 'If you could see our electricity bill, it would make your hair curl!'
9. to **have someone by the short hairs** – to have someone at a hopeless disadvantage, to have him in one's power.
10. to **split hairs / hair-splitting** – to make insignificant distinctions, to argue with exaggerated subtlety.
11. to **escape by a hair's breadth** / to **be saved by a hair's breadth** – to escape very narrowly, by a tiny distance. 'She was only saved from falling under the train by a hair's breadth.'
12. **to a hair** – accurate or exact to the last detail.

## FACE

13. to **be two-faced** – to support both parties in a dispute at the same time, to agree with a person to his face but disagree with him behind his back. 'Paul praised my painting while sitting for me, but I found out that he had made fun of it behind my back. He is very two-faced!'
14. to **put a bold face on** something – to behave without any embarrassment or shame. 'When Peter was accused of thc thcft, hc put a bold facc on it, sat down, and lit a cigar before replying.'
15. **bare-faced** – open, shameless, daring; almost always used in connection with 'insolence', 'impudence', 'cheek' and words with similar meanings. 'He had the bare-faced impudence to ask me for a loan ten minutes after we had been introduced!' cf. **'as bold as brass' 119/5**.
16. to **put the best face on something** – to accept a setback or defeat gracefully. 'Simon put the best face on his dismissal, saying that he had intended to take another job anyway.'
17. to **face a thing out** – to insist that one is in the right, often unreasonably.

    to **look in the face** – to confront bravely. 'After the crash of his business, the future was extremely bleak; nevertheless, he looked it in the face.'
18. to **stare in the face** – to be certain, to be clearly unavoidable. 'Bankruptcy has been staring Tom in the face for a long time, but he won't admit it.'
19. to **make faces** (colloquial) – to grimace. 'The little boy made faces at his aunt when she wasn't looking.'
20. to **pull a face** – to make a grimace which may express disgust, anger, derision or dismay.

    to **pull/make a long face** – to look dismal. 'When I told him that he would have to pay for all the damage out of his own pocket, he made a long face.'
21. to **keep a straight face** – to look as if you really believe a story or are in agreement with the speaker, when in reality you would like to laugh. 'When he told me he was going to photo-

graph the Loch Ness monster, it was all I could do to keep a straight face.'

1. **let's face it** – don't let us deceive ourselves. 'Let's face it, William will never get into College, not in a hundred years.'
2. to **face up to** – to confront a problem realistically without deluding oneself as to the nature of the difficulties. 'You must face up to the fact that we have no money.'
3. **on the face of it** – to all appearances, assuming that the facts have been correctly stated. 'On the face of it, your partner is clearly in the wrong, but have you told me the whole story?'
4. to **have the face to** – to be insolent enough to. 'After I had caught Mark stealing my crystal bowl, he had the face to ask me if he could keep it as a souvenir.'
5. to **show one's face** – to appear, to make one's presence known. 'I wonder she dare show her face here, after the way she has behaved.'
6. **to one's face** – in one's presence instead of behind someone's back. 'Let him make his accusations to my face!'
7. to **set one's face against** – to oppose strongly. 'He has set his face against any change in our plans.'
8. **at face value** – at its nominal or official value. 'The face value of an Elizabeth II sovereign is only £1, but its real value is at least £100.'
9. to **face both ways** – to support both contestants at the same time.
10. to **face about** – to change one's mind, to adopt a contrary opinion.
11. a **slap in the face** – a rebuff or snub. 'It was a slap in the face not inviting her old friend Sandra to her birthday party.'
12. to **lose face** – to be humiliated.
13. to **save face** – not to lose respect, to avoid humiliation.

a **face-saving formula** – a form of words that seeks to avoid humiliation for the defeated party.

14. to **put a new face on** something – to show something in a different light. 'Higg's presence at the house on the night of the crime has put a new face on the investigation.'
15. to **laugh in** someone's **face** – to mock. 'I told him he was to blame for the accident, but he laughed in my face and told me I must be joking.'
16. to **laugh on the other side of one's face** – to change from exultation to dismay. 'Andrew was looking forward to a few days' freedom, but he'll laugh on the other side of his face when he hears Joyce has gone away for good.'
17. to **wipe the smile off** someone's **face** – to destroy someone's complacency. 'Arnold has been boasting that he is the best heavyweight in our unit, but I'll soon wipe the smile off his face.'
18. to **fly in the face of** – to ignore the facts or logic of an argument, to deny or contradict unreasonably. 'You are flying in the face of all the authorities on this subject.'
19. to **throw in** someone's **face** – to reproach someone for a blunder or fault. 'Alice threw her husband's disgrace in his face.'
20. to **fall flat on one's face** – to make a dismal failure of something. 'A couple of years ago, Steven bought the book shop at the corner but, not having any experience of running a shop, he fell flat on his face.'
21. his/her **face fell** – he/she looked dismayed.
22. **her face is her fortune** – her beauty is her only asset.
23. **faceless men** – anonymous, unfeeling men. This phrase is used with special reference to civil servants who often use their traditional anonymity to escape responsibility for their actions.

## EYE

1. to **see eye to eye** – to be in agreement with someone, usually over a wide range of subjects. 'We found it difficult to live together because we don't see eye to eye.'
2. to **be up to the eyes/ears** – to be overwhelmed with, to have an excessive amount. 'I am up to the eyes in work', 'He is up to his eyes in debt.'
3. to **have an eye on the main chance** (derogatory) – to be alert to any opportunity for betterment. 'She was a shrewd woman; she never did a kindness without a good reason, and she always had an eye on the main chance.'
4. to **meet one's eye** – to look straight in the face. 'He could not meet my eyes, but blushed and turned away from me.'
5. there is **more** in something **than meets the eye** – there is some hidden significance. 'Mrs Lewis rang up to say she and her husband couldn't come to dinner today. She said she had a cold, but I think she's offended with us. There is more in this than meets the eye.'
6. to **cast an eye over** – to read through very quickly, to check.
7. **easy on the eye** – attractive, pretty. 'Julie would stand out anywhere with her looks – she is easy on the eye, isn't she?'
8. **beauty is in the eye of the beholder** – there is no objective test for judging beauty; it is only a matter of opinion. Sometimes said to console a girl when she feels dissatisfied with her looks.
9. to be **all eyes** – to be very attentive. 'When she got up to sing, her admirer was all eyes.'
10. **through the eyes of . . .** – from the point of view of . . . 'When you play chess, you should look at the game through the eyes of your opponent.'
11. to **open the eyes to** – to make someone aware of a truth, usually some unpleasant fact. 'I opened his eyes to his wife's unfaithfulness.'
12. to be **an eye-opener** – to be a revelation. The phrase suggests a sudden surprise, which may be good or bad. 'Charles had always had romantic ideas about being a cowboy, so his first day at the ranch was a real eye-opener for him.'
13. **with one's eyes open** – fully aware of the risk one is running. 'He went into it with his eyes open, so he can't complain now if things go wrong.'
14. **with one's eyes shut** – with no difficulty or need for any assistance. 'I know my way to her house so well that I could take you there with my eyes shut.'
15. to **have an eye for** – to have good judgement of something. 'She has an eye for horses; she has bred them all her life.'
16. to **get one's eye in** – to get accustomed to the conditions so that one can display one's skill. 'Once he's got his eye in, he is very difficult to beat.' The reference is to ball games like cricket in which a player has to adjust his sight to the movement of the ball.
17. to **have/keep an eye on** – to watch carefully. 'You must keep an eye on that girl. She is very wild, and is not to be trusted on her own.'
18. to **have a roving eye** – to be always looking for a pretty face. 'It's a pity, Anne's husband has a roving eye and always seems to be with a pretty girl!'
19. to **shut one's eyes to** – to ignore or to pretend ignorance of someone's faults. 'She shut her eyes to all his short-comings, although my brother was always pointing them out to her.'
20. **with an eye to** – with the aim of. 'I studied French with an eye to getting a job in one of the big fashion houses in Paris.'

1. to **see with one's own eyes** – to witness, to experience oneself without having to rely on anyone else's testimony. 'You can take my word for it; I saw it with my own eyes.'
2. **not to believe one's eyes** – to doubt the reality of what one has seen. 'When my sister returned from the beauty parlour, she was so changed that I couldn't believe my eyes.' cf. **'not to believe one's ears' 85/15**.
3. to **cry one's eyes out** – to weep so much that one can't weep any more.
4. to **catch the eye** / to **be eye-catching** – to attract attention. 'With her splendid figure and her elegant gown, she soon caught the eye of the judges.'
5. **an eyeful** – attractive. 'She's an eyeful, isn't she. Really pretty!'
6. that's **one in the eye for** – a snub or rebuff. 'She didn't invite him to her birthday party. That was one in the eye for him!'
7. **my eye!** – rubbish, humbug. 'That's all my eye! Edward isn't ill at all, he is only putting it on.'
   **eye-wash** – humbug, hypocritical nonsense.
8. **in the twinkling of an eye** – very quickly.
9. to **see out of the corner of one's eye** – to notice, usually for only a second, while one's attention is directed elsewhere. 'As I was entering the restaurant, I saw John out of the corner of my eye, jumping on a bus.'
10. **wide-eyed** – wide-open eyes that express surprise or innocence.
11. a **private eye** – a private detective. 'The police don't like private eyes as a rule, but they had to admit that Hugh was a first-class investigator.'
12. to **clap eyes on** – to see or meet. Nearly always negative. 'I've never clapped eyes on you before!'
13. to **cock the eye** – to look at knowingly. 'As soon as the Vicar began to speak about the drinking in the village, she cocked an eye at me, and I felt myself going red in the face.'
14. to **keep one's eyes skinned** – to be extremely vigilant and alert.
15. to **make eyes at** – to gaze amorously at.
16. to **see with half an eye** – to realize at once. 'You could see with half an eye that Bob and Ruth weren't happy.'
17. the **naked eye** – without the aid of spectacles or a telescope. 'On a fine day, you can see the Bowden Rocks with the naked eye.'
18. to view **with a beady eye** – to look doubtfully or critically at someone. 'When I asked the boss for a day off so that I could nurse my sick mother, he viewed me with a beady eye.'
19. to be **starry-eyed** – to be full of fancies, to have a lot of impracticable ideas.
20. to **give the glad eye** – to give a loving or flirtatious look at someone.
21. the **evil eye** / to **have an evil eye** on someone – a menacing, ominous look. In Voodoo, the evil eye casts its spell over the intended victim, even when they are separated by hundreds of miles.
22. **in the public eye** – very much in the news, much discussed.
23. **in one's mind's eye** – in one's imagination. 'In my mind's eye, I can still see him knocking out his pipe on the mantelpiece, although he's been dead these twenty years.'
24. to **have bigger eyes than one's stomach** – to over-eat, to be a glutton.
25. **an eye for an eye, a tooth for a tooth** – a like punishment, a punishment that is as severe as the crime but not more so, in accordance with both the Muslim and Judaic laws. It has come to be used in the sense of revenge.
26. to **throw dust in** someone's **eyes** –

to mislead or deceive someone wilfully.

1. **the eye of the typhoon** – the centre of the typhoon in the sky.
2. **eye-ball to eye-ball** – direct confrontation between two enemies.

## EYELID

3. not to **bat an eyelid** – to show no feeling or concern. 'No matter how outrageously the boy behaved, his father never batted an eyelid but just went on reading his newspaper.'
4. to **hang on by one's eyelids** – to hang by a thread, to maintain only a precarious hold.

## EYEBROW

5. a **high-brow** – someone with an intellectual approach to literature and art. The high-brow is interested in style rather than content, and in ideas rather than action.

   a **low-brow** – a person who has no intellectual interests. He likes a story with plenty of action, looks for a pleasant tune in music, and prefers a painting that tells a story.
6. to **raise the eyebrows** – to express surprise, sometimes mild disapproval. 'When her boss ordered flowers for the manageress, the secretary raised her eyebrows.'
7. to **knit one's brows** – to concentrate. 'He knitted his eyebrows as he tried to work out a solution to the puzzle.'
8. to **be steeped to the eyebrows** – to be totally immersed in a subject. 'Since his childhood he had been steeped to the eyebrows in Greek mythology.'
9. **by the sweat of one's brow** – by very hard work, either physical or mental, without anyone's help. 'He reached his present position, not by influence, but by the sweat of his brow.'

## NOSE

10. to **nose about** – to pry, to make all sorts of inquiries. 'The inspector has been nosing about among my father's documents all the morning.'
11. to **nose out** – to discover a secret.
12. to **be nosy** – to be inquisitive, to ask too many questions.

    a **nosy parker** – someone who is forever asking questions about one's business and one's private life. A busybody.
13. to **poke one's nose into someone else's business** – to pry, to interfere in another person's private business. 'He has been poking his nose into my affairs again.'
14. to **get up someone's nose** (slang) – to exasperate, irritate. 'Harry gets up my nose with his never-ending complaints.'
15. **under one's nose** – something that happens very close to a person without his knowing. 'He stole my watch from right under my nose.'
16. a **nose for** (trouble, etc.) – a gift for smelling out trouble. 'That journalist has a nose for the latest scandal.'
17. to **follow one's nose** – to go straight ahead or by instinct. 'She couldn't be bothered to explain how to get there. She told me just to follow my nose.'
18. to **be led by the nose** – to be completely dominated by, totally influenced by. 'The secretary led her boss by the nose until she had spent all his money.'
19. to **pay through the nose** – to pay an excessive price. 'I had to pay through the nose for that desk. I could have got it for a fraction of the price anywhere else.'
20. to **rub someone's nose in it** – to draw someone's attention repeatedly to a past blunder. 'It was bad enough for poor Kenneth, losing all that money,

without you rubbing his nose in it all the time.'

1. to **look down one's nose** – to regard with distaste or disdain. 'He looked down his nose at the youth for wearing his hair long.'
2. to **turn up one's nose** at something – to despise. 'She turns up her nose at Frinton and Bournemouth. Nothing but the Riviera is good enough for her.'
3. **with one's nose in the air** – in a snobbish manner. 'Judy never greets me; she always has her nose in the air.'
4. to **see beyond the end of one's nose** – to look beyond one's immediate surroundings, to use one's imagination and intelligence. 'He has no imagination. He can't see beyond the end of his nose.'
5. to **put** someone's **nose out of joint** – to upset or replace a favourite. 'Jenny is to replace Sally as the boss's confidential secretary. That will put Sally's nose out of joint!'
6. to **cut off one's nose to spite one's face** – to injure or deprive oneself while trying to hurt someone else. 'He was determined to punish his son, so he cancelled the cruise he had booked. But it was a case of cutting off his nose to spite his face, because his son went to Cornwall, leaving his father to be miserable at home.'
7. to **keep one's nose clean** (slang) – to keep out of trouble. 'Life in the army can be quite pleasant, provided you obey orders and keep your nose clean.'
8. to **keep/put one's nose to the grindstone** – to work hard and long at the same job without any rest. 'With so many debts to pay off, he'll just have to keep his nose to the grindstone for the next few years.'
9. to **make a long nose at** someone/to **thumb one's nose at** someone – to show contempt for a person or institution. 'When you are making £100,000 a year, you can thumb your nose at convention.' cf. **'to cock a snook at' 68/3**.
10. **hard-nosed** – shrewd, tough, unsentimental.
11. a **nose-dive** – a vertical dive by an aeroplane. 'The aeroplane went into a nose-dive and crashed into the ground.'
12. to **get a bloody nose** – to suffer an unpleasant rebuff.
13. a **Roman nose** – a rather large, bulbous nose.
14. a **Greek nose** – a straight nose that extends down from the forehead in a straight line.

## EAR

15. **long ears** – an inquisitive person who is always asking questions.
16. to **have sharp ears for any gossip** – alert to any gossip, not to miss any scandal.
17. a **thick ear** – a swollen ear, the result of being struck hard on the ear. 'The school bully threatened Martin with a thick ear.'
18. to **come to our ears** – to come to our knowledge, to learn of.
19. **coming out at the ears** – having something in superabundance. 'Jack has found so much oil, it's coming out at his ears.'
20. to **gain the ear** – to arouse someone's interest on one's behalf. 'Now that I have gained the chairman's ear, we shouldn't have any more difficulty.'
21. to **lend an ear** – to pay attention, to listen. 'If you will lend me your ear for a minute, I will explain how the burglar alarm works.'
22. to **play it by ear** – to use one's intuition, to improvise. '"I'm new to

this school; so I'll have to play it by ear for the first few lessons," the teacher said.' The phrase derives from playing a piece of music without looking at the musical score.

1. **in one ear and out the other** – heard without making any impression. 'Everything I say to that boy goes in one ear and out the other.'
2. **a word in the ear** – advice given in confidence.
3. to **be all ears** – to listen very attentively. 'What you say is very interesting. I'm all ears.'
4. to **have one's ear to the ground** – to be well-informed on what is going on, to be alert to future developments. 'Paul is always the first to know what's happening in the office. He keeps his ear to the ground.'
5. to be **still wet behind the ears** – to be naïve, inexperienced. 'He will be no match for them; he is still wet behind the ears.' The phrase has its origin in children's neglect to dry themselves behind the ears.
6. **'Are your ears burning?'** – Do you feel embarrassed to hear yourself talked about?
7. to **tickle the ears** – to flatter, to please. 'She said you were very handsome – yes, I thought that would tickle your ears.'
8. to **set** people **by the ears** – to stir up mischief. 'During his short stay, Philip set us all by the ears. We had no peace until he had gone.'
9. to **box the ears** – to strike the ears hard, usually as a punishment.
10. to be **out on one's ear** – to be ejected or sacked, often violently. 'The heckler was soon out on his ear, once he started interrupting the speaker.'
11. to **prick up one's ears** – to listen alertly, become suddenly interested in what is being said. 'He pricked up his ears when they mentioned the salary.' The idea comes from the pricking up of a dog's ears when it hears an unfamiliar sound.
12. to **grate on the ear** – to make a harsh, disagreeable sound. 'The lecturer's voice grated on the ears of his students.'
13. an **ear-splitting noise** – an unbearably loud noise.
14. to be **up to the ears in** work/debt – to have a huge amount of work/debts.
15. to be **unable to believe one's ears** – to be astounded at what one has heard. 'When Anne told me she had been married to my brother two years ago, I couldn't believe my ears.' cf. **'not to believe one's eyes' 82/2.**

## MOUTH

16. to look **down in the mouth** – to look depressed, dejected, in low spirits. 'Henry was looking very down in the mouth today; his wife and children had just left for their holiday leaving him to look after the house.'
17. to have a **big mouth** – to speak a lot in a loud voice, to boast.
18. to **shoot off one's mouth** – to talk loudly and indiscreetly. 'Alex was shooting his mouth off in the pub last night about his domestic problems; he should keep all that to himself.'
19. a **mouthful** – a long and difficult name. 'Andrei Andreivitch, that's a mouthful, isn't it?'
20. to **be mealy-mouthed** – to describe something evil with undue mildness. 'If the man is a scoundrel, then say so; why be so mealy-mouthed about it?'
21. a **loose mouth** – an indiscreet person.
22. to **stand convicted out of one's own mouth** – to condemn oneself with one's own words.
23. to **leave a nasty taste in the mouth** – to

leave an unpleasant impression with someone. 'She apologized profusely for making such an accusation against me, and we shook hands at once, but what she had said left a nasty taste in my mouth.'

1. to **put words into** someone's **mouth** – to accuse someone of saying things that he has not said. '"I never said that," the witness protested angrily. "You are putting words into my mouth."'
2. to **take the words out of** someone's **mouth** – to say something before the other person has had time to say it himself. '"This is an appalling play," I said. "You've taken the words out of my mouth. Let's go," Alan replied.'
3. to **open one's mouth too wide** (vulgar) – to ask for too much money. 'My plumber has started opening his mouth too wide. I shall have to find someone else.'
4. to **make one's mouth water** – to tantalize. 'He made my mouth water showing me all his beautiful carpets. I wish I had enough money to buy one!'
5. to **foam at the mouth** – to be overcome with fury, to be so angry as to lose all control over oneself. 'When the football squashed his prize dahlias, the gardener foamed at the mouth with rage.' The foam is the rush of saliva from the mouth.
6. **out of the mouths of babes and sucklings** – the truth is often spoken by children without their being aware of it.
7. **by word of mouth** – through the spoken word, as opposed to the written word. 'Many herbal remedies have been passed down by word of mouth from one generation of gypsies to the next.'
8. the **gift of the gab** – the gift of fluent speech. 'With your gift of the gab you should do well as a lawyer.' Gab derives from Gaelic 'gob' meaning 'mouth', but is only used in this phrase.

## JAW

9. a **glass jaw** – a glaring weakness which renders a person extremely vulnerable to attack. Mainly used in boxing. cf. 'to have **feet of clay' 104/10, 'Achilles' heel' 195/8**, 'a **chink in one's armour' 210/7**.
10. to **jaw away** (school slang) – to speak without interruption. 'Jaw, jaw is better than war, war' (Churchill) – to negotiate, even if it takes a long time, is better than making war.
11. out of **the jaws of death** – from the very brink of death. This phrase is often used with the verb 'snatch'. 'He was snatched from the jaws of death by his friend.'

## WHISKER

12. **within a whisker** – by a very narrow margin. 'We were within a whisker of being defeated. The result couldn't have been closer.'

## LIP

13. to **have one's lips sealed** – to be obliged to keep silent, to keep a confidence or secret.
14. to **bite one's lip** – to regret having said something indiscreet. 'She bit her lip for having made such a clumsy mistake.'
15. **none of your lip!** (colloquial) – don't be cheeky/impudent.
16. to **put a finger to one's lips** – to make a sign to keep quiet.
17. to **curl the lip** – to show contempt.
18. to **keep a stiff upper lip** – to suffer in

silence, to suppress all emotion. 'Lewis suffered dreadfully but he kept a stiff upper lip throughout his ordeal.' From the poem, 'A stiff upper lip', by Phoebe Cary (1824–74).

1. to **pay lip service** – to respect a principle or custom in theory but to ignore it in practice. 'He pays lip service to his wife's wishes but, once she has gone away, he reverts to his old way of life.'
2. to **lick/smack one's lips** – to exult at the prospect of an appetizing meal or other future event to be enjoyed.
3. to be **tight-lipped** – unwilling to say more than is absolutely necessary. 'He was very tight-lipped about his future plans.'
4. to **hang on** someone's **lips** – to listen attentively to every word a person is saying, to give him one's entire attention.

TOOTH

5. to **cut a tooth** – (of a young tooth) to pierce the gum.
6. to have a **sweet tooth** – to have a liking for sweet food, sugar, honey, ice-cream, etc. 'Nicola has such a sweet tooth; it makes it very difficult for her to slim.'
7. to **go over with a fine tooth-comb** – to make a most thorough and painstaking examination.
8. to be **long in the tooth** – old, too old, older than one cares to admit. 'He's a bit long in the tooth for her, isn't he? He must be at least sixty!'
9. the **toothless lion** – a warrior who no longer has the strength to defend himself, someone who has grown feeble and impotent.

TEETH

10. **milk teeth** – the first teeth.
11. to **cut one's wisdom / eye-teeth** – to acquire sense or discretion.
12. to **give one's eye-teeth for** – to wish with all one's heart for, to be prepared to make any sacrifice for. 'I would give my eye-teeth for your job. You have a job in a million!'
13. to **show one's teeth** – to make threats or express hostility. 'Our landlord has always been such a kind, easy-going man, but when I accidentally smashed his window he really showed his teeth.'
14. to **give teeth to** – to give a person or organization special powers and sanctions. 'We must give the Ombudsman teeth so that he can enforce his decisions.'
15. to **get one's teeth into** – to concentrate all one's energy on. 'Short stories are all very well, but I prefer a novel – something I can get my teeth into.'
16. to **get the bit between the teeth** – to throw off all restraint in achieving one's objective. 'Malcolm is determined to buy the house, whatever it costs. Once he gets the bit between his teeth, it is useless to argue with him.' The rider can control his horse by pulling on the bit in the horse's mouth. However, once the horse gets the bit between its teeth, the rider can no longer control it.
17. **in the teeth of** – against the strong resistance of. 'Henry married the girl in the teeth of her parents' disapproval.'
18. to be **fed up to the teeth / back teeth** – to be exasperated beyond endurance. 'I'm fed up to the back teeth with all his complaints.' cf. **'to have a bellyful' 99/13**.
19. to **be kicked in the teeth** – to suffer a severe blow from someone from whom you least expect it. 'After I had given her son all those private lessons for nothing, she cut me dead at the

party last night. It was a real kick in the teeth.'

1. to **set one's teeth on edge** – to grate or jar on the nerves. 'Her voice sets my teeth on edge, like scraping a plate with a knife.'

2. to **grind one's teeth** – to express one's fury. 'Herbert ground his teeth when he heard his daughter was going to marry his junior clerk.'

3. to **cast in the teeth** – to reproach a person to his face for some blunder or fault. 'She cast his drunkenness in his teeth.'

4. to **gnash one's teeth** – to regret bitterly, either one's own mistakes or the success of somebody of whom one is jealous. 'He gnashed his teeth at the idea of Michael marrying his old girlfriend.' A biblical phrase, '. . . there shall be weeping and gnashing of teeth' (Matthew VIII, 12).

5. to **grit one's teeth** – to suppress one's feelings when suffering a painful or frightening experience. 'He gritted his teeth and dived into the cold water.'

6. to **lie through one's teeth** – to lie shamelessly. 'If Richard told you that he was a rich man, he was lying through his teeth. Why, only yesterday he asked me to lend him £50!'

7. to **draw someone's teeth** – to render a dangerous person harmless. 'The Prime Minister drew the teeth of the Opposition by announcing that there had been a drop of a quarter of a million in the number of the unemployed.'

## TONGUE

8. to have a **sharp tongue** – to have a pointed, barbed way of speaking.

9. to be **loose-tongued** – to be garrulous, indiscreet.

10. to **give tongue to** – to express in words, cry out. (From the sound made by hounds when hunting.)

11. to **keep a civil tongue in one's head** – to speak respectfully to one's superiors. 'The director ordered his manager to keep a civil tongue in his head.' A little old-fashioned.

12. **with the tongue in one's cheek** – words spoken insincerely. 'When he congratulated Martin on his twenty years' public service, he must have had his tongue in his cheek, because he is always talking about Martin's bad work in the office.'

13. to **wag one's tongue** – to talk behind someone's back, to gossip.

    to **set tongues wagging** – to give cause for gossip through one's indiscretions.

14. to **get one's tongue round** – to have difficulty in saying a word. 'Hypothesize? I can hardly get my tongue round it.'

15. to have a **tongue that runs away with one** – to talk too much, to be indiscreet. 'How your tongue ran away with you last night, Roy! You shouldn't have talked about your father like that to a stranger.'

16. to **hold one's tongue** – to say nothing, to be discreet. 'If I tell him something in confidence, do you think he can be trusted to hold his tongue?'

17. a **slip of the tongue** – a mistake in one's speech, through carelessness or, more often, a conflict of wishes. An example: a chairman in his welcoming speech to his co-directors declared the meeting closed instead of open because he didn't want to see them (*Psychopathology of Everyday Life* by Sigmund Freud).

18. **I could have bitten my tongue off** – I was angry with myself for having said something (usually something tactless or stupid). 'I thought my joke

would amuse our guests but, instead, there was an embarrassed silence. I could have bitten my tongue off.'

1. to give someone **the rough edge of one's tongue** – to reprimand someone harshly. 'If he doesn't mend his ways, I shall give him the rough edge of my tongue, and he'll be sorry he was so impertinent.'
2. to have a **dirty tongue** to use bad language.
3. **on the tip of one's tongue** – (1) to be on the point of saying something. 'It was on the tip of my tongue to tell Mervyn that I had already read the book he had given me, but I stopped myself just in time.' (2) very nearly remembered. 'Her name was on the tip of my tongue just now; it will come back to me.' This use is almost always confined to the names of people or places.
4. **tongue-tied** – unable to speak through shyness or fear. 'The student stood tongue-tied in front of the examiners.'
5. **Have you lost your tongue?** – Why can't you speak? Addressed to someone who is speechless, silent.
6. to **find one's tongue** – to regain one's speech. 'Oh, you've found your tongue again, have you?'

## THROAT

7. to have a **lump in one's throat** – to feel sad, to be on the verge of tears. 'When I waved good-bye to Angela, I had a lump in my throat. I had grown very fond of her.'
8. to have **the words stick in one's throat** – to find it impossible to say the words, owing to dislike, pride or prejudice. 'I wanted to congratulate him, but I disliked him so much that the words stuck in my throat.'
9. to **force/ram down one's throat** – to force a belief or idea upon someone. 'It's a mistake to force your own ideas down his throat. He is old enough to think for himself.'
10. to **jump down one's throat** – to criticize someone for some trifling mistake, to speak sharply to. 'However carefully the student spoke, the teacher jumped down his throat.'
11. **at each other's throats** – deadly enemies, constantly fighting each other. 'The two brothers will never make peace; they have been at each other's throats for the last twenty years.'
12. to **slit one's throat** – to damage one's own interests. 'You would be slitting your throat if you reduced your prices still further.' It can also be used to express a strong negative attitude. 'I would rather slit my throat than work together with that rogue Maynard.'
13. **cut-throat competition** – ruthless competition by any method, fair or foul. 'You will find it difficult to open a shop in the High Street. There is a lot of cut-throat competition in this town.'

## CHEEK

14. **to give** someone **cheek / to cheek** someone – to show disrespect to anyone in authority, or senior. 'The girl gave cheek to the teacher.'

    to **have a cheek** – to be extremely disrespectful towards someone. 'He has a cheek. The minute we were introduced, he asked me for a loan.'
15. **the cheek of the devil** – uninhibited insolence. 'She has the cheek of the devil, asking her boss to post her letter for her.'
16. **none of your cheek** – don't be impertinent to me. 'Don't give me any of your cheek.'
17. to **turn the other cheek** – to submit to violence, not to resist the blows of one's oppressor. The charity of the

Christian ethic, which distinguishes it from many other religions. 'Resist not evil. Whoever shall smite thee on thy right cheek, turn to him the other also' (Matthew V.39).

1. **cheek by jowl with** – very close to one another.

CHIN

2. **'Chin up!'** – take courage, don't despair.
3. to **stick one's chin out** – to persist in one's own opinion, to defy other people's wishes. 'It was a stupid idea of the boss's, but I'm not going to stick my chin out.'
4. to **lead with one's chin** – to lay oneself open to a dangerous counter-attack when attacking an opponent. 'You were leading with your chin when you accused Williams of lying. You might have known he would say the same to you.' A boxer leads with the chin when he drops his guard as he moves forward.
5. to **take (it) on the chin** – to undergo a painful experience or punishment with courage. 'Rolf had a hard time when he was a recruit in the army but he took it all on the chin.'
6. to **have a chin-wag** – to have a talk or chat.

NECK

7. **neck and neck** – absolutely level. The phrase is taken from horse-racing.
8. **on the neck of** – immediately following.
9. to **get it in the neck** – to be severely punished.
10. **it's neck or nothing** – one must risk everything, one must gamble all on one throw.
11. to **stick one's neck out** – to make predictions which may be falsified by events.
12. to **chance one's neck** – to risk one's reputation by accepting responsibility, often when there is no need to. cf. 'to **chance one's arm' 91/17**.
13. to **break one's neck** – to be in a tremendous hurry. Used with such adverbs as almost, nearly, practically. 'You might have told me you weren't coming. I nearly broke my neck getting to the station in time to meet your train.'

    **at breakneck speed** – recklessly, dangerously fast.
14. to **save** someone's **neck** – to help someone out of a very unpleasant situation. 'If I hadn't taken the blame, you would have got the sack. This isn't the first time I have saved your neck.'
15. to **rubber-neck** – to listen to somebody else's conversation or read his newspaper over his shoulder.
16. to **breathe down someone's neck** (slang) – to supervise someone very closely. 'I would like the job much better if the boss wasn't breathing down my neck all the time.'
17. to be **up to one's neck in** something – to be deeply implicated in a crime or trouble. 'You knew very well what we were doing. You are in this up to your neck.'
18. **neck and crop** – entirely, the whole body. Nearly always used in connection with 'throwing out'. 'The man was ejected from the building, neck and crop.' cf. **'bag and baggage' 176/7**.
19. to **carry a millstone round one's neck** – to be burdened with a responsibility from which it is impossible to free oneself. 'My brother-in-law, who depends on us financially, has been a millstone round my neck ever since we married.'

1. to **come a cropper** – to fail disastrously. 'Even the most experienced businessman can come a cropper.' A hunting phrase meaning to fall heavily from a horse. The crop is the head.

## SHOULDER

2. to **carry/have on one's shoulders** – to bear responsibility for, to have to answer for. 'He had on his shoulders the whole burden of his father's debts.'
3. to **shoulder out** – to grab someone else's job.
4. to **shoulder the blame** – to accept full responsibility.
5. **straight from the shoulder** – frank, outspoken.
   to **give it** to someone **straight from the shoulder** – to tell someone the plain truth without sparing his feelings.
6. to **give** someone **the cold shoulder** – to treat someone with marked coldness, to ignore him in a noticeable manner. 'When I greeted Lucy this morning, she pretended not to see me. I wonder why she is giving me the cold shoulder.'
7. to **rub shoulders with** – to meet frequently, or to come into frequent contact with, a person.
8. to **have broad shoulders** – to be able to bear the full weight of one's responsibilities.
9. a **chip on the shoulder** – a grievance on one's mind which colours one's attitude to life. 'Steven has had a chip on the shoulder ever since he was thrown out of the army.'
10. to **put one's shoulder to the wheel** – to throw all one's energy into a task.
11. **a shoulder to cry on** – someone you can rely upon to offer sympathy and comfort in a time of sorrow or depression, a good friend. 'If you ever want a shoulder to cry on, you know where to come.'

## ARM

12. to receive/welcome **with open arms** – to accept/greet with great willingness, without any hesitation.
13. **at arm's length** – at a distance. 'Alan wanted to get to know Helen better, but she kept him at arm's length.'
14. to stand **with arms akimbo** – to stand with each fist on the hip bones, with the elbows pushed forward, a posture which may express shock or anger. The word 'akimbo' is derived from the Icelandic, 'Keng' ('into a crook') with the English doublet 'bow' unnecessarily added to it.
15. a **right arm** – the main supporter to whom one first turns for help when there is difficulty or trouble. 'Since Mother's death, Susan has been Father's right arm.'
16. **one would give one's right arm to . . .** – one would make a great sacrifice in order to . . . 'I would give my right arm to see Janet again.'
17. to **chance one's arm** – to take a big risk. cf. **'to chance one's neck'** which has much the same meaning **90/12**.
18. **with one arm tied behind one's back** – without the slightest difficulty, in spite of a huge disadvantage. 'Why, my man could beat yours with one arm tied behind his back!' Originally used of boxers. Now used to indicate a decisive superiority in any competitive situation.
19. **arm-twisting** – threatening, putting pressure on someone. 'After some arm-twisting by the management, the men withdrew their claim for a massive increase, for fear of the factory closing down.'

## ELBOW

1. **at one's elbow** – within very easy reach. 'I have all the books I want at my elbow.'
2. **elbow-room** – space in which to move. 'I haven't got any elbow-room in this tiny office.'
3. to **elbow one's way through** – to push opposition to one side.
4. to **give someone the elbow** – to get rid of someone. 'Hughes isn't worth his wages; it's time we gave him the elbow.'
5. **More power to your elbow!** – to wish someone success in what he is trying to do. 'Alan deserves a lot more money for the job he's doing. More power to his elbow.'
6. **elbow-grease** (colloquial) – energy, industry and sweat.
7. to be **out at elbows** – shabby, poorly dressed; sometimes used with 'down at heel', to describe someone whose clothes are patched or torn.
8. to **lift the elbow** – to be a habitual drinker. 'Have you noticed? Peter lifts the elbow!'

## WRIST

9. a **slap on the wrist** – a mild, ineffective punishment.

   **wrist-slap diplomacy** – a punishment inflicted by one government on another, which is too small and ineffective to serve any useful purpose. Diplomatic illnesses and cancellations of state visits both come into this category.

## HAND

10. to be **a great hand at** something – skilful; generally used in an ironic sense. 'He is a great hand at giving advice, but when it comes to doing some work, he is not so good.'
11. a **dab hand** – to be clever at doing something, often something of a practical nature. 'Why don't you let me decorate your sitting-room for you; I'm a dab hand at decorating.'
12. a **free hand** – complete freedom, without any interference or restriction. 'My husband has given me a free hand as to how I bring the children up.'
13. an **old hand** – experienced, skilful. 'He'll finish the fence for you very quickly. He is an old hand at that kind of work.'
14. to be **even-handed** – to be fair, unbiased, equally critical of both parties to a dispute.
15. to be **high-handed** – to be tyrannical, unwilling to listen to reason.
16. to **give** someone **the glad hand** – to give a warm and friendly welcome to someone. An Americanism.
17. to be **under-handed** – to be unfair, dishonourable. 'That was an under-handed trick he played on you, telling you your friends were at the airport waiting for you, when they were not.'
18. to **come away empty-handed** – to return with nothing to show for one's efforts. 'He went on a business trip to Rome and came back empty-handed.'
19. to be **short-handed** – to be short of assistance. 'We are very short-handed just now. Three of our staff are ill.'
20. a **handful** – a person who is always up to some mischief, in need of strict supervision. 'Their small son was quite a handful while they were on holiday.'
21. to **have one's hands full** – to be fully occupied, to be unable to accept any fresh work. 'I have my hands full running the business, so I've had to resign from the village council.'
22. to **have only one pair of hands** – to be incapable of working any faster. 'I can't look after the children and cook

the dinner at the same time; I've only got one pair of hands.'

1. to be **tied/bound hand and foot** – to have obligations which severely restrict one's freedom. 'I'd love to take a holiday with you but I'm tied hand and foot to my business.'

   to **have one's hands tied** – similar in meaning to the above, but a little less emphatic. 'I'm not allowed to advance you any money without your father's permission. I'm sorry I can't oblige you, but my hands are tied.'

2. **hands off** – do not interfere.
3. a **cool hand** – someone with good nerves, calm, not easily flustered. 'When the staff walked out, the boss sat down and lit a cigar. He's a cool hand all right.'
4. **with an open hand** – generously. 'Whenever we asked Mr Jones for money for the charity, he responded with an open hand.'
5. **with a heavy hand** – severely, oppressively. 'We were brought up with a heavy hand. None of us dared contradict our parents.'
6. to **hold a good hand / a bad hand** – to hold good cards / bad cards. 'You dealt me a good hand, but Martin has had one bad hand after another.'
7. one's **right-hand man** – someone's principal support and adviser.
8. a **left-handed compliment** – an apparent compliment which is really just the opposite. '"Your sister is very well preserved, isn't she? She doesn't look a day over forty." "My sister is thirty-five!"'
9. **close at hand** – within easy reach. 'If you need help, we are always close at hand.'
10. **at first hand** – direct from the person concerned and not from someone else. 'I got the news at first hand, so I know it's true.'
11. **at second hand** – indirectly, from somebody not immediately concerned. 'I have only received the news second hand, so it may not be reliable.'
12. **second hand** – sold for the second time, no longer new, having been used already.
13. to **have/hold the whip hand** – to have someone in one's power.
14. to have **clean hands** – to be above reproach. 'He who seeks equity must come to court with clean hands' (a legal maxim).
15. **when the left hand doesn't know what the right hand is doing** – when the activities of an organization are not properly co-ordinated and, as a result, there is confusion. 'My offer was accepted by the director but refused by the manager. The left hand of Vernon's doesn't know what the right hand is doing.'
16. to **soil/dirty one's hands** – to do something dishonest or shameful. 'I wouldn't soil my hands doing business with that firm; they are cheating the public.'
17. to **give a slow handclap to** – to show one's disapproval of a public speaker.
18. a **backhander** – (1) a sudden surprise blow given with the back of the hand; which can also be used metaphorically; (2) a bribe.
19. to **hand it to someone** – to give someone credit for something he has done. 'I'm sorry Philip has failed his examination again, but you've got to hand it to him for trying.'

    **'I've got to hand it to you'** – I must congratulate you.

20. to **work hand in hand** – to work together in close agreement.
21. to **make a poor hand at** – to work unskilfully at something. 'I should make a poor hand at doing your job. Book-keeping is not in my line.'

1. **with a strong hand** – firmly, vigorously, severely. 'The officer dealt with the man's insubordination with a strong hand.'
2. to **gain the upper hand** – to obtain a decisive advantage over someone, to master him. 'He was much stronger than his opponent and soon gained the upper hand.'
3. to **accept with both hands** – to accept most eagerly. 'If I'd been in your place, I'd have accepted his offer with both hands. You won't get a better one.'
4. to **join hands** – to unite with, work together with. 'We must join hands with our friends in Europe.'
5. to **go down on one's hands and knees** – to beg most humbly. 'I won't go down on my hands and knees to him, no matter how important he is.'
6. a **hand-out** (colloquial) – a free distribution of money, goods, etc., which may amount to bribery. 'When Lewis was leader of the local Council, there were plenty of hand-outs to his friends.'
7. to **hand down** – to bequeath, as a rule from one generation to the next. 'That gold watch has been handed down to us from our great-grandfather.'
8. to **have in hand** – (1) to put money on one side, or in reserve, usually for a special purpose. 'I have £300 in hand, in case the job works out dearer than they estimated.' (2) to attend to a job. 'We have the matter in hand and will inform you as soon as the work has been completed.'
9. to **get** something **in hand** – to have under control. 'I am making the holiday arrangements now, so you needn't worry. I have got everything in hand.'
10. to be **out of hand** – (1) to be undisciplined, out of control, ill-behaved. 'When his son was in Paris, the boy got out of hand and ran up big gambling debts.' (2) without any discussion. 'He refused the offer out of hand, and broke off negotiations.'
11. to **take in hand** – to take control of someone, usually for some particular purpose. 'He is ten kilos overweight. The dietician is taking him in hand.'
12. to **get one's hand in** – to regain one's skill. 'After a couple of games, you'll soon get your hand in.'
13. **off-hand** – (1) without referring to one's notes or records. 'I can't tell you off-hand, but, as soon as I get back to the office, I'll telephone you.' (2) casual, lacking in respect. 'She was off-hand with me, and went on with her housework while I was speaking.'
14. to be **in one's hands** – to be under one's control, to be one's own responsibility. 'It is in your hands now whether or not you succeed. I can't help you any more.'
15. to **have on one's hands** – to have a responsibility to attend to, often an irksome one. 'I shall have their boy on my hands all through his summer holidays.'
16. to have something **taken off one's hands** – to be relieved of an irksome responsibility. 'I am grateful to you for taking Judy off my hands. She was getting too much for me.'
17. to **raise/lift one's hand to** – to strike. 'I've never raised my hand to him, but one day I shall if he goes on like this!' cf. **'to lay hands on' 95/10**.
18. **hand-to-hand fighting** – fighting at close quarters with the enemy, with bayonets, knives or even fists.
19. to be **behindhand** – to be late in paying a debt or in completing a task. '"You've got badly behindhand with the work!" "Yes, we've had a lot of orders this month, and we can't keep up with the work."'

1. to **keep one's hand in** – to retain one's skill by practising. 'Mike keeps his hand in during the winter on the indoor tennis courts.'
2. to **have a hand in** something – to play a part in something, bear some of the responsibility for. This is often used in reference to something illicit. 'I suspect he has had a hand in the robbery, although I can't prove it.'
3. to **show one's hand** – to make one's intentions clear. 'When I asked Digby if he was planning to take over our company, he pretended to be very surprised. He doesn't want to show his hand yet.' The idiom comes from card-playing, e.g. from bridge in which it is important for the players not to show their cards during the bidding.
4. to **try one's hand** – to see how well one can do in an activity, instead of just watching others. 'Why don't you try your hand at weaving? You might do just as well as us.'
5. to **shake hands on it** – to signify one's assent to an agreement.
6. to **wash one's hands of** something – to absolve oneself from responsibility. 'That boy is quite impossible. From now on I wash my hands of him!' The allusion is to Pontius Pilate who washed his hands in a bowl of water in order to show that they were innocent of the blood of Jesus Christ (Matthew XXVII, 24).
7. to have **blood on one's hands** – to be responsible for the injury or death of a person. 'I don't think we should stop the surgeon operating; we don't want the patient's blood on our hands.'
8. to **sit on one's hands** – to wait passively, without doing anything.
9. to **win hands down** – to win very easily, by a large margin.
10. to **lay hands on** – to strike. 'If you lay hands on me, I will charge you with assault.' cf. 'to **raise/lift one's hand to**' **94/17**.

    to **lay hands on** also has two negative meanings: (1) to seize, arrest. 'The police have not yet laid hands on the wanted man.' (2) to find an object that has been mislaid. 'I know it's somewhere in the office, but I can't lay my hands on it.'
11. to **give a hand** with – to help, usually for only a short time. 'Please give me a hand with the suitcase. It's rather heavy.'
12. to **hold one's hand** – to refrain from taking any action, on receiving certain assurances. 'If you undertake to pay us by Tuesday, we will hold our hand.'
13. to **throw in one's hand** – to yield, to stop trying. 'When he was told that his men had called a strike, Fison threw in his hand and closed the factory.' From card-playing, when a player who had been dealt a bad hand threw his cards on the table and stopped playing.
14. to be **on one's hands** (commercial) – to be lying in the shop unsold. 'The antique furniture is still on our hands, we just cannot get rid of it.'
15. to **play into** someone's **hands** – to use the tactics which most benefit one's opponent/enemy. 'You should never have confided your business troubles to your competitors. Now they can make matters worse for you. You have played into their hands.'
16. to **overplay one's hand** – to press one's advantage too far. The phrase is derived from games of cards where a player with good cards bids or calls higher than the hand justifies.
17. to **turn one's hand to** – to turn one's attention to, to apply oneself to, to attempt. 'Everything your father turns his hand to, he does well.'
18. to **force** someone's **hand** – to bring pressure to bear on someone. 'I didn't

want to mention your name but, by going to the police, they forced my hand.'

1. to **stir a hand** – to help, make an effort. 'It's time you stirred a hand!'
2. to **be caught with one's hand/fingers in the till** – to be caught stealing from one's employer. 'You would think I had been caught with my hand in the till from the way my boss talks to me.'
3. **Hand on heart / Cross my heart and let me die** – I promise you, I am telling you the truth. 'I didn't smoke one cigarette while you were out. Hand on heart!'
4. **hand over fist** – (1) very rapidly. 'My son is very bright. He is making progress hand over fist.' (2) to make money very fast. 'Since Andrew started his own business, he has been making money hand over fist.' The phrase has probably been taken from rope-climbing, when the free hand is passed over and above the fist that is holding the rope.
5. to **wait on** someone **hand and foot** – to serve somebody with complete dedication. 'I was waited on hand and foot; I only had to ring a bell and a servant came to my room in a few seconds.'
6. to live **from hand to mouth** – to make only enough money to supply one's immediate needs, not to know where one's future income is coming from. 'I'm sick of this hand-to-mouth existence; I think I'll look for a regular job.'
7. to **bite the hand that feeds you** – to injure the person on whom you depend for your living. 'You shouldn't have criticized your father in front of his guests. You were biting the hand that feeds you!' (Edmund Burke, *Thought and Details on Scarcity*, 1800).
8. to **eat out of** someone's **hand** – to submit willingly to someone's wishes, to do anything to please someone. 'After our talk, Mary was eating out of my hands.' A tame animal will eat from its keeper's hand.
9. a **show of hands** – the taking of a vote by asking all those present who are in favour of a proposal to raise their hands.
10. **sleight of hand** – skilful trickery (often used humorously). 'With a sleight of hand, the Prime Minister was able to persuade the workers that they had won a victory over the employers, and the employers that they had got the better of the workers.' Literally, the clever use of the hands in conjuring and juggling.
11. to **know a place like the back/palm of one's hand** – to know a place intimately. 'I know London like the back of my hand.'
12. **all hands to the pumps** – Please help, everyone. It's urgent!
13. to be **man-handled** – to be moved by physical force. 'When I called for the money at Pearson's home, I was manhandled by his servants and thrown out of the house.'
14. to have **time hanging on one's hands** – to be in a state of boredom, when time passes slowly. 'Time hung heavy on the hotelier's hands in the winter when the tourists went home and her children were at boarding school.'
15. to **take one's life in one's hands** – to risk losing one's life. 'If you let him drive you there, you will be taking your life in your hands. He is the worst driver I've ever met.'
16. **with an iron hand** – with great severity. 'The leader crushed the rebellion with an iron hand.' cf. 'an **iron hand in a velvet glove' 172/10**.
17. to be **in good hands** – to be well looked after. 'If your mother goes to the Lavington Sanatorium, she will be in

good hands; the doctors and nurses there are really good.'

PALM

1. to **palm** someone **off with / be palmed off with** – to be offered something inferior. Usually used in a negative sense. 'They made me a much better offer to start with, so I'm not going to be palmed off with such a rotten job now.'
2. to **have** someone **in the palm of one's hand** – to have someone completely in one's power. A somewhat melodramatic expression.
3. to **grease** someone's **palm** – to bribe. Often used in connection with the bribing of minor officials.

   **palm oil** (colloquial) – money used for bribery, on the analogy of greasing the palms.

   to have an **itching palm** – to accept bribes eagerly. 'In that country the officials all have itching palms; they are only too anxious to take bribes.'

FIST

4. to **make a good fist of** – to write well about. 'Graham made a good fist of his Life of Henry VIII.'
5. to **be close-fisted** – to be miserly, stingy, mean. The term expresses a person's reluctance to open his fist and let go of the money he is holding.

THUMB

6. to have someone **under one's thumb** – to dominate, or domineer over. 'She has her son completely under her thumb. He would never dare contradict or disobey her.'
7. **rule of thumb** – a rough, practical calculation made without the benefit of theoretical knowledge or scientific measuring instruments. 'Although his methods are more or less rule of thumb, he gets excellent results.'
8. to **give the thumbs down** – to veto a plan or course of action. 'After consulting together for an hour, the Committee gave the thumbs down to the young architect's proposals.' The 'thumbs down' derives from the Roman Emperor Nero who gave the 'thumbs down' signal at the Colosseum when he wanted a defeated gladiator slain.
9. to **give the thumbs up** – a sign indicating a positive answer, good news or approval of a person or scheme. 'When I asked the young man whether he had enjoyed his evening with Jenny, he smiled and gave me the thumbs-up sign.'
10. to **thumb a lift / thumb one's way** – to ask for a lift from a vehicle driver.
11. to **twiddle one's thumbs** – to be idle, to have nothing to do. 'We had to twiddle our thumbs for an hour while Helen was getting dressed.'
12. to **stick out like a sore thumb** – to be conspicuous on account of some odd or peculiar feature. 'Why did you have to paint your house that colour? It sticks out from the others like a sore thumb.' cf. 'an **eye-sore' 128/6**.
13. to **thumb through** (the pages of a book) – to turn the pages of a book, usually without reading properly, but out of curiosity.
14. a **thumb-nail sketch** – a very abbreviated or miniature sketch – so small that it can be done on a thumb nail. 'The novelist only gave a thumb-nail sketch of his characters, as he thought their actions were more revealing than mere description of their appearance.'
15. to be **all thumbs / all fingers and**

**thumbs** – to be clumsy, as if each finger were a thumb, which would result in a loss of dexterity. 'I can't thread this needle; I am all thumbs today.'

## FINGER

1. to be **light-fingered** – to have a strong inclination to steal whenever the opportunity arises.
2. to **have money stick to one's fingers** – to wrongly keep money that belongs to someone else.
3. to **burn one's fingers** – to suffer the consequences of some error of judgement. 'I burned my fingers badly by investing money in your friend's company. I shan't make that mistake again.'
4. to **twist** someone **round one's little finger** – to know how to impose one's will over someone, or to have a strong influence on someone.
5. to have **at one's fingertips** – to be an expert in a subject, to know a subject to perfection. 'He has parliamentary procedure and the rules and traditions of the House of Commons at his fingertips.'
6. **to one's fingertips** – in every respect, completely. 'Evans never made a decision without consulting his book of rules first; he was a bureaucrat to his fingertips.'
7. to **keep one's fingers crossed** – to hope and pray for success. 'Good luck with your driving test; I'll keep my fingers crossed for you.' Making the sign of the cross – in this case with the fingers – was believed to preserve one from bad luck. Today, the phrase is only used light-heartedly.
8. **'I can't put my finger on it but . . .'** – I have a feeling that something is wrong, without knowing exactly what it is.
9. to **work one's fingers to the bone** – to work until one is exhausted.
10. to **slip through one's fingers** – to miss a good opportunity. 'I took too long making up my mind, and let the house slip through my fingers.'
11. to **snap one's fingers at** – to show contempt for a person or institution.
12. to **point the finger at** – to blame a person/organization for a blunder or crime. 'The finger has been pointed at the Government for the high level of unemployment.'
13. to **be able to count on the fingers / on the fingers of one hand** – to emphasize the smallness of a number by counting it on the fingers / fingers of one hand. 'You could count on the fingers of one hand the number of times old Westwood arrived late at the office during the thirty years he worked for the firm.'
14. to **lay a finger on** – to hurt or harm. 'If you lay a finger on the child, you will regret it.'
15. a **two-fingered gesture** – a rude gesture indicating contempt. The gesture is made with the palm of the hand facing inwards. Contrast the V-sign, which is made with two fingers but with the palm facing outwards.
16. to **put the finger on** – to determine or diagnose the cause. 'You've put your finger on it: too many late nights and parties. That's no way to prepare for an examination!'
17. **not to lift a finger** – to refuse to do the least thing to help. 'All the time we were staying there, the girl didn't lift a finger to help her mother.'
18. **pull/take your finger out** – get on with the job. 'Prince Philip appealed to British industry to pull its finger out.' The complete phrase is 'pull/take your finger out and get stuck in' (a naval phrase).

1. to **have more** (of something) **in one's little finger than someone else has in his whole body** – to be greatly superior in one quality (such as intelligence, knowledge, skill, ability, talent) to another person. 'Mary has more talent in her little finger than you have in your whole body, which isn't saying much!' Often said in the heat of an argument.

QUICK

2. to **cut to the quick** – to hurt someone's feelings very deeply. 'Robert was cut to the quick when his wife told him that she didn't want to go abroad with him.' The quick is the sensitive part of the flesh beneath the fingernail.

KNUCKLE

3. **too close to the knuckle** – too realistic for comfort, embarrassing. 'Genet's plays are too close to the knuckle to be entertaining.'
4. to **knuckle down** – to accept discipline.
5. to **knuckle under** – to submit to authority. The phrase suggests that the submission is unwilling.
6. to give someone a **rap on the knuckles** – to reprimand someone severely. 'He was given a rap on the knuckles for his bad work.' The person who gives the rap is always in a position or rank of superiority. This phrase is often abbreviated to **'take the rap'**, with the same meaning: 'Why should I take the rap for you?'

CHEST

7. to **play one's hand/cards close to one's chest** – to be secretive about one's plans. 'I know he is up to something, but he is playing his cards very close to his chest.' cf. 'to **keep one's own counsel' 230/15.**
8. to **get something off one's chest** – to talk freely about something one has concealed. 'It's been on my conscience for a long time but, now I've got it off my chest, I feel a lot better.'

BREAST

9. to **make a clean breast of** the matter – to make a full and complete confession. 'If you have stolen the money, you had better make a clean breast of it to your boss at once.'
10. to **beat one's breast** – to show remorse for one's mistakes. 'No wonder Peter is beating his breast; if he had remembered to post his coupon, he would have won the football pools.'

BOSOM

11. **bosom friends** – very close friends who confide all their secrets to each other (applicable to either sex). 'The two girls were bosom friends and kept nothing back from each other.'
12. to be **in the bosom of one's family** – to live with one's family, surrounded by one's parents and brothers and sisters.

BELLY

13. to **have a bellyful** – to be exasperated beyond endurance. cf. 'to **be fed up to the teeth / back teeth' 87/18**, and 'to **have a basinful' 155/13**.
14. a **pot-belly** – a large, protruding stomach. 'If you drink so much beer every day, you will get a pot-belly.'
15. a **belly-dance** – a dance in which the dancers rotate their hips in the manner of Hawaiian dancing girls.

## LAP

1. to **drop into someone's lap** – to acquire something easily, without the least effort. 'All the best things in life must be worked for – love, friendship, success . . . they won't drop into your lap.'
2. to live **in the lap of luxury** – to live in a state of great comfort and ease, having all one's material needs supplied without having to make any effort.
3. **in the lap of the gods** – completely unpredictable. 'I have no idea whether we shall win or not. It's in the lap of the gods.'

## BACK

4. to **back** – to support, morally, politically or financially; to show confidence in, to put one's money on. 'Peter is stronger than Alex and moves faster in the ring. I am backing him to win.'

   to **back a horse** – to wager money on a horse.
5. to **back up** – to give one's support to a person under attack or involved in a quarrel. 'Why didn't you back me up when they insulted me?'
6. to **back out of** – to withdraw from a promise or undertaking. Backing out is not so abrupt or decisive as the synonym 'breaking a promise'. Backing out often suggests a reluctant change of mind, accompanied by excuses and explanations. 'When he heard how much the scheme was going to cost, he backed out rather than pay the extra money.'
7. to **back down** – to yield, withdraw a demand. 'When I told him he could sue me if he wasn't satisfied, he backed down at once, pretending he hadn't been serious.'
8. a **back-up service** (commercial) – visiting a customer to check that the equipment sold him is working properly. 'This firm provided a back-up service free of charge.'
9. to **hold back** – to suppress or withhold news or information, to withhold support.
10. to **hang back** – to hesitate, remain passive when action is called for. 'When she was mugged in the street, her companions hung back because they were afraid of the robbers.'
11. to **give one's (full) backing** – to give one's (full) support to a person or a plan of action.
12. to **backfire** – to injure the author of a scheme instead of its intended victim. 'Your plan could backfire if the authorities get to hear of it.'
13. a **backlash** – a strong reaction to excessive provocation. 'If the judges continue handing out these ridiculously light sentences, there could be a nasty backlash from the public and people will take the law into their own hands.'
14. **Get off my back!** – Leave me alone! Stop making demands on me!
15. **behind one's back / when one's back is turned** – in a person's absence, without his knowledge. 'Christine has been saying some very nasty things about you behind your back, George.'
16. to **get one's own back** on someone – to revenge oneself on someone. 'I mean to get my own back for the injury he has done me, even if it takes me ten years.'
17. to **get** someone's **back up** – to provoke someone to anger. 'You really got his back up with your criticisms of his house.' From the idea of a cat being threatened by a dog, when the cat arches its back to show its anger.
18. the **backbone** – the main support. 'He has been the backbone of the team for the whole of the season.'

1. to **have no backbone** – to lack strength of purpose, to be morally submissive. 'That boy has no backbone. He gives in to the slightest opposition.'
2. **to the backbone** – completely, absolutely, without any question. 'She was a Tory to the backbone.'
3. **broken-backed** – damaged, lacking the ability or means to survive. 'It's been a broken-backed business ever since it lost its major customer.'
4. to **break the back of** a task – to finish the hardest part of a task. 'By the time his brother arrived, they had broken the back of the work, and there was little left for him to do.'
5. to **break one's back** – to exhaust oneself with overwork. 'I have broken my back trying to keep this business going, but I couldn't go on any longer.' cf. **'to work oneself to death' 42/5**.
6. to **stab in the back** – a forceful phrase for betrayal, indicating the indignation of the victim. 'He has been my best friend for the last twenty years. I would never have dreamed he would stab me in the back like that.'
7. **with one's back to the wall** – in a desperately dangerous situation from which there is no escape. On 18 April 1918, Field Marshal Haig gave this famous order to the Allied forces: 'With our backs to the wall and believing in the justice of our cause, each one must fight on to the end.'
8. to **make a rod for one's own back** – to create difficulties for oneself. 'Why did the silly man argue with the magistrate? He made a rod for his own back.'
9. to be **glad to see the back of** someone – to be glad to see the last of someone.
10. to have **a good background** / to have **no background** – to be from a good/poor family. 'I don't want her to marry Steven. He has no background.'
11. to **have a broad back** – to be willing to accept responsibility for other people's mistakes. 'Put all the blame on me if it makes you feel better. I have a broad back.'
12. **backscratching / you scratch my back and I'll scratch yours** – you praise me and I'll praise you; you help me and I'll help you.
13. to give someone a **pat on the back** – to praise or applaud, to congratulate, often in a mild manner. 'Although his plan had not completely succeeded, she gave him a pat on the back for having tried so hard.'
14. to **put one's back into** – to put all one's energy into a task.
15. to **back the field** – a betting phrase for wagering one's money against one particular horse – usually the favourite.
16. **the back of beyond** – a remote, inaccessible place. 'I wish you didn't live in the back of beyond.'
17. to **be backward** – (1) a slow learner, a slow developer. Often used in the phrase 'dull and backward'. 'He is thirteen years old, and they have put him in a class with ten-year-olds. His teacher tells me he is very backward for his age.' (2) the term can also be applied to a country or race. 'The villagers live in abject poverty and are very backward in their ways. Few of them can read or write.'

## BOTTOM

18. to **knock the bottom out of** an argument – to prove the falsity of an argument, to refute an argument. 'Pauline knocked the bottom out of our argument in a short but effective speech.'

## HIP

19. to have **one on the hip** – to gain a decisive advantage over one's opponent. A wrestling term.

1. to **smite hip and thigh** – a biblical phrase, meaning to make a merciless attack on the enemy.

LEG

2. **not a leg to stand on** – without any reasonable justification in a dispute, without the semblance of a case. 'Mark accused the doctor of negligence, but when he admitted he hadn't taken the medicine prescribed, he hadn't a leg to stand on.'
3. to be **on one's/its last legs** – to be on the point of collapse, worn out. 'Mr Jones hasn't enough money left to renew his stock; his business is on its last legs.'
4. a **leg-up** – a helping hand. 'He gave me a leg-up when I was starting work by introducing me to some new customers.'
5. to **stretch one's legs** – to take exercise by walking about after a period of inactivity. 'We've been sitting here all the morning. It's time we stretched our legs.'
6. to **pull someone's leg** – to play a joke on someone, to tell him some misleading story that momentarily shocks or frightens him but which amuses everybody else.

   a **leg-pull** – a joke or untrue story with the same meaning as above.
7. to **leg it** – (1) to run away, (2) to walk when other means of transport have failed.
8. to **shake a leg** – to take part in a dance.
9. to **show a leg** – to get up and be quick about it. 'If you want to catch your coach, you had better show a leg.' 'Show a leg!' is a naval order which dates from the days when sailors were allowed to have their wives on board ship with them. The order was given in order to distinguish between the sailors who had to get up and the women who were allowed to lie in.
10. to **be bow-legged** – to have one's legs bent outwards so that there is a big space between them. The opposite of 'knock-knees'.

KNEE

11. **on one's knees** – in a position of submission.
12. to **bend the knee** – to submit to a stronger force, to obey submissively.

    **on one's bended knees** – in a position of abject submission. 'My husband treated me so badly during our marriage that I wouldn't have him back if he came to me on his bended knees.'
13. to **bring to his/its knees** – to defeat or force to submit. 'The recession has brought our company to its knees.'
14. a **knee-jerk reaction** – an unthinking, automatic response. 'We got the usual knee-jerk reaction to our request for a rise in our salaries.' When the knee is tapped below the joint, it kicks involuntarily; this is known as the knee-jerk reflex.
15. **weak-kneed** – someone who is unable to resist pressure. 'He was so weak-kneed that he allowed the man to ransack his flat, although he was twice as big as the burglar.'

FOOT

16. **My foot!** – a comment expressing disbelief. 'Paul's too weak to carry his suitcase upstairs! Too weak, my foot! He's twice as strong as I was at his age.'
17. to **put one's foot in it** – to cause embarrassment with a tactless remark. 'You put your foot in it when you told her how much you admired her husband. They were divorced last year!'

1. to **put one's foot down** – to impose one's authority, to call a halt to some action of which one disapproves. 'When his eighteen-year-old son wanted to start a business with his girl-friend, his father put his foot down and told him he wouldn't allow it.'

2. to have **a foot in both camps** – to have an interest in supporting both parties in a contest. 'Sooner or later, you'll have to choose between Labour and the Conservatives; you can't have a foot in both camps indefinitely.'

   to **have/get a foot in the door** – to have/gain access to a business, market, occupation, etc., in spite of opposition. 'Now we've got a foot in the door, we are hoping to open up a big market in China.' The commercial traveller puts his foot in the door to prevent the housewife from shutting it in his face, so that he can persuade her to buy his merchandise.

3. to **set on foot** – to initiate, to get things moving. 'The mothers of the district intend to set on foot plans for opening a kindergarten.'

4. to **start on the wrong foot** – to make a mistake at the very beginning (of a relationship). 'You started on the wrong foot, asking the boss for a week's leave only a few days after you had joined.' The reference is to starting to march with the right foot instead of the left.

5. to **put a foot wrong** – to make a mistake, to break the rules. 'Since Alan came out of prison, he hasn't put a foot wrong.'

6. to **wrong-foot** someone – to put someone at a disadvantage in a contest, to surprise him. 'Mr Jukes wrong-footed us by calling our manager as a witness. We hadn't expected him to do that.'

   to **catch** someone **on the wrong foot** – to take advantage of an opponent's mistake.

7. to be **on a friendly / good footing** – to enjoy a friendly relationship with someone.

   **on a firm footing** – on a solid foundation. 'We have put our business with Phillips on a firm footing.'

8. to be **light-footed** – to be nimble, light on one's toes. 'Although he is such a fat man, he is light-footed when he dances.'

9. **footloose and fancy free** – unattached, free of romantic ties.

10. to put one's **best foot forward** – to walk briskly, to walk faster, to hurry. Usually with the meaning of reaching a place by a particular time. 'If you want to catch your train, you'll have to put your best foot forward.'

11. to **follow in** someone's **footsteps** – to do the same as he. 'So, young man, you are going to follow in your father's footsteps and be a doctor!'

12. to **foot the bill** – to pay someone else's bill. 'Mr Brown had to foot the bill for his son's drunken escapades.' So called because the person called upon to pay was required to sign his name at the foot of the bill.

13. to **trample/tread underfoot** – to beat down all opposition, to crush the body and the spirit of one's enemy.

14. **with one foot in the grave** – so old or ill that one is on the point of dying. 'With one foot in the grave, I am afraid he is in no position to help you.'

## FEET

15. to **be on one's feet** – to stand, to be standing. The phrase is often used to emphasize the length of time the subject has been standing. 'The medical students have been on their feet all day long in the operating theatre.'

16. to **set** someone **on his feet** – to give someone a fresh start, to help him over his difficulties.

1. to **fall/land on one's feet** – to adjust oneself to new conditions (after a setback) with unexpected success. 'No sooner had he lost his job than he obtained another at twice the salary. He always falls on his feet.'
2. to **find one's feet** – to get adjusted, to settle down. 'The boy soon found his feet at his new school.'
3. to **drag one's feet** – to show reluctance. 'It's over a month since Hughes had the contract, but he hasn't signed it yet. I wonder why he is dragging his feet.'
4. to **walk someone off his feet/legs** – to walk a long way with a companion until he is exhausted. 'Whenever we go out together, Alan walks me off my feet.'
5. to be **rushed off one's feet** – to have so many claims on one's time that everything has to be done in a great hurry.
6. to **sweep off one's feet** – to make a swift conquest. 'She was so captivated with his good looks that he swept her off her feet within a few minutes of meeting her.'
7. to **get back on one's feet** – to make a full recovery, to become adjusted again. 'Once you've got back on your feet, you will feel quite differently about your work.' The idiom is often used in the sense of recovering from the effects of an illness.
8. to cast oneself **at** someone's **feet** – to throw oneself on the mercy of another, to submit to another person's will.
9. to have/get **cold feet** – to feel afraid to commit oneself to a decision or action which may prove risky or dangerous. 'Simon is getting cold feet about advancing you the money, now that your firm is in difficulties.'
10. to have **feet of clay** – to have an insecure base. The phrase is often used in reference to men or governments of seemingly great power which conceals some fatal weakness. Origin: biblical, Daniel II, 31–45. cf. **'Achilles' heel' 195/8**, 'a **glass jaw' 86/9**, 'a **chink in one's armour' 210/7**.
11. **under someone's feet** – in the way, obstructing one's movements. 'I can't cook the lunch with you under my feet all the time.'
12. to **have one's feet under the table** – to have a friend in whose home one is made welcome. cf. **'to hang up one's hat in a house' 173/12**.
13. to **cut the ground from under one's feet** – to take an opponent by surprise by suddenly depriving him of his advantage. 'When Nancy's father complained about the teaching at the school, the headmaster cut the ground from under his feet by announcing that Nancy had won a scholarship at Marlborough College.' cf. 'to **pull the rug from under one's feet' 152/5**, 'to **take the wind out of** someone's **sails' 30/13**.
14. to **stand on one's own (two) feet** – to be independent, self-reliant, in an economic or emotional sense. 'My son must get a job and learn to stand on his own two feet.'
15. to **put one's feet up / take the weight off one's feet** – to sit down and rest. Often said to a guest who has arrived after a tiring journey.
16. to **sit at a person's feet** – to listen with respect to an intellectual authority. 'We all admired Professor Stanton for his original thinking and sat at his feet when we were at the university.'
17. to **vote with one's feet** – to show one's dissatisfaction with one's country by leaving it instead of voting for better conditions. 'In the last twenty years, tens of thousands of people have voted with their feet in the hope of finding a better life elsewhere.'

1. to **think on one's feet** – the ability to speak in public, and to respond quickly to unexpected questions.

2. to **keep one's feet** – to avoid falling. 'After three glasses of whisky, he found it difficult to keep his feet.'

3. **with both feet on the ground / to have one's feet planted firmly on the ground** – free from fanciful, impractical ideas; sensible and practical. 'Margaret won't get carried away by a lot of silly notions; she has both feet on the ground.'

## HEEL

4. to be **down-at-heel** – to be shabbily dressed. Sometimes the phrase is combined with **'out at elbows'**. 'I found my friend sadly changed for the worse; he was down-at-heel and out-at-elbows.'

5. **well heeled** (derisive) – well paid. 'His henchmen were all well heeled.' The original meaning was 'well-armed'. The phrase is taken from cock-fighting, when cocks were fitted with metal spurs or 'heels'.

6. to **dig one's heels in** – to resist a request by all the means at one's disposal. 'When the parents told the headmaster they had decided to send their daughter to another school and demanded a refund of the fees, he dug his heels in and refused point blank.'

7. to **kick up one's heels** – to enjoy one's newly gained freedom. 'When the teachers at our school went on strike and walked out of the class-rooms, we kicked up our heels with joy.'

8. to **lay by the heel** – to arrest and subdue. The reference is to 'laying by the ankles' of petty criminals in the stocks in the Middle Ages.

9. to **come to heel** – to obey, to submit after being disciplined. 'Once I have talked to them, they will come to heel quickly enough. They will soon learn who is the master here!' From the command given to a dog to rejoin his master.

10. to **tread on the heels of / follow upon the heels of** – to follow close behind. 'The recession trod on the heels of the oil crisis.'

    to **be hard on** someone's **heels** – to walk close behind someone.

11. to **show a clean pair of heels** – to remove oneself from the scene as quickly as possible. 'As soon as I asked them for money, they showed a clean pair of heels!'

    to **take to one's heels** – to run away.

12. to **turn on one's heel** – to turn round abruptly.

13. to **kick/cool one's heels** – to be kept waiting a long time. 'I had to kick my heels outside his office for an hour.'

## TOE

14. a **toe-hold** – a small and precarious entry, often used in a business sense. 'He gained a toe-hold in Japan, but it will take him some time to consolidate his position.'

15. to **toe the line** – to obey the rules and regulations. The phrase implies that the person 'toeing the line' is being pressured, against his will. 'Unless he toes the line, he will be expelled from the party.'

16. to **tread on** someone's **toes** – to offend someone with a tactless remark. 'You trod on his toes when you told him his novel was very promising. He has been five years writing it!'

17. to **keep** someone **on his toes** – to keep someone alert and attentive. 'The sergeant-major kept the recruits on their toes by continually firing orders at them.'

18. to **go/walk on tip-toe / to tip-toe** – to

walk on the tips of the toes. 'When their mother was ill, the children tiptoed up and down the stairs so as not to wake her.'

## BRAIN

1. to have the **brain of a pigeon** (colloquial) – to be quite brainless. Pigeons are supposed to have a very small brain.
2. **hare-brained** – wild, mad.
   a **hare-brained scheme** – a wild, mad scheme.
3. to **be scatterbrained** – to be careless and disorganized. 'I hope he won't forget the theatre tickets. He is so scatterbrained.'
4. a **brainwave** – a sudden insight into a problem, a flash of inspiration. 'She didn't know what to wear at the fancy-dress ball. Then she had a brainwave; she put on her oldest clothes, smeared some soot on her face and went as Cinderella.'
5. **a brainstorm** – a violent reaction with loss of emotional control. 'When he was told that all his possessions had been destroyed in the fire, he had a brainstorm.'
   a **brainstorming session** – a meeting at which all the members are encouraged to contribute suggestions and solutions, however far-fetched, to a problem.
6. **brain-washing** – to control a person's thinking and ideas by psychological and physical torture, disorientation and other forms of coercion.
7. **Brains Trust** – a panel of intelligent people who express their views on questions of current interest put to them by television or radio audiences.
8. the **Brain Drain** – the emigration from Britain to America of many college and university graduates who were tempted by the higher salaries and better facilities in the USA.
9. to **have something on the brain** – to have an obsession, to be preoccupied with an idea that won't give one any rest. 'Our plumber has fishing on the brain. He talks about it all day long.'
10. to **pick** someone's **brains** – to enlist the aid of someone more clever or expert in a given subject. 'This is much too difficult for me. Do you mind if I pick your brains?'
11. to **rack/cudgel one's brains** – to make a great intellectual effort by, for example, working for a long time on a problem, or trying to recollect some forgotten experience, name, etc.
12. to **turn** someone's **brain** – to madden or drive insane. 'The news that his daughter had married a criminal turned his brain.'

## NERVE

13. to **have the nerve to . . .** – to have the impudence to . . . 'When I caught him helping himself to the things in my larder, he had the nerve to ask me where the mayonnaise was.' cf. 'to **have the gall to' 113/17**.
14. to **nerve oneself to / nerve oneself for . . .** – to brace oneself mentally to . . . 'He nerved himself to ask his boss for a rise.'
15. to **get on** someone's **nerves** – to exasperate someone by the repetition of some irritating action. 'Her never-ending complaints got on my nerves.'
16. a **bag of nerves** – someone who is unable to control his anxiety or irritability. 'Since her divorce, Pamela has been a bag of nerves.'
17. to be a **strain on one's nerves** – to be a source of intense irritation or anxiety. 'Living with two other men in one cell was a great strain on all our nerves.'

1. **not to know what nerves are** – to be fearless, to be free from fear. 'He goes at tremendous speeds on the race-track without any fear. He doesn't know what nerves are!'
2. to have **nerves of steel** – to have very strong nerves, to have nerves that are strong enough to withstand any fear.
3. to have a **fit of nerves** – to have an uncontrollable bout of anxiety.
4. to **live on one's nerves** – to be in such a nervous state that one's whole life is affected. 'Since the car accident when she was badly injured, she has been living on her nerves.'
5. to **strain every nerve** – to exert oneself to the utmost. 'He strained every nerve to remain cool and collected and not to let his fingers shake when he opened the telegram.'
6. to **lose one's nerve** – to be reduced by fear to a state of helplessness. 'After hitting an air shot on the first tee in front of a big crowd, Henry lost his nerve and bolted.'

## VEIN

7. **in the same vein** – in the same style or mood. 'He wrote many stories in the same vein, humorous and light-hearted.'

## FLESH

8. **in the flesh** – in bodily form. 'I knew him better than any of you. In fact, I saw him in the flesh just before he died.'
9. **flesh and blood** – human, with all the weaknesses of human nature.
10. **one's own flesh and blood** – one's parents, brothers and sisters and one's children. 'You can't cut yourself off from your son; after all, he is your own flesh and blood.'
11. to **flesh out** – to add weight to, to make more substantial. 'You can flesh your article out by adding a descriptive passage.'
12. to **put on flesh** – to put on weight. 'Harold has put on a lot of flesh since he was here last. He'll have to cut down on cakes and sugar.'
13. **more than flesh can stand** – more than human nature can endure. 'To expect him to work six weeks on end without a break was asking too much. It was more than flesh could stand.'
14. to **make one's flesh creep** – to frighten or horrify with some dreadful tale. The allusion is to 'the fat boy' in Charles Dickens's *Pickwick Papers*.
15. to **have one's pound of flesh** – to exact what is due, to the very last ounce. 'All right, if you are going to insist on your pound of flesh, I'll work for you all next weekend, although you've paid me little enough for the work.' From Shakespeare's *The Merchant of Venice*.
16. to **press the flesh** – to canvass support in an election campaign by mixing with the voters, shaking hands, kissing babies and so on. 'I've done my share of pressing the flesh for the last six months; now I want a rest.' An American phrase.
17. **flesh-pots / the flesh-pots of Egypt** – great luxury, the finest food and drink. A biblical allusion to the captivity of the Israelites in Egypt (Exodus XVI, 3).
18. the **sins of the flesh** – love of physical pleasure like eating, drinking, fornication. 'The priest told his parishioners to resist temptation and fight against the sins of the flesh.'
19. **the spirit is willing but the flesh is weak** – because of our human frailties, we are not always able to resist the demands made on us by our bodies, even when we want to. Often used

facetiously: 'I wanted to get up at six o'clock this morning and study, but I just couldn't. The spirit was willing but the flesh was weak!'

1. to go **the way of all flesh** – to die. 'However rich and important they are, they will go the way of all flesh like the rest of us.'

## SKIN

2. to **save one's skin** – to escape from a disagreeable predicament. 'She saved his skin by telling the police he had spent the evening with her.'
3. to **escape with a whole skin** – to escape without injury.
4. to escape **by the skin of one's teeth** – to have a very narrow escape. 'That was a near thing! I only escaped being conscripted into the army by the skin of my teeth.'
5. to **jump out of one's skin** – to receive a tremendous shock. 'She nearly jumped out of her skin when she unlocked her front door and found a burglar standing in her hall.'
6. to **be in someone else's skin** – often used negatively to indicate some kind of trouble. 'I wouldn't be in his skin if he paid me £1,000.' cf. 'to **be in another's shoes' 168/5**.
7. to **get under one's skin** – to exasperate, to irritate. 'I can't stand the way he patronizes us. He gets under my skin.'
8. to be **all skin and bones** – to be undernourished, very thin. 'We must give that stray cat some food. It's all skin and bones.'
9. **skin-deep** – superficial, shallow. 'Her emotions were only skin-deep. She was incapable of any deep feeling.'
10. to **be thick-skinned / have a thick skin** – to be insensitive to criticism, insults, or the broadest of hints. 'Don't worry, you won't hurt his feelings. He is very thick-skinned.'
11. to **be thin-skinned** – to be oversensitive to criticism, to take offence at the slightest provocation. 'I didn't mean him to take my remarks personally. He is very thin-skinned!'
12. to be a **skin-flint** – to be mean, miserly. 'You won't get a penny out of him. He's a real skin-flint.'
13. to **skin alive** – to punish very severely. 'If Paul finds out that you've been using his movie camera, he'll skin you alive.' cf. 'to **come down on** someone **like a ton of bricks' 144/12**.

## BONE

14. a **lazy bones** / to be **bone idle** – slothful, idle. 'His son is a lazy bones. He never gets up before lunch!'
15. a **bone of contention** – an unresolved quarrel or dispute. 'The ownership of the ancestral home has been a bone of contention between the two brothers for the last twenty years.' The phrase derives from two dogs fighting over a bone.
16. to **feel it in one's bones** – to have a premonition that something (probably unpleasant) is about to happen, although one cannot give a reason for it. 'I am certain that something terrible will happen to Barbara very soon. I can't explain why, I just feel it in my bones.'
17. to **have a bone to pick with someone** – to have cause for making a complaint to someone. 'I have a bone to pick with you. My sister saw you take a £5 note out of my handbag this morning.'
18. to **make no bones of/about** – to speak very frankly, without holding anything back. 'I'll make no bones about it: my father was from a working-class family.'

1. the **bare bones** – just the essentials but no more. 'Those are the bare bones of the system. I'll fill you in on the details later.'
2. to **cut to the bone** – to reduce to an absolute minimum, to eliminate all inessentials. 'We have cut our housekeeping to the bone, but we still have a struggle to pay the bills.'
3. to be **bone dry / as dry as a bone** – to lack moisture. 'I can't grow anything in my garden. The soil is bone dry.' The same idiom can be used humorously for wanting a drink very badly. 'Let's stop at the pub; I'm as dry as a bone.'
4. to **bone up on** (slang) – to work hard on. 'If you are going to get a job in Italy, you had better bone up on the language.'

## SKELETON

5. a **skeleton in the cupboard** – a source of embarrassment and shame to a family, which is kept secret from strangers. 'I'm sure there is a skeleton in the Wellards' cupboard. Don't they have a relative who has been in prison?'
6. a **skeleton at the feast** – a reminder of sorrow or trouble on even the merriest occasions.
7. a **skeleton key** – a special key that will unlock many doors, a master key. 'Don't worry if you have lost your bedroom key. Reception has a skeleton key.'
8. **skeleton staff/crew**, etc. – a much-reduced staff, crew, etc., which is capable of maintaining the minimum service required for the organization to function.

## MARROW

9. **chilled to the marrow** – freezing cold, frozen through and through. 'We had better turn up the heating. Jack was chilled to the marrow, watching that football match.'

## SINEW

10. **the sinews of war** – the means to wage a war: money, arms, etc. 'Without the sinews of war, we have no power to defend our rights.'

## LIMB

11. to be **out on a limb** – having taken the initiative, to find oneself without effective support. 'As soon as the organizers saw they were out on a limb, they cancelled their campaign.'
12. to **escape with life and limb** – to escape without any broken bones.
13. a **danger to life and limb** – anything which threatens the health and security of other people. 'The way you drive your car is a danger to life and limb.'

## MUSCLE

14. **not to move a muscle** – to be immobile, motionless. 'All the time we were watching the sentry, he didn't move a muscle.'
15. to **use one's muscle** – to use superior strength. 'The printers have used their muscle to obtain far higher wages than they deserve.'

    to **carry a lot of muscle** – to make one's influence felt. 'The money you earn today depends on the muscle your union carries, nothing else.'
16. to **muscle in** – to take away the business of a competitor by force, or by the use of unethical methods. 'It's a good idea, but Philpot's will muscle in on you if they can. They are quite ruthless.'
17. to be **muscle-bound** – to have stiff,

unwieldy muscles, as a result of excessive exercise and training. 'The crew practised too hard at the beginning of the season, with the result that they were muscle-bound on the day of the race.'

## BLOOD

1. a **man of blood** – a man of violence.
2. to **make bad blood** between – to cause two people to quarrel with one another. 'He made bad blood between the two brothers.'
3. to be **after/out for one's blood** – to seek revenge. The idiom can be used humorously: 'Now that you have beaten him in the finals, Tom is after your blood.'
4. to **get one's blood up** – to become enraged. 'He is furious with the way they behaved to the old woman. They have got his blood up.'
5. **it makes one's blood boil** – it exasperates one beyond endurance. 'It made my blood boil to see him stealing our roses and then presenting them to his girl-friend.'
6. to **shed blood** – to kill or wound.
   to **shed one's blood** – to be wounded or killed in a war. 'They shed their blood that we might live.'
7. to **sweat blood** (slang) – to work until one is exhausted. 'I've sweated blood to make a success of your company and you haven't given me a word of thanks!'
8. to act **in cold blood** – to act coldly and deliberately, with premeditation. 'The jury found that the man had murdered his wife in cold blood, not in the heat of the moment.'
9. to **make the blood run cold / to chill the blood** – to terrify someone. 'The sight of the masked man climbing through her bedroom window was enough to make Julie's blood run cold.'
10. to act **in hot blood** – to act in anger, to be motivated by passion, not reason.
11. to be **hot-blooded** – passionate, easily aroused to either anger or amorousness.
12. a **full-blooded attack / to make a full-blooded attack** – to attack with one's whole strength, keeping nothing in reserve. 'He has made a full-blooded attack upon your policy, your character and your motives.'
13. to **draw blood** – to make a damaging attack on a person's pride or reputation. 'The Minister has been forced to write an angry letter to the *Daily Telegraph* in reply to our article. We have drawn blood!'
14. to **give** someone/something **a blood transfusion** – to give fresh life to, to reinvigorate. 'North Sea Oil has given Britain a blood transfusion, and only just in time.'
15. to **bring in new/young blood** – to employ people with fresh ideas. 'Now that they have brought in new blood, the marketing should be more energetic.'
16. a **blood-sucker** – a person who obtains money by blackmail or extortion.
17. **you can't get blood out of a stone** – you won't get pity or sympathy from someone who is completely unfeeling. 'It's no good appealing to Uncle Joe. You can't get blood out of a stone.'
18. **blood money** – the reward paid for information that secures the death or betrayal of a person.
19. a **blood-bath** – murder and bloodshed on a large scale. 'The revolutionaries are demanding a blood-bath.'
20. **blood and iron policies** – the attainment of political objectives by the use of brute force. 'Blood and iron was at the core of Bismarck's *Realpolitik*.'

1. **blood will tell** – one's innate qualities will come to the surface sooner or later. 'The adopted child was given the same opportunities as the other children, but he turned out completely different from them. Blood will tell.'
2. **it runs in the blood** – it is an inherited quality. 'The Mayers have been distinguished doctors for generations. It runs in the blood.'
3. **blood is thicker than water** – the ties between relations are closer than those between friends.

## HEART

4. **be of good heart** – take courage, don't lose hope!
5. **in good heart** – in good spirits, cheerful.
6. to **do one's heart good** – to cheer up, make one happy. 'It does my heart good to watch the children opening their Christmas presents.'
7. **after one's own heart** – with one's full approval and admiration. 'Saving the baby seals from the fishermen was an action after my own heart.'

   a man/woman **after my own heart** – the kind of man/woman whom I most admire. 'Peter is a man after my own heart. He fights for what he believes in and never gives up.'
8. to **steel one's heart against** – to suppress one's natural pity. 'He steeled his heart against the cries for help of the sick children.'
9. a **heart of stone** – pitiless, unfeeling. 'To turn away your own son! You must have a heart of stone!'
10. **with a light heart** – cheerfully, happily, in a carefree manner. 'I came home with a light heart. I had paid off all my debts at last.'
11. **with a sinking heart** – with growing dismay. 'The schoolboy listened to his examination results with a sinking heart. He realized that he would never get into university.'
12. to be **sick at heart** – to feel very miserable about something. 'When we saw our champion being knocked about in the boxing ring, we all felt sick at heart.'
13. to **break one's heart** – to suffer a personal loss from which it is impossible to recover, to be reduced to a state of complete despair.
14. a **heart-throb** – a charismatic personality, one who captivates members of the opposite sex.
15. a **hearty** – a low-brow, someone lacking in intellectual tastes, loud-mouthed and vulgar.
16. to **be hearty** – to be noisy and boisterous.
17. **the heart of the matter** – the essential problem.
18. **heart and soul** – passionately, in a totally committed way. 'Charles worked heart and soul for the cause.'
19. to **put one's heart (and soul) into** something – to work at something with energy and enthusiasm. 'Research is tiring and laborious work. If you can't put your heart into it, you should try something else.'
20. **one's heart is not in it** – to be not interested in or to feel unenthusiastic about something. 'In the last few weeks your heart hasn't been in your work. Would you like to talk to me about it?'
21. **from the bottom of one's heart** – with the utmost sincerity, most deeply. 'I wish you every success from the bottom of my heart.'
22. **at heart** – fundamentally. 'He has many faults, but at heart he is a very decent young man.'

    to **have at heart** – to feel deeply about; to be extremely concerned about. 'I am sure your mother has your best interests at heart.' The phrase can be used with 'health', 'happiness', 'safety', etc.

1. a **heart-to-heart talk** – a confidential and serious discussion between two people about some personal problem. 'I had a heart-to-heart talk with Lucy's father about our plans to marry, and my prospects.'
2. to **take heart** – to be encouraged. 'You can take heart from Robert's success. If he can pass the exam, so can you!'
3. to **take to heart** – (1) to take something badly, to be very much hurt by. 'When Martin forgot his date with Susan, she took it very much to heart.' (2) to take a warning very seriously. 'I hope you will take to heart what I have told you.'
4. to **take to one's heart** – to accept someone with love and joy. 'The people have taken Your Royal Highness to their hearts.'
5. to **give one heart** – to encourage, make one bold. 'You have given me heart. I'll try again.'
6. to **put (fresh) heart into** – to encourage, to give someone confidence. 'After so many failures, I was going to give up, but you have put fresh heart into me.'
7. **have a heart!** – the phrase is used as a plea in reply to some unreasonable demand. 'I've already typed thirty letters for you today, and now you want me to do another thirteen. Have a heart!'
8. to **have no heart** – to be unfeeling, inhumane. 'A man who shoots dumb animals can't have any heart at all.'
9. to **find it in one's heart to** – to be generous enough to . . . 'If you can find it in your heart to forgive Jenny, you will never regret it.'

   **not to have the heart to** – not to be able to . . . 'I didn't have the heart to tell Peter the bad news on his birthday and spoil his fun.'
10. to **lose heart** – to lose courage, to despair. 'When the skating champion tumbled on the ice, he lost heart and did not complete his programme.'
11. to **lose one's heart to** – to fall in love with. 'She lost her heart to the new arts teacher.'
12. **in one's heart of hearts** – if one is absolutely honest with oneself. 'In his heart of hearts, he knew that he wasn't cut out to be a lawyer, despite his academic success.'
13. **with all my heart** – with the utmost sincerity, with all best wishes. 'I hope with all my heart that your marriage will be a happy one.'
14. **close to one's heart** – especially valued by someone. 'The work you are doing for the sick children has always been close to his heart.'
15. to **learn (off) by heart** – to know a piece so well that one can recite it from memory. 'Our teacher makes us learn everything off by heart.'
16. to **set one's heart upon** – to want above all else, to have an intense longing to . . . 'His grandfather has set his heart on sending the boy to his old school.'
17. to **allow the heart to rule the head** – to be influenced by one's emotions and not by one's reason. 'In business, it is a mistake to allow the heart to rule the head.'
18. **to one's heart's content** – to one's complete satisfaction. 'There's a piano in your room, and you can play it to your heart's content. No one will disturb you.'
19. a **change of heart** – a change of mind or decision, prompted by a change in one's feelings. 'His father was against the marriage at first, but, after getting to know the girl better, he had a change of heart.'

1. **my heart goes out to** – I feel intense pity and sympathy for. 'My heart goes out to the victims of the bomb explosion.'
2. **one's heart bleeds for** someone – to feel extremely sorry for someone. Often used ironically: 'I'm sorry you won't be taking your usual holiday in the Bahamas this year. My heart bleeds for you.'
3. to **eat one's heart out** – to suffer intense grief, often resulting from failure or disappointment, especially over the loss of a person's love. 'Elizabeth has been eating her heart out ever since Dennis broke off their engagement.'
4. **with one's heart in one's mouth** – in a state of great fear. 'When the postman handed me the telegram, my heart was in my mouth.'
5. to **have one's heart in the right place** – to be kind and well-meaning. This idiom is almost always used when appearances are to the contrary. 'He may be a bit of a show-off sometimes, but his heart is in the right place.'
6. to **warm the cockles of one's heart** – to raise someone's spirits, to gratify. 'It warmed the cockles of her heart to have all the children and grandchildren seated at her dining-table at Christmas time.'
7. to **pour out one's heart** – to confide all one's sorrows, fears, anxieties, hopes and joys to another person. 'When we were alone, she poured out her heart to me about her broken marriage.'
8. to **have heart failure** (colloquial) – to suffer a great shock, to be demoralized. 'It was the audacity of its contents which gave them heart failure and persuaded them to surrender . . .' (*New Statesman*).
9. **one heartbeat from the Presidency** – on the death of the American President the immediate assumption of office by the Vice-President without any action by the legislature or judiciary.

## STOMACH

10. to have a **strong stomach** – to be not easily shocked or disgusted. 'You'll need a strong stomach if you are going to be a surgeon.'
11. to **have no stomach for** – to have no courage for, no desire for. 'He hated quarrelling and had no stomach for a fight.'
12. to **turn the stomach** – to disgust, to nauseate. 'Your hypocrisy turns my stomach.'
13. to **stomach** (an insult, etc.) – to accept, to submit to. 'If you want to be his friend, you'll have to stomach his insults.'
14. **on an empty stomach** – a stomach that lacks food. 'You must take these pills on an empty stomach.'
15. to have a **sinking feeling in the pit of one's stomach** – to have a great fear, a premonition of disaster.

## GALL

16. **as bitter as gall** – extreme bitterness. Gall is the old synonym of bile, the bitter liquid secreted into the stomach by the liver.
17. to **have the gall to . . .** (colloquial) – to have the impudence to . . . 'Sandra had the gall to ask for her job back two days after we had sacked her for dishonesty.' cf. 'to **have the nerve to**' **106/13**.
18. to **dip one's pen in gall** – to write with venom and bitter sarcasm.
19. **gall and wormwood** – that which arouses the most bitter resentment. Both words stand as symbols of extreme bitterness. 'It was gall and

wormwood for him to have to make a public withdrawal of his accusations.'

## BILE

1. to be **full of bile** – to be full of resentment and bitterness. 'His speeches were full of bile.' 'His opponents aroused his bile.'

## SPLEEN

2. to be **filled with spleen** – to be filled with anger and vexation. 'In his autobiography, he vented his spleen on all his enemies.'

## GUT

3. to **have the guts to . . .** – to have the courage to . . . 'He didn't have the guts to stand by his friend when he was in trouble.'

## KIDNEY

4. **of the same kidney** – of the same character, of the same type. It usually has a bad meaning. 'Have nothing to do with those two prisoners; they both have violent characters and long records. They are men of the same kidney.'

   **of another kidney** – of a different character, of a different type. 'Roberts has nothing in common with Taylor. Roberts enjoys classical music, while Taylor listens to pop. Roberts is a man of another kidney.'

## LIVER

5. **yellow-livered** (a term of abuse) – cowardly. There was a superstition that a coward's liver contained no blood; hence the phrases **yellow-livered, white-livered, lily-livered,** etc. cf. 'to **be yellow' 18/10**.

## BODY

6. to **have body** – to have weight or substance. 'That wine has body, as well as bouquet and clarity.'

   to **have no body** – to be lacking in substance. 'Richard's novel was quite amusing but very light; it had no body.'

7. to **be a nobody** – to be a person of no significance, no importance. 'I won't take orders from a nobody like Smith.'

8. a **busybody** – someone who meddles, or pries into other people's affairs. 'My neighbour has been asking me a lot of questions about my girl-friend. He is an appalling busybody.'

9. to **keep body and soul together** – to support life. 'When I left home, work was difficult to find, and I earned hardly enough to keep body and soul together.'

10. a **body-blow** to all one's hopes – a very severe blow, a disastrous blow. 'Failing to qualify after so many years' study dealt a body-blow to all her hopes.'

## FIGURE

11. to **cut a poor figure** – to look foolish. 'I must have cut a poor figure in front of the guests. I had quite forgotten how to dance.'

12. **a figure of fun** – an object of ridicule. 'When he was younger, the boys treated the master with respect, but now he's only a figure of fun.'

# 12. MIND

MIND

1. **mind over matter** – the triumph of willpower and courage over physical pain or infirmity. 'Whether a patient recovers from a dangerous illness often depends on his own willpower. It's a case of mind over matter as a rule.'
2. to **make up one's mind** – to come to a decision. 'I have made up my mind to sell my house and go abroad.'
3. to **have a good mind** to do something – to have a strong inclination. The phrase usually expresses irritation. 'He has behaved so badly, I've a good mind not to go to his party.' More often than not, the inclination is suppressed.
4. to **be in one's right mind** – to be sane. 'No one in his right mind would do a thing like that!'
5. to be **out of one's mind/senses** – to be extremely stupid or insane. 'You must have been out of your mind to talk like that to your boss.'

   to **be driven out of one's mind** – to be driven insane with worry, fear, suspicion, anxiety, etc. The phrase is often used with the adverbs 'nearly', and 'almost'.
6. to **have in mind** – to consider or propose. 'Yes, we have a number of four-bedroom houses on our books. What price did you have in mind?'
7. **an open mind** – an unprejudiced mind, one that is receptive to new ideas. 'I have an open mind whether to take him on. I will decide after I have seen him.'

   **a closed mind** – a mind that is prejudiced, one that is not receptive to new ideas. 'Rupert has a closed mind on the subject of politics, so you are wasting your time arguing with him about it.'
8. the **master-mind** – the person in charge of an operation, the originator of the plan on which the success of the operation depends. 'The police believe they know the master-mind behind the bank robbery.'
9. to **call to mind** – to recall, remember. Usually used negatively. 'I can't call to mind his ever having mentioned it, but he may have done so.'
10. to **cast one's mind back** – to make a conscious effort to recall an incident. 'Can you cast your mind back to the day you first visited him?'
11. to **know one's (own) mind** – to have a clear and firm conviction, usually as to what should be done. 'He never had any doubts about being a doctor; he always knew his own mind.'

    **not to know one's own mind** – to be undecided, usually as to what should be done. 'It would be a mistake putting Jim in charge; he never knows his own mind.'
12. to **have a mind of one's own** – to be capable of making decisions without depending on other people's opinions. 'Why do you always ask your father what to do? Surely you are old enough to have a mind of your own.'
13. to **be in two minds** (over a matter) – to be undecided. 'I could see the advantages and disadvantages of living in New Zealand. I was in two minds about moving there.'
14. to **change one's mind** – to change one's decision or opinion.
15. **mind you** – even so, all the same. 'Paul did wrong. Mind you, many people would have done the same in his place.' (An interjection used to qualify a statement.)
16. to **set one's mind on** – to be absolutely determined on a course of action. 'I

can see you have set your mind on taking the job, so I won't try to dissuade you.'

1. to be **of one mind** – to be unanimous, to be of the same opinion.
2. **to my mind** – in my opinion. The phrase is often used to indicate a difference of opinion. 'I know you won't agree with me but, to my mind, the whole idea was a mistake.'
3. to **put/give one's mind** to – to concentrate on. 'If he would only put his mind to his studies, he could be a brilliant scholar.'
4. to **bear/keep in mind** – to pay heed to, to take into consideration. 'You must bear in mind that Alan is very young.'
5. to **cross one's mind** – to occur to one, to have a momentary thought. 'It did cross my mind that the maid might have stolen the money.'
6. to **slip one's mind** – to forget, usually as a result of carelessness rather than a defective memory. 'It quite slipped my mind that Maureen was coming to tea today.'
7. to **prey/weigh on one's mind** – to worry, preoccupy or make one feel guilty. 'My unkindness to the old woman weighed on my mind for a long time.'
   to **have** something **on one's mind** – to be worried, preoccupied or feel guilty about something. 'I can see you have something on your mind; would you like to tell me about it?'
8. **a weight off one's mind** – relief from an anxiety or feeling of guilt. 'It was a weight off my mind to know that he was being well looked after.'
9. to **put** someone's **mind at rest** – to dispel someone's anxiety. 'I can put your mind at rest – your wife is out of danger.'
10. to be **easy in mind** – to be calm, to be free from anxiety.
11. to **put to the back of one's mind** – to dismiss (an idea) from one's mind for the time being.
12. to **get** something **out of one's mind** – to free oneself from an idea. 'I have made a terrible mistake and now I can't get it out of my mind.'
13. to **take one's mind off** something – to seek distraction from one's troubles. 'There is nothing like a good book to take one's mind off one's troubles.'
14. to **speak one's mind** – to speak very frankly. 'He said exactly what he thought; he spoke his mind.'
15. to **give** someone **a piece of one's mind** – to scold someone severely, to tell someone what one thinks of him. 'When James didn't trouble to see the girl home after the party, I gave him a piece of my mind.'
16. **presence of mind** – a quick response in an emergency. 'When the child fell out of the moving train, she had the presence of mind to pull the emergency cord.'
17. to **make the mind boggle** – to astonish. The alternative phrase is 'the mind boggles'. 'The mind boggles at the bills he ran up in such a short time.'
18. to **broaden the mind** – to develop new interests. 'Why don't you learn a foreign language and travel? That will broaden your mind.'

## MENTAL

19. **mental** (colloquial) – mad or idiotic.
20. a **mental block** – a psychological obstruction to the free flow of ideas. 'Whenever the psychiatrist asks me questions about my childhood, I have a mental block.'
21. **quick/slow in the uptake** – quick or slow to understand. 'I kept looking at my watch, but he made no move to leave; he must be a little slow in the uptake.'

## WIT, WITS

1. to have **quick wits / to be quick-witted** – to have a quick understanding, to be quick with an answer.

   to be **slow-witted** – to be slow in understanding.
2. to be **half-witted** – to be mentally sub-normal, or idiotic. 'It's a half-witted idea emigrating with no money or contacts.'
3. to **addle the wits** – to make someone incapable of using his brain, to make him stupid. 'I think George's two years at the Foreign Office must have addled his wits.' The verb 'addle, addled', means rotten, muddle, confuse, from the Anglo-Saxon word 'Adela' meaning mud.
4. to **have/keep one's wits about one** – to be alert and resourceful 'If he hadn't had his wits about him, he might have been drowned.'
5. to **live by/on one's wits** – to resort to expedients from day to day for a living rather than take a regular job.
6. **out of one's wits** – mentally disturbed, mentally disabled or senile.

   to **frighten** someone **out of his wits** – to terrify someone so much that he is unable to think properly. 'That alsatian of the Masons frightens me out of my wits whenever I pass their house; they should keep it chained up.'
7. **at one's wits' end** – in despair of finding a solution to one's problems.

   to **drive** someone **to his wits' end** – to drive someone to despair. 'The boy was so slow that he drove his teacher to his wits' end.'

## SENSE, SENSES

8. **out of one's senses** – mad.

   to **take leave of one's senses** – to go mad. 'Have you taken leave of your senses? The wedding is tomorrow; you can't possibly cancel it now!'
9. to **come to one's senses** – to start behaving sensibly again. 'You should warn John that you will stop his allowance unless he behaves himself; then he will come to his senses.'

   to **bring** someone **to his senses** – to persuade someone to stop behaving foolishly.
10. a **sense of loss** – a feeling of sadness that a person or thing is irretrievably lost. 'When Lucy saw her younger brother off to India, she felt a strong sense of loss and wondered whether she would ever see him again.'
11. a **sense of proportion** – the ability to see things in their proper perspective. 'So you have failed your examination, but there are worse things in life than failing exams; you mustn't lose your sense of proportion.'

## REASON

12. to **listen to reason** – to adopt a sensible approach to a question without being influenced by one's emotions. 'I warned you that the idea would never work; what a pity you wouldn't listen to reason.'
13. **it stands to reason** – there is only one conclusion to be drawn. 'It stands to reason that if the railway is losing money, fares should be reduced to attract more passengers.'
14. **without rhyme or reason** – nonsensical, illogical. 'At first, I could see no rhyme or reason in Gertrude Stein's writing, but later I changed my mind about her.'

## CONSCIENCE

15. **in all conscience** – taking a fair and reasonable view. The phrase is often used to emphasize one's doubts about the reasonableness of a demand. 'I should have thought that his charges were high enough in all conscience

without his asking for any extra money.'

1. to **make** something **a matter of conscience** – to be guided by one's sense of right and wrong. 'I agree with you that many laws are unjust, but if you make every law a matter of conscience you will end up in gaol!'
2. **conscience money** – money paid anonymously to ease one's conscience, for example when income tax has been evaded.

## MORAL, ERR AND FAULT

3. a **moral certainty** – such a strong probability as to exclude almost any doubt. 'This time next year, it is a moral certainty that we shall be living in America.'
4. **moral support** – encouragement which stops short of physical or financial help. 'I am making my first speech at our local debating society. I hope you'll be there to give me moral support.'
5. a **moral victory** – a defeat that should by rights have been a victory. 'We played better football than Honiton and would have won easily if two of our men hadn't been injured. Honiton agreed with us that it was a moral victory for our side.'
6. to **err on the right side** – to make a mistake which benefits someone else. 'You are not late; in fact you are erring on the right side coming in at half past eight instead of nine.'

   a **fault on the right side** – a mistake which benefits someone else. 'Molly got the account wrong. We owe her £80, not £60. At least, it's a fault on the right side.'

## CHARACTER

7. **in character** – in accordance with a person's usual behaviour; in a way anyone knowing him would expect.

   **out of character** – not in accordance with a person's usual behaviour; in a way anyone knowing him would not expect. 'I was surprised Francis was so rude to you; it was completely out of character.'
8. **(quite) a character** – peculiar, eccentric. 'Mr Fraser goes out in long flowing yellow and scarlet robes. Yesterday, he stopped the traffic in the Strand. He is quite a character.'

## PURPOSE, DESIRE, WILLING, WILL

9. **to all intents and purposes** – in essence, effectively. 'To all intents and purposes, the property was a complete loss; only the kitchen remained, the rest of the house having been burned to the ground.'
10. to be **at cross-purposes** – to have a misunderstanding because of conflicting intentions. 'I am afraid we are at cross-purposes; I am offering you a job, not asking you for one.'
11. to **leave a lot to be desired** – to be unsatisfactory in many respects. 'Although the hotel charges were very high, the cuisine and service left a lot to be desired.'
12. to **show willing** – to show that one is ready to co-operate even if one has no desire to. 'You may not want to strike, but you should show willing to protect your rights.'
13. **with a will** – with strength and determination. 'When the old man was attacked by the mugger, he defended himself with a will.'
14. **willy-nilly** (literary) – whether one wishes it or not. 'Paul wanted to keep aloof from his companions but, willy-nilly, he was drawn into their revels.' Willy-nilly is a corruption of 'will he,

nill he', 'nill he' deriving from Anglo-Saxon 'nillan', short for 'ne willan', not to wish.

## WISE, WISER

1. to **be wise to** – to be fully aware of, to be alert to. 'He is wise to all their tricks; he won't let them make use of him.'

   to **put** someone **wise to** – to make someone aware of the facts, to warn him as to the true position. 'I thought I had better put you wise as to what's going on here. Your conduct is being criticized in the officers' mess.'

2. to be **wise after the event** – to know what should have been done to prevent something happening when it has already taken place. 'Aren't you being wise after the event? How could we have known that the burglar would get in by the window on the second floor?' cf. 'to **second-guess' 216/20**.

3. **none the wiser** – knowing no more than one did before. 'I have spent six hours interrogating witnesses and I am none the wiser.'

## COURAGE, BOLD AND VIRTUE

4. to **have the courage of one's convictions** – to declare one's principles openly, regardless of the danger to oneself or to one's reputation. 'I don't agree with you, but I admire you for having the courage of your convictions.' cf. 'to **stand up and be counted' 222/5**.

5. **as bold as brass** – impertinent, shameless. 'Harry asked me what my income was the first time we met. The man is as bold as brass.' cf. **'barefaced' 79/15**.

6. to **make a virtue of necessity** – to turn an unwanted obligation into a positive advantage. 'I am being sent to North Europe. I didn't want to move but they are going to teach me skiing free of charge; so I'll be making a virtue of necessity.'

## KINDNESS, KINDLY, GENEROUS

7. to **kill with kindness** – to spoil someone's character, especially a child's, by indulging all his wishes and not correcting his faults. 'They've sent their daughter to a modern school where she can do exactly as she likes, and where punishments are forbidden. The teachers are killing her with kindness.'

8. **not to take kindly to** – not to welcome or approve (only used in the negative). 'These men and women are experienced teachers; I am afraid they won't take kindly to being told how to do their job by your inspector.'

9. **generous to a fault** – excessively generous, so generous as to cause difficulties or embarrassment. 'Matthew is generous to a fault; people are always taking advantage of him.'

## PROUD, PRIDE

10. to **do** someone **proud** – to treat someone with great generosity. 'Meg's parents did us proud; they treated us to a box at Wyndham's Theatre followed by dinner at Claridge's.'

11. to **swallow one's pride** – to submit humbly, to accept a humiliation. 'You made a mistake resigning in a temper like that. You had better swallow your pride and ask the boss to take you back.'

## CRUEL, MERCIES, PITY

12. to be **cruel to be kind** – to inflict pain on or punish a person in order to rid him of a distressing habit or fault. 'Mrs Fry warned her daughter that if

she continued taking drugs, she would turn her out of the house. She explained she had to be cruel to be kind.'

1. to **leave a person to** someone's **tender mercies** – to abandon a person to rough, brutal treatment. 'I could see at once that Harry's new guardian was a bully, and I was sorry to leave the boy to his tender mercies.'
2. **more's the pity** – so much the worse, that only makes it worse; generally used as a rejoinder to an excuse or explanation. '"I didn't send you a Christmas card this year. I haven't sent one to any of my friends." "More's the pity", replied Joan.'

## GRACE

3. a **saving grace** – one good quality which redeems many faults. 'Anne is lazy, untidy and disrespectful; her one saving grace is that she is good with the children.'
4. **with a good/bad grace** – in a good-humoured/ill-humoured manner. 'Rose paid me back the money, but with a bad grace as if I had done her a wrong.'
5. to **fall from grace** – to lose favour. 'Since smashing up Lady Robinson's car, I have fallen from grace, and expect very soon to lose my job.'

## PATIENCE, FAITH AND CHARITY

6. to **try the patience of a saint** – to be so tiresome or stupid that even the most tolerant and easy-going of people would get annoyed. 'If I've explained it to you once, I've explained it a hundred times. You would try the patience of a saint!' cf. 'to **try the patience of Job' 194/7**.
7. **in (all) good faith** – honestly and sincerely. 'I acted in good faith when I sold you that washing-machine. So far as I knew, it was in perfect condition.'

   **in bad faith** – dishonestly.
8. an **article of faith** – a crucial element in someone's philosophy. 'It is an article of faith among Conservatives that competition should be encouraged and state monopolies should be abolished.'
9. **as cold as charity** – hard and unfeeling. A reference to the cold, unsympathetic way charity is sometimes dispensed to the poor and needy.

## HAPPY, HUMOUR, BORED

10. a **happy event** – the birth of a child. 'Will your daughter be back in England for the happy event, or are you going to look after her in Germany?'
11. a **happy medium** – a middle way which avoids extremes. 'You should take plenty of exercise but avoid anything too strenuous like tennis or squash. Golf would be a happy medium for a man of your age.'
12. a **happy hunting-ground** – a place which offers good chances of success for hunters, collectors and other people with special interests. 'The International Club was always considered a happy hunting-ground for young men who were looking for a girl-friend.' 'The happy hunting-grounds' was the name given by the American Indians to their life after death.
13. to be **out of humour** – to be in an ill-humour, in a bad mood. 'William is out of humour this morning because he didn't get a letter from his daughter.'
14. **bored stiff / bored to tears** – very much bored, uninterested. 'I am bored stiff by many of the television programmes.'

## FANCY AND DREAM

1. to **take a fancy to** someone/something – to take a sudden liking to someone/something. 'You do take a fancy to the most extraordinary things. Where are we going to put a palm tree in this tiny flat?'

   to **take** someone's **fancy** – to attract. 'I don't really know why I bought it; it just took my fancy.'

2. to **fancy oneself** – to have a high opinion of one's looks or of one's abilities, to be conceited. 'Derek fancies himself as a ladies' man, but he spends too much time admiring himself in the mirror for my liking.' cf. 'to **think that one is God's gift to' 44/6**.

3. **a flight of fancy** – a free, unrestricted use of the imagination. 'Jack's play has nothing to say about our social or political problems. It is a flight of fancy, nothing else.'

4. **not dream of** – not think of, not consider. The phrase is used in order to make an emphatic denial. 'I wouldn't dream of charging you a fee for doing your portrait; please accept it as a gift.'

5. to **go like a dream** – to move with power and smoothness. The phrase is usually applied to cars, yachts or aeroplanes.

## LOVE

6. **a labour of love** – a work done without payment, either for its own sake or for the sake of a loved one. 'Miss Watts had worked for three years on the tapestry; it was a labour of love done for the church.'

7. **love in a cottage** – a love match or marriage which is not supported by sufficient means to keep a couple in comfort.

8. **love-birds** – two people who are very much in love with each other. 'Mr and Mrs Sanders still walk hand in hand, although they are over sixty; they are still love-birds.'

9. there's **no love lost** between them – two people who dislike each other very much. The original meaning was the exact opposite. Goldsmith writes in *She Stoops to Conquer* (I, v): 'As for mumures, Mother, we grumble a little now and then, to be sure. But there's no love lost between us' (meaning that none of the love between them was wasted).

10. **not for love or money** – not at any price. 'The London hotels are booked out at this time of the year; you can't get a room for love or money.'

11. to **play for love** – to play a game without gambling on it. 'I never gamble, but I'll play you for love if you like.'

## HATE AND FURY

12. a **pet hate/aversion** – a special dislike. 'My pet hate is the shift-workers who march past our house singing at the top of their voices at three o'clock in the morning on their way to work.'

13. **fast and furious** – excited, wild, noisy. 'Bill and Alison danced the waltz fast and furious round the room until they became too giddy to go on.'

14. **like fury** – with demonic energy and determination. 'After being a goal down, we played like fury and beat the champions 2–0.'

15. **all the rage** – in great demand, the height of fashion. 'Please, Mother, let's have a video. All our friends have one; it's all the rage.'

16. **with a vengeance** – in far greater measure than one expected or wanted. 'When the weather finally broke, it rained with a vengeance every day and all day for the next two weeks.'

## SHAME, CRYING, DOUBT

1. **Shame on you!** – you should be ashamed of yourself. 'Do you mean to say you let Doris carry all her luggage down the stairs without helping her? Shame on you!'
2. a **crying shame** – a great wrong that calls for action. 'It's a crying shame that the children should be separated from one another because of their parents' divorce.'

   a **crying need** – an urgent need that demands action.
3. to **put** someone **to shame** – to make someone feel inferior by showing up his faults. 'While you were sunning yourselves in Tenerife, Vivien worked over Christmas without once complaining. She has put you all to shame.'
4. a **nagging doubt** – a doubt that continually troubles the conscience. 'I had a nagging doubt whether we had been right to send William abroad with no one to accompany him when he was only thirteen.'
5. to **give** someone **the benefit of the doubt** – to accept the most charitable explanation of someone's actions. 'Very well, Mrs Brown, we will give you the benefit of the doubt this time, but in future please make sure you have paid for everything in your bag before you leave the shop.'

## FEAR, AFRAID, SCARE

6. **without fear or favour** – completely fair, without prejudice or fear of threats. 'It's expensive going to law, but one thing you can be certain of: your case will be heard without fear or favour.'
7. there's **not much fear of . . .** – it's not very likely that . . . (used in reference to future events). 'The only way to save our jobs would be for all of us to accept a ten per cent cut in our wages, but there's not much fear of that happening, worse luck.'
8. **in fear and trembling** – in a state of great fear, shaking with fear. 'When the boss sent for me, I went to his office in fear and trembling, but he only wanted to praise my work.'
9. to be **afraid of one's own shadow** – to be afraid to meet people, to be shy and timid. 'It's no good inviting Pam to your party. She never goes anywhere; I do believe the poor girl would be afraid of her own shadow.'
10. **scared stiff** – terrified, overcome with fear. 'When the alsatian leapt at me, I was scared stiff and couldn't move.'
11. to **scare the pants off** someone – to give someone a terrible fright. 'Spending the night in the haunted room of that castle would scare the pants off me.'

## SORROW, GRIEF AND MISERY

12. **more in sorrow than in anger** – with feelings of sadness and disappointment rather than anger (at someone's wrongdoing). 'When Kenneth told his wife that he had gambled away her money, she looked at him more in sorrow than in anger.'
13. to **drown one's sorrows** – to drink heavily to console oneself for a setback or misfortune. 'Margaret has just told me she won't be seeing me again, so I am drowning my sorrows.'
14. **in a sorry state** – in a pitiful condition. 'When I called on Oliver, I found him in a sorry state; he was lying in great pain on the floor.'
15. to **come to grief** – to fail disastrously. 'Owing to his lack of experience, all Gerald's ventures came to grief.'
16. to **put** someone **out of his misery** – to put an end to someone's suspense by giving him the information he

was hoping for. 'The doctor has put me out of my misery; there's nothing wrong with my lungs.' The original meaning was to kill a sick or injured animal that was suffering unnecessarily.

## SUFFER AND WOE

1. to **suffer fools gladly** (almost always used in the negative) – to tolerate stupidity in others. 'Alan is too impatient to suffer fools gladly.'

2. **woe betide you** – you will be sorry . . . 'Woe betide you if you miss your interview. You won't get another chance.' The phrase is sometimes used humorously. 'Betide' means 'happen to' and derives from Anglo-Saxon 'tide', 'time', 'hour'. It is only used in this phrase.

## DUMPS AND DAMPER

3. **in the dumps / down in the dumps** – depressed, miserable. 'Yvonne has been in the dumps ever since her brother went to Canada.' 'Dump' is a cognate of Dutch 'dompen' to quench, extinguish, and English 'damp'. Cf. 'a **wet blanket' 149/9**.

4. to **put a damper on** someone – to discourage or depress someone cf. **'in the dumps' 123/3**, 'a **wet blanket' 149/9**.

   to **put a damper on** an idea, enthusiasm, hope – to discourage someone's idea, enthusiasm or hope. 'I wish John weren't so negative; he puts a damper on all my ideas.' cf. 'to **pour cold water on' 25/9**.

## JOY AND HOPE

5. to be someone's **pride and joy** – to be the special object of someone's love and pride. 'The bird sanctuary which the old man had built himself was the pride and joy of his life.'

6. to **wish** someone **joy of** a person/thing – to express pleasure at being rid of a person/thing one doesn't like. An ironic comment on the person/thing one has been parted from. 'So Mrs Anderson has deserted us for Dr Boyd; I wish him joy of her!' 'I'm not sorry to have lost my new brooch; it was always pricking me. I wish the finder joy of it!'

7. to **get no joy from** – to get no help from. 'I've been looking everywhere for a room; I tried the information bureau, but got no joy from them.' cf. 'to **get no change out of' 243/1**.

8. to **hope against hope** – to keep on hoping even though there are no longer any grounds for hope. 'We were hoping against hope that Grandfather would get better, although the doctor had given him up.'

9. a **fond hope** – a foolish hope. 'The old man nourished the fond hope that his grandson would qualify as a doctor, although the boy had no interest in medicine.' 'Fond' derives from East Friesian 'fone', 'fon' meaning a girl, weakling, simpleton; hence foolish, whose meaning it has retained to the present day but only in this phrase,

10. to **pin one's hopes on** – to rely on a single thing or person for the fulfilment of one's hopes. 'We are pinning our hopes on a new German drug to cure our son.'

## FEELINGS

11. to **feel small** – to feel humiliated or ashamed. 'When Martin found he hadn't enough money to pay the bill, he felt very small.'

12. to **get the feel of** – to become accustomed to. 'After hammering away all day on the manual typewriter, it took me a little time to get the feel of the electric one.'

13. to **feel out of it** – to feel as if one

doesn't belong. 'All the guests at the party were teenagers. I was much too old and felt quite out of it.'

1. to **get the feeling that** – to suspect without understanding the reason. 'I get the feeling, Marion, that you don't want to come out with me.'
2. to acquire a **feeling for** something – to develop a sympathy for something. 'If you want to speak a foreign language well, you must acquire a feeling for it.'
3. to **feel the draught/pinch** – to suffer discomfort through lack of money. 'Now that people are short of money, the shops in the High Street are feeling the draught/pinch.'
4. **no hard feelings** – no ill-feelings or resentment. 'Since we don't agree, wouldn't it be better for us to part, with no hard feelings on either side?'
5. to **have mixed feelings** about – to be undecided, to feel regret as well as pleasure about a certain course of action. 'When my parents decided to emigrate to Australia, I had mixed feelings about going.'
6. to **vent one's feelings on** – to find an outlet for one's anger in; to divert one's anger on to. 'Just because you didn't get an increase in your salary, you needn't vent your feelings on me!'
7. **not to feel oneself** – to feel slightly unwell or depressed. 'I am sorry if I was a little short with you just now; I don't feel myself today.'

# 13. ILLNESSES AND AILMENTS

## BLIND

1. to be **blinded by hatred** – to hate to such an extent that one's judgement of a person is distorted.
2. to **turn a blind eye to** – deliberately to overlook a fault in another person, which one does not wish to acknowledge, even to oneself. 'The old man adored his grandson and always turned a blind eye to his misbehaviour.'
3. to **have a blind spot for** – to have uncritical enthusiasm for. 'Most parents have a blind spot for their children, and ignore their faults.'
4. a **blind date** – an introduction to an unknown person arranged by an agency or a third party.
5. a **blind-alley occupation / job** – one that offers no chance of promotion. It is always unskilled and therefore badly paid in the long run.
6. **the blind leading the blind** – an ironic comment on leaders who are as ignorant and incompetent as the people they are leading. From the Bible (Matthew XV, 14) 'And if the blind lead the blind, both shall fall into the ditch.'

## DEAF

7. to **turn a deaf ear to** – to refuse to listen, usually to some request for help.
8. to **fall on deaf ears** – to meet with no response, to be ignored.
9. a **dialogue of the deaf** – a fruitless discussion, one in which all the participants have closed minds and are unreceptive to any rational argument.
10. to be **as deaf as a door-post** – completely deaf. Sometimes said of a person who is not conscious of his deafness. 'He's as deaf as a door-post but he gets very angry if you shout at him.'
11. a **deafening silence** – a silence which expresses more embarrassment than any words could do. 'When Jack asked the bride at the wedding reception whether she had been married before, there was a deafening silence.' One can also say: **the silence was deafening**.
12. **hard of hearing** – having difficulty in hearing.

## DUMB

13. to **strike dumb** – to render someone speechless with surprise.
    to **be struck dumb** – to be made speechless with astonishment.
14. **dumb insolence** (a military phrase) – an insolent attitude conveyed by a subordinate towards a superior in rank without any words being uttered.
15. **the dumb millions** – the masses who have no say in the way they are governed.
16. **our dumb friends** – our animal friends.
17. **dumb animals** – a phrase used in pity because animals are unable to complain of ill-treatment.
18. a **dumb blonde** – (Americanism) – a girl who is good-looking but lacking in intelligence. The Americans use the word 'dumb' in the sense of 'stupid' in the same way as the Germans use the cognate 'dumm'.
19. a **dumb-waiter** – an arrangement of revolving shelves introduced in the eighteenth century for replacing servants in the drawing-room. The object of the device was to ensure

greater privacy rather than save labour.

## LAMENESS

1. a **lame excuse** – an excuse that is weak and unconvincing.
2. to **tread on** someone's **corns** – to mention a very delicate or sensitive subject, to speak tactlessly. 'You trod on his corns last night when you asked about his wife. Didn't you know, she has run off with his junior partner?'
3. **crippling taxes** – a tax that is so high that it discourages businessmen from expanding their enterprises or taking risks.
4. a **fractured sentence** – a sentence in which the subject and the object have been separated by one or more subordinate clauses, e.g. 'I wanted, when I was staying with my friends in Massachusetts, in the spring of 1983, to pay a visit to the Niagara Falls' instead of: 'When I was staying with my friends in Massachusetts in the spring of 1983, I wanted to pay a visit to the Niagara Falls.'

## FEVER AND COLDS

5. **at fever heat/pitch** – with the utmost exertion and excitement. 'The children worked at fever heat to get their play ready in time for Christmas.'
6. **not to be sneezed at** – not to be despised, considerable. 'An income of £30,000 a year is not to be sneezed at, even today.'
7. to **cough up** (vulgar) – to pay up.

## INFECTIONS

8. an **infectious laugh** – a laugh that is quickly echoed by the other people present. 'His laugh was so infectious that we all joined in, even though we didn't understand the joke.'
9. to **plague** someone – to pester someone with constant requests.
10. to **avoid like the plague** – to keep something you consider harmful or dangerous at as great a distance from you as possible. 'If you want to write well, you must avoid jargon like the plague.'
11. **a plague on both your houses** – a phrase of disgust with both parties in a contest. It is often said by Liberals and Social Democrats about the two major parties in British politics, the Conservative and Labour parties. The reference is to Shakespeare's *Romeo and Juliet* (III, i, 96).

## OTHER AFFLICTIONS

12. **intellectual myopia** – a phrase recently coined for stupidity.

    **a myopic view of a problem** – a short-sighted or narrow-minded conception of a problem.
13. to have **teething trouble** – to have initial difficulties that stem from inexperience or novelty of design. 'When we bought our new television set, the salesman warned us that we might have teething trouble with it, since the design of the model was a new and complicated one.' The reference is to the pain associated with the cutting of a tooth. cf. 'to **have growing pains**' **128/2**.
14. to be **stiff-necked** – to be very obstinate, impossible to argue with; unwilling to listen to reason. cf. **'pig-headed'** **59/6**.
15. to **cramp** someone's **style** – to hinder or spoil what someone is trying to do. 'My husband loves to entertain our guests with his funny stories but, when Father comes to dinner, Alan always forgets what he wants to say. I don't know why, but Father seems to cramp his style.'
16. to **work in spasms** – to work irregu-

larly, some days many hours on end and some days not at all.

1. **with a jaundiced eye** – with a sour, disapproving look. 'Having already lost a lot of his money on his wife's wild schemes, Philip viewed her new project with a jaundiced eye.'
2. a **measly reward** – a mean, miserly reward.
3. a **rash** of new ideas, etc. – one (idea) very quickly following another.
4. to **have itching fingers** – to have a strong impulse to hit someone. 'My fingers were itching to smack Peter's face.'
5. **warts and all** – with all its faults and imperfections, a realistic portrayal. The modern artist tries to render a true likeness, 'warts and all', and avoid flattering his subject. The phrase comes from Oliver Cromwell's statement that he wanted his portrait to show him accurately, 'warts and all'.
6. an **anaemic character** – a weak, subdued character.
7. to get **dizzy with success** – success has often been compared with climbing to the top of a pole, when it would be natural to feel dizzy on looking down.
8. to **play the giddy goat** – to behave wildly, irresponsibly. Goats have always been associated with wildness and lack of control.
9. **verbal diarrhoea** (colloquial) – compulsive talkativeness. 'Hewitt spoke to the conference for three hours, scarcely pausing to draw breath; a bad case of verbal diarrhoea.'
10. **with a sting in its tail** – a speech or article that reserves its venom until the end.
11. **only a hiccup / a mere hiccup** – only a small, temporary setback in one's progress, or in a relationship with someone. 'We look forward to doing a lot of business with you; your dispute with our director was only a hiccup.'
12. a **barren harvest** – a worthless reward.
13. **cancerous growth** – a pathological tendency to grow and spread. 'In the last few years there has been a cancerous growth in drug-taking which has affected all sections of society.'
14. **sick humour / a sick joke** – humour that is morbid or sadistic; for example, when an armless person is given a tennis racquet for his birthday.
15. to **pile on the agony** – to aggravate the pain. 'There was no need to tell Dennis he would have to get a job now that he has failed his exams and can't go to university. That was piling on the agony.'
16. to **add insult to injury** – to aggravate a wrong that one has done someone by adding another. 'Having failed to pay the doctor's bill, the patient then complained about his treatment to the medical association. He added insult to injury.'
17. to **lick one's wounds** – to console oneself after a severe blow.

## ACHES

18. to **be a headache** – to be a great trial to other people, due to one's misbehaviour and bad temper.
19. to **belly-ache** (Australian) – to complain continually. The phrase is now becoming fashionable in Great Britain.

## PAINS

20. to be **a fool for one's pains** – to work hard, or try to help someone else without proper reward or acknowledgement. 'Only £10 for all that work! You were a fool for your pains!'
21. to be **at pains / to take pains to** – to

exert oneself to, to make a great effort to. 'The teacher took pains to correct the girl's pronunciation.' 'They were all at pains to make me feel at home, and I soon forgot I was homesick.'

1. a **pain in the neck** (slang) – a pest, a real nuisance, a source of continuous annoyance. 'That man has been a pain in the neck ever since we took him on. He quarrels with all our customers and staff.'
2. to have **growing pains** – just as a child has 'growing pains' in its limbs, so an industry may have 'growing pains' when it has difficulties in getting itself established on a profitable basis. cf. **'teething trouble' 126/13**.

## SORES

3. to **be sore about** – to feel aggrieved about. 'He is still sore about Vivien going out with Norman.'
4. a **sore spot** – a subject about which someone is particularly sensitive. 'You shouldn't have mentioned his father's bankruptcy. You touched a sore spot with him.'
5. a **sight for sore eyes** – an object of outstanding beauty, capable of inspiring the most jaded observer.
6. an **eye-sore** – hideous, offensive to the eye. 'The new building was an eye-sore, quite out of place in its surroundings.' cf. 'to **stick out like a sore thumb' 97/12**.
7. to **open old sores** – to revive old quarrels. 'Why did you talk to Martin about Father's will? What was the point of opening old sores?'

## MADNESS

8. **midsummer madness** – madness has always been associated with the full moon, so that the midsummer heat, combined with the full moon, was the time when madness was at its fullest intensity.
9. there is **method in his madness** – although he seems to be acting illogically, he has, in fact, a purpose in everything he does. 'Our approach to our clients may surprise you at first, but you will soon see there is method in our madness.' (See Shakespeare's *Hamlet*, II, ii, 211.)
10. **hopping mad** – absolutely furious. 'When the bus went all the way at walking pace, the passengers were hopping mad with the driver.'
11. to **throw a fit** – to experience an attack of nerves, brought on by shock, anxiety, rage, etc. 'Your father would throw a fit if he knew what you were up to!'
12. **by fits and starts** – irregularly, spasmodically. 'Mary works by fits and starts. One day she will work for ten hours; the next two days she won't work at all.'
13. a **mania for** (fresh air, fast driving, stamp-collecting, etc.) – an overwhelming desire for or interest in some object or activity.
14. a **schizoid attitude to** – mixed or contradictory feelings and views about a particular topic. Schizoid is a psychiatric term meaning a dissociation between the reason and the emotions.
15. the **lunatic fringe** – the fanatics in a political party who seek to impose their extremist policies on the country by force.

## ILLNESS

16. to be **ill at ease with** – to feel awkward in the presence of someone. 'Bernard always felt ill at ease when he was with his father; he never understood why.'
17. a **diplomatic illness** – a sham illness to provide an excuse for non-

attendance at a party or function. Diplomatic illnesses are sometimes pleaded in order to extricate someone from an embarrassing situation; at other times, to express annoyance or resentment.

## MEDICINE AND HEALTH

1. to give someone **a dose/taste of his own medicine** – to treat a wrongdoer in the same way as he has his victims. 'While Johnson was breaking into the vicarage, his own flat was burgled. He was given a taste of his own medicine!'
2. a **bitter pill to swallow** – to be obliged to accept a great disappointment or humiliation. 'It was a bitter pill for him to swallow when he discovered that after twenty years of marriage his wife did not love him.'
3. to **give a clean bill of health** – after a medical check-up, to inform someone that he is in good physical condition. 'Now that the doctor has given me a clean bill of health, I can start training for the European Championship.'

# 14. RELATIONS

## RELATIONS

1. **poor relations** – relatives who are despised for their lack of money. The phrase is often applied to people who beg from their richer relations; but it can also be used ironically. 'My sister-in-law is a terrible snob. She always makes me feel like a poor relation when I visit her.'
2. **relations are rather strained** – a change for the worse in the feelings of two persons or parties towards one another, e.g. between the USA and Soviet Russia; a cooling-off of a friendship, usually brought about by some unresolved problem or dispute. 'Since I told my fiancée that I wanted to take a job in America, our relations have been rather strained.'

## FAMILY

3. a **family man** – a man whose interests are in his home, rather than outside it, e.g. in his career, or in sport, socializing, etc.
4. to **be family** – someone who is entitled to special consideration because he is one of the family. 'We always keep a room free for Pamela; she is family.'
5. **in the family way** (vulgar) – pregnant.
6. a **person of family** – born into a good family.
7. a **family doctor** – a doctor who attends the family when they are ill.
8. the **head of the family** – usually the father or, in his absence, the eldest son.
9. to **run in the family** – (of a characteristic or talent) to pass from one generation to the next. 'Jack's three children are all musical, just like their father; it must run in the family.'

## MARRIAGE

10. **marriage lines** – a marriage certificate.
11. a **shot-gun marriage** – one that the couple are forced into by circumstances beyond their control (for example, the pregnancy of the bride). It has come to mean any partnership that is forced on the parties. 'There may well be a shot-gun marriage between the trade unions and small business if the economic depression continues.' This is an American idiom which owes its origin to the old days when a young man who had seduced a girl would be forced by her angry parents to marry her at the point of a shot-gun.

## KINDRED

12. **kindred spirits** – two people who share the same ideas and interests. 'Anne and I must be kindred spirits; we have the same views on everything.'

## WIFE

13. a **fish-wife** – a woman who is vulgar and uses bad language.
14. an **old wives' tale** – an old story or belief that has no foundation in fact, a myth. Here are a few examples of old wives' tales: that a drowning man rises to the surface twice before sinking for the last time; that children suffer from 'growing pains'; that you will catch a cold if you sit about in wet socks; and that musical people learn a foreign language quicker than unmusical people.
15. **like Caesar's wife** – above suspicion (of any crime or immoral behaviour). Only used of important public figures.

'Ministers of the Crown must be like Caesar's wife. If their private lives give rise to scandal, they are expected to resign.' When asked why Caesar divorced his wife, he replied: 'I wished my wife to be not so much as suspected' (Caesar, Roman *Apothegms*).

## FATHER

1. a **father figure** – a man who takes the place of a father. He may play the part of a father to a young man, as Dr Johnson did to Boswell, or to a whole nation, as President Tito did to Yugoslavia.
2. **the father of** literature, history, modern psychology, etc. – the originator or the first example of. Chaucer is the father of English literature. Freud is the father of psycho-analysis.
3. **the wish is father to the thought** – we believe what we wish to believe – a common human failing.
4. **when Father turns, we all turn** – an ironic comment on the type of leader who, as he changes his views, expects his followers to do the same. The phrase is based on the idea of a man sleeping in one bed with his wife and children, who expects them all to turn over when he does so.
5. to be **gathered to one's fathers** (biblical) – to die.
6. **the sins of the fathers are visited on the sons** (biblical) – later generations suffer the consequences of their ancestors' vices.
7. **like father, like son** – resemblance of the son to the father from the intellectual or emotional point of view.
8. **the child is father of the man** – the child's behaviour indicates how the character of the man will develop. 'The childhood shows the man / As morning shows the day' (Milton, *Paradise Regained*, Book IV, 1.220). 'The child is father of the man' (Wordsworth, 'My heart leaps up when I behold . . .').
9. **on the father's/mother's side** – a relative of the father, for example the father's parents, or his brother, sister or cousin, etc. The same applies to the mother.
10. to **stand godfather** – to pay the bills, godfathers being people from whom one expects generous gifts.

## DADDY

11. a **sugar daddy** – a rich old man who keeps a girl young enough to be his daughter.
12. **Big Daddy** – a father who is very protective of his daughter.

## MOTHER

13. **'Like motherhood, we are all for it'** – to declare one's support for a policy which has the support of everybody; like saying: 'I'm in favour of a fair and just society.'
14. **mother tongue** – the first language one learns to speak.
15. a **mother-complex** – an unhealthy or abnormal emotional tie between the son and his mother, resulting in the son's emotional dependence on the mother and coolness towards other women.
16. a **mother's boy/darling** – a boy who is indulged or spoilt by his mother.
17. the **wicked step-mother** – step-mothers are often regarded as wicked by the step-children who look upon them as intruders.
18. a **fairy god-mother** – a person who provides one with every possible blessing. 'You've been a real fairy god-mother to me.' A figure of speech taken from fairy stories in which a woman with supernatural powers pro-

tects the interests of the young heroine.

1. **the mother and father of** – the biggest and the worst. 'I'm sorry I can't go out with you tonight. I've got the mother and father of a toothache.'

## CHILD

2. **child's play** – a simple task for anyone who has the gift or experience to accomplish it. 'It was child's play to teach the boy English, he was so quick and intelligent.'
3. **Spare the rod and spoil the child** – without strict discipline, a child's character will be ruined by his parents' indulgence. A Victorian adage which has been rejected by later generations of parents.
4. **child of nature** – someone who is innately good, even if unpolished.
5. a **child wife** – a wife who is too young to carry out her duties, for example David Copperfield's first wife (in *David Copperfield* by Charles Dickens).
6. a **brain-child** (colloquial) – one's original idea. It can be used in a derogatory way when the speaker disclaims responsibility for an idea that has failed in practice. 'The new shift system at the office was the manager's brain-child, not mine. He is to blame for its failure.'
7. **second childhood** – the simple-mindedness of old age which resembles in some ways the mind of a child.

## BABY

8. a **cry-baby** – someone who cries or complains at the smallest provocation. 'That boy cries out whenever he is touched. He's a real cry-baby.'
9. **baby-face** – round cheeks, innocent air and adolescent appearance, though advanced in years.
10. to **baby-sit** – to look after a baby or small children while the parents are out. This is done by a **baby-sitter**.
11. to **throw out the baby with the bath water** – to destroy the good while trying to eliminate the bad. 'When the new director dismissed a large number of his staff to make the company more profitable, he also got rid of some of his best engineers. He had thrown out the baby with the bath water.'
12. to **be left holding the baby** – to be forced to take over someone else's responsibility. 'When the firm started to lose money, Harry resigned, and I was left holding the baby.'
13. a **baby-snatcher** (derogatory) – a woman who has a boy-friend much younger than herself.
14. **the babes in the wood** – innocent, naïve people lacking in experience and over-trustful. 'We've been doing this work for many years; we aren't exactly babes in the wood.'
15. a **babe-in-arms** – someone who is completely naïve and inexperienced in the ways of the world. 'How can John think of starting a business at his age! He is only a babe-in-arms.'

## SON

16. he is **his father's son** – he resembles his father in character.
17. the **prodigal son** – someone who returns home after a long absence, and is received with great joy by his family despite his past behaviour. Today, the phrase is used in a humorous sense. 'Are you going to kill the fatted calf for the prodigal son, Tom?' The allusion is to the parable of the prodigal son in Luke XV, 30.
18. **son of the soil** – a person who has been

brought up on the land, e.g. a farm labourer.

1. a **son of a bitch** (vulgar) – an Americanism meaning a mean, nasty man who will take unfair advantage of you to further his own ends.
2. a **natural son/daughter** – an illegitimate son/daughter.

## DAUGHTER

3. a **daughter language** – a language which has been derived from an older one; for example the Romance languages, French, Italian, Spanish, etc., from Latin.

## BROTHER

4. the **brotherhood of man** – human society considered as one big family.
5. **Big Brother** – in George Orwell's novel *1984*, Big Brother is the dictator of an imaginary country who dominates the lives of all its citizens. Big Brother is able to observe each citizen through an electronic eye, so that there is no escaping him, however cautiously his opponents conspire against him. Big Brother has become a symbol of power and tyranny against whom it is useless to struggle.
6. **'Am I my brother's keeper?'** – often used as a disclaimer of responsibility for the actions of one's close associates. From Genesis IV, 9: 'And the Lord said unto Cain, Where is Abel thy brother; and he said I know not. Am I my brother's keeper?'
7. **brothers in arms** – originally fellow soldiers, but used metaphorically in the sense of participants in the same struggle.

## TWIN

8. a **twin-set** – matching jumper and cardigan.

## COUSIN

9. **country cousins** – people from the country rather than the town, who are presumed to be ignorant and unsophisticated.

## GRANDMOTHER

10. **don't teach your grandmother to suck eggs** – don't try to instruct someone who is more experienced than you.

## AUNT

11. an **Aunt Sally** – an object of ridicule whose policies have failed or become unpopular. 'The Prime Minister, Mrs Thatcher, has no intention of allowing the Home Secretary to be made an Aunt Sally for the increase in crime this year.' An Aunt Sally was originally a female effigy stuck on the end of a pole at which sticks and stones were thrown with the object of knocking the pipe out of its mouth; hence an object of derision.

## UNCLE

12. **Uncle Sam** – a nickname for the typical American. cf. **'John Bull of England' 192/12**.
13. **Uncle Tom** – a derisive term used by black nationalists for black people who collaborate with the white authorities. Uncle Tom was the black hero of *Uncle Tom's Cabin*, a story by Harriet Beecher Stowe.
14. **Uncle Tom Cobbleigh and all** – all and sundry, including the most ordinary people you can think of.

## BACHELOR

15. a **bachelor girl** – an unmarried girl.
16. a **bachelor's wife** – the perfect wife in the mind of the unmarried man.

## WIDOW

1. a **grass widow** – a woman whose husband is away temporarily. Originally, an unmarried woman who has lived with one or more men. The phrase suggests illicit relations out of doors rather than in the marriage bed.

   a **golf widow** – a woman whose husband spends much of his time on the golf course, so that she is alone for most of the day.

2. **not for widows and orphans** – not for investors of limited means who cannot afford to take risks with their money.

3. a **merry widow** – merry because she is now free to make new friends and have a merry time. The reference is to Franz Lehár's operetta 'The Merry Widow'.

4. **the widow's mite** – although the gift was very small, it had more moral worth coming from a poor woman than a bigger gift from a rich one. From Christ's parable, Mark XII, 42.

5. **widow's weeds** – a widow's mourning dress. 'Her widow's weeds become her.'

# 15. TOWN AND AROUND

## TOWN

1. to **go to town** – to spend one's money recklessly. 'The Howards have really gone to town on a house for their daughter. They have bought her an absolute beauty.' **'Go to town'** is an American colloquialism referring to the people who come into town from the countryside to spend their money. It was originally used about cowboys and ranch hands.
2. a **man about town** – a sociable man who attends many fashionable parties and has a wide circle of wealthy friends. 'My brother has become quite a man about town; when he was young, he hated going to parties.
3. a **lady of the town** – a woman of loose morals.
4. the **talk of the town** – someone whose behaviour and wild way of life give rise to gossip and scandal-mongering. 'You had better behave yourself, Pauline. You are becoming the talk of the town.'

   **it's the talk of the town** – it's the most talked-about or fashionable place or thing.
5. a **ghost town** – a town that is no longer inhabited.

## STREET

6. to **take to the streets** – to demonstrate against authority, to make a show of force. 'The students took to the streets in support of the health workers' claim for higher wages.'
7. to **go on the streets** – to work as a prostitute.
8. **streets ahead of** – far superior to, very much in advance of. 'You are streets ahead of us in technology.'
9. **not in the same street** – far inferior to, in no way comparable. 'All right, I'll have a game with you, but you know very well I'm not in the same street as you.'
10. the **man in the street** – the ordinary, typical man and woman. 'We are doing market research work, and we want the reaction of the man in the street to our suggestions.'
11. to **go back to Civvy Street** – to return to civilian life after serving in the armed forces. 'What are you going to do when you go back to Civvy Street?'
12. **in Queer Street** – in financial trouble, in debt. 'If we go on spending money like this, we shall soon be in queer street.' 'Queer Street' may be a corruption of Carey Street where the Courts in Bankruptcy are situated.
13. **grub street** – an inferior writer, inferior writing. '. . . any mean production is called grubstreet' (Dr Johnson, *Dictionary*). Grub Street near Moorfields in the East End of London (now Milton Street) was inhabited in the seventeenth century by a group of inferior writers and literary hacks.
14. **right up my street** – that's a subject I'm very familiar with. 'I'll be glad to advise Brian about his advertising. Advertising and publicity are right up my street.'

## ROAD

15. **one for the road** – a final drink before one leaves a social gathering.
16. to **take to the road** – to become a tramp. 'I would rather take to the road than work in an office from 9 till 5 each day. I want to be free.'
17. **at the end of the road** – (1) towards the end of one's life. 'I have come to the

end of the road, my dear; the doctor has given me only another six months.' (2) finally, last of all.

1. **at the cross-roads** – at a point in one's life when important decisions have to be made. 'Peter and Sue are at the cross-roads; they will have to decide very soon whether to make their home in England or emigrate.'

DEAD END

2. a **dead end** – leading nowhere.
   a **dead end job** – a job with no prospects or advancement, similar in meaning to a **'blind alley job' 125/5**.

WAY

3. to **pave the way for** – to create the necessary conditions for . . . , usually followed by some event. 'World War II paved the way for the independence of India.'
4. to **go all the way** with – to be in complete agreement with. 'I'm not sure whether I would go all the way with you, but I certainly sympathize with your aims.'
5. **way out** – (1) quite wrong, totally mistaken. 'You are way out in your calculations. The holiday will cost £300, not £200.' (2) out of the ordinary, bizarre. 'Some of the costumes at the party were way out, especially the exotic pyjamas which would have been more suitable for the bedroom.'
6. to **rub someone up the wrong way** – to be tactless, to say the very thing that is certain to annoy someone. 'You certainly rubbed Mrs Parker up the wrong way, telling her you don't like Sussex. She has lived there all her life and adores the county.'
7. to **go about something the wrong way** – to use the wrong method or approach to achieve an object. 'If you wanted Howard to back your project you went about it the wrong way contradicting him at dinner.'
8. **at the parting of the ways** – a time when it is best to separate. 'I am so sorry, Tim, but I'm afraid we've come to a parting of the ways. We are only making each other unhappy.' From the Bible, Ezekiel XXI, 21: 'For the king of Babylon stood at the parting of the way, at the head of the two ways . . .'
9. to **go one's own way** – to follow one's inclinations, to rely on one's own judgement and ignore other people's. 'All right, Tom, go your own way, if that's how you feel about it, but I wish you would listen to us just once.'
10. to **have a way with one** – to have a natural charm, which is very persuasive. 'Jenny certainly has a way with her. I found myself agreeing with everything she said.'
11. to **have come a long way** – to have accomplished a great deal. 'You've come a long way since we last met. You were a clerk then, and now you own your own factory.'
12. **in a big way** – on a large scale. 'Ian is very ambitious, he does everything in a big way.'
    **in a small way** – on a small scale, only to a small extent. 'If you could help me, even in a small way, I should be most grateful.'
13. to **find out the hard way** – to learn the truth from one's own painful experience. 'We warned you that you wouldn't like boarding school but you wouldn't listen. Now you've found out the hard way.'
14. to **make way for** – to surrender one's position to someone else. 'You've done a wonderful job for the Company, but we think, Sir, that at the age of seventy it is only fair you should make way for a younger man.'

1. to **have it one's own way** – to insist on doing what one wants despite arguments to the contrary. 'Have it your own way, Hugh, but if things go wrong, don't blame us.'
2. to **have it both ways** – to support two incompatible arguments or courses of action at the same time. 'If you want an absolutely safe investment, then you can't expect a high rate of interest. You can't have it both ways.'
3. to **cut both ways** – to have advantages and disadvantages at the same time. 'This new drug will relieve your arthritis, but you must put up with the side-effects; it cuts both ways.'
4. **set in one's ways** – having fixed ideas and habits. 'Turner is too set in his ways to adopt your ideas; you had better look for a younger man.'
5. to **look the other way** – to pretend not to see, to overlook a breach of the rules or some irregularity. 'Even a disciplinarian like the sergeant-major has to look the other way sometimes.'
6. **on its way out** – becoming unfashionable. 'The mini-skirt was already on its way out by 1969.'
7. to **pay one's way** – to support oneself without having to borrow money. 'Many American students pay their way through college by taking a part-time job.'
8. to **mend one's ways** – to change one's behaviour or habits, for the better. 'If you want your uncle to help you, you'll have to mend your ways. That will mean cutting out night clubs and starting to study seriously.'
9. a **way of life** – a set of principles according to which one lives one's life. 'Alan soon got used to the Muslim way of life, but his sister found it more difficult.'
10. to **see one's way to** – to feel justified in. 'After Peter's ingratitude to her, his cousin didn't see her way to giving him any more help.'
11. to **go out of one's way** to – to put oneself to some trouble to . . . , to make a special effort to . . . 'When we visited London, our hosts went out of their way to make our stay enjoyable.'
12. **no way** (colloquial American English) – out of the question, impossible. '"Could you please lend me £50?" "No way, I haven't got that much myself."'
13. **by the way** – incidentally, which reminds me. 'I'm sorry your cousin is ill. By the way, have you got his new address? I have some letters for him.'
14. **there are no two ways about it** – there is no other possibility or explanation. 'When you are in the army, you have to obey orders, no matter how unreasonable or stupid they may be. There are no two ways about it.'
15. to **stand in someone's way** – to obstruct or hinder someone in his aims. 'If you want to take a job abroad, don't let me stand in your way.'
16. **in a bad way** – physically or mentally in a serious condition. 'Your brother has had an accident. Will you go to the hospital at once; he's in a bad way.'
17. **not to know which way to turn** – to be in desperate difficulties. 'I was stranded in New York one winter without money or friends; I didn't know which way to turn until the British Consulate helped me out.'
18. to **put business** someone's **way** – to be the means of placing custom or orders with someone. 'If you are interested, I can put some business your way.'
19. to **fall by the wayside** – to fail to achieve one's aim, because of laziness, lack of strength or distractions. This phrase is generally used humorously. 'My father put me into accountancy, but I am sorry to say I was one of

those who fell by the wayside.' The allusion is to Luke VIII, 5: 'A Sower went out to sow his seed, and as he sowed, some fell by the wayside; and it was trodden down and the fowls of the air devoured it'.

## LANE

1. to **go down memory lane** – to revive old memories. 'Let's be sentimental, Joan, and go down memory lane this afternoon.'

## RIVER

2. to **sell down the river** – to betray, to act deceitfully towards. 'When we went back to the bookie's office to collect our winnings, he had already run off with the stakes; he had sold us down the river.' The phrase was first used by the black slaves who were sold by their owners to plantation owners further down the Mississippi, where conditions were usually much harsher.

## BRIDGE

3. to **cross one's bridges before one comes to them** – to worry unnecessarily about something that may never happen. 'I don't know why you are worrying about Father catching one of those tropical diseases in Africa. His company hasn't decided yet whether to send him to Africa. Don't cross your bridges before you come to them.'
4. **that's (all) water under the bridge** – that is all past now, and there is nothing that can be done about it. 'Yes, it's a pity you didn't accept Fred's offer, but it's useless to reproach yourself now. It's all water under the bridge.'
5. to **pull up the drawbridge** – to keep visitors out in order to ensure privacy for oneself and one's family. 'We enjoy entertaining, but at Christmas we like to pull up the drawbridge and be on our own.'

## AVENUE

6. to **explore every avenue** – to make the most thorough inquiry. 'We are exploring every avenue to obtain the information you are asking for.'

## TOWER

7. an **ivory tower** – a haven from the harsh realities of life. 'Living in your ivory tower at Oxford, you can't imagine, can you, what it's like to go hungry?' The term 'tour d'ivoire' (ivory tower) was first used by Sainte-Beuve (1837) to describe the retreat of the French poet, Vigny.
8. a **tower of strength** – a person one can always turn to for sympathy and support in times of trouble. 'When my parents' marriage broke up, my eldest sister was a tower of strength to the children. We couldn't have managed without her.'

## EXHIBITION

9. to **make an exhibition of oneself** – to invite public ridicule or contempt by one's behaviour. 'I wish Henry wouldn't make an exhibition of himself shouting at the waiter like that. It is so embarrassing.'

## MUSEUM

10. a **museum piece** – something antiquated or worn-out. 'We can't go to Scotland in that museum piece. Surely the car-hire company can do better than that!' The literal meaning is a specimen of an earlier civilization exhibited in a museum.

## PUBLIC HOUSE

1. to have someone **over a barrel** – to have a person in one's power, so that he can be forced to do whatever is asked of him. 'The boss has got you over a barrel. If you don't withdraw your accusations, he will take you to court, and if you do withdraw, you will lose the respect of the staff.'
2. to **scrape the bottom of the barrel** – to content oneself with poor quality when all other possibilities have been exhausted. 'Dorothy must have scraped the bottom of the barrel to have married a man like that!'

## MARKET

3. a **captive market** – a monopoly of an essential product or service which the consumer is obliged to accept without exercising his normal freedom of choice. 'We can ask any price we like for our water supply; we have a captive market.'
4. to be a **drug on the market** – to find no customers, something for which there is no demand. 'Gramophone records have become a drug on the market since cassettes were introduced.'
5. to be **in the market for** – to be interested in obtaining or buying something. 'We are not in the market for diamonds at present.'
6. to **play the market** – to speculate in the buying and selling of stocks and shares or commodities. 'Herbert calls it playing the market; I call it gambling.'
7. to **put something on the market** – to offer something for sale. 'We have decided to leave London, so we are putting our house on the market.'

   to **come on the market** – to be offered for sale.
8. to **corner the market** – to obtain a monopoly of the supply of particular goods or services. 'Once a government has cornered the market, as for instance in gas or electricity, there is always a huge rise in prices.'
9. a **rising/falling market** – a rising/falling demand for goods or services which will be reflected in their prices.
10. to **price oneself out of the market** – to ask so much more money for one's services or products that customers go elsewhere. 'The school fees you are charging are so high that you are in danger of pricing yourself out of the market.'
11. to **spoil the market for** – to reduce the demand for services or products by lowering their quality or putting too many on offer. 'The dishonest advertising agencies will spoil the market for the good ones.'
12. to **flood the market** – to offer services or goods far in excess of the demand for them.
13. to **drive a hard bargain** – to come to an agreement on one's own terms without making any worthwhile concessions. 'You drive a hard bargain, but I suppose I'll have to accept your offer.'
14. **under the counter** – of goods illegally sold in shops, secretly, without the knowledge of the authorities. 'Johnson always sold the stolen jewellery under the counter to clients who could be trusted not to go to the police.'
15. to **have no truck with** – to have no dealings with, not to tolerate. 'I'll have no truck with their demands for a higher wage.' 'Truck' originally meant to exchange goods for services, to barter, to have dishonest dealings with someone.

## HILL

16. **up hill and down dale** – everywhere. Idiomatically, this phrase is only used with verbs like look for, search for,

hunt for. 'Wherever have you been all this time? We have been looking for you up hill and down dale.'

1. **as old as the hills** – very old indeed. 'That car of yours is as old as the hills. Don't you think you ought to buy a new one?'

2. to **go downhill** – to suffer a decline in one's health or fortunes. 'Poor Bill, he has gone steadily downhill since he lost his job.'

   to **go down** – to suffer a decline in its reputation, quality or appearance. This is only used of things, not people, especially of neighbourhoods and districts. 'This was one of the most fashionable districts in London, but it has gone right down in the last ten years.'

## TRACK

3. to be **on the right/wrong track** – to make / not to make progress in one's search for . . . 'The police believe that they are at last on the right track in their hunt for the murderers.' 'If you think I had anything to do with it, you're on the wrong track.'

4. to **keep track of** – to keep oneself informed of someone's movements, activities, etc. 'I try to keep track of all my old school friends, but it isn't easy.'

   to **lose track of** – not to be informed of the movements, etc., of someone. 'Joyce has been married so many times that I've quite lost track.'

   to **lose (all) track of time** – not to be aware of the passage of time.

5. to **make tracks for** – to leave quickly for. 'It's getting late. We had better make tracks for home.'

6. a **track record** – a record of one's successes/failures. 'I think we should consider Holmes for the headmastership. His track record for getting his pupils into the universities is very good.'

7. **in one's tracks** – in the very place where one is standing at a particular moment. 'Hugh was on the point of hitting his son when his wife entered the room; that stopped him in his tracks!'

8. to **cover one's tracks** – to conceal traces of one's movements. 'The bank robbers have covered their tracks very cleverly.'

## PATH

9. to **keep to the straight and narrow (path)** – to resist temptation and lead a virtuous life. 'As a clergyman, I am naturally expected to keep to the straight and narrow path, but it hasn't always been easy.' The phrase comes from the Bible (Matthew VII, 14): 'Because strait is the gate, and narrow is the way which leadeth into life, and few there be that find it!'

10. to **beat a path to** a place – to visit in large numbers. 'Now that Vivien has become famous, all sorts of people will be beating a path to her door.' The path to a place is beaten flat by the feet of so many people.

11. to **cross** someone's **path** – (1) to meet someone accidentally. 'Since I left school, I haven't crossed Smith's path, and I can't say I have any wish to.' (2) to thwart someone. 'If Jones crosses your path again, let me know and I'll put a stop to his interference.'

## PITCH

12. to **queer someone's pitch** – to thwart or spoil someone's plans. 'The War Office queered our pitch by posting me overseas twenty-four hours before our wedding day.' 'Queer' is used as a verb only in this phrase. The pitch

refers to the pitching of a tent in which a street vendor could carry on his business or a circus performer could entertain the public. Sometimes the police would order these tented structures to be taken down, thus 'queering someone's pitch'.

## TRANSPORT AND TRAFFIC

1. to be **a slow coach** – to be very slow in one's actions, to keep one's companions waiting impatiently. 'What a slow coach you are! Do hurry up; everyone is waiting for you!'
2. to **jump the queue** – to try to seize an advantage without waiting one's turn. 'Everyone queues up in England. You'd make yourself very unpopular if you jumped the queue.'
3. to **miss the bus** – to lose an opportunity. 'I am fifty years old but I still haven't been promoted. Now it's too late; I've missed the bus.' cf. 'to **miss the boat' 180/1**.
4. to **tell** someone **where to get off** – to give someone a stern rebuke. 'When Joe started lecturing me on how to paint, I soon told him where to get off. He seemed to forget that I've had years of experience at it and he is only a beginner.' The phrase refers to the bus-conductor's right to order any passenger off a bus if he makes trouble.
5. to **fall off the back of a lorry** – a euphemism for 'to be stolen'. 'I wonder where Philip got that crate of very expensive wine. Did it fall off the back of a lorry?'
6. a **backseat driver** – someone who offers unwanted advice to the person in charge, while having no responsibility himself for the way a task is performed. 'We'd manage much better without the help of backseat drivers like Williams.' The phrase refers to the passenger in the back of a car, who is always telling the driver what to do.

# 16. THE HOUSE

## HOUSE

1. to **keep open house** – to be at home to visitors at all times; to offer them hospitality regardless of who they are.
2. a **rough house** – a fight, a violent disturbance. 'The soldiers are getting very aggressive. We had better leave before there is a rough house.'
3. a **full house** – a theatre that is fully attended.

   an **empty house** – an empty theatre. 'The ageing actress refused to retire, even though she was playing to empty houses.'
4. **The House of God** – a church or chapel.
5. to be **houseproud** – to take pride in keeping one's house clean and tidy. 'Anne is so houseproud, her drawing-room is like a shop window.'
6. a **household word** – something that is familiar to every household in the country.
7. a **drink on the house** – a drink that is paid for by the landlord of the public house. 'Have another; it's on the house.'
8. **in the best houses** – in the best society. The phrase suggests a country house with a retinue of servants to which the most distinguished people are invited.
9. a **house of cards** – an idea that has no foundation in fact, a wildly impracticable idea. 'His schemes for the future are no more than a house of cards that may topple over any moment.'
10. a **house of ill-fame** – a brothel.
11. a **madhouse** – one in which there is great commotion and disorder. 'I'll never visit my friend again. There was so much noise all through the night that it was impossible to sleep. It was a madhouse!'
12. **house arrest** – confinement to one's own home by order of the authorities.
13. to **bring the house down** – to receive resounding applause. 'The Prime Minister made a powerful speech which brought the house down.' The reference is to the applause of a theatre audience.
14. to **shout the house down / don't shout the house down** – to make a terrible commotion. 'I can't study while our brother is shouting the house down.'
15. to **cry/shout something from the housetops** – to tell everyone. 'If I'd known you were going to shout it from the housetops, I wouldn't have said anything.' The phrase derives from the East where the roofs are normally flat and are used as meeting places for the family.
16. a **house-warming party** – a party given in celebration of the new owners taking possession of their house.
17. to get on **like a house on fire** – to be in whole-hearted agreement with someone. The idiom suggests that the relationship of the two people grows in warmth. 'We have a great deal in common and work very well together. We are getting on like a house on fire.'
18. to be **as safe as houses** – to be absolutely safe. 'Your money will be quite safe in that company. It's well managed and it has huge assets. It's as safe as houses.'
19. to **have the run of the house** – to have free access to every room in the house. 'You can have the run of the house while we are on holiday.'
20. to **eat** someone **out of house and home** – to eat an excessive amount of one's host's food. 'My son William has a terrible appetite. At the rate he is going, he will eat us all out of house and home.'

1. to **set/put one's house in order** – to correct one's own mismanagement, often used with reference to business. 'Before we criticize others, we ought to put our own house in order.'

HOME

2. to **be/feel at home with** – to be on familiar ground, to be well informed on a given subject.
3. to **be 'at home' to people** – to be willing and prepared to receive friends in one's home.

   an **'at home'** – a meeting in one's own house of selected guests.
4. **not at home** – a euphemism for not wishing to receive an unwelcome guest. 'The maid was instructed to tell John Lane that her mistress was not at home.'
5. a **home from home** – a place or situation where one feels completely happy and at ease, where one is treated like one of the family.
6. to be **homesick** – to have a painful longing for one's own home and family.
7. the **last home** – the last resting-place, i.e. the grave.
8. to be **home and dry** – to have succeeded in one's aim. '"If the accused can prove he was at his mother's between 2 p.m. and 4 p.m., then he is home and dry", said the judge to defending counsel.'
9. to **do one's homework** – to be properly prepared, to master the facts before presenting one's case. 'Counsel paused for a few minutes to look at his papers before resuming his speech. It was obvious he hadn't done his homework.'
10. to **bring** something **home** to a person – to make someone aware of the truth, often painfully. 'His wife's nervous breakdown brought it home to Donald how cruel he had been to her.' This idiom is often connected with the idea of punishment.
11. a **home truth** – a statement that hurts someone because it tells him of a fault or weakness of which he is ashamed.
12. **nothing to write home about** – nothing special or out of the ordinary. 'Mary plays the piano quite competently but she's nothing to write home about. We were expecting much more.' The phrase suggests that a person's expectations have been disappointed.
13. to **romp home** – to leave all the others in the race far behind.
14. to **home in on** – (of a missile) to seek out and destroy a moving target after it has been launched.

WALL

15. to **go to the wall** – to fail, go bankrupt or collapse.

    **the weakest go to the wall** – the weakest are forced out of business by their more powerful competitors.
16. to drive someone **up the wall** – to irritate someone unbearably. 'When Alec talks about all the illnesses he has had, he drives me up the wall.'
17. **walls have ears** – you must be very careful what you say because someone may be eavesdropping. There is always a danger of being overheard, however private the conversation may be.
18. **within these four walls** – in confidence.
19. the **writing on the wall** – a warning of impending doom. 'Sanders & Duke are dismissing their staff. I am afraid the writing is on the wall for them.' From the Bible, Daniel V. 31.

STONE

20. to **stonewall** – to defend oneself with great caution in order to avoid mis-

takes and thus deny one's opponent any advantage. Originally, cricket slang for playing purely defensively, by blocking every ball and making no attempt to score.

1. to **leave no stone unturned** – to spare no effort to attain one's ends.
2. **only a stone's throw from** here – within easy calling distance, a very short walk.
3. to **break stones** – to do useless, unrewarding work.
4. a **stony stare** – to stare without any recognition or feeling.
5. to be **stony-broke** (slang) – to have no money.
6. to be **stone deaf** – to be completely deaf.
7. the water was **stone cold** – the water was devoid of any warmth.
8. to **lay the corner-stone** – to complete the most essential part of a work. The corner-stone is the most important part of the building.
9. to **cast the first stone** – to make the first accusation. From the New Testament, John VIII. 7: 'Let those among you who are without sin cast the first stone.'

## BRICK

10. a **brick** / a **regular brick** (slang) – a kind-hearted, unselfish person. 'Jean looked after the children all the time I was in hospital. She is a regular brick.'
11. to **drop a brick** – to make a tactless remark unintentionally. 'Have you ever seen such a horrible colour for a car? It's your car! Oh dear, I have dropped a brick, haven't I?'
12. to come down on someone **like a ton of bricks** – to punish someone with great severity. 'If Brian catches you reading his diary, he'll come down on you like a ton of bricks.' cf. 'to **skin alive' 108/13**.
13. **like talking to a brick wall** – to waste one's breath trying to persuade someone who is too obstinate to listen to reason. 'He is so dogmatic; it's like talking to a brick wall arguing with him.'
14. to **knock one's head against a brick wall** – to waste time and energy attempting the impossible. 'I told you that you would never get Alan to change his mind. You have been knocking your head against a brick wall!'
15. to **see through a brick wall** – to understand a truth which is beyond the grasp of ordinary people.
16. to **make bricks without straw** – to try to achieve some result with inadequate means. 'We were unable to give you an opinion because you didn't give us the information we needed. We can't make bricks without straw.' The reference is to the captivity of the Israelites in biblical times when they were commanded by the Egyptians to make bricks without straw: 'There is no straw given unto thy servants and they say to us make brick . . .' Exodus V. 16.
17. **'redbrick'** – a modern or recently built university, as distinct from the traditional universities like Oxford, Cambridge and St Andrews whose colleges were built of stone. The term is sometimes used in a derogatory sense.

## ROOF

18. to **raise the roof** – to arouse tremendous applause.
19. to **hit the roof / to go through the roof** – to be furiously angry, to explode with rage. 'When I told my father I had crashed his car, he went through the roof.'

## TILE

1. to **have a tile loose** – to be mentally deficient. 'If Sheila believes that, she must have a tile loose!'
2. to be **(out) on the tiles** – to be out all hours of the night, drinking and having a good time. 'I'll give George a piece of my mind when he gets home. He's been on the tiles again.'

## CHIMNEY, GUTTER, DRAIN AND PIPE

3. to **smoke like a chimney** – to smoke cigarettes incessantly.
4. **out of the gutter** – from the lowest and poorest family; without any education or breeding; with nothing to commend one socially.
5. a **guttersnipe** – a hooligan, someone of very bad character. The snipe is a bird that lives on the refuse in the gutters.
6. to **go down the drain** – to be irretrievably lost, usually as a result of waste or extravagance. 'He gambled away all his inheritance; every penny went down the drain.'
7. **in the pipe-line** – in preparation, not yet complete. 'John has two more novels in the pipe-line.'

## PILLAR AND PEDESTAL

8. to be driven **from pillar to post** – to be driven all over the place; to find it impossible to settle down.
9. a **pillar of society** – a prominent, important member of the community who can be relied upon to give it his support.
10. to **put on a pedestal** – to credit someone with qualities that he/she does not possess, to consider someone to be above criticism. 'It is a pity that Helen puts all her friends on a pedestal. Sooner or later she is disillusioned, and all her friendships end in disappointment and bitterness.'

## CORNER

11. to **drive** someone **into a corner** – to deprive an opponent of any possibility of retreat. The phrase is often used in boxing.
12. **in a tight corner** – in a dangerous position from which it is difficult to escape.
13. to **fight one's corner** – to fight hard for one's own interests. 'A minister will always resist cuts in public money for his own department. I don't blame a minister for fighting his corner' (former Premier James Callaghan on TV, 1981).
14. a **hole-and-corner affair** – a love affair between two people that is kept secret to avoid shocking public opinion.
15. to **turn the corner** – to make a recovery, often said with reference to health or finance. 'The doctor says that Mary has turned the corner and is out of danger.'
16. to **cut (off) a corner** – to achieve one's objective by breaking or stretching a rule to one's own advantage.
17. to **knock the corners off** someone – to make someone conform in his behaviour to the accepted pattern. 'I wouldn't worry about Peter being a problem child; once he gets to boarding school, they will soon knock the corners off him.'
18. to **stand** someone **in a corner** – to rebuke a subordinate publicly. 'The Prime Minister stood the young Under Secretary in the corner for attacking government policies in a newspaper article.' It used to be the custom in primary schools to stand children in the corner for misbehaving in class.

1. **all the corners of the earth** – every part of the earth.

DOOR

2. to **shut the door in** someone's **face** – to terminate any further negotiations. **to slam the door in** someone's **face** is the same as above, but more violent.
3. to **show** someone **the door** – to request someone to leave.
4. to let someone/something **in through the back door** – to introduce a measure in a way which one's opponents will not notice. 'The private motor-car has not been abolished yet, but there has been a great deal of back-door legislation making its use more expensive and less enjoyable – by increasing road tax, restricting parking facilities, making driving tests more difficult and so on.'
5. to **lay at** someone's **door** – to blame a person for something that has gone badly wrong. 'The delay in bringing relief to the victims of the earthquake was laid at the door of the government.'
6. to **leave a door open** – to offer an opportunity for further discussion.
7. to **open the door to** – to create an opportunity for some abuse. 'When a government acts as an agent for private business, it opens the door to bribery.'
8. **behind closed doors** – in complete privacy. Often used in the sense of denying a hearing to an interested party. 'The decision was reached behind closed doors and so was contrary to natural justice.'
9. to be **next door to** something – so close as to be almost identical. 'To suppress the truth about dry-rot in the house was next door to fraud.'

HINGE

10. to **hinge on** – to depend on. 'His future career will hinge on his success in the June examinations.'

KEY

11. to have **the key of the door** – to have free access to the house. A privilege granted to the children when their parents think that they are old enough to be trusted.
12. a **latch-key child** – a child who has been given a key to let himself into his home after school while his parents are still out at work. 'Most of the pupils who get into trouble at our school are latch-key children.'
13. **keyed up** – in a state of nervous expectation, as one would feel before making an important speech. 'He was all keyed up, knowing that his big moment had arrived.'
14. **the key to the problem** – the essential means of solving a problem.
15. the **key position** – a position of vital strategic importance.
16. the **key word** – the word that is needed for breaking a code.
17. a **key industry** – an essential industry without which other industries cannot function properly.

BELL

18. to be **as sound as a bell** – to be in the best of health; in this context 'sound' is a cognate of the German 'gesund', meaning healthy. cf. **'as fit as a fiddle' 238/11**.
19. **that rings a bell** – that sounds familiar, I've heard that before.

WINDOW AND SHUTTER

20. **window shopping** – looking at articles in a shop-window without buying anything.

1. **window-dressing** – to display things of little or no value so that their deficiencies are concealed. 'The Chairman manipulated the figures very cleverly to conceal the company's heavy losses. It was all window-dressing.' One dresses a window by arranging the merchandise to the best advantage so that it will attract the attention of the passers-by.

2. to **put all one's goods in the window** – to show off all one's good qualities without holding anything in reserve. To be immodest.

3. to **put up the shutters** – to close a house or business; to go into liquidation.

## FLOOR

4. to **cross the floor of the House** – to change political parties, to take one's seat on the opposite side of the House. The reference is to the House of Commons. 'Winston Churchill crossed the floor of the House twice during his parliamentary career.'

5. to **wipe the floor with** – to defeat decisively, to humiliate one's opponent.

6. to **have/take the floor** – (1) to be the centre of attention, when everyone is listening to you. (2) to start dancing.

7. to **fall through the floor** – to collapse. 'The dollar has fallen through the floor.'

   to **sink through the floor** – to feel extremely embarrassed. 'When she asked me in front of all the guests why I had been expelled from school, I was so embarrassed I could have sunk through the floor.' By sinking through the floor, the subject would no longer be visible and would thus avoid any further embarrassment.

8. to **get in on the ground floor** – to join forces with an enterprise that is still in an early stage of development with a view to profiting later.

9. **floor show** – a cabaret which is performed on the floor of a club or restaurant as opposed to the stage of a theatre.

## CORRIDOR AND STAIRS

10. the **corridors of power** – that part of Whitehall where the Civil Service Establishment wields power. From a novel of the same name, by C. P. Snow.

11. **backstairs** – something underhanded, e.g. backstairs intrigue/gossip/influence, etc. 'As a result of a backstairs intrigue, he got a well-paid job in one of the Ministries.' Originally, in a large house, one staircase was for the family and their guests, and a second staircase was for their servants.

## GATE AND FENCE

12. a **gate-crasher** – an uninvited guest.

    to **gate-crash** – to gain admittance to a party without having been invited.

13. **between you, me and the gate-post** – what I am telling you must not go any further, it is a secret.

14. to **sit on the fence** – to be unwilling to commit oneself to either party in a dispute.

15. to **come down on the right/wrong side of the fence** – to ally oneself with the successful/unsuccessful party in a dispute.

16. to **rush one's fences** – to take premature action, to take action without proper preparation. 'Aren't you rushing your fences proposing to Christine? You've only known her a week.' The phrase is taken from show jumping.

17. to **mend one's fences** – to improve relations with someone by removing the cause of the annoyance or dispute.

'If we want to trade with that country, we had better mend our fences with it without delay.' When fences are broken, disputes between neighbours often arise over their rights to the land.

ROOMS

1. to **prefer** someone's **room to his company** – to like someone for his money rather than for his own sake.

HALL

2. to **have the hallmarks of** – to show a person's characteristics. 'The article wasn't signed but it had all the hallmarks of S. Smith.' Literally, to bear the stamp of the Goldsmith's Company which certifies the standard of the gold or silver article tested.
3. **Liberty Hall** – a state of chaos, a place where people may do just as they please. 'I would never send my son to that school – no discipline there at all – pure Liberty Hall!' From Goldsmith's *She Stoops to Conquer*, Act II.
4. **in the hall of fame** – the imaginary hall in which all the famous characters in history are placed.

KITCHEN

5. **kitchen talk** – uneducated talk, consisting for the most part of gossip and idle chatter. 'That is only kitchen talk.'
6. **'If the kitchen is too hot, you should get out of it'** – if you find the responsibilities of office too nerve-racking, you should relinquish your post. Quoted by Harry S. Truman during his presidency of the United States.
7. **kitchen cabinet** – a group of advisers at the disposal of the Prime Minister, whose salaries are financed privately. These advisers are not civil servants but have access in some cases to Cabinet Minutes and other confidential documents. The term was first used in 1829 when Andrew Jackson, the American President, dismissed large numbers of civil servants and installed his own friends at the White House as his personal advisers.

CELLAR

8. to **have a good cellar** – to possess a cellar that is stocked with plenty of good wine.

## 17. FURNITURE AND HOUSEHOLD ARTICLES

### FURNITURE

1. **part of the furniture** – a person whose presence is ignored because he no longer plays any part in the life of a family or enjoys their respect. 'I've been a servant here for fifty years, but no one thought of telling me that we are moving. But then, I'm only a part of the furniture.'

### BED

2. a **good bedside manner** – a manner that inspires a patient with confidence in the doctor; a willingness to listen to the patient's complaints, and to reassure him whenever it is possible.
3. to **get out of bed on the wrong side** – to get up in a bad temper. 'What's the matter with you this morning, Paul? You got out of bed on the wrong side, didn't you?'
4. to **featherbed** – to cushion an industry from the effects of rising costs or competition from abroad by means of government grants and subsidies.
5. a **bed of nails** – a duty or situation which brings much annoyance or pain to a person. 'With my boss changing his instructions from one day to the next, my job has become a bed of nails.'
6. a **hotbed** (of vice, sedition, reaction) – a place where the tendency in question is nourished and developed. 'In biblical times, Sodom and Gomorrah were hotbeds of vice.'

### PILLOW AND BOLSTER

7. **pillow talk** – confidences exchanged between husbands and wives or between lovers when they are in bed.
8. to **bolster up** – to give one's support to a weak or unconvincing theory, argument, etc. 'Although Reed bolstered up his theory with many new arguments, he got no support from the experts.' The bolster is used as an under-pillow for supporting the sleeper's head.

### BLANKET

9. a **wet blanket** – one who spoils other people's fun by ill-humour or excessive seriousness, a depressing influence. The idiom has its origin in the seventeenth century when farmers used wet blankets for extinguishing fires in their cornfields. Later, by association of ideas, spoilsports and killjoys were dubbed 'wet blankets'. cf. **'in the dumps / down in the dumps' 123/3**, 'to **put a damper on someone' 123/4**.
10. to be **born the wrong side of the blanket** – to be illegitimate.
11. a **blanket regulation** – one that is applied to all alike, regardless of differences in size, quality and so on. 'If the Minister applies this blanket regulation to every school, he will destroy many of the best.'

### TABLE

12. **table talk** – light conversation, talk that avoids any serious or gloomy topic.
13. to **keep the table laughing** – to keep one's guests at table entertained.
    to **set the table in a roar** – to set the guests at table laughing uproariously at a joke or story.
14. to **keep a good table** – to provide a good cuisine and excellent wine.
15. **table manners** – polite, considerate

behaviour at meals. George Mikas remarked that the French have a good table, and that the English have good table manners.

1. to **turn the tables** – to reverse the position, to seize the advantage from one's opponent. 'The Rangers were three goals down at half-time, but in the second half they turned the tables on Wandsworth and won by 5–3.' The idiom originates in the one-time custom of turning the table round in the middle of a game of chess or draughts, so that the player who had the inferior position could then take advantage of the stronger position of his opponent.
2. to put a proposal **on the table** – to make a definite offer in the course of negotiations.
3. to **table a motion** – to put forward a proposal for debate.
4. a **round-table conference** – a conference at which the participants can confer on equal terms, the shape of the table ensuring that none of the seats take precedence.
5. **High table** – the table in a college that is reserved for the President, the Fellows and the most distinguished guests.
6. to **drink** someone **under the table** – to defeat one's companion in a drinking contest.

## CHAIR AND ARMCHAIR

7. to **take the chair** – to act as chairman at a meeting, to take charge of the meeting.
8. to **address the Chair** – to direct one's remarks to the Chairman.
9. to **appeal to the Chair** – to ask for the protection of the Chairman.
10. **playing musical chairs** – a children's game. Idiomatically, it means the shuffling of portfolios among the same ministers in a government to avoid the unpleasantness of making dismissals.
11. an **armchair strategist** – one who plans a military operation from the security of his own home without having to fight.
12. an **armchair critic** – one who is in a position to criticize the way a job is done, without being involved in the work himself. His criticism therefore tends to be vague and unrealistic.
13. an **armchair traveller** – someone who looks at travel films on television or reads books on travelling from the comfort of his armchair instead of visiting the countries himself. 'It's much safer to be an armchair traveller – and cheaper, too.'

## SEAT

14. a **hot seat** – a position of responsibility carrying great risks. 'The President of the United States is in the hot seat of world power.'
15. to **keep a seat warm for** someone – to keep a job until another person is ready to take it. 'Martin should have resigned his office this year, but he is staying on an extra year to keep the seat warm for you.'
16. to **take a back seat** – to retire from the active conduct of a concern and let someone else take control. 'I've been managing this company for the last twenty years; it's time I took a back seat.'
17. to **lose one's seat** – to lose a position of influence. The phrase often refers to a seat on a committee, local council or in Parliament.
18. a **seat of learning** – a retreat for scholars where learning is an end in itself, like the universities.
19. **the seat of the trouble** – the source of the difficulty or pain.

## STOOL

1. to **fall between two stools** – to fail through hesitation between two different courses of action, or through trying to combine both. 'Holmes fell between the stools of philosophy and mathematics. Having divided his time equally between both subjects, he left university without a degree in either.'
2. a **stool-pigeon** – someone employed to inform on his companions.
3. the **stool of repentance** – a low seat in Scottish churches on which sinners were set in full view of the congregation. The phrase may be used to indicate that someone has fallen into disfavour with the authorities.

## BENCH

4. to be **on the bench** – to be a judge or magistrate.
   to **be raised to the bench** – to be appointed to a judgeship either in the High Court or the County Court.

## DESK

5. a **desk general** – a general whose experience has been limited to administration, and who has had no battle experience. In World War II General Eisenhower was dismissed by his critics as a 'desk general' before the invasion of Europe in June 1944.

## CUPBOARD

6. **cupboard love** – a display of affection motivated by selfish interest. 'Jane's dog always gives me a wonderful welcome but I'm afraid it's only cupboard love.'

## SHELF

7. to be **on the shelf** – to have reached an age when a woman is unlikely to receive a proposal of marriage.
8. to **shelve** (a plan or proposal) – to postpone (a plan or proposal) indefinitely, often with the idea of putting it out of one's mind for good.

## DRAWER

9. **not out of the top drawer** (almost always used negatively) – not a lady or a gentleman.

## CURTAIN

10. **it's curtains for . . .** (slang) – it's the end of, or the finish of . . . 'It will be curtains for Norman if he doesn't find the money by next Wednesday.'
11. to **draw a curtain over** – to pass discreetly over an incident, to suppress it. This is done when the scene is too painful or embarrassing to relate. cf. 'to **draw a veil over' 174/12**.
12. to **suffer a curtain lecture** – to be scolded in bed by an irate wife.
13. **the iron curtain** – the military and political barrier which separates the Western democracies from the Warsaw Pact countries. The phrase first appeared in Dr Goebbels' diaries but was made famous by Winston Churchill in numerous speeches made after World War II.

## CARPET

14. to **sweep** something **under the carpet** – to banish from one's mind a subject that is unpleasant or embarrassing, to discourage its discussion. 'Sooner or later, you'll have to discuss Jane's marriage; it's no good sweeping the whole thing under the carpet.'
15. to be **carpeted** – to be rebuked by

one's employer. Origin: in the old days when there was a carpet only in the boss's office, an employee stood on the carpet to hear complaints about his work, or to be dismissed.

1. to **roll out the red carpet** – to treat a new arrival as a very important person. 'He had a wonderful tour of the United States. Everywhere he went, they rolled out the red carpet for him.'
2. to **bite the carpet** – to be very angry. 'He was so angry at the news that he almost bit the carpet.'
3. a **carpet-bagger** – a candidate for election who has no roots or interest in the constituency he wishes to represent. The original meaning was a Unionist financier or adventurer who exploited the cheap labour in the American South after the Civil War. The carpet bags carried by these adventurers were bags made of carpet material.
4. **like a magic carpet** – as if one could be transported by magic to any place one wanted to visit. The phrase is often used in a sarcastic sense. 'I'm sorry we can't deliver the furniture before next week. We haven't got a magic carpet.'

## RUG

5. to **pull the rug from under one's feet / under one** – to take one's opponent by surprise by suddenly depriving him of his advantage. 'Thomas got fifty customers to sign a complaint against the manager, but when he presented the petition to the company, they pulled the rug from under his feet by announcing the manager had already retired.' cf. 'to **cut the ground from under one's feet' 104/13** 'to **take the wind out of** someone's **sails' 30/13**.

## PICTURE AND FRAME

6. to **put** someone **in the picture** – to bring someone up to date with the latest developments. 'As you are new to this particular project, I had better put you in the picture before we go any further.'
7. a **perfect picture** – (1) a full and accurate description. 'The author has given us a perfect picture of Tasmania.' (2) lovely to look at. 'The bride was a perfect picture.'
8. to be **the picture of health** – to exhibit all the qualities of a healthy person: rosy cheeks, glistening skin, shining eyes, etc.
9. a **frame-up** – the fabrication of evidence with the object of incriminating an innocent party. 'Can you help me? I've been framed.'

## CANDLE

10. **not fit to hold a candle to / cannot hold a candle to** – not fit to compare with someone, to be in every way inferior. 'He paints quite well but he isn't fit to hold a candle to his brother.' The literal meaning was not fit to hold a light for the person doing the work to see by.
11. **the game is not worth the candle** – not worth the effort or money. 'I have tried to reorganize the company, but it's hopeless. It isn't worth the candle.'
12. to **burn the candle at both ends** – to exhaust one's energy recklessly, to allow oneself insufficient rest or sleep. Often said of students who prepare hastily for an examination by working late into the night and getting up early in the morning to resume their studies. The night is thus shortened at both ends like the candle.
13. **candle-end economies** – small paltry economies that serve no purpose. 'The government should stop making candle-end economies which only annoy the public.'

## CUP AND MUG

1. **my cup was full** – my happiness/bitterness was complete.
2. **in one's cups** – getting drunk. 'Matthew can be quite aggressive when he's in his cups.'
3. to **mug up** (slang) – to learn as fast as one possibly can, almost always in preparation for an examination.

## BOTTLE AND CRYSTAL

4. to **hit the bottle** – to drink too much (alcohol). 'Whenever my husband has a bad day at the office, he hits the bottle.'
5. to be **on the bottle** – to be a habitual drinker. 'She's been on the bottle ever since her husband died.'
6. to **bottle up** one's feelings, anger, etc. – to suppress one's feelings, to prevent them coming to the surface.
7. a **bottle-neck** – (1) an accumulation of unfinished goods in a factory whose production is interrupted owing to shortages of labour or materials. (2) the narrow part of a street in which the passage of traffic is constricted and delays consequently occur.
8. **crystal clear** – transparently clear, so that there is no room for misunderstanding. 'I thought I had made it crystal clear that I was very much opposed to your idea.'

## PLATE, DISH AND SAUCER

9. to have **enough on one's plate** – to have enough work or responsibility. 'I should have thought she had enough on her plate without playing nursemaid to her niece.'
10. to **be handed** something **on a plate** – to obtain an important advantage without having had to work for it in the usual way. 'Peter was handed the directorship on a plate; his uncle is the chairman of the company!'
11. **What a dish!** – what an attractive, beautiful person.
12. to **dish out** (slang) – to supply in plentiful measure. 'They enjoy dishing out advice.'
13. **a flying saucer** – possibly an unidentified object from another planet, but its existence has never been proved.

## KNIFE AND FORK

14. an **accent you could cut with a knife** – a very strong accent, one that is immediately noticeable. 'As soon as he opened his mouth, I knew he was a Yorkshireman. You could have cut his accent with a knife.'
15. to be/walk **on a knife-edge** – to be in the uncomfortable position of having to please both parties in a dispute. 'My two best friends are having a fierce quarrel. I have to walk on a knife-edge between them.'
16. **under the knife** – on the operating table.

    to **have a horror of the knife** – to be in great fear of an operation.
17. a **fork in the road** – the junction of two divergent roads.
18. to **fork out** – to pay out money on behalf of another person who has accumulated a big bill.

## SPOON

19. to be **spoon-fed** – to be given so much assistance that the subject has no need to make any effort on his own behalf. 'The nationalized industries have been spoon-fed for so long that they no longer care whether they give value for money, or make a profit or loss.'
20. to be awarded **the wooden spoon**

(ironical) – to get a bad mark for doing something wrong, in contrast with winning the gold or silver spoon. 'Richard got the wooden spoon for failing to stand up for his members.' The wooden spoon is similar to the booby prize, wood being material of very small value. Formerly, a custom at Cambridge University when a wooden spoon was awarded to the student who did worst in the examinations.

1. to **need a long spoon** – to need extreme caution in one's dealings with an evil person. 'If you do business with Roberts, you will need a long spoon; he is a terrible liar.' The phrase is derived from the proverb: 'He needs a long spoon who sups with the devil'.
2. to **count one's spoons** – to make sure one's guest hasn't stolen any valuables, the suggestion being that the guest is a bad character. 'The more he talked of his honour, the faster we counted the spoons' (Emerson in *Conduct of Life*, 1860).

## SIEVE

3. to have **a memory like a sieve** – to have a very bad memory. 'When it comes to people's names, I have a memory like a sieve.' The sieve, being full of holes, is unable to retain liquid poured into it. Similarly a bad memory is incapable of retaining information, impressions, etc.

## POT

4. to **go to pot** – to ruin oneself or one's prospects. 'Harry has let his business go to pot.'
5. to **take pot luck** – to eat whatever has been cooked just for the family. This is often said to an unexpected guest.
6. to **keep the pot boiling** – (1) to keep things moving at a lively pace, to maintain the momentum. 'If you want to keep the pot boiling, you'd better think of a new game or the children will get bored.' (2) to maintain one's living standards. 'While Father is looking for a new job, Mother is working part-time to keep the pot boiling.'
7. a **pot-boiler** – work that is well below the level of the writer's ability, done for the sake of making money quickly. Pot-boilers are often produced quickly by well-known writers to capitalize on their reputation.
8. **in the melting pot** – in a fluid condition when the outcome is still uncertain. 'In mid-term, with more than three million unemployed, the fortunes of the government were in the melting pot.' From the title of a novel by Israel Zangwill.
9. a case of **the pot calling the kettle black** – to blame someone for a fault that one has oneself in equal or greater degree.
10. a **pot of money** – a large sum of money obtained all at once from speculation or gambling.

    to have **pots of money** (slang) – to be in possession of a fortune. 'He spends every winter at St Moritz. His father has got pots of money.'
11. a **pot shot** – a shot taken at a sitting target, considered unsporting.
12. a **pot hunter** – someone who takes part in sporting events for the sake of the prizes and not for the fun of it.
13. a **tin-pot** (army slang) – a self-important official who inspects an active unit in the army and expects a lot of ceremony and fuss.
14. **pot** (slang) – soft drugs, like marijuana.

## PAN

15. a **flash in the pan** – a chance success which is unlikely to be repeated.

'Robin's book was a great success, but he hasn't written one since; I'm afraid it was only a flash in the pan.'

1. **out of the frying-pan into the fire / to jump out of the frying-pan into the fire** – to exchange a bad situation for one that is even worse. 'Rolf changed his job because he wanted more freedom, but in his new job he couldn't leave the office without the manager's permission. It was a case of out of the frying-pan into the fire.'

## GRILL

2. to **grill** someone – to interrogate someone very intensively, with the object of breaking a person's resistance and extracting a full confession.

## POKER

3. **as stiff as a poker** – unyielding, unresponsive.

## BUCKET

4. to **kick the bucket** (slang) – to die. One explanation of the phrase is that the suicide kicks away the bucket on which he is standing after he has tied the rope round his neck.

## BROOM AND BRUSH

5. **new brooms sweep cleaner** – a new manager will often make many reforms to justify his appointment and impress the staff with his importance.
6. to **have a brush with** – to come into conflict with someone else. 'He had a brush with the law yesterday.'
7. a **brush-off** – the dropping or rejection of a friend. 'After I had waited an hour for her, she rang up to say she didn't want to see me again. It was a real brush-off.'
8. to **brush to one side/aside** – to ignore or make little of.

   to **brush over** – to disregard. 'When I told him I hadn't enough money to repay him, he brushed over the incident with a wave of his hand.'
9. to be **tarred with the same brush** – to be suspected of having the same faults as one's relations or associates. 'Just because Dennis has been in prison, no one will have anything to do with his brothers and sister. They have all been tarred with the same brush.'
10. to **brush up** one's French, Spanish, etc. – to renew one's knowledge of a subject; often used in connection with a foreign language that has been neglected. 'I'll be staying in Hamburg for the next four weeks to brush up my German.'
11. a **toothbrush moustache** – a short, bristly moustache.

## SINK AND BASIN

12. a **sink of iniquity** – a place of vice and corruption. 'The Vicar denounced the village as a sink of iniquity.'
13. to **have a basinful** (vulgar) – to suffer from an excess of a thing or person. 'Tom has spent the whole day telling me his travelling stories. I've had a basinful of them.' cf. 'to **have a bellyful' 99/13**, 'to **be fed up to the teeth/back teeth' 87/18**.

## TAP

14. **on tap** – always available, like water from a tap.

## SPONGE AND SOAP

15. to **throw up the sponge** – to admit defeat, to be guilty of cowardice. The phrase is taken from boxing, when the second throws the sponge into the

ring to indicate that his man is unable to go on with the fight.

1. to **sponge on** someone – to squeeze money out of another person without giving him anything in return.
2. to **soft soap** (slang) – to conciliate a person one has wronged with false reassurances and compliments. cf. **'soothing syrup' 159/15**.
3. **soap opera** – an inferior play in serial form on radio or television.
4. **soap-box oratory** – speaking in public on a make-shift platform or soap-box. 'If you want to enjoy soap-box oratory, you should go next Sunday to Speaker's Corner in Hyde Park.'

## PEG

5. **square pegs in round holes** – people who are not suitable for their work or surroundings. 'That man should never have become a lawyer. He's a square peg in a round hole.'
6. to **take down a peg** – to reduce someone's self-importance, deflate his pride. The idiom suggests corrective action which falls short of total humiliation. 'The office-boy has been taking too much on himself lately. He was beginning to forget his position. I had to take him down a peg this morning.'
7. a **peg to hang** something **on** – an opportunity or excuse for discussion. 'The inspector said that he only used grammar in his English language classes as a peg for conversation, and that grammar had no value in itself.'

## HANDLE

8. to **fly off the handle** – to lose one's temper, speak violently, to lose one's self-control. 'When I told Harry that I would have to charge him for the work I had done for him, he flew off the handle and started to shout at me.' cf. 'to **go up in the air' 24/15**.
9. to **have a handle to one's name** – to have a title of rank or honour, such as Viscount, Lord, Professor, or of courtesy, such as Mr or Mrs. 'Please remember I have a handle to my name. I am Mr Chapman to you.'
10. to **give a handle to** – to provide evidence for rumour-mongers and gossips.
11. to **be good at handling people** – to know how to deal with people. The phrase has a commercial sense, and often suggests the idea of making use of people to suit one's own interests.

# 18. FOOD

## MILK

1. to **milk** – to swindle or cheat. 'The tourists were milked by the souvenir sellers.'
2. **the milk of human kindness** – compassion, sympathy. 'Pamela is clever and hard-working but she lacks the milk of human kindness.'
3. it's **no use crying over spilt milk** – it is useless to regret one's past mistakes. We cannot undo the past.
4. **milk and water** – insipid, feeble. 'These milk and water policies won't help the country. We need something more drastic.'
5. a **land of milk and honey** – a land overflowing with the good things of life, a land abounding in riches.
6. **mother's milk** – that which supplies an essential need. 'The professor's revolutionary ideas were mother's milk to his students.'

   to **imbibe with one's mother's milk** – to adopt instinctively. 'He imbibed a hatred of the old order with his mother's milk.'

## CREAM

7. to **cream off / to skim the cream** – to take the best. 'Oxford and Cambridge are still creaming off the most brilliant scholars, despite all the social changes that have taken place since the end of the war.'
8. **the cream** of society, etc. – the aristocracy, the most highly favoured class. The phrase is often used ironically. From the French: 'la crème de la crème.'

## CHEESE

9. to be **as different as chalk and cheese** – to be completely different, to have nothing in common. 'You'd never think that Paul and Sue were brother and sister. They are as different as chalk and cheese.'
10. **cheese-parings** – objects of no more value than cheese-parings, junk or trash. 'When the old man died, they found only cheese-parings in his house.'

    to **be cheese-paring** – to be extremely mean, to give grudgingly. 'The father was so cheese-paring with his son's pocket money that the boy hadn't enough money to buy a table-tennis bat.'
11. to be **cheesed off** (slang) – to be fed-up, bored, disgruntled.
12. **hard cheese!** – bad luck! 'That was hard cheese spraining your ankle just at the start of your holiday.' The phrase usually indicates a lack of sympathy for the victim.

## EGGS

13. to have **egg on one's face** – to be humiliated. 'Paul couldn't understand Marie-Louise when she asked him a simple question in French, although he has always boasted that he can speak French fluently. When he left, he had egg all over his face.'
14. a **bad egg** – a bad character, a rascal. 'We are so worried; our daughter has made friends with a very bad egg.'
15. an **egg-head** (American English) – an intellectual, probably from the belief that a long head with a high forehead, i.e. an egg-shaped head, is a sign of superior intelligence.

1. to **tread upon eggs** – to broach a subject with the utmost delicacy, as if treading on eggs.
2. **as sure as eggs is eggs** – absolutely certain, as certain as night follows day.
3. **don't put all your eggs in one basket** – don't invest all your money in one thing, but spread your risks.
4. **you can't make an omelette without breaking eggs** – you can't achieve anything in this life without causing somebody pain.
5. to **over-egg the cake** – to exaggerate very badly. 'When Jones told the Chairman that it was a privilege to work for him, and then called for a vote of thanks for him from his workmates, we all felt that he was over-egging the cake.'
6. to **unscramble** – to undo, to change back. 'Now that so much money has been spent on the plans, it will be difficult to unscramble them.' The reference is to scrambling eggs; once they have been scrambled, they cannot be cooked in any other way.

## BUTTER

7. to **butter up** – to flatter, to pay insincere compliments to someone. 'The boys buttered up the new master in the hope of getting less homework.'
8. to **spread the butter too thick** – to flatter, to exaggerate one's praise.
9. **butter-fingers** – someone who lets something slip between his fingers as if they were made of butter. 'That's the third time you've dropped the ball. What a butter-fingers you are!'
10. to look **as if butter wouldn't melt in one's mouth** – to look very innocent, although one is not innocent at all. 'He looked as if butter wouldn't melt in his mouth, but he didn't take me in. I knew he had done it.'
11. a **butter mountain** – the name given to the huge reserve of butter maintained by the EEC in order to ensure that the butter brought to market is not sold too cheaply. Note the similarity to the term **'wine lake'** which serves to maintain the prices of wine in the EEC.

## FAT

12. **the fat will be in the fire** – there will be an explosion of anger. This happens when news of someone's misbehaviour gets out. 'If Father hears you've been gambling on the Stock Exchange with his money, the fat will be in the fire.' The derivation is from the spitting and spluttering of a fire when fat is thrown into it.
13. **to live on/off the fat of the land** – to live in the most luxurious conditions.
14. **a fat lot** (ironical) – nothing at all, none at all. 'A fat lot they care whether you get well or not.' 'A fat lot of good that will do you.'

## BREAD

15. the **bread-winner** – the wage-earner who supports the family. 'With Father ill, our eldest brother has become the bread-winner of the family.'
16. **on the bread-line** – in a state of great poverty, when one is obliged to queue up for one's ration of food. It has come to mean poverty in general.
17. to **take the bread out of** someone's **mouth** – to deprive someone of his living. 'If you open your shop next door to Harry's, you will be taking the bread out of his mouth.'
18. one's **bread and butter** – one's living. 'I can't afford to give it up. It's my bread and butter.'

1. **the bread and butter of a business** – the main source of a business's income. 'The business they are doing with Japan is coming along nicely, but the bread and butter is with Europe.'
2. to **quarrel with one's bread and butter** – to find fault with one's livelihood. 'I wouldn't quarrel with your husband's bread and butter if I were you. If he gives up his job, you will have nothing to live on!'
3. to **know which side one's bread is buttered** – to know where one's interest lies. 'However much he sympathizes with you, he won't say anything to offend his boss. He knows which side his bread is buttered.'
4. to **have one's bread buttered on both sides** – to have a very easy life, to obtain an easy comfortable living.
5. a **bread and butter letter** – a thank-you letter for hospitality from a departed guest.

LOAF

6. **'Use your loaf!'** (vulgar) – 'Use your brain', 'Think'.

SANDWICH

7. to **sandwich between / in between** – to squash between, insert between. 'On the flight, I was sandwiched in between two very fat passengers so that I scarcely had room to raise my fork to my mouth.'
8. a **sandwich course** – a course which provides practical instruction as well as lectures on theory, the practical being 'sandwiched' between the theoretical.
9. a **sandwich man** – a man who carries advertising boards both in front and behind; so called because the man is sandwiched between the two boards.

TOAST

10. to be **as warm as toast** – to be comfortably warm, very warm.
11. to **have** someone **on toast** – to have someone in one's power, to enjoy a decisive advantage over someone, usually in consequence of some mistake he has made. 'Now, I've got you on toast. You must do as I say.'

CRUMB

12. a **crumb of comfort** – a small consolation, a small mercy. 'One crumb of comfort is that, although he will be bedridden, he can continue with his writings.'

HONEY AND SYRUP

13. to be **as sweet as honey** – to be unnaturally sweet, perhaps from some ulterior motive. 'The girls were as sweet as honey as long as I did what they wanted.' cf. 'to **be as sweet as pie' 161/2**.
14. **the honeymoon is over** – criticism which was muted for the first few weeks (of a new government's term of office, a new appointment, and so on) now becomes unrestrained. The allusion is to the change in attitude of the newly married couple which often occurs when the honeymoon is over.
4. **soothing syrup** – words designed to comfort rather than tell the truth. cf. **'soft soap' 156/2**.

JAM

16. to be **in a jam** – to be in great difficulties, to be in a mess, like a fly caught in a jar of jam from which it is unable to extricate itself.
17. **money for jam** – money that is made with no effort. 'All I had to do was to walk up and down the room and smile

at the customers. It was money for jam.'

1. **'It's jam tomorrow, jam yesterday, but never jam today!'** – You are always boasting about what you have given us in the past and what you are going to give us in the future. Unfortunately, nothing ever comes of your promises, and we are still as badly off as ever.

## SUGAR AND SWEETS

2. to **sugar the pill** – to make something which is unpleasant seem less so. 'I shall sugar the pill by sending Owen on a week's paid holiday before I make him redundant.'
3. a **toffee-nosed** person (mildly derogatory) – an upper-class person. A 'toffee-nose' is one that points upwards in a snobbish, disdainful manner.
4. 'I can't jump **for toffee**' – 'I jump very badly', the idea behind the phrase being 'I couldn't jump well, even if you offered me a toffee to do it'.
5. a **lollipop man, lollipop lady** – nickname for a traffic warden who escorts children across the road.
6. **chocolate box** – a face which possesses pretty features but is lacking in individuality or distinction, the kind of 'pretty' face one sees on the lid of a chocolate box. 'She was a nice chocolate box – nothing more.'

## CAKE, PANCAKE, BUN AND BISCUIT

7. **you can't have your cake and eat it** – you have a choice, meaning either/or, not both. 'You must make up your mind whether you want to buy a house with Uncle Tom's legacy, or invest the money. You can't have your cake and eat it.'
8. **a piece of cake** – something very easy to do, requiring little or no effort. 'The General Knowledge examination was terribly easy. It was a piece of cake.'
9. **icing on the cake** – an extra incentive which is not necessary, but gives a great deal of pleasure. 'If they send me to Saudi Arabia, I shall get a salary increase of 25% with my promotion, but the icing on the cake will be a two months' paid holiday every two years.'
10. a **slice of the cake** – a share of the profits. 'After such a wonderful year, your workers will want a slice of the cake.'
11. to **go like hot cakes** – to sell very quickly, to be snapped up. 'The new line in sports cars is going like hot cakes; there is a crazy demand for them.'
12. to **fall as flat as a pancake** – to have no effect at all. Sometimes abbreviated to **'fall flat'**. 'The joke fell flat; nobody laughed.'
13. hair done **in a bun** – with the hair piled up in the shape of a bun.
14. **That takes the biscuit!** – used ironically for something scarcely credible because it is so absurd. 'That takes the cake. The teacher has proposed to his granddaughter's schoolfriend.'

## PIE

15. **pie in the sky** – hopes and dreams that will never be realized. 'Universal brotherhood and peace is a wonderful ideal but, I am afraid, it is all pie in the sky.' cf. **'castles in the air' 24/13**, and **'castles in Spain' 186/8**.
16. to **eat humble pie** – to submit or apologize humbly. 'After boasting that he would win the boxing tournament, he had to eat humble pie when he was knocked out in the first round.' 'Humble pie' was made from the offal

of deer and offered to the footmen at a banquet.

1. to have **a finger in every pie** – to take a meddlesome interest in many affairs. 'When Mark heard there was to be a jumble sale, he was soon busy organizing the stalls. He has a finger in every pie.'
2. to be **as sweet as pie** – very charming, often used sarcastically. 'She could be as sweet as pie if she wanted to get something out of me'. cf. 'to **be as sweet as honey' 159/13**.
3. **promises are like pie-crust** – promises are made to be broken (a cynical view). From the fairy story 'The Beauty and the Beast'.

PUDDING

4. **the proof of the pudding is in the eating** – the test is whether it works or not. 'The yacht has elegant lines all right, but how will she sail? The proof of the pudding will be in the eating.'

PORRIDGE

5. **save your breath to cool your porridge** – the words used to scold someone who has given unwanted advice. 'Well, Friar, spare your breath to cool your porridge; come let us talk with deliberation, fairly and softly' (Rabelais: *Works* (1552), Book V, Chapter 28).

SPAGHETTI

6. **spaghetti junction** – the centre of a whole network of roads near Birmingham – so called because the pattern of the roads resembles spaghetti.

MEAT

7. **easy meat** – something easily and quickly accomplished or someone easily vanquished. 'The "A" level mathematics examination was easy meat for Ruth; she got full marks in every paper.'
8. **there's a lot of meat in it** – something which gives one plenty to think about. 'I like a novel with plenty of meat in it, for instance Tolstoy's *War and Peace*.'
9. **strong meat** – material that is difficult to accept or appreciate. 'He took his son to a play by Aristophanes – strong meat for a boy of twelve.'
10. **It must have been meat and drink to you** – it must have given you enormous satisfaction. Often used when a person's critics acknowledge they have been in the wrong. 'The apologies of her old rival were meat and drink to her.' cf. **'music to one's ears' 238/4**.
11. **one man's meat is another man's poison** – what favours one person, injures another. 'The epidemic kept the young doctor busy all day. One man's meat is another man's poison.'
12. to **make mincemeat of** someone (colloquial) – to win a devastating victory over an opponent. 'She made mincemeat of his arguments. Under her cross-examination, his case collapsed.' The idea comes from chopping meat up into tiny pieces and serving it as mince.
13. to **beef about** (Australian colloquialism) – to complain about.
14. **as dead as mutton** – completely dead. Similar to **'as dead as Queen Anne' 193/15**, and **'as dead as a door-nail' 211/10**.
15. **mutton dressed as lamb** – an older woman who dresses up to look like a young one. The phrase can be extended to ideas. 'Their ideas are exactly the same as twenty years ago; only the jargon has changed. Mutton dressed as lamb.'
16. to **talk tripe** – to talk utter nonsense. As well as being slang, the phrase can

be very rude. 'I don't agree with a word you are saying. You are talking tripe.' Tripe is the lining of a cow's stomach, and is considered a delicacy in the north of England.

1. **salami tactics** – achieving one's objective in small steps, like cutting salami up into slices.
2. to **stew in one's own juice** – to take the consequences of one's own actions. 'How many times have I told you not to borrow money? This time I am not going to help you out. You can stew in your own juice.'
3. to **bring home the bacon** – to succeed, achieve one's aim, to supply the needs of one's family. 'With all his faults, her husband certainly brings home the bacon. She can't complain on that score.'
4. to **save** someone's **bacon** – to get someone out of a difficulty. 'If you hadn't hidden me in your cupboard, I should have been terribly embarrassed. You really saved my bacon.'
5. **ham-fisted/ham-handed** – clumsy with one's hands. 'That girl is too ham-fisted to wait at table. She drops everything.'

## SOUP, SAUCE AND GRAVY

6. to be **in the soup** – to be in trouble. 'If you lose our passports, we shall be in the soup!'
7. to **soup up** (slang) – to make an engine more powerful by tuning it up. A souped-up version of an engine is one that has been developed into a racing model.
8. **a mess of potage** – something of little or no value. 'They have sold their comrades for a mess of potage' (Arthur Scargill, President of the National Union of Miners, referring to the working miners in the coal strike, December 1984). The allusion is to Esau's birthright which he sold to his brother Jacob for a mess of potage, Genesis XXV, 33.
9. **don't give me any of your sauce!** – don't give me any impertinence, insolence, cheek.
10. **to join/get on the gravy train** – to take one's share of the rewards. 'When a new party comes to power, there is always a scramble to join the gravy-train.'

## SALT

11. to be **above/below the salt** (humorous) – to be in favour/out of favour with one's host or hostess. 'Since his rudeness to his sister-in-law, Donald no longer sits above the salt when he visits his brother at Maybrick Hall.' In the old days when the family and the servants ate at the same table, the salt was placed half-way up the table to mark the dividing line between them. The master of the house sat with his family and guests 'above the salt', and their servants, including the governess and tutor, sat 'below the salt'.
12. to **eat salt with** – to enjoy a person's hospitality. There is a tradition among the Arabic people that you may not accept someone's hospitality and abuse him afterwards. 'If you eat salt with your Arab host, he will provide you with his benevolent protection.'
13. to **salt away** – to hide away, used in reference to money secretly hoarded. 'He must have salted away the best part of a fortune in the last ten years of his life.'
14. to **take with a pinch of salt** – to believe only a part of what you have been told, to allow for considerable exaggeration. This phrase is a translation from the Latin 'cum grano salis' which has the same meaning.

1. to **rub salt in a wound** – to add deliberately to someone's misery, to make an injury even worse. 'As you have just given your tenant a week's notice, I wouldn't ask him to clean up the flat before he leaves. You will only be rubbing salt in the wound.'
2. **worth one's salt** – worth one's pay, worth having. 'Any boy worth his salt wants to get into the school football team.'

   **not worth one's salt** – not worth one's pay. The phrase is taken from the Latin word 'salarium', which meant the salt money that was paid to Roman soldiers instead of their salt. A man not worth his salt was considered worthless.
3. the **salt of the earth** – God's elect, God's own people. The phrase comes from Matthew V.13, in reference to Our Lord's disciples: 'You are the salt of the earth.' The distinction has been claimed by many people since the time those words were spoken.
4. an **old salt** – an old sailor, one whose skin has absorbed a lot of salt from the sea.

## PEPPER AND MUSTARD

5. to **pepper** someone with questions – to put many questions quickly to someone. The questioning is similar to sprinkling pepper on one's food; the holes in the pepper-pot determine the way the pepper comes out.
6. **as keen as mustard** – very keen, full of enthusiasm.

## PICKLE

7. to be **in a pickle** – to be in chaotic disorder, to be in a mess. 'Your bedroom is in such a pickle, I wonder you can find anything in it.'

   to be **in a nice/fine pickle** – to be in trouble; used ironically for an awkward situation. 'We'd have been in a fine pickle if we had missed the last bus home.'

## GINGER

8. to **ginger up** – to put life into, to stir up. 'The new manager was determined to ginger up his staff if they didn't work harder.'
9. a **ginger group** – a group within a political party that tries to prod it into bolder and more energetic action. The '92 Group' is the ginger group of the Conservative Party.
10. to **take the gilt off the gingerbread** – to spoil or rob something of its main attractiveness. 'I spent a pleasant holiday with my aunt, but on the last day I overheard her saying to her housekeeper: "What a strain the visit has been." That took the gilt off the gingerbread.'

## FRUIT

11. to **bear fruit** – to produce results.
12. **stolen fruit / forbidden fruit** – a sin which is regarded as a pleasure. 'Forbidden fruit is always the most desirable.' The phrase is connected with the forbidden fruit in the Garden of Eden, taken by Adam in disobedience of God's commandment.
13. **Dead Sea fruit** – a thing of great promise which turns out to be worthless. 'Poor Andrew, he never got his invention to work; after five years of ceaseless effort, he had only produced Dead Sea fruit.' The reference is to the legendary apples of Sodom, which grew on the shores of the Dead Sea. The apples were very beautiful but would dissolve into ashes as soon as they were touched or tasted.

## ORANGE AND LEMON

1. to **squeeze the orange until the pips squeak** – to extract information by questioning someone until he is exhausted.
2. a **sucked orange** – someone who has served his purpose and is no longer wanted. 'After working twenty years for the company, Alex was discarded like a sucked orange.'
3. **the answer's a lemon** – a joking retort to a long, complicated problem which is not worth the time and effort needed to solve it.

## APPLE

4. **as sure as God made little apples** – with absolute certainty, as sure as night follows day.
5. the **rotten apple** – the one bad person among a number of good ones. 'His youngest son was the rotten apple.'
6. to **upset the apple cart** – to spoil a carefully laid plan. 'That has upset the apple cart! We can't go away while the men are on strike.'
7. to be **the apple of one's eye** – to be the one for whom a person has the tenderest affection. 'He loved his sons, but his daughter was the apple of his eye.'
8. to be **in apple-pie order** – to be clean, tidy, well organized. 'The room is in apple-pie order for our guest.'

## BANANA

9. a **banana skin** – a pitfall for the unwary which makes the victim look ridiculous. 'The government has slipped on too many banana skins for its own good.'
10. a **banana republic** – a republic whose governments are repeatedly overthrown and replaced by new ones, equally unstable.
11. to **go bananas** – to get into a rage, to lose all control over oneself.

## GOOSEBERRY

12. to **play gooseberry** – to accompany a pair of lovers, to be a chaperone to them. 'I am not playing gooseberry to you two. You will be perfectly all right without me.'

## RASPBERRY

13. to **give a raspberry** – to give someone a rebuke (slightly dated).

## GRAPE

14. **sour grapes** – to disparage something because it is unattainable. 'It is sour grapes to say you wouldn't accept the car, even if it were given you. Of course you would!' From Aesop's fable of the Fox and Grapes.
15. I heard it **through the grapevine** – the grapevine is a source of information, rumours, gossip, which is forever churning out new items. 'I heard it through the grapevine that the boss and his secretary are getting married at the end of the month.'
16. to **wither on the vine** – to die through neglect (with special reference to ideas or proposals). 'Our new manager had lots of ideas about reorganizing the business. Instead of arguing with him, we allowed his proposals to wither on the vine.'

## PLUM, CHERRY AND PEACH

17. a **plum** role/job, etc. – the most desired, the very best.

    to **land a plum job** – to obtain, by good luck or good management, the most sought-after job.
18. a **plummy voice** – an upper-class voice which is either affected by the

speaker, or which sounds affected to the listener.

1. to take **two bites at a cherry** – to make a second attempt, having failed the first time.
2. a **peach / she's a peach** (slang) – an outstandingly beautiful girl, stunningly attractive.

PRUNE

3. to **prune** a book, thesis or story – to eliminate all unnecessary words and passages.
4. **prunes and prisms** – a mincing way of speaking (from *Little Dorrit* by Charles Dickens).

FIG

5. **not worth a fig** – worth nothing at all. cf. **'not worth a straw' 48/11**.
6. **not to care a fig / not to give a fig for** – to care nothing for. 'I don't care a fig (I don't give a fig) for his opinions.'

VEGETABLES

7. to be a **vegetable** – to be alive but without the proper use of one's faculties. 'If he had survived the head injuries he got in the crash, he would have been a vegetable for the rest of his life.'

BEAN

8. to be **full of beans** – to be bursting with energy and health, to be in high spirits.
9. to **give someone beans** – to rebuke someone, to give someone a good thrashing.
10. to **spill the beans** – to talk indiscreetly, to let information slip out. 'She has spilt the beans about your engagement. It will be all over the town by now.'
11. **not to have a bean** – to have no money, to be penniless.
12. **not worth a bean / a row of beans** – worthless.
13. to **know how many beans make five** – to be alert, shrewd. From the custom of teaching small children to count with beans.

PEA

14. a **pea-souper** – a thick yellow fog. 'I can't see my hand in front of me. It's a real pea-souper!'
15. to be **as like as two peas** – to be indistinguishable from one another. 'The twin boys are as like as two peas.'
16. **as easy as shelling peas** – something so easy that it requires no skill or effort. cf. **'as easy as falling off a log' 51/2**.

OTHER VEGETABLES

17. the **stick and carrot policy** – rewarding success and punishing failure, just as one rewards a donkey for obedience and punishes it for disobedience. 'In every school, no matter how progressive, the stick and carrot policy is employed. The good children are rewarded and the bad children are punished.'
18. to drop something **like a hot potato** – to withdraw quickly from a commitment as soon as one discovers how embarrassing it could become. 'When he heard that his brother-in-law was an alcoholic, he dropped his temperance campaign like a hot potato.'
19. to **know one's onions** – to know one's job, to be extremely capable. 'If you want any information, ask Mrs Jones to give you a demonstration. She knows her onions.'

1. to **mushroom** – to multiply very fast. Almost always used in a bad sense. 'The number of travel agencies has mushroomed in the last ten years.' The mushroom is a vegetable that is well known for its phenomenal rate of growth.
2. **as red as a beetroot** – red with embarrassment, or from excessive heat.
3. a **cauliflower ear** – an ear that has been permanently swollen and disfigured as a result of having been repeatedly struck. Often a feature of veteran boxers.
4. **fine words butter no parsnips** – actions are more important than words; speeches are no substitute for hard work. 'When I was dismissed, the boss gave me a marvellous reference, but what's the good of that, now I can't get a job! Fine words butter no parsnips.'
5. **as cool as a cucumber** – serene, calm, undisturbed when under stress. 'While the rest of us were getting tremendously excited, she remained as cool as a cucumber and went on with her sewing as if nothing special had happened.'
6. **salad days** – inexperienced youth. 'My salad days / When I was green in judgement' (Shakespeare, *Antony and Cleopatra*, I. v).
7. **the pumpkin has not turned into a coach** – the early promise has not been fulfilled, and disenchantment has followed. In the fairy story of Cinderella, the fairy godmother turned Cinderella's pumpkin into a golden coach to convey her to the palace ball.

## NUT AND PEANUT

8. to be **nuts about** someone – to be madly enthusiastic, infatuated with. 'You know, don't you, that he is nuts about you.'
9. to be **off one's nut / to be nuts** – to be mad, insane. 'You mean to tell me you left all our money on the bus. You must be off your nut!' Nut is slang for head, so the phrase has the same meaning as 'off one's head'.
10. a **nut-case** (colloquial) – a mad person. 'Don't waste your time explaining it to her. She's a nut-case.'
11. **a hard nut to crack** – a tough, intractable problem or person to overcome. 'He is a difficult man to convince. You will find him a hard nut to crack.'
12. to **put in a nutshell** – to explain in a few words, to give a bare summary. 'That's right – we are broke. You've put it in a nutshell.'
13. to **pay peanuts** – to pay a ridiculously small sum of money. 'They pay him a salary of £6,000 a year; that's peanuts for a man of his experience and qualifications!'

## TEA

14. **not one's cup of tea** – not to one's taste. 'I was offered quite a well-paid job in the City, but the work wouldn't have been my cup of tea.'
15. **that's another cup of tea** – that's another matter, that puts a different complexion on it.
16. **I wouldn't do it for all the tea in China** – I wouldn't do it whatever you offered me. 'I wouldn't live with them for all the tea in China.'

## WINE

17. to **wine and dine** – to entertain on a lavish scale.
18. **good wine needs no bush** – if your products are good, they will speak for themselves without needing to be advertised. The bush was the bunch of ivy hung outside which advertised the vintner's business.

1. to put **new wine in old bottles** – to put new ideas into an old framework which cannot accommodate them. 'Some physicists tried to put Einstein's theory of relativity into a Newtonian framework – like putting new wine into old bottles.'

## BEER

2. **small beer** – people or things of trifling importance. 'He didn't trouble to acknowledge our greeting. Now that he has become famous, we are only small beer!'
3. **'Life isn't all beer and skittles'** – Life is not just a game; it has a serious side to it as well.' From *Tom Brown's School-days* by Thomas Hughes (1822–96).

## MEAL AND PICNIC

4. a **square meal** – a substantial meal. 'Kenneth is terribly thin, isn't he? He looks as if he could do with a square meal.'
5. to **make a meal of** it (colloquial) – to make an unnecessary fuss about someone's mistake. 'All right, we should have warned you earlier, but there's no need for you to make a meal of it.'
6. it's **a picnic** – something very pleasant which costs no effort. 'Last year's play was a picnic to produce compared with this year's.'

   **no picnic** – something that is both difficult and disagreeable. '"You must put up with a lot of hardship and discomfort. War is no picnic," the Major told his soldiers.'

## BITE AND EAT

7. to **bite off more than one can chew** – to undertake more than one can fulfil. 'I shall have to cancel some of my orders; I've bitten off more than I can chew.'
8. to **eat one's words** – to suffer a humiliation by having to withdraw a statement that has been proved wrong. 'Our critics said that we would never make a success of our magazine; now that we have proved them wrong, they will have to eat their words.'
9. to be **eaten up with jealousy** – to be consumed with jealousy, obsessed with jealousy. 'Maureen told me that if I bought a large car, she would drop me. The poor woman is eaten up with jealousy.'

## TASTE

10. **in good taste** – in a pleasing, agreeable manner.

    **in bad taste** – in a vulgar, offensive manner. 'All his jokes were in bad taste.'

## 19. CLOTHES

### SHOE

1. **where the shoe pinches** – the source of the discomfort. 'Helen is bringing up four children on £30 a week with no help from her husband, so she knows where the shoe pinches.'
2. to work **on a shoe-string** – to run a business with practically no capital. 'We had to work on a shoe-string, with hardly any staff.'
3. to **step into another person's shoes** – to replace a person, taking over his responsibilities (often someone who is occupying an important position). 'I hope that, by the time you retire, your son will be old enough to step into your shoes.'
4. to step into a **dead man's shoes** – to benefit from the death of a person by inheritance or by taking over his job.
5. to be **in another's shoes** – to be in someone else's situation. 'Betty told me you smashed up the car last night. I shouldn't like to be in your shoes when Father hears about it.' cf. 'to **be in someone else's skin' 108/6**.
6. to **shake in one's shoes** – to tremble with fear. 'He shook in his shoes when he heard he was wanted by the police.'

### BOOT

7. **the boot is on the other foot** – the circumstances are the other way round. 'The boot is on the other foot. It was your son who stole the money from the beggar, and not the beggar who stole from your son.'
8. to **boot out of a job** – to dismiss someone on the spot, without ceremony.
9. to **pull oneself up by one's own bootstraps** – to make one's way by one's own exertions without help from anyone.
10. to **lick** someone's **boots** – to flatter someone in a servile manner to obtain an advantage, to fawn on someone. 'It's nauseating the way he licks his boss's boots all the time.'

    a **bootlicker** – a person who does this.
11. **too big for one's boots** (slang) – conceited, pleased with oneself. 'Ever since that boy won the tennis tournament, he has been too big for his boots. He needs putting in his place.'
12. **Smarty-boots** – a know-all, someone who knows all the answers.
13. to **have one's heart in one's boots / to have one's heart sink into one's boots** – to be dismayed, to be in despair. 'When I saw the nurse's face, my heart sank into my boots.'
14. **as tough as old boots** – to be extremely tough, strong and unaffected by severe conditions. 'I wouldn't worry about Stephen if I were you. He's as tough as old boots and can look after himself.'
15. to be **booted and spurred** (humorous) – to be ready for action.
16. to **hang up one's boots** – to retire. 'I'll be hanging up my boots next year. I think I deserve a rest after running the business for thirty years.' The allusion is to the football player who hangs up his boots after the match.
17. to **die with one's boots on** – to die while still at work. Originally a military phrase, meaning to die in battle.
18. to **put the boot in** – to make a brutal attack on someone when he is at a serious disadvantage. 'After ransacking the widow's house, the burglars put the boot in by smashing up the place.'

## SOCK

1. to **pull up one's socks** (slang) – to work harder, to reform. 'You've had another bad school report. If you don't pull up your socks, you will have to work in the holidays.'
2. to **sock** a person / **to sock on the jaw** (slang) – to hit someone hard.
3. to **put a sock in it** (slang) – to keep quiet, to hold one's tongue.

## STOCKING

4. a **Christmas stocking** – it is the custom in England for children to hang their stockings at the end of their beds on Christmas Eve for Father Christmas to fill with Christmas presents. The custom is based on the belief that Father Christmas comes down the chimney of the child's bedroom.

## DRESS

5. to **dress up** – (1) to dress with the greatest possible care, usually for a special occasion (2) to wear fancy-dress costume.
6. a **fancy-dress ball/dinner** – a ball or dance at which the guests are dressed in the costumes of historic or fictional characters or anything else that takes their fancy.
7. to **dress down / to give** someone **a dressing-down** – to reprimand severely. 'The Colonel dressed the regiment down for their untidy appearance.'
8. **dressed to kill** – to be sumptuously dressed with the object of arousing interest or making a seduction. cf. **'dressed up to the nines' 218/13**.
9. **the dress circle** – the seats on the first floor of the theatre overlooking the stalls – so called because it was the custom for the audience in the dress circle to wear evening dress.
10. to **dress the soil / ground** – to make the soil ready for sowing and planting. 'The gardener has been dressing the soil – hoeing and raking in compost in time for the spring sowing.'
11. to **dress a fowl**, etc. – to pluck a fowl, clean and prepare it for cooking.

    to **dress a lobster** – to prepare a lobster for the dining-table.

## SKIRT

12. to **hide behind a woman's skirts** – to try to avoid the consequences of one's actions by putting the blame on a woman. 'Mary was acting on your instructions, and now that things have gone wrong you are hiding behind her skirts.'
13. a **skirt / a piece of skirt** (slang) – any young woman.
14. to like a **bit of skirt** – to enjoy the companionship of women. The phrase always has a sexual significance.

    to **run after anyone in skirts** – to chase women, to womanize. Neither of these phrases is in good taste.
15. to **skirt round** – to talk round a subject, to avoid the main issue.
16. to **skirt the coast** – to sail close to the coast to avoid squalls.
17. to live **on the outskirts** – to live on or near the boundary of a town.

## FROCK

18. to **unfrock a priest** – to expel a priest from the church for misconduct, neglect of duties, immorality and so on.

## PETTICOAT

19. to be under **petticoat government** – to be ruled by a woman domestically, socially, economically or politically.

'We haven't had a petticoat government since Queen Victoria.'

## FRILLS

1. **without frills** – the essence, without adornment. 'I would like a simple, straightforward account of what happened, without the frills, please.'

## APRON

2. to be **tied to a woman's apron-strings** – to be emotionally dependent on a woman, often used in reference to boys and young men. 'It's time that young man left home; he is tied too much to his mother's apron-strings.'

## PANTS

3. to **bore the pants off** someone – to bore someone very much. 'For goodness sake, don't invite Major Williams; he will bore the pants off our guests.'

## TROUSERS

4. to **wear the trousers** – to be the dominant party in the marriage, to command or rule. The idiom is more often used when the wife dominates her husband. 'From her wedding day until her death, she wore the trousers.'

## SHIRT

5. to **keep one's shirt** on – keep calm, don't get excited or angry. cf. 'to **keep one's hair on' 79/4**.
6. to **put one's shirt on** something – to wager or bet on. 'I am putting my shirt on that horse. It is certain to win.' The idea behind the idiom is that it is such a strong runner that you can put your last remaining possession on it in complete safety.
7. **without a shirt to one's back** – in dire poverty, with practically no possessions.
8. to **put on a hair-shirt** – to punish oneself for some sin. Politically, to sacrifice one's present comforts in order to strengthen the economy of the country. 'Mrs Thatcher is preparing to gamble her political life on the present hair-shirt policy to get through the next two to three years' (*Daily Mail*, 6 October 1982). Some monks put on hair-shirts to do penance.
9. a **stuffed shirt** – someone who is always on his dignity, a pompous bore.
10. to be **shirty** – to be in a bad temper. A word which usually implies that the person in question is being unreasonable. 'Don't get shirty with me; I didn't take your book.'

## SUIT

11. to be in one's **birthday suit** – to be naked, just as one was born.

## JACKET

12. an **Eton jacket** – a short jacket reaching only as far as the waist, similar to the jacket worn by junior boys at Eton College.
13. to put someone **in a strait-jacket** – to restrict someone's freedom. 'I feel as though I were in a strait-jacket; I can't do anything at that school without asking permission first.' A strait-jacket is a tight-fitting waistcoat that is put on violent patients to restrict their movements.
14. **strait-laced** – strict, puritanical, keeping one's feelings under strict control. 'You had better be careful what you say to Julian. He is strait-laced and easily shocked.' Literally, having the laces in the corset pulled very tight,

so that the wearer has a stiff rigid posture.

## TIE

1. the **old school tie** – the badge of former public school pupils. In the eyes of many people, the old school tie has become a symbol of class privilege which provides an elite with important social and business advantages. This charge is hotly denied by advocates of the public school system.

## COLLAR

2. a **dog-collar** – the name given to the collar worn by the clergy; so called because of its resemblance to a dog's collar.
3. to be **hot under the collar** – to be angry, excited. 'There's no reason for you to get hot under the collar. No one has stolen your room key; there it is on the hook.'
4. to **collar someone** – (1) to tackle, grab someone by his collar. (2) (school slang) – to help yourself to something without the permission of the owner.

## CUFF

5. **off the cuff** – without prior thought. 'In a case like this, off-the-cuff advice is useless. You must make a careful study of the problem before deciding what to do.'
6. to **cuff / give** someone **a cuff** – to slap or strike a light blow.

## BRACE

7. **'Brace up!'** – a command often used in the army, meaning: 'Stand up straight, and pay attention!'
8. **brace yourself for a shock** – prepare yourself for a shock so that, when it comes, you won't be overwhelmed.

## BELT

9. to hit **below the belt** – to make a mean or unfair attack. 'When he made fun of his opponent's deafness, he was roundly condemned for hitting him below the belt.' The idiom originates in boxing, hitting below the belt being expressly forbidden by the Queensberry Rules.
10. to have **under one's belt** – to have an achievement already to one's credit. 'Gerald already has two novels under his belt.'
11. to **tighten the belt / to pull in one's belt** – to make economies, eat less when food or money is scarce. Applicable to nations as well as individuals. 'The Chancellor warned the nation it would have to pull in its belt if the balance of trade figures showed no improvement.'
12. to **belt away / to belt along** (colloquial) – to drive very fast.
13. to **belt up** (slang) – to keep quiet or stop talking (rude).
14. to **belt** someone (slang) – to hit someone hard.

## CLOAK

15. **under the cloak of** – under the guise or pretence of. 'Under the cloak of assisting the Vicar, he did a lot of business with the parishioners.'
16. a **cloak and dagger play** – a Victorian melodrama of mystery and intrigue.
17. a **cloak and dagger operation** – an operation in espionage, involving secrecy, danger and often undercover violence and assassination.

## GOWN

1. **Town and Gown** – the age-old feud between the undergraduates at Oxford and Cambridge, and the townspeople.

## COAT

2. to **cut one's coat according to one's cloth** – to live within the limits of one's income. Often said of someone who has suffered a big drop in his earnings and who will be obliged to accept a lower standard of living. 'Now her husband has lost his job, she will be obliged to cut her coat according to her cloth.'
3. to **ride on / hang on** someone's **coat-tails** – to advance one's own career by associating with someone who is currently achieving quick promotion. 'If you want promotion, all you have to do is to ride on Crane's coat-tails; he's the favourite of the boss.'
4. to **be dragged by one's coat-tails** – to be forced against one's will into taking a particular action. 'But Britain is being dragged by its coat-tails into lining up with France and Germany . . .' (Gordon Greig, Political Editor, reporting on the GATT negotiations from Geneva, *Daily Mail*, 25 November 1982).
5. to **trail one's coat** – to provoke a fight. Trailing one's coat-tails, in the hope that someone would tread on them and thus give one the excuse to start a fight, used to be popular, especially in Ireland.
6. to **be a turncoat / to turn one's coat** – to change sides in a dispute, to betray one's principles.

## GLOVE

7. to be **hand in glove with** – to be in very close co-operation with someone else, almost always in a bad sense. 'The two of them were working hand in glove, and were arrested by the police together.'
8. to **fit like a glove** – (1) to fit perfectly, to follow the contours of the body exactly. 'She looks very elegant in her ski-suit. It fits her like a glove.' (2) to describe exactly. 'The description in the *Police Gazette* fitted the suspect like a glove.'
9. to treat someone **with kid gloves** – to treat someone with the utmost gentleness and tact, so as not to cause offence. The significance of the phrase lies in the fact that leather made from kid skin is of the softest texture.
10. **an iron hand in a velvet glove** – forceful action concealed in mild, restrained words. cf. **'with an iron hand' 96/16**.
11. to fight **with the gloves off** – to fight ruthlessly, without showing mercy. Boxing is normally conducted with the gloves on.

## GAUNTLET

12. to **throw down the gauntlet** – to challenge someone to a contest. 'Gauntlet' is derived from the French word 'gant', meaning a glove. In medieval times, one knight would challenge another by throwing down his gauntlet (glove). cf. 'to **throw one's hat into the ring' 173/6.**

    to **take up the gauntlet** – to accept the challenge by picking up the gauntlet (glove).
13. to **run the gauntlet** – to submit to a punishing ordeal. The phrase has been taken from the custom in the army and public schools of making an offender run between two lines of soldiers or schoolboys who would beat him with straps, sticks, etc., in order to demonstrate their disapproval of his misconduct.

## HAT

1. a **bad hat** – a bad character.
2. to pass **round the hat** – to ask for money.
3. to **talk through one's hat** – to talk nonsense.
4. **I'll eat my hat if I'm wrong!** – a promise to do something impossible if one is wrong – in other words, a declaration of absolute confidence in the correctness of one's judgement. 'I'll eat my hat if he hasn't passed his exam this time.'
5. to **take off one's hat to** someone – to show one's admiration for someone by (figuratively) taking off one's hat. 'I take off my hat to him for having the courage of his convictions, even if I don't always agree with him.' Removing one's hat has always been the traditional way of showing respect.
6. to **throw one's hat into the ring** – to challenge one's rivals to a contest for office. It is similar in meaning to the medieval custom of **throwing down the gauntlet**, see **172/12**.
7. **that's old hat** – that is old-fashioned, out of date. 'Everything he told me was old hat. I've heard it all a hundred times before.'
8. **at the drop of a hat** – without warning, without any special reason. 'She is quite capable of deserting you whenever she feels like it – at the drop of a hat.'
9. to **keep** something **under one's hat** – to keep something secret, confidential. 'I was told this in confidence, so I'd be grateful if you would keep it under your hat.' The allusion is to the art of the magician who conceals a number of articles under his hat in the performance of his act.
10. to **wear different hats**, e.g. Judge's hat, director's hat, politician's hat, etc. – the role played by a person at any particular time. 'When he speaks from the pulpit, he is wearing his clergyman's hat. When he writes a newspaper article, he is wearing his journalist's hat.'
11. to **get one's bowler-hat / to be bowler-hatted** – to be dismissed from the armed services. The phrase is much used in the army, despite the virtual disappearance of the bowler-hat, except in the City.
12. to **hang up one's hat in a house** – to be accepted as one of the family. cf. 'to **have one's feet under the table**' **104/12**.
13. to **knock into a cocked hat** – to defeat decisively, to smash. 'I don't fancy taking him on in a fight. He would knock me into a cocked hat.'
14. a **hat trick** – to score three victories in succession. 'Bjorn Borg did the hat trick in 1978 by winning the Men's Singles Championship at Wimbledon for the third time in succession!' From taking three wickets in successive balls in cricket.
15. **as mad as a hatter** – completely insane. Taken from *Alice's Adventures in Wonderland* by Lewis Carroll.

## CAP

16. **that caps it all! / to cap it all** – (1) to give something the finishing touch, to crown a person's achievements. 'He capped a wonderful year by winning a scholarship at Balliol.' (2) that is the limit! 'You were expelled from school, you lost your job, and now you are in trouble with the police. That caps it all!'
17. to **put on one's thinking cap** – to give something the most careful thought. 'I don't know what the answer is to your problem. I shall have to put on my thinking cap.'
18. to **wear a dunce's cap** – to be scoffed at for one's stupidity. It used to be the custom in schools to put a big conical hat on the head of the most stupid

pupil or 'dunce' and hold him up to the mockery of the class.

1. a **mad-cap** – a crazy, reckless person. 'He took that corner at over a hundred miles an hour. He is a real madcap!'
2. a **night-cap** – a drink taken last thing at night before going to bed.
3. a **feather in one's cap** – something one can be proud of, that does one credit. 'That's a feather in his cap, being asked to perform for them twice in one year!'
4. **If the cap fits, wear it** – no one is making any accusations against you, but if you are to blame, then by all means say so! Often used in reply to someone who claims he is being falsely accused, and is becoming aggressive.
5. to **throw up one's cap / to throw one's cap in the air** – to rejoice, to exult.
6. to **go cap in hand** – to beg humbly for favours or money. 'Why should I go cap in hand to him? I have a right to the money.'
7. to **set one's cap at** – to flirt with a man with the object of friendship or marriage. 'That girl sets her cap at all the tradesmen who call at our house. She is mad keen to marry, and not particular whom she does.'
8. to **cap a story** – (1) to finish off someone else's story for him. (2) to go one better with a story of one's own. 'Whenever I try to tell a story, he interrupts and caps it before I have finished.'
9. **cap and bells** – the badge of the professional clown or jester. 'Evelyn Waugh's immodest proposals, though they masquerade in cap and bells, are totally in earnest. He is an ironic writer only in the lightest social sense' (taken from Jonathan Raban's review of Gallacher's book on Evelyn Waugh, *New Statesman*, 23 December 1977).

### BONNET

10. to have a **bee in one's bonnet** – to be obsessed with a strange idea. 'Joan has a bee in her bonnet about illnesses; she thinks they only exist in the mind, so that it's a waste of time calling in the doctor.'

### VEIL

11. to **take the veil** – to become a nun.
12. to **draw a veil over** – to hide the facts, maintain a complete silence over. 'I will draw a veil over the events that followed, in order to spare the lady's feelings.' cf. 'to **draw a curtain over**' **151/11**.

### WIG

13. a **big-wig** – a very important, influential person. 'She must have invited a big-wig or she wouldn't have spent so much on the dinner.'

### BLOOMER

14. to **make a bloomer** – to make a very bad mistake that arouses merriment. A bloomer was originally a garment for ladies which covered the hips and thighs. Introduced into the USA by Mrs Amelia Bloomer in 1849, it never caught on as a fashion. To make a bloomer may therefore have originated in the idea of doing anything which exposed one to public ridicule like, for instance, being seen in one's underwear, i.e. one's bloomers!

### SLEEVE

15. to **laugh up one's sleeve** – to conceal one's amusement at the discomfiture of someone. 'Martin pretended to be so sympathetic when you lost the game, but I am sure he was laughing up his sleeve at you.' When wide,

loose sleeves were worn, one could 'laugh up one's sleeve' without being detected.

1. **nothing up my sleeve** – in an open, frank manner with nothing hidden or secret. 'You can trust me. I have told you the whole truth and I promise you I have nothing up my sleeve.' Conjurors conceal cards, birds, small animals, etc., up their sleeves when performing their tricks.

2. to **wear one's heart on one's sleeve** – to show one's feelings too obviously, to lack self-control in concealing them. 'I always know when Anne has quarrelled with her boy-friend. She wears her heart on her sleeve.' From Shakespeare's *Othello*, I, i: 'But I will wear my heart upon my sleeve / For daws to peck at'.

## BUTTON

3. **as bright as a button** – intelligent, lively; often used in reference to small children.

   **as cute as a button** – an American colloquialism with the same meaning.

4. to **button-hole** someone – to delay someone on his way in order to talk to him. The phrase comes from the habit of grasping a man by his button-hole so as to gain his attention.

5. to **press the button** – (1) to press the fatal button which would unleash a nuclear war. (2) to set in motion various kinds of machinery (administrative or otherwise). 'When you press buttons in Whitehall, things really do start to move' (said by Harold Wilson in November 1964, soon after being elected to power).

6. to have something **buttoned up** – an idiom much used in the army, meaning that all the necessary preparations have been made. 'Our unit is being sent overseas at the end of the week. Everything has been buttoned up.'

## POCKET

7. to be **in pocket** – to show a gain after deduction of all expenses.

   to be **out of pocket** – to show a loss after deduction of all expenses. 'The money he paid me for looking after his children wasn't enough. At the end of the school holidays I was £100 out of pocket.'

   **out-of-pocket expenses** – expenses incurred in doing a job, which may or may not have been foreseen.

8. to **line one's pocket** – to make an unlawful profit. 'The government officials lined their pockets with bribes and commissions.'

9. to **pick** someone's **pocket** – to steal money from someone's pocket without being noticed.

10. to **put one's hand in one's pocket** – to pay out of one's own resources. 'The soldiers were given a splendid welcome by the people in the pub and didn't have to put their hands in their pockets once during the whole evening.'

11. to **pocket** something – to take possession of something one is usually not entitled to. 'The beggar saw a £5 note in the road and, after looking round, he pocketed the money.'

12. to **pocket an insult** – to accept an insult without protest. 'I am not going to pocket his insults any longer.'

13. to **pocket one's pride** – to submit to a humiliation. 'The agent walked about my house giving orders to my staff as if he owned the place; but although I felt very offended, I pocketed my pride in order not to lose the contract.'

14. to **have** someone **in one's pocket** – to have someone under one's control. The phrase derives from the days of the 'pocket borough' when some constituencies contained only a handful of voters, under the control of one

man who was able to decide the outcome of the election and send his own Member to Parliament. The owner of the borough was said to 'have it in his pocket'. Pocket boroughs were abolished by the Reform Act of 1832.

## PURSE

1. **purse-proud** – proud of one's wealth.
2. to **hold the purse-strings** – to keep the finances under one's control. 'She let her husband do the talking, but she held the purse-strings.'
3. to **loosen one's purse-strings** – to give one's money, make money available. The idiom often suggests that the donor is mean and has been persuaded against his inclination to spend his money.
4. to **dig (deep) into one's purse** – to pay out more money when one hasn't very much left. 'A ski-ing holiday in Switzerland! I don't like to ask Father to dig into his purse again just after he's paid all those bills.'
5. to **put up a purse** – to collect a sum of money for the giving of a prize.
6. **out of the public purse** – out of the taxpayers' money. 'Money from the public purse is soon spent, with nothing to show for it.'

## BAG

7. **bag and baggage** – completely, without anything left behind. 'The angry landlady threw her student-lodger out of her house, bag and baggage.' First used in this sense by Gladstone when he called for the expulsion of the Turkish army from Bulgarian soil, 'bag and baggage'. cf. **'neck and crop' 90/18**.
8. to be a **bag of bones** – to be reduced to almost a skeleton through illness or undernourishment. 'When I saw the dog last, he was a bag of bones. I hope he'll put some flesh on in his new home.'
9. **it's in the bag** – we have as good as accomplished our objective. 'After three hours with the director, I was offered a position in the firm. It's in the bag!'
10. to **pack one's bags** – to leave as the result of a quarrel, usually with one's employer. 'When I told Martina that she would have to pay for all the broken china, she packed her bags and left.'
11. a **mixed bag** – a collection of people / objects of very uneven quality. 'The passengers on the cruise were a mixed bag. We were disappointed.'

## SUITCASE

12. a **suitcase economy** – an economy that suffers from raging inflation. The phrase comes from the inflation in Germany after World War I, when prices were so high that people were obliged to carry huge quantities of banknotes in their suitcases to do their shopping.

## RAG

13. the **local rag** – the local newspaper. Local newspapers, especially in London, are rightly or wrongly looked down on. Hence the phrase.
14. the **rag-tag and bob-tail** – the poorest of the poor. People dressed in rags and tatters.
15. to feel **like a wet rag** (colloquial) – to feel completely exhausted.
16. **glad rags** – a woman's best clothes, usually worn for a special occasion. 'You'd better put your glad rags on, Mary. I've invited the Admiral and his wife to dinner.'
17. **from rags to riches** – from extreme

poverty to great affluence. 'It was like a fairy story. After a few months in America, he had gone from rags to riches.' The opposite of this, **from riches to rags**, is sometimes used humorously.

## CLOTH

1. to **respect the cloth** – to show the respect that is due to a clergyman, 'the cloth' being the traditional name for the clergy.
2. **in sackcloth and ashes** (facetious) – showing extreme remorse and penitence for one's wrongdoing. 'I must have been in a bad mood when I reviewed Anne's book. I shall have to go to her in sackcloth and ashes and beg her forgiveness.' In biblical times, it was the custom for sinners to wear sackcloth and sprinkle ashes over their hair to make a public show of their penitence. Sackcloth is made from flax or hemp – the coarsest of material.
3. to **steal** someone's **clothes** – to adopt someone else's ideas and pass them off as your own. A favourite phrase in politics when one party is said to steal the clothes of the other.

## SILK

4. to **take silk** – to become a Queen's Counsel at the British Bar and wear a silk robe in Court in place of a Junior Counsel's stuff gown.

## LINEN

5. to **wash one's dirty linen in public** – to advertise in public the moral lapses and difficulties of one's private life. 'Of course, your brother has behaved very badly to you, but you will only make matters worse by washing your dirty linen in public.'

## COTTON AND WOOL

6. to **cotton on to** (colloquial) – to grasp, understand. 'When the tourist forgot to tip the chambermaid, she went back to his room and said good-bye to him a second time. He cottoned on to her meaning at once, and handed her a £5 note.'
7. to **wrap** someone **up in cotton wool** – to pamper, to be over-protective, generally used in reference to a child. 'It's time you stopped wrapping Ronald up in cotton wool and let him play with other children.'
8. to **pull the wool over** someone's **eyes** – to deceive, mislead, cheat. 'You certainly pulled the wool over our eyes with that sob-story of yours!'
9. to be **woolly-headed** – to be unclear or muddled in one's thinking.
10. to be **wool-gathering** – to let one's mind wander. 'Henry must have been wool-gathering or he would never have crashed the car. He always drives very carefully.'
11. **dyed-in-the-wool** – holding fixed and unalterable opinions. 'It's no good arguing with my uncle; he is a dyed-in-the-wool Conservative.' The literal meaning is that the wool has been dyed in its raw condition so that the dye is indelible.

## PATCH AND SEW

12. to **patch up a quarrel** – to put an end to a quarrel without going into the rights and wrongs of the dispute. 'It's time we patched up our quarrel with Johnson, otherwise we shall lose a lot of business.'
13. **not a patch on . . .** – nothing like as good as . . . 'I play tennis reasonably well but I'm not a patch on my brother.' A patch is a piece of cloth sewn on to a garment to cover a hole. The patch is of minor

importance compared with the garment itself.

1. to **sew up** – to come to an agreement on all the details of a plan. 'Now that the agreement has been sewn up, we can begin to work.'

THREAD

2. to **lose the thread** – to be unable to follow an argument, either because it is too hard to understand or because the listener's concentration has failed.
3. to **pick up the threads** – to resume one's work after a period of inactivity. 'It will be difficult for Alex to pick up the threads after neglecting his book for so long.'
4. to **hang by a thread** – to be in a precarious position. 'After the collision with the lorry, Oliver's life hung by a thread.'
5. to **wear** someone's **patience thread-bare/thin** – to exhaust someone's patience. 'I'm sorry I can't continue with the lessons. After three months, Toby has worn my patience thread-bare.' When an article of clothing is worn out, the threads of the material show.

# 20. SHIPS

SHIP

1. **all shipshape** – everything in good order, all neat and clean. 'The rooms are all shipshape for our guests.' The phrase was originally 'all shipshape and Bristol fashion', meaning that the ship was properly prepared for sea. The port of Bristol was well known for its efficiency in preparing ships for sea.
2. **when my ship comes home** – when I get rich, when I make my fortune. 'When my ship comes home, we'll buy that house by the sea.'
3. **ships in the night / ships that pass in the night** – casual acquaintances and friendships that last only a very short time. 'A pity you've been posted overseas just when we've met. Ships in the night!'
4. to **spoil a ship for a ha'porth of tar** – to lose a great deal for the sake of a small economy. 'What a pity you didn't use some good wood-preserver on that cedarwood of yours; then it wouldn't have warped. It was a case of spoiling the ship for a ha'porth of tar.' The 'ship' in the idiom is actually 'sheep', the two words being pronounced the same in some parts of England. In former times, sheep were smeared with tar to protect them from disease. cf. **'penny wise pound foolish' 244/2.**
5. **like rats leaving the sinking ship** – like traitors who desert the losing side in a contest. Rats are said to have a premonition when a ship is about to sink, and to leave it.
6. to **go down with the ship** – to stay at one's post until the bitter end. There was a tradition that the captain should go down with his ship. When the *Titanic* sank (1912), both the captain and the designer went down with the ship, although they were offered places in the life-boats. In modern times, the rule has been relaxed, and the captain is expected to be the last to leave the ship.
7. **the ship of the desert** – the camel. The journey of the camel across the desert has been compared with the voyage of a ship. Both are dependent on their own resources during the journey.
8. **spick and span** – clean, neat, tidy. 'Everything is spick and span now for our visitor. It has taken me all the morning to get his room ready.' A nautical phrase meaning that, on a new ship, every spick (nail) and span (chip) is new.
9. **in the wake of** – immediately after, in consequence of. 'In the wake of their electoral defeat in 1983, the divisions in the Labour Party came out into the open.' The wake is the track of smooth water left by a moving ship.

BOAT

10. **in the same boat** – to suffer the same predicament as somebody else. 'We are affected by rising prices just as much as you; we are all in the same boat.'
11. to **push the boat out** (somewhat dated) – to join one's friends in a celebration. It used to be the custom to have a celebration before starting on a voyage.
12. to **rock the boat** – to hinder the success of a concern in which one is involved. 'For goodness sake, don't criticize the management in front of our customers; you won't help us by rocking the boat.'
13. to **burn one's boats** – to commit oneself to a course of action that cannot possibly be changed. 'Now you have resigned your position in the com-

pany, you can't ask them for it back; you have burned your boats.'

1. to **miss the boat** – to miss an important opportunity. 'I'm afraid my husband is too old at sixty to be promoted; he has missed the boat.' cf. 'to **miss the bus' 141/3**.

## SAIL

2. to **sail through** – to succeed without any difficulty. 'Philip simply sailed through his exams – no trouble at all.'
3. **plain sailing** – an easy, uncomplicated plan of action. 'Nobody is opposing your application; it should be plain sailing for you from now on.' The term was originally 'plane sailing', meaning that the sailing was as simple as if you were sailing on a flat instead of a spherical plane.
4. to **sail into** someone – to scold or attack someone. 'Without more ado, Geoffrey sailed into the man with his fists.'
5. to **trim one's sails** – to change one's views, to withdraw them in the face of opposition. The full phrase was 'to trim the sails before the wind', meaning to adjust one's sails when the direction of the wind changed. In politics, a **'trimmer'** is someone who will change his principles under pressure of circumstances.
6. to **sail against the wind** – to oppose the prevailing view. 'Andrew never minded how much opposition he provoked; he liked sailing against the wind.'
7. to **strike one's sails** – to submit to a more powerful opponent, to accept humiliation. From the custom in the days of sail of a smaller ship lowering its sails as a sign of defeat by another ship.
8. **the cut of** someone's **jib** – someone's appearance. 'Since you ask me, I don't like the cut of his jib. I think Margaret has made a most unfortunate choice.' The jib is the foremost sail of a ship and derives from Dutch 'gijpen', (of sails) 'to turn suddenly'.

## BEAM

9. **broad in the beam** – broad-hipped.
10. **on one's beam ends** – in extreme financial difficulties, very short of money. 'Can you lend me some money, I'm on my beam ends.' A ship is on its beam ends just before it goes under.

## BOARD

11. to **go overboard** – to be extravagant. 'A Chippendale dining-suite and a Chinese carpet; you have gone overboard with your dining-room, haven't you?'
12. to **go by the board** – to manage without, often used in the sense of sacrificing everything to one purpose. 'Everything went by the board – holidays, new clothes, entertaining, lunches out – in order to get Vivien into college.' The original meaning was to throw unwanted articles overboard, i.e. over the side of the ship.
13. to **take on board** – to tolerate or acknowledge the truth of an idea. 'Today, people are taking on board the view that unemployment is a worldwide phenomenon and not the fault of any particular government.'

## OTHER PARTS OF THE SHIP

14. a **shot across the bows** – a warning signal. 'We've had a shot across the bows from the solicitor, warning us not to repeat our accusations.' A shot across the bows was a cannon-ball warning a ship either to surrender or to turn about.

1. to **clear the decks** – to get ready for action. 'We are clearing the decks for the launching of our new campaign.' The derivation is from naval warfare when the decks are cleared of any unnecessary objects which could obstruct the free movement of personnel and weapons during the action.
2. to **batten down the hatches** – to take every possible precaution to preserve one's money. A phrase that is much used by financial correspondents, meaning that when there has been a bad fall on the Stock Exchange, the only thing to do is to wait for the market to recover. When there is a storm at sea, the hatches, i.e. the openings in the ship's deck, are closed and secured to prevent the water getting in and sinking the ship.
3. **Davy Jones' locker** – the sea bed which receives the bodies of drowned sailors. 'Jones' is thought to be a corruption of 'Jonah', who was swallowed by a whale.
4. the **sheet anchor** – the basis of someone's livelihood, what he relies upon when everything else fails. 'I earn some money from my compositions, but the music lessons are my sheet anchor.'
5. to **throw a life-line** – to help somebody who is in trouble. The life-line is thrown from a ship to a person in danger of drowning.
6. to **show** someone / **know the ropes** – to be familiar with the way a business is organized. 'You'll find everything strange at first, but Carter will show you the ropes.' From the ropes used for sailing a ship.

## BERTH, TACK AND LEEWAY

7. to **give** someone **a wide berth** – to avoid someone's company, to keep a good distance away from someone. 'If you quarrel with Jakes, he can get very nasty; I would give him a wide berth if I were you.' The berth is the space in which a ship rides at anchor.
8. to be **on the right/wrong tack** – to take the line that leads to the right/wrong conclusion. If one took the wrong line in sailing, one went in the wrong direction.
9. to **make up leeway** – to compensate for time that has been wasted. 'You have a lot of leeway to make up, if you want to pass your examinations in June.' The leeway is the distance that the ship has deviated from its proper course.

## COAST AND SEA

10. **the coast is clear** – there is no danger of interference from the authorities. Much in use at schools when the pupils are on the look-out for a teacher. This was a smuggling term which meant that the coast was free from coastguards.
11. a **sea change** – a fundamental change, a transformation. 'The Prime Minister is convinced that there will soon be a sea change in the relations between East and West.'
12. **at sea / all at sea** – bewildered, confused. 'After listening a few minutes to their conversation, I was all at sea. Botany is not my subject.'
13. to **find one's sea-legs** – to adjust oneself to the roll and pitch of the ship. 'Once you've been on board a day or two, you'll soon find your sea-legs.' cf. 'to **be a good sailor' 232/12**.

## CANOE, BARGE AND ARK

14. to **paddle one's own canoe** – to use one's own ability and efforts to make one's way without anyone's help. 'In future I will paddle my own canoe

without asking for my parents' support.'

1. **not to touch with a barge-pole** – to dislike somebody or something intensely, to avoid. 'That man is a thoroughly disreputable character. I wouldn't touch him with a barge-pole.' cf. **'not to touch** someone **with a pair of tongs' 212/3**.
2. **out of the ark** – excessively old, ancient. 'Wherever did you get that wardrobe from? It looks as if it had come out of the ark!' The reference is to Noah's ark which Noah and his family built to escape from the Great Flood (described in Genesis).

## WRECK

3. a **nervous wreck** – mentally and physically exhausted. 'I feel a nervous wreck after looking after Jenny's children.'

# 21. THE WORLD AND ITS PLACES

WORLD

1. **it's a small world** – to be surprised at meeting a person one knows in an unexpected place. 'Fancy meeting you here, in the middle of a highland moor! It's a small world!'
2. to **make/get the best of both worlds** – to enjoy the advantages of two different situations or ways of life. 'As a day-pupil at a nearby boarding-school, Peter has the benefit of a good education, while enjoying the advantages of living at home with his parents. He gets the best of both worlds.'
3. to **carry the world before one** – to enjoy a resounding success. 'Stephen carried the world before him with his new invention.'
4. to **set the world on fire** – to achieve fame. 'I see you've set the world on fire with your latest symphony, Jack!' cf. **'not to set the Thames on fire' 185/3.**

   to **make a noise in the world** – to be talked about, to become famous.
5. to **come up in the world** – to improve one's professional and social standing. 'You've come up in the world since we last met.'

   to **come down in the world** – to lose one's professional and social standing.
6. to **make one's way in the world / to make one's way** – to advance in one's job. 'My three sons are all making their way in the world without any help from me.'
7. a **man of the world** – a man with a good understanding of men and women, and experienced in the ways of the world. 'If you are in trouble, Valerie, would you like to talk to my father; he is a man of the world and very understanding.'
8. to **take the world as one finds it** – to adapt oneself to the ways of the world without trying to change it, to respect social convention. 'It's best to take the world as you find it, then you won't be disappointed.'
9. **for all the world like** somebody/something – exactly like . . . 'Angela stood there in her mother's long white dress, for all the world like her mother when she was Angela's age.'

   **for all the world as if** – just like; e.g. 'When I visited my old university, I felt for all the world as if I were back in my student days.'
10. **not for all the world** – in no circumstances. 'I wouldn't leave London for all the world.'
11. **it's not the end of the world** – things could be worse. 'It's disappointing not getting into university but it's not the end of the world. You have a good job waiting for you.'
12. to **do** someone **a world of good** – to make a huge improvement to someone. 'You don't look well, Susan. Three weeks at the sea-side will do you the world of good.'
13. **on top of the world** – elated by one's own success. 'No one thought Tony would win the by-election; he is on top of the world.'
14. **out of this world** (slang) – fantastically beautiful, marvellous. 'Just wait until you have seen the house. We must buy it; it is out of this world.'
15. **with the best will in the world** – no matter how much one tries. 'With the best will in the world, we can't help you if you won't co-operate with us.'
16. **the old world** – Europe, Asia and Africa, as distinct from North and South America.
17. **in a world of one's own** – in a make-

believe world of one's own, in a world of fantasy. 'I don't think my sister recognizes me any more. She is living in a world of her own.'

1. **dead to the world** – in a deep sleep, very difficult to awaken. 'Alec must have drunk an awful lot. He is lying on his bed, dead to the world.'
2. **the world to come** – the life after death.

## PLACE, PLACES

3. **in place** – suitable, appropriate.
   **out of place** – unsuitable, inappropriate. 'The elegantly dressed woman felt out of place at the party where all the other women were wearing jeans.'
4. **all over the place** – in disorder, untidy. '"Keep to your positions," the football manager shouted angrily at the players. "You are all over the place!"'
5. to **keep** someone **in his place** – to keep in order, to keep under control. 'The teacher only had to look at the children to keep them in their place.'
6. to **put** someone **in his place** – to discourage familiarity. 'When the young lad took the lady by the hand, she promptly took her hand away from his, intending to put him in his place.'
7. **there's a time and place for everything** – a good thing can be spoilt by bad timing or an unsuitable setting. 'I love the Moonlight Sonata, but I should hate to hear it at breakfast! There's a time and place for everything.'
8. **not to be one's place to** (always used in the negative) – not to be right or proper to . . . '"It's not my place to give you advice," the clerk said to the manager.'
9. to **know one's place** – to accept the limits of one's position in society. In England up to the beginning of World War II, there was a deferential society in which everyone had a certain place or station in life, and respected their social superiors. This has now been largely replaced by an egalitarian society, with people claiming the same rights and privileges as the upper classes.
10. **a place in the sun** – a share of the good things in life. 'No one can dispute with us the place in the sun which is rightly ours' (said by Kaiser Wilhelm II, the German emperor, in 1911 during the Agadir crisis).
11. **pride of place** – the best position, often the most central or conspicuous, for the honoured guest, the most valuable objet d'art, and so on. 'He had a number of interesting ornaments on his mantelpiece, but pride of place was given to a silver snuff-box he had inherited from his father.'
12. to **fall into place** – to make sense, to follow a logical order. 'The work was difficult at first but, after a few weeks, everything fell into place.'
13. **in high places** – having power and influence. 'You had better be careful how you talk to me; I have friends in high places.'
14. to **come to the right place** – (1) to approach the best person for advice or help. (2) (vulgar) to sound a warning. 'If you are looking for trouble, you have come to the right place!' meaning: 'If you don't behave yourself, you'll be sorry.'

## IN LONDON

15. to **put** someone **in Chancery** – (1) to hold a person's head under one arm, leaving you free to punch him. (2) to put someone into an awkward position from which it is difficult to extricate himself. The reference is to the Court of Chancery which at one time had a reputation for delaying lawsuits and ruining the parties in dispute.

1. **the old lady of Threadneedle Street** – a nickname for the Bank of England.
2. to **talk Billingsgate** – to talk like fishmongers at Billingsgate. Billingsgate was formerly the principal fish market in London, and notorious for its bad language.
3. **not to set the Thames on fire** – not to distinguish oneself in any way, to be quite ordinary. 'Martin gets a lot of pleasure from his painting but I'm afraid he'll never set the Thames on fire.' cf. 'to **set the world on fire' 183/4**.
4. to **be/end up in Carey Street** – to go bankrupt. 'We shall end up in Carey Street at the rate we are spending money.' The Courts in Bankruptcy are situated in Carey Street, off the Strand.
5. **bedlam** – a mad commotion. 'The chairman was quite unable to keep order. Everyone was on his feet shouting and swearing. Absolute bedlam!' Bedlam, a corruption of 'Bethlehem', was the name of a mad house in the Middle Ages. (Today it would be called a mental hospital.)
6. **You are not at the Ritz!** – the Ritz is a hotel in Piccadilly (London) which has made a name for the excellence of its cooking and accommodation. When servicemen complained about the bad cooking in the army during World War II, they were often told that there was a war on and that they were not 'at the Ritz'.

IN ENGLAND

7. to **send to Coventry** – to punish someone for disloyalty to his companions or workmates by refusing to speak to him. 'Sending to Coventry' is a common practice in schools and trade unions. The idiom has its origin in the Civil War between King Charles I and Parliament (1642–6). In his *History of the Great Rebellion*, Volume 2, VI, 83, Clarendon says that Royalist prisoners captured at Birmingham were sent to Coventry, a Parliamentary stronghold, where some of them were beheaded; whence the association of 'sending to Coventry' with the punishment of disloyalty, which later took the form of not speaking to the offender.
8. to **carry coals to Newcastle** – to bring a thing to a place which is famous for its production, like trying to sell wine to the French, or kimonos to the Japanese, and so on.
9. a **Norfolk dumpling** – a person who is dull and stupid. The inhabitants of East Anglia have this reputation, for reasons which are not apparent.

IN SCOTLAND

10. **off to Gretna Green** – couples who were under age (in English law) would run away together to get married at Gretna Green, a small town on the English–Scottish border. The conditions for marrying under Scottish law being less strict than under English, this was a favourite device for couples who had not obtained the consent of their parents.

IN IRELAND

11. to be **full of Blarney / to talk Blarney** – to make wild promises, to flatter and deceive. The Irish have a reputation for making wild promises. From kissing the Blarney Stone in Killarney.
12. **beyond the Pale** – socially unacceptable; any form of serious misbehaviour. 'I won't invite those boys; I saw them throwing stones at Jane yesterday. They are beyond the Pale.' The word 'Pale' is derived from the Latin 'palus', a stake, stakes having been used, in the fourteenth century, to mark out the boundary between

the land settled by the British colonists in Ireland and the rest of the country. The people living beyond the Pale were regarded by the colonists as uncivilized. The same phrase was adopted by the English in their own country to indicate people of 'inferior class', who were not received in polite society. There was also a Pale of Settlement for the Jews in Czarist Russia from 1792.

## IN BELGIUM

1. to **meet your Waterloo** – to suffer a final, decisive defeat. The phrase has been taken from Napoleon's defeat by Wellington and Blücher at the Battle of Waterloo. It is usually applied to an unexpected defeat after a string of successes.

## IN ITALY

2. **Rome was not built in a day** – nothing of value has ever been achieved without great effort.
3. to **fiddle while Rome burns** – to occupy oneself with trifles during a crisis. Legend has it that the Emperor Nero fiddled while Rome burned.
4. **all roads lead to Rome** – Rome has always possessed a special importance – as capital of the ancient world, then as capital of Christendom. As the seat of the papacy, Rome commands the allegiance of six hundred million Catholics.
5. **See Naples and die** – Naples is the most beautiful city in the world and, when you have seen Naples, you may die happy. There is a small town near Naples called Mori, the Italian for 'die', where thousands once died of typhoid and cholera, so this is a joke phrase.
6. **the Venice of the North** – there are three cities in the north of Europe which boast that they are comparable with Venice: Bruges, Amsterdam and Stockholm.
7. to **cross the Rubicon** – to do something irrevocable. In ancient Rome, generals were guilty of treason if they failed to disband their armies before crossing the Rubicon. Caesar took the decision to cross the Rubicon with his army to seize power.

## OTHER COUNTRIES IN EUROPE

8. **castles in Spain** – unreal wealth and splendour which only exists in the mind of the dreamer. cf. **'castles in the air' 24/13, 'pie in the sky' 160/15**.
9. **the gnomes of Zurich** – Swiss bankers, so called because they were the guardians of huge treasures under the earth, i.e. in the vaults of their banks. The name was intended humorously.
10. an **Olympian detachment** – an impersonal, unemotional view of human conflict. From Olympus, the home of the Greek gods where Zeus reigned. The gods of ancient Greece were endowed with all the human passions and weaknesses – love, jealousy, vindictiveness and anger; so the modern meaning of the idiom has changed.
11. a **Marathon** – a long-drawn-out contest, an event which calls for great endurance. 'The conference began at eight this morning and went on all day until eleven o'clock at night. It was a real Marathon!' The name has been taken from the Battle of Marathon between the Greeks and the Persians, fought in 490 BC. The messenger, who announced the result of the battle, fell dead on his arrival in Athens after running nearly 23 miles.

## IN THE EAST

12. **Sodom and Gomorrah** – synonym for a centre of vice (Genesis XVII, 19).

1. the **Gadarene Swine** – to stampede with the herd (or crowd) to destruction. From the Bible, when Jesus told the people how the evil spirit that had been cast out entered the Gadarene swine, causing them to hurl themselves in a fit of madness over the edge of the cliff to their destruction (Matthew VIII, 28–34).
2. a **perfect Babel / a Babel of sounds** – an uproar in many different languages.
3. **the walls of Jericho didn't fall down in a day** – if you want to defeat your enemy, you will have to fight very hard.
4. **like the walls of Jericho** – any sudden unexpected collapse. 'To Ferdy, they [the English hostesses] fell like the walls of Jericho!' (from Somerset Maugham's Short Stories, Volume 2, 'The Alien Corn'). The allusion is to the collapse of the walls of Jericho when the Israelites blew their horns outside the city.
5. **'His road to Damascus', 'Her road to Damascus'** – a dramatic change of mind on some burning issue. When Saul of Tarsus, who had for a long time been a vigorous persecutor of the Christians, was on the road to Damascus, he heard the voice of God and immediately became an ardent disciple of Christ, adopting the name of Paul.
6. **Mecca** – a place which has a strong appeal for the enthusiast. 'Between the wars, Paris was the Mecca of painters and artists.' Mecca is the birthplace of the prophet Mohammed, and a holy place for Muslims.

## IMAGINARY PLACES

7. an **El Dorado** – an imaginary country where the traveller can make a fortune without any effort.
8. to **live in Eden** – a place of sheer bliss and delight. The place where Adam and Eve were created.
9. to **consign to Limbo** – to put out of one's mind once and for all. Limbo was a place adjoining hell which accommodated unbaptized infants.
10. **in the land of Nod** – asleep. Note the related phrase 'to **nod off**', meaning to fall asleep.
11. **Shangri-la / like Shangri-la** – a state of mind lacking in drive or interest, dull placidity. Shangri-la is the paradise described in James Hilton's *Lost Horizon* (1933) up in the mountains of a Buddhist country. In Hilton's city, the people lived in perfect peace and serenity, with no quarrelling or strife, but also with an absence of emotion or ambition.
12. a **fool's paradise** – a comfortable but false illusion which could have deceived only a fool. 'I knew all along that the business would never recover. You have been living in a fool's paradise all these years!'

# 22. LANGUAGES AND NATIONALITIES

LANGUAGE

1. to **pick up a language** – to learn a language by listening to native speakers talking together, without taking lessons or studying the grammar.
2. a **second language** – the first foreign language that one learns. Hundreds of millions of people have learned English as a second language. Usually the English learn French as their second language.
3. **bad/strong language** – language that is full of swear-words and obscene expressions.
4. to **talk the same language** – to share a common background with the person one is speaking to, to share the same problems and difficulties. 'We have both been running English language schools for the last twenty years. We talk the same language.'
5. to **use the language of violence** – to resort to intimidation and force instead of common sense or the Courts. 'I know you have been treated disgracefully, but to write threatening letters is to use the language of violence.'
6. to **murder a language** – to make every conceivable mistake in the course of learning a foreign language. One school of thought holds that in order to learn a language one must 'murder' it first, because practice is more important than theory.
7. a **dead language** – a language that is no longer spoken today, except by scholars, theologians and experts. The classical languages of ancient Greek, Latin and Sanskrit are dead languages. Cornish is a dead language; the last person known to have spoken it was Dolly Pentreath (1685–1778).

ENGLISH

8. **broken English**/French/Spanish, etc. – badly spoken English/French/Spanish, etc., containing many mistakes in grammar and pronunciation.
9. **Queen's English** – correct, grammatical English. It may be spoken in any accent, provided it is clear and intelligible.
10. **received English** – a phrase coined by Professor Daniel Jones for the socially most acceptable accent. It is the only accent that is not tied to any particular region but is local to the whole country. Jones called it 'received' because at one time this pronunciation was an essential condition for being received in the best society.
11. **pidgin English** – a corrupt, simplified form of English used by many people in Papua New Guinea and the Far East for trading. cf. **'dog-Latin' 54/2**.
12. **plain English** – (1) blunt, outspoken English. 'I told him in plain English what I thought of his idea', meaning I expressed my disapproval frankly and forcefully. (2) good, clear, easily understood English as opposed to the jargon that is sometimes employed by civil servants. We give below an example of bureaucratic English which we have rendered into plain English.

    Bureaucratic English: A distinction should be made at an age appropriate to the background and nationality of the student, below which the concept of the course should be for juveniles and above it for young adults (British Tourist Authority, 1979 BLE/1980).

    Plain English: The courses should take into account the ages, background and nationality of the students.
13. **the English disease** – the calling of

strikes, both official and unofficial, without reasonable justification.

## WELSH

1. to **welsh on** someone – to trick or swindle someone, to break a promise, often in connection with some business. At one time, Welsh bookies had a reputation for running off with the punters' stakes. (That is how the English explain the phrase. It reflects the hostility in former times between the Welsh and the English.)

## DUTCH

2. to **go Dutch** – each person pays his own bill in a restaurant. A practice favoured by students or young people who are working.
3. a **Dutch party** – a party to which each guest contributes some food or drink.
4. **double Dutch** – nonsense, meaningless words. 'I didn't understand a single word. It was all double Dutch to me.'
5. to **talk to someone like a Dutch uncle** – to lecture with excessive seriousness.
6. **Dutch courage** – false courage acquired by drinking. 'I ordered myself a double whisky to give myself some Dutch courage.'
7. **I'm a Dutchman if . . .** – a way of denying a supposition. 'If you're right, I'm a Dutchman', means I am quite sure you are wrong.
8. a **Dutch auction** – an auction at which the starting price is pitched high and then slowly reduced until a bid is made.

## OTHER NATIONALITIES

9. **Prussian efficiency** – a general term for all the qualities associated with the history of Prussia: energy, thoroughness, industry, patience and discipline.
10. **Teutonic thoroughness** – especially characteristic of Prussia. The Germans have always had a reputation for studiousness, theoretical analysis and research in depth, in contrast with Anglo-Saxon empiricism.
11. to **take French leave** – to leave without first obtaining permission. The French have a similar saying to the English: 'filer à l'anglaise'.
12. **French letter** – a contraceptive.
13. **Gallic humour** – humour that is logical and intellectual, wit rather than humour.
14. to **make a Roman holiday** – to organize a gruesome spectacle for the public. The words are from a quotation from Byron's *Childe Harolde's Pilgrimage*, IV cxli: '. . . butchered to make a Roman holiday'. Public executions and whippings would both come into this category.
15. **When in Rome, do as the Romans do** – you should adopt the manners and customs of the people you are living with. First said in a slightly different form by St Ambrose (Epistle 36, II Kings VI 18): 'When I am in Milan, I do as they do in Milan. But when I go to Rome, I do as Rome does!'
16. **when Greek meets Greek** – when two men of formidable strength engage in combat, the contest will be hard fought and severe.
17. a **Greek gift** – a gift which brings only trouble and sorrow. The reference is to Vergil's *Aeneid* II, 'I fear the Greeks, even when they bring gifts'.
18. **It's all Greek to me** – I can't understand a word of it, it's like listening to a foreign language (from Shakespeare's *Julius Caesar*, I, ii: 'But for my own part, it was Greek to me').
19. **'Young Turks'** – young agitators, young militants who are in a hurry to

make changes in the established order.

1. a **Bohemian life** – in some countries, the name 'Bohemian' was a synonym for 'gypsy' in the mistaken belief that gypsies came from Bohemia. It means an irregular, unconvential way of life, and is often applied to writers and artists.
2. **Bohemian tastes/dress** – bright, colourful, unconventional tastes or dress.
3. the **Russian soul** – a vague, unfulfilled yearning for a better, spiritual life which would bring consolation and relief to the suffering masses. Copiously described and dramatized in the works of Dostoyevsky and other Russian novelists of the nineteenth century.
4. **Russian roulette** – gamblers would stake their lives by putting a bullet in one of the six chambers of a revolver, spinning the chamber then holding it to their head and pressing the trigger.
5. a **Tartar** (term of abuse) – a grim, uncivilized, bad-tempered person who makes a lot of trouble. The Tartars are Asiatics of Turkish origin, and are said to be notorious for their savagery in war.
6. to **catch a Tartar** – to take prisoner a man who makes so much trouble that one regrets ever having captured him.
7. the **Amazons** – active, assertive women in different walks of life. The Amazons were a legendary tribe of women who fought on horseback against the ancient Greeks. They were renowned for their bravery in battle.
8. **Spartan simplicity** – absolute simplicity in one's way of life, the simplest diet and the avoidance of luxury or comfort in any form. The phrase has been taken from the Spartans, who were the most disciplined and austere people in ancient Greece.
9. **Spartan endurance** – great fortitude and discipline – a characteristic of the Spartan way of life.
10. **like the laws of the Medes and the Persians** – unchangeable.
11. a **Trojan horse** – an enemy concealed within. 'I think it would be dangerous to elect that man to the board; he could be a Trojan horse.'
12. a **Parthian shot** – a cutting remark made by someone on leaving, which gives the victim no opportunity of retaliating. It often means one final insult in addition to many others, with the idea of getting in the last word. The Parthian horsemen used to shoot at their enemy while retreating at full speed from them.
13. a **Philistine / to have Philistine tastes** – someone without cultural interests. The phrase was coined by Matthew Arnold but is really a misnomer because the Philistines who lived around 1200 BC were highly cultured, combining discipline and efficiency with a taste for luxury.
14. a **good Samaritan** – someone who goes out of his way to help a stranger in distress, although the stranger has no claim on him. The phrase has been taken from Christ's parable of the Good Samaritan, Luke X, 29.
15. **there are too many chiefs and not enough Indians** – there are too many highly paid directors and managers, and not enough men to carry out the orders.
16. the **Mandarin mentality** – Mandarin was the name given to the officials in the Chinese Civil Service who had ruled China for centuries before the Communist Revolution. The Mandarin mentality means the mentality of the ruling class, self-satisfied, domineering and very conscious of its superiority to the rest of the country.

# 23. NAMES

## NAME

1. **one's good name** – one's reputation. 'He had a good name for honest dealing.'

2. a **bad name** – a bad reputation. 'That hotel has a bad name for its accommodation and food.'

   to **give** someone **a bad name** – to do harm to someone's reputation. 'You'll give us a bad name if you talk to our customers like that!'

3. to **have a name for** – to be well known for. 'He has a name for his wit.'

4. to **make a name for oneself** – to distinguish oneself, usually used in a good sense. 'Arthur has made a name for himself in physics.'

5. to **know by name** – to know a person's name, but not to know him to speak to.

6. to **call** someone **names** – to address someone insultingly.

7. to **clear one's name** – to be acquitted of a serious accusation. 'The inquiry cleared Peter's name of all blame for the death of his patient.'

8. to **win a name for** – to be well known for. 'He has won a name for his rowdiness and bad manners.'

9. to pass **by the name of** – to assume the name of. 'He used to pass by the name of Thorn. His real name is Jones.'

10. to **lend one's name to** – to allow the use of one's name in support of a campaign or crusade.

11. **in the name of** – at the command of. 'In the name of the law, let me pass!'

12. **what's in a name?** – a name by itself has no significance. It is the associations which give it meaning. Shakespeare makes the same point: 'What's in a name? That which we call a rose / By any other name would smell as sweet' (*Romeo and Juliet*, II, ii).

13. to **name names** – to make accusations against certain people. 'I don't want to name names, but I will if the stealing doesn't stop.'

14. **maiden name** – a wife's family name prior to her marriage.

15. **nickname** – an extra name often coined by friends or school fellows to describe some physical characteristic, such as 'Tubby', 'Fatty', 'Ginger', 'Sandy', 'Tiny'. The word is derived from Middle English 'ekename', eke meaning other or additional.

16. a **household name** – a name familiar to every household in the country.

17. to **drag** someone's **name through the mud** – to damage someone's reputation by denigrating him in public.

18. to **drop names** / **name-dropping** – mentioning the names (especially the Christian names) of important people in one's conversation to give the impression that one is friendly with them.

19. **no names, no packdrill** – it's better not to mention the people involved because one doesn't wish to make trouble for them. 'Just as I was locking up the office, I overheard someone telephoning a friend in Tokyo. No names, no packdrill.' Packdrill was a punishment used in the British Army which obliged offenders to march up and down with heavy packs on their backs.

## BOYS' NAMES: JACK

20. **I'm all right, Jack!** – the slogan of the self-seeking opportunist who will forget his friends for the sake of his own interests.

21. a **jack in office** – a self-assertive official who misuses his authority.

22. to be a **cheap jack** – to sell shoddy

goods; to indulge in mean, dishonest tricks to sell one's goods.

1. **every man jack of them** – every single one. 'All the men on the building site went on strike, including the foreman, every man jack of them.'
2. to **climb like a steeplejack** – to be agile in climbing and sure-footed.
3. **Jack is as good as his master** – there is no difference between the boss and the worker. We are all equal and we should all have equal rights.
4. a **Jack of all trades** – a man who knows a little of many jobs but none properly. The phrase derives from 'A Jack of all trades is a master of none'.
5. **Jack Sprat** – a small, undersized boy or man. The sprat is a very small fish. From the nursery rhyme: 'Jack Sprat could eat no fat and his wife could eat no lean, but 'twixt them both they licked the platter clean.'
6. **every Jack has his Jill** – every man can find the right woman if he looks for her. (From the nursery rhyme, 'Jack and Jill went up the hill . . .')
7. **before one could say Jack Robinson** – in a moment, before one could turn round. The phrase was used, probably for the first time, by Fanny Burney, in her novel *Evelina* (1778), Letter 82, 'I'd do it as soon as say Jack Robinson.'
8. **Jack/Jack Tar** (nickname) – an ordinary sailor.
9. a **jack-in-the-box** – a toy man who springs out of a box as soon as the lid is lifted. Sometimes used as an idiomatic comparison. 'They were jumping to their feet like jacks in the box on points or order.'
10. to **hit the jackpot** – to get a huge return on one's money all at once; to make a lucky gamble. The phrase is taken from the card game Poker when one scoops the pool.
11. to **jack up** – to increase suddenly. 'By installing new machinery, they were able to jack up production by more than half.' One jacks up a car by raising up one end of it to change a wheel.

## JOHN, ROGER, PETER, PAUL AND OTHER BOYS' NAMES

12. **John Bull** – he is supposed to personify the typical Englishman, having been described by Arbuthnot in his *History of John Bull* in 1727: 'The Englishman is honest, straightforward, irascible, bold and quarrelsome, plain-dealing and independent.' cf. **'Uncle Sam' 133/12**.
13. to hoist **the Jolly Roger** – to challenge the authority of the state. The Jolly Roger is the black flag of piracy.
14. to **rob Peter to pay Paul** – to give to one person what rightfully belongs to another. 'To reduce income tax by doubling VAT is to rob Peter to pay Paul.'
15. to be a **Peter Pan** – to be a male adult who mentally remains fixated on his childhood. Peter Pan was the boy in Barrie's play of the same name who never wanted to grow up.
16. to be a **Paul Pry** – someone who is always interfering in other people's affairs, an objectionable busybody.
17. a **doubting Thomas** – a sceptic, someone who will believe only the evidence of his own eyes. Thomas, a disciple of Christ, was unwilling to believe in His resurrection until he had seen the marks left by the nails on the hands of Christ.
18. **Tommy / Tommy Atkins** – a generic name given to the English infantry soldiers in World War I.
19. a **peeping Tom** – a voyeur, a man who takes pleasure in looking secretly at nude women.

1. **tommy-rot** (slang) – the most utter nonsense. 'He's talking tommy-rot as usual.'
2. a **tomboy** – a young girl, below the age of adolescence, who behaves like a boy, preferring the company of boys and their games.
3. **Tom, Dick and Harry** any nonentity. 'I'm not going out with any Tom, Dick or Harry. If Ronald doesn't invite me, I won't go out at all.'
4. a **simple Simon** – someone who is easily taken in. From the nursery rhyme: 'Simple Simon met a pieman going to the fair . . .'
5. a **proper Charlie** – a fool. The name refers to the pensioners who were employed by King Charles I. These men had a reputation for stupidity.
   to **make a Charlie of** someone – to make a fool of someone.
6. to **take the micky out of** – to make fun of someone.
7. a **smart Alec** – a disagreeable know-all.
8. **And Bob's your uncle!** – now you have what you want. When the young Balfour was given a ministerial post by his uncle, Lord Robert Salisbury, the Prime Minister, members of the opposition said 'Bob's your uncle', meaning that with such an uncle he could have whatever he wanted.
9. a **silly Billy** – a foolish fellow. The nickname for William IV who was considered none too bright. This phrase is often used in the plural form. 'The silly Billies in the Ministry!'
10. **jerry-built** – a badly built house without a foundation.
11. to **gerrymander** – to manipulate the boundaries of a parliamentary constituency so as to gain an unfair advantage, e.g. by transferring a large number of one's opponents to another constituency. Gerry was a governor of Massachusetts.
12. to give **a Roland for an Oliver** – to give as good as one gets, to retaliate effectively.
13. a **Valentine** – a letter or card sent anonymously by a man to a girl on St Valentine's day expressing love and admiration.

## GIRLS' NAMES

14. **plain Jane** – a plain girl.
15. **as dead as Queen Anne / 'Queen Anne is dead'** – said in reply to news that is no longer new. 'Did you say your brother is engaged to Judy? Yes and Queen Anne is dead. I knew about their engagement weeks ago.' cf. **'as dead as mutton' 161/14, 'as dead as a door-nail' 211/10.**
16. **not on your Nelly** – a derisive refusal. 'Not on your Nelly, you won't catch me doing that.'
17. **Lady Bountiful** – a country lady who gave half her money to charity. '"I am not going to play Lady Bountiful with tax-payers' money," was said by Mrs Thatcher soon after becoming Prime Minister.'

## BIBLICAL NAMES

18. the **old Adam** – the primitive, sinful nature of a man which is concealed under a veneer of good breeding and education.
19. **not to know** someone **from Adam** – to have no knowledge or recollection of someone. 'I can't think why the man by the window keeps waving at me; I don't know him from Adam!'
20. **the mark of Cain** – the stain of a crime or misdeed on one's reputation. 'You will bear the mark of Cain for the rest of your life for your cruelty to her children.' The allusion is to the murder of Abel by his brother, Cain. 'And

the Lord set a mark upon Cain lest any finding him should kill him' (Genesis IV. 9).

1. to **raise Cain** – to create a terrible row, to explode with anger. 'He will raise Cain when he hears his son has been expelled from school.' So called because the name of Cain is associated with the most violent temper.
2. to be a **Daniel come to judgement** – to show judgement and wisdom beyond one's years. 'A Daniel come to judgement, yea, a Daniel! O wise young judge, how I do honour thee!' (Shakespeare, *The Merchant of Venice*, IV, i).
3. they are **like David and Jonathan** – inseparable friends. A perfect friendship (2 Samuel I, 26).
4. a **David and Goliath situation** – a situation in which one adversary is hopelessly outmatched by the other. 'How can you possibly compete with the shop across the road. They have a hundred times more capital than you. It's a David and Goliath situation.'
5. a **Jeremiah** – one who always sees everything in the gloomiest light. 'What a Jeremiah you are. You are always prophesying disaster!' Jeremiah was a prophet of gloom of the Old Testament.
6. the **worship of Mammon** – an excessive love of wealth which is pursued at the cost of one's duty to family and friends. Mammon is a synonym of avarice and the worship of money. 'You cannot serve God and Mammon' (Luke XVI, 13).
7. to **try the patience of Job** – to provoke even the most patient person. 'I've explained it to you a hundred times and you still don't understand! You would try the patience of Job!' Job was afflicted with every possible calamity but learned from God to bear his misfortunes with courage and patience. From the Old Testament. cf. 'to **try the patience of a saint**' **120/6**.
8. a **Job's comforter** – someone who calls to offer sympathy but makes matters worse by blaming the bereaved person for what has happened. 'I was so sorry to learn of your little boy's death. What a pity he was never inoculated.' In the Book of Job (Old Testament), Job is reproached by his friends for bringing calamity on himself by his disobedience to God.
9. to **out-herod Herod** – to exceed Herod in cruelty and wickedness. It was King Herod who had the babes of Bethlehem put to death (Matthew II, 16). The phrase comes from Shakespeare: 'I would have such a fellow shipped for o'erdoing Termagant; it outherods Herod' (*Hamlet*, III, 2, 1).
10. to **play Judas** – to be a traitor. Judas Iscariot betrayed Jesus for thirty pieces of silver.
11. **the kiss of Judas** – any display of affection whose purpose is to conceal an act of treachery. It was the kiss of Judas that betrayed Jesus to the Roman soldiers (Matthew XXVI, 49).
12. a **piece of Jesuitry** – a very subtle argument, full of sophistry and logic carried to extremes.

## CLASSICAL AND MYTHICAL NAMES

13. an **Adonis** – any young man of striking beauty. The phrase is sometimes used as a light-hearted compliment. 'With an Adonis like Mark at your side, you had better watch out. Half the girls in Tonbridge will be after him!'
14. **beyond the dreams of Croesus** – unimaginable riches. Croesus, King of Lydia 560–546 BC, was reputed to be the richest man of all time.
15. a **Janus** – having two faces, front and back, with contradictory expressions.

The phrase comes from the Roman god who guarded doors and gates. 'Descartes (the French philosopher, 1596–1660) was a Janus with one face smiling at the conventional wisdom, and the other sceptical of it' (from Frederic Raphael's review of Bernard Williams's *Descartes: The Project of Pure Inquiry*).

1. to **play Cupid** – to play the matchmaker. Cupid (Greek: Eros), son of Venus (Aphrodite), was the god of love. He is represented in fable as a boy of great beauty, with wings, carrying a bow and arrows.
2. **opening Pandora's box** – accepting a dangerous present which will bring every conceivable ill upon one's head. From the Greek myth which relates how Pandora, the first woman ever made, was given a box by the gods whose contents when released would afflict the human race ever after.
3. to be **as old as Methuselah** – the name is a symbol of longevity and the phrase is often used humorously; for example, 'That joke is as old as Methuselah.' Methuselah is a mythical figure who was reputed to have lived for 969 years.
4. **Homer sometimes nods** – even the greatest of mortals errs from time to time. Horace excuses Homer's occasional drowsiness in view of the great length of his poem.
5. **platonic love** – pure love between men and women in which there is no sexuality. The phrase occurs at the end of the *Symposium* when Plato refers to the non-sexual love that Socrates felt for young men.
6. **socratic method** – the rigorous logical analysis that the Greek philosopher, Socrates, applied to every problem.
7. a **caesarean operation / a caesarean** – the cutting of the abdomen to effect delivery of the child, as with Julius Caesar. Caesarean is derived from the Latin 'caesus', the past participle of 'caedere', meaning to cut.
8. **Achilles' heel** – the one and only weakness, but a fatal one. 'Brian could have been a rich man today had it not been for his gambling, his Achilles' heel.' From the legend of Achilles whose body, when a baby, was immersed by his nurse in the river Styx to make him invulnerable (the *Iliad* of Homer). cf. 'a **chink in one's armour' 210/7**, 'to **have feet of clay' 104/10**.
9. **Herculean efforts** – immense, almost superhuman efforts. Hercules earned immortality for himself by accomplishing twelve enormously difficult tasks set him by the Argive king. 'It will need Herculean efforts to master French in six months.'
10. the **sword of Damocles / like the sword of Damocles hanging over one** – the danger that looms ahead and threatens our well-being. 'The danger of war hangs over humanity like the sword of Damocles.' From the legend of King Dionysius, who made his courtier Damocles sit under a sword that hung from the ceiling by a single hair, in order to demonstrate to him the precariousness of a king's life which he so much envied.
11. the **Midas touch** – a person is said to have 'the Midas touch' when all his business ventures prosper spectacularly. The phrase comes from the legend of Midas, King of Phrygia, whose prayer that anything he touched might turn to gold was granted by the gods as a reward for his hospitality to Dionysius's tutor.
12. to **cut the Gordian knot** – to take decisive action in order to gain one's ends. There was an ancient legend that the first person to untie the Gordian knot would gain the empire of Asia. Many travellers had failed to unravel the knot, but Alexander of Macedonia solved the problem by

cutting the knot with his sword, and then went on to win all Asia in accordance with the legend.

1. a **Procrustean bed** – a harsh, inhumane system into which the individual is fitted by force, regardless of his own needs or wishes. The phrase is taken from the name of the Greek robber who forced his victims to lie on a couch. If they were too long, he chopped off their feet, and if they were too short, he stretched their bodies to the required length. The phrase is often used in political debate.
2. **like a Sphinx** – an expressionless face which conceals a secret.
3. the **Oedipus complex** – the association of patricidal fantasies and feelings of guilt in the mind of the young boy; a concept of the Freudian school of psycho-analysis based on the ancient Greek myth of Oedipus, who unwittingly slew his father and married his mother.

## NAMES FROM LITERATURE

4. an **Aladdin's cave** – a place full of riches and good things. 'It was like an Aladdin's cave for a poor country boy.'
5. like a **Rip van Winkle** – a man who lives in the past, and is out of touch with modern life. 'You might have got the house for that price twenty years ago but not today. Where have you been living all this time? You are a real Rip van Winkle!' In Washington Irving's fable, Rip van Winkle falls asleep for twenty years, and when he awakes, he finds his house deserted; he is bewildered and lost.
6. **Lilliputian** – fussy, small-minded people. Taken from Dean Swift's *Gulliver's Travels*, whose purpose was to show how small-minded we all are by portraying mankind as a race of pygmies preoccupied with the pettiest pursuits.
7. to be a **Shylock** – to be a ruthless, pitiless money-lender who will extract the last penny from his debtor. Taken from Shakespeare's *Merchant of Venice.*
8. a **Don Juan** – a man who is always falling in and out of love, one who has an insatiable love for women. 'He's a real Don Juan.' A notorious rake of the fourteenth century, Don Juan is the legendary hero of many stories, plays and poems. He is the central figure in Mozart's *Don Giovanni* and Byron's *Don Juan.*
9. a **Jekyll and Hyde personality** – someone who alternates great kindness and nobility of character with extreme brutality and barbarism. The phrase is taken from Robert Louis Stevenson's novel which depicts the good Dr Jekyll changing into the evil Mr Hyde. The character created by Stevenson was intended as a symbol of the struggle between good and evil in each one of us.
10. **like a Micawber/Micawberish** – someone who makes no provision for the future and hopes something will turn up. Taken from a character in Dickens's *David Copperfield.*
11. **Pipsqueak** – a small unimportant man who irritates people with his bossy manner. 'I'm not going to be pushed around by that Pipsqueak!' From the name Pip.
12. **Robin Hood policies** – the policy of taking money from the rich and giving it to the poor. Robin Hood was the name of the legendary outlaw who lived with his men in Sherwood Forest in the thirteenth century and was reputed to rob the king's officers in order to help the peasants.
13. **the Cinderella of** – the least admired. 'Woodwork has always been the

Cinderella of the Arts.' The phrase is taken from the fairy tale in which Cinderella was forced to drudge all day at home while her step-mother and two step-sisters enjoyed themselves at palatial balls.

1. **like Alice in Wonderland** – an imaginary world where the inhabitants are all insane, and the laws of logic and reason have been suspended. 'First, I am blamed for taking the girl out, then the next day, I am blamed for not taking her out. It's like Alice in Wonderland.' From *Alice's Adventures in Wonderland* by Lewis Carroll.

2. to be **as pleased as Punch** – absolutely delighted, usually with oneself over some achievement. 'My daughter is as pleased as Punch. She has just had an article published in the *Daily Mail.*' Punch is always portrayed as laughing or singing with pleasure at his own escapades.

3. a **Frankenstein monster** – the product of an inventor's imagination which destroys his creator. The phrase is taken from the famous horror story by Mary Shelley about a young student, Frankenstein, which describes how he made a monster which became so powerful that it eventually destroyed him. Parallels have been drawn with modern scientific discoveries, particularly in the biogenetic field.

4. a **Heath Robinson affair** – any machine that has been made amateurishly. 'Who ever installed your water-heater? It's a Heath Robinson affair!' W. Heath Robinson (1872–1944) illustrated the most complicated contraptions in the humorous magazine *Punch* and elsewhere.

5. **waiting for Godot** – waiting for ever because Godot never comes. From the play *Waiting for Godot* by Samuel Beckett.

## POLITICAL AND HISTORICAL NAMES

6. **Rabelaisian wit** – the earthy humour characteristic of the great French writer François Rabelais (1494–1553).

7. **Machiavellian cunning** – the most subtle, unprincipled cunning. In his treatise on state-craft, *The Prince*, Machiavelli tried to establish the principles of political power which he maintained were based on realism rather than conventional morality. Machiavelli's book foreshadowed Bismarck's 'Realpolitik' in the nineteenth century.

8. like the **Luddites** – a term of abuse for anybody who opposes the introduction of labour-saving machinery which may threaten his livelihood. The phrase comes from the 'Luddite' mechanics who attempted to destroy the new machinery in the Midlands and North of England which had been installed to replace their handicrafts, 1811–16.

9. **on a Napoleonic scale** – on a huge, ambitious scale.

10. a **maverick** – someone who is wild, reckless, out of control. Originally, an unbranded calf, named after a Texan ranger of that name who did not brand his cattle. Later, the name was given to politicians who refused to give allegiance to the party leadership.

11. to **boycott** – to coerce a person by forbidding any social or commercial relations with him. In 1880, the Irish Land League resolved that anyone buying the farm of an evicted tenant should be treated like a leper. The first victim of this policy was Captain Boycott who had defied the League and was consequently 'boycotted'. The term 'boycott' was later extended to similar action taken against organ-

izations or countries, and has been used in this way ever since.

1. **Custer's last stand** – any man who goes down to defeat in a spectacular manner. Custer was an American general whose troops were wiped out in an Indian ambush.

2. a **Blimpish point of view** – any reactionary or unprogressive point of view that harks back to the pre-war period in Britain. Colonel Blimp, a red-faced elderly colonel, invented by David Low, the celebrated cartoonist, was a familiar figure of fun in the 1930s.

3. to have **Hobson's choice** – to have no choice at all. 'You advertise a wide choice of holidays but you are only offering me one! It is Hobson's choice!' Tobias Hobson, a seventeenth-century Cambridge carrier, who hired out horses to the undergraduates of the university, never allowed his customers to choose a horse but insisted on their taking the horse nearest the stable door, so that they had no choice at all.

4. **Occam's razor** – the ruthless analysis of a problem which eliminates all superfluous factors. Occam of Ockham, Surrey (died 1349), held that entities must not be needlessly multiplied and that we were only entitled to generalize from experience.

5. **Parkinson's Law** – the title of a book by C. Northcote Parkinson in which he makes fun of the civil service. Parkinson's Law states: (1) the work done is in inverse proportion to the number of civil servants employed, and (2) public expenditure rises to accommodate the growth in bureaucracy. In other words, the more civil servants the state employs, the more work they will make in order to justify their existence and their salaries.

## JONES

6. **keeping up with the Joneses** – trying to maintain the same standards of material comfort as one's neighbours, who are represented by the very ordinary name of Jones. 'Just because our neighbours have bought a Daimler, that's no reason why we should buy one. I have no intention of keeping up with the Joneses.'

# 24. MONARCHY AND PARLIAMENT

KING

1. **fit for a king** – suitable for a king's use. 'That was a wonderful dinner you gave me – fit for a king.'
2. a **king-pin** – the most important person in any organization. 'You'd better not quarrel with Johnson; he's the king pin on the local Council.' In the game of skittles, the king-pin is the most important piece.
3. the **king of the castle** – the most important person in the locality. From the children's game of the same name; one child stands on top of a sandcastle while the other children try to knock him off.
4. a **king's ransom** – a huge, excessively large sum of money. 'You'd have to pay a king's ransom for a house that size looking on to the sea.' Originally, the money that had to be paid for the release of a captured king.

KINGDOM

5. to **send/blow to kingdom come** – to send/blow to the next world, to kill. The kingdom is the Kingdom of God. 'If the bomb explodes, we shall all be sent to kingdom come.'

QUEEN

6. to **queen/lord it** – to domineer over, to take advantage of one's rank to humiliate someone. 'I don't like the way your friend Doris queens it over the other girls in the office. Who does she think she is!'

PRINCE

7. **the prince of liars** – the biggest liar of all, the worst of liars. 'Peter is an awful liar but he is nothing compared with your brother, who must be the prince of liars.' The reference is to the Devil.
8. **like *Hamlet* without the Prince** – said when the most important person at an event is absent. 'To have the last day of the party conference without the leader would be like *Hamlet* without the Prince.'
9. **put not your trust in princes** – men of power and influence can be just as fickle and unreliable as the rest of us. 'I am not in the least surprised that the boss has forgotten about your promotion. Put not your trust in princes.' The reference is to Psalms CXLVI, 3.

LORD

10. to **live like a lord** – to live in great luxury with the best food and wine, and be waited upon by many servants. 'I don't know where he gets the money from, but he seems to be living like a lord.'
11. **as drunk as a lord** – very drunk indeed. 'When I arrived at the party last night, your boy-friend was already as drunk as a lord.' Lords had a reputation for drunkenness, because they had so much money and nothing to spend it on except their own pleasure.

ROYAL

12. a **battle royal** – a tremendous battle worthy of a contest between two kings. 'There was a battle royal going on between the two grandmothers who each wanted to look after the baby during the mother's absence.'
13. the **royal road to** – the easiest and quickest way to. 'There is no royal

road to freedom; you have to fight for it.'

1. a **royal welcome** – a splendid welcome, one that is fit for a king. 'When we arrived at a small village in Lapland, we were surprised at the royal welcome the villagers gave us.'
2. **right royal** – splendid, marvellous. 'Right royal' can also be used ironically in the sense of terrible or appalling. 'You made a right royal mess of the business while I was away; it will take months to put it right.'

## KNIGHT

3. a **knight in shining armour** – a man of great nobility and gallantry who will defend our rights without asking anything in return. 'If you want my advice, I'm afraid you'll have to pay for it; I'm a solicitor, not a knight in shining armour.'

## THRONE

4. **the power behind the throne** – someone with real, as opposed to nominal or symbolic, power. 'If you want a job in that company, you'd better apply to the secretary, not to the chairman. The secretary is the power behind the throne.'

## CROWN

5. to **crown it all** – on top of everything else. 'Harry left his briefcase in the train, was told off by his boss for arriving late at the office, and, to crown it all, found that his house had been burgled when he got home.'

## COURT

6. **a friend at court** – someone in an influential position, who is able to help you. 'I'm not worried about the consequences; I have a friend at court.'

## CEREMONY

7. to **stand on ceremony** – to do something in the manner prescribed by custom or etiquette. 'Don't wait to be asked but help yourselves to the cakes. There's no need to stand on ceremony.'

## THE UPPER CLASS

8. **'U' and 'Non-U'** – upper class and non upper class, based on Nancy Mitford's system of distinguishing social classes according to the words they use. For example: it is 'U' to say lavatory, and 'Non-U' to say toilet; 'U' to say napkin, 'Non-U' serviette; 'U' to have a bath, 'Non U' to take a bath.
9. the **upper crust** (humorous) – the aristocracy. 'Joan is from the upper crust; you can tell by the way she walks and talks.'

## PARLIAMENT

10. **the Mother of Parliaments** – the oldest Parliament in the world, a distinction that is claimed by the Parliaments in Westminster, the Isle of Man and the Swiss cantons; but, in England, the phrase is a synonym for Westminster.
11. a **hung parliament** – one in which no single party commands a clear majority, and government can only be carried on by a coalition.
12. a **maiden speech** – the first speech a member makes in Parliament.
13. to **lobby an MP** – to canvass an MP for support of one's case by going to Parliament and requesting to speak to him.
14. to **make a U-turn** – to pursue a policy in government that is directly

opposed to one's party's election promises. **'There will be no U-turn'** means that there will be no change in policy. At the Conservative Party Conference in October 1981 Margaret Thatcher declared: 'The lady's not for turning', meaning that there would be no relaxation in the Government's fight against inflation. (This was also a pun on the title of Christopher Fry's play *The Lady's Not For Burning*, about Joan of Arc.)

1. to **paper over the cracks** – to pretend that agreement on all important issues has been reached. 'Now that the election is approaching, the party managers are papering over the cracks to impress the voters.' Papering over the cracks is a common device for concealing the structural weaknesses of a house from a buyer.
2. to **go/appeal to the country** – to call a general election.
3. a **floating voter** – a voter at a general election who has not decided which party to vote for. Having no strong opinions, he will be pushed in this direction or that like someone floating on the water.
4. to **win by a landslide** (American colloquialism) – to win an election by an overwhelming majority of seats. A landslide denotes a fundamental shift in the political and social attitudes of the electorate. In 1945 in Britain, Labour won by a landslide; in 1980, Ronald Reagan won the presidential election in one of the biggest landslides in the history of America.
5. to **rig the poll** – to conduct a poll fraudulently, as by managing the poll in one's own interests instead of putting it under the control of an independent authority.
6. to **climb/jump on the bandwaggon** – to join a popular trend for the sake of material advantage. 'When Krugerrands rose quickly in value, many investors jumped on the bandwaggon and bought as many as they could in the hope of making an easy profit.' The reference is to the custom in America of putting a band on a waggon to advertise a politician's campaign at election time. When it becomes clear who is going to win, many of the local leaders will 'jump on the bandwaggon' to show their support in the hope of obtaining a well-paid job in the newly elected administration.
7. to **kick** someone **upstairs** – to promote someone who has proved unsatisfactory to a position of nominal importance without responsibility where he can do no harm. This is done when it would be embarrassing to dismiss or demote him. Senior Cabinet Ministers are sometimes 'kicked upstairs' to the House of Lords to save them from humiliation.
8. a **hue and cry** – an outcry, public protest and opposition to an unpopular measure of the government.

   to **raise a hue and cry** – to organize opposition to an unpopular measure. 'The opposition raised a hue and cry against the government's decision to increase the salaries of the top civil servants.' Originally (*c.* 1584), the hue and cry was a system for the pursuit and arrest of criminals in which all citizens were obliged to take part (from French 'huer', meaning to shout).
9. a **witch-hunt** – a campaign against a group of dissidents within a party for advocating views that are contrary to official policy. There have been similar witch-hunts against homosexuals who occupy positions of trust in the security services. The term takes its name from the witch-hunts in the Middle Ages when thousands of young women in Europe were denounced for practising witchcraft, and burned at the stake.

1. to **be beaten at the hustings** – to lose an election to Parliament. The hustings are the open-air meetings at which the rival candidates argue their case. Husting is an Icelandic word formed by 'hus', meaning house, and 'thing', meaning an assembly.

# 25. WAR AND PEACE

## WAR

1. **all's fair in love and war** – conventional morality does not apply to the most important activities in life.
2. to be **in the wars** – to suffer from a number of minor mishaps to one's health, all at the same time. 'A cut lip, a stiff neck and now a sore throat! You *are* in the wars, Tim!'
3. **on the war-path** – in an aggressive mood, in search of one's enemy in order to start a fight with him.
4. a **war of nerves** – constant attacks on the nerves of one's opponent, as by making propaganda against him and writing abusive letters to him. 'John and his neighbour are fighting a war of nerves against each other.'
5. a **cold war** – a diplomatic and economic struggle reflecting a high state of tension between the two power blocs which stops short of armed conflict. 'There are signs that the cold war between the West and Soviet Russia will soon be resumed.'
6. a **shooting war** – an outbreak of fighting. A shooting war is often contrasted with a cold war, when the hostility of the adversaries is limited to economic and diplomatic measures.

## BATTLE, FIGHT

7. a **pitched battle** – a battle in which large forces on both sides are committed. This phrase is used in contrast with 'skirmishes' or 'guerilla warfare'.
8. **half the battle** – the first steps in accomplishing a difficult task which often decide the outcome. 'We have got the best equipment for the job; that is half the battle.'
9. to **fight a losing battle** – to engage in a struggle which one cannot hope to win. 'We all fight a losing battle with age; it's better to grow old gracefully.'
10. a **running battle/fight** – a long-protracted dispute. 'William has had a running battle/fight with his local council about the rates ever since he bought his house.' The phrase comes from naval warfare. A running battle is one that takes place between two hostile fleets while they are on the move, one advancing and the other retreating.
11. to **fight shy of** – to avoid, to keep away from. 'Paul fought shy of the law courts because the costs were so ruinously high.'
12. to **put up a good fight** – to fight hard, to be a worthy opponent. 'Although we lost the match, we put up a good fight, losing by three goals to one.'
13. to **spoil for a fight** – to seize on any pretext for a fight. 'When you pay our landlord the rent, be careful how you speak to him. He is spoiling for a fight with you.'
14. to **take the fight out of** someone – to defeat one's enemy so severely that he has no wish to continue the fight.

    to have **plenty of fight left in one** – despite a bad defeat, to be willing and able to continue the fight.
15. a **fighting chance** – a fair chance, a reasonable chance. 'Harry is very ill, but he still has a fighting chance of pulling through.'
16. to **fight it out** – to settle a dispute by fighting. 'Those boys have been quarrelling the whole term and no amount of argument is going to settle the matter. The best thing is for them to fight it out.'

1. **fighting fit** (colloquial) – in excellent physical condition. 'Andrew is fighting fit and ready to start work again.' This phrase derives from cock-fighting.
2. to **show fight** – to accept a challenge, to indicate one's willingness to fight. 'We've had a letter from the defendant. He disputes your claim and he is showing plenty of fight.'
3. to **fight tooth and nail** – to fight with the utmost ferocity. 'Our son has been accused of stealing from another boy. We are going to fight tooth and nail to defend him.'
4. to **go on the offensive** – to change one's tactics from defence to attack in a contest or argument. 'Now we have refuted Anderson's accusations, it's time we went on to the offensive and attacked him.'
5. to be **on the defensive** – to be extremely sensitive to criticism, to imagine an insult when none is intended. 'I haven't accused you of anything, Henry. Why are you so much on the defensive?'
6. to **throw** someone **on the defensive** – to seize the initiative from one's opponent and turn from defence to attack. 'The manager was complaining about my work, but I threw him on the defensive by reminding him that he had absented himself for two weeks without permission.'
7. to **blunt the attack** – to weaken the attack of one's opponent, to reduce its effect. 'At the meeting, Johnson was very critical of Hazel Smith's record, but she was able to blunt his attack by showing that he had a private grievance against her.'
8. to **go for the jugular** – to attack one's opponent in the most vulnerable place. 'Harold Wilson, ex-Premier, said that during his political career he always went for the jugular.'
9. to **open (up) a new front** – to shift one's attack to a new target, to approach a problem from a new angle. 'The replacement of a human heart by an artificial one opens up a new front in the treatment of heart diseases.'
10. to **take the line of least resistance** – (1) when on the attack, to avoid obstacles so as to keep moving forward; a very effective strategy in World War II. (2) to avoid opposition of any kind and to submit to other people's demands. 'Henry always took the line of least resistance with his wife and did whatever she wanted.'
11. to **beat a retreat** – to withdraw, to abandon a position one has taken up. 'When Roger heard that there was going to be a collection, he beat a hasty retreat.'
12. to **make a tactical retreat** – to retreat with the object of advancing later in more favourable circumstances. 'Simmonds is not pressing his claim to our land, but I think he is only making a tactical retreat. He is trying to obtain more evidence, then he will go back to the Court.'
13. to **steal a march on** – to obtain an advantage over an opponent by making a sudden surprise move. 'Davis & Hay have stolen a march on us by starting their spring sales on the same day as we open our new shop.'
14. to **give** someone **his/her marching orders** – to dismiss, to terminate someone's employment abruptly. 'Claude didn't get in until three o'clock this morning. If she does that again, I shall give her her marching orders.'
15. a **trouble-shooter** – an expert in industrial/diplomatic relations who is called in to mediate between the parties to a dispute. 'We shall need a trouble-shooter to settle our dispute with the boss.'
16. to **shoot down** – to demolish, to refute

an argument. 'If you put forward that argument, the judge will shoot it down at once.'

1. to **shoot a line** (slang) – to tell a wildly exaggerated story in order to create an impression or mislead. 'Jerry was shooting a line that his parents are friends of the American president, but no one believed him.'

2. to **shoot from the hip** – to be quick with an answer. 'I'm not going to get into an argument with Sue again; she is very sharp, and she shoots straight from the hip.' This comes from the American Wild West, when firing the first shot was essential for survival.

3. **quick on the draw** – quick to attack, or defend oneself from, an enemy. The reference is to the drawing of their pistols by American cowboys when their lives would depend on the speed of their reaction to the approach of an enemy.

4. to **go over the top** – to act rashly, wildly. 'At the auction, Mary had £50 to spend, but when she saw a painting by her favourite artist, she went over the top and bid £100 for it.' The reference is to World War I when soldiers had to go over the top of their trenches in order to move forward and attack their enemy.

5. to **leave oneself wide open** – to offer an easy target to one's opponent/enemy. 'If you complain about the noise your neighbour makes, you will leave yourself wide open when you give a party for your son's twenty-first birthday.'

6. a **pincer movement** – an attack from two opposite directions. Often used humorously. 'Let's make a pincer movement on Father about our summer holidays. You tell him you are fed up with the South Coast, and I'll show him some photographs of Crete.'

7. a **Pyrrhic victory** – an apparent victory which in fact is no victory at all. The phrase comes from the victory won by King Pyrrhus at Asculum in 279 BC which cost him many of his best men. After the battle Pyrrhus remarked: 'One more such victory and we are finished.'

8. a **sitting target** – a target that is vulnerable to attack. 'The teaching profession is a sitting target for criticism and always has been.' cf. 'a **sitting duck' 68/16**.

9. **bang/plumb on target** – right in the centre of the target, a perfect aim.

10. **an uphill struggle** – something that costs a great deal of effort and shows very little result. 'It's an uphill struggle teaching Henry Greek; he has no aptitude for languages.'

11. to use **brute force** – to use physical strength rather than one's intelligence. 'Jones was the better boxer of the two but was overwhelmed by brute force.'

12. to **hold the fort** – to accept responsibilities in the absence of the person in charge. 'I have to meet my friend this afternoon. Could you hold the fort for me until I get back?' A military phrase meaning to hold one's position and not retreat.

## PEACE

13. to **hold one's peace** – to keep silent. 'I shall hold my peace until I have had the opportunity to study the facts of the case.'

14. to **make one's peace** – to put an end to a quarrel. 'It's time you made your peace with Betty. You and she have always been such good friends.'

15. a **peace offering** – a gift made with the object of ending a quarrel and restoring a friendship.

16. **peace at any price** – the avoidance of war or violence, whatever the cost.

The phrase applies not only to nations but also to private relationships. 'It's no good asking Father to support you in your row with the headmaster. Father is for peace at any price.'

1. **peace of mind** – inward serenity. 'Please telephone us as soon as you arrive. We shall have no peace of mind until we hear from you.'

# 26. WEAPONS

WEAPON

1. a **double-edged weapon** – a weapon which cuts both ways so that it may harm as well as benefit the user, particularly in an argument. 'If you reduce your children's pocket money, you will save money but they will hate you. It's a double-edged weapon!'

GUN

2. to **carry too many guns** – to possess strong superiority over one's opponent. 'In the debate, the proposers of the motion carried too many guns for us: they had a better grasp of the facts, and they were more experienced in public speaking.'
3. to **go down with all guns firing** – to suffer defeat fighting manfully to the very end. 'Robin was knocked out in the fifth round, but he went down with all guns firing.'
4. to **stick to one's guns** – to defend one's position against strong opposition. 'Alan has been asked by his boss to withdraw his complaints, but he is sticking to his guns.'
5. to **go great guns** – to act with energy and efficiency. 'Grandfather is going great guns and his business is booming.'
6. to **spike** someone's **guns** – to spoil someone's plans, to prevent him realizing them. 'When we heard the Simpsons were planning to buy the house next door to us to extend their shop, we spiked their guns by buying the house ourselves.' The spike (obsolete term for nail) was pushed into the barrel of the gun to stop it firing properly.
7. to bring up **the heavy guns/artillery** – the important people, the leaders. 'At the by-election, all the heavy guns were brought up to support the rival candidates.'
8. to **gun for** someone – to plot revenge on someone. 'Davey is gunning for us for taking his customers away from him.'
9. **calibre** – the relative worth of someone's mind or character. 'Sally is a nice girl with plenty of common sense but I shouldn't have thought she was university calibre.' Literally, the internal diameter of a gun.

POWDER, LOCK, STOCK, BARREL

10. to **keep one's powder dry** – to hold oneself ready for action as soon as the need arises. 'Colonel Williams is sure to attack you in the local newspaper. In the meantime, all you can do is to wait and keep your powder dry.' Powder meant gunpowder, which it was necessary to keep dry for effective use (somewhat dated).
11. **not worth powder and shot** – not worth making the effort (rather old-fashioned but still in use). 'It's not worth powder and shot writing to the Minister. There is nothing he can do to help you.'
12. **lock, stock and barrel** – everything, with nothing excluded. 'Mr Hobson was obliged to sell the house and contents, lock, stock and barrel.' The lock, stock and barrel are the three parts of a gun.

SWORD AND LANCE

13. to **cross swords with** – to fight or quarrel with. 'Jackson is a hot-tempered man; I wouldn't cross swords with him, if I were you.'

1. to **measure swords with** someone – to test one's strength against someone else. In duels, the swords were measured by the seconds in order to check that they were of the same length.
2. to **beat one's sword into a ploughshare** – to turn from war to peaceful pursuits. From the Old Testament: 'They shall beat their swords into ploughshares, . . . nation shall not lift up sword against nation . . .' (Isaiah II, 4).
3. to **break a lance with** – to have an argument with. 'It's a pleasure to break a lance with Tom; he is a very good-humoured man.'

## DAGGER, KNIFE AND STILETTO

4. **at daggers drawn** – in open enmity, ready to attack one's enemy. 'The two brothers have been at daggers drawn for many years.' When the dagger has been drawn from its scabbard, it can be used at once without any further preparation.
5. to **look daggers at** – to look with hatred or fury at someone. 'Mrs Jessop looked daggers at her little son when he repeated to her guest what she had been saying about him behind his back.'
6. to **have one's knife in** someone – to bear malice towards someone, to bear a strong grudge against him. 'The manager has got his knife in me; he is making my life a misery.'
7. to **put the knife in** – to deal one's enemy a fatal blow. 'When you published Kenneth's letter, you put the knife in; his career is finished.'
8. **the knives are out for . . .** a number of people are waiting for the opportunity to strike at their enemy. A phrase that is often used in politics, for example about an ex-prime minister who is blamed for the defeat of his party at the polls.
9. **stiletto heels** – high pointed metal heels on women's shoes. 'Marie-Louise, will you please take off your shoes. Your stiletto heels are cutting our carpet into ribbons.'

## SABRE, STEEL AND HILT

10. to **rattle the sabre / sabre rattling** – to make threatening noises, to attempt to frighten one's opponent/enemy into doing what one wants. 'Don't let Mr Ash frighten you. It's only sabre rattling.'
11. to **use cold steel** – to use bayonets or knives. 'Wars are no longer won by cold steel but by superior fire-power.'
12. **up to the hilt** – completely, to the very limit. 'Under the guarantee, your rights are protected up to the hilt.' The allusion is to the penetration of the full length of the sword into a body right up to the handle (hilt).

## ARMS

13. **up in arms** – in open revolt, as by demonstrating, shouting insults, etc. 'The students were up in arms when they heard that their privileges had been withdrawn.'
14. **armed to the teeth** – fully armed, armed with a variety of weapons so that one is prepared for any attack.

## SHOT AND TRIGGER

15. **like a shot** – at once, without the slightest hesitation. 'I would change jobs like a shot if I were twenty years younger.'
16. a **long shot** – an attempt to find an answer with very little information to assist one. 'It may be a long shot but I think Harry will marry again soon.'

1. a **shot in the dark** – a wild, random guess, one that has as little chance of being right as hitting a target in the dark.
2. **no more shots in the locker** – at the end of one's resources. The derivation of the phrase is from the lockers on board a warship in which the ammunition was stored.
3. to **call the shots** – to make the decisions. 'If you want anything done, you'd better ask Mary's housekeeper. She calls the shots in this house.'
4. a **shot in the arm** – a strong encouragement, a stimulus. 'North Sea Oil has been a shot in the arm for the economy of Great Britain.' A shot in the arm means an injection which stimulates the patient and gives him fresh energy.
5. to **have a shot** – to have a try and see how well you do. 'Table tennis is such an easy game. Why don't you have a shot at it?'
6. **trigger-happy** – willing to use force on the slightest pretext. 'The workers have gone on strike without warning us. They are in a trigger-happy mood.'
7. to **trigger off** – to precipitate, to be the immediate, as opposed to the fundamental, cause. 'It is feared that a big increase in wages for the miners might trigger off similar wage claims throughout the country.'

## BULLET AND BOMB

8. to **bite the bullet** (colloquial) – to accept with courage the prospect of a fight or unpleasant experience. 'Now that Father is dead, we must bite the bullet and learn to put up with hardship.'
9. to **come as a bombshell** – to astonish, to dumbfound. 'The news that their father had left home came as a bombshell to his wife and children.'
10. to **cost a bomb** – to cost a huge amount of money. 'A Persian carpet for our sitting-room would cost a bomb. It's out of the question.'
11. to **go like a bomb** – (1) to sell in huge numbers. 'Our fur-lined boots are going like a bomb now the cold weather is coming on.' (2) (of transport) to travel very fast.

## ARROW, BOLT, BOW

12. to **shoot one's last arrow** – to be left without resources in a contest. 'There are no further steps you can take against Mr Brown; you have shot your last arrow.'

    to **shoot one's bolt** – to spend one's resources prematurely in a contest. 'Jack attacked his opponent with all his strength but, by the fifth round, he had shot his bolt, and retired soon afterwards.'
13. **bolt upright** – absolutely straight. It is used to describe a sitting position. Bolt was the old English word for a short arrow for a cross-bow; hence, bolt upright means as straight as an arrow, and often expresses surprise.
14. to **draw the long bow** – to exaggerate.

## OTHER WEAPONS

15. **hoist with his own petard** (literary) – injured or harmed by one's own weapon; ensnared in a trap intended for someone else. 'The strikers threatened to bankrupt their boss unless their wages were doubled. Their demand was granted, but the firm went bankrupt and they all lost their jobs. They had been hoist with their own petard.' (Shakespeare, *Hamlet*, III, iv: 'For 'tis sport, to have the engineer / Hoist with his own petard'.) The petard was a small bomb which was exploded to make a breach in a wall. Sometimes the military engineer

firing the petard was blown up with it.

1. **cannon-fodder** – men who are regarded by the high command as unimportant enough to sacrifice in war. 'I would keep out of the infantry if I were you; they are only cannon-fodder.' Fodder is the food fed to the animals on a farm.
2. to **hold a pistol to** someone's **head** – to use a dangerous threat to achieve one's ends. 'I shall have to accept the workers' demands or close the factory. They are holding a pistol to my head.'
3. to **bury the hatchet** – to end a feud with one's enemy. The reference is to the old custom of the American Indians who buried all their weapons so that they might not be reminded of past quarrels when they smoked the pipe of peace with their old enemies.
4. a **hatchet man** – a person who is expert at destroying the reputation of an opponent. 'Harvey is a marvellous hatchet man but he never says anything constructive.'

   a **hatchet job / the hatchet work** – the task of destroying the reputation of an opponent.
5. a **battle-axe** – a domineering, aggressive woman, one who likes to take charge of any activity. A battle-axe with its long handle was used as a weapon in the Middle Ages. It is not clear why the term should be applied only to women.
6. to **take up the cudgels** on behalf of a person or cause – to defend a person or cause with great energy and determination. 'Now that the editor of the local newspaper has taken up the cudgels for your campaign, you have a good chance of success.' The cudgel is a thick stick or club.
7. a **chink in** someone's **armour** – a defect or weakness in someone which makes him vulnerable to attack. 'Robin was very sure of himself, but he had a chink in his armour: mention the name Yates and he would start shouting and swearing.' cf. **'Achilles' heel' 195/8**, **'a glass jaw' 86/9**, **'to have feet of clay' 104/10**.

# 27. TOOLS

## TOOLS

1. **it's a poor workman who quarrels with his tools** (proverb) – the inefficient and idle often put the blame for their failure on their tools, or the conditions in which they work. 'Jack blamed the school textbooks for failing his examinations although his class-mates were successful. It's a poor workman who quarrels with his tools.'
2. to **down tools** – to refuse to work, to go on strike.

## SCREW

3. to **put a screw / the screws on** someone – to put pressure on someone, usually with the object of extracting money. In former times, the thumbscrew was a common instrument of torture. By turning the screw, one could increase the pressure on the victim until the pain became unbearable. Hence: to **tighten the screw,** to **give the screw another turn,** and to **screw** something **out of a person.**
4. to **have a screw loose** (slang) – to be slightly mad, not quite sane. Often used humorously to express incredulity at someone's actions.
5. to **screw up one's courage** – to make up one's mind to do something courageous or daring, to overcome one's reluctance to act. 'Colin screwed up his courage and asked his boss for a rise in his wages.'
6. to **have one's head screwed on the right way** – to be sensible and intelligent. The very opposite of 'to **have a screw loose**' **211/4.**

## NAIL

7. **as hard as nails** – unrelenting, without feeling or sentiment.
8. to **pay on the nail** – to pay on the exact date that money becomes due.
9. to **drive a nail into one's coffin** – to make a blunder which will destroy one's reputation or happiness. 'If you resign from the Party, you will only be driving a nail into your coffin.'

   to **drive a nail/another nail/a final nail into** someone's **coffin** – to do someone an injury which will destroy his reputation or happiness. 'I've had a disastrous year anyway, but Joan's memoirs have driven the final nail into my coffin.'
10. **as dead as a door-nail** – dead beyond any doubt. It can apply to causes and campaigns, as well as people. 'The campaign for spelling reform is as dead as a door-nail.' cf. **'as dead as mutton' 161/14, 'as dead as Queen Anne' 193/15.**
11. to **nail a lie** – to produce certain, unquestionable proof of a lie. 'That's one lie we have nailed. I wonder how many more lies the witness has told.'
12. to **hit the nail on the head** – to find exactly the right answer to a problem in one or two words.

## HAMMER AND TONGS

13. to **come under the hammer** – to be sold by an auctioneer, to be put up for auction. The auctioneer indicates his acceptance of a bid by striking the table with his hammer.
14. to **hammer a point home** – to emphasize a point one has made in an argument by repeating it with great force.
15. to **hammer out** a scheme – to decide on a scheme after the most thorough and intensive examination of the difficulties, often in the course of discussion and argument.

1. to go for someone **hammer and tongs** – to quarrel furiously with someone. 'At the meeting the hecklers were going for the speaker hammer and tongs until the chairman threatened to have them turned out.'

   to **go hammer and tongs at** a job – to work at a job with all one's might.
2. to **take a sledgehammer to crack a nut** – to use unnecessary force to achieve one's object. 'Surely, to disconnect a customer's electricity because he owes the Electricity Board £3 was taking a sledgehammer to crack a nut.'
3. **not to touch** someone **with a pair of tongs** – to avoid someone at all costs, said of someone with an evil reputation. cf. **'not to touch with a bargepole' 182/1**.

## SPADE AND RAKE

4. to **call a spade a spade** – to speak plainly and bluntly, to tell the plain truth without bothering with polite phrases. 'In Yorkshire we don't use flowery language; we call a spade a spade.'
5. **the spadework** – the hard, detailed work. 'Peter's research workers took two years on the spadework before he was able to start on his book.'
6. **as thin as a rake** – very thin. The comparison is probably based on the thin prongs of the rake.
7. to **rake up** the past, the ashes, old quarrels, etc. – to remind someone of disagreeable events in the past, to revive unpleasant memories. 'Why rake up the past? I thought it was all over and forgotten.'
8. to **rake in** the money – to make money very fast, to make huge profits. 'George's shop is raking the money in with their new product.'
9. a **rake-off** – an introduction fee, a commission. A rake-off implies that there is something dishonest about the transaction; for example, when an information bureau, which states that it gives the public free and independent advice, takes commissions from the businesses it recommends.

## OTHER TOOLS

10. to **throw a spanner in the works** – deliberately to obstruct or ruin the results of someone's efforts. 'You threw a spanner in the works, didn't you, telling the manager your father wasn't paying him enough.'
11. to **have an axe to grind** – to allow one's private interest to affect the advice one gives. 'The principle of reducing fares to reverse the decline in the number of passengers was supported by many independent transport specialists with no political axes to grind' (The *Observer* Profile, 12 December 1982).
12. to **axe a job** – to abolish a job in order to save money. The job may be in the private or the public sector.

    to **be axed** – to lose one's job, to be made redundant for the sake of economy. 'Paul is afraid he'll be axed from the navy; he'll be fifty next April.'
13. **the nuts and bolts** – the practical considerations. 'We have talked enough about theory. It's time we considered the nuts and bolts.' The nuts and bolts are what hold the machinery together. They play a humble but essential part in any enterprise.
14. **by hook or by crook** – by any means whatsoever, lawful or unlawful. 'Hugh will make money by hook or by crook; he won't let anybody stop him.'
15. to **swallow hook, line and sinker/anchor** – to believe every detail of a story. 'Ted is the most credulous per-

son I have ever met. He swallowed my explanation hook, line and sinker.' From the fish that swallows the angler's hook, line and sinker, 'swallow' being a colloquialism for 'believe'.

1. to be **hooked on** – to be caught, to become addicted to a person or object. One can be hooked on a drug, tobacco, a hobby, a sport, or anything else that gives pleasure. A woman may hook a man and marry him.
2. to **let** someone **off the hook** – to release someone from an obligation, promise or admission of guilt. 'Now you have accepted Jackson's apology, you have let him off the hook.'
3. to be **on tenterhooks** – to be in a state of acute suspense, waiting for news/results. 'We've been on tenterhooks the whole morning waiting for the results of the X-rays.' The term 'tenterhooks' means tenting or canvas that has been stretched by hooks, thus producing a state of tension.

## TROWEL

4. to **lay** something **on with a trowel** – to flatter grossly, to exaggerate one's praise. 'You were laying it on with a trowel, weren't you, when you told Angela she had a divinely beautiful voice!' The phrase comes from Shakespeare, 'Well said; that was laid on with a trowel' (*As You Like It*, I, ii, 113).

## WEDGE

5. **the thin end of the wedge** – a small concession which is used to obtain a very big and costly one. 'If we give our workers an increase of 5 per cent in a bad year when we've made a loss, how much will they want in a good year? It's the thin end of the wedge.'

## TACKS

6. to **get down to brass tacks** – to concentrate on the essentials. 'Let's get down to brass tacks, shall we? How much is each of you prepared to put into the project?'

# 28. NUMBERS

## NUMBER, NUMBERS

1. an **opposite number** – someone who holds a corresponding post in another firm, company, etc.
2. a **back number** – (1) someone who is no longer active in his work, retired or semi-retired. 'I'd have been glad to advise you, but I haven't practised for the last ten years. I'm afraid I am a bit of a back number!' (2) any magazine or newspaper which has appeared prior to the current issue.
3. **one's number is up** – all hope for a person has been abandoned, one is doomed. 'His number is up' – he is finished, doomed.
4. to take **care of number one** – to put one's own interest before that of other people, an egoistic outlook.
5. **time out of number** – again and again, so frequently as to be uncountable.
6. **one's days are numbered** – one is approaching the end of one's life, or time in office, etc.
7. **in round numbers** – an approximate number, a number which is measured in tens, hundreds, thousands, and which does not include the numbers in between.
8. **safety in numbers** – protection provided by numerical superiority. 'I don't mind my daughter going out with a group, but I don't want her to be alone with one man. There is safety in numbers.'

## SINGLE

9. to do something **single-handed** – to accomplish a task without anyone else's help. Literally, to do something with only one hand.

## QUARTER

10. to have a **bad quarter of an hour** – to have a very unpleasant experience for a short period.
11. **no quarter was given** – no mercy was shown, no man's life was spared. One interpretation is that 'quarter' refers to the quarters, i.e. the lodging, given to prisoners of war by the victorious army. Hence 'no quarter given' meant 'no prisoners taken'.

## HALF

12. to **go halves** – to take an equal share with somebody else.
13. to **do** something **by halves** – to do something without finishing it, superficially, unenthusiastically. Also used in the negative: 'He doesn't do a thing by halves' – he is extremely thorough in everything he does.
14. **not half** (cockney) – very much indeed, with great pleasure. '"Would you like a glass of beer?" "Not half!"'
15. to **meet half-way** – to make concessions to another person's position in a disagreement, to make a fair compromise. 'I do think you might meet us half-way, Lilian. We have agreed to go with you to the theatre, but why must it be the evening performance? What's wrong with the matinee?'
16. **one's better half** (colloquial) – a humorous reference to one's wife.
17. to **have half a chance** – a very slight chance. 'If I had half a chance, I would go to America.'
18. to **have half a mind** – to feel somewhat inclined to do something, but without any real conviction.
19. a **half-baked idea** – an idea that has not been properly thought out; colloquially: a stupid idea.

a **half-baked boy/girl** (slang) – a foolish, stupid boy or girl.

1. to **go off at half-cock** – to execute a plan before the necessary preparations have been completed. 'Our attack went off at half-cock. We should have waited until we had won the support of our colleagues.' The phrase is taken from the inadvertent firing of a gun when the hammer is set at half-cock.
2. the flag **at half-mast** – the flag that flies half-way down as a sign of respect for an important person who has died.
3. **half-way house** – a compromise between two conflicting systems. 'The college was a half-way house between a school and a university. There were no regular lessons but we were not allowed out without permission.'

## ONE

4. **A.1.** – (1) the best possible. (2) in a military sense, enjoying perfect health.
5. to **be at one** – to be in full agreement (in the case of several people, to be unanimous).
6. to be **one too many for** someone – to outmatch somebody, to outwit him. 'When it comes to business, your sister is one too many for me.'
7. to **be the last one to** – to be the least likely to. 'You're the last one I would have expected to behave like that.'
8. to **have a one-track mind** – to be totally absorbed in a single topic. 'Harry has a one-track mind; he only thinks about sex.'
9. **one-sided** – to the advantage of one person and not the other, e.g. a **one-sided agreement** – an agreement which favours one party and not the other.

   to **be one-sided** – to be unfair or prejudiced.
10. to **go one better** – to outdo someone else. 'When Jack heard I had invited Mervyn to tea, he invited him to dinner. Jack always goes one better than me!'
11. **one-off** – once only. 'His novel has been selling very well but I doubt whether he can repeat his success. It was a one-off effort.'
12. to **take one with another** – to balance the advantages and disadvantages.
13. **it's all one to him** – it's all the same to him, he doesn't care.
14. **back to square one** – back to the very beginning of some task or enterprise as a result of a setback. 'My secretary has left my one and only manuscript in the taxi, so I'll have to write the book all over again. It's back to square one!' The allusion is to the game of Ludo when a player is sent back to square one if he lands on the wrong square.
15. a **one-armed bandit** – a gambling machine in which coins are inserted, usually 'fixed' so that the gambler loses his money. Hence the name 'bandit'.
16. to be a **one-man band** – to do all the work oneself without employing staff.

## FIRST

17. **first come, first served** – whoever arrives first has a right to be served first. '"Why do you always serve Mr Wood before me?" "Because Mr Wood always arrives before you. First come, first served."'
18. **first and last** – more important than any other consideration.
19. **there's always a first time for everything** – just because something has not happened in the past is no reason for thinking it will never happen in the future.

1. **at first sight** – the first impression, superficially. 'He fell in love with her at first sight.'
2. **first thing** – before doing anything else. 'I'll let you have the results first thing Monday morning.'
   **not to know the first thing about** something – to know nothing whatever about something. 'My father doesn't know the first thing about cooking.'
3. to **give the first refusal** – to give a person the first opportunity of accepting an offer, before others are considered. 'He's given us the first refusal of his house.'
4. to **get a first** – to obtain a first-class honours degree on graduation at a university.
5. **first fruit** – first benefits from one's work. From the first fruit that is ripe for picking.

## ONCE

6. **once and for all** – for the last time. 'Once and for all, the answer is no! I'm not going to pay you any more money.'
7. to **give** someone or something **the once-over** – to give someone or something a quick or superficial examination.
8. **once/twice removed** – refers to family relationships between cousins. My cousin once removed is my first cousin's child. My cousin twice removed is my second cousin's child.

## TWO

9. to **put two and two together** – to draw an obvious conclusion.
   **two and two make four** – an obvious conclusion from the facts.
10. **two's company, three's none** – when there are three in a company there is always a tendency for two of them to make friends at the expense of the third. cf. **'three's a crowd' 217/14**.
11. a **two-edged compliment** – a comment which can be understood in two contradictory ways, one of which is to the disadvantage of the person praised. An example might be: 'He has a phenomenal memory. He can remember every word of his old speeches.'
12. to have **two strings to one's bow** / to have **a second string to one's bow** – to have two means of achieving an objective. If the first fails, you can try the second. The allusion is to the second string that bowmen kept in reserve.
13. **not to care two hoots** – to be totally indifferent.
14. **not to give two pins for** someone – not to have any care or regard for that person.

## SECOND

15. to **come off second best** – to lose a fight or a contest.
16. to be **second-rate** – to be in an inferior class, e.g. a second-rate mind, a second-rate painter, a second-rate teacher.
17. to **be a good/bad second** – to run close behind the leader / a long way behind the leader.
18. **one's second self** – another person whose character, tastes and outlook are identical to one's own.
19. **second nature** – what can be done instinctively, without thought.
   to **become second nature** – to become habitual, almost instinctive. 'Bobby lies for the sake of lying. It has become second nature to him.'
20. to **second-guess** (American) – to give oneself credit for predicting an event correctly after it has already happened. 'Larry Speakes spent much of

last week angrily criticizing doctors who were now "second-guessing" about the original decision not to test the President immediately in 1984' (*Observer*, 21 July 1985). cf. 'to **be wise after the event' 119/2**.

1. to **play second fiddle** – to play a subordinate part, to be second in command. 'I am tired of playing second fiddle to William. I am every bit as good as he is.'
2. to **have second thoughts** – to change one's mind. 'He was going to buy the house but, when he saw the neighbourhood, he had second thoughts.'
3. **second sight** – the possession of extrasensory perception.

DOUBLE

4. to **see double** – to hallucinate under the influence of drink, drugs or disease.
5. to **be** someone's **double** – to resemble someone so closely that one can be mistaken for the other.
6. **double-talk** – talk that is calculated to mislead. Promises made dishonestly.
7. to **double-think** – this is a variation on double-talk and means the ability to hold two contradictory opinions simultaneously. From George Orwell's *1984* (written in 1948).
8. **double-quick** – at great speed. The phrase is derived from the command 'double', meaning run.
9. **double time** – twice the normal rate of pay; for example, double the normal wage when the work is done outside the usual working hours.
10. to **double back** – to turn round and retrace one's footsteps.
11. a **double-barrelled name** – two surnames joined by a hyphen.
12. **in double harness** – two people working together.

THREE

13. a **three-cornered fight** – a contest (e.g. for Parliament) in which three candidates participate.
14. **three's a crowd** – when two people want to be together, a third person will be in the way. cf. **'two's company, three's nonc' 216/10.**
15. **'Yes, Sir, yes, Sir, three bags full!'** – sometimes said of a person who is only too anxious to please, indicating a servile or submissive attitude. Taken from the nursery rhyme: 'Baa, Baa, black sheep, have you any wool?'
16. **the three R's** – Reading, Writing and Arithmetic, the three subjects which are taught in all elementary schools and are considered an essential part of anyone's education.
17. **the three wise monkeys** – these are a symbol of discretion because they see no evil, hear no evil and speak no evil.

THIRD

18. **third degree** – the pressure put on suspects by the police in some states by means of exhausting interrogation and intimidation in order to obtain information and confessions.

FOUR, FOURTH

19. **a foursome** – two partners who play against two other partners, especially at golf.
20. to **make up a four** – to join three others in a game, as in Bridge or tennis.
21. **the fourth dimension** – an imaginary dimension in addition to length, breadth and height.
22. **the fourth estate** – the Press, the other three estates being the Monarchy, Parliament and the Church.

## FIVE, FIFTH

1. **two and two make five in your case** – you have drawn the wrong conclusion.
2. **the fifth column** – a wartime phrase meaning those people in an occupied country who collaborated with the invaders.

## SIX, SIXTH

3. **six of one and half a dozen of the other** – there is no difference at all between one course of action and another.
4. **at sixes and sevens** – bewildered or hopelessly confused, chaotic. The phrase comes from the figures on the dice which were once used in gaming.
5. to **hit for six** – to deal an enemy a crushing blow. 'We hit the newspaper for six! For libelling us, the Court awarded us damages of £40,000 plus all our costs.' This is a cricketing metaphor: a batsman scores six runs when he hits the ball over the boundary line without it touching the ground first.
6. **six of the best** – six strokes with the cane, a school punishment. The phrase is sometimes used as the headline of a newspaper report: 'Six of the best – Mrs Todd gave birth yesterday to sextuplets. All are doing well.'
7. **sixth form** – the top form in any school.
8. **sixth sense** – a supernatural sense, a special intuition in addition to the five senses (sight, hearing, touch, smell, taste).

## SEVEN, SEVENTH

9. the **seven deadly sins** – in the Christian religion these are: pride, envy, anger, lust, sloth, avarice and gluttony.
10. **seven-league boots** – this phrase which is derived from fairy tales means boots which will carry the wearer seven leagues (21 miles) at a step.
11. **in (the) seventh heaven** – a state of exaltation, bliss or ecstasy. The seventh heaven in the Muslim religion is the dwelling of Allah; in Judaism it is the home of God and the highest angels. cf. **'on Cloud Nine' 30/1**.

## EIGHT

12. to have **one over the eight** – to get drunk, so called because eight drinks are usually enough to intoxicate anyone.

## NINE

13. to be **dressed up to the nines** – to be dressed for a special occasion, to be dressed to perfection. 'Up to the nines' is a corruption of medieval English 'to the eyne' – 'to the eyes', meaning from head to foot. cf. **'dressed to kill' 169/8**.
14. **a stitch in time saves nine** (proverb) – a prompt correction saves a lot of labour and time later.
15. a **nine-days wonder** – something very sensational or scandalous which will be forgotten after a short time.
16. to **bowl over like ninepins** – to overcome with little or no resistance. 'The unexpected results of the election bowled them over like ninepins. They all sat silent and dejected.'
17. **possession is nine points of the law** – a legal maxim meaning that it is easier to defend one's possession of an object than to dispossess someone else.

## TEN, TENTH

18. **ten out of ten** – full marks, ten marks being the maximum marks given in English schools. 'I gave Andrew ten

out of ten for his last novel. It was faultlessly written.'

1. **ten to one** – nine chances in ten that something will happen.
2. the **submerged tenth** – the lowest and most under-privileged social class.

ELEVEN, ELEVENTH

3. **elevenses** – tea or coffee or other refreshments taken at eleven o'clock in the morning.
4. **at the eleventh hour** – at the last possible moment, only just in time to save the situation.

TWELVE, DOZEN AND TEEN

5. a **baker's dozen** – thirteen. Formerly, bakers were fined for giving short weight. In order to avoid the trouble of weighing their loaves, they threw in one extra to make sure their loaves were up to the required weight.
6. to **talk nineteen to the dozen** – to talk very fast without stopping in order to prevent others from interrupting, to be excited.
7. **in one's teens** – a boy or girl aged from 13 to 19 years of age.

THIRTEEN

8. **thirteen at table** – this is considered unlucky by many people who believe that the first person to rise from a table of thirteen will die. The superstition is based on 'The Last Supper' when Jesus and the twelve Apostles were seated at the table, and Judas Iscariot, the thirteenth man, went out and hanged himself after betraying Christ.

SEVENTEEN

9. **sweet seventeen** – the age of sweetness and charm in a girl.

NINETEEN

10. the **nineteenth hole** – the bar in a golf club, a humorous phrase because there are only eighteen holes on a golf course.

TWENTY, TWENTY-ONE AND TWENTY-TWO

11. the **Roaring Twenties** – the period immediately following World War I when young men and women were enjoying a new freedom. Girls wore short skirts, smoked and danced the Charleston.
12. a **21st birthday party** – a coming of age party when the boy/girl is acknowledged by the parents to have reached adulthood.
13. a **Catch-22 situation** – a dilemma from which it is impossible to escape. 'The public are calling for less crowding in our prisons; at the same time they are demanding longer prison sentences for crimes of violence. It is a Catch-22 situation.' From *Catch 22* by Joseph Heller (1961).

THIRTY AND FORTY

14. the **hungry Thirties** – the 1930s were a period of depression and unemployment when many workers went hungry.
15. **forty winks** – a nap taken after lunch.
16. **fair, fat and forty** – refers to the middle-aged spread in women (Sir Walter Scott, *St Ronan's Well*, Ch. 7).

FIFTY AND SIXTY

17. **fifty-fifty** – in equal proportions, half and half, often used in reference to chance. 'The chances of his recovering from the operation are only fifty-fifty.'

1. the **wrong/right side of fifty** – over fifty years of age / under fifty years of age.
2. the **Swinging Sixties** – the 1960s which ushered in the 'permissive Society', 'the pill' and the 'mini-skirt'. It was a new era when young people threw off traditional restraints on sexual behaviour and expression. The word 'swinging' is connected with the swinging hips of the young woman.

## NINETY

3. the **Naughty Nineties** – the period from 1890 to the end of the century which was dominated by the aesthetic philosophy of 'Art for Art's Sake' of Wilde, Beardsley and others. The exponents of this philosophy were notorious for their dandyism and decadence.

## HUNDRED

4. **a hundred-and-one reasons** – many, many reasons which the speaker does not wish to enumerate.
5. **I've told you a hundred times** – I've told you over and over again. 'If I've told you once, I've told you a hundred times.'
6. **not in a hundred years** – never.
7. **not a hundred miles away** – very near here, closer than one might think. The phrase is used when the speaker does not wish to give an exact location.

## ONE THOUSAND

8. **one in a thousand** – very remarkable. 'She's one in a thousand' – she has a very splendid character.
   a **wife in a thousand** – an outstandingly good wife.
9. **a thousand and one** – a huge number. 'He has a thousand and one ideas.'

## MILLION

10. a **chance in a million** – either no chance at all or a very slim chance, a tremendous fluke.
    **not one chance in a million** – completely impossible.

# 29. SCHOOL AND EDUCATION

## SCHOOL

1. to **tell tales out of school** – to talk maliciously about a person's private affairs behind his back. 'I don't want to hear any more. Don't tell tales out of school.' In this context 'out of school' means after class, when the tale-bearer has the opportunity to speak to the teacher alone.
2. a **hard school** – a strict training. 'He was brought up in a hard school which stood him in good stead later when he explored the Antarctic.'
3. a man **of the old school** – someone whose education and point of view is based on traditional principles and loyalties. 'He is a strict disciplinarian and expects his men to work hard, but he never asks them to do more than he does himself. He is a man of the old school.'
4. a **different school of thought** – a different body of opinion. When a problem has not been resolved with any certainty – in philosophy, science or art – then rival groups or schools may form which advocate a variety of theories, as for example the empirical, idealistic and marxist schools in philosophy.

## CLASS

5. **top/bottom of the class** – to excel / to do badly in a particular field or subject. 'I would recommend Mr Vernon for the post; he is good at management and top of the class in administration.'
6. **in a class of one's own** – to be incomparably better than one's companions in a particular subject or skill. 'If you want a specialist in tax law, I would suggest we brief Mr Williams QC; he is in a class of his own.'

## LESSON

7. an **object lesson** – a model of how something should / should not be done. 'The way the little boy acted when the burglar attacked his mother is an object lesson to us all.'
8. to **teach** someone **a lesson** – to punish or make someone feel sorry. 'The losses you made on the Stock Exchange last year should have taught you a lesson.'

   **let that be a lesson to you** – let's hope you will take warning from this unpleasant experience.

## ANSWERS

9. a **straight answer** – a clear, simple and unambiguous answer. 'Are you going to lend me the money or not? I'd like a straight answer.'
10. to **know all the answers** – (1) to be an expert. (2) to take a smug satisfaction in one's knowledge and cleverness. 'George doesn't trouble to follow the lessons, he thinks he knows all the answers.'
11. to **answer back** – to answer insolently when corrected or rebuked. 'If you answer the teachers back, you will soon be in trouble.'

## READING AND WRITING

12. to **read between the lines** – to draw conclusions about the writer's feelings from the manner and tone of the work and not from his actual words. 'Reading between the lines of Miss Prout's reference, I have the impression that her employer was not satisfied with her work, although he doesn't actually say so.'
13. to **read** something **into** a document,

letter, etc. – to put words into a work to suggest a meaning that was not intended by the author. 'We said the brochures should be ready by the end of March, but we didn't promise anything; you are reading more into our letter than we intended.'

1. to **write** something **off** – to acknowledge that something no longer has any value. 'Malcolm's house was burned to the ground and he has written it off completely.' This is a book-keeping phrase for cancelling the value of an item shown in the accounts as an asset.

   to **write** someone **off** – (1) to acknowledge that someone is no longer capable of useful work in his/her occupation. 'It is too early to write Edwards off; he has had a disappointing season but he is still capable of championship tennis, once his health improves.' (2) to dismiss someone's chances of survival. 'After three days of intensive search, there is no trace of the missing mountaineers and their chances of survival have been written off.'

## SUMS

2. to **do one's sums** – to make one's calculations or estimate. 'In the course of the Minister's speech, it soon became clear that he had not done his sums.'

   to **get one's sums right** – to make a correct calculation or estimate. 'The borough treasurer was criticized by the Chairman for not getting his sums right.'

3. to **reckon without one's host** – to make one's plans or calculations without taking other people's views into account, to ignore possible opposition. Originally, to calculate the bill at an inn without asking the landlord for the bill.

4. to **take** someone's **measure** – to judge someone's character and abilities, his strengths and weaknesses. 'If I have taken Lever's measure, he is just the man we want for the job.'

5. to **stand up and be counted** – to declare one's principles openly, whatever the cost to one's career or reputation. 'If you wish to help our cause, it is time for you to stand up and be counted.' cf. 'to **have the courage of one's convictions' 119/4**.

6. **count me out** – I do not agree with you and do not wish to be counted among your supporters.

## GEOMETRY

7. to **draw the line** – to set a limit to one's tolerance. 'I don't mind Carol bringing her friends home but I draw the line at strangers she's picked up in the bus.'

8. to **draw a parallel** – to point to similarities between two (historic) events or phenomena. 'It is difficult to draw a parallel between the ancient and the modern world.'

9. to **go off at a tangent** – to introduce an irrelevant subject in the course of a discussion. 'It's impossible to discuss anything with Molly; she will keep going off at a tangent.'

## CIRCLE

10. to **go round in circles** – to think for a long time about a problem without getting any nearer to a solution. 'We've been arguing for the last half-hour about what we are going to do and we are just going round in circles.'

11. to **come full circle** – to return to one's starting point. 'After making and losing a fortune in America, Tom

returned to his old job at Barclays. He had come full circle.'

1. a **vicious circle** – a chain of events in which the cause of the difficulty / disorder produces an effect which intensifies the cause. 'I didn't have enough lodgers to pay the rates (tax) on my house. To pay the rates I had to sell some of the furniture. Without the furniture I lost some of my lodgers. As a result, I have less money than before to pay the rates; so I have to sell more of my furniture again. It's a vicious circle.'

SQUARE

2. to **square the circle** – to try to do the impossible. 'You'll never solve the problem; it's like trying to square a circle!'
3. **fair and square** – with the utmost frankness. 'I told Marion fair and square what I thought of her behaviour.'
4. a **square deal** – fair treatment. 'Tom always gave his workers a square deal.'
5. to **square accounts** – to revenge oneself on someone. 'Wallis has treated me with contempt in front of my friends; I intend to square accounts with him.'
6. to **square an account** – to pay a bill.
7. **all square** – a golfing phrase, meaning that the score is even. 'Dick won the eleventh hole to make them all square.'
8. **on the square** – (1) honest, straightforward, dependable. 'Miles has always been on the square with me; you can trust him to act fairly.' (2) to be a Freemason. Freemasonry is a secret religious society which goes back to medieval times when a group of stonemasons are believed to have founded it.

HISTORY

9. to **make history** – to do something important, for which one will be remembered. 'Professor Beloff has made history by establishing the first private university in Britain.'

   to **go down in history** – (of events, people) to be sufficiently important to be remembered or recorded. 'Alexander Bell has gone down in history as the inventor of the telephone.'
10. **ancient history** – something that is already familiar to everyone, nothing new. 'You've already told me that John and Mary are getting married; that's ancient history!'

GEOGRAPHY

11. to **put a place on the map** – to bring a place to the attention of the public, to make a place well-known. 'When the American film star returned to her birthplace, she put the small village on the map.'

ART

12. to **keep a low profile** – to avoid attracting attention, to be inconspicuous. 'I had no idea my proposal would arouse so much hostility. I had better keep a low profile for the next few months.'
13. **no oil painting** – not at all good-looking. 'Fred has plenty of girlfriends, although he is no oil painting.'

SLATE

14. to **wipe the slate clean** – to give someone another chance and overlook past offences. 'The judge told the prisoner that if he accepted the job offered him, he would wipe the slate clean.' The idiom has its origin in the former

custom in schools of chalking up on a slate the names of pupils who had misbehaved. When the pupils had been punished, the slate was wiped clean.

## COPYBOOK

1. to **blot one's copybook** – to make a serious mistake, which damages one's record. 'If you hadn't blotted your copybook borrowing the boss's car, you would have been promoted by now.'

## MARKS

2. to **give** someone **full marks** for – to give someone credit for a faultless achievement. 'Christine Bowles deserves full marks for the excellence of her latest biography.'

   to **give** someone **no marks** – to give someone no credit for his work. One can award marks on a ten-point scale in the same way as marks are awarded in English schools. 'I give the local council only five out of ten for its plan to clean up the town centre.'

## SNEAK AND EGG ON

3. a **sneaking sympathy** – a sympathy for someone or something that one is reluctant to admit. 'I have a sneaking sympathy for middle-aged housewives who are brought before me for shoplifting although, as a magistrate, I shouldn't talk like that.' The word 'sneak' means to complain about a fellow pupil behind his back to the teacher, and make trouble for him.
4. to **egg** someone **on** – to encourage someone to do wrong, as for example by breaking rules. 'You shouldn't have egged Stephen on to play that joke on Mr Gibbs. Now he'll be in trouble.' The derivation is from Icelandic 'egg' meaning edge, so that the literal meaning is to put someone on the edge.

## RULES AND PUNISHMENTS

5. a **hard and fast rule** – a rule that is strictly enforced and cannot be changed or varied in any circumstances. 'We have a hard and fast rule about wearing uniform at our school and we cannot make an exception for your son.'
6. to **rule with a rod of iron** – to use the utmost severity in maintaining order. 'Jack told us how his step-father ruled the family with a rod of iron; the teachers at school were quite gentle by comparison.'
7. to **kiss the rod** – to accept punishment meekly and submissively. 'If the boss expects me to kiss the rod the way the others do, he is making a mistake.'
8. to **haul over the coals** – to rebuke severely. 'I was hauled over the coals for taking the day off yesterday. I won't do that again!' The phrase meant originally to torture a person by holding him over burning coal.
9. to **be whacked** (colloquial) – to be exhausted. 'I feel completely whacked after spending the day with Jill shopping in the West End.' To 'whack' is slang for to beat or cane. cf. **'dead beat' 43/3**.
10. a **fair whack** (colloquial) – a fair share. 'If the Company can afford an increase of 15 per cent for the directors, I don't see why we shouldn't get a fair whack of the profits too!'
11. a **whacking/thumping/whopping lie** – a huge, obvious lie. 'That's a whacking lie of the Manager to say I am idle; I'm the first to arrive at the office and the last to leave.' The explanation for these phrases may be that whacking/thumping/whopping were regarded as a fit punishment for telling lies. The

verbs 'whack', 'thump' and 'whop' mean to beat.

1. a **whipping-boy** – someone who is made responsible for the mistakes and faults of another. 'The Cranes got badly sun-burned on their Pacific cruise and tried to make the travel agency the whipping-boy for their mishap for not warning them how hot the climate would be in those parts.' The whipping-boy was a boy who was educated with a prince and whipped whenever the prince deserved punishment, because tutors were not permitted to hit a child of the royal blood.

## BOY

2. a **new boy** – someone who is new to a position of employment or a place of work. 'I'd be grateful if you could please explain the office routine to me; I'm a new boy here.' Boys in their first term at school (in particular, boarding school) are referred to as new boys.
3. the **old boy network** – an association of ex-public school boys, i.e. old boys, who obtain jobs for one another on the basis of their common background, rather than merit.

# 30. WORK AND OCCUPATIONS

## WORK

1. to **have one's work cut out** – to accomplish a task only with the greatest difficulty. 'We shall have our work cut out to get the house ready in time for the wedding reception.' Literally, to work to a plan prepared by someone else.
2. to **make light work of** – to accomplish a task very easily, with little effort or trouble. 'Vivien made light work of her O-level papers; they were much easier than she had expected.'
3. to **work to rule** – to obey the rule-book (i.e. one's working instructions), with exaggerated care, so as to bring about a slow-down in the service; a tactic of the trade unions for putting pressure on the employer.
4. to **work wonders / to work like magic** – to have an astonishing effect. 'That medicine the doctor prescribed for me has worked wonders for my rheumatism; I have no pain now.'
5. to **make short work of** someone/something – to dispose of someone or something very quickly and easily. 'Rupert jumped on the burglar from behind and made short work of him.' 'The children made short work of the Christmas pudding, which disappeared very quickly.'
6. to **work off steam** – to find an outlet for one's energy or feelings. 'In the afternoons, the boys work off steam on the football field.'
7. a **nasty piece of work** – someone of bad character, false and cruel. 'I am sorry you are going out with Beaney. He is a nasty piece of work.'
8. a **glutton for** work/punishment – someone who welcomes the opportunity of working hard for long hours. 'Don't tell me you've brought your work home after nine hours at the office; you are a glutton for work!'

## JOB

9. to **have a job** (colloquial) – to have difficulty in doing something. 'I had a job making Pierre understand me. My French is very weak and he doesn't know any English.'
10. an **inside job** – a burglary committed with the assistance of an employee or relation of the person robbed. 'It must have been an inside job, otherwise how could the thieves have known where the jewellery was hidden?'
11. a **put-up job** – something arranged beforehand with a deceitful or criminal purpose. 'We were burgled two days after the new window-cleaner started work. The police think it was a put-up job.'
12. **just the job** – exactly what is wanted. 'Your car is just the job for London – cheap to run, and small enough to park anywhere.'
13. **it's a good job** – it's a good thing; it's lucky that. 'It's a good job you weren't at home when Jim called; he was in such a bad temper.'
14. to **make the best of a bad job** – to try to gain as much advantage as possible from an unsatisfactory situation. 'At least the post will give you the opportunity to learn Spanish. Why don't you make the best of a bad job instead of grumbling all the time.'
15. to **give** something **up as a bad job** – to abandon an attempt to do something because it is too difficult or impossible. 'Having failed the driving test three times, Ralph gave it up as a bad job.'

1. **jobs for the boys** – the giving of the best positions by those in authority to their relations, friends and supporters. Selection for the jobs is based on favour not merit.

## PROFESSION

2. **the oldest profession** – prostitution.

## OCCUPATIONS: THE CHURCH

3. to **go into the church** – to be ordained as a priest in the church.
4. a **broad church** – an organization which tolerates a wide range of ideas and policies among its supporters. 'The traditional Labour Party has always been a broad church with room for social democrats and Marxists.'
5. **as poor as a church-mouse** – very poor, because there is little or no food in most churches for mice to feed on. As the Germans have the same phrase in their language: 'So arm wie eine Kirchenmaus', it is possible that the Saxons introduced it to Britain in the fifth- or sixth-century invasions.
6. **high priest** – the leading exponent of a theory or doctrine. 'Sigmund Freud was the high priest of psychoanalysis.'
7. **take a pew** – make yourself comfortable, sit down. Often said casually by the host to a visitor who can only stay a short time. The pew is the bench that is fixed to the floor of the church for seating the congregation. It has no place in a private house, so its use is a little facetious.
8. **the Vicar of Bray** – a sixteenth-century vicar who changed his views in accordance with the views of each new government. The phrase is occasionally used to describe anyone who changes his views for profit.
9. **like the curate's egg** – a euphemism for something that is bad or unsatisfactory. It derives from a joke in *Punch*: a young curate on being asked whether his egg was good replied: 'It is good in parts.' He was too polite to tell his host that his egg was bad.
10. **benefit of clergy** – a privilege enjoyed by members of the Church in the Middle Ages which exempted them from criminal prosecution in the King's Courts, the Ecclesiastical Courts being much more lenient. The privilege was much abused and almost anybody who could read was able to claim 'benefit of clergy'.
11. the **parish pump / parish pump politics** – (1) a preoccupation with trivialities. (2) a derogatory term for local government and council meetings. 'I am tired of parish pump politics. We should be talking about our wages, not petty problems like canteen meals.'
12. to **give** someone **short shrift** – to treat someone curtly, impatiently. 'The Colonel gave his men's complaints short shrift.' 'Short shrift' was originally the short time allowed a prisoner for making his confession before execution. 'Shrift' meant confession and derives from Anglo-Saxon 'scrift', with the same meaning.
13. to **bear one's cross** – to bear suffering, affliction or annoyance. The suffering is usually the fault of someone else. 'To be under-estimated by men is the biggest cross I have had to bear' (Barbara Taylor Bradford, *Woman of Substance*).
14. an **odour of sanctity** – an overpowering atmosphere of piety and virtuous living. 'Although I was made welcome at the vicarage, there was an odour of sanctity about the place which made me uncomfortable.' The

allusion is to a legend in the Middle Ages that when the saints were buried, their bodies gave off a sweet-smelling odour, which came to be known as the odour of sanctity.

1. to **make a martyr of oneself** (derogatory) – to make unnecessary sacrifices in order to win sympathy and pity from one's friends. 'Why shouldn't you take a holiday like the rest of the staff? Are you trying to make a martyr of yourself?'
2. a **holier-than-thou** attitude/expression – to behave as though one were more virtuous than one's companions. 'Yes, I didn't get home until half-past two this morning, but you have come in later than that, so you needn't look at me with that holier-than-thou expression.'
3. **the holy of holies** – the most private room in a house. 'This is my husband's holy of holies where he can work without fear of being disturbed.' The Holy of Holies was the name given to the innermost apartment of the Jewish Temple where the Ark of the Covenant was kept. Only the high priest could enter this room on the Day of Atonement (Yom Kippur).
4. a **holy terror** – someone who causes a public disturbance by his rowdy misbehaviour. The term is often applied to a child who gets out of control and runs wild. 'That boy has become a holy terror to the whole neighbourhood, running his bicycle up and down the pavement all day long.'
5. to **take holy orders** – to be ordained as a priest in the Anglican Church. 'My son has just taken holy orders. He always wanted to be a priest.'
6. to **preach to the converted** – to waste one's persuasive powers on someone who is already of one's own opinion. 'I should like blood sports to be made illegal just as much as you. You are preaching to the converted.'
7. to **count one's blessings** – to remember all the advantages that one enjoys, especially when complaining about the annoyances of present-day conditions. 'Yes, it must have been disappointing not getting the job, but you should count your blessings: good health, a happy home, and a nice circle of friends.'
8. a **mixed blessing** – something that should bring joy but suffers from serious drawbacks. 'We were delighted when Mervyn gave us the puppy, but it has proved a mixed blessing; it has done so much damage to the furniture and curtains.'
9. to **give one's blessing to** – to give one's approval of. 'Although Julie is only sixteen, her parents have given us their blessing, and we are to be married in May.'
10. a **blessing in disguise** – what at first appears to be a misfortune turns out later to be a boon. 'Perhaps your son's failure to get into a university may be a blessing in disguise. He'll have no difficulty getting a job, and by the time he's 21 he'll have three years of practical experience behind him.'
11. to **take as Gospel** – to believe something to be true with absolute certainty. 'You must believe me; I'm telling you the Gospel truth.' The Gospel consists of the first four books of the New Testament (by Matthew, Mark, Luke and John) which describe the life and teaching of Christ.
12. to **give/quote chapter and verse** – to produce evidence in support of one's statements. 'I can't quote chapter and verse for what I am saying; you'll just have to believe me.' The whole of the Bible is divided into chapters and verses; so that when a priest gives 'chapter and verse' as the authority for his statements, they can be immediately verified.
13. a **baptism of fire** – someone's first test,

often painful. 'I have to visit a patient, so Dr Wake will have to take surgery; that will be his baptism of fire.' A baptism of fire is the first experience a soldier has of gun-fire.

1. **for one's sins** (humorous) – as a punishment for one's wrong-doing. 'I'm a teacher, for my sins.' Although the phrase is used humorously, it often implies dissatisfaction with one's occupation.
2. to **cover a multitude of sins** – to include a great number of undesirable possibilities. 'She calls herself a consultant on personal problems, but that could cover a multitude of sins.'
3. to be **thankful for small mercies** – to be thankful for the small advantages and consolations that can be set against a misfortune or setback. 'Almost all the furniture was destroyed but we were able to save the jewellery. I suppose we should be thankful for small mercies.'
4. **'That's your funeral!'** (colloquial and impolite) – that is your misfortune. 'You can't expect me to reduce your bill because your house has been burgled; that's your funeral!'

## THE LAW

5. to **take the law into one's own hands** – to seek justice by using force or the threat of force without resorting to the law courts.
6. to be **a law unto oneself** – to live in accordance with one's own principles and ignore the law. In practice, this amounts to putting oneself above the law. 'You can't apply ordinary standards to that man. He is a law unto himself.' From Romans II, 14 (New Testament): 'These, having not the law, are a law unto themselves.'
7. **the rule of law** – the application of the law to all alike (institutions, local government, etc.), irrespective of differences in power or wealth.
8. to keep **on the right side of the law** – to obey the law but without troubling whether one's actions are honest or moral.

   to be **on the wrong side of the law** – to disobey the law. It is possible to get on the wrong side of the law unintentionally or through ignorance.
9. **the long arm of the law** – criminals are never safe from the law which has all the resources of the state behind it.
10. **in the eyes of the law** – the legal position, as distinct from the commonsense point of view. 'If a stranger enters your room and sits on your bed, he has done you no wrong in the eyes of the law unless he uses force.'
11. to **lay down the law** – to be dogmatic and prejudiced on matters of opinion. 'It's no fun arguing with you; you lay down the law every time, and that's the end of the discussion.'
12. to keep **within the letter of the law** – to obey the law in every particular while defeating its spirit. 'There's nothing I can do about the noise my neighbour makes; he switches his radio off every night at the stroke of ten. In that way he can keep within the letter of the law and, at the same time, prevent me getting any peace.'
13. **the law of the jungle** – no law at all because, in the jungle, the strongest animals prevail over the weaker. Some economists have compared the Free Market economy with the law of the jungle.
14. a **loophole in the law** – a way of avoiding the effect of the law without breaking it, when the language of the law is inaccurate or ambiguous.
15. to **call in the law** – to request the assistance of the police to protect one's rights against criminal action.
16. the **unwritten law** – a law which is

generally recognized, although it has not been committed to writing. Custom has the force of law in many parts of the world, even when it is not part of the written law. There is also an unwritten law of criminals, such as the trial and execution of men and women who betray their accomplices to the police.

1. to **have the law on** someone – to prosecute, to take legal proceedings against. 'I'll have the law on you for the damage you have done to my property.'
2. to go **beyond the law** – to go beyond the reach of the law, outside the jurisdiction. 'We can't sue him now. He is in Brazil and beyond the law.'
3. to **go to law** – to take proceedings in a court of law in defence of one's rights. 'I don't *want* to go to law, but I shall have to if he doesn't offer me fair compensation.'
4. **necessity knows no law** – someone who is desperate cannot be expected to keep the law.
5. **'The law is an ass'** – the laws of the land are often unfair and stupid. The quotation is from *Oliver Twist* by Charles Dickens, when the beadle protested at being dismissed from his post.
6. the **law does not concern itself with trifles** – the courts will not listen to petty grievances, such as claims for a few pence or complaints that the neighbours' children make rude gestures over the garden fence. The derivation is from the Roman maxim '*de minimis non curat lex*'.
7. to be **laughed out of court** – to make such an absurd claim that it arouses derision instead of sympathy. 'The demands of the union leaders were so ridiculous that they were laughed out of court by the workers themselves.'
8. to put oneself **out of court** – to take any action which disqualifies one from receiving a benefit or advantage. 'By talking like that to the secretary about the boss, you have put yourself out of court for any promotion.' In a lawsuit, a party may 'put himself out of court' if he behaves improperly, for example if he tries to bribe the judge or jury or threatens the other party with physical violence.
9. **special pleading** – an unfair way of arguing which consists in giving the words (e.g. of a contract) an unreal meaning to suit one's own case.
10. an **open and shut case** – a case whose outcome can be predicted with absolute certainty. 'There is no such thing as an open and shut case. Going to law is always a gamble.'
11. a **cast-iron case** – an irrefutable case, one that cannot possibly be disproved. 'You have a cast-iron case; I would advise you to sue without further delay.' Cast iron is iron in a molten condition which is poured into a mould, where it is cooled and sets solid.
12. to be **as sober as a judge** – to be absolutely sober. Judges have a reputation for sobriety and seriousness.
13. a **Philadelphia lawyer** – one who is celebrated for his acuteness and quickness.
14. a **barrack-room lawyer** (derogatory) – a soldier without legal training who uses the Queen's Regulations to promote his own interests and make life uncomfortable for his military superiors. Such people are always disliked by their commanding officers.
15. to **keep one's own counsel** – to keep one's thoughts to oneself. 'There are times when it is wiser to keep one's own counsel. Even the best of friends may talk.' cf. 'to **play one's cards close to one's chest' 99/7**.
16. **the devil's advocate** – an official appointed by the Catholic Church to

refute the claims put forward for admitting a person to the calendar of saints. Counsel at conference with their clients sometimes play the part of devil's advocate to test them and, if possible, to anticipate the arguments of the other side.

1. an **honest broker** – an intermediary who brings two parties in dispute together in a fair and impartial manner without showing favour to either side. 'At the Congress of Berlin in 1876, Bismarck played honest broker to Russia and Turkey.'
2. **no respecter of persons** – to treat everyone equally, notwithstanding differences in rank or importance. 'Your senior position won't help you; the judges are no respecters of persons.' A biblical reference, Acts X, 34: 'Then Peter opened his mouth and said, Of a truth I perceive that God is no respecter of persons.'
3. a **gentleman's agreement** – an agreement that has no legal force but is based solely on the honour of the parties involved. 'We have a gentleman's agreement. When you are dealing with Malcolm, that is as good as a signed contract.'
4. a **sore trial** – a painful, disagreeable experience. 'The children were a sore trial to their mother and gave her no peace, only annoyance and hard work.'
5. **trial and error** – the use of experiment to find the correct solution to a problem by eliminating all the incorrect ones.
6. a **trial of strength** with – a contest to determine which of the two participants is the stronger. 'In 1972 and 1973 the government and the miners had a trial of strength; the miners won both times.'
7. to **have a raw deal** – to suffer an injustice. 'Only £100 compensation for all your injuries! You've had a raw deal.' The phrase comes from the dealing out of cards (at card games).
8. to **put** someone **in the dock** – to make accusations against someone.

   **not to be in the dock** – not to have to defend oneself against an accusation. 'You are forgetting that *we* are not in the dock; *you* were responsible for what happened, not us.'
9. to make a **snap judgement** – to make a quick judgement without taking all the facts into account. 'It wouldn't be fair to you to give you a snap judgement on the telephone. If you would like to make an appointment, that will give me time to study your case.'
10. to **sit in judgement on** (derogatory) – to criticize and pass judgement on the behaviour of other people. 'You have no right to sit in judgement on Mary for coming home late; you aren't her father, and it's no concern of yours when she gets in.'
11. to **do oneself justice** – to realize one's true potential, to do work which reflects one's true abilities. 'When Roy takes an examination, he is always in such a state of nerves that he never does himself justice.'

    to **do** someone/something **justice** – to be fair in one's treatment and judgement of someone or something. 'Your portrait of Sue is a reasonable likeness but, in my opinion, doesn't do justice to her charm and vivacity.' 'I'd better not eat anything now or I shan't be able to do justice to your mother's delicious cooking this evening!'
12. **poetic justice** – a misfortune which punishes a wrong-doer just as if it had been intended by divine providence. 'It was poetic justice that, after refusing his best friend a loan of £50, Mason was mugged on his way home and was robbed of twice that amount.'
13. to **hold no brief for** – to have nothing to say in defence of. 'I hold no brief

for Stewart, but he has a right to a fair trial.' The brief is the bundle of papers relating to a client's case which is passed over to Counsel by the solicitor.

1. to **read the riot act** – to threaten someone (usually a child) with severe punishment unless he stops his misconduct immediately. 'We were having a wonderful party, when the landlord suddenly appeared and read us the riot act. He threatened to give us notice if we didn't stop the commotion.' Under the Riot Act (1715) if twelve or more people make a riot, a magistrate may read the Riot Act to them, calling on them to disperse. If the riot continues for more than one hour, they are then guilty of a felony.

2. **the small print** – conditions which may not be noticed by one party to a contract because they appear in the small print. 'The typewriter had a 24-month guarantee. However, when I read the small print, I discovered the guarantee was null and void unless I had it serviced by the suppliers every year at a cost of £70 a time!'

3. **without prejudice** – without making any admission. If a letter in a legal dispute is marked 'without prejudice' the contents are treated as confidential, and the letter may not be shown to the judge. The writer of the letter can then make an offer, without fear that his letter will be used against him in court if his offer is refused by the other party.

4. to **sign one's own death-warrant** – to bring about one's own destruction or collapse. 'You have depended on your brother for your livelihood for the last twenty years. By quarrelling with him, you have signed your own death warrant.' Before execution of a convicted murderer, it was necessary for the responsible authority to sign the death-warrant.

5. to **send** someone **down** – to send someone to prison after he has been convicted and sentenced.

## MEDICINE

6. to **doctor** something – to add to, to dilute or otherwise interfere, as by poisoning, with the quality of wine, spirits or other drinks. The term usually has a sinister meaning.

7. to **doctor the accounts** – to falsify the accounts in order to make them appear better (or worse) than they really are.

8. **just what the doctor ordered** – exactly what is needed. 'A glass of iced lemonade? After two hours of tennis in the hot sun, that's just what the doctor ordered!'

9. to **hold a surgery** – of a Member of Parliament: to listen to the complaints of his constituents and, if necessary, take up their case with the appropriate Minister. The phrase has its origin in the doctor's surgery where the patients go for treatment.

10. to **nurse one's energy** – to keep one's energy in reserve, to save it for an important occasion.

11. to **nurse a grievance** – to feel resentment against someone or something. 'Having been dismissed from the Foreign Office, Peter nursed a grievance against it all his life.'

## THE NAVY AND AIR FORCE

12. to be **a good sailor** – to adjust quickly to the movement of a ship at sea, without being sea-sick. cf. 'to **find one's sea-legs' 181/13**.

    to be **a bad sailor** – to be frequently sea-sick. 'Nelson was a bad sailor all his life.'

13. **a sailor has a wife in every port** – sailors have always had a reputation

for promiscuity, owing to their long absences from home.

1. **Tell that to the marines!** – Don't expect me to believe that! The phrase was originally: 'Tell that to the horse marines!' There is no such thing as a horse marine, so it is a joke phrase.
2. to be a **sky pilot** (colloquial) – a clergyman.
3. to **drop the pilot** – to dismiss an expert adviser. The classic example was the dismissal of the German Chancellor, Bismarck, by Kaiser Wilhelm II in 1891.
4. a **pilot scheme** – an experiment to test the demand for a product without incurring heavy expenditure on its production or sale. 'Before you spend a lot of money on your invention, you should try a pilot scheme to see whether there is any interest in the idea.' A pilot is a guide who steers ships into and out of harbour.

## THE ARMY

5. to **come the old soldier** – to offer advice on how to do a job instead of doing it oneself, to claim superior knowledge because of one's long experience of the work. 'You needn't come the old soldier with me. I've been in the job as long as you.'
6. to **soldier on** – to persevere, despite setbacks and defeats. Soldiers are expected to fight on, even when they suffer defeats. 'The Government is expected to soldier on until the end of its term, although it has lost its majority in the House, and popular support in the country.'
7. **soldiers of fortune** – men who offer their services to any state; mercenaries.
8. to **swear like a trooper** – to use lurid language when swearing such as an ordinary soldier is supposed to do.
9. to **get a rocket** (slang) – to receive a severe reprimand. 'Mary got a rocket from her boss for coming back from her holiday two days late.' 'Rocket' is a military term for a self-propelled missile.
10. to **fall into line** – to conform to routine or custom. 'Naturally, you'll be expected to fall into line in your uncle's office, just like the rest of the staff.'

    to **fall out of line** – not to conform to routine or custom. Both phrases are military, deriving from the falling into/out of line of soldiers on parade.
11. **when the balloon goes up** (slang) – when events become critical. 'Have you any idea what you'll do if the balloon goes up and the company goes bust?'
12. **spit and polish** – emphasis on appearances rather than on more serious matters. 'We do 90 per cent of our business on the telephone, so we don't have to waste time on spit and polish, or trying to impress our customers with expensive wallpaper.'
13. to **pass muster** – to reach an acceptable standard, to pass inspection. 'I'm afraid I'm not a brilliant cook but the dinner should pass muster.' The 'muster' was the assembling of men for inspection, and introduction into the army or navy.
14. to **muster up one's courage/strength** – to summon up or marshal one's courage or strength. 'I could barely muster up courage to ask for a rise, although I had a right to one.' Soldiers were mustered up or collected for the defence of the country.
15. the **top brass** – the most important people in an organization. 'The top brass are coming up from London to inspect the factory, so we had better clean the place up.' In the army, the generals and staff officers at the War Office are often referred to as the top brass.

1. to **pull rank** – to remind people in an organization of one's senior position. 'I didn't like the way the managing director's wife pulled rank at the office party. I didn't see why I should give up my seat to her.' In the army, officers pull rank when they act with stiff formality off duty.
2. to **close ranks** – to unite in defence of a common interest. 'Commuters are at last closing ranks against the policies of British Rail because of the high fares.' A military phrase for uniting in the face of attack by the enemy.
3. to **break ranks** – to fail to maintain unity with one's comrades. 'If we break ranks now, that will be the end of our fight for a fair wage.' Soldiers break ranks when they retreat against orders.

## THE POLICE

4. **off** someone's **beat** (colloquial) – outside one's subject. 'I'm sorry, chemistry is off my beat; I'm a physicist.' The phrase comes from the police constable's beat – the area he has to patrol when he is on duty.
5. **not to have a clue** (slang) – to be unable to account for a fact, problem, etc. 'I haven't a clue why I have been picked for this job.' A clue is a fact which may point to the solution of an investigation, in particular the investigation of a crime.

## OTHER OCCUPATIONS

6. to **shepherd** someone – to guide, take care of. 'The verger shepherded us to our pews immediately behind the bridegroom.'
7. to **shepherd one's flock** – (of a priest) to attend to the spiritual needs of his parishioners.
8. the **poacher turned gamekeeper** – said of anyone with a dubious record who has been appointed to a post of trust and responsibility. 'The Irish were among the most lawless of the earlier immigrants to the US. But today the majority of American policemen are of Irish stock. The poacher turned gamekeeper!'
9. to be **as hungry as a hunter** – to be very hungry. Hunters are presumed to be hungry because of all the exercise they are obliged to take in order to catch their quarry.
10. to be **an old maid** – to be a spinster long past marriageable age.

    to be **old-maidish** – to be like an old spinster in character: fussy, prudish, gossipy.
11. **What's cooking?** (slang) – I wonder what is going to happen. What are they scheming? 'When I went into the dining-room, I could tell from the expression on the men's faces that something was cooking.'
12. a **butcher** – someone who uses brute force instead of intelligence. 'The operation was a disaster. The man behaved like a butcher, not a surgeon.'
13. **stick to your last** – concentrate on your own speciality, and don't tell me how to do mine. 'Administrators should stick to their lasts' (Winston Churchill during World War II). The phrase comes from the old adage: Cobbler, stick to your last. The last is a wooden model of a foot used by shoemakers for shaping boots and shoes. cf. **'every man to his trade' 237/1**.
14. **tailor-made** – specially designed to suit a person's particular needs. 'These language courses have been tailor-made for business executives.'
15. **like a tailor's dummy** – an effeminate or immaculately dressed man, a dandy; used in a disparaging sense.
16. **not to care a tinker's cuss** – not to

attach any value to . . . 'I don't care a tinker's cuss for her principles.'

1. to **tinker with** – to deal superficially with. 'It is only tinkering with the problem to give her sedatives. She should be examined by a specialist to find out the root cause of her illness.'

2. a **busman's holiday** – to spend one's time on holiday doing the same work as one does for a living. 'The teacher spent his summer holiday teaching at his friends' school in Italy. It was a real busman's holiday for him.'

3. an **empire-builder** – a civil servant who seeks to increase the size of his department at the expense of the taxpayer. It was originally used to describe the soldiers, explorers and administrators who extended the frontiers of the British Empire.

4. to be **taken to the cleaners** / to be **cleaned out** – to lose all one's money in business or gambling. 'We have been properly taken to the cleaners this time; we haven't a penny left.'

5. to **make a clean sweep** – to rid oneself completely of a thing or person that no longer serves a useful purpose. 'I have made a clean sweep of all my old papers that have been taking up too much space.'

6. to **come out in the wash** – of mistakes, difficulties and so on, to be soon forgotten, although they were embarrassing at the time. The reference is to the stains which disappear in the wash.

7. **'That won't wash!'** – 'Nobody is going to believe that!' The phrase is used with reference to explanations or excuses that are weak and unconvincing. 'That excuse Philip made for not keeping his appointment won't wash. If his train had really been stuck two hours in the tunnel, the story would have been in the papers.'

8. **everything is grist to his mill** – he can turn to good advantage everything you offer him. 'Your husband is a celebrity now, Mrs Holmes, so anything you tell us about him will interest our readers – everything is grist to our mill.'

9. to **put** someone **through the mill** – to subject someone to harsh training or unpleasant experiences. 'The army recruits were really put through the mill for the first three months of their training.'

to **go through the mill** – to undergo harsh training or unpleasant experiences. cf. 'to **go/put through the hoop**' **260/8**.

10. to be **on a treadmill** – to be employed on exhausting never-ending work. 'The meals run into one another. No sooner have I cooked one meal than I have to start on the next. I am on a treadmill.' In the old days, treadmills were used in prisons as a punishment.

11. **yeoman service** – steady, effective service, a help in time of need. 'My manager has given me yeoman service for many years. I shall be sorry to lose him.' The phrase comes from Shakespeare: 'It did one yeoman's service' (*Hamlet*, V, ii, 36), and refers to the military service of the yeomen in England's armies. The yeomen in Shakespeare's days were small middle-class farmers.

12. to **jockey for position** – to manoeuvre for advantage. Newly elected councillors jockey for positions in the most important committees, just as jockeys jostle one another for the best positions on the racecourse.

13. a **cowboy outfit** (American colloquialism) – an unscrupulous business which exploits and swindles its customers. And so one reads of **'cowboy airlines'**, **'cowboy contractors'**, **'cowboy language schools'** (meaning the bad ones).

## BEGGAR, THIEF, HEWERS AND CARRIERS

1. to **beggar description** – to be so remarkable or appalling that no words can describe it. 'The conditions in which the family are living are absolutely horrible; they beggar description.' The phrase 'It beggared all description' appears in Shakespeare's *Antony and Cleopatra* (II, ii, 199) with reference to Cleopatra, but is always used today in a bad sense.
2. to **go begging** – to be unwanted. 'Large numbers of jobs which no one seems to want are going begging at top London hotels' (*Daily Mail*, 23 May 1983).
3. to **beg the question** – to assume what one is trying to prove. 'The statement that travelling is good because it broadens the mind begs the question whether travelling does broaden the mind.'
4. **as thick as thieves** – on very close, friendly terms with one another. There is a similar phrase in German: 'dicke Freunde', meaning thick, i.e. close friends.
5. a **den of thieves** – a meeting place for criminals of all sorts. The phrase can be used as a term of abuse for a place.
6. **no honour among thieves** – criminals will not hesitate to give one another away to the police if they believe it is to their advantage.
7. the **hewers of wood and carriers of water** – used humorously today to emphasize the lowliness of a person's calling. 'It's no good asking me to explain your X-rays. I'm only a hewer of wood and carrier of water.' The hewers of wood and carriers of water were the bondsmen, i.e. slaves, referred to in the Old Testament (Joshua IX, 21).

## CUSTOMER

8. an **ugly customer / rough customer** – a bad character who may become violent unless he gets what he wants.
9. a **slippery customer** – a deceitful person who will cheat and swindle to achieve his object.

## SHOP

10. to **shop** (slang) – to get somebody into trouble by reporting him to the authorities. 'I don't want to shop you, but I will do so if I catch you stealing the men's food again.'
11. to **talk shop** – to restrict one's conversation to one's own specialized subject. 'When two doctors get together, they always talk shop.'
12. **the other shop** – the rival establishment.
13. to **come to the wrong shop** – to apply to the wrong person.
14. to **shut up shop** – (1) to stop work, to cease business for the day. 'It has turned half-past five. It's time we shut up shop.' (2) to go out of business.
15. to be **all over the shop** – to lie untidily all over the place.
16. **shoplifting** – stealing articles from a shop. 'Shoplifters always say they did it on the spur of the moment!'
17. **shop floor** – the workers on the factory floor, as opposed to the office workers and management.

    **shop floor politics** – action by the trade-union officials in a factory to obtain higher wages for the shop floor or factory workers by, for example, ordering a go-slow, or calling a strike.
18. to **shop around** – to go from shop to shop in search of the best bargain. 'You are paying too much for your meat. You should shop around like me.'

## TRADE

1. **every man to his trade** – keep to your own job and don't meddle in other people's. cf. **'stick to your last' 234/13**.
2. to be **in trade** – to engage in an unlearned, commercial occupation, as distinct from a profession.
3. **the tricks of the trade** – methods, dodges, short cuts and so on which are only learned with experience. 'That's a trick of the trade you can't learn out of a book or at college.'
4. to **trade on** – to take unfair advantage of someone's weakness to further one's own ends. 'He trades on his lameness to win sympathy.'
5. to **trade in** – to use an old article in part exchange for a new one, paying the difference in value in cash. 'I traded in my old car for a new one and got a 25 per cent discount.'
6. to **trade up** – to improve the quality of one's merchandise, thereby justifying an increase in prices. 'As they were unable to extend their premises, the chairman proposed a policy of trading up.'
7. **in the trade** – among people employed in the trade.
8. **known in the trade as . . .** – to use a word that is peculiar to the trade in question. For example: in the theatre, actors and actresses, who are out of work, are said to be 'resting'; in business, salesmen who praise their merchandise 'talk up' its value; and advertisers, who exaggerate the value of their products and services, are said to 'puff' them.

## BUSINESS

9. to **make** something **one's business** – to make it one's own responsibility. 'I will make it my business to see that he gets the job finished in good time.'
10. to **mean business** – to show that one's intentions are serious. 'He must mean business. He has paid £500 on account.'
11. to have **no business** in a place / **no business** to do something – to have no right to be in a place, no right to do a particular thing.
12. **Mind your own business!** – attend to your own affairs and don't concern yourself with mine.
13. to **send** someone **about his business** – to dismiss curtly, to end an interview abruptly.
14. **unfinished business** – scores still to settle with one's enemies.
15. **not to be in the business of** – to have no intention of . . . 'We are not in the business of dismantling the coal industry' (Norman Siddall, ex-Chairman of the National Coal Board).
16. a **bad business** – said when something has gone badly wrong. 'On his arrival he was robbed of all his money; a bad business!'

## AT WORK

17. a **sleeping partner** – a partner who has invested capital in a firm but plays no part in its management. 'It's no good going to Mr Parsons for advice; he is only a sleeping partner.'
18. **the top of the ladder** – the summit of one's career or profession. 'If you want to get to the top of the ladder, you must work like a demon, and be completely ruthless.' Benjamin Disraeli likened the premiership to 'the top of the greasy pole'.
19. to be sent on a **fool's errand** – to be sent on a pointless errand, one that has no purpose.
20. to **get the message** (slang) – to understand a warning or threat. 'I was polite but I made it clear we couldn't wait

any longer for our money. He got the message all right.'

1. to be **in a rut** – to lead a boring, monotonous way of life which is difficult to change because it is so well established. 'I'm doing exactly the same work now as I was doing fourteen years ago. It's too late now for me to get out of the rut.' The reference is to the groove made by cartwheels in a soft road.
2. to **sack / to get the sack** – to dismiss / to be dismissed. 'Harry got the sack for taking time off without permission.' In earlier times, workmen brought their tools in a sack to their place of work and on dismissal they were given back their sacks; hence, to get the sack.
3. a **rich man's hobby** – an occupation that enjoys a certain prestige but brings no money in. Before World War II, farming was described as a rich man's hobby because it was so uneconomic. The Bar was also so described shortly after the war because briefs were so scarce.

## THE MUSIC SHOP

4. **music to one's ears** (colloquial) – the pleasure one feels on receiving a piece of good news, especially news of the discomfiture of an old enemy. 'I hear Matthew has had to resign from the Ministry. That must be music to your ears, Tom!' cf. **'meat and drink' 161/10**.
5. to **face the music** – to answer for the consequences of one's actions. 'We have just received a complaint about you from the Dean of your College, Jack; you will have to face the music next term.'
6. to **blow one's own trumpet** – to praise oneself publicly, to boast about one's achievements. 'You have to blow your own trumpet in business. If you don't, no one else will.'
7. to **beat the drum for** someone – to campaign noisily on somebody's behalf, to advertise his services energetically. 'While I'm in Hong Kong, I'll beat the drum for you; so you'll get plenty of publicity.'
8. to **drum** something **into** someone – to impress an idea forcefully on someone. 'It's been drummed into them ever since they were small that their country is the best in the world.'
9. to be **drummed out** – to be dismissed in a humiliating manner. 'It is shameful the way Dean cheats his customers. He would have been drummed out of any decent company years ago.' The reference is to the dismissal of an officer from his regiment for dishonourable conduct; the dismissal takes effect in front of the soldiers with the drums beating.
10. to **fiddle / to be on the fiddle** – to swindle, often by falsifying the accounts. 'I'm sure that Robert is on the fiddle; otherwise he couldn't afford all those holidays on the Riviera on his salary.'
11. **as fit as a fiddle** – to be in excellent health. 'I've worked for twenty years without a holiday and I'm as fit as a fiddle!' cf. **'as sound as a bell' 146/18**.
12. to **harp on the same string** – to make the same point over and over again. 'I wish you wouldn't harp on the same string every time I light a cigarette. I know smoking is bad for the health, but I won't give it up!'
13. to **whistle in the dark** – to talk optimistically in order to keep up one's courage. 'Have you got any evidence, Frank, for believing things are going to improve, or are you just whistling in the dark?'
14. to **whistle for it** – to ask in vain for the repayment of one's money. 'I'm afraid you've seen the last of your money, Paul. You can whistle for it as far as Richard is concerned.'

1. to **blow the whistle on** – to denounce publicly an illegal or dishonest activity. 'It's time the authorities blew the whistle on these chain-letters, because they really amount to taking money under false pretences.' The reference is to football when the referee blows his whistle to stop foul play.
2. to **pull out all the stops** – to make a tremendous effort. 'When the airport told us Mary's luggage had been lost, Father pulled out all the stops to get it back for her.' The stops refer to organ stops. When the organist pulls out all the stops, the organ is being played at full volume. The church organ is the most powerful of all musical instruments.
3. to **soft-pedal** – to understate the importance of, to moderate. 'The workers are soft-pedalling their demands in case the company goes bankrupt and they lose their jobs.' When the soft pedal is down, the piano plays more quietly.
4. to **strike the right note** – to behave in a manner that is suited to the occasion. 'In his address to the men, the army chaplain struck just the right note; he was serious without being grim and friendly without being familiar.' The reference is to a musical note.
5. to **strike a chord** – to remind one of something. 'This book I am reading strikes a chord; I must have read it before, many years ago.'
6. to **compare notes** – to exchange ideas and opinions. The reference is to musical notation.
7. **out of tune with** – out of sympathy with, having nothing in common with. 'I don't think Paul enjoyed the African tour; he was out of tune with his companions.'
8. to **call the tune** – to impose one's will. 'You must do what your uncle asks. He is paying for your training so he has a right to call the tune.' From the proverb: He who pays the piper calls the tune.
9. **to the tune of** (colloquial) – the excessive amount of . . . 'Martin was charged by the hotel to the tune of £650 a week.'
10. to **be / not to be tuned in to** – to be / not to be in sympathy with. 'The teacher was not tuned in to the feelings of his pupils.' The reference is to the tuning in of a radio to a frequency.

## VOCAL AND DANCE MUSIC

11. to **change one's tune** – to change one's manner, usually after being disappointed or humiliated; but it can also be used when one has been proved wrong. 'Father said I would never make a painter, but he'll have to change his tune now that I've won first prize at the County Exhibition.'
12. to **sing** someone's **praises** – to speak very highly of someone, to praise him enthusiastically. 'Julie was singing your praises this afternoon. You must have made a very good impression on her.'
13. to **sing** (to the police) (slang) – to inform on one's criminal associates. The larger part of police evidence is supplied by the criminals themselves in the hope of getting lighter sentences.
14. to **sing for one's supper** – to do some unaccustomed work to pay one's keep. 'If Jackie wants to stay on with us after she has finished here, she will have to sing for her supper. I'm not giving her free board and lodging.'
15. to **go for a song** – to be sold for a very small sum. 'The house went for a song because the owner had to raise money quickly.'
16. to **make a song and dance about** – to make an unnecessary fuss about. 'I

don't know why Mrs Scott should have made such a song and dance about her daughter coming home at three o'clock in the morning. Angela is nineteen years old and not a little girl any longer.'

1. to **dance attendance on** someone – to be over-anxious to please and assist someone. 'I don't know why Lady Miriam should expect me to dance attendance on her all day. I'm only a friend of the family, not her servant.'
2. to **lead** someone **a (pretty) dance** – to put someone to a great deal of trouble before agreeing to what he wants. 'I must say Mr Vincent led me a pretty dance. I've never worked so hard in my life to win a customer.'
3. to **waltz home** – to win easily. 'With two of Fulham's team off the field with injuries, the Rangers should have waltzed home.'

## THE PRESS

4. to have **a good/bad press** – to be reported on favourably/unfavourably in the newspapers. 'The Government have been getting a bad press recently for their handling of the unemployment problem.'
5. **the gutter press** – newspapers that depend on scandal, sex and violence to promote their sales.
6. a **press campaign** – an organized attempt by newspapers to promote a cause rather than report – and comment on – the news.
7. **on the record** – officially authorized for publication. When information has been given on the record, it is 'attributable', i.e. the name of the informant may be given, and he will accept responsibility for the story.

   **off the record** – not authorized for publication, given in confidence and 'non-attributable', meaning that the name of the informant may not be used by the newspaper.
8. to **sit on a story** – to delay publication of a story. A newspaper may sit on a story in order to obtain confirmation from an independent source, or to await a more favourable opportunity for publication.
9. **a tall story** – a story that is so improbable that it will not be believed by the readers of the newspaper. 'That's a tall story! Show me your evidence.'
10. to **kill a story** – to suppress publication of a story. This may happen if the government objects to publication on security grounds, or if the editor believes that publication could damage the interests of the country.
11. to **meet a deadline** – to have a story ready for publication by a specified date. The 'deadline' refers to the Andersonville prisoner-of-war camp in the American Civil War, which had a 'deadline' marked out round its perimeter; any prisoner of war caught crossing the deadline would be shot on sight.
12. to **dot the i's and cross the t's** – to pay meticulous attention to detail so as to make oneself absolutely clear. From the confusion which arises when the letters 'i' and 't' are not properly written.
13. to **mind one's p's and q's** – to be on one's best behaviour, to take great care not to cause offence. 'If you are having tea with Aunt Jane, you had better mind your p's and q's; she takes offence very quickly.' The p's and q's refer to the type that the compositor sets up for printing.
14. a **free lance** – an independent, self-employed person, who works on his own initiative and is his own master. A free lance journalist or reporter contributes articles to a number of national or provincial newspapers

without being tied to any particular one.

1. **in the know** – having access to information that is not available to the ordinary citizen. Being in the know depends primarily on having reliable sources of information.

## THE BOOK TRADE

2. **in my book** – it is a matter of principle, in my opinion. 'In my book, you don't complain about the staff to the boss until you have discussed it with them first.' The book is an imaginary book of rules that everyone follows.
3. to **bring** someone **to book** – to make someone answer for his misdeeds. 'We must bring these criminals to book; they deserve severe punishment.'
4. to **throw the book at** someone – to charge someone with as many offences as one possibly can. For example, a housebreaker who attacks the landlord can be charged with unlawful entry, trespass, malicious damage to property, assault and battery. The book consists of the various sections of the Statutory Law under which the accused is charged.
5. to **read** someone **like a book** – to know exactly what someone is thinking, even before he has spoken. 'When Sally comes to my office, it is always to ask for money. No matter how carefully she leads up to the subject, I can read her like a book.'
6. to **cook the books** – to falsify the accounts for a dishonest purpose. 'I don't believe the company made anything like that profit. Peter has been cooking the books so that he can get a good price for the business.' A clever cook can conceal the basic ingredients of a dish by adding all kinds of spices.
7. to **suit / not to suit one's book** – to serve one's own interest – not to serve one's own interest. 'It may not suit his book to take the carpet back. He may not find another customer for it so quickly.'
8. to **go by the book** – to act in strict accordance with the rules and regulations, without taking personal factors into account. 'Edward would have been happier in the Civil Service than in business. Whatever the circumstances, he always goes by the book.'
9. a **closed book** – a subject about which one knows nothing, a mystery. 'Astronomy is a closed book to me.'
10. to **speak volumes / to speak volumes for** – (1) to be full of meaning. 'When the landlady showed Ralph his room, he was too polite to make any comment, but the expression on his face spoke volumes.' (2) to do a person or thing credit. 'Jack failed his examination three times before he finally passed; that speaks volumes for his determination.'

# 31. MONEY AND VALUABLES

## MONEY

1. **money down the drain** – money wasted. 'Why do you spend all your money on a hobby like model trains; it's all money down the drain.'
2. to be **in the money / to be rolling in money** – to be extremely rich.
3. to have money **burn a hole in one's pocket** – to be in possession of more money than one is used to and to be unable to stop oneself spending it. 'James can't wait to spend all that money you gave him; it is burning a hole in his pocket.'
4. a **money spinner** – a means of making money quickly with very little effort. It usually refers to ideas or projects.
5. a **licence to print money** – a business that is so profitable that it is like having permission to print money. These words were spoken by Lord Thomson when he took over the Independent Broadcasting Authority at its inception in 1967. cf. 'to **coin money**' **243/2**.
6. **hush-money** – money paid to someone in return for keeping silent about a crime.
7. **ready money** – money that is immediately available.
8. to **knock some money off** – to offer a reduction in price.
9. to **spend money like water** – to spend large sums of money recklessly without considering the cost.
10. to **throw good money after bad** – to try to recover money one has invested in an unsuccessful business by paying in still more, even though there is no chance of getting the money back. 'I wouldn't lend Henry any more money now he's lost so many of his customers. It would be throwing good money after bad.'
11. to **throw money at** something – to finance (usually at the taxpayers' expense) a business or enterprise which is losing money. 'You won't make the company efficient by throwing money at it. The only solution is to replace the management.'
12. **money is no object** – the amount of money spent is of no importance in comparison with the object desired.
13. to **put one's money where one's mouth is** – to give practical assistance to a cause one has been openly supporting by, for instance, contributing money to it. 'You have made so many speeches denouncing cruelty to animals. Isn't it time you put your money where your mouth is?'
14. to **give** someone **a run for his money** – to put someone to a great deal of trouble before he gets what he wants. 'The visiting team beat us in the end but we gave them a run for their money.'
15. to **have a run for one's money** – to get plenty of enjoyment for one's efforts, even if one doesn't achieve everything one hoped for.
16. **for my money** – if I had to make the choice. 'For my money, this bottle of champagne is better value than the others, even though it is a good deal more expensive.'

## CASH

17. to **cash in on** – to take advantage of. 'The dwarf cashed in on his abnormality to advance his career in the theatre.'
18. **hard cash** – money that consists of banknotes and coins as opposed to cheques. 'The advertising agency won't accept cheques any more, only hard cash.'

## CHANGE

1. to **get no change out of** – to get no help or satisfaction from. 'We complained to our neighbour about the behaviour of his children but we got no change out of him.' cf. 'to **get no joy from**' **123/7.**

## COIN

2. to **coin money** – to make so much money from one's business that it is almost the same as minting it oneself. cf. 'a **licence to print money' 242/5**.
3. to **pay back in the same coin** – to retaliate by using the same method. 'Jukes has attacked us in his advertising overseas; we will pay him back in the same coin.'
4. **the other side of the coin** – the opposite standpoint, showing the disadvantages as against the advantages. 'Flying has enormous advantages over other means of transport; it is not only much faster but much less tiring. The other side of the coin is that it is boring and takes all the novelty out of travelling.'
5. to **coin a phrase** – to invent a phrase in order to express a new idea. Hundreds of new phrases are coined every year, such as: software, meaning the contents of a computer program; hardware, the computer itself; video TV, for the storing and reproduction of TV programmes; to hijack, to seize an aeroplane for political or economic ends. All these phrases have been made out of existing words which are used in a new form.

## MINT

6. **in mint condition** – as good as new, perfect. 'These books are as good as the day they were printed; they are in mint condition.' The reference is to coins newly produced at the Royal Mint.

## CHEQUE

7. a **blank cheque** – permission to do whatever one considers desirable or necessary. 'I've been given a blank cheque to modernize the company's equipment.'

## PENNY

8. to **make an honest penny** – to make an honest living through hard work.
9. to **turn up like a bad penny** – a bad character who returns just when one was hoping to be rid of him.
10. **the penny drops** – the point of a remark is at last understood after a great deal of difficulty. 'I don't know how many times I told my husband that I was bored with fishing, but when he found me asleep over the rod one day, the penny dropped at last. He never took me fishing again.'
11. to **go/be two a penny** – to be in such plentiful supply that the pay offered is very small. 'You had better think of another way to make a living; artists are two a penny.'
12. **a penny for your thoughts** – what are you thinking about? May I know, or is it private? The person addressed is usually lost in thought. The phrase goes back to the sixteenth century.
13. **not to have / to be unable to rub two pennies together** – to be penniless, without any money; often said of someone who started without any money and got rich quickly. 'When I first met Tom three years ago, he couldn't rub two pennies together; look at him now!'
14. **not to care two pence for** – to be totally indifferent to. 'I don't care two pence what Martin thinks.' Two pence is almost valueless today.
15. to **cost a pretty penny** (colloquial) – to cost a considerable sum of money. 'It

will cost you a pretty penny to take Jackson to Court if you lose.'

1. to **spend a penny** – to pay a penny for the use of a public toilet. The price has risen in the last few years, but the phrase remains the same.

2. **penny wise pound foolish** – by trying to save a little one can lose a large sum. 'Herbert insisted on taking the bus to London Airport instead of a taxi. As a result, he missed his flight and had to pay £150 extra for a later one. Penny wise pound foolish!' cf. 'to **spoil a ship for a ha'porth of tar' 179/4**.

3. a **penny-farthing organization** – an organization that is managed inefficiently for lack of money or resources. 'We would have won the election if we had had a computer and a properly staffed office instead of the penny-farthing organization we had to make do with.' The farthing was worth one quarter of the old penny, and was abolished when the decimal currency was introduced in 1971.

4. **more kicks than halfpence** – criticism or punishment instead of gratitude. 'I get more kicks than halfpence for looking after my sister's dog when she is away on holiday. She always complains that I spoil the dog and give it too much to eat.'

## SHILLING

5. to **cut off with a shilling** – to disinherit a son. In the old days it was the custom for a father, who had been displeased with his son, to pay him a shilling and tell him to leave.

## DOLLAR

6. to **bet one's bottom dollar** – to be absolutely certain that something is going to happen or not going to happen. 'If my stockbroker recommends a share, you can bet your bottom dollar that it will go down.' The bottom dollar is the dollar at the bottom of a stack of banknotes, so if one bets one's bottom dollar, that means all the money in one's possession.

7. the **million /64 million dollar question** – the question that everybody would dearly like to know the answer to.

## GOLD

8. a **gold-digger** – an adventuress who obtains money from men by making use of her physical attraction.

9. **as good as gold** – very well behaved. Often said of a child who has been looked after by a relative or friend in the absence of the parents.

10. a **gold-mine** – a lucrative source of income. 'This business could be a gold mine if it were properly developed.'

11. **worth one's weight in gold** – someone whose services are considered invaluable. Often said of a trusted servant, or employee who cannot be easily replaced.

12. to **have a heart of gold** – to be a kind, generous, forgiving person whose qualities are much appreciated.

13. **a crock of gold** – a large reserve of money which will support one in old age.

    **the crock of gold at the end of the rainbow** – a treasure that is unattainable, a mere dream.

14. **fool's gold** – a worthless product or venture which is mistaken by foolish or ignorant people for something of great value. 'A firm which fell victim to a "fool's gold" swindle has collapsed with debts of £500,000 and the loss of 50 jobs' (*Daily Mail*, 21 January 1985). Literally, iron pyrites which, being yellow in colour, are sometimes mistaken for gold.

## SILVER

1. to **cross one's palm with silver** – to bribe someone.
2. **thirty pieces of silver** – the money paid to Judas Iscariot for betraying Jesus Christ. This phrase is used as a symbol of betrayal.

## DIAMOND

3. **a rough diamond** – someone whose kindness is concealed by a rough, unpolished manner. 'Jane's boy-friend is a bit of a rough diamond, but he's very nice when you get to know him.' A rough diamond is a diamond before it has been cut and polished.
4. **diamond cut diamond** – a contest between two equally sharp or cunning people. 'The two experts argued fiercely with each other the whole afternoon. It was diamond cut diamond.' The diamond is the hardest substance in the world, so it can only be cut by another diamond.

# 32. GAMES AND SPORTS

GAME

1. **the name of the game** is . . . – the outstanding feature or characteristic is . . . ; often said of a business, institution or school. 'The name of the game at our school is science.'
2. **two can play at that game / that's a game that two can play at** – in a contest, the opponent can use the same weapon or tactics. 'If you complain to the landlord about the noise, I will complain about the people you bring in at all hours; that's a game that two can play at.'
3. a **dirty game** – unfair, unethical behaviour. 'That's a dirty game of yours, threatening your men with dismissal unless they work overtime.'
4. to **have the game in one's hands** – to enjoy a decisive advantage over one's opponent. Said of card games when one has a winning hand.
5. to **know what** someone's **game is** – to understand what someone is scheming. 'You don't deceive me; I know what your game is!'
6. to **give the game away** – accidentally to betray one's purposes. 'Philip told the girl there was a spider just behind her, but his smile gave the game away.'
7. to be **game to the end** – to show courage to the end. 'Hammersmith were easily beaten by the Rangers, but they were game right up to the end of the match.'
8. to **play the game** – to be fair and honest in one's dealings with other people.
9. to **play a waiting game** – to act with caution, waiting for one's opponent to make a mistake.
10. to be **on one's game / off one's game** – to be in good form / to be below one's usual form, when playing a game.
11. **the game is up** – the deception has been exposed. 'The game is up; would you like to make a statement now?'
12. to **put** someone **off his game** – to spoil someone's game, to cause him to play badly. 'I wish you wouldn't photograph me all the time; you are putting me off my game.'
13. a **winning game** – a venture with a strong probability of success. 'Judging by his past successes, Paul is playing a winning game.'

    a **losing game** – a venture with little chance of success. 'You are playing a losing game competing with such a large and well-established company.'
14. a **deep game** – a secret plan or scheme. 'Stephen is playing a deep game; he won't talk about it to anyone.'
15. a **mug's game** – an activity which would only appeal to a fool. 'Crime is a mug's game; criminals always get caught in the end.'
16. a **completely new ballgame** – a totally different situation in which to continue the contest or struggle. 'I have just heard the police will be charging your son with pushing drugs in addition to being in possession of them. We are now in a completely new ballgame.'
17. a **game of chance** – a gamble whose outcome depends on chance, not on skill. 'If you play a game of chance, you can always blame your bad luck when you lose.'
18. to **beat** someone **at his own game** – to compete successfully with someone in his own specialized field. 'Heinrich Schliemann, the discoverer of the ancient city of Troy, had had no training in archaeology, but he beat the experts at their own game.'

1. **'So that's the game!'** – So that's what you are trying to do!
2. to **play games with** someone – to conceal, in a teasing or cruel manner. 'Stop playing games with me and tell me what you want!'
3. **on the game** – engaged in prostitution.
4. **fair game** – a legitimate target for attack or ridicule. 'Recruits in the army are fair game for the non-commissioned officers.' The phrase comes from the shooting of birds in the open season when they have a chance of escaping and are therefore fair game.
5. **game, set and match** – the decisive point which wins an argument or debate. 'So you do agree with me! Game, set and match to me.' This is the final point in tennis that wins the player a match in a tournament or championship.
6. a **slanging match** – a fierce argument conducted in abusive language.

## SPORT

7. to be **a good sport** – to act honourably and fairly, not to complain when one is beaten.

   to be **a bad sport** – to act dishonourably and unfairly, to complain and make excuses when one is beaten.
8. **a sporting chance** – a fair or reasonable chance. 'The examiner didn't give me a sporting chance to answer his questions. He went on to the next question before I could get the words out.'

## TO PLAY

9. to **play oneself in** – to get accustomed to the conditions before attempting anything bold or daring. 'The new Minister only expressed his opinion after he had played himself in and learned the routine of the department.'
10. to **play** someone **up** – (1) to tease or annoy. 'That little girl is playing her mother up; she is only pretending to be ill so that her mother will give her some extra attention.' (2) in the medical sense: when a part of the body causes pain from time to time. 'In the damp weather my left leg plays me up.'
11. to **play down** – to make little of, to discount. 'When I complained to the doctor about the pain in my elbow, I could tell he was trying to play it down.'
12. to **play hard to get** – to feign reluctance or unwillingness. 'Yvonne has refused your invitation to dinner again! Don't be discouraged; she is only playing hard to get.'
13. to **play safe** – to be extremely cautious, to avoid any risk. 'If you want to be sure of catching your aeroplane, you had better play safe and allow yourself two hours to get to the airport.'
14. to **play up to** – to flatter, with the object of gaining some advantage. 'I wonder why Campbell has been playing up to Lady Soames all the evening; he never does anything without a reason.'
15. to **play along with** – to pretend to co-operate with someone for a limited period. 'If you have any proof that your boss is breaking the law, let us know. In the meantime, play along with him.'
16. **played out** – out of date, no longer in fashion. 'There are signs that TV is played out as the main source of entertainment in the home now that video has come in.'
17. to **play fast and loose** with someone – to alternate warmth with coldness in a person's affection. 'John has been

playing fast and loose with Susan for months; she should find herself another boy-friend.'

1. to **play the fool** – to amuse oneself and one's companions joking and clowning.
2. to **play it cool** / to **keep one's cool** – to act calmly, in a restrained manner. 'Whatever you do, don't lose your temper with Paul; just play it cool.'
3. to **play havoc with** – to damage, ruin or destroy. 'Tony's chicken-pox has played havoc with his complexion. I hope he will lose the scars one day.' Havoc is derived from the military command 'Havock' of medieval times, meaning 'Kill all without quarter'.
4. to **play upon words** – to pun, to make a joke by using a word in a double sense. e.g. Question: 'When is a door not a door?' Answer: 'When it is ajar.' (ajar = only a little open; a jar = a container, e.g. a jar of jam.)
5. to **play one person off against another** – to make mischief between two people, often in order to divert their annoyance from oneself. 'Don't take any notice of what Stanley says; he is trying to play us off against each other.'
6. to **play upon** someone's **feelings, sympathy, etc.** – to arouse someone's feelings in order to make use of him. 'Don't let him play on your sympathy, Monica. He is only trying to get some money out of you.'
7. **foul play** – an act of violence (or treachery) which may result in murder. 'The girl has been missing seven days from her home; the police suspect foul play.'
8. to **toy with** an idea – to consider a possibility but only half seriously. 'I toyed once with the idea of emigrating to Canada, but rejected it almost at once because of the climate.'

## FOOTBALL AND OTHER BALL GAMES

9. to **kick off** – to start. 'The quizmaster kicked off by asking the first contestant where he came from.' The phrase comes from football, when the centre forward gives the ball the first kick to start the game.
10. to **kick over the traces** – to throw off all restraint. 'George is £2,000 in debt. He has been kicking over the traces again.' The traces are the harness a horse tries to get rid of so that it can kick more freely.
11. **a kick-back / a kick-back commission** – the commission paid to someone for introducing a client to an agency. The commission is usually split in equal shares between the agency and the person making the introduction. The 'kick-back' is not disclosed to the client, such payments being probably illegal. The phrase comes from football when a player kicks the ball back to one of his own side to prevent the other side getting possession of it.
12. a **political football** – a cause which is good in itself but which has become a political issue so that it is no longer judged on its own merits. 'What a pity, vivisection has become a political football.'
13. **the ball is in your court** – it is your turn to take the next step (in a negotiation, dispute, etc.). 'They have offered us £500 compensation. Are you going to accept or refuse their offer? The ball is in your court.' The reference is to tennis when the ball falls in a player's court and it is in his turn to hit the ball back.
14. to **play ball** (American colloquialism) – to co-operate with. 'If he won't play ball, we can always find someone who will.'
15. to **have the ball at one's feet** – to have the initiative, to have the opportunity one has been waiting for. 'Now that

the boss has put him in charge, Andrew has the ball at his feet.'

1. **on the ball** – alert, quick, and very keen. 'I am very pleased with my new assistant. You don't have to say anything to him twice; he is on the ball all the time.'

2. to **keep the ball rolling** – to keep the interest alive. 'At the meeting, the chairman kept the ball rolling by inviting each person to ask questions.'

## CRICKET

3. **'That's not cricket!'** – that's not fair, not honourable. 'When I caught Sam listening in to their conversation on the extension, I told him in no uncertain terms that that was not cricket!'

4. to **catch out** – to find someone in the act of doing wrong. 'Tim was caught out by his teacher playing truant yesterday.' In cricket, a batsman is dismissed if the ball he has hit is caught by a fielder; he is then said to be caught out.

5. to **play a straight bat** – to act in an honest, straightforward manner. 'You can trust Mike; he always plays a straight bat.'

6. **off one's own bat** – without asking for anyone's assistance or permission. 'You shouldn't have invited Mr and Mrs Robinson to dinner off your own bat like that. You should have spoken to your parents first.' From cricket, meaning the score made by one player in a game.

7. to **bat on a sticky wicket** – to take action in unfavourable conditions. 'We have been batting on a sticky wicket all the morning; it was obvious that the judge was against us.' From cricket, when the ground is damp from the rain, and the bowler has the batsman at a disadvantage.

8. **a long stop** – a last resort, a person one can rely upon when everyone else has failed. 'Would you mind guaranteeing my loan from the bank? You can be the long stop.' In cricket, the long stop is the player who stands behind the wicket keeper to stop the ball if he misses it.

9. to be **100 not out** – to be a hundred years old and still alive. The reference is to a player's innings when a batsman has made 100 runs and is still in the game.

10. to **have had a good innings** – to have had a long life, marriage or career. 'I suppose I can't complain; I'm eighty years old and sound in health and mind. I've had a good innings.' The innings is the time the batsman spends at the wicket scoring runs.

11. to be **bowled out / bowled over** – to be taken completely by surprise, to be unable to explain one's actions. 'Poor Angela, she was bowled out by the first question on the TV show, and it was such an easy one, too.' The phrase comes from cricket, the batsman being dismissed when the ball hits his stumps.

12. to be **stumped** – to be baffled, to be unable to solve a problem or answer a question. 'When my pupils asked me for the meaning of "mundungus", I was stumped for an answer. I only remembered later that it meant bad tobacco.'

## GOLF

13. to **stymie / to be stymied** – to obstruct or hinder / to be obstructed or hindered. 'I was planning to sell the house, but my sister has stymied me by letting some rooms.' A stymie is a golfing term meaning that a player can stymie his opponent's ball by interposing his own between it and the hole.

## KITE

1. to **fly a kite** – to put forward an idea (usually in a ministerial speech) to test public reaction. If the reaction is favourable, the idea may be adopted; if it is not, the idea can be disowned. A kite is a framework of paper and cardboard that is flown at the end of a string, in the wind. The kite gives an indication of the direction and strength of the wind. The toy is so called because it hovers like the bird of the same name.

## BOXING

2. to **keep up / to drop one's guard** – to keep one's defences in a state of readiness / to neglect one's defences. 'History shows that countries that drop their guard are often overrun by stronger and more aggressive ones.'
3. to **pull one's punches** – to struggle half-heartedly. 'If we are to compete successfully with Phillips, we can't afford to pull our punches; we must be ruthless.' A boxing term meaning to strike with less than one's full weight, to strike with a light blow.
4. to **beat** someone **to the punch** – to obtain an advantage over someone before he has time to do the same to you. 'Our book came out a week before Turner's. I'm glad we beat him to the punch.'
5. to **win a round** – to inflict a temporary but not a decisive defeat on the enemy. 'We have won a round, but we still have a hard struggle ahead of us.' A boxing match between amateurs is divided into 3 rounds, and between professionals 6–15 rounds.
6. to **win on points** – to win a useful advantage without crushing one's opponent. 'At the College debate, we won narrowly on points.' In a boxing match the contestants are given points at the end of each round, and the one who has scored more points at the end of the fight is the winner, unless the match has been terminated by a knock-out.

## SKATING

7. to **put/get one's skates on** (colloquial) – to hurry up.
8. to **skate over** – to deal superficially with. 'When I discussed our project with my partner, he expressed his approval while skating over the difficulties.'

## ROWING

9. **not to pull one's weight** – to leave one's share of the work to others. 'If Baxter doesn't pull his weight, we would be better off without him. He is putting too much strain on the rest of us.' A rowing phrase for moving the oar through the water without putting one's weight behind the stroke.
10. to **put one off one's stroke** – to distract someone from what he is doing. 'I wish you wouldn't criticize my driving; you are putting me off my stroke.'

## ARCHERY

11. **wide of the mark** – inaccurate, wrong. 'The auctioneer's estimate was wide of the mark. He overvalued the necklace by nearly half.'
12. to **hit/miss the mark** – to get something right/wrong. 'How extraordinary! When Madame Vernet told Julie's fortune, she hit the mark every time.' The mark is the target in archery.
13. to **overshoot the mark** – to exceed the limit. 'You overshot the mark, didn't you? You spent £300 more than your grant.'
14. **nearer/closer to the mark** – almost

correct. 'When you said that unemployment would go above four million, you were nearer the mark than you realized.'

SHOOTING

1. to **shoot the (traffic) lights** – to drive a vehicle past the lights when they are showing red or amber.
2. to **shoot off** – to commence proceedings. 'Tom shot off by welcoming the delegates to the conference.'

HUNTING

3. to give someone **a fair crack of the whip** – to give someone a fair opportunity, a fair share, e.g. of time or attention. 'You can say a lot in five minutes. I thought the chairman gave you a fair crack of the whip.'
4. to be **at bay** – to be beset by a danger from which there is no escape. 'The robbers are at bay and the police are calling on them to give themselves up.'

   to **keep at bay** – to prevent a danger from materializing when one is already under threat, but usually for only a short time. 'The medicine won't cure the arthritis in your thumb but it will keep it at bay.' The 'bay' means the baying of the hounds in pursuit of their quarry.
5. **in full cry** – in eager pursuit. 'A pity you said that about Sandra in your book. Her relations and friends are in full cry.' The reference is to the barking of the hounds as they approach their quarry.

ANGLING

6. to **rise to the bait** – to respond to a hint, temptation or provocation in the way hoped for. 'Whenever I want to infuriate Dennis, I make a violent attack on modern art. He rises to the bait every time.' The reference is to fish which rise to the surface of the water for food.

CYCLING

7. to **ride in tandem** with – to work in perfect harmony with. 'The twins ride in tandem; they manage the office without a hint of disagreement, and smile approval of each other throughout the day.'
8. to **back-pedal** – to withdraw quickly from an offer or statement one has made. 'Simpson promised he would look after our dog if we wanted to take a holiday, but now he is back-pedalling on his offer.'

RIDING

9. to **take for a ride** – to make a fool of, to cheat. 'I wish I hadn't paid Hughes all that money in advance; he has taken me for a ride.'
10. to **ride roughshod over** someone – to show a complete lack of consideration for a person's wishes or feelings, to treat him with harshness. 'The landlord has ridden roughshod over us; we asked him for a month's notice, and he has given us twenty-four hours to get out.' The shoes of a horse that is roughshod have the heads of the nails projecting to prevent slipping.
11. to **ride for a fall** – to bring disaster on oneself by behaving in an arrogant or provocative manner. 'Since Brian became the boss he has made a lot of enemies among the staff; I'm afraid he is riding for a fall.'
12. to keep someone **on the trot** – to keep someone busy, always on the move. 'The sightseers kept me on the trot all day long. I am exhausted.'
13. to **trot out** – to exhibit for approval.

'When I asked the official for information about language schools in London, she trotted out a number of brochures, commenting on each with great enthusiasm.' The phrase comes from trotting a horse to show off its paces in front of a customer.

1. to **win in a canter / an easy canter** – to win easily, without having to make any real effort. 'Hazel Smith won the election in an easy canter.' A canter is short for a Canterbury gallop, the slow easy pace that the pilgrims are supposed to have ridden on their way to Canterbury.
2. to **saddle with / to be saddled with** – to burden someone with responsibility for / to be burdened with a responsibility for. 'On the death of my father, I was saddled with the debts of his estate.'
3. to **remain in the saddle** – to remain in a position of authority. 'Despite the attempts by the clergy in the diocese to remove him, the bishop remained in the saddle until his death.'
4. to keep someone **on a tight rein** – to keep someone under strict control. 'Andy's father keeps him on a tight rein; he has to account to his father for every penny he spends.'
5. to be **back in harness** – to be restored to one's employment or office. Often said of someone returning to work after recovering from an illness. 'I am so glad to be back in harness. I'm miserable when I'm away from my work.'
6. to **die in harness** – to continue to work until the day of one's death. 'I hope I die in harness; I shouldn't know what to do with myself if I retired.'
7. to **win one's spurs** – to win recognition for outstanding ability. Originally, to gain a knighthood in recognition of one's courage in battle. The knight was then presented with a pair of gilt spurs. cf. 'to **win one's colours' 15/6.**

## SWIMMING AND DIVING

8. to **swim with / against the stream** – to think or act in accordance with / contrary to the views of the majority. 'Original thinkers seldom swim with the stream.'
9. **it's sink or swim** – in a desperate situation, one must resort to desperate remedies. 'I had to dismiss half our staff this morning; we are simply not earning enough to pay the wages; it's sink or swim for us.'
10. to be **in the swim** – to be active in – or aware of – what's going on. 'You didn't know that Lloyd has resigned from the government? You can't be in the swim any more.'
11. to **dive in at the deep end** – to be put to the test without any preparation. 'I'm a great believer in diving in at the deep end. The sooner young barristers get into court the better.'

## JUMPING

12. to be **for / to be due for the high jump** (slang) – to incur a severe punishment. 'If Mrs Brown finds out that Yvette has been wearing her clothes, she will be for the high jump.'
13. to **jump at an opportunity** – to accept an opportunity eagerly. 'I am sure that Diane would jump at the opportunity of learning French in such pleasant surroundings.'
14. to **jump the gun** – to take premature action, with the object of gaining an unfair advantage. 'You jumped the gun, didn't you, calling here at this hour of the morning? Mrs Graham will be making a statement to the press at three o'clock this afternoon.' The reference is to a sportsman who starts the race before the gun has been fired.
15. to **jump to conclusions** – to draw an inference from insufficient evidence.

'Aren't you jumping to conclusions? Just because I have taken Jenny out a couple of times this week, it doesn't mean that I want to marry her.'

1. to be **one jump ahead** – to be in a position to anticipate the words or actions of someone else. 'I know exactly what he is going to say before he is half-way through his sentence. I am always one jump ahead of him.'

## SKIPPING

2. **to skip** – to do without, to dispense with. 'Shall we skip the introduction and start the game?' The literal meaning is to jump lightly over something.

## RUNNING

3. to **run rings round** someone (slang) – to outmatch someone decisively. 'Amanda is a useful tennis player but her brother Ted can run rings round her.' From athletics, when one competitor runs so much faster than his rival that he can make a circle round him and still reach the winning post first.
4. **in the long run** – ultimately, looking a long time ahead. 'In the long run it is surely better to have your own house, even if it means having to pay a big mortgage for it.'

   **in the short run** – in the near future, looking only a short time ahead. 'In the short run, it is better to enjoy oneself while one can.'
5. **hit-and-run** – to knock someone down and drive away without stopping. 'They should increase the penalties for hit-and-run offences.'
6. a **running commentary** – a continuous account of an event while it is taking place. 'While the two boys were fighting together outside the girls' bedroom, Margaret gave her sister a running commentary.'
7. to **make the running** – to take the lead, to be the most prominent in any activity. 'All the Robsons were talented writers, but it was the mother who made the running with her magnificent biographies.'
8. to be **in/out of the running** for – to have a chance / no chance. 'Martin's headmaster has just told us that Martin is in the running for a scholarship, but he won't say more at the moment.'
9. to be **run down** – to be lacking in vitality and energy, easily tired. 'You look run down to me; you could do with a good holiday.'
10. to **run** someone **down** – to speak ill of / to find fault with someone. 'Joe is always running me down; I wonder what he's got against me?'
11. the **runner-up** – a competitor who comes second to the winner. 'Contrary to all expectations, Miss United Kingdom, the hot favourite for the Miss World Contest, had to be satisfied with being the runner-up to Miss France.'
12. to **run out of steam** – to lose vigour / momentum. 'Our new magazine did very well at first – we had lots of new ideas we wanted to experiment with – but after the first six numbers, we ran out of steam.'
13. to be **on the run** – to be in flight from. 'The jail-breakers are on the run, but it is only a question of time before they are caught.'
14. to **run** someone / something **close** – to rival, to compete strongly with. 'You are always saying how stupid our Director is, but I must say his Deputy runs him very close!'
15. to **run away with an idea** – to make a hasty assumption which is not supported by the facts. 'You shouldn't run away with the idea that because

you haven't been elected chairman, we don't appreciate your services to the association.'

1. to be **an also-ran** – to be a failure. 'Hugh was an also-ran in everything he tried to do and deeply resented his failure.' The phrase refers to horse racing: an also-ran is a horse that comes past the winning post after the first three.
2. **the first hurdle** – the first obstacle to one's plans. 'The first hurdle will be to obtain planning permission from the local council before we start building the new extension.'

## LEAPING

3. **by leaps and bounds** – with great rapidity. 'Since Tom has been taking private lessons in maths, he has progressed by leaps and bounds.'
4. a **leap in the dark** – a hazardous undertaking whose results cannot be predicted. 'When Baden-Powell started the Boy Scout movement in 1908, he could have had no idea that it would be such a success; it was a leap in the dark.'
5. to **leap to mind** – to suggest itself immediately to one, usually through an association of ideas. 'When William told us that his school-days had been the happiest time of his life, the memory of his being tossed in a blanket in the school dormitory leapt to my mind.'

## CLIMBING

6. to **climb down** – to withdraw an assertion or accusation one has energetically upheld, to accept a defeat. 'You had better climb down while there is still time, or you may find yourself in court.'

## CHESS

7. an **opening gambit** – the first step in a dispute or contest. 'Harvey's opening gambit was to call an emergency meeting.' In chess, the phrase means the offer of a sacrifice in the opening of a game in order to obtain a positional or tactical advantage. The idiom and the chess term do not therefore correspond in meaning. The 'opening gambit' (gambito) was first recorded in 1561 by the Spanish chess player, Ruy Lopez.
8. to **checkmate** – to make a move which puts an end at once to one's opponent's plans. 'Our main competitors have checkmated us by taking us over.' Checkmate is a chess term meaning a decisive attack on the opponent's King which brings the game to a finish.
9. **only a pawn (in the game)** – only a person of very minor importance who is manipulated by stronger forces. 'We none of us have any say in our future; we are just pawns, nothing more.' In chess, the pawns are the weakest pieces which are often sacrificed in attacks on the opponent.
10. a **stalemate** – a position in which neither party to a dispute can take effective steps against the other. In chess, stalemate occurs when one of the players is unable to move any of his pieces.

## CRIBBAGE

11. to **leave in the lurch** – to desert someone in need of one's help. 'James was only asking for a small loan. How could you have left such an old friend in the lurch!' In cribbage, the loser was said to be 'in the lurch' when the winner scored 61 before he had scored 31.

## GAMES OF CARDS

1. to be **a card / quite a card** – to be a notable character, to be eccentric. 'Old Mr Williams is quite a card, isn't he? He walks his dog up and down the road at all hours of the day and night.'
2. **one's leading/trump card** – one's strongest point, one's main strength. 'Jane's leading card was her charm. She played it time and again to good effect.'
3. to **play one's best card** – to employ the best means at one's disposal to get the desired result. 'In the court action Ian played his best card by calling a surprise witness.'
4. to **play one's cards well** – to act with skill and good judgement, to make the most of one's chances. 'At the interview, Jack played his cards well by trying to show how he could be useful to the company.'
5. to **hold all the cards in one's hands** – to be in a position to dictate the conditions. 'You will have to do as he says; he is holding all the cards in his hands.'
6. to **show one's cards** – to show one's intentions. 'I wouldn't show your cards if I were you. In business it is often best to keep one's intentions to oneself.'
7. **on the cards** – likely to happen, possible. 'It's on the cards that Julian will be getting married soon.' The phrase comes from fortune-telling, when the future is read in the cards.
8. to **have a card up one's sleeve** – to have some surprise or secret in reserve, unknown to one's adversary. The idiom is taken from cheating at cards, when a player conceals an ace up his sleeve.
9. to **stack the cards** against someone – to place obstacles in the way of someone's success. 'If you start a business, I'm afraid you will find the cards stacked against you. You have very little capital, and hardly any experience.'
10. to **put one's cards on the table** – to make one's intentions clear. 'Richard told me he was going to put his cards on the table but I had the impression that he was hiding something from me.'
11. **one's long suit** – one's principal strength. 'I'll be glad to help your daughter with her O-levels in history. History was always my long suit.'
12. to **follow suit** – to do exactly the same as the person immediately preceding you. 'When their host began to attack the government, Brian got up and left the room; soon afterwards, the other guests followed suit.' In many card games, a player is obliged to play a card of the same suit as the last card that has been played.
13. to **trump** someone's **ace** – to counter a strong argument / action of one's opponent with an argument / action that is even stronger. 'When the application of William Morris, the motor car manufacturer, to join a golf club was refused by its members, he trumped their ace by buying the club.'
14. to **trump up a charge** – to concoct a charge against someone by producing false evidence. 'All these charges against me have been trumped up. There isn't a word of truth in any of them.' The word derives from the French 'tromper' meaning to deceive.
15. to **come / turn up trumps** – to prove surprisingly helpful. 'Our neighbour has never had anything to do with us, but when Nancy had a bad fall, he turned up trumps, rang the hospital and gave her first aid.'
16. to **play one's last trump** – to use one's last asset. 'When Mark was made redundant as a chemist, there was noth-

ing for it but to play his last trump and return to his old school as a teacher.'

1. **a poker face** – a face that shows no expression so that one's feelings remain concealed. 'I never know whether Henry is pleased or annoyed; he has a real poker face.' The phrase comes from the card game of the same name.

## BOARD

2. to be **above-board** – to be honest, respectable. The 'board' is the table on which the card games were played. When the players had their hands 'above board', they couldn't change the cards or cheat. It follows that, if someone is 'above-board', you can rely on him not to cheat you.
3. to **sweep the board** – to vanquish all one's opponents and win all the prizes.

## DICING

4. **no dice** (slang) – no luck, no success. 'Sorry, no dice. I can't lend you any money this time.'
5. **as straight as a die** – absolutely honest and fair. A 'die' was originally the single form of dice, but is obsolete except in the phrases 'straight as a die' and 'the die is cast'.
6. **the die is cast** – the gamble has been taken and is irrevocable. The words used by Julius Caesar in 49 BC when he crossed the Rubicon.

## THE FAIRGROUND

7. **in full swing** – of social events, going off well, a success. 'When we arrived, the party was already in full swing.'
8. **what you lose on the swings you gain on the roundabouts** – there is nothing to be said for or against a particular course of action because the advantages and disadvantages are evenly balanced. 'You eat better at the Victoria Hotel, but then it's much further from the beach than the Cavendish; what you lose on the swings you gain on the roundabouts.'

## 33. THE THEATRE

### SHOW

1. to **steal the show** – to capture all the attention. 'At the garden party, the innocent charm of her beautiful teen-age daughter stole the show from the hostess.'
2. **the show must go on** – one must fulfil one's obligations whatever the cost to one's own feelings. 'I am so sorry that your husband has lost his job, but you cannot cancel your campaign now; the show must go on.' There is a tradition in the theatre that the show must go on, whatever happens, except in the case of accident or illness.
3. to **give the show away** – to tell everyone what is going to happen. 'Father will be making an announcement after dinner to the guests, but I won't tell you what about; that would be giving the show away.'
4. **good show** – well done, splendid. 'So you will be able to come to the party. Good show!' (rather dated but still in use).

   **it's a bad show** – disappointing news, very wrong. 'It's a bad show Alan wasn't given leave to come; what a mean way to treat him.'
5. to **get the show on the road** – to put an idea into effect, to get something organized. 'You deserve the credit for getting the show on the road.' The 'show' was originally the theatrical company on tour.
6. **only a side-show** – an activity of only incidental importance. 'The company's work in Australia is only a side-show; the bulk of the business is in London.' In a circus, there used to be side-shows like the 'strong man', the bearded lady and the freaks who were on display in the intervals of the performance but were not part of it.
7. a **show-down** – a show of strength to settle a dispute and force a person to withdraw or apologize. 'If that lout doesn't stop annoying my sister, I'll have a show-down with him.' The reference is to poker when the players lay down their cards on the table face upwards to show the strength of their hands.

### SCENE

8. **behind the scenes** – out of the public view. 'There is always a lot of manoeuvring behind the scenes before a new government is formed.' A theatrical term for all the work done behind the stage by the electricians, make-up artists, costume designers and so on (which the audience does not see).
9. to **make a scene** – to give way to one's emotions, especially anger or grief, in a dramatic manner. 'The bill is much too high, but for goodness sake let's pay it rather than make a scene.'
10. to **set the scene for** – to describe the background to an event (historic, literary, sporting, etc.). 'Before he began his lecture on the Battle of Jutland, Mr Walker set the scene for the naval cadets by describing the background to the action.'
11. to **come on the scene** – to appear, to make one's presence felt. 'Until Marx and Engels came on the scene, no one had attached any importance to the class war.'

### STAGE

12. **stage-fright** – the fear experienced when speaking in front of an audience. 'Although John prepared his sermons with great care, he always had a moment or two of stage-fright when he addressed the congregation.'

A theatrical term for the nervousness of actors / actresses on the stage, especially when they are appearing for the first time. cf. **'first-night nerves' 259/3**.

1. a **stage-whisper** – a whisper that is intended to be heard by others, as a whisper on the stage is intended to be heard by the audience. 'During the headmaster's end-of-term speech, his wife would entertain the boys with her stage whispers which could be heard all over the assembly room.'
2. to **stage-manage** – to plan in detail an operation or important event. 'At the annual conference of the party, one delegate complained that the speeches had been stage-managed.' In the theatre, every detail of the production is stage-managed.
3. to **stage a recovery / a come-back** – to repeat one's earlier success, after retirement or failure. 'The majority of athletes who try to stage a come-back are unsuccessful.'
4. to **upstage** a rival – to divert attention from a rival, to put him at a disadvantage. 'The managing director resented the way Forbes was trying to upstage him at the board meeting.' An actor is upstaged when he is obliged to turn his back on the audience in order to speak to his colleague upstage, i.e. at the back of the stage. When this happens, the attention of the audience is centred on the rival upstage, and the actor at the front of the stage is at a disadvantage.

## PART

5. to **throw oneself into a part** – to accept with enthusiasm a duty that has been laid on one. 'Having been unexpectedly appointed chairman of the Housing Committee on the local council, Patrick threw himself into the part with all his energy.'
6. to **look the part** of – to resemble a particular type of person in manner and appearance. 'You may hate being a captain in the Royal Artillery, but you certainly look the part.'
7. to **play a part** – (1) to assist in an activity or project, to co-operate in. 'Tom played an important part in starting the local youth club.' (2) to assume a false role, to pretend to be somebody one is not. 'Jeremy plays the part of the caring nephew to perfection, but don't let him fool you; it's her money he's after.'

## PLAY, PIECE AND ROLE

8. **as good as a play** – as entertaining as a performance at the theatre. 'It was most amusing to watch Hobson wriggling under your cross-examination – as good as a play.' A comment allegedly made by Charles II on a debate in the House of Lords.
9. **the villain of the piece** – the real cause of the evil. 'There is no doubt that inflation is the villain of the piece; it has bankrupted thousands of small businesses and even put state industries in danger.' A theatrical phrase for the wicked character in a drama.
10. to **cast** someone **in the role of the villain** – to fix blame on someone, to hold him responsible for a wrong. 'Since you have cast me in the role of the villain, I hope you will give me the opportunity to reply to your accusations.' The reference is to the distribution of roles among the actors/actresses in a theatre company.

## ACT

11. to **put on an act** – to dissimulate, to act in a way that is deliberately misleading. 'That boy is putting on an act; I don't believe he has hurt himself at all.'

1. to **get in on the act** – to imitate someone else in the hope of obtaining the same advantages. 'I have been making a good living from my mushroom growing, and now I see that my neighbour is getting in on the act, too.'
2. to **get/put one's act together** – to get oneself organized. 'You had better get your act together before you lose any more customers.' This phrase comes from the circus when the members of a troupe get their act ready for the performance.

SOME MORE FROM THE THEATRE

3. **first-night nerves** – an attack of nerves that some people experience when taking part in a public event, especially when it is for the first time. 'Winston Churchill often suffered from first-night nerves on the eve of an important debate in the House of Commons.' 'First-night nerves' refers to the nervousness felt by the actors/actresses the first night a play is performed in public. cf. **'stage-fright' 257/12**.
4. to **take one's cue from** – to follow someone else's example. 'When we were staying with the Garners, we noticed that the children took their cue from the eldest boy; when he began to laugh, they would all laugh, too.' In the theatre the cue is a gesture or word spoken by one actor which serves as a warning signal for another to say his words.
5. **a dress-rehearsal for** – a final preparation for. 'In the early part of the twentieth century, five years at a public school was a dress-rehearsal for military service on the Western Front.' A dress-rehearsal is the final rehearsal when actors wear the costumes in which they will appear at the performance.
6. to be **in the limelight** – to be the centre of public attention. Limelight usually has the meaning of an intense but passing attention. 'My son was in the limelight for a few days for challenging the school bully, but the excitement soon died down.' The limelight was used in the nineteenth century for lighting the stage. It would focus on one actor on the stage, leaving the others in the dark. Limelight is produced by heating lime in a hot flame.
7. to **play to the gallery** – to court the applause of the uneducated by showing off in front of them. 'Although Borotra was one of the most brilliant tennis players of all time, he sometimes played to the gallery.' The cheapest seats in the theatre are in the gallery.
8. to **ring the curtain down** – to put an end to; used in connection with life, marriage, career, happiness, business, plans, etc. 'The scandal rang the curtain down on a promising career.' In former times a bell was rung at the end of each act as a signal for the curtain to be lowered.
9. to **pull strings** – to make use of private influence to obtain favours. 'I've had no promotion, although I've been ten years in the service. Can't you pull a string for me?' From puppeteering, i.e. the manipulation of puppets by pulling the strings.
10. **If I had a magic wand . . .** – a picturesque way of expressing a vain wish. 'If I had a magic wand, I would do away with unemployment this very moment.' In fairy stories and pantomimes, the fairy godmother accomplishes good by waving her magic wand and making a wish which is immediately realized.

TRICKS

11. **a bag of tricks / the whole bag of tricks** (colloquial) – all a person's tools or

equipment. 'I've no idea where the plumber has gone, but I'm sure he'll be back; he has left his whole bag of tricks in the bathroom.' The term comes from the conjuror's bag in which he carries his equipment for the performance of his tricks.

1. to **do a vanishing trick / one of his vanishing tricks** – to disappear suddenly when it suits someone's purpose. 'The day before the rent was due, Andy did one of his vanishing tricks.' The allusion is to the magician's art of causing a person to disappear and reappear again.
2. **that should do the trick** – that should serve our purpose. 'I've stopped the bleeding and bandaged the wound; that should do the trick until you get him to hospital.'
3. to **have a trick** – to have a habit or mannerism. 'It sounds as if the man you were talking to was Paul, because Paul has the same trick of repeating himself.'
4. to **be/get up to one's old tricks again** – to use a device (generally dishonest) that one has used successfully in the past. 'So Philip has been up to his old tricks again. It's extraordinary how many people fall for his hard-luck story.'
5. to **know a trick or two / a thing or two** – to acquire a certain cunning in the course of one's experience. 'You learn a trick or two after twenty years in business.'
6. to **play a confidence trick on** someone – to tell someone a falsehood to get money out of him. So called because the success of the trick depends on winning the confidence of the victim.

## THE CIRCUS

7. to **walk a tight-rope** – to act with the greatest possible caution in an extremely delicate situation. 'The two teenage boys are always quarrelling with each other, so their mother has to walk a tight-rope between them.'
8. **to go/put through the hoop** – to undergo / to subject someone to a harsh discipline. 'The lieutenant really put us through the hoop when we joined the ship.' At circuses, lions, tigers and leopards are put through the hoop for the entertainment of the audience. cf. 'to **go through the mill' 235/9**.
9. to **have / not to have a crystal ball** – to have / not to have the means to predict the future. This phrase is often used ironically, for example: 'If I knew, Inspector Francis, how much money my company will be making this time next year, I should be only too pleased to let you know. Unfortunately, I don't have a crystal ball.' The reference is to the crystal ball used by fortune-tellers.

# 34. WORD AND WORDS

WORD

1. **a man of his word** – a trustworthy man who will do what he promises.

2. **a word to the wise** – one word of advice or even a hint is enough for an intelligent man. The derivation is from the Latin 'verbum sat sapienti', a word is enough to the wise.

3. **as good as one's word** – to do exactly what one has promised. Often said when the promise is unlikely to be kept. 'I didn't think for one moment Bob would keep his promise but he was as good as his word'.

4. to **break one's word** – to fail to do what one has promised. cf. to **go back on one's word.**

5. **from the word go** – right from the very beginning. 'From the word go Smithers has made trouble for us.'

6. to **give one's word** – to pledge one's honour on the truth of one's word.

7. to **give the word to** – (of officers in the armed services and the police) to command – 'The Major gave his men the word to open fire on the enemy.'

8. to **go back on one's word** – to change one's mind about keeping a promise in a way which causes great indignation. 'You can't go back on your word now; without the loan you promised us, we shall lose all our savings.'

9. to **have a word with someone** – to have a brief conversation with someone.

10. to **have the last word** – (1) to insist one is in the right in an argument. 'Denis is so argumentative; he will always have the last word.' (2) to take the final decision. 'I like your cost-cutting idea but you had better talk it over with the Manager; he has the last word.' (3) the most authoritative source of information on a subject. 'Gilbert has the last word on the life of Winston Churchill, having written many volumes on his chosen subject.'

11. **his word is law** – he must be obeyed. 'When we were children, our father expected us to do what he told us without questioning his orders. His word was law.'

12. **I don't believe a word of it** – the whole story is a lie from start to finish.

13. **in a word** – very briefly. 'Our son is bored with the office work, he dislikes his colleagues and he quarrels with the boss. In a word, he hates the job.'

14. to **keep one's word** – to do what one has promised.

15. to **leave word** – to leave a message. 'They left word for Anne at the hospital to come back later.'

16. **mum's the word** – don't talk about it to anyone. This is a secret between the two of us; 'mum' is used here to describe the expressive sound made by a person when his lips are closed. The word 'mum' is related to the verb mumble, to speak weakly, and to mummers who, in earlier times, entertained at Christmas parties in dumb shows.

17. **my word** – an explanation of surprise. 'My word!, this is the second time you've had a rise in your wages this year. Aren't you doing well!'

18. **my word is my bond** – my word is as good as a signed contract. 'You can rely on my promise, even though it is not in writing. My word is my bond.'

19. **not the word for it** – an inadequate or unsufficiently strong description. 'Impolite is not the word for it, he was downright insulting!'

1. **not to get in a word edgeways** – to find it impossible to take part in a conversation because the other person is talking continuously.

2. to **preach the word** – to preach the gospel of Jesus Christ.

3. to **put in a good word for someone** – to praise or recommend someone to a third party, who is in a position to help him. 'I would like the job Mrs Hornby is advertising. When you see her tomorrow, can you put in a good word for me.'

4. **say the word** – you only need to ask, and your wishes will be carried out. 'Say the word, and I'll marry you tomorrow.'

5. **send word** – send a message. 'As soon as you arrive, send word that you are safe.'

6. **spread the word** – inform as many people as possible. 'Jack Dickson will be speaking at the town hall at eight o'clock on Saturday. Spread the word.'

7. to **take someone at his word** – to act on the literal meaning of someone's words without making sure that he means to be taken seriously. 'I told Stephen to be sure to visit us if ever he came to Spain. Two weeks later, he arrived at our villa with six suitcases. He had taken me at my word.'

8. to **take someone's word for it** – to believe that he is speaking the truth without making further inquiries. 'Don't take my word for it – you can see for yourself.'

9. the **buzz word** – the fashionable word. 'The buzz word is 'community', e.g. 'community services', 'community care', 'community health', the 'European Community', the 'Chinese community', the 'community centre', and 'community singing'.

10. the **last word in** – the very best and most up-to-date. 'The hotel is the last word in luxury and elegance.'

11. the **operative word** – the most important word. 'You can take any route you like but please drive carefully. The operative word is carefully.'

12. **upon my word** – an exclamation expressing surprise (usually unpleasant) or impatience. 'Upon my word, what is the matter with our Managing Clerk? He is always ill – he must be a hypochondriac!'

13. the **word is** – a rumour, usually well founded, that something will happen. 'The word is that next month we shall be ordered overseas.'

14. **word came** – information was received.

15. **word for word** – literally. 'I translated the passage word for word from German into English.'

16. **word of honour** – (first person). I pledge my honour that I am telling the truth. cf. to **give one's word 261/6**.

17. **word perfect** – able to recite every word of a poem, part etc. without a mistake.

18. **word splitting** – (derogatory) making subtle distinctions, for example distinguishing between 'governance' and 'government', 'gentlemanly' and 'gentlemanlike', 'preciseness' and 'precision'. cf. to **'split hairs' 79/10**.

## WORDS

19. a **man of few words** – a man who avoids conversation whenever he can. Sometimes used as a euphemism for an unsociable person.

    a **man of many words** – a garrulous person, one who prefers three words when one would have done.

1. **actions speak louder than words** – 'The clergyman had often preached against the sin of drunkenness. One day, he was arrested for being drunk and disorderly. Actions speak louder than words.'
2. to **bandy words** – to enter into an argument with someone. 'Don't bandy words with that man. He is a violent character.
3. **be lost for words** – to be so astonished or shocked that one is unable to put one's feelings into words. cf. **words fail me 263/17.**
4. **big words** – boastful words. 'We shall beat the champions easily.' 'Big words.'
5. **empty words** – meaningless words. 'Sam telephoned this morning to apologize for his behaviour last night.' 'Empty words!'
6. **famous last words** – a humorous comment predicting disaster for an impractical undertaking. 'With modern technology, we can climb Everest in half the time it took Hillary in 1953.' 'Famous last words!'
7. **hang upon someone's words** – to pay slavish attention to what someone is saying. 'Sharon is full of admiration for Paul and hangs upon his words.' 'Words' may be replaced by 'lips' with the same meaning.
8. to **have words with** – to quarrel with. 'Ever since my sister had words with our neighbour, he hasn't spoken to us.'
9. **in other words** – put in another way in order to summarize what the speaker/writer has said or to deduce his true intention from the words he has used. 'Anne is sorry she can't come with us to France but the crossing always makes her feel sick and the trip would be too expensive.' 'In other words, she doesn't want to come with us!'
10. **let the words stand** – make no change. 'The editor is satisfied with the original wording of your article. Let the words stand.'
11. **mark my words** – listen carefully to what I am telling you. 'Mark my words, the boy will ruin himself before he is forty,' said by George V about his son, Edward Prince of Wales, shortly before the death of the King.
12. **not in so many words** – not actually said, although it was clearly meant. 'Did Margaret refuse your offer of help?' 'Not in so many words, but it was obvious from her manner that she did not want any help from me.'
13. **not to mince one's words** – to speak bluntly without troubling to be tactful. 'I won't mince my words: you are rude to the staff and insolent to the Manager; you will have to go.'
14. **too (adjective) for words** – too (adjective) to be expressed in words. 'Because of the epidemic we can't leave the hospital. It is too sickening for words.' Many adjectives can be used with this idiom, most of which express the speaker's feelings, e.g., beautiful, ugly, frightful, boring, annoying, exasperating, sickening, disgusting and disappointing.
15. **waste words on someone** – waste time and effort speaking to someone. 'Don't waste words on that man; he isn't interested in our complaint.'
16. **to weigh one's words** – to choose one's words with the greatest care. 'When you are being interviewed for a job, you must weigh your words before answering the questions they put to you.'
17. **words fail me** – I cannot express my feelings in words. 'When I try to describe my experience in the prison camp, words fail me.' cf. **be lost for words 263/3.**

# INDEX

*Possessives and plurals of nouns follow immediately after the singular unless there is a spelling change within the word. Thus* **day's** *and* **days** *follow* **day** *and precede* **daylight**; *but* **men** *follows* **memory**, *not* **man** *and* **man's**.

C

## E

## H

## I

## Q



## R

## T

## Y

PENGUIN REFERENCE

# *The New Penguin Dictionary of Abbreviations*

Rosalind Fergusson was born in Liverpool in 1953 and obtained her degree in French from Exeter University. From here she took a teaching certificate and became an assistant teacher at a school in West Sussex. From 1978 to 1984 she worked for Market House Books where she trained as an assistant editor and rose to the position of Senior Editor. During this time she worked on a range of reference books. Since leaving Market House Books she has worked as a freelance editor.

Her other publications include *The Penguin Dictionary of Proverbs* (1983), *The Penguin Rhyming Dictionary* (1985), *Choose your Baby's Name* (1987), *The Hamlyn Dictionary of Quotations* (1989), *The Penguin Dictionary of English Synonyms and Antonyms* (1992), *Chambers Dictionary of Foreign Words and Phrases* (1995) and *Cassell Dictionary of English Idioms* (1999). Rosalind Fergusson has also edited and co-edited a number of dictionaries and reference books, and has contributed to *The Bloomsbury Good Word Guide* (1988) and *Brewer's Dictionary of 20th-Century Phrase and Fable* (1991), among others.

Rosalind Fergusson is married and lives in Kent. Her leisure interests include walking, sailing and music.

*The New Penguin Dictionary of*

# *Abbreviations*

**From A to zz**

*Rosalind Fergusson*

PENGUIN BOOKS

PENGUIN BOOKS

Published by the Penguin Group
Penguin Books Ltd, 80 Strand, London WC2 0RL, England
Penguin Putnam Inc., 375 Hudson Street, New York, New York 10014, USA
Penguin Books Australia Ltd, 250 Camberwell Road, Camberwell, Victoria 3124, Australia
Penguin Books Canada Ltd, 10 Alcorn Avenue, Toronto, Ontario, Canada M4V 3B2
Penguin Books India (P) Ltd, 11, Community Centre, Panscheel Park, New Delhi – 110 017, India
Penguin Books (NZ) Ltd, Cnr Rosedale and Airborne Roads, Albany, Auckland, New Zealand
Penguin Books (South Africa) (Pty) Ltd, 24 Sturdee Avenue, Rosebank 2196, South Africa

Penguin Books Ltd, Registered Offices: 80 Strand, London WC2 0RL, England

www.penguin.com

First published 2000
20



Set in ITC Stone
Typeset by Rowland Phototypesetting Ltd, Bury St Edmunds, Suffolk
Printed in England by Clays Ltd, St Ives plc

# *Contents*

# Introduction

*The New Penguin Dictionary of Abbreviations* contains over 40,000 entries, listed under more than 20,000 headwords. Abbreviations abound in all walks of modern life, and no dictionary of abbreviations can hope to be fully comprehensive, but users of this book should find in its pages most of the abbreviations they are likely to encounter, whether they are reading a magazine, listening to the news, browsing on the Internet, buying a house, or applying for a job.

Abbreviations fall into five main categories. There are *shortenings*, in which a word is simply truncated, as in **Co.** and **technol.**; *contractions*, which contain the first and last letters of the full word, as in **Ltd** and **Dr**; *initialisms*, made up of the first letters of a series of words, as in **BBC** and **e.g.**; *acronyms*, in which the first letters or syllables of a name or phrase are pronounced as a word, as in **NATO** and **Ofsted**; and *symbols*, which often belong to the fields of science and technology and may or may not be related to the words they represent, such as **km** and **Pb** (meaning 'lead'). The scope of *The New Penguin Dictionary of Abbreviations* has been broadened to include some items that are not classified as abbreviations in many standard dictionaries because they are – or have become – part of the English language as words in their own right, such as the acronyms **radar** and **laser** and informal short forms such as **fridge** and **pub**.

Abbreviations are perhaps most frequently used to save time and space in writing and printing, and the form that they take may vary from person to person, or from publication to publication. Some acronyms can appear in print either as a lower-case word with a capital initial or as a string of capitals, as in **Unesco** or **UNESCO**. Initialisms may often be capital or lower-case, with or without full stops or other punctuation, as in **ASAP** or **a.s.a.p.** (In *The New Penguin Dictionary of Abbreviations* we have tended to prefer the all-capital form of acronyms, unless an alternative form is known to be more frequent or favoured by the organization concerned; for lower-case initialisms we have usually retained the full stops.) Many users of British English signal the difference between shortenings and contractions by putting a full stop at the end of the former but not the latter, a convention that has been followed in this dictionary.

## Order of entries

The abbreviations are listed in alphabetical order. Where two or more abbreviations differ only in capitalization and/or punctuation, all the forms containing capitals precede those in lower case, and unpunctuated forms precede those with slashes, full stops, spaces, etc. Abbreviations containing numbers follow those made up of the letter or letters before (or after) the number: **3M** comes between **M**, **m.**, etc. and **MA**, and **Y2K** comes between **Y**, **y.**, etc. and **YA**. The ampersand symbol has been alphabetized as 'and', so **R&A** follows **RANCOM**.

Within each entry, the full forms are listed in character-by-character alphabetical order, ignoring any letters or words in brackets.

# *Some Useful Groups of Abbreviations*

## *Abbreviations used in advertisements*

*personal*

| | | | |
|---|---|---|---|
| **ALA** | all letters answered | **PA** | photograph appreciated |
| **ALAWP** | all letters answered with photograph | **SOH** | sense of humour |
| **ARA** | all replies answered | **TDH** | tall, dark and handsome |
| **GL** | good-looking | **TLEH** | true love and everlasting happiness |
| **GSOH** | good sense of humour | **VGL** | very good-looking |
| **n/m** | not married | **VGSOH** | very good sense of humour |
| **NS** | nonsmoker | **VYAH** | very young at heart |
| **n/s** | nonsmoker | **WLTM** | would like to meet |
| **NSP** | nonsmoker preferred | **YAH** | young at heart |
| **NTW** | no time wasters | | |
| **OHAC** | own house and car | | |

*for cars*

| | | | |
|---|---|---|---|
| **a/b** | airbag(s) | **FAR** | front arm rests |
| **a/con.** | air conditioning | **FSH** | full service history |
| **AT** | automatic transmission | **g/box** | gearbox |
| **AW** | alloy wheels | **h'back** | hatchback |
| **b/bar** | bull-bar | **HFS** | heated front seats |
| **b/kit** | body kit | **HLW** | headlamp wipers |
| **C/C** | cruise control | **HLWW** | headlamp wash and wipe |
| **CDL** | central door locking | **HRW** | heated rear window |
| **ch.** | chassis | **HWW** | headlamp wash and wipe |
| **CL** | central locking | **IRL** | infrared (remote) locking |
| **c/lock.** | central locking | **IS** | independent suspension |
| **COL** | centrally operated locking | **l.h.d.** | left-hand drive |
| **EDS** | electrically adjusted driver's seat | **LSW** | lights spray and wipe |
| **EFW** | electric front windows | **LUD** | leather-upholstered dashboard |
| **EPS** | electrically positioned seats | **LW&S** | lights wipe and spray |
| **ESC** | electric seat control; etched security code | **MDS** | memory-adjusted driver's seat |
| | | **mlg.** | mileage |
| **ESR** | electric sunroof | **MSR** | manual sunroof |
| **EW** | electric windows | **OBC** | on-board computer |

| | | | |
|---|---|---|---|
| **OTG** | outside temperature gauge | **s/hist.** | service history |
| **p.a.s.** | power-assisted steering | **spd** | speed |
| **PS** | power steering | **s/r** | sunroof |
| **PW** | power windows | **s/roof** | sunroof |
| **r/belt** | rear seat belt | **s/susp.** | sports suspension |
| **r.h.d.** | right-hand drive | **T&T** | taxed and tested |
| **RHR** | rear head restraints | **WW** | walnut wood (trim) |

*for houses, flats, etc.*

| | | | |
|---|---|---|---|
| **balc.** | balcony | **lhld** | leasehold |
| **bath.** | bathroom | **lnge** | lounge |
| **bed.** | bedroom | **LU** | lock-up |
| **bedrm** | bedroom | **magnif.** | magnificent |
| **beds** | bedrooms | **mais.** | maisonette |
| **bung.** | bungalow | **mod.** | modernized |
| **c&c** | carpets and curtains | **OCH** | oil central heating |
| **CH** | central heating | **o'lkng** | overlooking |
| **c.h.** | central heating | **o.p.** | open-plan |
| **clkrm** | cloakroom | **ORP** | off-road parking |
| **conserv.** | conservatory | **OSCH** | off-peak (or overnight) storage central heating |
| **CW** | cavity wall | | |
| **det.** | detached | **OSP** | off-street parking |
| **d-f** | double-fronted | **p/b** | purpose-built |
| **DG** | double glazed (or glazing) | **p.p.** | planning permission |
| **DR** | dining room | **ptr** | porter |
| **ens.** | en suite | **rec.** | reception room |
| **EOT** | end of terrace | **recpt.** | reception room |
| **e/s** | en suite | **rest.** | restored |
| **FCH** | full central heating | **rm** | room |
| **FF** | fixtures and fittings; fully fitted | **SD** | semi-detached |
| | | **sh.** | shower |
| **FGCH** | full gas central heating | **shwr** | shower |
| **F/H** | freehold | **sit.** | sitting room |
| **fhld** | freehold | **sitt.** | sitting room |
| **FTB** | first-time buyer | **SOF** | share of freehold |
| **fttgs** | fittings | **spac.** | spacious |
| **GCH** | gas central heating | **s/pool** | swimming pool |
| **g/f** | ground floor | **SSTC** | sold subject to contract |
| **GFCH** | gas-fired central heating | **STC** | subject to contract |
| **gge** | garage | **t&s** | toilet and shower |
| **K** | kitchen | **terrd** | terraced |
| **k&b** | kitchen and bathroom | **unmod.** | unmodernized |
| **kit.** | kitchen | **util.** | utility room |
| **lge** | lounge | **W/W** | wall-to-wall |
| **L/H** | leasehold | | |

*for rented accommodation, hotels, etc.*

| | | | |
|---|---|---|---|
| **B** | bathroom | **BBEM** | bed, breakfast and evening meal |
| **b.** | bedroom | | |
| **BB** | bed and breakfast | **DBB** | dinner, bed and breakfast |
| **BBB** | bed, breakfast and bath | **ED** | evening dinner |

| | | | |
|---|---|---|---|
| **EM** | evening meal | **SD** | spin dryer |
| **ens.** | en suite | **sh.** | shower |
| **e/s** | en suite | **shwr** | shower |
| **f.** | furnished | **SWF** | single white female |
| **FB** | full board | **SWM** | single white male |
| **f.b.** | full board | **SWPF** | single white professional female |
| **FF** | fully furnished | **SWPM** | single white professional male |
| **f/furn** | fully furnished | **t&s** | toilet and shower |
| **furn.** | furnished | **u/f** | unfurnished |
| **p.a.x.** | per annum, exclusive | **unfurn.** | unfurnished |
| **penthse** | penthouse | **WM** | washing machine |
| **SC** | self-contained | | |
| **s/c** | self-catering; self-contained | | |

*general*

| | | | |
|---|---|---|---|
| **a/nw** | as new | **o.v.n.o.** | or very near offer |
| **g.c.** | good condition | **P/E** | part exchange |
| **immac.** | immaculate | **POA** | price on application |
| **neg.** | negotiable | **pt ex.** | part exchange |
| **o.b.o.** | or best offer | **PX** | part exchange |
| **OIEO** | offers in excess of | **v.g.c.** | very good condition |
| **OIRO** | offers in the region of | **WM** | well maintained |
| **o.n.o.** | or near(est) offer | **WTP** | willing to pay |
| **o/o** | offers over | | |

## *Abbreviations used on the Internet*

| | |
|---|---|
| **.ac.uk** | UK academic institution (in Internet address) |
| **AFK** | away from the keyboard (in Internet chat) |
| **ANSI** | American National Standards Institute |
| **ARPANET** | Advanced Research Projects Agency Network |
| **ASCII** | American Standard Code for Information Interchange |
| **.at** | Austria (in Internet address) |
| **ATK** | at the keyboard (in Internet chat) |
| **ATM** | asynchronous transfer mode; at the moment (in Internet chat and e-mail) |
| **.au** | Australia (in Internet address) |
| **BBL** | be back later (in Internet chat) |
| **BBS** | be back soon (in Internet chat); bulletin board system |
| **BCNU** | be seein' you (in Internet chat) |
| **.be** | Belgium (in Internet address) |
| **BITNET** | Because It's Time Network |
| **BRB** | be right back (in Internet chat) |
| **BTDT** | been there, done that (in Internet chat) |
| **BTW** | by the way (in Internet chat and e-mail) |
| **.ca** | Canada (in Internet address) |
| **.com** | (US) commercial organization (in Internet address) |
| **.co.uk** | UK commercial organization (in Internet address) |
| **.de** | Germany (in Internet address) |
| **.dk** | Denmark (in Internet address) |
| **DL** | download |

| | |
|---|---|
| **DNS** | domain name system |
| **EBCDIC** | extended binary-coded decimal-interchange code |
| **EOF** | end of file |
| **EOM** | end of message |
| **.es** | Spain (in Internet address) |
| **FAQ** | frequently asked question |
| **FOAF** | friend of a friend |
| **FOHCL** | falls off her/his chair laughing (in Internet chat) |
| **.fr** | France (in Internet address) |
| **FTP** | file-transfer protocol |
| **FWIW** | for what it's worth (in Internet chat and e-mail) |
| **GIF** | graphics interchange format |
| **GMTA** | great minds think alike (in Internet chat) |
| **.gov** | government (in Internet address) |
| **.gov.uk** | UK government (in Internet address) |
| **.gr** | Greece (in Internet address) |
| **.hk** | Hong Kong (in Internet address) |
| **HTML** | hypertext markup language |
| **HTTP** | hypertext transfer protocol |
| **IAB** | Internet architecture board |
| **IAP** | Internet access provider |
| **.ie** | Ireland (in Internet address) |
| **IETF** | Internet Engineering Task Force |
| **IMHO** | in my humble opinion (in Internet chat and e-mail) |
| **IMO** | in my opinion (in Internet chat and e-mail) |
| **IOW** | in other words (in Internet chat and e-mail) |
| **IP** | Internet protocol |
| **IRC** | Internet relay chat |
| **IRL** | in real life (in Internet chat) |
| **ISDN** | Integrated Services Digital Network |
| **ISP** | Internet service provider |
| **.it** | Italy (in Internet address) |
| **IVL** | in virtual life (in Internet chat) |
| **.jp** | Japan (in Internet address) |
| **LOL** | laughs out loud (in Internet chat) |
| **.lu** | Luxembourg (in Internet address) |
| **.mil** | US military (in Internet address) |
| **MIME** | multipurpose Internet mail extension |
| **.mod.uk** | Ministry of Defence (in Internet address) |
| **MUD** | multi-user dungeon (or dimension) (in game) |
| **.mx** | Mexico (in Internet address) |
| **.net** | network (in Internet address) |
| **.nl** | Netherlands (in Internet address) |
| **NNTP** | net(work) news transfer protocol |
| **.nz** | New Zealand (in Internet address) |
| **.org** | noncommercial organization (in Internet address) |
| **OTOH** | on the other hand (in Internet chat and e-mail) |
| **PC** | personal computer |
| **POP** | point of presence; post office protocol |
| **PPP** | point-to-point protocol |
| **.pt** | Portugal (in Internet address) |
| **ROTFL** | rolls on the floor laughing (in Internet chat) |

| | |
|---|---|
| **.ru** | Russia (in Internet address) |
| **.sg** | Singapore (in Internet address) |
| **SGML** | standard generalized markup language |
| **SLIP** | serial line Internet protocol |
| **SMTP** | simple mail transfer protocol |
| **TCP** | transmission control protocol |
| **TCP/IP** | transmission control protocol/Internet protocol |
| **.uk** | United Kingdom (in Internet address) |
| **UL** | upload |
| **URL** | Uniform Resource Locator (address of Internet location) |
| **.us** | United States of America (in Internet address) |
| **WAIS** | wide-area information service |
| **WAN** | wide-area network |
| **WLAN** | wireless local area network |
| **WWW** | World Wide Web |
| **wysiwyg** | what you see is what you get |
| **XML** | extensible markup language |

## *Foreign business abbreviations*

| | |
|---|---|
| **a.** | *accepté* (French: accepted); *akzeptiert* (German: accepted) |
| **A/B** | *Aktiebolaget* (Swedish: joint-stock company) |
| **a.B** | *auf Bestellung* (German: on order) |
| **abb.** | *abbuono* (Italian: allowance, discount) |
| **abl** | *abril* (Spanish: April) |
| **a.b.s.** | *aux bons soins (de)* (French: care of, c/o) (in postal addresses) |
| **a/c** | *ai cuidado (de)* (Portuguese: care of, c/o) (in postal addresses) |
| **a.c.** | *à compte* (French: on account); *année courante* (French: this year) |
| **a cta** | *a cuenta* (Spanish: on account) |
| **AG** | *Aktiengesellschaft* (German: public limited company, plc) |
| **ago.** | *agosto* (Italian or Spanish: August) |
| **Akt** | *Aktiebolaget* (Swedish: joint-stock company) |
| **Aktb** | *Aktiebolaget* (Swedish: joint-stock company) |
| **a.l.** | *après livraison* (French: after delivery) |
| **AM** | *assurance mutuelle* (French: mutual insurance) |
| **anme** | *anonyme* (French: limited liability; of company) |
| **AP** | *à protester* (French: to be protested; on bill of exchange) |
| **Apr.** | *April* (German: April) |
| **apr.** | *aprile* (Italian: April) |
| **A/S** | *Aksjeselskap* (Norwegian: limited company, Ltd); *Aktieselskab* (Danish: joint-stock company) |
| **a/s de** | *aux soins (de)* (French: care of, c/o) (in postal addresses) |
| **ASP** | *accepté sous protêt* (French: accepted under protest) |
| **ASPC** | *accepté sous protêt pour compte* (French: accepted under protest for account) |
| **Aug.** | *August* (German: August) |
| **av.** | *avril* (French: April) |
| **b. à p.** | *billets à payer* (French: bills payable) |
| **b. à r.** | *billets à recevoir* (French: bills receivable) |
| **Best.** | *Bestellung* (German: order) |
| **b.p.f.** | *bon pour francs* (French: value in francs) |

| | |
|---|---|
| **BV** | *Besloten Vennootschap* (Dutch: limited company, Ltd) |
| **Ca** | *compagnia* (Italian: company, Co.); *companhia* (Portuguese: company, Co.); *compañia* (Spanish: company, Co.) |
| **CAF** | *coût, assurance, fret* (French: cost, insurance, freight, CIF) |
| **c/c** | *compte courant* (French: current account); *conto corrente* (Italian: current account) |
| **ccc** | *cwmni cyfyngedig cyhoeddus* (Welsh: public limited company, plc) |
| **cedex** | *courrier d'entreprise à distribution exceptionnelle* (French: special business postal code) |
| **Cia** | *compagnia* (Italian: company, Co.); *companhia* (Portuguese: company, Co.); *compañia* (Spanish: company, Co.) |
| **Cie** | *compagnie* (French: company, Co.) |
| **CO** | *compte ouvert* (French: open account) |
| **cour.** | *courant* (French: current, this month, inst.) (in correspondence) |
| **ct** | *courant* (French: current, this month, inst.) (in correspondence) |
| **dbre** | *diciembre* (Spanish: December) |
| **déc.** | *décembre* (French: December) |
| **Dez.** | *Dezember* (German: December) |
| **dic.** | *dicembre* (Italian: December) |
| **dim.** | *dimanche* (French: Sunday) |
| **d.M** | *dieses Monats* (German: this month, inst.) |
| **Do.** | *Donnerstag* (German: Thursday) |
| **dom.** | *domenica* (Italian: Sunday); *domingo* (Spanish: Sunday) |
| **Dtg** | *Dienstag* (German: Tuesday) |
| **EGmbH** | *Eingetragene Gesellschaft mit beschränkter Haftung* (German: registered limited company) |
| **eno** | *enero* (Spanish: January) |
| **e.o.o.e.** | *erreur ou omission exceptée* (French: errors and omissions excepted) |
| **Fa** | *Firma* (German: firm, business) |
| **fa** | *factura* (Spanish: invoice) |
| **f. à b.** | *franco à bord* (French: free on board) |
| **facta** | *factura* (Spanish: invoice) |
| **fbro** | *febrero* (Spanish: February) |
| **febb.** | *febbraio* (Italian: February) |
| **Febr.** | *Februar* (German: February) |
| **fév.** | *février* (French: February) |
| **Fr.** | *Frau* (German: Mrs) |
| **Fre.** | *Freitag* (German: Friday) |
| **fre** | *facture* (French: invoice) |
| **Frk.** | *Fröken* (Swedish: Miss); *Frøken* (Danish or Norwegian: Miss) |
| **Frl.** | *Fräulein* (German: Miss) |
| **genn.** | *gennaio* (Italian: January) |
| **Ges.** | *Gesellschaft* (German: company, society) |
| **gio.** | *giovedì* (Italian: Thursday) |
| **giu.** | *giugno* (Italian: June) |
| **GmbH** | *Gesellschaft mit beschränkter Haftung* (German: limited company, Ltd) |
| **H/F** | *Hlutafjelagid* (Icelandic: limited company, Ltd) |
| **Hr** | *Herr* (German: Mr, Sir) |
| **Jan.** | *Januar* (German: January) |
| **janv.** | *janvier* (French: January) |
| **jeu.** | *jeudi* (French: Thursday) |
| **juev.** | *jueves* (Spanish: Thursday) |

| | |
|---|---|
| **juil.** | *juillet* (French: July) |
| **jul.** | *julio* (Spanish: July) |
| **jun.** | *junio* (Spanish: June) |
| **KG** | *Kommanditgesellschaft* (German: limited partnership) |
| **KK** | *Kabushiki Kaisha* (Japanese: joint-stock company) |
| **Komp.** | *Kompanie* (German: company) |
| **Kto** | *Konto* (German: account) |
| **Lda** | *Sociedade de responsabilidade limitada* (Portuguese: limited company, Ltd) |
| **liv.** | *livraison* (French: delivery) |
| **L/L** | *Lutlang* (Norwegian: limited company, Ltd) |
| **l/o** | *leur ordre* (French: their order) |
| **l.R** | *laufen der Rechnung* (German: current account) |
| **lu.** | *luglio* (Italian: July) |
| **lun.** | *lundi* (French: Monday); *lunedì* (Italian: Monday); *lunes* (Spanish: Monday) |
| **M** | *Monsieur* (French: Mr, Sir) |
| **magg.** | *maggio* (Italian: May) |
| **mar.** | *mardi* (French: Tuesday); *martedì* (Italian: Tuesday); *martes* (Spanish: Tuesday); *marzo* (Italian or Spanish: March) |
| **mbH** | *mit beschränkter Haftung* (German: with limited liability) (of company) |
| **m.c.** | *mois courant* (French: current month) |
| **mer.** | *mercoledì* (Italian: Wednesday); *mercredi* (French: Wednesday) |
| **miér.** | *miércoles* (Spanish: Wednesday) |
| **Mit.** | *Mittwoch* (German: Wednesday) |
| **Mlle** | *Mademoiselle* (French: Miss) |
| **Mme** | *Madame* (French: Mrs) |
| **Mmes** | *Mesdames* (French: plural of Mme) |
| **moms** | *mervaerdiomsaetningsskat* (Danish: value-added tax); *mervardesomsattningsskatt* (Swedish: value-added tax) |
| **Mon.** | *Montag* (German: Monday) |
| **Mpy** | *Maatschappij* (Dutch: company, Co.) |
| **nbre** | *noviembre* (Spanish: November) |
| **Nov.** | *November* (German: November) |
| **nov.** | *novembre* (French or Italian: November) |
| **NV** | *Naamloze Vennootschap* (Dutch: public limited company, plc) |
| **obre** | *octobre* (French: October) |
| **oct.** | *octubre* (Spanish: October) |
| **OHG** | *Offene Handelsgesellschaft* (German: partnership) |
| **Okt.** | *Oktober* (German: October) |
| **ott.** | *ottobre* (Italian: October) |
| **p.A** | *per Adresse* (German: care of, c/o) (in postal addresses) |
| **p. Adr.** | *per Adresse* (German: care of, c/o) (in postal addresses) |
| **SA** | *sociedad anónima* (Spanish: (public) limited company, plc or Ltd); *sociedade anónima* (Portuguese: (public) limited company, plc or Ltd); *società anonima* (Italian: (public) limited company, plc or Ltd); *société anonyme* (French: (public) limited company, plc or Ltd) |
| **sab.** | *sabato* (Italian: Saturday) |
| **sáb.** | *sábado* (Spanish: Saturday) |
| **Sam.** | *Samstag* (German: Saturday) |
| **sam.** | *samedi* (French: Saturday) |
| **Sarl** | *société à responsabilité limitée* (French: limited company, Ltd) |
| **Sas** | *società in accomandita semplice* (Italian: limited partnership) |

| | |
|---|---|
| **sbre** | *septiembre* (Spanish: September) |
| **S en C** | *sociedad en comandita* (Spanish: limited partnership); *société en commandite* (French: limited partnership) |
| **S en NC** | *société en nom collectif* (French: partnership) |
| **Sept.** | *September* (German: September) |
| **sept.** | *septembre* (French: September) |
| **sett.** | *settembre* (Italian: September) |
| **s.f.** | *sans frais* (French: no expenses) |
| **So.** | *Sonntag* (German: Sunday) |
| **Soc.** | *società* (Italian: company) |
| **SpA** | *società per azioni* (Italian: public limited company, plc) |
| **sprl** | *société de personnes à responsabilité limitée* (French: limited company, Ltd) |
| **SRC** | *sociedad regular colectiva* (Spanish: partnership) |
| **Srl.** | *società a responsabilità limitata* (Italian: limited company, Ltd) |
| **Sté** | *société* (French: company, Co.) |
| **t.p.** | *tout payé* (French: all (expenses) paid) |
| **TVA** | *taxe à la valeur ajoutée* (French: value-added tax, VAT) |
| **ven.** | *vendredi* (French: Friday); *venerdì* (Italian: Friday) |
| **Ver.** | *Verein* (German: association, company) |
| **vier.** | *viernes* (Spanish: Friday) |
| **z.H** | *zu Händen* (German: for the attention of, f.a.o., care of, c/o) (in postal addresses) |

## *Symbols for chemical elements*

| | | | |
|---|---|---|---|
| **Ac** | actinium | **Dy** | dysprosium |
| **Ag** | silver (from Latin *argentum*) | **Er** | erbium |
| **Al** | aluminium | **Es** | einsteinium |
| **Am** | americium | **Eu** | europium |
| **Ar** | argon | **F** | fluorine |
| **As** | arsenic | **Fe** | iron (from Latin *ferrum*) |
| **At** | astatine | **Fm** | fermium |
| **Au** | gold (from Latin *aurum*) | **Fr** | francium |
| **B** | boron | **Ga** | gallium |
| **Ba** | barium | **Gd** | gadolinium |
| **Be** | beryllium | **Ge** | germanium |
| **Bh** | bohrium | **H** | hydrogen |
| **Bi** | bismuth | **Ha** | hahnium |
| **Bk** | berkelium | **He** | helium |
| **Br** | bromine | **Hf** | hafnium |
| **C** | carbon | **Hg** | mercury (from Latin *hydrargyrum*) |
| **Ca** | calcium | | |
| **Cd** | cadmium | **Ho** | holmium |
| **Ce** | cerium | **Hs** | hassium |
| **Cf** | californium | **I** | iodine |
| **Cl** | chlorine | **In** | indium |
| **Cm** | curium | **Ir** | iridium |
| **Co** | cobalt | **K** | potassium (from Latin *kalium*) |
| **Cr** | chromium | | |
| **Cs** | caesium | **Kr** | krypton |
| **Cu** | copper (from Latin *cuprum*) | | |

| | | | |
|---|---|---|---|
| **Ku** | kurchatovium (alternative name for rutherfordium) | **Re** | rhenium |
| | | **Rf** | rutherfordium |
| **La** | lanthanum | **Rh** | rhodium |
| **Li** | lithium | **Rn** | radon |
| **Lr** | lawrencium | **Ru** | ruthenium |
| **Lu** | lutetium | **S** | sulphur |
| **Md** | mendelevium | **Sb** | antimony (from Latin *stibium*) |
| **Mg** | magnesium | | |
| **Mn** | manganese | **Sc** | scandium |
| **Mo** | molybdenum | **Se** | selenium |
| **Mt** | meitnerium | **Sg** | seaborgium |
| **N** | nitrogen | **Si** | silicon |
| **Na** | sodium (from Latin *natrium*) | **Sm** | samarium |
| | | **Sn** | tin (from Latin *stannum*) |
| **Nb** | niobium | **Sr** | strontium |
| **Nd** | neodymium | **Ta** | tantalum |
| **Ne** | neon | **Tb** | terbium |
| **Ni** | nickel | **Tc** | technetium |
| **No** | nobelium | **Te** | tellurium |
| **Np** | neptunium | **Th** | thorium |
| **O** | oxygen | **Ti** | titanium |
| **Os** | osmium | **Tl** | thallium |
| **P** | phosphorus | **Tm** | thulium |
| **Pa** | protactinium | **U** | uranium |
| **Pb** | lead (from Latin *plumbum*) | **V** | vanadium |
| **Pd** | palladium | **W** | tungsten (from former name wolfram) |
| **Pm** | promethium | | |
| **Po** | polonium | **Xe** | xenon |
| **Pr** | praseodymium | **Y** | yttrium |
| **Pt** | platinum | **Yb** | ytterbium |
| **Pu** | plutonium | **Zn** | zinc |
| **Ra** | radium | **Zr** | zirconium |
| **Rb** | rubidium | | |

## *UK vehicle registration letters*

| | | | |
|---|---|---|---|
| **AA** | Bournemouth | **AP** | Brighton |
| **AB** | Worcester | **AR** | Chelmsford |
| **AC** | Coventry | **AS** | Inverness |
| **AD** | Gloucester | **AT** | Hull |
| **AE** | Bristol | **AU** | Nottingham |
| **AF** | Truro | **AV** | Peterborough |
| **AG** | Hull | **AW** | Shrewsbury |
| **AH** | Norwich | **AX** | Cardiff |
| **AJ** | Middlesbrough | **AY** | Leicester |
| **AK** | Sheffield | **AZ** | Belfast |
| **AL** | Nottingham | **BA** | Manchester |
| **AM** | Swindon | **BB** | Newcastle upon Tyne |
| **AN** | Reading | **BC** | Leicester |
| **AO** | Carlisle | **BD** | Northampton |

| | | | |
|---|---|---|---|
| **BE** | Lincoln | **DJ** | Liverpool |
| **BF** | Stoke-on-Trent | **DK** | Manchester |
| **BG** | Liverpool | **DL** | Portsmouth |
| **BH** | Luton | **DM** | Chester |
| **BJ** | Ipswich | **DN** | Leeds |
| **BK** | Portsmouth | **DO** | Lincoln |
| **BL** | Reading | **DP** | Reading |
| **BM** | Luton | **DR** | Exeter |
| **BN** | Manchester | **DS** | Glasgow |
| **BO** | Cardiff | **DT** | Sheffield |
| **BP** | Portsmouth | **DU** | Coventry |
| **BR** | Newcastle upon Tyne | **DV** | Exeter |
| **BS** | Aberdeen | **DW** | Cardiff |
| **BT** | Leeds | **DX** | Ipswich |
| **BU** | Manchester | **DY** | Brighton |
| **BV** | Preston | **DZ** | Antrim |
| **BW** | Oxford | **EA** | Dudley |
| **BX** | Haverfordwest | **EB** | Peterborough |
| **BY** | northwest London | **EC** | Preston |
| **BZ** | Down | **ED** | Liverpool |
| **CA** | Chester | **EE** | Lincoln |
| **CB** | Manchester | **EF** | Middlesbrough |
| **CC** | Bangor | **EG** | Peterborough |
| **CD** | Brighton | **EH** | Stoke-on-Trent |
| **CE** | Peterborough | **EJ** | Haverfordwest |
| **CF** | Reading | **EK** | Liverpool |
| **CG** | Bournemouth | **EL** | Bournemouth |
| **CH** | Nottingham | **EM** | Liverpool |
| **CJ** | Gloucester | **EN** | Manchester |
| **CK** | Preston | **EO** | Preston |
| **CL** | Norwich | **EP** | Swansea |
| **CM** | Liverpool | **ER** | Peterborough |
| **CN** | Newcastle upon Tyne | **ES** | Dundee |
| **CO** | Exeter | **ET** | Sheffield |
| **CP** | Huddersfield | **EU** | Bristol |
| **CR** | Portsmouth | **EV** | Chelmsford |
| **CS** | Glasgow | **EW** | Peterborough |
| **CT** | Lincoln | **EX** | Norwich |
| **CU** | Newcastle upon Tyne | **EY** | Bangor |
| **CV** | Truro | **EZ** | Belfast |
| **CW** | Preston | **FA** | Stoke-on-Trent |
| **CX** | Huddersfield | **FB** | Bristol |
| **CY** | Swansea | **FC** | Oxford |
| **CZ** | Belfast | **FD** | Dudley |
| **DA** | Birmingham | **FE** | Lincoln |
| **DB** | Manchester | **FF** | Bangor |
| **DC** | Middlesbrough | **FG** | Brighton |
| **DD** | Gloucester | **FH** | Gloucester |
| **DE** | Haverfordwest | **FJ** | Exeter |
| **DF** | Gloucester | **FK** | Dudley |
| **DG** | Gloucester | **FL** | Peterborough |
| **DH** | Dudley | **FM** | Chester |

| | | | |
|---|---|---|---|
| **FN** | Maidstone | **HS** | Glasgow |
| **FO** | Gloucester | **HT** | Bristol |
| **FP** | Leicester | **HU** | Bristol |
| **FR** | Preston | **HV** | central London |
| **FS** | Edinburgh | **HW** | Bristol |
| **FT** | Newcastle upon Tyne | **HX** | central London |
| **FU** | Lincoln | **HY** | Bristol |
| **FV** | Preston | **HZ** | Tyrone |
| **FW** | Lincoln | **IA** | Antrim |
| **FX** | Bournemouth | **IB** | Armagh |
| **FY** | Liverpool | **IJ** | Down |
| **FZ** | Belfast | **IL** | Fermanagh |
| **GA** | Glasgow | **IW** | Londonderry |
| **GB** | Glasgow | **J** | Durham |
| **GC** | southwest London | **JA** | Manchester |
| **GD** | Glasgow | **JB** | Reading |
| **GE** | Glasgow | **JC** | Bangor |
| **GF** | southwest London | **JD** | central London |
| **GG** | Glasgow | **JE** | Peterborough |
| **GH** | southwest London | **JF** | Leicester |
| **GJ** | southwest London | **JG** | Maidstone |
| **GK** | southwest London | **JH** | Reading |
| **GL** | Truro | **JI** | Tyrone |
| **GM** | Reading | **JJ** | Maidstone |
| **GN** | southwest London | **JK** | Brighton |
| **GO** | southwest London | **JL** | Lincoln |
| **GP** | southwest London | **JM** | Reading |
| **GR** | Newcastle upon Tyne | **JN** | Chelmsford |
| **GS** | Luton | **JO** | Oxford |
| **GT** | southwest London | **JP** | Liverpool |
| **GU** | southeast London | **JR** | Newcastle upon Tyne |
| **GV** | Ipswich | **JS** | Inverness |
| **GW** | southeast London | **JT** | Bournemouth |
| **GX** | southeast London | **JU** | Leicester |
| **GY** | southeast London | **JV** | Lincoln |
| **GZ** | Belfast | **JW** | Birmingham |
| **HA** | Dudley | **JX** | Huddersfield |
| **HB** | Cardiff | **JY** | Exeter |
| **HC** | Brighton | **JZ** | Down |
| **HD** | Huddersfield | **K** | Liverpool |
| **HE** | Sheffield | **KA** | Liverpool |
| **HF** | Liverpool | **KB** | Liverpool |
| **HG** | Preston | **KC** | Liverpool |
| **HH** | Carlisle | **KD** | Liverpool |
| **HJ** | Chelmsford | **KE** | Maidstone |
| **HK** | Chelmsford | **KF** | Liverpool |
| **HL** | Sheffield | **KG** | Cardiff |
| **HM** | central London | **KH** | Hull |
| **HN** | Middlesbrough | **KJ** | Maidstone |
| **HO** | Bournemouth | **KK** | Maidstone |
| **HP** | Coventry | **KL** | Maidstone |
| **HR** | Swindon | **KM** | Maidstone |

| | | | |
|---|---|---|---|
| **KN** | Maidstone | **MT** | northeast London |
| **KO** | Maidstone | **MU** | northeast London |
| **KP** | Maidstone | **MV** | southeast London |
| **KR** | Maidstone | **MW** | Swindon |
| **KS** | Edinburgh | **MX** | southeast London |
| **KT** | Maidstone | **MY** | southeast London |
| **KU** | Sheffield | **MZ** | Belfast |
| **KV** | Coventry | **NA** | Manchester |
| **KW** | Sheffield | **NB** | Manchester |
| **KX** | Luton | **NC** | Manchester |
| **KY** | Sheffield | **ND** | Manchester |
| **KZ** | Antrim | **NE** | Manchester |
| **LA** | northwest London | **NF** | Manchester |
| **LB** | northwest London | **NG** | Norwich |
| **LC** | northwest London | **NH** | Northampton |
| **LD** | northwest London | **NJ** | Brighton |
| **LE** | northwest London | **NK** | Luton |
| **LF** | northwest London | **NL** | Newcastle upon Tyne |
| **LG** | Chester | **NM** | Luton |
| **LH** | northwest London | **NN** | Nottingham |
| **LJ** | Bournemouth | **NO** | Chelmsford |
| **LK** | northwest London | **NP** | Worcester |
| **LL** | northwest London | **NR** | Leicester |
| **LM** | northwest London | **NS** | Glasgow |
| **LN** | northwest London | **NT** | Shrewsbury |
| **LO** | northwest London | **NU** | Nottingham |
| **LP** | northwest London | **NV** | Northampton |
| **LR** | northwest London | **NW** | Leeds |
| **LS** | Edinburgh | **NX** | Dudley |
| **LT** | northwest London | **NY** | Cardiff |
| **LU** | northwest London | **NZ** | Londonderry |
| **LV** | Liverpool | **OA** | Birmingham |
| **LW** | northwest London | **OB** | Birmingham |
| **LX** | northwest London | **OC** | Birmingham |
| **LY** | northwest London | **OD** | Exeter |
| **LZ** | Armagh | **OE** | Birmingham |
| **MA** | Chester | **OF** | Birmingham |
| **MB** | Chester | **OG** | Birmingham |
| **MC** | northeast London | **OH** | Birmingham |
| **MD** | northeast London | **OI** | Belfast |
| **ME** | northeast London | **OJ** | Birmingham |
| **MF** | northeast London | **OK** | Birmingham |
| **MG** | northeast London | **OL** | Birmingham |
| **MH** | northeast London | **OM** | Birmingham |
| **MJ** | Luton | **ON** | Birmingham |
| **MK** | northeast London | **OO** | Chelmsford |
| **ML** | northeast London | **OP** | Birmingham |
| **MM** | northeast London | **OR** | Portsmouth |
| **MO** | Reading | **OS** | Glasgow |
| **MP** | northeast London | **OT** | Portsmouth |
| **MR** | Swindon | **OU** | Bristol |
| **MS** | Edinburgh | **OV** | Birmingham |

| | | | |
|---|---|---|---|
| **OW** | Portsmouth | **SA** | Aberdeen |
| **OX** | Birmingham | **SB** | Glasgow |
| **OY** | northwest London | **SC** | Edinburgh |
| **OZ** | Belfast | **SCY** | Truro (Isles of Scilly) |
| **PA** | Guildford | **SD** | Glasgow |
| **PB** | Guildford | **SE** | Aberdeen |
| **PC** | Guildford | **SF** | Edinburgh |
| **PD** | Guildford | **SG** | Edinburgh |
| **PE** | Guildford | **SH** | Edinburgh |
| **PF** | Guildford | **SJ** | Glasgow |
| **PG** | Guildford | **SK** | Inverness |
| **PH** | Guildford | **SL** | Dundee |
| **PJ** | Guildford | **SM** | Carlisle |
| **PK** | Guildford | **SN** | Dundee |
| **PL** | Guildford | **SO** | Aberdeen |
| **PM** | Guildford | **SP** | Dundee |
| **PN** | Brighton | **SR** | Dundee |
| **PO** | Portsmouth | **SS** | Aberdeen |
| **PP** | Luton | **ST** | Inverness |
| **PR** | Bournemouth | **SU** | Glasgow |
| **PS** | Aberdeen | **SV** | Carlisle |
| **PT** | Newcastle upon Tyne | **SW** | Glasgow |
| **PU** | Chelmsford | **SX** | Edinburgh |
| **PV** | Ipswich | **SZ** | Down |
| **PW** | Norwich | **TA** | Exeter |
| **PX** | Portsmouth | **TB** | Liverpool |
| **PY** | Middlesbrough | **TC** | Bristol |
| **PZ** | Belfast | **TD** | Manchester |
| **RA** | Nottingham | **TE** | Manchester |
| **RB** | Nottingham | **TF** | Reading |
| **RC** | Nottingham | **TG** | Cardiff |
| **RD** | Reading | **TH** | Swansea |
| **RE** | Stoke-on-Trent | **TJ** | Liverpool |
| **RF** | Stoke-on-Trent | **TK** | Exeter |
| **RG** | Newcastle upon Tyne | **TL** | Lincoln |
| **RH** | Hull | **TM** | Luton |
| **RJ** | Manchester | **TN** | Newcastle upon Tyne |
| **RK** | northwest London | **TO** | Nottingham |
| **RL** | Truro | **TP** | Portsmouth |
| **RM** | Carlisle | **TR** | Portsmouth |
| **RN** | Preston | **TS** | Dundee |
| **RO** | Luton | **TT** | Exeter |
| **RP** | Northampton | **TU** | Chester |
| **RR** | Nottingham | **TV** | Nottingham |
| **RS** | Aberdeen | **TW** | Chelmsford |
| **RT** | Ipswich | **TX** | Cardiff |
| **RU** | Bournemouth | **TY** | Newcastle upon Tyne |
| **RV** | Portsmouth | **TZ** | Belfast |
| **RW** | Coventry | **UA** | Leeds |
| **RX** | Reading | **UB** | Leeds |
| **RY** | Leicester | **UC** | central London |
| **RZ** | Antrim | **UD** | Oxford |

| | | | |
|---|---|---|---|
| **UE** | Dudley | **WD** | Dudley |
| **UF** | Brighton | **WE** | Sheffield |
| **UG** | Leeds | **WF** | Sheffield |
| **UH** | Cardiff | **WG** | Sheffield |
| **UI** | Londonderry | **WH** | Manchester |
| **UJ** | Shrewsbury | **WJ** | Sheffield |
| **UK** | Birmingham | **WK** | Coventry |
| **UL** | central London | **WL** | Oxford |
| **UM** | Leeds | **WM** | Liverpool |
| **UN** | Exeter | **WN** | Swansea |
| **UO** | Exeter | **WO** | Cardiff |
| **UP** | Newcastle upon Tyne | **WP** | Worcester |
| **UR** | Luton | **WR** | Leeds |
| **US** | Glasgow | **WS** | Bristol |
| **UT** | Leicester | **WT** | Leeds |
| **UU** | central London | **WU** | Leeds |
| **UV** | central London | **WV** | Brighton |
| **UW** | central London | **WW** | Leeds |
| **UX** | Shrewsbury | **WX** | Leeds |
| **UY** | Worcester | **WY** | Leeds |
| **UZ** | Belfast | **WZ** | Belfast |
| **VA** | Peterborough | **XI** | Belfast |
| **VB** | Maidstone | **XZ** | Armagh |
| **VC** | Coventry | **YA** | Taunton |
| **VE** | Peterborough | **YB** | Taunton |
| **VF** | Norwich | **YC** | Taunton |
| **VG** | Norwich | **YD** | Taunton |
| **VH** | Huddersfield | **YE** | central London |
| **VJ** | Gloucester | **YF** | central London |
| **VK** | Newcastle upon Tyne | **YG** | Leeds |
| **VL** | Lincoln | **YH** | central London |
| **VM** | Manchester | **YJ** | Brighton |
| **VN** | Middlesbrough | **YK** | central London |
| **VO** | Nottingham | **YL** | central London |
| **VP** | Birmingham | **YM** | central London |
| **VR** | Manchester | **YN** | central London |
| **VS** | Luton | **YO** | central London |
| **VT** | Stoke-on-Trent | **YP** | central London |
| **VU** | Manchester | **YR** | central London |
| **VV** | Northampton | **YS** | Glasgow |
| **VW** | Chelmsford | **YT** | central London |
| **VX** | Chelmsford | **YU** | central London |
| **VY** | Leeds | **YV** | central London |
| **VZ** | Tyrone | **YW** | central London |
| **WA** | Sheffield | **YX** | central London |
| **WB** | Sheffield | **YY** | central London |
| **WC** | Chelmsford | **YZ** | Londonderry |

## *International vehicle registration marks*

| | |
|---|---|
| **A** | Austria |
| **AFG** | Afghanistan |
| **AL** | Albania |
| **AND** | Andorra |
| **AUS** | Australia |
| **AZ** | Azerbaijan |
| **B** | Belgium |
| **BD** | Bangladesh |
| **BDS** | Barbados |
| **BF** | Burkina Faso |
| **BG** | Bulgaria |
| **BIH** | Bosnia-Herzegovina |
| **BOL** | Bolivia |
| **BR** | Brazil |
| **BRN** | Bahrain |
| **BRU** | Brunei |
| **BS** | Bahamas |
| **BUR** | Myanmar (from former name Burma) |
| **BVI** | British Virgin Islands |
| **BY** | Belarus (from alternative name Byelorussia) |
| **BZ** | Belize |
| **C** | Cuba |
| **CAM** | Cameroon |
| **CDN** | Canada |
| **CH** | Switzerland (from French *Confédération Helvétique* or Latin *Confederatio Helvetica*) |
| **CI** | Côte d'Ivoire (Ivory Coast) |
| **CL** | Sri Lanka (from former name Ceylon) |
| **CO** | Colombia |
| **CR** | Costa Rica |
| **CY** | Cyprus |
| **CZ** | Czech Republic |
| **D** | Germany (from German *Deutschland*) |
| **DK** | Denmark and Greenland |
| **DOM** | Dominican Republic |
| **DY** | Benin (from former name Dahomey) |
| **DZ** | Algeria (from Arabic *Djazïr*) |
| **E** | Spain (from Spanish *España*) |
| **EAK** | (East Africa) Kenya |
| **EAT** | (East Africa) Tanzania |
| **EAU** | (East Africa) Uganda |
| **EAZ** | (East Africa) Tanzania (formerly Zanzibar) |
| **EC** | Ecuador |
| **ES** | El Salvador |
| **EST** | Estonia |
| **ET** | (Arab Republic of) Egypt |
| **ETH** | Ethiopia |
| **F** | France |
| **FIN** | Finland |
| **FJI** | Fiji |
| **FL** | Liechtenstein (from German *Fürstentum Liechtenstein*) |
| **FR** | Faeroe Islands |
| **G** | Gabon |
| **GB** | Great Britain |
| **GBA** | Alderney |
| **GBG** | Guernsey |
| **GBJ** | Jersey |
| **GBM** | Isle of Man |
| **GBZ** | Gibraltar |
| **GCA** | Guatemala (Central America) |
| **GE** | Georgia |
| **GH** | Ghana |
| **GR** | Greece |
| **GUY** | Guyana |
| **H** | Hungary |
| **HK** | Hong Kong |
| **HKJ** | (Hashemite Kingdom of) Jordan |
| **HR** | Croatia (from Croatian *Hrvatska*) |
| **I** | Italy |
| **IL** | Israel |
| **IND** | India |
| **IR** | Iran |
| **IRL** | Ireland |
| **IRQ** | Iraq |
| **IS** | Iceland (from Icelandic *Ísland*) |
| **J** | Japan |
| **JA** | Jamaica |
| **K** | Cambodia (from former name Kampuchea) |
| **KS** | Kyrgyzstan |
| **KWT** | Kuwait |

| | |
|---|---|
| **KZ** | Kazakhstan |
| **L** | Luxembourg |
| **LAO** | Laos |
| **LAR** | Libya (Arab Republic) |
| **LB** | Liberia |
| **LS** | Lesotho |
| **LT** | Lithuania |
| **LV** | Latvia |
| **M** | Malta |
| **MA** | Morocco |
| **MAL** | Malaysia |
| **MC** | Monaco |
| **MD** | Moldova |
| **MEX** | Mexico |
| **MK** | Macedonia |
| **MOC** | Mozambique (from Portuguese *Moçambique*) |
| **MS** | Mauritius |
| **MW** | Malawi |
| **N** | Norway |
| **NA** | Netherlands Antilles |
| **NAM** | Namibia |
| **NAU** | Nauru |
| **NEP** | Nepal |
| **NGR** | Nigeria |
| **NIC** | Nicaragua |
| **NL** | Netherlands |
| **NZ** | New Zealand |
| **P** | Portugal |
| **PA** | Panama |
| **PE** | Peru |
| **PK** | Pakistan |
| **PL** | Poland |
| **PNG** | Papua New Guinea |
| **PY** | Paraguay |
| **Q** | Qatar |
| **RA** | (Republic of) Argentina |
| **RB** | (Republic of) Botswana |
| **RC** | Taiwan (Republic of China) |
| **RCA** | Central African Republic (from French *République Centrafricaine*) |
| **RCB** | (Republic of) Congo (from former name Congo-Brazzaville) |
| **RCH** | (Republic of) Chile |
| **RG** | (Republic of) Guinea |
| **RH** | (Republic of) Haiti |
| **RI** | (Republic of) Indonesia |
| **RIM** | (Islamic Republic of) Mauritania (from French *République Islamique de Mauritanie*) |
| **RL** | (Republic of) Lebanon |
| **RM** | (Republic of) Madagascar |
| **RMM** | (Republic of) Mali |
| **RN** | (Republic of) Niger |
| **RO** | Romania |
| **ROK** | (Republic of) Korea |
| **ROU** | (Republic of) Uruguay |
| **RP** | (Republic of the) Philippines |
| **RSM** | (Republic of) San Marino |
| **RU** | (Republic of) Burundi (from former name Urundi) |
| **RUS** | Russia |
| **RWA** | Rwanda |
| **S** | Sweden |
| **SA** | Saudi Arabia |
| **SD** | Swaziland |
| **SGP** | Singapore |
| **SK** | Slovakia |
| **SLO** | Slovenia |
| **SME** | Suriname |
| **SN** | Senegal |
| **SO** | Somalia |
| **SUD** | Sudan |
| **SY** | Seychelles |
| **SYR** | Syria |
| **T** | Thailand |
| **TCH** | Chad (from French *Tchad*) |
| **TG** | Togo |
| **TJ** | Tajikistan |
| **TM** | Turkmenistan |
| **TN** | Tunisia |
| **TR** | Turkey |
| **TT** | Trinidad and Tobago |
| **UA** | Ukraine |
| **USA** | United States of America |
| **V** | Vatican City State |
| **VN** | Vietnam |
| **WAG** | (West Africa) Gambia |
| **WAL** | (West Africa) Sierra Leone |
| **WD** | (Windward Islands) Dominica |
| **WG** | (Windward Islands) Grenada |
| **WL** | (Windward Islands) St Lucia |
| **WS** | (Western) Samoa |

| | | | |
|---|---|---|---|
| **WV** | (Windward Islands) St Vincent | **Z** | Zambia |
| **YAR** | Yemen (Arab Republic) | **ZA** | South Africa (from Afrikaans *Zuid Afrika*) |
| **YU** | Yugoslavia | **ZW** | Zimbabwe |
| **YV** | Venezuela | | |

## *UK postcodes*

| | | | |
|---|---|---|---|
| **AB** | Aberdeen | **HA** | Harrow |
| **AL** | St Albans | **HD** | Huddersfield |
| **B** | Birmingham | **HG** | Harrogate |
| **BA** | Bath | **HP** | Hemel Hempstead |
| **BB** | Blackburn | **HR** | Hereford |
| **BD** | Bradford | **HU** | Hull |
| **BH** | Bournemouth | **HX** | Halifax |
| **BL** | Bolton | **IG** | Ilford |
| **BN** | Brighton | **IM** | Isle of Man |
| **BR** | Bromley | **IP** | Ipswich |
| **BS** | Bristol | **IV** | Inverness |
| **BT** | Belfast | **JE** | Jersey |
| **CA** | Carlisle | **KA** | Kilmarnock |
| **CB** | Cambridge | **KT** | Kingston-upon-Thames |
| **CF** | Cardiff | **KW** | Kirkwall (Orkney) |
| **CH** | Chester | **KY** | Kirkcaldy |
| **CM** | Chelmsford | **L** | Liverpool |
| **CO** | Colchester | **LA** | Lancaster |
| **CR** | Croydon | **LD** | Llandrindod Wells |
| **CT** | Canterbury | **LE** | Leicester |
| **CV** | Coventry | **LL** | Llandudno |
| **CW** | Crewe | **LN** | Lincoln |
| **DA** | Dartford | **LS** | Leeds |
| **DD** | Dundee | **LU** | Luton |
| **DE** | Derby | **M** | Manchester |
| **DG** | Dumfries | **ME** | Medway |
| **DH** | Durham | **MK** | Milton Keynes |
| **DL** | Darlington | **ML** | Motherwell |
| **DN** | Doncaster | **N** | north London |
| **DT** | Dorchester | **NE** | Newcastle upon Tyne |
| **DY** | Dudley | **NG** | Nottingham |
| **E** | east London | **NN** | Northampton |
| **EC** | east central London | **NP** | Newport |
| **EH** | Edinburgh | **NR** | Norwich |
| **EN** | Enfield | **NW** | northwest London |
| **EX** | Exeter | **OL** | Oldham |
| **FK** | Falkirk | **OX** | Oxford |
| **FY** | Blackpool | **PA** | Paisley |
| **G** | Glasgow | **PE** | Peterborough |
| **GL** | Gloucester | **PH** | Perth |
| **GU** | Guildford | **PL** | Plymouth |
| **GY** | Guernsey | **PO** | Portsmouth |

| | | | |
|---|---|---|---|
| **PR** | Preston | **TD** | Galashiels |
| **RG** | Reading | **TF** | Telford |
| **RH** | Redhill | **TN** | Tonbridge |
| **RM** | Romford | **TQ** | Torquay |
| **S** | Sheffield | **TR** | Truro |
| **SA** | Swansea | **TS** | Cleveland |
| **SE** | southeast London | **TW** | Twickenham |
| **SG** | Stevenage | **UB** | Uxbridge |
| **SK** | Stockport | **W** | west London |
| **SL** | Slough | **WA** | Warrington |
| **SM** | Sutton (Surrey) | **WC** | west central London |
| **SN** | Swindon | **WD** | Watford |
| **SO** | Southampton | **WF** | Wakefield |
| **SP** | Salisbury | **WN** | Wigan |
| **SR** | Sunderland | **WR** | Worcester |
| **SS** | Southend-on-Sea | **WS** | Walsall |
| **ST** | Stoke-on-Trent | **WV** | Wolverhampton |
| **SW** | southwest London | **YO** | York |
| **SY** | Shrewsbury | **ZE** | Lerwick |
| **TA** | Taunton | | |

## *US postcodes (zip codes)*

| | | | |
|---|---|---|---|
| **AK** | Alaska | **MT** | Montana |
| **AL** | Alabama | **NC** | North Carolina |
| **AR** | Arkansas | **ND** | North Dakota |
| **AZ** | Arizona | **NE** | Nebraska |
| **CA** | California | **NH** | New Hampshire |
| **CO** | Colorado | **NJ** | New Jersey |
| **CT** | Connecticut | **NM** | New Mexico |
| **DC** | District of Columbia | **NV** | Nevada |
| **DE** | Delaware | **NY** | New York |
| **FL** | Florida | **OH** | Ohio |
| **GA** | Georgia | **OK** | Oklahoma |
| **HI** | Hawaii | **OR** | Oregon |
| **IA** | Iowa | **PA** | Pennsylvania |
| **ID** | Idaho | **RI** | Rhode Island |
| **IL** | Illinois | **SC** | South Carolina |
| **IN** | Indiana | **SD** | South Dakota |
| **KS** | Kansas | **TN** | Tennessee |
| **KY** | Kentucky | **TX** | Texas |
| **LA** | Louisiana | **UT** | Utah |
| **MA** | Massachusetts | **VA** | Virginia |
| **MD** | Maryland | **VT** | Vermont |
| **ME** | Maine | **WA** | Washington |
| **MI** | Michigan | **WI** | Wisconsin |
| **MN** | Minnesota | **WV** | West Virginia |
| **MO** | Missouri | **WY** | Wyoming |
| **MS** | Mississippi | | |

# A

**A** [fishing port] Aberdeen; [physics] absolute (temperature); academician; academy; [card games] ace; acre; acreage; adjutant; admiral; [cinema] adult (former film classification); [education] advanced (as in **A level**); air; *Altesse* (French: Highness); [music] alto; amateur; America; American; ammeter (in circuit diagrams); [Bible] Amos; ampere; ampere-turn; analog; [botany] androecium (in floral formula); angstrom; [horticulture] annual; anode; answer; anterior; April; area; armoured; art; arterial road (as in **A27**); article; artillery; assault (as in **A-day**); assistant; associate; athletic; atom(ic) (as in **A-bomb**); atomic weight; August; Australia; Australian; [international vehicle registration] Austria; *avancer* (French: go faster) (on clock or watch regulator); [medicine] blood group; [education] highest grade or mark; managerial or professional (occupational group); [physics] mass number; [music] note of scale; ten (in hexadecimal notation)

***A*** [physics] absorbance; [chemistry] activity; [chemistry] affinity; [mathematics] area

**a** *année* (French: year); *annus* (Latin: year); are (unit of area); atto- (indicates $10^{-18}$, as in **am** = attometre)

***a*** [physics] acceleration; [physics] amplitude

**a.** about; absent; accepted; [finance] *accepté* (French: accepted) (on bill of exchange); acre; acreage; acting; [grammar] active; actual; address; adjective; advance; advanced; afternoon; age; [finance] *akzeptiert* (German: accepted) (on bill of exchange); [music] alto; amateur; *anno* (Latin: in the year); anonymous; answer; *ante* (Latin: before); anterior; *aqua* (Latin: water); arrive; arriving; [baseball] assist

**A0** [paper size] 841 × 1189 mm

**A1** [paper size] 594 × 841 mm; in first-class condition

**A2** [paper size] 420 × 594 mm; [civil aircraft marking] Botswana

**a2** [music] *a due* (Italian: for two (instruments or voices))

**A3** [paper size] 297 × 420 mm; [civil aircraft marking] Tonga

**A4** [paper size] 210 × 297 mm

**A5** [paper size] 148 × 210 mm; [civil aircraft marking] Bhutan

**A6** [paper size] 105 × 148 mm; [civil aircraft marking] United Arab Emirates

**A7** [paper size] 74 × 105 mm; [civil aircraft marking] Qatar

**A8** [paper size] 52 × 74 mm

**A9** [paper size] 37 × 52 mm

**A9C** [civil aircraft marking] Bahrain

**A10** [paper size] 26 × 37 mm

**A40** [civil aircraft marking] Oman

**3A** [civil aircraft marking] Monaco

**5A** [civil aircraft marking] Libya

**9A** [civil aircraft marking] Croatia

**AA** [cinema] accompanied by adult (former film classification); achievement age; administrative assistant; advertising agency; Advertising Association; [taxation] age allowance; air attaché; Alcoholics Anonymous; [fishing port] Alloa; American Aviation; [biochemistry] amino acid; Anglers' Association; [military] anti-aircraft; Architectural Association; Army Act; [biochemistry] ascorbic acid; Associate in Accounting; Associate in Agriculture; Associate in Arts; Association of Agriculture; *Astronautica Acta* (journal of IAF); [physics] atomic absorption; [physics] atomic adsorption; Augustinians of the Assumption; Australian Army; author's alteration; Automobile Association; [vehicle registration] Bournemouth

**a.a.** absolute alcohol; acting appointment; after arrival; [shipping] always afloat; approximate absolute; area administrator; arithmetic average; attendance allowance; author's alteration

**AAA** [medicine] abdominal aortic aneurysm; [USA] Agricultural Adjustment Act; [USA] Agricultural Adjustment Administration; Allied Artists of America; Amateur Athletic Association; American Accounting Association; American Automobile Association; [biochemistry] amino acid analogue; [military] anti-aircraft artillery; [USA] Army Audit Agency; Association of Average Adjusters; Australian Association of Accountants; Australian Automobile Association; Automobile Association of America

**AAAA** Amateur Athletic Association of America; American Association of Advertising Agencies; Associated Actors and Artistes of America; Australian Association of Advertising Agencies

**AAAC** all-aluminium alloy conductor

**AAAI** American Association for Artificial Intelligence

**AAAL** American Academy of Arts and Letters

**AAAM** American Association of Aircraft Manufacturers

**AA&QMG** Assistant Adjutant and Quartermaster-General

**AAAS** American Academy of Arts and Sciences; American Academy of Asian Studies; American Association for the Advancement of Science; Associate of the American Antiquarian Society

**AAB** Aircraft Accident Board; Association of Applied Biologists

**AABC** American Amateur Baseball Congress

**AABL** Associated Australian Banks in London

**AABM** Australian Association of British Manufacturers

**AABT** American Association of Behavior Therapists

**AABW** Antarctic Bottom Water

**AAC** Aeronautical Advisory Council; Agricultural Advisory Council; [US air force] Alaskan Air Command; amateur athletic club; *anno ante Christum* (Latin: in the year before Christ); Army Air Corps; [electronics] automatic amplitude control

**AACB** [USA] Aeronautics and Astronautics Coordinating Board; Association of African Central Banks

**AACC** American Association of Clinical Chemists; [aeronautics] area-approach control centre

**AACP** American Association for Child Psychiatry; Anglo-American Council on Productivity

**AACR** [bibliography] Anglo-American Cataloguing Rules

**AACS** Aberdeen-Angus Cattle Society; [USA] Airways and Air Communications Service; [computing] automated-access control system

**AAD** [medicine] atlantoaxial dislocation

**AADC** air aide-de-camp; [USA] Army–Air Defense Command

**AADFI** Association of African Development Finance Institutions

**AADS** [USA] Army–Air Defense System

**AAE** American Association of Engineers

**AAEC** Australian Atomic Energy Commission

**AAEE** Aircraft and Armament Experimental Establishment

**AAeE** Associate in Aeronautical Engineering

**AAES** Association of Agricultural Education Staffs; Australian Army Education Service

**AAEW** [military] Atlantic airborne early warning

**AAF** Allied Air Forces; [USA] Army Air Forces

**AAFC** [military] anti-aircraft fire control

**AAFCE** Allied Air Forces in Central Europe

**AAFIS** Army and Air Force Intelligence Staff

**AAFNE** Allied Air Forces in Northern Europe

**AAFSE** Allied Air Forces in Southern Europe

**AAG** Air Adjutant-General; Assistant Adjutant-General; Association of American Geographers
**AAgr** Associate in Agriculture
**AAGS** Association of African Geological Surveys
**AAHPER** American Association for Health, Physical Education, and Recreation
**AAIA** Associate of the Association of International Accountants; Associate of the Australian Institute of Advertising; Association of American Indian Affairs
**AAIB** Air Accidents Investigation Branch
**AAII** Associate of the Australian Insurance Institute
**AAIL** American Academy and Institute of Arts and Letters
**AAL** [meteorology] above aerodrome level; Academy of Art and Literature; [USA] Arctic Aeromedical Laboratory; Association of Assistant Librarians
**AALA** American Association for Laboratory Accreditation
**AALD** Australian Army Legal Department
**AALL** American Association of Law Libraries
**AAM** air-to-air missile; American Association of Microbiology; American Association of Museums; Anti-Apartheid Movement; Association of Assistant Mistresses in Secondary Schools; Australian Air Mission
**AAMI** [medicine] age-associated memory impairment
**AAMW** [USA] Association of Advertising Men and Women
**AAMWS** Australian Army Medical Women's Service
**AANA** Australian Association of National Advertisers
**A&A** additions and amendments
**A&AEE** Aeroplane and Armament Experimental Establishment
**a&b** assault and battery
**A&C** addenda and corrigenda
**A&E** [medicine] accident and emergency (hospital department)
**a&h** [insurance] accident and health
**A&I** [USA] Agricultural and Industrial (college)
**a&i** [insurance] accident and indemnity
**A&M** [USA] Agricultural and Mechanical (college); Ancient and Modern (hymn book)
**A&N** Army and Navy (stores or club)
**A&NI** Andaman and Nicobar Islands
**A&P** [commerce] advertising and promotion; [New Zealand] Agricultural and Pastoral (show or association)
**A&R** artists and recording; artists and repertoire (as in **A&R man**)
**a&r** assault and robbery
**a&s** [insurance] accident and sickness
**A&SH** [military] Argyll and Sutherland Highlanders
**A&W** alive and well
**AANS** Australian Army Nursing Service
**AAO** American Association of Orthodontists; Anglo-Australian Observatory
**aaO** *am angeführten Orte* (German: at the place quoted)
**AAOC** Australian Army Ordnance Corps
**AAOM** American Academy of Occupational Medicine
**AAP** affirmative action programme; [US astronautics] Apollo Applications Program; Association of American Publishers; Australian Associated Press (news agency)
**AAPA** Advertising Agency Production Association; American Association of Port Authorities
**AAPB** American Association of Pathologists and Bacteriologists
**AAPC** All African People's Conference
**AAPE** American Academy of Physical Education
**AAPG** American Association of Petroleum Geologists
**AAPHI** Associate of the Association of Public Health Inspectors
**AAPM** American Association of Physicists in Medicine
**AAPS** American Association for the Promotion of Science
**AAPSO** Afro-Asian People's Solidarity Organization
**AAPSS** American Academy of Political and Social Science
**AAPSW** Associate of the Association of Psychiatric Social Workers
**AAPT** American Association of Physics Teachers
**AAR** Association of American Railroads
**a.a.r.** after action report; [insurance]

against all risks; aircraft accident record; aircraft accident report; average annual rainfall

**AARP** American Association of Retired Persons

**AAS** *Academiae Americanae Socius* (Latin: Fellow of the American Academy (of Arts and Sciences)); *Acta Apostolicae Sedis* (Latin: Acts of the Apostolic See) (publication of Roman Catholic Church); American Academy of Sciences; American Antiquarian Society; American Astronautical Society; American Astronomical Society; Andersen air sampler; Army Air Service; Associate in Applied Science; Association of Architects and Surveyors; Association of Asian Studies; atomic absorption spectrometry; Australian Academy of Science; Auxiliary Ambulance Service

**AASA** Associate of the Australian Society of Accountants

**AASB** [aeronautics] aerodynamically air-staged burner; American Association of Small Businesses

**AASC** Allied Air Support Command; Australian Army Service Corps

**AASF** Advanced Air Striking Force

**AASG** Association of American State Geologists

**A'asia** Australasia

**AASM** Associated African States and Madagascar (treaty)

**AASR** Airport and Airways Surveillance Radar

**AASS** *Americanae Antiquarianae Societatis Socius* (Latin: Associate of the American Antiquarian Society)

**AAT** [psychology] achievement anxiety test; Anglo-Australian Telescope (Siding Spring, Australia); Association of Accounting Technicians; [medicine] asymptomatic autoimmune thyroiditis; Australian Antarctic Territory

**AATA** Anglo-American Tourist Association

**AATNU** *Administration de l'assistance technique des Nations Unies* (French: United Nations Technical Assistance Administration)

**AATT** American Association of Textile Technology

**AATTA** Arab Association of Tourism and Travel Agents

**AATUF** All-African Trade Union Federation (replaced by OATUU)

**AAU** [USA] Amateur Athletic Union; Association of American Universities

**AAUN** American Association for United Nations; Australian Association for United Nations

**AAUP** American Association of University Presses; American Association of University Professors

**AAUW** American Association of University Women

**AAV** [medicine] adeno-associated virus; assault amphibious vehicle

**AAVC** Australian Army Veterinary Corps

**AAVS** American Anti-Vivisection Society

**AAWC** Australian Advisory War Council

**AAZPA** American Association of Zoological Parks and Aquariums

**AB** [UK postcode] Aberdeen; [fishing port] Aberystwyth; able-bodied seaman; advisory board; air board; airborne; [US air force] Airman Basic; Alberta; *Alliance balkanique* (French: Balkan Alliance); ammonia for bees (used to treat stings); antiballistic (missile); [medicine] asthmatic bronchitis; [baseball] at bat; [USA] Bachelor of Arts (from Latin *Artium Baccalaureus*); [medicine] blood group; [vehicle registration] Worcester

**A/B** [commerce] *Aktiebolaget* (Swedish: joint-stock company)

**Ab** antibody

**a.B** [commerce] *auf Bestellung* (German: on order)

**a/b** airbag(s) (in car advertisement); airborne

**ab.** about; abridgment

**a.b.** anchor bolt; [baseball] at bat

**ABA** Amateur Boxing Association; American Badminton Association; American Bankers' Association; American Bar Association; American Basketball Association (became part of NBA); American Book Award; American Booksellers Association; Antiquarian Booksellers Association; Associate in Business Administration; Association of British Archaeologists; Australian Bankers' Association

**ABAA** Antiquarian Booksellers Association of America
**ABAC** Association of British Aero Clubs and Centres
**ABB** [accounting] activity-based budgeting
**Abb.** Abbess; Abbey; Abbot
**abb.** abbey; [commerce] *abbuono* (Italian: allowance, discount)
**ABBA** Amateur Basketball Association; American Board of Bio-Analysis
**abbr.** abbreviated; abbreviation
**abbrev.** abbreviated; abbreviation
**ABC** [accounting] activity-based costing (as in **ABC method**); Advance Booking Charter (airline ticket); advanced biomedical capsule; Aerated Bread Company; air bridge to Canada; [medicine] airway, breathing, circulation (in first aid); America–Britain–Canada; American book-prices current; American Broadcasting Companies; analysis of benefits and costs; animal birth control; Arab Banking Corporation; Argentina–Brazil–Chile; Aruba, Bonaire, Curaçao (group of islands); Associated British Cinemas; [computing] Atanasoff–Berry computer; atomic, biological, and chemical (weapons or warfare); Audit Bureau of Circulation; Australian Broadcasting Corporation; [computing] automatic binary computer; automatic brake control
**ABCA** American Business Communication Association; Army Bureau of Current Affairs
**ABCB** Association of Birmingham Clearing Banks
**ABCC** Association of British Chambers of Commerce; Association of British Correspondence Colleges
**ABCD** [military] American, British, Chinese, Dutch (in World War II); atomic, biological and chemical protection and damage control
**ABCFM** American Board of Commissioners for Foreign Missions
**ABCM** Associate of the Bandsmen's College of Music
**ABD** [US military] advanced base depot; all but dissertation (of higher degree candidate); average body dose (of radiation)
**abd** abdicated; abridged
**abd.** abdicate; abdomen; abdominal
**ABDA** [military] American, British, Dutch, Australian (in World War II)
**abdom.** abdomen; abdominal
**ABDP** Association of British Directory Publishers
**ABE** acetone–butanol–ethanol (solvent)
**ABEd** [USA] Bachelor of Arts in Education
**Aber.** Aberdeen; Aberdonian
**ABERCOR** Associated Banks of Europe Corporation
**ABF** [informal] absolute bloody final (drink); Actors' Benevolent Fund; Associated British Foods
**Abf.** *Abfahrt* (German: departure)
**ABFD** Association of British Factors and Discounters
**ABFM** American Board of Foreign Missions
**ABGB** [Austria] *Allgemeines Bürgerliches Gesetzbuch* (German: General Civil Code)
**abgk.** *abgekürzt* (German: abbreviated)
**ABGWIU** [USA] Aluminum Brick and Glass Workers International Union
**ABH** actual bodily harm
**Abh.** *Abhandlungen* (German: transactions, treatises)
**ABI** [computing] application binary interface; Associate of the Institute of Book-keepers; Association of British Insurers
**ABIA** Association of British Introduction Agencies
**ab init.** *ab initio* (Latin: from the beginning)
**ABINZ** Associate of the Bankers' Institute of New Zealand
**ABL** atmospheric boundary layer
**abl** *abril* (Spanish: April)
**abl.** [grammar] ablative
**ABLA** American Business Law Association
**ablat.** [grammar] ablative
**ABLJ** adjustable buoyancy lifejacket
**ABLS** Association of British Library Schools; [USA] Bachelor of Arts in Library Science
**ABM** antiballistic missile; Associate in Business Management; Australian Board of Missions; automatic batch mix
**ABMA** Army Ballistic Missile Agency

**ABMAC** Association of British Manufacturers of Agricultural Chemicals
**ABMEWS** antiballistic missile early warning system
**ABMPM** Association of British Manufacturers of Printers' Machinery
**ABMT** [medicine] autologous bone marrow transplant(ation)
**ABN** [chemistry] acid–base–neutral; Anti-Bolshevik Bloc of Nations
**Abn** Aberdeen
**abn** airborne
**ABNE** Association for the Benefit of Noncontract Employees
**ABO** American Board of Ophthalmology; American Board of Orthodontics; American Board of Otolaryngology; [medicine] blood group system
**ABOF** Association of British Organic Fertilizers
**ABOG** American Board of Obstetrics and Gynecology
**A-bomb** atomic bomb
**ABOS** American Board of Oral Surgery; American Board of Orthopedic Surgery
**ABP** American Board of Pathology; American Board of Pediatrics; American Board of Peridontology; American Board of Prosthodontics; [biochemistry] androgen-binding protein; [medicine] arterial blood pressure; Associated Book Publishers; Associated British Ports
**Abp** Archbishop
**ABPA** Australian Book Publishers' Association
**ABPC** American Book Publishers' Council; Associated British Picture Corporation
**ABPI** Association of the British Pharmaceutical Industry
**ABPN** American Board of Psychiatry and Neurology; Association of British Paediatric Nurses
**ABPO** Advanced Base Personnel Officer
**ABPS** American Board of Plastic Surgery
**ABPVM** Association of British Plywood and Veneer Manufacturers
**ABR** American Board of Radiology; [medicine] auditory brainstem recording
**abr.** abridge; abridged; abridgment
**ABRACADABRA** Abbreviations and Related Acronyms Associated with Defense, Astronautics, Business and Radio-electronics (US publication)
**ABRC** Advisory Board for the Research Councils
**ABRES** advanced ballistic re-entry system
**ABRO** Animal Breeding Research Organization; Army in Burma Reserve of Officers
**ABRS** Association of British Riding Schools
**ABRSM** Associated Board of the Royal Schools of Music
**ABRV** [military] advanced ballistic re-entry vehicle
**ABS** acrylonitrile–butadiene–styrene (type of plastic); [chemistry] alkyl benzene sulphonate; American Bible Society; American Board of Surgery; American Bureau of Shipping; *Antiblockiersystem* (German: antilocking system (for brakes)); antilock braking system; Architects' Benevolent Society; Association of Broadcasting Staff; Australian Bureau of Statistics
**abs.** absence; absent; absolute; absolutely; absorbent; abstract
**a.b.s.** *aux bons soins* (*de*) (French: care of, c/o) (in postal addresses)
**ABSA** Association of Business Sponsorship of the Arts
**abse. re.** [law] *absente reo* (Latin: the defendant being absent)
**abs. feb.** [medicine] *absente febre* (Latin: when there is no fever)
**ABSIE** American Broadcasting Station in Europe (in World War II)
**ABSM** Associate of the Birmingham School of Music
**ABSM(TTD)** Associate of the Birmingham School of Music (Teacher's Training Diploma)
**absol.** absolute; absolutely
**abs. re.** [law] *absente reo* (Latin: the defendant being absent)
**abstr.** abstract; abstracted
**abs. visc.** absolute viscosity
**ABSW** Association of British Science Writers
**ABT** advanced backplane technology; [computing] advanced bi-CMOS technology; Association of Building Technicians
**Abt.** *Abteilung* (German: division, part)
**abt** about

**ABTA** Allied Brewery Traders' Association; Association of British Travel Agents Limited; Australian British Trade Association

**ABTAC** Australian Book Trade Advisory Committee

**ABTUC** All-Burma Trade Union Congress

**ABU** Asian Broadcasting Union; Assembly of the Baptist Union

**A-BU** Anglo-Belgian Union

**abv.** above

**ABWR** [nuclear technology] advanced boiling-water reactor

**AC** [chemistry] activated carbon; [chemistry] activated charcoal; [medicine] acute cholecystitis; adult contemporary (music); [computing] advanced CMOS; aero club; Air Command; Air Commodore; air conditioning; air control; Air Corps; Air Council; aircraftman; Alcohol Concern; Alpine Club; [physics] alternating current; Ambulance Corps; analogue computer; analytical chemist; angular correlation; annual conference; *ante Christum* (Latin: before Christ, BC); [law] Appeal Case; appeal court; *appellation contrôlée* (French: name controlled) (wine classification); Army Corps; Army Council; artillery college; Arts Council; Assistant Commissioner; athletic club; Atlantic Charter; *Auditor Camerae* (Latin: Auditor of the Papal Treasury); *Azione Cattolica* (Italian: Catholic Action) (social organization); Companion of the Order of Australia; [vehicle registration] Coventry

**A/C** account; account current; air conditioning; aircraft; aircraftman

**Ac** [chemistry] acetyl; [chemical element] actinium

***Ac*** [meteorology] altocumulus

**aC** *antes de Cristo* (Portuguese: before Christ, BC); *avanti Cristo* (Italian: before Christ, BC)

**a/c** account; account current; *ai cuidado* (*de*) (Portuguese: care of, c/o) (in postal addresses)

**ac.** acre; activity

**a.c.** *a capo* (Italian: new line); *à compte* (French: on account); advisory committee; [physics] alternating current; *année courante* (French: this year); *anno corrente* (Latin: this year); [medicine] *ante cibum* (Latin: before meals) (in prescriptions); [finance] *assegno circolare* (Italian: banker's draft); author's correction

**ACA** [telecommunications] adjacent-channel attenuation; advanced combat aircraft; Agricultural Cooperative Association; American Camping Association; American Canoe Association; Anglers' Cooperative Association; Arts Council of America; Associate of the Institute of Chartered Accountants; Association of Consulting Actuaries; Australian Consumers' Association; Australian Council for Aeronautics

**ACAA** Agricultural Conservation and Adjustment Administration; American Coal Ash Association

**ACAB** [USA] Army Contract Adjustment Board

**Acad.** Academy

**acad.** academic; academy

**Acad. fran.** *Académie française* (French: French academy)

**ACADI** *Association des cadres dirigeants de l'industrie* (French: Association of Industrial Executives)

**ACAE** Advisory Council for Adult and Continuing Education

**ACAL** Advanced Computer Architecture Laboratory

**AC&U** [USA] Association of Colleges and Universities

**ACAO** Assistant County Advisory Officer

**Acap.** Acapulco

**ACARD** Advisory Council for Applied Research and Development

**ACAS** Advisory, Conciliation, and Arbitration Service; Assistant Chief of Air Staff

**ACB** *Association canadienne des bibliothèques* (French: Canadian Library Association)

**ACBG** [medicine] aorto-coronary bypass graft

**ACBS** Accrediting Commission for Business Schools

**ACBSI** Associate of the Chartered Building Societies Institute

**ACBWS** automatic chemical–biological warning system

**ACC** [New Zealand] Accident Compensation Corporation; [computing] accumulator; [medicine] acute cardiovascular collapse; Administrative Coordination Committee; advanced communication course; Agricultural Credit Corporation Limited; Anglican Consultative Council; annual capital charge; army cadet college; Army Catering Corps; Assistant County Commissioner (in Scouting); Associated Chemical Companies; Association of County Councils

**acc.** accelerate; acceleration; accent; [commerce] acceptance; [commerce] accepted; [music] accompanied (by); [music] accompaniment; according (to); account; accountant; [grammar] accusative

**ACCA** Aeronautical Chamber of Commerce of America; Agricultural Central Cooperative Association; Associate of the Chartered Association of Certified Accountants; Association of Certified and Corporate Accountants

**ACCC** Association of Canadian Community Colleges

**ACCD** American Coalition of Citizens with Disabilities

**acce** [commerce] acceptance

**accel.** [music] *accelerando* (Italian: with increasing speed)

**access.** accessory

**ACCHAN** Allied Command Channel (in NATO)

**ACCM** Advisory Council for the Church's Ministry

**ACCO** Association of Child Care Officers

**accom.** accommodation

**accomp.** accompanied; accompaniment; accompany

**ACCP** American College of Chest Physicians

**accred.** accredited

**ACCS** Associate of the Corporation of Secretaries (formerly Associate of the Corporation of Certified Secretaries)

**ACCT** Association of Cinematograph, Television and Allied Technicians

**acct** account; accountant

**acct.** accounting

**acctd** accented

**accum.** accumulative

**accus.** [grammar] accusative

**accy** accountancy; accuracy

**ACD** [medicine] acid citrate dextrose (as in **ACD solution**); [medicine] acquired cystic disease of the kidney

**acd** accord

**ACDA** Advisory Committee on Distinction Awards; [USA] Arms Control and Disarmament Agency; Aviation Combat Development Agency

**ACDAS** automatic control and data acquisition system

**AC/DC** [physics] alternating current/direct current; [informal] bisexual

**ACDCM** Archbishop of Canterbury's Diploma in Church Music

**ACdre** Air Commodore

**ACDS** Assistant Chief of Defence Staff

**acdt** accident

**ACE** [astronomy] Advanced Composition Explorer; advanced computing environment; [engineering] advanced cooled engine; Advisory Centre for Education; [medicine] alcohol–chloroform–ether (anaesthetic); Allied Command Europe; American Council on Education; [medicine] angiotensin-converting enzyme (as in **ACE inhibitor**); [USA] Army Corps of Engineers; Association for the Conservation of Energy; Association of Conference Executives; Association of Consulting Engineers; Association of Cultural Exchange; Australian College of Education; [computing] Automatic Computing Engine

**ACEA** Action Committee for European Aerospace

**ACEd.** Associate in Commercial Education

**ACEEE** American Council for an Energy-Efficient Economy

**ACEF** Australian Council of Employers' Federations

**ACER** Australian Council for Educational Research

**ACERT** Advisory Council for the Education of Romanies and other Travellers

**ACET** Advisory Committee on Electronics and Telecommunications; [medicine] Aids care, education and treatment

**acet.** acetate; acetone

**ACEWEX** Allied Command Europe Weather Exchange

**ACF** *Académie Canadienne Française* (French: French Canadian Academy); [South Africa] Active Citizen Force; Army

Cadet Force; *Automobile Club de France* (French: Automobile Club of France)
**ACFA** Army Cadet Force Association
**ACFAS** *Association canadienne-française pour l'avancement des sciences* (French: French-Canadian Association for the Advancement of Science)
**ACFHE** Association of Colleges of Further and Higher Education
**ACFI** Associate of the Clothing and Footwear Institute
**acft** aircraft
**ACG** *An Comunn Gaidhealach* (Gaelic: The Gaelic Society); Assistant Chaplain-General; automatic control gear
**ACGB** Arts Council of Great Britain
**ACGBI** Automobile Club of Great Britain and Ireland
**ACGI** Associate of the City and Guilds (of London) Institute
**ACGME** Accreditation Council for Graduate Medical Education
**ACGS** Assistant Chief of the General Staff
**ACH** [banking] automated clearing house
**ach** [building] air changes per hour
**ACHR** American Convention on Human Rights
**AChS** Associate of the Society of Chiropodists
**ACI** *Alliance coopérative internationale* (French: International Cooperative Alliance); Alloy Castings Institute; American Concrete Institute; army council instruction; Associate of the Institute of Commerce; *Automobile Club d'Italia* (Italian: Automobile Club of Italy)
**ACIA** Associate of the Corporation of Insurance Agents; [computing] asynchronous communications interface adapter
**ACIAA** Australian Commercial and Industrial Artists' Association
**ACIArb** Associate of the Chartered Institute of Arbitrators
**ACIB** Associate of the Chartered Institute of Bankers; Associate of the Corporation of Insurance Brokers
**ACIC** [USA] Aeronautical Charting and Information Center
**ACIGS** Assistant Chief of the Imperial General Staff
**ACII** Associate of the Chartered Insurance Institute
**ACILA** Associate of the Chartered Institute of Loss Adjusters
**ACINF** [USA] Advisory Committee on Irradiated and Novel Foods
**ACIOPJF** *Association catholique internationale des œuvres de protection de la jeune fille* (French: International Catholic Girls' Society)
**ACIS** American Committee for Irish Studies; Associate of the Institute of Chartered Secretaries and Administrators (formerly Associate of the Chartered Institute of Secretaries)
**ACIT** Associate of the Chartered Institute of Transport
**ACJP** airways corporations joint pensions
**ACK** [telecommunications] acknowledgment
**ack.** acknowledge; acknowledgment
**ack-ack** anti-aircraft (from former phonetic alphabet for AA)
**ackgt** acknowledgment
**ackt** acknowledgment
**ACL** [computing] access control list; action-centred leadership; Analytical Chemistry Laboratory; Atlas Computer Laboratory
**ACLA** Anti-Communist League of America
**ACLANT** Allied Command Atlantic
**ACLC** Air Cadet League of Canada
**ACLP** Association of Contact Lens Practitioners
**ACLS** American Council of Learned Societies
**ACLS** automatic carrier landing system
**ACLU** American Civil Liberties Union; American College of Life Underwriters
**ACM** Air Chief Marshal; air combat manœuvring; American Campaign Medal; asbestos-containing material; [USA] Assistant Chief of Mission; Association for Computing Machinery; authorized controlled material
**ACMA** Agricultural Cooperative Managers' Association; Associate of the Chartered Institute of Management Accountants
**ACMC** Association of Canadian Medical Colleges
**ACME** [USA] Advisory Council on Medical Education; [USA] Association of Consulting Management Engineers

**ACMET** Advisory Council on Middle East Trade

**ACMF** [USA] Air Corps Medical Forces; Allied Central Mediterranean Forces; Australian Commonwealth Military Forces

**ACMM** Associate of the Conservatorium of Music, Melbourne

**ACMP** Advisory Committee on Marine Pollution; Assistant Commissioner of the Metropolitan Police

**acmp.** accompany

**ACMRR** Advisory Committee on Marine Resources Research

**ACMT** American College of Medical Technologies

**ACN** [chemistry] alkane carbon number; American College of Neuropsychiatrists; *ante Christum natum* (Latin: before the birth of Christ)

**a.c.n.** all concerned notified

**ACNA** [USA] Advisory Council on Naval Affairs; Arctic Institute of North America

**ACNS** Assistant Chief of Naval Staff; Associated Correspondents News Service

**ACNY** Advertising Club of New York

**ACO** Admiralty Compass Observatory; Association of Children's Officers

**AC of S** Assistant Chief of Staff

**ac.o.g.** aircraft on ground

**ACom** Associate in Commerce

**AComm** Associate in Commerce

**a/con.** air conditioning (in car advertisement)

**ACOPS** Advisory Commission on Pollution of the Sea

**ACOR** American Center for Oriental Research

**ACORD** Advisory Council on Research and Development

**ACORN** *A Classification of Residential Neighbourhoods* (directory); [computing] associative content retrieval network; [computing] automatic checkout and recording network

**ACOS** Advisory Committee on Safety; American College of Osteopathic Surgeons; Assistant Chief of Staff

**ACOST** Advisory Council on Science and Technology

**ACP** advanced computer program; advanced computer project; African, Caribbean and Pacific (countries); American College of Pharmacists; American College of Physicians; Associate of the College of Preceptors; Association of Circus Proprietors of Great Britain; Association of Clinical Pathologists; *Automóvel Clube de Portugal* (Portuguese: Automobile Club of Portugal)

**ACPM** American Congress of Physical Medicine and Rehabilitation

**ACPO** Association of Chief Police Officers

**acpt.** [commerce] acceptance

**ACPU** auxiliary computer power unit

**acq.** acquire; acquisition; acquittal

**ACR** Admiral Commanding Reserves; advanced capabilities radar; aircraft control room; American College in Rome; [aeronautics] approach control radar; Association of College Registrars; audio cassette recorder

**ACRB** *Aero-Club royal de Belgique* (French: Royal Belgian Aero Club)

**acrd** accrued

**ACRE** Action with Communities in Rural England; Advisory Committee on Releases to the Environment; automatic climatological recording equipment

**ACRF** Advanced Computing Research Facility

**acrg.** acreage

**ACRI** [USA] Air-Conditioning and Refrigeration Institute

**ACRL** [USA] Association of College and Research Libraries

**acron.** acronym

**ACRR** American Council on Race Relations

**ACRS** [taxation] accelerated cost recovery system; Advisory Committee on Reactor Safeguards

**ACS** [aeronautics] active control system; Admiral Commanding Submarines; Admiralty computing service; advanced communications system; air-conditioning system; airport catering services; [aeronautics] altitude control system; American Cancer Society; American Ceramic Society; American Chemical Society; American College of Surgeons; assembly control system; Associate in Commercial Science; Association of Caribbean States; Association of Commonwealth Students; Australian

Computer Society; [finance] automated confirmation service; [computing] automated control system

**ACSA** Allied Communications Security Agency; Associate of the Institute of Chartered Secretaries and Administrators

**ACSE** [Australia] Association of Consulting Structural Engineers

**ACSEA** Allied Command South East Asia

**ACSL** [computing] advanced continuous simulation language; assistant Cub Scout leader

**ACSM** American Congress on Surveying and Mapping

**ACSN** Association of Collegiate Schools of Nursing

**ACSPA** Australian Council of Salaried and Professional Associations

**a/cs pay.** accounts payable

**a/cs rec.** accounts receivable

**ACSS** [printing] automated colour separation system

**ACSTT** Advisory Committee on the Supply and Training of Teachers

**ACT** activated-complex theory; [aeronautics] active control technology; advance corporation tax; [computing] advanced CMOS with TTL inputs; advanced coal technology; Advisory Council on Technology; Agricultural Central Trading Limited; Air Council for Training; American College Test; [computing] analogical circuit technique; Associate of the College of Technology; Associated Container Transportation; Association of Corporate Treasurers; Australian Capital Territory; Australian College of Theology

**act.** acting; [grammar] active; activities; actor; actual; actuary

**a cta** *a cuenta* (Spanish: on account)

**ACTC** Art Class Teacher's Certificate

**actg** acting

**ACTH** [biochemistry] adrenocorticotrophic hormone

**ACTO** Advisory Council on the Treatment of Offenders

**ACTP** American College Testing Program

**ACTS** [USA] Acoustic Control and Telemetry System; Action of Churches Together in Scotland; Australian Catholic Truth Society

**ACTT** Association of Cinematograph, Television and Allied Technicians (became part of BECTU)

**ACTU** Australian Council of Trade Unions

**ACTWU** [USA] Amalgamated Clothing and Textile Workers Union

**ACU** Actors' Church Union; American Congregational Union; Asian Clearing Union; Association of Commonwealth Universities; Auto-Cycle Union; [computing] automatic calling unit

**ACUA** Association of Cambridge University Assistants

**ACUE** American Committee of United Europe

**.ac.uk** UK academic institution (in Internet address)

**ACUS** Atlantic Council of the United States

**ACV** actual cash value; air-cushion vehicle; Associate of the College of Violinists; Associated Commercial Vehicles

**ACW** agricultural crop waste; Air Command and Warning; Air Control and Warning; aircraftwoman; [physics] alternating continuous wave; automatic car wash

**ACWS** aircraft control and warning system

**ACWW** Associated Country Women of the World

**ACY** average crop yield

**AD** [insurance] accidental damage; *Acción Democrática* (Spanish: Democratic Action Party) (in Venezuela); accumulated dose (of radiation); [military] active duty; administrative department; [military] air defence; air dried; [currency] Algerian dinar; [medicine] Alzheimer's disease; *anno Domini* (Latin: in the year of the Lord, AD) (in dates); [fishing port] Ardrossan; armament depot; art director; assembly district; assistant director; Australian Democrat (or Democrats); autograph document; average deviation; Dame of the Order of Australia; [vehicle registration] Gloucester

**A-D** Albrecht Dürer (German artist)

**A/D** aerodrome; after date; [computing] analog–digital (conversion or converter)

**a.D** *ausser Dienst* (German: retired, on half pay)

**ad** [US short form] advantage (in tennis); [short form] advertisement

**ad.** adapt; adaptation; adapted; adapter; [medicine] *addantur* (Latin: let there be added) (in prescriptions); [medicine] *adde* (Latin: add) (in prescriptions); [grammar] adverb; advertisement

**.ad** Andorra (in Internet address)

**a.d.** after date; *ante diem* (Latin: before the day); autograph document

**ADA** [medicine] adenosine deaminase (as in **ADA deficiency**); Agricultural Development Association; [USA] Air Defense Agency; Aluminium Development Association; American Dental Association; American Diabetes Association; Americans for Democratic Action; Association of Drainage Authorities; Atomic Development Authority; Australian Dental Association

**ADAA** Art Dealers Association of America

**ADAD** [USA] automatic telephone dialing–announcing device

**adag.** [music] *adagio* (Italian: slowly)

**adap.** adapted

**Adapt** Access for Disabled People to Arts Today

**ADAPTS** [USA] Air-Deliverable Antipollution Transfer System (in Coast Guard)

**ADAS** Agricultural Development and Advisory Service; [computing] automatic data acquisition system; [computing] auxiliary data annotation set

**ADAWS** [military] action data automation and weapons systems; Assistant Director of Army Welfare Services

**A-day** assault day

**ADB** accidental death benefit; African Development Bank; Asian Development Bank; Associate of the Drama Board; [USA] Bachelor of Domestic Arts

**ADC** advanced developing country (or countries); [telecommunications] advice of duration and charge; aerodrome control; [Jamaica] Agricultural Development Corporation; aide-de-camp; [medicine] Aids dementia complex; Aid to Dependent Children; [USA] Air Defense Command; amateur dramatic club; [computing] analog–digital converter; apparent diffusion coefficient; Art Directors' Club; Assistant District Commissioner (in Scouting); Association of District Councils; [computing] automated distribution control; automatic digital calculator

**ADCC** [USA] Air Defense Control Center

**ADCCP** [computing] advanced data communication control procedure

**ADCI** American Die Casting Institute

**ADCM** Archbishop of Canterbury's Diploma in Church Music

**ADCONSEN** [USA] advice and consent of the Senate

**ADCP** personal aide-de-camp (to the monarch)

**ADCT** Art Directors' Club, Toronto

**ADD** [aeronautics] airstream direction detector; [medicine] attention deficit disorder

**add.** [medicine] *addantur* (Latin: let there be added) (in prescriptions); [medicine] *adde* (Latin: add) (in prescriptions); addenda; addendum; addition; additional; address; addressed

**ADDC** [USA] Air Defense Direction Center

**ADDF** Abu Dhabi Defence Force

**addl** additional

**addn** addition

**addnl** additional

**addsd** addressed

**ADEF** *Agence d'évaluation financière* (French: financial rating agency)

**ad effect.** [medicine] *ad effectum* (Latin: until effective) (in prescriptions)

**ADEME** Assistant Director, Electrical and Mechanical Engineering

**ad eund.** *ad eundem gradum* (Latin: to the same degree)

**ADF** [Australia] approved deposit fund; Asian Development Fund; Australian Defence Force; [navigation] automatic direction finder

**a.d.f.** after deducting freight

**ad fin.** *ad finem* (Latin: at the end, near the end)

**ADFManc** Art and Design Fellow, Manchester

**ADFW** Assistant Director of Fortifications and Works

**ADG** Assistant Director-General

**ADGB** Air Defence of Great Britain

**ADGMS** Assistant Director-General of Medical Services

**ad gr. acid.** [medicine] *ad gratam aciditatem* (Latin: to an agreeable acidity) (in prescriptions)
**ad gr. gust.** [medicine] *ad gratam gustum* (Latin: to an agreeable taste) (in prescriptions)
**ADH** [biochemistry] antidiuretic hormone; Assistant Director of Hygiene; Association of Dental Hospitals
**ADHD** [medicine] attention deficit hyperactivity disorder
**ad h.l.** *ad hunc locum* (Latin: at this place, on this passage)
**ADI** [medicine] acceptable daily intake (of toxic substance); approved driving instructor
**ad inf.** *ad infinitum* (Latin: to infinity)
**ad init.** *ad initium* (Latin: at the beginning)
**ad int.** *ad interim* (Latin: in the meantime)
**ADIZ** [USA] air defense identification zone
**ADJ** [meteorology] adjacent
**adj.** adjacent; [grammar] adjective; adjoining; [mathematics] adjoint; adjourned; adjudged; adjunct; [insurance, banking] adjustment; adjutant
**AdjA** [USA] Adjunct in Arts
**ADJAG** Assistant Deputy Judge Advocate-General
**Adj-Gen** Adjutant-General
**adjt** adjutant
**Adjt-Gen** Adjutant-General
**ADL** [electronics] acoustic delay line; [medicine] activities of daily living (or life); [computing] ADA design language; [USA] Anti-Defamation League (of B'nai B'rith); Assistant Director of Labour
**ad lib.** *ad libitum* (Latin: according to pleasure, freely)
**ad loc.** *ad locum* (Latin: at the place, on this passage)
**ADLP** Australian Democratic Labor Party
**ADM** Advanced Diploma in Midwifery; annual delegate meeting; Association of Domestic Management; atomic demolition munitions; average daily membership
**Adm.** Admiral; Admiralty
**adm.** administration; administrative; administrator; admission; admitted
**ADMA** American Drug Manufacturers' Association; [USA] Aviation Distributors' and Manufacturers' Association
**admin** [short form] administration
**admin.** administration; administrative; administrator
**Adml** Admiral
**ADMO(CA)** Assistant Director of the Meteorological Office (Civil Aviation)
**ADMOS** [computing] automatic device for mechanical order selection
**admov.** [medicine] *admoveatur* (Latin: let it be applied) (in prescriptions)
**Adm. Rev.** *Admodum Reverendus* (Latin: Very Reverend)
**ADMS** Assistant Director of Medical Services
**ADMT** Association of Dental Manufacturers and Traders of the United Kingdom
**admx** administratrix
**ADN** *Allgemeiner deutscher Nachrichtendienst* (German news agency)
**ADNA** Assistant Director of Naval Accounts
**ADNC** Assistant Director of Naval Construction
**ad neut.** [medicine] *ad neutralizandum* (Latin: until neutral)
**ADNI** Assistant Director of Naval Intelligence
**ADNOC** Abu Dhabi National Oil Company
**ADNS** Assistant Director of Nursing Services
**ADO** [USA] advanced development objective; air defence officer; assistant district officer; Association of Dispensing Opticians; automotive diesel oil
**ADOF** Assistant Director of Ordnance Factories
**ADOS** Assistant Director of Ordnance Services
**ADP** [biochemistry] adenosine diphosphate; air defence position; [physics] area density of particles; Association of Dental Prosthesis; [computing] automatic data processing
**ADPA** Associate Diploma of Public Administration
**ADPCM** [computing] adaptive differential pulse code modulation
**ADPLAN** advanced planning

**ADPR** Assistant Director of Public Relations
**ADPSO** Association of Data Processing Service Organizations
**ADR** accident data recorder; [law] alternative dispute resolution; [stock exchange] American Depository Receipt
**ADRA** Animal Diseases Research Association (Edinburgh)
**ADS** [computing] accurately defined systems; advanced dressing station; [USA] air defense sector; American Dialect Society; [engineering] articulated drill string; Astrophysics Data System; [engineering] automatic depressurization system
**A.d.S.** *Académie des sciences* (French: Academy of Sciences)
**a.d.s.** autograph document signed
**ad s.** [law] *ad sectam* (Latin: at the suit of)
**ad saec.** *ad saeculum* (Latin: to the century)
**ADS&T** Assistant Director of Supplies and Transport
**ad sat.** [medicine] *ad saturandum* (Latin: to saturation)
**ADSOC** [USA] Administrative Support Operations Center
**ADSS** Association of Directors of Social Services; Australian Defence Scientific Service
**ADST** [finance] approved deferred share trust
**adst. feb.** [medicine] *adstante febre* (Latin: when fever is present)
**ADT** American District Telegraph; Assistant Director of Transport; Atlantic Daylight Time; [electronics] automatic double tracking; average daily traffic
**ADTECH** advanced decoy technology
**ADTS** Automated Data and Telecommunications Service
**ad us.** *ad usum* (Latin: according to the custom)
**ad us. ext.** [medicine] *ad usum externum* (Latin: for external use) (in prescriptions)
**Adv.** Advent; Advocate
**adv.** advance; [grammar] adverb; [grammar] adverbial; *adversus* (Latin: against); advertisement; advertising; advice; advise; adviser; advisory; advocate
**ad val.** *ad valorem* (Latin: according to value)
**advb** [grammar] adverb
**adven.** adventure
**adv. pmt** advance payment
**ADVS** Advanced Diploma in Voice Studies; Assistant Director of Veterinary Services
**advt** advertisement
**advv.** [grammar] adverbs
**ADW** air defence warning; Assistant Director of Works
**ADWE&M** Assistant Director of Works, Electrical and Mechanical
**ADX** [computing] automatic data exchange; [telecommunications] automatic digital exchange
**AE** account executive; [physics] acoustic emission; adult education; aeronautical engineer; aeronautical engineering; [taxation] age exemption; *Agence Europe* (news agency); agricultural engineer; agricultural engineering; Air Efficiency Award; *Aktiebolaget Atomenergi* (Swedish: Atomic Energy Corporation); All England; American English; army education; Associate in Education; Associate in Engineering; atomic energy; [photography] autoexposure; [vehicle registration] Bristol; pen-name of George Russell (Irish poet)
**ae.** [numismatics] *aeneus* (Latin: made of copper); *aetatis* (Latin: at the age of, aged)
**.ae** United Arab Emirates (in Internet address)
**AEA** [physics] acoustic emission analysis; [USA] Actors' Equity Association; [engineering] air entraining agent; American Economic Association; [USA] Atomic Energy Act; Atomic Energy Authority
**AEAA** *Asociación de Escritores y Artistas Americanos* (Spanish: Association of Spanish-American Writers and Artists)
**AEAF** Allied Expeditionary Air Force
**AE&MP** Ambassador Extraordinary and Minister Plenipotentiary
**AE&P** Ambassador Extraordinary and Plenipotentiary
**AEAUSA** Adult Education Association of the United States of America
**AEB** Area Electricity Board; Associated Examining Board

**AEBP** atmospheric equivalent boiling point

**AEC** [insurance] additional extended cover(age); Agricultural Executive Council; American Express Company; Army Electronics Command; Associated Equipment Company; Association of Education Committees; [USA] Atomic Energy Commission; [South Africa] Atomic Energy Corporation; [USA] Atomic Energy Council; [photography] automatic exposure control

**a.e.c.** at earliest convenience

**AECB** [USA] Atomic Energy Control Board

**AECCG** African Elephant Conservation Coordinating Group

**AECI** African Explosives and Chemical Industries; Associate of the Institute of Employment Consultants

**AECL** Atomic Energy of Canada Limited

**AED** advanced electronics design; Algol Extended for Design (computer programming language); Association of Engineering Distributors; automated engineering design; Doctor of Fine Arts (from Latin *Artium Elegantium Doctor*)

**AEd** Associate in Education

**AEDE** *Association européenne des enseignants* (French: European Teachers' Association)

**AEDOT** Advanced Energy Design and Operation Technologies

**AEDP** [USA] Alternative Energy Development Program

**AEDS** [USA] Association for Educational Data Systems; Atomic Energy Detection Systems

**AEDU** Admiralty Experimental Diving Unit

**AEE** airborne evaluation equipment; Atomic Energy Establishment

**AeE** aeronautical engineer

**AEEC** [USA] Airlines Electronic Engineering Committee

**AEEE** [Canada] Army Equipment Engineering Establishment

**AEEN** *Agence européenne pour l'energie nucléaire* (French: European Agency for Atomic Energy)

**AEEU** Amalgamated Engineering and Electrical Union

**AEF** Allied Expeditionary Force; American Expeditionary Force(s); Australian Expeditionary Force

**A-effect** [theatre] alienation effect

**AEFM** *Association européenne des festivals de musique* (French: European Association of Music Festivals)

**AEG** *Allgemeine Elektrizitäts-Gesellschaft* (German manufacturer of electrical goods)

**a.e.g.** *ad eundem gradum* (Latin: to the same degree); [bookbinding] all edges gilt

**AEGIS** Aid for the Elderly in Government Institutions; [computing] an existing general information system

**AEGM** Anglican Evangelical Group Movement

**AEH** A(lfred) E(dward) Housman (British poet)

**AEI** [USA] Alternative Energy Institute; American Express International; Associated Electrical Industries; *Association des écoles internationales* (French: International Schools Association)

**AEIOU** *Austriae Est Imperare Orbi Universi* (Latin: it is given to Austria to rule the whole world); *Austria Erit In Orbe Ultima* (Latin: Austria will be the world's last survivor)

**AEJ** Association for Education in Journalism

**AEL** Admiralty Engineering Laboratory; aeronautical engine laboratory; aircraft engine laboratory; Associated Engineering Limited; automation engineering laboratory

**AELE** *Association européenne de libre-échange* (French: European Free Trade Association, EFTA)

**AELTC** All England Lawn Tennis Club

**AEM** Air Efficiency Medal; analytical electron microscope (or microscopy)

**AEMT** Association of Electrical Machinery Trades

**AEMU** [astronautics] Advanced Extra-vehicular Mobility Unit

**AEn** Associate in English

***Aen.*** *The Aeneid* (epic poem by Virgil)

**aen.** [numismatics] *aeneus* (Latin: made of copper)

**AENA** All England Netball Association

**AEng** Associate in Engineering

**AEO** Assistant Education Officer; Assistant

Experimental Officer; Association of Exhibition Organizers
**AEP** *Agence européenne de productivité* (French: European Production Agency); American Electric Power
**AEPI** American Educational Publishers Institute
**aeq.** *aequalis* (Latin: equal)
**AER** Army Emergency Reserve
**aer.** aeronautics; aeroplane
**AERA** American Educational Research Association; Associate Engraver, Royal Academy
**aera.** aeration
**AERE** Atomic Energy Research Establishment (Harwell)
**AerE** aeronautical engineer
**AERI** Agricultural Economics Research Institute (Oxford University)
**AERNO** aeronautical equipment reference number
**AERO** Air Education and Recreation Organization
**aero.** aeronautic(al)
**Aeroflot** Aero Flotilla (Russian airline company)
**aeron.** aeronautic(al); aeronautics
**aerosp.** aerospace
**AES** advanced energy system; [USA] Aerospace Electrical Society; Agricultural Economics Society (Reading University); [USA] Airways Engineering Society; [physics] atomic emission spectrum; Audio Engineering Society
**Aes.** Aesop (ancient Greek writer of fables)
**AESE** [USA] Association of Earth Science Editors
**AESL** [USA] Aerospace Energy Systems Laboratory
**aesth.** aesthetics
**AET** Associate in Electrical (or Electronic) Technology
**aet.** *aetatis* (Latin: at the age of, aged)
**a.e.t.** after extra time
**aetat.** *aetatis* (Latin: at the age of, aged)
**AEU** Amalgamated Engineering Union (became part of AEEU); American Ethical Union
**AEV** aerothermodynamic elastic vehicle; air evacuation; [microbiology] avian erythroblastosis virus
**AEW** Admiralty Experimental Works; airborne early warning (aircraft)
**AEW&C** airborne early warning and control
**AEWHA** All England Women's Hockey Association
**AEWLA** All England Women's Lacrosse Association
**AEWS** advanced earth satellite weapons system; aircraft early warning system
**AF** *Académie française* (French: French Academy); Admiral of the Fleet; air force; [USA] Air Foundation; Anglo-French; *Armée française* (French: French Army); Associated Fisheries; Associate Fellow; audiofrequency; [photography] autofocus; automatic (smoke) filter; [vehicle registration] Truro
**A/F** antiflooding; as found (in auction catalogue)
**Af** [currency] afgháni (used in Afghanistan)
**Af.** Africa; African; Afrikaans; [currency] Aruban florin
**a/f** [commerce] *a favor* (Spanish: in favour); as found (in auction catalogue)
**.af** Afghanistan (in Internet address)
**a.f.** advanced freight; [commerce] *a favor* (Spanish: in favour); *anno futuro* (Latin: next year); audiofrequency
**AFA** [nuclear technology] advanced fuel assembly; African Football Association; Air Force Act; [USA] Air Force Association; Amateur Fencing Association; Amateur Football Alliance; American Foundrymen's Association; Associate in Fine Arts; Associate of the Faculty of Actuaries
**AFAC** American Fisheries Advisory Committee
**AFAEP** Association of Fashion Advertising and Editorial Photographers
**AFAFC** [USA] Air Force Accounting and Finance Center
**AFAIAA** Associate Fellow of the American Institute of Aeronautics and Astronautics
**AFAIM** Associate Fellow of the Australian Institute of Management
**AFAITC** [USA] Armed Forces Air Intelligence Training Center
**AFAL** [USA] Air Force Astronautical Laboratory
**AFAM** Ancient Free and Accepted Masons

**AF&AM** Ancient Free and Accepted Masons
**AFAS** *Association française pour l'avancement des sciences* (French: French Association for the Advancement of the Sciences)
**AFASIC** Association for all Speech-Impaired Children
**AFB** [USA] Air Force Base; American Federation for the Blind
**AFBD** Association of Futures Brokers and Dealers
**AFBF** American Farm Bureau Federation
**AFBMD** [USA] Air Force Ballistic Missile Division
**AFBPsS** Associate Fellow of the British Psychological Society
**AFBS** American and Foreign Bible Society
**AFC** Air Force Cross; amateur football club; American Football Conference; [immunology] antibody-forming cell; association football club; Australian Flying Corps; automatic flight control; automatic frequency control; average fixed costs
**a.f.c.** automatic flight control; automatic frequency control
**AFCAI** Associate Fellow of the Canadian Aeronautical Institute
**AFCE** Associate in Fuel Technology and Chemical Engineering; automatic flight control equipment
**AFCEA** [USA] Armed Forces Communications and Electronics Association
**AFCent** Allied Forces in Central Europe
**AFCO** Admiralty Fleet Confidential Order
**afco** [engineering] automatic fuel cut-off
**AFCRL** [USA] Air Force Cambridge Research Laboratories
**AFCS** Air Force Communications Service; automatic flight control system
**AFCU** American and Foreign Christian Union
**AFCW** Association of Family Case Workers
**AFD** accelerated freeze dried; accelerated freeze drying; air force depot; [USA] Doctor of Fine Arts
**AFDC** [USA] Aid to Families with Dependent Children
**AFDCS** Association of First Division Civil Servants (formerly FDA)
**AFDM** [engineering] advanced fluid-dynamics model
**AFDS** Air Fighting Development Squadron
**AFEA** American Farm Economics Association; American Film Export Association
**AFEE** Airborne Forces Experimental Establishment
**AFEIS** Advanced Further Education Information Service
**AFERO** Asia and the Far East Regional Office
**AFES** Admiralty Fuel Experimental Station
**AFESC** [USA] Air Force Engineering and Services Center
**AFESD** Arab Fund for Economic and Social Development
**AFEX** [USA] Air Forces Europe Exchange; [USA] Armed Forces Exchange
**AFF** [photography] aberration-free focus
**aff.** affairs; affectionate; affectionately; affiliate; affiliated; affirmative; affix
**affil.** affiliate; affiliated
**Aff.IP** Affiliate of the Institute of Plumbing
**AFFL** Agricultural Finance Federation Limited
**afft** affidavit
**AFFTC** [USA] Air Force Flight Test Center
**AFG** [international vehicle registration] Afghanistan
**Afg.** Afghan; Afghanistan
**AFGE** American Federation of Government Employees
**Afgh.** Afghan; Afghanistan
**Afghan.** Afghanistan
**AFGL** [USA] Air Force Geophysics Laboratory
**AFGM** American Federation of Grain Millers
**AFH** American Foundation for Homeopathy
**AFHC** Air Force Headquarters Command
**AFHQ** Allied Forces Headquarters; Armed Forces Headquarters
**AFI** American Film Institute
**AFIA** American Foreign Insurance Association; Apparel and Fashion Industry
**AFIAP** *Artiste de la Fédération internationale de l'art photographique* (French: Artist of the International Federation of Photographic Art)

**AFICD** Associate Fellow of the Institute of Civil Defence
**AFII** American Federation of International Institutes
**AFIIM** Associate Fellow of the Institution of Industrial Managers
**AFIMA** Associate Fellow of the Institute of Mathematics and its Applications
**AFIPS** American Federation of Information Processing Societies (Incorporated)
**AFK** away from the keyboard (in Internet chat)
**AFL** [computing] abstract family of languages; Air Force List; American Federation of Labor; American Football League; *Associação de Futebol de Lisboa* (Portuguese: Lisbon Football Association)
**AFLA** Amateur Fencers' League of America; Asian Federation of Library Associations
**AFLC** [USA] Air Force Logistics Command
**AFL-CIO** American Federation of Labor and Congress of Industrial Organizations
**aflt** afloat
**AFM** [engineering] abrasive flow machining; Air Force Medal; American Federation of Musicians of the United States and Canada; assistant field manager; Associated Feed Manufacturers; [physics] atomic force microscope (or microscopy); [telecommunications] audiofrequency modulation
**AFMA** Armed Forces Management Association; Artificial Flower Manufacturers' Association of Great Britain
**AFMDC** [USA] Air Force Missile Development Center
**AFMEC** African Methodist Episcopal Church
**AFMed** Allied Forces in Mediterranean
**afmo** *afectísimo* (Spanish: very affectionately) (in correspondence)
**AFMTC** [USA] Air Force Missile Test Center
**AFN** American Forces Network; Armed Forces Network; Association of Free Newspapers
**AFNIL** *Agence francophone pour la numérotation internationale du livre* (French: French Agency for International Book Numbering, ISBN)
**AFNOR** *Association française de normalisation* (French: French Standardization Association)
**AFNorth** Allied Forces in Northern Europe
**AFO** Admiralty Fleet Order; army forwarding officer
**AFOAR** [USA] Air Force Office of Aerospace Research
**AFOAS** [USA] Air Force Office of Aerospace Sciences
**AF of M** American Federation of Musicians of the United States and Canada
**AFOM** Associate of the Faculty of Occupational Medicine
**AFOSR** [USA] Air Force Office of Scientific Research
**AFP** *Agence France Presse* (French news agency); [medicine] alpha-fetoprotein
**AFPRB** Armed Forces Pay Review Board
**AFR** accident frequency rate; air-fuel ratio; automatic fingerprint recognition
**AFr.** Anglo-French
**Afr.** Africa; African; Afrikaans
**AFRA** American Farm Research Association
**AFRAeS** Associate Fellow of the Royal Aeronautical Society
**AFRC** Agricultural and Food Research Council (formerly ARC)
**Afrik.** Afrikaans
**AFRO** African Regional Office
**AFRTS** [USA] Armed Forces Radio and Television Service
**AFS** Advanced Flying School; air force station; Alaska Ferry Service; American Field Service; Army Fire Service; Atlantic Ferry Service; auxiliary fire service
**AFSA** American Foreign Service Association; [USA] Armed Forces Security Agency
**AFSBO** American Federation of Small Business Organizations
**AFSC** Air Force Systems Command; American Friends Service Committee; Armed Forces Staff College
**AFSCME** American Federation of State, County and Municipal Employees
**afsd** aforesaid
**AFSIL** Accommodation for Students in London
**AFSLAET** Associate Fellow of the Society

of Licensed Aircraft Engineers and Technologists

**AFSouth** Allied Forces in Southern Europe

**AFT** American Federation of Teachers; axial-flow turbine

**aft.** after; afternoon

**AFTA** ASEAN Free Trade Area

**AFTE** American Federation of Technical Engineers

**AFTM** American Foundation of Tropical Medicine; [computing] anonymous file transfer protocol

**AFTN** Aeronautical Fixed Telecommunications Network

**aftn** afternoon

**AFTR** American Federal Tax Reports

**AFTRA** American Federation of Television and Radio Artists

**AFU** advanced flying unit

**AFULE** Australian Federated Union of Locomotive Enginemen

**AFV** armoured fighting vehicle; armoured force vehicle

**AFVG** [aeronautics] Anglo-French variable geometry

**AFVPA** Advertising Film and Videotape Producers' Association

**AFW** army field workshop

**AFWAL** [USA] Air Force Wright Aeronautical Laboratories

**AG** Accountant-General; Action Group Party (in Nigeria); Adjutant-General; Agent-General (of colonies); air gunner; [commerce] *Aktiengesellschaft* (German: public limited company, plc); *Alberghi per la Gioventù* (Italian: Youth Hostels); art gallery; Attorney-General; [vehicle registration] Hull

**Ag** antigen; [chemical element] silver (from Latin *argentum*)

**Ag.** August

**ag.** against; agent; agreement; agricultural; agriculture

**.ag** Antigua and Barbuda (in Internet address)

**a.g.** anti-gas

**AGA** air-to-ground-to-air; *Aktiebolaget Gasaccumulator* (Swedish gas company, original manufacturer of stoves); Amateur Gymnastics Association; American Gas Association; American Genetic Association; [obstetrics] appropriate for gestational age; Australian Garrison Artillery

**AGAC** American Guild of Authors and Composers

**AGACS** automatic ground-to-air communications system

**AGARD** Advisory Group for Aerospace Research and Development (in NATO)

**a.g.b.** a good brand; any good brand

**AGBI** Artists' General Benevolent Institution

**AGC** [USA] advanced graduate certificate; American Grassland Council; [electronics] automatic gain control

**AGCA** [aeronautics] automatic ground-controlled approach

**AGCAS** Association of Graduate Careers Advisory Service

**AGCC** Arab Gulf Cooperation Council

**AGCL** [aeronautics] automatic ground-controlled landing

**AGCM** [meteorology] atmospheric general circulation model

**agcy** agency

**agd** agreed

**a.g.d.** [engineering] axial gear differential

**AGDC** [Freemasonry] Assistant Grand Director of Ceremonies

**AGDL** Attorney-General of the Duchy of Lancaster

**AGE** Admiralty Gunnery Establishment; aerospace ground equipment; Associate in General Education; automatic guidance electronics

**AgE** agricultural engineer

**AGES** Association of Agricultural Education Staffs

**AGF** Adjutant-General to the Forces; army ground forces

**Agfa** *Aktiengesellschaft für Anilinfabrikation* (German chemical company)

**ag. feb.** [medicine] *aggrediente febre* (Latin: when the fever increases)

**agg.** aggregate

**aggr.** aggregate

**AGH** Australian General Hospital

**AGI** [USA] adjusted gross income (in tax returns); American Geographical Institute; American Geological Institute; annual general inspection; *Artistes graphiques internationaux* (French: International Graphic Artists); Associate of the Institute of Certificated Grocers

**AGIP** *Agenzia Generale Italiana Petroli* (Italian oil company)
**agit.** [medicine] *agitatum* (Latin: shaken)
**agit. ante sum.** [medicine] *agita ante sumendum* (Latin: shake before taking) (in prescriptions)
**Agitprop** *Agitpropbyuro* (Russian: Agitation and Propaganda Bureau) (former bureau of Soviet Communist Party)
**AGK** *Astronomische Gesellschaft Katalog* (German: Astronomical Society Catalogue)
**AGL** above ground level
**aglm.** agglomerate
**AGM** advisory group meeting; [medicine] African green monkey; air-to-ground missile; annual general meeting; Award of Garden Merit (Royal Horticultural Society award)
**AGMA** American Guild of Musical Artists; Athletic Goods Manufacturers' Association
**AGN** [astronomy] active galactic nucleus
**agn** again; agnomen
**agnos.** agnostic
**ago.** *agosto* (Italian or Spanish: August)
**AGOR** Auxiliary-General Oceanographic Research
**AGP** Academy of General Practice; [computing] accelerated graphics port; [computing] advanced graphics port; aviation general policy
**AGPA** American Group Psychotherapy Association
**AGPL** *Administração-Geral do Pôrto de Lisboa* (Portuguese: Port of Lisbon Authority)
**AGR** [nuclear technology] advanced gas-cooled reactor; Association of Graduate Recruiters
**agr.** agreed; agreement; agricultural; agriculture; agriculturist
**AGRA** Army Group Royal Artillery; Association of Genealogists and Record Agents
**AGREE** Advisory Group on Reliability of Electronic Equipment
**AGRF** American Geriatric Research Foundation
**agric.** agricultural; agriculture; agriculturist
**AGRM** Adjutant-General, Royal Marines
**agron.** agronomy
**AGS** [astronautics] abort guidance system; aircraft general standard; Air Gunnery School; Alpine Garden Society; American Geographical Society; Associate in General Studies
**AGSM** Associate of the Guildhall School of Music (and Drama); Australian Graduate of the School of Management
**AGSRO** Association of Government Supervisors and Radio Officers
**AGSS** American Geographical and Statistical Society
**agst** against
**AGT** advanced gas turbine; Art Gallery of Toronto; [USA] Association of Geology Teachers
**agt** agent; agreement
**AGU** American Geophysical Union
**AGV** [pharmacology] aniline gentian violet; automated guided vehicle; [electronics] autonomous guided vehicle
**AGVA** American Guild of Variety Artists
**AGW** actual gross weight
**AGWAC** Australian Guided Weapons and Analogue Computer
**AGWY** [insurance] Atlantic, Gulf, West Indies
**agy** agency
**AH** *anno Hebraico* (Latin: in the Jewish year); *anno Hegirae* (Latin: in the year of the Hegira) (in Muslim calendar); [insurance] Antwerp–Hamburg coastal ports; [fishing port] Arbroath; [chemistry] aromatic hydrocarbon; [medicine] artificial hyperglycaemia; [vehicle registration] Norwich
**a.h.** [shipping] after hatch; [shipping] aft hatch; ampere-hour; armed helicopter
**AHA** American Heart Association; American Historical Association; American Hospitals Association; area health authority; Australian Hotels Association
**AHAM** [USA] Association of Home Appliance Manufacturers
**AH&FITB** Agricultural, Horticultural and Forestry Industry Training Board
**AHAUS** Amateur Hockey Association of the United States
**AHC** Accepting Houses Committee; American Horticultural Council; Army Hospital Corps
**AHD** *American Heritage Dictionary*

**ahd** ahead
**AHDL** [medicine] alveolar hydatid disease of the liver
**AHE** [USA] Associate in Home Economics; [USA] Association for Higher Education
**AHEM** Association of Hydraulic Equipment Manufacturers
**AHF** [medicine] antihaemophilic factor
**AHG** [medicine] antihaemophilic globulin
**AHGMR** Ad Hoc Group on Missile Reliability
**AHI** American Health Institute; American Hospital Institute
**AHIL** [USA] Association of Hospital and Institutional Libraries
**AHL** American Hockey League
**a.h.l.** *ad hunc locum* (Latin: at this place, on this passage)
**AHMC** Association of Hospital Management Committees
**AHMPS** Association of Headmistresses of Preparatory Schools
**AHMS** American Home Mission Society
**AHNCV** Area of High Nature Conservation Value
**AHP** [engineering] absorption heat pump; assistant house physician
**ahp** air horsepower
**AHPR** Association of Health and Pleasure Resorts
**AHQ** Air Headquarters; Allied Headquarters; Army Headquarters
**a.h.r.** acceptable hazard rate (in risk analysis)
**AHRC** Australian Humanities Research Council
**AHRHS** Associate of Honour of the Royal Horticultural Society
**AHRIH** [New Zealand] Associate of Honour of the Royal Institute of Horticulture
**AHS** adult health study; American Helicopter Society; *anno humanae salutis* (Latin: in the year of human salvation); annual housing survey; assistant house surgeon
**AHSA** American Horse Shows Association
**AHSB** Authority, Health and Safety Branch (of Atomic Energy Authority)
**AHSM** Associate of the Institute of Health Services Management
**AHT** absorption heat transformer; acoustic homing torpedo; Animal Health Trust; Association of Highway Technicians
**a.h.v.** *ad hanc vocem* (Latin: at this word) (in reference book)
**AHWA** Association of Hospital and Welfare Administrators
**AI** Admiralty instruction; Admiralty Islands; [computing] Adobe Illustrator; air interception; air interdiction; *Altesse Impériale* (French: Imperial Highness); American Institute; Amnesty International; *anno inventionis* (Latin: in the year of the discovery); Anthropological Institute; Army Intelligence; artificial insemination; artificial intelligence
**a.i.** *ad interim* (Latin: for the meantime)
**AIA** Abrasive Industries Association; [USA] Aerospace Industries Association; American Institute of Aeronautics; American Institute of Architects; American Insurance Association; Anglo-Indian Association; Archeological Institute of America; Associate of the Institute of Actuaries; Association of International Accountants; Association of International Artists; automated image analysis; [New Zealand] Aviation Industry Association
**AIAA** Aircraft Industries Association of America; American Institute of Aeronautics and Astronautics; Association of International Advertising Agencies
**AIAB** Associate of the International Association of Book-keepers
**AIAC** Air Industries Association of Canada; *Association internationale d'archéologie classique* (French: International Association for Classical Archaeology)
**AIAE** Associate of the Institution of Automobile Engineers
**AIAgrE** Associate of the Institution of Agricultural Engineers
**AIAL** Associate Member of the International Institute of Arts and Letters
**AIAS** Australian Institute of Agricultural Science
**AIB** [insurance] accidents investigation branch (of insurance company); American Institute of Banking; Association of Independent Businesses; *Associazione Italiana Biblioteche* (Italian: Italian Library Association)
**AIBA** *Association internationale de boxe*

*amateur* (French: International Amateur Boxing Association)

**AIBC** Architectural Institute of British Columbia

**AIBD** Associate of the Institute of British Decorators; Association of International Bond Dealers

**AIBM** *Association internationale des bibliothèques musicales* (French: International Association of Music Libraries)

**AIBP** Associate of the Institute of British Photographers

**AIBS** American Institute of Biological Sciences

**AIBScot** Associate of the Institute of Bankers in Scotland

**AIC** Agricultural Improvement Council; Agricultural Institute of Canada; American Institute of Chemists; artificial insemination centre; Art Institute of Chicago

**AICA** Associate Member of the Commonwealth Institute of Accountants; *Association internationale des critiques d'art* (French: International Association of Art Critics)

**AICB** *Association internationale contre le bruit* (French: International Association Against Noise)

**AICBM** anti-intercontinental ballistic missile

**AICC** All India Congress Committee

**AICE** American Institute of Chemical Engineers; American Institute of Consulting Engineers; Associate of the Institution of Civil Engineers

**AIChE** American Institute of Chemical Engineers

**AICMA** *Association internationale des constructeurs de matériel aérospatial* (French: International Association of Aerospace Equipment Manufacturers)

**AICRO** Association of Independent Contract Research Organizations

**AICS** Associate of the Institute of Chartered Shipbrokers; *Association internationale du cinéma scientifique* (French: International Scientific Film Association)

**AICTA** Associate of the Imperial College of Tropical Agriculture

**AICV** armoured infantry combat vehicle

**AID** [medicine] acute infectious disease; Aeronautical Inspection Directorate; [USA] Agency for International Development; agricultural industrial development; Aircraft Intelligence Department; American Institute of Decorators; American Institute of Interior Designers; Army Intelligence Department; [medicine] artificial insemination by donor; *Association internationale pour le développement* (French: International Development Association)

**AIDA** *Association internationale de droit africain* (French: International African Law Association); *Association internationale de la distribution alimentaire* (French: International Association of Food Distribution); [marketing] attention, interest, desire, action (of customer)

**AIDAS** Agricultural Industry Development Advisory Service

**AIDD** American Institute for Design and Drafting

**AIDF** African Industrial Development Fund

**AIDL** [New Zealand] Auckland Industrial Development Laboratory

**AIDP** Associate of the Institute of Data Processing; *Association internationale de droit pénal* (French: International Association of Penal Law)

**AIDS** accident information display system; [medicine] acquired immune deficiency syndrome; aircraft integrated data system; air force intelligence data-handling system

**Aids** [medicine] acquired immune deficiency syndrome

**AIEA** *Agence internationale de l'énergie atomique* (French: International Atomic Energy Agency)

**AIED** *Association internationale des étudiants dentaires* (French: International Association of Dental Students)

**AIEE** Associate of the Institution of Electrical Engineers; *Association des instituts d'études européennes* (French: Association of Institutes for European Studies)

**AIEP** [USA] Association of Independent Electricity Producers

**AIF** *Alliance internationale des femmes* (French: International Alliance of Women); [USA] Atomic Industrial Forum; Australian Imperial Forces

**AIFA** Associate of the International Faculty of Arts
**AIFF** Associate of the Institute of Freight Forwarders
**AIFireE** Associate of the Institution of Fire Engineers
**AIFM** *Association internationale des femmes médecins* (French: International Association of Women Doctors)
**AIG** Adjutant Inspector-General; Assistant Inspector-General; Assistant Instructor of Gunnery
**AIGA** American Institute of Graphic Arts
**AIGCM** Associate of the Incorporated Guild of Church Musicians
**AIGS** Agricultural Investment Grant Schemes
**AIH** all in hand; [medicine] artificial insemination by husband; *Association internationale de l'hôtellerie* (French: International Hotel Association)
**AIHA** American Industrial Hygiene Association
**AIIA** Australian Institute of International Affairs
**AIIE** American Institute of Industrial Engineers
**AIIExE** Associate of the Institution of Incorporated Executive Engineers
**AIInfSc** Associate of the Institute of Information Scientists
**AIITech** Associate Member of the Institute of Industrial Technicians
**AIJD** *Association internationale des juristes démocrates* (French: International Association of Democratic Lawyers)
**AIJPF** *Association internationale des journalistes de la presse féminine et familiale* (French: International Association of Women's Press Journalists)
**AIL** air intelligence liaison; Associate of the Institute of Linguists
**AILAS** [aeronautics] automatic instrument-landing approach system
**AILO** air intelligence liaison officer
**AILocoE** Associate of the Institution of Locomotive Engineers
**AIM** Africa Inland Mission; Alternative Investment Market; American Indian Movement (civil-rights organization); American Institute of Management; Amsterdam International Market; analytical ion microscopy; Australian Inland Mission (in Presbyterianism); Australian Institute of Management
**a.i.m.a.** as interest may appear
**AIMarE** Associate of the Institute of Marine Engineers
**AIMCO** [USA] Association of Internal Management Consultants
**AIME** American Institute of Mechanical Engineers; American Institute of Mining Engineers
**AIMechE** Associate of the Institution of Mechanical Engineers
**AIMI** Associate of the Institute of the Motor Industry
**AIMM** Australasian Institute of Mining and Metallurgy
**AIMO** Association of Industrial Medical Officers
**AIMPA** *Association internationale de météorologie et de physique de l'atmosphère* (French: International Association of Meteorology and Atmospheric Physics)
**AIMS** Association for Improvement in Maternity Services
**AIMU** American Institute of Marine Underwriters
**AIN** American Institute of Nutrition
**AINEC** All-India Newspaper Editors' Conference
**AInstP** Associate of the Institute of Physics
**AInstPI** Associate of the Institute of Patentees and Inventors
**AINucE** Associate of the Institution of Nuclear Engineers
**AIP** American Institute of Physics; Associate of the Institute of Plumbing; Association of Independent Producers
**AIPA** Associate of the Institute of Practitioners in Advertising; *Association internationale de psychologie appliquée* (French: International Association of Applied Psychology)
**AIPO** American Institute of Public Opinion
**AIPR** Associate of the Institute of Public Relations
**AIPS** *Association internationale de la presse sportive* (French: International Sports Press Association); astronomical image-processing system
**AIQS** Associate of the Institute of Quantity Surveyors

**AIR** All India Radio; American Institute of Refrigeration

**a-i-r** artist-in-residence

**AIRA** [USA] air attaché

**AIRC** Association of Independent Radio Companies

**AIRCENT** Allied Air Forces, Central Europe

**AIRCOM** airways communications system

**air con.** air conditioning

**AIRG** Agency for Intellectual Relief in Germany

**AIRH** *Association internationale de recherches hydrauliques* (French: International Association of Hydraulic Research)

**AIRPASS** aircraft interception radar and pilots attack sight system

**AIRS** [physics, electronics] acoustic-imaging recognition system

**AIRTE** Associate of the Institute of Road Transport Engineers

**AIRTO** Association of Independent Research and Technology Organizations

**AIS** [commerce] agreed industry standard; androgen insensitivity syndrome; Anglo-Italian Society; *Association internationale de sociologie* (French: International Sociological Association); Australian Illawarra Shorthorn (breed of cattle)

**AISA** Associate of the Incorporated Secretaries Association

**AISE** *Association internationale des sciences économiques* (French: International Economics Association)

**AISI** American Iron and Steel Institute

**AISJ** *Association internationale des sciences juridiques* (French: International Association of Legal Science)

**AISS** *Association internationale de la sécurité sociale* (French: International Social Security Association)

**AIST** [USA] Agency of Industrial Science and Technology

**AIStructE** Associate of the Institution of Structural Engineers

**AIT** *Alliance internationale de tourisme* (French: International Tourism Alliance); [meteorology] artificial ionospheric turbulence; Asian Institute of Technology; Association of HM Inspectors of Taxes; Association of Investment Trusts

**AITA** *Association internationale du théâtre d'amateurs* (French: International Amateur Theatre Association)

**AITC** *Association internationale des traducteurs de conférence* (French: International Association of Conference Translators); Association of Investment Trust Companies

**AITO** Association of Independent Tour Operators

**AIU** *Association internationale des universités* (French: International Association of Universities)

**AIV** *Association internationale de volcanologie* (French: International Association of Volcanology)

**AIW** (International Union of) Allied Industrial Workers of America; Atlantic-Intercoastal Waterway (from Cape Cod to Florida Bay)

**AIWC** All-India Women's Conference

**AIWEM** Associate of the Institution of Water and Environmental Management

**AIWM** American Institute of Weights and Measures

**AIX** [computing] advanced interactive executive

**AJ** ankle jerk; [telecommunications] anti-jam; *Archaeological Journal*; Associate in Journalism; [vehicle registration] Middlesbrough

**AJA** American of Japanese ancestry; Anglo-Jewish Association; Australian Journalists' Association

**AJAG** Assistant Judge Advocate-General

**AJC** Australian Jockey Club

**AJCC** American Joint Committee on Cancer

**AJE** [accounting] adjusting journal entry

**AJEX** Association of Jewish Ex-Service Men and Women

**AJPM** *ad Jesum per Mariam* (Latin: to Jesus through Mary)

**AJR** Association of Jewish Refugees; Australian Jurist Reports

**AJY** Association for Jewish Youth

**AK** above knee; [US postcode] Alaska; automatic Kalashnikov (type of rifle, as in **AK-47**); Knight of the Order of Australia; [vehicle registration] Sheffield

**a.k.a.** also known as

**Akad.** *Akademie* (German: academy)
**AKC** American Kennel Club; Associate of King's College (London)
**AKEL** *Anorthotikon Komma Ergazomanou Laou* (Greek: Progressive Party of the Working People) (in Cyprus)
**AKOE** Anti-Killer Organization of Expatriates (in Cyprus)
**AKR** auroral kilometric radiation (from the earth)
**Akt** [commerce] *Aktiebolaget* (Swedish: joint-stock company)
**Aktb** [commerce] *Aktiebolaget* (Swedish: joint-stock company)
**Aktieb** [commerce] *Aktiebolaget* (Swedish: joint-stock company)
**AL** Abraham Lincoln (US president); [medicine] activity of living; Admiralty letter; [US postcode] Alabama; [international vehicle registration] Albania; *América Latina* (Spanish: Latin America); [baseball] American League; American Legion; Anglo-Latin; *anno lucis* (Latin: in the year of light); army list; [vehicle registration] Nottingham; [UK postcode] St Albans
**Al** [chemical element] aluminium
**al.** alcohol; alcoholic; *alia* (Latin: other things); *alii* (Latin: others)
**.al** Albania (in Internet address)
**a.l.** [finance] allotment letter; [commerce] *après livraison* (French: after delivery); autograph letter
**ALA** Air Licensing Authority; all letters answered (in personal advertisement); American Library Association; Associate in Liberal Arts; Associate of the Library Association; Association of London Authorities; Authors' League of America
**Ala.** Alabama
**ALAA** Associate of the Library Association of Australia
**ALAC** Artificial Limb and Appliance Centre
**ALACP** American League to Abolish Capital Punishment
**ALADI** *Asociación Latino-Americana de Integración* (Spanish: Latin-American Integration Association)
**ALAI** *Association littéraire et artistique internationale* (French: International Literary and Artistic Association)
**ALA-ISAD** American Library Association–Information Science and Automation Division
**ALAM** Associate of the London Academy of Music (and Dramatic Art)
**ALAP** as low as practicable (referring to radiation level or dose)
**ALARA** as low as reasonably achievable (referring to radiation level or dose)
**Alas.** Alaska
**ALAWP** all letters answered with photograph (in personal advertisement)
**Alb.** Albania; Albanian; Alberta; Albion
**alb.** [medicine] albumin
**Alba** Alberta
**Alban.** *Albanensis* (Latin: (Bishop) of St Albans)
**ALBM** air-launched ballistic missile
**Albq.** Albuquerque
**ALBSU** Adult Literacy and Basic Skills Unit
**ALC** Agricultural Land Commission
**alc.** alcohol
**a.l.c.** à la carte
**ALCAN** Aluminium Company of Canada
**ALCD** Associate of the London College of Divinity
**alch.** alchemy
**ALCM** air-launched cruise missile; Associate of London College of Music
**ALCS** Authors' Lending and Copyright Society
**ALD** [medicine] adrenoleukodystrophy; [computing] automatic line drawing
**Ald.** Alderman
**ALDEV** African Land Development
**Aldm.** Alderman
**ALE** [insurance] additional living expense; Association for Liberal Education
**A level** [education] Advanced level
**ALF** Animal Liberation Front; Arab Liberation Front (in Iraq); automatic letter facer (machine for sorting mail)
**ALFSEA** Allied Land Forces South-East Asia
**ALG** [medicine] antilymphocyte globulin
**Alg.** Algeria; Algerian; Algiers
**alg.** algebra; algebraic
**a.l.g.** advanced landing ground
**ALGES** Association of Local Government Engineers and Surveyors
**ALGFO** Association of Local Government Financial Officers
**Algol** [computing] algorithmic language

**ALH** Australian Light Horse
**ALI** American Library Institute; Argyll Light Infantry; Associate of the Landscape Institute
**ALICE** Autistic and Language-Impaired Children's Education
**align.** alignment
**ALJ** Administration Law Judge; Australian Law Journal
**ALJR** Australian Law Journal Reports
**alk.** alkali; alkaline
**ALL** [medicine] acute lymphatic leukaemia
**ALLC** Association for Literary and Linguistic Computing
**alleg.** allegation; allegorical; allegory
**All H.** All Hallows
**all'ingr.** *all'ingrosso* (Italian: wholesale)
**allo** [music] *allegro* (Italian: quickly)
**all'ott.** [music] *all'ottava* (Italian: an octave higher)
**All S.** All Souls
**All SS** All Saints
**ALM** [medicine] alveolar lining material; Association of Lloyd's Members; audio-lingual method (in foreign-language teaching); Master of the Liberal Arts (from Latin *Artium Liberalium Magister*)
**ALN** [medicine] axillary lymph nodes
**ALNA** *Armée de libération nationale d'Angola* (French: Angolan National Liberation Army)
**ALO** air liaison officer; allied liaison officer
**ALOE** A Lady of England (pen-name of Charlotte M. Tucker, British novelist)
**ALP** American Labor Party; Australian Labor Party; automated language processing; automated learning process; [USA] automated library program
**alp.** alpine
**ALPA** Air Line Pilots' Association
**ALPAL** [computing] A Livermore Physics Applications Language
**alph.** alphabetic(al)
**alphanum.** alphanumeric
**ALPO** Association of Land and Property Owners; Association of Lunar and Planetary Observers
**ALPSP** Association of Learned and Professional Society Publishers
**ALPURCOMS** all-purpose communications system
**ALR** American Law Reports
**alr** *aliter* (Latin: otherwise)
**ALRC** Anti-Locust Research Centre
**ALRI** airborne long-range input
**ALS** accident localization system; Agricultural Land Service; [medicine] amyotrophic lateral sclerosis; [immunology] antilymphocytic serum; [aeronautics] approach lighting system(s); Associate of the Linnean Society; autograph letter signed; automated library system
**a.l.s.** autograph letter signed
**Alsat.** Alsatian
**al seg.** [music] *al segno* (Italian: to the sign, at the sign)
**ALSEP** Apollo Lunar Surface Experiment Package
**ALT** Agricultural Land Tribunal
**Alt** [computing] alternate (key)
**Alt.** *Altesse* (French: Highness)
**alt.** alteration; altered; alternate; alternative; alternator; altimeter; altitude; [music] alto
**Alta** Alberta
**alt. dieb.** [medicine] *nis diebus* (Latin: every other day)
**alter.** alteration
**alt. hor.** [medicine] *alternis horis* (Latin: every other hour)
**alt. noct.** [medicine] *alternis noctibus* (Latin: every other night)
**ALTPR** Association of London Theatre Press Representatives
**ALTU** Association of Liberal Trade Unionists
**ALU** [computing] arithmetic and logic unit
**alum.** aluminium; alumna(e); alumnus (or alumni)
**ALV** [microbiology] avian leucosis virus
**ALWR** [nuclear technology] advanced light-water reactor
**AM** Academy of Management; administrative memorandum; [astronautics] airlock module; air mail; Air Marshal; Air Ministry; Albert Medal; Alpes-Maritimes (French department); [radio] amplitude modulation; [physics] angular momentum; *anno mundi* (Latin: in the year of the world); *annus mirabilis* (Latin: year of wonders, 1666); *ante meridiem* (Latin: before noon); area manager;

army manual; assistant manager; Associate Member; [insurance] *assurance mutuelle* (French: mutual insurance); *Ave Maria* (Latin: Hail Mary); Award of Merit; [USA] Master of Arts (from Latin *Artium Magister*); Member of the Order of Australia; [vehicle registration] Swindon

**Am** [chemical element] americium

**Am.** America; American; [Bible] Amos

**aM** *am Main* (German: on the River Main) (in place-names)

**am** attometre

**a/m** above-mentioned

**am.** amateur; ammeter; ammunition

**.am** Armenia (in Internet address)

**a.m.** [radio] amplitude modulation; *ante meridiem* (Latin: before noon)

**AMA** against medical advice; American Management Association; American Marketing Association; American Medical Association; American Missionary Association; American Motorcycle Association; Assistant Masters Association; Associate of the Museums Association; Association of Metropolitan Authorities; Australian Medical Association

**AMAB** Army Medical Advisory Board

**AMAE** American Museum of Atomic Energy

**amal.** amalgamated

**amalg.** amalgamated

**AMAmIEE** Associate Member of the American Institute of Electrical Engineers

**AMARC** Associated Marine and Related Charities

**AMASCE** Associate Member of the American Society of Civil Engineers

**amat.** amateur

**AMAusIMM** Associate Member of the Australasian Institute of Mining and Metallurgy

**AMB** Air Ministry bulletin; [USA] Airways Modernization Board

**Amb.** Ambassador; ambulance

**AMBAC** Associate Member of the British Association of Chemists

**Ambas.** Ambassador

**ambig.** ambiguity; ambiguous

**AMBIM** Associate Member of the British Institute of Management

**AMC** [USA] Aerospace Manufacturers' Council; Agricultural Mortgage Corporation Limited; American Motors Corporation; [USA] Army Missile Command; [USA] Army Mobile Command; [USA] Army Munitions Command; Art Master's Certificate; Association of Management Consultants; Association of Municipal Corporations

**AMCA** Architectural Metal Craftsmen's Association

**AMCIB** Associate Member of the Corporation of Insurance Brokers

**AMCIOB** Associate Member of the Chartered Institute of Building

**AMCL** Association of Metropolitan Chief Librarians

**AMCS** airborne missile control system

**AMCT** Associate of the Manchester College of Technology

**am. cur.** [law] *amicus curiae* (Latin: friend of the court)

**AMD** acid-mine drainage; Admiralty machinery depot; aerospace medical division; [meteorology] air movement data; Army Medical Department

**amd** amend

**AMDB** Agricultural Machinery Development Board

**AMDEA** Association of Manufacturers of Domestic Electrical Appliances

**AMDEC** Agricultural Marketing Development Executive Committee

**AMDG** *ad majorem Dei gloriam* (Latin: to the greater glory of God) (motto of Jesuits)

**amdt** amendment

**AME** [USA] Advanced Master of Education; African Methodist Episcopal; Association of Municipal Engineers

**AMEC** Australian Minerals and Energy Council

**AMEDS** [USA] Army Medical Service

**AMEE** Admiralty Marine Engineering Establishment; Association of Managerial Electrical Executives

**AMEIC** Associate Member of the Engineering Institute of Canada

**AMEM** African Methodist Episcopal Mission

**Am. Emb.** American Embassy

**AMEME** Association of Mining Electrical and Mechanical Engineers

**amend.** amendment
**amendt** amendment
**Amer.** America; American
**Amer. Ind.** American Indian
**Amer. Std** American Standard
**AMES** Air Ministry Experimental Station; Association of Marine Engineering Schools
**AMet** Associate of Metallurgy
**AMETS** Association for Management Education and Training in Scotland
**AMEWA** Associated Manufacturers of Electric Wiring Accessories
**Amex** American Express; American Stock Exchange
**AMEZC** African Methodist Episcopal Zion Church
**AMF** Allied Mobile Force (of NATO); Australian Marine Force; Australian Military Forces
**AMG** Allied Military Government
**amg** among
**a.m.g.** [aeronautics] automatic magnetic guidance
**AMGO** Assistant Master-General of Ordnance
**AMGOT** Allied Military Government of Occupied Territory (in World War II)
**AMI** [medicine] acute myocardial infarction; American Meat Institute; American Military Institute; Ancient Monuments Inspectorate; *Association Montessori internationale* (French: International Montessori Association)
**a.m.i.** [military] advanced manned interceptor; [aeronautics] air mileage indicator
**AMIAE** Associate Member of the Institution of Automobile Engineers
**AMIAP** Associate Member of the Institution of Analysts and Programmers
**AMIBF** Associate Member of the Institute of British Foundrymen
**AMICE** Associate Member of the Institution of Civil Engineers
**AMICEI** Associate Member of the Institution of Civil Engineers of Ireland
**AMIChemE** Associate Member of the Institution of Chemical Engineers
**AMICW** Associate Member of the Institute of Clerks of Works of Great Britain
**AMIED** Associate Member of the Institution of Engineering Designers
**AmIEE** American Institute of Electrical Engineers
**AMIEI** Associate Member of the Institution of Engineering Inspection
**AMIEx** Associate Member of the Institute of Export
**AMIFireE** Associate Member of the Institution of Fire Engineers
**AMIGasE** Associate Member of the Institution of Gas Engineers
**AMIHT** Associate Member of the Institution of Highways and Transportation
**AMII** Association of Musical Instrument Industries
**AMIIE** Associate Member of the Institution of Incorporated Engineers
**AMIIM** Associate Member of the Institution of Industrial Managers
**AMILocoE** Associate Member of the Institution of Locomotive Engineers
**AMIMarE** Associate Member of the Institute of Marine Engineers
**AMIMechE** Associate Member of the Institution of Mechanical Engineers
**AMIMGTechE** Associate Member of the Institution of Mechanical and General Technician Engineers
**AMIMI** Associate Member of the Institute of the Motor Industry
**AMIMM** Associate Member of the Institution of Mining and Metallurgy
**Am. Ind.** American Indian
**AMinlsTech** Associate in Minerals Technology
**AMInstBE** Associate Member of the Institution of British Engineers
**AMInstR** Associate Member of the Institute of Refrigeration
**AMINucE** Associate Member of the Institution of Nuclear Engineers
**AMIOP** Associate Member of the Institute of Printing
**AMIPA** Associate Member of the Institute of Practitioners in Advertising
**AMIPRE** Associate Member of the Incorporated Practitioners in Radio and Electronics
**AMIQA** Associate Member of the Institute of Quality Assurance
**AMIRA** Australian Mineral Industries Research Association
**AMIRSE** Associate Member of the Institute of Railway Signalling Engineers

**AMIStructE** Associate Member of the Institution of Structural Engineers
**AMITA** Associate Member of the Industrial Transport Association
**AMIWEM** Associate Member of the Institution of Water and Environmental Management
**AMJ** *Assemblée mondiale de la jeunesse* (French: World Assembly of Youth)
**AML** abandoned mine land; [medicine] acute myeloid leukaemia; Admiralty materials laboratory; [New Zealand] applied mathematics laboratory
**AMLS** [USA] Master of Arts in Library Science
**AMM** antimissile missile; assistant marketing manager; *Association médicale mondiale* (French: World Medical Association)
**amm.** ammunition
**AMMA** Assistant Masters' and Mistresses' Association
**AMMI** American Merchant Marine Institute
**amn** ammunition
**AMNECInst** Associate Member of the North East Coast Institution of Engineers and Shipbuilders
**AMNILP** Associate Member of the National Institute of Licensing Practitioners
**AMO** Air Ministry order; area medical officer; assistant medical officer; Association of Managerial Officers
**AMOB** automatic meteorological oceanographic buoy
**AMORC** Ancient Mystical Order Rosae Crucis (= Rosicrucians)
**amort.** amortization
**AMOS** automatic meteorological observing station
**AMP** [biochemistry] adenosine monophosphate; Air Member for Personnel (in RAF); Associated Master Plumbers and Domestic Engineers; Australian Mutual Provident Society
**amp** [short form] ampere; [short form] amplifier
**amp.** amperage; ampere; amplification; amplified; amplifier; amplitude
**AMPAS** [USA] Academy of Motion Picture Arts and Sciences
**AMPC** [USA] automatic message processing center; auxiliary military pioneer corps
**amph.** amphibian; amphibious
**AMPHIBEX** amphibious exercise
**ampl.** amplifier
**AMPS** [finance] auction market preferred stock; automatic message processing system
**AMPSS** advanced manned precision strike system
**AMQ** American medical qualification
**AMR** Atlantic missile range; automated meter reading; automatic message routing
**AMRAAM** advanced medium-range air-to-air missile
**AMRINA** Associate Member of the Royal Institution of Naval Architects
**Amrit.** Amritsar
**AMRO** Association of Medical Record Officers
**AMRS** Air Ministry radio station
**AMS** accident-monitoring system; [USA] Agricultural Marketing Service; American Mathematical Society; American Meteorological Society; American Microscopical Society; American Musicological Society; Ancient Monuments Society; [astronautics] Apollo mission simulator; army map service; army medical services; army medical staff; assistant military secretary; Australian medical services; automatic music search
**AMSA** advanced manned strategic aircraft
**AMSAM** antimissile surface-to-air missile
**Am. Sam.** American Samoa
**AMSE** Associate Member of the Society of Engineers
**AMSEF** anti-minesweeping explosive float
**AMSERT** Associate Member of the Society of Electronic and Radio Technicians
**AMSGA** Association of Manufacturers and Suppliers for the Graphic Arts
**AMSL** above mean sea level
**AMSO** Air Member for Supply and Organization (in RAF); Association of Market Survey Organizations
**AMSST** Associate Member of the Society of Surveying Technicians
**Amst.** Amsterdam
**Amstrad** Alan Michael Sugar Trading (computer manufacturer)

**AMSW** [USA] Master of Arts in Social Work
**AMT** Academy of Medicine, Toronto; airmail transfer; Air Member for Training (in RAF); [USA] alternative minimum tax; area management team; Associate in Mechanical Technology; Associate in Medical Technology; Association of Marine Traders; [USA] Master of Arts in Teaching
**amt** amount
**AMTA** Association of Multiple Travel Agents
**AMTC** Art Master's Teaching Certificate
**AMTDA** Agricultural Machinery Tractor Dealers' Association
**AMTE** Admiralty Marine Technology Establishment
**AMTI** airborne moving target indicator
**AMTRI** Advanced Manufacturing Technology Research Institute
**AMTS** Associate Member of the Television Society
**AMU** Associated Metalworkers' Union; [USA] Associated Midwestern Universities; Association of Master Upholsterers
**amu** [physics] atomic mass unit
**AMUA** Associate of Music, University of Adelaide
**AMus** Associate in Music
**AMusD** Doctor of Musical Arts
**AMusLCM** Associate in Music, London College of Music
**AMusTCL** Associate in Music, Trinity College of Music, London
**AMV** *Association mondiale vétérinaire* (French: World Veterinary Association); [microbiology] avian myeloblastosis virus
**AMVAP** Associated Manufacturers of Veterinary and Agricultural Products
**AMVERS** automated merchant vessel report system
**AMVETS** American Veterans (of World War II etc.)
**AMW** average molecular weight
**AN** [chemistry] acid number; [chemistry] ammonium nitrate; Anglo-Norman; [medicine] antenatal; Associate in Nursing; [physics] audible noise; [medicine] avascular necrosis; [civil aircraft marking] Nicaragua; [vehicle registration] Reading
**A/N** advice note; alphanumeric
**An** [chemistry] actinon
**An.** Annam
**an.** *anno* (Latin: in the year); anonymous; answer
**.an** Netherlands Antilles (in Internet address)
**a.n.** above named
**ANA** All Nippon Airways; American Nature Association; American Neurological Association; American Newspaper Association; American Numismatic Association; American Nurses' Association; [commerce] Article Number Association; [USA] Associate National Academician; Association of Nurse Administrators; Australian Natives' Association
**anaes.** anaesthesia; anaesthetic
**anag.** anagram
**anal.** analogous; analogy; analyse; analysis; analytic(al)
**ANAPO** *Allianza Nacional Popular* (Spanish: National Popular Alliance) (in Colombia)
**ANARE** Australian National Antarctic Research Expedition
**anat.** anatomic(al); anatomy
**ANC** advanced nuclear computer; African National Congress; Army Nurse Corps; Australian Newspapers Council
**anc.** ancient
**anch.** anchored
**ANCUN** Australian National Committee for the United Nations
**AND** [international vehicle registration] Andorra
**And** [astronomy] Andromeda
**and.** [music] *andante* (Italian: at moderate speed)
**ANDB** [USA] Air Navigation Development Board
**ANDI** [medicine] abnormal development and involution
**ANEC** American Nuclear Energy Council
**ANECInst** Associate of the North East Coast Institution of Engineers and Shipbuilders
**ANERI** [USA] Advanced Nuclear Equipment Research Institute
**ANF** [USA] Advanced Nuclear Fuels (Corporation); antinuclear factor; Atlantic Nuclear Force; [medicine] atrial natriur-

etic factor; Australian National Flag Association
**ANG** [USA] Air National Guard; Australian Newspaper Guild
**Ang.** Anglesey; *Anglice* (Latin: in English)
**ang.** angle; angular
**ANGB** [USA] Air National Guard Base
**Angl.** *Angleterre* (French: England); Anglican; Anglicized
**Anglo-Fr.** Anglo-French
**Anglo-Ind.** Anglo-Indian
**Anglo-Ir.** Anglo-Irish
**Anglo-L** Anglo-Latin
**Anglo-Sax.** Anglo-Saxon
**ANGUS** Air National Guard of the United States
**Anh.** *Anhang* (German: appendix) (of book etc.)
**anhyd.** [chemistry] anhydrous
**anhydr.** [chemistry] anhydrous
**ANI** *Agência Nacional de Informações* (Portuguese: National Information Agency); American Nuclear Insurers
**anim.** [music] *animato* (Italian: in a lively manner)
**Ank.** *Ankunft* (German: arrival)
**ANL** Anti-Nazi League; *Archaeological News Letter*; [USA] Argonne National Laboratory; [engineering] automatic noise limiting; National Library of Australia
**ANM** Admiralty Notices to Mariners
**Anm.** *Anmerkung* (German: note) (in book etc.)
**anme** [commerce] *anonyme* (French: limited liability) (of company)
**ANN** [telecommunications] all-figure numbers now; [computing] artificial neural network
**ann.** annals; *anni* (Latin: years); *anno* (Latin: in the year); annual; annuity
**ANNA** [USA] Army–Navy–NASA–Air Force satellite
**anniv.** anniversary
**annot.** annotate; annotation; annotator
**annuit.** annuitant
**annul.** annulled; annulment
**Annunc.** Annunciation
**ANO** [USA] Association of Nuclear Operators
**anon.** anonymous; anonymously
**ANOVA** [mathematics] analysis of variance
**ANP** advanced nursing practice; aircraft nuclear propulsion; *Algemeen Nederlands Persbureau* (Dutch news agency); ammonium nitrate–phosphate (fertilizer); Australian National Party
**ANPA** American Newspaper Publishers' Association; Australian National Publicity Association
**anr** another
**anrac** aids navigation radio control
**ANRC** American National Red Cross; Australian National Research Council
**ANRE** advanced nuclear rocket engine
**ANRPC** Association of Natural Rubber Producing Countries
**ANS** [physics] advanced neutron source; American Nuclear Society; Army News Service; Army Nursing Service; [computing] artificial neural system; Astronomical Netherlands Satellite; [anatomy] autonomic nervous system
**ans.** answer
**a.n.s.** autograph note signed
**ANSA** *Agenzia Nazionale Stampa Associata* (Italian news agency); Independent Union for Abbey National Staff (formerly Abbey National Staff Association)
**ANSI** American National Standards Institute
**ANSI–SPARC** American National Standards Institute/Systems Planning and Requirements Committee
**ANSL** Australian National Standards Laboratory
**ANSP** Academy of Natural Sciences of Philadelphia; Australian National Socialist Party
**ANSR** [nuclear technology] advanced neutron-source reactor
**ANSTI** African Network of Scientific and Technological Institutions
**ANSTO** Australian Nuclear Science and Technology Organization
**Ant** [astronomy] Antlia
**Ant.** Antarctica; Antigua; Antrim
**ant.** antenna; anterior; anticipated; antilogarithm; antiquarian; antique; antiquity; antonym
**ANTA** American National Theater and Academy; Australian National Travel Association
**Antarc.** Antarctic
**anthol.** anthology

**anthrop.** anthropological; anthropology
**anthropol.** anthropological; anthropology
**Antig.** Antigua
**antilog** [short form] antilogarithm
**antiq.** antiquarian; antiquities
**antiq.** antiquity
**Ant. Lat.** antique Latin
**ant. ld** antique laid (paper)
**anton.** antonym
**ANTOR** Association of National Tourist Office Representatives
**Antr.** Antrim
**ant. wo.** antique wove (paper)
**ANU** Australian National University
**a/nw** as new (in advertisement)
**ANWR** Arctic National Wildlife Refuge
**anx** annex
**ANZ** Australia and New Zealand
**ANZAAS** Australia and New Zealand Association for the Advancement of Science
**Anzac** Australia and New Zealand Army Corps (in World War I)
**ANZAM** Australia, New Zealand and Malaysia (defence strategy)
**ANZAMRS** Australia and New Zealand Association for Medieval and Renaissance Studies
**ANZCAN** Australia, New Zealand and Canada
**ANZIA** Associate of the New Zealand Institute of Architects
**ANZUK** Australia, New Zealand and United Kingdom (defence force)
**ANZUS** Australia, New Zealand and the United States (defence alliance)
**AO** accountant officer; Air Officer; air ordnance; *anno ordinis* (Latin: in the year of the order); [chemistry] anthracene oil; area office; army order; Australian Opera; [vehicle registration] Carlisle; Officer of the Order of Australia
**A/O** [accounting] account of; and others
**aO** *an der Oder* (German: on the River Oder) (in place-names)
**a/o** [accounting] account of
**.ao** Angola (in Internet address)
**AOA** activity-on-arrow; [USA] Administration on Aging; Aerodrome Owners' Association; Air Officer in charge of Administration; American Ordnance Association; American Orthopedic Association; American Osteopathic Association; American Overseas Association
**AOB** advanced operational base; Antediluvian Order of Buffaloes; any other business
**a.o.b.** any other business; at or below
**AOC** Air Officer Commanding; *anno orbis Conditi* (Latin: in the year of the Creation); any other colour; *appellation d'origine contrôlée* (French: name of origin controlled) (wine classification); Army Ordnance Corps; Artists of Chelsea
**AOCB** any other competent business
**AOC-in-C** Air Officer Commanding-in-Chief
**AOCM** [US air force] aircraft out of commission for maintenance
**AOD** acousto-optic device; advanced ordnance depot; Ancient Order of Druids; Army Ordnance Department
**AOER** Army Officers' Emergency Reserve
**AOF** *Afrique Occidentale Française* (French: French West Africa); Ancient Order of Foresters; Australian Olympic Federation
**A of F** Admiral of the Fleet
**AOFP** absolute open-flow potential
**A of S** Academy of Science
**AOG** aircraft on ground
**AOH** Ancient Order of Hibernians
**AoI** aims of industry
**aoi** angle of incidence
**a.o.i.v.** [engineering] automatically operated inlet valve
**A-OK** [USA] all OK
**AOL** [USA] absent over leave; Admiralty Oil Laboratory; America Online (Internet service provider); [USA] Atlantic Oceanographic Laboratories; [Canada] Atlantic Oceanographic Laboratory
**AOM** amorphous organic matter
**AON** activity-on-node
**AONB** area of outstanding natural beauty
**AOP** Association of Optical Practitioners
**AOPU** Asian Oceanic Postal Union
**AOQ** average outgoing quality
**AOQL** average outgoing quality limit
**AOR** [music] adult-oriented rock; [US law] advice of rights; [USA] album-oriented radio; [music] album-oriented rock
**aor** angle of reflection

**a/or** and/or
**aor.** aorist
**AOS** [astronautics] acquisition of signal; American Opera Society; American Ophthalmological Society; Ancient Order of Shepherds; automated office system
**AOSIS** Association of Small Island States
**AOSO** advanced orbiting solar observatory
**AOSS** *Americanae Orientalis Societatis Socius* (Latin: Fellow of the American Oriental Society)
**AOSTRA** Alberta Oil Sands Technology and Research Authority
**AOSW** Association of Official Shorthand Writers
**AOT** [engineering] allowed outage time; [engineering] allowed out-of-service time
**AOTA** American Occupational Therapy Association
**AOU** American Ornithologists' Union
**AOV** any other variety
**AP** [insurance] additional premium; [grammar] adjective phrase; aerosol particle; [USA] airplane; [USA] Air Police; air pollution; air publication (of Ministry of Defence); *Alianza Popular* (Spanish: Popular Alliance) (political party); [USA] American plan (for payment of hotel bills); [surveying] *Amsterdamsch Peil* (German: Amsterdam level) (mean level used in parts of northern Europe); Andhra Pradesh; [medicine] angina pectoris; [medicine] anterior pituitary; [medicine] anteroposterior; antipersonnel; [commerce] *à protester* (French: to be protested) (on bill of exchange); armour-piercing; [computing] array processor; [medicine] arterial (blood) pressure; Associated Presbyterian; Associated Press (news agency); atomic power; authority to pay; authority to purchase; automotive products; [insurance] average payable; [vehicle registration] Brighton; [civil aircraft marking] Pakistan
**Ap.** apostle; Apostolic; April
**ap.** apostle; apothecaries' (weight or measure); apothecary; apparent; apparently; *apud* (Latin: in the works of, according to)
**a.p.** above proof; [insurance] additional premium; advanced post; [medicine] *ante prandium* (Latin: before meals) (in prescriptions); [mathematics] arithmetical progression; author's proof
**APA** [taxation] additional personal allowance; Alaska Power Authority; [Australia] All Parties Administration; [computing] all points addressable (as in **APA mode**); American Philological Association; American Physicists Association; American Pilots Association; American Press Association; American Protestant Association; American Psychiatric Association; American Psychological Association; [telecommunications] annular phased array; Associate in Public Administration; Association for the Prevention of Addiction; Association of Public Analysts; Australian Physiotherapy Association; *Austria Presse Agentur* (Austrian news agency)
**APACL** Asian People's Anti-Communist League
**APACS** Association for Payment Clearing Services
**APAE** Association of Public Address Engineers
**apart.** apartment
**APB** Accounting Principles Board; [USA] all-points bulletin (police alert); Auditing Practices Board
**APBA** American Power Boat Association
**APBF** Accredited Poultry Breeders' Federation
**APC** [engineering] advanced process control; air-pollution control; All People's Congress (in Sierra Leone); American Philatelic Congress; [immunology] antigen-presenting cell; Appalachian Power Company; armoured personnel carrier; aspirin, phenacetin and caffeine; Assistant Principal Chaplain; Associated Portland Cement; Auditing Practices Committee; automatic phase control; [electronics] automatic power control; automatic public convenience
**a.p.c.** average propensity to consume
**APCA** [USA] Air Pollution Control Association; Anglo-Polish Catholic Association
**APCIMS** Association of Private Client Investment Managers and Stockbrokers
**APCK** Association for Promoting Christian Knowledge (in Church of Ireland)
**APCN** *anno post Christum natum* (Latin: in the year after the birth of Christ)

**APCO** Association of Pleasure Craft Operators
**APCOL** All-Pakistan Confederation of Labour
**APD** Administrative Planning Division; [USA] Air Pollution Division; Army Pay Department
**apd** approved
**APDC** Apple and Pear Development Council
**Ap. Deleg.** Apostolic Delegate
**AP/DOS** [computing] advanced pick/disk operating system
**APE** Amalgamated Power Engineering; automatic photomapping equipment; [physics] available potential energy
**APEC** Asia-Pacific Economic Cooperation Conference
**APEX** advance-purchase excursion (reduced fare on train or aeroplane); Association of Professional, Executive, Clerical and Computer Staff (became part of GMB)
**APF** Association for the Propagation of the Faith
**APFC** Asia-Pacific Forestry Commission
**APG** [US air force] air proving ground
**APGA** American Public Gas Association
**APH** A(lan) P(atrick) Herbert (British writer and politician); [medicine] antepartum haemorrhage; [biochemistry] anterior pituitary hormone
**aph.** aphorism
**APHA** American Public Health Association
**APHC** Association of Plumbing and Heating Contractors
**aphet.** aphetic
**APHI** Association of Public Health Inspectors
**APHIS** [USA] Animal and Plant Health Inspection Service
**API** air-pollution index; air-position indicator; American Petroleum Institute (as in **API scale** for measuring specific gravity of petroleum products); [computing] application program(mer) interface; *Association phonétique internationale* (French: International Phonetic Association); atmospheric pressure ionization
**APIS** Army Photographic Intelligence Service
**ap. J-C** *après Jésus-Christ* (French: after Jesus Christ, AD)
**APL** Alberta Power Limited; alternating polarization laser; [USA] Applied Physics Laboratory (Johns Hopkins University); [computing] A Programming Language
**Apl** April
**APLA** Azanian People's Liberation Army
**APLE** Association of Public Lighting Engineers
**APM** [USA] Academy of Physical Medicine; airborne particulate matter; Assistant Paymaster; Assistant Provost-Marshal; [astronomy] automatic plate-measuring machine
**APMC** Allied Political and Military Commission
**APMG** Assistant Postmaster-General
**APMI** Associate of the Pensions Management Institute
**apmt** appointment
**APNEC** All-Pakistan Newspaper Employees' Confederation
**APO** Acting Pilot Officer; African People's Organization; Armed Forces Post Office; Army Post Office; Asian Productivity Organization
**apo.** apogee
**Apoc.** Apocalypse; Apocrypha; Apocryphal
**Apocr.** Apocrypha; Apocryphal
**apog.** apogee
**Apos.** Apostolic
**apos.** apostrophe
**APOTA** automatic positioning telemetering antenna
**apoth.** apothecary
**APP** African People's Party (became part of KANU); [computing] application portability profile
**App.** Apostles
**app.** apparatus; apparent; apparently; appeal; appended; appendix (of book); applied; appointed; appointment; appreciated; apprentice; approval; approved; approximate; approximately
**APPA** African Petroleum Producers Association
**appar.** apparatus; apparent; apparently
**app. crit.** *apparatus criticus* (Latin: critical apparatus) (list of variant readings)
**appd** approved

**APPITA** Australian Pulp and Paper Industries Technical Association
**appl** appeal
**appl.** appellant; applicable; applied
**appos.** appositive
**APPR** [USA] Army Package Power Reactor
**appr.** apprentice; approved
**appro** [short form] approval
**approx.** approximate; approximately; approximation
**apps** appendices
**appt** appoint; appointment
**apptd** appointed
**APPU** Australian Primary Producers' Union
**appurts** appurtenances
**appx** appendix (of book)
**APR** Accredited Public Relations Practitioner; annual percentage rate (of interest); annual progress report; annual purchase rate (on hire purchase)
**Apr.** April; *April* (German: April)
**apr.** *aprile* (Italian: April)
**APRA** Air Public Relations Association
**APRC** *anno post Romam conditam* (Latin: in the year from the foundation of Rome)
**A/Prin.** Assistant Principal
**apr. J-C** *après Jésus-Christ* (French: after Jesus Christ, AD)
**APRS** [navigation] acoustic position reference system; Association for the Protection of Rural Scotland; Association of Professional Recording Studios
**APS** [Australia] Aborigines' Protection Society; Advanced Photo System; Algeria Press Service (news agency); American Peace Society; American Philatelic Society; American Philosophical Society; American Physics Society; American Physiological Society; American Protestant Society; Arizona Public Service (Company); army postal service; assistant private secretary; Associate of the Pharmaceutical Society; Associate of the Philosophical Society
**Aps** [astronomy] Apus
**a.p.s.** autograph poem signed; average propensity to save
**APSA** American Political Science Association; Associate of the Photographic Society of America; Australian Political Studies Association
**APSE** [computing] Ada programming support environment
**APSL** Acting Paymaster Sublieutenant
**APST** Association of Professional Scientists and Technologists
**APSW** Association of Psychiatric Social Workers
**APT** advanced passenger train; advanced process technology; [nautical] after peak tank; [medicine] alum-precipitated (diphtheria) toxoid; Association of Polytechnic Teachers; Association of Printing Technologists; Association of Private Traders; automatic picture transmission (from satellite)
**apt** apartment
**APTC** Army Physical Training Corps
**APTI** Association of Principals of Technical Institutions
**APTIS** all-purpose ticket-issuing systems
**APTS** [astronautics] Automatic Picture Transmission Subsystem
**APTU** African Postal and Telecommunications Union
**APU** acute psychiatric unit; Arab Postal Union; [education] Assessment of Performance Unit; [aeronautics] auxiliary power unit
**APUC** Association for Promoting Unity of Christendom
**APUD** amine-precursor uptake and decarboxylation (as in **APUD cell**)
**a.p.v.** adjusted present value
**APWA** All Pakistan Women's Association; American Public Welfare Association; American Public Works Association
**APWR** [nuclear technology] advanced pressurized-water reactor
**APWU** American Postal Workers Union
**apx.** approximately
**AQ** [psychology] accomplishment quotient; [psychology] achievement quotient; [military] Administration and Quartering
**Aq.** [horticulture] aquatic
**aq.** *aqua* (Latin: water); aqueous
**.aq** Antarctica (in Internet address)
**aq. bull.** [pharmacology] *aqua bulliens* (Latin: boiling water)
**AQC** Associate of Queen's College (London)

**aq. cal.** [pharmacology] *aqua calida* (Latin: warm water)
**aq. com.** [pharmacology] *aqua communis* (Latin: tap water)
**aq. dest.** [pharmacology] *aqua destillata* (Latin: distilled water)
**aq. ferv.** [pharmacology] *aqua fervens* (Latin: hot water)
**aq. frig.** [pharmacology] *aqua frigida* (Latin: cold water)
**AQI** air-quality index
**AQL** acceptable quality level
**Aql** [astronomy] Aquila
**AQMG** Assistant Quartermaster-General
**aq. m. pip.** [pharmacology] *aqua menthae piperitae* (Latin: peppermint water)
**AQPS** *autre que pur sang* (French: other than pure blood) (in horse-breeding)
**aq. pur.** [pharmacology] *aqua pura* (Latin: pure water)
**Aqr** [astronomy] Aquarius
**aq. tep.** [pharmacology] *aqua tepida* (Latin: tepid water)
**aque.** aqueduct
**AR** [psychology] accomplishment ratio; account receivable; [psychology] achievement ratio; acid resisting; acrylic rubber; [medicine] acute rejection; [physiology] adrenergic receptor; advice of receipt; *Agencja Robotnicza* (Polish workers' news agency); [USA] airman recruit; *Altesse Royale* (French: Royal Highness); [physiology] androgen receptor; *Anna Regina* (Latin: Queen Anne); *anno regni* (Latin: in the year of the reign); annual register; *Annual Register of World Events*; annual report; [taxation] annual return; [medicine] aortic regurgitation; [numismatics] *argentum* (Latin: silver); [US postcode] Arkansas; Army Regulation(s); artificial respiration; [image technology] aspect ratio; Assistant Resident; Associated Rediffusion; Autonomous Region; Autonomous Republic; [fishing port] Ayr; [vehicle registration] Chelmsford
**Ar** [chemical element] argon
**Ar.** Arab; Arabia; Arabian; Arabic; Aramaic
**aR** *am Rhein* (German: on the River Rhine) (in place-names)
**a/r** [insurance] all risks
**ar.** arrival; arrive(s); arrived
**.ar** Argentina (in Internet address)
**a.r.** [insurance] all risks; *anno regni* (Latin: in the year of the reign)
**ARA** Aircraft Research Association; all replies answered (in personal advertisement); Amateur Rowing Association; American Railway Association; Army Rifle Association; Associate of the Royal Academy; Association of the River Authorities; [New Zealand] Auckland Regional Authority
**Arab.** Arabia; Arabian; Arabic
**ARAC** Associate of the Royal Agricultural College
**arach.** arachnology
**ARACI** Associate of the Royal Australian Chemical Institute
**ARAD** Associate of the Royal Academy of Dancing
**ARAeS** Associate of the Royal Aeronautical Society
**ARAIA** Associate of the Royal Australian Institute of Architects
**ARAM** Associate of the Royal Academy of Music
**Aram.** Aramaic
**ARAMCO** Arabian-American Oil Company
**ARAS** Associate of the Royal Astronomical Society
**ARB** Air Registration Board (in civil aviation); Air Research Bureau
**arb.** arbiter; arbitrageur; arbitrary; arbitration; arbitrator
**ARBA** Associate of the Royal Society of British Artists
**ARBE** *Académie royale des beaux-arts, école supérieure des arts décoratifs et école supérieure d'architecture de Bruxelles* (French: Brussels Royal Academy of Fine Arts)
**arbor.** arboriculture
**ARBS** Associate of the Royal Society of British Sculptors
**ARC** Aeronautical Research Council; Agricultural Research Council (former name of AFRC); [medicine] Aids-related complex; American Red Cross; [USA] Ames Research Center; Archaeological Resource Centre (York); Architects' Registration Council; Arthritis and Rheumatism Council; Astrophysical Research Consortium; Atlantic Research Corporation
**arc.** [music] *arcato* (Italian: bowed);

[music] *coll'arco* (Italian: with the bow)

**ARCA** Associate of the Royal Cambrian Academy; Associate of the Royal Canadian Academy of Arts; Associate of the Royal College of Art

**ARCamA** Associate of the Royal Cambrian Academy

**arccos** [mathematics] arc cosine

**arccosec** [mathematics] arc cosecant

**arccot** [mathematics] arc cotangent

**Arch.** Archbishop; Archdeacon; Archduke

**arch.** archaic; archaism; archery; archipelago; architect; architectural; architecture

**archaeol.** archaeology

**Archbp** Archbishop

**Archd.** Archdeacon; Archduke

**archit.** architect; architectural; architecture

**archt** architect

**ARCIC** Anglican/Roman Catholic International Commission

**ARCM** Associate of the Royal College of Music

**Arcnet** attached resource computing network

**ARCO** Associate of the Royal College of Organists

**ARCO(CHM)** Associate of the Royal College of Organists with Diploma in Choir Training

**ARCOS** Anglo-Russian Cooperative Society

**ARCPsych** Associate of the Royal College of Psychiatrists

**ARCS** Associate of the Royal College of Science; Associate of the Royal College of Surgeons (of England); Australian Red Cross Society

**arcsec** [mathematics] arc secant; arc second

**arcsin** [mathematics] arc sine

**ARCST** Associate of the Royal College of Science and Technology (Glasgow)

**arctan** [mathematics] arc tangent

**ARCUK** Architects' Registration Council of the United Kingdom

**ARCVS** Associate of the Royal College of Veterinary Surgeons

**ARD** [medicine] acute radiation disease; [medicine] acute respiratory disease

**ARDC** [USA] Air Research and Development Command

**ARDEC** [USA] Army Research Development and Engineering Center

**ARDMS** automated route design and management system

**ARDS** [medicine] adult respiratory distress syndrome

**ARE** activated reactive evaporation; Admiralty Research Establishment; Arab Republic of Egypt; Associate of the Royal Society of Painter-Printmakers (formerly Associate of the Royal Society of Painter-Etchers and Engravers)

**ARELS** Association of Recognized English Language Schools

**ARENA** *Aliança Renovadora Nacional* (Spanish: National Renewal Alliance) (in Brazil)

**ARF** [medicine] acute renal failure; [medicine] acute respiratory failure; Advertising Research Foundation

**Arg.** [heraldry] argent; Argentina; Argentine; Argentinian; Argyll(shire)

**aRh.** *am Rhein* (German: on the River Rhine) (in place-names)

**ARHA** Associate of the Royal Hibernian Academy

**ARHS** Associate of the Royal Horticultural Society

**ARI** [medicine] acute respiratory infection

**Ari** [astronomy] Aries

**ARIA** automated radioimmunoassay

**ARIAS** Associate of the Royal Incorporation of Architects in Scotland

**ARIBA** Associate of the Royal Institute of British Architects

**ARICS** Professional Associate of the Royal Institution of Chartered Surveyors

**ARIEL** Automated Real-time Investments Exchange Limited (former share-dealing system)

**ARIMA** [computing] autoregressive integrated moving average

**ARINA** Associate of the Royal Institution of Naval Architects

**ARIPHH** Associate of the Royal Institute of Public Health and Hygiene

**ARIS** advanced range instrumentation ship

**Arist.** Aristotle (ancient Greek philosopher)

**Aristoph.** Aristophanes (ancient Greek dramatist)

**arith.** arithmetic; arithmetical; arithmetician

**Ariz.** Arizona
**Ark.** Arkansas
**ARL** Admiralty Research Laboratory; Aeronautical Research Laboratory; Arctic Research Laboratory; [USA] Association of Research Libraries; Australian Rugby League
**ARLA** Association of Residential Letting Agents
**ARLL** [computing] advanced run length limited
**ARM** [USA] adjustable-rate mortgage; *Alliance réformée mondiale* (French: Worldwide Presbyterian Alliance); antiradar missile; antiradiation missile; [medicine] artificial rupture of membranes; atomic resolution microscope; Australian Republican Movement
**ArM** Master of Architecture (from Latin *Architecturae Magister*)
**Arm.** Armagh; Armenia; Armenian; Armorica; Armorican
**ARMA** Association of Residential Managing Agents; [computing] autoregressive moving average
**ARMCM** Associate of the Royal Manchester College of Music
**armd** armoured
**ARMIT** Associate of the Royal Melbourne Institute of Technology
**ARMS** Action for Research into Multiple Sclerosis; Associate of the Royal Society of Miniature Painters
**ARNA** Arab Revolution News Agency
**ARO** army routine order; Asian Regional Organization; Associate Member of the Register of Osteopaths
**AROD** airborne remote operated device
**AROS** African Regional Organization for Standardization
**ARP** [US finance] adjustable rate preferred (stock); air-raid precautions; Associated Reformed Presbyterian
**arp.** [music] *arpeggiato* (Italian: played as arpeggio); [music] arpeggio
**ARPA** Advanced Research Projects Agency (former name of DARPA)
**ARPANET** [computing] Advanced Research Projects Agency Network
**ARPO** Association of Resort Publicity Officers
**ARPS** Associate of the Royal Photographic Society; Association of Railway Preservation Societies
**ARR** accounting rate of return; *anno regni Reginae* (Latin: in the year of the Queen's reign); *anno regni Regis* (Latin: in the year of the King's reign); Association of Radiation Research
**arr.** [music] arranged (by); [music] arrangement; [music] arranger; arrival; arrive(s); arrived
**ARRC** Associate of the Royal Red Cross
**arrd** arrived
**arron.** *arrondissement* (French: administrative district)
**ARRS** American Roentgen Ray Society
**ARS** [medicine] acute radiation syndrome; [USA] Agricultural Research Service; American Records Society; American Recreation Society; American Rocket Society; *anno reparatae salutis* (Latin: in the year of our redemption); [medicine] aortic regurgitation and stenosis; Army Radio School
**ARSA** Associate of the Royal Scottish Academy; Associate of the Royal Society of Arts
**ARSAP** [USA] Advanced Reactor Severe Accident Program
**ARSCM** Associate of the Royal School of Church Music
**ARSH** Associate of the Royal Society of Health
**ARSL** Associate of the Royal Society of Literature
**ARSM** Associate of the Royal School of Mines
**ARSR** air route surveillance radar
**ARSW** Associate of the Royal Scottish Water Colour Society
**ART** [computing] algebraic reconstruction technique; [computing] automated reasoning tool
**Art.** Artemis (ancient Greek goddess)
**art.** article; artificer; artificial; artillery; artist
**ARTC** air route traffic control
**artic** [short form] articulated truck
**artic.** articulated
**artif.** artificer
**art. pf** artist's proof
**arty** artillery
**ARU** American Railway Union; [computing] audio response unit

**ARV** [medicine] Aids-associated retrovirus; [Bible] American (Standard) Revised Version
**ARVA** Associate of the Rating and Valuation Association
**ARWA** Associate of the Royal West of England Academy
**ARWS** Associate of the Royal Watercolour Society
**AS** Academy of Science; Admiral Superintendent; [education] Advanced Supplementary (as in **AS level**); air speed; air staff; [insurance] all sections; [music] *al segno* (Italian: to the sign, at the sign); [geology] aluminium silicate; American Samoa; [computing] analogue states; Anglo-Saxon; *anno salutis* (Latin: in the year of salvation); *anno Salvatoris* (Latin: in the year of the Saviour); antisubmarine; assistant secretary; assistant surgeon; Associate in Science; [vehicle registration] Inverness; [taxation] personal allowance
**A/S** account sales; [education] Advanced Supplementary (as in **A/S level**); [banking] after sight; [commerce] *Aksjeselskap* (Norwegian: limited company, Ltd); [commerce] *Aktieselskab* (Danish: joint-stock company); alongside
**As** [chemical element] arsenic
***As*** [meteorology] altostratus
**As.** Asia; Asian; Asiatic
**a.s.** account sales; aggregate supply
**ASA** Acoustical Society of America; [USA] Addiction Services Agency; Advertising Standards Authority; Amateur Swimming Association; American Sociological Association; American Standards Association; American Statistical Association; Army Sailing Association; [USA] Associate of the Society of Actuaries; Australian Society of Accountants
**ASAA** Associate of the Society of Incorporated Accountants and Auditors
**ASAB** Association for the Study of Animal Behaviour
**ASAI** Associate of the Society of Architectural Illustrators
**ASAM** Associate of the Society of Art Masters
**AS&TS of SA** Associated Scientific and Technical Societies of South Africa
**ASAP** as soon as possible; automated shipboard aerological programme
**a.s.a.p.** as soon as possible
**ASAT** [military] antisatellite (interceptor)
**ASB** Accounting Standards Board; [South Africa] *Afrikaanse Studentebond* (Afrikaans: South African students' union); Alternative Service Book (in Church of England); American Society of Bacteriologists; [medicine] anencephaly and spina bifida
**asb.** asbestos
**a.s.b.** aircraft safety beacon
**ASBAH** Association for Spina Bifida and Hydrocephalus
**ASBM** air-to-surface ballistic missile
**ASBSBSW** Amalgamated Society of Boilermakers, Shipwrights, Blacksmiths and Structural Workers
**ASC** Accounting Standards Committee; Administrative Staff College (Henley); [USA] Air Service Command; altered state of consciousness; American Society of Cinematographers; Anglo-Soviet Committee; Asian Socialist Conference
**ASc** Associate in Science
**Asc.** [astrology] Ascendant
**asc.** ascend; ascent
**ASCA** Associate of the Society of Company and Commercial Accountants
**ASCAB** Armed Services Consultant Approval Board
**ASCAP** American Society of Composers, Authors, and Publishers
**ASCC** Accounting Standards Steering Committee; Association of Scottish Climbing Clubs; [computing] Automatic Sequence Controlled Calculator
**ASCE** American Society of Civil Engineers
**ASCII** [computing] American Standard Code for Information Interchange
**ASCM** Australian Student Christian Movement
**ASCS** [engineering] advanced Stirling conversion system
**ASCU** [USA] Association of State Colleges and Universities
**ASD** [engineering] adjustable speed drive; Admiralty Salvage Department; [engineering] antislip drive; Armament Supply Department; [medicine] atrial septal defect
**Asda** Associated Dairies

**ASDAR** aircraft-to-satellite data relay
**ASDC** Associate of the Society of Dyers and Colourists
**ASDE** Airport Surface Detection Equipment
**a/s de** *aux soins de* (French: care of, c/o) (in postal addresses)
**ASDIC** Allied Submarine Detection Investigation Committee (early form of sonar); [USA] Armed Services Documents Intelligence Center
**ASE** Admiralty Signal Establishment; American Stock Exchange; [physics] amplified spontaneous emission; Army School of Education; Associate of the Society of Engineers; Association for Science Education; automotive Stirling engine
**ASEA** Association of South East Asia
**ASEAN** Association of South East Asian Nations
**ASEC** [USA] Applied Solar Energy Corporation
**ASEE** American Society for Engineering Education; Association of Supervisory and Executive Engineers (became part of IIExE)
**ASF** [computing] aspect source flag; Associate of the Institute of Shipping and Forwarding Agents
**ASG** Acting Secretary-General; Assistant Secretary-General
**ASGB** Aeronautical Society of Great Britain; Anthroposophical Society of Great Britain
**ASGBI** Anatomical Society of Great Britain and Ireland
**asgd** assigned
**asgmt** assignment
**ASH** Action on Smoking and Health
**ashp** airship
**ASHRAE** American Society of Heating, Refrigeration and Air-Conditioning Engineers
**ASI** airspeed indicator; *Association soroptimiste internationale* (French: Soroptimist International Association)
**ASIA** Airlines Staff International Association
**ASIC** [electronics] application-specific integrated circuit
**ASIF** Amateur Swimming International Federation
**ASIO** Australian Security Intelligence Organization
**ASIP** [astronomy] all-sky imaging photometer
**ASIRC** [USA] Aquatic Sciences Information Retrieval Center (Rhode Island)
**ASIS** [astronautics] abort sensing and implementation system; American Society for Information Science
**ASL** above sea level; Acting Sublieutenant; Advanced Student in Law; American Sign Language; American Soccer League; assistant Scout leader
**ASLA** American Society of Landscape Architects
**ASLB** [USA] Atomic Safety and Licensing Board
**ASLE** American Society of Lubrication Engineers
**ASLEF** Associated Society of Locomotive Engineers and Firemen
**ASLEP** [astronautics] Apollo surface lunar experiments package
**AS level** [education] Advanced Supplementary level
**A/S level** [education] Advanced Supplementary level
**ASLIB** Association for Information Management (formerly Association of Special Libraries and Information Bureaux)
**ASLO** American Society of Limnology and Oceanography; Australian Scientific Liaison Office
**ASLP** Amalgamated Society of Lithographic Printers
**ASLW** Amalgamated Society of Leather Workers
**ASM** Acting Sergeant-Major; air-to-surface missile; [computing] algorithmic state machine; American Society for Metals; assistant sales manager; assistant Scoutmaster; assistant stage manager; assistant station master; Association of Senior Members
**ASME** American Society of Mechanical Engineers; Association for the Study of Medical Education
**As. Mem.** Associate Member
**ASMO** Arab Organization for Standardization and Metrology
**ASMP** American Society of Magazine Photographers

**ASN** army service number; average sample number
**ASNE** American Society of Newspaper Editors
**ASO** Air Staff Officer; American Symphony Orchestra; area supplies officer
**ASOS** automatic storm observation service
**ASP** [commerce] *accepté sous protêt* (French: accepted under protest); [US air force] aerospace plane; African Special Project (of IUCN); Afro-Shirazi Party (in Tanzania); American selling price; [USA] Anglo-Saxon Protestant; Astronomical Society of the Pacific
**ASPA** Australian Sugar Producers' Association
**ASPAC** Asian and Pacific Council
**ASPC** [commerce] *accepté sous protêt pour compte* (French: accepted under protest for account); Association of Swimming Pool Contractors
**ASPCA** American Society for the Prevention of Cruelty to Animals
**ASPEP** Association of Scientists and Professional Engineering Personnel
**ASPF** Association of Superannuation and Pension Funds
**ASPI** [computing] advanced SCSI programming interface
**ASR** airport surveillance radar; air-sea rescue; [meteorology] altimeter setting region; answer, send and receive; [computing] automatic send and receive
**ASRE** Admiralty Signal and Radar Establishment
**A/SRS** air-sea rescue service
**ASS** automatic space station
**Ass.** Associate; Associated; Association
**ass.** assembly; assistance; assistant; association; assurance
**ASSC** Accounting Standards Steering Committee
**Ass-Com-Gen** Assistant-Commissary-General
**ASSET** [US air force] aero-thermodynamic-elastic structural systems environmental tests
**ASSGB** Association of Ski Schools in Great Britain
**assigt** assignment
**assim.** assimilate; assimilated
**assmt** assessment
**assn** association
**assoc.** associate; associated; association
**AssocEng** Associate of Engineering
**AssocMCT** Associateship of Manchester College of Technology
**assocn** association
**AssocSc** Associate in Science
**ASSR** Autonomous Soviet Socialist Republic
**asst** assistant
**asstd** assorted
**ASSU** American Sunday School Union
**assy** assembly
**Assyr.** Assyrian
**AST** above-ground storage tank; advanced supersonic transport; air service training; assured shorthold tenancy; Atlantic Standard Time; automated screen trading; automatic station tuning
**ASTA** American Society of Travel Agents; [New Zealand] Auckland Science Teachers' Association
**ASTC** Administrative Service Training Course; Associate of the Sydney Technical College
**ASTIA** [USA] Armed Services Technical Information Agency
**ASTM** American Society for Testing and Materials
**ASTMS** Association of Scientific, Technical and Managerial Staffs
**ASTOR** antisubmarine torpedo ordnance rocket
**ASTP** Apollo–Soyuz test project
**astr.** astronomer; astronomical; astronomy
**ASTRO** [USA] Air Space Travel Research Organization
**astro.** astronautics; astronomer; astronomy
**astrol.** astrologer; astrological; astrology
**astron.** astronomer; astronomical; astronomy
**astrophys.** astrophysical
**Ast. T** astronomical time
**ASU** American Students Union; Arab Socialist Union
**ASUA** Amateur Swimming Union of the Americas
**ASV** aircraft-to-surface vessel; [Bible] American Standard Version; [microbiology] avian sarcoma virus

**ASVA** Associate of the Incorporated Society of Valuers and Auctioneers
**ASVU** Army Security Vetting Unit
**ASW** Amalgamated Society of Wood Workers; antisubmarine warfare; antisubmarine work; Association of Scientific Workers; Association of Social Workers
**ASWDU** Air Sea Warfare Development Unit
**ASWE** Admiralty Surface Weapons Establishment
**AT** achievement test; administrative trainee; Advanced Technologies; [immunology] agglutination test; alternative technology; *Angling Times*; antitank; apparent time; [USA] appropriate technology; arrival time; [medicine] ataxia telangiectasia; Atlantic Time; [education] attainment target; Australia Telescope; automatic transmission (in car advertisement); [vehicle registration] Hull
**A/T** American terms
**At** ampere-turn; [chemical element] astatine; [informal] (member of the) Auxiliary Territorial Service
**at.** atmosphere; atomic; [navigation] attitude; attorney
**.at** Austria (in Internet address)
**ATA** [computing] Advanced Technologies attachment; [nuclear technology] advanced test accelerator; Air Transport Association; Air Transport Auxiliary; American Translators' Association; Amusement Trades Association; Animal Technicians' Association; Associate Technical Aide; Atlantic Treaty Association
**ATAC** Air Transport Advisory Council
**ATAE** Association of Tutors in Adult Education
**ATAF** Allied Tactical Air Force
**ATAM** Association for Teaching Aids in Mathematics
**AT&T** American Telephone and Telegraph Company
**Atapi** [computing] Advanced Technologies attachment packet interface
**ATAS** Air Transport Auxiliary Service
**ATB** advanced technology bomber; all-terrain bike; at the time of the bomb(ing)
**ATBM** antitactical ballistic missile
**ATC** acid-treated coal; air traffic control; Air Training Command; Air Training Corps; Air Transport Command; [law] Annotated Tax Cases; Art Teacher's Certificate; [computing] authorization to copy (software); automatic temperature control; automatic train control
**a.t.c.** average total costs
**ATCC** air traffic control centre
**ATCE** [astronautics] ablative thrust chamber engine
**atchd** attached
**ATCL** Associate of Trinity College of Music, London
**ATCO** Air Traffic Control Officer
**ATCRBS** air traffic control radar beacon system
**ATCSP** Association of Teachers of the Chartered Society of Physiotherapy
**ATD** actual time of departure; advanced technology development; Art Teacher's Diploma; Australian Tax Decisions
**ATDS** Association of Teachers of Domestic Science
**ATE** Amusement Trades Exhibition; Automatic Telephone and Electric (Company); [electronics] automatic test equipment
**ATEC** Air Transport Electronics Council
**a tem.** [music] *a tempo* (Italian: in time)
**ATF** [nuclear technology] accelerator test facility; [nuclear technology] advanced toroidal facility
**ATFS** Association of Track and Field Statisticians
**ATG** [medicine] antithymocyte globulin
**ath.** athlete; athletic
**ATHE** Association of Teachers in Higher Education
**Athen.** Athenian
**athl.** athlete; athletic
**ATI** Associate of the Textile Institute; Association of Technical Institutions
**ATII** Associate of the Taxation Institute, Incorporated (member of Chartered Institute of Taxation)
**ATK** at the keyboard (in Internet chat)
**ATL** [insurance] actual total loss; [medicine] adult T-cell leukaemia; Association of Teachers and Lecturers; [computing] automated (or automatic) tape library
**Atl.** Atlantic
**ATLAS** [astronomy] airborne tunable laser absorption spectrometer; [USA] Argonne tandem-linac accelerator system; auto-

matic tabulating, listing and sorting package; automatic telephone line address system

**ATLB** Air Transport Licensing Board

**ATLV** [medicine] adult T-cell leukaemia virus

**ATM** [computing] Adobe Type Manager; air training memorandum; antitank missile; approved testing material; Association of Teachers of Management; Association of Teachers of Mathematics; [computing] asynchronous transfer mode; at the moment (in Internet chat and e-mail); [banking] automated teller machine

**atm** atmosphere (unit of pressure)

**atm.** atmospheric

**ATMS** assumption-based truth maintenance system

**ATN** [medicine] acute tubular necrosis; [mathematics] arc tangent; [telecommunications] augmented transition network

**ATNA** Australasian Trained Nurses' Association

**ATNF** Australia Telescope National Facility

**at. no.** atomic number

**ATO** Ammunition Technical Officer (bomb-disposal officer); [aeronautics] assisted take-off

**A to A** air-to-air

**A to J** [New Zealand] Appendices to Journals (of parliament)

**ATOL** Air Travel Organizers' Licence

**ATP** [biochemistry] adenosine triphosphate; [aeronautics] advanced turboprop; [commerce] aid trade provision; Air Technical Publications; Associated Theatre Properties; Association of Tennis Professionals; [railways] automatic train protection

**ATPAS** Association of Teachers of Printing and Allied Subjects

**ATPC** Association of Tin Producing Countries

**ATPG** automatic test-pattern generation

**ATPL(A)** Airline Transport Pilot's Licence (Aeroplanes)

**ATPL(H)** Airline Transport Pilot's Licence (Helicopters)

**ATR** [nuclear technology] advanced test reactor; [nuclear technology] advanced thermal reactor; [aeronautics] air turbo-ram (jet engine); [radar] anti-transmit-receive (as in **ATR tube**); Association of Teachers of Russian; [military] automatic target recognition

**ATRAN** automatic terrain recognition and navigation

**a.t.r.i.m.a.** [law] as their respective interests may appear

**ATS** [Australia] Amalgamated Television Services; American Temperance Society; American Tract Society; American Transport Service; [medicine] antitetanus serum; [USA] Army Transport Service; Associate of Theological Study; automated trade system; Auxiliary Territorial Service (in World War II)

**a.t.s.** [law] at the suit of

**ATSC** Associate of the Tonic Sol-Fa College

**ATSDR** [USA] Agency for Toxic Substances and Disease Registry

**ATSIS** [computing] automated technical-specification information system

**ATSS** Association for the Teaching of Social Sciences

**ATT** antitetanus toxoid

**att.** attached; attention; attorney

**Att-Gen** Attorney-General

**attn** attention; for the attention of

**attrac.** attractive

**attrib.** attribute; attributed (to); attribution; [grammar] attributive; attributively

**atty** attorney

**Atty-Gen** Attorney-General

**ATU** [USA] Amalgamated Transit Union

**ATUC** African Trade Union Confederation

**ATV** all-terrain vehicle; Associated Television

**at. wt** atomic weight

**AU** [USA] Actors' Union; [printing] all up (i.e. all set in type); angstrom unit; arithmetic(al) unit; astronomical unit; [vehicle registration] Nottingham

**Au** [chemical element] gold (from Latin *aurum*)

**.au** Australia (in Internet address)

**AUA** [finance] agricultural unit of account (in EU); American Unitarian Association; American Urological Association

**AUBC** Association of Universities of the British Commonwealth

**AUBTW** Amalgamated Union of Building Trade Workers
**AUC** *ab urbe condita* (Latin: (in the year) from the founding of the city (of Rome)); *anno urbis conditae* (Latin: in the year from the founding of the city (of Rome)); [mathematics] area under the curve (on graph); Association of Underwater Contractors; Australian Universities Commission
**AUCAS** Association of University Clinical Academic Staff
**aud.** audit; audited; auditor
**Aud-Gen** Auditor-General
**AUEW** Amalgamated Union of Engineering Workers (became part of AEEU)
**Aufl.** *Auflage* (German: edition)
**AUFW** Amalgamated Union of Foundry Workers
**Aug.** August; *August* (German: August)
**aug.** augment; [grammar] augmentative; augmented
**augm.** augment; [grammar] augmentative; *augmenté* (French: enlarged)
**AUI** [computing] attachment unit interface
**AULLA** Australasian Universities Language and Literature Association
**AUM** air-to-underwater missile
**AUMLA** Australian Universities Modern Language Association
**a.u.n.** *absque ulla nota* (Latin: with no identifying mark)
**AUO** African Unity Organization
**AUP** Aberdeen University Press; acceptable use policy; Australian United Press (news agency)
**Aur** [astronomy] Auriga
**AUS** Army of the United States; assistant undersecretary; [international vehicle registration] Australia
**Aus.** Australia; Australian; Austria; Austrian
**AUSA** Association of the United States Army
**Ausg.** *Ausgabe* (German: edition)
**Aust.** Australia; Australian; Austria; Austrian
**Austral.** Australasia; Australasian; Australia; Australian
**AUT** Association of University Teachers
**Aut.** *Autriche* (French: Austria)
**aut.** autograph; autumn
**AUTA** Association of University Teachers of Accounting
**AUTEC** [US navy] Atlantic Underwater Test Evaluation Center
**auth.** authentic; author; authority; authorize; authorized
**Auth. Ver.** [Bible] Authorized Version
**AUTIF** Association of Unit Trusts and Investment Funds
**auto.** automatic; automobile; automotive
**autobiog.** autobiographical; autobiography
**autog.** autograph
**AUT(S)** Association of University Teachers (Scotland)
**a.u.w.** all-up-weight
**AUWE** Admiralty Underwater Weapons Establishment
**AUX** [linguistics] auxiliary verb
**aux.** auxiliary
**AV** [chemistry] acid value; [finance] *ad valorem* (Latin: according to value); [photography] aperture value; Artillery Volunteers; [medicine] atrioventricular (as in **AV node**); audiovisual; [numismatics] *aurum* (Latin: gold); [Bible] Authorized Version; average value; [vehicle registration] Peterborough
**Av.** Avenue; *Avocat* (French: lawyer)
**a/v** [finance] *ad valorem* (Latin: according to value)
**av.** avenue; average; avoirdupois; *avril* (French: April)
**a.v.** *annos vixit* (Latin: (he/she) lived . . . years); [finance] asset value
**AVA** Alberta Veterinary Association; Amateur Volleyball Association (of Great Britain); audiovisual aids; Audiovisual Association; Australian Veterinary Association
**avail.** available
**AVB** [medicine] atrioventricular block
**AVC** additional voluntary contribution (to pension scheme); American Veterans' Committee; [electronics] automatic volume control
**av. C** *avanti Cristo* (Italian: before Christ, BC)
**a.v.c.** [electronics] automatic volume control; average variable costs
**Av. Cert.** Aviator's Certificate

**AVCM** Associate of Victoria College of Music
**AVCO** [accounting] average cost
**AVD** Army Veterinary Department
**avdp.** avoirdupois
**Ave.** Avenue
**ave.** average
**AVF** [US military] all-volunteer force
**avg.** average
**AVGAS** aviation gasoline
**avge** [cricket] average
**AVI** Association of Veterinary Inspectors; audio-video interleaved; automatic vehicle identification
**avia.** aviation
**av. J-C** *avant Jésus-Christ* (French: before Jesus Christ, BC)
**AVL** [computing] Adel'son-Vel'skii-Landis (as in **AVL tree**); automatic vehicle location
**AVLA** Audio Visual Language Association
**AVLIS** atomic vapour laser isotope separation
**AVM** Air Vice-Marshal; [medicine] arteriovenous malformation; automatic vending machine
**AVMA** Action for the Victims of Medical Accidents; Automatic Vending Machine Association
**AVN** [medicine] atrioventricular node
**avn** aviation
**AVO** administrative veterinary officer; average vehicle occupancy
**avoir.** avoirdupois
**AVR** Army Volunteer Reserve
**AVRI** Animal Virus Research Institute
**AVRO** A. V. Roe and Company Limited (aircraft manufacturer)
**AVRP** audiovisual recording and presentation
**AVS** Anti-Vivisection Society
**AVSL** assistant Venture Scout leader
**AVTRW** Association of Veterinary Teachers and Research Workers
**AW** added water (in food); Alfred Wainwright (British walker and writer); alloy wheels (in car advertisement); Armstrong Whitworth (aircraft manufacturer); Articles of War; atomic warfare; [vehicle registration] Shrewsbury
**a/w** actual weight; airworthy; artwork
**.aw** Aruba (in Internet address)
**a.w.** actual weight; [shipping] all water; atomic weight
**AWACS** airborne warning and control system
**AWAM** Association of West African Merchants
**AWAS** Australian Women's Army Service
**AWB** [South Africa] *Afrikaner Weerstandsbeweging* (Afrikaans: Afrikaner Resistance Movement) (right-wing political party); Agricultural Wages Board; [USA] air waybill; Australian Wages Board
**AWC** Allied Works Council; [USA] Army War College; Australian Wool Corporation
**AWE** Atomic Weapons Establishment
**AWEA** American Wind Energy Association
**AWeldI** Associate of the Welding Institute
**AWG** American Wire Gauge; Art Workers' Guild
**AWHA** Australian Women's Home Army
**AWJ** [engineering] abrasive water jet
**AWL** absent with leave
**AWMC** Association of Workers for Maladjusted Children
**AWNL** Australian Women's National League
**AWO** American Waterways Operators (Incorporated)
**AWOL** absent without (official) leave
**AWP** amusements with prizes (in British Gaming Acts); annual wood production
**AWPR** Association of Women in Public Relations
**AWR** Association for the Study of the World Refugee Problem
**AWRA** Australian Wood Realization Agency
**AWRE** Atomic Weapons Research Establishment
**AWS** [geology] acoustic well sounding; Agricultural Wholesale Society; American Welding Society; automatic warning system
**AWSA** American Water Ski Association
**AWU** Australian Workers' Union
**AX** [vehicle registration] Cardiff
**ax.** axiom
**AXAF** Advanced X-ray Astrophysical Facility (at NASA)

**AY** [vehicle registration] Leicester
**AYH** American Youth Hostels
**AYM** [Freemasonry] Ancient York Mason
**Ayr.** Ayrshire
**AZ** [US postcode] Arizona; [international vehicle registration] Azerbaijan; [vehicle registration] Belfast
**az.** azimuth; azure
**.az** Azerbaijan (in Internet address)
**Azapo** [South Africa] Azanian People's Organization
**az. ld** [printing] azure laid (paper)
**Azo.** Azores
**AZT** [medicine] azidothymidine (used to treat Aids)
**az. wo.** [printing] azure wove (paper)

# B

**B** administrative or professional (occupational group); Bachelor; [currency] baht (used in Thailand); [currency] balboa (used in Panama); [fishing port] Ballina; Baptist; Baron; [physics] baryon number; [chemistry] base-catalysed reaction; [music] bass; [music] basso; bathroom (in accommodation advertisement); battle; Baumé (temperature scale); bay (on map); *Beatus* (Latin: Blessed); [fishing port] Belfast; [international vehicle registration] Belgium; Benediction; best (wrought iron); Bey; Bible; billion; [UK postcode] Birmingham; Bishop; [chess] bishop; black (soft pencil lead); Blessed; [medicine] blood group; blue; board; boatswain; [currency] bolívar (used in Venezuela); bomber (aircraft) (as in **B-52**); [immunology] bone marrow (as in **B-cell**); book; [chemical element] boron; breadth; Britain; British; brotherhood; [photography] B-setting (shutter setting); building; [civil aircraft marking] China; eleven (in hexadecimal notation); [music] note of scale; of secondary importance (as in **B-side**); secondary road (as in **B5053**); [education] second highest grade or mark; [civil aircraft marking] Taiwan
**b** [physics] barn (unit of nuclear cross-section); [meteorology] blue sky; [physics] bottom (quark flavour)
**b.** bag; bale; ball; barrel; base; [music] bass; [music] basso; bath; batsman; bay; beam; bedroom (in accommodation advertisement); before; billion; *bis* (Latin: twice); bitch; bloody; book; born; bound; [medicine] bowels; [cricket] bowled (by); breadth; brother; [informal] bugger; bust; by; [cricket] bye
**B0** [paper size] 1000 × 1414 mm
**B1** [paper size] 707 × 1000 mm
**B2** [paper size] 500 × 707 mm
**B3** [paper size] 353 × 500 mm
**B4** [paper size] 250 × 353 mm
**B5** [paper size] 176 × 250 mm
**B6** [paper size] 125 × 176 mm
**B7** [paper size] 88 × 125 mm
**B8** [paper size] 62 × 88 mm
**B9** [paper size] 44 × 62 mm
**B10** [paper size] 31 × 44 mm
**2B** double black (very soft pencil lead)
**3B** [civil aircraft marking] Mauritius; treble black (very soft pencil lead)
**5B** [civil aircraft marking] Cyprus
**BA** able-bodied seaman; Bachelor of Arts; [fishing port] Ballantrae; [finance] bank acceptance; [finance] banker's acceptance; [UK postcode] Bath; [medicine] biliary atresia; [USA] *Biological Abstracts*; Board of Agriculture; Booksellers' Association (of Great Britain and Ireland); [chemistry] boric acid; British Academy; British Airways; British America; British Association (for the Advancement of Science); [medicine] bronchial asthma; Buenos Aires; [computing] bus automaton; [vehicle registration] Manchester
**Ba** [chemical element] barium
**.ba** Bosnia-Herzegovina (in Internet address)
**b.a.** [taxation] balancing allowance; blind approach
**BAA** Bachelor of Applied Arts; Booking Agents' Association of Great Britain; British Accounting Association; British

Airports Authority; British Archaeological Association; British Astronomical Association
**BAA&A** British Association of Accountants and Auditors
**BAAB** British Amateur Athletic Board
**BA(Admin)** Bachelor of Arts in Administration
**BAAF** British Agencies for Adoption and Fostering
**BAAL** British Association for Applied Linguistics
**BA(Art)** Bachelor of Arts in Art
**BAAS** British Association for the Advancement of Science
**Bab.** Babylonia; Babylonian
**BABIE** British Association for Betterment of Infertility and Education
**BABS** [aeronautics] beam approach beacon system; [aeronautics] blind approach beacon system
**BAC** biologically active compound(s); blood-alcohol concentration; blood-alcohol content; British Aircraft Corporation; British Association of Chemists; [medicine] bronchoalveolar cell(s); Business Archives Council
**BAc** Bachelor of Acupuncture
**Bac.** Baccalauréat (French school-leaving examination); *Baccalaureus* (Latin: Bachelor)
**BACAH** British Association of Consultants in Agriculture and Horticulture
**BACAN** British Association for the Control of Aircraft Noise
**BACAT** barge aboard catamaran; barge canal traffic
**BAcc** Bachelor of Accountancy
**bach.** bachelor
**BACIE** British Association for Commercial and Industrial Education
**BACM** British Association of Colliery Management
**BACO** British Aluminium Company (Limited)
**BACS** Bankers Automated Clearing System
**bact.** bacteria; bacterial; bacteriological; bacteriology; bacterium
**bacteriol.** bacteriological; bacteriology
**BAD** base air depot; British Association of Dermatology
**BADA** British Antique Dealers' Association
**BADGE** base air defence ground environment
**BAdmin** Bachelor of Administration
**BAE** Bachelor of Aeronautical Engineering; Bachelor of Arts in Education; Badminton Association of England; Belfast Association of Engineers; [USA] Bureau of Agricultural Economics
**BAe** British Aerospace
**BAEA** British Actors' Equity Association
**BAEC** Bangladesh Atomic Energy Commission; British Agricultural Export Council
**BA(Econ)** Bachelor of Arts in Economics
**BA(ED)** Bachelor of Arts in Environmental Design
**BA(Ed)** Bachelor of Arts in Education
**BAEF** Belgian-American Educational Foundation
**BAF** biological aerated filter; British Athletics Federation
**BAFM** British Association of Forensic Medicine; British Association of the Friends of Museums
**BAFMA** British and Foreign Maritime Agencies
**BAFO** British Air Forces of Occupation; British Army Forces Overseas
**BAFRA** British Antique Furniture Restorers' Association
**BAFSC** British Association of Field and Sports Contractors
**BAFSV** British Armed Forces Special Vouchers
**BAFTA** British Academy of Film and Television Arts
**BAG** Bank Action Group
**BAGA** British Amateur Gymnastics Association
**BAGB** Bicycle Association of Great Britain
**BAgEc** Bachelor of Agricultural Economics
**BAgr** Bachelor of Agriculture
**BAgrSc** Bachelor of Agricultural Science
**Bah.** Bahamas
**BAHA** British Association of Hotel Accountants
**BAHOH** British Association for the Hard of Hearing
**BAHS** British Agricultural History Society

**BAI** Bachelor of Engineering (from Latin *Baccalaureus Artis Ingeniariae*); [military] battlefield air interdiction; Book Association of Ireland; [medicine] bronchial arterial infusion
**BAIE** British Association of Industrial Editors
**BAIR** British Airports Information Retrieval
**BAJ** Bachelor of Arts in Journalism
**BAL** blood alcohol level; British anti-lewisite (antidote to gas and metal poisoning); [medicine] bronchoalveolar lavage
**Bal.** Ballarat
**bal.** [accounting] balance
**balc.** balcony (in property advertisement)
**BALH** British Association for Local History
**ball.** ballast; ballistics
**BALPA** British Air Line Pilots' Association
**bals.** balsam
**Balt.** Baltic; Baltimore
**balun** [telecommunications] balanced unbalanced (transformer)
**BAM** Bachelor of Applied Mathematics; Bachelor of Arts in Music
**BaM** [medicine] barium meal
**BAMA** British Aerosol Manufacturers' Association; British Amsterdam Maritime Agencies; British Army Motoring Association
**BAMBI** ballistic missile boost intercept
**BAMTM** British Association of Machine Tool Merchants
**BA(Mus)** Bachelor of Arts in Music
**BAMW** British Association of Meat Wholesalers
**BAN** British Association of Neurologists
**Ban.** Bangor; Bantu
**BANC** British Association of National Coaches; British Association of Nature Conservationists
**Banc. Sup.** [law] *Bancus Superior* (Latin: higher bench, Queen's Bench, King's Bench)
**B&B** bed and breakfast
**B&C** [insurance] building and contents
**B&D** bondage and discipline; bondage and domination
**b&e** beginning and ending
**B&FBS** British and Foreign Bible Society
**B&Q** (Richard) Block and (David) Quayle (British founders of chain of DIY stores)
**B&S** brandy and soda; Browne and Sharpe (wire gauge)
**B&W** black and white
**B&WE** Bristol and West of England
**BANS** British Association of Numismatic Societies
**BANZARE** British, Australian, New Zealand Antarctic Research Expedition
**BAO** Bachelor of Arts in Obstetrics; Bankruptcy Annulment Order; British American Oil
**BAOD** British Airways Overseas Division
**BA of E** Badminton Association of England
**BAOMS** British Association of Oral and Maxillofacial Surgeons
**BAOR** British Army of the Rhine
**Bap.** Baptist
**bap.** baptize; baptized
**b. à p.** *billets à payer* (French: bills payable)
**BAPA** British Amateur Press Association
**BAPC** British Aircraft Preservation Council
**BAPCO** Bahrain Petroleum Company
**BA(PE)** Bachelor of Arts in Physical Education
**BAPL** Bettis Atomic Power Laboratory
**BAPLA** British Association of Picture Libraries and Agencies
**BAPM** British Association of Physical Medicine
**BAppArts** Bachelor of Applied Arts
**BAppSc** Bachelor of Applied Science
**BAppSc(MT)** Bachelor of Applied Science (Medical Technology)
**BAPS** beacon automated processing system (for lighthouses); British Association of Paediatric Surgeons; British Association of Plastic Surgeons
**BAPT** British Association for Physical Training
**Bapt.** Baptist
**bapt.** baptism; baptized
**BAR** [computing] base address register; *Book Auction Records*; British Association of Removers; Browning Automatic Rifle; [computing] buffer address register
**Bar.** Baritone; Barrister; [Bible] Baruch (book of Apocrypha)
**bar.** baritone; barleycorn (former unit of

length); barometer; barometric; barrel; barrister

**b. à r.** *billets à recevoir* (French: bills receivable)

**BARB** British Association of Rose Breeders; British Audience Research Bureau; Broadcasters' Audience Research Board

**Barb.** Barbados

**barbie** [Australian short form] barbecue

**BARC** British Automobile Racing Club

**BArch** Bachelor of Architecture

**BArchE** Bachelor of Architectural Engineering

**barg.** bargain

**barit.** baritone

**BARLA** British Amateur Rugby League Association

**BARP** British Association of Retired Persons

**BARR** British Association of Rheumatology and Rehabilitation

**Barr.** Barrister

**BARS** [commerce] behaviourally anchored rating scales; British Association of Residential Settlements

**Bart** Baronet

**Bart's** St Bartholomew's Hospital (London)

**BAS** Bachelor of Agricultural Science; Bachelor of Applied Science; British Antarctic Survey

**BASA** British Architectural Students' Association; British Australian Studies Association

**BASAF** British and South Africa Forum

**BASC** British Association for Shooting and Conservation

**BASc** Bachelor of Agricultural Science; Bachelor of Applied Science

**BASCA** British Academy of Songwriters, Composers and Authors

**BASF** *Badische Anilin- und Soda-Fabrik* (German chemical and electronics company)

**BASI** British Association of Ski Instructors

**Basic** beginners' all-purpose symbolic instruction code (computer programming language); British-American scientific international commercial (as in **Basic English**)

**BASMA** Boot and Shoe Manufacturers' Association and Leather Trades Protection Society

**bass. con.** [music] *basso continuo* (Italian: continuous bass)

**BASW** British Association of Social Workers

**BAT** best available technology; British Aerial Transport; British-American Tobacco Company; [medicine] brown adipose tissue

**Bat.** Batavia

**bat.** battalion; battery; battle

**BATF** [USA] Bureau of Alcohol, Tobacco and Firearms

**bath.** bathroom (in property advertisement)

**BA(Theol)** Bachelor of Arts in Theology

**bathrm** bathroom (in property advertisement)

**BATO** [aeronautics] balloon-assisted take-off

**BA(TP)** Bachelor of Arts in Town and Country Planning

**BATS** [ecology] biosphere–atmosphere transfer scheme

**batt.** battalion; [military] battery

**battn** battalion

**BAU** British Association Unit; business as usual

**BAUA** Business Aircraft Users' Association

**BAUS** British Association of Urological Surgeons

**Bav.** Bavaria; Bavarian

**b. à v.** [finance] *bon à vue* (French: good at sight)

**BAWA** British Amateur Wrestling Association

**BAWLA** British Amateur Weightlifters' Association

**BAYS** British Association of Young Scientists

**BB** bail bond; balloon barrage; bank book; bed and breakfast (in accommodation advertisement); best best (wrought iron); [UK postcode] Blackburn; Blue Book; B'nai B'rith (Jewish society); Boys' Brigade; Brigitte Bardot (French actress); double black (very soft pencil lead); [vehicle registration] Newcastle upon Tyne

**Bb.** bishops

**bb.** books

**.bb** Barbados (in Internet address)

**b.b.** ball bearing; bearer bonds; [nautical] below bridges

**BBA** Bachelor of Business Administration; [obstetrics] born before arrival; British Backgammon Association; British Bankers' Association; British Beekeepers' Association; British Bloodstock Association; British Board of Agrément; British Bobsleigh Association

**BBAC** British Balloon and Airship Club

**b/bar** bull-bar (in car advertisement)

**BBB** bed, breakfast and bath (in accommodation advertisement); [USA] Better Business Bureau; [physiology] blood–brain barrier; treble black (very soft pencil lead)

**BBBC** British Boxing Board of Control

**BBC** British Broadcasting Corporation

**BBCC** British Bottle Collectors' Club

**BBCCS** British Beer Can Collectors Society

**BBCM** Bandmaster of the Bandsmen's College of Music

**BBCMA** British Baby Carriage Manufacturers' Association

**BBCS** British Beer Mat Collectors Society; British Butterfly Conservation Society

**BBEM** bed, breakfast and evening meal (in accommodation advertisement)

**BBF** British Baseball Federation

**BBFC** British Board of Film Classification (formerly British Board of Film Censors)

**BBI** British Bottlers' Institute

**BBIP** *British Books in Print*

**BBIRA** British Baking Industries' Research Association

**B Bisc.** Bay of Biscay

**BBL** be back later (in Internet chat); British Bridge League

**bbl** barrel

**BBMA** British Brush Manufacturers' Association; British Button Manufacturers' Association

**BBMC** British Board of Marbles Control

**BBQ** barbecue

**BBQC** British Board of Quality Control

**BBS** Bachelor of Business Science; Bachelor of Business Studies; be back soon (in Internet chat); [computing] bulletin board system

**BBSR** Bermuda Biological Station for Research

**BBSRC** Biotechnology and Biological Sciences Research Council

**BBT** [medicine] basal body temperature

**BC** Bachelor of Chemistry; Bachelor of Commerce; Bachelor of Surgery (from Latin *Baccalaureus Chirurgiae*); badminton club; [taxation] balancing charge; bank clearing; bankruptcy court; basketball club; [music] *basso continuo* (Italian: continuous bass); Battery Commander; battle cruiser; bayonet cap (on light bulb); before Christ (in dates); bicycle club; billiards club; bills for collection; birth control; bishop and confessor; [medicine] blood consumption; board of control; boat club; boating club; [biochemistry] body composition; [astronomy] bolometric correction; Bomber Command; borough council; bowling club; bowls club; boxing club; boys' club; Bristol Channel; British Coal; British Columbia; British Commonwealth; British Council; [medicine] bronchial carcinoma; budgeted cost; [education] Burnham Committee; [vehicle registration] Leicester

**B/C** bills for collection

**b.c.** [music] *basso continuo* (Italian: continuous bass); blind copy; bulk carrier

**BCA** [New Zealand] Bachelor of Commerce and Administration; Book Club Associates; Boys' Clubs of America; British-Caribbean Association; [angling] British Casting Association; British Chicken Association; British Chiropractic Association

**BCAB** Birth Control Advisory Bureau; British Computer Association for the Blind

**BCAC** British Conference on Automation and Computation

**BC&T** [USA] Bakery, Confectionery and Tobacco Workers International Union

**BCAP** British Code of Advertising Practice

**BCAR** British Civil Airworthiness Requirements; British Council for Aid to Refugees

**BCAS** British Compressed Air Society

**BCAT** Birmingham Centre for Art Therapies

**BCBC** British Cattle Breeders' Club; British Citizens Band Council

**BCC** [medicine] basal-cell carcinoma; British Caravanners Club; British Coal Corporation (replacement for NCB); British Colour Council; British Copy-

right Council; British Council of Churches; British Crown Colony; Bus and Coach Council
**b.c.c.** blind carbon copy
**BCCA** British Cyclo-Cross Association
**BCCG** British Cooperative Clinical Group
**BCCI** Bank of Credit and Commerce International
**BCD** [USA] bad conduct discharge; [computing] binary coded decimal; [astronomy] blue compact dwarf
**BCDP** [medicine] balloon catheter dilation of the prostate
**BCDTA** British Chemical and Dyestuffs Traders' Association
**BCE** Bachelor of Chemical Engineering; Bachelor of Civil Engineering; before Christian Era (in dates); before Common Era (in dates); Board of Customs and Excise
**BCEAO** *Banque centrale des états de l'Afrique de l'Ouest* (French: Central Bank of West African States)
**BCECC** British and Central European Chamber of Commerce
**BCF** battle cruiser force; billion cubic feet; British Chess Federation; British Cycling Federation; [chemistry] bromochlorodifluoromethane (used in fire extinguishers); [textiles] bulked continuous filament; [USA] Bureau of Commercial Fisheries
**BCFA** British–China Friendship Association
**BCG** [medicine] bacille Calmette–Guérin (vaccine against tuberculosis); [medicine] ballistocardiography; [astronomy] blue compact galaxy
**BCGA** British Commercial Gas Association; British Cotton Growing Association
**BCH** [computing] Bose–Chaudhuri–Hocquenghem (code)
**BCh** Bachelor of Surgery (from Latin *Baccalaureus Chirurgiae*)
**bch** branch; bunch
**BChD** Bachelor of Dental Surgery (from Latin *Baccalaureus Chirurgiae Dentalis*)
**BChE** Bachelor of Chemical Engineering
**BChemEng** Bachelor of Chemical Engineering
**BChir** Bachelor of Surgery (from Latin *Baccalaureus Chirurgiae*)
**BCINA** British Commonwealth International Newsfilm Agency
**BCIRA** British Cast-Iron Research Association
**BCIS** Building Cost Information Service; *Bureau central international de séismologie* (French: International Central Bureau of Seismology)
**BCK** [fishing port] Buckie
**BCL** Bachelor of Canon Law; Bachelor of Civil Law
**BCM** [USA] Boston Conservatory of Music; British Commercial Monomark; British Consular Mail
**BCMA** British Colour Makers' Association; British Columbia Medical Association; British Complementary Medicine Association; British Country Music Association
**BCMD** biological and chemical munitions disposal
**BCMF** British Ceramic Manufacturers' Federation
**BCMG** Birmingham Contemporary Music Group
**BCMS** Bible Churchmen's Missionary Society
**BCN** British Commonwealth of Nations
**bcn** beacon
**BCNU** be seein' you (in Internet chat)
**BCNZ** Broadcasting Corporation of New Zealand
**BCO** [medicine] bilateral carotid (artery) occlusion; British College of Optometrists (or Ophthalmic Opticians)
**BCOG** British College of Obstetricians and Gynaecologists
**BCom** Bachelor of Commerce
**BComm** Bachelor of Commerce
**BComSc** Bachelor of Commercial Science
**BCP** Book of Common Prayer; Bulgarian Communist Party (former name of BSP)
**BCPC** British Crop Protection Council
**BCPIT** British Council for the Promotion of International Trade
**BCPL** [computing] Basic Combined Programming Language; [computing] Basic Computer Programming Language
**BCPMA** British Chemical Plant Manufacturers' Association
**BCR** battlefield casualty replacement
**BCRA** British Carbonization Research Association; British Ceramic Research Association

**BCRC** British Cave Rescue Council; British Columbia Research Council

**BCRD** British Council for the Rehabilitation of the Disabled

**BCRU** British Committee on Radiological Units

**BCRUM** British Committee on Radiation Units and Measurements

**BCS** Bachelor of Chemical Science; Bachelor of Commercial Science; [physics] Bardeen–Cooper–Schrieffer (theory of superconductivity); battle cruiser squadron; Bengal Civil Service; British Calibration Service; British Cardiac Society; British Computer Society; British Crossbow Society; [USA] Bureau of Criminal Statistics

**BCSA** British Constructional Steelwork Association

**bcst** broadcast

**BCT** Belfast Chamber of Trade; [medicine] body computer tomograph; Building Conservation Trust

**BCTA** British Canadian Trade Association; British Children's Theatre Association

**BCTGA** British Christmas Tree Growers Association

**BCTV** [microbiology] beet curly top virus

**BCU** [cinema] big close-up; British Canoe Union; British Commonwealth Union

**BCURA** British Coal Utilization Research Association

**BCVA** British Columbia Veterinary Association

**BCWMA** British Clock and Watch Manufacturers' Association

**BCYC** British Corinthian Yacht Club

**BD** Bachelor of Divinity; [currency] Bahraini dinar; [international vehicle registration] Bangladesh; battle dress; [physics] beam deflection; [fishing port] Bideford; [medicine] bile duct; [commerce] bill(s) discounted; bomb disposal; [medicine] bone density; [astronomy] Bonner Durchmusterung (star catalogue); boom defence; [UK postcode] Bradford; *Bundesrepublik Deutschland* (German: Federal Republic of Germany); [vehicle registration] Northampton

**B/D** bank draft; banker's draft; [commerce] bill(s) discounted; [book-keeping] brought down

**Bd** *Band* (German: volume); [computing] baud; Board; Boulevard

**bd** board; [printing] bold; [finance] bond; [bookbinding] bound; broad

**b/d** barrels per day; [book-keeping] brought down

**bd.** bundle

**.bd** Bangladesh (in Internet address)

**b.d.** [commerce] bill(s) discounted; [medicine] *bis (in) die* (Latin: twice a day) (in prescriptions)

**BDA** Bachelor of Domestic Arts; Bachelor of Dramatic Art; bomb damage assessment; British Deaf Association; British Decorators Association; British Dental Association; British Diabetic Association; British Dyslexia Association

**BDBJ** Board of Deputies of British Jews

**BDC** Book Development Council

**b.d.c.** [engineering] bottom dead centre

**BDCC** British Defence Coordinating Committee

**Bde** *Bände* (German: volumes); Brigade

**BDentSc** Bachelor of Dental Science

**BDes** Bachelor of Design

**BDF** [computing] backward differentiation formulae (as in **BDF methods**); Ballroom Dancers Federation; Botswana Defence Force

**BDFA** British Dairy Farmers' Association

**bd ft** board foot (unit of timber length)

**BDG** [bookbinding] binding

**BDG/ND** [bookbinding] binding, no date (given)

**BDH** British Drug Houses

**BDI** British Dyslexia Institute; *Bundesverband der deutschen Industrie* (German: Federal Association of German Industry)

**b.d.i.** bearing deviation indicator; both dates (or days) included

**BDL** below detectable limits; British Drama League

**bdl.** bundle

**bdle** bundle

**BDM** births, deaths, marriages; bomber defence missile; branch delegates' meeting

**BDMA** British Direct Marketing Association; British Disinfectant Manufacturers' Association

**BDMAA** British Direct Mail Advertising Association

**Bdmr** Bandmaster

**BDNF** [medicine] brain-derived neurotrophic factor
**BDO** Boom Defence Officer; British Darts Organization
**BDP** breakdown pressure
**Bdr** Bombardier; Brigadier
**BDRA** British Drag Racing Association
**bdrm** bedroom (in property or accommodation advertisement)
**BDS** Bachelor of Dental Surgery; [international vehicle registration] Barbados; bomb disposal squad; British Deer Society; British Dragonfly Society; British Driving Society
**bds** [bookbinding] boards; bundles
**b.d.s.** [medicine] *bis (in) die sumendus* (Latin: to be taken twice a day) (in prescriptions)
**BDSA** [USA] Business and Defense Services Administration
**BDSc** Bachelor of Dental Science
**BDST** British Double Summer Time
**BDU** [astronomy] baryon-dominated universe; bomb disposal unit
**BDV** breakdown voltage; [accounting] budget day value
**Bdx** Bordeaux
**BE** Bachelor of Economics; Bachelor of Education; Bachelor of Engineering; Bank of England; [fishing port] Barnstaple; best estimate; bill of exchange; [computing] binary encounter; [physics] binding energy; [USA] Board of Education; borough engineer; [physics] Bose–Einstein; British Element; British Embassy; British Empire; [vehicle registration] Lincoln
**B/E** bill of entry; bill of exchange
**Be** [chemical element] beryllium
**Bé** Baumé (temperature scale)
**be.** *bezüglich* (German: with reference to)
**.be** Belgium (in Internet address)
**b.e.** bill of entry; bill of exchange; binding edge
**BEA** British East Africa; British Epilepsy Association; British Esperanto Association; British European Airways (former airline company)
**BEAB** British Electrical Approvals Board
**BEAC** *Banque des états de l'Afrique centrale* (French: Bank of Central African States)
**BEAIRE** British Electrical and Allied Industries' Research Association
**BEAM** [medicine] brain electrical activity mapping
**BEAMA** (Federation of) British Electrotechnical and Allied Manufacturers' Associations
**bearb.** *bearbeitet* (German: compiled, edited)
**BEAS** British Educational Administration Society
**BEC** Building Employers' Confederation; *Bureau européen du café* (French: European Coffee Bureau); [USA] Bureau of Employees' Compensation
**BEc** Bachelor of Economics
**bec.** because
**BECA** British Exhibition Contractors' Association
**Bech.** Bechuanaland (former name of Botswana)
**BE(Chem)** Bachelor of Chemical Engineering
**BECO** booster-engine cut-off
**BEcon** Bachelor of Economics
**BEcon(IA)** Bachelor of Economics in Industrial Administration
**BEcon(PA)** Bachelor of Economics in Public Administration
**BECTU** Broadcasting, Entertainment, Cinematograph and Theatre Union
**BEd** Bachelor of Education
**bed.** bedroom (in property advertisement)
**BEDA** British Electrical Development Association; Bureau of European Designers' Associations
**BEd(Com)** Bachelor of Education in Commerce
**BEd(HEc)** Bachelor of Education in Home Economics
**BEd(N)** Bachelor of Education in Nursing
**BEd(PE)** Bachelor of Education in Physical Education
**bedrm** bedroom (in property advertisement)
**Beds** Bedfordshire
**beds** bedrooms (in property advertisement)
**BEd(Sc)** Bachelor of Education in Science
**BEE** Bachelor of Electrical Engineering
**Beeb** [short form] British Broadcasting Corporation

**BEEL** biological equivalent exposure limit (of radiation)
**BEF** British Equestrian Federation; British Expeditionary Force
**bef.** before
**b.e.f.** blunt end first
**BEFA** British Emigrant Families Association
**BEG** [USA] Bureau of Economic Geology
**beg.** beginning
**BEHA** British Export Houses Association
**BEI** Bachelor of Engineering (Dublin); *Banque européenne d'investissement* (French: European Investment Bank, EIB)
**Beibl.** *Beiblatt* (German: supplement)
**BEIC** British Egg Industry Council
**beigeb.** *beigebunden* (German: bound, in with something else)
**beil.** *beiliegend* (German: enclosed)
**BEIR** biological effects of ionizing radiation
**BEL** British Electrotechnical Committee
**Bel.** Belgian; Belgium
**bel ex.** *bel exemplaire* (French: fine copy) (of book or engraving)
**Belf.** Belfast
**Belfox** Belgian Futures and Options Exchange
**Belg.** Belgian; Belgic; Belgium
**BEM** British Empire Medal; bug-eyed monster
**BEMA** British Essence Manufacturers' Association
**BEMAC** British Exports Marketing Advisory Committee
**BEMAS** British Education Management and Administration Society
**BEMB** British Egg Marketing Board
**BEME** Brigade Electrical and Mechanical Engineer
**BEMSA** British Eastern Merchant Shippers' Association
**BEN** [electronics] broadband electrostatic noise
**ben.** *benedictio* (Latin: blessing); benediction
**Bend.** Bendigo (Australia)
**BenDr** *Bachelier en droit* (French: Bachelor of Law)
**benef.** benefice
**Benelux** Belgium, Netherlands, Luxembourg
**BEng** Bachelor of Engineering
**Beng.** Bengal; Bengali
**BEngr** Bachelor of Engraving
**BenH** *Bachelier en humanité* (French: Bachelor of Humanities)
**BEO** Base Engineer Officer
**BEPC** British Electrical Power Convention
**beq.** bequeath
**beqt** bequest
**Ber.** Berlin
**BERCO** British Electric Resistance Company
**Berks** Berkshire
**Berl.** Berlin
**Berm.** Bermuda
**BERSA** British Elastic Rope Sports Association
**Berw.** Berwick(shire)
**BES** Bachelor of Engineering Science; Bachelor of Environmental Studies; Biological Engineering Society; British Ecological Society; Business Expansion Scheme (replaced by EIS)
**bes.** *besonders* (German: especially)
**BESA** British Esperanto Scientific Association
**BèsA** *Bachelier ès arts* (French: Bachelor of Arts)
**BESI** bus electronic scanning indicator
**BèsL** *Bachelier ès lettres* (French: Bachelor of Letters)
**BESO** British Executive Service Overseas
**BESS** Bank of England Statistical Summary; bottom environmental sensing system (in oceanography)
**BèsS** *Bachelier ès sciences* (French: Bachelor of Science)
**BEST** British Expertise in Science and Technology (database)
**Best.** [commerce] *Bestellung* (German: order)
**BET** British Electric Traction Company; buildings energy technology
**bet.** between
**BETA** Broadcasting and Entertainment Trades Alliance (became part of BECTU); Business Equipment Trades' Association
**BETAA** British Export Trade Advertising Association
**BETRO** British Export Trade Research Organization
**betw.** between

**BEU** [engineering] batch extraction unit; Benelux Economic Union
**BEUC** *Bureau européen des unions de consommateurs* (French: European Bureau of Consumers' Unions)
**BEV** Black English Vernacular
**BeV** [USA] billion electronvolts
**bev.** bevel; beverage
**BEVA** British Exhibition Venues' Association
**BEXA** British Exporters Association
**bez.** *bezahlt* (German: paid); *bezüglich* (German: with reference to)
**bezw.** *beziehungsweise* (German: respectively)
**BF** Bachelor of Forestry; [fishing port] Banff; *Banque de France* (French: Bank of France); [currency] Belgian franc; black face (sheep); blast furnace; [informal] bloody fool; body fat; breathing frequency; British Funds; [international vehicle registration] Burkina Faso; [vehicle registration] Stoke-on-Trent
**B/F** bring forward; [book-keeping] brought forward
**bf** brief
**b/f** bring forward; [book-keeping] brought forward
**.bf** Burkina Faso (in Internet address)
**b.f.** bankruptcy fee; base frequency; beer firkin; [informal] bloody fool; [printing] bold face; bona fide
**BFA** Bachelor of Fine Arts; British Film Academy
**BFAP** British Forces Arabian Peninsula
**BFASS** [nuclear technology] BWR fuel assembly sealing system
**b'fast** breakfast
**BFAWU** Bakers', Food and Allied Workers' Union
**BFBB** British Federation of Brass Bands
**BFBPW** British Federation of Business and Professional Women
**BFBS** British and Foreign Bible Society; British Forces Broadcasting Service
**BFCA** British Federation of Commodity Associations
**BFCS** British Friesian Cattle Society
**BFEBS** British Far Eastern Broadcasting Service
**BFET** [electronics] ballistic field-effect transistor
**BFFA** British Film Fund Agency
**BFFC** British Federation of Folk Clubs
**BFFS** British Federation of Film Societies
**BFG** Big Friendly Giant (in children's book by Roald Dahl)
**BFI** British Film Institute
**BFIA** British Flower Industry Association
**BFMA** British Farm Mechanization Association
**BFMF** British Federation of Music Festivals; British Footwear Manufacturers' Federation
**BFMIRA** British Food Manufacturing Industries' Research Association
**BFMP** British Federation of Master Printers
**BFN** [informal] bye for now
**Bfn** Bloemfontein; British Forces Network
**BFO** beat-frequency oscillator
**BFor** Bachelor of Forestry
**BForSc** Bachelor of Forestry Science
**BFP** Bureau of Freelance Photographers
**BFPA** British Film Producers' Association
**BFPC** British Farm Produce Council
**BFPO** British Forces Post Office
**BFr** [currency] Belgian franc
**BFS** [mining] blast-furnace slag; British Fuchsia Society
**BFSA** British Fire Services' Association
**BFSS** British and Foreign Sailors' Society; British Field Sports Society
**BFT** biofeedback training
**BFTA** British Fur Trade Alliance
**BFUW** British Federation of University Women
**BFV** [military] Bradley fighting vehicle
**BG** Birmingham (Wire) Gauge; blood group; Brigadier-General; British Guiana (former name of Guyana); [international vehicle registration] Bulgaria; [vehicle registration] Liverpool
**bg** [commerce] bag
**b/g** bonded goods
**.bg** Bulgaria (in Internet address)
**b.g.** [horseracing] bay gelding
**BGA** [USA] Better Government Association; British Gliding Association; British Graduates Association
**BGB** *Bürgerliches Gesetzbuch* (German: code of civil law)
**BGC** bank giro credit
**BGCS** Botanic Gardens Conservation Secretariat

**BGEA** Billy Graham Evangelistic Association
**BGenEd** Bachelor of General Education
**BGF** [Australia] Banana Growers' Federation
**BGH** [biochemistry] bovine growth hormone
**BGIRA** British Glass Industry Research Association
**BGL** Bachelor of General Laws
**b.g.l.** below ground level
**bglr** bugler
**BGM** Bethnal Green Museum
**BGMA** British Gear Manufacturers' Association
**BGMV** [microbiology] bean golden mosaic virus
**BGRB** British Greyhound Racing Board
**BGS** Brigadier General Staff; British Geological Survey; British Geriatrics Society; British Goat Society; Brothers of the Good Shepherd
**bgt** bought
**BGV** below-ground vault
**BH** base hospital; [astronomy] black hole; [fishing port] Blyth; [UK postcode] Bournemouth; [metallurgy] Brinell hardness; British Honduras (former name of Belize); British Hovercraft; Burlington House (London) (home of Royal Academy); [vehicle registration] Luton
**B/H** bill of health
**Bh** [chemical element] bohrium
**b/h** barrels per hour
**.bh** Bahrain (in Internet address)
**b.h.** [informal] bloody hell
**BHA** [mining] bottom-hole assembly; British Handball Association; British Homeopathic Association; British Humanist Association
**B'ham** Birmingham
**BHB** British Hockey Board
**BHC** [medicine] benign hereditary chorea; benzene hexachloride (insecticide); British High Commissioner
**bhd** beachhead; billhead; bulkhead
**BHDF** British Hospital Doctors' Federation
**BHE** Bachelor of Home Economics
**B'head** Birkenhead
**BHF** British Hardware Federation; British Heart Foundation
**Bhf** *Bahnhof* (German: railway station)
**BHGA** British Hang Gliding Association
**BHI** British Horological Institute; *Bureau hydrographique international* (French: International Hydrographic Bureau)
**BHL** biological half-life
**Bhm** Birmingham
**BHMRA** British Hydromechanics' Research Association
**BHN** [metallurgy] Brinell hardness number
**BHort** Bachelor of Horticulture
**BHortSc** Bachelor of Horticultural Science
**BHP** [Australia] Broken Hill Proprietary
**bhp** brake horsepower
**bhpric** bishopric
**BHQ** Brigade Headquarters
**BHRA** British Hydromechanics' Research Association
**BHRCA** British Hotels, Restaurants and Caterers' Association
**BHS** boys' high school; British Home Stores; British Horse Society
**BHT** [electronics] bipolar heterojunction transistor; [mining] bottom-hole temperature
**BHTA** British Herring Trade Association
**Bhu.** Bhutan
**BHy** Bachelor of Hygiene
**BI** background information; Bahama Islands; Balearic Islands; base ignition; Befrienders International; Bermuda Islands; [medicine] bone injury; bulk issue
**Bi** [chemical element] bismuth
**.bi** Burundi (in Internet address)
**BIA** British Institute of Acupuncture; British Insurance Association; British Ironfounders' Association; [USA] Bureau of Indian Affairs
**BIAA** British Industrial Advertising Association
**BIAC** Business and Industry Advisory Committee
**BIAE** British Institute of Adult Education
**BIAS** Bristol Industrial Archaeological Society
**BIAT** British Institute of Architectural Technologists
**BIATA** British Independent Air Transport Association
**BIB** [military] baby incendiary bomb
**Bib.** Bible; Biblical

**bib.** [medicine] *bibe* (Latin: drink); biblical; *bibliothèque* (French: library)
**BIBA** British Insurance Brokers' Association (former name of BIIBA)
**BIBC** British Isles Bowling Council
**BIBF** British and Irish Basketball Federation
**bibl.** biblical; bibliographer; bibliographical; bibliography
**biblio.** bibliography
**bibliog.** bibliographer; bibliographical; bibliography
**BIBRA** British Industrial Biological Research Association
**BIC** Bahá'i International Community; [electronics] biased ion collector; *Bureau international du cinéma* (French: International Cinema Bureau); Butter Information Council
**bicarb** [short form] bicarbonate of soda
**BICC** Berne International Copyright Convention; British Insulated Callender's Cables Limited
**BICE** *Bureau international catholique de l'enfance* (French: International Catholic Child Bureau)
**BICEMA** British Internal Combustion Engine Manufacturers' Association
**BICEP** British Industrial Collaborative Exponential Programme
**BICERI** British Internal Combustion Engine Research Institute
**BICFET** [electronics] bipolar inversion-channel field-effect transistor
**bi-CMOS** [electronics] (merged) bipolar/complementary metal oxide semiconductor
**BICS** British Institution of Cleaning Science
**BID** Bachelor of Industrial Design; Bachelor of Interior Design; [medicine] brought in dead
**b.i.d.** [medicine] *bis in die* (Latin: twice a day) (in prescriptions)
**BIDS** British Institute of Dealers in Securities
**BIE** Bachelor of Industrial Engineering; [mathematics] boundary integral equation; *Bureau international d'éducation* (French: International Bureau of Education); *Bureau international des expositions* (French: International Exhibition Bureau)
**BIEE** British Institute of Energy Economics
**bien.** biennial
**bienn.** biennial
**BIET** British Institute of Engineering Technology
**BIF** [geology] banded iron formation; British Industries Fair
**BIFFEX** Baltic International Freight Futures Market (formerly Baltic International Freight Futures Exchange)
**BIFU** Banking, Insurance and Finance Union
**BIH** [medicine] benign intracranial hypertension; [international vehicle registration] Bosnia-Herzegovina; *Bureau international de l'heure* (French: International Time Bureau)
**BIHA** British Ice Hockey Association
**BIIBA** British Insurance and Investment Brokers' Association (formerly BIBA)
**bike** [short form] bicycle
**BIM** [mathematics] boundary integral method; British Institute of Management; British Insulin Manufacturers
**bim.** *bimestrale* (Italian: bimonthly); *bimestre* (Italian: two-month period)
**BIMA** [astronomy] Berkeley–Illinois–Maryland Association (array)
**BIMBO** buy-in management buyout
**BIMCAM** British Industrial Measuring and Control Apparatus Manufacturers' Association
**BIN** *Bulletin of International News*
**bin.** [mathematics] binary
**BINC** Building Industries' National Council
**bind.** binding
**BIO** [Canada] Bedford Institute of Oceanography
**biochem.** biochemical; biochemistry
**biodeg.** biodegradable
**biog.** biographer; biographical; biography
**biogeog.** biogeography
**biol.** biological; biologist; biology
**BIOS** [computing] basic input–output system; Biological Investigation of Space; [astronautics] biological satellite; British Intelligence Objectives Subcommittee
**BIOT** British Indian Ocean Territory
**BIP** Botswana Independence Party; British

Industrial Plastics; British Institute in Paris
**BIPCA** *Bureau international permanent de chimie analytique pour les matières destinées à l'alimentation de l'homme et des animaux* (French: Permanent International Bureau of Analytical Chemistry of Human and Animal Food)
**BIPL** Burmah Industrial Products Limited
**BIPM** *Bureau international des poids et mésures* (French: International Bureau of Weights and Measures)
**BIPP** [medicine] bismuth iodoform paraffin paste (formerly applied to wounds); British Institute of Practical Psychology
**BIR** Board of Inland Revenue; British Institute of Radiology
**BIRD** *Banque internationale pour la reconstruction et le développement* (French: International Bank for Reconstruction and Development, IBRD)
**BIRF** Brewing Industry Research Foundation
**Birm.** Birmingham
**BIRMO** British Infra-Red Manufacturers' Organization
**BIRS** British Institute of Recorded Sound
**BIS** Bank for International Settlements; British Information Services; British Interplanetary Society; *Bureau international du scoutisme* (French: Boy Scouts International Bureau); business information system
**bis.** bissextile
**BISA** British International Studies Association
**Bisc.** Biscayan
**BISF** British Iron and Steel Federation
**BISFA** British Industrial and Scientific Film Association
**bish.** bishop
**bis in 7d.** [medicine] *bis in septem diebus* (Latin: twice a week) (in prescriptions)
**BISPA** British Independent Steel Producers' Association
**BISRA** British Iron and Steel Research Association
**BISYNC** [computing] binary synchronous communications
**BIT** *Bureau international du travail* (French: International Labour Office)
**bit** [computing] binary digit
**bit.** bitumen; bituminous
**BITA** British Industrial Truck Association
**bitm.** bituminous
**BITNET** [computing] Because It's Time Network
**BITO** British Institution of Training Officers
**BITOA** British Incoming Tour Operators' Association
**bitum.** bituminous
**BIU** Bermuda Industrial Union; *Bureau international des universités* (French: International University Bureau)
**biv.** bivouac
**BIWF** British–Israel World Federation
**BIWS** Bureau of International Whaling Statistics
**BIZ** *Bank für internationalen Zahlungsausgleich* (German: Bank for International Settlements)
**BJ** Bachelor of Journalism; [vehicle registration] Ipswich
**.bj** Benin (in Internet address)
**BJA** British Judo Association
**BJCEB** British Joint Communications Electronics Board
**BJJ** [electronics] boundary Josephson junction
**BJJA** British Ju Jitsu Association
**BJOS** *British Journal of Occupational Safety*
**BJP** [India] Bharatiya Janata Party
**BJSM** British Joint Services Mission
**BJT** [electronics] bipolar junction transistor
**BJTRA** British Jute Trade Research Association
**BJur** Bachelor of Jurisprudence
**BJuris** Bachelor of Jurisprudence
**BK** [fishing port] Berwick-on-Tweed; [trademark] Burger King; [vehicle registration] Portsmouth
**Bk** [chemical element] berkelium
**bk** backwardation; bank; bark; barrack; black; block; book; break
**BKA** British Karate Association; *Bundeskriminalamt* (German: criminal investigations office)
**bkble** bookable
**bkcy** bankruptcy
**BKD** [medicine] bacterial kidney disease
**bkd** blackboard; booked
**bkfst** breakfast
**bkg** banking; booking; book-keeping

**bkgd** background
**b/kit** body kit (in car advertisement)
**bkkg** book-keeping
**bklr** [printing] black letter
**bklt** booklet
**Bklyn** [USA] Brooklyn
**bkm** buckram
**bkpg** book-keeping
**bkpt** bankrupt
**bkrpt** bankrupt
**bks** barracks; books
**BKSTS** British Kinematograph, Sound and Television Society
**bkt** basket; bracket; bucket
**BL** Bachelor of Law; Bachelor of Letters; Bachelor of Literature; Barrister-at-Law; base line; bill lodged; bill of lading; [printing] black letter; [medicine] blood lead; Boatswain Lieutenant; Bodleian Library (Oxford); [UK postcode] Bolton; [fishing port] Bristol; British Legion; British Leyland (former vehicle manufacturer); British Library; [medicine] Burkitt's lymphoma; [vehicle registration] Reading
**B/L** bill of lading
**Bl.** *Blatt* (German: newspaper); Blessed
**bl** barrel
**bl.** bale; black; blue
**b.l.** bill of lading; breech-loading (rifle)
**BLA** Bachelor of Landscape Architecture; Bachelor of Liberal Arts; British Legal Association; British Liberation Army
**BLACC** British and Latin American Chamber of Commerce
**BLAISE** British Library Automated Information Service
**BLAVA** British Laboratory Animals Veterinary Association
**BLB** [horticulture] bacterial leaf blight; [medicine] Boothby, Lovelace and Bulbulian (nasal oxygen mask)
**BLBSD** British Library, Bibliographic Services Division
**BLC** British Lighting Council
**bld** [printing] bold (face)
**bldg** building
**BLDSC** British Library, Document Supply Centre
**BLE** [USA] Brotherhood of Locomotive Engineers
**bleaters** [informal] born losers expending all their energy rubbishing success
**BLESMA** British Limbless Ex-Servicemen's Association
**BLEU** Belgo-Luxembourg Economic Union; [aeronautics] Blind Landing Experimental Unit
**BLG** *Burke's Landed Gentry*
**BLH** British Legion Headquarters
**BLHSS** British Library, Humanities and Social Sciences
**BLI** British Lighting Industries
**BLib** Bachelor of Library Science
**BLibSc** Bachelor of Library Science
**BLIC** *Bureau de liaison des industries du caoutchouc de la CE* (French: Rubber Industries Liaison Bureau of the EU)
**BLIS** [USA] Bibliographic Literature Information System
**Bliss** baby life support systems; [military] bend, low silhouette, irregular shape, small, secluded (pilots' escape technique)
**BLit** Bachelor of Literature
**BLitt** Bachelor of Letters (from Latin *Baccalaureus Litterarum*)
**blk** black; blank; block; bulk
**BLL** Bachelor of Laws
**BLLD** British Library, Lending Division
**BLM** blind landing machine; [USA] Bureau of Land Management
**BLMA** British Lead Manufacturers' Association
**BLMAS** Bible Lands Missions' Aid Society
**BLMRA** British Leather Manufacturers' Research Association
**BLNL** British Library Newspaper Library
**BLOF** British Lace Operatives' Federation
**BLOX** [finance] block order exposure system
**BLP** Barbados Labour Party
**b.l.r.** breech-loading rifle
**BLRA** British Launderers' Research Association
**BLRD** British Library, Reference Division
**BLRG** [astronomy] broad-line radio galaxy
**BLS** Bachelor of Library Science; basic life support; *benevolenti lectori salutem* (Latin: greeting to the well-wishing reader); Branch Line Society; [USA] Bureau of Labor Statistics
**BLSN** [meteorology] blowing snow
**BLT** bacon, lettuce and tomato (sandwich)
**blt** built

**BLV** [microbiology] bovine leukaemia virus; British Legion Village
**Blvd** Boulevard
**BLWA** British Laboratory Ware Association
**BLWN** [electronics] band-limited white noise
**BM** Bachelor of Medicine; Bachelor of Music; bandmaster; [medicine] basal metabolism; base metal; *beatae memoriae* (Latin: of blessed memory); *Beata Maria* (Latin: Blessed Mary); [surveying] benchmark; Bishop and Martyr; *bonae memoriae* (Latin: of happy memory); [medicine] bone marrow; [computing] Boyer–Moore (algorithm); brigade major; British Monomark; British Museum; [fishing port] Brixham; bronze medal; bronze medallist; [USA] Bureau of Mines; [vehicle registration] Luton
**b.m.** *bene merenti* (Latin: to the well-deserving); [horseracing] black mare; board measure (of wood); [medicine] bowel movement; breech mechanism (of firearm)
**BMA** Bahrain Monetary Agency; British Manufacturers' Association; British Medical Association; British Midland Airways
**BMath** Bachelor of Mathematics
**BMATT** British Military Advisory and Training Team
**BMBF** British Mountain Bike Federation
**BMC** [medicine] bone marrow cell(s); [medicine] bone mineral content (or concentration); Book Marketing Council; British Match Corporation; British Medical Council; British Metal Corporation; British Motor Corporation (vehicle manufacturer); British Mountaineering Council; British Museum Catalogue (of 15th-century books)
**BMCIS** Building Maintenance Cost Information Service
**BMD** ballistic missile defence; births, marriages and deaths; [medicine] bone mineral density
**BMDM** [medicine] bone-marrow-derived macrophage(s); British Museum Department of Manuscripts
**BMDO** [USA] Ballistic Missile Defense Organization
**Bmdr** Bombardier
**BME** Bachelor of Mechanical Engineering; Bachelor of Mining Engineering; Bachelor of Music Education; [medicine] benign myalgic encephalomyelitis
**BMEC** British Marine Equipment Council
**BMed** Bachelor of Medicine
**BMedSci** Bachelor of Medical Science
**BMEF** British Mechanical Engineering Federation
**BMEG** Building Materials Export Group
**BMEO** British Middle East Office
**BMEP** [engineering] brake mean effective pressure
**BMet** Bachelor of Metallurgy
**BMetE** Bachelor of Metallurgical Engineering
**BMEWS** ballistic missile early warning system
**BMF** Builders Merchants Federation
**BMFA** Boston Museum of Fine Arts
**BMH** British Military Hospital
**BMI** ballistic missile interceptor; Birmingham and Midland Institute; body-mass index; Broadcast Music Incorporated
**BMJ** *British Medical Journal*
**BML** Bachelor of Modern Languages; British Museum Library
**BMM** British Military Mission
**BMMA** Bacon and Meat Marketing Association
**b.m.o.** business machine operator
**B'mouth** Bournemouth
**BMP** biochemical methane potential; biochemical methane production; [computing] bitmap (format)
**bmp** brake mean power
**BMPA** British Metalworking Plantmakers' Association
**BMPS** British Musicians' Pension Society
**BMR** [physiology] basal metabolic rate
**BMRA** Brigade Major Royal Artillery
**BMRB** British Market Research Bureau
**BMRMC** British Motor Racing Marshals' Club
**BMRR** [USA] Brookhaven Medical Research Reactor
**BMS** Bachelor of Marine Science; Baptist Missionary Society; British Mycological Society; building management system; business modelling system
**BMSE** Baltic Mercantile and Shipping Exchange

**BMT** basic motion time-study; bone-marrow transplant; borehole-mining tool; British Mean Time
**BMTA** British Motor Trade Association
**BMus** Bachelor of Music
**BMusEd** Bachelor of Music Education
**BMV** Blessed Mary the Virgin; [microbiology] brome mosaic virus
**BMW** *Bayerische Motorenwerke* (German vehicle manufacturer)
**BMWE** [USA] Brotherhood of Maintenance of Way Employees
**BMWS** ballistic missile weapon system
**BMX** bicycle motocross
**BN** Bachelor of Nursing; bank note; [astronomy] Becklin–Neugebauer (object); [fishing port] Boston; [UK postcode] Brighton; Britten–Norman (aircraft); [vehicle registration] Manchester
**Bn** Baron; Battalion
**bn** bassoon; battalion; beacon; been; billion; born
**.bn** Brunei (in Internet address)
**BNA** British Naturalists' Association; British North America; [insurance] British North Atlantic; British Nursing Association
**BNAF** British North Africa Force
**BNB** [physiology] blood–nerve barrier; *British National Bibliography*
**BNBC** British National Book Centre
**BNC** [computing] bayonet nut couplers; [linguistics] British National Corpus
**BNCAR** British National Committee for Antarctic Research
**BNCC** British National Committee for Chemistry
**BNCI** *Banque nationale pour le commerce et l'industrie* (French: National Bank for Commerce and Industry) (in Madagascar)
**BNCM** *Bibliothèque nationale du conservatoire de musique* (French: National Library of Music) (in Paris)
**BNCS** British National Carnation Society
**BNCSAA** British National Committee on Surface-Active Agents
**BNCSR** British National Committee on Space Research
**BND** *Bundesnachrichtendienst* (German: national intelligence service)
**B/ND** [bookbinding] binding, no date (given)
**BNDD** [USA] Bureau of Narcotics and Dangerous Drugs
**Bndr** Bandmaster
**BNEC** British National Export Council; British Nuclear Energy Conference
**BNES** British Nuclear Energy Society
**BNF** [computing] Backus–Naur form; [computing] Backus normal form; [pharmacology] British National Formulary; British Nuclear Fuels; British Nutrition Foundation
**BnF** *Bibliothèque nationale de France* (French: National Library of France)
**BNFC** British National Film Catalogue
**BNFL** British Nuclear Fuels Limited
**BNFMF** British Non-Ferrous Metals Federation
**BNGA** British Nursery Goods Association
**BNGM** British Naval Gunnery Mission
**BNHQ** battalion headquarters
**bnkg** banking
**BNL** *Banca Nazionale del Lavoro* (Italian: National Bank of Labour); Brookhaven National Laboratory
**BNM** *Bureau national de métrologie* (French: National Bureau of Metrology)
**BNO** [medicine] bowels not opened
**BNOC** British National Oil Corporation; British National Opera Company
**BNP** *Banque nationale de Paris* (French: National Bank of Paris); Barbados National Party; British National Party
**BNS** Bachelor of Natural Science; Bathymetric Navigation System; British Numismatic Society; buyer no seller
**BNSC** British National Space Centre
**BNSc** Bachelor of Nursing Science
**BNTA** British Numismatic Trade Association
**BNurs** Bachelor of Nursing
**BNX** British Nuclear Export Executive
**bnzn** [chemistry] benzoin
**BO** Bachelor of Oratory; biological oceanography; [informal] body odour; [fishing port] Borrowstounness (Bo'ness); [medicine] bowels opened; box office; branch office; [vehicle registration] Cardiff
**B/O** [book-keeping] brought over; buyer's option
**b/o** [book-keeping] brought over
**.bo** Bolivia (in Internet address)
**b.o.** back order; blackout; broker's order; buyer's option

**BOA** British Olympic Association; British Optical Association; British Orthopaedic Association; broad ocean area
**BOAC** British Overseas Airways Corporation (former airline company)
**BOAD** *Banque ouest-africaine de développement* (French: West African Development Bank)
**BOA(Disp)** British Optical Association, Dispensing Certificate
**BOAI** [medicine] balloon occluded arterial infusion
**BOAT** byroad open to all traffic
**BOBA** British Overseas Banks' Association
**BOBMA** British Oil Burner Manufacturers' Association
**BOBS** Board of Banking Supervision
**BOC** [computing] beginning of cycle; [computing] bimodal optical computer; British Oxygen Corporation; Burmah Oil Company
**BOCE** Board of Customs and Excise
**BOCM** British Oil and Cake Mills Limited
**BOD** biochemical oxygen demand
**Bod.** Bodleian Library (Oxford)
**Bodl.** Bodleian Library (Oxford)
**BODMAS** brackets, of, division, multiplication, addition, subtraction (mnemonic for order of arithmetical operations)
**Body** British Organ Donor Society
**BOE** Bank of England; Board of Education; [building] brick on edge (as in **BOE sill**)
**BOF** basic oxygen furnace; [computing] beginning of file; British Orienteering Federation; British Overseas Fairs
**B of E** Bank of England
**B of H** Band of Hope Union
**BOGMC** Bangladesh Oil, Gas and Minerals Corporation
**Boh.** Bohemia; Bohemian
**BOHA** [medicine] balloon occlusion hepatic angiography
**BOJ** Bank of Japan
**BOL** beginning of life; [international vehicle registration] Bolivia
**Bol.** (Simon) Bolívar (South American statesman); Bolivia; Bolivian
**bol.** [medicine] bolus (large pill)
**BOLTON** better on lips than on notepaper (on envelope of love letter)
**BOM** bill of materials; [USA] Bureau of Mines
**Bom.** Bombay
**b.o.m.** bill of materials
**Bomb.** Bombardier; Bombay
**BomCS** Bombay Civil Service
**BomSC** Bombay Staff Corps
**BON** British Organization of Non-Parents
**bon** *bataillon* (French: battalion)
**BONUS** [finance] Borrower's Option for Notes and Underwritten Standby
**Boo** [astronomy] Bootes
**BOP** [chemistry] basic oxygen process; [mining] blowout preventer; *Boy's Own Paper*
**BOptom** Bachelor of Optometry
**BOQ** [US military] bachelor officers' quarters; base officers' quarters
**BOr** Bachelor of Orientation
**bor.** borough
**BORAD** British Oxygen Research and Development Association
**boro.** borough
**BOS** basic oxygen steelmaking; [computing] business operating system
**bos'n** boatswain
**Bos Pops** [USA] Boston Pops Orchestra
**BOSS** Bioastronautic Orbiting Space Station; [South Africa] Bureau of State Security
**Boswash** [USA] Boston–Washington, DC (urban area)
**BOT** [computing] beginning of tape (marker); Board of Trade (became part of DTI)
**bot** bought
**bot.** botanic(al); botanist; botany; bottle; bottom
**BOTB** British Overseas Trade Board
**BOU** British Ornithologists' Union
**Boul.** Boulevard
**BOV** brown oil of vitriol (commercial sulphuric acid)
**BOWO** Brigade Ordnance Warrant Officer
**BP** Bachelor of Pharmacy; Bachelor of Philosophy; back projection; (Robert) Baden Powell (founder of Scout movement); barometric pressure; [finance] basis point; [military] beach party; before present (in dates); be prepared (motto of Scout movement); [shipping] between perpendiculars; [medicine] blood pressure; *Blue Peter* (television programme);

*Boerenpartij* (Dutch: Farmers' Party); boiling point; British Patent; British Petroleum; British Pharmacopoeia; British Public; [vehicle registration] Portsmouth

**B/P** bills payable

**Bp** Bishop

**b/p** bills payable; blueprint

**bp.** baptized; birthplace

**b.p.** below proof (of alcohol); bills payable; [medicine] blood pressure; boiling point; *bonum publicum* (Latin: the public good)

**BPA** Bachelor of Professional Arts; *Bahnpostamt* (German: railway post office); [USA] Biological Photographic Association; Bookmakers' Protection Association; British Paediatric Association; British Parachute Association; British Philatelic Association; [USA] Brookhaven (National Laboratory) Plant Analyzer; [USA] Business Publications Audit of Circulation

**BPAA** British Poster Advertising Association

**BPAGB** Bicycle Polo Association of Great Britain

**BPAS** British Pregnancy Advisory Service

**b.p.b.** bank post bills

**BPBF** British Paper Box Federation

**BPBIRA** British Paper and Board Industry Research Association

**BPBMA** British Paper and Board Makers' Association

**BPC** Book Prices Current; British Pharmaceutical Codex; British Pharmacopoeia Commission; British Printing Corporation; British Productivity Council; [USA] Business and Professional Code

**BPCA** British Pest Control Association

**BPCC** British Printing and Communication Corporation

**bpcd** barrels per calendar day

**BPCF** British Precast Concrete Federation

**BPCR** Brakes on Pedal Cycle Regulations

**BPCRA** British Professional Cycle Racing Association

**BPd** Bachelor of Pedagogy

**bpd** barrels per day

**BPDB** Bangladesh Power Development Board

**BPDMS** [military] basic point defence missile system

**BPE** Bachelor of Physical Education

**BPEd** Bachelor of Physical Education

**BPF** bottom pressure fluctuation; British Plastics Federation; British Polio Fellowship

**b.p.f.** [commerce] *bon pour francs* (French: value in francs)

**BPG** Broadcasting Press Guild

**BPH** Bachelor of Public Health; [medicine] benign prostatic hypertrophy (or hyperplasia)

**BPh** Bachelor of Philosophy

**bph** barrels per hour

**BPharm** Bachelor of Pharmacy

**BPhil** Bachelor of Philosophy

**BPI** Booksellers' Provident Institution; British Pacific Islands

**bpi** [computing] bits per inch; [computing] bytes per inch

**BPICA** *Bureau permanent international des constructeurs d'automobiles* (French: International Permanent Bureau of Motor Manufacturers)

**BPIF** British Printing Industries' Federation

**Bpl.** Barnstaple

**bpl.** birthplace

**bpm** barrels per minute; [music] beats per minute

**BPMA** British Premium Merchandise Association; British Pump Manufacturers' Association

**BPMF** British Postgraduate Medical Federation; British Pottery Manufacturers' Federation

**BPO** base post office; Berlin Philharmonic Orchestra

**BPOE** Benevolent and Protective Order of Elks

**BPP** Botswana People's Party

**BPPMA** British Power-Press Manufacturers' Association

**BPR** business process re-engineering

**BPRA** Book Publishers' Representatives' Association

**BPRO** Blind Persons Resettlement Officer

**BPS** [medicine] blood-pool scintigraphy; border patrol sector; border patrol station; British Pharmacological Society; British Psychological Society; [USA] Bureau of Professional Standards (Internal Affairs)

**BPs** Bachelor of Psychology

**bps** [computing] bits per second; [computing] bytes per second
**BPsS** British Psychological Society
**Bp Suff.** Bishop Suffragan
**BPsych** Bachelor of Psychology
**BPT** Bachelor of Physiotherapy; battle practice target; British Petroleum Tanker
**bpt** [computing] bits per track
**BPV** [microbiology] bovine papilloma virus
**BQ** *bene quiescat* (Latin: may he/she rest well)
**Bq** becquerel (unit of radioactivity)
**bq.** barque
**BQA** British Quality Association
**BQMS** Battery Quartermaster-Sergeant
**bque** barque
**BR** [law] *Bancus Reginae* (Latin: Queen's Bench); [law] *Bancus Regis* (Latin: King's Bench); bioaccumulation ratio; [medicine] blink reflex; [education] block release; book of reference; [international vehicle registration] Brazil; [nuclear technology] breeder reactor; breeding ratio; [physics] bremsstrahlung radiation; [fishing port] Bridgwater; British Rail; [UK postcode] Bromley; (poly)butadiene rubber; butyl rubber; [vehicle registration] Newcastle upon Tyne
**B/R** bills receivable; Bordeaux or Rouen (in grain trade); [insurance] builders' risks
**Br** [currency] birr (used in Ethiopia); Bombardier; [chemical element] bromine; [Roman Catholic Church] Brother; [military] Bugler
**Br.** Branch; Brazil; Breton; Britain; British
**br.** bearing; branch; bridge; brief; brig; bronze; brother; brown
**.br** Brazil (in Internet address)
**b.r.** bank rate; bills receivable
**BRA** Bee Research Association; Brigadier Royal Artillery; British Records Association; British Rheumatism and Arthritis Association
**bra** [short form] brassière
**BRAD** *British Rates and Data* (directory of publications)
**Brad.** Bradford
**Br. Am.** British America
**BRAS** ballistic rocket air suppression
**Braz.** Brazil; Brazilian
**Brazza.** Brazzaville
**BRB** be right back (in Internet chat); [medicine] blood retinal barrier
**BRC** [USA] base residence course; Biological Records Centre (Nature Conservancy Council); British Radio Corporation; business reply card
**Br. C** British Columbia
**brch** branch
**BRCS** British Red Cross Society
**BRD** [fishing port] Broadford; [USA] Building Research Division (National Bureau of Standards)
**brd** board
**BRDC** British Racing Drivers' Club
**brdcst** broadcast
**BRE** Bachelor of Religious Education; British Rail Engineering; Building Research Establishment
**Brec.** Brecon
**b. rec.** bills receivable
**BREL** British Rail Engineering Limited
**BREMA** British Radio Equipment Manufacturers' Association
**Bren** Brno and Enfield (places of manufacture of Bren gun)
**Br'er** Brother
**Bret.** Breton
**brev.** brevet; *breveté* (French: patent); *brevetto* (Italian: patent)
**brew.** brewer; brewery; brewing
**BRF** Bible Reading Fellowship; British Road Federation
**brf** [law] brief
**BRFC** [angling] British Record Fish Committee
**brg** bearing
**br. g.** [horseracing] brown gelding
**BRI** *Banque des règlements internationaux* (French: Bank for International Settlements, BIS); [computing] basic-rate ISDN; [USA] Biological Research Institute; [USA] Brain Research Institute
**Br. I** British India; British Isles
**Brig.** Brigade; Brigadier
**Brig-Gen** Brigadier-General
**brill** [short form] brilliant
**brill.** [music] *brillante* (Italian: brilliant)
**BRIMEC** British Mechanical Engineering Confederation
**BRINCO** British Newfoundland Corporation Limited
**Brisb.** Brisbane

**Brist.** Bristol
**Brit.** Britain; Britannia; British; Briton
**Brit. Mus.** British Museum
**Brit. Pat.** British Patent
**brk** brick
**brkf.** breakfast
**brklyr** bricklayer
**brkt** bracket
**brkwtr** breakwater
**BRL** Ballistic Research Laboratory; [USA] Bible Research Library
**brl** barrel
**BRM** [computing] binary-rate multiplier; [medicine] biological response modifier; British Racing Motors
**BRMA** Board of Registration of Medical Auxiliaries; British Rubber Manufacturers' Association
**BRMCA** British Ready-Mixed Concrete Association
**BRMF** British Rainwear Manufacturers' Federation
**BRN** [international vehicle registration] Bahrain
**brn** brown
**BRNC** Britannia Royal Naval College
**brng** [navigation] bearing; burning
**BRO** brigade routine order
**Bro.** Brotherhood
**bro.** brother
**brom.** [chemistry] bromide
**Bros.** Brothers
**bros.** brothers
**BRP** biological reclamation process
**BRS** British Record Society; British Road Services; Building Research Station
**BRSA** British Rail Staff Association
**BRSCC** British Racing and Sports Car Club
**BRT** *Belgische Radio en Televisie* (Belgian broadcasting company); [shipping] *Brutto-Registertonnen* (German: gross register tons)
**brt** bright
**BRTA** British Racing Toboggan Association; British Regional Television Association; British Road Tar Association
**BRU** [international vehicle registration] Brunei
**Brum** Brummagem (informal name for Birmingham)
**Brunsw.** Brunswick
**BRurSc** Bachelor of Rural Science
**Brux.** *Bruxelles* (French: Brussels)
**BRW** British Relay Wireless
**bry.** bryology
**bryol.** bryology
**brz.** bronze
**BS** [vehicle registration] Aberdeen; [USA] Bachelor of Science; Bachelor of Surgery; [international vehicle registration] Bahamas; battleship; battle squadron; [fishing port] Beaumaris; below specification; Bibliographical Society; bill of sale; [computing] binary state; Biochemical Society; Blackfriars Settlement; Blessed Sacrament; [medicine] blood sugar; Boy Scouts; [angling] breaking strain (of line); [medicine] breath sounds; [UK postcode] Bristol; [aeronautics] Bristol Siddeley; British Standard; British Steel (plc); Budgerigar Society; building society; [slang] bullshit; [computing] bus switch
**B/S** bill of sale; [commerce] bill of store
**Bs** [currency] bolívar (used in Venezuela)
**bs** bags; bales
**.bs** Bahamas (in Internet address)
**b.s.** backstage; balance sheet; bill of sale; [slang] bullshit
**BSA** Bachelor of Science in Agriculture; Bachelor of Scientific Agriculture; Bibliographical Society of America; Birmingham Small Arms Company; [medicine] body surface area; [medicine] bovine serum albumin; Boy Scouts' Association; Boy Scouts of America; British School at Athens; British Speleological Association; Building Societies' Association
**BSAA** Bachelor of Science in Applied Arts; British School of Archaeology at Athens
**BSAC** British Sub-Aqua Club
**BSAdv** Bachelor of Science in Advertising
**BSAE** Bachelor of Science in Aeronautical Engineering; Bachelor of Science in Agricultural Engineering
**BSAeEng** Bachelor of Science in Aeronautical Engineering
**BSAgE** Bachelor of Science in Agricultural Engineering
**BSAgr** Bachelor of Science in Agriculture
**BS&W** basic (or bottom) sediment and water
**BSAP** British Society of Animal Production

**BSArch** Bachelor of Science in Architecture
**BSAS** British Ship Adoption Society
**BSAVA** British Small Animals Veterinary Association
**BSB** British Satellite Broadcasting (became part of BSkyB); British Standard brass (screw thread)
**Bsb.** Brisbane
**BSBA** Bachelor of Science in Business Administration
**BSBC** British Social Biology Council
**BSBI** Botanical Society of the British Isles
**BSBus** Bachelor of Science in Business
**BSC** Bachelor of Science in Commerce; Bengal Staff Corps; Bibliographical Society of Canada; [computing] binary symmetric channel; [computing] binary synchronous communications; Biomedical Sciences Corporation; British Safety Council; British Shoe Corporation; British Society of Cinematographers; British Standard Channel; British Stationery Council; British Steel Corporation; British Sugar Corporation; British Supply Council; Broadcasting Standards Council; Building Societies Commission
**BSc** Bachelor of Science
**bsc** basic
**BSCA** British Swimming Coaches' Association; [USA] Bureau of Security and Consular Affairs
**BSc(A)** Bachelor of Science in Agriculture
**BSc(Acc)** Bachelor of Science in Accounting
**BSc(Ag)** Bachelor of Science in Agriculture
**BScApp** Bachelor of Applied Science
**BSc(Arch)** Bachelor of Science in Architecture
**BSCC** British Society of Clinical Cytology; British Synchronous Clock Conference
**BSc(ChemE)** Bachelor of Science in Chemical Engineering
**BScD** Bachelor of Dental Science
**BSc(Dent)** Bachelor of Science in Dentistry
**BSCE** Bachelor of Science in Civil Engineering
**BSc(Econ)** Bachelor of Science in Economics
**BSc(Ed)** Bachelor of Science in Education
**BSc(Eng)** Bachelor of Science in Engineering
**BSChE** Bachelor of Science in Chemical Engineering
**BSc(Hort)** Bachelor of Science in Horticulture
**BScMed** Bachelor of Medical Science
**BSc(Nutr)** Bachelor of Science in Nutrition
**BSCP** British Standard Code of Practice
**BSCRA** British Steel Castings Research Association
**BScSoc** Bachelor of Social Science
**BScTech** Bachelor of Technical Science
**BSD** Bachelor of Science in Design; ballistic system division; [computing] Berkeley Systems Distribution; British Society of Dowsers; British Space Development
**BSDes** Bachelor of Science in Design
**b.s.d.l.** boresight datum line
**BSE** Bachelor of Science in Education; Bachelor of Science in Engineering; [veterinary science] bovine spongiform encephalopathy; [medicine] breast self-examination
**b.s.e.** base support equipment
**BSEc** Bachelor of Science in Economics
**BSECP** Black Sea Economic Cooperation Project
**BSEd** Bachelor of Science in Education
**BSEE** Bachelor of Science in Electrical Engineering; Bachelor of Science in Elementary Education
**BSEEng** Bachelor of Science in Electrical Engineering
**BSEIE** Bachelor of Science in Electronic Engineering
**BSEM** Bachelor of Science in Engineering of Mines
**BSEng** Bachelor of Science in Engineering
**BSES** Bachelor of Science in Engineering Sciences; British Schools Exploring Society
**BSF** Bachelor of Science in Forestry; British Salonica Force; British Shipping Federation (Limited); British Slag Federation; British Standard fine (screw thread); British Stone Federation
**BSFA** British Science Fiction Association; British Steel Founders' Association
**b.s.f.c.** brake specific fuel consumption
**BSFL** British Shipping Federation Limited

**BSFM** Bachelor of Science in Forestry Management
**BSFor** Bachelor of Science in Forestry
**BSFS** Bachelor of Science in Foreign Service; British Soviet Friendship Society
**BSFT** Bachelor of Science in Fuel Technology
**BSG** British Standard Gauge
**b.s.g.d.g.** *breveté sans garantie du gouvernement* (French: patented without government guarantee)
**BSGE** Bachelor of Science in General Engineering
**BSH** British Society of Hypnotherapists; British Standard Hardness
**bsh.** bushel
**BSHA** Bachelor of Science in Hospital Administration
**BSHE** Bachelor of Science in Home Economics
**BSHEc** Bachelor of Science in Home Economics
**BSHS** British Society for the History of Science
**BSHyg** Bachelor of Science in Hygiene
**BSI** British Sailors' Institute; British Standards Institution; Building Societies' Institute
**BSIA** British Security Industry Association
**BSIB** Boy Scouts International Bureau
**BSIC** British Ski Instruction Council
**BSIE** Bachelor of Science in Industrial Engineering
**BSIP** British Solomon Islands Protectorate
**BSIRA** British Scientific Instrument Research Association
**BSIS** Business Sponsorship Incentive Scheme
**BSIU** British Society for International Understanding
**BSJ** Bachelor of Science in Journalism
**BSJA** British Show Jumping Association
**bsk.** basket
**bskt** basket
**BSkyB** British Sky Broadcasting
**BSL** Bachelor of Sacred Literature; Bachelor of Science in Linguistics; [medicine] bacterial skin lesion; Boatswain Sublieutenant; British Sign Language
**Bs/L** bills of lading
**BSLS** Bachelor of Science in Library Science
**BSM** Bachelor of Sacred Music; Bachelor of Science in Medicine; Battery Sergeant-Major; branch sales manager; British School of Motoring; [USA] bronze star medal
**BSMA** British Skate Makers' Association
**BSME** Bachelor of Science in Mechanical Engineering; Bachelor of Science in Mining Engineering
**BSMedTech** Bachelor of Science in Medical Technology
**BSMet** Bachelor of Science in Metallurgy
**BSMetE** Bachelor of Science in Metallurgical Engineering
**BSMGP** British Society of Master Glass-Painters
**BSMT** Bachelor of Science in Medical Technology
**bsmt** basement
**BSMV** [microbiology] barley stripe mosaic virus
**BSN** Bachelor of Science in Nursing
**BSNE** Bachelor of Science in Nuclear Engineering
**BSNS** Bachelor of Naval Science
**BSO** base supply officer; Boston Symphony Orchestra; Bournemouth Symphony Orchestra; Business Statistics Office
**BSocSc** Bachelor of Social Science
**BSOT** Bachelor of Science in Occupational Therapy
**BSP** Bachelor of Science in Pharmacy; Bering Sea Patrol; [computing] binary space-partitioning (as in **BSP tree**); Birmingham School of Printing; [printing] bleached sulphite pulp; British Standard pipe (screw thread); Bulgarian Socialist Party (formerly BCP); business systems planning
**BSPA** Bachelor of Science in Public Administration
**BSPE** Bachelor of Science in Physical Education
**BSPH** Bachelor of Science in Public Health
**BSPhar** Bachelor of Science in Pharmacy
**BSPharm** Bachelor of Science in Pharmacy
**BSPhTh** Bachelor of Science in Physical Therapy
**BSPT** Bachelor of Science in Physical Therapy
**BSR** Birmingham Sound Reproducers;

[medicine] blood sedimentation rate; Board for Social Responsibility (in Church of England); British School at Rome

**BSRA** British Ship Research Association; British Society for Research on Ageing; British Sound Recording Association

**BSRAE** British Society for Research in Agricultural Engineering

**BSRC** [USA] Biological Serial Record Center

**BSRT** Bachelor of Science in Radiological Technology

**BSS** Bachelor of Secretarial Science; Bachelor of Social Science; [medicine] balanced salt solution; basic safety standards; Bibliothèque Saint-Sulpice (Montreal library); [geology] borehole seismic system; British Sailors' Society; British Standard size; British Standards Specification

**BSSA** Bachelor of Science in Secretarial Administration

**BSSc** Bachelor of Social Science

**BSSE** Bachelor of Science in Secondary Education

**BSSG** [USA] Biomedical Sciences Support Grant

**BSSO** British Society for the Study of Orthodontics

**BSSS** Bachelor of Science in Secretarial Studies; Bachelor of Science in Social Science; British Society of Soil Science

**BST** Bachelor of Sacred Theology; bovine somatotrophin; British Standard Time; British Summer Time; bulk supply tariff

**B/St** bill of sight

**BSTA** British Surgical Trades' Association

**BSTC** British Student Travel Centre

**bstd** bastard

**bstr** booster

**bstr rkt** booster rocket

**BSU** [engineering] bench scale unit

**BSurv** Bachelor of Surveying

**BSW** Bachelor of Social Work; British Standard Whitworth (screw thread)

**b.s.w.** barrels of salt water

**BSWB** Boy Scouts World Bureau

**BSWE** British Scouts in Western Europe

**BSWIA** British Steel Wire Industries' Association

**BT** Bachelor of Teaching; Bachelor of Theology; basic trainer; basic training; [psychology] behaviour therapy; [UK postcode] Belfast; [medicine] benign tumour; bishop's transcript; British Telecommunications (plc) (formerly British Telecom); [vehicle registration] Leeds

**Bt** [currency] baht (used in Thailand); Baronet; [military] brevet

**bt** beat; benefit; bent; bought

**.bt** Bhutan (in Internet address)

**BTA** Billiards Trade Association; [USA] Blood Transfusion Association; British Theatre Association; British Tourist Authority (formerly British Travel Association); British Tuberculosis Association

**BTAC** [computing] binary tree algebraic computation

**BTASA** Book Trade Association of South Africa

**BTB** [medicine] blood–tumour barrier; [medicine] breakthrough bleeding

**BTBA** British Tenpin Bowling Association

**BTBS** Book Trade Benevolent Society

**BTC** [USA] Bankers' Trust Company; [USA] basic training center; British Textile Confederation; British Transport Commission

**btca** *biblioteca* (Spanish: library)

**BTCC** Board of Transportation Commissioners of Canada

**BTCh** Bachelor of Textile Chemistry

**BTCP** Bachelor of Town and Country Planning

**BTCV** British Trust for Conservation Volunteers

**b.t.d.** bomb testing device

**BTDB** Bermuda Trade Development Board

**b.t.d.c.** [engineering] before top dead centre

**BTDT** been there, done that (in Internet chat)

**BTE** Bachelor of Textile Engineering

**bté** *breveté* (French: patent)

**BTEC** Business and Technology Education Council

**BTech** Bachelor of Technology

**BTechEd** Bachelor of Technical Education

**BTechFood** Bachelor of Food Technology

**BTEF** Book Trade Employers' Federation

**BTEMA** British Tanning Extract Manufacturers' Association

**BTEX** benzene, toluene, ethylbenzene and xylene (solvents)
**BTF** British Trawlers Federation; British Turkey Federation
**b.t.f.** balance to follow; barrels of total fuel; bomb tail fuse
**BTG** British Technology Group
**BTH** British Thomson-Houston Company
**BTh** Bachelor of Theology
**bth** bath; berth
**bth.** bathroom (in property or accommodation advertisement)
**BTHMA** British Toy and Hobby Manufacturers' Association
**BthU** British thermal unit
**BTI** *British Technology Index*
**BTIA** British Tar Industries' Association
**btk** buttock
**btl.** bottle
**BTM** bromotrifluoromethane (used in firefighting)
**btm** bottom
**BTMA** British Typewriter Manufacturers' Association
**BTN** Brussels Tariff Nomenclature
**btn** baton; button
**BTO** big-time operator; British Trust for Ornithology; Brussels Treaty Organization (replaced by WEU)
**BTP** Bachelor of Town Planning
**BTR** [physics] bimetric theory of relativity; *British Tax Review*; British Telecommunications Research
**BTRA** Bombay Textile Industry's Research Association
**BTRP** Bachelor of Town and Regional Planning
**btry** [military] battery
**BTS** Blood Transfusion Service; British Telecommunications Systems
**Btss** Baronetess
**BTTA** British Thoracic and Tuberculosis Association
**BTU** Board of Trade unit; [USA] British thermal unit
**Btu** British thermal unit
**BTUC** Bahamas Trade Union Congress
**BTW** by the way (in Internet chat and e-mail)
**btw.** between
**btwn** between
**BTX** benzene, toluene and xylene (solvents)
**bty** [military] battery
**BU** Bakers, Food and Allied Workers Union; Baptist Union (of Great Britain and Ireland); Brown University (Rhode Island); [fishing port] Burntisland; [vehicle registration] Manchester
**Bu.** Bureau
**bu.** bureau; bushel
**b.u.** base unit; [finance] break-up
**BuAer** [USA] Bureau of Aeronautics
**BUAF** British United Air Ferries
**BUA of E** Badminton Umpires' Association of England
**BUAV** British Union for the Abolition of Vivisection
**BUC** Bangor University College
**buck.** buckram
**Bucks** Buckinghamshire
**BUCOP** *British Union Catalogue of Periodicals*
**Bud.** Buddhism; Buddhist
**bud.** budget
**Budd.** Buddhism; Buddhist
**BuDocks** [US navy] Bureau of Yards and Docks
**Budpst** Budapest
**BUF** British Union of Fascists
**BUIC** back-up interceptor control
**BUJ** Bachelor of Canon and Civil Law (from Latin *Baccalaureus Utriusque Juris*)
**bul.** bulletin
**Bulg.** Bulgaria; Bulgarian
**bull.** bulla (seal on papal bull); bulletin; [medicine] *bulliat* (Latin: let it boil)
**buloga** business logistics game
**BULVA** Belfast and Ulster Licensed Vintners' Association
**BuMed** [US navy] Bureau of Medicine and Surgery
**BUN** [medicine] blood urea nitrogen
**Buna** [trademark] butadiene and natrium (synthetic rubber)
**BUNAC** British Universities North America Club
**BUNCH** Burroughs, Univac, NCR, Control Data, Honeywell (computer manufacturers)
**bung.** bungalow (in property advertisement)
**BuOrd** [US navy] Bureau of Ordnance
**BUP** British United Press
**BUPA** British United Provident Association (company providing health insurance)

**BuPers** [US navy] Bureau of Naval Personnel
**BuPubAff** [USA] Bureau of Public Affairs
**BUR** [international vehicle registration] Myanmar (from former name Burma)
**Bur.** Burma; Burmese
**bur.** bureau; buried
**BuRec** [USA] Bureau of Reclamation
**burg.** burgess; burgomaster
**burl.** burlesque
**Burm.** Burma; Burmese
**BURMA** be undressed ready, my angel (on envelope of love letter)
**burp** [informal] bankrupt unemployed rejected person
**Burs.** Bursar
**bus** [short form] omnibus
**bus.** bushel; business
**BuS&A** [US navy] Bureau of Supply and Accounts
**BUSF** British Universities' Sports Federation
**bush.** bushel
**BuShips** [US navy] Bureau of Ships
**bus. mgr** business manager
**BUSWE** British Union of Social Work Employees
**but.** butter; button
**buy.** buyer; buying
**BV** *Beata Virgo* (Latin: Blessed Virgin); *Beatitudo Vestra* (Latin: Your Holiness); *bene vale* (Latin: farewell); [commerce] *Besloten Vennootschap* (Dutch: limited company, Ltd); Bible Version (of Psalms); Blessed Virgin; [medicine] blood vessel; [medicine] blood volume; [shipping] *Bureau Veritas* (French shipping classification society); [vehicle registration] Preston
**b.v.** balanced voltage; [accounting] book value
**BVA** British Veterinary Association
**BVD** [veterinary science] bovine virus diarrhoea
**BVetMed** Bachelor of Veterinary Medicine
**BVetSc** Bachelor of Veterinary Science
**BVI** [international vehicle registration] British Virgin Islands
**BVJ** *British Veterinary Journal*
**BVK** *Bundesverdienstkreuz* (German: Federal Cross of Merit)
**BVM** Bachelor of Veterinary Medicine; *Beata Virgo Maria* (Latin: Blessed Virgin Mary); Blessed Virgin Mary
**BVMA** British Valve Manufacturers' Association
**BVMS** Bachelor of Veterinary Medicine and Surgery
**BVO** *Bundesverdienstorden* (German: Federal Order of Merit)
**BVP** British Visitors' Passport; British Volunteer Programme
**BVRLA** British Vehicle Rental and Leasing Association Limited
**BVS** Bachelor of Veterinary Surgery
**BVSc** Bachelor of Veterinary Science
**BVSc&AH** Bachelor of Veterinary Science and Animal Husbandry
**bvt** brevet
**BW** bacteriological warfare; [fishing port] Barrow; Bath and Wells (bishop's see); biological warfare; black and white; Black Watch; Board of Works; body water; [medicine] body weight; bonded warehouse; British Waterways; business week; [vehicle registration] Oxford
**B/W** black and white
**b/w** black and white
**.bw** Botswana (in Internet address)
**b.w.** *bitte wenden* (German: please turn over, PTO); bridleway(s)
**BWA** backward wave amplifier; Baptist World Alliance; British Waterworks Association; British West Africa
**B-way** [USA] Broadway
**BWB** British Waterways Board
**BWC** [USA] Board of War Communications; British War Cabinet
**BWCC** British Weed Control Conference
**BWD** [veterinary science] bacillary white diarrhoea
**bwd** backward
**BWF** British Whiting Federation; British Wool Federation
**BWG** Birmingham Wire Gauge
**BWI** British West Indies
**BWIA** British West Indian Airways
**BWIR** British West India Regiment
**BWISA** British West Indies Sugar Association
**bwk** brickwork; bulwark
**BWM** British War Medal
**BWMA** British Woodwork Manufacturers' Association
**BWMB** British Wool Marketing Board

**BWO** backward wave oscillator
**BWP** basic war plan
**BWPA** backward wave power amplifier; British Waste Paper Association; British Word Preserving Association
**bwpd** barrels of water per day
**bwph** barrels of water per hour
**BWPUC** British Wastepaper Utilization Council
**BWR** [nuclear technology] boiling-water reactor
**BWS** [medicine] battered wife (or woman) syndrome; British Watercolour Society
**BWSF** British Water Ski Federation
**BWTA** British Women's Temperance Association
**BWU** Barbados Workers' Union
**BWV** [music] *Bach Werke-Verzeichnis* (German: Catalogue of (J. S.) Bach's Works)
**b.w.v.** back water valve
**BWVA** British War Veterans of America
**BWWA** British Waterworks Association
**BX** [US air force] Base Exchange; British Xylonite; [vehicle registration] Haverfordwest
**bx** box
**BY** [international vehicle registration] Belarus (from alternative name Byelorussia); [vehicle registration] northwest London
**By** Barony
**.by** Belarus (in Internet address)
**b.y.** billion years
**BYDV** [microbiology] barley yellow dwarf virus
**BYO** bring your own
**Byo** Bulawayo
**BYOB** bring your own beer; bring your own booze; bring your own bottle
**BYOG** bring your own girl
**byr** billion years
**BYT** [informal] bright young things
**BYU** [USA] Brigham Young University
**Byz.** Byzantine; Byzantium
**BZ** [international vehicle registration] Belize; B'nai Zion; Brazil; British Zone; [vehicle registration] Down
**Bz** [chemistry] benzene (used in formulae)
**.bz** Belize (in Internet address)
**BZH** Brittany (from Breton *Breizh*)
**bzw.** *beziehungsweise* (German: respectively)

# C

**C** *Caballeros* (Spanish: gentlemen); Caesar; *caldo* (Italian: hot); *caliente* (Spanish: hot); *calle* (Spanish: street); [geology] Cambrian; [civil aircraft marking] Canada; [informal] cancer; candle; canon; canto; Cape; Captain; [chemical element] carbon; [geology] Carboniferous; Cardinal; [USA] cargo transport (aircraft); [chess] castle; catechism; Catholic; Celsius; Celtic; centigrade; [theatre] centre (of stage); century; Chancellor; Chancery; *chaud* (French: hot); chief; Christ; Christian; circuit; *ciudad* (Spanish: town); [card games] clubs; [slang] cocaine; cold (water); Commander; Command Paper (1870–99) (in parliamentary procedure); commended; Commodore; Companion; [immunology] complement; Confessor; [pharmacology] *congius* (Latin: gallon); Congregation; Congregational; Congress; Conservative; contract; copyright; [fishing port] Cork; [botany] corolla (in floral formula); Corps; coulomb; council; Count; [music] countertenor; county; coupon; cross; [paper size] crown; cruiser; [international vehicle registration] Cuba; curacy; curate; current (electricity); [Roman numeral] hundred; [music] note of scale
***C*** [physics] capacitance; [physics] charm quantum number; [physics] compliance; [physics] heat capacity; [chemistry] molecular concentration
**©** copyright
**c** centi- (indicates one-hundredth, as in **cl** = centilitre); [physics] charm (quark flavour); [chemistry] concentration; [mathematics] constant; cubic; [Roman numeral] hundred

**c** [physics] specific heat capacity; [physics] speed of light in vacuum

**c.** canine (tooth); capacity; *caput* (Latin: chapter); carat; carbon (paper); carton; case; [baseball] catcher; cathode; cattle; [cricket] caught (by); [currency] cent (hundredth of dollar etc.); [currency] centavo (hundredth of peso etc.); [currency] centime (hundredth of franc etc.); central; centre; century; chairman; chairwoman; chapter; charge; chest; child; church; [medicine] *cibus* (Latin: meal); *circiter* (Latin: approximately); *circum* (Latin: around); city; class; cloudy; cold; collected; college; colt; compound; conductor; constable; consul; *contra* (Latin: against); contralto; contrast; convection; copy; copyright; court; cousin; crowned; [medicine] *cum* (Latin: with) (in prescriptions); cup; currency; current (electricity); cycle(s)

***c.*** *circa* (Latin: about) (in dates)

**c/-** [Australia, New Zealand] care of (in postal addresses); case; coupon; currency

**C1** supervisory or clerical (occupational group)

**C2** [civil aircraft marking] Nauru; skilled manual (occupational group)

**C3** [civil aircraft marking] Andorra

**C³I** [military] command, control, communications and intelligence

**C4** Channel Four (television company); [paper size] crown quarto (7.5 × 10 in)

**C5** Channel Five (television company); [civil aircraft marking] Gambia

**C6** [civil aircraft marking] Bahamas

**C8** [paper size] crown octavo (5 × 7.5 in)

**C9** [civil aircraft marking] Mozambique

**C16** [paper size] crown 16mo (3.75 × 5 in)

**C32** [paper size] crown 32mo (2.5 × 3.75 in)

**3C** [civil aircraft marking] Equatorial Guinea

**CA** [US postcode] California; Canadian army; capital account; [taxation] capital allowances; cardiac arrest; [fishing port] Cardigan; [UK postcode] Carlisle; Caterers' Association; Catholic Association; [chemistry] cellulose acetate; Central America; certificate of airworthiness; chargé d'affaires; [Scotland] Chartered Accountant; *Chemical Abstracts*; [vehicle registration] Chester; chief accountant; [genetics] chromosomal aberration; chronological age; Church Army; Church Assembly; citric acid; city architect; city attorney; civil affairs; civil aviation; Classical Association; clean air; coast artillery; College of Arms; commercial agent; community association; Companies Act; [USA] Confederate Army; constituent assembly; consular agent; Consumers' Association; [medicine] contrast angiography; Contributions Agency; controlled atmosphere; controller of accounts; cooperative agreement; *Corps d'armée* (French: Army Corps); county alderman; county architect; Court of Appeal; Croquet Association; Crown Agent; Cruising Association; [commerce] current assets

**C/A** capital account; credit account; current account

**Ca** [chemical element] calcium; [commerce] *compagnia* (Italian: company, Co.); [commerce] *companhia* (Portuguese: company, Co.); [commerce] *compañia* (Spanish: company, Co.)

**Ca.** California; Canada; Canadian

**ca** centiare (unit of area)

**c/a** cash account

**ca.** [medicine] carcinoma; [law] case(s)

***ca.*** *circa* (Latin: about) (in dates)

**.ca** Canada (in Internet address)

**c.a.** [commerce] capital asset; [engineering] close annealed; [music] *coll'arco* (Italian: with the bow); [physics] *corriente alterna* (Spanish: alternating current); [physics] *courant alternatif* (French: alternating current)

**CAA** Campaign for the Abolition of Angling; Canadian Authors' Association; [commerce] Capital Allowances Act; Central African Airways Corporation; [USA] Civil Aeronautics Administration; [USA] Civil Aeronautics Administrator; Civil Aviation Authority; Clean Air Act; Commonwealth Association of Architects; [USA] Community Action Agency; Concert Artists' Association; [medicine] coronary artery aneurysm; Cost Accountants' Association; County Agricultural Adviser

**CAAA** Canadian Association of Advertising Agencies

**CAADRP** civil aircraft airworthiness data recording program
**CAAE** Canadian Association of Adult Education
**CAAIS** computer-aided (or -assisted) action information system(s)
**CAAR** compressed-air accumulator rocket
**CAARC** Commonwealth Advisory Aeronautical Research Council
**CAAT** Campaign Against Arms Trade; [Canada] College of Applied Arts and Technology; [accounting] computer-aided (or -assisted) audit technique
**CAAtt** Civil Air Attaché
**CAAV** Central Association of Agricultural Valuers
**CAB** Canadian Association of Broadcasters; [chemistry] cellulose acetate butyrate; Citizens' Advice Bureau; [USA] Civil Aeronautics Board; Commonwealth Agricultural Bureaux (former name of CABI)
**cab.** cabalistic; cabin; cabinet; cable
**CABAS** City and Borough Architects' Society
**CABEI** Central American Bank for Economic Integration
**CABG** [medicine] coronary artery bypass graft
**CABI** CAB International (formerly Commonwealth Agricultural Bureaux)
**CABM** Commonwealth of Australia Bureau of Meteorology
**CABMA** Canadian Association of British Manufacturers and Agencies
**CABS** [medicine] coronary artery bypass surgery
**cabtmkr** cabinetmaker
**CAC** Campaign Against Censorship; Canadian Armoured Corps; Central Advisory Committee; Central Arbitration Committee; [USA] Climate Analysis Center; Colonial Advisory Council; *Compagnie des agents de change* (French: stockbrokers' association); [USA] Consumer Advisory Council; County Agricultural Committee
**CACA** Canadian Agricultural Chemicals Association
**CAC&W** continental aircraft control and warning
**CACC** Civil Aviation Communications Centre; Council for the Accreditation of Correspondence Colleges (former name of ODLQC)
**CACD** computer-aided (or -assisted) circuit design
**CACDS** Centre for Advanced Computing and Decision Support
**CACE** Central Advisory Council for Education
**CACGP** Commission on Atmospheric Chemistry and Global Pollution
**CACLB** Churches' Advisory Committee on Local Broadcasting
**CACM** Central Advisory Council for the Ministry; Central American Common Market
**CACSD** computer-aided (or -assisted) control system design
**CACUL** Canadian Association of College and University Libraries
**CAD** cash against documents; [USA] civil air defense; *comité d'aide au développement* (French: development assistance committee); compact audio disc; computer-aided (or -assisted) design; computer-aided (or -assisted) drawing; contract award date; [medicine] coronary artery disease; Crown Agent's Department
**Cád.** Cádiz
**cad.** *cadauno* (Italian: each); [medicine] cadaver; [music] cadenza; cadet
**c.a.d.** cash against disbursements; cash against documents
**c-à-d** *c'est-à-dire* (French: that is to say)
**cadav.** [medicine] cadaver
**CADC** central air-data computer; colour analysis display computer
**CADCAM** computer-aided (or -assisted) design and manufacture
**CADD** computer-aided (or -assisted) drafting and design
**CADF** Commutated Antenna Direction Finder
**CADIN** [USA] continental air defense integration north
**CADIS** computer-aided (or -assisted) design information system
**CADMAT** computer-aided (or -assisted) design, manufacture and testing
**CADO** [USA] central air documents office
**CADPO** communications and data-processing operation

**CADPOS** communications and data-processing operations system
**CADS** computer-aided (or -assisted) design system
**CAE** Canadian Aviation Electronics; Chartered Automobile Engineer; *cóbrese al entregar* (Spanish: cash on delivery, COD); [Australia] College of Advanced Education; computer-aided (or -assisted) education; computer-aided (or -assisted) engineering
**Cae** [astronomy] Caelum
**CAEC** Central American Economic Community; County Agricultural Executive Committee
**CAEM** *Conseil d'assistance économique mutuelle* (French: Council for Mutual Economic Aid, COMECON)
**CAER** Conservative Action for Electoral Reform
**Caern.** Caernarvon(shire)
**Caerns** Caernarvonshire
**CAES** compressed-air energy storage
**Caes.** Caesar
**CAEU** Council of Arab Economic Unity
**CAF** [medicine] cardiac assessment factor; Central African Federation; charities aid foundation; charities aid fund; clerical, administrative and fiscal; [commerce] cost and freight; [commerce] *coût, assurance, fret* (French: cost, insurance, freight, CIF)
**caf.** cafeteria
**c.a.f.** [commerce] cost and freight; [commerce] *coût, assurance, fret* (French: cost, insurance, freight, c.i.f.)
**CAFE** [USA] Corporate Average Fuel Economy (fuel consumption standard for cars)
**CAFEA-ICC** Commission on Asian and Far Eastern Affairs of the International Chamber of Commerce
**CAFIC** Combined Allied Forces Information Centre
**c.a.f.m.** commercial air freight movement
**Cafod** Catholic Fund for Overseas Development
**CAFR** [accounting] comprehensive annual financial report
**CAFS** [computing] content-addressable file system
**CAFU** civil aviation flying unit
**CAG** Canadian Association of Geographers; [US navy] carrier air group; [USA] civil air guard; commercial arbitration group; Commercial Artists' Guild; Concert Artists' Guild
**CAGI** [USA] Compressed Air and Gas Institute
**CAGR** [nuclear technology] civil advanced gas-cooled reactor; [nuclear technology] commercial advanced gas-cooled reactor
**CAGS** [USA] Certificate of Advanced Graduate Study
**CAH** [medicine] chronic active hepatitis; [medicine] congenital adrenal hyperplasia; [chemistry] cyanacetic hydrazide
**CAI** Canadian Aeronautical Institute; *Club Alpino Italiano* (Italian: Italian Alpine Club); colour alteration indices; computer-aided (or -assisted) instruction; Confederation of Aerial Industries Limited; [chemical engineering] controlled air incineration (or incinerator); [forestry] current annual increment
**Cai.** Caithness
**CAIRC** [USA] Caribbean Air Command
**CAISM** Central Association of Irish Schoolmistresses
**CAISSE** computer-aided (or -assisted) information system on solar energy
**Caith.** Caithness
**CAL** computer-aided (or -assisted) learning; Continental Airlines; [computing] conversational algebraic language; [USA] Cornell (University) Aeronautical Laboratory
**Cal** kilocalorie (from alternative name Calorie)
**Cal.** Calcutta; Caledonia; Calends; California
**cal** calorie
**cal.** [music] *calando* (Italian: lowering, falling away); calendar; calibre
**CALA** Civil Aviation Licensing Act
**CALANS** Caribbean and Latin American News Service
**Calc.** Calcutta
**Calç.** *Calçada* (Portuguese: street)
**calc.** calculate; calculated; calculation; calculator; calculus
**cald** calculated
**CALE** Canadian Army Liaison Executive
**Calg.** Calgary
**calg** calculating
**calibr.** calibrate; calibration

**Calif.** California
**Cal. Mac.** Caledonian MacBrayne (Scottish ferry company)
**caln** calculation
**CALPA** Canadian Air Line Pilots' Association
**Caltech** California Institute of Technology
**Caltex** California Texas Petroleum Corporation
**Calv.** (John) Calvin (French theologian); Calvinism; Calvinistic
**Calz.** *Calzada* (Spanish: boulevard)
**CAM** [international vehicle registration] Cameroon; [computing] cellular automata machine; commercial air movement; Commonwealth Association of Museums; communication, advertising and marketing (as in **CAM Foundation**); computer-aided (or -assisted) manufacture; [computing] content-addressable memory; continuous air monitor
**Cam** [astronomy] Camelopardalis
**Cam.** Cambodia; Cambodian; Cambrian; Cambridge; Cameroon
**cam.** camber; camouflage
**CAMA** Civil Aerospace Medical Association
**CAMAL** continuous airborne missile-launched and low-level system
**Camb.** Cambrian; Cambridge(shire)
**Cambs** Cambridgeshire
**CAMC** Canadian Army Medical Corps
**CAMD** [chemistry] computer-aided (or -assisted) molecular design
**CAMDA** Car and Motorcycle Drivers' Association
**CAMDS** chemical agent munitions disposal system
**CAMM** computer-aided (or -assisted) maintenance management
**CAMRA** Campaign for Real Ale
**CAMRIC** Campaign for Real Ice Cream
**CAMS** Certificate of Advanced Musical Study; [engineering] computer-aided (or -assisted) manipulation system
**CaMV** [microbiology] cauliflower mosaic virus
**CAMW** Central Association for Mental Welfare
**CAN** Committee on Aircraft Noise; customs-assigned number
**Can.** Canada; Canadian; Canal; Canberra; Canon; Canonry; *Cantoris* (Latin: of the precentor) (side of church choir)
**can.** canal; cancel; cannon; canon; canto; canton
**CANA** Caribbean News Agency; Clergy Against Nuclear Arms
**Canad.** Canada; Canadian
**Canc.** *Cancellarius* (Latin: Chancellor)
**canc.** cancellation; cancelled
**CANCIRCO** Cancer International Research Cooperative
**CAND** Campaign Against Nuclear Dumping
**cand.** candidate
**C&A** Clemens and Auguste (Breeninkmeyer) (Dutch founders of chain store)
**c&b** [cricket] caught and bowled (by)
**c&c** carpets and curtains (in property advertisement); command and control
**c&d** collection and delivery
**C&E** Customs and Excise
**c&e** consultation and education
**c&f** cost and freight
**C&G** Cheltenham and Gloucester (Building Society); City and Guilds
**C&I** commerce and industry; commercial and industrial
**c&i** cost and insurance
**C&J** clean and jerk (in weightlifting)
**c&m** care and maintenance
**c&p** carriage and packing; [bookbinding] collated and perfect
**c&r** convalescence and rehabilitation
**CANDU** [nuclear technology] Canadian Deuterium Uranium Reactor
**C&W** country and western (music)
**C&W Ck** caution and warning (system) check
**CANEL** [USA] Connecticut Advanced Nuclear Engineering Laboratory
**Can. Fr.** Canadian French
**Can. I** Canary Islands
**CANO** chief area nursing officer
**Can. Pac.** Canadian Pacific
**CANSG** Civil Aviation Navigational Services Group
**Cant.** Canterbury; [Bible] Canticles; Cantonese
**cant.** cantilever
**Cantab.** *Cantabrigiensis* (Latin: of Cambridge (University))
**canton.** [military] cantonment

**CANTRAN** cancel in transmission
**Cantuar.** *Cantuariensis* (Latin: (Archbishop) of Canterbury)
**CANUS** [military] Canada–United States
**canv.** canvas
**CAO** chief accountant officer; chief administrative officer; county advisory officer; county agricultural officer; Crimean Astrophysical Laboratory
**CAORB** Civil Aviation Operational Research Branch
**CAORG** Canadian Army Operational Research Group
**CAOT** Canadian Association of Occupational Therapy
**CAP** Canadian Association of Physicists; [genetics] catabolite activator protein; Church Action on Poverty; [USA] civil air patrol; Code of Advertising Practice; College of American Pathologists; [USA] combat air patrol; Common Agricultural Policy (in EU); [USA] Community Action Program; computer-aided (or -assisted) planning; computer-aided (or -assisted) production
**Cap** [astronomy] Capricornus
**Cap.** Captain
**cap.** capacity; [medicine] *capiat* (Latin: let him/her take) (in prescriptions); capital; capitalize; capital letter; *capitulum* (Latin: chapter, heading); *caput* (Latin: chapter, heading); foolscap
**c.a.p.** *codice di avviamento postale* (Italian: postcode number)
**CAPA** Canadian Association of Purchasing Agents
**CAPAC** Composers', Authors' and Publishers' Association of Canada
**CAPCOM** capsule communicator (in NASA)
**CAPD** [medicine] continuous ambulatory peritoneal dialysis
**CAPE** Clifton Assessment Procedures for the Elderly
**CAPM** [accounting] capital asset pricing model; computer-aided (or -assisted) production management
**Capn** Captain
**CAPO** Canadian Army Post Office; Chief Administrative Pharmaceutical Officer
**CAPP** computer-aided (or -assisted) process planning
**Capric.** Capricorn
**CAPS** Captive Animals' Protection Society; [USA] Center for Analysis of Particle Scattering
**caps.** capital letters; capsule
**Capt.** Captain
**capt.** caption
**CAR** Canadian Association of Radiologists; Central African Republic; Civil Air Regulations; [aeronautics] cloudtop altitude radiometer; [nuclear technology] collisionally activated reaction; [Australia] *Commonwealth Arbitration Reports*; [finance] compound annual return; compounded annual rate (of interest); computer-aided (or -assisted) retrieval; [computing] contents of address register
**Car** [astronomy] Carina
**Car.** Carlow; *Carolus* (Latin: Charles)
**car.** carat
**CARA** combat air rescue aircraft
**CARAC** Civil Aviation Radio Advisory Committee
**CARAF** Christians Against Racism and Fascism
**CARB** California Air Resources Board
**carb** [short form] carburettor
**carb.** carbon; [chemistry] carbonate
**CARD** Campaign Against Racial Discrimination; compact automatic retrieval device; computer-augmented road design
**Card.** Cardinal
**card.** cardinal
**CARDE** Canadian Armament Research and Development Establishment
**Cards** Cardiganshire (former name of Ceredigion)
**CARE** Christian Action for Research and Education; [psychology] communicated authenticity, regard, empathy; computer-aided (or -assisted) risk evaluation; continuous aircraft reliability evaluation; Cooperative for American Relief Everywhere; Cottage and Rural Enterprises
**CAREC** Caribbean Epidemiology Centre
**Carib.** Caribbean
**CARIBANK** Caribbean Investment Bank
**CARICAD** Caribbean Centre for Administration Development
**CARICOM** Caribbean Community and Common Market
**CARIFTA** Caribbean Free Trade Area

**Carliol.** *Carlioliensis* (Latin: (Bishop) of Carlisle)
**Carms** Carmarthenshire
**carn.** carnival
**Carns** Caernarvonshire
**Carp.** Carpathian (Mountains); Carpentaria
**carp.** carpenter; carpentry
**carr. fwd** [commerce] carriage forward
**CARS** Canadian Arthritis and Rheumatism Society
**CART** collision avoidance radar trainer
**cart.** cartage; carton
**Carth.** Carthage
**cartog.** cartographer; cartographic; cartography
**CAS** Cambridge Antiquarian Society; Carib Advertising Services (in Guyana); Centre for Administrative Studies; CERN Accelerator School; [USA] Certificate of Advanced Studies; Chemical Abstracts Service; Chief of Air Staff; Children's Aid Society; close air support; [aeronautics] collision avoidance system; *Connecticutensis Academiae Socius* (Latin: Fellow of the Connecticut Academy of Arts and Sciences); controlled airspace; [medicine] coronary arterial stenosis
**Cas** [astronomy] Cassiopeia
**cas.** castle; casual; casualty
**CASA** [USA] Coal Advisory Service Association; Contemporary Art Society of Australia
**CA(SA)** Chartered Accountant (South Africa)
**ca. sa.** [law] *capias ad satisfaciendum* (Latin: writ of execution)
**CASAC** [USA] Clean Air Scientific Advisory Committee
**CASE** Campaign for State Education; Centre for Advanced Studies in Environment; [USA] Committee on Academic Science and Engineering; computer-aided (or -assisted) software engineering; computer-aided (or -assisted) system engineering; Confederation for the Advancement of State Education; Cooperative Awards in Science and Engineering
**casevac** [military] casualty evacuation
**cash.** cashier
**CASI** Canadian Aeronautics and Space Institute
**CASIG** Careers Advisory Service in Industry for Girls
**CASLE** Commonwealth Association of Surveying and Land Economy
**Caspar** [physics] Cambridge analog simulator for predicting atomic reactions
**cass.** cassette
**CAST** Consolidated African Selection Trust
**Cast.** Castile; Castilian
**CASTE** Civil Aviation Signals Training Establishment
**CASU** Cooperative Association of Suez Canal Users
**CASW** [USA] Council for the Advancement of Scientific Writing
**CAT** Centre for Alternative Technology; [psychology] Children's Apperception Test; Civil Air Transport; cleanup and treatment; [aeronautics] clear-air turbulence; College of Advanced Technology; compressed-air tunnel; [medicine] compute(rize)d axial tomography (as in **CAT scanner**); computer-aided (or -assisted) teaching; computer-aided (or -assisted) testing; [medicine] computer-aided (or -assisted) tomography; computer-aided (or -assisted) trading; computer-aided (or -assisted) training; computer-aided (or -assisted) translation; computer-aided (or -assisted) typesetting; low charges, easy access, fair terms (as in **CAT standard** for ISAs)
**Cat.** Catalan; Catholic; Catullus (Roman poet)
**cat** [short form] catalytic converter; [short form] catamaran
**cat.** catalogue; catamaran; [medicine] cataplasm (poultice); catapult; catechism; category; cattle
**CATA** Commonwealth Association of Tax Administration
**catachr.** catachresis; catachrestic
**Catal.** Catalan; Catalonian
**CATC** Commonwealth Air Transport Commission
**CATCC** Canadian Association of Textile Colorists and Chemists
**CATE** Committee for the Accreditation of Teacher Education
**Cath.** Cathedral; Catholic
**cath.** cathedral; cathode

**CATI** computer-aided (or -assisted) telephone interviewing
**CATOR** Combined Air Transport Operations Room
**CATRA** Cutlery and Allied Trades Research Association
**CATS** [education] credit accumulation transfer scheme
**CATU** Ceramic and Allied Trade Union
**CATV** community antenna television (= cable television)
**caus.** causation; causative
**CAV** constant air-volume (control system); [computing] constant angular velocity; [law] *curia advisari vult* (Latin: the court wishes to consider it) (used in reports when judgment follows hearing); [medicine] cyclophosphamide, adriamycin and vincristine (used in chemotherapy)
**Cav.** *Cavaliere* (Italian: Knight); Cavalry; Cavan
**cav.** cavalier; cavalry; [law] caveat
**CAVD** Completion, Arithmetic Problems, Vocabulary, Following Directions (intelligence test)
**CAVI** *Centre audio-visuel international* (French: International Audio-Visual Centre)
**Caviar** Cinema and Video Industry Audience Research
**CAWU** Clerical and Administrative Workers' Union (became part of GMB)
**Cay.** Cayenne; Cayman Islands
**CAYA** Catholic Association of Young Adults
**CB** [civil aircraft marking] Bolivia; [UK postcode] Cambridge; Cape Breton (Canada); carbon black; carte blanche; cash book; cavalry brigade; [USA] Census Bureau; [theatre] centre back (of stage); centre of buoyancy; chemical and biological (weapons or warfare); Chief Baron; chlorobromomethane (used in firefighting); Citizens' Band (radio); Coal Board; [law] Common Bench; Companion of the Order of the Bath; [physics] conduction band; confidential book (in Royal Navy); confined to barracks; construction battalion; *contrabasso* (Italian: double bass); cost-benefit; county borough; [chemistry] covalent bonding; currency bond; [vehicle registration] Manchester
**Cb** [chemical element] columbium (former name of niobium)
***Cb*** [meteorology] cumulonimbus
**c/b** [cricket] caught and bowled; cost-benefit
**c.b.** cash book; cast brass; centre of buoyancy; circuit breaker; compass bearing; continuous breakdown
**CBA** [physics] colliding-beam accelerator; Commercial Bank of Australia; Commonwealth Broadcasting Association; [USA] Community Broadcasters' Association; cost-benefit analysis; Council for British Archaeology
**CBAA** Canadian Business Aircraft Association
**CB&PGNCS** circuit breaker and primary guidance navigation control system
**CBAT** [USA] College Board Achievement Test
**CBB** Campaign for Better Broadcasting
**CBBC** Children's BBC
**CBC** Canadian Broadcasting Corporation; Caribbean Broadcasting Company; [USA] Children's Book Council; [Australia] Christian Brothers' College; [computing] cipher block chaining; [medicine] complete blood count; county borough council
**CBCRL** Cape Breton Coal Research Laboratory
**CBCS** [Australia] Commonwealth Bureau of Census and Statistics
**CBD** cash before delivery; central business district; [anatomy] common bile duct
**c.b.d.** cash before delivery
**CBDC** Cape Breton Development Corporation
**CBE** chemical, biological and environmental (weapons or warfare); Commander of the Order of the British Empire; Council for Basic Education
**CBEL** *Cambridge Bibliography of English Literature*
**CBEVE** Central Bureau for Educational Visits and Exchanges
**CBF** Central Board of Finance; [medicine] cerebral blood flow
**CBI** Cape Breton Island; computer-based information; computer-based instruction; Confederation of British Industry; [USA] *Cumulative Book Index*
**c.b.i.** complete background investigation

**CBIM** Companion of the British Institute of Management
**CBiol** Chartered Biologist
**CBIS** computer-based information system
**CBIV** computer-based interactive video-disc
**CBJO** Coordinating Board of Jewish Organizations
**cbk** chequebook
**CBL** commercial bill of lading; computer-based learning; [meteorology] convective boundary layer
**cbl.** cable
**CBM** Californian Business Machines; confidence building measure; conveyor belt monitor(ing)
**CBMIS** computer-based management information system
**CBMM** Council of Building Materials Manufacturers
**CBMPE** Council of British Manufacturers of Petroleum Equipment
**CBMS** [USA] Conference Board of Mathematical Sciences
**CBNM** [USA] Central Bureau for Nuclear Measurements
**CBNS** Commander British Navy Staff
**CBO** Conference of Baltic Oceanographers; [USA] Congressional Budget Office; Counter-Battery Officer
**Cbo** Colombo (Sri Lanka)
**CBOE** Chicago Board of Options Exchange
**C-bomb** cobalt bomb
**CBOT** Chicago Board of Trade
**CBPC** Canadian Book Publishers' Council
**CBQ** civilian bachelor quarters
**CBR** [USA] Center for Brain Research; chemical, bacteriological and radiation (weapons or warfare); [aeronautics] cloud base recorder; [immunology] complement-binding reaction; [medicine] complete bed rest; [computing] constant bit rate; [astronomy] cosmic background radiation; crude birth rate
**CBRI** [India] Central Building Research Institute
**CBS** Canadian Biochemical Society; *Centraal Bureau voor de Statistiek* (Dutch: Central Statistical Bureau); Church Building Society; [medicine] citrate-buffered saline; [computing] close binary system; [USA] Columbia Broadcasting System; [medicine] computerized bone scanning; [Roman Catholic Church] Confraternity of the Blessed Sacrament
**CBSA** Clay Bird Shooting Association
**CBSI** Chartered Building Societies Institute
**CBSM** conveyor-belt service machine
**CBSO** City of Birmingham Symphony Orchestra
**CBT** Chicago Board of Trade; computer-based teaching; computer-based training
**CBU** Clearing Banks Union; [commerce] completely built-up (goods for immediate use)
**c.b.u.** cluster(ed) bomb unit; [commerce] completely built-up (goods for immediate use)
**CBV** [medicine] cerebral blood volume
**CBW** chemical and biological warfare
**CBX** [telecommunications] company branch exchange
**CBZ** coastal boundary zone
**CC** [vehicle registration] Bangor; Cape Colony; Caribbean Commission; central committee; Chamber of Commerce; Charity Commission; chess club; chief clerk; [civil aircraft marking] Chile; circuit court; city council; city councillor; [insurance] civil commotion; civil court; [physics] close coupling; closed circuit (transmission); collision course; colour centre; [photography] colour conversion; [photography] colour correction; community council; [genetics] compact chromosome; Companion of the Order of Canada; company commander; [electronics] compensating current; computer code; concave; [military] confined to camp; consular clerk; [commerce] continuation clause; control computer; [medicine] corpus callosum; [medicine] corpus cardiacum; [physics] correction coil; [physics] *corriente continua* (Spanish: direct current); Countryside Commission; county clerk; county commissioner; county council; county councillor; county court; [electronics] coupled channel; credit card; cricket club; croquet club; Crown Clerk; cruise control (in car advertisement); cruising club; Curate in Charge; cushion craft; cycling club
**C/C** cruise control (in car advertisement)

**Cc** [meteorology] cirrocumulus
**cc** carbon copy (or copies); cruise control (in car advertisement); cubic centimetre
**c/c** *compte courant* (French: current account); *conto corrente* (Italian: current account)
**cc.** centuries; chapters
**c.c.** carbon copy (or copies); cash credit; change course; chronometer correction; close control; colour code; *compte courant* (French: current account); *conto corrente* (Italian: current account); contra credit; [physics] *courant continu* (French: direct current); cubic centimetre
**CCA** Canadian Construction Association; [US navy] carrier-controlled approach; Chief Clerk of the Admiralty; [USA] Circuit Court of Appeals; [medicine] common carotid artery; Commonwealth Correspondents' Association; [USA] Consumers' Cooperative Association; continental control area; [USA] Council for Colored Affairs; County Councils' Association; [USA] County Court of Appeals; current-cost accounting
**CCAB** Canadian Circulations Audit Board; Consultative Committee of Accountancy Bodies
**CCAFS** [USA] Cape Canaveral Air Force Station
**CCAHC** Central Council for Agricultural and Horticultural Cooperation
**CCAM** Canadian Congress of Applied Mechanics
**CCAMLR** Commission for the Conservation of Antarctic Marine Living Resources
**CCAT** Central Council for the Amateur Theatre
**CCB** [South Africa] Civil Cooperation Bureau
**c.c.b.** cubic capacity of bunkers
**CCBI** Council of Churches for Great Britain and Ireland
**CCBN** Central Council for British Naturism
**CCBW** Committee on Chemical and Biological Warfare
**CCC** Camping and Caravanning Club (of Great Britain and Ireland); Canadian Chamber of Commerce; Central Control Commission; Central Criminal Court; [USA] Chemical Control Corporation; [USA] Civilian Conservation Corps; Club Cricket Conference; Commodity Credit Corporation; *Conseil de coopération culturelle* (French: European Council for Cultural Cooperation); Council for the Care of Churches; county cricket club; cross-country club; Customs Cooperation Council
**ccc** [commerce] *cwmni cyfyngedig cyhoeddus* (Welsh: public limited company, plc)
**CCCA** Cocoa, Chocolate and Confectionery Alliance; Corps Commander, Coast Artillery
**CCCBR** Central Council of Church Bell Ringers
**CCCC** Charity Christmas Card Council
**CCCI** [military] command, control, communications and intelligence
**CCCM** Central Committee for Community Medicine
**CCCO** Committee on Climatic Changes and the Ocean
**CCCP** *Soyuz Sovietskikh Sotsialisticheskikh Respublik* (Russian: Union of Soviet Socialist Republics, USSR) (transcription of Cyrillic characters, transliterated as SSSR)
**CCCR** [medicine] closed-chest cardiac resuscitation; Coordinating Committee for Cancer Research
**CCCS** Commonwealth and Continental Church Society
**CCD** Central Council for the Disabled; [electronics] charge-coupled device; *Conseil de coopération douanière* (French: Customs Cooperation Council)
**CCDA** [USA] Commercial Chemical Development Association
**CCE** [chemistry] carbon-chloroform extract; Chartered Civil Engineer; compound-cycle engine; *Conseil des communes d'Europe* (French: Council of European Municipalities); [USA] Council of Construction Employers; [accounting] current cash equivalent; [electronics] current-carrying element
**c.c.e.i.** composite cost-effectiveness index
**CCETSW** Central Council for Education and Training in Social Work
**CCETT** *Centre commun d'études de télédiffusion et télécommunications* (French:

Television and Telecommunications Research Centre)

**CCF** central computing facility; central control function; Combined Cadet Force; common-cause failure; Common Cold Foundation; concentrated complete fertilizer; [medicine] congestive cardiac failure; [Canada] Cooperative Commonwealth Federation; [statistics] cross-correlation function

**CCFA** Combined Cadet Force Association

**CCFD** [statistics] complementary cumulative frequency distribution

**CCFL** [electronics] counter-current flow limit

**CCFM** Combined Cadet Forces Medal

**CCFP** Certificate of the College of Family Physicians

**CCG** Control Commission for Germany

**CCGB** Cycling Council of Great Britain

**c.c.h.** commercial clearing house; cubic capacity of holds

**CCHE** Central Council for Health Education

**CChem** Chartered Chemist

**CCHF** Children's Country Holidays Fund

**CCHMS** Central Committee for Hospital Medical Services

**CCI** Calculated Cetane Index; *Chambre de commerce internationale* (French: International Chamber of Commerce)

**CCIA** Commission of the Churches on International Affairs; [USA] Consumer Credit Insurance Association

**CCIC** *Comité consultatif international du coton* (French: International Cotton Advisory Committee)

**CCIE** [computing] Cisco Certified Internetworking Expert

**CCIR** Catholic Council for International Relations; *Comité consultatif international des radiocommunications* (French: International Radio Consultative Committee)

**CCIS** command control information system

**CCITT** *Comité consultatif international télégraphique et téléphonique* (French: International Telegraph and Telephone Consultative Committee)

**CCITU** Coordinating Committee of Independent Trade Unions

**CCIVS** Coordinating Committee for International Voluntary Service

**CCJ** circuit court judge; Council of Christians and Jews; county court judge; [medicine] cranio-cervical junction

**CCJO** Consultative Council of Jewish Organizations

**CCK** [biochemistry] cholecystokinin

**CCL** Canadian Congress of Labour; [USA] commodity control list

**CCLGF** Consultative Committee on Local Government Finance

**CCLRC** Council for the Central Laboratory of the Research Councils

**CCM** [medicine] caffeine clearance measurement; [physics] constant current modulation; [physics] controlled carrier modulation; Cornish Chamber of Mines

**CCMA** Call Centre Management Association; Commander, Corps Medium Artillery; Contract Cleaning and Maintenance Association

**CCMD** [USA] Carnegie Committee for Music and Drama; [physics] continuous-current monitoring device

**CCMS** Committee on the Challenge of Modern Society (in NATO)

**CCN** [meteorology] cloud condensation nuclei; command control number; contract change notice; contract change notification

**CCNDT** Canadian Council for Non-Destructive Technology

**CCNR** Consultative Committee for Nuclear Research (in Council of Europe)

**CCNSC** [USA] Cancer Chemotherapy National Service Center

**CCNY** Carnegie Corporation of New York; City College of the City University of New York

**CCO** Central Coding Office; current-controlled oscillator

**CCOA** County Court Officers' Association

**CCOFI** California Cooperative Oceanic Fisheries Investigations

**CCP** Chinese Communist Party; Code of Civil Procedure; Committee on Commodity Problems; Court of Common Pleas; [nuclear technology] critical compression pressure

**c.c.p.** credit-card purchase

**CCPE** Canadian Council of Professional Engineers

**CCPF** *Comité central de la propriété forestière*

*de la CE* (French: Central Committee on Forest Property for the EU)

**CCPI** Cyanamid Canada Pipeline Incorporated

**CCPIT** China Committee for the Promotion of International Trade

**CCPL** [USA] Computer Center Program Library

**CCPO** *Comité central permanent de l'opium* (French: Permanent Central Opium Board)

**CCPR** Central Council of Physical Recreation

**CCPS** Consultative Committee for Postal Studies

**CCR** cassette camera recorder; [USA] Commission of Civil Rights; Common Centre of Research; [law] contract change request; [medicine] cranial cavity ratio; critical compression ratio

**CCRA** Commander Corps of Royal Artillery

**CCRE** Commander Corps of Royal Engineers

**CCREME** Commander Corps of Royal Electrical and Mechanical Engineers

**CCRSigs** Commander Corps of Royal Signals

**CCRU** [USA] Common Cold Research Unit

**CCS** [computing] calculus of communicating systems; Canadian Cancer Society; Canadian Ceramic Society; casualty clearing station; child-care service; collective call sign; [USA] Combined Chiefs of Staff; controlled combustion system

**CCSA** Canadian Committee on Sugar Analysis

**CCSATU** Coordinating Council of South African Trade Unions

**CCSC** Central Consultants and Specialists Committee (in BMA)

**CCSD** [computing] coupled-cluster single and double

**CCSEM** computer-controlled scanning electron microscope (or microscopy)

**CCSS** centrifugally cast stainless steel

**CCST** [USA] Center for Computer Sciences and Technology

**CCSU** Council of Civil Service Unions

**CCT** [medicine] cerebral circulation time; [USA] clean coal technology; common customs tariff (in EU); compulsory competitive tendering; [electronics] contact charge-transfer; correct corps time; [medicine] cranial compute(rize)d tomography

**CCTA** Central Computer and Telecommunications Agency; *Commission de coopération technique pour l'Afrique* (French: Commission for Technical Cooperation in Africa); Coordinating Committee of Technical Assistance

**CCTG** constant concentration tracer gas (system)

**CCTR** [nuclear technology] cassette compact toroid reactor

**CCTS** [USA] Canaveral Council of Technical Societies; Combat Crew Training Squadron

**CCTV** closed-circuit television

**CCU** [medicine] coronary care unit

**CCUS** Chamber of Commerce of the United States

**CCV** [aeronautics] control-configured vehicle

**CCW** [nuclear technology] component cooling water; Curriculum Council for Wales

**ccw.** counterclockwise

**CCWS** [nuclear technology] component cooling water system

**CD** [vehicle registration] Brighton; Canadian Forces Decoration; [electronics] carrier density; certificate of deposit; [law] Chancery Division; Civil Defence; civil disobedience; closing date; [immunology] cluster of differentiation; coal dust; College Diploma; [Jamaica] Commander of the Order of Distinction; commercial dock; compact disc; Conference on Disarmament (of UN); confidential document; [USA] Congressional District; [medicine] contagious disease; [image technology] contrast detail; [astronomy] Córdoba Durchmusterung (star catalogue); [nuclear technology] core damage; *Corps diplomatique* (French: Diplomatic Corps); countdown; [Freemasonry] Court of Deliberation; cross-dresser (= transvestite); [electronics] current density

**C/D** consular declaration; customs declaration

**Cd** [chemical element] cadmium; [military]

Command; Command Paper (1900–18) (in parliamentary procedure); [military] Commissioned

**cd** candela (unit of luminous intensity); *ciudad* (Spanish: city); command; cord; could

**c/d** [book-keeping] carried down

**c.d.** [book-keeping] carried down; cash discount; [finance] cum dividend (i.e. with dividend)

**CDA** Canadian Dental Association; *Centre de données astronomiques* (French: Centre for Astronomical Data); [South Africa] Christian Democratic Alliance; Civil Defence Act; College Diploma in Agriculture; [computing] compound document architecture; [Canada] Conference of Defence Associations; Copper Development Association

**CDAA** Churches Drought Action in Africa

**CDAAA** Committee to Defend America by Aiding the Allies

**CD&G** compact disc and graphics

**Cd Armn** Commissioned Airman

**CDAS** Civil Defence Ambulance Service

**CDB** [computing] comprehensive database

**Cd B** Commissioned Boatswain

**cdbd** cardboard

**Cd Bndr** Commissioned Bandmaster

**CDC** Canada Development Corporation; canister decontamination cell (or chamber); [chemistry] carbon derived from coal; Caribbean Defence Command; [USA] Center for Disease Control; [USA] Combat Development Command; [computing] command and data-handling console; Commissioners of the District of Columbia; [computing] common development cycle; Commonwealth Development Corporation; Control Data Corporation (computer manufacturer); cost determination committee; [electronics] critical density of current

**Cd CO** Commissioned Communication Officer

**Cd Con.** Commissioned Constructor

**CDD** [USA] certificate of disability for discharge; [electronics] charge-density distribution

**CDDI** [computing] copper distributed data interface

**CDE** chemical defence ensemble; compact disc erasable

**CD-E** compact disc erasable

**CDEE** Chemical Defence Experimental Establishment

**C de G** *Croix de Guerre* (French: War Cross) (military decoration)

**CDEM** crop disease environment monitor

**Cd Eng.** Commissioned Engineer

**CDEU** Christian Democratic European Union

**CDF** [computing] central database facility; Collider Detector at Fermilab; [nuclear technology] core-damage frequency

**c.d.f.** [statistics] cumulative distribution function

**CDFC** Commonwealth Development Finance Company

**Cdg.** Cardigan

**Cd Gr** Commissioned Gunner

**CDH** College Diploma in Horticulture; [medicine] congenital disease of the heart; [medicine] congenital dislocation of the hip

**CDHS** California Department of Health Services

**CDI** compact disc interactive

**CD-I** compact disc interactive

**CDIC** [USA] Carbon Dioxide Information Center

**CDIF** [computing] CASE data interchange format

**Cd In. O** Commissioned Instructor Officer

**CDipAF** Certified Diploma in Accounting and Finance

**c. div.** [finance] cum dividend (i.e. with dividend)

**CDL** Central Dockyard Laboratory (in Ministry of Defence); central door locking (in car advertisement); [chemistry] coal-derived liquid; Council of the Duchy of Lancaster; [Australia] County and Democratic League

**Cdl** Cardinal

**CDLD** [medicine] chronic diffuse liver disease

**CDM** [astronomy] cold dark matter (as in **CDM theory**)

**Cd MAA** Commissioned Master-at-Arms

**CDN** [international vehicle registration] Canada; *Chicago Daily News*

**Cdn** Canadian

**cDNA** [biochemistry] complementary DNA

**Cd O** Commissioned Officer

**Cdo** Commando
**Cd Obs.** Commissioned Observer
**Cd OE** Commissioned Ordnance Engineer
**CDOI** Colorado Department of Institutions
**Cd OO** Commissioned Ordnance Officer
**CDOS** [computing] concurrent disk operating system
**CDP** Committee of Directors of Polytechnics
**CDPE** continental daily parcels express
**CDPS** [computing] compound document protocol specification
**CDR** carbon dioxide research; Committees for the Defence of the Revolution (in Cuba); compact disc recordable; [computing] contents of decrement register; critical design review; crude death rate
**CD-R** [computing] compact disc recordable
**Cdr** Commander; Conductor
**CDRA** Committee of Directors of Research Associations
**Cd Rad. O** Commissioned Radio Officer
**CDRB** Canadian Defence Research Board
**CDRC** Civil Defence Regional Commissioner
**CDRD** [USA] Carbon Dioxide Research Division
**Cdre** Commodore
**CDRF** Canadian Dental Research Foundation
**CDRH** [USA] Center for Devices and Radiological Health
**CDRI** [India] Central Drug Research Institute
**CD-ROM** [computing] compact disc read-only memory
**CD-ROM XA** [computing] CD-ROM extended architecture
**CDRS** Civil Defence Rescue Service
**CD-RW** [computing] compact disc rewritable
**CDS** Chief of the Defence Staff; Civil Defence Services
**CDSC** Communicable Disease Surveillance Centre
**CDSE** computer-driven simulation environment
**Cd Sh.** Commissioned Shipwright
**CDSO** Companion of the Distinguished Service Order
**Cd SO** Commissioned Stores Officer; Commissioned Supply Officer
**CDT** Carnegie Dunfermline Trust; [USA, Canada] Central Daylight Time; craft, design and technology (school subject)
**Cdt** Cadet; Commandant
**Cdt Mid.** Cadet Midshipman
**CDTV** [computing] Commodore Dynamic Total Vision; compact-disc television
**CDU** *Christlich-Demokratische Union* (German: Christian Democratic Union) (political party)
**CDUCE** Christian Democratic Union of Central Europe
**CDV** [microbiology] canine distemper virus; Civil Defence Volunteers; compact-disc video; current domestic value
**c.d.v.** *carte-de-visite* (French: visiting card)
**CDW** [USA] collision damage waiver (in car insurance)
**c.d.w.** chilled drinking water; cold drinking water
**Cd Wdr** Commissioned Wardmaster
**CD-WO** [computing] compact disc write once
**CDWR** California Department of Water Resources
**CDWS** Civil Defence Wardens' Service
**Cdz** Cádiz
**CE** Canada East; carbon equivalent; centre of effort; [medicine] cerebral embolism; Chancellor of the Exchequer; chemical engineer; chief engineer; Christian Endeavour; Christian Era (in dates); Church of England; [computing] circular error; civil engineer; [medicine] clinical evaluation; [fishing port] Coleraine; Combustion Engineering (Incorporated); [education] Common Entrance; Common Era (in dates); *Communauté européenne* (French: European Community); community education; compass error; compression engine; [computing] computing efficiency; contrast-enhanced (of picture image); Corps of Engineers; Council of Europe; counter-espionage; [electronics] current efficiency; [vehicle registration] Peterborough
**Ce** [chemical element] cerium
**c.e.** [law] *caveat emptor* (Latin: let the buyer beware); centre of effort; [computing] circular error; compass error; critical examination

**CEA** Canadian Electrical Association; [medicine] carcino-embryonic antigen; Central Electricity Authority; Cinematograph Exhibitors Association; Combustion Engineering Association; *Comité européen des assurances* (French: European Insurance Committee); [commerce] commodity exchange authority; *Confédération européenne de l'agriculture* (French: European Confederation of Agriculture); Conference of Educational Associations; control electronics assembly; [USA] Council of Economic Advisors; Council of Educational Advance

**CEAA** [USA] Center for Editions of American Authors; Council of European-American Associations

**CEAC** [USA] Citizens Energy Advisory Committee; *Commission européenne de l'aviation civile* (French: European Civil Aviation Commission)

**CEB** Central Electricity Board

**CEBAR** chemical, biological and radiological warfare

**CEC** California Energy Commission; Canadian Electrical Code (of standardization); Catholic Education Council; Central Ethical Committee (in BMA); Centre for Economic Cooperation (in UN); Church Education Corporation; Civil Engineering Corps; Clothing Export Council; Commission of the European Communities; Commonwealth Economic Committee; Commonwealth Education Conference; Commonwealth Engineering Conference; Community Education Centre; Council for Exceptional Children

**CECA** *Communauté européenne du charbon et de l'acier* (French: European Coal and Steel Community)

**CECD** *Confédération européenne du commerce de détail* (French: European Confederation of Retail Trades)

**CECE** Committee for European Construction Equipment

**CECG** Consumers in the European Community Group

**CECLES** *Conseil européen pour la construction de lanceurs d'engins spatiaux* (French: European Space Launching Development Organization)

**CECS** Church of England Children's Society; civil engineering computing system; Communications Electronics Coordination Section

**CED** Committee for Economic Development; computer entry device; [USA] Council for Economic Development

**CEDA** Committee for Economic Development of Australia

**CEDAR** coupling, energetics and dynamics of atmospheric regions

**CEDC** Committee on Economic Cooperation among Developing Countries

**CEDEL** *Centrale de livraison de valeurs mobilières* (French: eurobond settlement service)

**cedex** *courrier d'entreprise à distribution exceptionnelle* (French: special business postal code)

**CEDI** *Centre européen de documentation et d'information* (French: European Documentation and Information Centre)

**CEDIC** Church Estates Development and Improvement Company

**CEDO** Centre for Educational Development Overseas

**CEDR** Centre for Dispute Resolution

**CEE** Central Engineering Establishment; Certificate of Extended Education; *Commission économique pour l'Europe* (French: Economic Commission for Europe); *Commission internationale de réglementation en vue de l'approbation de l'équipement électrique* (French: International Commission on Rules for the Approval of Electrical Equipment); Common Entrance Examination; *Communauté économique européenne* (French: European Economic Community); Council for Environmental Education

**CEEA** *Communauté européenne de l'énergie atomique* (French: European Atomic Energy Community)

**CEEB** [USA] College Entrance Examination Board

**CEEC** Council for European Economic Cooperation

**CEED** Centre for Economic and Environmental Development

**CEEP** *Centre européen d'études de population* (French: European Centre for Population Studies)

**CEF** Canadian Expeditionary Force; Chinese Expeditionary Force; [chemistry] crystalline electric field
**CEFTA** Central European Free Trade Area
**CEFTRI** [India] Central Food Technological Research Institute
**CEG** *collège d'enseignement général* (French: college of general education); Computer Education Group
**CEGB** Central Electricity Generating Board
**CEGGS** Church of England Girls' Grammar School
**CEGS** Church of England Grammar School
**CEI** [Switzerland] *Centre d'études industrielles* (French: Centre for Industrial Studies); *Commission électrotechnique internationale* (French: International Electrotechnical Commission); Committee for Environmental Information; communications-electronics instructions; cost-effectiveness index; Council of Engineering Institutions
**CEIF** Council of European Industrial Federations
**CEIR** Corporation for Economic and Industrial Research
**CEL** [USA] Constitutional Educational League
**Cel.** Celsius
**cel.** celebrate; celebrated; celebration; celery; [music] celesta; celibate
**CELA** Council for Exports to Latin America
**CELC** Commonwealth Education Liaison Committee
**celeb** [short form] celebrity
**celest.** celestial
**CELEX** *Communitatis Europeae Lex* (Latin: European Community Law) (computerized documentation system)
**CELJ** Conference of Editors of Learned Journals
**cello** [short form] violoncello
**Cels.** Celsius
**CELSS** controlled ecological life-support system
**Celt.** Celtic
**CEM** *Companhia Electricidade de Macáu* (Macao electricity company); [physics] continuous emission monitoring; cost and effectiveness method; [astronautics] crew-escape module
**cem.** cement; cemetery
**CEMA** Canadian Electrical Manufacturers' Association; Catering Equipment Manufacturers' Association; Conveyor Equipment Manufacturers' Association; Council for Economic Mutual Assistance; Council for the Encouragement of Music and the Arts
**CEMAC** Committee of European Associations of Manufacturers of Active Electronic Components; *Communauté économique et monétaire de l'Afrique central* (French: Central African Economic and Monetary Community)
**CEMAP** *Commission européenne des méthodes d'analyse des pesticides* (French: Collaborative Pesticides Analytical Committee)
**CEMF** [electronics] counter-electromotive force
**CEMLA** *Centro de Estudios Monetarios Latino-Americanos* (Spanish: Latin-American Centre for Monetary Studies)
**CEMR** Council of European Municipalities and Regions
**CEMS** Church of England Men's Society
**CEN** *Comité européen de normalisation* (French: European Standardization Committee)
**Cen** [astronomy] Centaurus
**cen.** central; centre; century
**CEND** Civil Engineers for Nuclear Disarmament
**CENELEC** *Comité européen de normalisation électrotechnique* (French: European Electrotechnical Standardization Committee)
**CEng** Chartered Engineer
**cens.** censor; censored; censorship
**cent.** [currency] centavo (hundredth of peso etc.); [currency] centesimo (hundredth of peso etc.); centigrade; [currency] centime (hundredth of franc etc.); central; centrifugal; *centum* (Latin: hundred); century
**CENTA** Combined Edible Nut Trade Association
**CENTAG** Central (European) Army Group (in NATO)
**centenn.** centennial
**centig.** centigrade
**Cento** Central Treaty Organization
**CEO** chief education officer; chief execu-

tive officer; Confederation of Employee Organizations
**CEOA** Central European Operating Agency (in NATO)
**CEP** [computing] circular error probability
**Cep** [astronomy] Cepheus
**CEPCEO** *Comité d'études des producteurs de charbon d'Europe occidentale* (French: Western European Coal Producers' Association)
**CEPES** *Comité européen pour le progrès économique et social* (French: European Committee for Economic and Social Progress)
**CEPIS** Council of European Professional Informatics Societies
**CEPO** Central European Pipeline Office
**CEPR** Centre for Economic Policy Research
**CEPS** Central European Pipeline System; Centre for European Policy Studies; Cornish Engine Preservation Society
**CEPT** *Conférence européenne des administrations des postes et des télécommunications* (French: European Conference of Postal and Telecommunications Administrations)
**CEQ** [USA] Council on Environmental Quality
**CEQA** [USA] California Environmental Quality Act
**CER** carbon dioxide evolution rate; carbon dioxide exchange rate; [Australia, New Zealand] closer economic relations; Community of European Railways
**cer.** ceramic
**ceram.** ceramic
**CERC** [USA] Center for Energy Research Computation; Civil Engineering Research Council
**CERCA** Commonwealth and Empire Radio for Civil Aviation
**CERCLA** [USA] Comprehensive Environmental Response, Compensation and Liability Act
**Cerdip** [computing] ceramic dual in-line package
**CERES** [USA] Coalition for Environmentally Responsible Economies; Consumers for Ethics in Research Group
**CERG** Conservative European Reform Group
**CERI** Centre for Educational Research and Innovation (of OECD)
**CERL** Central Electricity Research Laboratories
**CERN** *Conseil européen pour la recherche nucléaire* (French: European Organization for Nuclear Research)
**CERP** *Centre européen des relations publiques* (French: European Centre of Public Relations)
**CERT** Charities Effectiveness Review Trust; computer emergency response team
**cert** [short form] certainty
**cert.** certain; certificate; certificated; certification; certified; certify
**CertCAM** Certificate in Communication, Advertising and Marketing
**CertEd** Certificate in Education
**CertHE** Certificate in Higher Education
**certif.** certificate; certificated; certified
**cert. inv.** certified invoice
**cerv.** [medicine] cervical
**CES** [USA] Center for Energy Studies; Centre for Environmental Studies; Christian Evidence Society; *collège d'enseignement secondaire* (French: college of secondary education); community energy system; cost-estimating system
**CESAR** [USA] Center for Engineering Systems Advanced Research
**CESC** Conference on European Security and Cooperation
**CESE** [USA] Center for Earth Science and Engineering
**CESP** Confederation of European Socialist Parties
**CESR** [USA] Cornell electron storage ring
**CESSAC** Church of England Soldiers', Sailors' and Airmen's Clubs
**CESSI** Church of England Sunday School Institution
**CEST** Centre for Exploitation of Science and Technology
**Cestr.** *Cestrensis* (Latin: (Bishop) of Chester)
**CET** Central European Time; *collège d'enseignement technique* (French: college of technical education); Common External Tariff; Council for Educational Technology
**Cet** [astronomy] Cetus
**CETA** [USA] Comprehensive Employment and Training Act
**CETEX** Committee on Extra-Terrestrial Exploration

**CETHV** Council for the Education and Training of Health Visitors
**CETI** communications with extraterrestrial intelligence
**CETO** Centre for Educational Television Overseas
**cet. par.** *ceteris paribus* (Latin: other things being equal)
**CETS** chemical energy transmission systems; Church of England Temperance Society
**CEU** Christian Endeavour Union
**CEUS** Central and Eastern United States
**CEUSA** Committee for Exports to the United States of America
**CEVS** [USA] controlled environment vitrification system
**CEWC** Council for Education in World Citizenship
**CEWMS** Church of England Working Men's Society
**Cey.** Ceylon
**CEYC** Church of England Youth Council
**Ceyl.** Ceylon
**CEZMS** Church of England Zenana Missionary Society
**CF** calibration factor; [civil aircraft marking] Canada; Canadian Forces; capacity factor; [fishing port] Cardiff; [UK postcode] Cardiff; [commerce] carried forward; centre of flotation; Chaplain to the Forces; charcoal-filtered; *Comédie Française* (French national theatre); Commonwealth Fund; [currency] Comorian franc; compensation fee; [medicine] conventional fractionation radiotherapy; Corresponding Fellow; cost and freight; [chemistry] crystal field (as in **CF theory**); [medicine] cystic fibrosis; [vehicle registration] Reading
**Cf** [chemical element] californium
**Cf.** [Roman Catholic Church] Confessions
**c/f** [book-keeping] carried forward; cost and freight
**cf.** [bookbinding] calfskin; *confer* (Latin: compare)
**.cf** Central African Republic (in Internet address)
**c.f.** [music] *cantus firmus* (Latin: fixed song); [book-keeping] carried forward; [sports] centre field; [baseball] centre fielder; [sports] centre forward; centre of flotation; *chemin de fer* (French: railway); communication factor; context free; cost and freight; cubic feet
**CFA** Canadian Federation of Agriculture; Canadian Field Artillery; Canadian Forestry Association; cash-flow accounting; [USA] Chartered Financial Analyst; Commission of Fine Arts; Commonwealth Forestry Association; *Communauté financière africaine* (French: African Financial Community, as in **CFA franc**); [medicine] complete Freund's adjuvant; Consumer Federation of America; Contract Flooring Association Limited; Cookery and Food Association; Council for Acupuncture; Council of Foreign Affairs; [electrical engineering] cross-field amplifier; [medicine] cryptogenic fibrosing alveolitis
**CFAF** [currency] CFA franc (used in some countries of Africa)
**CFAL** current food additives legislation
**CFAM** cogeneration feasibility analysis model
**CFAP** Canadian Foundation for the Advancement of Pharmacy
**CFAR** constant false alarm rate
**CFAT** Carnegie Foundation for the Advancement of Teaching
**CFB** [computing] cipher feedback; [USA] Consumer Fraud Bureau; Council of Foreign Bondholders
**CFBAC** Central Fire Brigade Advisory Council (of England and Wales)
**CFBS** Canadian Federation of Biological Sciences
**CFC** carbon-fibre composite; chlorofluorocarbon (chemical harmful to ozone layer); [microbiology] colony-forming cell; Common Fund for Commodities (in UN); *Congregatio Fratrum Christianorum* (Latin: Congregation of Christian Brothers); consolidation freight classification
**CFCE** *Conseil des fédérations commerciales d'Europe* (French: Council of European Commercial Federations)
**CFD** [computing] compact floppy disk; [engineering] computational fluid dynamics
**cfd** cubic feet per day
**CFDC** Canadian Film Development Corporation
**CFDT** *Confederation française démocratique*

*du travail* (French: Democratic Federation of Labour)

**CFE** Central Fighter Establishment; College of Further Education; [microbiology] colony-forming efficiency; [physics] control fuel element; Conventional (Armed) Forces in Europe (as in **CFE treaty**)

**CFF** *Chemins de fer fédéraux suisses* (French: Swiss federal railways); [computing] critical flicker frequency; [physics] critical fusion frequency

**CFFLS** [USA] Consortium for Fossil Fuel Liquefaction Science

**c.f.g.** cubic feet of gas

**cfh** cubic feet per hour

**CFHT** Canada–France–Hawaii Telescope (Mauna Kea, Hawaii)

**CFI** Campaign for Freedom of Information; chief flying instructor; cost, freight and insurance; Court of First Instance (in EU)

**c.f.i.** cost, freight and insurance

**CFL** Canadian Football League; ceasefire line; Central Film Library

**CFLP** Central Fire Liaison Panel

**CFM** Cadet Forces Medal; [chemistry] chlorofluoromethane; Council of Foreign Ministers

**cfm** confirm; cubic feet per minute

**cfm.** confirmation

**CfN** Council for Nature

**CFO** [meteorology] Central Forecasting Office; chief financial officer; chief fire officer

**c.f.o.** calling for orders; channel for orders

**CFOA** Chief Fire Officers' Association

**CFOD** Catholic Fund for Overseas Development

**CFP** Common Fisheries Policy (of EU); *Communauté financière du Pacifique* (French: Pacific Financial Community, as in **CFP franc**); *Compagnie française des pétroles* (French petroleum company)

**CFPF** [currency] CFP franc (used in some countries of Pacific)

**CFPP** coal-fired power plant

**CFR** [USA] Code of Federal Regulations; Commander of the Order of the Federal Republic of Nigeria; [nuclear technology] commercial fast reactor; [engineering] Cooperative Fuel Research (Committee) (as in **CFR engine**); [medicine] coronary flow reserve; [metallurgy] corrosion-fatigue resistance; Council on Foreign Relations

**cfr** chauffeur

**cfr.** *confronta* (Italian: compare)

**CFRI** [USA] Central Fuel Research Institute

**CFRP** carbon-fibre reinforced plastic

**CFS** central flying school; [medicine] chronic fatigue syndrome; Clergy Friendly Society; [telecommunications] combination frequency signal; [computing] common file system

**cfs** cubic feet per second

**CFSAN** [USA] Center for Food Safety and Applied Nutrition

**CFSL** Central Forensic Science Laboratory

**CFSP** Common Foreign and Security Policy (in EU)

**CFSTI** [USA] Clearinghouse for Federal Scientific and Technical Information

**CFT** *Compagnie française de télévision* (French television company); [medicine] complement fixation test; [engineering] cross-flow turbine; Cystic Fibrosis Trust

**cft** craft

**CFTB** Commonwealth Forestry and Timber Bureau

**CFTC** [USA] Commodity Futures Trading Commission; Commonwealth Fund for Technical Cooperation

**cftmn** craftsman

**CFU** [microbiology] colony-forming unit

**CFV** continuous-flow ventilation

**CFWI** County Federation of Women's Institutes

**CFX** [Roman Catholic Church] *Congregatio Fratrum Xaverianorum* (Latin: Congregation of Xaverian Brothers)

**CG** [vehicle registration] Bournemouth; Captain-General; Captain of the Guard; centre of gravity; Chaplain-General; [aeronautics] cloud-to-ground; coastguard; Coldstream Guards; [US army] Commanding General; Commissary-General; computer graphics; concentration guide; conjugate gradient; Consul-General; Covent Garden (opera house); *Croix de Guerre* (French: War Cross) (military decoration)

**C-G** Chaplain-General

**cg** centigram

**.cg** (Republic of) Congo (in Internet address)

**c.g.** centre of gravity
**CGA** [commerce] cargo's proportion of general average; Certified General Accountant; [USA] Coast Guard Academy; [USA] Coast Guard Auxiliary; [computing] colour graphics adapter; Community of the Glorious Ascension; Country Gentlemen's Association
**CGAT** City Gallery Arts Trust
**CGB** Commonwealth Geographical Bureau
**CGBR** central government borrowing requirement
**CGC** [USA] Coast Guard cutter; Commonwealth Games Council; *Confédération générale des cadres* (French: General Confederation of Executive Staff ); Conspicuous Gallantry Cross
**CGD** [medicine] chronic granulomatous disease
**CGDK** Coalition Government of Democratic Kampuchea
**CGE** Conservative Group for Europe
**cge** carriage; charge
**cge fwd** carriage forward
**cge pd** carriage paid
**CGF** Commonwealth Games Federation
**CGH** Cape of Good Hope; computer-generated hologram
**CGI** Catholic Guides of Ireland; chief ground instructor; chief gunnery instructor; City and Guilds Institute; commercial grade item; [computing] common gateway interface; computer graphics interface
**c.g.i.** corrugated galvanized iron
**CGIA** City and Guilds (of London) Insignia Award
**CGIAR** Consultative Group in International Agricultural Research
**CGIL** *Confederazione Generale Italiana del Lavoro* (Italian: General Italian Confederation of Labour)
**CGLI** City and Guilds of London Institute
**CGM** computer graphics metafile; Conspicuous Gallantry Medal
**cgm** centigram
**CGMW** Commission for the Geological Map of the World
**cgo** cargo; [finance] contango
**CGOU** [USA] Coast Guard Oceanographic Unit
**CGP** College of General Practitioners
**CGPM** *Conférence générale des poids et mesures* (French: General Conference of Weights and Measures); *Conseil général des pêches pour la Méditerranée* (French: General Fisheries Council for the Mediterranean)
**CGPS** Canadian Government Purchasing System
**CGRI** [India] Central Glass and Ceramic Research Institute
**CGRM** Commandant-General, Royal Marines
**CGRO** Compton Gamma Ray Observatory
**CGS** central gunnery school; Chief of the General Staff; Coast and Geodetic Survey; [US army] Commissary General of Subsistence; Cottage Gardens Society
**cgs** centimetre-gram-second (as in **cgs units**)
**CGSB** Canadian Government Specifications Board
**CGSC** [USA] Command and General Staff College
**CGSS** [USA] Command and General Staff School
**CGSUS** Council of Graduate Schools in the United States
**CGT** capital gains tax; ceramic gas turbine; closed gas turbine; *Compagnie générale transatlantique* (French shipping company); compressed-gas turbometer; *Confederación general del trabajo* (Spanish: General Confederation of Labour) (in Argentina); *Confédération générale du travail* (French: General Confederation of Labour)
**CGTB** Canadian Government Travel Bureau
**CGT-FO** *Confédération générale du travail–force ouvrière* (French: General Confederation of Labour/Workers' Force)
**c.g.u.** ceramic glazed units
**CH** [military] Captain of the Horse; [Freemasonry] Captain of the Host; Carnegie Hall; central heating (in property advertisement); [medicine] cerebral haemorrhage; chapter house; [fishing port] Chester; [UK postcode] Chester; Christ's Hospital; clearing house; Companion of Honour; [medicine] contact hypersensitivity; [astronomy] coronal hole; corporate hospitality; custom(s) house; [vehicle registration] Nottingham; [inter-

national vehicle registration] Switzerland (from French *Confédération Helvétique* or Latin *Confederatio Helvetica*)

**C/H** central heating (in property advertisement)

**Ch.** chairman; chairwoman; Chaldean; Chaldee; Chamber; Champion; Chancellor; Chancery; Chapter; Chile; Chilean; China; Chinese; *Chirurgiae* (Latin: of Surgery) (in academic degrees); Christ; [Bible] Chronicles; Church

**ch** [mathematics] hyperbolic cosine

**.ch** Switzerland (in Internet address)

**ch.** chain (crochet stitch); chain (unit of length); chaldron (unit of capacity); *chambre(s)* (French: room(s)); champion; chaplain; chapter; charge(s); chart; [horseracing] chase; chassis (in car advertisement); [chess] check; cheese; chemical; chemistry; cheque; [horseracing] chestnut; *cheval-vapeur* (French: horsepower); chief; child; children; choir; choke; church

**c.h.** candle hour; central heating (in property advertisement); [sports] centre half; clearing house; club house; compass heading; court house; custom(s) house

**CHA** Catholic Hospital Association; Chest and Heart Association; Community Health Association; Countrywide Holidays Association

**Cha** [astronomy] Chamaeleon

**chacom** chain of command

**Chal.** Chaldaic; Chaldean; Chaldee

**chal.** chaldron (unit of capacity); *chaleur* (French: heat); challenge

**Chald.** Chaldaic; Chaldean; Chaldee

**Chamb.** Chamberlain; Chambers

**Chan.** Chancellor; Chancery

**chan.** chancel; channel

**Chanc.** Chancellor; Chancery

**CHANCOM** Channel Committee (in NATO)

**chap.** chapel; chaplain; chaplaincy; chapter

**CHAPS** Clearing House Automated Payment System

**chapt.** chapter

**CHAR** Campaign for Homeless People (formerly Campaign for the Homeless and Rootless)

**char.** character; characteristic; characterize; charity; charter

**charc.** charcoal

**CHAS** Catholic Housing Aid Society

**Chas.** Charles

**Chauc.** (Geoffrey) Chaucer (English poet)

**CHB** Companion of Honour of Barbados; [medicine] complete heart block

**ChB** Bachelor of Surgery (from Latin *Chirurgiae Baccalaureus*); [USA] Chief of the Bureau

**Chb.** Cherbourg

**CHC** child health clinic; choke coil; Clerk to the House of Commons; Community Health Council; [USA] Confederate High Command; [chemistry] cyclohexylamine carbonate

**ch. cent.** *chauffage central* (French: central heating)

**Ch. Clk** Chief Clerk

**CHD** [medicine] congenital heart disease; [medicine] coronary heart disease

**ChD** Doctor of Chemistry; Doctor of Surgery (from Latin *Chirurgiae Doctor*)

**Ch. Div.** [law] Chancery Division

**CHDL** computer hardware description language

**CHE** Campaign for Homosexual Equality

**ChE** chemical engineer; chief engineer

**CHEAR** Council on Higher Education in the American Republics

**CHEC** Commonwealth Human Ecology Council

**Cheka** *Chrezvychainaya Comissiya* (Russian: Special Commission (for fighting counter-revolution and sabotage)) (former Soviet security organization)

**CHEL** *Cambridge History of English Literature*

**Chelm** Cheltenham

**CHEM** chemical health effects (assessment) methodology

**chem.** chemical; chemically; chemist; chemistry

**ChemE** chemical engineer

**Ches.** Cheshire

**CHESS** [USA] Cornell high-energy synchrotron source

**Chev.** Chevalier

**chev.** chevron

**CHF** Carnegie Hero Fund; [medicine] congestive heart failure

**ChF** Chaplain of the Fleet

**chf** chief

**ch. fwd** charges forward

**chg.** change; charge
**chgd** charged
**chge** charge
**chgph.** choreographer; choreographic; choreography
**Chi.** Chicago; Chichester; China; Chinese
**Chic.** Chicago
**Chich.** Chichester
**Chicom** Chinese communist
**childn** children
**CHILL** [computing] CCITT high-level language
**Chin.** China; Chinese
**CHIPS** Clearing House Inter-Bank Payments System
**CHIRP** Confidential Human Incidence Reporting Programme (civil aviation safety scheme)
***Chi. Trib.*** *Chicago Tribune*
**chiv.** chivalry
**Ch. J** Chief Justice
**Ch. K** Christ the King
**chk** check
**chkd** checked
**chkpt** checkpoint
**chkr** checker
**Chl** [botany] chlorophyll
**chl.** chloride; chloroform
**Ch. Lbr** chief librarian
**ChLJ** Chaplain of the Order of St Lazarus of Jerusalem
**chlo.** chloride; chloroform
**CHLW** [nuclear technology] commercial high-level waste
**ChM** Master of Surgery (from Latin *Chirurgiae Magister*)
**chm.** chairman; [chess] checkmate; choirmaster
**CHMC** [USA] Children's Hospital Medical Center
**chmn** chairman
**CHMR** [USA] Center for Hazardous Materials Research
**CHNT** Community Health Nurse Tutor
**CHO** Confederation of Healing Organizations; Crop Husbandry Officer
**cho.** choral; chorister; chorus
**choc.** chocolate
**Ch. of S** Chamber of Shipping
**Ch. of the F** Chaplain of the Fleet
**CHOGM** Commonwealth Heads of Government Meeting
**choirm.** choirmaster
**chor.** choral; chorister; chorus
**CHP** chemical heat pump; combined heat and power; *Cumhuriyet Halk Partisi* (Turkish: Republican People's Party)
**ch. pd** charges paid
**ch. ppd** charges prepaid
**CHQ** Commonwealth Headquarters (of Girl Guides Association); [military] Corps Headquarters
**chq.** cheque
**Chr.** Christ; Christian; Christianity; Christmas; [Bible] Chronicles
**CHRI** Commonwealth Human Rights Initiative
**chrm.** chairman
**Chron.** [Bible] Chronicles
**chron.** chronicle; chronological; chronologically; chronology; chronometry
**chronol.** chronological; chronologically; chronology
**Chrs** Chambers
**CHS** Canadian Hydrographic Service; Church Historical Society; [computing] cylinders, heads and sectors
**chs** chapters
**CHSA** Chest, Heart and Stroke Association
**CHSC** Central Health Services Council
**ch'ship** championship
**Ch. Skr** chief skipper
**ChStJ** Chaplain of the Order of St John of Jerusalem
**c.h.t.** cylinder-head temperature
**chtg** charting
**ch. v.** check valve
**c.h.w.** constant hot water
**chwdn** churchwarden
**chyd** churchyard
**Chy Div.** [law] Chancery Division
**CI** [medicine] cardiac index; [medicine] cerebral infarction; Channel Islands; [Freemasonry] Chapter of Instruction; chemical inspectorate; chemical ionization; Chief Inspector; chief instructor; [astronomy] Colour Index; [medicine] combined injury; [chemistry] combustion index; Commonwealth Institute; Communist International; compression-ignition (as in **CI engine**); [statistics] confidence interval; [chemistry] configuration interaction; consular invoice; [commerce] continuous improvement; [photography] contrast index;

[astronomy] coronal index (of solar activity); [engineering] corrosion inhibitor; [international vehicle registration] Côte d'Ivoire (Ivory Coast); counter-intelligence; (Imperial Order of the) Crown of India

**Ci** curie (unit of radioactivity)

***Ci*** [meteorology] cirrus

**.ci** Côte d'Ivoire (Ivory Coast, in Internet address)

**c.i.** cast iron

**CIA** Cancer Information Association; cash in advance; [USA] Central Intelligence Agency; Chemical Industries' Association; Chief Inspector of Armaments; *Conseil international des archives* (French: International Council on Archives); Corporation of Insurance Agents; Culinary Institute of America

**Cia** [commerce] *compagnia* (Italian: company, Co.); [commerce] *companhia* (Portuguese: company, Co.); [commerce] *compañia* (Spanish: company, Co.)

**CIAA** *Centre international d'aviation agricole* (French: International Agricultural Aviation Centre); Coordinator of Inter-American Affairs

**CIAB** [USA] Coal Industry Advisory Board; *Conseil international des agences bénévoles* (French: International Council of Voluntary Agencies)

**CIAC** Construction Industry Advisory Council

**CIAgrE** Companion of the Institution of Agricultural Engineers

**CIAI** Commerce and Industry Association Institute

**CIAL** Corresponding Member of the International Institute of Arts and Letters

**CIAPG** *Confédération internationale des anciens prisonniers de guerre* (French: International Confederation of Former Prisoners of War)

**CIArb** Chartered Institute of Arbitrators

**CIAS** Conference of Independent African States

**CIB** Campaign for an Independent Britain; Central Intelligence Board; Chartered Institute of Bankers (formerly IOB); Corporation of Insurance Brokers; [New Zealand] Criminal Investigation Branch

**CIBS** Chartered Institute of Building Services (former name of CIBSE); Chartered Institution of Building Societies

**CIBSE** Chartered Institution of Building Services Engineers (formerly CIBS)

**CIC** Capital Issues Committee; Chemical Institute of Canada; Cinema International Corporation; [immunology] circulating immune complexes; [USA] Combat Information Center; Commander-in-Chief; [USA] Command Information Center; Commonwealth Information Centre; [USA] Counterintelligence Corps; [USA] Critical Issues Council

**Cic.** (Marcus Tullius) Cicero (Roman orator)

**CICA** Canadian Institute of Chartered Accountants

**CICADA** central instrumentation control and data acquisition

**CICAR** Cooperative Investigations of the Caribbean and Adjacent Regions

**CICB** Criminal Injuries Compensation Board

**CICC** [electronics] cable-in-conduit conductor; *Conférénce internationale des charités catholiques* (French: International Conference of Catholic Charities)

**Cicestr.** *Cicestrensis* (Latin: (Bishop) of Chichester)

**CICG** *Centre international du commerce de gros* (French: International Centre for Wholesale Trade)

**CICHE** Committee for International Cooperation in Higher Education

**CICI** Confederation of Information Communication Industries

**CICP** [USA] Committee to Investigate Copyright Problems

**CICR** *Comité international de la Croix-Rouge* (French: International Committee of the Red Cross)

**CICRC** *Commission internationale contre le régime concentrationnaire* (French: International Commission Against Concentration Camp Practices)

**CICRIS** Cooperative Industrial and Commercial Reference and Information Service

**CICS** [computing] customer information control system

**CICT** *Conseil international du cinéma et de*

*la télévision* (French: International Film and Television Council)

**CID** [electronics] charge injection device; Committee for Imperial Defence; Council of Industrial Design; Criminal Investigation Department

**CIDA** Canadian International Development Agency; *Comisión interamericano de desarrollo agricola* (Spanish: Inter-American Committee for Agricultural Development); *Comité intergouvernemental du droit d'auteur* (French: Intergovernmental Copyright Committee)

**CIDADEC** *Confédération internationale des associations d'experts et de conseils* (French: International Confederation of Associations of Experts and Consultants)

**CIDE** *Comisión de inversion y desarrollo económico* (Spanish: Commission for Investment and Economic Development) (in Uruguay)

**CIDESA** *Centre international de documentation économique et sociale africaine* (French: International Centre for African Social and Economic Documentation)

**CIDNP** chemically induced dynamic nuclear polarization

**CIDOC** [Mexico] Centre for Intercultural Documentation

**CIE** captain's imperfect entry; *Centre international de l'enfance* (French: International Children's Centre); *Commission internationale de l'éclairage* (French: International Commission on Illumination, ICI); Companion of the Order of the Indian Empire; *Confédération internationale des étudiants* (French: International Confederation of Students); [Ireland] *Córas Iompair Éireann* (Gaelic: Transport Organization of Ireland)

**Cie** [commerce] *compagnie* (French: company, Co.)

**CIEC** *Centre international d'études criminologiques* (French: International Centre of Criminological Studies); *Commission internationale de l'état civil* (French: International Commission on Civil Status)

**CIEE** Companion of the Institution of Electrical Engineers

**CIEO** Catholic International Education Office

**CIEPS** *Conseil international de l'éducation physique et sportive* (French: International Council of Sport and Physical Education)

**CIF** Canadian Institute of Forestry; *Clube internacional de futebol* (Portuguese: International Football Club); *Conseil international des femmes* (French: International Council of Women); [commerce] cost, insurance and freight

**c.i.f.** [commerce] cost, insurance and freight

**CIFA** Corporation of Insurance and Financial Advisers

**c.i.f.c.** [commerce] cost, insurance, freight and commission

**c.i.f.c.i.** [commerce] cost, insurance, freight, commission and interest

**CIFE** Colleges and Institutes for Further Education; *Conseil des fédérations industrielles d'Europe* (French: Council of European Industrial Federations); *Conseil international du film d'enseignement* (French: International Council for Educational Films)

**c.i.f.e.** [commerce] cost, insurance, freight and exchange

**c.i.f.i.** [commerce] cost, insurance, freight and interest

**CIFJ** *Centre international du film pour la jeunesse* (French: International Centre of Films for Children)

**c.i.f.L.t.** [commerce] cost, insurance and freight, London terms

**CIG** *Comité international de géophysique* (French: International Geophysical Committee)

**cig** [short form] cigarette

**CIGA** *Compagnia Italiana dei Grandi Alberghi* (Italian hotel company)

**CIGAR** [nuclear technology] channel inspection and gauging apparatus of reactors

**CIGAS** Cambridge Intercollegiate Graduate Application Scheme

**CIGasE** Companion of the Institution of Gas Engineers

**CIGR** *Commission internationale du génie rural* (French: International Commission of Agricultural Engineering)

**CIGS** Chief of the Imperial General Staff

**CIH** Certificate in Industrial Health; Chartered Institute of Housing; [medicine] chronic inactive hepatitis

**CIHA** *Comité international d'histoire de l'art* (French: International Committee on the History of Art)
**CIHE** Council for Industry and Higher Education
**CII** Centre for Industrial Innovation (of University of Strathclyde); Chartered Insurance Institute; *Conseil international des infirmières* (French: International Council of Nurses)
**CIIA** Canadian Institute of International Affairs; *Commission internationale des industries agricoles* (French: International Commission for Agricultural Industries)
**CIIR** Catholic Institute for International Relations
**CIJ** Chartered Institute of Journalists; *Commission internationale de juristes* (French: International Commission of Jurists)
**CIL** Confederation of Irish Labour
**CILB** *Commission internationale de lutte biologique contre les ennemis des plantes* (French: International Commission for Biological Control)
**CILECT** *Centre international de liaison des écoles de cinéma et de télévision* (French: International Association of National Film Schools)
**CILG** Construction Industry Information Liaison Group
**CIM** Canadian Institute of Mining; Chartered Institute of Marketing; China Inland Mission; Commission for Industry and Manpower; computer input on microfilm; computer-integrated manufacturing; *Conférence islamique mondial* (French: World Muslim Conference); *Conseil international de la musique* (French: International Music Council); Cooperative Investment Management
**CIMA** Chartered Institute of Management Accountants; [USA] Construction Industry Manufacturers' Association
**CIMarE** Companion of the Institute of Marine Engineers
**CIMAS** continuous iron-making and steel-making
**CIMB** Construction Industry Manpower Board
**CIME** *Comité intergouvernemental pour les migrations européennes* (French: Intergovernmental Committee for European Migration); Council of Industry for Management Education
**CIMechE** Companion of the Institution of Mechanical Engineers
**CIMGTechE** Companion of the Institution of Mechanical and General Technician Engineers
**CIMM** Canadian Institute of Mining and Metallurgy
**CIMPM** *Comité international de médecine et de pharmacie militaires* (French: International Committee of Military Medicine and Pharmacy)
**CIMS** [USA] chemical information management systems
**CIMTP** *Congrès international de médecine tropicale et de paludisme* (French: International Congress of Tropical Medicine and Malaria)
**CIN** [medicine] cervical intraepithelial neoplasia (in cervical smear); *Commission internationale de numismatique* (French: International Numismatic Commission)
**C-in-C** Commander-in-Chief
**CINCENT** Commander-in-Chief Allied Forces Central Europe
**CINCLANT** Commander-in-Chief Atlantic
**CINCNORTH** Commander-in-Chief Allied Forces Northern Europe
**CINCPAC** Commander-in-Chief Pacific
**CINCSOUTH** Commander-in-Chief Allied Forces Southern Europe
**CINFO** Chief of Information
**Cinn.** Cincinnati
**CINO** Chief Inspector of Naval Ordnance
**CINR** [USA] Central Institute for Nuclear Research
**CINS** [USA] child(ren) in need of supervision
**CInstR** Companion of the Institute of Refrigeration
**CIO** Church Information Office; *Comité international olympique* (French: International Olympic Committee); *Commission internationale d'optique* (French: International Commission for Optics); [USA] Congress of Industrial Organizations
**CIOB** Chartered Institute of Building (formerly IOB)
**CIOMS** Council for International Organizations of Medical Sciences
**CIOS** Combined Intelligence Objectives

Subcommittee; *Conseil international pour l'organisation scientifique* (French: International Committee of Scientific Management)

**CIOT** Chartered Institute of Taxation

**CIP** [mining] carbon-in-pulp; Cataloguing in Publication; *Centre d'information de la presse* (Belgian news agency); [engineering] cold isostatic pressing; Common Industrial Policy (of EU); [engineering] constant-injection pressure

**CIPA** Canadian Industrial Preparedness Association; Chartered Institute of Patent Agents

**CIPFA** Chartered Institute of Public Finance and Accountancy

**CIPL** *Comité international permanent des linguistes* (French: International Standing Committee of Linguists)

**CIPM** *Commission internationale des poids et mesures* (French: International Committee on Weights and Measures); [USA] Council for International Progress in Management

**CIPO** *Comité international pour la préservation des oiseaux* (French: International Committee for Bird Preservation)

**CIPP** *Conseil indo-pacifique des pêches* (French: Indo-Pacific Fisheries Council)

**CIPR** *Commission internationale de protection contre les radiations* (French: International Commission on Radiological Protection)

**CIPS** Central Illinois Public Service (Company); Chartered Institute of Purchasing and Supply; Choice in Personal Safety

**CIPSH** *Conseil international de la philosophie et des sciences humaines* (French: International Council for Philosophy and the Humanities)

**CIR** Canada India reactor; Commission (or Council) on Industrial Relations; Commissioners of Inland Revenue; cost information report; [computing] current instruction register

**Cir** [astronomy] Circinus

**cir.** circle; circuit; circular; circulation; circumference; circus

***cir.*** *circa* (Latin: about) (in dates)

**CIRA** Conference of Industrial Research Associations

**circ.** circle; circuit; circular; circulation; circumcision; circumference; circus

***circ.*** *circa* (Latin: about) (in dates)

**CIRCCE** *Confédération internationale de la représentation commerciale de la communauté européenne* (French: International Confederation of Commercial Representation in the European Community)

**circs** [short form] circumstances

**circum.** circumference

**CIRF** *Centre international d'information et de recherche sur la formation professionelle* (French: International Vocational Training Information and Research Centre); Corn Industries Research Foundation

**CIRIA** Construction Industry Research and Information Association

**CIRIEC** *Centre international de recherches et d'information sur l'économie collective* (French: International Centre of Research and Information on Collective Economy)

**CIRP** *Collège international pour recherche et production* (French: International Institution for Production Engineering Research)

**CIRRPC** [USA] Committee on Interagency Radiation Research and Policy Coordination

**CIRS** [computing] cross-interleaved Reed-Solomon (as in **CIRS scheme**)

**CIRT** Community Initiative Research Trust

**CIS** [medicine] carcinoma in situ; cataloguing in source; [USA] Catholic Information Society; [USA] Center for International Studies; Central Information Service on Occupational Health and Safety (of RoSPA); Chartered Institute of Secretaries (former name of ICSA); Coal Industry Society; [medicine] combined-injury syndrome; Commonwealth of Independent States (former Soviet republics); Cooperative Insurance Society

**CISA** Canadian Industrial Safety Association

**CISAC** Centre for International Security and Arms Control; *Confédération internationale des sociétés d'auteurs et compositeurs* (French: International Confederation of Societies of Authors and Composers)

**CISBH** *Comité international de standardis-*

*ation en biologie humaine* (French: International Committee for Standardization in Human Biology)
**CISC** complex instruction-set chip; complex instruction-set computer
**CISCO** City Group for Smaller Companies; Civil Service Catering Organization
**CIS-COBOL** [computing] compact interactive standard Cobol
**CISF** *Confédération internationale des sages-femmes* (French: International Confederation of Midwives)
**CISL** *Confédération internationale des syndicats libres* (French: International Confederation of Free Trade Unions); *Confederazione Italiana Sindacati Lavoratori* (Italian: Italian Confederation of Workers' Trade Unions)
**CISM** *Conseil international du sport militaire* (French: International Military Sports Council)
**CISPR** *Comité international spécial des perturbations radioélectriques* (French: International Special Committee on Radio Interference)
**CISS** Centre for International Sports Studies; *Conseil international des sciences sociales* (French: International Social Science Council)
**Cist.** Cistercian
**CISTI** Canadian Institute for Scientific and Technological Information
**CISV** Children's International Summer Village Association
**CIT** [USA] California Institute of Technology; [USA] Carnegie Institute of Technology; [New Zealand] Central Institute of Technology; Chartered Institute of Transport; [astronomy] circumstellar imaging telescope; *Comité international des transports par chemin de fer* (French: International Railway Transport Committee); [nuclear technology] compact ignition tokamak; *Compagnia Italiana Turismo* (Italian tourism company)
**cit.** citadel; citation; cited; citizen; citrate
**c.i.t.** compression in transit
**CITB** Construction Industry Training Board
**CITC** Canadian Institute of Timber Construction; Construction Industry Training Centre
**CITEL** Committee for Inter-American Telecommunications
**CITES** Convention on International Trade in Endangered Species
**CITI** *Confédération internationale des travailleurs intellectuels* (French: International Confederation of Professional and Intellectual Workers)
**cito disp.** [medicine] *cito dispensatur* (Latin: let it be dispensed quickly) (in prescriptions)
**CITV** Children's Independent Television
**CIU** Club and Institute Union
**CIUS** *Conseil international des unions scientifiques* (French: International Council of Scientific Unions)
**CIUSS** Catholic International Union for Social Service
**CIV** City Imperial Volunteers; *Commission internationale du verre* (French: International Glass Commission)
**civ.** civil; civilian; civilization; civilize
**CivE** civil engineer
**civvies** [short form] civilian clothes
**civvy** [short form] civilian (as in **civvy street**)
**CIW** [USA] Carnegie Institute of Washington
**CIWF** Compassion in World Farming
**CIX** commercial Internet exchange
**CJ** Chief Justice; [vehicle registration] Gloucester
**cj.** conjectural
**CJA** Commonwealth Journalists' Association; Criminal Justice Act
**CJCC** Commonwealth Joint Communications Committee
**CJD** [medicine] Creutzfeld–Jakob disease
**CJEC** Court of Justice of the European Communities
**CJM** *Code de justice militaire* (French: Code of Military Justice); [Roman Catholic Church] Congregation of Jesus and Mary; *Congrès juif mondial* (French: World Jewish Congress)
**CK** [trademark] Calvin Klein; certified kosher; [fishing port] Colchester; [vehicle registration] Preston
**ck** cask; check; cook
**CKD** [computing] centre for key distribution; [commerce] completely knocked down (of goods sold in parts)
**ckout** checkout

**ckpt** cockpit
**ckw.** clockwise
**CL** calendar line; [fishing port] Carlisle; cathode luminescence; central locking (in car advertisement); civil law; Civil Lord; [Belgium] Commander of the Order of Leopold; common law; Communication Lieutenant; confidence limits; craft loss; critical list; [medicine] cruciate ligament; [vehicle registration] Norwich; [international vehicle registration] Sri Lanka (from former name Ceylon)
**Cl** [chemical element] chlorine
**cl** centilitre; council
**c/l** cash letter; craft loss
**cl.** claim; clarinet; class; classical; classics; classification; clause; clearance; clergy; clergyman; clerk; climb; close; closet; closure; cloth; clove
**.cl** Chile (in Internet address)
**c.l.** carload; central locking (in car advertisement); centre line; *cum laude* (Latin: with praise); cut lengths
**CLA** Canadian Library Association; Canadian Lumbermen's Association; Copyright Licensing Agency; Country Landowners' Association
**Cla.** Clackmannan(shire)
**Clack.** Clackmannan(shire)
**CL(ADO)** Contact Lens Diploma of the Association of Dispensing Opticians
**CLAM** chemical ramjet low-altitude missile
**CLAN** [computing] cordless local-area network
**CLAP** [USA] Citizens Lobbying Against Prostitution
**CLAPA** Cleft Lip and Palate Association
**Clar.** [heraldry] Clarenceux (King of Arms)
**clar.** [printing] clarendon (typeface); clarinet
**Clarnico** Clark, Nichols and Coombes (Limited) (confectionery manufacturers)
**CLASS** Computer-based Laboratory for Automated School Systems
**class.** classic; classical; classification; classified; classify
**clav.** [music] clavier
**CLAW** Consortium of Local Authorities in Wales
**CLB** [USA] Cape Lookout Bight (North Carolina); Church Lads' Brigade
**CLC** Canadian Labour Congress; Chartered Life Underwriter of Canada; Commonwealth Liaison Committee
**CLCB** Committee of London Clearing Banks
**CLCr** Communication Lieutenant-Commander
**CLD** [medicine] chronic liver disease; Doctor of Civil Law
**cld** [stock exchange] called; cancelled; cleared; coloured; cooled; could
**CLE** Council of Legal Education
**CLEA** Council of Local Education Authorities
**CLEAPSE** Consortium of Local Education Authorities for the Provision of Science Equipment
**cler.** clerical
**cl. gt** [bookbinding] cloth gilt
**CLH** *Croix de la Légion d'Honneur* (French: Cross of the Legion of Honour)
**CLI** [computing] command-line interface; cost-of-living index
**CLIC** Cancer and Leukaemia in Children
**clim.** climate; climatic
**CLIMAP** Climate: Long-range Interpretation, Mapping and Prediction (international project)
**clin.** clinic; clinical
**CLit** Companion of Literature
**CLitt** Companion of Literature
**CLJ** *Cambridge Law Journal*; Commander of the Order of St Lazarus of Jerusalem
**clk** clerk; clock
**clkrm** cloakroom (in property advertisement)
**clks** cloaks (= cloakroom)
**clkw.** clockwise
**CLL** [medicine] chronic lymphatic leukaemia
**cl. L** classical Latin
**CLLR** International Symposium on Computing in Literary and Linguistic Research
**Cllr** Councillor
**CLM** coal–liquid mixture; conservation and load management
**clm** column
**CLML** *Current List of Medical Literature*
**CLNS** [computing] connectionless network service
**CLO** chief liaison officer; cod liver oil

**Clo.** Close (in road name)
**clo.** closet; clothing
**cloakrm** cloakroom (in property advertisement)
**c/lock.** central locking (in car advertisement)
**CLP** China Light and Power (Company Limited); [computing] concurrent logic programming; Constituency Labour Party; [computing] constraint logic programming
**CLPA** Common Law Procedure Acts
**CLR** Central London Railway; City of London Rifles; computer-language recorder; [USA] Council on Library Resources
**clr** clear; colour; cooler
**CLRAE** Conference of Local and Regional Authorities of Europe
**clrm** classroom
**CLRU** Cambridge Language Research Unit
**CLS** Certificate in Library Science; Christian Literature Society; [statistics] classical least-squares; [statistics] constrained least-squares; Courts of London Sessions
**cls.** close
**CLSB** Committee of London and Scottish Bankers
**CLT** *Canadian Law Times*; *Compagnie Luxembourgeoise de Télédiffusion* (European media company); computer-language translator
**CLU** Chartered Life Underwriter
**CLV** [microbiology] carnation latent virus; [microbiology] cassava latent virus; [computing] constant linear velocity
**clvd** clavichord
**CM** Canadian Militia; Catholic Mission; [USA] Central Maine; central meridian; [physics] centre of mass; Certificated Master; Certificate of Merit; Certified Master; [UK postcode] Chelmsford; church mission; church missionary; circulation manager; [USA] Cleveland Museum (of Art); combustion modification; [astronautics] command module; Common Market; [music] common metre; complex mixture; composite material; condition monitoring; [computing] configuration management; [Roman Catholic Church] Congregation of the Mission; contrast medium (in radiology); [nuclear technology] core meltdown; corporate membership; Corresponding Member; court martial; [microbiology] culture medium; [vehicle registration] Liverpool; Master of Surgery (from Latin *Chirurgiae Magister*); Member of the Order of Canada
**Cm** Command Paper (1987– ); [chemical element] curium
**cM** [genetics] centimorgan
**cm** centimetre
**.cm** Cameroon (in Internet address)
**c.m.** *carat métrique* (French: metric carat); *causa mortis* (Latin: by reason of death); [physics] centre of mass; [music] common metre; [medicine] *cras mane* (Latin: tomorrow morning)
**CMA** Cable Makers' Association; [chemistry] calcium magnesium acetate; Canadian Medical Association; Catering Managers' Association; [USA] Certificate of Management Accounting; Chartered Management Accountant; Church Music Association; civil–military affairs; coal–mineral analysis; [USA] Colorado Mining Association; Commonwealth Medical Association; Communication Managers' Association; cost and management accountant; Country Music Association; Court of Military Appeals
**CMa** [astronomy] Canis Major
**CMAC** Catholic Marriage Advisory Council
**CMACP** *Conseil mondial pour l'assemblée constituante des peuples* (French: World Council for the People's World Convention)
**CMAS** Clergy Mutual Assurance Society; *Confédération mondiale des activités subaquatiques* (French: World Underwater Federation)
**CMB** Central Medical Board; Central Midwives Board; Chase Manhattan Bank; [chemistry] chemical mass balance; coastal motor boat; [astronomy] cosmic microwave background
**CMBHI** Craft Member of the British Horological Institute
**CMBI** Caribbean Marine Biological Institute
**cmbt** combat
**CMC** Canadian Marconi Company; Canadian Meteorological Centre; Canadian

Music Council; [chemistry] carboxymethyl cellulose; Catholic Media Council; Central Manpower Committee; ceramic-matrix composite; [USA] certified management consultant; Collective Measures Committee (of UN); Commandant of the Marine Corps; Conservation Monitoring Centre

**CMCW** Calvinistic Methodist Church of Wales

**CMD** [astronomy] colour-magnitude diagram; [music] common metre double; conventional munitions disposal; [physics] cryogenic magnetic detector

**Cmd** Command Paper (1919–56) (in parliamentary procedure)

**cmdg** commanding

**Cmdr** Commander

**Cmdre** Commodore

**Cmdt** Commandant

**CME** Chicago Mercantile Exchange; *Conférence mondiale de l'énergie* (French: World Power Conference); [astronomy] coronal mass ejection; [USA] cost and manufacturability expert

**CMEA** Council for Mutual Economic Assistance

**CMF** Cement Makers' Federation; Central Mediterranean Force; [Australia] Citizen Military Forces; Coal Merchants' Federation; [physics] coherent memory filter; Commonwealth Military Forces; [physics] compressed magnetic field; [Roman Catholic Church] *Cordis Mariae Filii* (Latin: Missionary Sons of the Immaculate Heart of Mary)

**CMG** Commission on Marine Geology; Companion of the Order of St Michael and St George; Computer Management Group

**CMH** Campaign for the Mentally Handicapped; combined military hospital; [USA] Congressional Medal of Honor

**CMHA** Canadian Mental Health Association

**CMHC** [Canada] Central Mortgage and Housing Corporation

**CMHR** combustion modified highly resilient

**CMI** [medicine] cell-mediated immunity; *Comité maritime international* (French: International Maritime Committee); *Commission mixte internationale pour la protection des lignes de télécommunication et des canalisations* (French: Joint International Committee for the Protection of Telecommunication Lines and Ducts); Commonwealth Mycological Institute; computer-managed instruction

**CMi** [astronomy] Canis Minor

**CMIA** Coal Mining Institute of America

**CMIPS** [computing] common management information protocol/service

**CMIR** [USA] Center for Medical Imaging Research

**CMJ** Church's Ministry among the Jews

**CML** Central Music Library; [medicine] chronic myeloid leukaemia; computer-managed learning; Council of Mortgage Lenders; [computing] current mode logic

**cml** commercial

**CMLA** Chief Martial Law Administrator

**CMLJ** Commander of Merit of the Order of St Lazarus of Jerusalem

**CMM** [computing] capability and maturity model; [Canada] Commander of the Order of Military Merit

**CMMA** [USA] Coal Mining Management College; Concrete Mixer Manufacturers' Association

**cmn** commission

**Cmnd** Command Paper (1957–86) (in parliamentary procedure)

**cmnr** commissioner

**CMO** Central Merchandising Office (in Zambia); chief medical officer; [USA] collateralized mortgage-backed obligation; [astronomy] compact massive object

**CMOPE** *Confédération mondiale des organisations de la profession enseignante* (French: World Confederation of Organizations of the Teaching Profession)

**CMOS** [electronics] complementary metal oxide semiconductor; [electronics] complementary metal oxide silicon

**CMP** [USA] Central Maine Power Company; Christian Movement for Peace; [astronautics] command module pilot; Commissioner of the Metropolitan Police; cost of maintaining project

**cmp.** compromise

**cmpd** compound

**CMPDI** [USA] Central Mine Planning and Design Institute

**cm. pf.** cumulative preference (shares); cumulative preferred (shares)

**Cmpn** Companion
**CMR** Cape Mounted Rifles; central meter reading; cerebral metabolic rate; [electronics] common mode rejection
**CMRA** Chemical Marketing Research Association
**CMRC** [USA] Coal Mining Research Company
**CMRO** County Milk Regulations Officer
**CMRR** [electronics] common mode rejection ratio
**CMRS** [USA] Central Mining Research Station
**CMS** Catholic Missionary Society; [USA] Center for Measurement of Science; central materials supply; Certificate in Management Studies; Church Missionary Society; [computing] conversational monitor system
**c.m.s.** [medicine] *cras mane sumendus* (Latin: to be taken tomorrow morning) (in prescriptions)
**CMSER** [USA] Commission on Marine Science, Engineering and Resources
**CM/SM** [astronautics] command module service module
**cmt** cement
**CMV** [medicine] cerebral major vessel; [medicine] conventional mechanical ventilation; [microbiology] cucumber mosaic virus; [medicine] cytomegalovirus
**CMY** [computing] cyan, magenta, yellow
**CMYK** [computing] cyan, magenta, yellow, black
**CMZS** Corresponding Member of the Zoological Society
**CN** [fishing port] Campbeltown; Canadian National (Railway); [chemistry] cellulose nitrate; Chinese Nationalists; [chemistry] chloracetophenone; *Code Napoléon* (French: Napoleonic Code); common network; [physics] compound nucleus; [physics] condensation nucleus; Confederate Navy; [commerce] credit note; [civil aircraft marking] Morocco; [vehicle registration] Newcastle upon Tyne
**C/N** [ecology] carbon–nitrogen (as in **C/N ratio**); circular note; consignment note; contract note; [insurance] cover note; [commerce] credit note
**Cn** [ecclesiastical] Canon
**.cn** China (in Internet address)
**c.n.** [medicine] *cras nocte* (Latin: tomorrow night)
**CNA** Canadian Nuclear Association; [US navy] Center for Naval Analyses; Central News Agency (in Taiwan); [USA] Chemical Notation Association; [astronomy] cosmic noise absorption; Cyprus News Agency
**CNAA** Council for National Academic Awards
**CNADS** Conference of National Armaments Directors (in NATO)
**CNAR** Chief of Naval Air Services; [finance] compound net annual rate
**CNC** computerized numerical control
**Cnc** [astronomy] Cancer
**CNCIEC** China National Coal Import and Export Corporation
**Cncl** Council
**Cnclr** Councillor
**CNCMH** Canadian National Committee for Mental Hygiene
**cncr.** concurrent
**CND** Campaign for Nuclear Disarmament
**CNDC** Cherished Numbers Dealers Association; China Nuclear Data Centre
**CNE** *Comisión nacional de energía* (Spanish: National Energy Commission)
**CNEAF** coal, nuclear, electric and alternate fuels
**CN(Eng)O** Chief Naval Engineering Officer
**CNES** *Centre national d'études spatiales* (French: National Space Centre)
**CNF** Challis National Forest; Commonwealth Nurses' Federation
**CNFD** [USA] Commercial Nuclear Fuel Division
**CNG** compressed natural gas; consolidated natural gas
**CNI** Chief of Naval Information; Companion of the Nautical Institute
**CNIP** Ciskei National Independence Party
**CNIPA** Committee of National Institutes of Patent Agents
**CNL** Canadian National Library; [Australia] Commonwealth National Library; [USA] Crocker Nuclear Laboratory
**cnl** cancel
**CNLA** [USA] Council of National Library Associations
**CNLS** [statistics] complex nonlinear least-square

**CNM** [USA] Certified Nurse-Midwife
**CNN** Cable News Network; Certified Nursery Nurse
**CNO** chief nursing officer; Chief of Naval Operations
**CNP** Chief of Naval Personnel; Council for National Parks
**CNR** Canadian National Railway; Civil Nursing Reserve; *Conseil national de la révolution* (French: National Revolutionary Council) (in Burkina Faso); Council of National Representatives
**cnr** corner
**CNRE** [USA] cooperative networks on rural energy
**CNRS** *Centre national de la recherche scientifique* (French: National Centre for Scientific Research)
**CNS** [anatomy] central nervous system; [USA] Cherokee Nuclear Station; Chief of Naval Staff; China News Service (news agency); Community Nursing Services; Congress of Neurological Surgeons
**c.n.s.** [medicine] *cras nocte sumendus* (Latin: to be taken tomorrow night) (in prescriptions)
**CNSI** [USA] Chem-Nuclear Systems Incorporated
**CNSLD** chronic nonspecific lung disease
**CNSSO** Chief Naval Supply and Secretariat Officer
**CNT** Canadian National Telegraphs; celestial navigation trainer; [USA] Center for Neighborhood Technology; Commission for the New Towns; *Confederación nacional del trabajo* (Spanish: National Confederation of Labour)
**cntn** contain
**cntr** container
**cntr.** contribute; contribution
**cnvt** convict
**CO** Cabinet Office; [fishing port] Caernarvon; [medicine] cardiac output; careers officer; central office; chief officer; clerical officer; [UK postcode] Colchester; [international vehicle registration] Colombia; [US postcode] Colorado; [military] combined operations; commanding officer; command order; Commissioner of Oaths; Commonwealth Office (became part of FCO); [finance] *compte ouvert* (French: open account); conscientious objector; criminal offence; Crown Office; [electronics] current oscillations; [vehicle registration] Exeter
**C/O** case oil; cash order; certificate of origin
**Co** [chemical element] cobalt
**Co.** Coalition; Colorado; Company; County
**c/o** care of (in postal addresses); [bookkeeping] carried over; change over
**.co** Colombia (in Internet address)
**co.** [navigation] course
**c.o.** [medicine] complains of; [bookkeeping] carried over
**$CO_2$** carbon dioxide
**COA** change of address; College of Aeronautics; [medicine] condition on admission
**coad.** coadjutor
**Coal.** Coalition
**COAS** Council of the Organization of American States
**coax** [short form] coaxial cable
**c.o.b.** close of business
**COBE** [astronomy] Cosmic Background Explorer
**Cobol** [computing] common business-oriented language
**c.o.b.q.** *cum omnibus bonis quiescat* (Latin: may he/she rest with all good souls)
**Cobra** Cabinet Office Briefing Room
**COC** Chamber of Commerce; Clerk of the Chapel; [USA] combat operations center; [medicine] combined oral contraceptive; Corps of Commissionaires
**coc.** cocaine
**COCA** [USA] consent order and compliance agreement
**COCAST** Council for Overseas Colleges of Arts, Science and Technology
**COCEMA** *Comité des constructeurs européens de matériel alimentaire* (French: Committee of European Machinery Manufacturers for the Food Industries)
**coch.** [medicine] *cochleare* (Latin: spoonful)
**coch. amp.** [medicine] *cochleare amplum* (Latin: heaped spoonful)
**cochl.** [medicine] *cochleare* (Latin: spoonful)
**coch. mag.** [medicine] *cochleare magnum* (Latin: tablespoonful)

**coch. med.** [medicine] *cochleare medium* (Latin: dessertspoonful)
**coch. parv.** [medicine] *cochleare parvum* (Latin: teaspoonful)
**COCI** Consortium on Chemical Information
**COCOM** Coordinating Committee for Multinational Export Controls
**COCOMO** [computing] constructive cost model
**COD** cash on delivery; cause of death; Chamber of Deputies; chemical oxygen demand; [USA] collect on delivery; *Concise Oxford Dictionary*
**Cod.** Codex
**cod.** codex; codicil; codification
**c.o.d.** cargo on deck; cash on delivery; [USA] collect on delivery
**CODAG** [engineering] combined diesel and gas turbine
**CODAN** [telecommunications] carrier-operated device anti-noise
**CODASYL** [computing] Conference on Data Systems Languages
**CODATA** Confederation of Design and Technology Associations
**codd.** codices
**codec** [computing] coder-decoder
**Codesh** Convention for a Democratic South Africa
**CODIPHASE** [computing] coherent digital phased array system
**CODOG** [engineering] combined diesel or gas turbine
**CODOT** *Classification of Occupations and Directory of Occupational Titles*
**COE** Chamber Orchestra of Europe; *Conseil oecuménique des églises* (French: World Council of Churches); [USA] Corps of Engineers; cost of electricity; cost of energy
**COED** computer-operated electronic display; *Concise Oxford English Dictionary*
**co-ed** [short form] coeducational
**coeff.** coefficient
**CoEnCo** Committee for Environmental Conservation
**COESA** [USA] Committee on Extension to the Standard Atmosphere
**COF** *Comité olympique française* (French: French Olympic Committee)
**C of A** Certificate of Airworthiness; College of Arms
**COFACE** [commerce] *Compagnie française pour l'assurance du commerce extérieur* (French: French export credit guarantee company)
**C of B** confirmation of balance
**C of C** Chamber of Commerce
**C of E** Church of England; Council of Europe
**C of ECS** Church of England Children's Society
**C of F** Chaplain of the Fleet; chief of finance; [engineering] coefficient of friction
**C of G** centre of gravity
**C of GH** Cape of Good Hope
**COFI** Committee on Fisheries
**C of I** Church of Ireland
**C of L** City of London
**C of M** [aeronautics] Certificate of Maintenance
**C of S** Chief of Staff; Church of Scotland; conditions of service
**COG** Cleansing Officers' Guild
**CoG** centre of gravity
**cog.** cognate; cognizant; cognomen
**c.o.g.** centre of gravity
**COGAG** [engineering] combined gas and gas turbine
**COGB** certified official government business
**COGECA** *Comité général de la coopération agricole des pays de la CE* (French: General Committee for Agricultural Cooperation in the EU Countries)
**Cogene** Committee on Genetic Experimentation
**COGLA** Canada Oil and Gas Lands Administration
**COGMA** Concrete Garage Manufacturers' Association
**COGS** [astronautics] continual orbital guidance system; [accounting] cost of goods sold
**coh.** coheir
**c.o.h.** cash on hand
**COHSE** Confederation of Health Service Employees (became part of Unison)
**COI** Central Office of Information; certificate of origin and interest; *Commission océanographique intergouvernementale* (French: Intergovernmental Oceanographic Commission); [USA] cost of illness
**COIC** Canadian Oceanographic Identifica-

tion Centre; Careers and Occupational Information Centre
**COID** Council on International Development
**CoID** Council of Industrial Design (former name of Design Council)
**COIE** Committee on Invisible Exports
**COIF** Control of Intensive Farming
**COIL** chemical oxygen–iodine laser
**COIN** [USA] counter-insurgency
**COINS** [USA] Committee on Improvement of National Statistics
**COJO** Conference of Jewish Organizations
**COL** centrally operated locking (in car advertisement); computer-oriented language; cost of living
**Col** [astronomy] Columba
**Col.** Colombia; Colombian; Colonel; Colorado; [Bible] Colossians
**col.** collect; collected; collection; collector; college; collegiate; colon; colonial; colony; colour; coloured; column
**COLA** Camping and Outdoor Leisure Association; [USA] cost-of-living adjustment (in employment contract)
**Col. Comdt** Colonel Commandant
**COLD** [medicine] chronic obstructive lung disease
**Coling** International Conference on Computational Linguistics
**Coll.** College
**coll.** collateral; colleague; collect; collected; collection; collective; collector; college; collegiate; colloquial; colloquialism; [medicine] collyrium (eyewash)
**collab.** collaborate; (in) collaboration (with); collaborator
**collat.** collateral; collaterally
**collect.** collective; collectively
**colloq.** colloquial; colloquialism; colloquially
**coll'ott.** [music] *coll'ottava* (Italian: in octaves)
**collr** collector
**colly** colliery
**Colo.** Colorado
**colog.** cologarithm
**Coloss.** [Bible] Colossians
**Col. P** [advertising] colour page
**COLS** [computing] communications for online systems
**cols** columns
**Col-Sgt** Colour-Sergeant
**COM** coal–oil mixture; [US navy] Commander; [chemistry] complex organic mixture; computerized operations management; computer output on microfiche (or microfilm)
**Com** [astronomy] Coma Berenices
**Com.** Commander; Commissary; Commissioner; Committee; Commodore; Commonwealth; Communist
**com.** comedy; comic; comma; commentary; commerce; commercial; commission; commissioner; committee; common; commoner; commonly; commune; communicate; communicated; communication(s); community
**.com** (US) commercial organization (in Internet address)
**COMA** Committee on Medical Aspects of Food Policy
**COMAF** *Comité des constructeurs de matériel frigorifique de la CE* (French: Committee of Refrigerating Plant Manufacturers of the EU)
**COMAL** [computing] common algorithmic language
**COMAR** [USA] Code of Maryland Air Regulations
**COMARE** [USA] Committee on Medical Aspects of Radiation in the Environment
**COMART** Commander, Marine Air Reserve Training
**comb.** combination; combine; combined; combining; combustible; combustion
**Comd.** Commander
**comd** command
**comd.** commanding
**COMDEV** Commonwealth Development Finance Company
**Comdg** [military] Commanding
**Comdr** Commander
**Comdt** Commandant
**COME** Chief Ordnance Mechanical Engineer
**COMECON** Council for Mutual Economic Assistance
**Comet** Committee for Middle East Trade; computer-operated management evaluation technique
**COMEX** [USA] Commodity Exchange (New York)
**COMEXO** Committee for Exploitation of the Oceans
**comfy** [short form] comfortable

**Com-Gen** Commissary-General
**COMIBOL** *Corporación Minera de Bolivia* (Bolivian state mining company)
**Cominform** Communist Information Bureau
**COMINT** communications intelligence
**Comintern** Communist International
**coml** commercial
**COMLOGNET** [US air force] combat logistics network
**Comm.** Commander; Commodore
**comm.** commentary; commerce; commercial; commercially; committee; commonwealth; communal; communication
**Commd** [military] Commissioned
**commem.** commemoration; commemorative
**Commiss.** Commissary
**Commissr** Commissioner
**Commn** Commission
**commn** commission
**Commnd** [military] Commissioned
**Commr** Commissioner
**comms** communications
**commun.** communication; community
**Commy** Commissary
**COMO** Committee of Marketing Organizations
**Comp.** Companion (of institute or institution)
**comp.** companion; comparative; compare; comparison; compass; compensation; compete; competition; competitive; competitor; compilation; compiled; compiler; complete; compose; composer; composite; composition; compositor; compound; compounded; comprehensive; compression; comprising
**COMPAC** Commonwealth Trans-Pacific Telephone Cable
**compar.** comparative; comparison
**compd** compound
**Comp-Gen** Comptroller-General
**compl.** complement; complete; compliment; complimentary
**complt** complainant; complaint
**compo.** composition
**compr.** compressive
**Compsac** International Computer Software and Applications Conference
**compt** compartment
**Compt.** Comptroller
**Comptr** Comptroller
**Comr** Commissioner
**Com. Rom.** Common Romance (language)
**comsat** communications satellite
**ComSec** Commonwealth Secretariat
**COMSER** Commission on Marine Science and Engineering Research (in UN)
**Com. Teut.** Common Teutonic (language)
**Com. Ver.** [Bible] Common Version
**Com. W Ger.** Common West Germanic (language)
**Comy-Gen** Commissary-General
**Con.** Conformist; Conservative; [finance] Consols; Constable; [military] Constructor; Consul; [music] contralto
**con.** concentration; concerning; concerto; conclusion; conditioning; confidence; conics; *conjunx* (Latin: wife); connection; conservation; consolidate; consolidated; [finance] consols; continue; continued; *contra* (Latin: against); convenience; conversation
**CONAC** [USA] Continental Air Command
**CONAD** [USA] Continental Air Defense Command
**CONARC** [USA] Continental Army Command
**CONBA** Council of National Beekeeping Associations of the United Kingdom
**conbd** contributed
**Con. C** Constructor Captain
**conc.** concentrate; concentrated; concentration; concerning; concerto; concise
**concd** concentrated
**concg** concentrating
**conch.** conchology
**conchie** [short form] conscientious objector
**concn** concentration
**Con. Cr** Constructor Commander
**concr.** concrete
**con. cr.** [book-keeping] contra credit
**cond.** condense; condensed; condenser; condition; conditional; conduct; conducted; conductivity; conductor
**condr** conductor
**con esp.** [music] *con espressione* (Italian: with expression)
**con espr.** [music] *con espressione* (Italian: with expression)
**conf.** confection; confectionery; *confer* (Latin: compare); conference; confession; confessor; confidential

**confab** [short form] confabulation
**Confed.** Confederacy; Confederate; Confederation
**confed.** confederate; confederated; confederation
**Cong.** Congregational; Congregationalist; Congress; Congressional
**cong.** [pharmacology] *congius* (Latin: gallon); congregation; congregational
**Cong. R** [USA] Congressional Records
**Cong. Rec.** [USA] Congressional Records
**CONGU** Council of National Golf Unions
**CONI** *Comitato Olimpico Nazionale Italiano* (Italian: Italian National Olympic Committee)
**con. inv.** consular invoice
**conj.** conjecture; [grammar] conjugation; [grammar] conjunction; conjunctive
**Con. L** Constructor Lieutenant
**CONLAN** [computing] consensus language
**Con. LCr** Constructor Lieutenant-Commander
**Conn.** Connecticut
**conn.** connect; connected; connection; connotation
**conq.** conquer; conquered; conqueror; conquest
**CONS** [computing] connection-oriented network service
**Cons.** Conservative; Conservatoire; Conservatorium; Conservatory; Constable; Constitution; Consul
**cons.** consecrate; consecrated; consecration; consecutive; consequence; conservation; conservative; conserve; consider; consigned; consignment; consolidated; consonant; constable; constitution; constitutional; construction; consul; consult; consulting
**con. sec.** conic section
**Conserv.** Conservatoire; Conservatorium; Conservatory
**conserv.** conservatory (in property advertisement)
**cons. et prud.** *consilio et prudentia* (Latin: by counsel and prudence)
**consgt** consignment
**consid.** consideration
**Con. SL** Constructor Sub-Lieutenant
**consol.** consolidated
**consols** [short form] consolidated annuities (or stock)
**Const.** Constable; Constitution
**const.** constable; constant; constituency; constitution; constitutional; construction
**constit.** constituent
**constl** constitutional
**constr.** construct; construction; construe
**cont.** container; containing; contents; continent; continental; continue; continued; [music] continuo; continuum; *contra* (Latin: against); contract; contraction; control; controller
**contag.** contagious
**contbd** contraband
**contbg** contributing
**cont. bon. mor.** *contra bonos mores* (Latin: contrary to good manners)
**contd** contained; continued
**contemp.** contemporary
**contg** containing
**contn** continuation
**contr.** contract(s); contracted; contraction; contralto; contrary; contrast; contrasted; control; controller
**contr. bon. mor.** *contra bonos mores* (Latin: contrary to good manners)
**cont. rem.** [medicine] *continuantur remedia* (Latin: let the medication be continued) (in prescriptions)
**contrib.** contributed; contributing; contribution; contributor
**CONUS** continental United States
**Conv.** Convocation
**conv.** convenience; convenient; convent; convention; conventional; conversation; conversion; converter; convertible
**convce** conveyance
**COOC** [insurance] contact with oil or other cargo
**co-op** [short form] cooperative (society or store)
**COP** [New Zealand] Certificate of Proficiency (university pass); coefficient of performance (in thermodynamics); [USA] community-oriented policing; custom of port
**Cop.** Copernican; Coptic
**cop.** copper; copulative; copyright; copyrighted
**COPA** *Comité des organisations professionnelles agricoles de la CE* (French: Committee of Agricultural Organizations in the EU)

**COPAL** Cocoa Producers' Alliance
**COPD** [medicine] chronic obstructive pulmonary disease
**Copec** Conference on Christian Politics, Economics and Citizenship
**COPPSO** Conference of Professional and Public Service Organizations
**copr.** copyright
**COPS** Council of Polytechnic Secretaries
**Copt.** Coptic
**coptr** copartner
**COPUOS** Committee on the Peaceful Uses of Outer Space
**COPUS** Committee on the Public Understanding of Science
**COR** Committee of the Regions (in EU)
**Cor.** [Bible] Corinthians; Coroner
**cor.** corner; cornet; [music] *corno* (Italian: horn); coroner; *corpus* (Latin: the body); correct; corrected; correction; correlative; correspondence; correspondent; corresponding; corrupt
**Coral** [computing] common real-time application language
**Corat** Christian Organizations Research and Advisory Trust
**CORBA** [computing] common object request broker architecture
**CORD** [medicine] chronic obstructive respiratory disease
**Corda** Coronary Artery Disease Research Association
**CORE** [USA] Congress of Racial Equality
**CORES** computer-aided (or -assisted) order routing and execution system (in Tokyo Stock Exchange)
**CORGI** Council for Registered Gas Installers
**Cor. Mem.** Corresponding Member
**Corn.** Cornish; Cornwall
***Cornh.*** *Cornhill Magazine*
**corol.** corollary
**coroll.** corollary
**Corp.** Corporal; Corporation
**Corpl** Corporal
**Corpn** Corporation
**corr.** correct; corrected; correction; corrective; correlative; *corrente* (Italian: current); correspond; correspondence; correspondent; corresponding; corrigenda; corrugated; corrupt; corrupted; corruption
**CORRA** Combined Overseas Rehabilitation Relief Appeal
**correl.** correlative
**corresp.** correspondence; corresponding
**Corresp. Mem.** Corresponding Member
**corrupt.** corruption
**CORS** Chief of the Regulating Staff
**Cors.** Corsica; Corsican
**Cor. Sec.** corresponding secretary
**CORSO** [New Zealand] Council of Organizations for Relief Services Overseas
**CORT** Council of Regional Theatres; Council of Repertory Theatres
**cort.** cortex
**COS** [commerce] cash on shipment; Chamber of Shipping; Charity Organization Society; Chief of Staff; Cinema Organ Society
**CoS** Chief of Staff
**Cos.** Companies; Counties
**cos** [mathematics] cosine
**c.o.s.** [commerce] cash on shipment
**COSA** Colliery Officials and Staffs Association; [accounting] cost of sales adjustment
**co. sa** *come sopra* (Italian: as above)
**COSAG** [shipping] combined steam turbine and gas turbine
**COSAR** compression scanning array radar
**COSATI** Committee on Scientific and Technical Information
**COSATU** Congress of South African Trade Unions
**COSBA** Computer Services and Bureaux Association
**COSE** [computing] common open software environment
**COSEC** Coordinating Secretariat of the National Union of Students
**cosec** [mathematics] cosecant
**cosech** [mathematics] hyperbolic cosecant
**COSFPS** Commons, Open Spaces and Footpaths Preservation Society
**cosh** [mathematics] hyperbolic cosine
**COSHEP** Committee of Scottish Higher Education Principals
**COSHH** Control of Substances Hazardous to Health
**CoSIRA** Council for Small Industries in Rural Areas
**COSLA** Convention of Scottish Local Authorities
**COSMD** Combined Operations Signals Maintenance Division

**cosmog.** cosmogony; cosmographical; cosmography
**COSMOS** Coast Survey Marine Observation System
**co. so.** *come sopra* (Italian: as above)
**COSPAR** Committee on Space Research
**Coss.** *Consules* (Latin: Consuls)
**COSSAC** Chief of Staff to Supreme Allied Commander
**COSSEC** Cambridge, Oxford and Southern School Examinations Council
**COST** Committee for Overseas Science and Technology
**COT** [physics] change of temperature
**CoT** College of Technology
**cot** [mathematics] cotangent
**cotan** [mathematics] cotangent
**COTC** Canadian Officers' Training Corps
**coth** [mathematics] hyperbolic cotangent
**COTR** [USA] contracting officers' technical representative
**Cots** Childlessness Overcome Through Surrogacy
**COTT** [South Africa] Central Organization for Technical Training
**couch.** [heraldry] couchant
**.co.uk** UK commercial organization (in Internet address)
**Coun.** Council; Councillor; Counsellor
**cour.** *courant* (French: current, this month, inst.) (in correspondence)
**COV** [statistics] coefficient of variation; [chemistry] concentrated oil of vitriol; [electronics] corona onset voltage; [statistics] covariance; [genetics] crossover value
**Cov.** Coventry
**cov.** [statistics] covariance; covenant
**covers** [mathematics] coversed sine
**cov. pt** [cricket] cover point
**COW** character-oriented windows
**COWAR** Committee on Water Research
**COWPS** [USA] Council on Wages and Price Stability
**Coy** [military] company
**COZI** communications zone indicator
**CP** [civil aircraft marking] Bolivia; [medicine] Campylobacter pylori (bacterium causing gastric illness); Canadian Pacific (Railway); Canadian Press (news agency); Cape Province (former South African province); Captain of the Parish (in Isle of Man); [navigation] cardinal point; *casella postale* (Italian: post office box); [computing] central processor; [aeronautics] centre of pressure; centrifugal pump; [medicine] cerebral palsy; [surveying] change point; [physics] charge parity; charter party; chemically pure; Chief of Police; Chief Patriarch; [medicine] chronic pancreatitis; [medicine] cisplatin (used to treat cancer); civil power; civil procedure; Clarendon Press; Clerk of the Peace; code of procedure; *Codice Penale* (Italian: Penal Code); College of Preceptors; colour printing (as in **CP filter**); [military] Command Post; commercial paper; Common Pleas; Common Prayer; Communist Party; community physician; community programme; *Companhia dos Caminhos de Ferro Portugueses* (Portuguese railway company); [stock exchange] concert party; condensation product; conference paper; conference proceedings; [Roman Catholic Church] *Congregatio Passionis* (Latin: Congregation of the Passion); [India] Congress Party; [South Africa] Conservative Party; convict prison; corporal punishment; [Australia] Country Party (former name of National Party); county primary (school); Court of Probate; [biochemistry] creatine phosphate; [physics] cross polarization; current paper; [vehicle registration] Huddersfield
**C/P** charter party
**Cp.** [Roman Catholic Church] compline
**cp.** compare
**c.p.** candlepower; carriage paid; [aeronautics] centre of pressure; chemically pure; constant pressure
**CPA** Canadian Pharmaceutical Association; Canadian Psychological Association; central planning area; [USA] Certified Public Accountant; Chartered Patent Agent; Chick Producers' Association; [insurance] claims payable abroad; Clyde Port Authority; Commonwealth Parliamentary Association; Communist Party of Australia; Construction Plant Association; Contractors' Plant Association; contract price adjustment; cost planning and appraisal; Council of Provincial Associations; [computing] critical path analysis

**CPAC** Collaborative Pesticides Analytical Committee; Consumer Protection Advisory Committee
**CPAG** Child Poverty Action Group; [USA] Collision Prevention Advisory Group
**CPAI** Canvas Products Association International
**C Pal.** Crystal Palace
**CPAM** Committee of Purchasers of Aircraft Material
**CPAS** Catholic Prisoners' Aid Society; Church Pastoral Aid Society
**CPB** [medicine] cardiopulmonary bypass; [book-keeping] casual payments book; Central Planning Bureau; Communist Party of Britain
**CPBF** Campaign for Press and Broadcasting Freedom
**CPC** [USA] City Planning Commission; city police commissioner; Clerk of the Privy Council; [medicine] clinicopathological conference; Communist Party of China; Conservative Political Centre
**CPCIZ** *Comité permanent des congrès internationaux de zoologie* (French: Standing Committee of International Zoological Congresses)
**CPCU** [USA] Chartered Property and Casualty Underwriter
**CPD** [astronomy] Cape Photographic Durchmusterung (star catalogue); [medicine] chronic pulmonary disease; [electronics] contact potential difference; continuing professional development
**cpd** compound
**c.p.d.** [commerce] charterers pay dues
**CPDL** Canadian Patents and Developments Limited
**CPDM** Centre for Physical Distribution Management
**CPE** Certificate of Physical Education; [USA] Certified Property Exchanger; [medicine] chronic pulmonary emphysema; College of Physical Education; [law] Common Professional Examination; *Congrès du peuple européen* (French: Congress of European People); contractor performance evaluation; [microbiology] cytopathic effect
**CPEA** Catholic Parents' and Electors' Association; [USA] Cooperative Program for Educational Administration
**c. pén.** *code pénal* (French: penal code)
**CPEQ** Corporation of Professional Engineers of Quebec
**CPF** contributory pension fund
**CPFF** cost plus fixed fee
**CPFS** Council for the Promotion of Field Studies
**CPG** Coronary Prevention Group
**CPGB** Communist Party of Great Britain
**CPH** Certificate in Public Health
**cph** cycles per hour
**CPHA** Canadian Public Health Association
**CPhys** Chartered Physicist
**CPI** chief pilot instructor; Communist Party of India; consumer price index
**cpi** [printing] characters per inch
**CPJI** *Cour permanente de justice internationale* (French: Permanent Court of International Justice)
**CPL** Cats' Protection League; central public library; Colonial Products Laboratory; [computing] combined programming language; commercial pilot's licence
**Cpl** Corporal
**cpl** [printing] characters per line
**CPM** [USA] Certified Property Manager; Colonial Police Medal; [music] common particular metre; Communist Party of Malaya; computer program module; [computing] critical path method
**CP/M** [trademark] Control Program for Microcomputers
**cpm** [computing] characters per minute; cycles per minute
**CPMEE&W** Council for Postgraduate Medical Education in England and Wales
**CPN** *Communistische Partij van Nederland* (Dutch: Netherlands Communist Party); community psychiatric nurse
**Cpn** Copenhagen
**cpn** coupon
**CPNA** Council of Photographic News Agencies
**Cpnhgn** Copenhagen
**CPNZ** Communist Party of New Zealand
**CPO** cancel previous order; [chemistry] catalytic partial oxidation; Chief Petty Officer; command pay office; Commonwealth Producers' Organization; compulsory purchase order; county planning officer; crime prevention officer

**CPP** chemical processing plant; Convention People's Party (in Ghana); [computing] critical path plan(ning); current purchasing power (as in **CPP accounting**)
**c.p.p.** controllable pitch propeller
**CPPA** Canadian Pulp and Paper Association
**CPPCC** Chinese People's Political Consultative Conference
**CPPS** [computing] critical path planning and scheduling
**CPR** Canadian Pacific Railway; [medicine] cardiopulmonary resuscitation
**CPRC** Central Price Regulation Committee
**CPRE** Council for the Protection of Rural England
**CPRS** Central Policy Review Staff
**CPRW** Council for the Protection of Rural Wales
**CPS** Centre for Policy Studies; cents per share; [USA] Certified Professional Secretary; Church Patronage Society; Clerk of Petty Sessions; Commonwealth Public Service; Communist Party of Syria; Congregational Publishing Society; Crown Prosecution Service; *Custos Privati Sigilli* (Latin: Keeper of the Privy Seal)
**cps** [computing] characters per second; cycles per second
**CPSA** Civil and Public Services Association; Clay Pigeon Shooting Association
**CPSC** [USA] Consumer Product Safety Commission
**CPSS** Certificate in Public Service Studies
**CPSU** Communist Party of the Soviet Union
**CPsychol** Chartered Psychologist
**CPT** Canadian Pacific Telegraphs; [physics] charge parity–time; cost per thousand; [computing] critical path technique
**Cpt.** Captain
**cpt** cockpit; counterpoint
**CPTB** Clay Products Technical Bureau
**CPU** central packaging unit; [computing] central processing unit; collective protection unit; Commonwealth Press Union
**CPUSA** Communist Party of the United States of America
**CPVE** Certificate of Pre-vocational Education
**CQ** [military] charge of quarters; conditionally qualified
**CQM** Chief Quartermaster; Company Quartermaster
**CQMS** Company Quartermaster-Sergeant
**CQR** *Church Quarterly Review*
**CQS** Court of Quarter Sessions
**CQSW** Certificate of Qualification in Social Work
**CR** *Carolina Regina* (Latin: Queen Caroline); *Carolus Rex* (Latin: King Charles); carriage return; carrier's risk; cash receipts; central railway; central registry; Chief Ranger; [medicine] chronic rejection; *Civis Romanus* (Latin: Roman citizen); [USA] Commendation Ribbon; Community of the Resurrection (Anglican monastic order); company's risk; [medicine] complete regression; [medicine] complete remission; [engineering] compression ratio; [medicine] computed radiography; [chemistry] concentration ratio; [psychology] conditioned reflex; [psychology] conditioned response; conference report; Congo red (dye); consciousness raising; control relay; cosmic rays; [international vehicle registration] Costa Rica; crease-resistant; credit; credit rating; credit report; [statistics] critical ratio; [UK postcode] Croydon; current rate; *Custos Rotulorum* (Latin: Keeper of the Rolls); [vehicle registration] Portsmouth; [civil aircraft marking] Portugal
**Cr** [chemical element] chromium; Commander; Councillor; cruiser
**c/r** company's risk
**cr.** created; creation; credit; creditor; creek; [music] *crescendo* (Italian: with increasing loudness); crew; crimson; crown; cruise; *crux* (Latin: cross)
**.cr** Costa Rica (in Internet address)
**c.r.** *con riserva* (Italian: with reservations); [finance] cum rights (i.e. with rights)
**CRA** California Redwood Association; Canadian Rheumatism Association; [Northern Ireland] Civil Rights Association; Coal Research Association of New Zealand; Commander of the Royal Artillery; Commercial Rabbit Association; composite research aircraft; corrosion-resistant alloy
**CrA** [astronomy] Corona Australis
**CrAA** Commander-at-Arms

**CRAC** Careers Research and Advisory Centre; Central Religious Advisory Committee; Construction Research Advisory Council

**CRAD** Committee for Research into Apparatus for the Disabled

**CRAE** Committee for the Reform of Animal Experimentation

**CRAeS** Companion of the Royal Aeronautical Society

**CRAF** [USA] Civil Reserve Air Fleet

**CRAMRA** Convention on the Regulation of Antarctic Mineral Resource Activities

**cran.** craniology

**craniol.** craniology

**craniom.** craniometry

**CRASC** Commander of the Royal Army Service Corps

**CRB** Central Radio Bureau

**CrB** [astronomy] Corona Borealis

**CRC** [printing] camera-ready copy; Cancer Research Campaign; child-resistant closure; Civil Rights Commission; coal rank code; Community Relations Council; [printing] composing room chapel; [USA] Coordinating Research Council; cycle racing club; [computing] cyclic redundancy check

**CRCC** Canadian Red Cross Committee

**CRCH** central register and clearing house

**CRCP** Certificant of the Royal College of Physicians

**CRCS** Certificant of the Royal College of Surgeons (of England)

**CRD** [medicine] chronic respiratory disease; Crop Research Division

**CRDEC** [USA] Chemical Research, Development and Engineering Center

**CRDF** cathode-ray direction-finding

**CRE** [USA] Coal Research Establishment; Commander of the Royal Engineers; Commercial Relations and Exports; Commission for Racial Equality; cumulative radiation effect

**CREFAL** *Centro Regional de Educación Fundamental para la América Latina* (Spanish: Regional Centre of Fundamental Education for Latin America)

**Cres.** Crescent (in road name)

**cres.** [music] *crescendo* (Italian: with increasing loudness)

**cresc.** [music] *crescendo* (Italian: with increasing loudness)

**CRF** [finance] capital recovery factor; [medicine] chronic renal failure; [medicine] coagulase reacting factor; [biochemistry] corticotrophin-releasing factor

**crg.** carriage

**CRH** [biochemistry] corticotrophin-releasing hormone

**CRI** Caribbean Research Institute; Children's Relief International; [medicine] chronic renal insufficiency; [photography] colour reversal intermediate; [USA] Cray Research Incorporated; *Croce Rossa Italiana* (Italian: Italian Red Cross)

**CRIB** Current Research in Britain

**CRIC** [Roman Catholic Church] Canons Regular of the Immaculate Conception; Commercial Radio International Committee

**crim.** criminal

**crim. con.** [law] criminal conversation (i.e. adultery)

**criminol.** criminology

**CRIS** [medicine] clinical radiology imaging system; [computing] command retrieval information system; current research information system

**crit.** criterion; critic; critical; critically; criticism

**Crk** Cork (Ireland)

**CRL** [Roman Catholic Church] Canons Regular of the Lateran; Certified Record Librarian; Certified Reference Librarian; Chemical Research Laboratory

**CRM** [USA] Central Rocky Mountains; certified reference material; counter-radar missile; count-rate meter; cruise missile

**CRMA** Cotton and Rayon Merchants' Association

**CRMF** Cancer Relief Macmillan Fund

**CRMP** Corps of Royal Military Police

**crn** crown

**crn.** crane

**CRNA** Campaign for the Restoration of the National Anthem and Flag; Clinical Research Nurses' Association

**CRNCM** Companion of the Royal Northern College of Music

**CRNSS** Chief of the Royal Naval Scientific Service

**CRO** cathode-ray oscilloscope (or oscillograph); Cave Rescue Organization of Great Britain; chief recruiting officer; Commonwealth Relations Office (became part of FCO); community relations officer; Companies Registration Office; compulsory rights order; Criminal Records Office

**Croat.** Croatia; Croatian

**CRP** *Calendarium Rotulorum Patentium* (Latin: Calendar of the Patent Rolls); [Roman Catholic Church] Canons Regular of Prémontré; capacity requirement plan; [India] Central Reserve Police; coordinated research programme

**CRPL** [USA] Central Radio Propagation Laboratory

**CRPPH** [USA] Committee on Radiation Protection and Public Health

**CRR** constant ratio rule; Curia Regis Roll

**CRS** Catholic Record Society; Cereals Research Station; cold-rolled steel; Cooperative Retail Society; cosmic radio source

**CRSI** [USA] Concrete Reinforcing Steel Institute

**CRT** cathode-ray tube; [mathematics] Chinese remainder theorem; combat readiness training; composite rate tax

**Crt** Court; [astronomy] Crater

**CRTC** Canadian Radio-Television Commission

**crtkr** caretaker

**CRTS** Commonwealth Reconstruction Training Scheme

**CRU** civil resettlement unit; [computing] control register user

**Cru** [astronomy] Crux

**Crv** [astronomy] Corvus

**crypto.** cryptographic; cryptography

**cryst.** crystal; crystalline; crystallography

**crystallog.** crystallography

**crystd** crystallized

**crystn** crystallization

**CRZZ** *Centralna Rada Związków Zawadowych* (Polish: Central Council of Trade Unions)

**CS** [medicine] Caesarean section; [chemistry] calcium silicate; capital stock; carbon steel; (Ben) Carson and (Roger) Stoughton (as in **CS gas**); [biochemistry] casein; cast steel; Certificate in Statistics; Chartered Surveyor; Chemical Society; Chief of Staff; chief secretary; [computing] chip select; Christian Science; Christian Scientist; city surveyor; civil servant; Civil Service; Clerk of Session; Clerk to the Signet; [medicine] clinical stage; close shot; close support; College of Science; [mining] colliery screened; [psychology] conditioned stimulus; [USA] Confederate States; [Roman Catholic Church] Congregation of Salesians; [physics] coolant system; Cooperative Society; cotton seed; county surveyor; Court of Session; [fishing port] Cowes; credit sales; cruiser squadron; *Custos Sigilli* (Latin: Keeper of the Seal); [vehicle registration] Glasgow; [civil aircraft marking] Portugal

**C/S** channel shank (buttons); cycles per second

**Cs** [chemical element] caesium

**Cs** [meteorology] cirrostratus

**c/s** cases; cycles per second

**cs.** case; census; consul

**c.s.** capital stock; *come sopra* (Italian: as above)

**CSA** Canadian Standards Association; Casualty Surgeons' Association; Channel Swimming Association; Child Support Agency; Common Services Agency; [USA] Community Services Administration; [Canada] Computer Science Association; Confederate States Army; Confederate States of America

**CSAA** Child Study Association of America

**CSAB** Civil Service Appeal Board

**CSAE** Canadian Society of Agricultural Engineering

**CSAP** Canadian Society of Animal Production

**CSAR** Communication Satellite Advanced Research

**CSB** Bachelor of Christian Science; [engineering] calcium silicate brick; Central Statistical Board; [medicine] chemical stimulation of the brain

**CSBF** Civil Service Benevolent Fund

**CSBGM** Committee of Scottish Bank General Managers

**CSBM** [military] confidence- and security-building measures

**CSC** Civil Service Commission; Commonwealth Science Council; Comprehensive Schools Committee; [Belgium] *Confédération des syndicats chrétiens* (French: Federation of Christian Trade Unions); Conspicuous Service Cross (replaced by DSC)

**csc** [mathematics] cosecant
**CSCB** Committee of Scottish Clearing Bankers
**CSCBS** Commodore Superintendent, Contract-Built Ships
**CSCC** Civil Service Commission of Canada; Council of Scottish Chambers of Commerce
**CSCE** Conference on Security and Cooperation in Europe (former name of OSCE)
**CSCFE** Civil Service Council for Further Education
**CSCW** computer-supported cooperative working
**CSD** Chartered Society of Designers (formerly SIAD); Civil Service Department; Commonwealth Society for the Deaf; [engineering] constant speed drive; Cooperative Secretaries Diploma; Doctor of Christian Science
**CSDE** Central Servicing Development Establishment (in RAF)
**CSE** Campaign for State Education; Central Signals Establishment; Certificate of Secondary Education (replaced by GCSE); [computing] cognitive systems engineering; Council of the Stock Exchange
**cse** course
**CSEA** [USA] Civil Service Employees Association
**C-section** [medicine] Caesarean section
**CSED** [US navy] coordinated ship electronics design
**CSEU** Confederation of Shipbuilding and Engineering Unions
**CSF** [medicine] cerebrospinal fluid; Coil Spring Federation; [medicine] colony-stimulating factor
**CSFA** Canadian Scientific Film Association
**CSFE** Canadian Society of Forest Engineers
**CSG** Catholic Social Guild; Companion of the Order of the Star of Ghana; [computing] constructive solid geometry
**CSGA** Canadian Seed Growers' Association
**CS gas** tear gas invented by (Ben) Carson and (Roger) Stoughton
**CSH** [chemistry] calcium silicate hydrate
**csh** cash
**CSI** Chartered Surveyors' Institution; Church of South India; *Commission sportive internationale* (French: International Sporting Commission); [image technology] compact source iodide (as in **CSI lamp**); Companion of the Order of the Star of India; [USA] Construction Specifications Institute
**CSICC** Canadian Steel Industries Construction Council
**CSIP** Committee for the Scientific Investigation of the Paranormal
**CSIR** Council for Scientific and Industrial Research
**CSIRA** Council for Small Industries in Rural Areas
**CSIRO** Commonwealth Scientific and Industrial Research Organization (Australia)
**CSJ** *Christian Science Journal*
**csk** cask; countersink
**CSL** [Australia] Commonwealth Serum Laboratories; Communication Sub-Lieutenant; computer simulation language; [computing] control and simulation language; Cub Scout leader
**CSLATP** Canadian Society of Landscape Architects and Town Planners
**CSLO** Canadian Scientific Liaison Office; Combined Services Liaison Officer
**CSLT** Canadian Society of Laboratory Technologists
**CSM** [medicine] cerebrospinal meningitis; *Christian Science Monitor*; Christian Socialist Movement; [astronautics] command service module; Commission for Synoptic Meteorology; Committee on Safety of Medicines; Company Sergeant-Major; [USA] corn, soya, milk (food supplement)
**CSMA** [computing] carrier sense multiple access; Chemical Specialities Manufacturers' Association; Civil Service Motoring Association
**CSMA/CD** [computing] carrier sense multiple access, collision detection (network protocol)
**CSMMG** Chartered Society of Massage and Medical Gymnastics
**CSMTS** Card Setting Machine Tenters' Society
**CSN** Confederate States Navy
**CSNI** [USA] Committee on the Safety of Nuclear Installations

**CSO** Caltech Submillimeter Observatory; Central Selling Organization; Central Statistical Office; chief scientific officer; Chief Signal Officer; Chief Staff Officer; Colonial Secretary's Office; [image technology] colour separation overlay; Command Signals Officer; Commonwealth Scientific Office; community service order

**CSP** Chartered Society of Physiotherapy; Civil Service of Pakistan; [computing] communicating sequential processes; Congregation of Saint Paul; Council for Scientific Policy

**CSPAA** *Conférence de solidarité des pays afro-asiatiques* (French: Afro-Asian People's Solidarity Conference)

**CSPCA** Canadian Society for the Prevention of Cruelty to Animals

**CSPR** [chemistry] chlorosulphonated polyethylene rubber

**CSR** [Australia] Colonial Sugar Refining Company; combat-stress reaction; Czechoslovak Socialist Republic

**CSS** [computing] centralized structure store; Certificate in Social Service; computer systems simulator; (member of the) Congregation of the Holy Ghost (from Latin *Sanctus Spiritus*); Council for Science and Society

**CSSA** Civil Service Supply Association

**CSSB** Civil Service Selection Board

**CSSDA** [USA] Council for Social Science Data Archives

**CSSR** [Roman Catholic Church] *Congregatio Sanctissimi Redemptoris* (Latin: Congregation of the Most Holy Redeemer, the Redemptorists)

**CSSS** Canadian Soil Science Society

**CST** [USA] Central Standard Time; College of Science and Technology; College of Speech Therapists; convulsive shock therapy

**CSTA** Canadian Society of Technical Agriculturists; [New Zealand] Canterbury Science Teachers' Association

**CSTI** Council of Science and Technology Institutes

**CStJ** Commander of the Most Venerable Order of the Hospital of St John of Jerusalem

**CSU** [medicine] catheter specimen of urine; Central Services Unit; Central Statistical Unit; *Christlich-Soziale Union* (German: Christian Social Union) (German political party); Civil Service Union; Colorado State University; [engineering] constant speed unit

**CSV** [computing] comma-separated variables; community service volunteer

**CSW** [USA] Certified Social Worker; continuous seismic wave

**CSYS** [Scotland] Certificate of Sixth Year Studies

**CT** cable transfer; Candidate in Theology; [UK postcode] Canterbury; Cape Town; [fishing port] Castletown; [medicine] cell therapy; [USA] Central Time; [medicine] cerebral thrombosis; [medicine] cerebral tumour; certifi(cat)ed teacher; Civic Trust; code telegrams; College of Technology; commercial traveller; *commissario tecnico* (Italian: sports coach); [medicine] compute(rize)d tomography (as in **CT scan**); [US postcode] Connecticut; [medicine] coronary thrombosis; corporation tax; counter trade; [electrical engineering] current transformer; cycle time; [vehicle registration] Lincoln

**C/T** Californian Terms (in grain trade)

**Ct** Count; Court

**ct** carat; caught; [currency] cent (hundredth of dollar etc.); [currency] centime (hundredth of franc etc.); circuit; *courant* (French: current, this month, inst.) (in formal correspondence); court; credit; current

**Ct.** Canton; Connecticut; [music] countertenor

**ct.** *centum* (Latin: hundred); certificate; crate

**CTA** Cable Television Association; Camping Trade Association; Canadian Tuberculosis Association; Caribbean Technical Assistance; Caribbean Tourist Association; Catering Teachers' Association; [chemistry] cellulose triacetate; Channel Tunnel Association; Chaplain Territorial Army; Chicago Transit Authority; Commercial Travellers' Association; [USA] commodities trading advisor; [medicine] compute(rize)d tomographic angiography; [medicine] compute(rize)d tomographic arteriography

**c.t.a.** [law] *cum testamento annexo* (Latin: with the will annexed)
**CTAU** Catholic Total Abstinence Union
**CTB** Commonwealth Telecommunications Board; comprehensive test ban
**CTBT** comprehensive test ban treaty
**CTC** Canadian Transport Commission; [chemistry] carbon tetrachloride; centralized traffic control; Central Training Council; [USA] Citizens' Training Corps; city technology college; Civil Technical Corps; Commando Training Centre; *Confederación de Trabajadores Cubanos* (Spanish: Confederation of Cuban Workers); *Congrès du travail du Canada* (French: Canadian Labour Congress); corn trade clauses; crushing, tearing and curling (machine); Cyclists' Touring Club
**CTD** central training depot; [electronics] charge-transfer device; classified telephone directory
**ctd** coated; continued; crated
**CTE** [physics] coefficient of thermal expansion
**Cte** *Comte* (French: Count)
**CTEB** Council of Technical Examining Bodies
**Ctesse** *Comtesse* (French: Countess)
**CTETOC** Council for Technical Education and Training for Overseas Countries
**CText** Chartered Textile Technologist
**CTF** Catholic Teachers' Federation; Chaplain to the Territorial Forces; coal-tar fuels
**ctf.** certificate; certify
**ctge** cartage; cartridge; cottage
**CTH** Corporation of Trinity House
**CTI** computer telephony integration
**CTIO** Cerro Tololo Inter-American Observatory (Chile)
**CTL** constant tensile load; [insurance] constructive total loss; [medicine] cytotoxic T-lymphocyte
**ctl** central
**CTM** [medicine] compute(rize)d tomographic myelography
**CTMB** Canal Transport Marketing Board
**CTN** confectioner, tobacconist and newsagent
**ctn** carton; [mathematics] cotangent
**CTNC** Committee on Transnational Corporations (in UN)
**CTO** [philately] cancelled to order; Central Telegraph Office; Central Treaty Organization; chief technical officer
**CTOL** [aeronautics] conventional take-off and landing
**CTP** *Confederación de Trabajadores del Peru* (Spanish: Peruvian Confederation of Labour)
**ctpt** [music] counterpoint
**ctptal** [music] contrapuntal
**ctptst** [music] contrapuntist
**CTR** certified test record; controlled thermonuclear reaction; controlled thermonuclear research
**ctr.** centre; contribution; contributor
**CTRA** Coal Tar Research Association
**Ctrl** [computing] control (key)
**CTRP** *Confederación de Trabajadores de la Républica de Panama* (Spanish: Confederation of Workers of the Republic of Panama)
**CTS** [medicine] carpal tunnel syndrome; Catholic Truth Society; characteristic time scale; [computing] clear to send; [medicine] compute(rize)d tomographic scanner; Consolidated Tin Smelters
**cts** cents; certificates; crates
**CTSA** Crucible and Tool Steel Association
**CTT** capital transfer tax
**CTTB** Central Trade Test Board (of RAF)
**Cttee** committee
**CTTH** Cathedrals Through Touch and Hearing
**CTTSC** Certificate in the Teaching and Training of Subnormal Children
**CTU** Conservative Trade Unionists
**CTUC** Commonwealth Trade Union Council
**CTUS** Carnegie Trust for the Universities of Scotland
**CTV** cable television; Canadian Television Network Limited; *Confederación de Trabajadores de Venezuela* (Spanish: Confederation of Venezuelan Workers)
**CTVM** Centre for Tropical Veterinary Medicine
**CTZ** control traffic zone (around airport)
**CU** Cambridge University; Christian Union; Church Union; [photography] close-up; Congregational Union (of England and Wales); [computing] control unit; Cooperative Union; [USA] Cornell University; [civil aircraft marking] Cuba;

Customs Union; [vehicle registration] Newcastle upon Tyne
**Cu** [chemical element] copper (from Latin *cuprum*)
***Cu*** [meteorology] cumulus
**cu.** cubic
**.cu** Cuba (in Internet address)
**CUA** Canadian Underwriters' Association; Catholic University of America; Colour Users' Association; [computing] common user access; Conference of University Administrators
**CUAC** Cambridge University Athletic Club; Cambridge University Automobile Club
**CUAFC** Cambridge University Association Football Club
**CUAS** Cambridge University Agricultural Society; Cambridge University Air Squadron
**cub.** cubic
**CUBC** Cambridge University Boat Club; Cambridge University Boxing Club
**CUC** Canberra University College; Coal Utilization Council
**CUCC** Cambridge University Cricket Club
**CUDAT** Community Urban Development Assistance Team
**CUDS** Cambridge University Dramatic Society
**CUEP** Central Unit on Environmental Pollution
**CUEW** Congregational Union of England and Wales
**CUF** *Catholicarum Universitatum Foederatio* (Latin: Federation of Catholic Universities); common university fund
**CUG** closed user group
**CUGC** Cambridge University Golf Club
**CUHC** Cambridge University Hockey Club
**cuis.** cuisine
**CUKT** Carnegie United Kingdom Trust
**CUL** Cambridge University Library
**cul.** culinary
**CULS** [finance] convertible unsecured loan stock
**CULTC** Cambridge University Lawn Tennis Club
**CUM** Cambridge University Mission
**cum.** [finance] cumulative
**Cumb.** Cumberland
**cum div.** [finance] cum dividend (i.e. with dividend)
**cum pref.** [finance] cumulative preference (shares)
**CUMS** Cambridge University Musical Society
**CUNA** Credit Union National Association
**CUNY** City University of New York
**CUOG** Cambridge University Opera Group
**CUP** Cambridge University Press; [currency] Cuban peso
**cur.** currency; current
**CURAC** [Australia] Coal Utilization Research Advisory Committee
**cur. adv. vult** [law] *curia advisari vult* (Latin: the court wishes to consider it) (used in reports when judgment follows hearing)
**CURE** Care, Understanding and Research (drug addiction organization)
**curt** current (month)
**CURUFC** Cambridge University Rugby Union Football Club
**CURV** [US navy] cable-controlled undersea recovery vehicle
**CUS** Catholic University School
**CUSO** Canadian University Services Overseas
**CUSRPG** Canada–United States Regional Planning Group (in NATO)
**cust.** custard; custodian; custody
**custod.** custodian
**CUTF** Commonwealth Unit Trust Fund
**CUTS** [computing] cassette users' tape specification; [computing] computer users' tape system
**CV** calorific value; [medicine] cardiovascular; [astronomy] cataclysmic variable; *cavallo vapore* (Italian: horsepower); *cavalos vapor* (Portuguese: horsepower); [medicine] cerebrovascular; *cheval-vapeur* (French: horsepower); [statistics] coefficient of variation; [mathematics] collective vector; common valve; [Bible] Common Version; [medicine] contrast ventriculography; [finance] convertible; [UK postcode] Coventry; [Canada] Cross of Valour; [chemistry] crystal violet; curriculum vitae; [vehicle registration] Truro
**cv.** [botany] cultivar
**.cv** Cape Verde (in Internet address)
**c.v.** *cheval-vapeur* (French: horsepower); chief value; [medicine] *cras vespere* (Latin: tomorrow evening); curriculum

vitae; *cursus vitae* (Latin: course of life)
**CVA** [medicine] cerebrovascular accident (i.e. stroke); [USA] Columbia Valley Authority
**CVC** capacitance-voltage characteristics; current-voltage characteristics
**CVCP** Committee of Vice-Chancellors and Principals (of UK universities)
**CVD** [medicine] cerebrovascular disease; [electronics] chemical vapour deposition; common valve development
**c.v.d.** [commerce] cash versus documents
**CVE** Certificate of Vocational Education; Council for Visual Education
**CVEsc** [currency] Cape Verde escudo
**CVI** chemical vapour infiltration; [medicine] common variable immunodeficiency
**CVJ** [engineering] constant velocity joint (in motor vehicles)
**CVK** centre vertical keel
**CVL** Central Veterinary Laboratory
**CVM** Company of Veteran Motorists
**CVn** [astronomy] Canes Venatici
**CVO** Commander of the Royal Victorian Order
**CVP** [medicine] central venous pressure; [Belgium] *Christelijk Volkspartif* (Flemish: Christian Social Party)
**CVS** [medicine] cardiovascular system; [medicine] chorionic villus sampling; Council of Voluntary Service
**CVSNA** Council of Voluntary Service National Association
**CVT** [mathematics] canonical variational theory; [chemistry] chemical vapour transport; [engineering] continuously variable transmission (in motor vehicles)
**cvt.** [finance] convertible
**Cvt Gdn** Covent Garden
**CVWS** combat vehicle weapons system
**CVWW** Council of Voluntary Welfare Work
**CW** Canada West; [physics] carrier wave; cavity wall (in property advertisement); chemical warfare; chemical weapons; child welfare; clerk of works; cold-worked (metals); commercial weight; Commissions and Warrants (department of Admiralty); complete with; continuous wave (as in **CW radar**); [UK postcode] Crewe; [physics] Curie–Weiss (law); [vehicle registration] Preston
**c/w** [cycling] chainwheel
**cw.** clockwise
**c.w.** continuous weld
**CWA** Catering Wages Act; chemical warfare agent; [USA] Civil Works Administration; [USA] Clean Water Act; [Australia] Country Women's Association; Crime Writers' Association
**CWB** Canadian Wheat Board; Central Wages Board
**CWBW** chemical warfare/biological (or bacteriological) warfare
**CWC** Catering Wages Commission; Commonwealth of World Citizens
**CWD** civilian war dead
**CWDE** Centre for World Development Education
**C'wealth** Commonwealth
**CWF** coal–water fuel
**CWG** Cooperative Women's Guild
**CWGC** Commonwealth War Graves Commission (formerly IWGC)
**CWINC** [India] Central Waterways, Irrigation and Navigation Commission
**CWIS** [computing] campus-wide information service
**CWL** Catholic Women's League
**Cwlth** Commonwealth
**CWM** Council for World Mission
**CWME** Commission on World Mission and Evangelism
**CWNA** Canadian Weekly Newspapers Association
**CWO** Chief Warrant Officer
**c.w.o.** cash with order
**CWOIH** Conference of World Organizations Interested in the Handicapped
**CWP** Christian Workers' Party (in Malta); [USA] Communist Workers' Party
**CWR** continuous welded rail
**CW radar** continuous-wave radar
**CWS** coal–water slurry; Cooperative Wholesale Society; Court Welfare Service
**CWT** central war time
**cwt** hundredweight
**CWU** Chemical Workers' Union; Communication Workers' Union
**CX** [vehicle registration] Huddersfield; [civil aircraft marking] Uruguay
**cx** [medicine] cervix; convex

**CXR** chest X-ray
**CXT** Common External Tariff
**CY** calendar year; [fishing port] Castlebay; [international vehicle registration] Cyprus; [vehicle registration] Swansea
**cy** capacity; currency; cycle(s)
**.cy** Cyprus (in Internet address)
**cyath.** [medicine] *cyathus* (Latin: glassful)
**cyath. vin.** [medicine] *cyathus vinarius* (Latin: wineglassful)
**cyber.** cybernetics
**cyc.** cycle(s); cycling; cyclopedia; cyclopedic
**CYCA** Clyde Yacht Clubs Association
**cyclo.** cyclopedia
**CYEE** Central Youth Employment Executive
**Cyg** [astronomy] Cygnus
**CYL** Communist Youth League
**cyl.** cylinder; cylindrical
**Cym.** Cymric
**CYMS** Catholic Young Men's Society
**CYO** [USA] Catholic Youth Organization
**Cyp.** Cyprian; Cypriot; Cyprus
**CYS** Catholic Youth Services
**CYSA** Community Youth Services Association
**CYWU** Community Youth Workers' Union
**CZ** [vehicle registration] Belfast; Canal Zone; [international vehicle registration] Czech Republic
**Cz** [geology] Cenozoic
**.cz** Czech Republic (in Internet address)
**CZMA** [USA] Coastal Zone Management Act

# D

**D** [currency] dalasi (used in Gambia); *Damen* (German: ladies); [geology] darcy (permeability coefficient of rock); December; defence (as in **D notice**); Democrat; Democratic; [paper size] demy; Department; destroyer; Detective; *Deus* (Latin: God); [chemistry] deuterium; [music] Deutsch (catalogue of Schubert's works); *Deutschland* (German: Germany); [geology] Devonian; [card games] diamonds; digital; dimension; dimensional (as in **3-D**); [currency] dinar; dioptre; director; *diretto* (Italian: through train); distinguished; doctor; *dogana* (Italian: customs); Dom (title of monks); *Dominus* (Latin: Lord, God, Christ); Don (Spanish title for men); [currency] dông (used in Vietnam); *douane* (French: customs); Dowager; [fishing port] Dublin; Duchess; Duke; Dutch; [Roman numeral] five hundred; [civil aircraft marking] Germany; [international vehicle registration] Germany (from German *Deutschland*); [music] note of scale; [medicine] rhesus antigen (as in **anti-D**); semiskilled or unskilled (occupational group)
***D*** absorbed dose (of radiation); diameter; [chemistry] diffusion coefficient; [physics] dispersion; [aeronautics] drag; [physics] electric flux density; [physics] electric flux displacement
**d** day; deci- (indicates one-tenth, as in **dl** = decilitre); [physics] deuteron; [music] do(h) (in tonic sol-fa); [physics] down (quark flavour); [meteorology] drizzle; [Roman numeral] five hundred; (old) pence (from Latin *denarii*); (old) penny (from Latin *denarius*)
***d*** [chemistry] dextrorotatory; diameter; relative density
**d.** dam (in animal pedigree); damn; date; daughter; day; deacon; dead; deceased; [dentistry] deciduous; decision; decree; degree; delete; deliver; delivery; delta; density; depart(s); departure; depth; deputy; desert; deserted; deserter; *destro* (Italian: right); diameter; died; dime (= ten cents); [currency] dinar; discharge; distance; dividend; [currency] dollar; [medicine] dose; [currency] drachma; drama; *droite* (French: right); dump
**D2** [civil aircraft marking] Angola
**D2T2** [computing] dye diffusion thermal transfer
**D4** [civil aircraft marking] Cape Verde
**D6** [civil aircraft marking] Comoros Islands
**3D** [civil aircraft marking] Swaziland

**3-D** three-dimensional
**DA** [currency] Algerian dinar; [vehicle registration] Birmingham; [UK postcode] Dartford; Daughters of America; deed of arrangement; Defence Act; delayed action (bomb); [USA] Department of Agriculture; Depressives Anonymous; deputy advocate; deputy assistant; design automation; destructive analysis; developmental age; Diploma in Anaesthetics (or Anaesthesia); Diploma in Art; direct action; [chemistry] dissolved acetylene; [USA] District Attorney; Doctor of Arts; doesn't answer; [medicine] dopamine; [fishing port] Drogheda; duck's arse (hairstyle)
**D/A** [commerce] days after acceptance; [commerce] delivery on acceptance; deposit account; digital-to-analogue (converter); [commerce] documents against acceptance
**D-A** digital–analogue (converter)
**Da** dalton (unit of atomic mass)
**Da.** Danish
**da** deca- (indicates 10, as in **dal** = decalitre)
**d/a** [commerce] days after acceptance; deposit account; discharge afloat; [commerce] documents against acceptance
**DAA** *défense anti-aérienne* (French: antiaircraft defence); [chemistry] diacetone acrylamide; [chemistry] diacetone alcohol; Diploma of the Advertising Association
**DAA&QMG** Deputy Assistant Adjutant and Quartermaster-General
**DAAG** Deputy Assistant Adjutant-General
**DA&QMG** Deputy Adjutant and Quartermaster-General
**DAAS** data acquisition and analysis system
**DAB** daily audience barometer; *Deutsches Apothekerbuch* (German: German Pharmacopoeia); *Dictionary of American Biography*; digital audio broadcasting
**DABN** [medicine] diffuse acute bacterial nephritis
**DAC** data analysis and control; Development Assistance Committee (of OECD); [computing] digital–analogue converter
**DAc** Doctor of Acupuncture
**d.a.c.** [insurance] deductible average clause; direct air cycle
**DACC** Dangerous Air Cargoes Committee
**DACG** Deputy Assistant Chaplain-General
**dachs.** dachshund
**DACOR** data correction
**dact.** dactyl
**DAD** deputy assistant director
**DADG** Deputy Assistant Director-General
**DAdmin** Doctor of Administration
**DAE** [USA] Department of Atomic Energy; *Dictionary of American English*; differential algebraic equation; Diploma in Advanced Engineering; Director of Army Education
**DAEP** Division of Atomic Energy Production
**DAER** Department of Aeronautical and Engineering Research
**DAF** [USA] Department of the Air Force; dissolved air flotation; *Doorne Automobielfabriek* (Dutch vehicle manufacturer); dry ash-free (coal)
**d.a.f.** described as follows
**DAFS** Department of Agriculture and Fisheries for Scotland
**DAG** Deputy Adjutant-General; *Deutsche Angestellten-Gewerkschaft* (German: German Salaried Employees' Union); development assistance group; [Ireland] Divorce Action Group
**dag** decagram
**DAGMAR** [commerce] defining advertising goals for measured advertising results
**DAgr** Doctor of Agriculture
**DAgrSc** Doctor of Agricultural Science
**DAH** [medicine] disordered action of the heart
**DAI** disease activity index; distributed artificial intelligence
**d.a.i.** death from accidental injuries
**DAJAG** Deputy Assistant Judge Advocate-General
**Dak.** Dakota
**DAL** direct acid leaching
**dal** decalitre
**DALR** [meteorology] dry adiabatic lapse rate
**dal S** [music] *dal segno* (Italian: (repeat) from the sign)
**DAM** Diploma in Ayurvedic Medicine
**dam** decametre
**dam.** damage
**DAMS** [USA] defense against missiles

system(s); deputy assistant military secretary
**DAN** (People's) Direct Action Network
**Dan.** [Bible] Daniel; Danish
**D&AD** Designers and Art Directors Association
**D&B** discipline and bondage; Dun and Bradstreet (financial reports)
**D&C** dean and chapter; [medicine] dil(a-t)ation and curettage (of cervix and uterus)
**D&D** death and dying; drunk and disorderly
**D&G** Dolce e Gabbana
**D&HAA** Dock and Harbour Authorities' Association
**d&p** developing and printing
**d&s** demand and supply
**D&V** [medicine] diarrhoea and vomiting
**DAO** district advisory officer
**DAOT** Director of Air Organization and Training
**DAP** Director of Administrative Planning; [computing] distributed array processor; [electronics] donor–acceptor pair; Draw a Person (psychological test)
**d.a.p.** do anything possible; documents against payment
**DAP&E** Diploma in Applied Parasitology and Entomology
**DAPM** Deputy Assistant Provost-Marshal
**DAppSc** Doctor of Applied Science
**DAPS** Director of Army Postal Services
**DAQMG** Deputy Assistant Quartermaster-General
**DAR** Daughters of the American Revolution; [USA] Defense Aid Reports; direct absorption receiver (of solar radiation); [Canada] Directorate of Atomic Research
**DArch** Doctor of Architecture
**DARD** Directorate of Aircraft Research and Development
**DARE** demand and resource evaluation
**DARPA** [USA] Defense Advanced Research Projects Agency (formerly ARPA)
**DArt** Doctor of Art
**DAS** [computing] data-acquisition system; development advisory service; Director of Armament Supply; double algebraic sum; Dramatic Authors' Society
**d.a.s.** [commerce] delivered alongside ship
**DASA** [USA] Defense Atomic Support Agency; Domestic Appliance Service Association
**DASC** [USA] Direct Air Support Centre
**DASc** Doctor of Agricultural Science
**DASD** [computing] direct-access storage device; Director of Army Staff Duties
**DASH** drone antisubmarine helicopter
**dash** [short form] dashboard
**DASM** delayed-action space missile
**Dass** Depressives Associated
**DAT** [medicine] dementia of the Alzheimer type; digital audio tape
**dat.** [grammar] dative
**DATA** Draughtsmen's and Allied Technician's Association
**Datacom** data communications
**Datanet** data network
**Datastor** data storage
**Datran** data transmission
**Datrec** data recording
**DATV** digitally assisted television
**dau.** daughter
**DAV** Disabled American Veterans
**DAvMed** Diploma in Aviation Medicine
**DAW** Drama Association of Wales; [nuclear technology] dry active waste
**DAWS** Director of Army Welfare Services
**DAX** [stock exchange] *Deutsche Aktienindex* (German: German share price index)
**DAyM** Doctor of Ayurvedic Medicine
**DB** Bachelor of Divinity (from Latin *Divinitatis Baccalaureus*); dark blue; database; [book-keeping] daybook; deals and battens (timber); delayed broadcast (in radio and television); *Deutsche Bundesbahn* (German: German Federal Railway); *Deutsche Bundesbank* (German: German Federal Bank); dock brief; Domesday Book; double-barrelled; [vehicle registration] Manchester
**D/B** [book-keeping] daybook
**Db** [currency] dobra (used in São Tomé and Príncipe)
**dB** decibel
**d.b.** [book-keeping] daybook; [music] double bass; double bed; double-breasted; drawbar (on tractors etc.)
**DBA** [computing] database administration; [computing] database administrator; [medicine] dihydrodimethylbenzopyranbutyric acid (used to

treat sickle-cell anaemia); Doctor of Business Administration; doing business as (or at)
**d.b.a.** doing business as (or at)
**DBB** deals, battens and boards (timber); *Deutscher Beamtenbund* (German: German Civil Servants' Association) (trade union); dinner, bed and breakfast (in accommodation advertisement)
**DBC** Deaf Broadcasting Council
**DBE** Dame Commander of the Order of the British Empire; design-basis event
**DBEATS** dispatch payable both ends on all time saved
**DBELTS** dispatch payable both ends on lay time saved
**DBH** [forestry] diameter at breast height
**DBib** Douay Bible
**DBIU** [Canada] Dominion Board of Insurance Underwriters
**dbk** disembark; drawback
**dbkn** debarkation
**dbl.** double
**dble** double
**DBM** Diploma in Business Management
**DBMC** Danish Bacon and Meat Council
**DBMS** [computing] database management system
**DBMT** [medicine] displacement bone-marrow transplantation
**Dbn** Durban (South Africa)
**DBO** Diploma of the British Orthoptic Board
**dbre** *diciembre* (Spanish: December)
**DBS** direct broadcasting by satellite; direct-broadcast satellite
**DBST** Double British Summer Time
**dbt** debit
**DBW** desirable body weight
**DC** [music] *da capo* (Italian: from the head) (instruction to repeat from beginning); Daughters of Charity of St Vincent de Paul; death certificate; decimal currency; *Democrazia Cristiana* (Italian: Christian Democratic Party); [USA] Dental Corps; depth charge; deputy chief; deputy commissioner; deputy consul; deputy counsel; Detective Constable; [computing] device coordinates; diagnostic centre; diplomatic corps; [physics] direct current; Disarmament Conference; Disciples of Christ; district commissioner; district council; district court; District of Columbia; [US postcode] District of Columbia; Doctor of Chiropractic; [commerce] documents against cash; Douglas Commercial (aircraft) (as in **DC10**); [theatre] down centre (of stage); [vehicle registration] Middlesbrough
**D/C** [insurance] deviation clause
**dC** *depois de Cristo* (Portuguese: after Christ, AD); *dopo Cristo* (Italian: after Christ, AD)
**d.c.** dead centre; [physics] direct current; [printing] double column; [music] double crotchet; [navigation] drift correction
**DCA** [USA] Defense Communications Agency; [Australia] Department of Civil Aviation; [computing] document content architecture
**DCAe** Diploma of the College of Aeronautics
**DCAO** deputy county advisor officer
**DCAS** Deputy Chief of Air Staff; Divorce Conciliation and Advisory Service
**DCB** Dame Commander of the Order of the Bath; double cantilever beam
**DCBE** [medicine] double-contrast barium enema
**DCC** Deputy Chief Constable; digital compact cassette; Diocesan Consistory Court; Diploma of Chelsea College
**DCCC** Domestic Coal Consumers Council
**DCD** [USA] Department of Community Development; Diploma in Chest Diseases; [electronics] drain-current drift
**dcdr** decoder
**DCE** [computing] data communications equipment; design and construction error; Diploma in Chemical Engineering; Doctor of Civil Engineering; domestic credit expansion
**DCEP** Diploma in Child and Educational Psychology
**DCF** [accounting] discounted cash flow
**DCG** Deputy Chaplain-General; direct coal gasification
**dcg** dancing
**DCGS** Deputy Chief of the General Staff
**DCh** Diploma in Child Health; Doctor of Surgery (from Latin *Doctor Chirurgiae*)
**DChD** Doctor of Dental Surgery
**DChE** Doctor of Chemical Engineering
**DCI** Detective Chief Inspector; direct com-

puter interviewing; [computing] display control interface; [advertising] double column inch; ductile cast iron

**d.c.i.** [advertising] double column inch

**DCJ** [USA] district court judge

**DCL** Distillers' Company Limited; Doctor of Civil Law

**dcl.** [cricket] declaration; [cricket] declared

**DCLI** Duke of Cornwall's Light Infantry

**DCLJ** Dame Commander of the Order of St Lazarus of Jerusalem

**DClSc** Doctor of Clinical Science

**DCM** Diploma in Community Medicine; Distinguished Conduct Medal; district court martial; Doctor of Comparative Medicine

**DCMG** Dame Commander of the Order of St Michael and St George

**DCMS** Department for Culture, Media and Sport; Deputy Commissioner Medical Services

**DCnL** Doctor of Canon Law

**DCNS** Deputy Chief of Naval Staff

**DCO** Duke of Cambridge's Own (regiment)

**DC of S** Deputy Chief of Staff

**d. col.** [printing] double column

**DComL** Doctor of Commercial Law

**DComm** Doctor of Commerce

**DCompL** Doctor of Comparative Law

**DCP** Diploma in Clinical Pathology; Diploma in Clinical Psychology; Diploma in Conservation of Paintings

**DCPA** [USA] Defense Civil Preparedness Agency

**DCPath** Diploma of the College of Pathologists

**DCR** Diploma of the College of Radiographers

**DCrim** Doctor of Criminology

**DCS** Deputy Chief of Staff; Deputy Clerk of Session(s); [physics] differential cross section; digital camera system; Doctor of Christian Science; Doctor of Commercial Sciences; [medicine] dorsal column stimulator

**DCSO** deputy chief scientific officer

**DCST** Deputy Chief of Supplies and Transport

**DCT** [computing] discrete cosine transform; Doctor of Christian Theology; [medicine] dynamic compute(rize)d tomography

**dct** document

**DCV** [accounting] direct charge voucher

**DCVO** Dame Commander of the Royal Victorian Order

**DCW** dead carcass weight; domestic cold water

**DD** [insurance] damage done; dangerous drug; [banking] demand draft; [USA] Department of Defense; deputy director; deputy directorate; Diploma in Dermatology; [banking] direct debit; *direttissimo* (Italian: fast train); discharged dead; dishonourable discharge; Doctor of Divinity (from Latin *Divinitatis Doctor*); *dono dedit* (Latin: gave as a gift); [paper size] double demy; [computing] double density (disk); [medicine] Duchenne dystrophy; [UK postcode] Dundee; [vehicle registration] Gloucester

**D/D** [commerce] delivered at docks; [banking] demand draft; dock dues

**D/d** days after date; [commerce] delivered

**Dd.** *Deo dedit* (Latin: gave to God)

**dd** dated; dedicated; delivered; drilled

**d.d.** days after date; *de dato* (Latin: today's date); delayed delivery; [commerce] delivered at docks; [banking] demand draft; detergent dispersant; dry dock; due date; due day

**DDA** Dangerous Drugs Act; Disabled Drivers' Association

**D-Day** Day Day (i.e. specified day, esp. date of Allied invasion of Europe)

**DDBMS** distributed database management system

**DDC** Dewey Decimal Classification (for library books); [medicine] dideoxycytidine (used to treat Aids); [computing] direct digital control; [computing] display data channel

**DDCMP** [computing] digital data communication message protocol

**DDD** *dat, dicat, dedicat* (Latin: gives, devotes and dedicates); deadline delivery date; *dono dedit dedicavit* (Latin: gave and dedicated as a gift)

**DDDS** Deputy Director of Dental Services

**DDE** [computing] direct data entry; Dwight David Eisenhower (US president); dynamic data exchange

**DDG** Deputy Director-General

**DDGAMS** Deputy Director-General, Army Medical Services

**DDH** Diploma in Dental Health
**DDI** [medicine] dideoxyinosine (used to treat Aids); Divisional Detective Inspector
**d.d. in d.** [medicine] *de die in diem* (Latin: from day to day)
**DDL** [computing] data definition language; [computing] data description language; Deputy Director of Labour; digital data link
**DDM** Diploma in Dermatological Medicine; Doctor of Dental Medicine
**DDME** Deputy Director of Mechanical Engineering
**DDMI** Deputy Director of Military Intelligence
**DDMOI** Deputy Director of Military Operations and Intelligence
**DDMS** Deputy Director of Medical Services
**DDMT** Deputy Director of Military Training
**DDNI** Deputy Director of Naval Intelligence
**DDO** Diploma in Dental Orthopaedics; district dental officer
**DDOS** Deputy Director of Ordnance Services
**DDP** [computing] distributed data processing
**DDPH** Diploma in Dental Public Health
**DDPR** Deputy Director of Personal Services; Deputy Director of Postal Services; Deputy Director of Public Relations
**DDR** *Deutsche Demokratische Republik* (German: German Democratic Republic, the former East Germany); Diploma in Diagnostic Radiology
**DDRA** Deputy Director, Royal Artillery
**DDRB** Doctors' and Dentists' Review Body
**DDRD** Deputy Directorate of Research and Development
**DDS** deep diving system; Deputy Directorate of Science; Dewey Decimal System (for classifying library books); [pharmacology] diaminodiphenyl sulphone (= dapsone, drug used to treat skin disease); digital data storage; Director of Dental Services; Doctor of Dental Science; Doctor of Dental Surgery
**dd/s** delivered sound
**DDSc** Doctor of Dental Science
**DDSD** Deputy Director of Staff Duties
**DDSM** [USA] Defense Distinguished Service Medal
**DDSR** Deputy Director of Scientific Research
**DDST** Deputy Director of Supplies and Transport
**DDT** dichlorodiphenyltrichloroethane (insecticide)
**DDTL** dreary desk-top lunch
**DDVS** Deputy Director of Veterinary Services
**DDWE&M** Deputy Director of Works, Electrical and Mechanical
**DE** *Dáil Éireann* (Gaelic: Assembly of Ireland) (lower chamber of Irish parliament); deflection error; [US postcode] Delaware; Department of Employment; [UK postcode] Derby; [military] destroyer escort; destruction efficiency; diesel engine; direct electrolysis; Doctor of Engineering; Doctor of Entomology; [paper size] double elephant; [fishing port] Dundee; [vehicle registration] Haverfordwest
**.de** Germany (in Internet address)
**d.e.** deckle edge; diesel-electric; [fencing] direct elimination; [book-keeping] double entry
**DEA** [computing] data encryption algorithm; Department of Economic Affairs (former government department); Department of External Affairs; [USA] Drug Enforcement Administration; [USA] Drug Enforcement Agency
**Dea.** Deacon; Dean
**deb** [short form] debutante
**deb.** debenture; debit; debut
**debil.** debilitating; debilitation
**deb. stk** debenture stock
**DEC** dental examination centre; [USA] Department of Environmental Conservation; Digital Equipment Corporation; Disasters Emergency Committee; Dollar Export Council
**DEc** Doctor of Economics
**Dec.** *Decani* (Latin: of the dean) (side of church choir); *Decanus* (Latin: dean); December; [architecture] Decorated
**dec** [astronomy] declination
**dec.** deceased; decimal; declaration; declare; declared; [grammar] declension; decorated; decoration; decorative;

decrease; [music] *decrescendo* (Italian: with decreasing loudness)
**déc.** *décembre* (French: December)
**decaf** [short form] decaffeinated (coffee)
**decasyll.** decasyllabic; decasyllable
**decd** deceased
**decel.** deceleration
**decid.** deciduous
**decis.** decision
**decl.** [grammar] declension
**decn** decontamination
**decom.** decommission
**DEcon** Doctor of Economics
**DEconSc** Doctor of Economic Science
**DECR** [meteorology] decrease
**decr.** decrease
**decresc.** [music] *decrescendo* (Italian: with decreasing loudness)
**decrim.** decriminalization
**DED** Department of Economic Development (Northern Ireland)
**DEd** Doctor of Education
**ded.** dedicate; dedicated; dedication; deduce; deduct; deduction
**de d. in d.** [medicine] *de die in diem* (Latin: from day to day)
**deduct.** deduction; deductive
**DEE** Diploma in Electrical Engineering
**DEED** [USA] Department of Energy and Economic Development
**DEEP** Directly Elected European Parliament
**def.** defecate; defecation; defect; defection; defective; defector; defence; defendant; deferred; deficit; define; definite; definition; definitive; deflagrate; deflect; deflection; defoliate; defrost; defunct; *defunctus* (Latin: deceased)
**def. art.** [grammar] definite article
**DEFCON** [military] defence readiness condition
**defect.** defective
**defl.** deflate; deflation; deflect; deflection
**deft** defendant
**DEG** [meteorology] degrees
**deg.** degree
**degen.** degeneration
**degr.** degradation; degree
**dehyd.** dehydration
**DEI** Dutch East Indies (former name of Indonesia)
**Del** [computing] delete (key); [astronomy] Delphinus
**Del.** Delaware; Delhi
**del.** delegate; delegation; delete; deletion; *delineavit* (Latin: (he/she) drew it); deliver; delivered; delivery
**deld** delivered
**deleg.** delegate; delegation
**deli** [short form] delicatessen
**delib.** deliberate; deliberation
**deliq.** deliquescent
**DElo** Doctor of Elocution
**delv.** deliver; delivered; delivery
**dely** delivery
**Dem.** Democrat; Democratic
**dem.** demand; demerara; democracy; democratic; demolish; demolition; [grammar] demonstrative; demurrage
**DEME** Directorate of Electrical and Mechanical Engineering
**demo** [short form] demonstration
**demob** [short form] demobilization; [short form] demobilize
**demon.** demonstrate; [grammar] demonstrative
**demons.** [grammar] demonstrative
**demonstr.** [grammar] demonstrative
**DEMS** defensively equipped merchant ships
**DemU** [Northern Ireland] Democratic Unionist
**demur.** demurrage
**DEN** District Enrolled Nurse
**DEn** Department of Energy; Doctor of English
**Den.** Denbighshire; Denmark; Denver
**den.** denier; denotation; denote; denoted; dental; dentist; dentistry
**DenD** *Docteur en droit* (French: Doctor of Law)
**dend.** dendrology
**dendrochron.** dendrochronology
**dendrol.** dendrological; dendrology
**DEng** Doctor of Engineering
**DEngS** Doctor of Engineering Science
**DenM** *Docteur en médecine* (French: Doctor of Medicine)
**DenMed** *Docteur en médecine* (French: Doctor of Medicine)
**denom.** denomination
**DENR** [USA] Department of Energy and Natural Resources
**dens.** density
**DEnt** Doctor of Entomology
**dent.** dental; dentist; dentistry; denture

**DEOVR** Duke of Edinburgh's Own Volunteer Rifles
**DEP** Department of Employment and Productivity; [USA] Department of Environmental Protection
**dep.** depart(s); department; departure; dependant; dependency; dependent; deponent; depose; deposed; deposit; deposition; depositor; depot; deputize; deputized; deputy
**dép.** *département* (French: department, administrative division); *député* (French: deputy, member of parliament)
**Depca** International Study Group for the Detection and Prevention of Cancer
**dept** department; deponent
**dept.** deputy
**deptn** deputation
**DER** [USA] Department of Environmental Resources
**der.** *derecha* (Spanish: right); derivation; derivative; derive; derived; *dernier* (French: last)
**Derby.** Derbyshire
**Derbys** Derbyshire
**dereg.** deregulation
**deriv.** derivation; derivative; derive; derived
**DERL** derived emergency reference level (of radiation)
**derm.** dermatitis; dermatology
**dermat.** dermatology
**dermatol.** dermatology
**derog.** derogatory
**DERR** Duke of Edinburgh's Royal Regiment
**derv** diesel-engined road vehicle (diesel oil used as transport fuel)
**DES** [computing] data encryption standard; Department of Education and Science (former government department); [pharmacology] diethylstilboestrol (synthetic hormone); Director of Educational Services
**Des** Deaconess
**des.** desert; design; designate; designated; designation; designer; desirable; desire; dessert
**desc.** descend; descendant; descent; describe; description
**descr.** description
**desid.** *desideratum* (Latin: something wanted)
**desig.** designate
**DèsL** *Docteur ès lettres* (French: Doctor of Letters)
**desp.** despatch; despatched
**DesRCA** Designer of the Royal College of Art
**des res** [short form] desirable residence
**DèsS** *Docteur ès sciences* (French: Doctor of Science)
**DèsSc** *Docteur ès sciences* (French: Doctor of Science)
**DèsScPol** *Docteur ès sciences politiques* (French: Doctor of Political Science)
**dest.** destination; destroyer
**destn** destination
**DET** [linguistics] determiner; [pharmacology] diethyltryptamine (hallucinogen); direct energy transfer
**Det** Detective
**det.** detach; detached (in property advertisement); detachment; detail; determine; [grammar] determiner; [medicine] *detur* (Latin: let it be given)
**Det. Con.** Detective Constable
**Det. Insp.** Detective Inspector
**detn** detention; determination
**detox** [short form] detoxification
**DETR** Department of the Environment, Transport and the Regions
**Det. Sgt** Detective Sergeant
**Det. Supt** Detective Superintendent
**Deut.** [Bible] Deuteronomy
**Dev.** Devon(shire)
**dev.** develop; developed; developer; development; deviate; [navigation] deviation
**Devon.** Devonshire
**devp** develop
**devpt** development
**devs** devotions
**DEW** directed-energy weapon; distant early warning
**Dez.** *Dezember* (German: December)
**DF** Dean of Faculty; [nuclear technology] decontamination factor; Defender of the Faith; [telecommunications] direction finder; [telecommunications] direction-finding; [currency] Djibouti franc; Doctor of Forestry; [paper size] double foolscap; [vehicle registration] Gloucester
**d-f** double-fronted (in property advertisement)
**df.** draft

**d.f.** [commerce] dead freight; drinking fountain
**DFA** [USA] Department of Foreign Affairs; Diploma in Foreign Affairs; Doctor of Fine Arts
**DFC** Distinguished Flying Cross
**DFD** [computing] dataflow diagram; data function diagram
**DFDS** *Det Forende Dampskibs-Selskab* (Danish shipping company)
**DfEE** Department for Education and Employment
**DFHom** Diploma of the Faculty of Homoeopathy
**DFID** Department for International Development
**Dfl** [currency] Dutch guilder (from alternative name florin)
**DFLP** Democratic Front for the Liberation of Palestine
**DFLS** Day Fighter Leaders' School
**DFM** Diploma in Forensic Medicine; Distinguished Flying Medal
**dfndt** defendant
**DFR** [nuclear technology] Dounreay fast reactor
**d.f.r.** decreasing failure rate
**DFS** disease-free survival; [computing] disk filing system
**DFSc** Doctor of Financial Science
**DFT** dual-flow turbine
**dft** defendant; draft
**DFW** Director of Fortifications and Works
**DG** *Dei gratia* (Latin: by the grace of God); *Deo gratias* (Latin: thanks be to God); dependence graph; *Deutsche Grammophon* (German record company); differential geometry; [navigation] directional gyro; Directorate-General; Director-General; double glazed (in property advertisement); double glazing (in property advertisement); Dragoon Guards; [UK postcode] Dumfries; [vehicle registration] Gloucester
**dg** decigram
**DGA** Director-General, Aircraft; Directors' Guild of America
**DGAA** Distressed Gentlefolk's Aid Association
**DGAME** Director-General, Army Medical Services
**DGAS** Double Glazing Advisory Service
**DGB** *Deutscher Gewerkschaftsbund* (German: German Trade Union Federation)
**DGC** Diploma in Guidance and Counselling
**DGCA** Director-General of Civil Aviation
**DGCE** Directorate-General of Communications Equipment
**DGD** Director, Gunnery Division
**DGD&M** Director-General, Dockyards and Maintenance
**DGE** Directorate-General of Equipment
**DGEME** Director-General, Electrical and Mechanical Engineering
**DGI** Director-General of Information; Director-General of Inspection
**DGLP(A)** Director-General, Logistic Policy (Army)
**DGM** Diploma in General Medicine; Director-General of Manpower
**DGMS** Director-General of Medical Services
**DGMT** Director-General of Military Training
**DGMW** Director-General of Military Works
**Dgn** Dragoon
**DGO** Diploma in Gynaecology and Obstetrics
**DGP** Director-General of Personnel; Director-General of Production
**DGPS** Director-General of Personal Services
**DGR** Dante Gabriel Rossetti (British poet and painter); Director of Graves Registration
**DGS** Diploma in General Studies; Diploma in General Surgery; Diploma in Graduate Studies; Directorate-General of Signals; Director-General, Ships
**DGSRD** Directorate-General of Scientific Research and Development
**DGT** Director-General of Training
**DGW** Director-General of Weapons; Director-General of Works
**DH** [fishing port] Dartmouth; [sports] dead heat; De Havilland (aircraft); Department of Health; [baseball] designated hitter; [currency] dirham (used in Morocco); district heating; Doctor of Humanities; [electronics] double heterostructure; [vehicle registration] Dudley; [UK postcode] Durham

**Dh** [currency] dirham (used in United Arab Emirates)
**d.h.** *das heisst* (German: that is, i.e.); [sports] dead heat
**DHA** Department of Humanitarian Affairs (of UN); district health authority
**DHC** Domestic Heating Council
**Dhc** *Doctor honoris causa* (Latin: Honorary Doctor)
**DHDS** Dolmetsch Historical Dance Society
**DHHS** [USA] Department of Health and Human Services
**DHL** Doctor of Hebrew Letters; Doctor of Hebrew Literature; Doctor of Humane Letters
**DHMSA** Diploma in the History of Medicine (Society of Apothecaries)
**DHO** damped harmonic oscillator; district headquarters; divisional headquarters
**DHR** [nuclear technology] decay heat removal
**DHS** Diploma in Horticultural Science; Doctor of Health Sciences
**DHSA** Diploma in Health Service Administration
**DHSS** Department of Health and Social Security (former government department)
**DHumLit** Doctor of Humane Letters
**DHW** domestic hot water
**DHyg** Doctor of Hygiene
**DI** Defence Intelligence; Department of the Interior; Detective Inspector; [medicine] diabetes insipidus; direct injection; Director of Infantry; district inspector; divisional inspector; [medicine] donor insemination; [paper size] double imperial; drill instructor
**Di** didymium
**Di.** [currency] dinar
**di.** diameter
**d.i.** daily inspection; *das ist* (German: that is, i.e.); de-ice; diplomatic immunity; document identifier
**DIA** [USA] Defense Intelligence Agency; Design and Industries Association; Diploma in International Affairs; Driving Instructors Association
**dia.** diagnose; diagram; dialect; diameter
**diag.** diagnose; diagnosis; diagonal; diagram
**dial.** dialect; dialectal; dialectic; dialectical; dialogue
**diam.** diameter
**diamat** dialectical materialism (in philosophy and economics)
**DIANE** Direct Information Access Network for Europe
**diap.** [music] diapason
**diaph.** diaphragm
**DIAS** Dublin Institute of Advanced Science
**DIC** Diamond Information Centre; Diploma of (Membership of the) Imperial College (of Science and Technology); [medicine] disseminated intravascular coagulation; [chemistry] dissolved inorganic carbon; drunk in charge
**dic.** *dicembre* (Italian: December)
**DIChem** Diploma in Industrial Chemistry
**dicot.** dicotyledon
**dict.** dictate; dictated; dictation; dictator; dictionary
**DICTA** Diploma of Imperial College of Tropical Agriculture
**DIDS** [electronics] donor-impurity density of states
**DIE** Designated Investment Exchange; Diploma in Industrial Engineering; Diploma of the Institute of Engineering
**dieb. alt.** [medicine] *diebus alternis* (Latin: on alternate days)
**DIEL** (Advisory Committee on Telecommunications for) Disabled and Elderly People
**DIEME** Directorate of Inspection of Electrical and Mechanical Equipment
**diet.** dietary; dietetics; dietician
**DIF** [computing] data interchange format; District Inspector of Fisheries
**dif.** differ; differential
**diff.** differ; difference; different; differential
**diff. calc.** differential calculus
**diffr.** diffraction
**diffu.** diffusion
**DIG** Deputy Inspector-General; disablement income group
**dig.** digest (compilation); digestion; digestive; digit; digital
**DIH** Diploma in Industrial Health
**DIIR** digital image-intensifier radiography
**Dij.** Dijon
**DIL** [electronics] dual in-line

**dil.** dilute; diluted; dilution
**diln** dilution
**DIM** Diploma in Industrial Management
**dim.** *dimanche* (French: Sunday); dimension; *dimidium* (Latin: half); diminish; [music] *diminuendo* (Italian: with diminishing loudness); diminutive
**dimin.** [music] *diminuendo* (Italian: with diminishing loudness); diminutive
**Dimm** [computing, electronics] dual in-line memory module
**DIMS** [computing] data and information management system
**DIN** *Deutsches Industrie Normen* (German: German Industry Standard); *Deutsches Institut für Normung* (German: German Standards Institute); [computing] digital imaging network
**Din** [currency] dinar
**din.** dining car; dining room (in property advertisement); dinner
**DIng** Doctor of Engineering (from Latin *Doctor Ingeniariae*)
**dinky** [informal] double (or dual) income, no kids (yet)
**DInstPA** Diploma of the Institute of Park Administration
**DIO** district intelligence officer
**dio.** diocese
**dioc.** diocesan; diocese
**dioc. syn.** diocesan synod
**DIP** [computing] document image processing; [electronics] dual in-line package; [electronics] dual in-line pin
**Dip.** Diploma
**dip.** diploma
**DipAD** Diploma in Art and Design
**DipAe** Diploma in Aeronautics
**DipAgr** Diploma in Agriculture
**DipALing** Diploma in Applied Linguistics
**DipAM** Diploma in Applied Mechanics
**DipAppSc** Diploma in Applied Science
**DipArch** Diploma in Architecture
**DipArts** Diploma in Arts
**DipASE** Diploma in Advanced Study of Education, College of Preceptors
**DipAvMed** Diploma in Aviation Medicine
**DipBA** Diploma in Business Administration
**DipBac** Diploma in Bacteriology
**DipBMS** Diploma in Basic Medical Sciences
**DipBS** Diploma in Fine Art, Byam Shaw School
**DipCAM** Diploma in Communication, Advertising and Marketing (of CAM Foundation)
**DipCC** Diploma of the Central College
**DipCD** Diploma in Child Development; Diploma in Civic Design
**DipCE** Diploma in Civil Engineering
**DipChemEng** Diploma in Chemical Engineering
**DipCom** Diploma in Commerce
**DipDHus** Diploma in Dairy Husbandry
**DipDP** Diploma in Drawing and Painting
**DipDS** Diploma in Dental Surgery
**DipEcon** Diploma in Economics
**DipEd** Diploma in Education
**DipEl** Diploma in Electronics
**DipEng** Diploma in Engineering
**DipESL** Diploma in English as a Second Language
**DipEth** Diploma in Ethnology
**DipFA** Diploma in Fine Arts
**DipFD** Diploma in Funeral Directing
**DipFE** Diploma in Further Education
**DipFor** Diploma in Forestry
**DipGSM** Diploma in Music, Guildhall School of Music (and Drama)
**DipGT** Diploma in Glass Technology
**DipHA** Diploma in Hospital Administration
**DipHE** Diploma in Higher Education; Diploma in Highway Engineering
**DipHSc** Diploma in Home Science
**diphth.** diphthong
**DipHum** Diploma in Humanities
**DipJ** Diploma in Journalism
**DipL** Diploma in Languages
**dipl.** diploma; diplomacy; diplomat; diplomatic
**DipLA** Diploma in Landscape Architecture
**DipLib** Diploma in Librarianship
**DipLSc** Diploma in Library Science
**DipM** Diploma in Marketing
**DipMechE** Diploma in Mechanical Engineering
**DipMet** Diploma in Metallurgy
**DipMFOS** Diploma in Maxillofacial and Oral Surgery
**DipMusEd** Diploma in Musical Education
**DipN** Diploma in Nursing

**DipNEd** Diploma in Nursery School Education
**DipO&G** Diploma in Obstetrics and Gynaecology
**DipOL** Diploma in Oriental Learning
**DipOrth** Diploma in Orthodontics
**DipPA** Diploma in Public Administration
**DipP&OT** Diploma in Physiotherapy and Occupational Therapy
**DipPharmMed** Diploma in Pharmaceutical Medicine
**DipPhysEd** Diploma in Physical Education
**DipQS** Diploma in Quantity Surveying
**DipRADA** Diploma of the Royal Academy of Dramatic Art
**DipREM** Diploma in Rural Estate Management
**DIPS** digital image-processing system
**DipS&PA** Diploma in Social and Public Administration
**DipSMS** Diploma in School Management Studies
**DipSoc** Diploma in Sociology
**DipSpEd** Diploma in Special Education
**DipSS** Diploma in Social Studies
**DipSW** Diploma in Social Work
**DipT** Diploma in Teaching
**DipTA** Diploma in Tropical Agriculture
**DipT&CP** Diploma in Town and Country Planning
**DipTech** Diploma in Technology
**DipTEFL** Diploma in the Teaching of English as a Foreign Language
**DipTh** Diploma in Theology
**DipTP** Diploma in Town Planning
**DipTPT** Diploma in Theory and Practice of Teaching
**DIR** [photography] developer inhibitor release
**dir.** direct; directed; direction; director; [currency] dirham
**Dir-Gen** Director-General
**DIS** [USA] Defense Intelligence School; Development Information System
**dis.** disabled; discharge; disciple; discipline; disconnect; discontinue; discontinued; discount; dispense; distance; distant; distribute
**disab.** disability
**disabil.** disability
**disag.** disagreeable
**disb.** disbursement
**disc.** disciple; discipline; discount; discover; discovered; discoverer; discovery
**disch.** discharge
**disco** [short form] discotheque
**discont.** discontinued
**discr.** discretion
**disemb.** disembark; disembarkation
**DISH** [medicine] diffuse idiopathic skeletal hyperostosis
**dishon.** dishonest; dishonourable; dishonourably
**disloc.** dislocation
**dismac** [military] digital scene-matching area correlation sensors
**disp.** dispensary; dispensation; dispense; disperse; dispersion; disputed
**displ.** displacement
**diss.** dissenter; dissertation; dissolve
**dist.** distance; distant; distilled; distinguish; distinguished; distribute; distributor; district
**Dist. Atty** [USA] District Attorney
**distr.** distribution; distributor
**distrib.** distributive
**DistTP** Distinction in Town Planning
**DIT** [medicine] desferrioxamine infusion test; Detroit Institute of Technology; double income tax (as in **DIT relief**)
**DITB** Distributive Industry Training Board
**Div.** Divine; Divinity
**div** [mathematics] divergence
**div.** diversion; divide; divided; dividend; divine; [music] *divisi* (Italian: divided) (referring to musical parts); division; divisor; divorce; divorced
**div. in par. aeq.** [medicine] *dividatur in partes aequales* (Latin: let it be divided into equal parts) (in prescriptions)
**divn** division
**divnl** divisional
**DIY** do-it-yourself
**DJ** dinner jacket; Diploma in Journalism; disc jockey; [USA] district judge; divorce judge; Doctor of Law (from Latin *Doctor Juris*); [finance] Dow Jones; dust jacket (of book); [vehicle registration] Liverpool
**d.J** *der Jüngere* (German: the Younger, Junior); *dieses Jahres* (German: of this year)
**.dj** Djibouti (in Internet address)
**DJAG** Deputy Judge Advocate-General
**DJF** Disc Jockeys Federation
**DJI** [finance] Dow Jones Index

**DJIA** [finance] Dow Jones Industrial Average
**DJS** Doctor of Juridical Science
**DJT** Doctor of Jewish Theology
**DJTA** [finance] Dow Jones Transportation Average
**DJUA** [finance] Dow Jones Utilities Average
**DJur** Doctor of Law (from Latin *Doctor Juris*)
**DK** [international vehicle registration] Denmark and Greenland; Dorling Kindersley (publishing company); [fishing port] Dundalk; [vehicle registration] Manchester
**dk** dark; deck; dock; duck
**.dk** Denmark (in Internet address)
**DKB** [computing] distributed knowledge base
**dkhse** deckhouse
**DKNY** [trademark] Donna Karan New York
**Dkr** [currency] Danish krone
**DKS** Deputy Keeper of the Signet
**dkt** docket
**dkyd** dockyard
**DL** [UK postcode] Darlington; [fishing port] Deal; Deputy Lieutenant; [physics] detection limit; diesel; [psychology] difference limen; [electronics] distribution line; Doctor of Laws (from Latin *Doctor Legum*); dog licence; [physics] dose level; [book-keeping] double ledger; [theatre] down left (of stage); [computing] download (on Internet); driving licence; [vehicle registration] Portsmouth
**D/L** data link; demand loan
**dl** decilitre
**DLA** diffusion limited aggregation
**DLC** Diploma of Loughborough College; divisional land commissioner; Doctor of Celtic Literature; [theatre] down left centre (of stage)
**d.l.c.** direct lift control
**DLCO-EA** Desert Locust Control Organization for Eastern Africa
**dld** delivered
**d.l.d.** deadline date
**DLE** [medicine] discoid lupus erythematosus
**DLES** Doctor of Letters in Economic Studies
**DLett** *Docteur ès lettres* (French: Doctor of Letters)
**DLF** Disabled Living Foundation
**DLG** David Lloyd George (British statesman)
**DLI** Durham Light Infantry
**D-Lib** [USA] Liberal Democrat
**DLit** Doctor of Literature
**DLitt** Doctor of Letters (from Latin *Doctor Litterarum*)
**DLittS** Doctor of Sacred Letters
**DLJ** Dame of Justice of the Order of St Lazarus of Jerusalem
**DLL** [computing] dynamic link library
**DLM** [genetics] dominant lethal mutation
**DLO** dead letter office (former name of RLO); Diploma in Laryngology and Otology; Diploma in Laryngology and Otorhinolaryngology; dispatch loading only
**DLOY** Duke of Lancaster's Own Yeomanry
**DLP** Democratic Labour Party
**DLR** Docklands Light Railway
**dlr** dealer
**DLS** debt liquidation schedule; Doctor of Library Science; Dominion Land Surveyor
**DLSc** Doctor of Library Science
**DLT** Dave Lee Travis (British disc jockey)
**dlvd** delivered
**dlvr** deliver
**dlvy** delivery
**DLW** Diploma in Labour Welfare
**dly** daily
**DM** [vehicle registration] Chester; *Daily Mail*; [astronomy] dark matter; deputy master; design manual; [currency] Deutschmark; [medicine] diabetes mellitus; [medicine] diastolic murmur; [physics] dipole moment; direct mail; Director of Music; dispersion measures; [computing] distributed memory; district manager; *Docteur en médecine* (French: Doctor of Medicine); Doctor of Mathematics; Doctor of Medicine; Doctor of Music
**d.M** *dieses Monats* (German: this month, inst.)
**dm** decimetre
**.dm** Dominica (in Internet address)
**DMA** Defence Manufacturers' Association; Diploma in Municipal Administration; [computing] direct memory access
**DMAC** [computing] direct memory access

control; [television] duobinary multiplexed analogue component

**DM&CW** Diploma in Maternity and Child Welfare

**DMath** Doctor of Mathematics

**DMC** direct manufacturing costs; district medical committee

**DMD** [computing] digital micromirror device; Doctor of Dental Medicine; Doctor of Mathematics and Didactics; Doctor of Medical Dentistry; [medicine] Duchenne muscular dystrophy

**dmd** demand

**DME** Diploma in Mechanical Engineering; [computing] direct machine environment; [aeronautics] distance-measuring equipment; [computing] distributed management environment; [electronics] dropping mercury electrode

**DMed** Doctor of Medicine

**DMet** Doctor of Metallurgy; Doctor of Meteorology

**DMF** decayed, missing and filled (teeth); Disabled Motorists Federation; [electronics] dose-modifying factor

**DMFOS** Diploma in Maxillofacial and Oral Surgery

**dmg.** damage

**DMGO** Divisional Machine-Gun Officer

**DMGT** [genetics] DNA-mediated gene transfer

**DMHS** Director of Medical and Health Services

**DMI** [computing] desktop management interface; Director of Military Intelligence

**DMin** Doctor of Ministry

**DMJ** Diploma in Medical Jurisprudence

**DMJ(Path)** Diploma in Medical Jurisprudence (Pathology)

**DML** [computing] data-manipulation language; Defence Medal for Leningrad (former Soviet decoration); Doctor of Modern Languages

**dml.** demolish

**DMLJ** Dame of Merit of the Order of St Lazarus of Jerusalem

**DMLS** Doppler microwave landing system

**DMLT** Diploma in Medical Laboratory Technology

**DMM** Defence Medal for Moscow (former Soviet decoration); [medicine] diffuse malignant mesothelioma

**dmn** dimension

**dmnl** dimensional

**DMO** Defence Medal for Odessa (former Soviet decoration); [astronomy] diffuse massive object; Director of Military Operations; district medical officer

**DMO&I** Director, Military Operations and Intelligence

**DMP** Diploma in Medical Psychology; Director of Manpower Planning

**DMPB** Diploma in Medical Pathology and Bacteriology

**DMR** Diploma in Medical Radiology; Director of Materials Research

**DMRD** Diploma in Medical Radiological Diagnosis; Directorate of Materials Research and Development

**DMRE** Diploma in Medical Radiology and Electrology

**DMRT** Diploma in Medical Radiotherapy

**DMS** [computing] database management system; [computing] data management system; [mining] dense-medium separation; Diploma in Management Studies; Directorate of Military Survey; Director of Medical Services; *Dis manibus sacrum* (Latin: consecrated to the souls of the departed); Doctor of Medical Science; Doctor of Medicine and Surgery

**DMs** Doc(tor) Martens (trademark for brand of lace-up boots)

**DMSA** [medicine] dimercaptosuccinic acid (used in diagnosis)

**DMSO** [medicine] dimethylsulphoxide (used in ointments)

**DMSSB** Direct Mail Services Standard Board

**dmst.** demonstration; demonstrator

**dmstn** demonstration

**dmstr** demonstrator

**DMSV** Defence Medal for Sevastopol (former Soviet decoration)

**DMT** [pharmacology] dimethyltryptamine (hallucinogen); Director of Military Training

**DMTF** [computing] desktop management task force

**DMU** [commerce] decision-making unit; directly managed unit (of hospital in NHS)

**DMus** Doctor of Music

**DMV** [USA] Department of Motor Vehicles; *Docteur en médecine vétérinaire*

(French: Doctor of Veterinary Medicine)
**DMZ** demilitarized zone
**DN** [commerce] debit note; *de novo* (Latin: from the beginning); Diploma in Nursing; *Dominus noster* (Latin: our Lord); [UK postcode] Doncaster; [vehicle registration] Leeds
**D/N** [commerce] debit note
**Dn** Deacon; *Don* (Spanish: Mr); Dragoon
**dn** down; dozen
**DNA** [USA] Defense Nuclear Agency; [genetics] deoxyribonucleic acid; *Det Norske Arbeiderpartiet* (Norwegian: Norwegian Labour Party); *Deutscher Normenausschuss* (German: German Standards Committee); [medicine] did not attend; Director of Naval Accounts; District Nursing Association
**Dna** *Doña* (Spanish: Mrs)
**DNAase** [biochemistry] deoxyribonuclease
**DNAD** Director of Naval Air Division
**DNase** [biochemistry] deoxyribonuclease
**DNB** *Dictionary of National Biography*
**DNC** [nuclear technology] delayed-neutron counting; Director of Naval Construction; [computing] distributed numerical control
**DND** Director of Navigation and Direction
**DNE** Diploma in Nursing Education; Director of Naval Equipment; Director of Nurse Education; Dounreay Nuclear Establishment
**dne** *douane* (French: customs)
**DNES** Director of Naval Education Service
**DNF** [sports] did not finish (in race)
**DNH** Department of National Heritage
**DNHW** [USA] Department of National Health and Welfare
**DNI** Director of Naval Intelligence
**DNJC** *Dominus noster Jesus Christus* (Latin: Our Lord Jesus Christ)
**DNMS** Director of Naval Medical Services
**DNO** Director of Naval Ordnance; district naval officer; district nursing officer; divisional nursing officer
**DNP** declared national programme; dynamic nuclear polarization
**DNPDE** Dounreay Nuclear Power Development Establishment
**DNPP** *Dominus Noster Papa Pontifex* (Latin: Our Lord the Pope)
**DNR** [USA] Department of Natural Resources; Director of Naval Recruitment; [medicine] do not resuscitate
**Dnr** [currency] dinar
**DNS** Department for National Savings; [computing] domain name system
**dns** downs (on map)
**DNSA** Diploma in Nursing Service Administration
**DNT** Director of Naval Training
**DNWA** Director of Naval Weather Service
**DO** defence order; [finance] deferred ordinary (shares); [commerce] delivery order; Diploma in Ophthalmology; Diploma in Osteopathy; [grammar] direct object; [commerce] direct order; dissolved oxygen; district office; district officer; divisional office; divisional officer; Doctor of Optometry; Doctor of Oratory; Doctor of Osteopathy; [fishing port] Douglas; drawing office; [vehicle registration] Lincoln
**D/O** [commerce] direct order
**d/o** [commerce] delivery order
**Do.** *Donnerstag* (German: Thursday)
**do.** ditto
**.do** Dominican Republic (in Internet address)
**DOA** date of availability; [medicine] dead on arrival; [USA] Department of the Army; dissolved-oxygen analyser
**DOAE** Defence Operational Analysis Establishment (of MOD)
**DOB** date of birth
**d.o.b.** date of birth
**DObstRCOG** Diploma in Obstetrics of the Royal College of Obstetricians and Gynaecologists
**DOC** *denominazione di origine controllata* (Italian: name of origin controlled) (wine classification); [USA] Department of Commerce; direct operating cost; [chemistry] dissolved organic carbon; District Officer Commanding
**Doc.** Doctor
**doc** [short form] doctor
**doc.** document(s)
**d.o.c.a.** date of current appointment
**d.o.c.e.** date of current enlistment
**DocEng** Doctor of Engineering
**DOCG** *denominazione di origine controllata garantita* (Italian: name of origin guaranteed controlled) (wine classification)

**docu.** document; documentary; documentation

**DOD** date of death; [USA] Department of Defense; died of disease

**d.o.d.** date of death

**DOE** [USA] Department of Energy; Department of the Environment; depends on experience (in job advertisement); Director of Education

**d.o.e.** depends on experience (in job advertisement)

**DOF** [science] degrees of freedom

**D of Corn. LI** Duke of Cornwall's Light Infantry

**D of H** degree of honour

**D of L** Duchy of Lancaster

**D of S** Director of Stores

**DOG** Directory of Opportunities for Graduates

**DOH** Department of Health

**DOHC** double overhead cam(shaft); dual overhead cam(shaft)

**DOHS** [USA] Department of Health Services

**DOI** Department of Industry; [USA] Department of the Interior; died of injuries; Director of Information

**DOJ** [USA] Department of Justice

**DOL** [USA] Department of Labor; Doctor of Oriental Learning

**dol.** [music] *dolce* (Italian: sweetly, gently); [currency] dollar

**dolciss.** [music] *dolcissimo* (Italian: very sweetly, very gently)

**DOM** date of marriage; *Deo Optimo Maximo* (Latin: to God, the best, the greatest); *département d'outre mer* (French: overseas department); [informal] dirty old man; dispersed organic material; dissolved organic material; [international vehicle registration] Dominican Republic; *Dominus omnium magister* (Latin: God the master of all)

**Dom.** Dominica; Dominical; [Roman Catholic Church] Dominican; *Dominus* (Latin: Lord)

**dom.** domain; *domenica* (Italian: Sunday); domestic; domicile; dominant; *domingo* (Spanish: Sunday); dominion

**d.o.m.** date of marriage

**Dom. Bk** Domesday Book

**Dom. Proc.** [law] *Domus Procerum* (Latin: House of Lords)

**DOMS** Diploma in Ophthalmic Medicine and Surgery

**Domsat** domestic communications satellite

**DON** [USA] Department of the Navy; Diploma in Orthopaedic Nursing; [chemistry] dissolved organic nitrogen

**Don.** Donegal

**don.** *donec* (Latin: until)

**Doneg.** Donegal

**DOpt** Diploma in Ophthalmic Optics

**DOR** Director of Operational Requirements

**Dor** [astronomy] Dorado

**Dor.** Dorian; Doric

**DORA** Defence of the Realm Act

**dorm** [short form] dormitory

**Dors.** Dorset

**DOrth** Diploma in Orthodontics; Diploma in Orthoptics

**DOS** date of sale; day of sale; [USA] Department of State; Diploma in Orthopaedic Surgery; Directorate of Overseas Surveys; Director of Ordnance Services; [computing] disk-operating system; Doctor of Ocular Science

**dos.** dosage

**DOSV** deep ocean survey vehicle

**DOT** Department of Overseas Trade; Department of Transport; [USA] Department of Transportation; designated order turnaround (in New York Stock Exchange); [computing] digital optical tape; Diploma in Occupational Therapy; [medicine] directly observed therapy; [physiology] dissolved oxygen tension

**dot.** [law] dotation (= endowment)

**dott.** *dottore* (Italian: doctor)

**DOV** double oil of vitriol (sulphuric acid)

**DOW** died of wounds

**Dow.** Dowager

**dow.** dowager

**doz.** dozen

**DP** data processing; decimal pitch; [chemistry] degree of polymerization; delivery point; Democratic Party; diametral pitch; Diploma in Psychiatry; (by) direction of the president; Director of Photography; disabled person; displaced person; Doctor of Philosophy; domestic prelate; [law] *Domus Procerum* (Latin: House of Lords); durable press; duty paid; [computing] dynamic programming; [vehicle registration] Reading

**D/P** delivery on payment; delivery papers; [commerce] documents against payment; [commerce] documents against presentation

**dp** deep

**d.p.** damp-proof; damp-proofed; damp-proofing; deep penetration; departure point; [finance] depreciation percentage; direct port; double paper; [baseball] double play; dry powder; dual purpose

**DPA** Data Protection Authority; *Deutsche Presse Agentur* (German news agency); Diploma in Public Administration; discharged prisoners' aid; [USA] Doctor of Public Administration

**d.p.a.** deferred payment account

**DPAA** Draught Proofing Advisory Association

**DPAS** Discharged Prisoners' Aid Society

**DPath** Diploma in Pathology

**DPB** [finance] deposit pass book

**DPC** Defence Planning Committee (in NATO)

**d.p.c.** damp-proof course

**DPCM** [telecommunications] differential pulse code modulation

**DPCP** Department of Prices and Consumer Protection

**DPCS** data personal communications service

**DPD** Data Protection Directive; Diploma in Public Dentistry; [statistics] discrete probability distributions

**DPE** Diploma in Physical Education

**DPEc** Doctor of Political Economy

**DPed** Doctor of Pedagogy

**DPH** Diploma in Public Health; Director of Public Health; [USA] Doctor of Public Health

**DPh** Doctor of Philosophy

**DPharm** Doctor of Pharmacy

**DPHD** Diploma in Public Health Dentistry

**DPhil** Doctor of Philosophy

**DPHN** Diploma in Public Health Nursing

**DPhysMed** Diploma in Physical Medicine

**DPI** Department of Public Information

**dpi** [computing] dots per inch

**dpl.** diploma; diplomat; duplex

**DPM** data processing manager; Deputy Prime Minister; Deputy Provost-Marshal; Diploma in Psychological Medicine

**DPMI** [computing] DOS/Protected Mode Interface

**DPMS** [computing] display power management system

**DPO** distributing post office; district pay office

**d.p.o.b.** date and place of birth

**DPolSc** Doctor of Political Science

**DPP** [insurance] deferred payment plan; Diploma in Plant Pathology; Director of Public Prosecutions; [US finance] direct participation program

**DPR** Data Protection Register; Director of Public Relations

**DPRK** Democratic People's Republic of Korea (North Korea)

**DPS** Dales Pony Society; Director of Personal Services; Director of Postal Services; Doctor of Public Service

**dps** dividend per share

**DPSA** Diploma in Public and Social Administration

**DPSK** [computing] differential phase shift keying

**DPSN** Diploma in Professional Studies in Nursing

**DPsSc** Doctor of Psychological Science

**DPsy** *Docteur en psychologie* (French: Doctor of Psychology)

**DPsych** Diploma in Psychiatry; Doctor of Psychology

**DPT** [medicine] dental pantomogram; [medicine] diphtheria, pertussis (whooping cough), tetanus (vaccine)

**dpt** department; deponent; deposit; depot

**dpty** deputy

**DPU** data processing unit

**DPW** Department of Public Works

**dpx** duplex

**DQ** dispersion quotient; [sports] disqualified; [sports] disqualify; [civil aircraft marking] Fiji

**d.q.** direct question

**DQDB** [computing] distributed queue dual bus

**DQMG** Deputy Quartermaster-General

**DQMS** Deputy Quartermaster-Sergeant

**DR** [USA] Daughters of the Revolution; [navigation] dead reckoning; [physics] decay ratio; defence regulation; *Deutsches Reich* (German: German

Empire); dining room (in property advertisement); Diploma in Radiology; discount rate; dispatch rider; dispersion relation; district railway; district registry; [paper size] double royal; [fishing port] Dover; [theatre] down right (of stage); dry riser (for firefighter's hose); Dutch Reformed (Church); dynamic relaxation; [vehicle registration] Exeter

**D/R** deposit receipt

**Dr** Director; Doctor; [currency] drachma

**Dr.** Drive (in road name)

**dr** debtor; door; dram; [meteorology] drizzle and rain

**dr.** debit; drachm; [currency] drachma; drama; draw; drawer; drawn; dresser; driver; drum; drummer

**d.r.** deficiency report; design requirements; development report; document report

**DRA** de-rating appeals

**Dra** *Doctora* (Spanish: Doctor (female)); *Doutora* (Portuguese: Doctor (female)); [astronomy] Draco

**DRAC** Director, Royal Armoured Corps

**DrAgr** Doctor of Agriculture

**DRAM** [computing] dynamic random-access memory

**dram.** drama; dramatic; dramatist

**dram. pers.** *dramatis personae* (Latin: characters in the play)

**DRAO** Dominion Radio Astrophysical Observatory

**Drav.** Dravidian (language)

**DRAW** [computing] direct read after write

**draw.** drawing room (in property advertisement)

**DrBusAdmin** Doctor of Business Administration

**DRC** [theatre] down right centre (of stage); Dutch Reformed Church

**DrChem** Doctor of Chemistry

**DRCOG** Diploma of the Royal College of Obstetricians and Gynaecologists

**DRCPath** Diploma of the Royal College of Pathologists

**DRCS** [computing] dynamically redefinable character set

**DRCST** Diploma of the Royal College of Science and Technology (Glasgow)

**DRD** Diploma in Restorative Dentistry

**DRDW** [computing] direct read during write

**DRE** [medicine] digital rectal examination; Director of Religious Education; Doctor of Religious Education

**DRelEd** Doctor of Religious Education

**DrEng** Doctor of Engineering

**DRG** [medicine] diagnosis-related group

**drg** drawing

**DRK** *Deutsches Rotes Kreuz* (German: German Red Cross)

**DRLS** dispatch-rider letter service

**DRM** Diploma in Radiation Medicine; Diploma in Resource Management

**DrMed** Doctor of Medicine

**drn** drawn

**DrNatSci** Doctor of Natural Science

**DRO** daily routine order; disablement resettlement officer; divisional routine order

**DrOecPol** Doctor of Political Economics (from Latin *Doctor Oeconomiae Politicae*)

**DRP** dividend reinvestment plan

**DrPH** Doctor of Public Health

**DrPhil** Doctor of Philosophy

**DrPolSci** Doctor of Political Science

**DRS** Diploma in Religious Studies

**DRSAMD** Diploma of the Royal Scottish Academy of Music and Drama

**DRSE** [medicine] drug-related side effects

**DRSN** [meteorology] drifting snow

**DRT** [psychology] diagnostic rhyme test

**DrTheol** Doctor of Theology

**Dr. und Vrl.** *Druck und Verlag* (German: printed and published (by))

**DRurSc** Doctor of Rural Science

**DRV** dietary reference values

**DRW** [computing] draw format

**drx.** [currency] drachma

**DS** [music] *dal segno* (Italian: (repeat) from the sign); [finance] debenture stock; defect score; [physics] defect size; dental surgeon; Department of State; deputy secretary; Detective Sergeant; [physics] diffractive system; Directing Staff; [medicine] disseminated sclerosis; Doctor of Science; Doctor of Surgery; [computing] double-sided (disk); [medicine] Down's syndrome; driver seated (vehicle); [fishing port] Dumfries; [vehicle registration] Glasgow

**D/S** [medicine] dextrose saline

**Ds** *Deus* (Latin: God); *Dominus* (Latin: Lord, Master)

**ds.** *destro* (Italian: right)

**d.s.** date of service; daylight saving; days after sight; day's sight; document signed
**DSA** [medicine] digital subtraction angiography; Diploma in Social Administration; *Docteur ès sciences agricoles* (French: Doctor of Agricultural Science); Down's Syndrome Association; Driving Standards Agency
**DSAC** Defence Scientific Advisory Council
**DSAO** Diplomatic Service Administration Office
**DSASO** Deputy Senior Air Staff Officer
**DSB** *Dansk Statsbaner* (Danish: Danish State Railways); Drug Supervisory Body (of UN)
**DSC** Discovery Channel; Distinguished Service Cross (replacement for CSC); Doctor of Surgical Chiropody
**DSc** Doctor of Science
**DScA** *Docteur ès sciences agricoles* (French: Doctor of Agricultural Science); *Docteur ès sciences appliquées* (French: Doctor of Applied Sciences)
**DSc(Agr)** Doctor of Science in Agriculture
**DSc(Eng)** Doctor of Science in Engineering
**DSc(For)** Doctor of Science in Forestry
**DSCHE** Diploma of the Scottish Council for Health Education
**DScMil** Doctor of Military Science
**DScTech** Doctor of Technical Science
**DSD** Director of Signals Division; Director of Staff Duties
**dsDNA** [biochemistry] double-stranded deoxyribonucleic acid
**DSDP** deep-sea drilling project
**DSE** Doctor of Science in Economics
**Dsf** Düsseldorf
**dsgn** design
**dsgn.** designer
**DSIR** [New Zealand] Department of Scientific and Industrial Research
**DSL** district Scout leader; Doctor of Sacred Letters
**DSM** deputy stage manager; *Diagnostic and Statistical Manual* (of American Psychiatric Association); [computing] digital storage medium; Directorate of Servicing and Maintenance; Distinguished Service Medal; Doctor of Sacred Music
**dsmd** dismissed
**DSN** [astronautics] Deep-Space Network
**DSO** (Companion of the) Distinguished Service Order; District Staff Officer
**DSocSC** Doctor of Social Science(s)
**DSP** Democratic Socialist Party; [electronics] digital signal processing; [electronics] digital signal processor; *Docteur ès sciences politiques* (French: Doctor of Political Science); dye sublimation printing
**d.s.p.** *decessit sine prole* (Latin: died without issue)
**dspl** disposal
**d.s.p.l.** *decessit sine prole legitima* (Latin: died without legitimate issue)
**d.s.p.m.** *decessit sine prole mascula* (Latin: died without male issue)
**d.s.p.m.s.** *decessit sine prole mascula superstite* (Latin: died without surviving male issue)
**dspn** disposition
**d.s.p.s.** *decessit sine prole superstite* (Latin: died without surviving issue)
**d.s.p.v.** *decessit sine prole virile* (Latin: died without male issue)
**d.s.q.** discharged to sick quarters
**DSR** [commerce] debt service ratio; [medicine] digital subtraction radiography; Director of Scientific Research; [medicine] dynamic spatial reconstructor
**DSRD** Directorate of Signals Research and Development
**DSS** [computing] decision support system; Department of Social Security; Director of Social Services; Doctor of Holy (or Sacred) Scripture (from Latin *Doctor Sacrae Scripturae*); Doctor of Social Science
**Dss** Deaconess
**DSSc** Diploma in Sanitary Science; Doctor of Social Science
**DST** Daylight Saving Time; deep-sleep therapy; Director of Supplies and Transport; Doctor of Sacred Theology; Double Summer Time; [mining] drill-stem test
**dstn** destination
**D Surg.** Dental Surgeon
**DSW** [New Zealand] Department of Social Welfare; Doctor of Social Welfare; Doctor of Social Work
**DT** *Daily Telegraph*; damage-tolerant; data transmission; daylight time; [medicine] dead from tumour; delirium tremens; dental technician; [USA] Department of

Transportation; [USA] Department of Treasury; destructive testing; [US informal] detective; [nuclear technology] deuterium–tritium; Director of Transport; Doctor of Divinity (or Theology) (from Latin *Doctor Theologiae*); [UK postcode] Dorchester; [vehicle registration] Sheffield

**d.t.** delirium tremens; double throw

**DTA** [physics] differential thermal analysis; Diploma in Tropical Agriculture; Distributive Trades' Alliance

**DTAM** data transfer, access and manipulation

**d.t.b.a.** [commerce] date to be advised

**DTC** Department of Technical Cooperation; [USA] Depository Trust Company; Diamond Trading Company; [medicine] differentiated thyroid carcinoma; Diploma in Textile Chemistry; Docklands Transportation Consortium

**DTCD** [USA] Department of Technical Cooperation for Development; Diploma in Tuberculosis and Chest Diseases

**DTD** Diploma in Tuberculous Diseases; Director of Technical Development; document type definition

**dtd** dated

**d.t.d.** [medicine] *detur talis dosis* (Latin: let such a dose be given) (in prescriptions)

**DTDP** ditridecyl phthalate (PVC plasticizer)

**DTE** [computing] data terminal equipment

**DTech** Doctor of Technology

**DTF** Dairy Trade Federation; Domestic Textiles Federation

**Dtg** *Dienstag* (German: Tuesday)

**DTH** [immunology] delayed-type hypersensitivity; Diploma in Tropical Hygiene

**DTh** Doctor of Divinity (or Theology) (from Latin *Doctor Theologiae*)

**DTheol** Doctor of Divinity (or Theology) (from Latin *Doctor Theologiae*)

**DThPT** Diploma in Theory and Practice of Teaching

**DTI** Department of Trade and Industry

**DTIC** [medicine] dacarbazine (used to treat cancer)

**DTL** [electronics] diode-transistor logic; down the line (in shooting)

**DTM** Diploma in Tropical Medicine

**Dtm.** Dortmund

**DTMH** Diploma in Tropical Medicine and Hygiene

**dto** *direito* (Portuguese: right)

**DTOD** Director of Trade and Operations Division

**DTP** [computing] desktop publishing

**DTPA** [medicine] diethylenetriamine-pentaacetic acid (used in diagnosis)

**DTPH** Diploma in Tropical Public Health

**DTR** [photography] diffusion-transfer reversal; Diploma in Therapeutic Radiology; double taxation relief

**DTRP** Diploma in Town and Regional Planning

**DTRT** [meteorology] deteriorating

**DTS** [medicine] dual tracer scintigraphy

**DTs** [informal] delirium tremens

**DTV** digital television

**DTVM** Diploma in Tropical Veterinary Medicine

**DU** [vehicle registration] Coventry; [physics] depleted uranium; died unmarried; Doctor of the University; [medicine] duodenal ulcer

**Du.** Ducal; Duchy; Duke; Dutch

**DUART** [computing, electronics] dual universal asynchronous receiver transmitter

**Dub.** Dublin

**dub.** dubious; *dubitans* (Latin: doubting)

**Dubl.** Dublin

**DUC** [meteorology] dense upper cloud

**DUI** [USA] driving under the influence (of alcohol or drugs)

**Dumf.** Dumfries and Galloway

**Dun.** Dundee

**Dunelm.** *Dunelmensis* (Latin: (Bishop) of Durham)

**DUniv** Doctor of the University

**duo.** [paper size] duodecimo

**DUP** [Northern Ireland] Democratic Unionist Party; *Docteur de l'Université de Paris* (French: Doctor of the University of Paris)

**dup.** duplicate

**Dur.** Durban; Durham

**DUS** Diploma of the University of Southampton

**DUSC** [US air force] deep underground support center

**Dut.** Dutch

**DUV** damaging ultraviolet (radiation)

**DV** defective vision; *Deo volente* (Latin: God willing); Diploma in Venereology;

direct vision; distinguished visitor; district valuer; [Bible] Douay Version; double vision; [vehicle registration] Exeter
**DVA** [medicine] digital video angiography; Diploma in Veterinary Anaesthesia; Dunkirk Veterans' Association
**DV&D** Diploma in Venereology and Dermatology
**DVC** [microbiology] direct viable count
**DVD** [computing] digital versatile disc; digital video disc
**DVD-R** [computing] digital versatile disc recordable
**DVE** Diploma in Vocational Education
**DVH** Diploma in Veterinary Hygiene
**DVI** [computing] digital video imaging; [computing] digital video interactive
**DVLA** Driver and Vehicle Licensing Agency
**DVLC** Driver and Vehicle Licensing Centre (Swansea)
**DVM** digital voltmeter; Doctor of Veterinary Medicine
**d.v.m.** *decessit vita matris* (Latin: died in the lifetime of the mother)
**DVMS** Doctor of Veterinary Medicine and Surgery
**DVO** district veterinary officer
**d.v.p.** *decessit vita patris* (Latin: died in the lifetime of the father)
**DVPH** Diploma in Veterinary Public Health
**DVR** Diploma in Veterinary Radiology; [computing] discrete-variable representation
**DVS** Doctor of Veterinary Surgery
**DVSc** Doctor of Veterinary Science
**DVSci** Doctor of Veterinary Science
**DVT** [medicine] deep-vein thrombosis
**DW** [vehicle registration] Cardiff; [chemistry] deionized water; [commerce] dock warrant
**D/W** [commerce] dock warrant
**d/w** dust wrapper
**d.w.** dead weight; delivered weight
**DWA** driving without awareness
**DWAS** Doctor Who Appreciation Society
**d.w.c.** deadweight capacity
**dwel.** dwelling
**DWEM** [USA] dead white European male
**dwg** drawing; dwelling
**DWI** [USA] driving while intoxicated; Dutch West Indies (former name of Netherlands Antilles)
**DWR** Duke of Wellington's Regiment
**dwr** drawer
**dwt** pennyweight
**d.w.t.** deadweight tonnage
**DWU** [USA] Distillery, Wine and Allied Workers International Union
**DX** [photography] daylight exposure; [vehicle registration] Ipswich; [telecommunications] long-distance
**DXF** data exchange format
**DXR** [medicine] deep X-ray
**DXRT** [medicine] deep X-ray therapy
**DXS** diagnostic X-ray spectrometry
**DY** [international vehicle registration] Benin (from former name Dahomey); [vehicle registration] Brighton; dockyard; [UK postcode] Dudley
**Dy** [chemical element] dysprosium
**dy** delivery; [paper size] demy
**DYB** do your best (Scout motto)
**Dyd** dockyard
**dyn** dyne
**dyn.** dynamic; dynamics; dynamite; dynamo; dynasty
**DYS** Duke of York's Royal Military School
**DZ** [international vehicle registration] Algeria (from Arabic *Djazïr*); [vehicle registration] Antrim; Doctor of Zoology; [meteorology] drizzle; [military] drop zone
**dz.** dozen
**.dz** Algeria (in Internet address)
**DZool** Doctor of Zoology
**D-Zug** *Durchgangszug* (German: express train)

# E

**E** casual workers (occupational group); Earl; [astronomy] earth; [electrical engineering] earth; east; Easter; eastern; [UK postcode] east London; [slang] ecstasy (drug); Edinburgh; efficiency; Egypt; Egyptian; [chemistry] electromeric effect; electronic (as in **E-commerce**); [chemistry] elimination reaction; [astronomy] elliptical galaxy; elocution; [currency] emalangeni (used in Swaziland); eminence; enemy; engineer; engineering; England; English; [numismatics] English shilling; envoy; equator; *España* (Spanish: Spain); EU-recognized food additive (as in **E120** = cochineal); European; evening; evensong; exa- (indicates $10^{18}$, as in **Em** = exametre); [fishing port] Exeter; [music] note of scale; [international vehicle registration] Spain (from Spanish *España*); [logic] universal negative categorical proposition

***E*** [physics] electric field strength; [chemistry] electrode potential; [physics] electromotive force; [physics] energy; [physics] illuminance; [physics] irradiance

**e** [mathematics] base of natural logarithm; electromotive; [physics] electron; electronic (as in **e-text**); [physics] positron; [meteorology] wet air

***e*** [mathematics] eccentricity (of ellipse); [physics] electron charge; [chemistry] equatorial conformation (of molecules); [physics] proton charge

**e.** edition; educated; elder; eldest; electric; electricity; electromotive; engineer; engineering; Erlang (unit of traffic intensity in telephony); [baseball] error; evening; excellence; excellent

**EA** [vehicle registration] Dudley; early antigen; East Anglia; economic adviser; educational age; effective action; effective agent (as in **EA content**); electrical artificer; *Ente Autonomo* (Italian: Autonomous Corporation); [Freemasonry] Entered Apprentice; enterprise allowance; environmental assessment; Evangelical Alliance; experimental area; exposure age

**E/A** enemy aircraft; experimental aircraft

**ea.** each

**EAA** Edinburgh Architectural Association; Electrical Appliance Association; [USA] Engineer in Aeronautics and Astronautics; [chemistry] eth(yl)ene acrylic acid

**EAAA** European Association of Advertising Agencies

**EAAC** European Agricultural Aviation Centre

**EAAFRO** East African Agriculture and Forestry Research Organization

**EAAP** European Association for Animal Production

**EAB** [medicine] extra-anatomic bypass

**EAC** East African Community; Educational Advisory Committee; Engineering Advisory Council; European Atomic Commission

**EACA** East Africa Court of Appeal; [medicine] epsilon aminocaproic acid

**EACC** East Asia Christian Conference

**EACSO** East African Common Services Organization

**ead.** *eadem* (Latin: the same (woman))

**eaed.** *eaedem* (Latin: the same (women))

**EAEG** European Association of Exploration Geophysicists

**EAES** European Atomic Energy Society

**EAF** electric-arc furnace

**e.a.f.** emergency action file

**EAFFRO** East African Freshwater Fisheries Research Organization

**EAG** Economists Advisory Group

**EAGGF** European Agricultural Guidance and Guarantee Fund (in EU)

**EAHF** [medicine] eczema, asthma, hay fever

**EAK** [international vehicle registration] (East Africa) Kenya

**EAM** *Ethniko Apelentherotiko Metopo* (Greek: National Liberation Front) (in World War II)

**EAMF** European Association of Music Festivals

**EAMFRO** East African Marine Fisheries Research Organization

**EAMTC** European Association of Management Training Centres
**EAN** [chemistry] effective atomic number; [computing] European Academic Network; European Article Number (computer coding for retail goods)
**e&e** each and every
**E&O** errors and omissions
**E&OE** errors and omissions excepted
**e.a.o.n.** except as otherwise noted
**EAP** East Africa Protectorate; Edgar Allan Poe (US writer); [USA] employee-assistance program; English for academic purposes
**EAPC** Euro-Atlantic Partnership Council (in NATO, replacement for NACC)
**EAPR** European Association for Potato Research
**EAPROM** [computing] electrically alterable programmable read-only memory
**EAR** employee advisory resource; employee attitude research; [engineering] energy-absorbing resin
**EARCCUS** East African Regional Committee for Conservation and Utilization of Soil
**EARN** [computing] European Academic and Research Network
**EAROM** [computing] electrically alterable read-only memory
**EAROPH** East Asia Regional Organization for Planning and Housing
**EAS** electronic article surveillance; [medicine] endotoxin-activated serum; [aeronautics] equivalent air speed; [aeronautics] estimated air speed
**EASA** Entertainment Arts Socialist Association
**EASEP** [astronautics] Early Apollo Scientific Experiments Package
**EASHP** European Association of Senior Hospital Physicians
**east.** eastern
**EASTROPAC** Eastern Tropical Pacific
**EAT** earliest arrival time; [medicine] Ehrlich ascites tumour; Employment Appeals Tribunal; estimated arrival time; [medicine] experimental autoimmune thyroiditis; [international vehicle registration] (East Africa) Tanzania
**EATRO** East African Trypanosomiasis Research Organization
**EAU** [international vehicle registration] (East Africa) Uganda
**EAVRO** East African Veterinary Research Organization
**EAW** Electrical Association for Women; equivalent average words
**EAX** [telecommunications] electronic automatic exchange
**EAZ** [international vehicle registration] (East Africa) Tanzania (formerly Zanzibar)
**EB** electricity board; electron beam; electronic book; *Encyclopaedia Britannica*; [medicine] epidermolysis bullosa (skin disease); Epstein–Barr (virus); [currency] Ethiopian birr; Evans blue (dye); [vehicle registration] Peterborough
**Eb** [computing] exabyte
**e-b** estate-bottled
**EBA** English Bowling Association
**EB&RA** Engineer Buyers' and Representatives' Association
**e.b.a.r.** edited beyond all recognition
**EBC** English Benedictine Congregation; European Billiards Confederation; European Brewery Convention
**EBCDIC** [computing] extended binary-coded decimal-interchange code
**e-beam** electron beam
**EBICON** [physics] electron-bombardment-induced conductivity
**EBIT** [accounting] earnings before interest and tax
**EBL** electron-beam lithography; European Bridge League
**EBM** electron-beam machining; [medicine] expressed breast milk
**EBMC** English Butter Marketing Company
**EbN** east by north
**EBNF** [computing] extended Backus normal form
**Ebor.** *Eboracensis* (Latin: (Archbishop) of York); *Eboracum* (Latin: York)
**EBR** electron-beam recording; [nuclear technology] experimental breeder reactor
**EBRA** Engineer Buyers' and Representatives' Association
**EBRD** European Bank for Reconstruction and Development
**EBS** emergency bed service; emergency

broadcast system; engineered barrier system; English Bookplate Society
**EbS** east by south
**EBT** [medicine] electron-beam therapy
**EBU** English Bridge Union; European Badminton Union; European Boxing Union; European Broadcasting Union
**EBV** [medicine] Epstein–Barr virus
**EBWR** [nuclear technology] experimental boiling-water reactor
**EC** East Caribbean; [UK postcode] east central London; east coast; Eastern Command; Ecclesiastical Commissioner; [international vehicle registration] Ecuador; [physics] eddy current; educational committee; education committee; [chemistry] effective concentration; electricity council; electrolytic corrosion; electronic computer; emergency commission; [medicine] endothelial cell; Engineering Corps; [biochemistry] Enzyme Commission (in enzyme code number); Episcopal Church; Established Church; [chemistry] eth(yl)ene carbonate; [Canada] *Étoile du Courage* (French: Star of Courage); European Commission; European Community; executive committee; [vehicle registration] Preston; [civil aircraft marking] Spain
**Ec.** Ecuador
**.ec** Ecuador (in Internet address)
**ec.** earth closet; enamel-coated; enamel-covered; error correction; *exempli causa* (Latin: for example); extended coverage; extension course
**ECA** Early Closing Association; Economic Commission for Africa; [USA] Economic Cooperation Administration; Educational Centres Association; Electrical Contractors' Association; European Congress of Accountants
**ECAC** Engineering College Administrative Council; European Civil Aviation Conference
**ECAFE** Economic Commission for Asia and the Far East (former name of ESCAP)
**ECAS** Electrical Contractors' Association of Scotland
**ECAT** [medicine] emission compute(rize)d axial tomography
**ECB** electronic codebook; electronic components board; European Central Bank
**ECBS** engineering of computer-based systems
**ECC** [electrical engineering] earth continuity conductor; [physics] emergency core cooling (or coolant); energy-conscious construction; [computing] error-correction code; European Cultural Centre
**Ecc.** *Eccellenze* (Italian: Excellency)
**ecc.** *eccetera* (Italian: et cetera, etc.)
**Ecc. Hom.** *Ecce Homo* (Latin: behold the man)
**ECCI** European Confederation for Commerce and Industry plc
**Eccl.** [Bible] Ecclesiastes
**eccl.** ecclesiastic(al)
**Eccles.** [Bible] Ecclesiastes
**eccles.** ecclesiastic(al)
**Ecclus.** [Bible] Ecclesiasticus (book of Apocrypha)
**ECCM** [military] electronic counter-countermeasure(s)
**ECCP** European Committee on Crime Problems
**ECCS** [physics] emergency core cooling system
**ECCU** English Cross-Country Union
**ECD** early closing day; [electronics] electrostatic charge decay; [computing] enhanced colour display; estimated completion date
**ECE** Economic Commission for Europe
**ECF** [US medicine] extended-care facility; extracellular fluid
**ECFA** European Committee for Future Accelerators
**ECFMG** Educational Council for Foreign Medical Graduates
**ECFMS** Educational Council for Foreign Medical Students
**ECG** [medicine] electrocardiogram; [medicine] electrocardiograph; Export Credit Guarantee
**ECGB** East Coast of Great Britain
**ECGC** Empire Cotton Growing Corporation
**ECGD** Export Credits Guarantee Department
**ech.** echelon
**ECHP** [USA] Environmental Compliance and Health Protection

**ECHR** European Commission on Human Rights; European Court of Human Rights
**ECI** East Coast of Ireland; energy-cost indicator
**ECIA** European Committee of Interior Architects
**ECITO** European Central Inland Transport Organization
**ECJ** European Court of Justice
**ECL** [physics] emergency cooling limit; [electronics] emitter-coupled logic
**ECLAC** Economic Commission for Latin America and the Caribbean
**eclec.** eclectic; eclecticism
**ecli.** eclipse; ecliptic
**ECLO** [electronics] emitter-coupled logic operator
**ECLOF** Ecumenical Church Loan Fund
**ECLSS** environmental control and life-support system
**ECM** electric coding machine; electrochemical machining; [military] electronic countermeasure(s); energy conservation measure; environmental corrosion monitor; extended core memory
**ECMA** [geology] East Coast Magnetic Anomaly; European Computer Manufacturers' Association
**ECME** Economic Commission for the Middle East
**ECMF** Electric Cable Makers' Federation
**ECMO** [medicine] extracorporeal membrane oxygenation
**ECMRA** European Chemical Market Research Association
**ECMT** European Conference of Ministers of Transport
**ECMWF** European Centre for Medium-range Weather Forecast
**ECN** epoxy–cresol–novolak (synthetic resin)
**ECNSW** Electricity Commission of New South Wales
**ECO** energy conservation opportunity; English Chamber Orchestra; European Coal Organization
**eco.** ecological; ecology
**ECODU** European Control Data Users
**ECoG** [medicine] electrocochleography; electrocorticogram
**ecol.** ecological; ecology
**E coli** *Escherichia coli* (Latin: name of bacterium)
**Ecol. Soc. Am.** Ecological Society of America
**ECOM** electronic computer-originated mail
**ECOMOG** ECOWAS Monitoring Group (peacekeeping force)
**econ.** economic(al); economics; economist; economy
***Econ. J*** *Economic Journal*
***Econ. R*** *Economic Review*
**ECOR** [USA] Engineering Committee on Ocean Resources
**ECOSOC** Economic and Social Council (of UN)
**ECOVAST** European Council for the Village and Small Town
**ECOWAS** Economic Community of West African States
**ECP** [finance] Euro-commercial paper; European Committee on Crop Protection; *Evangelii Christi Praedicator* (Latin: Preacher of the Gospel of Christ)
**ECPA** Electric Consumers Protection Act
**ECPD** [USA] Engineers' Council for Professional Development
**ECPS** European Centre for Population Studies
**ECQAC** Electronic Components Quality Assurance Committee
**ECR** electronic cash register
**ECS** emergency cooling (or coolant) system; environmental control system; European Communications Satellite; European Components Service
**ECSC** European Coal and Steel Community (predecessor of EU)
**ECST** European Convention on the Suppression of Terrorism
**ECT** [medicine] electroconvulsive therapy; [medicine] emission-compute(rize)d tomography
**ECTA** Electrical Contractors' Trading Association
**ECTD** [USA] Emission Control Technology Division
**ECTF** Enterprise Computer Telephony Forum
**ECU** English Church Union; environmental control unit; European Chiropractic Union; European Currency Unit;

European Customs Union; [photography] extreme close-up
**ecu** European Currency Unit
**Ecua.** Ecuador; Ecuadorian
**ECUK** East Coast of the United Kingdom
**ECUSA** Episcopal Church of the United States of America
**ECV** [obstetrics] external cephalic version
**ECWA** Economic Commission for Western Asia
**ECWEC** European Community Wind Energy Conference and Exhibition
**ECWS** English Civil War Society
**ECY** European Conservation Year
**ECYO** European Community Youth Orchestra
**ED** [USA] Doctor of Engineering; economic dispatch; Education Department; [pharmacology] effective dose; Efficiency Decoration; election district; [physics] electromagnetic dissociation; [electronics] electron device; [physics, chemistry] electron diffraction; [medicine] embryonic day; Employment Department; [medicine] end-diastole; [medicine] end-diastolic; entertainments duty; equilibrium dialysis; equivalent dose (of radiation); European Democrat; evening dinner (in accommodation advertisement); [finance] ex dividend; existence doubtful; experimental detector; [medicine] extensive disease; [finance] extra dividend; [vehicle registration] Liverpool
**Ed.** Edinburgh; Editor
**ed.** *edile* (Italian: building); *edilizia* (Italian: building); edited; edition; editor; educated; education
**éd.** *édition* (French: edition)
**e.d.** edge distance; enemy dead; error detecting; excused duty; extra duty
**EDA** [USA] Economic Development Administration; Electrical Development Association; electronic design automation; *Eniea Dimokratiki Aristera* (Greek: Union of the Democratic Left) (political party)
**e.d.a.** early departure authorized
**ED&S** *English Dance and Song* (publication of EFDSS)
**EDAS** [computing] enhanced data-acquisition system
**EDB** ethene dibromide (fuel additive)
**EdB** Bachelor of Education
**EDBS** [computing] expert database system
**EDC** Economic Development Committee; Engineering Design Centre; [computing] error-detection code; ethylene dichloride; European Defence Community; [obstetrics] expected date of confinement
**e.d.c.** error detection and correction; extra dark colour
**EDD** *English Dialect Dictionary*; exactly delayed detonator; [obstetrics] expected date of delivery
**EdD** Doctor of Education
**edd.** *ediderunt* (Latin: published by); *editiones* (Latin: editions)
**EDE** effective dose equivalent (of radiation)
**EDF** *Électricité de France* (French electricity corporation); [USA] Environmental Defense Fund; European Development Fund
**EDG** emergency diesel generator; European Democratic Group
**EDHE** experimental data handling equipment
**EDI** [computing] electronic data interchange
**Edin.** Edinburgh
**Ed. in Ch.** Editor in Chief
**EDIP** European Defence Improvement Programme (in NATO)
**EDIS** Engineering Data Information System
**edit.** edited; edition; editor; *editore* (Italian: publisher); editorial
**EDL** economic discard limits; [chemistry] electrical double layer; electrodeless discharge lamp
**e.d.l.** edition de luxe
**EDM** [chemistry] electrical-discharge machining; electric dipole moment; [surveying] electronic distance measurement; [physics] energy-density model
**EdM** Master of Education
**EDMA** European Direct Marketing Association
**Edm. & Ips.** (Bishop of) St Edmundsbury and Ipswich
**Edmn** Edmonton
**edn** edition
**Ednbgh** Edinburgh

**EDNS** expected demand not supplied
**EDO** [computing] extended data out
**e.d.o.c.** effective date of change
**EDO DRAM** [computing] extended data out dynamic random-access memory
**EDP** [physics] electron-diffraction pattern; [computing] electronic data processing; emergency defence plan; [medicine] end-diastolic pressure
**EDPS** [computing] electronic data-processing system
**EDPT** [computing] enhanced-drive parameter table
**EDR** electronic decoy rocket; Electronic Dictionary Research; European Depository Receipts; except during rain (following pollen count)
**EDRF** [medicine] endothelium-derived relaxing factor
**EDRP** European Demonstration Reprocessing Plant (for nuclear fuel)
**EDS** electrically adjusted driver's seat (in car advertisement); Electronic Data Systems Corporation; English Dialect Society; [computing] exchangeable disk store
**EdS** Education Specialist
**EDSAC** [computing] Electronic Delay Storage Automatic Calculator
**EDSAT** Educational Television Satellite
**EDSP** Exchange Delivery Settlement Price
**EDSS** expert decision-support system
**ED/st** electrically adjusted driver's seat (in car advertisement)
**EDT** [USA, Canada] Eastern Daylight Time; energy design technique
**EDTA** European Dialysis and Transplant Association
**EDU** European Democratic Union
**.edu** US educational institution (in Internet address)
**educ.** educated; education; educational
**educn** education
**EDV** [medicine] end-diastolic volume
**EDVAC** Electronic Discrete Variable Automatic Computer
**Edw.** Edward
**EE** Early English; Eastern Electricity; edge-to-edge; electrical engineer; electrical engineering; electron emission; electronic engineer; electronic engineering; employment exchange; environmental education; environmental engineering; Envoy Extraordinary; errors excepted; explosive emission; expressed emotion; [vehicle registration] Lincoln
**e.e.** errors excepted; eye and ear
**.ee** Estonia (in Internet address)
**EEA** Electronic Engineering Association; European Economic Area
**EEAIE** Electrical, Electronic and Allied Industries, Europe
**EE&MP** Envoy Extraordinary and Minister Plenipotentiary
**EEB** European Environmental Bureau
**EEC** [physics] energy–energy correlation; English Electric Company; European Economic Community (predecessor of EU); [electronics] explosive-emission cathode
**EECA** European Electronic Component Manufacturers' Association
**EECS** electrical-energy conversion system
**EED** effective equivalent dose (of radiation); electro-explosive device
**EEDC** Economic Development Committee for the Electronics Industry
**EEF** Egyptian Expeditionary Force; Engineering Employers' Federation; equivalent-energy function
**EEG** [medicine] electroencephalogram; [medicine] electroencephalograph; Essence Export Group
**EEI** [USA] Edison Electric Institute; [USA] Environmental Equipment Institute
**EEIBA** Electrical and Electronic Industries Benevolent Association
**EEMJEB** Electrical and Electronic Manufacturers' Joint Education Board
**EEMS** [computing] enhanced expanded memory specification
**EEMUA** Engineering Equipment and Materials Users Association
**E Eng.** Early English
**EENT** [medicine] eye, ear, nose and throat
**EEO** Energy Efficiency Office; equal employment opportunity
**EEOC** [USA] Equal Employment Opportunities Commission
**EEPLD** [computing] electrically erasable programmable logic device
**EEPROM** [computing] electrically erasable programmable read-only memory
**EER** energy–efficiency ratio
**EERI** [USA] Earthquake Engineering Research Institute

**EEROM** [computing] electrically erasable read-only memory
**EES** European Exchange System
**EET** Eastern European Time
**EETPU** Electrical, Electronic, Telecommunications and Plumbing Union (became part of AEEU)
**EETS** Early English Text Society
**EEZ** exclusive economic zone
**EF** edge-to-face; educational foundation; education foundation; [genetics] elongation factor; emergency fleet; [physics] enrichment factor; expectant father; expeditionary force; experimental flight; extra fine; [vehicle registration] Middlesbrough
**EFA** engine fault analysis; [biochemistry] essential fatty acid; Eton Fives Association; European Fighter Aircraft
**EFB** energy from biomass
**EFC** European Federation of Corrosion; European Forestry Commission
**EFCE** European Federation of Chemical Engineering
**EFCT** European Federation of Conference Towns
**EFD** [engineering] early fault detection
**EFDSS** English Folk Dance and Song Society
**EFF** Electronic Frontier Foundation; European Furniture Federation
**eff.** *effetto* (Italian: bill, promissory note); efficiency; effigy
**EFG** electric-field gradient
**EFGF** [electronics] epitaxial ferrite-garnet film
**EFI** electronic fuel injection
**EFIS** [aeronautics] electronic flight-information system
**EFL** English as a foreign language; external financial limit
**EFM** [medicine] electronic fetal monitor; European Federalist Movement
**EFNS** Educational Foundation for Nuclear Science
**EFP** [mathematics] Einstein–Fokker–Planck (differential equation); [photography] electronic field production; [commerce] exchange of futures for physicals; explosively formed penetrator; explosively formed projectile
**EFPD** effective full-power day
**EFPH** effective full-power hour
**EFPW** European Federation for the Protection of Waters
**EFPY** effective full-power year
**EFR** [astronomy] emerging flux region; [telecommunications] Enhanced Full Rate (for voice quality on mobile phone); [nuclear technology] European Fast Reactor; [nuclear technology] experimental fast reactor
**EFRC** [USA] Edwards Flight Research Center
**EFSA** European Federation of Sea Anglers
**EFSC** European Federation of Soroptimist Clubs
**EFT** electronic funds transfer
**EFTA** European Free Trade Association
**EFTC** Electrical Fair Trading Council
**EFTPOS** electronic funds transfer at point of sale
**EFTS** electronic funds transfer system; elementary flying training school
**EFTU** Engineering and Fastener Trade Union
**EFU** energetic feed unit; European Football Union
**EFVA** Educational Foundation for Visual Aids
**EFW** electric front windows (in car advertisement); energy from waste
**EG** Engineers Guild; equivalent grade; [chemistry] ethylene glycol; [vehicle registration] Peterborough
**Eg.** Egypt; Egyptian; Egyptologist; Egyptology
**.eg** Egypt (in Internet address)
**e.g.** *ejusdem generis* (Latin: of a like kind); *exempli gratia* (Latin: for example)
**EGA** Elizabeth Garrett Anderson (women's hospital); [computing] enhanced graphics adapter; European Golf Association
**EGARD** environmental gamma-ray and radon detector
**EGAS** Educational Grants Advisory Service
**EGCI** Export Group for the Construction Industries
**EGCS** English Guernsey Cattle Society
**EGD** epithermal gold deposit
**EGEAS** Electric Generating Expansion Analysis System
**EGF** [medicine] epidermal growth factor

**EGFR** [medicine] epidermal growth factor receptor
**EGIFO** Edward Grey Institute of Field Ornithology (Oxford)
**EGL** Engineers Guild Limited
**EGM** Empire Gallantry Medal (replaced by GC); European Glass Container Manufacturers' Committee; extraordinary general meeting
**EGmbH** [commerce] *Eingetragene Gesellschaft mit beschränkter Haftung* (German: registered limited company)
**EGO** eccentric (orbit) geophysical observatory
**EGR** [finance] earned growth rate; exhaust gas recirculation (as in **EGR valve**)
**EGSP** electronics glossary and symbol panel
**EGT** [physics] Einstein-invariant gauge theory (of gravitation)
**e.g.t.** exhaust gas temperature
**EGU** English Golf Union; [chemistry] external gelation of uranium
**EGYPT** eager to grab your pretty tits (on envelope of love letter)
**Egypt.** Egyptian
**Egyptol.** Egyptologist; Egyptology
**EH** [UK postcode] Edinburgh; [music] English horn (= cor anglais); [medicine] essential hypertension; [vehicle registration] Stoke-on-Trent
**eh.** *ehrenhalber* (German: honorary)
**EHC** effective heat capacity (of building); European Hotel Corporation; [medicine] external heart compression
**EHF** European Hockey Federation; experimental husbandry farm; [radio] extremely high frequency
**EHG** electro-hydraulic governor
**EHL** [physics] effective half-life
**EHO** environmental health officer
**EHP** electric and hybrid propulsion
**ehp** effective horsepower; electric horsepower
**EHR** Environmental Hazard Ranking; [USA] Environmental Health Services; European hybrid spectrometer; extra-high strength
**EHT** [electronics] extra-high tension
**EHV** electric and hybrid vehicle; extra-high voltage
**EHWS** extreme high water springs (level of tide)
**EI** earth (atmosphere) interface; East Indian; East Indies; electrical insulation; electromagnetic interaction; electron impact; electron ionization; [finance] endorsement irregular; energy intake; environmentally induced illness; [photography] exposure index; external irradiation; [civil aircraft marking] (Republic of) Ireland
**EIA** East Indian Association; economic impact assessment; [USA] Electrical Industries Association; [USA] Electronic Industries Association; Engineering Industries Association; environmental impact analysis; environmental impact assessment; Environmental Investigation Agency; [medicine] enzyme immunoassay; [medicine] exercise-induced asthma
**EIB** European Investment Bank; Export–Import Bank
**EIC** East India Company; Electrical Industries' Club; Engineering Institute of Canada
**EICM** employer's inventory of critical manpower
**EICS** East India Company's Service
**EID** East India Dock; [military] Electrical Inspection Directorate
**EIDCT** Educational Institute of Design, Craft and Technology
**E-IDE** enhanced integrated-drive electronics
**EIEE** [medicine] early infantile epileptic encephalopathy
**EIEMA** Electrical Installation Equipment Manufacturers' Association
**EIF** Elderly Invalids Fund
**EIFAC** European Inland Fisheries Advisory Committee
**EIIR** *Elizabetha Secunda Regina* (Latin: Queen Elizabeth the Second)
**E-in-C** Engineer-in-Chief
**E Ind.** East Indies
**einschl.** *einschliesslich* (German: including, inclusive)
**Einw.** *Einwohner* (German: inhabitant)
**EIO** extended interaction oscillator
**EIPC** European Institute of Printed Circuits
**EIR** [taxation] earned income relief; [computing] error-indicating recording

**EIRMA** European Industrial Research Management Association
**EIS** economic information system; Educational Institute of Scotland; effluent information system; energy information system; Enterprise Investment Scheme (replacement for BES); environmental impact statement; epidemic intelligence service
**EISA** [computing] enhanced industry standard architecture; [computing] extended industry standard architecture
**EITB** Engineering Industry Training Board
**EITF** [USA] Emerging Issues Task Force
**EIU** Economist Intelligence Unit
**EIVT** European Institute for Vocational Training
**EJ** elbow jerk; exajoule; [vehicle registration] Haverfordwest; [civil aircraft marking] (Republic of) Ireland
**ej.** *ejemplo* (Spanish: example)
**EJC** [USA] Engineers' Joint Council
**EJMA** English Joinery Manufacturers' Association
**ejusd.** *ejusdem* (Latin: of the same)
**EK** [civil aircraft marking] Armenia; East Kilbride; *Enosis Kentron* (Greek: Centre Union) (political party); [vehicle registration] Liverpool
**eK** *etter Kristi* (Norwegian: after Christ, AD)
**Ekco** E. K. Cole (manufacturer of electrical goods)
**EKD** *Evangelische Kirche in Deutschland* (German: Protestant Church in Germany)
**EKG** [USA] electrocardiogram; [USA] electrocardiograph; *Elektrokardiogramme* (German: electrocardiogram)
**EL** [vehicle registration] Bournemouth; [music] easy listening; electrical laboratory; electroluminescent; electronics laboratory; Engineer Lieutenant; epitaxial layer; Everyman's Library; explosive limit; [medicine] extracorporeal lithotripsy; [civil aircraft marking] Liberia
**el.** elect; elected; electric(al); electricity; element; elevated; elevated railway; elevation; elongation
**ELA** electronic learning aid; Eritrean Liberation Army
**ELAS** *Ethnikos Laikos Apeleutherotikos Stratos* (Greek: Hellenic People's Army of Liberation) (in World War II)
**elas.** elasticity
**ELB** Bachelor of English Literature
**ELBS** English Language Book Society
**ELC** Early Learning Centre (chain of educational toyshops); Environment Liaison Centre (Nairobi)
**ELD** economic load distribution
**eld.** elder; eldest
**ELDC** economic load dispatching centre; equivalent load duration curve
**ELDO** [astronautics] European Launcher Development Organization (became part of ESA)
**ELEC** European League for Economic Cooperation
**elec.** election; elector; electoral; electric(al); electrician; electricity; electron; electronic; [medicine] electuary
**elect.** election; elector; electoral; electric(al); electrician; electricity; electron; electronic; [medicine] electuary
**electr.** electrical; electrically
**Electra** Electrical, Electronics and Communications Trades Association
**electron.** electronic; electronically; electronics
**elem.** element(s); elementary
**elev.** elevation; elevator
**ELF** Eritrean Liberation Front; European Landworkers' Federation; [radio] extra-low frequency; [radio] extremely low frequency
**e.l.f.** early lunar flare
**ELG** [astronomy] emission-line galaxy
**ELH** [biochemistry] egg-laying hormone
**ELI** [sports] electronic line indicator
**Eli.** Elias; Elijah
**Elien.** *Eliensis* (Latin: (Bishop) of Ely)
**Elint** [military] electronic intelligence
**ELISA** [medicine] enzyme-linked immunosorbent assay
**elix.** [medicine] elixir
**Eliz.** Elizabethan
**ELLA** European Long Lines Agency
**ellipt.** elliptical
**ELMA** electromechanical aid
**Elmint** [military] electromagnetic intelligence
**elo.** elocution; eloquence
**ELOISE** European Large Orbiting Instrumentation for Solar Experiments
**E Long.** east longitude
**elong.** elongate; elongated; elongation

**ELP** equivalent local potential
**ELR** [meteorology] environment lapse rate; exceptional leave to remain (for asylum-seekers); export licensing regulations
**ELS** Electronic Lodgement Service
**elsewh.** elsewhere
**ELSIE** electronic speech information equipment
**ELSS** emergency life support system
**ELT** English language teaching (for foreign learners); European letter telegram
**ELU** English Lacrosse Union
**ELV** expendable launch vehicle; extra-low voltage
**ELWS** extreme low water springs (level of tide)
**ely** easterly
**EM** Earl Marshal; Edward Medal; [physics] effective mass; Efficiency Medal; electrical and mechanical; electromagnetic; electromotive; electronic mail; electron microscope (or microscopy); emission measure; engineering model; Engineer of Mines; [genetics] enhanced mutagenesis; enlisted man; environmental modelling; equipment module; European Movement; evaluation model; evening meal (in accommodation advertisement); expectation maximization; [vehicle registration] Liverpool; Master of the Horse (from Latin *Equitum Magister*)
**Em.** Eminence
**em.** emanation; embargo; eminent
**e.m.** electromagnetic; emergency maintenance; expanded metal; external memorandum
**EMA** effective medium approximation; [immunology] epithelial membrane antigen; European Marketing Association; European Monetary Agreement; Evangelical Missionary Alliance
**EMAD** engine maintenance and disassembly
**e-mail** electronic mail
**EMAS** [computing] Edinburgh multiaccess system; Employment Medical Advisory Service
**EMB** [USA] Energy Mobilization Board
**Emb.** Embankment (London); Embassy
**emb.** embargo; embossed
**EMBL** European Molecular Biology Laboratory
**EMBO** European Molecular Biology Organization
**embr.** embroider; embroidery
**embryol.** embryological; embryology
**EMC** [USA] Einstein Medical Center; [computing] electromagnetic compatibility; Energy Management Centre; Energy Management Company; [USA] Engineering Manpower Commission; environmental monitoring and compliance
**EMCB** earth-mounded concrete bunker
**EMCC** European Municipal Credit Community
**EMCCC** European Military Communications Coordinating Committee
**EMCOF** European Monetary Cooperation Fund
**EMCS** energy monitoring and control system
**EME** East Midlands Electricity
**Emer.** Emeritus
**emer.** emergency
**EMet** Engineer of Metallurgy
**EMEU** East Midlands Educational Union
**EMF** electromagnetic force; electromotive force; European Metalworkers' Federation; European Motel Federation
**emf** electromotive force
**EMFI** [USA] Energy and Mineral Field Institute
**EMG** [medicine] electromyogram; [medicine] electromyograph
**EMI** [USA] Earth Mechanics Institute; Electric and Musical Industries (Limited) (recording company); [computing] electromagnetic interference; European Monetary Institute
**EMIC** emergency maternity and infant care
**EMK** *elektromotorische Kraft* (German: electromotive force)
**EML** Environmental Measurement(s) Laboratory; Everyman's Library
**EMLA** [medicine] eutectic mixture of local anaesthetics (as in **EMLA cream**)
**E Mn E** Early Modern English
**EMNRD** Energy, Minerals and Natural Resources Department
**e.m.o.s.** earth's mean orbital speed
**EMP** ecological monitoring programme; electromagnetic pulse; electronic

materials programme; environmental management (or monitoring) plan; environmental monitoring programme
**Emp.** Emperor; Empire; Empress
**emp.** [medicine] *emplastrum* (Latin: plaster); employed; employer; employment
**emp. agcy** employment agency
**empld** employed
**EMR** Eastern Mediterranean Region; electromagnetic radiation
**EMRIC** [USA] Educational Media Research Information Center
**EMRS** East Malling Research Station
**EMS** emergency management system; emergency medical service; energy management system; European Monetary System; [computing] expanded memory specification; [computing] expanded memory support
**EMSA** Electron Microscopy Society of America
**EMSC** [USA] Electrical Manufacturers' Standards Council
**EMT** [physics] effective-mass theory; emergency medical technician
**EMTA** Electro-Medical Trade Association
**EMU** electrical multiple unit; electromagnetic unit; European monetary union (in EU); [astronautics] extravehicular mobility unit
**emu** electromagnetic unit
**EMV** [accounting] expected monetary value
**EMW** energy from municipal waste
**EN** [meteorology] El Niño; *Emissora Nacional* (Portuguese: national broadcasting); [UK postcode] Enfield; English Nature (replacement for NCC); Enrolled Nurse; *Estrada Nacional* (Portuguese: national highway); Euro Norm (European standard); exceptions noted; extrapolation number; [vehicle registration] Manchester
**En.** Engineer; English
**en.** enemy
**ENA** Eastern News Agency (Bangladesh); Eastern North America; *École nationale d'administration* (French: national school of administration) (college for top civil servants); English Newspaper Association
**ENAB** Evening Newspaper Advertising Bureau
**enam.** enamel; enamelled
**ENB** English National Ballet; English National Board for Nursing, Midwifery and Health Visiting
**ENC** equivalent noise charge
**enc.** enclosed; enclosure
**ENCA** European Naval Communications Agency
***Enc. Brit.*** *Encyclopaedia Britannica*
**encl.** enclosed; enclosure
**ency.** encyclopedia; encyclopedic; encyclopedism; encyclopedist
**encyc.** encyclopedia; encyclopedic
**encycl.** encyclopedia; encyclopedic
**END** European Nuclear Disarmament
**ENDO** Ethiopian National Democratic Organization
**endow.** endowment
**endp.** endpaper
**ENDS** Euratom Nuclear Documentation System
**ENE** east-northeast
**ENEA** European Nuclear Energy Agency
**ENF** European Nuclear Force
**ENG** [television] electronic news gathering; Enrolled Nurse (General) (formerly SEN)
**Eng.** England; English
**eng.** engine; engineer; engineering; engraved; engraver; engraving
**EngD** Doctor of Engineering
**engg** engineering
**Eng. hn** [music] English horn (= cor anglais)
**engin.** engineer; engineering
**Engl.** England; English
**engr** engineer; engraver
**engr.** engrave; engraved; engraving
**EngScD** Doctor of Engineering Science
**EngTech** Engineering Technician
**ENIAC** Electronic Numerical Integrator and Calculator (first electronic calculator)
**ENIT** *Ente Nazionale Industrie Turistiche* (Italian: National Tourist Authority)
**enl.** enlarge; enlarged; enlargement; enlisted
**ENM** Enrolled Nurse (Mental)
**ENMH** Enrolled Nurse (Mental Handicap)
**ENO** English National Opera
**eno** *enero* (Spanish: January)

**ENP** electronic number plate
**ENR** Energy and Natural Resources
**ENS** empty nest syndrome; European Nuclear Society
**Ens.** [music] Ensemble; Ensign
**ens.** [music] ensemble; en suite (in property or accommodation advertisement)
**ENSA** Entertainments National Service Association (in World War II)
**ENSDF** Evaluated Nuclear Structure Data File
**ENSO** [meteorology] El Niño southern oscillation
**ENT** [medicine] ear, nose and throat
**Ent.** [theatre] enter (stage direction)
**ent.** entertainment; entomological; entomology; entrance
**entom.** entomological; entomology
**entomol.** entomological; entomology
**Ent. Sta. Hall** entered at Stationers' Hall (registration of copyright pre-1924)
**E-number** code number of EU-recognized food additive
**Env.** Envoy
**env.** envelope; environment; environmental; environs
**Env. Ext.** Envoy Extraordinary
**EO** Eastern Orthodox (Church); education officer; [physics] electro-optic(al); emergency operation; employers' organization; Engineer Officer; entertainments officer; equal opportunities; executive officer; executive order; experimental officer; [vehicle registration] Preston
**e.o.** *ex officio* (Latin: by right of office)
**EOA** [USA] Essential Oil Association; examination, opinion and advice
**EOARDC** [USA] European Office of the Air Research and Development Command
**EOB** [computing] end of block; executive office building
**EOC** electron-optical camera; [USA] Emergency Operating Center; [USA] Emergency Operations Center; [physics] end of charge; end of cycle; Equal Opportunities Commission
**Eoc** [geology] Eocene
**EOD** [computing] end of data; [military] explosive ordnance demolition; [military] explosive ordnance disposal
**e.o.d.** entry on duty; every other day
**EOE** enemy-occupied Europe; equal opportunity employer; errors and omissions excepted; European Options Exchange
**EOF** [USA] Emergency Operating Facility; [USA] Emergency Operations Facility; [computing] end of file
**EOG** [medicine] electrooculogram
**e.o.h.p.** except otherwise herein provided
**EOJ** [computing] end of job
**Eoka** *Ethniki Organosis Kypriakou Agonos* (Greek: National Organization of the Cypriot Struggle)
**EOL** end of life
**EOLM** electro-optical light modulator
**EOM** Egyptian Order of Merit; [computing] end of message (on Internet); extractable organic material; extractable organic matter
**e.o.m.** [commerce] end of the month; every other month
**EONR** European Organization for Nuclear Research
**e.o.o.e.** [commerce] *erreur ou omission exceptée* (French: errors and omissions excepted)
**EOP** [microbiology] efficiency of plating; emergency operating procedure
**EOPH** Examined Officer of Public Health
**EOQ** [accounting] economic order quantity
**EOQC** European Organization for Quality Control
**EOQL** end of qualified life
**EOR** [astronautics] earth-orbit rendezvous; [computing] end of record; enhanced oil recovery
**EORI** [USA] Economic Opportunity Research Institute
**EORTC** European Organization for Research into the Treatment of Cancer
**EOS** [physics] equation of state; [computing] erasable optical storage; European Orthodontic Society
**EOT** [computing] end of tape; end of terrace (in property advertisement); [computing] end of transmission
**e.o.t.** enemy-occupied territory
**EOTP** European Organization for Trade Promotion
**EP** early picture; educational psychologist; [electronics] electrically conducting polymer; electroplate; electroplated; electrostatic precipitator; end point; environmental protection; [navigation]

estimated position; European Parliament; expanded polystyrene; extended-play (record); extraction procedure; Extraordinary and Plenipotentiary; [civil aircraft marking] Iran; [vehicle registration] Swansea

**Ep.** *Episcopus* (Latin: Bishop); [Bible] Epistle

**e.p.** easy projection; *editio princeps* (Latin: first edition); electrically polarized; endpaper; engineering personnel; [chess] *en passant* (French: in passing); [navigation] estimated position; extreme pressure

**EPA** educational priority area; Emergency Powers Act; Employment Protection Act; energy-performance assessment; [USA] Environmental Protection Agency; European Productivity Agency

**EPAA** [USA] Emergency Petroleum Allocation Act

**EPACCI** Economic Planning and Advisory Council for the Construction Industries

**EPAQ** electronic parts of assessed quality

**EPB** equivalent pension benefit

**EPC** Economic and Planning Council; Educational Publishers' Council; evaporative pattern-casting (in foundry)

**EPCA** [USA] Energy Policy and Conservation Act; energy production and consumption account; European Petro-Chemical Association

**EPCOT** Experimental Prototype Community of Tomorrow (Florida)

**EPD** earliest practicable date

**EPDA** Emergency Powers Defence Act

**EPDC** [USA] Electric Power Development Company

**EPEA** Electrical Power Engineers' Association

**EPF** emulsified petroleum fuel; European Packaging Federation

**EPFM** elastic-plastic fracture mechanics

**EPG** [USA] Electronic Proving Ground; [medicine] electropalatogram; [medicine] electropalatology; Emergency Procedure Guideline(s); Eminent Persons Group

**EPGS** electric power generating system

**Eph.** [Bible] Ephesians

**Ephes.** [Bible] Ephesians

**EPI** echo planar imaging; electronic position indicator

**EPIC** Engineering and Production Information Council; European Prospective Investigation into Cancer

**Epict.** Epictetus (ancient Greek philosopher)

**epid.** epidemic

**epil.** epilogue

**Epiph.** Epiphany

**EPIRB** [navigation] emergency position indicator radio beacon

**Epis.** Episcopal; Episcopalian; [Bible] Epistle

**Episc.** Episcopal; Episcopalian

**Epist.** [Bible] Epistle

**epit.** epitaph; epitome

**EPL** exact power law

**EPLD** [computing] erasable programmable logic device

**EPLF** Eritrean People's Liberation Front

**EPM** electron-probe microanalysis; extract of particulate matter

**EPMA** electron-probe microanalysis

**EPMI** Esso Production Malaysia Incorporated

**EPN** elemental point number

**EPNdB** effective perceived noise decibels

**EPNG** El Paso Natural Gas Company

**EPNS** electroplated nickel silver; English Place-Name Society

**EPO** [medicine] erythropoietin

**EPOC** Eastern Pacific Oceanic Conference

**Epoch** End Physical Punishment of Children

**EPOS** [commerce] electronic point of sale (as in **EPOS system**)

**EPP** [physiology] endplate potential; [computing] enhanced parallel port; European People's Party; executive pension plan; [computing] extended parallel port

**EPPO** European and Mediterranean Plant Protection Organization

**EPPT** [computing] European printer performance test

**EPPV** electropneumatic proportional valve

**EPR** electron paramagnetic resonance; ethylene–propylene rubber

**EPRDF** Ethiopian People's Revolutionary Democratic Front

**EPRI** [USA] Electric Power Research Institute

**EPROM** [computing] erasable programmable read-only memory

**EPS** electrically positioned seats (in car

advertisement); electric(al) power system; [USA] Environmental Protection Service

**eps** earnings per share

**EPSP** [physiology] excitatory postsynaptic potential

**EPSRC** Engineering and Physical Sciences Research Council

**EPSS** electrical power supervision system

**EPT** [medicine] early pregnancy test; Environmental Protection Technology; ethylene–propylene terpolymer (synthetic rubber); excess profits tax

**EPTA** Expanded Programme of Technical Assistance (in UN)

**Ep. tm** [law] Epiphany term

**EPU** European Payments Union

**Epus** *Episcopus* (Latin: Bishop)

**EPW** earth-penetrator weapon; enemy prisoner of war

**EQ** educational quotient; [electronics] equalize; equipment qualification; [electronics] equivalence (as in **EQ gate**)

**Eq.** Equerry

**eq.** equal; equate; equation; equator; equatorial; equipment; equitable; equity; equivalent

**EQA** [commerce] European Quality Award

**EQC** external quality control

**EQD** Electrical Quality Assurance Directorate

**EQDB** equipment qualification data bank

**EQI** exhaust quality index

**eqn** equation

**eqn.** equine

**eqpt** equipment

**Equ** [astronomy] Equuleus

**equil.** equilibrium

**EQUIP** equipment usage information programme

**equip.** equipment

**equiv.** equivalent

**ER** [railways] Eastern Region; East Riding (of Yorkshire); *Eduardus Rex* (Latin: King Edward); efficiency report; *Elizabetha Regina* (Latin: Queen Elizabeth); [medicine] emergency room; engine room; [computing] entity relationship; evaporation residue; [civil aircraft marking] Moldova; [vehicle registration] Peterborough

**Er** [chemical element] erbium

**er** elder

**.er** Eritrea (in Internet address)

**e.r.** echo ranging; effectiveness report; electronic reconnaissance; emergency request; emergency rescue; established reliability; external resistance

**ERA** [baseball] earned run average; [USA] Economic Regulatory Administration; Education Reform Act; Electrical Research Association; electronic reading automation; Electronic Rentals Association; [USA] Emergency Relief Administration; engine-room artificer; [computing] entity relationship attribute; [USA] Equal Rights Amendment; European Ramblers' Association; Evangelical Radio Alliance

**ERAB** Energy Research Advisory Board

**ERAMS** Environmental Radiation Ambients Monitoring System

**Eras.** (Desiderius) Erasmus (Dutch humanist)

**Erasmus** European Community Action Scheme for the Mobility of University Students

**ERB** electric roller blind

**ERBM** extended-range ballistic missile

**ERC** Economic Research Council; Electronics Research Council; Employment Rehabilitation Centre; [medicine] endoscopic retrograde cholangiography; [USA] Energy Research Corporation

**ERC&I** Economic Reform Club and Institute

**ERCB** [USA] Energy Resources Conservation Board

**ERCP** [medicine] endoscopic retrograde cholangiopancreatography

**ERCS** emergency response computer system

**ERD** elastic recoil detection; Emergency Reserve Decoration; emergency return device; environmental radiation data; equivalent residual dose (of radiation); extrapolated response dose

**ERDA** [electronics] elastic recoil detection analysis; [Australia] Electrical and Radio Development Association; [USA] Energy Research and Development Administration

**ERDAF** [USA] Energy Research and Development in Agriculture and Food

**ERDE** Engineering Research and Development Establishment; Explosives

Research and Development Establishment

**ERDF** European Regional Development Fund

**ERDIC** Energy Research, Development and Information Centre

**ERDL** Engineering Research and Development Laboratory

**ERDS** emergency response data system

**ERE** *Ethniki Rizospastiki Enosis* (Greek: National Radical Union) (political party); extent of reaction effect

**erec.** erection

**ERFA** European Radio Frequency Agency

**ERG** electrical resistance gauge; [medicine] electroretinogram

**ERGOM** European Research Group on Management

**ergon.** ergonomic; ergonomics

**ERI** *Eduardus Rex et Imperator* (Latin: Edward King and Emperor)

**Eri** [astronomy] Eridanus

**ERIC** [USA] Educational Resources Information Center; energy rate input controller

**ERIM** Environmental Research Institute of Michigan

**ERIS** Emergency Response Information System; [astronautics] Exo-atmospheric Re-entry Vehicle Interceptor Subsystem

**ERISA** [USA] Employee Retirement Income Security Act

**Erit.** Eritrea

**ERL** Energy Research Laboratory

**Erl.** *Erläuterung* (German: explanatory note)

**ERLL** [computing] enhanced run length limited

**ERM** [finance] Exchange Rate Mechanism

**erm.** ermine

**Ernie** electronic random number indicator equipment (selecting winning premium bonds)

**ERO** European Regional Organization of the International Confederation of Free Trade Unions

**EROM** [computing] erasable read-only memory

**EROPA** Eastern Regional Organization for Public Administration

**EROS** earth resources observation satellite; [astronautics] experimental reflection orbital shot

**ERP** [medicine] endoscopic retrograde pancreatography; [commerce] enterprise resource planning; [biochemistry] enzyme-releasing peptide; European Recovery Programme

**e.r.p.** effective radiated power

**ERPF** [medicine] effective renal plasma flow

**ERR** energy release rate

**erron.** erroneous; erroneously

**ERS** earnings-related supplement; earth resources satellite; emergency radio service; emergency response system; engine repair section; Ergonomics Research Society; [USA] Experimental Research Society

**ERT** *Elliniki Radiophonia Tileorasis* (Greek: Hellenic National Radio and Television); excess retention tax

**ERTA** [USA] Economic Recovery and Tax Act

**ERTS** Earth Resources Technology Satellite; European Rapid Train System

**ERU** English Rugby Union

**ERV** [Bible] English Revised Version; [medicine] exercise radionuclide ventriculography

**ERW** enhanced radiation weapon

**erw.** *erweitert* (German: enlarged, extended)

**erweit.** *erweitert* (German: enlarged, extended)

**ES** [vehicle registration] Dundee; Econometric Society; Education Specialist; [chemistry] electronic structure; electrostatic; [international vehicle registration] El Salvador; [medicine] endoscopic sphincterotomy; [medicine] end-systole; [medicine] end-systolic; energy spectrum; engine-sized (paper); Entomological Society; [civil aircraft marking] Estonia; [mining] exploratory shaft

**Es** [chemical element] einsteinium

**e/s** en suite (in property or accommodation advertisement)

**es.** *esempio* (Italian: example)

**.es** Spain (in Internet address)

**e.s.** eldest son; electrical sounding; electric starting; [medicine] *enema saponis* (Latin: soap enema)

**ESA** Ecological Society of America; Educational Supply Association; electrostatic sector analyser; energy system analysis; Entomological Society of America; environmentally sensitive area; European Space Agency; Euthanasia Society of America

**ESAAB** [USA] Energy System Acquisition Advisory Board

**ESAF** enhanced structural adjustment facility (in IMF)

**ESANZ** Economic Society of Australia and New Zealand

**ESAR** electronically steerable array radar

**ESB** electrical stimulation of the brain; [USA] Electricity Supply Board; electric storage battery; Empire State Building; English Speaking Board; environmental specimen bank

**ESBA** English Schools' Badminton Association

**ESBBA** English Schools' Basket Ball Association

**ESBTC** [USA] European Space Battery Test Center

**ESC** Economic and Social Council (of UN); electric seat control (in car advertisement); electronic stills camera; electronic structural correlator; [USA] Energy Security Corporation; Energy Study Centre (Netherlands); English Stage Company; English Steel Corporation; Entomological Society of Canada; etched security code (in car advertisement); European Space Conference; [computing] extended core storage

**Esc** [computing] escape (key); [currency] escudo

**esc.** *escompte* (French: discount); escutcheon

**ESCA** [physical chemistry] electron spectroscopy for chemical analysis; English Schools' Cricket Association; English Schools' Cycling Association

**ESCAP** Economic and Social Commission for Asia and the Pacific (formerly ECAFE)

**ESCB** European System of Central Banks

**ESCC** [engineering] external stress corrosion cracking

**ESCCD** electrical short-circuit current decay

**eschat.** eschatology

**ESCO** Educational, Scientific and Cultural Organization (of UN)

**ESCOM** Electricity Supply Commission of South Africa

**ESCR** external standard channel ratio

**ESD** echo-sounding device; electromagnetic shower detector; [computing] electrostatic discharge; [USA] Environmental Sciences Division; Euratom Safeguards Directorate

**Esd.** [Bible] Esdras (books of Apocrypha)

**Esda** electrostatic deposition analysis; electrostatic document analysis

**ESDAC** European Space Data Centre

**ESDI** enhanced small-device interface

**ESE** east-southeast; engineers stores establishment

**ESECA** [USA] Energy Supply and Environmental Coordination Act

**ESEF** Electrotyping and Stereotyping Employers' Federation

**ESES** environmentally sound energy system

**ESF** European Science Foundation

**ESG** Education Support Grant; English Standard Gauge

**ESH** Environmental Safety and Health; equivalent standard hours; European Society of Haematology

**ESI** electricity supply industry; environment sensitivity index

**ESITB** Electricity Supply Industry Training Board

**Esk.** Eskimo

**ESL** English as a second language

**e.s.l.** expected significance level

**ESLAB** European Space Research Laboratory

**ESMA** Electrical Sign Manufacturers' Association

**ESN** educationally subnormal

**esn.** essential

**ESNS** educationally subnormal, serious

**esntl** essential

**ESNZ** Entomological Society of New Zealand

**ESO** Energy Services Operator; European Southern Observatory (Chile)

**ESOC** European Space Operations Centre

**ESOL** English for speakers of other languages

**ESOMAR** European Society for Opinion Surveys and Market Research

**ESOP** employee share-ownership plan; [USA] employee stock-option plan

**ESOT** employee share-ownership trust
**ESP** electric submersible pump(ing); [commerce] emotional selling proposition; English for special purposes; English for specific purposes; extrasensory perception
**Esp.** *Espagne* (French: Spain); *España* (Spanish: Spain); Esperanto
**esp.** especially; [music] *espressivo* (Italian: expressively)
**espec.** especially
**espg.** espionage
**espr.** [music] *espressivo* (Italian: expressively)
**espress.** [music] *espressivo* (Italian: expressively)
**ESPRIT** European strategic programme for research and development in information technology
**Esq.** Esquire
**ESQA** English Slate Quarries Association
**esqo** *esquerdo* (Portuguese: left)
**Esqr.** Esquire
**ESR** electric sunroof (in car advertisement); [physics] electron-spin resonance; [medicine] erythrocyte sedimentation rate
**ESRC** Economic and Social Research Council (formerly SSRC); Electricity Supply Research Council
**ESRD** [medicine] end-stage renal disease
**ESRF** [medicine] end-stage renal failure
**ESRIN** European Space Research Institute
**ESRO** European Space Research Organization (became part of ESA)
**ESRS** European Society for Rural Sociology
**ESS** energy storage system; evolutionarily stable strategy
**Ess.** Essex
**ess.** essence; [pharmacology] *essentia* (Latin: essence); essential
**ESSA** English Schools' Swimming Association; [USA] Environmental Science Services Administration
**Esso** Standard Oil (phonetic spelling of initials)
**EST** earliest start time; [USA, Canada] Eastern Standard Time; electric-shock treatment; electroshock therapy; [nuclear technology] ellipsoidal shell tokamak; [international vehicle registration] Estonia
**Est.** Established; Estonia; Estonian
**est.** establish; established; [law] estate; estimate; estimated; estimation; estimator; estuary
**estab.** establish; established; establishment
**ESTEC** European Space Technology Centre
**estg** estimating
**Esth.** [Bible] Esther
**ESTI** European Space Technology Institute
**estn** estimation
**ESU** electrostatic unit; English-Speaking Union
**esu** electrostatic unit
**ESV** [astronautics] earth satellite vehicle; [engineering] emergency shutdown valve; [medicine] end-systolic volume
**ESWL** [medicine] extracorporeal shockwave lithotripsy
**ET** [USA] Eastern Time; educational therapy; [international vehicle registration] (Arab Republic of) Egypt; [chemistry] electron transfer; [physics, chemistry] electron transition; [nuclear technology] elongated tokamak; [medicine] embryo transfer; emerging technology (in NATO); Employment Trainee; Employment Training (for unemployed); emptying time; English text; English translation; ephemeris time; [physics] equation of time; [civil aircraft marking] Ethiopia; [electronics] excitation transport; extraterrestrial; [vehicle registration] Sheffield
**.et** Ethiopia (in Internet address)
**e.t.** electric telegraph; engineering time; entertainment tax; exchange telegraph
**ETA** Entertainment Trades' Alliance; estimated time of arrival; European Teachers' Association; *Euzkadi ta Askatasuna* (Basque: Basque Nation and Liberty) (separatist organization)
**Étab.** *Établissement* (French: (business) establishment)
**ETAC** Education and Training Advisory Council
**et al.** *et alibi* (Latin: and elsewhere); *et alii* (Latin: and others)
**ETB** English Tourist Board
**ETC** Eastern Telegraph Company; European Translation Centre
**etc.** *et cetera* (Latin: and the other things)

**ETCTA** Electrical Trades Commercial Travellers' Association
**ETD** estimated time of departure; [telecommunications] extension trunk dialling
**ETE** estimated time en route; evacuation-time estimate; Experimental Tunnelling Establishment
**ETF** [banking] electronic transfer of funds
**ETH** [Switzerland] *Eidgenössische technische Hochschule* (German: Federal Institute of Technology); [international vehicle registration] Ethiopia
**Eth.** Ethiopia; Ethiopian; Ethiopic
**eth.** ether; ethical; ethics
**ethnog.** ethnographical; ethnography
**ethnol.** ethnological; ethnology
**ETI** estimated time of interception; extraterrestrial intelligence
**e.t.i.** elapsed time indicator
**ETJC** Engineering Trades Joint Council
**e.t.k.m.** every test known to man
**ETMA** English Timber Merchants' Association; European Television Magazine Association
**ETO** European Theatre of Operations (in World War II); European Transport Organization
**e.t.o.** estimated time off
**ETOP** [USA] Environmental Threat and Opportunity Profile
**e.t.p.** estimated turning (or turnaround) point
**ETR** [nuclear technology] engineering test reactor; estimated time of return; [nuclear technology] experimental test reactor; [nuclear technology] experimental thermonuclear reactor
**Etr.** Etruscan
**ETS** earth thermal storage; [USA] Educational Testing Service; [biochemistry] electron-transport system; estimated time of sailing; [US military] estimated time of separation (i.e. discharge); [medicine] exercise thallium scintigraphy; expiration of time of service
**ETSA** Electricity Trust of South Australia
**et seq.** *et sequens* (Latin: and the following); *et sequentia* (Latin: and those that follow)
**et seqq.** *et sequentia* (Latin: and those that follow)
**ETSI** European Telecommunications Standards Institute
**e.t.s.p.** entitled to severance pay
**et sqq.** *et sequentia* (Latin: and those that follow)
**ETSU** Energy Technology Support Unit
**ETTA** English Table Tennis Association
**ETTU** European Table Tennis Union
**ETU** Electrical Trades Union; experimental test unit
**ETUC** European Trade Union Confederation
**ETUI** European Trade Union Institute
**et ux.** *et uxor* (Latin: and wife)
**ETV** educational television; engine test vehicle
**ety.** etymological; etymologist; etymology
**etym.** etymological; etymologist; etymology
**etymol.** etymological; etymologist; etymology
**EU** [vehicle registration] Bristol; *Estados Unidos* (Portuguese or Spanish: United States); *États-Unis* (French: United States); European Union; Evangelical Union; [medicine] excretory urography; experimental unit
**Eu** [chemical element] europium
**EUA** *Estados Unidos da América* (Portuguese: United States of America); *Estados Unidos de América* (Spanish: United States of America); *États-Unis d'Amérique* (French: United States of America); [finance] European unit of account; [medicine] examination under anaesthesia
**Euc.** Euclid (ancient Greek mathematician)
**Eucl.** Euclid (ancient Greek mathematician)
**EUCOM** [US military] European Command
**EUDISED** European Documentation and Information Service for Education
**EUFTT** European Union of Film and Television Technicians
**eugen.** eugenics
**EUI** energy utilization index; energy utilization intensity
**EUL** Everyman's University Library
**EUM** *Estados Unidos Mexicanos* (Spanish: Mexico)
**EUMETSAT** European Meteorological Satellite System
**EUP** English Universities Press

**euph.** euphemism; euphemistic; euphemistically
**EUR** *Esposizione Universale di Roma* (Italian: Roman Universal Exhibition)
**Eur.** Europe; European
**Euratom** European Atomic Energy Authority (predecessor of EU)
**Eureca** [astronautics] European retrievable carrier
**Eur. Ing.** European Engineer (from the word for engineer in several European languages)
**Eurip.** Euripides (ancient Greek dramatist)
**EURO** European Regional Office
**EUROCAE** European Organization for Civil Aviation Electronics
**EUROCEAN** European Oceanographic Association
**EUROCHEMIC** European Company for the Chemical Processing of Irradiated Fuels
**EUROCOM** European Coal Merchants' Union
**EUROM** European Federation for Optics and Precision Mechanics
**EURONET** European data-transmission network
**EUROP** European Railway Wagon Pool
**Europol** European Police Office
**EUROSPACE** European Industrial Space Study Group
**EUROTOX** European Standing Committee for the Protection of Populations against the Risks of Chronic Toxicity
**EUS** Eastern United States
**Eus.** Eusebius of Caesarea (ecclesiastical historian)
**Euseb.** Eusebius of Caesarea (ecclesiastical historian)
**EUV** [physics] extreme ultraviolet
**EUVE** [astronomy] Extreme Ultraviolet Explorer
**EUW** European Union of Women
**EV** [vehicle registration] Chelmsford; electric vehicle; [Bible] English Version; [astronautics] entry vehicle; [medicine] equilibrium venography; [medicine] erythrocyte volume; [accounting] expected value; [image technology] exposure value
**eV** *eingetragener Verein* (German: registered society); electronvolt
**ev.** *evangelisch* (German: Protestant)
**e.v.** efficient vulcanization
**EVA** Electric Vehicle Association of Great Britain; Engineer Vice-Admiral; [chemistry] ethene and vinyl acetate; [astronautics] extravehicular activity
**evac.** evacuate; evacuated; evacuation
**eval.** evaluate; evaluated; evaluation
**evan.** evangelical; evangelist
**evang.** evangelical; evangelist
**evap** [short form] evaporated milk
**evap.** evaporate; evaporated; evaporation; evaporator
**evce** evidence
**EVCS** [astronautics] extravehicular communications system
**EVFU** [computing] electronic vertical format unit
**evg** evening
**EVGA** [computing] enhanced video graphics array
**evid.** evidence
**evng** evening
**evol.** evolution; evolutionary; evolutionist
**EVR** electronic video recording and reproduction
**EVT** Educational and Vocational Training
**EVW** European Voluntary Workers
**evy** every
**EW** [civil aircraft marking] Belarus; early warning; electric windows (in car advertisement); electronic warfare; [USA] enlisted woman; [vehicle registration] Peterborough
**e.w.** each way (in betting)
**EWA** [USA] Education Writers' Association
**EWF** Electrical Wholesalers' Federation; European Welding Federation
**EWICS** European Workshop for Industrial Computer Systems
**EWL** evaporative water loss
**EWO** educational welfare officer; essential work order; European Women's Orchestra
**EWP** emergency war plan
**EWR** early-warning radar
**EWS** emergency water supply; emergency welfare service
**EWSF** European Work Study Federation
**EX** [UK postcode] Exeter; [civil aircraft marking] Kyrgyzstan; [vehicle registration] Norwich
**Ex.** Exeter; [Bible] Exodus

**ex.** examination; examine; examined; examiner; example; excellent; except; excepted; exception; excess; exchange; exclude; excluding; exclusive; excursion; excursus (literary digression); execute; executed; executive; executor; exempt; exercise; export; express; extended; extension; extra; extract
**exag.** exaggerate; exaggerated; exaggeration
**exam** [short form] examination
**exam.** examine; examiner
**examd** examined
**examg** examining
**examn** examination
**ex aq.** [medicine] *ex aqua* (Latin: from water)
**ex b.** [finance] ex bonus (i.e. without bonus)
**Exc.** Excellency
**exc.** excellent; except; excepted; exception; exchange; excommunication; *excudit* (Latin: (he/she) engraved it); excursion
**ex cap.** [finance] ex capitalization (i.e. without capitalization)
**excel.** excellent
**Exch.** Exchequer
**exch.** exchange; exchequer
**excl.** exclamation; exclamatory; exclude; excluding; exclusive
**exclam.** exclamation; exclamatory
**ex cp.** [finance] ex coupon (i.e. without interest on coupon)
**exd** examined
**ex div.** [finance] ex dividend (i.e. without dividend)
**exec.** execute; execution; executive; executor
**execx** executrix
**exempl.** *exemplaire* (French: copy (of publication))
**exes** expenses
**ex. g.** *exempli gratia* (Latin: for example)
**ex. gr.** *exempli gratia* (Latin: for example)
**exh.** exhaust; exhibition
**exhbn** exhibition
**exhib.** exhibit; exhibition; exhibitioner; exhibitor
**Ex-Im** [USA] Export-Import Bank
**Eximbank** [USA] Export-Import Bank
**ex int.** [banking] ex interest (i.e. without interest)
**ex lib.** *ex libris* (Latin: from the books (of), from the library (of))
**ex n.** [stock exchange] ex new (of shares)
**Exod.** [Bible] Exodus
**ex off.** *ex officio* (Latin: by right of office)
**Exon.** *Exonia* (Latin: Exeter); *Exoniensis* (Latin: (Bishop) of Exeter)
**exor** executor
**EXP** Exchange of Persons Office (in UNESCO); [meteorology] expected
**exp** [mathematics] exponential
**exp.** expand; expansion; expedition; expense(s); experience; experiment; experimental; expiration; expire; expired; expiry; export; exportation; exported; exporter; exposed; express; expression; expurgated
**ex p.** [law] *ex parte* (Latin: on behalf of one party)
**expdn** expedition
**exper.** experimental
**expl.** explain; explanation; explanatory; explosion; explosive
**exploit.** exploitation
**expn** exposition
**exp. o.** experimental order
**expr.** express; expression
**expt** experiment
**exptl** experimental
**exptr** exporter
**expurg.** expurgate; expurgated
**exr** executor
**exrx** executrix
**exs** expenses
**ext.** extend; extension; extent; exterior; external; externally; extinct; extra; extract; extraction; [medicine] *extractum* (Latin: extract); extreme
**EXTEL** Exchange Telegraph (news agency)
**exten.** extension
**EXTEND** Exercise Training for the Elderly and/or Disabled
**ext. liq.** *extractum liquidum* (Latin: liquid extract)
**extn** extension
**extr.** extraordinary
**extrad.** extradition
**EXW** ex works (i.e. from the factory)
**exx** examples; executrix
**EY** [vehicle registration] Bangor; [civil aircraft marking] Tajikistan
**EYC** European Youth Campaign
**EYR** East Yorkshire Regiment

**EZ** [vehicle registration] Belfast; [US informal] easy; [civil aircraft marking] Turkmenistan

**Ez.** [Bible] Ezra

**Ezek.** [Bible] Ezekiel

**Ezr.** [Bible] Ezra

# F

**F** Fahrenheit; fail; false; family; farad; fast (on clock or watch regulator); Father; fathom; [fishing port] Faversham; February; Federation; Fellow; female; [grammar] feminine; *ferrovia* (Italian: railway); [medicine] *fiat* (Latin: let it be made); fiction; [USA] fighter (aircraft) (as in **F-111**); [genetics] filial generation; [horseracing] filly; finance; fine; fleet; [chemical element] fluorine; [photography] f-number (as in **F16**); Fokker (aircraft); folio; foolscap; [sports] Formula (as in **F1**); [sports] foul; [currency] franc; [civil aircraft marking] France; [international vehicle registration] France; *Frauen* (German: women); *freddo* (Italian: cold); French; [ecclesiastical] *Frère* (French: Brother); Friday; *frio* (Portuguese or Spanish: cold); *froid* (French: cold); [music] note of scale

***F*** [physics] Faraday constant; [physics] force

**f** [music] fa(h) (in tonic sol-fa); [numismatics] face value; femto- (indicates $10^{-15}$, as in **fm** = femtometre); [photography] f-number (as in **f4**); [meteorology] fog; foreign

***f*** [physics] focal length; [music] *forte* (Italian: loudly); [physics] frequency; [physical chemistry] fugacity; [mathematics] function; [biochemistry] furanose

**f.** facing; fair; farthing (quarter of old penny); father; fathom; feet; female; [grammar] feminine; [horseracing] filly; fine; [horseracing] firm; flat; fluid; folio; following (page); foot; for; forecastle; [botany] form (in classification of plants); formula; [sports] foul; founded; [currency] franc; freehold; from; front; fuck; furlong; furlough; furnished (in accommodation advertisement); [currency] guilder (from alternative name florin)

**FA** [statistics] factor analysis; Factory Act; Faculty of Actuaries; family allowance; [slang] Fanny Adams (i.e. nothing); farm adviser; [chemistry] fatty acid; field activities; field allowance; field ambulance; field artillery; filtered air; Finance Act; financial adviser; fine art; [immunology] fluorescent antibody; [building] fly ash; [biochemistry] folic acid; [biochemistry] folinic acid; Football Association; freight agent; [slang] fuck all (i.e. nothing); [building] fuel ash; [nuclear technology] fuel assembly; [metallurgy] furnace annealing; [vehicle registration] Stoke-on-Trent

**Fa** *Firma* (German: firm, business); Florida

**Fa.** Faeroes

**fa** *factura* (Spanish: invoice)

**f.a.** [slang] Fanny Adams (i.e. nothing); fire alarm; first aid; first attack; [commerce] free alongside; [optics] free aperture; freight agent; friendly aircraft; [slang] fuck all (i.e. nothing); fuel–air (ratio)

**FAA** [USA] Federal Aviation Administration; Fellow of the Australian Academy (of Science); Film Artistes' Association; Fleet Air Arm; [biochemistry] free amino acid; [insurance] free of all averages

**FAAAS** Fellow of the American Academy of Arts and Sciences; Fellow of the American Association for the Advancement of Science

**FAAC** Food Additives and Contaminants Committee

**FAARM** Fellow of the American Academy of Reproductive Medicine

**FAAV** Fellow of the Central Association of Agricultural Valuers

**FAB** [physics, electronics] fast-atom beam; [physics, electronics] fast-atom bombardment; Flour Advisory Bureau; French–American–British; fuel-air bomb

**fab** [short form] fabulous

**fab.** fabric; fabricate; [commerce] *fabrication* (French: make, manufacture)
**f.a.b.** first aid box
**f. à b.** [commerce] *franco à bord* (French: free on board)
**fabbr.** *fabbrica* (Italian: factory)
**FABMDS** [USA] field army ballistic missile defense system
**fabr.** fabricate; fabrication
**Fab. Soc.** Fabian Society
**fabx** fire alarm box
**FAC** Federation of Agricultural Cooperatives; [military] forward air controller
**Fac.** Faculty
**fac.** façade; facial; facility; facsimile; factor; factory; faculty
**f.a.c.** fast as can; [insurance] *franc d'avarie commune* (French: free of general average)
**FACC** [USA] Ford Aerospace and Communication Corporation
**FACCP** Fellow of the American College of Chest Physicians
**FACD** Fellow of the American College of Dentistry
**FACE** Fellow of the Australian College of Education; field artillery computer equipment; Fight Against Cuts in Education; [USA] Financial Advertising Code of Ethics
**FACEM** Federation of the Associations of Colliery Equipment Manufacturers
**FACerS** Fellow of the American Ceramic Society
**facet.** facetious
**FACG** Fellow of the American College of Gastroenterology
**facil.** facility
**FACMTA** [USA] Federal Advisory Council on Medical Training
**FACOG** Fellow of the American College of Obstetricians and Gynecologists
**FACOM** Fellow of the Australian College of Occupational Medicine
**FACP** Fellow of the American College of Physicians; Fellow of the American College of Radiology
**FACRM** Fellow of the Australian College of Reproductive Medicine
**FACS** Fellow of the American College of Surgeons; [immunology] fluorescence-activated cell sorter
**facs.** facsimile
**facsim.** facsimile
**FACT** Federation Against Copyright Theft; fully automatic compiler-translator
**fact.** *factura* (Spanish: invoice)
**facta** *factura* (Spanish: invoice)
**FAD** [biochemistry] flavin adenine dinucleotide
**f.a.d.** free air delivered
**FADEC** [computing] fully authorized digital engine control
**FADO** Fellow of the Association of Dispensing Opticians
**FAE** [military] fuel-air explosive(s)
**Faer.** Faeroes
**FAGO** Fellowship in Australia in Obstetrics and Gynaecology
**FAGS** Federation of Astronomical and Geophysical Services; Fellow of the American Geographical Society
**Fah.** Fahrenheit
**Fahr.** Fahrenheit
**FAI** *Fédération aéronautique internationale* (French: International Aeronautical Federation); Football Association of Ireland; fresh-air inlet
**FAIA** Fellow of the American Institute of Architects; Fellow of the Association of International Accountants; Fellow of the Australian Institute of Advertising
**FAIAA** Fellow of the American Institute of Aeronautics and Astronautics
**FAIAS** Fellow of the Australian Institute of Agricultural Science
**FAIB** Fellow of the Australian Institute of Builders
**FAIC** Fellow of the American Institute of Chemists
**FAIE** Fellow of the Australian Institute of Energy
**FAII** Fellow of the Australian Insurance Institute
**FAIM** Fellow of the Australian Institute of Management
**FAK** [shipping] freights all kinds
**Fak.** *Faktura* (German: invoice)
**Falk. I** Falkland Islands
**Falk. Is.** Falkland Islands
**FALN** *Fuerzas Armadas de Liberación Nacional* (Spanish: Armed Forces of National Liberation) (in Puerto Rico)
**FAM** Free and Accepted Masons
**fam.** familiar; family

**FAMA** Fellow of the American Medical Association; Fellow of the Australian Medical Association; Foundation for Mutual Assistance in Africa

**FAMEME** Fellow of the Association of Mining Electrical and Mechanical Engineers

**FAmNucSoc** Fellow of the American Nuclear Society

**FAMS** Fellow of the Ancient Monuments Society; Fellow of the Indian Academy of Medical Sciences

**f&a** fore and aft

**F&AP** [insurance] fire and allied perils

**F&C** full and change (tides)

**F&D** freight and demurrage

**f&d** fill and drain; freight and demurrage

**f&f** fixtures and fittings

**F&Gs** [bookbinding] folded and gathered pages

**F&M** [veterinary science] foot and mouth (disease)

**F&T** [insurance] fire and theft

**FANY** First Aid Nursing Yeomanry

**FAO** Fleet Accountant Officer; Food and Agriculture Organization (of the United Nations)

**f.a.o.** finish all over; for the attention of

**FAP** [USA] Family Assistance Program; fixed action pattern (in ethology); *Força Aérea Portuguesa* (Portuguese: Portuguese Air Force); [insurance] *franc d'avarie particulière* (French: free of particular average)

**FAPA** Fellow of the American Psychiatric Association; Fellow of the American Psychological Association

**FAPHA** Fellow of the American Public Health Association

**FAQ** [commerce] free alongside quay; [computing] frequently asked question (used on Internet)

**f.a.q.** [commerce] fair average quality; [commerce] free alongside quay

**f.a.q.s.** [commerce] fair average quality of season

**FAR** false alarm rate; [USA] Federal Aviation Regulation(s); [insurance] free (of claim) for accident reported; front arm rests (in car advertisement)

**far.** farriery; farthing (quarter of old penny)

**FArborA** Fellow of the Arboricultural Association

**FARE** Federation of Alcoholic Rehabilitation Establishments

**FARELF** Far East Land Forces

**FAS** Faculty of Architects and Surveyors; Federation of American Scientists; Fellow of the Anthropological Society; Fellow of the Antiquarian Society; [medicine] fetal alcohol syndrome; [commerce] free alongside ship

**f.a.s.** firsts and seconds; [commerce] free alongside ship

**FASA** Fellow of the Australian Society of Accountants

**FASB** [USA] Financial Accounting Standards Board

**FASc** Fellow of the Indian Academy of Sciences

**fasc.** [anatomy] fascicle (bundle of fibres); fascicule (instalment of printed work)

**FASCE** Fellow of the American Society of Civil Engineers

**FASE** Fellow of the Antiquarian Society, Edinburgh

**FASEB** Federation of American Societies for Experimental Biology

**FASI** Fellow of the Architects' and Surveyors' Institute

**FASS** Federation of the Associations of Specialists and Subcontractors

**FAST** factor analysis system; fast automatic shuttle transfer; Federation Against Software Theft; first atomic ship transport; forecasting and assessment in science and technology (in EU)

**fastnr** fastener

**FAT** [computing] file allocation table

**fath.** fathom

**FATIS** Food and Agriculture Technical Information Service (of OEEC)

**FAU** Friends' Ambulance Unit

**FAusIMM** Fellow of the Australasian Institute of Mining and Metallurgy

**fav.** favour; favourite

**FAVO** Fleet Aviation Officer

**FAWA** Federation of Asian Women's Associations

**FAX** fuel-air explosion

**fax** [short form] facsimile

**FB** [vehicle registration] Bristol; Fenian Brotherhood; film badge (for radiation protection); fire brigade; fisheries board; fishery board; [railways] flat bottom;

flying boat; [medicine] foreign body; Forth Bridge; Free Baptist; full board (in accommodation advertisement)

**F-B** full-bore

**f.b.** flat bar; fog bell; freight bill; full board (in accommodation advertisement); [sports] fullback

**FBA** Farm Buildings Association; [USA] Federal Bar Association; Federation of British Artists; Federation of British Astrologers; Fellow of the British Academy; fluorescent brightening agent (in detergent); Freshwater Biological Association

**FBAA** Fellow of the British Association of Accountants and Auditors

**f 'ball** football

**f.b.c.** [insurance] fallen building clause

**FBCM** Federation of British Carpet Manufacturers

**FBCO** Fellow of the British College of Optometrists (or Ophthalmic Opticians)

**FBCS** Fellow of the British Computer Society

**f.b.c.w.** [insurance] fallen building clause waiver

**fbd** freeboard

**FBEA** Fellow of the British Esperanto Association

**FBEC(S)** Fellow of the Business Education Council (Scotland)

**FBFM** Federation of British Film Makers

**FBH** fire brigade hydrant

**FBHI** Fellow of the British Horological Institute

**FBHS** Fellow of the British Horse Society

**FBHTM** Federation of British Hand Tool Manufacturers

**FBI** [USA] Federal Bureau of Investigation; Federation of British Industries

**FBIBA** Fellow of the British Insurance Brokers' Association

**FBIM** Fellow of the British Institute of Management

**FBINZ** Fellow of the Bankers' Institute of New Zealand

**FBIPP** Fellow of the British Institute of Professional Photography

**FBIS** Fellow of the British Interplanetary Society

**FBL** [aeronautics] fly-by-light (aircraft control using optical fibres)

**FBM** fleet ballistic missile

**FBMA** Food and Beverage Managers' Association

**f.b.o.** for the benefit of

**FBOA** Fellow of the British Optical Association

**FBOU** Fellow of the British Ornithologists' Union

**FBP** [chemistry] final boiling point; [biochemistry] folate-binding protein

**FBPS** Fellow of the British Phrenological Society

**FBPsS** Fellow of the British Psychological Society

**FBR** [nuclear technology] fast breeder reactor

**fbr.** fibre

**FBRAM** Federation of British Rubber and Allied Manufacturers

**fbro** *febrero* (Spanish: February)

**FBS** Fellow of the Botanical Society; [medicine] fetal bovine serum; [military] forward-based system

**FBSC** Fellow of the British Society of Commerce

**FBSE** Fellow of the Botanical Society, Edinburgh

**FBSM** Fellow of the Birmingham School of Music

**FBSS** [medicine] failed back-surgery syndrome

**FBT** *Fédération des bourses du travail* (French: Federation of Labour Exchanges) (French trade union); fringe benefit tax

**FBU** Fire Brigades Union

**FBu** [currency] Burundi franc

**FBW** [aeronautics] fly-by-wire (aircraft control using electronic circuits)

**f.b.y.** future budget year

**FC** [Australia] Federal Cabinet; [Freemasonry] fellow craft; fencing club; *ferrocarril* (Spanish: railway); *fidei commissum* (Latin: bequeathed in trust); *fieri curavit* (Latin: the donor directed this to be done) (on monuments); fifth column; Fighter Command; fire cock; fire control; Fishmongers' Company; football club; Forestry Commission; [medicine] free cholesterol; Free Church; fuel cell; [medicine] full course (of treatment); [meteorology] funnel cloud; [vehicle registration] Oxford

**f.c.** [baseball] fielder's choice; filing

cabinet; *fin courant* (French: at the end of this month); fixed charge; [printing] follow copy; for cash

**FCA** [USA] Farm Credit Administration; Federation of Canadian Artists; Fellow of the Institute of Chartered Accountants

**FCAATSI** [Australia] Federal Council for the Advancement of Aborigines and Torres Strait Islanders

**FC-AL** [computing] fibre channel arbitrated loop

**FCAnaes** Fellow of the College of Anaesthetists

**fcap** foolscap

**FCAR** [insurance] free of claim for accident reported

**FCASI** Fellow of the Canadian Aeronautics and Space Institute

**FCB** [computing] file control block

**FCBA** Federal Communications Bar Association; Fellow of the Canadian Bankers' Association

**FCBSI** Fellow of the Chartered Building Societies Institute

**FCC** [USA] Federal Communications Commission; Federal Council of Churches; first-class certificate

**FCCA** Fellow of the Chartered Association of Certified Accountants

**FCCEA** Fellow of the Commonwealth Council for Educational Administration

**FCCEd** Fellow of the College of Craft Education

**FCCS** Fellow of the Corporation of Secretaries (formerly Fellow of the Corporation of Certified Secretaries)

**FCCSET** [USA] Federal Coordinating Council on Science, Engineering and Technology

**FCCT** Fellow of the Canadian College of Teachers

**FCD** First Chief Directorate (of KGB)

**FCDA** [USA] Federal Civil Defense Administration

**FCEC** Federation of Civil Engineering Contractors

**FCFC** Free Church Federal Council

**FCFI** Fellow of the Clothing and Footwear Institute

**fcg** facing

**FCGB** Forestry Commission of Great Britain

**FCGI** Fellow of the City and Guilds (of London) Institute

**FCH** full central heating (in property advertisement)

**FChS** Fellow of the Society of Chiropodists

**FCI** *Fédération cynologique internationale* (French: International Federation of Kennel Clubs); Fellow of the Institute of Commerce

**FCIA** Fellow of the Corporation of Insurance Agents; Foreign Credit Insurance Association

**FCIArb** Fellow of the Chartered Institute of Arbitrators

**FCIB** Fellow of the Chartered Institute of Bankers; Fellow of the Corporation of Insurance Brokers

**FCIBSE** Fellow of the Chartered Institution of Building Services Engineers

**FCIC** [USA] Federal Crop Insurance Corporation; Fellow of the Chemical Institute of Canada

**FCII** Fellow of the Chartered Insurance Institute

**FCILA** Fellow of the Chartered Institute of Loss Adjusters

**FCIM** Fellow of the Chartered Institute of Marketing

**FCIOB** Fellow of the Chartered Institute of Building

**FCIPA** Fellow of the Chartered Institute of Patent Agents

**FCIPS** Fellow of the Chartered Institute of Purchasing and Supply

**FCIS** Fellow of the Institute of Chartered Secretaries and Administrators (formerly Fellow of the Chartered Institute of Secretaries)

**FCIT** Fellow of the Chartered Institute of Transport; Four Countries International Tournament (in basketball)

**FCIV** Fellow of the Commonwealth Institute of Valuers

**FCMA** Fellow of the Chartered Institute of Management Accountants

**FCMS** Fellow of the College of Medicine and Surgery

**FCMSA** Fellow of the College of Medicine of South Africa

**FCNA** Fellow of the College of Nursing, Australia

**fcng** facing

**FCO** Farmers' Central Organization; fire-control officer; Foreign and Commonwealth Office
**fco** [commerce] *franco* (French: free of charge)
**f. co.** [printing] fair copy
**FCOG(SA)** Fellow of the South African College of Obstetrics and Gynaecology
**FCollP** Fellow of the College of Preceptors
**FCOphth** Fellow of the College of Ophthalmologists
**FCOT** Fellow of the College of Occupational Therapists
**FCP** [engineering] fatigue-crack propagation; Fellow of the College of Clinical Pharmacology; Fellow of the College of Preceptors
**fcp** foolscap
**FCPA** Fellow of the Canadian Psychological Association; [USA] Foreign Corrupt Practices Act
**FCPO** Fleet Chief Petty Officer
**FCPS** Fellow of the College of Physicians and Surgeons
**FCS** Federation of Conservative Students; [medicine] fetal calf serum
**fcs** francs
**f.c.s.** [insurance] warranted free of capture, seizure, arrest, detainment and the consequences thereof
**FCSA** Fellow of the Institute of Chartered Secretaries and Administrators
**FCSD** Fellow of the Chartered Society of Designers
**FCSP** Fellow of the Chartered Society of Physiotherapy
**f.c.s.r.c.c.** [insurance] warranted free of capture, seizure, arrest, detainment and the consequences thereof, and damage caused by riots and civil commotions
**FCST** [USA] Federal Council for Science and Technology; Fellow of the College of Speech Therapists
**FCT** [Australia] Federal Capital Territory; Fellow of the Association of Corporate Treasurers
**FCTB** Fellow of the College of Teachers of the Blind
**FCTU** Federation of Associations of Catholic Trade Unionists
**fcty** factory
**FCU** fighter control unit
**FD** [vehicle registration] Dudley; *Fidei Defensor* (Latin: Defender of the Faith); financial director; [computing] finite difference; fire department; fleet duties; [fishing port] Fleetwood; [medicine] folate deficiency; free delivery; Free Democrat
**fd** field; fiord; ford; forward; found; founded; fund
**f.d.** flight deck; focal distance; free delivery; free discharge; free dispatch
**FDA** First Division Association (former name of AFDCS); [USA] Food and Drug Administration
**FD&C** [USA] Food, Drug and Color Regulations
**FDC** [USA] Fire Detection Center; [philately] first-day cover; [numismatics] *fleur de coin* (French: mint condition)
**FDDI** [computing] fibre distributed data interface
**FDF** Food and Drink Federation
**fdg** funding
**FDHO** Factory Department, Home Office
**FDI** *Fédération dentaire internationale* (French: International Dental Federation)
**FDIC** [USA] Federal Deposit Insurance Corporation; Food and Drink Industries Council
**FDIF** *Fédération démocratique internationale des femmes* (French: Women's International Democratic Federation)
**FDM** [computing] finite-difference method; [telecommunications] frequency-division multiplexing
**FDO** Fleet Dental Officer; [taxation] for declaration (purposes) only
**FDP** *Freie Demokratische Partei* (German: Free Democratic Party)
**FDR** Franklin Delano Roosevelt (US president); *Freie Demokratische Republik* (German: Free Democratic Republic, the former West Germany)
**fdr** founder
**fdry** foundry
**FDS** Fellow in Dental Surgery; [aeronautics] flight-director system
**FDSRCPSGlas** Fellow in Dental Surgery of the Royal College of Physicians and Surgeons of Glasgow
**FDSRCS** Fellow in Dental Surgery of the Royal College of Surgeons (of England)

**FDSRCSE** Fellow in Dental Surgery of the Royal College of Surgeons of Edinburgh
**FE** Far East; [fishing port] Folkestone; foreign editor; further education; [vehicle registration] Lincoln
**Fe** [chemical element] iron (from Latin *ferrum*)
**f.e.** first edition; for example
**FEA** [USA] Federal Energy Administration; [USA] Federal Executive Association; *Fédération internationale pour l'éducation artistique* (French: International Federation for Art Education); [mathematics] finite-element analysis
**FEAF** Far East Air Force
**FEANI** *Fédération européenne des associations nationales d'ingénieurs* (French: European Federation of National Associations of Engineers)
**FEB** [USA] Fair Employment Board; functional electronic block
**Feb.** February
**febb.** *febbraio* (Italian: February)
**Febr.** *Februar* (German: February)
**FEBS** Federation of European Biochemical Societies
**Feby** February
**FEC** [USA] Federal Election(s) Commission; First Edition Club; *Fondation européenne de la culture* (French: European Cultural Foundation)
**fec.** *fecit* (Latin: (he/she) made it)
**FECB** Foreign Exchange Control Board
**FECDBA** Foreign Exchange and Currency Deposit Brokers' Association
**FECI** Fellow of the Institute of Employment Consultants
**FED** Federal Reserve System
**Fed.** Federal; Federalist; Federated; Federation
**fed.** federal; federated
**FEDC** Federation of Engineering Design Consultants
**FedEx** [trademark] Federal Express
**FEER** [banking] fundamental equilibrium exchange rate
**FEF** Far East Fleet
**FEI** *Fédération équestre internationale* (French: International Equestrian Federation); [USA] Financial Executive Institute
**FEIDCT** Fellow of the Educational Institute of Design Craft and Technology
**FEIS** Fellow of the Educational Institute of Scotland
**FEL** free-electron laser
**FELF** Far East Land Forces
**Fell.** Fellow
**FeLV** [microbiology] feline leukaemia virus
**FEM** [physics] field-emission microscope (or microscopy); [mathematics] finite-element method
**fem.** female; [grammar] feminine
**f. ém.** *force électromotrice* (French: electromotive force, emf)
**FEMA** [USA] Federal Emergency Management Agency
**fenc.** fencing
**FEng** Fellow of the Fellowship of Engineering; Fellow of the Royal Academy of Engineering
**FENSA** Film Entertainments National Service Association
**FEO** Fleet Engineer Officer
**FEOGA** *Fonds européen d'orientation et de garantie agriculturel* (French: European Agricultural Guidance and Guarantee Fund) (in EU)
**FEP** fluorinated ethene propene (plastic)
**FEPA** [USA] Fair Employment Practices Act
**FEPC** [USA] Fair Employment Practices Committee
**FEPEM** Federation of European Petroleum Equipment Manufacturers
**Fer.** Fermanagh
**FERA** [USA] Federal Emergency Relief Administration
**FERC** [USA] Federal Energy Regulatory Commission
**FERDU** Further Education Review and Development Unit
**Ferm.** Fermanagh
**ferr.** *ferrovia* (Italian: railway)
**ferv.** [pharmacology] *fervens* (Latin: boiling)
**FES** Federation of Engineering Societies; Fellow of the Entomological Society; Fellow of the Ethnological Society; F(rederick) E(dwin) Smith, Earl of Birkenhead (British statesman); [fencing] foil, épée and sabre
**Fest.** Festival
**FET** [USA] federal estate tax; [USA] federal excise tax; field-effect transistor; fossil-energy technology

**FEU** Further Education Unit
**feud.** feudal; feudalism
**FEV** [medicine] forced expiratory volume
**fév.** *février* (French: February)
**FEX** [US navy] fleet exercise
**FF** [vehicle registration] Bangor; *Felicissimi Fratres* (Latin: Most Fortunate Brothers); Fellows; *Fianna Fáil* (Gaelic: Warriors of Ireland) (Irish political party); [military] field force; fixtures and fittings (in property advertisement); [USA] Ford Foundation; [currency] (French) franc; [military] frontier force; fully fitted (in property advertisement); fully furnished (in accommodation advertisement)
***ff*** [music] *fortissimo* (Italian: very loudly)
**f/f** fully fitted (in property advertisement); fully furnished (in accommodation advertisement)
**ff.** *fecerunt* (Latin: (they) made it); folios; following (pages or lines); forms
**f.f.** factory fitted; fixed focus; fully fashioned
**FFA** Fellow of the Faculty of Actuaries; Fellow of the Institute of Financial Accountants; [biochemistry] free fatty acid; Future Farmers of America
**f.f.a.** free foreign agency; [commerce] free from alongside (ship)
**FFARACS** Fellow of the Faculty of Anaesthetists of the Royal Australasian College of Surgeons
**FFARCS** Fellow of the Faculty of Anaesthetists of the Royal College of Surgeons (of England)
**FFARCSI** Fellow of the Faculty of Anaesthetists of the Royal College of Surgeons in Ireland
**FFAS** Fellow of the Faculty of Architects and Surveyors
**FFB** Fellow of the Faculty of Building
**FFC** Foreign Funds Control
**FFCM** Fellow of the Faculty of Community Medicine
**FFCMI** Fellow of the Faculty of Community Medicine of Ireland
**FFD** Fellow of the Faculty of Dental Surgeons
**FFDRCSI** Fellow of the Faculty of Dentistry of the Royal College of Surgeons in Ireland
**FFF** Free French Forces
***fff*** [music] *fortississimo* (Italian: as loudly as possible)
**FFHC** Freedom from Hunger Campaign
**FFHom** Fellow of the Faculty of Homoeopathy
**FFI** Fellow of the Faculty of Insurance; Finance for Industry; free from infection; French Forces of the Interior
**FFJ** Franciscan Familiar of Saint Joseph
**FFL** *Forces françaises libres* (French: Free French Forces)
**ffly** faithfully
**FFOM** Fellow of the Faculty of Occupational Medicine
**FFPath** Fellow of the Faculty of Pathologists
**FFPHM** Fellow of the Faculty of Public Health Medicine
**FFPM** Fellow of the Faculty of Pharmaceutical Medicine
**FFPS** Fauna and Flora Preservation Society; Fellow of the Faculty of Physicians and Surgeons
**FFR** Fellow of the Faculty of Radiologists
**FFr** [currency] French franc
**Ffr** [currency] French franc
**FFRR** full-frequency range recording
**FFS** [Algeria] *Front des Forces Socialistes* (French: Socialist Forces Front)
**FFSS** full-frequency stereophonic sound
**FFT** [computing] fast Fourier transform; [computing] final form text
**f/furn** fully furnished (in accommodation advertisement)
**FFV** [USA] First Families of Virginia
**FFWM** free-floating wave meter
**FFY** Fife and Forfar Yeomanry
**ffy** faithfully
**FG** [vehicle registration] Brighton; Federal Government; *Fine Gael* (Gaelic: Tribe of the Gaels) (Irish political party); fire guard; [engineering] flue gas; [meteorology] fog; foot guards; *frais généraux* (French: overheads); full gilt
**fg** fog
**f.g.** [sports] field goal; fine grain; [commerce] fully good
**FGA** Fellow of the Gemmological Association; [insurance] free of general average
**FGCH** full gas central heating (in property advertisement)
**FGCM** field general court martial
**FGDS** *Fédération de la gauche démocrate et*

*socialiste* (French: Federation of the Democratic and Socialist Left)
**f.g.f.** [commerce] fully good, fair
**FGI** *Fédération graphique internationale* (French: International Graphical Federation); Fellow of the Institute of Certificated Grocers
**Fgn** Foreign
**FGO** Fleet Gunnery Officer
**Fg Off.** Flying Officer
**FGS** Fellow of the Geological Society
**FGSM** Fellow of the Guildhall School of Music (and Drama)
**FGT** [USA] federal gift tax
**fgt** freight
**FGTB** *Fédération générale du travail de Belgique* (French: Belgian General Federation of Labour)
**FH** [fishing port] Falmouth; [medicine] family history; field hospital; fire hydrant; fly half (in rugby); [medicine] fetal heart; [vehicle registration] Gloucester
**F/H** freehold (in property advertisement)
**f.h.** [medicine] *fiat haustus* (Latin: let a draught be made); foghorn; forehatch; forward hatch
**FHA** [USA] Farmers' Home Administration; [USA] Federal Housing Administration; Finance Houses Association
**FHAS** Fellow of the Highland and Agricultural Society of Scotland
**FHB** [informal] family hold back
**FHCIMA** Fellow of the Hotel Catering and Institutional Management Association
**FHH** [medicine] fetal heart heard
**FHI** *Fédération haltérophile internationale* (French: International Weightlifting Federation)
**FHLB** [USA] Federal Home Loan Bank
**FHLBA** [USA] Federal Home Loan Bank Administration
**FHLBB** [USA] Federal Home Loan Bank Board
**fhld** freehold (in property advertisement)
**FHLMC** [USA] Federal Home Loan Mortgage Corporation
**FHM** *For Him Magazine*
**FHNH** [medicine] fetal heart not heard
**f/hold** freehold (in property advertisement)
**fhp** friction horsepower
**FHR** [Australia] Federal House of Representatives; [medicine] fetal heart rate
**FHS** Fellow of the Heraldry Society
**FHSA** Family Health Services Authority
**FHSM** Fellow of the Institute of Health Services Management
**FHWA** [USA] Federal Highway Administration
**FI** Faeroe Islands; Falkland Islands; Fiji Islands; fire insurance; [engineering] flow injection
**.fi** Finland (in Internet address)
**f.i.** for instance; [commerce] free in
**FIA** [USA] Federal Insurance Administration; *Fédération internationale de l'automobile* (French: International Automobile Federation); Fellow of the Institute of Actuaries; Fitness Industry Association; [commerce] full interest admitted
**FIAA** *Fédération internationale athlétique d'amateur* (French: International Amateur Athletic Federation)
**FIAA&S** Fellow of the Incorporated Association of Architects and Surveyors
**FIAAS** Fellow of the Institute of Australian Agricultural Science
**FIAB** *Fédération internationale des associations de bibliothécaires* (French: International Federation of Library Associations and Institutions); Fellow of the International Association of Bookkeepers
**FIAF** *Fédération internationale des archives du film* (French: International Federation of Film Archives)
**FIAgrE** Fellow of the Institution of Agricultural Engineers
**FIAI** *Fédération internationale des associations d'instituteurs* (French: International Federation of Teachers' Associations); Fellow of the Institute of Industrial and Commercial Accountants
**FIAJ** *Fédération internationale des auberges de la jeunesse* (French: International Youth Hostel Federation)
**FIAL** Fellow of the International Institute of Arts and Letters
**FIAM** Fellow of the Institute of Administrative Management; Fellow of the International Academy of Management
**FIAP** *Fédération internationale de l'art photographique* (French: International Federation of Photographic Art); Fellow of the Institution of Analysts and Programmers
**FIAPF** *Fédération internationale des associ-*

*ations de producteurs de films* (French: International Federation of Film Producers' Associations)

**FIAS** [USA] Fellow of the Institute of the Aerospace Sciences

**FIASc** Fellow of the Indian Academy of Sciences

**Fiat** *Fabbrica Italiana Automobili Torino* (Italian car manufacturer)

**fib.** [anatomy] fibula

**f.i.b.** free into barge; free into bond; free into bunker

**FIBA** *Fédération internationale de basketball amateur* (French: International Amateur Basketball Federation); Fellow of the Institute of Business Administration (Australia)

**FIBD** Fellow of the Institute of British Decorators

**FIBiol** Fellow of the Institute of Biology

**FIBOR** [finance] Frankfurt Inter-Bank Offered Rate

**FIBOT** Fair Isle Bird Observatory Trust

**FIBP** Fellow of the Institute of British Photographers

**FIBScot** Fellow of the Institute of Bankers in Scotland

**FIBST** Fellow of the Institute of British Surgical Technicians

**FIC** Falkland Islands Company; Fellow of Imperial College (London); Fellow of the Institute of Chemistry; frequency interference control

**fic.** fiction; fictional; fictitious

**FICA** [USA] Federal Insurance Contributions Act; Fellow of the Commonwealth Institute of Accountants; Food Industries Credit Association

**FICAI** Fellow of the Institute of Chartered Accountants in Ireland

**FICC** *Fédération internationale de camping et de caravanning* (French: International Federation of Camping and Caravanning); *Fédération internationale des ciné-clubs* (French: International Federation of Film Societies)

**FICCI** Federation of Indian Chambers of Commerce and Industry

**FICD** Fellow of the Indian College of Dentists; Fellow of the Institute of Civil Defence

**FICE** Fellow of the Institution of Civil Engineers

**FICFor** Fellow of the Institute of Chartered Foresters

**FIChemE** Fellow of the Institution of Chemical Engineers

**FICI** Fellow of the Institute of Chemistry in Ireland

**FICM** Fellow of the Institute of Credit Management

**FICS** Fellow of the Institute of Chartered Shipbrokers; Fellow of the International College of Surgeons

**FICSA** Federation of International Civil Servants' Associations

**fict.** *fictilis* (Latin: made of pottery); fiction; fictional; fictitious

**FICW** Fellow of the Institute of Clerks of Works of Great Britain

**FID** Falkland Islands Dependencies; *Fédération internationale de documentation* (French: International Federation for Documentation); *Fédération internationale du diabète* (French: International Diabetes Federation); Fellow of the Institute of Directors; field intelligence department

**fid.** fidelity; fiduciary

**FIDA** Fellow of the Institute of Directors, Australia

**Fid. Def.** *Fidei Defensor* (Latin: Defender of the Faith)

**FIDDI** [computing] fibre-distributed data interface

**FIDE** *Fédération internationale des échecs* (French: International Chess Federation); Fellow of the Institute of Design Engineers

**FIDO** Film Industry Defence Organization; [US astronautics] Flight Dynamics Officer; Fog Investigation Dispersal Operation (in World War II)

**FIDP** Fellow of the Institute of Data Processing

**FIE** *Fédération internationale d'escrime* (French: International Fencing Federation)

**FIE(Aust)** Fellow of the Institution of Engineers, Australia

**FIED** Fellow of the Institution of Engineering Designers

**FIEE** Fellow of the Institution of Electrical Engineers

**FIEEE** [USA] Fellow of the Institute of Electrical and Electronics Engineers

**FIEI** Fellow of the Institution of Engineers in Ireland

**FIEJ** *Fédération internationale des éditeurs de journaux* (French: International Federation of Newspaper Publishers)

**FIET** *Fédération internationale des employés, techniciens et cadres* (French: International Federation of Commercial, Clerical and Technical Employees)

**FIEx** Fellow of the Institute of Export

**FIFA** *Fédération internationale de football association* (French: International Federation of Association Football); *Fédération internationale du film d'art* (French: International Federation of Art Films); Fellow of the International Faculty of Arts

**fi. fa.** *fieri facias* (Latin: have it done) (writ of execution)

**FIFCLC** *Fédération internationale des femmes de carrières libérales et commerciales* (French: International Federation of Business and Professional Women)

**FIFDU** *Fédération internationale des femmes diplômées des universités* (French: International Federation of University Women)

**FIFF** Fellow of the Institute of Freight Forwarders

**FIFireE** Fellow of the Institution of Fire Engineers

**FIFO** first in, first out

**FIFSP** *Fédération internationale des fonctionnaires supérieurs de police* (French: International Federation of Senior Police Officers)

**FIFST** Fellow of the Institute of Food Science and Technology

**FIG** *Fédération internationale de gymnastique* (French: International Gymnastic Federation)

**Fig.** Figure (book illustration)

**fig.** figurative; figuratively; figure

**FIGasE** Fellow of the Institution of Gas Engineers

**FIGC** *Federazione Italiana Gioco Calcio* (Italian: Italian Football Association)

**FIGCM** Fellow of the Incorporated Guild of Church Musicians

**FIGED** *Fédération internationale des grandes entreprises de distribution* (French: International Federation of Distributors)

**FIGO** *Fédération internationale de gynécologie et d'obstétrique* (French: International Federation of Gynaecology and Obstetrics)

**FIGRS** Fellow of the Irish Genealogical Research Society

**FIH** *Fédération internationale de hockey* (French: International Hockey Federation); *Fédération internationale des hôpitaux* (French: International Hospital Federation); Fellow of the Institute of Hygiene; [image technology] focused-image holography

**FIHE** Fellow of the Institution of Health Education

**FIHort** Fellow of the Institute of Horticulture

**FIHospE** Fellow of the Institute of Hospital Engineering

**FIHT** Fellow of the Institution of Highways and Transportation

**FII** franked investment income

**FIIA** Fellow of the Institute of Internal Auditors

**FIIC** Fellow of the International Institute for Conservation of Historic and Artistic Works

**FIIE** Fellow of the Institution of Incorporated Engineers

**FIIM** Fellow of the Institution of Industrial Managers

**FIInfSc** Fellow of the Institute of Information Scientists

**FIInst** Fellow of the Imperial Institute

**FIISec** Fellow of the International Institute of Security

**FIITech** Fellow of the Institute of Industrial Technicians

**FIJ** *Fédération internationale de judo* (French: International Judo Federation); *Fédération internationale des journalistes* (French: International Federation of Journalists)

**FIL** *Fédération internationale de laiterie* (French: International Dairy Federation); Fellow of the Institute of Linguists

**fil.** filament; fillet; filter; filtrate

**FILA** *Fédération internationale de lutte amateur* (French: International Amateur Wrestling Federation)

**FILE** Fellow of the Institute of Legal Executives

**FILO** first in, last out

**FILT** *Fédération internationale de lawn*

*tennis* (French: International Lawn Tennis Federation)

**FIM** *Fédération internationale des musiciens* (French: International Federation of Musicians); *Fédération internationale motocycliste* (French: International Motorcycle Federation); Fellow of the Institute of Materials; field-ion microscope (or microscopy)

**FIMA** Fellow of the Institute of Mathematics and its Applications

**FIMarE** Fellow of the Institute of Marine Engineers

**FIMBRA** Financial Intermediaries, Managers and Brokers Regulatory Association

**FIMC** Fellow of the Institute of Management Consultants

**FIMechE** Fellow of the Institution of Mechanical Engineers

**FIMGTechE** Fellow of the Institution of Mechanical and General Technician Engineers

**FIMH** Fellow of the Institute of Military History

**FIMI** Fellow of the Institute of the Motor Industry

**FIMIT** Fellow of the Institute of Musical Instrument Technology

**FIMM** Fellow of the Institution of Mining and Metallurgy

**FIMP** *Fédération internationale de médecine physique* (French: International Federation of Physical Medicine)

**FIMS** *Fédération internationale de médecine sportive* (French: International Federation of Sporting Medicine); Fellow of the Institute of Mathematical Statistics

**FIN** [international vehicle registration] Finland

**Fin.** Finland; Finnish

**fin.** *ad finem* (Latin: at the end, towards the end); final; finance; financial; financier; *finis* (Latin: the end); finish

**FINA** *Fédération internationale de natation amateur* (French: International Amateur Swimming Federation)

**f.i.n.a.** following items not available

**Findus** Fruit Industries Limited

**Finn.** Finnish

**Fin. Sec.** financial secretary

**FInstAM** Fellow of the Institute of Administrative Management

**FInstB** Fellow of the Institution of Buyers

**FInstCh** Fellow of the Institute of Chiropodists

**FInstD** Fellow of the Institute of Directors

**FInstE** Fellow of the Institute of Energy

**FInstF** Fellow of the Institute of Fuel

**FInstLEx** Fellow of the Institute of Legal Executives

**FInstMC** Fellow of the Institute of Measurement and Control

**FInstO** Fellow of the Institute of Ophthalmology

**FInstP** Fellow of the Institute of Physics

**FInstPet** Fellow of the Institute of Petroleum

**FInstPI** Fellow of the Institute of Patentees and Inventors

**FInstR** Fellow of the Institute of Refrigeration

**FInstSMM** Fellow of the Institute Sales and Marketing Management

**FINucE** Fellow of the Institution of Nuclear Engineers

**f.i.o.** for information only; [commerce] free in and out

**FIOA** Fellow of the Institute of Acoustics

**FIOP** Fellow of the Institute of Printing

**FIP** *Fédération internationale de philatélie* (French: International Philatelic Federation); *Fédération internationale pharmaceutique* (French: International Pharmaceutical Federation); Fellow of the Institute of Plumbing

**FIPA** *Fédération internationale des producteurs agricoles* (French: International Federation of Agricultural Producers); Fellow of the Institute of Practitioners in Advertising

**FIPENZ** Fellow of the Institution of Professional Engineers, New Zealand

**FIPG** Fellow of the Institute of Professional Goldsmiths

**FIPR** Fellow of the Institute of Public Relations

**FIPS** [computing] Federal International Processing Standards

**FIQ** *Fédération internationale de quilleurs* (French: International Bowling Federation); Fellow of the Institute of Quarrying

**FIQA** Fellow of the Institute of Quality Assurance

**FIQS** Fellow of the Institute of Quantity Surveyors

**FIR** far-infrared radiation; fuel-indicator reading
**fir.** firkin
**f.i.r.** flight information region; floating-in rate; fuel-indicator reading
**FIRA** *Fédération internationale de rugby amateur* (French: International Amateur Rugby Federation); Furniture Industry Research Association
**FIREE(Aust)** Fellow of the Institute of Radio and Electronics Engineers (Australia)
**FIRSE** Fellow of the Institute of Railway Signalling Engineers
**FIRST** Far Infrared and Submillimetre Telescope; [computing] Forum of Incident and Response Teams
**FIRTE** Fellow of the Institute of Road Transport Engineers
**FIS** Family Income Supplement; farm improvement scheme; *Fédération internationale de sauvetage* (French: International Life Saving Federation); *Fédération internationale de ski* (French: International Ski Federation); Fellow of the Institute of Statisticians; [Algeria] *Front Islamique du Salut* (French: Islamic Salvation Front)
**f.i.s.** flight information service; free into store
**FISA** *Fédération internationale de sport automobile* (French: International Motor Sport Federation); *Fédération internationale des sociétés d'aviron* (French: International Rowing Federation); Fellow of the Incorporated Secretaries Association; Finance Industry Standards Association
**FISE** *Fédération internationale syndicale de l'enseignement* (French: International Federation of Teachers' Unions); Fellow of the Institution of Sales Engineers; *Fonds international de secours à l'enfance* (French: United Nations Children's Fund, UNICEF)
**fish.** fishery; fishes; fishing
**FIST** Fellow of the Institute of Science Technology
**FISTC** Fellow of the Institute of Scientific and Technical Communicators
**FIStructE** Fellow of the Institution of Structural Engineers
**FISU** *Fédération internationale du sport universitaire* (French: International University Sports Federation)
**FISVA** Fellow of the Incorporated Society of Valuers and Auctioneers
**FISW** Fellow of the Institute of Social Work
**FIT** [USA] federal income tax; *Fédération internationale des traducteurs* (French: International Federation of Translators)
**f.i.t.** [commerce] free in truck; free of income tax
**FITA** *Fédération internationale de tir à l'arc* (French: International Archery Federation)
**FITCE** *Fédération des ingénieurs des télécommunications de la CE* (French: Federation of Telecommunications Engineers in the EU)
**FITD** Fellow of the Institute of Training and Development
**FITE** Fellow of the Institution of Electrical and Electronics Technician Engineers
**FITS** [astronomy] flexible image transport system
**FITT** *Fédération internationale de tennis de table* (French: International Table Tennis Federation)
**FITW** [USA] federal income tax withholding
**FIUO** for internal use only
**FIVB** *Fédération internationale de volley-ball* (French: International Volleyball Federation)
**f.i.w.** [commerce] free in(to) wagon
**FIWC** Fiji Industrial Workers' Congress
**FIWEM** Fellow of the Institution of Water and Environmental Management
**FIWSc** Fellow of the Institute of Wood Science
**fix.** fixture(s)
**fixt.** fixture(s)
**FJ** [vehicle registration] Exeter
**Fj.** Fjord
**.fj** Fiji (in Internet address)
**FJA** Future Journalists of America
**Fjd** Fjord
**FJI** Fellow of the Institute of Journalists; [international vehicle registration] Fiji
**FK** [vehicle registration] Dudley; [UK postcode] Falkirk; [astronomy] *Fundamental Katalog* (German: Fundamental Catalogue)
**fk** fork

**.fk** Falkland Islands (in Internet address)
**f.k.** flat keel
**FKC** Fellow of King's College (London)
**FKCHMS** Fellow of King's College Hospital Medical School
**Fkr** [currency] Faeroese krone
**FL** Flag Lieutenant; Flight Lieutenant; [US postcode] Florida; football league; [international vehicle registration] Liechtenstein (from German *Fürstentum Liechtenstein*); [vehicle registration] Peterborough
**Fl.** Flanders; Flemish
**fl.** *fleuve* (French: river); floor; [medicine] *flores* (Latin: flowers) (powdered drug); [currency] florin; *floruit* (Latin: flourished) (of famous person whose dates (of birth and death) are not known); flourish; flourished; fluid; [music] flute; [currency] guilder (from alternative name florin)
**f.l.** *falsa lectio* (Latin: false reading)
**FLA** Fellow of the Library Association; *fiat lege artis* (Latin: let it be done by the rules of the art); Film Laboratory Association; Finance and Leasing Association; Future Large Aircraft (design project)
**Fla** Florida
**flag.** [music] flageolet
**FLAI** Fellow of the Library Association of Ireland
**flak** *Fliegerabwehrkanone* (German: aircraft defence gun)
**FLCD** [electronics] ferroelectric liquid-crystal display
**FLCM** Fellow of the London College of Music
**FLCO** Fellow of the London College of Osteopathy
**fld** failed; field; filed; fluid
**fldg** folding
**fl. dr.** fluid dram
**Flem.** Flemish
**flex.** flexible
**flg** flagging; flooring; flying; following
**FLHS** Fellow of the London Historical Society
**FLI** Fellow of the Landscape Institute
**FLIA** Fellow of the Life Insurance Association
**Flint.** Flintshire
**FLIP** [US navy] floating instrument platform
**FLIR** [military] forward-looking infrared
**Flli** *Fratelli* (Italian: Brothers)
**FLN** [Algeria] *Front de Libération Nationale* (French: National Liberation Front)
**FLOOD** [USA] fleet observation of oceanographic data
**flops** [computing] floating-point operations per second (measure of computer power)
**Flor.** Florence; Florentine; Florida
**flor.** [currency] florin; *floruit* (Latin: flourished) (of famous person whose dates (of birth and death) are not known)
**fl. oz** fluid ounce
**f.l.p.** [aeronautics] fault location panel
**fl. pl.** [botany] *flore pleno* (Latin: with double flowers)
**FLQ** [Canada] *Front de Libération du Québec* (French: Quebec Liberation Front) (French-speaking separatists)
**flr** floor
**flr.** failure; [currency] florin
**FLRA** [USA] Federal Labor Relations Authority
**flrg** flooring
**fl. rt.** flow rate
**FLS** Fellow of the Linnean Society
**FLSA** [USA] Fair Labor Standards Act
**flst** flautist
**F/Lt** Flight Lieutenant
**Flt** Flight (in air force rank)
**flt** flat; flight
**Flt Cmdr** Flight Commander
**fltg** floating
**Flt Lt** Flight Lieutenant
**Flt Off.** Flight Officer
**Flt Sgt** Flight Sergeant
**flu** [short form] influenza
**fluc.** fluctuant; fluctuate; fluctuated; fluctuating; fluctuation
**fluor.** fluorescent; fluoridation; fluoride; fluorspar
**fly.** [boxing] flyweight
**FM** [vehicle registration] Chester; [computing] facilities management; [electrical engineering] field magnet; Field Marshal; [aeronautics] figure of merit; Flight Mechanic; foreign mission; *Fraternitas Medicorum* (Latin: Fraternity of Physicians); *fraternité mondiale* (French: world brotherhood); freemason; [radio] frequency modulation; Friars Minor

**Fm** [chemical element] fermium
**fm** farm; fathom; femtometre; from
**.fm** Micronesia (in Internet address)
**f.m.** face measurement; facial measurement; [advertising] facing matter; *femmes mariées* (French: married women); [medicine] *fiat mistura* (Latin: let a mixture be made) (in prescriptions); fine measure; fine measurement; [radio] frequency modulation
**FMA** Farm Management Association; Fellow of the Museums Association; Food Machinery Association
**fman** foreman
**FMANU** *Fédération mondiale des associations pour les Nations Unies* (French: World Federation of United Nations Associations)
**FMANZ** Fellow of the Medical Association of New Zealand
**FMAO** farm machinery advisory officer
**FMAS** Foreign Marriage Advisory Service
**FMB** Farmers' Marketing Board (in Malawi); [USA] Federal Maritime Board; Federation of Master Builders
**FMC** [USA] Federal Maritime Commission; Fellow of the Medical Council; Forces Motoring Club; Ford Motor Company
**FMCE** Federation of Manufacturers of Construction Equipment
**FMCG** fast-moving consumer goods
**FMCP** Federation of Manufacturers of Contractors' Plant
**FMCS** [USA] Federal Mediation and Conciliation Service
**FMCW** [electronics] frequency modulated continuous wave
**FMD** [veterinary science] foot and mouth disease
**fmd** formed
**FMDV** [microbiology] foot and mouth disease virus
**FMEA** failure mode and effect analysis
**FMES** Fellow of the Minerals Engineering Society
**FMF** [medicine] Fiji Military Forces; Fleet Marine Force(s); fetal movements felt; Food Manufacturers' Federation
**FMFPAC** [USA] Fleet Marine Forces, Pacific
**FMG** Federal Military Government (in Nigeria); [currency] franc malgache (used in Madagascar)
**FMI** Fellow of the Motor Industry; *Filii Mariae Immaculatae* (Latin: Sons of Mary Immaculate)
**FMIG** Food Manufacturers' Industrial Group
**FMk** [currency] Finnish markka
**Fmk** Finnmark
**fml** formal
**FMLN** *Farabundo Martí Liberación Nacional* (Spanish: Farabundo Martí National Liberation Front) (guerrilla movement in El Salvador)
**FMN** [biochemistry] flavin mononucleotide
**fmn** formation
**FMO** Fleet Medical Officer; Flight Medical Officer
**FMPA** *Fédération mondiale pour la protection des animaux* (French: World Federation for the Protection of Animals)
**fmr** farmer; former
**fmrly** formerly
**FMRS** Foreign Member of the Royal Society
**FMS** Federated Malay States; *Fédération mondiale des sourds* (French: World Federation of the Deaf); Fellow of the Institute of Management Studies; Fellow of the Medical Society; [computing] flexible manufacturing system; [aeronautics] flight management system(s)
**FMSA** Fellow of the Mineralogical Society of America
**FMTS** field maintenance test station
**FMV** [computing] full-motion video
**FMVSS** [USA] Federal Motor Vehicle Safety Standards
**FN** [vehicle registration] Maidstone
**f.n.** footnote
**FNA** Fellow of the Indian National Science Academy; French North Africa
**f.n.a.** for necessary action
**FNAEA** Fellow of the National Association of Estate Agents
**FNAL** Fermi National Accelerator Laboratory
**FNB** Federal Narcotics Bureau
**FNCB** [USA] First National City Bank
**FNCO** Fleet Naval Constructor Officer
**fnd** found; foundered
**fnd.** foundation

**fndd** founded
**fndr** founder
**fndry** foundry
**FNECInst** Fellow of the North East Coast Institution of Engineers and Shipbuilders
**FNI** *Fédération naturiste internationale* (French: International Naturist Federation); Fellow of the Nautical Institute
**FNIF** Florence Nightingale International Foundation
**FNILP** Fellow of the National Institute of Licensing Practitioners
**FNL** Friends of the National Libraries
**FNLA** *Frente Nacional de Libertação de Angola* (Portuguese: National Front for the Liberation of Angola)
**FNMA** [USA] Federal National Mortgage Association
**FNO** Fleet Navigation Officer
**FNU** *Forces des Nations Unies* (French: United Nations Forces)
**f-number** [photography] ratio of focal length to aperture
**FNWC** [USA] Fleet Numerical Weather Center
**FNZIA** Fellow of the New Zealand Institute of Architects
**FO** federal official; Field Officer; [commerce] firm offer; First Officer; Flag Officer (in Royal Navy); Flying Officer; Foreign Office (became part of FCO); [commerce] formal offer; [military] forward observer; [music] full organ; [vehicle registration] Gloucester
***Fo*** [physics] Fourier number
**fo** *firmato* (Italian: signed)
**f/o** [commerce] for orders; full out
**fo.** folio
**.fo** Faeroe Islands (in Internet address)
**f.o.** fast operating; [commerce] free overside; fuel oil
**FOAF** friend of a friend (used on Internet)
**FOB** [medicine] faecal occult blood; [commerce] free on board
**FOBFO** Federation of British Fire Organizations
**FOBS** [military] fractional orbital bombardment system
**FOBTSU** [military] forward observer target survey unit
**FOC** [commerce] free of charge; free of claims
**FoC** father of the chapel (in printing or publishing trade union)
**FOCL** fibre-optic communications line
**FOCOL** Federation of Coin-Operated Launderettes
**FOCUS** Focus on Computing in the United States
**FOD** finger of death (in computer game); [aeronautics] foreign object damage (of aircraft engine); free of damage
**FODA** Fellow of the Overseas Doctors' Association
**FOE** [USA] Fraternal Order of Eagles
**FoE** Friends of the Earth
**FOF** [stock exchange] Futures and Options Fund
**FOFA** follow-on forces attack
**FOFATUSA** Federation of Free African Trade Unions of South Africa
**F of F** Firth of Forth
**FOH** [theatre] front of house
**FOHCL** falls off her/his chair laughing (in Internet chat)
**FOI** [USA] freedom of information
**FOIA** [USA] Freedom of Information Act
**FOIC** Flag Officer in Charge
**f.o.k.** [stock exchange] fill or kill (i.e. carry out or cancel)
**FOL** [New Zealand] Federation of Labour
**fol.** folio; follow; followed; following
**folg** following
**foll.** followed; following
**FOM** [statistics] figure of merit
**FOMC** [USA] Federal Open Market Committee
**FONA** Flag Officer, Naval Aviation
**FONAC** Flag Officer, Naval Air Command
**FOP** forward observation post
**FOQ** [commerce] free on quay
**FOR** Fellowship of Operational Research; flying objects research; [commerce] free on rail
**For** [astronomy] Fornax
**For.** [currency] forint (used in Hungary)
**for.** foreign; foreigner; forensic; forest; forester; forestry; [music] *forte* (Italian: loudly)
**FORATOM** *Forum atomique européen* (French: European Atomic Forum)
**FORES** floor order routing and execution system (in Tokyo Stock Exchange)
**FOREST** Freedom Organization for the Right to Enjoy Smoking Tobacco

**FOREX** foreign exchange
**formn** formation
**form. wt** [chemistry] formula weight
**for. rts** foreign rights
**fort.** fortification; fortified; fortify
**f.o.r.t.** [commerce] full out rye terms
**Fortran** formula translation (computer programming language)
**Forts.** *Fortsetzung* (German: continuation)
**forz.** [music] *forzando* (Italian: with force)
**FOS** Fisheries Organization Society; [finance] free of stamp; [commerce] free on ship; [commerce] free on station; [commerce] free on steamer
**FOSDIC** [computing] film optical sensing device
**FOT** [commerce] free of tax; [commerce] free on truck
**Found.** Foundation
**found.** foundry
**FOV** field of view
**FOW** [commerce] first open water; [commerce] free on wagon
**FOX** Futures and Options Exchange
**FP** Federal Parliament; field punishment; filter paper; fireplug; [insurance] fire policy; [nuclear technology] fission product; [insurance] floating policy; [optics] focal plane; [Australia] forensic pathologist; former pupil; [veterinary science] fowl pest; Free Presbyterian; freezing point; fresh paragraph; fully paid; [computing] functional programming; [vehicle registration] Leicester
**Fp.** frontispiece
**fp** foolscap
***fp*** [music] *forte-piano* (Italian: loudly (then) softly)
**fp.** fireplace
**f.p.** [medicine] *fiat pilula* (Latin: let a pill be made) (in prescriptions); [medicine] *fiat potio* (Latin: let a drink be made) (in prescriptions); fine paper; [cricket] fine point; fixed price; flameproof; [chemistry] flash point; footpath; foot-pound; [sports] forward pass; freezing point; fresh paragraph; full point; fully paid (shares)
**FPA** Family Planning Association; Film Production Association of Great Britain; Fire Protection Association; [astronomy] first point of Aries; [computing] floating-point accelerator; Foreign Press Association; [insurance] free of particular average
**f.p.b.** fast patrol boat
**f.p.b.g.** fast patrol boat with guided missiles
**FPC** family planning clinic; Family Practitioner Committee; [USA] Federal Power Commission; Federation of Painting Contractors; fish protein concentrate; Flowers Publicity Council
**f.p.c.** for private circulation
**FPEA** Fellow of the Physical Education Association
**FPF** *Federação Portuguesa de Futebol* (Portuguese: Portuguese Football Federation)
**FPGA** [computing] field-programmable gate array
**FPHA** [USA] Federal Public Housing Authority
**FPhyS** Fellow of the Physical Society
**FPI** [USA] Federal Prison Industries
**FPIA** Fellow of the Plastics Institute of Australia
**FPLA** [computing, electronics] field-programmable logic array
**fpm** feet per minute
**FPMI** Fellow of the Pensions Management Institute
**FPMR** [USA] Federal Property Management Regulation
**FPO** field post office; fire prevention officer; [US navy] fleet post office
**FPRC** Flying Personnel Research Committee
**FPROM** [computing] field-programmable read-only memory; [computing] fusible-link programmable read-only memory
**FPS** Fellow of the Pharmaceutical Society; Fellow of the Philharmonic Society; Fellow of the Philological Society; Fellow of the Philosophical Society; Fellow of the Physical Society; [USA] Fluid Power Society
**fps** feet per second; foot-pound-second (as in **fps units**); [photography] frames per second
**fpsps** feet per second per second
**FPT** [commerce] fixed price tender; [nautical] forepeak tank
**FPU** [computing] floating point unit
**f.q.** [finance] fiscal quarter
**FQDN** [computing] fully qualified domain name

**FQS** [USA] Federal Quarantine Service
**FR** [international vehicle registration] Faeroe Islands; Federal Republic; Federal Reserve (System); fighter reconnaissance; [chemistry] fluorine rubber; *Forum Romanum* (Latin: Roman Forum); [fishing port] Fraserburgh; freight release; frequency rate; [nuclear technology] fusion reactor; [vehicle registration] Preston
**F/R** folio reference
**Fr** [ecclesiastical] Father; [chemical element] francium; [Roman Catholic Church] *Frater* (Latin: Brother)
**Fr.** France; *Fratelli* (Italian: Brothers); *Frau* (German: Mrs); French; Friar; Friday
**fr.** fragment; frame; [currency] franc; free; frequent; frequently; from; front; fruit; [botany] fruiting
**.fr** France (in Internet address)
**f.r.** *folio recto* (Latin: on the right-hand page)
**FRA** [finance] forward rate agreement
**Fra** [Roman Catholic Church] *Frate* (Italian: Brother)
**f.r.a.** flame retardant additive
**FRACDS** Fellow of the Royal Australian College of Dental Surgeons
**FRACGP** Fellow of the Royal Australian College of General Practitioners
**FRACI** Fellow of the Royal Australian Chemical Institute
**FRACMA** Fellow of the Royal Australian College of Medical Administrators
**FRACO** Fellow of the Royal Australian College of Ophthalmologists
**FRACOG** Fellow of the Royal Australian College of Obstetricians and Gynaecologists
**FRACP** Fellow of the Royal Australasian College of Physicians
**FRACS** Fellow of the Royal Australasian College of Surgeons
**FRAD** Fellow of the Royal Academy of Dancing
**FRAeS** Fellow of the Royal Aeronautical Society
**FRAgSs** Fellow of the Royal Agricultural Societies
**FRAHS** Fellow of the Royal Australian Historical Society
**FRAI** Fellow of the Royal Anthropological Institute
**FRAIA** Fellow of the Royal Australian Institute of Architects
**FRAIC** Fellow of the Royal Architectural Institute of Canada
**FRAM** Fellow of the Royal Academy of Music; [computing] ferroelectric random-access memory
**FRAME** Fund for the Replacement of Animals in Medical Experiments
**Franc.** Franciscan
**f.r. & c.c.** [insurance] free of riot and civil commotions
**Frank.** Frankish
**FRAP** *Frente de Acción Popular* (Spanish: Popular Action Front) (in Chile)
**FRAPI** Fellow of the Royal Australian Planning Institute
**FRAS** Fellow of the Royal Asiatic Society; Fellow of the Royal Astronomical Society
**FRASE** Fellow of the Royal Agricultural Society of England
**frat.** fraternity; fraternize
**FRATE** [railways] formulae for routes and technical equipment
**fraud.** fraudulent
**FRB** [USA] Federal Reserve Bank; [USA] Federal Reserve Board; Fisheries Research Board of Canada; *Frente de la Revolución Boliviana* (Spanish: Bolivian Revolutionary Front)
**FRBS** Fellow of the Royal Botanic Society; Fellow of the Royal Society of British Sculptors
**FRC** [USA] Federal Radiation Council; [USA] Federal Radio Commission; Financial Reporting Council; Flight Research Center (at NASA)
**FRCA** Fellow of the Royal College of Art
**Fr-Can** French-Canadian
**FRCD** Fellow of the Royal College of Dentists of Canada; [banking] floating-rate certificate of deposit
**FRCGP** Fellow of the Royal College of General Practitioners
**FRCM** Fellow of the Royal College of Music
**FRCN** Fellow of the Royal College of Nursing
**FRCO** Fellow of the Royal College of Organists
**FRCO(CHM)** Fellow of the Royal College

of Organists with Diploma in Choir Training
**FRCOG** Fellow of the Royal College of Obstetricians and Gynaecologists
**FRCP** Fellow of the Royal College of Physicians
**FRCPA** Fellow of the Royal College of Pathologists of Australasia
**FRCPath** Fellow of the Royal College of Pathologists
**FRCPE** Fellow of the Royal College of Physicians of Edinburgh
**FRCPI** Fellow of the Royal College of Physicians of Ireland
**FRCPSGlas** Fellow of the Royal College of Physicians and Surgeons of Glasgow
**FRCPsych** Fellow of the Royal College of Psychiatrists
**FRCR** Fellow of the Royal College of Radiologists
**FRCS** Fellow of the Royal College of Surgeons (of England)
**FRCSE** Fellow of the Royal College of Surgeons of Edinburgh
**FRCSEd** Fellow of the Royal College of Surgeons of Edinburgh
**FRCSI** Fellow of the Royal College of Surgeons in Ireland
**FRCSoc** Fellow of the Royal Commonwealth Society
**FRCVS** Fellow of the Royal College of Veterinary Surgeons
**frd** friend
**FR Dist.** [USA] Federal Reserve District
**Fre.** *Freitag* (German: Friday); French
**fre** *facture* (French: invoice)
**FREconS** Fellow of the Royal Economic Society
**FRED** Fast Reactor Experiment, Dounreay; figure reading electronic device; financial reporting exposure draft
**Free.** [USA] freeway
**FREGG** Free Range Egg Association
**FREI** Fellow of the Real Estate Institute (Australia)
**Frelimo** *Frente de Libertação de Moçambique* (Portuguese: Mozambique Liberation Front)
**freq.** frequency; frequent; [grammar] frequentative; frequently
**FRES** Federation of Recruitment and Employment Services; Fellow of the Royal Entomological Society
**FRESH** foil research hydrofoil
**FRG** Federal Republic of Germany
**Fr. G** French Guiana
**FRGS** Fellow of the Royal Geographical Society; Fellow of the Royal Geographical Society of Australasia
**frgt** freight
**FRHB** Federation of Registered House Builders
**FRHistS** Fellow of the Royal Historical Society
**Frhr** *Freiherr* (German: Baron)
**FRHS** Fellow of the Royal Horticultural Society
**FRI** Fellow of the Royal Institution; Food Research Institute
**Fri.** Fribourg; Friday
**FRIA** Fellow of the Royal Irish Academy
**FRIAI** Fellow of the Royal Institute of the Architects of Ireland
**FRIAS** Fellow of the Royal Incorporation of Architects in Scotland; Fellow of the Royal Institute for the Advancement of Science
**FRIBA** Fellow of the Royal Institute of British Architects
**fric.** friction; frictional
**FRICS** Fellow of the Royal Institution of Chartered Surveyors
**frict.** friction; frictional
**fridge** [short form] refrigerator
**FRIH** [New Zealand] Fellow of the Royal Institute of Horticulture
**FRIIA** Fellow of the Royal Institute of International Affairs
**FRIN** Fellow of the Royal Institute of Navigation
**FRINA** Fellow of the Royal Institution of Naval Architects
**FRIPA** Fellow of the Royal Institute of Public Administration
**FRIPHH** Fellow of the Royal Institute of Public Health and Hygiene
**Fris.** Friesland; Frisian
**Frk.** *Fröken* (Swedish: Miss); *Frøken* (Danish or Norwegian: Miss)
**FRL** full repairing lease
**Frl.** *Fräulein* (German: Miss)
**frld** foreland; freehold (in property advertisement)
**frm** from
**FRMCM** Fellow of the Royal Manchester College of Music

**FRMCS** Fellow of the Royal Medical and Chirurgical Society
**FRMedSoc** Fellow of the Royal Medical Society
**FRMetS** Fellow of the Royal Meteorological Society
**FRMS** Fellow of the Royal Microscopical Society
**FRN** [finance] floating-rate note
**FRNCM** Fellow of the Royal Northern College of Music
**FRNS** Fellow of the Royal Numismatic Society
**FRNSA** Fellow of the Royal Navy School of Architects
**FRO** Fellow of the Register of Osteopaths; Fire Research Organization; [insurance] fire risk only
**f.r.o.f.** [insurance] fire risk on freight
**Frolinat** *Front de Libération Nationale Tchadienne* (French: Chad National Liberation Front)
**front.** frontispiece
**frontis.** frontispiece
**FRP** fibreglass-reinforced plastic; fibre-reinforced plastic; fuel-reprocessing plant
**frpf** fireproof
**FRPharmS** Fellow of the Royal Pharmaceutical Society
**FRPS** Fellow of the Royal Photographic Society
**FRPSL** Fellow of the Royal Philatelic Society, London
**FRQ** [meteorology] frequent
**frq.** frequent
**FRR** Financial Reporting Release
**FRRP** Financial Reporting Review Panel
**FRS** [USA] Federal Reserve System; Fellow of the Royal Society; Ffestiniog Railway Society; Financial Reporting Standard; fuel research station
**Frs.** Frisian
**FRSA** Fellow of the Royal Society of Arts
**FRSAI** Fellow of the Royal Society of Antiquaries of Ireland
**FRSAMD** Fellow of the Royal Scottish Academy of Music and Drama
**FRSC** Fellow of the Royal Society of Canada; Fellow of the Royal Society of Chemistry
**FRSCan** Fellow of the Royal Society of Canada
**FRSCM** Fellow of the Royal School of Church Music
**FRSE** Fellow of the Royal Society of Edinburgh
**FRSGS** Fellow of the Royal Scottish Geographical Society
**FRSH** Fellow of the Royal Society of Health
**FRSL** Fellow of the Royal Society of Literature
**FRSM** Fellow of the Royal Society of Medicine
**FRSNZ** Fellow of the Royal Society of New Zealand
**FRSS** Fellow of the Royal Statistical Society
**FRSSA** Fellow of the Royal Scottish Society of Arts; Fellow of the Royal Society of South Africa
**FRSSI** Fellow of the Royal Statistical Society of Ireland
**FRSSS** Fellow of the Royal Statistical Society of Scotland
**FRST** Fellow of the Royal Society of Teachers
**FRSTM&H** Fellow of the Royal Society of Tropical Medicine and Hygiene
**frt** freight
**frt fwd** freight forward
**FRTPI** Fellow of the Royal Town Planning Institute
**frt ppd** freight prepaid
**FRTS** Fellow of the Royal Television Society
**Fru** [biochemistry] fructose
**frum** *fratrum* (Latin: of the brothers)
**frust.** [medicine] *frustillatim* (Latin: in small portions)
**FRVA** Fellow of the Rating and Valuation Association
**FRVC** Fellow of the Royal Veterinary College
**frwk** framework
**frwy** freeway
**FRZSScot** Fellow of the Royal Zoological Society of Scotland
**FS** [vehicle registration] Edinburgh; Fabian Society; Faraday Society; feasibility study; *Ferrovie dello Stato* (Italian: State Railways); field security; financial secretary; financial statement; Fleet Surgeon; Flight Sergeant; Foreign Service; [USA] Forest Service; Free State; Friendly Society

**fs.** facsimile

**f.s.** factor of safety; *faire suivre* (French: please forward); far side; film strip; fire station; flight service; flying saucer; flying status; foot-second

**FSA** [USA] Farm Security Agency; [USA] Federal Security Agency; [USA] Fellow of the Society of Actuaries; Fellow of the Society of Antiquaries; Field Survey Association; Financial Services Act; Financial Services Authority; [computing] finite-state automaton; foreign service allowance; Friendly Societies Act

**f.s.a.** fuel storage area

**FSAA** Fellow of the Society of Incorporated Accountants and Auditors

**FSAE** Fellow of the Society of Art Education; Fellow of the Society of Automotive Engineers

**FSAI** Fellow of the Society of Architectural Illustrators

**FSAM** Fellow of the Society of Art Masters

**FSAScot** Fellow of the Society of Antiquaries of Scotland

**FSB** Federation of Small Businesses

**FSBI** Fellow of the Savings Bank Institute

**FSBR** Financial Statement and Budget Report

**FSC** [USA] Federal Supreme Court; Field Studies Council; [Roman Catholic Church] *Fratres Scholarum Christianorum* (Latin: Brothers of the Christian Schools, Christian Brothers); Friends Service Council

**FSCA** Fellow of the Society of Company and Commercial Accountants

**FSD** full-scale deflection (of measuring instrument)

**FSDC** Fellow of the Society of Dyers and Colourists

**FSE** Fellow of the Society of Engineers; field support equipment

**FSF** Fellow of the Institute of Shipping and Forwarding Agents; Free Software Foundation

**FSFMV** [computing] full-screen, full-motion video

**FSG** Fellow of the Society of Genealogists

**FSGT** Fellow of the Society of Glass Technology

**FSgt** Flight Sergeant

**FSH** [biochemistry] follicle-stimulating hormone; full service history (in car advertisement)

**FSHM** Fellow of the Society of Housing Managers

**FSI** *Fédération spirite internationale* (French: International Spiritualist Federation); Free Sons of Israel

**FSK** [telecommunications] frequency shift keying

**FSL** First Sea Lord; Folger Shakespeare Library

**FSLAET** Fellow of the Society of Licensed Aircraft Engineers and Technologists

**FSLIC** [USA] Federal Savings and Loan Insurance Corporation

**FSLN** *Frente Sandinista de Liberación Nacional* (Spanish: Sandinista National Liberation Front) (in Nicaragua)

**FSLTC** Fellow of the Society of Leather Technologists and Chemists

**FSM** *Fédération syndicale mondiale* (French: World Federation of Trade Unions); [electronics] flying-spot microscope; [USA] Free Speech Movement

**FSMC** Freeman of the Spectacle-Makers' Company

**FSME** Fellow of the Society of Manufacturing Engineers

**FSN** federal stock number

**FSO** field security officer; Fleet Signals Officer; Foreign Service Officer

**FSP** field security police; foreign service pay

**FSR** Field Service Regulations; *Fleet Street Patent Law Reports*

**FSRP** Fellow of the Society for Radiological Protection

**FSS** Fellow of the Royal Statistical Society; [Algeria] *Front des forces socialistes* (French: Socialist Forces Front)

**FSSI** Fellow of the Statistical Society of Ireland

**FSSU** Federated Superannuation Scheme for Universities

**FST** flatter squarer tube (for computer or TV screen)

**FSTD** Fellow of the Society of Typographic Designers

**FSU** family service unit

**FSUC** Federal Statistics Unit Conference

**FSVA** Fellow of the Incorporated Society of Valuers and Auctioneers

**FT** *Financial Times*; [obstetrics] full term

(of pregnancy); [vehicle registration] Newcastle upon Tyne
**Ft** [currency] forint (used in Hungary); Fort
**ft** feet (unit of length); feint; [medicine] *fiat* (Latin: let there be made); foot (unit of length); fort
**ft.** fortification; fortify
**f.t.** formal training; full term(s)
**FTA** [medicine] fluorescent treponemal antibody; Free Trade Agreement; Free Trade Area; Freight Transport Association; Future Teachers of America
**FTA Index** Financial Times Actuaries Share Index
**FTAM** [computing] file transfer, access and management
**FTASI** Financial Times Actuaries All-Share Index
**FTAT** Furniture, Timber and Allied Trades Union
**FTB** first-time buyer (in property advertisement); fleet torpedo bomber
**FTBD** [obstetrics] full term, born dead
**ftbrg.** footbridge
**FTC** [USA] Federal Trade Commission; [USA] flight test center; flying training command; Full Technological Certificate (of City and Guilds Institute)
**FTCD** Fellow of Trinity College, Dublin
**FTCL** Fellow of Trinity College of Music, London
**FTD** foreign technology division
**FTDA** Fellow of the Theatrical Designers and Craftsmen's Association
**f.t.e.** full-time equivalent
**FTESA** Foundry Trades Equipment and Supplies Association
**FTFL** [computing] fixed-to-fixed-length (code)
**FTG** Fuji Texaco Gas
**ftg** fitting
**fth.** fathom
**fthm** fathom
**FTI** Fellow of the Textile Institute
**FT Index** Financial Times Ordinary Share Index
**ft-lb** foot-pound
**Ft Lieut.** Flight Lieutenant
**FTM** flying training manual; [medicine] fractional test meal
**ft mist.** [medicine] *fiat mistura* (Latin: let a mixture be made) (in prescriptions)
**FTND** [obstetrics] full term, normal delivery
**FTO** Fleet Torpedo Officer
**FT Ord.** Financial Times (Industrial) Ordinary Share Index
**FTP** [computing] file-transfer protocol (used on Internet)
**FTPA** Fellow of the Town and Country Planning Association
**ft pulv.** [medicine] *fiat pulvis* (Latin: let a powder be made) (in prescriptions)
**FTS** Fellow of the Tourism Society
**FTS** flying training school
**ft/s** feet per second
**ft/s$^2$** feet per second per second
**FTSC** Fellow of the Tonic Sol-Fa College
**FTSE 100** Financial Times Stock Exchange 100 Index (also called Footsie)
**FTT** [medicine] failure to thrive
**fttgs** fittings (in property advertisement)
**fttr** fitter
**FTU** Federation of Trade Unions (in Hong Kong); [photography] Freeman time-unit
**FTVL** [computing] fixed-to-variable-length (code)
**FTW** [commerce] tree-trade wharf
**FTZ** Free Trade Zone
**FU** Farmers' Union; [photography] Freeman time-unit; *Freie Universität* (German: Free University (of Berlin)); [vehicle registration] Lincoln
**f.u.** follow-up
**FUACE** *Fédération universelle des associations chrétiennes d'étudiants* (French: World Student Christian Federation)
**FUEN** Federal Union of European Nationalities
**FUMIST** Fellow of the University of Manchester Institute of Science and Technology
**fund.** fundamental
**FUO** [medicine] fever of uncertain origin
**fur.** furlong; furnished (in accommodation advertisement); further
**furn.** furnace; furnish; furnished (in accommodation advertisement); furniture
**fus.** fuselage; fusilier
**fut.** future; [finance] futures
**FUW** Farmers' Union of Wales
**FV** [vehicle registration] Preston
**f.v.** fire vent; fishing vessel; flush valve; *folio verso* (Latin: on the left-hand page)

**FVC** [medicine] forced vital capacity (in breathing tests)
**FVRDE** Fighting Vehicle Research and Development Establishment
**FW** [chemistry] formula weight; fresh water; [vehicle registration] Lincoln
**FWA** Factories and Workshops Act; Family Welfare Association; [USA] Federal Works Agency; Fellow of the World Academy of Arts and Sciences; Free Wales Army
**FWAG** Farming and Wildlife Advisory Group
**FWB** Free Will Baptists
**f.w.b.** four-wheel brake; four-wheel braking
**FWCC** Friends' World Committee for Consultation
**fwd** forward
**f.w.d.** four-wheel drive; fresh water damage; front-wheel drive
**fwdg** forwarding
**FWeldI** Fellow of the Welding Institute
**FWFM** Federation of Wholesale Fish Merchants
**f.w.h.** flexible working hours
**FWI** Federation of West Indies; French West Indies
**FWIW** for what it's worth (in Internet chat and e-mail)
**FWL** Foundation of World Literacy
**FWO** Federation of Wholesale Organizations; Fleet Wireless Officer
**FWPCA** [USA] Federal Water Pollution Control Administration
**FWS** fighter weapons school; fleet work study
**FWSG** farm water supply grant
**fwt** [boxing] featherweight
**f.w.t.** fair wear and tear
**FX** [vehicle registration] Bournemouth; foreign exchange; Francis Xavier (Spanish Jesuit missionary); [theatre] sound effects (phonetic spelling of 'effects'); [cinema] special effects (phonetic spelling of 'effects')
**fxd** fixed; foxed
**fxg** fixing
**fxle** [nautical] forecastle
**FY** [UK postcode] Blackpool; [USA, Canada] fiscal year; [fishing port] Fowey; [vehicle registration] Liverpool
**f.y.a.** first-year allowance
**FYC** Family and Youth Concern
**FYI** for your information
**FYM** farmyard manure
**FYP** [economics] Five-Year Plan
**FYROM** Former Yugoslav Republic of Macedonia
**FZ** [vehicle registration] Belfast; [meteorology] freezing; Free Zone; French Zone
**fz.** [music] *forzando* (Italian: accentuating strongly); [music] *forzato* (Italian: accentuated strongly)
**FZA** [USA] Fellow of the Zoological Academy
**FZGB** Federation of Zoological Gardens of Great Britain and Ireland
**FZS** Fellow of the Zoological Society
**F-Zug** *Fernschnellzug* (German: long-distance express train)

# G

**G** [international vehicle registration] Gabon; [fishing port] Galway; gauss (unit of magnetic flux density); [cinema] general exhibition (film classification in Australia and USA); German; Germany; giga- (indicates $10^9$, as in **GW** = gigawatt); [computing] giga- (indicates $2^{30}$, as in **GB** = gigabyte); [UK postcode] Glasgow; [biochemistry] glycine; good; [currency] gourde (used in Haiti); [slang] grand (= 1,000 (pounds, dollars, etc.)); gravity (as in **G-force**); Great; green; Group; [biochemistry] guanine; [biochemistry] guanosine; [currency] guaraní (used in Paraguay); Guernsey; Gulf; [botany] gynoecium (in floral formula); [music] note of scale; [civil aircraft marking] United Kingdom
***G*** [physics] conductance; [physics] gravitational constant

**g** [physics] acceleration of free fall; [meteorology] gale; gallon; gas; [chemistry] gaseous; [physics] gluon; [mathematics] grade; gram; grav (unit of acceleration); [physics] gravitational acceleration; gravity
***g*** [physics] degeneracy
**g.** garage; *gauche* (French: left); gauge; gelding; gender; general; [grammar] genitive; geographical; gilt; goal; goalkeeper; gold; good; government; grand; great; green; grey; *gros(se)* (French: large); guardian; guide; [currency] guilder; [currency] guinea; gunnery
**G3** [economics] Group of Three (most powerful western industrialized nations)
**G$^3$** [electronics] gadolinium gallium garnet
**G5** [finance] Group of Five (nations stabilizing exchange rates)
**G7** [economics] Group of Seven (leading industrialized nations)
**G10** [finance] Group of Ten (nations lending money to IMF)
**G24** [economics] Group of Twenty-Four (richest industrialized nations)
**G77** [economics] Group of Seventy-Seven (developing nations)
**9G** [civil aircraft marking] Ghana
**GA** Gaelic Athletic (Club); Gamblers Anonymous; garrison artillery; General Accident (property and insurance company); general administrator; general agent; [linguistics] General American; [medicine] general anaesthesia; [medicine] general anaesthetic; General Assembly (of UN); general assignment; [insurance] general average; Geographical Association; Geologists' Association; [US postcode] Georgia; [obstetrics] gestational age; [vehicle registration] Glasgow; [netball] goal attack; government actuary; graphic arts
**G/A** [insurance] general average; ground-to-air
**Ga** [chemical element] gallium; Georgia
**Ga.** Gallic
**g/a** ground-to-air
**.ga** Gabon (in Internet address)
**g.a.** [insurance] general average
**GAA** [Ireland] Gaelic Athletic Association
**GAAP** generally accepted accounting principles
**GAAR** [taxation] general anti-avoidance rule
**GAAS** generally accepted auditing standards
**GAB** general arrangements to borrow (in IMF)
**Gab.** Gabon
**GABA** [biochemistry] gamma-aminobutyric acid (neurotransmitter)
**Gae.** Gaelic
**Gael.** Gaelic
**GAFTA** Grain and Free Trade Association
**GAI** General Assembly of International Sports Federations; [USA] guaranteed annual income; Guild of Architectural Ironmongers
**Gal.** [Bible] Galatians; Galicia; Galway
**gal.** gallon
**gall.** gallery; gallon
**GALT** [medicine] gut-associated lymphoid tissue
**galv.** galvanic; galvanize; galvanized; galvanometer
**GAM** guided aircraft missile
**Gam.** Gambia
**G&AE** [accounting] general and administrative expense(s)
**G&O** [medicine] gas and oxygen (in anaesthetic)
**G&S** (William Schwenck) Gilbert and (Arthur) Sullivan (British writers of comic operettas)
**G&T** gin and tonic
**GAO** [USA] General Accounting Office
**GAP** general assembly programme; great American public; [economics] gross agricultural product
**GAPAN** Guild of Air Pilots and Air Navigators
**GAR** Grand Army of the Republic (in American Civil War); guided aircraft rocket
**gar.** garage; garrison
**gard.** garden
**GARIOA** government aid and relief in occupied areas
**GARP** Global Atmospheric Research Programme
**GASC** German-American Securities Corporation
**GASCO** General Aviation Safety Committee
**GASP** Group Against Smokers' Pollution

**gast.** gastric
**gastroent.** gastroenterological; gastroenterology
**GATB** General Aptitude Test Battery
**GATCO** Guild of Air Traffic Control Officers
**GATT** General Agreement on Tariffs and Trade (replaced by WTO)
**GAUFCC** General Assembly of Unitarian and Free Christian Churches
**GAV** [accounting] gross annual value
**GAW** Global Atmosphere Watch; guaranteed annual wage
**GAWF** Greek Animal Welfare Fund
**GAYE** give as you earn
**gaz.** gazette; gazetteer
**GB** [medicine] gall bladder; gas board; [computing] gigabyte; Girls' Brigade; [vehicle registration] Glasgow; government and binding; Great Britain; [international vehicle registration] Great Britain; guide book; gunboat
**Gb** [computing] gigabyte; gilbert (unit of magnetomotive force)
**GBA** [international vehicle registration] Alderney; Governing Bodies Association
**GB&I** Great Britain and Ireland
**GBCW** Governing Body of the Church in Wales
**GBDO** Guild of British Dispensing Opticians
**GBE** (Dame or Knight) Grand Cross of the Order of the British Empire
**g.b.e.** gilt bevelled edge
**GBF** gay black female
**GBG** [international vehicle registration] Guernsey
**GBGSA** Governing Bodies of Girls' Schools Association
**GBH** grievous bodily harm
**GBJ** [international vehicle registration] Jersey
**GBM** gay black male; [international vehicle registration] Isle of Man
**GBNE** Guild of British Newspaper Editors
**g.b.o.** goods in bad order
**g/box** gearbox (in car advertisement)
**GBP** British pounds; [biochemistry] glutamate-binding protein; great British public
**GBRE** General Board of Religious Education
**GBS** George Bernard Shaw (Irish dramatist); [computing] Gragg–Burlisch–Stoer (method)
**GBSM** Graduate of Birmingham and Midland Institute School of Music
**GBT** Green Bank Telescope
**GBTA** Guild of Business Travel Agents
**GBZ** [international vehicle registration] Gibraltar
**GC** [astronomy] galactic centre; gas chromatography; gas council; [chemistry] gel chromatography; [astronomy] General Catalogue; George Cross (replacement for EGM); gliding club; Goldsmiths' College; golf club; good conduct; government chemist; Grand Chancellor; Grand Chaplain; Grand Chapter; Grand Conductor; Grand Cross; [vehicle registration] southwest London
**g.c.** going concern; good condition (in advertisement)
**GCA** Girls' Clubs of America; Global Commission on Aids; [aeronautics] ground-controlled approach; [international vehicle registration] Guatemala (Central America)
**G Capt.** Group Captain
**GCB** (Dame or Knight) Grand Cross of the Order of the Bath
**GCBS** General Council of British Shipping
**GCC** Game Conservancy Council; Gas Consumers' Council; Gulf Cooperation Council
**GCD** general and complete disarmament; [mathematics] greatest common divisor
**GCE** General Certificate of Education; [USA] General College Entrance
**GCF** [mathematics] greatest common factor
**GCFR** [nuclear technology] gas-cooled fast reactor
**GCH** gas central heating (in property advertisement); Guild Certificate of Hairdressing
**GCHQ** Government Communications Headquarters
**GCI** [aeronautics] ground-controlled interception
**GCIE** (Knight) Grand Commander of the Order of the Indian Empire
**GCIU** [USA] Graphic Communications International Union
**GCL** [aeronautics] ground-controlled

landing; Guild of Cleaners and Launderers

**GCLH** Grand Cross of the Legion of Honour

**GCLJ** (Knight) Grand Cross of the Order of St Lazarus of Jerusalem

**GCM** [meteorology] general circulation model; general court martial; Good Conduct Medal; [statistics] greatest common measure; [mathematics] greatest common multiple

**GCMG** (Dame or Knight) Grand Cross of the Order of St Michael and St George

**GCO** Gun Control Officer (in Royal Navy)

**GCON** Grand Cross of the Order of the Niger

**GCR** [nuclear technology] gas-cooled reactor; [computing] grey component replacement; ground-controlled radar; [computing] group code recording

**GCRN** General Council and Register of Naturopaths

**GCRO** General Council and Register of Osteopaths

**GCSE** General Certificate of Secondary Education (replacement for CSE and GCE O level)

**GCSG** (Knight) Grand Cross of the Order of St Gregory the Great

**GCSI** (Knight) Grand Commander of the Order of the Star of India

**GCSJ** (Knight) Grand Cross of the Order of St John of Jerusalem

**GCStJ** (Bailiff or Dame) Grand Cross of the Order of St John of Jerusalem

**GCVO** (Dame or Knight) Grand Cross of the Royal Victorian Order

**GD** [obstetrics] gestational day; [vehicle registration] Glasgow; [electronics] glow discharge; [netball] goal defence; Graduate in Divinity; Grand Duchess; Grand Duchy; Grand Duke; Gunnery Division

**Gd** [chemical element] gadolinium

**gd** good; granddaughter; ground

**.gd** Grenada (in Internet address)

**g.d.** general duties; gravimetric density

**GDA** Glasgow Development Agency

**GDBA** Guide Dogs for the Blind Association

**GDC** General Dental Council; General Dynamics Corporation

**Gde** [currency] gourde (used in Haiti)

**GDI** [computing] graphical device interface; [economics] gross domestic income

**Gdk** Gdansk

**gdn** garden; guardian

**Gdns** Gardens

**GDP** [economics] gross domestic product

**GDPA** General Dental Practitioners' Association

**GDR** German Democratic Republic (the former East Germany)

**Gds** Guards

**gds** goods

**Gdsm.** Guardsman

**GDT** graphic display terminal

**GDU** graphic display unit

**GE** garrison engineer; gastroenterology; general election; [USA] General Electric (Company); [international vehicle registration] Georgia; [vehicle registration] Glasgow; [fishing port] Goole; [astronomy] greatest elongation; gross energy

**Ge** [chemical element] germanium

**.ge** Georgia (in Internet address)

**g.e.** [bookbinding] gilt edges

**GEA** Garage Equipment Association

**geb.** *geboren* (German: born); *gebunden* (German: bound)

**GEBCO** general bathymetric chart of the oceans

**Gebr.** *Gebrüder* (German: brothers)

**GEC** General Electric Company

**GED** general educational development

**Gedcom** [computing] genealogical data communications

**GEF** Global Environment Facility

**gegr.** *gegründet* (German: founded)

**gel.** gelatin(e); gelatinous

**GEM** genetically engineered microorganism; [computing] graphics environment manager; ground effect machine; guidance evaluation missile; Guild of Experienced Motorists

**Gem** [astronomy] Gemini

**GEMS** Global Environmental Monitoring System (in UN)

**Gen.** General; [Bible] Genesis; Geneva; Genoa

**gen** [short form] (general) information

**gen.** gender; genealogy; general; generally; generator; generic; genetic; gen-

etics; genital; [grammar] genitive; genuine; [biology] genus
**gen. av.** [insurance] general average
**gend.** *gendarme* (French: police officer)
**geneal.** genealogy
**genit.** genital; [grammar] genitive
**Genl** General
**genn.** *gennaio* (Italian: January)
**gent** [short form] gentleman
**GEO** geostationary earth orbit; geosynchronous earth orbit
**Geo.** George
**geod.** geodesy; geodetic
**geog.** geographer; geographic(al); geography
**geol.** geologic(al); geologist; geology
**geom.** geometer; geometric(al); geometry
**GEON** gyro-erected optical navigation
**geophys.** geophysical; geophysics
**geopol.** geopolitical; geopolitics
**GEOREF** World Geographic Reference System
**GEOS** geodetic orbiting satellite
**GER** gross energy requirement
**Ger.** German; Germany
**ger.** [grammar] gerund; [grammar] gerundive
**Gerbil** Great Education Reform Bill
**GES** Global Epidemiological Surveillance and Health Situation (of WHO)
**Ges.** [commerce] *Gesellschaft* (German: company, society)
**GESP** generalized extrasensory perception
**GEST** Grants for Education, Support and Training
**gest.** *gestorben* (German: deceased)
**Gestapo** *Geheime Staatspolizei* (German: secret state police) (in Nazi Germany)
**GET** [medicine] gastric emptying time
**GETT** [USA] Grants Equal To Tax
**GeV** gigaelectronvolt
**GEW** gram-equivalent weight
**gez.** *gezeichnet* (German: signed)
**GF** General Foods Limited; girlfriend; glass fibre; government form; gradient freezing; growth factor; Guggenheim Foundation; [currency] Guinea franc; [vehicle registration] southwest London
**g/f** ground floor (in property advertisement)
**g.f.a.** [commerce] good fair average; [commerce] good freight agent
**GFCH** gas-fired central heating (in property advertisement)
**GFCM** General Fisheries Council for the Mediterranean
**GFD** geophysical fluid dynamics
**GFG** *Good Food Guide*
**GFH** George Frederick Handel (German composer)
**GFOF** [stock exchange] Geared Futures and Options Fund
**GFR** German Federal Republic; [medicine] glomerular filtration rate
**GFS** Girls' Friendly Society
**GFT** Glasgow Film Theatre
**GFTU** [USA] General Federation of Trade Unions
**GFWC** General Federation of Women's Clubs
**GG** [medicine] gamma globulin; Girl Guides; [vehicle registration] Glasgow; Governor-General; great gross (= 144 dozen); Grenadier Guards
**g.g.** gas generator
**GGC** generalized genetic code
**ggd** great-granddaughter
**gge** garage (in property advertisement)
**GGF** Glass and Glazing Federation
**GGG** [electronics] gadolinium gallium garnet
**g.gr.** great gross (= 144 dozen)
**ggs** great-grandson
**GGSM** Graduate of the Guildhall School of Music (and Drama)
**GH** general hospital; [international vehicle registration] Ghana; [fishing port] Grangemouth; [military] Green Howards; Greenwich Hospital; [biochemistry] growth hormone; [vehicle registration] southwest London
**.gh** Ghana (in Internet address)
**GHA** [astronomy] Greenwich hour angle
**GHB** gamma hydroxybutyrate (bodybuilding drug)
**GHCIMA** Graduate of the Hotel Catering and Institutional Management Association
**g.h.e.** ground handling equipment
**GHI** Good Housekeeping Institute
**GHMS** Graduate in Homoeopathic Medicine and Surgery

**GHOST** global horizontal sounding technique (for collection of atmospheric data)
**GHQ** [military] General Headquarters
**GHRH** [biochemistry] growth-hormone-releasing hormone
**GHS** girls' high school
**GHz** gigahertz
**GI** galvanized iron; gastrointestinal; [USA] general issue; generic issue; Gideons International; (Royal) Glasgow Institute (of the Fine Arts); [USA] government issue; Government of India; [biochemistry] growth inhibitor; US soldier (from government (or general) issue)
**Gi** gilbert (unit of magnetomotive force)
**gi.** gill (unit of liquid measure)
**.gi** Gibraltar (in Internet address)
**g.i.** galvanized iron
**GIA** Garuda Indonesian Airways
**GIB** Gulf International Bank
**Gib.** Gibraltar
**GIBiol** Graduate of the Institute of Biology
**GIC** *Guilde internationale des coopératrices* (French: International Cooperative Women's Guild)
**GIEE** Graduate of the Institute of Electrical Engineers
**GIF** [computing] graphics interchange format; [biochemistry] growth-hormone inhibiting factor
**GIFT** [medicine] gamete intrafallopian transfer (infertility treatment)
**gig** [short form, computing] gigabyte
**GIGO** [computing] garbage in, garbage out
**GIMechE** Graduate of the Institution of Mechanical Engineers
**GINO** [computing] graphical input output
**GInstAEA** Graduate of the Institute of Automotive Engineer Assessors
**GINucE** Graduate of the Institution of Nuclear Engineers
**gio.** *giovedì* (Italian: Thursday)
**GIP** glazed imitation parchment (paper)
**GIPME** Global Investigation of Pollution in the Marine Environment
**GIS** [computing] geographical information system; [computing] geological information system; Global Information Solutions
**GISS** Goddard Institute for Space Studies
**GITB** Gas Industry Training Board
**giu.** *giugno* (Italian: June)
**GIUK** Greenland, Iceland, United Kingdom
**GJ** [vehicle registration] southwest London
**GJD** [Freemasonry] Grand Junior Deacon
**GK** goalkeeper; [fishing port] Greenock; [vehicle registration] southwest London
**Gk** Greek
**GKA** Garter King of Arms
**GKC** G(ilbert) K(eith) Chesterton (British writer)
**GKN** Guest, Keen and Nettlefold (engineering company)
**GKS** [computing] graphical kernel system
**GL** [shipping] *Germanischer Lloyd* (German shipping classification society); [UK postcode] Gloucester; good-looking (in personal advertisement); [printing] gothic letter; government laboratory; [Freemasonry] Grand Lodge; Grand Luxe (car); ground level; gun licence; [vehicle registration] Truro
**Gl.** Gloria (doxology)
**gl** gill (unit of liquid measure)
**g/l** grams per litre
**gl.** glass; gloss
**.gl** Greenland (in Internet address)
**4GL** [computing] fourth-generation language
**GLAB** Greater London Arts Board
**glab.** [botany] glabrous
**Glam.** Glamorgan
**glam** [informal] greying, leisured, affluent, married
**gland.** glandular
**Glas.** Glasgow; Glaswegian
**glau.** [botany] glaucous
**glauc.** [medicine] glaucoma
**glaz.** glazed; glazing
**GLB** gay, lesbian, bisexual; Girls' Life Brigade
**GLC** [chemistry] gas–liquid chromatography; Greater London Council (former local authority); ground-level concentration (of radioactive material); Guild of Lettering Craftsmen
**GLCM** Graduate of the London College of Music; ground-launched cruise missile
**gld.** [currency] guilder
**GLDP** Greater London Development Plan
**GLM** graduated length method (in skiing)

**GLOBECOM** [US air force] Global Communications System
**GLOMEX** Global Oceanographic and Meteorological Experiment
**GLORIA** Geological Long Range ASDIC
**Glos** Gloucestershire
**gloss.** glossary
**Gloucestr.** *Gloucestriensis* (Latin: (Bishop) of Gloucester)
**GLS** [Freemasonry] Grand Lodge of Scotland
**GLT** greetings letter telegram
**glt** [bookbinding] gilt
**GM** [physics] Geiger–Müller (as in **GM counter**); general manager; general merchandise; [computing] General Midi; general mortgage; General Motors Corporation; genetically modified; Geological Museum; geometric mean; George Medal; gold medal; gold medallist; Grand Marshal; Grand Master; [education] grant maintained; guided missile; [vehicle registration] Reading
**gm** gram
**.gm** Gambia (in Internet address)
**gm²** grams per square metre (unit of weight of paper)
**GMAG** Genetic Manipulation Advisory Group
**G-man** [USA] government man (FBI agent)
**GMB** General, Municipal, Boilermakers and Allied Trades Union; Grand Master Bowman (in archery); Grand Master of the Order of the Bath
**g.m.b.** good merchantable brand
**GMBE** Grand Master of the Order of the British Empire
**GmbH** [commerce] *Gesellschaft mit beschränkter Haftung* (German: limited company, Ltd)
**GMC** general management committee; General Medical Council; [astronomy] giant molecular cloud; Guild of Memorial Craftsmen
**Gmc** Germanic
**GMF** Glass Manufacturers' Federation
**GMIE** Grand Master of the Order of the Indian Empire
**GMKP** Grand Master of the Knights of St Patrick
**GMMG** Grand Master of the Order of St Michael and St George
**GMO** genetically modified organism
**GMP** [USA] Glass, Molders, Pottery, Plastics and Allied Workers International Union; Grand Master of the Order of St Patrick; [economics] gross material product; Gurkha Military Police
**g.m.q.** good merchantable quality
**GMR** ground-mapping radar
**GMRT** Giant Metre-wave Radio Telescope
**GMS** [education] grant-maintained status
**GMSC** General Medical Services Committee
**GMSI** Grand Master of the Order of the Star of India
**GMST** Grant-Maintained Schools Trust; [astronomy] Greenwich Mean Sidereal Time
**GMT** Greenwich Mean Time
**GMTA** great minds think alike (in Internet chat)
**GMTV** Good Morning Television
**GMV** [microbiology] golden mosaic virus
**GMW** gram-molecular weight
**GN** [USA] Graduate Nurse; [fishing port] Granton; [vehicle registration] southwest London
**gn** grandnephew; grandniece
**gn.** [currency] guinea
**.gn** Guinea (in Internet address)
**GNA** Ghana News Agency; Guinea News Agency; Guyana News Agency
**GNAS** Grand National Archery Society
**GNC** General Nursing Council (replaced by UKCC)
**gnd** ground
**GNMA** [USA] Government National Mortgage Association
**GNP** [economics] gross national product
**GNR** *Guarda Nacional Republicana* (Portuguese: National Republican Guard)
**Gnr** Gunner
**GnRH** [biochemistry] gonadotrophin-releasing hormone
**gns** guineas
**GNTC** Girls' Nautical Training Corps
**GNVQ** General National Vocational Qualification
**GO** gas operated; General Office; General Officer; [military] general order; [music] great organ; Group Officer; [vehicle registration] southwest London
**g.o.a.** gone on arrival

**g.o.b.** good ordinary brand
**GOC** General Officer Commanding; General Optical Council; Greek Orthodox Church
**GOC-in-C** General Officer Commanding-in-Chief
**GOCO** government-owned, contractor-operated
**GOE** General Ordination Examination
**GOES** [USA] Geostationary Operational Environmental Satellite
**GOM** Grand Old Man
**GONG** [astronomy] Global Oscillations Network Group
**GOP** *Girls' Own Paper*; [USA] Grand Old Party (i.e. the Republican Party)
**Gopa** Government Oil and Pipeline Agency
**GORD** [medicine] gastro-oesophageal reflux disease
**Gos.** *Gosudarstvo* (Russian: state) (in former USSR)
**GOSIP** [computing] government open systems interconnection profile
**Gosplan** *Gosudarstvennaya Planovaya Comissiya* (Russian: State Planning Commission) (in former USSR)
**Gosud.** *Gosudarstvo* (Russian: state) (in former USSR)
**Goth.** Gothic
**gou.** [currency] gourde (used in Haiti)
**Gov.** Government; Governor
**gov.** government; governor
**.gov** government (in Internet address)
**Gov-Gen** Governor-General
**Govt** Government
**govt** government
**.gov.uk** UK government (in Internet address)
**GOX** gaseous oxygen
**GP** Gallup Poll; gas-permeable (contact lenses); [medicine] general paralysis; [music] general pause; general practitioner; general purpose; general-purpose computer; *Gloria Patri* (Latin: Glory to the Father); government property; graduated pension; Graduate in Pharmacy; *grande passion* (French: great passion); grand passion; Grand Prix; gross profit; [vehicle registration] south-west London
**gp** group
**g.p.** [printing] galley proofs; [mathematics] geometrical progression; [printing] great primer
**GPA** General Practitioners' Association; [US education] grade point average
**GPALS** Global Protection Against Limited Strikes (reduced form of SDI)
**GPC** general purposes committee
**g.p.c.** good physical condition (in advertisement)
**Gp Capt** Group Captain
**gpcd** gallons per caput per day
**Gp Comdr** Group Commander
**gpd** gallons per day
**GPDST** Girls' Public Day School Trust
**GPh** Graduate in Pharmacy
**gph** gallons per hour
**GPHI** Guild of Public Health Inspectors
**GPI** [medicine] general paralysis of the insane
**GPIB** [computing] general-purpose interface bus
**GPKT** Grand Priory of the Knights of the Temple
**GPM** [USA] graduated payment mortgage; [Freemasonry] Grand Past Master
**gpm** gallons per minute
**GPMU** Graphical, Paper and Media Union (became part of NATSOPA)
**GPO** General Post Office; [USA] Government Printing Office
**GPR** *genio populi Romani* (Latin: to the genius of the Roman people); ground-penetrating radar
**GPS** Global Positioning System; Graduated Pension Scheme; [Australia] Great Public Schools
**gps** gallons per second
**GPSS** General Purpose System Simulator
**GPT** Guild of Professional Toastmasters
**GPU** General Postal Union (former name of UPU); [USA] General Public Utilities Corporation; *Gosudarstvennoye Politicheskoye Upravlenie* (Russian: State Political Administration) (former Soviet secret police)
**GQ** [military] general quarters
**.gq** Equatorial Guinea (in Internet address)
**GQG** *Grand Quartier Général* (French: General Headquarters)
**GR** gamma ray; general reconnaissance; [physics] general relativity; general reserve; *Georgius Rex* (Latin: King

George); [fishing port] Gloucester; grand recorder; [international vehicle registration] Greece; ground rent; *Gulielmus Rex* (Latin: King William); Gurkha Rifles; [vehicle registration] Newcastle upon Tyne

**Gr** Gunner

**Gr.** Great; Greater; Grecian; Greece; Greek; Grove (in road name)

**gr.** grade; grain (unit of weight); gram; grammar; grand; great; greater; grey; gross; ground; group

**.gr** Greece (in Internet address)

**GRA** Game Research Association; Greyhound Racing Association

**GRACE** group routing and charging equipment

**grad.** gradient; grading; gradual; graduate; graduated

**GradIAE** Graduate of the Institution of Automobile Engineers

**GradInstBE** Graduate of the Institution of British Engineers

**GradInstP** Graduate of the Institute of Physics

**GradInstR** Graduate of the Institute of Refrigeration

**GradSE** Graduate of the Society of Engineers

**gram.** grammar; grammarian; grammatical

**GRAS** [USA] generally regarded as safe

**GRB** [astronomy] gamma-ray burst; Gas Research Board

**GRBI** Gardeners' Royal Benevolent Institution

**Gr. Br.** Great Britain

**Gr. Brit.** Great Britain

**GRBS** Gardeners' Royal Benevolent Society

**GRC** General Research Corporation

**Gr. Capt** Group Captain

**GRCM** Graduate of the Royal College of Music

**GRDF** Gulf Rapid Deployment Force

**GRE** [USA] Graduate Record Examination; grant-related expenditure; Guardian Royal Exchange Assurance plc

**GRF** [biochemistry] growth-hormone releasing factor

**gr.f.** [horseracing] grey filly

**GRI** *Georgius Rex Imperator* (Latin: George King and Emperor); [New Zealand] guaranteed retirement income

**GRID** gay-related immunodeficiency; Global Resource Information Database

**Gr-L** Graeco-Latin

**grm** gram

**GRN** goods received note

**Grn** Green (in road name)

**grn** green

**GRO** Gamma Ray Observatory; General Register Office; Greenwich Royal Observatory

**Gro.** Grove

**gro.** gross

**GROBDM** General Register Office for Births, Deaths and Marriages

**gro. t.** gross ton; gross tonnage

**GRP** glass(fibre)-reinforced plastic (or polyester)

**grp** group

**GRS** [astronomy] Great Red Spot (on Jupiter)

**grs** grains; gross

**GRSC** Graduate of the Royal Society of Chemistry

**GRSE** Guild of Radio Service Engineers

**GRSM** Graduate of the Royal Schools of Music

**gr. t.** gross ton

**g.r.t.** gross registered tonnage

**GRU** *Glavnoye Razvedyvatelnoye Upravleniye* (Russian: Central Intelligence Office) (in former USSR)

**Gru** [astronomy] Grus

**gr. wt** gross weight

**g.r.y.** [finance] gross redemption yield

**GS** General Schedule (in US civil service); general secretary; general service; [military] General Staff; geographical survey; geological survey; [netball] goal shooter; gold standard; grammar school; [aeronautics] ground speed; [vehicle registration] Luton

**Gs** gauss (unit of magnetic flux density); [currency] guaraní (used in Paraguay)

**gs** grandson; guineas

**GSA** [USA] General Services Administration; Girl Scouts of America; Girls' Schools Association; Glasgow School of Art

**GS&WR** [Ireland] Great Southern and Western Railway

**GSB** Government Savings Bank

**GSC** [chemistry] gas–solid chromatography; General Service Corps; [USA] General Staff Corps
**GSD** general supply depot; [astronomy] Greenwich sidereal gate
**GSE** ground service equipment; ground support equipment
**GSEE** *Geniki Synomospondia Ergaton Hellados* (Greek: Greek General Confederation of Labour)
**GSGB** Geological Survey of Great Britain; Golf Society of Great Britain
**GSI** [medicine] genuine stress incontinence
**GSL** Geological Society of London; group Scout leader; [USA] guaranteed student loan
**GSM** Garrison Sergeant-Major; general sales manager; General Service Medal; global system for mobile communications; (Member of the) Guildhall School of Music (and Drama)
**gsm** grams per square metre (unit of weight of paper)
**g.s.m.** [commerce] good sound merchantable (quality)
**GSMD** (Member of the) Guildhall School of Music and Drama
**GSO** General Staff Officer
**GSOH** good sense of humour (in personal advertisement)
**GSP** glass(fibre)-strengthened polyester; Good Service Pension; [economics] gross social product
**G-spot** Gräfenburg spot (erogenous zone)
**GSR** galvanic skin reflex; galvanic skin response
**GSS** geostationary satellite; global surveillance system; Government Statistical Service
**GST** [Canada, New Zealand] goods and services tax; [astronomy] Greenwich Sidereal Time
**g. st.** [knitting] garter stitch
**GSVQ** General Scottish Vocational Qualification
**GSW** gunshot wound
**GT** gas turbine; [physics] gauge theory; Good Templar; [Freemasonry] Grand Tiler; *Gran Turismo* (Italian: Grand Touring) (sports car); greetings telegram; [vehicle registration] southwest London
**gt** [bookbinding] gilt; great
**gt.** [medicine] *gutta* (Latin: a drop)
**.gt** Guatemala (in Internet address)
**g.t.** gas tight; [bookbinding] gilt top; gross tonnage
**GTA** gas–tungsten arc
**Gt Br.** Great Britain
**Gt Brit.** Great Britain
**GTC** [Scotland] General Teaching Council; Girls' Training Corps; [commerce] good till cancelled (or countermanded); Government Training Centre
**GTCL** Graduate of Trinity College of Music, London
**gtd** guaranteed
**g.t.e.** [bookbinding] gilt top edge
**gtee** guarantee
**GTH** [biochemistry] gonadotrophic hormone
**GTI** GT Injection (sports car)
**gtm** good this month
**GTO** *Gran Turismo Omologato* (Italian: homologated GT) (sports car)
**GTR** general theory of relativity
**gtr** greater
**GTS** gas turbine ship; [USA] General Theological Seminary
**GTT** [medicine] glucose tolerance test
**gtt.** [medicine] *guttae* (Latin: drops); [medicine] *guttatim* (Latin: drop by drop)
**g.t.w.** good this week
**GU** [medicine] gastric ulcer; [medicine] genitourinary; [fishing port] Guernsey; [UK postcode] Guildford; [vehicle registration] southeast London
**Gu.** Guinea
**gu.** [currency] guinea; [heraldry] gules (= red)
**guar.** guarantee; guaranteed
**Guat.** Guatemala
**GUI** Golfing Union of Ireland; [computing] graphical user interface
**gui.** guitar
**GUIDO** [US astronautics] Guidance Officer
**guil.** [currency] guilder
**Guin.** Guinea
**Gulag** *Glavnoye Upravleniye Lagerei* (Russian: Central Administration for Camps) (former Soviet labour camp system)
**GUM** [medicine] genitourinary medicine; *Gosudarstvenni Universalni Magazin* (Russian: Universal State Store)

**gun.** gunnery; gunpowder
**GUR** [medicine] glucose utilization rate
**GUS** Great Universal Stores
**GUT** [physics] grand unified theory
**guttat.** [medicine] *guttatim* (Latin: drop by drop)
**guv** [short form] governor
**g.u.v.** *gerecht und vollkommen* (German: correct and complete)
**GUY** [international vehicle registration] Guyana
**GV** *grande vitesse* (French: high speed (train)); [vehicle registration] Ipswich
**g.v.** gravimetric volume; gross valuation
**GVH** [medicine] graft versus host
**GVHD** [medicine] graft-versus-host disease
**gvt** government
**GVW** gross vehicle weight
**GW** George Washington (US president); gigawatt; [fishing port] Glasgow; gross weight; guided weapon(s); [vehicle registration] southeast London
**.gw** Guinea-Bissau (in Internet address)
**GW-Basic** [computing] gee whizz beginners' all-purpose symbolic instruction code
**GWF** gay white female
**GWH** gigawatt-hour
**GWM** gay white male
**GWP** Government White Paper; [economics] gross world product
**GWR** Great Western Railway
**Gwyn.** Gwynedd
**GX** [vehicle registration] southeast London
**GY** [fishing port] Grimsby; [UK postcode] Guernsey; [vehicle registration] southeast London
**Gy** gray (unit of radiation dose)
**.gy** Guyana (in Internet address)
**gym** [short form] gymnasium; [short form] gymnastics
**gyn.** gynaecological; gynaecology
**gynaecol.** gynaecological; gynaecology
**GZ** [vehicle registration] Belfast; ground zero
**G-Z** [astronomy] Giacobini–Zinner (comet)

# H

**H** [advertising] half page; harbour; hard (pencil lead); hardness; [card games] hearts; [immunology] heavy; height; henry (unit of electric inductance); herbaceous; [slang] heroin; [medicine] histamine receptor; [biochemistry] histidine; Holy; [music] horn; hospital; hour; [fishing port] Hull; [international vehicle registration] Hungary; hydrant; [chemical element] hydrogen
***H*** [physics, medicine] dose equivalent; [physics] Hamiltonian; [physics, photography] light exposure; [physics] magnetic field strength
**h** [meteorology] hail; hecto- (indicates 100, as in **hg** = hectogram); hour
***h*** [physics] heat transfer coefficient; height; [physics] Planck constant
**h.** hand; harbour; hard; hardness; heat; height; high; hip; [sports] hit; horizontal; [music] horn; horse; hot; hour; house; hundred; husband
**H4** [civil aircraft marking] Solomon Islands
**2H** double hard (pencil lead)
**3H** treble hard (pencil lead)
**5H** [civil aircraft marking] Tanzania
**9H** [civil aircraft marking] Malta
**HA** [vehicle registration] Dudley; [medicine] haemagglutination; [horticulture] hardy annual; [UK postcode] Harrow; Hautes-Alpes (French department); health authority; heavy artillery; high altitude; Highway(s) Act; [biochemistry] histamine; Historical Association; Hockey Association; [astronomy] hour angle; [geology] humic acid; [civil aircraft marking] Hungary; Hydraulic Association of Great Britain
**Ha** [chemical element] hahnium
**Ha.** Haiti; Haitian; Hawaii; Hawaiian
**ha** hectare
**h.a.** heir apparent; high angle (in gunnery); *hoc anno* (Latin: in this year)
**HAA** heavy anti-aircraft; [immunology] hepatitis-associated antigen

**HA&M** *Hymns Ancient and Modern*
**HAB** high-altitude bombing
**Hab.** [Bible] Habakkuk
**hab.** habitat; habitation
**hab. corp.** [law] habeas corpus (type of writ)
**habt** *habeat* (Latin: let him have)
**HAC** high-alumina cement; Honourable Artillery Company
**HACSG** Hyperactive Children's Support Group
**h.a.d.** hereinafter described
**haem.** haemoglobin; haemorrhage
**HAF** Hellenic Air Force
**Hag.** [Bible] Haggai
**hagiol.** hagiology
**HAI** [medicine] haemagglutination inhibition; Health Action International; [medicine] hospital-acquired infection
**HAIL** Hague Academy of International Law
**Hak. Soc.** Hakluyt Society
**Hal** [computing] hard-array logic
**hal.** halogen
**Hal. Orch.** Hallé Orchestra
**Ham.** Hamburg
**Han.** Hanover; Hanoverian
**H&C** hot and cold (water)
**H&E** *Health and Efficiency*; heredity and environment
**h&f** heated and filtered (swimming pool)
**h&j** [printing] hyphenation and justification
**h&t** hardened and tempered; hospitalization and treatment
**H&W** Harland and Wolff (shipbuilding company); Hereford and Worcester
**Hants** Hampshire (from Old English name of county)
**HAO** hydrogenated anthracene oil
**HAP** hazardous air pollutant
**HAPA** Handicapped Adventure Playground Association
**h. app.** heir apparent
**HAPPA** Horses and Ponies Protection Association
**HaPV** [microbiology] hamster polyomavirus
**har.** harbour
**HARCVS** Honorary Associate of the Royal College of Veterinary Surgeons
**HARM** high-speed anti-radiation missile
**harm.** harmonic; harmony
**harp.** harpoon; harpsichord
**HART** [New Zealand] Halt All Racist Tours (sports organization)
**Harv.** [USA] Harvard University
**HAS** Headmasters' Association of Scotland; Health Advisory Service; Helicopter Air Service; Hospital Advisory Service
**HASAWA** Health and Safety at Work Act
**HASTE** Helicopter Ambulance Service to Emergencies
**HAT** housing action trust; housing association trust
**haust.** [medicine] *haustus* (Latin: draught)
**HAV** [medicine] hepatitis A virus
**HAWT** horizontal-axis wind turbine
**haz.** hazard; hazardous
**HAZOP** [computing] hazard and operability study
**HB** [vehicle registration] Cardiff; hard black (pencil lead softer than H); [horticulture] hardy biennial; His Beatitude; House of Bishops; [civil aircraft marking] Switzerland and Liechtenstein
**Hb** [biochemistry] haemoglobin
**h.b.** [sports] halfback; handbook; hardback (of books); homing beacon; human being
**HbA** [biochemistry] adult haemoglobin
**HBAB** [medicine] hepatitis B antibody
**h'back** hatchback (in car advertisement)
**HBAg** [medicine] hepatitis B antigen
**HBC** [electrical engineering] high breaking capacity; Historic Buildings Council; Hudson's Bay Company
**HBCU** [USA] Historically Black Colleges and Universities
**HBD** had (or has) been drinking
**hbd** hardboard; headboard
**h.b.d.** hereinbefore described
**HBF** [medicine] hepatic blood flow; House-Builders' Federation
**HbF** [biochemistry] fetal haemoglobin
**Hbf.** *Hauptbahnhof* (German: central station)
**HBIG** [medicine] hepatitis B immunoglobulin
**HBJ** Harcourt Brace Jovanovich
**hbk** hardback (of books)
**HBLV** [medicine] human B-lymphotropic virus
**HBM** Her/His Britannic Majesty('s)

**HBMC** Historic Buildings and Monuments Commission for England
**HBO** hyperbaric oxygen
**h/board** hardboard; headboard
**H-bomb** hydrogen bomb
**HBP** [medicine] high blood pressure
**HBPF** High Blood Pressure Foundation
**hbr** harbour
**HBS** Harvard Business School
**HbS** [biochemistry] sickle-cell haemoglobin
**HBT** [electronics] heterojunction bipolar transistor
**Hbt** Hobart
**HBV** [medicine] hepatitis B virus
**HBWTA** Home Brewing and Winemaking Trade Association
**hby** hereby
**HC** [vehicle registration] Brighton; [civil aircraft marking] Ecuador; Hague Convention; Hairdressing Council; hard copy; Headmasters' Conference; Headteachers' Conference; health certificate; Heralds' College; High Church; High Commission; High Commissioner; High Court; higher certificate; highly commended; [computing] high-speed CMOS; *Highway Code*; hockey club; Holy Communion; home counties; *hors concours* (French: outside the competition); House of Clergy; House of Commons; house of correction; housing centre; housing corporation
**H/C** [insurance] held covered; hot and cold (water)
**h.c.** habitual criminal; hand control; heating cabinet; high capacity; *honoris causa* (Latin: for the sake of honour, honorary); hot and cold (water)
**HCA** Hospital Caterers' Association
**HCAAS** Homeless Children's Aid and Adoption Society
**hcap** handicap
**HCB** House of Commons Bill
**HCBA** Hotel and Catering Benevolent Association
**HCC** Housing Consultative Council for England
**h.c.c.** hydraulic cement concrete
**h.c.d.** high current density
**h.c.e.** human-caused error
**HCEC** Hospital Committee of the European Community
**HCF** high-calorific fuel; high carbohydrate and fibre; [mathematics] highest common factor; Honorary Chaplain to the Forces
**h.c.f.** hundred cubic feet
**HCFC** hydrochlorofluorocarbon
**HCG** [biochemistry] human chorionic gonadotrophin
**HCH** Herbert Clark Hoover (US president); hexachlorocyclohexane (insecticide)
**HCI** Hotel and Catering Institute; human–computer interaction (or interface)
**HCIL** Hague Conference on International Law
**HCIMA** Hotel Catering and Institutional Management Association
**HCITB** Hotel and Catering Industry Training Board
**HCJ** High Court of Justice; Holy Child Jesus
**h.c.l.** high cost of living
**HCM** Her Catholic Majesty; High Court Master; His Catholic Majesty
**HCO** Harvard College Observatory; higher clerical officer
**HCOPIL** Hague Conference on Private International Law
**HCP** House of Commons Paper
**hcp** handicap
**HCPT** Historic Churches Preservation Trust
**hcptr** helicopter
**HCR** High Chief Ranger; [USA] highway contract route
**HCS** Home Civil Service
**h.c.s.** high-carbon steel
**HCSA** Hospital Consultants and Specialists Association
**HCT** [computing] high-speed CMOS with TTL inputs
**HCVC** Historic Commercial Vehicle Club
**HCVD** [medicine] hypertensive cardiovascular disease
**h.c.w.** hot and cold water
**HD** heavy duty; [medicine] herniated disc; high density; high dose (of radiation); (51st) Highland Division; Hilda Doolittle (US poet); [medicine] Hodgkin's disease; home defence; honourable discharge; Hoover Dam; [UK postcode] Huddersfield; [vehicle registration] Huddersfield; [chemistry] hydrogen–deuterium

**H/D** [shipping] Havre–Dunkirk
**hd** hand; head
**h.d.** heavy duty; high density; [medicine] *hora decubitus* (Latin: at bedtime) (in prescriptions)
**HDA** [Australia] Hawkesbury Diploma in Agriculture; high-duty alloy; Hospital Doctors' Association
**HDATZ** high-density air traffic zone
**hdbk** handbook; hardback (of books)
**HDC** [medicine] high-dose chemotherapy; [law] holder in due course
**HDCD** high-density CD-ROM
**HDCR** Higher Diploma of the College of Radiographers
**HDD** [computing] hard disk drive; [aeronautics, computing] head-down display; heavy-duty diesel; Higher Dental Diploma
**hdg** heading
**HDipEd** Higher Diploma in Education
**HDK** husbands don't know
**hdkf** handkerchief
**HDL** [computing] hardware description language; [biochemistry] high-density lipoprotein
**hdl.** handle
**HDLC** [biochemistry] high-density lipoprotein cholesterol; [computing] high-level data link control
**hdle** handle; [horseracing] hurdle
**hdlg** handling
**hdlr** handler
**HDM** high-duty metal
**HDN** [medicine] haemolytic disease of the newborn
**hdn** harden
**HDP** heavy-duty petrol; [chemistry] high-density polyeth(yl)ene
**HDPE** [chemistry] high-density polyeth(yl)ene
**hdqrs** headquarters
**HDR** high dose rate (of radiation); hot dry rock
**HDRA** Henry Doubleday Research Association
**HDTV** high-definition television
**HDU** haemodialysis unit
**HDV** heavy-duty vehicle; [medicine] hepatitis delta virus
**hdw.** [computing] hardware
**hdwd** hardwood; headword
**HE** [medicine] hepatic encephalopathy; Her Excellency; high energy; higher education; high explosive; His Eminence; His Excellency; home establishment; horizontal equivalent; hydraulic engineer; [vehicle registration] Sheffield
**He** [chemical element] helium
**He.** Hebrew
**h.e.** heat engine; *hic est* (Latin: this is); hub end
**HEA** Health Education Authority; Horticultural Education Association
**HEAO** High Energy Astronomy Observatory; High Energy Astrophysical Observatory
**Heb.** Hebraic; Hebrew; [Bible] Hebrews
**Hebr.** Hebrew; [Bible] Hebrews; Hebridean; Hebrides
**HEC** (*école des*) *hautes études commerciales* (French: (college of) higher commercial studies); Health Education Council; Higher Education Corporation; [chemistry] hydroxyethyl cellulose
**HECTOR** [nuclear technology] heated experimental carbon thermal oscillator reactor
**HEDCOM** [US air force] headquarters command
**HEF** high-energy fuel
**HEFA** Human Embryo and Fertilization Authority
**HEFC** Higher Education Funding Council
**HEH** Her/His Exalted Highness
**h.e.i.** high-explosive incendiary
**HEIC** Honourable East India Company
**HEICS** Honourable East India Company's Service
**heir app.** heir apparent
**heir pres.** heir presumptive
**HEL** high-energy laser
**hel.** helicopter
**heli.** helicopter
**Hellen.** Hellenic; Hellenism; Hellenistic
**HELLP** [medicine] haemolysis, elevated liver enzymes, low platelet count (as in **HELLP syndrome**)
**helo** [short form] helicopter; [short form] heliport
**HELP** helicopter electronic landing path; Help Establish Lasting Peace
**HEMM** heavy earth-moving machinery
**HEMS** helicopter-based emergency medical services

**HEMT** [electronics] high-electron-mobility transistor
**HEO** [astronautics] high earth orbit; higher executive officer
**HEP** [statistics] human error probability; hydroelectric power
**HEPC** [USA] hydroelectric power commission
**HEPCAT** helicopter pilot control and training
**Her** [astronomy] Hercules
**Her.** Hereford(shire)
**her.** heraldic; heraldry; [law] *heres* (Latin: heir)
**HERA** high-explosive rocket-assisted
**HERALD** [nuclear technology] Highly Enriched Reactor, Aldermaston
**herb.** herbaceous; herbalist; herbarium
**hered.** hereditary; heredity
**HERI** Higher Education Research Institute
**herm.** hermetic; hermetically
**Herod.** Herodotus (ancient Greek historian)
**herp.** herpetologist; herpetology
**herpet.** herpetologist; herpetology
**herpetol.** herpetologist; herpetology
**Herts** Hertfordshire
**HERU** Higher Education Research Unit
**HET** heavy-equipment transporter
**heterocl.** heteroclite
**heterog.** heterogeneous
**HEU** highly enriched uranium
**heur.** heuristic
**HEW** [USA] Department of Health, Education and Welfare (replaced by HHS)
**hex** [computing] hexadecimal (notation)
**hex.** hexachord; hexagon; hexagonal
**hexa.** hexamethylene tetramine (synthetic rubber)
**hexag.** hexagonal
**HF** hard firm (pencil lead); [radio] high frequency; Holy Father; home fleet; home forces; [vehicle registration] Liverpool
**H/F** [commerce] *Hlutafjelagid* (Icelandic: limited company, Ltd)
**Hf** [chemical element] hafnium
**hf** half
**h.f.** hold fire; [military] horse and foot
**Hfa** Haifa (Israel)
**HFARA** Honorary Foreign Associate of the Royal Academy
**hf bd** [bookbinding] half bound
**HFC** high-frequency current; [chemistry] hydrofluorocarbon
**hf cf** [bookbinding] half calf
**hf cl.** [bookbinding] half cloth
**HFDF** high-frequency direction-finder
**HFEA** Human Fertility and Embryology Authority
**h.f.m.** hold for money
**hf mor.** [bookbinding] half morocco
**HFO** heavy fuel oil; high-frequency oscillator
**HFR** [nuclear technology] high-flux reactor
**hfr** heifer
**HFRA** Honorary Foreign Member of the Royal Academy
**HFRO** Hill Farming Research Organization
**HFS** heated front seats (in car advertisement)
**Hft** *Heft* (German: part (of book))
**HG** [UK postcode] Harrogate; Haute-Garonne (French department); Her Grace; High German; high grade; His Grace; Holy Ghost; Home Guard; Horse Guards; [vehicle registration] Preston
**Hg** [chemical element] mercury (from Latin *hydrargyrum*)
**hg** hectogram
**hgb.** haemoglobin
**HGC** [computing] Hercules graphics card
**HGCA** Home Grown Cereals Authority
**hgd** hogshead
**HGDH** Her/His Grand Ducal Highness
**HGG** [biochemistry] human gammaglobulin; [medicine] hypogammaglobulinaemia
**HGH** [biochemistry] human growth hormone
**HGHSC** Home Grown Herbage Seeds Committee
**HGMM** Hereditary Grand Master Mason
**hgr** hangar; hanger
**hgt** height
**HGTAC** Home Grown Timber Advisory Committee
**HGTMC** Home Grown Timber Marketing Corporation
**HGV** heavy goods vehicle (replaced by LGV)
**HGW** heat-generating water; H(erbert) G(eorge) Wells (British writer)
**hgwy** highway
**HH** [vehicle registration] Carlisle; double hard (pencil lead); [civil aircraft marking]

Haiti; [fishing port] Harwich; [physics, chemistry] heavy hydrogen; Her Highness; Her Honour; (Member of the) Hesketh Hubbard Art Society; His Highness; His Holiness; His Honour

**hh** hands (unit of height of horses)

**HHA** [horticulture] half-hardy annual; Historic Houses Association

**HHB** [horticulture] half-hardy biennial

**HHD** [USA] Doctor of Humanities (from Latin *Humanitatum Doctor*); [medicine] hypertensive heart disease

**hhd** hogshead

**HHDWS** heavy handy deadweight scrap

**HHFA** [USA] Housing and Home Finance Agency

**HHH** treble hard (pencil lead)

**HHI** Highland Home Industries

**hhld** household

**HHNK** [medicine] hyperglycaemic hyperosmolar nonketoacidotic (diabetic coma)

**H-Hour** Hour Hour (i.e. specified time, esp. of commencement of operation)

**HHP** [horticulture] half-hardy perennial

**HHS** [USA] Department of Health and Human Services (replacement for HEW)

**HHV** [medicine] human herpes virus

**HHW** household hazardous waste

**HI** [civil aircraft marking] Dominican Republic; [US postcode] Hawaii; Hawaiian Islands; hearing impaired; [surveying] height of instrument; *hic iacet* (Latin: here lies) (on tombstone); high intensity

**Hi.** Hindi

**HIA** Housing Improvement Association

**h.i.a.** hold in abeyance

**hi. ac.** high accuracy

**HIAS** [USA] Hebrew Immigrant Aid Society

**HIB** Herring Industry Board

**Hib** [medicine] *Haemophilus influenzae* type B (as in **Hib vaccine**)

**Hib.** Hibernia; Hibernian

**HICAT** high-altitude clear air turbulence

**Hi. Com.** High Command; High Commission; High Commissioner

**HIDB** Highlands and Islands Development Board

**HIE** Highlands and Islands Enterprise

**hier.** hieroglyphics

**hi-fi** [short form] high fidelity (equipment)

**HIH** Her/His Imperial Highness

**HIL** [chemistry] hazardous immiscible liquid

**HILAC** [nuclear technology] heavy-ion linear accelerator

**HILAT** high-latitude (satellite)

**HIM** Her/His Imperial Majesty

**Hind.** Hindi; Hindu; Hindustan; Hindustani

**HIP** [USA] health-insurance plan; [accounting] human information processing

**HIPAR** high-power acquisition radar

**hipot** high potential

**Hipp.** Hippocrates (ancient Greek physician)

**HIPPI** [computing] high-performance parallel processor interface

**HIPS** high-impact polystyrene (synthetic plastic)

**hi-rel** high reliability

**hi-res** [physics] high resolution

**HIS** *hic iacet sepultus* (or *sepulta*) (Latin: here lies buried) (on tombstone)

**hist.** histology; historian; historic(al); history

**histn** historian

**histol.** histological; histologist; histology

**hi-tech** [short form] high technology

**Hitt.** Hittite

**HIUS** Hispanic Institute of the United States

**HIV** [medicine] human immunodeficiency virus (formerly LAV)

**HIV-P** [medicine] HIV-positive

**HJ** [vehicle registration] Chelmsford; *hic jacet* (Latin: here lies) (on tombstone); high jump; Hilal-e-Jurat (Pakistani honour); *Hitler Jugend* (German: Hitler Youth)

**HJBT** [electronics] heterojunction bipolar transistor

**HJS** *hic jacet sepultus* (or *sepulta*) (Latin: here lies buried) (on tombstone)

**HJSC** Hospital Junior Staff Council

**HK** [vehicle registration] Chelmsford; [civil aircraft marking] Colombia; Hong Kong; [international vehicle registration] Hong Kong; House of Keys (parliament of Isle of Man); [taxation] housekeeper allowance

**.hk** Hong Kong (in Internet address)

**hkf** handkerchief

**HKI** Helen Keller International
**HKJ** [international vehicle registration] (Hashemite Kingdom of) Jordan
**HL** hard labour; [fishing port] Hartlepool; Haute-Loire (French department); honours list; House of Laity; House of Lords; [civil aircraft marking] Republic of Korea; [vehicle registration] Sheffield
**Hl.** *Heilige(r)* (German: Saint)
**hl** hectolitre
**h.l.** *hoc loco* (Latin: in this place)
**HLA** [immunology] human lymphocyte antigen
**HLBB** [USA] Home Loan Bank Board
**HLD** Doctor of Humane Letters
**HLE** [physics] high-level exposure (to radiation)
**HLG** Historic Landscapes Group
**HLHSR** [computing] hidden-line/hidden-surface removal
**HLI** Highland Light Infantry
**HLL** [computing] high-level language
**h/lmp** headlamp
**HLNW** high-level nuclear waste
**HLPR** Howard League for Penal Reform
**hlpr** helper
**HLRW** high-level radioactive waste
**HLS** Harvard Law School
**HLW** headlamp wipers (in car advertisement); high-level waste
**HLWN** highest low water neaps (level of tide)
**HLWW** headlamp wash and wipe (in car advertisement)
**HM** [vehicle registration] central London; harbour master; [music] harmonic mean; Haute-Marne (French department); [chemistry] hazardous material; headmaster; headmistress; heavy metal; Her Majesty('s); His Majesty('s); home mission
**hm** hectometre
**h.m.** hallmark; *hoc mense* (Latin: in this month)
**HMA** Head Masters' Association; [computing] high-memory area
**HMAC** Her/His Majesty's Aircraft Carrier
**HMAS** Her/His Majesty's Australian Ship
**HMBDV** Her/His Majesty's Boom Defence Vessel
**HMC** Headmasters' and Headmistresses' Conference; Her/His Majesty's Customs; Historical Manuscripts Commission; Horticultural Marketing Council; Hospital Management Committee; Household Mortgage Corporation
**HMCA** Hospital and Medical Care Association
**HMCG** Her/His Majesty's Coast Guard
**HMCIC** Her/His Majesty's Chief Inspector of Constabulary
**HMCIF** Her/His Majesty's Chief Inspector of Factories
**HMCN** Her/His Majesty's Canadian Navy
**HMCS** Her/His Majesty's Canadian Ship
**HMCSC** Her/His Majesty's Civil Service Commissioners
**HMD** [computing] head-mounted display; Her/His Majesty's Destroyer
**hmd** humid
**HMF** [chemistry] heavy-metal fluoride; Her/His Majesty's Forces
**HMFI** Her/His Majesty's Factory Inspectorate
**HMG** heavy machine gun; Her/His Majesty's Government; [medicine] human menopausal gonadotrophin
**HMHS** Her/His Majesty's Hospital Ship
**HMI** Her/His Majesty's Inspector (of schools); Her/His Majesty's Inspectorate (of schools); [computing] human–machine interface
**HMIC** Her/His Majesty's Inspectorate of Constabulary
**HMIED** Honorary Member of the Institution of Engineering Designers
**HMIP** Her/His Majesty's Inspectorate of Pollution
**HMIT** Her/His Majesty's Inspector of Taxes
**HML** Her/His Majesty's Lieutenant
**HMLR** Her/His Majesty's Land Registry
**HMML** Her/His Majesty's Motor Launch
**HMMS** Her/His Majesty's Mine Sweeper
**HMNZS** Her/His Majesty's New Zealand Ship
**HMO** [USA] health maintenance organization
**HMOCS** Her/His Majesty's Overseas Civil Service
**HMP** Her/His Majesty's Prison; *hoc monumentum posuit* (Latin: (he/she) erected this monument)
**h.m.p.** handmade paper
**HMRT** Her/His Majesty's Rescue Tug
**HMS** [mining] heavy media separation;

Her/His Majesty's Service; Her/His Majesty's Ship
**h.m.s.** hours, minutes, seconds
**HMSO** Her/His Majesty's Stationery Office (replaced by The Stationery Office)
**hmstd** homestead
**HMT** Her/His Majesty's Trawler; Her/His Majesty's Treasury; Her/His Majesty's Tug
**HMV** His Master's Voice (music company)
**HMW** high molecular weight
**HMWA** Hairdressing Manufacturers' and Wholesalers' Association
**HMXB** [astronomy] high-mass X-ray binary
**HN** [vehicle registration] Middlesbrough
**hn** [music] horn
**.hn** Honduras (in Internet address)
**h.n.** [medicine] *hac nocte* (Latin: tonight)
**HNC** [education] Higher National Certificate
**HND** [education] Higher National Diploma
**hndbk** handbook
**hndlg** handling
**hndlr** handler
**HNL** [physics] helium–neon laser
**hnRNA** [biochemistry] heterogeneous nuclear ribonucleic acid
**hnRNP** [biochemistry] heterogeneous nuclear ribonucleoprotein
**Hnrs** Honours
**HO** [vehicle registration] Bournemouth; [law] habitual offender; head office; Home Office; hostilities only; Hydrographic Office
**Ho** [chemical element] holmium
**ho.** house
**h.o.** hold over
**hobgoblin** [informal] help, our budget's gone beyond the limits of our income
**HOC** heavy organic chemical
**HoC** House of Commons
**h.o.c.** held on charge
**HOCRE** Home Office Central Research Establishment
**HoD** head of department
**H of C** House of Commons
**H of K** House of Keys
**H of L** House of Lords
**H of R** [USA] House of Representatives
**HoL** House of Lords
**Hol** [geology] Holocene
**Hol.** Holland
**hol.** holiday
**HOLC** [USA] Home Owners' Loan Corporation
**Holl.** Holland
**HOLLAND** hope our love lasts and never dies (on envelope of love letter)
**Holmes** Home Office Large Major Enquiry System (crime-investigation computer)
**hols** [short form] holidays
**Hom.** Homer (ancient Greek poet)
**homoeo.** homoeopath; homoeopathic; homoeopathy
**Hon.** Honorary; Honorary Member; Honourable
**hon.** honorary; honour; honourable
**Hond.** Honduran; Honduras
**Hono.** Honolulu
**Hons** Honours
**Hon. Sec.** honorary secretary
**HOOD** [computing] hierarchical object-oriented design
**hopeful** [informal] hard-up old person expecting full useful life
**Hor** [astronomy] Horologium
**Hor.** Horace (Roman poet)
**hor.** horizon; horizontal; horology
**hor. decub.** [medicine] *hora decubitus* (Latin: at bedtime) (in prescriptions)
**HoReCa** (International Union of National Associations of) Hotel, Restaurant and Café Keepers
**horol.** horological; horologist; horology
**hort.** horticultural; horticulturalist; horticulture
**hortic.** horticultural; horticulture
**HORU** Home Office Research Unit
**Hos.** [Bible] Hosea
**hosp.** hospital
**HOT** Hawk and Owl Trust
**HOTOL** [astronautics] horizontal take-off and landing
**HOV** high-occupancy vehicle
**how.** howitzer
**HP** [vehicle registration] Coventry; Handley Page (aircraft); [horticulture] hardy perennial; Hautes-Pyrénées (French department); [UK postcode] Hemel Hempstead; [trademark] Hewlett-Packard (computer manufacturer); high performance; high power; high pressure; high priest; Himachal Pradesh; hire purchase; hot-pressed (paper); house phys-

ician; Houses of Parliament; [horticulture] hybrid perpetual (rose); [civil aircraft marking] Panama

**hp** horsepower

**h.p.** half pay; heir presumptive; high power (electricity); hire purchase; horizontally polarized

**HPA** Hospital Physicists' Association

**HPC** [medicine] history of present complaint

**hpch.** harpsichord

**hpd** harpsichord

**HPF** [computing] highest priority first

**HPFS** [computing] high-performance filing system

**HPGL** [trademark, computing] Hewlett-Packard graphics language

**HPIB** [trademark, computing] Hewlett-Packard interface bus

**HPk** Hilal-e-Pakistan (Pakistani honour)

**HPLC** [chemistry] high-performance liquid chromatography; [chemistry] high-pressure liquid chromatography

**HPPA** Horses and Ponies Protection Association

**HPRU** Handicapped Persons Research Unit

**HPS** Highland Pony Society; high-pressure steam; high-protein supplement

**HPT** high-pressure turbine

**HPTA** Hire Purchase Trade Association

**HPV** [medicine] human papilloma virus

**HQ** headquarters

**h.q.** headquarters; *hoc quaere* (Latin: look for this)

**HQA** Hilal-i-Quaid-i-Azam (Pakistani honour)

**HQBA** headquarters base area

**HQMC** [USA] Headquarters, Marine Corps

**HR** [international vehicle registration] Croatia (from Croatian *Hrvatska*); [medicine] heart rate; [UK postcode] Hereford; Highland Regiment; [optics] high resolution; Home Rule; Home Ruler; [baseball] home run; [civil aircraft marking] Honduras; [USA] House of Representatives; human resources; [vehicle registration] Swindon

**H-R** [astronomy] Hertzsprung–Russell (diagram)

**Hr** *Herr* (German: Mr, Sir); Hussar

**hr** [meteorology] hail and rain; hour

**.hr** Croatia (in Internet address)

**h.r.** [baseball] home run

**HRA** [USA] Health Resources Administration

**HRC** [chemistry] high-resolution chromatography; Holy Roman Church

**HRCA** Honorary Royal Cambrian Academician

**HRCT** [medicine] high-resolution compute(rize)d tomography

**HRE** Holy Roman Emperor; Holy Roman Empire

**HREM** high-resolution electron microscope (or microscopy)

**HRG** high-resolution graphics

**HRGC** [chemistry] high-resolution gas chromatography

**HRGI** Honorary Member of the Royal Glasgow Institute of the Fine Arts

**HRH** Her/His Royal Highness

**HRHA** Honorary Member of the Royal Hibernian Academy

**HRI** Honorary Member of the Royal Institute of Painters in Water Colours

**HRIP** *hic requiescit in pace* (Latin: here rests in peace) (on tombstone)

**HRM** human resource management

**Hrn** *Herren* (German: Messrs, Sirs, Gentlemen)

**HROI** Honorary Member of the Royal Institute of Oil Painters

**HRP** Home Responsibilities Protection; [military] human remains pouch

**HRR** [taxation] higher reduced rate

**HRS** Human Rights Society

**hrs** hours

**HRSA** Honorary Member of the Royal Scottish Academy

**hrsg.** *herausgegeben* (German: edited, published)

**HRSW** Honorary Member of the Royal Scottish Water Colour Society

**HRT** [medicine] hormone replacement therapy

**HRTEM** high-resolution transmission electron microscope (or microscopy)

**HRW** heated rear window (in car advertisement)

**HS** [vehicle registration] Glasgow; Haute-Saône (French department); Hawker Siddeley (aircraft); *hic sepultus* (or *sepulta*) (Latin: here is buried) (on tombstone); high school; Home Secretary; hospital ship; house surgeon; [numismatics] sesterce (Roman coin); [civil aircraft marking] Thailand

**Hs** [chemical element] hassium

**Hs.** *Handschrift* (German: manuscript)

**hs** [medicine] hail and snow

**h.s.** highest score; *hoc sensu* (Latin: in this sense); [medicine] *hora somni* (Latin: at bedtime) (in prescriptions)

**HSA** [USA] Health Systems Agency; [medicine] human serum albumin; Humane Slaughter Association

**HSAB** [chemistry] hard and soft acids and bases

**HSB** [computing] hue, saturation, brightness

**HSBC** Hongkong and Shanghai Banking Corporation

**HSC** [medicine] haemopoietic stem cell; Health and Safety Commission; [Australia] Higher School Certificate

**HSD** heat-storage device; high-speed diesel

**HSDU** hospital sterilization and disinfection unit

**HSE** Health and Safety Executive; *hic sepultus* (or *sepulta*) *est* (Latin: here is buried) (on tombstone)

**hse** house

**hsekpr** housekeeper

**hsg** housing

**HSH** Her/His Serene Highness

**HSI** [computing] human–system interaction (or interface)

**HSL** [computing] hue, saturation, lightness; Huguenot Society of London

**HSLA** high strength, low alloy (steel)

**HSM** Her Serene Majesty; [computing] hierarchical storage management; His Serene Majesty

**HSO** Hamburg Symphony Orchestra

**HSP** [medicine] heat-shock protein

**HSR** [genetics] homogeneously staining region

**HSS** high-speed steel; *Historicae Societatis Socius* (Latin: Fellow of the Historical Society)

**Hss.** *Handschriften* (German: manuscripts)

**HSSU** hospital sterile supply unit

**HST** Harry S Truman (US president); Hawaii Standard Time; highest spring tide; high-speed train; Hubble Space Telescope; hypersonic transport

**HSV** [medicine] herpes simplex virus

**HSWA** [USA] Hazardous and Solid Waste Act; [USA] Hazardous and Solid Waste Amendments

**HT** [vehicle registration] Bristol; [sports] half time; Hawaii Time; heat-treated; heat treatment; high temperature; [electrical engineering] high tension; high tide; high treason; [horticulture] hybrid tea (rose)

**ht** heat; height

**h/t** [printing] half-title

**.ht** Haiti (in Internet address)

**h.t.** [sports] half time; halftone; heavy tank; *hoc tempore* (Latin: at this time); *hoc titulo* (Latin: under this title)

**HTA** Help the Aged; Horticultural Traders' Association; Household Textile Association

**h.t.b.** high-tension battery

**HTC** [physics] heat-transfer coefficient

**htd** heated

**Hte** *Haute* (French: high) (in place-names)

**htg** heating

**HTGR** [nuclear technology] high-temperature gas-cooled reactor

**HTLV** [medicine] human T-cell lymphotropic virus

**HTM** heat-transfer medium

**HTML** [computing] hypertext markup language (used on Internet)

**HTOL** [astronautics] horizontal take-off and landing

**HTR** [nuclear technology] high-temperature reactor

**htr** heater

**H Trin.** Holy Trinity

**HTS** high-temperature superconductivity; high-temperature superconductor; high-tensile steel

**Hts** Heights (in place-names)

**h.t.s.** half-time survey; high-tensile steel

**HTT** heavy tactical transport

**HTTP** [computing] hypertext transfer protocol (used on Internet)

**HTTR** [nuclear technology] high-temperature test reactor

**HTV** Harlech Television

**ht wkt** [cricket] hit wicket

**HU** [vehicle registration] Bristol; Harvard University; [UK postcode] Hull

**.hu** Hungary (in Internet address)

**HUAC** House (of Representatives) Un-American Activities Committee
**HUD** [aeronautics, computing] head-up display; [USA] (Department of) Housing and Urban Development
**Hugo** Human Genome Organization
**HUJ** Hebrew University of Jerusalem
**HUKFORLANT** [US navy] hunter-killer forces, Atlantic
**HUKS** [US navy] hunter-killer submarine
**Hum.** humanities (academic subject)
**hum.** human; humane; humanism; humanity; humble; humorous
**HUMINT** [military] human intelligence
**HUMRRO** Human Resources Research Office
**HUMV** [military] human light vehicle
**hund.** hundred
**Hung.** Hungarian; Hungary
**Hunts** Huntingdonshire
**HUP** Harvard University Press
**hur.** hurricane
**Huridocs** International Human Rights Information and Documentation System
**hurr.** hurricane
**Husat** Human Science and Advanced Technology Research Institute
**husb.** husband; husbandry
**HV** [vehicle registration] central London; health visitor; [anatomy] hepatic vein; high velocity; high voltage; *hoc verbum* (Latin: this word); [civil aircraft marking] Vatican City State
**HVAC** heating, ventilation and air conditioning; high-voltage alternating current
**HVAR** high-velocity aircraft rocket
**HVCA** Heating and Ventilating Contractors' Association
**HVCert** Health Visitor's Certificate
**HVDC** high-voltage direct current
**HVEM** high-voltage electron microscope (or microscopy)
**HVP** hydrolysed vegetable protein
**HVT** [physics] half-value thickness; health visitor teacher
**hvy** heavy
**HW** [vehicle registration] Bristol; hazardous waste; high water; hot water
**h/w** herewith; husband and wife
**h.w.** [cricket] hit wicket
**HWL** Henry Wadsworth Longfellow (US poet); high-water line
**HWLB** high water, London Bridge
**HWM** high-water mark
**HWONT** high water, ordinary neap tides
**HWOST** high water, ordinary spring tides
**HWR** [nuclear technology] heavy-water reactor
**HWS** hot water system; hurricane warning system
**HWW** headlamp wash and wipe (in car advertisement); [engineering] hot-and-warm worked
**hwy** highway
**HX** [vehicle registration] central London; [UK postcode] Halifax
**HXR** hard X-ray
**HY** [vehicle registration] Bristol
**Hy.** Henry
**hy** heavy; highway
**Hya** [astronomy] Hydra
**hyb.** hybrid
**HyCoSy** [medicine] hysterosalpingo-contrast sonography
**hyd.** hydrate; hydraulic; hydrographic
**hydrog.** hydrographic
**hydt** hydrant
**hyg.** hygiene; hygienic
**Hyi** [astronomy] Hydrus
**hyp.** hypodermic; [mathematics] hypotenuse; hypothesis; hypothetical
**hyperb.** hyperbole; hyperbolic
**hypo** [short form] hypodermic (syringe)
**hypoth.** hypothesis; hypothetical
**HZ** [civil aircraft marking] Saudi Arabia; [vehicle registration] Tyrone
**Hz** hertz

# I

**I** *Iesus* (Latin: Jesus); *Imperator* (Latin: Emperor); *Imperatrix* (Latin: Empress); Imperial; *Imperium* (Latin: Empire); [advertising] (single column) inch; incumbent; Independence; Independent; India; Indian; [chemistry] inductive effect; *Infidelis* (Latin: infidel); information; inspector; Institute; instructor; intelligence; interceptor; International; interpreter; [chemical element] iodine; Ireland; Irish; Island; Isle; issue; Italian; [civil aircraft marking] Italy; [international vehicle registration] Italy; [Roman numeral] one

***I*** [physics] electric current; [chemistry] ionic strength; [physics, chemistry] ionization potential; [physics] luminous intensity; [physics] moment of inertia (in mechanics); [physics] radiant intensity; [mathematics] unit matrix

**i** [mathematics] imaginary number (square root of −1); [Roman numeral] one

***i*** [physics] instantaneous current

**i.** *id* (Latin: that); incisor (tooth); indicate; [banking] interest; [grammar] intransitive; island

**3i** Investors in Industry

**IA** [vehicle registration] Antrim; Incorporated Accountant; Indian Army; infected area; information anxiety; [taxation] initial allowance; Institute of Actuaries; Inter-American; [computing] International Alphabet (as in **IA5**); [medicine] intra-arterial; [US postcode] Iowa

**I/A** Isle of Anglesey

**Ia** Iowa

**i.A** *im Auftrage* (German: by order of)

**i.a.** immediately available; *in absentia* (Latin: while absent); [aeronautics] indicated altitude; initial appearance

**IAA** indoleacetic acid (plant hormone); Institute of Industrial Administration; International Academy of Astronautics; International Actuarial Association; International Advertising Association

**IAAA** Irish Amateur Athletic Association; Irish Association of Advertising Agencies

**IAAE** [USA] Institution of Automotive and Aeronautical Engineers

**IAAF** International Amateur Athletic Federation

**IAAP** International Association of Applied Psychology

**IAAS** Incorporated Association of Architects and Surveyors

**IAB** Industrial Advisory Board; Industrial Arbitration Board; Inter-American Bank; Internet architecture board

**IABA** International Association of Aircraft Brokers and Agents

**IABO** International Association of Biological Oceanography

**IAC** [USA] Industrial Advisory Council; Institute of Amateur Cinematographers

**i.a.c.** integration, assembly and checkout

**IACA** Independent Air Carriers' Association

**IACB** International Advisory Committee on Bibliography (in UNESCO)

**IACCP** Inter-American Council of Commerce and Production

**IACOMS** International Advisory Committee on Marine Sciences

**IACP** International Association for Child Psychiatry and Allied Professions; International Association of Chiefs of Police; [USA] International Association of Computer Programmers

**IACR** Institute of Arable Crops Research

**IACS** International Annealed Copper Standard

**IADB** Inter-American Defense Board; Inter-American Development Bank

**IADR** International Association for Dental Research

**IAE** [USA] Institute of Atomic Energy; Institute of Automotive Engineers; Institution of Automobile Engineers

**IAEA** International Atomic Energy Agency

**IAEC** Israel Atomic Energy Commission

**IAECOSOC** Inter-American Economic and Social Council

**IAEE** International Association of Energy Economists

**IAF** Indian Air Force; Indian Auxiliary Force; International Archery Federation; International Astronautical Federation

**i.a.f.** [aeronautics] interview after flight

**IAFD** International Association on Food Distribution

**IAG** International Association of Geodesy; International Association of Geology; International Association of Gerontology

**IAGB&I** Ileostomy Association of Great Britain and Ireland

**IAgrE** Institution of Agricultural Engineers

**IAH** International Association of Hydro-

geologists; International Association of Hydrology
**IAHA** Inter-American Hotel Association
**IAHM** Incorporated Association of Headmasters
**IAHP** International Association of Horticultural Producers
**IAHR** International Association for Hydraulic Research; International Association for the History of Religions
**IAI** International African Institute
**IAL** Imperial Airways Limited; Imperial Arts League; [computing] international algorithmic language; Irish Academy of Letters
**IALA** International African Law Association; International Association of Lighthouse Authorities
**IALL** International Association of Law Libraries
**IALS** International Association of Legal Science
**IAM** Institute of Administrative Management; Institute of Advanced Motorists; Institute of Aviation Medicine; [anatomy] internal auditory meatus; [USA] International Association of Machinists and Aerospace Workers; International Association of Meteorology; International Association of Microbiologists
**IAMA** Incorporated Advertising Managers' Association
**IAMAP** International Association of Meteorology and Atmospheric Physics
**IAMC** Indian Army Medical Corps
**IAML** International Association of Music Libraries
**IAMS** International Association of Microbiological Societies; International Association of Microbiological Studies
**IANC** International Airline Navigators' Council
**I&D** [medicine] incision and drainage
**I&O** intake and output
**IANE** Institute of Advanced Nursing Education
**IANEC** Inter-American Nuclear Energy Commission
**IAO** Incorporated Association of Organists
**IAOC** Indian Army Ordnance Corps
**IAOS** Irish Agricultural Organization Society
**IAP** International Academy of Pathology; Internet access provider
**IAPA** Inter-American Press Association
**IAPB** International Association for the Prevention of Blindness
**IAPC** International Auditing Practices Committee
**IAPG** International Association of Physical Geography
**IAPH** International Association of Ports and Harbours
**IAPO** International Association of Physical Oceanography
**IAPS** Incorporated Association of Preparatory Schools
**IAPSO** International Association for the Physical Sciences of the Oceans
**IAPT** International Association for Plant Taxonomy
**IAR** instruction address register
**IARA** Inter-Allied Reparations Agency
**IARC** Indian Agricultural Research Council; International Agency for Research on Cancer
**IARD** International Association for Rural Development
**IARF** International Association for Religious Freedom
**IARI** Indian Agricultural Research Institute
**IARO** Indian Army Reserve of Officers
**IARU** International Amateur Radio Union
**IAS** [computing] immediate access store; Indian Administrative Service (formerly ICS); [aeronautics] indicated air speed; [USA] Institute for Advanced Studies; [USA] Institute of the Aerospace Sciences; [aeronautics] instrument approach system; International Accounting Standard
**IASA** International Air Safety Association
**IASC** Indian Army Service Corps; International Accounting Standards Committee
**IASH** International Association of Scientific Hydrology
**IASI** Inter-American Statistical Institute
**i.a.s.o.r.** ice and snow on runway
**IASS** International Association for Scandinavian Studies; International Association of Soil Science
**IAT** International Atomic Time
**i.a.t.** inside air temperature

**IATA** International Air Transport Association; International Amateur Theatre Association
**IATUL** International Association of Technological University Libraries
**IAU** International Association of Universities; International Astronomical Union
**IAUPL** International Association of University Professors and Lecturers
**IAV** International Association of Vulcanology
**IAVG** International Association for Vocational Guidance
**IAW** International Alliance of Women
**i.a.w.** in accordance with
**IAWPRC** International Association on Water Pollution Research and Control
**IB** [vehicle registration] Armagh; in bond; incendiary bomb; industrial business; information bureau; instruction book; intelligence branch; International Baccalaureate; International Bank (for Reconstruction and Development); invoice book
**ib.** *ibidem* (Latin: in the same place) (indicating reference cited earlier)
**IBA** Independent Bankers' Association; Independent Broadcasting Authority (replacement for ITA); Industrial Bankers' Association; [taxation] industrial buildings allowances; International Bar Association; International Bowling Association; Investment Bankers' Association
**IBAA** Investment Bankers' Association of America
**IBAE** Institution of British Agricultural Engineers
**IBB** Institute of British Bakers; International Bowling Board; Invest in Britain Bureau
**IBBR** [finance] interbank bid rate
**IBC** International Broadcasting Corporation
**IBD** Incorporated Institute of British Decorators and Interior Designers; [medicine] inflammatory bowel disease; [electronics] ion-beam deposition
**IBE** Institution of British Engineers; International Bureau of Education (became part of UNESCO)
**IBEL** [finance] interest-bearing eligible liability
**IBEW** [USA] International Brotherhood of Electrical Workers
**IBF** Institute of British Foundrymen; International Badminton Federation; international banking facility; International Boxing Federation
**IBG** Incorporated Brewers Guild; Institute of British Geographers; [computing] interblock gap
**IBI** [book-keeping] invoice book inwards
**IBID** international bibliographical description
**ibid.** *ibidem* (Latin: in the same place) (indicating reference cited earlier)
**IBiol** Institute of Biology
**IBK** Institute of Book-keepers
**IBM** intercontinental ballistic missile; International Business Machines (Corporation) (computer manufacturer)
**IBMBR** [finance] interbank market bid rate
**IBO** [book-keeping] invoice book outwards
**IBP** initial boiling point; Institute of British Photographers; International Biological Programme
**IBPAT** [USA] International Brotherhood of Painters and Allied Trades
**IBRC** Insurance Brokers Registration Council
**IBRD** International Bank for Reconstruction and Development (World Bank)
**IBRO** International Bank Research Organization; International Brain Research Organization
**IBS** Institute of Bankers in Scotland; [medicine] irritable bowel syndrome
**IBScot** Institute of Bankers in Scotland
**IBST** Institute of British Surgical Technicians
**IBT** International Brotherhood of Teamsters, Chauffeurs, Warehousemen and Helpers of America
**IBTE** Institute of British Telecommunications Engineers
**IBWM** International Bureau of Weights and Measures
**IC** identity card; *Iesus Christus* (Latin: Jesus Christ); [grammar] immediate constituent; [immunology] immune complex; Imperial College (of Science and Technology, London); [astronomy] Index Catalogue; industrial court; information centre; [electronics] integrated

circuit; Intelligence Corps; [engineering] internal-combustion (engine); [chemistry] ion chromatography; [physics] ionization chamber

**I-C** Indo-China

**i/c** in charge; in command

**i.c.** index correction; instrument correction; internal communication

**ICA** ignition control additive (for motor vehicles); Industrial Caterers' Association; Institute of Chartered Accountants (in England and Wales); Institute of Company Accountants; Institute of Contemporary Arts; [medicine] internal carotid artery; International Cartographic Association; International Chefs' Association; International Coffee Agreement; International Colour Authority; International Commercial Arbitration; International Commission on Acoustics; International Commodity Agreement; International Cooperation Administration; International Cooperative Alliance; International Council on Archives; International Court of Arbitration; International Cyclist Association; invalid care allowance

**ICAA** Invalid Children's Aid Association

**ICAE** International Commission on Agricultural Engineering

**ICAEW** Institute of Chartered Accountants in England and Wales

**ICAI** Institute of Chartered Accountants in Ireland; International Commission for Agricultural Industries

**ICAM** Institute of Corn and Agricultural Merchants

**ICAN** International Commission for Air Navigation

**IC&CY** Inns of Court and City Yeomanry

**ICAO** International Civil Aviation Organization

**ICAP** Institute of Certified Ambulance Personnel; International Congress of Applied Psychology

**ICAR** Indian Council of Agricultural Research

**ICAS** Institute of Chartered Accountants of Scotland; International Council of Aeronautical Sciences; International Council of Aerospace Sciences

**ICB** Institute of Comparative Biology

**ICBA** International Community of Booksellers' Associations

**ICBD** International Council of Ballroom Dancing

**ICBHI** Industrial Craft (Member) of the British Horological Institute

**ICBM** intercontinental ballistic missile

**ICBN** International Code of Botanical Nomenclature

**ICBP** International Council for Bird Preservation

**ICC** [USA] Indian Claims Commission; intercounty championship; International Chamber of Commerce; International Children's Centre; International Congregational Council; International Convention Centre (Birmingham); International Correspondence Colleges; International Cricket Conference (formerly Imperial Cricket Conference); [USA] Interstate Commerce Commission

**ICCB** Intergovernmental Consultation and Coordination Board

**ICCC** International Conference of Catholic Charities

**ICCE** International Council of Commerce Employers

**ICCF** International Correspondence Chess Federation

**ICCH** International Commodities Clearing House

**ICCPR** International Covenant on Civil and Political Rights (of UN)

**ICCROM** International Centre for Conservation at Rome

**ICCS** International Centre of Criminological Studies

**ICD** Institute of Cooperative Directors; International Classification of Diseases (published by WHO)

**ICDO** International Civil Defence Organization

**ICE** [medicine] ice, compress, elevation (treatment for bruised limbs); [computing] in-circuit emulator; Institute of Chartered Engineers; Institution of Civil Engineers; internal-combustion engine; International Cultural Exchange

**Ice.** Iceland; Icelander; Icelandic

**ICED** International Council for Educational Development

**ICEF** International Council for Educational Films
**ICEI** Institution of Civil Engineers of Ireland
**Icel.** Iceland; Icelander; Icelandic
**ICeram** Institute of Ceramics (became part of Institute of Materials)
**ICES** International Council for the Exploration of the Sea
**ICETT** Industrial Council for Educational and Training Technology
**ICF** Industrial and Commercial Finance Corporation; [nuclear technology] inertial-confinement fusion; International Canoe Federation; International Chess Federation
**ICFTU** International Confederation of Free Trade Unions
**icg** icing
**ICGS** interactive computer-graphics system; International Catholic Girls' Society
**ich.** ichthyology
**ICHCA** International Cargo Handling Coordination Association
**IChemE** Institution of Chemical Engineers
**ICHEO** Inter-University Council for Higher Education Overseas
**ICHPER** International Council for Health, Physical Education and Recreation
**ichth.** ichthyology
**ichthyol.** ichthyologist; ichthyology
**ICI** Imperial Chemical Industries; International Commission on Illumination; [USA] Investment Casting Institute
**ICIA** International Credit Insurance Association
**ICIANZ** Imperial Chemical Industries, Australia and New Zealand
**ICID** International Commission on Irrigation and Drainage
**ICIDH** International Classification of Impairments, Disabilities and Handicaps (published by WHO)
**ICJ** International Commission of Jurists; International Court of Justice
**ICJW** International Council of Jewish Women
**ICL** International Computers Limited; International Confederation of Labour
**ICLA** International Committee on Laboratory Animals
**ICM** Institute for Complementary Medicine; Institute of Credit Management; Intergovernmental Committee for Migrations (of UN); International Confederation of Midwives; [astronomy] intracluster medium; Irish Church Missions
**ICMMP** International Committee of Military Medicine and Pharmacy
**ICMS** International Centre for Mathematical Sciences (Edinburgh)
**ICN** *in Christi nomine* (Latin: in Christ's name); infection control nurse; International Council of Nurses
**ICNA** Infection Control Nurses' Association
**ICNB** International Code of Nomenclature of Bacteria
**ICNCP** International Code of Nomenclature of Cultivated Plants
**ICNV** International Code of Nomenclature of Viruses
**ICO** Institute of Careers Officers; International Coffee Organization; Islamic Conference Organization
**ICOM** International Council of Museums
**ICOMOS** International Council of Monuments and Sites
**ICON** indexed currency option note
**icon.** iconographical; iconography
**ICOR** Intergovernmental Conference on Oceanic Research (in UNESCO)
**ICorrST** Institution of Corrosion Science and Technology
**ICP** [medicine] intracranial pressure
**ICPA** International Commission for the Prevention of Alcoholism; International Cooperative Petroleum Association
**ICPHS** International Council for Philosophy and Humanistic Studies
**ICPO** International Criminal Police Organization (= Interpol)
**ICPU** International Catholic Press Union
**ICQ** [accounting] internal control questionnaire
**ICR** [computing] intelligent character recognition
**ICRC** International Committee of the Red Cross
**ICRF** Imperial Cancer Research Fund
**ICRP** International Commission on Radiological Protection

**ICRU** International Commission on Radiation Units (and Measurements)
**ICRUM** International Commission on Radiation Units and Measurements
**ICS** Imperial College of Science and Technology (London); Indian Civil Service (former name of IAS); instalment credit selling; Institute of Chartered Shipbrokers; International Chamber of Shipping; International College of Surgeons; international consultancy service; [finance] investors' compensation scheme
**ICSA** Institute of Chartered Secretaries and Administrators (formerly CIS)
**ICSB** International Congress of Small Businesses
**ICSH** [biochemistry] interstitial-cell-stimulating hormone
**ICSI** [medicine] intracytoplasmic sperm injection (infertility treatment)
**ICSID** International Council of Societies of Industrial Design
**ICSLS** International Convention for Safety of Life at Sea
**ICSPE** International Council of Sport and Physical Education
**ICST** Imperial College of Science and Technology (London)
**ICSU** International Council of Scientific Unions (in UNESCO)
**ICTA** International Council of Travel Agents
**ICTP** International Centre for Theoretical Physics
**ICTU** Irish Congress of Trade Unions
**ICTV** International Committee on Taxonomy of Viruses
**ICU** [medicine] intensive care unit; international code use (in signalling)
**ICVA** International Council of Voluntary Agencies
**ICW** Institute of Clerks of Works of Great Britain; International Congress of Women; [telecommunications] interrupted continuous wave
**i.c.w.** in connection with
**ICWA** Indian Council of World Affairs; Institute of Cost and Works Accountants
**ICWG** International Cooperative Women's Guild
**ICWU** [USA] International Chemical Workers Union
**ICYF** International Catholic Youth Federation
**ICZN** International Code of Zoological Nomenclature
**ID** [US postcode] Idaho; identification; identify; identity; infectious disease(s); information department; inside diameter; Institute of Directors; intelligence department; [medicine] intradermal; [currency] Iraqi dinar
**Id.** Idaho
**id.** *idem* (Latin: the same (man))
**.id** Indonesia (in Internet address)
**i.d.** inside diameter
**IDA** Industrial Diamond Association; International Development Association (affiliate of World Bank); Irish Dental Association; Islamic Democratic Association
**IDB** illicit diamond buyer; illicit diamond buying; Industrial Development Bank; [Northern Ireland] Industrial Development Board; Inter-American Development Bank; Internal Drainage Board
**IDC** industrial development certificate; insulation displacement connector
**ID card** identification card
**IDD** [medicine] insulin-dependent diabetes; [telecommunications] international direct dialling
**IDDA** Interior Decorators and Designers Association
**IDDD** [telecommunications] international direct distance dialling
**IDDM** [medicine] insulin-dependent diabetes mellitus
**IDE** [computing] integrated drive electronics; [computing] intelligent drive electronics; [computing] interactive development environment
**iden.** identification; identify; identity
**ident.** identification; identify; identity
**IDF** International Dairy Federation; International Democratic Fellowship; International Dental Federation; International Diabetes Federation
**IDIB** Industrial Diamond Information Bureau
**IDL** [biochemistry] intermediate-density lipoprotein; international date line; international driver's licence
**IDLH** immediately dangerous to life and health

**IDMS** [computing] integrated data-management system
**IDN** *in Dei nomine* (Latin: in God's name); [computing] integrated data network
**IDP** Institute of Data Processing; [computing] integrated data processing; International Driving Permit; [astronomy] interplanetary dust particle(s)
**IDPM** Institute of Data Processing Management
**IDR** [finance] International Depository Receipt
**IDRC** International Development Research Centre
**IDS** Income Data Services; Industry Department for Scotland; Institute of Development Studies
**IDSM** Indian Distinguished Service Medal
**IDT** industrial design technology
**IDV** International Distillers and Vintners
**IE** [medicine] immunoelectrophoresis; index error; Indian Empire; Indo-European (languages); Institute of Engineers and Technicians (became part of IIE); [chemistry] ion exchange; [chemistry] ionization energy; [fishing port] Irvine
**.ie** Ireland (in Internet address)
**i.e.** *id est* (Latin: that is); inside edge
**IEA** Institute of Economic Affairs; Institution of Engineers, Australia; International Economic Association; International Energy Agency; International Ergonomics Association
**IE(Aust)** Institution of Engineers, Australia
**IEC** industrial energy conservation; integrated environmental control; International Electrotechnical Commission
**IED** improvised explosive device; Information Engineering Directorate; Institution of Engineering Designers
**IEDD** improvised explosive device disposal
**IEE** [USA] Institute of Energy Economics; Institution of Electrical Engineers
**IEEE** Institute of Electrical and Electronics Engineers
**IEEIE** Institution of Electrical and Electronics Incorporated Engineers (became part of IIE)
**IEF** Indian Expeditionary Force
**IEHO** Institution of Environmental Health Officers
**IEI** Industrial Engineering Institute; Institution of Engineers of Ireland
**IEM** inborn error of metabolism
**IEME** Inspectorate of Electrical and Mechanical Engineering
**IEng** Incorporated Engineer
**IER** Institute of Environmental Research
**IERE** Institution of Electronic and Radio Engineers (became part of IEE)
**IES** Indian Educational Service; Institution of Engineers and Shipbuilders in Scotland
**IET** interest equalization tax
**IETF** Internet Engineering Task Force
**IEW** intelligence and electronic warfare
**IExpE** Institute of Explosives Engineers
**IF** [nuclear technology] inertial fusion; [baseball] infield; [biochemistry] inhibitory factor; [genetics] initiation factor; [sports] inside forward; Institute of Fuel; [medicine] interferon; [electronics] intermediate frequency
**i-f** in-flight
**i.f.** information feedback; *ipse fecit* (Latin: (he) did it himself)
**IFA** [medicine] immunofluorescence assay; Incorporated Faculty of Arts; independent financial adviser; instrumented fuel assembly; International Federation of Actors; International Fertility Association; International Fiscal Association; Irish Football Association
**IFAA** Independent Financial Advisers Association
**IFAC** International Federation of Automatic Control
**IFAD** International Fund for Agricultural Development
**IFALPA** International Federation of Air Line Pilots' Associations
**IFAP** International Federation of Agricultural Producers
**IFATCA** International Federation of Air Traffic Controllers' Associations
**IFAW** International Fund for Animal Welfare
**IFB** [finance] invitation for bid
**IFBPW** International Federation of Business and Professional Women
**IFC** International Finance Corporation

(affiliate of World Bank); [USA, Canada] International Fisheries Commission
**IFCATI** International Federation of Cotton and Allied Textile Industries
**IFCC** International Federation of Camping and Caravanning; International Federation of Children's Communities
**IFCCPTE** International Federation of Commercial, Clerical, Professional and Technical Employees
**IFCO** International Fisheries Cooperative Organization
**IFCTU** International Federation of Christian Trade Unions
**IFE** [computing] intelligent front end
**IFF** [radar] Identification, Friend or Foe; [computing] image file format; Institute of Freight Forwarders; [computing] interchange file format
**iff** [logic, mathematics] if and only if
**IFFA** International Federation of Film Archives
**IFFPA** International Federation of Film Producers' Associations
**IFFS** International Federation of Film Societies
**IFFTU** International Federation of Free Teachers' Unions
**IFGA** International Federation of Grocers' Associations
**IFGO** International Federation of Gynaecology and Obstetrics
**IFHE** International Federation of Home Economics
**IFHP** International Federation for Housing and Planning
**IFIP** International Federation for Information Processing
**IFireE** Institution of Fire Engineers
**IFJ** International Federation of Journalists
**IFL** International Friendship League
**IFLA** International Federation of Landscape Architects; International Federation of Library Associations
**IFM** International Falcon Movement
**IFMC** International Folk Music Council
**IFMSA** International Federation of Medical Students' Associations
**IFOR** Implementation Force (NATO-led peacekeeping force in Bosnia, replaced by SFOR); International Fellowship of Reconciliation
**IFORS** International Federation of Operational Research Societies
**Ifox** Irish Futures and Options Exchange
**IFP** [South Africa] Inkatha Freedom Party
**IFPA** Industrial Film Producers' Association
**IFPAAW** International Federation of Plantation, Agricultural and Allied Workers
**IFPCS** International Federation of Unions of Employees in Public and Civil Services
**IFPM** International Federation of Physical Medicine
**IFPW** International Federation of Petroleum (and Chemical) Workers
**IFR** [aeronautics] instrument flying regulations; [nuclear technology] integral fast reactor
**IFRB** International Frequency Registration Board
**IFS** Indian Forest Service; Institute for Fiscal Studies; International Federation of Surveyors; Irish Free State; [computing] iterated function system
**IFSPO** International Federation of Senior Police Officers
**IFST** Institute of Food Science and Technology
**IFSW** International Federation of Social Workers
**IFTA** International Federation of Teachers' Associations; International Federation of Travel Agencies
**IFTC** International Film and Television Council
**IFTU** International Federation of Trade Unions (replaced by WFTU)
**IFUW** International Federation of University Women
**IFWEA** International Federation of Workers' Educational Associations
**IFWL** International Federation of Women Lawyers
**IG** [UK postcode] Ilford; imperial gallon; Indo-Germanic (languages); industrial group; [astronomy] inertial guidance; inner guard; Inspector-General; Instructor in Gunnery; Irish Guards
**Ig** [immunology] immunoglobulin
**ig.** ignition
**IGA** International Geographical Association; International Golf Association

**IGADD** Intergovernmental Authority on Drought and Development
**IGasE** Institution of Gas Engineers
**IGBT** [computing] insulated-gate bipolar transistor
**IGC** Intergovernmental Conference
**IGCM** Incorporated Guild of Church Musicians
**IGD** illicit gold dealer
**IGES** [computing] initial graphics exchange specification
**IGF** Inspector-General of Fortifications; [medicine] insulin-like growth factor; International Gymnastic Federation
**IGFA** International Game Fish Association
**IGFET** [electronics] insulated-gate field-effect transistor
**IGH** Incorporated Guild of Hairdressers
**IGM** [chess] International Grandmaster
**ign.** ignite(s); ignition; *ignotus* (Latin: unknown)
**IGO** intergovernmental organization
**IGPP** Institute of Geophysics and Planetary Physics
**IGRS** Irish Genealogical Research Society
**IGS** Imperial General Staff; independent grammar school
**IGU** International Gas Union; International Geographical Union
**IGWF** International Garment Workers' Federation
**IGY** International Geophysical Year
**IH** *iacet hic* (Latin: here lies) (on tombstone); industrial hygiene; [computing] interrupt handler; [fishing port] Ipswich
**IHA** International Hotel Association
**IHAB** International Horticultural Advisory Bureau
**IHB** International Hydrographic Bureau
**IHC** [New Zealand] intellectually handicapped child; Intercontinental Hotels Corporation
**IHCA** International Hebrew Christian Alliance
**IHD** [medicine] ischaemic heart disease
**IHEU** International Humanist and Ethical Union
**IHF** Industrial Hygiene Foundation; International Hockey Federation; International Hospitals Federation
**IHospE** Institute of Hospital Engineering
**ihp** indicated horsepower
**IHR** Institute of Historical Research
**IHRB** International Hockey Rules Board
**IHS** *Iesous* (Greek: Jesus) (from first three letters of name in Greek alphabet); *Iesus Hominum Salvator* (Latin: Jesus Saviour of Mankind); *in hoc signo* (Latin: in this sign)
**IHSM** Institute of Health Services Management
**IHT** inheritance tax; Institution of Highways and Transportation
**IHU** Irish Hockey Union
**IHVE** Institute of Heating and Ventilation Engineers
**II** [electronics] image intensifier; [electronics] ion implantation
**IIA** International Institute of Agriculture
**IIAC** Industrial Injuries Advisory Council
**IIAL** International Institute of Arts and Letters
**IIAS** International Institute of Administrative Sciences
**IIB** *Institut international des brevets* (French: International Patent Institute)
**IIBD&ID** Incorporated Institute of British Decorators and Interior Designers
**IID** [medicine] insulin-independent diabetes; [electronics] ion-implantation doping
**iid.** *iidem* (Latin: the same (men))
**i.i.d.** [statistics] independent identically distributed (random variables)
**IIE** Institute for International Education; Institution of Incorporated Engineers (in Electronic, Electrical and Mechanical Engineering); International Institute of Embryology
**IIEP** International Institute of Educational Planning
**IIExE** Institution of Incorporated Executive Engineers
**IIF** [computing] image interchange facility
**IIHF** International Ice Hockey Federation
**III** International Institute of Interpreters
**IIL** [electronics] integrated injection logic
**IIM** Institution of Industrial Managers
**IInfSc** Institute of Information Scientists
**IIP** *Institut international de la presse* (French: International Press Institute); International Ice Patrol; International Institute of Philosophy
**IIR** [chemistry] isobutylene-isoprene rubber

**IIRS** [Ireland] Institute for Industrial Research and Standards
**IIS** Institute of Information Scientists; International Institute of Sociology
**IISO** Institution of Industrial Safety Officers
**IISS** International Institute of Strategic Studies
**IIT** Indian Institute of Technology
**IIW** International Institute of Welding
**IJ** [vehicle registration] Down
**i.J** *im Jahre* (German: in the year)
**IKBS** [computing] intelligent knowledge-based system
**IL** [vehicle registration] Fermanagh; [US postcode] Illinois; Ilyushin (aircraft); [sports] inside left; Institute of Linguists; [aeronautics] instrument landing; [immunology] interleukin; [international vehicle registration] Israel
**I/L** import licence
**.il** Israel (in Internet address)
**i.l.** inside leg
**ILA** Individual Learning Account (for vocational training); [physics] induction linear accelerator; Institute of Landscape Architects; [aeronautics] instrument landing approach; International Law Association; International Longshoremen's Association
**ILAA** International Legal Aid Association
**ILAB** International League of Antiquarian Booksellers
**ILAE** International League Against Epilepsy
**ILBM** [computing] interleaved bit map
**ILC** International Law Commission (of UN)
**ILD** [medicine] interstitial lung disease
**ILE** Institution of Locomotive Engineers
**ILEA** Inner London Education Authority
**ILEC** Inner London Education Committee
**ILF** International Landworkers' Federation
**ILGA** Institute of Local Government Administration
**ILGWU** [USA] International Ladies' Garment Workers' Union
**Ill.** Illinois
**ill.** illustrate; illustrated; illustration; illustrator; *illustrissimus* (Latin: most distinguished)
**illegit.** illegitimate
**illit.** illiterate
**illum.** illuminate; illuminated; illumination
**illus.** illustrate; illustrated; illustration; illustrator
**illust.** illustrate; illustrated; illustration; illustrator
**ILN** *Illustrated London News*
**ILO** industrial liaison officer; International Labour Office (of UN); International Labour Organization
**i.l.o.** in lieu of
**ILocoE** Institution of Locomotive Engineers
**ILP** Independent Labour Party
**ILR** Independent Law Reports; independent local radio
**ILRM** International League for the Rights of Man
**ILS** Incorporated Law Society; [aeronautics] instrument landing system; [statistics] inverse least-squares
**i.l.t.** in lieu thereof
**ILTF** International Lawn Tennis Federation
**ILU** Institute of London Underwriters
**ILW** [nuclear technology] intermediate-level waste
**ILY** I love you
**IM** Indian Marines; Institute of Materials; Institute of Metals (became part of Institute of Materials); interceptor missile; [chess] International Master; [medicine] intramuscular; [UK postcode] Isle of Man
**Im.** Imperial
**IMA** Indian Military Academy; Institute of Mathematics and its Applications; International Music Association; Irish Medical Association
**imag.** imaginary; imagination; imagine
**IM&AWU** [USA] International Molders' and Allied Workers' Union
**IMarE** Institute of Marine Engineers
**IMAS** International Marine and Shipping Conference
**IMB** Institute of Marine Biology
**IMC** [photography] image motion compensation; Institute of Management Consultants; Institute of Measurement and Control; [aeronautics] instrument meteorological conditions; International Maritime Committee; International Missionary Council; International Music Council

**IMCO** Intergovernmental Maritime Consultative Organization (former name of IMO)
**IME** Institute of Medical Ethics
**IMEA** Incorporated Municipal Electrical Association
**IMechE** Institution of Mechanical Engineers
**I Meth.** Independent Methodist
**IMF** International Monetary Fund; International Motorcycle Federation; interplanetary magnetic field (in astrophysics)
**IMG** [computing] image file format
**IMGTechE** Institution of Mechanical and General Technician Engineers
**IMHO** in my humble opinion (in Internet chat and e-mail)
**IMinE** Institution of Mining Engineers (became part of IMM)
**IMINT** [military] image intelligence (from aerial photographs)
**imit.** imitate; imitation; imitative
**IMM** Institution of Mining and Metallurgy; International Mercantile Marine; International Monetary Market
**imm.** immediately
**immac.** immaculate (in advertisement)
**immed.** immediate
**IMMTS** Indian Mercantile Marine Training Ship
**immun.** immunity; immunization; immunology
**IMO** in my opinion (in Internet chat and e-mail); International Maritime Organization (formerly IMCO); International Meteorological Organization; International Miners' Organization
**IMP** [computing] interface message processor (in network); [card games] International Match Point (in bridge); interplanetary measurement probe
**Imp.** *Imperator* (Latin: Emperor); *Imperatrix* (Latin: Empress); Imperial
**imp.** imperative; imperfect; imperial; impersonal; implement; import; important; imported; importer; impression; imprimatur; *imprimeur* (French: printer); *imprimé* (French: printed); imprint; improved; improvement
**IMPA** International Master Printers' Association
**IMPACT** implementation, planning and control technique
**impce** importance
**imper.** imperative
**imperf.** imperfect; [philately] imperforate (of stamps)
**impers.** impersonal
**impf.** imperfect
**impft** imperfect
**imp. gal.** imperial gallon
**imposs.** impossible
**IMPR** [meteorology] improving
**impreg.** impregnate; impregnated; impregnation
**improp.** improper; improperly
**impt** important
**imptd** imported
**imptr** importer
**IMR** individual medical report; infant mortality rate; Institute of Medical Research
**IMRA** Industrial Marketing Research Association
**IMRAN** international marine radio aids to navigation
**IMRO** Investment Management Regulatory Organization
**IMS** Indian Medical Service; industrial methylated spirit; [trademark, computing] Information Management System; Institute of Management Services; International Musicological Society
**IMT** International Military Tribunal
**IMU** International Mathematical Union
**IMunE** Institution of Municipal Engineers (became part of Institution of Civil Engineers)
**IMVS** [Australia] Institute of Medical and Veterinary Science
**IMW** Institute of Masters of Wine; intermediate molecular weight
**IN** [US postcode] Indiana; Indian Navy
**In** [chemical element] indium
**In.** India; Indian; Instructor
**in.** inch
**.in** India (in Internet address)
**INA** Indian National Army; Institution of Naval Architects; International Newsreel Association; Iraqi News Agency
**INAO** *Institut national des appellations d'origine des vins et eaux-de-vie* (French authority controlling wine production)
**inaud.** inaudible

**inaug.** inaugural; inaugurate; inaugurated; inauguration
**inbd** inboard
**Inbucon** International Business Consultants
**INC** *in nomine Christi* (Latin: in the name of Christ); Indian National Congress; International Numismatic Commission
**Inc.** Incorporated (after US company name)
**inc.** include; included; including; inclusive; income; incomplete; incorporate; incorporated; increase; increment; incumbent
**INCA** International Newspaper Colour Association
**incalz.** [music] *incalzando* (Italian: hastening)
**INCB** International Narcotics Control Board (of UN)
**incho.** [law] inchoate
**incid.** incidental
**incl.** inclination; incline; include(s); included; including; inclusive
**incldg** including
**incls.** inclusive
**incog.** incognito
**incomp.** incomplete
**incompat.** incompatibility; incompatible
**incorp.** incorporated; incorporation
**incorr.** incorrect
**INCPEN** Industry Committee for Packaging and the Environment
**INCR** [meteorology] increase
**incr.** increase; increased; increasing; increment
**incumb.** incumbent
**incun.** incunabula
**IND** [international vehicle registration] India; *in nomine Dei* (Latin: in the name of God); [US pharmacology] investigational (or investigative) new drug
**Ind** [astronomy] Indus
**Ind.** Independent; India; Indian; Indiana; Indies
**ind.** independence; independent; index; indicate; indication; indicative; indigenous; indigo; indirect; indirectly; industrial; industry
**in d.** [medicine] *in dies* (Latin: daily)
**indecl.** [grammar] indeclinable
**indef.** indefinite
**indep.** independence; independent
**indic.** indicating; indicative; indicator
**Ind. Imp.** *Indiae Imperator* (Latin: Emperor of India); *Indiae Imperatrix* (Latin: Empress of India)
**indiv.** individual
**individ.** individual
**Ind. Meth.** Independent Methodist
**Indo-Eur.** Indo-European
**Indo-Ger.** Indo-Germanic
**Indon.** Indonesia; Indonesian
**indre** indenture
**induc.** inductance; induction
**indust.** industrial; industrialized; industrious; industry
**ined.** *ineditus* (Latin: unpublished)
**INER** Institute of Nuclear Energy Research
**INET** Institute of Nuclear Energy Technology
**in ex.** *in extenso* (Latin: in full)
**INF** intermediate-range nuclear forces; International Naturist Federation; International Nuclear Force
**Inf.** Infantry
**inf.** infant; infectious; inferior; [grammar] infinitive; influence; informal; information; *infra* (Latin: below); [medicine] *infusum* (Latin: infusion)
**infin.** [grammar] infinitive
**infirm.** infirmary
**infl.** inflammable; inflated; inflect; inflection; [botany] inflorescence; influence; influenced
**infm.** information
**info** [short form] information
**infra dig** [short form] *infra dignitatem* (Latin: beneath one's dignity, undignified)
**Ing.** *Ingenieur* (German: engineer)
**Ingl.** *Inghilterra* (Italian: England)
**INGO** international nongovernmental organization
**INH** [pharmacology] isonicotinic acid hydrazide (= isoniazid, drug used to treat tuberculosis)
**Inh.** *Inhaber* (German: proprietor); *Inhalt* (German: contents)
**inhab.** inhabitant
**INI** *in nomine Iesu* (Latin: in the name of Jesus)
**init.** initial; initially; *initio* (Latin: in the beginning)
**INJ** *in nomine Jesu* (Latin: in the name of Jesus)

**inj.** injection; injury
**INLA** International Nuclear Law Association; Irish National Liberation Army
**in lim.** *in limine* (Latin: at the outset)
**in loc.** *in loco* (Latin: in the place (of))
**in loc. cit.** *in loco citato* (Latin: in the place cited)
**Inmarsat** International Maritime Satellite Organization
**in mem.** *in memoriam* (Latin: to the memory (of))
**inn.** [cricket] innings
**INO** Inspectorate of Naval Ordnance
**inorg.** inorganic
**INP** Institute of Nuclear Physics
**in pr.** *in principio* (Latin: in the beginning)
**in pro.** in proportion
**inq.** inquest; inquiry; inquisition
**INR** independent national radio (as in **INR licence**); Index of Nursing Research
**INRI** *Iesus Nazarenus Rex Iudaeorum* (Latin: Jesus of Nazareth King of the Jews)
**INS** [USA] Immigration and Naturalization Service; Indian Naval Ship; inertial navigation system; International News Service; [fishing port] Inverness
**Ins** [computing] insert (key)
**ins.** inches; inscribe; inscription; insert; inspection; inspector; insular; insulate; insulated; insulation; insurance
**in s.** in situ
**INSA** Indian National Science Academy
**INSAG** International Nuclear Safety Advisory Group
**insce** insurance
**inscr.** inscribe; inscription
**INSEA** International Society for Education through Art
**INSEAD** *Institut européen d'administration des affaires* (French: European Institute of Administrative Affairs)
**insep.** inseparable
**INSET** [education] in-service (education and) training
**insol.** insoluble
**insolv.** insolvent
**Insp.** Inspector; Inspectorate
**insp.** inspect; inspected; inspection; inspector
**Insp-Gen** Inspector-General
**INST** *in nomine Sanctae Trinitatis* (Latin: in the name of the Holy Trinity)
**Inst.** Institute; Institution
**inst.** instance; instant; instant (= this month, used in formal correspondence); instantaneous; institute; institution; instruct; instruction; instructor; instrument; instrumental
**INSTAB** Information Service on Toxicity and Biodegradability (relating to water pollution)
**InstAct** Institute of Actuaries
**InstBE** Institution of British Engineers
**InstCE** Institution of Civil Engineers
**InstD** Institute of Directors
**InstE** Institute of Energy
**InstEE** Institution of Electrical Engineers
**InstF** Institute of Fuel
**instl.** installation
**InstMM** Institution of Mining and Metallurgy
**Instn** Institution
**instn** institution
**InstP** Institute of Physics
**InstPet** Institute of Petroleum
**InstPI** Institute of Patentees and Inventors
**InstR** Institute of Refrigeration
**instr.** instruction; instructor; instrument; instrumental
**INSTRAW** United Nations International Research and Training Institute for the Advancement of Women
**InstSMM** Institute of Sales and Marketing Management
**InstT** Institute of Transport
**INT** Isaac Newton Telescope (La Palma)
**int.** intelligence; intercept; interest; interim; interior; [grammar] interjection; intermediate; internal; international; interpret; interpretation; interpreter; interval; [grammar] intransitive; [music] introit
**.int** international (in Internet address)
**INTAL** Institute for Latin American Integration (Buenos Aires)
**int. al.** *inter alia* (Latin: among other things)
**int. comb.** internal combustion
**Intelsat** International Telecommunications Satellite Organization
**intens.** intensifier; intensify; intensive
**inter.** intermediate
**intercom** [short form] intercommunication (system)

**interj.** [grammar] interjection
**internat.** international
**interp.** interpreter
**Interpol** International Criminal Police Organization
**interrog.** interrogate; interrogation; [grammar] interrogative; interrogatively
**intl** international
**INTO** Irish National (Primary) Teachers' Organization
**intr.** [grammar] intransitive
**intrans.** [grammar] intransitive
**in trans.** in transit
**intro** [short form] introduction
**intro.** introduce; introduction; introductory
**introd.** introduce; introduction; introductory
**INTUC** Indian National Trade Union Congress
**INucE** Institution of Nuclear Engineers
**Inv.** Inverness
**inv.** *invenit* (Latin: (he/she) designed it); invent; invented; invention; inventor; inventory; inverse; inversion; invert; investment; invoice
**inv. et del.** *invenit et delineavit* (Latin: (he/she) designed and drew it)
**invty** inventory
**IO** India Office; [grammar] indirect object; inspecting officer; integrated optics; intelligence officer
**I/O** [computing] input/output; inspecting order
**Io.** Iowa
**IOA** Institute of Acoustics
**IOB** Institute of Bankers (former name of CIB); Institute of Biology; Institute of Book-keepers; Institute of Brewing; Institute of Building (former name of CIOB)
**IOC** Intergovernmental Oceanographic Commission; International Olympic Committee
**IOCU** International Organization of Consumers' Unions
**IOD** injured on duty; Institute of Directors
**IODE** [Canada] Imperial Order of Daughters of the Empire
**IOE** International Organization of Employers
**IOF** Independent Order of Foresters; Institute of Fuel; International Oceanographic Foundation; International Orienteering Federation
**IOFB** [medicine] intraocular foreign body
**I of E** Institute of Export
**I of M** Isle of Man
**I of W** Isle of Wight
**IOGT** International Order of Good Templars
**IOJ** Institute of Journalists; International Organization of Journalists
**IOM** Indian Order of Merit; Institute of Materials; Institute of Medicine; Isle of Man
**IOMTR** International Office for Motor Trades and Repairs
**Ion.** Ionic
**IONARC** Indian Ocean National Association for Regional Cooperation
**IOO** Inspecting Ordnance Officer
**IOOF** Independent Order of Oddfellows
**IOP** [computing] input/output processor; Institute of Painters in Oil Colours; Institute of Petroleum; Institute of Physics; Institute of Plumbing; Institute of Printing; [medicine] intraocular pressure
**IOPAB** International Organization for Pure and Applied Biophysics
**IOPCW** International Organization for the Prohibition of Chemical Weapons
**IOR** Independent Order of Rechabites
**IOS** [computing] integrated office system
**IoS** *Independent on Sunday*
**IOSCO** International Organization of Securities Commissions
**IOSM** Independent Order of the Sons of Malta
**IOT** Institute of Transport
**IOU** Industrial Operations Unit; I owe you
**IOW** in other words (in Internet chat and e-mail); Isle of Wight
**IP** [electronics] image processing; Imperial Preference; India Paper; [baseball] innings pitched; [medicine] in-patient; [electrical engineering] input primary; instalment plan; Institute of Petroleum; Institute of Plumbing; International Pharmacopoeia; [computing] Internet protocol; [chemistry] ionization potential; [UK postcode] Ipswich
**i.p.** identification point; incentive pay; indexed and paged; initial phase; [electrical engineering] input primary
**IPA** India Pale Ale; Insolvency Prac-

titioners' Association; Institute of Park Administration; Institute of Practitioners in Advertising; International Phonetic Alphabet; International Phonetic Association; International Poetry Archives (Manchester); International Police Academy; International Police Association; International Publishers' Association

**IPAA** International Petroleum Association of America; International Prisoners' Aid Association

**IPARS** International Programmed Airline Reservation System

**IPBM** interplanetary ballistic missile (in computer game)

**IPC** [astronomy] imaging proportional counter; International Petroleum Company; International Polar Commission; International Publishing Corporation; [computing] interprocess communication; Iraq Petroleum Company

**IPCA** International Pest Control Association

**IPCC** Intergovernmental Panel on Climatic Change (of UN)

**IPCS** Institution of Professional Civil Servants; [computing] intelligent process-control system

**IPD** individual package delivery; [law] *in praesentia dominorum* (Latin: in the presence of the Lords (of Session)) (Scotland); Institute of Personnel and Development; [medicine] intermittent peritoneal dialysis

**IPE** Institution of Plant Engineers; International Petroleum Exchange

**IPF** [medicine] interstitial pulmonary fibrosis; Irish Printing Federation

**IPFC** Indo-Pacific Fisheries Council

**IPG** Independent Publishers' Guild; Industrial Painters' Group

**IPH** [medicine] idiopathic portal hypertension; industrial process heat(ing)

**iph** impressions per hour

**IPHE** Institution of Public Health Engineers

**IPI** [computing] image processing and interchange; Institute of Patentees and Inventors; Institute of Professional Investigators; International Press Institute

**i.p.i.** *in partibus infidelium* (Latin: in the regions of unbelievers)

**IPL** [computing] information processing language; [computing] initial program load

**IPlantE** Institution of Plant Engineers

**IPLO** Irish People's Liberation Organization

**IPM** [Freemasonry] immediate past master; Institute of Personnel Management

**ipm** inches per minute; inches per month

**IPMS** Institute of Professionals, Managers and Specialists

**IPO** [US stock exchange] initial public offering (flotation on market); [computing] input-process-output; Israel Philharmonic Orchestra

**IPP** Institute for Plasma Physics; [medicine] intermittent positive pressure (in ventilation)

**IPPF** International Planned Parenthood Federation

**IPPR** Institute for Public Policy Research

**IPPS** Institute of Physics and the Physical Society

**IPPV** [medicine] intermittent positive-pressure ventilation

**IPR** Institute of Public Relations

**IPRA** International Public Relations Association

**IPRE** Incorporated Practitioners in Radio and Electronics

**IProdE** Institution of Production Engineers (became part of IEE)

**IPS** Indian Police Service; Indian Political Service; International Confederation for Plastic Surgery; [astronomy] interplanetary scintillations; Inter Press Service (Italian news agency); [computing] interpretative programming system

**Ips.** Ipswich

**ips** inches per second; [computing] instructions per second

**IPSA** International Political Science Association

**IPSE** [computing] integrated project support environment

**IPSP** [physiology] inhibitory post-synaptic potential

**IPT** Institute of Petroleum Technologies; interpersonal therapy

**IPTO** [astronautics] independent power take-off

**IPTPA** International Professional Tennis Players' Association
**IPTS** [physics] International Practical Temperature Scale
**IPU** Inter-Parliamentary Union
**IPX** Internet package exchange
**ipy** inches per year
**IQ** Institute of Quarrying; intelligence quota; international quota
**.iq** Iraq (in Internet address)
**i.q.** *idem quod* (Latin: the same as)
**IQA** Institute of Quality Assurance
**IQS** Institute of Quantity Surveyors
**IR** [meteorology] ice on runway; incidence rate; index register; industrial relations; informal report; information retrieval; infrared (radiation); Inland Revenue; [sports] inside right; inspector's report; Institute of Refrigeration; instrument reading; international registration; [international vehicle registration] Iran; [currency] Iranian rial; [chemistry] isoprene rubber
**Ir** [chemical element] iridium
**Ir.** Ireland; Irish
**i.R** *im Ruhestand* (German: retired, emeritus)
**.ir** Iran (in Internet address)
**i.r.** inside radius
**IRA** [USA] individual retirement account; Institute of Registered Architects; Irish Republican Army
**IRAD** Institute for Research on Animal Diseases
**IRAF** [astronomy] image reduction and analysis facility
**IRAM** *Institut de radioastronomie millimétrique* (French: Institute of Millimetre Radioastronomy)
**Iran.** Iranian
**i.r.a.n.** inspect and repair as necessary
**IRAS** Infrared Astronomical Satellite
**IRB** industrial revenue bond; Irish Republican Brotherhood
**IRBM** intermediate-range ballistic missile
**IRC** Industrial Reorganization Corporation; Infantry Reserve Corps; interdisciplinary research centre (of EPSRC); International Red Cross; international reply coupon; International Research Council; Internet relay chat
**IRCert** Industrial Relations Certificate
**IRD** International Research and Development Company
**IRDA** Industrial Research and Development Authority; Infra-Red Data Association
**IRE** [USA] Institute of Radio Engineers
**Ire.** Ireland
**IREE(Aust)** Institution of Radio and Electronics Engineers (Australia)
**Irel.** Ireland
**IRF** International Road Federation; International Rowing Federation
**IRFB** International Rugby Football Board
**IRFU** Irish Rugby Football Union
**IRI** Institution of the Rubber Industry (became part of Institute of Materials); *Istituto per la Ricostruzione Industriale* (Italian: Industrial Reconstruction Institute)
**irid.** iridescent
**IRIS** International Research and Information Service
**Iris** infrared intruder system
**IRL** in real life (in Internet chat); infrared (remote) locking (in car advertisement); [international vehicle registration] Ireland
**IRLS** [navigation] interrogation recording location system
**IRM** Islamic Republic of Mauritania; [geology] isothermal remanent magnetization
**IRN** Independent Radio News
**IRO** industrial relations officer; Inland Revenue Office; International Refugee Organization; International Relief Organization
**iron.** ironic(al)
**IRPA** International Radiation Protection Association
**IRQ** [computing] interrupt request; [international vehicle registration] Iraq
**IRR** infrared radiation; Institute of Race Relations; [finance] internal rate of return
**irr.** [finance] irredeemable; irregular
**irreg.** irregular; irregularly
**IRRI** International Rice Research Institute
**IRRV** Institute of Revenues, Rating and Valuation
**IRS** [computing] information retrieval system; [USA] Internal Revenue Service
**IRSF** Inland Revenue Staff Federation (became part of PTC)

**IRTE** Institute of Road Transport Engineers

**IRTF** Infrared Telescope Facility (Mauna Kea, Hawaii)

**IRU** industrial rehabilitation unit; International Relief Union; International Road Transport Union

**IRWC** International Registry of World Citizens

**IS** [international vehicle registration] Iceland (from Icelandic *Ísland*); independent suspension (in car advertisement); Industrial Society; information science; information system; [electrical engineering] input secondary; [genetics] insertion sequence; internal security; International Society of Sculptors, Painters and Gravers; Irish Society

**Is.** [Bible] Isaiah; Islam; Islamic; Island(s); Isle(s); Israel; Israeli

**.is** Iceland (in Internet address)

**i.s.** [electrical engineering] input secondary

**ISA** Independent Schools' Association; Individual Savings Account (replacement for TESSA); [computing] Industry Standard Architecture; International Sociological Association; [aeronautics] International Standard Atmosphere (formerly Interim Standard Atmosphere); International Standards in Auditing

**Isa.** [Bible] Isaiah

**ISAB** Institute for the Study of Animal Behaviour

**ISAC** Industrial Safety Advisory Council

**ISAM** [computing] indexed sequential access method

**ISAS** [Japan] Institute of Space and Astronautical Science

**ISBA** Incorporated Society of British Advertisers

**ISBN** International Standard Book Number (replacement for SBN)

**ISC** Imperial Service College (Haileybury); Imperial Staff College; Indian Staff Corps; [medicine] intermittent self-catheterization; International Seismological Centre; International Student Conference; International Sugar Council; [Freemasonry] International Supreme Council

**ISCE** International Society of Christian Endeavour

**ISCM** International Society for Contemporary Music

**ISCO** Independent Schools Careers Organization; International Standard Classification of Occupations

**ISD** international standard depth; international subscriber dialling

**ISDA** International Swaps and Derivatives Association

**ISDN** [computing, telecommunications] Integrated Services Digital Network

**ISE** Indian Service of Engineers; Institution of Structural Engineers; International Stock Exchange

**ISEE** [astronomy] International Sun–Earth Explorer

**ISF** [computing] integrated systems factory; International Shipping Federation; International Spiritualist Federation

**ISGE** International Society of Gastroenterology

**ISH** International Society of Haematology

**ISHS** International Society for Horticultural Science

**ISI** Indian Standards Institution; International Statistical Institute; Iron and Steel Institute (became part of Institute of Materials)

**ISIS** Independent Schools Information Service; International Shipping Information Services

**ISJC** Independent Schools Joint Council

**ISK** [currency] Icelandic króna

**isl.** island; isle

**ISM** *Iesus Salvator Mundi* (Latin: Jesus Saviour of the World); Imperial Service Medal; Incorporated Society of Musicians; [astronomy] interstellar medium

**ISMA** International Securities Market Association

**ISME** International Society for Musical Education

**ISMRC** Inter-Services Metallurgical Research Council

**ISO** Imperial Service Order; Infrared Space Observatory; International Organization for Standardization (from Greek *iso-* meaning 'equal', chosen as a multilingual abbreviation); International Sugar Organization

**ISOL** [meteorology] isolated

**isol.** isolate; isolated; isolation

**ISP** Institute of Sales Promotion; [computing] instruction set processor; International Study Programme; Internet service provider
**ISPA** International Society for the Protection of Animals; International Sporting Press Association
**ISPEMA** Industrial Safety (Personal Equipment) Manufacturers' Association
**ISQ** *in statu quo* (Latin: in the same state)
**ISR** information storage and retrieval; Institute of Social Research; International Society for Radiology; [computing] interrupt service routine
**ISRB** Inter-Services Research Bureau
**ISRD** International Society for Rehabilitation of the Disabled
**ISRO** International Securities Regulatory Organization
**ISS** Institute for Strategic Studies; Institute of Space Sciences; Institute of Space Studies; International Social Service(s); interstellar scintillations
**iss.** issue; issued
**ISSA** International Social Security Association
**ISSC** International Social Science Council
**ISSN** International Standard Serial Number
**ISSS** International Society of Soil Science
**IST** Indian Standard Time; information sciences technology; Institute of Science Technology; [medicine] insulin shock therapy
**ISTC** Institute of Scientific and Technical Communicators; Iron and Steel Trades Confederation
**ISTD** Imperial Society of Teachers of Dancing
**ISTEA** Iron and Steel Trades Employers' Association
**isth.** isthmus
**IStructE** Institution of Structural Engineers
**ISU** International Seamen's Union; International Shooting Union; International Skating Union
**ISV** independent software vendor; International Scientific Vocabulary
**ISVA** Incorporated Society of Valuers and Auctioneers
**ISWG** Imperial Standard Wire Gauge
**IT** ignition temperature; income tax; [USA] Indian Territory; industrial tribunal; infantry training; information technology; [law] Inner Temple; [physics] International Table (as in **IT calorie**); Investment Trust
**It** [short form] Italian vermouth
**It.** Italian; Italy
**it.** italic (type)
**.it** Italy (in Internet address)
**i.t.** in transit; inspection tag; internal thread (of tool)
**ITA** Independent Television Authority (replaced by IBA); industrial and technical assistance; Industrial Transport Association; Information Technology Agreement; Initial Teaching Alphabet; Institute of Air Transport; Institute of Travel Agents
**ITAI** Institution of Technical Authors and Illustrators
**Ital.** Italian; Italy
**ital.** italic (type)
**ITALY** I trust and love you (on envelope of love letter)
**ITAR** Information Telegraph Agency of Russia
**ITB** Industry Training Board; International Time Bureau; Irish Tourist Board
**ITC** Imperial Tobacco Company; Independent Television Commission; Industrial Training Council; International Tin Council; International Trade Centre; [meteorology] intertropical confluence; [USA] investment tax credit
**i.t.c.** installation time and cost
**ITCA** Independent Television Contractors' Association
**ITCZ** [meteorology] intertropical convergence zone
**ITDA** [military] indirect target damage assessment
**ITE** Institute of Terrestrial Ecology
**ITEME** Institution of Technician Engineers in Mechanical Engineering
**ITER** [nuclear technology] international thermonuclear engineering reactor; [nuclear technology] international tokamak engineering reactor
**ITF** [accounting] integrated test facility; International Tennis Federation; International Trade Federations; International Transport Workers' Federation

**ITGWF** International Textile and Garment Workers' Federation
**itin.** itinerary
**ITMA** Institute of Trade Mark Agents; *It's That Man Again* (former radio comedy series)
**ITN** Independent Television News
**ITO** [electronics] indium–tin oxide; International Trade Organization
**ITS** Industrial Training Service; [USA] Intermarket Trading System; International Trade Secretariat
**ITT** [medicine] insulin tolerance test; International Telephone and Telegraph Corporation
**ITTF** International Table Tennis Federation
**ITU** [computing] intelligent thermal update; [medicine] intensive therapy unit; International Telecommunication Union; International Temperance Union; International Typographical Union
**ITV** Independent Television; [USA] instructional television
**ITVA** International Television Association
**ITWF** International Transport Workers' Federation
**IU** immunizing unit; [pharmacology] international unit(s); *Izquierda Unida* (Spanish: United Left) (political party)
**IUA** International Union against Alcoholism; International Union of Architects
**IUAA** International Union of Advertisers' Associations
**IUAES** International Union of Anthropological and Ethnological Sciences
**IUAI** International Union of Aviation Insurers
**IUAO** International Union for Applied Ornithology
**IUAPPA** International Union of Air Pollution Prevention Associations
**IUB** International Union of Biochemistry; International Universities Bureau
**IUBS** International Union of Biological Sciences
**IUCD** [medicine] intrauterine contraceptive device
**IUCN** International Union for the Conservation of Nature and Natural Resources
**IUCr** International Union of Crystallography
**IUCW** International Union for Child Welfare
**IUD** [medicine] intrauterine death; [medicine] intrauterine (contraceptive) device
**IUE** [astronomy] International Ultraviolet Explorer; [USA] International Union of Electronic, Electrical, Salaried, Machine and Furniture Workers
**IUF** International Union of Food and Allied Workers' Associations
**IUFO** International Union of Family Organizations
**IUFRO** International Union of Forest Research Organizations
**IUGG** International Union of Geodesy and Geophysics
**IUGR** [medicine] intrauterine growth retardation
**IUGS** International Union of Geological Sciences
**IUHPS** International Union of the History and Philosophy of Science
**IUI** [medicine] intrauterine insemination
**IULA** International Union of Local Authorities
**IUMF** *institut universitaire de formation des maîtres* (French: university institute for advanced teacher education)
**IUMI** International Union of Marine Insurance
**IUMSWA** Industrial Union of Marine and Shipbuilding Workers of America
**IUNS** International Union of Nutritional Sciences
**IUOE** [USA] International Union of Operating Engineers
**IUP** *institut universitaire professionnel* (French: vocational university institute); [medicine] intrauterine pressure
**IUPAB** International Union of Pure and Applied Biophysics
**IUPAC** International Union of Pure and Applied Chemistry
**IUPAP** International Union of Pure and Applied Physics
**IUPS** International Union of Physiological Sciences
**IUS** [astronautics] inertial upper stage; International Union of Students; [medi-

cine] intrauterine system (contraceptive device)
**IUSP** International Union of Scientific Psychology
**IUSY** International Union of Socialist Youth
**IUT** *institut universitaire de technologie* (French: university institute of technology); [medicine] intrauterine transfusion
**IUTAM** International Union of Theoretical and Applied Mechanics
**IV** interactive video; [chemistry] intermediate valency; [medicine] intravenous; [medicine] intravenously; [UK postcode] Inverness; invoice value
**i.V** *in Vertretung* (German: by proxy)
**i.v.** increased value; initial velocity; [medicine] intravenous; [medicine] intravenously; invoice value
**IVA** individual voluntary arrangement (in bankruptcy proceedings); invalidity allowance
**IVB** invalidity benefit
**IVBF** International Volleyball Federation
**IVC** [medicine] inferior vena cava; intervarsity club
**IVF** [medicine] in vitro fertilization
**IVL** in virtual life (in Internet chat)
**IVM** illuminated vanity mirror
**IVP** [medicine] intravenous pyelogram
**IVR** international vehicle registration
**IVS** International Voluntary Service
**IVT** [astronautics] intravehicular transfer; [medicine] intravenous transfusion
**IVU** International Vegetarian Union
**IW** inspector of works; Isle of Wight; [vehicle registration] Londonderry
**i.w.** indirect waste; inside width
**IWA** Inland Waterways Association; Institute of World Affairs
**IWC** International Whaling Commission; International Wheat Council
**IWD** Inland Waterways and Docks
**IWEM** Institution of Water and Environmental Management (replacement for IWPC)
**IWGC** Imperial War Graves Commission (former name of CWGC)
**IWM** Imperial War Museum
**IWO** Institute of Welfare Officers; Institution of Water Officers
**IWPC** Institute of Water Pollution Control (replaced by IWEM)
**IWS** International Wool Secretariat
**IWTA** Inland Water Transport Association
**IWW** Industrial Workers of the World; International Workers of the World
**IX** *Iesous Christos* (Greek: Jesus Christ) (from initial letters in Greek alphabet)
**IY** Imperial Yeomanry
**IYHF** International Youth Hostels Federation
**IYRU** International Yacht Racing Union
**iyswim** if you see what I mean
**IZ** I Zingari (cricket club)
**IZS** [medicine] insulin zinc suspension (used to treat diabetes)

# J

**J** [engineering] advance ratio; [vehicle registration] Durham; [card games] jack; Jacobean; [mathematics] Jacobian determinant; *Jahr* (German: year); January; [international vehicle registration] Japan; [fishing port] Jersey; Jesus; jet; Jew; Jewish; [immunology] joining region (of immunoglobulin chain); [slang] joint (of cannabis); joule; Journal; Judaic; Judaism; *judex* (Latin: judge); Judge; July; June; [geology] Jurassic; Justice
***J*** [physics] angular momentum; [physics] magnetic polarization; [physics] sound intensity
**j** imaginary number (square root of –1)
**j.** *jour* (French: day); *juris* (Latin: of law); *jus* (Latin: law)
**J2** [civil aircraft marking] Djibouti
**J3** [civil aircraft marking] Grenada
**J5** [civil aircraft marking] Guinea-Bissau
**J6** [civil aircraft marking] St Lucia
**J7** [civil aircraft marking] Dominica
**9J** [civil aircraft marking] Zambia

**JA** [international vehicle registration] Jamaica; [civil aircraft marking] Japan; joint account; Judge Advocate; Justice of Appeal; [vehicle registration] Manchester
**J/A** joint account
**Ja.** January
**JAA** Japan Aeronautic Association; Jewish Athletic Association
**Jaat** [military] joint air attack team
**JAC** Joint Advisory Committee (of UN); [USA] Joint Apprenticeship Committee; [USA] Junior Association of Commerce
**Jac.** Jacobean
**JACARI** Joint Action Commission Against Racial Interference
**JACNE** Joint Advisory Committee on Nutritional Education
**JACT** Joint Association of Classical Teachers
**JAD** Julian Astronomical Day
**JADB** [USA] Joint Air Defense Board
**JAEC** Japan Atomic Energy Commission; Joint Atomic Energy Committee (of US Congress)
**JAF** Judge Advocate of the Fleet
**JAFC** Japan Atomic Fuel Corporation
**Jafo** [military slang] just another fucking observer
**JAG** Judge Advocate-General
**Jag** [short form] Jaguar (car)
**JAIEG** Joint Atomic Information Exchange Group
**JAL** jet approach and landing (chart)
**Jam.** Jamaica; Jamaican; [Bible] James
**JAMA** *Journal of the American Medical Association*
**Jan.** *Januar* (German: January); January
**jan.** janitor
**J&K** Jammu and Kashmir
**j. & w.o.** [insurance] jettisoning and washing overboard
**JANET** [computing] Joint Academic Network
**janv.** *janvier* (French: January)
**Jap.** Japan; Japanese
**jap.** japanned
**jar.** jargon
**JARE** Japanese Antarctic Research Expedition
**JAS** Jamaica Agricultural Society; Junior Astronomical Society
**Jas.** [Bible] James
**jastop** [aeronautics] jet-assisted stop
**JAT** *Jugoslovenski Aero-Transport* (Yugoslav airline company)
**JATCC** Joint Aviation Telecommunications Coordination Committee
**JATCRU** joint air traffic control radar unit
**JATO** [aeronautics] jet-assisted take-off
**JATS** joint air transportation service
**jaund.** jaundice
**Jav.** Java; Javanese
**jav.** [athletics] javelin
**JB** Bachelor of Laws (from Latin *Juris Baccalaureus*); junior beadle; [vehicle registration] Reading
**Jb.** *Jahrbuch* (German: yearbook, annual)
**j.b.** jet bomb; joint board; junction box
**JBAA** *Journal of the British Archaeological Association*
**JBC** Jamaica Broadcasting Corporation; Japan Broadcasting Corporation
**JBCNS** Joint Board of Clinical Nursing Studies
**Jber.** *Jahresbericht* (German: annual report)
**JBES** Jodrell Bank Experimental Station
**JBL** *Journal of Business Law*
**JBS** [USA] John Birch Society
**JC** [vehicle registration] Bangor; Jesus Christ; *Jewish Chronicle*; Jockey Club; Julius Caesar (Roman emperor); [USA] Junior Chamber (of Commerce) (applied to members); [USA] junior college; [law] jurisconsult (legal adviser); Justice Clerk; justiciary case; juvenile court
**J-C** *Jésus-Christ* (French: Jesus Christ)
**j.c.** joint compound
**JCAC** [USA] Joint Civil Affairs Committee
**JCAR** Joint Commission on Applied Radioactivity
**JCB** Bachelor of Canon Law (from Latin *Juris Canonici Baccalaureus*); Bachelor of Civil Law (from Latin *Juris Civilis Baccalaureus*); Joseph Cyril Bamford (manufacturer of excavating machines)
**JCC** Joint Consultants' Committee; Joint Consultative Committee; Junior Chamber of Commerce
**JCD** Doctor of Canon Law (from Latin *Juris Canonici Doctor*); Doctor of Civil Law (from Latin *Juris Civilis Doctor*)
**JCHMT** Joint Committee on Higher Medical Training
**JCHST** Joint Committee on Higher Surgical Training

**JCI** Junior Chamber International
**JCL** [computing] job-control language; Licentiate in Canon Law (from Latin *Juris Canonici Licentiatus*); Licentiate in Civil Law (from Latin *Juris Civilis Licentiatus*)
**JCMC** Joint Conference on Medical Conventions
**JCMD** Joint Committee on Mobility for the Disabled
**JCMT** James Clerk Maxwell Telescope
**JCNAAF** Joint Canadian Navy-Army-Air Force
**JC of C** Junior Chamber of Commerce
**JCP** Japan Communist Party
**JCR** junior combination room (in university or college); junior common room (in university or college)
**JCS** Jersey Cattle Society of the United Kingdom; Joint Chiefs of Staff; Joint Commonwealth Societies; *Journal of the Chemical Society*
**jct.** junction
**jctn** junction
**JCWI** Joint Council for the Welfare of Immigrants
**JD** [vehicle registration] central London; Diploma in Journalism; Doctor of Jurisprudence (or Laws) (from Latin *Jurum Doctor*); [currency] Jordanian dinar; [astronomy] Julian date; junior deacon; junior dean; jury duty; [USA] Justice Department; juvenile delinquent
**jd** joined
**JDA** Japan Defence Agency
**JDB** Japan Development Bank
**JDipMA** Joint Diploma in Management Accounting Services
**JDL** [USA] Jewish Defense League
**JDM** [medicine] juvenile diabetes mellitus
**JDS** [accounting] Joint Disciplinary Scheme
**j.d.s.** job data sheet
**JE** [UK postcode] Jersey; [vehicle registration] Peterborough
**JEA** Jesuit Educational Association; Joint Engineering Association
**j.e.a.** joint export agent
**JEB** Joint Examining Board
**JEC** Joint Economic Committee (of US Congress)
**JECFI** Joint Expert Committee on Food Irradiation
**JECI** *Jeunesse étudiante catholique internationale* (French: International Young Catholic Students)
**JEDEC** Joint Electronic Devices Engineering Council
**JEIDA** Japanese Electronic Industry Development Association
**Jer.** [Bible] Jeremiah; Jersey; Jerusalem
**JERC** Joint Electronic Research Committee
**JERI** Japan Economic Research Institute
**jerob.** jeroboam (large wine bottle)
**Jes.** Jesus
**JESA** Japanese Engineering Standards Association
**JESSI** Joint European Submicron Silicon Initiative
**JET** [nuclear technology] Joint European Torus (Culham, Oxfordshire); Joint European Transport
**Jet.** jetsam; jettison
**JETCO** Jamaican Export Trading Company; Japan Export Trading Company
**JETP** *Journal of Experimental and Theoretical Physics*
**JETRO** Japan External Trade Organization
**jett.** jettison
**jeu.** *jeudi* (French: Thursday)
**JF** [vehicle registration] Leicester
**J/F** [book-keeping] journal folio
**JFET** [electronics] junction field-effect transistor
**JFK** John Fitzgerald Kennedy (US president)
**JFM** *Jeunesse fédéraliste mondiale* (French: Young World Federalists)
**JFTC** Joint Fur Trade Committee
**JFU** Jersey Farmers' Union
**JG** [vehicle registration] Maidstone
**Jg.** *Jahrgang* (German: year's issues (of magazine))
**j.g.** junior grade
**JGTC** Junior Girls' Training Corps
**JGW** [Freemasonry] Junior Grand Warden
**JH** [numismatics] Jubilee head (of Queen Victoria); [biochemistry] juvenile hormone; [vehicle registration] Reading
**Jh.** *Jahresheft* (German: annual volume); *Jahrhundert* (German: century)
**j.h.a.** job hazard analysis
**JHDA** Junior Hospital Doctors' Association
**JHMO** junior hospital medical officer
**JHS** *Jesus Hominum Salvator* (Latin: Jesus

Saviour of Men); [USA] junior high school
**JHU** [USA] Johns Hopkins University
**JI** Journalists' Institute; [vehicle registration] Tyrone
**JIB** joint intelligence bureau
**JIC** joint industrial council; [USA] joint intelligence center; [USA] joint intelligence committee; just in case
**JICNARS** Joint Industry Committee for National Readership Surveys
**JICRAR** Joint Industry Committee for Radio Audience Research
**JICTAR** Joint Industry Committee for Television Advertising Research
**JIE** Junior Institute of Engineers
**JIM** Japan Institute of Metals
**JINS** [USA] juvenile(s) in need of supervision
**JINucE** Junior Member of the Institution of Nuclear Engineers
**JIOA** joint intelligence objectives agency
**JIS** Jamaica Information Service; Japan Industrial Standard; Jewish Information Society; joint intelligence staff
**JIT** [commerce] just-in-time (manufacturing system)
**JIU** joint inspection unit
**JJ** jaw jerk; (Sir) Joseph John Thomson (British physicist); [electronics] Josephson junction; Judges; Justices; [vehicle registration] Maidstone
**JK** [vehicle registration] Brighton
**JKG** John Kenneth Galbraith (US economist)
**jkt** jacket
**j.k.t.** job knowledge test
**JL** [vehicle registration] Lincoln
**Jl.** July
**jl** journal
**JLA** Jewish Lads' Brigade; Jewish Librarians' Association
**JLC** [USA] Jewish Labor Committee
**JLP** Jamaica Labour Party
**JM** [vehicle registration] Reading
**.jm** Jamaica (in Internet address)
**JMA** Japanese Meteorological Agency
**JMB** J(ames) M(atthew) Barrie (Scottish writer); Joint Matriculation Board
**JMBA** *Journal of the Marine Biological Association*
**JMC** Joint Mathematical Council of the United Kingdom
**JMCS** Junior Mountaineering Club of Scotland
**JMJ** [Roman Catholic Church] Jesus, Mary and Joseph
**JMPR** Joint Meeting on Pesticide Residues (of WHO)
**JMSAC** Joint Meteorological Satellite Advisory Committee
**JN** [vehicle registration] Chelmsford
**Jn** Junction
**jn** join; junction
**jn.** junior
**JNA** Jordan News Agency
**JNC** joint negotiating committee
**jnc.** junction
**JND** just noticeable difference
**JNEC** Jamaican National Export Corporation
**JNF** Jewish National Fund
**Jnl** Journal
**jnl** journal
**jnlst** journalist
**JNR** Japanese National Railways
**Jnr** Junior
**jnr** junior
**j.n.s.** just noticeable shift
**jnt** joint
**JNTO** Japan National Tourist Organization
**jnt stk** joint stock
**JO** job order; *Journal Officiel* (French: Official Gazette); junior officer; [vehicle registration] Oxford
**.jo** Jordan (in Internet address)
**Jo. Bapt.** John the Baptist
**Joburg** [short form] Johannesburg
**JOC** *Jeunesse ouvrière chrétienne* (French: Young Christian Workers); [USA] joint operations center
**joc.** jocose; jocular
**JOD** [medicine] juvenile onset diabetes
**j.o.d.** joint occupancy date
**J of E** *Journal of Education*
**JOG** junior offshore group (in yachting)
**Johan.** Johannesburg
**join.** joinery
**Jon.** [Bible] Jonah
**Jos.** Joseph
**Josh.** [Bible] Joshua
**JOT** joint observer team
**jour.** journal; journalist; journey; journeyman
**JOVIAL** [computing] Jules' own version of

international algorithmic language (named after Jules Schwarz)

**JP** jet-propelled; jet propulsion; Justice of the Peace; [vehicle registration] Liverpool

**.jp** Japan (in Internet address)

**JPA** Jamaica Press Association

**JPC** joint planning council; joint production council; Judge of the Prize Court

**JPCAC** Joint Production, Consultative and Advisory Committee

**JPEG** Joint Photographic Expert Group

**JPL** Jet Propulsion Laboratory (California); *Journal of Planning Law*

**JPMO** Jersey Potato Marketing Organization

**Jpn** Japan

**JPRS** [USA] Joint Publications Research Service

**JPS** jet-propulsion system; [USA] Jewish Publications Society; Joint Parliamentary Secretary; joint planning staff; Junior Philatelic Society

**JPTO** [astronautics] jet-propelled take-off

**JR** *Jacobus Rex* (Latin: King James); joint resolution; Judges' Rules; Jurist Reports; [vehicle registration] Newcastle upon Tyne

**Jr** Junior; juror

**jr** *jour* (French: day); junior

**jr.** journal

**JRA** [medicine] juvenile rheumatoid arthritis

**JRAI** *Journal of the Royal Anthropological Institute*

**JRC** Junior Red Cross

**JS** [vehicle registration] Inverness; [USA] Japan Society; [law] judgment summons; [law] judicial separation

**JSA** jobseekers' allowance

**JSAWC** Joint Services Amphibious Warfare Centre

**JSB** joint-stock bank

**JSC** Johnson Space Center (Texas)

**JSD** Doctor of Juristic Science; [computing] Jackson system development

**JSDC** Joint Service Defence College

**JSE** Johannesburg Stock Exchange

**Jsey** Jersey

**JSLS** Joint Services Liaison Staff

**JSP** [trademark, computing] Jackson Structured Programming; Japan Socialist Party

**JSPS** Japan Society for the Promotion of Science

**JSS** Jacob Sheep Society; joint services standard

**JSSC** Joint Services Staff College; joint shop stewards' committee

**J-stars** joint surveillance and targeting acquisition radar system

**JT** [vehicle registration] Bournemouth

**jt** joint

**j.t.** [law] joint tenancy

**JTC** Junior Training Corps

**Jt Ed.** joint editor

**JTIDS** Joint Tactical Information Distribution Systems

**jtly** jointly

**JTMP** [computing] job transfer and manipulation protocol

**JTO** [aeronautics] jump take-off

**JTS** job training standards

**JTUAC** Joint Trade Union Advisory Committee

**JU** [vehicle registration] Leicester

**Ju.** June

**j.u.** joint use

**JUD** Doctor of Canon and Civil Law (from Latin *Juris Utriusque Doctor*)

**Jud.** Judaea; [Bible] Judah; Judaism; Judge; [Bible] Judges; [Bible] Judith (book of Apocrypha)

**jud.** judgment; judicial; judo

**Judg.** [Bible] Judges

**judgt** judgment

**juev.** *jueves* (Spanish: Thursday)

**JUGFET** [electronics] junction-gate field-effect transistor

**juil.** *juillet* (French: July)

**Jul.** July

**jul.** *julio* (Spanish: July)

**Jun.** June; Junior

**jun.** *junio* (Spanish: June); junior

**junc.** junction

**jun. part.** junior partner

**Junr** Junior

**JurD** Doctor of Law (from Latin *Juris Doctor*)

**jurisd.** jurisdiction

**jurisp.** jurisprudence

**jus.** justice

**JUSMAG** Joint United States Military Advisory Group

**juss.** [grammar] jussive

**Just.** Justinian (Byzantine emperor)

**just.** justice
**Juv.** (Decimus Junius) Juvenal(is) (Roman poet)
**juv.** juvenile
**JUWTFA** Joint Unconventional Warfare Task Force, Atlantic
**jux.** juxtaposed; juxtaposition
**JV** [commerce] joint venture; [anatomy] jugular vein; [USA] junior varsity; [vehicle registration] Lincoln
**Jv.** Java; Javanese
**JVS** Jewish Vegetarian and Natural Health Society
**JW** [vehicle registration] Birmingham; Jehovah's Witness(es); junior warden
**JWB** Jewish Welfare Board; joint wages board
**JWEF** Joinery and Woodwork Employers' Federation
**JWG** joint working group
**jwlr** jeweller
**j.w.o.** [insurance] jettisoning and washing overboard
**JWPAC** Joint Waste Paper Advisory Council
**JWS** Joint Warfare Staff
**JWV** Jewish War Veterans
**JX** [vehicle registration] Huddersfield; Jesus Christ
**JY** [vehicle registration] Exeter; [civil aircraft marking] Jordan
**Jy** jansky (unit used in astronomy); July; jury
**JZ** [vehicle registration] Down

# K

**K** [botany] calyx (in floral formula); [international vehicle registration] Cambodia (from former name Kampuchea); [geology] Cretaceous; *Kalt* (German: cold); [physics] kaon; kelvin (unit of thermodynamic temperature); [immunology] killer (as in **K-cell**); [computing] kilo- (indicates 1,024, as in **KB** = kilobyte); [currency] kina (used in Papua New Guinea); King('s); [chess, card games] king; [currency] kip (used in Laos); [music] Kirkpatrick (catalogue of Domenico Scarlatti's works); [fishing port] Kirkwall; kitchen (in property advertisement); Knight; knighthood; [music] Köchel (catalogue of Mozart's works); *koel* (Dutch: cold); [currency] krona (used in Sweden); [currency] króna (used in Iceland); [currency] krone (used in Denmark and Norway); [currency] kwacha (used in Zambia); [currency] kyat (used in Myanmar); [vehicle registration] Liverpool; [chemical element] potassium (from Latin *kalium*); [astronomy] solar constant; [baseball] strikeout; thousand (from prefix kilo-)
***K*** [physics] bulk modulus; [ecology] carrying capacity; [chemistry] equilibrium constant; [physics] kinetic energy; [physics] luminous efficacy
**k** [mathematics] constant; [mathematics] curvature; kilo- (indicates 1,000, as in **kg** = kilogram); [computing] kilo- (indicates 1,024, as in **kbyte** = kilobyte)
***k*** radius of gyration (in mechanics); [chemistry] rate coefficient; [chemistry] rate constant; [physics] thermal conductivity
**k.** [USA] karat; keel; killed; king; kingdom; knight; [knitting] knit; knot; [currency] kopek (hundredth of rouble); kosher
**K9** [military] canine (referring to army dogs)
**9K** [civil aircraft marking] Kuwait
**KA** [UK postcode] Kilmarnock; King of Arms; Knight of St Andrew, Order of Barbados; [vehicle registration] Liverpool
**KADU** Kenya African Democratic Union (became part of KANU)
**KAI** Keep America Independent
**KAK** *Kungliga Automobil Klubben* (Swedish: Royal Automobile Club)
**Kal.** *Kalendae* (Latin: calends, first day of month)
**Kan.** Kansas
**k&b** kitchen and bathroom (in property advertisement)
**Kans.** Kansas

**KANTAFU** Kenya African National Traders' and Farmers' Union
**KANU** Kenya African National Union
**KANUPP** Karachi Nuclear Power Plant
**KAO** Kuiper Airborne Observatory
**kao.** kaolin
**Kap.** [finance] *Kapital* (German: capital); *Kapitel* (German: chapter)
**KAR** King's African Rifles
**Kar.** Karachi
**Karel.** Karelia; Karelian
**Kash.** Kashmir
**KB** [computing] kilobyte; King's Bench; [chess] kings' bishop; Knight Bachelor; [knitting] knit into back of stitch; [computing] knowledge base; *Koninkrijk België* (Flemish: Kingdom of Belgium); [vehicle registration] Liverpool
**kb** kilobar (unit of pressure)
**KBC** [law] King's Bench Court
**KBD** [law] King's Bench Division
**kbd** keyboard
**KBE** Knight Commander of the Order of the British Empire
**KBES** [computing] knowledge-based expert system
**Kbhvn** *København* (Danish: Copenhagen)
**Kbl** Kabul
**KBP** [chess] king's bishop's pawn
**KBS** Knight of the Blessed Sacrament; [computing] knowledge-based system
**KBW** King's Bench Walk (Temple, London)
**kbyte** [computing] kilobyte
**KC** Kansas City; Kennel Club; King's College; King's Counsel; King's Cross (London); Knight Commander; Knight of the Crescent (in Turkey); Knights of Columbus; [vehicle registration] Liverpool
**kc** kilocycle(s per second) (unit of frequency)
**KCA** *Keesing's Contemporary Archives*
**kcal** kilocalorie
**KCB** Knight Commander of the Order of the Bath
**KCC** (Knight) Commander of the Order of the Crown (Belgium and the Congo Free State)
**K-cell** [immunology] killer cell
**KCH** King's College Hospital (London); Knight Commander of the Hanoverian Order
**KCHS** Knight Commander of the Order of the Holy Sepulchre
**KCIE** Knight Commander of the Order of the Indian Empire
**KCL** King's College, London
**KCLJ** Knight Commander of the Order of St Lazarus of Jerusalem
**KCMG** Knight Commander of the Order of St Michael and St George
**KCMS** [trademark] Kodak colour management system
**KCNA** Korean Central News Agency
**Kcs** [currency] koruna (used in Czech Republic)
**kc/s** kilocycles per second (unit of frequency)
**KCSA** Knight Commander of the Military Order of the Collar of St Agatha of Paterna
**KCSG** Knight Commander of the Order of St Gregory the Great
**KCSI** Knight Commander of the Order of the Star of India
**KCSJ** Knight Commander of the Order of St John of Jerusalem (Knights Hospitallers)
**KCSS** Knight Commander of the Order of St Silvester
**KCVO** Knight Commander of the Royal Victorian Order
**KD** kiln dried; knock down (at auction); [commerce] knocked down (of goods sold in parts); *Kongeriget Danmark* (Danish: Kingdom of Denmark); [currency] Kuwaiti dinar; [vehicle registration] Liverpool
**kd** killed
**KDC** [computing] key distribution centre; [commerce] knocked-down condition (of goods sold in parts)
**KDD** [computing] knowledge discovery in databases
**KDF** *Kraft durch Freude* (German: Strength through Joy) (Nazi holiday scheme)
**KDG** King's Dragoon Guards
**KDM** *Kongelige Danske Marine* (Danish: Royal Danish Navy)
**KE** kinetic energy; kinetic equation; [vehicle registration] Maidstone
**.ke** Kenya (in Internet address)
**KEAS** [aeronautics] knots equivalent air speed
**Kef.** Keflavik (Iceland)

**KEH** King Edward's Horse
**Ken.** Kensington; Kentucky; Kenya
**Kent.** Kentucky
**KEO** King Edward's Own
**Ker.** Kerry
**keV** kiloelectronvolt
**KEY** keep extending yourself
**KF** [vehicle registration] Liverpool
**KFA** Keep-Fit Association; Kenya Farmers' Association
**KFAED** Kuwait Fund for Arab Economic Development
**KFAT** National Union of Knitwear, Footwear and Apparel Trades
**KFC** [trademark] Kentucky Fried Chicken
**KFL** Kenya Federation of Labour
**Kfm.** *Kaufmann* (German: merchant)
**kfm.** *kaufmännisch* (German: commercial)
**KFOR** Kosovo Force (NATO-led peace-keeping force)
**Kfz.** *Kraftfahrzeug* (German: motor vehicle)
**KG** [vehicle registration] Cardiff; Knight of the Order of the Garter; [commerce] *Kommanditgesellschaft* (German: limited partnership)
**kg** keg; kilogram
**.kg** Kyrgyzstan (in Internet address)
**KGB** *Komitet Gosudarstvennoi Bezopasnosti* (Russian: Committee of State Security) (former Soviet secret police)
**KGC** Knights of the Golden Circle (US antifederal organization)
**Kgf.** *Kriegsgefangener* (German: prisoner-of-war)
**kgf** [physics] kilogram-force
**KGFR** [medicine] kidney glomerular filtration rate
**Kgl.** *Königlich* (German: Royal)
**Kgn** Kingston (Jamaica)
**KGS** known geological structure
**Kgs** [Bible] Kings
**KGV** Knight of Gustavus Vasa (Swedish decoration)
**KH** [vehicle registration] Hull; kennel huntsman; [astronautics] keyhole (as in **KH-11**, name of NASA satellite); King's Hussars; Knight of the Hanoverian Order
**.kh** Cambodia (in Internet address)
**KHC** King's Honorary Chaplain
**KHDS** King's Honorary Dental Surgeon
**KHM** King's Harbour Master
**KHNS** King's Honorary Nursing Sister
**KHP** King's Honorary Physician
**KHS** King's Honorary Surgeon; Knight of the Order of the Holy Sepulchre
**kHz** kilohertz
**.ki** Kiribati (in Internet address)
**KIA** killed in action
**KIAS** [aeronautics] knots indicated air speed
**kid.** kidney
**kil.** kilderkin (brewing cask size)
**Kild.** Kildare
**kild.** kilderkin (brewing cask size)
**Kilk.** Kilkenny
**Kinc.** Kincardineshire
**kind.** kindergarten
**kingd.** kingdom
**Kinr.** Kinross
**KIO** Kuwait Investment Office
**Kirk.** Kirkcudbrightshire
**KISS** keep it short and simple; [informal] keep it simple, stupid; [stock exchange] Kurs Information Service System
**kit.** kitchen (in property advertisement)
**kitch.** kitchen (in property advertisement)
**KJ** [medicine] knee jerk; Knight of St Joachim; [vehicle registration] Maidstone
**kJ** kilojoule
**KJV** [Bible] King James Version
**KK** [commerce] *Kabushiki Kaisha* (Japanese: joint-stock company); [vehicle registration] Maidstone
**KKK** Ku Klux Klan
**KKt** [chess] king's knight
**KKtP** [chess] king's knight's pawn
**KL** [astronomy] Kleinmann–Low (as in **KL nebula**); Kuala Lumpur; [vehicle registration] Maidstone
**kl** kilolitre
**KLA** Kosovo Liberation Army
**klax.** klaxon
**KLH** Knight of the Legion of Honour
**KLJ** Knight of the Order of St Lazarus of Jerusalem
**KLM** *Koninklijke Luchtvaart Maatschappij* (Dutch airline company)
**KLS** [medicine] kidney, liver, spleen
**KLSE** Kuala Lumpur Stock Exchange
**KM** King's Medal; Knight of Malta; [vehicle registration] Maidstone
**km** kilometre
**.km** Comoros (in Internet address)

**KMF** [currency] Comorian franc
**km/h** kilometres per hour
**KMO** Kobe Marine Observatory (Japan)
**KMP** [computing] Knuth–Morris–Pratt (algorithm)
**kmph** kilometres per hour
**KMT** Kuomintang (Chinese Nationalist Party)
**KN** [chess] king's knight; [numismatics] King's Norton (Birmingham mint mark); *Kongeriket Norge* (Norwegian: Kingdom of Norway); [vehicle registration] Maidstone
**kn** knot (unit of speed); [currency] krona (used in Sweden); [currency] krone (used in Denmark and Norway)
**KNA** Kenya News Agency; *Kongelig Norsk Automobil-klubb* (Norwegian: Royal Norwegian Automobile Club)
**KNM** *Kongelige Norske Marine* (Norwegian: Royal Norwegian Navy)
**KNP** [chess] king's knight's pawn; Kruger National Park (South Africa)
**KNPC** Kuwait National Petroleum Company
**Knt** Knight
**KO** [informal] knock out; [informal] knockout; [vehicle registration] Maidstone
**k.o.** keep off; keep out; kick-off (in football); [informal] knock out; [informal] knockout
**KOC** Kuwait Oil Company
**KOD** [navigation] kick-off drift
**K of C** Knights of Columbus
**K of K** (Lord) Kitchener of Khartoum (British field marshal)
**K of P** [USA] Knights of Pythias
**KOM** Knight of the Order of Malta
**Komintern** *Kommunisticheskii Internatsionál* (Russian: Communist International)
**Komp.** [commerce] *Kompanie* (German: company)
**Komsomol** *Kommunisticheskii Soyuz Molodezhi* (Russian: Communist Union of Youth)
**kop.** [currency] kopek (hundredth of rouble)
**Kor.** Koran; Korea; Korean
**KORR** King's Own Royal Regiment
**KOSB** King's Own Scottish Borderers
**KOYLI** King's Own Yorkshire Light Infantry
**KP** King's Parade; [chess] king's pawn; [US military] kitchen police; Knight of the Order of St Patrick; [vehicle registration] Maidstone
**.kp** North Korea (in Internet address)
**k.p.** key personnel
**kpc** kiloparsec (unit of astronomical distance)
**KPD** *Kommunistische Partei Deutschlands* (German: German Communist Party)
**KPDR** Korean People's Democratic Party
**KPFSM** King's Police and Fire Service Medal
**kpg** kilometres per gallon
**kph** kilometres per hour
**KPM** King's Police Medal
**KPMG** (Piet) Klynveld, (William Barclay) Peat, (James) Marwick, (Reinhard) Goerdeler (founding members of international accounting group)
**Kpmtr** [music] *Kapellmeister* (German: conductor)
**KPNLF** Khmer People's National Liberation Front
**KPNO** Kitt Peak National Observatory (Arizona)
**KPP** Keeper of the Privy Purse
**kpr** keeper
**KPTT** [medicine] kaolin partial thromboplastin time
**KPU** Kenya People's Union
**KR** King's Regiment; [military] King's Regulations; [chess] king's rook; [vehicle registration] Maidstone
**Kr** [currency] króna (used in Iceland); [chemical element] krypton
**kr.** [currency] krona (used in Sweden); [currency] krone (used in Denmark and Norway)
**.kr** Republic of Korea (in Internet address)
**KRC** Knight of the Red Cross
**KRE** Knight of the Order of the Red Eagle
**KRL** [computing] knowledge representation language
**KRP** [chess] king's rook's pawn
**KRR** King's Royal Rifles
**KRRC** King's Royal Rifle Corps
**KS** [vehicle registration] Edinburgh; [US postcode] Kansas; [medicine] Kaposi's sarcoma; King's Scholar; King's School; Kipling Society; Kitchener Scholar;

*Konungariket Sverige* (Swedish: Kingdom of Sweden); [international vehicle registration] Kyrgyzstan

**KSA** Kitchen Specialists Association

**KSC** Kennedy Space Center (Florida); King's School, Canterbury; Knight of St Columba

**KSF** key success factor

**KSG** Knight of the Order of St Gregory the Great

**Ksh** [currency] Kenya shilling

**KSI** Knight of the Order of the Star of India

**KSJ** Knight of the Order of St John of Jerusalem (Knights Hospitallers)

**KSL** [medicine] kidney, spleen, liver

**KSLI** King's Shropshire Light Infantry

**KSM** Korean Service Medal; *Kungliga Svenska Marinen* (Swedish: Royal Swedish Navy)

**KSS** Knight of the Order of St Silvester

**KSSU** KLM, SAS, Swissair, UTA (international airline organization)

**KStJ** Knight of the Order of St John of Jerusalem (Knights Hospitallers)

**KSU** Kansas State University

**KT** [UK postcode] Kingston-upon-Thames; Knight of the Order of the Thistle; Knight Templar; [meteorology] knot; [vehicle registration] Maidstone

**Kt** knight

**kt** [USA] karat; kilotonne; knot (unit of speed)

**Kt Bach.** Knight Bachelor

**Kto** [banking] *Konto* (German: account)

**KU** [vehicle registration] Sheffield

**Ku** [chemical element] kurchatovium (alternative name for rutherfordium)

**KUB** [medicine] kidney, ureter, bladder

**KUTD** keep up to date

**Kuw.** Kuwait

**KV** [vehicle registration] Coventry; [music] *Köchel Verzeichnis* (German: Köchel catalogue) (catalogue of Mozart's works)

**kV** kilovolt

**KW** [UK postcode] Kirkwall (Orkney); [vehicle registration] Sheffield

**kW** kilowatt

**.kw** Kuwait (in Internet address)

**KWAC** key word and context

**kWh** kilowatt hour

**KWIC** key word in context

**KWOC** key word out of context

**KWP** Korean Workers' Party

**KWT** [international vehicle registration] Kuwait

**KX** [vehicle registration] Luton

**KY** [US postcode] Kentucky; [fishing port] Kirkcaldy; [UK postcode] Kirkcaldy; *Kol Yisrael* (Israeli broadcasting station); [vehicle registration] Sheffield

**Ky** Kentucky

**ky.** [currency] kyat (used in Myanmar)

**kybd** keyboard

**Kyr.** *Kyrie eleison* (Greek: Lord have mercy) (ecclesiastical invocation)

**KZ** [vehicle registration] Antrim; [international vehicle registration] Kazakhstan; [military] killing zone

**.kz** Kazakhstan (in Internet address)

**Kzrl** [currency] kwanza (used in Angola)

# L

**L** [Roman numeral] fifty; [electrical engineering] inductor; [politics] Labour; Lady; Lake; lambert (former unit of luminance); [military] Lancers; [linguistics] language; large; Latin; law; League; learner (driver) (as in **L-plate**); lecturer; left; [currency] lempira (used in Honduras); lethal; *liber* (Latin: book); [politics] Liberal; Licentiate; Lieutenant; [aeronautics] lift; [immunology] light; [fishing port] Limerick; line (of text); linear; link; [currency] lira; litre; [electrical engineering] live; [UK postcode] Liverpool; Loch; *locus* (Latin: place); Lodge (of fraternal organization); London; Lord; [sports] lost; Lough; low; [international vehicle registration] Luxembourg; [currency] pound sterling (from Latin *libra*); [theatre] stage left

***L*** [physics] angular momentum; [chemistry] Avogadro constant; [physics] Lagrangian function; [physics] latent heat;

length; [biochemistry] linking number; longitude; [physics] luminance; [astronomy] luminosity; [physics] radiance; [electrical engineering] self-inductance; [physics] sound intensity

**l** [Roman numeral] fifty; [music] la(h) (in tonic sol-fa); [meteorology] lightning; [chemistry] liquid; [currency] lira; litre; [currency] pound sterling (from Latin *libra*)

***l*** [chemistry] laevorotatory; length; [physics] lepton number

**l.** lake; land; large; late; lateral; latitude; law; leaf; league; leasehold; left; legitimate; length; light; line (of text); link; literate; little; loch; long; lost; lough; low

**4L** [civil aircraft marking] Georgia

**9L** [civil aircraft marking] Sierra Leone

**LA** [UK postcode] Lancaster; [photography] large aperture; Latin America; Latin American; law agent; leave allowance; [medicine] left atrial; [medicine] left atrium; legal adviser; Legislative Assembly; letter of authority; Library Association; Licensing Act; licensing authority; Lieutenant-at-Arms; [physics] linear accelerator; [computing] linear arithmetic; Literate in Arts; Liverpool Academy; [fishing port] Llanelly; Lloyd's agent; local agent; local anaesthetic; local association; local authority; long acting; Los Angeles; [US postcode] Louisiana; low altitude; [vehicle registration] northwest London

**La** [chemical element] lanthanum; Louisiana

**La.** Lancastrian; Lane

**la.** last

**.la** Laos (in Internet address)

**l.a.** landing account; leading article; [medicine] *lege artis* (Latin: as directed) (in prescriptions); lighter than air

**LAA** [USA] League of Advertising Agencies; Library Association of Australia; Libyan Arab Airlines; Lieutenant-at-Arms; [USA] Life Assurance Advertisers; light anti-aircraft

**LAADS** [USA] Los Angeles Air Defense Sector

**LAAOH** Ladies' Auxiliary, Ancient Order of Hibernians

**LAAR** liquid-air accumulator rocket

**LAB** Legal Aid Board; [chemistry] linear alkyl benzene; load aboard barge; low-altitude bombing

**Lab.** [USA] Laborite; [politics] Labour; Labrador

**lab** [short form] laboratory; [short form] labrador (dog)

**lab.** label; laboratory; labour; labourer

**LABA** [USA] Laboratory Animal Breeders' Association

**LABBS** Ladies' Association of British Barbershop Singers

**LAC** Laboratory Animals Centre; Landscape Advisory Committee; leading aircraftman; Licentiate of the Apothecaries' Company; London Athletic Club; [finance] long-run average cost

**Lac** [astronomy] Lacerta

**lac.** lacquer; lactation

**LACES** London Airport cargo electronic processing scheme; [USA] Los Angeles Council of Engineering Societies

**LACONIQ** [computing] laboratory computer online inquiry

**LACS** League Against Cruel Sports

**LACSA** *Lineas Aéreas Costarricenses* (Costa Rican airline company)

**LACSAB** Local Authorities' Conditions of Service Advisory Board

**LACW** leading aircraftwoman

**LAD** [linguistics] language acquisition device; light aid detachment

**ladar** laser detection and ranging

**Ladp** Ladyship

**L Adv.** Lord Advocate

**LAE** [mathematics] linear algebraic equation

**laev.** [medicine] *laevus* (Latin: left)

**LAF** *L'Académie française* (French: the French Academy)

**LaF** Louisiana French

**LAFC** Latin American Forestry Commission

**La Font.** (Jean de) La Fontaine (French writer)

**LAFTA** Latin American Free Trade Association (former name of LAIA)

**lag.** lagoon

**LAH** Licentiate of the Apothecaries' Hall (Dublin)

**Lah.** Lahore

**LAHS** low altitude, high speed

**LAI** [botany] leaf area index; Library

Association of Ireland; *Logos Agencia de Información* (Spanish news agency)
**LAIA** Latin American Integration Association (formerly LAFTA)
**LAK** [medicine] lymphokine-activated killer (cell) (used to treat cancer)
**LAL** *Laboratoire de l'accélérateur linéaire* (French: Linear Accelerator Laboratory)
**lali** [informal] lonely aged low income
**LAM** London Academy of Music (and Dramatic Art); Master of the Liberal Arts (from Latin *Liberalium Artium Magister*)
**Lam.** Lamarck (French naturalist); [Bible] Lamentations
**lam.** laminate; laminated; lamination
**LAMA** Locomotive and Allied Manufacturers' Association of Great Britain
**Lamb.** Lambeth
**LAMC** Livestock Auctioneers' Market Committee of England and Wales
**LAMCO** Liberian-American-Swedish Mineral Corporation
**LAMDA** London Academy of Music and Dramatic Art
**LAMIDA** Lancashire and Merseyside Industrial Development Association
**LAMP** low-altitude manned penetration; [USA] Lunar Analysis and Mapping Program
**LAMS** launch acoustic measuring system
**LAMSAC** Local Authorities' Management Services and Computer Committee
**LAN** *Linea Aérea Nacional (de Chile)* (Chilean airline company); local apparent noon; [computing] local area network
**LANBY** large automatic navigation buoy
**Lanc.** Lancaster; [military] Lancers
**Lancs** Lancashire
**L&D** loans and discounts; loss and damage
**L&ID** London and India Docks
**L&NRR** [USA] Louisville and Nashville Railroad
**L&NWR** London and North-Western Railway
**L&SWR** London and South-Western Railway
**l&w** living and well
**L&YR** Lancashire and Yorkshire Railway
**Lan. Fus.** Lancashire Fusiliers
**Lang.** Languedoc
**lang.** language
**LANICA** *Lineas Aéreas de Nicaragua* (Nicaraguan airline company)
**LANL** [USA] Los Alamos National Laboratory
**LANRAC** Land Army Reunion Association Committee
**LanR(PWV)** Lancashire Regiment (Prince of Wales' Volunteers)
**LANSA** *Lineas Aéreas Nacionales SA* (Peruvian airline company)
**Lantirn** [military] low-altitude navigation and targeting infrared system
**LAO** [international vehicle registration] Laos; Licentiate in the Art of Obstetrics
**LAOAR** [US air force] Latin American Office of Aerospace Research
**LAP** [USA] Laboratory of Aviation Psychology; *Lineas Aéreas Paraguayas* (Paraguayan airline company); [computing] link access protocol
**Lap.** Lapland; Lappish
**LAPD** Los Angeles Police Department
**LAPES** low-altitude parachute extraction system
**LAPO** Los Angeles Philharmonic Orchestra
**LAPT** London Association for the Protection of Trade
**LAR** [botany] leaf area ratio; [international vehicle registration] Libya (Arab Republic); [taxation] life assurance relief; [computing] limit address register
**LARA** light armed reconnaissance aircraft
**larg.** [music] *largamente* (Italian: broadly); *largeur* (French: width); [music] *largo* (Italian: broad, slow)
**LARO** Latin American Regional Office
**LARSP** Language Assessment, Remediation and Screening Procedure
**laryngol.** laryngologist; laryngology
**LAS** Land Agents' Society; large astronomical satellite; League of Arab States; Legal Aid Society; London Archaeological Service; Lord Advocate of Scotland; low-altitude satellite; lower airspace
**LASER** London and South Eastern Library Region
**laser** light amplification by stimulated emission of radiation
**LASH** [commerce] lighter aboard ship
**LASL** [USA] Los Alamos Scientific Laboratory

**LASMO** London and Scottish Marine Oil
**LASP** low-altitude space platform
**LASS** lighter-than-air submarine simulator
**LAT** local apparent time; *Los Angeles Times*
**Lat.** Latin; Latvia; Latvian
**lat.** latent; lateral; latitude; *latus* (Latin: wide)
**LATCC** London air traffic control centre
**LATCRS** London air traffic control radar station
**lat. ht** latent heat
**LATS** [medicine] long-acting thyroid stimulator
**Latv.** Latvia
**Latvn** Latvian
**lau.** laundry
**LAUK** Library Association of the United Kingdom
**laun.** launched
**LAUTRO** Life Assurance and Unit Trust Regulatory Organization
**LAV** light armoured vehicle; *Lineas Aéreas Venezolanas* (Venezuelan airline company); [medicine] lymphadenopathy-associated virus (former name of HIV)
**lav** [short form] lavatory
**LAW** League of American Writers; light anti-tank weapon
**law.** lawyer
**Lawn** [computing] local area wireless network
**LAWRS** limited airport weather reporting system
**lax.** laxative
**LB** Bachelor of Letters (or Literature) (from Latin *Litterarum Baccalaureus*); late bottled (wine); [international vehicle registration] Liberia; light bomber; local board; [vehicle registration] northwest London
**L.b.** *Lectori benevolo* (Latin: to the kind reader)
**lb** binary logarithm; pound (unit of weight, from Latin *libra*)
**.lb** Lebanon (in Internet address)
**l.b.** landing barge; [sports] left back; [cricket] leg bye; letter box; link belt
**LBA** late booking agent (= ticket tout); linear-bounded automaton; [computing] logical block address
**LB&SCR** London, Brighton and South Coast Railway
**LBB** [engineering] leak before break
**LBBB** [medicine] left bundle branch block
**LBC** Land Bank Commission; London Broadcasting Company
**Lbc.** Lübeck
**LBCH** London Bankers' Clearing House
**LBCM** Licentiate of the Bandsmen's College of Music; London Board of Congregational Ministers
**LBD** League of British Dramatists
**L/Bdr** Lance-Bombardier
**LBF** [medicine] liver blood flow
**lbf** pound-force
**lb-ft** pound-foot
**LBH** length, breadth, height
**LBI** [astronomy] long baseline interferometry
**LBJ** Lyndon Baines Johnson (US president)
**LBL** [medicine] lymphoblastic lymphoma
**LBO** [commerce] leveraged buyout
**LBP** length between perpendiculars
**lbr** labour; lumber
**LBS** Libyan Broadcasting Service; lifeboat station; London Business School
**L.b.s.** *Lectori benevolo salutem* (Latin: to the kind reader, greeting)
**LBSM** Licentiate of Birmingham and Midland Institute School of Music
**LBV** landing barge vehicle; late bottled vintage (port); [astronomy] luminous blue variable
**LBW** live body weight
**lbw** [cricket] leg before wicket
**LC** Cross of Leo; landing craft; [medicine] Langerhans cells; Leander Club; Legislative Council; letter of credit; level crossing (on map); [USA] Library of Congress; Lieutenant-Commander; [chemistry] linear chain; [electronics] linear contact; [military slang] line crosser (i.e. defector); [chemistry] liquid chromatography; [electronics] liquid crystal; livestock commissioner; Lord Chamberlain; Lord Chancellor; Lower Canada; Lutheran Council of Great Britain; [vehicle registration] northwest London
**L/C** letter of credit
**l/c** letter of credit
**.lc** St Lucia (in Internet address)
**l.c.** label clause; law courts; lead covered;

leading cases; left centre; legal currency; letter card; letter of credit; *loco citato* (Latin: in the place (already) cited); low-calorie; low-carbon; [printing] lower case

**LCA** Library Club of America; Licensed Company Auditor; [computing] logic cell array; low-cost automation

**LCAD** London Certificate in Art and Design

**LCAP** [computing] loosely coupled array of processors

**LCB** [theatre] left centre back (of stage); [USA] Liquor Control Board; London Convention Bureau; Lord Chief Baron

**l.c.b.** longitudinal centre of buoyancy

**LCC** [electronics] leadless chip carrier; Legalize Cannabis Campaign; [accounting] life-cycle cost(ing); load-carrying capability; London Chamber of Commerce; London County Council (former local authority)

**LCCC** [USA] Library of Congress Catalog Card

**LCD** [electronics] liquid-crystal display; Lord Chamberlain's Department; Lord Chancellor's Department; lower court decisions; [mathematics] lowest common denominator

**LCDT** London Contemporary Dance Theatre

**LCE** Licentiate in Civil Engineering; London Commodity Exchange

**lce** lance

**LCF** Law Centres Federation; [mathematics] lowest common factor

**l.c.f.** longitudinal centre of flotation

**l.c.g.** longitudinal centre of gravity

**LCGB** Locomotive Club of Great Britain

**LCH** London Clearing House

**LCh** Licentiate in Surgery (from Latin *Licentiatus Chirurgiae*); Lord Chancellor

**LChir** Licentiate in Surgery (from Latin *Licentiatus Chirurgiae*)

**LCIGB** Locomotive and Carriage Institution of Great Britain and Ireland

**LCIOB** Licentiate of the Chartered Institute of Building

**LCJ** Lord Chief Justice

**LCL** [US commerce] less-than-carload lot; [commerce] less-than-container load; Licentiate in Canon Law

**l.c.l.** lower control limit

**LCLS** Livestock Commission Levy Scheme

**LCM** landing craft mechanized; [mathematics] least common multiple; [computing] life-cycle management; London College of Music; [mathematics] lowest common multiple

**LCN** [aeronautics] load classification number; local civil noon

**Lcn** Lincoln

**LCO** landing craft officer; launch control officer

**L/Corp.** Lance-Corporal

**LCP** last complete programme; least-cost planning; Licentiate of the College of Preceptors; [chemistry] liquid-crystal polymer; London College of Printing; low-cost production

**LCP&SA** Licentiate of the College of Physicians and Surgeons of America

**LCP&SO** Licentiate of the College of Physicians and Surgeons of Ontario

**L/Cpl** Lance-Corporal

**LCPS** Licentiate of the College of Physicians and Surgeons

**l/cr.** *lettre de crédit* (French: letter of credit)

**LCS** London Cooperative Society

**LCSAJ** [computing] linear code sequence and jump

**LCSP** London and Counties Society of Physiologists

**LCST** Licentiate of the College of Speech Therapists

**LCT** landing craft tank; local civil time

**LCU** [photography] large close-up

**LCV** Licentiate of the College of Violinists

**LD** Doctor of Letters (or Literature) (from Latin *Litterarum Doctor*); Lady Day; *laus Deo* (Latin: praise be to God); [education, psychology] learning difficulties; [education, psychology] learning-disabled; legal dose (or dosage); *lepide dictum* (Latin: wittily said); [pharmacology] lethal dose (as in $\mathbf{LD}_{50}$, dose killing 50% of test group); Liberal and Democratic; Liberal Democrat(s); [currency] Libyan dinar; Licentiate in Divinity; Light Dragoons; *Litera Dominicalis* (Latin: Dominical letter); [UK postcode] Llandrindod Wells; London Docks; low density; Low Dutch; [vehicle registration] northwest London

**L/D** letter of deposit

**Ld** Limited (company); Lord (in titles)

**ld** land; [printing] lead; load
**l.d.** light difference; line of departure; line of duty
**LDA** Lead Development Association
**Lda** [commerce] *Sociedade de responsabilidade limitada* (Portuguese: limited company, Ltd)
**l.d.b.** light distribution box
**LDC** less developed country; local distribution company
**l.d.c.** long-distance call; lower dead centre
**LDDC** London Docklands' Development Corporation
**LDEF** [astronomy] long duration exposure facility
**LDEG** *laus Deo et gloria* (Latin: praise and glory be to God)
**LDentSc** Licentiate in Dental Science
**L'derry** Londonderry
**Ldg** Leading (in military rank)
**ldg** landing; leading; loading; lodging
**Ldge** Lodge
**Ld'H** *Légion d'Honneur* (French: Legion of Honour)
**LDiv** Licentiate in Divinity
**ldk** lower deck
**LDL** [biochemistry] low-density lipoprotein
**ldmk** landmark
**LDN** less developed nation
**Ldn** London
**LDOS** Lord's Day Observance Society
**LDP** Liberal Democratic Party; [finance] London daily price; long-distance path
**Ldp** Ladyship; Lordship
**LDPE** low-density polyethylene (packaging material)
**LDR** Liberal, Democratic and Reform Goup (in European Parliament); low dose rate
**ldr** leader; ledger; lodger
**ldry** laundry
**LDS** Latter-Day Saints; *laus Deo semper* (Latin: praise be to God for ever); Licentiate in Dental Surgery
**lds** loads
**LDSc** Licentiate in Dental Science
**LDT** [finance] licensed deposit taker
**LDV** Local Defence Volunteers (i.e. Home Guard)
**LDWA** Long Distance Walkers' Association
**LDX** long-distance xerography
**LDY** Leicestershire and Derbyshire Yeomanry
**LE** labour exchange (former name for jobcentre); [UK postcode] Leicester; London Electricity; low energy; [medicine] lupus erythematosus; [vehicle registration] northwest London
**Le** [currency] leone (used in Sierra Leone)
**Le.** Lebanese; Lebanon
**l.e.** leading edge; left eye; library edition; light equipment; limited edition; low explosive
**LEA** local education authority
**lea.** league; leather; leave
**LEAJ** [USA] Law Enforcement and Administration of Justice
**LEAP** Life Education for the Autistic Person; lift-off elevation and azimuth programmer; Loan and Educational Aid Programme
**LEB** London Electricity Board; [astronautics] low-energy booster
**Leb.** Lebanese; Lebanon
**LEC** Local Employment Committee; Local Enterprise Company
**lect.** *lectio* (Latin: lesson); lecture; lecturer
**lectr** lecturer
**LED** [electronics] light-emitting diode
**led.** ledger
**LEDC** Lighting Equipment Development Council
**LEFM** linear elastic fracture mechanics
**leg.** legal; legate; legation; [music] *legato* (Italian: bound, smoothly); legion; legislation; legislative; legislature; legitimate
**legg.** [music] *legg(i)ero* (Italian: light, rapid)
**legis.** legislation; legislative; legislature
**legit** [short form] legitimate
**Leics** Leicestershire
**Leip.** Leipzig
**Leit.** Leitrim
**LEL** Laureate in English Literature; [physics] linear energy loss
**LEM** [astronautics] lunar excursion module
**LEMA** Lifting Equipment Manufacturers' Association
**LENTA** London Enterprise Agency
**LEO** [astronautics] low earth orbit; Lyons Electronic Office (early computer)
**LEP** [physics] large electron-positron (collider) (at CERN)

**Lep** [astronomy] Lepus
**LEPMA** [USA] Lithographic Engravers' and Plate Makers' Association
**LEPORE** [USA] long-term and expanded program of oceanic research and exploration
**LEPRA** Leprosy Relief Association
**LEPT** long-endurance patrolling torpedo
**LES** launch escape system; Liverpool Engineering Society
**LèsL** *Licencié ès lettres* (French: Bachelor of Arts)
**LESS** least-cost estimating and scheduling
**LèsS** *Licencié ès sciences* (French: Bachelor of Science)
**LEST** large earth-based solar telescope
**LET** [physics] linear energy transfer
**let.** letter
**LETS** Local Employment and Trade System; Local Exchange and Trading System (community bartering system)
**LEU** [physics] low-enriched uranium
**LEV** [astronautics] lunar excursion vehicle
**Lev.** Levant; [Bible] Leviticus
**Levit.** [Bible] Leviticus
**LEX** land exercise
**lex.** lexicon
**lexicog.** lexicographer; lexicographical; lexicography
**LEY** Liberal European Youth
**LF** Lancashire Fusiliers; line feed; [radio] low frequency; [astronomy] luminosity function; [currency] Luxembourg franc; [vehicle registration] northwest London
**Lf** limit of flocculation (in toxicology)
**lf** leaf
**l.f.** ledger folio; life float; [printing] light face
**LFA** less favoured area; local freight agent
**LFB** London Fire Brigade
**LFBC** London Federation of Boys' Clubs
**LFC** low-frequency current; Lutheran Free Church
**LFCDA** London Fire and Civil Defence Authority
**LFD** least fatal dose; low-fat diet
**LFE** laboratory for electronics
**Lfg** *Lieferung* (German: delivery)
**LFO** low-frequency oscillator
**lft** leaflet
**LFTU** landing force training unit
**LG** [vehicle registration] Chester; Lady Companion of the Order of the Garter; landing ground; Lewis gun; Lieutenant-General; Life Guards; (David) Lloyd George (British statesman); *London Gazette*; Low German
**lg** common logarithm; long
**lg.** lagoon; large
**LGAR** [USA] Ladies of the Grand Army of the Republic
**LGB** Local Government Board
**LGBC** Local Government Boundary Commission for England
**LGC** lunar (module) guidance computer
**lge** large; league; lounge (in property advertisement)
**LGEB** Local Government Examination Board
**L-Gen** Lieutenant-General
**LGer** Low German
**LGIO** Local Government Information Office
**LGk** Late Greek
**LGM** little green men; Lloyd's Gold Medal
**LGO** [USA] Lamont Geological Observatory
**LGPRA** Local Government Public Relations Association
**LGR** leasehold ground rent; local government reports
**LGr** Late Greek
**LGSM** Licentiate of the Guildhall School of Music (and Drama)
**LGTB** Local Government Training Board
**lgth** length
**lg tn** long ton
**LGU** Ladies' Golf Union
**LGV** large goods vehicle (replacement for HGV)
**LH** left hand; left handed; [fishing port] Leith; licensing hours; Licentiate in Hygiene; [military] Light Horse; [biochemistry] luteinizing hormone; [vehicle registration] northwest London
**L/H** leasehold (in property advertisement)
**l.h.** [sports] left half; left hand; left handed
**LHA** landing helicopter assault; local health authority; local hour angle; Lord High Admiral; lower hour angle
**l.h.b.** [sports] left halfback
**LHC** [physics] Large Hadron Collider (at CERN); Lord High Chancellor

**LHCIMA** Licentiate of the Hotel Catering and Institutional Management Association
**LHD** Doctor of Humanities (or Literature) (from Latin *Litterarum Humaniorum Doctor*)
**l.h.d.** left-hand drive (in car advertisement)
**LHDC** lateral homing depth charge
**LHeb** Late Hebrew
**lhld** leasehold (in property advertisement)
**LHMC** London Hospital Medical College
**LHO** livestock husbandry officer
**lhr** lumen-hour
**LHRC** Light and Health Research Council
**LH-RH** [biochemistry] luteinizing-hormone-releasing hormone
**LHS** left hand side
**LHSM** Licentiate of the Institute of Health Services Management
**LHT** Lord High Treasurer
**LHWN** lowest high water neaps (level of tide)
**LI** Leeward Islands; Liberal International; [USA] Licentiate in Instruction; Light Infantry; [law] Lincoln's Inn; [fishing port] Littlehampton; Long Island (New York)
**Li** [chemical element] lithium
**li.** link; [currency] lira
**.li** Liechtenstein (in Internet address)
**l.i.** letter of introduction; longitudinal interval
**LIA** [USA] Laser Industry Association; [USA] Lead Industries Association; Leather Industries of America; Lebanese International Airways; Life Insurance Association
**LIAB** Licentiate of the International Association of Book-keepers
**LIAT** London International Arbitration Trust
**Lib** [astronomy] Libra
**Lib.** [politics] Liberal; Liberia; Liberian; Libya; Libyan
**lib.** *liber* (Latin: book); liberation; liberty; librarian; library; libretto
**LIBA** Lloyd's Insurance Brokers' Association
**lib. cat.** library catalogue
**Lib. Cong.** [USA] Library of Congress
**Lib Dem** [short form] Liberal Democrat
**LIBER** *Ligue des bibliothèques européennes de recherche* (French: League of European Research Libraries)
**LIBID** [finance] London Inter-Bank Bid Rate
**LIBOR** [finance] London Inter-Bank Offered Rate
**libst** librettist
**LIC** Lands Improvement Company; [electronics] linear integrated circuit
**Lic.** *Licenciado* (Spanish: Bachelor) (in academic degrees); Licentiate (in academic degrees)
**lic.** licence; licensed
**LicAc** Licentiate of Acupuncture
**LicMed** Licentiate in Medicine
**LicTheol** Licentiate in Theology
**LICW** Licentiate of the Institute of Clerks of Works of Great Britain
**lidar** light detection and ranging
**LIDC** Lead Industries Development Council
**LIE** loss of independent existence
**Lieut.** Lieutenant
**Lieut-Cdr** Lieutenant-Commander
**Lieut-Col** Lieutenant-Colonel
**Lieut-Com** Lieutenant-Commander
**Lieut-Gen** Lieutenant-General
**Lieut-Gov** Lieutenant-Governor
**LIF** [medicine] left iliac fossa; [computing] low insertion force
**LIFFE** London International Financial Futures (and Options) Exchange
**LIFireE** Licentiate of the Institution of Fire Engineers
**LIFO** last in, first out
**Lig.** Liguria; Limoges
**LIHG** *Ligue internationale de hockey sur glace* (French: International Ice Hockey Federation)
**LILO** last in, last out
**LIM** linear-induction motor; [computing] Lotus, Intel, Microsoft
**Lim.** Limerick
**lim.** limit; limited
**LIMEAN** [finance] London Inter-Bank Mean Rate
**limo** [short form] limousine
**lin.** lineal; linear; liniment
**linac** [physics] linear accelerator
**Lincs** Lincolnshire
**ling.** linguistic; linguistics
**Linn.** (Carolus) Linnaeus (Swedish botanist); Linnean

**lino** [short form] linoleum
**LInstP** Licentiate of the Institute of Physics
**LIOB** Licentiate of the Institute of Building
**LIP** life insurance policy; [medicine] lymphocytic interstitial pneumonitis
**LIPA** Liverpool Institute for the Performing Arts
**LIPM** Lister Institute of Preventive Medicine
**lips** [computing] logical inferences per second
**liq.** liquid; liquor
**LIRA** Linen Industry Research Association
**LIRMA** London International Insurance and Reinsurance Market Association
**LIS** laser isotope separation
**Lis.** Lisbon
**LISA** *Library and Information Science Abstracts*
**LISC** Library and Information Services Council
**LISM** Licentiate of the Incorporated Society of Musicians
**LISP** list processing (computer programming language)
**Lit** [currency] Italian lira
**lit.** literal; literally; literary; literature; litre; litter; little; liturgy
**LitB** Bachelor of Letters (or Literature) (from Latin *Litterarum Baccalaureus*)
**lit crit** [short form] literary criticism
**LitD** Doctor of Letters (or Literature) (from Latin *Litterarum Doctor*)
**Lith.** Lithuania; Lithuanian
**lith.** lithograph; lithography
**litho.** lithograph; lithographic; lithography
**lithog.** lithograph; lithographic; lithography
**lithol.** lithology
**Lit. Hum.** *Literae Humaniores* (Latin: Humane Letters) (classics degree at Oxford University)
**LitM** Master of Letters (or Literature) (from Latin *Litterarum Magister*)
***Lit. Sup.*** (*Times*) *Literary Supplement*
**LittB** Bachelor of Letters (or Literature) (from Latin *Litterarum Baccalaureus*)
**LittD** Doctor of Letters (or Literature) (from Latin *Litterarum Doctor*)
**LittM** Master of Letters (or Literature) (from Latin *Litterarum Magister*)
**liturg.** liturgical; liturgy
**LIUNA** Laborers' International Union of North America
**Liv.** Liverpool; Livy (Roman historian)
**liv.** [commerce] *livraison* (French: delivery)
**liv. st.** *livre sterling* (French: pound sterling)
**Lix** [computing] legal information exchange
**LJ** [vehicle registration] Bournemouth; *Library Journal*; [athletics] long jump; Lord Justice
**l.j.** life jacket
**LJA** Lady Jockeys' Association
**LJC** London Juvenile Courts
**LJJ** Lords Justices
**LK** [fishing port] Lerwick; [vehicle registration] northwest London
**Lk** [currency] lek (used in Albania)
**.lk** Sri Lanka (in Internet address)
**lkd** locked
**lkg** locking
**lkge** leakage
**lkr** locker
**LL** Late Latin; Law Latin; *Law List*; laws; lending library; lend-lease; limited liability; [mathematics, physics] linear-linear; lines (of text); [fishing port] Liverpool; [UK postcode] Llandudno; London Library; Lord Lieutenant; Lords; [medicine] lower limb; Low Latin; [vehicle registration] northwest London
**L/L** [commerce] *Lutlang* (Norwegian: limited company, Ltd)
**ll.** leaves; *leges* (Latin: laws); lines (of text)
**l.l.** live load; *loco laudato* (Latin: in the place cited with approval); lower left; lower limit
**LLA** Lady Literate in Arts
**LL.AA.II.** *Leurs Altesses Impériales* (French: Their Imperial Highnesses)
**LL.AA.RR.** *Leurs Altesses Royales* (French: Their Royal Highnesses)
**LLB** Bachelor of Laws (from Latin *Legum Baccalaureus*)
**l.l.c.** lower left centre
**LLCM** Licentiate of the London College of Music
**LLCO** Licentiate of the London College of Osteopathy

**LLD** Doctor of Laws (from Latin *Legum Doctor*)
**Llds** [insurance] Lloyd's
**LLE** low-level exposure (to radiation)
**LL.EE.** *Leurs Éminences* (French: Their Eminences); *Leurs Excellences* (French: Their Excellencies)
**LLett** Licentiate of Letters
**LLI** Lord Lieutenant of Ireland
**l.l.i.** latitude and longitude indicator
**LLL** Licentiate in Laws; loose leaf ledger; [computing] low-level language; [computing] low-level logic
**LLLW** [nuclear technology] liquid low-level waste
**LLM** Master of Laws (from Latin *Legum Magister*)
**LLMCom** Master of Laws in Commercial Law
**LL.MM.** *Leurs Majestés* (French: Their Majesties)
**LLN** [USA] League for Less Noise
**LLNL** [USA] Lawrence Livermore National Laboratory
**LLNW** low-level nuclear waste
**LLRW** low-level radioactive waste
**LLS** [astronautics] lunar logistics system
**LLSV** [astronautics] lunar logistics system vehicle
**LLU** lending library unit
**LLV** [astronautics] lunar logistics vehicle
**LLW** [nuclear technology] low-level waste
**LM** Legion of Merit; Licentiate in Medicine; Licentiate in Midwifery; Licentiate in Music; light microscopy; liquid metal; [electrical engineering] load management; London Museum; [music, prosody] long metre; [Scotland] Lord Marquis; Lord Mayor; [astronautics] lunar module; [currency] Maltese lira; [vehicle registration] northwest London
**l.M** *laufenden Monats* (German: of the current month)
**lm** lumen (unit of luminous flux)
**l.m.** land mine; light metal; *locus monumenti* (Latin: place of the monument)
**LMA** Linoleum Manufacturers' Association; low moisture avidity
**LMBC** Liverpool Marine Biological Committee
**LMC** [astronomy] Large Magellanic Cloud; [nuclear technology] liquid-metal coolant; Lloyd's Machinery Certificate; local medical committee
**LMCC** Licentiate of the Medical Council of Canada
**LMD** local medical doctor; [music, prosody] long metre double
**lmd** leafmould
**LME** London Metal Exchange
**LMed** Licentiate in Medicine
**LMFBR** [nuclear technology] liquid-metal-cooled fast breeder reactor
**LMG** light machine gun
**LMI** [USA] Logistics Management Institute
**LMi** [astronomy] Leo Minor
**LMO** lens-modulated oscillator; light machine oil
**LMP** [medicine] last menstrual period; [astronautics] lunar module pilot
**LMR** [nuclear technology] liquid-metal reactor; [railways] London Midland Region
**LMRCP** Licentiate in Midwifery of the Royal College of Physicians
**LMRSH** Licentiate Member of the Royal Society of Health
**LMRTPI** Legal Member of the Royal Town Planning Institute
**LMS** Latin Mass Society; Licentiate in Medicine and Surgery; [education] local management of schools; London Mathematical Society; London Medical Schools; London Missionary Society; London, Midland and Scottish (Railway); [medicine] loss of memory syndrome
**LMSR** London, Midland and Scottish Railway
**LMSSA** Licentiate in Medicine and Surgery of the Society of Apothecaries
**LMT** [physics] length, mass, time; [astronomy] local mean time
**LMus** Licentiate in Music
**LMVD** [New Zealand] Licensed Motor Vehicle Dealer
**LMW** low molecular weight
**LMX** [insurance] London Market Excess of Loss (at Lloyd's)
**LMXB** [astronomy] low-mass X-ray binary
**LN** [fishing port] King's Lynn; [UK postcode] Lincoln; liquid nitrogen; [medicine] lymph node; [vehicle registration]

northwest London; [civil aircraft marking] Norway
**Ln.** Lane
**ln** natural logarithm (from Latin *logarithmus naturalis*)
**LNat** Liberal National
**LNB** low noise blocker (on satellite dish)
**LNC** League of Nations Covenant
**LNER** London and North Eastern Railway
**LNG** liquefied natural gas
**lnge** lounge (in property advertisement)
**LNLC** Ladies' Naval Luncheon Club
**Lnrk** Lanark
**LNS** land navigation system
**LNT** liquid-nitrogen temperature
**LNU** League of Nations Union
**LNWR** London and North Western Railway
**LO** *Landsorganisationen i Sverige* (Swedish: General Federation of Swedish Trade Unions); launch operator; liaison officer; [fishing port] London; London office; [vehicle registration] northwest London
**Lo.** Lord
**l/o** [commerce] *leur ordre* (French: their order)
**lo.** loam; local
**l.o.** lubricating oil
**LOA** leave of absence; length over all; light observation aircraft
**l.o.a.** length over all
**LOB** [baseball] left on base; line of balance; Location of Offices Bureau
**LOBAL** long-base-line buoy
**LOBAR** long-base-line radar
**LOC** launch operations centre; [USA] Library of Congress; [meteorology] locally
**loc.** local; location; [grammar] locative
**l.o.c.** letter of credit; line(s) of communication
**LOCA** [nuclear technology] loss-of-coolant accident
**loc. cit.** *loco citato* (Latin: in the place (already) cited)
**loc. laud.** *loco laudato* (Latin: in the place cited with approval)
**locn** location
**loco.** locomotion; locomotive
**loc. primo cit.** *loco primo citato* (Latin: in the place first cited)
**LOD** limit(s) of detection
**LOF** loss of flow; loss of fluid; loss of function
**L of C** [USA] Library of Congress; line(s) of communication
**L of N** League of Nations
**LOFT** low-frequency radio telescope
**log** [short form] logarithm
**log.** logic; logical; logistic
**LOH** light observation helicopter
**LOI** [Northern Ireland] Loyal Orange Institution; lunar orbit insertion
**LOL** laughs out loud (in Internet chat); [Northern Ireland] Loyal Orange Lodge
**LOLA** library on-line acquisition; lunar orbit landing approach
**LOM** [USA] Loyal Order of Moose
**LOMA** [USA] Life Office Management Association
**Lomb.** Lombard; Lombardy
**lombard** [informal] loads of money but a right dickhead
**Lon.** London; Londonderry
**lon.** longitude
**Lond.** London; Londonderry
**Londin.** *Londiniensis* (Latin: (Bishop) of London)
**Long.** Longford
**long.** longitude
**longl** longitudinal
**Lonrho** [finance] London Rhodesian
**LOOM** [USA] Loyal Order of Moose
**l.o.p.** [navigation] line of position
**LOPAR** low-power acquisition radar
**loq.** *loquitur* (Latin: (he/she) speaks)
**LOR** light output ratio; lunar orbit rendezvous
**LORAC** long-range accuracy
**LORAD** long-range active detection
**LORAN** long-range navigation
**LORAPH** long-range passive homing system
**LORCS** League of Red Cross and Red Crescent Societies
**LORV** low observable re-entry vehicle
**LOS** Latin Old Style; Law of the Seas; line of sight; loss of signal
**LOSS** large-object salvage system
**LOT** large orbital telescope; *Polskie Linie Lotnicze* (Polish airline company)
**lot.** lotion
**LOTC** [finance] London over-the-counter market
**Lou.** Louisiana
**LOX** liquid oxygen
**loy.** loyal; loyalty

**LOYA** League of Young Adventurers
**LP** Labour Party; Lady Provost; large paper (edition of book); [paper size] large post; last post; legal procurator; Liberal Party; life policy; limited partnership; [computing] linear programming; liquid petroleum; liquid propellant; long play (on video recorder); long-playing (record); Lord Provost; low pressure; [medicine] lumbar puncture; [vehicle registration] northwest London
**Lp** Ladyship; Lordship
**L/P** letterpress; life policy
**lp** limp
**l.p.** last paid; latent period; launch platform; [printing] long primer (type size); low pressure
**LPA** Leather Producers' Association for England; Local Productivity Association
**LPC** leaf protein concentrate (in nutrition); Legal Practice Course; Lord President of the Council
**l.p.c.** low pressure chamber
**LPE** [electronics] liquid-phase epitaxy; London Press Exchange
**LPEA** Licentiate of the Physical Education Association
**LPed** Licentiate in Pedagogy
**LPF** [computing] League for Programming Freedom
**LPG** liquefied petroleum gas
**LPGA** Ladies' Professional Golf Association
**LPh** Licentiate in Philosophy
**lpi** lines per inch
**LPLC** low-pressure liquid chromatography
**lpm** lines per millimetre; lines per minute
**LPN** [USA] Licensed Practical Nurse
**LPNA** [USA] Lithographers' and Printers' National Association
**LPO** local post office; local purchasing officer; London Philharmonic Orchestra
**L'pool** Liverpool
**LPRP** Laotian People's Revolutionary Party
**LPS** London Philharmonic Society; Lord Privy Seal
**LPSO** Lloyd's Policy Signing Office
**LPU** low pay unit
**lpw** lumens per watt
**Lpz.** Leipzig
**LQ** [civil aircraft marking] Argentina; [computing] letter quality (of printing); [mathematics] linear-quadratic
**l.q.** *lege quaeso* (Latin: please read)
**lqdr** liquidator
**LQR** *Law Quarterly Review*
**LQT** [commerce] Liverpool quay terms
**LR** [fishing port] Lancaster; Land Registry; Law Report; left-(to-)right; Lloyd's Register (of Shipping); Lowland Regiment; Loyal Regiment; [vehicle registration] northwest London
**Lr** Lancer; [chemical element] lawrencium; ledger; [currency] lira
**l.R** *laufen der Rechnung* (German: current account)
**lr** ledger; [currency] lira; lower
**.lr** Liberia (in Internet address)
**l.r.** landing report; log run; long range; long run
**LRA** Local Radio Association
**LRAC** Law Reports, Appeal Cases; [finance] long-run average cost
**LRAD** Licentiate of the Royal Academy of Dancing
**LRAM** Licentiate of the Royal Academy of Music
**LRB** London Residuary Body; London Rifle Brigade
**LRC** Labour Representation Committee; Langley Research Center (in NASA); Leander Rowing Club; London Rowing Club; [computing] longitudinal redundancy check
**LRCh** Law Reports, Chancery Division
**LRCM** Licentiate of the Royal College of Music
**LRCP** Licentiate of the Royal College of Physicians
**LRCPE** Licentiate of the Royal College of Physicians of Edinburgh
**LRCPI** Licentiate of the Royal College of Physicians of Ireland
**LRCPSGlas** Licentiate of the Royal College of Physicians and Surgeons of Glasgow
**LRCS** League of Red Cross Societies; Licentiate of the Royal College of Surgeons (of England)
**LRCSE** Licentiate of the Royal College of Surgeons of Edinburgh
**LRCSI** Licentiate of the Royal College of Surgeons in Ireland

**LRCVS** Licentiate of the Royal College of Veterinary Surgeons
**LREC** [medicine] Local Research Ethics Committee
**LRHL** Law Reports, House of Lords
**LRIBA** Licentiate of the Royal Institute of British Architects
**LRKB** Law Reports, King's Bench
**LRM** language reference manual
**LRP** Law Reports, Probate Division; long-range planning
**LRPS** Licentiate of the Royal Photographic Society
**LRQB** Law Reports, Queen's Bench
**LRR** [taxation] lower reduced rate
**LRS** Land Registry Stamp; Lloyd's Register of Shipping
**Lrs** Lancers
**LRSC** Licentiate of the Royal Society of Chemistry
**LRSM** Licentiate of the Royal Schools of Music
**LRT** light rail transit; London Regional Transport; long-range transport
**LRTF** long-range theatre nuclear forces
**LRTI** [medicine] lower respiratory tract infection
**LRU** least recently used; line replaceable unit
**LRV** light rail vehicle; lunar roving vehicle
**LRWES** long-range weapons experimental station
**LS** [vehicle registration] Edinburgh; Law Society; leading seaman; [UK postcode] Leeds; legal seal; [international vehicle registration] Lesotho; letter service; Licensed Surveyor; Licentiate in Surgery; [psychology] liminal sensitivity; Linnean Society; [law] *locus sigilli* (Latin: the place of the seal); London Scottish; London Sinfonietta; [cinema] long shot; loudspeaker
**ls** litres per second
**.ls** Lesotho (in Internet address)
**l.s.** landing ship; left side; letter signed; local sunset; [law] *locus sigilli* (Latin: the place of the seal); long sight; low speed; lump sum
**LSA** Land Settlement Association; leading supply assistant; learning support assistant; Licence in Agricultural Sciences; Licentiate of the Society of Apothecaries
**LSAA** Linen Supply Association of America
**LS&GCM** Long Service and Good Conduct Medal
**LSB** [computing] least significant bit; London School Board
**LSC** Licentiate in Sciences; [chemistry] liquid–solid chromatography; London Salvage Corps; Lower School Certificate
**l.s.c.** *loco supra citato* (Latin: in the place cited above)
**LScAct** Licentiate in Actuarial Science
**LSCF** [statistics] least squares curve fitting
**LSCS** [obstetrics] lower segment Caesarean section
**LSD** League of Safe Drivers; [computing] least significant digit; *librae, solidi, denarii* (Latin: pounds, shillings, pence); Lightermen, Stevedores and Dockers; [pharmacology] lysergic acid diethylamide (hallucinogen, from German *Lysergsäure-Diäthylamid*)
**l.s.d.** *librae, solidi, denarii* (Latin: pounds, shillings, pence)
**lsd li.** leased line
**LSE** [chemistry] liquid–solid extraction; [chemistry] liquid–solvent extraction; London School of Economics and Political Science; London Stock Exchange
**lse** lease
**l.s.e.** limited signed edition
**L/Sgt** Lance-Sergeant
**LSHTM** London School of Hygiene and Tropical Medicine
**LSI** Labour and Socialist International; [electronics] large-scale integration
**LSJ** London School of Journalism
**LSJM** *laus sit Jesu et Mariae* (Latin: praise be to Jesus and Mary)
**LSL** landing ship logistic; low-speed logic
**LSM** laser scanning microscope; [mathematics, physics] least-squares method; [electrical engineering] linear synchronous motor
**l.s.m.** *litera scripta manet* (Latin: the written word remains)
**LSO** London Symphony Orchestra
**LSS** large-scale structure; large-scale system; Licentiate in Sacred Scripture; life-saving station (or service); life-support system
**LSSc** Licentiate in Sanitary Science

**LST** landing ship (for) tanks; landing ship (for) transport; Licentiate in Sacred Theology; [astronomy] local sidereal time; local standard time
**l.s.t.** local standard time
**LSU** Louisiana State University
**LSW** lights spray and wipe (in car advertisement)
**LSZ** [New Zealand] limited speed zone
**LT** lawn tennis; leading telegraphist; letter telegram; [medicine] leukotriene; Licentiate in Teaching; Licentiate in Theology; [international vehicle registration] Lithuania; London Transport; [fishing port] Lowestoft; low temperature; [electrical engineering] low tension; [vehicle registration] northwest London; [currency] Turkish lira
**Lt** Lieutenant; [military] Light
**lt** light
**.lt** Lithuania (in Internet address)
**l.t.** landed terms; landing team; large tug; local time; locum tenens (person standing in for another); long ton; loop test
**LTA** Lawn Tennis Association; lighter than air (of aircraft); London Teachers' Association
**LTAA** Lawn Tennis Association of Australia
**LT&SR** London, Tilbury and Southend Railway
**LTB** London Tourist Board; London Transport Board
**l.t.b.** low-tension battery
**LTBT** Limited Test Ban Treaty
**LTC** lawn tennis club
**Lt-Cdr** Lieutenant-Commander
**LTCL** Licentiate of Trinity College of Music, London
**Lt-Col** Lieutenant-Colonel
**Lt-Com** Lieutenant-Commander
**Ltd** Limited (after company name)
**LTDP** long-term defence programme
**LTE** [astronomy] local thermodynamic equilibrium; London Transport Executive
**LTF** Lithographic Technical Foundation
**ltg** lettering; lighting
**ltge** [commerce] lighterage
**Lt-Gen** Lieutenant-General
**Lt-Gov** Lieutenant-Governor
**LTH** light training helicopter; [biochemistry] luteotrophic hormone
**LTh** Licentiate in Theology
**LTheol** Licentiate in Theology
**lthr** leather
**LTI** Licentiate of the Textile Institute
**LTIB** Lead Technical Information Bureau
**Lt Inf.** Light Infantry
**LTL** [US commerce] less-than-truckload lot
**LTM** Licentiate in Tropical Medicine; London Terminal Market; long-term memory
**ltn.** lightning
**LTO** leading torpedo operator
**LTOM** London Traded Options Market
**LTP** [biochemistry] lipid-transfer protein; [science] long-term potentiation
**LTR** [genetics] long terminal repeat
**ltr** letter; lighter; litre
**LTRA** Lands Tribunal Rating Appeals
**LtRN** Lieutenant, Royal Navy
**LTRS** Low Temperature Research Station
**LTSC** Licentiate of Tonic Sol-Fa College
**LTTE** Liberation Tigers of Tamil Eelam (in Sri Lanka)
**LTU** *Lufttransport-Unternehmen GmbH* (German airline company)
**LU** Liberal Unionist; lock-up (in property advertisement); loudness unit; [UK postcode] Luton; [vehicle registration] northwest London
**Lu** [chemical element] lutetium
**Lu.** Lucerne
**l/u** [shipping] laid up; [shipping] lying up
**lu.** *luglio* (Italian: July)
**.lu** Luxembourg (in Internet address)
**LUA** Liverpool Underwriting Association
**lub.** lubricant; lubricate; lubrication
**lubr.** lubricant; lubricate; lubrication
**LUC** London Underwriting Centre
**LUCOM** lunar communication system
**LUD** leather-upholstered dashboard (in car advertisement)
**LUG** light utility glider; [computing] local users group
**lug.** luggage; lugger
**LUHF** [electronics] lowest useful high frequency
**LULOP** *London Union List of Periodicals*
**LUM** lunar excursion module
**lum.** lumbago; lumber; luminous
**LUMAS** lunar mapping system
**lun.** *lundi* (French: Monday); *lunedì*

(Italian: Monday); *lunes* (Spanish: Monday)
**LUNCO** Lloyd's Underwriters Non-Marine Claims Office
**LUOTC** London University Officers' Training Corps
**Lup** [astronomy] Lupus
**l/up** lock-up
**LUS** Land Utilization Survey
**LUSCS** [obstetrics] lower uterine segment Caesarean section
**LUSI** lunar surface inspection
**lusing.** [music] *lusingando* (Italian: coaxing, caressing)
**LUT** [computing] look-up table
**Luth.** Lutheran
**Lux.** Luxembourg; Luxembourger
**lux.** luxurious; luxury
**LV** [civil aircraft marking] Argentina; [international vehicle registration] Latvia; [medicine] left ventricle; [medicine] left ventricular; licensed victualler; [meteorology] light and variable; [vehicle registration] Liverpool; luncheon voucher
**Lv** [currency] lev (used in Bulgaria)
**lv.** leave (of absence); *livre* (French: book)
**.lv** Latvia (in Internet address)
**l.v.** low voltage
**LVA** Licensed Victuallers' Association
**LVF** [medicine] left ventricular function
**LVI** *laus Verbo Incarnato* (Latin: praise to the Incarnate Word); low viscosity index
**LVLO** Local Vehicle Licensing Office
**LVN** [USA] Licensed Vocational Nurse
**LVO** Lieutenant of the Royal Victorian Order
**LVS** Licentiate in Veterinary Science
**lvs** leaves
**LVT** landing vehicle, tracked
**LW** light weight; [radio] long wave; low water; [vehicle registration] northwest London
**Lw** [chemical element] lawrencium (former symbol, replaced by Lr)
**lw** lumens per watt
**l.w.** [sports] left wing
**LWA** London Weighting Allowance; London Welsh Association
**LW&S** lights wipe and spray (in car advertisement)
**l.w.b.** long wheelbase (in car advertisement)
**LWEST** low water equinoctial spring tide
**LWF** Lutheran World Federation
**LWL** length at waterline (of boat or ship); [shipping] load waterline
**LWM** low water mark
**LWONT** low water ordinary neap tides
**LWOST** low water ordinary spring tides
**LWR** [nuclear technology] light-water reactor
**LWRA** London Waste Regulation Authority
**LWT** London Weekend Television
**LWV** [USA] League of Women Voters
**LX** electricians (phonetic spelling of 'elecs'); electrics (phonetic spelling of 'elecs'); [civil aircraft marking] Luxembourg; [vehicle registration] northwest London
**lx** lux (unit of light)
**Lxmbrg** Luxembourg
**LXX** [Bible] Septuagint (Roman numeral for 70)
**LY** [civil aircraft marking] Lithuania; [fishing port] Londonderry; [vehicle registration] northwest London
**Ly.** Lyon
**.ly** Libya (in Internet address)
**l.y.** light year
**Lyn** [astronomy] Lynx
**Lyr** [astronomy] Lyra
**lyr.** lyric; lyrical; lyrics
**LZ** [vehicle registration] Armagh; [civil aircraft marking] Bulgaria

# M

**M** [printing] em; [currency] (ma)loti (used in Lesotho); [aeronautics] Mach (followed by number); *Magister* (Latin: Master); magistrate; Majesty; [international vehicle registration] Malta; [UK postcode] Manchester; Manitoba; March; [currency] mark; Marquess; Marquis; martyr; [grammar] masculine;

Master; [cinema] mature audience (film classification in Australia); May; medal; medieval; medium (size); mega- (indicates one million, as in **MHz** = megahertz); [computing] mega- (indicates $2^{20}$, as in **MB** = megabyte); Member; [chemistry] mesomeric effect; [astronomy] Messier Catalogue; [chemistry] metal (in chemical formula); Methodist; [music] metronome; metropolitan; *mezzo* (Italian: half); Middle; [fishing port] Milford; militia; million; minesweeper; minim (unit of liquid measure); Monday; [economics] monetary aggregate (in measures of money supply); *Monsieur* (French: Mr, Sir); *Monte* (Italian: Mount); mother; motorway (as in **M6**); mountain; mud (on chart); [Roman numeral] thousand

***M*** [astronomy] absolute magnitude; [physics] magnetic quantum number; [physics] magnetization; mass; molar mass; [physics] moment (of a force); [electrical engineering] mutual inductance

**m** [printing] em; [music] me (in tonic sol-fa); metre; milli- (indicates one-thousandth, as in **mm** = millimetre); million; [meteorology] mist; [Roman numeral] thousand

***m*** [astronomy] apparent magnitude; [physics] magnetic moment; [physics] magnetic quantum number; [chemistry] mass; [chemistry] molality

**m.** [cricket] maiden (over); male; *manipulus* (Latin: handful); mare; [currency] mark; married; [grammar] masculine; master; mate; measure; medical; medicine; medium; memorandum; meridian; *meridies* (Latin: noon); meridional; midday; middle; mile; [currency] mill (thousandth of dollar); *mille* (French: thousand); minim (unit of liquid measure); minor; minute; [medicine] *misce* (Latin: mix); mixture; moderate; *mois* (French: month); molar (tooth); month; moon; morning; *mort(e)* (French: dead); *morto* (Italian: dead); mountain

**3M** Minnesota Mining and Manufacturing Company

**9M** [civil aircraft marking] Malaysia

**MA** [vehicle registration] Chester; Magistrates' Association; [USA] Manpower Administration; [USA] Maritime Administration; [US postcode] Massachusetts; Master of Arts; Mathematical Association; medieval archaeology; [psychology] mental age; Middle Ages; Military Academy; military assistant; military attaché; *Missionarius Apostolicus* (Latin: Apostolic Missionary); mobility allowance; [international vehicle registration] Morocco; Mountaineering Association; Museums Association

***Ma*** [aeronautics] Mach number

**Ma.** *Mater* (Latin: Mother)

**mA** milliampere

**m/a** [book-keeping] my account

**.ma** Morocco (in Internet address)

**m.a.** manufacturing assembly; map analysis; menstrual age

**MAA** Manufacturers' Agents Association of Great Britain; Master-at-Arms; Mathematical Association of America; Member of the Architectural Association; Motor Agents' Association; [USA] Mutual Aid Association; [USA] Mutual Assurance Association

**MAAAS** Member of the American Academy of Arts and Sciences

**MAAF** Mediterranean Allied Air Forces

**ma'am** madam

**MAAT** Member of the Association of Accounting Technicians

**MAB** monoclonal antibody

**MABP** [medicine] mean arterial blood pressure

**MABS** [USA] marine air base squadron

**MAC** maximum allowable concentration; [computing] media access control; [television] multiplexed analogue component(s); [USA] Municipal Assistance Corporation

**MAc** Master of Accountancy

**Mac.** Macao; [Bible] Maccabees (books of Apocrypha)

**mac** [short form] mackintosh

**MACA** Mental After Care Association

**MACC** military aid to the civilian community

**Macc.** [Bible] Maccabees (books of Apocrypha)

**MACE** Member of the Association of Conference Executives; Member of the Australian College of Education

**Maced.** Macedonia; Macedonian

**mach.** machine; machinery; machinist
**MACHO** [astronomy] massive astrophysical compact halo object
**MACM** Member of the Association of Computing Machines
**macroecon.** macroeconomics
**MACS** Member of the American Chemical Society
**MAD** magnetic anomaly detection; maintenance, assembly and disassembly; [psychology] major affective disorder; [commerce] mean absolute deviation; [military] mutual assured destruction
**Mad.** Madeira
**Madag.** Madagascar
**MADD** Mothers Against Drunk Driving
**MADO** Member of the Association of Dispensing Opticians
**Madr.** Madras; Madrid
**MAE** Master of Aeronautical Engineering; Master of Art Education; Master of Arts in Education
**m.a.e.** mean absolute error
**MA(Econ)** Master of Arts in Economics
**MA(Ed)** Master of Arts in Education
**MAEE** Marine Aircraft Experimental Establishment
**maesto.** [music] *maestoso* (Italian: majestic)
**MAFA** Manchester Academy of Fine Arts
**MAFF** Ministry of Agriculture, Fisheries and Food
**MAG** Motorcycle Action Group
**MAg** Master of Agriculture
**Mag.** Magnificat (canticle); Magyar
**mag** [short form] magazine
**mag.** magazine; magnesium; magnet; magnetic; magnetism; magneto; magnitude; magnum
**MAgEc** Master of Agricultural Economics
**magg.** *maggio* (Italian: May); [music] *maggiore* (Italian: major) (key or scale)
**maglev** magnetic levitation (for high-speed train)
**magn.** magnetic; magnetism
**magnif.** magnificent (in property advertisement)
**MAGPI** [medicine] meatal advancement and glanuloplasty (surgical operation)
**MAgr** Master of Agriculture
**MAgrSc** Master of Agricultural Science
**mah.** mahogany
**mahog.** mahogany
**MAI** Master of Engineering (from Latin *Magister in Arte Ingeniaria*); [forestry] mean annual increment; Member of the Anthropological Institute
**MAIAA** Member of the American Institute of Aeronautics and Astronautics
**MAIB** Marine Accidents Investigation Branch
**MAICE** Master of the American Institute of Consulting Engineers
**MAIChE** Master of the American Institute of Chemical Engineers
**maint.** maintenance
**mais.** maisonette (in property advertisement)
**MAISE** Member of the Association of Iron and Steel Engineers
**Maj.** [military] Major
**maj.** major; majority
**Maj-Gen** Major-General
**MAL** [international vehicle registration] Malaysia
**Mal** *Maréchal* (French: Field Marshal)
**Mal.** [Bible] Malachi; Malay; Malaya; Malayan; Malaysia; Malaysian; Malta; Maltese
**MALD** Master of Arts in Law and Diplomacy
**mall.** malleable
**MAM** [computing] multiple allocation memory
**MAMBO** Mediterranean Association for Marine Biology and Oceanography
**MAMEME** Member of the Association of Mining Electrical and Mechanical Engineers
**MAN** [computing] metropolitan area network
**Man.** Manchester; Manila; Manitoba
**man.** management; manager; managing; manual; manually; manufacture; manufacturer; manufacturing
**MAnaes** Master of Anaesthesiology
**Manch.** Manchester; Manchuria
**mand.** [law] mandamus (High Court order); mandatory; mandolin
**M&A** [finance] mergers and acquisitions
**M&B** May and Baker (pharmaceutical company); mild and bitter (beer); Mills and Boon (publishing company)
**M&E** music and effects
**M&G** Mercantile and General (insurance company)

**Man. Dir.** managing director
**m&r** maintenance and repairs
**M&S** Marks and Spencer plc (chain store)
**m&s** maintenance and supply
**Man. Ed.** managing editor
**MANF** May, August, November, February (end of financial quarters)
**manf.** manufacture; manufactured; manufacturer
**mang. B** manganese bronze
**Manit.** Manitoba
**man. op.** manually operated
**man. pr.** [medicine] *mane primo* (Latin: first thing in the morning)
**Mans.** Mansion(s)
**manuf.** manufacture; manufactured; manufacturer; manufacturing
**manufac.** manufacture; manufactured; manufacturer; manufacturing
**Manweb** Merseyside and North Wales Electricity Board
**MAO** Master of Arts in Obstetrics; [biochemistry] monoamine oxidase
**MAOI** [pharmacology] monoamine oxidase inhibitor (antidepressant)
**MAOT** Member of the Association of Occupational Therapists
**MAOU** Member of the American Ornithologists' Union
**MAP** major air pollutant; [computing] manufacturing automation protocol; maximum average price; [medicine] mean arterial (blood) pressure; medical aid post; Member of the Association of Project Managers; Ministry of Aircraft Production; [USA] modified American plan (for payment of hotel bills)
**MAPI** [computing] messaging application program interface
**MAppArts** Master of Applied Arts
**MAppSc** Master of Applied Science
**MAPsS** Member of the Australian Psychological Society
**MAR** [taxation] marginal age relief; Master of Arts in Religion; [computing] memory address register
**Mar.** March
**mar.** *mardi* (French: Tuesday); [music] marimba; marine; maritime; marriage; married; *martedì* (Italian: Tuesday); *martes* (Spanish: Tuesday); *marzo* (Italian: March); *marzo* (Spanish: March)
**MARAC** Member of the Australasian Register of Agricultural Consultants
**MARC** [bibliography] machine-readable cataloguing
**marc.** [music] *marcato* (Italian: marked, emphasizing each note)
**MArch** Master of Architecture
**March.** Marchioness
**MArchE** Master of Architectural Engineering
**marg** [short form] margarine
**marg.** margin; marginal
**marit.** maritime
**mar. lic.** marriage licence
**MARMAP** [USA] Marine Resources Monitoring Assessment and Prediction
**Marq.** Marquess; Marquis
**MARS** meteorological automatic reporting station (or system)
**mart** market
**mart.** martyr
**MARV** [military] manœuvrable re-entry vehicle
**MAS** Malaysian Airline System; Master of Agricultural Science; Master of Applied Science; Medical Advisory Service; Military Agency for Standardization
**mas.** [grammar] masculine
**MASC** Member of the Australian Society of Calligraphers
**MASc** Master of Applied Science
**masc.** [grammar] masculine
**MASCE** Member of the American Society of Civil Engineers
**mascon** [astronomy] mass concentration
**maser** microwave amplification by stimulated emission of radiation
**MASH** [USA] mobile army surgical hospital
**MASI** Member of the Architects' and Surveyors' Institute
**MASME** Member of the American Society of Mechanical Engineers
**MA(SS)** Master of Arts in Social Sciences
**Mass.** Massachusetts
**MASTA** Medical Advisory Service for Travellers Abroad
**MAT** [insurance] marine, aviation and transport; Master of Arts in Teaching
**mat.** maternity; matinée; matins; [printing] matrix; mature; [finance] maturity
**MATA** multiple answering teaching aid

**MATh** Master of Arts in Theology
**math** [US and Canadian short form] mathematics
**math.** mathematical; mathematically; mathematician; mathematics
**maths** [short form] mathematics
**MATIF** *marché à terme des instruments financiers* (French: financial futures market)
**matr.** matrimonial; *matrimonium* (Latin: marriage)
**matric** [short form] matriculation (former school examination)
**MATS** [US air force] Military Air Transport Service
**MATSA** Managerial Administrative Technical Staff Association
**Matt.** [Bible] Matthew
**MATTS** [military] multiple airborne target trajectory system
**MATV** master antenna television
**MAU** [computing] multi-station access unit
**Maur.** Mauritian; Mauritius
**Mau Rs** [currency] Mauritian rupee
**MAusIMM** Member of the Australasian Institute of Mining and Metallurgy
**MAW** [USA] marine air wing; [military] medium assault weapon
**MAX** maximum
**max.** maxim; maximum
**MAYC** Methodist Association of Youth Clubs
**MB** Bachelor of Medicine (from Latin *Medicinae Baccalaureus*); Bachelor of Music (from Latin *Musicae Baccalaureus*); [vehicle registration] Chester; Manitoba; maritime board; marketing board; mark of the Beast; maternity benefit; [Canada] Medal of Bravery; medical board; [computing] megabit; [computing] megabyte; metropolitan borough; millibar (unit of atmospheric pressure); motor barge; motorboat; municipal borough
**mb** millibar (unit of atmospheric pressure)
**m.b.** magnetic bearing; main battery; medium bomber; [medicine] *misce bene* (Latin: mix well); motor barge; motorboat
**MBA** Master of Business Administration
**Mba** Mombasa
**MBAC** Member of the British Association of Chemists
**MBAcC** Member of the British Acupuncture Council
**mbar** millibar (unit of atmospheric pressure)
**MBASW** Member of the British Association of Social Workers
**MBC** metropolitan borough council; mountain bike club; municipal borough council
**m.b.c.** [medicine] maximum breathing capacity
**MBCO** Member of the British College of Optometrists (or Ophthalmic Opticians)
**MBCPE** Member of the British College of Physical Education
**MBCS** Member of the British Computer Society
**MBD** [medicine] minimal brain dysfunction
**MBdgSc** Master of Building Science
**MBE** Member of the Order of the British Empire; [electronics] molecular-beam epitaxy
**MBF** Musicians Benevolent Fund
**MBG** microemulsion-based gel
**MBH** [astronomy] massive black hole
**mbH** [commerce] *mit beschränkter Haftung* (German: with limited liability) (of company)
**MBHI** Member of the British Horological Institute
**MBI** [finance] management buy-in
**MBIAT** Member of the British Institute of Architectural Technologists
**MBIFD** Member of the British Institute of Funeral Directors
**MBIM** Member of the British Institute of Management
**MBK** [military] missing, believed killed
**MBKSTS** Member of the British Kinematograph, Sound and Television Society
**MBL** [medicine] menstrual blood loss
**MBM** Master of Business Management
**MBNOA** Member of the British Naturopathic and Osteopathic Association
**MBNQA** [commerce] Malcolm Baldridge National Quality Award
**MBO** [finance] management buyout; [commerce] management by objectives
**MBOU** Member of the British Ornithologists' Union
**MBP** [medicine] mean blood pressure
**MBPICS** Member of the British

Production and Inventory Control Society
**MBPsS** Member of the British Psychological Society
**MBR** [astronomy] microwave background radiation
**mbr** member
**MBRF** [military] mutual and balanced force reduction
**MBS** Manchester Business School
**MBSc** Master of Business Science
**MBT** [military] main battle tank; [medicine] mean body temperature
**MBuild** Master of Building
**MBWA** [commerce] management by wandering around
**Mbyte** [computing] megabyte
**MC** machinery certificate; magistrates' court; [navigation] magnetic course; marginal cost; [USA] Marine Corps; [USA] Maritime Commission; marriage certificate; Master of Ceremonies; Master of Surgery (from Latin *Magister Chirurgiae*); medical certificate; [USA] Medical Corps; [astrology] *Medium Caeli* (Latin: Midheaven); [USA] Member of Congress; Member of Council; mess committee; Methodist Church; military college; Military Cross; Missionaries of Charity; [astronomy] molecular cloud; [chemistry] molecular cluster; [international vehicle registration] Monaco; [politics] Monday Club; Monte Carlo; Morse code; motor contact; [vehicle registration] northeast London
**M/C** Manchester; [finance] marginal credit
**Mc** megacycle
**m/c** machine; motorcycle
**.mc** Monaco (in Internet address)
**m.c.** *mois courant* (French: current month); motorcycle
**MCA** Management Consultants' Association; Manufacturing Chemists' Association; Maritime and Coastguard Agency; Master of Commerce and Administration; Matrimonial Causes Act; [trademark, computing] micro channel architecture; monetary compensatory amount(s); Motor Cycle Association; [electronics] multichannel analyser; multicriteria analysis; [electronics] multiple channel analyser; multiple classification analysis
**MCAB** [USA] Marine Corps air base
**MCAM** Member of the CAM Foundation
**MC&G** mapping, charting and geodesy
**MCANW** Medical Campaign Against Nuclear Weapons
**MCAV** [computing] modified constant angular velocity
**MCB** [USA] Marine Corps Base; Master of Clinical Biochemistry; [computing] memory control block; Metric Conversion Board; miniature circuit breaker; [military] multiple-cratering bomblets
**MCBSI** Member of the Chartered Building Societies Institute
**MCC** Manchester Computer Centre; Marylebone Cricket Club; Maxwell Communications Corporation; Melbourne Cricket Club; member of the county council; metropolitan county council; [navigation] mid-course correction; Motor Caravanners' Club
**MCCA** Minor Counties Cricket Association
**MCCC** Middlesex County Cricket Club
**MCCD RCS** Member in Clinical Community Dentistry of the Royal College of Surgeons (of England)
**MCCU** [medicine] mobile coronary care unit
**MCD** Master of Civic Design; [medicine] mean cell diameter; [medicine] mean corpuscular diameter; Movement for Christian Democracy
**MCDS** management control data system
**MCE** Master of Chemical Engineering; Master of Civil Engineering
**MCFP** [Canada] Member of the College of Family Physicians
**MCG** Melbourne Cricket Ground
**MCGA** [computing] multicolour graphics array
**MCGB** Master Chef of Great Britain
**McGU** McGill University (Canada)
**MCH** [medicine] mean cell haemoglobin; [medicine] mean corpuscular haemoglobin; [biochemistry] melanin-concentrating hormone
**MCh** Master of Surgery (from Latin *Magister Chirurgiae*)
**Mch.** Manchester
**MCHC** [medicine] mean cell haemoglobin concentration; [medicine] mean corpuscular haemoglobin concentration

**MChD** Master of Dental Surgery (from Latin *Magister Chirurgiae Dentalis*)
**MChE** Master of Chemical Engineering
**MChemA** Master in Chemical Analysis
**MChemEng** Master of Chemical Engineering
**MChir** Master of Surgery (from Latin *Magister Chirurgiae*)
**MChOrth** Master of Orthopaedic Surgery (from Latin *Magister Chirurgiae Orthopaedicae*)
**MChS** Member of the Society of Chiropodists
**mcht** merchant
**mchy** machinery
**mCi** millicurie (unit of radioactivity)
**m.c.i.** malleable cast iron
**MCIBSE** Member of the Chartered Institution of Building Services Engineers
**MCIM** Member of the Chartered Institute of Marketing
**MCIOB** Member of the Chartered Institute of Building
**MCIS** Member of the Institute of Chartered Secretaries and Administrators (formerly Member of the Chartered Institute of Secretaries)
**MCIT** Member of the Chartered Institute of Transport
**MCL** Master of Civil Law; maximum contamination levels
**MClinPsychol** Master of Clinical Psychology
**MClSc** Master of Clinical Science
**MCLV** [computing] modified constant linear velocity
**MCM** [mathematics] Monte Carlo method; [computing] multichip module; multistage conventional munitions
**MCMES** Member of the Civil and Mechanical Engineers' Society
**MCO** Managed Care Organization
**Mco** Morocco
**mcol.** musicological; musicologist; musicology
**MCollH** Member of the College of Handicrafts
**MCom** Master of Commerce
**MCommH** Master of Community Health
**MConsE** Member of the Association of Consulting Engineers
**MCOphth** Member of the College of Ophthalmologists
**MCP** male chauvinist pig; [USA] Master of City Planning; Member of Colonial Parliament; Member of the College of Preceptors
**MCPO** Master Chief Petty Officer
**MCPP** Member of the College of Pharmacy Practice
**MCPS** Mechanical Copyright Protection Society; Member of the College of Physicians and Surgeons
**m.c.q.** multiple-choice question
**MCR** mass communications research; [engineering] maximum continuous rating; [medicine] metabolic clearance rate; middle common room (in university or college); mobile control room
**MCS** Madras Civil Service; Malayan Civil Service; Marine Conservation Society; Master of Commercial Science; Military College of Science; monitoring and control system; [electronics] multichannel scaler
**Mc/s** megacycles per second
**MCSD** [computing] Microsoft Certified Solutions Developer
**MCSE** Microsoft Certified Systems Engineer
**MCSP** Member of the Chartered Society of Physiotherapy
**MCST** Member of the College of Speech Therapists
**MCT** mainstream corporation tax; Member of the Association of Corporate Treasurers
**MCU** main control unit; [photography] medium close-up
**MCV** [medicine] mean cell volume; [medicine] mean corpuscular volume
**MCW** [telecommunications] modulated continuous wave
**MD** Doctor of Medicine (from Latin *Medicinae Doctor*); [music] *main droite* (French: right hand); malicious damage; managing director; [music] *mano destra* (Italian: right hand); map distance; market day; [US postcode] Maryland; medical department; [banking] memorandum of deposit; mentally deficient; mess deck; Middle Dutch; military district; minidisc (audio recording); [international vehicle registration] Moldova; molecular dynamics; Monroe Doctrine; [medicine] muscular dystrophy; musical

director; [vehicle registration] northeast London
**Md** Maryland; [chemical element] mendelevium
**M/d** [commerce] months after date
**.md** Moldova (in Internet address)
**MDA** [pharmacology] methylenedioxyamphetamine (= ice, hallucinogenic drug); minimum detectable activity; minimum detectable amount; [computing] monochrome display adapter; [finance] multiple discriminant analysis; Muscular Dystrophy Association
**MDAM** [computing] multidimensional access memory
**MD&A** [commerce] management discussion and analysis
**MDAP** [USA] Mutual Defense Assistance Program
**M-day** [USA] mobilization day
**MDB** *Movimento Democrático Brasileiro* (Portuguese: Brazilian Democratic Movement)
**MdB** *Mitglied des Bundestages* (German: Member of the Bundestag)
**MDC** metropolitan district council; minimum detectable concentration; modification and design control; more developed country
**MDD** minimum detectable dose
**Mddx** Middlesex
**MDentSc** Master of Dental Science
**MDes** Master of Design
**MDF** Manic Depression Fellowship; medium-density fibreboard
**MDG** Medical Director-General
**MDHB** Mersey Docks and Harbour Board
**m. dict.** [medicine] *more dicto* (Latin: in the manner directed) (in prescriptions)
**MDip** Master of Diplomacy
**mdise** merchandise
**MDiv** Master of Divinity
**MDL** minimum detectable level
**mdl** model
**Mdlle** *Mademoiselle* (French: Miss)
**Mdm** Madam
**MDMA** [pharmacology] methylenedioxymethamphetamine (= ecstasy, hallucinogenic drug)
**Mdme** *Madame* (French: Mrs)
**mdn** median
**MDNS** [computing] managed data network service
**mdnt** midnight
**MDP** Mongolian Democratic Party
**MDQ** minimum detectable quantity
**MDR** [computing] memory data register; minimum daily requirement
**MDRAM** [computing] multibank dynamic random-access memory
**MDS** main dressing station; Master of Dental Surgery; memory-adjusted driver's seat (in car advertisement); microprocessor development system
**MDSc** Master of Dental Science
**mdse** merchandise
**MD/st** memory-adjusted driver's seat (in car advertisement)
**MDT** [computing] mean downtime; [USA] Mountain Daylight Time
**MDU** Medical Defence Union
**MDu** Middle Dutch
**MDV** Doctor of Veterinary Medicine
**MDW** Military Defence Works
**Mdx** Middlesex
**ME** [US postcode] Maine; managing editor; marine engineer; marine engineering; [USA] marriage encounter; Master of Education; Master of Engineering; mechanical engineer; mechanical engineering; [USA] Medical Examiner; [UK postcode] Medway; [medicine] metabolizable energy; Methodist Episcopal; Middle East; Middle Eastern; Middle English; military engineer; milled edge; mining engineer; mining engineering; [fishing port] Montrose; [physics] Mössbauer effect; Most Excellent; [medicine] myalgic encephalomyelitis; [vehicle registration] northeast London
**Me** Maine; *Maître* (French: Master) (title of lawyer); Messerschmitt (German aircraft); [chemistry] methyl (used in formulae)
**m.e.** [bookbinding] marbled edges; maximum effort; mobility equipment; [bookbinding] mottled edges
**MEA** Member of the European Assembly; Middle East Airlines
**MEAF** Middle East Air Force
**meas.** measurable; measure; measurement
**MEB** Midlands Electricity Board
**MEC** [finance] marginal efficiency of capital; Master of Engineering Chemistry; Member of the Executive Council;

Methodist Episcopal Church; Middle East Command; minimum effective concentration
**MEc** Master of Economics
**MECAS** Middle East Centre for Arab Studies
**mech.** mechanic; mechanical; mechanically; mechanics; mechanism; mechanize; mechanized
**MechE** mechanical engineer
**ME(Chem)** Master of Chemical Engineering
**MECI** Member of the Institute of Employment Consultants
**MECO** [astronautics] main engine cut off
**MEcon** Master of Economics
**MED** maximum equivalent dose; [pharmacology] minimum effective dose; [chemistry] molecular electronic device; [New Zealand] Municipal Electricity Department
**MEd** Master of Education
**Med** [short form] Mediterranean
**Med.** Mediterranean
**med.** medal; medallist; median; medical; medicine; medieval; medium
**Medit.** Mediterranean
**med. jur.** medical jurisprudence
**MEDLARS** [USA] Medical Literature Analysis and Retrieval System
**Med. Lat.** Medieval Latin
**MedRC** Medical Reserve Corps
**MedScD** Doctor of Medical Science
**med. tech.** medical technician; medical technology
**MEE** Master of Electrical Engineering
**ME(Elec)** Master of Electrical Engineering
**MEF** Mediterranean Expeditionary Force; Middle East Force
**meg** [short form, computing] megabyte
**MEIC** Member of the Engineering Institute of Canada
**Mej.** *Mejuffrouw* (Dutch: Miss)
**MEK** methyl ethyl ketone (solvent)
**Melan.** Melanesia; Melanesian
**Melb.** Melbourne
**MELF** Middle East Land Forces
**Mem.** Member
**mem.** member; *memento* (Latin: remember); memoir(s); memorandum; memorial; memory
**ME(Mech)** Master of Mechanical Engineering
**memo** [short form] memorandum
**MEN** [medicine] multiple endocrine neoplasia
**Men** [astronomy] Mensa
**MENA** Middle East News Agency
**Mencap** Royal Society for Mentally Handicapped Children and Adults
**MEng** Master of Engineering
**MENS** [medicine] multiple endocrine neoplasia syndromes
**menst.** menstrual; menstruation
**mensur.** mensuration
**ment.** mental; mention; mentioned
**mentd** mentioned
**MEO** Marine Engineering Officer
**MEP** *Mahajana Eksath Peramuna* (Sinhalese: People's United Front) (in Sri Lanka); Master of Engineering Physics; mean effective pressure; Member of the European Parliament
**MEPA** Master of Engineering and Public Administration
**Mer.** Merionethshire
**mer.** mercantile; merchandise; *mercoledì* (Italian: Wednesday); *mercredi* (French: Wednesday); mercury; meridian; meridional
**Merc** [short form] Mercedes (car)
**merc.** mercantile; mercury
**MERCOSUR** *Mercado Común del Sur* (Spanish: Southern (American) Common Market)
**MERLIN** [astronomy] Multi-Element Radio-linked Interferometer Network
**MERU** Maharishi European Research University
**MèsA** *Maître ès arts* (French: Master of Arts)
**MESc** Master of Engineering Science
**MESFET** [electronics] metal-semiconductor field-effect transistor
**Messrs** *Messieurs* (French: gentlemen, sirs) (plural of Mr in English)
**Met** [short form] Metropolitan Opera House (New York); [short form] Metropolitan Police
**Met.** Meteorological (as in **Met. Office**)
**met.** metallurgical; metallurgist; metallurgy; metaphor; metaphoric(al); metaphysical; metaphysics; meteorological; meteorology; metronome; metropolitan
**metall.** metallurgical; metallurgist; metallurgy

**metaph.** metaphor; metaphoric(al); metaphysical; metaphysics
**METAR** Meteorological Airfield Report
**met. bor.** metropolitan borough
**MetE** metallurgical engineer
**meteor.** meteorological; meteorology
**meteorol.** meteorological; meteorology
**Meth.** Methodist
**meths** [short form] methylated spirits
**M-et-L** Maine-et-Loire (French department)
**M-et-M** Meurthe-et-Moselle (French department)
**m. et n.** [medicine] *mane et nocte* (Latin: morning and night) (in prescriptions)
**MetR** Metropolitan Railway (London)
**metro** [short form] metropolitan railway
**metrol.** metrological; metrology
**metrop.** metropolis; metropolitan
**metropol.** metropolis; metropolitan
**metsat** meteorological satellite
**MeV** megaelectronvolt
**Mev.** *Mevrouw* (Dutch: Mrs)
**MEW** [finance] measure of economic welfare; [military] microwave early warning (system)
**MEX** [international vehicle registration] Mexico
**Mex.** Mexican; Mexico
**MEXE** Military Engineering Experimental Establishment
**Mex. Sp.** Mexican Spanish
**MEZ** *Mitteleuropäische Zeit* (German: Central European Time)
**mez.** [music] *mezza* (Italian: half, medium); [music] *mezzo* (Italian: half, medium)
**mezzo.** mezzotint
**MF** machine finish (on paper); machine finished (paper); magnetic field; Master of Forestry; [radio] medium frequency; melamine-formaldehyde (as in **MF resin**); Middle French; mill finish; [US slang] motherfucker; [telecommunications] multifrequency; [vehicle registration] northeast London
**M/F** male or female
**mF** millifarad
***mf*** [music] *mezzo forte* (Italian: moderately loudly)
**MFA** Master of Fine Arts; Multi-Fibre Arrangement
**MFAMus** Master of Fine Arts in Music
**MFARCS** Member of the Faculty of Anaesthetists of the Royal College of Surgeons (of England)
**MFB** Metropolitan Fire Brigade
**MFC** Mastership in Food Control; motor-fuel consumption
**MFCM** Member of the Faculty of Community Medicine
**MFD** minimum fatal dose
**mfd** manufactured
**mfg** manufacturing
**MFH** Master of Foxhounds; mobile field hospital
**MFHom** Member of the Faculty of Homoeopathy
**MFlem** Middle Flemish
**mflops** [computing] millions of floating-point operations per second (measure of computer power)
**MFM** [computing] modified frequency modulation
**MFN** most favoured nation (in trade agreement)
**MFOM** Member of the Faculty of Occupational Medicine
**MFP** [physics] mean free path
**MFPA** Mouth and Foot Painting Artists
**MFr** Middle French
**mfr** manufacturer
**mfr.** manufacture
**mfre** manufacture
**MFS** Master of Food Science; Master of Foreign Study
**mfst** manifest
**MFT** [computing] master file table
**m. ft** [medicine] *mistura fiat* (Latin: let a mixture be made) (in prescriptions)
**m.f.t.** motor freight tariff
**MFV** motor fleet vehicle; motor fleet vessel
**MG** machine glazed (paper); machine gun; [music] *main gauche* (French: left hand); Major-General; [building] make good; Morris Garages (sports car manufacturer); motor generator; [medicine] myasthenia gravis; [vehicle registration] northeast London
**Mg** [chemical element] magnesium
**mg** milligram
**.mg** Madagascar (in Internet address)
**MGA** Major-General in charge of Administration

**m.g.a.w.d.** make good all works disturbed (in commercial contract)
**MGB** metropolitan green belt; *Ministerstvo Gosudarstvennoi Bezopasnosti* (Russian: Ministry of State Security) (former Soviet secret police); motor gunboat
**MGC** Machine Gun Corps; Marriage Guidance Council (former name of Relate)
**mgd** million gallons per day
**MGDS RCS** Member in General Dental Surgery of the Royal College of Surgeons (of England)
**mge** message
**MGGS** Major-General, General Staff
**MGI** Member of the Institute of Certificated Grocers
**MGk** Medieval Greek; Modern Greek
**M Glam.** Mid Glamorgan
**MGM** Metro-Goldwyn-Mayer (film studio); mobile guided missile
**mgmt** management
**MGN** Mirror Group Newspapers
**MGO** Master General of the Ordnance; Master of Gynaecology and Obstetrics
**MGP** manufactured-gas plant
**MGR** [nuclear technology] modular gas-cooled reactor
**MGr** Medieval Greek; Modern Greek
**Mgr** Manager; *Monseigneur* (French: my lord); [Roman Catholic Church] Monsignor
**mgr** manager
**Mgrs** Managers; *Monseigneurs* (French: my lords); [Roman Catholic Church] Monsignors
**mgs** metre-gram-second
**mgt** management
**MH** [navigation] magnetic heading; [nautical] main hatch; marital history; Master of Horse; Master of Horticulture; Master of Hounds; Master of Hygiene; [USA] Medal of Honor; medical history; mental health; [fishing port] Middlesbrough; military hospital; Ministry of Health; [vehicle registration] northeast London
**mH** millihenry (unit of electric inductance)
**.mh** Marshall Islands (in Internet address)
**MHA** [USA] Master of Hospital Administration; [Australia, Canada] Member of the House of Assembly; [USA] Mental Health Administration; Methodist Homes for the Aged
**MHC** [immunology] major histocompatibility complex
**MHCIMA** Member of the Hotel Catering and Institutional Management Association
**MHD** [physics] magnetohydrodynamics
**MHE** Master of Home Economics
**MHeb** Middle Hebrew
**MHF** massive hydraulic fracture (or fracturing); [radio] medium high frequency
**MHG** Middle High German
**MHK** Member of the House of Keys (in Isle of Man)
**MHLG** Ministry of Housing and Local Government
**M Hon.** Most Honourable
**MHortSc** Master of Horticultural Science
**MHR** [USA, Australia] Member of the House of Representatives
**MHRA** Modern Humanities Research Association
**MHRF** Mental Health Research Fund
**MHS** medical history sheet; Member of the Historical Society; [computing] message-handling service (or system)
**MHTGR** [nuclear technology] modular high-temperature gas-cooled reactor
**MHum** Master of Humanities
**MHW** mean high water (level of tide)
**MHWN** mean high water neaps (level of tide)
**MHWS** mean high water springs (level of tide)
**MHy** Master of Hygiene
**MHz** megahertz
**MI** malleable iron; [civil aircraft marking] Marshall Islands; medical inspection; [US postcode] Michigan; Military Intelligence (as in **MI5**); Ministry of Information; [biology] mitotic index; moment of inertia; mounted infantry; [medicine] myocardial infarction
**Mi.** Minor; Mississippi
**mi.** mile; [currency] mill (thousandth of dollar); minute
**MI5** Military Intelligence, section five (popular name for UK counterintelligence agency)
**MI6** Military Intelligence, section six (popular name for UK intelligence and espionage agency)
**MIA** Master of International Affairs; [mili-

tary] missing in action; [Australia] Murrumbidgee Irrigation Area
**MIAA&S** Member of the Incorporated Association of Architects and Surveyors
**MIAgrE** Member of the Institution of Agricultural Engineers
**MIAM** Member of the Institute of Administrative Management
**MIAP** Member of the Institution of Analysts and Programmers
**MIAS** Member of the Institute of Accounting Staff
**MIB** [computing] management information base
**MIBE** Member of the Institution of British Engineers
**MIBF** Member of the Institute of British Foundrymen
**MIBiol** Member of the Institute of Biology
**MIBK** methyl isobutyl ketone (solvent)
**MIBritE** Member of the Institution of British Engineers
**MIBScot** Member of the Institute of Bankers in Scotland
**Mic** [astronomy] Microscopium
**Mic.** [Bible] Micah
**MICE** Member of the Institution of Civil Engineers
**MICEI** Member of the Institution of Civil Engineers of Ireland
**MICFor** Member of the Institute of Chartered Foresters
**Mich.** Michaelmas; Michigan
**MIChemE** Member of the Institution of Chemical Engineers
**MICorrST** Member of the Institution of Corrosion Science and Technology
**MICR** [computing] magnetic ink character recognition
**Micro** Micronesia; Micronesian; Multinational Initiative for the Use of Computers in Research Organizations
**micro.** microscope; microscopic; microscopist; microscopy
**microbiol.** microbiology
**micros.** microscope; microscopic; microscopist; microscopy
**MICS** Member of the Institute of Chartered Shipbrokers
**MICU** [medicine] mobile intensive care unit
**MICV** [military] mechanized infantry combat vehicle
**MID** minimum infective dose
**Mid.** Midlands; Midshipman
**mid.** middle; midnight
**MIDAS** [computing] measurement information and data analysis system; missile defence alarm system
**Middx** Middlesex
**MIDELEC** Midlands Electricity Board
**Midi** musical instrument digital interface
**Midl.** Midlands; Midlothian
**Mid. Lat.** Middle Latin
**MIDPM** Member of the Institute of Data Processing Management
**midw.** midwest; midwestern
**MIE(Aust)** Member of the Institution of Engineers, Australia
**MIED** Member of the Institution of Engineering Designers
**MIEE** Member of the Institution of Electrical Engineers
**MIEEE** [USA] Member of the Institute of Electrical and Electronics Engineers
**MIEI** Member of the Institution of Engineering Inspection
**MIE(Ind)** Member of the Institution of Engineers, India
**miér.** *miércoles* (Spanish: Wednesday)
**MIES** Member of the Institution of Engineers and Shipbuilders, Scotland
**MIEx** Member of the Institute of Export
**MIExpE** Member of the Institute of Explosives Engineers
**MIF** [computing] management information format; [immunology] migration inhibition factor; milk in first (in pouring tea); Miners' International Federation
**MIFA** Member of the Institute of Field Archaeologists
**MIFF** Member of the Institute of Freight Forwarders
**MIFireE** Member of the Institute of Fire Engineers
**MIG** metal-inert gas (as in **MIG welding**); mortgage indemnity guarantee
**MiG** Mikoyan and Gurevich (designers of Soviet fighter aircraft)
**MIGA** Multilateral Investment Guarantee Agency (affiliate of World Bank)
**MIGasE** Member of the Institution of Gas Engineers

**MIGeol** Member of the Institution of Geologists
**MIH** Master of Industrial Health
**MIHort** Member of the Institute of Horticulture
**MIHT** Member of the Institution of Highways and Transportation
**MIIE** Member of the Institution of Industrial Engineers
**MIIM** Member of the Institution of Industrial Managers
**MIInfSc** Member of the Institute of Information Sciences
**MIISec** Member of the International Institute of Security
**MIL** Member of the Institute of Linguists; [USA] one million
**Mil.** Milan
**mil.** mileage; military; militia
**.mil** US military (in Internet address)
**Mil. Att.** Military Attaché
**MILGA** Member of the Institute of Local Government Administrators
**milit.** military
**mill.** million
**MILocoE** Member of the Institution of Locomotive Engineers
**Milw.** Milwaukee
**MIM** Member of the Institute of Materials
**MIMarE** Member of the Institute of Marine Engineers
**MIMC** Member of the Institute of Management Consultants
**MIMD** [computing] multiple instruction, multiple data
**MIME** multipurpose Internet mail extension
**MIMechE** Member of the Institution of Mechanical Engineers
**MIMGTechE** Member of the Institution of Mechanical and General Technician Engineers
**MIMI** Member of the Institute of the Motor Industry
**MIMM** Member of the Institution of Mining and Metallurgy
**MIMS** *Monthly Index of Medical Specialities*
**MIN** minimum
**Min.** Minister; Ministry
**min.** mineralogical; mineralogy; minim (unit of liquid measure); minimum; mining; ministerial; minor; minute
**mineral.** mineralogical; mineralogy
**Minn.** Minnesota
**Min. Plen.** Minister Plenipotentiary
**Min. Res.** Minister Resident(iary)
**MINS** [USA] minor(s) in need of supervision
**MInstAM** Member of the Institute of Administrative Management
**MInstBE** Member of the Institution of British Engineers
**MInstD** Member of the Institute of Directors
**MInstE** Member of the Institute of Energy
**MInstEnvSci** Member of the Institute of Environmental Sciences
**MInstMC** Member of the Institute of Measurement and Control
**MInstMM** Member of the Institution of Mining and Metallurgy
**MInstP** Member of the Institute of Physics
**MInstPet** Member of the Institute of Petroleum
**MInstPI** Member of the Institute of Patentees and Inventors
**MInstPkg** Member of the Institute of Packaging
**MInstR** Member of the Institute of Refrigeration
**MInstRA** Member of the Institute of Registered Architects
**MInstTM** Member of the Institute of Travel Managers in Industry and Commerce
**MInstWM** Member of the Institute of Wastes Management
**MINucE** Member of the Institution of Nuclear Engineers
**Mio** [geology] Miocene
**MIOSH** Member of the Institution of Occupational Safety and Health
**MIP** marine insurance policy; maximum investment plan; Member of the Institute of Plumbing; monthly investment plan
**m.i.p.** mean indicated pressure
**MIPA** Member of the Institute of Practitioners in Advertising
**MIPD** Member of the Institute of Personnel and Development
**MIPR** Member of the Institute of Public Relations
**mips** [computing] millions of instructions per second

**MIQ** Member of the Institute of Quarrying
**MIQA** Member of the Institute of Quality Assurance
**MIR** [taxation] mortgage interest relief
**MIr** Middle Irish
**MIRA** Member of the Institute of Registered Architects; Motor Industry Research Association
**MIRAS** [taxation] mortgage interest relief at source
**MIRD** medical internal radiation dose
**MIRT** Member of the Institute of Reprographic Technicians
**MIRTE** Member of the Institute of Road Transport Engineers
**MIRV** [military] multiple independently targeted re-entry vehicle
**MIS** management information system; manufacturing information system; marketing information system; Member of the Institute of Statisticians; meteorological information system; Mining Institute of Scotland
**Mis** [geology] Mississippian
**misc.** miscellaneous; miscellany
**MISD** [computing] multiple instruction, single data
**MISFET** [electronics] metal-insulator-semiconductor field-effect transistor
**Miss.** Mission; Missionary; Mississippi
**mist.** *mistura* (Latin: mixture)
**mistrans.** mistranslation
**MIStructE** Member of the Institution of Structural Engineers
**MIT** Massachusetts Institute of Technology
**Mit.** *Mittwoch* (German: Wednesday)
**MITA** Member of the Industrial Transport Association
**MITD** Member of the Institute of Training and Development
**MITE** Member of the Institution of Electrical and Electronics Technician Engineers
**MITI** [Japan] Ministry of International Trade and Industry
**MITL** magnetically insulated transmission line
**MITT** Member of the Institute of Travel and Tourism
**mitts** minutes of telecommunications traffic
**MIU** Maharishi International University
**MIWEM** Member of the Institution of Water and Environmental Management
**mixt.** mixture
**MJ** [vehicle registration] Luton; megajoule; Ministry of Justice
**MJA** Medical Journalists' Association
**MJD** management job description
**MJI** Member of the Institute of Journalists
**MJQ** Modern Jazz Quartet
**MJS** Member of the Japan Society
**MJSD** March, June, September, December (end of financial quarters)
**MJur** Master of Law (from Latin *Magister Juris*)
**MK** [international vehicle registration] Macedonia; [currency] Malawi kwacha; [UK postcode] Milton Keynes; [vehicle registration] northeast London
**Mk** mark (model of car etc.); Mark; [currency] markka (used in Finland)
**mk** [currency] mark
**.mk** Macedonia (in Internet address)
**mkd** marked
**MKO** Mauna Kea Observatory (Hawaii)
**mks** [currency] marks; metre-kilogram-second (as in **mks units**)
**mksA** metre-kilogram-second-ampere (as in **mksA system**)
**mkt** market
**ML** Licentiate in Medicine (from Latin *Medicinae Licentiatus*); Licentiate in Midwifery; Master of Law(s); Master of Letters; [statistics] maximum likelihood; Medieval Latin; [fishing port] Methil (Scotland); [UK postcode] Motherwell; motor launch; muzzle-loading (gun); [vehicle registration] northeast London
**ml** mail; millilitre
**.ml** Mali (in Internet address)
**m.l.** machine language; mean level; minelayer
**MLA** [accounting] mandatory liquid assets; Master Locksmiths Association; Master of Landscape Architecture; Master of the Liberal Arts; Medical Library Association; Member of the Legislative Assembly; [USA] Modern Language Association
**MLArch** Master of Landscape Architecture
**MLC** Meat and Livestock Commission; [Australia, India] Member of the Legisla-

tive Council; [medicine] mixed lymphocyte culture
**MLCOM** Member of the London College of Osteopathic Medicine
**MLD** Master of Landscape Design; [pharmacology] mean lethal dose; [pharmacology] minimum lethal dose
**mld** mould; moulded
**mldg** moulding
**m.l.e.** maximum loss expectancy
**MLF** *Mouvement de libération des femmes* (French: Women's Liberation Movement); [military] multilateral (nuclear) force
**MLG** Middle Low German
**mlg.** mileage (in car advertisement)
**MLib** Master of Library Science
**MLibSc** Master of Library Science
**MLitt** Master of Letters (from Latin *Magister Litterarum*)
**MLK** Martin Luther King (US civil-rights leader)
**Mlle** *Mademoiselle* (French: Miss)
**MLNS** [medicine] mucocutaneous lymph node syndrome
**MLO** military liaison officer; [microbiology] mycoplasma-like organism(s)
**MLR** [banking] minimum lending rate; [medicine] mixed lymphocyte reaction; *Modern Language Review*; [statistics] multiple linear regression
**MLRS** multiple-launch rocket system
**MLS** main-line station; Master of Library Science; [cinema] medium long shot; Member of the Linnean Society; [aeronautics] microwave landing system; mixed language system; multi-language system
**MLSO** medical laboratory scientific officer
**MLV** [microbiology] murine leukaemia virus
**MLW** mean low water (level of tide)
**MLWN** mean low water neaps (level of tide)
**MLWS** mean low water springs (level of tide)
**MM** [music] Maelzel's metronome (indication of tempo); maintenance manual; Majesties; [medicine] malignant melanoma; Martyrs; [Freemasonry] Master Mason; Master Mechanic; Master of Music; Medal of Merit; mercantile marine; *Messieurs* (French: gentlemen, sirs) (plural of M (Monsieur) in French); Military Medal; [medicine] mucus membrane; music master; [vehicle registration] northeast London
**mm** millimetre
**.mm** Myanmar (in Internet address)
**m.m.** made merchantable; *mutatis mutandis* (Latin: with the necessary changes)
**MMA** Metropolitan Museum of Art; [astronomy] Millimeter Array; Music Masters' Association
**MMath** Master of Mathematics
**MMB** Milk Marketing Board (replaced by Milk Marque)
**MMC** metal-matrix composite; Monopolies and Mergers Commission
**MMD** Movement for Multiparty Democracy (in Zambia)
**MMDA** [USA] money market deposit account
**MMDS** [radio] multipoint microwave distribution system
**MME** Master of Mechanical Engineering; Master of Mining Engineering; Master of Music Education
**Mme** *Madame* (French: Mrs)
**MMechE** Master of Mechanical Engineering
**MMed** Master of Medicine
**MMedSci** Master of Medical Science
**Mmes** *Mesdames* (French: plural of Mme)
**MMet** Master of Metallurgy
**MMetE** Master of Metallurgical Engineering
**mmf** [physics] magnetomotive force
**MMG** [military] medium machine gun
**MMGI** Member of the Mining, Geological and Metallurgical Institute of India
**mmHg** millimetre(s) of mercury (unit of pressure)
**MMI** [computing] man–machine interface; Municipal Mutual Insurance
**MMin** Master of Ministry
**MMM** [Canada] Member of the Order of Military Merit
**mmol** millimole
**MMP** [biochemistry] matrix metalloproteinase (enzyme); Military Mounted Police; mixed member proportional (system of proportional representation)
**m.m.p.** [chemistry] mixture melting point
**MMPI** [psychology] Minnesota Multiphasic Personality Inventory

**MMQ** minimum manufacturing quantity
**MMR** [medicine] mass miniature radiography; [medicine] measles, mumps and rubella (vaccine)
**MMRBM** mobile medium-range ballistic missile
**MMS** Marine Meteorological Services; Member of the Institute of Management Services; Methodist Missionary Society; Moravian Missionary Society; multimission modular spacecraft
**MMSA** Master of Midwifery of the Society of Apothecaries
**MMSc** Master of Medical Science
**MMT** methylcyclopentadienyl manganese tricarbonyl (fuel additive); Multiple Mirror Telescope (Arizona)
**MMU** [computing] memory management unit; [finance] million monetary units
**MMus** Master of Music
**MMusEd** Master of Musical Education
**MMX** multimedia extension
**MN** magnetic north; [fishing port] Maldon; Master of Nursing; Merchant Navy; [US postcode] Minnesota
**Mn** [chemical element] manganese; Modern (language)
**mn** *maison* (French: house); million
**mn.** midnight
**.mn** Mongolia (in Internet address)
**m.n.** *mutato nomine* (Latin: with the name changed)
**MNA** Master of Nursing Administration; Member of the National Assembly (of Quebec)
**MNAD** Multinational Airmobile Division (of NATO)
**MNAEA** Member of the National Association of Estate Agents
**MNAS** [USA] Member of the National Academy of Sciences
**MNC** major NATO command; multinational company
**MND** Ministry of National Defence; [medicine] motor neurone disease
**MNE** multinational enterprise
**MnE** Modern English
**MNECInst** Member of the North East Coast Institution of Engineers and Shipbuilders
**mng** managing
**MnGk** Modern Greek
**mngmt** management
**MnGr** Modern Greek
**mngr** manager
**MNI** Member of the Nautical Institute
**MNIMH** Member of the National Institute of Medical Herbalists
**Mnl.** Manila
**mnm** minimum
**MNOS** [electronics] metal-nitride-oxide semiconductor
**MNP** microcomputer networking protocol
**MNR** marine nature reserve; mean neap rise (of tide); Mozambique National Resistance
**Mnr** *Mijnheer* (Dutch: Mr, Sir)
**MNSc** Master of Nursing Science
**MNT** mean neap tide
**MNurs** Master of Nursing
**MO** mail order; manually operated; mass observation; Master of Obstetrics; Master of Oratory; medical officer; medical orderly; Meteorological Office; military operations; [US postcode] Missouri; *modus operandi* (Latin: method of operating); [chemistry] molecular orbital; money order; monthly order; motor-operated; municipal officer; [vehicle registration] Reading
**Mo** [computing] magneto-optical; [chemical element] molybdenum
**Mo.** Missouri; Monday
**m-o** months old
**mo.** moment; month; mouth
**m.o.** mail order; *modus operandi* (Latin: method of operating); money order
**MOA** memorandum of agreement; Ministry of Aviation
**MO&G** Master of Obstetrics and Gynaecology
**MOB** movable object block
**mob.** mobile; mobilization; mobilize
**MOBS** multiple orbit bombardment system (nuclear weapons)
**MOC** management and operating contractor; [international vehicle registration] Mozambique (from Portuguese *Moçambique*)
**MoC** mother of the chapel (in printing or publishing trade union)
**MOD** mail-order department; Ministry of Defence; Ministry of Overseas Development
**mod** [computing, mathematics] modulo

**mod.** model; moderate; [music] *moderato* (Italian: at a moderate tempo); modern; modernization; modernized (in property advertisement); modification; modified; [mathematics] modulus
**mod cons** [short form] modern conveniences
**mod. dict.** [medicine] *modo dicto* (Latin: as directed) (in prescriptions)
**modem** [computing] modulator demodulator
**MODFET** [electronics] modulation-doped field-effect transistor
**modif.** modification; modified
**mod. praes.** [medicine] *modo praescripto* (Latin: as directed) (in prescriptions)
**Mods** [short form] Honour Moderations (at Oxford University)
**modto** [music] *moderato* (Italian: at a moderate tempo)
**MODU** mobile offshore drilling unit
**.mod.uk** Ministry of Defence (in Internet address)
**MOEH** Medical Officer for Environmental Health
**MOF** [medicine] multiple organ failure
**M of A** Ministry of Agriculture, Fisheries and Food
**M of W** Ministry of Works
**MOH** Master of Otter Hounds; Medical Officer of Health; Ministry of Housing (and Local Government)
**MOHLG** Ministry of Housing and Local Government
**MOHLL** [computing] machine-oriented high-level language
**MOI** military operations and intelligence; Ministry of Information; Ministry of the Interior
**MOL** [astronautics] manned orbital laboratory; Ministry of Labour
**mol** mole (unit of amount of substance)
**mol.** molecular; molecule
**Mold.** Moldavia; Moldavian; Moldova
**Moldv.** Moldavia; Moldavian; Moldova
**mol. wt** molecular weight
**MOM** milk of magnesia
**m.o.m.** middle of month
**MOMA** Museum of Modern Art
**MOMI** Museum of the Moving Image
**MOMIMTS** Military and Orchestral Instrument Makers' Trade Society
**moms** *mervaerdiomsaetningsskat* (Danish: value-added tax); *mervardesomsattningsskatt* (Swedish: value-added tax)
**Mon** [astronomy] Monoceros
**Mon.** Monaco; Monaghan; Monday; Monegasque; Monmouth(shire); *Montag* (German: Monday); Montana
**mon.** monastery; monastic; monetary; monitor; monsoon; month
**Monag.** Monaghan
**MONEP** *Marché des options négotiables de Paris* (French: Paris traded option market)
**Mong.** Mongolia; Mongolian
**Mongol.** Mongolia; Mongolian
**Monm.** Monmouth(shire)
**monog.** monogram; monograph
**Mons.** *Monsieur* (French: Mr)
**Mont.** Montana; Montgomeryshire
**Montgom.** Montgomeryshire
**Montr.** Montreal
**MOO** [computing] multiuser object-oriented
**m.o.p.** mother-of-pearl
**MOPA** [electronics] master oscillator power amplifier
**MOPH** [USA] Military Order of the Purple Heart
**MOPS** Mail Order Protection Scheme
**MOR** middle-of-the-road; [engineering] modulus of rupture
**Mor.** Moroccan; Morocco
**mor.** [music] *morendo* (Italian: dying away); [bookbinding] morocco
**MORC** Medical Officer Reserve Corps
**mor. dict.** [medicine] *more dicto* (Latin: as directed) (in prescriptions)
**Mori** Market and Opinion Research Institute (as in **Mori poll**)
**morn.** morning
**morph.** morphological; morphology
**morphol.** morphological; morphology
**mor. sol.** [medicine] *more solito* (Latin: in the usual way) (in prescriptions)
**mort.** mortal; mortality; mortar; mortgage; mortuary
**MOS** magneto-optical system; [electronics] metal oxide semiconductor; [electronics] metal oxide silicon; Ministry of Supply
**Mos.** Moscow; Moselle
**mos.** months
**MOSFET** [electronics] metal-oxide-silicon field-effect transistor

**MOST** [electronics] metal-oxide-silicon transistor
**MOT** Ministry of Transport (as in **MOT test**)
**mot.** motor; motorized
**MOTNE** meteorological operational telecommunications network
**MOU** memorandum of understanding
**MOUS** [medicine] multiple occurrence of unexplained symptoms
**MOUSE** [military] minimum orbital unmanned satellite of the earth (used to gather information)
**MOV** [engineering] motor-operated valve
**mov.** [music] *movimento* (Italian: movement, motion)
**MOVE** Men Over Violence (organization counselling wife-batterers)
**movt** movement
**MOW** [New Zealand] Ministry of Works; Movement for the Ordination of Women
**MOX** mixed oxide (as in **MOX fuel**)
**Moz.** Mozambique
**MP** Madhya Pradesh; [metallurgy] martensitic phase; medium pressure; melting point; Member of Parliament; [physiology] membrane potential; [cartography] Mercator's projection; metal pollutant; Methodist Protestant; Metropolitan Police; mile post (on map); Military Police; Military Policeman; *mille passuum* (Latin: 1,000 paces) (Roman mile); Minister Plenipotentiary; miscellaneous papers; miscellaneous publications; Mounted Police; Mounted Policeman; [vehicle registration] north-east London
**M/P** memorandum of partnership
***mp*** [music] *mezzo piano* (Italian: moderately softly)
**m.p.** meeting point; melting point; mile post (on map); months after payment; mooring post
**MPA** Master of Professional Accounting; Master of Public Administration; Master Printers Association; Member of the Parliamentary Assembly of Northern Ireland; Music Publishers' Association
**MPAA** Motion Picture Association of America
**MPAGB** Modern Pentathlon Association of Great Britain
**MPB** male pattern baldness; [USA] Missing Persons Bureau
**MPC** mathematics, physics, chemistry; maximum permissible concentration; Metropolitan Police College; Metropolitan Police Commissioner; multimedia personal computer
**MPD** maximum permissible dose
**MPE** Master of Physical Education; maximum permissible exposure (to radiation); maximum possible error
**MPEA** Member of the Physical Education Association
**MPEG** [computing] Moving Picture Expert Group
**MPer** Middle Persian
**MPF** [medicine] maturation-promoting factor
**MPG** [education] main professional grade (basic salary); *Max-Planck-Gesellschaft zur Förderung der Wissenschaften* (German: Max Planck Society for the Advancement of Science)
**mpg** miles per gallon
**MPH** Master of Public Health
**MPh** Master of Philosophy
**mph** miles per hour
**MPharm** Master of Pharmacy
**MPhil** Master of Philosophy
**MPI** Max Planck Institute; maximum permissible intake
**m.p.i.** mean point of impact
**MPIA** Master of Public and International Affairs
**MPIR** Max Planck Institute for Radio Astronomy
**MPL** maximum permissible level
**MPLA** *Movimento Popular de Libertação de Angola* (Portuguese: Popular Movement for the Liberation of Angola)
**mpm** metres per minute
**MPO** management and personnel office; Metropolitan Police Office; military post office; mobile printing office; mobile publishing office
**MPP** [computing] massively parallel processor; Member of the Provincial Parliament (of Ontario)
**m.p.p.** most probable position
**MPR** *Majelis Permusyawaratan Rakyat* (Bahasa Indonesian: People's Consultative Assembly); maximum permitted

radiation; Mongolian People's Republic
**MPRISA** Member of the Public Relations Institute of South Africa
**MPRP** Mongolian People's Revolutionary Party
**MPS** manufacturer's part specification; marginal propensity to save; master production schedule; Medical Protection Society; Member of the Pharmaceutical Society; Member of the Philological Society; Member of the Physical Society; [medicine] mucopolysaccharide (as in **MPS disease**)
**MPs** Master of Psychology
**mps** metres per second
**MPsSc** Master of Psychological Science
**MPsych** Master of Psychology
**MPsyMed** Master of Psychological Medicine
**MPTA** Municipal Passenger Transport Association
**MPU** Medical Practitioners Union; [computing] microprocessor unit
**MPV** multipurpose vehicle
**Mpy** [commerce] *Maatschappij* (Dutch: company, Co.)
**MQ** [photography] metol-quinol (developing fluid)
**mq.** mosque
**Mqe** Martinique
**MR** magnetic resonance (as in **MR scan**); [computing] magneto-resistive; [fishing port] Manchester; map reference; [law] Master of the Rolls; match rifle; [commerce] mate's receipt; mental retardation; metabolic rate; Middlesex Regiment; Minister Resident(iary); motivation(al) research; motorways regulations; municipal reform; [vehicle registration] Swindon
**Mr** Master; Mister
**.mr** Mauritania (in Internet address)
**m.r.** memorandum receipt
**MRA** Maritime Royal Artillery; Moral Rearmament
**MRAC** Member of the Royal Agricultural College
**MRACP** Member of the Royal Australasian College of Physicians
**MRACS** Member of the Royal Australasian College of Surgeons
**MRadA** Member of the Radionic Association
**MRAeS** Member of the Royal Aeronautical Society
**MRAF** Marshal of the Royal Air Force
**MRAIC** Member of the Royal Architectural Institute of Canada
**MRAO** Mullard Radio Astronomy Observatory
**MRAS** Member of the Royal Academy of Science; Member of the Royal Asiatic Society; Member of the Royal Astronomical Society
**MRB** Mersey River Board
**MRBM** medium-range ballistic missile
**MRBS** Member of the Royal Botanic Society
**MRC** Medical Registration Council; Medical Research Council; Medical Reserve Corps; Model Railway Club
**MRCA** multirole combat aircraft
**MRCGP** Member of the Royal College of General Practitioners
**MRC-LMB** Medical Research Council Laboratory of Molecular Biology
**MRCO** Member of the Royal College of Organists
**MRCOG** Member of the Royal College of Obstetricians and Gynaecologists
**MRCP** Member of the Royal College of Physicians
**MRCPA** Member of the Royal College of Pathologists of Australia
**MRCPath** Member of the Royal College of Pathologists
**MRCPE** Member of the Royal College of Physicians of Edinburgh
**MRCPI** Member of the Royal College of Physicians of Ireland
**MRCPSGlas** Member of the Royal College of Physicians and Surgeons of Glasgow
**MRCPsych** Member of the Royal College of Psychiatrists
**MRCS** Member of the Royal College of Surgeons (of England)
**MRCSE** Member of the Royal College of Surgeons of Edinburgh
**MRCSI** Member of the Royal College of Surgeons in Ireland
**MRCVS** Member of the Royal College of Veterinary Surgeons
**MRD** machine-readable dictionary; minimal residual disease
**MRE** Master of Religious Education; [mili-

tary] meal(s) ready to eat; Member of the Royal Society of Painter-Printmakers (formerly Member of the Royal Society of Painter-Etchers and Engravers); Microbiological Research Establishment; Mining Research Establishment

**MRes** Master of Research

**MRG** Minority Rights Group

**MRGS** Member of the Royal Geographical Society

**MRH** Member of the Royal Household

**MRHS** Member of the Royal Horticultural Society

**MRI** [medicine] magnetic resonance image; [medicine] magnetic resonance imaging; Member of the Royal Institution

**MRIA** Member of the Royal Irish Academy

**MRIAI** Member of the Royal Institute of the Architects of Ireland

**MRICS** Member of the Royal Institution of Chartered Surveyors

**MRIN** Member of the Royal Institute of Navigation

**MRINA** Member of the Royal Institution of Naval Architects

**MRIPHH** Member of the Royal Institute of Public Health and Hygiene

**mrkr** marker

**MRM** mechanically recovered meat (in food processing)

**MRMetS** Member of the Royal Meteorological Society

**MRN** materials return note

**mRNA** [biochemistry] messenger ribonucleic acid

**mrng** morning

**MRO** Member of the Register of Osteopaths

**MRP** manufacturer's recommended price; Master of Regional Planning; [commerce] material requirements planning

**MRPharmS** Member of the Royal Pharmaceutical Society

**MRRP** manufacturer's recommended retail price

**MRS** Market Research Society; [computing] monitored retrievable storage

**MRs** [currency] Mauritian rupee

**Mrs** Mistress

**MRSC** Member of the Royal Society of Chemistry

**MRSH** Member of the Royal Society of Health

**MRSL** Member of the Royal Society of Literature

**MRSM** Member of the Royal Society of Medicine; Member of the Royal Society of Musicians of Great Britain

**MRSPP** Member of the Royal Society of Portrait Painters

**MRST** Member of the Royal Society of Teachers

**MRT** [medicine] magnetic resonance tomography; mass rapid transit

**MRTPI** Member of the Royal Town Planning Institute

**MRU** manpower research unit; mobile repair unit

**MRUSI** Member of the Royal United Service Institution

**MRV** [military] multiple re-entry vehicle

**MRVA** Member of the Rating and Valuation Association

**MS** [vehicle registration] Edinburgh; [physics] magnetic susceptibility; mail steamer; [astronomy] main sequence; [music] *mano sinistra* (Italian: left hand); manuscript; [physics, chemistry] mass spectrometer; [physics, chemistry] mass spectrometry; [USA] Master of Science; Master of Surgery; [international vehicle registration] Mauritius; media studies; medical staff; [photography] medium shot; *memoriae sacrum* (Latin: sacred to the memory of) (on tombstone); Mess Sergeant; [photography] mid-shot; milestone (on map); minesweeper; Ministry of Supply; [US postcode] Mississippi; [medicine] mitral stenosis; [USA] motor ship; [medicine] multiple sclerosis; municipal surveyor

**Ms** Miss or Mrs

**ms** millisecond

**m/s** metres per second; [finance] months after sight

**ms.** manuscript

**m.s.** mail steamer; margin of safety; maximum stress; mild steel

**m/s²** metres per second per second (unit of acceleration)

**MSA** Malaysia-Singapore Airways; Master of Science and Arts; Master of Science in Agriculture; Media Studies Association; Member of the Society of Apothecaries;

Merchant Shipping Act; metropolitan statistical area; Mineralogical Society of America; Motor Schools Association of Great Britain Limited; motorway service area; [USA] Mutual Security Agency

**MSAE** [USA] Master of Science in Aeronautical Engineering; [USA] Member of the Society of Automotive Engineers

**MSAgr** Master of Science in Agriculture

**MS&R** Merchant Shipbuilding and Repairs

**MSArch** Master of Science in Architecture

**MSB** Maritime Safety Board; Metropolitan Society for the Blind; [computing] most significant bit

**MSBA** Master of Science in Business Administration

**MSBus** Master of Science in Business

**MSByte** [computing] most significant byte

**MSC** major subordinate command (in NATO); Manchester Ship Canal; Manpower Services Commission; medical staff corps; Metropolitan Special Constabulary

**MSc** Master of Science

**msc.** miscellaneous

**m.s.c.** moved, seconded and carried

**MSc(Ag)** Master of Science in Agriculture

**MScApp** Master of Applied Science

**MSc(Arch)** Master of Science in Architecture

**MSc(ChemE)** Master of Science in Chemical Engineering

**MScD** [USA] Doctor of Medical Science; Master of Dental Science

**MSCE** Master of Science in Civil Engineering

**MSc(Econ)** Master of Science in Economics

**MSc(Ed)** Master of Science in Education

**MSChE** Master of Science in Chemical Engineering

**MSc(Hort)** Master of Science in Horticulture

**MSCI Index** [finance] Morgan Stanley Capital International World Index

**MScMed** Master of Medical Science

**MSc(Nutr)** Master of Science in Nutrition

**MSCP** Master of Science in Community Planning

**MScTech** Master of Technical Science

**MSD** Doctor of Medical Science; Master of Science in Dentistry; Master Surgeon Dentist; [computing] most significant digit

**MSDent** Master of Science in Dentistry

**MS-DOS** [trademark, computing] Microsoft Disk Operating System

**MSE** Master of Science in Education; Master of Science in Engineering; Member of the Society of Engineers

**MSEd** Master of Science in Education

**MSEE** Master of Science in Electrical Engineering

**MSEM** Master of Science in Engineering Mechanics; Master of Science in Engineering of Mines

**MSF** Manufacturing, Science and Finance (Union); Master of Science in Forestry; *Médecins sans frontières* (French: Doctors Without Frontiers) (charity); minesweeping flotilla

**MSFC** [USA] Marshall Space Flight Center

**MSG** monosodium glutamate (food additive)

**msg.** message

**Msgr** *Monseigneur* (French: my lord); [Roman Catholic Church] Monsignor

**msgr** messenger

**MSgt** [US military] Master Sergeant

**MSH** Master of Staghounds; [biochemistry] melanocyte-stimulating hormone

**MSHE** Master of Science in Home Economics

**MSHEc** Master of Science in Home Economics

**Mshl** Marshal

**MSHyg** Master of Science in Hygiene

**MSI** [electronics] medium-scale integration; Member of the Securities Institute; *Movimento Sociale Italiano* (Italian: Italian Social Movement)

**MSIE** Master of Science in Industrial Engineering

**MSJ** Master of Science in Journalism

**MSL** Master of Science in Linguistics; mean sea level

**MSLS** Master of Science in Library Science

**MSM** Master of Sacred Music; Master of Science in Music; Meritorious Service Medal

**MSME** Master of Science in Mechanical Engineering

**MSMed** Master of Medical Science

**MSMetE** Master of Science in Metallurgical Engineering
**MSMus** Master of Science in Music
**MSN** Master of Science in Nursing; [trademark, computing] Microsoft Network
**MSO** Member of the Society of Osteopaths
**MSocIS** *Membre de la société des ingénieurs et scientifiques de France* (French: Member of the Society of Engineers and Scientists of France)
**MSocSc** Master of Social Science(s)
**MSP** matched sale–purchase agreement; [trademark, computing] Microsoft Paint
**MSPE** Master of Science in Physical Education
**MSPH** Master of Science in Public Health
**MSPhar** Master of Science in Pharmacy
**MSPharm** Master of Science in Pharmacy
**MSPHE** Master of Science in Public Health Engineering
**MSQ** managing service quality
**MSR** [computing] magnetic stripe reader; main supply route; manual sunroof (in car advertisement); mean spring rise (of tide); Member of the Society of Radiographers; [military] missile-site radar
**MSRP** [USA] manufacturer's suggested retail price
**MSS** manuscripts; [computing] mass storage system; Master of Social Science; Master of Social Service; Member of the Royal Statistical Society; [medicine] midstream specimen (of urine)
**mss** manuscripts
**MSSc** Master of Social Science
**MSSE** [USA] Master of Science in Sanitary Engineering
**MST** Master of Sacred Theology; Master of Science in Teaching; mean spring tide; mean survival time; [USA] Mountain Standard Time
**MSt** Master of Studies
**mst** measurement
**MStat** Master of Statistics
**MSTD** Member of the Society of Typographic Designers
**Mstr** Master
**MSTS** [US navy] Military Sea Transportation Service
**MSU** [medicine] midstream specimen of urine
**MSUL** Medical Schools of the University of London
**MSurv** Master of Surveying
**MSurvSc** Master of Surveying Science
**MSW** magnetic surface wave(s); Master of Social Welfare; Master of Social Work; medical social worker; municipal solid waste
**MSw** Middle Swedish
**MSX** [trademark, computing] Microsoft extended Basic
**MSY** maximum sustainable yield (of natural resource)
**MT** machine translation; magnetic tape; mail transfer; [medicine] malignant tumour; mandated territory; [fishing port] Maryport; mass transport; mean time; mechanical transport; megaton (unit of explosive power); [currency] metical (used in Mozambique); [law] Middle Temple; [US postcode] Montana; motor tanker; motor transport; [USA] Mountain Time; [vehicle registration] northeast London
**M/T** empty; mail transfer
**Mt** [chemical element] meitnerium; Mount
**Mt.** Mountain
**mt.** megaton (unit of explosive power); mountain
**.mt** Malta (in Internet address)
**m.t.** metric ton; missile test
**MTA** [computing] message transfer agent; minimum terms agreement; Music Teachers' Association; Music Trades' Association
**MTB** motor torpedo boat; mountain bike
**MTBE** methyl tertiary-butyl ether (fuel additive)
**MTBF** [computing] mean time between failures
**MTBI** [computing] mean time between incidents
**MTC** Mechanized Transport Corps; Music Teacher's Certificate
**MTCA** Ministry of Transport and Civil Aviation
**MTD** maximum tolerated dose; mean temperature difference; Midwife Teacher's Diploma; moving target detector
**mtd** mounted
**mtDNA** [biochemistry] mitochondrial deoxyribonucleic acid

**MTech** Master of Technology
**MTEFL** Master in the Teaching of English as a Foreign Language
**MTFA** medium-term financial assistance
**MTG** [USA] methanol to gasoline
**mtg** meeting; mounting
**mtg.** mortgage
**mtgd** mortgaged
**mtge** mortgage
**mtgee** mortgagee
**mtgor** mortgagor
**MTh** Master of Theology
**mth** month
**MTI** [radar] moving target indicator (or indication)
**MTL** mean tide level
**mtl** material
**mtl.** *monatlich* (German: monthly)
**MTM** methods-time measurement
**MTN** [finance] medium-term note; multilateral trade negotiations
**mtn** motion; mountain
**MTNA** Music Teachers' National Association
**MTO** made to order; mechanical transport officer
**MTP** Master of Town Planning
**MTR** minimum time rate
**mtr** meter
**Mt Rev.** Most Reverend (title of archbishop)
**MTS** Master of Theological Studies; Merchant Taylors' School; [computing] Michigan terminal system; motor transport service; [USA] multichannel television sound
**Mts** Mountains; Mounts
**MTT** [electronics] mean transit time
**MTTR** mean time to repair; mean time to restore
**MTU** [computing] magnetic tape unit; [computing] maximum transfer unit; [US air force] missile training unit
**MTV** motor torpedo vessel; [USA] music television
**MU** maintenance unit; marginal utility; monetary unit; Mothers' Union; Musicians' Union; [vehicle registration] northeast London
**m/u** make-up
**.mu** Mauritius (in Internet address)
**MUC** Missionary Union of the Clergy
**MU car** [US railways] multiple-unit car
**MUD** [computing] multi-user dungeon (or dimension) (in game)
**MUF** [telecommunications] maximum usable frequency
**MUFTI** [military] minimum use of force tactical intervention
**MUG** [computing] multi-user game
**MUGA** [medicine] multiple-gated arteriography (as in **MUGA scan**)
**Multics** [trademark] Multiplexed Information and Computing Service
**mun.** municipal; municipality; munitions
**munic.** municipal; municipality
**MUniv** Master of the University
**Mus** [astronomy] Musca
**mus.** museum; music; musical; musician
**musa** multiple unit steerable aerial (or antenna)
**MusB** Bachelor of Music (from Latin *Musicae Baccalaureus*)
**MusD** Doctor of Music (from Latin *Musicae Doctor*)
**MusM** Master of Music (from Latin *Musicae Magister*)
**musn** musician
**mut.** mutilate; mutilated; mutual
**MUX** multiplexer
**MV** market value; megavolt; merchant vessel; [chemistry] mixed valence; motor vessel; muzzle velocity (of gun); [vehicle registration] southeast London
**mV** millivolt
**mv** [music] *mezza voce* (Italian: half voice, softly)
**.mv** Maldives (in Internet address)
**m.v.** market value; mean variation; merchant vessel; motor vessel
**MVB** Bachelor of Veterinary Medicine
**MVD** Doctor of Veterinary Medicine; *Ministerstvo Vnutrennikh Del* (Russian: Ministry of Internal Affairs) (former Soviet police organization); [medicine] mitral valve disease
**MVEE** Military Vehicles and Engineering Establishment
**MVetMed** Master of Veterinary Medicine
**MVetSc** Master of Veterinary Science
**MVL** motor-vehicle licence
**mvmt** movement
**MVO** Member of the Royal Victorian Order
**MVP** most valuable player; most valued player

**MVRA** Motor Vehicle Repairers Association
**MVS** Master of Veterinary Science
**MVSc** Master of Veterinary Science
**mvt** movement
**MW** [international vehicle registration] Malawi; Master of Wine; [radio] medium wave; megawatt; Middle Welsh; [nuclear technology] mixed waste; molecular weight; Most Worshipful; Most Worthy; [vehicle registration] Swindon
**mW** milliwatt
**.mw** Malawi (in Internet address)
**MWA** Mystery Writers of America
**MWC** municipal waste combustion
**MWeldI** Member of the Welding Institute
**MWF** Medical Women's Federation
**MWG** music wire gauge
**MWGM** [Freemasonry] Most Worshipful Grand Master; [Freemasonry] Most Worthy Grand Master
**MWh** megawatt hour
**MWI** municipal waste incineration; municipal waste incinerator
**MWIA** Medical Women's International Association
**MWO** Meteorological Watch Office
**MWP** mechanical wood pulp
**MWPA** Married Women's Property Act
**MX** missile-experimental; [vehicle registration] southeast London
**Mx** maxwell (unit of magnetic flux); Middlesex
**.mx** Mexico (in Internet address)
**mxd** mixed
**mxm** maximum
**MY** motor yacht; [vehicle registration] southeast London
**my.** myopia; myopic
**.my** Malaysia (in Internet address)
**m.y.** million years
**myc.** mycological; mycology
**mycol.** mycological; mycology
**MYOB** [informal] mind your own business
**MYRA** [finance] multiyear rescheduling agreement
**myst.** mysteries; mystery
**myth.** mythical; mythological; mythology
**mythol.** mythological; mythology
**MZ** [vehicle registration] Belfast
**Mz** [geology] Mesozoic
**.mz** Mozambique (in Internet address)

# N

**N** [printing] en; [chess] knight; [currency] naira (used in Nigeria); National; Nationalist; navigation; Navy; neap (tide); near; [electrical engineering] neutral; New; [fishing port] Newry; newton (unit of force); [currency] ngultrum (used in Bhutan); [chemical element] nitrogen; Norse; north; northern; [UK postcode] north London; [international vehicle registration] Norway; November; nuclear; [physics] nucleon; [law] nullity; nurse; nursing; [civil aircraft marking] United States of America
***N*** [physics] neutron number; [physics, chemistry] number (of molecules etc.)
**n** [printing] en; nano- (indicates $10^{-9}$, as in **nm** = nanometre); [physics] neutron
***n*** [genetics] haploid chromosome number; [mathematics] indefinite number; [chemistry] normal; [physics, chemistry] number density (of atoms etc.); [physics] principal quantum number; [optics] refractive index; [physics] rotational frequency
**n.** nail (former unit of length); name; nasal; *natus* (Latin: born); nautical; naval; near; negative; nephew; nerve; [commerce] net; [grammar] neuter; neutral; new; night; [grammar] nominative; noon; norm; normal; *nostro* (Italian: our); note; *notre* (French: our); [grammar] noun; *nous* (French: we, us); number
**'n'** and (as in **fish 'n' chips**)
**5N** [civil aircraft marking] Nigeria
**9N** [civil aircraft marking] Nepal
**NA** [vehicle registration] Manchester; Narcotics Anonymous; [USA] National Academician; National Academy; National Airlines; National Archives; National Army; National Assembly; nautical almanac; naval architect; naval attaché;

naval auxiliary; [international vehicle registration] Netherlands Antilles; [engineering] neutral axis; [banking] new account; [medicine] *Nomina Anatomica* (Latin: Anatomical Names) (official terminology); [biochemistry] noradrenaline; North America; North American; [optics] numerical aperture; nursing auxiliary

**N/A** [banking] new account; no account; [banking] no advice; [banking] non-acceptance; not applicable; not available

**Na** Nebraska; [chemical element] sodium (from Latin *natrium*)

**n/a** not applicable; not available

**.na** Namibia (in Internet address)

**NAA** [USA] National Aeronautic Association; National Association of Accountants; [USA] National Automobile Association; Nursing Auxiliaries' Association

**n.a.a.** [shipping] not always afloat

**NAAA** National Alliance of Athletic Associations

**NAACP** [USA] National Association for the Advancement of Colored People

**NAAFA** National Association to Aid Fat Americans

**NAAFI** Navy, Army and Air Force Institutes

**NAAQS** [USA] National Ambient Air Quality Standard

**NAAS** National Agricultural Advisory Service

**NAB** National Advisory Body for Public Sector Higher Education; National Alliance of Businessmen; National Assistance Board (former government department); [USA] National Association of Broadcasters; National Australia Bank; naval air base; naval amphibious base; New American Bible; News Agency of Burma

**NABC** National Association of Boys' Clubs

**NABS** National Advertising Benevolent Society

**NAC** National Advisory Council; National Agricultural Centre; [USA] National Airways Corporation; National Anglers' Council; National Archives Council; National Association for the Childless; [geology] North American craton; North Atlantic Council (in NATO)

**NACA** [USA] National Advisory Committee for Aeronautics

**NACAB** National Association of Citizens' Advice Bureaux

**NACC** North Atlantic Cooperation Council (in NATO, replaced by EAPC)

**NACCAM** National Coordinating Committee for Aviation Meteorology

**NACCB** National Accreditation Council for Certification Bodies

**NACEIC** National Advisory Council on Education for Industry and Commerce

**NACF** National Art Collections Fund

**NACM** National Association of Colliery Managers

**NACNE** National Advisory Committee on Nutrition Education

**NACO** National Association of Cooperative Officials

**NACODS** National Association of Colliery Overmen, Deputies and Shotfirers

**NACOSS** National Approval Council for Security Systems

**NACRO** National Association for the Care and Resettlement of Offenders

**NACS** National Association of Chimney Sweeps

**NACST** National Advisory Council on the Training and Supply of Teachers

**NAD** [USA] National Academy of Design; naval aircraft department; naval air division; [medicine] no abnormality detected; no appreciable difference; not on active duty

**nad.** nadir

**NADC** naval aide-de-camp

**NADEC** National Association of Development Education Centres

**NADFAS** National Association of Decorative and Fine Arts Societies

**NADGE** NATO Air Defence Ground Environment

**NADOP** [USA] North American Defense Operational Plan

**NADW** North Atlantic deep water

**NADWARN** [USA] Natural Disaster Warning System

**NAE** [USA] National Academy of Engineering; naval aircraft establishment

**NAEA** National Association of Estate Agents

**NAEP** [USA] National Assessment of Educational Progress

**NAEW** NATO Airborne Early Warning
**NAf** [currency] Netherlands Antilles guilder (from alternative name florin)
**NAFD** National Association of Funeral Directors
**NAFO** National Association of Fire Officers; Northwest Atlantic Fisheries Organization
**NAFTA** New Zealand and Australia Free Trade Agreement; North American Free Trade Agreement; North Atlantic Free Trade Area
**NAG** National Association of Goldsmiths
**Nag.** Nagasaki
**n.a.g.** net annual gain
**NAGC** National Association for Gifted Children
**NAGS** National Allotments and Gardens Society
**Nah.** [Bible] Nahum
**NAHA** National Association of Health Authorities
**Nahal** *No'ar Halutzi Lohem* (Hebrew: Pioneer and Military Youth) (in Israel)
**NAHAT** National Association of Health Authorities and Trusts
**NAHB** [USA] National Association of Home Builders
**NAHT** National Association of Head Teachers
**NAI** nonaccidental injury
**NAIR** [USA] national arrangements for incidents involving radioactivity
**NAIRU** [economics] nonaccelerating inflation rate of unemployment
**NAITA** National Association of Independent Travel Agents
**NAK** [telecommunications] negative acknowledgment
**NAL** [USA] National Aerospace Laboratory
**NALC** [USA] National Association of Letter Carriers
**NALGO** National and Local Government Officers' Association (became part of Unison)
**NALHM** National Association of Licensed House Managers
**NAM** [international vehicle registration] Namibia; [USA] National Association of Manufacturers
**N Am.** North America; North American
**NAMAS** National Measurement and Accreditation Service
**NAMB** National Association of Master Bakers
**NAMCW** National Association of Maternal and Child Welfare
**NAMH** National Association for Mental Health (former name of MIND)
**NAMMA** NATO MRCA Management Agency
**NAMS** [USA] national air-monitoring sites
**NAN** News Agency of Nigeria
**NANC** non-adrenergic non-cholinergic
**N&Q** notes and queries
**n&v** [medicine] nausea and vomiting
**NAO** National Audit Office
**NAP** National Association for the Paralysed
**Nap.** Naples; Napoleon (Bonaparte) (French emperor); Napoleonic
**NAPA** [USA] National Association of Performing Artists
**NAPF** National Association of Pension Funds
**naph.** [chemistry] naphtha
**NAPLPS** [computing] North American presentation level protocol syntax
**NAPO** National Association of Probation Officers; National Association of Property Owners
**NAPT** National Association for the Prevention of Tuberculosis
**NAPV** National Association of Prison Visitors
**NAR** [botany] net assimilation rate
**nar.** narrow
**narc.** narcotic; narcotics
**NARM** natural and accelerator-produced radioactive material
**NAS** [USA] National Academy of Sciences; National Adoption Society; National Association of Schoolmasters (became part of NAS/UWT); naval air station; Noise Abatement Society; nursing auxiliary service
**NASA** [USA] National Aeronautics and Space Administration
**NASCAR** [USA] National Association for Stock Car Auto Racing
**NASD** National Amalgamated Stevedores and Dockers; [USA] National Association of Securities Dealers
**NASDA** [Japan] National Space Development Agency

**NASDAQ** [USA] National Association of Securities Dealers Automated Quotations (system)
**Nash.** Nashville
**NASL** North American Soccer League
**Nass.** Nassau
**NAS/UWT** National Association of Schoolmasters/Union of Women Teachers
**NASW** [USA] National Association of Social Workers
**NAT** National Arbitration Tribunal
**Nat.** Natal; National; Nationalist
**nat.** national; nationalist; native; natural; naturalize; naturalized; nature; naturist; *natus* (Latin: born)
**N At.** North Atlantic
**n.a.t.** normal allowed time
**NATCS** National Air Traffic Control Service
**NATE** National Association for the Teaching of English
**NATFHE** National Association of Teachers in Further and Higher Education
**nat. hist.** natural history
**Nativ.** Nativity
**natl** national
**NATLAS** National Testing Laboratory Accreditation Scheme
**NATM** New Austrian Tunnelling Method
**NATO** North Atlantic Treaty Organization
**nat. phil.** natural philosophy
**NATS** National Air Traffic Services; [USA] Naval Air Transport Service
**NatScD** Doctor of Natural Science
**nat. sci.** natural science(s)
**NATSOPA** National Society of Operative Printers, Graphical and Media Personnel (formerly National Society of Operative Printers and Assistants)
**N Att.** naval attaché
**NATTKE** National Association of Theatrical, Television and Kinematographic Employees
**NATTS** National Association of Trade and Technical Schools
**natur.** naturalist
**NatWest** National Westminster Bank plc
**NAU** [international vehicle registration] Nauru
**naut.** nautical
**NAV** [finance] net asset value (of organization)
**nav.** naval; navigable; navigation; navigator
**NAVAIR** [USA] Naval Air Systems Command
**Nav. E** naval engineer
**navig.** navigable; navigation; navigator
**NAVS** National Anti-Vivisection Society
**NAVSAT** navigational satellite
**NAWB** National Association of Workshops for the Blind
**NAWC** National Association of Women's Clubs
**NAWO** National Alliance of Women's Organizations
**NAYC** Youth Clubs UK (formerly National Association of Youth Clubs)
**NAYPIC** National Association of Young People in Care
**NAYT** National Association of Youth Theatres
**naz.** *nazionale* (Italian: national)
**Nazi** *Nationalsozialisten* (German: National Socialist)
**NB** [vehicle registration] Manchester; narrow bore; naval base; Nebraska; [medicine] needle biopsy; [physics] neutral beam; New Brunswick; North Britain (i.e. Scotland); *nota bene* (Latin: note well)
**Nb** [chemical element] niobium
***Nb*** [meteorology] nimbus
**n.b.** [cricket] no ball; *nota bene* (Latin: note well)
**NBA** [USA] National Basketball Association; [USA] National Book Award; [USA] National Boxing Association; National Building Agency; Net Book Agreement; North British Academy
**NBC** [USA] National Basketball Committee; National Book Council (former name of NBL); National Boys' Club; [USA] National Broadcasting Company; National Bus Company; nuclear, biological and chemical (weapons or warfare)
**NBCD** [computing] natural binary-coded decimal
**NBD** [statistics] negative binomial distribution
**NbE** north by east
**NBER** [USA] National Bureau of Economic Research
**n.b.g.** [informal] no bloody good

**NBI** National Benevolent Institution; [medicine] no bone injury
**NBK** National Bank of Kuwait
**NBL** National Book League (formerly NBC)
**n.b.l.** [informal] not bloody likely
**NBP** [chemistry] normal boiling point
**NBPI** National Board for Prices and Incomes (replacement for PIB)
**NBR** National Buildings Record; [chemistry] nitrile-butadiene rubber
**nbre** *noviembre* (Spanish: November)
**NBRI** National Building Research Institute
**NBS** [USA] National Bureau of Standards; Newcastle Business School
**NBTS** National Blood Transfusion Service
**NBV** [accounting] net book value (of asset)
**NbW** north by west
**NC** [vehicle registration] Manchester; National Certificate; National Congress; National Council; [education] National Curriculum; Nature Conservancy; New Caledonia; New Church; nickel–cadmium (battery); nitrocellulose; [chemistry] nitrogen compound; [meteorology] no change; no charge; normally closed; North Carolina; [US postcode] North Carolina; Northern Command; numerical control; numerically controlled; [USA] Nurse Corps
**N/C** new charter; nitrocellulose; no charge
**NCA** National Certificate of Agriculture; National Childminding Association; National Cricket Association; no copies available
**NCAA** [USA] National Collegiate Athletic Association; Northern Counties Athletic Association
**NCACC** National Civil Aviation Consultative Committee
**NCAR** [USA] National Center for Atmospheric Research (Colorado)
**NCARB** [USA] National Council of Architectural Registration Boards
**NCB** National Children's Bureau; National Coal Board (replaced by BCC); Nippon Credit Bank; [insurance] no-claim(s) bonus
**NCBA** National Cattle Breeders' Association
**NCBAE** [insurance] no-claim(s) bonus as earned
**NCBW** nuclear, chemical and biological warfare
**NCC** [USA] National Climatic Center; National Computing Centre; National Consumer Council; [USA] National Council of Churches; [education] National Curriculum Council; Nature Conservancy Council (replaced by EN)
**NCCA** National Carpet Cleaners Association
**NCCI** National Committee for Commonwealth Immigrants
**NCCJ** National Conference of Christians and Jews
**NCCL** National Council for Civil Liberties (former name of Liberty)
**NCCS** national command and control system; National Council for Civic Responsibility
**NCCVD** National Council for Combating Venereal Diseases
**NCD** naval construction department
**n.c.d.** [informal] no can do
**NCDAD** National Council for Diplomas in Art and Design
**NCDL** National Canine Defence League
**NCERT** National Council for Educational Research and Training
**NCET** National Council for Educational Technology
**NCFT** National College of Food Technology
**NCH** National Children's Home; National Clearing House
**n.Chr.** *nach Christus* (German: after Christ, AD)
**NCI** [USA] National Cancer Institute; [finance] New Community Instrument
**n.c.i.** no common interest
**NCIC** National Cancer Institute of Canada; [USA] National Crime Information Center
**NCIS** National Criminal Intelligence Service
**NCL** National Carriers Limited; National Central Library; National Chemical Laboratory; National Church League
**NCLC** National Council of Labour Colleges
**NCN** National Council of Nurses
**NCNA** New China News Agency
**NCNC** National Convention of Nigeria and the Cameroons; National Conven-

tion of Nigerian Citizens (political party)

**NCO** noncommissioned officer

**NCP** National Car Parks (Limited); [Australia] National Country Party (former name of National Party); national cycling proficiency; [computing] network control protocol

**n.c.p.** [engineering] normal circular pitch

**NCPL** National Centre for Programmed Learning

**NCPS** noncontributory pension scheme

**NCPT** [USA] National Congress of Parents and Teachers

**NCR** National Cash Register (Company Limited); no carbon required (of paper)

**NCRE** Naval Construction Research Establishment

**NCRL** National Chemical Research Laboratory

**NCRP** [USA] National Council on Radiation Protection and Measurement

**NCS** [USA] National Communications System

**NCSC** [Australia] National Companies and Securities Commission; [USA] National Computer Security Center

**NCSE** National Council for Special Education

**NCSS** National Council of Social Service

**NCT** National Chamber of Trade; National Childbirth Trust; [medicine] neutron-capture therapy; [medicine] neutron compute(rize)d tomography

**NCTA** [USA] National Community Television Association

**NCTE** [USA] National Council of Teachers of English

**NCU** National Communications Union (became part of CWU); National Cyclists' Union

**n.c.u.p.** no commission until paid

**NCV** no commercial value

**NCVCCO** National Council of Voluntary Child Care Organizations

**NCVO** National Council of Voluntary Organizations

**NCVQ** National Council for Vocational Qualifications

**NCW** National Council of Women (of Great Britain)

**ND** [vehicle registration] Manchester; national debt; National Diploma; Naturopathic Diploma; [photography] neutral density; no date; nondelivery; North Dakota; [US postcode] North Dakota

**N-D** *Notre-Dame* (French: Our Lady) (in church names)

**Nd** [chemical element] neodymium

**n.d.** [photography] neutral density; next day (delivery); no date; no decision; no deed; no delay; no demand; nondelivery; not dated; not deeded; [banking] not drawn; [informal] nothing doing

**NDA** National Dairymen's Association; National Diploma in Agriculture; [engineering] nondestructive analysis; [engineering] nondestructive assay

**NDAC** [USA] National Defense Advisory Commission

**N Dak.** North Dakota

**NDB** [aeronautics] nondirectional beacon

**NDC** National Dairy Council; NATO Defence College; [computing] normalized device coordinates

**NDCS** National Deaf Children's Society

**NDD** National Diploma in Dairying; National Diploma in Design

**NDE** near-death experience; [engineering] nondestructive evaluation; [engineering] nondestructive examination

**NDF** National Diploma in Forestry

**NDH** National Diploma in Horticulture

**NDIC** National Defence Industries Council

**Ndl.** Netherlands

**NDN** National District Nurse Certificate

**NDP** National Democratic Party; [economics] net domestic product; [Canada] New Democratic Party

**n.d.p.** [engineering] normal diametric pitch

**NDPB** nondepartmental public body

**NDPS** National Data Processing Service

**NDR** [electronics] negative differential resistance; [electronics] negative differential resistivity; nondomestic rates; *Norddeutscher Rundfunk* (German: North German Radio)

**NDRC** National Defence Research Committee

**NDSB** Narcotic Drugs Supervisory Body (of UN)

**NDT** [engineering] nondestructive testing; [commerce] nondistributive trade

**NDTA** [USA] National Defense Transportation Association
**NDU** Nursing Development Unit
**NDV** [microbiology] Newcastle disease virus
**NE** [vehicle registration] Manchester; national emergency; National Executive; naval engineer; [US postcode] Nebraska; [fishing port] Newcastle upon Tyne; [UK postcode] Newcastle upon Tyne; new edition; New England; news editor; [banking] no effects (= no funds); northeast; northeastern; nuclear energy; nuclear explosion; nuclear explosive
**Ne** [chemical element] neon
**Ne.** Nepal; Nepalese; Nepali; Netherlands
**n/e** new edition; [banking] no effects (= no funds); [accounting] not entered
**.ne** Niger (in Internet address)
**n.e.** not essential; not exceeding
**NEA** [USA] National Education Association; [USA] National Endowment for the Arts; North East Airlines
**NEAC** New English Art Club
**NEACP** [USA] National Emergency Airborne Command Post (pronounced 'kneecap')
**NEAF** Near East Air Force
**NEAFC** North-East Atlantic Fisheries Commission
**Neapol.** Neapolitan
**NEARELF** Near East Land Forces
**NEB** [USA] National Electricity Board; [USA] National Energy Board; National Enterprise Board; New English Bible
**Neb.** Nebraska
**NEBOSH** National Examination Board in Occupational Safety and Health
**Nebr.** Nebraska
**NEBSS** National Examinations Board for Supervisory Studies
**NEC** [USA] National Economic Council; [USA] National Electric Code; National Electronics Council; National Equestrian Centre; National Executive Committee; National Exhibition Centre (Birmingham); National Extension College (Cambridge); [medicine] necrotizing enterocolitis; [Japan] Nippon Electric Company
**nec.** necessary
**n.e.c.** not elsewhere classified
**NECCTA** National Educational Closed Circuit Television Association
**NECInst** North East Coast Institution of Engineers and Shipbuilders
**necr.** necrosis
**necrol.** necrology
**NED** [medicine] no evidence of disease
**NEDC** National Economic Development Council (also called Neddy); North East Development Council
**NEDO** National Economic Development Office
**NEEB** North Eastern Electricity Board
**NEF** National Energy Foundation; [acoustics] noise exposure forecast (value)
**neg.** negation; negative; negatively; negligence; negotiable (in job advertisement); negotiate; negotiation
**NEH** National Endowment for the Humanities
**Neh.** [Bible] Nehemiah
**NEI** Netherlands East Indies
**n.e.i.** *non est inventa* (Latin: (she) has not been found); *non est inventum* (Latin: (it) has not been found); *non est inventus* (Latin: (he) has not been found); not elsewhere indicated
**NEL** [USA] National Electronics Laboratory; National Engineering Laboratory
**nem. con.** *nemine contradicente* (Latin: nobody opposing, unanimously)
**nem. dis.** *nemine dissentiente* (Latin: nobody opposing, unanimously)
**NE/n.d.** [bibliography] new edition, no date given
**N Eng.** New England; northern England
**neol.** neologism
**NEP** [international vehicle registration] Nepal; New Economic Policy (in USSR in 1920s)
**Nep.** Nepal; Nepalese; Nepali; Neptune
**n.e.p.** new edition pending
**NEPA** [USA] National Environmental Policy Act
**NEPP** [USA] National Energy Policy Plan
**NEQ** [computing] nonequivalence (as in **NEQ gate**)
**NERA** [USA] National Emergency Relief Administration
**NERC** National English Rabbit Club; Natural Environment Research Council
**NERIS** National Educational Resources Information Service

**NES** National Eczema Society
**n.e.s.** not elsewhere specified
**NESC** [USA] National Electric Safety Code
**NESTOR** [nuclear technology] neutron source thermal reactor
**NET** [USA] National Educational Television; [nuclear technology] Next European Torus
**.net** network (in Internet address)
**n.e.t.** not earlier than
**Neth.** Netherlands
**Neth. Ant.** Netherlands Antilles
**n. et m.** [medicine] *nocte et mane* (Latin: night and morning) (in prescriptions)
**neurol.** neurological; neurology
**neut.** [grammar] neuter; neutral; neutralize; neutralized; neutralizer
**Nev.** Nevada
**NEW** [US economics] net economic welfare
**Newf.** Newfoundland
**New M** New Mexico
**news.** newsagency; newsagent
**New Test.** New Testament
**NF** [vehicle registration] Manchester; *Nationale Front* (German: National Front); [US pharmacology] National Formulary; National Front; [medicine] neurofibromatosis; New Forest; Newfoundland; New French; [banking] no funds; [telecommunications] noise factor; [telecommunications] noise figure; Norman French (language)
**N/F** [banking] no funds
**n.f.** [engineering] near face; [informal] no fool; [grammar] noun feminine
**NFA** National Farmers' Association; National Federation of Anglers; [USA] National Food Administration; [USA] National Futures Association; no fixed abode; no fixed address
**n.f.a.** no further action
**NFAL** National Foundation of Arts and Letters
**NFB** National Film Board (of Canada)
**NFBPM** National Federation of Builders' and Plumbers' Merchants
**NFBTE** National Federation of Building Trades Employers
**NFC** [USA] National Football Conference; National Freight Consortium
**n.f.c.** not favourably considered
**NFCO** National Federation of Community Organizations
**NFD** Newfoundland; no fixed date
**Nfd** Newfoundland
**NFDM** nonfat dry milk
**NFER** National Foundation for Educational Research
**NFFC** National Film Finance Corporation
**NFFE** [USA] National Federation of Federal Employees
**NFFO** non-fossil-fuel obligation (for electricity companies)
**NFFPT** National Federation of Fruit and Potato Trades
**NFHA** National Federation of Housing Associations
**NFI** National Federation of Ironmongers
**NFL** [USA, Canada] National Football League
**Nfld** Newfoundland
**n.f.m.** nearest full moon; next full moon
**NFMPS** National Federation of Master Printers in Scotland
**NFMS** National Federation of Music Societies
**NFO** National Freight Organization
**NFPW** National Federation of Professional Workers
**n.f.r.** no further requirements
**NFRC** National Federation of Roofing Contractors
**NFRN** National Federation of Retail Newsagents
**NFS** National Fire Service; National Flying Services; National Forest Service; [computing] network filing service; [computing] network filing system; not for sale
**NFSE** National Federation of the Self-Employed
**NFT** National Film Theatre
**NFTS** National Film and Television School
**NFU** National Farmers' Union
**NFUW** National Farmers' Union of Wales
**NFWI** National Federation of Women's Institutes
**NFYFC** National Federation of Young Farmers' Clubs
**NG** [railways] narrow gauge; National Gallery; National Government; [USA] National Guard; National Guardsman; New Granada; [medicine] new growth; New Guinea; nitroglycerine; [Free-

masonry] Noble Grand; [Freemasonry] Noble Guard; no go; no good; North Germanic; [vehicle registration] Norwich; [UK postcode] Nottingham
**Ng** [geology] Neogene
**Ng.** Norwegian
**.ng** Nigeria (in Internet address)
**n.g.** no good; not given
**NGA** National Glider Association; National Graphical Association (became part of GPMU)
**NGC** [USA] National Grid Company; [astronomy] New General Catalogue
**NGF** [biochemistry] nerve growth factor
**NGk** New Greek
**NGL** [chemistry] natural-gas liquid(s)
**NGNP** [economics] nominal gross national product
**NGO** [USA] National Gas Outlet; [India] nongazetted officer; nongovernmental organization
**NGR** [international vehicle registration] Nigeria
**NGr** New Greek
**NGRC** National Greyhound Racing Club
**NGRS** Narrow Gauge Railway Society
**NGS** National Galleries of Scotland; National Geographic Society; nuclear generating station
**NGT** National Guild of Telephonists
**ngt** *négociant* (French: merchant)
**NGTE** National Gas Turbine Establishment
**NGU** [medicine] nongonococcal urethritis
**NGV** natural-gas vehicle
**NH** National Hunt; naval hospital; New Hampshire; [US postcode] New Hampshire; [vehicle registration] Northampton; northern hemisphere; Northumberland Hussars
**NHA** National Horse Association of Great Britain; [USA] National Housing Agency
**NHBC** National Housebuilding Council
**NHBRC** National House-Builders' Registration Certificate
**NHC** National Hunt Committee
**NHD** Doctor of Natural History
**NHeb** New Hebrew
**N Heb.** New Hebrides
**NHF** National Hairdressers' Federation
**NHG** New High German
**NHI** National Health Insurance
**NHK** *Nippon Hoso Kyokai* (Japanese: Japanese Broadcasting Corporation)
**NHL** [USA] National Hockey League; [medicine] non-Hodgkin lymphoma
**NHLBI** [USA] National Heart, Lung and Blood Institute
**NHMF** National Heritage Memorial Fund
**NHMRCA** National Health and Medical Research Council of Australia
**NHO** Navy Hydrographic Office
**nhp** nominal horsepower
**NHR** National Housewives Register; National Hunt Rules
**NHS** National Health Service
**NHSTA** National Health Service Training Authority
**NHTPC** National Housing and Town Planning Council
**NI** National Insurance; Native Infantry; naval instructor; Naval Intelligence; new impression; News International; [computing] noninterfaced; Northern Ireland; North Island (New Zealand)
**Ni** [chemical element] nickel
**.ni** Nicaragua (in Internet address)
**NIA** [USA] National Intelligence Authority; Newspaper Institute of America
**NIAAA** Northern Ireland Amateur Athletic Association
**NIAB** National Institute of Agricultural Botany
**NIACRO** Northern Ireland Association for the Care and Resettlement of Offenders
**NIAE** National Institute of Agricultural Engineering
**NIAID** National Institute of Allergy and Infectious Diseases
**Nibmar** no independence before majority African rule
**NIBSC** National Institute for Biological Standards Control
**NIC** National Incomes Commission; National Insurance contribution(s); network interface card; newly industrialized country; [international vehicle registration] Nicaragua
**Nic.** Nicaragua; Nicaraguan
**n.i.c.** not in contract
**Nica.** Nicaragua; Nicaraguan
**NiCad** nickel–cadmium (battery)
**NICAM** [electronics] near-instantaneous companded audio multiplex (for coding sound signals digitally)

**Nicar.** Nicaragua; Nicaraguan
**NiCd** nickel–cadmium (battery)
**NICEC** National Institute for Careers Education and Counselling
**NICEIC** National Inspection Council for Electrical Installation Contracting
**NICF** Northern Ireland Cycling Federation
**NICG** Nationalized Industries Chairmen's Group
**NICRA** Northern Ireland Civil Rights Association
**NICS** Northern Ireland Civil Service
**NICU** [medicine] neonatal intensive care unit
**NID** National Institute for the Deaf; [India] National Institute of Design; Naval Intelligence Division; Northern Ireland District
**NIDC** Northern Ireland Development Council
**NIDD** [medicine] non-insulin-dependent diabetes
**NIES** Northern Ireland Electricity Service
**NIESR** National Institute of Economic and Social Research
**NIF** [finance] note issuance facility
**NIFES** National Industrial Fuel Efficiency Service
**NIFO** next in, first out
**NIFTP** [computing] network independent file transfer protocol
**Nig.** Nigeria; Nigerian
**NIH** [USA] National Institutes of Health; North Irish Horse (former regiment)
**NIHCA** Northern Ireland Hotels and Caterers Association
**NIHE** [Ireland] National Institute for Higher Education
**NII** Nuclear Installations Inspectorate
**NIIP** National Institute of Industrial Psychology
**NILP** Northern Ireland Labour Party
**NIMA** National Infomercial Marketing Association
**nimby** [informal] not in my back yard
**NIMH** National Institute of Medical Herbalists; [USA] National Institute of Mental Health
**n. imp.** new impression
**NIMR** National Institute for Medical Research
**NIN** national information network
**NINO** no inspector, no operator (system)
**NIO** National Institute of Oceanography
**NIOSH** [USA] National Institute for Occupational Safety and Health
**Nip.** Nippon; Nipponese
**nip.** [engineering] nipple
**ni. pri.** *nisi prius* (Latin: unless previously)
**NIR** non-ionizing radiation; Northern Ireland Railways
**N Ir.** Northern Ireland
**NIRA** [USA] National Industrial Recovery Act
**NIRC** National Industrial Relations Court
**N Ire.** Northern Ireland
**NIREX** Nuclear Industry Radioactive Waste Executive
**NIRS** [USA] National Institute of Radiological Sciences
**NIS** [currency] (new) Israeli shekel
**n.i.s.** not in stock
**NISA** National Independent Supermarkets' Association
**NISC** National Industrial Safety Committee
**NIST** [USA] National Institute of Standards and Technology
**NISTRO** Northern Ireland Science and Technology Regional Organization
**NISW** National Institute for Social Workers
**NIT** national intelligence test; negative income tax
**NITB** Northern Ireland Tourist Board
**NIV** New International Version (of Bible)
**NIWAAA** Northern Ireland Women's Amateur Athletic Association
**NJ** [vehicle registration] Brighton; New Jersey; [US postcode] New Jersey; [informal] nose job
**n.J** *nächsten Jahres* (German: next year)
**NJA** National Jewellers' Association
**NJAC** National Joint Advisory Council
**NJC** National Joint Council
**NJCC** National Joint Consultative Committee
**NJNC** National Joint Negotiating Committee
**NK** [vehicle registration] Luton; [immunology] natural killer (as in **NK-cell**); not known
**NKC** [immunology] natural killer cell
**NKGB** *Narodny Komissariat Gosudarstvennoi Bezopasnosti* (Russian: People's

Commissariat of State Security) (former Soviet secret police)
**NKr** [currency] Norwegian krone
**NKVD** *Narodny Komissariat Vnutrennikh Del* (Russian: People's Commissariat of Internal Affairs) (former Soviet police organization)
**NL** National Labour; [USA] National League (baseball); National Liberal; Navy League; Navy List; [international vehicle registration] Netherlands; [vehicle registration] Newcastle upon Tyne; New Latin; no liability (after Australian company name); north latitude
**Nl** National
**.nl** Netherlands (in Internet address)
**n.l.** [printing] new line; *non licet* (Latin: it is not permitted); *non liquet* (Latin: it is not clear)
**N Lat.** north latitude
**NLB** National Library for the Blind
**NLBD** National League for the Blind and Disabled
**NLC** National Liberal Club; National Library of Canada
**NLCB** National Lottery Charities Board
**NLCS** North London Collegiate School
**NLD** National League for Democracy (in Myanmar)
**NLF** National Labour Federation; National Liberal Federation; National Liberation Front; National Loans Fund
**n.l.f.** nearest landing field
**NLI** National Library of Ireland
**NLLST** National Lending Library for Science and Technology
**NLM** National Library of Medicine
**NLMC** National Labour Management Council
**NLN** National League for Nursing
**n.l.n.** no longer needed
**NLO** naval liaison officer
**NLP** [computing] natural language processing; Natural Law Party; [USA] neighborhood loan program; [computing] neurolinguistic programming
**NLQ** [computing] near letter quality (of printing)
**NLR** [astronomy] narrow-line region
**NLRB** [USA] National Labor Relations Board
**NLS** National Library of Scotland
**n.l.t.** not later than; not less than
**NLW** National Library of Wales
**nly** northerly
**NLYL** National League of Young Liberals
**NM** [vehicle registration] Luton; national marketing; nautical mile; New Mexico; [US postcode] New Mexico; nuclear medicine
**N/m** [commerce] no mark(s) (on bill of lading)
**Nm.** *Nachmittag* (German: afternoon); [advertising] next matter
**n.M** *nächsten Monats* (German: next month)
**nm** nanometre
**n/m** not married (in personal advertisement)
**nm.** nutmeg
**n.m.** nautical mile; new moon; [medicine] *nocte et mane* (Latin: night and morning) (in prescriptions); nonmetallic; [grammar] noun masculine
**NMA** National Management Association; National Medical Association
**NMB** National Maritime Board
**NMC** National Marketing Council; [USA] National Meteorological Center
**n.m.c.** no more credit
**N Mex.** New Mexico
**NMFS** [USA] National Marine Fisheries Service
**NMHA** National Mental Health Association
**NMHF** [USA] National Mental Health Foundation
**NMI** [computing] non-maskable interrupt
**n mile** nautical mile
**NMP** [economics] net material product
**NMR** nuclear magnetic resonance
**NMRI** [medicine] nuclear magnetic resonance imaging
**NMS** [USA] National Market System; National Museums of Scotland; [stock exchange] Normal Market Size
**NMSQT** [USA] National Merit Scholarship Qualifying Test
**NMSS** [USA] National Multiple Sclerosis Society
**n.m.t.** not more than
**NMTF** National Market Traders' Federation
**NMU** National Maritime Union
**NMW** national minimum wage
**NN** [fishing port] Newhaven; no name;

[UK postcode] Northampton; [vehicle registration] Nottingham
**N/N** [banking] not to be noted
**nn.** names; notes; nouns
**NND** [medicine] neonatal death
**NNE** north-northeast
**NNEB** National Nursery Examination Board
**NNF** Northern Nurses' Federation
**NNHT** Nuffield Nursing Homes Trust
**NNI** noise and number index (for aircraft noise); noise nuisance index
**NNMA** Nigerian National Merit Award
**NNOM** Nigerian National Order of Merit
**NNP** [economics] net national product
**NNR** national nature reserve
**NNSA** [USA] National Nuclear Safety Administration
**NNT** nuclear nonproliferation treaty
**NNTP** [computing] net(work) news transfer protocol
**NNTR** no need to return
**NNW** north-northwest
**NO** [vehicle registration] Chelmsford; natural order; naval officer; naval operations; navigation officer; New Orleans; Nuffield Observatory (Jodrell Bank, Cheshire); nursing officer
**N/O** [banking] no orders
**No** [chemical element] nobelium
**No.** north; northern; Norway; Norwegian; number (from Latin *numero*, ablative of *numerus*, or French *numéro*)
**no.** north; northern; number (from Latin *numero*, ablative of *numerus*, or French *numéro*)
**.no** Norway (in Internet address)
**n.o.** normally open; [cricket] not out
**NOA** National Opera Association; National Orchestral Association; not otherwise authorized
**NOAA** [USA] National Oceanic and Atmospheric Administration
**NOAO** [USA] National Optical Astronomy Observatories
**NOB** naval operating base
**nob.** *nobis* (Latin: for our part, on our part); noble
**NOC** National Olympic Committee; not otherwise classified
**n.o.c.** notation of content; not otherwise classified
**NOCD** [informal] not our class, dear
**No. Co.** northern counties
**noct.** [medicine] *nocte* (Latin: at night) (in prescriptions)
**NOD** Naval Ordnance Department; night observation device
**NODA** National Operatic and Dramatic Association
**NODC** non-OPEC developing country
**NOE** nuclear Overhauser effect
**n.o.e.** notice of exception; not otherwise enumerated
**NOERC** North of England Regional Consortium
**n.o.h.p.** not otherwise herein provided
**n.o.i.b.n.** not otherwise indexed by name
**NOIC** Naval Officer in Charge
**NOISE** [USA] National Organization to Insure a Sound-controlled Environment
**n.o.k.** next of kin
**NOL** [USA] Naval Ordnance Laboratory
**nol. con.** [law] *nolo contendere* (Latin: I do not wish to contend)
**nol. pros.** [law] *nolle prosequi* (Latin: to be unwilling to prosecute)
**nom.** nomenclature; nominal; nominated; nomination; [grammar] nominative
**nom. cap.** [finance] nominal capital
**nomen.** nomenclature
**nomin.** nominal; nominated; nomination; [grammar] nominative
**nom. nov.** *nomen novum* (Latin: new name)
**NOMSS** [USA] National Operational Meteorological Satellite System
**noncom.** noncommissioned
**Noncon.** Nonconformist
**non cul.** *non culpabilis* (Latin: not guilty)
**non obst.** *non obstante* (Latin: notwithstanding)
**non pros.** [law] *non prosequitur* (Latin: he does not prosecute)
**non rep.** [medicine] *non repetatur* (Latin: do not repeat) (in prescriptions)
**non seq.** *non sequitur* (Latin: it does not follow (logically))
**nonstand.** nonstandard
**nonstd** nonstandard
**non-U** not upper-class
**NOP** National Opinion Poll; not our publication
**n.o.p.** not otherwise provided (for)

**NOPWC** National Old People's Welfare Council
**NOR** [biology] nucleolar-organizing region
**Nor** [astronomy] Norma
**Nor.** Norman; Normandy; north; northern; Norway; Norwegian; Norwich
**nor.** normal; north; northern
**NORAD** North American Air Defense Command
**Norf.** Norfolk
**NORM** not operationally ready maintenance
**Norm.** Norman; Normandy
**norm.** normal; normalized
**NORML** [USA] National Organization for the Reform of Marijuana Laws
**NORS** not operationally ready supply (or supplies)
**Northants** Northamptonshire
**Northd** Northumberland
**Northumb.** Northumberland
**Norvic.** *Norvicensis* (Latin: (Bishop) of Norwich)
**Norw.** Norway; Norwegian
**Norweb** North Western Electricity Board
**NORWICH** knickers off ready when I come home (on envelope of love letter)
**NOS** *Nederlandse Omroep Stichting* (Dutch: Netherlands Broadcasting Corporation); [computing] network operating system
**Nos.** numbers
**nos.** numbers
**n.o.s.** not otherwise specified
**NOSC** [US navy] Naval Ordnance Systems Command
**Not.** Notary
**not.** notice
**NOTAR** no-tail rotor (of aircraft)
**NOTB** National Ophthalmic Treatment Board
**Nottm** Nottingham
**Notts** Nottinghamshire
**notwg** notwithstanding
**nouv.** *nouveau* (French: new); *nouvelle* (French: new)
**Nov.** November; *November* (German: November)
**nov.** novel; novelist; *novembre* (Italian: November); *novembre* (French: November); novice; novitiate
**NOW** [USA] National Organization for Women; [US banking] negotiable order of withdrawal; New Opportunities for Women
**NoW** *News of the World*
**NOX** nitrogen oxide(s)
**n.o.y.** not out yet
**noz.** nozzle
**NP** Nationalist Party; national park; National Party; National Power plc; net profit; neuropsychiatric; neuropsychiatry; [UK postcode] Newport; New Providence (Bahamas); nitro proof (in firearms); Nobel Prize; [chemistry] nonpolar; Notary Public; [grammar] noun phrase; nurse practitioner; [vehicle registration] Worcester
**Np** napalm; neap (tide); neper (unit used in telecommunications); [chemical element] neptunium
**np** neap (tide); new pence (used in 1970s, after decimalization)
**n/p** net proceeds
**.np** Nepal (in Internet address)
**n.p.** near point; [law] net personalty; net proceeds; [printing] new paragraph; new pattern; nickel-plated; *nisi prius* (Latin: unless previously); [medicine] *nomen proprium* (Latin: its own name) (in prescriptions); nonparticipating; [bibliography] no place of publication (given); no printer; no publisher; normal pitch; not paginated; nursing procedure
**NPA** National Park Authority; National Pigeon Association; New People's Army (in Philippines); Newspaper Publishers' Association
**NPACI** National Production Advisory Council on Industry
**NPBA** National Pig Breeders' Association
**NPC** [China] National People's Congress; [USA] National Petroleum Council; National Ports Council; [USA] National Press Club; no-player character (in computer game); [computing] normalized projection coordinates; Northern People's Congress (in Nigeria)
**NPCS** Narrowband Personal Communications Service
**NPD** *Nationaldemokratische Partei Deutschlands* (German: National Democratic Party of Germany); [marketing] new product development; [astronomy] north polar distance

**NPF** National Progressive Front (in Syria); Newspaper Press Fund
**n.p.f.** not provided for
**NPFA** National Playing Fields Association
**NPG** National Portrait Gallery; Nuclear Planning Group (in NATO)
**NPGH** [education] National Professional Qualification for Headship
**NPH** [chemistry] normal paraffin hydrocarbon
**NPh** nuclear physics
**NPHT** Nuffield Provincial Hospitals Trust
**NPK** nitrogen, phosphorus and potassium (in fertilizers, from chemical symbols)
**NPL** National Physical Laboratory (Teddington, Middlesex)
**n. pl.** [grammar] noun plural
**NPN** [medicine] nonprotein nitrogen
**n.p.n.a.** [commerce] no protest for non-acceptance
**NPO** New Philharmonia Orchestra
**n.p.o.** [medicine] *ne per oris* (Latin: not by mouth)
**n.p. or d.** no place or date
**NPP** nuclear power plant
**n.p.p.** no passed proof
**NPR** [USA] National Public Radio; noise power ratio
**NPRA** National Petroleum Refiners Association
**NPS** National Portrait Society; nuclear power source; nuclear power station
**n.p.s.** nominal pipe size; no prior service
**NPT** (Nuclear) Non-Proliferation Treaty
**NPTA** National Pest Technicians' Association
**NPU** National Pharmaceutical Union; National Postal Union; [medicine] not passed urine
**n.p.u.** *ne plus ultra* (Latin: not more beyond) (i.e. extremity, culmination or perfection)
**NPV** [finance] net present value; [finance] no par value (of shares)
**NPW** nuclear-powered warship
**n.q.a.** [finance] net quick assets
**NQOC** [informal] not quite our class
**NR** [vehicle registration] Leicester; National Register; natural rubber; naval rating; Navy Regulations; [insurance] no risk; North Riding (former division of Yorkshire); [UK postcode] Norwich
**Nr** *Nummer* (German: number)
**nr** near; number
**.nr** Nauru (in Internet address)
**n.r.** net register; [insurance] no risk
**NRA** National Reclamation Association; [USA] National Recovery Administration; National Recreation Area; [USA] National Rehabilitation Association; National Rifle Association; National Rivers Authority; nuclear-reaction analysis
**n.r.a.** never refuse anything
**NRAA** National Rifle Association of America
**NRAO** [USA] National Radio Astronomy Observatory
**NRC** National Redemption Council (in Ghana); National Research Council; [USA] Nuclear Regulatory Commission
**NRCA** National Retail Credit Association
**NRCC** National Research Council of Canada
**NRD** National Registered Designer; National Register of Designers
**NRDC** National Research Development Corporation; [USA] Natural Resources Defense Council
**NRDS** [medicine] neonatal respiratory distress syndrome
**NREM** [physiology] non-rapid eye movement (as in **NREM sleep**)
**NREN** [computing] National Research and Education Network
**NRF** National Relief Fund
**NRFL** Northern Rugby Football League
**NRI** National Resources Institute
**NRK** *Norsk Rikskringkasting* (Norwegian broadcasting company)
**NRL** National Reference Library; [USA] Naval Research Laboratory
**NRM** National Resistance Movement (in Uganda)
**NRMA** [Australia] National Roads and Motorists Association
**nrml** normal
**NROR** [finance] normal rate of return
**NROTC** Naval Reserve Officer Training Corps
**NRP** nuclear reprocessing plant
**NRPB** National Radiological Protection Board
**NRR** net reproduction rate (of populations); Northern Rhodesia Regiment

**NRS** National Readership Survey; National Rose Society
**NRs** [currency] Nepalese rupee
**n.r.t.** net registered tonnage
**NRTA** [USA] National Retired Teachers Association
**NRV** [finance] net realizable value; non-return valve
**Nrw.** Norwegian
**NRZ** [computing] nonreturn to zero
**NS** [vehicle registration] Glasgow; *Nachschrift* (German: postscript, PS); [computing] Nassi–Schneidermann (as in **NS chart**); National Service; National Society; natural science; naval service; [fishing port] New Ross; new series; Newspaper Society; New Style (in dates); nonsmoker (in personal advertisement); Nova Scotia; nuclear science; nuclear ship; Numismatic Society
**N/S** nonsmoker (in personal advertisement)
**N-S** *Notre-Seigneur* (French: Our Lord)
***Ns*** [meteorology] nimbostratus
**ns** nanosecond
**n/s** news-sheet; nonsmoker (in personal advertisement); [banking] not sufficient (funds)
**n.s.** near side; new series; nickel steel; not satisfactory; not significant; not specified; [banking] not sufficient (funds)
**NSA** [USA] National Security Agency; [USA] National Shipping Authority; National Skating Association; [USA] National Standards Association; [USA] National Student Association; New Society of Artists; non-sterling area
**NSACS** National Society for the Abolition of Cruel Sports
**NSAE** National Society of Art Education
**NSAFA** National Service Armed Forces Act
**NSAID** [pharmacology] nonsteroidal anti-inflammatory drug
**NSB** National Savings Bank; [USA] National Science Board
**NSBA** National Sheep Breeders' Association
**NSC** National Safety Council; National Savings Certificate(s); [USA] National Security Council; National Sporting Club; National Steel Corporation
**NSCA** National Society for Clean Air
**NSCC** [USA] National Securities Clearing Corporation
**NSCR** National Society for Cancer Relief
**NSD** naval supply depot; nominal standard dose; normal spontaneous delivery
**NSDAP** *Nationalsozialistische Deutsche Arbeiterpartei* (German: National Socialist German Workers' Party, Nazis)
**NSERC** [USA] Natural Sciences and Engineering Research Council
**NSF** [USA] National Science Foundation; [banking] not sufficient funds; Nuclear Structure Facility (Daresbury, Cheshire)
**n.s.f.** [banking] not sufficient funds
**NSFGB** National Ski Federation of Great Britain
**NSG** [education] nonstatutory guidelines (relating to National Curriculum)
**NSGT** non-self-governing territory (or territories)
**NSHEB** North of Scotland Hydroelectric Board
**NSI** [USA] National Security Information
**n. sing.** [grammar] noun singular
**NSL** National Sporting League
**NSM** new smoking material; non-stipendiary minister
**NSO** National Solar Observatory; Naval Staff Officer
**NSP** nonsmoker preferred (in personal advertisement)
**NSPCC** National Society for the Prevention of Cruelty to Children
**NSPE** [USA] National Society of Professional Engineers
**n.s.p.f.** not specifically (or specially) provided for
**NSRA** National Small-Bore Rifle Association
**NSS** national sample survey; National Secular Society; New Shakespeare Society; [medicine] normal saline solution
**NSSA** National School Sailing Association
**NSSU** National Sunday School Union
**NST** Newfoundland Standard Time
**NSTC** Nova Scotia Technical College
**NSTP** Nuffield Science Teaching Project
**NSU** [medicine] nonspecific urethritis
**NSW** New South Wales
**NSY** New Scotland Yard
**NT** [Ireland] National Teacher; National Theatre; National Trust; neap tide(s);

[fishing port] Newport; new technology; New Testament; New Translation; Northern Territory (Australia); not titled; [card games] no-trump(s) (in bridge); Nurse Teacher; [vehicle registration] Shrewsbury

**n.t.** net terms; net tonnage; normal temperature

**NTA** [USA] National Technical Association; National Training Award; net tangible assets

**NTB** [economics] non-tariff barrier

**NTC** [physics] negative temperature coefficient

**NTD** [informal] not top drawer

**NTDA** National Trade Development Association

**NTEU** [USA] National Treasury Employees Union

**NTFS** new technology filing system

**ntfy** notify

**NTG** North Thames Gas

**NTGB** North Thames Gas Board

**NTGk** New Testament Greek

**Nth** North

**Nthb.** Northumberland

**nthn** northern

**NTI** noise transmission impairment

**NTIA** [USA] National Telecommunications and Information Administration

**NTL** [electronics] non-threshold logic

**n.t.l.** no time lost

**NTM** [economics] non-tariff measure

**NTO** naval transport officer

**n.t.o.** not taken out

**NTP** normal temperature and pressure

**n.t.p.** normal temperature and pressure; no title page

**NTS** National Trust for Scotland; Nevada Test Site; not to scale

**NTSB** [USA] National Transportation Safety Board

**NTSC** [USA] National Television System Committee (US broadcasting system)

**NTT** New Technology Telescope

**NTUC** National Trades Union Congress (in Singapore)

**NTV** Nippon Television

**NTVLRO** National Television Licence Records Office

**NTW** no time wasters (in personal advertisement)

**nt wt** net weight

**NU** name unknown; National Union; *Nations Unies* (French: United Nations, UN); natural uranium; Northern Union; [vehicle registration] Nottingham; number unobtainable

**Nu** [currency] ngultrum (used in Bhutan)

**n.u.** name unknown; number unobtainable

**NUAAW** National Union of Agricultural and Allied Workers

**NUBE** National Union of Bank Employees

**nuc.** nuclear

**nucl.** nuclear

**NUCPS** National Union of Civil and Public Servants (became part of PTC)

**NUCUA** National Union of Conservative and Unionist Associations

**nud.** nudism; nudist

**NUDAGO** National Union of Domestic Appliances and General Operatives

**NUDETS** nuclear detection system

**NUI** National University of Ireland

**NUIW** National Union of Insurance Workers

**NUJ** National Union of Journalists

**NUJMB** Northern Universities Joint Matriculation Board

**NUKFAT** National Union of Knitwear, Footwear and Apparel Trades

**NUL** [USA] National Urban League

**NULMW** National Union of Lock and Metal Workers

**NUM** National Union of Mineworkers; New Ulster Movement

**Num.** [Bible] Numbers

**num.** number; numeral(s); numerical; numerological; numerologist; numerology; numerous

**NUMAST** National Union of Marine, Aviation and Shipping Transport Officers

**Numb.** [Bible] Numbers

**numis.** numismatic; numismatics; numismatist

**numism.** numismatic; numismatics; numismatist

**NUOS** Naval Underwater Ordnance Station

**NUPE** National Union of Public Employees (became part of Unison)

**NUR** National Union of Railwaymen (became part of RMT)

**NURBS** [computing] nonuniform rational B-splines

**NUS** National Union of Seamen (became part of RMT); National Union of Students
**NUT** National Union of Teachers
**N-u-T** Newcastle-upon-Tyne
**NUTG** National Union of Townswomen's Guilds
**NUTN** National Union of Trained Nurses
**nutr.** nutrition
**NUU** New University of Ulster
**NV** [commerce] *Naamloze Vennootschap* (Dutch: public limited company, plc); needle valve; [US postcode] Nevada; New Version; nonvintage (wine); [finance] nonvoting (shares); [shipping] *Norske Veritas* (Norwegian shipping classification society); [vehicle registration] Northampton
**N/V** nonvintage (wine); [banking] no value
**n.v.** nonvoting
**NVALA** National Viewers' and Listeners' Association
**NVB** National Volunteer Brigade
**NVC** nonverbal communication
**n.v.d.** no value declared
**NVG** [military] night-vision goggles
**NVGA** [USA] National Vocational Guidance Association
**NVI** nonvalue indicator (postage stamp)
**NVM** Nativity of the Virgin Mary; [chemistry] nonvolatile matter
**NVQ** National Vocational Qualification
**NVRAM** [computing] nonvolatile random-access memory
**NVRS** National Vegetable Research Station
**NW** [vehicle registration] Leeds; net worth; North Wales; northwest; northwestern; [UK postcode] northwest London
**n.w.** net weight; no wind
**NWC** National War College
**NWEB** North Western Electricity Board
**Nwfld** Newfoundland
**NWFP** North-West Frontier Province (Pakistan)
**NWG** national wire gauge
**NWGA** National Wool Growers' Association
**NWI** Netherlands West Indies (former name of Netherlands Antilles)
**NWIDA** North West Industrial Development Association
**NWS** [USA] National Weather Service; normal water surface
**NWT** Northwest Territories (Canada)
**nwt** nonwatertight
**n. wt** net weight
**NWTV** North West Television
**NX** [vehicle registration] Dudley
**NY** [vehicle registration] Cardiff; new year; New York; [US postcode] New York
**NYA** [USA] National Youth Administration
**NYC** New York City
**NYCSCE** New York Coffee, Sugar and Cocoa Exchange
**NYD** [medicine] not yet diagnosed
**NYFE** New York Futures Exchange
**nyl.** nylon
**NYMEX** New York Mercantile Exchange
**NYMT** National Youth Music Theatre
**NYO** National Youth Orchestra
**NYOS** National Youth Orchestra of Scotland
**NYP** not yet published
**NYPD** New York Police Department
**NYR** not yet returned
**NYS** New York State
**NYSE** New York Stock Exchange
**NYT** National Youth Theatre; *New York Times*
**NYU** New York University
**NZ** [vehicle registration] Londonderry; neutral(ity) zone; New Zealand; [international vehicle registration] New Zealand
**.nz** New Zealand (in Internet address)
**NZBC** New Zealand Broadcasting Corporation
**NZDSIR** New Zealand Department of Scientific and Industrial Research
**N Zeal.** New Zealand
**NZEF** New Zealand Employers' Federation; New Zealand Expeditionary Force (in both world wars)
**NZEFIP** New Zealand Expeditionary Force in the Pacific (in World War II)
**NZEI** New Zealand Educational Institute
**NZFL** New Zealand Federation of Labour
**NZIA** New Zealand Institute of Architects
**NZLR** New Zealand Law Reports
**NZMA** New Zealand Medical Association
**NZPA** New Zealand Press Association
**NZRFU** New Zealand Rugby Football Union
**NZRN** New Zealand Registered Nurse

# O

**O** [medicine] blood group; observe; observer; [obstetrics] occiput; occupation; Ocean; [pharmacology] *octarius* (Latin: pint); [printing] octavo; October; [medicine] *oculus* (Latin: eye); Oddfellows; *oeste* (Portuguese or Spanish: west); office; officer; Ohio; old; operation; [genetics] operator; [slang] opium; orange; [computing, mathematics] order; Order (of monks, knights, etc.); ordinary; [geology] Ordovician; Orient; *Osten* (German: east); [music] *ottava* (Italian: octave); *ouest* (French: west); [cricket] over; *ovest* (Italian: west); owner; [chemical element] oxygen

**o** [computing, mathematics] order; [meteorology] overcast

**o'** of

**o.** occasional; [printing] octavo; off; old; only; *optimus* (Latin: best); order; organ; [music] *ottava* (Italian: octave); [baseball] out; over; overseer; owner

**6O** [civil aircraft marking] Somalia

**7O** [civil aircraft marking] Yemen

**OA** [vehicle registration] Birmingham; objective analysis; office address; office automation; Officers' Association; *Officier d'Académie* (French: Officer of the Academy); [banking] old account; [chemistry] oleic acid; operational analysis; [medicine] osteoarthritis; overall

**O/A** [banking] old account

**o/a** on account (of); on or about

**o.a.** overall

**OAA** *Organisation pour l'alimentation et l'agriculture* (French: Food and Agriculture Organization, FAO); Outdoor Advertising Association of Great Britain

**OACI** *Organisation de l'aviation civile internationale* (French: International Civil Aviation Organization, ICAO)

**OAD** [medicine] obstructive airways disease

**o.a.d.** overall depth

**OAG** [USA] Official Airline Guide

**o.a.h.** overall height

**o. alt. hor.** [medicine] *omnibus alternis horis* (Latin: every other hour)

**OAMDV** *omnia ad majorem Dei gloriam* (Latin: all to the greater glory of God)

**OANA** Organization of Asian News Agencies

**O&A** October and April (on bills)

**O&C** Oxford and Cambridge (Schools Examination Board)

**o&c** onset and course

**O&E** [USA] Operations and Engineers (or Engineering)

**O&G** obstetrics and gynaecology

**O&M** Ogilvie and Mather (advertising agency); organization and method(s)

**O&O** Oriental and Occidental Steamship Company; owned and operated

**OAO** one and only; Orbiting Astronomical Observatory

**o.a.o.** off and on

**OAP** old age pension; old age pensioner

**OAPC** [USA] Office of Alien Property Custodian

**OAPEC** Organization of Arab Petroleum Exporting Countries

**OAR** [Roman Catholic Church] Order of Augustinian Recollects

**OAr** Old Arabic

**OAS** [military] offensive air support; on active service; *Organisation de l'armée secrète* (French: Secret Army Organization); Organization of American States

**OASIS** optimal aircraft sequencing using intelligent systems

**OAT** outside air temperature

**OATC** Oceanic Air Traffic Control

**OATG** outside air temperature gauge

**OATUU** Organization of African Trade Union Unity (replacement for AATUF)

**OAU** Organization of African Unity

**OB** [vehicle registration] Birmingham; [fishing port] Oban; observed bearing; [USA] obstetric; [USA] obstetrician; [USA] obstetrics; [theatre] off-Broadway; official board; Old Bailey; old bonded (whisky); old boy; Order of Barbados; order of battle; Order of the Bath;

[insurance] ordinary business (in life assurance); ordnance board; outside broadcast; [civil aircraft marking] Peru

**Ob.** [Bible] Obadiah

**o/b** on or before

**ob.** *obiit* (Latin: (he/she) died); *obiter* (Latin: incidentally); obligation; oboe; observation; obsolete; obstetric; obstetrics

**o.b.** ordinary building (grade of timber)

**OBA** optical bleaching agent (in detergent)

**Obad.** [Bible] Obadiah

**ÖBB** *Österreichische Bundesbahnen* (German: Federal Railways of Austria)

**obb.** [music] *obbligato* (Italian: essential (part))

**obbl.** [music] *obbligato* (Italian: essential (part))

**OBC** old boys' club; on-board computer (in car advertisement)

**OBD** [medicine] organic brain disease

**ob. dk** observation deck

**obdt** obedient

**OBE** (Officer of the) Order of the British Empire; out-of-the-body experience

**OBEV** *Oxford Book of English Verse*

**ob-gyn** obstetrics-gynaecology

**OBI** Order of British India

**obit** [short form] obituary

**obj.** object; objection; objective

**objn** objection

**obl.** obligation; oblige; oblique; oblong

**OBLI** Oxford and Buckinghamshire Light Infantry

**OBM** [surveying] Ordnance benchmark

**OBO** ore-bulk-oil (ship)

**o.b.o.** or best offer (in advertisement)

**Obogs** [military] on-board oxygen-generating system

**ob. ph.** [surveying] oblique photograph (or photography)

**obre** *octobre* (French: October)

**OBS** [medicine] organic brain syndrome

**Obs.** Observatory

***Obs.*** *The Observer*

**obs.** obscure; observation; observatory; observe; observed; observer; obsolete; obstacle; obstetric; obstetrician; obstetrics; obstruction

**obsc.** obscure

**obscd** obscured

**OBSF** [accounting] off balance sheet finance

**obsol.** obsolescent; obsolete

**ob.s.p.** *obiit sine prole* (Latin: died without issue)

**obst** oboist

**obstet.** obstetric; obstetrician; obstetrics

**obstn** obstruction

**obt** obedient

**obtd** obtained

**OBU** offshore banking unit; One Big Union

**OBV** ocean boarding vessel

**obv.** obverse

**OC** [vehicle registration] Birmingham; Observer Corps; [USA] Office of Censorship; officer commanding; Officer in Charge; [electrical engineering] operating characteristic; operations centre; [pharmacology] oral contraceptive; Order in Council; (Officer of the) Order of Canada; orienteering club; [philately] original cover; Oslo Convention; Ottawa Convention; overseas command; overseas country

**Oc.** Ocean

**o/c** officer commanding; overcharge

**o.c.** office copy; official classification; [architecture] on centre; only child; [shipping] open charter; open cover; *opere citato* (Latin: in the work cited); over-the-counter

**OCA** Old Comrades Association

**oca.** [music] ocarina

**OCAM** *Organisation commune africaine et malgache* (French: African and Malagasy Common Organization)

**OCarm.** Order of Carmelites

**OCart.** Order of Carthusians

**OCAS** Organization of Central American States

**OCAW** [USA] Oil, Chemical and Atomic Workers International Union

**occ.** occasion; occasional; occasionally; occident; occidental; occupation; occupied; occurrence

**occas.** occasional; occasionally

**occn** occasion

**OCD** [medicine] obsessive compulsive disorder; [USA] Office of Civil Defense; [computing] on-line communications driver; *Ordinis Carmelitarum Discalceatorum* (Latin: of the Order of Discalced

Carmelites); *Ordo Carmelitarum Discalceatorum* (Latin: Order of Discalced Carmelites)

**OCDE** *Organisation de coopération et de développement economiques* (French: Organization for Economic Cooperation and Development, OECD)

**OCDM** [USA] Office of Civil Defense Mobilization

**OCDS** [Canada] Overseas College of Defence Studies

**O/Cdt** Officer-Cadet

**oceanog.** oceanography

**OCelt** Old Celtic

**OCF** Officiating Chaplain to the Forces

**OCH** oil central heating (in property advertisement)

**och.** ochre

**OCNL** [meteorology] occasional

**OCorn** Old Cornish

**OCPSF** organic chemicals, plastics and synthetic fibres

**OCR** [computing] optical character reader; [computing] optical character recognition; *Ordinis Cisterciensium Reformatorum* (Latin: of the Order of Reformed Cistercians); *Ordo Cisterciensium Reformatorum* (Latin: Order of Reformed Cistercians, Trappists)

**OCS** [USA] Officer Candidate School; Old Church Slavonic; outer continental shelf

**OCSC** Office of the Civil Service Commissioners

**OCSO** Order of Cistercians of the Strict Observance (= Trappists)

**ocst** [meteorology] overcast

**Oct** [astronomy] Octans

**Oct.** October

**oct.** [music] octave; [printing] octavo; *octubre* (Spanish: October)

**OCTU** Officer Cadet Training Unit

**OCTV** open-circuit television

**OCU** Operational Conversion Unit

**OCUC** Oxford and Cambridge University Club

**OCV** open-circuit voltage

**OD** Doctor of Ophthalmology; Doctor of Optometry; Doctor of Osteopathy; [vehicle registration] Exeter; [civil aircraft marking] Lebanon; [medicine] *oculus dexter* (Latin: right eye); officer of the day; Old Dutch; [military] olive drab; operations division; [Jamaica] (Officer of the) Order of Distinction; ordinary seaman; ordnance datum (standard sea level); ordnance department; ordnance depot; organization development; other denominations; outside diameter; overdose

**O/D** on deck; [banking] on demand; [banking] overdraft; [banking] overdrawn

**o/d** on deck; overdose

**od.** *oder* (German: or)

**o.d.** [medicine] *oculus dexter* (Latin: right eye); [military] olive drab; optical density; outside diameter

**ODA** [computing] office document architecture; [computing] open (or office) document architecture; [medicine] operating department assistant; Overseas Development Administration (former government department)

**ODan** Old Danish

**ODAS** Ocean Data Station

**ODC** Order of Discalced Carmelites

**ODCh** Chaplain for Other Denominations

**ODE** [mathematics] ordinary differential equation

**ODECA** *Organización de estados centroamericanos* (Spanish: Organization of Central American States, OCAS)

**ODESSA** Ocean Data Environmental Sciences Services Acquisition; *Organisation der SS-Angehörigen* (German: Organization of SS Members)

**ODETTE** Organization for Data Exchange through Tele-Transmission in Europe

**ODI** [computing] open datalink interface; Overseas Development Institute

**ODLQC** Open and Distance Learning Quality Council (formerly CACC)

**ODO** outdoor officer (at customs)

**ODP** official development planning; [computing] open distributed processing; open-door policy; overall development planning

**ODV** [informal] brandy (phonetic spelling of French name *eau de vie*)

**OE** [civil aircraft marking] Austria; [vehicle registration] Birmingham; [USA] Office of Education; Old English; Old Etonian; [medicine] on examination; Order of Excellence (in Guyana); original error; outboard engine

**Oe** oersted (unit of magnetic field strength)
**o.e.** omissions excepted; open end
**OEA** Overseas Education Association; oxygen-enriched air
**OEC** oxygen-enriched combustion
**OECD** Organization for Economic Cooperation and Development (replacement for OEEC)
**OECS** Organization of Eastern Caribbean States
**OED** *Oxford English Dictionary*
**OEEC** Organization for European Economic Cooperation (replaced by OECD)
**OEF** Organization of Employers' Federations and Employers in Developing Countries
**OEIC** open-ended investment company
**OEL** occupational exposure limit (of radiation)
**OEM** [computing] original equipment manufacturer
**OEO** [USA] Office of Economic Opportunity
**OEP** [USA] Office of Economic Preparedness
**OER** Officers' Emergency Reserve; Organization for European Research
**OES** ocean energy system(s); [USA] Office of Economic Stabilization; Order of the Eastern Star; Organization of European States
**OET** Office of Education and Training
**OF** [vehicle registration] Birmingham; Oddfellows; oil-filled; oil-fired; [printing] old face (type); Old French; operating forces; operational forces; Order of the Founder (of Salvation Army); oxidizing flame
**o.f.** optional form; outside face
**OFA** [medicine] oncofetal antigen
**O factor** [psychology] oscillation factor
**OFB** [computing] output feedback
**OFEMA** *Office français d'exportation de matériel aéronautique* (French: French Office for the Export of Aeronautical Material)
**Off.** Offaly
**off.** offer; offered; offering; office; officer; official; officinal
**Offer** Office of Electricity Regulation
**offg** offering; officiating
**offic.** official; officially
**offl** official
**offr** officer
**Ofgas** Office of Gas Supply
**OFHC** [engineering] oxygen-free high-conductivity copper
**Oflag** *Offizierslager* (German: officers' (prisoner-of-war) camp)
**OFlem** Old Flemish
**Oflot** Office of the National Lottery
**OFM** Order of Friars Minor (= Franciscans); *Ordo Fratrum Minorum* (Latin: Order of Friars Minor)
**OFMCap.** Order of Friars Minor Capuchin
**OFMConv.** Order of Friars Minor Conventual
**OFR** Order of the Federal Republic of Nigeria
**OFr** Old French
**OFris** Old Frisian
**OFS** Orange Free State
**Ofsted** Office for Standards in Education
**OFT** Office of Fair Trading
**Oftel** Office of Telecommunications
**Ofwat** Office of Water Services
**OG** [vehicle registration] Birmingham; [astronomy] object glass; officer of the guard; [architecture] ogee; Olympic Games; [US slang] original gangster (criminals' term of respect); original gravity (in brewing); [philately] original gum; outside guard
**o.g.** [philately] original gum; [sports] own goal
**OGael** Old Gaelic
**ÖGB** *Österreichischer Gewerkschaftsbund* (German: Austrian Federation of Trade Unions)
**OGCM** [meteorology] ocean general circulation model
**OGD** [medicine] oesophagogastroduodenoscopy
**OGL** [commerce] open general licence
**OGM** ordinary general meeting
**OGO** Orbiting Geophysical Observatory
**OGPU** *Obyedinyonnoye Gosudarstvennoye Politicheskoye Upravleniye* (Russian: United State Political Administration) (former Soviet police organization)
**OGS** Oratory of the Good Shepherd; [electronics] oxide glassy (or glasslike) semiconductor
**OH** [vehicle registration] Birmingham; [civil aircraft marking] Finland; [US post-

code] Ohio; [numismatics] old head (of Queen Victoria)

**o.h.** observation helicopter; office hours; [medicine] *omni hora* (Latin: hourly); on hand; open hearth; overhead

**OHAC** own house and car (in personal advertisement)

**OHBMS** On Her/His Britannic Majesty's Service

**OHC** overhead cam(shaft) (in car advertisement)

**OHD** [medicine] organic heart disease

**OHDETS** over-horizon detection system

**OHG** [commerce] *Offene Handelsgesellschaft* (German: partnership); Old High German

**OHMS** On Her/His Majesty's Service

**OHN** occupational health nurse

**OHNC** occupational health nursing certificate

**OHP** overhead projector

**OHS** occupational health service; [metallurgy] open-hearth steel

**OHV** overhead valve

**OI** [vehicle registration] Belfast; office instruction; Old Irish; operating instructions; [medicine] osteogenesis imperfecta

**OIC** Officer in Charge; *Organisation internationale du commerce* (French: International Trade Organization, ITO); Organization of the Islamic Conference

**OIcel** Old Icelandic

**OIEO** offers in excess of (in advertisement)

**OIG** *organisation intergouvernementale* (French: intergovernmental organization)

**OII** [physics] optical imaging instrument

**OILC** Offshore Industry Liaison Committee

**OIPC** *Organisation internationale de police criminelle* (French: International Criminal Police Organization, Interpol)

**OIr** Old Irish

**OIRO** offers in the region of (in advertisement)

**OIRT** *Organisation internationale de radiodiffusion et télévision* (French: International Radio and Television Organization)

**OIS** organizer industrial safety; overnight indexed swap

**OIT** *Organisation internationale du travail* (French: International Labour Organization, ILO)

**OIt** Old Italian

**OJ** [vehicle registration] Birmingham; *Official Journal* (of EU); orange juice; Order of Jamaica

**o.j.** open joint; open joist

**OJAJ** October, January, April, July (end of financial quarters)

**OJCS** Office of the Joint Chiefs of Staff

**Ojocs** [horseracing] overnight declaration of jockeys

**OJR** old Jamaica rum

**OJT** on-the-job training

**OK** all correct (perhaps from facetious misspelling 'oll korrekt'); [vehicle registration] Birmingham; [civil aircraft marking] Czech Republic; [US postcode] Oklahoma

**o.k.a.** otherwise known as

**OKH** *Oberkommando der Heeres* (German: Army High Command) (in World War II)

**Okla** Oklahoma

**Okt.** *Oktober* (German: October)

**OL** [vehicle registration] Birmingham; [medicine] *oculus laevus* (Latin: left eye); [UK postcode] Oldham; Old Latin; [computing] on-line; operating licence; (Officer of the) Order of Leopold; Ordnance Lieutenant; [sports] outside left; overflow level; overhead line

**Ol.** Olympiad; Olympic

**ol.** [medicine] *oleum* (Latin: oil)

**o.l.** [medicine] *oculus laevus* (Latin: left eye)

**OLC** oak-leaf cluster (US military decoration)

**Old Test.** Old Testament

**OLE** [computing] object linking and embedding

**O level** [education] Ordinary level (replaced by GCSE)

**OLG** Old Low German

**Oli** [geology] Oligocene

**o'lkng** overlooking (in property advertisement)

**OLQ** officer-like qualities

**OLR** off-line reader

**OLRT** [computing] on-line real time

**OLS** [statistics] ordinary least squares

**OM** [vehicle registration] Birmingham; old man; optical microscopy; *Optimus*

*Maximus* (Latin: greatest and best) (Roman title for Jupiter); Order of Merit; ordnance map; organic matter; [civil aircraft marking] Slovakia
**Om.** Oman
**.om** Oman (in Internet address)
**o.m.** old measurement; [medicine] *omni mane* (Latin: every morning)
**OMA** [US finance] orderly marketing agreement
**OMB** [USA] Office of Management and Budget
**OMC** operation and maintenance costs
**OMCS** Office of the Minister for the Civil Service
**OMI** Oblate(s) of Mary Immaculate
**OMM** [Canada] (Officer of the) Order of Military Merit
**omn. hor.** [medicine] *omni hora* (Latin: every hour)
**omn. noct.** [medicine] *omni nocte* (Latin: every night)
**OMO** one-man operation (or operator) (of bus)
**OMR** [computing] optical mark reading (or reader)
**OMRS** Orders and Medals Research Society
**OMS** [computing] object management system; [astronautics] orbital manœuvring system; *Organisation mondiale de la santé* (French: World Health Organization, WHO)
**o.m.s.** output per man shift
**OMT** [computing] object modelling technique
**OMV** open-market value
**ON** [vehicle registration] Birmingham; octane number; Old Norse; Ontario; [Jamaica] Order of the Nation; orthopaedic nurse
**o.n.** [medicine] *omni nocte* (Latin: every night)
**ONC** Ordinary National Certificate; Orthopaedic Nursing Certificate
**OND** Ophthalmic Nursing Diploma; Ordinary National Diploma; [medicine] other neurological disorders
**ONERA** *Office national d'études et de recherches aérospatiales* (French: National Office of Aerospace Study and Research)
**ONF** Old Norman French; Old Northern French
**ONG** *organisation non-gouvernementale* (French: nongovernmental organization)
**ONGC** [USA] Oil and Natural Gas Commission
**ONI** Office of Naval Intelligence
**o.n.o.** or near(est) offer (in advertisement)
**onomat.** onomatopoeia; onomatopoeic
**ONorw** Old Norwegian
**ONR** [USA] Office of Naval Research
**ONS** Office for National Statistics
**ONT** ordinary neap tide
**Ont.** Ontario
**ONZ** Order of New Zealand
**OO** [civil aircraft marking] Belgium; [vehicle registration] Chelmsford; observation officer; [informal] once-over; operation order; orderly officer
**o/o** offers over (in advertisement); on order; order of
**OOBE** out-of-the-body experience
**OOD** [computing] object-oriented design; officer of the day; officer of the deck
**OODBMS** [computing] object-oriented database management system
**OOG** officer of the guard
**OOL** [computing] object-oriented language
**OON** Officer of the Order of the Niger
**o/o/o** out of order
**o.o.o.** of obscure origin
**OOP** [computing] object-oriented programming; out-of-pocket (expenses)
**OOT** out of town
**OOW** officer of the watch
**OP** [vehicle registration] Birmingham; observation point; observation post; old people; Old Persian; old prices; [insurance] open policy; [theatre] opposite prompt (side); *Ordinis Praedictatorum* (Latin: of the Order of Preachers); *Ordo Praedictatorum* (Latin: Order of Preachers, Dominicans); organophosphate; osmotic pressure; [informal] other people('s); out of print; [medicine] outpatient; over proof (of alcohol)
**Op.** [music] Opus (piece by composer)
**op** [short form] operation
**op.** opaque; opera; *opera* (Latin: works); operation; operational; operator; opinion; opposite; optical; *optimus* (Latin: best, excellent); *opus* (Latin: work)

**o.p.** old pattern; open pattern; open-plan (in property advertisement); [theatre] opposite prompt (side); out of print; over proof (of alcohol)
**OPA** [USA] Office of Price Administration (in World War II); Orbis Press Agency (Czech news agency)
**op art** [short form] optical art
**OPAS** Occupational Pensions Advisory Board
**OPB** Occupational Pensions Board
**OPC** [computing] optical photoconductor; ordinary Portland cement; [medicine] outpatient(s') clinic; Overseas Press Club of America
**op. cit.** *opere citato* (Latin: in the work cited)
**OPCON** operational control
**OPCS** Office of Population Censuses and Surveys
**OPD** [medicine] outpatient(s') department
**OPDAR** optical detection and ranging
**OPE** out-of-pocket expenses
**OPEC** Organization of (the) Petroleum Exporting Countries
**Op-Ed** [USA] opposite editorial (page) (in newspaper)
**OPEIU** [USA] Office and Professional Employees International Union
**OPEP** *Organisation des pays exportateurs de pétrole* (French: Organization of Petroleum Exporting Countries, OPEC)
**OPers** Old Persian
**OPEX** operational, executive and administrative personnel (in UN)
**OPG** [dentistry] orthopantomogram
**OPg** Old Portuguese
**opg** opening
**Oph** [astronomy] Ophiuchus
**oph.** ophthalmic
**ophthal.** ophthalmic; ophthalmologist; ophthalmology
**ophthalmol.** ophthalmologist; ophthalmology
**OPIC** [USA] Overseas Private Investment Corporation
**opl** operational
**OPM** [USA] Office of Personnel Management; [informal] other people's money; output per man
**opm** operations per minute
**OPMA** Overseas Press and Media Association
**opn** operation; opinion; option
**o.p.n.** *ora pro nobis* (Latin: pray for us)
**OPO** one-person operation (of bus); one-person operator (of bus)
**OPol** Old Polish
**OPP** oriented polypropene (film); out of print at present
**Opp.** [music] Opuses (pieces by composer)
**opp.** *opera* (Latin: works); opportunity; oppose; opposed; opposite; opposition
**oppy** opportunity
**OPQ** occupational personality questionnaire
**OPr** Old Provençal
**opr** operator
**opr.** operate
**OPRAF** Office of Passenger Rail Franchising
**OProv** Old Provençal
**OPruss** Old Prussian
**OPS** Office of Public Service
**ops** [short form] operations
**OPT** optimized production technology
**opt.** [grammar] optative; optic(al); optician; optics; optimal; *optime* (Latin: best, excellently); optimum; option; optional
**OptD** Doctor of Optometry
**OPV** [medicine] oral poliomyelitis vaccine
**OQ** (Officer of the) National Order of Quebec
**OR** [statistics] odds ratio; official receiver; official referee; Old Roman; [currency] Omani rial; [US medicine] operating room; operational (or operations) requirement; operational (or operations) research; orderly room; [US postcode] Oregon; [military] other ranks; [sports] outside right; [insurance] owner's risk; [vehicle registration] Portsmouth
**ÖR** *Österreichischer Rundfunk* (German: Austrian Radio) (broadcasting service)
**or** other
**or.** orange; oratorio; orient; oriental; orientalist; original
**o.r.** operationally risky; operational (or operations) requirement; operations room; out of range; overhaul and repair; [insurance] owner's risk
**Oracle** [trademark] optional reception of announcements by coded line electronics (teletext service)
**orat.** oration; orator; oratorical; oratorically; oratorio; oratory

**ORB** oceanographic research buoy; omnidirectional radio beacon
**o.r.b.** [insurance] owner's risk of breakage
**ORBIS** orbiting radio beacon ionospheric satellite
**ORBIT** on-line retrieval of bibliographical information
**ORC** [USA] Officers' Reserve Corps; Overseas Research Council
**ORCA** Ocean Resources Conservation Association
**orch.** orchestra; orchestral; orchestrated (by); orchestration
**orchd** orchestrated (by)
**orchid** [informal] one recent child, heavily in debt
**ord.** ordain; ordained; order; ordinal; ordinance; ordinary; ordnance
**o.r.d.** [insurance] owner's risk of damage
**ordn.** ordnance
**ORE** occupational radiation exposure
**Ore.** Oregon
**Oreg.** Oregon
**ORELA** Oak Ridge Electron Linear Accelerator
**ORESCO** Overseas Research Council
**ORF** [genetics] open reading frame
**o.r.f.** [insurance] owner's risk of fire
**org.** organ; organic; organism; organist; organization; organize; organized; organizer
**.org** noncommercial organization (in Internet address)
**ORGALIME** *Organisme de liaison des industries métalliques européennes* (French: Liaison Group for the European Metal Industries)
**organ.** organic; organization
**orgst** organist
**orgzn** organization
**Ori** [astronomy] Orion
**orient.** oriental; orientalist
**orig.** origami; origin; original; originally; originate; originated
**ORIT** *Organización regional interamericana de trabajadores* (Spanish: Inter-American Regional Organization of Workers)
**Ork.** Orkney (Islands)
**Orkn.** Orkney (Islands)
**ORL** [medicine] otorhinolaryngology (= ear, nose and throat (ENT))
**o.r.l.** [insurance] owner's risk of leakage
**orn.** ornament; ornamental; ornithology
**ornith.** ornithological; ornithology
**ornithol.** ornithological; ornithology
**ORNL** Oak Ridge National Laboratory
**OROM** [computing] optical read-only memory
**ORP** off-road parking (in property advertisement)
**orph.** orphan; orphanage
**ORR** Office of the Rail Regulator
**o.r.r.** owner's risk rates
**ORS** [geology] Old Red Sandstone; Operational Research Society
**ors** others
**ORSL** Order of the Republic of Sierra Leone
**ORSORT** Oak Ridge School of Reactor Technology
**ORT** [medicine] oral rehydration therapy; [USA] Organization for Rehabilitation by Training
**ORTF** *Office de radiodiffusion-télévision française* (French: French Radio and Television Organization) (former state broadcasting service)
**Orth.** Orthodox
**orth.** orthographic(al); orthography; orthopaedic; orthopaedics
**ORuss** Old Russian
**ORV** off-road vehicle
**OS** [vehicle registration] Glasgow; [medicine] *oculus sinister* (Latin: left eye); Old Saxon; Old School; old series; Old Side; Old Style (in dates); [computing] operating system; Ordinary Seaman; Ordnance Survey; out of stock; outsize (clothing)
**Os** [chemical element] osmium
**o/s** on sale; out of service; out of stock; outsize (clothing); [banking] outstanding
**o.s.** ocean station; [medicine] *oculus sinister* (Latin: left eye); oil switch; old series; only son; on station; outside
**OSA** [USA] Office of the Secretary of the Army; Official Secrets Act; [printing] old style antique (type); Order of St Augustine (= Augustinians); *Ordinis Sancti Augustini* (Latin: of the Order of St Augustine); *Ordo Sancti Augustini* (Latin: Order of St Augustine, Augustinians); Overseas Sterling Area
**OSAF** [USA] Office of the Secretary of the Air Force

**OS&W** [building] oak, sunk and weathered
**OSax** Old Saxon
**OSB** Order of St Benedict (= Benedictines); *Ordinis Sancti Benedicti* (Latin: of the Order of St Benedict); *Ordo Sancti Benedicti* (Latin: Order of St Benedict, Benedictines)
**OSC** on-site cover; Order of St Clare (= Poor Clares)
**osc.** oscillator
**OScan** Old Scandinavian
**OScand** Old Scandinavian
**OSCAR** Orbital Satellites Carrying Amateur Radio; Organization for Sickle Cell Anaemia Research
**OSCE** Organization for Security and Cooperation in Europe (formerly CSCE)
**OSCH** off-peak (or overnight) storage central heating (in property advertisement)
**OSD** [USA] Office of the Secretary of Defense; Order of St Dominic (= Dominicans)
**OSE** operational support equipment
**OSerb** Old Serbian
**OSF** [computing] Open Software Federation; Order of St Francis (= Franciscans); *Ordinis Sancti Francisci* (Latin: of the Order of St Francis); *Ordo Sancti Francisci* (Latin: Order of St Francis, Franciscans)
**OSFC** Order of St Francis, Capuchin
**OSHA** [USA] Occupational Safety and Health Administration
**OSI** [USA] Office of Scientific Integrity; on-site inspection; [computing] open systems interconnection
**O/Sig** Ordinary Signalman
**OSJ** on a secret journey
**OSL** Old Style Latin
**OSl** Old Slavonic
**Osl.** Oslo
**OSlav** Old Slavonic
**OSM** Order of the Servants of Mary (= Servites)
**OSN** [USA] Office of the Secretary of the Navy
**OSNC** Orient Steam Navigation Company
**OSO** orbiting solar observatory
**OSP** off-street parking (in property advertisement)
**OSp** Old Spanish
**o.s.p.** *obiit sine prole* (Latin: died without issue)
**OSR** [USA] Office of Science and Research
**OSRB** Overseas Service Resettlement Bureau
**OSRD** [USA] Office of Scientific Research and Development
**OSRO** Office for Special Relief Operations
**OSS** Office for the Supervision of Solicitors; [USA] Office of Space Sciences (in NASA); [USA] Office of Strategic Services (in World War II)
**O.SS.S.** *Ordinis Sanctissimi Salvatoris* (Latin: of the Order of the Most Holy Saviour); *Ordo Sanctissimi Salvatoris* (Latin: Order of the Most Holy Saviour, Bridgettines)
**O.SS.T.** *Ordinis Sanctissimae Trinitatis Redemptionis Captivorum* (Latin: of the Order of the Most Holy Trinity for the Redemption of Captives); *Ordo Sanctissimae Trinitatis Redemptionis Captivorum* (Latin: Order of the Most Holy Trinity for the Redemption of Captives, Trinitarians)
**OST** [USA] Office of Science and Technology; ordinary spring tide
**osteo.** osteopath; osteopathic; osteopathy
**OSTI** [USA] Office of Scientific and Technical Information; [USA] Organization for Social and Technological Innovation
**OStJ** (Officer of the) Order of St John of Jerusalem
**OSU** Order of St Ursula (= Ursulines)
**OSUK** Ophthalmological Society of the United Kingdom
**OSV** ocean station vessel
**OSw** Old Swedish
**OT** occupational therapist; occupational therapy; off time; Old Testament; Old Teutonic; [medicine] operating theatre; [Australia] Overland Telegraph (from Adelaide to Darwin); overseas trade; overtime; [vehicle registration] Portsmouth
**OTA** Office of Technology Assessment
**OTAN** *Organisation du traité de l'Atlantique nord* (French: North Atlantic Treaty Organization, NATO)
**OTASE** *Organisation du traité de défense collective pour l'Asie du sud-est* (French: South-East Asia Treaty Organization, SEATO)
**OTB** [USA] off-track betting; oxide titanium bronze
**otbd** outboard

**OTC** [USA] officer in tactical command; Officers' Training Corps; Officers' Transit Camp; one-stop-inclusive tour charter; Organization for Trade Cooperation; over-the-counter (as in **OTC medicines**); [pharmacology] oxytetracycline (antibiotic)
**OTE** on-target earnings (in job advertisement); or the equivalent
**OTEC** ocean thermal-energy conversion
**OTeut** Old Teutonic
**OTF** [photography] off the film
**OTG** outside temperature gauge (in car advertisement)
**OTH** [telecommunications] over the horizon
**OTOH** on the other hand (in Internet chat and e-mail)
**otol.** otological; otology
**OTP** [computing] one-time programmable (EPROM)
**OTS** Office of Technical Services; Officers' Training School; [advertising] opportunities to see
**OTT** [medicine] oesophageal transit test; [informal] over the top
**Ott.** Ottawa
**ott.** [music] *ottava* (Italian: octave); *ottobre* (Italian: October)
**OTU** [biology] operational taxonomic unit; operation training unit
**OTurk** Old Turkish
**OU** [vehicle registration] Bristol; official use; Open University; Oxford University
**OUAC** Oxford University Appointments Committee; Oxford University Athletic Club
**OUAFC** Oxford University Association Football Club
**OUBC** Oxford University Boat Club
**OUCC** Oxford University Cricket Club
**OUDS** Oxford University Dramatic Society
**OUP** [Northern Ireland] Official Unionist Party; Oxford University Press
**OURC** Oxford University Rifle Club
**OURFC** Oxford University Rugby Football Club
**OURT** Order of the United Republic of Tanzania
**out.** outlet
**outbd** outboard
**OV** [vehicle registration] Birmingham
**Ov.** Ovid (Roman poet)
**ov.** ovary; over; overture
**ovbd** overboard
**o.v.c.** [law] other valuable consideration
**overlkg** overlooking (in property advertisement)
**ovfl.** overflow
**OVH** overhead projector
**ovhd** overhead
**ovld** overload
**OVNI** *objet volant non identifié* (French: unidentified flying object, UFO)
**o.v.n.o.** or very near offer (in advertisement)
**ÖVP** *Österreichische Volkspartei* (German: Austrian People's Party)
**ovpd** overpaid
**ovrd.** override
**OW** Office of Works; Old Welsh; old woman; [vehicle registration] Portsmouth
**O/W** oil in water (emulsion)
**o.w.** one way; out of wedlock
**OWC** Ordnance Weapons Command
**OWF** optimum working frequency
**OWI** [USA] Office of War Information (in World War II); [USA] operating (a motor vehicle) while intoxicated
**own.** owner
**OWRS** [USA] Office of Water Regulations and Standards
**OWS** ocean weather service; ocean weather ship; ocean weather station
**OX** [vehicle registration] Birmingham; [UK postcode] Oxford
**Ox.** Oxford
**Oxf.** Oxford(shire)
**Oxfam** Oxford Committee for Famine Relief
**Oxon.** Oxfordshire (from Latin *Oxonia*); *Oxoniensis* (Latin: of Oxford)
**OY** [civil aircraft marking] Denmark; [vehicle registration] northwest London
**oys.** oysters
**OZ** [vehicle registration] Belfast
**oz** ounce (from Italian *onza*)
**oz ap** apothecaries' ounce
**oz av** avoirdupois ounce
**oz avdp** avoirdupois ounce
**oz T** troy ounce

# P

**P** [civil aircraft marking] North Korea; [Roman Catholic Church] *Papa* (Latin: Pope); [genetics] parental generation; park; parking; parson; pass; passed; [US education] passing; pastor; *pater* (Latin: father); [chess] pawn; [music] pedal; pedestrian; pedestrian crossing; [horticulture] perennial; [ecclesiastical] *Père* (French: Father); [botany] perianth (in floral formula); period; [geology] Permian; personnel; peta- (indicates $10^{15}$, as in **Pm** = petametre); pharmacy (on non-prescription medicine); [currency] Philippine peso; [biochemistry] phosphate; [chemical element] phosphorus; [botany] phytochrome; pitch; [physics] poise; [computing] polynomial; [Roman Catholic Church] Pope; *populus* (Latin: people); port; [fishing port] Portsmouth; [international vehicle registration] Portugal; positive; post; postage; posterior; post office (on map); Presbyterian; President; priest; Prince; probate; pro-consul; [politics] Progressive; [theatre] prompt (side); proprietary (product); Protestant; public; [currency] pula (used in Botswana); pupil

***P*** [physics] dielectric polarization; [physics] parity; [physics] power; [physics] pressure; [genetics] promoter

**p** page; [currency] pence; [currency] penny; per; pico- (indicates $10^{-12}$, as in **ps** = picosecond); [physics] proton; [meteorology] shower

***p*** [physics] electric dipole moment; [physics] momentum (in vector equations); [chemistry] permanent dipole moment (of molecule); [music] *piano* (Italian: softly); [physics] pressure; [biochemistry] pyranose

**p.** page; pamphlet; paragraph; part; [grammar] participle; particle; *partim* (Latin: in part); pass; passed; [grammar] passive; [grammar] past; peak; pectoral (fin); per; *per* (Latin: by, for); perch (unit of measure for stone); [music] percussion; perennial; [grammar] person; [currency] peseta; [currency] peso; [currency] piastre; *pied* (French: foot); pint; pipe; *pius* (Latin: holy); plaster; polar; pole; *pondere* (Latin: by weight); population; port; positive; *post* (Latin: after); *pouce* (French: inch); *pour* (French: for, per); power; [grammar] present; *primus* (Latin: first); *pro* (Latin: for, in favour of); professional; [knitting] purl

**P2** [civil aircraft marking] Papua New Guinea

**P4** [civil aircraft marking] Aruba

**7P** [civil aircraft marking] Lesotho

**8P** [civil aircraft marking] Barbados

**PA** [vehicle registration] Guildford; [UK postcode] Paisley; Pakistan Army; [international vehicle registration] Panama; [chemistry] parent atom; Parents' Association; [insurance] particular average; Patients' Association; Pedestrians' Association; [US postcode] Pennsylvania; performance assessment; [medicine] pernicious anaemia; [insurance] personal accident; personal account; [taxation] personal allowance; personal appearance; personal assistant; [chemistry] phosphoric acid; photograph appreciated (in personal advertisement); [USA] physician assistant; Pierre Allain (brand of climbing boot); Piper Aircraft; [engineering] pitch angle; [medicine] plasminogen activator; political agent; *por autorización* (Spanish: by authority of); [astronomy] position angle; power amplifier; power of attorney; [Roman Catholic Church] Prefect Apostolic; press agent; Press Association; press attaché; private account; product analysis; programme assistant; [USA] prosecuting attorney; Protestant Alliance; [medicine] psoriatic arthritis; [USA] public accountant; public address (system); publicity agent; Publishers Association; [medicine] pulmonary artery; [engineering] pulsed annealing; purchasing agent

**P/A** [insurance] particular average; per-

sonal account; power of attorney; private account
**Pa** pascal (unit of pressure); Pennsylvania; [chemical element] protactinium
**p.A** *per Adresse* (German: care of, c/o) (in postal addresses)
**pa.** past
**.pa** Panama (in Internet address)
**p.a.** [grammar] participial adjective; *per annum* (Latin: yearly); permanent address; personal appearance
**PAA** Pan American Airways; [chemistry] peracetic acid; [chemistry] polyacrylic acid
**PAADC** Principal Air Aide-de-camp
**PABIAC** Paper and Board Industry Advisory Committee
**PABLA** problem analysis by logical approach
**PABX** [telecommunications] private automatic branch exchange
**PAC** [US air force] Pacific Air Command; Pan-African(ist) Congress; Pan-American Congress; [building] passive air cycle; Permanent Agricultural Committee (of ILO); [USA] political action committee; polymer–asphalt composite; [chemistry] powdered activated carbon; Public Accounts Committee; Public Assistance Committee; [stock exchange] put-and-call (option)
**P-A-C** [psychology] parent, adult, child
**Pac.** Pacific
**PACA** Public Art Commissions Agency
**PACAF** [US air force] Pacific Air Forces
**PACE** Parental Alliance for Choice in Education; performance and cost evaluation; Police and Criminal Evidence Act; precision analogue computing equipment; Protestant and Catholic Encounter
**Pacif.** Pacific
**PACOM** [USA] Pacific Command
**PACS** Pacific area communications system; [medicine] picture archiving and communication system
**PACT** Producers' Alliance for Cinema and Television
**PAD** [computing] packet assembler/disassembler; passive air defence; payable after death
**PaD** Pennsylvania Dutch
**pad.** padding; paddock; padlock
**PADAR** [military] passive detection and ranging
**PADLOC** [military] passive detection and location of countermeasures
**p. Adr.** *per Adresse* (German: care of, c/o) (in postal addresses)
**PADT** Public Art Development Trust
**p. ae.** [pharmacology] *partes aequales* (Latin: equal parts)
**paediat.** paediatrician; paediatrics
**PAF** [computing] peripheral address field; [medicine] platelet-activating factor; [Northern Ireland] Protestant Action Force
**p.a.f.** *puissance au frein* (French: brake horsepower)
**PAFC** phosphoric acid fuel cell
**PAg** Professional Agronomist
**PaG** Pennsylvania German
**PAGB** Poultry and Egg Producers' Association of Great Britain; Proprietary Association of Great Britain
**PAHO** Pan-American Health Organization
**PAI** [medicine] platelet accumulation index
**PAICV** *Partido Africano da Independencia de Cabo Verde* (Portuguese: African Party for the Independence of Cape Verde)
**PAIN** Parents Against Injustice
**paint.** painter; painting
**PAIS** [USA] Public Affairs Information Service
**PAISLEY** pants away if sexual liaison expected – yes! (on envelope of love letter)
**Pak.** Pakistan; Pakistani
**PakRs** [currency] Pakistan rupee
**PAL** [USA] Parcel Air Lift; [computing] peripheral availability list; [television] phase alternation line (European broadcasting system); Philippine Airlines; [USA] Police Athletic League; present atmospheric level; [computing, electronics] programmable array logic
**Pal** [geology] Palaeocene
**Pal.** Palace; Palestine; Palestinian
**pal.** palace; palaeography; palaeontology
**palaeob.** palaeobotanical; palaeobotany
**palaeobot.** palaeobotanical; palaeobotany
**palaeog.** palaeographic(al); palaeography
**palaeontol.** palaeontological; palaeontology

**PALS** [computing] permissive action link systems
**PAM** [telecommunications] pulse-amplitude modulation
**pam.** pamphlet
**PAMA** Pan-American Medical Association; Press Advertisement Managers' Association
**pamph.** pamphlet
**PAMR** Public Access Mobile Radio
**PAN** [Mexico] *Partido Acción Nacional* (Spanish: National Action Party); peroxyacetyl nitrate (pollutant of atmosphere); Pesticides Action Network; polyacrylonitrile (polymer)
**Pan.** Panama; Panamanian
**pan.** panchromatic; panoramic; pantomime; pantry
**PANA** Pan-African News Agency
**PANAFTEL** Pan-African Telecommunications Network
**Pan. Can.** Panama Canal
**P&E** plant and equipment
**P&F chart** point-and-figure chart
**P&G** Procter and Gamble
**P&L** profit and loss
**P&O** Peninsular and Oriental (shipping company)
**p&p** postage and packing
**P&RT** physical and recreational training
**P&S** [US stock exchange] purchase and sales
**PANN** Professional Association of Nursery Nurses
**PANS** procedures for air navigation services
**panto** [short form] pantomime
**PAO** [medicine] peak acid output; Prince Albert's Own (regiment); public affairs officer
**PAP** People's Action Party (in Singapore); *Polska Agencja Prasowa* (Polish news agency); [medicine] pulmonary arterial pressure
**Pap.** Papua; Papuan
**PAPS** periodic armaments planning system
**PAR** [military] perimeter acquisition radar; phased-array radar; [botany] photosynthetically active radiation; [computing] positive acknowledgment and retransmission; [aeronautics] precision approach radar; programme analysis review; [electronics] pulse acquisition radar
**Par.** Paraguay; Paraguayan
**par.** paragraph; parallax; parallel; paraphrase; parenthesis; parish; parochial
**p.a.r.** planed all round (in woodworking)
**Para.** Paraguay; Paraguayan
**para** [short form] paratrooper
**para.** parachute; paragraph
**parab.** parabola
**par. aff.** [pharmacology] *pars affecta* (Latin: to the affected part)
**Par. Ch.** parish church
**parch.** parchment
**paren.** parenthesis
**parens.** parentheses
**park.** parking
**Parl.** Parliament; Parliamentary
**parl.** parliament; parliamentary
**parl. agt** parliamentary agent
**parl. proc.** parliamentary procedure
**Parly Sec.** Parliamentary Secretary
**PARM** programme analysis for resource management
**part.** partial; participate; participation; [grammar] participial; [grammar] participle; particle; particular; partition; [grammar] partitive; partner; partnership
**part. aeq.** [pharmacology] *partes aequales* (Latin: in equal parts)
**PARU** [medicine] post-anaesthetic recovery unit
**PAS** public address system
**pas.** [grammar] passive
**p.a.s.** power-assisted steering (in car advertisement)
**PASCAL** *programme appliqué à la sélection et la compilation automatique de la littérature* (French: program applied to the selection and automatic compilation of literature)
**Pasok** *Panellenion Sozialistikon Kinema* (Greek: Panhellenic Socialist Movement)
**Pass.** Passover
**pass.** passage; passenger; *passim* (Latin: here and there throughout); [grammar] passive
**PASSIM** [USA] Presidential Advisory Staff on Scientific Management
**PAT** planned activities time; [banking] preauthorized automatic transfer; Professional Association of Teachers

**pat.** patent; patented; pattern
**p.a.t.** *poids atomique* (French: atomic weight)
**PATA** Pacific Air Travel Association
**Pata.** Patagonia; Patagonian
**patd** patented
**path.** pathological; pathology
**pathol.** pathological; pathology
**Pat. Off.** Patent Office
**pat. pend.** patent pending
**PAU** Pan American Union; programmes analysis unit
**Pav** [astronomy] Pavo
**pav.** pavilion
**PAW** plasma-arc welding; powered all the way
**PAWA** Pan American World Airways
**PAWC** Pan-African Workers' Congress
**PAWR** [USA] Public Authority for Water Resources
**PAX** [telecommunications] private automatic exchange
**p.a.x.** per annum, exclusive (in accommodation advertisement)
**PAYE** [taxation] pay as you earn; pay as you enter
**paymr** paymaster
**PAYP** pay as you play (at golf club)
**payt** payment
**PAYV** pay as you view
**PB** Bachelor of Philosophy (from Latin *Philosophiae Baccalaureus*); [vehicle registration] Guildford; passbook; permanent base; [athletics] personal best; *Pharmacopoeia Britannica* (Latin: British Pharmacopoeia); [pharmacology] phenobarbitone; plastic-bonded; Plymouth Brethren; pocket book; power brakes; Prayer Book; premium bond; Primitive Baptists; [USA] Publications Board; [knitting] purl into back of stitch
**Pb** [chemical element] lead (from Latin *plumbum*); [computing] petabyte
**p/b** purpose-built (in property advertisement); push-button
**p.b.** paperback (of books); [baseball] passed ball(s)
**PBA** [informal] poor bloody assistant; [USA] Professional Bowlers Association; [USA] Public Buildings Administration
**PBAB** please bring a bottle
**PBB** [chemistry] polybrominated biphenyl (constituent of plastics)
**PBC** powerboat club
**PBI** Peace Brigades International; [informal] poor bloody infantry; [medicine] protein-bound iodine
**pbk** paperback (of books)
**PBM** [surveying] permanent benchmark; play by mail (of games)
**PBMA** Plastic Bath Manufacturers' Association
**PBR** payment by results
**PBS** [medicine] phosphate-buffered saline; Public Broadcasting Service
**PBT** [accounting] pay-back time
**p.b.t.** [finance] profit before tax
**p.b.u.h.** peace be upon him
**PBX** [telecommunications] private branch exchange
**PC** [vehicle registration] Guildford; Panama Canal; [chemistry] paper chromatography; [chemistry] paraffin concentration; parish council; parish councillor; Parliamentary Commissioner (= ombudsman); *Partie Communiste* (French: Communist Party); Past Commander; Paymaster Captain; [Ireland] Peace Commissioner; [USA] Peace Corps; perpetual curate; personal computer; [military] pioneer corps; [engineering] pitch circle; *Plaid Cymru* (Welsh: Party of Wales); Police Constable; politically correct; political correctness; polo club; [chemistry] polycarbonate; polymer concrete; polyprop(yl)ene carbonate (plastic); Poor Clares (religious order); Portland cement; port of call; postcard; Post Commander; potentially correct; preparatory commission; Press Council; prestressed concrete; Prince Consort; [electronics] printed circuit; Prison Commission; Privy Council; Privy Counsellor; process control; [USA] professional corporation; [Canada] Progressive Conservative; [chemistry] prop(yl)ene carbonate; propositional calculus; public convenience (on map); pulverized coal; [microbiology] pure culture
**P/C** petty cash; photocopy; price(s) current
**pc** parsec (unit of astronomical distance)
**pc.** percentage; [printing] pica; piece; price
**p.c.** per cent; postcard; [medicine] *post*

*cibum* (Latin: after meals) (in prescriptions)

**PCA** Parliamentary Commissioner for Administration (= ombudsman); Parochial Clergy Association; [medicine] patient-controlled analgesia; Permanent Court of Arbitration; Police Complaints Authority; [statistics] principal component analysis; Professional Cycling Association

**PCAS** Polytechnics Central Admissions System (became part of UCAS)

**PC-AT** personal computer, advanced technologies

**PCB** petty cash book; [chemistry] polychlorinated biphenyl (constituent of plastics); [medicine] post-coital bleeding; [electronics] printed-circuit board; [insurance] private car benefits

**PCC** parochial church council; *Partido Comunista de Cuba* (Spanish: Communist Party of Cuba); political consultative committee; Press Complaints Commission; Privy Council cases; Professional Conduct Committee (disciplinary body of BMA)

**PCCS** Primate Captive Care Society

**PCD** [electronics] photo compact disc

**PC-DOS** [trademark, computing] Personal Computer Disk Operating System

**PCE** *Partido Comunista de España* (Spanish: Communist Party of Spain); Postgraduate Certificate of Education; [engineering] pyrometric cone equivalent

**pce** piece

**PCF** *Parti Communiste Français* (French: French Communist Party); pistol, centre fire (gun calibre)

**pcf** pounds per cubic foot

**PCFRE** Professional Council for Religious Education

**PCGC** pulverized coal gasification and combustion

**PCGG** Primary Care Group in Gynaecology

**PCGN** Permanent Committee on Geographical Names

**P Ch.** parish church

**PCI** *Partito Comunista Italiano* (Italian: Italian Communist Party) (former name of PDS); Pax Christi International; [computing] peripheral component interconnect; [computing] personal computer interface

**p.c.i.** pounds per cubic inch

**PCID** Pontifical Council for Inter-Religious Dialogue

**PCIFC** Permanent Commission of the International Fisheries Convention

**PCIJ** Permanent Court of International Justice

**PCIS** Period Cottage Improvement Society

**PCIUG** personal computer independent user group

**PCL** [computing] printer control language

**pcl** parcel

**PCM** photochemical machinery; [USA] plug-compatible manufacturer; polyatomic ceramic material; protein-calorie malnutrition; [telecommunications] pulse-code modulation

**pcm** per calendar month

**PCMA** Plastic Crate Manufacturers' Association; Potato Chip Manufacturers' Association

**PCMCIA** Personal Computer Memory Card International Association

**PCMI** photochromic microimage

**PCMO** Principal Colonial Medical Officer

**PCN** *Partido de Conciliación Nacional* (Spanish: National Conciliation Party) (in El Salvador); [computing] personal communications network

**PCOB** Permanent Central Opium Board (in UN)

**PCOD** [medicine] polycystic ovary disease

**PCP** Past Chief Patriarch; pentachlorophenol (wood preservative); [finance] permissible capital payment; [trademark, pharmacology] phencycl(ohexylpiper)idine (= angel dust, hallucinogenic drug); [medicine] *Pneumocystis carinii* pneumonia; polychloroprene (rubber); prime commercial paper

**PCPCU** Pontifical Council for Promoting Christian Unity

**PCPI** Parent Cooperative Preschools International; Permanent Committee on Patent Information (of WIPO)

**PCR** Pedestrian Crossings Regulations; [medicine] plasma clearance rate; politically correct retailing; [biochemistry] polymerase chain reaction

**PCRS** Poor Clergy Relief Society

**PCS** [electronics] plasma-current switch; [Scotland] Principal Clerk of Session
**pcs.** pieces; prices
**PCSP** Permanent Commission for the South Pacific
**PCT** [medicine] positron compute(rize)d tomography; product consistency test
**pct** per cent
**PCTCT** [accounting] profit chargeable to corporation tax
**PCTE** [computing] portable common tool environment
**PCTFE** polychlorotrifluoroeth(yl)ene (plastic coating)
**PCU** plant control unit; power control unit; power conversion unit; pressurization control unit
**p.c.u.** passenger car unit
**PCV** [medicine] packed cell volume; passenger-carrying vehicle; passenger-controlled vehicle; [USA] Peace Corps Volunteers; positive crankcase ventilation (in car); pressure containment vessel
**PCWPC** Permanent Committee of the World Petroleum Congress
**PCX** [computing] picture exchange format
**PC-XT** personal computer extended
**PCZ** Panama Canal Zone
**PCZST** Panama Canal Zone Standard Time
**PD** Doctor of Pharmacy (from Latin *Pharmaciae Doctor*); [vehicle registration] Guildford; [fishing port] Peterhead; *Pharmacopoeia Dublinensis* (Latin: Dublin Pharmacopoeia); polar distance; [USA] Police Department; port dues; *posdata* (Spanish: postscript, PS); postal district; preventive detainee; preventive detention; *Privatdozent* (German: unsalaried university teacher); probability of detection; production department; [Ireland] Progressive Democrat(s); progressive disease; [insurance] property damage; [USA] Public Defender; [computing] public domain (software)
**P/D** price–dividend (ratio)
**Pd** [chemical element] palladium
**pd** paid; passed
**p/d** postdated
**p.d.** *per diem* (Latin: daily); [engineering] pitch diameter; poop deck; postage due; postdated; [physics] potential difference; preliminary design; printer's devil
**PDA** [medicine] patent ductus arteriosus; [computing] personal digital assistant; *pour dire adieu* (French: to say goodbye); [navigation] predicted drift angle
**PDAD** Probate, Divorce and Admiralty Division (former High Court division)
**PdB** [USA] Bachelor of Pedagogy (from Latin *Pedagogiae Baccalaureus*)
**PDC** *Partido Demócrata Cristiano* (Spanish: Christian Democratic Party) (in El Salvador); personnel dispatch centre; personnel dispersal centre; Programme Delivery Control (for video recording); [engineering] pulse-discharge cleaning
**PDCI** *Parti Démocratique de la Côte d'Ivoire* (French: Democratic Party of Côte d'Ivoire)
**PDD** precise delay detonator
**PdD** [USA] Doctor of Pedagogy (from Latin *Pedagogiae Doctor*)
**PDE** [mathematics] partial differential equation; Projectile Development Establishment
**P-de-C** Pas-de-Calais (French department)
**P-de-D** Puy-de-Dôme (French department)
**PDF** [statistics] probability density function
**PDFLP** Popular Democratic Front for the Liberation of Palestine
**PDG** *Parti Démocratique de Guinée* (French: Democratic Party of Guinea); Paymaster Director-General; *président directeur général* (French: chairman and managing director)
**PDGF** [medicine] platelet-derived growth factor
**PDH** [computing] plesiochronous digital hierarchy
**PDI** [astronautics] powered descent initiation; product data interchange
**p.d.i.** predelivery inspection
**PDL** [computing] page definition language; [computing] page description language; poverty datum line; [computing] program design language
**pdl** poundal (unit of force)
**PDM** physical distribution management; [telecommunications] pulse-duration modulation
**PdM** [USA] Master of Pedagogy (from Latin *Pedagogiae Magister*)

**PDN** public data network
**pdn** production
**PDP** [computing] parallel distributed processing; program development plan (in NASA); programmed data processor (or processing)
**PDPA** People's Democratic Party of Afghanistan
**PDQ** [informal] pretty damn quick
**PDR** People's Democratic Republic; [astronomy] photodissociation region; [engineering] pitch-to-diameter ratio; precision depth recorder; price–dividend ratio
**PDRA** postdoctoral research assistant
**P/D ratio** price–dividend ratio
**PDRE** People's Democratic Republic of Ethiopia
**PDRY** People's Democratic Republic of Yemen
**PDS** Parkinson's Disease Society; *Partei Demokratischen Sozialismus* (German: Party of Democratic Socialism); *Partito Democratico della Sinistra* (Italian: Democratic Party of the Left) (formerly PCI); previously digested sludge; [computing] programming documentation standards
**PDSA** People's Dispensary for Sick Animals
**PDSR** Principal Director of Scientific Research
**PDT** Pacific Daylight Time; personal development technology; [medicine] photodynamic therapy
**PDTC** Professional Dancer's Training Course (Diploma)
**PDU** process-development unit
**PE** [vehicle registration] Guildford; peat extract; permissible error; [insurance] personal effects; [international vehicle registration] Peru; [UK postcode] Peterborough; [USA] petroleum engineer; *Pharmacopoeia Edinburgensis* (Latin: Edinburgh Pharmacopoeia); [computing] phase-encoded (tape format); physical education; plastic explosive; pocket edition; polyeth(yl)ene; [fishing port] Poole; Port Elizabeth (South Africa); [physics] potential energy; Presiding Elder; printer's error; [statistics] probable error; [computing] processing element; procurement executive; [USA] Professional Engineer; Protestant Episcopal; [medicine] pulmonary embolism
**P/E** part exchange (in advertisement); port of embarkation; price–earnings (ratio)
**.pe** Peru (in Internet address)
**p.e.** [law] personal estate; printer's error
**PEA** Physical Education Association of Great Britain and Northern Ireland
**PEAB** Professional Engineers' Appointments Bureau
**PEC** photoelectric cell; photoelectrochemical cell; Protestant Episcopal Church
**pec** [short form] pectoral (muscle)
**PECD** [electronics] photoelectric conversion device
**ped.** pedal; pedestal; pedestrian
**PedD** [USA] Doctor of Pedagogy (from Latin *Pedagogiae Doctor*)
**PEDir** Director of Physical Education
**Peeb.** Peebles(shire)
**PEEP** pilot's electronic eye-level presentation
**PEF** Palestine Exploration Fund; [US insurance] personal effects floater; [electronics] pulsed electric field
**PEFCO** Private Export Funding Corporation
**Peg** [astronomy] Pegasus
**PEI** [Canada] Prince Edward Island
**pej.** pejorative
**p.ej.** *por ejemplo* (Spanish: for example)
**Pek.** Peking
**PEL** permissible exposure level; permissible exposure limit
**Pembs** Pembrokeshire
**Pemex** *Petróleos Mexicanos* (Mexican oil company)
**PEN** International Association of Poets, Playwrights, Editors, Essayists and Novelists
**Pen** [geology] Pennsylvanian
**Pen.** Peninsula; Penitentiary
**pen.** penal; penetrate; penetration; peninsula; peninsular
**PEng** Member of the Society of Professional Engineers; [Canada] (Registered) Professional Engineer
**Penn.** Pennsylvania
**penol.** penology
**Pent.** [Bible] Pentateuch; Pentecost

**pent.** pentagon
**penthse** penthouse (in accommodation advertisement)
**PEO** [USA] Philanthropic Educational Organization
**PEP** [radio] peak envelope power; personal equity plan (savings scheme); political and economic planning
**PEPP** [USA] Professional Engineers in Private Practice
**PER** price–earnings ratio; Professional and Executive Recruitment; Professional Employment Register
**Per** [astronomy] Perseus
**Per.** Persia; Persian
**per.** percentile; period; person
**PERA** Production Engineering Research Association of Great Britain
**per an.** *per annum* (Latin: yearly)
**per ann.** *per annum* (Latin: yearly)
**P/E ratio** price–earnings ratio
**perc.** [music] percussion
**per con.** [book-keeping] *per contra* (Latin: on the other side)
**perd.** [music] *perdendosi* (Italian: dying away)
**perf.** perfect; perfection; perforate; perforated; perforation; performance; performed (by); performer
**perh.** perhaps
**peri.** perigee
**perig.** perigee
**perjy** perjury
**perk** [short form] percolate; [short form] perquisite
**PERL** [computing] practical extraction and report language; [medicine] pupils equal and react(ive) to light
**Perm** pre-embossed rigid magnetic technology
**perm** [short form] permanent wave; [short form] permutation
**perm.** permanent; permission
**PERME** Propellants, Explosives and Rocket Motor Establishment
**perp.** perpendicular; perpetual
**per pro.** *per procurationem* (Latin: through the agency of)
**Pers.** Persia; Persian
**pers.** person; personal; personally; perspective
**persp.** perspective
**PERT** [commerce] performance evaluation and review technique; [computing] program evaluation and review technique; programme evaluation and review technique; project evaluation and review technique
**pert.** pertaining
**Peruv.** Peruvian
**PES** [computing] programmable electronic system
**Pes.** [currency] peseta
**PESA** [medicine] percutaneous epididymal sperm aspiration
**PESC** Public Expenditure Survey Committee
**PESGB** Petroleum Exploration Society of Great Britain
**Pesh.** Peshawar (Pakistan)
**PEST** political, environmental, social and technological; Pressure for Economic and Social Toryism
**PET** polyeth(yl)ene terephthalate (packaging plastic); [medicine] positron emission tomography (as in **PET scanner**); [taxation] potentially exempt transfer; [medicine] pre-eclamptic toxaemia
**Pet.** [Bible] Peter; (Gaius) Petronius (Roman satirist)
**pet.** petrol; petroleum; petrological; petrologist; petrology
**PETA** People for Ethical Treatment of Animals
**Pet.E** [USA] petroleum engineer
**PETN** pentaerythritol tetranitrate (explosive)
**petn** petition
**PETP** [chemistry] polyeth(yl)ene terephthalate (polyester)
**petr.** petrification; petrify; petrology
**Petriburg.** *Petriburgensis* (Latin: (Bishop) of Peterborough)
**petro.** petrochemical
**petrochem.** petrochemical
**petrog.** petrography
**petrol.** petrological; petrology
**PETS** [computing] posting and enquiry terminal system
**P/Ex** part exchange (in advertisement)
**p.ex.** *par exemple* (French: for example, e.g.)
**PF** [vehicle registration] Guildford; Pagan Federation; panchromatic film; Patriotic Front; phenol–formaldehyde (as in **PF resin**); [building] plain face; power

factor; Procurator Fiscal; [finance] public funding; pulverized fuel

**Pf** [currency] Pfennig (hundredth of Deutschmark)

**pF** picofarad (unit of electrical capacitance)

**pf** [music] piano(forte); proof

***pf*** [music] *piano e forte* (Italian: softly and (then) loudly); [music] *più forte* (Italian: louder)

**pf.** perfect; [finance] preferred (stock)

**p.f.** pneumatic float; pro forma (invoice)

**PFA** Popular Flying Association; [USA] Private Fliers' Association; Professional Footballers' Association; pulverized fuel ash

**P factor** [psychology] preservation factor

**PFB** [building] preformed beam(s)

**PFBR** [nuclear technology] prototype fast breeder reactor

**PFC** polychlorinated fluorocarbon (synthetic resin); [US informal] poor foolish (or forlorn) civilian

**Pfc** [US military] Private first class

**pfce** performance

**PFD** personal flotation device; position fixing device

**Pfd** *Pfund* (German: pound)

**pfd** preferred

**pfd sp.** preferred spelling

**PFF** pathfinder force

**pfg** [currency] Pfennig (hundredth of Deutschmark)

**PFLO** Popular Front for the Liberation of Oman

**PFLP** Popular Front for the Liberation of Palestine

**PFLT** People's Front of Liberation Tigers (Sri Lankan separatist group)

**PFM** [telecommunications] pulse-frequency modulation

**PFMA** Pet Food Manufacturers Association

**PFP** Partnership for Peace (in NATO); personal financial planning; [South Africa] Progressive Federal Party

**PFPUT** Pension Fund Property Unit Trust

**PFR** [nuclear technology] prototype fast reactor

**PFRT** preliminary flight rating test

**PFSA** *pour faire ses adieux* (French: to say goodbye)

**PFSF** Parents for Safe Food

**PFT** [medicine] pulmonary function test

**PFV** *pour faire visite* (French: to make a call)

**pfx** [grammar] prefix

**PG** [vehicle registration] Guildford; [cinema] parental guidance (film classification); [Freemasonry] Past Grand; paying guest; postgraduate; Preacher-General; [US informal] pregnant; *prisonnier de guerre* (French: prisoner of war); Procurator-General; [pharmacology] prostaglandin

**Pg** [geology] Palaeocene

**Pg.** Portugal; Portuguese

**pg.** page

**.pg** Papua New Guinea (in Internet address)

**p.g.** pay group; paying guest; *persona grata* (Latin: acceptable person); proof gallon (of alcohol); proving ground

**PGA** [electronics] pin grid array; Power Generation Association; Prison Governors' Association; Professional Golfers' Association; [computing] programmable gate array; [biochemistry] pteroylglutamic acid (folic acid)

**p.g.c.** [navigation] per gyrocompass

**PGCE** Postgraduate Certificate of Education

**PGCert** Postgraduate Certificate

**PGD** [Freemasonry] Past Grand Deacon

**PGDip** Postgraduate Diploma

**PgDn** [computing] page down (key)

**PGDRS** psychogeriatric dependency rating scale

**PGF** [medicine] polypeptide growth factor

**PGG** Professional Gardeners' Guild

**PGJD** [Freemasonry] Past Grand Junior Deacon

**PGL** [medicine] persistent generalized lymphadenopathy (stage of Aids); [Freemasonry] Provincial Grand Lodge

**PGM** [Freemasonry] Past Grand Master; precision-guided missile (or munition)

**pgn** pigeon

**PGP** [computing] pretty good privacy

**PGR** [cinema] parental guidance recommended (film classification in Australia); population growth rate; [psychology] psychogalvanic response

**PGSD** [Freemasonry] Past Grand Senior Deacon

**p.g.t.** per gross ton

**PgUp** [computing] page up (key)
**PH** [vehicle registration] Guildford; [civil aircraft marking] Netherlands; [UK postcode] Perth; petroleum hydrocarbon; [fishing port] Plymouth; previous (medical) history; public health; public house (on map); [medicine] pulmonary hypertension; Purple Heart (US military decoration)
**Ph** [geology] Phanerozoic
**Ph.** Philosophy (in academic degrees)
**pH** [chemistry] potential of hydrogen ions (measure of acidity or alkalinity)
**ph** phot (unit of illumination)
**ph.** phase; philosopher; philosophy; phone
**.ph** Philippines (in Internet address)
**p.h.** [engineering] precipitation hardening
**PHA** [immunology] phytohaemagglutinin; Public Health Act; [USA] Public Housing Administration; [USA] public housing authority
**PHAB** Physically Handicapped and Able Bodied
**phal.** phalanx
**phar.** pharmaceutical; pharmacist; pharmacology; pharmacopoeia; pharmacy
**PharB** Bachelor of Pharmacy (from Latin *Pharmaciae Baccalaureus*)
**PharD** Doctor of Pharmacy (from Latin *Pharmaciae Doctor*)
**PharM** Master of Pharmacy (from Latin *Pharmaciae Magister*)
**pharm.** pharmaceutical; pharmacist; pharmacology; pharmacopoeia; pharmacy
**pharmacol.** pharmacological; pharmacology
**PharmB** Bachelor of Pharmacy (from Latin *Pharmaciae Baccalaureus*)
**pharm. chem.** pharmaceutical chemistry
**PharmD** Doctor of Pharmacy (from Latin *Pharmaciae Doctor*)
**PharmM** Master of Pharmacy (from Latin *Pharmaciae Magister*)
**PhB** Bachelor of Philosophy (from Latin *Philosophiae Baccalaureus*)
**ph. brz.** phosphor bronze
**PHC** pharmaceutical chemist; primary health care
**PHCA** Private Hire Car Association
**PHD** Doctor of Public Health
**PhD** Doctor of Philosophy (from Latin *Philosophiae Doctor*)
**PhDEd** Doctor of Philosophy in Education
**PHE** public health engineer
**Phe** [astronomy] Phoenix
**PhG** [USA] Graduate in Pharmacy
**PHI** permanent health insurance; public health inspector
**PHIBLANT** [US navy] Amphibious Forces, Atlantic
**PHIBPAC** [US navy] Amphibious Forces, Pacific
**PHIGS** [computing] programmers' hierarchical interactive graphics standard
**Phil.** Philadelphia; Philharmonic; [Bible] Philippians; Philippines
**phil.** philological; philology; philosopher; philosophical; philosophy
**Phila.** Philadelphia
**Philem.** [Bible] Philemon
**Phil. I** Philippine Islands
**Phil. Is.** Philippine Islands
**philol.** philological; philology
**philos.** philosopher; philosophical; philosophy
**Phil. Soc.** Philharmonic Society
***Phil. Trans.*** *Philosophical Transactions of the Royal Society of London*
**PhL** Licentiate in Philosophy (from Latin *Philosophiae Licentiatus*)
**PHLS** Public Health Laboratory Service
**PHLSB** Public Health Laboratory Service Board
**PhM** Master of Philosophy (from Latin *Philosophiae Magister*)
**PHN** public health nurse
**Phoen.** Phoenician; Phoenix
**phon.** phonetic; phonetically; phonetics; phonological; phonology
**phone** [short form] telephone
**phonet.** phonetic; phonetically; phonetics
**phonog.** phonography
**phonol.** phonological; phonology
**phot.** photograph; photographer; photographic; photography
**photog.** photograph; photographer; photographic; photography
**photom.** photometric(al); photometry
**php** pounds per horsepower; pump horsepower
**PHR** [engineering] power-to-heat ratio
**phr.** phrase; phraseology
**phren.** phrenological; phrenology

**phrenol.** phrenological; phrenology
**PHRG** Parliamentary Human Rights Group
**PHS** [USA] Public Health Service
**PHSA** Provincial Hospital Services Association
**PHTS** [USA] Psychiatric Home Treatment Service
**PHWR** [nuclear technology] pressurized heavy-water reactor
**phys.** physical; physically; physician; physicist; physics; physiological; physiology
**phys. ed.** physical education
**physio** [short form] physiotherapy
**physiog.** physiognomy; physiography
**physiol.** physiological; physiologist; physiology
**phys. sc.** physical science
**PI** [medicine] parainfluenza virus; Pasteur Institute; [mathematics] path integral; per inquiry; [US law] personal injury; petrol-injected; *Pharmacopoeia Internationalis* (Latin: International Pharmacopoeia); Philippine Islands; [civil aircraft marking] (Republic of the) Philippines; photographic interpretation; photographic interpreter; [US informal] pimp; [USA] principal investigator; Privacy International; private investigator; [accounting] profitability index; [computing] programmed instruction
**p.i.** [insurance] professional indemnity
**PIA** Pakistan International Airlines Corporation; [computing] peripheral interface adapter; Personal Investment Authority
**PIAC** Petroleum Industry Advisory Council
**piang.** [music] *piangendo* (Italian: plaintively)
**pianiss.** [music] *pianissimo* (Italian: very softly)
**piano** [short form] pianoforte
**PIARC** Permanent International Association of Road Congresses
**PIAT** [military] projector infantry antitank (weapon)
**PIB** Petroleum Information Bureau; Prices and Incomes Board (replaced by NBPI)
**PIBOR** [finance] Paris Inter-Bank Offered Rate
**PIBS** permanent interest-bearing share
**PIC** [computing] picture format; Poultry Industry Conference; [computing] problem isolation code; product of incomplete combustion; [computing] programmable interrupt controller
**Pic** [astronomy] Pictor
**pic** [short form] picture
**pic.** [music] piccolo; pictorial; picture
**PICC** Provisional International Computation Centre
**PICS** [computing] platform for Internet content selection
**pict.** pictorial; picture
**PICUTPC** Permanent and International Committee of Underground Town Planning and Construction
**PICV** Permanent International Commission of Viticulture
**PID** [medicine] pelvic inflammatory disease; [computing] personal identification device; [medicine] prolapsed intervertebral disc (= slipped disc)
**PIDE** *Polícia Internacional e de Defesa do Estado* (Portuguese: International Police for the Defence of the State) (former state security system)
**PIDS** [medicine] primary immune deficiency syndrome
**PIE** Proto-Indo-European
**PIF** [computing] program information file
**PIFA** Packaging and Industrial Films Association
**pigmt** pigment
**pigmtn** pigmentation
**PIH** Paintings in Hospitals; [medicine] pregnancy-induced hypertension
**PIK** payment in kind
**PIL** [computing] paper interchange language; payment in lieu; Pest Infestation Laboratory
**pil.** [medicine] *pilula* (Latin: pill) (in prescriptions)
**PILL** [computing] programmed instruction language learning
**PILOT** [computing] programmed inquiry, learning or teaching
**PIM** [computing] personal information manager; [telecommunications] pulse-interval modulation
**PIME** *Pontificium Institutum pro Missionibus Externis* (Latin: Pontifical Institute for Foreign Missions)
**PIMS** profit impact of market strategy

**PIN** personal identification number
**PINC** property income certificate
**P-in-C** Priest-in-Charge
**Pind.** Pindar (ancient Greek poet)
**PING** [computing] Packet Internet Groper
**PINS** [USA] person(s) in need of supervision
**pinx.** *pinxit* (Latin: (he/she) painted it)
**PIO** [computing] parallel input/output; photographic interpretation officer; [US military] public information office; [US military] public information officer
**PIPO** [computing] parallel in, parallel out
**pippy** [informal] person inheriting parent's property
**PIR** passive infrared
**PIRA** Paper Industries Research Association; Provisional Irish Republican Army
**PISO** [computing] parallel in, serial out
**PITB** Petroleum Industry Training Board
**PITCOM** Parliamentary Information Technology Committee
**PIX** [computing] picture exchange format
**pix** [short form] pictures
**pixel** [computing] picture element
**pizz.** [music] *pizzicato* (Italian: plucked)
**PJ** [vehicle registration] Guildford; [civil aircraft marking] Netherlands Antilles; petajoule; Presiding Judge; Probate Judge; [informal] pyjama(s)
**p.j.** physical jerks; [informal] pyjama(s)
**PK** [vehicle registration] Guildford; [civil aircraft marking] Indonesia and West Irian; [international vehicle registration] Pakistan; personal knowledge; psychokinesis
**pk** pack; park; peak; peck (unit of dry measure)
**pk.** package
**.pk** Pakistan (in Internet address)
**pkg** packing; parking
**pkg.** package
**pkge** package
**PKI** *Partai Komunis Indonésia* (Bahasa Indonesian: Indonesian Communist Party)
**PKP** *Polskie Koleje Państwowe* (Polish: Polish State Railways)
**pkt** packet; pocket
**PKTF** Printing and Kindred Trades Federation
**PKU** [medicine] phenylketonuria
**pkwy** [USA] parkway
**PL** [vehicle registration] Guildford; [insurance] partial loss; [insurance] passenger liability; patrol leader (in Scouts or Guides); Paymaster Lieutenant; [fishing port] Peel; *Pharmacopoeia Londiniensis* (Latin: Pharmacopoeia of London); [shipping] Plimsoll line; [UK postcode] Plymouth; Poet Laureate; [international vehicle registration] Poland; position line; Primrose League; [law] product liability; product licence (on medicinal product); programmed learning; [computing] programming language; public law; public library
**P/L** [insurance] partial loss; [law] product liability
**P-L** [astronomy] period–luminosity
**Pl.** Place (in road name); Plate(s) (book illustration); *Platz* (German: Square) (in road name)
**p/l** profit and loss
**pl.** place; plain; plate; platoon; [grammar] plural; pole (unit of length)
**.pl** Poland (in Internet address)
**PLA** [China] People's Liberation Army; Port of London Authority; Private Libraries Association; [computing, electronics] programmable logic array; [computing, electronics] programmed logic array
**Pla.** Plaza
**p.l.a.** passengers' luggage in advance
**PLAN** People's Liberation Army of Namibia
**plan.** planet; planetarium
**plas.** plaster; plastic
**plat.** plateau; platform; platinum; platonic; platoon
**platf.** platform
**PLATO** [computing] programmed logic for automatic teaching operation
**Plaut.** (Titus Maccius) Plautus (Roman dramatist)
**PLC** Poor Law Commissioners; [marketing] product life cycle; [computing] programmable logic controller; public limited company
**plc** public limited company
**PLCC** [computing] plastic leadless chip carrier
**PLCWTWU** Power Loom Carpet Weavers' and Textile Workers' Union
**plcy** policy
**PLD** potentially lethal damage; [computing] programmable logic device

**pld** payload
**Ple** [geology] Pleistocene
**pleb** [short form] plebeian
**Plen.** Plenipotentiary
**PLF** Palestine Liberation Front; [medicine] (serum) placental fementin
**plf** plaintiff
**plff** plaintiff
**PLG** private/light goods (vehicle)
**PLI** *Partito Liberale Italiano* (Italian: Italian Liberal Party); President of the Landscape Institute
**Pli** [geology] Pliocene
**PLJ** [trademark] pure lemon juice
**PLL** [computing] phase-locked loop
**PLM** Paris–Lyons–Mediterranean (railway); [telecommunications] pulse-length modulation
**PL/M** [computing] Programming Language for Microcomputers
**plmb.** plumber; plumbing
**plng** planning
**PLO** Palestine Liberation Organization
**PLP** Parliamentary Labour Party; Progressive Labour Party (in Bermuda); Progressive Liberal Party (in Bahamas)
**PLR** public lending right
**PLS** [statistics] partial least-squares; [computing] programmable logic sequencer
**Pls.** Plates (book illustrations)
**Pl. Sgt** Platoon Sergeant
**plsnt** pleasant
**PLSS** [astronautics] personal life-support system; [astronautics] portable life-support system
**plstc** plastic
**plstr** plasterer
**PLT** Princeton Large Torus (nuclear reactor)
**plt** pilot
**pltc.** political
**pltf** plaintiff
**PLU** [informal] people like us
**plu.** [grammar] plural
**PLUNA** *Primeras Lineas Uruguayas de Navegación Aérea* (Uruguayan airline company)
**plup.** [grammar] pluperfect
**plupf.** [grammar] pluperfect
**plur.** [grammar] plural; plurality
**Pluto** pipe line under the ocean (for fuel in World War II)
**Ply.** Plymouth
**plywd** plywood
**PL/Z** [computing] Programming Language Zilog
**PM** [vehicle registration] Guildford; Pacific mail; parachute mine; [music] particular metre; Past Master (of fraternity); Paymaster; [music] peculiar metre; [telecommunications] phase modulation; *piae memoriae* (Latin: of pious memory); Pipe Major; police magistrate; *polícia militar* (Portuguese: military police); *polizia militare* (Italian: military police); Pope and Martyr; Postmaster; *post meridiem* (Latin: after noon); postmortem (examination); powder metallurgy; predictive maintenance; preventive maintenance; Prime Minister; product manager; [music] proper metre; Provost Marshal
**Pm** [chemical element] promethium
**pm.** premium
**p.m.** permanent magnet; *post meridiem* (Latin: after noon); postmortem (examination); premolar (tooth)
**PMA** Pakistan Medical Association; [dentistry] papillary, marginal, attached (gingivitis); [pharmacology] paramethoxyamphetamine (hallucinogen); personal military assistant; [chemistry] phenylmercuric acetate; [chemistry] polymethyl acrylate; [USA] Purchasing Management Association
**PMAF** [USA] Pharmaceutical Manufacturers' Association Foundation
**PM&ATA** Paint Manufacturers' and Allied Trades Association
**PM&R** physical medicine and rehabilitation
**PMB** Potato Marketing Board
**PMBX** [telecommunications] private manual branch exchange
**PMC** Personnel Management Centre; [building] plaster-moulded cornice
**PMD** [USA] Program for Management Development
**PMDA** Pianoforte Manufacturers' and Distributors' Association
**PME** [electronics] protective multiple earthing
**PMF** probable maximum flood; [physics] pulsating magnetic field
**PMG** *Pall Mall Gazette*; Paymaster-General; [electrical engineering] permanent-magnet generator;

Postmaster-General; Provost Marshal-General
**PMH** previous medical history
**p.m.h.** per man-hour
**PMI** Pensions Management Institute
**pmk** postmark
**PML** Prime Minister's list; [insurance] probable maximum loss
**PMM** platinum-metal minerals; [telecommunications] pulse-mode multiplex
**PMMA** polymethylmethacrylate (synthetic resin)
**PMMS** Plainsong and Medieval Music Society
**PMN** [medicine] polymorphonuclear
**PMO** principal medical officer
**PMR** Pacific missile range; [medicine] polymyalgia rheumatica
**pmr** paymaster
**PMRAFNS** Princess Mary's Royal Air Force Nursing Service
**PMS** [printing] Pantone Matching System; [medicine] pregnant mare's serum; [medicine] premenstrual syndrome; President of the Miniature Society; [computing] processor-memory-switch (notation); project management system
**PMSG** [medicine] pregnant mare's serum gonadotrophin
**PMT** [photography] photomechanical transfer; [US finance] post-market trading; [medicine] premenstrual tension; project management team
**pmt** payment
**PMTS** [commerce] predetermined motion-time standards
**PMU** Pontifical Missionary Unit
**PMV** predicted mean vote
**PMX** [telecommunications] private manual exchange
**PN** [vehicle registration] Brighton; Pakistan Navy; [medicine] parenteral nutrition; [engineering] performance number; [astronomy] planetary nebula; [medicine] postnatal; [physics] post-Newtonian; [fishing port] Preston; [commerce] promissory note; [computing] pseudonoise; psychoneurotic
**P/N** part number; [commerce] promissory note
**p.n.** percussion note; percussive note; please note; [commerce] promissory note; [physics] proton number
**PNA** Pakistan National Alliance; paranitroaniline (dye); Philippines News Agency; Psychiatric Nurses Association
**Pna** Panama
**PNB** Philippine National Bank
**PNC** Palestinian National Council; People's National Congress (in Guyana)
**PND** [medicine] postnatal depression
**PNdB** perceived noise decibel
**pndg** pending
**PNEU** Parents' National Education Union
**pneu.** pneumatic
**pneum.** pneumatic
**PNG** Papua New Guinea; [international vehicle registration] Papua New Guinea
**p.n.g.** *persona non grata* (Latin: unacceptable person)
**PNI** [medicine] psychoneuroimmunology
**PNL** Pacific Northwest Laboratory
**pnl** panel
**PNLA** Palestine National Liberation Army
**PNLM** Palestine National Liberation Movement
**PNM** People's National Movement (in Trinidad and Tobago)
**PNO** principal nursing officer
**PNP** *Partido Nuevo Progresista* (Spanish: New Progressive Party) (in Puerto Rico); [Jamaica] People's National Party
**PnP** [computing] plug and play
**PNR** [physics] prompt nuclear reaction
**pnr** pioneer
**p.n.r.** prior notice required
**PNS** [anatomy] parasympathetic nervous system
**PNSB** [microbiology] purple nonsulphur bacteria
**Pnt.** [USA] Pentagon
**PNTO** principal naval transport officer
**pntr** painter
**PNV** *Partido Nacional Vasco* (Spanish: Basque National Party)
**pnxt** *pinxit* (Latin: (he/she) painted it)
**PNYA** Port of New York Authority
**Pnz.** Penzance
**PO** parcels office; parole officer; *par ordre* (French: by order); Passport Office; Patent Office; personnel officer; petty officer; philharmonic orchestra; pilot officer; [UK postcode] Portsmouth; [vehicle registration] Portsmouth; postal order; post office; power-operated; power oscillator; Province of Ontario;

public office; public officer; Pyrénées-Orientales (French department)
**Po** [chemical element] polonium
**p/o** printout
**p.o.** part of; [medicine] *per os* (Latin: by mouth) (in prescriptions); postal order; previous order(s)
**POA** price on application (in advertisement); primary optical area (in graphic design); Prison Officers' Association
**POAC** Post Office Advisory Council
**POB** Post Office Box
**PO Box** Post Office Box
**POC** port of call; [chemistry] product of combustion
**POD** payment on delivery; pay on death; pay on delivery; *Pocket Oxford Dictionary*; port of debarkation; [USA] Post Office Department
**POE** port of embarkation; port of entry
**POED** Post Office Engineering Department
**poet.** poetic(al); poetry
**POETS day** [slang] piss off early tomorrow's Saturday (facetious name for Friday)
**POEU** Post Office Engineering Union
**P of W** Prince of Wales
**POG** passion fruit, orange and guava (juice)
**POGO** Polar Orbiting Geophysical Observatory
**poi.** poison; poisonous
**POL** Patent Office Library; petrol(eum), oil and lubricants; [computing] problem-oriented language
**Pol.** Poland; Polish
**pol.** polar; polarize; polarized; police; political; politician; politics
**pol. ad.** political adviser
**pol. econ.** political economy
**pol. ind.** pollen index
**Polis** Parliamentary On-Line Information Service
**polit.** political; politics
**poll.** pollution
**pol. sci.** political science
**poly** [short form] polytechnic
**Poly.** Polynesia; Polynesian; Polytechnic
**Polyb.** Polybius (ancient Greek historian)
**Polyn.** Polynesia; Polynesian
**POM** particulate organic matter; prescription-only medicine (or medication)
**POMEF** Political Office Middle East Force
**PON** [computing] passive optical network
**PONI** product of Northern Ireland
**Ponsi** [military slang] person of no strategical importance
**pont. br.** pontoon bridge
**Ponti** [military slang] person of no tactical importance
**POO** Post Office order
**POOF** [computing] peripheral on-line oriented function
**POP** plaster of Paris; [computing] point of presence; point of purchase; Post Office preferred (size of stationery); [computing] post office protocol; [photography] printing-out paper; [pharmacology] progestogen-only pill; proof of purchase
**pop.** popular; popularly; population
**p.o.p.** point of purchase
**POPA** Property Owners Protection Association
**POPIN** Population Information Network
**POPL** [computing] principles of programming languages
**por.** porosity; porous; portion; portrait
**p.o.r.** pay(able) on receipt; pay(able) on return; port of refuge
**PORIS** Post Office Radio Interference Station
**porn** [short form] pornography
**Port.** Portugal; Portuguese
**port.** portable; portrait; portraiture
**POS** [grammar] part of speech; point of sale; [medicine] polycystic ovary syndrome; Port of Spain (Trinidad); [computing] product of sums
**pos.** position; positive; possession; [grammar] possessive
**POSAS** Patent Office Search and Advisory Service
**posn** position
**POSS** Palomar Observatory Sky Survey; passive optical surveillance system; prototype optical surveillance system
**poss.** possession; [grammar] possessive; possible; possibly
**POSSLQ** [US informal] person of the opposite sex sharing living quarters
**Possum** patient-operated selector mechanism (phonetic spelling of initials)
**POST** Parliamentary Office of Science and

Technology; point-of-sale terminal; [computing] power-on self test
**postgrad** [short form] postgraduate
**posth.** posthumous; posthumously
**posthum.** posthumous; posthumously
**pot.** potash; potassium; potential; potentiometer
**poul.** poultry
**POUM** *Partido Obrero de Unificación Marxista* (Spanish: Workers' Party of Marxist Unity)
**POUNC** Post Ofice Users' National Council
**POV** point of view
**p.o.v.** point of view; privately owned vehicle
**POW** please oblige with; Prince of Wales; prisoner of war
**POWAGOD** Prince of Wales' Advisory Group on Disability
**powd.** powder
**POY** [textiles] partially oriented yarn
**PP** [civil aircraft marking] Brazil; [vehicle registration] Luton; [geology] Pacific plate; parcel post; parish priest; parliamentary papers; *Partido Popular* (Spanish: Popular Party); *Pastor Pastorum* (Latin: Shepherd of the Shepherds); Past President; *Pater Patriae* (Latin: Father of his Country); *Patres* (Latin: Fathers); [medicine] pellagra-preventive; permanent pass; petrol point; [chemistry] phenolphthalein (alkalinity test); pilot plant; [chemistry] polyprop(yl)ene; [grammar] prepositional phrase; present pupil
***pp*** [music] *pianissimo* (Italian: very softly)
**pp.** pages
**p.p.** parcel post; [grammar] past participle; per person; *per procurationem* (Latin: through the agency of); planning permission (in property advertisement); play or pay; post(age) paid; [medicine] *post prandium* (Latin: after meals) (in prescriptions); prepaid; present position; privately printed
**PPA** Pakistan Press Association; *Parti Populaire Algérien* (French: Popular Party of Algeria); Periodical Publishers' Association; Pools Proprietors' Association; Pre-School Playgroups Association
**PPARC** Particle Physics and Astronomy Research Council
**PPB** paper, printing and binding; party political broadcast; planning-programming-budgeting (system); private posting box
**ppb** parts per billion
**PPBAS** planning-programming-budgeting-accounting system
**PPBS** planning-programming-budgeting system
**PPC** *Patres Conscripti* (Latin: Conscript Fathers) (members of Roman Senate); *pour prendre congé* (French: to take leave); Professional Purposes Committee; [medicine] progressive patient care; prospective parliamentary candidate; [USA] Public Power Corporation
**PPCLI** Princess Patricia's Canadian Light Infantry
**PPCS** [New Zealand] Primary Producers' Cooperation Society
**PPD** *Partido Popular Democrático* (Spanish: Popular Democratic Party) (in Puerto Rico); [medicine] purified protein derivative (of tuberculin)
**ppd** post(age) paid; prepaid
**PPE** personal protective equipment; philosophy, politics and economics (academic course)
**PPF** [US insurance] personal property floater
**PPFA** Planned Parenthood Federation of America
**PPG** Pacific proving grounds
**PPH** [USA] paid personal holidays; [medicine] postpartum haemorrhage
**pph.** pamphlet
**PPI** Pakistan Press International; [USA] patient package insert (instructions with prescribed medication); [radar] plan-position indicator; [insurance] policy proof of interest; [economics] producer price index
**p.p.i.** parcel post insured
**PPITB** Printing and Publishing Industry Training Board
**PPK** *Polizei Pistole Kriminal* (German: police criminal pistol)
**PPL** private pilot's licence
**pple** [grammar] participle
**PPLO** [microbiology] pleuropneumonia-like organism(s)
**PPM** [electronics] peak programme meter;

[telecommunications] pulse-position modulation

**ppm** pages per minute; parts per million

**PPMA** Produce Packaging and Marketing Association

**PPN** [computing] public packet network

**PPO** [US medicine] preferred-provider organization

**PPP** Pakistan People's Party; People's Progressive Party (in Gambia and Guyana); personal pension plan; [computing] point-to-point protocol; Private Patients Plan; psychology, philosophy and physiology (academic course); [economics] purchasing power parity

***ppp*** [music] *pianississimo* (Italian: as softly as possible)

**pppm** per person per month

**pppn** per person per night

**PPPS** *post post postscriptum* (Latin: third postscript)

**PPR** printed paper rate (of postage)

**ppr** paper; proper

**p.pr.** [grammar] participle present

**PPRA** Past President of the Royal Academy

**PPRBA** Past President of the Royal Society of British Artists

**PPRBS** Past President of the Royal Society of British Sculptors

**p.pro.** *per procurationem* (Latin: through the agency of)

**PPS** Parliamentary Private Secretary; [medicine] pelvic pain syndrome; *post postscriptum* (Latin: second postscript); [Australia] prescribed payments system; Principal Private Secretary; *Proceedings of the Prehistoric Society*; purchasing power standard

**PPT** *Parti Progressiste Tchadien* (French: Chad Progressive Party); [electrical engineering] peak power transfer

**ppt.** [chemistry] precipitate

**pptd** [chemistry] precipitated

**pptg** [chemistry] precipitating

**pptn** [chemistry] precipitation

**ppty** property

**PPU** Peace Pledge Union; Primary Producers' Union

**PQ** parliamentary question; [Canada] *Parti Québecois* (French: Quebec Party); personality quotient; Province of Quebec

**p.q.** preceding question; previous question

**PR** [vehicle registration] Bournemouth; parliamentary report; [medicine] partial remission; partial response; *Partido Radical* (Spanish: Radical Party) (in Chile); *Parti Républicain* (French: Republican Party); [computing] pattern recognition; payroll; percentile rank; performance ratio; [law] personal representative; photographic reconnaissance; Pipe Rolls (former public records); plotting and radar; *Populus Romanus* (Latin: the Roman people); postal regulations; preliminary report; Pre-Raphaelite; press release; press representative; [UK postcode] Preston; [boxing] prize ring; production rate; profit rate; progress report; project report; [politics] proportional representation; public relations; Puerto Rican; Puerto Rico; purchase request

**P/R** payroll

**Pr** [chemical element] praseodymium

**Pr.** *Praça* (Portuguese: Square) (in road name); Prince; Protestant; Provençal

**pr** painter; pair; paper; per; power

**pr.** prayer; [US finance] preferred (stock); [grammar] present; pressure; price; priest; print; printed; printer; printing; [grammar] pronoun; proof; proper; prove; provincial

**p.r.** parcel receipt; [medicine] *per rectum* (Latin: by the rectum) (in prescriptions)

**PRA** [medicine] plasma renin activity; President of the Royal Academy; probabilistic risk analysis; probabilistic risk assessment; [USA] Public Roads Administration

**prag.** pragmatic; pragmatism

**pram** [short form] perambulator

**PRB** People's Republic of Bulgaria; Pre-Raphaelite Brotherhood

**PRBS** President of the Royal Society of British Sculptors

**PRC** People's Republic of China; [medicine] plasma renin concentration; [USA] Postal Rate Commission; *post Romam conditam* (Latin: after the foundation of Rome); [USA] Price Regulation Committee

**PRCA** President of the Royal Cambrian Academy; Public Relations Consultants' Association

**prchst** parachutist
**PRCP** President of the Royal College of Physicians
**PRCS** President of the Royal College of Surgeons (of England)
**prcs** process
**prcst** precast
**PRE** petroleum refining engineer; President of the Royal Society of Painter Printmakers (formerly President of the Royal Society of Painter-Etchers and Engravers)
**Preb.** Prebend(ary)
**Prec.** Precentor
**prec.** preceding; precision
**PRECIS** preserved context index system
**pred.** [grammar] predicate; predicative; predicatively
**predic.** [grammar] predicate; predicative; predicatively
**Pref.** Prefect
**pref.** preface; prefatory; preferably; preference; preferred; [grammar] prefix
**prefab** [short form] prefabricated (building)
**prehist.** prehistoric(al); prehistory
**prej.** prejudice
**prel.** prelude
**Prela** *Prensa Latina* (Cuban news agency)
**prelim.** preliminary
**prem.** premature; premium
**premed** [short form] premedical (student); [short form] premedication
**prems** premises
**PrEng** [USA] Professional Engineer
**prep** [short form] preparation (for schoolwork); [short form] preparatory (school); [short form] prepare
**prep.** preparation; preparatory; [grammar] preposition
**prepd** prepared
**prepg** preparing
**prepn** preparation
**PREPP** Post-Registration Education and Practice Project (in nursing)
**Pres.** Presbyterian; President
**pres.** present; presentation; presidency; presidential; presumed; presumptive
**Presb.** Presbyterian
**press.** pressure
**PRESTO** [USA] program reporting and evaluation system for total operation
**presv.** preservation; preservative; preserve
**pret.** [grammar] preterite
**prev.** previous; previously
**PRF** Petroleum Research Fund; [electronics] pulse recurrence frequency; [electronics] pulse repetition frequency
**prf** proof
**prfnl** professional
**prfr** proofreader
**PRHA** President of the Royal Hibernian Academy
**PRI** [Mexico] *Partido Revolucionario Institucional* (Spanish: Institutional Revolutionary Party); *Partito Repubblicano Italiano* (Italian: Italian Republican Party); Penal Reform International; Plastics and Rubber Institute (became part of Institute of Materials); President of the Royal Institute of Painters in Water Colours; [computing] primary-rate ISDN
**pri.** primary; primate; primer; priority; private
**PRIA** President of the Royal Irish Academy
**PRIAS** President of the Royal Incorporation of Architects in Scotland
**PRIBA** President of the Royal Institute of British Architects
**PRII** Public Relations Institute of Ireland
**prim.** primary; primate; primer; primitive
**primip.** [obstetrics] primipara (woman who has given birth once)
**Prin.** Principal; Principality
**prin.** principal; principle
**Princ.** Principal; Principality
**princ.** principal; principle
**print.** printed; printer; printing
**PRISA** Public Relations Institute of South Africa
**PRISM** [USA] program reliability information system for management
**prism.** prismatic
**priv.** private; privative
**PRM** personal radiation monitor
**prm** premium
**PRML** [computing] partial-response maximum-likelihood
**prn** [medicine] *pro re nata* (Latin: when required) (in prescriptions)
**PRO** Public Record Office; public relations officer
**Pr. O** press officer
**Pro.** Provost

**pro** [short form] professional; [short form] prostitute
**pro.** procedure; proceed; procure; profession; professional; [finance] promissory (note)
**pro-am** [sports] professional–amateur
**prob.** probability; probable; probably; probate; probation; problem
**prob. off.** probation
**Proc.** Proceedings; Proctor
**proc.** procedure; proceedings; process; processed; processing
***Proc. Roy. Soc.*** *Proceedings of the Royal Society*
**prod.** produce; produced; producer; product; production
**Prof.** Professor
**prof.** profession; professional
**Prof. Eng.** [USA] Professional Engineer
**Pr. of Man.** [Bible] Prayer of Manasseh (book of Apocrypha)
**Prog.** [politics] Progressive
**prog** [short form] programme
**prog.** prognosis; [computing] program; programme; progress; progressive
**PROI** President of the Royal Institute of Oil Painters
**proj.** project; projectile; projection; projector
**prol.** prologue
**prole** [short form] proletarian
**PROLOG** programming in logic (computer programming language)
**PROM** [computing] programmable read-only memory
**prom** [short form] promenade
**prom.** prominent; promontory; promote; promoter; promotion
**pron.** [grammar] pronominal; [grammar] pronoun; pronounce; pronounceable; pronounced; pronouncement; pronouncing; pronunciation
**PRONED** Promotion of Non-Executive Directors
**pronunc.** pronunciation
**PROP** Preservation of the Rights of Prisoners
**prop** [short form] propeller; [short form] property (in theatre)
**prop.** proper; properly; property; proportion; proportional; proposition; proprietary; proprietor
**propl** proportional
**propn** proportion
**propr** proprietor
**props** [short form] properties (in theatre)
**PRORM** Pay and Records Office, Royal Marines
**PROS** preventive maintenance, repair and operational services
**pros.** prosecution; prosodical; prosody; [advertising] prospectus rate
**Pros. Atty** [USA] prosecuting attorney
**prosc.** proscenium
**prost.** [medicine] prostate; prostitution
**Prot.** Protectorate; Protestant
**pro tem.** *pro tempore* (Latin: for the time being)
**Prov.** Provençal; Provence; [Bible] Proverbs; Province; Provost
**prov.** proverb; proverbial; proverbially; province; provincial; provision; provisional
**Prov. GM** [Freemasonry] Provincial Grand Master
**prox.** *proximo* (Latin: in the next (month)) (used in formal correspondence)
**prox. acc.** *proxime accessit* (Latin: (he/she) came nearest (to the winner)) (referring to runner-up in competition)
**prox. luc.** *proxima luce* (Latin: on the day before)
**PRP** performance-related pay; petrol refilling point; profit-related pay
**pr.p.** [grammar] present participle
**pr. pr.** *praeter propter* (Latin: about, nearly)
**PRR** [electronics] pulse repetition rate
**PRS** Performing Right Society Limited; President of the Royal Society; Protestant Reformation Society
**PRs** [currency] Pakistan rupee
**prs** pairs
**PRSA** President of the Royal Scottish Academy; Public Relations Society of America
**prsd** pressed
**PRSE** President of the Royal Society of Edinburgh
**PRSH** President of the Royal Society of Health
**PRST** please return some time
**Pr.ST** [USA] Prairie Standard Time
**PRSW** President of the Royal Scottish Water Colour Society

**PRT** [USA] personal rapid transit; petroleum revenue tax
**PRTC** Princess Royal Trust for Carers
**prtg** printing
**PRU** photographic reconnaissance unit(s) (in RAF)
**PRUAA** President of the Royal Ulster Academy of Arts
**Prus.** Prussia; Prussian
**PRV** *pour rendre visite* (French: to return a call); pressure-reducing valve
**PRWA** President of the Royal West of England Academy
**PRWS** President of the Royal Watercolour Society
**PS** [vehicle registration] Aberdeen; paddle steamer; Parliamentary Secretary; *Partido Socialista* (Portuguese: Socialist Party); *Parti Socialiste* (French: Socialist Party); passenger steamer; Pastel Society; penal servitude; Permanent Secretary; [computing] personal system; Pharmaceutical Society; Philological Society; [linguistics] phrase structure; Physical Society; [electronics] plasma switch; Police Sergeant; [chemistry] polystyrene; postscript; power steering (in car advertisement); press secretary; private secretary; Privy Seal; [theatre] prompt side; [biochemistry] protein synthesis; Provost Sergeant; *Pubblica Sicurezza* (Italian: police); [USA] public school; [Australia] public service
**Ps.** Psalm; [Bible] Psalms
**ps** picosecond
**ps.** pieces; pseudonym
**p.s.** particle size; pull switch
**PSA** Passenger Shipping Association; Petty Sessions Area; Photographic Society of America; pleasant Sunday afternoon; Political Studies Association of the United Kingdom; President of the Society of Antiquaries; [Australia] Prices Surveillance Authority; probabilistic safety analysis; probabilistic safety assessment; Property Services Agency; [medicine] prostatic specific antigen; [New Zealand] Public Service Association; Public Services Authority
**PsA** [astronomy] Piscis Austrinus
**Psa.** Psalm; [Bible] Psalms
**PSAB** Public Schools Appointments Bureau
**PSAC** [USA] President's Science Advisory Committee; Production Statistics Advisory Committee
**PSAT** [USA] Preliminary Scholastic Aptitude Test
**PSB** pistol, small-bore; [Japan] Postal Savings Bureau; Prayer Book Society; Premium Savings Bond
**PSBA** Public School Bursars' Association
**PSBR** public sector borrowing requirement
**PSC** [Belgium] *Parti Social Chrétien* (French: Christian Social Party); Pipe Smokers' Council; [meteorology] polar stratospheric clouds; Professional Services Committee; [USA] Public Service Commission
**Psc** [astronomy] Pisces
**PSCD** patrol service central depot
**PSD** *Partido Social Democrata* (Portuguese: Social Democratic Party); *Parti Social Démocrate* (French: Social Democratic Party) (in Madagascar); pay supply depot; [law] Petty Sessional Division; [physics] position-sensitive detector; [USA] prevention of significant deterioration
**PSDI** *Partito Socialista Democratico Italiano* (Italian: Italian Democratic Socialist Party)
**PSDR** public sector debt requirement
**PSE** Pacific Stock Exchange; pale soft exudate (in meat processing); Pidgin Sign English; [computing] programming support environment; [computing] project support environment; psychological stress evaluator (lie detector)
**pseud.** pseudonym
**PSF** [image technology] point spread function
**psf** pounds per square foot
**PSG** [linguistics] phrase-structure grammar
**PSGB** Pharmaceutical Society of Great Britain
**PSHFA** Public Servants Housing Finance Association
**PSI** *Partito Socialista Italiano* (Italian: Italian Socialist Party); [education] personalized system of instruction; Pharmaceutical Society of Ireland; Policy Studies Institute
**psi** pounds per square inch
**psia** pounds per square inch, absolute

**psid** pounds per square inch, differential
**PSIF** Prison Service Industries and Farms
**psig** pounds per square inch, gauge
**PSIS** Permanent Secretaries Commission on the Intelligence Services
**PSIUP** *Partito Socialista Italiano di Unità Proletaria* (Italian: Italian Socialist Party of Proletarian Unity)
**PSK** [telecommunications] phase shift keying
**PSL** Paymaster Sublieutenant; [USA] Primary Standards Laboratory; [economics] private-sector liquidity; public-sector loan(s)
**PSL/PSA** [computing] problem statement language/problem statement analyser
**PSM** product sales manager
**PSMA** President of the Society of Marine Artists
**PSN** [computing] packet-switching network; [computing] packet switch node; [computing] public switched network
**PSNC** Pacific Steam Navigation Company
**PSO** Personal Staff Officer; principal scientific officer
**PSOE** *Partido Socialista Obrero Español* (Spanish: Spanish Workers Socialist Party)
**PSP** *Pacifistisch Socialistische Partij* (Dutch: Pacifist Socialist Party); [medicine] phenolsulphonphthalein (in kidney function test)
**PSPS** Paddle Steamer Preservation Society
**PSR** [commerce] profit-sharing ratio
**PSRAM** [computing] pseudo static random-access memory
**PSRO** [USA] Professional Standards Review Organization
**PSS** [computing] packet switching service; Palomar Sky Survey; Partially Sighted Society; [medicine] physiological saline solution; postscripts; power-system stabilizer; Printing and Stationery Service; professional services section
**Pss.** Psalms
**PSSC** Personal Social Services Council
**p.s.s.o.** [knitting] pass slipped stitch(es) over
**PST** [USA, Canada] Pacific Standard Time
**pstl** postal
**PSTN** [telecommunications] public switched telephone network
**PSU** *Partito Socialista Unitario* (Italian: Unitary Socialist Party); police support unit; [computing] power supply unit; process support unit
**p. surg.** plastic surgery
**PSV** public service vehicle
**PSW** [computing] processor status word; [computing] program status word; psychiatric social worker
**psych.** psychiatric; psychiatry; psychic(al); psychological; psychologist; psychology
**psychiat.** psychiatric; psychiatry
**psychoanal.** psychoanalysis; psychoanalytic(al)
**psychol.** psychological; psychologist; psychology
**PT** [civil aircraft marking] Brazil; [vehicle registration] Newcastle upon Tyne; [USA] Pacific Time; [USA] patrol torpedo (as in **PT boat**); [insurance] *perte totale* (French: total loss); [physics] perturbation theory; [physics] phase transition; physical therapist; physical therapy; physical training; physiotherapist; physiotherapy; [fishing port] Port Talbot; postal telegraph; post town; preferential treatment; [medicine] previously treated; Public Trustee; pupil teacher; purchase tax
**Pt** [chemical element] platinum; Point (in place-names); Port (in place-names)
**pt** part; patient; payment; pint; point; port
**pt.** [grammar] preterite
**.pt** Portugal (in Internet address)
**p.t.** part time; [grammar] past tense; point of turn(ing); primary target; *pro tempore* (Latin: for the time being)
**PTA** Parent–Teacher Association; Passenger Transport Authority; [medicine] percutaneous transluminal angioplasty; Pet Traders' Association; Piano Tuners' Association; [medicine] plasma thromboplastin antecedent; [medicine] post-traumatic amnesia; preferential trade area; Printing Trades Alliance; [medicine] prior to admission
**Pta** [currency] peseta; Pretoria
**ptbl.** portable; potable (= drinkable)
**PT boat** [USA] patrol torpedo boat
**PTBT** partial test-ban treaty
**PTC** [medicine] percutaneous transhepatic

cholangiography; personnel transfer capsule (in diving); photographic type composition; [medicine] plasma thromboplastin component; primary training centre; Public Services, Tax and Commerce Union
**Ptc** [geology] Pleistocene
**PTCA** [medicine] percutaneous transluminal coronary angioplasty
**PTD** permanent total disability
**ptd** painted; printed
**PTE** Passenger Transport Executive; post-test examination
**Pte** Plate (book illustration); [military] Private; [commerce] private (equivalent of Ltd after company name in India and elsewhere)
**pt ex.** part exchange (in advertisement)
**pt exch.** part exchange (in advertisement)
**PTFE** polytetrafluoroeth(yl)ene
**Ptg.** Portugal; Portuguese
**ptg** painting; printing
**PTH** [biochemistry] parathyroid hormone; [USA] public teaching hospital
**PTI** physical training instructor; Press Trust of India; [computing] public tool interface
**PTIA** Pet Trade and Industry Association
**PTM** [telecommunications] pulse-time modulation
**PTMA** phosphotungstomolybdic acid (used in pigments)
**PTN** [informal] pay through the nose; public telephone network; public transport(ation) network
**ptn** partition; portion
**ptnr** partner
**PTO** [USA] Patent and Trademark Office; please turn over; [astronautics] power take-off; public telecommunications operator; Public Trustee Office
**p.t.o.** please turn over
**ptp.** [grammar] past participle
**ptpg** participating
**pt/pt** [horseracing] point-to-point
**ptr** porter (in property advertisement); printer
**PTS** Philatelic Traders' Society; pressurized thermal shock; printing technical school
**Pts.** Portsmouth
**pts** parts; payments; pints; points; ports
**PTSD** [medicine] post-traumatic stress disorder
**pts/hr** parts per hour
**Ptsmth** Portsmouth
**PTT** [medicine] partial thromboplastin time; Postal, Telegraph and Telephone Administration; *Postes, télécommunications et télédiffusion* (French post office and telephone service)
**pt-tm** part-time
**PTU** Plumbing Trades Union
**PTUF** Professional Tennis Umpires' Federation
**PTV** [USA] public television
**p.t.w.** per thousand words
**Pty** [commerce] proprietary (equivalent of Ltd after company name in Australia, South Africa and elsewhere)
**pty** party
**PU** [vehicle registration] Chelmsford; [medicine] passed urine; [medicine] peptic ulcer; pick-up; [chemistry] polyurethane; [computing] processing unit; public utility
**Pu** [chemical element] plutonium
**p.u.** paid up
**pub** [short form] public house
**pub.** public; publican; publication; publicity; publish; published; publisher; publishing
**pubd** published
**pub. doc.** public document
**publ.** public; publican; publication; publicity; publish; published; publisher; publishing
**pubn** publication
**pubr** publisher
**pub. wks** public works
**PUC** papers under consideration; pick-up car; [USA] Public Utilities Commission
**PUD** pick-up and deliver; pick-up and delivery; [USA] planned unit development (large condominium)
**pud** [short form] pudding
**PUFA** polyunsaturated fatty acids
**pug.** pugilist
**PUHCA** [USA] Public Utility Holding Company Act
**pulv.** [pharmacology] *pulvis* (Latin: powder)
**p.u.m.s.** permanently unfit for military service
**pun.** punish; punishment

**punc.** punctuation
**punct.** punctuation
**Punj.** Punjab
**PUO** [medicine] pyrexia (fever) of unknown origin
**PUP** People's United Party; [USA] Princeton University Press; [Northern Ireland] Progressive Unionist Party
**Pup** [astronomy] Puppis
**pur.** purchase; purchased; purchaser; purification; purified; purify; purity; purple; pursuit
**purch.** purchase; purchased; purchaser
**purp.** purple
**PURV** powered underwater research vehicle
**PUS** Parliamentary Undersecretary; Permanent Undersecretary
**p.u.s.** permanently unfit for service
**PUVA** [medicine] psoralen ultraviolet A (used to treat psoriasis)
**PUWP** Polish United Workers' Party
**PV** [vehicle registration] Ipswich; patrol vessel; *petite vitesse* (French: low speed (train)); [sports] pole vault; positive vetting; [microbiology] potato virus; power voltage; pressure vessel; pressure–volume; profit–volume
**pv.** [microbiology] pathovar
**p.v.** [medicine] *per vaginam* (Latin: by the vagina) (in prescriptions)
**PVA** polyvinyl acetate (synthetic resin)
**PVC** [computing] permanent virtual circuit; polyvinyl chloride
**p.v.c.** pigment volume concentration (in paint)
**PVCu** polyvinyl chloride unplasticized
**PVD** [medicine] peripheral vascular disease; physical vapour deposition
**PVDA** *Partij van de Arbeid* (Dutch: Labour Party)
**PVF** polyvinyl fluoride (synthetic resin)
**PVFS** [medicine] postviral fatigue syndrome
**PVO** principal veterinary officer
**PVOA** Passenger Vehicle Operators' Association
**PVP** polyvinyl pyrrolidone (synthetic resin)
**PVR** premature voluntary retirement
**PVS** [medicine] persistent vegetative state; [USA] post-Vietnam syndrome; [medicine] postviral (fatigue) syndrome
**PVSM** [India] Param Vishisht Seva Medal
**PVT** pressure, volume, temperature
**Pvt.** [military] Private
**p.v.t.** *par voie télégraphique* (French: by telegraph)
**pvte** private
**PW** [vehicle registration] Norwich; [fishing port] Padstow; policewoman; power windows (in car advertisement); prisoner of war; public works; [electronics] pulse width
**p.w.** per week
**PWA** [medicine] person with Aids; [USA] Public Works Administration
**PWC** [USA] personal watercraft; postwar credits
**PWD** Public Works Department
**pwd** powered
**PWE** Political Welfare Executive
**PWG** Permanent Working Group (of European Junior Hospital Doctors)
**PWLB** Public Works Loan Board
**PWM** [telecommunications] pulse-width modulation
**PWO** Prince of Wales's Own (regiment)
**p.w.p.** price when perfect
**PWPS** Pure Water Preservation Society
**PWR** [nuclear technology] pressurized-water reactor
**pwr** power
**pwr sup.** power supply
**pwt** pennyweight
**PWV** Pretoria-Witwatersrand-Vereeniging (former name of Gauteng province)
**PX** part exchange (in advertisement); physical examination; please exchange; [vehicle registration] Portsmouth; [USA] Post Exchange (army or navy retail store); [telecommunications] private exchange
**pxt** *pinxit* (Latin: (he/she) painted it)
**PY** [vehicle registration] Middlesbrough; [international vehicle registration] Paraguay
**.py** Paraguay (in Internet address)
**PYB** [accounting] preceding-year basis
**PYO** pick your own (fresh produce)
**pyro.** pyrotechnics
**pyrotech.** pyrotechnical; pyrotechnics
**Pyx** [astronomy] Pyxis
**PZ** [vehicle registration] Belfast; [fishing port] Penzance; [civil aircraft marking] Suriname

**Pz** [geology] Palaeozoic
**PZI** [medicine] protamine zinc insulin (used to treat diabetes)
**PZS** President of the Zoological Society
**PZT** [astronomy] photographic zenith tube

# Q

**Q** [international vehicle registration] Qatar; quality; quantity; [nautical] quarantine; quarterly; Quartermaster; [advertising] quarter-page; Quarto (early Shakespearean text); [geology] Quaternary; Quebec; Queen('s); [chess] queen; Queensland; query; question; [currency] quetzal (used in Guatemala); queue; (Sir Arthur Thomas) Quiller-Couch (British writer)
***Q*** [electrical engineering] quality factor; [physics] quantity of electricity (i.e. electric charge); [physics] quantity of heat; [physics] quantity of light; [electrical engineering] reactive power; [chemical engineering] throughput
**q** [physics] quark; quintal (= 100 lb or 100 kg); [meteorology] squall
***q*** [physics] density of heat flow rate; [physics] electric charge
**q.** *quaere* (Latin: inquire); *quaque* (Latin: every); quart; quarter; quarterly; quarto; *quasi* (Latin: almost); queen; quench; query; question; quick; quire
**8Q** [civil aircraft marking] Maldives
**9Q** [civil aircraft marking] Democratic Republic of Congo (formerly Zaïre)
**QA** qualification approval; quality assurance; quarters allowance
**Q/A** qualification approval
**.qa** Qatar (in Internet address)
**q.a.** quick assembly
**QAB** Queen Anne's Bounty (in Church of England)
**QADS** quality-assurance data system
**QAIMNS** Queen Alexandra's Imperial Military Nursing Service
**QALY** quality-adjusted life year (used in assessment of treatment)
**QAM** [telecommunications] quadrature amplitude modulation
**Q&A** question and answer
**Qantas** Queensland and Northern Territory Aerial Service (Australian airline company)
**QARANC** Queen Alexandra's Royal Army Nursing Corps
**QARNNS** Queen Alexandra's Royal Naval Nursing Service
**QB** [USA, Canada] quarterback (in American and Canadian football); [law] Queen's Bench; [chess] queen's bishop
**Qbc** Quebec
**QBD** Queen's Bench Division
**QBE** [computing] query by example
**QBI** [informal] quite bloody impossible
**QBO** [meteorology] quasi-biennial oscillation
**Q-boat** query-boat (vessel of uncertain status, with concealed guns)
**QBP** [chess] queen's bishop's pawn
**QC** quality control; Quartermaster Corps; Queen's College; Queen's Consort; Queen's Counsel; [law] quit claim
**QCD** [physics] quantum chromodynamics
**QCE** quality-control engineering
**QCH** Queen Charlotte's Hospital
**QC Is.** Queen Charlotte Islands (Canada)
**qck** quick
**QCR** quality-control reliability
**QCT** quality-control technology; [medicine] quantitative compute(rize)d tomography
**QCVSA** Queen's Commendation for Valuable Service in the Air
**q.d.** [medicine] *quaque die* (Latin: every day) (in prescriptions); *quasi dicat* (Latin: as if one should say); *quasi dictum* (Latin: as if said); [medicine] *quater (in) die* (Latin: four times a day) (in prescriptions)
**QDRI** [USA] qualitative development requirement information
**q.d.s.** [medicine] *quater (in) die sumendus* (Latin: to be taken four times a day) (in prescriptions)
**QE** quantum electronics

**q.e.** *quod est* (Latin: which is)
**QE2** Queen Elizabeth II (passenger ship)
**QED** [physics] quantum electrodynamics; *quod erat demonstrandum* (Latin: which was to be proved)
**QEF** *quod erat faciendum* (Latin: which was to be done)
**QEH** Queen Elizabeth Hall (London)
**QEI** *quod erat inveniendum* (Latin: which was to be found out)
**QEO** Queen Elizabeth's Own (regiment)
**QER** *Quarterly Economic Review*
**QF** [electronics] quality factor; quick-firing
**QFA** [computing] quick file access
**QFD** [commerce] quality function deployment; [physics] quantum flavour-dynamics
**QFSM** Queen's Fire Service Medal
**QFT** [physics] quantum field theory
**QG** Quartermaster-General; *quartiere generale* (Italian: headquarters); *quartier-général* (French: headquarters)
**QGM** Queen's Gallantry Medal
**q.h.** [medicine] *quaque hora* (Latin: every hour) (in prescriptions)
**QHC** Queen's Honorary Chaplain
**QHDS** Queen's Honorary Dental Surgeon
**QHM** Queen's Harbour Master
**QHNS** Queen's Honorary Nursing Sister
**QHP** Queen's Honorary Physician
**QHS** Queen's Honorary Surgeon
**QI** quartz–iodine (as in **QI lamp**)
**QIC** [computing] Quarter Inch (Cartridge Standards) Committee; [computing] quarter inch cartridge
**q.i.d.** [medicine] *quater in die* (Latin: four times a day) (in prescriptions)
**QIP** *quiescat in pace* (Latin: may he/she rest in peace)
**QISAM** [computing] queued indexed sequential access method
**qk** quick
**QKt** [chess] queen's knight
**QKtP** [chess] queen's knight's pawn
**QL** Queen's Lancers; [computing] query language
**ql** quarrel; quintal (= 100 lb or 100 kg)
**q.l.** [medicine] *quantum libet* (Latin: as much as you please) (in prescriptions)
**Qld** Queensland
**QLF** [commerce] quality loss function
**q.lib.** [medicine] *quantum libet* (Latin: as much as you please) (in prescriptions)
**qlty** quality
**qly** quarterly
**QM** [physics] quantum mechanics; [physics] quark model; Quartermaster; Queen's Messenger
**qm.** *quomodo* (Latin: by what means)
**q.m.** [medicine] *quaque mane* (Latin: every morning) (in prescriptions)
**QMAAC** Queen Mary's Army Auxiliary Corps
**QMC** Quartermaster Corps; Queen Mary College (London) (became part of QMW)
**Q Mess.** Queen's Messenger
**QMG** Quartermaster-General
**QMGF** Quartermaster-General to the Forces
**QMR** qualitative material requirement
**Qmr** Quartermaster
**QMS** Quartermaster-Sergeant
**QMW** Queen Mary and Westfield College (London)
**QN** [chess] queen's knight
**Qn** Queen
**qn** question; quotation
**q.n.** [medicine] *quaque nocte* (Latin: every night) (in prescriptions)
**QNI** Queen's Nursing Institute
**QNP** [chess] queen's knight's pawn
**QNS** quantity not sufficient
**qnt** quintet
**qnty** quantity
**QO** qualified in ordnance (in Royal Navy); qualified officer
**QOCH** Queen's Own Cameron Highlanders
**QOOH** Queen's Own Oxfordshire Hussars
**QOR** qualitative operational requirement
**QP** qualification pay; [chess] queen's pawn; [computing] query processing
**q.p.** [medicine] *quantum placet* (Latin: as much as seems good) (in prescriptions)
**QPC** Qatar Petroleum Company
**q.pl.** [medicine] *quantum placet* (Latin: as much as seems good) (in prescriptions)
**QPM** Queen's Police Medal
**QPO** [astronomy] quasi-periodic oscillation
**QPR** Queen's Park Rangers (football club)
**QPS** Quaker Peace and Service
**Qq.** Quartos (early Shakespearian texts)
**qq.** questions

**qq.v.** *quae vide* (Latin: which (items) see) (multiple cross-reference)
**QR** [currency] Qatari riyal; *Quarterly Review*; [chess] queen's rook; [marketing] quick response
**qr** quarter
**qr.** quarterly; quire
**QRA** [military] quick reaction alert (of aircraft)
**QRIH** Queen's Royal Irish Hussars
**QRP** [chess] queen's rook's pawn
**QRR** Queen's Royal Rifles
**qrs** quarters
**QS** quadraphonic-stereophonic (audio equipment); quantity surveyor; quarantine station; quarter sessions; Queen's Scholar; [building] quick sweep
**q.s.** [medicine] *quantum sufficit* (Latin: as much as will suffice) (in prescriptions); quarter section (of land)
**QSAR** quantitative structure–activity relationship
**QSE** qualified scientist and engineer
**Q-ship** query-ship (vessel of uncertain status, with concealed guns)
**QSM** [New Zealand] Queen's Service Medal
**QSMR** quantitative structure–metabolism relationship
**QSO** [astronomy] quasi-stellar object; [New Zealand] Queen's Service Order
**QSS** [astronomy] quasi-stellar source
**QSTOL** [aeronautics] quiet short take-off and landing
**QSTS** quadruple screw turbine ship
**qt** quart; quartet
**qt.** quantity
**q.t.** [informal] quiet (as in **on the q.t.**)
**qtly** quarterly
**qto** quarto
**QTOL** [aeronautics] quiet take-off and landing
**qtr** quarter
**QTS** Qualified Teacher Status
**qty** quantity
**Qu.** Queen
**qu.** quart; quarter; quarterly; queen; query; question
**quad** [short form] quadrangle; [short form] quadraphonic; [short form] quadruplet
**quad.** quadrant; quadrilateral; quadruple; quadruplicate
**quadr.** quadruplicate
**quadrupl.** quadruplicate
**qual.** qualification; qualified; qualitative; quality
**qualgo** quasi-autonomous local government organization
**qualn** qualification
**quango** quasi-autonomous national government organization; quasi-autonomous nongovernmental organization
**quant.** quantitative; quantity
**quant. suff.** [medicine] *quantum sufficit* (Latin: as much as will suffice) (in prescriptions)
**quar.** quarter; quarterly
**quart.** quarter; quarterly
**quasar** [astronomy] quasi-stellar object
**quat.** quaternary; [medicine] *quattuor* (Latin: four) (in prescriptions)
**QUB** Queen's University, Belfast
**Que.** Quebec
**ques.** question
**questn.** questionnaire
**quin** [short form] quintuplet
**quint.** quintuplicate
**QUIP** [computing] query interactive processor
**quor.** quorum
**quot.** quotation; quoted
**quotid.** [medicine] *quotidie* (Latin: daily)
**q.v.** [medicine] *quantum vis* (Latin: as much as you wish) (in prescriptions); *quod vide* (Latin: which see) (cross-reference)
**QVR** Queen Victoria Rifles
**QWERTY** standard keyboard layout (from first six letters on upper row)
**QWL** quality of working life
**qy** quay; query
**qz** quartz

# R

**R** rabbi; [politics] Radical; [chemistry] radical (in formulae); radiology; radius; [USA] railroad; railway; [fishing port] Ramsgate; [currency] rand (used in South Africa); *rapido* (Italian: express train); [mathematics] ratio; [physics] Réaumur (temperature scale); *Recht* (German: law); [medicine] *recipe* (Latin: take) (in prescriptions); recommendation; rector; red; redactor; Regiment; *Regina* (Latin: Queen); registered; Regius (Professor); regular (clothing size); [navigation] relative; reliability; reply; report; Republic; Republican; reserve; [electrical engineering] resistance; [genetics] resistance; [chemistry] resonance effect; response (in liturgy); *Respublica* (Latin: Republic); [cinema] restricted (film classification in Australia and USA); *retarder* (French: slow down) (on clock or watch regulator); return (fare or ticket); reverse (in car); reward; *Rex* (Latin: King); [military] Rifles; right; river; road; roentgen (unit of electromagnetic radiation dose); Roman; Romania; Romanian; Rome; [chess] rook; rosary; [currency] rouble; route; Royal; *Rue* (French: Street); [sports] run(s); [currency] rupee; [theatre] stage right

® registered trademark

**r** [meteorology] rain; [music] ray (or re) (in tonic sol-fa); [biochemistry] ribonucleoside

***r*** internal resistance (in electricity); [mathematics, physics] position vector; radius; [mathematics] radius vector; [ecology] rate of increase

**r.** radius; [USA] railroad; railway; rain; range; rare; ratio; rear; [commerce] received; [medicine] *recipe* (Latin: take) (in prescriptions); [printing] recto (right-hand page); red; replacing; reply; reserve; residence; resides; response; retired; right; rises (referring to the sun); river; road; rod (unit of length); [currency] rouble; [card games] rubber; ruled; [sports] run(s); [currency] rupee

**4R** [civil aircraft marking] Sri Lanka

**5R** [civil aircraft marking] Madagascar

**8R** [civil aircraft marking] Guyana

**RA** [international vehicle registration] (Republic of ) Argentina; [vehicle registration] Nottingham; Racecourse Association; [meteorology] rain; Ramblers' Association; Rear-Admiral; reduction of area; Referees' Association (in football); [USA] Regular Army; *República Argentina* (Spanish: Argentine Republic); [USA] Resettlement Administration; [medicine] rheumatoid arthritis; [astronomy] right ascension; [medicine] right atrium; Road Association; Royal Academician; Royal Academy; Royal Artillery; Rural Action; [civil aircraft marking] Russia

**R/A** [finance] refer to acceptor (on bill of exchange); return to author

**Ra** [chemical element] radium

**ra.** radio

**RAA** Rabbinical Alliance of America; Regional Arts Association; Royal Academy of Arts; Royal Artillery Association; Royal Australian Artillery

**RAAF** Royal Australian Air Force; Royal Auxiliary Air Force

**RAAFNS** Royal Australian Air Force Nursing Service

**RAAMC** Royal Australian Army Medical Corps

**RAANC** Royal Australian Army Nursing Corps

**Rab.** Rabat (Morocco)

**Rabb.** Rabbinate; Rabbinic(al)

**RABDF** Royal Association of British Dairy Farmers

**RABI** Royal Agricultural Benevolent Institution

**RAC** Railway Association of Canada; Regional Advisory Committee (of TUC); Regional Advisory Council; Royal Aero Club (of the United Kingdom); Royal Agricultural College; Royal Armoured Corps; Royal Automobile Club

**RACA** Royal Automobile Club of Australia

**RACE** rapid automatic checkout equipment; Research and Development in

Advanced Communication Technologies for Europe

**RACGP** Royal Australian College of General Practitioners

**RAChD** Royal Army Chaplains' Department

**RACI** Royal Australian Chemical Institute

**RACO** Royal Australian College of Ophthalmologists

**RACOG** Royal Australian College of Obstetricians and Gynaecologists

**RACP** Royal Australasian College of Physicians

**RACS** Royal Arsenal Cooperative Society; Royal Australasian College of Surgeons

**RAD** radiation absorbed dose; [medicine] reflex anal dilation; Royal Academy of Dancing; Royal Albert Docks

**Rad.** [politics] Radical; Radnor(shire)

**rad** radian (unit of angle)

**rad.** radar; radiator; radical; radio; radiologist; radiology; radiotherapist; radiotherapy; radius; [mathematics, anatomy] radix

**r.a.d.** rapid automatic drill

**RADA** Royal Academy of Dramatic Art

**RADAR** Royal Association for Disability and Rehabilitation

**radar** radio detection and ranging

**RADAS** random access discrete address system

**RADC** Royal Army Dental Corps

**RADCM** radar countermeasure

**raddol.** [music] *raddolcendo* (Italian: becoming calmer)

**RAdm** Rear-Admiral

**radmon** radiological monitor(ing)

**radn** radiation

**RAE** Royal Aerospace Establishment (formerly Royal Aircraft Establishment); Royal Australian Engineers

**r.a.e.** radio astronomy explorer

**RAEC** Royal Army Educational Corps

**RAeroC** Royal Aero Club (of the United Kingdom)

**RAeS** Royal Aeronautical Society

**RAF** *Rote Armee Faktion* (German: Red Army Faction) (terrorist group); Royal Aircraft Factory; Royal Air Force

**RAFA** Royal Air Forces Association; Royal Australian Field Artillery

**RAFBF** Royal Air Force Benevolent Fund

**RAFES** Royal Air Force Educational Service

**RAFG** Royal Air Force Germany

**RAFMS** Royal Air Force Medical Services

**RAFR** Royal Air Force Regiment

**RAFRO** Royal Air Force Reserve of Officers

**RAFSAA** Royal Air Force Small Arms Association

**RAFSC** Royal Air Force Staff College; Royal Air Force Strike Command

**RAFT** [banking] revolving acceptance facility by transfer

**RAFTC** Royal Air Force Transport Command

**RAFVR** Royal Air Force Volunteer Reserve

**r.a.g.** river assault group

**RAGA** Royal Australian Garrison Artillery

**RAH** Royal Albert Hall

**RAHS** Royal Australian Historical Society

**RAI** *Radiotelevisione Italiana* (Italian broadcasting company, formerly *Radio Audizioni Italiane*); Royal Anthropological Institute; Royal Archaeological Institute

**RAIA** Royal Australian Institute of Architects

**RAIC** Royal Architectural Institute of Canada

**RAID** [computing] redundant array of independent (or inexpensive) disks

**Raj.** Rajasthan

**RAJAR** Radio Joint Audience Research

**RAK** random act of kindness

**RAL** Rutherford Appleton Laboratory (Harwell, Oxfordshire)

**rall.** [music] *rallentando* (Italian: slowing down)

**RALS** [aeronautics] remote augmented lift system

**RAM** [aeronautics] radar absorbing material; [computing] random-access memory; [USA] reverse-annuity mortgage; rocket-assisted motor; Royal Academy of Music; Royal Air Maroc (Moroccan airline company); [Freemasonry] Royal Arch Masons

**r.a.m.** relative atomic mass

**RAMAC** Radio Marine Associated Companies

**ramb.** rambler (rose)

**RAMC** Royal Army Medical Corps

**RAN** request for authority to negotiate; Royal Australian Navy

**RANC** Royal Australian Naval College

**RANCOM** random communication satellite
**R&A** Royal and Ancient (Golf Club) (St Andrews)
**R&B** rhythm and blues; ring and ball (game)
**R&CC** [insurance] riot and civil commotion
**R&D** research and development
**R&E** research and engineering
**R&I** *Regina et Imperatrix* (Latin: Queen and Empress); *Rex et Imperator* (Latin: King and Emperor)
**R&M** reliability and marketing
**r&m** reports and memoranda
**R&R** [medicine] rescue and resuscitation; rest and recreation; rock and roll
**R&T** research and technology
**RANN** [USA] Research Applied to National Needs
**RANR** Royal Australian Naval Reserve
**RANVR** Royal Australian Naval Volunteer Reserve
**RAOB** Royal Antediluvian Order of Buffaloes
**RAOC** Royal Army Ordnance Corps
**RAOU** Royal Australian Ornithologists' Union
**RAP** ready-assembled price; Regimental Aid Post; remedial action plan (or programme); [medicine] right atrial pressure
**rap.** rapid
**RAPC** Royal Army Pay Corps
**RAPID** Register for the Ascertainment and Prevention of Inherited Diseases
**RAPRA** Rubber and Plastics Research Association of Great Britain
**RAR** Royal Australian Regiment
**RARDE** Royal Armament Research and Development Establishment
**RARE** [computing] *Réseaux associés pour la recherche européenne* (French: Associated Networks for European Research)
**RARO** Regular Army Reserve of Officers
**RAS** [aeronautics] rectified air speed; Royal Agricultural Society; Royal Asiatic Society; Royal Astronomical Society
**RASC** Royal Army Service Corps (former name of RCT)
**RASE** Royal Agricultural Society of England
**raser** radio-frequency amplification by stimulated emission of radiation
**RAT** rocket-assisted torpedo
**rat.** rateable; rating; ration
**RATAN** radar and television aid to navigation
**RATO** rocket-assisted take-off
**RATP** *Régie autonome des transports parisiens* (French: Paris transport authority)
**RAuxAF** Royal Auxiliary Air Force
**RAVC** Royal Army Veterinary Corps
**RAWC** Radioactive Waste Coordinating Committee
**RAX** [telecommunications] rural automatic exchange
**RB** [international vehicle registration] (Republic of) Botswana; [vehicle registration] Nottingham; [astronomy] radiation belt; radiation burn; reconnaissance bomber (aircraft); representative body; *República Boliviana* (Spanish: Republic of Bolivia); review body; Rifle Brigade; *Ritzaus Bureau* (Danish news agency); Royal Ballet (formerly SWRB)
**Rb** [chemical element] rubidium
**r.b.** [sports] right back; rubber band
**RBA** Retail Book, Stationery and Allied Trades Employees Association; Royal Society of British Artists
**RBAF** Royal Belgian Air Force
**RBC** [medicine] red blood cell; [medicine] red blood (cell) count; Royal British Colonial Society of Artists
**RBE** relative biological effectiveness (of radiation)
**r/belt** rear seat belt (in car advertisement)
**RBerks** Royal Berkshire Regiment
**RBG** Royal Botanic Gardens (Kew)
**RBI** resource-based industry; right back inside (of skate); [baseball] run(s) batted in
**r.b.i.** require better information; [baseball] run(s) batted in
**RBK&C** Royal Borough of Kensington and Chelsea
**RBL** Royal British Legion
**rbl.** [currency] rouble
**RBN** Registry of Business Names
**RBn** radio beacon
**RBNA** Royal British Nurses' Association
**RBO** right back outside (of skate)
**RBP** [biochemistry] retinol-binding protein

**RBS** [medicine] radionuclide bone scintigraphy; Rare Breeds Society; Royal Botanical Society; Royal Society of British Sculptors
**RBSA** Royal Birmingham Society of Artists
**RBT** random breath-testing; [computing] remote batch terminal
**rbt** roundabout
**RBY** Royal Bucks Yeomanry
**RC** [vehicle registration] Nottingham; [cycling] racing club; radio/cassette (player); [medicine] red (blood) cell; [medicine] red corpuscle; Red Cross; Reformed Church; reinforced concrete; remote control; reproductive capacity; [USA] Republican Convention; research centre; reserve corps; [photography] resin-coated; [electronics] resistance-capacitance; [electronics] resistor-capacitor; [telecommunications] reversed charge; rifle club; [cycling] road club; Roman Catholic; [building] rough cutting; Royal College; Royal Commission; [international vehicle registration] Taiwan (Republic of China)
**R/C** recredited
**r.c.** radio code; radio coding; reinforced concrete; release clause; reverse course; right centre; rotary combustion; rubber-cushioned
**RCA** [international vehicle registration] Central African Republic (from French *République Centrafricaine*); Rabbinical Council of America; Racecourse Association; Radio Corporation of America; [medicine] right coronary artery; Royal Cambrian Academy; Royal Canadian Academy of Arts; Royal College of Art; Royal Company of Archers; Rural Crafts Association
**RCAC** Royal Canadian Armoured Corps
**RCAF** Royal Canadian Air Force
**RCamA** Royal Cambrian Academy
**RCAMC** Royal Canadian Army Medical Corps
**RCASC** Royal Canadian Army Service Corps
**RCB** [international vehicle registration] (Republic of) Congo (from former name Congo-Brazzaville); [theatre] right centre back (of stage)
**RCC** recovery control centre; [medicine] renal cell carcinoma; rescue coordination centre; Roman Catholic Chaplain; Roman Catholic Church; Rural Community Council
**RCCh** Roman Catholic Church
**RCD** *Rassemblement Constitutionnel Démocratique* (French: Democratic Constitutional Rally) (Tunisian political party); Regional Cooperation for Development (association of Asian countries); [electronics] residual current device
**rcd** received
**RCDC** Royal Canadian Dental Corps
**RCDS** Royal College of Defence Studies
**RCE** [engineering] rotary combustion engine
**RCF** Redundant Churches Fund
**r.c.f.** relative centrifugal force
**RCFCA** Royal Canadian Flying Clubs' Association
**RCGA** Royal Canadian Golf Association
**RCGP** Royal College of General Practitioners
**RCGS** Royal Canadian Geographical Society
**RCH** [international vehicle registration] (Republic of) Chile; railway clearing house
**RCHA** Royal Canadian Horse Artillery
**RCHM** Royal Commission on Historical Manuscripts; Royal Commission on Historical Monuments
**RCI** Radiochemical Inspectorate; Royal Canadian Institute
**r.c.i.** radar coverage indicator
**RCJ** Royal Courts of Justice
**RCL** Royal Canadian Legion; ruling case law
**RCM** radar countermeasures; radio countermeasures; [medicine] radiological contrast medium; regimental court martial; Royal College of Midwives; Royal College of Music
**RCMP** Royal Canadian Mounted Police (formerly RNWMP)
**RCN** Royal Canadian Navy; Royal College of Nursing
**RCNC** Royal Corps of Naval Constructors
**RCNR** Royal Canadian Naval Reserve
**RCNT** Registered Clinical Nurse Teacher
**RCNVR** Royal Canadian Naval Volunteer Reserve
**RCO** Royal College of Organists

**RCOG** Royal College of Obstetricians and Gynaecologists
**RCP** Revolutionary Communist Party; Royal College of Physicians; Royal College of Preceptors
**RCPath** Royal College of Pathologists
**RCPB** Revolutionary Communist Party of Great Britain
**RCPE** Royal College of Physicians of Edinburgh
**RCPEd** Royal College of Physicians of Edinburgh
**RCPI** Royal College of Physicians of Ireland
**RCPSG** Royal College of Physicians and Surgeons of Glasgow
**RCPsych** Royal College of Psychiatrists
**rcpt** receipt
**RCR** Royal College of Radiologists
**RCRP** Rape Counselling and Research Project
**RCS** reaction control system (in spacecraft); [nuclear technology] reactor cooling system; remote control system; Royal Choral Society; Royal College of Science; Royal College of Surgeons (of England); Royal Commonwealth Society; Royal Corps of Signals; Royal Counties Show
**RCSB** Royal Commonwealth Society for the Blind
**RCSC** Radio Components Standardization Committee
**RCSE** Royal College of Surgeons of Edinburgh
**RCSEd** Royal College of Surgeons of Edinburgh
**RCSI** Royal College of Surgeons in Ireland
**RCSLT** Royal College of Speech and Language Therapists
**RCSS** random communications satellite system
**RCT** randomized clinical trial; regimental combat team; Registered Clinical Teacher; remote control transmitter; Royal Corps of Transport (formerly RASC)
**rct** receipt; recruit
**RCU** remote control unit; road-construction unit; rocket-countermeasure unit
**rcvr** receiver
**RCVS** Royal College of Veterinary Surgeons
**RD** radiation dose; [metallurgy] radiation-induced defect; [vehicle registration] Reading; *récemment dégorgé* (French: recently disgorged) (in winemaking); [banking] refer to drawer (on cheque); [USA] Registered Dietician; *República Dominicana* (Spanish: Dominican Republic); research department; (Royal Naval and Royal Marine Forces) Reserve Decoration; Royal Dragoons; Rural Dean; [New Zealand] Rural Delivery
**R/D** [banking] refer to drawer (on cheque)
**Rd** Road
**rd** rendered; road; rod (unit of length); round; rutherford (unit of radioactivity)
**r.d.** [physics] relative density; *rive droite* (French: right bank); [shipping] running days
**RDA** *Rassemblement Démocratique Africain* (French: African Democratic Rally) (political party); recommended daily allowance (of nutrients etc.); recommended dietary allowance; Retail Distributors' Association; Riding for the Disabled Association; Royal Defence Academy; Royal Docks Association
**RD&D** research, development and demonstration
**RD&E** research, development and engineering
**RDAT** rotary-head digital audio tape
**RDB** [military] Research and Development Board; Royal Danish Ballet; Rural Development Board
**RDBMS** [computing] relational database management system
**RDC** Royal Defence Corps; [insurance] running-down clause; Rural Development Commission; rural district council
**RDCA** Rural District Councils' Association
**RDD** [US marketing] random digital dialing
**r.d.d.** required delivery date
**RDE** Research and Development Establishment; [chemistry] rotating-disc electrode
**RDF** radio direction finder (or finding); [US military] Rapid Deployment Force; refuse-derived fuel; Royal Dublin Fusiliers
**RDI** Royal Designer for Industry
**RDP** [South Africa] Reconstruction and Development Programme
**RDPL** [civil aircraft marking] Laos

**rdr** radar
**RDS** radio data system (for automatic tuning); Research Defence Society; [medicine] respiratory distress syndrome; Royal Drawing Society; Royal Dublin Society
**rds.** [shipping] roadstead
**RDT&E** research, development, testing and engineering
**RDV** rendezvous
**RDX** Research Department Explosive (= cyclonite)
**RDY** Royal Dockyard
**rdy** ready
**RDZ** radiation danger zone
**RE** [chemistry] rare earth; [USA] real estate; Reformed Episcopal; religious education; renewable energy; revised edition; Right Excellent; Royal Engineers; Royal Exchange; Royal Society of Painter-Printmakers (formerly Royal Society of Painter-Etchers and Engravers); [vehicle registration] Stoke-on-Trent
**R/E** [USA] real estate
**Re** [chemical element] rhenium; [currency] rupee
**r.e.** right eye
**REA** Radar and Electronics Association; request for engineer's authorization; Rubber Export Association; [USA] Rural Electrification Administration
**REAC** Regional Education Advisory Committee (of TUC)
**reac.** reactor
**REACH** Retired Executives' Action Clearing House
**REACT** research education and aid for children with potentially terminal illness
**Rear-Adm** Rear-Admiral
**reasm.** reassemble
**Réau.** Réaumur (temperature scale)
**REB** regional examining body
**REC** Railway Executive Committee; regional electricity company
**rec** [short form] recreation ground
**rec.** receipt; receive; received; [medicine] *recens* (Latin: fresh) (in prescriptions); recent; reception; reception room (in property advertisement); recipe; recognized; recommended; record; recorded; recorder; recording; recreation
**recap** [short form] recapitulate; [short form] recapitulation
**recce** [short form] reconnaissance; [short form] reconnoitre
**recd** received
**recep.** reception; reception room (in property advertisement)
**recept.** reception; reception room (in property advertisement)
**RECHAR** *Reconversion de bassins charbonniers* (French: Reconversion of Coal Fields) (EU funding programme)
**recip.** reciprocal; reciprocity
**recirc.** recirculate
**recit.** recitation; [music] recitative
**reclam.** reclamation
**recm.** recommend
**recmd** recommended
**RECMF** Radio and Electronic Component Manufacturers' Federation
**recog.** recognition; recognize
**recom.** recommend
**recon.** reconciliation; recondition; reconditioned; reconnaissance; reconnoitre; reconsign; reconsignment; reconstruct; reconstruction
**recond.** recondition; reconditioned
**REconS** Royal Economic Society
**reconst.** reconstruct; reconstruction
**recpt** receipt; reception; reception room (in property advertisement)
**recr** receiver
**rec. sec.** recording secretary
**Rect.** Rector; Rectory
**rect** receipt
**rect.** rectangle; rectangular; [medicine] *rectificatus* (Latin: rectified) (in prescriptions); rectify
**red.** [finance] redeemable; reduce; reduced; reduction
**redox** [chemistry] reduction–oxidation
**redup.** reduplicate; reduplication; reduplicative
**redupl.** reduplicate; reduplication; reduplicative
**REE** [chemistry] rare-earth element
**Ref.** Reformation; Reformatory; Reformed
**ref** [short form] referee
**ref.** refer; referee; reference; referred; refined; refining; reform; reformation; reformed; reformer; refrigerated ship; refund; refunding; refuse
**refash.** refashion; refashioned

**Ref. Ch.** Reformed Church
**refd** referred; refund
**refl.** reflect; reflection; reflective; reflex; [grammar] reflexive
**Reform.** Reformatory
**Ref. Pres.** Reformed Presbyterian
**refrig.** refrigerate; refrigerated; refrigeration; refrigerator
**Ref. Sp.** Reformed Spelling
**refurb.** refurbished
**Reg.** Regent; *Regina* (Latin: Queen); Regius (Professor)
**reg.** regiment; region; regional; register; registered; registrar; registration; registry; regular; regularly; regulation; regulator
**REGAL** [aeronautics] range and elevation guidance for approach and landing
**regd** registered
**Reg-Gen** Registrar-General
**Reg. Prof.** Regius Professor
**regr** registrar
**Regt** Regent; Regiment
**regtl** regimental
**Reg. TM** registered trademark
**REHAB** [medicine] Rehabilitation Evaluation of Hall and Baker
**rehab** [short form] rehabilitation
**reinf.** reinforce; reinforced
**reinfmt** reinforcement
**REIT** [USA] real-estate investment trust
**reit.** [printing] reiteration
**rej.** reject
**REL** recommended exposure limit (to radiation)
**rel.** relate; related; relating; relation; relative; relatively; release; released; relic; [bibliography] *relié* (French: bound); religion; religious; *reliquiae* (Latin: relics)
**relig.** religion; religious
**rel. pron.** [grammar] relative pronoun
**REM** [physiology] rapid eye movement (as in **REM sleep**); [chemistry] rare-earth metal
**rem** roentgen equivalent man (former unit of radioactivity)
**rem.** remainder; remains; remark(s); remission; remit; remittance
**REMC** Radio and Electronics Measurements Committee
**REME** Royal Electrical and Mechanical Engineers
**remitt.** remittance
**Ren.** Renaissance
**Renf.** Renfrew(shire)
**RENFE** *Red Nacional de Ferrocarriles Españoles* (Spanish: Spanish National Railway Network)
**REngDes** Registered Engineering Designer
**renv.** renovate; renovation
**REO** regional education officer
**REP** [USA] Recovery and Evacuation Program
**Rep.** Repertory (Theatre); [USA] Representative; Republic; Republican
**rep** [short form] repertory (theatre); [short form] representative
**rep.** repair; repeat; [theatre] repertory (company); [medicine] *repetatur* (Latin: let it be repeated) (in prescriptions); repetition; report; reported; reporter; represent; representative; representing; reprint
**REPC** Regional Economic Planning Council
**repl.** replace; replaced; replacement; replica; replicate
**repo.** repossess; repossession
**repr.** represent; representative; represented; representing; reprint; reprinted; reprinting
**repres.** represent; representative; represented; representing
**repro.** reproduced; reproduction
**rept** receipt; report
**Repub.** Republic; Republican
**repub.** republish; republished
**req.** request; require; required; requirement; requisition
**reqd** required
**reqn** requisition
**reqs** requires
**RER** renewable energy resource(s)
**RERO** Royal Engineers Reserve of Officers
**RES** renewable energy source; renewable energy system; [physiology] reticuloendothelial system; Royal Entomological Society of London
**res.** rescue; research; researcher; reservation; reserve; reserved; reservoir; reside; residence; resident; residential; resides; resigned; resolution
**resgnd** resigned
**resid.** residential; residual
**resig.** resignation

**resp.** respective; respectively; respiration; respondent; response; responsibility
**res. phys.** resident physician
**res. sec.** resident secretary
**Rest.** Restoration (historical period)
**rest.** restaurant; restoration; restored (in property advertisement); restraint; restrict; restricted; restriction
**RET** [computing] resolution enhancement technology
**Ret** [astronomy] Reticulum
**ret.** retain; retained; retainer; retire; retired; return; returned
**retd** retained; retired; returned
**R et I** *Regina et Imperatrix* (Latin: Queen and Empress); *Rex et Imperator* (Latin: King and Emperor)
**retnr** retainer
**RETRA** Radio, Electrical and Television Retailers' Association
**REV** [astronautics] re-entry vehicle
**Rev.** [Bible] Revelation; Revenue; Reverend; Review; Revised; Revolution
**rev** [short form] revolution
**rev.** revenue; reverse; reversed; review; reviewed; reviewer; revise; revised; revision; revolution; revolve; revolver; revolving
**rev. ac.** revenue account(s)
**Revd** Reverend
**rev. ed.** revised edition
**Rev. Stat.** Revised Statutes
**Rev. Ver.** Revised Version (of Bible)
**rew.** reward; rewind; rewired; rewiring
**REXX** [computing] restructured extended executor
**RF** radio frequency; reconnaissance fighter (aircraft); [military] regular forces; [genetics] release factor; [cartography] representative fraction; *République française* (French: French Republic); research foundation; [military] reserve force; Rockefeller Foundation; Royal Fusiliers; rugby football; [currency] Rwanda franc; [vehicle registration] Stoke-on-Trent
**Rf** [currency] rufiyaa (used in Maldives); [chemical element] rutherfordium
**rf** reef; [music] *rinforzando* (Italian: reinforcing)
**r.f.** radio frequency; range finder; rapid fire; [telecommunications] reception fair; relative flow; [medicine] rheumatic fever; [baseball] right field; [baseball] right fielder; rough finish (of paper)
**RFA** Royal Field Artillery; Royal Fleet Auxiliary; Rugby Fives Association
**RFAC** Royal Fine Art Commission
**RFC** [USA] Reconstruction Finance Corporation; [computing] request for comments; Royal Flying Corps; rugby football club
**RFD** radio-frequency device; reporting for duty; [USA] rural free delivery (postal service)
**RFDS** [Australia] Royal Flying Doctor Service
**RFE** Radio Free Europe
**RFH** Royal Festival Hall (London)
**RFI** radio-frequency interference; request for information; right forward inside (of skate)
**RFL** Rugby Football League
**RFN** Registered Fever Nurse
**Rfn** Rifleman
**RFO** right forward outside (of skate)
**RFP** [nuclear technology] reversed-field pinch
**r.f.p.** retired on full pay
**RFPC** [electronics] radio-frequency pulse compression
**RFQ** [commerce] request for quotation
**RFR** Royal Fleet Reserve
**rfrd** referred
**RFS** rear-facing seat; Registry of Friendly Societies; Royal Forestry Society
**RFSU** Rugby Football Schools' Union
**RFT** [computing] revisable form text; [astronomy] richest-field telescope
**RFTF** Retail Fruit Trade Federation
**RFU** Rugby Football Union
**rfz.** [music] *rinforzando* (Italian: reinforcing)
**RG** [international vehicle registration] (Republic of) Guinea; [vehicle registration] Newcastle upon Tyne; [UK postcode] Reading; reserve guard
**r.g.** *rive gauche* (French: left bank)
**RGA** remote geological analysis; residual-gas analyser; Royal Garrison Artillery; Royal Guernsey Artillery
**RGB** red, green, blue (in colour transmission etc.)
**RGBI** red, green, blue intensity
**rgd** registered; reigned
**rge** range

**R-Gen** Registrar-General
**RGG** Royal Grenadier Guards
**RGH** Royal Gloucestershire Hussars
**RGI** Royal Glasgow Institute of the Fine Arts
**RGJ** Royal Green Jackets
**RGN** Registered General Nurse (formerly SRN)
**Rgn** Rangoon
**rgn** region
**RGNP** [economics] real gross national product
**RGO** Royal Greenwich Observatory
**RGS** Royal Geographical Society
**RGSA** Royal Geographical Society of Australasia
**RGT** [physics] relativistic gravitational theory
**Rgt** Regiment
**rgtl** regimental
**RH** [international vehicle registration] (Republic of) Haiti; [vehicle registration] Hull; [UK postcode] Redhill; [meteorology] relative humidity; remote handling; right hand; right handed; [fishing port] Rochester; Royal Highlanders; Royal Highness; Royal Hospital
**Rh** [medicine] rhesus (factor) (as in **Rh negative**); [chemical element] rhodium
**r.h.** [sports] right half; right hand; right handed
**RHA** regional health authority; Road Haulage Association; Royal Hibernian Academy; Royal Horse Artillery
**RHAF** Royal Hellenic Air Force
**RHamps** Royal Hampshire Regiment
**rhap.** rhapsody
**RHAS** Royal Highland and Agricultural Society of Scotland
**RHB** regional hospital board
**r.h.b.** [sports] right halfback
**RHBNC** Royal Holloway and Bedford New College (London)
**r.h.d.** right-hand drive (in car advertisement)
**RHEL** Rutherford High Energy Laboratory
**rheo.** rheostat
**rheol.** rheological; rheology
**rhet.** rhetoric; rhetorical
**RHF** Royal Highland Fusiliers
**RHG** Royal Horse Guards
**RHHI** Royal Hospital and Home for Incurables
**RHistS** Royal Historical Society
**RHM** Ranks Hovis McDougall
**RHMS** Royal Hibernian Military School
**rhomb.** rhombic; rhomboid; rhombus
**rhp** rated horsepower
**RHQ** regimental headquarters
**RHR** rear head restraints (in car advertisement); Royal Highland Regiment
**r/h/r** rear head restraints (in car advertisement)
**RHS** Robin Hood Society; Royal Highland Show; Royal Historical Society; Royal Horticultural Society; Royal Humane Society
**r.h.s.** right-hand side; round-headed screw
**RHSI** Royal Horticultural Society of Ireland
**RHT** Railway Heritage Trust
**RHV** Registered Health Visitor
**RI** [international vehicle registration] (Republic of) Indonesia; radio interference; radioisotope; Railway Inspectorate; refractive index; Regimental Institute; *Regina et Imperatrix* (Latin: Queen and Empress); reinsurance; religious instruction; report of investigation; *Rex et Imperator* (Latin: King and Emperor); Rhode Island; [US postcode] Rhode Island; Rockwell International Corporation; Rotary International; Royal Institute of Painters in Water Colours; Royal Institution
**R/I** reinsurance
**r.i.** reflective insulation; rubber insulation
**RIA** [medicine] radioimmunoassay; Royal Irish Academy
**RIAA** Recording Industry Association of America
**RIAC** Royal Irish Automobile Club
**RIAF** Royal Indian Air Force
**RIAI** Royal Institute of the Architects of Ireland
**RIAM** Royal Irish Academy of Music
**RIAS** Royal Incorporation of Architects in Scotland
**RIASC** Royal Indian Army Service Corps
**RIB** Racing Information Bureau; rigid-hull inflatable boat; Rural Industries Bureau
**RIBA** Royal Institute of British Architects
**RIBI** Rotary International in Great Britain and Ireland
**RIC** [chemistry] radiation-induced change;

[physics] radiation-induced conductivity; Radio Industry Council; Royal Institute of Chemistry (former name of RSC); Royal Irish Constabulary
**RICA** Research Institute for Consumer Affairs
**RICE** rest, ice, compression, elevation (treatment for sports injuries)
**RICO** [USA] Racketeer Influenced and Corrupt Organizations Act
**RICS** Royal Institution of Chartered Surveyors
**RID** [physics] radiation-induced defect; [physics] radiation-induced diffusion
**RIE** [commerce] recognized investment exchange; Royal Indian Engineering College
**RIF** [military] reduction in force; Royal Inniskilling Fusiliers
**Rif. Brig.** Rifle Brigade
**RIFF** [computing] raster image file format
**RIGS** regionally important geological site
**RIIA** Royal Institute of International Affairs
**RILC** Racing Industry Liaison Committee
**RILKO** Research into Lost Knowledge Organization
**RIM** [international vehicle registration] (Islamic Republic of) Mauritania (from French *République Islamique de Mauritanie*); Royal Indian Marines
**RIMB** [South Africa] Research Institute for Medical Biophysics
**RIMNET** Radioactive Incident Monitoring Network
**RIN** [aeronautics] reference indicator number; Royal Indian Navy
**RINA** Royal Institution of Naval Architects
**rinf.** [music] *rinforzando* (Italian: reinforcing)
**RINVR** Royal Indian Naval Volunteer Reserve
**RIO** reporting in and out
**RIOP** Royal Institute of Oil Painters
**RIP** [computing] raster input processor; *requiescant in pace* (Latin: may they rest in peace); *requiescat in pace* (Latin: may he/she rest in peace); rest in peace
**rip.** [music] *ripieno* (Italian: filled, for all players)
**RIPA** Royal Institute of Public Administration
**RIPHH** Royal Institute of Public Health and Hygiene
**RIR** Royal Irish Regiment
**RIrF** Royal Irish Fusiliers
**RIS** Research Information Service
**RISC** reduced-instruction-set computer
**RIT** [psychology] Rorschach inkblot test
**rit.** [music] *ritardando* (Italian: slowing down); [music] *ritenuto* (Italian: held back)
**RITA** reusable interplanetary transport approach (vehicle)
**ritard.** [music] *ritardando* (Italian: slowing down)
**riten.** [music] *ritenuto* (Italian: held back)
**riv.** river
**RJ** [vehicle registration] Manchester; ramjet; road junction
**RJA** Royal Jersey Artillery
**RJE** [computing] remote job entry
**RJET** [computing] remote job entry terminal
**RJF** Reformed Jokers' Federation
**RJLI** Royal Jersey Light Infantry
**RJM** Royal Jersey Militia
**RK** [vehicle registration] northwest London; [medicine] radical keratotomy (used to treat myopia); religious knowledge
**RKKA** *Rabochekrest'yanshi Krasny* (Russian: Red Army of Workers and Peasants)
**RKO** Radio-Keith-Orpheum (US broadcasting and former film company)
**rky** rocky
**RL** [international vehicle registration] (Republic of) Lebanon; reference library; research laboratory; rocket launcher; Rugby League; [vehicle registration] Truro
**Rl** [currency] rouble; Royal
**RLC** Royal Logistic Corps
**RLD** [USA] retail liquor dealer
**RLF** Royal Literary Fund
**RLL** [computing] run length limited
**RLO** railway liaison officer; returned letter office (formerly DLO)
**RLPAS** Royal London Prisoners' Aid Society
**RLPO** Royal Liverpool Philharmonic Orchestra
**RLPS** Royal Liverpool Philharmonic Society
**RLS** Robert Louis Stevenson (Scottish writer)

**Rls** [currency] rial (used in Iran)
**RLSS** Royal Life Saving Society
**rlwy** railway
**rly** railway; relay
**RM** [vehicle registration] Carlisle; [international vehicle registration] (Republic of) Madagascar; radiation monitoring; radio monitoring; [computing] Reed-Muller (code); Registered Midwife (replacement for SCM); [currency] Reichsmark (formerly used in Germany); remote monitoring; resident magistrate; riding master; [UK postcode] Romford; Royal Mail; Royal Marines
**rm** ream; room
**RMA** Royal Marine Artillery; Royal Marines Association; Royal Military Academy (formerly RMC); Royal Musical Association
**RMC** regional meteorological centre; Royal Military College (former name of RMA)
**RMCC** Royal Military College of Canada
**RMCM** Royal Manchester College of Music
**RMCS** Royal Military College of Science
**r.m.d.** ready money down
**RMedSoc** Royal Medical Society (Edinburgh)
**RMetS** Royal Meteorological Society
**RMFVR** Royal Marine Forces Volunteer Reserves
**RMH** Royal Marsden Hospital (London)
**RMI** Resource Management Initiative (for NHS)
**RMIT** Royal Melbourne Institute of Technology
**RMLI** Royal Marine Light Infantry
**RMM** [international vehicle registration] (Republic of) Mali
**r.m.m.** [chemistry] relative molecular mass
**RMN** Registered Mental Nurse
**RMO** Regimental Medical Officer; regional medical officer; resident medical officer; Royal Marine Office
**RMP** Royal Marine Police; Royal Military Police
**RMPA** Royal Medico-Psychological Association
**RMR** Royal Marines Reserve
**RMRA** Royal Marines Rifle Association
**RMS** radiation-monitoring system; remote monitoring system; [mathematics] root mean square; Royal Mail Service; Royal Mail Ship; Royal Mail Steamer; Royal Medical Society; Royal Microscopical Society; Royal Society of Miniature Painters
**rms** [mathematics] root mean square; rooms (in property advertisement)
**RMSchMus** Royal Marines School of Music
**RMSM** Royal Military School of Music
**RMT** National Union of Rail, Maritime and Transport Workers
**RN** [international vehicle registration] (Republic of) Niger; [vehicle registration] Preston; Registered Nurse; *route nationale* (French: trunk road); Royal Naval; Royal Navy; [fishing port] Runcorn
**Rn** [chemical element] radon
**r.n.** [telecommunications] reception nil
**RNA** [biochemistry] ribonucleic acid; Romantic Novelists' Association; Royal Naval Association
**RNAS** Royal Naval Air Service; Royal Naval Air Station
**RNase** [biochemistry] ribonuclease
**RNAW** Royal Naval Aircraft Workshop
**RNAY** Royal Naval Aircraft Yard
**RNB** Royal Naval Barracks
**R 'n' B** rhythm and blues
**RNBS** Royal Naval Benevolent Society
**RNBT** Royal Naval Benevolent Trust
**RNC** [USA] Republican National Committee
**RNC** Royal Naval College
**RNCM** Royal Northern College of Music
**RND** Royal Naval Division
**rnd** round
**RNEC** Royal Naval Engineering College
**RNF** Royal Northumberland Fusiliers
**RNHA** Registered Nursing Home Association
**RNIB** Royal National Institute for the Blind
**RNID** Royal National Institute for the Deaf
**RNLAF** Royal Netherlands Air Force
**RNLI** Royal National Lifeboat Institution
**RNLO** Royal Naval Liaison Officer
**RNMDSF** Royal National Mission to Deep Sea Fishermen
**RNMH** Registered Nurse for the Mentally Handicapped

**RNMS** Royal Naval Medical School
**RNoN** Royal Norwegian Navy
**RNP** [biochemistry] ribonucleoprotein
**RNPFN** Royal National Pension Fund for Nurses
**RNR** Royal Naval Reserve
**R 'n' R** rock and roll
**RNRA** Royal Naval Rifle Association
**RNRS** Royal National Rose Society
**RNS** [stock exchange] Regulatory News Service; [mathematics] residue number system; Royal Numismatic Society
**rns** runs
**RNSA** Royal Naval Sailing Association
**RNSC** Royal Naval Staff College
**RNSR** Royal Naval Special Reserve
**RNSS** Royal Naval Scientific Service
**RNT** Registered Nurse Tutor; Royal National Theatre
**RNTE** Royal Naval Training Establishment
**RNTNEH** Royal National Throat, Nose and Ear Hospital
**RNTU** Royal Naval Training Unit
**RNVR** Royal Naval Volunteer Reserve
**RNVSR** Royal Naval Volunteer Supplementary Reserve
**RNWMP** [Canada] Royal Northwest Mounted Police (former name of RCMP)
**rnwy** runway
**RNXS** Royal Naval Auxiliary Service
**RNZAC** Royal New Zealand Armoured Corps
**RNZAF** Royal New Zealand Air Force
**RNZIR** Royal New Zealand Infantry Regiment
**RNZN** Royal New Zealand Navy
**RNZNVR** Royal New Zealand Naval Volunteer Reserve
**RO** [vehicle registration] Luton; radar observer; radar operator; radio operator; Radio Orchestra; [psychology] reality orientation; receiving office; receiving officer; receiving order; record(s) office; recruiting officer; regimental order; registered office; relieving officer; reserved occupation; returning officer; [chemistry] reverse osmosis; [currency] rial Omani; [international vehicle registration] Romania; [fishing port] Rothesay; Royal Observatory
**ro.** [printing] recto (right-hand page); roan
**.ro** Romania (in Internet address)
**r.o.** [rowing] rowed over; [cricket] run out
**ROA** Racehorse Owners' Association; [education] record of achievement; Reserve Officers' Association; [finance] return on assets
**ROAM** [finance] return on assets managed
**ROAR** right of admission reserved
**ROB** remaining on board
**ROC** [finance] return on capital; Royal Observer Corps
**ROCE** [finance] return on capital employed
**ROE** [finance] return on equity; Royal Observatory, Edinburgh
**ROF** Royal Ordnance Factory
**Roffen.** *Roffensis* (Latin: (Bishop) of Rochester)
**R of O** Reserve of Officers
**ROG** receipt of goods
**ROH** Royal Opera House (Covent Garden)
**ROI** region of interest; [finance] return on investment; Royal Institute of Oil Painters
**ROK** [international vehicle registration] (Republic of) Korea
**Rolls** [short form] Rolls-Royce (car)
**ROM** [computing] read-only memory; [medicine] rupture of membranes
**Rom.** Roman; Romance (language); Romania; Romanian; Romanic (language); [Bible] Romans
**rom.** roman (type)
**Rom. Cath.** Roman Catholic
**RONA** [finance] return on net assets
**ROP** [advertising] run of paper
**RORC** Royal Ocean Racing Club
**ro-ro** roll on, roll off (ferry)
**ROS** [computing] remote operations service
**Ros.** Roscommon
**Rosa** [computing] recognition of open systems achievement
**ROSAT** [astronomy] *Röntgenstrahlen Satellit* (German: X-ray satellite)
**Rosco** Road Operators' Safety Council
**ROSE** [computing] Research Open Systems in Europe
**ROSL** Royal Overseas League
**ROSLA** raising of school-leaving age
**RoSPA** Royal Society for the Prevention of Accidents
**ROT** Registered Occupational Therapist; remedial occupational therapy; rule of thumb

**Rot.** Rotterdam
**rot.** rotary; rotating; rotation; rotor
**ROTC** [USA] Reserve Officers' Training Corps
**ROTFL** rolls on the floor laughing (in Internet chat)
**ROU** [international vehicle registration] (Republic of) Uruguay
**rout.** routine
**ROV** remotely operated vehicle
**ROW** right of way; Rights of Women
**ROWPU** reverse osmosis water purification unit
**Rox.** Roxburghshire
**Roy.** Royal
**RP** [vehicle registration] Northampton; [civil aircraft marking] (Republic of the) Philippines; [international vehicle registration] (Republic of the) Philippines; radiation protection; [chemistry] reaction product; Received Pronunciation; recommended practice; recommended price; recovery phase; redundancy payment; Reformed Presbyterian; regimental police; regimental policeman; Registered Plumber; Regius Professor; reinforced plastic; reply paid; reprint; reprinting; *República Portuguesa* (Portuguese: Republic of Portugal); [US finance] repurchase agreement; research paper; [medicine] retinitis pigmentosa; [insurance] return (of) premium; *Révérend Père* (French: Reverend Father); rocket projectile; Royal Society of Portrait Painters; rules of procedure
**R/P** reprint; reprinting
**Rp** [currency] rupiah (used in Indonesia)
**r.p.** [telecommunications] reception poor; regimental policeman; reply paid
**RPA** radiation protection adviser; Rationalist Press Association; [education] record of personal achievement; Registered Plumbers' Association
**RPB** recognized professional body
**RPC** rapid Portland cement; [computing] remote procedure call; [USA] Republican Party Conference; request the pleasure of your company; Royal Pioneer Corps
**RPD** Doctor of Political Science (from Latin *Rerum Politicarum Doctor*); regional port director
**RPE** radio production executive; Reformed Protestant Episcopal; [medicine] retinal pigment epithelium (of eye)
**RPF** [medicine] renal plasma flow; [medicine] retroperitoneal fibrosis; Rwanda Patriotic Front
**RPG** [computing] report program generator; [military] rocket-propelled grenade; role-playing game
**rpg** rounds per gun
**rph** revolutions per hour
**RPhilS** Royal Philharmonic Society
**RPI** retail price index
**rplca** replica
**RPM** reliability performance measure; resale price maintenance; retail price maintenance
**rpm** revolutions per minute
**RPMS** Royal Postgraduate Medical School
**RPN** Registered Psychiatric Nurse; [computing, mathematics] reverse Polish notation
**RP/ND** reprinting, no date
**RPO** railway post office; regional personnel officer; Royal Philharmonic Orchestra
**RPQ** [commerce] request for price quotation
**RPR** *Rassemblement pour la République* (French: Rally for the Republic) (= Gaullists, formerly UDR)
**RPRA** Royal Pigeon Racing Association
**RPS** radiological protection service; rapid processing system; Royal Philharmonic Society; Royal Photographic Society
**rps** revolutions per second
**RPSGB** Royal Pharmaceutical Society of Great Britain
**RPSL** Royal Philatelic Society, London
**RPT** Registered Physiotherapist
**rpt** repeat; report; reprint
**RPV** [nuclear technology] reactor pressure vessel; [military] remotely piloted vehicle
**RQ** regraded quality (of tyre); remoulded quality (of tyre); [commerce] request for quotation; [medicine] respiratory quotient
**R/Q** [commerce] request for quotation
**RQL** reference quality level
**RQMS** Regimental Quartermaster-Sergeant
**rqmt** requirement
**rqr.** require; requirement
**RR** [vehicle registration] Nottingham; radiation resistance; [USA] railroad; Rem-

ington Rand (manufacturing company); research report; return rate; Right Reverend; [cycling] road race; [fishing port] Rochester; Rolls-Royce; [USA] rural route
**rr.** rare
**r.r.** ready reckoner
**RRA** Royal Regiment of Artillery
**RRB** Race Relations Board
**RRC** [cycling] Road Racing Club; Road Runners' Club; Royal Red Cross
**RRE** Royal Radar Establishment (former name of RSRE)
**RRF** [military] Rapid Reaction Force; Royal Regiment of Fusiliers
**RRI** Rowett Research Institute (Aberdeen)
**RRL** Registered Record Librarian; Road Research Laboratory
**RRM** [USA] renegotiable-rate mortgage
**rRNA** [biochemistry] ribosomal ribonucleic acid
**RRP** recommended retail price
**RR.PP.** *Révérends Pères* (French: Reverend Fathers)
**RRR** [USA] return receipt requested (of registered mail)
**RRS** Royal Research Ship
**RRT** rail rapid transit
**RS** [vehicle registration] Aberdeen; Rallye Sport; Received Standard (English); reconnaissance squadron; reconnaissance strike; recording secretary; recruiting service; [computing] Reed–Solomon (as in **RS code**); Reformed Spelling; remote sensing; research station; [medicine] respiratory system; [law] Revised Statutes; Royal Scots (regiment); Royal Society
**R/S** rejection slip
**Rs** [currency] rupee
**rs** [meteorology] rain and snow (i.e. sleet)
**r.s.** right side
**3Rs** reading, (w)riting and (a)rithmetic
**RSA** Republic of South Africa; [New Zealand] Returned Services Association; [computing] Rivest, Shamir and Adelman (as in **RSA cipher**); Road Safety Act; Royal Scottish Academician; Royal Scottish Academy; Royal Society for the Encouragement of Arts, Manufactures and Commerce; Royal Society of Arts; Royal Society of Australia
**RSAA** Royal Society for Asian Affairs
**RSAD** Royal Surgical Aid Society
**RSAF** Royal Small Arms Factory
**RSAI** Royal Society of Antiquaries of Ireland
**RSAMD** Royal Scottish Academy of Music and Drama
**RSAS** Royal Surgical Aid Society
**r.s.b.** range safety beacon
**RSC** Royal Shakespeare Company; Royal Society of Canada; Royal Society of Chemistry (formerly RIC); Rules of the Supreme Court
**RSCDS** Royal Scottish Country Dance Society
**rsch** research
**RSCJ** *Religiosae Sacratissimi Cordis Jesus* (Latin: Nuns of the Most Sacred Heart of Jesus, Sacred Heart Society)
**RSCM** Royal School of Church Music
**RSCN** Registered Sick Children's Nurse (formerly SRCN)
**RSD** recovery, salvage and disposal; Royal Society of Dublin
**rsdntl** residential
**RSE** Received Standard English; Royal Society of Edinburgh
**RSF** [building] rough sunk face; Royal Scots Fusiliers
**RSFS** Royal Scottish Forestry Society
**RSFSR** Russian Soviet Federative Socialist Republic (former official Soviet name of Russia)
**RSG** rate-support grant; recirculating steam generator; regional seat of government (in civil defence); Royal Scots Greys
**RSGB** Radio Society of Great Britain
**RSGS** Royal Scottish Geographical Society
**RSH** Royal Society of Health
**RSHA** *Reichssicherheitshauptamt* (German: Reich Security Central Office) (in Nazi Germany)
**RSI** regional staff inspector; [medicine] repetitive strain (or stress) injury; Royal Sanitary Institute
**RSJ** [building] rolled-steel joist
**RSL** [Australia] Returned Services League; Royal Society of Literature
**RSLA** raising of school-leaving age
**RSM** Regimental Sergeant-Major; regional sales manager; Royal School of Mines; Royal Society of Medicine; Royal Society of Musicians of Great Britain; [inter-

national vehicle registration] (Republic of) San Marino
**RSMA** Royal Society of Marine Artists
**RSME** Royal School of Military Engineering
**rsn** reason
**RSNA** Radiological Society of North America
**RSNC** Royal Society for Nature Conservation
**RSNO** Royal Scottish National Orchestra
**RSNT** Railway Staffs National Tribunal
**RSNZ** Royal Society of New Zealand
**RSO** Radio Symphony Orchestra; radiological safety officer; railway sorting office; railway suboffice; [military] range safety officer; Recruiting Staff Officer; resident surgical officer; Royal Scottish Orchestra (formerly SNO); rural suboffice
**RSocMed** Royal Society of Medicine
**r.s.p.** [cricket] rain stopped play
**RSPB** Royal Society for the Protection of Birds
**RSPBA** Royal Scottish Pipe Band Association
**RSPCA** Royal Society for the Prevention of Cruelty to Animals
**RSPE** Royal Society of Painter-Printmakers (formerly Royal Society of Painter-Etchers and Engravers)
**RSPP** Royal Society of Portrait Painters
**RSPS** Royal Scottish Pipers' Society
**rsq.** rescue
**RSRE** Royal Signals and Radar Establishment (formerly RRE)
**RSS** *Regiae Societatis Socius* (Latin: Fellow of the Royal Society); Royal Statistical Society
**RSSA** Royal Scottish Society of Arts
**RSSPCC** Royal Scottish Society for the Prevention of Cruelty to Children
**RSTM&H** Royal Society of Tropical Medicine and Hygiene
**rstr.** restricted
**RSU** road safety unit
**RSUA** Royal Society of Ulster Architects
**RSV** [medicine] respiratory syncytial virus; Revised Standard Version (of Bible); [microbiology] Rous sarcoma virus
**RSVP** *répondez s'il vous plaît* (French: please reply)
**rsvr** reservoir
**RSW** Royal Scottish Water Colour Society
**RSWC** right side up with care
**RSwN** Royal Swedish Navy
**RT** [vehicle registration] Ipswich; [medicine] radiation therapy; radio telegraph; radio telegraphy; radio telephone; radio telephony; reaction time; reading test; received text; return ticket; room temperature; round table; round trip
**R/T** radio telegraph; radio telegraphy; radio telephone; radio telephony
**rt** right
**RTA** reciprocal trade agreement(s); road traffic accident; Road Traffic Act
**RTB** return to base (as in **RTB warranty**)
**RTBA** rate to be agreed
**RTBF** *Radio-Télévision Belge de la Communauté Française* (Belgian broadcasting company)
**RTC** [computing] real-time clock; [India] Road Transport Corporation; Round Table Conference
**rtc.** ratchet
**rtd** retired; returned
**rtd ht** [cricket] retired hurt
**RTDS** [computing] real-time data system
**RTE** *Radio Telefis Éireann* (Irish broadcasting company); [computing] real-time execution
**rte** route
**RTECS** Registry of Toxic Effects of Chemical Substances
**RTF** *Radiodiffusion-Télévision Française* (European broadcasting company); [computing] rich text format
**RTFM** [slang, computing] read the fucking manual
**RTG** [astronomy] radioisotope thermoelectric generator; [physics] relativistic theory of gravitation
**rtg** rating
**Rt Hon.** Right Honourable
**RTI** [medicine] respiratory tract infection; Round Table International
**RTITB** Road Transport Industry Training Board
**RTK** right to know
**RTL** *Radio-Télé Luxembourg* (European broadcasting company); [computing] real-time language; [electronics] resistor-transistor logic

**RTM** [computing] read the manual; registered trademark
**rtn** retain; return
**rtng** returning
**RTO** [USA] railroad transportation officer; railway transport officer
**RTOL** [aeronautics] reduced take-off and landing
**RTP** [engineering] rated thermal power; [physics] room temperature and pressure
**RTPI** Royal Town Planning Institute
**RTR** Royal Tank Regiment
**RTRA** Road Traffic Regulation Act
**Rt Rev.** Right Reverend
**Rt Revd** Right Reverend
**RTS** Religious Tract Society; [computing] request to send; reserve tug service; Royal Television Society; Royal Toxophilite Society
**RTSA** Retail Trading Standards Association
**RTT** radioteletype
**RTTC** [cycling] Road Time Trials Council
**RTU** [military] return(ed) to unit
**RTV** real-time video
**RTW** ready to wear
**Rt W** Right Worshipful
**rty** rarity
**RTYC** Royal Thames Yacht Club
**RTZ** Rio Tinto Zinc Corporation Limited
**RU** [vehicle registration] Bournemouth; [international vehicle registration] (Republic of) Burundi (from former name Urundi); Readers' Union; [computing] registered user; reprocessed uranium; Rugby Union
**Ru** [chemical element] ruthenium
**Ru.** Russia; Russian
**.ru** Russia (in Internet address)
**RUA** Royal Ulster Academy of Painting, Sculpture and Architecture
**RUAS** Royal Ulster Agricultural Society
**rub.** rubber
**RUC** Royal Ulster Constabulary
**RUCR** Royal Ulster Constabulary Reserve
**rud.** rudder
**RUF** [banking] revolving underwriting facility
**RUG** [computing] restricted users group
**RUI** Royal University of Ireland
**RUKBA** Royal United Kingdom Beneficent Association
**rumpie** [informal] rural upwardly mobile professional
**RUPP** road used as public path
**RUR** Royal Ulster Regiment
**RURAL** Society for the Responsible Use of Resources in Agriculture and on the Land
**RUS** [international vehicle registration] Russia
**Rus.** Russia; Russian
**RUSI** Royal United Services Institute for Defence Studies (formerly Royal United Service Institution)
**RUSM** Royal United Service Museum
**Russ.** Russia; Russian
**Rut.** Rutland
**Rutd** Rutland
**RV** [vehicle registration] Portsmouth; rateable value; [USA] recreational vehicle; [astronautics] re-entry vehicle; rendezvous; research vessel; [medicine] residual volume; Revised Version (of Bible); Rifle Volunteers; [medicine] right ventricle; [medicine] right ventricular
**r.v.** [statistics] random variable; rendezvous
**RVA** Rating and Valuation Association
**RVC** Rifle Volunteer Corps; Royal Veterinary College
**RVCI** Royal Veterinary College of Ireland
**RVLR** Road Vehicles Lighting Regulations
**RVM** Royal Victorian Medal
**RVO** Royal Victorian Order
**RVR** runway visual range
**RVSVP** *répondez vite, s'il vous plaît* (French: please reply quickly)
**RVU** research vessel unit
**RW** [vehicle registration] Coventry; rainwater; right of way; Right Worshipful; Right Worthy; Royal Warrant; runway
**R/W** right of way
**Rw.** Rwanda; Rwandan
**r/w** read/write
**.rw** Rwanda (in Internet address)
**r.w.** [sports] right wing
**RWA** Race Walking Association; Royal West of England Academy; [international vehicle registration] Rwanda
**RWAFF** Royal West African Frontier Force
**R War. R** Royal Warwickshire Regiment
**RWAS** Royal Welsh Agricultural Society
**RWD** radioactive waste disposal
**r.w.d.** rear-wheel drive

**RWEA** Royal West of England Academy
**RWF** Radio Wholesalers' Federation; Royal Welch Fusiliers
**RWFCS** Red and White Friesian Cattle Society
**RwFr** [currency] Rwanda franc
**RWGM** [Freemasonry] Right Worshipful Grand Master
**RWGR** [Freemasonry] Right Worthy Grand Representative
**RWGS** [Freemasonry] Right Worthy Grand Secretary
**RWGT** [Freemasonry] Right Worthy Grand Templar; [Freemasonry] Right Worthy Grand Treasurer
**RWGW** [Freemasonry] Right Worthy Grand Warden
**RWIC** Rioja Wine Information Centre
**RWK** Queen's Own Royal West Kent Regiment
**RWM** radioactive waste management; [computing] read–write memory
**RWMAC** Radioactive Waste Management Advisory Committee
**RWP** rainwater pipe
**RWS** Royal Watercolour Society
**rwy** railway
**RX** [vehicle registration] Reading; [fishing port] Rye
**Rx** recording (in broadcasting)
**RY** [vehicle registration] Leicester; [fishing port] Ramsey
**ry** railway
**RYA** Royal Yachting Association
**RYC** in reply to your cable
**RYS** Royal Yacht Squadron
**RZ** [vehicle registration] Antrim
**r.z.** return to zero
**RZS** Royal Zoological Society
**RZSI** Royal Zoological Society of Ireland
**RZSS** Royal Zoological Society of Scotland
**RZSScot** Royal Zoological Society of Scotland

# S

**S** Sabbath; [heraldry] sable; [anatomy] sacral (of vertebrae); Saint; *San* (Italian: Saint); *Sankt* (German: Saint); *Santa* (Italian: Saint); *Santo* (Italian: Saint); *São* (Portuguese: Saint); satisfactory; Saturday; Saxon; [currency] Schilling; School; Scotland; Scottish; Sea; secondary; secret; secretary; section; *Seite* (German: page); Senate; *Señor* (Spanish: Mr); sentence; September; *sepultus* (Latin: buried); series; [UK postcode] Sheffield; ship; siemens (unit of electric conductance); signaller; signature; *Signor* (Italian: Mr); *Signora* (Italian: Mrs); [geology] Silurian; silver; [fishing port] Skibbereen; slow (on clock or watch regulator); small; [microbiology] smooth; Socialist; Society; *Socius* (Latin: Fellow) (used in titles); solar; [astronomy] solar mass; [music] soprano; south; southern; [card games] spades; [astronomy] spiral galaxy; square; staff; [law] statute; [microbiology] strain; submarine; [chemistry] substitution reaction; [currency] sucre (used in Ecuador); [chemical element] sulphur; summer; [shipping] summer (load line); sun; Sunday; Sweden; [international vehicle registration] Sweden
***S*** [electrical engineering] apparent power; [physics] entropy; [music] *segno* (Italian: sign); [chemistry] sinister; [physics] spin quantum number (of system); [physics] strangeness quantum number
**s** second; shilling(s) (from Latin *solidus*); [meteorology] snow; [music] soh (in tonic sol-fa); [chemistry] solid; [physics] strange (quark flavour)
***s*** [chemistry] secondary (isomer); [chemistry] sedimentation coefficient; [physics] specific entropy; [physics] spin quantum number; [chemistry] symmetric
**s/** *sur* (French: on) (in place-names)
**s.** school; sea; seaman; section; see; semi-; series; sermon; set; sets (referring to the sun); *siècle* (French: century); *siehe* (German: see); sign; signed; *sine* (Latin: without); single; [grammar] singular; *sinister* (Latin: left); *sinistra* (Italian: left); sire; sister; small; snow; society; solo; son; [music] soprano; spherical; steamer;

steel; stem; stock; [grammar] substantive; succeeded; suit; summer; sun; sunny; surplus

**S2** [civil aircraft marking] Bangladesh

**S4C** *Sianel 4 Cymru* (Welsh: Channel 4 Wales)

**S5** [civil aircraft marking] Slovenia

**S7** [civil aircraft marking] Seychelles

**SA** [vehicle registration] Aberdeen; Salvation Army; Saudi Arabia; [international vehicle registration] Saudi Arabia; Saudi Arabian; seaman apprentice; secret agent; [USA] Secretary of the Army; [horticulture] semiannual; senior administrator; sex appeal; [microbiology] simian agent; [medicine] sinoatrial (as in **SA node**); small arms; [commerce] *sociedad anónima* (Spanish: (public) limited company, plc or Ltd); [commerce] *sociedade anónima* (Portuguese: (public) limited company, plc or Ltd); [commerce] *società anonima* (Italian: (public) limited company, plc or Ltd); [commerce] *société anonyme* (French: (public) limited company, plc or Ltd); Society of Antiquaries; Society of Arts; Society of Authors; Soil Association; *Son Altesse* (French: Her/His Highness); South Africa; South African; South America; South American; South Australia; South Australian; special agent; spherical aberration; [computing] structured systems analysis; *Sturmabteilung* (German: storm troopers) (Nazi militia); subsistence allowance; surface area; surface-to-air (missile); [fishing port] Swansea; [UK postcode] Swansea; systems analysis; systems analyst

**S/A** subject to acceptance; subject to approval; [US banking] survivorship agreement

**Sa.** Saturday

**sa.** [heraldry] sable

**.sa** Saudi Arabia (in Internet address)

**s.a.** safe arrival; *secundum artem* (Latin: by skill, scientifically, in the standard way); see also; [horticulture] semiannual; sex appeal; *siehe auch* (German: see also); *sine anno* (Latin: without year, undated); [chemistry] soluble in alkali; storage area; subject to acceptance; subject to approval; subsistence allowance

**SAA** Scottish Archery Association; small arms ammunition; South African Airways; Speech Association of America; Standards Association of Australia; [chemistry] surface-active agent; [computing] systems application architecture

**SAAA** Scottish Amateur Athletic Association

**SAAAU** South African Amateur Athletic Union

**Saab** *Svensk Aeroplan Aktiebolag* (Swedish car and aircraft manufacturer)

**SAABS** Scottish Action Against Blood Sports

**SAAD** small arms ammunition depot

**SAAF** South African Air Force

**SAAFA** Special Arab Assistance Fund for Africa

**SAAO** South African Astronomical Observatory

**SAARC** South Asian Association for Regional Cooperation

**SAAU** South African Agricultural Union

**SAB** Science Advisory Board; Scientific Advisory Board; Society of American Bacteriologists; [music] soprano, alto, bass; South Atlantic Bight

**Sab.** Sabbath

**sab.** *sabato* (Italian: Saturday); sabbatical

**sáb.** *sábado* (Spanish: Saturday)

**SABA** Scottish Amateur Boxing Association

**Sabbat.** Sabbatical

**SABC** Scottish Association of Boys' Clubs; South African Broadcasting Corporation

**Sabena** *Société anonyme belge d'exploitation de la navigation aérienne* (Belgian airline company)

**SABIC** Society for the Advancement of Brain-Injured Children

**SABMIS** seaborne antiballistic missile intercept system

**sabo.** sabotage

**SABRA** South African Bureau of Racial Affairs

**SABS** South African Bureau of Standards

**SAC** Scientific Advisory Committee; Scottish Arts Council; Scottish Automobile Club; Senior Aircraftman; [finance] short-run average cost; small-arms club; South Atlantic Coast; (Post Office) Stamp Advisory Committee; [USA] State Athletic Commission; [USA] Strategic Air Command

**SACAB** Scottish Association of Citizens' Advice Bureaux
**SACEUR** Supreme Allied Commander Europe
**SACHR** Standing Advisory Commission on Human Rights
**SACL** South African Confederation of Labour
**SACLANT** Supreme Allied Commander Atlantic
**SACO** *Sveriges Akademikers Centralorganisation* (Swedish: Swedish Confederation of Professional Associations)
**SACP** South African Communist Party
**Sacr.** Sacramento; Sacrist
**SACRO** Scottish Association for the Care and Resettlement of Offenders
**SACSEA** Supreme Allied Command, Southeast Asia
**SACSIR** South African Council for Scientific and Industrial Research
**SACU** single-application computer user; Society for the Promotion of Anglo-Chinese Understanding; Southern African Customs Union
**SACW** Senior Aircraftwoman
**SAD** Scottish Action on Dementia; Scottish Association for the Deaf; [psychology] seasonal affective disorder; systems analysis and design
**SADC** Southern African Development Community
**SADCC** Southern African Development Coordination Conference
**SADF** South African Defence Force
**SADG** *Société des architectes diplômés par le gouvernement* (French: Society of Government-Certified Architects)
**SADI** Society of Approved Driving Instructors
**SADIE** scanning analogue to digital input equipment
**SADT** [trademark, computing] structured analysis and design technique
**SAE** self-addressed envelope; [USA] Society of Automotive Engineers (motor-oil viscosity scale); stamped addressed envelope
**s.a.e.** self-addressed envelope; stamped addressed envelope
**SAEF** Stock Exchange Automatic Execution Facility
**SAF** Scottish Athletic Federation; [USA] Secretary of the Air Force; Society of American Foresters; [USA] Strategic Air Force; structural adjustment facility (in IMF)
**SAFA** Scottish Amateur Football Association; South Africa Freedom Association
**s.a.f.e.** stamped addressed foolscap envelope
**S Afr.** South Africa; South African
**SAfrD** South African Dutch
**SAFU** Scottish Amateur Fencing Union
**SAG** [USA] Screen Actors' Guild
**SAGA** Scottish Amateur Gymnastics Association; Society of American Graphic Artists
**SAGB** Schizophrenia Association of Great Britain; Spiritualist Association of Great Britain
**SAGE** [military] semiautomatic ground environment
**SAGGA** Scout and Guide Graduate Association
**SAH** [medicine] subarachnoid haemorrhage; Supreme Allied Headquarters
**SAHC** Scottish Association of Health Councils
**SAHGB** Society of Architectural Historians of Great Britain
**SAHR** Society of Army Historical Research
**Sai.** Saigon
**SAIC** Scottish Agricultural Improvement Council
**SAID** sexual allegations in divorce
**SAIDS** simian acquired immune deficiency syndrome
**SAIF** South African Industrial Federation
**SAIMR** South African Institute of Medical Research
**SAIRR** South African Institute of Race Relations
**SAISSA** Scottish Amateur Ice Speed Skating Association
**SAL** South Arabian League; surface airlifted (mail)
**sal.** salary
**SALA** South African Library Association
**SALC** symmetry-adapted linear combinations
**Salop** Shropshire (from old name of county)
**SALP** South African Labour Party
**SALR** [meteorology] saturated adiabatic lapse rate; South African Law Reports

**SALT** Scottish Association for Language Teaching; Strategic Arms Limitation Talks; Strategic Arms Limitation Treaty
**Salv.** Salvador; Salvadorian
**salv.** salvage
**SAM** Scottish Aids Monitor; [USA] shared-appreciation mortgage; [USA] Space Available Mail; surface-to-air missile
**S Am.** South America; South American
**Sam.** Samaria; Samaritan; Samoa; Samoan; *Samstag* (German: Saturday); [Bible] Samuel
**sam.** *samedi* (French: Saturday)
**SAMA** Saudi Arabian Monetary Agency; Scottish Amateur Music Association
**Samar.** Samaritan
**SAMC** South African Medical Corps
**S Amer.** South America; South American
**SAMH** Scottish Association for Mental Health
**SAMU** *Service d'assistance médicale d'urgence* (French: emergency medical assistance service)
**SAN** styrene–acrylonitrile (polymer)
**san.** sanitary
**SANA** Scottish Anglers' National Association
**sanat.** sanatorium
**SANCAD** Scottish Association for National Certificates and Diplomas
**SAND** Scotland Against Nuclear Dumping
**sand.** sandwich
**s&d** search and destroy; song and dance
**S&F** [insurance] stock and fixtures
**s&f** [informal] shopping and fucking (popular fiction genre)
**S&FA** shipping and forwarding agents
**S&H** shipping and handling (charges)
**S&L** [USA] savings and loan association
**S&M** sadism and masochism; [insurance] stock and machinery
**s&m** sausages and mash
**S&P 500** [USA] Standard and Poors 500 Stock Index
**Sands** Stillbirth and Neonatal Death Society
**s&s** [informal] sex and shopping (popular fiction genre)
**s&sc** sized and supercalendered (paper)
**S&T** signalling and telecommunications; supply and transport
**S&TA** Salmon and Trout Association
**Sane** Schizophrenia – A National Emergency
**SANFP** Scottish Association for Natural Family Planning
**sanit.** sanitary; sanitation
**s.a.n.r.** subject to approval, no risk
**Sans.** Sanskrit
**sans.** [printing] sanserif
**Sansk.** Sanskrit
**SANZ** Standards Association of New Zealand
**SAO** Scottish Association of Opticians
**SAOS** Scottish Agricultural Organization Society
**SAP** South African Police
**s.a.p.** soon as possible
**SAPA** South African Press Association; South African Publishers' Association
**SAPC** Scottish Accident Prevention Council
**sapfu** [slang] surpassing all previous foul-ups
**sapl** [shipping] sailed as per list (referring to Lloyd's List)
**SAPT** Scottish Association for Public Transport
**SAR** search and rescue; *Son Altesse Royale* (French: Her/His Royal Highness); Sons of the American Revolution; South African Republic; [China] Special Administrative Region; [physics] specific absorption rate; synthetic aperture radar
**Sar.** Sarawak; Sardinia; Sardinian
**SARA** Scottish Amateur Rowing Association; Scottish Anti-Racist Alliance
**SARAH** search and rescue homing (radar system); [medicine] surgery assistant robot acting on the head (in brain surgery)
**SARBE** search and rescue beacon equipment
**Sarl** [commerce] *société à responsabilité limitée* (French: limited company, Ltd)
**SARM** Scottish Anti-Racist Movement
**SARs** Substantial Acquisition Rules (for mergers and takeovers)
**SARSAT** search and rescue satellite(-aided tracking)
**SA/RT** [computing] structured systems analysis for real time
**Sarum.** *Sarumensis* (Latin: (Bishop) of Salisbury)
**SAS** Scandinavian Airlines System; Small

Astronomical Satellite; *Societatis Antiquariorum Socius* (Latin: Fellow of the Society of Antiquaries); *Son Altesse Sérénissime* (French: Her/His Most Serene Highness); [military] Special Air Service; Statement of Auditing Standards

**Sas** [commerce] *società in accomàndita semplice* (Italian: limited partnership)

**SASA** Scottish Amateur Snooker Association; Scottish Amateur Swimming Association

**SASC** Small Arms School Corps

**SASE** [USA] self-addressed stamped envelope

**SASF** Salvation Army Students' Fellowship

**Sask.** Saskatchewan

**SASO** Senior Air Staff Officer; South African Students' Organization

**SASR** Special Air Service Regiment

**SASV** Scottish Association for the Speaking of Verse

**SAT** [USA] scholastic aptitude test; Senior Member of the Association of Accounting Technicians; ship's apparent time; South Australian Time; [education] standard assessment task

**S At.** South Atlantic

**Sat.** Saturday

**sat.** satellite; saturate; saturated

**SATB** [music] soprano, alto, tenor, bass

**SATCO** signal automatic air traffic control system

**SATEX** semiautomatic telegraph exchange

**SATIPS** Society of Assistant Teachers in Preparatory Schools

**satn** saturation

**SATRA** Shoe and Allied Trades Research Association

**SATRO** Science and Technology Regional Organization

**SATS** South African Transport Services

**S Aus.** South Australia; South Australian

**S Austral.** South Australia; South Australian

**SAV** [microbiology] simian adenovirus

**s.a.v.** sale at valuation; stock at valuation

**SAVS** Scottish Anti-Vivisection Society

**SAW** Scottish Association of Writers; [advertising] space at will; submerged arc welding; [telecommunications] surface acoustic wave

**SAWA** Scottish Amateur Wrestling Association

**SAWS** synoptic automatic weather station

**Sax.** Saxon; Saxony

**sax** [short form] saxophone

**sax.** saxophone

**SAYC** Scottish Association of Youth Clubs

**SAYE** save as you earn

**SB** Bachelor of Science (from Latin *Scientiae Baccalaureus*); [astronomy] barred spiral galaxy; [vehicle registration] Glasgow; sales book; [military] Sam Browne (officer's belt with diagonal strap); savings bank; selection board; Serving Brother (of order); [commerce] short bill (of exchange); sick bay; Signal Boatswain; signal book; simultaneous broadcast(ing); [chemical engineering] slurry bed; small business; [chemistry] sodium borate; South Britain (i.e. England and Wales); Special Branch; statute book; [medicine] stillborn; stretcher bearer; sub-branch

**Sb** [chemical element] antimony (from Latin *stibium*)

**sb** stilb (unit of luminance)

**sb.** [grammar] substantive

**.sb** Solomon Islands (in Internet address)

**s.b.** single-breasted; small bore (rifle); smooth bore; [baseball] stolen base(s)

**SBA** School of Business Administration; Scottish Basketball Association; sick-bay (or -berth) attendant; [USA] Small Business Administration; [aeronautics] standard beam approach

**SBAA** Sovereign Base Areas Administration

**SBAC** Society of British Aerospace Companies (formerly Society of British Aircraft Constructors)

**SBB** *Schweizerische Bundesbahnen* (German: Swiss Federal Railways)

**SBBNF** Ship and Boat Builders' National Federation

**SBC** School Broadcasting Council; single-board computer; [electrical engineering] small bayonet cap

**SBD** [slang] silent but deadly (breaking of wind); Soviet Block Division (of CIA); [electronics] surface-barrier diode

**SBE** Southern British English

**SbE** south by east

**SBGI** Society of British Gas Industries
**SBH** Scottish Board of Health
**SBIC** [USA] small business investment company
**SBL** Society of Biblical Literature; [electronics] surface boundary layer
**SBLI** [USA] savings bank life insurance
**SBM** single buoy mooring
**SBN** Standard Book Number (replaced by ISBN)
**SBNO** Senior British Naval Officer
**s'board** starboard
**SBOT** Sacred Books of the Old Testament
**SBP** [medicine] systolic blood pressure
**SBPR** Society for Back Pain Research
**SBR** [medicine] strict bed rest; styrene–butadiene rubber
**sbre** *septiembre* (Spanish: September)
**SBS** [medicine] sick building syndrome; [military] Special Boat Service
**SBSA** Scottish Board Sailing Association
**SBStJ** Serving Brother of the Order of St John of Jerusalem
**SBT** [shipping] segregated ballast tanks
**SBTD** Society of British Theatre Designers
**SBU** Scottish Badminton Union; strategic business unit
**SBV** seabed vehicle
**SbW** south by west
**SC** [vehicle registration] Edinburgh; safe custody; sailing club; Salvage Corps; [law] same case; [US military] Sanitary Corps; [Australia, New Zealand] School Certificate; Schools Council; [fishing port] Scilly; Security Council (of UN); self-contained (in accommodation advertisement); *Senatus Consultum* (Latin: decree of the Senate); Senior Counsel; service certificate; [law] Sessions Cases; shooting club; short course; Signal Corps; [printing] single column; [chemistry] single crystal; skating club; skiing club; small craft; social club; solar cell; South Carolina; [US postcode] South Carolina; [military] Southern Command; special case; Special Constable; Special Constabulary; sports club; Staff Captain; staff college; Staff Corps; standing committee; standing conference; [Canada] Star of Courage; statutory committee; [engineering] stress corrosion; [grammar] structural change; [medicine] subcutaneous; Suffolk and Cambridgeshire (regiment); supercalendered (paper); Supreme Court; surface contamination; swimming club
**Sc** [chemical element] scandium
***Sc*** [meteorology] stratocumulus
**Sc.** Scandinavia; Scandinavian; Science; Scotch; Scotland; Scots; Scottish; sculptor
**s/c** self-catering (in accommodation advertisement); self-contained (in accommodation advertisement); [commerce] *son compte* (French: (on) her/his account)
**sc.** scale; scene; science; scientific; *scilicet* (= namely, that is, from Latin *scire licet*); screw; scruple (unit of weight); *sculpsit* (Latin: (he/she) carved it); sculptor
**.sc** Seychelles (in Internet address)
**s.c.** salvage charges; self-contained (in property or accommodation advertisement); [printing] single column; [printing] small capital(s); steel casting; supercalendered (paper)
**SCA** Scottish Canoe Association; Scottish Chess Association; Scottish Council on Alcohol; Scottish Croquet Association; [medicine] sickle-cell anaemia; Suez Canal Authority; [computing] synchronous concurrent algorithm
**SCAAA** Southern Counties Amateur Athletic Association
**SCAARF** Scottish Combined Action Against Racism and Fascism
**Scada** system control and data acquisition
**SCAFA** Scottish Child and Family Alliance
**SCAHT** Scottish Churches Architectural Heritage Trust
**SCAN** suspected child abuse and neglect
**Scan.** Scandinavia; Scandinavian
**Scand.** Scandinavia; Scandinavian
**SCAO** Senior Civil Affairs Officer
**SCAP** Supreme Command Allied Powers; Supreme Commander Allied Powers
**SCAPA** Society for Checking the Abuses of Public Advertising
**s. caps** [printing] small capitals
**SCAR** Scientific Committee on Antarctic Research; Special Committee on Antarctic Research
**SCARA** selective compliance assembly robot arm
**Scarab** submerged craft assisting repair and burial

**SCARF** Sickle Cell Anaemia Research Foundation; [accounting] systems control and review file

**SCART** *Syndicat des constructeurs des appareils radio récepteurs et téléviseurs* (French: Syndicate of Radio and Television Manufacturers) (designers of plug-and-socket system used in home entertainment equipment)

**SCAT** [medicine] sheep-cell agglutination test

**SCB** Solicitors Complaints Bureau; [medicine] special-care baby; Speedway Control Board (in motorcycle racing)

**ScB** Bachelor of Science (from Latin *Scientiae Baccalaureus*)

**ScBC** Bachelor of Science in Chemistry

**ScBE** Bachelor of Science in Engineering

**SCBU** [medicine] special-care baby unit

**SCC** Scottish Churches Council; Scottish Consumer Council; Sea Cadet Corps; Society of Church Craftsmen; [medicine] squamous-cell carcinoma; [engineering] stress-corrosion cracking

**s.c.c.** [printing] single column centimetre; [electrical engineering] single cotton-covered (wire)

**SCCA** Scottish Consumer Credit Association; Society of Company and Commercial Accountants; Sports Car Club of America

**SCCAPE** Scottish Council for Commercial, Administrative and Professional Education

**SCCL** Scottish Council for Civil Liberties

**SCD** Scottish Council on Disability; [medicine] sickle-cell disease

**ScD** Doctor of Science (from Latin *Scientiae Doctor*)

**scd** scheduled

**SCDA** Scottish Community Drama Association

**SCDC** Schools Curriculum Development Committee

**ScDHyg** Doctor of Science in Hygiene

**ScDMed** Doctor of Science in Medicine

**SCE** schedule compliance evaluation; Scottish Certificate of Education; [genetics] sister-chromatid exchange

**sce.** scenario

**SCEC** Scottish Community Education Council

**SCET** Scottish Council for Educational Technology

**SCF** Save the Children Fund; Senior Chaplain to the Forces

**scf** standard cubic feet

**scfd** standard cubic feet per day

**scfh** standard cubic feet per hour

**scfm** standard cubic feet per minute

**SCG** Sydney Cricket Ground

**scg** scoring

**SCGB** Ski Club of Great Britain

**Sch.** [taxation] schedule; [currency] Schilling; School

**sch.** schedule; scholar; scholarship; scholastic; scholiast; *scholium* (Latin: note); school; schooner

**sched.** schedule

**schem.** schematic

**scherz.** [music] *scherzando* (Italian: joking, playfully)

**SchMusB** Bachelor of School Music

**schol.** scholar; scholarship; scholastic; scholiast; *scholium* (Latin: note)

**schr** schooner

**SCI** Scottish Central Institutions; Society of the Chemical Industry

**sci.** science; scientific

**s.c.i.** [printing] single-column inch

**SCIAF** Scottish Catholic International Aid Fund

**SCID** Scotland's Campaign against Irresponsible Drivers; [medicine] severe combined immune deficiency

**sci. fa.** *scire facias* (Latin: cause it to be known) ( judicial writ)

**sci-fi** [short form] science fiction

**scil.** *scilicet* (= namely, that is, from Latin *scire licet*)

**SCIT** Special Commissioners of Income Tax

**SCK** Servants of Christ the King

**SCL** Scottish Central Library; Student of Civil Law

**Scl** [astronomy] Sculptor

**SCLC** Scottish Child Law Centre; [medicine] small-cell lung cancer (or carcinoma); Southern Christian Leadership Conference

**SCLI** Somerset and Cornwall Light Infantry

**SCM** [stock exchange] smaller companies market; State Certified Midwife (replaced by RM); Student Christian Movement; summary court martial

**ScM** Master of Science (from Latin *Scientiae Magister*)

**SCMA** Society of Cinema Managers of Great Britain and Ireland (Amalgamated); Stilton Cheese Manufacturers' Association

**SCMAC** Scottish Catholic Marriage Advisory Council

**SCMES** Society of Consulting Marine Engineers and Ship Surveyors

**ScMHyg** Master of Science in Hygiene

**SCNE** Select Committee on National Expenditure

**SCNI** Sports Council for Northern Ireland

**SCNO** Senior Canadian Naval Officer

**Sco** [astronomy] Scorpius

**SCOBEC** Scottish Business Education Council

**SCODL** [computing] scan conversion object description language

**SCOFF** Society for the Conquest of Flight Fear

**Scolag** Scottish Legal Action Group

**S Con. Res.** [USA] Senate concurrent resolution

**SCONUL** Standing Conference of National and University Libraries

**SCOR** Scientific Committee on Oceanic Research; Standing Committee on Refugees

**Scot.** Scotch; Scotland; Scottish

**ScotBIC** Scottish Business in the Community

**SCOTEC** Scottish Technical Education Council

**SCOTUS** Supreme Court of the United States

**SCOTVEC** Scottish Vocational Educational Council (became part of SQA)

**SCOUT** [commerce] shared currency option under tender

**SCP** single-cell protein (in food technology); [Canada] Social Credit Party

**SCPC** [telecommunications] single channel per carrier

**SCPR** Scottish Council of Physical Recreation

**SCPS** Society of Civil and Public Servants

**SCR** [chemical engineering] selective catalytic reactor; senior combination room (in university or college); senior common room (in university or college); sequence control register; [electronics] silicon-controlled rectifier; small companies rate (of corporation tax)

**scr.** [finance] scrip; script; scruple (unit of weight)

**SCRAM** Scottish Campaign to Resist the Atomic Menace

**SCRE** Scottish Council for Racial Equality; Scottish Council for Research in Education

**SCREAM** Society for the Control and Registration of Estate Agents and Mortgage Brokers

**Script.** Scriptural; Scripture(s)

**SCS** Scottish Crime Squad; [USA] Soil Conservation Service; space communications system

**SCSA** signal computing system achitecture; Soil Conservation Society of America

**SCSI** small computer systems interface (pronounced 'scuzzy')

**SCSS** Scottish Council of Social Service

**Sct** [astronomy] Scutum

**SCTR** Standing Conference on Telecommunications Research

**SCU** Scottish Cricket Union; Scottish Cyclists' Union; [medicine] special care unit

**SCUA** Scottish Conservative and Unionist Association; Suez Canal Users' Association

**scuba** self-contained underwater breathing apparatus

**sculp.** *sculpsit* (Latin: (he/she) carved it); sculptor; sculptural; sculpture

**sculps.** *sculpsit* (Latin: (he/she) carved it)

**sculpt** *sculpsit* (Latin: (he/she) carved it)

**sculpt.** sculptor; sculptural; sculpture

**SCV** *Stato della Città del Vaticano* (Italian: Vatican City State)

**SCWS** Scottish Cooperative Wholesale Society

**SCY** [vehicle registration] Truro (Isles of Scilly)

**SCYA** Scottish Christian Youth Assembly

**SD** Diploma in Statistics; Doctor of Science (from Latin *Scientiae Doctor*); [vehicle registration] Glasgow; *salutem dicit* (Latin: (he/she) sends greeting); sea-damaged; [USA] Secretary of Defense; semi-detached (in property advertisement); *Senatus Decreto* (Latin: by decree of the Senate); send direct; [medicine] senile dementia; senior deacon; sequence date; [military] service dress; [commerce] short delivery; *Sicherheitsdienst* (German: Security Service) (in Nazi Germany); [finance] sight draft; Signal Department; Signal Division; [computing] single density (disk); South Dakota; [US postcode] South Dakota; special delivery; special duty; spin dryer (in accommodation advertisement); staff duties; stage door; [statistics] standard deviation; [USA] State Department; [grammar] structural description; submarine detector; [currency] Sudanese dinar; [fishing port] Sunderland; supply depot; [international vehicle registration] Swaziland

**S/D** [USA] school district; [finance] sight draft

**sd** said; sailed; [bookbinding] sewed; signed; sound

**.sd** Sudan (in Internet address)

**s.d.** safe deposit; same date; *sans date* (French: no date); semi-detached (in property advertisement); sense datum (in philosophy); several dates; [commerce] short delivery; *siehe dies* (German: see this); *sine die* (Latin: without a day (being fixed)); [statistics] standard deviation

**SDA** Scottish Darts Association; Scottish Development Agency; Scottish Dinghy Association; Scottish Diploma in Agriculture; Seventh Day Adventist(s); Social Democratic Alliance; spray-drying absorption (or absorber)

**S Dak.** South Dakota

**SD&T** staff duties and training

**SDAT** [medicine] senile dementia of the Alzheimer type

**S-DAT** stationary digital audio tape

**SDC** Society of Dyers and Colourists; submersible decompression chamber

**SDCGB** Square Dance Callers of Great Britain

**SDD** Scottish Development Department; [telecommunications] subscriber direct dialling

**SDECE** *Service de documentation étrangère et de contre-espionnage* (French counterintelligence agency)

**SDF** Social Democratic Federation

**SDG** *Soli Deo Gloria* (Latin: Glory to God Alone)

**SDH** [computing] synchronous digital hierarchy

**SDHE** spacecraft data-handling equipment

**SDI** selective dissemination of information; Strategic Defense Initiative (US Star Wars programme)

**SDIO** [USA] Strategic Defense Initiative Office

**SDL** special duties list

**sdl.** saddle

**SDLC** [computing] synchronous data link control

**SDLP** [Northern Ireland] Social Democratic and Labour Party

**SDMJ** September, December, March, June (end of financial quarters)

**SDO** senior dental officer; senior duty officer; station duty officer; subdivisional officer

**S Doc.** [USA] Senate document

**SDP** Social Democratic Party (former political party); [insurance] social, domestic and pleasure

**SDPM** [computing] software development process model

**SDR** special dispatch rider; *Suddeutscher Rundfunk* (German: South German Radio)

**SDRAM** [computing] synchronous dynamic random-access memory

**SDRs** [finance] special drawing rights (in IMF)

**SDRT** stamp duty reserve tax

**SDS** scientific data system; Sisters of the Divine Saviour; sodium dodecyl sulphate (detergent); *Sozialistischer Deutscher Studentenbund* (German: Federation of Socialist Students); [USA] strategic defense system; [USA] Students for a Democratic Society

**SDT** Society of Dairy Technology

**SDTU** Sign and Display Trades Union

**SDUK** Society for the Diffusion of Useful Knowledge

**SE** [vehicle registration] Aberdeen; [fishing port] Salcombe; sanitary engineering; Scottish Enterprise; Society of Engineers; [computing] software engineering; *Son Éminence* (French: His Eminence); *Son Excellence* (French: Her/His Excellency);

southeast; southeastern; [UK postcode] southeast London; Staff Engineer; Standard English; Stirling engine; stock exchange; [building] stopped end; [civil aircraft marking] Sweden

**S/E** stock exchange

**Se** [chemical element] selenium

**.se** Sweden (in Internet address)

**s.e.** single end; single ended; single engine; [book-keeping] single entry; special equipment; [statistics] standard error; straight edge

**SEA** Southeast Asia

**SEAAC** Southeast Asia Air Command

**SEAC** School Examination and Assessment Council; Southeast Asia Command; Standard Eastern Automatic Computer

**SEAL** [US navy] sea-air-land

**SEALF** Southeast Asia Land Forces

**SE&CR** South Eastern and Chatham Railway

**SEAQ** Stock Exchange Automated Quotations (System)

**SEAT** *Sociedad Española de Automoviles de Tourismo* (Spanish vehicle manufacturer)

**SEATO** Southeast Asia Treaty Organization

**SEATS** Stock Exchange Alternative Trading Service

**SEB** Scottish Education Board (became part of SQA); Southern Electricity Board

**SEC** Scottish Evangelistic Crusade; Secondary Examinations Council; [USA] Securities and Exchange Commission; [military] Southeastern Command

**Sec.** Secretary

**sec** [mathematics] secant; [short form] second

**sec.** second; secondary; seconded; secretary; section; sector; *secundum* (Latin: according to); security

**SECAM** [television] *séquentiel couleur à mémoire* (French: colour sequence by memory) (broadcasting system)

**SECC** Scottish Exhibition and Conference Centre

**Sec-Gen** Secretary-General

**sech** [mathematics] hyperbolic secant

**Sec. Leg.** Secretary of the Legation

**sec. leg.** *secundum legem* (Latin: according to law)

**sec. nat.** *secundum naturam* (Latin: according to nature, naturally)

**sec. reg.** *secundum regulam* (Latin: according to rule)

**sect.** section

**secy** secretary

**SED** Scottish Education Department; shipper's export declaration; *Sozialistische Einheitspartei Deutschlands* (German: Socialist Unity Party) (former East German Communist Party)

**sed.** sedative; sediment

**SEDAR** [navigation] submerged electrode detection and ranging

**sedt** sediment

**sedtn** sedimentation

**SEE** senior electrical engineer; Society of Environment Engineers

**Seeboard** Southeastern Electricity Board

**SEF** Shipbuilding Employers' Federation

**SEG** [taxation] Self Employment Group; socioeconomic grade

**seg.** segment; segregate; [music] *segue* (Italian: follows, comes after)

**SEIF** *Secretaria de Estado da Informação e Turismo* (Portuguese: State Information and Tourist Board)

**SEIS** submarine escape immersion suit

**seismol.** seismological; seismology

**SEIU** [USA] Service Employees International Union

**sel.** select; selected; selection; *selig* (German: deceased)

**Selk.** Selkirk

**SELNEC** Southeast Lancashire, Northeast Cheshire

**SEM** scanning electron microscope (or microscopy)

**Sem.** Seminary; Semitic

**sem.** semester; semicolon; seminary

**s.e.m.** [statistics] standard error of the mean

**semi** [short form] semi-detached house

**semp.** [music] *sempre* (Italian: always, still)

**s/empl.** self-employed

**SEN** special educational needs; State Enrolled Nurse (former name of ENG)

**Sen.** Senate; Senator; (Marcus Annaeus) Seneca (Roman writer); Senior

**sen.** senior; [music] *senza* (Italian: without)

**S en C** [commerce] *sociedad en comandita* (Spanish: limited partnership); [commerce] *société en commandite* (French: limited partnership)

**Sennac** Special Educational Needs National Advisory Council

**S en NC** [commerce] *société en nom collectif* (French: partnership)

**Senr** Senior

**sent.** sentence

**SEO** senior executive officer; senior experimental officer; Society of Educational Officers

**s.e.o.o.** *sauf erreur ou omission* (French: errors or omissions excepted)

**SEP** [USA] simplified employee pension

**Sep.** September; Septuagint

**sep.** [botany] sepal; separable; separate; separated; separation

**SEPA** Scottish Environment Protection Agency

**SEPM** Society of Economic Palaeontologists and Mineralogists

**sepn** separation

**SEPON** Stock Exchange Pool Nominees Limited

**Sept.** *September* (German: September); September; Septuagint

**sept.** *septem* (Latin: seven); *septembre* (French: September)

**seq.** sequel; sequence; *sequens* (Latin: the following (one) ); *sequente* (Latin: and in what follows); *sequitur* (Latin: it follows)

**seq. luce** [medicine] *sequenti luce* (Latin: on the following day) (in prescriptions)

**seqq.** *sequentia* (Latin: the following (ones) ); *sequentibus* (Latin: in the following (places) )

**Ser** [astronomy] Serpens

**ser.** serial; series; sermon; servant; service

**SERA** Socialist Environment and Resources Association

**Serb.** Serbia; Serbian

**SERC** Science and Engineering Research Council (formerly SRC)

**Serg.** Sergeant

**Sergt** Sergeant

**Serj.** Serjeant

**Serjt** Serjeant

**SERL** Services Electronics Research Laboratory

**SERLANT** [US navy] Service Forces, Atlantic

**SERPAC** [US navy] Service Forces, Pacific

**Serps** State Earnings-Related Pension Scheme

**SERT** Society of Electronic and Radio Technicians

**serv.** servant; service

**SES** Scientific Exploration Society; [USA] socioeconomic status; Stock Exchange of Singapore

**SESCO** secure submarine communications

**SESDAQ** Stock Exchange of Singapore Dealing and Automated Quotation System

**SESI** Stock Exchange of Singapore Index

**SESO** Senior Equipment Staff Officer

**sess.** session

**SET** Securities Exchange of Thailand; selective employment tax (former tax)

**SETI** [astronomy] search for extraterrestrial intelligence

**S-et-L** Saône-et-Loire (French department)

**S-et-M** Seine-et-Marne (French department)

**S-et-O** Seine-et-Oise (French department)

**Sets** Stock Exchange electronic trading system

**sett.** *settembre* (Italian: September)

**sev.** sever; several; severe

**sevl** several

**SEW** safety-equipment worker

**sew.** sewage; sewer; sewerage

**Sex** [astronomy] Sextans

**sex.** sextet; sexual

**Sexag.** Sexagesima

**sext.** sextant

**SF** [vehicle registration] Edinburgh; San Francisco; science fiction; Senior Fellow; [military] Sherwood Foresters; shipping federation; [telecommunications] signal frequency; [finance] sinking fund; Sinn Féin; Society of Friends; special facilities; special forces; [electrical engineering] standard frequency

**Sf** [currency] Suriname guilder (from alternative name florin)

**sf.** [music] *sforzando* (Italian: strengthening, strongly accented)

**s.f.** [baseball] sacrifice fly; [commerce] *sans frais* (French: no expenses); science fiction; [telecommunications] signal frequency; [finance] sinking fund; *sub finem* (Latin: towards the end)

**SFA** Scottish Football Association; Securities and Futures Authority; Small Farmers' Association; sulphated fatty alcohol (in detergent); [slang] sweet Fanny Adams (i.e. nothing); [slang] sweet fuck all (i.e. nothing)

**SFAC** Statement of Financial Accounting Concepts

**SFAS** Statement of Financial Accounting Standards

**SFB** *Sender Freies Berlin* (German: Broadcasting Station of Free Berlin)

**SFBMS** Small Farm Business Management Scheme

**SFC** specific fuel consumption (of jet engine)

**Sfc** [USA] Sergeant first class

**SFD** [obstetrics] small for dates (of baby)

**SFEP** Society of Freelance Editors and Proofreaders

**SFEU** Scottish Further Education Unit

**SFF** [computing] small form factor

**sfgd** safeguard

**SFHEA** Scottish Further and Higher Education Association

**SFI** *Société financière internationale* (French: International Finance Corporation)

**SFInstE** Senior Fellow, Institute of Energy

**SFL** Scottish Football League; [aeronautics] sequenced flashing lights (on runway)

**sfm** surface feet per minute

**SFO** Senior Flag Officer; Serious Fraud Office; Superannuation Funds Office

**SFOF** spaceflight operations facility (in NASA)

**SFOR** Sustaining (or Stabilization) Force (NATO-led peacekeeping force in Bosnia, replacement for IFOR)

**sfp** [music] *sforzato-piano* (Italian: strongly accented (then) soft)

**SFR** [finance] sinking fund rate of return

**SFr** [currency] Swiss franc

**SFSR** Socialist Federation of Soviet Republics

**SFT** supercritical fluid technology

**SFTCD** Senior Fellow of Trinity College, Dublin

**SFU** signals flying unit; suitable for upgrade (on airline ticket)

**sfz.** [music] *sforzando* (Italian: strengthening, strongly accented)

**SG** [vehicle registration] Edinburgh; *Sa Grâce* (French: Her/His Grace); *Sa Grandeur* (French: Her/His Highness); Scots Guards; Seaman Gunner; Secretary-General; *selon grandeur* (French: according to size) (on menus etc.); [US education] senior grade; [astronomy] Seyfert galaxy; ship and goods; Showmen's Guild of Great Britain; Society of Genealogists; Solicitor-General; spin-glass (type of crystal); [UK postcode] Stevenage; Surgeon-General

**Sg** [chemical element] seaborgium

**Sg.** Surgeon

**sg.** [grammar] singular

**.sg** Singapore (in Internet address)

**s.g.** specific gravity; steel girder

**SGA** Scottish Games Association; [obstetrics] small for gestational age; Society of Graphic Art

**SGB** *Schweizerischer Gewerkschaftsbund* (German: Swiss Federation of Trade Unions)

**SGBI** Schoolmistresses' and Governesses' Benevolent Institution

**SgC** Surgeon Captain

**SgCr** Surgeon Commander

**SGD** [Freemasonry] Senior Grand Deacon

**sgd** signed

**sgdg** *sans garantie du gouvernement* (French: without government guarantee) (of patent)

**Sge** [astronomy] Sagitta

**SGF** Scottish Grocers' Federation

**SGHWR** [nuclear technology] steam-generating heavy-water reactor

**sgl.** single

**S Glam.** South Glamorgan

**SgLCr** Surgeon Lieutenant-Commander

**sgle** single

**SGM** Sea Gallantry Medal

**SGML** [computing] standard generalized markup language

**SGO** Squadron Gunnery Officer

**SGOT** [medicine] serum glutamic oxaloacetic transaminase

**SGP** [international vehicle registration] Singapore

**SGPT** [medicine] serum glutamic pyruvic transaminase

**Sgr** [astronomy] Sagittarius

**SgRA** Surgeon Rear-Admiral

**SGRAM** [computing] synchronous graphics random-access memory

**SGT** Society of Glass Technology

**Sgt** Sergeant

**Sgt-Maj** Sergeant-Major
**SGTS** Scottish Gaelic Texts Society
**SGU** Scottish Gliding Union; Scottish Golf Union
**SgVA** Surgeon Vice-Admiral
**SGW** [Freemasonry] Senior Grand Warden
**SH** [vehicle registration] Edinburgh; [fishing port] Scarborough; Schleswig-Holstein; school house; scrum half (in rugby); sexual harassment; [meteorology] showers; [numismatics] small head; southern hemisphere
**Sh.** [military] Shipwright
**s/h** shorthand
**sh.** shall; [stock exchange] share; sheep; [bookbinding] sheet; shilling; shower (in property or accommodation advertisement)
**s.h.** [baseball] sacrifice hit; second-hand; shit-house; slant height; slope height
**SHA** Scottish Hockey Association; Secondary Heads Association; [astronomy, navigation] sidereal hour angle; special health authority; [mathematics] spherical harmonic analysis
**SHAC** Shelter Housing Aid Centre
**SHACT** Scottish Housing Associations Charitable Trust
**SHAEF** Supreme Headquarters Allied Expeditionary Forces (in World War II)
**Shak.** (William) Shakespeare (English writer)
**Shakes.** (William) Shakespeare (English writer)
**SH&MA** Scottish Horse and Motormen's Association
**SHAPE** Supreme Headquarters Allied Powers Europe (of NATO)
**SHC** [physics] specific heat capacity
**SHCJ** Society of the Holy Child Jesus
**shd** should
**SHE** safety, health and ergonomics
**S/HE** [shipping] Sundays and holidays excepted
**Shef.** Sheffield
**SHEFC** Scottish Higher Education Funding Council
**Sheff.** Sheffield
**Shet.** Shetland Islands
**Shetl.** Shetland Islands
**SHEX** [shipping] Sundays and holidays excepted
**SHF** [radio] superhigh frequency
**Sh.F** shareholders' funds
**SHGF** Scottish Hang-Gliding Federation
**SHHD** Scottish Home and Health Department
**shipmt** shipment
**shipt** shipment
**s/hist.** service history (in car advertisement)
**SHM** [physics] simple harmonic motion; Society of Housing Managers
**SHMIS** Society of Headmasters and Headmistresses of Independent Schools
**SHMO** senior hospital medical officer
**SHO** senior house officer
**SHORAN** short-range navigation
**SHP** [chemical engineering] selective hydrogenation process; [horticulture] single-flowered hardy perennial (rose); [horticulture] single-flowered hybrid perpetual (rose)
**shp** shaft horsepower
**shpg** shipping
**shpt** shipment
**SHQ** station headquarters; supreme headquarters
**shr.** share(s)
**shrap.** shrapnel
**SHRG** Scottish Homosexual Rights Group
**Shrops** Shropshire
**SHS** Shire Horse Society; Social History Society of the United Kingdom; *Societatis Historicae Socius* (Latin: Fellow of the Historical Society)
**SHT** [horticulture] single-flowered hybrid tea (rose)
**sht** [bookbinding] sheet
**shtg.** shortage
**SHU** Scottish Hockey Union
**s.h.v.** *sub hac voce* (Latin: under this word) (in reference book); *sub hoc verbo* (Latin: under this word) (in reference book)
**SHW** safety, health, and welfare
**shwr** shower (in property or accommodation advertisement)
**SI** Sandwich Islands (former name of Hawaii); seriously ill; Shetland Islands; Smithsonian Institution (Washington, DC); Socialist International; [USA] Society of Illustrators; South Island (New Zealand); Staff Inspector; (Order of the) Star of India; Staten Island (New York); statutory instrument (of government); styrene–isoprene (polymer); *Système*

*International* (*d'Unités*) (French: International System (of Units), as in **SI unit**)
**Si** [chemical element] silicon
**.si** Slovenia (in Internet address)
**s.i.** sum insured
**SIA** Securities Industry Association; Society of Investment Analysts; Spinal Injuries Association
**SIAC** [USA] Securities Industry Automation Corporation
**SIAD** Society of Industrial Artists and Designers (former name of CSD)
**SIAM** [USA] Society of Industrial and Applied Mathematics
**SIAS** Statement on Internal Auditing Standards
**SIB** Savings and Investment Bank; Securities and Investments Board; [medicine] self-injurious behaviour; Shipbuilding Industry Board; Special Investigation Branch (of police)
**Sib.** Siberia; Siberian
**SIBH** Society for the Interpretation of Britain's Heritage
**SIBOR** [finance] Singapore Inter-Bank Offered Rate
**SIC** [USA] Scientific Information Center; Standard Industrial Classification
**Sic.** Sicilian; Sicily
**sic.** [pharmacology] *siccus* (Latin: dry)
**SICAV** *société d'investissement à capital variable* (French: unit trust)
**SICOT** *Société internationale de chirurgie orthopédique et de traumatologie* (French: International Society of Orthopaedic Surgery and Traumatology)
**SID** Society for International Development; *Spiritus in Deo* (Latin: her/his spirit is with God); [radio] sudden ionospheric disturbance
**SIDA** Swedish International Development Authority; [medicine] *syndrome immunodéficitaire acquis* (French: acquired immune deficiency syndrome, Aids)
**SIDF** system independent data format
**SIDS** [medicine] sudden infant death syndrome (= cot death)
**SIEC** Scottish Industrial Estates Corporation
**SIESO** Society of Industrial and Emergency Service Officers
**SIF** selective identification feature; [engineering] stress-intensity factor
**SIFS** special instructors' flying school
**SIG** [numismatics] signature of engraver present; special interest group
**Sig.** *Signor* (Italian: Mr); *Signore* (Italian: Sir)
**sig.** signal; signature; *signetur* (Latin: let it be written, let it be labelled); significant; signification; signifies
**SIGAC** Scottish Industrial Groups Advisory Council
**SIGBI** Soroptimist International of Great Britain and Ireland
**sig. fig.** [mathematics] significant figures
**sigill.** *sigillum* (Latin: seal)
**SIGINT** signals intelligence (gathering network)
**SIGMA** Science in General Management
**Sigmn** Signalman
**sign.** signature
**signif.** significant; signifier
**sig. n. pro.** [medicine] *signa nomine proprio* (Latin: label with the proper name) (in prescriptions)
**Sig. O** Signal Officer
**SIH** Society for Italic Handwriting
**SIL** [electronics] single in-line; *Société internationale de la lèpre* (French: International Leprosy Association)
**Sil.** Silesia; Silesian
**SIM** self-inflicted mutilation; *Société internationale de musicologie* (French: International Musicological Society); survey information on microfilm
**sim.** similar; similarly; simile
**SIMA** Scientific Instrument Manufacturers' Association of Great Britain; Steel Industry Management Association; [psychology] system for identifying motivated abilities
**SIMC** *Société internationale pour la musique contemporaine* (French: International Society for Contemporary Music)
**Simca** *Société industrielle de mécanique et carrosserie automobiles* (French car manufacturer)
**SIMD** [computing] single instruction, multiple data
**SIME** Security Intelligence Middle East
**SIMEX** Singapore International Monetary Exchange
**SIMG** *Societas Internationalis Medicinae Gen-*

*eralis* (Latin: International Society of General Medicine)
**SIMM** [computing, electronics] single in-line memory module
**SIMPL** Scientific, Industrial and Medical Photographic Laboratories
**SIN** [accounting] stores issue note
**sin** [mathematics] sine
**sin.** sinecure; *sinistra* (Italian: left)
**sinbad** [informal] single income, no boyfriend, absolutely desperate
**Sing.** Singapore; Singaporean
**sing.** [grammar] singular; [medicine] *singulorum* (Latin: of each) (in prescriptions)
**Sinh.** Sinhalese
**sinh** [mathematics] hyperbolic sine
**SINS** ship's inertial navigation system
**SIO** senior intelligence officer; [computing] serial input/output
**SIOP** [USA] single integrated operations plan (for nuclear war)
**SIP** [computing] single in-line package; [USA] supplemental income plan
**SIPC** [USA] Securities Investor Protection Corporation
**SIPO** [computing] serial in, parallel out
**SIPRC** Society of Independent Public Relations Consultants
**SIPRI** Stockholm International Peace Research Institute
**SIPS** side impact protection system (in car bodywork)
**SIR** [taxation] small income relief
**Sir** [computing] serial infrared
**SIRA** Scientific Instrument Research Association
**SIRS** [medicine] systemic inflammatory response syndrome
**SIRTF** Space Infrared Telescope Facility
**SIS** Satellite Information Services; Secret Intelligence Service (= MI6); [New Zealand] Security Intelligence Service
**sis** [short form] sister
**sis.** sister
**SISD** Scottish Information Service for the Disabled; [computing] single instruction, single data
**SISO** [computing] serial in, serial out; [electronics] single input, single output
**SISS** submarine integrated sonar system
**SISTER** Special Institutions for Scientific and Technological Education and Research
**SIT** Society of Industrial Technology; Society of Instrument Technology; [engineering] spontaneous ignition temperature; [currency] tolar (used in Slovenia)
**sit.** sitting room (in property advertisement); situated; situation
**s.i.t.** stopping in transit; storing in transit
**SITA** *Société internationale de télécommunications aéronautiques* (French: International Society of Aeronautical Telecommunications); Students' International Travel Association
**SITC** Standard International Trade Classification
**sitcom** [short form] situation comedy
**SITC(R)** Standard International Trade Classification (Revised)
**SITPRO** Simpler Trade Procedures Board (formerly Simplification of International Trade Procedures)
**sits vac.** situations vacant
**sitt.** sitting room (in property advertisement)
**sit. vac.** situation(s) vacant
**SIUNA** Seafarers International Union of North America
**SI unit** *Système international* unit
**SIV** [microbiology] simian immunodeficiency virus
**SIW** self-inflicted wound
**SIWA** Scottish Inland Waterways Association
**SJ** [vehicle registration] Glasgow; Society of Jesus (= Jesuits); supersonic jet
**s.j.** [law] sub judice
**SJA** St John Ambulance
**SJAA** St John Ambulance Association
**SJAB** St John Ambulance Brigade
**SJC** standing joint committee; [USA] Supreme Judicial Court
**SJCRE** Scottish Joint Committee on Religious Education
**SJD** Doctor of Juridical (or Juristic) Science (from Latin *Scientiae Juridicae Doctor*)
**SJF** Scottish Judo Federation
**SK** [vehicle registration] Inverness; Saskatchewan; Sealed Knot (historical re-enactment society); [international vehicle registration] Slovakia; [UK postcode] Stockport
**Sk** [currency] Slovakian koruna
**sk** sack; sick

**sk.** sketch
**.sk** Slovakia (in Internet address)
**SKAMP** station keeping and mobile platform (unmanned boat)
**SKC** Scottish Kennel Club
**SKFA** Scottish Keep Fit Association
**Skm** Stockholm
**s.k.p.o.** [knitting] slip one, knit one, pass slipped stitch over
**Skr** Skipper; [currency] Swedish krona
**Skr.** Sanskrit
**Skt** Sanskrit
**SKU** [commerce] stock-keeping unit
**SL** [vehicle registration] Dundee; [insurance] salvage loss; Scout leader; sea level; Second Lieutenant; security list; Sergeant-at-Law; [building] short lengths; Sierra Leone; [UK postcode] Slough; Solicitor-at-Law; source language; southern league; south latitude; [commerce] specification limits; Squadron Leader; supplementary list
**Sl.** Slovak; Slovakian
**sl.** sleet; slightly; slip
**.sl** Sierra Leone (in Internet address)
**s.l.** [insurance] salvage loss; *secundum legem* (Latin: according to law); seditious libel; [bibliography] *sine loco* (Latin: without place (of publication)); support line
**SLA** School Libraries Association; Scottish Library Association; special landscape area (in conservation); [USA] Special Libraries Association; Symbionese Liberation Army
**SLAC** Stanford Linear Accelerator Center
**SLADE** Society of Lithographic Artists, Designers, Engravers and Process Workers
**SLAET** Society of Licensed Aircraft Engineers and Technologists
**Slam** standoff land-attack missile
**s.l.a.n.** [bibliography] *sine loco, anno vel nomine* (Latin: without place, year or name (of publisher))
**Slar** [military] side-looking airborne radar
**SLAS** Society for Latin American Studies
**SLASH** Scottish Local Authorities Special Housing Group
**S Lat.** south latitude
**Slav.** Slavic; Slavonian; Slavonic
**SLBM** submarine-launched ballistic missile
**SLC** Scottish Land Court; Scottish Law Commission; Scottish Leaving Certificate; Statute Law Committee; Surgeon Lieutenant-Commander
**SLCM** sea-launched cruise missile; ship-launched cruise missile; submarine-launched cruise missile
**SLD** self-locking device; Social and Liberal Democrats (former name of Liberal Democrats)
**sld** sailed; sealed; sold; solid
**S Ldr** Squadron Leader
**SLE** [medicine] systemic lupus erythematosus
**s.l. et a.** [bibliography] *sine loco et anno* (Latin: without place and year (of publication))
**S level** [education] Special level (formerly Scholarship level)
**SLF** Scottish Landowners' Federation
**s.l.f.** [telecommunications] straight-line frequency
**SLFP** Sri Lanka Freedom Party
**SLGA** Scottish Ladies' Golfing Association
**SLIC** [USA] (Federal) Savings and Loan Insurance Corporation
**SLIM** South London Industrial Mission
**SLIP** [computing] serial line Internet protocol
**Slipar** [military] short light pulse alerting receiver (in aircraft)
**SLLA** Scottish Ladies' Lacrosse Association
**SLLW** solid low-level (radioactive) waste
**SLM** ship-launched missile
**SLMA** [USA] Student Loan Marketing Association
**SLMC** Scottish Ladies' Mountaineering Club
**s.l.n.d.** [bibliography] *sine loco nec data* (Latin: without date or place (of publication))
**SLO** senior liaison officer; [international vehicle registration] Slovenia
**SLOA** Steam Locomotive Operators' Association
**SLOC** [computing] source lines of code
**SLP** Scottish Labour Party; [USA] Socialist Labor Party
**slp** slip
**s.l.p.** *sine legitime prole* (Latin: without lawful issue)
**SLR** satellite laser ranging; self-loading rifle; single-lens reflex (camera)

**SLRS** Sexual Law Reform Society
**SL Rs** [currency] Sri Lankan rupee
**SLS** sodium lauryl sulphate (detergent); Stephenson Locomotive Society
**SLSC** surf life-saving club
**SLSI** [electronics] super large-scale integration
**SLTA** Scottish Lawn Tennis Association; Scottish Licensed Trade Association
**Slud** [military slang] salivate, lachrymate, urinate, defecate (effects of chemical weapons)
**SLV** Society of Licensed Victuallers; space launch vehicle; standard launch vehicle
**SLW** solid low-level (radioactive) waste
**sly** slowly; southerly
**SM** [vehicle registration] Carlisle; Master of Science (from Latin *Scientiae Magister*); sadomasochism; sadomasochist; sales manager; *Sa Majesté* (French: Her/His Majesty); *sanctae memoriae* (Latin: of holy memory); *Seine Majestät* (German: Her/His Majesty); senior magistrate; Sergeant-Major; [USA] service mark (registered proprietary name); [astronautics] service module; shipment memorandum; [fishing port] Shoreham; [music] short metre; silver medal; silver medallist; Sisters of Mercy; Society of Miniaturists; Sons of Malta; Staff Major; stage manager; [astronomy] standard model; [USA] state militia; station master; stipendiary magistrate; strategic missile; *Sua Maestà* (Italian: Her/His Majesty); (officer qualified for) Submarine Duties; *Su Magestad* (Spanish: Her/His Majesty); Surgeon Major; [UK postcode] Sutton (Surrey); [medicine] systolic murmur
**Sm** [chemical element] samarium
**s/m** sadomasochism; sadomasochist
**sm.** small
**.sm** San Marino (in Internet address)
**SMA** [medicine] spinal muscular atrophy; [USA] Surplus Marketing Administration
**SMAC** Standing Medical Advisory Committee (of NHS)
**SMATV** satellite (or small) master antenna television
**SMAW** shielded metal-arc welding
**SMB** Bachelor of Sacred Music; *Sa Majesté Britannique* (French: Her/His Britannic Majesty)
**SMBA** Scottish Marine Biological Association
**SMBF** Scottish Musicians' Benevolent Fund
**SMBG** [medicine] self-monitoring of blood glucose (in diabetes)
**SMC** *Sa Majesté Catholique* (French: Her/His Catholic Majesty); School Meals Campaign; Scottish Mountaineering Club; Scottish Museums Council; [astronomy] Small Magellanic Cloud; [aeronautics] standard mean chord
**sm. caps** [printing] small capitals
**SMC(Disp)** Dispensing Certificate of the Worshipful Company of Spectacle Makers
**SMD** Doctor of Sacred Music; [medicine] senile macular degeneration; [music] short metre double; submarine mine depot; [electronics] surface-mounted device (on printed circuit board)
**SMDS** [computing] switched multi-megabit data service
**SME** *Sancta Mater Ecclesia* (Latin: Holy Mother Church); seismic-margin earthquake; [international vehicle registration] Suriname
**SMERSH** *Smert Shpionam* (Russian: death to spies) (section of KGB)
**SMEs** small and medium enterprises
**SMEX** [astronomy] Small Explorer
**SMG** Scottish Media Group; submachine gun
**SMGC** Scottish Marriage Guidance Council
**SMH** [fishing port] St Margaret's Hope (Orkney)
**SMHD** Higher Diploma in Ophthalmic Optics of the Worshipful Company of Spectacle Makers
**SMHI** Swedish Meteorological and Hydrological Institute
**SMHO** Sovereign Military Hospitaller Order (in Malta)
**SMI** *Sa Majesté Impériale* (French: Her/His Imperial Majesty); Swiss Market Index
**SMIA** Sheet Metal Industries Association
**SMIEEE** [USA] Senior Member of the Institute of Electrical and Electronics Engineers
**SMIRE** [USA] Senior Member of the Institute of Radio Engineers

**Smith. Inst.** Smithsonian Institution (Washington, DC)
**SMJ** Sisters of Mary and Joseph
**smk.** smoke
**SML** Science Museum Library
**sml** small; small, medium, large
**sml.** simulate; simulation; simulator
**SMLE** short magazine Lee-Enfield (rifle)
**SMM** Master of Sacred Music; *Sancta Mater Maria* (Latin: Holy Mother Mary)
**SMMB** Scottish Milk Marketing Board
**SMMT** Society of Motor Manufacturers and Traders Limited
**SMO** senior medical officer; Sovereign Military Order
**SMON** [medicine] subacute myelo-opticoneuropathy
**smorz.** [music] *smorzando* (Italian: becoming slower and softer)
**SMP** Society of Mural Painters; statutory maternity pay; [computing] symmetric multiprocessing
**s.m.p.** *sine mascula prole* (Latin: without male issue)
**SMPS** Society of Master Printers of Scotland; switched-mode power supply
**SMPTE** [USA] Society of Motion Picture and Television Engineers
**SMR** *Sa Majesté Royale* (French: Her/His Royal Majesty); standardized mortality ratio; standard Malaysian rubber; [medicine] standard metabolic rate; standard mortality rate
**SMRC** Scottish Motor Racing Club
**SMRE** Safety in Mines Research Establishment
**SMRTB** Ship and Marine Requirements Technology Board
**SMS** secondary modern school; Shipwrecked Mariners' Society; synchronous meteorological satellite
**SMSA** [USA] Standard Metropolitan Statistical Area
**SMSO** Senior Maintenance Staff Officer
**SMT** ship's mean time; [computing] surface mount technology
**SMTA** Scottish Motor Trade Association
**SMTF** Scottish Milk Trade Federation
**SMTO** senior mechanical transport officer
**SMTP** [computing] simple mail transfer protocol
**SMTWTFS** Sunday, Monday, Tuesday, Wednesday, Thursday, Friday, Saturday
**SMV** submentovertical (in radiology)
**SMW** standard metal window
**SMWIA** [USA] Sheet Metal Workers' International Association
**SMWS** Scottish Malt Whisky Society
**SN** [vehicle registration] Dundee; [fishing port] North Shields; [USA] Secretary of the Navy; [international vehicle registration] Senegal; Sergeant Navigator; shipping note; [meteorology] snow; [astronomy] supernova; [UK postcode] Swindon
**S/N** shipping note; [electronics] signal-to-noise (as in **S/N ratio**)
**Sn** [chemical element] tin (from Latin *stannum*)
**s/n** serial number; series number; service number
**sn.** senior; snow
**.sn** Senegal (in Internet address)
**s.n.** *secundum naturam* (Latin: according to nature, naturally); serial number; series number; service number; *sine nomine* (Latin: without name); *sub nomine* (Latin: under the (specified) name)
**SNA** Scottish Netball Association; [computing] systems network architecture
**snafu** [slang] situation normal, all fouled (or fucked) up
**SNAME** [USA] Society of Naval Architects and Marine Engineers
**SNAP** Shelter Neighbourhood Action Project; systems for nuclear auxiliary power
**SNB** [stock exchange] sellers no buyers
**SNBTS** Scottish National Blood Transfusion Service
**SNCB** *Société nationale des chemins de fer belges* (French: Belgian National Railways)
**SNCF** *Société nationale des chemins de fer français* (French: French National Railways)
**SND** Sisters of Notre Dame
**Snd** Sound (in place-names)
**SNECMA** *Société nationale d'étude et de construction de moteurs d'aviation* (French: national aeroengine research and construction company)
**SNF** solids, nonfat (in nutrition); spent nuclear fuel; [USA] strategic nuclear forces
**SNFA** Standing Naval Force, Atlantic
**SNFU** Scottish National Farmers' Union

**SNG** substitute natural gas; synthetic natural gas
**Sng.** Singapore
**SNH** Scottish National Heritage
**SNIF** [finance] short-term note issuance facility
**SNIG** sustainable noninflationary growth
**SNIPEF** Scottish and Northern Ireland Plumbing Employers' Federation
**SNL** Sandia National Laboratories (Albuquerque); standard nomenclature list
**SNLA** Scottish National Liberation Army
**SNLR** services no longer required
**SNLV** strategic nuclear launch vehicle
**SNM** [USA] Society of Nuclear Medicine; Somali National Movement
**SNMP** [computing] simple network management protocol
**SNO** Scottish National Orchestra (former name of RSO); senior naval officer; senior navigation officer; senior nursing officer
**SNOBOL** string oriented symbolic language (computer programming language)
**SNP** Scottish National Party
**SNPA** Scottish National Newspaper Proprietors' Association
**SNR** [electronics] signal-to-noise ratio; Society for Nautical Research; [astronomy] supernova remnant
**Snr** Senior
**Sñr** *Señor* (Spanish: Mr)
**snr** senior
**Snra** *Senhora* (Portuguese: Mrs)
**Sñra** *Señora* (Spanish: Mrs)
**Sñrta** *Señorita* (Spanish: Miss)
**SNSC** Scottish National Ski Council
**SNSS** School Natural Science Society
**SNTPC** Scottish National Town Planning Council
**SNTS** Society for New Testament Studies
**SNU** [astronomy] solar neutrino unit; Spiritualists' National Union
**Snug** Scottish Network Users' Group
**SO** [vehicle registration] Aberdeen; scientific officer; Scottish Office; section officer; senior officer; shale oil (residue); Signal Officer; [fishing port] Sligo; [computing] small outline; [international vehicle registration] Somalia; sorting office; [UK postcode] Southampton; [meteorology] southern oscillation; special order; Staff Officer; standing order; Stationery Office; statistical office; suboffice; supply officer; symphony orchestra
**S/O** section officer; seller's option; shipowner
**So.** *Sonntag* (German: Sunday); south; southern
**so.** sonata; south; southern
**.so** Somalia (in Internet address)
**s.o.** seller's option; shipping order; *siehe oben* (German: see above); strike out; substance of (weight of paper)
**SOA** Scottish Orienteering Association; state of the art
**SoA** Society of Authors
**SOAD** Staff Officer, Air Defence
**SOAP** [medicine] subjective, objective, analysis, plan (in patients' records)
**SOAS** School of Oriental and African Studies (University of London)
**SOB** [USA] Senate office building; [medicine] shortness of breath; [informal] silly old bastard; [informal] son of a bitch; state office building
**s.o.b.** [informal] son of a bitch
**SOBHD** Scottish Official Board of Highland Dancing
**SOC** Scottish Ornithologists' Club; [informal] slightly off colour
**Soc.** Socialist; [commerce] *società* (Italian: company); Society; Socrates (ancient Greek philosopher)
**soc.** social; socialist; society; sociology
**SocCE(France)** *Société des ingénieurs civils de France* (French: Society of Civil Engineers of France)
**Soc. Dem.** Social Democrat
**sociol.** sociological; sociologist; sociology
**SOCO** scene-of-crime officer
**SOCONY** Standard Oil Corporation of New York
**SOCS** Society of County Secretaries
**soc. sci.** social science; social scientist
**Socy** Society
**sod.** sodium
**SODAC** Society of Dyers and Colourists
**SODEPAX** Committee on Society, Development and Peace (from Latin *pax*)
**SODS** ship's operatic and dramatic society (in Royal Navy)
**SOE** Special Operations Executive (in World War II); state-owned enterprise

**SOED** Scottish Office Education Department; *Shorter Oxford English Dictionary*
**SOEID** Scottish Office Education and Industry Department
**SOES** [US finance] Small Order Execution System (of NASDAQ)
**SOF** share of freehold (in property advertisement); [chemistry] soluble organic fraction; [cinema] sound on a film
**SOFAA** Society of Fine Art Auctioneers
**sofar** sound fixing and ranging
**SOFCS** self-organizing flight-control system
**SOFFEX** Swiss Options and Financial Futures Exchange
**SOFIA** Stratospheric Observatory for Infrared Astronomy
**S of S** Secretary of State; [Bible] Song of Solomon; [Bible] Song of Songs
**S of Sol.** [Bible] Song of Solomon
**S of T** Sons of Temperance
**S of TT** School of Technical Training
**SOGAT** Society of Graphical and Allied Trades (became part of GPMU)
**SOH** sense of humour (in personal advertisement)
**SOHC** single overhead cam(shaft)
**SOHIO** Standard Oil of Ohio
**SOHO** Solar Heliospheric Observatory
**SoHo** small office/home office (furniture); [USA] South of Houston
**Sohyo** *Nihon Rodo Kumiai So Hygikai* (Japanese: General Council of Japanese Trade Unions)
**SO(I)** Staff Officer (Intelligence)
**SOIC** [electronics] small outline integrated circuit
**SO-in-C** Signal Officer-in-Chief
**SOL** [US slang] strictly (or shit) out of luck
**Sol.** Solicitor; [Bible] Song of Solomon
**sol.** solicitor; soluble; solution
**s.o.l.** [insurance] shipowner's liability
**Solace** Society of Local Authority Chief Executives
**Sol-Gen** Solicitor-General
**soln** solution
**solr** solicitor
**solv.** solvent
**soly** solubility
**SOM** Society of Occupational Medicine
**Som.** Somerset
**SOMA** Society of Mental Awareness
**SOME** Senior Ordnance Mechanical Engineer
**SOMPA** [USA] System of Multicultural Pluralistic Assessment (intelligence testing)
**Som.Sh.** [currency] Somali shilling
**sonar** sound navigation and ranging
**SONET** [computing] synchronous optical network
**SO(O)** Staff Officer (Operations)
**SOP** significant other person; sleeping-out pass; standard operating procedure; [computing] sum of products
**sop.** [music] soprano
**Soph.** Sophocles (ancient Greek writer)
**soph.** sophomore
**SOR** sale or return; Society of Radiographers
**SORD** submerged-object recovery device
**SORG** Stratospheric Ozone Review Group
**SORP** [accounting] Statement of Recommended Practice
**SOS** save our souls (international distress signal, letters chosen for ease and clarity of transmission in Morse code); Secretary of State; senior officers' school; services of supply
**s.o.s.** [medicine] *si opus sit* (Latin: if necessary) (in prescriptions)
**SOSc** Society of Ordained Scientists
**SoSh** [currency] Somali shilling
**sost.** [music] *sostenuto* (Italian: sustained)
**SOT** stay-on tab
**Soton** Southampton
**SOTS** Society for Old Testament Study
**Sou.** south; Southampton; southern
**sou.** south; southern
**SOV** [linguistics] subject-object-verb
**Sov.** Soviet
**sov.** sovereign
**s.o.v.** shut-off valve
**Sov. Un.** Soviet Union
**Soweto** Southwestern Townships (South Africa)
**SP** [vehicle registration] Dundee; [civil aircraft marking] Poland; *Saint-Père* (French: Holy Father); [UK postcode] Salisbury; *Sanctissimus Pater* (Latin: Most Holy Father); Self-Propelled (Antitank Regiment); service pistol; [military] service police; shore patrol; Sisters of Providence; Socialist Party; [building] soil pipe; spark(ing) plug; Staff Paymaster;

standard play (on video recorder); starting price (hence slang meaning 'latest information'); stirrup pump; [banking] stop payment; stop press; stretcher party; submarine patrol; *Summus Pontifex* (Latin: Supreme Pontiff, the pope); supply point; [finance] supra protest

**Sp.** Spain; Spaniard; Spanish

**sp.** space; special; specie; [biology] species; specific; specimen; speed; spelling; spirit; sport; *sposa* (Italian: wife)

**s.p.** self-propelled; [music] *senza pedale* (Italian: without pedal); *sine prole* (Latin: without issue); [electrical engineering] single phase; [advertising] special position; starting point; [banking] stop payment

**SPA** Saudi Press Agency; Scottish Pipers' Association; Scottish Pistol Association; Scottish Publishers' Association; [USA] Society for Personnel Administration; special protection area (for conservation of wild birds)

**SpA** [commerce] *società per azioni* (Italian: public limited company, plc)

**SPAA** Scottish Passenger Agents' Association

**SPAB** Society for the Protection of Ancient Buildings

**SPAC** Standing Pharmaceutical Advisory Committee (of NHS)

**spac.** spacious (in property advertisement)

**Sp. Am.** Spanish American

**Span.** Spaniard; Spanish

**SPANA** Society for the Protection of Animals in North Africa

**SPANDAR** space and range radar (in NASA)

**SPAR** member of US Coast Guard women's reserve (in World War II, from Latin motto *Semper paratus* = always ready); superprecision-approach radar

**Sp. Ar.** Spanish Arabic

**SPARC** [computing] scalable processor architecture

**SPARKS** Sport Aiding Medical Research for Kids

**SPAS** *Societatis Philosophicae Americanae Socius* (Latin: Fellow of the American Philosophical Society)

**SPATC** South Pacific Air Transport Council

**SPBA** Scottish Pipe Band Association

**SPBP** Society for the Preservation of Birds of Prey

**SPBW** Society for the Preservation of Beers from the Wood

**SPC** Secretariat of the Pacific Community; Society for the Prevention of Crime; Southern Pacific Commission (former name of the Pacific Community); [commerce] statistical process control; [telecommunications] stored program control

**SPCA** [USA] Society for the Prevention of Cruelty to Animals

**SPCK** Society for Promoting Christian Knowledge

**SPD** Salisbury Plain District; [astronomy] south polar distance; *Sozialdemokratische Partei Deutschlands* (German: Social Democratic Party of Germany)

**spd** speed (in car advertisement)

**s.p.d.** [finance] subject to permission to deal

**SPDA** single-premium deferred annuity

**SPDL** [computing] standard page description language

**SPE** Society for Pure English; [USA] Society of Petroleum Engineers; [electronics] solid-phase epitaxy

**SPEC** [Canada] Society for Pollution and Environmental Control; South Pacific Bureau for Economic Cooperation

**spec** [short form] specification; [short form] speculation (as in **on spec**)

**spec.** special; specialist; specially; specific; specifically; specification; specimen; spectrum

**special.** specialized

**specif.** specific; specifically; specification

**SPECmark** Systems Performance Evaluation Cooperative's benchmark

**specs** [short form] specifications; [short form] spectacles

**SPECT** [medicine] single photon emission compute(rize)d tomography

**SPECTRE** Special Executive for Counter-Intelligence, Revenge and Extortion (in James Bond stories by Ian Fleming)

**Sp.Ed.** [USA] Specialist in Education

**SPES** South Place Ethical Society

**SPET** [medicine] single photon emission tomography

**SPF** South Pacific forum; sun protection factor (in sunscreen)
**SPF/DB** [aeronautics] super-plastic forming/diffusion bonding (manufacturing method)
**SPG** Society for the Propagation of the Gospel (in Foreign Parts) (became part of USPG); Special Patrol Group
**s.p.g.** self-propelled gun
**SPGA** Scottish Professional Golfers' Association
**SPGB** Socialist Party of Great Britain
**sp. gr.** specific gravity
**sp. ht** specific heat
**SPI** [finance] selected period investment; [USA] Society of the Plastics Industry
**SPIRE** [navigation] spatial inertial reference equipment
**spirit.** [music] *spiritoso* (Italian: with spirit); spiritualism; spiritualistic
**SPIW** special-purposes individual weapon
**SPKC** Small Pig Keepers' Council
**s.p.l.** *sine prole legitima* (Latin: without legitimate issue)
**SPLA** Sudan People's Liberation Army
**SPM** scanning proton microscope; [music] short particular metre
**s.p.m.** *sine prole mascula* (Latin: without male issue)
**SPMO** senior principal medical officer
**SPMU** Society of Professional Musicians in Ulster
**SPN** stop press news
**SPNC** Society for the Promotion of Nature Conservation
**SPNM** Society for the Promotion of New Music
**SPNR** Society for the Promotion of Nature Reserves
**SPO** senior press officer
**SPÖ** *Sozialistische Partei Österreichs* (German: Austrian Socialist Party)
**SPOA** Scottish Prison Officers' Association
**SPOD** Sexual Problems of the Disabled
**SPOE** Society of Post Office Engineers
**Spool** simultaneous peripheral operation on-line
**s/pool** swimming pool (in property advertisement)
**Spore** Society for the Preservation of the Rainforest Environment
**SPOT** single property ownership trust
**SPP** [medicine] sub-pubic prostatectomy
**spp.** [biology] species (plural)
**SPQR** *Senatus Populusque Romanus* (Latin: the Senate and People of Rome); small profits and quick returns
**SPR** Society for Psychical Research; strategic petroleum reserve
**Spr** [military] Sapper
**spr.** spring; sprinkle; sprinkler; sprung
**SPRC** Society for the Prevention and Relief of Cancer
**SPREd** Society of Picture Researchers and Editors
**SPRI** Scott Polar Research Institute (Cambridge)
**SPRINT** solid-propellant rocket-intercept missile
**SPRL** Society for the Promotion of Religion and Learning
**sprl** [commerce] *société de personnes à responsabilité limitée* (French: limited company, Ltd)
**SPS** Scottish Painters' Society; [physics] Super Proton Synchrotron (at CERN); syndiotactic polystyrene (plastic)
**s.p.s.** *sine prole supersite* (Latin: without surviving issue)
**SPSL** Society for the Protection of Science and Learning
**SPSO** senior principal scientific officer
**SPSP** St Peter and St Paul
**spt** seaport; sport; support
**sptg** sporting
**SPTL** Society of Public Teachers of Law
**SPUC** Society for the Protection of the Unborn Child
**SPURV** self-propelled underwater research vehicle
**SPVD** Society for the Prevention of Venereal Disease
**sp. vol.** specific volume
**SQ** sick quarters; [meteorology] squall; [building] squint quoin; stereophonic-quadraphonic; survival quotient
**Sq.** Squadron; Square (in road name)
**sq.** sequence; *sequens* (Latin: the following (one)); squadron; square
**SQA** Scottish Qualifications Agency; [computing] software quality assurance
**sq cm** square centimetre
**sqd** squad
**Sqdn** Squadron
**sqdn** squadron
**Sqdn Ldr** Squadron Leader

**sq ft** square feet; square foot
**sq in** square inch
**sq km** square kilometre
**SQL** [computing] standard query language; [computing] structured query language
**sq m** square metre
**sq mi** square mile
**sq mm** square millimetre
**SQMS** Staff Quartermaster-Sergeant
**Sqn** Squadron
**sqn** squadron
**Sqn Ldr** Squadron Leader
**SqnQMS** Squadron Quartermaster-Sergeant
**SqnSM** Squadron Sergeant-Major
**SqO** Squadron Officer
**sqq.** *sequentia* (Latin: the following (ones))
**squid** [electronics] superconducting quantum interference device
**sq yd** square yard
**SR** [vehicle registration] Dundee; [currency] Saudi riyal; Saunders Roe (aircraft); [USA] Senate resolution; senior registrar; service rifle; [computing] set-reset; Socialist Revolutionary (Party) (in former USSR); Society of Radiographers; sodium ricinoleate (in toothpaste); [USA] Sons of the Revolution; [railways] Southern Region; [physics] special relativity; [military] Special Reserve; [taxation] standard rate; [psychology] stimulus–response; [fishing port] Stranraer; [UK postcode] Sunderland; *Sveriges Radio* (Swedish broadcasting corporation); [physics] synchrotron radiation; synthetic rubber
**S/R** sale or return
**Sr** *Senhor* (Portuguese: Mr, Sir); Senior; *Señor* (Spanish: Mr, Sir); *Signor* (Italian: Mr, Sir); Sir; Sister (title of nun); [chemical element] strontium
**sr** senior; steradian (unit of solid angle)
**s/r** sunroof (in car advertisement)
**.sr** Suriname (in Internet address)
**s.r.** self-raising; shipping receipt; short rate
**SRA** Squash Rackets Association
**Sra** *Senhora* (Portuguese: Mrs); *Señora* (Spanish: Mrs)
**SRAC** [finance] short-run average cost
**SRAM** short-range attack missile
**SRAM** [computing] static random-access memory
**SR&CC** [insurance] strikes, riot and civil commotion
**SRAP** Scottish Rent Assessment Panel
**SRB** solid rocket booster; [computing] source route bridge; [microbiology] sulphate-reducing bacteria
**SRBC** [medicine] sheep red blood cell(s)
**SRBM** short-range ballistic missile
**SRBP** synthetic resin-bonded paper
**SRC** sample return container; Science Research Council (former name of SERC); [commerce] *sociedad regular colectiva* (Spanish: partnership); solvent-refined coal; [chemistry] standard reference compound; [engineering] steam Rankine cycle; Students' Representative Council; Swiss Red Cross
**SRCC** [insurance] strikes, riot and civil commotion
**SRCh** State Registered Chiropodist
**SRCN** State Registered Children's Nurse (former name of RSCN)
**SRD** service rum diluted
**SRDE** Signals Research and Development Establishment
**SRE** *Sancta Romana Ecclesia* (Latin: Holy Roman Church)
**S Rept** [USA] Senate report
**S Res.** [USA] Senate resolution
**SRG** standard reformed gas; Strategic Research Group (market research company)
**SRHE** Society for Research into Higher Education
**SRI** *Sacrum Romanum Imperium* (Latin: Holy Roman Empire)
**SRIS** Science Reference Information Service
**Srl.** [commerce] *società a responsabilità limitata* (Italian: limited company, Ltd)
**SRls** [currency] Saudi riyal
**SRM** short-range missile; speed of relative movement
**SRN** State Registered Nurse (former name of RGN)
**SRNA** Shipbuilders and Repairers National Association
**sRNA** [biochemistry] soluble ribonucleic acid
**SRO** Scottish Record Office; [finance] self-regulatory organization; [microbiology]

sex-ratio organism; [USA] single room occupancy; sold right out; standing room only; Statutory Rules and Orders; Supplementary Reserve of Officers

**s/roof** sunroof (in car advertisement)

**SRP** Society of Recorder Players; State Registered Physiotherapist; suggested retail price; supply refuelling point

**SRPA** Squash Rackets Professional Association

**SRPS** Scottish Railway Preservation Society

**SRR** Society for Research in Rehabilitation

**SRS** Scottish Record Society; *Societatis Regiae Sodalis* (Latin: Fellow of the Royal Society)

**SRs** [currency] Seychelles rupee

**SRSA** Scientific Research Society of America

**SRSS** [mathematics] square-root sum of squares

**Srta** *Senhorita* (Portuguese: Miss); *Señorita* (Spanish: Miss)

**SRU** Scottish Rugby Union

**SRWS** Scottish Rights of Way Society

**SRY** Sherwood Rangers Yeomanry

**SS** [vehicle registration] Aberdeen; *Sacra Scriptura* (Latin: Holy Scripture); Saints; *Santa Sede* (Italian: Holy See); *Sa Sainteté* (French: His Holiness); *Schutzstaffel* (German: protection squad) (Nazi organization); secondary school; Secretary of State; secret service; security service; short sleeves; [computing] single-sided (disk); social security; [chemistry] sodium sulphate; [UK postcode] Southend-on-Sea; Staff Surgeon; stainless steel; standard size; steamship; [fishing port] St Ives; *Strada Statale* (Italian: National Highway); Straits Settlements; Sunday school; surface-to-surface (missile)

**S/S** same size (of illustrations); silk screen (printing); steamship

**SS.** Saints; *sanctissimus* (Latin: most holy)

**ss.** sections; [medicine] *semis* (Latin: half) (in prescriptions); subsection

**s.s.** screw steamer; *sensu stricto* (Latin: in the strict sense); [music] *senza sordini* (Italian: without mutes); simplified spelling; steamship; *supra scriptum* (Latin: written above)

**SSA** Scottish Schoolmasters' Association; [computing] serial storage architecture; [USA] Social Security Administration; Society of Scottish Artists; standard spending assessment (in local government)

**SSAC** Scottish Sub-Aqua Club; Social Security Advisory Committee

**SSADM** [computing] structured systems analysis and design method

**SSAE** stamped self-addressed envelope

**SSAFA** Soldiers', Sailors' and Airmen's Families Association

**SSAIB** Security Systems and Alarms Inspection Board

**SSAP** Statement of Standard Accounting Practice

**SSB** Bachelor of Sacred Scripture (from Latin *Sacrae Scripturae Baccalaureus*); [telecommunications] single-sideband (transmission); [USA] Social Security Board

**SSBN** [US navy] strategic submarine, ballistic nuclear

**SSC** Scottish Ski Club; Scottish Sports Council; Sculptors' Society of Canada; [India] Secondary School Certificate; Short Service Commission; [USA] small-saver certificate; *Societas Sanctae Crucis* (Latin: Society of the Holy Cross); [Scotland] Solicitor before the Supreme Court; Species Survival Commission; [physics] Superconducting Super Collider

**SScD** Doctor of Social Science

**SSD** Doctor of Sacred Scripture (from Latin *Sacrae Scripturae Doctor*); Social Services Department

**SS.D** *Sanctissimus Dominus* (Latin: Most Holy Lord, the pope)

**ssDNA** [biochemistry] single-stranded deoxyribonucleic acid

**SSE** Society of St Edmund; south-southeast

**SSEB** South of Scotland Electricity Board

**SSEC** Secondary School Examinations Council

**SSEES** School of Slavonic and East European Studies (University of London)

**SSEG** Scottish Solar Energy Group

**SSF** single-seater fighter (aircraft); Society of St Francis

**SSFA** Scottish Schools' Football Association; Scottish Steel Founders' Association

**SSgt** Staff Sergeant
**SSHA** Scottish Special Housing Association
**SSHC** Society to Support Home Confinement
**SSI** Scottish Symphony Orchestra; site of scientific interest; [electronics] small-scale integration; Social Services Inspectorate; Society of Scribes and Illuminators; [USA] supplemental security income
**SSJE** Society of St John the Evangelist
**SSL** Licentiate in Sacred Scripture (from Latin *Sacrae Scripturae Licentiatus*)
**SSLH** Society for the Study of Labour History
**SSM** Saturday, Sunday, Monday; [telecommunications] single-sideband modulation; Society of the Sacred Mission; [commerce] soft systems methodology; Staff Sergeant-Major; surface-to-surface missile
**SSMA** Stainless Steel Manufacturers' Association
**SSMH** Scottish Society for the Mentally Handicapped
**SSN** severely subnormal; [USA] Social Security number; Standard Serial Number
**SSO** senior scientific officer; senior supply officer; Staff Signal Officer; Station Staff Officer
**SSP** Scottish Socialist Party; statutory sick pay
**ssp.** [biology] subspecies
**SSPCA** Scottish Society for the Prevention of Cruelty to Animals
**SSPE** [medicine] subacute sclerosing panencephalitis
**SS.PP.** *Sancti Patres* (Latin: Holy Fathers)
**sspp.** [biology] subspecies (plural)
**SSPWB** Scottish Society for the Protection of Wild Birds
**SSQ** [military] station sick quarters
**SSR** secondary surveillance radar; Small Ships Register; Soviet Socialist Republic
**SSRA** Scottish Squash Rackets Association
**SSRC** Social Science Research Council (former name of ESRC)
**SSRI** [pharmacology] selective serotonin reuptake inhibitor (used to treat depression); [USA] Social Science Research Institute
**SSS** Secretary of State for Scotland; [USA] Selective Service System (for military mobilization); [medicine] sick sinus syndrome; Simplified Spelling Society; single-screw ship; [fishing port] South Shields; standard scratch score (in golf)
**SSSA** Scottish Salmon Smokers' Association; Scottish Schools' Swimming Association
**SSSI** site of special scientific interest
**SSSR** *Soyuz Sovietskikh Sotsialisticheskikh Respublik* (Russian: Union of Soviet Socialist Republics, USSR)
**SSStJ** Serving Sister, Order of St John of Jerusalem
**SSSU** Scottish Speed Skating Union
**SST** Scottish Scenic Trust; [telecommunications] single-sideband transmission; Society of Surveying Technicians; supersonic transport
**SSTA** Scottish Secondary Teachers' Association
**SSTC** sold subject to contract (in property advertisement)
**SSU** Sunday School Union
**s/susp.** sports suspension (in car advertisement)
**SSV** [microbiology] simian sarcoma virus
**SSW** Secretary of State for War; south-southwest; special security wing (of prison)
**SSWA** Scottish Society of Women Artists
**ST** [vehicle registration] Inverness; sanitary towel; septic tank; shipping ticket; (Hubble) Space Telescope; speech therapist; spring tide; Standard Time; [fishing port] Stockton; [UK postcode] Stoke-on-Trent; [civil aircraft marking] Sudan; Summer Time; *Sunday Times*; [building] surface trench; surtax
**St** Saint; stokes (unit of viscosity); Strait; Street
***St*** [meteorology] stratus
**St.** Statute; Strait; Street
**st** seat; strait; street
**st.** stanza; state; statement; statute; stem; [printing] stet (instruction to restore or retain deleted text); [knitting] stitch; stone (unit of weight); strait; street; strophe (division of verse); [cricket] stumped (by)
**s.t.** select time; short ton; static thrust; steam trawler

**STA** Sail Training Association; [USA] Science and Technology Agency; Scottish Typographical Association; Society of Typographic Arts; Swimming Teachers' Association

**Sta** *Santa* (Italian, Portuguese or Spanish: Saint (female))

**sta.** station; stationary

**StAAA** St Andrew's Ambulance Association

**stab.** stability; stabilization; stabilized; stabilizer; stable

**stacc.** [music] *staccato* (Italian: detached)

**Staffs** Staffordshire

**STAGS** Sterling Transferable Accruing Government Securities

**stalag** *Stammlager* (German: base camp) (World War II prisoner-of-war camp)

**STANAG** Standard NATO Agreement

**stand.** standard

**St And.** St Andrews (Scotland)

**STARCAT** Space Telescope Archive and Catalogue

**START** Strategic Arms Reduction Talks

**stat.** static; statics; [medicine] *statim* (Latin: immediately) (in prescriptions); stationary; statistic(s); statistical; statuary; statue; statute

**STATE** [military] simplified tactical approach and terminal equipment

**Stat. Hall** Stationers' Hall (London)

**stats** [short form] statistics

**STAUK** Seed Trade Association of the United Kingdom

**STB** Bachelor of Sacred Theology (from Latin *Sacrae Theologiae Baccalaureus*); Scottish Tourist Board

**stbd** starboard

**stbt** steamboat

**STC** Samuel Taylor Coleridge (British poet); satellite test centre; Senior Training Corps; Short-Title Catalogue; Standard Telephones and Cables Limited; state total cost; [India] State Trading Corporation; subject to contract (in property advertisement)

**STD** Doctor of Sacred Theology (from Latin *Sacrae Theologiae Doctor*); salinity-temperature-depth (sensor system); [medicine] sexually transmitted disease; Society of Typographic Designers; [computing] state transition diagram; [New Zealand] subscriber toll dialling; subscriber trunk dialling

**Std.** *Stunde* (German: hour)

**std** standard; started

**STE** Society of Telecom Executives

**Ste** *Sainte* (French: Saint (female))

**Sté** [commerce] *société* (French: company, Co.)

**STEL** short-term exposure level (of radiation); short-term exposure limit (of radiation)

**STEM** scanning transmission electron microscope (or microscopy)

**Sten** Shepherd and Turpin (inventors of Sten gun)

**sten.** stenographer; stenographic(al); stenography

**steno.** stenographer; stenographic(al); stenography

**stenog.** stenographer; stenographic(al); stenography

**STEP** Solar/Terrestrial Energy Programme; Special Temporary Employment Programme

**ster.** stereophonic; stereotype; sterling

**stereo** [short form] stereophonic

**stereo.** stereotype

**St. Ex.** Stock Exchange

**stg** seating; sterling

**StGB** *Strafgesetzbuch* (German: Penal Code)

**stge** storage

**STGWU** Scottish Transport and General Workers' Union

**STH** [biochemistry] somatotrophic hormone

**STh** Scholar in Theology

**Sth** South

**sthn** southern

**STI** Straits Times Index (of Singapore Stock Exchange)

**STIM** scanning transmission ion microscope

**STINGS** [aeronautics] stellar inertial guidance system

**stip.** stipend; stipendiary; stipulation

**Stir.** Stirling(shire)

**s.t.i.r.** surplus to immediate requirements

**stk** stock

**STL** Licentiate in Sacred Theology (from Latin *Sacrae Theologiae Licentiatus*); *Sacrae Theologiae Lector* (Latin: Reader in Sacred Theology); Standard Telecom-

munications Laboratories; [telecommunications] studio-to-transmitter link
**stlg** sterling
**STLO** Scientific Technical Liaison Office; Scientific Technical Liaison Officer
**STLV** [microbiology] simian T-lymphotropic virus
**STM** Master of Sacred Theology (from Latin *Sacrae Theologiae Magister*); scanning tunnelling microscope (or microscopy); scientific, technical and medical (as in **STM publishing**); [psychology] short-term memory; [computing] synchronous transfer module
**STMS** [finance] short-term monetary support (in EMS)
**stmt** statement
**stn** stain; station
**STO** sea transport officer; senior technical officer; standing order
**Sto** *Santo* (Portuguese: Saint)
**STOL** [aeronautics] short take-off and landing
**STOLVCD** [aeronautics] short take-off and landing, vertical climb and descent
**S'ton** Southampton
**STOP** Students Tired of Pollution; suction termination of pregnancy
**STOPP** Society of Teachers Opposed to Physical Punishment
**S to S** ship to shore; station to station
**STP** [informal] hallucinogenic drug related to mescaline (from its energizing effect, facetiously compared to that of the oil substitute STP); Professor of Sacred Theology (from Latin *Sacrae Theologiae Professor*); [trademark] scientifically treated petroleum (oil substitute); sewage treatment plant; [computing] shielded twisted pair; standard temperature and pressure
**s.t.p.** standard temperature and pressure
**STPMA** Scottish Theatrical Proprietors' and Managers' Association
**Str.** Strait; *Strasse* (German: Street); Street
**str** seater; steamer
**str.** straight; strait; street; strength; [music] string(s); [music] stringed; stringer (in journalism); [rowing] stroke (oar); strong; structural; structure
**s.t.r.** surplus to requirements
**STRAC** [USA] strategic air command; strategic army corps
**STRAD** signal transmitting, receiving and distribution
**Strad** [short form] Stradivarius (violin)
**stratig.** stratigraphy
**strd** stranded
**strep.** streptococcal; streptococcus
**STRG** Scottish Tory Reform Group
**STRICOM** [USA] Strike Command
**string.** [music] *stringendo* (Italian: compressing, with increasing speed)
**STROBE** satellite tracking of balloons and emergencies
**STS** Scottish Tartan Society; Scottish Text Society; [astronautics] space transportation system
**Sts** Saints
**STSF** Scottish Target Shooting Federation
**STSO** Senior Technical Staff Officer
**st. st.** [knitting] stocking stitch
**STTA** Scottish Table Tennis Association
**STUC** Scottish Trades Union Congress
**stud.** student
**Stuka** *Sturzkampfflugzeug* (German: dive bomber)
**STV** Scottish Television; single transferable vote; standard test vehicle; [USA] subscription television
**stvdr.** stevedore
**stwy** stairway
**SU** [civil aircraft marking] Egypt; [vehicle registration] Glasgow; Scripture Union; [fishing port] Southampton; Soviet Union; [physics] strontium unit
**Su.** Sudan; Sudanese; Sunday
**s.u.** set up; *siehe unten* (German: see below)
**SUA** [USA] State Universities Association
**SUB** [USA] supplemental unemployment benefits
**sub** [short form] sub-edit; [short form] submarine; [short form] subscription
**sub.** subaltern; [music] *subito* (Italian: immediately, suddenly); subject; [grammar] subjunctive; submarine; subordinate; subordinated; subscription; subsidiary; subsidy; subsistence; [grammar] substantive; substitute; suburb; suburban; subvention; subway
**SUBAW** Scottish Union of Bakers and Allied Workers
**subd.** subdivide; subdivision
**sub-ed.** sub-edit; sub-editor

**subj.** subject; subjective; subjectively; [grammar] subjunctive
**SUBLANT** [US navy] Submarine Forces, Atlantic
**Sub-Lieut.** Sub-Lieutenant
**Sub-Lt** Sub-Lieutenant
**subord.** [grammar] subordinate; [grammar] subordinating
**SUBPAC** [US navy] Submarine Forces, Pacific
**SUBROC** submarine rocket
**subs** [short form] subscription
**subs.** subsidence; subsidiary; subsistence
**subsc.** subscription
**subsec.** subsection
**subseq.** subsequent; subsequently
**subsp.** [biology] subspecies
**subspp.** [biology] subspecies (plural)
**subsq.** subsequent; subsequently
**subst.** [grammar] substantive; substantively; substitute; substitution
**substand.** substandard
**suc.** succeed; success; successor; suction
**succ.** succeed; succeeding; success; successive; successor
**SUD** [international vehicle registration] Sudan
**SUDS** [medicine] sudden unexplained death syndrome
**suf.** [grammar] suffix
**Suff.** Suffolk; Suffragan
**suff.** sufficient; [grammar] suffix
**suffoc.** suffocation
**Suffr.** Suffragan
**sug.** suggest; suggestion
**SUIT** Scottish and Universal Investment Trust
**suiv.** *suivant* (French: following)
**Sult.** Sultan
**SUM** surface-to-underwater missile
**sum.** [medicine] *sumat* (Latin: let her/him take it) (in prescriptions); [medicine] *sumendum* (Latin: let it be taken) (in prescriptions); summary; summer
**sums.** summons
**Sun.** Sunday
**Sund.** Sunday
**SUNFED** Special United Nations Fund for Economic Development
**SUNS** sonic underwater navigation system
**SUNY** State University of New York
**sup.** superficial; superfine; superior; superlative; [grammar] supine; supplement; supplementary; supply; support; supporter; *supra* (Latin: above); supreme
**sup. ben.** supplementary benefit
**Sup. Ct** Superior Court; Supreme Court
**Supdt** Superintendent
**super.** superficial; superfine; superior; supernumerary
**superl.** superlative
**SUPLO** Scottish Union of Power Loom Overlookers
**supp.** supplement; supplementary
**suppl.** supplement; supplementary
**Supp. Res.** Supplementary Reserve (of officers)
**supr** superior; supervisor
**supr.** superior; supreme
**Supt** Superintendent
**supvr** supervisor
**SUR** [commerce] set-up reduction
**Sur.** Surrey
**sur.** surface; surplus
**SURF** spent unreprocessed fuel
**surg.** surgeon; surgery; surgical
**Surg. Cdr** Surgeon Commander
**Surg. Comdr** Surgeon Commander
**Surg. Gen.** Surgeon General
**Surg. Lt-Cdr** Surgeon Lieutenant-Commander
**Surg. Maj.** Surgeon Major
**Surr.** Surrey
**surr.** surrender; surrogate
**surro.** surrogate
**SURV** standard underwater research vessel
**surv.** survey; surveying; surveyor; survive; surviving; survivor
**Surv-Gen** Surveyor-General
**SUS** Scottish Union of Students; Students' Union Society
**Sus.** [Bible] Susanna (book of Apocrypha); Sussex
**sus** [short form] suspicious
**SUSI** Sydney University Stellar Interferometer
**susp.** suspend; suspension
**Suss.** Sussex
**Sustrans** Sustainable Transport
**SUT** Society for Underwater Technology
**Suth.** Sutherland
**SUV** [USA] sport-utility vehicle
**SV** safety valve; *Sancta Virgo* (Latin: Holy Virgin); *Sanctitas Vestra* (Latin: Your Holi-

ness); [microbiology] simian virus; stroke volume (of engine)
**Sv** sievert (unit of radiation dose equivalent)
**s/v** [insurance] surrender value
**.sv** El Salvador (in Internet address)
**s.v.** sailing vessel; side valve; *sub verbo* (Latin: under the word) (in reference book); *sub voce* (Latin: under the word) (in reference book); [insurance] surrender value
**SVA** Scottish Volleyball Association
**SVC** [medicine] superior vena cava; [computing] supervisor call
**svc.** service
**svce** service
**SVD** [veterinary science] swine vesicular disease
**svg** saving
**SVGA** [computing] super video graphics array
**svgs** savings
**SVO** Scottish Variety Orchestra; [linguistics] subject-verb-object; superintending veterinary officer
**SVP** saturated vapour pressure
**s.v.p.** *s'il vous plaît* (French: (if you) please)
**SVQ** Scottish Vocational Qualification
**s.v.r.** [medicine] *spiritus vini rectificatus* (Latin: rectified spirit of wine) (in prescriptions)
**SVS** still-camera video system
**SVTP** sound velocity, temperature, pressure
**s.vv.** *sub verbis* (Latin: under the words) (in reference book)
**s.v.v.** *sit venia verbo* (Latin: pardon the expression)
**svy** survey
**SW** [vehicle registration] Carlisle; [vehicle registration] Glasgow; senior warden; shipper's weight; shock wave; [radio] short wave; small women's (clothing size); South Wales; southwest; southwestern; [UK postcode] southwest London; standard weight
**S/W** [computing] software
**Sw.** Sweden; Swedish; Swiss
**s/w** salt water; sea water; seaworthy
**sw.** switch
**s.w.** salt water; sea water
**Swab.** Swabia; Swabian
**SWACS** space warning and control system
**SWALK** sealed with a loving kiss (on envelope of love letter)
**SWANU** South West Africa National Union
**SWANUF** South West Africa National Union Front
**SWAP** Scottish Women Against Pornography
**SWAPO** South West Africa People's Organization
**SWAS** Submillimetre Wave Astronomy Satellite
**SWAT** [USA] Special Weapons and Tactics (police unit)
**SWB** [military] South Wales Borderers
**s.w.b.** short wheelbase (in car advertisement)
**swbd** switchboard
**SWCI** [computing] software configuration item
**swd** [bookbinding] sewed
**SWE** [USA] Society of Women Engineers
**SWEB** South Wales Electricity Board; Southwest Electricity Board
**Swed.** Sweden; Swedish
**SWET** Society of West End Theatre(s)
**SWF** single white female (in accommodation advertisement)
**SwF** [currency] Swiss franc
**SWFA** Scottish Women's Football Association
**SWG** Song Writers' Guild of Great Britain; standard wire gauge
**SWH** solar water heating
**SWHA** Scottish Women's Hockey Association
**SWIE** South Wales Institute of Engineers
**SWIFT** Society for Worldwide Interbank Financial Transactions
**Swing** [finance] Sterling Warrant into Gilt-edged Stock
**Swit.** Switzerland
**Switz.** Switzerland
**SWL** safe working load
**SWLA** Society of Wildlife Artists
**SWM** single white male (in accommodation advertisement)
**SWMF** South Wales Miners' Federation
**SWO** Station Warrant Officer
**SWOA** Scottish Woodland Owners' Association

**SWOPS** single-well oil-production system
**SWOT** [marketing] strengths, weaknesses, opportunities and threats (of new product)
**SWP** safe working pressure; Socialist Workers' Party
**SWPA** South-West Pacific Area
**SWPF** single white professional female (in accommodation advertisement)
**SWPM** single white professional male (in accommodation advertisement)
**SWR** [telecommunications] standing-wave ratio
**SWRB** Sadler's Wells Royal Ballet (former name of Royal Ballet)
**SWRI** Scottish Women's Rural Institute
**SWS** static water supply
**SWSWU** Sheffield Wool Shear Workers' Union
**SWT** Scottish Wildlife Trust
**Swtz.** Switzerland
**SWWJ** Society of Women Writers and Journalists
**SX** [vehicle registration] Edinburgh; [civil aircraft marking] Greece; soft X-rays; [shipping] Sundays excepted
**Sx** Sussex
**SXR** soft X-radiation; soft X-rays
**SXT** sextant
**SY** [international vehicle registration] Seychelles; [UK postcode] Shrewsbury; steam yacht; [fishing port] Stornoway
**Sy** supply; Surrey
**Sy.** Seychelles; Syria
**.sy** Syria (in Internet address)
***SYB*** *Statesman's Yearbook*
**S Yd** Scotland Yard
**Syd.** Sydney
**SYHA** Scottish Youth Hostels Association
**syl.** syllable; syllabus
**Sylk** [computing] symbolic link
**syll.** syllable; syllabus
**sym.** symbol; symbolic; symmetrical; symmetry; symphonic; symphony; symptom
**symp.** symposium
**symph.** symphony
**syn.** synchronize; synod; synonym; synonymous; synonymy; synthetic
**sync** [short form] synchronization (as in **out of sync**)
**sync.** synchronization; synchronize; synchronized; synchronous
**Syncom** synchronous communications satellite
**synd.** syndicate; syndicated
**synon.** synonymous
**synop.** synopsis
**synth.** [music] synthesizer; synthetic
**Sy PO** Supply Petty Officer
**SYR** [international vehicle registration] Syria
**Syr.** Syria; Syriac; Syrian
**syr.** [pharmacology] syrup
**sys.** system
**syst.** system; systematic
**SZ** [vehicle registration] Down
**sz.** size
**.sz** Swaziland (in Internet address)

# T

**T** [physics] surface tension; tablespoon(ful); [music] *tace* (Italian: be silent); tanker; target; [chemistry] tautomeric effect; [horticulture] tea (rose); teacher; telegraph; telegraphic; telephone; temperature; [music] tempo; temporary; [music] tenor; tera- (indicates $10^{12}$, as in **Tm** = terametre); Territorial; Territory; tesla (unit of magnetic flux density); Testament; [international vehicle registration] Thailand; thermometer; [advertising] third of a page (area of type); Thursday; [immunology] thymus (as in **T-cell**); time; torpedo; [photography] total light transmission (as in **T-number**); trainer (aircraft); [fishing port] Tralee; transaction(s); translation; transport; transportation; [obstetrics] transverse (presentation); Treasury; Trinity; [chemistry] tritium; [shipping] tropical (load line); true; Tuesday; Turkish; [knitting] twist
***T*** [physics] kinetic energy; [physics] period;

[physics] thermodynamic temperature; [engineering, physics] torque

**t** [astronomy] hour angle; [music] te (in tonic sol-fa); thickness; [meteorology] thunder; tonne; [physics] top (quark flavour)

***t*** Celsius temperature; [chemistry] tertiary (isomer); [chemistry] transport number

**t.** table; tabulated; [sports] tackle; taken (from); [commerce] tare; teaspoon(ful); teeth; temperature; [music] tempo; *tempore* (Latin: in the time of); [music] tenor; [grammar] tense; terminal; territorial; territory; thunder; time; *tome* (French: volume (of book)); ton; tonne; *tonneau* (French: ton); town; township; transit; [grammar] transitive; troy (weight); tun; turn

**T2** [civil aircraft marking] Tuvalu

**T3** [civil aircraft marking] Kiribati

**T7** [civil aircraft marking] San Marino

**5T** [civil aircraft marking] Mauritania

**7T** [civil aircraft marking] Algeria

**TA** [vehicle registration] Exeter; [taxation] table of allowances; [UK postcode] Taunton; [USA] teaching assistant; telegraphic address; temporary admission; [computing] terminal adapter; Territorial Army; [physics] thermal analysis; tithe annuity; training adviser; Training Agency (formerly TSA); [psychology] transactional analysis; [USA] transit authority; travel(ling) allowance; Tricycle Association

**T/A** technical assistant; temporary assistant

**Ta** [chemical element] tantalum

**ta.** tableau; tablet

**t.a.** target area; time and attendance; true altitude

**TAA** Territorial Army Association; test of academic aptitude; Trans-Australia Airlines; Transportation Association of America

**TA&VRA** Territorial Auxiliary and Volunteer Reserve Association

**TAB** tabulator (key) (on typewriter); Technical Assistance Board (of UN); Total Abstinence Brotherhood; [Australia, New Zealand] Totalizator Agency Board; [medicine] typhoid, paratyphoid A, paratyphoid B (vaccine)

**tab.** table; tableau; tablet; tabulate; tabulation; tabulator

**TABA** Timber Agents' and Brokers' Association of the United Kingdom

**TABMAC** The All British Martial Arts Council

**TAC** [US air force] Tactical Air Command; Technical Assistance Committee (of UN); Television Advisory Committee; The Athletics Congress; Theatres Advisory Council; Tobacco Advisory Committee; Trades Advisory Council

**Tac.** (Publius Cornelius) Tacitus (Roman historian)

**TACAN** tactical air navigation

**tach.** tachometer

**tacho** [short form] tachograph

**TACL** Training for Action-Centred Leadership

**TACMAR** tactical multifunction array radar

**TACS** tactical air-control system

**TACV** tracked air-cushion vehicle; *Transportes Aéreos de Cabo Verde* (Portuguese: Cape Verde airline company)

**Tads** [military] target acquisition and designation sight

**TAF** Tactical Air Force

**TAFE** technical and further education

**tafu** [slang] things are fouled (or fucked) up

**tafubar** [slang] things are fouled (or fucked) up beyond all recognition

**TAG** [USA] The Adjutant-General; Towpaths Action Group

**Tag.** Tagalog (language)

**T/Agt** [USA] transfer agent

**TAH** [medicine] total abdominal hysterectomy

**TAI** *temps atomique international* (French: International Atomic Time, IAT)

**Tai.** Taiwan

**TAL** [insurance] traffic and accident loss

**Tal.** Talmud

**tal.** *talis* (Latin: such)

**Talisman** [stock exchange] Transfer Accounting Lodgement for Investors and Stock Management

**tal. qual.** *talis qualis* (Latin: average quality)

**TAM** tactical air missile; Television Audience Measurement

**Tam.** Tamil (language)

**Tamba** Twins and Multiple Births Association
**tan** [mathematics] tangent
**TANCA** Technical Assistance to Non-Commonwealth Countries
**T&A** [US slang] tits and ass; [medicine] tonsillectomy and adenoidectomy; [medicine] tonsils and adenoids
**T&AFA** Territorial and Auxiliary Forces Association
**T&AVR** Territorial and Army Volunteer Reserve
**t&b** top and bottom
**T&CPA** Town and Country Planning Association
**T&E** test and evaluation; [informal] tired and emotional (i.e. drunk); travel and entertainment; trial and error
**T&G** Transport and General Workers' Union
**t&g** tongue(d) and groove(d) (in woodworking)
**t&o** taken and offered (in betting)
**t&p** [insurance] theft and pilferage
**T&RA** Tennis and Rackets Association
**T&S** transport and supply
**t&s** toilet and shower (in property or accommodation advertisement)
**T&SG** Television and Screenwriters' Guild
**T&T** taxed and tested (in car advertisement); Trinidad and Tobago
**Tang.** Tangier
**tanh** [mathematics] hyperbolic tangent
**TANS** terminal-area navigation system; Territorial Army Nursing Service (became part of QARANC)
**TANU** Tanganyika African National Union
**TAO** Technical Assistance Operations (of UN)
**TAOC** [USA] Tactical Air Operations Center
**TAP** [USA] Technical Assistance Program; *Transportes Aéreos Portugueses* (Portuguese airline company)
**Tapi** [trademark] telephony application programming interface
**Tapline** Trans-Arabian Pipeline Company
**TAPPI** [USA] Technical Association of the Pulp and Paper Industry
**TAPS** Trans-Alaska Pipeline System
**TAR** terrain-avoidance radar; Territorial Army Regulations; [accounting] throughput accounting ratio; thrust-augmented rocket
**tar.** tariff; tarpaulin
**TARA** Technical Assistant, Royal Artillery; Territorial Army Rifle Association
**TARAN** test and replace as necessary
**TARDIS** time and relative dimensions in space (Doctor Who's time machine used in BBC science fiction series)
**tarfu** [slang] things are really fouled (or fucked) up
**TARO** Territorial Army Reserve of Officers
**TARS** Technical Assistance Recruitment Service; The Arthur Ransome Society
**TAS** torpedo antisubmarine (course); [aeronautics] true air speed
**Tas.** Tasmania; Tasmanian
**TASI** [telecommunications] time-assignment speech interpolation
**TASM** tactical air-to-surface missile
**Tasm.** Tasmania; Tasmanian
**TASMO** tactical air support of maritime operations
**TASR** terminal area surveillance radar
**TASS** Technical, Administrative and Supervisory Section (of AEU); Transport Aircraft Servicing Specialist (in RAF)
**Tass** *Telegrafnoye Agentstvo Sovetskovo Soyuza* (Russian: Telegraph Agency of the Soviet Union)
**TAT** [psychology] thematic apperception test; [medicine] tired all the time; transatlantic telephone (cable)
**TATSA** transportation aircraft test and support activity
**Tau** [astronomy] Taurus
**TAUN** Technical Assistance of the United Nations
**TAURUS** [stock exchange] Transfer and Automated Registration of Uncertified Stock
**taut.** tautology
**t.-à-v.** *tout-à-vous* (French: yours ever) (at end of letter)
**tav.** tavern
**TAVR** Territorial and Army Volunteer Reserve
**TAVRA** Territorial Auxiliary and Volunteer Reserve Association
**t.a.w.** twice a week
**tax.** taxation
**taxn** taxation
**TB** [vehicle registration] Liverpool; [com-

puting] terabyte; torpedo boat; torpedo bomber; training battalion; training board; Treasury bill; [book-keeping] trial balance; [medicine] tubercle bacillus; [medicine] tuberculosis

**Tb** [computing] terabyte; [chemical element] terbium (formerly Tr)

**t.b.** [printing] take back; temporary buoy; [baseball] total bases; [book-keeping] trial balance; true bearing

**TBA** tyres, batteries and accessories

**t.b.a.** [commerce] to be advised; to be agreed; to be announced

**tb&s** top, bottom and sides

**TBCEP** tri-beta-chloroethyl phosphate (flame retardant)

**t.b.c.f.** to be called for

**TBD** torpedo-boat destroyer

**t.b.d.** to be decided; to be determined

**TBF** Teachers' Benevolent Fund

**TBI** [engineering] throttle-body injection; [medicine] total body irradiation

**T-bill** Treasury bill

**TBL** through bill of lading

**t.b.l.** [knitting] through back of loop

**TBM** tactical ballistic missile; [surveying] temporary benchmark; [medicine] tuberculous meningitis; tunnel-boring machine

**TBO** [aeronautics] time between overhauls; [theatre] total blackout

**T-bond** Treasury bond

**TBS** talk between ships (radio apparatus); [computing] tape backup system; tight building syndrome; training battle simulation

**tbs.** tablespoon(ful)

**tbsp.** tablespoon(ful)

**TBSV** [microbiology] tomato bushy stunt virus

**TBT** tributyl tin (antifouling agent in marine paint)

**TC** [vehicle registration] Bristol; Tank Corps; [USA] Tariff Commission; [law] Tax Cases; technical college; temporary clerk; Temporary Constable; tennis club; touring club; town clerk; town council; town councillor; training centre; training college; training corps; [military] Transport Command; traveller's cheque; [music] *tre corde* (Italian: three strings) (instruction to release soft pedal of piano); Trinity College; (Order of the) Trinity Cross (in Trinidad and Tobago); [meteorology] tropical cyclone; Trusteeship Council (of UN); tungsten carbide; [civil aircraft marking] Turkey; twin carburettors

**Tc** [chemical element] technetium

**tc.** [music] tierce (organ stop)

**t.c.** temperature control; terracotta; till cancelled; time check; [navigation] true course

**TCA** trichloroacetic acid (herbicide); [pharmacology] tricyclic antidepressant

**TCB** [US slang] take care of business; Thames Conservancy Board; [medicine] tumour cell burden

**TCBM** transcontinental ballistic missile

**TCC** [telecommunications] time compression coding; Transport and Communications Commission (of UN); Trinity College, Cambridge; [USA] Troop Carrier Command

**TCCB** Test and County Cricket Board

**TCD** Trinity College, Dublin

**TCDD** tetrachlorodibenzodioxin (environmental pollutant)

**TCE** trichloroeth(yl)ene (solvent)

**TCF** Temporary Chaplain to the Forces; time-correction factor; *Touring Club de France* (French: French Touring Club)

**tcf** [USA] trillion cubic feet (used to measure natural gas)

**TCFB** Transcontinental Freight Bureau

**TCGF** [immunology] T-cell growth factor

**TCH** [international vehicle registration] Chad (from French *Tchad*)

**tchg** teaching

**tchr** teacher

**TCI** *Touring Club Italiano* (Italian: Italian Touring Club)

**TCJCC** Trades Council Joint Consultative Committee

**TCL** Trinity College (of Music) London

**T-CLL** [medicine] T-cell chronic lymphatic leukaemia

**TCM** Trinity College of Music (London)

**TCMA** Telephone Cable Makers' Association

**TCO** test control office; *Tjänstemännens Centralorganisation* (Swedish: Central Organization of Salaried Employees) (Swedish trade union); Trinity College, Oxford

**TCP** [computing] transmission control

protocol; [trademark] trichlorophenylmethyliodisalicyl (antiseptic)
**TCPA** Town and Country Planning Association (or Act)
**TCP/IP** [computing] transmission control protocol/Internet protocol
**TCR** [immunology] T-cell receptor; [physics] temperature coefficient of resistance
**TCRE** [medicine] transcervical resection of the endometrium
**TCS** target cost system; [USA] traffic control station
**tctl** tactical
**TCU** [USA] Transportation, Communications, International Union
**TD** [UK postcode] Galashiels; [vehicle registration] Manchester; [military] Tactical Division; tank destroyer; [medicine] tard(at)ive dyskinesia; Teaching Diploma; [Ireland] *Teachta Dála* (Gaelic: Member of the Dáil); technical development; technical drawing; Territorial (Efficiency) Decoration (in Territorial Army); Tilbury Docks; torpedo depot; [sports] touchdown; [USA] traffic director; [USA] Treasury Department; trust deed; [currency] Tunisian dinar
**td.** touchdown
**.td** Chad (in Internet address)
**t.d.** technical data; [medicine] *ter in die* (Latin: three times a day) (in prescriptions); test data; time delay; tractor-drawn
**TDA** tax-deferred annuity; Timber Development Association
**TDB** *temps dynamique barycentrique* (French: barycentric dynamical time); total disability benefit
**TDC** Temporary Detective Constable; through-deck cruiser
**t.d.c.** [engineering] top dead centre
**TDD** telecommunications device for the deaf; Tubercular Diseases Diploma
**TDDL** [telecommunications] time-division data link
**TDE** total digestible energy
**TDG** Timeshare Developers Group; twist drill gauge
**TDH** tall, dark and handsome (in personal advertisement)
**TDK** *Tokyo Denkikagaku Kogyu KK* (Japanese electronics company)
**TDL** tunable diode laser
**TDM** telemetric data monitor; [telecommunications] time-division multiplexing
**TDMA** [telecommunications] time-division multiple access
**TDN** total digestible nutrients
**T-DNA** [genetics] transferred deoxyribonucleic acid
**TDP** technical development plan
**TDR** [computing] time domain reflectometer; [finance] Treasury deposit receipt
**t.d.r.** *touts droits réservés* (French: all rights reserved)
**TDRSS** tracking and data-relay satellite system
**TDS** [computing] tabular data stream
**t.d.s.** [medicine] *ter (in) die sumendus* (Latin: to be taken three times a day) (in prescriptions)
**TDT** [astronomy] terrestrial dynamical time
**TE** [vehicle registration] Manchester; telecommunications engineering; [biochemistry] trace element; trade expenses; [telecommunications] transverse electric
**Te** [chemical element] tellurium
**t/e** time-expired; twin-engined
**t.e.** thermal efficiency; tinted edge (of paper); trailing edge; trial and error; turbine engine
**TEA** Terminal Education Age
**TEAC** Technical Educational Advisory Council
**TEACH** Teacher Education Admissions Clearing House
**Tear** The Evangelical Alliance Relief (Fund)
**TEC** Training and Enterprise Council
**tec** [short form] detective
**tech** [short form] technical college
**tech.** technical; technically; technician; technique; technological; technology
**Tech(CEI)** Technician (Council of Engineering Institutions)
**techn** technician
**techn.** technical; technique
**technol.** technological; technologically; technologist; technology
**Tedco** Thames Estuary Development Company
**TEDIS** Trade Electronic Data Interchange System

**TEE** Telecommunications Engineering Establishment; Torpedo Experimental Establishment; total energy expenditure; [railways] Trans-Europe Express
**TEF** Textile Employers' Federation; toxicity equivalence factor
**TEFL** teaching (of) English as a foreign language
**t.e.g.** [bookbinding] top edges gilt
**Teh.** Tehran
**TEL** tetraethyl lead (petrol additive); [astronautics] transporter-erector-launcher
**Tel** [astronomy] Telescopium
**tel.** telegram; telegraph; telegraphic; telephone
**telecom.** telecommunication(s)
**teleg.** telegram; telegraph; telegraphic; telegraphy
**teleph.** telephone; telephony
**telex** teleprinter exchange
**telly** [short form] television
**TELNET** [computing] teletype network
**tel. no.** telephone number
**TELO** Tamil Eelam Liberation Organization
**TEM** Territorial Efficiency Medal; transmission electron microscope (or microscopy); [telecommunications] transverse electromagnetic
**TEMA** Telecommunications Engineering and Manufacturing Association
**temp** [short form] temporary (worker)
**temp.** temperance; temperate; temperature; [music] tempo; temporal; temporary; *tempore* (Latin: in the time of)
**Templar** tactical expert mission planner (military computer)
**temp. prim.** [music] *tempo primo* (Italian: at the original speed)
**tempy** temporary
**ten.** tenant; tenement; [music] tenor; [music] *tenuto* (Italian: held, sustained)
**tency** tenancy
**Tenn.** Tennessee
**TENS** [medicine] transcutaneous electrical nerve stimulation
**tepid** [informal] tastes expensive, pension inadequate, dammit
**TEPP** tetraethyl pyrophosphate (pesticide)
**Ter.** Terence (Roman writer); Terrace (in road name); Territorial; Territory
**ter.** terrace; territorial; territory
**terat.** teratology
**TERCOM** [aeronautics] terrain contour matching (or mapping)
**term.** terminal; terminate; termination; terminology
**Terr.** Terrace (in road name); Territorial; Territory
**terr.** terrace; territorial; territory
**terrd** terraced (in property advertisement)
**tert.** tertiary
**TES** thermal-energy storage; *Times Educational Supplement*
**Tesco** T. E. Stockwell and J. Cohen (supermarket chain)
**TESL** teaching (of) English as a second language
**TESOL** teaching of English to speakers of other languages
**TESSA** Tax-Exempt Special Savings Account (replaced by ISA)
**test.** testament; testator; testatrix; testimonial; testimony
**TET** Teacher of Electrotherapy
**T-et-G** Tarn-et-Garonne (French department)
**TETOC** technical education and training for overseas countries
**tet. tox.** tetanus toxin
**TEU** [shipping] twenty-foot equivalent unit
**Teut.** Teuton; Teutonic
**TeV** teraelectronvolt
**TEWT** [military] tactical exercise without troops
**Tex.** Texan; Texas
**text.** textile(s); textual
**text. rec.** *textus receptus* (Latin: the received text)
**TF** [civil aircraft marking] Iceland; [vehicle registration] Reading; task force; [UK postcode] Telford; Territorial Force; [electronics] thin film; [biochemistry] transcription factor; [shipping] tropical freshwater (load line)
**t.f.** tabulating form; tax-free; training film; *travaux forcés* (French: hard labour)
**TFA** Tenant Farmers' Association; [biochemistry] total fatty acids
**TFAP** Tropical Forestry Action Plan
**tfc** traffic
**TFD** [electronics] thin-film detector
**TFECG** Training and Further Education Consultative Group

**TFEL** [computing] thin-film electroluminescent display
**TFOF** Taxi Fleet Operators' Federation
**TFR** Territorial Force Reserve; total fertility rate
**tfr** transfer
**TFS** [medicine] testicular feminization syndrome
**TFSC** Turkish Federated State of Cyprus
**TFSK** Turkish Federated State of Kibris (Turkish name for Cyprus)
**TFSR** Tools for Self Reliance
**TFT** [electronics] thin-film transistor
**TFTA** Traditional Farm-Fresh Turkey Association
**TFTR** [nuclear technology] Tokamak Fusion Test Reactor
**TFU** telecommunications flying unit
**TFW** [military] tactical fighter wing
**TFX** tactical fighter experimental (aircraft)
**TG** [vehicle registration] Cardiff; [civil aircraft marking] Guatemala; Tate Gallery; temporary gentleman; [informal] thank God; [USA] Theater Guild; [international vehicle registration] Togo; Townswomen's Guild; training group; transformational-generative (grammar); transformational grammar; Translators' Guild
**tg** [mathematics] tangent
**.tg** Togo (in Internet address)
**t.g.** tail gear; [biology] type genus
**TGA** [chemistry] thermal gravimetric analysis
**TGAT** [education] Task Group on Assessment and Testing
**T-gate** [computing] ternary selector gate
**TGB** *très grande bibliothèque* (French: very large library) (popular name for French national library)
**t.g.b.** tongued, grooved and beaded (in woodworking)
**TGE** [medicine] transmissible gastroenteritis
**TGF** [medicine] transforming growth factor
**TGI** [marketing] Target Group Index
**TGIA** Toy and Giftware Importers' Association
**TGIF** [informal] thank God it's Friday
**TGM** torpedo gunner's mate
**TGMV** [microbiology] tomato golden mosaic virus
**T-group** training group
**TGT** [aeronautics] turbine gas temperature
**tgt** target
**TGV** *train à grande vitesse* (French: high-speed train)
**TGWU** Transport and General Workers' Union
**TH** [vehicle registration] Swansea; *Technische Hochschule* (German: technical college, technical university); [fishing port] Teignmouth; Territory of Hawaii; [numismatics] toothed border; town hall (on map); Toynbee Hall; Transport House; Trinity House
**Th** [chemical element] thorium
**Th.** Theatre; Theology; Thursday
**th.** thermal
**.th** Thailand (in Internet address)
**Thai.** Thailand
**thanat.** thanatology
**ThB** Bachelor of Theology (from Latin *Theologiae Baccalaureus*)
**THC** tetrahydrocannabinol (active component of cannabis); [New Zealand] Tourist Hotel Corporation
**THD** total harmonic distortion (in recording)
**ThD** Doctor of Theology (from Latin *Theologiae Doctor*)
**THE** Technical Help to Exporters (division of British Standards Institution)
**theat.** theatre; theatrical
**THELEP** Therapy of Leprosy
**Theoc.** Theocritus (ancient Greek poet)
**theol.** theologian; theological; theology
**Theoph.** Theophrastus (ancient Greek philosopher)
**theor.** theorem; theoretical; theory
**theoret.** theoretical
**theos.** theosophical; theosophist; theosophy
**therap.** therapeutic; therapeutics
**therapeut.** therapeutic; therapeutics
**therm.** thermometer; thermometry; thermostatic
**thermochem.** thermochemical; thermochemistry
**thermodyn.** thermodynamic; thermodynamics
**thermom.** thermometer; thermometry
**THES** *Times Higher Education Supplement*
**thes.** thesis
**thesp.** thespian

**Thess.** [Bible] Thessalonians; Thessaly
**THF** Trusthouse Forte plc
**THI** temperature–humidity index
**t.h.i.** time handed in
**thk** thick
**ThL** Licentiate in Theology
**ThM** Master of Theology (from Latin *Theologiae Magister*)
**tho'** though
**thor.** thoracic; thorax
**thoro.** thoroughfare
**Thos.** Thomas
**thou.** thousand
**thp** thrust horsepower
**THR** [medicine] total hip replacement
**thr** their
**thr.** through; thrust
**throt.** throttle
**ThSchol** Scholar in Theology
**THT** Terrence Higgins Trust
**Thu.** Thursday
**Thuc.** Thucydides (ancient Greek historian)
**Thur.** Thursday
**Thurs.** Thursday
**THWM** Trinity (House) high-water mark
**THz** terahertz
**TI** [civil aircraft marking] Costa Rica; technical inspection; technical institute; temperature indication; temperature indicator; Texas Instruments; thermal imaging; tourist information
**T/I** target identification; target indicator
**Ti** [chemical element] titanium
**Ti.** Tiberius (Roman emperor); Tibet
**TIA** Tax Institute of America; Telecommunications Industry Association; [medicine] transient ischaemic attack (minor stroke)
**TIB** tourist information bureau
**Tib.** Tibet; Tibetan
**TIBC** [medicine] total iron-binding capacity
**TIBOR** [finance] Tokyo Inter-Bank Offered Rate
**TIC** [law] taken into consideration; Timber Industries Confederation; total inorganic carbon; tourist information centre
**TICCIH** The International Committee for the Conservation of the Industrial Heritage
**t.i.d.** [medicine] *ter in die* (Latin: three times a day) (in prescriptions)
**TIE** Theatre in Education
**tier.** [music] tierce (organ stop)
**TIF** [computing] tagged image format; telephone influence factor; telephone interference factor; Theatre Investment Fund; [biochemistry] transcription initiation factor; *Transports internationaux par chemin de fer* (French: International Rail Transport)
**TIFF** [computing] tagged image file format
**TIG** tungsten inert gas (in welding)
**TIGR** Treasury Investment Growth Receipts (type of bond, pronounced 'tiger')
**TIH** Their Imperial Highnesses
**TIIAL** The International Institute of Applied Linguistics
**TIL** [medicine] tumour-infiltrating lymphocyte
**TILS** Technical Information and Library Service
**TIM** transient intermodulation distortion (in recording)
**Tim.** [Bible] Timothy
**t.i.m.** time is money
**timp.** [music] timpani
**timps** [short form] timpani
**TIMS** The Institute of Management Sciences
**TIN** [USA] taxpayer identification number
**TINA** [informal] there is no alternative (phrase originally associated with Margaret Thatcher)
**tinct.** tincture
**TIO** technical information officer
**TIP** [computing] terminal interface processor
**Tip.** Tipperary
**Tipp.** Tipperary
**TIR** [optics] total internal reflection; *Transport international routier* (French: International Road Transport)
**TIRC** Tobacco Industry Research Committee
**TIROS** television and infrared observation satellite
**TIS** technical information service
**tis.** tissue
**Tit.** [Bible] Titus
**tit.** title; titular

**TIU** Telecommunications International Union
**TJ** [civil aircraft marking] Cameroon; [vehicle registration] Liverpool; [international vehicle registration] Tajikistan; talk jockey; terajoule; [athletics] triple jump
**.tj** Tajikistan (in Internet address)
**TJR** [currency] Tajik rouble
**TK** [vehicle registration] Exeter
**Tk** [currency] taka (used in Bangladesh)
**tk** tank; truck
**tkg** taking
**tkgs** takings
**TKO** [boxing] technical knockout
**tkr** tanker
**tks** thanks
**tkt** ticket
**TL** [civil aircraft marking] Central African Republic; [vehicle registration] Lincoln; target language; [physics] thermoluminescence; [physics] thermoluminescent (as in **TL-dating**); Torpedo Lieutenant; [insurance] total loss; [US informal] trade-last (exchange of compliments); transmission line; [currency] Turkish lira
**T/L** [banking] time loan; [insurance] total loss
**Tl** [chemical element] thallium
**tl** [meteorology] thunder and lightning
**t.l.** test link; [engineering] thrust link; time length; title list; total load; [insurance] total loss; trade list
**TLA** three-letter abbreviation (or acronym); Toy Libraries Association
**TLB** [computing] translation look-aside buffer
**t.l.b.** temporary lighted buoy
**TLC** tender loving care; [chemistry] thin-layer chromatography; [medicine] total lung capacity; [Australia] Trades and Labour Council
**tld** tooled
**TLEH** true love and everlasting happiness (in personal advertisement)
**TLF** transferable loan facility
**TLG** Theatrical Ladies' Guild
**TLMI** The Leprosy Mission International
**TLO** technical liaison officer
**t.l.o.** [insurance] total loss only
**TLP** [astronomy] transient lunar phenomenon
**TLR** Times Law Reports; [photography] twin-lens reflex
**tlr** tailor; trailer
**TLRS** Tramway and Light Railway Society
**TLS** *Times Literary Supplement*; typed letter, signed
**tltr** translator
**TLU** [computing] table look-up
**TLV** [electronics] threshold-limit value
**TLWM** Trinity (House) low-water mark
**TM** [vehicle registration] Luton; tactical missile; technical manual; technical memorandum; test manual; Their Majesties; [telecommunications] tone modulation; trademark; trained man; training manual; transcendental meditation; [telecommunications] transverse magnetic; trench mortar; tropical medicine; [computing] Turing machine; [international vehicle registration] Turkmenistan
**Tm** [chemical element] thulium
**.tm** Turkmenistan (in Internet address)
**t.m.** temperature meter; true mean
**TMA** Theatrical Management Association; Trans-Mediterranean Airways (Lebanese airline company)
**TMB** travelling medical board
**TMBA** Twins and Multiple Births Association
**tmbr** timber
**TMC** [USA] Tanglewood Music Center; The Movie Channel
**TMD** [military] theatre missile defence
**TMI** [USA] Three Mile Island
**TMJ** [medicine] temporomandibular joint
**tmkpr** timekeeper
**TML** [chemistry] tetramethyl lead; [shipping] three-mile limit
**TMMG** Teacher of Massage and Medical Gymnastics
**TMO** telegraph(ic) money order
**TMP** thermomechanical pump
**TMPDF** Trade Marks, Patterns and Designs Federation
**tmpry** temporary
**tmr** timer
**TMS** Tramway Museum Society
**TMT** turbine motor train
**TMV** [microbiology] tobacco mosaic virus; true mean value
**TN** [civil aircraft marking] (Republic of)

Congo; [vehicle registration] Newcastle upon Tyne; [US postcode] Tennessee; [UK postcode] Tonbridge; tradename; [fishing port] Troon; true north; [international vehicle registration] Tunisia

**tn** ton; tonne; town; train; transportation

**.tn** Tunisia (in Internet address)

**t.n.** technical note; telephone number

**TNA** Tamil National Army

**TNC** Theatres National Committee; total numerical control; transnational corporation

**TNF** [military] theatre nuclear forces; [medicine] tumour necrosis factor

**TNG** [USA] The Newspaper Guild

**tng** training; turning

**TNIP** [South Africa] Transkei National Independence Party

**TNM** tactical nuclear missile; [medicine] tumour, node, metastasis

**T-note** [finance] Treasury note

**TNP** *Théâtre national populaire* (French: National Popular Theatre)

**TNPG** The Nuclear Power Group

**tnpk.** turnpike

**TNT** trinitrotoluene (explosive)

**TNTC** too numerous to count

**TNW** tactical nuclear warfare; [military] theatre nuclear weapon

**TO** [vehicle registration] Nottingham; [commerce] table of organization; tax officer; technical officer; telegraphic order; telegraph office; telephone office; telephone order; Torpedo Officer; trained operator; transport officer; [fishing port] Truro; turn over (page)

**T/O** turnover

**To.** Togo

**.to** Tonga (in Internet address)

**t.o.** take-off; [printing] take over; turnover

**TOB** temporary office building

**ToB** [cycling] Tour of Britain

**Tob.** [Bible] Tobit (book of Apocrypha)

**tob.** tobacco; tobacconist

**TobRV** [microbiology] tobacco ringspot virus

**TOC** total organic carbon

**Toc H** Talbot House (original headquarters of society, from former telegraphic code for TH)

**TOD** time of delivery; trade and operations division

**TOE** [physics] theory of everything

**t.o.e.** ton oil equivalent

**TOEFL** test(ing) of English as a foreign language

**TOET** test of elementary training

**TOF** [physics] time of flight

**TOFC** trailer on flat car (freight container)

**TOFPET** [medicine] time-of-flight positron-emission tomography

**tog.** together

**togr** together

**Tok.** Tokyo

**TOL** Tower of London

**TOM** *territoire d'outre mer* (French: overseas territory); total organic matter

**tom.** tomato; *tomus* (Latin: volume (of book))

**tomat.** tomato

**TOMCAT** theatre of operations missile continuous-wave antitank weapon

**TOMS** Total Ozone Mapping Spectrometer

**TON** total organic nitrogen

**tonn.** tonnage

**TOO** time of origin; [commerce] to order only

**TOP** [computing] technical office protocol; temporarily out of print; termination of pregnancy

**TOPIC** [stock exchange] Teletext Output Price Information Computer

**topog.** topographer; topographical; topography

**topol.** topological; topology

**TOPS** Theatre Organ Preservation Society; Training Opportunities Scheme

**TOR** Tertiary Order Regular of St Francis

**Tor.** Toronto

**t.o.r.** time of receipt; time of reception

**torn.** tornado

**torp.** torpedo

**t.o.s.** temporarily out of service; temporarily out of stock; terms of service

**TOSD** Tertiary Order of St Dominic

**TOSF** Tertiary Order of St Francis

**Toshiba** *Tokyo Shibaura Denki KK* (Japanese electrical corporation)

**tot.** total; totally

**t.o.t.** time on target; time over target

**TOTC** time-on-target computation (military computer)

**tote** [short form] totalizator

**TOTP** *Top of the Pops* (BBC television programme)

**tour.** tourism; tourist
**tourn.** tournament
**TOW** tube-launched optically tracked wire-guided (antitank missile); tug-of-war
**tox.** toxicological; toxicology
**toxicol.** toxicological; toxicologist; toxicology
**TP** [vehicle registration] Portsmouth; target practice; taxpayer; teaching practice; technical paper; technical publication; teleprinter; [computing] teleprocessing; [music] *tempo primo* (Italian: at the original speed); *tempore Paschale* (Latin: at Easter); test panel; [insurance] third party; town planner; town planning; [computing] transaction processing; Transvaal Province; treaty port; trig point; true position; turning point
**tp** township; troop
**t.p.** *timbre-poste* (French: postage stamp); title page; to pay; toilet paper; [commerce] *tout payé* (French: all (expenses) paid)
**TPA** [medicine] tissue plasminogen activator
**TPC** [USA] The Peace Corps; [Australia] Trade Practices Commission; Transaction Processing Council
**tpd** tons per day
**tph** tons per hour
**TPI** tax and price index; [computing] terminal phase initiation; [Australia] totally and permanently incapacitated; Town Planning Institute; transpolyisoprene (synthetic rubber); Tropical Products Institute
**tpi** [engineering] teeth per inch; [engineering, textiles] threads per inch; [shipping] tons per inch (immersion); [computing] tracks per inch; [engineering] turns per inch
**tpk.** turnpike
**TPLF** Tigrean People's Liberation Front
**TPM** third-party maintenance; [commerce] total productive management
**tpm** tons per minute
**TPN** [medicine] total parenteral nutrition
**TPO** travelling post office; Tree Preservation Order
**TPR** [medicine] temperature, pulse, respiration
**Tpr** Trooper
**tpr** teleprinter
**TPS** Tax Payers' Society; Thomas Paine Society; toughened polystyrene
**tpt** transport; trumpet
**tptr** trumpeter
**TQ** [banking] tel quel (exchange rate); [computing] text quality; [UK postcode] Torquay; [commerce] total quality
**TQM** [commerce] total quality management
**TR** [civil aircraft marking] Gabon; [vehicle registration] Portsmouth; target rifle; tariff reform; Telephone Rentals plc; *tempore reginae* (Latin: in the time of the queen); *tempore regis* (Latin: in the time of the king); Territorial Reserve; test run; Theodore Roosevelt (US president); tons registered; tracking radar; transmit–receive; [UK postcode] Truro; trust receipt; [international vehicle registration] Turkey
**T/R** transmitter–receiver
**Tr** [chemical element] terbium (former symbol, replaced by Tb); [geology] Triassic
**tr.** [medicine] *tinctura* (Latin: tincture); trace; track; tragedy; train; trainee; transaction(s); transfer; [grammar] transitive; translate; translated; translation; translator; transport; transportation; [printing] transpose; transposition; treasurer; [music] treble; [music] trill; troop; truck; trumpet; trumpeter; trust; trustee
**.tr** Turkey (in Internet address)
**TRA** [USA] Thoroughbred Racing Association
**TrA** [astronomy] Triangulum Australe
**trac.** tracer; tractor
**TRACALS** [aeronautics] traffic control and landing system
**TRACE** task reporting and current evaluation; [aeronautics] test equipment for rapid automatic checkout evaluation
**trad** [short form] traditional
**trad.** tradition; traditional; *traducteur* (French: translator); *traduction* (French: translation); *traduttore* (Italian: translator); *traduzione* (Italian: translation)
**TRADA** Timber Research and Development Association
**trag.** tragedian; tragedy; tragic
**TRAM** [medicine] transverse rectus abdom-

inus myocutaneus (breast reconstruction)
**TRAMPS** temperature regulator and missile power supply
**trannie** [short form] transistor (radio)
**Trans.** Transvaal
**trans.** transaction(s); transfer; transferred; transit; [grammar] transitive; transitory; translate; translated; translation; translator; transparent; transport; transportation; [printing] transpose; transposition; transverse
**transcr.** transcribed; transcription
**transf.** transfer; transference; transferred
**transl.** translate; translated; translation; translator
**translit.** transliterate; transliterated; transliteration
**transp.** transport; transportation; [printing] transpose
**trany** transparency
**trav.** travel; traveller; travels
**Trb.** Tribune
**trbn.** trombone
**TRC** Thames Rowing Club; Tobacco Research Council
**tr. co.** trust company
**tr. coll.** training college
**Trd** Trinidad
**TRDA** Timber Research and Development Association
**Treas.** Treasury
**treas.** treasurer; treasury
**trem** transport emergency (card) (carried by chemical tankers)
**trem.** [music] *tremolando* (Italian: trembling); [music] tremulant (organ device)
**TRF** [biochemistry] thyrotrophin-releasing factor; tuned radio frequency
**trf** tariff
**trf.** transfer
**TRG** Tory Reform Group
**trg** touring; training
**trg.** [music] triangle
**trge** [music] triangle
**TRH** Their Royal Highnesses; [biochemistry] thyrotrophin-releasing hormone
**TRI** Television Reporters International; [USA] Textile Research Institute; Thrombosis Research Institute
**Tri** [astronomy] Triangulum
**trib.** tribal; tribunal; tributary; tribute
**TRIC** Television and Radio Industries Club; [medicine] trachoma inclusion conjunctivitis
**trid.** [medicine] *triduum* (Latin: three days) (in prescriptions)
**trig** [short form] triangulation (as in **trig point**)
**trig.** trigger; trigonometric(al); trigonometry
**TRIGA** [engineering] training, research and isotope-production reactors – General Atomic
**trigon.** trigonometric(al); trigonometry
**trike** [short form] tricycle
**trim.** trimester
**Trin.** Trinidad; Trinidadian; Trinity
**Trip.** Tripos (final examination at Cambridge University)
**tripl.** triplicate
**trit.** triturate
**TRJ** turboramjet (engine)
**TRLFSW** tactical range landing-force support weapon
**trlr** trawler
**TRM** trademark
**trml** terminal
**t.r.n.** technical research note
**tRNA** [biochemistry] transfer ribonucleic acid
**TRNC** Turkish Republic of Northern Cyprus
**trng** touring; training
**TRO** [law] temporary restraining order
**TROBI** Tree Register of the British Isles
**trom.** trombone
**tromb.** trombone
**trombst** trombonist
**Tron** [computing] the real-time operating system nucleus
**trop.** tropic; tropical
**Trop. Can.** Tropic of Cancer
**Trop. Cap.** Tropic of Capricorn
**trop. med.** tropical medicine
**trp** troop
**TRRL** Transport and Road Research Laboratory
**TRS** [computing] term rewriting system; Torry Research Station (Scotland)
**trs.** transfer; [printing] transpose; trustees
**TRSB** time reference scanning beam
**trsd** transferred; transposed
**trsp.** transport
**TRSR** taxi and runway surveillance radar

**TRSSGM** tactical range surface-to-surface guided missile
**TRSSM** tactical range surface-to-surface missile
**trt** turret
**Truron.** *Truronensis* (Latin: (Bishop) of Truro)
**try.** truly
**TS** [UK postcode] Cleveland; [vehicle registration] Dundee; [music] *tasto solo* (Italian: one key alone); Television Society; Theosophical Society; Tolkien Society; tool steel; [slang] tough shit; [medicine] Tourette's syndrome; training ship; [chemistry] transition state; transsexual; Treasury Solicitor; [medicine] tuberous sclerosis; tub-sized (paper); [civil aircraft marking] Tunisia; typescript
**T/S** transshipment
**t.s.** temperature switch; tensile strength; test summary; till sale; turbine ship; twin screw; type specification
**TSA** The Securities Association Limited; [statistics] time-series analysis; total surface area; Training Services Agency (former name of TA); Training Support Agency; [medicine] tumour-specific antigen
**TSAPI** telephony services application programming interface
**TSB** Trustee Savings Bank
**TSBA** Trustee Savings Banks Association
**TSD** Tertiary of St Dominic
**TSDS** two-speed destroyer sweeper
**TSE** Tokyo Stock Exchange; Toronto Stock Exchange; [medicine] transmissible spongiform encephalopathy
**TSF** two-seater fighter
**TSFA** The Securities and Futures Authority
**tsfr** transfer
**TSgt** Technical Sergeant
**TSH** Their Serene Highnesses; [biochemistry] thyroid-stimulating hormone
**Tsh** [currency] Tanzanian shilling
**TSH-RF** [biochemistry] thyroid-stimulating-hormone-releasing factor
**TSH-RH** [biochemistry] thyroid-stimulating-hormone-releasing hormone
**tsi** tons per square inch
**TSO** The Stationery Office (replacement for HMSO); town sub-office; trading standards officer
**TSP** textured soya protein; [computing] travelling salesman problem
**tsp.** teaspoon(ful)
**TSR** tactical strike reconnaissance; terminate but stay resident (computer program); torpedo-spotter reconnaissance; Trans-Siberian Railway
**TSRB** Top Salaries Review Body
**TSS** time-sharing system; [medicine] toxic shock syndrome; turbine steamship; twin-screw steamship; typescripts
**TSSA** Transport Salaried Staffs Association
**tstr** tester
**t.s.u.** this side up
**TSV** [microbiology] tobacco streak virus
**t.s.v.p.** *tournez s'il vous plaît* (French: please turn over, PTO)
**TSW** Television South West
**TT** [civil aircraft marking] Chad; [vehicle registration] Exeter; [fishing port] Tarbert; technical training; teetotal; teetotaller; [banking] telegraphic transfer; [geology] Tertiary; tetanus toxoid; [cycling] time trial; torpedo tube; Tourist Trophy (motorcycle race); transit time; [international vehicle registration] Trinidad and Tobago; Trust Territories; tuberculin-tested (milk)
**.tt** Trinidad and Tobago (in Internet address)
**TTA** Teacher Training Agency; Travel Trade Association
**TTAW** Table Tennis Association of Wales
**TTB** tetragonal tungsten bronze
**TTBT** Threshold Test Ban Treaty
**TTC** teachers' training course; technical training centre; [military] Technical Training Command; [medicine] transcutaneous transhepatic cholangiography
**TTF** Timber Trade Federation
**TTFN** [informal] ta-ta for now
**TTL** [photography] through the lens; to take leave; [electronics] transistor-transistor logic; tribal trust land (in Zimbabwe)
**TTM** [commerce] time to market
**Tto** Toronto
**TTRA** Tourist Trophy Riders' Association
**TTS** teletypesetter; teletypesetting; [acoustics] temporary threshold shift; [computing] text-to-speech

**TTT** [cycling] team time trial; [banking] telegraphic transfer; Tyne Tees Television Limited
**TTTA** Timber Trade Training Association
**TTY** [USA] teletypewriter
**TU** [vehicle registration] Chester; [civil aircraft marking] Côte d'Ivoire (Ivory Coast); thermal unit; toxic unit; trade union; [telecommunications] traffic unit; training unit; [telecommunications, acoustics] transmission unit; Tupolev (former Soviet aircraft, as in **TU-144**)
**Tu.** Tudor; Tuesday
**TUA** Telecommunications Users' Association
**TUAC** Trade Union Advisory Committee
**tub.** [cycling] tubular (tyre)
**TUBCS** Trade Union Badge Collectors' Society
**TUBE** The Union of Bookmakers' Employees
**tuberc.** tubercular; tuberculosis
**TUC** Trades Union Congress
**Tuc** [astronomy] Tucana
**TUCC** Transport Users' Consultative Committee (or Council)
**TUCGC** Trades Union Congress General Council
**Tue.** Tuesday
**Tues.** Tuesday
**TUG** Telephone Users' Group
**TUI** Trade Unions International of Public and Allied Employees
**TUIAFPW** Trade Unions International of Agricultural, Forestry and Plantation Workers
**TUIREG** Trade Unions International Research and Education Group
**TUIWC** Trade Unions International of Workers in Commerce
**TUIWE** Trade Unions International of Workers in Energy
**TULF** Tamil United Liberation Front
**TULRA** Trade Union and Labour Relations Act
**TUM** Trades Union Movement
**TUPE** Transfer of Undertakings (Protection of Employment) Regulations
**TUR** [medicine] transurethral resection
**TURB** [meteorology] turbulence
**turb.** turbine
**Turk.** Turkey; Turkish
**TURP** [medicine] transurethral resection of the prostate
**turps** [short form] turpentine
**TV** [vehicle registration] Nottingham; television; [finance] terminal value; [informal] transvestite
**.tv** Tuvalu (in Internet address)
**t.v.** terminal velocity; test vehicle
**TVA** *taxe à la valeur ajoutée* (French: value-added tax, VAT); Tennessee Valley Authority
**TVE** Television Trust for the Environment
**TVEI** Technical and Vocational Educational Initiative
**Tvl** Transvaal
**tvl** travel
**TVO** tractor vaporizing oil
**TVP** textured vegetable protein (meat substitute)
**TVR** television rating; [physics] temperature variation of resistance; Trevor (Wilkinson) (founder of sports car company)
**TVRO** television receive only (type of aerial)
**TW** [vehicle registration] Chelmsford; [telecommunications] travelling wave (as in **TW antenna**); [UK postcode] Twickenham
**.tw** Taiwan (in Internet address)
**t.w.** tail wind
**TW3** *That Was The Week That Was* (former television comedy series)
**TWA** Thames Water Authority; time-weighted average; Trans-World Airlines
**TWh** terawatt hour
**TWI** The Welding Institute
**TWIF** Tug of War International Federation
**TWIMC** to whom it may concern
**TWN** teleprinter weather network
**TWO** this week only
**TWOC** taking without owner's consent (theft of car)
**twp** township
**TWR** Trans World Radio
**TWT** transonic wind tunnel; [electronics] travelling-wave tube
**TWU** Tobacco Workers' Union; Transport Workers' Union of America
**TWX** [USA] teletypewriter exchange service
**twy** twenty

**TX** [vehicle registration] Cardiff; [US postcode] Texas
**Tx** transmission (in broadcasting)
**tx** tax; taxation; thanks
**TY** [civil aircraft marking] Benin; [vehicle registration] Newcastle upon Tyne
**Ty** Territory
**ty** truly (in correspondence)
**TYC** Thames Yacht Club
**TYMV** [microbiology] turnip yellow mosaic virus
**t.y.o.** [horseracing] two-year-old
**typ.** typical; typically; typing; typist; typographer; typographic(al); typography
**typh.** typhoon
**typo** [short form] typographical error
**typo.** typographer; typographic(al); typography
**typog.** typographer; typographic(al); typography
**typw.** typewriter; typewriting; typewritten
**Tyr.** Tyrone
**Tyrol.** Tyrolean; Tyrolese
**TYVM** thank you very much
**TZ** [vehicle registration] Belfast; [civil aircraft marking] Mali
**.tz** Tanzania (in Internet address)

# U

**U** rate of heat loss; Union; Unionist; Unit; United; [cinema] universal (film classification); University; unsatisfactory; upper; [informal] upper class (as in **U and non-U**); [chemical element] uranium; urinal; Utah; you (phonetic spelling, as in **while U wait**)
***U*** [physics] potential difference
**u** [meteorology] ugly threatening sky; [chemistry] unified atomic mass unit; [physics] up (quark flavour)
***u*** [physics] instantaneous potential difference
**u.** uncle; *und* (German: and); unit; unsatisfactory; *unter* (German: under, among); upper; utility
**U3A** University of the Third Age
**5U** [civil aircraft marking] Niger
**9U** [civil aircraft marking] Burundi
**UA** [vehicle registration] Leeds; [international vehicle registration] Ukraine; Ulster Association; United Artists Corporation; University of Alabama
**U/a** [insurance] underwriting account
**.ua** Ukraine (in Internet address)
**u.a.** unauthorized absence; under age; *unter anderem* (German: among other things); *usque ad* (Latin: as far as)
**UAA** United Arab Airlines
**UAB** Unemployment Assistance Board; Universities Appointments Board; University of Alabama in Birmingham
**UABS** Union of American Biological Societies
**UAC** Ulster Automobile Club
**UADW** Universal Alliance of Diamond Workers
**UAE** United Arab Emirates
**UAI** *Union des associations internationales* (French: Union of International Associations)
**UAL** United Airlines
**UAM** underwater-to-air missile
**u&o** use and occupancy
**UAOD** United Ancient Order of Druids
**UAOS** Ulster Agricultural Organization Society
**UAP** United Australia Party
**UAPT** *Union africaine des postes et télécommunications* (French: African Postal and Telecommunications Union)
**UAR** United Arab Republic (former official name of Egypt)
**UARS** upper-atmosphere research satellite
**UART** [computing, electronics] universal asynchronous receiver/transmitter
**UAS** University Air Squadron
**u.a.s.** upper airspace
**UAU** Universities Athletic Union
**UAV** unmanned air vehicle
**UAW** [USA] United Automobile Workers (United International Union of Automobile, Aerospace and Agricultural Implement Workers of America)

**u.A.w.g.** *um Antwort wird gebeten* (German: an answer is requested)
**UB** [vehicle registration] Leeds; United Brethren; [UK postcode] Uxbridge
**UB40** registration card for unemployment benefit
**UBA** [medicine] ultrasonic bone analysis
**UBC** University of British Columbia (Vancouver)
**UBF** Union of British Fascists
**UBI** Understanding British Industry
**U-boat** German submarine (from German *Unterseeboot*)
**UBR** [taxation] Uniform Business Rate; University Boat Race
**UBS** United Bible Societies
**UBV** [astronomy] ultraviolet, blue, visual
**UC** [vehicle registration] central London; [music] *una corda* (Italian: one string) (instruction to use soft pedal of piano); under construction; undercover; University College; upcast shaft (in civil engineering); [theatre] up centre (of stage); Upper Canada; urban council; *urbe condita* (Latin: the city being built); [obstetrics] uterine contraction
**Uc** [cinema] universal, particularly suitable for children (film classification)
**u/c** [commerce] undercharge
**u.c.** [printing] upper case
**UCA** United Chemists' Association
**UCAE** Universities' Council for Adult Education
**UCAR** Union of Central African Republics
**UCAS** Universities and Colleges Admissions Service
**UCATT** Union of Construction, Allied Trades and Technicians
**u.c.b.** unless caused by
**UCBSA** United Cricket Board of South Africa
**UCC** Union Carbide Corporation; Universal Copyright Convention; University Computing Company
**UCCA** Universities' Central Council on Admissions (became part of UCAS)
**UCCD** United Christian Council for Democracy
**UCD** University College, Dublin; upper critical depth (in oceanography)
**UCET** Universities Council for Education of Teachers
**UCG** underground coal gasification
**UCH** University College Hospital (London)
**UCHD** usual childhood diseases
**UCI** *Union cycliste internationale* (French: International Cycling Union); United Cinemas International; University of California, Irvine
**UCITS** [finance] Undertakings for Collective Investment in Transferable Securities
**UCJG** *Alliance universelle des unions chrétiennes de jeunes gens* (French: World Alliance of Young Men's Christian Associations)
**UCL** University College London; upper control limit
**u.c.l.** [engineering] upper cylinder lubricant
**UCLA** University of California at Los Angeles
**UCM** University Christian Movement
**UCMJ** [USA] uniform code of military justice
**UCMSM** University College and Middlesex School of Medicine
**UCNS** Universities' Council for Non-academic Staff
**UCNW** University College of North Wales
**UCR** [psychology] unconditioned reflex; [psychology] unconditioned response; [computing] under-colour removal; [USA] Uniform Crime Report
**UCS** [psychology] unconditioned stimulus; Union of Concerned Scientists; [computing] universal multiple-octet coded character set; University College School (London); Upper Clyde Shipbuilders
**UCSB** University of California, Santa Barbara
**UCSD** University of California, San Diego
**UCSW** University College of South Wales
**UCTA** United Commercial Travellers' Association
**UCV** [USA] United Confederate Veterans
**UCW** Union of Communication Workers; University College of Wales
**UCWRE** Underwater Countermeasures and Weapons Research Establishment
**UD** [vehicle registration] Oxford; United Dairies
**U/D** [USA] under deed

**u.d.** unfair dismissal; [medicine] *ut dictum* (Latin: as directed) (in prescriptions)
**UDA** Ulster Defence Association
**UDAG** [USA] Urban Development Action Grant
**UDC** [USA] United Daughters of the Confederacy; universal decimal classification; Urban Development Corporation; urban district council
**u.d.c.** upper dead centre
**UDCA** Urban District Councils' Association
**UDE** Underwater Development Establishment
**UDEAC** *Union douanière et économique de l'Afrique centrale* (French: Central African Customs and Economic Union)
**UDEAO** *Union douanière des états d'Afrique d'Ouest* (French: Customs Union of West African States)
**UDF** Ulster Defence Force; [South Africa] Union Defence Force; Union of Democratic Forces (in Bulgaria); *Union pour la Démocratie Française* (French: French Democratic Union) (political party); [South Africa] United Democratic Front
**u.d.f.** *und die folgende* (German: and the following)
**u. dgl.** *und dergleichen* (German: and the like)
**UDHR** Universal Declaration of Human Rights
**UDI** unilateral declaration of independence
**UDM** Union of Democratic Mineworkers
**UDN** [veterinary science] ulcerative dermal necrosis (disease of fish)
**UDP** United Democratic Party
**UDR** Ulster Defence Regiment; *Union des démocrates pour la république* (French: Union of Democrats for the Republic) (former name of RPR)
**UDSR** *Union démocratique et socialiste de la résistance* (French: Democratic and Socialist Union of the Resistance)
**UDT** United Dominions Trust
**UDUP** Ulster Democratic Unionist Party
**UE** [vehicle registration] Dudley; university entrance (examination)
**UEA** Universal Esperanto Association; University of East Anglia
**UED** University Education Diploma
**UEF** *Union européenne des fédéralistes* (French: European Union of Federalists); *Union européenne féminine* (French: European Union of Women)
**u.e.f.** universal extra fine (screw)
**UEFA** Union of European Football Associations
**UEI** Union of Educational Institutions
**UEIC** United East India Company
**UEL** United Empire Loyalists
**UEMOA** *Union économique et monètaire ouest-africaine* (French: West African Economic and Monetary Union)
**UEO** *Union de l'Europe occidentale* (French: Western European Union, WEU); unit education(al) officer
**UEP** *Union européenne de paiements* (French: European Payments Union); [genetics] unit evolutionary period
**UEPS** *Union européenne de la presse sportive* (French: European Sports Press Union)
**UER** *Union européenne de radiodiffusion* (French: European Broadcasting Union, EBU); university entrance requirements; unsatisfactory equipment report
**UETA** [USA] universal engineer tractor, armoured
**UETRT** [USA] universal engineer tractor, rubber-tyred
**UF** [vehicle registration] Brighton; United Free (Church of Scotland); [India] United Front; urea–formaldehyde (as in **UF resin**); utilization factor (of electric light)
**u/f** unfurnished (in accommodation advertisement)
**UFA** *Universum Film-Aktiengesellschaft* (European media company); [biochemistry] unsaturated fatty acid
**UFAW** Universities Federation for Animal Welfare
**UFC** United Free Church (of Scotland); Universities Funding Council
**UFCW** [USA] United Food and Commercial Workers International Union
**UFF** Ulster Freedom Fighters
**uff.** *ufficiale* (Italian: official)
**UFFI** urea–formaldehyde foam insulation
**UFO** unidentified flying object
**u.f.p.** unemployed full pay
**UFT** [physics] unified field theory; [USA] United Federation of Teachers
**UFTAA** Universal Federation of Travel Agents' Association

**UFTU** Union of Free Trades Union (in Romania)
**UFU** Ulster Farmers' Union
**UFW** United Farm Workers of America
**UG** [vehicle registration] Leeds
**Ug.** Uganda; Ugandan
**u/g** underground
**.ug** Uganda (in Internet address)
**Ugan.** Uganda; Ugandan
**UGC** underground gasification of coal; University Grants Committee
**UGLE** [Freemasonry] United Grand Lodge of England
**UGT** *Unión General de Trabajadores* (Spanish: General Union of Workers)
**UGWA** United Garment Workers of America
**UH** [vehicle registration] Cardiff
**UHA** [South Africa] Union House of Assembly
**UHB** [informal] urban haute bourgeoisie
**UHCC** Upper House of the Convocation of Canterbury
**UHCY** Upper House of the Convocation of York
**UHF** [radio] ultrahigh frequency
**UHT** ultra-heat-treated (as in **UHT milk**); ultrahigh temperature
**UHV** ultrahigh vacuum; ultrahigh voltage
**UI** [vehicle registration] Londonderry; [USA] unemployment insurance; [computing] user interface
**u/i** under instruction
**u.i.** *ut infra* (Latin: as below)
**UIA** Union of International Associations
**UIAA** *Union internationale des associations d'alpinisme* (French: International Union of Mountaineering Associations)
**UIC** *Union internationale des chemins de fer* (French: International Union of Railways)
**UICC** *Union internationale contre le cancer* (French: International Union against Cancer)
**UICN** *Union internationale pour la conservation de la nature et ses resources* (French: International Union for Conservation of Nature and Natural Resources)
**UICPA** *Union internationale de chimie pure et appliquée* (French: International Union of Pure and Applied Chemistry, IUPAC)
**UIE** *Union internationale des étudiants* (French: International Union of Students)
**UIEO** Union of International Engineering Organizations
**UIHPS** *Union internationale d'histoire et de philosophie des sciences* (French: International Union of the History and Philosophy of Science)
**UIJS** *Union internationale de la jeunesse socialiste* (French: International Union of Socialist Youth)
**UIL** *Unione Italiana del Lavoro* (Italian: Italian Federation of Trade Unions); United Irish League
**UIMS** [computing] user-interface management system
**UIP** *Union internationale de patinage* (French: International Skating Union); *Union interparlementaire* (French: Inter-Parliamentary Union)
**UIPC** *Union internationale de la presse catholique* (French: International Catholic Press Union)
**UIPM** *Union internationale de pentathlon moderne* (French: International Modern Pentathlon Union)
**UIPPA** *Union internationale de physique pure et appliquée* (French: International Union of Pure and Applied Physics, IUPAP)
**UIS** *Union internationale de secours* (French: International Relief Union)
**UISB** *Union internationale des sciences biologiques* (French: International Union of Biological Sciences)
**UISM** *Union internationale des syndicats des mineurs* (French: Miners' Trade Unions International)
**UISPP** *Union internationale des sciences préhistoriques et prohistoriques* (French: International Union of Prehistoric and Prohistoric Sciences)
**UIT** *Union internationale des télécommunications* (French: International Telecommunications Union, ITU); unit investment trust
**UITF** [accounting] Urgent Issues Task Force
**UITP** *Union internationale des transports publics* (French: International Union of Public Transport)
**UIU** Upholsterers' International Union of North America

**UJ** [vehicle registration] Shrewsbury; Union Jack; [engineering] universal joint
**UJC** Union Jack Club (London)
**UJD** Doctor of Canon and Civil Law (from Latin *Utriusque Juris Doctor*)
**UK** [vehicle registration] Birmingham; United Kingdom; [civil aircraft marking] Uzbekistan
**.uk** United Kingdom (in Internet address)
**UKA** Ulster King of Arms; United Kingdom Alliance
**UK(A)** [athletics] United Kingdom Allcomers
**UKAC** United Kingdom Automation Council
**UKADGE** United Kingdom Air Defence Ground Environment
**UKAEA** United Kingdom Atomic Energy Authority
**UKAPE** United Kingdom Association of Professional Engineers
**UKBG** United Kingdom Bartenders' Guild
**UKCC** United Kingdom Central Council for Nursing, Midwifery and Health Visiting (replacement for GNC)
**UKCIS** United Kingdom Chemical Information Service
**UKCOSA** United Kingdom Council for Overseas Students' Affairs
**UKCSBS** United Kingdom Civil Service Benefit Society
**UKCTA** United Kingdom Commercial Travellers' Association
**UKDA** United Kingdom Dairy Association
**UKFBPW** United Kingdom Federation of Business and Professional Women
**UKgal** United Kingdom gallon
**UKIAS** United Kingdom Immigrants' Advisory Service
**UKIRT** United Kingdom Infrared Telescope (Mauna Kea, Hawaii)
**UKISC** United Kingdom Industrial Space Committee
**UKLF** United Kingdom Land Forces
**UKMF(L)** United Kingdom Military Forces (Land)
**UKMIS** United Kingdom Mission
**UK(N)** [athletics] United Kingdom National
**UKOOA** United Kingdom Offshore Operators Association
**UKOP** United Kingdom Oil Pipelines
**UKPA** United Kingdom Pilots' Association
**UKPIA** United Kingdom Petroleum Industry Association Limited
**Ukr.** Ukraine; Ukrainian
**UKSATA** United Kingdom South Africa Trade Association
**UKSLS** United Kingdom Services Liaison Staff
**UKSMA** United Kingdom Sugar Merchant Association Limited
**UKST** United Kingdom Schmidt Telescope (Siding Spring, Australia)
**UKW** *Ultrakurzwelle* (German: ultrashort wave)
**UL** [vehicle registration] central London; [fishing port] Ullapool; [USA] Underwriters' Laboratories (on electrical appliance labels); university library; [biochemistry] unsaturated lipid; [theatre] up left (of stage); [computing] upload (on Internet); [medicine] upper limb
**u.l.** upper left; upper limit
**ULA** [computing] uncommitted logic array
**ULC** [theatre] up left centre (of stage)
**ULCC** ultralarge crude carrier (oil tanker); University of London Computer Centre
**ULCI** Union of Lancashire and Cheshire Institutes
**ULF** [radio] ultralow frequency; upper limiting frequency
**ULICS** University of London Institute of Computer Science
**ULM** ultrasonic light modulator; universal logic module
**ULMS** underwater long-range missile system
**ULP** University of London Press
**ULS** [finance] unsecured loan stock
**ULSEB** University of London School Examinations Board
**ULT** United Lodge of Theosophists
**ult.** ultimate; ultimately; *ultimo* (Latin: in the last (month), of the last (month)) (used in formal correspondence)
**ulto** *ultimo* (Latin: in the last (month), of the last (month)) (used in formal correspondence)
**ult. praes.** [medicine] *ultimum praescriptum* (Latin: last prescribed)
**ULTRA** Unrelated Live Transplant Regulatory Authority
**ULV** ultralow volume

**UM** [vehicle registration] Leeds; [currency] ouguiya (used in Mauritania); unaccompanied minor (on aircraft); University of Minnesota
**u/m** undermentioned
**um.** unmarried
**UMA** *Union du Maghreb Arabe* (French: Arab Maghreb Union) (customs union)
**UMa** [astronomy] Ursa Major
**UMB** *Union mondiale de billard* (French: World Billiards Union); [computing] upper memory block
**umbl.** umbilical
**UMC** University of Missouri, Columbia
**UMCP** University of Maryland, College Park
**UMDS** United Medical and Dental Schools
**UMEJ** *Union mondiale des étudiants juifs* (French: World Union of Jewish Students)
**UMF** Umbrella Makers' Federation
**UMFC** United Methodist Free Churches
**UMi** [astronomy] Ursa Minor
**UMIST** University of Manchester Institute of Science and Technology
**UMNO** United Malaysia National Organization
**ump.** umpire
**UMT** universal military training
**UMTS** universal military training service (or system)
**UMW** United Mine Workers (of America)
**UMWA** United Mine Workers of America
**UN** [vehicle registration] Exeter; [civil aircraft marking] Kazakhstan; United Nations
**un.** unified; union; united; unsatisfactory
**UNA** United Nations Association
**UNAA** United Nations Association of Australia
**unab.** unabridged
**UNACC** United Nations Administrative Committee and Coordination
**unacc.** unaccompanied
**unaccomp.** unaccompanied
**UNACOM** universal army communication system
**unan.** unanimous
**UNARCO** United Nations Narcotics Commission
**unasgd** unassigned
**unatt.** unattached
**unattrib.** unattributed
**UNAUS** United Nations Association of the United States
**unauth.** unauthorized
**unauthd** unauthorized
**UNB** universal navigation beacon; University of New Brunswick
**unb.** unbound
**unbd** unbound
**UNBRO** United Nations Border Relief Operation
**UNC** [numismatics] uncirculated; *Union National Camerounaise* (French: Cameroon National Union); United Nations Command; University of North Carolina
**unc.** uncertain; uncle
**UNCAST** United Nations Confederation on the Applications of Science and Technology
**UNCC** United Nations Cartographic Commission
**UNCCP** United Nations Conciliation Commission for Palestine
**UNCDF** United Nations Capital Development Fund
**UNCED** United Nations Conference on Environment and Development
**UNCID** Uniform Rules of Conduct for Interchange of Trade Data by Teletransmission
**UNCIO** United Nations Conference on International Organization
**uncir.** uncirculated
**uncirc.** uncirculated
**UNCITRAL** United Nations Commission on International Trade Law
**unclas.** unclassified
**unclass.** unclassified
**UNCLE** United Network Command for Law and Enforcement (in 1960s television series *The Man from UNCLE*)
**UNCLOS** United Nations Conference on the Law of the Sea
**uncond.** unconditional
**uncor.** uncorrected
**UNCSTD** United Nations Conference on Science and Technology for Development
**UNCTAD** United Nations Conference on Trade and Development
**UND** University of North Dakota
**UNDC** United Nations Disarmament Commission

**UNDCP** United Nations Drug Control Programme
**undergrad** [short form] undergraduate
**UNDOF** United Nations Disengagement Observer Force (peacekeeping force in Syria)
**UNDP** United Nations Development Programme
**UNDRO** United Nations Disaster Relief Organization
**undsgd** undersigned
**undtkr** undertaker
**UNE** underground nuclear explosion
**UNEC** United Nations Education Conference
**UNECA** United Nations Economic Commission for Asia
**UNEDA** United Nations Economic Development Administration
**UNEF** United Nations Emergency Force
**UNEP** United Nations Environment Programme
**UNESCO** United Nations Educational, Scientific and Cultural Organization
**UNETAS** United Nations Emergency Technical Aid Service
**unexpl.** unexplained; unexploded; unexplored
**UNFAO** United Nations Food and Agriculture Organization
**UNFB** United Nations Film Board
**UNFC** United Nations Food Conference
**UNFICYP** United Nations (Peacekeeping) Force in Cyprus
**UNFPA** United Nations Fund for Population Activities
**unfurn.** unfurnished (in accommodation advertisement)
**ung.** [medicine] *unguentum* (Latin: ointment)
**UNGA** United Nations General Assembly
**UNHCR** United Nations High Commissioner for Refugees
**UNHQ** United Nations Headquarters
**UNI** *Ente Nazionale Italiano di Unificazione* (Italian: Italian Standards Association); United News of India
**uni** [short form] university
**UNIC** United Nations Information Centre
**UNICA** *Union internationale du cinéma d'amateurs* (French: International Union of Amateur Cinema)
**UNICE** *Union des industries de la communauté européenne* (French: Union of Industries of the European Community)
**UNICEF** United Nations Children's Fund (formerly United Nations International Children's Emergency Fund)
**UNICOM** universal integrated communication system
**UNIDO** United Nations Industrial Development Organization
**UNIDROIT** *Institut international pour l'unification du droit privé* (French: International Institute for the Unification of Private Law)
**unif.** uniform
**UNIFIL** United Nations Interim Force in Lebanon
**UNIKOM** United Nations Iraq–Kuwait Observation Mission (peacekeeping force)
**UNIMA** *Union internationale des marionettes* (French: International Union of Puppeteers)
**UNIO** United Nations Information Organization
**UNIP** United National Independence Party (in Zambia)
**UNIPEDE** *Union internationale des producteurs et distributeurs d'énergie électrique* (French: International Union of Producers and Distributors of Electrical Energy)
**UNIS** United Nations International School
**unis.** [music] unison
**UNISCAT** United Nations Expert Committee on the Application of Science and Technology
**UNISIST** Universal System for Information in Science and Technology
**Unit.** Unitarian; Unitarianism
**UNITA** *União Nacional para a Independência Total de Angola* (Portuguese: National Union for the Total Independence of Angola)
**UNITAR** United Nations Institute for Training and Research
**Univ.** Universalist; University
**univ.** universal; universally; university
**UNIVAC** universal automatic computer
**UNIX** [trademark] type of computer operating system (originally Unics, short for Uniplexed Information and Computing System)

**UNJSPF** United Nations Joint Staff Pension Fund
**unkn.** unknown
**UNLC** United Nations Liaison Committee
**UNM** University of New Mexico
**unm.** unmarried
**UNMC** United Nations Mediterranean Commission
**UNMIBH** United Nations Mission in Bosnia-Herzegovina (peacekeeping force)
**unmod.** unmodernized (in property advertisement)
**UNMOGIP** United Nations Military Observer Group in India and Pakistan (peacekeeping force)
**UNO** United Nations Organization
**UNOG** United Nations Office at Geneva
**UNOMA** United Nations Observer Mission in Angola (peacekeeping force)
**UNOMIG** United Nations Observer Mission in Georgia (peacekeeping force)
**UNOMIL** United Nations Observer Mission in Liberia (peacekeeping force)
**unop.** unopened; unopposed
**UNOSOM** United Nations Operation in Somalia
**UNOV** United Nations Office at Vienna
**UNP** United National Party (in Sri Lanka)
**unp.** unpaged; unpaid
**UNPA** United Nations Postal Administration
**UNPC** United Nations Palestine Commission
**unpd** unpaged; unpaid
**UNPREDEP** United Nations Preventive Deployment Force (peacekeeping force in FYROM)
**UNPROFOR** United Nations Protection Force (in former Yugoslavia)
**unpub.** unpublished
**unpubd** unpublished
**UNREF** United Nations Refugee Emergency Fund
**UNRISD** United Nations Research Institute for Social Development
**UNRRA** United Nations Relief and Rehabilitation Administration
**UNRWA** United Nations Relief and Works Agency (for Palestine Refugees in the Near East)
**unsat.** unsatisfactory; unsaturated
**UNSC** United Nations Security Council; United Nations Social Commission
**UNSCC** United Nations Standards Coordinating Committee
**UNSCCUR** United Nations Scientific Conference on the Conservation and Utilization of Resources
**UNSCOM** United Nations Special Commission
**UNSF** United Nations Special Fund for Economic Development
**UNSG** United Nations Secretary-General
**UNSR** United Nations Space Registry
**UNSSM** United Nations Special Services Medal
**unst.** unstable
**UNSW** University of New South Wales
**UNTAA** United Nations Technical Assistance Administration
**UNTAB** United Nations Technical Assistance Board
**UNTAC** United Nations Transitional Authority in Cambodia
**UNTAG** United Nations Transition Assistance Group (in Namibia)
**UNTAM** United Nations Technical Assistance Mission
**UNTC** United Nations Trusteeship Council
**UNTSO** United Nations Truce Supervision Organization (peacekeeping force)
**UNTT** United Nations Trust Territory
**UNU** United Nations University
**UNV** United Nations Volunteers
**UNWCC** United Nations War Crimes Commission
**UO** [vehicle registration] Exeter
**u.ö.** *und öfters* (German: and often)
**u.o.c.** ultimate operating capability
**UOD** ultimate oxygen demand (in water conservation)
**U of A** University of Alaska
**U of NC** University of North Carolina
**U of S** University of Saskatchewan
**U of T** University of Toronto
**UOM** Union of Myanmar
**UP** [vehicle registration] Newcastle upon Tyne; Ulster Parliament; Union Pacific; United Party; United Presbyterian; United Press (news agency); United Provinces (former name of Uttar Pradesh); University of Paris; University of Pennsylvania; University of Pittsburgh; Uni-

versity Press; unsaturated polyester; [USA] Upper Peninsula; Uttar Pradesh
**up.** upper
**u.p.** underproof (of alcohol)
**UPA** *Union postale arabe* (French: Arab Postal Union); United Productions of America (company producing animated films)
**UPC** Uganda People's Congress; *Union des Populations Camerounaises* (French: Union of the Populations of Cameroon); United Presbyterian Church; Universal Postal Convention; universal product code (bar code)
**UPD** united port district; Urban Planning Directorate
**upd** unpaid
**UPF** untreated polyurethane foam
**UPGC** University and Polytechnic Grants Committee
**UPGWA** United Plant Guard Workers of America
**uphd** uphold
**uphol.** upholsterer; upholstery
**UPI** United Press International
**UPIGO** *Union professionelle internationale des gynécologues et obstétriciens* (French: International Union of Professional Gynaecologists and Obstetricians)
**UPIU** [USA] United Paperworkers International Union
**UPNI** Unionist Party of Northern Ireland
**UPOA** Ulster Public Officers' Association
**UPOW** Union of Post Office Workers (became part of UCW)
**UPP** United Peasant Party (in Poland)
**UPPP** [medicine] uvulopalatopharyngoplasty
**UPR** [insurance] unearned premiums reserve; Union Pacific Railroad
**UPS** uninterruptible power supply; [trademark] United Parcel Service; United Publishers' Services
**UPU** Universal Postal Union (formerly GPU)
**UPUP** Ulster Popular Unionist Party
**uPVC** unplasticized polyvinyl chloride
**UPW** Union of Post Office Workers (became part of UCW)
**UR** [vehicle registration] Luton; [civil aircraft marking] Ukraine; [psychology] unconditioned reflex; [psychology] unconditioned response; uniform regulations; [theatre] up right (of stage); urban renewal
**Ur.** Urdu; Uruguay; Uruguayan
**ur.** [medicine] urine
**URA** Urban Regeneration Agency; [USA] Urban Renewal Administration
**Uran.** Uranus
**urb.** urban
**URBM** ultimate-range ballistic missile
**URC** United Reformed Church; [theatre] up right centre (of stage)
**Urd.** Urdu
**URF** *Union des services routiers des chemins de fer européens* (French: Union of European Railways Road Services); uterine relaxing factor
**urg.** urgent; urgently
**URI** [medicine] upper respiratory infection
**URL** [computing] Uniform Resource Locator (address of Internet location); Unilever Research Laboratory
**urol.** urologic(al); urology
**URSI** *Union radio scientifique internationale* (French: International Scientific Radio Union)
**URT** upper respiratory tract
**URTI** [medicine] upper respiratory tract infection
**URTU** United Road Transport Union
**Uru.** Uruguay; Uruguayan
**Urupabol** Uruguay, Paraguay and Bolivia (commission for international cooperation)
**URW** United Rubber, Cork, Linoleum and Plastic Workers of America
**US** [vehicle registration] Glasgow; *ufficio stampa* (Italian: press office); [medicine] ultrasonic scanning; [medicine] ultrasound scanning; [USA] Uncle Sam; [psychology] unconditioned stimulus; undersecretary; [USA] United Service; United States (of America); United States highway (as in **US66**); unsaleable
**u/s** unserviceable; useless
**.us** United States of America (in Internet address)
**u.s.** *ubi supra* (Latin: where (mentioned) above); *ut supra* (Latin: as above)
**USA** United States Army; United States of America; [international vehicle registration] United States of America; United Synagogue of America

**USA/ABF** United States of America Amateur Boxing Federation
**USAC** United States Air Corps; United States Auto Club
**USAEC** United States Atomic Energy Commission
**USAF** United States Air Force
**USAFA** United States Air Force Academy
**USAFC** United States Army Forces Command
**USAFE** United States Air Forces in Europe
**USAFI** United States Armed Forces Institute
**USAFR** United States Air Force Reserve
**USAID** United States Agency for International Development
**USAMC** United States Army Materiel Command
**USAMedS** United States Army Medical Service
**USAR** United States Army Reserve
**USASA** United States Army Security Agency
**USASigC** United States Army Signal Corps
**USASMC** United States Army Supply and Maintenance Command
**USAT** United States Army Transport
**USATDC** United States Army Training and Doctrine Command
**USATEC** United States Army Test and Evaluation Command
**USAWC** United States Army Weapons Command
**USB** [computing] universal serial bus
**USBC** United States Bureau of the Census
**USBM** United States Bureau of Mines
**USC** Ulster Special Constabulary; United Services Club; United Somali Congress; United States Code; United States Congress; United States of Colombia; University of South Carolina; University of Southern California
**USCA** United States Code Annotated
**USCC** United States Circuit Court
**USCCA** United States Circuit Court of Appeals
**USCG** United States Coast Guard
**USCGA** United States Coast Guard Academy
**USCGC** United States Coast Guard Cutter
**USCGR** United States Coast Guard Reserve
**USCGS** United States Coast and Geodetic Survey
**USCL** United Society for Christian Literature
**USCRC** United States Citizens Radio Council
**USCSC** United States Civil Service Commission
**USD** US dollars
**USDA** United States Department of Agriculture
**USDAW** Union of Shop, Distributive and Allied Workers
**USDOE** United States Department of Energy
**USEA** United States Energy Association
**U/sec.** Undersecretary
**USECC** United States Employees' Compensation Commission
**USES** United States Employment Service
**USF** United States Forces
**usf.** *und so fort* (German: and so on, etc.)
**USFL** United States Football League
**USG** United States Government; United States Standard Gauge
**USGA** United States Golf Association
**USgal** United States gallon
**USGPO** United States Government Printing Office
**USGS** United States Geological Survey
**Ush** [currency] Uganda shilling
**USHA** United States Housing Authority
**USI** United Schools International; United Service Institution; United States Industries
**USIA** United States Information Agency
**USIS** United States Information Service
**USITC** United States International Trade Commission
**USL** United States Legation; United States Lines
**USLTA** United States Lawn Tennis Association
**USM** ultrasonic machining; underwater-to-surface missile; United States Mail; United States Marines; United States Mint; [stock exchange] unlisted securities market
**USMA** United States Military Academy
**USMC** United States Marine Corps; United States Maritime Commission
**USMH** United States Marine Hospital
**USMS** United States Maritime Service
**USN** United States Navy

**USNA** United States National Army; United States Naval Academy
**USNC** United States National Committee
**USNG** United States National Guard
**USNI** United States Naval Institute
**USNO** United States Naval Observatory
**USNR** United States Naval Reserve
**USNRC** United States Nuclear Regulatory Commission
**USNS** United States Navy Ship
**USO** [USA] United Service Organization
**US of A** [informal] United States of America
**USP** unbleached sulphite pulp (for papermaking); [advertising] unique selling proposition (distinctive feature of product); United States Patent; United States Pharmacopeia
**USPat.** United States Patent
**USPC** Ulster Society for the Preservation of the Countryside
**USPCA** Ulster Society for the Prevention of Cruelty to Animals
**USPG** United Society for the Propagation of the Gospel
**USPHS** United States Public Health Service
**USPO** United States Post Office
**USPS** United States Postal Service
**USR** United States Reserves; Universities' Statistical Record
**USRA** [USA] Universities Space Research Association
**USRC** United States Reserve Corps
**USS** [medicine] ultrasound scanning; Undersecretary of State; *Union Syndicale Suisse* (French: Swiss Federation of Trade Unions); United States Senate; United States Service; United States Ship; United States Steamer; United States Steamship; Universities Superannuation Scheme
**USSAF** United States Strategic Air Force
**USSB** United States Shipping Board
**USSC** United States Supreme Court
**USSCt** United States Supreme Court
**USSR** Union of Soviet Socialist Republics
**USSS** United States Steamship
**UST** undersea technology
**USTA** United States Tennis Association; United States Trademark Association
**USTC** United States Tariff Commission
**USTS** United States Travel Service
**usu.** usual; usually
**USV** United States Volunteers
**USVA** United States Volleyball Association
**USVB** United States Veterans' Bureau
**USVI** United States Virgin Islands
**USW** [radio] ultrashort wave; ultrasonic waves; underwater sea warfare
**usw.** *und so weiter* (German: and so forth, etc.)
**USWA** United Steelworkers of America
**USWB** United States Weather Bureau
**USWI** United States West Indies; urban solid-waste incinerator
**UT** [vehicle registration] Leicester; ultrasonic testing; ultrasonic transducer; [India] Union Territory; unit trust; Universal Time (= GMT); University of Texas (at Austin); [medicine] urinary tract; [US postcode] Utah
**U/T** under trust
**Ut.** Utah
**ut.** untrained; utility
**u.t.** universal trainer; user test
**UTA** Ulster Transport Authority; *Union de Transports Aériens* (French airline company); Unit Trust Association
**UTC** Universal Time Coordinated; University Training Corps
**Utd** United
**UTDA** Ulster Tourist Development Association
**ut dict.** [medicine] *ut dictum* (Latin: as directed) (in prescriptions)
**utend.** [medicine] *utendus* (Latin: to be used)
**UTI** [medicine] urinary-tract infection
**util.** utility room (in property advertisement)
**ut inf.** *ut infra* (Latin: as below)
**UTK** University of Tennessee, Knoxsville
**UTP** [computing] unshielded twisted pair
**UTS** ultimate tensile strength
**ut sup.** *ut supra* (Latin: as above)
**UTU** Ulster Teachers' Union; [USA] United Transportation Union
**UTW** Union of Textile Workers
**UTWA** United Textile Workers of America
**UU** [vehicle registration] central London; Ulster Unionist
**u.U** *unter Umständen* (German: circumstances permitting)

**UUA** [USA] Unitarian Universalist Association
**UUCP** [computing] UNIX-to-UNIX copy
**UUM** underwater-to-underwater missile
**UUP** Ulster Unionist Party
**UUUC** United Ulster Unionist Coalition; United Ulster Unionist Council
**UUUP** United Ulster Unionist Party
**u.u.V** *unter üblichem Vorbehalt* (German: errors and omissions excepted)
**UV** [vehicle registration] central London; ultraviolet
**UVA** ultraviolet radiation of wavelength 320–380 nanometres
**UVAS** ultraviolet astronomical satellite
**uvaser** ultraviolet amplification by stimulated emission of radiation
**UVB** ultraviolet radiation of wavelength 280–320 nanometres
**UVF** Ulster Volunteer Force
**UVL** ultraviolet light
**UVR** ultraviolet radiation
**UW** [vehicle registration] central London; underwater; University of Washington; unladen weight
**U/W** [law] under will; underwriter
**u/w** underwater; unladen weight
**UWA** University of Western Australia
**UWC** Ulster Workers' Council
**UWCE** Underwater Weapons and Countermeasures Establishment
**UWI** University of the West Indies
**UWIST** University of Wales Institute of Science and Technology
**UWT** Union of Women Teachers (became part of NAS/UWT)
**UWUA** Utility Workers Union of America
**UWUSA** United Workers' Union of South Africa
**UX** [vehicle registration] Shrewsbury
**ux.** *uxor* (Latin: wife)
**UXB** unexploded bomb
**UY** Universal Youth; [vehicle registration] Worcester
**.uy** Uruguay (in Internet address)
**UZ** [vehicle registration] Belfast; University of Zürich
**Uz.** Uzbek; Uzbekistan
**.uz** Uzbekistan (in Internet address)

# V

**V** [Roman numeral] five; Valiant (aircraft) (as in **V bomber**); [chemical element] vanadium; [immunology] variable region (of immunoglobulin chain); [international vehicle registration] Vatican City State; [currency] vatu (used in Vanuatu); Venerable; *Vergeltungswaffe* (German: reprisal weapon, as in **V-1**, **V-2**); version; Very (in titles); very; vespers; *Via* (Italian: Street); Vicar; Vice (in titles); Victor (aircraft) (as in **V bomber**); victory (as in **V-sign**); Viscount; Viscountess; volt; [music] *volti* (Italian: turn over); voltmeter; Volunteer(s); Vulcan (aircraft) (as in **V bomber**)
***V*** electric potential; [physics] luminous efficiency; [physics] potential difference; [physics] potential energy; volume (capacity)
**v** [Roman numeral] five; variable absorption (in spectroscopy); [meteorology] (abnormally good) visibility; [physics] (instantaneous) voltage
***v*** [physics] instantaneous potential difference; [chemistry] specific volume; [physics] velocity; *versus* (Latin: against); [chemistry] vibrational quantum number
**v.** vacuum; vagrant; vale; valley; valve; vein; *vel* (Latin: or); ventilator; ventral; [grammar] verb; verbal; verse; version; [printing] verso (left-hand page); versus; vertical; very; via; vicar; vicarage; *vice* (Latin: in place of ); victory; *vide* (Latin: see); village; violin; virus; visibility; [medicine] vision; [grammar] vocative; [music] *voce* (Italian: voice); [music] voice; volcano; volume; *von* (German: of ) (in names); *votre* (French: your); vowel
**V-1** *Vergeltungswaffe 1* (German: reprisal weapon 1) (World War II flying bomb)

**V¹** [music] *violino primo* (Italian: first violin)
**V2** [civil aircraft marking] Antigua
**V-2** *Vergeltungswaffe 2* (German: reprisal weapon 2) (World War II ballistic missile)
**V²** [music] *violino secondo* (Italian: second violin)
**V3** [civil aircraft marking] Belize
**V5** [civil aircraft marking] Namibia
**V6** car engine with six cylinders arranged in V-shape
**V8** [civil aircraft marking] Brunei; car engine with eight cylinders arranged in V-shape
**5V** [civil aircraft marking] Togo
**6V** [civil aircraft marking] Senegal
**9V** [civil aircraft marking] Singapore
**VA** [vehicle registration] Peterborough; value-added; [commerce] value analysis; [medicine] ventricular arrhythmia; [USA] Veterans' Administration; Vicar Apostolic; Vice-Admiral; (Order of) Victoria and Albert; [US postcode] Virginia; [medicine] visual acuity; Voice of America; Volunteer Artillery; Volunteers of America; *Vostra Altezza* (Italian: Your Highness); *Votre Altesse* (French: Your Highness); *Vuestra Alteza* (Spanish: Your Highness)
**V/A** voucher attached
**Va** Virginia (US state)
**va** [music] viola
**.va** Vatican City State (in Internet address)
**v.a.** [commerce] value analysis; [grammar] verb active; [grammar] verbal adjective
**VAB** [astronautics] vehicle assembly building (of NASA)
**VABF** Variety Artists' Benevolent Fund
**VABM** [surveying] vertical angle benchmark
**VAC** vector analogue computer
**vac** [short form] vacation
**vac.** vacancy; vacant; vacation; vacuum
**vacc.** vaccination; vaccine
**VAD** Voluntary Aid Detachment
**VADAS** [medicine] voice-activated domestic appliance system
**V-Adm** Vice-Admiral
**VAF** Variety Artists' Federation
**VAFC** [computing] VESA advanced feature connector
**vag.** vagabond; vagina; vaginal; vagrancy; vagrant
**VAH** [USA] Veterans' Administration Hospital
**val.** valley; valuable; valuation; value; valued
**valid.** validate; validation
**valn** valuation
**Valpo** Valparaiso
**vamp.** vampire
**VAN** [computing] value-added network
**van** [short form] advantage (in tennis); [short form] vanguard
**van.** vanilla
**Vanc.** Vancouver
**V&A** Victoria and Albert Museum
**V&L** vodka and lime
**V&M** Virgin and Martyr
**V&T** vodka and tonic
**V&V** [computing] verification and validation
**VANS** [computing] value-added network service
**VAPI** [aeronautics] visual approach path indicator
**vapor.** vaporization
**VAR** [computing] value-added reseller; visual aural range; Volunteer Air Reserve; *Votre Altesse Royale* (French: Your Royal Highness)
**var.** variable; variant; variation; [botany] variety; variometer; various
**VARIG** *Viação Aérea Rio Grandense* (Portuguese: Brazilian airline company)
**var. lect.** *varia lectio* (Latin: variant reading)
**varn.** varnish
**VAS** [medicine] ventricular-atrial shunt
**vas.** vasectomy
**VASARI** [computing] Visual Art System for Archiving and Retrieval of Images
**vasc.** vascular
**Vascar** visual average speed computer and recorder
**VASI** [aeronautics] visual approach slope indicator
**VASP** *Viação Aérea São Paulo* (Portuguese: Brazilian airline company)
**VAT** value-added tax
**Vat.** Vatican
**VATE** versatile automatic test equipment
**Vat. Lib.** Vatican Library

**vaud.** vaudeville
**v. aux.** [grammar] auxiliary verb
**VAV** variable air volume (in air-conditioning system)
**VAWT** vertical-axis wind turbine
**VAX** [trademark, computing] virtual address extension (range of computers)
**VB** [vehicle registration] Maidstone; [chemistry] valence bond; volunteer battalion
**vb** [grammar] verb
**vb.** verbal
**v.b.** vehicle borne; vertical bomb
**VBI** [medicine] vertebrobasilar insufficiency
**vbl** verbal
**V bomber** Valiant bomber; Victor bomber; Vulcan bomber
**VBR** [computing] variable bit rate
**VBRA** Vehicle Builders and Repairers Association Limited
**VC** [vehicle registration] Coventry; [engineering] vapour compression; Vatican City; [cycling] velo club; [finance] venture capital; [USA] Veterinary Corps; Vice-Chairman; Vice-Chamberlain; Vice-Chancellor; Vice-Consul; Vickers Commercial (aircraft) (as in **VC10**); Victoria Cross; Viet Cong; [chemistry] vinyl chloride; [physiology] vital capacity
**vc.** (violon)cello
**.vc** St Vincent and the Grenadines (in Internet address)
**v.c.** valuation clause; vehicular communication; visual communication
**VCA** [chemistry] vinyl carbonate; [medicine] viral capsid antigen; [USA] Volunteer Civic Association
**VCAS** Vice-Chief of Air Staff
**VCC** Veteran Car Club of Great Britain; Vice-Chancellors' Committee
**VCCS** [electronics] voltage-controlled current source
**VCDS** Vice-Chief of the Defence Staff
**VCE** variable-cycle engine
**Vce** Venice
**VCG** vertical centre of gravity; Vice-Consul-General
**VCGS** Vice-Chief of the General Staff
**VCH** *Victoria County History* (reference book)
**v.Chr.** *vor Christus* (German: before Christ, BC)
**VCI** volatile corrosion inhibitor
**vcl.** (violon)cello; vehicle
**VCM** vinyl chloride monomer (plastic)
**vcm** vacuum
**VCNS** Vice-Chief of Naval Staff
**vcnty** vicinity
**VCO** [India] Viceroy's Commissioned Officer; voltage-controlled oscillator; voluntary county organizer (in Women's Institute)
**VCPI** [computing] virtual control program interface
**VCR** video cassette recorder; visual control room (at airfield)
**Vcr** Vancouver
**vcs** voices
**VCT** venture capital trust
**V Cz** Vera Cruz (Mexico)
**VD** [medicine] vascular dementia; venereal disease; Victorian Decoration; Volunteer Decoration
**vd** void
**v.d.** vapour density; various dates
**V-Day** Victory Day
**VDC** Volunteer Defence Corps
**Vdc** volts direct current
**VDF** [computing] voice data fax
**VDH** [medicine] valvular disease of the heart
**VDI** [computing] virtual device interface
**VDJ** video disc jockey
**VDM** *Verbi Dei Minister* (Latin: Minister of the Word of God); [computing] Vienna Development Method (notation)
**VDQS** *vin délimité de qualité supérieure* (French: superior-quality wine)
**VDR** variable-diameter rotor; video-disc recording
**VDRL** Venereal Disease Research Laboratory (test)
**VDS** variable-depth sonar
**VDT** [computing] visual display terminal; [computing] visual display unit
**VDW** [chemistry] van der Waals (as in **VDW force**)
**VE** [vehicle registration] Peterborough; [medicine] vaginal examination; [chemistry] valence electron; valve engineering; Victory in Europe (as in **VE Day**); vocational education; *Vostra Eccellenza* (Italian: Your Excellency); *Votre Éminence* (French: Your Eminence); *Vuestra Excelencia* (Spanish: Your Excellency)

**ve.** *veuve* (French: widow)
**.ve** Venezuela (in Internet address)
**VEB** *Volkseigener Betrieb* (German: People's Concern) (state-owned company in former East Germany)
**vec.** vector
**ved.** *vedova* (Italian: widow)
**VE Day** Victory in Europe Day (8 May 1945)
**veg** [short form] vegetable(s)
**veg.** vegetable; vegetarian; vegetation
**veh.** vehicle; vehicular
**Vel** [astronomy] Vela
**vel.** vellum; velocity; velvet
**Ven.** Venerable; Venetian; Venezuela; Venezuelan; Venice
**ven.** *vendredi* (French: Friday); veneer; *venerdì* (Italian: Friday); venereal; venery; venison; venom; venomous; ventral; ventricle
**Venet.** Venetian
**Venez.** Venezuela; Venezuelan
**vent.** ventilate; ventilation; ventriloquist
**Ver.** [commerce] *Verein* (German: association, company)
**ver.** verification; verify; vermilion; verse; version
**VERA** versatile reactor assembly; vision electronic recording apparatus
**verb.** *verbessert* (German: improved, revised)
**verb. et lit.** [law] *verbatim et literatim* (Latin: word for word and letter for letter)
**verb. sap.** *verbum sapienti* (*sat est*) (Latin: a word (is enough) to the wise)
**verb. sat** *verbum sapienti sat est* (Latin: a word is enough to the wise)
**Verf.** *Verfasser* (German: author)
**Verl.** *Verlag* (German: publisher)
**verm.** vermiculite; vermilion
**vern.** vernacular
**vers** [mathematics] versed sine; [mathematics] versine
**vers.** version
**vert.** vertebra; vertebral; vertical; vertigo
**VES** Voluntary Euthanasia Society
**ves.** [medicine] *vesica* (Latin: bladder); [medicine] *vesicula* (Latin: blister); [medicine] *vespere* (Latin: in the evening) (in prescriptions); vessel; vestry
**VESA** Video Electronics Standards Association
**vesp.** [medicine] *vespere* (Latin: in the evening) (in prescriptions)
**VESPER** Voluntary Enterprises and Services and Part-time Employment for the Retired
**vet** [US short form] veteran; [short form] veterinary surgeon
**vet.** veteran; veterinarian; veterinary
**Vet. Admin.** [USA] Veterans' Administration
**veter.** veteran; veterinarian; veterinary
**VetMB** Bachelor of Veterinary Medicine
**vet. sci.** veterinary science
**vet. surg.** veterinary surgeon; veterinary surgery
**VF** [vehicle registration] Norwich; [medicine] ventricular fibrillation; [Roman Catholic Church] Vicar Forane; video frequency; [telecommunications] voice frequency
**v.f.** very fair; very fine
**VFA** [Australia] Victorian Football Association; [chemistry] volatile fatty acid
**Vfat** [computing] virtual file allocation table
**VFD** [computing] vacuum fluorescent display; verified free distribution; [USA] volunteer fire department
**VFL** [Australia] Victorian Football League
**VFM** value for money; variable-frequency oscillator
**VFOAR** [US air force] Vandenberg Field Office of Aerospace Research
**VFR** [aeronautics] visual flight rules
**VFT** [Australia] very fast train
**VFU** [computing] vertical format unit
**VFW** [USA] Veterans of Foreign Wars
**vfy** verify
**VG** [vehicle registration] Norwich; *vaisseau de guerre* (French: warship); very good; Vicar-General; [Freemasonry] Vice Grand; *Votre Grâce* (French: Your Grace); *Votre Grandeur* (French: Your Highness)
**Vg.** [ecclesiastical] Virgin
**.vg** Virgin Islands (British) (in Internet address)
**v.g.** *verbi gratia* (Latin: for example); *verbigracia* (Spanish: for example); very good
**VGA** [computing] video graphics adapter; [computing] video graphics array
**v.g.c.** very good condition (in advertisement)
**VGH** very good health

**VGL** very good-looking (in personal advertisement)
**vgl.** *vergleiche* (German: compare)
**VGPI** [aeronautics] visual glide path indicator (in World War II)
**VGSOH** very good sense of humour (in personal advertisement)
**VH** [civil aircraft marking] Australia; [vehicle registration] Huddersfield; *Votre Hautesse* (French: Your Highness)
**v.h.** vertical height; very high
**v.h.b.** very heavy bombardment
**VHC** very highly commended
**VHD** [computing] very high density; video high density (system)
**VHE** very high energy
**VHF** very high fidelity (in sound recording); [radio] very high frequency
**VHLW** vitrified high-level (radioactive) waste
**VHN** [engineering] Vickers hardness number
**VHO** very high output
**VHP** [India] Vishwa Hindu Parishad (militant group)
**VHS** [trademark] Video Home System
**VHT** very high temperature
**VHV** very high vacuum
**VI** Vancouver Island; [cartography] vertical interval; Virgin Islands; virgo intacta; viscosity index; volume indicator
**.vi** Virgin Islands (US) (in Internet address)
**v.i.** [grammar] verb intransitive; *vide infra* (Latin: see below)
**VIA** [computing] versatile interface adapter; Visually Impaired Association
**viad.** viaduct
**VIASA** *Venezolana Internacional dè Aviácion, Sociedad Anónima* (Spanish: Venezuelan International Airways Limited)
**VIB** vertical integration building
**vib.** [music] vibraphone; vibrate; vibration
**VIC** Victoria Institute of Colleges
**Vic.** Vicar; Victoria; Victorian
**vic.** vicar; vicarage; vicinity; victory
**Vict.** Victorian
**VID** [computing] virtual image display
**vid.** *vide* (Latin: see); [law] *vidua* (Latin: widow)
**Vien.** Vienna; Viennese
**vier.** *viernes* (Spanish: Friday)
**VIF** variable import fee
**vig.** vignette
**vign.** vignette
**vil.** village
**vill.** village
**v. imp.** [grammar] verb impersonal
**v. imper.** [grammar] verb imperative
**VIN** [USA] vehicle identification number
**vin.** vinegar
**vind.** vindicate; vindication
**vini.** viniculture
**VIO** Veterinary Investigation Officer
**VIP** [medicine] vasoactive intestinal peptide; very important person
**VIR** *Victoria Imperatrix Regina* (Latin: Victoria Empress and Queen)
**Vir** [astronomy] Virgo
**Vir.** Virgil (Roman poet)
**vir.** *viridis* (Latin: green)
**Virg.** Virgil (Roman poet); Virginia (USA)
**v. irr.** [grammar] verb irregular
**Vis.** Viscount; Viscountess
**vis.** viscosity; visibility; visible; visiting; visual
**Visc.** Viscount; Viscountess
**visc.** viscosity
**Visct** Viscount; Viscountess
**VISS** VHS index search system
**VISTA** Volunteers in Service to America
**vit.** vital; vitamin; vitreous
**VITA** Volunteers for International Technical Assistance
**viti.** viticulture
**vitr.** *vitreum* (Latin: glass)
**vit. stat.** vital statistics
**viv.** [music] *vivace* (Italian: lively, animated)
**vivi.** vivisection
**vix.** *vixit* (Latin: (he/she) lived)
**viz** *videlicet* (Latin: namely)
**VJ** [vehicle registration] Gloucester; [Australia] Vaucluse Junior (yacht); Victory over Japan (as in **VJ Day**); video jockey
**v.J** *vorigen Jahres* (German: last year)
**VJ Day** Victory over Japan Day (15 August 1945)
**VK** [vehicle registration] Newcastle upon Tyne
**v.k.** vertical keel
**VL** [vehicle registration] Lincoln; Vulgar Latin
**vl.** violin
**v.l.** *varia lectio* (Latin: variant reading)

**VLA** [astronomy] Very Large Array (of radio telescopes in New Mexico)
**vla** [music] viola
**Vlad.** Vladivostok
**VLB** vertical-lift bridge; [computing] VESA local bus
**VLBA** [astronomy] very long baseline array
**VLBC** [shipping] very large bulk carrier
**VLBI** [astronomy] very long baseline interferometry
**VL-Bus** [computing] VESA local bus
**VLBW** [medicine] very low birth weight
**VLCC** [shipping] very large crude carrier
**VLCD** very low calorie diet
**VLDB** [computing] very large database
**VLDL** [biochemistry] very low-density lipoprotein
**VLE** [chemistry] vapour–liquid equilibrium
**vle** [music] violone (double-bass viol)
**VLF** [radio] very low frequency
**VLFMF** very low-frequency magnetic field
**VLIW** [computing] very long instruction word
**VLLW** very low-level (radioactive) waste
**vln** violin
**VLR** very long range (aircraft); Victoria Law Reports
**VLS** [physics] vapour–liquid–solid
**VLSI** [electronics] very large-scale integration
**VLT** very large telescope
**vltg.** voltage
**vlv.** valve; valvular
**VM** [vehicle registration] Manchester; [physics] velocity modulation; Victory Medal; Viet Minh; Virgin Mary; [computing] virtual machine; [computing] virtual memory; [chemistry] volatile matter; *Votre Majesté* (French: Your Majesty)
**v.M** *vorigen Monats* (German: of last month)
**VMC** [computing] VESA medium channel; [aeronautics] visual meteorological conditions
**VMCCA** Veteran Motor Car Club of America
**VM/CMS** [trademark, computing] virtual machine, conversational monitor system
**VMD** Doctor of Veterinary Medicine (from Latin *Veterinariae Medicinae Doctor*)
**VME** [trademark, computing] Versa Module Eurocard (bus)
**VMH** Victoria Medal of Honour (Royal Horticultural Society award)
**VMO** [astronomy] very massive object
**VMS** vertical marketing system; [computing] virtual machine system; Voluntary Medical Services
**v.m.t.** very many thanks
**VN** [vehicle registration] Middlesbrough; Vietnam; [international vehicle registration] Vietnam; Vietnamese
**vn** violin
**.vn** Vietnam (in Internet address)
**Vna** Vienna
**VNM** [Canada] Victoria National Museum
**VNTR** [genetics] variable number tandem repeat
**VO** [vehicle registration] Nottingham; valuation officer; verbal order; very old (brandy etc.); veterinary officer; (Royal) Victorian Order; voice-over
**vo.** [printing] verso (left-hand page)
**VOA** Voice of America; Volunteers of America
**VOC** Vehicle Observer Corps; volatile organic chemical; volatile organic compound
**voc.** vocal; vocalist; vocation; vocational; [grammar] vocative
**vocab.** vocabulary
**VOCAL** Voluntary Organizations Communication and Language
**vocat.** [grammar] vocative
**voc. ed.** vocational education
**voctl** vocational
**VOD** velocity of detonation
**VODAT** voice-operated device for automatic transmission
**VOH** Vehicle on Hire (certificate)
**Vol** [astronomy] Volans
**Vol.** volume (of book); Volunteer
**vol.** volatile; volcanic; volcano; volume; voluntary; volunteer
**volc.** volcanic; volcano
**Vols** volumes
**vols** volumes
**volum.** volumetric
**voly** voluntary
**VONA** vehicle of the new age (rapid shuttle)

**VOP** very oldest procurable (brandy etc.)
**VOR** [navigation] very-high-frequency omnidirectional radio range
**vorm.** *vormals* (German: formerly); *vormittags* (German: in the morning, a.m.)
**Vors.** *Vorsitzender* (German: chairman)
**vou.** voucher
**vox pop** [short form] *vox populi* (Latin: voice of the people)
**VP** [vehicle registration] Birmingham; [civil aircraft marking] British Colonies and Protectorates; [physics, chemistry] vapour phase; [building] vent pipe; [grammar] verb phrase; Vice-President; Vice-Principal; victory points; *vita patris* (Latin: during the life of her/his father)
**v.p.** [photography] vanishing point; vapour pressure; variable pitch; [grammar] verb passive
**VPC** *vente par correspondence* (French: mail order)
**vpd** vehicles per day
**vph** vehicles per hour
**v.ph.** vertical photography
**VPL** visible panty line
**vpm** vehicles per mile
**VPO** Vienna Philharmonic Orchestra
**Vpo** Valparaiso
**VPop** [computing] virtual point of presence
**VPP** [India] value payable post; [veterinary science] virus pneumonia of pigs; Volunteer Political Party
**VPRGS** Vice-President of the Royal Geographical Society
**VPRP** Vice-President of the Royal Society of Portrait Painters
**VPRS** Vice-President of the Royal Society
**vps** vibrations per second
**VPZS** Vice-President of the Zoological Society
**VQ** [civil aircraft marking] British Colonies and Protectorates
**VQMG** Vice-Quartermaster-General
**VR** [civil aircraft marking] British Colonies and Protectorates; [vehicle registration] Manchester; variant reading; [physics] velocity ratio; [medicine] ventricular reflux; Vicar Rural; *Victoria Regina* (Latin: Queen Victoria); [computing] virtual reality; voltage regulator; Volunteer Reserve; vulcanized rubber
**v.r.** variant reading; *vedi retro* (Italian: please turn over, PTO); [grammar] verb reflexive
**VRA** [USA] Vocational Rehabilitation Administration
**VRAM** [computing] video random-access memory
**VRB** [meteorology] variable
**VRC** Vehicle Research Corporation; Volunteer Rifle Corps
**VRD** Royal Naval Volunteer Reserve Officers' Decoration
**v. refl.** [grammar] verb reflexive
**V Rev.** Very Reverend
**VRG** [biochemistry] vaccinia rabies glycoprotein
**vrg** [meteorology] veering
**VRI** *Victoria Regina et Imperatrix* (Latin: Victoria Queen and Empress); [medicine] viral respiratory infection; [aeronautics] visual rule instrument (landing)
**VRM** [USA] variable-rate mortgage
**VRN** [finance] variable-rate note
**VRO** vehicle registration office
**Vry** Viceroy
**VS** [vehicle registration] Luton; [Freemasonry] Venerable Sage; veterinary surgeon; *vieux style* (French: Old Style) (in dates); [chemistry] volatile solid; [music] *volti subito* (Italian: turn over quickly); *Vostra Santità* (Italian: Your Holiness); *Votre Sainteté* (French: Your Holiness)
**vs.** versus
**v.s.** variable speed; *vide supra* (Latin: see above); [music] *volti subito* (Italian: turn over quickly)
**VSAM** [computing] virtual storage access method
**VSB** [telecommunications] vestigial sideband
**vsby** visibility
**VSC** Volunteer Staff Corps
**VSCC** Vintage Sports Car Club
**VSD** vendor's shipping document; [medicine] ventricular septal defect
**VSI** [navigation] vertical speed indicator
**VSL** Venture Scout leader
**VSM** [telecommunications] vestigial sideband modulation
**vsn** vision
**VSO** [linguistics] verb-subject-object (as in **VSO language**); [computing] very small outline; very superior old (brandy

etc.); Vienna State Opera; Voluntary Service Overseas
**VSOP** very special old pale (brandy etc.); very superior old pale (brandy etc.)
**VSQ** very special quality
**VSR** very short range; very special reserve (wine)
**VSS** [medicine] vital signs stable
**vst** violinist
**VSTOL** [aeronautics] vertical and short take-off and landing
**VSUK** Vegetarian Society of the United Kingdom Limited
**VSV** [medicine] vesicular stomatitis virus
**VSW** vitrified stoneware
**VSWR** [telecommunications] voltage standing-wave ratio
**VT** [civil aircraft marking] India; [vehicle registration] Stoke-on-Trent; variable time; [currency] vatu (used in Vanuatu); [medicine] ventricular tachycardia; [US postcode] Vermont
**Vt** Vermont
**v.t.** vacuum technology; variable transmission; [grammar] verb transitive
**VTC** Volunteer Training Corps; voting trust certificate
**VTE** [psychology] vicarious trial and error
**Vte** *Vicomte* (French: Viscount)
**Vtesse** *Vicomtesse* (French: Viscountess)
**VTFL** [computing] variable-to-fixed length (code)
**vtg** voting
**VTL** [computing] variable threshold logic
**VTMoV** [microbiology] velvet tobacco mottle virus
**VTO** [aeronautics] vertical take-off
**VTOHL** [aeronautics] vertical take-off, horizontal landing
**VTOL** [aeronautics] vertical take-off and landing
**VTOVL** [aeronautics] vertical take-off, vertical landing
**VTR** videotape recorder; videotape recording
**VTVL** [computing] variable-to-variable length (code)
**VU** [vehicle registration] Manchester; [medicine] varicose ulcer; [acoustics] volume unit
**.vu** Vanuatu (in Internet address)
**Vul** [astronomy] Vulpecula
**Vul.** Vulgate
**Vulg.** Vulgate
**vulg.** vulgar; vulgarly
**VV** [vehicle registration] Northampton
**vv.** verbs; verses; [music] (first and second) violins; [music] voices; volumes
**v.v.** vice versa; viva voce
**VVD** *Volkspartij voor Vrijheid en Democratie* (Dutch: People's Party for Freedom and Democracy)
**vve** *veuve* (French: widow)
**vv.ll.** *variae lectiones* (Latin: variant readings)
**VV.MM.** *Vos Majestés* (French: Your Majesties)
**VVO** very very old (brandy etc.)
**VW** [vehicle registration] Chelmsford; [computing] van Wijngaarden (grammar); Very Worshipful; *Volkswagen* (German vehicle manufacturer)
**VWH** Vale of the White Horse
**VX** [vehicle registration] Chelmsford
**vx** vertex
**VY** [vehicle registration] Leeds
**vy** very
**v.y.** [bibliography] various years
**VYAH** very young at heart (in personal advertisement)
**VZ** [vehicle registration] Tyrone
**VZIG** [immunology] varicella zoster hyperimmune globulin

# W

**W** [genetics] sex chromosome of birds and insects; [chemical element] tungsten (from former name wolfram); Wales; Warden; [fishing port] Waterford; watt; Wednesday; Welsh; Wesleyan; west; western; [UK postcode] west London; white; wide; widow; widowed; widower; width; [shipping] winter (load line);

women; women's (clothing size); [currency] won (used in Korea)
***W*** [engineering] load; [physics] weight; [physics] work
**w** [meteorology] dew
***w*** [chemistry] mass fraction
**w.** waist; wall; war; warm; waste; water; weather; week; weight; wet; white; [cricket] wicket; [cricket] wide; width; wife; win; wind; wire; with; woman; won; wooden; word; work; wrong
**5W** [civil aircraft marking] Samoa
**6W** [civil aircraft marking] Senegal
**WA** [vehicle registration] Sheffield; [UK postcode] Warrington; [US postcode] Washington; [USA] Welfare Administration; West Africa; West African; Western Australia; Westminster Abbey; [fishing port] Whitehaven; [netball] wing attack; [insurance] with average; [US banking] withholding agent; Woodworkers of America
**w.a.** with answers
**WAA** Women's Auxiliary Association
**WAAA** Women's Amateur Athletic Association
**WAAAF** Women's Auxiliary Australian Air Force
**WAAC** Women's Army Auxiliary Corps
**WAAE** World Association for Adult Education
**WAAF** Women's Auxiliary Air Force; Women's Auxiliary Australian Air Force
**WAAS** Women's Auxiliary Army Service; World Academy of Art and Science
**WAC** [USA] Women's Army Corps (in World War II); World Aeronautical Chart
**WACB** World Association for Christian Broadcasting
**WACC** [accounting] weighted average cost of capital; World Association for Christian Communications
**WACCC** Worldwide Air Cargo Commodity Classification
**WACSM** [USA] Women's Army Corps Service Medal
**WADEX** word and author index
**WADF** [USA] Western Air Defense
**WADS** wide-area data service
**w.a.e.** when actually employed
**WAF** West African Forces; [USA] Women in the Air Force
**w.a.f.** with all faults
**WAFC** West African Fisheries Commission
**W Afr.** West Africa; West African
**WAFS** [USA] Women's Auxiliary Ferrying Squadron; Women's Auxiliary Fire Service
**WAG** [international vehicle registration] (West Africa) Gambia; Writers' Action Group; Writers' and Artists' Guild
**WAGBI** Wildfowl Association of Great Britain and Ireland
**WAGGGS** World Association of Girl Guides and Girl Scouts
**WAIF** World Adoption International Fund
**WAIS** [psychology] Wechsler Adult Intelligence Scale; [computing] wide-area information service
**WAL** [international vehicle registration] (West Africa) Sierra Leone
**Wal.** Walloon
**WAM** wife and mother; work analysis and measurement; [USA] wrap-around mortgage
**WAN** [computing] wide-area network
**w&i** weighing and inspection
**W&L** [USA] Washington and Lee University
**W&M** William and Mary (joint sovereigns of England)
**W&S** whisky and soda
**w&t** wear and tear
**WANS** Women's Australian National Service
**WAOS** Welsh Agricultural Organization Society
**WAP** work assignment plan; work assignment procedure
**WAPC** Women's Auxiliary Police Corps
**WAPOR** World Association for Public Opinion Research
**WAR** West Africa Regiment
**War.** Warsaw; Warwick(shire)
**war.** warrant
**WARC** [USA] Western Air Rescue Center; World Administrative Radio Conference; World Alliance of Reformed Churches
**WARI** [Australia] Waite Agricultural Research Institute
**Warks** Warwickshire
**warn.** warning
**warr.** warranty

**warrty** warranty
**WASA** Welsh Amateur Swimming Association
**Wash.** Washington
**WASP** [USA] White Anglo-Saxon Protestant; [USA] Women Airforce Service Pilots
**WAST** Western Australia Standard Time
**WAT** [aeronautics] weight, altitude, temperature; [psychology] word association test
**Wat.** Waterford
**WATA** World Association of Travel Agencies
**WATFOR** [computing] University of Waterloo Fortran
**WATS** [USA] Wide Area Telephone Service
**W Aus.** Western Australia
**W Aust.** Western Australia
**WAV** [computing] waveform
**WAVES** [US navy] Women Accepted for Volunteer Emergency Service
**WAWF** World Association of World Federalists
**WAY** World Assembly of Youth
**WAYC** Welsh Association of Youth Clubs
**WB** [vehicle registration] Sheffield; warehouse book; Warner Brothers (film studio); water board; [telecommunications] waveband; [commerce] waybill; weather bureau; [psychology] Wechsler–Bellevue (Intelligence Scale); [insurance] weekly benefits; World Bank
**W/B** warehouse book; [telecommunications] waveband; [commerce] waybill
**Wb** weber (unit of magnetic flux)
**w.b.** wage board; waste ballast; water ballast; [commerce] waybill; wheel base; [knitting] wool back
**WBA** West Bromwich Albion (football club); whole-body activity; World Boxing Association
**WBAFC** [USA] Weather Bureau Area Forecast Center
**WBAN** [USA] Weather Bureau, Air Force and Navy
**WBC** [medicine] white blood cell; [medicine] white blood (cell) count; World Boxing Council
**WBF** World Bridge Federation
**WBGT** [meteorology] wet-bulb globe temperature; [meteorology] wet-bulb globe thermometer
**WBI** [medicine] whole-body irradiation
**w.b.i.** will be issued
**WbN** west by north
**WBR** [medicine] whole-body radiation
**WBS** [medicine] whole-body scan; [physics] wide-band spectrometer; [physics] wide-band spectrum
**WbS** west by south
**w.b.s.** [engineering] walking-beam suspension; [insurance] without benefit of salvage
**WBT** [meteorology] wet-bulb temperature
**WC** [vehicle registration] Chelmsford; walking club; war cabinet; war council; water closet (= toilet); Wesleyan chapel; [UK postcode] west central London; [military] Western Command; working capital; [computing] world coordinates
**W/C** Wing Commander
**w.c.** watch committee; water closet (= toilet); water cock; wheelchair; without charge
**WCA** Wholesale Confectioners' Alliance; Wildlife and Countryside Act; Women's Christian Association
**w.c.a.** worst-case analysis
**WCAT** Welsh College of Advanced Technology
**WCC** War Crimes Commission; World Council of Churches
**W/Cdr** Wing Commander
**WCEU** World Christian Endeavour Union
**WCF** World Congress of Faiths
**WCL** World Confederation of Labour
**WCP** World Climate Programme; World Council of Peace
**WCRA** [USA] Weather Control Research Association; Women's Cycle Racing Association
**WCT** World Championship Tennis
**WCTU** [USA, Canada] Women's Christian Temperance Union
**WCWB** World Council for the Welfare of the Blind
**WD** [international vehicle registration] (Windward Islands) Dominica; [vehicle registration] Dudley; War Department; [UK postcode] Watford; [fishing port] Wexford; [astronomy] white dwarf; [netball] wing defence; Works Department

**wd** ward; warranted; weed; wood; word; would; wound

**W/D** wind direction; [banking] withdrawal

**w/d** warranted; well developed

**2WD** two-wheel drive

**4WD** four-wheel drive

**WDA** Welsh Development Agency; Women's Diocesan Association; [taxation] writing-down allowance

**WDC** War Damage Commission; [USA] War Damage Corporation; Woman Detective Constable; World Data Centre

**w.d.f.** wood door and frame

**wdg** winding

**WDM** [telecommunications] wavelength division multiplex

**Wdr** Wardmaster

**WDS** Woman Detective Sergeant

**wd sc.** wood screw

**WDSPR** [meteorology] widespread

**WDV** [taxation] written-down value

**WE** [vehicle registration] Sheffield; War Establishment

**w/e** weekend; week ending

**WEA** (Royal) West of England Academy; Workers' Educational Association

**wea.** weapon; weather

**WE&FA** Welsh Engineers' and Founders' Association

**WEARCON** weather observation and forecasting control system

**WEC** wave energy converter; wind energy converter; World Energy Conference

**WECOM** [USA] Weapons Command

**Wed.** Wednesday

**WEDA** Wholesale Engineering Distributors' Association

**Wednes.** Wednesday

**Weds.** Wednesday

**w.e.f.** with effect from

**WEFC** World European Fisheries Conference

**WEFT** [aeronautics] wings, engine, fuselage, tail

**Wel.** Welsh

**weld.** welding

**Well.** Wellington (New Zealand)

**WEN** Women's Environmental Network

**w/end** weekend

**WES** Women's Engineering Society; World Economic Survey

**Wes.** Wesleyan

**WES/PNEU** Worldwide Education Service of Parents' National Educational Union

**west.** western

**Westm.** Westmeath; Westminster; Westmorland

**WET** Western European Time

**WETUC** Workers' Educational Trade Union Committee

**WEU** Western European Union (replacement for BTO)

**Wex.** Wexford

**Wexf.** Wexford

**WF** [vehicle registration] Sheffield; [UK postcode] Wakefield; [physics] wave function; [USA] Wells Fargo and Company; white female

**w.f.** [sports] wing forward; [knitting] wool forward; [printing] wrong font

**WFA** White Fish Authority; Women's Football Association; World Friendship Association

**WFB** World Fellowship of Buddhists

**WFC** World Food Council (of UN)

**WFD** World Federation of the Deaf

**w.fd** [knitting] wool forward

**WFDY** World Federation of Democratic Youth

**WFEO** World Federation of Engineering Organizations

**WFF** [logic] well-formed formula; World Friendship Federation

**WFGA** Women's Farm and Garden Association

**WFL** Women's Freedom League

**Wfl** Worshipful

**WFMH** World Federation for Mental Health

**WFMW** World Federation of Methodist Women

**WFN** World Federation of Neurology

**WFP** World Food Programme (of UN)

**WFPA** World Federation for the Protection of Animals

**WFSW** World Federation of Scientific Workers

**WFTC** Working Families Tax Credit

**WFTU** World Federation of Trade Unions (replacement for IFTU)

**WFUNA** World Federation of United Nations Associations

**WG** [international vehicle registration] (Windward Islands) Grenada; [vehicle registration] Sheffield; water gauge;

weight guaranteed; Welsh Guards; West Germanic (language group); [informal] W(illiam) G(ilbert) Grace (British cricketer); wire gauge; working group
**wg** weighing; wing
**w.g.** water gauge; weight guaranteed; wire gauge
**WGA** Writers' Guild of America
**WGC** Welwyn Garden City; World Gold Council; [Freemasonry] Worthy Grand Chaplain
**Wg/Cdr** Wing Commander
**WGer** West Germanic (language group)
**WGG** [Freemasonry] Worthy Grand Guardian; [Freemasonry] Worthy Grand Guide
**WGGB** Writers' Guild of Great Britain
**WGI** world geophysical interval
**w. gl.** wired glass
**W Glam.** West Glamorgan
**WGM** [Freemasonry] Worthy Grand Master
**WGmc** West Germanic (language group)
**WGPMS** warehouse gross performance measurement system
**WGS** [Freemasonry] Worthy Grand Sentinel
**WGU** Welsh Golfing Union
**WH** [vehicle registration] Manchester; water heater; [fishing port] Weymouth; [cycling] wheelers; [USA] White House; [banking] withholding
**Wh** watt hour
**w/h** [banking] withholding
**wh.** wharf; which; whispered; white
**w.h.** [sports] wing half
**WHA** World Health Assembly (of WHO); World Hockey Association
**W'hampton** Wolverhampton
**w.h.b.** wash-hand basin
**whd** warhead
**WhF** Whitworth Fellow
**whf** wharf
**whfg.** wharfage
**whfr** wharfinger
**Whi.** Whitehall (London)
**whis.** whistle
**whmstr** weighmaster
**WHO** [USA] White House Office; World Health Organization
**WHOA!** [USA] Wild Horse Organized Assistance
**WHOI** [USA] Woods Hole Oceanographic Institution
**whp** water horsepower
**whr** whether
**WHRA** World Health Research Centre
**whs.** warehouse
**WhSch** Whitworth Scholar
**whse** warehouse
**whsle** wholesale
**whsmn** warehouseman
**whsng** warehousing
**WHT** William Herschel Telescope (La Palma)
**WHTSO** Welsh Health Technical Services Organization
**w.h.y.** what have you
**WI** West Indian; West Indies; Windward Islands; [fishing port] Wisbech; [US postcode] Wisconsin; Women's Institute; wrought iron
**w.i.** [finance] when issued
**WIA** wounded in action
**WIBC** [USA] Women's International Bowling Congress
**WICA** Warsaw International Consumer Association
**Wick.** Wicklow
**WID** West India Docks (London)
**wid.** widow; widower
**WIDF** Women's International Democratic Federation
**WIF** West Indies Federation
**Wig.** Wigtownshire
**Wigorn.** *Wigorniensis* (Latin: (Bishop) of Worcester)
**wilco** will comply (in radio communications)
**WILPF** Women's International League for Peace and Freedom
**Wilts** Wiltshire
**WIMP** [physics] weakly interacting massive particle; [computing] windows, icons, menus and pointers
**WIN** [USA] Work Incentive
**Winch.** Winchester
**W Ind.** West Indian; West Indies
**Wind. I** Windward Islands
**Wings** [finance] warrants in negotiable government securities
**Winn.** Winnipeg
**wint.** winter
**Winton.** *Wintoniensis* (Latin: (Bishop) of Winchester)

**WIP** waste incineration plant; work in progress
**WIPO** World Intellectual Property Organization
**WIRA** Wool Industries Research Association
**WIRDS** weather information reporting and display system
**Wis.** Wisconsin
**WISC** [psychology] Wechsler Intelligence Scale for Children
**Wisd.** [Bible] Wisdom of Solomon (book of Apocrypha)
***Wisd.*** *Wisden* (*Cricketers' Almanack*)
**WISP** wide-range imaging spectrometer
**wit.** witness
**WITA** Women's International Tennis Association
**withdrl** withdrawal
**witht** without
**Wits.** Witwatersrand
**WIZO** Women's International Zionist Organization
**WJ** [vehicle registration] Sheffield
**WJC** World Jewish Congress
**WJEC** Welsh Joint Education Committee
**WK** [vehicle registration] Coventry; [fishing port] Wick
**Wk** Walk (in road name)
**wk** weak; week; work; wreck
**w.k.** warehouse keeper; well known
**wkg** working
**wkly** weekly
**WKN** [meteorology] weakening
**wkr** walker; worker; wrecker
**wks** weeks; works
**wks.** workshop
**wkt** [cricket] wicket
**WL** [vehicle registration] Oxford; [international vehicle registration] (Windward Islands) St Lucia; *wagon-lit* (French: sleeping car); waiting list; water line; wavelength; West Lothian; Women's Liberation
**W/L** wavelength
**wl** wool
**w.l.** water line
**WLA** Women's Land Army
**WLAN** [computing] wireless local area network
**WLB** [USA] War Labor Board
**Wld** World
**wld** would
**wldr** welder
**WLF** Women's Liberal Federation
**wl fwd** [knitting] wool forward
**WLGS** Women's Local Government Society
**WLHB** Women's League of Health and Beauty
**WLI** workload index
**WLM** Women's Liberation Movement
**Wln** Wellington (New Zealand)
**W Long.** west longitude
**W Loth.** West Lothian
**WLPSA** Wild Life Preservation Society of Australia
**WLR** Weekly Law Reports
**WLRI** World Life Research Institute
**WLS** [statistics] weighted least squares
**WLTBU** Watermen, Lightermen, Tugmen and Bargemen's Union
**WLTM** would like to meet (in personal advertisement)
**WLU** World Liberal Union
**WLUS** World Land Use Survey
**wly** westerly
**wlz** waltz
**WM** [vehicle registration] Liverpool; war memorial; washing machine (in accommodation advertisement); wattmeter; well maintained (in advertisement); white male; wire mesh; [Freemasonry] Worshipful Master
**W/M** [shipping] weight or measurement
**Wm.** William
**WMA** Working Mothers' Association; World Medical Association
**WMAA** Whitney Museum of American Art
**WMC** [USA] War Manpower Commission (in World War II); Ways and Means Committee; working men's club; Working Men's College; World Meteorological Centre; World Methodist Council
**WMCIU** Working Men's Club and Institute Union Limited
**WMF** [trademark, computing] Windows metafile format
**wmk** watermark
**WMM** World Movement of Mothers
**WMO** World Meteorological Organization
**WMP** with much pleasure
**WMS** Wesleyan Missionary Society; World Magnetic Survey

**WMTC** Women's Mechanized Transport Corps
**WN** [vehicle registration] Swansea; [UK postcode] Wigan; [fishing port] Wigtown
**WNA** [shipping] winter North Atlantic (load line)
**WNB** weekly news bill
**WNCCC** Women's Nationwide Cancer Control Campaign Limited
**w.n.d.p.** with no down payment
**wndw** window
**WNE** Welsh National Eisteddfod
**WNL** within normal limits
**WNLF** Women's National Liberal Federation
**WNO** Welsh National Opera
**WNP** Welsh National Party
**WNW** west-northwest
**WO** [vehicle registration] Cardiff; walkover; War Office; Warrant Officer; welfare officer; wireless operator; [fishing port] Workington; [commerce] written order
**w/o** without; [accounting] written off
**w.o.** walkover; *wie oben* (German: as mentioned above); [commerce] written order
**WOA** Wharf Owners' Association
**w.o.a.** without answers
**WOAR** Women Organized Against Rape
**w.o.b.** washed overboard
**WOC** [building] waiting on cement (setting)
**w.o.c.** without compensation
**WOCA** world outside centrally planned economic areas
**WOCS** [building] waiting on cement setting
**w.o.e.** without equipment
**WOF** [New Zealand] Warrant of Fitness (for vehicles)
**w.o.g.** water, oil or gas; with other goods
**w.o.l.** wharf-owner's liability
**WOM** wireless operator mechanic
**WOMAN** World Organization for Mothers of All Nations
**w.o.n.** [knitting] wool on needle
**WOO** Warrant Ordnance Officer; World Oceanographic Organization
**WoO** *Werke ohne Opuszahl* (German: works without opus number) (works by Beethoven not listed in standard catalogue)
**woopie** [informal] well-off older person
**w.o.p.** with other property; without personnel
**w.o.p.e.** without personnel or equipment
**WOR** without our responsibility
**Wor.** Worshipful
**WORC** [USA] Washington Operations Research Council
**Worcs** Worcestershire
**WORM** [computing] write once, read many (times)
**WOSAC** worldwide synchronization of atomic clocks
**WOSB** War Office Selection Board
**wotcha** [informal] wonderful old thing, considering her/his age
**WOW** waiting on weather; War On Want; Women Against the Ordination of Women
**WP** Warsaw Pact; weather permitting; West Point (US military academy); Western Province (South Africa); White Paper (government report); [USA] wire payment; [law] without prejudice; [vehicle registration] Worcester; word processing; word processor; working paper; working party; working pressure; [Freemasonry] Worthy Patriarch; [Freemasonry] Worthy President
**Wp.** Worship; Worshipful
**w.p.** waste paper; waste pipe; weather permitting; [baseball] wild pitch(es); will proceed; [law] without prejudice; word processing; word processor
**WPA** Water Polo Association; Western Provident Association; [insurance] with particular average; [USA] Work Progress Administration; [USA] Work Projects Administration; World Parliament Association; World Pool–Billiard Association; World Presbyterian Alliance
**WPB** [USA] War Production Board (in World War II); wastepaper basket
**w.p.b.** wastepaper basket
**WPBL** [USA] Women's Professional Basketball League
**WPBSA** World Professional Billiards and Snooker Association
**WPC** War Pension(s) Committee; Woman Police Constable; wood–plastic composite; wood–polymer composite; World Petroleum Congress
**WPCA** [USA] Water Pollution Control Administration

**WPCF** [USA] Water Pollution Control Federation
**WPE** white porcelain enamel
**WPFC** West Pacific Fisheries Commission
**Wpfl** Worshipful
**wpg** waterproofing
**WPGA** Women's Professional Golfers' Association
**WPHC** Western Pacific High Commission
**WPI** wholesale price index; World Press Institute
**WPL** warning-point level
**wpm** words per minute
**WPMSF** World Professional Marathon Swimming Federation
**wpn** weapon
**WPPSI** [psychology] Wechsler Preschool and Primary Scale of Intelligence
**WPRL** Water Pollution Research Laboratory
**w.p.s.** with prior service
**WPT** Women's Playhouse Trust
**WR** [vehicle registration] Leeds; wardrobe; ward room; warehouse receipt; war reserve; [medicine] Wassermann reaction; [railways] Western Region; West Riding (former division of Yorkshire); *Wilhelmus Rex* (Latin: King William); [astronomy] Wolf–Rayet (stars); [UK postcode] Worcester
**w.r.** warehouse receipt; [insurance] war risk; water repellent
**WRA** [USA] War Relocation Authority; Water Research Association; [horticulture] Wisley Rose Award
**WRAAC** Women's Royal Australian Army Corps
**WRAAF** Women's Royal Australian Air Force
**WRAC** Women's Royal Army Corps
**WRAF** Women's Royal Air Force
**WRAM** [computing] Windows random-access memory
**WRANS** Women's Royal Australian Naval Service
**WRAP** [USA] weapons readiness analysis program
**WRC** Water Research Centre; [USA] Welding Research Council
**WRE** [Australia] Weapons Research Establishment
**w. ref.** with reference (to)
**w. reg.** with regard (to)
**WRI** war risks insurance; Women's Rural Institute
**w.r.n.** [knitting] wool round needle
**WRNG** [meteorology] warning
**WRNR** Women's Royal Naval Reserve
**WRNS** Women's Royal Naval Service (hence informal name Wrens)
**wrnt** warrant
**WRO** Weed Research Organization
**w.r.o.** [insurance] war risks only
**WRP** Workers' Revolutionary Party
**WRRA** [cycling] Women's Road Records Association
**wrt** wrought (iron)
**w.r.t.** with respect to
**WRU** Welsh Rugby Union; Wesleyan Reform Union; who are you?
**WRVS** Women's Royal Voluntary Service (formerly WVS)
**WS** [vehicle registration] Bristol; [international vehicle registration] (Western) Samoa; [UK postcode] Walsall; water-soluble; weapon system; West Saxon; wind speed; [Scots law] Writer to the Signet [Scotland]
**.ws** Samoa (in Internet address)
**WSA** [USA] War Shipping Administration
**W Sam.** Western Samoa
**WSC** World Series Cricket
**WSCF** World Student Christian Federation
**WSF** Wake Shield Facility; [chemistry] water-soluble fraction
**w/shop** workshop
**WSI** Writers and Scholars International
**WSJ** *Wall Street Journal*
**WSL** Warren Spring Laboratory (Stevenage, Hertfordshire)
**WSM** Women's Suffrage Movement
**WSP** water supply point
**WSPU** Women's Social and Political Union
**WSSA** Welsh Secondary Schools Association
**WSTN** World Service Television News
**WSTV** World Service Television
**WSU** Wichita State University
**WSW** west-southwest
**WT** [vehicle registration] Leeds; Warrant Telegraphist (in Royal Navy); war transport; watertight; weekly takings; [fishing port] Westport; wireless telegraphy; wireless telephony; withholding tax

**W/T** wireless telegraphy; wireless telephony
**wt** warrant; watertight; weight; without
**WTA** winner takes all; Women's Tennis Association; World Transport Agency
**WTAA** World Trade Alliance Association
**WTAU** Women's Total Abstinence Union
**WTB** Welsh Tourist Board
**Wtb.** *Wörterbuch* (German: dictionary)
**WTC** Wheat Trade Convention
**WTD** watertight door
**wtd** wanted; warranted; watered
**Wtf.** Waterford
**WTG** wind turbine generator
**WTH** whole-tree harvesting
**wthr** weather
**WTIS** World Trade Information Service
**WTMH** watertight manhole
**WTN** Worldwide Television News
**WTO** Warsaw Treaty Organization; World Tourism Organization; World Trade Organization (replacement for GATT)
**WTP** willingness to pay; willing to pay (in advertisement)
**wtr** water; winter; writer
**WTRC** Wool Textile Research Council
**WTS** Women's Transport Service
**WTT** World Team Tennis
**WTTA** Wholesale Tobacco Trade Association of Great Britain and Northern Ireland
**WTTC** World Travel and Tourism Council
**WTUC** World Trade Union Conference
**WTUL** Women's Trade Union League
**WU** [vehicle registration] Leeds; Western Union
**WUCT** World Union of Catholic Teachers
**WUF** World Underwater Federation
**WUJS** World Union of Jewish Students
**WUPJ** World Union for Progressive Judaism
**WUS** World University Service
**WUSL** Women's United Service League
**WV** [vehicle registration] Brighton; [international vehicle registration] (Windward Islands) St Vincent; water valve; [US postcode] West Virginia; [UK postcode] Wolverhampton
**w/v** water valve; [chemistry] weight in volume (of solution)
**WVA** World Veterinary Association
**W Va** West Virginia
**WVD** *Wereldverbond van Diamant Bewerkers* (Dutch: Universal Alliance of Diamond Workers)
**wvd** waived
**WVF** World Veterans' Federation
**WVS** Women's Voluntary Service (former name of WRVS)
**WVT** water vapour transfer; water vapour transmission
**WVU** West Virginia University
**WW** [vehicle registration] Leeds; wall-to-wall (in property advertisement); walnut wood (trim) (in car advertisement); warehouse warrant; warrant writer; whitewall (tyre); *Who's Who*; World War; worldwide
**W/W** wall-to-wall (in property advertisement); warehouse warrant
**w/w** weight for weight
**WW1** World War One
**WW2** World War Two
**WWDC** World War Debt Commission
**WWDSHEX** [shipping] weather working days, Sundays and holidays excluded
**Wwe** *Witwe* (German: widow)
**WWF** Worldwide Fund for Nature (formerly World Wildlife Fund); World Wrestling Federation
**WWI** World War One
**WWII** World War Two
**WWMCCS** World Wide Military Command and Control System
**WWO** Wing Warrant Officer
**WWSSN** worldwide standard seismograph network
**WWSU** World Water Ski Union
**WWW** *Who Was Who*; World Weather Watch (of WMO); [computing] World Wide Web
**WWY** (Queen's Own) Warwickshire and Worcestershire Yeomanry
**WX** [vehicle registration] Leeds; women's extra (large) (clothing size)
**WY** [vehicle registration] Leeds; [fishing port] Whitby; [US postcode] Wyoming
**Wy** Way (in road name)
**Wy.** (John) Wycliffe (English religious reformer); Wyoming
**Wycl.** (John) Wycliffe (English religious reformer)
**Wyo.** Wyoming
**WYR** West Yorkshire Regiment

**wysiwyg** [computing] what you see is what you get

**WZ** [vehicle registration] Belfast; *Weltzeit* (German: universal time)

**Wz.** *Warenzeichen* (German: trademark)

**WZO** World Zionist Organization

# X

**X** Christ (transcription of Greek letter chi); Cross (as in **Charing X**); error; exchange; experiment; experimental; explosive; extension; extra; extraordinary; [cinema] for over-18s only (former film classification); [chemistry] halogen; kiss (on letter, card, etc.); location on map; [genetics] sex chromosome; [Roman numeral] ten; unknown person or thing; X-ray; xylonite (plastic)

***X*** [physics] exposure dose

**x** cross (as in **x-section**); [commerce] ex (= from); [finance] ex (= without); extra; [meteorology] hoar-frost; [Roman numeral] ten; trans- (as in **xformer**)

***x*** [mathematics] algebraic variable; [mathematics] (horizontal) coordinate (as in ***x*-axis**)

**3X** [civil aircraft marking] Guinea

**4X** [civil aircraft marking] Israel

**5X** [civil aircraft marking] Uganda

**XA** [civil aircraft marking] Mexico

**xa** [finance] ex all (i.e. without any benefits)

**XB** [civil aircraft marking] Mexico

**xb** [finance] ex bonus

**Xber** December

**XBT** expendable bathythermograph

**xbt** exhibit

**XC** [USA, Canada] cross-country (as in **XC skiing**); [civil aircraft marking] Mexico

**xc** [finance] ex capitalization; [finance] ex coupon (i.e. without interest on coupon)

**x.c.l.** [insurance] excess current liabilities

**xcp** [finance] ex coupon (i.e. without interest on coupon)

**xcpt** except

**XCT** [medicine] X-ray compute(rize)d tomography

**XD** [physics] X-ray diffraction

**xd** [finance] ex dividend

**x'd** crossed; executed

**xdiv** [finance] ex dividend

**XDR** extended dynamic range (of cassettes)

**Xdr** crusader

**Xe** [chemical element] xenon

**Xen.** Xenophon (ancient Greek historian)

**xf** extra fine

**xfer** transfer

**xfmr** transformer

**xg** crossing

**XGA** [computing] extended graphics array

**XG Midi** extended general musical instrument digital interface

**xhst** exhaust

**xhy** extra heavy

**XI** [vehicle registration] Belfast; [medicine] X-ray imaging

**xi** [finance] ex interest

**xin** [finance] ex interest

**XL** extra large (clothing size)

**xlnt** excellent

**x.l.w.b.** extra-long wheelbase

**XM** experimental missile

**Xmas** Christmas

**xmit** transmit

**XML** [computing] extensible markup language (used on Internet)

**XMS** [computing] extended memory specification

**xmsn** transmission

**xmtr** transmitter

**Xn** Christian

**xn** [finance] ex new (i.e. without right to new shares)

**x/nt** excellent

**Xnty** Christianity

**XO** cognac of superior quality; executive officer

**XP** Christ (transcription of Greek letters chi and rho); Christianity; express paid; [medicine] xeroderma pigmentosum

**x.p.** express paid

**xpl.** explosive

**xplt** exploit
**xpn** expansion
**xq** cross-question
**XR** X-ray(s)
**Xr** examiner
**xr** [finance] ex rights
**X-ray** electromagnetic radiation of very short wavelength (from originally unknown nature of this radiation)
**XRD** [physics] X-ray diffraction
**Xrds** crossroads
**XRE** X-ray emission
**x-ref.** cross-refer; cross-reference
**XRF** X-ray fluorescence
**XRM** [medicine] X-ray mammography
**XRMA** X-ray microprobe analysis
**XRT** [medicine] X-ray therapy
**XRT** [medicine] X-ray tomography
**xrts** [finance] ex rights
**XS** cross-section; excess
**xs** expenses
**XT** [civil aircraft marking] Burkina Faso; extended technology
**Xt** Christ
**xtal** crystal
**XTE** [astronomy] X-ray Timing Explorer
**X-tgd** [building] cross-tongued
**Xth** tenth
**Xtian** Christian
**xtra** extra
**xtry** extraordinary
**Xty** Christianity
**XU** [civil aircraft marking] Cambodia
**XUI** [computing] X user interface
**XUV** [astronomy] extreme ultraviolet
**xw** [finance] ex warrants
**x/wb** extra-long wheelbase
**XX** double-strength beer
**XXX** triple-strength beer
**XY** [civil aircraft marking] Myanmar (formerly Burma)
**xyl.** xylophone
**XZ** [vehicle registration] Armagh; [civil aircraft marking] Myanmar (formerly Burma)

# Y

**Y** [genetics] sex chromosome; [currency] yen (used in Japan); Yeomanry; [fishing port] Youghal; [chemical element] yttrium; [currency] yuan (used in China); Yugoslavia
***Y*** [physics] hypercharge
**y** [meteorology] dry air
***y*** [mathematics] algebraic variable; altitude; [mathematics] (vertical) coordinate (as in ***y*-axis**); [aeronautics] lateral axis
**y.** yacht; yard; year; yellow; young; youngest
**Y2K** Year 2000
**5Y** [civil aircraft marking] Alaska
**6Y** [civil aircraft marking] Jamaica
**9Y** [civil aircraft marking] Trinidad and Tobago
**YA** [civil aircraft marking] Afghanistan; [vehicle registration] Taunton; [insurance] York–Antwerp (Rules); [USA] young adult
**YABA** Young American Bowling Alliance
**YAC** [genetics] yeast artificial chromosome(s)
**YACC** [computing] yet another compiler-compiler
**YAG** [electronics] yttrium–aluminium garnet
**YAH** young at heart (in personal advertisement)
**YAL** Young Australia League
**Y&LR** York and Lancaster Regiment
**YAR** [international vehicle registration] Yemen (Arab Republic); [insurance] York–Antwerp Rules
**Y-ARD** Yarrow-Admiralty Research Department
**YAS** Yorkshire Agricultural Society
**YAVIS** [US informal] young, attractive, verbal, intelligent and successful
**YB** [vehicle registration] Taunton; yearbook
**Yb** [chemical element] ytterbium
**y.b.** [knitting] yarn back
**YC** [vehicle registration] Taunton; yacht club; [USA] Yale College; Young Conservative; youth club
**YCA** Youth Camping Association

**YC&UO** Young Conservative and Unionist Organization
**YCL** [USA] Young Communist League
**YCNAC** Young Conservative National Advisory Committee
**YCS** (International) Young Catholic Students
**yct** yacht
**YCW** [informal] you can't win; (International) Young Christian Workers
**YD** [vehicle registration] Taunton
**yd** yard (unit of length)
**y'day** yesterday
**ydg** yarding
**yds** yards (unit of length)
**YE** [vehicle registration] central London; [civil aircraft marking] Yemen; Your Excellency
**.ye** Yemen (in Internet address)
**YEA** [USA] Yale Engineering Association
**yearb.** yearbook
**YEB** Yorkshire Electricity Board
**yel.** yellow
**Yel. NP** [USA] Yellowstone National Park
**Yem.** Yemen; Yemeni
**YEO** Youth Employment Officer
**yeo.** yeoman; yeomanry
**YER** [finance] yearly effective rate (of interest)
**YES** Youth Employment Service; Youth Enterprise Scheme
**yesty** yesterday
**YF** [vehicle registration] central London
**y.f.** [knitting] yarn forward
**YFC** Young Farmers' Club; Youth for Christ
**YFCU** Young Farmers' Club of Ulster
**YFG** [electronics] yttrium–ferrite garnet
**YG** [vehicle registration] Leeds
**YH** [vehicle registration] central London; [fishing port] Yarmouth; [numismatics] young head (of Queen Victoria); youth hostel
**YHA** Youth Hostels Association
**YHANI** Youth Hostels Association of Northern Ireland
**YHVH** Hebrew name for God (the Tetragrammaton)
**YHWH** Hebrew name for God (the Tetragrammaton)
**YI** [civil aircraft marking] Iraq
**Yi.** Yiddish
**Yid.** Yiddish
**YIG** [electronics] yttrium–iron garnet
**YIP** [USA] Youth International Party
**Yippie** [US informal] member of Youth International Party
**YJ** [vehicle registration] Brighton; [civil aircraft marking] Vanuatu
**YK** [vehicle registration] central London; [civil aircraft marking] Syria
**YL** [vehicle registration] central London; [civil aircraft marking] Latvia; yield limit
**YLI** Yorkshire Light Infantry
**YM** [vehicle registration] central London
**YMBA** Yacht and Motor Boats Association
**YMCA** Young Men's Christian Association
**YMCath.A** [USA] Young Men's Catholic Association
**YMCU** Young Men's Christian Union
**YMFS** Young Men's Friendly Society
**YMHA** Young Men's Hebrew Association
**YMV** [microbiology] yellow mosaic virus
**YN** [vehicle registration] central London; [civil aircraft marking] Nicaragua
**YNP** [USA] Yellowstone National Park
**YO** [vehicle registration] central London; [UK postcode] York
**y.o.** [knitting] yarn over; year(s) old
**y.o.b.** year of birth
**YOC** Young Ornithologists' Club (of RSPB)
**y.o.d.** year of death
**y.o.m.** year of marriage
**YOP** Youth Opportunities Programme (former government scheme)
**Yorks** Yorkshire
**YP** [vehicle registration] central London; yield point (in mechanics); young people; young person; young prisoner
**y.p.** year's purchase
**YPA** Young Pioneers of America
**YPFB** *Yacimientos Petroliferos Fiscales Bolivianos* (Spanish: Bolivian state petroleum organization)
**YPSCE** [USA] Young People's Society of Christian Endeavour
**YPSL** [USA] Young People's Socialist League
**YPTES** Young People's Trust for Endangered Species
**YR** [vehicle registration] central London; [civil aircraft marking] Romania
**yr** year; younger; your
**YRA** Yacht Racing Association

**yrbk** yearbook
**YRls** [currency] Yemeni riyal
**yrly** yearly
**Yrs** Yours
**yrs** years
**YS** [civil aircraft marking] El Salvador; [vehicle registration] Glasgow; yield strength (in mechanics); Young Socialists
**Ys.** Yugoslavia; Yugoslavian
**YSA** Young Socialist Alliance
**YSAG** [electronics] yttrium–scandium–aluminium garnet
**YSO** [astronomy] young stellar object
**yst** youngest
**YT** [vehicle registration] central London; Yukon Territory
**yt** yacht
**YTD** [accounting] year to date
**YTS** Youth Training Scheme
**YTV** Yorkshire Television
**YTYTK** you're too young to know
**YU** [vehicle registration] central London; [USA] Yale University; [civil aircraft marking] Yugoslavia; [international vehicle registration] Yugoslavia
**.yu** Yugoslavia (in Internet address)
**Yugo.** Yugoslavia; Yugoslavian
**Yuk.** Yukon
**YUP** Yale University Press
**yuppie** [informal] young upwardly-mobile professional; [informal] young urban professional
**YV** [vehicle registration] central London; [civil aircraft marking] Venezuela; [international vehicle registration] Venezuela
**YVF** Young Volunteer Force
**YVFF** Young Volunteer Force Foundation
**YW** [vehicle registration] central London
**YWCA** Young Women's Christian Association
**YWCTU** Young Women's Christian Temperance Union
**YWF** Young World Federalists
**YWHA** Young Women's Hebrew Association
**YWS** Young Wales Society; Young Workers' Scheme
**YX** [vehicle registration] central London
**YY** [vehicle registration] central London
**YZ** [vehicle registration] Londonderry

# Z

**Z** [genetics] sex chromosome of birds and insects; [international vehicle registration] Zambia; *Zeit* (German: time); zero (as in **Z-hour**); [civil aircraft marking] Zimbabwe; Zion; Zionist; *Zoll* (German: customs); zone
***Z*** [physics] proton number
**z** [meteorology] haze
***z*** [mathematics] algebraic variable; [chemistry] charge number; [mathematics] coordinate (as in **z-axis**)
**z.** zenith; zero; zone
**ZA** [civil aircraft marking] Albania; [international vehicle registration] South Africa (from Afrikaans *Zuid Afrika*)
**za.** *zirca* (German: approximately)
**.za** South Africa (in Internet address)
**Zag.** Zagreb
**Zam.** Zambia
**ZAMS** [astronomy] zero-age main sequence
**Zan.** Zanzibar
**ZANU** Zimbabwe African National Union
**ZANU(PF)** Zimbabwe African National Union (Patriotic Front)
**Zanz.** Zanzibar
**ZAP** [military] zero anti-aircraft potential
**ZAPU** Zimbabwe African People's Union
**ZB** Zen Buddhism; Zen Buddhist
**z.B** *zum Beispiel* (German: for example, e.g.)
**ZBB** [US finance] zero-base(d) budgeting
**ZC** Zionist Congress
**ZCCT** Zoo Check Charitable Trust
**ZD** [electronics] Zener diode; [astronomy] zenith distance; zero defect(s)
**Z-DNA** [biochemistry] zigzagged deoxyribonucleic acid
**ZE** [UK postcode] Lerwick
**ZEBRA** [nuclear technology] zero-energy breeder-reactor assembly
**Zech.** [Bible] Zechariah

**ZEEP** [nuclear technology] zero-energy experimental pile
**ZEG** zero economic growth
**zen.** zenith
**ZENITH** [nuclear technology] zero-energy nitrogen-heated thermal reactor
**Zeph.** [Bible] Zephaniah
**zepp.** zeppelin
**ZETA** [nuclear technology] zero-energy thermonuclear apparatus (or assembly)
**ZETR** [nuclear technology] zero-energy thermal reactor
**ZF** zero frequency; [military] zone of fire
**ZFGBI** Zionist Federation of Great Britain and Ireland
**ZG** zero gravity; zoological gardens
**z-g** zero gravity
**ZH** zero hour
**z.H** *zu Händen* (German: for the attention of, f.a.o., care of, c/o)
**ZHR** [astronomy] zenithal hourly rate
**ZI** [military] zone of interior
**Ziana** Zimbabwe Inter-Africa News Agency
**ZIF** [electronics] zero insertion force
**ZIFT** [medicine] zygote intrafallopian transfer (infertility treatment)
**ZIL** [computing] zigzag in-line
**zip** [computing] zigzag in-line package; [USA] zone improvement plan (as in **zip code**, US postcode)
**ZK** [civil aircraft marking] New Zealand
**ZL** [civil aircraft marking] New Zealand
**Zl** [currency] zloty (used in Poland)
**ZM** [civil aircraft marking] New Zealand
**.zm** Zambia (in Internet address)
**ZN** [civil aircraft marking] New Zealand
**Zn** [chemical element] zinc
**ZO** Zionist Organization
**ZOA** Zionist Organization of America
**zod.** zodiac
**zoo** [short form] zoological garden
**zool.** zoological; zoologist; zoology
**ZP** [civil aircraft marking] Paraguay
**ZPG** zero population growth
**Zr** [chemical element] zirconium
**.zr** Democratic Republic of Congo (formerly Zaïre) (in Internet address)
**ZS** [civil aircraft marking] South Africa; Zoological Society
**Zs.** *Zeitschrift* (German: periodical, journal)
**ZSI** Zoological Society of Ireland
**ZSL** Zoological Society of London
**ZST** zone standard time
**ZT** [civil aircraft marking] South Africa; zone time
**z.T** *zum Teil* (German: partly)
**Ztg** *Zeitung* (German: newspaper)
**ZU** [civil aircraft marking] South Africa
**Zulu.** Zululand
**ZUM** Zimbabwe Unity Movement
**Zür** Zürich
**ZV** zoomed video
**ZW** [international vehicle registration] Zimbabwe
**zw.** *zwischen* (German: between, among)
**.zw** Zimbabwe (in Internet address)
**ZZ** [vehicle registration] vehicle temporarily imported by foreign visitor
**Zz.** [medicine] *zingiber* (Latin: ginger)
**z.Z** *zur Zeit* (German: at present)
**zz** zigzag

# READ MORE IN PENGUIN

In every corner of the world, on every subject under the sun, Penguin represents quality and variety – the very best in publishing today.

For complete information about books available from Penguin – including Puffins, Penguin Classics and Arkana – and how to order them, write to us at the appropriate address below. Please note that for copyright reasons the selection of books varies from country to country.

**In the United Kingdom**: Please write to *Dept. EP, Penguin Books Ltd, Bath Road, Harmondsworth, West Drayton, Middlesex UB7 0DA*

**In the United States**: Please write to *Consumer Services, Penguin Putnam Inc., 405 Murray Hill Parkway, East Rutherford, New Jersey 07073-2136.* VISA and MasterCard holders call 1-800-631-8571 to order Penguin titles

**In Canada**: Please write to *Penguin Books Canada Ltd, 10 Alcorn Avenue, Suite 300, Toronto, Ontario M4V 3B2*

**In Australia**: Please write to *Penguin Books Australia Ltd, 487 Maroondah Highway, Ringwood, Victoria 3134*

**In New Zealand**: Please write to *Penguin Books (NZ) Ltd, Private Bag 102902, North Shore Mail Centre, Auckland 10*

**In India**: Please write to *Penguin Books India Pvt Ltd, 11 Community Centre, Panchsheel Park, New Delhi 110017*

**In the Netherlands**: Please write to *Penguin Books Netherlands bv, Postbus 3507, NL-1001 AH Amsterdam*

**In Germany**: Please write to *Penguin Books Deutschland GmbH, Metzlerstrasse 26, 60594 Frankfurt am Main*

**In Spain**: Please write to *Penguin Books S. A., Bravo Murillo 19, 1°B, 28015 Madrid*

**In Italy**: Please write to *Penguin Italia s.r.l., Via Vittorio Emanuele 45/a, 20094 Corsico, Milano*

**In France**: Please write to *Penguin France, 12, Rue Prosper Ferradou, 31700 Blagnac*

**In Japan**: Please write to *Penguin Books Japan Ltd, Iidabashi KM-Bldg, 2-23-9 Koraku, Bunkyo-Ku, Tokyo 112-0004*

**In South Africa**: Please write to *Penguin Books South Africa (Pty) Ltd, P.O. Box 751093, Gardenview, 2047 Johannesburg*

# READ MORE IN PENGUIN

## PHILOSOPHY

**Brainchildren** Daniel C. Dennett

Philosophy of mind has been profoundly affected by this century's scientific advances, and thinking about thinking – how and why the mind works, its very existence – can seem baffling. Here eminent philosopher and cognitive scientist Daniel C. Dennett has provided an eloquent guide through some of the mental and moral mazes.

**Language, Truth and Logic** A. J. Ayer

The classic text which founded logical positivism and modern British philosophy, *Language, Truth and Logic* swept away the cobwebs and revitalized British philosophy.

**The Penguin Dictionary of Philosophy** Edited by Thomas Mautner

This dictionary encompasses all aspects of Western philosophy from 600 BC to the present day. With contributions from over a hundred leading philosophers, this dictionary will prove the ideal reference for any student or teacher of philosophy as well as for all those with a general interest in the subject.

**Labyrinths of Reason** William Poundstone

'The world and what is in it, even what people say to you, will not seem the same after plunging into *Labyrinths of Reason* . . . holds up the deepest philosophical questions for scrutiny in a way that irresistibly sweeps readers on' *New Scientist*

**Metaphysics as a Guide to Morals** Iris Murdoch

'This is philosophy dragged from the cloister, dusted down and made freshly relevant to suffering and egoism, death and religious ecstasy . . . and how we feel compassion for others' *Guardian*

**Philosophy Football** Mark Perryman

The amazing tale of a make-believe team, *Philosophy Football* is the story of what might have happened to the world's greatest thinkers if their brains had been in their boots instead of their heads . . .

# READ MORE IN PENGUIN

## LITERARY CRITICISM

**The Penguin History of Literature**

Published in ten volumes, *The Penguin History of Literature* is a superb critical survey of the English and American literature covering fourteen centuries, from the Anglo-Saxons to the present, and written by some of the most distinguished academics in their fields.

**New Bearings in English Poetry** F. R. Leavis

'*New Bearings in English Poetry* was the first intelligent account of the work of Eliot, Pound and Gerard Manley Hopkins to appear in English and it significantly altered critical awareness . . . Leavis gave to literary criticism a thoroughness and respectability that has never since been equalled' Peter Ackroyd, *Spectator*. 'The most influential literary critic of modern times' *Financial Times*

**The Uses of Literacy** Richard Hoggart

Mass literacy has opened new worlds to new readers. How far has it also been exploited to debase standards and behaviour? 'A vivid inside view of working-class culture and one of the most influential books of the post-war era' *Observer*

**Epistemology of the Closet** Eve Kosofsky Sedgwick

Through her brilliant interpretation of the readings of Henry James, Melville, Nietzsche, Proust and Oscar Wilde, Eve Kosofsky Sedgwick shows how questions of sexual definition are at the heart of every form of representation in this century. 'A signal event in the history of late-twentieth-century gay studies' Wayne Koestenbaum

**Dangerous Pilgrimages** Malcolm Bradbury

'This capacious book tracks Henry James from New England to Rye; Evelyn Waugh to a Hollywood as grotesque as he expected; Gertrude Stein to Spain to be mistaken for a bishop; Oscar Wilde to a rickety stage in Leadsville, Colorado . . . The textbook on the the transatlantic theme' *Guardian*

# READ MORE IN PENGUIN

## LITERARY CRITICISM

**The Practice of Writing** David Lodge

This lively collection examines the work of authors ranging from the two Amises to Nabokov and Pinter; the links between private lives and published works; and the different techniques required in novels, stage plays and screenplays. 'These essays, so easy in manner, so well-built and informative, offer a fine blend of creative writing and criticism' *Sunday Times*

**A Lover's Discourse** Roland Barthes

'May be the most detailed, painstaking anatomy of desire we are ever likely to see or need again ... The book is an ecstatic celebration of love and language ... readers interested in either or both ... will enjoy savouring its rich and dark delights' *Washington Post*

**The New Pelican Guide to English Literature** Edited by Boris Ford

The indispensable critical guide to English and American literature in nine volumes, erudite yet accessible. From the ages of Chaucer and Shakespeare, via Georgian satirists and Victorian social critics, to the leading writers of the twentieth century, all literary life is here.

**The Structure of Complex Words** William Empson

'Twentieth-century England's greatest critic after T. S. Eliot, but whereas Eliot was the high priest, Empson was the *enfant terrible* ... *The Structure of Complex Words* is one of the linguistic masterpieces of the epoch, finding in the feel and tone of our speech whole sedimented social histories' *Guardian*

**Vamps and Tramps** Camille Paglia

'Paglia is a genuinely unconventional thinker ... Taken as a whole, the book gives an exceptionally interesting perspective on the last thirty years of intellectual life in America, and is, in its wacky way, a celebration of passion and the pursuit of truth' *Sunday Telegraph*

# READ MORE IN PENGUIN

## LANGUAGE/LINGUISTICS

**Language Play** David Crystal

We all use language to communicate information, but it is language play which is truly central to our lives. Full of puns, groan-worthy gags and witty repartee, this book restores the fun to the study of language. It also demonstrates why all these things are essential elements of what makes us human.

**Swearing** Geoffrey Hughes

'A deliciously filthy trawl among taboo words across the ages and the globe' *Observer*. 'Erudite and entertaining' Penelope Lively, *Daily Telegraph*

**The Language Instinct** Stephen Pinker

'Dazzling . . . Pinker's big idea is that language is an instinct, as innate to us as flying is to geese . . . Words can hardly do justice to the superlative range and liveliness of Pinker's investigations' *Independent*. 'He does for language what David Attenborough does for animals, explaining difficult scientific concepts so easily that they are indeed absorbed as a transparent stream of words' John Gribbin

**Mother Tongue** Bill Bryson

'A delightful, amusing and provoking survey, a joyful celebration of our wonderful language, which is packed with curiosities and enlightenment on every page' *Sunday Express*. 'A gold mine of language-anecdote. A surprise on every page . . . enthralling' *Observer*

**Longman Guide to English Usage**
Sidney Greenbaum and Janet Whitcut

Containing 5000 entries compiled by leading authorities on modern English, this invaluable reference work clarifies every kind of usage problem, giving expert advice on points of grammar, meaning, style, spelling, pronunciation and punctuation.

# READ MORE IN PENGUIN

## REFERENCE

**The Penguin Dictionary of the Third Reich**
James Taylor and Warren Shaw

This dictionary provides a full background to the rise of Nazism and the role of Germany in the Second World War. Among the areas covered are the major figures from Nazi politics, arts and industry, the German Resistance, the politics of race and the Nuremberg trials.

**The Penguin Biographical Dictionary of Women**

This stimulating, informative and entirely new Penguin dictionary of women from all over the world, through the ages, contains over 1,600 clear and concise biographies on major figures from politicians, saints and scientists to poets, film stars and writers.

**Roget's Thesaurus of English Words and Phrases**
Edited by Betty Kirkpatrick

This new edition of Roget's classic work, now brought up to date for the nineties, will increase anyone's command of the English language. Fully cross-referenced, it includes synonyms of every kind (formal or colloquial, idiomatic and figurative) for almost 900 headings. It is a must for writers and utterly fascinating for any English speaker.

**The Penguin Dictionary of International Relations**
Graham Evans and Jeffrey Newnham

International relations have undergone a revolution since the end of the Cold War. This new world disorder is fully reflected in this new Penguin dictionary, which is extensively cross-referenced with a select bibliography to aid further study.

**The Penguin Guide to Synonyms and Related Words**
S. I. Hayakawa

'More helpful than a thesaurus, more humane than a dictionary, the *Guide to Synonyms and Related Words* maps linguistic boundaries with precision, sensitivity to nuance and, on occasion, dry wit' *The Times Literary Supplement*

# READ MORE IN PENGUIN

## REFERENCE

**The Penguin Dictionary of Troublesome Words** Bill Bryson

Why should you avoid discussing the *weather conditions*? Can a married woman be celibate? Why is it eccentric to talk about the aroma of a cowshed? A straightforward guide to the pitfalls and hotly disputed issues in standard written English.

**Swearing** Geoffrey Hughes

'A deliciously filthy trawl among taboo words across the ages and the globe' Valentine Cunningham, *Observer*, Books of the Year. 'Erudite and entertaining' Penelope Lively, *Daily Telegraph*, Books of the Year.

**Medicines: A Guide for Everybody** Peter Parish

Now in its seventh edition and completely revised and updated, this bestselling guide is written in ordinary language for the ordinary reader yet will prove indispensable to anyone involved in health care: nurses, pharmacists, opticians, social workers and doctors.

**Media Law** Geoffrey Robertson QC and Andrew Nichol

Crisp and authoritative surveys explain the up-to-date position on defamation, obscenity, official secrecy, copyright and confidentiality, contempt of court, the protection of privacy and much more.

**The Penguin Careers Guide**
Anna Alston and Anne Daniel; Consultant Editor: Ruth Miller

As the concept of a 'job for life' wanes, this guide encourages you to think broadly about occupational areas as well as describing day-to-day work and detailing the latest developments and qualifications such as NVQs. Special features include possibilities for working part-time and job-sharing, returning to work after a break and an assessment of the current position of women.

# READ MORE IN PENGUIN

## DICTIONARIES

Abbreviations
Ancient History
Archaeology
Architecture
Art and Artists
Astronomy
Biographical Dictionary of Women
Biology
Botany
Building
Business
Challenging Words
Chemistry
Civil Engineering
Classical Mythology
Computers
Contemporary American History
Curious and Interesting Geometry
Curious and Interesting Numbers
Curious and Interesting Words
Design and Designers
Economics
Eighteenth-Century History
Electronics
English and European History
English Idioms
Foreign Terms and Phrases
French
Geography
Geology
German
Historical Slang
Human Geography
Information Technology
International Finance
International Relations
Literary Terms and Literary Theory
Mathematics
Modern History 1789–1945
Modern Quotations
Music
Musical Performers
Nineteenth-Century World History
Philosophy
Physical Geography
Physics
Politics
Proverbs
Psychology
Quotations
Quotations from Shakespeare
Religions
Rhyming Dictionary
Russian
Saints
Science
Sociology
Spanish
Surnames
Symbols
Synonyms and Antonyms
Telecommunications
Theatre
The Third Reich
Third World Terms
Troublesome Words
Twentieth-Century History
Twentieth-Century Quotations

PENGUIN REFERENCE

# The Penguin Pocket English Dictionary

Robert Allen, the editor of this dictionary, is an experienced lexicographer and writer on language. After ten years on the *Oxford English Dictionary* he edited a major new edition of the *Concise Oxford Dictionary*, was an associate editor of the *Oxford Companion to the English Language*, and directed work on the *Chambers 21st Century Dictionary*. He has been a consultant for a number of major publishing houses, has written an updated version of *Fowler's Modern English Usage*, and writes articles in *English Today* and other journals. He is an honorary research fellow of the Department of English Language at the University of Glasgow.

# THE PENGUIN POCKET ENGLISH DICTIONARY

Consultant Editor
Robert Allen

PENGUIN BOOKS

PENGUIN BOOKS

Published by the Penguin Group
Penguin Books Ltd, 80 Strand, London WC2R 0RL, England
Penguin Group (USA) Inc., 375 Hudson Street, New York, New York 10014, USA
Penguin Group (Canada), 90 Eglinton Avenue East, Suite 700, Toronto, Ontario, Canada M4P 2Y3 (a division of Pearson Penguin Canada Inc.)
Penguin Ireland, 25 St Stephen's Green, Dublin 2, Ireland (a division of Penguin Books Ltd)
Penguin Group (Australia), 250 Camberwell Road, Camberwell, Victoria 3124, Australia (a division of Pearson Australia Group Pty Ltd)
Penguin Books India Pvt Ltd, 11 Community Centre, Panchsheel Park, New Delhi – 110 017, India
Penguin Group (NZ), 67 Apollo Drive, Rosedale, North Shore 0632, New Zealand (a division of Pearson New Zealand Ltd)
Penguin Books (South Africa) (Pty) Ltd, 24 Sturdee Avenue, Rosebank, Johannesburg 2196, South Africa

Penguin Books Ltd, Registered Offices: 80 Strand, London WC2R 0RL, England

www.penguin.com

First published as *The Penguin Pocket English Dictionary* 2004
This special sales edition published 2008
1



Set in Stone Sans and Stone Serif
Typeset by Columns Design Ltd, Reading, Berkshire
Printed in England by Clays Ltd, St Ives plc

# *Contents*

# Acknowledgments

*Consultant Editor*
Robert Allen

*Publishing Director*
Nigel Wilcockson

*Publisher*
Martin Toseland

*Lexicographers*
Stephen Curtis, Rosalind Fergusson

*Database Editor*
Rachael Arthur

*Proofreaders*
David Cumming, Rosalind Fergusson, Peter Horton

*Designer*
Richard Marston

*Database Systems*
Librios Ltd

*Typesetting*
Columns Design Ltd

# *Layout of Dictionary Entries*

*The display below shows the main features of a dictionary entry.*

| | |
|---|---|
| headword | **educate** *v* to teach or instruct in academic, moral, or social matters. ➤ **educator** *n.* |
| | **educated** *adj* **1** having had an education, *esp* a good one. **2** based on some knowledge or experience: *an educated guess.* |
| part of speech | **education** *n* **1** the act of educating or the process of being educated. **2** instruction in some subject. **3** the knowledge resulting from instruction. **4** the field of study that deals mainly with methods of teaching. ➤ **educational** *adj.* |
| definition | **Edwardian** *adj* of the reign of King Edward VII of England (1901–1910). |
| | **eel** *n* a long snakelike fish with a smooth slimy skin. |
| alternative spelling and inflected forms | **eerie or eery** *adj* (**-ier, -iest**) frighteningly strange or gloomy. ➤ **eerily** *adv.* |
| | **efface** *v* **1** to remove from a surface or make indistinct. **2** to make (oneself) inconspicuous. |
| idioms and phrases | **effect**[1] *n* **1** the result produced by a cause or action. **2** the extent to which a cause or action produces results. **3** the state of being operative: *come into effect.* **4** (*in pl*) personal movable property; goods. **5** (*often in pl*) something designed to enhance the drama, realism, or impressiveness of a play or film. * **for effect** in order to impress. **in effect** actually although not officially so. **take effect 1** to become operative. **2** to produce a result. |
| Usage note on points of grammar and language sensitivity | ***Usage note:*** Do not confuse this word with **affect,** which is a verb only. |
| | **effect**[2] *v* to bring about, carry out, or accomplish. |

**effective** *adj* **1** producing a decisive or desired effect. **2** impressive or striking. **3** actual or real, though not officially recognized. **4** in force; operative. ➤ **effectiveness** *n.*

**effectual** *adj* able to produce a desired effect; effective.

**effeminate** *adj* of a man: having qualities usu thought of as feminine. ➤ **effeminacy** *n.*

derived word with meaning deducible from headword

**effervesce** *v* of a liquid: to bubble and hiss as gas escapes.

**effervescent** *adj* **1** effervescing. **2** lively and exhilarated.

**effete** *adj* **1** marked by weakness and decadent overrefinement. **2** effeminate.

**efficacious** *adj formal* effective.

**efficacy** *n formal* effectiveness.

usage label

**efficient** *adj* **1** producing desired effects, *esp* with minimum waste. **2** of a person: briskly competent. ➤ **efficiency** *n*, **efficiently** *adv.*

**effigy** *n* (*pl* -ies) an image or representation of a person, *esp* a hated person.

noun plural form

**effluent** *n* fluid industrial refuse, sewage, etc discharged into the environment and causing pollution.

**effluvium** *n* (*pl* **effluvia**, **effluviums**) an offensive gas or smell.

## *Pronunciation*

Guidance on pronunciation is given within slashes // for words that cause particular difficulty. The characters used are those of the English alphabet with their normal values. The following special characters and combinations of characters are used:

dh as in **th**ey
kh as in lo**ch**
aw as in h**orn**, **aw**ful
ə as in **a**like, gard**e**n
eə as in h**air**, th**ere**
ie as in b**i**te, f**igh**t
iə as in b**eer**, h**ere**
oh as in b**o**ne, l**oa**n
oo as in b**oo**k, p**u**t
ooh as in b**oo**t, l**u**te
ow as in n**ow**, r**ou**t
uh as in b**ir**d, abs**ur**d

The main stress or emphasis in a word of more than one syllable is shown by the symbol ˈ and any secondary stress by the symbol ˌ.

## List of Abbreviations

Abbreviations in general use (such as AD and i.e.) are given in the main text. Special abbreviations are as follows:

| | | | | | |
|---|---|---|---|---|---|
| *abbr* | abbreviation | *derog* | derogatory | *part.* | participle |
| *adj* | adjective | *dimin.* | diminutive | *pers* | person |
| *adv* | adverb | *esp* | especially | *pl* | plural |
| *attrib* | attributive(ly) | *euphem* | euphemistic | *prep* | preposition |
| *Aus* | Australian | *fem* | feminine | *prob* | probably |
| *aux* | auxiliary (verb) | *fl* | floruit | *pron* | pronoun |
| *b.* | born | *interj* | interjection | *SAfr* | South Africa(n) |
| *Brit* | British | *intrans* | intransitive | *Scot* | Scottish |
| *c.* | circa | *irreg* | irregular(ly) | *sing.* | singular |
| *Can* | Canadian | *masc* | masculine | *specif* | specifically |
| *cent.* | century | *n* | noun | *superl* | superlative |
| *cents* | centuries | *NAmer* | North American | *trans* | transitive |
| *comb. form* | combining form | *N Eng* | Northern English | *usu* | usually |
| *compar* | comparative | *NZ* | New Zealand | *v* | verb |
| *conj* | conjunction | *orig* | originally | *v aux* | auxiliary verb |
| *d.* | died | | | | |

**A**[1] *or* **a** *n* (*pl* **A's** *or* **As** *or* **a's**) the first letter of the English alphabet. ✱ **from A to Z** from beginning to end.

**A**[2] *abbr* **1** ampere. **2** answer.

**a** *or* **an** *indefinite article* **1** used before a singular noun to denote a person or thing not previously specified. **2** one single. **3** every; per.

**AA** *abbr* **1** Alcoholics Anonymous. **2** Automobile Association.

**aardvark** *n* an African mammal with a long extendable tongue, large ears, that feeds on ants and termites.

**aback** ✱ **be taken aback** to be surprised or shocked.

**abacus** *n* (*pl* **abacuses**) an instrument for performing calculations by sliding beads as counters along rods or in grooves.

**abaft** *adv and prep* towards or at the stern of a ship.

**abandon**[1] *v* (**abandoned, abandoning**) **1** to give up completely. **2** to leave or desert (somebody or something) permanently. **3** to give (oneself) over to a feeling or emotion. ➤ **abandonment** *n.*

**abandon**[2] *n* freedom from constraint or inhibitions.

**abase** *v* to bring down in status or esteem. ➤ **abasement** *n.*

**abashed** *adj* ashamed or embarrassed. ➤ **abashment** *n.*

**abate** *v* to become less intense or widespread. ➤ **abatement** *n.*

**abattoir** *n* a slaughterhouse.

**abbess** *n* the superior of an abbey of nuns.

**abbey** *n* (*pl* **abbeys**) the buildings of a monastery or a former monastery.

**abbot** *n* the superior of a community of monks.

**abbreviate** *v* to make (a word or phrase) shorter.

**abbreviation** *n* a shortened form of a written word or phrase.

**ABC** *n* (*pl* **ABC's** *or* **ABCs**) **1** the alphabet. **2** the rudiments of a subject.

**abdicate** *v* to relinquish a power or duty, *esp* to give up the throne. ➤ **abdication** *n.*

**abdomen** *n* **1** the part of the body between the thorax and the pelvis containing the liver, gut, etc. **2** the rear part of the body of an insect or arthropod. ➤ **abdominal** *adj.*

**abduct** *v* to carry off secretly or by force. ➤ **abduction** *n,* **abductor** *n.*

**aberrant** *adj* deviating from what is right, usual, or natural. ➤ **aberrance** *n.*

**aberration** *n* **1** a departure from a normal state or moral standard. **2** an unsoundness or disorder of the mind.

**abet** *v* (**abetted, abetting**) to encourage or approve of somebody in doing wrong.

**abeyance** ✱ **in abeyance** temporarily suspended or out of use.

**abhor** *v* (**abhorred, abhorring**) to detest; to loathe.

**abhorrent** *adj* causing horror. ➤ **abhorrence** *n.*

**abide** *v* **1** (*usu* **cannot abide** *or* **could not abide**) to bear (somebody or something) patiently. **2** to remain stable or fixed. ✱ **abide by** to comply with (a rule or decision).

**ability** *n* (*pl* **-ies**) **1** the power to do something. **2** competence or skill.

**abject** *adj* **1** wretched or miserable. **2** humble or servile. ➤ **abjection** *n,* **abjectly** *adv.*

**abjure** *v* to renounce formally or on oath.

**ablaze** *adj and adv* burning strongly.

**able** *adj* (**abler, ablest**) **1** having the power, skill, or means to do something. **2** skilful or competent. ➤ **ably** *adv.*

**-able** *or* **-ible** *suffix* able to act or be acted on in some way: *breakable; reliable.* ➤ **-ably** *suffix.*

**able-bodied** *adj* physically strong and fit.

**ablutions** *n* a place with washing and toilet facilities.

**abnegate** *v* to relinquish or renounce. ➤ **abnegation** *n,* **abnegator** *n.*

**abnormal** *adj* deviating from the normal or average. ➤ **abnormality** *n,* **abnormally** *adv.*

**aboard** *prep and adv* on or onto a ship, aircraft, train, or vehicle.

**abode** *n formal* a home or residence.

**abolish** *v* to put an end to (a custom or institution). ➤ **abolition** *n.*

**abolitionist** *n* a person who wants to abolish a custom or institution. ➤ **abolitionism** *n.*

**A-bomb** *n* = ATOM BOMB.

**abominable** *adj* **1** causing disgust or hatred. **2** *informal* disagreeable or unpleasant. ➤ **abominably** *adv.*

**Abominable Snowman** *n* a large hairy manlike animal reported as existing high in the Himalayas. Also called YETI.

**abominate** *v* to hate or loathe.
**abomination** *n* **1** a detestable or shameful thing or action. **2** extreme disgust and hatred.
**aboriginal**[1] *adj* **1** growing or living in a place from the earliest times. **2** (**Aboriginal**) of Australian Aboriginals. ➤ **aboriginally** *adv.*
**aboriginal**[2] *n* **1** an aboriginal person, animal, or plant. **2** (**Aboriginal**) the indigenous people of Australia.
**Aborigine** *n* an Australian Aboriginal.
**abort**[1] *v* **1** to induce the abortion of (a foetus). **2** to expel a premature foetus. **3** to end (an activity) because of a fault or failure. **4** to fail to develop completely.
**abort**[2] *n* the premature termination of a mission or procedure, *esp* one involving a military aircraft or spacecraft.
**abortion** *n* **1** the induced expulsion of a foetus in order to terminate a pregnancy. **2** the spontaneous expulsion of a foetus before it is able to survive independently.
**abortive** *adj* fruitless; unsuccessful. ➤ **abortively** *adv.*
**abound** *v* **1** to exist in large numbers or in great quantity. **2** (+ in/with) to have a large number or amount of.
**about**[1] *adv* **1** on or to all sides; round. **2** here and there. **3** in succession or rotation. **4** approximately. **5** almost. **6** in the vicinity. ✱ **about to** on the verge of.
**about**[2] *prep* **1** with regard to or concerning. **2** approximately. **3** carried by or associated with. **4** in different parts of. **5** surrounding.
**about-turn**[1] (*NAmer* **about-face**) *n* **1** a turn to face the opposite direction. **2** a reversal of policy or opinion.
**about-turn**[2] (*NAmer* **about-face**) *v* to make an about-turn.
**above**[1] *adv* **1** in or to a higher place or position. **2** higher on the same page or on an earlier page. **3** in or to a higher rank or number.
**above**[2] *prep* **1** higher than the level of. **2** more than. **3** superior to in rank. ✱ **above all** before every other consideration; especially.
**abracadabra** *interj* used to accompany conjuring tricks.
**abrade** *v* to roughen or wear away by friction.
**abrasion** *n* **1** a process of wearing or rubbing away. **2** an area of scraped skin.
**abrasive**[1] *adj* **1** having a rough surface used for grinding or smoothing. **2** rude or unpleasant.
**abrasive**[2] *n* an abrasive substance, e.g. emery.
**abreast** *adj and adv* **1** side by side and facing in the same direction. **2** (+ of) up-to-date with trends or developments.
**abridge** *v* **1** to shorten (a book or other piece of writing). **2** to reduce or curtail (a right or privilege). ➤ **abridgment** *n.*
**abroad** *adv and adj* **1** in or to a foreign country. **2** over a wide area. **3** in wide circulation. **4** *dated* away from one's home; out of doors.
**abrogate** *v* to abolish (a law or agreement) by authoritative action. ➤ **abrogation** *n.*
**abrupt** *adj* **1** occurring without warning; unexpected. **2** unceremoniously curt. **3** rising or dropping sharply; steep. ➤ **abruptly** *adv,* **abruptness** *n.*
**abscess** *n* an accumulation of pus surrounded by inflamed tissue.
**abscond** *v* to leave secretly or hurriedly to avoid discovery or arrest. ➤ **absconder** *n.*
**abseil** *v* to descend a vertical surface by sliding down a rope secured from above and wound round the body.
**absence** *n* **1** the state of being absent. **2** a period of being absent. **3** (+ of) a lack of.
**absent**[1] *adj* **1** not present or attending. **2** not existing. **3** not paying attention. ➤ **absently** *adv.*
**absent**[2] *v* to take or keep (oneself) away.
**absentee** *n* somebody who is absent.
**absenteeism** *n* persistent unauthorized absence from work or school.
**absentminded** *adj* **1** unaware of one's surroundings or actions. **2** habitually forgetful.
**absinthe** *or* **absinth** *n* **1** = WORMWOOD. **2** a green liqueur flavoured with aniseed.
**absolute** *adj* **1** complete; perfect. **2** having no restriction or qualification. **3** independent of external references or comparisons.
**absolute zero** *n* the lowest temperature theoretically possible (–273.15°C).
**absolution** *n* forgiveness of sins pronounced by a priest.
**absolutism** *n* government by an absolute ruler or authority. ➤ **absolutist** *n and adj.*
**absolve** *v* **1** (*often* + of/from) to set free from an obligation or guilt. **2** to forgive (a sin or sinner).
**absorb** *v* **1** to take in (a liquid or gas). **2** to learn (information). **3** to make part of an existing whole; to incorporate. **4** to engage or occupy wholly. **5** to receive and transform (energy) without reflecting or transmitting it. ➤ **absorption** *n.*
**absorbent** *adj* able to absorb a liquid or gas. ➤ **absorbency** *n.*
**abstain** *v* **1** to refrain from something pleasant. **2** to choose not to vote. ➤ **abstainer** *n.*
**abstemious** *adj* not allowing oneself much food, drink, or enjoyment.
**abstention** *n* **1** abstaining. **2** an instance of abstaining from voting.
**abstinence** *n* voluntary forbearance, *esp* from drinking alcohol. ➤ **abstinent** *adj.*
**abstract**[1] *adj* **1** theoretical rather than practical. **2** of art: having little or no element of pictorial representation. **3** of a noun: naming a quality, state, or action rather than a thing.
**abstract**[2] *n* a summary of the main points, e.g. of a piece of writing.
**abstract**[3] *v* to remove, separate, or extract.
**abstracted** *adj* preoccupied or absentminded.

**abstraction** *n* **1** an abstract idea or term. **2** the act or process of abstracting something. **3** preoccupation or absentmindedness.

**abstruse** *adj* difficult to understand.

**absurd** *adj* **1** ridiculously unreasonable or incongruous. **2** lacking order, value, or meaning. ➤ **absurdity** *n*, **absurdly** *adv.*

**abundance** *n* a large quantity or amount.

**abundant** *adj* **1** occurring in large quantities. **2** (+ in) having plenty of. ➤ **abundantly** *adv.*

**abuse**[1] *v* **1** to put to a wrong or improper use. **2** to attack in words; to revile. **3** to harm or injure by wrong or cruel treatment. ➤ **abuser** *n.*

**abuse**[2] *n* **1** improper use or treatment. **2** strong condemnation or disapproval. **3** physical maltreatment. **4** a corrupt practice or custom.

**abusive** *adj* **1** involving verbal abuse; insulting. **2** involving physical abuse. **3** improper or corrupt. ➤ **abusively** *adv.*

**abut** *v* (**abutted, abutting**) **1** (+ on/upon) of an area: to touch (another area) along a boundary. **2** (+ on/against) to terminate at a point of contact with. **3** (+ on/upon) to lean on for support. ➤ **abutter** *n.*

**abysmal** *adj* extremely bad. ➤ **abysmally** *adv.*

**abyss** *n* **1** a deep chasm or void. **2** a wretched situation.

**AC** *abbr* **1** air conditioning. **2** alternating current.

**Ac** *abbr* the chemical symbol for actinium.

**acacia** *n* a tree or shrub with white or yellow flowers.

**academia** *or* **academe** *n* the academic environment or an academic community.

**academic**[1] *adj* **1** relating to formal study or education. **2** theoretical and impractical. ➤ **academically** *adv.*

**academic**[2] *n* a teacher or research student at a college or university.

**academy** *n* (*pl* **-ies**) **1** a college in which special subjects or skills are taught. **2** a society of learned people organized to promote the arts or sciences.

**acanthus** *n* (*pl* **acanthuses** *or* **acanthi**) a prickly plant or shrub with spiny leaves and white or purple flower spikes.

**a cappella** *or* **a capella** *adj and adv* of music: performed without instrumental accompaniment.

**accede** *v* (*usu* + to) **1** to give consent to. **2** to take up (an office or position, *esp* the throne). **3** to become a party to (an agreement or treaty).

**accelerate** *v* **1** to move faster. **2** to increase the speed of. ➤ **acceleration** *n.*

**accelerator** *n* **1** a pedal in a motor vehicle that controls the speed of the engine. **2** a substance that speeds up a chemical reaction. **3** in physics, an apparatus for giving high velocities to charged particles, e.g. electrons.

**accent**[1] *n* **1** a distinctive pattern of pronunciation and intonation. **2** prominence given to one syllable over others by stress or a change in pitch. **3** greater stress given to one musical note. **4** rhythmically significant stress on certain syllables of a verse. **5** a mark added to a letter to show how it should be pronounced. **6** special emphasis. ➤ **accentual** *adj.*

**accent**[2] *v* **1** to stress (a vowel, syllable, or word). **2** to mark (a word or letter) with an accent. **3** to emphasize.

**accentuate** *v* to accent or emphasize. ➤ **accentuation** *n.*

**accept** *v* **1** to agree to receive or undertake. **2** to agree to a suggestion. **3** to regard as proper or normal. **4** to recognize as true. ➤ **acceptance** *n.*

**acceptable** *adj* **1** good enough to be accepted. **2** welcome or pleasing. **3** tolerable. ➤ **acceptability** *n*, **acceptably** *adv.*

**access**[1] *n* **1** freedom to approach or reach somebody or something. **2** a means of approaching or entering.

**access**[2] *v* to gain access to.

**accessible** *adj* **1** of a place: capable of being reached. **2** in a form that can be grasped intellectually. **3** (+ to) able to be influenced by. ➤ **accessibility** *n*, **accessibly** *adv.*

**accession** *n* **1** the act of entering on a high office. **2** an item added to a library or museum.

**accessory** *or* **accessary** *n* (*pl* **accessories** *or* **accessaries**) **1** something extra that makes a thing more useful or attractive. **2** a person who helps someone commit a crime without taking part.

**accident** *n* **1** an unpleasant or harmful event that occurs by chance. **2** lack of intention; chance. **3** an unexpected happening.

**accidental** *adj* happening unexpectedly or by chance. ➤ **accidentally** *adv.*

**acclaim**[1] *v* to applaud or praise.

**acclaim**[2] *n* public praise or approval.

**acclamation** *n* loud or keen public praise or approval.

**acclimatize** *or* **-ise** *v* to adapt to a new climate or situation. ➤ **acclimatization** *n.*

**accolade** *n* a mark of acknowledgment or honour; an award.

**accommodate** *v* **1** to have adequate room for. **2** to provide with lodgings. **3** (+ to) to make fit or appropriate. **4** to oblige or give help or consideration to.

**accommodating** *adj* helpful or obliging.

**accommodation** *n* **1** a building or space in which somebody may live or work. **2** a settlement or agreement.

**accompaniment** *n* **1** an instrumental or vocal part supporting a principal voice or instrument. **2** an addition or complement.

**accompany** *v* (**-ies, -ied**) **1** to go with as an escort or companion. **2** to perform an accompaniment for a singer or musician. **3** to supplement (one thing) with another.

**accomplice** *n* somebody who helps another person to commit a crime.
**accomplish** *v* to manage or achieve (an undertaking).
**accomplished** *adj* skilled or proficient.
**accomplishment** *n* **1** successful completion or fulfilment. **2** an achievement or ability.
**accord**[1] *v* to grant or concede. ✱ **accord with** to be consistent with.
**accord**[2] *n* **1** agreement or conformity. **2** a formal treaty of agreement. ✱ **of one's own accord** on one's own initiative; voluntarily.
**accordance** *n* ✱ **in accordance with** agreeing with or conforming to.
**according** ✱ **according as** depending on how or whether. **according to** in a way that corresponds to.
**accordingly** *adv* **1** in an appropriate way. **2** consequently.
**accordion** *n* a musical instrument played by squeezing hand-operated bellows and pressing keys or buttons. ➤ **accordionist** *n.*
**accost** *v* to approach and speak to (a person) boldly or challengingly.
**account**[1] *n* **1** a description of facts or events. **2** a record of money received and spent. **3** a facility for keeping money in a bank or for buying goods on credit. **4** ✱ **on account of** due to; because of. **on no account/not on any account** under no circumstances. **on somebody's account** for somebody's sake. **take into account/take account of** to consider along with other factors.
**account**[2] *v* to consider or think of in a certain way. ✱ **account for 1** to give a reason for. **2** to be the explanation for.
**accountable** *adj* **1** (*often* + to/for) responsible; answerable. **2** able to be explained; explicable. ➤ **accountability** *n.*
**accountant** *n* a person who keeps financial accounts for a living.
**accoutrement** (*NAmer* **accouterment**) *n* (*usu in pl*) an additional item of equipment or dress.
**accredit** *v* (**accredited, accrediting**) **1** to give official authorization to. **2** to give credit or recognition to. **3** to attribute (words) to somebody. ➤ **accreditation** *n.*
**accretion** *n* **1** increase in size caused by natural growth or addition. **2** something added or formed extraneously.
**accrue** *v* (**accrues, accrued, accruing**) **1** (*often* + to) to come as an increase or addition. **2** of money: to be received periodically and accumulate. **3** to collect or accumulate. ➤ **accrual** *n.*
**accumulate** *v* **1** to collect together gradually. **2** to increase in quantity or number. ➤ **accumulation** *n,* **accumulative** *adj.*
**accumulator** *n* **1** *Brit* a rechargeable electric cell. **2** *Brit* a bet whereby the winnings from one event are staked on the next.
**accurate** *adj* **1** correct; free from error. **2** reaching the intended target. ➤ **accuracy** *n,* **accurately** *adv.*
**accursed** *or* **accurst** *adj* **1** under a curse; ill-fated. **2** *informal* detestable; irritating.
**accusation** *n* a charge of wrongdoing; an allegation.
**accusative** *adj* of a grammatical case expressing the direct object of a verb. ➤ **accusative** *n.*
**accuse** *v* (*often* + of) to charge with a fault or crime. ➤ **accuser** *n.*
**accustom** *v* to make used to through experience; to habituate.
**accustomed** *adj* **1** customary or habitual. **2** (+ to) in the habit of or used to.
**AC/DC** *abbr* alternating current/direct current.
**ace**[1] *n* **1** a playing card marked with one spot. **2** a service in tennis that an opponent cannot return. **3** *informal* an expert or leading performer. ✱ **within an ace of** on the point of; very near to.
**ace**[2] *adj informal* excellent.
**acerbic** *adj* **1** bitter or sour in taste. **2** sharp or vitriolic in speech. ➤ **acerbically** *adv,* **acerbity** *n.*
**acetate** *n* **1** a textile fibre made from cellulose acetate. **2** an audio recording disc coated with cellulose acetate.
**acetic acid** *n* a pungent liquid that gives vinegar its taste.
**acetone** *n* a volatile liquid used as a solvent.
**acetylene** *n* a colourless inflammable gas used *esp* as a fuel to produce a bright flame.
**ache**[1] *v* **1** to suffer a dull persistent pain. **2** (*often* + for) to yearn or long for something. ➤ **achy** *adj.*
**ache**[2] *n* a dull persistent pain.
**achieve** *v* **1** to accomplish successfully. **2** to obtain or win by effort. ➤ **achievable** *adj,* **achiever** *n.*
**achievement** *n* **1** something achieved; a feat. **2** successful completion or accomplishment.
**Achilles' heel** *n* a single weak or vulnerable point.
**Achilles tendon** *n* the tendon joining the muscles in the calf to the heelbone.
**acid**[1] *adj* **1** sour or sharp to the taste. **2** sharp in speech or manner. ➤ **acidity** *n.*
**acid**[2] *n* **1** a compound that turns litmus paper red and is capable of reacting with an alkali or other chemical base to form a salt. **2** *slang* the hallucinogenic drug LSD. ➤ **acidic** *adj.*
**acidify** *v* (**-ies, -ied**) to make or become acid.
**acid rain** *n* rain containing high levels of acid caused by pollution from burning fuel into the atmosphere.
**acid test** *n* a severe or crucial test.
**acknowledge** *v* **1** to admit to be true or valid. **2** to express gratitude or obligation for. **3** to

greet or show recognition of. **4** to confirm receipt of.

**acknowledgment** *or* **acknowledgement** *n* **1** something done or given in recognition of something received. **2** a declaration or avowal of a fact. **3** a mention of people to whom an author is indebted.

**acme** *n* the highest point or stage.

**acne** *n* a skin disorder characterized by red pustules. ➤ **acned** *adj.*

**acolyte** *n* an assistant or follower.

**acorn** *n* the nut of the oak, a smooth oval fruit in a cuplike base.

**acoustic** *adj* **1** of sound or the sense of hearing. **2** of a musical instrument having sound produced naturally. **3** deadening or absorbing sound. ➤ **acoustically** *adv.*

**acoustics** *pl n* **1** the science of sound. **2** the sound properties of a room.

**acquaint** *v* (+ with) to cause to know something; to make familiar with.

**acquaintance** *n* **1** personal knowledge or familiarity. **2** somebody one knows slightly.

**acquiesce** *v* (*often* + in) to submit or comply tacitly. ➤ **acquiescence** *n,* **acquiescent** *adj.*

**acquire** *v* **1** to gain or come into possession of. **2** to gain as a new characteristic or ability. ➤ **acquirement** *n.*

**acquisition** *n* **1** acquiring or gaining possession. **2** something or somebody acquired.

**acquisitive** *adj* fond of acquiring material possessions.

**acquit** *v* (**acquitted, acquitting**) **1** (*often* + of) to declare that somebody is not guilty of an offence. **2** to conduct (oneself) in a specified manner. ➤ **acquittal** *n.*

**acre** *n* a unit of area equal to 4840yd$^2$ (about 0.405ha). ➤ **acreage** *n.*

**acrid** *adj* **1** unpleasantly pungent. **2** acrimonious.

**acrimonious** *adj* characterized by personal hostility or bitterness. ➤ **acrimoniously** *adv.*

**acrimony** *n* caustic sharpness of manner or language. ➤ **acrimonious** *adj,* **acrimoniously** *adv.*

**acrobat** *n* an entertainer who performs gymnastic feats. ➤ **acrobatic** *adj,* **acrobatically** *adv.*

**acronym** *n* a word formed from the initial letters of other words, e.g. *Aids* from *acquired immune deficiency syndrome.*

**across**[1] *adv* **1** from one side to the other. **2** to or on the opposite side.

**across**[2] *prep* **1** from one side to the other of. **2** on the opposite side of.

**acrylic** *adj* made with acrylic acid, an unsaturated liquid acid, or its derivatives.

**act**[1] *n* **1** a thing done, or the process of doing something. **2** a formal record of something done or transacted. **3** a law passed by a legislative body. **4** a division of a play or opera. **5** each part or performance in an entertainment. **6** a display of affected behaviour; a pretence.

**act**[2] *v* **1** to take action; to do something. **2** to behave in a specified way. **3** (+ as) to perform a function. **4** to produce an effect. **5** (+ on) to do something in response to advice or instructions. **6** to play a role in a play or film.

**action**[1] *n* **1** practical activity directed towards a particular aim. **2** the state of functioning actively. **3** energetic activity. **4** a voluntary act. **5** the events in a story or play. **6** armed combat in war. **7** the operating part of a mechanism or device. **8** the manner in which something operates or moves. **9** a civil legal proceeding. ✱ **out of action** not working or functioning actively. **take action** to begin to act; to do something.

**action**[2] *v* to take action on.

**actionable** *adj* giving grounds for an action at law.

**action stations** *pl n* the positions taken up by forces for military action.

**activate** *v* to cause a device or process to start operating. ➤ **activation** *n.*

**active** *adj* **1** moving, working, or operating, not at rest. **2** full of activity; busy. **3** characterized by practical action and involvement. **4** having practical results; effective. **5** of a volcano: liable to erupt. **6** in grammar, of a verb: having as the subject the person or thing doing the action. ➤ **actively** *adv.*

**active service** *n* military service in a war.

**activist** *n* a person who advocates vigorous social or political action. ➤ **activism** *n.*

**activity** *n* (*pl* **-ies**) **1** a state in which things are happening or being done. **2** vigorous or energetic action. **3** a pursuit in which a person takes part.

**act of God** *n* a sudden event brought about by uncontrollable natural forces.

**actor** *n* **1** a person who takes part in a dramatic production. **2** a participant in an event or situation.

**actress** *n* a female actor.

**actual** *adj* existing or happening in fact.

**actuality** *n* (*pl* **-ies**) **1** the quality or state of being actual; reality. **2** (*often in pl*) an existing circumstance; a real fact.

**actualize** *v* to make (a plan, etc.) happen.

**actually** *adv* really; in fact.

**actuary** *n* (*pl* **-ies**) a person who calculates insurance risks and premiums. ➤ **actuarial** *adj.*

**actuate** *v* **1** to put (a device or machine) into action. **2** to incite to action; to motivate.

**acuity** *n* keenness of mental or physical perception.

**acumen** *n* keen judgment or ability in practical matters; shrewdness.

**acupuncture** *n* the puncturing of the body with needles to cure disease or relieve pain. ➤ **acupuncturist** *n.*

**acute** *adj* **1** intelligent and shrewd. **2** of a sense or feeling: intensely felt or perceived. **3** of something bad: serious or critical. **4** of an angle: measuring less than 90°. ➤ **acutely** *adv,* **acuteness** *n.*

**acute accent** *n* a mark (´) placed over certain vowels in some languages to show a particular vowel quality or stress.

**AD** *abbr* anno Domini, used to indicate that a date comes within the Christian era.

***Usage Note:*** AD *and* BC. *AD* is traditionally written before a number signifying a year: *AD 1625.* When referring to centuries, however, it is necessary to place *AD* at the end of the phrase: *in the third century AD. BC* always follows a date: *440 BC; the seventh century BC.*

**adage** *n* a maxim or proverb that embodies a general truth.

**adagio** *adj and adv* of a piece of music: performed in a slow gentle tempo.

**adamant** *adj* refusing to change one's mind; unyielding. ➤ **adamantly** *adv.*

**Adam's apple** *n* the projection in the front of the neck, more prominent in men.

**adapt** *v* (*often* + to) to make or become suited to different circumstances. ➤ **adaptability** *n,* **adaptable** *adj,* **adaptive** *adj.*

**adaptation** *n* **1** adapting or being adapted. **2** a play or film adapted from a novel or other medium.

**adapter** *or* **adaptor** *n* **1** a device for connecting two pieces of apparatus not orig intended to be joined. **2** a device for connecting several pieces of electrical apparatus to a single power point.

**add** *v* **1** to join to something else so as to bring about an increase or improvement. **2** to serve as an addition to something. **3** to say or write further. **4** (*often* + up) to combine into a single number.

**addendum** *n* (*pl* **addenda**) an extra item at the end of a book.

**adder** *n* a poisonous viper with a dark zigzag pattern along the back.

**addict**[1] *v* (*usu in passive*) **1** to cause to become dependent on a habit-forming drug. **2** to cause to indulge habitually or obsessively in (an activity). ➤ **addiction** *n,* **addictive** *adj.*

**addict**[2] *n* **1** somebody who is addicted to a drug. **2** an enthusiast or devotee.

**addition** *n* **1** the process of adding. **2** something or somebody added. ✱ **in addition** also; as well.

**additional** *adj* added or extra. ➤ **additionally** *adv.*

**additive** *n* a substance added to another in relatively small amounts.

**addled** *adj* **1** confused or muddled. **2** of an egg: rotten.

**address**[1] *v* **1** to mark directions for delivery on (a letter or package). **2** to speak or write directly to. **3** to communicate directly to somebody. **4** to greet by a prescribed form. **5** to deal with or apply oneself to. ➤ **addressee** *n.*

**address**[2] *n* **1** a place where a person lives or a building is situated. **2** the details of such a place. **3** a location in the memory of a computer where particular information is stored. **4** a prepared speech delivered to an audience.

**adduce** *v formal* to offer as evidence or proof. ➤ **adducible** *adj.*

**add up** *v* **1** to come to a total. **2** *informal* to be internally consistent; to make sense.

**adenoids** *pl n* a mass of tissue at the back of the pharynx that obstructs breathing when enlarged. ➤ **adenoidal** *adj.*

**adept**[1] *adj* highly skilled or proficient. ➤ **adeptly** *adv.*

**adept**[2] *n* a highly skilled person.

**adequate** *adj* sufficient or acceptable. ➤ **adequacy** *n,* **adequately** *adv.*

**adhere** *v* **1** to stick or hold fast. **2** to give support or loyalty to. **3** (+ to) to observe or follow exactly. ➤ **adherence** *n.*

**adherent**[1] *n* a supporter of a leader or cause.

**adherent**[2] *adj* sticking or holding fast.

**adhesion** *n* the action or state of adhering.

**adhesive**[1] *adj* sticky.

**adhesive**[2] *n* an adhesive substance.

**ad hoc** *adj and adv* for the particular purpose at hand only.

**adieu** *interj chiefly literary* goodbye.

**ad infinitum** *adv* without end or limit; indefinitely.

**adjacent** *adj* **1** (*often* + to) having a common boundary or border. **2** near or next to something or to one another.

**adjective** *n* a word that modifies a noun or pronoun by describing a particular characteristic of it. ➤ **adjectival** *adj.*

**adjoin** *v* to be next or joined to.

**adjourn** *v* **1** to suspend (a meeting) until a later time. **2** to defer for later consideration or resolution. **3** to move to another place. ➤ **adjournment** *n.*

**adjudge** *v* **1** to declare or judge formally. **2** to award or grant judicially.

**adjudicate** *v* **1** to decide judicially. **2** to act as judge in a competition. ➤ **adjudication** *n,* **adjudicator** *n.*

**adjunct** *n* something added as an incidental accompaniment.

**adjure** *v formal* to command or advise solemnly to do something.

**adjust** *v* **1** to regulate or modify slightly. **2** to adapt oneself to new conditions. **3** to decide the amount to be paid under an insurance policy. ➤ **adjustable** *adj,* **adjustment** *n.*

**adjutant** *n* a military officer who assists a commanding officer with administrative matters. ➤ **adjutancy** *n.*

**ad-lib**[1] *adj* spoken or performed without preparation.

**ad-lib**[2] *v* (**ad-libbed, ad-libbing**) to speak spontaneously; to improvise.

**ad-lib**[3] *n* an improvised speech, line, or performance.

**administer** *v* (**administered, administering**) **1** to manage or supervise. **2** to give (a remedy or punishment).

**administrate** *v* to manage or supervise the affairs of a business or country. ➤ **administrative** *adj.*

**administration** *n* **1** the business of running the affairs of a business or country. **2** a government in power.

**admirable** *adj* deserving the highest respect; excellent. ➤ **admirably** *adv.*

**admiral** *n* **1** the commander-in-chief of a fleet or navy. **2** a senior officer in the Royal Navy or US Navy.

**admire** *v* to admire or think highly of. ➤ **admirer** *n.*

**admissible** *adj* **1** acceptable or permissible. **2** entitled to enter a place.

**admission** *n* **1** acknowledgment that a fact or allegation is true. **2** being allowed to enter a place or join a group.

**admit** *v* (**admitted, admitting**) **1** to concede as true or valid. **2** (+ to) to make an acknowledgment of. **3** to allow to enter a place or join a group. **4** to take into a hospital for treatment.

**admittance** *n* **1** permission to enter a place. **2** access or entrance.

**admonish** *v* **1** to reprove gently. **2** to urge or warn. ➤ **admonition** *n,* **admonitory** *adj.*

**ad nauseam** *adv* to a tediously excessive degree.

**ado** *n* * **without more/further ado** without further delay.

**adolescent**[1] *adj* of the period of life between puberty and maturity. ➤ **adolescence** *n.*

**adolescent**[2] *n* an adolescent person.

**Adonis** *n* a strikingly handsome young man.

**adopt** *v* **1** to bring up (a child of other parents) as one's own child. **2** to take over or begin to use. **3** to vote to accept. ➤ **adoption** *n.*

**adoptive** *adj* of a parent: adopting a child.

**adorable** *adj* lovable or charming. ➤ **adorably** *adv.*

**adore** *v* **1** to admire or love greatly. **2** to worship or honour as a deity. ➤ **adoration** *n.*

**adorn** *v* to decorate with ornaments. ➤ **adornment** *n.*

**adrenal** *adj* **1** of the region of the kidneys. **2** of the adrenal glands.

**adrenal glands** *pl n* glands near the front of each kidney, secreting hormones and adrenalin.

**adrenalin** *or* **adrenaline** *n* a hormone produced by the adrenal gland in response to stress or excitement, increasing the heart rate and blood pressure.

**adrift** *adv and adj* **1** of a boat: drifting without power or steerage. **2** unfastened or unstuck.

**adroit** *adj* clever or skilful. ➤ **adroitly** *adv.*

**adulate** *v* to flatter or admire excessively. ➤ **adulation** *n,* **adulatory** *adj.*

**adult**[1] *adj* **1** fully developed and mature. **2** appropriate to adults. ➤ **adulthood** *n.*

**adult**[2] *n* an adult person.

**adulterate** *v* to corrupt or make impure. ➤ **adulteration** *n.*

**adulterer** *or* **adulteress** *n* a man or woman who commits adultery.

**adultery** *n* (*pl* **-ies**) voluntary sexual intercourse between a married person and somebody other than his or her spouse. ➤ **adulterous** *adj.*

**adumbrate** *v formal* **1** to outline broadly without details. **2** to foreshadow vaguely.

**advance**[1] *v* **1** to move forward in position or time. **2** to accelerate the growth or progress of. **3** to develop or make progress. **4** to raise in rank. **5** to supply (money or goods) ahead of time or as a loan. **6** to bring (an opinion or argument) forward for notice.

**advance**[2] *n* **1** a forward movement. **2** progress in development. **3** (*usu in pl*) a friendly or amorous approach. **4** money or goods supplied ahead of time. * **in advance** beforehand.

**advance**[3] *adj* **1** made, sent, or provided ahead of time. **2** going or situated ahead of others.

**advanced** *adj* **1** far on in time or course. **2** more complex or developed.

**advancement** *n* **1** promotion to a higher rank or position. **2** furtherance towards perfection or completeness. **3** forward movement or progress.

**advantage** *n* **1** a favourable or helpful factor or circumstance. **2** a benefit or gain. **3** the first point won in tennis after deuce. * **take advantage of somebody or something 1** to use something for one's benefit. **2** to impose on or exploit.

**Advent** *n* **1** the period from the fourth Sunday before Christmas to Christmas itself. **2** the coming of Christ to earth as a human being. **3** (**advent**) a coming into being; an arrival.

**adventitious** *adj* coming accidentally or unexpectedly.

**adventure** *n* **1** an undertaking involving danger and uncertainty. **2** an exciting or remarkable experience. ➤ **adventuresome** *adj.*

**adventurer** *or* **adventuress** *n* **1** somebody who enjoys adventures. **2** somebody who seeks wealth or position by unscrupulous means.

**adventurous** *adj* prepared to take risks or try new experiences. ➤ **adventurously** *adv.*

**adverb** *n* a word that modifies a verb, an adjective, another adverb, or a sentence, answering questions such as *how?*, *when?*, or *where?*
**adversarial** *adj* involving opposition or hostility.
**adversary** *n* (*pl* **-ies**) an enemy or opponent.
**adverse** *adj* unfavourable or harmful. ➤ **adversely** *adv.*
**adversity** *n* (*pl* **-ies**) a condition of suffering or hardship.
**advert** *n chiefly Brit, informal* an advertisement.
**advertise** *v* **1** to encourage sales of (a product or service) by emphasizing its qualities. **2** to announce publicly. **3** (+ for) to seek by means of advertising. ➤ **advertiser** *n.*
**advertisement** *n* something published or broadcast to advertise a product or service.
**advice** *n* guidance or recommendations about a decision or course of conduct.
**advisable** *adj* worthy of being recommended; prudent. ➤ **advisability** *n.*
**advise** *v* **1** to give advice to. **2** to recommend. **3** to give information to.
**advised** *adj* thought out; considered. ➤ **advisedly** *adv.*
**advisory** *adj* having the power to advise but not to decide.
**advocaat** /'advəkah/ *n* a sweet liqueur made with brandy and eggs.
**advocate**[1] *n* **1** somebody who pleads the cause of another before a tribunal or court. **2** *Scot* a barrister. **3** somebody who openly supports a cause or proposal.
**advocate**[2] *v* to recommend or plead in favour of (a cause or proposal). ➤ **advocacy** *n.*
**adze** (*NAmer* **adz**) *n* a cutting tool with the blade attached at right angles to the handle.
**aegis** *n* protection or support.
**aeon** *or* **eon** *n* an extremely long period of time.
**aerate** *v* **1** to combine or impregnate with a gas. **2** to make (a liquid) effervescent. ➤ **aeration** *n.*
**aerial**[1] *adj* **1** existing or occurring in the air or atmosphere. **2** operating overhead on elevated cables or rails. **3** of or involving aircraft.
**aerial**[2] *n* a metal rod or wire designed to transmit or receive radio or television signals.
**aerie** *n* see EYRIE.
**aerobatics** *n* the performance of stunts in an aircraft as the entertainment. ➤ **aerobatic** *adj.*
**aerobic** *adj* **1** to do with aerobics. **2** living or occurring only in the presence of oxygen.
**aerobics** *n* a system of physical exercises designed to improve respiration and circulation.
**aerodrome** *n chiefly Brit* a small airport or airfield.
**aerodynamics** *n* the dynamics of the motion of gases, e.g. air, and solid bodies moving through them. ➤ **aerodynamic** *adj.*
**aerofoil** *n chiefly Brit* a structure on an aircraft or vehicle for providing lift as the vehicle moves through the air.
**aeronautics** *n* the science or practice of flight. ➤ **aeronautical** *adj.*
**aeroplane** *n* a powered aircraft with fixed wings.
**aerosol** *n* **1** a suspension of fine solid or liquid particles in gas. **2** a substance dispersed from a pressurized container as an aerosol.
**aerospace** *n* the science or technology of flight in the earth's atmosphere and beyond.
**aesthete** (*NAmer* **esthete**) *n* somebody who appreciates beauty in art or nature.
**aesthetic**[1] (*NAmer* **esthetic**) *adj* to do with beauty or the appreciation of the beautiful. ➤ **aesthetically** *adv.*
**aesthetic**[2] *n* a set of principles on which the work of an artist or artistic movement is based.
**aesthetics** (*NAmer* **esthetics**) *n* **1** a branch of philosophy dealing with the nature of beauty and aesthetic taste. **2** the principles concerning beauty.
**afar** *adv* to or at a great distance.
**affable** *adj* pleasant and friendly. ➤ **affability** *n,* **affably** *adv.*
**affair** *n* **1** a particular or personal concern. **2** (*in pl*) commercial or public business. **3** a procedure or action. **4** a love affair. **5** a matter causing public controversy or scandal.
**affect**[1] *v* **1** to have an effect on. **2** to act on (somebody) so as to bring about a response.

***Usage Note:*** *Affect* is a verb that means 'to influence or change': *How will this affect my pension prospects? Effect* is most commonly used as a noun: *What effect will this have on my pension prospects?* It can also be used, slightly formally, as a verb meaning to 'bring about' or 'carry out': *The police effected an entry into the premises.*

**affect**[2] *v* **1** to pretend to feel or show (a quality). **2** to assume the character or attitude of. **3** to wear or use ostentatiously.
**affectation** *n* **1** an insincere or pretended display of a quality or feeling. **2** a deliberately assumed peculiarity of speech or behaviour.
**affected** *adj* **1** insincere or pretentious. **2** pretended for effect. ➤ **affectedly** *adv.*
**affection** *n* fondness or liking.
**affectionate** *adj* showing affection. ➤ **affectionately** *adv.*
**affidavit** *n* a sworn written statement for use as judicial proof.
**affiliate**[1] *v* **1** to attach (an organization) as a member or branch. **2** to connect or associate oneself with another. ➤ **affiliation** *n.*
**affiliate**[2] *n* an affiliated person or organization.
**affinity** *n* (*pl* **-ies**) **1** a natural liking for or understanding of somebody. **2** an attraction to or taste for something. **3** resemblance based on

relationship or causal connection. **4** a chemical attraction or biological relation.

**affirm** *v* **1** to validate or confirm. **2** to state positively. **3** to assert (e.g. a judgment of a lower court) as valid.

**affirmative**[1] *adj* stating that something is true or correct. ➤ **affirmatively** *adv.*

**affirmative**[2] *n* a word or statement expressing agreement or assent.

**affix**[1] *v* **1** to attach physically. **2** to add in writing.

**affix**[2] *n* a prefix or suffix.

**afflict** *v* **1** to distress severely. **2** to cause serious problems or trouble to. ➤ **affliction** *n.*

**affluent** *adj* wealthy. ➤ **affluence** *n.*

**afford** *v* **1** to have enough money or time for. **2** to be able to do without serious harm. **3** to provide or supply. ➤ **affordable** *adj.*

**affray** *n* a brawl in a public place.

**affront**[1] *n* an open insult.

**affront**[2] *v* to insult or offend.

**aficionado** /ə͵fishyə'nahdoh/ *n* (*pl* **aficionados**) a devotee or fan.

**afield** *adv* away or at a distance.

**aflame** *adj and adv* on fire.

**afloat** *adj and adv* **1** floating on the water. **2** free of debt.

**afoot** *adv and adj* happening or imminent.

**aforementioned** *adj* mentioned previously.

**afraid** *adj* (*often* + of/to) filled with fear.

**afresh** *adv* again or differently.

**African** *n* a person from Africa, *esp* a black person. ➤ **African** *adj.*

**Afrikaans** *n* a language of southern Africa developed from Dutch.

**aft** *adv and adj* towards or in the rear of a ship or aircraft.

**after**[1] *prep* **1** behind in place or order. **2** later than. **3** in search or pursuit of. **4** in accordance with. **5** in the manner of or in imitation of.

**after**[2] *adv* **1** in the rear; behind. **2** afterwards.

**after**[3] *conj* later than the time when.

**afterbirth** *n* the placenta and foetal membranes expelled from the womb after a birth.

**aftereffect** *n* an effect that follows later.

**afterlife** *n* an existence after death.

**aftermath** *n* the time or result following an unpleasant or disastrous event.

**afternoon** *n* the time between noon or lunchtime and evening. ➤ **afternoon** *adj.*

**aftershave** *n* a scented lotion for use on the face after shaving.

**afterthought** *n* an idea thought of or added later.

**afterwards** *or* **afterward** *adv* after that; subsequently.

**afterword** *n* = EPILOGUE.

**Ag** *abbr* the chemical symbol for silver.

**again** *adv* **1** once more. **2** so as to be as before. **3** in addition.

**against** *prep* **1** in opposition or hostility to. **2** in contact with. **3** opposite to the motion or course of. **4** in preparation or provision for. **5** in exchange for.

**agape** /ə'gayp/ *adj* wide open; gaping.

**agate** *n* a mineral used as a gem composed of quartz of various colours, often arranged in bands.

**age**[1] *n* **1** the length of time a person has lived or a thing existed. **2** a stage of life. **3** a period of past time dominated by a central figure or prominent feature. **4** a division of geological time, shorter than an epoch. **5** *informal* (*usu in pl*) a long time. ✱ **come of age** to reach legal adult status.

**age**[2] *v* (**ageing** *or* **aging**) **1** to become or start to look old. **2** to cause to seem old. **3** to mellow or ripen.

**aged** /'ayjid/ *adj* **1** of an advanced age. **2** /ayjd/ of a specified age.

**ageism** *or* **agism** *n* discrimination on grounds of age. ➤ **ageist** *adj and n.*

**ageless** *adj* timeless or eternal.

**agency** *n* (*pl* **-ies**) **1** an establishment that does a particular type of business. **2** an administrative department of a government. **3** intervention or instrumentality.

**agenda** *n* **1** a list of items for discussion at a meeting. **2** a plan of procedure.

**agent** *n* **1** a person who is authorized to act for another. **2** a representative of a government. **3** a spy. **4** something or somebody that produces an effect or exerts power.

**agent provocateur** /͵ahzhonhprə͵vokə'tuh/ *n* (*pl* **agents provocateurs**) a person employed to incite suspected people to action that will incriminate them.

**age of consent** *n* the age at which a person may legally consent to sexual intercourse.

**agglomeration** *n* a collection or mass of things.

**aggrandize** *or* **-ise** *v* to make more powerful or important. ➤ **aggrandizement** *n.*

**aggravate** *v* **1** to make worse or more severe. **2** *informal* to annoy or irritate. ➤ **aggravation** *n.*

**aggregate**[1] *adj* formed by combining separate elements into a whole.

**aggregate**[2] *v* to combine into a mass or whole.

**aggregate**[3] *n* **1** a mass of loosely associated parts. **2** the whole amount; the sum total. **3** a rock composed of closely packed mineral crystals or rock fragments. **4** sand, gravel, etc for mixing with cement to make concrete.

**aggression** *n* hostile or violent behaviour or attitudes. ➤ **aggressor** *n.*

**aggressive** *adj* **1** hostile or violent in behaviour or attitude. **2** forceful or dynamic. ➤ **aggressively** *adv.*

**aggrieved** *adj* showing or expressing resentment for unfair treatment.

**aghast** *adj* shocked or horrified.

**agile** *adj* **1** able to move easily and gracefully. **2** mentally quick and resourceful. ➤ **agilely** *adv*, **agility** *n*.

**agitate** *v* **1** to trouble or disturb. **2** to shake or stir. **3** to work to arouse public feeling about an issue. ➤ **agitation** *n*, **agitator** *n*.

**AGM** *abbr* annual general meeting.

**agnostic** *n* somebody who believes it is impossible to know whether God exists. ➤ **agnostic** *adj*, **agnosticism** *n*.

**ago** *adv* before now.

**agog** *adj* full of excitement or eagerness.

**agonize** *or* **-ise** *v* **1** to suffer, or cause to suffer, agony or anguish. **2** to make a great effort. **3** to worry excessively over a decision.

**agony** *n* (*pl* **-ies**) intense physical pain or mental suffering.

**agony column** *n* a column in a magazine or newspaper offering advice on readers' personal problems.

**agoraphobia** *n* abnormal fear of open spaces. ➤ **agoraphobic** *n and adj*.

**agrarian** *adj* to do with farming and agriculture.

**agree** *v* **1** to have the same opinion or judgment about something. **2** (*often* + to) to approve of something or consent to do something. **3** (*often* + with) to be compatible with; to correspond or be consistent. **4** (+ with) to suit somebody's health or constitution. **5** (*often* + on) to decide together about.

**agreeable** *adj* **1** to one's liking; pleasing. **2** willing to agree or consent. ➤ **agreeably** *adv*.

**agreement** *n* **1** a sharing of opinion or feeling. **2** correspondence or consistency. **3** consent. **4** a treaty or contract.

**agriculture** *n* the theory and practice of farming. ➤ **agricultural** *adj*, **agriculturally** *adv*.

**aground** *adv and adj* touching the shore or the bottom of a body of water.

**ague** *n* a malarial fever with attacks of chills and sweating.

**ahead** *adv and adj* **1** in front or in a forward direction. **2** in the future.

**ahoy** *interj* used at sea as a greeting or warning.

**aid**[1] *v* **1** to give help or assistance to. **2** to facilitate.

**aid**[2] *n* **1** help or assistance. **2** money or supplies given to a country in need. ✱ **in aid of** in order to help or support.

**aide** *n chiefly NAmer* an assistant to a political leader.

**Aids** *or* **AIDS** *n* a disease of the immune system, caused by the HIV virus.

**aikido** *n* a martial art resembling judo.

**ail** *v archaic* to give pain or trouble to.

**ailing** *adj* ill or unwell or chronically ill.

**ailment** *n* a mild illness.

**aim**[1] *v* **1** to point a weapon, camera, etc at an object or person. **2** to intend or try to do something.

**aim**[2] *n* **1** a clear intention or purpose. **2** the pointing of a weapon at a target. ➤ **aimless** *adj*, **aimlessly** *adv*.

**ain't** *contraction non-standard* **1** am not; are not; is not. **2** have not; has not.

**air**[1] *n* **1** the mixture of invisible gases that surrounds the earth. **2** empty unconfined space. **3** nothingness. **4** the supposed medium of transmission of radio waves. **5** a person's bearing or demeanour. **6** (*in pl*) an artificial or affected manner. **7** a tune or melody. ✱ **in the air** being generally spread round or hinted at. **on the air** being broadcast on radio or television. **up in the air** not yet settled; uncertain.

**air**[2] *v* **1** to express (an opinion) openly. **2** to broadcast on radio or television. **3** to expose to fresh air or warmth.

**air base** *n* a base for military aircraft.

**airborne** *adj* **1** carried in the air. **2** of an aircraft: in the air after taking off.

**airbrush**[1] *n* an atomizer for spraying paint.

**airbrush**[2] *v* to paint or spray with an airbrush.

**air conditioning** *n* an apparatus for controlling the temperature and quality of the air in a building or vehicle. ➤ **air-condition** *v*.

**aircraft** *n* (*pl* **aircraft**) an aeroplane, helicopter, or other vehicle that can fly.

**aircraft carrier** *n* a large warship serving as a base for aircraft.

**airfield** *n* an area of land where aircraft can take off and land.

**air force** *n* the branch of a country's armed forces that fights with aircraft.

**air gun** *n* a gun that propels a pellet by compressed air.

**air hostess** *n* a female member of the cabin crew on a passenger aircraft.

**airing** *n* exposure to discussion.

**airlift** *n* the transport of supplies or passengers by air from an otherwise inaccessible area. ➤ **airlift** *v*.

**airline** *n* a company that provides public air transport.

**airliner** *n* a large passenger aircraft.

**air lock** *n* **1** an airtight chamber, e.g. in a spacecraft or submerged vessel, that allows movement between two areas of different air pressure. **2** a stoppage of flow caused by the presence of air in circulating liquid.

**airmail** *n* mail transported by aircraft, or this system of transporting mail. ➤ **airmail** *v*.

**airman** *or* **airwoman** *n* (*pl* **airmen** *or* **airwomen**) a military pilot or crew member.

**airplane** *n chiefly NAmer* = AEROPLANE.

**airport** *n* an airfield with runways and associated buildings, used as a base for the transport of passengers and cargo by air.

**airship** *n* a gas-filled lighter-than-air aircraft that has its own means of propulsion and steering.

**airspace** *n* the area of the atmosphere above a nation and coming under its jurisdiction.
**airstrip** *n* a strip of ground where aircraft can take off and land.
**airtight** *adj* **1** not allowing air to pass through. **2** of an argument: unassailable.
**airwaves** *pl n* the supposed medium of radio and television transmission.
**airway** *n* **1** a designated route along which aircraft fly. **2** the passage through which air reaches the lungs.
**airworthy** *adj* of an aircraft: fit for operation in the air. ➤ **airworthiness** *n.*
**airy** *adj* (**-ier, -iest**) **1** spacious and well-ventilated. **2** showing lack of concern; flippant. **3** light and graceful. ➤ **airily** *adv.*
**airy-fairy** *adj chiefly Brit* whimsically unrealistic.
**aisle** *n* **1** a passage between rows of seats in a church or other public building. **2** a passage between rows of shelving in a shop.
**ajar** *adj and adv* of a door: slightly open.
**AKA** *or* **aka** *abbr* also known as.
**akimbo** *adj and adv* with the hands on the hips and the elbow turned outwards.
**akin** *adj* **1** descended from a common ancestor. **2** essentially similar or compatible.
**Al** *abbr* the chemical symbol for aluminium.
**alabaster** *n* a fine-textured white translucent stone often carved into ornaments.
**à la carte** *adv and adj* according to a menu that prices each item separately: compare TABLE D'HÔTE.
**alacrity** *n formal* promptness or cheerful readiness.
**alarm**[1] *n* **1** the fear resulting from the sudden sensing of danger. **2** a signal that warns or alerts, or an automatic device that produces such a signal. **3** = ALARM CLOCK.
**alarm**[2] *v* **1** to cause great fear or anxiety in. **2** to warn or alert. **3** to fit with an automatic alarm. ➤ **alarming** *adj,* **alarmingly** *adv.*
**alarm clock** *n* a clock that can be set to sound an alarm at a required time, used to wake somebody up.
**alarmist** *n* a person who needlessly alarms other people.
**alas** *interj* used to express unhappiness, pity, or disappointment.
**albatross** *n* (*pl* **albatrosses** *or* **albatross**) a very large web-footed seabird with long narrow wings related to the petrels.
**albeit** *conj formal* even though.
**albino** *n* (*pl* **-os**) a person or animal with deficient pigmentation resulting in white skin and hair, and eyes with a pink pupil. ➤ **albinism** *n.*
**album** *n* **1** a blank book for holding or displaying a collection, e.g. of stamps or photographs. **2** a collection of musical recordings issued on a single disc.
**albumen** *n* the white of an egg.
**alchemy** *n* (*pl* **-ies**) a medieval form of chemical science that sought to turn base metals into gold. ➤ **alchemic** *adj,* **alchemical** *adj,* **alchemist** *n.*
**alcohol** *n* **1** a colourless liquid, the intoxicating agent in fermented and distilled drinks and also used as a solvent. **2** drink containing alcohol.
**alcoholic**[1] *adj* **1** containing or caused by alcohol. **2** affected with alcoholism.
**alcoholic**[2] *n* somebody affected with alcoholism.
**alcoholism** *n* addiction to alcoholic drink.
**alcove** *n* a recess or arched opening. in a wall.
**alder** *n* a tree or shrub of the birch family with toothed leaves and catkins.
**alderman** *n* (*pl* **aldermen**) formerly in Britain, a senior member of a county or borough council.
**ale** *n* **1** beer. **2** an alcoholic drink made with malt and hops.
**alert**[1] *adj* **1** watchful; aware. **2** active; brisk. ➤ **alertly** *adv,* **alertness** *n.*
**alert**[2] *n* a warning of danger. * **on the alert** on the lookout for danger or opportunity.
**alert**[3] *v* to warn about a danger or opportunity.
**A level** *n* an examination at sixth-form level.
**alfalfa** *n* a plant of the pea family that is widely grown for fodder.
**alfresco** *or* **al fresco** *adj and adv* taking place in the open air.
**algae** *pl noun* aquatic plants that lack differentiated stems, roots, and leaves, e.g. seaweed.
**algebra** *n* a branch of mathematics in which letters and symbols represent various entities in equations and formulas. ➤ **algebraic** *adj.*
**algorithm** *n* a systematic mathematical procedure for making a calculation. ➤ **algorithmic** *adj.*
**alias**[1] *adv* otherwise called or known as.
**alias**[2] *n* an assumed name.
**alibi** *n* (*pl* **alibis**) a plea of having been elsewhere when a crime was committed, or evidence supporting such a claim.
**alien**[1] *adj* **1** belonging to another person, place, or thing; strange or foreign. **2** from another world; extraterrestrial. **3** differing in nature or character.
**alien**[2] *n* **1** a foreign-born resident. **2** a being from another world.
**alienate** *v* **1** to make hostile or indifferent. **2** to cause (affection or sympathy) to be withdrawn or diverted. **3** to convey or transfer (property or a right) to another.
**alight**[1] *v* **1** to dismount or disembark from a vehicle. **2** to descend from the air and settle. **3** (+ on) to discover or notice.
**alight**[2] *adj* **1** *chiefly Brit* on fire; ignited. **2** animated or alive.

**align** *v* **1** to bring into proper relative position, usu in a straight line. **2** to position (oneself) in relation to a party or cause. ➤ **alignment** *n.*

**alike[1]** *adj* showing close resemblance without being identical.

**alike[2]** *adv* in the same manner, form, or degree; equally.

**alimentary canal** *n* the passage from the mouth to the anus along which food passes.

**alimony** *n chiefly NAmer* = MAINTENANCE 2.

**alive** *adj* **1** having life; not dead. **2** still in existence or operation; active. **3** (+ to) realizing the existence of; aware of. **4** lively or animated.

**alkali** *n* (*pl* **alkalis**) **1** a soluble chemical base, *esp* a hydroxide or carbonate of an alkali metal, that combine with acids to form salts. **2** a soluble chemical salt that is present in some soils of dry regions and prevents the growth of crops. ➤ **alkaline** *adj.*

**all[1]** *adj* **1** the whole amount or quantity of. **2** every. **3** any whatever. **4** as much as possible. ✱ **all there** *informal* alert or shrewd.

**all[2]** *adv* **1** wholly or altogether. **2** to a supreme degree. **3** in scores: for each side. ✱ **all but** very nearly; almost. **all together** all at the same time or in the same place. **all too** emphatically so.

**all[3]** *pron* (*pl* **all**) everybody or everything. ✱ **all in all** taking everything into account. **in all** in total.

**Allah** *n* the name for the Muslim God.

**allay** *v* to reduce the severity of (pain, fear, or suffering).

**all clear** *n* a signal that a danger has passed.

**allegation** *n* a statement made without proof.

**allege** *v* to assert without proof. ➤ **alleged** *adj,* **allegedly** *adv.*

**allegiance** *n* loyalty to or support of a person, group, or cause.

**allegory** *n* (*pl* **-ies**) a story, poem, or picture that contains a symbolic meaning. ➤ **allegorical** *adj.*

**allegro** *adj and adv* of a piece of music: performed in a brisk lively manner.

**alleluia** *interj and n* see HALLELUJAH.

**allergic** *adj* **1** having an allergy. **2** inducing an allergy.

**allergy** *n* (*pl* **-ies**) extreme sensitivity to substances that have no such effect on the average individual.

**alleviate** *v* to relieve (a problem or anxiety). ➤ **alleviation** *n.*

**alley** *n* (*pl* **-eys**) **1** a narrow passageway between buildings. **2** a garden walk bordered by trees or a hedge. **3** a long narrow lane for bowling or playing skittles.

**alliance** *n* **1** an association or bond for mutual help between nations or groups, **2** a connection or relationship, *esp* by marriage.

**allied** *adj* **1** joined in alliance by agreement or treaty. **2** in close association; united. **3** related genetically.

**alligator** *n* a large aquatic reptile related to the crocodile but with a broader head.

**all in** *adj informal* tired out; exhausted.

**all-in** *adj* **1** *chiefly Brit* including all costs. **2** *Brit* said of wrestling: having almost no holds barred.

**alliteration** *n* the repetition of initial consonant sounds in neighbouring words or syllables for special effect. ➤ **alliterative** *adj.*

**allocate** *v* to apportion or distribute. ➤ **allocation** *n.*

**allot** *v* (**allotted, allotting**) **1** to apportion or assign. **2** to earmark or designate.

**allotment** *n* **1** *Brit* a small plot of land for growing flowers or vegetables. **2** the act of allotting or a share allotted.

**allow** *v* **1** to permit or make it possible for somebody to do something. **2** to assign (time or money) as a share or suitable amount. **3** to grant (a sum of money) as an allowance. **4** (+ for) to take into account. ➤ **allowable** *adj.*

**allowance** *n* **1** a share or portion allowed. **2** a sum paid to a person, usu at regular intervals. **3** an amount of income on which no tax is payable. ✱ **make allowances for** to take (mitigating circumstances) into account.

**alloy[1]** *n* **1** a mixture of metals or of a metal with a non-metal. **2** a metal mixed with a more valuable metal.

**alloy[2]** *v* **1** to mix (metals) to form an alloy. **2** to spoil by addition.

**all right[1]** *adv* well enough.

**all right[2]** *adj* **1** satisfactory or acceptable. **2** safe or well. **3** agreeable or pleasing.

**all-rounder** *n* somebody who is competent in many fields.

**all told** *adv* with everything or everybody taken into account.

**allude** *v* (+ to) to refer to indirectly; to mention in passing.

**allure[1]** *v* to entice by charm or attraction.

**allure[2]** *n* power of attraction or fascination.

**allusion** *n* **1** an implied or indirect reference. **2** alluding or hinting. ➤ **allusive** *adj.*

**alluvium** *n* (*pl* **alluviums** *or* **alluvia**) clay or silt deposited by running water. ➤ **alluvial** *adj.*

**ally[1]** *v* (**-ies, -ied**) **1** to join or unite with, *esp* for common benefit. **2** (*usu in passive*) to combine with. **3** (+ to) to relate by resemblance or common properties.

**ally[2]** *n* (*pl* **-ies**) **1** a state associated with another by treaty. **2** a person or group that helps, supports, or cooperates with another.

**alma mater** *n* a school, college, or university that one has attended.

**almanac** *or* **almanack** *n* an annual publication containing statistical information, *esp* a publication containing astronomical and meteorological data.
**almighty**[1] *adj* **1** (*often* **Almighty**) having absolute power over all. **2** having relatively unlimited power. **3** *informal* great in extent, seriousness, force, etc.
**almighty**[2] *adv informal* to a great degree, very.
**almond** *n* an edible oval nut obtained from a small tree of the rose family.
**almost** *adv* very nearly but not exactly.
**alms** *pl noun* money or food formerly given to help the poor.
**almshouse** *n Brit* a house for the poor, founded and financed by charity.
**aloe** *n* a succulent plant with thick leaves and tall spikes of flowers, and producing a juice used as a laxative.
**aloe vera** *n* a jelly-like extract from a species of aloe, used in cosmetic preparations and ointments.
**aloft** *adv* at or to a higher place; up in the air.
**alone** *adj and adv* **1** separated from others; isolated. **2** considered by itself. **3** free from interference or help.
**along**[1] *prep* **1** over the length of or in a line parallel with. **2** in the course of. **3** in accordance with.
**along**[2] *adv* forward; onward. ✱ **all along** all the time. **along with** in addition to.
**alongside**[1] *adv* along or at the side of something.
**alongside**[2] *prep* (*also* + of) side by side with or along the side of.
**aloof** *adj* distant or unsympathetic. ➤ **aloofness** *n.*
**alopecia** *n* abnormal loss of hair.
**aloud** *adv* with a normal speaking voice.
**alp** *n* **1** a high mountain. **2** in Switzerland, a mountainside pasture.
**alpaca** *n* (*pl* **alpacas** *or* **alpaca**) a type of mammal related to the llama, found in Peru, producing a fine wool.
**alpha** *n* the first letter of the Greek alphabet (Α, α).
**alphabet** *n* a set of letters used to write a language.
**alphabetical** *or* **alphabetic** *adj* in the order of the letters of the alphabet. ➤ **alphabetically** *adv.*
**alpha particle** *n* a positively charged nuclear particle, identical with the nucleus of a helium atom, ejected from radioactive substances: compare BETA PARTICLE.
**alpine** *adj* relating to or growing in mountainous regions.
**already** *adv* **1** before a particular time or the expected time. **2** previously.
**alright** *adv, adj, and interj* = ALL RIGHT[1].

***Usage Note:*** *All right* is often preferred.

**Alsatian** *n chiefly Brit* a large dog of a wolflike breed originating in Germany. Also called GERMAN SHEPHERD.
**also** *adv* as well; in additionally.
**also-ran** *n* an undistinguished person.
**altar** *n* **1** a table on which the communion bread and wine are consecrated in Christian churches. **2** a table-like structure on which offerings are made to a deity.
**alter** *v* to make or become different. ➤ **alteration** *n.*
**altercation** *n* an angry discussion or quarrel.
**alter ego** *n* (*pl* **alter egos**) **1** a side of somebody's character that is different from their usual character. **2** a close and trusted friend.
**alternate**[1] *adj* **1** of two things: occurring by turns. **2** forming an alternating series. **3** every other; every second. ➤ **alternately** *adv.*
**alternate**[2] *v* **1** of two things or people: to occur or do something by turns. **2** to interchange (one person or thing) with another. **3** to change repeatedly from one state or action to another. ➤ **alternation** *n.*
**alternating current** *n* an electric current that reverses its direction at regularly recurring intervals: compare DIRECT CURRENT.
**alternative**[1] *adj* **1** able to be used instead of something else. **2** different from the usual forms or kinds. ➤ **alternatively** *adv.*
**alternative**[2] *n* **1** another person or thing that could act as a replacement. **2** a choice between two or more possibilities.
**alternator** *n* an electric generator for producing alternating current.
**although** *conj* **1** in spite of the fact or possibility that; though. **2** but.
**altimeter** *n* an instrument for measuring altitude.
**altitude** *n* the height of an object or place above sea level.
**alto** *n* (*pl* **-os**) **1** a female singer with a range below that of a soprano. **2** an adult male singer with a range above that of a tenor.
**altogether** *adv* **1** completely; in every way. **2** with everything taken into account.
**altruism** *n* unselfish regard for others. ➤ **altruist** *n,* **altruistic** *adj.*
**alum** *n* a sulphate of aluminium with potassium.
**aluminium** (*NAmer* **aluminum**) *n* a light silver-white metallic element.
**alumnus** *n* (*pl* **alumni**) a former student of a particular school, college, or university.
**always** *adv* **1** at all times; continuously. **2** in all cases. **3** forever. **4** as a last resort.
**Alzheimer's disease** /ˈalts·hieməz/ *n* a disease leading to premature senile dementia.
**AM** *abbr* amplitude modulation.

**Am** *abbr* the chemical symbol for americium.

**am** *v* first person sing. present of BE.

**a.m.** *abbr* ante meridiem, before noon.

**amalgam** *n* **1** an alloy of mercury with another metal. **2** a mixture of different elements.

**amalgamate** *v* **1** to combine into a single body. **2** to combine or alloy (a metal) with mercury. ➤ **amalgamation** *n.*

**amanuensis** *n* (*pl* **amanuenses**) somebody employed to write from dictation or to copy a manuscript.

**amass** *v* **1** to collect or accumulate. **2** to bring together into a mass.

**amateur**[1] *n* **1** somebody who undertakes a sport or other activity as a pastime rather than a profession. **2** somebody who does something unskilfully. ➤ **amateurism** *n.*

**amateur**[2] *adj* **1** of or for amateurs rather than professionals. **2** inexpert.

**amateurish** *adj* not skilful or competent. ➤ **amateurishly** *adv.*

**amatory** *adj* expressing sexual love or desire.

**amaze** *v* to fill with wonder; to astound. ➤ **amazement** *n.*

**Amazon** *n* a tall strong or athletic woman.

**ambassador** *n* **1** a diplomat sent to a foreign country as a resident representative of a government or sovereign. **2** somebody who represents or promotes a cause. ➤ **ambassadorial** *adj.*

**amber** *n* **1** a hard yellowish translucent substance that is the fossilized resin of some extinct trees, used in jewellery. **2** a yellowish colour.

**ambergris** *n* a waxy substance from the intestines of sperm whales, used in perfumes.

**ambidextrous** *adj* able to use either hand with equal ease.

**ambience** *or* **ambiance** *n* a characteristic atmosphere in a place.

**ambient** *adj* relating to the immediate surroundings of a place.

**ambiguity** *n* (*pl* **-ies**) **1** an ambiguous or imprecise word or expression. **2** uncertainty of meaning.

**ambiguous** *adj* **1** capable of more than one interpretation. **2** vague; difficult to classify. ➤ **ambiguously** *adv.*

**ambit** *n* the scope or range of something; a limit.

**ambition** *n* a strong drive to achieve something, *esp* status or success.

**ambitious** *adj* **1** acting from or showing ambition. **2** motivated by a strong ambition and therefore difficult to achieve. ➤ **ambitiously** *adv.*

**ambivalence** *n* the state of having mixed attitudes or feelings towards a person or thing. ➤ **ambivalent** *adj.*

**amble**[1] *v* to move at a leisurely pace.

**amble**[2] *n* a leisurely walk.

**ambrosia** *n* **1** the food of the Greek and Roman gods. **2** something extremely pleasing to eat or smell.

**ambulance** *n* a vehicle for transporting injured or sick people to and from hospital.

**ambulatory** *adj* relating to or adapted for walking.

**ambush**[1] *v* to attack from a hidden position.

**ambush**[2] *n* a surprise attack from a hidden position.

**ameliorate** *v formal* to make better or more tolerable. ➤ **amelioration** *n.*

**amen** *interj* a word used at the end of a prayer with the meaning 'so be it'.

**amenable** *adj* willing to be persuaded. **2** capable of being judged or tested.

**amend** *v* to revise or make corrections to.

**amendment** *n* an alteration to a document or law.

**amends** ✱ **make amends** to compensate for a wrong.

**amenity** *n* (*pl* **-ies**) a facility that improves material comfort.

**American** *n* a native or inhabitant of America, *esp* the USA. ➤ **American** *adj.*

**American football** *n* a football game played with an oval ball between teams of eleven players, involving kicking and running with the ball and forward passing.

**American Indian** *n dated* a member of any of the indigenous peoples of America.

**amethyst** *n* a clear purple or violet variety of quartz used as a gemstone.

**amiable** *adj* friendly and pleasant. ➤ **amiability** *n,* **amiableness** *n,* **amiably** *adv.*

**amicable** *adj* friendly and peaceable. ➤ **amicably** *adv.*

**amid** *prep formal* in or to the middle of; among.

**amidships** *adv and adj* in or towards the middle part of a ship.

**amino acid** *n* any of the organic acids that are the chief components of proteins.

**amir** *n* see EMIR.

**amiss** *adv and adj* wrong; not in order. ✱ **not come/go amiss** to be appropriate or welcome. **take it/something amiss** to be offended or upset by something.

**amity** *n* friendly relations.

**ammeter** *n* an instrument for measuring electric current in amperes.

**ammo** *n informal* ammunition.

**ammonia** *n* a pungent colourless gas used in the manufacture of fertilizers, synthetic fibres, and explosives.

**ammonite** *n* an extinct sea mollusc that was common during the Mesozoic era.

**ammunition** *n* **1** a supply of bullets or shells for use in weapons. **2** points used to support an argument.

**amnesia** *n* loss of memory. ➤ **amnesiac** *adj and n.*

**amnesty** *n* (*pl* **-ies**) **1** a pardon granted to a large group of individuals, *esp* for political offences. **2** a period during which no legal action is taken against people who admit an offence and comply with conditions.

**amniotic fluid** *n* the fluid surrounding a foetus in the uterus.

**amoeba** (*NAmer* **ameba**) *n* (*pl* **amoebas** *or* **amoebae,** *NAmer* **amebas** *or* **amebae**) a single-celled organism that can change its shape.

**amok** *or* **amuck** *adv* ✱ **run amok** to act wildly or be completely out of control.

**among** *or* **amongst** *prep* **1** in midst of; surrounded by. **2** by or through the whole group of. **3** in the number or class of. **4** shared by.

**amoral** *adj* not concerned with or caring about moral principles or ethical judgments: compare IMMORAL. ➤ **amorality** *n.*

**amorous** *adj* showing or feeling sexual love or desire. ➤ **amorously** *adv.*

**amorphous** *adj* having no definite form; shapeless.

**amount**[1] *v* **1** (+ to) to add up to. **2** (+ to) to be equivalent to.

**amount**[2] *n* **1** a quantity. **2** the total of two or more quantities.

**ampere** /'ampeə/ *n* the basic SI unit of electric current.

**ampersand** *n* a sign (&) standing for the word *and.*

**amphetamine** *n* a synthetic drug used as a stimulant.

**amphibian** *n* **1** a frog, toad, newt, or other member of a class of cold-blooded vertebrates that live in the water when young and on land when fully developed. **2** a vehicle adapted to operate on both land and water. ➤ **amphibious** *adj.*

**amphitheatre** (*NAmer* **amphitheater**) *n* an open oval or circular building with rising tiers of seats ranged about an arena, used for sports and public spectacles.

**ample** *adj* (**ampler, amplest**) **1** enough or more than enough. **2** large or extensive. ➤ **amply** *adv.*

**amplifier** *n* an electronic device that increasess sounds or electrical signals.

**amplify** *v* (**-ies, -ied**) **1** to increase the strength or (a sound or electrical signal). **2** to expand (a statement) or make it clearer. ➤ **amplification** *n.*

**amplitude** *n* **1** largeness of size or scope; abundance. **2** the extent of a vibration or oscillation measured from the average position to a maximum.

**ampoule** (*NAmer* **ampul** *or* **ampule**) *n* a small sealed glass vessel holding a solution for hypodermic injection.

**amputate** *v* to remove (a limb) surgically. ➤ **amputation** *n.*

**amputee** *n* somebody who has had all or part of a limb amputated.

**amuck** *adv* see AMOK.

**amulet** *n* a small stone or piece of jewellery worn as a protection from harm.

**amuse** *v* **1** to appeal to the sense of humour of. **2** to entertain or interest.

**amusement** *n* **1** the act of amusing or being amused. **2** a pleasant diversion, *esp* a fairground entertainment.

**an** *indefinite article* used in place of *a* (see A) before words with an initial vowel sound.

**anabolic steroid** *n* a synthetic hormone that increases the size and weight of skeletal muscle.

**anachronism** *n* **1** the placing of people or things in a period to which they do not belong. **2** a person or thing that belongs or seems to belong to an older time. ➤ **anachronistic** *adj.*

**anaconda** *n* a large snake of the boa family that crushes its prey.

**anaemia** (*NAmer* **anemia**) *n* a condition in which the blood is deficient in red blood cells or haemoglobin, causing a lack of energy.

**anaesthetic** (*NAmer* **anesthetic**) *n* a substance that suppresses pain, so that surgery can be carried out.

**anaesthetize** *or* **-ise** (*NAmer* **anesthetize**) *v* to administer an anaesthetic to. ➤ **anaesthetist** *n.*

**anagram** *n* a word or phrase made by rearranging the letters of another.

**anal** *adj* relating to or in the region of the anus.

**analgesic** *n* a drug that relieves pain.

**analog** *adj* **1** of a computer: using data supplied in a stream of numbers represented by directly measurable quantities, e.g. voltages or mechanical rotations: compare DIGITAL. **2** of a clock or watch, etc: using a pointer or hands rather than having an electronic display: compare DIGITAL. **3** converting sound waves into a continuous electrical wave form to record sound: compare DIGITAL.

**analogous** *adj* **1** (*often* + to/with) similar in some respects. **2** of plant or animal parts: similar in function but having evolved separately and distinctly.

**analogue**[1] (*NAmer* **analog**) *n* something that is analogous to something else.

**analogue**[2] *adj* = ANALOG.

**analogy** *n* (*pl* **-ies**) an explanation or illustration of something that uses a comparison with something similar.

**analyse** (*NAmer* **analyze**) *v* **1** to make a close examination of (something) in order to determine its nature, content, or structure. **2** = PSYCHOANALYSE.

**analysis** *n* (*pl* **analyses**) **1** the examination and identification of the constituents of a complex whole and their relationship to one another. **2** the act or process of breaking something up into its constituent elements. **3** = PSYCHOANALYSIS.

**analyst** *n* **1** a person who analyses or is skilled in analysis. **2** a psychoanalyst.

**analytical** *or* **analytic** *adj* using analysis. ➤ **analytically** *adv.*

**anarchic** *or* **anarchical** *adj* **1** advocating anarchy or likely to bring about anarchy. **2** not adhering to conventions or expectations. ➤ **anarchically** *adv.*

**anarchist** *n* somebody who attacks the established social order or laws; a revolutionary. ➤ **anarchism** *n,* **anarchistic** *adj.*

**anarchy** *n* **1** a society with no government. **2** a state of lawlessness or disorder.

**anathema** *n* somebody or something that is hated.

**anatomy** *n* (*pl* **-ies**) **1** the scientific study of the structure of people, animals, and plants. **2** the structural make-up of an organism. ➤ **anatomical** *adj.* **anatomist** ➤ noun.

**ancestor** *n* **1** somebody from whom a person is descended. **2** an earlier type or model from which a more recent version has developed.

**ancestral** *adj* of or inherited from an ancestor.

**ancestry** *n* (*pl* **-ies**) a line of noble descent; a lineage.

**anchor**[1] *n* a heavy hook or other device dropped from a ship or boat to hold it in a particular place.

**anchor**[2] *v* **1** to hold in place with an anchor. **2** to secure firmly.

**anchorage** *n* a place where boats and ships can anchor.

**anchorite** *n* somebody who lives in seclusion for religious reasons.

**anchorman** *or* **anchorwoman** *n* (*pl* **anchormen**) in broadcasting, a person who links up with outside reporters from a central studio.

**anchovy** *n* (*pl* **-ies**) a small fish that resembles a herring, with a strong taste.

**ancien régime** /ˌonsi·an ray'zheem/ *n* (*pl* **anciens régimes**) a political or social system that has been superseded.

**ancient** *adj* **1** belonging to a remote period of history. **2** *informal* very old. ➤ **anciently** *adv.*

**ancillary** *adj* **1** giving support; auxiliary. **2** subordinate.

**and** *conj* **1** used to join words, clauses, or sentences. **2** used to express the addition of numbers.

**andante** *adj and adv* of a piece of music: performed moderately slowly.

**androgynous** *adj* combining male and female features. ➤ **androgyny** *n.*

**android** *n* in science fiction, an automaton with a human form.

**anecdotal** *adj* in the form of an anecdote, without evidence or proof. ➤ **anecdotally** *adv.*

**anemometer** *n* an instrument for measuring the speed of the wind.

**anemone** *n* **1** a plant with divided leaves and brightly coloured flowers. **2** = SEA ANEMONE.

**aneurysm** *or* **aneurism** *n* a swelling of a diseased blood vessel. ➤ **aneurysmal** *adj.*

**anew** *adv chiefly literary* **1** one more time; again. **2** in a new form or way.

**angel** *n* **1** a spiritual being, usu depicted in human form with wings, believed to serve as a messenger of God. **2** a good or loving person.

**angelica** *n* a plant with candied stalks used as a cake decoration.

**anger**[1] *n* a strong feeling of displeasure.

**anger**[2] *v* (**angered, angering**) to make or become angry.

**angina** *n* a disease with severe chest pain, caused by a deficiency of blood to the heart.

**angle**[1] *n* **1** a space formed by two lines or surfaces extending outwards from the same point or line. **2** a corner. **3** a position from which something is observed. **4** a way of thinking or asking about something. ➤ **angled** *adj.*

**angle**[2] *v* **1** to place or move in a slanting position. **2** to bend or shape into an angle. **3** to present (information) from a particular point of view.

**angle**[3] *v* **1** to fish with a hook and line. **2** (*usu* + for) to use indirect of devious means to get something. ➤ **angler** *n.*

**Anglican**[1] *adj* relating to the Church of England. ➤ **Anglicanism** *n.*

**Anglican**[2] *n* a member of the Church of England.

**anglicize** *or* **-ise** *v* to make English in character or form. ➤ **anglicization** *n.*

**Anglophile** *or* **Anglophil** *n* (*also* **anglophile**) somebody who admires England or Britain.

**Anglo-Saxon** *n* **1** a member of the Germanic peoples who conquered England in the fifth cent. **2** the Old English language. ➤ **Anglo-Saxon** *adj.*

**angora** *n* **1** a cat, goat, or rabbit with long soft hair. **2** a fabric made from Angora rabbit or goat hair.

**Angostura bitters** *n trademark* a bitter aromatic tonic added to alcoholic drinks as a flavouring.

**angry** *adj* (**-ier, -iest**) **1** feeling or showing anger. **2** caused by or expressing anger. **3** of a wound: painfully inflamed. ➤ **angrily** *adv.*

**angst** *n* a strong feeling of anxiety about the human condition.

**angstrom** *n* a unit of length equal to $10^{-10}$m, used in measuring electromagnetic radiation wavelength.

**anguish** *n* extreme mental distress or physical pain.

**angular** *adj* having or forming angles **1** placed at an angle. **2** of a person: lean and bony. ➤ **angularity** *n.*

**animal** *n* **1** a living creature that is able to move and respond to stimulation. **2** any living creature apart from a human being. **3** a mammal as distinct from a bird, fish,or insect. **4** a coarse, unfeeling, or cruel person.
**animate**[1] *v* **1** to make lively and interesting. **2** to create or film using the techniques of animation. **3** to give life to. ➤ **animator** *n.*
**animate**[2] *adj* possessing life; alive.
**animated** *adj* **1** lively or vivacious. **2** made using the techniques of animation. ➤ **animatedly** *adv.*
**animation** *n* **1** being lively or active. **2** the technique of filming a sequence of images or models in different positions so that they appear to be moving.
**animism** *n* attribution of souls to nature or natural phenomena. ➤ **animist** *n.*
**animosity** *n* (*pl* **-ies**) a strong feeling of hostility or resentment.
**animus** *n* ill will or hostility; animosity.
**anion** *n* a negatively charged ion.
**aniseed** *n* the seed of anise (a plant of the carrot family) used as a flavouring.
**ankle** *n* the joint between the foot and the leg.
**anklet** *n* a band or chain worn round the ankle.
**annals** *pl noun* a record of events, activities, etc, arranged in yearly sequence.
**anneal** *v* to toughen (metal or glass) by heating and gradual cooling it.
**annex**[1] *v* **1** to add as an extra part. **2** to incorporate (another country) within the domain of a state. ➤ **annexation** *n.*
**annex**[2] *or* **annexe** *n* **1** an extra building providing additional accommodation. **2** an addition to a document.
**annihilate** *v* to destroy entirely. ➤ **annihilation** *n.*
**anniversary** *n* (*pl* **-ies**) the date on which a notable event took place in an earlier year.
**annotate** *v* to provide (a text) with notes. ➤ **annotation** *n.*
**announce** *v* **1** to make known publicly. **2** to indicate in advance; to foretell. ➤ **announcement** *n.*
**annoy** *v* **1** to make mildly angry. **2** to bother or pester. **3** to be a source of irritation. ➤ **annoyance** *n.*
**annual**[1] *adj* **1** covering or lasting for the period of a year. **2** occurring once a year. **3** of a plant: completing the life cycle in one growing season. ➤ **annually** *adv.*
**annual**[2] *n* **1** a publication that appears once a year. **2** an annual plant.
**annuity** *n* (*pl* **-ies**) an amount payable each year to a person.
**annul** *v* (**annulled, annulling**) **1** to declare legally invalid. **2** to cancel or abolish. ➤ **annulment** *n.*
**annular** *adj* in the shape of a ring.
**annunciation** *n* (**the Annunciation**) the announcement by Gabriel to the Virgin Mary that she would be the mother of Jesus Christ celebrated by Christians on 25 March.
**anode** *n* the electrode by which electrons leave a device and enter an external circuit.
**anodize** *or* **-ise** *v* to coat (metal) with a protective film by means of electrolytic action.
**anodyne**[1] *adj* dully mild or inoffensive.
**anodyne**[2] *n* a painkilling drug.
**anoint** *v* to put oil on (somebody) as part of a religious ceremony.
**anomalous** *adj* deviating from what is usual or expected.
**anomaly** *n* (*pl* **-ies**) something that deviates from what is usual or expected.
**anon** *adv archaic or informal* in a short while; soon.
**anonymous** *adj* **1** having or giving no name. **2** nondescript. ➤ **anonymity** *n,* **anonymously** *adv,* **anonymousness** *n.*
**anorak** *n chiefly Brit* a short weatherproof coat with a hood.
**anorexia** *or* **anorexia nervosa** *n* a disorder with prolonged loss of appetite.
**another**[1] *adj* **1** being a different or additional one. **2** some other.
**another**[2] *pron* a different or additional one.
**answer**[1] *n* **1** a spoken or written reply to a question or statement. **2** the solution to a problem.
**answer**[2] *v* **1** to give an answer to. **2** to provide a solution to (a problem). **3** to act in response to. **4** (+ for) to be responsible or accountable for something. **5** (+ to) to have to explain oneself to (somebody). **6** to be adequate or usable.
**answerable** *adj* (+ to/for) responsible to somebody for something.
**answering machine** *n* a telephone device that responds to calls with a recorded reply and records messages spoken by callers.
**ant** *n* a small insect that lives in large organized groups.
**antacid** *n* a medicine that combats excessive acidity, *esp* in the stomach.
**antagonism** *n* open hostility or antipathy.
**antagonist** *n* an opponent or adversary. ➤ **antagonistic** *adj.*
**antagonize** *or* **-ise** *v* to cause to become antagonistic.
**Antarctic** *adj* of the South Pole or the surrounding region.
**anteater** *n* a mammal with a long snout and bushy tail that feeds chiefly on ants and termites.
**antecedent**[1] *n* **1** a preceding thing, event, or circumstance. **2** (*in pl*) family origins; ancestry.
**antecedent**[2] *adj* earlier in time or order.
**antedate** *v* to precede in time.

**antediluvian** *adj* **1** belonging to the period before the flood described in the Bible. **2** ridiculously out-of-date or antiquated.

**antelope** *n* (*pl* **antelopes** *or* **antelope**) a fast-running hoofed mammal native to Africa and Asia.

**antenatal** *adj* relating to pregnancy. ➤ **antenatally** *adv.*

**antenna** *n* **1** (*pl* **antennae** /-nee/) a long thin sense organ on the head of insects, crustaceans, and centipedes. **2** (*pl* **antennas** *or* **antennae**) an aerial.

**anterior** *adj* **1** before in time. **2** situated towards the front.

**anteroom** *n* an outer room that leads to a larger one.

**anthem** *n* **1** a solemn song sung as an expression of national identity. **2** a musical setting of a religious text.

**anther** *n* an organ at the tip of a flower's stamen that contains and releases pollen.

**anthill** *n* a mound of soil and leaves thrown up by ants or termites making a nest.

**anthology** *n* (*pl* **-ies**) a selection of literary or musical pieces or passages. ➤ **anthologist** *n.*

**anthracite** *n* a hard variety of coal that burns slowly and with a non-luminous flame.

**anthrax** *n* a disease of cattle and sheep caused by a spore-forming bacterium and capable of being transmitted to humans.

**anthropoid** *adj* resembling human beings in form or behaviour.

**anthropology** *n* the scientific study of human societies and behaviour. ➤ **anthropological** *adj,* **anthropologist** *n.*

**anthropomorphic** *adj* **1** having human form. **2** ascribing human characteristics to non-human things. ➤ **anthropomorphically** *adv,* **anthropomorphism** *n.*

**anti-** *or* **ant-** *prefix* against or opposing.

**antibiotic** *n* a substance that kills bacteria. ➤ **antibiotic** *adj.*

**antibody** *n* (*pl* **-ies**) a protein, e.g. a blood protein, that is produced by the body in response to a specific ANTIGEN (toxin, virus, etc).

**Antichrist** *n* (*often* **the Antichrist**) an enemy of Christ predicted to appear shortly before the end of the world.

**anticipate** *v* **1** to foresee and deal with in advance; to forestall. **2** to discuss or think about in advance or too early. **3** to use or spend before the right or natural time. **4** to look forward to. ➤ **anticipation** *n,* **anticipatory** *adj.*

**anticlimax** *n* an event that is strikingly less important or exciting than expected. ➤ **anticlimactic** *adj.*

**anticlockwise** *adj and adv* in a direction opposite to that in which the hands of a clock rotate.

**antics** *pl n* foolish or entertaining behaviour.

**anticyclone** *n* a system of winds that rotates about a centre of high atmospheric pressure, usually bringing calm, fine weather. ➤ **anticyclonic** *adj.*

**antidote** *n* a remedy that counteracts the effects of poison.

**antifreeze** *n* a substance added to a liquid to lower its freezing point.

**antigen** *n* a harmful substance that stimulates the body to produce an antibody.

**anti-hero** *n* (*pl* **anti-heroes**) a main character in a story, film, play, etc, who lacks traditional heroic qualities.

**antihistamine** *n* a drug that opposes the actions of histamine and is used *esp* for treating allergies.

**antimacassar** *n* a cover put over the backs or arms of furniture to protect it from grease and dirt.

**antimatter** *n* hypothetical matter composed of antiparticles.

**antimony** *n* a silver-white metallic chemical element used as a strengthening constituent of alloys.

**antipathy** *n* (*pl* **-ies**) (*often* + to) a deep-seated aversion or dislike.

**antiperspirant** *n* a substance used to reduce perspiration.

**antiphon** *n* a verse said or sung as part of a church service. ➤ **antiphonal** *adj.*

**Antipodes** *pl n* (**the Antipodes**) Australia and New Zealand. ➤ **Antipodean** *adj and n.*

**antiquarian** *adj* **1** relating to ancient relics. **2** said of books other works of art: old and rare.

**antiquated** *adj* outmoded or out-of-date.

**antique**[1] *adj* **1** valuable because of its age. **2** suggesting the style of an earlier period.

**antique**[2] *n* an object or work of art made in an earlier period and sought by collectors.

**antiquity** *n* (*pl* **-ies**) **1** ancient times. **2** the quality of being ancient. **3** (*in pl*) relics or monuments of ancient times.

**anti-Semitism** *n* hostility towards or discrimination against Jewish people. ➤ **anti-Semite** *n,* **anti-Semitic** *adj.*

**antiseptic** *adj* preventing the growth of micro-organisms that cause disease. ➤ **antiseptic** *n,* **antiseptically** *adv.*

**antisocial** *adj* **1** of a person or behaviour: causing annoyance to others. **2** tending to avoid the company of others; unsociable. ➤ **antisocially** *adv.*

**antithesis** *n* (*pl* **antitheses**) **1** somebody or something that is a direct opposite. **2** a contrast of ideas.

**antithetical** *or* **antithetic** *adj* directly opposed or contrary. ➤ **antithetically** *adv.*

**antler** *n* one of a pair of branched horns of a male deer.

**antonym** *n* a word that means the opposite of another. ➤ **antonymy** *n.*

**anus** *n* the opening through which solid waste matter leaves the body.
**anvil** *n* a heavy iron block on which metal is shaped by hammering.
**anxiety** *n* (*pl* **-ies**) **1** uneasiness of mind because of possible trouble or danger. **2** a cause of anxiety.
**anxious** *adj* **1** uneasy in the mind because of possible trouble or danger. **2** causing anxiety; worrying. **3** ardently or earnestly wishing to do something. ➤ **anxiously** *adv.*
**any**[1] *adj* one or some, no matter which.
**any**[2] *pron* (*pl* **any**) any person or thing.
**any**[3] *adv* to any extent or degree.
**anybody** *pron* any person.
**anyhow** *adv* **1** in a haphazard manner. **2** anyway.
**anyone** *pron* any person.
**anything** *pron* any thing whatever.
**anyway** *adv* **1** in any case; inevitably. **2** used when resuming a narrative. **3** nevertheless.
**anywhere**[1] *adv* in or to any place. ✱ **get anywhere**
**anywhere**[2] *n* any place.
**aorta** *n* the main artery carrying blood from the heart to be distributed by branch arteries throughout the body. ➤ **aortic** *adj.*
**apace** *adv* at a quick pace; swiftly.
**apart** *adv* **1** at a distance from something or somebody in space, time, or quality. **2** in or into two or more parts. ✱ **apart from** except for.
**apartheid** /ə'paht·(h)ayt, -(h)iet/ *n* a policy of racial segregation formerly operated in South Africa.
**apartment** *n* **1** *chiefly NAmer* a flat. **2** a suite of rooms used for living in. ➤ **apartmental** *adj.*
**apathetic** *adj* lacking interest; indifferent. ➤ **apathetically** *adv.*
**apathy** *n* lack of interest or enthusiasm.
**apatosaurus** *n* a large dinosaur with a long neck and tail and short forelegs, formerly called *brontosaurus.*
**ape**[1] *n* a large tailless primate belonging to the group which includes gorillas, chimpanzees, orang-utans, and gibbons.
**ape**[2] *v* to imitate closely but clumsily.
**aperitif** *n* an alcoholic drink taken before a meal to stimulate the appetite.
**aperture** *n* **1** an opening or gap. **2** the adjustable opening in a camera through which the light passes.
**apex** *n* (*pl* **apexes** *or* **apices**) the top or uppermost point; a tip.
**aphid** *n* a small insect that sucks the juices of plants, e.g. a greenfly.
**aphorism** *n* a pithy phrase expressing a truth.
**aphrodisiac** *n* a food, drink, or drug that stimulates sexual desire.
**apiary** *n* (*pl* **-ies**) a place where bees are kept.
**apiece** *adv* for each one; individually.
**aplenty** *adj archaic or literary* in abundance.
**aplomb** *n* calm self-assurance.
**apocalypse** *n* **1** a cataclysmic event. **2** (**the Apocalypse**) the ultimate destruction of the world, as depicted in the Book of Revelation in the Bible.
**apocalyptic** *or* **apocalyptical** *adj* momentous or catastrophic.
**apocryphal** *adj* of an account or story: probably untrue.
**apogee** *n* **1** the point farthest from the earth reached by the moon or a satellite in its orbit. **2** the farthest or highest point; the culmination.
**apolitical** *adj* having no interest in politics.
**apologetic** *adj* regretfully acknowledging a fault or failure; contrite. ➤ **apologetically** *adv.*
**apologia** *n* a reasoned defence of a faith, cause, or institution.
**apologist** *n* a person who speaks or writes in defence of something.
**apologize** *or* **-ise** *v* (*often* + for) to make an apology.
**apology** *n* (*pl* **-ies**) **1** a regretful admission of error or discourtesy. **2** (+ for) a poor substitute; a specimen.
**apoplectic** *adj* **1** relating to or causing apoplexy. **2** *informal* extremely angry.
**apoplexy** *n* (*pl* **-ies**) a stroke.
**apostasy** *n* (*pl* **-ies**) renunciation of a belief.
**apostate** *n* a person who renounces a belief. ➤ **apostate** *adj.*
**apostle** *n* **1** (*often* **Apostle**) an early Christian teacher sent out to preach the gospel. **2** an advocate, or supporter of a system, movement, etc.
**apostrophe** *n* a punctuation mark (') used to indicate the omission of letters or figures, the possessive case, or the plural of letters or figures.
**apothecary** *n* (*pl* **-ies**) *archaic* a pharmacist or pharmacy.
**apotheosis** *n* (*pl* **apotheoses**) a supreme example of something at its most developed.
**appal** (*NAmer* **appall**) *v* (**appalled, appalling**) to overcome with horror or dismay. ➤ **appalling** *adj,* **appallingly** *adv.*
**apparatus** *n* (*pl* **apparatuses** *or* **apparatus**) equipment designed for a particular use.
**apparel** *n literary* clothing.
**apparent** *adj* **1** easily seen or understood; evident. **2** seemingly real but not necessarily so. ➤ **apparently** *adv.*
**apparition** *n* an unusual or unexpected sight; *esp* the appearance of a ghost.
**appeal**[1] *n* **1** the power of arousing a sympathetic response; attraction. **2** an earnest plea or request. **3** a legal proceeding by which a case is brought to a higher court for review.
**appeal**[2] *v* (*often* + to) **1** to arouse a sympathetic response. **2** to make an earnest plea or request. **3** to take a case to a higher court for review.

**appealing** *adj* having appeal; attractive. ➤ **appealingly** *adv.*
**appear** *v* **1** to become visible or present. **2** to arrive. **3** to give the impression of being; to seem.
**appearance** *n* **1** an act of appearing or being present. **2** the way someone or something looks or seems.
**appease** *v* **1** to pacify or calm (somebody) by agreeing to what they want. **2** to assuage or allay (hunger, thirst, etc). ➤ **appeasement** *n.*
**appellation** *n literary* a name or title.
**append** *v* to attach or add as a supplement.
**appendage** *n* something added to something larger or more important.
**appendicitis** *n* inflammation of the appendix.
**appendix** *n* **1** (*pl* **appendixes**) a short tube that extends from the lower end of the large intestine. **2** ( *pl* **appendices** /-seez/) a supplement at the end of a book or other piece of writing.
**appertain** *v* **1** (*usu* + to) to relate to. **2** to be relevant.
**appetite** *n* **1** a desire to eat. **2** a strong desire or inclination.
**appetizer** *or* **appetiser** *n* a food or drink that stimulates the appetite.
**appetizing** *or* **appetising** *adj* appealing to the appetite.
**applaud** *v* to express approval by clapping or cheering.
**applause** *n* approval or admiration expressed by clapping.
**apple** *n* a round fruit with red or green skin and crisp white flesh. * **the apple of one's eye** somebody or something greatly cherished.
**appliance** *n* an instrument or device designed for a particular use.
**applicable** *adj* able to be applied; appropriate or related. ➤ **applicability** *n.*
**applicant** *n* a person who applies for something.
**application** *n* **1** a formal request or petition. **2** an act of applying. **3** a use to which something is put. **4** close attention; diligence. **5** a computer program that performs a particular function.
**applicator** *n* a device for applying a substance.
**applied** *adj* of a subject of study: put to practical use.
**appliqué** /ə'pleekay, aplee'kay/ *n* decorative work in which a cutout decoration is attached to a larger piece of material.
**apply** *v* (**-ies, -ied**) **1** to bring to bear or put to use. **2** to lay or spread on a surface. **3** to devote (oneself) to something. **4** (*usu* + to) to be relevant. **5** (*usu* + for/to) to make a formal request for something.
**appoint** *v* **1** to select for an office or position. **2** *formal* to decide on (a time) officially.
**appointment** *n* **1** an act of appointing. **2** an office or position to which somebody is appointed. **3** an arrangement for a meeting or other engagement.
**apportion** *v* **1** to divide or distribute. **2** to assign (blame). ➤ **apportionment** *n.*
**apposite** *adj* appropriate or apt.
**appraisal** *n* an act of appraising, e.g. a valuation of property or an assessment of an employee's performance.
**appraise** *v* **1** to evaluate the worth or status of. **2** to make a valuation of (property).

***Usage Note:*** Do not confuse this word with *apprise.*

**appreciable** *adj* large enough to notice; substantial. ➤ **appreciably** *adv.*
**appreciate** *v* **1** to recognize the value or importance of. **2** to esteem. **3** to realize or be aware of. **4** to increase in value.
**appreciation** *n* **1** recognition of the value of something. **2** admiration, approval, or gratitude. **3** an increase in value. **4** a favourable critical assessment.
**appreciative** *adj* showing appreciation; pleased or grateful. ➤ **appreciatively** *adv.*
**apprehend** *v* **1** to arrest or seize (a suspect). **2** to understand or perceive.
**apprehension** *n* **1** nervous anxiety or fear. **2** understanding; comprehension. **3** the arrest of a suspect.
**apprehensive** *adj* nervously fearful or uneasy. ➤ **apprehensively** *adv.*
**apprentice**[1] *n* a person who is learning a skill or trade from an employer. ➤ **apprenticeship** *n.*
**apprentice**[2] *v* (*usu in passive*) to employ as an apprentice.
**apprise** *or* **apprize** *v formal* to inform of something.

***Usage Note:*** Do not confuse this word with *appraise.*

**approach**[1] *v* **1** to draw close to. **2** to come near to in quality or character. **3** to make an offer or request to. **4** to begin to consider or deal with.
**approach**[2] *n* **1** a means of access. **2** a manner or method of doing something. **3** (*usu in pl*) an offer or request.
**approachable** *adj* friendly and easy to talk to.
**approbation** *n* **1** approval. **2** praise or commendation.
**appropriate**[1] *v* **1** to take possession of without approval. **2** (*often* + to) to set (money) apart for a purpose. ➤ **appropriation** *n.*
**appropriate**[2] *adj* suitable or apt. ➤ **appropriately** *adv.*
**approval** *n* **1** a favourable opinion or judgment. **2** formal or official permission. * **on approval** of goods: able to be returned if unsatisfactory.

**approve** *v* **1** (*often* + of) to take a favourable view. **2** to sanction or ratify. **3** to accept as satisfactory.

**approximate**[1] *adj* **1** nearly correct or exact. **2** of a term, etc: loose; inexact. ➤ **approximately** *adv.*

**approximate**[2] *v* **1** (*often* + to) to come close in quality or character. **2** (*often* + to) to average out. ➤ **approximation** *n.*

**appurtenances** *pl noun* things needed for an activity or purpose.

**après-ski** /ˌapray'skee/ *n* social activity after a day's skiing.

**apricot** *n* an oval orange-coloured fruit with soft juicy flesh.

**April** *n* the fourth month of the year.

**a priori** *adj and adv* using reasoning from self-evident propositions.

**apron** *n* **1** a garment tied round the waist and used to protect clothing. **2** the part of a theatre stage extending in front of the curtain. **3** a paved area at an airport, used for loading and moving aircraft.

**apropos** /aprə'poh/ *prep* (*also* + of) concerning; with regard to.

**apse** *n* a projecting and rounded part of a church or other building.

**apt** *adj* **1** likely to do something. **2** suited to a purpose. **3** keenly intelligent. ➤ **aptly** *adv,* **aptness** *n.*

**aptitude** *n* **1** a natural ability or talent. **2** (*usu* + for) fitness or suitability.

**aqualung** *n* an underwater breathing apparatus.

**aquamarine** *n* **1** a bluish green gemstone. **2** a pale bluish green colour.

**aquaplane** *v* of a vehicle: to slide out of control on the surface of a wet road.

**aquarium** *n* (*pl* **aquariums** *or* **aquaria**) a glass tank filled with water for keeping fish and other sea animals.

**Aquarius** *n* the eleventh sign of the zodiac (the Water Carrier).

**aquatic** *adj* **1** growing or living in water. **2** taking place in or on water.

**aqueduct** *n* a bridge-like structure built to carry a canal across a valley.

**aqueous** *adj* resembling or containing water.

**aquiline** *adj* **1** relating to or like an eagle. **2** of the human nose: hooked.

**Ar** *abbr* the chemical symbol for argon.

**Arab** *n* a member of a Semitic people of the Middle East and North Africa. ➤ **Arab** *adj,* **Arabian** *adj.*

**arabesque** *n* **1** a ballet posture in which the dancer is supported on one leg with one arm extended forwards and the other arm and leg backwards. **2** an intricate decorative design or style with intertwining motifs. **3** an ornamental musical passage.

**Arabic** *n* the Semitic language of the Arab peoples. ➤ **Arabic** *adj.*

**Arabic numeral** *n* any of the number symbols 0, 1, 2, 3, 4, 5, 6, 7, 8, 9.

**arable** *adj* of land: used or suitable for crop farming.

**arachnid** *n* an arthropod having a body in two segments, e.g. a spider or scorpion. ➤ **arachnid** *adj.*

**arachnophobia** *n* irrational fear of spiders.

**arbiter** *n* **1** a person or agency who settles disputes. **2** a person respected for authority in a subject.

**arbitrary** *adj* **1** based on whim or random choice rather than reason. **2** of power or or rule: despotic or tyrannical. ➤ **arbitrarily** *adv.*

**arbitrate** *v* **1** to act as an arbitrator. **2** to submit for decision to an arbitrator.

**arbitrator** *n* a person or group chosen to settle a dispute.

**arboreal** *adj* inhabiting or relating to trees.

**arboretum** *n* (*pl* **arboretums** *or* **arboreta**) a place where trees and shrubs are cultivated for study and display.

**arbour** (*NAmer* **arbor**) *n* a garden alcove formed by climbing plants or branches. ➤ **arboured** *adj.*

**arc**[1] *n* **1** a continuous portion of a curve. **2** the apparent path followed by a planet or other celestial body. **3** a luminous discharge of electricity across a gap in a circuit.

**arc**[2] *v* (**arced, arcing**) to form or move in an arc.

**arcade** *n* **1** a passageway or covered walk with shops on both sides. **2** a series of arches with their columns or piers.

**Arcadian** *adj* ideally quiet and rural; idyllic.

**arcane** *adj* secret and esoteric.

**arch**[1] *n* **1** a curved structure spanning an opening or supporting a structure. **2** the inner bony structure of the foot.

**arch**[2] *v* to form or bend into an arch.

**arch**[3] *adj* consciously or playfully sly or teasing. ➤ **archly** *adv,* **archness** *n.*

**archaeology** (*NAmer* **archeology**) *n* the study of the material remains of past human life and activities. ➤ **archaeological** *adj,* **archaeologist** *n.*

**archaeopteryx** *n* the oldest fossil bird, with the wings and feathers of a bird and the teeth and tail of a dinosaur.

**archaic** *adj* **1** old or antiquated. **2** belonging to an earlier time. ➤ **archaism** *n.*

**archangel** *n* a chief or principal angel.

**archbishop** *n* a bishop of the highest rank.

**archdeacon** *n* a senior member of the clergy with administrative functions.

**archer** *n* a person who shoots with a bow and arrows. ➤ **archery** *n.*

**archetype** *n* **1** an original pattern or model. **2** a perfect example. ➤ **archetypal** *adj.*

**archipelago** *n* (*pl* **-os** *or* **-oes**) a group of scattered islands.
**architect** *n* **1** a person who designs buildings. **2** a person who originates an idea or plan.
**architecture** *n* **1** the designing and erecting of buildings. **2** the design and structure of anything. ➤ **architectural** *adj.*
**architrave** *n* **1** in classical architecture, a beam resting on the capitals of the columns. **2** the frame round a a door or window.
**archive**[1] *n* a collection of historical documents and records. ➤ **archival** *adj.*
**archive**[2] *v* to collect in an archive.
**archivist** *n* a person who organizes archives.
**archway** *n* an arch with a passage or entrance beneath it.
**Arctic** *adj* relating to the North Pole or the surrounding region.
**ardent** *adj* eager or zealous. ➤ **ardently** *adv.*
**ardour** (*NAmer* **ardor**) *n* **1** intense or passionate feelings, **2** great enthusiasm.
**arduous** *adj* difficult or strenuous. ➤ **arduously** *adv.*
**are**[1] *v* second person sing. present or pl present of BE.
**are**[2] *n* a metric unit of area equal to $100m^2$.
**area** *n* **1** the extent of a surface measured in square units. **2** a piece of ground. **3** a particular space or surface. **4** a range of activity.
**arena** *n* **1** an enclosed area used for public entertainment. **2** a sphere of interest or activity.
**aren't** *contraction* **1** are not. **2** used in questions: am not.
**areola** *n* (*pl* **areolae**) a coloured ring round a nipple.
**argon** *n* a gaseous chemical element used in vacuum tubes and electric light bulbs.
**argot** *n* the jargon or slang of a particular group.
**arguable** *adj* able to be argued or disputed. ➤ **arguably** *adv.*
**argue** *v* (**argues, argued, arguing**) **1** to disagree in words; to bicker or quarrel. **2** to give reasons for or against something. ✱ **argue the toss** to dispute a settled decision. ➤ **arguer** *n.*
**argument** *n* **1** a quarrel or disagreement. **2** the act or process of arguing; debate. **3** a coherent reason or series of reasons offered as proof.
**argumentative** *adj* tending or liking to argue.
**aria** *n* (*pl* **arias**) an accompanied melody sung by one voice.
**arid** *adj* **1** of land: excessively dry from lack of rainfall. **2** dull or unproductive. ➤ **aridity** *n.*
**Aries** *n* the first sign of the zodiac (the Ram).
**arise** *v* (**arose, arisen**) **1** to originate from a source. **2** (*often* + from) to come into being or to the attention.
**aristocracy** *n* (*pl* **-ies**) hereditary nobility ranking socially above the ordinary or common people and below royalty.
**arithmetic** *n* a branch of mathematics dealing with real numbers and calculations. ➤ **arithmetical** *adj.*
**ark** *n* **1** in the Bible, the ship built by Noah to escape the Flood. **2** (**Ark/Ark of the Covenant**) the sacred chest containing the Ten Commandments. **3** (*also* **Holy Ark**) a repository for the scrolls of the Torah. ✱ **out of the ark** *informal* very antiquated.
**arm**[1] *n* **1** either of the human upper limbs extending from the shoulder to the hand. **2** a support for the forearm on a chair. **3** an inlet of water from the sea. **4** a division of a group or activity. ✱ **with open arms** with welcoming enthusiasm.
**arm**[2] *v* **1** to supply with weapons. **2** to provide with something that strengthens or protects. **3** to activate the fuse of (a bomb).
**armada** *n* (*pl* **armadas**) a fleet of warships.
**armadillo** *n* (*pl* **-os**) a burrowing South American mammal with a body and head encased in bony plates.
**Armageddon** *n* **1** the final battle between good and evil in the New Testament. **2** a vast decisive conflict.
**armament** *n* **1** (*often in pl*) the arms and equipment of a nation or military force. **2** preparation for war.
**armature** *n* **1** the central rotating part of an electric motor or generator. **2** a bar of iron placed across the poles of a magnet to close the circuit.
**armchair** *n* an upholstered chair with armrests.
**armed** *adj* having or using a gun.
**armed forces** *pl n* the army, navy and air force of a country.
**armistice** *n* a suspension of hostilities.
**armorial** *adj* relating to or bearing heraldic arms.
**armour** (*NAmer* **armor**) *n* **1** a covering of metal or chain mail worn by medieval soldiers in combat. **2** a protective covering for a military ship or aircraft. **3** armoured forces and vehicles.
**armourer** (*NAmer* **armorer**) *n* a person who repairs, assembles, and tests weapons or armour.
**armoury** (*NAmer* **armory**) *n* (*pl* **-ies**) a store of arms and military equipment.
**armpit** *n* the hollow between the arm and shoulder.
**arms** *pl noun* **1** weapons, *esp* guns. **2** a set of heraldic insignia. ✱ **up in arms** protesting strongly.
**army** *n* (*pl* **-ies**) **1** a large organized force for fighting on land. **2** a large crowd or group.
**aroma** *n* a pleasant smell. ➤ **aromatic** *adj.*
**aromatherapy** *n* the use of natural oils to relieve symptoms, promote healing, and reduce tension. ➤ **aromatherapist** *n.*
**arose** *v* past tense of ARISE.

**around**[1] *adv* **1** in the vicinity. **2** in various directions; to and fro. **3** approximately. **4** so as to face the opposite way. **5** so as to move in a circle.

**around**[2] *prep* **1** here and there in (a place). **2** so as to encircle.

**arouse** *v* **1** to stimulate (a feeling or response). **2** to rouse to action. **3** to excite sexually. **4** to awaken from sleep. ➤ ***arousal*** *n.*

**arpeggio** *n* (*pl* **-os**) a chord with notes that are played in quick succession.

**arraign** *v* to charge formally with an offence in a court of law. ➤ ***arraignment*** *n.*

**arrange** *v* **1** to put in order or into sequence. **2** to make preparations for. **3** to adapt (music) for different voices or instruments. ➤ ***arranger*** *n.*

**arrangement** *n* **1** a preparation or plan. **2** an informal agreement or settlement. **3** something made by arranging parts together. **4** a musical adaptation.

**arrant** *adj* complete; utter.

**array**[1] *v* **1** to set or place in order. **2** to dress or decorate impressively.

**array**[2] *n* **1** an imposing collection or large number. **2** an orderly arrangement.

**arrears** *pl n* an unpaid or overdue debt. * **in arrears 1** behind in the payment of a debt. **2** of rent or wages: paid at the end of each period.

**arrest**[1] *v* **1** to seize and keep in custody by legal authority. **2** to bring to a stop or make inactive.

**arrest**[2] *n* **1** the act of arresting somebody. **2** a sudden stopping.

**arresting** *adj* catching the attention; striking. ➤ ***arrestingly*** *adv.*

**arrival** *n* **1** the act or time of arriving. **2** somebody or something that has arrived.

**arrive** *v* **1** to reach a destination. **2** to come. **3** to achieve success. * **arrive at** to reach by effort or thought.

**arrogant** *adj* having or showing a feeling of superiority over others. ➤ ***arrogance*** *n,* ***arrogantly*** *adv.*

**arrogate** *v* to claim or take without justification. ➤ ***arrogation*** *n.*

**arrow** *n* **1** a slender pointed shaft with feathers at the end, shot from a bow. **2** a symbol shaped like an arrow, showing direction.

**arrowroot** *n* a starch obtained from a tropical plant, used as a thickening agent in cooking.

**arse** *n Brit, coarse slang* the buttocks or anus.

**arsenal** *n* a store of weapons and ammunition.

**arsenic** *n* a grey element that forms many poisonous compounds.

**arson** *n* the criminal act of intentionally setting fire to property. ➤ ***arsonist*** *n.*

**art**[1] *n* **1** the use of skill and creative imagination in producing visual representations. **2** paintings, sculptures, and other works produced by creative imagination. **3** an activity which requires imagination as well as practical knowledge. **4** (**the Arts**) the humanities as contrasted with science.

**art**[2] *v archaic* second person sing. present of BE.

**artefact** *or* **artifact** *n* a tool or other useful object made by human effort.

**artery** *n* (*pl* **-ies**) **1** any of the vessels that carry blood from the heart to the lungs and through the body. **2** a road or other important channel of communication.

**artesian well** *n* a well in which the water reaches the surface under its own pressure.

**artful** *adj* cunningly or deceitfully clever. ➤ ***artfully*** *adv.*

**arthritis** *n* inflammation and stiffness of the joints.

**arthropod** *n* an animal with a jointed body and limbs, such as an insect, spider, or crab.

**artichoke** *n* (*also* **globe artichoke**) the flower head of a tall thistle-like plant, used as a vegetable.

**article**[1] *n* **1** a particular or separate object. **2** a distinct piece of non-fictional writing in a magazine or newspaper. **3** a separate item in a document. **4** (*in pl*) a period of professional work with a firm undertaken by a trainee. **5** *a, an,* and *the,* used with nouns. * **article of faith** a strongly held belief.

**article**[2] *v* to employ as an apprentice.

**articulate**[1] *adj* **1** expressing oneself clearly. **2** clearly expressed. **3** having joints. ➤ ***articulacy*** *n,* ***articulately*** *adv.*

**articulate**[2] *v* **1** to say (words) or express (an idea) clearly. **2** to join (a body part) with a joint. **3** of bones: to fit together to form a joint. ➤ ***articulation*** *n.*

**artifact** *n* see ARTEFACT.

**artifice** *n* **1** an artful device or scheme. **2** clever or artful skill.

**artificer** *n* a skilled or artistic worker or designer.

**artificial** *adj* **1** made by human skill and labour imitating what is natural. **2** affected or insincere. ➤ ***artificiality*** *n,* ***artificially*** *adv.*

**artificial intelligence** *n* a capacity of computers or programs to emulate human behaviour or understanding.

**artificial respiration** *n* the forcing of air into and out of the lungs of somebody whose breathing has stopped.

**artillery** *n* (*pl* **-ies**) **1** heavy weapons used in land warfare. **2** a branch of an army using artillery.

**artisan** *n* a skilled manual worker.

**artist** *n* **1** a person who practises an imaginative art such as painting or sculpture. **2** a skilled performer.

**artiste** /ah'teest/ *n* a professional public entertainer.

**artistic** *adj* **1** showing creative skill. **2** characteristic of art or artists. ➤ ***artistically*** *adv.*

**artistry** *n* artistic quality or ability.

**artless** *adj* **1** sincere or natural. **2** free from deceit or artifice. ➤ **artlessly** *adv.*
**artwork** *n* the pictures and illustrations in a publication.
**arty** *adj* (**-ier, -iest**) showily or pretentiously artistic. ➤ **artily** *n.*
**Aryan** *n* **1** a member of an ancient people who appeared as invaders in North India in the second millennium BC. **2** in Nazi ideology, a white non-Jewish person of European origin. ➤ **Aryan** *adj.*
**As** *abbr* the chemical symbol for arsenic.
**as**[1] *adv* to the same degree or amount; equally; so.
**as**[2] *conj* **1** used in comparisons, often in pairs. **2** used to give a reason. **3** in accordance with. **4** while.
**as**[3] *prep* **1** in the capacity of. **2** used with certain verbs of regarding and describing.
**a.s.a.p.** *abbr* as soon as possible.
**asbestos** *n* a mineral of thin fibres, used to make non-combustible or chemically resistant materials.
**ascend** *v* **1** to move or slope upwards. **2** to rise from a lower level or degree.
**ascendant** *or* **ascendent** *adj* **1** rising. **2** superior or dominant. ➤ **ascendancy** *n.*
**ascension** *n* **1** the act of rising in position or degree. **2** (**Ascension**) in Christianity, Christ's ascent to heaven after the Resurrection.
**ascent** *n* **1** the act of going up. **2** a way up. **3** an advance in status.
**ascertain** *v* to find out or learn. ➤ **ascertainable** *adj.*
**ascetic** *or* **ascetical** *adj* **1** practising strict self-denial. **2** austere in appearance or manner. ➤ **asceticism** *n.*
**ascorbic acid** *n* a compound occurring in citrus fruits and green vegetables and essential for healthy connective tissue.
**ascribe** *v* to refer or attribute to a cause or source. ➤ **ascription** *n.*
**aseptic** *adj* **1** preventing infection. **2** free from micro-organisms.
**asexual** *adj* **1** having no sex or sex organs. **2** lacking sexual interest. ➤ **asexually** *adv.*
**ash**[1] *n* a tall tree of the olive family with tough elastic wood.
**ash**[2] *n* **1** the solid residue left when material has been burned. **2** (*in pl*) the remains of a dead body after cremation.
**ashamed** *adj* feeling shame or guilt.
**ashen** *adj* deadly pale from fear or shock.
**ashore** *adv* on or to the shore.
**ashram** *n* a Hindu religious retreat or sanctuary.
**Asian** *adj* relating to Asia or its people. ➤ **Asian** *n.*
**Asiatic** *adj* relating to Asia.
**aside**[1] *adv and adj* **1** to or towards the side. **2** out of the way. **3** in reserve for future use.
**aside**[2] *n* **1** an actor's speech supposedly not heard by other characters on stage. **2** a digression or incidental remark.
**asinine** *adj* extremely foolish or stupid.
**ask** *v* **1** to say something that calls for an answer. **2** to make a request of. **3** to provoke (an unpleasant consequence). **4** to invite. **5** (*often* + for) to make a request about or seek information from. **6** (+ after) to enquire about somebody's welfare.
**askance** ✱ **look askance at** to regard with disapproval or distrust.
**askew** *adv and adj* out of line; awry.
**aslant** *prep, adv, and adj* in a slanting direction.
**asleep** *adj* **1** in a state of sleep. **2** of a limb: numb.
**asp** *n* a small viper with an upturned snout.
**asparagus** *n* a spike-shaped shoot of a tall plant, used as a vegetable.
**aspect** *n* **1** a particular feature of a situation or plan. **2** appearance to the eye or mind. **3** the side of a building facing a particular direction.
**aspen** *n* a poplar with fluttering leaves.
**asperity** *n* (*pl* **-ies**) **1** roughness of manner. **2** unevenness.
**aspersion** *n* ✱ **cast aspersions on** to attack the reputation of.
**asphalt** *n* **1** a black substance like tar, **2** a composition from asphalt used for surfacing roads.

***Usage Note:*** Note the spelling with *as-* not *ash-*.

**asphyxia** *n* a lack of oxygen in the body resulting in unconsciousness or death.
**asphyxiate** *v* to make unconscious or kill by depriving of oxygen. ➤ **asphyxiation** *n.*
**aspic** *n* a savoury jelly of fish or meat stock.
**aspidistra** *n* a plant of the lily family with large leaves.
**aspirant** *n* somebody seeking to achieve an objective.
**aspirate**[1] /'aspirayt/ *v* **1** to pronounce (a vowel, consonant, or word) with a forceful exhalation of breath. **2** to draw or remove (e.g. blood) by suction. **3** *technical* to inhale.
**aspirate**[2] /'aspirət/ *n* **1** an independent /h/ sound, or the character representing this sound. **2** an aspirated consonant, e.g. the *p* of *pit.*
**aspiration** *n* a strong desire or ambition. ➤ **aspirational** *adj.*
**aspire** *v* (*usu* + to) to seek to achieve a particular objective.
**aspirin** *n* (*pl* **aspirin** *or* **aspirins**) a compound (acetylsalicylic acid) used in the form of a tablet to relieve pain and reduce fever.
**ass**[1] *n* **1** a long-eared hardy mammal related to and smaller than the horse. **2** a stupid or obstinate person.
**ass**[2] *n chiefly NAmer* = ARSE.

**assail** *v* **1** to attack violently with blows or words. **2** of a feeling: to prey on.
**assailant** *n* an attacker.
**assassin** *n* a murderer of a political or religious leader.
**assassinate** *v* to murder (a political or religious leader). ➤ **assassination** *n.*
**assault**[1] *n* **1** a violent attack. **2** an attempt to attack a fortified position.
**assault**[2] *v* to make an assault on.
**assault course** *n* an obstacle course for training soldiers.
**assay**[1] *n* analysis of an ore or drug, etc to determine its purity.
**assay**[2] *v* to analyse (an ore) for its purity.
**assemblage** *n* **1** a collection or gathering. **2** a three-dimensional collage.
**assemble** *v* **1** to come or bring together. **2** to fit together the parts of (a kit or model).
**assembly** *n* (*pl* **-ies**) **1** a group of people gathered together. **2** a legislative or deliberative body. **3** the fitting together of parts.
**assembly line** *n* a sequence of machines for assembling a product.
**assent**[1] *v* to agree to something.
**assent**[2] *n* formal agreement or approval.
**assert** *v* **1** to state or declare formally. **2** to demonstrate (a quality or attribute). **3** to insist on (a right or claim). ✱ **assert oneself** to compel recognition of one's rights.
**assertion** *n* a declaration or positive statement.
**assertive** *adj* self-confident and firm in dealing with others. ➤ **assertively** *adv,* **assertiveness** *n.*
**assess** *v* **1** to determine the rate or amount of. **2** to estimate the quality or worth of. ➤ **assessment** *n,* **assessor** *n.*
**asset** *n* **1** (*in pl*) the total property of a person or company. **2** a single item of property. **3** an advantage or resource.
**assiduity** *n* persistent application or diligence.
**assiduous** *adj* showing careful attention or application. ➤ **assiduously** *adv.*
**assign** *v* **1** to allot (something) to somebody. **2** to appoint to a particular role or task. **3** to transfer (property) to another person. **4** to ascribe as a motive or reason.
**assignation** *n* a secret meeting with a lover.
**assignment** *n* a specified task or amount of work assigned to somebody.
**assimilate** *v* **1** to take in or absorb (a substance). **2** to absorb and understand (information). **3** to make (one thing) similar to another. **4** to absorb (people or pinciples) into a different culture. ➤ **assimilation** *n.*
**assist** *v* to help (somebody).
**assistance** *n* help or support.
**assistant** *n* a person whose job is to help somebody.
**assize** *n* (*usu in pl*) a civil and criminal court formerly held in each English and Welsh county.
**associate**[1] *v* **1** to involve (a person or group) with another more powerful one. **2** to connect (somebody or something) mentally with a particular thing, quality, or feeling. **3** (*often* + with) to mix socially.
**associate**[2] *adj* **1** sharing a function or office with another. **2** having subordinate status.
**associate**[3] *n* **1** a fellow worker or colleague. **2** a person admitted to a subordinate degree of membership.
**association** *n* **1** an organization of people having a common interest. **2** a mental connection between sensations or ideas.
**Association Football** *n* football played with a round ball by teams of eleven players.
**assonance** *n* repetition of the vowel sounds in two or more words as an alternative to rhyme.
**assorted** *adj* consisting of various kinds.
**assortment** *n* a mixed collection of various kinds.
**assuage** *v* **1** to ease or lessen the intensity of (suffering or discomfort). **2** to relieve or satisfy (thirst or desire).
**assume** *v* **1** to take (something) as granted or true without proof. **2** to take on (a role or duty). **3** to pretend to have (a feeling or attitude). **4** to adopt (a new name or identity).
**assumption** *n* **1** a supposition that something is true. **2** a fact or statement taken for granted. **3** the act of laying claim to or taking possession of something. **4** (**Assumption**) the taking up of the Virgin Mary into heaven, celebrated by Christians on 15 August.
**assurance** *n* **1** a declaration that something is true. **2** freedom from doubt. **3** confidence of mind or manner. **4** *chiefly Brit* life insurance.
**assure** *v* **1** to inform positively that something is true. **2** to give confidence to. **3** to ensure. **4** to protect with life insurance.
**assured** *adj* **1** self-confident and sure of one's competence. **2** certain; guaranteed. ➤ **assuredly** *adv.*
**asterisk** *n* the sign (*) used as a reference mark.
**astern** *adv* behind or towards the rear of a ship or aircraft.
**asteroid** *n* a small rocky planet between Mars and Jupiter.
**asthma** *n* an allergic condition with laboured breathing and chest constriction. ➤ **asthmatic** *adj and n.*
**astigmatism** *n* a defect of the eye resulting in blurring of the image. ➤ **astigmatic** *adj.*
**astir** *adj* **1** in a state of bustle or excitement. **2** out of bed.
**astonish** *v* to affect with sudden wonder or surprise. ➤ **astonishment** *n.*
**astound** *v* to affect with bewilderment and wonder.

**astrakhan** /astrə'kan/ *n* **1** a woollen fabric with curled and looped pile. **2** wool of Russian origin.
**astral** *adj* relating to or consisting of stars.
**astray** *adv* **1** off the right path or route. **2** in error.
**astride**[1] *adv* with the legs wide apart.
**astride**[2] *prep* **1** with one leg on each side of. **2** extending over or across.
**astringent** *adj* **1** causing the soft tissues of the body to contract. **2** dry or caustic. ➤ **astringency** *n.*
**astrolabe** *n* an instrument formerly used to show the positions of the planets and stars.
**astrology** *n* the study of the supposed influences of the planets and their motions on human affairs. ➤ **astrologer** *n,* **astrological** *adj.*
**astronaut** *n* a person trained to travel in space.
**astronomical** *or* **astronomic** *adj* **1** relating to astronomy. **2** *informal* extremely large. ➤ **astronomically** *adv.*
**astronomy** *n* the scientific study of the stars, planets, and universe. ➤ **astronomer** *n.*
**astrophysics** *pl n* the scientific study of the physical nature of astronomical bodies and phenomena. ➤ **astrophysicist** *n.*
**astute** *adj* shrewd and perceptive. ➤ **astutely** *adv,* **astuteness** *n.*
**asunder** *adv literary* into parts or pieces.
**asylum** *n* **1** protection from arrest or danger. **2** a place of retreat and security. **3** *dated* an institution for the care of the mentally ill.
**asymmetric** *or* **asymmetrical** *adj* not symmetrical. ➤ **asymmetric** *adj,* **asymmetry** *n.*
**At** *abbr* the chemical symbol for astatine.
**at** *prep used to indicate:* **1** position in or movement towards a place. **2** time. **3** a rate or value. **4** the object of an action. **5** a state.
**atavistic** *adj* relating to or typical of ancestors.
**ate** *v* past tense of EAT.
**atheism** *n* the belief or doctrine that there is no God. ➤ **atheist** *n,* **atheistic** *adj adv.*
**athlete** *n* a person who is trained or skilled in exercises and sports, *esp* in athletics.
**athlete's foot** *n* a form of fungal infection of the feet affecting the skin between the toes.
**athletic** *adj* **1** relating to athletes or athletics. **2** vigorous or active. **3** muscular and well-proportioned. ➤ **athletically** *adv,* **athleticism** *n.*
**athletics** *pl n* the sport of running and other track and field events.
**athwart** *prep* across.
**-ation** *suffix* denoting an action or process.
**Atlantic** *adj* of or near the Atlantic Ocean.
**atlas** *n* a book of maps or charts.
**atmosphere** *n* **1** the gas enveloping the earth or other celestial body. **2** the air or climate of a locality. **3** a surrounding feeling or mood encountered in some environment. **4** a unit of pressure equal to the typical pressure of the air at sea level.
**atmospheric** *adj* **1** relating to the atmosphere of the earth. **2** having a strong aesthetic or emotional atmosphere. ➤ **atmospherically** *adv.*
**atmospherics** *pl n* lightning and other atmospheric phenomena that cause radio interference.
**atoll** *n* a coral reef surrounding a lagoon.
**atom** *n* **1** the smallest particle of an element that can exist. **2** a tiny particle; a bit.
**atom bomb** *or* **atomic bomb** *n* a bomb whose violent explosive power is due to the sudden release of atomic energy derived from the splitting of the nuclei of plutonium, uranium, etc by neutrons in a very rapid chain reaction.
**atomic** *adj* **1** relating to atoms, atom bombs, or atomic energy. **2** existing as separate atoms.
**atomize** *or* **-ise** *v* to reduce to minute particles or a fine spray.
**atonal** *adj* of music: not written in a particular key and using the notes of the chromatic scale impartially. ➤ **atonality** *n.*
**atone** *v* to make amends for a crime or wrong.
**atrium** *n* (*pl* **atria** *or* **atriums**) **1** an inner courtyard open to the sky or with a glazed roof. **2** either of the two upper chambers of the heart.
**atrocious** *adj* **1** extremely wicked or cruel. **2** *informal* very horrible or bad. ➤ **atrociously** *adv.*
**atrocity** *n* (*pl* **-ies**) **1** a wicked or cruel act. **2** *informal* something ugly; an eyesore.
**atrophy**[1] *n* (*pl* **-ies**) a wasting away or progressive decline of something. ➤ **atrophic** *adj.*
**atrophy**[2] *v* (**-ies, -ied**) to waste away or degenerate.
**attach** *v* **1** to join or fasten. **2** to ascribe or attribute. **3** to appoint (a person) to serve with an organization.

***Usage Note:*** Note the spelling with *-ach* not *-atch.*

**attaché** /ə'tashay/ *n* a technical expert on a diplomatic staff.
**attaché case** *n* a slim case used for carrying papers.
**attachment** *n* **1** the process of attaching. **2** a device for attaching to a machine or implement. **3** fondness or fidelity. **4** computer data sent with an email message.
**attack**[1] *v* **1** to try to hurt or injure. **2** to take the initiative against (an opponent or opposing team). **3** to criticize in a hostile way. **4** to have a harmful effect on. **5** to begin (a task) vigorously. ➤ **attacker** *n.*
**attack**[2] *n* **1** the act of attacking; an assault. **2** an act of attacking. **3** an onset of sickness or disease.
**attain** *v* **1** to achieve (an objective). **2** *formal* to reach (a certain age). ➤ **attainable** *adj.*
**attainment** *n* something achieved.

**attar** *n* a fragrant perfume obtained from rose petals.
**attempt**[1] *v* to make an effort to accomplish (something).
**attempt**[2] *n* an instance of attempting something.
**attend** *v* **1** to go to or be present at. **2** to look after or tend to. **3** to accompany in a formal role. **4** (+ to) to deal with a task or problem. **5** (*often* + to) to pay attention to what is being said or done. **6** (+ on) to result from something.
**attendance** *n* **1** the number of people present. **2** the number of times a person attends something.
**attendant**[1] *adj formal* (*often* + on/upon) accompanying or following.
**attendant**[2] *n* a person who performs a service for another.
**attention** *n* **1** application of the mind to an object of sense or thought. **2** (*usu in pl*) an act of civility or courtesy. **3** sympathetic consideration of the needs of others. **4** a formal position of readiness assumed by a soldier.
**attentive** *adj* **1** paying close attention. **2** concerned for the welfare of another. ➤ **attentively** *adv.*
**attenuate** *v* **1** to weaken or lessen the force of. **2** to make thinner. ➤ **attenuation** *n.*
**attest** *v* **1** to be proof of or bear witness to. **2** to affirm the truth or existence of. ➤ **attestation** *n.*
**attic** *n* a room or space in the roof of a building.
**attire**[1] *n formal* dress or clothing of a particular kind.
**attire**[2] *v formal* (*usu in passive*) to dress in a particular way.
**attitude** *n* **1** a way of regarding or thinking about a topic, person, etc. **2** a posture. **3** *informal* a confrontational or deliberately challenging manner.
**attitudinize** *or* **-ise** *v* to assume an affected mental attitude.
**attorney** *n* (*pl* **-eys**) **1** a person who has legal authority to act for another. **2** *NAmer* a lawyer.
**attract** *v* **1** to fascinate or arouse the affection or interest of. **2** to have the power to draw (things) towards itself. **3** to become the focus of (attention). **4** to be liable for (an obligation).
**attraction** *n* **1** an attractive quality or aspect. **2** the ability to draw a response. **3** something that draws visitors or spectators. **4** the power of attracting. **5** personal charm.
**attractive** *adj* **1** good-looking or sexually interesting. **2** arousing interest or pleasure. ➤ **attractively** *adv,* **attractiveness** *n.*
**attribute**[1] *n* a characteristic or quality.
**attribute**[2] *v* **1** to credit a person or group with (something). **2** (+ to) to put (a happening, etc) down to a particular cause. ➤ **attributable** *adj,* **attribution** *n.*
**attrition** *n* the process of weakening or exhausting an opponent by constant harassment. ➤ **attritional** *adj.*
**attune** *v* **1** to cause or allow (people or their bodies) to become accustomed to new circumstances. **2** (*often* + to) to train (the ear) to respond to certain sounds.
**atypical** *adj* not typical.
**Au** *abbr* the chemical symbol for gold.
**aubergine** *n* a large purple fruit used as a vegetable.
**auburn** *n* a reddish brown colour.
**auction**[1] *n* a public sale in which each item is sold to the buyer offering the highest bid.
**auction**[2] *v* to sell (property) at an auction.
**auctioneer** *n* an official who conducts an auction.
**audacious** *adj* **1** boldly daring. **2** insolent or presumptuous. ➤ **audaciously** *adv,* **audacity** *n.*
**audible** *adj* loud enough to be heard. ➤ **audibility** *n,* **audibly** *adv.*
**audience** *n* **1** a group of listeners or spectators at a theatre or concert or at a lecture. **2** a formal hearing or interview.
**audit**[1] *n* an official examination of company accounts.
**audit**[2] *v* (**audited, auditing**) to perform an audit on (accounts, etc).
**audition**[1] *n* a trial performance to assess the ability of a candidate for joining an orchestra, choir, etc.
**audition**[2] *v* to test (a performer) for a part.
**auditorium** *n* (*pl* **auditoria** *or* **auditoriums**) the part of a theatre or concert hall where the audience sits.
**auditory** *adj* relating to hearing or the ear.
**au fait** /oh'fay/ *adj* fully informed about or familiar with.
**auger** *n* a tool for boring holes.
**aught** *pron archaic* anything at all.
**augment** *v* to make or become greater or more numerous. ➤ **augmentation** *n.*
**augur** *v* to be a sign of (a future state or event).
**augury** *n* (*pl* **-ies**) an omen or portent.
**August** *n* the eighth month of the year.
**august** *adj* marked by dignity or grandeur.
**auk** *n* a diving seabird with a short neck and black-and-white plumage.
**aunt** *n* the sister of one's father or mother, or the wife of one's uncle.
**au pair** /oh 'peə/ *n* a young foreign woman who does domestic work for a family in return for accommodation.
**aura** *n* a distinctive atmosphere surrounding a person or place.
**aural** *adj* relating to the ear or hearing. ➤ **aurally** *adv.*
**aureole** *n* a circle of light surrounding the sun or moon when seen through thin cloud.
**au revoir** /oh rə'vwah/ *interj* goodbye.

**aurora borealis** *n* streamers of light sometimes seen in the sky over the North Pole.

**auspice** *n archaic* a favourable sign. * **under the auspices of** under the patronage or guidance of.

**auspicious** *adj* being a sign of likely success. ➤ **auspiciously** *adv.*

**Aussie** *n informal* an Australian.

**austere** *adj* **1** stern and forbidding in appearance and manner. **2** plain or simple. ➤ **austerely** *adv,* **austerity** *n.*

**Australian** *n* a native or inhabitant of Australia. ➤ **Australian** *adj.*

**authentic** *adj* know to be genuine or trustworthy. ➤ **authentically** *adv,* **authenticity** *n.*

**authenticate** *v* **1** to prove or declare to be genuine. **2** to corroborate (a story) independently. ➤ **authentication** *n.*

**author** *n* **1** the writer of a book or article. **2** the source or inventor of something. ➤ **authorship** *n.*

**authoritarian**[1] *adj* **1** enforcing strict obedience; **2** dictatorial.

**authoritarian**[2] *n* an authoritarian person.

**authoritative** *adj* **1** depending on good authority; definitive or reliable. **2** commanding respect and obedience. ➤ **authoritatively** *adv.*

**authority** *n* (*pl* **-ies**) **1** the power to issue orders and expect obedience. **2** (**the authorities**) people in command; the government or law-enforcers. **3** a government body that administers a public service or enterprise. **4** an individual or book regarded as an expert.

**authorize** *or* **-ise** *v* **1** to give (a person or body) powers to act in a certain way. **2** to allow (a proceeding or activity). ➤ **authorization** *n.*

**autism** *n* a mental disorder marked by acute difficulty in forming relations with other people. ➤ **autistic** *adj and n.*

**autobiography** *n* (*pl* **-ies**) an account of one's life written by oneself. ➤ **autobiographical** *adj.*

**autocracy** *n* (*pl* **-ies**) government by a single ruler with total power.

**autocrat** *n* **1** a person who rules with total power. **2** a dictatorial person. ➤ **autocratic** *adj,* **autocratically** *adv.*

**autograph**[1] *n* **1** a celebrity's handwritten signature as a memento. **2** an original manuscript or work of art.

**autograph**[2] *v* to write an autograph on.

**automate** *v* to convert (a machine or system) to automatic operation.

**automatic** *adj* **1** acting or done spontaneously or unconsciously. **2** resembling an automaton; mechanical. **3** able to operate without human intervention. **4** of a gun: able to fire repeatedly from a round of ammunition. **5** happening or implemented as a matter of course. ➤ **automatically** *adv.*

**automatic pilot** *n* a device for steering a ship or aircraft without human control.

**automaton** *n* (*pl* **automatons** *or* **automata**) **1** a robot. **2** a mechanism designed to respond to encoded instructions.

**automobile** *n chiefly NAmer* a motor car.

**automotive** *adj* relating to motor vehicles.

**autonomous** *adj* self-governing; independent. ➤ **autonomously** *adv.*

**autonomy** *n* (*pl* **-ies**) **1** self-government. **2** freedom to act independently.

**autopsy** *n* (*pl* **-ies**) a postmortem examination.

**autumn** *n chiefly Brit* the season between summer and winter. ➤ **autumnal** *adj.*

**auxiliary**[1] *adj* **1** subsidiary. **2** kept in reserve; extra.

**auxiliary**[2] *n* (*pl* **-ies**) a person, group, or device that is extra or kept in reserve.

**avail**[1] *v* **1** to help or benefit. **2** to be of use or advantage. * **avail oneself of** to make use of or take advantage of.

**avail**[2] *n* benefit; use. * **of little/no avail** in vain useless.

**available** *adj* **1** present or ready for use. **2** obtainable. ➤ **availability** *n.*

**avalanche** *n* **1** a mass of snow or ice falling rapidly down a mountain. **2** a sudden overwhelming rush.

**avant-garde** *adj* daringly modern or innovative.

**avarice** *n* extreme desire for wealth or gain. ➤ **avaricious** *adj.*

**avenge** *v* **1** to take vengeance on behalf of. **2** to exact satisfaction for (a wrong). ➤ **avenger** *n.*

**avenue** *n* **1** a broad street or road, *esp* one bordered by trees. **2** a way of doing something or making progress.

**aver** *v* (**averred, averring**) *formal* to declare positively.

**average**[1] *n* **1** a value obtained by adding several values together and dividing by the number of them. **2** a level typical of a group.

**average**[2] *adj* **1** in arithmetic and geometry, equalling a mean. **2** midway between extremes. **3** common or typical.

**average**[3] *v* to have (an amount) as an average.

**averse** *adj* (*usu* + to) strongly opposed to or disliking.

***Usage Note:*** Do not confuse this word with *adverse.*

**aversion** *n* a strong dislike or antipathy.

**avert** *v* **1** to turn away (the eyes). **2** to avoid or prevent (something unwelcome).

**avian** *adj* relating to birds.

**aviary** *n* (*pl* **-ies**) an enclosure for keeping birds.

**aviation** *n* the manufacture and operation of aircraft.

**aviator** *n dated* a pilot.

**avid** *adj* very eager or keen. ➤ **avidly** *adv,* **avidness** *n.*

**avionics** *pl noun* the use of electronic equipment in aircraft. ➤ **avionic** *adj.*

**avocado** *n* (*pl* **-os** *or* **-oes**) a pear-shaped fruit with a green flesh.

**avoid** *v* **1** to keep away from or shun. **2** to prevent the occurrence of. **3** to refrain from (doing something). ➤ **avoidable** *adj,* **avoidance** *n.*

**avoirdupois** /ˌavwahdooh'pwah, ˌavədə'poyz/ *n* the series of units of weight based on a pound of 16 ounces.

**avow** *v* **1** to declare with assurance. **2** to acknowledge openly. ➤ **avowal** *n,* **avowed** *adj.*

**avuncular** *adj* kindly or genial towards somebody younger.

**await** *v* **1** to wait for. **2** to be in store for.

**awake**[1] *v* (**awoke, awoken**) **1** to come out of sleep. **2** (*usu* + to) to become aware of. **3** to arouse from sleep.

**awake**[2] *adj* **1** not asleep. **2** (*usu* + to) aware of.

**awaken** *v* **1** to wake. **2** to wake up. **3** to stir up (a feeling).

**award**[1] *v* to confer or bestow (something deserved or complimentary).

**award**[2] *n* **1** something that is conferred as an honour or reward. **2** the act of awarding something.

**aware** *adj* knowing about or conscious of something. ➤ **awareness** *n.*

**awash** *adj* covered or flooded with water.

**away**[1] *adv* **1** at a distance. **2** into a secure place. **3** out of existence. **4** constantly or without interruption.

**away**[2] *adj* of a sports fixture: played at the opponent's ground.

**awe**[1] *n* a feeling of dread and wonder.

**awe**[2] *v* to fill with awe.

**awesome** *adj* **1** inspiring awe. **2** *informal* impressive. ➤ **awesomely** *adv.*

**awful** *adj* **1** extremely unpleasant. **2** *informal* used as an intensive: *an awful headache.* **3** *archaic* inspiring awe. ➤ **awfully** *adv.*

**awhile** *adv* for a short time.

**awkward** *adj* **1** difficult to use or handle. **2** lacking dexterity; clumsy. **3** lacking social grace and assurance. **4** causing or feeling embarrassment. ➤ **awkwardly** *adv.*

**awl** *n* a pointed tool for making small holes.

**awning** *n* a canavs cover used to protect something from the weather.

**awoke** *v* past tense of AWAKE[1].

**awoken** *v* past part. of AWAKE[1].

**AWOL** *adj* absent without leave.

**awry** *adv and adj* out of the right position or course; amiss.

**axe**[1] (*NAmer* **ax**) *n* **1** a tool with a large heavy blade, used for chopping. **2** (**the axe**) a drastic reduction or removal. ✱ **have an axe to grind** to have a private purpose to pursue.

**axe**[2] (*NAmer* **ax**) *v* to cancel or dismiss abruptly.

**axiom** *n* a principle or rule generally recognized as true.

**axis** *n* (*pl* **axes**) **1** a straight line about which a body or figure can rotate. **2** a reference line in a system of coordinates. **3** (**Axis**) the alliance between Germany and Italy in World War II.

**axle** *n* a shaft on which a wheel rotates.

**ayatollah** /ie·ə'tolə/ *n* a leader of Shiite Muslims in Iran.

**aye** *or* **ay** *interj archaic or dialect* yes.

**azalea** *n* a rhododendron with bright flowers.

**azimuth** *n* the direction of a star in relation to the observer, measured as the angle from a point on the horizon due north or south.

**azure** *n* **1** sky blue. **2** in heraldry, blue.

**B**[1] *or* **b** *n* (*pl* **B's** *or* **Bs** *or* **b's**) the second letter of the English alphabet.

**B**[2] *abbr* the chemical symbol for boron.

**BA** *abbr* Bachelor of Arts.

**Ba** *abbr* the chemical symbol for barium.

**baa**[1] *v* (**baas, baaed** *or* **baa'd, baaing**) to make the bleat of a sheep.

**baa**[2] *n* (*pl* **baas**) the bleating sound of a sheep.

**babble**[1] *v* **1** to utter meaningless or unintelligible sounds. **2** to talk foolishly; to chatter.

**babble**[2] *n* meaningless or unintelligible sounds.

**babe** *n* **1** *chiefly literary* an infant or baby. **2** *informal* a girl or woman.

**babel** *n* a scene of noise or confusion.

**baboon** *n* a large monkey with a long doglike muzzle and a medium-length tail.

**baby**[1] *n* (*pl* **-ies**) **1** a very young child or animal, *esp* one that has recently been born. **2** (*used before a noun*) comparatively small of its type. **3** a childish or immature person. ➤ **babyhood** *n*, **babyish** *adj*.

**baby**[2] *v* (**-ies, -ied**) to treat with excessive or inappropriate care.

**babysit** *v* (**babysitting,** *past tense and past part.* **babysat**) to look after a child while the parents are out. ➤ **babysitter** *n*.

**baccalaureate** *n* a qualification in some countries to allow students to enter higher education.

**baccarat** /'bakərah/ *n* a card game in which players bet against the dealer.

**bacchanalia** *pl n* a drunken feast; an orgy. ➤ **bacchanalian** *adj*.

**bachelor** *n* **1** an unmarried man. **2** a recipient of a first degree from a university. ➤ **bachelorhood** *n*.

**bacillus** *n* (*pl* **bacilli**) a rod-shaped bacterium that causes disease.

**back**[1] *n* **1** the rear part of the human body from the neck to the end of the spine. **2** the upper part of an animal's body. **3** the side or surface behind the front or face. **4** a defensive player in a team game. ✱ **back to front** in such a way that the back and the front are reversed in position. **behind somebody's back** without a person's knowledge or permission. **get/put somebody's back up** to annoy or irritate somebody. **the back of beyond** *informal* a remote place. **turn one's back on** to reject or deny (somebody or something).

**back**[2] *adv* **1** to or at the rear. **2** in or into a reclining position. **3** in or into the past. **4** nearer the beginning. **5** to or in a place from which somebody or something came. **6** to or towards a former state. **7** in return or reply. ✱ **back and forth** backwards and forwards repeatedly.

**back**[3] *adj* **1** at or in the back. **2** distant from a central or main area; remote.

**back**[4] *v* **1** to give support to. **2** to provide a musical accompaniment for. **3** to drive (a vehicle) backwards. **4** to be at or form the back of. **5** to place a bet on (a competitor in a race). **6** of the wind: to shift anticlockwise. **7** (+ on/onto) of a building: to have its back adjacent to or closely facing. ➤ **backer** *n*.

**back-bencher** *n* an MP who does not hold a post in the government or opposition.

**backbiting** *n* mean and spiteful talk.

**backbone** *n* **1** the spine. **2** the most substantial part of something. **3** firmness of character.

**backchat** *n* *chiefly Brit* rude or impertinent remarks.

**backdate** *v* **1** to apply retrospectively. **2** to date (a document) with an earlier date than the actual date.

**backdoor** *adj* using unfair or underhand methods.

**back down** *v* to concede defeat.

**backdrop** *n* **1** a painted cloth hung at the back of a theatre stage. **2** a setting for an event.

**backfire** *v* **1** of an engine: to make a loud bang when fuel ignites prematurely. **2** to cause difficulty by having the reverse of the expected effect.

**backgammon** *n* a board game for two players played with dice and counters.

**background** *n* **1** the scenery or ground behind something. **2** the part of a painting or photograph that depicts what lies behind objects in the foreground. **3** the conditions forming a setting for an experience. **4** information that helps to explain a problem or situation. **5** a person's experience and upbringing.

**backhand** *n* a stroke in tennis, squash, etc made with the back of the hand turned in the direction of the stroke.

**backhanded** *adj* of a compliment: apparently complimentary but with an uncomplimentary edge to it.

**backhander** *n* **1** a backhanded blow or stroke. **2** *informal* a bribe.

**backing** *n* **1** financial support or aid. **2** endorsement. **3** something forming a back or reverse side. **4** the musical or vocal accompaniment to a song or singer.

**backlash** *n* a strong adverse reaction to a political or social development.

**backlog** *n* an accumulation of things still needing to be done.

**back off** *v* to withdraw from a confrontation.

**back out** *v* to withdraw from a commitment.

**backpack** *n* a rucksack. ➤ **backpacker** *n.*

**backpedal** *v* (**backpedalled, backpedalling,** *NAmer* **backpedaled, backpedaling**) to withdraw from a previous opinion or stand.

**backroom** *adj* done or working behind the scenes.

**backside** *n informal* the buttocks.

**backslapping** *n* excessive cordiality or praising.

**backsliding** *n* lapsing after a period of improvement.

**backstage** *adj and adv* behind the stage out of view of the audience.

**backstreet** *n* a quiet or minor street in a town.

**backstroke** *n* a swimming stroke performed on the back using reverse overarm strokes and kicking movements of the feet.

**backtrack** *v* **1** to retrace a path or course. **2** to reverse one's position or stand.

**back-up** *n* **1** support. **2** a copy of computer data made for security.

**back up** *v* **1** to give support to. **2** in computing, to make a security copy of (data). **3** of traffic: to form a queue behind a hazard or congestion.

**backward** *adj* **1** directed or turned towards the back. **2** not developed as far as normal.

**backwards** (*NAmer* **backward**) *adv* **1** towards the back. **2** with the back foremost. **3** in a reverse direction or towards the beginning. **4** perfectly; thoroughly. **5** towards the past. **6** towards or into a worse state. ✱ **bend/fall/lean over backwards** to make extreme efforts.

**backwash** *n* the backward movement of a receding wave.

**backwater** *n* **1** an area of stagnant water. **2** an isolated or backward place or condition.

**backwoods** *n* a remote or culturally backward area.

**bacon** *n* cured and salted or smoked meat cut from the side of a pig.

**bacteria** *n* pl of BACTERIUM.

**bacterium** *n* a microscopic organism living in organic matter and often carrying disease.

**bad** *adj* (**worse, worst**) **1** poor or inadequate in quality; below an acceptable standard. **2** morally objectionable. **3** mischievous or disobedient. **4** (*often* + at) unskilful or incompetent. **5** disagreeable or unpleasant. **6** (+ for) injurious or harmful. **7** worse than usual; severe. **8** unwell. **9** unhealthy or diseased. **10** (*often* + about) regretful or remorseful. **11** of a debt: not going to be paid. **12** *chiefly NAmer, informal* excellent. ✱ **not bad** *informal* quite good.

**bade** *v* past tense of BID[1].

**badge** *n* **1** a token of membership in a society or group. **2** an emblem awarded for a particular accomplishment.

**badger**[1] *n* a black or dark grey mammal with white striped facial markings, active at night and living underground.

**badger**[2] *v* to harass or annoy persistently.

**badinage** *n* playful repartee or banter.

**badlands** *pl n* a barren region marked by extensive rock erosion.

**badly** *adv* **1** in an unsatisfactory or unpleasant way. **2** unkindly; cruelly. **3** unsuccessfully. **4** severely. **5** very much. ✱ **badly off** poor.

**badminton** *n* a game played with light rackets and a shuttlecock that is volleyed over a net.

**baffle** *v* to puzzle or perplex. ➤ **bafflement** *n.*

**bag**[1] *n* **1** a flexible container for storing or carrying things. **2** a handbag or shoulder bag. **3** a sagging of the skin under the eyes. **4** *chiefly Brit, informal* (*in pl*) a great deal; lots. **5** *informal, derog* an old woman. **6** *informal* a person; special interest. ✱ **in the bag** *informal* as good as achieved. ➤ **bagful** (*pl* **bagfuls**) *n.*

**bag**[2] *v* (**bagged, bagging**) **1** to swell out or bulge. **2** to hang loosely. **3** to put into a bag. **4** to get possession of. **5** *informal* to steal. **6** to take (animals) as game.

**bagatelle** *n* **1** a game in which balls are struck up a board past obstacles into holes. **2** something unimportant or of little value.

**bagel** /'baygl/ *n* a hard ring-shaped bread roll.

**baggage** *n* luggage for travel.

**baggy** *adj* (**-ier, -iest**) loose or puffed out.

**bagpipe** *or* **bagpipes** *n* a wind instrument with pipes, played by squeezing air through from a bag.

**baguette** /ba'get/ *n* a long thin French loaf.

**bail**[1] *n* **1** money paid as security that a person released from custody will return to stand trial. **2** temporary release by payment of bail.

**bail**[2] *v* to release on payment of bail.

**bail**[3] *n* in cricket, each of the two crosspieces that rest on the stumps to form the wicket.

**bail**[4] *or* **bale** *v* **1** (*usu* + out) to clear (water) from a ship or boat. **2** (*usu* + out) to jump from an aircraft, using a parachute. **3** (*usu* + out) to rescue somebody in danger or difficulty.

**bailey** *n* (*pl* **-eys**) the outer wall of a castle.

**bailiff** *n* **1** *chiefly Brit* an official who serves writs and seizes property on which rent is owed. **2** *chiefly Brit* somebody who manages an estate or farm.

**bailiwick** *n* the area of jurisdiction of a bailiff.

**bait**[1] *n* something put on a hook or trap to lure an animal.

**bait**[2] *v* **1** to provoke or tease. **2** to harass (a chained animal) with dogs. **3** to provide with bait.

**baize** *n* a green woollen cloth used as a covering for billiard tables.

**bake** *v* **1** to cook (food) in an oven. **2** to dry or harden by heat. **3** to become extremely hot.

**baker** *n* a person who bakes and sells bread and cakes. * **a baker's dozen** thirteen.

**bakery** *n* (*pl* **-ies**) a place where bread is made and sold.

**baking soda** *n* sodium bicarbonate.

**balaclava** *n* a close-fitting woollen hood that covers the head leaving the face free.

**balance**[1] *n* **1** stability produced by even distribution of weight on each side of a vertical axis. **2** the ability to retain a physical equilibrium. **3** mental and emotional steadiness. **4** equilibrium between contrasting elements. **5** equality between the totals of the two sides of an account. **6** the difference between credits and debits in an account. **7** something left over. **8** a weighing instrument consisting of a beam pivoted at the centre with pans suspended from the ends. * **in the balance** with the fate or outcome still to be determined. **on balance** all things considered. ➤ **balanced** *adj.*

**balance**[2] *v* **1** to make or become in a position or state of balance. **2** to compare the relative value or importance of the factors in (a situation). **3** of accounts: to have the debit and credit totals equal. **4** to counterbalance or offset.

**balance of payments** *n* the difference between a country's payments for imports and receipts for exports.

**balance sheet** *n* a statement of the financial state of an organization.

**balcony** *n* (*pl* **-ies**) **1** a platform with a railing built out from the wall of a building. **2** a gallery inside a theatre or other building.

**bald** *adj* **1** having no hair on the head. **2** of a tyre: having little or no tread. **3** plainly or bluntly expressed. ➤ **baldly** *adv,* **baldness** *n.*

**balderdash** *n* nonsense.

**balding** *adj* becoming bald.

**bale**[1] *n* a large bundle of cloth, paper, or hay.

**bale**[2] *v* to tie into bales or bundles.

**bale**[3] *n and verb Brit* see BAIL[4].

**baleen** *n* whalebone.

**baleful** *adj* pernicious or menacing. ➤ **balefully** *adv.*

**balk** (*Brit* **baulk**) *v* **1** (*usu* + at) to stop short and refuse to go on. **2** (*often* + at) to refuse abruptly. **3** to check or thwart.

**ball**[1] *n* **1** a solid or hollow spherical object used in a game or sport. **2** a delivery or play of the ball in a game. **3** *coarse slang* (*in pl*) the testicles. * **on the ball** knowledgeable and competent; alert.

**ball**[2] *v* to form or gather into a ball.

**ball**[3] *n* a large formal gathering for social dancing. * **have a ball** *informal* to enjoy oneself.

**ballad** *n* **1** a rhythmic poem or song that tells a story. **2** a slow, romantic or sentimental popular song.

**ballast** *n* **1** heavy material carried in a ship or airship to improve stability. **2** broken stone laid in a bed for railway lines or the lower layer of roads.

**ball bearing** *n* a bearing of steel balls that roll with minimal friction in a groove between a shaft and a support.

**ballcock** *n* an automatic valve in a cistern controlled by the rise and fall of a float.

**ballerina** *n* a female ballet dancer.

**ballet** *n* a form of artistic dancing based on conventional positions and steps, usu performed to music. ➤ **balletic** *adj.*

**ballistic** *adj* **1** relating to the movement of projectiles under their own momentum and the force of gravity. **2** *informal* violently angry.

**ballistic missile** *n* a missile guided in ascent and falling freely on its target.

**ballistics** *pl n* the science of the movement of projectiles.

**balloon**[1] *n* **1** a baglike container filled with hot air or a gas lighter than air so as to rise and float in the atmosphere. **2** an inflatable coloured rubber bag used as a toy or decoration. **3** an outline enclosing words spoken or thought by a character in a cartoon.

**balloon**[2] *v* **1** to ascend or travel in a balloon. **2** (*often* + out) to swell or puff out. **3** to increase rapidly.

**ballot**[1] *n* **1** an election in which votes are cast in secret. **2** the number of votes cast.

**ballot**[2] *v* (**balloted, balloting**) **1** (*often* + for) to vote by ballot. **2** to ask (people) to vote.

**ballpoint** *or* **ballpoint pen** *n* a pen having a tiny rotating ball as the writing point.

**ballroom** *n* a large room for formal dancing.

**ballroom dancing** *n* formal dancing by couples.

**ballyhoo** *n* noisy talk or fuss.

**balm** *n* **1** an aromatic and medicinal resin. **2** something that soothes or heals.

**balmy** *adj* (**-ier, -iest**) of weather: pleasantly mild.

**baloney** *or* **boloney** *n* (*pl* **-eys**) nonsense.

**balsa** *n* (*also* **balsa wood**) the strong light wood of a tropical American tree, used in making models.

**balsam** *n* an oily resin obtained from certain plants, or a medicinal preparation containing it.

**baluster** *n* each of the upright supports for a rail.

**balustrade** *n* a row of balusters topped by a rail.

**bamboo** *n* a tropical giant grass with strong hollow stems.
**bamboozle** *v* **1** to deceive or cheat. **2** to confuse or mystify.
**ban**[1] *v* (**banned, banning**) to prohibit or forbid officially.
**ban**[2] *n* a legal or social prohibition.
**banal** *adj* lacking originality or novelty; dull. ➤ **banality** *n*, **banally** *adv*.
**banana** *n* a long curved fruit growing in bunches, with a thick yellow skin and soft pulpy flesh.
**band**[1] *n* **1** a narrow strip of material used as trimming on an article of dress. **2** a strip distinguishable by colour, texture, or composition. **3** a strip or belt serving to join or hold things together or to transmit motion. **4** a range of radio wavelengths.
**band**[2] *v* **1** (*often* + together) to unite for a common purpose. **2** to fasten with a band. **3** to mark with a band.
**band**[3] *n* **1** a group of musicians playing jazz, pop, rock, or marching music. **2** a group of people sharing an interest or purpose.
**bandage**[1] *n* a strip of fabric used to dress and bind up wounds.
**bandage**[2] *v* to bind or dress with a bandage.
**bandanna** *n* a large patterned piece of cloth worn round the head.
**b and b** *abbr* (*often* **B and B**) *Brit* bed and breakfast.
**bandit** *n* a member of a band of armed robbers. ➤ **banditry** *n*.
**bandolier** *or* **bandoleer** *n* a belt worn across the chest with pockets or loops for cartridges.
**bandstand** *n* a roofed outdoor stand for a brass band.
**bandwagon** *n* a fashionable cause or activity.
**bandwidth** *n* a range of frequencies used in radio transmission and telecommunications.
**bandy**[1] *v* (**-ies, -ied**) (*often* + about) to use or make reference to in a glib or offhand manner. ✱ **bandy words** to argue angrily.
**bandy**[2] *adj* (**-ier, -iest**) of a person's legs: bowed.
**bane** *n* a cause of ruin or trouble.
**bang**[1] *v* **1** to strike sharply. **2** to cause to make a loud sharp or metallic noise.
**bang**[2] *n* **1** a sudden loud noise. **2** a resounding blow. **3** a burst of energy or activity.
**bang**[3] *adv informal* **1** right or directly. **2** exactly.
**banger** *n Brit* **1** a firework that explodes with a loud bang. **2** *informal* a sausage. **3** *informal* an old usu dilapidated car.
**bangle** *n* a rigid ornamental bracelet.
**banish** *v* **1** to send (somebody) permanently away from a place as a punishment. **2** to dispel (an unpleasant thought) from one's mind. ➤ **banishment** *n*.
**banister** *or* **bannister** *n* **1** (*also in pl*) a handrail with its upright supports at the edge of a staircase. **2** an upright support of such a handrail.
**banjo** *n* (*pl* **-os** *or* **-oes**) a stringed musical instrument with a round flat body and long neck. ➤ **banjoist** *n*.
**bank**[1] *n* **1** a mound of earth or snow. **2** a mass of cloud or fog. **3** the rising ground bordering a lake or river or forming the embankment along a road or railway. **4** a slope.
**bank**[2] *v* **1** (*often* + up) to rise in or form a bank. **2** of an aircraft: to incline laterally.
**bank**[3] *n* **1** an establishment for keeping, lending, and issuing money and for the transmission of funds. **2** a collection of something kept available for use. **3** a container for collecting materials for recycling.
**bank**[4] *v* to deposit (money) in a bank. ✱ **bank on** to rely on.
**bank**[5] *n* **1** a group or series of objects arranged together. **2** a row of keys on a typewriter or computer keyboard.
**bankable** *adj* popular and therefore likely to be a source of profit.
**bank holiday** *n* a public holiday when banks and some businesses are closed.
**banknote** *n* money in paper form.
**bankroll**[1] *n* **1** a roll of banknotes. **2** *NAmer* a supply of money; funds.
**bankroll**[2] *v* to finance.
**bankrupt**[1] *adj* legally declared to be incapable of paying outstanding debts.
**bankrupt**[2] *n* a bankrupt person.
**bankrupt**[3] *v* to make bankrupt.
**banner**[1] *n* a usu square or oblong flag bearing heraldic arms or a symbolic design, held up high.
**banner**[2] *adj NAmer* distinguished from all others, *esp* in excellence: *a banner year for business*.
**bannister** *n* see BANISTER.
**banns** *pl n* the public announcement in church of a proposed marriage.
**banquet**[1] *n* a large and elaborate ceremonial meal.
**banquet**[2] *v* (**banqueted, banqueting**) to provide or entertain with a banquet.
**banshee** *n* a female spirit in Gaelic folklore whose wailing warns of death.
**bantam** *n* a small domestic fowl.
**banter**[1] *n* light-hearted teasing or badgering.
**banter**[2] *v* to speak or act playfully or wittily.
**bap** *n Brit* a soft round bread roll.
**baptism** *n* the Christian sacrament of admission to the church by sprinkling with or immersion in water. ➤ **baptismal** *adj*.
**baptism of fire** *n* a severe initial experience.
**Baptist** *adj* belonging to a Protestant denomination which baptizes full adult believers rather than babies. ➤ **Baptist** *n*.
**baptize** *or* **-ise** *v* **1** to administer baptism to. **2** to give a name to at baptism.

**bar**[1] *n* **1** a long firm piece of hard material. **2** something that obstructs or prevents progress or action. **3** a counter at which alcoholic drinks are served, or a room or premises containing this. **4** in a court of law, the dock or the railing that encloses the dock. **5** (*usu* **the Bar**) *Brit* the profession or body of barristers. **6** a straight stripe or band. **7** a group of notes and rests in music, marked on each side by a line. * **behind bars** in prison.

**bar**[2] *v* (**barred, barring**) **1** to fasten with a bar. **2** to shut in or out. **3** to prevent or forbid. ➤ **barred** *adj.*

**bar**[3] *prep* except for.

**barb** *n* **1** a sharp projection extending backwards from the point of an arrow, fishhook, etc. **2** a pointedly critical remark.

**barbarian** *n* **1** a person belonging to a land, culture, or people regarded as uncivilized or inferior. **2** a cruel or uncivilized person.

**barbaric** *adj* **1** vicious and cruel. **2** unsophisticated or uncivilized. ➤ **barbarically** *adv.*

**barbarism** *n* **1** primitive or unsophisticated social or intellectual condition. **2** merciless cruelty.

**barbarous** *adj* **1** mercilessly cruel. **2** lacking culture or refinement.

**barbecue**[1] *n* **1** an outdoor meal at which food is cooked over a charcoal fire. **2** a piece of equipment for use at a barbecue.

**barbecue**[2] *v* (**barbecues, barbecued, barbecuing**) to cook on a barbecue.

**barbed** *adj* **1** having barbs. **2** of a remark: sarcastic or spiteful.

**barbed wire** *n* twisted wires with sharp points set along them.

**barbel** *n* **1** a thin projecting organ on the lips of some fishes. **2** a freshwater fish with four barbels on its upper jaw.

**barbell** *n* a bar with adjustable weighted discs attached to each end, used for weight-lifting.

**barber** *n* a person who cuts and styles men's hair and shaves or trims beards.

**barbiturate** *n* a sedative drug used in the treatment of epilepsy and formerly in sleeping pills.

**bar code** *n* an identifying code printed on a product for sale, consisting of parallel lines of varying thickness that can be read by an electronic scanner.

**bard** *n* **1** *archaic or literary* a poet who sang or recited verses about heroes. **2** a poet. **3** (**the Bard**) Shakespeare. ➤ **bardic** *adj.*

**bare**[1] *adj* **1** not wearing any clothes. **2** lacking a natural or usual covering. **3** open to view; exposed. **4** unfurnished or empty. **5** having nothing left over or added; mere. **6** not disguised or embellished in any way. ➤ **bareness** *n.*

**bare**[2] *v* to reveal or uncover.

**bareback** *or* **barebacked** *adv and adj* on the back of a horse without a saddle.

**barefaced** *adj* lacking scruples; shameless.

**bargain**[1] *n* **1** something bought at a very favourable price. **2** an agreement between people to help or support each other. * **into the bargain** in addition.

**bargain**[2] *v* (*often* + with) to negotiate over the terms of a purchase or agreement. * **bargain for** to be prepared for. **bargain on** to expect.

**barge**[1] *n* a long flat-bottomed boat used for transporting goods on inland waterways.

**barge**[2] *v* **1** to move clumsily or forcefully. **2** (+ in/into) to intrude noisily or clumsily.

**baritone** *n* a male singer having a voice between base and tenor.

**barium** *n* a silver-white soft metallic chemical element.

**bark**[1] *v* **1** to make the short loud cry of a dog. **2** to speak loudly or angrily. * **bark up the wrong tree** to proceed under a misapprehension.

**bark**[2] *n* the sound made by a barking dog.

**bark**[3] *n* the tough exterior covering of a tree.

**bark**[4] *v* to scrape the skin off (the knee or shin) by accident.

**barley** *n* (*pl* **-eys**) a cereal grass used in foods and for cattle feed.

**barley sugar** *n* a brittle sweet made of boiled sugar .

**barman** *n* (*pl* **barmen**) somebody who serves drinks in a bar.

**bar mitzvah** /bah 'mitsvə/ *n* the religious ceremony marking the time when a Jewish boy takes on adult duties and responsibilities at the age of 13.

**barmy** *adj* (**-ier, -iest**) *informal* foolish or slightly mad.

**barn** *n* a large farm building for storage.

**barnacle** *n* a marine crustacean that is fixed to rocks or floating objects.

**barn dance** *n* a social gathering with country dancing.

**barnstorm** *v chiefly NAmer* to travel staging theatrical performances or conducting a political campaign.

**barnyard** *n NAmer* a farmyard.

**barometer** *n* **1** an instrument for measuring atmospheric pressure in order to predict the weather. **2** a gauge of fluctuations in public opinion. ➤ **barometric** *adj.*

**baron** *n* **1** a member of the lowest rank of the peerage in Britain. **2** formerly, a feudal tenant who received his rights and title directly from the sovereign in return for his allegiance.

**baroness** *n* **1** the wife or widow of a baron. **2** a woman having the rank of a baron.

**baronet** *n* a man holding a title below a baron and above a knight. ➤ **baronetcy** *n.*

**baroque** *adj* of a 17th-cent. ornamental style of European art, architecture, and music.

**barrack** *v chiefly Brit* to jeer or scoff at (a player or performer).

**barracks** *pl n* a group of buildings providing accommodation for soldiers.

**barracuda** *n* (*pl* **barracudas** *or* **barracuda**) a predatory fish of warm seas.

**barrage**[1] *n* **1** a continuous bombardment of intensive artillery fire. **2** an overwhelming series of questions or complaints. **3** *Brit* an artificial dam placed in a watercourse or estuary.

**barrage**[2] *v* to overwhelm with questions or complaints.

**barrel** *n* **1** a cylindrical container for liquids, with bulging sides and flat ends. **2** the tube of a gun, from which the bullet is fired. * **over a barrel** *informal* in a weak position.

**barrel organ** *n* a street organ with a revolving cylinder played by turning a handle.

**barren** *adj* **1** incapable of producing offspring. **2** of a tree: habitually failing to fruit. **3** of land: not productive. **4** lacking interest or information.

**barricade**[1] *n* an obstruction thrown up to block a road or entrance.

**barricade**[2] *v* to block or defend with a barricade.

**barrier** *n* something that prevents entry or progress.

**barring** *prep* except for.

**barrister** *n Brit* a lawyer who has the right to plead as an advocate in a lawcourt.

**barrow**[1] *n* a cart with two wheels and shafts for pushing it.

**barrow**[2] *n* a large mound of earth or stones over an ancient grave.

**bartender** *n chiefly NAmer* a barman.

**barter**[1] *v* to trade by exchanging goods without the use of money.

**barter**[2] *n* trade by bartering.

**basalt** *n* a dark igneous rock.

**base**[1] *n* **1** the bottom or lowest part of something; a support or foundation. **2** a side or face of a geometrical figure on which it is regarded as standing. **3** the fundamental part of something; a basis on which other activities or institutions depend. **4** a centre from which a start is made in an activity or from which operations proceed. **5** the locality or installations on which a military force relies for supplies or from which it starts operations. **6** the number with reference to which a number system is constructed. **7** any of the stations at each of the four corners of the inner part of a baseball field to which a batter must run in turn in order to score a run. **8** a chemical compound capable of taking up a hydrogen ion from or donating an unshared pair of electrons to an acid to form a salt.

**base**[2] *v* **1** to make or serve as a base for. **2** (*usu* + on/upon) to use as a base or basis for; to found. **3** (*usu* + in/at) to have (a place) as an operational base.

**base**[3] *adj* **1** lacking higher values; degrading. **2** lacking or showing a lack of moral values such as honour, chivalry, or loyalty. **3** of a metal: of comparatively low value and having relatively inferior properties.

**baseball** *n* a game played with a bat and ball between two teams on a field with four bases arranged in a diamond marking the course a batsman must run to score.

**baseball cap** *n* a close-fitting round cap with a large peak.

**baseless** *adj* not supported by fact; unfounded.

**baseline** *n* **1** a basis or starting point for measurements or comparisons. **2** the back line at each end of a court in tennis, badminton, or volleyball.

**basement** *n* the part of a building wholly or partly below ground level.

**bases**[1] *n* pl of BASE[1].

**bases**[2] *n* pl of BASIS.

**bash**[1] *v informal* **1** to strike violently. **2** (*often* + up) to make a violent physical attack on.

**bash**[2] *n informal* **1** a heavy blow. **2** *chiefly Brit* (*often* + at) an attempt. **3** a party.

**bashful** *adj* self-consciously shy or timid. ➤ **bashfully** *adv.*

**basic**[1] *adj* **1** forming the base or essence; fundamental. **2** simple; elementary. **3** having the character of a chemical base. ➤ **basically** *adv.*

**basic**[2] *n* (*usu in pl*) a fundamental fact or principle.

**basil** *n* an aromatic plant of the mint family with leaves used as a herb in cooking.

**basilica** *n* an oblong building used in ancient Rome as a place of assembly or as a lawcourt, or an early Christian church similar to this.

**basilisk** *n* **1** a mythical reptile with a fatal breath and glance. **2** a crested tropical American lizard related to the iguanas.

**basin** *n* **1** a rounded open container used for holding liquid. **2** a bowl used for mixing food. **3** a depression in the surface of the land or ocean floor. **4** the region drained by a river and its tributaries.

**basis** *n* (*pl* **bases**) the principal component of something.

**bask** *v* **1** to lie enjoying warmth or sunshine. **2** (*usu* + in) to enjoy favour or approval.

**basket** *n* **1** a rigid receptacle made of interwoven strips of wicker or wood. **2** a net, open at the bottom and suspended from a metal ring, that constitutes the goal in basketball.

**basketball** *n* a team game in which players score goals by throwing a ball through a raised basket.

**bass**[1] *n* (*pl* **basses** *or* **bass**) an edible spiny-finned sea and freshwater fish.

**bass**[2] *n* **1** a male singer with a voice of the lowest range. **2** a double bass or bass guitar. **3** the lower portion of the audio frequency range. ➤ **bassist** *n.*

**bass**[3] *adj* **1** of low pitch. **2** deep or grave in tone.
**bass clef** *n* a musical clef placing the F below middle C on the fourth line of the staff.
**basset hound** *n* a hunting dog of a short-legged breed with a long body and drooping ears.
**bassoon** *n* a large woodwind musical instrument of the oboe family. ➤ **bassoonist** *n.*
**bastard** *n* **1** *offensive or archaic* a child of unmarried parents. **2** *informal* an offensive or disagreeable person.
**bastardize** *or* **-ise** *v* to debase.
**baste**[1] *v* to sew with loose stitches.
**baste**[2] *v* to pour fat and juices over (meat) during cooking.
**baste**[3] *v* to beat soundly; to thrash.
**bastion** *n* **1** a projecting part of a fortification. **2** something considered as providing defence or protection.
**bat**[1] *n* **1** awooden implement used for hitting the ball in sports and games. **2** an implement like a rounded bat for guiding aircraft on the ground. ✱ **off one's own bat** through one's own efforts.
**bat**[2] *v* (**batted, batting**) **1** to strike or hit with a bat. **2** to take one's turn at batting.
**bat**[3] *n* **1** a nocturnal flying mammal. **2** (**old bat**) *derog* a disagreeable old woman.
**bat**[4] *v* (**batted, batting**) to blink (an eye) in surprise or emotion. ✱ **not bat an eyelid** not to be at all surprised.
**batch**[1] *n* a quantity of goods produced at one time.
**batch**[2] *v* to gather (things) together or process as a batch.
**bated** ✱ **with bated breath** in a state of nervous suspense.
**bath**[1] *n* **1** a large open container for filling with water and lying in for washing. **2** an act of washing in a bath. **3** (*usu in pl*) a building containing a swimming pool or rooms for bathing.
**bath**[2] *v Brit* to wash in a bath.
**bathe**[1] *v* **1** to wash in a bath. **2** *chiefly Brit* to swim for pleasure. **3** to wash or clean with water or other liquid. **4** to suffuse with light. ➤ **bather** *n.*
**bathe**[2] *n Brit* an act of swimming.
**bathos** *n* a sudden change from something serious to something trivial. ➤ **bathetic** *adj.*
**bathroom** *n* **1** a room containing a bath or shower and usu a washbasin and toilet. **2** *NAmer* a toilet.
**batik** *n* a method of hand-printing by coating with wax the parts to be left undyed.
**baton** *n* **1** a small stick with which a conductor directs a band or orchestra. **2** a stick passed by the runners in a relay team. **3** a short stick carried as a symbol of military rank. **4** a long metal rod twirled by a drum major.
**batsman** *n* (*pl* **batsmen**) a player who bats or is batting in cricket.
**battalion** *n* **1** a military unit composed of a headquarters and two or more companies. **2** a large number of troops, people, or things.
**batten**[1] *n* a thin narrow strip of squared timber, plastic, or metal.
**batten**[2] *v* (*often* + down) to fasten (*esp* a ship's hatches) with battens.
**batten**[3] *v* (+ on/upon) to thrive at the expense of somebody else.
**batter**[1] *v* to strike heavily and repeatedly; to break or damage with heavy persistent blows. ➤ **battered** *adj.*
**batter**[2] *n* a mixture of flour, egg, and milk or water, used for making pancakes or coating food for frying. ➤ **battered** *adj.*
**batter**[3] *n* in baseball, etc, the player who is batting.
**battery** *n* (*pl* **-ies**) **1** a source of power consisting of two or more cells connected together to provide an electric current. **2** a number of similar things connected or used together. **3** *chiefly Brit* a series of cages or compartments for raising poultry. **4** the unlawful use of force or violence on a person without their consent. **5** a fortified gun emplacement.
**battle**[1] *n* **1** an extensive fight between opposing armed forces. **2** an extended struggle or controversy.
**battle**[2] *v* **1** to fight vigorously. **2** to struggle to do something. ➤ **battler** *n.*
**battle-axe** *n* **1** a large axe used formerly in warfare. **2** a domineering older woman.
**battledress** *n* uniform worn by soldiers in battle.
**battlefield** *or* **battleground** *n* a piece of ground where a battle is fought.
**battlement** *n* a parapet on a wall, with gaps originally used for firing through.
**battleship** *n* a heavily armed warship.
**batty** *adj* (**-ier, -iest**) *informal* eccentric or crazy.
**bauble** *n* a trinket or trifle.
**baulk** *v Brit* see BALK.
**bauxite** *n* a mineral that is the principal ore of aluminium.
**bawdy** *adj* (**-ier, -iest**) boisterously or humorously indecent. ➤ **bawdiness** *n.*
**bawl** *v* to cry or shout out. ➤ **bawl** *n.*
**bawl out** *v chiefly NAmer, informal* to reprimand loudly or severely.
**bay**[1] *n* a wide curving inlet of a sea or lake.
**bay**[2] *n* a small evergreen tree of the laurel family with leaves used for flavouring.
**bay**[3] *n* **1** a special area or compartment within a larger structure. **2** a structure projecting from the wall of a building. **3** a section of wall between two columns or buttresses.
**bay**[4] *adj* of a horse: reddish brown.

**bay**[5] *v* **1** of a dog: to bark fiercely. **2** (+ for) to demand insistently. * **hold/keep at bay** to prevent from coming close to or affecting one.
**bayonet**[1] *n* a blade attached to the muzzle of a firearm and used in hand-to-hand combat.
**bayonet**[2] *v* (**bayoneted, bayoneting**) to stab with a bayonet.
**bay window** *n* a window projecting outwards from the wall.
**bazaar** *n* **1** a market in the Middle East. **2** a sale to raise money for charity.
**bazooka** *n* a short-range antitank rocket launcher.
**BBC** *abbr* British Broadcasting Corporation.
**BC** *abbr* **1** used after a date: before Christ. **2** British Columbia.

***Usage Note:*** *BC* comes after the date, e.g. *133BC*.

**Be** *abbr* the chemical symbol for beryllium.
**be** *v* (*sing. present* **am, are, is,** *pl present* **are,** *first and third person sing. past* **was,** *second person sing. past and pl past* **were,** *past part.* **been**) **1** to exist or be present. **2** to occur in time. **3** to have a specified state, function, or value. **4** used instead of *go* or *come* in the perfect tense: *I've been to New York.* ➤ *verb aux.* **1** used with a present participle to form continuous or progressive tenses. **2** used with a past participle to form the passive voice. **3** used with *to* and an infinitive to express a wish or future action: *You are not to worry.* * **be oneself** to behave normally or naturally. **the be-all and end-all** the most important factor or part.
**beach**[1] *n* the shore of a sea or lake, covered by sand or pebbles.
**beach**[2] *v* to bring ashore from the water.
**beachcomber** *n* a person who searches a beach for useful or saleable objects.
**beacon** *n* **1** a signal fire lit at the top of a hill. **2** a light or signal used to guide shipping or aircraft.
**bead** *n* **1** a small piece of wood or glass, threaded on a string or wire to make a necklace. **2** a drop of liquid. ➤ **beaded** *adj.*
**beadle** *n* a minor parish official.
**beady** *adj* (**-ier, -iest**) of the eyes: small and round, and vigilant.
**beagle** *n* a hound of a breed with short legs and a smooth coat.
**beak** *n* a bird's hard projecting mouth structure. ➤ **beaked** *adj.*
**beaker** *n* **1** a tall drinking vessel without a handle. **2** a cylindrical flat-bottomed vessel used by chemists and pharmacists.
**beam**[1] *n* **1** a long piece of heavy timber used in building. **2** a bar for balancing on in gymnastics. **3** the width of a ship at its widest part. **4** a ray or shaft of light or other radiation. **5** a radio signal transmitted continuously in one direction as an aircraft navigation aid. * **off beam** wrong; irrelevant.
**beam**[2] *v* **1** to smile broadly. **2** to transmit (a broadcast signal). **3** to emit a bright light.
**bean** *n* **1** a seed of a climbing plant, growing in a pod and used as a vegetable. **2** *informal* the smallest possible amount. * **full of beans** lively or energetic.
**beanbag** *n* **1** a small bag filled with beans, used in games or as a toy. **2** a large loosely stuffed cushion used as an informal low chair.
**bear**[1] *n* **1** a large heavy mammal with long shaggy hair and a short tail. **2** a surly, uncouth, or shambling person.
**bear**[2] *v* (**bore, borne**) **1** to carry or transport. **2** to behave in a particular way. **3** to have or show as a feature. **4** to give birth to. **5** of a plant or tree: to produce (fruit or flowers). **6** to support the weight of. **7** to tolerate. **8** to sustain or incur (e.g. a cost). **9** to go in a specified direction. **10** (+ on) to be relevant to something. **11** (+ with) to show patience or indulgence towards somebody. * **bear fruit** to have good results. **bear in mind** to remember or consider. ➤ **bearable** *adj,* **bearably** *adv,* **bearer** *n.*
**beard**[1] *n* a growth of hair on the lower part of a man's face. ➤ **bearded** *adj.*
**beard**[2] *v* to confront boldly or defiantly.
**bear down** *v* * **bear down on 1** to approach purposefully or threateningly. **2** to weigh heavily on.
**bearing** *n* **1** a person's manner of standing, moving, or behaving. **2** (*often in pl*) a machine part in which another part turns or slides. **3** the compass direction of a course or of one point with respect to another. **4** (*in pl*) comprehension of one's position or situation. **5** (*usu* + on) connection or relevance to something. **6** an emblem or figure on a heraldic shield.
**bear out** *v* to confirm or substantiate.
**bear up** *v* to remain cheerful or resolute in a difficult situation.
**beast** *n* **1** an animal, *esp* a large or wild animal. **2** a cruel or contemptible person.
**beast of burden** *n* an animal used to carry loads.
**beat**[1] *v* (**beat, beaten**) **1** (*often* + up) to hit repeatedly, *esp* so as to inflict pain. **2** to strike repeatedly in order to produce a noise or signal. **3** to mix (food) by stirring. **4** to shape or flatten thin by repeated blows. **5** to overcome or defeat (an opponent). **6** to surpass. **7** of a heart or pulse: to pulsate. **8** *informal* to bewilder or baffle. * **beat about the bush** to fail to come to the point. **beat it** *informal* to hurry away. **beat somebody to it** to act ahead of somebody. **off the beaten track** remote or isolated.
**beat**[2] *n* **1** a pulsation or throb. **2** a sound produced by beating. **3** metrical or rhythmic stress in poetry or music. **4** an area patrolled by a police officer.
**beat**[3] *adj informal* exhausted.

**beatific** *adj* blissfully happy. ➤ **beatifically** *adv.*
**beatify** *v* (**-ies, -ied**) to authorize the veneration of (a dead person) by the Roman Catholic Church by giving the title 'Blessed'. ➤ **beatification** *n.*
**beatnik** *n* in the 1950s and 1960s, a young person who rejected established society.
**beat up** *v* to assault and harm by repeated punching or kicking.
**beat-up** *adj informal* dilapidated or worn out.
**beau** *n* (*pl* **beaux** *or* **beaus**) *chiefly NAmer* a boyfriend.
**beautician** *n* somebody who gives beauty treatments.
**beautiful** *adj* **1** producing aesthetic or sensual pleasure. **2** generally enjoyable and good; excellent. ➤ **beautifully** *adv.*
**beautify** *v* (**-ies, -ied**) to make beautiful.
**beauty** *n* (*pl* **-ies**) **1** a quality that gives pleasure to the senses. **2** a beautiful woman. **3** a brilliant or extreme example of something. **4** a particularly advantageous or excellent quality.
**beaver**[1] *n* a large semiaquatic rodent with webbed hind feet and a broad flat tail.
**beaver**[2] *v* (*also* + away) to work energetically.
**becalm** *v* (*usu in passive*) to keep (a sailing vessel) motionless by lack of wind.
**because** *conj* for the reason that; since.
**beck**[1] *n N Eng* a brook; *esp* a pebbly mountain stream.
**beck**[2] ✱ **at somebody's beck and call** constantly ready to obey somebody.
**beckon** *v* **1** to summon or signal somebody to come. **2** to look appealing.
**become** *v* (**became, become**) **1** to begin to be. **2** to suit or be suitable for. ✱ **become of** to happen to.
**becquerel** *n* the SI unit of radiation.
**bed**[1] *n* **1** a piece of furniture for sleeping on. **2** sleep, or a time for sleeping. **3** a plot of ground prepared for plants. **4** the bottom of a body of water. **5** a supporting surface or structure. ✱ **go to bed with** to have sexual intercourse with.
**bed**[2] *v* (**bedded, bedding**) **1** (*often* + down) to provide with a bed. **2** (*often* + down) to go to bed. **3** (*often* + out) to plant (seedlings, etc) in beds.
**bedclothes** *pl n* the covers used on a bed.
**bedding** *n* **1** bedclothes. **2** straw used as a bed for livestock.
**bedevil** *v* (**bedevilled, bedevilling,** *NAmer* **bedeviled, bedeviling**) to be a continual problem or nuisance to.
**bedlam** *n* a place or state of uproar and confusion.
**bedpan** *n* a shallow vessel used as a toilet by a person in bed.
**bedraggled** *adj* looking limp and untidy.
**bedridden** *adj* confined to bed by illness or old age.
**bedrock** *n* **1** a layer of solid rock under the soil. **2** the basis of something.
**bedroom** *n* a room for sleeping in.
**bed-sit** *n or* **bed-sitter** *Brit, informal* a rented room used as both a sitting room and bedroom, often also with cooking facilities.
**bedsore** *n* a sore caused by prolonged pressure on part of the body of a bedridden invalid.
**bedspread** *n* an ornamental cloth cover for a bed.
**bedstead** *n* the framework of a bed.
**bee** *n* a winged insect kept in a hive for the honey that it produces. ✱ **a bee in one's bonnet** an obsessive idea. **the bee's knees** *informal* somebody or something that is outstandingly good.
**beech** *n* a hardwood deciduous tree with smooth grey bark.
**beef**[1] *n* **1** meat from a bullock, cow, or bull. **2** (*pl* **beeves,** *NAmer* **beefs**) a full-grown ox, cow, or bull, *esp* when fattened for food. **3** *informal* a complaint.
**beef**[2] *v* **1** *informal* (*usu* + up) to add weight or strength to. **2** *informal* to complain.
**beefburger** *n* a hamburger.
**beefy** *adj* (**-ier, -iest**) brawny or powerful.
**beehive** *n* a structure for keeping bees.
**beeline** ✱ **make a beeline for** to hurry directly towards.
**Beelzebub** *n* the Devil.
**been** *v* past part. of BE.
**beep**[1] *n* a sound from a horn or electronic device, that serves as a signal or warning.
**beep**[2] *v* to make a beep. ➤ **beeper** *n.*
**beer** *n* an alcoholic drink brewed from fermented malt flavoured with hops.
**beeswax** *n* a yellowish substance secreted by bees for constructing honeycombs, used as a wood polish.
**beet** *n* a plant with a swollen root used as a vegetable or a source of sugar.
**beetle**[1] *n* an insect with hard coverings over its wings.
**beetle**[2] *v Brit, informal* (*often* + off) to move swiftly.
**beetroot** *n* (*pl* **beetroots** *or* **beetroot**) *chiefly Brit* a beet with a red edible root used as a vegetable.
**befall** *v* (**befell, befallen**) of something unwelcome: to affect or happen to.
**befit** *v* (**befitted, befitting**) to be appropriate or suitable for. ➤ **befitting** *adj.*
**before**[1] *adv* **1** earlier in time. **2** so as to be in advance of others; ahead.
**before**[2] *prep* **1** in front of. **2** earlier than. **3** in a higher or more important position than. **4** in preference to.
**before**[3] *conj* **1** earlier than the time when. **2** rather than.
**beforehand** *adv and adj* ahead of time.
**befriend** *v* to seek to be a friend of.

**befuddled** *adj* muddled or confused.
**beg** *v* (**begged, begging**) **1** to ask for alms or charity. **2** to ask for earnestly. **3** of a dog: to sit up and hold out its forepaws. * **beg the question** to assume something as established or proved without justification. **go begging** to be available but unwanted.
**beget** *v* (**begetting, begot,** *archaic* **begat, begotten**) *archaic* **1** to produce (offspring) as the father. **2** to cause (an effect). ➤ **begetter** *n.*
**beggar**[1] *n* **1** a person who lives by asking for money or food. **2** a very poor person. **3** *informal* a person of a specified kind: *a lucky beggar* ➤ **beggary** *n.*
**beggar**[2] *v* to make very poor.
**begin** *v* (**beginning, began, begun**) **1** to do the first part of an action; to start. **2** to bring or come into existence. **3** (+ with) to have as a starting point. **4** to come first in. ➤ **beginner** *n.*
**begonia** *n* a plant with bright flowers, cultivated as an ornamental garden and house plant.
**begrudge** *v* **1** to give reluctantly. **2** to envy (somebody) the pleasure or enjoyment of something.
**beguile** *v* to please or charm, often deceptively.
**behalf** * **on behalf of 1** in the interest of. **2** as a representative of.
**behave** *v* **1** to act in a specified way. **2** to conduct oneself properly.
**behaviour** (*NAmer* **behavior**) *n* **1** the way in which a person behaves. **2** the way in which something functions. ➤ **behavioural** *adj.*
**behead** *v* to execute (somebody) by cutting off their head.
**behemoth** *n* a huge and monstrous creature.
**behest** *n* a command or urgent request.
**behind**[1] *adv* **1** in or towards the back. **2** in a place now departed from. **3** in a secondary or inferior position. **4** (*usu* + in/with) in arrears. **5** (*usu* + with) late.
**behind**[2] *prep* **1** at or to the rear of. **2** remaining after. **3** obscured by. **4** less advanced than. **5** not keeping up with (a plan or schedule). **6** responsible for (something unwelcome). **7** supporting and helping.
**behind**[3] *n informal* the buttocks.
**behold** *v* (*past tense and past part.* **beheld**) to see or admire. ➤ **beholder** *n.*
**beholden** *adj* (*usu* + to) under an obligation for a favour or gift.
**behove** *v* to be necessary or advantageous for.
**beige** *adj* of a yellowish grey colour.
**being** *n* **1** life or existence. **2** the essential qualities of somebody or something. **3** a living thing; *esp* a person.
**bejewelled** (*NAmer* **bejeweled**) *adj* decorated with jewels.
**belated** *adj* delayed beyond the usual time. ➤ **belatedly** *adv.*
**belay** *n* in mountain climbing, a rope securing a climber.
**belch**[1] *v* **1** to expel gas from the stomach through the mouth. **2** to emit (smoke, steam, etc) violently.
**belch**[2] *n* an act of belching.
**beleaguer** *v* **1** to harass. **2** to besiege. **beleaguered** *adj.*
**belfry** *n* (*pl* **-ies**) a room in which a bell is hung in the bell tower of a church.
**belie** *v* (**belies, belied, belying**) **1** to give a false impression of. **2** to show to be false.
**belief** *n* **1** something widely believed. **2** conviction of the truth or reality of something. **3** trust in somebody or something.
**believe** *v* **1** to consider (something) to be true or (somebody) to be telling the truth. **2** to have as an opinion. **3** to have a firm religious faith. **4** (*often* + in) to have a firm conviction as to the reality or goodness of something. ➤ **believable** *adj,* **believer** *n.*

***Usage Note:*** Note the spelling *-ie-*.

**belittle** *v* to undermine the value or importance of.
**bell** *n* **1** a hollow metallic device that makes a ringing sound when struck. **2** the sound of a bell as a signal. **3** something with the shape of a bell.
**belladonna** *n* **1** deadly nightshade. **2** an extract of deadly nightshade containing atropine.
**belle** *n* a beautiful young woman.
**bellicose** *adj* aggressive and fond of fighting. ➤ **bellicosity** *n.*
**belligerence** *n* **1** an aggressive attitude or disposition. **2** the state of being at war.
**belligerent**[1] *adj* **1** engaged in war. **2** aggressive or combative.
**belligerent**[2] *n* a country or person engaged in war.
**bellow**[1] *v* **1** to make a loud deep roar. **2** to shout in a deep voice.
**bellow**[2] *n* **1** a bellowing sound. **2** a loud deep shout.
**bellows** *pl n* (*treated as sing.*) a device with handles and pleated expandable sides used to create a current of air to fan a fire.
**belly**[1] *n* (*pl* **-ies**) **1** the abdomen. **2** the undersurface of an animal's body. **3** the stomach and associated organs. **4** an internal cavity; the interior.
**belly**[2] *v* (**-ies, -ied**) (*often* + out) to swell or fill.
**bellyache**[1] *n* colic.
**bellyache**[2] *v informal* to complain peevishly. ➤ **bellyacher** *n.*
**belly flop** *n* a dive into water in which the front of the body strikes flat against the surface.
**belong** *v* **1** (+ to) to be somebody's property. **2** to be in a proper situation or position. **3** (+ to)

to be attached by birth, allegiance, or membership. **4** (+ to) to be an attribute or function of a person or thing.

**belongings** *pl n* possessions.

**beloved**[1] *adj* dearly loved.

**beloved**[2] *n* a dearly loved person.

**below**[1] *adv* **1** in or to a lower place or position. **2** lower on the same page or on a following page.

**below**[2] *prep* **1** lower than the level of. **2** less than. **3** inferior to in rank.

**belt**[1] *n* **1** a strip of leather or material worn round the waist to hold clothing or a weapon. **2** an endless band of material for transmitting motion and power or conveying objects. **3** an area characterized by some distinctive feature. **4** *informal* a heavy blow. ✱ **below the belt** unfairly. **tighten one's belt** to reduce expenditure. **under one's belt** successfully attained or accomplished. ➤ **belted** *adj.*

**belt**[2] *v* **1** to fasten with a belt. **2** *informal* to strike or hit hard. **3** *informal* (*usu* + out) to sing in a forceful manner or style. **4** *informal* to move or act vigorously or violently.

**belt up** *v Brit, informal* to stop talking.

**bemoan** *v* to express regret or displeasure over.

**bemused** *adj* confused or bewildered.

**bench**[1] *n* **1** a long seat for two or more people. **2** (*often* **the Bench**) a judge's seat in court. **3** a long worktable. **4** (**the bench**) seating for substitute players at a sports match.

**bench**[2] *v* **1** to exhibit (a dog) at a show. **2** *NAmer* to remove (a player) from or keep them out of a game.

**benchmark** *n* a standard or point of reference.

**bend**[1] *v* (*past tense and past part.* **bent**) **1** to move into or out of a curve or angle. **2** to make submissive; to subdue. **3** to incline the body, *esp* in submission; to bow. **4** (*often* + to) to yield or compromise. **5** to alter or modify (a rule) to make it more acceptable.

**bend**[2] *n* **1** a curved part of a road or stream. **2** (**the bends**) (*treated as sing. or pl*) = DECOMPRESSION SICKNESS. ✱ **round the bend** *informal* mad or crazy.

**bender** *n informal* a drinking spree.

**beneath**[1] *prep* **1** in or to a lower position than. **2** directly under. **3** not suitable to; unworthy of. **4** under the control or influence of.

**beneath**[2] *adv* in or to a lower position.

**benediction** *n* a blessing in public worship.

**benefactor** *n* a person who gives financial or other aid.

**benefice** *n* an ecclesiastical office to which an income is attached. ➤ **beneficed** *adj.*

**beneficiary**[1] *n* (*pl* **-ies**) a person who benefits from the terms of a a trust or will.

**beneficiary**[2] *adj* of a benefice.

**benefit**[1] *n* **1** an advantage or helpful thing. **2** good or welfare. **3** (*also in pl*) financial help provided by the state to those in need. **4** a payment provided by a pension scheme or insurance policy. **5** a game or social event to raise funds for a person or cause.

**benefit**[2] *v* (**benefited, benefiting**) **1** to be useful or profitable to. **2** to receive a benefit.

***Usage Note:*** Note the spellings *benefited* and *benefiting* with one *t*.

**benevolent** *adj* **1** disposed to do good; charitable. **2** characterized by goodwill. ➤ **benevolence** *n.*

**benighted** *adj* intellectually, morally, or socially unenlightened.

**benign** *adj* **1** gentle or gracious. **2** favourable or mild. **3** of a tumour: not malignant.

**bent**[1] *v* past tense and past part. of BEND[1].

**bent**[2] *adj* **1** not straight or even; curved. **2** (+ on) determined to. **3** *Brit, informal* corrupt; dishonest.

**bent**[3] *n* a special talent or interest.

**benzene** *n* a liquid found in petroleum and used as a solvent.

**bequeath** *v* **1** to leave (personal property) in a will. **2** to transmit or hand down. ➤ **bequeathal** *n.*

**bequest** *n* **1** a legacy. **2** the act of bequeathing.

**berate** *v* to scold or condemn angrily.

**bereave** *v* (*past part.* **bereaved** *or* **bereft**) (**be bereaved**) to suffer loss by the death of a loved person. ➤ **bereavement** *n.*

**bereft** *adj* deprived or robbed of; completely without.

**beret** *n* a round flat cloth cap.

**bergamot** *n* an essential oil found in some oranges and used as a flavouring.

**beriberi** *n* a disease caused by a lack of vitamin B1.

**berk** *n Brit, slang* a stupid person.

**berry** *n* (*pl* **-ies**) a small, pulpy, edible fruit without a stone.

**berserk** ✱ **go berserk** to become wildly frenzied.

**berth**[1] *n* **1** a place for sleeping on a ship or train. **2** a place in a harbour for a ship. ✱ **give a wide berth to** to remain at a safe distance from.

**berth**[2] *v* **1** of a ship: to dock. **2** to allot a berth to.

**beryllium** *n* a steel-grey light metallic chemical element.

**beseech** *v* (**beseeched** *or* **besought**) to ask earnestly or pleadingly.

**beset** *v* (**besetting,** *past tense and past part.* **beset**) **1** to trouble constantly. **2** to surround and attack.

**beside** *prep* **1** by the side of. **2** in comparison with. **3** unconnected with. ✱ **beside oneself** extremely agitated or worried.

**besides**[1] *adv* **1** in addition. **2** moreover.

**besides**[2] *prep* **1** other than. **2** as an addition to.

**besiege** *v* **1** to surround with armed forces. **2** to crowd round. **3** to importune with questions or complaints.

**besmirch** *v* to sully or soil.
**besotted** *adj* **1** infatuated. **2** drunk or intoxicated.
**bespoke** *adj Brit* made to individual requirements.
**best**[1] *adj* **1** of the highest quality or most excellent type. **2** most appropriate or advisable. * **the best part of** most of something.
**best**[2] *adv* **1** in the best manner; to the best extent or degree. **2** as a preference or ideal. * **had best** would be well advised to do something.
**best**[3] *n* (**the best**) what is most excellent or desirable. * **get the best of** to defeat or get an advantage over. **make the best of** to get some benefit from (an unfavourable situation).
**best**[4] *v* to outdo or outwit (somebody).
**bestial** *adj* brutally cruel.
**bestiality** *n* brutally cruel behaviour.
**bestir** *v* (**bestirred, bestirring**) to rouse (oneself) to action.
**best man** *n* a male friend or relative who attends the bridegroom at a wedding.
**bestow** *v* (*usu* + on/upon) to present as a gift or honour. ➤ **bestowal** *n.*
**bestrew** *v* (**bestrewed, bestrewed** *or* **bestrewn**) *literary* **1** to strew (something) somewhere. **2** (+ with) to lie scattered over (a place): *The ground was bestrewn with leaves.*
**bestride** *v* (**bestrode, bestridden**) **1** to ride or stand astride. **2** to tower over; to dominate.
**bestseller** *n* a book or other product that achieves a high level of sales. ➤ **bestselling** *adj.*
**bet**[1] *n* **1** the act of risking a sum of money or other stake on the forecast outcome of a future event, e.g. a race or contest. **2** a stake. **3** an opinion or belief. **4** a person or thing likely to be successful.
**bet**[2] *v* (**betting, bet** *or* **betted**) **1** (*usu* + on) to stake (an amount of money) as a bet. **2** to make a bet with. **3** *informal* to be convinced that (a guess or prediction) is true.
**beta** *n* the second letter of the Greek alphabet (Β, β).
**beta-blocker** *n* a drug used to treat high blood pressure.
**beta particle** *n* an electron or positron emitted from the nucleus of an atom during beta decay: compare ALPHA PARTICLE.
**bête noire** *n* (*pl* **bêtes noires**) a person or thing strongly detested.
**betide** *v* * **woe betide** used as a warning of retribution or punishment.
**betoken** *v* **1** to show. **2** to presage or portend.
**betray** *v* **1** to give up or reveal (somebody or something) to an enemy by treachery. **2** to be disloyal to. **3** to show (a feeling) inadvertently. **4** to disclose (a secret). ➤ **betrayal** *n.*
**betrothed** *adj* engaged to be married.
**better**[1] *adj* **1** of a higher quality. **2** more appropriate or advisable. **3** improved in health; partly or wholly recovered from an illness or injury. * **better off** enjoying better circumstances, *esp* financially. **get the better of** to overcome or defeat.
**better**[2] *adv* **1** in a way that is more excellent or desirable. **2** to a greater degree; more. * **had better** would be well advised (to do something).
**better**[3] *v* to surpass or improve on. * **better oneself** to improve one's living conditions or social status.
**betterment** *n* improvement.
**between**[1] *prep* **1** in or into the time or space that separates. **2** in intermediate relation to. **3** from one to the other of (two places). **4** through the common action of. **5** in shares to each of. * **between you and me** in confidence.
**between**[2] *adv* in or into an intermediate space or interval.
**betwixt** *adv and prep archaic* between. * **betwixt and between** in a midway position; neither one thing nor the other.
**bevel**[1] *n* a sloping or slanting edge or surface, usu between two other surfaces meeting at right angles.
**bevel**[2] *v* (**bevelled, bevelling,** *NAmer* **beveled, beveling**) to cut or shape to a bevel.
**beverage** *n* a drink.
**bevy** *n* (*pl* **-ies**) a group of people.
**bewail** *v* to express deep sorrow for.
**beware** *v* to be wary of (a threat or danger).
**bewilder** *v* to perplex or confuse.
**bewitch** *v* **1** to attract or charm. **2** to cast a spell over.
**beyond**[1] *prep* **1** on or to the farther side of. **2** out of the reach of. **3** in a degree or amount surpassing. **4** out of the comprehension of.
**beyond**[2] *adv* on or to the farther side.
**beyond**[3] *n* (**the beyond**) something that lies outside the scope of ordinary experience; *specif* life after death, the hereafter.
**Bi** *abbr* the chemical symbol for bismuth.
**biannual** *adj* occurring twice a year. ➤ **biannually** *adv.*
**bias** *n* **1** an inclination to favour or disfavour certain people or things. **2** a line diagonal to the grain of a fabric. **3** the tendency of a bowl to take a curved path when rolled.
**bias binding** *n* a narrow folded strip of fabric cut on the bias used for hemming, to cover raw edges, or for decoration.
**biased** *adj or* **biassed** having a bias; prejudiced.
**biathlon** *n* an athletic contest consisting of cross-country skiing and rifle shooting.
**bib** *n* **1** a cloth or plastic covering placed over a child's front to protect the clothes while it is eating. **2** a small rectangular section of a garment above the waist.

**bible** *n* **1** (**the Bible**) the sacred book of Christians, comprising the Old Testament and the New Testament. **2** an authoritative book.

**biblical** *adj* of or in accordance with the Bible. ➤ **biblically** *adv.*

**bibliography** *n* (*pl* **-ies**) a list of books and articles relating to a particular topic. ➤ **bibliographer** *n,* **bibliographical** *adj.*

**bibliophile** *n* a collector of books.

**bibulous** *adj* prone to over-indulgence in alcoholic drinks.

**bicameral** *adj* having two legislative chambers.

**bicarbonate** *n* an acid carbonate; *esp* SODIUM BICARBONATE.

**bicentenary** *n* (*pl* **-ies**) the celebration of a 200th anniversary.

**biceps** *n* a large muscle at the front of the upper arm that bends the arm at the elbow.

**bicker** *v* to engage in petty bad-tempered argument.

**bicycle**[1] *n* a two-wheeled pedal-driven vehicle with handlebars and a saddle. ➤ **bicyclist** *n.*

**bicycle**[2] *v* to ride a bicycle.

**bid**[1] *v* (**bidding, bid** *or* **bade, bid** *or* **bidden**) **1** to offer (a price) for payment or acceptance, e.g. at an auction. **2** to make a bid of or in (a suit at cards). **3** to make an attempt to do something. ➤ **bidder** *n.*

**bid**[2] *n* **1** an act of bidding. **2** an offer of a price.

**biddable** *adj* easily led or controlled; docile.

**biddy** *n* (*pl* **-ies**) *informal* an old woman.

**bide** *v archaic or dialect* to remain for a while. ✱ **bide one's time** to wait patiently for an opportunity to act.

**bidet** *n* a low basin used for washing the genitals and anus.

**biennial** *adj* **1** occurring every two years. **2** of a plant: growing for two years and then dying.

**bier** *n* a stand for a corpse or coffin before burial.

**biff**[1] *n informal* a whack or blow.

**biff**[2] *v informal* to hit sharply or roughly.

**bifocal** *adj* of a lens: having one part that corrects for near vision and one for distant vision.

**big** *adj* (**bigger, biggest**) **1** large in size, amount, number, or scale. **2** important in influence, standing, or wealth. **3** of a sibling: older or grown-up. **4** of great force or intensity. **5** magnanimous or generous.

**bigamy** *n* the crime of marrying while legally married to another person. ➤ **bigamist** *n,* **bigamous** *adj.*

**big bang** *n* **1** the theoretical explosion of material from which the universe originated. **2** a sudden reorganization or change.

**big end** *n Brit* the end of an engine's connecting rod nearest the crankpin.

**big game** *n* large animals hunted or fished for sport.

**bighead** *n informal* a conceited person. ➤ **bigheaded** *adj.*

**bigot** *n* an unpleasantly prejudiced and intolerant person. ➤ **bigoted** *adj,* **bigotry** *n.*

**big top** *n* the main tent of a circus.

**bigwig** *n informal* an important person.

**bijou** *adj* small and attractively elegant.

**bike**[1] *n informal* a bicycle or motorcycle.

**bike**[2] *v* to ride a bicycle or motorcycle.

**biker** *n* a member of a gang of motorcyclists.

**bikini** *n* a woman's two-piece swimsuit.

**bilateral** *adj* having two sides or parts.

**bilberry** *n* (*pl* **-ies**) a bluish edible soft fruit.

**bile** *n* **1** a fluid secreted by the liver to aid the digestion of fats. **2** a tendency to become angry.

**bilge** *n* **1** the lowest part of a ship's hull. **2** *informal* nonsense.

**bilingual** *adj* **1** able to use two languages fluently. **2** expressed in two languages.

**bilious** *adj* **1** suffering from a feeling of nausea. **2** relating to bile.

**bilk** *v* to cheat by swindling.

**bill**[1] *n* **1** an itemized statement of charges. **2** a draft of a law presented to a law-making body. **3** a programme of entertainment in a theatre or cinema. **4** *chiefly NAmer* a banknote. ✱ **fill/fit the bill** to be suitable.

**bill**[2] *v* **1** to submit a bill of charges to. **2** (+ as) to announce or proclaim to be something.

**bill**[3] *n* **1** the beak of a bird. **2** a narrow piece of land projecting into the sea.

**bill**[4] *v* ✱ **bill and coo** to caress and talk lovingly.

**billboard** *n chiefly NAmer* a large board for advertisements.

**billet**[1] *n* a private home where soldiers are given board and lodging.

**billet**[2] *v* (**billeted, billeting**) (*often* + on) to provide (soldiers) with a billet.

**billet-doux** /ˌbiliˈdooh, ˌbeeyay/ *n* (*pl* **billets-doux**) a love letter.

**billhook** *n* a pruning tool having a blade with a hooked point.

**billiards** *n* a game played with three balls, in which scores are made by causing the cue ball to hit the other two balls in succession.

**billing** *n* the relative prominence given to each performer in advertising programmes.

**billion** *n* a thousand millions or 1,000,000,000 ($10^9$). ➤ **billionth** *adj and n.*

**billionaire** *n* somebody whose wealth is estimated at a billion or more pounds or dollars.

**billow**[1] *n* **1** a large wave in the open sea. **2** a swirling mass of flame or smoke.

**billow**[2] *v* to rise or swell out in billows.

**billy** *n* (*pl* **-ies**) a metal can with a handle and lid, used for outdoor cooking.

**billy goat** *n informal* a male goat.

**bimbo** *n* (*pl* **-os**) *informal, derog* an attractive but unintelligent young woman.

**bin**[1] *n* **1** *Brit* a container for rubbish. **2** a large container used for storage.

**bin**[2] *v* (**binned, binning**) to discard or throw away.

**binary** *adj* **1** relating to a system of numbers that has two as its base and uses only the digits 0 and 1. **2** involving a choice of two alternatives (e.g. on or off). **3** consisting of two things or parts.

**bind**[1] *v* (*past tense and past part.* **bound**) **1** (*also* + up) to tie together, or make secure by tying. **2** to put under an obligation or legal requirement. **3** (*often* + up) to enclose by wrapping something round. **4** to stick together. **5** to strengthen or decorate with a band or binding. **6** to apply a binding to (a book). **7** to form a cohesive mass. **8** to become unable to move or operate freely.

**bind**[2] *n informal* a nuisance or annoyance.

**binder** *n* **1** a cover for holding sheets of paper. **2** a person who binds books. **3** a harvesting machine that binds straw into bundles.

**bindi** *n* (*pl* **bindis**) a decorative mark in the middle of the forehead, worn by Indian women.

**binding**[1] *n* **1** a covering that fastens the leaves of a book together. **2** a narrow strip of fabric used to finish raw edges.

**binding**[2] *adj* (*often* + on) imposing an obligation.

**bind over** *v* to impose a specific legal obligation on.

**bindweed** *n* a twining plant such as convolvulus.

**binge**[1] *n informal* a period of excessive eating or drinking.

**binge**[2] *v* (**binged, bingeing**) *informal* to eat or drink excessively.

**bingo**[1] *interj* used to express sudden success or welcome surprise.

**bingo**[2] *n* a game in which players mark off numbers on a card as they are randomly called out, the winner being the first to complete a card.

**binocular** *adj* relating to or using both eyes.

**biobank** *n* a collection of genetic material established to facilitate research, *esp* into genetic links to disease.

**biochemistry** *n* the study of the chemical processes in living organisms. ➤ **biochemical** *adj*, **biochemist** *n*.

**biodegradable** *adj* capable of being broken down into simpler harmless products by the action of bacteria and other living organisms.

**biodiversity** *n* the variety of living species in the world or a particular environment.

**biofeedback** *n* the technique of making involuntary bodily processes perceptible to the senses so that they can be affected by conscious mental control.

**biography** *n* (*pl* **-ies**) **1** an account of a person's life. **2** biographical writing as a literary genre. ➤ **biographer** *n*, **biographical** *adj*.

**biological** *adj* **1** relating to biology or living organisms. **2** acting on or produced by living organisms. **3** of a detergent: containing an enzyme. ➤ **biologically** *adv*.

**biology** *n* the study of the life processes of living organisms. ➤ **biologist** *n*.

**biometric** *adj* **1** relating to records of a person's fingerprints, iris image, voice pattern, etc. **2** relating to the use of such data as a means of identification, as in an identify card.

**bionic** *adj* **1** of an artificial body part: designed to replace or simulate a living part. **2** *informal* **having exceptional powers**.

**biopsy** *n* (*pl* **-ies**) the removal and examination of tissue from the living body.

**biorhythm** *n* (*usu in pl*) a periodic cycle of biological activity affecting mood and behaviour. ➤ **biorhythmic** *adj*.

**bipartite** *adj* **1** consisting of two parts. **2** affecting both parties to a treaty.

**biped** *n* a two-footed animal. ➤ **bipedal** *adj*.

**biplane** *n* an aeroplane with two pairs of wings, one above the other.

**bipolar** *adj* **1** having positive and negative electrical poles. **2** characterized by two opposed statements or views. ➤ **bipolarity** *n*.

**birch**[1] *n* **1** a deciduous tree with a thin bark that peels readily. **2** (**the birch**) punishment by flogging with a bundle of birch twigs.

**birch**[2] *v* to flog with a birch.

**bird** *n* **1** an animal with feathers, a beak, and wings, laying eggs and usually able to fly. **2** *chiefly Brit, informal* a girlfriend or young woman. ✱ **the birds and the bees** *informal* the facts of sex and sexual reproduction.

**birdie** *n* **1** a small bird. **2** a golf score of one stroke less than par on a hole.

**bird of prey** *n* a bird that feeds on carrion or on meat taken by hunting.

**bird's-eye view** *n* a view from above.

**Biro** *n* (*pl* **-os**) *trademark* a kind of ballpoint pen.

**birth** *n* **1** the emergence of a new individual from the body of its parent. **2** family origin and social status. **3** a beginning or start. ✱ **give birth** to produce a baby as a mother.

**birth control** *n* use of contraception and other means to control the number of children born.

**birthday** *n* an anniversary of the day a person was born.

**birthmark** *n* a blemish existing on the skin at birth.

**birthrate** *n* the number of live births per unit of population.

**birthright** *n* something to which a person is entitled by being born into a particular family, nation, etc.

**biscuit** *n* **1** *Brit* a small flat crisp sweet or savoury cake. **2** a light yellowish brown colour.

**bisect** *v* to divide into two parts. ➤ **bisection** *n*.

**bisexual**[1] *adj* **1** sexually attracted to both sexes. **2** possessing characteristics of both sexes. ➤ **bisexuality** *n.*
**bisexual**[2] *n* a bisexual person.
**bishop** *n* **1** a senior member of the Christian clergy, typically governing a diocese. **2** a chess piece that moves diagonally across the board.
**bismuth** *n* a heavy brittle reddish white metallic element used in alloys.
**bison** *n* (*pl* **bison**) a large ox with a shaggy mane and a humped back.
**bistro** *n* (*pl* **-os**) a small bar or restaurant.
**bit**[1] *n* **1** a small piece or quantity of something. **2** (**a bit**) a short period or distance. **3** a small coin. ✻ **a bit** *informal* somewhat; rather. **bit by bit** by small amounts. **bits and pieces/bobs** miscellaneous things of little value. **do one's bit** *Brit* to make one's personal contribution to a task or cause.
**bit**[2] *n* a unit of computer information corresponding to a choice between two alternatives (e.g. *on* or *off*).
**bit**[3] *n* **1** a bar of metal attached to a horse's bridle and inserted in its mouth. **2** a piece of a tool for drilling or boring. **have the bit between one's teeth** to act with determination.
**bit**[4] *v* past tense and past part. of BITE[1].
**bitch**[1] *n* **1** a female dog. **2** *slang* a spiteful and domineering woman. **3** *informal* something difficult or unpleasant.
**bitch**[2] *v informal* **1** to make malicious or spiteful comments. **2** to complain.
**bitchy** *adj* (**-ier, -iest**) *informal* malicious or spiteful. ➤ **bitchiness** *n.*
**bite**[1] *v* (**bit, bitten**) **1** to seize or cut into with the teeth or jaws. **2** to sting with a fang or other specialized part of the body. **3** to take a strong hold of; to grip. **4** to have an effect. ✻ **be bitten by/with something** to have great enthusiasm for. **bite somebody's head off** to speak to or scold somebody angrily. **bite the bullet** to endure stoically something unpleasant that cannot be avoided. **bite the dust 1** to fall dead, *esp* in a fight. **2** to collapse or be destroyed.
**bite**[2] *n* **1** an act of biting. **2** a wound made by biting. **3** the amount of food taken with one bite. **4** a strong grip. **5** sharpness or pungency of taste.
**biting** *adj* **1** of a wind: strong and intensely cold. **2** of a remark: unkind or sarcastic.
**bit part** *n* a minor acting role.
**bitter**[1] *adj* **1** having a sharp or sour taste. **2** intense or severe. **3** showing or stemming from great dislike or resentment. **4** of a wind: intensely cold. **5** characterized by or causing severe grief or regret. ➤ **bitterly** *adv,* **bitterness** *n.*
**bitter**[2] *n Brit* a bitter beer heavily flavoured with hops.
**bittersweet** *adj* **1** bitter and sweet at the same time. **2** pleasant but with elements of sadness.
**bitty** *adj* (**-ier, -iest**) scrappy or disjointed. ➤ **bittily** *adv.*
**bitumen** *n* tar or other black sticky substance obtained from petroleum and used in surfacing roads. ➤ **bituminous** *adj.*
**bivalve** *n* an aquatic mollusc having a shell composed of two valves.
**bivouac**[1] *n* a temporary encampment under little or no shelter.
**bivouac**[2] *v* (**bivouacked, bivouacking**) to camp in a bivouac.
**bizarre** *adj* odd or eccentric. ➤ **bizarrely** *adv.*
**Bk** *abbr* the chemical symbol for berkelium.
**blab**[1] *v* (**blabbed, blabbing**) **1** to reveal (a secret). **2** to talk indiscreetly or thoughtlessly. ➤ **blabber** *n.*
**blab**[2] *n* somebody who blabs.
**blabber** *v* (**blabbered, blabbering**) **1** to babble. **2** to talk indiscreetly.
**black**[1] *adj* **1** of the darkest colour. **2** relating to people having dark skin pigmentation. **3** of coffee or tea: served without milk or cream. **4** sinister or evil. **5** indicative of hostility or disapproval. **6** showing a financial profit: compare RED[1]. **7** characterized by grim or grotesque humour. ➤ **blackness** *n.*
**black**[2] *n* **1** a black colour. **2** a black person. ✻ **in the black** financially in credit.
**black**[3] *v* **1** to make black. **2** *chiefly Brit* to declare (e.g. a business or industry) subject to boycott by trade-union members.
**black-and-blue** *adj* darkly discoloured from bruising.
**black-and-white** *adj* **1** reproducing visual images in black, white, and tones of grey. **2** evaluating things in extremes.
**blackball** *v* **1** to vote against (a candidate for membership). **2** to ostracize.
**black belt** *n* a black belt worn by an expert in a martial art.
**blackberry** *n* (*pl* **-ies**) a black edible fruit that grows on a prickly shrub.
**blackbird** *n* a bird with black feathers and an orange beak.
**blackboard** *n* a hard smooth board used for writing on with chalk.
**black box** *n* an aircraft's flight recorder.
**blackcurrant** *n* a small black edible soft fruit.
**black economy** *n* illegal or unofficial business activity.
**blacken** *v* **1** to make or become black. **2** to injure or destroy (somebody's reputation).
**black eye** *n* an area of bruising round the eye.
**blackfly** *n* a small dark-coloured insect that feeds on plants.
**blackguard** *n* a coarse or unscrupulous person; a scoundrel.
**blackhead** *n* a small dark-coloured oily plug blocking a pore on the face.

**black hole** *n* an area in space with an intense gravitational field, from which no radiation can escape.
**black ice** *n Brit* transparent slippery ice on a road.
**blackleg** *n chiefly Brit* a worker who continues working during an official strike.
**blacklist**[1] *n* a list of people or organizations who are disapproved of or are to be boycotted.
**blacklist**[2] *v* to put on a blacklist.
**black magic** *n* magic performed by invoking evil spirits.
**blackmail**[1] *n* **1** extortion with the threat of exposing secret or compromising information. **2** political or moral pressure to do something undesirable.
**blackmail**[2] *v* to subject to blackmail. ➤ **blackmailer** *n*.
**black mark** *n* a mark of censure or disapproval.
**black market** *n* illicit trade in violation of official regulations. ➤ **black marketeer** *n*.
**blackout** *n* **1** a period of darkness enforced as a precaution against air raids. **2** a sudden loss of electrical power. **3** a temporary loss of consciousness. **4** a holding back or suppression of something. **5** a brief loss of radio signal.
**black out** *v* to become unconscious.
**black pudding** *n chiefly Brit* a dark sausage made from suet and pigs' blood.
**black sheep** *n* a disreputable member of a family or organization.
**blacksmith** *n* somebody who works iron at a forge. ➤ **blacksmithing** *n*.
**black spot** *n Brit* a stretch of road on which accidents occur frequently.
**blackthorn** *n* a spiny shrub with hard wood and small white flowers.
**black widow** *n* a venomous spider of which the female is black with a red mark on the underside.
**bladder** *n* **1** a sac in animals in which urine collects before being discharged. **2** an air-filled rubber bag inside a ball.
**blade** *n* **1** the cutting part of a knife, razor, or other tool. **2** a long narrow leaf of a grass or cereal. **3** the runner of an ice skate. **4** the broad flattened part of an oar, paddle, bat, propeller, etc.
**blag** *v* (**blagged, blagging**) **1** *Brit, informal* to rob with violence. **2** to steal. **3** to bluff. ➤ **blagger** *n*.
**blame**[1] *v* **1** to hold responsible for wrongdoing or misfortune. **2** to find fault with.
**blame**[2] *n* **1** responsibility for wrongdoing or misfortune. **2** disapproval or reproach. ➤ **blameless** *adj*, **blameworthy** *adj*.
**blanch** *v* **1** to make or become pale. **2** to scald (almonds) to remove the skin. **3** to prepare (vegetables) by plunging them briefly in boiling water.
**blancmange** *n* a sweetened and flavoured dessert made from cornflour and milk.
**bland** *adj* **1** without character or excitement; dull or insipid. **2** of food: with little flavour or texture. **3** showing no emotion or anxiety.
**blandishments** *pl n* pleasing things said to coax or flatter somebody.
**blank**[1] *adj* **1** with nothing marked, written, or recorded on it. **2** not filled in. **3** dazed or nonplussed. **4** showing no expression. **5** temporarily without memory or understanding. **6** absolute or unqualified. ➤ **blankly** *adv*, **blankness** *n*.
**blank**[2] *n* **1** an empty space to be filled in on a form. **2** a void, without thought, memory, or understanding. **3** a vacant or uneventful period. **4** a piece of material prepared to be made into something, e.g. a key or coin. **5** a gun cartridge containing powder but no bullet. * **draw a blank** to obtain no positive results.
**blanket**[1] *n* **1** a large thick piece of fabric used as a warm covering. **2** a thick covering or layer.
**blanket**[2] *v* (**blanketed, blanketing**) to cover with a thick layer.
**blanket**[3] *adj* applying generally.
**blank out** *v* to hide or erase.
**blank verse** *n* verse with no rhyme.
**blare**[1] *v* **1** to emit a loud harsh sound. **2** to proclaim loudly or sensationally.
**blare**[2] *n* a loud harsh sound.
**blarney** *n* **1** pleasing but insincere talk or flattery. **2** nonsense.
**blasé** /'blahzay/ *adj* indifferent to pleasure or excitement because of over-familiarity.
**blaspheme** *v* to use a holy or sacred name with impiety. ➤ **blasphemer** *n*.
**blasphemy** *n* (*pl* **-ies**) disrespect for a holy or sacred name. ➤ **blasphemous** *adj*.
**blast**[1] *n* **1** an explosion or violent detonation. **2** a violent wave of increased atmospheric pressure produced by this. **3** a strong gust of wind. **4** a violent outburst. **5** the sound made by a wind instrument or whistle. * **at full blast** at top speed or full capacity.
**blast**[2] *v* **1** to shatter, remove, or open with an explosive. **2** to destroy (hopes, etc). **3** to curse or denounce.
**blast**[3] *interj Brit, informal* used to express annoyance.
**blast furnace** *n* a furnace for converting iron ore into iron, using currents of air under pressure.
**blast off** *v* of a spacecraft or missile: to leave the launching pad.
**blatant** *adj* obvious and unashamed. ➤ **blatancy** *n*, **blatantly** *adv*.
**blather**[1] *n* foolish voluble talk.
**blather**[2] *v* (**blathered, blathering**) to talk foolishly or volubly. ➤ **blatherer** *n*.
**blaze**[1] *n* **1** an intensely burning flame or fire. **2** intense direct light. **3** a dazzling display. **4** a

sudden outburst. ✱ **like blazes** *informal* intensely.

**blaze[2]** *v* **1** to burn or shine strongly. **2** to be conspicuously brilliant. **3** (+ away) to shoot rapidly and repeatedly.

**blaze[3]** *n* a broad white mark on a horse's face.

**blaze[4]** *v* ✱ **blaze a trail 1** to mark out a path or way. **2** to lead or be a pioneer in some activity.

**blazer** *n* a jacket with patch pockets, worn for casual wear or as part of a school uniform.

**blazon** *v* to proclaim widely and ostentatiously.

**bleach[1]** *v* to make whiter or remove the colour from (e.g. fabric) by chemical or physical means.

**bleach[2]** *n* a strong chemical substance used in bleaching.

**bleak** *adj* **1** barren and exposed. **2** cold or raw. **3** lacking in warmth or kindness. **4** of circumstances: not hopeful or encouraging. **5** severely simple or austere. ➤ **bleakly** *adv*, **bleakness** *n.*

**bleary** *adj* (**-ier, -iest**) **1** of the eyes or vision: dull and indistinct from fatigue or sleep. **2** poorly outlined or defined. ➤ **blearily** *adv.*

**bleat[1]** *v* **1** to make the cry of a sheep or goat. **2** to talk complainingly or feebly.

**bleat[2]** *n* the cry of a sheep or goat.

**bleed[1]** *v* (*past tense and past part.* **bled**) **1** to emit or lose blood. **2** formerly in medicine, to remove or draw blood from. **3** (+ for) to feel anguish, pain, or sympathy. **4** of colour or dye: to flow over into an adjoining area. **5** to extort money from. **6** to drain the vitality or lifeblood from. **7** to let out liquid or gas from (a container).

**bleed[2]** *n* an act or instance of bleeding.

**bleep[1]** *n* a short high-pitched sound made by an electronic device.

**bleep[2]** *v* **1** to emit a bleep. **2** to summon by means of a bleeping device. ➤ **bleeper** *n.*

**blemish[1]** *n* **1** a flaw or disfiguring mark. **2** a defect of character.

**blemish[2]** *v* to spoil the appearance of.

**blench** *v* to draw back or flinch from fear or pain.

**blend[1]** *v* **1** to mix or combine separate constituents. **2** (*often* + in) to produce a harmonious effect.

**blend[2]** *n* a mixture.

**blender** *n* an electrical device for grinding or mixing food.

**bless** *v* **1** to consecrate by a prayer or religious rite. **2** to invoke divine care for. **3** to confer prosperity or happiness on.

**blessed** *adj* **1** holy and venerated. **2** bringing pleasure or contentment. ➤ **blessedly** *adv.*

**blessing** *n* **1** the invocation of God's favour upon a person. **2** the words used in this. **3** approval or moral support. **4** something conducive to happiness or welfare.

**blew** *v* past tense of BLOW[1].

**blight[1]** *n* **1** a disease of plants resulting in withering. **2** something that impairs or destroys. **3** a condition of disorder or decay.

**blight[2]** *v* **1** to affect (e.g. a plant) with blight. **2** to impair or destroy.

**blighter** *n chiefly Brit, informal* a troublesome or unfortunate person or thing.

**blind[1]** *adj* **1** unable to see. **2** (*often* + to) unable to perceive clearly or judge rationally. **3** acting or done without adequate knowledge or judgment. **4** having only one opening or outlet. ✱ **turn a blind eye** to overlook mistakes or wrongdoing. ➤ **blindly** *adv*, **blindness** *n.*

**blind[2]** *v* **1** to make blind. **2** (*often* + to) to rob of judgment or discernment.

**blind[3]** *n* **1** a flexible screen for covering a window. **2** a cover or subterfuge.

**blind date** *n* a date between people who have not previously met.

**blindfold[1]** *v* to cover the eyes of (somebody) with a piece of material.

**blindfold[2]** *n* a piece of cloth tied around a person's head to prevent them from seeing.

**blindfold[3]** *adj and adv* wearing a blindfold.

**blinding** *adj* **1** of light: overpoweringly bright. **2** extremely obvious. ➤ **blindingly** *adv.*

**blindman's buff** *n* a game in which a blindfolded player tries to catch other players.

**blind spot** *n* **1** a point in the retina of the eye that is not sensitive to light. **2** a part of a visual field that cannot be seen. **3** an area in which one lacks knowledge or discrimination.

**blink[1]** *v* **1** to close and open the eyes rapidly or involuntarily. **2** to shine intermittently.

**blink[2]** *n* an act of blinking. ✱ **on the blink** *informal* not working properly.

**blinker[1]** *n* **1** a warning or signalling light that flashes on and off. **2** (*in pl*) something that restricts understanding or awareness. **3** *chiefly Brit* each of two flaps over a horse's eyes to prevent it from seeing to the sides.

**blinker[2]** *v* **1** to put blinkers on (a horse). **2** to restrict or lessen the understanding or awareness of. ➤ **blinkered** *adj.*

**blip[1]** *n* **1** a bleep. **2** an image on a radar screen. **3** a brief deviation from the norm; an aberration.

**blip[2]** *v* (**blipped, blipping**) to deviate briefly from the norm.

**bliss** *n* complete happiness. ➤ **blissful** *adj*, **blissfully** *adv.*

**blister[1]** *n* **1** a raised part of the outer skin containing watery liquid. **2** a bubble or raised spot on a surface.

**blister[2]** *v* to be affected with blisters.

**blistering** *adj* **1** of heat: extremely intense or severe. **2** of speed: extremely fast.

**blithe** *adj* **1** cheerful and light-hearted. **2** casual or heedless. ➤ **blithely** *adv.*

**blithering** *adj informal* **1** stupid. **2** talking nonsense.

**blitz**[1] *n* **1** an intensive aerial bombardment. **2** a period of intensive action.
**blitz**[2] *v* **1** to attack in a blitz. **2** to deal with by intensive action.
**blizzard** *n* a severe snowstorm with a strong wind.
**bloat** *v* to swell with gas or liquid. ➤ **bloated** *adj.*
**bloater** *n* a salted smoked herring or mackerel.
**blob** *n* **1** a small drop of a sticky substance. **2** an amorphous shape. ➤ **blobby** *adj.*
**bloc** *n* an alliance of nations for a common purpose.
**block**[1] *n* **1** a large building divided into separate functional units. **2** a rectangular area of buildings enclosed by streets. **3** a compact solid piece of material. **4** an obstacle or blockage.
**block**[2] *v* **1** to be a barrier that obstructs (a passage, road, pipe, etc). **2** to hinder the movement or progress of.
**blockade**[1] *n* the surrounding of an enemy area to prevent people and supplies from passing in and out.
**blockade**[2] *v* to subject to a blockade.
**blockage** *n* something that causes something to be blocked.
**blockbuster** *n informal* something particularly outstanding or effective.
**block capitals** *pl n* plain capital letters.
**bloke** *n chiefly Brit, informal* a man.
**blonde**[1] *or* **blond** *adj* **1** *esp* of hair: golden or pale yellow. **2** having blonde hair.
**blonde**[2] *or* **blond** *n* a woman with blonde hair.
**blood**[1] *n* **1** the red fluid that circulates in the arteries and veins of a vertebrate animal. **2** family background; ancestors. ✱ **in one's blood** part of a person's character or life. **one's blood is up** one is ready for a fight.
**blood**[2] *v* to give an initiating experience to.
**bloodbath** *n* a slaughter or massacre.
**blood-curdling** *adj* horrifying.
**blood group** *n* any of the classes by which human blood is classified.
**bloodhound** *n* a large hound used for tracking and following a scent.
**bloodless** *adj* **1** without the shedding of blood. **2** lacking in spirit or vitality. **3** of the complexion: pale from lack of blood.
**bloodletting** *n* **1** the draining of blood as a former medical treatment. **2** conflict with bloodshed.
**blood pressure** *n* the pressure exerted by the blood as it passes through blood vessels.
**bloodshed** *n* the killing or injuring of people.
**bloodshot** *adj* of an eye: having the white part tinged with red.
**blood sport** *n* a sport in which animals are hunted or killed.
**bloodstream** *n* the blood circulating in the body.
**bloodthirsty** *adj* eager for bloodshed.
**blood vessel** *n* any of the veins, arteries, or capillaries through which the blood circulates.
**bloody**[1] *adj* (**-ier, -iest**) **1** covered with blood. **2** involving bloodshed. **3** murderous or bloodthirsty. **4** *informal* used to express annoyance.
**bloody**[2] *v* (**-ies, -ied**) to cover or mark with blood.
**bloody-minded** *adj* obstructive and unhelpful.
**bloom**[1] *n* **1** a flower. **2** the state of having flowers. **3** a time of freshness and vigour. **4** a rosy or healthy complexion. **5** a light coating on some fruits and leaves.
**bloom**[2] *v* **1** to produce flowers. **2** to support abundant plant life. **3** to flourish.
**bloom**[3] *n* a thick bar of hammered or rolled iron or steel.
**bloomer** *n* **1** *informal* a foolish blunder. **2** *chiefly Brit* a long loaf marked with diagonal cuts.
**bloomers** *pl n* **1** a former women's costume consisting of a short skirt and loose trousers gathered at the ankles. **2** women's full loose knickers.
**blossom**[1] *n* **1** the flower of a plant. **2** the mass of flowers on a tree or shrub.
**blossom**[2] *v* (**blossomed, blossoming**) **1** to bloom. **2** to develop or flourish.
**blot**[1] *n* **1** a spot of ink or other liquid. **2** a fault or bad act.
**blot**[2] *v* (**blotted, blotting**) **1** to spot or stain. **2** to dry with an absorbent material. **3** to spoil (one's reputation) by committing an error or wrongdoing. ✱ **blot one's copybook** to spoil a good record or reputation.
**blotch**[1] *n* an irregular spot or mark. ➤ **blotchy** *adj.*
**blotch**[2] *v* to mark with blotches.
**blot out** *v* **1** to obscure or eclipse. **2** to exclude from one's mind.
**blotter** *n* a piece of blotting paper.
**blotting paper** *n* absorbent paper for drying or soaking up ink.
**blouse**[1] *n* a loose-fitting woman's upper garment like a shirt.
**blouse**[2] *v* **1** to fall in folds. **2** to make (e.g. part of a piece of clothing) fall in folds.
**blouson** *n* a short loose jacket gathered at the waist.
**blow**[1] *v* (**blew, blown**) **1** of air or wind: to move perceptibly. **2** to send a current of air through the mouth or nose. **3** to force air through (a musical instrument) to produce a sound. **4** of a tyre: to burst and lose the air inside it. **5** of a fuse: to break when overloaded. **6** *informal* to explode or detonate. **7** to burst or destroy with explosives. **8** to shape (e.g. glass or bubbles) by the action of blown air. **9** *informal* to waste (a chance of success). **10** *informal* to spend (money) extravagantly. **11** *informal* to reveal (a

secret or disguise). **12** *informal* to leave hurriedly. ✱ **blow hot and cold** to vary unpredictably in one's support for something; to vacillate. **blow one's own trumpet** to boast. **blow one's top** *informal* to lose one's temper.

**blow**[2] *n* **1** an act of blowing. **2** a strong wind or windy storm.

**blow**[3] *n* **1** a hard hit delivered with the hand or a weapon. **2** a shock or misfortune. ✱ **come to blows** to start fighting; to end up as a fight.

**blowfly** *n* (*pl* **-ies**) a fly that deposits eggs in meat.

**blowhole** *n* a nostril in the top of the head of a whale or dolphin.

**blowout** *n* **1** *informal* a large meal or other lavish entertainment. **2** the bursting of a tyre or fuse. **3** an uncontrolled eruption of an oil or gas well.

**blow over** *v* of a difficulty: to pass without harm.

**blowsy** *or* **blowzy** *adj* (**-ier, -iest**) *esp* of a woman: slovenly and overweight.

**blowtorch** *or* **blowlamp** *n* a portable burner that produces an intense flame.

**blow up** *v* **1** to shatter or destroy by an explosion. **2** to exaggerate. **3** to inflate with air or gas. **4** to enlarge (a photograph). ➤ **blowup** *n.*

**blowy** *adj* (**-ier, -iest**) windy.

**blub** *v* (**blubbed, blubbing**) *informal* to sob uncontrollably.

**blubber**[1] *n* **1** the fat of whales and seals. **2** *informal* body fat. ➤ **blubbery** *adj.*

**blubber**[2] *v informal* to sob uncontrollably.

**bludgeon**[1] *n* a heavy club used as a weapon.

**bludgeon**[2] *v* **1** to hit or beat with a bludgeon. **2** (*also* + into) to force (somebody) to do something.

**blue**[1] *adj* **1** of the colour of a clear sky. **2** low in spirits. **3** depressing or dismal. **4** indecent or pornographic. **5** *Brit* politically conservative. ✱ **once in a blue moon** very rarely.

**blue**[2] *v* (**blues, blued, blueing** *or* **bluing**) *Brit, informal* to spend (money) wastefully.

**bluebell** *n* a plant with blue bell-shaped flowers.

**blueberry** *n* (*pl* **-ies**) a dark blue fruit produced by a shrub of the heath family.

**blue blood** *n* high or noble birth. ➤ **blue-blooded** *adj.*

**bluebottle** *n* a large fly with an iridescent blue body.

**blue cheese** *n* cheese marked with veins of mould.

**blue chip** *n* a high-quality stock that is a sound investment. ➤ **blue-chip** *adj.*

**blue-collar** *adj* relating to manual work and workers.

**blueprint**[1] *n* **1** a plan or drawing done in white on a blue background. **2** a programme of action.

**blueprint**[2] *v* **1** to make a blueprint of (a plan, etc). **2** to plan out (a programme of action).

**blues** *n* (*pl* **blues**) **1** (**the blues**) low spirits; melancholy. **2** (*often* **the blues**) a melancholy style of music which originated among American blacks. ➤ **bluesy** *adj.*

**bluestocking** *n derog* a woman with intellectual or literary interests.

**blue tit** *n* a bird with a bright blue crown and yellow underside.

**blue whale** *n* a large bluish whale found *esp* in northern European waters.

**bluff**[1] *v* to deceive by a pretence of strength or confidence.

**bluff**[2] *n* an act or instance of bluffing. ✱ **call somebody's bluff** to challenge (somebody) to prove a claim one believes to be untrue.

**bluff**[3] *adj* good-naturedly frank and outspoken.

**bluff**[4] *n* a high steep bank or cliff.

**blunder**[1] *v* **1** to move unsteadily or confusedly. **2** to make a blunder.

**blunder**[2] *n* a careless or clumsy mistake.

**blunderbuss** *n* an obsolete short gun with a a flared muzzle.

**blunt**[1] *adj* **1** without a sharp edge or point. **2** direct and straightforward in manner. ➤ **bluntly** *adv.*

**blunt**[2] *v* to make or become blunt.

**blur**[1] *n* **1** something vague or indistinct. **2** a smear or stain. ➤ **blurry** *adj.*

**blur**[2] *v* (**blurred, blurring**) to make or become indistinct or confused.

**blurt out** *v* to say abruptly and impulsively.

**blush**[1] *v* to become red in the face from modesty or embarrassment.

**blush**[2] *n* **1** an instance of blushing. **2** a red or rosy tint.

**blusher** *n* a cream or powder for adding colour to the cheeks.

**bluster**[1] *v* **1** to talk or act in a showy manner. **2** of wind or rain: to blow in stormy gusts. ➤ **blustery** *adj.*

**bluster**[2] *n* loud boastful or threatening talk.

**boa** *n* **1** a large snake that crushes its prey. **2** a long fluffy stole of fur or feathers.

**boa constrictor** *n* a large American boa.

**boar** *n* **1** a male pig. **2** a wild pig with large tusks.

**board**[1] *n* **1** a long thin narrow piece of sawn timber. **2** a flat piece of material with a surface designed for a special purpose. **3** a group of people managing an organization or enterprise. **4** provision of daily meals. ✱ **go by the board** to be rejected or overlooked. **on board** aboard.

**board**[2] *v* **1** to go aboard a ship, train, aircraft, or vehicle. **2** to come alongside and attack (a ship). **3** (+ over/up) to cover with boards. **4** to live in school as a boarder.

**boarder** *n* a resident pupil at a boarding school.

**board game** *n* a game that is played by moving pieces on a special board.
**boarding house** *n* a lodging house that supplies meals.
**boarding school** *n* a school at which meals and lodging are provided.
**boardroom** *n* a room in which a board of directors meets.
**boast**[1] *n* an act of self-praise. ➤ **boastful** *adj*, **boastfully** *adv*, **boastfulness** *n*.
**boast**[2] *v* **1** to praise oneself or one's achievements openly. **2** to have or display as a source of pride.
**boat** *n* **1** a small open vessel for travelling across water. **2** a boat-shaped dish. * **in the same boat** in the same situation.
**boater** *n* a straw hat with a flat crown and a brim.
**boatswain** *or* **bosun** *or* **bo's'n** *n* an officer responsible for maintenance and equipment on a ship.
**bob**[1] *v* (**bobbed, bobbing**) **1** to move repeatedly up and down. **2** to curtsy briefly.
**bob**[2] *n* a short quick bobbing movement.
**bob**[3] *n* **1** a short straight hanging hairstyle for women. **2** a hanging ball or weight on a plumb line or kite's tail.
**bob**[4] *v* (**bobbed, bobbing**) to cut (hair) in a bob.
**bob**[5] *n* (*pl* **bob**) *Brit, informal* a shilling.
**bobbin** *n* a cylinder or spindle for holding yarn or thread.
**bobble** *n* a small fluffy ball made from pieces of wool.
**bobby** *n* (*pl* **-ies**) *Brit, informal, dated* a police officer.
**bobsleigh** *n chiefly Brit* a sledge used for racing down an ice-covered slope.
**bode** *v* * **bode ill/well** to be a bad or good sign for the future.
**bodge** *v Brit, informal* to make or repair clumsily.
**bodice** *n* **1** the upper part of a woman's dress. **2** formerly, a woman's corset-like undergarment.
**bodily**[1] *adj* **1** relating to the body. **2** physical or actual, as distinct from spiritual.
**bodily**[2] *adv* **1** involving the whole body. **2** in bodily form; in the flesh.
**bodkin** *n* a blunt thick needle with a large eye.
**body** *n* (*pl* **-ies**) **1** the physical structure of a person or animal. **2** a corpse. **3** the main part of a human or animal body. **4** the main part of a building. **5** an expanse of water. **6** a star or planet. **7** a material object. **8** a group of people or things working or acting together. **9** firmness or fullness of texture or substance.
**body bag** *n* a bag in which a dead body is placed for transportation.
**body blow** *n* **1** a hard punch on the body. **2** a serious setback.
**body-building** *n* strengthening the body and developing a muscular physique. ➤ **body-builder** *n*.
**bodyguard** *n* an escort who protects a person from bodily harm.
**body language** *n* the unconscious expressing of feelings by looks and movements.
**body shop** *n* a workshop where bodywork of vehicles is repaired.
**body stocking** *n* a light one-piece garment covering the trunk.
**bodywork** *n* the outer structure of a vehicle.
**Boer** /ˈbawə, ˈboh·ə/ *n* a South African of Dutch descent.
**boffin** *n chiefly Brit, informal* a scientist or technical expert.
**bog** *n* an area of wet spongy ground. ➤ **boggy** *adj*.
**bog down** *v* **1** to cause (a vehicle) to sink into soft ground. **2** to hinder with complications or obstructions.
**bogey** *or* **bogy** *n* (*pl* **-eys** *or* **-ies**) **1** a golf score of one stroke over par on a hole. **2** a spectre or ghost. **3** a source of recurring fear. **4** *Brit, informal* a piece of dried nasal mucus.
**bogeyman** *or* **bogyman** *n* (*pl* **bogeymen** *or* **bogymen**) a frightening evil spirit.
**boggle** *v informal* (+ at) to hesitate from fear or scruples. * **the mind boggles** used in mock bewilderment or ironic speculation: goodness knows.
**bogie** *or* **bogy** *n* (*pl* **-ies**) *chiefly Brit* a swivelling framework with one or more pairs of wheels and springs to carry and guide one end of a railway vehicle.
**bogus** *adj* spurious or sham.
**Bohemian** *n* a writer or artist living an unconventional life. ➤ **Bohemian** *adj*.
**boil**[1] *v* **1** of a fluid: to reach a temperature at which it bubbles and changes into vapour. **2** to cook (food) in boiling water. **3** to heat (a vessel) until its contents boil. * **boil down to** to amount in essence to.
**boil**[2] *n* (**the boil**) the act or state of boiling; boiling point.
**boil**[3] *n* a pus-filled swelling of the skin.
**boiler** *n* a tank in which water is heated and stored.
**boiler suit** *n chiefly Brit* a pair of overalls used for messy or oily work.
**boisterous** *adj* noisily and cheerfully rough. ➤ **boisterously** *adv*.
**bold** *adj* **1** showing a fearless adventurous spirit. **2** impudent or presumptuous. **3** conspicuous. **4** of type: darker and thicker than normal. ➤ **boldly** *adv*, **boldness** *n*.
**bole** *n* the trunk of a tree.
**bolero** /bəˈleəroh/ *n* (*pl* **-os**) a Spanish dance in triple time.
**boll** *n* the seed pod of cotton or similar plants.

**bollard** *n* **1** *Brit* a short post used to guide vehicles or prevent their access. **2** a post on a wharf for fastening mooring lines.

**Bolshevik** *n* a member of the party that seized power in Russia in 1917. ➤ **Bolshevism** *n.*

**bolshie** *or* **bolshy** *adj* (**-ier, -iest**) *Brit, informal* stubborn and uncooperative. ➤ **bolshiness** *n.*

**bolster**[1] *n* a long pillow or cushion.

**bolster**[2] *v* to strengthen or support.

**bolster**[3] *n* a heavy chisel used for cutting bricks or stone slabs.

**bolt**[1] *n* **1** a sliding bar or rod used to fasten a door. **2** a metal rod or pin for fastening objects together. **3** a rod or bar that closes the breech of a gun. **4** a short blunt arrow shot from a crossbow. **5** a lightning stroke. ✱ **bolt from the blue** something totally unexpected and unwelcome. **bolt upright** with a straight back.

**bolt**[2] *v* **1** to move rapidly; to flee. **2** of plants: to produce seed prematurely. **3** to secure or fasten with a bolt. **4** to swallow (food) hastily.

**bolt**[3] *n* an attempt to escape or flee. ✱ **make a bolt for** to dash towards (a door, etc).

**bolt-hole** *n chiefly Brit* a place to escape to and find refuge in.

**bomb**[1] *n* **1** a device that explodes and causes widespread damage. **2** (**the bomb**) nuclear weapons. ✱ **cost a bomb** *Brit, informal* to be very expensive. **go like a bomb** *informal* to move very fast.

**bomb**[2] *v* **1** to attack with bombs. **2** *informal* to be a failure. **3** *Brit, informal* to move very fast.

**bombard** *v* **1** to attack with heavy artillery or with bombs. **2** (*usu* + with) to direct an unremitting flow of questions or facts at. **3** to subject (a substance) to the impact of electrons or other particles. ➤ **bombardment** *n.*

**bombardier** *n* **1** a non-commissioned officer in the British artillery. **2** a US bomber-crew member who releases the bombs.

**bombast** *n* pretentious inflated speech or writing. ➤ **bombastic** *adj.*

**bomber** *n* **1** an aircraft designed for dropping bombs. **2** somebody who throws or plants bombs.

**bombshell** *n* **1** an astounding occurrence or piece of news. **2** *informal* a stunningly attractive woman.

**bona fide** /ˌbohnə ˈfiedi/ *adj* genuine or real.

**bonanza** *n* an unexpected supply of wealth or prosperity.

**bonbon** *n* a sweet.

**bond**[1] *n* **1** something that binds or restrains. **2** an adhesive or cementing material. **3** the adhesion achieved between surfaces cemented together. **4** something that unites or binds. **5** a feeling or purpose that unites people. **6** a binding agreement or contract. **7** a certificate of intention to pay the holder a specified sum, with or without other interest, on a specified date.

**bond**[2] *v* **1** to fasten or secure together. **2** to form a strong close emotional bond.

**bondage** *n* **1** slavery or serfdom. **2** sexual gratification involving the physical restraint of one partner.

**bone**[1] *n* **1** the hard material of which the skeleton of vertebrates is chiefly composed, or a piece of this. **2** a hard substance resembling bone. **3** a hard strip used to stiffen a corset or dress. ✱ **bone of contention** a cause of argument. **feel in one's bones** to know instinctively or intuitively. **have a bone to pick with** *informal* to have a cause of complaint against. **make no bones about** to have no hesitation in. **near/close to the bone** of a remark: risqué, indecent, or too close to the truth. ➤ **boneless** *adj.*

**bone**[2] *v* to remove the bones from (fish or meat).

**bone china** *n* a translucent white hard-paste porcelain.

**bone-dry** *adj* completely dry.

**bone-idle** *adj* thoroughly lazy.

**bone meal** *n* fertilizer or feed made of ground bones.

**bonfire** *n* a large open-air fire.

**bongo** *n* (*pl* **-os** *or* **-oes**) each of a pair of small drums played with the hands.

**bonhomie** /ˈbonəmee, bonəˈmee/ *n* good-natured friendliness.

**bonk**[1] *v informal* **1** to hit or knock. **2** *Brit* to have sexual intercourse with.

**bonk**[2] *n informal* **1** a light blow or hit. **2** *Brit* an act of sexual intercourse.

**bonkers** *adj Brit, informal* mad or crazy.

**bonnet** *n* **1** a woman's or child's hat, tied under the chin. **2** *Brit* the hinged metal covering over the engine of a motor vehicle.

**bonny** *adj* (**-ier, -iest**) *chiefly Scot, N Eng* fresh-looking and attractive.

**bonsai** /ˈbonsie/ *n* (*pl* **bonsai**) the art of growing miniature trees.

**bonus** *n* (*pl* **bonuses**) **1** something extra or unexpected. **2** an extra sum of money paid to employees or shareholders.

**bon voyage** /bon vwahˈyahj, -ˈyahzh/ *interj* good wishes to somebody starting on a journey.

**bony** *adj* (**-ier, -iest**) **1** consisting of or resembling bone. **2** full of bones. **3** skinny or scrawny.

**boo**[1] *interj* used to express disapproval or to startle or frighten.

**boo**[2] *v* (**boos, booed, booing**) to show disapproval by shouting 'boo!'

**boob**[1] *n Brit, informal* a stupid mistake or blunder.

**boob**[2] *v Brit, informal* to make a stupid mistake.

**boob**[3] *n informal* a woman's breast.

**booby**[1] *n* (*pl* **-ies**) *informal* an awkward foolish person.

**booby**[2] *n* (*pl* **-ies,**) *informal* a woman's breast.

**boogie**[1] *n informal* a dance to rock music.
**boogie**[2] *v* (**boogies, boogied, boogieing**) *informal* to dance to rock music.
**book**[1] *n* **1** a set of written, printed or blank sheets bound together down one edge. **2** a printed work in this form. **3** a major division of a literary work. **4** (*in pl*) financial records or accounts. ✻ **by the book** following rules or guidelines exactly. **throw the book at** to reprimand or punish severely.
**book**[2] *v* **1** to reserve or hire in advance. **2** to take the name of (an offender) with a view to prosecution or other action.
**bookcase** *n* a piece of furniture with shelves for holding books.
**book club** *n* an association that offers books to its members at a discount.
**booked up** *adj* fully booked.
**bookend** *n* a support placed at the end of a row of books.
**bookie** *n informal* a bookmaker.
**book in** *v* to register on arrival at a hotel.
**bookish** *adj* fond of reading and studying.
**bookkeeper** *n* a person who records the accounts or transactions of a business. ➤ **bookkeeping** *n.*
**booklet** *n* a small slim book with a paper cover.
**bookmaker** *n* a person who receives and pays bets. ➤ **bookmaking** *n.*
**bookmark** *n* **1** a strip of card or leather used to mark a place in a book. **2** a computing facility for recording the address of a file or web page for future access.
**bookworm** *n informal* a person who enjoys reading and study.
**boom**[1] *n* **1** a booming deep low sound or cry. **2** a rapid and widespread expansion of economic activity.
**boom**[2] *v* **1** to make a deep low sound or cry. **2** to experience rapid economic growth.
**boom**[3] *n* **1** a spar at the foot of a mainsail. **2** a long movable arm carrying a microphone. **3** a cable or line of spars forming a barrier across a river or harbour mouth.
**boomerang** *n* a bent piece of wood shaped so that it curves round and returns when thrown.
**boon** *n* a benefit or blessing.
**boor** *n* a coarse or insensitive person. ➤ **boorish** *adj.*
**boost**[1] *v* **1** to increase or raise the level of. **2** to encourage or give a fillip to.
**boost**[2] *n* **1** an increase in amount. **2** a support or encouragement.
**booster** *n* **1** a supplementary dose of vaccine renewing the effectiveness of an earlier dose. **2** an auxiliary engine which provides extra thrust to a rocket or spacecraft. **3** a device that increases voltage or amplifies an electrical signal.
**boot**[1] *n* **1** a piece of footwear that extends above the ankle. **2** *informal* a kick. **3** *Brit* the luggage compartment of a motor car. **4** (**the sack**) *informal* dismissal from employment.
**boot**[2] *v* **1** to kick roughly. **2** *informal* (+ out) to eject or discharge (a person) summarily. **3** to start (a computer).
**boot**[3] ✻ **to boot** besides; as well.
**bootee** *n* **1** a baby's boot-shaped sock. **2** a woman's short boot.
**booth** *n* **1** a stall or stand for the sale or exhibition of goods. **2** a small enclosure affording privacy for telephoning, voting, etc.
**bootleg** *adj* **1** of alcoholic drink or recordings: smuggled or illegally produced. **2** of trousers: having legs that flare slightly at the bottom.
**booty** *n* (*pl* **-ies**) **1** plunder taken in war. **2** a rich gain or prize.
**booze**[1] *n informal* alcoholic drink, *esp* spirits.
**booze**[2] *v informal* to drink alcohol heavily.
**bop**[1] *n chiefly Brit, informal* **1** a dance to popular music. **2** a disco or dance.
**bop**[2] *v* (**bopped, bopping**) *informal* to dance to popular music. ➤ **bopper** *n.*
**bop**[3] *v* (**bopped, bopping**) *informal* to punch smartly.
**bop**[4] *n informal* a punch.
**boracic** *adj* containing boron.
**borage** *n* a coarse hairy herb with blue flowers.
**borax** *n* natural or synthetic hydrated sodium borate used *esp* as a flux and cleansing agent.
**border**[1] *n* **1** an outer part or edge. **2** a boundary or frontier. **3** a narrow flower bed along the edge of grass. **4** an ornamental design at the edge of something.
**border**[2] *v* **1** to form a border along the edge of. **2** of a country or region: to adjoin (another country or region). **3** (+ on) to be close to a feeling or state.
**borderline** *adj* verging on one or other place or state.
**bore**[1] *v* **1** to make (a hole) in something using a drill. **2** to hollow out (a gun barrel). ➤ **borer** *n.*
**bore**[2] *n* **1** the hollow interior of a gun's barrel. **2** the interior diameter of a tube.
**bore**[3] *n* a dull or tedious person or situation.
**bore**[4] *v* to make (somebody) weary by being dull or monotonous. ➤ **bored** *adj,* **boring** *adj.*
**bore**[5] *n* a tidal flood that moves rapidly up an estuary.
**bore**[6] *v* past tense of BEAR[2].
**boredom** *n* the state of being bored.
**borehole** *n* a hole drilled in the earth to find water or oil.
**boric acid** *n* a white crystalline solid acid used *esp* as an antiseptic.
**born** *adj* **1** brought into existence by birth. **2** having a natural ability or aptitude: *a born teacher.* **3** (+ of) resulting from (e.g. a feeling or cause).
**born-again** *adj* recently converted to Christianity or some other belief.
**borne** *v* past part. of BEAR[2].

**boron** *n* a metalloid chemical element found in nature only in combination.

**borough** *n* **1** an urban area in Britain with powers of local self-government granted by royal charter. **2** a local-government area of London. **3** a political division of New York City.

**borrow** *v* **1** to take or receive (something) with the intention or requirement of returning it. **2** to get (a sum of money) from a bank under an arrangement to pay it back, usu with interest. ➤ **borrower** *n.*

**Borstal** *n Brit* formerly, a penal institution providing training for young offenders.

**bosom** *n* **1** the front of the human chest; *esp* the female breasts. **2** the deep heart or centre of something, e.g. the family.

**boss**[1] *n informal* a person who exercises control or authority.

**boss**[2] *v informal* to give orders to in a domineering manner.

**boss**[3] *n* **1** a stud or knob at the centre of a shield. **2** the enlarged part of a shaft, on which a wheel is mounted. **3** the middle part of a propeller.

**bossa nova** *n* a Brazilian dance similar to the samba.

**boss-eyed** *adj Brit, informal* having a squint; cross-eyed.

**bossy** *adj* (**-ier, -iest**) *informal* domineering or dictatorial. ➤ **bossiness** *n.*

**bosun** *n* see BOATSWAIN.

**botany** *n* the study of plant life. ➤ **botanical** *adj,* **botanist** *n.*

**botch** *v informal* **1** to repair in a makeshift or inept way. **2** to bungle.

**both**[1] *adj* affecting or involving the one as well as the other of two people or things.

**both**[2] *pron* the one as well as the other of two people or things.

**bother**[1] *v* **1** to disturb or distract. **2** to cause to be troubled or perplexed. **3** to cause discomfort or pain to. **4** to take the trouble to do something. **5** to concern oneself about something.

**bother**[2] *n* **1** unnecessary fuss or effort. **2** a cause of difficulty or fuss.

**bothersome** *adj* causing bother; annoying.

**bottle**[1] *n* **1** a glass or plastic container with a narrow neck, used for liquids. **2** *Brit, informal* courage.

**bottle**[2] *v* **1** to store (liquid) in a bottle. **2** *Brit* to preserve (fruit) in glass jars.

**bottleneck** *n* a narrow stretch of road where the flow of traffic is impeded.

**bottle out** *v informal* to lose one's nerve.

**bottle up** *v* to restrain (an emotion).

**bottom**[1] *n* **1** the underside of something, or the surface on which it rests. **2** the buttocks or rump. **3** the lowest or deepest part or place. **4** the lowest position or last place in order of precedence. **5** (*also in pl*) the lower part of a two-piece garment. ✱ **get to the bottom of** to find out the truth or basis of.

**bottom**[2] *v* of a submarine: to reach the sea bed.

**bottom**[3] *adj* relating to or situated at the bottom or lower part of something. ➤ **bottommost** *adj.*

**bottom line** *n* (**the bottom line**) *informal* the crucial factor.

**bottom out** *v* of a bad situation: to reach its worst point and level out.

**botulism** *n* an acute form of food poisoning caused by a toxin in food.

**boudoir** /'boohdwah/ *n* a woman's bedroom or private room.

**bouffant** /'boohfong/ *adj* of hair: puffed out in a rounded shape.

**bougainvillea** *or* **bougainvillaea** *n* a tropical climbing plant with bright floral bracts.

**bough** *n* a main branch of a tree.

**bought** *v* past tense and past part. of BUY[1].

**boulder** *n* a large stone or rock.

**boulevard** *n* a broad avenue.

**bounce**[1] *v* **1** to cause (a ball, etc) to rebound. **2** to rebound after striking a surface. **3** to move with a springing step. **4** *informal* of a cheque: to be returned by a bank because there are not enough funds in the payer's account. **5** *Brit, informal* to coerce into doing something.

**bounce**[2] *n* **1** a sudden leap or bound. **2** a rebound. **3** verve or liveliness.

**bouncer** *n* a person employed in a nightclub to remove disorderly people.

**bouncy** *adj* (**-ier, -iest**) **1** bouncing readily. **2** buoyant; exuberant.

**bound**[1] *adj* **1** going somewhere specified: *bound for home.* **2** confined to a place: *housebound.* **3** certain or sure to do something. **4** placed under legal or moral obligation: *duty-bound.*

**bound**[2] *n* (*usu in pl*) **1** a limiting line or boundary. **2** something that limits or restrains. ✱ **out of bounds 1** outside the permitted limits. **2** of the ball in team sport: outside the area of play.

**bound**[3] *v* **1** to set limits to. **2** to form the boundary of (a country, region, etc).

**bound**[4] *n* **1** a leap or jump. **2** a bounce.

**bound**[5] *v* **1** to move by leaping. **2** to rebound or bounce.

**bound**[6] *v* past tense and past part. of BIND[1].

**boundary** *n* (*pl* **-ies**) **1** a dividing line that indicates or fixes a limit or extent. **2** a border or frontier.

**boundless** *adj* limitless.

**bounteous** *adj* giving or given freely. ➤ **bounteously** *adv.*

**bountiful** *adj* **1** generous; liberal. **2** abundant; plentiful. ➤ **bountifully** *adv.*

**bounty** *n* **1** a financial reward paid for the capture of a criminal or outlaw. **2** *literary* something given generously. **3** *literary* generosity.

**bouquet** *n* **1** a bunch of flowers. **2** a distinctive fragrance.

**bourbon** *n* an American whisky distilled from maize with malt and rye.
**bourgeois** *adj* belonging to or characteristic of the middle class.
**bourgeoisie** /booəzhwah'zee/ *n* the middle class.
**bout** *n* **1** a spell of activity. **2** a boxing or wrestling match. **3** an attack of an illness.
**boutique** *n* a small fashionable shop selling clothes or other specialized goods.
**bouzouki** /boo'zoohki/ *n* (*pl* **bouzoukis**) a Greek stringed instrument resembling a mandolin.
**bovine**[1] *adj* **1** relating to cattle. **2** slow, stolid, or dull.
**bovine**[2] *n* an ox or related animal.
**bow**[1] *v* **1** to bend the head or upper body in respect or greeting. **2** to submit or yield to something or somebody. * **bow and scrape** to act in an obsequious manner.
**bow**[2] *n* a bending of the head or body in respect or greeting. * **take a bow** to acknowledge applause or praise.
**bow**[3] *n* **1** a knot tied with two loops and two free ends. **2** a weapon for shooting arrows, consisting of a strip of wood or other flexible material held bent by a taut cord at the two ends. **3** a rod with horsehairs stretched from end to end, used for playing a stringed instrument.
**bow**[4] *n* (*also in pl*) the front end of a ship.
**bowdlerize** *or* **-ise** *v* to remove parts from (a book) because they are considered indecent or offensive.
**bowel** *n* **1** (*in pl*) the intestines. **2** the large intestine or the small intestine. **3** (*in pl*) the innermost parts of something.
**bower** *n* **1** a shelter in a garden. **2** an attractive dwelling or retreat.
**bowl**[1] *n* **1** a round deep dish for holding or mixing food. **2** the hollow rounded part of something. **3** a bowl-shaped geographical region or formation.
**bowl**[2] *n* **1** a weighted shaped ball used in the game of bowls. **2** a ball used in skittles or tenpin bowling. **3** (*in pl*) a game played outdoors on a green, in which players roll bowls as close as possible to a target bowl.
**bowl**[3] *v* **1** to roll (a ball) in a game of bowls. **2** to deliver (a ball) to a batsman in cricket. **3** of a bowler: to dismiss (a batsman in cricket) by hitting the wicket. **4** (*often* + along) to travel quickly.
**bowlegged** *adj* having legs that curve outwards at the knees.
**bowler**[1] *n* the person who bowls in a team sport.
**bowler**[2] *n* a man's stiff felt hat with a rounded crown and narrow brim.
**bowling** *n* a game in which balls are rolled at one or more objects.
**bowl over** *v informal* to impress or astonish.
**bow tie** *n* a short tie fastened in a bow.
**bow window** *n* a curved bay window.
**box**[1] *n* **1** a flat-sided container with a lid. **2** a small compartment for a group of people, e.g. in a theatre or sports ground. **3** (**the box**) *chiefly Brit, informal* television. **4** a space or area marked out with straight lines or as a grid.
**box**[2] *v* **1** to enclose in a box. **2** to confine or restrict.
**box**[3] *v* **1** to engage in boxing. **2** to slap (somebody's ears) with the hand.
**box**[4] *n* a punch or slap on the ear.
**box**[5] *n* an evergreen shrub or small tree used for hedges.
**boxer**[1] *n* a person who engages in boxing.
**boxer**[2] *n* a dog of a breed having short brown hair and a flat pug-like face.
**boxer shorts** *pl n* men's loose-fitting underpants.
**boxing** *n* the sport of attack and defence with the fists enclosed in thickly padded gloves.
**Boxing Day** *n* 26 December, observed as a public holiday.
**box number** *n* the number of a box at a post office, for delivering and collecting mail.
**box office** *n* the place in a cinerma or theatre where tickets are sold.
**boxroom** *n Brit* a small storage room in a house.
**boxy** *adj* (**-ier, -iest**) **1** resembling a box; boxlike. **2** of a room: cramped or poky.
**boy** *n* a male child or young person. ➤ **boyhood** *n*, **boyish** *adj*.
**boycott**[1] *v* to refuse to have dealings with or trade with, as a protest or penalty.
**boycott**[2] *n* an act of boycotting.
**boyfriend** *n* a regular male companion or lover.
**Br** *abbr* the chemical symbol for bromine.
**bra** *n* a woman's undergarment for supporting the breasts.
**brace**[1] *n* **1** a diagonal piece of structural material that serves to strengthen. **2** an appliance for supporting a weak leg or other body part. **3** a dental fitting for correcting irregular teeth. **4** a rope attached to a yard on a ship that swings the yard horizontally to trim the sail. **5** a mark ({ or }) used to connect words or items to be considered together. **6** a pair. **7** (*also* **brace and bit**) a crank-shaped drilling instrument that holds a bit.
**brace**[2] *v* **1** to prepare (oneself, or a part of one's body) for receiving an impact. **2** to prepare (oneself) for something unpleasant. **3** to support with a brace.
**bracelet** *n* an ornamental band or chain worn round the wrist.
**braces** *pl n Brit* a pair of elasticated straps worn over the shoulders and attached to the trousers to keep them up.

**bracing** *adj* refreshing or invigorating.
**bracken** *n* a large coarse fern of moorland areas.
**bracket**[1] *n* **1** each of a pair of marks ( ), [ ], < >, or { }, used to enclose matter in writing or printing. **2** a social group. **3** a projecting fixture that supports a load or strengthens an angle.
**bracket**[2] *v* (**bracketed, bracketing**) **1** to place (written or printed matter) within brackets. **2** (+ together) to put (people or things) in the same category.
**brackish** *adj* of water: slightly salty.
**bract** *n* a small leaf near a flower or floral axis.
**brag**[1] *v* (**bragged, bragging**) to talk boastfully.
**brag**[2] *n* a card game resembling poker.
**braggart** *n* a loud arrogant boaster.
**braid**[1] *v* **1** to plait (hair). **2** to decorate with ribbon or braid.
**braid**[2] *n* **1** a plaited strip of cord or ribbon. **2** a length of plaited hair. **3** a narrow plait of hair.
**Braille** *n* a system of writing or printing for the blind, with characters made up of raised dots.
**brain**[1] *n* **1** the organ of thought and neural coordination enclosed within the skull. **2** (*in pl*) intelligence. **3** *informal* an intelligent or intellectual person. **4** (**the brain/the brains**) *informal* the chief planner of an organization or enterprise. * **on the brain** *informal* constantly recurring in one's head.
**brain**[2] *v informal* to hit hard on the head.
**brainchild** *n* something that results from a particular person's creative imagination.
**brain drain** *n informal* the loss of highly qualified people through emigration.
**brainless** *adj* stupid or foolish.
**brainstorm** *n informal* a mental abberation or lapse in concentration.
**brainwash** *v* to attempt to instil beliefs into (somebody), or change existing beliefs, by systematic repetition.
**brain wave** *n* **1** a rhythmic fluctuation of voltage between parts of the brain. **2** *informal* a sudden bright idea.
**brainy** *adj* (**-ier, -iest**) *informal* intelligent.
**braise** *v* to cook (meat) slowly by frying it briefly and then stewing it at a low heat.
**brake**[1] *n* (*also in pl*) a device for slowing down or stopping a vehicle.
**brake**[2] *v* to apply a brake on a vehicle.
**brake**[3] *n* an open carriage drawn by horses.
**brake**[4] *n* **1** a toothed instrument used for crushing flax and hemp. **2** (*also* **brake harrow**) a machine formerly used for breaking up large clumps of earth.
**bramble** *n* a prickly rambling shrub, *esp* a blackberry. ➤ **brambly** *adj.*
**bran** *n* the broken husk of cereal grain separated from the flour or meal by sifting.
**branch**[1] *n* **1** a thick shoot growing from the trunk of a tree. **2** a road, railway line, or river that deviates from a main one. **3** a division of a family, organization, or group. **4** a section of a subject of study.
**branch**[2] *v* **1** to put out branches. **2** to spring from a main stem.
**branch out** *v* to try new activities or experiences.
**brand**[1] *n* **1** a product identified by name as made by a single firm or manufacturer. **2** a mark made on farm animals by burning with a hot iron, e.g. to designate ownership. **3** a charred or smouldering piece of wood.
**brand**[2] *v* **1** to mark with a hot iron. **2** to identify (goods) with a brand name. **3** to stigmatize (somebody, or their conduct).
**brandish** *v* to shake or wave (a weapon, etc) menacingly or ostentatiously.
**brand name** *n* a maker's name for a product.
**brand new** *adj* completely new.
**brandy** *n* (*pl* **-ies**) a spirit made by distilling wine or fermented fruit juice.
**brash** *adj* **1** aggressively self-assertive. **2** tastelessly showy. ➤ **brashly** *adv,* **brashness** *n.*
**brass** *n* **1** an alloy of copper and zinc. **2** the brass instruments of an orchestra. **3** *Brit* a brass memorial tablet set into the wall or floor of a church. **4** a round flat brass ornament for a horse's harness. **5** (*also* **the top brass**) *informal* the people in authority.
**brass band** *n* a band consisting of brass instruments.
**brasserie** *n* a small informal French-style restaurant.
**brassy** *adj* (**-ier, -iest**) **1** shamelessly bold or showy. **2** resembling brass in colour.
**brat** *n informal* an ill-disciplined child. ➤ **brattish** *adj.*
**bravado** *n* bold conduct intended to impress or deceive people.
**brave**[1] *adj* showing courage. ➤ **bravely** *adv.*
**brave**[2] *v* to face or endure (unpleasant or dangerous conditions) with courage.
**brave**[3] *n dated* a Native American warrior.
**bravery** *n* courage or valour.
**bravo**[1] *interj* used by an audience to applaud a performer.
**bravo**[2] *n* (*pl* **-os** *or* **-oes**) a villain or desperado; *esp* a hired assassin.
**bravura** /brə'v(y)ooərə/ *n* **1** a flamboyant brilliant style of performance. **2** a display of daring.
**brawl**[1] *v* to quarrel or fight noisily.
**brawl**[2] *n* a noisy quarrel or fight.
**brawn** *n* **1** muscular strength. **2** *Brit* pork trimmings pressed into a mould.
**bray** *v* to utter the loud harsh cry of a donkey. ➤ **bray** *n.*
**brazen**[1] *adj* **1** shamelessly bold. **2** *literary* resembling or made of brass. ➤ **brazenly** *adv.*
**brazen**[2] * **brazen it out** to face danger, trouble, or criticism with defiance or impudence.

**brazier**[1] /'brayzi·ə, 'brayzhə/ *n* **1** a receptacle or stand for holding burning coals. **2** *NAmer* a barbecue.

**brazier**[2] *n* a person who works in brass.

**brazil nut** *n* a large three-sided nut.

**breach**[1] *n* **1** a violation of a law or obligation. **2** a gap made in a wall or barrier. **3** a temporary quarrel or disagreement. * **step into the breach** to replace somebody who has been suddenly prevented from doing a job.

**breach**[2] *v* **1** to make a breach in (a wall or barrier). **2** to break or violate (a law or agreement).

**bread** *n* **1** a food made from flour or meal which is baked and leavened with yeast. **2** *informal* money.

**bread and butter** *n* one's means of sustenance or livelihood.

**breadcrumb** *n* a small fragment of bread.

**breadline** *n* * **on the breadline** *Brit* earning barely enough for survival.

**breadth** *n* **1** the distance from side to side of something. **2** wide range or scope.

**breadwinner** *n* the member of a family whose income provides the chief means of support.

**break**[1] *v* (**broke, broken**) **1** to separate into pieces from a blow, mishap, etc. **2** to stop working. **3** to fracture (a limb), or to become fractured. **4** to fail to keep (an agreement or rule). **5** to defeat or crush. **6** to reduce the impact of (a fall). **7** to interrupt (a journey) for a rest or diversion. **8** to exceed or surpass. **9** to solve (a code). **10** to make (news) known to people. **11** of news: to become known. **12** of the day: to begin at dawn. **13** of weather: to change after a settled period. **14** of a storm: to develop suddenly. **15** of a person: to give way under pressure. **16** in tennis, to win a game against (an opponent's service). **17** of a boy's voice: to deepen at puberty. * **break even** to recoup an initial investment or outlay. **break into** to start an activity. **break loose** to escape. **break the back of** to complete the most difficult part of. **break the bank** to cause financial ruin. **break wind** to release gas from the anus. **break with** to end a relationship with after a quarrel. ➤ **breakable** *adj.*

**break**[2] *n* **1** an act or action of breaking. **2** a place where something is broken. **3** a gap. **4** a brief rest or respite. **5** a dash or rush. **6** *informal* an opportunity or a stroke of good luck. **7** in tennis, an instance of breaking an opponent's service. **8** in snooker, a sequence of successful shots or strokes. **9** in jazz, a short ornamental passage between phrases.

**breakage** *n* **1** something that has been broken. **2** the action of breaking something.

**breakaway** *n* **1** somebody or something that breaks away. **2** a breaking away from a group or tradition.

**break away** *v* **1** to escape. **2** to separate from a main group.

**breakdown** *n* **1** a failure to function. **2** a physical or nervous collapse. **3** the process of decomposing. **4** a classification or detailed analysis.

**break down** *v* **1** to fail or stop working. **2** of an agreement, talks, etc: to fail or become unworkable. **3** to give way to feelings. **4** to cause to collapse. **5** to separate into components or elements.

**breaker** *n* a wave breaking into foam.

**breakfast**[1] *n* the first meal of the day.

**breakfast**[2] *v* to eat breakfast.

**break in** *v* **1** to enter a building by force. **2** to intrude or interrupt. **3** to train (a horse) to carry a rider. **4** to use (new shoes) until they become comfortable.

**break-in** *n* an act of forcing an entry into a building.

**breakneck** *adj* dangerously fast.

**break off** *v* **1** to stop abruptly. **2** to discontinue (a connection or relationship).

**break out** *v* **1** of something unwelcome: to start suddenly. **2** to escape from confinement.

**breakthrough** *n* a sudden advance or discovery.

**break up** *v* **1** to bring or come to an end. **2** to break into pieces. **3** to finish an activity and disperse.

**breakwater** *n* a barrier protecting a harbour or beach from the sea.

**bream** *n* (*pl* **breams** *or* **bream**) a silvery freshwater fish with a deep narrow body.

**breast**[1] *n* **1** either of the two milk-producing organs on a woman's chest. **2** the front part of the body between the neck and the abdomen.

**breast**[2] *v* **1** to confront resolutely. **2** to meet or lean against with the breast or front.

**breastbone** *n* a narrow flat bone extending down the chest, to which some of the ribs are attached.

**breast-feed** *v* (*past tense and past part.* **breast-fed**) to feed (a baby) with milk from the breast.

**breaststroke** *n* a swimming stroke performed by pushing the arms forward then sweeping them out and back, while kicking the legs out and back.

**breath** *n* **1** air inhaled and exhaled in breathing. **2** an act of breathing. **3** a slight movement of air. **4** a slight indication. * **out of breath** breathing very rapidly from strenuous exercise. **under one's breath** in a whisper.

**breathalyse** *or* **breathalyze** *v* to test (a driver's breath) with a breathalyser.

**breathalyser** *or* **breathalyzer** *n* a device used to test the alcohol level in a driver's blood.

**breathe** *v* **1** to draw air into the lungs and expel it. **2** to let air or moisture out. **3** to say or express.

**breather** *n informal* a short break in an activity.

**breathless** *adj* **1** gasping for breath after strenuous exercise. **2** gripping or intense. ➤ **breathlessly** *adv.*
**breathtaking** *adj* extremely exciting or thrilling. ➤ **breathtakingly** *adv.*
**breathy** *adj* (**-ier, -iest**) accompanied by audible breathing.
**breech** *n* the part of a firearm at the rear of the barrel.
**breech birth** *n* a birth in which the baby's feet or buttocks emerge first.
**breeches** *pl n* knee-length trousers fastened at the knees.
**breed**[1] *v* (*past tense and past part.* **bred**) **1** to produce offspring by sexual union. **2** to propagate (plants or animals). **3** to produce or engender.
**breed**[2] *n* **1** a particular group of animals or plants having similar characteristics. **2** a class or kind.
**breeder reactor** *n* a nuclear reactor in which more radioactive fuel is produced than is consumed.
**breeding** *n* good behaviour regarded as resulting from family background.
**breeze**[1] *n* **1** a light wind. **2** *informal* something easily done.
**breeze**[2] *v* to come or go casually or nonchalantly.
**breeze-block** *n* a building block made from ashy residue mixed with sand and cement.
**breezy** *adj* (**-ier, -iest**) **1** fresh and windy. **2** brisk and cheerful. ➤ **breezily** *adv.*
**brethren** *n* pl of BROTHER, used in religious contexts.
**breve** *n* a musical note with the time value of two semibreves.
**brevity** *n* **1** conciseness of expression. **2** shortness of duration.
**brew**[1] *v* **1** to make (beer) by fermentation. **2** to make (tea) by infusion in hot water. **3** (*often* + up) to contrive or plot. ➤ **brewer** *n.*
**brew**[2] *n* a brewed drink.
**brewery** *n* (*pl* **-ies**) a place in which beer is brewed.
**briar** *n* see BRIER.
**bribe**[1] *v* to offer money or other inducement to persuade (somebody) to do something illegal or wrong.
**bribe**[2] *n* something offered to bribe somebody.
**bribery** *n* the practice of giving a bribe.
**bric-a-brac** *n* miscellaneous small articles or curios.
**brick**[1] *n* **1** a rectangular block of baked clay used in building. **2** a small block used as a children's toy. ✱ **bricks and mortar** buildings and housing.
**brick**[2] *v* (+ up) to enclose or pave with bricks.
**brickbat** *n* a critical or hostile remark.
**bricklayer** *n* a person who is employed to lay bricks.
**bridal** *adj* of or for a bride or wedding.
**bride** *n* a woman at the time of her wedding.
**bridegroom** *n* a man at the time of his wedding.
**bridesmaid** *n* a woman or girl who attends a bride.
**bridge**[1] *n* **1** a structure spanning a river or road or other obstacle. **2** the upper bony part of the nose. **3** an arch supporting the strings of a musical instrument. **4** an enclosed platform on a ship for the captain and officers. **5** a denture filling a gap.
**bridge**[2] *v* to make a bridge over or across (a river or road).
**bridge**[3] *n* a card game for four players, with bidding.
**bridgehead** *n* an advanced position in enemy territory, taken as a foothold for further advance.
**bridle**[1] *n* a framework of leather straps attached to a horse's head and used to control it.
**bridle**[2] *v* **1** to put a bridle on (an animal). **2** to restrain or control. **3** to show hostility or resentment.
**bridleway** *n* a path with right of way for horse riding.
**Brie** /bree/ *n* a cream-coloured soft French cheese.
**brief**[1] *adj* **1** short in length or time. **2** using few words. **3** of clothing: covering only a small area. ➤ **briefly** *adv.*
**brief**[2] *n* **1** a set of instructions describing a task and setting its limits. **2** a statement of a client's case drawn up for legal counsel. **3** *Brit, informal* a barrister or solicitor assigned to a case.
**brief**[3] *v* to provide with instructions or information for a task.
**briefcase** *n* a flat rectangular case for carrying papers.
**briefing** *n* a meeting for giving instructions or information.
**briefs** *pl n* short underpants.
**brier** *or* **briar** *n* a plant with woody and thorny or prickly stems.
**brig** *n* a two-masted square-rigged sailing ship.
**brigade** *n* **1** a large section of an army including a headquarters and several fighting units. **2** *informal* a group of people who have a particular point of view.
**brigadier** *n* an officer in the British Army ranking below a major general.
**brigand** *n* a member of a gang of bandits.
**bright** *adj* **1** radiating a lot of light; shining. **2** lively and cheerful. **3** of a colour: bold and brilliant. **4** quick to learn or understand. **5** promising success or good fortune. ➤ **brightly** *adv,* **brightness** *n.*
**brighten** *v* (*often* + up) to make or become brighter or happier.
**brill** *n* (*pl* **brill**) a flatfish related to the turbot.

**brilliant** *adj* **1** very bright or bold. **2** having great intellectual ability. **3** strikingly impressive or distinctive. **4** *Brit, informal* of high quality; good. ➤ **brilliance** *n,* **brilliantly** *adv.*

**brim**[1] *n* **1** the edge or rim of a container. **2** the projecting edge of a hat.

**brim**[2] *v* (**brimmed, brimming**) to be full to the brim.

**brimful** *adj* full to the brim.

**brimstone** *n archaic* = SULPHUR.

**brindled** *or* **brindle** *adj* of an animal: having dark streaks on a grey or tawny background.

**brine** *n* **1** a solution of salty water. **2** sea water.

**bring** *v* (*past tense and past part.* **brought**) **1** to carry or convey to a place. **2** to cause to reach a particular condition. **3** to force (oneself) to do something. **4** to cause to occur; to lead to. **5** to present or initiate.

**bring about** *v* to cause to happen.

**bring down** *v* **1** to reduce. **2** to cause the collapse of (a government).

**bring in** *v* **1** to earn (an amount of income). **2** to introduce (a measure).

**bring off** *v* to achieve successfully.

**bring on** *v* **1** to cause (a feeling or symptom) to occur. **2** to help to make progress.

**bring out** *v* **1** to publish or produce. **2** to emphasize or make more obvious.

**bring round** (*NAmer* **bring around**) *v* **1** to persuade (somebody) to adopt a particular opinion. **2** to revive (an unconscious person).

**bring up** *v* **1** to educate and look after (a child). **2** to raise for consideration.

**brink** *n* **1** the edge of land at the top of a steep place or by water. **2** the point at which something is about to happen.

**brinkmanship** *n* the art of going to the very brink of conflict, danger, etc before drawing back.

**briny**[1] *n* (**the briny**) *Brit, informal* the sea.

**briny**[2] *adj* (**-ier, -iest**) salty.

**brio** *n* enthusiasm and liveliness.

**brioche** *n* a light, slightly sweet French bread roll.

**brisk** *adj* **1** energetic and fast. **2** fresh and invigorating. **3** sharp in tone or manner. ➤ **briskly** *adv.*

**brisket** *n* a joint of beef cut from the breast.

**brisling** *n* (*pl* **brislings** *or* **brisling**) a small herring.

**bristle**[1] *n* a short stiff hair.

**bristle**[2] *v* **1** of hair or fur: to rise and stand stiffly erect. **2** to react peevishly or resentfully.

**bristly** *adj* (**-ier, -iest**) **1** resembling bristles. **2** covered with bristles.

**British**[1] *n* (**the British**) (*treated as pl*) the people of Britain.

**British**[2] *adj* of Britain or its people.

**Briton** *n* a native or inhabitant of Britain.

**brittle** *adj* **1** hard and easily broken. **2** of the voice: light and thin in tone.

**broach** *v* **1** to raise (a subject) for discussion. **2** to pierce (a container).

**broad** *adj* **1** large in size or extent from side to side. **2** of a specified size in width. **3** widely applicable or applied. **4** relating to the main features and not details. **5** clear or easily noticed. **6** extending far; vast. **7** of an accent: marked. **8** of humour: coarse. ➤ **broadly** *adv.*

**broad bean** *n* a large flat green bean.

**broadcast**[1] *v* (*past tense* **broadcast,** *past part.* **broadcast** *or* **broadcasted**) **1** to transmit (a television or radio programme). **2** to make widely known. ➤ **broadcaster** *n.*

**broadcast**[2] *n* a radio or television programme.

**broaden** *v* to make or become broad or broader.

**broad-minded** *adj* tolerant of other views or forms of behaviour.

**broadsheet** *n* a newspaper printed on large folded sheets.

**broadside** *n* **1** a forceful verbal or written attack. **2** formerly, the firing together of all the guns on one side of a ship.

**brocade** *n* a rich fabric woven with raised patterns. ➤ **brocaded** *adj.*

**broccoli** *n* a vegetable with a green or purplish flower head.

**brochure** *n* a small pamphlet containing promotional material.

**brogue**[1] *n* a stout shoe with decorative perforations in the leather.

**brogue**[2] *n* a dialect or regional accent.

**broil** *v* **1** *NAmer* to grill (food). **2** to become extremely hot.

**broke**[1] *v* past tense of BREAK[1].

**broke**[2] *adj informal* having no money.

**broken**[1] *v* past part. of BREAK[1].

**broken**[2] *adj* of language: hesitant and containing errors.

**broken-down** *adj* in a state of disrepair; dilapidated.

**brokenhearted** *adj* overcome by sorrow or grief.

**broken home** *n* a family that has been affected by separation of the parents.

**broker**[1] *n* **1** an agent who negotiates contracts of purchase and sale. **2** an intermediary in business or politics.

**broker**[2] *v* to negotiate (a deal).

**bromide** *n* a compound of bromine.

**bromine** *n* a non-metallic chemical element with a pungent vapour.

**bronchial** *adj* relating to the tubes leading from the windpipe to the lungs.

**bronchitis** *n* inflammation of the bronchial tubes.

**bronco** *n* (*pl* **-os**) a wild or partially broken horse of the American West.

**brontosaurus** *n* a former name for apatosaurus.

**bronze**[1] *n* **1** a yellowish brown alloy of copper and tin. **2** a sculpture made of bronze. **3** a yellowish brown colour.

**bronze**[2] *v* **1** to give the appearance of bronze to. **2** to make brown or suntanned.

**Bronze Age** *n* (**the Bronze Age**) the period of human history in which bronze and copper tools and weapons were common, coming between the Stone Age and the Iron Age.

**bronze medal** *n* a medal of bronze awarded for third place in a competition.

**brooch** *n* an ornament fastened to clothing with an attached pin.

**brood**[1] *n* **1** a group of young birds or animals born or hatched at one time. **2** *humorous* the children of a family.

**brood**[2] *v* **1** of a bird: to sit on eggs to hatch them. **2** to worry at length about something unpleasant. **3** to hover menacingly.

**broody** *adj* (**-ier, -iest**) **1** of a hen: ready to hatch eggs. **2** *informal* of a woman: feeling a strong desire to have a baby. **3** constantly occupied with melancholy thoughts. ➤ **broodily** *adv.*

**brook**[1] *n* a small stream.

**brook**[2] *v formal* to tolerate.

**broom** *n* **1** a long-handled brush for sweeping. **2** a shrub with small leaves and showy yellow flowers.

**broomstick** *n* a brush of twigs on a long thin handle, ridden by a witch in children's stories.

**bros.** *or* **Bros.** *abbr* brothers.

**broth** *n* a soup or stock in which meat, fish, cereal grains, or vegetables have been cooked.

**brothel** *n* a premises in which prostitutes can be visited.

**brother** *n* **1** a man or boy having the same parents as another person. **2** a male colleague. **3** a male member of a religious order. ➤ **brotherly** *adj.*

**brotherhood** *n* **1** the state of being brothers. **2** a religious body founded for a particular purpose. **3** fellowship or friendship between human beings.

**brother-in-law** *n* (*pl* **brothers-in-law**) **1** the brother of one's husband or wife. **2** the husband of one's sister.

**brought** *v* past tense and past part. of BRING.

**brow** *n* **1** the forehead. **2** an eyebrow. **3** the top point of a hill.

**browbeat** *v* (**browbeat, browbeaten**) to intimidate with persistent threats.

**brown**[1] *adj* **1** of the colour of wood or soil, between red and yellow. **2** of dark or tanned complexion.

**brown**[2] *v* to make brown by cooking.

**browned-off** *adj informal* annoyed or disheartened.

**brownfield** *adj* of a site: located in an urban area where buildings previously stood.

**brownie** *n* **1** (**Brownie**) a member of the junior section of the Guides Assoication, for girls aged from seven to ten. **2** a small square of rich chocolate cake. **3** in stories, a goblin believed to perform household chores secretly at night.

**browse**[1] *v* **1** to look idly through a book or mass of things. **2** of animals: to nibble at leaves or other vegetation. **3** to look at (the contents of computer data).

**browse**[2] *n* a period of browsing.

**browser** *n* **1** a person or animal that is browsing. **2** a computer program for viewing information on the World Wide Web.

**bruise**[1] *n* **1** an area of discoloration on the skin, caused by a blow or injury. **2** an area of discoloration caused by damage to plant tissue.

**bruise**[2] *v* **1** to inflict a bruise on. **2** to be damaged by a bruise.

**bruiser** *n informal* a large burly person.

**brunch** *n* a meal eaten in the late morning, combining breakfast and lunch.

**brunette** (*NAmer* **brunet**) *n* a girl or woman with dark brown hair.

**brunt** *n* the principal force of an attack or a blow.

**brush**[1] *n* **1** an implement of hair, bristle, or wire set into a handle and used for grooming hair, painting, or cleaning. **2** an act of brushing. **3** a momentary touch or contact. **4** a conductor that makes electrical contact between a stationary part and a moving part. **5** the bushy tail of a fox.

**brush**[2] *v* **1** to clean or groom with a brush. **2** to apply (paint) with a brush. **3** to remove with sweeping strokes. **4** to touch lightly.

**brush**[3] *n* scrub vegetation, or land covered with it.

**brush**[4] *n* a brief antagonistic encounter or skirmish.

**brush off** *v* to dismiss in an offhand way.

**brush up** *v* to renew one's skill in.

**brushwood** *n* undergrowth of broken twigs and small branches.

**brusque** *adj* blunt or abrupt in manner or speech. ➤ **brusquely** *adv.*

**Brussels sprout** *n* a bud of a plant of the cabbage family, used as a vegetable.

**brutal** *adj* **1** cruel and violent. **2** harsh or severe. **3** unpleasantly direct or uncompromising. ➤ **brutalism** *n,* **brutality** *n,* **brutally** *adv.*

**brutalize** *or* **-ise** *v* **1** to make brutal or unfeeling. **2** to treat brutally.

**brute**[1] *n* **1** a cruel and violent person. **2** a large aggressive animal. ➤ **brutish** *adj.*

**brute**[2] *adj* **1** purely physical. **2** cruel or savage.

**bryony** *n* (*pl* **-ies**) a climbing plant with large leaves and red or black fruit.

**BSE** *abbr* bovine spongiform encephalopathy, a fatal disease of cattle affecting the central nervous system.

**BSI** *abbr* British Standards Institution.

**BST** *abbr* British Summer Time.

**Btu** *or* **BTU** *abbr* British thermal unit.

**bubble**[1] *n* **1** a small body of gas within a liquid or solid. **2** a thin transparent film of liquid inflated with air or vapour. **3** a transparent dome.

**bubble**[2] *v* **1** to form or produce bubbles. **2** to be highly excited.

**bubble gum** *n* chewing gum that can be blown into bubbles.

**bubbly**[1] *adj* (**-ier, -iest**) **1** full of bubbles. **2** lively and in good spirits.

**bubbly**[2] *n informal* champagne.

**bubonic plague** *n* a highly infectious and fatal form of plague.

**buccaneer** *n* **1** a pirate. **2** an unscrupulous adventurer. ➤ **buccaneering** *adj.*

**buck**[1] *n* **1** a male animal, *esp* a male deer or rabbit. **2** *archaic* a fashionable young man.

**buck**[2] *v* **1** of a horse: to spring into the air with the back curved. **2** to fight against or refuse to comply with; to oppose.

**buck**[3] *n* a plunging leap by a horse.

**buck**[4] *n NAmer, Aus, NZ, informal* a dollar.

**bucket**[1] *n* **1** an open container with a handle, used for holding or carrying liquids. **2** a tool or part of a machine shaped like a bucket. **3** *informal* (*in pl*) large quantities. ➤ **bucketful** (*pl* **bucketfuls**) *n.*

**bucket**[2] *v* (**bucketed, bucketing**) to move about jerkily or recklessly.

**buckle**[1] *n* a fastening consisting of a rigid rim with a hinged pin.

**buckle**[2] *v* **1** to fasten with a buckle. **2** to bend or warp under stress.

**buckle down** *v* to apply oneself vigorously.

**buckshot** *n* a coarse lead shot used for shooting large animals.

**buck up** *v* **1** to become encouraged or more cheerful. **2** to hurry up.

**buckwheat** *n* a plant with pinkish white flowers and seeds used to make flour.

**bucolic** *adj* relating to pastoral or country life.

**bud**[1] *n* a small growth on the stem of a plant that develops into a flower, leaf, or shoot.

**bud**[2] *v* (**budded, budding**) of a plant: to produce buds.

**Buddhism** *n* a religion or philosophy based on the teaching of Gautama Buddha. ➤ **Buddhist** *n and adj.*

**budding** *adj* in an early and usu promising stage of development.

**buddleia** *n* a shrub or tree with showy clusters of yellow or violet flowers.

**buddy** *n* (*pl* **-ies**) *chiefly NAmer, informal* a friend or colleague.

**budge** *v* (*usu in negative contexts*) **1** to move a little. **2** to change an opinion.

**budgerigar** *n* a small Australian bird often kept in captivity.

**budget**[1] *n* **1** a statement of income and expenditure over a period. **2** the amount of money available for or required for a particular purpose. **3** (**the Budget**) a statement of the government's financial position presented annually by a country's finance minister. **4** (*used before a noun*) simple and inexpensive. ➤ **budgetary** *adj.*

**budget**[2] *v* (**budgeted, budgeting**) to plan or provide for the use of available resources.

**budgie** *n informal* a budgerigar.

**buff**[1] *n* **1** a pale yellowish brown colour. **2** *informal* somebody who has a keen interest in a subject. * **in the buff** *informal* naked.

**buff**[2] *v* to polish or shine with a soft cloth.

**buffalo** *n* (*pl* **buffaloes** *or* **buffalo**) **1** an American bison. **2** a large African ox with a short mane and large curving horns.

**buffer**[1] *n* **1** a spring-loaded metal disc on a railway vehicle or at the end of a railway track, for absorbing shocks. **2** a device that serves to protect or cushion against shock. **3** a temporary storage area in a computer.

**buffer**[2] *n Brit, informal* a silly or ineffectual man.

**buffet**[1] *n* **1** a self-service meal set out on tables or a sideboard. **2** a counter where refreshments are sold.

**buffet**[2] *v* (**buffeted, buffeting**) to batter or strike repeatedly.

**buffoon** *n* an absurd but amusing person. ➤ **buffoonery** *n.*

**bug**[1] *n* **1** a tiny insect. **2** *informal* a microorganism, or a disease caused by one. **3** a fault in a computer program. **4** a hidden listening device.

**bug**[2] *v* (**bugged, bugging**) **1** *informal* to bother or annoy. **2** to plant a listening device in.

**bugbear** *n* a cause of concern or difficulty.

**bug-eyed** *adj* with protruding eyes.

**bugger**[1] *n coarse slang* **1** a disagreeable or contemptible person. **2** *chiefly Brit* a cause of annoyance or difficulty. **3** a man who has anal intercourse.

**bugger**[2] *v coarse slang* **1** (*often* + up) to damage or ruin. **2** *Brit* (+ around/about) to behave foolishly or annoyingly. **3** to have anal intercourse with.

**buggery** *n* anal intercourse.

**buggy** *n* (*pl* **-ies**) **1** a lightweight foldable pushchair. **2** a small open motor vehicle. **3** a light one-horse carriage.

**bugle** *n* a valveless brass instrument like a small trumpet. ➤ **bugler** *n.*

**build**[1] *v* (*past tense and past part.* **built**) **1** to construct by putting materials together. **2** (+on) to develop (a plan or idea). **3** to increase gradually. ➤ **builder** *n.*

**build**[2] *n* the physical proportions of a person or animal.

**build in** *v* to construct or develop as an integral part.
**building** *n* **1** a permanent structure with walls and a roof. **2** the business or act of building structures.
**building society** *n* an organization providing financial services for members and making mortgage loans.
**buildup** *n* **1** a gradual increase. **2** advance praise or publicity.
**build up** *v* **1** to accumulate or develop. **2** to develop gradually by increments.
**built** *v* **1** past tense and past part. of BUILD[1]. **2** proportioned or formed in a specified way.
**built-in** *adj* forming part of a larger structure.
**built-up** *adj* occupied by many houses and other buildings.
**bulb** *n* **1** a short stem base of a plant, with one or more buds enclosed in overlapping leaves, from which the roots develop. **2** (*also* **light bulb**) a glass bulb with a filament and gas, giving light when an electric current is passed through it. **3** a part shaped like a bulb.
**bulbous** *adj* **1** round like a bulb. **2** of a plant: growing from bulbs.
**bulge**[1] *n* **1** a swelling or convex curve on a flat surface. **2** *informal* a temporary increase or expansion.
**bulge**[2] *v* to swell or curve outwards.
**bulimia** *n* an emotional disorder with periods of compulsive overeating alternating with fasting or self-induced vomiting. ➤ **bulimic** *adj and n.*
**bulk**[1] *n* **1** the volume or size of something. **2** a large or heavy mass. **3** (+ of) the main or greater part. **4** dietary fibre; roughage. * **in bulk** in large amounts or quantities.
**bulk**[2] *v* **1** (*often* + out) to swell or thicken. **2** to appear as an unwelcome factor.
**bulkhead** *n* an internal partition or wall in an aircraft or ship.
**bulky** *adj* (**-ier, -iest**) large and cumbersome.
**bull**[1] *n* **1** an adult male bovine animal. **2** an adult male elephant, whale, or other large animal. * **take the bull by the horns** to face up to a problem.
**bull**[2] *n* a papal edict.
**bull**[3] *n informal* nonsense.
**bulldog** *n* a sturdy breed of dog with a short neck and wide head.
**bulldoze** *v* to clear or demolish.
**bulldozer** *n* a vehicle with caterpillar tracks and a broad horizontal blade at the front, for clearing ground.
**bullet** *n* **1** a small projectile fired from a gun. **2** a large dot in in printing.
**bulletin** *n* **1** a brief news item or broadcast. **2** a journal published at regular intervals.
**bullfight** *n* a public spectacle in which a bull is taunted and killed. ➤ **bullfighter** *n,* **bullfighting** *n.*
**bullfinch** *n* a finch with a rosy red breast and throat.
**bullfrog** *n* a large frog with a deep croak.
**bullion** *n* gold or silver in bars.
**bullish** *adj* energetically optimistic or enterprising.
**bullock** *n* a young castrated bull.
**bullring** *n* an arena for bullfights.
**bull's-eye** *n* the centre of a target, or a shot that hits it.
**bull terrier** *n* a short-haired breed of terrier.
**bully**[1] *n* (*pl* **-ies**) a person who habitually intimidates weaker people.
**bully**[2] *v* (**-ies, -ied**) to intimidate.
**bulrush** *n* a grasslike plant growing in wet areas.
**bulwark** *n* **1** a defensive wall or barrier. **2** (*usu in pl*) the side of a ship above the upper deck.
**bum**[1] *n Brit, informal* the buttocks.
**bum**[2] *adj informal* bad or worthless.
**bum**[3] *n NAmer, informal* **1** an idler or loafer. **2** a homeless vargant.
**bum**[4] *v* (**bummed, bumming**) *chiefly NAmer, informal* (+ around) to spend time idly.
**bumble** *v* to speak or act in a faltering or confused manner. ➤ **bumbler** *n.*
**bumblebee** *n* a large bee with a loud hum.
**bumf** *or* **bumph** *n chiefly Brit, informal* unwanted documents and printed information.
**bump**[1] *v* **1** to strike or knock with force. **2** to collide with. **3** to move in a series of bumps or jolts. * **bump into** to meet unexpectedly.
**bump**[2] *n* **1** a sudden blow or jolt. **2** a swelling or protuberance.
**bumper**[1] *n* a bar fitted at either end of a motor vehicle for absorbing shock.
**bumper**[2] *adj* unusually large or fine.
**bumpkin** *n* an awkward and unsophisticated country person.
**bump off** *v informal* to murder.
**bumptious** *adj* unpleasantly self-assertive.
**bump up** *v informal* to increase.
**bumpy** *adj* (**-ier, -iest**) **1** covered with bumps. **2** marked by jolts.
**bun** *n* **1** a small bread roll or cake. **2** a tight knot of hair at the back of the head.
**bunch**[1] *n* **1** a compact group of things loosely held together. **2** *informal* a group of people. ➤ **bunchy** *adj.*
**bunch**[2] *v* (*often* + up) to form into a bunch.
**bundle**[1] *n* **1** a collection of things held loosely together. **2** *informal* a large sum of money.
**bundle**[2] *v* **1** to form into a bundle or package. **2** *informal* to hustle or hurry unceremoniously. **3** (+ into) to force hastily into a container or vehicle.
**bung**[1] *n* a stopper in the hole of a cask.
**bung**[2] *v* **1** (*often* + up) to block or close. **2** *chiefly Brit, informal* to throw or put clumsily.
**bungalow** *n* a house with one storey.

**bungee jumping** *n* the sport of diving from a high place to which the feet are attached by an elastic cord.
**bungle**[1] *v* to do clumsily; to botch. ➤ **bungler** *n.*
**bungle**[2] *n* something done clumsily.
**bunion** *n* an inflamed swelling on the big toe.
**bunk**[1] *n* a narrow built-in bed.
**bunk**[2] *v* (*often* + down) to sleep in a makeshift bed.
**bunk**[3] *n informal, dated* nonsense.
**bunk**[4] * **do a bunk** *chiefly Brit, informal* to escape hurriedly.
**bunker** *n* **1** a bin or compartment for storing fuel. **2** a fortified underground shelter. **3** a sand-filled hazard on a golf course.
**bunk off** *v chiefly Brit, informal* to play truant from school.
**bunny** *n* (*pl* **-ies**) *informal* a rabbit.
**Bunsen burner** *n* a gas burner used in laboratories.
**bunting**[1] *n* a small bird with a short strong beak.
**bunting**[2] *n* flags and streamers used as outdoor decorations.
**buoy**[1] *n* a moored float serving as a navigational aid.
**buoy**[2] *v* (+ up) to raise the spirits of.

***Usage Note:*** Note the spelling *buoy* not *bouy.*

**buoyant** *adj* **1** capable of floating. **2** cheerful and resilient. ➤ **buoyancy** *n.*
**burble**[1] *v* **1** to make a bubbling sound. **2** to speak rapidly or ramblingly.
**burble**[2] *n* **1** a burbling sound. **2** rapid or rambling speech.
**burden**[1] *n* **1** a heavy load or thing to be carried. **2** an oppressive or troubling duty or responsibility.
**burden**[2] *v* to load or oppress with a burden.
**burdensome** *adj* oppressive or troublesome.
**bureau** /ˈbyooərroh/ *n* (*pl* **bureaus** *or* **bureaux**) **1** a government department. **2** a public office or agency. **3** *Brit* a writing desk with a sloping top. **4** *NAmer* a low chest of drawers.
**bureaucracy** *n* (*pl* **-ies**) **1** government based on fixed rules and a hierarchy of authority. **2** excessive official procedure. ➤ **bureaucratic** *adj.*
**bureaucrat** *n* a government official who follows procedures rigidly.
**burgeon** *v* **1** to send forth new growth. **2** to grow and expand rapidly.
**burger** *n* a hamburger.
**burgher** *n archaic* an inhabitant of a borough or town.
**burglar** *n* somebody who commits burglary.
**burglary** *n* (*pl* **-ies**) the offence of burgling a building.
**burgle** *v* to steal from (a building).
**Burgundy** *n* (*pl* **-ies**) a red or white wine from Burgundy in France.
**burial** *n* the burying of a dead body.
**burlesque** *n* **1** a literary or dramatic work that imitates or ridicules. **2** *NAmer* a variety show.
**burly** *adj* (**-ier, -iest**) strongly and heavily built.
**burn**[1] *v* (*past and past part.* **burned** *or* **burnt**) **1** to undergo or cause to undergo combustion by fire. **2** to damage or become damaged by exposure to fire or heat. **3** of a fire: to consume fuel and give off heat. **4** (+ with) to experience a strong emotion or desire. * **burn one's bridges/boats** to commit oneself to a course of action. **burn one's fingers** see FINGER[1]. **burn the candle at both ends** to be active at night as well as by day.
**burn**[2] *n* an injury resulting from burning.
**burn**[3] *n chiefly Scot* a small stream.
**burner** *n* the part of a fuel-burning device that produces the flame.
**burning** *adj* **1** on fire or very hot. **2** ardent or intense. **3** urgent.
**burnish** *v* to make shiny or lustrous by rubbing.
**burnout** *n* extreme exhaustion caused by overwork and stress.
**burnt** *v chiefly Brit* past tense and past part. of BURN[1].
**burp**[1] *n informal* a belch.
**burp**[2] *v informal* to belch.
**burr**[1] *n* **1** a rough or prickly covering of a fruit or seed. **2** a rough edge. **3** the rolled pronunciation of /r/ made at the back of the throat or the front of the mouth.
**burr**[2] *v* to make a whirring sound.
**burrow**[1] *n* a hole or passage in the ground made by a small animal.
**burrow**[2] *v* **1** to make (a hole or passage) by tunnelling. **2** to conceal oneself under something. **3** to search as if by digging.
**bursar** *n chiefly Brit* an official in charge of the financial affairs of an institution.
**bursary** *n* (*pl* **-ies**) a grant of money awarded to a student.
**burst**[1] *v* (*past tense and past part.* **burst**) **1** to break suddenly and violently apart or into pieces. **2** (+ into/out) to give vent suddenly to laughter or tears. **3** (+ into) to begin suddenly and forcefully. **4** to emerge or appear suddenly. **5** (+ with) to be filled to the point of breaking or overflowing.
**burst**[2] *n* **1** a sudden outbreak or eruption. **2** a brief period of effort or exertion. **3** an act of bursting.
**bury** *v* (**-ies, -ied**) **1** to place or hide in the earth or underground. **2** to conceal. **3** (+ in) to engross (oneself). * **bury the hatchet** to settle a disagreement.
**bus**[1] *n* (*pl* **buses,** *NAmer* **busses**) **1** a large motor vehicle that carries passengers along a

fixed route. **2** a conductor carrying data from one part of a computer to another.

**bus**[2] *v* (**bused** *or* **bussed, busing** *or* **bussing**) to travel or transport by bus.

**busby** *n* (*pl* **-ies**) a tall ceremonial fur hat worn by members of some regiments.

**bush**[1] *n* **1** a shrub with a woody stem and thickly growing branches. **2** (*usu* **the bush**) a large wild area in Africa or Australia.

**bush**[2] *or* **bushing** *n* an insulated lining through which an electrical wire passes.

**bush baby** *n* a small African primate with large eyes and ears.

**bushel** *n* **1** a unit of volume for dry goods and for liquids, equal to 8 imperial gallons (about 36.4l). **2** a US unit of volume, equal to 64 US pints (about 30.3l).

**bushy** *adj* (**-ier, -iest**) **1** growing thickly. **2** overgrown with bushes.

**business** *n* **1** commercial activity. **2** a commercial or industrial enterprise. **3** one's regular employment. **4** an immediate task or objective. **5** a matter that concerns one. ✱ **mean business** to speak or act with serious intent.

**businesslike** *adj* efficient and systematic.

**businessman** *or* **businesswoman** *n* (*pl* **businessmen** *or* **businesswomen**) a person who is engaged in business.

**busk** *v* to play music in the street to collect money from passers-by. ➤ **busker** *n.*

**bust**[1] *n* **1** a woman's breasts. **2** a sculpture of the head, neck, and shoulders.

**bust**[2] *v* (*past tense and past part.* **busted** *or* **bust**) *informal* **1** to break or smash. **2** *chiefly NAmer* to arrest or raid.

**bust**[3] *adj informal* **1** broken. **2** bankrupt.

**bust**[4] *n informal* **1** a police raid or arrest. **2** a period of economic collapse.

**bustle**[1] *v* **1** to move briskly and ostentatiously. **2** to be full of people and activity.

**bustle**[2] *n* noisy and energetic activity.

**bustle**[3] *n* a pad or framework formerly worn by women to give extra fullness at the back of a skirt.

**bust-up** *n informal* a quarrel or brawl.

**busty** *adj* (**-ier, -iest**) *informal* of a woman: having large breasts.

**busy**[1] *adj* (**-ier, -iest**) **1** fully engaged in an activity. **2** full of activity; bustling. ➤ **busily** *adv.*

**busy**[2] *v* (**-ies, -ied**) to occupy (oneself).

**busybody** *n* (*pl* **-ies**) a meddlesome person.

**but**[1] *conj* used to join words, clauses, or sentences to express reservation: *poor but proud.* ✱ **but for** were it not for: *He might have died but for your help.*

**but**[2] *prep* with the exception of; other than: *all but one.*

**butane** *n* an inflammable gas obtained from petroleum or natural gas and used as a fuel.

**butch** *adj informal* aggressively masculine.

**butcher**[1] *n* **1** a person who slaughters animals for their meat. **2** a person who sells or deals in meat. **3** a ruthless or brutal killer of people.

**butcher**[2] *v* **1** to slaughter and prepare (an animal) for sale. **2** to kill (people) indiscriminately. **3** to spoil or ruin. ➤ **butchery** *n.*

**butler** *n* the chief male servant of a household.

**butt**[1] *v* to strike or push with the head or horns.

**butt**[2] *n* a blow or thrust with the head or horns.

**butt**[3] *n* **1** the thicker end of a tool or weapon. **2** the unsmoked remnant of a cigar or cigarette. **3** *NAmer, informal* the buttocks.

**butt**[4] *n* **1** an object of abuse or ridicule. **2** a target in archery or shooting.

**butt**[5] *v* **1** to place end to end. **2** (+ against/on to) to adjoin.

**butt**[6] *n* a large barrel.

**butter**[1] *n* a pale yellow fatty substance made by churning milk or cream.

**butter**[2] *v* to spread or coat with butter.

**butter bean** *n* a large dried bean of a tropical plant.

**buttercream** *n* a creamy cake filling made with butter and icing sugar.

**buttercup** *n* a wild plant with bright yellow cup-shaped flowers.

**butterfingers** *n* (*pl* **butterfingers**) *informal* somebody who tends to drop things.

**butterfly** *n* (*pl* **-ies**) **1** an insect with large, broad, brightly coloured wings. **2** a frivolous person. **3** a swimming stroke performed by moving both arms together forwards out of the water and then sweeping them back. **4** *informal* (*in pl*) a queasy feeling caused by nervous tension.

**buttermilk** *n* **1** the liquid left after butter has been churned. **2** slightly sour milk made by adding bacteria to milk.

**butterscotch** *n* a brittle toffee made from brown sugar, and butter.

**butter up** *v informal* to charm or persuade with flattery.

**buttery**[1] *n* (*pl* **-ies**) *Brit* a room in a college, in which food and drink are sold.

**buttery**[2] *adj* similar to or containing butter.

**butt in** *v* to intrude or interrupt.

**buttock** *n* the back of a hip that forms one of the two fleshy parts on which a person sits.

**button**[1] *n* **1** a small disc secured to a piece of clothing and fastened by passing it through a buttonhole or loop. **2** a knob on a piece of equipment that is pressed to activate a function.

**button**[2] *v* (*often* + up) to fasten with buttons.

**buttonhole**[1] *n* **1** a slit or loop on a piece of clothing, through which a button is passed. **2** *Brit* a flower worn in the buttonhole of a lapel.

**buttonhole**[2] *v informal* to seek out and detain in conversation.

**buttress**[1] *n* **1** a supporting structure built

against a wall or building. **2** a projecting part of a mountain or rock cliff.

**buttress**[2] *v* **1** to support with a buttress. **2** to give support or strength to.

**buxom** *adj* of a woman: with an attractively rounded figure and large breasts.

**buy**[1] *v* (*past tense and past part.* **bought**) **1** to pay for (something) in order to own it. **2** to obtain by making a sacrifice. **3** *informal* to believe or accept (something said or proposed). ➤ **buyer** *n.*

**buy**[2] *n informal* a purchase.

**buyout** *n* the purchase of all the shares in a business.

**buzz**[1] *v* **1** to make a continuous low humming sound. **2** to be filled with activity or conversation. **3** to move in a hurried or busy manner. **4** to summon or signal with a buzzer.

**buzz**[2] *n* **1** a continuous low humming sound. **2** a flurry of activity or excitement. **3** *informal* rumour or gossip. **4** a signal conveyed by a buzzer or bell. **5** *informal* a telephone call. **6** *informal* a thrill.

**buzzard** *n* **1** *chiefly Brit* a large hawk with broad wings and a soaring flight. **2** *chiefly NAmer* a large bird of prey.

**buzzer** *n* an electrical device that makes a buzzing sound.

**buzz off** *v informal* to go away.

**buzzword** *n informal* a technical word or phrase that has become fashionable.

**by**[1] *prep* **1** through the action or creation of. **2** near to. **3** up to and beyond. **4** during: *by night.* **5** not later than. **6** by means of. **7** in conformity with.

**by**[2] *adv* past.

**bye**[1] *n* **1** the right of a competitor to proceed to the next round when there is no opponent or the opponent has withdrawn. **2** in cricket, a run scored off a ball that passes the batsman without contact.

**bye**[2] *interj informal* used as an expression of farewell.

**by-election** *n Brit* a mid-term election to fill a vacancy in a constituency.

**bygone**[1] *adj* belonging to an earlier time. * **let bygones be bygones** to forgive past quarrels.

**bygone**[2] *n* a domestic or industrial implement of an early and now disused type.

**bylaw** *or* **byelaw** *n* a law made by a local authority and valid only within its area.

**by-line** *n* **1** a line in a newspaper or magazine article naming the author. **2** a goal line on a football pitch.

**bypass**[1] *n* **1** a road built to take traffic round a town centre. **2** a passage created surgically between two blood vessels to divert blood.

**bypass**[2] *v* **1** to go round by means of a bypass. **2** to neglect or ignore.

**byplay** *n* action apart from the main action of a film or play.

**by-product** *n* **1** something produced in the manufacture of something else. **2** a secondary result.

**byre** *n Brit* a cow shed.

**bystander** *n* somebody present but not involved in a situation or event.

**byte** *n* in computing, a unit equal to a string of eight adjacent bits (binary digits).

**byway** *n* a quiet or minor road.

**byword** *n* **1** a saying or proverb. **2** a noteworthy or typical example of a quality.

**Byzantine** *adj* **1** of the ancient city of Byzantium or its empire. **2** excessively complex. **3** characterized by trickery and deception.

**C**[1] *or* **c** *n* (*pl* **C's** *or* **Cs** *or* **c's**) the third letter of the English alphabet.

**C**[2] *abbr* **1** Celsius. **2** centigrade. **3** century.

**C**[3] *abbr* the chemical symbol for carbon.

**Ca** *abbr* the chemical symbol for calcium.

**cab** *n* **1** a taxi. **2** a compartment for the driver of a train, bus, or large vehicle. **3** formerly, a horse-drawn carriage used for hire.

**cabal** *n* a clandestine political faction.

**cabaret** /ˈkabəray/ *n* a stage show at a nightclub.

**cabbage** *n* **1** the leaves of a plant with a a dense round head, used as a vegetable. **2** *informal* an inactive or apathetic person.

**caber** *n* a tree trunk thrown in the Scottish sport of tossing the caber.

**cabin** *n* **1** a private room or compartment on a ship. **2** the passenger compartment in an aircraft. **3** a small simple wooden house.

**cabinet** *n* **1** a cupboard usu with doors and shelves for storing or displaying articles. **2** an upright case housing a radio, television, etc. **3** (*often* **Cabinet**) a body consisting of the prime minister and senior ministers.

**cabinetmaker** *n* a craftsman who makes furniture in wood.

**cable** *n* **1** a strong thick rope of fibre or metal. **2** a set of electrical wires surrounded by a sheath.

**cable car** *n* a small cabin hanging from a cable, carrying passengers up and down a mountainside.

**cable television** *n* a television service to subscribers via a cable.

**caboodle** * **the whole caboodle** *informal* the whole lot.

**caboose** *n* *NAmer* a wagon for the crew, attached to a goods train.

**cabriolet** /ˌkabriohˈlay/ *n* a car with a folding or removable roof.

**cacao** *n* (*pl* **-os**) the seeds of a South American tree used in making cocoa and chocolate.

**cache** *n* a hiding place, *esp* for provisions or weapons.

**cachet** *n* prestige or esteem.

**cackle**[1] *v* **1** to make the squawking cry of a hen. **2** to talk or laugh noisily.

**cackle**[2] *n* **1** a cackling noise made by a hen. **2** a cackling laugh.

**cacophony** *n* (*pl* **-ies**) a discordant combination of sounds. ➤ **cacophonous** *adj.*

**cactus** *n* (*pl* **cacti** *or* **cactuses**) a plant with a fleshy stem and scales or spines instead of leaves.

**cad** *n* *dated* a dishonourable man. ➤ **caddish** *adj.*

**cadaver** *n* a corpse, *esp* one intended for dissection.

**cadaverous** *adj* unhealthily pale or thin.

**caddie**[1] *or* **caddy** *n* (*pl* **-ies**) somebody who carries a golfer's clubs and gives advice.

**caddie**[2] *or* **caddy** *v* (**-ies, -ied**) to work as a caddie.

**caddy**[1] *n* (*pl* **-ies**) a small container for tea.

**caddy**[2] *n* see CADDIE[1].

**caddy**[3] *v* see CADDIE[2].

**cadence** *n* **1** the rhythmic flow and intonations of speech. **2** in music, a sequence of chords moving to a harmonic close.

**cadenza** *n* an elaborate solo passage in a concerto.

**cadet** *n* **1** a trainee officer in the armed forces or the police force. **2** a young person receiving basic military training.

**cadge** *v* *informal* to ask for and get (something) one does not deserve.

**cadmium** *n* a bluish white metallic chemical element used in batteries.

**cadre** *n* a group of trained people forming the nucleus of a military force or political organization.

**Caesar** *n* a title for a Roman emperor.

**Caesarean section** (*NAmer* **Cesarean section**) *n* an operation for delivering a baby by cutting through the mother's abdominal wall.

**café** *n* *chiefly Brit* a small restaurant serving light meals and drinks.

**cafeteria** *n* a self-service restaurant.

**cafetière** /kafˈtyeə/ *n* a coffee pot with a plunger used to force the grounds to the bottom.

**caffeine** *n* a stimulant occurring naturally in tea and coffee.

**caftan** *n* see KAFTAN.

**cage**[1] *n* an enclosure with bars for confining or carrying animals.

**cage**[2] *v* **1** to put or keep in a cage. **2** to confine as if in a cage.

**cagey** *or* **cagy** *adj* (**-ier, -iest**) *informal* hesitant about speaking or committing oneself. ➤ **cagily** *adv,* **caginess** *n.*

**cagoule** *or* **kagoul** *n* a lightweight waterproof jacket with a hood.
**cahoots** * **in cahoots** *informal* working together secretly.
**caiman** *n* see CAYMAN.
**cairn** *n* **1** a pile of stones built as a memorial or landmark. **2** a breed of small terrier with coarse hair.
**cajole** *v* to persuade with flattery or deception. ➤ **cajolery** *n.*
**cake**[1] *n* **1** a sweet baked food made from a mixture of flour, sugar, fat, and eggs. **2** a flat round mass of savoury food.
**cake**[2] *v* **1** to cover and encrust. **2** to form or harden into a mass.
**calabrese** *n* a type of sprouting broccoli.
**calamine** *n* a pink powder used in soothing or cooling lotions.
**calamity** *n* (*pl* **-ies**) an extremely grave event; a disaster. ➤ **calamitous** *adj.*
**calcify** *v* (**-ies, -ied**) **1** to harden with calcium carbonate or other calcium compounds. **2** to convert into a solid compound of calcium.
**calcium** *n* a silver-white metallic chemical element.
**calcium carbonate** *n* a chemical compound occurring naturally as chalk, marble, and limestone, etc.
**calculate** *v* **1** to determine by mathematical processes. **2** to reckon or estimate. **3** (+ on) to count or rely on. ➤ **calculable** *adj.*
**calculated** *adj* planned to accomplish a purpose; intentional.
**calculating** *adj* devious or scheming.
**calculation** *n* **1** the process or result of calculating. **2** studied care in planning.
**calculator** *n* an electronic device for making mathematical calculations.
**calculus** *n* a branch of mathematics dealing with rates of change of functions.
**caldron** *n* see CAULDRON.
**calendar** *n* **1** a system for fixing the length and divisions of the year. **2** a chart or table showing the days of the year. **3** a chronological list of events or activities.
**calf**[1] *n* (*pl* **calves** *or* **calfs**) **1** a young cow or bull. **2** the young of some other large animals, e.g. the elephant or whale.
**calf**[2] *n* (*pl* **calves**) the fleshy back part of the leg below the knee.
**calibrate** *v* **1** to mark the graduations of (a gauge or thermometer). **2** to determine the correct reading of (a scale or instrument) by comparison with a standard. ➤ **calibration** *n.*
**calibre** (*NAmer* **caliber**) *n* **1** the internal diameter of a gun barrel or bullet. **2** degree of quality or ability.
**calico** *n* (*pl* **-oes** *or* **-os**) **1** white or unbleached cotton cloth. **2** *NAmer* brightly printed cotton fabric.
**caliper** *n NAmer* see CALLIPER.
**caliph** *or* **calif** *n* formerly, a secular and spiritual Islamic leader.
**calk** *n* see CAULK.
**call**[1] *v* **1** to cry out loudly. **2** to cry out to (somebody) to attract attention. **3** of a bird or animal: to utter a characteristic note or cry. **4** to telephone. **5** to summon to a meeting. **6** to use a name or description for. **7** (*often* + in/by/round) to make a short visit. **8** to stop at a particular place. * **call for** to need or demand. **call on/upon** to require (somebody) to do something. **call the shots/tune** to be in control. **call to account** to demand an explanation from. ➤ **caller** *n.*
**call**[2] *n* **1** an act of calling with the voice. **2** the cry of a bird or animal. **3** a request or command to come. **4** need or justification. **5** a strong inner prompting. **6** a short visit. **7** an act of telephoning. * **on call** ready to be used or summoned when needed.
**call centre** *n* an office dealing with large numbers of telephone enquiries for an organization.
**call girl** *n* a prostitute making appointments by telephone.
**calligraphy** *n* the art of producing decorative handwriting. ➤ **calligrapher** *n,* **calligraphic** *adj.*
**calling** *n* **1** a profession or occupation. **2** a strong inner impulse.
**calliper** (*NAmer* **caliper**) *n* **1** (*usu in pl*) a measuring instrument with two hinged arms. **2** a support for the human leg.
**callisthenics** (*NAmer* **calisthenics**) *pl n* rhythmic bodily exercises. ➤ **callisthenic** *adj.*
**call off** *v* to cancel (an arrangement).
**callous** *adj* cruelly insensitive. ➤ **callously** *adv.*
**callow** *adj* immature and lacking experience.
**call up** *v* to summon for military service.
**callus** *n* (*pl* **calluses**) a hard thickened area on skin or bark.
**calm**[1] *adj* **1** free from anger, nervousness, or excitement. **2** quiet or still. ➤ **calmly** *adv,* **calmness** *n.*
**calm**[2] *n* a calm state.
**calm**[3] *v* (*often* + down) to make or become calm.
**calorie** *or* **calory** *n* (*pl* **-ies**) a unit for measuring energy.
**calorific** *adj* relating to the energy-producing content of food or fuel.
**calumniate** *v formal* to make false statements about.
**calumny** *n* (*pl* **-ies**) a maliciously false statement about somebody.
**calve** *v* to give birth to (a calf).
**calves**[1] *n* pl of CALF[1].
**calves**[2] *n* pl of CALF[2].
**calypso** *n* (*pl* **-os**) a style of West Indian music with improvised lyrics on topical themes.
**calyx** *n* (*pl* **calyxes** *or* **calyces**) the outer leafy part of a flower surrounding the bud.

**cam** *n* a wheel or shaft with a projecting part that transforms circular motion into back-and-forth motion.

**camaraderie** *n* a spirit of good humour and trust among friends.

**camber** *n* a slight arching or curved shape given to a flat surface such as a road.

**cambric** *n* a fine white linen or cotton fabric.

**camcorder** *n* a video camera with a built-in video recorder.

**came** *v* past tense of COME.

**camel** *n* a mammal with a long neck and either one or two humps on its back, used for riding in desert regions.

**camellia** *n* a shrub with glossy leaves and bright flowers.

**cameo** *n* (*pl* **-os**) **1** a piece of jewellery carved with a contrasting raised design of a head in profile. **2** a short piece of writing highlighting a plot or character. **3** a small dramatic role played by a well-known actor.

**camera** *n* a device for taking photographs or moving images. ✱ **in camera** in private, often in a judge's private rooms.

**camisole** *n* a short bodice worn as an undergarment by women.

**camomile** *or* **chamomile** *n* a strong-scented plant with leaves and flowers that are used in herbal remedies.

**camouflage**[1] *n* **1** the disguising of military personnel and equipment so that they blend in with their surroundings. **2** clothing and other covering used for this purpose. **3** animal markings and colouring that match the natural surroundings.

**camouflage**[2] *v* to conceal or disguise with camouflage.

**camp**[1] *n* **1** an area of ground where tents or other temporary shelters are erected. **2** a place with accommodation and other facilities for troops, holidaymakers, prisoners, etc. **3** the members of a political party or supporters of a particular cause.

**camp**[2] *v* **1** to pitch or occupy a camp. **2** to live temporarily in a tent or other outdoor accommodation. ➤ **camper** *n.*

**camp**[3] *adj informal* **1** exaggeratedly effeminate. **2** deliberately and outrageously affected or inappropriate.

**camp**[4] *v* ✱ **camp it up** *informal* to act or behave in a camp manner.

**campaign** *n* **1** a series of military operations forming a distinct phase of a war. **2** a series of coordinated actions for achieving a particular result.

**campanology** *n* the art of bell ringing. ➤ **campanologist** *n.*

**camp bed** *n* a small collapsible bed.

**camphor** *n* a chemical compound obtained from the camphor tree and used as a liniment and insect repellent.

**campus** *n* (*pl* **campuses**) **1** the grounds and buildings of a university. **2** *NAmer* the grounds of a school or college.

**camshaft** *n* a shaft to which cams are attached.

**can**[1] *v aux* (*third person sing. present tense* **can**, *past tense* **could**) **1** to be able to. **2** to have permission to. **3** to have a certain tendency.

**can**[2] *n* a cylindrical metal container for food or drink.

**can**[3] *v* (**canned, canning**) to preserve food or drink) in a can.

**Canadian** *n* a native or inhabitant of Canada. ➤ **Canadian** *adj.*

**canal** *n* **1** an artificial waterway for ships or boats. **2** any channel or watercourse used for drainage or irrigation. **3** a tubular passage in an animal or plant.

**canapé** *n* a small piece of bread or pastry with a savoury topping.

**canard** *n* a false report or story.

**canasta** *n* a card game for four players using two full packs plus jokers.

**cancan** *n* an energetic stage dance with high kicks.

**cancel** *v* (**cancelled, cancelling,** *NAmer* **canceled, canceling**) **1** to decide that (something arranged) will not take place. **2** to annul or revoke. **3** to mark (a ticket or postage stamp) to show that it has been used. **4** (*often* + out) to match in force or effect; to counterbalance or offset. ➤ **cancellation** *n.*

**cancer** *n* **1** a malignant tumour that develops when cells multiply in an unlimited way. **2** the medical condition that is characterized by this. **3** a spreading evil in a person, society, etc. **4** (**Cancer**) the fourth sign of the zodiac. ➤ **cancerous** *adj.*

**candela** *n* the basic SI unit of luminous intensity.

**candelabrum** *n* (*pl* **candelabra**) a branched candlestick or lamp with several lights.

**candid** *adj* frank or sincere. ➤ **candidly** *adv.*

**candidate** *n* **1** somebody who applies for a job or award. **2** somebody who is taking an examination. **3** somebody or something regarded as deserving or suitable for something. ➤ **candidacy** *n.*

**candied** *adj* of fruit: preserved in a heavy syrup.

**candle** *n* a cylindrical length of wax with a wick that is burned to give light. **not worth the candle** not justified by the result.

**candlestick** *n* a holder for a candle.

**candlewick** *n* a fabric made with thick soft cotton yarn cut in a raised tufted pattern.

**candour** (*NAmer* **candor**) *n* sincerity or frankness.

**candy** *n* **1** crystallized sugar formed by boiling down sugar syrup. **2** *chiefly NAmer* sweets.

**candy floss** *n Brit* a light fluffy mass of spun sugar, wound round a stick.

**cane**[1] *n* **1** a hollow stem of some reeds and grasses. **2** a length of cane used as a walking stick or for beating somebody.
**cane**[2] *v* to beat with a cane. ➤ **caning** *n.*
**canine**[1] *adj* resembling or being a member of the dog family.
**canine**[2] *n* a pointed tooth next to each incisor.
**canister** *n* a small round container for storage.
**canker** *n* **1** an ulcer or spreading sore. **2** an area of dead tissue in a plant. **3** an inflammatory disease of animals. **4** a source of spreading corruption or evil. ➤ **cankerous** *adj.*
**cannabis** *n* the dried leaves of hemp plants, used as a drug.
**canned** *adj* **1** sold or preserved in a can. **2** *informal* drunk.
**cannelloni** *pl n* rolls of pasta served with a filling of meat, vegetables, or cheese.
**cannery** *n* (*pl* **-ies**) a factory for canning foods.
**cannibal** *n* a human being who eats human flesh. ➤ **cannibalism** *n,* **cannibalistic** *adj.*
**cannibalize** *or* **-ise** *v* to dismantle (e.g. a machine) for spare parts.
**cannon** *n* (*pl* **cannons** *or* **cannon**) **1** a large gun on a carriage, used formerly in warfare. **2** an automatic shell-firing gun mounted in an aircraft or tank.
**cannonball** *n* a metal or stone ball for firing from a cannon.
**cannon fodder** *n* soldiers seen as expendable in war.
**cannot** *contraction* can not.
**canny** *adj* (**-ier, -iest**) cautious and shrewd; astute. ➤ **cannily** *adv.*
**canoe**[1] *n* a long light narrow boat with pointed ends, propelled with a paddle.
**canoe**[2] *v* (**canoes, canoed, canoeing**) to travel in a canoe. ➤ **canoeist** *n.*
**canon**[1] *n* **1** a regulation or dogma decreed by a church council. **2** an accepted rule or criterion. **3** a body of principles or standards. **4** an authoritative list of books accepted as Holy Scripture. **5** the authentic works of a writer. **6** a musical composition in which a melody is repeated by parts entering in succession and overlapping.
**canon**[2] *n* a clergyman attached to a cathedral.
**canonical** *adj* **1** conforming to a general rule; orthodox. **2** conforming to canon law. **3** accepted as authentic.
**canonize** *or* **-ise** *v* to recognize (a dead person) officially as a saint. ➤ **canonization** *n.*
**canon law** *n* the law governing a church.
**canoodle** *v informal* to kiss and cuddle amorously.
**canopy** *n* (*pl* **-ies**) **1** a cloth covering hung over a bed or throne. **2** an ornamental rooflike structure. **3** the lifting or supporting surface of a parachute. **4** the spreading leafy branches at the top of a forest.
**cant**[1] *n* **1** insincere or hypocritical talk suggesting piety. **2** the jargon of a specific group.
**cant**[2] *n* slope or slanting surface.
**cant**[3] *v* to tilt or slope.
**can't** *contraction* can not.
**cantaloupe** *or* **cantaloup** *n* a type of melon with a hard rind and orange flesh.
**cantankerous** *adj* ill-natured or quarrelsome.
**cantata** *n* a musical setting of a religious text, comprising choruses, solos, recitatives, and interludes.
**canteen** *n* **1** a restaurant in a school or factory. **2** *Brit* a box for holding cutlery. **3** a small water flask used by soldiers or campers.
**canter**[1] *n* a gait of a horse that is smoother and slower than a gallop.
**canter**[2] *v* (**cantered, cantering**) to move or ride at a canter.
**canticle** *n* a hymn based on a text from the Bible and used in services of worship.
**cantilever** *n* a projecting beam or member supported at only one end. ➤ **cantilevered** *adj,.*
**canto** *n* (*pl* **-os**) a major division of a long poem.
**canton** *n* a territorial division of a country.
**canvas** *n* (*pl* **canvases** *or* **canvasses**) **1** a strong closely woven cloth used for making sails, tents, etc. **2** a cloth surface for painting in oils. **3** the floor of a boxing or wrestling ring.
**canvass** *v* to visit (voters) to seek political support or to find out their opinions. ➤ **canvasser** *n.*
**canyon** *n* a deep valley or gorge.
**cap**[1] *n* **1** a soft close-fitting hat with a peak and no brim. **2** *chiefly Brit* a head covering awarded to a member of a sports team. **3** a cover or lid for a container. **4** an upper financial limit. **5** a small container holding an explosive charge that bangs when struck. **6** *Brit* a contraceptive diaphragm fitting over the cervix of the womb. **7** a protective covering for the external part of a tooth. * **cap in hand** in a deferential manner.
**cap**[2] *v* (**capped, capping**) **1** to provide or protect with a cap. **2** to form a cap over. **3** *chiefly Brit* to select (a player) for a sports team. **4** to follow (something) with a better example. **5** to impose an upper financial limit on (e.g. a tax or charge).
**capability** *n* (*pl* **-ies**) the ability to do something.
**capable** *adj* **1** able or competent. **2** (+ of) having the ability or propensity to do something. ➤ **capably** *adv.*
**capacious** *adj* able to hold a great deal; roomy.
**capacitance** *n* the ability to store an electric charge.
**capacitor** *n* a component in an electrical circuit that can store an electric charge.
**capacity** *n* (*pl* **-ies**) **1** the maximum amount that can be contained or produced. **2** the power

or ability to do something. **3** a position or role that somebody has.

**cape[1]** *n* a short cloak.

**cape[2]** *n* an area of land jutting out into the sea.

**caper[1]** *v* to leap about playfully.

**caper[2]** *n* **1** a playful or carefree leap. **2** a high-spirited escapade or prank.

**caper[3]** *n* (*usu in pl*) the flower bud or berry of a shrub, pickled and used as a seasoning.

**capillarity** *n* the pressure on the surface of a liquid in contact with a solid, e.g. in a fine-bore tube, raising or lowering it.

**capillary[1]** *n* (*pl* **-ies**) a blood vessel connecting small arteries with veins.

**capillary[2]** *adj* **1** slender and elongated, like a hair. **2** of a tube, passage, etc: having a very fine bore.

**capillary action** *n* the force on a liquid in a tube, making it rise or fall.

**capital[1]** *n* **1** a city serving as a seat of government. **2** wealth or goods used to produce further wealth or goods. **3** the excess of the assets of a business over its liabilities. **4** a capital letter. * **make capital out of** to turn (a situation) to one's advantage.

**capital[2]** *adj* **1** punishable by death. **2** of a letter: of the series used to begin sentences or proper names, e.g. *A, B, C* rather than *a, b, c*. **3** *dated* excellent.

**capital[3]** *n* the top part of a pillar or column.

**capitalism** *n* an economic system based on private ownership and control of the means of production. ➤ **capitalist** *n and adj.*

**capitalize** *or* **-ise** *v* **1** (+ on) to gain by turning (something) to advantage. **2** to supply capital for. **3** to convert into capital. **4** to write or print (in capitals or with an initial capital. ➤ **capitalization** *n.*

**capital punishment** *n* the punishment of a crime by death.

**capitulate** *v* to surrender or cease resisting. ➤ **capitulation** *n.*

**capon** *n* a castrated male chicken fattened for eating.

**cappuccino** /kapoo'cheenoh/ *n* (*pl* **-os**) frothy coffee made with steamed milk.

**caprice** *n* a sudden unexpected change of mind.

**capricious** *adj* changing mood suddenly or unpredictably. ➤ **capriciously** *adv.*

**Capricorn** *n* the tenth sign of the zodiac (the Goat).

**capsicum** *n* a fleshy fruit of a tropical plant, used as a vegetable.

**capsize** *v* of a boat: to overturn in the water.

**capstan** *n* a rotating cylinder or shaft on which rope or cable is wound.

**capsule** *n* **1** a gelatin shell enclosing a dose of a medicine. **2** a small compartment or container.

**captain[1]** *n* **1** a person in command of a ship or civil aircraft. **2** a naval officer ranking below a commodore. **3** an army officer ranking below a major. **4** a leader of a team. ➤ **captaincy** *n.*

**captain[2]** *v* to be captain of.

**caption** *n* **1** a comment or description accompanying a pictorial illustration. **2** a piece of text appearing on a film or television screen.

**captivate** *v* to fascinate or charm irresistibly. ➤ **captivating** *adj.*

**captive[1]** *adj* **1** taken and held prisoner. **2** confined and unable to escape. ➤ **captivity** *n.*

**captive[2]** *n* somebody who has been taken prisoner.

**captor** *n* somebody who takes another as captive.

**capture[1]** *n* **1** the act of gaining control or possession. **2** somebody or something that has been captured. **3** the storing of data on a computer.

**capture[2]** *v* **1** to take captive. **2** to represent or preserve in words, pictures, etc. **3** to remove (a piece) from the playing board by the rules of a game. **4** to store (data) in a computer.

**capybara** *n* (*pl* **capybaras**) a large South American rodent.

**car** *n* **1** a motor vehicle designed for carrying a small number of people. **2** a railway carriage.

**carafe** *n* a glass bottle with a flaring lip and open top, used for serving wine.

**caramel** *n* **1** sugar or syrup heated to a brown colour and used as a colouring and flavouring. **2** a chewy soft toffee.

**carapace** *n* a hard case on the back of a turtle, crab, etc.

**carat** *n* **1** a unit of weight used for precious stones. **2** (*NAmer chiefly* **karat**) a unit of fineness for gold.

**caravan** *n* **1** *Brit* a vehicle designed to be towed and for living in when parked. **2** a group of travellers on a journey through a desert.

**caraway** *n* the seeds of an aromatic plant, used in cookery.

**carbide** *n* a chemical compound of carbon with a metallic element.

**carbine** *n* a light automatic rifle.

**carbohydrate** *n* a compound of carbon, hydrogen, and oxygen, forming a major class of energy providing animal foods.

**carbolic** *or* **carbolic acid** *n* a chemical compound used as a disinfectant.

**carbon** *n* a chemical element occurring naturally as diamond and graphite or forming a constituent of organic compounds. ➤ **carbonaceous** *adj.*

**carbonate[1]** *n* a salt or ester of carbonic acid.

**carbonate[2]** *v* **1** to convert (something) into a carbonate. **2** to impregnate (a drink) with carbon dioxide.

**carbon copy** *n* **1** a copy made with carbon paper. **2** a duplicate or exact replica.

**carbon dating** *n* a method of dating organic material by recording the deterioration of carbon 14 in it.
**carbon dioxide** *n* a gas formed by the burning and decomposition of organic substances and absorbed by plants in photosynthesis.
**carbonic acid** *n* a weak acid that is a solution of carbon dioxide in water.
**carbon monoxide** *n* a toxic gas formed by the incomplete combustion of carbon.
**carbon paper** *n* thin paper coated with dark pigment, used to make a copy of a document.
**Carborundum** *n trademark* an abrasive material.
**carbuncle** *n* **1** a painful inflammation of the skin. **2** a red gemstone.
**carburettor** *or* **carburetter** (*NAmer* **carburetor**) *n* a device for mixing the fuel with air in an internal-combustion engine.
**carcass** *or* **carcase** *n* the body of a slaughtered animal.
**carcinogen** *n* a susbtance that causes cancer. ➤ **carcinogenic** *adj.*
**carcinoma** *n* (*pl* **carcinomas** *or* **carcinomata**) a cancerous tumour originating in the skin or tissue lining a body cavity. ➤ **carcinomatous** *adj.*
**card**[1] *n* **1** thin cardboard or stiff paper. **2** a postcard, greetings card, visiting card. **3** a playing card. **4** a game played with playing cards. **5** a rectangular piece of plastic with machine-readable information, used to withdraw cash, make payment, etc. **6** *informal* an amusing or eccentric person. ✱ **get one's cards** *Brit, informal* to be dismissed/resign from employment. **on the cards** possible or likely.
**card**[2] *v* to disentangle (fibres) with a toothed implement before spinning.
**cardamom** *n* the fruit and seeds of a plant of the ginger family, used as a spice or condiment.
**cardboard** *n* a stiff material made from paper pulp.
**cardiac** *adj* relating to the heart.
**cardigan** *n* a knitted garment with buttons down the front.
**cardinal**[1] *n* **1** a high official of the Roman Catholic Church who takes part in the election of a new pope. **2** a deep scarlet colour.
**cardinal**[2] *adj* of primary importance; fundamental.
**cardinal number** *n* a number used in counting, e.g. one, two, three, etc.
**cardiograph** *n* an instrument for recording movements of the heart. ➤ **cardiography** *n.*
**cardiology** *n* the branch of medical science concerned with the heart and its diseases. ➤ **cardiologist** *n.*
**cardiovascular** *adj* relating to the heart and blood vessels.
**cardsharp** *n* a cheat at cards.
**care**[1] *n* **1** a cause for anxiety. **2** close attention or effort. **3** attention to or provision for the welfare of somebody or something. **4** charge or supervision. **5** *Brit* legal responsibility for children by a local authority. **6** a sense of loving protection. ✱ **care of** at the address of (somebody other than the addressee). **take care of** to deal with or look after.
**care**[2] *v* **1** to be concerned about something or somebody. **2** to feel an interest or involvement. **3** (+ for) to have a liking or taste for. **4** to wish (to do something).
**careen** *v* of a ship: to lean over to one side.
**career**[1] *n* a field of employment to which a person devotes much of their working life, hoping to make progress in it.
**career**[2] *v* to move swiftly in an uncontrolled way.
**careerist** *n* somebody who is primarily intent on advancing their career. ➤ **careerism** *n.*
**carefree** *adj* free from anxiety or responsibility.
**careful** *adj* **1** exercising or taking care. **2** marked by attentive concern. **3** cautious or prudent. ➤ **carefully** *adv.*
**careless** *adj* **1** not taking enough care. **2** indifferent or unconcerned. ➤ **carelessly** *adv,* **carelessness** *n.*
**carer** *n Brit* a person who looks after somebody who is ill, elderly, or disabled.
**caress**[1] *n* **1** a gentle or loving touch or stroke. **2** a kiss.
**caress**[2] *v* to touch or stroke lightly and lovingly.
**caretaker** *n* a person who looks after a school or other public building.
**careworn** *adj* showing the effects of anxiety.
**cargo** *n* (*pl* **-oes** *or* **-os**) goods carried by a ship, aircraft, or vehicle.
**Caribbean** *adj* of the Caribbean Sea and its islands.
**caribou** *n* (*pl* **caribou**) a large North American deer with broad branching antlers.
**caricature**[1] *n* a picture or description that comically or grotesquely exaggerates the appearance or main features of a person or thing.
**caricature**[2] *v* to make a caricature of.
**caries** *n* (*pl* **caries**) decay of a tooth or bone.
**carmine** *n* a rich crimson or scarlet colour.
**carnage** *n* great slaughter.
**carnal** *adj* relating to sexual pleasures and appetites.
**carnation** *n* a plant with fragrant red, pink, or white flowers.
**carnelian** *n* see CORNELIAN.
**carnival** *n* a festival with music, dancing, and processions.
**carnivore** *n* a flesh-eating mammal.
**carnivorous** *adj* eating meat.

**carob** *n* the edible pod of a Mediterranean tree, used as the source of a chocolate substitute.
**carol**[1] *n* a Christmas song or hymn.
**carol**[2] *v* (**carolled, carolling,** *NAmer* **caroled, caroling**) **1** to sing carols. **2** to sing joyfully. ➤ **caroller** *n.*
**carotene** *n* an orange or red pigment found in carrots and a source of vitamin A.
**carotid artery** *n* either of the arteries that supply the head with blood.
**carouse** *v* to take part in a drinking spree or drunken revel.
**carousel** *or* **carrousel** *n* **1** a merry-go-round. **2** a rotating delivery system for baggage at an airport.
**carp**[1] *n* (*pl* **carp**) a large edible freshwater fish.
**carp**[2] *v informal* (+ at) to complain or find fault peevishly.
**carpal** *adj* of or forming part of the wrist.
**carpel** *n* the female reproductive organ of a flowering plant.
**carpenter** *n* a person who builds with wood. ➤ **carpentry** *n.*
**carpet**[1] *n* **1** a floor covering made of a heavy woven material. **2** a thick layer. ✱ **on the carpet** being reprimanded.
**carpet**[2] *v* (**carpeted, carpeting**) to cover with a carpet.
**carpetbag** *n* a travelling bag made of carpet-like fabric.
**carpet bomb** *v* to bomb (an area) thoroughly.
**carport** *n* an open-sided shelter for a car.
**carriage** *n* **1** *Brit* a railway passenger vehicle. **2** a horse-drawn passenger vehicle. **3** a movable part of a machine that supports another part. **4** the carrying or conveying of goods. **5** the manner of bearing the body.
**carriage clock** *n* a small clock in a glass-sided frame.
**carriageway** *n Brit* the part of a road used by vehicles.
**carrier** *n* **1** an organization that transports goods or people. **2** a bag with handles for carrying shopping. **3** a device or mechanism that carries something. **4** a messenger. **5** a person or animal that can transmit a disease while being immune to it themselves.
**carrion** *n* dead and putrefying flesh.
**carrot** *n* **1** a long orange root vegetable. **2** a promised reward or advantage.
**carry** *v* (**-ies, -ied**) **1** to move or transport from one place to another. **2** to wear or have on one's person. **3** to support the weight of. **4** to bear or transmit (a disease). **5** to accept (blame or responsibility). **6** to have as a consequence or attribute. **7** to win acceptance of. **8** to broadcast or publish (a feature or story). **9** of sounds: to be audible at a distance. ✱ **be/get carried away** to lose self-control. **carry the can** *informal* to accept blame or responsibility. **carry the day** to win or prevail.
**carrycot** *n Brit* a transportable bed with handles, for carrying a baby.
**carry forward** *v* to transfer a total to a new column or account.
**carry off** *v* **1** to take away by force. **2** to perform successfully.
**carry on** *v* **1** to conduct or manage. **2** to continue. **3** *informal* to behave in a rowdy or improper manner. **4** *Brit, informal* to have a love affair.
**carry-on** *n Brit, informal* a fuss.
**carry out** *v* to perform (a task).
**carry over** *v* **1** to postpone. **2** = CARRY FORWARD.
**carry through** *v* to complete (a task).
**cart**[1] *n* **1** an open vehicle used for transporting loads. **2** a small wheeled container for pushing by hand.
**cart**[2] *v* **1** to carry or convey in a cart. **2** *informal* (+ off) to take or drag away by force. **3** *informal* to carry something heavy) with difficulty.
**carte blanche** /ˌkaht 'blonhsh/ *n* full discretionary power.
**cartel** *n* an association of commercial enterprises aimed at limiting competition by agreeing to keep prices high.
**carthorse** *n* a strong horse used for pulling heavy loads.
**cartilage** *n* a firm tissue that becomes mostly converted into bone in adults and forms structures such as the external ear and the larynx. ➤ **cartilaginous** *adj.*
**cartography** *n* the science of drawing maps and charts. ➤ **cartographer** *n,* **cartographic** *adj.*
**carton** *n* a container of cardboard or plastic.
**cartoon** *n* **1** a satirical drawing in a newspaper or magazine. **2** a series of drawings telling a story or narrative. **3** an animated film made from a sequence of drawings. **4** a preparatory design or drawing. **cartoonist** *n.*
**cartridge** *n* **1** a tube containing a bullet and explosive, for firing from a gun. **2** a case holding ink, magnetic tape, or photographic film for inserting into a device.
**cartridge paper** *n* thick paper for drawing on.
**cartwheel** *n* **1** a sideways handspring with arms and legs extended. **2** a wheel of a cart.
**carve** *v* **1** to cut and shape (wood or stone). **2** to cut (meat) into pieces or slices.
**carvery** *n* (*pl* **-ies**) *chiefly Brit* a buffet or restaurant where roast meat is carved for customers.
**carving** *n* an object carved from wood or stone.
**Casanova** *n* a promiscuous and unscrupulous male lover.
**casbah** *n* see KASBAH.
**cascade**[1] *n* **1** a small waterfall, *esp* one of a series. **2** a series or succession of stages, processes, etc in which each item derives from, is triggered by, or acts on the product of the one before. **3** an arrangement of fabric that falls in a

wavy line. **4** something that comes suddenly in large amounts.

**cascade**[2] *v* to fall or pour in a cascade, or in large amounts.

**case**[1] *n* **1** a situation or set of circumstances. **2** a situation requiring investigation or action. **3** an instance. **4** a suit or action in a court of law. **5** the evidence or arguments supporting a conclusion. **6** in grammar, a form of a noun, pronoun, or adjective indicating its grammatical relation to other words. * **in case** for use or as a precaution if something happens.

**case**[2] *n* **1** a box or receptacle for holding something. **2** an outer covering. **3** *chiefly Brit* a suitcase. **4** a box together with its contents. **5** a shallow divided tray for holding printing type.

**case**[3] *v* **1** to enclose in a case; to encase. **2** *informal* to inspect or study (a place) before robbing it.

**casement** *n* a window that opens on hinges at the side.

**cash**[1] *n* **1** money in notes and coins. **2** money paid at the time of purchase.

**cash**[2] *v* to pay or obtain cash for (a cheque, money order, etc).

**cash crop** *n* a crop produced for sale.

**cashew** *n* the edible kidney-shaped nut of a tropical American tree.

**cash flow** *n* the flow of money into and out of a business.

**cashier**[1] *n* a person who handles payments and receipts in a shop, bank, etc.

**cashier**[2] *v* to dismiss from service in the armed forces.

**cash in** *v* **1** to convert into cash. **2** (+ on) to exploit financially.

**cashmere** *n* fine wool from the undercoat of the Kashmir goat.

**cash register** *n* a machine used in a shop to record the amount of a sale and hold the money received.

**casing** *n* **1** an outer cover or shell. **2** a frame round a door or window.

**casino** *n* (*pl* **-os**) a building or room used for gambling.

**cask** *n* a large barrel for holding liquids.

**casket** *n* **1** a small chest or box for jewels. **2** *chiefly NAmer* a coffin.

**cassava** *n* the fleshy edible rootstock of a tropical plant, used as food.

**casserole**[1] *n* **1** a heatproof covered dish for cooking food in an oven. **2** a stew cooked in a casserole.

**casserole**[2] *v* to cook in a casserole.

**cassette** *n* a sealed case containing magnetic tape or film for inserting into a player or camera.

**cassock** *n* an ankle-length garment worn by Christian clergy and choristers.

**cassowary** *n* (*pl* **-ies**) a large flightless bird found in New Guinea and Australia.

**cast**[1] *v* (*past and past part.* **cast**) **1** to throw with force. **2** to direct (one's eyes or mind). **3** to send forth or emit. **4** to cause (doubt) to occur. **5** to cause (a spell) to have an effect. **6** to record (a vote). **7** to discard or shed. **8** to assign the parts for (a play or film) or select (an actor) for a role. **9** to shape (metal, plastic, etc) in a mould. **10** to throw out a line and bait with a fishing rod. **11** (+ about/around) to look or search.

**cast**[2] *n* **1** the performers in a dramatic production. **2** a reproduction, e.g. of a statue, formed by casting. **3** an impression taken from an object with a molten or plastic substance. **4** = PLASTER[1] 3. **5** the act or an instance of casting something. **6** a slight squint in the eye. **7** the excrement of an earthworm or a pellet regurgitated by a bird. **8** a shape or appearance.

**castanets** *pl n* a pair of small wooden or plastic shells clicked together in the hand by flamenco dancers.

**castaway** *n* a person who is cast adrift or ashore after a shipwreck.

**caste** *n* any of the hereditary social groups in Hinduism.

**castellated** *adj* having battlements like a castle.

**castigate** *v formal* to punish or reprimand severely. ➤ **castigation** *n.*

**casting vote** *n* a deciding vote cast by a presiding officer in the event of a tie.

**cast iron** *n* a hard alloy of iron and carbon cast in a mould.

**castle** *n* **1** a large fortified building or set of buildings. **2** = ROOK[3]. * **castles in the air** unrealistic schemes.

**cast off** *v* to unfasten or untie a boat or a line.

**cast-off** *adj* given up or discarded.

**castor** *or* **caster** *n* **1** a small wheel set in a swivel mounting on the base of a piece of furniture. **2** a container with a perforated top for sprinkling sugar, flour, or salt.

**castor oil** *n* a laxative oil made from the seeds of a tropical plant.

**castor sugar** *n* fine white sugar.

**castrate** *v* **1** to remove the testes of (a male animal). **2** to deprive of vitality or effect. ➤ **castration** *n.*

**casual** *adj* **1** existing or occurring by chance. **2** occurring without regularity; occasional. **3** of workers: employed for irregular periods. **4** nonchalant or offhand. **5** of clothes: designed for informal wear. ➤ **casually** *adv.*

**casualty** *n* (*pl* **-ies**) **1** a person killed or injured in action or in an accident. **2** a person or thing that has been injured or lost. **3** the accident and emergency department of a hospital.

**casuistry** *n* the false application of general principles to particular instances.

**cat** *n* **1** a small furry mammal kept as a pet. **2** a wild animal of the same family as this. **3** *informal* a malicious woman. * **let the cat out of**

**the bag** to divulge a secret inadvertently. **the cat's whiskers** *informal* an excellent person or thing. **put/set the cat among the pigeons** to cause trouble.

**cataclysm** *n* an event marked by violent upheaval or destruction. ➤ **cataclysmic** *adj.*

**catacomb** *n* an underground cemetery of galleries with recesses for tombs.

**catalepsy** *n* a trancelike state in which the body remains rigid and immobile for prolonged periods. ➤ **cataleptic** *adj and n.*

**catalogue**[1] (*NAmer* **catalog**) *n* **1** a list of items arranged systematically. **2** a series of unwelcome things.

**catalogue**[2] (*NAmer* **catalog**) *v* (**catalogue, catalogued, cataloguing,** *NAmer* **catalogs, cataloged, cataloging**) to list in a catalogue.

**catalyse** (*NAmer* **catalyze**) *v* to cause the catalysis of (a chemical reaction).

**catalysis** *n* a change in the rate of a chemical reaction induced by a catalyst.

**catalyst** *n* **1** a substance that increases the rate of a chemical reaction but itself remains unchanged. **2** somebody or something that causes an important event. ➤ **catalytic** *adj.*

**catalytic converter** *n* a device in a motor vehicle that reduces the polluting substances in exhaust fumes.

**catamaran** *n* a boat with twin hulls side by side.

**catapult**[1] *n* **1** *chiefly Brit* a Y-shaped stick with a piece of elastic material fixed between the two prongs, used for shooting small stones. **2** formerly, a military device used for hurling missiles. **3** a device for launching an aircraft at flying speed.

**catapult**[2] *v* **1** to throw or launch by means of a catapult. **2** to move suddenly or abruptly.

**cataract** *n* **1** a large steep waterfall. **2** a clouding of the lens of the eye, causing blurred vision.

**catarrh** *n* inflammation of a mucous membrane in the nose and throat, causing an excess of mucus.

**catastrophe** *n* a sudden momentous or tragic event. ➤ **catastrophic** *adj,* **catastrophically** *adv.*

**catatonia** *n* **1** a form of schizophrenia marked by catalepsy. **2** = CATALEPSY. ➤ **catatonic** *adj and n.*

**cat burglar** *n* a burglar who enters buildings by climbing up them.

**catcall**[1] *n* a loud or shrill cry expressing disapproval.

**catcall**[2] *v* to make a catcall.

**catch**[1] *v* (*past tense and past part.* **caught**) **1** to capture or seize (a person or animal), *esp* after pursuing them. **2** to take or entangle in a snare. **3** to discover (somebody) unexpectedly. **4** to become or cause to become entangled, fastened, or stuck. **5** to intercept and keep hold of (a moving object). **6** of a container: to take in and retain. **7** to become infected with (a disease). **8** to hit or strike. **9** to be struck or affected by. **10** to attract or arrest (somebody's attention). **11** to take or get momentarily or quickly. **12** to be in time for. **13** to grasp with the senses or the mind. **14** to capture a likeness of. **15** of a fire: to start to burn. ✱ **catch sight of** to see (something or somebody) suddenly or momentarily.

**catch**[2] *n* **1** the total quantity caught at one time. **2** the act of catching. **3** a game in which a ball is thrown and caught. **4** a device for fastening a door or window. **5** a concealed difficulty or snag. **6** *informal* an eligible marriage partner. **7** a break in the voice, *esp* one caused by emotion.

**catch-22** *n* a predicament from which there is no escape because this depends on mutually exclusive prior conditions.

**catchment area** *n* **1** the area from which a river, lake, reservoir, etc gets its water. **2** the area from which the pupils of a school or patients of a hospital are drawn.

**catch on** *v informal* **1** to become popular. **2** to understand or become aware.

**catch out** *v* to expose or detect in wrongdoing or error.

**catchphrase** *n* a well-known phrase associated with a particular person or group.

**catch up** *v* **1** to succeed in reaching (somebody ahead). **2** to complete (remaining or overdue work).

**catchword** *n* a word or expression associated with an idea or principle.

**catchy** *adj* (**-ier, -iest**) of a tune: easy to remember.

**catechism** *n* a summary of religious doctrine in the form of questions and answers.

**categorical** *adj* absolute and unqualified. ➤ **categorically** *adv.*

**categorize** *or* **-ise** *v* to put into a category; to classify. ➤ **categorization** *n.*

**category** *n* (*pl* **-ies**) a division or group of people or things within a system of classification.

**cater** *v* **1** (*often* + for) to provide and serve a supply of prepared food. **2** (+ for/to) to supply what is required or desired by. ➤ **caterer** *n.*

**caterpillar** *n* the wormlike larva of a butterfly or moth.

**caterwaul** *v* to make a loud wailing cry.

**catgut** *n* a tough cord made from the intestines of sheep and used for the strings of musical instruments.

**catharsis** *n* (*pl* **catharses**) **1** releasing of the emotions through drama. **2** the process of bringing repressed ideas and feelings to consciousness during psychoanalysis. ➤ **cathartic** *adj.*

**cathedral** *n* the principal church of a diocese.

**Catherine wheel** *n* a firework in the form of a flat spinning coil.

**catheter** *n* a flexible tube inserted into a hollow body part to draw off fluid.

**cathode** *n* **1** the electrode by which electrons leave an external circuit and enter a device. **2** the electrode in a thermionic valve that emits the electrons.

**cathode-ray tube** *n* a vacuum tube in which a beam of electrons is projected onto a screen e.g. to produce a television picture.

**catholic** *adj* **1** comprehensive or universal. **2** broad in tastes or interests. **3** (**Catholic**). **4** Roman Catholic. ➤ **Catholicism** *n.*

**cation** *n* a positively charged ion.

**catkin** *n* a spike of flowers hanging from a tree, e.g. a willow or hazel.

**catnap** *n* a brief period of sleep during the day.

**Catseye** *n trademark* each of a series of small reflecting studs set in the road to mark the middle or edge of the carriageway.

**cat's-paw** *n* somebody used by another as a tool or dupe.

**catsuit** *n* a tightly fitting one-piece garment combining top and trousers.

**cattery** *n* (*pl* **-ies**) a place for the breeding or care of cats.

**cattle** *pl n* cows and oxen.

**catty** *adj* (**-ier, -iest**) spiteful or malicious. ➤ **cattily** *adv.*

**catwalk** *n* **1** a narrow stage extending into the audience at a fashion show. **2** a narrow walkway.

**Caucasian** *adj* of the white race of humankind as classified according to physical features. ➤ **Caucasian** *n.*

**caucus** *n* (*pl* **caucuses**) **1** a closed political meeting to decide on policy. **2** a group of people forming a faction within a larger organization.

**caught** *v* past tense of CATCH[1].

**caul** *n* a membrane covering the head of a foetus at birth.

**cauldron** *or* **caldron** *n* a large metal cooking pot.

**cauliflower** *n* a vegetable of the cabbage family with a white flower head.

**caulk** *or* **calk** *n* waterproof material used as a filler and sealant.

**causal** *adj* being or expressing a cause. ➤ **causally** *adv.*

**causation** *n* **1** the process of causing. **2** the relationship between cause and effect.

**cause**[1] *n* **1** somebody or something that brings about an effect. **2** a reason or motive. **3** a principle or movement worth defending or supporting.

**cause**[2] *v* to be the cause of; to make happen.

**causeway** *n* a raised road or path across wet ground.

**caustic** *adj* **1** capable of destroying or eating away by chemical action. **2** sarcastic or cutting.

**caustic soda** *n* = SODIUM HYDROXIDE.

**cauterize** *or* **-ise** *v* to sear or burn (a wound) with a hot iron to stop bleeding or destroy infection.

**caution**[1] *n* **1** prudent forethought to minimize risk. **2** an official warning given to somebody who has committed a minor offence.

**caution**[2] *v* **1** to warn or advise caution to. **2** to give a legal caution to. **3** to admonish or reprove.

**cautionary** *adj* serving as a warning.

**cautious** *adj* careful or prudent. ➤ **cautiously** *adv.*

**cavalcade** *n* a procession of people on horseback or in vehicles.

**cavalier**[1] *n* **1** formerly, a gallant gentleman. **2** (**Cavalier**) a supporter of Charles I of England in the Civil War.

**cavalier**[2] *adj* offhand or dismissive in attitude.

**cavalry** *n* (*pl* **-ies**) the mounted troops of an army. ➤ **cavalryman** *n.*

**cave**[1] *n* a natural hollow chamber underground or in the side of a hill or cliff.

**cave**[2] *v* to explore underground caves. ➤ **caver** *n.*

**caveat** *n formal* a warning or reservation.

**cave in** *v* **1** to collapse. **2** to submit.

**cavern** *n* a large underground chamber or cave.

**cavernous** *adj* oppressively large and spacious.

**caviar** *or* **caviare** *n* the salted roe of a sturgeon or other large fish.

**cavil**[1] *v* (**cavilled, cavilling,** *NAmer* **caviled, caviling**) (*often* + at) to raise trivial objections.

**cavil**[2] *n* a trivial objection.

**cavity** *n* (*pl* **-ies**) **1** a hollowed-out space within a mass. **2** an area of decay in a tooth.

**cavort** *v* to prance or leap about.

**caw** *v* to utter the harsh cry of the crow. ➤ **caw** *n.*

**cayenne** *n* a pungent red pepper made from dried chillies.

**cayman** *or* **caiman** *n* (*pl* **caymans** *or* **cayman**) an American reptile closely related to the alligators.

**CBE** *abbr Brit* Commander of the (Order of the) British Empire.

**cc** *abbr* **1** carbon copy. **2** cubic centimetre.

**CCTV** *abbr* closed-circuit television.

**CD** *abbr* **1** compact disc. **2** diplomatic corps.

**Cd** *abbr* the chemical symbol for cadmium.

**CD-ROM** *n* a compact disc on which large amounts of data can be stored for use by a computer.

**Ce** *abbr* the chemical symbol for cerium.

**cease** *v* to come or bring to an end.

**cease-fire** *n* a suspension of hostilities.

**ceaseless** *adj* continuing without stopping. ➤ **ceaselessly** *adv.*

**cedar** *n* a tall evergreen tree of the pine family.

**cede** *v* to yield or surrender (territory or power).

**cedilla** *n* a mark (¸) placed under a *c* in French to change its sound from /k/ to /s/.

**ceilidh** /'kayli/ *n* a Scottish or Irish party with traditional country dancing and music.

**ceiling** *n* **1** the overhead inside surface of a room. **2** an upper limit on prices, expenditure, etc.

***Usage Note:*** Note the spelling *-ei-*.

**celebrate** *v* **1** to mark an occasion with special activities. **2** to mark (a holy day or feast day) ceremonially. ➤ **celebration** *n,* **celebratory** *adj.*

**celebrity** *n* (*pl* **-ies**) **1** a famous person. **2** the state of being famous.

**celeriac** *n* a type of celery with a large edible root.

**celestial** *adj* **1** of or relating to heaven. **2** of or in the sky.

**celibate** *adj* abstaining from sexual relations. ➤ **celibacy** *n.*

**cell** *n* **1** a small room in a prison, convent, or monastery. **2** the smallest unit of living matter. **3** a compartment of a honeycomb or a receptacle for seeds in a plant. **4** a subversive political group within a larger organization. **5** a vessel for generating electricity by chemical action.

**cellar** *n* **1** an underground room used for storage. **2** a stock of wine.

**cello** *n* (*pl* **-os**) a large stringed musical instrument of the violin family that is held upright between the player's knees. ➤ **cellist** *n.*

**Cellophane** *n trademark* thin transparent material for wrapping.

**cellular** *adj* **1** relating to or consisting of cells. **2** of a phone or radio system: based on 'cells' or areas each having its own transmitter.

**cellulite** *n* a type of body fat that produces a dimpled effect on the skin.

**celluloid** *n* a transparent plastic photographic film.

**cellulose** *n* a carbohydrate derived from plant cell walls and used to make paper, rayon, paint, and cellophane.

**cellulose acetate** *n* a chemical compound formed by the action of acetic acid on cellulose and used for making textile fibres, packaging sheets, photographic films, and varnishes.

**Celsius** *adj* of a scale of temperature on which water freezes at 0° and boils at 100°.

**Celt** *or* **Kelt** *n* a member of a pre-Roman people livingin Britain and parts of Europe.

**Celtic**[1] *or* **Keltic** *adj* of the Celts or their languages.

**Celtic**[2] *or* **Keltic** *n* a group of languages including Welsh, Cornish, Breton, Irish and Scottish Gaelic, and Manx.

**cement**[1] *n* **1** a powder containing lime and clay, used as the binding agent in mortar and concrete. **2** concrete or mortar. **3** a substance used for sticking objects together.

**cement**[2] *v* **1** to join or fix with cement. **2** to make firm and strong.

**cemetery** *n* (*pl* **-ies**) a burial ground.

**cenotaph** *n* a monument in honour of members of the armed forces killed in war.

**censer** *n* a covered incense burner used in religious rituals.

**censor**[1] *n* an official who examines publications and films and removes parts that are unacceptable or offensive.

**censor**[2] *v* to remove unacceptable parts of (a publication or film). ➤ **censorship** *n.*

***Usage Note:*** Do not confuse this word with *censure.*

**censorious** *adj* severely critical.

**censure**[1] *n* strong disapproval or condemnation.

**censure**[2] *v* to criticize or disapprove of.

**census** *n* (*pl* **censuses**) an official counting of the population.

**cent** *n* a unit of currency worth 100th of the dollar or other monetary unit.

**centaur** *n* a mythological creature with the head, arms, and upper body of a man, and the lower body and back legs of a horse.

**centenarian** *n* somebody who has reached the age of 100 years.

**centenary** *n* (*pl* **-ies**) a 100th anniversary.

**centennial**[1] *adj* **1** marking a 100th anniversary. **2** occurring every 100 years.

**centennial**[2] *n* a 100th anniversary.

**center** *n and v NAmer* see CENTRE[1], CENTRE[2].

**centigrade** *adj* of a scale of 100 degrees, *esp* the Celsius scale of temperature.

**centilitre** (*NAmer* **centiliter**) *n* a metric unit of capacity equal to 100th of a litre (about 0.35fl oz).

**centime** *n* a unit of currency worth 100th of a franc.

**centimetre** (*NAmer* **centimeter**) *n* a metric unit of length equal to 100th of a metre (about 0.4in.).

**centipede** *n* a long animal with a flattened segmented body and many legs.

**central** *adj* **1** at or near the centre. **2** of primary importance; principal. **3** having overall power or control. ➤ **centrally** *adv.*

**centralize** *or* **-ise** *v* to bring (power or authority) under central control. ➤ **centralization** *n.*

**centre**[1] (*NAmer* **center**) *n* **1** the middle point or part of something. **2** a building in which a particular activity is concentrated. **3** the part of a town or city where most of the shops, banks, offices, etc are situated. **4** a focus of attention or activity. **5** (*often* **Centre**) a political group holding moderate views.

**centre**[2] *v* **1** (+ on/round/around) to have as a centre; to focus on. **2** to place or fix in a centre.

**centre back** *n* a player or position in football in the middle of the defence.
**centrefold** *n* an illustration or feature occupying the two centre pages of a magazine.
**centre forward** *n* a player or position in football in the middle of the forward line.
**centre of gravity** *n* the point from which the mass of a body may be considered to act.
**centrepiece** *n* the most important or outstanding item.
**centrifugal force** *n* a force that appears to act outwardly on an object moving on a circular path.
**centurion** *n* an officer commanding a century in the ancient Roman army.
**century** *n* (*pl* **-ies**) **1** a period of 100 years. **2** a score of 100 runs made by a cricketer in one innings. **3** a unit of 100 men in the ancient Roman army.
**cephalic** *adj* relating to the head.
**ceramic** *adj* made from clay by firing at high temperatures.
**ceramics** *pl n* the process of making ceramic articles.
**cereal** *n* **1** a plant yielding grain suitable for food. **2** the edible grain of such a plant. **3** a breakfast food made from grain.
**cerebellum** *n* (*pl* **cerebellums** *or* **cerebella**) a part of the brain that projects at the back of the skull.
**cerebral** *adj* **1** of the brain or cerebrum. **2** intellectual, or appealing to the intellect.
**cerebral palsy** *n* a disability involving speech disturbance and lack of muscular coordination.
**cerebrum** *n* (*pl* **cerebrums** *or* **cerebra**) the expanded front portion of the brain.
**ceremonial**[1] *adj* marked by or used in ceremony. ➤ **ceremonially** *adv.*
**ceremonial**[2] *n* a prescribed system of formalities or rituals.
**ceremonious** *adj* devoted to form and ceremony; punctilious. ➤ **ceremoniously** *adv.*
**ceremony** *n* (*pl* **-ies**) **1** a formal act or series of acts prescribed by ritual or convention. **2** established procedures of civility or politeness. * **stand on ceremony** to act in a formally correct manner.
**cerise** *adj* of a light purplish red colour.
**cerium** *n* a grey soft metallic chemical element.
**certain**[1] *adj* **1** assured in one's mind. **2** established beyond doubt or question. **3** able to be relied on; inevitable. **4** of a known but unspecified character. **5** named but not known. * **for certain** without doubt.
**certain**[2] *pron* some; unspecified ones.
**certainly** *adv* **1** undoubtedly; definitely. **2** yes; of course.
**certainty** *n* (*pl* **-ies**) **1** something indisputable or inevitable. **2** somebody or something that cannot fail. **3** the quality or state of being certain.
**certifiable** *adj* **1** able to be certified. **2** *informal* insane.
**certificate** *n* a document officially stating a particular qualification or achievement of the holder. ➤ **certification** *n.*
**certify** *v* (**-ies, -ied**) **1** to confirm officially in writing. **2** to declare officially to be insane.
**certitude** *n* the state of being or feeling certain.
**cervical** *adj* relating to the cervix.
**cervical smear** *n* a test for signs of cancer in cells from the cervix.
**cervix** *n* (*pl* **cervices**) the narrow outer end of the uterus.
**cessation** *n* a stop or ending.
**cession** *n* yielding of rights or territory.
**cesspool** *n* an underground basin for sewage.
**cetacean** *n* a mammal such as a whale, dolphin, or porpoise.
**Cf** *abbr* the chemical symbol for californium.
**cf.** *abbr* compare.
**CFC** *abbr* chlorofluorocarbon, a gas formerly used in aerosols and refrigerators and thought to harm the ozone layer.
**CFE** *abbr* College of Further Education.
**chador** *n* a cloth worn round the head and top part of the body by some Muslim women.
**chafe** *v* **1** to make or become sore by rubbing. **2** to rub (something) so as to wear it away. **3** to warm (part of the body) by rubbing. **4** to feel irritation or discontent.
**chaff**[1] *n* husks and other debris separated from the seed in threshing grain.
**chaff**[2] *v* to tease good-naturedly.
**chaffinch** *n* a finch with a reddish breast and white wing bars.
**chagrin**[1] *n* a feeling of humiliating disappointment.
**chagrin**[2] *v* (*usu in passive*) to disappoint or annoy.
**chain**[1] *n* **1** a series of connected links used for support or restraint, or to form a boundary or barrier. **2** a unit of length equal to 66ft (about 20.12m). **3** a series of linked or connected things.
**chain**[2] *v* (*often* + up/down) to fasten or restrict with a chain.
**chain mail** *n* flexible armour made of interlinked metal rings.
**chain reaction** *n* **1** a series of related events, each one initiating the next. **2** a chemical or nuclear reaction yielding energy or products that cause further reactions.
**chain saw** *n* a power saw with teeth linked in a continuous revolving chain.
**chain-smoke** *v* to smoke continuously by lighting one cigarette from the butt of the previous one.
**chain store** *n* each of a series of shops under the same ownership.
**chair**[1] *n* **1** a seat for one person, with legs, a

back, and sometimes arms. **2** a professorship. **3** the chairperson at a meeting.
**chair**[2] *v* to preside as chairperson at (a meeting).
**chair lift** *n* a ski lift with seats for passengers.
**chairman** *or* **chairwoman** *n* (*pl* **chairmen** *or* **chairwomen**) somebody who presides over a meeting or board of directors. ➤ **chairmanship** *n.*
**chairperson** *n* (*pl* **chairpersons**) a person who presides at a meeting.
**chaise longue** *n* (*pl* **chaises longues**) a low sofa with a partial backrest and only one armrest, for reclining on.
**chalet** *n* **1** a wooden house with a steep roof and overhanging eaves, common in rural Switzerland. **2** a cabin at a holiday camp.
**chalice** *n* a large drinking cup or goblet.
**chalk**[1] *n* **1** a soft white limestone. **2** a piece of chalklike material used for writing and drawing. ✱ **not by a long chalk** by no means. ➤ **chalky** *adj.*
**chalk**[2] *v* **1** to write or mark with chalk. **2** (+ up) to achieve as a success.
**challenge**[1] *v* **1** to invite or call to fight or compete. **2** to dispute the validity or truth of. **3** to order to provide proof of identity. **4** to test the ability of. ➤ **challenger** *n.*
**challenge**[2] *n* **1** an invitation to fight or compete. **2** a calling to account or into question. **3** a command to halt and prove identity. **4** a formal objection. **5** something demanding or stimulating.
**challenging** *adj* testing one's ability in a stimulating way.
**chamber** *n* **1** an enclosed space or cavity. **2** a legislative or judicial body. **3** a reception room in an official building. **4** *archaic* a bedroom. **5** (*in pl*) a set of rooms used by barristers. **6** (*usu in pl*) a room where a judge hears private cases. **7** the part of a gun that holds the charge or cartridge.
**chamberlain** *n* **1** a chief officer of a royal or noble household. **2** a treasurer of a corporation.
**chambermaid** *n* a woman who cleans and tidies bedrooms in a hotel.
**chamber music** *n* classical music written for a small group of instruments.
**chamber pot** *n* a bowl for urine and faeces, kept in a bedroom.
**chameleon** *n* a small lizard that can change the colour of its skin to match its surroundings.
**chamfer** *v* to cut a narrow angled surface on the edge of (a piece of wood). ➤ **chamfer** *n.*
**chamois** *n* (*pl* **chamois**) **1** a small antelope of Europe and the Caucasus. **2** a soft leather made from the skin of the chamois or sheep.
**chamomile** *n* see CAMOMILE.
**champ**[1] *v* to munch noisily. ✱ **champ at the bit** to be impatient.
**champ**[2] *n informal* a champion in a sport or game.
**champagne** *n* **1** a white sparkling wine from the Champagne region of France. **2** a pale golden cream colour.
**champion**[1] *n* **1** the winner of a competitive event. **2** an active supporter of a person or cause. **3** formerly, a person who did battle on behalf of another.
**champion**[2] *v* to protect or fight for as a champion.
**champion**[3] *adj chiefly N Eng, informal* excellent or splendid.
**championship** *n* **1** a contest to find a champion. **2** the position or title of champion.
**chance**[1] *n* **1** an element in existence that makes events unpredictable. **2** an event without an observable cause. **3** an opportunity. ✱ **by chance** without planning or intention. **take a chance/chances** to do something risky.
**chance**[2] *adj* happening by chance.
**chance**[3] *v* **1** to take place or come about by chance. **2** (+ on/upon) to find by chance. **3** to take a risk with.
**chancel** *n* the part of a church near the altar.
**chancellor** *n* **1** the chief minister of state in some European countries. **2** the titular head of a British university.
**Chancellor of the Exchequer** *n* the British government minister in charge of public finances.
**chancer** *n Brit, informal* an unprincipled opportunist.
**chancy** *adj* (**-ier, -iest**) uncertain or risky.
**chandelier** *n* a branched ornamental lighting fixture suspended from a ceiling.
**chandler** *n* a dealer in supplies for ships and boats.
**change**[1] *v* **1** to make or become different. **2** (*often* + over) to replace (one thing) with another. **3** to convert into something else. **4** to give (money of one currency) in exchange for an equivalent amount in another currency. **5** to put on fresh clothes. ✱ **change hands** to become the property of somebody else.
**change**[2] *n* **1** a process of becoming different. **2** an alternative set of clothes. **3** money returned when a payment exceeds the amount due. **4** coins of low denominations.
**changeable** *adj* **1** likely to vary. **2** capable of being altered or exchanged. **3** unpredictable or fickle.
**changeling** *n* a child believed to have been left in place of a human child by fairies.
**change-over** *n* a conversion to a different system or function.
**channel**[1] *n* **1** a narrow region of sea between two land masses. **2** the bed of a stream of water. **3** the navigable part of a river or harbour. **4** a path for communication or information. **5** a band of frequencies for radio or television transmission, e.g. from a radio or television

station. **6** a television station. **7** a gutter, groove, or furrow.

**channel**[2] *v* (**channelled, channelling,** *NAmer* **channeled, channeling**) **1** to direct towards a particular purpose. **2** to convey through a channel.

**chant**[1] *v* to sing or recite in a rhythmic monotonous tone.

**chant**[2] *n* **1** a repetitive melody used for liturgical singing. **2** a psalm or canticle sung in this way. **3** a rhythmic monotonous utterance, recitation, or song.

**Chanukah** *n* see HANUKKAH.

**chaos** *n* **1** a state of utter confusion. **2** a confused mass. ➤ **chaotic** *adj*, **chaotically** *adv*.

**chap** *n informal* a man or fellow.

**chapati** *or* **chapatti** *n* (*pl* **chapatis** *or* **chapattis**) in Indian cookery, a flat round piece of unleavened bread.

**chapel** *n* **1** a room or small church used for prayer or worship. **2** a part of a church set aside with its own altar. **3** the members of a printing trade union.

**chaperon**[1] *or* **chaperone** *n* an older woman who accompanies an unmarried younger woman on social occasions.

**chaperon**[2] *or* **chaperone** *v* to act as chaperon to.

**chaplain** *n* a clergyman attached to a branch of the armed forces, an institution, or a private family. ➤ **chaplaincy** *n*.

**chapped** *adj* of the skin: cracked and sore from exposure to the wind or cold.

**chapter** *n* **1** a major division of a book. **2** a significant period or sequence of events. **3** the canons of a cathedral or collegiate church, or the members of a religious house. **4** a local branch of a society or fraternity.

**char**[1] *v* (**charred, charring**) to burn slightly.

**char**[2] *n Brit, informal* a woman employed to clean in a private house.

**character** *n* **1** the qualities that distinguish a particular person or thing from others. **2** a person portrayed in a novel, film or play. **3** *informal* an interesting or eccentric person. **4** a person's good reputation. **5** moral strength or integrity. **6** a letter or other symbol used in writing or printing. ➤ **characterful** *adj*, **characterless** *adj*.

**characteristic**[1] *adj* typical of a particular person or thing. ➤ **characteristically** *adv*.

**characteristic**[2] *n* a distinguishing trait or quality.

**characterize** *or* **-ise** *v* **1** to describe the character or quality of. **2** to distinguish. ➤ **characterization** *n*.

**charade** *n* **1** a game in which a word or phrase is acted out for other players to guess. **2** a ridiculous pretence.

**charcoal** *n* **1** a black porous carbon prepared by partly burning wood. **2** fine charcoal used in pencil form for drawing. **3** a dark grey colour.

**chard** *n* a vegetable with large dark green leaves and succulent stalks.

**charge**[1] *v* **1** to ask (a price) or ask for payment from (somebody). **2** to accuse (somebody) of having committed an offence. **3** (*often* + with) to entrust with a task or responsibility. **4** to command or exhort with right or authority. **5** to rush forward in attack. **6** to load or fill. **7** (*often* + up) to store electrical energy in (a battery). **8** to fill (somebody or something) with passionate emotion, feeling, etc. ➤ **chargeable** *adj*.

**charge**[2] *n* **1** a price asked or paid for something. **2** a formal accusation. **3** an instruction or command. **4** an obligation or requirement. **5** supervision or custody. **6** somebody or something committed to another's care. **7** a rush forwards in attack. **8** the quantity that something is intended to receive and hold, *esp* the quantity of explosive for a gun or cannon. **9** a basic property of matter responsible for electrical activity and characterized as negative or positive. **10** a definite quantity of electricity held by a battery. ✻ **in charge** in control or command.

**charge card** *n* a card issued by a large shop for buying goods on credit.

**chargé d'affaires** /ˌshahzhay daˈfeə/ *n* (*pl* **chargés d'affaires**) **1** a diplomat who deputizes for an ambassador or minister. **2** a diplomatic representative inferior in rank to an ambassador.

**charger** *n* **1** a device used to charge a battery. **2** a horse for battle or parade.

**chargrill** *v* to grill (food) quickly over charcoal.

**chariot** *n* a two-wheeled horse-drawn vehicle used in ancient warfare and racing. ➤ **charioteer** *n*.

**charisma** *n* the special appeal or charm of an individual that inspires loyalty and enthusiasm.

**charitable** *adj* **1** liberal in giving to the poor; generous. **2** merciful or kind in judging others. ➤ **charitably** *adv*.

**charity** *n* (*pl* **-ies**) **1** kindly generosity and helpfulness shown to those in need. **2** an institution set up to help those in need. **3** money or other help given to those in need.

**charlatan** *n* somebody who pretends to have special knowledge or ability.

**charm**[1] *n* **1** the quality of alluring or delighting others. **2** a particularly pleasing or attractive quality or feature. **3** an act or phrase believed to have magic power. **4** something worn to ward off evil or attract good fortune. **5** a small ornament worn on a bracelet or chain. ➤ **charmless** *adj*.

**charm**[2] *v* **1** to delight with attractive qualities or manner. **2** to gain (something) or influence (somebody) by the use of personal charm. **3** to affect as if by magic. **4** to control (an animal) by the use of rituals. ➤ **charmer** *n.*

**charming** *adj* extremely pleasing or delightful. ➤ **charmingly** *adv.*

**charnel house** *n* a place formerly used for depositing dead bodies or bones.

**chart**[1] *n* **1** a sheet giving information in the form of a table or graph. **2** a map used for sea or air navigation. **3** (**the charts**) a weekly list of best-selling pop records.

**chart**[2] *v* **1** to make a chart of. **2** to mark or record on a chart. **3** to outline the course or progress of.

**charter**[1] *n* **1** a document that defines the rights of a city, educational or professional institution, or company. **2** a special privilege or exemption. **3** a lease of a ship or aircraft for a particular use or group. **4** (*used before a noun*) relating to such a lease: *charter flights.*

**charter**[2] *v* (**chartered, chartering**) **1** to grant a charter to. **2** to hire a ship or aircraft.

**chartered** *adj* officially qualified for membership of a professional institution.

**chary** *adj* (**-ier, -iest**) cautious and wary. ➤ **charily** *adv.*

**chase**[1] *v* **1** to follow rapidly in order to catch. **2** to rush or hurry. **3** *chiefly Brit* (+ up) to try to find or contact.

**chase**[2] *n* **1** an act of chasing. **2** (**the chase**) hunting. **3** unenclosed land set aside for breeding animals.

**chase**[3] *v* to engrave with raised or incised work.

**chaser** *n* a strong alcoholic drink taken after a milder one.

**chasm** *n* **1** a deep cleft in the earth. **2** a big difference or disagreement.

**chassis** *n* (*pl* **chassis**) **1** the framework supporting the body of a vehicle. **2** a frame supporting a piece of equipment.

**chaste** *adj* **1** not having sexual intercourse, or sexual intercourse outside marriage. **2** pure in thought and behaviour.

**chasten** *v* **1** to correct by punishment or rebuke. **2** to subdue or restrain.

**chastise** *v* **1** to punish, *esp* by beating. **2** to criticize severely. ➤ **chastisement** *n.*

**chastity** *n* the state of being chaste.

**chasuble** *n* a sleeveless outer vestment worn by a priest.

**chat**[1] *v* (**chatted, chatting**) to talk informally.

**chat**[2] *n* informal conversation.

**château** /'shatoh/ *n* (*pl* **châteaus** *or* **châteaux**) a large country house in France.

**chattel** *n* an item of personal property.

**chatter**[1] *v* **1** to talk idly or incessantly. **2** of teeth: to click together repeatedly from cold.

**chatter**[2] *n* **1** idle talk or conversation. **2** the sound or action of chattering.

**chatterbox** *n informal* somebody who likes to chatter.

**chat up** *v Brit, informal* to talk to in a flirtatious or scheming way.

**chauffeur**[1] *or* **chauffeuse** *n* a person employed to drive somebody in a private car.

**chauffeur**[2] *v* to act as driver for (somebody).

**chauvinism** *n* **1** undue belief in the superiority of one's own group, cause, etc. **2** excessive or blind patriotism. ➤ **chauvinist** *n and adj,* **chauvinistic** *adj.*

**cheap** *adj* **1** low in price. **2** charging a low price. **3** of inferior quality or worth. **4** gained with little effort or by dubious means. ➤ **cheaply** *adv.*

**cheapen** *v* to reduce the value or quality of.

**cheapskate** *n informal* a miserly or stingy person.

**cheat**[1] *v* **1** to violate the rules of a game or competition dishonestly. **2** to deceive or swindle. **3** to deprive (somebody) of something by deceit or fraud. **4** (+ on) to be sexually unfaithful to.

**cheat**[2] *n* **1** somebody who cheats. **2** a trick or fraud.

**check**[1] *n* **1** a test of the accuracy, state, or quality of something. **2** a pause or stoppage. **3** somebody or something that restrains. **4** in chess, exposure of a king to direct attack. **5** a pattern of squares of alternating colours. **6** *NAmer* a bill in a restaurant. **7** under restraint or control.

**check**[2] *v* **1** to test or inspect for satisfactory condition, accuracy, or quality. **2** to slow or bring to a stop. **3** to restrain or block the progress of. **4** in chess, to put (the opposing king) in check. **5** *chiefly NAmer* (*often* + out) to tally. ✱ **check up on** to make inquiries about. ➤ **checkable** *adj.*

**checker**[1] *v* see CHEQUER[2].

**checker**[2] *n informal* see CHEQUER[1].

**check in** *v* to arrive and register at a hotel or airport. ➤ **check-in** *n.*

**checklist** *n* a list of checks to be made or tasks to be done.

**checkmate** *n* in chess, the act of putting an opponent's king in check from which escape is impossible. ➤ **checkmate** *v.*

**checkout** *n* **1** a cash desk at a supermarket or large shop. **2** the act of checking out of a hotel etc.

**check out** *v* **1** to complete the formalities for leaving a hotel. **2** to get information about.

**checkpoint** *n* a place where travellers are checked for security.

**checkup** *n* a routine medical or dental examination.

**Cheddar** *n* a hard smooth-textured cheese.

**cheek**[1] *n* **1** the side of the face below the eye. **2** insolent boldness or impudence. **3** *informal* a buttock. ✱ **cheek by jowl** close together.

**cheek**[2] *v informal* to speak rudely to.

**cheekbone** *n* the bone forming the rounded part of the face below the eye.
**cheeky** *adj* (**-ier, -iest**) impudent or insolent. ➤ **cheekily** *adv.*
**cheep** *n* a faint shrill sound made by a young bird. ➤ **cheep** *v.*
**cheer**[1] *n* **1** a shout of joy, congratulation, or encouragement. **2** happiness or gaiety.
**cheer**[2] *v* **1** to shout with pleasure or, in applause. **2** to acclaim or encourage by shouting. **3** (*often* + up) to make or become happier or more hopeful.
**cheerful** *adj* **1** full of good spirits; happy. **2** ungrudging. **3** conducive to good spirits. ➤ **cheerfully** *adv*, **cheerfulness** *n.*
**cheerleader** *n* in North America, somebody who leads organized cheering at sports events.
**cheerless** *adj* gloomy or miserable.
**cheers** *interj* used as a drinking toast or an informal farewell or expression of thanks.
**cheery** *adj* (**-ier, -iest**) cheerful and optimistic. ➤ **cheerily** *adv.*
**cheese** *n* a food made from processed milk curds.
**cheesecake** *n* a dessert with a filling of cream cheese on a biscuit or pastry base.
**cheesecloth** *n* a lightweight loosely woven cotton fabric.
**cheesy** *adj* (**-ier, -iest**) **1** resembling cheese. **2** *informal* poor in quality and taste.
**cheetah** *n* a long-legged spotted African cat that can run very fast.
**chef** *n* a cook in a restaurant or hotel.
**chemical**[1] *adj* **1** used in or produced by chemistry. **2** involving or made from chemicals. ➤ **chemically** *adv.*
**chemical**[2] *n* a substance produced by a chemical process.
**chemise** *n* a woman's loose-fitting dress or undergarment.
**chemist** *n* **1** *Brit* a pharmacist. **2** *Brit* a retail shop where medicines and other articles, e.g. cosmetics and films, are sold. **3** somebody who studies chemistry.
**chemistry** *n* **1** a science that deals with the composition and properties of substances and the transformations they undergo. **2** the composition and chemical properties of a substance. **3** a natural attraction between people.
**chemotherapy** *n* the use of chemical agents in the treatment of cancer.
**chenille** *n* a soft velvety fibre or the fabric made from it.
**cheque** (*NAmer* **check**) *n chiefly Brit* a written order for a bank to pay money to a named person or account.
**cheque card** *n* a card guaranteeing payment on a cheque.
**chequer**[1] (*NAmer* **checker**) *n* (*also in pl*) a pattern of squares of alternating colours.
**chequer**[2] (*NAmer* **checker**) *v* (**chequered, chequering,** *NAmer* **checkered, checkering**) to mark with squares of alternating colours.
**cherish** *v* **1** to feel or show affection for. **2** to keep or nurture with care and affection. **3** to keep in the mind.
**cheroot** *n* a cigar cut square at both ends.
**cherry** *n* (*pl* **-ies**) **1** a smooth red or blackish fruit with sweet flesh and a hard stone. **2** a bright red colour.
**cherub** *n* **1** (*pl* **cherubim**) a biblical attendant of God often represented with large wings, a human head, and an animal body. **2** (*pl* **cherubs**) a winged chubby child in painting and sculpture. **3** an innocent-looking chubby and pretty young person. ➤ **cherubic** *adj.*
**chervil** *n* an aromatic plant with leaves used as a herb and vegetable.
**chess** *n* a board game for two players with the object of putting the opponent's king into checkmate.
**chest** *n* **1** a storage box with a lid. **2** the part of the body enclosed by the ribs and breastbone. **3** the front of the body from the neck to the waist. * **get something off one's chest** to admit or confess something.
**chesterfield** *n* a padded leather sofa with arms and back of the same height.
**chestnut** *n* **1** an edible nut with shiny brown skin. **2** a reddish brown colour. **3** a horse chestnut. **4** *informal* an often repeated joke or story.
**chest of drawers** *n* a piece of furniture with a set of drawers.
**chesty** *adj* (**-ier, -iest**) inclined to or suffering from catarrh.
**chevron** *n* **1** a V-shaped sleeve badge indicating the wearer's rank. **2** a V-shaped heraldic design with the point uppermost. **3** (*in pl*) a row of V-shaped stripes marked on a road.
**chew**[1] *v* **1** to grind or gnaw with the teeth. **2** (+ over) to consider at length. * **chew the fat** *informal* to chat informally.
**chew**[2] *n* **1** the act of chewing. **2** a sweet for chewing.
**chewing gum** *n* a flavoured gum for chewing.
**chewy** *adj* tough and difficult to chew.
**chi** *n* the 22nd letter of the Greek alphabet (X, χ).
**chic** *adj* (**chicer, chicest**) elegant and fashionable.
**chicane** *n* a series of tight turns in a motor-racing track.
**chicanery** *n* clever trickery or deception.
**chick** *n* **1** a newly hatched chicken or bird. **2** *informal* a young woman.
**chicken**[1] *n* **1** the common domestic fowl. **2** *informal* a coward.
**chicken**[2] *adj informal* scared or cowardly.
**chicken feed** *n informal* an insignificant amount of money.

**chicken out** *v informal* (*often* + of) to lose one's nerve.
**chickenpox** *n* an infectious disease marked by a rash of small blisters.
**chickweed** *n* a plant with small leaves that occurs as a weed.
**chicory** *n* (*pl* **-ies**) **1** a plant with edible thick roots and leaves used in salads. **2** the root of this plant, used as a coffee additive.
**chide** *v* (*past tense* **chided** *or* **chid,** *past part.* **chided** *or* **chidden**) to rebuke or scold.
**chief**[1] *n* the head of an organization or group of people.
**chief**[2] *adj* **1** of the highest rank. **2** of greatest importance; main.
**chiefly** *adv* **1** principally or especially. **2** mostly or mainly.
**chieftain** *n* the leader of a tribe or clan.
**chiffon** *n* a sheer silky fabric.
**chignon** *n* a smooth knot of hair worn at the nape of the neck.
**Chihuahua** *n* a dog of a very small breed with a round head and large ears.
**chilblain** *n* an inflammatory sore on the feet or hands, caused by exposure to cold.
**child** *n* (*pl* **children**) **1** a young person between infancy and youth. **2** a son or daughter. ➤ **childhood** *n.*
**childbirth** *n* the process of giving birth to a child.
**childish** *adj* **1** of a child or childhood. **2** silly or immature.
**childlike** *adj* marked by the innocence and trust associated with children.
**childminder** *n chiefly Brit* a person who looks after other people's children.
**chill**[1] *v* **1** to make or become cold. **2** to frighten or horrify. **3** to dispirit. **4** *informal* (also + out) to relax. ➤ **chillingly** *adv.*
**chill**[2] *n* **1** an unpleasant sensation of coldness. **2** a feverish cold. **3** a moderate degree of cold.
**chill**[3] *adj* unpleasantly cold.
**chilli** (*NAmer* **chili**) *n* (*pl* **chillies,** *NAmer* **chilies**) the pod of a hot pepper used as a flavouring or spice.
**chilly** *adj* (**-ier, -iest**) **1** unpleasantly cold. **2** aloof or unfriendly.
**chime**[1] *n* **1** a musically tuned set of bells. **2** a set of hanging metal bars or tubes sounding like bells when struck. **3** (*usu in pl*) a musical ringing sound.
**chime**[2] *v* **1** to make a musical ringing sound. **2** (*usu* + together/with) to be or act in accord.
**chimera** *or* **chimaera** *n* (*pl* **chimeras** *or* **chimaeras**) **1** (**Chimera, Chimaera**) in Greek mythology, a fire-breathing female monster with a lion's head, a goat's body, and a serpent's tail. **2** an unrealizable hope or dream. ➤ **chimerical** *adj.*
**chimney** *n* (*pl* **-eys**) a vertical structure for carrying off smoke and extending above a roof.
**chimney breast** *n* a projecting part of an inside wall enclosing a chimney.
**chimpanzee** *n* an African ape with black coloration.
**chin** *n* the lower portion of the face below the mouth. ✱ **keep one's chin up** to remain cheerful.
**china** *n* fine porcelain or crockery.
**china clay** *n* a soft white clay for making porcelain.
**chinchilla** *n* a small South American rodent with soft pearly-grey fur.
**Chinese** *n* (*pl* **Chinese**) **1** a native or inhabitant of China. **2** a group of languages spoken in China, including Mandarin. ➤ **Chinese** *adj.*
**chink**[1] *n* **1** a narrow slit or fissure. **2** a means of evasion or escape.
**chink**[2] *n* a short sharp metallic sound.
**chink**[3] *v* to make a sharp ringing sound.
**chino** *n* (*pl* **-os**) **1** a cotton twill fabric. **2** (*in pl*) trousers made of chino.
**chintz** *n* a printed plain-weave fabric of glazed cotton.
**chintzy** *adj* **1** made or decorated with chintz. **2** gaudy and cheap.
**chip**[1] *n* **1** a small thin flat piece cut or flaked off a hard substance. **2** a flaw left after a chip is removed. **3** *chiefly Brit* a strip of potato fried in deep fat. **4** *NAmer* a potato crisp. **5** a counter used as a token in gambling games. **6** an integrated circuit or microchip. **7** a short high shot with a ball.
**chip**[2] *v* (**chipped, chipping**) **1** (*often* + off/away) to cut or break (a small piece) from something. **2** to break off in small pieces. **3** to kick or hit (a ball, pass, etc) in a short high arc. **4** *Brit* to cut (potatoes) into chips.
**chipboard** *n* a board made from compressed wood chips.
**chip in** *v informal* to contribute to or interrupt in a conversation.
**chipmunk** *n* a small striped American squirrel.
**chipolata** *n* a small sausage.
**chipper** *adj informal* cheerful and bright.
**chiropody** *n* the care and treatment of the feet. ➤ **chiropodist** *n.*
**chiropractic** *n* a system of healing using manipulation of the spinal column and other body structures. ➤ **chiropractor** *n.*
**chirp**[1] *v* of a small bird or insect: to make a short shrill sound.
**chirp**[2] *n* a chirping sound.
**chirpy** *adj* (**-ier, -iest**) *informal* lively and cheerful. ➤ **chirpily** *adv.*
**chisel**[1] *n* a metal tool with a cutting edge, used in shaping wood, stone, or metal.
**chisel**[2] *v* (**chiselled, chiselling,** *NAmer* **chiseled, chiseling**) to cut or work with a chisel.
**chit**[1] *n* a small young woman.
**chit**[2] *n* a small slip of paper with a note of money owed.

**chivalrous** *adj* **1** courteous and considerate to women. **2** honourable or generous. ➤ **chivalrously** *adv.*

**chivalry** *n* **1** the spirit or customs of medieval knighthood. **2** courteous behaviour towards women. **3** chivalrous conduct.

**chive** *n* (*usu in pl*) a plant with long thin leaves used to flavour and garnish food.

**chivvy** *or* **chivy** *v* (**-ies, -ied**) *informal* to harass or pester.

**chloride** *n* a compound of chlorine with another element or radical.

**chlorinate** *v* to treat (water) with chlorine. ➤ **chlorination** *n.*

**chlorine** *n* a chemical element that is a pungent greenish yellow gas.

**chloroform[1]** *n* a liquid used as a solvent and formerly as an anaesthetic.

**chloroform[2]** *v* to administer chloroform to make unconscious.

**chlorophyll** (*NAmer also* **chlorophyl**) *n* the green colouring matter of plants that enables them to absorb sunlight.

**chloroplast** *n* a part of a green plant that contains chlorophyll and is the site of photosynthesis.

**chock** *n* a wedge or block placed under a wheel or door to prevent it from moving.

**chock-a-block** *adj and adv* crowded or tightly packed.

**chocolate** *n* **1** a sweet food prepared from ground roasted cacao seeds. **2** a sweet made or coated with chocolate. **3** a drink made by mixing chocolate with hot water or milk. **4** dark brown.

**choice[1]** *n* **1** the act of choosing. **2** the power of choosing. **3** somebody or something chosen. **4** a sufficient number and variety to choose from.

**choice[2]** *adj* **1** of high quality. **2** selected with care.

**choir** *n* **1** an organized group of singers. **2** the part of a church between the sanctuary and the nave.

**choirboy** *or* **choirgirl** *n* a boy or girl singer in a church choir.

**choke[1]** *v* **1** to stop (somebody) breathing by compressing or obstructing the windpipe, or by poisoning the air. **2** to become unable to breathe. **3** (*often* + back/down) to suppress (tears) or prevent the expression of (emotion). **4** (*also* + up) to make or become speechless with emotion.

**choke[2]** *n* **1** the act or sound of choking. **2** a valve in a petrol engine for controlling the mixture of fuel and air.

**choker** *n* a short necklace or decorative band fitting closely round the throat.

**cholera** *n* an epidemic disease marked by severe disorders of the stomach and intestines.

**choleric** *adj formal* angry or irate.

**cholesterol** *n* a steroid present in animal and plant cells and thought to be a factor in hardening of the arteries.

**chomp** *v* to chew noisily.

**choose** *v* (**chose, chosen**) **1** to decide on and take (somebody or something) from several alternatives. **2** to decide (to do something).

**choosy** *or* **choosey** *adj* (**-ier, -iest**) fastidious in making choices.

**chop[1]** *v* (**chopped, chopping**) **1** (*usu* + off/down) to cut into or sever by a blow or repeated blows of a sharp instrument. **2** (*often* + up) to cut into pieces. **3** to strike with a short sharp blow.

**chop[2]** *n* **1** a forceful blow or cutting stroke. **2** a small cut of meat often including part of a rib. **3** (**the chop**) *informal* an abrupt dismissal or cancellation.

**chop[3]** *v* (**chopped, chopping**) *esp* of the wind: to change direction. ✻ **chop and change** *Brit* to keep changing one's mind, plans, etc.

**chopper** *n* **1** *Brit* a short-handled axe or cleaver. **2** *informal* a helicopter. **3** *informal* (*in pl*) teeth.

**choppy** *adj* (**-ier, -iest**) of the sea: rough with small waves.

**chopstick** *n* each of two slender sticks used in oriental countries for eating food.

**choral** *adj* accompanied with or designed for singing by a choir.

**chorale** *n* a traditional hymn or psalm for singing in church.

**chord** *n* a combination of notes sounded together. ✻ **strike/touch a chord** produce a sympathetic response.

**chore** *n* a routine or tedious task.

**choreograph** *v* to compose or arrange the steps and dances for (a ballet or piece of music). ➤ **choreographer** *n,* **choreography** *n.*

**chorister** *n* a choirboy or choirgirl.

**chortle** *v* to laugh or chuckle.

**chorus[1]** *n* **1** an organized group of singers who sing the choral parts of music, opera, or musicals. **2** a composition sung by a chorus. **3** a section of a song or hymn repeated at intervals.

**chorus[2]** *v* (**choruses, chorused, chorusing**) to sing or utter (something) together.

**chose** *v* past tense of CHOOSE.

**chosen** *v* past part. of CHOOSE.

**choux pastry** *n* a light pastry used for profiteroles, eclairs, etc.

**Christ** *n* a title given by Christians to Jesus.

**christen** *v* **1** to give a name to (a baby) at baptism. **2** *informal* to use for the first time.

**Christian[1]** *n* a follower of Christianity.

**Christian[2]** *adj* relating to Christianity or Christians.

**Christianity** *n* the religion based on the life and teachings of Jesus Christ and the New Testament.

**Christian name** *n* a forename.

**Christmas** *n* a festival of the Christian Church commemorating the birth of Christ, held on 25 December.

**Christmas tree** *n* an evergreen tree decorated with lights and trinkets at Christmas.

**chromatic** *adj* **1** relating to colour. **2** of a musical scale: based entirely on semitones. **3** of music: using intervals or notes outside the diatonic scale.

**chrome** *n* a plating of chromium.

**chromium** *n* a blue-white metallic element used in alloys.

**chromosome** *n* a gene-carrying body that contains DNA and protein and is found in the cell nucleus.

**chronic** *adj* **1** of an illness or difficulty: lasting for a long time. **2** suffering from a long-lasting disease. **3** habitual or persistent. **4** *Brit, informal* very bad. ➤ **chronically** *adv.*

**chronicle**[1] *n* **1** an account of events arranged chronologically. **2** a narrative.

**chronicle**[2] *v* to record (events) in chronological order. ➤ **chronicler** *n.*

**chronological** *adj* arranged in or according to the order in which things happen. ➤ **chronologically** *adv.*

**chronology** *n* (*pl* **-ies**) **1** the study of the dating of past events and the evidence for this. **2** a system of dates for past events.

**chronometer** *n* an instrument for measuring time.

**chrysalis** *n* (*pl* **chrysalises**) a pupa of a butterfly or moth.

**chrysanthemum** *n* a garden plant with brightly coloured flowers.

**chub** *n* a freshwater fish of the carp family.

**chubby** *adj* (**-ier, -iest**) round and plump. ➤ **chubbiness** *n.*

**chuck**[1] *v* **1** *informal* to toss or throw casually. **2** (*often* + out/away) to discard. **3** to pat or tap gently.

**chuck**[2] *n* a pat or nudge under the chin.

**chuck**[3] *n* a device for holding a drill or other working piece in a tool or lathe.

**chuckle**[1] *v* to laugh inwardly or quietly.

**chuckle**[2] *n* a quiet laugh.

**chuff** *v* to move with the sound of a steam engine.

**chuffed** *adj Brit, informal* very pleased.

**chug** *v* (**chugged, chugging**) to move with a repeated heavy sound like a labouring engine. ➤ **chug** *n.*

**chum** *n informal, dated* a friend or mate.

**chump** *n* **1** a cut of meat taken from between the loin and hindleg. **2** *informal* a foolish person.

**chunk** *n* a thick or solid lump.

**church** *n* **1** a building for public Christian worship. **2** (**the Church**) the whole body of Christians. **3** a Christian denomination.

**churchyard** *n* an enclosed piece of ground surrounding a church.

**churlish** *adj* uncooperative and unfriendly. ➤ **churlishly** *adv.*

**churn**[1] *n* **1** a vessel for agitating milk or cream to make butter. **2** *Brit* a large metal container for transporting milk.

**churn**[2] *v* **1** to agitate (milk or cream) to make butter. **2** to stir or agitate (liquid) violently. **3** to be in violent motion.

**churn out** *v chiefly informal* to produce routinely and in large quantities.

**chute** *n* **1** an inclined channel down which things pass to a lower level. **2** a slide into a swimming pool.

**chutney** *n* a spicy relish containing fruits, vegetables, sugar, vinegar, and spices.

**chutzpah** *n informal* brazen audacity.

**CIA** *abbr NAmer* Central Intelligence Agency.

**ciabatta** /chə'bahtə/ *n* (*pl* **ciabattas**) a flat Italian bread made with olive oil.

**cicada** /si'kahdə/ *n* (*pl* **cicadas**) an insect that produces a shrill singing noise.

**CID** *abbr Brit* Criminal Investigation Department.

**cider** *n* an alcoholic drink of fermented apple juice.

**cigar** *n* a roll of tobacco leaf for smoking.

**cigarette** (*NAmer also* **cigaret**) *n* a cylinder of cut tobacco rolled in paper for smoking.

**cilium** *n* (*pl* **cilia**) an eyelash or other minute hairlike part.

**cinch** *n informal* something very easy or certain.

**cinder** *n* a piece of partly burned coal or wood.

**cinema** *n* **1** *chiefly Brit* a theatre where films are shown. **2** the film industry.

**cinematic** *adj* to do with films or the cinema.

**cinematography** *n* the art or science of cinema photography. ➤ **cinematographer** *n.*

**cinnamon** *n* a spice obtained from the dried bark of an Asian tree.

**cipher**[1] *or* **cypher** *n* **1** a code. **2** a key to a code. **3** a nonentity.

**cipher**[2] *or* **cypher** *v* (**ciphered** *or* **cyphered, ciphering** *or* **cyphering**) to put into code.

**circa** *prep* approximately.

**circadian** *adj* of a biological activity: occurring in day-long periods or cycles.

**circle**[1] *n* **1** a shape in the form of a closed curved line every point of which is the same distance from the centre. **2** a balcony or tier of seats in a theatre. **3** a group of people sharing a common interest or activity.

**circle**[2] *v* **1** to move in a circle. **2** to enclose in a circle.

**circuit** *n* **1** a closed loop enclosing an area, or the area enclosed. **2** a racetrack. **3** a regular tour of an official round an assigned area. **4** a complete path of an electric current. **5** a system of electrical components connected so as to allow the passage of current. **6** a regular series of sports events or competitions.

**circuitous** *adj* indirect in route or method.

**circuitry** *n* (*pl* **-ies**) a system of electrical circuits.

**circular[1]** *adj* **1** having the form of a circle. **2** of a letter or advertising material: intended for circulation to a number of people. ➤ **circularity** *n.*

**circular[2]** *n* a letter or leaflet intended for wide distribution.

**circulate** *v* **1** to follow a course round an area. **2** to flow freely. **3** to become well known or widely available. **4** to go from group to group at a social gathering.

**circulation** *n* **1** movement through a system or circuit. **2** the movement of blood through the vessels of the body induced by the pumping action of the heart. **3** the passing of things from one person to another. **4** the number of copies of a publication sold over a given period.

**circumcise** *v* to cut off the foreskin of (a male) or the clitoris of (a female). ➤ **circumcision** *n.*

**circumference** *n* **1** the perimeter of a circle. **2** the external boundary or distance round something.

**circumflex** *n* a mark (ˆ) over a vowel in some languages to show a particular vowel sound.

**circumlocution** *n* the use of an unnecessarily large number of words to express an idea.

**circumnavigate** *v* to travel by sea or air round the earth. ➤ **circumnavigation** *n.*

**circumscribe** *v* to restrict the range or activity of.

**circumspect** *adj* careful to consider all circumstances. ➤ **circumspection** *n.*

**circumstance** *n* **1** a fact or detail relating to an event, story, etc. **2** (*usu in pl*) the situation one finds oneself in and for which one is not responsible. **3** (*in pl*) one's financial or material situation. ✱ **in/under the circumstances** considering the situation.

**circumstantial** *adj* of evidence: tending to prove a fact indirectly by proving related events or circumstances. ➤ **circumstantially** *adv.*

**circumvent** *v* to find a way round (a difficulty). ➤ **circumvention** *n.*

**circus** *n* (*pl* **circuses**) **1** a group of performers, including acrobats and clowns, who entertain with trained animals. **2** (**Circus**) *Brit* a large open road junction in a town enclosed by a circle of buildings.

**cirrhosis** *n* hardening of the liver.

**cirrus** *n* (*pl* **cirri**) a wispy white cloud formation occurring at high altitudes.

**CIS** *abbr* Commonwealth of Independent States (formed in succession to the USSR).

**cistern** *n* **1** a water reservoir for a toilet. **2** a tank at the top of a house or building. **3** *chiefly NAmer* a tank, usu underground, for storing rainwater.

**citadel** *n* a fortress that commands a city.

**citation** *n* **1** an act of quoting. **2** a quotation. **3** an official mention of something praiseworthy.

**cite** *v* **1** to quote for authority. **2** to refer to or name officially.

**citizen** *n* **1** a member of a state, *esp* a native or naturalized one. **2** an inhabitant of a city or town. ➤ **citizenship** *n.*

**citric acid** *n* an acid occurring in lemons, limes, and other sharp-tasting fruits.

**citrus** *n* (*pl* **citruses**) any of a group of juicy fruits, including the orange, lemon, lime, and grapefruit.

**city** *n* (*pl* **-ies**) **1** a large town, *esp* (in Britain) one that has been created by charter and has a cathedral. **2** (**the City**) *Brit* the financial and commercial area of London.

**city-state** *n* an autonomous state consisting of a city and surrounding territory.

**civet** *n* **1** an African and Asian cat with a long body and short legs. **2** a musky-smelling perfumed obtained from the civet.

**civic** *adj* of a city or citizenship.

**civil** *adj* **1** courteous and polite. **2** involving the general public as opposed to the military or clergy. **3** relating to private rights as distinct from criminal proceedings. ➤ **civilly** *adv.*

**civil engineer** *n* an engineer who designs large-scale public works, e.g. roads and bridges. ➤ **civil engineering** *n.*

**civilian** *n* somebody who is not a member of the armed forces or the police. ➤ **civilian** *adj.*

**civility** *n* (*pl* **-ies**) **1** courtesy or politeness. **2** (*usu in pl*) a polite act or remark.

**civilization** *or* **-isation** *n* **1** a high level of cultural and technological development. **2** the culture characteristic of a particular time or place. **3** the process of becoming civilized.

**civilize** *or* **-ise** *v* **1** to bring to a technically and socially advanced stage of development. **2** to educate or refine. ➤ **civilized** *adj.*

**civil liberty** *n* an individual's right or freedom in relation to the state.

**civil rights** *pl n* the rights of citizens, *esp* to equality between races or groups.

**civil servant** *n* a member of a civil service.

**civil service** *n* (*treated as sing. or pl*) the administrative service of a government or international agency.

**civil war** *n* war between citizens of the same country.

**CJD** *abbr* Creutzfeldt-Jakob disease, a progressive disease characterized by dementia and muscular wasting, of which one variant is thought to be linked to BSE.

**Cl** *abbr* the chemical symbol for chlorine.

**cl** *abbr* centilitre.

**clack[1]** *v* **1** to make an abrupt striking sound. **2** *informal* to chatter.

**clack[2]** *n* a sound of clacking.

**clad** *v* past tense and past part. of CLOTHE.
**cladding** *n* a thin protective covering or overlay.
**claim**[1] *v* **1** to ask for as a right. **2** to require or demand. **3** to take as the rightful owner. **4** to assert; to maintain without proof. **5** to end (somebody's life). **6** (+ for) to make a claim under the terms of an insurance policy. ➤ **claimant** *n.*
**claim**[2] *n* **1** an assertion open to challenge. **2** a demand for something due. **3** an act of claiming under an insurance policy. **4** (+ to/on) a right or title to something.
**clairvoyance** *n* the ability to perceive matters beyond the range of ordinary perception. ➤ **clairvoyant** *adj and n.*
**clam** *n* a large mollusc with a tightly closed hinged shell.
**clamber** *v* (**clambered, clambering**) to climb awkwardly or with difficulty. ➤ **clamberer** *n.*
**clammy** *adj* (**-ier, -iest**) **1** unpleasantly damp and clinging. **2** of the weather: humid.
**clamour**[1] (*NAmer* **clamor**) *n* **1** noisy shouting. **2** a loud continuous noise. **3** (*often* + against/for) insistent public support or protest. ➤ **clamorous** *adj.*
**clamour**[2] (*NAmer* **clamor**) *v* **1** to make a din. **2** (*usu* + for) to make one's wishes or views known loudly and insistently.
**clamp**[1] *n* **1** a device that holds two or more things firmly together. **2** a device placed round the wheel of an illegally parked vehicle to immobilize it.
**clamp**[2] *v* to hold or fasten with a clamp.
**clamp down** *v* to impose restrictions.
**clam up** *v informal* to become silent.
**clan** *n* **1** a group of related families of Scottish descent. **2** a group of people united by a common interest. ➤ **clansman** *n,* **clanswoman** *n.*
**clandestine** *adj* held or done in secret. ➤ **clandestinely** *adv.*
**clang** *v* to make a loud metallic sound. ➤ **clang** *n.*
**clank** *v* to make a sharp metallic sound. ➤ **clank** *n.*
**clannish** *adj* associating only with a select group of similar background or interests.
**clap**[1] *v* (**clapped, clapping**) **1** to strike (the hands) together repeatedly in applause. **2** to applaud (a person or an act). **3** to strike (somebody) with the flat of the hand in a friendly way. **4** to put (something or somebody) forcefully or suddenly in a certain place or condition. **5** to impose (e.g. a restriction). ✱ **clap hold of** *informal* to seize forcefully.
**clap**[2] *n* **1** the act or sound of clapping hands. **2** a loud sound of thunder. **3** a friendly slap.
**clapped out** *adj Brit, informal* old and worn out.
**clapper** *n* the tongue of a bell.
**clapperboard** *n* in filming, a hinged board banged together to synchronize the beginning and end of each take.
**claret** *n* a dry red Bordeaux wine.
**clarify** *v* (**-ies, -ied**) **1** to make or become easier to understand. **2** to make (liquid) clear by freeing it from suspended matter. **3** to melt (butter) to make it clear. ➤ **clarification** *n.*
**clarinet** *n* a woodwind instrument with a single reed, a flared end, and holes stopped by keys. ➤ **clarinettist** *n.*
**clarion**[1] *n* a medieval trumpet, or the sound of one.
**clarion**[2] *adj* loud and clear.
**clarity** *n* the quality or state of being clear.
**clash**[1] *n* **1** a noisy metallic sound of collision. **2** a conflict or hostile encounter.
**clash**[2] *v* **1** to make a clash. **2** to come into conflict. **3** to form a displeasing combination. **4** to be incompatible or irreconcilable.
**clasp**[1] *n* **1** a device for holding objects or parts together. **2** an embrace.
**clasp**[2] *v* **1** to fasten with a clasp. **2** to enclose and hold with the arms. **3** to seize with the hand.
**clasp knife** *n* a knife with a single folding blade.
**class**[1] *n* **1** a group in society sharing the same economic or social status. **2** the system of differentiating society by classes. **3** *informal* high quality; elegance. **4** a regular group of students being taught. **5** a lesson at a school or college. **6** a distinct group of things sharing common characteristics.
**class**[2] *v* to classify or grade.
**classic**[1] *adj* **1** serving as a standard of excellence. **2** traditional and enduring. **3** being an archetypal example of some particular thing or occurrence.
**classic**[2] *n* **1** a work of lasting excellence. **2** (**Classics**) the study of Greek and Latin literature, history, and philosophy.
**classical** *adj* **1** relating to the ancient Greek and Roman world. **2** relating to music of the traditional European forms including orchestral music, chamber music, and opera. **3** constituting an early influential approach to a subject that becomes standard. ➤ **classically** *adj.*
**classicism** *n* **1** adherence to traditional standards having universal and lasting worth. **2** the principles or style embodied in classical literature, art, or architecture.
**classicist** *n* a scholar or student of Classics.
**classification** *n* **1** systematic arrangement of things in defined groups. **2** a class or category.
**classified** *adj* **1** of information, documents, etc: withheld from general circulation for reasons of security. **2** of newspaper or magazine advertisements: organized according to their subjects.

**classify** *v* (**-ies, -ied**) **1** to arrange in classes. **2** (*often* + as) to assign to a category. **3** to designate (a document, information, etc) as secret. ➤ **classifiable** *adj.*

**classroom** *n* a room in a school where classes are held.

**classy** *adj* (**-ier, -iest**) *informal* elegant and stylish.

**clatter** *v* **1** to make a loud rattling or banging noise. **2** to move or go noisily. ➤ **clatter** *n.*

**clause** *n* **1** a group of words containing a subject and verb and forming part of a sentence. **2** a distinct article or condition in a formal document.

**claustrophobia** *n* abnormal fear of being in confined spaces. ➤ **claustrophobic** *adj.*

**clavicle** *n* a shoulder bone linking the shoulder blade and breastbone; the collarbone.

**claw**[1] *n* **1** a sharp curved nail on an animal's toe. **2** a pincer on the end of some limbs of a shellfish, scorpion, etc. **3** a tool or device resembling a claw.

**claw**[2] *v* to scratch or dig with the claws or fingernails.

**clay** *n* **1** an earthy material, soft when moist but hard when fired, used for making bricks and pottery. **2** thick and clinging earth or mud. ➤ **clayey** *adj.*

**clean**[1] *adj* **1** free or relatively free from dirt. **2** habitually keeping oneself clean. **3** free from contamination or disease. **4** producing little or no radioactive fallout. **5** not obscene. **6** unused or unmarked. **7** having no record of wrongdoing or offences. **8** of an action: smooth and effective. ➤ **cleaner** *n,* **cleanly** *adv.*

**clean**[2] *adv* all the way; completely.

**clean**[3] *v* **1** to make clean. **2** (*often* + out) to strip or empty (something).

**clean**[4] *n* an act of cleaning.

**clean-cut** *adj* clean and neat in appearance.

**cleanliness** *n* care in keeping things or one's person clean. ➤ **cleanly** *adj.*

**cleanse** *v* to clean or purify thoroughly. ➤ **cleanser** *n.*

**clean-shaven** *adj* with the beard and moustache shaved off.

**clear**[1] *adj* **1** easy to understand. **2** easy to see or hear. **3** transparent. **4** of the air or sky: free from cloud, mist, or dust. **5** free from obstructions or interruptions. **6** (+ of) not touching. **7** free from doubt. ✱ **in the clear** free of suspicion or danger. ➤ **clearly** *adv.*

**clear**[2] *adv* **1** clearly. **2** *chiefly NAmer* all the way.

**clear**[3] *v* **1** to free from obstructions or unwanted things. **2** to evacuate (an area or building). **3** (*often* + off/up/away) to remove or dispose of (something). **4** to go over (an obstacle) without touching it. **5** in football, to kick (the ball) away from the goal as a defensive measure. **6** to free from accusation or blame. **7** (*often* + off) to settle or discharge (a debt). **8** to deal with (work) until it is finished or settled. **9** to put (a cheque) through a clearing house. **10** to authorize or cause to be authorized. **11** (*often* + up) of the weather: to become fine again. ✱ **clear the air** to remove tension or hostility by open discussion. **clear the decks** to prepare for action.

**clearance** *n* **1** the removal of obstructions or unwanted things. **2** clear space allowing one thing to pass another. **3** official authorization. **4** in football, a kick to clear the ball.

**clear-cut** *adj* easily seen or understood.

**clearing** *n* an area of land cleared of wood and brush.

**clear off** *v informal* to go away.

**clear up** *v* **1** to remove (dirt or mess). **2** to tidy by removing unwanted things. **3** to provide a solution for (a problem or mystery). **4** of an illness, etc: to be cured or alleviated.

**clearway** *n Brit* a road on which vehicles may stop only in an emergency.

**cleat** *n* **1** a projecting piece on a shoe, for providing a grip. **2** a wedge-shaped piece serving as a support or check. **3** a fitting with projecting horns, for securing a rope.

**cleavage** *n* **1** the hollow space between a woman's breasts. **2** a split or division.

**cleave**[1] *v* (*past tense* **clove** *or* **cleft** *or* **cleaved,** *past part.* **cloven** *or* **cleft** *or* **cleaved**) **1** to split along the grain. **2** to create (a path) as if by cutting.

**cleave**[2] *v* (*past tense* **cleaved** *or archaic* **clave**) **1** (+ to) to stick firmly and loyally. **2** (+ to) to be devoted.

**cleaver** *n* a butcher's chopping implement with a large heavy blade.

**clef** *n* a sign placed on a musical stave to indicate the pitch of the notes following it.

**cleft**[1] *n* **1** a space or opening made by splitting. **2** a hollow between ridges or protuberances.

**cleft**[2] *v* past tense and past part. of CLEAVE[1].

**cleft lip** *n* a harelip.

**cleft palate** *n* a congenital split in the roof of the mouth.

**clematis** *n* a climbing plant with white, pink, or purple flowers.

**clement** *adj* **1** of the weather: pleasantly mild. **2** merciful or lenient. ➤ **clemency** *n.*

**clementine** *n* a small citrus fruit with bright orange skin.

**clench** *v* **1** to close or hold together (the fists or teeth) tightly. **2** to grip or clutch firmly. **3** of a set of muscles: to contract suddenly.

**clerestory** *n* (*pl* **-ies**) the part of an outside wall of a church that rises above an adjoining roof.

**clergy** *n* the priests or ministers of a Christian Church.

**clergyman** *or* **clergywoman** *n* (*pl* **clergymen** *or* **clergywomen**) an ordained priest or minister.

**cleric** *n* a Christian minister or religious leader.

**clerical** *adj* **1** relating to routine office work such as typing and filing. **2** relating to the clergy.

**clerk** *n* **1** a person who keeps records or accounts or does general office work. **2** an official who keeps records for a council or court.

**clever** *adj* (**cleverer, cleverest**) **1** mentally quick and intelligent. **2** skilful or adroit with the hands or body. ➤ **cleverly** *adv*, **cleverness** *n.*

**cliché** *n* a hackneyed idea or expression. ➤ **clichéd** *adj.*

**click**[1] *n* **1** a light sharp sound made by hard parts locking into one another. **2** in computing, an action of pressing and releasing a mouse button.

**click**[2] *v* **1** to produce or make (something) produce a click. **2** in computing, to press and release (a button on a mouse). **3** *informal* to become friendly or successful. **4** *Brit* to be suddenly recognized.

**client** *n* somebody who uses the services of a professional person or organization.

**clientele** *n* the clients of a business, shop, etc.

**cliff** *n* a steep high face of rock on the coast.

**cliffhanger** *n* an episode in a story ending in extreme suspense.

**climacteric** *n* **1** the menopause, or a corresponding period in men. **2** a major turning point or critical stage.

**climate** *n* **1** the average weather conditions in a particular area over a long period. **2** the prevailing state of affairs or feelings of a group or period. ➤ **climatic** *adj.*

**climax**[1] *n* **1** the highest point or point of maximum intensity. **2** a sexual orgasm. ➤ **climactic** *adj.*

**climax**[2] *v* to come or bring to a climax.

**climb**[1] *v* **1** to go up to or down from a higher position. **2** of a plant: to ascend while growing. **3** to go gradually upwards; to rise. **4** to slope upwards. **5** to get into or out of a confined space with effort.

**climb**[2] *n* **1** an act of climbing. **2** a route up a mountain. **3** a steep slope or ascent.

**climb down** *v* to withdraw from a position in an argument. ➤ **climbdown** *n.*

**climbing frame** *n Brit* a framework of bars for children to climb on.

**clime** *n chiefly literary* (*usu in pl*) a region of the earth having a particular climate.

**clinch**[1] *v* **1** to make final; to settle. **2** to fasten (a nail) by turning it over and flattening it. **3** *informal* to embrace or hug.

**clinch**[2] *n* **1** a tight hold or embrace. **2** a fastening with a clinched nail.

**cling** *v* (*past tense and past part.* **clung**) **1** (+ to/onto) to hold on tightly. **2** (+ to/onto) to stick to. **3** to have a strong emotional dependence. **4** (+ to) to remain convinced of something. ➤ **clingy** *adj.*

**clingfilm** *n* a thin clear plastic film used for wrapping food.

**clinic** *n* a place where medical treatment or advice is given.

**clinical** *adj* **1** relating to the medical observation and treatment of patients. **2** analytic or detached in attitude. **3** of aplace: severely plain and functional. ➤ **clinically** *adv.*

**clink** *v* to make or cause to make a slight sharp sound. ➤ **clink** *n.*

**clinker** *n* stony matter left by a fire.

**clip**[1] *v* (**clipped, clipping**) to clasp or fasten with a clip.

**clip**[2] *n* **1** a device that grips or holds things. **2** a piece of jewellery held in position by a spring clip.

**clip**[3] *v* (**clipped, clipping**) **1** to cut (hair or wool) with shears or scissors. **2** to cut off the end or outer part of. **3** to hit with a sharp blow.

**clip**[4] *n* **1** a sharp blow. **2** a short excerpt from a film or broadcast. **3** *informal* a rapid pace or speed.

**clipboard** *n* a small writing board with a spring clip for holding papers.

**clipped** *adj* of speech: tersely quick and distinct.

**clipper** *n* **1** (*usu in pl*) an implement for trimming hair or nails. **2** a fast sailing ship.

**clipping** *n* **1** a piece cut or trimmed from something. **2** an extract cut from a newspaper or magazine.

**clique** *n* an exclusive group of people. ➤ **cliquey** *adj.*

**clitoris** *n* an organ at the front of the vulva that is a centre of sexual sensation in females.

**cloak**[1] *n* **1** a long sleeveless outer garment that hangs loosely. **2** something that conceals.

**cloak**[2] *v* to cover or hide.

**cloak-and-dagger** *adj* involving melodramatic intrigue and secrecy.

**cloakroom** *n* **1** a room in which clothing or bags may be left. **2** *chiefly Brit* a room with a toilet.

**clobber**[1] *n Brit, informal* clothing or paraphernalia.

**clobber**[2] *v informal* to hit with force.

**cloche** *n* **1** a cover used for outdoor plants. **2** a woman's soft close-fitting rounded hat.

**clock**[1] *n* **1** a device for indicating or measuring time. **2** *informal* a speedometer or other metering device. ✱ **round the clock** all day and night.

**clock**[2] *v* **1** *esp* in sports, to time with a stopwatch or electric timing device. **2** to register (a time, distance, or speed) on a recording device. **3** *Brit, informal* (*often* + up) to achieve (a time, speed, etc). **4** *Brit, informal* to see or observe.

**clock in** *or* **clock on** *v* to record the time of arriving at work.

**clock out** *or* **clock off** *v* to record the time of leaving work.
**clockwise** *adv and adj* in a direction in which the hands of a clock rotate.
**clockwork** *n* a mechanism with toothed gearwheels and powered by a coiled spring. * **like clockwork** smoothly and with no hitches.
**clod** *n* **1** a lump of earth or clay. **2** *informal* a clumsy or stupid person.
**clodhopper** *n informal* **1** a large heavy shoe. **2** an awkward or clumsy person.
**clog**[1] *n* a shoe with a thick wooden sole.
**clog**[2] *v* (**clogged, clogging**) (*often* + up) to block or become blocked.
**cloister** *n* a covered passage along the wall of a courtyard in a church, monastery, college, etc.
**cloistered** *adj* **1** surrounded with a cloister. **2** sheltered from everyday life.
**clomp** *v* to walk heavily or clumsily.
**clone**[1] *n* **1** an asexually produced individual identical to its parent. **2** *informal* an exact or very close copy.
**clone**[2] *v* **1** to cause (a cell or organism) to grow as a clone. **2** to make a copy of.
**close**[1] *adj* **1** near in space or time. **2** of relatives: near in relationship. **3** intimate or affectionate. **4** of a connection: strong. **5** of a resemblance: showing only small variations. **6** having little space in between; dense. **7** of a game or contest: evenly contested. **8** very careful and concentrated. **9** of the weather: hot and stuffy. **10** secretive or reticent. **11** mean with money. * **at close quarters** in a position close to somebody or something. ➤ **closely** *adv.*
**close**[2] *adv* (**closer, closest**) in or into a close position or manner. * **close on** almost.
**close**[3] *n* **1** *Brit* a road closed at one end. **2** *Brit* the precinct of a cathedral.
**close**[4] *v* **1** to move in a position to cover an opening. **2** to cover or shut. **3** to prevent access to (a road or entrance). **4** to bring or come to an end. **5** (*often* + down) of a business, etc: to suspend or stop operations. **6** of a shop: to stop trading for the day. **7** (*often* + on/in on) to come closer to (somebody), in order to challenge them. ➤ **closable** *adj.*
**close**[5] *n* the end or conclusion of something.
**close call** *n* a narrow escape.
**closed** *adj* **1** not open. **2** not allowing entry; blocked. **3** of a system or society: forming a self-contained unit; self-sufficient. **4** limited or restricted.
**closed-circuit television** *n* a television system or installation used for surveillance in a building or area.
**closed shop** *n* an establishment which employs only union members.
**close in** *v* (*often* + on) to approach and surround a place.
**close-knit** *adj* bound together by strong ties of familiarity and affection.
**close season** *n Brit* a period during which fishing or hunting is not allowed, or a sport is not played.
**close shave** *n informal* a narrow escape.
**closet**[1] *n* **1** a small or private room. **2** *chiefly NAmer* a cupboard.
**closet**[2] *v* (**closeted, closeting**) to shut away in a private place.
**close up** *v* to become closer together.
**close-up** *n* a photograph or film sequence taken at close range.
**closure** *n* **1** the act of closing. **2** the closing by voting of a debate in a legislative body. **3** a device that closes or seals a container.
**clot**[1] *n* **1** a coagulated mass produced by clotting of blood. **2** a viscous lump formed by coagulation of cream or other liquid. **3** *Brit, informal* a foolish person.
**clot**[2] *v* (**clotted, clotting**) to form clots.
**cloth** *n* (*pl* **cloths**) **1** a fabric made by weaving or knitting fibres. **2** a piece of cloth used for a particular purpose. **3** (**the cloth**) the clergy.
**clothe** *v* (*past tense and past part.* **clothed** *or* **clad**) **1** to cover with clothing. **2** to provide with clothes.
**clothes** *pl n* articles of cloth or other material worn to cover the body.
**clothing** *n* clothes.
**clotted cream** *n* a thick cream made by heating and cooling whole milk and then skimming the top.
**cloud**[1] *n* **1** a mass of water particles at a great height in the air. **2** a light billowy mass of smoke or dust in the air. **3** a feeling of gloom. * **under a cloud** disliked or under suspicion. **with one's head in the clouds** out of touch with reality.
**cloud**[2] *v* **1** (+ over/up) to become cloudy. **2** of facial features: to become troubled or anxious. **3** to make or become blurred or unclear.
**cloudburst** *n* a sudden heavy fall of rain.
**cloud-cuckoo-land** *n* a fantasy world.
**cloudy** *adj* (**-ier, -iest**) **1** overcast with clouds. **2** not clear or transparent.
**clout**[1] *n* **1** *informal* a heavy blow. **2** *informal* power or influence.
**clout**[2] *v informal* to hit forcefully.
**clove**[1] *n* a small bulb that makes up a larger bulb of garlic.
**clove**[2] *n* the dried unopened flower bud of a tropical tree, used as a spice.
**clove**[3] *v* past tense of CLEAVE[1].
**clove hitch** *n* a knot used to secure a rope to a spar or another rope.
**cloven** *v* past part. of CLEAVE[1].
**cloven hoof** *n* the divided hoof of a sheep, cow, or other animals.
**clover** *n* a plant with leaves that have three leaflets and flowers in dense heads. * **in clover** in luxury.

**clown**[1] *n* **1** a comic entertainer in a circus. **2** a person who jokes and fools about. ➤ **clownish** *adj.*
**clown**[2] *v* (*usu* + about/around) to behave in a comic or silly way.
**cloy** *v* of something normally pleasing: to satiate with an excess. ➤ **cloying** *adj.*
**club**[1] *n* **1** an association of people who enjoy a common interest or activity. **2** premises available for members to stay, eat, or socialize. **3** a nightclub. **4** a thick heavy stick used as a hand weapon. **5** a stick used to hit the ball in golf. **6** (*in pl*) the suit in a pack of playing cards that is marked with black figures in the shape of a clover leaf.
**club**[2] *v* (**clubbed, clubbing**) **1** to beat or strike with a club or other heavy weapon. **2** (+ together) to share a cost or expense. **3** *informal* to visit nightclubs.
**club foot** *n* a misshapen foot twisted out of position from birth.
**clubhouse** *n* a building used for a club's activities.
**cluck** *v* to make the guttural sound of a hen. ➤ **cluck** *n.*
**clue** *n* **1** something that provides evidence to solve a problem or mystery. **2** a phrase or anagram that has to be solved as part of a crossword puzzle. * **not have a clue 1** to know nothing. **2** to be incompetent.
**clued-up** *adj informal* well informed.
**clueless** *adj informal* completely ignorant or incompetent.
**clump**[1] *n* **1** a group of trees or bushes growing close together. **2** a compact mass or cluster. **3** a heavy tramping sound.
**clump**[2] *v* **1** to form clumps. **2** to tread clumsily and noisily.
**clumsy** *adj* (**-ier, -iest**) **1** awkward and ungraceful in movement. **2** lacking tact or subtlety. ➤ **clumsily** *adv,* **clumsiness** *n.*
**clung** *v* past tense and past part. of CLING.
**clunk** *v* to make the dull sound of one heavy object striking another. ➤ **clunk** *n.*
**cluster**[1] *n* a compact group of similar things or people.
**cluster**[2] *v* (**clustered, clustering**) to form a cluster or into a cluster.
**clutch**[1] *v* **1** to grasp or hold tightly. **2** (*often* + at) to try to grasp and hold.
**clutch**[2] *n* **1** the act of grasping or seizing firmly. **2** (*in pl*) control or possession. **3** a device that connects and disconnects the engine and the wheels in a vehicle.
**clutch**[3] *n* a nest of eggs laid at one time, or a brood of chicks hatched from them.
**clutter**[1] *v* to fill or cover untidily with scattered things.
**clutter**[2] *n* an untidy scattering of things.
**Cm** *abbr* the chemical symbol for curium.
**cm** *abbr* centimetre.
**Co** *abbr* the chemical symbol for cobalt.
**co.** *or* **Co.** *abbr* **1** company. **2** county.
**co-** *prefix* with or together: *coexist; co-pilot.*
**coach**[1] *n* **1** *chiefly Brit* a comfortable single-deck bus used for long-distance travel. **2** a railway carriage. **3** somebody who gives training in a sport. **4** a person who gives private lessons in a subject.
**coach**[2] *v* **1** to train in a sport. **2** to give private lessons to.
**coagulate** *v* of a liquid: to thicken or curdle. ➤ **coagulant** *n,* **coagulation** *n.*
**coal** *n* a black solid mineral consisting of carbonized vegetable matter and used as a fuel.
**coalesce** *v* to fuse into a whole. ➤ **coalescence** *n.*
**coalface** *n* the exposed seam in a coalmine.
**coalfield** *n* a region in which deposits of coal occur.
**coalition** *n* a temporary alliance of political parties to form a government.
**coalmine** *n* a mine from which coal is extracted. ➤ **coalminer** *n.*
**coal tar** *n* tar obtained from coal.
**coarse** *adj* **1** rough in texture or tone. **2** composed of large particles. **3** crude or unrefined in manners or language. ➤ **coarsely** *adv.*
**coarse fish** *n chiefly Brit* any freshwater fish not belonging to the salmon family.
**coarsen** *v* to make or become coarse.
**coast**[1] *n* **1** the edge of land where it reaches the sea. **2** the land near a shore. * **the coast is clear** there is no danger. ➤ **coastal** *adj.*
**coast**[2] *v* **1** to move downhill by the force of gravity. **2** to move along without, or as if without, further application of propulsive power. **3** to proceed easily without making any special effort or becoming greatly involved. **4** to sail along the shore.
**coaster** *n* **1** a small mat for resting drinks on. **2** a ship that sails from port to port along a coast.
**coastguard** *n* an official or organization that keeps guard over coastal waters.
**coastline** *n* the outline of the land at a coast.
**coat**[1] *n* **1** a full-length outer garment with sleeves. **2** the external covering of hair or fur on an animal. **3** a layer of paint or other liquid covering.
**coat**[2] *v* to cover or spread with a protective or enclosing layer. ➤ **coater** *n.*
**coat of arms** *n* (*pl* **coats of arms**) a heraldic design belonging to a particular family or institution.
**coax** *v* **1** to urge or influence gently. **2** to manipulate into a desired condition.
**coaxial** *adj* **1** of a cable: having a central wire insulated from another wire wrapped round it. **2** using or connected to a coaxial cable. ➤ **coaxially** *adv.*

**cob** *n* **1** a male swan. **2** the core on which sweet corn grows. **3** a cobnut. **4** a horse of a short-legged stocky breed. **5** *Brit* a small rounded loaf.
**cobalt** *n* a silver-white metallic chemical element used in alloys.
**cobber** *n Aus, informal* a friend.
**cobble**[1] *v* **1** to repair or make shoes. **2** (+ together) to make or assemble roughly or hastily.
**cobble**[2] *n* a small rounded stone used for paving a street. ➤ **cobbled** *adj.*
**cobbler** *n* **1** a person who makes and mends shoes. **2** *NAmer* a deep fruit pie with a thick crust. **3** *Brit* stewed meat with rounds of pastry.
**cobnut** *n* the nut of a hazel tree.
**cobra** *n* a poisonous Asiatic and African snake with grooved fangs.
**cobweb** *n* a spider's web.
**cocaine** *n* an addictive alkaloid drug obtained from coca leaves.
**coccyx** *n* (*pl* **coccyges** *or* **coccyxes**) a small triangular bone at the base of the spinal column.
**cochineal** *n* a red dye used as a colouring agent for food.
**cochlea** *n* (*pl* **cochleae**) a coiled part of the inner ear filled with liquid through which sound waves are transmitted.
**cock**[1] *n* **1** the male of the domestic fowl or other birds. **2** *coarse slang* the penis.
**cock**[2] *v* **1** to turn or tip to one side. **2** to draw back and set the hammer of (a gun) for firing. **3** to turn up (the brim of a hat). * **cock a snook** to react with disdain or defiance.
**cockade** *n* a rosette or knot of ribbon worn on the hat as a badge.
**cock-a-hoop** *adj informal* delighted.
**cock-and-bull story** *n* an improbable story.
**cockatoo** *n* (*pl* **cockatoos**) a large parrot with a crest and brightly coloured plumage.
**cockcrow** *n literary* dawn.
**cockerel** *n* a young male domestic fowl.
**cocker spaniel** *n* a small spaniel with long ears and a silky coat.
**cock-eyed** *adj informal* **1** askew. **2** foolish or crazy.
**cockle** *n* an edible mollusc with a ribbed shell.
**cockney** *n* (*pl* **-eys**) **1** a native of the East End of London. **2** the dialect or accent of East London.
**cockpit** *n* **1** a space in the fuselage of an aircraft or spacecraft for the pilot and crew. **2** the driver's compartment in a racing car.
**cockroach** *n* an insect like a beetle with a flattened body and long antennae.
**cocksure** *adj informal* arrogantly self-confident.
**cocktail** *n* **1** an alcoholic drink of mixed spirits or of spirits mixed with flavourings. **2** a mixture of different things.
**cocky** *adj* (**-ier, -iest**) *informal* self-confident in an arrogant or cheeky way.
**cocoa** *n* a drink made from roasted and powdered cacao seeds.
**coconut** *n* the large oval fruit of a tropical palm, with a hard hairy outer husk, thick edible white flesh, and sweet milk.

***Usage Note:*** Note the spelling *coco* not *cocoa.*

**coconut shy** *n* a funfair stall at which people throw balls to knock down coconuts on stands.
**cocoon**[1] *n* **1** a silk envelope which an insect larva forms about itself when passing the pupa stage. **2** a protective covering like a cocoon.
**cocoon**[2] *v* to wrap in a cocoon.
**cod** *n* (*pl* **cod**) a large grey sea fish used for food.
**coda** *n* a distinct concluding section to a piece of music.
**coddle** *v* **1** to cook (eggs) slowly in liquid. **2** to treat (a person or animal) with excessive care.
**code**[1] *n* **1** a system of letters, numbers, or symbols used to represent and replace the normal ones for secrecy. **2** a system of numbers and symbols for conveying instructions to a computer. **3** a body of laws. **4** a set of rules or principles governing behaviour. ➤ **coded** *adj.*
**code**[2] *v* to put into the form of a code.
**codeine** *n* a derivative of morphine used to relieve pain.
**codger** *n informal* an elderly man.
**codicil** *n* a clause added to a will to modify an existing part.
**codify** *v* (**-ies, -ied**) to organize (laws or rules) in a systematic form. ➤ **codification** *n.*
**cod-liver oil** *n* an oil obtained from the liver of the cod and used as a source of vitamins A and D.
**codpiece** *n* formerly, a pouch covering an opening in the front of men's breeches.
**codswallop** *n chiefly Brit, informal* nonsense.
**co-education** *n* the education of students of both sexes at the same school. ➤ **co-educational** *adj.*
**coefficient** *n* **1** a number placed before the variable factor or factors in an algebraic expression and multiplying them. **2** a number that serves as a measure of some property.
**coerce** *v* **1** (*often* + into) to compel (somebody) to do something. **2** to restrain by authority or force. ➤ **coercion** *n.*
**coexist** *v* **1** to exist together or at the same time. **2** to live together harmoniously. ➤ **coexistence** *n.*
**C of E** *abbr* Church of England.
**coffee** *n* a drink made from the roasted seeds of a tropical shrub.
**coffee table** *n* a low table placed in a living room.
**coffer** *n* **1** a chest or box for valuables. **2** (*usu in pl*) a treasury or exchequer.

**coffin** *n* a box or chest for the burial or cremation of a corpse.

**cog** *n* **1** a tooth on the rim of a wheel or gear. **2** a toothed wheel that engages with others to transmit motion.

**cogent** *adj* of an argument: clear and convincing. ➤ **cogency** *n*, **cogently** *adv.*

**cogitate** *v formal* to think carefully about something. ➤ **cogitation** *n.*

**cognac** /'konyak/ *n* a French brandy from the Cognac region of France.

**cognition** *n* the process of acquiring knowledge through perception, awareness, and judgment. ➤ **cognitive** *adj.*

**cognizance** *or* **cognisance** *n* **1** *formal* the ability to perceive or understand. **2** notice or heed.

**cognoscenti** /konyoh'shenti/ *pl n* people having expert knowledge in a subject.

**cohabit** *v* (**cohabited, cohabiting**) to live together as unmarried sexual partners. ➤ **cohabitation** *n.*

**cohere** *v* **1** to hold together firmly. **2** to be logically consistent.

**coherent** *adj* **1** able to speak clearly and understandably. **2** of an argument: logically consistent. ➤ **coherence** *n*, **coherently** *adv.*

**cohesion** *n* **1** the process of acting or working together effectively. **2** the act of cohering. ➤ **cohesive** *adj.*

**cohort** *n* **1** a division of a Roman legion. **2** a group of individuals sharing certain characteristics.

**coif**[1] *n* a close-fitting cap worn by nuns under a veil.

**coif**[2] *v* (**coiffed, coiffing,** *NAmer* **coifed, coifing**) to arrange (hair) by brushing or combing.

**coiffure** *n* a hairstyle. ➤ **coiffured** *adj.*

**coil**[1] *v* **1** to wind (something long) into rings or spirals. **2** to move in a circular or winding course. **3** to form a coil.

**coil**[2] *n* **1** a length of rope, cable, etc gathered into loops. **2** a spiral of wire used for providing electrical resistance or supplying a high voltage. **3** a contraceptive device in the form of a small coil fitted into the womb.

**coin**[1] *n* a small disc of metal used as money.

**coin**[2] *v* **1** to make (coins) by stamping metal. **2** to invent (a new word or phrase). **3** to make or earn (a lot of money).

**coinage** *n* **1** coins collectively. **2** the coins in use in a particular country. **3** a new word or phrase.

**coincide** *v* **1** to occur at the same time or place. **2** to have the same form or nature; to correspond.

**coincidence** *n* **1** the chance occurrence of two or more events at the same time or place. **2** a state of correspondence. ➤ **coincidental** *adj*, **coincidentally** *adv.*

**coitus** *n technical* sexual intercourse. ➤ **coital** *adj.*

**coke**[1] *n* a solid porous fuel that remains after gases have been driven from coal by heating.

**coke**[2] *n informal* cocaine.

**colander** *or* **cullender** *n* a perforated bowl for washing or draining food.

**cold**[1] *adj* **1** having a low temperature. **2** of a person or manner: aloof and unemotional. **3** depressing or cheerless. **4** dead or unconscious. **5** retaining only faint scents or traces. **6** far from a goal or solution being sought. **7** unprepared. * **give somebody the cold shoulder** to be unfriendly. **in cold blood** with premeditation; deliberately. **leave somebody cold** to fail to impress somebody. ➤ **coldly** *n.*

**cold**[2] *n* **1** a condition of low temperature. **2** cold weather. **3** an infection characterized by a runny nose and sneezing. * **out in the cold** ignored or neglected.

**cold-blooded** *adj* **1** done or acting without feeling; ruthless. **2** having a body temperature approximating to that of the environment.

**cold feet** *pl n informal* a loss of nerve.

**cold sore** *n* a blister round or inside the mouth, caused by a viral infection.

**cold turkey** *n informal* unpleasant symptoms suffered by somebody who has stopped taking a narcotic drug.

**cold war** *n* (**the Cold War**) the period of hostility between the Western and Soviet blocs between 1945 and 1989.

**coleslaw** *n* a salad of chopped raw cabbage and carrots mixed with mayonnaise.

**colic** *n* abdominal pain in the intestines caused by obstruction or wind. ➤ **colicky** *adj.*

**collaborate** *v* **1** to work together on a common project. **2** to cooperate with an enemy. ➤ **collaboration** *n*, **collaborative** *adj*, **collaboratively** *adv*, **collaborator** *n.*

**collage** *n* a composition made of pieces of different materials fixed to a surface.

**collapse**[1] *v* **1** to fall down or break completely. **2** to fail suddenly and completely. **3** to suffer a breakdown through exhaustion or disease. **4** to fold down into a more compact shape. ➤ **collapsible** *adj.*

**collapse**[2] *n* **1** an instance of collapsing. **2** a sudden failure or breakdown.

**collar**[1] *n* **1** a band of fabric round the neckline of a garment. **2** a band fitted round the neck of a pet animal. **3** a ring or round flange to restrain motion or hold something in place. **4** a cut of bacon from the neck of a pig.

**collar**[2] *v informal* to seize or apprehend.

**collarbone** *n* the clavicle.

**collate** *v* to collect and compare (information).

**collateral**[1] *adj* **1** secondary or less important. **2** sharing the same ancestry but not in a direct line of descent.

**collateral**[2] *n* property pledged by a borrower to secure a loan.

**colleague** *n* a fellow worker.

**collect** *v* **1** to bring together. **2** to exact (payments) from a number of sources. **3** to come together in a group. **4** to fetch (something or somebody) from a place. **5** to regain control of (one's thoughts).

**collected** *adj* **1** calm and composed. **2** assembled from a number of sources.

**collection** *n* **1** the act or process of collecting. **2** an accumulation of objects gathered for study or exhibition. **3** a range of similar clothing products presented to the public.

**collective**[1] *adj* **1** of individuals considered as one group. **2** made or held in common by a group of individuals. ➤ **collectively** *adv.*

**collective**[2] *n* **1** a collective body or group. **2** an organization or business owned by those who work in it.

**college** *n* **1** a building used for an educational or religious purpose. **2** *Brit* an independent institution forming part of a university. **3** an institution offering vocational or technical instruction.

**collegiate** *adj* **1** relating to or comprising a college. **2** of a university: made up of separate colleges.

**collide** *v* **1** to come together forcibly. **2** to come into conflict.

**collier** *n* **1** a coalminer. **2** a ship for transporting coal.

**colliery** *n* (*pl* **-ies**) a coalmine and its associated buildings.

**collision** *n* an act or instance of colliding; a clash.

**colloquial** *adj* in the style of familiar and informal speech; conversational. ➤ **colloquially** *adv.*

**colloquy** *n* (*pl* **-ies**) **1** a formal conversation or dialogue. **2** a religious conference.

**collude** *v* to cooperate with somebody secretly. ➤ **collusion** *n.*

**collywobbles** *pl n informal* **1** discomfort in the stomach. **2** a nervous or anxious feeling.

**cologne** *n* scented toilet water.

**colon**[1] *n* the part of the large intestine that extends to the rectum. ➤ **colonic** *adj.*

**colon**[2] *n* a punctuation mark (:) used to introduce a quotation, a list of items, or an expansion or explanation of the words it follows.

**colonel** *n* an officer in the army or US air force ranking below brigadier or brigadier general.

**colonial**[1] *adj* **1** relating to or characteristic of a colony. **2** possessing or composed of colonies.

**colonial**[2] *n* an inhabitant of a colony.

**colonialism** *n* the policy or practice by a state of acquiring control over other countries or peoples. ➤ **colonialist** *n and adj.*

**colonist** *n* an inhabitant of a colony.

**colonize** *or* **-ise** *v* **1** to establish a colony in (a place). **2** of plants and animals: to begin to live and breed in (a new area or environment). ➤ **colonization** *n.*

**colonnade** *n* a row of columns placed at regular intervals and supporting a roof.

**colony** *n* (*pl* **-ies**) **1** a body of settlers living in a new territory that is subject to control by the settlers' parent state. **2** the territory settled or controlled in this way. **3** a group of individuals with common interests or origins living close together. **4** a distinguishable localized population within a species.

**coloration** (*Brit also* **colouration**) *n* **1** colouring or complexion. **2** an arrangement or range of colours.

**colossal** *adj* very large or great. ➤ **colossally** *adv.*

**colossus** *n* (*pl* **colossuses** *or* **colossi**) **1** a statue of gigantic size. **2** a person or thing of great size or importance.

**colostomy** *n* (*pl* **-ies**) the surgical formation of an artificial anus in the wall of the abdomen after a shortening of the colon.

**colour**[1] (*NAmer* **color**) *n* **1** a visual sensation, e.g. of things being red, blue, etc, caused by the wavelength of perceived light. **2** a hue, e.g. red or blue, or such hues in general, as opposed to black, white, and grey. **3** a pigment or other substance that gives colour when applied to an object. **4** the use of colours by a painter. **5** the skin pigmentation characteristic of a particular race. **6** the tint characteristic of good health. **7** (*usu in pl*) an identifying badge or uniform. **8** vitality or interest.

**colour**[2] (*NAmer* **color**) *v* **1** to give colour to. **2** to misrepresent or distort. **3** to influence or affect. **4** to blush.

**colour-blind** *adj* unable to distinguish certain colours. ➤ **colour blindness** *n.*

**coloured**[1] (*NAmer* **colored**) *adj* **1** having colour. **2** marked by exaggeration or bias. **3** *offensive* of a race other than white.

**coloured**[2] (*NAmer* **colored**) *n* (*often* **Coloured**) *offensive* a person of mixed descent.

**colourfast** *adj* having colour that will not fade or run.

**colourful** (*NAmer* **colorful**) *adj* **1** having striking colours. **2** full of variety or interest. ➤ **colourfully** *adv.*

**colouring** (*NAmer* **coloring**) *n* **1** the application or combination of colours. **2** the effect produced by colours. **3** something that produces colour.

**colourist** (*NAmer* **colorist**) *n* a painter who uses colour in special ways.

**colourless** (*NAmer* **colorless**) *adj* **1** lacking colour. **2** dull or uninteresting.

**colt** *n* a young male horse.

**coltish** *adj* frisky or playful.

**column** *n* **1** a round pillar with a capital and a base. **2** a long narrow formation of soldiers, vehicles, etc in rows. **3** a vertical section of printing on a page. **4** a regular feature in a newspaper or magazine.

**columnist** *n* a writer of a newspaper or magazine column.

**coma** *n* (*pl* **comas**) a state of prolonged deep unconsciousness.

**comatose** *adj* in a state of coma.

**comb**[1] *n* **1** a toothed instrument used for arranging or holding the hair. **2** a toothed device used in separating or ordering textile fibres. **3** a fleshy crest on the head of a domestic fowl or a related bird. **4** a honeycomb.

**comb**[2] *v* **1** to draw a comb through (the hair) to arrange it. **2** to prepare (wool or cotton) for use in manufacturing by cleaning and arranging its fibres with a comb. **3** to search systematically.

**combat**[1] *n* **1** a fight or contest. **2** active fighting in a war.

**combat**[2] *v* (**combated** *or* **combatted, combating** *or* **combatting**) to act to prevent (something bad or unwelcome).

**combatant**[1] *n* a person or state engaged in or prepared for combat.

**combatant**[2] *adj* actively participating in combat.

**combative** *adj* eager to fight or contend.

**combe** *n Brit* see COOMB.

**combination** *n* **1** an act or the process of combining things. **2** a collection of people or things that have been combined or brought together. **3** the sequence of letters or numbers that will open a combination lock.

**combination lock** *n* a lock operated by entering a specific combination of letters or numbers.

**combine**[1] *v* **1** to bring together; to unite or mix. **2** to act together.

**combine**[2] *n* a combination of people or organizations for commercial activities.

**combine harvester** *n* a harvesting machine that cuts, threshes, and cleans grain while moving over a field.

**combust** *v* to burn or be burned.

**combustible** *adj* able to catch fire easily.

**come** *v* (**came, come**) **1** to move in a direction towards the speaker. **2** to arrive or occur. **3** to happen. **4** to move into a certain state: *to come loose*. **5** to reach a certain position or limit. **6** to be available in a specified form. **7** *informal* to have an orgasm. * **come across 1** to produce a specified impression. **2** to meet or find by chance. **come by** to manage to get. **come clean** *informal* to admit everything. **come into** to inherit (money or property). **come of** to result from. **come over** to affect (somebody) suddenly and strangely. **come to 1** to recover consciousness. **2** to reach a total. **come upon** to meet (somebody) by chance.

**come about** *v* **1** to occur or take place. **2** of a ship: to change course.

**comeback** *n* **1** a return to former success or popularity. **2** *informal* a sharp or witty reply.

**comedian** *n* an entertainer who aims at making people laugh.

**comedown** *n informal* **1** a loss of rank or dignity. **2** a disappointment.

**come down** *v* **1** to decrease in amount or value. **2** of an aircraft: to land or crash.

**comedy** *n* (*pl* **-ies**) **1** a play, film, etc of light and amusing character. **2** a ludicrous or farcical event or series of events.

**come-hither** *adj* of a look: flirtatious.

**come in** *v* to be useful.

**comely** *adj* (**-ier, -iest**) pleasing in appearance.

**come off** *v* to succeed, or to finish as specified.

**come on** *v* **1** to advance or begin by degrees. **2** to make an entrance.

**come out** *v* **1** to be published or made public. **2** to declare oneself in favour of or opposed to something. **3** to end up as specified. **4** to declare one's homosexuality. **5** *Brit, dated* to make one's first appearance in society as a debutante. * **come out with** to say (something) unexpected.

**come over** *v* **1** to make a casual visit. **2** to change sides. **3** to be affected by a feeling.

**come round** *v* **1** to recover consciousness. **2** to be persuaded to adopt an opinion.

**comestibles** *pl n formal* food.

**comet** *n* a moving celestial body consisting of an icy nucleus surrounded by a trailing cloud of gas and dust.

**come up** *v* to arise or occur.

**comeuppance** *n informal* a deserved rebuke or punishment.

**comfort**[1] *n* **1** contented well-being; physical ease. **2** consolation or encouragement in time of trouble or worry.

**comfort**[2] *v* to cheer or console. ➤ **comforter** *n*.

**comfortable** *adj* **1** providing or enjoying physical comfort. **2** of a win or success: achieved with ease. **3** free from stress or tension. ➤ **comfortably** *adv*.

**comfy** *adj* (**-ier, -iest**) *informal* comfortable.

**comic**[1] *adj* **1** of or marked by comedy. **2** causing laughter or amusement.

**comic**[2] *n* **1** a comedian. **2** a children's magazine containing strip cartoons.

**comical** *adj* causing laughter from being ridiculous or funny. ➤ **comically** *adv*.

**comma** *n* a punctuation mark (,) used to separate parts of a sentence or list.

**command**[1] *v* **1** to give an order to. **2** to be able to ask for and receive. **3** to overlook or dominate. **4** to have military charge of.

**command**[2] *n* **1** an authoritative order. **2** the ability or power to control; mastery. **3** the authority or right to command. **4** a computer instruction that actuates the performance of a function. **5** the unit or personnel under a commander.

**commandant** *n* a commanding officer.

**commandeer** *v* to seize for military purposes.

**commander** *n* **1** a person having command. **2** a naval officer ranking below a captain.

**commander-in-chief** *n* (*pl* **commanders-in-chief**) an officer in supreme command of an armed force.

**commanding** *adj* **1** having command or authority. **2** deserving respect and obedience. **3** dominating or having priority.

**commandment** *n* a rule or law, *esp* one of the Ten Commandments.

**commando** *n* (*pl* **-os**) a soldier trained to carry out raids.

**commemorate** *v* to mark or formally remember (an event or a person). ➤ **commemoration** *n*, **commemorative** *adj*.

***Usage Note:*** Note the spelling with *-mm-* and then *-m-*.

**commence** *v* to start or begin.

**commencement** *n* a beginning.

**commend** *v* **1** to praise or approve of. **2** to recommend as worthy of confidence or notice. **3** to entrust for care or preservation. ➤ **commendable** *adj*, **commendation** *n*.

**commendable** *adj* deserving praise; admirable. ➤ **commendably** *adv*.

**commensurable** *adj* having a common measure. ➤ **commensurably** *adv*.

**commensurate** *adj* **1** (*usu* + with) approximately equal in measure or extent. **2** (*often* + to/with) corresponding in size or amount.

**comment[1]** *n* **1** a remark expressing an opinion or attitude. **2** discussion of a topical issue.

**comment[2]** *v* **1** to make a comment. **2** (+ on) to explain or interpret.

**commentary** *n* (*pl* **-ies**) **1** a systematic series of explanations or interpretations. **2** a series of spoken comments describing an event as it happens.

**commentate** *v* to give a commentary of an event.

**commerce** *n* the buying and selling of goods.

**commercial[1]** *adj* **1** involving or relating to commerce. **2** having a good financial prospect. **3** supported by advertising. ➤ **commercially** *adv*.

**commercial[2]** *n* a television or radio advertisement.

**commercialism** *n* **1** commercial institutions or methods. **2** excessive emphasis on profit.

**commercialize** *or* **-ise** *v* **1** to make commercial. **2** to exploit for profit. ➤ **commercialization** *n*.

**commiserate** *v* to feel or express sympathy. ➤ **commiseration** *n*.

**commissar** *n* a Communist party official responsible for teaching party principles and ideals.

**commission[1]** *n* **1** an authorization or command to perform a task. **2** a group of people directed to perform some duty. **3** a percentage fee paid to an agent or employee. **4** a formal warrant granting various powers. **5** military rank above a certain level. **6** authority to act as agent for another. ✱ **out of commission** out of use or working order.

**commission[2]** *v* **1** to order or appoint (somebody) to perform a task or function. **2** to order (a task) to be done. **3** to put into working order.

**commissionaire** *n* *chiefly Brit* a uniformed attendant at a hotel, theatre, etc.

**commissioner** *n* **1** a member or the head of a commission. **2** the government representative in an area.

**commit** *v* (**committed, committing**) **1** to carry out (a wrong act). **2** to obligate or bind (oneself) to a course of action or a set of beliefs. **3** to assign to a particular course or use. **4** to entrust (something or somebody) to somebody's care. **5** to place in a prison or psychiatric hospital.

**commitment** *n* **1** an agreement or pledge to do something. **2** an engagement or obligation. **3** loyalty to a system of thought or action. **4** an act of committing to a charge or trust.

***Usage Note:*** Note the spelling with *-mm-* and then one *-t-*.

**committal** *n* **1** the sending of somebody to prison or a psychiatric hospital, or for trial. **2** the burial of a body.

**committee** *n* **1** a body of people appointed for a purpose by a larger organization. **2** a body of people delegated to report on some matter.

***Usage Note:*** Note the spelling with *-mm-* and *-tt-*.

**commode** *n* an upright chair with a removable seat covering a chamber pot.

**commodious** *adj* *formal* comfortably or spacious.

**commodity** *n* (*pl* **-ies**) **1** something that can be bought and sold. **2** something useful or valuable.

**commodore** *n* **1** the senior captain of a merchant shipping line. **2** the chief officer of a yacht club.

**common[1]** *adj* **1** occurring or appearing frequently. **2** of the most familiar kind. **3** widespread or general. **4** characterized by a lack of privilege or special status. **5** simply satisfying accustomed criteria and no more. **6** lacking refinement. **7** belonging to or shared by two or more individuals. **8** of the community at large; public. **9** in grammar, belonging to a gender that includes masculine and feminine. * **common or garden** ordinary or everyday. ➤ **commonly** *adv.*

**common²** *n* an area of land available for public recreation. * **in common 1** shared together. **2** used jointly.

**common denominator** *n* **1** in mathematics, a number into which the denominators of several fractions can be divided with no remainder. **2** a common feature or theme.

**commoner** *n* a member of the common people and not of noble rank.

**common ground** *n* shared opinions.

**common market** *n* (**the Common Market**) the economic association that became the European Union.

**common noun** *n* a noun that designates any one of a class of beings or things.

**commonplace¹** *adj* ordinary or unremarkable.

**commonplace²** *n* an obvious or trite observation.

**common room** *n chiefly Brit* a room in a school or college for the recreational use of staff or students.

**commons** *pl n* **1** (**the Commons**) the House of Commons. **2** the common people as a political group.

**common sense** *n* sound and prudent judgment. ➤ **commonsensical** *adj.*

**commonwealth** *n* **1** an independent state; a republic. **2** (**the Commonwealth**) an association consisting of the UK and states that were formerly British colonies.

**commotion** *n* **1** a disturbance or tumult. **2** noisy confusion and bustle.

**communal** *adj* shared or used in common by members of a group or community. ➤ **communally** *adv.*

**commune¹** *n* a community of individuals or families sharing possessions.

**commune²** *v* (*usu* + with) to communicate intimately.

**communicable** *adj* of a disease: able to be transmitted to others.

**communicant** *n* a church member who receives Communion.

**communicate** *v* **1** to convey or share information about something. **2** to cause (something) to pass from one person to another. **3** of rooms: to give access to each other. **4** to receive Communion. ➤ **communicator** *n.*

**communication** *n* **1** the exchange of knowledge or information. **2** a verbal or written message. **3** (*in pl*) a system of travelling or communicating information.

**communicative** *adj* tending to communicate; talkative.

**communion** *n* **1** intimate fellowship or rapport. **2** a body of Christians having a common faith. **3** (*often* **Communion**) the religious service consecrating and receiving the Eucharist in Christian churches.

**communiqué** *n* an official announcement.

**communism** *n* **1** a politcal theory or system advocating elimination of private property. **2** (**Communism**) a system based on revolutionary Marxist socialism, followed in China and formerly in the Soviet Union. ➤ **communist** *n and adj.*

**community** *n* (*pl* **-ies**) **1** a group of people living in a particular area or sharing the same religion, ethnic group, etc. **2** a group of individuals sharing a profession or activity. **3** a body of people or nations having a common history or common interests.

**community care** *n* the provision of care to enable people to stay in their own community rather than in a hospital or institution.

**community service** *n* work undertaken by offenders for the benefit of the community, as an alternative to a prison term.

**commute** *v* **1** to travel regularly between home and work. **2** to exchange (a penalty) for a less severe one. ➤ **commuter** *n.*

**compact¹** *adj* **1** having parts or units closely packed or joined. **2** efficiently occupying a small space.

**compact²** *v* to press into a small space.

**compact³** *n* a small slim case for face powder.

**compact⁴** *n* an agreement or contract.

**compact disc** *n* a small disc on which sound or information is stored in digital form.

**companion** *n* **1** a person who accompanies or spends time with somebody else. **2** something belonging to a pair or set of matching things. ➤ **companionship** *n.*

**companionable** *adj* friendly and sociable.

**company** *n* (*pl* **-ies**) **1** a business or commercial organization. **2** friendly association with other people. **3** companions or associates. **4** visitors or guests. **5** a group of people or things. **6** a unit of soldiers. **7** an organization of musical or dramatic performers.

**comparable** *adj* **1** capable of or suitable for comparison. **2** approximately equivalent; similar. ➤ **comparably** *adv.*

**comparative** *adj* **1** considered in comparison to something else. **2** involving comparison between different branches of a subject. **3** in grammar, denoting a degree of comparison expressing a higher degree or quantity, e.g. *smaller*. ➤ **comparatively** *adv.*

**compare** *v* **1** (*usu* + to) to represent as similar to another thing or person. **2** (*often* + to/with) to examine the character or qualities of (something or somebody) in order to discover resemblances or differences. **3** (+ with) to be similar.

**comparison** *n* **1** the comparing of one thing or person to or with another. **2** identity or similarity of features.

**compartment** *n* **1** a part into which an enclosed space is divided. **2** a separate division or section.

**compartmentalize** *or* **-ise** *v* to separate into compartments or categories.

**compass**[1] *n* **1** an instrument that indicates directions, typically by having a needle that points to magnetic north. **2** (*usu in pl*) an instrument for drawing circles, consisting of two arms joined at one end by a pivot. **3** range or scope.

**compass**[2] *v archaic* **1** to encompass. **2** to travel round (a place).

**compassion** *n* sympathetic concern for the hardships of others.

**compassionate** *adj* **1** having or showing compassion. **2** of leave: granted because of special distressing circumstances. ➤ **compassionately** *adv.*

**compatible** *adj* **1** (*often* + with) capable of existing or living together in harmony. **2** of equipment: able to be used in combination. ➤ **compatibility** *n.*

**compatriot** *n* a person from the same country.

**compel** *v* (**compelled, compelling**) **1** to drive or force (somebody) to do something. **2** to cause (something) to occur.

**compelling** *adj* having an irresistible power of attraction. ➤ **compellingly** *adv.*

**compendium** *n* (*pl* **compendiums** *or* **compendia**) **1** a set of information on a subject. **2** a collection of indoor games and puzzles.

**compensate** *v* **1** (*often* + for) to make a payment or give a benefit to (somebody) to make amends for something disadvantageous or unpleasant. **2** to have an equal and opposite effect to. **3** (+ for) to supply an equivalent. ➤ **compensatory** *adj.*

**compensation** *n* **1** a payment for damage or loss. **2** something that counterbalances a disadvantage.

**compere**[1] *n Brit* the presenter of a radio or television programme or a variety show.

**compere**[2] *v Brit* to be a compere for.

**compete** *v* (*often* + with) to strive against others for an objective.

**competent** *adj* **1** having or done with adequate ability. **2** legally qualified to deal with a particular matter. ➤ **competence** *n,* **competently** *adv.*

**competition** *n* **1** the process of competing; rivalry. **2** an organized test of skill, performance, etc. **3** people who are competing with an individual or organization.

**competitive** *adj* **1** relating to or based on competition. **2** inclined or desiring to compete. **3** at least as good as those offered by rivals. ➤ **competitively** *adv.*

**competitor** *n* a person or thing that competes; a contestant or rival.

**compilation** *n* **1** the act or process of compiling. **2** something compiled from different sources.

**compile** *v* to collect or compose from various materials.

**complacent** *adj* smugly uncritical of oneself or one's concerns. ➤ **complacency** *n,* **complacently** *adv.*

**complain** *v* **1** to express feelings of discontent. **2** to say that one has a pain or symptom.

**complainant** *n* in law, a plaintiff.

**complaint** *n* **1** an expression of discontent. **2** something that is the cause of protest. **3** a minor illness or disease.

**complaisant** *adj* inclined to please or comply. ➤ **complaisance** *n.*

**complement**[1] *n* **1** something that completes a whole or adds extra features. **2** the quantity required to make something complete.

***Usage Note:*** Do not confuse this word with *compliment.*

**complement**[2] *v* to add to or enhance (something).

**complementary** *adj* **1** serving to complete or enhance something. **2** of medicine: not forming part of conventional scientific practice.

**complete**[1] *adj* **1** having all necessary parts; whole or entire. **2** fully carried out; thorough. **3** total or absolute. **4** totally competent or skilled in an activity. ➤ **completely** *adv.*

**complete**[2] *v* **1** to bring to an end; to finish doing. **2** to make whole or perfect. **3** to mark the end of. **4** to execute or fulfil. **5** to enter information on (a form). ➤ **completion** *n.*

**complex**[1] *adj* **1** composed of two or more parts. **2** hard to separate, analyse, or solve. ➤ **complexity** *n.*

**complex**[2] *n* **1** a whole made up of interrelated parts. **2** a set of buildings forming a unit. **3** a group of repressed feelings that adversely affects personality and behaviour.

**complexion** *n* **1** the appearance of the skin of a person's face. **2** the overall aspect or character of something.

**compliance** *n* the act of complying with the wishes of others. ➤ **compliant** *adj.*

**complicate** *v* to make complex or difficult.

**complicated** *adj* **1** difficult to analyse, understand, or explain. **2** consisting of parts intricately combined.

**complication** *n* **1** intricacy or complexity. **2** the act of making something difficult or intricate. **3** a complex or intricate feature or element. **4** a factor or issue that occurs unexpectedly and affects a situation. **5** a secondary disease or condition developing in the course of a primary disease or condition.

**complicit** *adj* participating in a wrongful act.

**complicity** *n* association or participation in a wrongful act.

**compliment**[1] *n* **1** an expression of esteem or admiration. **2** (*in pl*) best wishes; regards.

***Usage Note:*** Do not confuse this word with *complement.*

**compliment**[2] *v* (*often* + on) to pay a compliment to.
**complimentary** *adj* **1** expressing or containing a compliment. **2** given free of charge.
**comply** *v* (**-ies, -ied**) **1** (*usu* + with) to do as somebody asks. **2** (*usu* + with) to meet a certain standard.
**component**[1] *n* a constituent part, *esp* of a machine.
**component**[2] *adj* of parts: helping to constitute a whole.
**comportment** *n formal* bearing or demeanour.
**compose** *v* **1** to create (a work of art, *esp* music or poetry). **2** to form (something) by putting it together. **3** (*usu in passive*) to form the substance of (something). **4** to calm or settle (oneself).
**composite**[1] *adj* made up of distinct parts or constituents.
**composite**[2] *n* a composite material.
**composition** *n* **1** a piece of writing or music. **2** the act or process of composing works of art. **3** a mixture of various elements or ingredients. **4** the way in which the parts of something make up the whole.
**compositor** *n* a printer who sets type.
**compos mentis** *adj* of sound mind.
**compost** *n* decayed organic matter used as a fertilizer.
**composure** *n* calmness of mind or bearing.
**compound**[1] *n* **1** something formed by a union of elements or parts. **2** in chemistry, a distinct substance formed by combination of chemical elements in fixed proportion.
**compound**[2] *adj* **1** made from a union of separate elements or parts. **2** of a bone fracture: causing the bone to pierce the skin.
**compound**[3] *v* **1** to put together (parts) to form a whole; to combine. **2** to augment or add to (something bad).
**compound**[4] *n* an enclosed area containing a group of buildings.
**comprehend** *v* to grasp the nature or meaning of.
**comprehensible** *adj* able to be comprehended; intelligible.
**comprehension** *n* **1** the process of or capacity for understanding. **2** *Brit* an exercise testing understanding of a passage.
**comprehensive**[1] *adj* **1** including everything involved or all aspects of something. **2** wide-ranging in scope. **3** *Brit* relating to the education of children of all abilities in one type of secondary school. ➤ **comprehensively** *adv.*
**comprehensive**[2] *n Brit* a comprehensive school.
**compress**[1] *v* **1** to press or squeeze together. **2** to force into a smaller space. ➤ **compression** *n.*
**compress**[2] *n* a pad pressed on to a part of the body to ease the pain and swelling of a bruise.
**compressor** *n* a machine for compressing gases.
**comprise** *v* **1** to be made up of. **2** to make up or constitute.
**compromise**[1] *n* **1** a settlement reached by each side conceding points. **2** a state of opinion or action intermediate between extremes.
**compromise**[2] *v* **1** to come to agreement by mutual concession. **2** to expose to discredit or danger. **3** to go against (one's principles) for expediency.
**comptroller** *n* a public finance officer.
**compulsion** *n* **1** being compelled to do something. **2** a strong impulse to perform an irrational act.
**compulsive** *adj* caused by or suffering from a psychological compulsion. ➤ **compulsively** *adv.*
**compulsory** *adj* required to be done by a law or rule.
**compunction** *n* anxiety arising from a feeling of guilt; remorse.
**computation** *n* **1** a process or system of calculating. **2** the use or operation of a computer. ➤ **computational** *adj.*
**compute** *v* to calculate (a quantity or number).
**computer** *n* an electronic device that can store, retrieve, and process data according to programmed instructions.
**computerize** *or* **-ise** *v* **1** to equip with computers. **2** to carry out by means of a computer.
**comrade** *n* **1** a friend or associate; a member of the same organization. **2** a fellow soldier. ➤ **comradeship** *n.*
**con** *n informal* a confidence trick.
**concatenate** *v* to link together in a series or chain. ➤ **concatenation** *n.*
**concave** *adj* hollowed or rounded inwards like the inside of a bowl.
**conceal** *v* **1** to place out of sight. **2** (*often* + from) to prevent disclosure or recognition of. ➤ **concealment** *n.*
**concede** *v* **1** to accept as true, valid, or accurate. **2** to acknowledge grudgingly or hesitantly. **3** to grant or yield (a right or privilege). **4** to allow (a goal or point by an opponent) through error.
**conceit** *n* **1** excessively high opinion of oneself. **2** *literary* a fanciful idea.
**conceited** *adj* having an excessively high opinion of oneself. ➤ **conceitedly** *adv.*
**conceivable** *adj* able to be conceived in the mind; imaginable. ➤ **conceivably** *adv.*
**conceive** *v* **1** to become pregnant with (a baby). **2** to visualize or imagine.

***Usage Note:*** Note the spelling *-ei-*.

**concentrate**[1] *v* **1** (*often* + on) to focus or direct (the mind or attention) on something. **2** to gather into one body or mass. **3** to make (a solution) stronger.

**concentrate**[2] *n* something in concentrated form, *esp* food.

**concentration** *n* **1** the process of concentrating on something. **2** a concentrated mass or thing. **3** the relative amount of a substance in a mixture or a solution.

**concentration camp** *n* a camp where political prisoners are confined.

**concentric** *adj* of shapes: having a common centre. ➤ **concentrically** *adv*, **concentricity** *n*.

**concept** *n* a thought or notion conceived in the mind. ➤ **conceptual** *adj*, **conceptually** *adv*.

**conception** *n* **1** the process of conceiving a baby; the beginning of pregnancy. **2** a general idea or concept. **3** the originating of something in the mind.

**conceptualize** *or* **-ise** *v* to form an idea of in the mind.

**concern**[1] *v* **1** to be about; to relate to. **2** to involve or have an influence on. **3** to be a cause of trouble or distress to. **4** to engage or occupy (oneself).

**concern**[2] *n* **1** something that relates to or involves one. **2** anxiety or a cause of anxiety. **3** a matter for consideration. **4** a business or organization.

**concerned** *adj* anxious or troubled.

**concerning** *prep* relating to.

**concert** *n* **1** a public performance of music. **2** agreement. ✱ **in concert** working together.

**concerted** *adj* **1** planned or done together; combined. **2** performed in unison.

**concertina**[1] *n* a small hexagonal musical instrument of the accordion family.

**concertina**[2] *v* (**concertinas, concertinaed, concertinaing**) to collapse or fold up like the bellows of a concertina.

**concerto** *n* (*pl* **concertos** *or* **concerti**) a piece of music for an orchestra and one or more soloists.

**concession** *n* **1** the act of conceding something. **2** a reduction in price for people in certain categories. **3** a grant or right made in return for services. **4** a small shop or business operating on the premises of a larger business. ➤ **concessionary** *adj*.

**conch** *n* (*pl* **conchs** *or* **conches**) a large mollusc with a spiral shell.

**concierge** *n* a doorkeeper or caretaker in a large building.

**conciliate** *v* **1** to appease or pacify. **2** *formal* to reconcile (people). ➤ **conciliation** *n*, **conciliatory** *adj*.

**concise** *adj* brief and clear, with a minimum of detail. ➤ **concisely** *adv*, **conciseness** *n*.

**conclave** *n* a private meeting or assembly.

**conclude** *v* **1** to bring or come to an end. **2** to arrive at (an opinion) by reasoning. **3** to reach an agreement on.

**conclusion** *n* **1** the act of concluding. **2** a final summing up of an argument or essay. **3** a reasoned judgment. **4** a result or outcome.

**conclusive** *adj* putting an end to debate or a question; decisive. ➤ **conclusively** *adv*.

**concoct** *v* **1** to prepare (food) from various ingredients. **2** to devise or invent (a story or excuse). ➤ **concoction** *n*.

**concomitant** *adj formal* accompanying in a subordinate or incidental way.

**concord** *n* **1** a state of agreement or harmony. **2** a treaty or covenant.

**concordance** *n* an alphabetical index of the principal words in a book or text.

**concordat** *n* a compact or agreement.

**concourse** *n* a large open space in a building or where roads or paths meet.

**concrete**[1] *adj* **1** real or tangible. **2** specific or particular.

**concrete**[2] *n* a building material made by mixing cement, sand and gravel with water.

**concrete**[3] *v* to cover or set with concrete.

**concubine** *n* in a polygamous society, a woman who lives with a man in addition to his lawful wife or wives.

**concur** *v* (**concurred, concurring**) **1** (*often* + with) to express agreement. **2** of events: to coincide.

**concurrent** *adj* operating or occurring at the same time. ➤ **concurrence** *n*, **concurrently** *adv*.

**concussion** *n* temporary unconsciousness caused by a blow to the head. ➤ **concussed** *adj*.

**condemn** *v* **1** to declare (a person or an action) to be utterly wrong or bad. **2** to sentence to death. **3** (*usu* + to) to cause to suffer something unpleasant. **4** to declare unfit for use. ➤ **condemnation** *n*.

**condensation** *n* **1** droplets of water formed on a cold surface when water vapour in the air cools and becomes liquid. **2** the process of changing from a vapour or gas to a liquid.

**condense** *v* **1** to make denser or more compact; to compress. **2** to change from a vapour or gas to a liquid.

**condensed milk** *n* milk thickened by evaporation and sweetened.

**condescend** *v* **1** to adopt a patronizing attitude of superiority. **2** to descend to less formal or dignified action or speech. **3** to agree to do something thought to be unworthy. ➤ **condescending** *adj*, **condescendingly** *adv*, **condescension** *n*.

**condiment** *n* a flavouring for food, such as pepper or mustard.

**condition**[1] *n* **1** the state of something with regard to appearance or fitness for use. **2** a defective state of health. **3** a state of physical fitness. **4** (*in pl*) attendant circumstances. **5** something that is necessary for something else to exist or occur. * **on condition that** providing that.

**condition**[2] *v* **1** to train (a person or animal) to act or respond in a particular way. **2** to put into a proper state for work or use. **3** to give a certain condition to. **4** to make subject to or dependent on a condition.

**conditional** *adj* **1** subject to a condition or conditions. **2** in grammar, expressing a condition, often with the word 'if'. ➤ **conditionally** *adv.*

**conditioner** *n* a substance applied to hair or fabric to improve its condition.

**condole** *v* (+ with) to express sympathy.

**condolence** *n* **1** sympathy with somebody in sorrow. **2** (*also in pl*) an expression of sympathy.

**condom** *n* a rubber sheath worn over the penis during sexual intercourse to prevent conception.

**condominium** *n* (*pl* **condominiums**) *NAmer* a block of individually owned apartments.

**condone** *v* to pardon or overlook (an offence).

**condor** *n* a large South American vulture.

**conducive** *adj* (+ to) likely to bring about a desirable result.

**conduct**[1] *n* **1** a mode or standard of personal behaviour. **2** the act or manner of directing an operation.

**conduct**[2] *v* **1** to guide or escort (somebody) somewhere. **2** to carry on or direct (an operation). **3** to convey (water or other fluid material) in a channel, pipe, etc. **4** to act as a medium for transmitting (heat or light). **5** to behave (oneself) in a specified manner. **6** to direct the performance or execution of (a musical or artistic work).

**conductance** *n* the ability of a material to conduct electricity.

**conductor** *n* **1** a person who directs the performance of a group of musicians. **2** a substance or body capable of transmitting electricity or heat. **3** a collector of fares on a bus. **4** *chiefly NAmer* a guard in charge of a train.

**conduit** *n* **1** a channel for conveying fluid. **2** a tube protecting electric wires or cables.

**cone** *n* **1** the tapering fruit of a coniferous tree. **2** a solid figure tapering evenly to a point from a circular base. **3** a cone-shaped wafer for holding a portion of ice cream.

**coney** *n* = CONY.

**confect** *v* to prepare (something elaborate) from assorted materials.

**confection** *n* **1** an elaborately prepared item of sweet food. **2** an elaborately contrived article of dress.

**confectionery** *n* (*pl* **-ies**) sweets and chocolate.

**confederacy** *n* (*pl* **-ies**) **1** an alliance of independent states. **2** (**the Confederacy**) the eleven southern states that withdrew from the USA in 1860–61.

**confederate**[1] *adj* **1** united in a league; allied. **2** (**Confederate**) belonging or relating to the Confederacy.

**confederate**[2] *n* an ally or accomplice.

**confederate**[3] *v* to unite in a confederacy.

**confederation** *n* a league or alliance of states.

**confer** *v* (**conferred, conferring**) **1** to bestow (an honour or award) on somebody. **2** (*often* + with) to consult or discuss. ➤ **conferral** *n.*

**conference** *n* a formal meeting of people, e.g. members of a certain profession, for discussions.

**confess** *v* **1** to admit (a wrongdoing). **2** to acknowledge reluctantly. **3** to acknowledge one's sins to a priest.

**confession** *n* **1** an acknowledgement of a wrongdoing. **2** a disclosure of one's sins in confidence to a priest.

**confessional** *n* an enclosed cubicle in a church where a priest hears confessions.

**confessor** *n* a priest who hears confessions and gives absolution.

**confetti** *n* small pieces of coloured paper for throwing over the bride and groom at a wedding.

**confidant** *or* **confidante** *n* a friend that one can confide in.

**confide** *v* (+ in) to tell secrets and other private matters to somebody.

**confidence** *n* **1** faith or trust in something or somebody. **2** a feeling that one's powers or abilities are sufficient. **3** certainty or strong expectation. **4** a secret. * **in confidence** as private or secret information.

**confidence trick** *n* a swindle performed by gaining the victim's confidence.

**confident** *adj* **1** characterized by confidence or assurance. **2** (*also* + of) full of conviction; certain. ➤ **confidently** *adv.*

**confidential** *adj* intended to be kept secret. ➤ **confidentiality** *n,* **confidentially** *adv.*

**configuration** *n* an arrangement of parts relative one to another.

**configure** *v* to arrange (things) in a certain way relative to one another.

**confine** *v* **1** (*often* + to) to restrict within certain limits. **2** to shut (somebody) up. **3** of an illness or injury: to keep (somebody) in bed or a wheelchair.

**confined** *adj* of a space: cramped or enclosed.

**confinement** *n* **1** a state of being confined. **2** the time when a woman is about to give birth.

**confirm** *v* **1** to establish the correctness of (a report, fear, etc). **2** (+ in) to vindicate or strengthen (somebody) in a belief, etc. **3** to be evidence of or prove. **4** to commit oneself definitely to (an arrangement). **5** to administer the rite of confirmation to.

**confirmation** *n* **1** confirming proof; corroboration. **2** the confirming of an arrangement. **3** a religious ceremony admitting a person to full membership of a Christian church.

**confirmed** *adj* fixed in habit or attitude.

**confiscate** *v* to seize (property) by authority. ➤ **confiscation** *n.*

**conflagration** *n* a large and disastrous fire.

**conflate** *v* to combine (two or more things) into one. ➤ **conflation** *n.*

**conflict**[1] *n* **1** a sharp disagreement or clash. **2** mental struggle resulting from incompatible impulses. **3** a prolonged hostile encounter.

**conflict**[2] *v* to be incompatible or in opposition; to clash.

**confluence** *n* the meeting of two rivers or streams.

**conform** *v* **1** to be obedient or compliant. **2** (+ to/with) to accord with a certain standard or pattern.

**conformist** *n* a person who conforms to an accepted view or practice.

**conformity** *n* **1** correspondence with a certain model or standard. **2** (+ to) behaviour that is in compliance with a convention or specified requirements. **3** similarity in form.

**confound** *v* **1** to surprise or disconcert. **2** to prove (an argument or prediction) wrong. **3** to defeat or overthrow (a person or plan).

**confront** *v* **1** of a problem, etc: to require attention from (somebody). **2** to face up to and tackle (a problem or an opponent). **3** to present (somebody) with unwelcome facts.

**confrontation** *n* a state of hostile opposition or argument. ➤ **confrontational** *adj.*

**confuse** *v* **1** to bewilder or perplex. **2** to make more incomprehensible. **3** (*often* + with) to mistake (one person or thing) for another. ➤ **confusable** *adj.*

**confused** *adj* **1** bewildered. **2** disorganized or muddled.

**confusion** *n* **1** a state of being confused. **2** disorder or panic.

**confute** *v* **1** to defeat in argument. **2** to refute (an argument). ➤ **confutation** *n.*

**conga** *n* a dance performed by a group in single file.

**congeal** *v* to become solid during cooking or freezing; to coagulate.

**congenial** *adj* agreeably suited to one's nature or tastes.

**congenital** *adj* **1** of a disease or abnormality: existing from birth. **2** *informal* having an ingrained tendency to be a certain thing.

**conger eel** *n* a large edible sea eel.

**congested** *adj* **1** heavily crowded with people or traffic. **2** of the lungs or respiratory system: blocked by mucus. **3** of other parts of the body: over-full of blood. ➤ **congestion** *n.*

**conglomerate**[1] *v* to gather into a mass; to accumulate. ➤ **conglomeration** *n.*

**conglomerate**[2] *n* **1** a composite mixture. **2** a large business company formed from acquisitions of other firms.

**congratulate** *v* (+ on) to express pleasure to (somebody) at their success or good fortune. ➤ **congratulation** *n,* **congratulatory** *adj.*

**congratulations** *pl n* good wishes expressed at somebody's success or good fortune.

**congregate** *v* to gather together.

**congregation** *n* **1** an assembly of people for religious worship. **2** a collection of people or things.

**congress** *n* **1** a formal meeting or programme of meetings between delegates. **2** (**Congress**) the supreme legislative body of the USA and some other countries. **3** *formal* the act or action of coming together and meeting. ➤ **congressional** *adj.*

**congruent** *adj* **1** in agreement or harmony. **2** geometrically identical size and shape. ➤ **congruence** *n.*

**conical** *adj* having the shape of a cone.

**conifer** *n* a tree that bears cones. ➤ **coniferous** *adj.*

**conjecture**[1] *n* a conclusion or opinion based on incomplete evidence. ➤ **conjectural** *adj.*

**conjecture**[2] *v* **1** to guess. **2** to form a conjecture.

**conjoin** *v formal* to unite or join.

**conjugal** *adj* relating to marriage or married people.

**conjugate** *v* to give the inflections of (a verb). ➤ **conjugation** *n.*

**conjunction** *n* **1** in grammar, a word such as *and, or, but, if,* or *when,* that joins words or clauses. **2** in astrology, the apparent meeting or passing of two or more planets in the same part of the sky. **3** occurrence together in time or space.

**conjunctivitis** *n* inflammation of the membrane lining the eyelid.

**conjure** *v* **1** (+ up) to produce from one's imagination or by using one's creative powers. **2** (+ up) of a word, sensation, etc: to evoke (ideas, images, etc). **3** to perform conjuring tricks.

**conk** *n informal Brit* the nose.

**conker** *n* the hard shiny brown nut of the horse chestnut tree.

**conk out** *v informal* **1** of a machine: to break down. **2** of a person: to faint or fall asleep.

**conman** *n* (*pl* **conmen**) *informal* a person who swindles with confidence tricks.

**connect** *v* **1** to link together. **2** (*often* + with) to associate (two things) mentally. **3** to constitute a link or relationship between. **4** to link (two callers) by telephone. ➤ **connective** *adj,* **connectively** *adv,* **connectivity** *n.*

**connection** (*Brit* **connexion**) *n* **1** something that connects; a link. **2** a relationship or association. **3** a train, bus, plane, etc, that one transfers to to continue a journey. **4** (*also in pl*) somebody connected to one by friendship, professional interests, etc.

**connive** *v* **1** (*often* + in/at) to ignore or secretly support a wrong. **2** (*often* + with) to cooperate secretly to do wrong. ➤ **connivance** *n.*

**connoisseur** /konəˈsuh/ *n* an expert judge in matters of taste or appreciation.

**connotation** *n* something suggested by a word as distinct from its direct meaning.

**connote** *v* of a word: to convey (ideas or feelings) in addition to its explicit meaning.

**connubial** *adj* concerning marriage or the relationship between husband and wife.

**conquer** *v* **1** to defeat and gain control over (a country or its people) by force. **2** to overcome or master (a challenge or weakness). ➤ **conqueror** *n.*

**conquest** *n* **1** the act or process of conquering. **2** a conquered territory. **3** a person who has been won over by love or sexual attraction.

**conscience** *n* the consciousness of the moral quality of one's conduct or intentions.

**conscientious** *adj* meticulous or careful in one's work; hard-working. ➤ **conscientiously** *adv.*

**conscious** *adj* **1** aware of one's surroundings and responding to them. **2** (+ of) aware of something. **3** of an action: intentional, deliberate. ➤ **consciously** *adv,* **consciousness** *n.*

**conscript**[1] *n* a person who has been called for military service.

**conscript**[2] *v* to enlist compulsorily for military service. ➤ **conscription** *n.*

**consecrate** *v* **1** to make or declare sacred by a solemn ceremony. **2** to ordain to a religious office. ➤ **consecration** *n.*

**consecutive** *adj* following in order without gaps. ➤ **consecutively** *adv.*

**consensual** *adj* relating to consent or consensus. ➤ **consensually** *adv.*

**consensus** *n* general agreement; unanimity.

***Usage Note:*** Note the spelling with *-sus* not *-cus.*

**consent**[1] *v* **1** to give assent or approval to something. **2** to agree (to do something).

**consent**[2] *n* approval or acquiescence.

**consequence** *n* **1** a result or effect. **2** importance or relevance.

**consequent** *adj* **1** *formal* (+ to) following as a result or effect. **2** observing logical sequence; rational. ➤ **consequently** *adv,* **consequential** *adj.*

**conservation** *n* **1** preservation and protection of the environment and its natural resources. **2** the preservation of historic or archaeological artefacts or sites. **3** in physics, the conserving of a quantity. ➤ **conservationist** *n.*

**conservative**[1] *adj* **1** holding established views and tending to resist change. **2** (**Conservative**) relating to a political party associated with support of established institutions. **3** moderate or cautious. ➤ **conservatism** *n,* **conservatively** *adv.*

**conservative**[2] *n* **1** (**Conservative**) a supporter of a Conservative party. **2** a person who holds traditional views.

**conservatory** *n* (*pl* **-ies**) a room with a glass roof and large windows, built on to a house.

**conserve**[1] *v* **1** to keep in a state of safety or wholeness. **2** to maintain (a resource) and avoid wasteful use of it.

**conserve**[2] *n* a jam made from boiled fruit.

**consider** *v* **1** to think about carefully. **2** to deem or judge. **3** to have sympathetic regard for. **4** to have in mind.

**considerable** *adj* **1** worth consideration; significant. **2** large in extent or degree. ➤ **considerably** *adv.*

**considerate** *adj* showing concern for the welfare of others. ➤ **considerately** *adv.*

**consideration** *n* **1** careful thought. **2** a factor taken into account in making a decision. **3** the bearing of something in mind. **4** concern for others. **5** a payment for a service.

**considering**[1] *prep and adv* taking into account.

**considering**[2] *conj* in view of the fact that.

**consign** *v* **1** to entrust (something) to somebody's care. **2** to commit (something) to a place where it will be got rid of.

**consignment** *n* a batch of goods for delivery.

**consist** *v* **1** (+ of) to be made up or composed of. **2** (+ in) to be essentially.

**consistency** *n* (*pl* **-ies**) **1** the degree of thickness or firmness of a substance. **2** the quality of not varying or of being consistent.

**consistent** *adj* **1** not varying over a period of time. **2** (*often* + with) in agreement; not contradictory. **3** logically coherent. ➤ **consistently** *adv.*

**consolation** *n* **1** comfort received by somebody who has suffered loss or disappointment. **2** something that affords comfort.

**consolation prize** *n* a prize given to a competitor who just fails to win a main prize.

**console**[1] *v* to comfort (somebody) in grief or disappointment. ➤ **consolable** *adj.*

**console**[2] *n* **1** a panel, or switchboard housing a set of controls. **2** an electronic device for playing computerized video games.

**consolidate** *v* **1** to strengthen or make more stable. **2** to combine (several elements) into a unit. ➤ **consolidation** *n.*

**consommé** *n* a thin clear soup made from meat broth.

**consonance** *n formal* harmony or agreement.

**consonant**[1] *n* a letter representing one of the speech sounds, e.g. /p/, /g/, /n/, /l/, /s/, /r/, characterized by constriction or closure at one or more points in the breath channel.

**consonant**[2] *adj formal* (+ with) in agreement or harmony with.

**consort**[1] *n* **1** a husband or wife, *esp* of a reigning monarch. **2** a companion.

**consort**[2] *n* a group of musicians performing together.

**consort**[3] *v formal* (+ with) to keep regular company with.

**consortium** *n* (*pl* **consortia** *or* **consortiums**) a temporary combination of businesses.

**conspicuous** *adj* **1** obvious to the eye or mind. **2** attracting attention. ➤ **conspicuously** *adv.*

**conspiracy** *n* (*pl* **-ies**) a secret plot to do wrong.

**conspire** *v* **1** to plot secretly with others to do wrong. **2** of circumstances: to seem to be acting together to produce undesirable results.

**constable** *n Brit* a police officer of the lowest rank.

**constabulary** *n* (*pl* **-ies**) a local police force.

**constant**[1] *adj* **1** faithful and resolute. **2** invariable or uniform. **3** continually occurring or recurring; regular. ➤ **constancy** *n,* **constantly** *adv.*

**constant**[2] *n* **1** a number that has a fixed value. **2** something that stays the same in a given situation.

**constellation** *n* a group of stars forming patterns identified with mythical figures.

**consternation** *n* a state of confused dismay.

**constipated** *adj* affected by constipation.

**constipation** *n* difficulty in emptying the bowels because of compacted faeces.

**constituency** *n* (*pl* **-ies**) an electoral district or the body of voters resident in it.

**constituent**[1] *n* **1** an essential part; a component. **2** a member of an MP's constituency.

**constituent**[2] *adj* serving to form a unit or whole.

**constitute** *v* **1** of a group of people or things: to compose (something) together. **2** to be or amount to. **3** to establish or set up.

**constitution** *n* **1** the body of principles and laws of a nation, state, or social group. **2** the act of establishing or setting up. **3** the physical and mental make-up of a person. ➤ **constitutionless** *adj.*

**constitutional** *adj* **1** relating to or in accordance with the constitution of a state or society. **2** relating to the constitution of body or mind. ➤ **constitutionally** *adv.*

**constrain** *v* **1** of circumstances: to force (somebody) to do something. **2** to restrict or inhibit.

**constraint** *n* a constraining force or check.

**constrict** *v* **1** to make (a passage or opening) narrow. **2** to compress or squeeze. **3** to limit or inhibit. ➤ **constriction** *n.*

**constrictor** *n* a snake that kills its prey by crushing it.

**construct**[1] *v* **1** to build or erect. **2** to form (a theory or hypothesis).

**construct**[2] *n* a developed idea or concept.

**construction** *n* **1** the process of constructing. **2** a building or other structure. **3** a particular interpretation.

**constructive** *adj* **1** of a criticism, suggestion, etc: positive and helpful. **2** inferred rather than explicit. ➤ **constructively** *adv.*

**construe** *v* (**construes, construed, construing**) to interpret (something) in a certain way. ➤ **construal** *n.*

**consul** *n* **1** an official appointed by a government to reside in a foreign country and look after the interests of citizens of the appointing country. **2** either of two elected chief magistrates of the Roman republic. ➤ **consular** *adj.*

**consulate** *n* the office of a consul.

**consult** *v* **1** to seek the advice or opinion of (a professional person). **2** to look up (a reference book, etc). **3** to deliberate together; to confer. ➤ **consultation** *n,* **consultative** *adj.*

**consultancy** *n* (*pl* **-ies**) **1** an agency that provides consulting services. **2** the post of a consultant.

**consultant** *n* **1** an expert who gives professional advice or services. **2** a senior British hospital doctor.

**consume** *v* **1** to eat or drink (food or drink). **2** to use or use up (a fuel or other resource). **3** of fire: to destroy completely. **4** (*usu in passive*) of an emotion: to obsess (somebody).

**consumer** *n* somebody who uses goods or services.

**consumerism** *n* the promotion and protection of the consumer's interests. ➤ **consumerist** *n and adj.*

**consummate**[1] *adj* **1** extremely skilled and accomplished. **2** of the highest degree. ➤ **consummately** *adv.*

**consummate**[2] *v* **1** to make (a marriage) complete by sexual intercourse. **2** to complete (a business deal). ➤ **consummation** *n.*

**consumption** *n* **1** the process of consuming. **2** an amount consumed. **3** *dated* a wasting disease, *esp* tuberculosis of the lungs.

**contact**[1] *n* **1** the action of physically touching. **2** meeting or communication. **3** a useful business acquaintance or relationship. **4** an individual who has been in association with an infected person. **5** an electrical connection or junction.

**contact**[2] *v* to communicate with. ➤ **contactable** *adj.*

**contact lens** *n* a thin lens placed over the cornea of the eye to correct a sight defect.

**contagion** *n* the transmission of a disease from one person to another by contact.

**contagious** *adj* **1** of a disease: communicable by contact. **2** of a person: suffering from a contagious disease. **3** of a mood or attitude: tending to communicate itself to others.

**contain** *v* **1** to have or hold (something) within itself. **2** to comprise or include. **3** to keep (something) within limits. **4** to check or restrain.

**container** *n* **1** a box, tin, etc that contains things. **2** a large metal case for transporting.

**containment** *n* the action of keeping something harmful or unwelcome under control.

**contaminate** *v* **1** to render impure or unfit for use. **2** to make radioactive. ➤ **contamination** *n.*

**contemplate** *v* **1** to consider or meditate on. **2** to look at attentively. **3** to consider as a course of action.

**contemporaneous** *adj* existing or happening in the same period of time. ➤ **contemporaneously** *adv.*

**contemporary**[1] *adj* **1** happening or existing in the same period of time. **2** modern or fashionable.

**contemporary**[2] *n* (*pl* **-ies**) a person living or active in the same period of time as another.

**contempt** *n* **1** a feeling one has that somebody or something is bad or worthless. **2** (**contempt of court**) the offence of wilful disrespect for a court. ✱ **beneath contempt** utterly despicable.

**contemptible** *adj* deserving contempt. ➤ **contemptibly** *adv.*

**contemptuous** *adj* showing or expressing contempt. ➤ **contemptuously** *adv.*

**contend** *v* **1** to struggle or compete. **2** (+ with) to try to overcome difficulties. **3** to debate or argue. **4** to maintain or assert. ➤ **contender** *n.*

**content**[1] *adj* happy or satisfied. ➤ **contentment** *n.*

**content**[2] *v* to satisfy or appease.

**content**[3] *n* a state of happy satisfaction. ✱ **to one's heart's content** as much as one wants.

**content**[4] *n* **1** (*in pl*) the things that are contained in something. **2** (*in pl*) the topics treated in a book. **3** the matter dealt with in a literary work, lecture, etc, as distinct from its form or style. **4** the amount or proportion of a specified material contained in something.

**contented** *adj* **1** satisfied or happy. **2** willing to accept a situation. ➤ **contentedly** *adv.*

**contention** *n* **1** strong disagreement or rivalry. **2** a point advanced in a debate. ✱ **in contention** contending for a prize or success.

**contentious** *adj* likely to cause disagreement or controversy. ➤ **contentiously** *adv.*

**contest**[1] *n* **1** a struggle for superiority or victory. **2** a competition or competitive event.

**contest**[2] *v* **1** to stand as a candidate in (an election). **2** to dispute (a claim or decision). **3** (+ with/against) to strive or vie.

**contestant** *n* a participant in a contest.

**context** *n* **1** the parts surrounding a written or spoken word or passage that clarify its meaning. **2** the conditions in which something exists or occurs. ➤ **contextual** *adj.*

**contiguous** *adj* **1** in contact. **2** touching along a line or at a point; adjacent. **3** next or near in time or sequence.

**continent**[1] *n* **1** a large division of land on the globe (Europe, Asia, Africa, N and S America, Australia, and Antarctica). **2** (**the Continent**) Europe regarded from the British Isles.

**continent**[2] *adj* **1** able to control the bladder and bowels. **2** exercising self-restraint. ➤ **continence** *n.*

**continental**[1] *adj* relating to or characteristic of a continent, *esp* Europe.

**continental**[2] *n* an inhabitant of a continent, *esp* Europe.

**continental breakfast** *n* a light breakfast of bread rolls and coffee.

**contingency** *n* (*pl* **-ies**) **1** an event that may occur but cannot be definitely predicted; an eventuality. **2** the absence of certainty in the occurrence of events.

**contingent**[1] *adj* **1** subject to chance or unforeseen causes. **2** (+ on/upon) dependent on or conditioned by.

**contingent**[2] *n* a group of people forming part of a larger body.

**continual** *adj* happening constantly: *continual interruptions.* ➤ **continually** *adv.*

***Usage Note:*** Do not confuse this word with *continuous.*

**continuation** *n* **1** the process of continuing. **2** resumption after an interruption. **3** something that continues or adds to something.

**continue** *v* **1** to maintain without interruption; to carry on (doing something). **2** to resume (an activity) after interruption. **3** to remain or endure. **4** to say something further.

**continuity** *n* (*pl* **-ies**) **1** uninterrupted connection or succession. **2** persistence without essential change. **3** uninterrupted duration in time. **4** a film script or scenario giving the details of the sequence of individual shots. **5** speech or music used to link parts of a radio or television programme.

**continuous** *adj* continuing uninterrupted; unbroken: *a continuous humming.* ➤ **continuously** *adv.*

***Usage Note:*** Do not confuse this word with *continual.*

**continuum** *n* (*pl* **continua**) **1** a continuous succession of parts that are not distinguishable. **2** a sequence of minute gradations between extremes.

**contort** *v* to twist (something) out of shape. ➤ **contortion** *n.*

**contortionist** *n* a performer who contorts the body into strange postures.

**contour**[1] *n* **1** an outline of a curving or irregular figure. **2** a line on a map connecting points of equal elevation or height.

**contour**[2] *v* **1** to shape the contour or outline of. **2** to construct in conformity to a contour.

**contraband** *n* goods that have been brought out of or into a country illegally.

**contraception** *n* the use of contrceptives to prevent pregnancy.

**contraceptive** *n* a device or drug that aims at preventing a woman becoming pregnant. ➤ **contraceptive** *adj.*

**contract**[1] *n* **1** a legally binding agreement. **2** *informal* an arrangement for the murder of somebody by a hired killer. ➤ **contractual** *adj.*

**contract**[2] *v* **1** to reduce to a smaller size. **2** to draw together or tighten. **3** to shorten (a word) by omitting letters. **4** to establish or undertake by legal contract. **5** to catch (a disease). **6** to incur (a debt).

**contraction** *n* **1** the process of contracting. **2** the periodic contracting of the muscles of the womb during childbirth. **3** a shortening of a word.

**contractor** *n* a person who contracts to do work, *esp* a builder.

**contradict** *v* **1** to state the opposite of (a statement or speaker). **2** to deny the truthfulness of (a statement or speaker).

**contradiction** *n* **1** the act of contradicting. **2** a statement or series of statements containing contradictory parts. **3** opposition of factors inherent in a system or situation.

**contradictory** *adj* **1** incompatible or inconsistent with one another. **2** of propositions: logically such that only one can be true.

**contradistinction** *n* a distinction made by contrasting qualities.

**contraflow** *n* a temporary two-way traffic-flow system introduced on one carriageway of a motorway while the other is closed off.

**contralto** *n* (*pl* **-os**) a female singer with the lowest singing voice.

**contraption** *n* a strange or complicated device or gadget.

**contrapuntal** *adj* relating to musical counterpoint.

**contrariwise** *adv* in an opposite direction or way.

**contrary**[1] *adj* **1** completely different or opposed in nature or meaning. **2** /kən'treəri/ stubbornly inclined to oppose the wishes of others. **3** of the wind or weather: unfavourable. **4** /kən'treəri/ opposite in position or direction.

**contrary**[2] *n* ✱ **on the contrary** just the opposite.

**contrast**[1] *n* **1** comparison of similar objects to set off their dissimilar qualities. **2** a person or thing against which another may be contrasted. **3** juxtaposition of dissimilar elements in a work of art. **4** the degree of difference between the lightest and darkest parts of a photograph, television picture, etc.

**contrast**[2] *v* **1** (+ with) to be different or opposite. **2** to compare (two things) in respect to differences.

**contravene** *v* of a person or act: to break (a law or principle). ➤ **contravention** *n.*

**contretemps** /'konhtrətonh, 'kon-/ *n* (*pl* **contretemps**) a minor disagreement or quarrel.

**contribute** *v* **1** to give something towards a common cause or objective. **2** (+ to) to help bring about an end or result. ➤ **contribution** *n*, **contributor** *n.*

**contributory** *adj* **1** helping to cause something. **2** contributing to a common fund or enterprise. **3** of a pension scheme or insurance plan: contributed to by both employers and employees.

**contrite** *adj* sorry for a wrongdoing. ➤ **contritely** *n.*

**contrivance** *n* **1** the process of contriving something. **2** an ingenious device or a plan.

**contrive** *v* **1** to devise or plan (something) with ingenuity. **2** to manage (to do something foolish).

**contrived** *adj* of art, language, etc: unnatural or forced.

**control**[1] *v* (**controlled, controlling**) **1** to supervise and direct (something). **2** to operate (a machine). **3** to restrain (oneself or one's emotions). **4** to regulate (the finances of an organization, etc). ➤ **controllable** *adj*, **controllability** *n*, **controller** *n.*

**control**[2] *n* **1** power or authority to control. **2** the activity or situation of controlling. **3** the direction and coordination of business activities. **4** mastery in the use of a tool or technique. **5** restraint or reserve. **6** a thing or person used as a gauge for checking something else. **7** (*in pl*) the devices and mechanisms used to regulate the operation of a machine or system. **8** an organization that directs a space flight. ✱ **in control** having control or command. **out of control** dangerously unrestrained.

**control tower** *n* a tall airport building from which movements of aircraft are controlled.

**controversial** *adj* likely to cause controversy. ➤ **controversially** *adv.*

**controversy** *n* (*pl* **-ies**) **1** debate or disagreement on an important matter. **2** a dispute over a specific issue.

**contumely** *n formal* contemptuous language or treatment.

**contusion** *n* a bruise.

**conundrum** *n* (*pl* **conundrums**) **1** a riddle, *esp* one involving a pun. **2** an intricate and difficult problem.

**conurbation** *n* a large urban area, formed when the suburbs of two or more towns merge.

**convalesce** *v* to recover gradually after illness or injury. ➤ **convalescence** *n*, **convalescent** *adj and n.*
**convection** *n* the transfer of heat by the movement of a heated gas or liquid in relation to a colder part.
**convector** *n* a heater in which heated air circulates by convection.
**convene** *v* to assemble for a meeting. ➤ **convener** *n*, **convenor** *n.*
**convenience** *n* **1** ease of use or access. **2** personal comfort or advantage. **3** a useful appliance or service. **4** *Brit* a public toilet.
**convenient** *adj* **1** suited to personal comfort or easy use. **2** suited to a particular situation. **3** near at hand; easily accessible. ➤ **conveniently** *adv.*
**convent** *n* a community of nuns.
**convention** *n* **1** accepted social custom or practice. **2** a generally agreed principle. **3** an agreement between states. **4** an assembly or conference.
**conventional** *adj* **1** conforming to or sanctioned by convention. **2** lacking originality or individuality. **3** of warfare: not using nuclear weapons. ➤ **conventionally** *adv.*
**converge** *v* **1** to move together towards a common point. **2** (+ on/upon) to come together in a common interest or focus. ➤ **convergence** *n*, **convergent** *adj.*
**conversant** *adj* (+ with) fully acquainted or familiar with facts, principles, etc.
**conversation** *n* an informal verbal exchange. ➤ **conversational** *adj.*
**converse**[1] *v* to have a conversation.
**converse**[2] *adj* opposite in order or relation. ➤ **conversely** *adv.*
**converse**[3] *n* a situation, fact, etc that is the opposite of something else.
**conversion** *n* **1** the process of converting, or something converted. **2** a building that has been altered to a different purpose. **3** the adoption of a new or different religious faith. **4** in rugby, successful kick at goal awarded after a try.
**convert**[1] *v* **1** to change (something) from one form or function to another. **2** to alter (a building) to a new purpose. **3** to persuade (somebody) to follow a principle, religious belief, etc. **4** in rugby, to complete (a try) by successfully kicking a conversion.
**convert**[2] *n* a person who has undergone a religious conversion.
**convertible**[1] *adj* **1** capable of being converted. **2** of a car: having a top that can be lowered.
**convertible**[2] *n* a convertible car.
**convex** *adj* curved or rounded outwards like the outside of a bowl.
**convey** *v* **1** to take or carry from one place to another. **2** to communicate (a feeling or idea). **3** in law, to transfer (property or rights) to another person.
**conveyance** *n* **1** the conveying of something. **2** a means of transport. **3** the legal transfer of rights to property. ➤ **conveyancing** *n.*
**conveyor belt** *n* a moving belt or set of linked plates for moving objects from one part of a building to another.
**convict**[1] *v* to prove and declare (somebody) to be guilty of a crime.
**convict**[2] *n* a person who has been convicted of a crime and imprisoned.
**conviction** *n* **1** a strongly held persuasion or belief. **2** the state of being convinced. **3** the process of convicting someone of a crime, or an instance of this.
**convince** *v* **1** to cause (somebody) to believe or accept something. **2** to persuade (somebody) to follow a course of action.
**convincing** *adj* **1** serving to convince. **2** of a victory, etc: secured by a large margin. ➤ **convincingly** *adv.*
**convivial** *adj* **1** sociable or friendly. **2** enjoying good company. ➤ **conviviality** *n.*
**convoluted** *adj* **1** complex and difficult to understand. **2** *technical* having twists or coils.
**convolution** *n* **1** a twist or coil. **2** something intricate or complicated.
**convoy** *n* (*treated as sing. or pl*) a group of ships or vehicles travelling together.
**convulse** *v* **1** to cause (a person) to be shaken violently by spasms of rage, laughter, etc. **2** to be convulsed. ➤ **convulsive** *adj.*
**convulsion** *n* **1** an involuntary contraction or series of contractions of the muscles. **2** a violent disturbance. **3** (*in pl*) an uncontrolled fit of laughter.
**cony** *or* **coney** *n* (*pl* **conies** *or* **coneys**) a rabbit.
**coo** *v* (**coos, cooed, cooing**) **1** to make the low soft cry of a dove or pigeon. **2** to talk lovingly or appreciatively. ➤ **coo** *n.*
**cook**[1] *v* **1** to prepare food for eating by heating it. **2** of food: to be cooked by heating. **3** *informal* to falsify (financial accounts) in order to deceive. ➤ **cooking** *n.*
**cook**[2] *n* a person who cooks food.
**cooker** *n Brit* **1** an appliance for cooking food, with an oven, hot plates, and a grill. **2** *informal* an apple or other fruit suitable only for cooking.
**cookery** *n* (*pl* **-ies**) the art or practice of cooking.
**cookie** *n* **1** *NAmer* a sweet biscuit. **2** *informal* a person of a specified type: *a tough cookie.* **3** in computing, data downloaded from an Internet website to identify a user on future visits.
**cool**[1] *adj* **1** moderately cold. **2** bringing relief from heat. **3** unfriendly or lacking enthusiasm. **4** calm and self-controlled. **5** *informal* used as an intensive: *a cool million.* **6** *informal* fashion-

able or attractive. **7** *informal* very good. ➤ **coolly** *adv,* **coolness** *n.*

**cool**[2] *v* to make or become cool.

**cool**[3] *n informal* poise or composure.

**coolant** *n* a liquid or gas used in cooling an engine or machine.

**coomb** *n* a valley or hollow on a hillside or running up from a coast.

**coon** *n NAmer* a raccoon.

**coop**[1] *n* a small enclosure for poultry.

**coop**[2] *v* (*usu* + up) to confine in a small space.

**cooper** *n* a person who makes or repairs barrels and casks.

**cooperate** *or* **co-operate** *v* **1** to act or work together for a common purpose. **2** to do or agree to what is asked. ➤ **cooperation** *n.*

**cooperative**[1] *or* **co-operative** *adj* **1** showing a willingness to work with others. **2** of an organization: owned by and operated for the benefit of its members. ➤ **cooperatively** *adv.*

**cooperative**[2] *or* **co-operative** *n* a cooperative organization or business.

**co-opt** *v* **1** of a committee or other body: to choose or elect (somebody) as a member. **2** to appropriate (an idea). ➤ **co-option** *n.*

**coordinate**[1] *or* **co-ordinate** *v* **1** to combine (diverse elements) into a common condition or action. **2** to combine or act together harmoniously. ➤ **coordinator** *n.*

**coordinate**[2] *or* **co-ordinate** *n* in mathematics, a set of numbers used to specify the location of a point on a line or surface, or in space.

**coordinate**[3] *or* **co-ordinate** *adj* equal in rank or importance.

**coordinated** *or* **co-ordinated** *adj* able to move one's body efficiently and effectively.

**coordination** *or* **co-ordination** *n* **1** the process of coordinating. **2** the ability to move one's body efficiently and effectively.

**coot** *n* a water bird with dark plumage and a white bill.

**cop**[1] *n informal* a police officer. ✱ **not much cop** *Brit, informal* fairly bad.

**cop**[2] *v* (**copped, copping**) *informal* **1** to capture or arrest. **2** to suffer (something bad or unwelcome). ✱ **cop it 1** *Brit, informal* to be in serious trouble. **2** *Brit, informal* to be killed.

**cope**[1] *v* to deal effectively with something difficult or awkward.

**cope**[2] *n* a long vestment worn by a priest on special occasions.

**copier** *n* a machine for making copies of documents.

**co-pilot** *n* a second pilot in an aircraft.

**coping** *n* a sloping, course of brick or stone on the top of a wall.

**copious** *adj* abundant or plentiful. ➤ **copiously** *adv.*

**cop-out** *n informal* avoidance of a responsibility.

**cop out** *v informal* to avoid a responsibility.

**copper**[1] *n* **1** a reddish metallic chemical element. **2** a reddish brown colour. **3** *Brit* a coin or token made of copper or bronze.

**copper**[2] *n Brit, informal* a police officer.

**copper-bottomed** *adj Brit* completely reliable.

**copperplate** *n* a style of fine handwriting marked by lines of contrasting thickness.

**coppice** *n* a woodland area in which the trees are regularly cut back to promote growth.

**copse** *n* a small area of trees.

**copulate** *v* to have sexual intercourse. ➤ **copulation** *n.*

**copy**[1] *n* (*pl* **-ies**) **1** something made to imitate or be identical to something else. **2** a single specimen of a book, CD, etc. **3** material ready to be printed and published.

**copy**[2] *v* (**-ies, -ied**) **1** to make a copy of. **2** to imitate. **3** to model oneself on.

**copycat** *n informal* somebody who slavishly copies another.

**copy-edit** *v* (**copy-edited, copy-editing**) to prepare (manuscript copy) for printing by correcting errors and making the style consistent. ➤ **copy editor** *n.*

**copyright**[1] *n* the exclusive right to publish or perform a literary, musical, or artistic work for a fixed period.

**copyright**[2] *v* to secure a copyright on (a literary, musical, or artistic work).

**copywriter** *n* a writer of copy for advertising or publicity. ➤ **copywriting** *n.*

**coquette** *n* a woman who flirts with men. ➤ **coquetry** *n,* **coquettish** *adj.*

**coracle** *n* a small round boat made of waterproof material over a wicker frame.

**coral** *n* a hard substance produced by certain marine invertebrate animals.

**cor anglais** /ˌkawr'ongglay, kawrong'glay/ *n* (*pl* **cors anglais**) a woodwind musical instrument of the oboe family, with a rounded end.

**corbel** *n* a projection from a wall which supports a weight. ➤ **corbelled** *adj.*

**cord** *n* **1** a length of of several strands of thread or yarn woven or twisted together. **2** an electric flex. **3** corduroy. **4** (*in pl*) trousers made of corduroy. ➤ **cordless** *adj.*

**cordial**[1] *adj* **1** warm and affable. **2** sincerely or deeply felt. ➤ **cordiality** *n,* **cordially** *adv.*

**cordial**[2] *n* **1** *Brit* a non-alcoholic sweetened fruit drink. **2** *NAmer* a liqueur.

**cordite** *n* a smokeless explosive.

**cordon**[1] *n* a line of troops, police, preventing access to an area.

**cordon**[2] *v* (+ off) to form a cordon round.

**cordon bleu** /ˌkawdonh 'bluh/ *adj* of cookery: of the highest standard.

**corduroy** *n* a cotton pile fabric with lengthways ribs.

**core**[1] *n* **1** the central part of some fruits. **2** the essential or central part of something.

**core**[2] *v* to remove a core from (fruit).
**co-respondent** *n* a person alleged to have committed adultery with the respondent in a divorce case.
**corgi** *n* (*pl* **corgis**) a dog of a breed with short legs and a fox-like head.
**coriander** *n* a plant of the carrot family with leaves and seeds used in cooking.
**cork**[1] *n* **1** the tough outer tissue of a type of oak tree. **2** a cork stopper for a bottle.
**cork**[2] *v* to fit or close (a bottle) with a cork.
**corker** *n informal* a very good example of a person or thing.
**corkscrew**[1] *n* an implement for removing corks from bottles.
**corkscrew**[2] *v* to move or twist in a spiral.
**corm** *n* a rounded thick underground base of some plants.
**cormorant** *n* a dark-coloured seabird with a long neck and hooked bill.
**corn**[1] *n* **1** *chiefly Brit* the most important cereal crop of a region. **2** *NAmer, Aus, NZ* maize. **3** *informal* something trite or sentimental.
**corn**[2] *n* a painful hardening of the skin on the top of a toe.
**cornea** *n* the transparent membrane covering the iris and pupil of the eye.
**corned beef** *n* beef preserved in brine.
**cornelian** *or* **carnelian** *n* a hard reddish mineral used in jewellery.
**corner**[1] *n* **1** the point or angle where converging lines, edges, or sides meet. **2** the place where two streets or roads meet. **3** in football, a free kick from a corner of the pitch, awarded to the attacking team. **4** the part of a boxing or wrestling ring in which a fighter rests between rounds. **5** a private or remote place. **6** an awkard or difficult situation.
**corner**[2] *v* **1** to drive (a person or animal) into a place of no escape. **2** to detain and talk to (somebody). **3** to gain control of (an economic market) by acquiring a substantial supply of a commodity. **4** to go round a corner in a road.
**cornerstone** *n* **1** a block of stone forming the base of a corner of a building. **2** the most basic part of something.
**cornet** *n* **1** a brass musical instrument resembling a trumpet but shorter. **2** *Brit* an ice cream cone.
**cornflour** *n Brit* ground flour made from maize.
**cornflower** *n* a plant with narrow leaves and blue, purple, or white flowers.
**cornice** *n* an ornamental plaster moulding between the wall and ceiling of a room.
**cornucopia** *n* a plentiful supply or store.
**corny** *adj* (**-ier, -iest**) **1** *informal* sentimental and trite. **2** overused and hackneyed.
**corolla** *n* the petals of a flower.
**corollary** *n* (*pl* **-ies**) **1** a conclusion drawn from a proved proposition. **2** a natural consequence or association.
**corona** *n* (*pl* **coronas** *or* **coronae**) **1** a coloured circle of light seen round the sun, the moon, or a star. **2** the outermost part of the atmosphere of the sun and other stars.
**coronary**[1] *adj* relating to the arteries and veins that supply the heart with blood.
**coronary**[2] *or* **coronary thrombosis** *n* (*pl* **coronaries** *or* **coronary thromboses**) a blockage in an artery of the heart.
**coronation** *n* the ceremony of crowning a sovereign.
**coroner** *n* a public officer who enquires into the cause of a sudden or suspicious death.
**coronet** *n* **1** a small crown. **2** an ornamental wreath or band for the head.
**corpora** *n* pl of CORPUS.
**corporal**[1] *n* a non-commissioned army officer ranking below sergeant.
**corporal**[2] *adj* of or affecting the body.
**corporal punishment** *n* physical punishment, e.g. caning.
**corporate** *adj* **1** relating to companies or businesses. **2** of or belonging to a body of individuals.
**corporation** *n* **1** a body of people authorized to act as a single person with its own legal identity. **2** (*treated as sing. or pl*) the municipal authorities of a British town or city.
**corporeal** *adj* **1** relating to a physical material body; not spiritual. **2** not immaterial or intangible; substantial.
**corps** *n* (*pl* **corps**) **1** an army unit consisting of two or more divisions organized for a particular purpose. **2** a body of people engaged in a specific activity.
**corpse**[1] *n* a dead body, *esp* a dead human body.
**corpse**[2] *v informal* to stifle laughter with difficulty, e.g. on a solemn occasion or while acting in a play.
**corpulent** *adj* excessively fat; obese. ➤ **corpulence** *n.*
**corpus** *n* (*pl* **corpora** *or* **corpuses**) a collection of writings or texts.
**corpuscle** *n* a blood cell.
**corral**[1] *n NAmer* an enclosure for livestock.
**corral**[2] *v* (**corralled, corralling**) *chiefly NAmer* to enclose (livestock) in a corral.
**correct**[1] *adj* **1** true or right. **2** conforming to an accepted standard or to an ideology. ➤ **correctly** *adv*, **correctness** *n.*
**correct**[2] *v* **1** to make or set right. **2** to alter so as to remove an error or imperfection. **3** to point out the faults in.
**correction** *n* **1** the process of correcting. **2** a change made in order to correct something. **3** punishment.
**corrective** *adj* intended to correct.

**correlate** *v* **1** to relate to and affect one another. **2** to bring together for comparison.
**correlation** *n* **1** a relationship between things having a mutual effect. **2** the act or an instance of correlating two things.
**correspond** *v* **1** to conform or be compatible. **2** to be equivalent or similar. **3** to communicate by exchanging letters.
**correspondence** *n* **1** letters, or communication by letter. **2** agreement or similarity.
**correspondence course** *n* a course of study in which students send and receive material by post.
**correspondent** *n* **1** a person who communicates by letter. **2** a newspaper or broadcasting journalist who reports on a particular subject.
**corridor** *n* **1** a passage with doors leading into rooms. **2** a strip of land through foreign-held territory. **3** a restricted path for air traffic.
**corroborate** *v* to support (a claim or an opinion) with evidence or authority. ➤ **corroboration** *n*, **corroborative** *adj*.
**corrode** *v* **1** to eat or wear away (metal) by chemical action. **2** to weaken or destroy gradually. ➤ **corrosion** *n*.
**corrosive**[1] *adj* **1** causing corrosion. **2** harmful or destructive.
**corrosive**[2] *n* a substance that causes corrosion.
**corrugate** *v* to fold into ridges and grooves. ➤ **corrugated** *adj*, **corrugation** *n*.
**corrupt**[1] *adj* **1** open to or characterized by bribery or other improper conduct. **2** morally degenerate. **3** of computer data: damaged and unusable. **4** of a text: containing errors. ➤ **corruptly** *adv*.
**corrupt**[2] *v* to make corrupt. ➤ **corruptible** *adj*.
**corruption** *n* **1** the process of corrupting. **2** improper or immoral conduct.
**corsage** *n* a small posy of flowers pinned to a woman's dress.
**corset** *n* a supporting undergarment for the middle part of a woman's body.
**cortège** *or* **cortege** *n* a funeral procession.
**cortex** *n* (*pl* **cortices**) the outer part of an organ of the body, *esp* of the brain.
**coruscate** *v literary* to flash or sparkle. ➤ **coruscating** *adj*.
**corvette** *n* a small armed escort ship.
**cos** *abbr* cosine.
**cosh**[1] *n Brit* a short heavy stick used as a weapon.
**cosh**[2] *v Brit* to hit with a cosh.
**cosine** *n* in mathematics, the ratio in a right-angled triangle between the side adjacent to a particular angle and the hypotenuse.
**cos lettuce** *n* a crisp variety of lettuce with long leaves.
**cosmetic**[1] *n* a preparation designed to be applied to the skin or hair to improve its appearance or texture.
**cosmetic**[2] *adj* **1** intended to improve beauty, e.g. of the hair or complexion. **2** affecting or improving something superficially without substantial change. ➤ **cosmetically** *adv*.
**cosmic** *adj* relating to the universe.
**cosmonaut** *n* a Russian astronaut.
**cosmopolitan** *adj* **1** composed of people or elements from many parts of the world. **2** having worldwide rather than provincial scope or bearing.
**cosmos** *n* the universe as an orderly system.
**Cossack** *n* a member of a people of South Russia and the Ukraine famous for skilful horseriding.
**cosset** *v* (**cosseted, cosseting**) to treat (a person or animal) in an excessively protective way.
**cost**[1] *n* **1** the price paid or charged for something. **2** the expenditure of effort or sacrifice made to achieve something. **3** the loss or penalty incurred in gaining something. **4** (*in pl*) legal expenses. ✱ **at all costs** regardless of the price or difficulties.
**cost**[2] *v* (*past tense and past part.* cost) **1** to have a price of (a specified amount). **2** to cause (somebody) to suffer or lose something. **3** (*past tense and past part.* costed) to estimate or set the cost of.
**co-star**[1] *n* a performer who has equal billing with another performer in a film or play.
**co-star**[2] *v* (**co-starred, co-starring**) **1** to appear as a co-star in a film or play. **2** to feature (an actor) as a co-star.
**cost-effective** *adj* economically worthwhile.
**costermonger** *n Brit, dated* a person who sells fruit or vegetables from a street barrow or stall.
**costly** *adj* (**-ier, -iest**) **1** expensive or valuable. **2** achieved with considerable sacrifice.
**costume**[1] *n* a set of clothing belonging to a specific time, place, or character.
**costume**[2] *v* to provide with a costume.
**costume jewellery** *n* inexpensive imitation jewellery.
**costumier** (*NAmer* **costumer**) *n* a person who deals in or makes costumes, e.g. for theatrical productions.
**cosy**[1] (*NAmer* **cozy**) *adj* (**-ier, -iest**) **1** affording warmth and comfort; snug. **2** *informal* suggesting close association or connivance. ➤ **cosily** *adv*, **cosiness** *n*.
**cosy**[2] (*NAmer* **cozy**) *n* (*pl* **-ies**) a cover for a teapot or boiled egg, to keep it hot.
**cosy up** (*NAmer* **cozy up**) *v* (**-ies, -ied**) *informal* (*usu* + to) to seek friendship or intimacy in a self-serving way.
**cot** *n Brit* a small bed for a baby or young child, with high sides of vertical bars.
**cot death** *n Brit* the unexplained death of a baby while asleep.
**coterie** *n* a small exclusive group of people.
**cottage** *n* a small house in the country.
**cottage cheese** *n* a soft white cheese made from the curds of skimmed milk.

**cotter pin** *n* a pin for fastening parts of a mechanism together.
**cotton** *n* **1** a soft white fibrous substance surrounding the seeds of a tropical plant. **2** yarn or fabric made of cotton.
**cotton wool** *n* **1** *Brit* fluffy soft material in balls or pads, used for cleaning the skin. **2** *NAmer* raw cotton.
**cotyledon** *n* the first leaf developed by the embryo of a seed plant.
**couch**[1] *n* a long upholstered piece of furniture for sitting or lying on.
**couch**[2] *v* to phrase in a specified manner.
**couch potato** *n informal* somebody who watches a lot of television.
**cougar** *n NAmer* a puma.
**cough**[1] *v* **1** to expel air from the lungs with an explosive noise. **2** *Brit, informal* to reveal information.
**cough**[2] *n* **1** an act or sound of coughing. **2** a condition marked by repeated or frequent coughing. ➤ **cougher** *n.*
**cough mixture** *n Brit* a medicated liquid used to relieve coughing.
**cough up** *v* **1** to expel (mucus) by coughing. **2** *informal* to produce or hand over (money or information) unwillingly.
**could** *v aux* the past tense of CAN[1].
**couldn't** *contraction* could not.
**coulomb** *n* the SI unit of electric charge.
**council** *n* **1** an elected or appointed body with administrative or legislative powers. **2** a locally elected body administering a city, county, or district.
**council house** *n* a house rented to tenants by a local council.
**councillor** (*NAmer* **councilor**) *n* a member of a council. ➤ **councillorship** *n.*

***Usage Note:*** Do not confuse this word with *counsellor.*

**counsel**[1] *n* **1** formal or personal advice. **2** a barrister or other lawyer engaged in a court case.
**counsel**[2] *v* (**counselled, counselling,** *NAmer* **counseled, counseling**) **1** to advise. **2** to give (somebody) help with psychological or personal problems. ➤ **counselling** *n.*
**counsellor** (*NAmer* **counselor**) *n* **1** a person who gives professional advice or guidance. **2** *NAmer* a barrister.

***Usage Note:*** Do not confuse this word with *councillor.*

**count**[1] *v* **1** to find the total number of. **2** to name the numbers in order. **3** to include in a reckoning. **4** to think of (somebody or something) as having a particular quality or function. **5** (+ in/out) to include or exclude. **6** to have value or importance. ✱ **count on 1** to look forward to (something) as certain. **2** to rely on (somebody).
**count**[2] *n* **1** the act of counting. **2** a total obtained by counting. **3** in law, a charge in an indictment. **4** a specific point under consideration; an issue. ✱ **out for the count 1** in boxing, knocked down and unable to rise again during a count of ten. **2** *informal* unconscious or deeply asleep.
**count**[3] *n* a European nobleman.
**countdown** *n* a continuous count down to zero of the time remaining before an event.
**countenance**[1] *n* a person's face as an indication of mood or character.
**countenance**[2] *v* to allow or tolerate.
**counter**[1] *n* **1** a level surface over which goods are sold or food is served. **2** a small disc used in counting or in board games. **3** a person or machine that counts. ✱ **under the counter** obtained by illegal or surreptitious means.
**counter**[2] *v* **1** to act in opposition to; to oppose. **2** to challenge attacks or arguments.
**counter**[3] *adv* (+ to) in an opposite direction.
**counteract** *v* to lessen or neutralize the ill effects of. ➤ **counteractive** *adj.*
**counterattack**[1] *or* **counter-attack** *n* an attack made in reply to an attack.
**counterattack**[2] *or* **counter-attack** *v* to make a counterattack.
**counterbalance**[1] *n* **1** a weight that balances another. **2** a force or influence that offsets or checks an opposing force.
**counterbalance**[2] *v* to oppose or balance with an equal weight or force.
**counterespionage** *or* **counter-espionage** *n* activities directed towards detecting and thwarting enemy espionage.
**counterfeit**[1] *adj* made in imitation of something with intent to deceive or defraud.
**counterfeit**[2] *n* a forgery.
**counterfeit**[3] *v* to imitate or copy fraudulently.
**counterfoil** *n chiefly Brit* the part of a cheque, ticket, etc that is kept as a record or receipt.
**counterintelligence** *or* **counter-intelligence** *n* activity designed to block an enemy's sources of information; counterespionage.
**countermand** *v* to revoke (a command) by a contrary order.
**countermeasure** *n* a measure designed to counter a danger or difficulty.
**counterpane** *n* a bedspread.
**counterpart** *n* a person or thing with the same function or characteristics as another.
**counterpoint** *n* **1** the combination of two or more independent melodies into a single harmonic texture. **2** one or more independent melodies added above or below a given melody.
**counterproductive** *adj* having effects opposite to those intended.
**countersign** *v* to add a signature to (a docu-

ment) as a witness to another signature. ➤ **countersignature** *n.*

**countersink** *v* (*past tense and past part.* **countersunk**) **1** to enlarge the exposed surface of (a hole) so that the head of a bolt or screw will fit into it. **2** to set the head of (a bolt or screw) into the surface.

**countertenor** *n* a male singer having a voice higher than tenor.

**countervail** *v* to counterbalance the effect of; to offset.

**countess** *n* **1** the wife or widow of an earl or count. **2** a woman who has the rank of earl or count in her own right.

**countless** *adj* too numerous to be counted; innumerable.

**countrified** *or* **countryfied** *adj* rural in style or manner.

**country** *n* (*pl* **-ies**) **1** a political state or nation or its territory. **2** rural as opposed to urban areas. **3** an expanse of land. * **go to the country** *Brit* to hold a general election.

**country music** *n* folk music of the southern USA.

**countryside** *n* a rural area.

**county** *n* (*pl* **-ies**) each of the principal territorial divisions of Britain and some other countries or states for administrative purposes.

**county town** *n Brit* the administrative centre of a county.

**coup** /kooh/ *n* (*pl* **coups**) **1** (*also* **coup d'état** /koohday'tah/) the violent overthrow of a government from within a country. **2** a sudden brilliant stroke or act.

**coupe** *n* a dessert of fruit and ice cream served in a shallow dish.

**coupé** *n* a two-door car with a fixed roof and a sloping rear.

**couple**[1] *n* **1** two things considered together; a pair. **2** two people who are married or living together. **3** *informal* an indefinite small number; a few. **4** in mechanics, two forces that together cause rotation.

**couple**[2] *v* **1** to link or fasten. **2** to copulate.

**couplet** *n* a unit of two successive rhyming lines of verse.

**coupling** *n* a device that connects adjacent parts or objects, e.g. electrical circuits or railway carriages.

**coupon** *n* **1** a voucher that entitles the holder to a discount or other benefit. **2** a part of a printed advertisement that can be cut out and filled in to make an enquiry or enter a competition.

**courage** *n* mental or moral strength to confront danger, suffering, or difficulty.

**courageous** *adj* having or showing courage; brave. ➤ **courageously** *adv.*

**courgette** *n Brit* a variety of small vegetable marrow used as a vegetable.

**courier** *n* **1** a person who collects and delivers parcels and documents. **2** a person employed to assist tourists abroad.

**course**[1] *n* **1** the path over which something moves. **2** a movement or progression in space or time. **3** the direction of travel of an aircraft. **4** the usual procedure or normal action of something. **5** a chosen manner of conducting oneself; a plan of action. **6** a series of lessons or lectures relating to a subject. **7** a part of a meal served at one time. **8** a medical treatment administered over a period. **9** an area of land marked out for a sport, e.g. golf or racing. **10** a layer of brick or masonry in a wall.

**course**[2] *v* **1** of a liquid: to run or flow. **2** to hunt or pursue (hares) with dogs.

**court**[1] *n* **1** an official assembly of people authorized to hear judicial cases. **2** a place in which such a court is held. **3** a space marked off for playing tennis or other ball games. **4** a space enclosed by buildings. **5** the residence or the family and retinue of a sovereign.

**court**[2] *v* **1** *dated* to seek the affections of; to woo. **2** to seek to win the favour or support of. **3** to act in a way that provokes (a bad outcome).

**court card** *n Brit* a king, queen, or jack in a pack of cards.

**courteous** *adj* showing respect and consideration; polite. ➤ **courteously** *adv.*

**courtesan** *n* a prostitute with wealthy or upper-class clients.

**courtesy** *n* (*pl* **-ies**) **1** polite and courteous behaviour. **2** a courteous act or expression. * **by courtesy of** through the generosity or permission of.

**courtier** *n* an attendant or companion to a king or queen.

**courtly** *adj* (**-ier, -iest**) elegant and refined.

**court-martial**[1] *n* (*pl* **courts-martial** *or* **court-martials**) **1** a court that tries members of the armed forces. **2** a trial by such a court.

**court-martial**[2] *v* (**court-martialled, court-martialling,** *NAmer* **court-martialed, court-martialing**) to try by court-martial.

**courtship** *n* **1** a period of courting. **2** the courting rituals of animals. **3** the process of courting favour.

**court shoe** *n Brit* a plain woman's shoe with high heels and no fastenings.

**couscous** *n* a North African dish of steamed ground wheat.

**cousin** *n* a child of one's uncle or aunt.

**couture** *n* the business of designing and making fashionable custom-made women's clothing.

**couturier** *or* **couturière** *n* a person who makes and sells couture clothes.

**cove** *n* a small sheltered inlet or bay.

**coven** *n* a group or gathering of witches.

**covenant** *n* **1** a formal agreement or contract. **2** an agreement to make regular payments to a charity.

**cover**[1] *v* **1** to place or set something over (a thing) to conceal or protect it. **2** to lie or spread over. **3** to extend thickly or conspicuously over the surface of. **4** to hide from sight or knowledge. **5** to travel (a specified distance). **6** of an amount of money: to be enough to pay for. **7** to include or take into account. **8** to report news about. **9** to have as one's field of activity. **10** to insure or provide protection against (a risk or contingency). **11** to protect (somebody) by being in a position to fire at an attacker. **12** of a male animal: to copulate with (a female animal). **13** to record a cover version of (a song). **14** (+ for) to act as a substitute for. * **cover one's tracks** to conceal evidence of one's past actions. ➤ **covering** *n.*

**cover**[2] *n* **1** something put over to conceal or give protection. **2** a jacket for a book. **3** natural shelter for an animal. **4** shelter or protection from attack. **5** a pretext or disguise. **6** *Brit* protection under an insurance policy. **7** a place setting in a restaurant. **8** (*also* **cover version**) a new version of a pop song previously recorded by another performer. * **break cover** to leave shelter and face pursuit.

**coverage** *n* **1** an area or amount covered. **2** inclusion within the scope of something.

**cover charge** *n* a charge for service in a restaurant.

**covering letter** *n* a letter explaining an enclosed item.

**coverlet** *n* a bedspread.

**covert**[1] *adj* not openly shown or acknowledged; secret. ➤ **covertly** *adv.*

**covert**[2] *n* a thicket providing cover for game.

**cover-up** *n* an attempt to conceal an error or a crime.

**covet** *v* (**coveted, coveting**) to long to have (something that belongs to somebody else). ➤ **covetous** *adj.*

**covey** *n* (*pl* **-eys**) a small flock of game birds.

**cow**[1] *n* **1** the mature female animal of domestic cattle. **2** a mature female of other large animals. **3** *informal* an unpleasant woman. * **till the cows come home** for ever.

**cow**[2] *v* to intimidate with threats or a show of strength.

**coward** *n* somebody who lacks courage or resolve. ➤ **cowardice** *n,* **cowardly** *adj.*

**cowboy** *n* **1** a man on horseback who herds cattle in North America. **2** *informal* an incompetent or dishonest trader.

**cower** *v* to crouch down or shrink away in fear.

**cowl** *n* **1** a monk's hood or long hooded cloak. **2** a chimney covering designed to improve ventilation. **3** a cowling.

**cowling** *n* a removable metal covering over an engine.

**cowrie** *or* **cowry** *n* (*pl* **-ies**) a sea mollusc with a glossy shell.

**cowslip** *n* a plant of the primrose family with fragrant yellow flowers.

**cox**[1] *n* a person who steers a racing boat and directs the rowers.

**cox**[2] *v* to be cox of (a boat).

**coxcomb** *n archaic* a conceited foolish person.

**coxswain** *n* **1** a cox of a racing rowing boat. **2** a sailor who commands a ship's boat.

**coy** *adj* **1** self-consciously shy or unassuming. **2** provocatively playful or coquettish. **3** showing reluctance to reveal details of a sensitive issue. ➤ **coyly** *adv.*

**coyote** *n* (*pl* **coyotes** *or* **coyote**) a wolflike wild dog of North America.

**coypu** *n* (*pl* **coypus** *or* **coypu**) a South American rodent like a beaver.

**cozy**[1] *adj NAmer* see COSY[1].

**cozy**[2] *n NAmer* see COSY[2].

**Cr** *abbr* the chemical symbol for chromium.

**crab** *n* a sea crustacean with a broad flat shell and pincers at the front.

**crab apple** *n* a small wild sour apple.

**crabbed** *adj* **1** of writing: difficult to read or understand. **2** morose or peevish.

**crabby** *adj* (**-ier, -iest**) bad-tempered.

**crack**[1] *v* **1** to make or cause (something) to make a sudden sharp noise. **2** to break or split without coming apart. **3** to break (something) with a crack. **4** to tell (a joke). **5** to work out (a code or mystery). **6** to break into (a safe). **7** of the voice: to change pitch suddenly. **8** to collapse emotionally under stress.

**crack**[2] *n* **1** a sudden sharp loud noise. **2** a narrow opening where something has split or broken. **3** a sharp resounding blow. **4** *informal* a witty remark. **5** *informal* an attempt at something. **6** (*also* **crack cocaine**) *informal* a strong and addictive variety of cocaine.

**crack**[3] *adj informal* very able or skilled: *a crack shot.*

**crackdown** *n informal* a period of harsh treatment of bad behaviour or wrongdoing.

**crack down** *v informal* (+ on) to deal harshly with.

**cracker** *n* **1** a paper tube that makes a cracking noise when pulled sharply apart and contains a toy and a paper hat. **2** a firecracker. **3** a thin savoury biscuit. **4** *Brit, informal* something or somebody exceptional.

**crackers** *adj chiefly Brit, informal* mad or eccentric.

**cracking** *adv informal, dated* exceptionally good or fast.

**crackle**[1] *v* to make a series of small cracking noises.

**crackle**[2] *n* a crackling noise. ➤ **crackly** *adj.*

**crackling** *n* the crisp skin of roast pork.

**crackpot** *n informal* a crazy or eccentric person.

**crack up** *v informal* **1** to suffer an emotional breakdown. **2** to laugh uncontrollably.

**cradle**[1] *n* **1** a baby's bed or cot on rockers. **2** a supporting framework of wood or metal. **3** a place where something important originates.

**cradle**[2] *v* to shelter or hold protectively.

**craft**[1] *n* **1** an activity or trade requiring manual dexterity or artistic skill. **2** skill in making or executing something; dexterity. **3** (*pl* **craft** *or* **crafts**) a boat, ship, aircraft, or spacecraft. **4** skill in deception.

**craft**[2] *v* to make using skill and dexterity.

**craftsman** *or* **craftswoman** *n* (*pl* **craftsmen** *or* **craftswomen**) a man or woman who practises a skilled craft. ➤ **craftsmanship** *n.*

**crafty** *adj* (**-ier, -iest**) showing subtlety and guile. ➤ **craftily** *adv.*

**crag** *n* a steep rugged rock or cliff.

**cram** *v* (**crammed, cramming**) **1** to pack or jam (a container) tight. **2** (+ in/into) to thrust forcefully into something. **3** *informal* to eat voraciously. **4** to study intensively for an examination.

**crammer** *n Brit, informal* a school that prepares students intensively for an examination.

**cramp**[1] *n* **1** a painful spasmodic contraction of a muscle. **2** (*in pl*) severe abdominal pain.

**cramp**[2] *n* a device used to hold timbers or blocks of stone together.

**cramp**[3] *v* **1** to affect with cramp. **2** to confine or restrain.

**cramped** *adj* **1** too small or crowded for comfort. **2** of handwriting: small and hard to read.

**crampon** *n* a spiked metal frame fitted to a boot for climbing on ice or hard snow.

**cranberry** *n* (*pl* **-ies**) a sour red berry used in sauces and jellies.

**crane**[1] *n* **1** a machine with a swinging arm or a hoisting apparatus, used for moving heavy weights. **2** a tall wading bird.

**crane**[2] *v* to stretch (the neck) in order to see better.

**crane fly** *n* a fly with wide wings and long legs.

**cranium** *n* (*pl* **craniums** *or* **crania**) the part of the skull that encloses the brain. ➤ **cranial** *adj.*

**crank**[1] *n* **1** a part of an axle or shaft bent at right angles to convert back-and-forth motion into circular motion. **2** an eccentric person.

**crank**[2] *v* **1** (*often* + up) to turn a crank, or to start (an engine) using a crank. **2** (+ up) to increase in intensity.

**crankshaft** *n* a shaft driven by a crank.

**cranky** *adj* (**-ier, -iest**) **1** *informal* odd or eccentric. **2** *NAmer* bad-tempered.

**cranny** *n* (*pl* **-ies**) a small crack or slit.

**crap**[1] *n coarse slang* **1** excrement. **2** nonsense; rubbish.

**crap**[2] *v* (**crapped, crapping**) *coarse slang* to defecate.

**crap**[3] *adj coarse slang* of poor quality.

**crape** *n* black artificial silk, formerly used for mourning clothes.

**craps** *pl n* (*treated as sing. or pl*) a gambling game played with two dice.

**crash**[1] *v* **1** to break or smash violently and noisily. **2** to make or cause to make a crashing sound. **3** to damage (a vehicle or aircraft) in a collision. **4** of a vehicle or aircraft: to collide with another vehicle or the ground and be damaged. **5** to move or force (one's way) somewhere noisily. **6** of a computer system: to fail and become inoperative. **7** of shares: to fall suddenly in value. **8** *informal* to enter (a party, etc) without being invited. **9** *informal* (*also* + out) to go to sleep.

**crash**[2] *n* **1** a loud noise. **2** the noise of things smashing. **3** the act of crashing; a violent collision. **4** a sudden decline or failure.

**crash**[3] *adj* designed to achieve a rapid result: *a crash diet.*

**crash helmet** *n* a padded helmet worn to protect the head.

**crash-land** *v* of an aircraft: to land clumsily in an emergency.

**crass** *adj* insensitive and coarse. ➤ **crassly** *adv.*

**crate**[1] *n* **1** a wooden framework or box for holding or transporting goods. **2** *informal* an old dilapidated vehicle.

**crate**[2] *v* to pack in a crate.

**crater** *n* a bowl-shaped depression in the ground caused by an impact or explosion or forming the mouth of a volcano.

**cravat** *n* a decorative band worn round the neck by men.

**crave** *v* **1** to have a strong desire for. **2** *formal* to ask for.

**craven** *adj* cowardly. ➤ **cravenly** *adv.*

**craving** *n* a strong desire or longing.

**craw** *n* the crop of a bird or insect.

**crawl**[1] *v* **1** to move slowly on hands and knees. **2** to move or progress slowly or laboriously. **3** to be swarming with creeping or unwelcome things. **4** of the skin: to have an unpleasant sensation as of insects crawling over it. **5** *informal* (*often* + to) to behave obsequiously.

**crawl**[2] *n* **1** the act or an instance of crawling. **2** slow or laborious motion. **3** a swimming stroke performed with alternating overarm strokes while kicking the legs.

**crayfish** *n* (*pl* **crayfish** *or* **crayfishes**) a freshwater crustacean like a small lobster.

**crayon**[1] *n* a stick of coloured chalk or wax used for drawing.

**crayon**[2] *v* to draw with a crayon.

**craze** *n* a short-lived popular enthusiasm; a fad.

**crazed** *adj* **1** mad or crazy. **2** having a mesh of fine cracks.

**crazy** *adj* (**-ier, -iest**) *informal* **1** insane or eccentric. **2** foolish or impractical. **3** (+ about) very fond of or enthusiastic about. ➤ **crazily** *adv,* **craziness** *n.*

**crazy paving** *n* a paved surface of irregular flat stones.
**creak**[1] *v* to make a grating or squeaking noise.
**creak**[2] *n* a creaking sound. ➤ **creaky** *adj.*
**cream**[1] *n* **1** the thick yellowish part of milk which forms a surface layer when milk is allowed to stand. **2** a food prepared with or resembling cream. **3** a biscuit, chocolate, etc filled with whipped cream or a soft preparation resembling it. **4** a thick liquid cosmetic applied to the skin. **5** (**the cream**) (+ of) the best part or members of a group. **6** a pale yellowish white colour. ➤ **creamy** *adj.*
**cream**[2] *v* **1** to prepare (food) with a cream sauce. **2** to mash (vegetables) with added milk or cream. **3** to work or blend (butter and sugar) to the consistency of cream. **4** (*also* + off) to take (the best part of something).
**cream cheese** *n* a mild soft cheese.
**creamery** *n* (*pl* **-ies**) an establishment where butter and cheese are made.
**crease**[1] *n* **1** a ridge or line made in fabric, paper, etc by crushing or folding. **2** a line marked on a cricket pitch.
**crease**[2] *v* **1** to make creases in (cloth or paper). **2** to become creased. **3** *chiefly Brit, informal* (*often* + up) to double up with laughter.
**create** *v* **1** to bring into existence. **2** to produce or cause. **3** to invest (somebody) with a new form or rank. **4** *Brit, informal* to make a loud fuss.
**creation** *n* **1** something created. **2** an original work of art. **3** the world. **4** (**the Creation**) the act of making the universe.
**creative** *adj* **1** showing the ability or power to create. **2** having the quality of something imaginatively created. ➤ **creatively** *adv,* **creativeness** *n,* **creativity** *n.*
**creator** *n* **1** a person who creates something. **2** (**the Creator**) God.
**creature** *n* an animate being, *esp* a non-human one.
**creature comforts** *pl n* material things that provide comfort.
**crèche** *n Brit* a centre where young children are looked after while their parents are at work.
**credence** *n* acceptance of something as true or real.
**credential** *n* (*usu in pl*) a letter or other document that gives proof of identity or status.
**credible** *adj* able to be believed; likely or reasonable. ➤ **credibly** *adv.*

***Usage Note:*** Do not confuse this word with *creditable.*

**credit**[1] *n* **1** a source of honour or repute. **2** acknowledgment or approval. **3** influence derived from enjoying the confidence of others; standing. **4** the balance in a person's favour in an account. **5** an amount or sum placed at a person's disposal by a bank and usu to be repaid with interest. **6** time given for payment for goods or services. **7** an entry in an account recording money received. **8** (*usu in pl*) an acknowledgment of a contributor at the beginning or end of a film or television programme. **9** recognition that a student has fulfilled a course requirement. ✱ **in credit** having money avaiable for use. **on credit** with the cost charged to an account and paid later.
**credit**[2] *v* (**credited, crediting**) **1** to believe (something). **2** to place an amount to the credit of (an account). **3** (+ with) to ascribe favourable characteristics to. **4** (+ to) to attribute (e.g. an invention, a saying, etc) to.
**creditable** *adj* deserving acknowledgment even if not successful. ➤ **creditably***adv.*

***Usage Note:*** Do not confuse this word with *credible.*

**credit card** *n* a card allowing the holder to obtain goods and services on credit.
**creditor** *n* a person to whom a debt is owed.
**credo** *n* (*pl* **-os**) a statement of beliefs.
**credulous** *adj* too ready to believe. ➤ **credulity** *n,* **credulously** *adv.*
**creed** *n* **1** a set of religious beliefs. **2** a tenet or set of tenets. **3** a statement of beliefs.
**creek** *n* **1** a small narrow inlet of a lake or sea. **2** *NAmer* a stream or brook. ✱ **up the creek** *informal* in bad trouble.
**creel** *n* a basket for newly caught fish.
**creep**[1] *v* (*past tense and past part.* **crept**) **1** to move along with the body close to the ground. **2** to go very slowly. **3** to move cautiously or quietly. **4** *informal* to behave in a servile manner.
**creep**[2] *n* **1** a creeping movement. **2** *Brit, informal* an ingratiatingly servile or unlikeable person. ✱ **give one the creeps** *informal* to unnerve or disgust one.
**creeper** *n* a plant growing along a surface.
**creepy** *adj* (**-ier, -iest**) **1** producing a sensation of fear or apprehension. **2** *informal* slightly sinister or unpleasant.
**cremate** *v* to reduce (a dead body) to ashes by burning. ➤ **cremation** *n.*
**crematorium** *n* (*pl* **crematoriums** *or* **crematoria**) a place where dead bodies are cremated.
**crème de la crème** /ˌkrem də lah ˈkrem/ *n* (the crème de la crème) the very best or most exclusive.
**crenellation** *n* an indentation in a battlement.
**Creole** *n* **1** a person of European descent in the West Indies or Spanish America. **2** a descendant of French or Spanish settlers in the USA. **3** a person of mixed French or Spanish and black descent. **4** (**creole**) a language based on a combination of an African and a European language.
**creosote** *n* a brownish oily liquid obtained from coal tar and used as a wood preservative.

**crepe** *or* **crêpe** *n* **1** (*also* crape) a light crinkled fabric. **2** a thin pancake.
**crept** *v* past tense and past part. of CREEP[1].
**crepuscular** *adj formal* relating to or resembling twilight.
**crescendo** *n* (*pl* **crescendos** *or* **crescendi**) a gradual increase in volume in a musical passage.
**crescent** *n* **1** a narrow rounded shape coming to a point at each end. **2** *Brit* a curved street.
**cress** *n* a plant with mildly pungent leaves, used in salads.
**crest**[1] *n* **1** a showy tuft or projection on the head of a bird or other animal. **2** a plume on a helmet. **3** a symbol of a family or organization above the shield in a coat of arms. **4** the ridge or top of a wave, roof, or mountain. ➤ **crested** *adj.*
**crest**[2] *v* to reach the crest of (a hill, ridge, wave, etc).
**crestfallen** *adj* disheartened or dejected.
**cretin** *n* a foolish person. ➤ **cretinous** *adj.*
**crevasse** *n* a deep wide crack in a glacier.
**crevice** *n* a narrow opening resulting from a split or crack.
**crew**[1] *n* **1** the personnel of a ship or boat, excluding the captain and officers. **2** the people who work on an aircraft or train. **3** a number of people working together.
**crew**[2] *v chiefly Brit* past tense of CROW[2].
**crew**[3] *v* **1** to serve as a member of a crew on (a ship, aircraft, etc). **2** to provide with a crew.
**crew cut** *n* a short bristly haircut.
**crew neck** *n* a round neckline on a knitted pullover.
**crib**[1] *n* **1** *chiefly NAmer* a child's cot. **2** a cattle stall. **3** a manger or rack for animal fodder. **4** a literal translation of a text used by students. **5** the card game cribbage.
**crib**[2] *v* (**cribbed, cribbing**) to copy (somebody else's work) dishonestly.
**cribbage** *n* a card game for two to four players.
**crick**[1] *n* a painful stiff feeling in the muscles of the neck or back.
**crick**[2] *v* to cause a crick in (the neck or back).
**cricket**[1] *n* a team game played with a bat and ball on a large field with two wickets near its centre. ➤ **cricketer** *n.*
**cricket**[2] *n* a leaping insect noted for the chirping sounds produced by the male.
**cried** *v* past tense and past part. of CRY[1].
**crime** *n* **1** a violation of a law. **2** a grave offence against morality. **3** criminal activity. **4** *informal* something deplorable or disgraceful.
**criminal**[1] *adj* **1** relating to or guilty of a crime. **2** *informal* disgraceful. ➤ **criminality** *n,* **criminally** *adv.*
**criminal**[2] *n* a person who has committed or been convicted of a crime.
**crimp** *v* **1** to make (the hair) wavy or curly. **2** to pinch or press (material) together to seal or join it.
**crimson** *n* a deep purplish red colour.
**cringe** *v* **1** to shrink or cower in fear. **2** to feel acute embarrassment.
**crinkle**[1] *v* **1** to wrinkle. **2** to cause (something) to crinkle.
**crinkle**[2] *n* a small wrinkle. ➤ **crinkly** *adj.*
**crinoline** *n* a full skirt or hooped petticoat formerly worn by women.
**cripple**[1] *n offensive* a lame or partly disabled person.
**cripple**[2] *v* **1** to make (somebody) a cripple. **2** to impair mentally or emotionally. **3** to hamper or severely limit (a person, operation, etc).
**crisis** *n* (*pl* **crises**) **1** a time of acute difficulty or danger. **2** the turning point in an acute disease.
**crisp**[1] *adj* **1** brittle or easily crumbled. **2** desirably firm and fresh. **3** decisive or sharp in manner. **4** of the weather: cold and fresh. ➤ **crisply** *adv.*
**crisp**[2] *n Brit* a thin slice of fried potato.
**crispbread** *n* a plain dry biscuit made from rye or other grain.
**crisscross**[1] *adj* marked with a pattern or network of intersecting lines.
**crisscross**[2] *v* **1** to pass back and forth across. **2** to mark with intersecting lines.
**criterion** *n* (*pl* **criteria** *or* **criterions**) a standard on which a judgment may be based.

***Usage Note:*** Note that *criteria* is the plural form: *these criteria not this criteria.*

**critic** *n* **1** a person who evaluates works of art, literature, or music. **2** a person who tends to judge harshly.
**critical** *adj* **1** inclined to criticize severely. **2** consisting of or involving criticism. **3** involving careful evaluation. **4** crucial or decisive. **5** in a state of crisis or danger. ➤ **critically** *adv.*
**criticism** *n* **1** an instance of criticizing or disapproving. **2** a critical observation or remark. **3** a detailed or reasoned assessment; a critique.
**criticize** *or* **-ise** *v* **1** to find fault with. **2** to evaluate (a literary or artistic work).
**critique** *n* a critical estimate or discussion.
**croak** *v* **1** to give the cry of a frog or crow. **2** to speak in a hoarse voice. **3** *informal* to die. ➤ **croak** *n,* **croaky** *adj.*
**crochet**[1] *n* the art of making designs by drawing a yarn or thread into a pattern of interlocked loops using a hooked needle.
**crochet**[2] *v* (**crocheted, crocheting**) to make (a garment or design) by crochet.
**crock**[1] *n Brit, informal* **1** an elderly infirm person. **2** an old broken-down vehicle.
**crock**[2] *n* a thick earthenware pot or jar.
**crock**[3] *v informal* **1** (*also* + up) to injure, weaken, or disable (somebody or something): *I've crocked my back.* **2** *NAmer* to make (somebody)

drunk: *The man was crocked.* **3** *informal* (*also* + up) to break down; to collapse.

**crockery** *n* earthenware or china tableware.

**crocodile** *n* **1** a large reptile with a thick skin, long jaws, and a long body with a tail. **2** *Brit* a line of people or schoolchildren walking in pairs.

**crocodile tears** *pl n* insincere or affected sorrow.

**crocus** *n* (*pl* **crocuses** *or* **croci**) a spring plant with a single brightly-coloured flower.

**croft** *n* a small farm, *esp* in Scotland, worked by a tenant. ➤ **crofter** *n.*

**croissant** *n* a flaky crescent-shaped roll.

**crone** *n* a withered old woman.

**crook**[1] *n* **1** an implement having a bent or hooked shape. **2** a shepherd's staff or bishop's crozier. **3** a bend or curve. **4** *informal* a criminal.

**crook**[2] *v* to bend or curve.

**crooked** *adj* **1** having a crook or curve; bent. **2** *informal* not morally straightforward; dishonest.

**croon** *v* to sing in a low or soft voice. ➤ **crooner** *n.*

**crop**[1] *n* **1** a plant grown and harvested for food. **2** a group or quantity appearing at any one time. **3** a short riding whip. **4** a short haircut. **5** a pouch in a bird's gullet in which food is stored and prepared for digestion.

**crop**[2] *v* (**cropped, cropping**) **1** to trim or cut short. **2** of an animal: to graze on (grass, etc). **3** to cut and harvest (mature plant produce).

**cropper** ✱ **come a cropper** *informal* to fall or fail dramatically.

**crop up** *v informal* to happen or appear unexpectedly.

**croquet** *n* a game in which wooden balls are driven by mallets through a series of hoops.

**croquette** *n* a small roll of minced meat or vegetable fried in breadcrumbs.

**crosier** *or* **crozier** *n* a bishop's staff like a shepherd's crook.

**cross**[1] *n* **1** a figure formed by two intersecting lines (+ or x). **2** a cross-shaped upright stake used in antiquity for executions. **3** (**the Cross**) the cross on which Christ was crucified. **4** a monument or badge in the form of a cross. **5** a cross-bred animal or plant. **6** a person or thing that combines characteristics of two different types. **7** the act of crossing the ball in football. ✱ **at cross purposes** misunderstanding each other or having different objectives. **make the sign of the cross** to indicate the shape of the Cross on one's front.

**cross**[2] *v* **1** to go across or from one side to the other of. **2** to lie or be situated across. **3** of a line, road, etc: to intersect (another). **4** to pass simultaneously in opposite directions. **5** (+ off/out/through) to cancel (an item) by drawing a line across it. **6** to draw two parallel lines across (a cheque) to restrict payment to a named account. **7** to finish off (a letter *t* or *f*) with the horizontal bar. **8** in sitting, to put (the arms or legs) so that one is resting on the other. **9** to make the sign of the cross in front of (oneself). **10** to oppose or frustrate (somebody). **11** to produce (an animal or plant) by mixing two breeds. **12** to kick or pass (the ball) across the field in football. ✱ **cross swords** (*often* + with) to come into conflict.

**cross**[3] *adj* angry or annoyed. ➤ **crossly** *adv.*

**crossbar** *n* **1** a transverse bar between the uprights of a football goal. **2** a bar extending from the handlebars of a bicycle to the saddle.

**crossbow** *n* a mechanical bow formerly used to fire bolts in warfare.

**crossbreed**[1] *v* (*past tense and past part.* **crossbred**) to produce (an animal or plant) by mixing two breeds.

**crossbreed**[2] *n* an animal or plant produced by crossbreeding.

**cross-check** *v* to check (information) by referring to more than one source.

**cross-country** *adj and adv* **1** over countryside rather than by roads. **2** across the whole of a country.

**cross-dressing** *n* the wearing of clothing of the opposite sex. ➤ **cross-dresser** *n.*

**cross-examine** *v* to question (a witness) testifying for the other side in a law case. ➤ **cross-examination** *n.*

**cross-eyed** *adj* having one or both eyes squinting inwards.

**cross-fertilize** *or* **-ise** *v* to fertilize (a plant) by joining the ova with pollen or sperm from a different individual of the same species. ➤ **cross-fertilization** *n.*

**crossfire** *n* **1** firing from two or more points in crossing directions. **2** rapid or heated interchange.

**crossing** *n* **1** part of a road marked for pedestrians to cross. **2** a place where roads or railway lines cross. **3** a journey across a stretch of water.

**cross-legged** *adv and adj* sitting on the floor with ankles crossed and knees bent outwards.

**crossover** *n* **1** a crossing. **2** the changing of style from one type of music to another.

**cross-question** *v* to question or cross-examine intensively.

**cross-reference** *n* a reference from one part of a book to another, for additional information.

**crossroads** *pl n* a place where two or more roads cross.

**cross-section** *n* **1** a surface made by cutting across something at right angles to its length. **2** a representative sample of a group.

**crosswise** *or* **crossways** *adv* so as to cross something; across.

**crossword** *n* a puzzle in which words are entered horizontally and vertically in a pattern of numbered squares according to clues.

**crotch** *n* **1** the angle of the body between the inner thighs. **2** a fork in a tree. ➤ **crotched** *adj.*
**crotchet** *n Brit* a musical note with the time value of half a minim.
**crotchety** *adj informal* bad-tempered.
**crouch**[1] *v* to lower the body by bending one's knees and bending the upper body forward.
**crouch**[2] *n* a crouching position.
**croup**[1] *n* a children's disease of the larynx, causing rasping breathing.
**croup**[2] *n* the rump of a horse.
**croupier** *n* a person who runs the gaming tables in a casino.
**crouton** *n* a small cube of crisp bread served with soup or used as a garnish.
**crow**[1] *n* a large black bird with a loud cry. * **as the crow flies** in a direct line across country.
**crow**[2] *v* (*past tense* **crowed** *or* **crew,** *past part.* **crowed**) **1** to make the shrill cry of a cock. **2** (+ over) to boast about a success or gloat over another's discomfort.
**crowbar** *n* an iron or steel bar with a flattened end, used as a lever.
**crowd**[1] *n* **1** a large number of people gathered together. **2** a particular social group.
**crowd**[2] *v* **1** to collect in large numbers. **2** to fill (a place). **3** to force or thrust into a small space. **4** (+ off/out of) to push (others) out of the way. **5** to press close to (somebody).
**crown**[1] *n* **1** a round metal headdress worn by a sovereign. **2** (**the Crown**) the sovereign as head of state. **3** a wreath or band worn on the head as a symbol of victory. **4** a mark of honour or victory. **5** the topmost part of something. **6** the part of a tooth visible outside the gum, or an artificial substitute for it. **7** the high point or culmination. **8** a former British coin worth five shillings (25 pence).
**crown**[2] *v* **1** to place a crown on the head of (somebody), *esp* as a symbol of investiture. **2** to recognize as the leader in a particular field, *esp* a sport. **3** *literary* to form the top of. **4** to bring to a successful conclusion. **5** to put an artificial crown on (a tooth). **6** *informal* to hit on the head.
**crow's-foot** *n* (*pl* **crow's-feet**) a wrinkle round the outer corners of the eyes.
**crow's nest** *n* a high lookout platform on a ship's mast.
**crozier** *n* see CROSIER.
**crucial** *adj* **1** essential to resolve a crisis. **2** very important or significant. ➤ **crucially** *adv.*
**crucible** *n* a vessel for melting a substance at a high temperature.
**crucifix** *n* a representation of Christ on the cross.
**crucifixion** *n* **1** execution by crucifying. **2** (**Crucifixion**) the crucifying of Christ.
**cruciform** *adj* forming a cross.
**crucify** *v* (**-ies, -ied**) **1** to execute (somebody) by fastening them to a cross. **2** *informal* to criticize ruthlessly.
**crud** *n informal* **1** dirt or mess. **2** nonsense. ➤ **cruddy** *adj.*
**crude** *adj* **1** in a natural unprocessed state. **2** coarse or vulgar. **3** rough or inexpert. ➤ **crudely** *n.*
**cruel** *adj* (**crueller, cruellest,** *NAmer* **crueler, cruelest**) **1** liking to inflict pain or suffering; pitiless. **2** painful. ➤ **cruelly** *adv.*
**cruelty** *n* (*pl* **-ies**) **1** being cruel. **2** cruel behaviour.
**cruet** *n* **1** *Brit* a small container for salt, pepper, mustard, etc at table. **2** *Brit* a set of cruets on a stand.
**cruise**[1] *v* **1** to travel by sea for pleasure. **2** to go about without any definite destination. **3** of a vehicle: to travel at a steady speed.
**cruise**[2] *n* a sea voyage for pleasure.
**cruiser** *n* **1** a yacht or motor boat with passenger accommodation. **2** a large fast warship.
**crumb** *n* **1** a small fragment of bread, cake, biscuit, or cheese. **2** a small amount.
**crumble**[1] *v* **1** to break into small pieces. **2** to disintegrate. ➤ **crumbly** *adj.*
**crumble**[2] *n* a dessert of stewed fruit with a crumbly topping.
**crummy** *or* **crumby** *adj* (**-ier, -iest**) *informal* disagreeable or inferior; squalid.
**crumpet** *n* **1** a small round unsweetened cake that is eaten toasted. **2** *Brit, informal* women collectively as sexual objects.
**crumple** *v* **1** to crush out of shape. **2** to make or become creased or wrinkled. **3** to collapse.
**crunch**[1] *v* **1** to chew or bite with a noisy crushing sound. **2** to make or move with a crushing sound.
**crunch**[2] *n* **1** a crunching sound or action. **2** (**the crunch**) *informal* the decisive situation or moment.
**crusade**[1] *n* **1** (*usu* **the Crusades**) a series of medieval Christian military expeditions to win the Holy Land from the Muslims. **2** a reforming enterprise enthusiastically undertaken.
**crusade**[2] *v* to take part in a crusade. ➤ **crusader** *n.*
**crush**[1] *v* **1** to deform or flatten by pressing. **2** to reduce to particles by pounding or grinding. **3** to subdue or overwhelm.
**crush**[2] *n* **1** a crowd of people in a small space. **2** a soft fruit drink. **3** *informal* a strong infatuation.
**crust**[1] *n* **1** the hardened surface of a loaf of bread. **2** the pastry cover of a pie. **3** a hard or brittle surface layer. **4** the outer rocky layer of the earth. **5** a deposit built up on the inside of a wine bottle.
**crust**[2] *v* to form a crust on.
**crustacean** *n* a sea creature with a hard shell, e.g. a lobster or crab.

**crusty** *adj* (**-ier, -iest**) **1** having a hard well-baked crust. **2** morose or surly.
**crutch** *n* **1** a long stick of wood or metal used to support an injured person in walking. **2** a prop or support. **3** a person's crotch.
**crux** *n* (*pl* **cruxes**) an essential or decisive point.
**cry**[1] *v* (**-ies, -ied**) **1** to shed tears; to weep or sob. **2** to call loudly. **3** of a bird or animal: to utter its call. **4** *informal* (+ out for) to require or suggest strongly a certain response or treatment. * **a crying shame** something very regrettable.
**cry**[2] *n* (*pl* **-ies**) **1** a spell of shedding tears. **2** a loud call or shout. **3** a general public demand or complaint. **4** the call of an animal or bird. * **in full cry** in pursuit.
**cry off** *v* to call off an arrangement.
**cryogenics** *pl n* the branch of physics dealing with very low temperatures. ➤ **cryogenic** *adj.*
**crypt** *n* an underground chamber beneath a church.
**cryptic** *adj* **1** mysterious or secret. **2** obscure in meaning. ➤ **cryptically** *adv.*
**crystal** *n* **1** a piece of a natural solid material with plane faces symmetrically arranged. **2** a clear transparent mineral, *esp* colourless quartz. **3** a fine clear glass.
**crystalline** *adj* like or made of crystal.
**crystallize** *or* **-ise** *v* **1** to form crystals. **2** to give (a thought) a definite form. **3** to coat or preserve(fruit) with sugar. **4** to become crystallized.
**Cs** *abbr* the chemical symbol for caesium.
**Cu** *abbr* the chemical symbol for copper.
**cu.** *abbr* cubic.
**cub** *n* **1** the young of a fox, bear, lion, or other flesh-eating mammal. **2** (**Cub** *or* **Cub Scout**) a member of the junior branch of the Scout Association.
**cubbyhole** *n* a small room or enclosed space.
**cube**[1] *n* **1** a three-dimensional shape with six equal square faces. **2** the result of multiplying a number by itself twice.
**cube**[2] *v* **1** to multiply (a number) by itself twice. **2** to cut (food) into small cubes.
**cube root** *n* the number that produces a given number when cubed.
**cubic** *adj* **1** having the shape of a cube. **2** three-dimensional. **3** used before a unit of length: denoting a volume equal to that of a cube whose edges are of the specified unit.
**cubicle** *n* a small partitioned space or compartment.
**cubism** *n* an art movement that used geometric patterns to show perspectives from several aspects at the same time. ➤ **cubist** *n and adj.*
**cubit** *n* an ancient unit of length based on the length of the forearm.
**cuckoo**[1] *n* (*pl* **cuckoos**) **1** a greyish brown bird that lays its eggs in the nests of other birds. **2** the two-note call of the cuckoo.
**cuckoo**[2] *adj informal* crazy or eccentric.
**cucumber** *n* a long green fruit eaten raw in salads.
**cud** *n* partly digested food brought up into the mouth by a ruminating animal to be chewed again.
**cuddle**[1] *v* **1** to hold close in the arms and hug for warmth or comfort or in affection. **2** (*often* + up to) to nestle or lie close.
**cuddle**[2] *n* an act of cuddling.
**cuddly** *adj* (**-ier, -iest**) attractively soft and plump.
**cudgel**[1] *n* a short heavy club. * **take up the cudgels** to engage vigorously in a defence.
**cudgel**[2] *v* (**cudgelled, cudgelling,** *NAmer* **cudgeled, cudgeling**) to beat with a cudgel.
**cue**[1] *n* **1** a signal to a performer to begin a speech or action. **2** a signal or hint prompting action. * **on cue** at exactly the right time.
**cue**[2] *v* (**cuing, cueing**) **1** to give a cue to; to prompt. **2** to set audio or video equipment to play (a preselected section of a recording).
**cue**[3] *n* a long tapering rod for striking the ball in billiards, snooker, or pool.
**cue**[4] *v* (**cuing, cueing**) to strike (a ball) with a cue.
**cuff**[1] *n* **1** a fold or band at the end of a sleeve which encircles the wrist. **2** *chiefly NAmer* a turned-up hem of a trouser leg. * **off the cuff** without preparation. ➤ **cuffed** *adj.*
**cuff**[2] *v* to strike with the palm of the hand.
**cuff**[3] *n* a blow with the hand.
**cuff link** *n* a device of two linked parts used to fasten a shirt cuff.
**cuisine** /kwi'zeen/ *n* a partiuclar manner of preparing or cooking food.
**cul-de-sac** *n* (*pl* **culs-de-sac** *or* **cul-de-sacs**) a street or path that is closed at one end.
**culinary** *adj* relating to cookery.
**cull** *v* **1** to reduce the population of (animals) by selective killing. **2** to select (a body of people or things) from a source or a range of sources. ➤ **cull** *n.*
**culminate** *v* (*often* + in) to reach the highest or decisive point. ➤ **culmination** *n.*
**culottes** /kyoo'lots/ *pl n* women's full knee-length shorts.
**culpable** *adj* deserving blame. ➤ **culpability** *n,* **culpably** *adv.*
**culprit** *n* a person who is guilty of an offence or wrong.
**cult** *n* **1** a system of religious beliefs and ritual, or its followers. **2** a religion regarded as unorthodox or spurious. **3** great devotion among a group to a particular person, idea, or thing.
**cultivate** *v* **1** to prepare or use (land) for the growing of crops. **2** to grow (a plant or crop) on a large scale. **3** to grow (bacteria, tissue, etc) in a culture. **4** to improve or refine (one's mind). **5** to seek or affect (a manner or quality). **6** to

encourage or foster the friendship of. ➤ **cultivation** *n.*

**cultural** *adj* **1** relating to the arts and education. **2** relating to a society's culture and traditions. ➤ **culturally** *adv.*

**culture** *n* **1** the development of the mind, *esp* by education. **2** intellectual and artistic enlightenment. **3** the customary beliefs, social forms, etc of a people or group. **4** the cultivation of living cells, viruses, etc in prepared nutrient media.

**cultured** *adj* **1** well educated; cultivated. **2** of a pearl: grown under controlled conditions by inserting a foreign body in the oyster.

**culvert** *n* a small passage taking water under a road or railway.

**cum** *prep* combined with; along with.

**cumbersome** *adj* heavy and unwieldy.

**cumin** *or* **cummin** /'kumin/ *n* the seeds of a plant, used as a flavouring.

**cummerbund** *n* a broad sash worn round the waist as part of a man's formal evening wear.

**cumulative** *adj* increasing by successive additions. ➤ **cumulatively** *adv.*

**cuneiform** /'kyoohnifawm/ *adj* of ancient writing: using wedge-shaped characters.

**cunning**[1] *adj* **1** clever in a deceitful way; crafty. **2** ingenious. ➤ **cunningly** *adv,* **cunningness** *n.*

**cunning**[2] *n* craftiness.

**cup**[1] *n* **1** a small bowl-shaped drinking vessel with a handle on one side. **2** an ornamental metal cup with two handles awarded as a prize in a sports competition. **3** a sports competition with a cup as prize. **4** something resembling a cup in shape. **5** either of two parts of a bra that are shaped to fit over the breasts. ✱ **one's cup of tea** *informal* exactly what one likes. ➤ **cupful** *n* (*pl* **cupfuls**).

**cup**[2] *v* (**cupped, cupping**) **1** to curve (one's hands) into the shape of a cup. **2** to curve one's hands round (something).

**cupboard** /'kubəd/ *n* a piece of furniture with a door, used for storage.

**cupid** *n* **1** (**Cupid**) the Roman god of sexual love, depicted as a winged naked boy holding a bow and arrow. **2** a representation of Cupid in art.

**cupidity** *n* excessive desire for wealth or possessions.

**cupola** /'kyoohpələ/ *n* a small domed structure built on top of a roof.

**cur** *n* **1** a mongrel or inferior dog. **2** *informal* a surly or cowardly man.

**curate** *n* an assistant to a rector or priest in a parish.

**curate's egg** *n Brit* something with both good and bad parts.

**curative** *adj* used to cure disease.

**curator** *n* a person in charge of a museum or gallery.

**curb**[1] *n* **1** a check or restraint. **2** a chain or strap used to restrain a horse, attached to the sides of the bit and passing below the lower jaw. **3** *chiefly NAmer* = KERB.

**curb**[2] *v* to check or control.

**curd** *n* (*also in pl*) the thick part of coagulated milk used as a food or made into cheese.

**curdle** *v* to separate into solid curds or lumps and liquid.

**cure**[1] *n* **1** a drug or treatment that gives relief or recovery from an illness. **2** relief or recovery from an illness. **3** something that puts right a wrong or difficulty.

**cure**[2] *v* **1** to restore to health. **2** to bring about recovery from (an illness or other disorder). **3** to rectify (a harmful or troublesome situation). **4** to free from something objectionable or harmful. **5** to preserve (meat or fish) by salting, drying, or smoking. ➤ **curable** *adj.*

**curfew** *n* **1** a regulation requiring people to be indoors by a stated time. **2** the time at which a curfew begins, or the period during which it is in effect.

**curie** *n* a unit of radioactivity.

**curio** *n* (*pl* **-os**) an object that is considered unusual or rare.

**curiosity** *n* (*pl* **-ies**) **1** desire to know something. **2** inquisitiveness. **3** a strange, interesting, or rare object, fact, etc.

**curious** *adj* **1** eager to learn and find things out. **2** inquisitive. **3** strange or unusual. ➤ **curiously** *adv.*

**curl**[1] *v* **1** to form into waves or coils. **2** to adopt or grow in a twisted or spiral shape. **3** to move in curves or spirals.

**curl**[2] *n* **1** a curled lock of hair. **2** something with a spiral or coiled form. **3** a curling movement.

**curler** *n* a small roller on which hair is wound for curling.

**curlew** *n* (*pl* **curlews** *or* **curlew**) a wading bird with long legs and a long curved bill.

**curling** *n* a team game in which players slide heavy flat stones over ice towards a marked circle.

**curmudgeon** *n* a bad-tempered old man. ➤ **curmudgeonly** *adj.*

**currant** *n* a small seedless dried grape.

***Usage Note:*** Do not confuse this word with *current.*

**currency** *n* (*pl* **-ies**) **1** a system of money used as a medium of exchange. **2** the state of being in general use.

**current**[1] *adj* **1** occurring now or belonging to the present time. **2** generally accepted or used. ➤ **currently** *adv.*

***Usage Note:*** Do not confuse this word with *currant.*

**current**[2] *n* **1** a body of water, air, etc that moves in a certain direction. **2** a flow of electricity.

**current account** *n Brit* a bank account allowing immediate payments and withdrawals.

**curriculum** *n* (*pl* **curricula** *or* **curriculums**) the courses offered by an educational institution. ➤ **curricular** *adj.*

**curriculum vitae** /'veetie/ *n* (*pl* **curricula vitae**) a summary of a person's career and qualifications.

**curry**[1] *v* (**-ies, -ied**) **1** to groom the coat of (a horse). **2** to dress (tanned leather). * **curry favour** to seek approval by flattery or attention.

**curry**[2] *n* (*pl* **-ies**) a dish of Indian origin, seasoned with hot spices and sauces.

**curry**[3] *v* (**-ies, -ied**) to flavour or cook (food) with hot spices and sauces.

**curse**[1] *n* **1** an appeal to a deity invoking harm or injury on somebody. **2** a swearword or other offensive expression. **3** a cause of misfortune.

**curse**[2] *v* **1** to doom or damn with a curse. **2** to swear or use offensive language. **3** to bring evil upon.

**cursor** *n* **1** a movable pointer on a computer or radar screen, indicating the position where input will take effect. **2** a transparent slide locating marks on a slide rule.

**cursory** *adj* rapid and superficial. ➤ **cursorily** *adv.*

**curt** *adj* rude or brusque. ➤ **curtly** *adv.*

**curtail** *v* to limit or cut short. ➤ **curtailment** *n.*

**curtain**[1] *n* **1** a piece of fabric hung at a window or at the front of a theatre stage, forming a screen when pulled across. **2** *informal* (*in pl*) death or catastrophe.

**curtain**[2] *v* to cover or screen with a curtain.

**curtsy**[1] *or* **curtsey** *n* (*pl* **-ies**) a woman's or girl's gesture of respect made by flexing the knees with one leg behind the other.

**curtsy**[2] *or* **curtsey** *v* (**-ies, -ied**) to make a curtsy.

**curvaceous** *adj* having an attractively curved figure.

**curvature** *n* **1** the fact or extent of being curved. **2** an abnormal curving of the spine.

**curve**[1] *v* to deviate gradually from a straight line or course.

**curve**[2] *n* a curving line or surface. ➤ **curvy** *adj.*

**cushion**[1] *n* **1** a soft pillow or padded bag used for sitting or leaning on. **2** a pad along the inside of a billiard table. **3** something that mitigates the effects of disturbances or disorders. ➤ **cushiony** *adj.*

**cushion**[2] *v* **1** to furnish with a cushion or cushions. **2** to protect against force or shock. **3** to mitigate the effects of (something unpleasant).

**cushy** *adj* (**-ier, -iest**) *informal* easy or effortless.

**cusp** *n* **1** either horn of a crescent moon. **2** a pointed projection formed by or arising from the intersection of two arcs. **3** a point on the grinding surface of a tooth. * **on the cusp** between one state and another.

**custard** *n* a thick sweetened sauce made with milk and eggs or a preparation of cornflour.

**custodial** *adj* **1** involving imprisonment. **2** relating to guardianship or custody.

**custodian** *n* a person who guards and protects.

**custody** *n* **1** care or guardianship. **2** imprisonment or detention.

**custom** *n* **1** an established or socially accepted practice. **2** (*in pl*) duties imposed on imports or exports, or the officials that collect them. **3** *chiefly Brit* the use of a business by its customers.

**customary** *adj* established by or according to custom; usual. ➤ **customarily** *adv.*

**custom-built** *adj* built to individual specifications.

**customer** *n* **1** a person who buys a commodity or service. **2** an individual with a specified unfavourable quality: *an awkward customer.*

**customize** *or* **-ise** *v* to build or adjust (something) to individual requirements.

**cut**[1] *v* (**cutting,** *past tense and past part.* **cut**) **1** to penetrate or make an opening in (something) with a sharp object. **2** to shorten, divide, or detach by cutting. **3** to make or shape by cutting. **4** to reduce the amount of. **5** to shorten or edit. **6** to break or interrupt (a flow, supply, etc). **7** to cross or intersect. **8** to divide (a pack of cards) into two parts. **9** to ignore deliberately or spitefully. **10** to switch off (an engine or machine). **11** to stop filming or recording. **12** to change from one sound or image to another. **13** to go by a shorter route. * **cut both ways 1** to be equally valid for and against an argument. **2** of a procedure: to have advantages and disadvantages. **cut corners** to do something cheaply or quickly by making risky economies. **cut no ice** to fail to impress or make a difference. **cut one's teeth** to get early experience of an activity. **cut short** to interrupt (a speaker).

**cut**[2] *n* **1** an opening or wound made with an edged instrument. **2** a reduction or economy. **3** the style in which the hair or a piece of clothing is cut. **4** something cut or cut off. **5** a piece of meat cut from a carcass. **6** *informal* a share. **7** a sharp blow or stroke. **8** a version of an edited film. * **a cut above** superior to. **cut and thrust** a competitive and stimulating environment.

**cut-and-dried** *adj* completely decided and unalterable.

**cutaneous** *adj* relating to or affecting the skin.

**cutback** *n* a reduction or decrease.

**cut back** *v* to reduce expenditure.

**cut down** *v* **1** to make (something growing) fall by cutting through it. **2** to reduce or restrict an activity, expenditure, etc.

**cute** *adj* **1** *informal* appealingly attractive or pretty. **2** shrewd; knowing. ➤ **cutely** *adv.*

**cut glass** *n* glass with patterns cut into its surface.

**cuticle** *n* **1** dead skin round the base and sides of a fingernail or toenail. **2** the outer layer of a hair.

**cut in** *v* **1** to interrupt. **2** to pull in too closely after overtaking a vehicle. **3** of a device: to start functioning automatically.

**cutlass** *n* a short curved sword used formerly by sailors.

**cutlery** *n* knives, forks, and spoons for cutting and eating food.

**cutlet** *n* **1** a small slice of meat from the neck. **2** a fried cake of minced meat or vegetables.

**cutoff** *n* a stopping-point or limit.

**cut off** *v* **1** to remove by cutting. **2** to stop the supply of. **3** to block access to. **4** to disconnect during a telephone call. **5** to disinherit.

**cutout** *n* **1** something cut out from a larger piece. **2** a device that stops the flow of an electric current or the operation of a machine.

**cut out** *v* **1** to make by cutting from a larger piece. **2** to eliminate or exclude. **3** to stop doing (something). **4** of an engine: to stop operating. * **be cut out for** be suited to. **cut it out** *informal* to stop doing something.

**cutter** *n* **1** a person or implement that cuts. **2** a ship's boat for carrying stores or passengers. **3** a light fast boat.

**cutthroat**[1] *n dated* a murderous thug.

**cutthroat**[2] *adj* ruthless or unprincipled.

**cutting**[1] *n* **1** a piece cut from a newspaper or magazine. **2** a piece cut from a plant for growing into a new plant. **3** an excavation through high ground, for a railway, road, etc.

**cutting**[2] *adj* **1** of a remark: likely to hurt or offend. **2** of wind: piercingly cold. * **the cutting edge** the most advanced or ambitious stage of an activity.

**cuttlefish** *n* a sea mollusc like a squid, having ten arms.

**CV** *abbr* curriculum vitae.

**cwt** *abbr* hundredweight.

**cyan** *n* a greenish blue colour.

**cyanide** *n* an extremely poisonous salt.

**cybernetics** *pl n* the comparative study of the automatic control systems in the nervous system of humans and in machines such as computers. ➤ **cybernetic** *adj.*

**cyberspace** *n* the notional environment in which electronic network communication takes place.

**cyclamen** /'sikləmən/ *n* a plant with drooping pink, red, or white flowers.

**cycle**[1] *n* **1** a series of related events happening in a set order. **2** one complete performance of a periodic process, e.g. a vibration or electrical oscillation. **3** a group of poems, plays, novels, operas, or songs on a particular theme. **4** a bicycle.

**cycle**[2] *v* to ride a bicycle.

**cyclic** *adj* occurring in cycles.

**cyclone** *n* **1** a system of winds rotating about a centre of low atmospheric pressure and often bringing rain. **2** a violent storm. ➤ **cyclonic** *adj.*

**cygnet** *n* a young swan.

**cylinder** *n* **1** a three-dimensional shape with circular cross-section and parallel sides. **2** the piston chamber in a steam or internal-combustion engine.

**cymbal** *n* a percussion instrument consisting of a concave brass plate that produces a clashing tone when struck with a stick or against another cymbal.

**cynic** /'sinik/ *n* **1** a person who doubts the existence of human sincerity or of any motive other than self-interest. **2** a person who is habitually pessimistic or sardonic. ➤ **cynicism** *n.*

**cynical** *adj* **1** doubting the existence of human sincerity. **2** motivated by selfish interests. ➤ **cynically** *adv.*

**cypher**[1] *n* see CIPHER[1].

**cypher**[2] *v* see CIPHER[2].

**cypress** *n* an evergreen tree with overlapping leaves resembling scales.

**Cypriot** /'sipri·ət/ *or* **Cypriote**/-oht/ *n* **1** a native or inhabitant of Cyprus. **2** the form of Greek spoken on Cyprus. ➤ **Cypriot** *adj.*

**Cyrillic** *n* the alphabet used for writing Russian and other Slavic languages.

**cyst** *n* a sac of watery liquid or gas developing abnormally in a plant or animal.

**cystic** *adj* **1** containing a cyst or cysts. **2** of the bladder or gall bladder. **3** enclosed in a cyst.

**cystic fibrosis** *n* a hereditary disease marked *esp* by faulty digestion and difficulty in breathing.

**cystitis** *n* inflammation of the bladder.

**cytoplasm** *n* the substance of a plant or animal cell outside the nucleus.

**czar** *n* see TSAR.

**Czech** /chek/ *n* **1** a native or inhabitant of the Czech Republic or formerly of Czechoslovakia. **2** the Slavonic language of the Czechs. ➤ **Czech** *adj.*

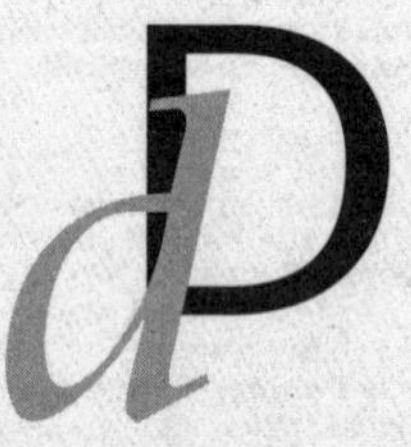

**D**[1] *or* **d** *n* (*pl* **D's** *or* **Ds** *or* **d's**) **1** the fourth letter of the English alphabet. **2** the Roman numeral for 500.

**D**[2] *abbr* the chemical symbol for deuterium.

**'d** *contraction* **1** had. **2** would.

**DA** *abbr NAmer* district attorney.

**dab**[1] *v* (**dabbed, dabbing**) **1** to touch lightly and repeatedly. **2** to apply (a liquid or powder) with light strokes.

**dab**[2] *n* **1** a small amount of something soft or moist. **2** a gentle touch or stroke.

**dabble** *v* **1** to dip (the fingers or toes) in water and move them about. **2** (*often* + in) to have a casual or superficial involvement or interest. ➤ **dabbler** *n.*

**dab hand** *n Brit, informal* a person who is skilful at something; an expert.

**dace** *n* (*pl* **dace**) a small European freshwater fish.

**dachshund** /'daksənd/ *n* a dog of a breed having a long body, short legs, and long drooping ears.

**dad** *n informal* one's father.

**daddy** *n* (*pl* **-ies**) *informal* one's father.

**daddy longlegs** *n* (*pl* **daddy longlegs**) *Brit* a crane fly.

**daffodil** *n* a plant having yellow flowers with elongated trumpet-shaped centres.

**daffy** *adj* (**-ier, -iest**) *informal* crazy or foolish. ➤ **daffiness** *n.*

**daft** *adj chiefly Brit, informal* silly or foolish.

**dagger** *n* a short knife used as a stabbing weapon.

**daguerreotype** *or* **daguerrotype** /də'gerətiep/ *n* an early photograph produced on a silver-covered plate.

**dahlia** /'dayli·ə, 'daylyə/ *n* an ornamental garden plant with showy flowers.

**daily**[1] *adj* of or occurring every day or every weekday.

**daily**[2] *adv* every day.

**daily**[3] *n* (*pl* **-ies**) *informal* a newspaper published daily from Monday to Saturday.

**dainty**[1] *adj* (**-ier, -iest**) **1** delicately beautiful or graceful. **2** fastidious, *esp* about food. ➤ **daintily** *adv.*

**dainty**[2] *n* (*pl* **-ies**) something pleasant to eat; a delicacy.

**dairy** *n* (*pl* **-ies**) **1** a place where milk is processed and butter or cheese is made. **2** (*used before a noun*) involving milk or other dairy products.

**dais** /'day·is/ *n* a raised platform in a large room, e.g. for a speaker.

**daisy** *n* (*pl* **-ies**) a common small European plant whose flowers have yellow centres and slim white petals.

**dale** *n* a valley.

**dally** *v* (**-ies, -ied**) **1** to waste time; to dawdle. **2** (+ with) to behave flirtatiously with. ➤ **dalliance** *n.*

**Dalmatian** *n* a large dog of a short-haired breed with a white coat with black or brown spots.

**dam**[1] *n* a barrier built across a watercourse to hold back and store the water.

**dam**[2] *v* (**dammed, damming**) **1** to build a dam across (a river). **2** to block ( a flow of something).

**dam**[3] *n* a female parent of a domestic animal.

**damage**[1] *n* **1** loss or harm resulting from injury. **2** (*in pl*) compensation in money imposed by law for loss or injury.

**damage**[2] *v* **1** to cause damage to. **2** to become damaged. ➤ **damaging** *adj.*

**damask** *n* a lustrous fabric with patterns woven into a plain background.

**dame** *n* **1** (**Dame**) in the UK, the title of, and form of address for, a woman who has been given an honour equivalent to a knighthood. **2** *Brit* the part of a comic old woman in a pantomime, usu played by a male actor. **3** *NAmer, informal* a woman.

**damn** *v* **1** to condemn to eternal punishment in hell. **2** to condemn as worthless. **3** to curse. ✱ **damn all** *Brit, informal* nothing at all.

**damnable** /'damnəbl/ *adj* **1** very bad. **2** deserving damnation.

**damnation** /dam'naysh(ə)n/ *n* condemnation to hell.

**damned** *adj* (**damnedest**) *informal* used as an intensive.

**damp**[1] *adj* slightly or moderately wet.

**damp**[2] *n* moisture or humidity.

**damp**[3] *v* **1** to make damp. **2** (*often* + down) to restrain, decrease or make less intense.

**damp course** *n* a horizontal damp-resistant layer near the ground in a masonry wall.

**dampen** *v* **1** to make damp. **2** to reduce in strength or intensity.

**damper** *n* **1** a small felted block that stops the vibration of a piano string. **2** a valve or plate in the flue of a furnace for regulating the draught. * **put a damper on** to have a dulling or restraining influence on.

**damp squib** *n Brit* something that proves to be less effective or impressive than expected.

**damsel** *n archaic or literary* a young unmarried woman.

**damson** *n* a small purple fruit similar to a plum.

**dance**[1] *v* **1** to move the body in a rhythmic way, *esp* in a set sequence of steps and in time to music. **2** to move quickly and lightly. ➤ **dancer** *n.*

**dance**[2] *n* **1** a series of steps and bodily movements, usu in time to music. **2** a social event with dancing. **3** a piece of music for dancing to.

**dandelion** *n* a common plant with yellow flowers and downy seed heads.

**dander** * **get/have one's dander up** *informal* to lose one's temper.

**dandle** *v* to move (a baby or small child) up and down in one's arms or on one's knee.

**dandruff** *n* dead skin that comes off the scalp in small white or greyish scales.

**dandy**[1] *n* (*pl* **-ies**) a man obsessively concerned with looking fashionable. ➤ **dandified** *adj.*

**dandy**[2] *adj* (**-ier, -iest**) *chiefly NAmer, informal* very good.

**Dane** *n* a native or inhabitant of Denmark.

**danger** *n* **1** exposure to the possibility of injury, pain, or loss. **2** a cause of danger. **3** the possibility of something unwelcome.

**dangerous** *adj* able or likely to do harm or inflict injury. ➤ **dangerously** *adv.*

**dangle** *v* **1** to hang or swing loosely. **2** to offer enticingly. ➤ **dangly** *adj.*

**dank** *adj* unpleasantly moist or wet.

**dapper** *adj* of a man: neat and spruce in dress.

**dapple**[1] *v* to mark (a surface) with patches of varying shade.

**dapple**[2] *n* a spot or patch of a colour different from its background.

**dare**[1] *v* **1** to have sufficient courage or boldness to do something. **2** to challenge (somebody) to do something. * **I dare say/daresay** it is likely or probable that.

**dare**[2] *n* a challenge to do something bold or rash.

**daredevil** *n* somebody who is recklessly bold.

**daring**[1] *adj* adventurously bold in action or thought. ➤ **daringly** *adv.*

**daring**[2] *n* adventurous boldness.

**dark**[1] *adj* **1** with little or no light. **2** of a colour: not light or pale. **3** of the hair or complexion: not fair. **4** secret or mysterious. **5** sinister or evil. **6** dismal or sad. ➤ **darkly** *adv,* **darkness** *n.*

**dark**[2] *n* **1** the absence of light; darkness. **2** night or nightfall. * **in the dark** in a state of ignorance.

**Dark Ages** *pl n* the period of European history from the fall of the Roman Empire (AD 476) to about 1000, perceived as devoid of culture or learning.

**darken** *v* **1** to make or become dark or darker. **2** of something unwelcome: to spoil or blight. **3** to make or become unhappy or angry.

**dark horse** *n* **1** somebody or something that is little known about. **2** a secretive person.

**darkroom** *n* a room with subdued light for handling and processing photographic materials.

**darling**[1] *n* **1** used as an affectionate form of address. **2** a dearly loved person.

**darling**[2] *adj* **1** dearly loved. **2** charming.

**darn**[1] *v* to mend (knitted material) by stitching up holes.

**darn**[2] *n* a darned area of a garment.

**darn**[3] *or* **darned** *adj informal, euphem* damned.

**dart**[1] *n* **1** a small pointed projectile with flights of feather or plastic, used as a weapon or in the game of darts. **2** a tapering fold put in a garment to shape it. **3** a quick movement or dash.

**dart**[2] *v* to move suddenly or rapidly.

**darts** *pl n* (*usu treated as sing.*) an indoor game in which darts are thrown at a round board marked in numbered sections.

**dash**[1] *v* **1** to move with speed or haste. **2** to hurl with great force. **3** to destroy (a hope or plan).

**dash**[2] *n* **1** a punctuation mark (–) used to indicate a break or an omission. **2** a hasty movement or journey. **3** *chiefly NAmer* a sprint. **4** a small amount of a substance. **5** panache or stylishness. **6** = DASHBOARD.

**dashboard** *n* an instrument panel in a car or other vehicle.

**dashing** *adj* **1** vigorous and spirited. **2** smart and stylish in dress.

**dash off** *v* to write (something) hurridly.

**dastardly** *adj dated* despicably malicious or cowardly.

**data** *pl n* **1** factual information used as a basis for reasoning, discussion, or calculation. **2** the numbers, characters, etc stored and processed by a computer.

***Usage Note:*** *Data* is, strictly speaking, a plural noun with the singular form *datum*, but it is increasingly used as a singular mass noun like *information* or *news*: *The data is currently being processed.*

**database** *n* a large structured set of data held in a computer.

**date**[1] *n* **1** a particular day of the month or year, identified by a number. **2** the time at which an event occurred or will occur. **3** *informal* an appointment, *esp* a romantic or social engagement, or the person one goes to meet. **4** a show or concert, *esp* one of a series performed in different venues. * **to date** up to now.

**date**[2] *v* **1** to determine the date of. **2** to mark with a date. **3** *informal* to go on a date or dates with. **4** to have been in existence for a specified time. **5** to become old-fashioned. ➤ **datable** *or* **dateable** *adj.*

**date**[3] *n* a small brown oval fruit with a sweet taste, eaten fresh or dried.

**dated** *adj* out of date or old-fashioned.

**dative** *adj* of a grammatical case expressing an indirect object. ➤ **dative** *n.*

**datum** *n* (*pl* **data**) a piece of information used as a basis for reasoning, measuring or calculating.

**daub**[1] *v* to apply, or cover (a surface) with, a soft thick substance crudely. ➤ **dauber** *n.*

**daub**[2] *n* **1** a mixture of plaster or clay and straw, used with wattle to build a wall. **2** a smear. **3** a crude painting.

**daughter** *n* **1** a girl or woman having the relation of child to parent. **2** a female descendant.

**daughter-in-law** *n* (*pl* **daughters-in-law**) the wife of one's son.

**daunt** *v* to discourage or dishearten. ➤ **daunting** *adj.*

**dauntless** *adj* courageous and fearless.

**dawdle** *v* to move slowly or lackadaisically.

**dawn**[1] *n* **1** the first appearance of light in the morning. **2** a first appearance or beginning.

**dawn**[2] *v* **1** of the day, to begin to grow light. **2** to begin to appear or develop. **3** (*usu* + on) to be realized or begin to be understood.

**dawn chorus** *n* birdsong in the early morning.

**day** *n* **1** a period of 24 hours beginning at midnight. **2** the period of daylight between sunrise and sunset. **3** the hours spent daily at work, school, etc. **4** (*also in pl*) a particular time or period in the past. ✱ **call it a day** to stop work or activity for the time being. **day in, day out** continually for a long time. **these days** in the present times.

**daybreak** *n* dawn.

**daydream**[1] *n* a pleasant fantasy or reverie indulged in while awake.

**daydream**[2] *v* to have a daydream.

**daylight** *n* **1** the light of the sun during the day. **2** dawn.

**daylight robbery** *n Brit, informal* exorbitant pricing or charging.

**daze**[1] *v* to stupefy or stun.

**daze**[2] *n* a state of confusion or shock.

**dazzle**[1] *v* **1** to blind temporarily with a sudden bright light. **2** to impress or overwhelm. ➤ **dazzling** *adj.*

**dazzle**[2] *n* sudden blinding brightness.

**dB** *abbr* decibel(s).

**DC** *abbr* **1** direct current. **2** District of Columbia (US postal abbreviation).

**de-** *prefix* denoting removal, or the reversal of an action: *decapitate, deactivate.*

**deacon** *n* **1** in some Christian Churches, an ordained minister ranking below a priest. **2** a lay minister in various Protestant Churches.

**deactivate** *v* to make (e.g. a bomb) inactive or ineffective.

**dead**[1] *adj* **1** no longer alive. **2** of a body part: numb. **3** unresponsive. **4** of equipment: no longer working. **5** no longer used, active, or relevant. **6** *informal* lacking in activity or interest. **7** *informal* complete or absolute.

**dead**[2] *n* the time when something is at its most intense.

**dead**[3] *adv* **1** absolutely or exactly. **2** *Brit, informal* very.

**deadbeat** *n informal* an idle person.

**dead duck** *n informal* somebody or something that is unlikely to succeed.

**deaden** *v* **1** to reduce the resonance of (a sound). **2** to make (pain, etc) less intense. **3** to numb (a part of the body).

**dead end** *n* **1** a street or passage without an exit. **2** a situation in which no progress can be made.

**deadhead** *v chiefly Brit* to remove dead flower heads from (a plant).

**dead heat** *n* a race or contest where two or more competitors finish level.

**deadline** *n* a date or time before which something must be completed.

**deadlock** *n* **1** a situation in which no progress can be made. **2** *Brit* a lock that can be opened and shut only by a key.

**deadlocked** *adj* brought to a standstill by irreconcilable disagreements.

**dead loss** *n* a useless person or thing.

**deadly**[1] *adj* (**-ier, -iest**) **1** likely or able to cause death. **2** vicious, malicious, or irreconcilable. **3** unerring. **4** *informal* dull or tedious.

**deadly**[2] *adv* extremely.

**deadpan** *adj and adv* without feeling or expression.

**dead reckoning** *n* the calculation of the position of a ship or aircraft from the record of the course and distance travelled.

**dead ringer** *n* a person or thing strongly resembling another.

**deadweight** *n* **1** the weight of an inert person or object. **2** the total weight of a ship's contents, including cargo, fuel, passengers, etc.

**deadwood** *n* unproductive people or things.

**deaf** *adj* **1** unable to hear, or having deficient hearing. **2** (+ to) unwilling to listen to. ✱ **fall on deaf ears** to be ignored. ➤ **deafness** *n.*

**deafen** *v* to overpower with noise.

**deal**[1] *v* (*past tense and past part.* **dealt** /delt/) **1** to distribute (cards) in a game. **2** (+ out) to distribute or apportion. **3** to administer or inflict (e.g. a blow). **4** (*often* + in) to sell or trade in commercially. **5** *informal* to buy and sell drugs illegally. ✱ **deal with 1** to take action with regard to. **2** to cope with. **3** to have business relations with. **4** to be concerned with (a theme or subject).

**deal**[2] *n* **1** an agreement. **2** a particular kind of treatment. **3** the process of distributing cards in

a game. * **a good/great deal 1** a lot. **2** considerably.
**deal**[3] *n* fir or pine timber.
**dealer** *n* **1** a person who deals in goods or services. **2** a person who deals in shares, securities, etc, through an agent. **3** a drugs pusher. **4** the player who deals the cards in a game. ➤ **dealership** *n.*
**dealings** *pl n* business or personal relationships.
**dean** *n* **1** the head of the chapter of a collegiate or cathedral church. **2** the head of a university division, faculty, or school. ➤ **deanery** *n.*
**dear**[1] *adj* **1** much loved; precious or cherished. **2** used as a polite form of address in letters. **3** sweet; appealing. **4** expensive.
**dear**[2] *n* **1** used as an affectionate form of address. **2** a lovable person.
**dearly** *adv* **1** very much. **2** at a great cost.
**dearth** *n* a scarcity.
**death** *n* **1** the end of life. **2** an instance of dying. **3** the state of being dead. **4** extinction or disappearance. * **at death's door** seriously ill. **like death warmed up** *informal* looking very ill.
**death knell** *n* **1** the ringing of a bell to mark a death. **2** a sign of the ending of something.
**deathly** *adj* (**-ier, -iest**) suggestive of death.
**death penalty** *n* punishment by execution.
**death row** *n* a part of a prison containing the cells of those condemned to death.
**deathwatch beetle** *n* a small beetle that bores into woodwork making an ominous ticking sound.
**debacle** /di'bahkəl/ *n* a complete failure.
**debar** *v* (**debarred, debarring**) (+ from) to prevent from doing something.
**debase** *v* to lower in status, quality or value. ➤ **debasement** *n.*
**debatable** *adj* open to debate; questionable.
**debate**[1] *n* **1** a formal discussion of a motion. **2** an argument or controversy.
**debate**[2] *v* **1** to discuss a question by considering opposed arguments. **2** to consider from different viewpoints.
**debauch** *v* to corrupt or pervert.
**debauchery** *n* unrestrained indulgence in sensual pleasures. ➤ **debauched** *adj,* **debauchee** *n.*
**debilitate** *v* to make weak and lifeless.
**debility** *n* weakness or infirmity.
**debit**[1] *n* **1** an entry in an account recording money owed. **2** a charge against a bank account.
**debit**[2] *v* (**debited, debiting**) **1** to record (an amount) as a debit. **2** of a bank: to take (a sum of money) from an account as payment.
**debit card** *n* a bank card enabling purchases to be charged electronically to the holder's account.
**debonair** *adj* **1** suave or urbane. **2** lighthearted or nonchalant. ➤ **debonairly** *adv.*
**debrief** *v* to interrogate (a soldier, diplomat, etc) about a mission. ➤ **debriefing** *n.*
**debris** /'debri/ *n* **1** scattered remains or rubbish left after something has been broken down. **2** an accumulation of fragments of rock.
**debt** *n* **1** money owed or due. **2** the state of owing money or gratitude.
**debtor** *n* somebody who owes a debt.
**debug** *v* (**debugged, debugging**) **1** to climinate malfunctions in (computer software or equipment). **2** to remove concealed listening devices from (a place).
**debunk** *v* to expose as false or exaggerated.
**debut**[1] /'dayb(y)ooh/ *n* a first public appearance.
**debut**[2] *v* (**debuted, debuting**) to make a debut.
**debutant** *n* somebody making a debut.
**debutante** *n* an aristocratic young woman making her formal entrance into society.
**decade** *n* a period of ten years.
**decadent** *adj* **1** marked by moral or cultural decline. **2** self-indulgent in an immoral way. ➤ **decadence** *n.*
**decaffeinated** *adj* of coffee: having had most of the caffeine removed.
**decagon** *n* a polygon with ten angles and ten sides.
**decahedron** *n* (*pl* **decahedra** *or* **decahedrons**) a polyhedron with ten faces.
**decamp** *v* to depart secretly or suddenly.
**decant** *v* to pour (liquid) from one vessel into another.
**decanter** *n* an ornamental glass bottle into which an alcoholic drink is decanted.
**decapitate** *v* to cut off the head of. ➤ **decapitation** *n.*
**decathlon** *n* an athletic contest in which each competitor takes part in ten events. ➤ **decathlete** *n.*
**decay**[1] *v* **1** to rot or decompose. **2** to decrease gradually in soundness or vigour.
**decay**[2] *n* **1** the state or process of decaying. **2** decayed material or tissue.
**decease** *n formal* death.
**deceased**[1] *n* (*pl* **deceased**) (**the deceased**) *formal* a person who has recently died.
**deceased**[2] *adj formal* recently dead.
**deceit** *n* **1** the act or practice of deceiving. **2** an attempt to deceive.
**deceitful** *adj* having a tendency to deceive. ➤ **deceitfully** *adv.*
**deceive** *v* to cause to accept as true something that is false. ➤ **deceiver** *n.*

***Usage Note:*** Note the spelling with *-ei-*.

**decelerate** *v* to slow down. ➤ **deceleration** *n.*
**December** *n* the twelfth month of the year.
**decency** *n* (*pl* **-ies**) **1** behaviour that conforms to normal standards of propriety. **2** (*usu in pl*) a standard of propriety.

**decennial** *adj* **1** lasting for ten years. **2** occurring every ten years.
**decent** *adj* **1** conforming to normal standards of propriety. **2** adequate or satisfactory. **3** *chiefly Brit, informal* kind or helpful. **4** *informal* sufficiently clothed to be seen without impropriety. ➤ **decently** *adv.*
**decentralize** *or* **-ise** *v* to redistribute functions and powers from a central authority to regional authorities. ➤ **decentralization** *n.*
**deception** *n* **1** the act of deceiving or the state of being deceived. **2** something that deceives.
**deceptive** *adj* having the power to deceive.
**deceptively** *adv* **1** so as to disguise the reality; misleadingly: *Her voice was deceptively calm.* **2** despite appearances to the contrary: *a deceptively spacious room.*
**decibel** *n* a unit for expressing the intensity of sounds or the power of an electric signal.
**decide** *v* **1** to make a definite choice or come to a firm conclusion. **2** to influence (somebody) to make a choice. **3** to settle the outcome of.
**decided** *adj* **1** definite. **2** unhesitating; firm. ➤ **decidedly** *adv.*
**decider** *n* a final point or additional contest that decides who wins a competition.
**deciduous** *adj* of a tree: having leaves that are shed seasonally.
**decimal**[1] *adj* **1** based on the number ten. **2** divided into units that are tenths, hundredths, etc of one another.
**decimal**[2] *n* a fraction that is expressed by a dot followed by digits for the number of tenths, hundredths, etc.
**decimal place** *n* the position of a digit to the right of a decimal point.
**decimal point** *n* the dot placed between a decimal fraction and a whole number.
**decimate** *v* **1** to kill a large number from among (a group or population). **2** to destroy a large part of. ➤ **decimation** *n.*
**decipher** *v* **1** to convert (something coded) into intelligible form. **2** to make out the meaning of (something obscure).
**decision** *n* **1** a choice or conclusion reached after considering various alternatives. **2** promptness and firmness in deciding.
**decisive** *adj* **1** of crucial importance in determining the outcome of something. **2** unambiguously settling an issue. **3** having the ability to make firm decisions. ➤ **decisively** *adv,* **decisiveness** *n.*
**deck**[1] *n* **1** a platform dividing a ship's hull horizontally, *esp* the top platform, open to the air. **2** a floor in e.g. a bus, or a wooden platform, e.g. in a garden. **3** the upper operating surface of a record player. **4** *NAmer* a pack of playing cards. **5** (**the deck**) *informal* the ground or floor.
**deck**[2] *v* **1** (*often* + out) to decorate or adorn. **2** *informal* to knock down.
**deck chair** *n* a folding chair made of canvas stretched over a wooden frame.
**decking** *n* material used to make a deck.
**declaim** *v* to speak loudly and dramatically or pompously.
**declamation** *n* the art or act of declaiming. ➤ **declamatory** *adj.*
**declaration** *n* **1** an emphatic announcement or formal statement. **2** the act of declaring.
**declare** *v* **1** to make known formally or explicitly. **2** to make evident. **3** to make a full statement of (something taxable or dutiable). **4** of a cricket captain or team: to end the team's innings before all the batsmen are out. ✱ **declare oneself** admit one's intentions.
**declassify** *v* (**-ies, -ied**) to declare (e.g. documents, information) no longer secret.
**declension** *n* **1** a schematic arrangement of noun, adjective, or pronoun inflections. **2** a class of nouns or adjectives with the same inflectional forms.
**decline**[1] *v* **1** to become gradually smaller, less strong, or less good. **2** to refuse, *esp* courteously. **3** to slope downwards or descend. **4** in grammar, to list the inflectional forms of (a noun, pronoun, or adjective).
**decline**[2] *n* **1** a gradual reduction or change for the worse. **2** the period when something is approaching its end.
**declivity** *n* (*pl* **-ies**) *formal* a descending slope.
**decode** *v* to convert (a coded message) into intelligible language. ➤ **decoder** *n.*
**décolletage** /daykol'tahzh/ *n* the low-cut neckline of a dress.
**décolleté** /daykol'tay, day'koltay/ *adj* of a dress: low-necked.
**decommission** *v* to take (a ship, weapon, nuclear reactor etc) out of service.
**decompose** *v* to decay or rot. ➤ **decomposition** *n.*
**decompress** *v* **1** to release from pressure or compression. **2** to return (computer data) to its normal size after compression. ➤ **decompression** *n.*
**decompression sickness** *n* a condition suffered by deep-sea divers who surface too quickly, caused by the expansion of nitrogen bubbles in the blood and tissue.
**decongestant** *n* a drug that relieves *esp* nasal congestion. ➤ **decongestant** *adj.*
**deconstruct** *v* **1** to analyse (e.g. a film or text) by treating its elements as having meanings independent of the work as a whole. **2** to dismantle. ➤ **deconstruction** *n.*
**decontaminate** *v* to rid of contamination, e.g. radioactivity. ➤ **decontamination** *n.*
**decor** *or* **décor** *n* the style and layout of interior decoration and furnishings.
**decorate** *v* **1** to give a more attractive appearance by adding colour or ornament. **2** to apply

paint, wallpaper, etc to (a room or building). **3** to award a medal or honour to.

**decoration** *n* **1** the act or process of decorating. **2** an ornament. **3** a badge of honour, *esp* a medal.

**decorative** *adj* serving to decorate; ornamental. ➤ **decoratively** *adv.*

**decorator** *n* somebody whose job is painting and wallpapering rooms or buildings.

**decorous** *adj* marked by propriety and good taste. ➤ **decorously** *adv.*

**decorum** *n* behaviour that is in accordance with propriety and good taste.

**decoy**[1] *n* **1** something used to lure a person or animal into a trap. **2** somebody or something used to divert the attention, e.g. of an enemy.

**decoy**[2] *v* to lure by a decoy.

**decrease**[1] *v* to make or become progressively less in size, number, or intensity.

**decrease**[2] *n* **1** the process of decreasing. **2** the amount by which something decreases.

**decree**[1] *n* **1** an order, *esp* one having legal force. **2** a judicial decision, *esp* in an equity, probate, or divorce court.

**decree**[2] *v* (**decrees, decreed, decreeing**) to command or impose by decree.

**decrepit** *adj* **1** weakened, *esp* by the infirmities of old age. **2** worn-out, ruined, or in disrepair. ➤ **decrepitude** *n.*

**decriminalize** *or* **-ise** *v* to stop treating as a criminal offence.

**decry** *v* (**-ies, -ied**) to express strong disapproval of.

**decrypt** *v* to decode.

**dedicate** *v* **1** to make a long-term commitment of (e.g. oneself, one's time) to a particular goal. **2** to set apart for a specific use. **3** to address (a book, song, etc) to somebody as a mark of esteem or affection. ➤ **dedicatee** *n,* **dedicatory** *adj.*

**dedicated** *adj* **1** devoted to a cause, ideal, or purpose. **2** given over to a particular purpose.

**dedication** *n* **1** commitment to achieving a particular purpose, ideal, etc. **2** the act of dedicating. **3** words used to dedicate a book, song, etc to somebody.

**deduce** *v* to establish (a fact, the truth, etc) by reasoning and making use of the information available.

**deduct** *v* to subtract (an amount) from a total. ➤ **deductible** *adj.*

**deduction** *n* **1** the act of deducting. **2** an amount that is deducted. **3** the act of deducing. ➤ **deductive** *adj.*

**deed** *n* **1** something that is done. **2** an illustrious act. **3** in law, a document containing a transfer, bargain, or contract.

**deem** *v formal* to judge or consider to be.

**deep**[1] *adj* **1** extending far downwards, inwards, or back from a surface or area. **2** having a specified extension in this direction. **3** of a colour: rich and dark; dark. **4** of a sound: having a low pitch. **5** intellectually demanding or difficult to understand. **6** capable of serious and significant thought. **7** intense or extreme. **8** in sport, near or towards the outer limits of the playing area. * **go off the deep end** to become very excited or angry. ➤ **deeply** *adv.*

**deep**[2] *n* (**the deep**) the sea.

**deepen** *v* to make or become deeper.

**deep freeze** *n* a freezer.

**deep-fry** *v* (**-ies, -ied**) to fry (food) by complete immersion in hot fat or oil.

**deer** *n* (*pl* **deer**) a ruminant mammal with antlers, *esp* in the male.

**deerstalker** *n* a close-fitting hat with peaks at the front and the back and ear-flaps.

**deface** *v* to spoil the external appearance of.

**de facto**[1] /day 'faktoh/ *adv* in reality; actually.

**de facto**[2] *adj* existing in fact; effective.

**defame** *v* to injure the reputation of (somebody) by libel or slander. ➤ **defamation** *n,* **defamatory** *adj.*

**default**[1] *n* **1** failure to do something required by law, e.g. to pay debts or appear in court. **2** a pre-selected option or setting, e.g. in computing, that remains in effect until cancelled. * **by default** in the absence of an alternative.

**default**[2] *v* **1** (*often* + on) to fail to meet an obligation, *esp* a financial one. **2** to revert to a pre-selected option or setting.

**defeat**[1] *v* **1** to win a victory over. **2** to frustrate (e.g. a hope). **3** to prevent (a motion, bill) from being passed.

**defeat**[2] *n* **1** failure to win. **2** a contest, battle, etc in which one is the loser. **3** the act of defeating.

**defeatism** *n* resignation to defeat. ➤ **defeatist** *n and adj.*

**defecate** *v* to discharge faeces from the bowels. ➤ **defecation** *n.*

**defect**[1] *n* a fault or shortcoming.

**defect**[2] *v* to desert a cause or party, often in favour of another. ➤ **defection** *n,* **defector** *n.*

**defective** *adj* unable to function properly; faulty.

**defence** (*NAmer* **defense**) *n* **1** the act of defending. **2** a means or method of defending, or a defensive structure. **3** an argument in support or justification. **4** a defendant's case. **5** the lawyers representing a defendant in a court. **6** in sport, defending players or moves. ➤ **defenceless** *adj.*

**defend** *v* **1** to protect from attack. **2** to attempt to retain (a military position, sporting title, or parliamentary seat) that others wish to gain. **3** to maintain (something) by argument against opposition or criticism. **4** in sport, to attempt to prevent an opponent from scoring, e.g. by protecting a goal. **5** to act as legal representative in court for (an accused or defendant). ➤ **defender** *n.*

**defendant** *n* a party against whom a criminal charge or civil claim is made.

**defensible** *adj* capable of being defended by argument or in a war.

**defensive** *adj* **1** serving to defend or protect. **2** sensitive to criticism and eager to justify one's own actions or views. * **on the defensive** having to defend oneself against attack or criticism. ➤ **defensively** *adv,* **defensiveness** *n.*

**defer**[1] *v* (**deferred, deferring**) to postpone (an action, decision, etc). ➤ **deferment** *n,* **deferral** *n.*

**defer**[2] *v* (**deferred, deferring**) (*usu* + to) to acknowledge somebody's superiority or allow their opinion to prevail.

**deference** *n* the respect due to a superior or an elder.

**deferential** *adj* **1** respectful. **2** obsequious. ➤ **deferentially** *adv.*

**defiance** *n* bold resistance or disobedience.

**defiant** *adj* boldly resisting or disobeying. ➤ **defiantly** *adv.*

**deficiency** *n* (*pl* **-ies**) **1** inadequacy. **2** a lack or shortage.

**deficient** *adj* **1** (*usu* + in) lacking in some necessary quality or element. **2** inadequate.

**deficit** *n* **1** a deficiency in amount or quality. **2** an excess of expenditure over revenue or of liabilities over assets.

**defile**[1] *v* to make unclean or impure.

**defile**[2] *n* a narrow passage or gorge.

**define** *v* **1** to describe the essential nature or scope of. **2** to set forth the meaning of (e.g. a word). **3** to fix or mark the limits of. **4** to make clear or precise in outline. ➤ **definable** *adj.*

**definite** *adj* **1** free of ambiguity or uncertainty. **2** clearly apparent. **3** having distinct or certain limits. ➤ **definitely** *adv.*

**definite article** *n* the word *the.*

**definition** *n* **1** a statement of what a word or phrase means. **2** the act of defining. **3** distinctness of outline or detail, e.g. in a photograph.

**definitive** *adj* **1** serving to provide a final solution. **2** authoritative and apparently exhaustive. ➤ **definitively** *adv.*

**deflate** *v* **1** to release air or gas from (e.g. a balloon or a tyre). **2** to reduce in self-confidence or self-importance. **3** to cause deflation in (an economy or price levels).

**deflation** *n* **1** the act of deflating. **2** a reduction in the amount of money and credit available in an economy, and a resulting decline in economic activity and price levels. ➤ **deflationary** *adj.*

**deflect** *v* to turn from a straight course or fixed purpose. ➤ **deflection** *n.*

**deflower** *v dated or literary* to deprive (a woman) of her virginity.

**defoliate** *v* to deprive (a tree or an area) of leaves. ➤ **defoliant** *n,* **defoliation** *n.*

**deforest** *v* to clear (an area) of forests. ➤ **deforestation** *n.*

**deform** *v* to spoil the form or appearance of. ➤ **deformed** *adj,* **deformation** *n.*

**deformity** *n* (*pl* **-ies**) **1** the state of being deformed. **2** a physical blemish or distortion; a disfigurement.

**defraud** *v* to cheat (somebody) of something, *esp* money.

**defray** *v* to provide for the payment of (an expense).

**defrock** *v* to unfrock (e.g. a priest).

**defrost** *v* **1** to thaw out (frozen food). **2** to free (a refrigerator or freezer) from ice.

**deft** *adj* marked by facility and skill. ➤ **deftly** *adv,* **deftness** *n.*

**defunct** *adj* **1** no longer existing or in use. **2** dead.

**defuse** *v* **1** to remove the fuse from (a mine, bomb, etc). **2** to make (a situation) less dangerous or tense.

**defy** *v* (**-ies, -ied**) **1** to resist by refusing to obey. **2** to challenge. **3** to do something considered impossible.

**degenerate**[1] *adj* having sunk to a lower and usu morally or physically corrupt state. ➤ **degeneracy** *n.*

**degenerate**[2] *n* a degenerate person.

**degenerate**[3] *v* to pass from a better to a worse state. ➤ **degeneration** *n,* **degenerative** *adj.*

**degrade** *v* **1** to cause to lose self-respect or the respect of others. **2** to reduce the quality of. **3** in chemistry, to cause to decompose or disintegrate. ➤ **degradable** *adj,* **degrader** *n.*

**degree** *n* **1** the extent or level of an action, condition, or relation. **2** an amount or measure. **3** a division of a scale of measurement, *esp* a unit for measuring temperature. **4** a 360th part of the circumference of a circle. **5** an academic title conferred on university students who successfully complete a course.

**dehumanize** *or* **-ise** *v* to deprive of human qualities or personality.

**dehumidify** *v* (**-ies, -ied**) to remove moisture from (e.g. air). ➤ **dehumidifier** *n.*

**dehydrate** *v* **1** to remove water from (a chemical compound, foodstuff, etc). **2** to cause to lose water or body fluids. ➤ **dehydrated** *adj,* **dehydration** *n.*

**de-ice** *v* to keep free from ice or rid of ice.

**deify** /'deeifie, 'day-/ *v* (**-ies, -ied**) to worship or treat as a god. ➤ **deification** *n.*

**deign** *v* to see fit to do something that one is usually too proud to do.

**deity** /'deeiti, 'day-/ *n* (*pl* **-ies**) **1** a god or goddess. **2** (**the Deity**) God.

**déjà vu** /ˌdayzhah 'vooh/ *n* the illusion of remembering scenes and events when they are experienced for the first time.

**dejected** *adj* cast down; depressed. ➤ **dejection** *n.*

**delay**[1] *n* the time during which something is delayed.
**delay**[2] *v* **1** to put off to a later time. **2** to detain or hinder for a time. **3** to fail to act or move immediately.
**delectable** *adj* highly pleasing; delightful or delicious. ➤ **delectably** *adv.*
**delectation** *n formal* delight or enjoyment.
**delegate**[1] *n* a person delegated to represent or act for somebody else, e.g. at a conference.
**delegate**[2] *v* **1** to entrust (e.g. a duty or responsibility) to somebody else. **2** to appoint as one's representative. **3** to assign responsibility or authority to other people.
**delegation** *n* **1** a group of people chosen to represent others. **2** the act of delegating.
**delete** *v* to eliminate by erasing. ➤ **deletion** *n.*
**deleterious** /deli'tiəri·əs/ *adj formal* harmful or detrimental.
**deli** *n* (*pl* **delis**) *informal* a delicatessen.
**deliberate**[1] *adj* **1** characterized by awareness of the nature of an action and its consequences; intentional. **2** slow or unhurried. ➤ **deliberately** *adv.*
**deliberate**[2] *v* to ponder or discuss carefully and thoroughly before reaching a decision.
**deliberation** *n* **1** careful and serious thought or consideration. **2** slow and careful movement or action. ➤ **deliberative** *adj.*
**delicacy** *n* (*pl* **-ies**) **1** daintiness. **2** fragility. **3** refined sensibility in feeling, perception, or conduct. **4** something pleasing to eat that is considered rare or luxurious.
**delicate** *adj* **1** very finely made. **2** easily damaged. **3** pleasing to the senses in a mild or subtle way. **4** marked by extreme precision. **5** having or showing extreme sensitivity. **6** requiring tact or careful treatment. **7** weak or sickly. ➤ **delicately** *adv.*
**delicatessen** *n* a shop where delicacies and foreign foods, e.g. cooked meats, are sold.
**delicious** *adj* **1** highly pleasing to the sense of taste. **2** delightful. ➤ **deliciously** *adv.*
**delight**[1] *v* **1** to take great pleasure in. **2** to give enjoyment to.
**delight**[2] *n* **1** great pleasure or satisfaction. **2** something that gives great pleasure.
**delighted** *adj* highly pleased. ➤ **delightedly** *adv.*
**delightful** *adj* highly pleasing; charming. ➤ **delightfully** *adv.*
**delineate** *v* to describe or depict in sharp or vivid detail. ➤ **delineation** *n.*
**delinquency** *n* (*pl* **-ies**) antisocial or illegal conduct.
**delinquent**[1] *n* somebody who has behaved in an antisocial or criminal way.
**delinquent**[2] *adj* guilty of wrongdoing.
**deliquesce** *v* to dissolve gradually in water attracted and absorbed from the air. ➤ **deliquescence** *n,* **deliquescent** *adj.*
**delirious** *adj* **1** suffering from delirium. **2** wildly joyful; ecstatic. ➤ **deliriously** *adv.*
**delirium** *n* **1** confusion, disordered speech, hallucinations, etc, occurring as a mental disturbance. **2** frenzied excitement or emotion.
**deliver** *v* **1** to bring or take to a specified place or person. **2** (*often* + up) to surrender. **3** to guide (e.g. a blow) to an intended target. **4** to utter or pronounce (a speech, verdict, etc). **5** to set free. **6** to assist in the birth of (a baby). **7** (*often* **be delivered of**) to give birth to (a baby). **8** *informal* to produce the promised, desired, or expected results.
**deliverance** *n* liberation or rescue.
**delivery** *n* (*pl* **-ies**) **1** the act of delivering something. **2** an item or items delivered at one time. **3** the act of giving birth. **4** an instance of throwing or bowling, *esp* in cricket.
**dell** *n* a small secluded hollow or valley.
**delphinium** *n* (*pl* **delphiniums**) a garden plant with blue or purple flowers in showy spikes.
**delta** *n* **1** a triangular area at the mouth of a river formed by deposited silt. **2** the fourth letter of the Greek alphabet (Δ, δ).
**delude** *v* to mislead the mind or judgment of; to deceive.
**deluge**[1] *n* **1** a great flood. **2** an overwhelming amount or number.
**deluge**[2] *v* **1** to overwhelm or swamp. **2** to flood.
**delusion** *n* a false belief or impression. ➤ **delusional** *adj.*
**de luxe** *adj* of superior quality.
**delve** *v* **1** to make a careful search for information. **2** to reach inside something and search about in it. **3** *archaic* to dig.
**demagnetize** *or* **-ise** *v* to remove magnetic properties from.
**demagogue** (*NAmer* **demagog**) *n* **1** an agitator who makes use of popular prejudices in order to gain power. **2** a leader of the common people in ancient times.
**demand**[1] *n* **1** a claim or forceful request. **2** (*in pl*) requirements. **3** desire or need, *esp* of consumers for a product. ✱ **in demand** sought after; popular. **on demand** whenever asked for.
**demand**[2] *v* **1** to ask for in an authoritative or peremptory way. **2** to call for urgently or insistently. **3** to require.
**demanding** *adj* **1** needing much effort or skill. **2** difficult to please.
**demarcate** *v* to mark the limits of.
**dematerialize** *or* **-ise** *v* to lose material form; to vanish.
**demean** *v* to degrade or debase.
**demeanour** (*NAmer* **demeanor**) *n* behaviour towards others, or outward manner.
**demented** *adj* insane; crazy.

**dementia** *n* a state of chronic mental impairment, characterized by memory failure and personality changes.

**demerara sugar** *n* brown cane sugar from the West Indies.

**demerit** *n* a fault or defect.

**demigod** *or* **demigoddess** *n* a mythological superhuman being with less power than a god.

**demilitarize** *or* **-ise** *v* to strip (an area) of military forces, weapons, etc. ➤ **demilitarization** *n.*

**demimonde** *n* a class of people, *esp* courtesans and kept women, on the fringes of respectable society.

**demise** *n* **1** *technical or euphem* death. **2** the end of something, e.g. an industry.

**demist** *v Brit* to remove mist from (e.g. a car windscreen). ➤ **demister** *n.*

**demo** *n* (*pl* **demos**) *informal* **1** a political demonstration. **2** a version of a computer game or piece of recorded music used for demonstration purposes.

**demob** *v* (**demobbed, demobbing**) *chiefly Brit, informal* to demobilize (troops).

**demobilize** *or* **-ise** *v* to release at the end of a period of military service. ➤ **demobilization** *n.*

**democracy** *n* (*pl* **-ies**) **1** a form of government in which the supreme power is exercised by the people. **2** a state governed in this way. **3** control of a group by its own members or a majority of them.

**democrat** *n* **1** an adherent of democracy. **2** (**Democrat**) a member of the Democratic party of the USA.

**democratic** *adj* **1** practising or favouring democracy. **2** (*often* **Democratic**) denoting a political party of the USA associated with policies of social reform and internationalism. ➤ **democratically** *adv.*

**democratize** *or* **-ise** *v* to make (a state or organization) democratic. ➤ **democratization** *n.*

**demography** *n* the statistical study of human populations. ➤ **demographic** *adj.*

**demolish** *v* **1** to destroy, smash, or tear down. **2** to defeat or refute (an argument). **3** *informal* to devour (food). ➤ **demolition** *n.*

**demon** *n* **1** an evil supernatural being; a devil. **2** (*used before a noun*) very forceful or enthusiastic.

**demoniac** *or* **demoniacal** *adj* = DEMONIC.

**demonic** *adj* **1** of or resembling a demon or evil spirit. **2** intense or frenzied.

**demonize** *or* **-ise** *v* to make seem evil or wicked.

**demonstrable** *adj* capable of being demonstrated. ➤ **demonstrably** *adv.*

**demonstrate** *v* **1** to show clearly. **2** to prove or make clear by reasoning, evidence, or example. **3** to show how something is done by doing it. **4** to take part in a political demonstration. ➤ **demonstrator** *n.*

**demonstration** *n* **1** the act of demonstrating. **2** a mass meeting, procession, etc to display group feelings about grievances or political issues.

**demonstrative** *adj* **1** inclined to display feelings openly. **2** (+ of) demonstrating something to be real or true. ➤ **demonstratively** *adv.*

**demoralize** *or* **-ise** *v* to weaken the morale or self-respect of. ➤ **demoralizing** *adj.*

**demote** *v* to reduce to a lower grade or rank. ➤ **demotion** *n.*

**demotivate** *v* to make less motivated to do something.

**demur**[1] *v* (**demurred, demurring**) to show hesitation about accepting something.

**demur**[2] *n* hesitation or objection.

**demure** *adj* (**demurer, demurest**) reserved or modest. ➤ **demurely** *adv.*

**demystify** *v* (**-ies, -ied**) to make less mysterious; to clarify.

**den** *n* **1** the lair of a wild animal. **2** a centre of secret or unlawful activity. **3** a comfortable usu secluded room.

**denationalize** *or* **-ise** *v* to remove from the ownership or control of the state.

**denial** *n* **1** an assertion that an allegation or statement is false. **2** a refusal to satisfy a request or desire. **3** in psychology, an unconscious refusal to acknowledge feelings or thoughts that may be painful.

**denier** *n* a unit of fineness for silk, rayon, or nylon yarn.

**denigrate** *v* to make negative or critical statements about, usu unjustly. ➤ **denigration** *n.*

**denim** *n* **1** a durable usu blue cotton fabric used for jeans and work clothes. **2** (*in pl*) denim clothes; *esp* jeans.

**denizen** *n literary or humorous* an inhabitant or resident.

**denominate** *v formal* to give a name to.

**denomination** *n* **1** a distinctive group within a religious faith. **2** a value shown on a coin or stamp. **3** *formal* a name or designation.

**denominator** *n* the part of a vulgar fraction below the line, indicating how many parts the numerator is divided into.

**denote** *v* **1** to indicate or mean. **2** to be a sign or symbol of.

**denouement** /day'noohmonh/ *n* the final part of a literary work in which all the complications of the plot are resolved.

**denounce** *v* **1** to condemn, *esp* publicly. **2** to inform against or accuse.

**dense** *adj* **1** marked by compactness or a crowding together of its parts. **2** *informal* stupid. ➤ **densely** *adv.*

**density** *n* (*pl* **-ies**) **1** the state of being dense. **2** the mass of a substance per unit of volume. **3**

the average number of individuals per unit of space.

**dent**[1] *n* a depression made by a blow or pressure.

**dent**[2] *v* **1** to make a dent in. **2** to affect adversely.

**dental** *adj* relating to the teeth or dentistry.

**dentine** (*NAmer* **dentin**) *n* a calcium-containing material, similar to bone, of which a tooth is composed.

**dentist** *n* somebody who treats diseases of, and injuries to, the teeth, mouth, and gums. ➤ **dentistry** *n.*

**denture** *n* **1** an artificial replacement for one or more teeth. **2** (*in pl*) a set of false teeth.

**denude** *v* to strip of all covering.

**denunciation** *n* the act of denouncing, or a public condemnation.

**deny** *v* (**-ies, -ied**) **1** to declare to be untrue or invalid. **2** to refuse to give or permit something to (somebody). **3** to refuse to grant (e.g. a request or access). * **deny oneself** to refrain from self-indulgence or pleasure.

**deodorant** *n* a substance that masks unpleasant smells, *esp* body odour.

**deodorize** *or* **-ise** *v* to remove an unpleasant smell from.

**depart** *v* **1** to go away; to leave. **2** (*usu* + from) to do something different from what is usual or was prearranged.

**departed** *adj euphem* having died.

**department** *n* **1** a major division of a government, institution, or business. **2** a major administrative subdivision, e.g. in France. **3** *informal* a distinct sphere, e.g. of activity or thought; an area of responsibility. ➤ **departmental** *adj.*

**department store** *n* a large shop with several different sections selling different types of goods.

**departure** *n* the act of departing; a going-away.

**depend** *v* **1** (*usu* + on/upon) to be determined by a particular condition or action. **2** (+ on/upon) to rely.

**dependable** *adj* reliable or trustworthy. ➤ **dependability** *n,* **dependably** *adv.*

**dependant** (*NAmer* **dependent**) *n* a person who relies on another person, *esp* for financial support.

***Usage Note:*** *Dependent* is an adjective and *dependant* is a noun meaning 'a dependent person'.

**dependency** *n* (*pl* **-ies**) **1** a territorial unit under the jurisdiction of a nation but not formally annexed to it. **2** dependence.

**dependent** *adj* **1** relying on somebody or something else for support or help. **2** (*often* + on/upon) determined or conditioned by. **3** having a need for something, e.g. a drug.

***Usage Note:*** See note at DEPENDANT.

**depict** *v* **1** to represent by a picture. **2** to describe. ➤ **depiction** *n.*

**depilate** *v* to remove hair from (a part of the body). ➤ **depilation** *n,* **depilatory** *adj.*

**deplete** *v* to lessen markedly in quantity or content. ➤ **depletion** *n.*

**deplorable** *adj* extremely bad. ➤ **deplorably** *adv.*

**deplore** *v* to regret or disapprove of strongly.

**deploy** *v* **1** to spread out (e.g. troops or ships), *esp* in battle formation. **2** to bring into action. ➤ **deployment** *n.*

**depopulate** *v* to reduce greatly the population of (an area). ➤ **depopulation** *n.*

**deport** *v* to expel (e.g. an alien) legally from a country. ➤ **deportation** *n.*

**deportment** *n Brit* the manner in which one stands, sits, or walks; posture.

**depose** *v* to remove from a position of authority, e.g. the throne.

**deposit**[1] *v* (**deposited, depositing**) **1** to place for safekeeping or as a pledge. **2** to put (money) in a bank. **3** to put down in a particular place. **4** to let (e.g. sediment) fall and form a layer.

**deposit**[2] *n* **1** money given as a pledge or down payment. **2** money or valuables deposited in a bank. **3** matter deposited by a natural process.

**deposition** *n* **1** removal from a position of authority. **2** a sworn statement presented as evidence. **3** an act or process of depositing.

**depository** *n* (*pl* **-ies**) a storehouse where things are put for safekeeping.

**depot** *n* **1** *Brit* a place where buses or trains are kept, or taken for maintenance. **2** *NAmer* a railway or bus station. **3** a place for storing goods.

**deprave** *v* to corrupt morally. ➤ **depraved** *adj.*

**depravity** *n* moral corruption.

**deprecate** *v* **1** to express disapproval of, *esp* mildly or regretfully. **2** to disparage.

**depreciate** *v* **1** to lessen in value. **2** to belittle or disparage. ➤ **depreciation** *n.*

**depredation** *n* (*usu in pl*) an act of plundering or robbery.

**depress** *v* **1** to sadden or dispirit. **2** to lessen the activity or strength of. **3** to push or press down.

**depressant** *n* a drug that slows down natural functions. ➤ **depressant** *adj.*

**depressed** *adj* **1** very sad or dispirited, *esp* suffering from depression. **2** suffering from economic depression.

**depression** *n* **1** a mental disorder marked by inactivity, difficulty in thinking and concentration, and *esp* by sadness. **2** an unhappy state or mood. **3** a period of low economic activity and rising levels of unemployment. **4** a lowered or sunken place. **5** an area of low atmospheric pressure that usually brings bad weather. **6** the act of depressing.

**depressive** *adj* **1** tending to depress. **2** characterized by psychological depression.

**deprivation** *n* **1** hardship caused by lack of basic necessities such as food or shelter. **2** the act of depriving somebody of something.

**deprive** *v* (*usu* + of) to prevent from making use of or benefiting from something.

**deprived** *adj* lacking the necessities of life.

**dept** *abbr* department.

**depth** *n* **1** the measurement downwards from a surface. **2** the distance from front to back. **3** a part that is far from the outside or surface. **4** a profound or intense state, e.g. of thought or feeling: *the depths of despair.* **5** the degree of intensity of a feeling. **6** the quality of having or containing far-reaching insights and great wisdom. ✱ **out of one's depth 1** in water that is deeper than one's height. **2** faced with a situation beyond one's ability to deal with.

**depth charge** *n* an explosive device for use underwater against submarines.

**deputation** *n* a small group of people chosen to represent the members of a larger group.

**depute** *v* to appoint (somebody) to do something on one's behalf.

**deputize** *or* **-ise** *v* (*usu* + for) to act as a deputy.

**deputy** *n* (*pl* **-ies**) a person appointed as a substitute for another.

**derail** *v* **1** to cause (a train) to leave the rails. **2** to throw off course. ➤ **derailment** *n.*

**derange** *v* **1** to disarrange. **2** to make insane. ➤ **derangement** *n.*

**deranged** *adj* mad or insane.

**derby** *n* (*pl* **-ies**) **1** (**the Derby**) a flat race for three-year-old horses held annually at Epsom. **2** a sporting match against a major local rival.

**deregulate** *v* to remove from government control or management. ➤ **deregulation** *n.*

**derelict**[1] *adj* **1** left to decay; abandoned or ruined. **2** *chiefly NAmer* lacking a sense of duty; negligent.

**derelict**[2] *n* a down-and-out.

**dereliction** *n* **1** conscious neglect, *esp* of duty. **2** a decaying or ruined state.

**deride** *v* to mock or scorn (something).

**de rigueur** /dəri'guh/ *adj* required by fashion or etiquette.

**derision** *n* scorn or ridicule.

**derisive** *adj* mocking or scornful. ➤ **derisively** *adv.*

**derisory** *adj* **1** ridiculously small and inadequate. **2** derisive.

**derivation** *n* **1** the fact of being obtained or originating from a particular source. **2** the formation of a word from another word or root.

**derivative**[1] *adj* made up of derived elements; not original.

**derivative**[2] *n* something derived, e.g. a word formed by derivation.

**derive** *v* **1** to obtain or receive, *esp* from a specified source. **2** (+ from) to come, result, or originate from.

**dermatitis** *n* a disease or inflammation of the skin.

**dermatology** *n* the branch of medicine dealing with the skin and skin diseases. ➤ **dermatological** *adj,* **dermatologically** *adv,* **dermatologist** *n.*

**derogatory** *adj* expressing a low opinion; insulting or disparaging.

**derrick** *n* **1** a hoisting apparatus with a swivelling beam, similar to a crane. **2** a framework over an oil well for supporting drilling tackle.

**derring-do** *n archaic or literary* daring action.

**dervish** *n* a member of a Muslim religious order noted for its energetic whirling dances that lead to a trance.

**descant** *n* an additional melody sung or played above the main tune.

**descend** *v* **1** to pass from a higher to a lower level. **2** to incline, lead, or extend downwards. **3** (*usu* **be descended from**) to have as an ancestor. **4** (+ on/upon) to make a sudden attack on, or a sudden disconcerting visit to. **5** (+ to) to lower or degrade oneself.

**descendant** *n* somebody descended from a particular ancestor.

**descent** *n* **1** the act or process of descending. **2** a downward slope. **3** family origins or lineage.

**describe** *v* **1** to give an account of in words. **2** to trace the outline of.

**description** *n* **1** an account in words. **2** the act of describing. **3** a kind or sort.

**descriptive** *adj* serving to describe, *esp* vividly. ➤ **descriptively** *adv.*

**descry** *v* (**-ies**, **-ied**) *formal* to notice or see, *esp* at a distance.

**desecrate** *v* to treat (something sacred) irreverently or contemptuously. ➤ **desecration** *n.*

**desegregate** *v* to eliminate racial segregation in (e.g. a school). ➤ **desegregation** *n.*

**deselect** *v* of a constituency political party: to refuse to readopt (somebody) as a parliamentary candidate. ➤ **deselection** *n.*

**desensitize** *or* **-ise** *v* to make less sensitive.

**desert**[1] *n* **1** a barren region incapable of supporting much life. **2** a place that is deprived of something important: *a cultural desert.*

***Usage Note:*** The noun *desert* has the stress on the first syllable; the verb *desert* has the stress on the second. Do not confuse these with *dessert* (sweet course), which has the stress on the second syllable.

**desert**[2] *n* (*usu in pl*) deserved reward or punishment: *just deserts.*

**desert**[3] *v* **1** to abandon (somebody), *esp* somebody to whom one owes a duty. **2** to quit one's post, military service, etc without leave or justification. ➤ **deserter** *n*, **desertion** *n*.

**deserted** *adj* left empty of people.

**deserve** *v* to be worthy of (a reward, punishment, or particular type of treatment). ➤ **deservedly** *adv*.

**deserving** *adj* worthy of something, *esp* financial aid.

**déshabillé** /dayza'beeay/ *or* **deshabille** /-'beel, disə'beel/ *n* the state of being partially or carelessly dressed.

**desiccate** *v* to remove moisture from, *esp* as a means of preservation.

**design**[1] *v* **1** to draw the plans for (e.g. a building). **2** to devise for a specific purpose.

**design**[2] *n* **1** a drawing showing how something is to be constructed. **2** the act of producing such a plan. **3** a decorative pattern. **4** a particular purpose held in view. **5** deliberate purposeful planning. * **have designs on** to wish to obtain, often dishonestly.

**designate**[1] *v* **1** to nominate for a particular office or duty. **2** to call by a distinctive name or title.

**designate**[2] *adj* chosen for an office but not yet installed: *ambassador designate*.

**designation** *n* **1** a distinguishing name or title. **2** the act of indicating or identifying.

**designer** *n* **1** somebody who designs *esp* manufactured objects. **2** (*used before a noun*) made by a well-known fashion designer: *designer jeans*.

**desirable** *adj* **1** worth having as advantageous or beneficial. **2** attractive, *esp* sexually. ➤ **desirability** *n*.

**desire**[1] *v* **1** to long or hope for. **2** to wish to have sexual relations with.

**desire**[2] *n* **1** a longing or craving, *esp* a sexual longing. **2** something desired.

**desirous** *adj formal* (*usu* + of/to) eagerly wanting; desiring.

**desist** *v formal* (*often* + from) to cease to proceed or act.

**desk** *n* **1** a table with a sloping or horizontal surface, designed for writing and reading. **2** a counter at which cashiers, receptionists, etc work.

**desktop** *n* **1** the working surface of a desk. **2** a compact computer suitable for use on a desk. **3** the visible screen on a VDU, on which icons, the cursor, etc are displayed.

**desolate**[1] *adj* **1** barren, lifeless, or uninhabited. **2** extremely unhappy.

**desolate**[2] *v* **1** to make barren or lifeless. **2** (**be desolated**) to be extremely unhappy. ➤ **desolation** *n*.

**despair**[1] *v* (*often* + of) to lose all hope or confidence. ➤ **despairing** *adj*.

**despair**[2] *n* utter loss of hope.

**despatch**[1] *v* see DISPATCH[1].

**despatch**[2] *n* see DISPATCH[2].

**desperado** *n* (*pl* **-oes** *or* **-os**) *dated* a reckless or violent criminal.

**desperate** *adj* **1** in despair because beyond hope. **2** reckless because of despair. **3** (*often* + for) suffering extreme need. **4** fraught with extreme danger. **5** violent or dangerous. ➤ **desperately** *adj*, **desperation** *n*.

***Usage Note:*** Note the spelling with *-er-*.

**despicable** *adj* morally contemptible. ➤ **despicably** *adv*.

**despise** *v* to regard with contempt or distaste.

**despite** *prep* notwithstanding; in spite of. * **despite oneself** in spite of one's intentions, wishes, character, etc.

**despoil** *v* to plunder or pillage.

**despondent** *adj* extremely discouraged or dejected. ➤ **despondency** *n*, **despondently** *adv*.

**despot** *n* a ruler with absolute power. ➤ **despotic** *adj*, **despotism** *n*.

**dessert** *n* a sweet course or dish served at the end of a meal.

***Usage Note:*** See note at DESERT[1].

**dessertspoon** *n* a spoon intermediate in size between a teaspoon and a tablespoon.

**destabilize** *or* **-ise** *v* to make (a government, an economy, etc) unstable.

**destination** *n* a place where a journey is set to end, or to which something is sent.

**destine** *v* **1** (*usu* **be destined for/to do**) to designate or set apart for a particular purpose or fate: *She was destined for great things*. **2** (**be destined for**) be going to a place: *freight destined for various English ports*.

**destiny** *n* (*pl* **-ies**) **1** the power held to determine the course of events. **2** a person's fate or future course of life.

**destitute** *adj* lacking the basic necessities of life; extremely poor. ➤ **destitution** *n*.

**destroy** *v* **1** to demolish or ruin. **2** to put an end to. **3** to kill (an animal) humanely.

**destroyer** *n* **1** somebody or something that destroys. **2** a small fast multi-purpose warship.

**destruction** *n* the act of destroying.

**destructive** *adj* **1** causing destruction. **2** of criticism, etc: pointing out faults without offering ideas for improvement. ➤ **destructively** *adv*.

**desultory** *adj* **1** passing aimlessly from one subject or activity to another. **2** happening on and off.

**detach** *v* **1** to separate (something), *esp* from a larger object, organization, or group. **2** to keep (oneself) emotionally detached. ➤ **detachable** *adj*.

***Usage Note:*** Note the spelling with *-ach* not *-atch*.

**detached** *adj* **1** separate; not connected to e.g. another house. **2** of a person: free from prejudice or emotional involvement.

**detachment** *n* **1** freedom from bias or emotional involvement. **2** a section of a body of troops, ships, etc, designated for a special mission.

**detail**[1] *n* **1** (*usu in pl*) an individual relevant part or fact. **2** such small parts or facts collectively. **3** a small part of a work of art considered in isolation. **4** a small military detachment selected for a particular task. * **in detail** item by item; thoroughly.

**detail**[2] *v* **1** to describe in detail. **2** to assign to a particular task.

**detailed** *adj* marked by abundant detail or thorough treatment.

**detain** *v* **1** to delay. **2** to hold in custody.

**detainee** *n* a person held in custody, *esp* for political reasons.

**detect** *v* **1** to discover the existence or discern the presence of. **2** to discover (a crime or criminal). ➤ **detectable** *adj*, **detection** *n*.

**detective** *n* a police officer or other person engaged in investigating crimes.

**detector** *n* a device used to detect the presence of e.g. radiation, smoke, or metal.

**détente** *or* **detente** *n* a relaxation of strained relations, e.g. between hostile nations.

**detention** *n* **1** the act of detaining, *esp* in custody. **2** *chiefly Brit* a period during which a pupil is kept in school after normal hours as a punishment.

**deter** *v* (**deterred, deterring**) **1** (*often* + from) to discourage or prevent (somebody) from doing something. **2** to prevent (something) happening. ➤ **deterrence** *n*, **deterrent** *adj*.

**detergent** *n* a cleansing agent; *esp* a chemical one.

**deteriorate** *v* to grow worse. ➤ **deterioration** *n*.

**determination** *n* **1** firmness and persistence in carrying out one's intentions. **2** the act of determining something.

**determine** *v* **1** to regulate or condition the nature or scope of. **2** to ascertain or work out. **3** to settle or decide conclusively or authoritatively.

**determined** *adj* firm; resolute. ➤ **determinedly** *adv*.

**determiner** *n* **1** something or somebody that determines. **2** a basic type of word, such as *this*, *that*, *my*, *his*, etc, that comes before a noun and any descriptive adjective applied to that noun.

**deterrent** *n* something that deters, e.g. nuclear weapons held by one nation to deter another from attacking it.

**detest** *v* to feel intense dislike for.

**detestable** *adj* arousing or deserving intense dislike.

**detestation** *n* extreme dislike.

**dethrone** *v* to remove (*esp* a monarch) from a position of power or authority.

**detonate** *v* **1** to cause (a bomb, etc) to explode. **2** of a bomb, etc: to explode. ➤ **detonation** *n*.

**detonator** *n* a device used for detonating a high explosive.

**detour**[1] *n* a roundabout route that is an alternative to a shorter or planned route.

**detour**[2] *v* to make a detour.

**detoxify** *v* (**-ies, -ied**) **1** to remove a poison or toxin from. **2** to treat for dependency on alcohol or drugs.

**detract** *v* (+ from) to make less valuable, interesting, etc.

**detractor** *n* a person who denigrates somebody or their ideas or beliefs.

**detriment** *n* injury or damage.

**detritus** *n* debris or waste material.

**deuce** *n* **1** a score of 40 all in tennis, after which two consecutive points are needed to win a game. **2** (**the deuce**) *informal* the devil.

**Deutschmark** /'doychmahk/ *or* **Deutsche Mark** /'doychə mahk/ *n* the basic monetary unit of Germany before the Euro.

**devalue** *v* **1** to reduce the exchange value of (money). **2** to lessen the value or reputation of. ➤ **devaluation** *n*.

**devastate** *v* **1** to reduce (a place) to ruin. **2** to overwhelm (somebody), e.g. with grief or horror. ➤ **devastation** *n*.

**devastating** *adj* **1** causing great destruction. **2** shocking; horrifying. **3** *informal* extremely attractive or impressive. ➤ **devastatingly** *adv*.

**develop** *v* (**developed, developing**) **1** to go through a process of natural growth or evolution. **2** to cause to grow, mature, or increase. **3** to become gradually visible or apparent. **4** to unfold (an idea) gradually or in detail. **5** to show signs of (an illness). **6** to use chemicals to produce a visible image on (a photograph). **7** to acquire gradually: *He developed a taste for good wine*. **8** to build on or change the use of (land).

**development** *n* **1** the act of developing. **2** an innovation or new product. **3** something which changes a situation. **4** an area of new building. ➤ **developmental** *adj*.

**deviant**[1] *adj* deviating from a norm. ➤ **deviance** *n*.

**deviant**[2] *n* a person whose sexual or social behaviour differs markedly from the norm.

**deviate** *v* to stray, *esp* from a principle, norm, or straight course.

**device** *n* **1** a piece of equipment designed for a special purpose. **2** a scheme to trick or deceive. **3** a heraldic symbol. * **leave somebody to their own devices** to leave somebody to do as they please.

**devil** *n* **1** (*usu* **the Devil**) the supreme spirit of evil in Jewish and Christian belief. **2** a malignant spirit; a demon. **3** an extremely cruel or wicked person. **4** *informal* a person of the specified type: *You're a lucky devil.* **5** (**the devil**) *informal* something provoking, difficult, or trying. ✱ **the devil to pay** a lot of trouble.

**devilish** *adj* **1** characteristic of a devil; wicked. **2** mischievous. ➤ **devilishly** *adv.*

**devil-may-care** *adj* heedless of authority or convention.

**devilment** *n* wild mischief.

**devilry** *n* **1** mischief. **2** action performed with the help of the devil.

**devil's advocate** *n* a person who champions the less accepted cause, *esp* for the sake of argument.

**devious** *adj* **1** of a person: not straightforward or wholly sincere. **2** roundabout or circuitous. ➤ **deviously** *adv,* **deviousness** *n.*

**devise** *v* to formulate (a plan) in the mind; to invent.

**devoid** *adj* (+ of) totally without.

**devolution** *n* the surrender of powers to regional or local authorities by a central government.

**devolve** *v* **1** (*usu* + on/upon/to) to surrender (power) by devolution. **2** (*usu* + on/upon/to) to be passed, usu as an obligation or responsibility.

**devote** *v* (+ to) to set apart for, or give over entirely to.

**devoted** *adj* **1** very loving. **2** loyally attached. **3** dedicated. ➤ **devotedly** *adv.*

**devotee** *n* **1** an enthusiast. **2** a person devoted to a particular religious cult or practice.

**devotion** *n* **1** great love, affection, or dedication. **2** the act of devoting. **3** religious zeal; piety. **4** (*usu in pl*) a special act of prayer or supplication. ➤ **devotional** *adj.*

**devour** *v* **1** to eat (food) up greedily or ravenously. **2** *literary* to swallow up. **3** (**be devoured**) to be preoccupied or absorbed. **4** to take in eagerly through the mind or senses.

**devout** *adj* **1** devoted to religion; pious. **2** sincere; genuine. ➤ **devoutly** *adv.*

**dew** *n* moisture that condenses on cool surfaces, *esp* at night.

**dewlap** *n* a hanging fold of skin under the neck of an animal, e.g. a cow.

**dewy** *adj* (**-ier, -iest**) moist with dew, or as if with dew.

**dexterity** *n* skill, *esp* in using the hands.

**dexterous** *or* **dextrous** *adj* skilful, *esp* with the hands. ➤ **dexterously** *adv.*

**diabetes** *n* an illness characterized by the secretion of excessive amounts of urine, *esp* diabetes mellitus in which the body is unable to process sugar as a result of not producing enough insulin.

**diabetic**[1] *adj* affected with diabetes.

**diabetic**[2] *n* a person affected with diabetes.

**diabolical** *adj* **1** of the devil. **2** *chiefly Brit, informal* dreadful; appalling. ➤ **diabolically** *adv.*

**diadem** *n* a crown.

**diagnose** *v* to recognize (a disease, etc) by signs and symptoms. ➤ **diagnostic** *adj.*

**diagnosis** *n* (*pl* **diagnoses**) **1** the act of identifying a disease from its signs and symptoms. **2** the investigation of the cause or nature of a problem.

**diagonal**[1] *adj* **1** of a line: straight and slanting. **2** joining two opposite or nonadjacent angles of a rectangle or other figure. ➤ **diagonally** *adv.*

**diagonal**[2] *n* a diagonal line.

**diagram** *n* a line drawing, made for mathematical or scientific purposes or to show the arrangement of parts. ➤ **diagrammatic** *adj.*

**dial**[1] *n* **1** a face with marks or numbers on which something is measured by a pointer, *esp* the face of a clock. **2** a disc-shaped control mechanism, *esp* for selecting numbers on a telephone.

**dial**[2] *v* (**dialled, dialling,** *NAmer* **dialed, dialing**) to operate a dial, or press buttons, to select (a telephone number).

**dialect** *n* a variety of a language, usu differing in grammar and vocabulary from the standard, used by a particular regional or social group. ➤ **dialectal** *adj.*

**dialectic** *n* (*usu in pl*) systematic reasoning or argument that juxtaposes opposed ideas and seeks to resolve their conflict. ➤ **dialectical** *adj.*

**dialogue** (*NAmer* **dialog**) *n* **1** a conversation between two or more people. **2** the conversational element in a literary work. **3** discussion between two groups with conflicting interests.

**dialysis** *n* (*pl* **dialyses**) the use of a membrane to separate out substances in solution, *esp* the purification of blood by such means in a kidney machine.

**diamanté** *n* **1** sparkling particles, or fabric decorated with these. **2** (*used before a noun*) decorated with diamanté.

**diameter** *n* a straight line passing through the centre of a circle or sphere, or the length of this line.

**diametric** *or* **diametrical** *adj* completely opposed or opposite. ➤ **diametrically** *adv.*

**diamond**[1] *n* **1** a precious stone formed of very hard crystalline carbon. **2** a square or rhombus turned so that it rests on one of its angles. **3** a playing card marked with red diamond-shaped figures.

**diamond**[2] *adj* marking a 60th anniversary: *diamond wedding.*

**diaper** *n NAmer* a nappy.

**diaphanous** *adj* of fabrics: so fine as to be almost transparent.

**diaphragm** *n* **1** the layer of muscle separating the chest and abdominal cavities in mammals.

**2** a contraceptive cap that fits over the cervix. **3** a device that controls the amount of light entering a camera lens. **4** a thin vibrating disc in a sound-reproduction system, e.g. in an earphone.

**diarist** *n* somebody who keeps a diary.

**diarrhoea** (*NAmer* **diarrhea**) *n* abnormally frequent bowel movements with fluid faeces.

**diary** *n* (*pl* **-ies**) a book containing a daily record of personal experiences or observations, or for noting appointments, etc.

**diatonic** *adj* relating to a standard major or minor musical scale of eight notes to the octave.

**diatribe** *n* a lengthy piece of bitter and abusive criticism.

**dice**[1] *n* (*pl* **dice**) a small cube marked on each face with from one to six spots, used in various games.

**dice**[2] *v* to cut (food) into small cubes. * **dice with death** to take a big risk.

**dicey** *adj* (**dicier, diciest**) *informal* risky; unpredictable.

**dichotomy** *n* (*pl* **-ies**) a sharp division or contrast, between two things.

**dicky** *adj* (**-ier, -iest**) *Brit, informal* weak or unsound.

**dictate**[1] *v* **1** to read out the text of (a letter, etc) for someone else to write down. **2** (*often* + to) to give orders authoritatively or overbearingly. **3** to impose or control the nature, scope, etc of with authority. ➤ **dictation** *n.*

**dictate**[2] *n* an authoritative rule, principle, or command.

**dictator** *n* an absolute ruler, *esp* an oppressive and unconstitutional one. ➤ **dictatorial** *adj.*

**dictatorship** *n* a state or form of government where absolute power is wielded by one person.

**diction** *n* **1** choice of words in speech or writing. **2** pronunciation of words in speaking.

**dictionary** *n* (*pl* **-ies**) a reference book that lists words alphabetically and gives their meanings or their equivalents in a foreign language.

**dictum** *n* (*pl* **dicta** *or* **dictums**) an authoritative statement on some topic.

**did** *v* past tense of DO[1].

**didactic** *adj* intended to teach something, *esp* a moral lesson.

**diddle** *v informal* to cheat or swindle.

**didgeridoo** *n* (*pl* **didgeridoos**) an Australian wind instrument consisting of a long wooden tube.

**didn't** *contraction* did not.

**die**[1] *v* (**dies, died, dying**) **1** to stop living. **2** (*also* + out) to cease to exist; to become extinct. **3** (*often* + away) to become weaker or fainter, or to cease. **4** (*also* + for) to long keenly or desperately. **5** (+ of) to be almost overwhelmed with (e.g. boredom). * **never say die** *informal* never give up. **to die for** *informal* excellent or desirable.

**die**[2] *n* **1** (*pl* **dice**) a dice. **2** (*pl* **dies**) a tool for pressing or moulding materials or impressing a design on e.g. coins. * **the die is cast** the irrevocable decision or step has been taken.

**die away** *v* to become weaker or fainter, then disappear.

**die-cast** *v* (*past tense and past part.* **die-cast**) to make (an object) by forcing molten plastic, metal, etc into a die.

**die down** *v* to diminish or subside.

**die-hard** *n* **1** a person who strongly resists change. **2** (*used before a noun*) strongly resisting change.

**die off** *v* to die one by one.

**die out** *v* **1** to become extinct. **2** to cease to exist, be done, etc.

**diesel** *n* **1** an internal-combustion engine in which the fuel is ignited by the heat generated by compressing the air in the cylinders. **2** a diesel-engined vehicle. **3** a heavy mineral oil used as fuel in diesel engines.

**diet**[1] *n* **1** the food habitually eaten by a person or animal. **2** the kind and amount of food prescribed for a special purpose, *esp* losing weight. **3** (*used before a noun*) of food or drinks: low in calories or fat content.

**diet**[2] *v* (**dieted, dieting**) to eat and drink sparingly, *esp* to lose weight.

**dietary** *adj* **1** of a diet. **2** present in the food a person eats.

**dietitian** *or* **dietician** *n* a specialist in diet and nutrition.

**differ** *v* **1** (+ from) to be unlike. **2** of people: to disagree.

**difference** *n* **1** unlikeness between two or more people or things. **2** a disagreement or dispute. **3** a remainder left after subtracting one number from another. **4** a significant effect on a situation.

**different** *adj* **1** partly or totally unlike. **2** distinct. **3** other. **4** *informal* unusual; special. ➤ **differently** *adv.*

***Usage Note:*** **different from/to/than**. The preferred combination is *different from*. British English also accepts *different to*. *Different than* is acceptable only in American English.

**differential**[1] *adj* of or involving a difference.

**differential**[2] *n* **1** the amount by which the rate of pay differs for workers doing comparable types of work. **2** in mathematics, a very small change in the value of a variable. **3** an arrangement of gears that allows one of a pair of driving wheels to turn faster than the other when cornering.

**differentiate** *v* **1** to show the difference in (things). **2** to distinguish between (different things). ➤ **differentiation** *n.*

**difficult** *adj* **1** hard to do, make, carry out, or understand. **2** hard to deal with, manage, or please.

**difficulty** *n* (*pl* **-ies**) **1** the state of being difficult. **2** (*often in pl*) a cause of trouble or embarrassment; a problem.
**diffident** *adj* lacking in self-confidence; shy. ➤ **diffidence** *n*, **diffidently** *adv.*
**diffract** *v* to cause (a beam of light) to split into bands as it passes the edge of an opaque body, through narrow slits, etc. ➤ **diffraction** *n.*
**diffuse**[1] *adj* **1** not concentrated; scattered. **2** lacking conciseness; verbose.
**diffuse**[2] *v* **1** to spread out. **2** of atomic particles: to become intermingled in a substance as a result of their spontaneous movements. ➤ **diffusion** *n.*
**dig**[1] *v* (**digging,** *past tense and past part.* **dug**) **1** to turn up, loosen, or remove earth. **2** to hollow out (a hole or tunnel) by removing earth. **3** (*often* + into) to search for information. **4** to poke or prod. **5** *slang, dated* to appreciate. ➤ **digger** *n.*
**dig**[2] *n* **1** a thrust or poke. **2** *informal* a cutting or snide remark. **3** an archaeological excavation site. **4** *chiefly Brit, informal* (*in pl*) lodgings.
**digest**[1] *v* **1** to convert (food) into a form the body can use. **2** to assimilate mentally. ➤ **digestible** *adj.*
**digest**[2] *n* a summary, abridgment, or compilation of essential information.
**digestion** *n* the process or capability of digesting something, *esp* food.
**digestive** *adj* relating to digestion.
**digestive biscuit** *or* **digestive** *n Brit* a slightly sweet biscuit made from wholemeal flour.
**dig in** *v* **1** of a soldier: to dig defensive positions. **2** *informal* to hold stubbornly to a position. **3** *informal* to begin eating. ✱ **dig one's heels in** *informal* to refuse to move or change one's mind.
**digit** *n* **1** an element that can be used in forming a number, *esp* an Arabic numeral from 0 to 9. **2** a finger or toe.
**digital** *adj* **1** presented, stored, or manipulated in the form of numerical digits. **2** of a computer: operating with numbers expressed as discrete pulses representing digits in binary notation. **3** of a clock or watch: presenting information in the form of numerical digits rather than by a pointer and a dial. **4** of sound recording: involving the conversion of sounds into digital form to reduce background noise and distortion. **5** relating to fingers or toes. ➤ **digitally** *adv.*
**digital pen** *n* a pen that makes a digital record of what is written for later downloading onto a computer or transmission by mobile phone.
**digitize** *or* **-ise** *v* to put (data, etc) into digital form.
**dignified** *adj* showing or having dignity.
**dignify** *v* (**-ies, -ied**) to confer dignity or distinction on.
**dignitary** *n* (*pl* **-ies**) a person of high rank.
**dignity** *n* **1** composure and self-control. **2** the quality of being worthy or esteemed. **3** a high opinion of oneself.
**dig out** *v* **1** to remove by digging. **2** to search for and find.
**digress** *v* to turn aside from the main subject in writing or speaking. ➤ **digression** *n.*
**dig up** *v* **1** to remove by digging. **2** to discover by searching.
**dike**[1] *n* see DYKE[1].
**dike**[2] *n informal, derog* see DYKE[2].
**diktat** *n* a dictatorial order or ruling.
**dilapidated** *adj* decayed or fallen into partial ruin. ➤ **dilapidation** *n.*
**dilate** *v* to become wider or wider open. ➤ **dilation** *n.*
**dilatory** *adj* **1** intended to cause delay. **2** slow, tardy.
**dilemma** *n* **1** a situation involving choice between two equally unsatisfactory alternatives. **2** *informal* a seemingly insoluble problem.
**dilettante** /dili'tanti/ *n* (*pl* **dilettantes** *or* **dilettanti**) a person with a superficial interest in an art or a branch of knowledge.
**diligent** *adj* hard-working and conscientious. ➤ **diligence** *n*, **diligently** *adv.*
**dill** *n* a herb used in flavouring foods, e.g. pickles.
**dillydally** *v* (**-ies, -ied**) *informal* to waste time by loitering; to dawdle.
**dilute**[1] *v* **1** to make (a liquid) thinner or weaker by adding more liquid. **2** to make less powerful or effective by adding other elements. ➤ **dilution** *n.*
**dilute**[2] *adj* weak; diluted.
**dim**[1] *adj* (**dimmer, dimmest**) **1** giving out a weak or insufficient light. **2** seen or remembered indistinctly. **3** not seeing clearly. **4** *informal* unintelligent. ✱ **take a dim view of** to have an unfavourable attitude to. ➤ **dimly** *adv.*
**dim**[2] *v* (**dimmed, dimming**) to make or become dim.
**dime** *n* a coin worth ten US cents.
**dimension** *n* **1** a measurement giving the length, breadth or height of an object. **2** (*in pl*) size or scope. **3** an aspect. ➤ **dimensional** *adj.*
**diminish** *v* to make or become gradually less.
**diminution** *n* a diminishing or decrease.
**diminutive**[1] *adj* exceptionally small; tiny.
**diminutive**[2] *n* a word or affix, e.g *-ette*, indicating a smaller-sized version of something.
**dimmer** *n* a device for regulating the brightness of electric lighting.
**dimple** *n* a slight indentation, *esp* in the cheek or chin. ➤ **dimpled** *adj.*
**dimwit** *n informal* a stupid person. ➤ **dimwitted** *adj.*
**din**[1] *n* a loud continued discordant noise.

**din²** *v* (**dinned, dinning**) ✱ **din something into** to instil something into (somebody) by perpetual repetition.

**dine** *v* to eat dinner.

**diner** *n* **1** somebody who is dining. **2** *NAmer* a small restaurant, often beside the road. **3** *chiefly NAmer* a dining car.

**dinghy** *n* (*pl* **-ies**) **1** a small open sailing boat. **2** a small inflatable rubber boat.

**dingo** *n* (*pl* **-oes** *or* **-os**) a wild dog of Australia.

**dingy** *adj* (**-ier, -iest**) **1** dirty; discoloured. **2** gloomy; dim.

**dinky** *adj* (**-ier, -iest**) *chiefly Brit, informal* neat and dainty.

**dinner** *n* **1** the principal meal of the day taken either in the evening or at midday. **2** a formal evening meal.

**dinner jacket** *n* a jacket, usu black, for men's semi-formal evening wear.

**dinosaur** *n* **1** an extinct, typically very large reptile of a type that existed from 245 to 65 million years ago. **2** a person or organization that is outdated and reluctant to change.

**dint** ✱ **by dint of** by means or application of.

**diocese** *n* the area under the jurisdiction of a bishop. ➤ **diocesan** *adj.*

**diode** *n* a semiconductor device having only two terminals.

**dioxide** *n* an oxide containing two atoms of oxygen.

**dip¹** *v* (**dipped, dipping**) **1** to plunge or immerse in a liquid. **2** to drop or decrease, often temporarily and by a small amount. **3** to lower (something) and then raise it again. **4** to lower (the beam of headlights) so as to reduce glare. **5** (+ in/into) to reach (a hand, etc) into a container to take something out. **6** to slope down. ✱ **dip into 1** to make inroads into for funds or supplies. **2** to read superficially.

**dip²** *n* **1** the act of dipping. **2** a brief bathe. **3** a soft mixture into which food is dipped before being eaten. **4** a brief drop or downward slope followed by a rise.

**diphtheria** *n* an acute infectious disease marked by the formation of a false membrane in the throat, causing difficulty in breathing.

**diphthong** *n* a sound that combines two vowels in one syllable, e.g. /oy/ in *toy*.

**diploma** *n* a certificate awarded for a qualification, usu in a specialized subject.

**diplomacy** *n* **1** the art of conducting international relations. **2** skill and tact in dealing with people.

**diplomat** *n* **1** a person, e.g. an ambassador, employed in diplomacy. **2** a tactful person.

**diplomatic** *adj* **1** of diplomats or international relations. **2** employing tact and conciliation. ➤ **diplomatically** *adv.*

**dipper** *n* **1** a small bird that swims underwater to feed. **2** something, e.g. a long-handled cup, used for dipping.

**dippy** *adj* (**-ier, -iest**) *informal* crazy; eccentric.

**dipsomania** *n* alcoholism. ➤ **dipsomaniac** *n.*

**dipstick** *n* **1** a graduated rod for measuring the depth of a liquid, *esp* the oil in a car. **2** *informal* a stupid person.

**dire** *adj* **1** desperately urgent. **2** *informal* dreadful; awful.

**direct¹** *v* **1** to control the activities or course of. **2** to control the way (a film, play, or broadcast) is performed. **3** to order or instruct. **4** to show or point out the way for. **5** to cause to turn, move, or point in a particular direction. **6** to address or aim (a remark).

**direct²** *adj* **1** going from one point to another in space without deviation or interruption; straight. **2** going by the shortest way. **3** stemming immediately from a source. **4** operating without an intervening agency. **5** frank; straightforward.

**direct³** *adv* **1** by the shortest way. **2** without an intervening agency.

**direct current** *n* an electric current flowing in one direction only.

**direct debit** *n* an order to a bank to pay sums not specified in advance from one's account to another account at specified times.

**direction** *n* **1** the line or course along which somebody or something moves or is aimed. **2** the point towards which somebody or something faces. **3** the act of directing. **4** guidance or supervision. **5** (*in pl*) explicit instructions on how to do something or get to a place. ➤ **directional** *adj.*

**directive** *n* an authoritative instruction from an official body.

**directly¹** *adv* **1** in a direct manner. **2** immediately; soon.

**directly²** *conj chiefly Brit, informal* immediately after; as soon as.

**director** *n* **1** the head of an organized group or administrative unit. **2** a member of a management board of a company. **3** somebody who supervises the artistic and technical aspects of a film or play. ➤ **directorial** *adj,* **directorship** *n.*

**director-general** *n* (*pl* **directors-general** *or* **director-generals**) the senior director of a large organization.

**directory** *n* (*pl* **-ies**) **1** an alphabetical or classified list, e.g. of names, addresses, telephone numbers, etc. **2** a list of the files contained in a computer disk.

**dirge** *n* **1** a song of grief or lamentation, *esp* to accompany a funeral. **2** an unduly slow or mournful piece of music.

**dirigible** *n* an airship.

**dirk** *n* a dagger, formerly used by Scottish Highlanders.

**dirt** *n* **1** a filthy or soiling substance. **2** earth; soil. **3** *informal* excrement. **4** *informal* obscene or pornographic material. **5** *informal* scandalous gossip. * **treat like dirt** *informal* to treat very badly.

**dirty**[1] *adj* (**-ier, -iest**) **1** not clean or pure. **2** base, dishonest, or unsporting. **3** low; despicable: *a dirty trick*. **4** indecent; obscene. **5** of the weather: rough or stormy. **6** conveying resentment or disgust: *a dirty look*.

**dirty**[2] *v* (**-ies, -ied**) to make or become dirty.

**dis-** *prefix* denoting removal, exclusion, or the opposite of (a specified action): *disarm; disbar; disappear.*

**disability** *n* (*pl* **-ies**) **1** an inability to do something because of physical or mental impairment. **2** a handicap.

**disable** *v* **1** to impair physically; to cripple. **2** to make incapable of operating.

**disabled** *adj* **1** having physical disabilities. **2** incapable of operating.

**disabuse** *v* (*usu* + of) to free from a mistaken impression.

**disadvantage**[1] *n* something which causes one to be in an unfavourable position. ➤ **disadvantageous** *adj.*

**disadvantage**[2] *v* to place at a disadvantage.

**disadvantaged** *adj* underprivileged, *esp* socially.

**disaffected** *adj* discontented and resentful, *esp* towards authority. ➤ **disaffection** *n.*

**disagree** *v* **1** (*often* + with) to differ in opinion. **2** to be unlike or at variance with. **3** (+ with) to have a bad effect on. ➤ **disagreement** *n.*

**disagreeable** *adj* **1** unpleasant; objectionable. **2** ill-tempered.

**disallow** *v* **1** to prohibit. **2** to refuse to recognize the validity of.

**disappear** *v* **1** to cease to be visible. **2** to cease to exist. **3** *informal* to leave or depart, *esp* secretly. ➤ **disappearance** *n.*

**disappoint** *v* to fail to meet the expectations or hopes of, and to sadden by so doing. ➤ **disappointed** *adj*, **disappointing** *adj.*

***Usage Note:*** Note the spelling with *-s-* and *-pp-*.

**disappointment** *n* **1** a sad feeling caused by being disappointed. **2** somebody or something that disappoints.

**disapprobation** *n formal* disapproval.

**disapprove** *v* to have or express an unfavourable opinion of. ➤ **disapproval** *n*, **disapproving** *adj.*

**disarm** *v* **1** to deprive of weapons. **2** to reduce or abolish weapons and armed forces. **3** to make (a bomb, etc) harmless, *esp* by removing a fuse or warhead. **4** to dispel the hostility or suspicion of, *esp* through personal charm. ➤ **disarming** *adj.*

**disarmament** *n* the relinquishment or reduction of weapons and armed forces.

**disarrange** *v* to disturb the arrangement or order of. ➤ **disarrangement** *n.*

**disarray**[1] *n* a lack of order or sequence; disorder.

**disarray**[2] *v* to throw into disorder.

**disassociate** *v* = DISSOCIATE.

**disaster** *n* **1** a sudden event bringing great damage, loss, or destruction. **2** a great misfortune. **3** *informal* a failure. ➤ **disastrous** *adj.*

**disavow** *v formal* to deny knowledge of or responsibility for. ➤ **disavowal** *n.*

**disband** *v* **1** of a group: to break up and separate. **2** to break up (a group).

**disbar** *v* (**disbarred, disbarring**) to deprive (a barrister) of the right to practise.

**disbelief** *n* mental rejection of something as untrue.

**disbelieve** *v* not to believe or believe in.

**disburse** *v* to pay out (money), *esp* from a fund. ➤ **disbursement** *n.*

**disc** (*NAmer* **disk**) *n* **1** a thin flat circular object. **2** a computer disk. **3** a cartilaginous disc between the spinal vertebrae. **4** a gramophone record.

***Usage Note:*** *Disc* is the correct spelling in British English, except in the context of computers where *disk* is preferred.

**discard**[1] *v* to get rid of as useless or superfluous.

**discard**[2] *n* something discarded, e.g. a playing card.

**discern** *v* **1** to detect with one of the senses, *esp* to see, often with difficulty. **2** to perceive mentally. ➤ **discernible** *adj.*

**discerning** *adj* showing insight and understanding. ➤ **discernment** *n.*

**discharge**[1] *v* **1** to dismiss from employment or service. **2** to release from custody or care. **3** to fulfil (a debt or obligation). **4** to send or pour out (a liquid or gas). **5** to shoot (a firearm).

**discharge**[2] *n* **1** the act of discharging. **2** something discharged or emitted.

**disciple** *n* **1** a person who learns from a teacher or instructor. **2** a follower of Christ during his life on earth, *esp* any of Christ's twelve apostles.

**disciplinarian** *n* a person who enforces strict discipline.

**disciplinary** *adj* undertaken to enforce order or correct conduct.

**discipline**[1] *n* **1** order obtained by enforcing obedience, e.g. in a school or army. **2** self-control. **3** training designed to produce obedience and self-control. **4** a field of study.

**discipline**[2] *v* **1** to punish (a person or animal) for the sake of discipline. **2** to train (a person or animal) in obedience and self-control.

**disciplined** *adj* showing obedience, order, or self-control.

**disc jockey** *n* a person who plays recorded music on a radio programme or at a nightclub or party.

**disclaim** *v* to deny or disavow.

**disclaimer** *n* **1** a denial or repudiation. **2** a denial of legal responsibility.

**disclose** *v* **1** to make (information) known. **2** to expose to view.

**disclosure** *n* **1** something disclosed; a revelation. **2** the act of disclosing.

**disco** *n* (*pl* **-os**) **1** a discotheque. **2** a party with dancing to recorded music. **3** a type of soul-based dance music popular in the 1970s.

**discolour** (*NAmer* **discolor**) *v* to change, or cause to change, colour for the worse; to stain. ➤ **discoloration** *n*, **discolouration** *n*.

**discomfit** *v* (**discomfited, discomfiting**) to cause perplexity and embarrassment to. ➤ **discomfiture** *n*.

**discomfort**[1] *n* mental or physical unease.

**discomfort**[2] *v* to make uncomfortable or uneasy.

**discompose** *v formal* to disturb the composure of. ➤ **discomposure** *n*.

**disconcert** *v* to startle and unsettle; to fluster.

**disconnect** *v* **1** to break the connection between two things or of something to e.g. a power supply. **2** to cut off the supply of e.g. electricity or the telephone to (a person, etc). **3** to cut (somebody) off during a telephone call. ➤ **disconnection** *n*.

**disconsolate** *adj* dejected; downcast.

**discontent** *n* dissatisfaction.

**discontented** *adj* unhappy; dissatisfied. ➤ **discontentment** *n*.

**discontinue** *v* (**discontinues, discontinued, discontinuing**) **1** to cease or stop. **2** to cease production of. ➤ **discontinuation** *n*.

**discontinuous** *adj* lacking continuity; interrupted. ➤ **discontinuity** *n*.

**discord** *n* **1** lack of agreement or harmony; conflict. **2** a combination of musical sounds that strikes the ear as harsh or unpleasant.

**discordant** *adj* **1** musically dissonant or unpleasant. **2** disagreeing; at variance.

**discotheque** *n* a nightclub for dancing to recorded music.

**discount**[1] *n* **1** a reduction in the price of goods or in the amount payable on a debt, etc. **2** (*used before a noun*) selling or sold at reduced prices.

**discount**[2] *v* **1** to make a deduction from (a price). **2** to leave out of account as unreliable, unimportant, or irrelevant.

**discourage** *v* **1** to make less confident or less willing to undertake something. **2** to hinder or deter, *esp* by showing disapproval. ➤ **discouragement** *n*, **discouraging** *adj*.

**discourse**[1] *n* **1** talk, conversation, or continuous text. **2** a formal speech or piece of writing.

**discourse**[2] *v literary* (+ on/upon) to express one's ideas in speech or writing.

**discourteous** *adj* rude or impolite.

**discourtesy** *n* (*pl* **-ies**) rudeness, incivility, or a rude action.

**discover** *v* **1** to find by searching or by chance. **2** to be the first to see, find, or know about. **3** to realize or find out.

**discovery** *n* (*pl* **-ies**) **1** the act of discovering something. **2** somebody or something discovered.

**discredit**[1] *v* (**discredited, discrediting**) **1** to reject as untrue. **2** to cast doubt on the trustworthiness or reputation of (a person or their ideas, work, etc).

**discredit**[2] *n* loss of reputation, or a discredited state.

**discreditable** *adj* bringing discredit or disgrace; shameful.

**discreet** *adj* **1** careful and reliable, *esp* unlikely to betray secrets. **2** subtle; trying not to attract attention. ➤ **discreetly** *adv*.

**discrepancy** *n* (*pl* **-ies**) an inconsistency between two accounts, etc.

**discrete** *adj* individually distinct. ➤ **discretely** *adv*.

**discretion** *n* **1** the quality of being discreet. **2** the freedom to act as one sees fit.

**discretionary** *adj* left to or exercised at one's own discretion.

**discriminate** *v* **1** (+ between) to make a distinction between (two things). **2** (+ against) to treat differently and *esp* unfavourably on the grounds of race, sex, religion, etc.

**discriminating** *adj* discerning in matters of taste, etc.

**discrimination** *n* **1** prejudicial treatment, e.g. on the grounds of race or sex. **2** the recognition of the difference between one thing and another. **3** good judgment, *esp* in matters of taste.

**discriminatory** *adj* showing discrimination, *esp* of an unfavourable kind.

**discursive** *adj* **1** of a person's writing style, etc: ranging over a variety of topics, often unsystematically. **2** relating to discourse of various kinds.

**discus** *n* a solid disc, thrown in athletic contests.

**discuss** *v* **1** to consider (a topic) in speech or writing. **2** to talk about (an issue, problem, etc) so as to make decisions.

**discussion** *n* **1** a conversation or debate about something. **2** a consideration of a topic in writing.

**disdain**[1] *n* the feeling one has for something one despises; scorn.

**disdain**[2] *v* **1** to regard with disdain. **2** to refuse (to do something) because of disdain.

**disease** *n* a condition that impairs a vital function in a living animal or plant. ➤ **diseased** *adj*.

**disembark** *v* to alight from a ship, plane, etc. ➤ **disembarkation** *n*.

**disembodied** *adj* **1** existing apart from the body. **2** coming from an invisible source: *a disembodied voice.*

**disembowel** *v* (**disembowelled, disembowelling,** *NAmer* **disemboweled, disemboweling**) to remove the entrails of.

**disempower** *v* (**disempowered, disempowering**) to deprive (a person or group) of initiative or confidence.

**disenchant** *v* to disillusion. ➤ **disenchanted** *adj,* **disenchantment** *n.*

**disenfranchise** *v* to deprive of the right to vote.

**disengage** *v* **1** to release or detach from something that holds or entangles. **2** to remove (troops) from combat areas. ➤ **disengagement** *n.*

**disentangle** *v* **1** to free from an entanglement. **2** to unravel (tangled wool, string, etc).

**disestablish** *v* to deprive (*esp* a national Church) of established status.

**disfavour** (*NAmer* **disfavor**) *n* disapproval or dislike.

**disfigure** *v* to spoil the appearance of. ➤ **disfigurement** *n.*

**disgorge** *v* **1** to allow to stream out. **2** to vomit (food) from the stomach. **3** to give up (dishonestly acquired funds).

**disgrace**[1] *v* to bring reproach or shame to.

**disgrace**[2] *n* **1** loss of favour, honour, or respect. **2** somebody or something shameful.

**disgraceful** *adj* shameful or shocking. ➤ **disgracefully** *adv.*

**disgruntled** *adj* aggrieved and dissatisfied.

**disguise**[1] *v* **1** to change the appearance of (a person or thing) to conceal their identity. **2** to hide the true state or character of.

**disguise**[2] *n* **1** a costume or other means of concealing one's identity. **2** the state of being disguised.

**disgust**[1] *n* a feeling of loathing, revulsion, or moral outrage.

**disgust**[2] *v* to arouse repugnance or indignation in (somebody). ➤ **disgusted** *adj,* **disgusting** *adj.*

**dish** *n* **1** a shallow open vessel for holding or serving food. **2** (**the dishes**) the utensils used in preparing and serving a meal. **3** a type of food prepared in a particular way. **4** something resembling a dish in shape. **5** *informal* an attractive person.

**disharmony** *n* lack of harmony.

**dishearten** *v* to cause to lose enthusiasm or morale. ➤ **disheartening** *adj.*

**dishevelled** (*NAmer* **disheveled**) *adj* unkempt or untidy in appearance.

**dishonest** *adj* not honest, truthful, or sincere. ➤ **dishonesty** *n.*

**dishonour**[1] (*NAmer* **dishonor**) *n* a state of shame or disgrace.

**dishonour**[2] (*NAmer* **dishonor**) *v* **1** to treat in a disrespectful manner. **2** to bring shame on. **3** of a bank, etc: to refuse to pay (a cheque, etc).

**dishonourable** (*NAmer* **dishonorable**) *adj* base or shameful.

**dish out** *v* **1** to serve out (food) from a dish, pan, etc. **2** *informal* to give (advice, criticism, etc) freely.

**dish up** *v* **1** to serve (food) onto dishes. **2** to present (facts or information).

**dishwasher** *n* an electrical machine that washes dishes.

**dishwater** *n* water used to wash dishes.

**dishy** *adj* (**-ier, -iest**) *chiefly Brit, informal* very attractive.

**disillusion**[1] *v* to disappoint (somebody) by revealing the unpleasant truth about somebody or something they admire. ➤ **disillusioned** *adj.*

**disillusion**[2] *n* the state of being disillusioned.

**disincentive** *n* something that discourages action or effort.

**disinclination** *n* unwillingness to do something.

**disinclined** *adj* unwilling to do something.

**disinfect** *v* to cleanse (a place, etc) by destroying harmful micro-organisms. ➤ **disinfection** *n.*

**disinfectant** *n* a chemical that destroys harmful micro-organisms.

**disinformation** *n* deliberately false or misleading information.

**disingenuous** *adj* insincere, especially in pretending ignorance of something one knows about.

**disinherit** *v* (**disinherited, disinheriting**) to deprive (an heir) of the right to inherit.

**disintegrate** *v* **1** to break into fragments or constituent elements. **2** to lose unity or cohesion.

**disinter** *v* (**disinterred, disinterring**) to dig up (something buried).

**disinterest** *n* **1** lack of self-interest; impartiality. **2** *non-standard* lack of interest.

**disinterested** *adj* **1** free from selfish motives; impartial. **2** *non-standard* uninterested.

***Usage Note:*** Do not use this word to mean 'not interested'; use *uninterested* for this.

**disjointed** *adj* lacking an orderly sequence; incoherent.

**disjunction** *n* **1** a lack of coordination; a mismatch. **2** a cleavage or separation.

**disk** *n* **1** (*Brit also* **disc**) a round plate coated with a magnetic substance for storing computer data. **2** *chiefly NAmer* = DISC.

***Usage Note:*** See note at DISC.

**disk drive** *n* a device that enables a computer to transfer data to, and retrieve it from, magnetic disks.

**diskette** *n* a floppy disk.
**dislike**[1] *n* **1** a feeling of aversion or disapproval. **2** something one dislikes. * **take a dislike to**
**dislike**[2] *v* to regard with dislike.
**dislocate** *v* **1** to displace (a bone) from its normal position in a joint. **2** to disrupt the normal order or working of. ➤ **dislocation** *n.*
**dislodge** *v* to force out of a fixed position.
**disloyal** *adj* not loyal; unfaithful. ➤ **disloyalty** *n.*
**dismal** *adj* **1** causing or expressing gloom or sadness. **2** *informal* incompetent. ➤ **dismally** *adv.*
**dismantle** *v* to take to pieces.
**dismay**[1] *v* to fill with consternation or sadness.
**dismay**[2] *n* consternation or sadness.
**dismember** *v* **1** to cut or tear off the limbs of (a person or animal). **2** to divide up (a territory, etc) into parts. ➤ **dismemberment** *n.*
**dismiss** *v* **1** to order or allow to leave. **2** to discharge from employment or service. **3** to reject (a suggestion, etc) as unworthy of serious consideration. **4** of a judge: to refuse a further hearing to (a court case). **5** in cricket, to bowl out (a batsman or side). ➤ **dismissal** *n.*
**dismissive** *adj* of somebody's attitude: disparaging or disdainful. ➤ **dismissively** *adv.*
**dismount** *v* to get off a horse, bicycle, etc.
**disobedient** *adj* refusing or failing to obey. ➤ **disobedience** *n.*
**disobey** *v* to fail to obey (somebody, an order, etc).
**disorder** *n* **1** lack of order; confusion. **2** breach of the peace or public order. **3** an abnormal physical or mental condition. ➤ **disordered** *adj.*
**disorderly** *adj* **1** untidy or disarranged. **2** unruly, violent, or disruptive.
**disorganized** *adj* **1** lacking coherence or system. **2** of a person: unmethodical.
**disorientate** *v* (*often* **be disorientated**) to confuse by depriving of the normal sense of position and relationship to one's surroundings. ➤ **disorientation** *n.*
**disown** *v* to repudiate any connection with (a relative, *esp* one's own child, a belief, etc).
**disparage** *v* to speak slightingly of. ➤ **disparaging** *adj.*
**disparate** *adj* quite separate and distinct.
**disparity** *n* (*pl* **-ies**) difference or inequality.
**dispassionate** *adj* not influenced by strong feeling; impartial. ➤ **dispassionately** *adv.*
**dispatch**[1] *or* **despatch** *v* **1** to send (a letter, etc) somewhere. **2** to send (personnel) to carry out a particular task. **3** to carry out (a task) rapidly or efficiently. **4** *euphem* to kill.
**dispatch**[2] *or* **despatch** *n* **1** a message; *esp* a diplomatic or military message. **2** promptness and efficiency. **3** the act of dispatching.
**dispel** *v* (**dispelled, dispelling**) to drive away or disperse (fears, doubts, depression, etc).
**dispensable** *adj* that can be dispensed with; inessential.
**dispensary** *n* (*pl* **-ies**) a part of a hospital or chemist's shop where drugs, medical supplies, etc are dispensed.
**dispensation** *n* **1** an exemption from a law, vow, etc, *esp* one granted by the Roman Catholic Church. **2** the act of dispensing. **3** the religious system prevailing during a particular period.
**dispense** *v* **1** to distribute in portions. **2** to prepare and give out (drugs, medicine, etc on prescription). **3** to administer (law or justice). **4** (+ with) to get rid of or do without.
**disperse** *v* **1** to spread or distribute widely. **2** of a crowd, etc: to break up and leave in different directions. **3** to cause (fog, etc) to vanish. ➤ **dispersal** *n,* **dispersion** *n.*
**dispirit** *v* (**dispirited, dispiriting**) to dishearten. ➤ **dispirited** *adj,* **dispiriting** *adj.*
**displace** *v* **1** to take the place of. **2** to remove or force from its usual or proper place.
**displacement** *n* **1** the act of displacing. **2** the volume or weight of water displaced by a ship floating in it, used as a measure of the ship's size. **3** the difference between the initial position of a body and any later position.
**display**[1] *v* **1** to set out or expose to view. **2** of a computer, etc: to show (information) on screen. **3** to demonstrate (a quality).
**display**[2] *n* **1** a public presentation, e.g. a performance or exhibition. **2** the displaying of something, e.g. the demonstration of a type of behaviour or feeling. **3** ostentation; showing off. **4** an electronic device for presenting data on screen.
**displease** *v* to annoy or upset.
**displeasure** *n* disapproval or annoyance.
**disport** *v archaic* to amuse (oneself) actively; to frolic.
**disposable** *adj* **1** designed to be used once and then thrown away. **2** of financial resources: available for use.
**disposal** *n* the act of getting rid of something. * **at one's disposal** available for one's use.
**dispose** *v* **1** to put (things or personnel) in position. **2** (+ of) to transfer or sell to somebody else. **3** (+ of) to get rid of (rubbish or waste).
**disposed** *adj* **1** willing to do something. **2** having a particular attitude to somebody or something.
**disposition** *n* **1** a person's temperament. **2** a tendency or inclination. **3** a particular arrangement of people or things.
**dispossess** *v* **1** to deprive of possession or occupancy. **2** in football, etc, to deprive (an opponent) of the ball. ➤ **dispossession** *n.*
**disproportionate** *adj* out of proportion. ➤ **disproportionately** *adv.*
**disprove** *v* to prove (a statement, etc) to be false.

**disputation** *n* debate or argument.
**disputatious** *adj* argumentative.
**dispute**[1] *v* **1** (*often* + about) to argue. **2** to call (a statement, claim etc) into question. **3** to contest (e.g. a leading position) with somebody. ➤ **disputable** *adj.*
**dispute**[2] *n* a quarrel or disagreement, *esp* between workers and management.
**disqualify** *v* (**-ies, -ied**) to make or declare unfit or ineligible to do something. ➤ **disqualification** *n.*
**disquiet** *n* anxiety or worry. ➤ **disquieting** *adj.*
**disquisition** *n* a long or elaborate discussion or essay on a subject.
**disregard**[1] *v* to pay no attention to.
**disregard**[2] *n* lack of attention; neglect.
**disrepair** *n* the state of being in need of repair.
**disrepute** *n* lack of good reputation or respectability.
**disrespect** *n* lack of respect or politeness. ➤ **disrespectful** *adj.*
**disrobe** *v* to undress.
**disrupt** *v* **1** to throw into disorder. **2** to interrupt the continuity of (a schedule, etc). ➤ **disruption** *n,* **disruptive** *adj.*
**dissatisfy** *v* (**-ies, -ied**) to disappoint or fail to satisfy. ➤ **dissatisfied** *adj.*
**dissect** *v* **1** to cut (an animal or plant) into pieces, *esp* for scientific examination. **2** to analyse (a literary work, etc) in detail. ➤ **dissection** *n.*

***Usage Note:*** Note the spelling with *-ss-*.

**dissemble** *v* to conceal facts, intentions, or feelings under some pretence.
**disseminate** *v* to spread (ideas, information, etc) about freely or widely. ➤ **dissemination** *n.*
**dissension** *n* disagreement in opinion that makes for discord.
**dissent**[1] *v* **1** to differ in opinion. **2** to reject the doctrines of an established Church. **3** in sport: to show disagreement with a referee's verdict. ➤ **dissenter** *n.*
**dissent**[2] *n* disagreement *esp* with religious doctrine or political policy.
**dissertation** *n* a long detailed essay, *esp* one submitted for a degree, diploma, etc.
**disservice** *n* an action which works to somebody's disadvantage.
**dissident**[1] *n* a person who rebels against government policy or established opinion. ➤ **dissidence** *n.*
**dissident**[2] *adj* opposed to official policy.
**dissimilar** *adj* not similar; unlike. ➤ **dissimilarity** *n.*
**dissimulate** *v* to conceal or disguise one's real feelings or motives. ➤ **dissimulation** *n.*
**dissipate** *v* **1** to dispel or scatter. **2** to use up (money, energy, etc) aimlessly or foolishly.
**dissipated** *adj* dissolute; debauched.
**dissociate** *v* **1** to declare (oneself) to have no connection with or responsibility for somebody or something. **2** to separate (two ideas) in the mind.
**dissolute** *adj* morally unrestrained; debauched.
**dissolution** *n* **1** the act of dissolving. **2** the termination of an association or union, *esp* a marriage. **3** the breaking up of an assembly, etc.
**dissolve** *v* **1** to terminate (a partnership, *esp* a marriage) officially. **2** to break up (an assembly, etc). **3** to cause (a substance) to pass into solution. **4** (*usu* + into) to be emotionally overcome.
**dissonant** *adj* not harmonious; discordant.
**dissuade** *v* (+ from) to deter or discourage by persuasion. ➤ **dissuasion** *n.*
**distaff** *n* in spinning, a staff for holding the flax, wool, etc that is to be spun.
**distaff side** *n* the female side of a family.
**distance**[1] *n* **1** the space between two points or places, or the length of this. **2** a far-off point. **3** wide separation or remoteness. * **go the distance** to keep going until the end of a contest, etc. **keep one's distance** to avoid getting involved.
**distance**[2] *v* to keep (oneself) aloof from a situation, etc.
**distant** *adj* **1** a certain distance away. **2** remote in space or time. **3** not closely related. **4** reserved or aloof in personal relationships. ➤ **distantly** *adv.*
**distaste** *n* aversion to something.
**distasteful** *adj* causing distaste; offensive.
**distemper**[1] *n* a viral disease of dogs, with fever and coughing.
**distemper**[2] *n* a type of paint used mainly for walls.
**distend** *v* to cause (a part of the body, e.g. the belly) to swell from internal pressure. ➤ **distension** *n.*
**distil** (*NAmer* **distill**) *v* (**distilled, distilling**) **1** to produce (a liquid) in purified form by heating it till it evaporates and then cooling it again. **2** to make (whisky or other spirits) by this method. **3** to extract the essential matter from (previously amassed material). ➤ **distillation** *n,* **distiller** *n.*
**distillery** *n* (*pl* **-ies**) a factory where whisky, etc is distilled.
**distinct** *adj* **1** different or separate. **2** readily perceptible to the senses or mind; clear. ➤ **distinctly** *adv.*
**distinction** *n* **1** a difference between things that are similar but not the same. **2** outstanding merit or special talent. **3** the highest level of excellence in passing an exam.
**distinguish** *v* **1** (+ between/from) to recognize the difference between (two or more things). **2** to perceive; to make out. **3** of a feature, etc: to serve to identify (a person or thing). **4** to do

something to make (oneself) notable. ➤ **distinguishable** *adj.*

**distinguished** *adj* **1** characterized by eminence or excellence. **2** dignified in manner or appearance.

**distort** *v* **1** to cause to take on an abnormal shape. **2** to alter the true meaning of (words, a statement, etc). ➤ **distortion** *n.*

**distract** *v* to draw (somebody or their attention) away from the task in hand, etc. ➤ **distracting** *adj.*

**distracted** *adj* **1** not able to concentrate on the matter in hand, etc. **2** crazy; out of one's mind.

**distraction** *n* **1** something that distracts one's attention. **2** an amusement or activity.

**distraught** *adj* mentally agitated; frantic.

**distress**[1] *n* **1** mental or physical anguish. **2** a state of danger or desperate need.

**distress**[2] *v* to cause distress to (somebody). ➤ **distressing** *adj.*

**distribute** *v* **1** to divide among a number of recipients. **2** (*usu* **be distributed**) to scatter over an area. **3** to supply (goods) to retail outlets.

**distribution** *n* **1** the act of distributing. **2** the position, arrangement, or frequency of occurrence of things dispersed in space or time.

**distributor** *n* **1** a person or company that manages the distribution of goods. **2** an apparatus for directing current to the sparking plugs of an internal-combustion engine.

**district** *n* an area or region with a particular character.

**distrust**[1] *n* suspicion or lack of trust. ➤ **distrustful** *adj.*

**distrust**[2] *v* to regard as untrustworthy or unreliable.

**disturb** *v* **1** to break in upon or interrupt. **2** to alter the position or arrangement of. **3** to destroy the peace of mind or composure of. ➤ **disturbing** *adj.*

**disturbance** *n* **1** the act of disturbing. **2** an interruption. **3** a riot or outbreak of public disorder.

**disturbed** *adj* suffering from emotional or mental instability.

**disunite** *v* to divide or cause to differ in opinion. ➤ **disunited** *adj.*

**disuse** *n* the state of no longer being used.

**ditch**[1] *n* a long narrow excavation for defence, drainage, irrigation, etc.

**ditch**[2] *v* **1** of a pilot or aircraft: to make a forced landing on water. **2** *informal* to get rid of or abandon (a plan, project, etc).

**dither** *v* to act nervously or indecisively.

**ditto** *n* **1** used to avoid repeating a word: the same. **2** a mark („ or ") used to indicate repetition usu of the word directly above.

**ditty** *n* (*pl* **-ies**) a short simple song.

**diuretic** *adj* of a drug: acting to increase the flow of urine.

**diurnal** *adj* occurring during the day or daily.

**diva** /'deevə/ *n* (*pl* **divas**) a principal female opera singer.

**divan** *n* **1** a long low couch, usu without arms or back. **2** a bed without a head or foot board.

**dive**[1] *v* (*past tense and past part.* **dived** *or NAmer* **dove**) **1** to plunge into water headfirst. **2** to swim underwater using breathing equipment. **3** of a submarine: to submerge. **4** of a bird or an aircraft: to descend steeply through the air. **5** to move quickly, *esp* downwards or under cover.

**dive**[2] *n* **1** a headlong plunge into water. **2** a steep descent by an aircraft. **3** *informal* a disreputable bar or meeting place. **4** a ploy in football in which a player falls over deliberately and pretends to have been fouled.

**dive-bomb** *v* to bomb (a place) while making a steep dive towards the target.

**diver** *n* **1** a person who dives as a competitive sport or who works or explores underwater. **2** a large fish-eating diving bird.

**diverge** *v* **1** to move in different directions from a common point. **2** (*often* + from) to differ in character or opinion. ➤ **divergence** *n,* **divergent** *adj.*

**diverse** *adj* **1** different or unlike. **2** varied or assorted.

**diversify** *v* (**-ies, -ied**) **1** to make (things) diverse. **2** of a company: to engage in varied types of business or production to reduce risk. ➤ **diversification** *n.*

**diversion** *n* **1** a turning aside from a course or activity. **2** a detour for traffic when the usual route is closed. **3** an amusement or pastime. **4** something that draws the attention away from the main scene of activity. ➤ **diversionary** *adj.*

**diversity** *n* (*pl* **-ies**) **1** the condition of having differences. **2** a variety or assortment.

**divert** *v* **1** to redirect from one course or use to another. **2** to distract. **3** to entertain or amuse (somebody).

**divest** *v* **1** (+ of) to dispossess of property, authority, title, etc. **2** (+ of) to rid or free (oneself) of something oppressive.

**divide**[1] *v* **1** to separate into parts, branches, groups, etc. **2** to share (something) between recipients. **3** to be what separates (one thing and another). **4** to provoke disagreement between (people, groups, etc). **5** in mathematics, to find out how many times a larger number will contain a smaller one.

**divide**[2] *n* a line of division; a split.

**dividend** *n* **1** a sum of money to be divided and distributed, *esp* the part of a company's profits payable to shareholders. **2** an individual shareholder's portion of this. **3** (*usu in pl*) a reward or benefit.

**divider** *n* **1** (*in pl*) a compasslike instrument used for measuring. **2** a partition used to separate parts of a room.

**divination** *n* the art of trying to foresee the future, e.g. by using supernatural powers.

**divine**[1] *adj* **1** of or from God or a god. **2** *informal* delightful or superb. ➤ **divinely** *adv.*

**divine**[2] *v* **1** to discover, perceive, or foresee intuitively or by supernatural means. **2** to locate (water or minerals) using a rod. ➤ **diviner** *n.*

**divinity** *n* (*pl* **-ies**) **1** the quality or state of being divine. **2** a male or female deity. **3** theology.

**divisible** *adj* **1** capable of being divided. **2** of a number: that can be divided by another without remainder.

**division** *n* **1** the act of dividing. **2** a part into which a whole is divided. **3** a major army formation. **4** an administrative or operating unit of an organization. **5** a competitive class or category, e.g. of a football league. **6** a dividing line or partition. **7** disagreement or disunity. ➤ **divisional** *adj.*

**division sign** *n* the mathematical symbol (÷) used to indicate division.

**divisive** *adj* tending to cause disunity or dissension.

**divorce**[1] *n* the legal dissolution of a marriage.

**divorce**[2] *v* **1** to end marriage with (one's spouse) by divorce. **2** to dissociate (one thing) from another.

**divorcee** /divaw'see/ *n* a divorced person.

**divot** *n* a piece of turf, *esp* one struck out by a golfer making a shot.

**divulge** *v* to make known or reveal (a confidence or secret).

**Diwali** /di'wahli/ *or* **Divali** /di'vahli/ *n* the Hindu or Sikh Festival of Lights, celebrating the end of the monsoon.

**DIY** *n chiefly Brit* amateur repair and building work around the home.

**dizzy**[1] *adj* (**-ier, -iest**) **1** experiencing a whirling sensation in the head and a tendency to lose balance. **2** *informal* foolish or silly. ➤ **dizzily** *adv,* **dizziness** *n.*

**dizzy**[2] *v* (**-ies, -ied**) to make dizzy; to bewilder.

**DJ** *n* (*pl* **DJs**) **1** = DISC JOCKEY. **2** = DINNER JACKET.

**DNA** *n* the material, deoxyribonucleic acid, in the nuclei of cells that makes up genes.

**do**[1] *v* (**did, done**) **1** to effect or perform (an action or activity). **2** to make or provide. **3** to have a particular effect: *A rest will do you good.* **4** to work at for a living or as a course of study. **5** to be adequate or acceptable. **6** to achieve (a particular speed). **7** to serve (a number of years) in prison. ➤ *v aux* **1** used to form questions and negative statements. **2** used for emphasis: *I do hope you can come.* **3** used as a substitute for a verb already mentioned: *I am earning more than I did last year.* ✱ **do away with** *informal* abolish or kill. **do out of** to deprive of unjustly. **do without** to manage in spite of not having. **have done with** to have no further concern with. **to do with** concerned with.

**do**[2] *n* (*pl* **dos** *or* **do's**) **1** (*usu in pl*) something one ought to do: *dos and don'ts.* **2** *chiefly Brit, informal* a party or festive occasion.

**docile** *adj* easily led or managed. ➤ **docility** *n.*

**dock**[1] *n* an enclosed body of water in a port, where a ship can moor for unloading, repair work, etc.

**dock**[2] *v* **1** of a ship: to go into a dock. **2** of spacecraft: to join together while in space.

**dock**[3] *n* the prisoner's enclosure in a criminal court.

**dock**[4] *v* **1** to cut (an animal's tail) short. **2** to take away (a specified amount) from wages, a score etc.

**dock**[5] *n* a coarse weed with leaves used to alleviate nettle stings.

**docker** *n* a person employed in loading and unloading ships.

**docket** *n* a document recording the contents of a shipment or the payment of customs duties.

**dockyard** *n* a place where ships are built or repaired.

**doctor**[1] *n* **1** a person qualified to practise medicine. **2** a holder of the highest academic degree conferred by a university.

**doctor**[2] *v* (**doctored, doctoring**) **1** to give medical treatment to. **2** to adapt, modify, or add to (something), often for a dishonest purpose. **3** *euphem* to castrate or spay (a dog or cat).

**doctoral** *adj* relating to a doctorate.

**doctorate** *n* the highest academic degree, awarded by a university for original postgraduate research.

**doctrinaire** *adj* concerned with abstract theory and ignoring practical considerations.

**doctrine** *n* a principle, or the set of principles, underlying a branch of knowledge or system of belief. ➤ **doctrinal** *adj.*

**document**[1] *n* a written or printed paper, or electronic record, giving information about or proof of something.

**document**[2] *v* to record (e.g. an event) in detail.

**documentary**[1] *adj* **1** consisting of documents. **2** presenting or based on factual material.

**documentary**[2] *n* (*pl* **-ies**) a broadcast or film that presents a factual account of a subject.

**documentation** *n* documents providing evidence, instructions, support for a claim, etc.

**dodder** *v* to walk feebly and unsteadily. ➤ **doddery** *adj.*

**doddle** *n chiefly Brit, informal* a very easy task.

**dodecagon** *n* a polygon with twelve angles and twelve sides.

**dodecahedron** *n* (*pl* **dodecahedrons** *or* **dodecahedra**) a polyhedron with twelve faces.

**dodge** *v* **1** to shift position suddenly, e.g. to avoid a blow. **2** to evade (a duty, etc) usu in an underhand way.

**dodgem** *n* a small electric car designed to be bumped into others as a funfair amusement.
**dodgy** *adj* (**-ier, -iest**) *chiefly Brit, informal* **1** shady or dishonest. **2** risky or dangerous. **3** liable to collapse or break down.
**dodo** *n* (*pl* **-oes** *or* **-os**) a large extinct flightless bird that formerly lived on Mauritius.
**doe** *n* **1** the adult female fallow deer. **2** the adult female of various mammals, e.g. the rabbit.
**does** *v* third person sing. present tense of DO[1].
**doesn't** *contraction* does not.
**doff** *v* to take off (one's hat) as a greeting or sign of respect.
**dog[1]** *n* **1** a four-legged flesh-eating domesticated mammal, kept as a pet, for hunting, or to work. **2** a member of the dog family, e.g. a wolf, jackal, or fox. **3** (*often used before a noun*) a male dog, wolf, fox, etc. * **go to the dogs** *informal* to decline or deteriorate.
**dog[2]** *v* (**dogged, dogging**) **1** to pursue (somebody) closely. **2** of something unwanted: to haunt (somebody).
**dog collar** *n informal* a clerical collar.
**dog-eared** *adj* **1** of a book: having pages with turned-down corners. **2** worn or shabby.
**dog-end** *n informal* a cigarette end.
**dogfight** *n* a fight between aircraft, usu at close quarters.
**dogfish** *n* (*pl* **dogfishes** *or* **dogfish**) a small long-tailed shark.
**dogged** /'dogid/ *adj* stubbornly determined. ➤ **doggedly** *adv.*
**doggerel** *n* verse that lacks any poetic quality.
**doggo** * **lie doggo** to stay quiet and motionless, to avoid detection.
**doggy paddle** *n* a simple form of swimming in which the arms paddle and the legs kick.
**doghouse** *n chiefly NAmer* a dog kennel. * **in the doghouse** *informal* in disgrace.
**dog in the manger** *n* a person who selfishly deprives others of something he or she does not need.
**dogleg** *n* a sharp bend, e.g. in a road.
**dogma** *n* a doctrine, or body of doctrines, authoritatively stated by a Church.
**dogmatic** *adj* **1** of statements or opinions: insisted on as if authoritative. **2** of a person: inclined to make dogmatic statements. ➤ **dogmatically** *adv.*
**dogsbody** *n* (*pl* **-ies**) *chiefly Brit, informal* a person who carries out routine or menial work for others.
**dogtooth** *n* an architectural moulding resembling dog's teeth.
**doily** *n* (*pl* **-ies**) a small decorative lacy mat, placed under cakes, biscuits, etc on a plate.
**do in** *v informal* **1** to kill. **2** to exhaust (somebody).
**doings** *n chiefly Brit, informal* a word used to refer to an unspecified fitting, tool, etc.
**doldrums** *pl n* * **in the doldrums 1** in a state of depression. **2** of the economy: stagnating.
**dole** *n Brit, informal* the government unemployment benefit.
**doleful** *adj* sad or mournful. ➤ **dolefully** *adv.*
**dole out** *v* to hand out or distribute.
**doll** *n* **1** a child's toy in the form of a human being. **2** *informal* an attractive person, *esp* a woman.
**dollar** *n* the basic monetary unit of the USA, Canada, Australia, and various other countries.
**dollop[1]** *n* a soft shapeless blob, *esp* of food.
**dollop[2]** *v* (**dolloped, dolloping**) (+ out) to serve out (food) carelessly or clumsily.
**dolour** (*NAmer* **dolor**) *n* mental suffering or anguish.
**dolphin** *n* a small whale with its snout elongated into a beak.
**dolphinarium** *n* (*pl* **dolphinariums** *or* **dolphinaria**) an establishment where dolphins perform in public in a large pool.
**dolt** *n* an extremely stupid person.
**domain** *n* **1** a territory over which control is exercised. **2** a sphere of influence or activity. **3** a group of Internet addresses with the same suffix.
**dome** *n* **1** a hemispherical roof or vault. **2** a dome-shaped structure or building with a dome-shaped roof.
**domestic** *adj* **1** of, for, or devoted to the home or the family. **2** of one's own country; not foreign. **3** of an animal: tame, or bred by human beings for a specific purpose, e.g. food or hunting. ➤ **domestically** *adv.*
**domesticate** *v* to bring (an animal) under human control, e.g. for carrying loads, hunting, or food. ➤ **domestication** *n.*
**domesticity** *n* home or family life.
**domicile[1]** *n* a home; *esp* a person's permanent home for legal purposes.
**domicile[2]** *v* (**be domiciled**) to live in a particular country or place.
**dominant** *adj* **1** controlling or prevailing over all others. **2** of a position: commanding a view from a superior height. ➤ **dominance** *n.*
**dominate** *v* **1** to exert controlling influence or power over. **2** to overlook from a superior height. ➤ **domination** *n.*
**domineer** *v* to exercise arbitrary or overbearing control. ➤ **domineering** *adj.*
**dominion** *n* **1** the power or right to rule. **2** the territory of a ruler. **3** (*often* **Dominion**) a self-governing nation of the British Commonwealth.
**domino** *n* (*pl* **-oes** *or* **-os**) **1** a flat rectangular block with a face divided into two equal parts that are either blank or bear from one to six dots. **2** (*in pl*) a game played with a set of 28 dominoes.
**don[1]** *n* a university teacher, *esp* at Oxford or Cambridge.

**don**[2] *v* (**donned, donning**) to put on (an item of clothing).
**donate** *v* **1** to make a gift of (money, etc), *esp* to a charitable cause. **2** to give (blood, semen, organs, etc) for use in the medical treatment of others.
**donation** *n* something donated, *esp* money.
**done**[1] *v* past part. of DO[1].
**done**[2] *adj* **1** completed. **2** of food: cooked sufficiently. **3** physically exhausted. **4** socially acceptable or expected.
**done**[3] *interj* used when accepting a deal or bet.
**doner kebab** /'dohnə, 'donə/ *n* slices of spiced lamb cut from a large block grilled on a spit.
**donkey** *n* (*pl* **-eys**) a domesticated animal of the horse family with long ears.
**donkey jacket** *n* a thick hip-length jacket and with a strip of leather or plastic across the shoulders.
**donkey's years** *pl n chiefly Brit, informal* a very long time.
**donor** *n* a person who donates something.
**don't** *contraction* do not.
**donut** *n NAmer* a doughnut.
**doodle**[1] *v* to draw in a bored or aimless manner.
**doodle**[2] *n* an aimless scribble or sketch.
**doom**[1] *n* an unhappy, terrible, or unavoidable fate.
**doom**[2] *v* to cause to fail or be ruined.
**doomsday** *n* the end of the world, or some remote point in the future.
**door** *n* a hinged or sliding panel closing the entrance to a building, room, or vehicle. * **out of doors** in or into the open air.
**doorman** *n* (*pl* **doormen**) an employee who stands at the entrance to a hotel, theatre, etc to assist people going in or out.
**doormat** *n* **1** a mat placed at a doorway for wiping dirt from shoes. **2** *informal* a very submissive person.
**doorstep** *n* a step in front of an outer door.
**doorstop** *n* a device for holding a door open.
**dope**[1] *n* **1** a drug given illegally to a racehorse, greyhound, etc to make it run faster or slower. **2** *slang* marijuana, opium, or another illegal drug. **3** *informal* a stupid person.
**dope**[2] *v* to administer an illegal or narcotic drug to.
**dopey** *or* **dopy** *adj* (**-ier, -iest**) **1** sleepy or drugged. **2** *informal* stupid.
**doppelgänger** /'doplgengə, -gangə/ *n* a ghostly counterpart of a living person.
**Doppler effect** *n* a change in the apparent frequency of sound or light waves when the source and the observer move closer together or farther apart.
**dorm** *n informal* = DORMITORY 1.
**dormant** *adj* **1** asleep or inactive, e.g. during hibernation. **2** temporarily showing no signs of activity or growth.
**dormer** *or* **dormer window** *n* a window set vertically in a a sloping roof.
**dormitory** *n* (*pl* **-ies**) **1** a large room containing a number of beds. **2** (*often used before a noun*) a residential community whose inhabitants commute to their places of work.
**dormouse** *n* (*pl* **dormice**) a small rodent that resembles a mouse with a long bushy tail.
**dorsal** *adj* relating to the back or top surface: compare VENTRAL.
**dose**[1] *n* **1** a measured quantity of medicine to be taken at one time. **2** a quantity of radiation administered or absorbed.
**dose**[2] *v* to give a dose of medicine to.
**dosh** *n Brit, informal* money.
**doss** *v chiefly Brit, informal* **1** (*often* + down) to sleep rough or in a makeshift bed. **2** to be lazy or a shirker.
**dossier** /'dosi·ə, 'dosiay/ *n* a file of papers containing a detailed report or information.
**dot**[1] *n* a small round spot or mark. * **on the dot** exactly; precisely. **the year dot** *Brit, informal* a very long time ago.
**dot**[2] *v* (**dotted, dotting**) **1** to mark with a dot or dots. **2** to scatter marks, objects, etc at random over (an area).
**dotage** *n* a period of mental decline in old age.
**dotcom** *n* a company that operates exclusively or mainly on the Internet.
**dote** *v* (+ on/upon) to show great or excessive fondness for. ➤ **doting** *adj.*
**dotty** *adj* (**-ier, -iest**) *informal* eccentric, crazy, or absurd, often in an endearing way.
**double**[1] *adj* **1** consisting of two similar parts. **2** of twice the usual size, quantity, etc. **3** designed for two people. **4** having two interpretations; ambiguous. ➤ **doubly** *adv.*
**double**[2] *n* **1** something twice the usual amount, number, size, etc. **2** somebody who closely resembles another person. **3** somebody who replaces an actor in scenes calling for special skills. * **at the double** very quickly.
**double**[3] *adv* to twice the extent or amount.
**double**[4] *v* **1** to make or become twice as much or as many. **2** to fold into two thicknesses. **3** (+ up/over) to bend over, e.g. in pain or laughter. **4** (+ back) to turn back on one's course. **5** (+ as) to serve the additional purpose of. **6** (+ for) to be a stand-in or substitute for.
**double agent** *n* a spy pretending to serve one government while actually serving another.
**double-barrelled** *adj* **1** of a firearm: having two barrels. **2** of a surname: having two parts.
**double bass** *n* the largest and lowest-pitched instrument of the violin family.
**double bed** *n* a bed for two people.
**double-breasted** *adj* of a coat, jacket, etc: having a large overlapping front, usu with two sets of buttons and buttonholes.
**double chin** *n* a chin with a fleshy fold under it.

**double cream** *n* thick heavy cream containing a high proportion of fat.

**double-cross** *v* to betray or cheat while pretending to help.

**double-dealing** *n* underhand or deceitful action. ➤ **double-dealer** *n.*

**double-decker** *n* something with two levels or layers, *esp* a bus with two floors.

**double Dutch** *n informal* unintelligible or nonsensical language.

**double entendre** /ˌdoohbl on'ton(h)dr/ *n* (*pl* **double entendres** /ˌdoohbl on'ton(h)dr/) an ambiguous expression, one of whose meanings is usu risqué.

**double figures** *pl n* the numbers from 10 to 99.

**double glazing** *n* windows having two panes of glass separated by an air space. ➤ **double-glaze** *v.*

**double jeopardy** *n* the act of prosecuting a person for the same offence twice.

**double-jointed** *adj* of a person: having exceptionally flexible joints.

**doubles** *pl n* a game between two pairs of players, e.g. in tennis.

**double standard** *n* an *esp* moral principle applied more rigorously to one group than another.

**doublet** *n* a man's close-fitting jacket of the 15th to 17th cents.

**double take** *n* a delayed reaction to a surprising situation.

**doubloon** *n* a former Spanish gold coin.

**doubt**[1] *v* **1** to be uncertain about; to feel inclined to disbelieve. **2** to consider unlikely.

**doubt**[2] *n* **1** uncertainty. **2** an inclination not to believe something. ✱ **no doubt** certainly; probably.

**doubtful** *adj* **1** causing doubt; open to question. **2** uncertain; unconvinced. **3** unlikely. **4** of questionable worth or honesty. ➤ **doubtfully** *adv.*

**doubtless** *adv* **1** without doubt; certainly. **2** probably.

**douche** /doohsh/ *n* a jet of fluid, directed on or into part of the body, *esp* the vagina.

**dough** *n* **1** a stiff mixture of flour and liquid used to make bread, pastry, etc. **2** *informal* money.

**doughnut** (*NAmer also* **donut**) *n* a small round or ring-shaped cake of deep-fried yeast dough.

**doughty** /'dowti/ *adj* (**-ier, -iest**) *chiefly literary or humorous* bold and resolute.

**do up** *v* **1** to wrap or fasten. **2** *informal* to repair or refurbish.

**dour** /dooə, 'dowə/ *adj* **1** stern or harsh. **2** gloomy; sullen.

**douse** *or* **dowse** *v* **1** to drench with liquid. **2** to extinguish (a flame, light, etc).

**dove**[1] /duv/ *n* **1** a bird similar to but smaller than the domestic pigeon. **2** an advocate of peace, negotiation, or compromise.

**dove**[2] /dohv/ *v NAmer* past tense of DIVE[1].

**dovecot** *or* **dovecote** *n* a structure with nesting compartments for domestic pigeons.

**dovetail**[1] *n* a joint formed by fitting a wedge-shaped projection into a similarly shaped cavity.

**dovetail**[2] *v* **1** to join (wood) by means of dovetails. **2** to fit together neatly or conveniently.

**dowager** *n* **1** a widow holding property or a title from her deceased husband. **2** a dignified elderly woman.

**dowdy** *adj* (**-ier, -iest**) old-fashioned or dull in appearance, clothing etc.

**dowel** *n* a wooden or metal pin used to hold components together.

**down**[1] *adv* **1** at or towards a relatively low level. **2** in or into a lying or sitting position. **3** *chiefly Brit* away from the capital of a country or a university city. **4** southwards. **5** in or into a relatively worse condition. **6** into a state of relatively low intensity, heat, volume, etc. **7** to a lower amount, price, figure, or rank. **8** in writing. **9** from an earlier time.

**down**[2] *adj* **1** directed or going downwards. **2** depressed; dejected. **3** of a computer system: temporarily out of action. ✱ **down to 1** attributed to. **2** the responsibility of.

**down**[3] *prep* **1** in a downward direction along, through, etc. **2** at or to a position further along. **3** *Brit, informal* to; at: *I'm going down the shops.*

**down**[4] *v informal* to drink or swallow quickly.

**down**[5] *n* fine soft feathers or hairs.

**down**[6] *n* (*usu in pl*) a rounded ridge or hill, *esp* in southern England.

**down-and-out** *adj* destitute and homeless.

**downbeat** *adj* **1** pessimistic; gloomy. **2** relaxed; informal.

**downcast** *adj* **1** dejected or depressed. **2** directed downwards.

**downer** *n* **1** *informal* a depressing experience or situation. **2** *slang* a depressant drug.

**downfall** *n* a sudden loss of power or status.

**downgrade** *v* to lower in rank or importance.

**downhearted** *adj* discouraged or dejected.

**downhill**[1] *adv* towards the bottom of a hill or slope. ✱ **go downhill** to decline or deteriorate.

**downhill**[2] *adj* going or sloping downhill.

**download** *v* to transfer (programs or data) from one computer to another.

**down-market** *adj* designed to appeal to less wealthy or sophisticated consumers.

**down payment** *n* an initial payment for something bought on credit.

**downplay** *v* to treat as being less significant than it is.

**downpour** *n* a heavy fall of rain.

**downright**[1] *adv* thoroughly; altogether.

**downright**[2] *adj* **1** absolute; thorough. **2** plain or blunt.

**downriver** *adv and adj* towards the mouth of a river.
**downside** *n* a drawback or undesirable feature.
**Down's syndrome** *n* a chromosomal disorder causing intellectual impairment and distinctive physical characteristics.
**downstairs** *adv and adj* on or to a lower floor.
**downstream** *adv and adj* in the direction of the flow of a stream.
**down-to-earth** *adj* practical or realistic.
**downtown** *adv and adj chiefly NAmer* of, to, or in the central part of a town or city.
**downtrodden** *adj* oppressed by those in power.
**down under** *adv informal* in or to Australia or New Zealand.
**downward** *adj* moving or extending downwards.
**downwards** *adv* from a higher to a lower place or level.
**downwind** *adv and adj* in the direction towards which the wind is blowing.
**downy** *adj* (**-ier, -iest**) covered in soft fluffy feathers or fine hairs.
**dowry** *n* (*pl* **-ies**) the money or property that a woman brings to her husband in marriage.
**dowse**[1] *v* to search for hidden water or minerals with a divining rod.
**dowse**[2] *v* see DOUSE.
**doyen** *or* **doyenne** *n* the most experienced or highly respected member of a group.
**doze**[1] *v* to sleep lightly.
**doze**[2] *n* a short light sleep.
**dozen** *n* (*pl* **dozens** *or* **dozen**) **1** a group of twelve. **2** (*in pl*) an indefinitely large number. * **talk nineteen to the dozen** *Brit* to talk non-stop and very quickly.
**DPhil** *abbr* Doctor of Philosophy.
**Dr** *abbr* doctor.
**drab** *adj* (**drabber, drabbest**) **1** dull or cheerless. **2** of a dull brown or grey colour.
**draconian** *adj* of laws, measures, etc: extremely severe.
**draft**[1] *n* **1** a preliminary sketch or version. **2** (*used before a noun*) constituting a preliminary version or sketch. **3** an order for the payment of money drawn by one person or bank on another. **4** *chiefly NAmer* conscription for military service.
**draft**[2] *v* **1** to produce a draft of (a letter, design, etc). **2** to select for a particular job or purpose. **3** *NAmer* to conscript for military service.
**drag**[1] *v* (**dragged, dragging**) **1** to pull along slowly or with difficulty. **2** to cause to trail along a surface. **3** to move (e.g. an icon) across a computer screen. **4** to search (a body of water) with a large net or hook. **5** to pass or proceed laboriously or tediously. **6** *informal* (+ on) to draw smoke from (a cigarette, pipe, etc) into the mouth. * **drag one's feet/heels** to act in a deliberately slow manner.
**drag**[2] *n* **1** the retarding force acting on a body moving through air, water, etc. **2** *informal* an inhalation of cigarette, pipe, or cigar smoke. **3** *informal* women's clothing worn by a man. **4** *informal* a dull or boring person or experience.
**dragnet** *n* a net drawn along the bottom of a body of water or the ground to catch fish or small game.
**dragon** *n* a mythical monster usu represented as a winged, fire-breathing reptile.
**dragonfly** *n* (*pl* **-ies**) a long slender-bodied insect with two pairs of delicate wings.
**dragoon**[1] *n* a soldier belonging to a cavalry unit.
**dragoon**[2] *v* to force to do something.
**drag out** *v* to prolong unduly.
**drag race** *n* an acceleration contest between cars over a short course. ➤ **drag racing** *n.*
**drain**[1] *v* **1** to draw off (liquid) gradually. **2** of liquid: to flow off gradually. **3** to empty by allowing liquid to drain away. **4** to empty (e.g. a glass) by drinking the contents. **5** to exhaust physically or emotionally.
**drain**[2] *n* **1** a pipe or other means by which liquid is drained away. **2** something that uses up energy or resources. * **go down the drain** to be wasted.
**drainage** *n* **1** the process of draining. **2** a system of drains.
**draining board** *n Brit* a slightly sloping surface beside a sink, on which washed dishes are placed to drain.
**drainpipe** *n* a pipe that carries rainwater from a roof.
**drake** *n* a male duck.
**dram** *n chiefly Scot* a tot of spirits, usu whisky.
**drama** *n* **1** a play. **2** plays collectively or as a genre. **3** an exciting or emotionally charged situation.
**dramatic** *adj* **1** characteristic of drama or acting. **2** vivid or exciting. **3** striking in appearance or effect. ➤ **dramatically** *adv.*
**dramatics** *pl n* the study or practice of acting and stage management.
**dramatist** *n* a writer of plays.
**dramatize** *or* **-ise** *v* **1** to adapt (e.g. a novel) for performance by actors. **2** to exaggerate the seriousness, excitement, etc of. ➤ **dramatization** *n.*
**drank** *v* past tense of DRINK[1].
**drape**[1] *v* **1** to cover with cloth or clothing hanging in loose folds. **2** to place (oneself, one's arm, etc) casually on, over, or around something.
**drape**[2] *n* **1** a piece of drapery. **2** *chiefly NAmer* (*usu in pl*) a curtain.
**draper** *n chiefly Brit, dated* a person who sells fabrics and haberdashery.
**drapery** *n* (*pl* **-ies**) cloth, clothing, etc arranged in loose folds.

**drastic** *adj* radical in effect; severe. ➤ **drastically** *adv.*

**draught**[1] (*NAmer* **draft**) *n* **1** a current of air in an enclosed space. **2** an act of drinking or inhaling, or a portion drunk or inhaled. **3** the act of drawing liquid, e.g. from a cask. **4** the depth of water a vessel requires to float in.

**draught**[2] (*NAmer* **draft**) *adj* **1** of an animal: used for drawing loads. **2** of beer or cider: served from the barrel.

**draughts** *pl n Brit* a board game for two players each of whom moves twelve disc-shaped pieces across a chessboard.

**draughtsman** *or* **draughtswoman** (*NAmer* **draftsman** *or* **draftswoman**) *n* (*pl* **draughtsmen** *or* **draughtswomen**) **1** a person who draws technical plans and sketches. **2** an artist skilled in drawing.

**draughty** (*NAmer* **drafty**) *adj* (**-ier, -iest**) of a room, house, etc: having cold draughts blowing through it.

**draw**[1] *v* (**drew, drawn**) **1** to produce (a picture, diagram, portrait, etc) by making lines on a surface. **2** to pull or haul (a vehicle, etc). **3** to move (somebody) in a particular direction. **4** to pull (curtains) to an open or closed position. **5** (*often* + out) to bring out of a container, sheath, etc. **6** to take in (a breath). **7** to attract: *to draw the crowds.* **8** to bring about (a response): *drew gasps from the crowd.* **9** to reach (a conclusion). **10** to receive (a salary). **11** (*often* + out) to take (money) from a bank account. **12** to select, often at random, from among things offered. **13** to have equal scores at the end of (a game). **14** to come or go steadily. ✱ **draw on/upon** to use as a source of supply. **draw the line** to fix a limit for an activity.

**draw**[2] *n* **1** a random process of choosing, e.g. in a lottery or raffle, or in organizing a sports competition. **2** a contest that ends with the scores even. **3** something that attracts public attention or a large audience. **4** a sucking action on something held between the lips, e.g. a pipe.

**drawback** *n* an undesirable feature; a disadvantage.

**drawbridge** *n* a bridge that can be raised or let down, e.g. over a castle moat.

**drawer** *n* **1** /draw/ an open-topped storage box that slides out of a piece of furniture. **2** /'draw·ə/ somebody who draws something. **3** /'draw·ə/ the person who writes a cheque. **4** /drawz/ *dated or humorous* (*in pl*) knickers or underpants.

**draw in** *v* of successive days: to grow shorter.

**drawing** *n* a representation of something in lines made with pencil, crayon, etc.

**drawing pin** *n Brit* a pin with a broad flat head used *esp* to fasten sheets of paper to boards.

**drawing room** *n* a formal reception room.

**drawl**[1] *v* to speak slowly or lazily with prolonged vowels.

**drawl**[2] *n* a drawling manner of speaking.

**drawn**[1] *v* past part. of DRAW[1].

**drawn**[2] *adj* **1** looking strained, tired, or ill. **2** of a game, competition, etc: ended in a draw.

**draw on** *v* to approach.

**draw out** *v* **1** to extend (a process) beyond its normal duration. **2** to encourage (somebody) to speak freely. **3** of successive days: to grow longer.

**drawstring** *n* a string or tape that can be pulled to close a bag, tighten clothes, etc.

**draw up** *v* **1** to prepare (a document or proposal). **2** to come to a halt.

**dray** *n* a strong low cart, used *esp* by brewers.

**dread**[1] *v* **1** to be extremely apprehensive about. **2** to fear greatly.

**dread**[2] *n* great fear or apprehension.

**dreadful** *adj* **1** extremely unpleasant or shocking. **2** very disagreeable. **3** extreme. ➤ **dreadfully** *adv.*

**dreadlocks** *pl n* long plaited or tightly curled locks of hair worn *esp* by male Rastafarians.

**dream**[1] *n* **1** a series of images or emotions occurring during sleep. **2** a state of absentmindedness. **3** a strongly desired goal; an ambition. **4** something especially beautiful, excellent, etc. **5** (*used before a noun*) perfect.

**dream**[2] *v* (*past tense and past part.* **dreamed** *or* **dreamt** /dremt/) **1** to have a dream. **2** to indulge in daydreams or fantasies. **3** to consider as a possibility; to imagine. ➤ **dreamer** *n.*

**dream up** *v informal* to devise or invent.

**dreamy** *adj* (**-ier, -iest**) **1** given to daydreaming or fantasy. **2** suggestive of a dream. **3** *informal* very pleasing or attractive. ➤ **dreamily** *adv.*

**dreary** *adj* (**-ier, -iest**) causing feelings of cheerlessness or gloom; dull. ➤ **drearily** *adv,* **dreariness** *n.*

**dredge**[1] *n* a machine for removing earth, mud, etc, esp from the bottom of a waterway.

**dredge**[2] *v* **1** (*often* + up/out). **2** to deepen (e.g. a waterway) with a dredge. **3** *informal* (+ up) to bring to light by thorough searching. ➤ **dredger** *n.*

**dregs** *pl n* **1** sediment contained in or deposited by a liquid. **2** the most undesirable part.

**drench** *v* to make thoroughly wet.

**dress**[1] *v* **1** to put clothes on (oneself or somebody else). **2** to put on clothing. **3** to choose or wear one's clothes in a particular way or for a particular purpose. **4** to make more attractive by decorating, arranging, grooming, etc. **5** to apply dressings or medicaments to (e.g. a wound). **6** to prepare (food) for cooking or eating.

**dress**[2] *n* **1** a woman's one-piece outer garment including both top and skirt. **2** clothing, *esp* garments suitable for a particular occasion or time.

**dressage** /'dresahzh/ *n* the performance by a trained horse of precise movements in response to its rider.

**dress circle** *n* the first or lowest curved tier of seats in a theatre.

**dress down** *v* **1** to reprove severely. **2** to wear informal clothes. ➤ **dressing down** *n.*

**dresser** *n* a sideboard with a high back with open shelves for holding dishes.

**dressing** *n* **1** a usu cold sauce for adding to food, *esp* salads. **2** material applied to cover a wound, sore, etc.

**dressing gown** *n* a loose robe worn *esp* over nightclothes.

**dressing room** *n* a room used chiefly for dressing, *esp* for changing costumes in a theatre.

**dressing table** *n* a table with drawers and a mirror for use while applying make-up, combing one's hair, etc.

**dressmaker** *n* a person who makes clothes for female clients. ➤ **dressmaking** *n.*

**dress rehearsal** *n* a full rehearsal in costume and under performance conditions shortly before the first performance of a play, etc.

**dress up** *v* to dress in formal or smart clothes or in a particular costume.

**dressy** *adj* (**-ier, -iest**) of clothes: stylish, smart, or formal.

**drew** *v* past tense of DRAW[1].

**dribble**[1] *v* **1** to fall or flow in drops or in a thin stream. **2** to let saliva trickle from the mouth. **3** in football, hockey, basketball, etc, to propel (a ball) by successive slight taps or bounces.

**dribble**[2] *n* **1** a small trickling flow. **2** an act of dribbling in sport.

**dribs and drabs** *pl n informal* small usu scattered amounts.

**dried** *v* past tense and past part. of DRY[2].

**drier**[1] *or* **dryer** *n* a machine for drying something.

**drier**[2] *adj* compar of DRY[1].

**drift**[1] *v* **1** to be carried along by a current of water or air. **2** to move in an aimless or casual way. **3** of snow, leaves, etc: to pile up under the force of wind.

**drift**[2] *n* **1** the motion of drifting. **2** a gradual shift in attitude. **3** a mass of snow, leaves, etc deposited by wind. **4** a general underlying meaning.

**drifter** *n* somebody who travels about aimlessly.

**driftwood** *n* wood floating on water or cast up on a beach.

**drill**[1] *v* **1** to make (a hole) with a drill. **2** to drill a hole in. **3** to fix in somebody's mind by repetitive instruction. **4** to train in military drill.

**drill**[2] *n* **1** a boring tool for making a hole in a solid substance. **2** military training in marching, the handling of arms, etc. **3** an exercise to improve skill by regular practice. **4** *chiefly Brit, informal* the approved or correct procedure.

**drily** *or* **dryly** *adv* in a subtly ironic way.

**drink**[1] *v* (**drank, drunk**) **1** to swallow (a liquid), usu for refreshment or nourishment. **2** to drink alcohol, *esp* habitually or to excess. **3** (+ in) to take in avidly. ✱ **drink to** to drink a toast to. ➤ **drinkable** *adj,* **drinker** *n.*

**drink**[2] *n* **1** liquid suitable for drinking. **2** alcoholic drink. **3** a portion of liquid for drinking.

**drink-driving** *n Brit* the crime of driving a vehicle while under the influence of alcohol. ➤ **drink-driver** *n.*

**drip**[1] *v* (**dripped, dripping**) to let (liquid) fall in drops.

**drip**[2] *n* **1** a drop of liquid. **2** the act of falling in drops. **3** a device used to administer drugs or nutrients in solution slowly into a vein. **4** *informal* a weak or insipid person.

**drip-feed** *v* to put liquid into gradually.

**dripping**[1] *n* the fat that runs out from meat during roasting.

**dripping**[2] *adj* extremely wet.

**drive**[1] *v* (**drove, driven**) **1** to direct the course of (a vehicle). **2** to transport in a vehicle. **3** to propel by physical force. **4** to apply pressure on (somebody) to act in a certain way. **5** to provide the motive power for (a machine or engine). ✱ **be driving at** to be implying or suggesting. ➤ **driver** *n.*

**drive**[2] *n* **1** a journey or trip in a car. **2** a private road giving access to a building, *esp* a private house. **3** a motivating instinctual need. **4** great zeal in pursuing one's ends. **5** a campaign. **6** a powerful shot in golf, cricket, etc.

**drivel** *n* foolish or childish nonsense.

**drizzle**[1] *v* **1** to rain in small drops or very lightly. **2** to let (liquid) fall in minute drops.

**drizzle**[2] *n* a fine misty rain.

**droll** *adj* amusing, *esp* in an odd way.

**dromedary** *n* (*pl* **-ies**) a one-humped camel.

**drone**[1] *n* **1** a male bee whose sole function is to mate with the queen. **2** a remote-controlled aircraft, missile, or ship. **3** a droning sound.

**drone**[2] *v* **1** to make a deep murmuring or buzzing sound. **2** (*often* + on) to talk persistently and tediously.

**drool** *v* **1** to let saliva dribble from the mouth. **2** (*often* + over) to make an effusive show of pleasure.

**droop**[1] *v* **1** to hang or bend downwards. **2** to become tired or depressed.

**droop**[2] *n* the condition or appearance of drooping. ➤ **droopy** *adj.*

**drop**[1] *n* **1** a round or pear-shaped mass of falling liquid. **2** a minute quantity, *esp* of liquid. **3** a small globular sweet. **4** a fall, decrease, or decline. **5** a parachute descent, or the things dropped by parachute. ✱ **at the drop of a hat** without hesitation; promptly.

**drop**[2] *v* (**dropped, dropping**) **1** to fall or cause to fall vertically. **2** to fall in a state of collapse. **3** to become weaker or less. **4** to give up or abandon (an idea, accusation, friendship, etc). **5** to leave out of a team, etc. **6** to set down (passengers or cargo) from a vehicle, ship, etc. **7** to lose (a point or game) in a series.

**drop kick** *n* a kick made, e.g. in rugby, by dropping a ball and kicking it as it rebounds.

**droplet** *n* a small drop of liquid.

**drop off** *v* **1** to fall asleep, *esp* unintentionally. **2** to become less.

**dropout** *n* **1** somebody who withdraws from conventional society. **2** a student who fails to complete a course.

**drop out** *v* **1** to withdraw from an activity. **2** to adopt an alternative lifestyle.

**droppings** *pl n* animal excrement.

**dross** *n* waste or rubbish. ➤ **drossy** *adj.*

**drought** /drowt/ *n* a prolonged period with little or no rainfall.

**drove**[1] *n* **1** a group of animals moving together. **2** (*also in pl*) a crowd of people moving together.

**drove**[2] *v* past tense of DRIVE[1].

**drown** *v* **1** to die or cause to die through suffocation by submersion in water. **2** to submerge, *esp* by a rise in the water level. **3** (*often* + out) to cause (a sound) not to be heard by making a loud noise.

**drowsy** *adj* (**-ier, -iest**) sleepy. ➤ **drowsily** *adv,* **drowsiness** *n.*

**drub** *v* (**drubbed, drubbing**) **1** to beat severely. **2** to defeat decisively. ➤ **drubbing** *n.*

**drudge** *n* a person who does hard, menial, or monotonous work.

**drudgery** *n* hard, menial, or monotonous work.

**drug**[1] *n* **1** a substance intended for the treatment or prevention of disease. **2** a substance that has a particular effect on the body, e.g. a stimulant. **3** something that causes addiction.

**drug**[2] *v* (**drugged, drugging**) to administer a drug to.

**drugstore** *n chiefly NAmer* a pharmacy, *esp* one that also sells refreshments and other goods.

**druid** *n* (*often* **Druid**) a member of an ancient Celtic order of priests.

**drum**[1] *n* **1** a hollow cylindrical percussion instrument that is played by beating with sticks or the hands. **2** the sound made by striking a drum, or any similar sound. **3** a cylindrical container or mechanical part.

**drum**[2] *v* (**drummed, drumming**) **1** to beat a drum. **2** to throb or sound rhythmically. **3** (*usu* + into) to instil (an idea or lesson) by constant repetition.

**drum and bass** *n* a type of modern dance music characterized by insistent drum beats and low bass lines.

**drumstick** *n* **1** a stick for beating a drum. **2** a fowl's leg between the thigh and foot when cooked.

**drunk**[1] *v* past part. of DRINK[1].

**drunk**[2] *adj* under the influence of alcohol.

**drunk**[3] *n* a person who is drunk, *esp* habitually.

**drupe** *n* a fruit, e.g. a cherry or plum, with a stone enclosed by a fleshy layer.

**dry**[1] *adj* (**drier** *or* **dryer, driest** *or* **dryest**) **1** not or no longer wet. **2** of wine, etc: not sweet. **3** uninteresting. **4** marked by a matter-of-fact, ironic, or terse manner of expression. ➤ **dryness** *n.*

**dry**[2] *v* (**-ies, -ied**) **1** to make or become dry. **2** to preserve by removing moisture.

**dry-clean** *v* to clean (a fabric, garment, etc) with organic solvents rather than water. ➤ **dry cleaner** *n,* **dry cleaning** *n.*

**dryer** *n* see DRIER[1].

**dry ice** *n* solidified carbon dioxide used *esp* to produce the theatrical effect of white mist.

**dryly** *adv* see DRILY.

**dry rot** *n* a decay of seasoned timber caused by fungi.

**dry run** *n* a rehearsal or trial.

**drystone** *adj* of a wall: constructed of stone without the use of mortar.

**dry up** *v* of a supply: to dwindle and stop.

**dual** *adj* **1** consisting of two parts or elements. **2** having a double nature. ➤ **duality** *n.*

**dual carriageway** *n chiefly Brit* a road that has traffic travelling in two or more, usu separated lanes in each direction.

**dualism** *n* **1** the state of being dual. **2** a theory that considers reality to consist of two independent and contrasting principles, e.g. mind and matter. ➤ **dualist** *n,* **dualistic** *adj.*

**dub**[1] *v* (**dubbed, dubbing**) **1** to call by an unofficial name or nickname. **2** to confer knighthood on, *esp* by ceremonial touching on the shoulder with a sword.

**dub**[2] *v* **1** to provide (a film, television broadcast, etc) with a new soundtrack, *esp* in a different language. **2** (*often* + in) to add (sound effects, music, etc) to a film or broadcast. ➤ **dubbing** *n.*

**dubbin** *n* a grease used for softening and waterproofing leather.

**dubious** *adj* **1** doubtful; uncertain. **2** of questionable quality or origin. ➤ **dubiously** *adv.*

**ducal** *adj* of a duke or duchy.

**ducat** *n* a gold coin formerly used in many European countries.

**duchess** *n* **1** the wife or widow of a duke. **2** a woman having the rank of a duke.

**duchy** *n* (*pl* **-ies**) the territory of a duke or duchess.

**duck**[1] *n* (*pl* **ducks** *or* **duck**) **1** a swimming bird with a short neck, short legs, webbed feet, and a broad flat beak. **2** a female duck: compare DRAKE.

**duck**[2] *v* **1** to lower one's head or body suddenly, e.g. to avoid being seen or hit. **2** to thrust momentarily under water. **3** to evade (a duty, question, responsibility, etc).

**duck**[3] *n* a score of nought, *esp* in cricket.

**duck-billed platypus** *n* = PLATYPUS.

**duckboard** *n* (*usu in pl*) a wooden board used to make a path over muddy ground.

**duckling** *n* a young duck.

**duct** *n* **1** a pipe or channel that carries air, power lines, telephone cables, etc. **2** a bodily tube that carries a glandular secretion.

**ductile** *adj* of metals: capable of being drawn out or hammered thin.

**dud**[1] *n informal* **1** something that fails to perform as it should. **2** (*in pl*) clothes.

**dud**[2] *adj informal* ineffectual.

**dude** *n chiefly NAmer, informal* a man.

**dudgeon** *n* ✱ **in high dudgeon** in a state of great indignation.

**due**[1] *adj* **1** owed or owing as a debt. **2** owed or owing as a natural or moral right. **3** proper or appropriate. **4** expected in the prearranged or normal course of events. ✱ **due to 1** ascribable to. **2** because of. **in due course** after a normal passage of time.

**due**[2] *n* **1** something that rightfully belongs to somebody. **2** (*in pl*) fees; charges. ✱ **give somebody their due** to give somebody the credit they deserve.

**due**[3] *adv* directly or exactly.

**duel**[1] *n* **1** a formal combat with weapons fought between two people to settle a quarrel or point of honour. **2** a conflict between usu evenly matched people, ideas, or forces.

**duel**[2] *v* (**duelled, duelling,** *NAmer* **dueled, dueling**) to fight a duel.

**duet** *n* **1** a composition for two performers. **2** a performance by two musicians, singers, dancers, etc.

**duff** *adj Brit, informal* not working; useless.

**duffel bag** *n* a cylindrical canvas bag closed by a drawstring.

**duffel coat** *n* a hooded coat made of heavy woollen material, usu fastened with toggles.

**duffer** *n informal* an incompetent or clumsy person.

**dug**[1] *v* past tense and past part. of DIG[1].

**dug**[2] *n* an udder, teat or nipple.

**dugout** *n* **1** a boat made by hollowing out a log. **2** a shelter dug in the ground, *esp* for troops. **3** a shelter at the side of a sports ground where trainers, substitutes, etc sit.

**duke** *n* **1** a member of the highest rank of the British peerage. **2** a sovereign ruler of a European duchy. ➤ **dukedom** *n.*

**dulcet** *adj* of sounds: sweetly pleasant or soothing.

**dulcimer** /ˈdulsimə/ *n* a musical instrument played by striking its strings with light hammers.

**dull**[1] *adj* **1** boring or uninteresting. **2** cloudy or overcast. **3** lacking brightness or intensity. **4** slow in perception or understanding. ➤ **dullness** *n,* **dully** *adv.*

**dull**[2] *v* to make or become dull.

**dullard** *n* a stupid or insensitive person.

**duly** *adv* in a due manner, time, or degree; properly.

**dumb** *adj* **1** lacking the power of speech; mute. **2** unwilling or temporarily unable to speak. **3** *chiefly NAmer, informal* stupid. ➤ **dumbly** *adv.*

**dumbbell** *n* a short bar with adjustable weights at each end used for weight training.

**dumb down** *v informal* to make less intellectually challenging.

**dumbfound** *v* to amaze.

**dumbstruck** *adj* too astonished to speak.

**dumb waiter** *n* a small lift for conveying food and dishes from the kitchen to the dining area of a restaurant.

**dumdum** *n* a bullet that expands on impact and inflicts a severe wound.

**dummy** *n* (*pl* **-ies**) **1** an imitation or copy of something used as a substitute, for demonstration purposes, etc. **2** a model of the human body used e.g. for fitting or displaying clothes. **3** *chiefly Brit* a rubber or plastic teat given to babies to suck. **4** *informal* a dull or stupid person. **5** the act of deceiving an opponent in sports by pretending to pass or release the ball.

**dummy run** *n* a rehearsal or trial run.

**dump**[1] *v* **1** to unload or deposit (something unwanted, e.g. refuse). **2** to deposit carelessly or heavily. **3** to get rid of unceremoniously or irresponsibly.

**dump**[2] *n* **1** a place where discarded materials are dumped. **2** an accumulation of military materials or the place where they are stored. **3** *informal* an unpleasant or dilapidated place.

**dumpling** *n* a small round mass of dough cooked by boiling or steaming, often in a stew.

**dumps** *pl n* ✱ **down in the dumps** *informal* gloomy; despondent.

**dumpy** *adj* (**-ier, -iest**) of a person: short and thick in build.

**dun** *n* a brownish grey colour.

**dunce** *n* a stupid person or slow learner.

**dune** *n* a ridge of sand piled up by the wind.

**dung** *n* the excrement of an animal.

**dungarees** *pl n* a one-piece outer garment consisting of trousers and a bib with shoulder straps.

**dungeon** *n* a dark underground prison.

**dunk** *v* **1** to dip (a biscuit, a piece of bread, etc) into liquid, e.g. a drink or soup, before eating it. **2** to submerge temporarily in water.

**dunnock** *n* a small dull-coloured European bird.

**duo** *n* (*pl* **-os**) **1** a pair of people or things, *esp* a pair of performers. **2** a duet.

**duodenum** *n* (*pl* **duodena** *or* **duodenums**) the first part of the small intestine, extending from the stomach to the jejunum.
**dupe**[1] *n* somebody who is easily deceived or cheated.
**dupe**[2] *v* to cheat or deceive.
**duple** *adj* of musical rhythm: having two beats per bar.
**duplex** *n* **1** *NAmer* a house divided into two flats. **2** *NAmer, Aus* a semi-detached house.
**duplicate**[1] *adj* **1** consisting of two corresponding or identical parts. **2** being the same as another.
**duplicate**[2] *n* **1** either of two things that exactly resemble each other. **2** a copy.
**duplicate**[3] *v* **1** to make an exact copy of. **2** to repeat or equal. ➤ **duplication** *n.*
**duplicity** *n* malicious deception in thought, speech, or action. ➤ **duplicitous** *adj.*
**durable** *adj* able to be used for a long time without deteriorating. ➤ **durability** *n.*
**duration** *n* the time during which something exists or lasts.
**duress** *n* **1** compulsion by threat, violence, or imprisonment. **2** forcible restraint or restriction.
**during** *prep* **1** throughout the whole duration of. **2** at some point in the course of.
**dusk** *n* the darker part of twilight.
**dusky** *adj* (**-ier, -iest**) **1** somewhat dark in colour. **2** shadowy; gloomy.
**dust**[1] *n* **1** fine dry particles of any solid matter. **2** the fine particles of waste that settle on household surfaces.
**dust**[2] *v* **1** to make free of dust, e.g. by wiping or brushing. **2** (+ down/off) to prepare to use again, *esp* after a long period of disuse. **3** to sprinkle with fine particles.
**dustbin** *n Brit* a large container for holding household refuse.
**dustcart** *n Brit* a vehicle for collecting household refuse.
**duster** *n* a cloth for removing dust from household surfaces.
**dustman** *n* (*pl* **dustmen**) *Brit* somebody employed to remove household refuse.
**dustpan** *n* a shovel-like utensil into which household dust and litter is swept.
**dust-up** *n informal* a quarrel or fight.
**Dutch** *n* **1** (**the Dutch**) (*treated as pl*) the people of the Netherlands. **2** the language of the people of the Netherlands. ✱ **go Dutch** to divide expenses equally. ➤ **Dutch** *adj.*
**Dutch courage** *n* courage induced by drinking alcohol.
**dutiable** *adj* subject to a duty.
**dutiful** *adj* motivated by or expressive of a sense of duty. ➤ **dutifully** *adv.*
**duty** *n* (*pl* **-ies**) **1** a task or function arising from one's position or job. **2** official service or business. **3** a moral or legal obligation. **4** a tax, e.g. on imports or the transfer of property. ✱ **on/off duty** engaged or not engaged in one's usual work.
**duty-bound** *adj* morally or legally obliged.
**duty-free** *adj* exempt from duty.
**duvet** /'doohvay/ *n* a large quilt, used in place of an upper sheet and blankets.
**DVD** *abbr* digital videodisc (or digital versatile disc), a disc with a large capacity for storing audio, video, or other information.
**dwarf**[1] *n* (*pl* **dwarfs** *or* **dwarves**) **1** a person of abnormally small stature. **2** an animal or plant that is much smaller than normal size. **3** in mythology, a small human-like creature often depicted as having magical powers.
**dwarf**[2] *v* to cause to appear smaller or less significant by comparison.
**dwell** *v* (*past tense and past part.* **dwelt** *or* **dwelled**) *formal* to live; to reside. ✱ **dwell on/upon** to think, write, or speak about at length.
**dwelling** *n formal* a place, e.g. a house or flat, in which people live.
**dwindle** *v* to become steadily less in quantity or size.
**Dy** *abbr* the chemical symbol for dysprosium.
**dye**[1] *n* a substance used to colour something.
**dye**[2] *v* (**dyes, dyed, dyeing**) to impart a new and often permanent colour to (e.g. fabric or hair) with a dye.
**dyed-in-the-wool** *adj* uncompromising or unchanging.
**dying** *v* present part. of DIE[1].
**dyke**[1] *or* **dike** *n* **1** a watercourse or ditch. **2** a bank, usu of earth, constructed to control or confine water.
**dyke**[2] *or* **dike** *n informal, derog* a lesbian.
**dynamic** *adj* **1** of physical force or energy in motion. **2** marked by continuous activity or change. **3** energetic and forceful. **4** relating to variation in sound intensity or volume. ➤ **dynamically** *adv.*
**dynamics** *pl n* **1** the branch of mechanics that deals with forces and their relation to motion. **2** a pattern of change or growth, or the forces that produce it. **3** variation in the intensity of sound, *esp* in music.
**dynamism** *n* the quality of being energetic and forceful.
**dynamite**[1] *n* **1** a blasting explosive made of nitroglycerine. **2** *informal* somebody or something that has a potentially dangerous or spectacular effect.
**dynamite**[2] *v* to blow up or destroy with dynamite.
**dynamo** *n* (*pl* **-os**) a machine for converting mechanical into electrical energy.
**dynasty** *n* (*pl* **-ies**) **1** a succession of hereditary rulers. **2** a powerful group or family that main-

tains its position for a considerable time. ➤ **dynastic** *adj.*

**dysentery** /ˈdis(ə)ntri/ *n* an infection of the intestines characterized by severe diarrhoea.

**dysfunctional** *adj* **1** not functioning properly. **2** characterized by the breakdown of social behaviour and relationships.

**dyslexia** *n* difficulties with reading, writing, and spelling, caused by a neurological disorder. ➤ **dyslexic** *adj and n.*

**dyspepsia** *n* indigestion.

**dyspeptic** *adj* **1** relating to or having dyspepsia. **2** ill-tempered.

**E**[1] *or* **e** *n* (*pl* **Es** *or* **E's** *or* **e's**) the fifth letter of the English alphabet.

**E**[2] *abbr* **1** East. **2** Eastern.

**E**[3] *n* (*pl* **Es** *or* **E's**) **1** the drug Ecstasy. **2** an Ecstasy tablet.

**e-** *prefix* electronic; using the Internet: *email, e-commerce.*

**each**[1] *adj and pron* every one of the individuals within a group, considered separately.

**each**[2] *adv* to or for each.

**eager** *adj* showing keen desire or interest. ➤ **eagerly** *adv.*

**eagle** *n* **1** a large bird of prey noted for its strength, size, and keenness of vision. **2** a golf score of two strokes less than par on a hole.

**eagle-eyed** *adj* having very good eyesight.

**ear**[1] *n* **1** the organ of hearing in humans and other vertebrates. **2** sensitivity to musical tone and pitch. **3** sympathetic attention. * **be all ears** to listen very attentively. **play it by ear** to act according to circumstances.

**ear**[2] *n* the seed-bearing spike of a cereal plant.

**earache** *n* pain in the ear.

**eardrum** *n* a vibrating membrane in the ear that responds to sound waves.

**earl** *n* a member of the British peerage ranking below a marquess and above a viscount. ➤ **earldom** *n.*

**early** *adj and adv* (**-ier, -iest**) **1** before the usual or expected time. **2** near the beginning of a period of time or series.

**earmark** *v* to designate (e.g. funds) for a specific use or recipient.

**earmuffs** *pl n* a pair of ear coverings worn as protection against cold or noise.

**earn** *v* **1** to receive (money) as return for work done or services rendered. **2** to deserve (a title, reward, etc) because of one's behaviour or efforts.

**earnest** *adj* determined and serious. * **in earnest** serious or sincere; wholeheartedly. ➤ **earnestly** *adv.*

**earnings** *pl n* money or other income earned.

**earphone** *n* a device worn directly over or in the ear that reproduces sound from a radio, personal stereo, etc.

**earpiece** *n* the part of an instrument, e.g. a telephone, held to the ear.

**earplug** *n* a device inserted into the the ear for protection against water, loud noise, etc.

**earring** *n* an ornament attached to the lobe or edge of the ear.

**earshot** *n* the range within which something, *esp* the unaided voice, may be heard: *out of earshot.*

**earth**[1] *n* **1** (*often* **Earth**) the planet on which we live. **2** land or solid ground. **3** soil. **4** *chiefly Brit* an electrical connection to the ground, used to carry current safely from a circuit in the event of a fault. **5** the lair of a fox, badger, etc. * **go to earth** to go into hiding.

**earth**[2] *v chiefly Brit* to connect (an electrical device) to earth.

**earthen** *adj* made of earth or baked clay.

**earthenware** *n* ceramic ware made of clay fired at a low temperature.

**earthling** *n* an inhabitant of the earth, *esp* in science fiction.

**earthly** *adj* **1** characteristic of the earth or human life on earth. **2** possible: *no earthly reason.*

**earthquake** *n* a sudden violent earth tremor caused by pressures within the earth's crust.

**earthwork** *n* an embankment, fortification, etc made of earth.

**earthworm** *n* a common hermaphroditic worm that lives in the soil.

**earthy** *adj* (**-ier, -iest**) **1** resembling earth or soil. **2** dealing frankly or cheerfully with sex and bodily functions.

**earwig**[1] *n* a small insect with a slender body and a pair of appendages like forceps at its rear end.

**earwig**[2] *v* (**earwigged, earwigging**) *informal* to eavesdrop.

**ease**[1] *n* **1** lack of difficulty in doing something; effortlessness. **2** freedom from pain, anxiety, embarrassment, or constraint. **3** rest or relaxation.

**ease**[2] *v* **1** to make (pain, suffering, etc) less severe or intense. **2** to manoeuvre gently or carefully. **3** (*often* + off/up) to decrease in activity, intensity, severity, etc.

**easel** *n* a frame for supporting something, *esp* an artist's canvas.

**east**[1] *n* **1** the direction of sunrise, 90° clockwise from north. **2** regions or countries lying to the east. ➤ **eastbound** *adj and adv.*

**east**[2] *adj and adv* **1** at or towards the east. **2** of the wind: blowing from the east.

**Easter** *n* a Christian feast commemorating Christ's resurrection, observed on a Sunday between 21 March and 25 April.

**Easter egg** *n* a chocolate egg given as a present at Easter.

**easterly** *adj and adv* **1** in an eastern position or direction. **2** of a wind: blowing from the east.

**eastern** *adj* **1** in or towards the east. **2** (*often* **Eastern**) relating to countries or continents east of Europe, or their traditions.

**Easterner** *n* a person from the eastern part of a country.

**eastward** *adj and adv* towards the east; in a direction going east. ➤ **eastwards** *adv.*

**easy** *adj* (**-ier, -iest**) **1** causing or involving little difficulty. **2** marked by peace, comfort, or freedom from constraint. **3** free from pain, annoyance, or anxiety. **4** *chiefly Brit, informal* not having strong preferences on a particular issue. * **go easy on 1** to be lenient with. **2** to be sparing with. **take it easy** to relax or rest. ➤ **easily** *adv,* **easiness** *n.*

**easygoing** *adj* relaxed and tolerant.

**easy listening** *n* music that is undemanding and pleasant to listen to.

**eat** *v* (**ate, eaten**) **1** to put (food) in the mouth and swallow it. **2** (+ away/into/through) to destroy, erode, or corrode gradually. **3** (+ into) to use a great deal of (a limited resource). **4** *informal* to worry or annoy (somebody). * **eat one's words** to retract what one has said. ➤ **eatable** *adj.*

**eatery** *n* (*pl* **-ies**) *informal* a restaurant.

**eau de cologne** /ˌoh də kəˈlohn/ *n* (*pl* **eaux de cologne** /ˌoh/) a variety of toilet water with a characteristic perfume.

**eaves** *pl n* the lower border of a roof that overhangs the wall.

**eavesdrop** *v* (**eavesdropped, eavesdropping**) to listen secretly to what is said in private.

**ebb**[1] *n* the flowing out of the tide towards the sea. * **at a low ebb** in a poor state.

**ebb**[2] *v* **1** of tidal water: to recede from the highest level. **2** (*often* + away) to decline or disappear gradually.

**ebony** *n* **1** a hard heavy black wood from a tropical tree. **2** a dark brown or black colour. ➤ **ebony** *adj.*

**ebullient** *adj* full of liveliness and enthusiasm. ➤ **ebullience** *n.*

**EC** *abbr* **1** European Commission. **2** European Community.

**eccentric**[1] /ikˈsentrik/ *adj* unusual, unconventional, and, usu amusingly, odd. ➤ **eccentrically** *adv,* **eccentricity** *n.*

**eccentric**[2] *n* an eccentric person.

**ecclesiastical** *adj* relating to the Church.

**echelon** /ˈeshəlon/ *n* a level or grade, e.g. of authority or responsibility, in some organized field of activity.

**echo**[1] /ˈekoh/ *n* (*pl* **-oes**) **1** the repetition of a sound caused by the reflection of sound waves. **2** the reflection by an object of transmitted radar signals. ➤ **echoey** *adj.*

**echo**[2] *v* (**echoes, echoed, echoing**) **1** to produce an echo. **2** to produce a continuing effect. **3** to repeat or imitate (somebody or somebody's words).

**echo chamber** *n* a room with sound-reflecting walls used for making acoustic measurements and for producing echoing sound effects, *esp* in radio broadcasting.

**éclair** *or* **eclair** /iˈkleə, ayˈkleə/ *n* a small cylindrical cake of choux pastry filled with cream and topped with chocolate icing.

**éclat** /ayˈklah/ *n* brilliant or conspicuous success.

**eclectic** *adj* selecting elements from a variety of sources, methods, or styles.

**eclipse**[1] *n* **1** the total or partial obscuring of one celestial body by another. **2** a falling into obscurity or decay.

**eclipse**[2] *v* **1** to cause an eclipse of (a celestial body). **2** to surpass (a person, achievement, etc).

**eco-friendly** *adj* not harmful to the environment.

**E. coli** /ˈkohlie/ *n* a bacterium that can sometimes cause severe food poisoning.

**ecology** *n* the interrelationship of living organisms and their environments, or the scientific study of this. ➤ **ecological** *adj,* **ecologist** *n.*

**economic** *adj* **1** relating to economics or an economy. **2** profitable. ➤ **economically** *adv.*

**economical** *adj* **1** thrifty. **2** efficient; not wasting money, fuel, etc. ➤ **economically** *adv.*

**economics** *pl n* a social science concerned with the production, distribution, and consumption of goods and services. ➤ **economist** *n.*

**economize** *or* **-ise** *v* (*often* + on) to be frugal or not wasteful.

**economy** *n* (*pl* **-ies**) **1** the system whereby a country produces and sells goods and services and creates wealth. **2** thrifty and efficient use of money or resources. **3** an instance of economizing; a saving. **4** (*often used before a noun*) a cheaper standard of travel.

**ecosystem** *n* a community of plants and animals and its environment, functioning as an ecological unit in nature.

**Ecstasy** *n* an illegal drug taken recreationally for its stimulant and euphoric effects.

**ecstasy** *n* (*pl* **-ies**) **1** a feeling of great joy or happiness. **2** a state of frenzied emotion.

***Usage Note:*** Note the spelling *-asy* not *-acy*.

**ecstatic** *adj* extremely happy or enthusiastic. ➤ **ecstatically** *adv.*

**ectoplasm** *n* a substance supposed to emanate from a spiritualist medium in a state of trance and in which a spirit manifests itself.

**ecumenical** *adj* **1** representing several different Churches. **2** promoting worldwide Christian unity.

**eczema** /ˈeksimə/ *n* an inflammatory condition of the skin characterized by itching and oozing blisters.

**eddy**[1] *n* (*pl* **-ies**) a current of water, air, etc running counter to the main current and causing a small whirlpool.

**eddy**[2] *v* (**-ies, -ied**) to move in an eddy or with circular motion.

**edelweiss** /ˈaydlvies/ *n* a small perennial Alpine plant covered in dense white hairs.

**edema** *n NAmer* see OEDEMA.

**Eden** *n* **1** the garden where, according to Genesis, Adam and Eve lived before the Fall. **2** a paradise.

**edge**[1] *n* **1** the line where an object or area begins or ends; a border. **2** a line where two surfaces of a solid meet. **3** the cutting side of a blade. * **have the edge on/over somebody** to have an advantage over somebody. **on edge** anxious or nervous.

**edge**[2] *v* **1** to provide with an edge. **2** to move gradually or cautiously.

**edgeways** *or* **edgewise** *adv* with the edge foremost; sideways. * **get a word in edgeways** to be allowed to contribute to a conversation.

**edgy** *adj* (**-ier, -iest**) tense, anxious, or irritable.

**edible** *adj* fit to be eaten as food.

**edict** *n* an official public decree or command.

**edifice** *n* a building, *esp* a large or massive structure.

**edify** *v* (**-ies, -ied**) to instruct and improve, *esp* in moral knowledge. ➤ **edification** *n*, **edifying** *adj*.

**edit**[1] *v* (**edited, editing**) **1** to alter (e.g. written material), *esp* to condense or improve it. **2** to assemble (e.g. a film or recording) by deleting, inserting, and rearranging material. **3** to be the editor of (a newspaper or periodical).

**edit**[2] *n* an editorial change or correction.

**edition** *n* **1** the form in which a text is published. **2** a number of copies published at one time or place. **3** a particular broadcast or instalment of a radio or television programme.

**editor** *n* **1** a person in overall charge of the content of a newspaper, magazine, book by various writers, or radio or television programme. **2** a person who edits text, films, recordings, etc.

**editorial**[1] *adj* of or written by an editor. ➤ **editorially** *adv*.

**editorial**[2] *n* a newspaper or magazine article giving the opinions of the editor.

**educate** *v* to teach or instruct in academic, moral, or social matters. ➤ **educator** *n*.

**educated** *adj* **1** having had an education, *esp* a good one. **2** based on some knowledge or experience: *an educated guess*.

**education** *n* **1** the act of educating or the process of being educated. **2** instruction in some subject. **3** the knowledge resulting from instruction. **4** the field of study that deals mainly with methods of teaching. ➤ **educational** *adj*.

**Edwardian** *adj* of the reign of King Edward VII of England (1901–1910).

**eel** *n* a long snakelike fish with a smooth slimy skin.

**eerie** *or* **eery** *adj* (**-ier, -iest**) frighteningly strange or gloomy. ➤ **eerily** *adv*.

**efface** *v* **1** to remove from a surface or make indistinct. **2** to make (oneself) inconspicuous.

**effect**[1] *n* **1** the result produced by a cause or action. **2** the extent to which a cause or action produces results. **3** the state of being operative: *come into effect*. **4** (*in pl*) personal movable property; goods. **5** (*often in pl*) something designed to enhance the drama, realism, or impressiveness of a play or film. * **for effect** in order to impress. **in effect** actually although not officially so. **take effect 1** to become operative. **2** to produce a result.

***Usage Note:*** Do not confuse this word with *affect*, which is a verb only.

**effect**[2] *v* to bring about, carry out, or accomplish.

**effective** *adj* **1** producing a decisive or desired effect. **2** impressive or striking. **3** actual or real, though not officially recognized. **4** in force; operative. ➤ **effectiveness** *n*.

**effectual** *adj* able to produce a desired effect; effective.

**effeminate** *adj* of a man: having qualities usu thought of as feminine. ➤ **effeminacy** *n*.

**effervesce** *v* of a liquid: to bubble and hiss as gas escapes.

**effervescent** *adj* **1** effervescing. **2** lively and exhilarated.

**effete** *adj* **1** marked by weakness and decadent overrefinement. **2** effeminate.

**efficacious** *adj formal* effective.

**efficacy** *n formal* effectiveness.

**efficient** *adj* **1** producing desired effects, *esp* with minimum waste. **2** of a person: briskly competent. ➤ **efficiency** *n*, **efficiently** *adv*.

**effigy** *n* (*pl* **-ies**) an image or representation of a person, *esp* a hated person.

**effluent** *n* liquid industrial refuse, sewage, etc discharged into the environment and causing pollution.

**effluvium** *n* (*pl* **effluvia, effluviums**) an offensive gas or smell.

**effort** *n* **1** conscious exertion of physical or

mental power. **2** a serious attempt; a try. **3** something produced by exertion or trying.

**effortless** *adj* involving no effort; done easily and without strain. ➤ **effortlessly** *adv.*

**effrontery** *n* the quality of being shamelessly bold; insolence.

**effusion** *n* **1** an act of emitting or pouring out. **2** an unrestrained expression of feelings in words.

**effusive** *adj* unduly emotionally demonstrative, *esp* in speech; gushing. ➤ **effusively** *adv.*

**e.g.** *abbr* for example.

**egalitarian** *adj* believing in social, political, and economic equality among human beings. ➤ **egalitarian** *n,* **egalitarianism** *n.*

**egg** *n* **1** a reproductive cell enclosed in a hard or soft casing, produced by a female bird, fish, or reptile. **2** = OVUM. **3** the egg of domestic poultry, etc, used as food. **4** *dated, informal* a person. * **have egg on one's face** to be made to look foolish.

**egghead** *n derog or humorous* an intellectual or highbrow.

**egg on** *v* to incite to action.

**eggplant** *n chiefly NAmer* an aubergine.

**ego** *n* (*pl* **egos**) **1** self-esteem. **2** excessive self-esteem. **3** in psychoanalytic theory, a part of the mind that mainly controls a person's sense of identity, behaviour and relations with reality.

**egocentric** *adj* self-centred or selfish.

**egoism** *n* self-seeking or self-centredness. ➤ **egoist** *n,* **egoistic** *adj.*

**egomania** *n* extreme self-centredness.

**egotism** *n* **1** the practice of talking about oneself too much. **2** extreme self-importance. ➤ **egotist** *n,* **egotistic** *adj.*

**egregious** *adj* conspicuously or shockingly bad.

**egress** *n formal* **1** going or coming out. **2** an exit.

**egret** *n* a species of heron that has long plumes during the breeding season.

**Eid** /eed/ *n* a Muslim festival marking the end of the fast of Ramadan.

**eider** *n* (*pl* **eiders** *or* **eider**) a large northern sea duck with fine soft down.

**eiderdown** *n chiefly Brit* a thick warm quilt filled with feathers or other insulating material.

**eight** *n* **1** the number 8. **2** an eight-person racing boat or its crew. ➤ **eight** *adj.*

**eighteen** *adj and n* the number 18. ➤ **eighteenth** *adj and n.*

**eighth** *adj and n* **1** having the position in a sequence corresponding to the number eight. **2** one of eight equal parts of something.

***Usage Note:*** Note the spelling with *-h-* before *-th.*

**eighty** *adj and n* (*pl* **-ies**) **1** the number 80. **2** (*in pl*) the numbers 80 to 89. ➤ **eightieth** *adj and n.*

**eisteddfod** *n* (*pl* **eisteddfods** *or* **eisteddfodau**) a Welsh-language competitive festival of music and poetry.

**either**[1] *adj* **1** both of the two: *on either side of the path.* **2** being the one or the other of two: *Take either road.*

**either**[2] *pron* the one or the other.

**either**[3] *conj* used to indicate that what immediately follows is the first of two or more alternatives.

**either**[4] *adv* for that matter; likewise: *I can't drive and I can't ride a bike either.*

**ejaculate** *v* **1** to eject (semen) from the body in orgasm. **2** *formal* to utter suddenly and vehemently. ➤ **ejaculation** *n.*

**eject** *v* **1** to drive or throw out, *esp* by physical force. **2** to escape from an aircraft by using the ejector seat. ➤ **ejection** *n.*

**ejector seat** *n* an emergency escape seat that propels its occupant out of an aircraft.

**eke out** *v* **1** to make (a supply) last longer by using it frugally. **2** to make (e.g. a living) laboriously or precariously.

**elaborate** *adj* **1** planned with great care and attention to detail. **2** marked by complexity and wealth of detail. ➤ **elaborately** *adv.*

**élan** /ay'lonh, ay'lan/ *n* vigorous spirit or enthusiasm; verve.

**elapse** *v* of a period of time: to pass by.

**elastic**[1] *adj* **1** of a material: capable of resuming its former shape after being stretched, squashed, etc. **2** flexible or adaptable. ➤ **elasticity** *n.*

**elastic**[2] *n* an easily stretched material made of yarns containing rubber.

**elasticated** *adj* of fabric: made stretchy by the insertion of elastic.

**elastic band** *n Brit* = RUBBER BAND.

**elated** *adj* filled with joy or pride.

**elation** *n* a feeling of great joy or pride.

**elbow**[1] *n* **1** the joint between the human forearm and upper arm. **2** (**the elbow**) *informal* an abrupt rejection or dismissal.

**elbow**[2] *v* **1** to shove aside with one's elbow. **2** to strike with one's elbow.

**elbow grease** *n informal* hard work to clean something.

**elder**[1] *adj* older.

**elder**[2] *n* **1** somebody who is older. **2** somebody having authority by virtue of age and experience. **3** an official of a Presbyterian, Quaker, etc congregation.

**elder**[3] *n* a common shrub or small tree with white flowers and black or red berries.

**elderly** *adj* rather old.

**eldest** *adj* oldest.

**elect**[1] *v* **1** to select by vote for an office, position, etc. **2** *formal* to choose to do something. ➤ **electable** *adj.*

**elect**[2] *adj* **1** picked out in preference to others. **2** chosen for office but not yet installed.

**election** *n* **1** a procedure for electing somebody, e.g. to public office. **2** the act of electing or fact of being elected.
**electioneering** *n* **1** activities aimed at getting a person or party elected to political office. **2** insincere or unscrupulous election campaigning.
**elective** *adj* **1** chosen or filled by election. **2** that can be freely selected; optional.
**elector** *n* somebody qualified to vote in an election.
**electoral** *adj* relating to elections or electors.
**electoral roll** *n* the official list of those who are entitled to vote in an election.
**electorate** *n* a body of electors.
**electric**[1] *adj* **1** of, producing, or operated by electricity. **2** thrilling. **3** (*often* + with) tense.
**electric**[2] *n* (*in pl*) electrical parts or electric circuitry.
**electrical** *adj* of, using, or producing electricity. ➤ **electrically** *adv.*
**electric blue** *n* a bright slightly greenish blue.
**electric chair** *n* a chair used to electrocute criminals condemned to death.
**electrician** *n* somebody who installs or repairs electrical equipment.
**electricity** *n* **1** a form of energy derived from charged particles. **2** electric current or electric charge. **3** contagious excitement.
**electric shock** *n* the violent effect on the nerves and muscles caused by electricity passing through the body.
**electric storm** *n* a thunderstorm.
**electrify** *v* (**-ies, -ied**) **1** to charge with electricity. **2** to equip for the use of electric power. **3** to excite or thrill. ➤ **electrification** *n.*
**electroconvulsive therapy** *n* a treatment for serious mental disorder, *esp* severe depression, in which an electric current is passed through the brain.
**electrocute** *v* to execute or kill by electric shock. ➤ **electrocution** *n.*
**electrode** *n* a conductor that makes electrical contact with a non-metallic part of a circuit, e.g. the acid in a car battery.
**electrolysis** *n* **1** the process of passing an electric current through a solution to separate out the solution's constituents. **2** the destruction of hair roots, warts, moles, etc by an electric current. ➤ **electrolytic** *adj.*
**electrolyte** *n* a non-metallic electric conductor, e.g. battery acid.
**electromagnet** *n* a metal core, surrounded by a coil of wire, which is magnetized when an electric current is passed through the wire.
**electromagnetic** *adj* relating to electromagnets and the interaction of electricity and magnetism. ➤ **electromagnetism** *n.*
**electromotive** *adj* producing an electric current.
**electron** *n* an elementary particle carrying a negative electrical charge, which occurs in atoms outside the nucleus.
**electronic** *adj* **1** relating to electrons or electronics. **2** involving devices, e.g. transistors or microchips, in which a flow of electrons is controlled by a voltage. **3** involving computers or other electronic systems. ➤ **electronically** *adv.*
**electronic mail** *n* email.
**electronics** *pl n* **1** the branch of physics dealing with the behaviour and effects of electrons in transistors, microchips, etc. **2** the circuits, devices, etc of a piece of electronic equipment.
**electron microscope** *n* a microscope in which a highly magnified image is produced by a beam of electrons.
**electroplate** *v* to plate (an object) with a metallic coating by electrolysis.
**elegant** *adj* **1** gracefully refined, dignified, or stylish. **2** of ideas: simple and ingenious. ➤ **elegance** *n,* **elegantly** *adv.*
**elegiac** *adj* **1** characteristic of an elegy. **2** expressing sorrow, often for something past.
**elegy** *n* (*pl* **-ies**) a song, poem, or other work expressing sorrow, *esp* for a dead person.
**element** *n* **1** in chemistry, a fundamental substance consisting of atoms of only one kind. **2** a constituent part that makes up a whole. **3** a specified group within a human community. **4** a small quantity; a hint. **5** the part of an electric device, e.g. a kettle, that contains the heating wire. **6** a substance, air, water, fire, or earth, formerly believed to compose the physical universe. **7** the state or sphere natural to someone or something. **8** (*in pl*) the weather *esp* bad weather.
**elemental** *adj* **1** fundamental. **2** of or resembling a powerful force of nature.
**elementary** *adj* of or dealing with the basic elements of something; simple.
**elephant** *n* a very large mammal having a muscular trunk instead of a snout and two long ivory tusks, found in Africa and South Asia.
**elephantine** *adj* **1** huge or massive. **2** clumsy or ponderous.
**elevate** *v* **1** to lift up. **2** to raise in rank or status.
**elevated** *adj* **1** raised above a surface. **2** on a high moral or intellectual plane; lofty.
**elevation** *n* **1** the height to which something is elevated, *esp* above sea level. **2** the act of elevating. **3** a scale drawing of the front, back, or side of a building.
**elevator** *n* **1** *chiefly NAmer* = LIFT[2] 1. **2** an endless belt with scoops or buckets for raising grain, liquids, etc. **3** *NAmer* a building for storing grain. **4** a movable horizontal part of the tailplane of an aircraft for controlling climb and descent.

**eleven** *n* **1** the number 11. **2** a cricket, football, or hockey team. ➤ **eleven** *adj,* **eleventh** *adj and n.*

**eleven-plus** *or* **11-plus** *n* an examination taken, *esp* formerly, at the age of 10–11 to determine which type of British state secondary school a child should attend.

**elevenses** *pl n Brit* light refreshment taken in the middle of the morning.

**eleventh hour** *n* (**the eleventh hour**) the latest possible time.

**elf** *n* (*pl* **elves**) a fairy, *esp* a small mischievous one.

**elfin** *adj* small and delicate.

**elicit** *v* (**elicited, eliciting**) (*often* + from) to call forth or draw out (e.g. a response or reaction).

**elide** *v* to omit (e.g. a vowel or syllable) in speaking or writing.

**eligible** *adj* **1** qualified to do or receive something. **2** desirable, *esp* as a marriage partner. ➤ **eligibility** *n.*

**eliminate** *v* **1** to get rid of completely. **2** to remove (a competitor, team, etc) from a competition by defeating them. ➤ **elimination** *n.*

**elision** *n* omission of a vowel or syllable, e.g. reducing *I am* to *I'm*.

**elite** *or* **élite** *n* a group considered to be intellectually, professionally, or socially superior.

**elitism** *or* **élitism** *n* **1** the belief in leadership by an elite. **2** the belief that some people are superior and deserve special treatment. ➤ **elitist** *n and adj.*

**elixir** *n* a substance believed to have magical properties, *esp* that of prolonging life indefinitely.

**Elizabethan** *adj* of the reign of Queen Elizabeth I of England (1558–1603).

**elk** *n* (*pl* **elks** *or* **elk**) the largest deer of Europe and Asia.

**ellipse** *n* a flattened circle.

**ellipsis** *n* (*pl* **ellipses**) **1** the omission of words needed to make a construction grammatically complete. **2** a mark (e.g. ... or *** or —), indicating the omission of letters or words.

**elliptical** *adj* **1** of or shaped like an ellipse. **2** of or marked by ellipsis. **3** of speech or writing: extremely or excessively concise, usu through omitting words.

**elm** *n* a large tree with serrated leaves.

**elocution** *n* the art of effective public speaking, *esp* of good diction.

**elongate** *v* to make or become longer. ➤ **elongated** *adj.*

**elope** *v* to run away secretly with a lover, usu with the intention of getting married.

**eloquence** *n* fluent, forceful, and persuasive speech.

**eloquent** *adj* **1** fluent, forceful, and persuasive in the use of language. **2** vividly expressive or revealing. ➤ **eloquently** *adv.*

**else** *adv* **1** different from the person, place, etc previously mentioned: *somewhere else*. **2** also; besides. ✱ **or else** if not; otherwise.

**elsewhere** *adv* in or to another place.

**elucidate** *v* to make clear, *esp* by explanation. ➤ **elucidation** *n.*

**elude** *v* **1** to avoid cunningly or adroitly. **2** to escape the memory or notice of.

**elusive** *adj* difficult to find, catch, obtain, or remember.

**elver** *n* a young eel.

**elves** *n* pl of ELF.

**emaciated** *adj* excessively thin or feeble. ➤ **emaciation** *n.*

**email**[1] *or* **e-mail** *n* **1** a system for transmitting messages from one computer to another, usu-through a modem and telephone line. **2** a message sent in this way.

**email**[2] *or* **e-mail** *v* to send (a message, document, etc) by email.

**emanate** *v* **1** to come out from a source. **2** to send out or give off.

**emancipate** *v* to free from slavery or restrictions imposed by society or law. ➤ **emancipation** *n.*

**emasculate** *v* **1** to deprive of effectiveness or strength. **2** to castrate. **3** to rob (a man) of his male identity or role. ➤ **emasculation** *n.*

**embalm** *v* to treat (a dead body) in order to protect it against decay.

**embankment** *n* a raised structure to hold back water or to carry a road or railway.

**embargo**[1] *n* (*pl* **-oes**) a legal prohibition, *esp* on commerce.

**embargo**[2] *v* (**embargoes, embargoed, embargoing**) to place an embargo on.

**embark** *v* **1** to go on board a ship or aircraft. **2** (+ on) to make a start on. ➤ **embarkation** *n.*

**embarrass** *v* **1** to cause to experience awkward self-consciousness or shame. **2** to involve in financial difficulties. ➤ **embarrassed** *adj,* **embarrassing** *adj,* **embarrassment** *n.*

***Usage Note:*** Note the spelling with *-rr-* and *-ss-*.

**embassy** *n* (*pl* **-ies**) the official residence or offices of an ambassador.

**embattled** *adj* **1** hemmed in by adversaries, difficulties, etc. **2** involved in battle.

**embed** *or* **imbed** *v* (**embedded** *or* **imbedded, embedding** *or* **imbedding**) to fix firmly or deeply in surrounding matter.

**embellish** *v* **1** to make beautiful by adding ornaments; to decorate. **2** to make (speech or writing) more interesting by adding fictitious detail.

**ember** *n* a glowing fragment of coal or wood in a dying fire.

**embezzle** *v* to take (money or property entrusted to one's care) fraudulently for one's own use. ➤ **embezzler** *n.*

**embittered** *adj* feeling bitter or resentful.

**emblazon** *v* **1** to display conspicuously on. **2** to decorate with a heraldic or other emblem.
**emblem** *n* a design or symbol used as an identifying mark.
**emblematic** *adj* acting as an emblem or symbol.
**embody** *v* (**-ies, -ied**) **1** to represent (an idea or belief) in a concrete and perceptible form. **2** (+ in) to make (e.g. ideas or principles) part of a body or system. ➤ **embodiment** *n.*
**embolden** *v* to make bold or courageous.
**embolism** *n* the sudden obstruction of a blood vessel by a clot or air bubble.
**emboss** *v* to carve a raised design on (a surface).
**embrace**[1] *v* **1** to take and hold in one's arms as a sign of affection. **2** to take up (a cause or opportunity) eagerly. **3** to include as an integral part.
**embrace**[2] *n* the act of embracing.
**embrocation** *n* a liquid rubbed into the skin, *esp* to relieve pain.
**embroider** *v* **1** to ornament (e.g. cloth or a garment) with decorative stitches. **2** to embellish with exaggerated or fictitious details.
**embroidery** *n* (*pl* **-ies**) **1** the art of embroidering. **2** embroidered work.
**embroil** *v* to involve in conflict or difficulties. ➤ **embroilment** *n.*
**embryo** *n* (*pl* **-os**) an animal in the early stages of growth before birth or hatching, *esp* an unborn baby less than eight weeks old.
**embryonic** *adj* **1** relating to an embryo. **2** in an early stage of development.
**emend** *v* to remove errors from (a text).
**emerald** *n* **1** a bright green gemstone. **2** a bright green colour. ➤ **emerald** *adj.*
**emerge** *v* **1** to come out into view. **2** to become known. **3** to survive a difficult or unpleasant experience.
**emergency** *n* (*pl* **-ies**) an unforeseen and potentially dangerous occurrence that calls for immediate action.
**emergent** *adj* in the early stages of development.
**emeritus** *adj* retaining a title on an honorary basis after retirement.
**emery board** *n* a strip of cardboard or wood coated with abrasive powder and used as a nail file.
**emetic** *adj* causing vomiting.
**emigrant** *n* a person who emigrates.
**emigrate** *v* to leave one's country for permanent residence abroad. ➤ **emigration** *n.*
**émigré** *or* **emigré** /'emigray/ *n* a person who emigrates, *esp* for political reasons.
**eminence** *n* **1** a position of prominence or superiority. **2** a person of high rank or attainments.
**eminent** *adj* **1** conspicuous or notable. **2** highly regarded; distinguished. ➤ **eminently** *adv.*
**emir** *or* **amir** *n* a ruler of a Muslim state.
**emissary** *n* (*pl* **-ies**) a person sent on a mission to represent a government or head of state.
**emission** *n* **1** the act of emitting. **2** something emitted, e.g. fumes or radiation.
**emit** *v* (**emitted, emitting**) **1** to send out or give off (e.g. light, smoke, or radiation). **2** to make (a sound).
**emollient** *adj* **1** softening or soothing, *esp* to the skin. **2** making a situation calmer.
**emolument** *n formal* a salary or fee.
**emotion** *n* **1** a strong feeling, e.g. anger, fear, or joy. **2** such feelings collectively. **3** instinctive feelings as opposed to reason.
**emotional** *adj* **1** relating to the emotions. **2** feeling or expressing emotion. **3** inclined to show excessive emotion. ➤ **emotionally** *adv.*
**emotive** *adj* arousing or appealing to emotion.
**empathize** *or* **-ise** *v* (*usu* + with) to understand and share the feelings of another person.
**empathy** *n* the capacity for understanding and sharing another's feelings.
**emperor** *n* the ruler of an empire.
**emphasis** *n* (*pl* **emphases**) **1** special importance given to something, *esp* in speaking or writing. **2** special stress given to a word or sound.
**emphasize** *or* **-ise** *v* to give emphasis to.
**emphatic** *adj* **1** spoken with or marked by emphasis. **2** clear or definite. ➤ **emphatically** *adv.*
**emphysema** *n* a disorder of the lungs, causing breathlessness.
**empire** *n* **1** a large group of countries under the authority of a single ruler or state. **2** an extensive territory or enterprise controlled by a single person or entity.
**empirical** *adj* based on experience or experiment rather than theory. ➤ **empirically** *adv,* **empiricism** *n,* **empiricist** *n.*
**emplacement** *n* a prepared position for large guns to fire from.
**employ** *v* **1** to pay (somebody) in return for their work. **2** to give (somebody) a task or occupation. **3** to use (something) for a specific purpose.
**employee** *n* somebody employed by another for wages or a salary.
**employer** *n* a person or company that employs people.
**employment** *n* **1** the act of employing. **2** paid work. **3** a job or occupation.
**emporium** *n* (*pl* **emporiums** *or* **emporia**) a large shop or commercial centre.
**empower** *v* **1** to give authority or power to. **2** to give (somebody) the confidence to act on their own initiative. ➤ **empowerment** *n.*

**empress** *n* **1** the wife or widow of an emperor. **2** a woman having the rank of emperor.
**empty**[1] *adj* (**-ier, -iest**) **1** containing nothing, *esp* lacking typical contents. **2** not inhabited. **3** lacking substance, meaning, or sincerity; hollow. ➤ **emptiness** *n.*
**empty**[2] *v* (**-ies, -ied**) **1** to remove the contents of. **2** to become empty. **3** of a river: to flow into a sea or lake.
**empty**[3] *n* (*pl* **-ies**) a bottle or other container that has been emptied.
**emu** *n* a flightless Australian bird, related to but smaller than the ostrich.
**emulate** *v* to imitate closely, *esp* in order to equal. ➤ **emulation** *n.*
**emulsify** *v* (**-ies, -ied**) to convert (e.g. an oil) into an emulsion.
**emulsion** *n* **1** a substance consisting of one liquid dispersed in droplets throughout another. **2** a light-sensitive coating for photographic film. **3** a type of water-based paint used *esp* on walls and ceilings.
**enable** *v* **1** to provide with the means or opportunity to do something. **2** to make possible.
**enact** *v* **1** to make (e.g. a bill) into law. **2** to perform (a role, scene, etc). ➤ **enactment** *n.*
**enamel**[1] *n* **1** a usu opaque glassy coating applied to the surface of metal, glass, or pottery. **2** a white substance forming a hard layer on teeth. **3** a paint that dries with a glossy appearance.
**enamel**[2] *v* (**enamelled, enamelling,** *NAmer* **enameled, enameling**) to cover or decorate with enamel.
**enamoured** (*NAmer* **enamored**) *adj* (*usu* + of/with) fond of or in love with a person or thing.
**en bloc** /onh 'blok/ *adv and adj* all together; in a mass.
**encamp** *v* to set up a camp, or place (people) in a camp.
**encampment** *n* a camp, *esp* a large one for troops.
**encapsulate** *v* **1** to express in a concise form. **2** to enclose in a capsule.
**encase** *v* to enclose in a case.
**encephalitis** *n* inflammation of the brain.
**enchant** *v* **1** to cast a spell on. **2** to attract and delight. ➤ **enchanter** *n,* **enchantment** *n,* **enchantress** *n.*
**enchanting** *adj* charming; delightful.
**encircle** *v* to form a circle round.
**enclave** *n* a unit of one country's territory enclosed within another country.
**enclose** *v* **1** to include in a package or envelope, *esp* along with something else. **2** to shut in or surround completely.
**enclosure** *n* **1** a fenced-off area of ground. **2** an area reserved for certain spectators in a sports ground. **3** something included with a letter in the same envelope.
**encode** *v* to convert (a message) into code.
**encompass** *v* **1** to encircle or enclose. **2** to include, *esp* in a comprehensive manner.
**encore** *n* an additional or repeated performance at the request of the audience.
**encounter**[1] *v* **1** to meet, *esp* unexpectedly. **2** to be faced with.
**encounter**[2] *n* **1** a chance meeting. **2** a clash between hostile factions or people.
**encourage** *v* **1** to inspire with confidence or hope. **2** to give support or approval to (e.g. a process or action). ➤ **encouragement** *n,* **encouraging** *adj.*
**encroach** *v* **1** (+ on/upon) to intrude gradually on somebody's possessions or rights. **2** (*often* + on/upon) to advance beyond the proper limits. ➤ **encroachment** *n.*
**encrust** *v* to cover with a hard or decorative layer.
**encrypt** *v* to convert into code. ➤ **encryption** *n.*
**encumber** *v* to impede or weigh down.
**encumbrance** *n* an impediment or burden.
**encyclopedia** *or* **encyclopaedia** *n* a work containing general information on all branches of knowledge.
**encyclopedic** *or* **encyclopaedic** *adj* comprehensive.
**end**[1] *n* **1** the point at which something stops, is completed, or ceases to exist. **2** the last part of something. **3** either of the parts farthest from the middle of something long. **4** death or destruction. **5** a goal or purpose. **6** either half of a sports field, court, etc. **7** (**the end**) *informal* something or somebody particularly unpleasant. ✱ **in the end** eventually. **make ends meet** to cope financially. **no end 1** exceedingly. **2** a huge quantity. **on end** in an upright position.
**end**[2] *v* **1** to bring or come to an end. **2** (*often* + up) to reach a particular situation, condition, place, etc eventually.
**endanger** *v* to put in danger.
**endangered** *adj* at risk, *esp* threatened with extinction.
**endear** *v* (*often* + to) to cause to become beloved or admired. ➤ **endearing** *adj.*
**endearment** *n* a word or phrase expressing affection.
**endeavour**[1] (*NAmer* **endeavor**) *v* to attempt (to do something).
**endeavour**[2] (*NAmer* **endeavor**) *n* **1** serious determined effort. **2** an attempt or undertaking.
**endemic** *adj* **1** of a disease, prevalent within a particular area or group of people. **2** of a species, native to a particular region.
**ending** *n* the final part of something, e.g. a book, film, etc.
**endive** *n* a plant resembling a lettuce, whose bitter leaves are used in salads.

**endless** *adj* **1** being or seeming without end. **2** extremely numerous. ➤ **endlessly** *adv.*

**endocrine** *adj* of a gland: producing secretions that are discharged directly into the bloodstream.

**endorphin** *n* a natural painkiller secreted by the brain.

**endorse** *or* **indorse** *v* **1** to express approval of or support for publicly. **2** to sign the back of (a cheque, bill, etc) as an instruction regarding payment. **3** *Brit* to record details of a motoring offence on (a driver's licence). ➤ **endorsement** *n.*

**endow** *v* **1** to provide with a continuing source of income, often by bequest. **2** to provide with an ability or attribute.

**endowment** *n* **1** money or property given to an institution or person to provide them with an income. **2** a natural ability or characteristic.

**endowment mortgage** *n* a mortgage that is paid back by the money received when a life insurance policy matures.

**endpaper** *n* a folded sheet of paper pasted to the front or back inside cover of a book.

**endurance** *n* the ability to withstand hardship, adversity, or stress.

**endure** *v* **1** to undergo (e.g. a hardship), *esp* without giving in. **2** to tolerate. **3** to last.

**enema** *n* an injection of liquid into the intestine through the anus, e.g. to ease constipation.

**enemy** *n* (*pl* **-ies**) **1** a person who is opposed to or seeking to harm somebody or something. **2** a nation or military force with whom one is at war.

**energetic** *adj* marked by energy or vigour. ➤ **energetically** *adv.*

**energize** *or* **-ise** *v* to give energy or enthusiasm to.

**energy** *n* (*pl* **-ies**) **1** the natural strength and vitality required for action. **2** (*in pl*) physical and mental powers. **3** fuel and other sources of power, *esp* electricity.

**enervate** *v* to lessen the mental or physical vitality of. ➤ **enervated** *adj,* **enervating** *adj.*

**enfant terrible** /ˌonfonh teˈreeblə/ *n* (*pl* **enfants terribles**) a person whose outspoken remarks or unconventional actions cause controversy.

**enfeeble** *v* to make weak.

**enfold** *v* **1** (*usu* + in) to envelop. **2** to embrace.

**enforce** *v* **1** to cause (a rule or law) to be obeyed. **2** to impose or compel (e.g. obedience). ➤ **enforceable** *adj,* **enforced** *adj,* **enforcement** *n,* **enforcer** *n.*

**enfranchise** *v* **1** to give the right of voting to. **2** to set free, *esp* from slavery.

**engage** *v* **1** to attract and hold (somebody's thoughts, attention, etc). **2** (+ in) to participate or become involved. **3** to arrange to employ. **4** of a mechanical part: to interlock with (another part).

**engaged** *adj* **1** involved in activity; occupied. **2** pledged to be married. **3** *chiefly Brit* of a telephone line: already in use.

**engagement** *n* **1** an agreement to marry. **2** an appointment. **3** a hostile encounter between military forces. **4** the state of being involved in something.

**engaging** *adj* attractive or pleasing.

**engender** *v* to cause to exist or develop.

**engine** *n* **1** a machine for converting energy into mechanical force and motion. **2** a railway locomotive.

**engineer**[1] *n* **1** a person who is trained in engineering. **2** a person who maintains or operates an engine. **3** *NAmer* a driver of a railway locomotive.

**engineer**[2] *v* **1** to design or construct as an engineer. **2** to contrive or plan, usu with subtlety.

**engineering** *n* the study of the design and construction of machines, structures, etc.

**English** *n* **1** the Germanic language spoken in Britain, the USA, and most Commonwealth countries. **2** (**the English**) (*used as pl*) the people of England. ➤ **English** *adj.*

**engorge** *v* to make swollen with blood, water, etc.

**engrained** *adj* see INGRAINED.

**engrave** *v* **1** to cut (a design or lettering) on metal or stone. **2** to impress deeply on somebody's mind. ➤ **engraver** *n.*

**engraving** *n* **1** a print made from an engraved surface. **2** the art of cutting designs on hard surfaces.

**engross** *v* to occupy all the time and attention of.

**engulf** *v* **1** to flow over and completely cover. **2** to overwhelm.

**enhance** *v* to improve the value, desirability, or attractiveness of. ➤ **enhancement** *n.*

**enigma** *n* somebody or something hard to understand or explain. ➤ **enigmatic** *adj,* **enigmatically** *adv.*

**enjoin** *v formal* to order (somebody) to do something.

**enjoy** *v* **1** to take pleasure in. **2** to have the use or benefit of. ✱ **enjoy oneself** to take pleasure in what one is doing. ➤ **enjoyment** *n.*

**enjoyable** *adj* giving pleasure.

**enlarge** *v* **1** to make or become larger. **2** (+ on/upon) to speak or write at greater length.

**enlargement** *n* **1** a photographic print that is larger than the negative or an earlier print. **2** the act of enlarging.

**enlighten** *v* to give knowledge or spiritual insight to. ➤ **enlightenment** *n.*

**enlightened** *adj* rational, well-informed, and free from prejudice.

**enlist** *v* **1** to enrol for duty in the armed forces. **2** to secure and employ (somebody, resources, etc) in advancing a cause, etc. ➤ **enlistment** *n.*

**enliven** *v* **1** to make more lively or interesting. **2** to make more cheerful.

**en masse** /onh 'mas/ *adv* in a body; as a whole.

**enmesh** *v* to entangle as in a net.

**enmity** *n* (*pl* **-ies**) a feeling or state of hostility or hatred.

**ennoble** *v* **1** to make finer or more dignified. **2** to raise to the nobility.

**ennui** *n* weariness and dissatisfaction resulting from boredom.

**enormity** *n* (*pl* **-ies**) **1** the state of being enormous. **2** great wickedness. **3** a terribly wicked act.

**enormous** *adj* extraordinarily large. ➤ **enormously** *adv.*

**enough**[1] *adj* fully adequate in quantity, number, or degree.

**enough**[2] *adv* **1** to a fully adequate degree. **2** to a moderate degree.

**enough**[3] *pron* a sufficient quantity or number.

**enquire** *or* **inquire** *v* **1** to seek information by questioning; to ask. **2** (*often* + into) to make an investigation. ✱ **enquire after** to ask about the health, etc of.

***Usage Note:*** *Enquire* is the commoner British English spelling; *inquire* is generally used in American English.

**enquiry** *or* **inquiry** *n* (*pl* **-ies**) **1** a request for information. **2** a systematic investigation.

**enrage** *v* to make very angry.

**enrapture** *v* to fill with delight.

**enrich** *v* **1** to make wealthy or wealthier. **2** to improve or enhance, *esp* by adding additional ingredients. ➤ **enrichment** *n.*

**enrol** (*NAmer* **enroll**) *v* (**enrolled, enrolling**) to register as a member or student. ➤ **enrolment** *n.*

**en route** /on 'rooht/ *adv and adj* on or along the way.

**ensconce** *v* to settle (e.g. oneself) comfortably or snugly.

**ensemble** *n* **1** a group that works together as a whole. **2** a complete outfit of matching garments. **3** a group of actors, musicians, etc who perform together.

**enshrine** *v* to preserve as sacred and protect from change.

**enshroud** *v* to cover and conceal completely.

**ensign** *n* a flag flown *esp* by a ship.

**enslave** *v* **1** to reduce to slavery. **2** to make dependent on. ➤ **enslavement** *n.*

**ensnare** *v* **1** to catch in a snare. **2** to lure into a situation from which there is no escape.

**ensue** *v* (**ensues, ensued, ensuing**) to take place afterwards or as a result.

**en suite** /on 'sweet/ *adv and adj* of a room: opening off another room.

**ensure** *v* to make sure or certain.

***Usage Note:*** Do not confuse this word with *insure*, which means 'to take out insurance on'.

**entail** *v* to involve as a necessary accompaniment or result.

**entangle** *v* **1** to cause to become tangled. **2** to involve in a difficult situation. ➤ **entanglement** *n.*

**entente** *n* a friendly relationship between two or more countries.

**enter** *v* **1** to go or come into (a place). **2** to record (a piece of information) in a diary, account, computer file etc. **3** to become a member of. **4** to register as contestant in a competition. **5** (+ into/on/upon) to embark on something. ✱ **enter into 1** to make oneself a party to or in (e.g. an agreement). **2** to be a factor in.

**enterprise** *n* **1** a project or undertaking. **2** a business organization. **3** boldness and initiative.

**enterprising** *adj* marked by boldness and initiative; resourceful.

**entertain** *v* **1** to give enjoyment or amusement to. **2** to show hospitality to. **3** to have in one's mind (a doubt, suggestion, etc).

**entertainment** *n* **1** something that is enjoyable to watch or take part in. **2** the act of entertaining.

**enthral** (*NAmer* **enthrall**) *v* (**enthralled, enthralling**) to hold the complete interest and attention of; to captivate.

***Usage Note:*** Note the spelling with *-al* and not *-all.*

**enthrone** *v* to place on a throne, *esp* to mark the beginning of a period in office. ➤ **enthronement** *n.*

**enthuse** *v* **1** to make enthusiastic. **2** to show enthusiasm.

**enthusiasm** *n* keen interest and excited admiration.

**enthusiast** *n* somebody who is extremely interested in and attached to a cause or pursuit.

**entice** *v* to tempt or lure by arousing hope or desire. ➤ **enticement** *n,* **enticing** *adj.*

**entire** *adj* having no element or part left out; whole.

**entirely** *adv* **1** wholly or completely. **2** solely.

**entirety** *n* the whole or total. ✱ **in its entirety** with nothing omitted.

**entitle** *v* **1** to give a title to. **2** to give the right to do or have something. ➤ **entitlement** *n.*

**entity** *n* (*pl* **-ies**) something that has separate and distinct existence.

**entomb** *v* **1** to place (e.g. a body) in a tomb. **2** to shut away.

**entomology** *n* the study of insects. ➤ **entomological** *adj,* **entomologist** *n.*

**entourage** *n* a group of attendants or associates of an important person.

**entrails** *pl n* internal organs, *esp* the intestines.

**entrance**[1] /'entrəns/ *n* **1** the act of entering. **2** a means or place of entry. **3** right or permission to enter.

**entrance**[2] /in'trahns/ *v* to fill with delight or wonder. ➤ **entrancing** *adj.*
**entrant** *n* somebody who enters a contest, profession, etc.
**entrap** *v* (**entrapped, entrapping**) **1** to catch in a trap. **2** to trick into making a compromising statement or committing a crime. ➤ **entrapment** *n.*
**entreat** *v* to beg or plead with or for.
**entreaty** *n* (*pl* **-ies**) a humble or heartfelt plea.
**entrée** *or* **entree** *n* **1** *chiefly Brit* a dish served before the main course of a formal dinner. **2** the principal dish of a meal. **3** right of entry or access.
**entrench** *or* **intrench** *v* **1** to establish (something) so solidly that it is difficult to change. **2** to dig and occupy trenches for defence. ➤ **entrenchment** *n.*
**entrepreneur** *n* somebody who sets up a business and assumes the risks of running it. ➤ **entrepreneurial** *adj.*
**entropy** *n* a measure of the amount of energy that is unavailable for doing work in a thermodynamic system.
**entrust** *v* **1** (+ with) to give (somebody) the responsibility of looking after or dealing with something. **2** (+ to) to put (something) into somebody's care.
**entry** *n* (*pl* **-ies**) **1** the act of entering. **2** the right or privilege of entering. **3** a door, gate, hall, or other way in. **4** a record made in a diary, account book, index, etc.
**entwine** *v* to twine together or round.
**E number** *n* a number with the letter E in front of it, used to denote a particular additive to food.
**enumerate** *v* to list or name one by one. ➤ **enumeration** *n.*
**enunciate** *v* **1** to articulate distinctly. **2** to state or formulate precisely. ➤ **enunciation** *n.*
**envelop** *v* (**enveloped, enveloping**) to wrap, cover, or surround completely. ➤ **envelopment** *n.*
**envelope** *n* **1** a flat container, usu of folded and gummed paper, e.g. for a letter. **2** a wrapper, cover, or casing, e.g. the gasbag of an airship.
**enviable** *adj* worthy of envy; highly desirable. ➤ **enviably** *adv.*
**envious** *adj* feeling or showing envy. ➤ **enviously** *adv.*
**environment** *n* **1** the objects or conditions by which somebody or something is surrounded. **2** (**the environment**) the natural surroundings and plant and animal life, among which people live. ➤ **environmental** *adj,* **environmentally** *adv.*
**environmentalism** *n* concern for the protection or quality of the natural environment. ➤ **environmentalist** *n.*
**environs** *pl n* the area surrounding something.
**envisage** *v* **1** to have a mental picture of. **2** to consider as a possibility in the future.
**envoy** *n* **1** a diplomatic agent, *esp* one ranking immediately below an ambassador. **2** a messenger or representative.
**envy**[1] *n* (*pl* **-ies**) **1** a wish to possess an advantage enjoyed by somebody else. **2** somebody or something that is envied.
**envy**[2] *v* (**-ies, -ied**) to feel envy for.
**enzyme** *n* a protein produced by living cells that promotes biochemical reactions without undergoing change itself.
**eon** *n* see AEON.
**epaulette** (*NAmer* **epaulet**) *n* an ornamental strip attached to the shoulder of a garment, *esp* a military uniform.
**ephemera** *pl n* items of short-lived duration, use, or interest.
**ephemeral** *adj* lasting a very short time.
**epic**[1] *n* **1** a long narrative poem recounting the deeds of a legendary or historical figure or the events in a nation's history. **2** a novel, film, etc that resembles an epic.
**epic**[2] *adj* **1** of an epic. **2** extending beyond the usual in size or scope. **3** heroic.
**epicentre** (*NAmer* **epicenter**) *n* the part of the earth's surface directly above the origin of an earthquake.
**epicure** *n* a connoisseur of food or wine. ➤ **epicurean** *n and adj.*
**epidemic** *n* **1** an outbreak of a disease affecting many individuals within a population or region. **2** a sudden rapid spread of something undesirable.
**epidermis** *n* **1** the outer layer of the skin of an animal that covers the dermis. **2** a protective surface layer of cells in plants. ➤ **epidermal** *adj.*
**epidural** *n* an injection of local anaesthetic into the canal housing the spinal cord, *esp* during childbirth.
**epiglottis** *n* a thin plate of cartilage behind the tongue that folds back to cover the entrance to the larynx during swallowing.
**epigram** *n* **1** a short witty or satirical poem. **2** a concise, witty remark or saying. ➤ **epigrammatic** *adj.*
**epigraph** *n* **1** an engraved inscription. **2** a quotation at the beginning of a book, chapter, etc.
**epilepsy** *n* a disorder affecting the electrical rhythms of the brain and resulting in convulsive attacks and loss of consciousness. ➤ **epileptic** *n and adj.*
**epilogue** *n* a concluding section of a literary work commenting on the main theme or revealing the later fate of the characters.
**epiphany** *n* (*pl* **epiphanies**) **1** (**Epiphany**) the coming of the Magi to see the infant Christ, commemorated on 6 January. **2** a revelation of the nature or meaning of something.

**episcopacy** *n* (*pl* **-ies**) **1** government of the Church by bishops. **2** the bishops of a Church or country.

**episcopal** *adj* **1** of a bishop. **2** governed by bishops. **3** (**Episcopal**) of the Anglican Church in the USA or Scotland.

**episcopalian** *adj* **1** of or supporting the episcopal form of Church government. **2** (**Episcopalian**) of the Episcopal Church.

**episode** *n* **1** a distinct event that is part of a larger series, e.g. in history or somebody's life. **2** an instalment of a serialized literary work, radio or television programme, etc.

**episodic** *adj* **1** made up of separate episodes. **2** occasional or sporadic.

**epistemology** *n* the philosophical study of knowledge.

**epistle** *n* **1** a letter. **2** (**Epistle**) any of the letters from the apostles adopted as books of the New Testament.

**epistolary** *adj* **1** of letters or letter-writing. **2** written in the form of a series of letters.

**epitaph** *n* a commemorative inscription on a tombstone or monument.

**epithet** *n* a descriptive word or phrase accompanying or replacing the name of a person or thing.

**epitome** *n* a typical or ideal example.

**epitomize** *or* **-ise** *v* to serve as a typical or ideal example of.

**epoch** *n* an extended period of historical time with its own distinctive character.

**eponym** *n* **1** a word, e.g. *cardigan*, derived from a person's name. **2** a person after whom something is named.

**eponymous** *adj* denoting a character in a film, book, etc, whose name is in its title.

**epsilon** *n* the fifth letter of the Greek alphabet (Ε, ϵ).

**equable** *adj* **1** even-tempered or placid. **2** free from extremes or sudden changes. ➤ **equably** *adv.*

**equal**[1] *adj* **1** of the same quantity, size, value, or status as another. **2** identical for each member of a group. **3** evenly balanced or matched. **4** (+ to) capable of meeting the requirements of (e.g. a task). ➤ **equally** *adv.*

**equal**[2] *v* (**equalled, equalling,** *NAmer* **equaled, equaling**) **1** to be equal to. **2** to achieve the same standard as.

**equality** *n* the state of being equal, *esp* of having the same rights and status as others.

**equalize** *or* **-ise** *v* **1** to make equal. **2** to bring the scores level, e.g. in a football match. ➤ **equalization** *n,* **equalizer** *n.*

**equanimity** *n* evenness of temper; composure.

**equate** *v* to treat or regard as equal.

**equation** *n* **1** a statement of the equality of two mathematical expressions. **2** an expression representing a chemical reaction by means of chemical symbols. **3** the act of equating.

**equator** *n* the imaginary circle around the earth, equidistant from the two poles, that divides the northern and southern hemispheres.

**equatorial** *adj* **1** of, at, or near the equator. **2** of climate: consistently hot and rainy.

**equerry** *n* (*pl* **-ies**) an officer of the British royal household in personal attendance on a member of the royal family.

**equestrian**[1] *adj* of horses or horse riding. ➤ **equestrianism** *n.*

**equestrian**[2] *n* a person who rides on horseback.

**equidistant** *adj* equally distant.

**equilateral** *adj* of e.g. a triangle: with all its sides of equal length.

**equilibrium** *n* (*pl* **equilibria**) **1** a state of balance between opposing forces. **2** a state of physical balance. **3** a calm intellectual or emotional state.

**equine** *adj* of or resembling a horse.

**equinoctial** *adj* **1** relating to or occurring at an equinox. **2** relating to the equator.

**equinox** *n* either of the two times each year, around 21 March and 23 September, when day and night are of equal length.

**equip** *v* (**equipped, equipping**) **1** to provide with appropriate tools, supplies, etc. **2** to provide with the necessary abilities and intellectual or emotional resources for something.

**equipment** *n* the tools and resources needed for a particular purpose.

**equitable** *adj* fair and just. ➤ **equitably** *adv.*

**equity** *n* (*pl* **-ies**) **1** fairness. **2** a system of natural justice developed to supplement common law. **3** the value of a property when monetary claims against it, e.g. mortgages, have been subtracted. **4** the value of shares issued by a company.

**equivalent**[1] *adj* **1** equal in force, amount, or value. **2** corresponding or virtually identical in effect, function, or meaning. ➤ **equivalence** *n,* **equivalently** *adv.*

**equivalent**[2] *n* something or somebody that is equivalent.

**equivocal** *adj* subject to two or more interpretations; ambiguous. ➤ **equivocally** *adv.*

**equivocate** *v* to use equivocal language, *esp* in order to deceive or avoid committing oneself. ➤ **equivocation** *n.*

**Er** *abbr* the chemical symbol for erbium.

**-er**[1] *suffix* forming the comparative of adjectives and adverbs: *hotter; sooner.*

**-er**[2] *suffix* denoting somebody or something that performs an action: *recorder; baker.*

**era** *n* a historical period typified by some characteristic feature.

**eradicate** *v* to destroy or do away with completely. ➤ **eradication** *n.*

**erase** *v* **1** to rub out (something written). **2** to remove (recorded matter) from a tape. **3** to remove from existence or memory completely.

**eraser** *n* something, e.g. a piece of rubber or a felt pad, used to erase pencil, chalk, etc.

**ere** *prep and conj literary* before.

**erect**[1] *adj* **1** upright and rigidly straight. **2** in a state of physiological erection. ➤ **erectly** *adv*, **erectness** *n*.

**erect**[2] *v* **1** to build. **2** to establish; to set up.

**erectile** *adj* capable of physiological erection. ➤ **erectility** *n*.

**erection** *n* **1** a process in which a limp body part, *esp* the penis, becomes firm through being dilated with blood. **2** something erected, *esp* a building. **3** the act of erecting.

**ergo** *adv* therefore.

**ergonomics** *pl n* a science concerned with the relationship between human beings and their working environment.

**ERM** *abbr* exchange-rate mechanism.

**ermine** *n* (*pl* **ermines** *or* **ermine**) **1** a stoat that has a white winter coat. **2** the winter fur of this animal.

**erode** *v* **1** to wear away by the action of water, wind, etc. **2** to diminish or destroy by degrees.

**erogenous** *adj* of part of the body: sensitive to sexual stimulation.

**erosion** *n* the process of eroding.

**erotic** *adj* concerned with or arousing sexual desire. ➤ **erotically** *adv*.

**erotica** *pl n* literature or art with an erotic theme.

**eroticism** *n* **1** an erotic quality or character. **2** sexual arousal or excitement.

**err** *v* **1** to make a mistake. **2** to do wrong.

**errand** *n* a short trip to attend to some business, often for somebody else.

**errant** *adj* **1** *formal* doing wrong. **2** *archaic* travelling in search of adventure.

**erratic** *adj* lacking consistency or regularity; unpredictable. ➤ **erratically** *adv*.

**erratum** *n* (*pl* **errata**) **1** an error in a printed work, shown with its correction. **2** (*in pl*) a list of such errors and corrections inserted into a publication.

**erroneous** *adj* incorrect. ➤ **erroneously** *adv*.

**error** *n* **1** a mistake or inaccuracy. **2** the state of being wrong.

**ersatz** *adj* denoting an artificial and inferior substitute or imitation.

**erstwhile** *adj* former; previous.

**erudite** *adj* possessing or displaying extensive knowledge; learned. ➤ **erudition** *n*.

**erupt** *v* **1** of a volcano: to release lava, steam, etc suddenly and violently. **2** to become suddenly active or violent. **3** to become violently angry. **4** of a rash, spot, etc: to appear on the skin.

**Es** *abbr* the chemical symbol for einsteinium.

**escalate** *v* to increase in amount, intensity, or seriousness, usu rapidly. ➤ **escalation** *n*.

**escalator** *n* a power-driven set of stairs on an endless belt.

**escalope** *or* **escallop** /'eskəlop/ *n* a thin slice of meat coated with egg and breadcrumbs, and fried.

**escapade** *n* a reckless and often mischievous adventure.

**escape**[1] *v* **1** to get away, *esp* from confinement or restraint. **2** of gases, liquids, etc: to leak out gradually. **3** to avoid a threatening evil, danger, etc. **4** to fail to be noticed or recalled by. ➤ **escapee** *n*, **escaper** *n*.

**escape**[2] *n* **1** the act of escaping. **2** a means of escape.

**escapism** *n* activity or entertainment intended to take one's mind off unpleasant realities. ➤ **escapist** *adj and n*.

**escapology** *n* the theatrical art of escaping from restraints such as chains, handcuffs, or locked boxes. ➤ **escapologist** *n*.

**escarpment** *n* a long steep slope separating two comparatively level surfaces.

**eschew** *v formal* to avoid habitually.

**escort**[1] *n* **1** one or more people, cars, ships, etc accompanying somebody or something to give protection or show courtesy. **2** a person who accompanies another person socially.

**escort**[2] *v* to accompany as an escort.

**escutcheon** *n* a shield on which a coat of arms is displayed.

**Eskimo** *n* (*pl* **Eskimos** *or* **Eskimo**) a member of an indigenous people of northern Canada, Greenland, Alaska, and eastern Siberia.

**esoteric** *adj* understood by or restricted to a small group, *esp* of the specially initiated.

**ESP** *abbr* extrasensory perception.

**espadrille** *n* a flat sandal with a canvas upper and rope sole.

**especial** *adj* **1** particularly special. **2** distinctly personal.

**especially** *adv* **1** in particular. **2** very much.

**espionage** *n* the use of spies to obtain information.

**esplanade** *n* a level open stretch of paved or grassy ground, *esp* along a shore.

**espouse** *v* to take up and support (a cause, belief, etc). ➤ **espousal** *n*.

**espresso** *n* coffee brewed by forcing steam through finely ground coffee beans.

***Usage Note:*** Note the spelling with *esp-* and not *exp-*.

**esprit de corps** /də 'kaw/ *n* a spirit of loyalty and common purpose uniting the members of a group.

**espy** *v* (**-ies, -ied**) *literary* to catch sight of.

**Esq.** *abbr* Esquire.

**esquire** *n Brit* used instead of Mr as a man's courtesy title and usu placed after the surname.

**-ess** *suffix* denoting a female person or animal: *actress; lioness*.

**essay**[1] *n* **1** a short piece of prose writing on a specific topic. **2** *formal* an attempt. ➤ **essayist** *n.*
**essay**[2] *v formal* to attempt.
**essence** *n* **1** the most important qualities of an individual being or thing, those that make it what it is. **2** the special qualities of a plant, drug, etc, extracted in concentrated form, and used to make e.g. a perfume or flavouring. ✱ **of the essence** of the utmost importance.
**essential**[1] *adj* **1** of the utmost importance; necessary. **2** fundamental or inherent. ➤ **essentially** *adv.*
**essential**[2] *n* something indispensable or fundamental.
**essential oil** *n* an oil with a characteristic odour extracted from a plant for use in perfumes and flavourings.
**-est** *suffix* forming the superlative of adjectives and adverbs: *nearest; dirtiest.*
**establish** *v* **1** to make stable, secure, or permanent. **2** to bring into existence. **3** to place (somebody, e.g. oneself) in a permanent or secure position. **4** to put beyond doubt; to prove.
**establishment** *n* **1** the act of establishing. **2** a place of business or residence with its furnishings and staff. **3** (**the Establishment**) the group of institutions and people who control public life and support the existing order of society.
**estate** *n* **1** a large landed property, usu with a house on it. **2** *Brit* an area devoted to buildings of a particular type, e.g. housing, or commercial or retail premises. **3** the assets and liabilities left by somebody at death.
**estate agent** *n chiefly Brit* a person who sells land, houses, and flats for clients.
**estate car** *n Brit* a car with a rear door opening onto a large luggage compartment.
**esteem**[1] *v* to admire and respect.
**esteem**[2] *n* admiration and respect.
**ester** *n* a chemical compound formed by the reaction between an acid and an alcohol.
**esthetic** *adj NAmer* see AESTHETIC[1].
**estimable** *adj* worthy of esteem.
**estimate**[1] *n* **1** a rough calculation. **2** a statement of the expected cost of a job. **3** an opinion or judgment.
**estimate**[2] *v* **1** to make an estimate of. **2** to judge or conclude. ➤ **estimation** *n.*
**estranged** *adj* of a husband or wife: no longer living with his or her spouse.
**estrogen** *n NAmer* see OESTROGEN.
**estuary** *n* (*pl* **-ies**) a sea inlet at the mouth of a river.
**eta** *n* the seventh letter of the Greek alphabet (Η, η).
**et al** *adv* and others.
**etc** *abbr* et cetera.
**et cetera** *adv* and other things; and so forth.
**etch** *v* **1** to produce (a picture or letters) on metal or glass by the corrosive action of an acid. **2** to delineate or imprint clearly.
**etching** *n* **1** the art of printing from an etched metal plate. **2** a picture produced by etching.
**eternal** *adj* **1** lasting or existing for ever. **2** *informal* incessant or interminable. ➤ **eternally** *adv.*
**eternity** *n* (*pl* **-ies**) **1** infinite time. **2** *informal* a seemingly endless time.
**ethane** *n* a gas obtained from petroleum or natural gas and used as a fuel.
**ether** *n* **1** an inflammable liquid used *esp* as a solvent and formerly as a general anaesthetic. **2** *literary* the sky or upper regions of the atmosphere.
**ethereal** *adj* **1** intangible. **2** unusually delicate and light. **3** *literary* celestial; heavenly.
**ethic** *n* **1** (*also in pl*) a set of moral principles or values governing the conduct of an individual or group. **2** (*in pl*) the study of the nature of moral principles and judgments.
**ethical** *adj* **1** conforming to accepted standards of conduct or morality. **2** relating to ethics. ➤ **ethically** *adv.*
**ethnic** *adj* **1** relating to the basic factors, e.g. race, culture, or language, that a group of people have in common. **2** belonging to a particular group by birth or descent. **3** of a traditional, *esp* peasant or non-Western, culture. ➤ **ethnically** *adv,* **ethnicity** *n.*
**ethnic cleansing** *n* the systematic removal of all members of a particular ethnic group from a region.
**ethnic minority** *n* an ethnic group that constitutes a minority of the population of a country.
**ethos** *n* the guiding beliefs of a person, institution, etc.
**ethyl** *n* a chemical group ($CH_3CH_2$) derived from ethane and present in alcohol.
**etiquette** *n* the conventionally accepted standards of proper social or professional behaviour.
**etymology** *n* (*pl* **-ies**) the history of the origin and development of a word. ➤ **etymological** *adj.*
**EU** *abbr* European Union.
**Eu** *abbr* the chemical symbol for europium.
**eucalyptus** *n* (*pl* **eucalyptuses** *or* **eucalypti**) an Australasian evergreen tree.
**Eucharist** *n* **1** the Christian sacrament in which consecrated bread and wine are consumed in accordance with Christ's injunctions at the Last Supper. **2** the consecrated bread and wine consumed in the Eucharist. ➤ **Eucharistic** *adj.*
**eugenics** *pl n* a science dealing with the improvement of the hereditary qualities of a race, e.g. by careful selection of parents.

**eulogize** *or* **eulogise** *v* to praise highly in speech or writing.
**eulogy** *n* (*pl* **-ies**) a speech or piece of writing in praise of somebody or something.
**eunuch** *n* a castrated man.
**euphemism** *n* a mild or indirect expression substituted for an offensive or unpleasant one. ➤ **euphemistic** *adj*, **euphemistically** *adv*.
**euphonious** *adj* pleasing to the ear. ➤ **euphoniously** *adv*.
**euphonium** *n* a brass musical instrument resembling a tuba but smaller.
**euphony** *n* (*pl* **-ies**) a pleasing or sweet sound.
**euphoria** *n* an intense feeling of well-being or elation. ➤ **euphoric** *adj*.
**Eurasian** *adj* **1** of mixed European and Asian origin. **2** relating to or from Europe and Asia considered as a single landmass.
**eureka** *interj* used to express triumph at a discovery.
**euro** *n* (*pl* **-os**) the single European currency used by many member countries of the European Union.
**European**[1] *adj* **1** of, from, or relating to Europe. **2** relating to the European Union. ➤ **Europeanism** *n*.
**European**[2] *n* **1** a native or inhabitant of Europe. **2** a person of European origin; a white person.
**European Union** *n* an economic and political association of European states.
**euthanasia** *n* the mercy killing of incurably sick or injured individuals.
**evacuate** *v* **1** to remove (people) from a dangerous place. **2** to vacate (a dangerous place). **3** to discharge urine, faeces, etc from the body. ➤ **evacuation** *n*.
**evacuee** *n* a person evacuated from a dangerous place.
**evade** *v* **1** to avoid, *esp* by skill or deception. **2** to avoid facing up to or answering. **3** to fail to pay (taxes, etc).
**evaluate** *v* to determine the amount, value, or significance of. ➤ **evaluation** *n*.
**evanescent** *adj chiefly literary* tending to dissipate or vanish like vapour. ➤ **evanescence** *n*.
**evangelical**[1] *adj* **1** of or in accordance with the Christian message in the four Gospels. **2** (*often* **Evangelical**) denoting a Protestant denomination emphasizing salvation by faith, personal conversion, and the authority of Scripture. **3** fervent; zealous. ➤ **evangelicalism** *n*.
**evangelical**[2] *n* (*often* **Evangelical**) a member of an evangelical denomination.
**evangelist** *n* **1** (*often* **Evangelist**) a writer of any of the four Gospels. **2** a person who preaches the Christian gospel and seeks converts. **3** a person with crusading zeal. ➤ **evangelistic** *adj*.
**evangelize** *or* **-ise** *v* to preach the Christian gospel to and seek to convert.
**evaporate** *v* **1** to change from liquid to vapour. **2** to disappear or fade. ➤ **evaporation** *n*.
**evaporated milk** *n* unsweetened milk concentrated by partial evaporation.
**evasion** *n* the act or a means of evading something or somebody.
**evasive** *adj* **1** intended to avoid something. **2** tending to avoid committing oneself; equivocal. ➤ **evasively** *adv*.
**eve** *n* **1** the evening or day before a special day, *esp* a religious holiday. **2** the period immediately preceding an event. **3** *chiefly literary* the evening.
**even**[1] *adj* **1** flat or level. **2** smooth. **3** without variation; uniform. **4** of a person's temper: calm; equable. **5** equal. **6** fair. **7** in equilibrium; balanced. **8** of a number: exactly divisible by two. ✱ **get even with somebody** take revenge on somebody. ➤ **evenly** *adv*, **evenness** *n*.
**even**[2] *v* (*often* + up/out) to make or become even.
**even**[3] *adv* used to emphasize something: *even better than last time*. ✱ **even if/though** in spite of the possibility or fact that. **even so** in spite of that.
**even**[4] *n archaic or literary* the evening.
**evenhanded** *adj* fair; impartial.
**evening** *n* the latter part of the day and early part of the night.
**evening star** *n* the planet Venus, seen in the western sky at sunset.
**evensong** *n* (*often* **Evensong**) the daily evening service of the Anglican Church.
**event** *n* **1** a happening or occurrence, *esp* an important one. **2** a public or social occasion. **3** any of the contests in a sporting programme. ✱ **in the event of/that** if the specified thing should happen.
**eventful** *adj* marked by noteworthy or exciting occurrences.
**eventual** *adj* taking place at an unspecified later time; ultimately resulting. ➤ **eventually** *adv*.
**eventuality** *n* (*pl* **-ies**) a possible, *esp* unwelcome, event or outcome.
**ever** *adv* **1** at any time. **2** always: *an ever-growing need*. **3** used as an intensive: *why ever not?*
**evergreen** *adj* **1** having leaves that remain green throughout the year. **2** always retaining popularity.
**everlasting** *adj* **1** lasting for all time. **2** continuing for a very long time. **3** tediously persistent. ➤ **everlastingly** *adv*.
**evermore** *adv archaic or literary* always; forever.
**every** *adj* **1** all, without exception, of a group larger than two. **2** each or all possible: *She was given every chance*. **3** once in each: *every 5000 miles*. ✱ **every now and then/so often/once in a while** at intervals; occasionally. **every other** each alternate.
**everybody** *pron* every person.

**everyday** *adj* **1** daily. **2** encountered routinely; ordinary.
**everyone** *pron* every person.
**everything** *pron* **1** all that exists. **2** all that is necessary or that relates to the subject. **3** something of the greatest importance.
**everywhere** *adv* **1** in, at, or to every place. **2** in many places.
**evict** *v* to remove (a tenant) from rented accommodation or land by a legal process. ➤ **eviction** *n.*
**evidence**[1] *n* **1** outward sign or indication. **2** something that gives reason for believing or agreeing with something; *esp* information used by a court to arrive at the truth. ✱ **in evidence** to be seen; conspicuous.
**evidence**[2] *v* to show.
**evident** *adj* clear; obvious. ➤ **evidently** *adv.*
**evil**[1] *adj* **1** not morally good; sinful or wicked. **2** disagreeable or offensive: *an evil smell.* ➤ **evilly** *adv.*
**evil**[2] *n* **1** wickedness; sin. **2** something that is socially harmful or morally wrong.
**evince** *v formal* to show clearly; to reveal.
**eviscerate** *v* to disembowel.
**evocative** *adj* evoking something, e.g. a memory or image, strongly.
**evoke** *v* **1** to call forth. **2** to bring to mind. ➤ **evocation** *n.*
**evolution** *n* **1** a theory that existing types of animals and plants are derived from preexisting types by natural selection. **2** a process of change and development, *esp* a gradual and peaceful one. ➤ **evolutionary** *adj.*
**evolve** *v* **1** to work out or develop gradually. **2** of a species: to develop by natural evolution.
**ewe** *n* a female sheep.
**ewer** *n* a wide-mouthed pitcher or jug.
**ex** *n informal* a former spouse, boyfriend, or girlfriend.
**ex-** *prefix* **1** out of; outside. **2** denoting deprivation or removal. **3** former: *the ex-president.*
**exacerbate** *v* to make worse; to aggravate. ➤ **exacerbation** *n.*
**exact**[1] *adj* **1** precise or accurate. **2** marked by thorough consideration of all details. ➤ **exactitude** *n,* **exactness** *n.*
**exact**[2] *v* to demand and obtain by force, threats, etc. ➤ **exaction** *n.*
**exacting** *adj* making rigorous demands, *esp* requiring careful attention and accuracy.
**exactly** *adv* **1** accurately; precisely. **2** altogether; entirely. **3** used to express complete agreement.
**exaggerate** *v* **1** to say or believe that (something) is greater, better, etc than it is. **2** to make more pronounced than normal. ➤ **exaggeration** *n.*
**exalt** *v* **1** to raise to a high rank or status. **2** to praise highly.
**exaltation** *n* **1** intense happiness. **2** the act of exalting.
**exam** *n* an examination, *esp* associated with a course of study.
**examination** *n* **1** a close inspection. **2** an exercise designed to test knowledge or proficiency. **3** the act of examining.
**examine** *v* **1** to inspect closely. **2** to investigate the health of (a patient). **3** to test the knowledge, proficiency, etc of. ➤ **examinee** *n,* **examiner** *n.*
**example** *n* **1** something representative of the group or type to which it belongs. **2** somebody or something that may be copied by other people. **3** something that illustrates a general rule.
**exasperate** *v* to anger or irritate intensely. ➤ **exasperating** *adj,* **exasperation** *n.*
**excavate** *v* **1** to form (e.g. a hole or tunnel) by digging. **2** to dig out and remove (e.g. soil or earth). **3** to expose (e.g. archaeological remains) to view by digging away a covering. ➤ **excavation** *n.*
**exceed** *v* **1** to be greater than or superior to. **2** to go beyond the limits of.
**exceedingly** *adv* very; extremely.
**excel** *v* (**excelled, excelling**) **1** (*often* + at/in) to be extremely good at. **2** *formal* to be better than. ✱ **excel oneself** to do something better than ever before.
**excellency** *n* (*pl* **-ies**) (**Excellency**) used as a title for certain high dignitaries of State and Church.
**excellent** *adj* outstandingly good. ➤ **excellence** *n,* **excellently** *adv.*
**except**[1] *prep* excluding. ✱ **except for 1** with the exception of. **2** but for.
**except**[2] *conj* only; but.
**except**[3] *v* to exclude.
**excepting** *prep* = EXCEPT[1].
**exception** *n* **1** the act of excepting. **2** somebody or something that is left out, *esp* a case to which a rule does not apply. ✱ **take exception to** to object to.
**exceptionable** *adj formal* likely to cause disapproval; objectionable.
**exceptional** *adj* **1** unusual. **2** not average; superior. ➤ **exceptionally** *adv.*

***Usage Note:*** Do not confuse *exceptional* meaning 'unusual' or 'outstanding' and *exceptionable* meaning 'objectionable'.

**excerpt** *n* a passage taken from a book, musical composition, film, etc, e.g. for quoting.
**excess** *n* **1** an amount that is more than necessary, prescribed, or desirable. **2** (*also in pl*) unrestrained behaviour or immoderate indulgence. **3** an amount an insured person agrees to pay towards a claim. **4** (*used before a noun*) denoting an amount that is more than normal or

allowed: *excess baggage.* ✱ **in excess of** more than.

**excessive** *adj* exceeding normal or desirable limits. ➤ **excessively** *adv.*

**exchange**[1] *n* **1** the act of giving one thing for another. **2** a brief interchange of words or blows. **3** the conversion of one currency into another. **4** an organized market for trading in securities or commodities. **5** equipment controlling the connection of telephone calls between many different lines.

**exchange**[2] *v* to give (something) in return for something received as an equivalent.

**exchange rate** *n* the value of a unit of one currency expressed in units of another.

**exchequer** *n* **1** (*often* **Exchequer**) *Brit* the department of state in charge of the national revenue. **2** a national or royal treasury.

**excise**[1] *n* a tax levied on the manufacture, sale, or consumption of a commodity within a country.

**excise**[2] *v* **1** to remove (something) by cutting it out, *esp* surgically. **2** to delete (e.g. a passage of text). ➤ **excision** *n.*

**excitable** *adj* easily excited. ➤ **excitability** *n.*

**excite** *v* **1** to cause to feel pleasurably stimulated, enthusiastic, or expectant. **2** to arouse sexually. **3** to provoke (an action or response). **4** to increase the activity of (an organ, tissue, etc); to stimulate. ➤ **excitation** *n*, **excited** *adj*, **exciting** *adj*, **excitingly** *adv.*

**excitement** *n* **1** a feeling of lively, pleasurable eagerness or anticipation. **2** something that produces this feeling. **3** the act of exciting or arousing.

**exclaim** *v* to cry out.

**exclamation** *n* a word or remark uttered suddenly. ➤ **exclamatory** *adj.*

**exclude** *v* **1** to decide not to include or consider. **2** to bar from participation. **3** to shut out.

**exclusion** *n* **1** the act of excluding; the fact of being left out. **2** something not covered by a contract, insurance policy, etc.

**exclusive**[1] *adj* **1** limited to a single individual, a particular group, etc. **2** excluding others from participation, membership, or entry. **3** stylish and expensive. **4** whole or undivided: *gave her his exclusive attention.* **5** (+ of) not including. ➤ **exclusively** *adv*, **exclusiveness** *n.*

**exclusive**[2] *n* an interview, article, etc published by only one newspaper or broadcast by only one television channel or radio station.

**excommunicate** *v* to deprive officially of the rights of church membership. ➤ **excommunication** *n.*

**excoriate** *v* **1** to wear away the skin of. **2** *formal* to censure scathingly. ➤ **excoriation** *n.*

**excrement** *n* faeces.

**excrescence** *n* an abnormal outgrowth or enlargement.

**excreta** *pl n* excrement.

**excrete** *v* to discharge (waste) from the body. ➤ **excretion** *n*, **excretory** *adj.*

**excruciating** *adj* **1** causing great pain; agonizing. **2** intensely embarrassing. **3** very bad or tedious. ➤ **excruciatingly** *adv.*

**exculpate** *v* to clear from blame or guilt.

**excursion** *n* a short pleasure trip, e.g. for sightseeing.

**excuse**[1] *v* **1** to try to remove blame from (somebody, oneself). **2** to be an acceptable reason for; to justify. **3** to forgive entirely. **4** to overlook as unimportant. **5** to allow to leave. **6** *Brit* to free from a duty. ✱ **excuse oneself** to announce politely that one is leaving. ➤ **excusable** *adj.*

**excuse**[2] *n* **1** a reason given to explain or justify a fault, mistake, etc. **2** a pretext. **3** (*in pl*) an expression of regret for failure to do something or for one's absence. **4** *informal* (+ for) a very poor example of.

**ex-directory** *adj Brit* not listed in a telephone directory at the subscriber's request.

**execrable** *adj* detestable or appalling.

**execrate** *v* to detest utterly; to abhor. ➤ **execration** *n.*

**execute** *v* **1** to put into effect (a plan, order, etc). **2** to put to death as a punishment. **3** to carry out or perform (e.g. a movement). **4** in computing, to run (a file, program, etc).

**execution** *n* **1** the act of carrying something out. **2** the act of putting somebody to death as a punishment.

**executioner** *n* a person legally appointed to carry out capital punishment.

**executive**[1] *adj* concerned with carrying out laws, decisions, plans, etc, rather than formulating them.

**executive**[2] *n* **1** a person with administrative or managerial responsibility. **2** a person or group that controls an organization. **3** the executive branch of a government.

**executor** *n* a person appointed to carry out the provisions of another person's will.

**exegesis** *n* (*pl* **exegeses**) an explanation or critical interpretation of a text.

**exemplar** *n* somebody or something that serves as a typical example or ideal model.

**exemplary** *adj* **1** worthy of imitation; outstanding. **2** of a punishment: serving as a warning.

**exemplify** *v* (**-ies, -ied**) **1** to serve as an example of. **2** to illustrate with an example. ➤ **exemplification** *n.*

**exempt**[1] *adj* free from some liability or requirement to which others are subject.

**exempt**[2] *v* to make exempt; to excuse. ➤ **exemption** *n.*

**exercise**[1] *n* **1** physical exertion for the sake of maintaining bodily fitness. **2** an activity or test intended to develop or display a physical or mental skill. **3** something done for a particular purpose. **4** the use of a power or right.

**exercise**[2] *v* **1** to engage in physical exertion for the sake of fitness. **2** to use or exert (e.g. a right). **3** to cause anxiety, alarm, or indignation in.
**exercise book** *n* a booklet of blank pages used for written work in schools.
**exert** *v* to bring (strength or authority) to bear on a situation. ✻ **exert oneself** to make an effort. ➤ **exertion** *n.*
**exeunt** *v* used as a stage direction instructing more than one character to leave the stage.
**exfoliate** *v* **1** to cast (skin or bark) off in scales, layers, etc. **2** to remove surface cells, layers, etc from (the skin). ➤ **exfoliation** *n.*
**exhale** *v* **1** to breathe out. **2** to emit (gas or vapour). ➤ **exhalation** *n.*
**exhaust**[1] *v* **1** to tire out. **2** to consume entirely; to use up. **3** to deal with (a subject) so fully that there is no more to say about it. ➤ **exhaustible** *adj.*
**exhaust**[2] *n* **1** used gases or vapour expelled from an engine. **2** the pipe or system through which these gases escape.
**exhaustion** *n* **1** extreme tiredness. **2** the act of exhausting.
**exhaustive** *adj* dealing with every aspect of a subject; comprehensive. ➤ **exhaustively** *adv.*
**exhibit**[1] *v* (**exhibited, exhibiting**) **1** to show (a work of art, etc) publicly. **2** to show (a feeling, symptom, etc) outwardly.
**exhibit**[2] *n* **1** something exhibited, e.g. in a museum. **2** something produced as evidence in a court of law.
**exhibition** *n* **1** a public showing, e.g. of works of art. **2** the act of exhibiting. ✻ **make an exhibition of oneself** to behave foolishly in public.
**exhibitionism** *n* behaviour intended to attract attention to oneself. ➤ **exhibitionist** *n.*
**exhilarate** *v* **1** to make very happy or cheerful. **2** to enliven or invigorate. ➤ **exhilarating** *adj,* **exhilaration** *n.*
**exhort** *v* to urge or advise strongly.
**exhortation** *n* a strongly worded appeal to somebody to do something.
**exhume** *v* to dig (something buried, *esp* a dead body) up again.
**exigency** *n* (*pl* **-ies**) *formal* **1** an emergency. **2** desperate or urgent nature.
**exigent** *adj formal* requiring immediate aid or action.
**exiguous** *adj formal* excessively scanty; meagre.
**exile**[1] *n* **1** a state of banishment from one's country or home. **2** somebody who is sent into exile.
**exile**[2] *v* to send into exile.
**exist** *v* **1** to have being or life, or to be real. **2** to live at an inferior level.
**existence** *n* **1** the state of existing or being. **2** a manner of living.
**existential** *adj* **1** of or grounded in existence. **2** relating to existentialism. ➤ **existentially** *adv.*
**existentialism** *n* a philosophical movement characterized by enquiry into human beings' experience of themselves in relation to the world, *esp* insofar as they are free individuals, responsible for their own moral choices in a universe where there are no absolute concepts of right and wrong. ➤ **existentialist** *n and adj.*
**exit**[1] *v* (**exited, exiting**) **1** used as a stage direction to tell a particular character to leave the stage. **2** to leave or depart.
**exit**[2] *n* **1** a way out of a room or building. **2** the act of going out, away, or off stage. **3** a point at which vehicles can leave a major road, roundabout, etc.
**exit poll** *n* a survey of voting trends conducted by questioning people as they leave a polling station.
**exodus** *n* a mass departure; an emigration.
**exonerate** *v* **1** to free from blame. **2** (*often* + from) to relieve of a responsibility. ➤ **exoneration** *n.*
**exorbitant** *adj* of prices, demands, etc: much greater than is reasonable. ➤ **exorbitantly** *adv.*
**exorcize** *or* **-ise** *v* to expel (an evil spirit) from a person or place. ➤ **exorcism** *n,* **exorcist** *n.*
**exotic** *adj* **1** introduced from another country. **2** strikingly or excitingly different or unusual. ➤ **exotically** *adv,* **exoticism** *n.*
**expand** *v* **1** to make or become larger, greater, etc. **2** (*often* + on) to speak or write at greater length. **3** to grow genial; to become more sociable. ➤ **expandable** *adj,* **expander** *n.*
**expanse** *n* a wide area of something.
**expansive** *adj* **1** covering a large area. **2** genial and freely communicative. ➤ **expansively** *adv.*
**expat** *n informal* = EXPATRIATE.
**expatiate** *v* (*usu* + on/upon) to speak or write at length on.
**expatriate** *n* a person who lives outside their native country.
**expect** *v* **1** to consider (an event) probable or certain. **2** to consider (e.g. respect, obedience) to be reasonable or due. **3** to consider (somebody) to be duty-bound or obligated to do something. **4** to look forward to or be waiting for. **5** to be waiting for the arrival of. ✻ **be expecting** *informal* to be pregnant.
**expectancy** *n* (*pl* **-ies**) **1** expectation, *esp* eager or joyful expectation. **2** the expected amount or length of something.
**expectant** *adj* **1** having, showing, or characterized by expectation. **2** of a woman: pregnant. ➤ **expectantly** *adv.*
**expectation** *n* **1** the state of expecting something; anticipation. **2** (*also in pl*) something expected.

**expectorant** *n* a medicine that promotes the bringing up of phlegm from the throat or lungs.

**expectorate** *v* to eject (phlegm or similar matter) from the throat or lungs by coughing or spitting.

**expedient**[1] *adj* **1** suitable for achieving a particular end. **2** characterized by concern with what is advantageous rather than what is right or ethical. ➤ **expediency** *n.*

**expedient**[2] *n* a means to an end, *esp* a makeshift or improvised one.

**expedite** *v formal* to hasten the progress of.

**expedition** *n* a journey undertaken for a specific purpose, e.g. for exploration. ➤ **expeditionary** *adj.*

**expeditious** *adj formal* prompt and efficient. ➤ **expeditiously** *adv.*

**expel** *v* (**expelled, expelling**) **1** to drive or force out. **2** to force to leave a school, society, etc.

**expend** *v* to spend or use up (e.g. time, care, or attention) on dealing with somebody or something.

**expendable** *adj* **1** not intended to be kept or re-used. **2** regarded as available for sacrifice in order to accomplish an objective.

**expenditure** *n* **1** the act of spending money. **2** the amount of money spent.

**expense** *n* **1** financial outlay; cost. **2** (*in pl*) the charges incurred by an employee in performing their duties. **3** a cause of expenditure. ✻ **at somebody's expense** with somebody paying the bill or suffering the consequences. **at the expense of** disregarding or damaging.

**expensive** *adj* costing a great deal of money. ➤ **expensively** *adv.*

**experience**[1] *n* **1** direct participation or observation. **2** the knowledge or skill derived from direct involvement with something over a period of time. **3** something personally encountered or undergone. **4** the sum total of events encountered during an individual life.

**experience**[2] *v* to have experience of.

**experienced** *adj* skilful or wise as a result of experience.

**experiment**[1] *n* **1** a controlled scientific operation carried out to make a discovery, test a hypothesis, or illustrate a known law. **2** a procedure or policy that has not been tried before.

**experiment**[2] *v* to carry out an experiment or experiments. ➤ **experimentation** *n.*

**experimental** *adj* **1** used as a means of trying something out. **2** based on or relating to scientific experiments. **3** innovative and unconventional. ➤ **experimentally** *adv.*

**expert**[1] *adj* showing special skill or knowledge derived from training or experience. ➤ **expertly** *adv.*

**expert**[2] *n* a person who has special skill or knowledge in a particular field.

**expertise** *n* skill in or knowledge of a particular field.

**expiate** *v* to make amends for (a sin, crime, etc). ➤ **expiation** *n.*

**expire** *v* **1** of e.g. a permit: to cease to be valid. **2** of a period: to come to an end. **3** *formal* to die. **4** to breathe (air) out from the lungs.

**expiry** *n* a termination, *esp* of a period of validity.

**explain** *v* **1** to make plain or understandable, *esp* by giving details. **2** to give the reason for. ✻ **explain oneself** to clarify the reasons for one's conduct. ➤ **explanation** *n.*

**explanatory** *adj* serving to explain.

**expletive** *n* an obscenity or profanity.

**explicable** *adj* capable of being explained.

**explicit** *adj* **1** clear and unambiguous. **2** graphically frank or detailed. ➤ **explicitly** *adv.*

**explode** *v* **1** to burst violently as a result of pressure or a chemical or nuclear reaction. **2** to expand suddenly. **3** to give expression violently and usu noisily to emotion. **4** to demonstrate the falsity of (a belief or theory).

**exploit**[1] *n* a notable or heroic action.

**exploit**[2] *v* **1** to use or develop (resources, materials, etc) fully. **2** to take unfair advantage of. ➤ **exploitation** *n,* **exploitative** *adj.*

**explore** *v* **1** to travel through (an unfamiliar place), *esp* for purposes of discovery. **2** to examine or enquire into thoroughly. ➤ **exploration** *n,* **exploratory** *adj,* **explorer** *n.*

**explosion** *n* **1** the act of exploding. **2** a rapid large-scale expansion or increase.

**explosive**[1] *adj* **1** capable of exploding. **2** threatening to cause trouble or controversy. **3** sudden, rapid, and powerful. ➤ **explosively** *adv.*

**explosive**[2] *n* an explosive substance.

**exponent** *n* **1** somebody that expounds, advocates, or exemplifies something. **2** a skilled practitioner of an art, etc. **3** a symbol written above and to the right of a number to indicate that it is to be multiplied by itself that many times, e.g. $2^3 = 2 \times 2 \times 2$.

**exponential** *adj* **1** involving a a mathematical exponent. **2** increasing with accelerating rapidity. ➤ **exponentially** *adv.*

**export**[1] *v* **1** to send (a commodity) to another country for purposes of trade. **2** to take (an idea, custom, etc) to another country. ➤ **exportation** *n,* **exporter** *n.*

**export**[2] *n* **1** something exported. **2** the act of exporting.

**expose** *v* **1** to lay open to view; to uncover or display. **2** to lay open to attack, danger, etc. **3** to subject (a photographic film) to the action of light. **4** to bring (something shameful) to public notice. * **expose oneself** to engage in indecent exposure.

**exposé** *n* **1** a formal exposition of facts. **2** an exposure of something discreditable.

**exposition** *n* **1** the art of expounding or explaining. **2** a large public exhibition. **3** the first part of a musical composition in which the themes are presented.

**expostulate** *v formal* to remonstrate with somebody, *esp* in order to dissuade them. ➤ **expostulation** *n.*

**exposure** *n* **1** the fact of being exposed, *esp* to something harmful or unpleasant. **2** lack of protection from cold weather. **3** the act of exposing a sensitized photographic film to light. **4** a section of a film with one picture on it. **5** the disclosure *esp* of something shameful or criminal. **6** publicization, *esp* by means of the mass media.

**expound** *v* to state and explain (an idea, theory, etc) carefully.

**express**[1] *v* **1** to show or make known in words or by other means. **2** to force out (air or liquid) by pressure.

**express**[2] *adj* **1** firmly and explicitly stated. **2** specific. **3** travelling at high speed, usu with few stops along the way. **4** *Brit* designated to be delivered without delay.

**express**[3] *adv* by express.

**express**[4] *n* **1** an express train. **2** *Brit* an express delivery service.

**expression** *n* **1** the act or a means of expressing. **2** a significant word or phrase. **3** a look on somebody's face that indicates their feelings. **4** a mathematical or logical symbol or combination of symbols. ➤ **expressionless** *adj.*

**expressionism** *n* a style in art, literature, or music that attempts to depict subjective emotions and responses to objects and events. ➤ **expressionist** *n and adj.*

**expressive** *adj* vividly expressing something. ➤ **expressively** *adv,* **expressiveness** *n,* **expressivity** *n.*

**expropriate** *v* to deprive of owner's rights to a piece of property, *esp* with official sanction. ➤ **expropriation** *n.*

**expulsion** *n* the act of expelling.

**expunge** *v formal* to erase or obliterate completely.

**expurgate** *v* to remove objectionable parts from (a text) before publication. ➤ **expurgation** *n.*

**exquisite** *adj* **1** extremely beautiful, and usu delicate. **2** keenly sensitive, *esp* in feeling. **3** acute or intense. ➤ **exquisitely** *adv.*

**extant** *adj* still or currently existing.

**extemporary** *adj* spoken, done, etc on the spur of the moment without preparation.

**extempore** /ik'stempəri/ *adj and adv* spoken or done without preparation.

**extemporize** *or* **-ise** *v* to improvise or make something up on the spur of the moment.

**extend** *v* **1** to lengthen or enlarge. **2** to prolong in time. **3** to continue over a particular distance, area, or length of time. **4** to hold out or stretch out (e.g. one's hand or arm). **5** to give or offer. ➤ **extendable** *adj,* **extendible** *adj,* **extensible** *adj.*

**extended family** *n* a family unit that includes three or more generations of near relatives living close together.

**extension** *n* **1** the act of extending. **2** a part added to make something longer or larger, e.g. an extra room or rooms added to a building. **3** an extra telephone connected to the principal line.

**extensive** *adj* **1** extending over a large area. **2** large-scale. ➤ **extensively** *adv.*

**extent** *n* **1** the distance or area over which something extends. **2** the scale or scope of something. **3** the degree to which something is applicable.

**extenuate** *v* to lessen the seriousness of (a crime, etc) by providing a reason or excuse for it. ➤ **extenuating** *adj,* **extenuation** *n.*

**exterior**[1] *adj* on the outside or an outside surface.

**exterior**[2] *n* **1** an exterior part or surface; outside. **2** an outward appearance.

**exterminate** *v* to destroy or kill off completely. ➤ **extermination** *n,* **exterminator** *n.*

**external**[1] *adj* **1** on or intended for the outside. **2** arising or acting from outside. **3** relating to dealings with foreign countries or other organizations. ➤ **externally** *adv.*

**external**[2] *n* (*usu in pl*) an external feature or aspect.

**externalize** *or* **-ise** *v* to express (e.g. a feeling) in externally visible form.

**extinct** *adj* **1** no longer existing as a species. **2** of a volcano: no longer active.

**extinguish** *v* **1** to cause (a flame, fire, etc) to cease burning. **2** to put out (a light). **3** to destroy completely. ➤ **extinguisher** *n.*

**extirpate** *v* to remove or destroy completely. ➤ **extirpation** *n.*

**extol** (*NAmer* **extoll**) *v* (**extolled, extolling**) to praise highly.

**extort** *v* to obtain (e.g. money or a confession) by force or threats. ➤ **extortion** *n.*

**extortionate** *adj* of a price: excessive or exorbitant. ➤ **extortionately** *adv.*

**extra**[1] *adj* more than is due, usual, or necessary.

**extra**[2] *n* **1** something extra, e.g. an additional charge. **2** somebody hired to act in a group scene in a film or stage production.

**extra**[3] *adv* beyond the usual size or amount.
**extra-** *prefix* outside; beyond: *extramural.*
**extract**[1] *v* **1** to pull out from within something. **2** to obtain, *esp* against resistance or with effort. **3** to separate out (e.g. a mineral) by a physical or chemical process.
**extract**[2] *n* **1** a short passage taken from a book, film, etc. **2** a substance containing the essential constituents of e.g. an aromatic plant in concentrated form.
**extraction** *n* **1** the act of extracting. **2** ancestry or origin.
**extractor fan** *n* a type of ventilator designed to expel fumes, stale air, etc.
**extradite** *v* to hand (somebody) over to a foreign country to stand trial for an offence committed there. ➤ **extradition** *n.*
**extramarital** *adj* of sexual relations: occurring outside marriage.
**extramural** *adj chiefly Brit* for students of a university, college, etc who do not attend on a full-time basis.
**extraneous** *adj* **1** not forming an essential or vital part; irrelevant. **2** coming from the outside.
**extraordinaire** *adj* (*used after a noun*) outstanding: *a decorator extraordinaire.*
**extraordinary** *adj* **1** highly exceptional; remarkable. **2** held for a special reason: *an extraordinary general meeting.* ➤ **extraordinarily** *adv.*
**extrapolate** *v* to use (known data or experience) as a basis for working out something unknown. ➤ **extrapolation** *n.*
**extrasensory perception** *n* perception by means other than the known senses, e.g. by telepathy and clairvoyance.
**extraterrestrial**[1] *adj* from outside the earth or its atmosphere.
**extraterrestrial**[2] *n* an extraterrestrial being.
**extravagant** *adj* **1** wasteful, *esp* of money. **2** unreasonably high in price. **3** lacking in moderation and restraint. **4** excessively elaborate or showy. ➤ **extravagance** *n,* **extravagantly** *adv.*
**extravaganza** *n* a lavish or spectacular show.
**extreme**[1] *adj* **1** existing in a very high degree. **2** not moderate; doctrinaire. **3** exceedingly severe or drastic. **4** situated at the farthest possible point from a centre. ➤ **extremely** *adv.*
**extreme**[2] *n* **1** something situated at one end or the other of a range. **2** (*also in pl*) a very pronounced or extreme degree. **3** (*also in pl*) an extreme measure.
**extremist** *n* somebody who holds extreme views.
**extremity** *n* (*pl* **-ies**) **1** the furthest part or point. **2** (*also in pl*) a human hand or foot. **3** extreme misfortune or danger or death.
**extricate** *v* to disentangle with considerable effort.
**extrinsic** *adj* not forming part of or belonging to a thing; extraneous.
**extrovert** *n* a gregarious or outgoing person: compare INTROVERT. ➤ **extrovert** *adj.*
**extrude** *v* **1** to force or push out. **2** to shape (metal, plastic, etc) by forcing it through a die. ➤ **extrusion** *n.*
**exuberant** *adj* **1** joyously unrestrained and enthusiastic. **2** abundant or luxuriant. ➤ **exuberance** *n,* **exuberantly** *adv.*
**exude** *v* **1** to ooze out or allow (a liquid or smell) to ooze out. **2** to display (a quality, feeling, etc) in abundance.
**exult** *v* to rejoice openly and triumphantly. ➤ **exultant** *adj,* **exultantly** *adv,* **exultation** *n.*
**eye**[1] *n* **1** an organ of sight. **2** the faculty of sight, perception, or appreciation: *an eye for beauty.* **3** the hole through the head of a needle. **4** a loop, *esp* one of metal into which a hook is inserted. **5** an undeveloped bud, e.g. on a potato. **6** a calm area in the centre of a storm, hurricane, etc. * **be all eyes** to watch intently. **have/keep one's eye on** to watch *esp* constantly and attentively. **in the eye/eyes of** in the judgment or opinion of. **make eyes at** to ogle. **more than meets the eye** more than is at first apparent. **see eye to eye** to have a common viewpoint; to agree. **with an eye to** having as an aim or purpose.
**eye**[2] *v* (**eyes, eyed, eyeing** *or* **eying**) to look at *esp* carefully.
**eyeball** *n* the more or less spherical capsule of the eye of a vertebrate animal. * **eyeball to eyeball** *informal* face to face, *esp* with hostility.
**eyebrow** *n* the ridge over the eye or the line of hair that grows on it.
**eyeful** *n informal* **1** an attractive person. **2** a look or gaze.
**eyeglass** *n* a lens worn to aid vision.
**eyelash** *n* the fringe of hair edging the eyelid or a single hair of this fringe.
**eyelet** *n* **1** a small reinforced hole that a cord, lace, etc may be passed through. **2** a small metal ring to reinforce an eyelet.
**eyelid** *n* a movable lid of skin and muscle that can be closed over the eyeball.
**eyeliner** *n* a cosmetic for emphasizing the outline of the eyes.
**eye-opener** *n informal* something surprising and revelatory.
**eyepiece** *n* the lens looked through at the eye end of an optical instrument.
**eyeshade** *n* a small shield, fastened to the head, that shades the eyes from strong light.
**eye shadow** *n* a coloured cream applied to the eyelids to accentuate the eyes.
**eyesight** *n* the ability to see.

**eyesore** *n* something offensive to the sight, *esp* an ugly building.

**eyetooth** *n* (*pl* **eyeteeth**) a canine tooth of the upper jaw.

**eye up** *v informal* to look at (somebody) in order to assess their sexual attractiveness.

**eyewash** *n* **1** *informal* nonsense. **2** lotion for the eyes.

**eyewitness** *n* a person who sees an event take place.

**eyrie** *or* **aerie** *n* the nest of a bird of prey.

**F**[1] *or* **f** *n* (*pl* **F's** *or* **Fs** *or* **f's**) the sixth letter of the English alphabet.

**F**[2] *abbr* Fahrenheit.

**F**[3] *abbr* the chemical symbol for fluorine.

**FA** *abbr* Football Association.

**fable** *n* **1** a short story intended to convey a moral. **2** a legendary story of supernatural happenings.

**fabled** *adj* **1** famous or legendary. **2** fictitious.

**fabric** *n* **1** a pliable material made by weaving or knitting; cloth. **2** the floor, walls, and roof of a building. **3** the underlying structure of an organization or society.

**fabricate** *v* **1** to invent or create (facts), *esp* to deceive. **2** to manufacture (a product) from various parts. ➤ **fabrication** *n.*

**fabulous** *adj* **1** incredible or extraordinary. **2** *informal* excellent. **3** told of in or based on fable. ➤ **fabulously** *adv.*

**facade** *or* **façade** *n* **1** the front of a building. **2** a false or superficial appearance.

**face**[1] *n* **1** the front part of the human head from the chin to the forehead. **2** a facial expression, *esp* a grimace. **3** a front, upper, or outer surface. **4** in geometry, each of the plane surfaces of a solid. **5** the side of a mountain or cliff. **6** one aspect of something. ✱ **on the face of it** at first glance; apparently.

**face**[2] *v* **1** to have the face or front turned in a specific direction. **2** to meet or deal with (a situation or problem) firmly. **3** to have the prospect of (something unpleasant). **4** to cover the front or surface of. ✱ **face the music** to confront unpleasant consequences. **face up to** to confront (a difficulty or problem).

**facecloth** *n* a small cloth for washing the face.

**face down** *v* to prevail against (somebody) by defiant confrontation.

**faceless** *adj* lacking identity; anonymous.

**face-lift** *n* **1** an operation to remove wrinkles or sagging skin. **2** a renovation or overhaul.

**face-pack** *n* a cream or paste applied to the face to improve the complexion and remove impurities.

**face-saving** *adj* serving to preserve one's dignity or reputation.

**facet** *n* **1** a plane surface of a cut gem. **2** an aspect of something.

**facetious** *adj* inappropriately humorous or flippant. ➤ **facetiously** *adv.*

**face value** *n* **1** the value indicated on a coin or postage stamp. **2** the apparent value or significance of something.

**facia** *n chiefly Brit* see FASCIA.

**facial**[1] *adj* relating to the face. ➤ **facially** *adv.*

**facial**[2] *n* a beauty treatment for the face.

**facile** *adj* **1** indicating a lack of thought; superficial and glib. **2** easily or readily accomplished or performed.

**facilitate** *v* to make (a task or procedure) easier. ➤ **facilitation** *n.*

**facility** *n* (*pl* **-ies**) **1** a building, piece of equipment, or resource designed to provide a particular service. **2** a natural ability or aptitude.

**facing** *n* **1** a lining at the edge of a garment, for stiffening or ornament. **2** an ornamental or protective layer applied to a wall.

**facsimile** *n* **1** an exact copy of printed material. **2** a fax.

**fact** *n* **1** an actual event or occurrence. **2** a piece of information. **3** reality or truth. ✱ **the facts of life** information about sexual reproduction. **in fact** in reality; actually.

**faction** *n* a minority group within a party. ➤ **factional** *adj.*

**factious** *adj* caused by or inclined to dissension.

---

***Usage Note:*** Do not confuse this word with *fractious.*

---

**factitious** *adj* produced artificially; sham or unreal.

**factor**[1] *n* **1** a condition, force, or fact that contributes to a result. **2** in mathematics, one of two or more numbers that can be multiplied together to produce a given number. **3** formerly, in biology, a gene. **4** a substance in the blood that causes it to clot. **5** a person who acts for another; an agent.

**factor**[2] *v* to express (a number) as the product of factors. ✱ **factor in/out** to include or exclude as a matter to be considered.

**factory** *n* (*pl* **-ies**) a building containing machinery used for manufacturing.

**factory farming** *n* a system of dairy or meat farming that uses intensive production methods.

**factotum** *n* (*pl* **factotums**) a person employed to carry out many types of work.

**factual** *adj* restricted to or based on fact. ➤ **factually** *adv.*

**faculty** *n* (*pl* **-ies**) **1** an inherent capability or function. **2** a natural aptitude or talent. **3** *chiefly Brit* a group of related departments in a university.

**fad** *n* **1** a short-lived interest or craze. **2** an idiosyncratic taste or habit. ➤ **faddish** *adj,* **faddy** *adj.*

**fade**[1] *v* **1** to disappear gradually; to vanish. **2** to lose freshness or colour. **3** of an image or sound: to come gradually into or out of view or hearing.

**fade**[2] *n* an instance of fading.

**faeces** (*NAmer* **feces**) *pl n* bodily waste discharged from the bowels. ➤ **faecal** *adj.*

**fag**[1] *n Brit, informal* a cigarette.

**fag**[2] *n chiefly Brit, informal* **1** a tiring or tedious task. **2** a pupil at a public school who does tasks for an older pupil.

**fag**[3] *v* (**fagged, fagging**) *chiefly Brit, informal* to work hard.

**faggot** *n* **1** *Brit* a fried mass of minced meat and herbs. **2** a bundle of sticks used as fuel. **3** *chiefly NAmer, informal, derog* a male homosexual.

**Fahrenheit** *adj* of a scale of temperature on which water freezes at 32° and boils at 212°.

**fail**[1] *v* **1** to be unsuccessful at something. **2** to neglect to do something. **3** to stop functioning. **4** to be insufficient or inadequate. **5** to weaken or die away. **6** to become bankrupt or insolvent. **7** to be unable to reach the required standard in an examination. **8** to judge (somebody or something) as having failed a test or examination. **9** to disappoint or prove inadequate for.

**fail**[2] *n* a mark indicating the failing of an examination. * **without fail** whatever the circumstances.

**failing**[1] *n* a defect in character.

**failing**[2] *prep* in the absence or default of.

**failsafe** *adj* **1** of a machine: designed to return to a safe condition in the event of failure or breakdown. **2** foolproof.

**failure** *n* **1** lack of success. **2** an unsuccessful person or thing. **3** an instance of failing to perform something expected. **4** an instance of failing to function normally.

**faint**[1] *adj* **1** not easy to see or hear. **2** slight. **3** on the point of losing consciousness. ➤ **faintly** *adv.*

**faint**[2] *v* to lose consciousness briefly.

**faint**[3] *n* a brief loss of consciousness.

**faint-hearted** *adj* lacking courage or resolve; timid.

**fair**[1] *adj* **1** honest and just. **2** conforming with the rules; allowed. **3** of hair or complexion: light in colour. **4** moderately good or large. **5** of weather: fine and dry. **6** of wind: favourable. ➤ **fairness** *n.*

**fair**[2] *n* **1** an outdoor event with sideshows and amusements. **2** an exhibition for promoting products of a particular type. **3** a gathering of buyers and sellers.

**fair copy** *n* the final corrected version of a document.

**fair game** *n* a person or thing open to legitimate attack or ridicule.

**fairground** *n* an area where an outdoor fair is held.

**fairing** *n* a smooth structure intended to reduce air resistance on a vehicle or aircraft.

**fairly** *adv* **1** impartially or honestly. **2** in a proper or legal manner. **3** to a moderate degree. **4** positively.

**fair trade** *n* trade that supports producers in developing countries.

**fairway** *n* the mown part of a golf course between a tee and a green.

**fair-weather friend** *n* a friend who is loyal only in untroubled times.

**fairy** *n* (*pl* **-ies**) a small mythical being in human form with magical powers.

**fairy godmother** *n* in fairy stories, a woman who comes to the aid of the heroine or hero.

**fairy lights** *pl n* small coloured electric lights hung up for decoration.

**fairy story** *n* **1** a children's story about magical or imaginary people and places. **2** a made-up account or excuse.

**fait accompli** /ˌfayt əˈkompli/ *n* something accomplished that cannot be changed.

**faith** *n* **1** complete confidence or belief. **2** a system of religious beliefs. **3** belief in the traditional doctrines of a religion.

**faithful**[1] *adj* **1** loyal or steadfast. **2** true to the facts; accurate. ➤ **faithfully** *adv.*

**faithful**[2] *n* (*treated as pl*) (**the faithful**) the people who belong to a religion.

**faithless** *adj* disloyal or untrustworthy.

**fake**[1] *adj* not genuine; counterfeit.

**fake**[2] *n* a person or thing that is not genuine.

**fake**[3] *v* **1** to forge or counterfeit. **2** to pretend to have (an illness or emotion).

**fakir** *n* a Muslim or Hindu holy man.

**falcon** *n* a hawk with long pointed wings.

**falconry** *n* the art of training falcons to pursue game. ➤ **falconer** *n.*

**fall**[1] *v* (**fell, fallen**) **1** to descend freely by the force of gravity. **2** to collapse to the ground. **3** to hang down. **4** of a place: to be defeated or captured. **5** of a government: to lose office. **6** to become less or weaker. **7** to pass into a new state or condition: *to fall in love.* **8** to occur at a specified time. **9** to come within the scope or limits of something. * **fall for 1** *informal* to fall in love with. **2** *informal* to be deceived by (a trick, etc). **fall into place** to begin to make sense or progress. **fall on** to attack suddenly or fiercely. **fall over oneself** *informal* to make great efforts. **fall short** to fail to achieve a goal or target. **fall to** to be the responsibility of.

**fall**[2] *n* **1** an instance of falling. **2** something that falls or has fallen. **3** *NAmer* autumn. **4** a drop in height. **5** (*in pl*) a steep waterfall. **6** a downward slope. **7** a decrease in quantity or value. **8** a collapse or defeat.

**fallacy** *n* (*pl* **-ies**) **1** a mistaken idea. **2** a false argument. ➤ **fallacious** *adj.*

**fallback** *n* an alternative or reserve option if the main one fails.

**fall back** *v* to retreat. ✱ **fall back on** to have recourse to in difficulty.

**fall behind** *v* to fail to keep up.

**fall down** *v* **1** to collapse or drop to the ground. **2** to fail to meet expectations.

**fall guy** *n informal* a scapegoat.

**fallible** *adj* capable of being wrong. ➤ **fallibility** *n.*

**fall in** *v* **1** to sink or collapse inwards. **2** of a soldier: to take a place in a formation. ✱ **fall in with 1** to concur with (an arrangement). **2** to encounter and join (a group).

**fall off** *v* **1** to become detached and drop to the ground. **2** to become less or weaker.

**Fallopian tube** *n* either of the pair of tubes conducting the egg from the ovary to the uterus in female mammals.

**fallout** *n* **1** radioactive particles resulting from a nuclear explosion. **2** unfavourable secondary results or effects.

**fall out** *v* **1** to have a disagreement. **2** to happen in a certain way.

**fallow** *adj* **1** of land: left unsown after ploughing. **2** of a sow: not pregnant.

**fall through** *v* to fail to be carried out.

**false** *adj* **1** untrue or incorrect. **2** not according to law or rules; invalid. **3** intended to deceive; artificial. **4** illusory. **5** disloyal or treacherous. ➤ **falsely** *adv,* **falseness** *n,* **falsity** *n.*

**false alarm** *n* a warning that proves to be groundless.

**falsehood** *n* **1** an untrue statement; a lie. **2** absence of truth or accuracy.

**false pretences** *pl n* acts or claims intended to deceive.

**falsetto** *n* (*pl* **-os**) a high-pitched male voice.

**falsify** *v* (**-ies, -ied**) to make (information, etc) false. ➤ **falsification** *n.*

**falter** *v* **1** to hesitate in purpose or action. **2** to lose strength or effectiveness. **3** to move or speak unsteadily.

**fame** *n* the state of being famous.

**famed** *adj* famous.

**familial** *adj* relating to a family.

**familiar**[1] *adj* **1** frequently seen or experienced; common or well-known. **2** (+ with) having knowledge of. **3** close or intimate. ➤ **familiarity** *n.*

**familiar**[2] *n* **1** an intimate associate; a companion. **2** a spirit that waits on a witch.

**familiarize** *or* **-ise** *v* to make (somebody) familiar with something. ➤ **familiarization** *n.*

**family** *n* (*pl* **-ies**) **1** a group of parents and their children. **2** the children of a parent or parents. **3** a group of people related by descent or marriage. **4** a group of related things. **5** in biology, a category above genus and below order.

**family planning** *n* control of the number of children born in a family by means of contraception.

**family tree** *n* a diagram showing a family's history and relationships.

**famine** *n* an extreme scarcity of food.

**famished** *adj informal* very hungry.

**famous** *adj* **1** well-known. **2** *informal, dated* excellent or first-rate. ➤ **famously** *adv.*

**fan**[1] *n* **1** a device of rotating vanes, for producing a current of air. **2** a folding semicircular device that is waved to and fro to cool the face.

**fan**[2] *v* (**fanned, fanning**) **1** to cause a current of air to blow on. **2** to drive (something) away by waving. **3** to spread out in the shape of an open fan. **4** to increase the intensity of (a fire) by agitating the air around it. **5** to stir up or stimulate (an emotion).

**fan**[3] *n* a supporter or admirer of a sport or celebrity.

**fanatic** *n* a person who is excessively enthusiastic about a religion, cause, or activity. ➤ **fanatical** *adj,* **fanatically** *adv,* **fanaticism** *n.*

**fan belt** *n* a belt driving the cooling fan of a motor vehicle.

**fancier** *n* a person who breeds a specified kind of animal: *a pigeon fancier.*

**fanciful** *adj* **1** existing in fancy only; imaginary. **2** marked by fancy or whim; elaborate or contrived. ➤ **fancifully** *adv.*

**fancy**[1] *v* (**-ies, -ied**) **1** to feel a liking or desire for. **2** to consider (somebody or something) likely to do well. **3** to believe or imagine. ✱ **fancy oneself** *informal* to have a high opinion of one's own worth, ability, etc. ➤ **fanciable** *adj.*

**fancy**[2] *adj* (**-ier, -iest**) **1** of a fine quality. **2** highly decorated or decorative.

**fancy**[3] *n* (*pl* **-ies**) **1** a liking based on whim rather than reason. **2** a notion or whim. **3** a mental image. **4** capricious use of imagination. **5** the power of mental conception in art.

**fancy dress** *n* unusual or amusing dress worn at some parties.

**fancy-free** *adj* free because not involved in an amorous relationship.

**fandango** *n* (*pl* **-os**) a lively Spanish dance for two people.

**fanfare** *n* **1** a flourish of brass instruments on a ceremonial occasion. **2** a showy display.

**fang** *n* **1** a tooth by which an animal seizes and holds its prey. **2** a tooth of a venomous snake.

**fanlight** *n* a semicircular window over a door or window.

**fanny** *n* (*pl* **-ies**) **1** *Brit, coarse slang* the female genitals. **2** *NAmer, informal* the buttocks.
**fantasize** *or* **-ise** *v* to form imaginative ideas about something desirable.
**fantastic** *adj* **1** unreal or imaginary. **2** so extreme as to be incredible. **3** strange or unrealistic. **4** *informal* wonderful; excellent. ➤ **fantastical** *adj*, **fantastically** *adv.*
**fantasy** *n* (*pl* **-ies**) **1** the process of creating extravagant mental images or daydreams. **2** a fantastic design or idea. **3** imaginative fiction or drama characterized by strange or unrealistic elements.
**fanzine** *n* a magazine for fans of a sports team or performer.
**far**[1] *adv* (**farther** *or* **further, farthest** *or* **furthest**) **1** to or at a large distance in space or time. **2** by a broad interval. **3** (+ from) in total contrast to. **4** to or at a considerable distance or degree. **5** very much. ✱ **a far cry from** totally different to. **as far as** to the extent that. **by far** by a considerable margin. **go far** to be successful in life. **go too far** to behave in an unacceptable way. **so far** up to the present.
**far**[2] *adj* (**farther** *or* **further, farthest** *or* **furthest**) **1** remote in space, time, or degree. **2** extreme.
**farad** *n* the SI unit of electrical capacitance.
**faraway** *adj* **1** situated at a great distance; remote. **2** dreamy or abstracted.
**farce** *n* **1** a comedy based on an improbable plot. **2** a ridiculous or nonsensical situation. **3** a travesty or mockery.
**farcical** *adj* ludicrous or absurd. ➤ **farcically** *adv.*
**fare**[1] *n* **1** the price charged to travel on public transport. **2** a paying passenger. **3** food provided for a meal.
**fare**[2] *v* **1** *formal* to get along; to succeed or do. **2** to happen.
**Far East** *n* China, Japan, Indochina, and other countries of east Asia.
**farewell**[1] *interj archaic* goodbye.
**farewell**[2] *n* an act of leave-taking.
**farfetched** *adj* exaggerated and improbable.
**far-flung** *adj* remote or widely spread.
**farm**[1] *n* **1** an area of land and associated buildings for growing crops or raising animals. **2** a farmhouse. **3** an area of water used to breed fish.
**farm**[2] *v* **1** to engage in the production of crops or livestock. **2** to cultivate or rear (crops or livestock) on a farm. **3** to manage and cultivate (land) as farmland or as a farm. **4** (+ out) to allocate (work) to several people. ➤ **farmed** *adj*, **farming** *n.*
**farmer** *n* somebody who owns or runs a farm.
**farmhouse** *n* a house on a farm.
**farrago** *n* (*pl* **-oes** *or* **-os**) a confused collection.
**farrier** *n* a blacksmith who shoes horses.
**farrow**[1] *n* a litter of pigs.
**farrow**[2] *v* of a sow: to give birth to (piglets).
**fart**[1] *v informal* to expel wind from the anus.
**fart**[2] *n informal* **1** an expulsion of wind from the anus. **2** a tiresome or unpleasant person.
**farther**[1] *adv* at or to a greater distance; further.
**farther**[2] *adj* more distant or remote; further.
**farthest**[1] *adj* most distant in space or time; furthest.
**farthest**[2] *adv* to or at the greatest distance in space or time; furthest.
**farthing** *n* a former British coin, worth a quarter of an old penny.
**fascia** (*chiefly Brit* **facia**) *n* **1** a flat horizontal piece of stone or board, under projecting eaves. **2** a nameplate over the front of a shop. **3** *chiefly Brit* the dashboard of a motor vehicle.
**fascinate** *v* to arouse the interest or curiosity of. ➤ **fascination** *n.*
**fascism** *n* **1** a political system that is aggressively nationalistic and supports a centralized autocratic government. **2** *informal* brutal or intolerant dictatorial control. ➤ **fascist** *n and adj.*
**fashion**[1] *n* **1** a prevailing custom or style. **2** the prevailing style of dress, or the business of producing it. **3** a manner or way. ✱ **after a fashion** in an approximate or rough way. **in/out of fashion** fashionable or unfashionable.
**fashion**[2] *v* to give shape or form to.
**fashionable** *adj* conforming to the latest custom or fashion. ➤ **fashionably** *adv.*
**fast**[1] *adj* **1** moving or able to move at a high speed. **2** needing only a short time; accomplished quickly. **3** of a clock or watch: showing a time later than the actual time. **4** of a colour: not liable to fade. **5** firmly fixed or attached.
**fast**[2] *adv* **1** quickly. **2** in a firm or fixed manner. **3** sound or deeply: *fast asleep.*
**fast**[3] *v* to go without foods or drink for a time.
**fast**[4] *n* an act or time of fasting.
**fasten** *v* **1** to attach or secure. **2** to fix or direct (something) steadily. **3** (+ on) to choose and concentrate on.
**fastener** *or* **fastening** *n* a device used to fasten a piece of clothing.
**fastidious** *adj* **1** difficult to satisfy or please. **2** showing or demanding great delicacy or care. ➤ **fastidiously** *adv.*
**fastness** *n* **1** the quality of being fixed. **2** the durability of a dyed colour. **3** a fortified or secure place.
**fat**[1] *n* **1** animal tissue consisting of greasy or oily matter. **2** a solid or semisolid substance derived from animal tissue, as distinct from an oil.
**fat**[2] *adj* (**fatter, fattest**) **1** having an unusually large amount of fat. **2** large or thick. **3** profitable or substantial. ✱ **a fat chance** *informal* no chance at all. ➤ **fatness** *n.*
**fatal** *adj* **1** causing death. **2** bringing ruin. ➤ **fatally** *adv.*

**fatalism** *n* the belief that events are predetermined and outside the control of human beings. ➤ **fatalist** *n*, **fatalistic** *adj*.
**fatality** *n* (*pl* **-ies**) a death resulting from a war or disaster.
**fat cat** *n informal, derog* a wealthy businessman.
**fate**[1] *n* **1** a power beyond human control that is believed to determine events. **2** an outcome, *esp* one that is unpleasant and inevitable.
**fate**[2] *v* ✱ **be fated** to be certain to turn out in a particular way.
**fateful** *adj* having momentous unpleasant or deadly consequences.
**father**[1] *n* **1** a male parent. **2** a male ancestor. **3** a priest. **4** somebody who originates or institutes something. ➤ **fatherhood** *n*.
**father**[2] *v* to be the father of.
**father-in-law** *n* (*pl* **fathers-in-law**) the father of one's husband or wife.
**fatherland** *n* one's native land.
**fatherly** *adj* affectionate and caring.
**fathom**[1] *n* a unit of length for measuring the depth of water, equal to 6ft (about 1.83m).
**fathom**[2] *v* (*often* + out) to consider and begin to understand.
**fatigue**[1] *n* **1** physical or nervous tiredness. **2** the tendency of a material to break under repeated stress. **3** manual or menial military work. **4** (*in pl*) the uniform or work clothing worn on fatigue.
**fatigue**[2] *v* (**fatigues, fatigued, fatiguing**) to weary or exhaust.
**fatten** *v* (*often* + up) to make or become fatter.
**fatty**[1] *adj* (**-ier, -iest**) **1** containing large amounts of fat. **2** oily; greasy. ➤ **fattiness** *n*.
**fatty**[2] *n* (*pl* **-ies**) *informal* a fat person.
**fatuous** *adj* foolish and useless. ➤ **fatuity** *n*, **fatuously** *adv*.
**fatwa** *n* a legal opinion given by an Islamic religious authority.
**faucet** *n chiefly NAmer* a tap.
**fault**[1] *n* **1** a failing or defect. **2** responsibility for wrongdoing or failure. **3** a misdemeanour or mistake. **4** in tennis, a service that does not land in the prescribed area. **5** a fracture in the earth's crust. **6** a break in rock structures caused by strain. ✱ **at fault** liable for blame. **to a fault** excessively. ➤ **faultless** *adj*.
**fault**[2] *v* to find a fault in.
**faulty** *adj* (**-ier, -iest**) having a fault or defect.
**faun** *n* in Roman mythology a figure with a human body and a goat's horns and legs.
**fauna** *n* the animal life of a region or period.
**faux pas** /ˌfoh ˈpah/ *n* (*pl* **faux pas** /ˌfoh ˈpahz/) a social blunder.
**favour**[1] (*NAmer* **favor**) *n* **1** positive approval or liking. **2** partiality or favouritism. **3** an act of kindness. ✱ **in favour of 1** in agreement or sympathy with. **2** to the advantage of. **3** out of preference for.
**favour**[2] (*NAmer* **favor**) *v* **1** to regard or treat with favour. **2** (+ by/with) to do a favour or kindness for. **3** to show partiality towards; to prefer.
**favourable** (*NAmer* **favorable**) *adj* **1** expressing or winning approval. **2** disposed to favour; partial. **3** successful. ➤ **favourably** *adv*.
**favourite**[1] (*NAmer* **favorite**) *n* **1** a preferred person or thing. **2** the competitor thought most likely to win.
**favourite**[2] (*NAmer* **favorite**) *adj* preferred to all the others.
**favouritism** (*NAmer* **favoritism**) *n* the showing of unfair favour.
**fawn**[1] *n* **1** a young deer. **2** a light brown colour.
**fawn**[2] *v* (+ on/upon) to court favour with somebody by flattery.
**fax**[1] *n* **1** a copy of a document that is scanned and transmitted electronically over a telephone line. **2** a machine for sending and receiving faxes.
**fax**[2] *v* to send a fax to.
**faze** *v informal* to disturb or disconcert.
**FBI** *abbr NAmer* Federal Bureau of Investigation.
**FC** *abbr* Football Club.
**Fe** *abbr* the chemical symbol for iron.
**fear**[1] *n* **1** an unpleasant emotion caused by awareness of danger. **2** a reason for alarm; a danger. ➤ **fearless** *adj*.
**fear**[2] *v* **1** to be afraid of. **2** to be anxious or regretful about. **3** (+ for) to be apprehensive.
**fearful** *adj* **1** full of fear; afraid. **2** showing or arising from fear. **3** causing fear. **4** *informal* extremely bad or great. ➤ **fearfully** *adv*.
**fearsome** *adj* **1** causing fear. **2** awesome or frightening. ➤ **fearsomely** *adv*.
**feasible** *adj* **1** capable of being done or carried out. **2** *informal* reasonable or likely. ➤ **feasibility** *n*, **feasibly** *adv*.
**feast**[1] *n* **1** a grand or elaborate meal. **2** a periodic religious observance.
**feast**[2] *v* to have or take part in a feast. ✱ **feast one's eyes on** to look appreciatively at.
**feat** *n* **1** a notable or courageous act or achievement. **2** an act of skill or ingenuity.
**feather**[1] *n* a light horny growth that forms part of the external covering of a bird's body, consisting of a shaft with two sets of interlocking barbs. ✱ **a feather in one's cap** an achievement or distinction in which one can take pride. ➤ **feathery** *adj*.
**feather**[2] *v* to turn (an oar) so that the blade is horizontal when lifting it from the water. ✱ **feather one's nest** to provide for oneself, *esp* dishonestly.
**feature**[1] *n* **1** a prominent or distinctive part or characteristic. **2** a part of the face. **3** (*in pl*) the face. **4** the main film on a cinema programme. **5** an important article or story in a newspaper or magazine. ➤ **featureless** *adj*.

**feature**[2] *v* **1** to give special prominence to. **2** to have as a characteristic or feature. **3** (+ in) to play an important part.
**febrile** *adj* symptomatic of a fever; feverish.
**February** *n* (*pl* **-ies**) the second month of the year.

***Usage Note:*** Note the spelling with *-br-*.

**feces** *pl n NAmer* see FAECES.
**feckless** *adj* **1** ineffectual or weak. **2** worthless or irresponsible.
**fecund** *adj* fruitful or prolific. ➤ **fecundity** *n.*
**fed** *v* past tense and past part. of FEED[1].
**federal** *adj* **1** of a system of government in which constituent states subscribe to a central government while retaining self-government in local matters. **2** of the central government of a federation. **3** loyal to the federal government of the USA in the American Civil War. ➤ **federalism** *n,* **federalist** *n and adj,* **federally** *adv.*
**federate** *v* to join in a federation. ➤ **federate** *adj.*
**federation** *n* **1** a group of states forming a federal union. **2** a union of organizations. **3** the act of forming a federal union.
**fee** *n* a sum of money paid *esp* for entrance or for a professional service.
**feeble** *adj* **1** lacking in strength; weak. **2** deficient in authority or force. ➤ **feebly** *adv.*
**feed**[1] *v* (*past tense and past part.* **fed**) **1** to give food to. **2** to provide regular food for. **3** to provide something essential to the growth, sustenance, or operation of. **4** to satisfy or gratify (a feeling). **5** to supply continuously for use or processing. **6** (*usu* + off/on/upon) to eat or be satisfied by.
**feed**[2] *n* **1** an instance of feeding or eating. **2** food for livestock.
**feedback** *n* **1** information given to the originator about the results of an action or process. **2** the return to the input of a part of the output of a machine or system, e.g. noise fed back to a microphone.
**feeder** *n* **1** a person or animal that feeds in a specified way. **2** a device or apparatus for supplying food. **3** a device feeding material into or through a machine. **4** a road, railway, airline, or aircraft that links remote areas with the main transport system.
**feel**[1] *v* (*past tense and past part.* **felt**) **1** to handle or touch (something) to examine or explore it. **2** to perceive by a physical sensation. **3** to give a particular sensation when touched. **4** to experience (an emotion or physical sensation). **5** to be affected by. **6** to be aware of (something) without direct experience. **7** to believe or think. **8** (+ for) to have sympathy or pity for. * **feel like** to have a passing fancy for. **feel up to** to be well or fit enough to.
**feel**[2] *n* **1** the sense of feeling or touch. **2** sensation or feeling. **3** the quality of a thing as imparted through touch. **4** a particular quality or atmosphere. **5** intuitive skill or knowledge.
**feeler** *n* **1** an animal's feeling organ. **2** (*usu in pl*) a cautious attempt to ascertain the views of others.
**feeling**[1] *n* **1** an emotional state or reaction. **2** (*in pl*) susceptibility to impression; sensibility. **3** a conscious recognition; a sense. **4** an opinion or belief. **5** bodily consciousness or awareness. **6** capacity to respond emotionally. **7** the sensation of touching or being touched.
**feeling**[2] *adj* **1** expressing emotion or sensitivity. **2** able to feel or respond emotionally; sensitive. **3** easily moved emotionally; sympathetic.
**feet** *n* pl of FOOT[1].
**feign** *v* **1** to give a false appearance or impression of. **2** to pretend (something).
**feint**[1] *n* a mock blow or attack made as a diversion.
**feint**[2] *v* to make a feint.
**feint**[3] *adj* of rulings on paper: faint or pale.
**feisty** *adj* (**-ier, -iest**) *informal* spirited and determined.
**felicitations** *pl n* congratulations.
**felicitous** *adj formal* very well suited or expressed.
**felicity** *n* (*pl* **-ies**) *formal* **1** great happiness. **2** in the ability to use art or language effectively. **3** an apt expression.
**feline**[1] *adj* **1** of cats or the cat family. **2** resembling a cat.
**feline**[2] *n* a member of the cat family.
**fell**[1] *v* past tense of FALL[1].
**fell**[2] *v* to cut or knock down.
**fell**[3] *n* a rugged stretch of high moorland, *esp* in northern England.
**fell**[4] *adj* * **at one fell swoop** all at once.
**fellow** *n* **1** *informal* a man or a boy. **2** an equal in rank, power, or character. **3** either of a pair; a mate. **4** (*usu in pl*) a comrade or associate. **5** (*used before a noun*) belonging to the same group: *fellow travellers.* **6** *Brit* a member of a learned society. **7** an incorporated member of a college.
**fellowship** *n* **1** friendly relations between people. **2** community of interest or experience. **3** the state of being a fellow or associate. **4** a group of people with similar interests; an association. **5** the position of a college fellow.
**felon** *n* somebody who has committed a felony.
**felony** *n* (*pl* **-ies**) a serious crime. ➤ **felonious** *adj.*
**felt**[1] *n* a cloth made by compressing wool or fur.
**felt**[2] *v* past tense and past part. of FEEL[1].
**felt-tip pen** *n* a pen with a soft felt writing tip.
**female**[1] *adj* **1** relating to the sex that bears offspring or produces eggs. **2** of a plant or flower: having an ovary but no stamens. **3** designed with a hollow part for receiving a corresponding male part.
**female**[2] *n* a female animal, person, or plant.

**feminine** *adj* **1** female. **2** characteristic of women. **3** of the gender that includes most words or grammatical forms referring to females. ➤ **femininity** *n.*

**feminism** *n* the advocacy or furtherance of women's rights and interests. ➤ **feminist** *n and adj.*

**feminize** *or* **-ise** *v* **1** to give a feminine quality to. **2** to cause to take on feminine characteristics. ➤ **feminization** *n.*

**femme fatale** /ˌfam fəˈtahl/ *n* (*pl* **femmes fatales**) a seductive and dangerous woman.

**femur** *n* (*pl* **femurs** *or* **femora**) the thighbone. ➤ **femoral** *adj.*

**fen** *n* an area of low marshy or flooded land.

**fence[1]** *n* **1** a barrier of wire or boards enclosing an area. **2** an upright obstacle to be jumped by a horse. **3** *informal* a receiver of stolen goods. * **sit on the fence** to remain undecided or uncommitted.

**fence[2]** *v* **1** (*usu* + in) to enclose (an area) with a fence. **2** (*usu* + off) to separate (an area) with a fence. **3** *informal* to receive or sell (stolen goods). **4** to practise fencing. ➤ **fencer** *n.*

**fencing** *n* **1** the sport of attack and defence with a sword or foil. **2** fences, or material used for building them.

**fend** *v* (+ for) to provide a livelihood for somebody, *esp* oneself.

**fender** *n* **1** a cushion of rope or wood hung over the side of a ship to absorb impact. **2** a low metal guard to prevent coal spilling from a fire. **3** *NAmer* a wing or mudguard of a vehicle.

**feng shui** /ˌfung ˈshway, ˌfeng ˈshooh·i/ *n* a Chinese system of rules for the position and arrangement of a building, room, etc, according to the flow of energy in the environment.

**fennel** *n* a plant cultivated for its aromatic seeds and foliage.

**feral** *adj* **1** of an animal: not or no longer domesticated, wild. **2** fierce or savage.

**ferment[1]** *v* **1** of a substance: to undergo a chemical breakdown, e.g. by the action of bacteria. **2** to cause (a state of agitation). ➤ **fermentation** *n.*

**ferment[2]** *n* a state of unrest or upheaval.

**fern** *n* (*pl* **ferns** *or* **fern**) a flowerless plant with leaflike fronds. ➤ **ferny** *adj.*

**ferocious** *adj* extremely fierce or violent. ➤ **ferociously** *adv,* **ferociousness** *n,* **ferocity** *n.*

**ferret[1]** *n* a small fierce animal used for hunting small rodents or rabbits. ➤ **ferrety** *adj.*

**ferret[2]** *v* (**ferreted, ferreting**) **1** *informal* (+ about/around) to search about or around. **2** to hunt with ferrets.

**ferret out** *v informal* to find (information) by searching.

**Ferris wheel** *n* a fairground amusement consisting of a large upright revolving wheel with seats round the rim.

**ferrous** *adj* containing iron.

**ferrule** *n* a metal ring or cap on the end of a stick, umbrella, etc.

**ferry[1]** *v* (**-ies, -ied**) **1** to carry by boat or ship over a body of water. **2** to convey by car from one place to another.

**ferry[2]** *n* (*pl* **-ies**) a boat or ship that carries passengers and vehicles across a body of water.

**fertile** *adj* **1** of land or soil: capable of producing or bearing fruit; productive. **2** of the mind: imaginative or inventive. **3** of a person or animal: capable of breeding or reproducing. **4** of an egg: capable of growing or developing. ➤ **fertility** *n.*

**fertilize** *or* **-ise** *v* **1** to make (an ovule, egg, etc) capable of developing into a new individual by uniting with a male germ cell. **2** to apply a fertilizer to. ➤ **fertilization** *n.*

**fertilizer** *or* **-iser** *n* a substance used to make soil more fertile.

**fervent** *adj* showing deep emotion. ➤ **fervently** *adv.*

**fervid** *adj* passionately intense. ➤ **fervidly** *adv.*

**fervour** (*NAmer* **fervor**) *n* passionate intensity of feeling.

**festal** *adj* relating to a festival.

**fester** *v* **1** of a wound: to generate pus. **2** of food: to putrefy or rot. **3** to become worse; to intensify.

**festival** *n* **1** a time marked by special celebration. **2** a programme of cultural events or entertainment. **3** a religious feast.

**festive** *adj* **1** of or suitable for a feast or festival. **2** joyous or merry.

**festivity** *n* (*pl* **-ies**) **1** festive activity; a party or celebration. **2** a festival.

**festoon[1]** *n* a decorative hanging chain or strip.

**festoon[2]** *v* to decorate with festoons.

**fetal** *adj* = foetal (see FOETUS).

**fetch[1]** *v* **1** to go or come after (something or somebody) and bring them back. **2** to be sold for (a specified price).

**fetch[2]** *n* **1 a** the distance along open water or land over which the wind blows. **b** the distance traversed by waves without obstruction. **2** the act or an instance of fetching. **3** *archaic* a trick or stratagem.

**fetching** *adj* attractive or becoming.

**fetch up** *v informal* to arrive or come to rest.

**fete[1]** *or* **fête** *n Brit* an outdoor bazaar or other event held to raise money.

**fete[2]** *or* **fête** *v* to honour or celebrate extravagantly.

**fetid** *or* **foetid** *adj* having an unpleasant smell; stinking.

**fetish** *n* **1** an object believed to have magical power. **2** a form of sexual desire related to an object or bodily part.

**fetlock** *n* **1** a projection bearing a tuft of hair on the back of a horse's leg above the hoof. **2** the joint of the limb or tuft of hair at the fetlock.

**fetter**[1] *n* **1** a shackle for the feet. **2** (*usu in pl*) something that confines; a restraint.

**fetter**[2] *v* **1** to put fetters on. **2** to shackle or restrain.

**fettle** *n* a state of physical or mental fitness.

**fettuccine** /fetəˈcheeni/ *pl n* pasta in narrow ribbons.

**fetus** *n* see FOETUS.

**feud**[1] *n* a lasting state of hostilities.

**feud**[2] *v* to carry on a feud.

**feudal** *adj* of feudalism. ➤ **feudally** *adv.*

**feudalism** *n* the medieval social system in which vassals held land from a lord in return for allegiance and service.

**fever** *n* **1** a rise of body temperature above the normal. **2** a state of intense emotion or activity. ➤ **feverish** *adj.*

**fevered** *adj* **1** hot or flushed with fever. **2** agitated or excited.

**few**[1] *adj* **1** amounting to only a small number. **2** (**a few**) some but not many. ✱ **few and far between** scarce.

**few**[2] *n* **1** (*pl*) not many. **2** (**the few**) an exclusive group of people.

**fey** *adj* **1** unworldly and irresponsible. **2** able to see into the future.

**fez** *n* (*pl* **fezzes**) a red brimless hat with a flat top, worn by men in some Muslim countries.

**ff** *abbr* following pages.

**fiancé** *or* **fiancée** *n* a man or woman to whom a person is engaged to be married.

**fiasco** *n* (*pl* **-os**) a complete and ignominious failure.

**fiat** *n* an authoritative order or decree.

**fib**[1] *n informal* a trivial or childish lie.

**fib**[2] *v* (**fibbed, fibbing**) *informal* to tell a fib. ➤ **fibber** *n.*

**fibre** (*NAmer* **fiber**) *n* **1** an elongated tapering plant cell with thick walls. **2** a filament composing part of the intercellular matrix of connective tissue. **3** an elongated contractile cell of muscle tissue. **4** a slender natural or manufactured thread or filament, e.g. of wool or cotton. **5** material made of fibres. **6** the part of food that helps digestion. **7** strength or fortitude. ➤ **fibrous** *adj.*

**fibreboard** *n* a building material made by compressing wood fibres.

**fibreglass** *n* **1** a tough material made from glass fibres. **2** a combination of this with synthetic resins.

**fibre optics** *pl n* the use of glass or plastic fibres to transmit information as optical signals. ➤ **fibre-optic** *adj.*

**fibrillation** *n* **1** the forming of fibres or fibrils. **2** rapid irregular contractions of muscle fibres of the heart resulting in a lack of synchronization between heartbeat and pulse.

**fibula** *n* (*pl* **fibulae** *or* **fibulas**) the outer of the two bones between the knee and ankle.

**fickle** *adj* inconsistent in one's loyalties.

**fiction** *n* **1** literature describing imaginary people and events. **2** something untrue or invented. ➤ **fictional** *adj.*

**fictionalize** *or* **-ise** *v* to make into fiction.

**fictitious** *adj* invented or unreal.

**fiddle**[1] *n* **1** *informal* a violin. **2** *Brit, informal* a dishonest practice or swindle.

**fiddle**[2] *v* **1** to move one's hands or fingers restlessly. **2** *Brit* to falsify (accounts, etc). **3** *Brit* to get or contrive by cheating or deception. ✱ **fiddle with** *informal* to tamper or meddle with. ➤ **fiddler** *n.*

**fiddly** *adj* (**-ier, -iest**) *Brit, informal* intricate or awkward to use.

**fidelity** *n* **1** the quality of being faithful; loyalty. **2** accuracy in detail or reproduction.

**fidget**[1] *v* (**fidgeted, fidgeting**) to move or act restlessly or nervously. ➤ **fidgety** *adj.*

**fidget**[2] *n* **1** somebody who fidgets. **2** (*usu in pl*) restlessness.

**fief** *n* formerly, a feudal estate. ➤ **fiefdom** *n.*

**field**[1] *n* **1** an enclosed area of land used for cultivation or pasture. **2** a large expanse of ice. **3** an outdoor area marked for a game or sport. **4** an area of activity or knowledge. **5** (**the field**) the participants in a sports activity. **6** a region or space in which a given effect, e.g. magnetism, exists. **7** the area visible through an optical instrument.

**field**[2] *v* **1** to try to intercept (a ball struck in cricket or baseball). **2** to deal with (a question) by giving an impromptu answer. **3** to put (a team) into the field of play. ➤ **fielder** *n.*

**field day** *n* a time of freedom to enjoy oneself.

**field event** *n* an athletic event that is not a race, e.g. discus.

**field marshal** *n* an officer of the highest rank in the British army.

**field sport** *n* an open-air sport such as hunting or shooting.

**fiend** *n* **1** a demon. **2** a person of great wickedness or cruelty. **3** *informal* an enthusiast or devotee of an activity.

**fiendish** *adj* **1** extremely cruel or wicked. **2** extremely wicked or unpleasant. **3** *informal* difficult or complex. ➤ **fiendishly** *adv.*

**fierce** *adj* **1** violently hostile or aggressive. **2** extremely intense or severe. ➤ **fiercely** *adv,* **fierceness** *n.*

**fiery** *adj* (**-ier, -iest**) **1** consisting of or looking like fire. **2** showing strong emotion or spirit; passionate. **3** irascible.

**fiesta** *n* **1** a religious festival in Spain or Latin America. **2** a festive occasion.

**fife** *n* a small flute used in military bands.

**fifteen** *adj and n* the number 15. ➤ **fifteenth** *adj and n.*

**fifth** *adj and n* **1** having the position in a sequence corresponding to the number five. **2** one of five equal parts of something. ➤ **fifthly** *adv.*

**fifty** *adj and n* (*pl* **-ies**) **1** the number 50. **2** (*in pl*) the numbers 50 to 59. ➤ **fiftieth** *adj and n.*

**fig** *n* a fleshy fruit with many seeds.

**fight**[1] *v* (*past tense and past part.* **fought**) **1** to contend in battle or physical combat. **2** to disagree verbally; to argue. **3** (*often* + for/against) to strive or struggle. **4** to contend against or try to prevent. * **fight shy of** to avoid facing or getting.

**fight**[2] *n* **1** an act or spell of fighting. **2** a heated argument. **3** a protracted struggle for an objective.

**fighter** *n* **1** somebody or something that fights. **2** a fast manoeuvrable military aircraft.

**fighting chance** *n* a small chance that may be realized with an effort.

**fighting fit** *adj* in excellent health.

**fight off** *v* to ward off or repel by fighting or resisting.

**figment** *n* something fabricated or imagined.

**figurative** *adj* **1** characterized by or using figures of speech, *esp* metaphor. **2** representing by a figure or likeness. ➤ **figuratively** *adv.*

**figure**[1] *n* **1** a number symbol, *esp* an Arabic one. **2** bodily shape or form, *esp* of a woman. **3** an important or well-known person. **4** a diagram or pictorial illustration. **5** a geometrical diagram or shape.

**figure**[2] *v* **1** (*often* + in) to take an important or conspicuous part. **2** to calculate. **3** *informal* to seem reasonable or expected. **4** *chiefly NAmer, informal* to regard or consider (something). **5** to represent or portray by a figure or outline. * **figure on** *informal* to take into consideration.

**figurehead** *n* **1** an ornamental carved figure on a ship's bow. **2** a head or chief in name only.

**figure of speech** *n* a form of expression used to convey a special meaning or effect, e.g. metaphor.

**figure out** *v informal* **1** to discover or determine. **2** to solve or fathom.

**figure skating** *n* skating in distinctive circular patterns.

**figurine** *n* a small statue of a human figure.

**filament** *n* **1** a single threadlike object or part. **2** a slender conductor in an electric light bulb, made to glow by the passage of an electric current. **3** the stalk of a stamen that bears the anther.

**filbert** *n* a sweet hazelnut with a thick shell.

**filch** *v informal* to steal or pilfer.

**file**[1] *n* **1** a box or folder for keeping papers in order. **2** a collection of letters and documents on a subject. **3** a collection of data stored under one name in a computer.

**file**[2] *v* **1** to store or organize (papers) in files. **2** to submit or record (a lawsuit) officially.

**file**[3] *n* a row of people, animals, or things arranged one behind the other.

**file**[4] *v* to walk or move one behind the other.

**file**[5] *n* a steel tool with a rough surface for shaping or smoothing.

**file**[6] *v* to shape or smooth with a file.

**filial** *adj* relating to a son or daughter's relationship to a parent.

**filibuster** *n* the use of delaying tactics in a legislative assembly.

**filigree** *or* **filagree** *n* delicate ornamental work in fabric or metal.

**filing** *n* (*usu in pl*) a metal fragment rubbed off in filing.

**fill**[1] *v* **1** to make or become full. **2** to stop up or plug (a hole or gap). **3** to satisfy or fulfil (a need or requirement). **4** to spread through or occupy the whole of. **5** to exercise or appoint somebody to (an office or post).

**fill**[2] *n* as much as one needs or can tolerate.

**filler** *n* a substance used to fill holes or increase the bulk of something.

**fillet**[1] (*NAmer* **filet**) *n* **1** a fleshy boneless piece of meat. **2** a long slice of fish with the bones removed. **3** a narrow strip of material used as a headband. **4** a narrow flat architectural moulding.

**fillet**[2] *v* (**filleted, filleting**) **1** to remove the bones from (a fish). **2** to cut (meat or fish) into fillets.

**fill in** *v* **1** *Brit* to complete (a form). **2** (*often* + on) to give (somebody) information. **3** (*often* + for) to act as a temporary substitute.

**filling**[1] *n* something used to fill a hole or container.

**filling**[2] *adj* of food: pleasantly satisfying.

**fillip** *n* a boost or stimulus.

**fill out** *v* **1** to become fatter. **2** *chiefly NAmer* to complete (a form).

**filly** *n* (*pl* **-ies**) **1** a young female horse. **2** *informal* a lively young woman.

**film**[1] *n* **1** a roll or strip of plastic coated with a light-sensitive emulsion for taking photographs or moving pictures. **2** a thin transparent sheet of plastic used as a wrapping. **3** a story, documentary, etc, recorded on film for showing in cinemas or on television. **4** a thin layer or covering.

**film**[2] *v* **1** to make a film of. **2** (*often* + over) to become covered with a thin layer.

**filmy** *adj* (**-ier, -iest**) **1** resembling or made of film. **2** covered with a mist or film.

**filter**[1] *n* **1** a substance or device that allows liquid or gas to pass through and separates out solid matter. **2** a device or material for suppressing light or sound waves of certain frequencies. **3** *Brit* a signal that allows traffic to turn left or right while the main flow is stopped.

**filter**[2] *v* **1** to pass or move through a filter. **2** of information: to become known gradually. **3** *Brit* of traffic: to turn left or right from the main flow.

**filth** *n* **1** dirt or refuse. **2** obscene or pornographic material.

**filthy** *adj* (**-ier, -iest**) **1** extremely or offensively dirty. **2** vile or lewd. **3** *informal* of the weather: stormy. **4** *informal* of books or magazines: obscene or pornographic. * **filthy rich** extremely wealthy.

**filtrate** *n* material that has passed through a filter.

**filtration** *n* the process of passing liquid through a filter.

**fin** *n* **1** a flattened appendage on a fish or whale, used in propelling or guiding the body. **2** a flattened projecting part attached to a vessel or aircraft to guide or stabilize it. **3** a flipper used in underwater swimming.

**final**[1] *adj* **1** being the last; occurring at the end. **2** conclusive or unchangeable.

**final**[2] *n* **1** the last game in a sport or competition, which determines the overall winner. **2** (*in pl*) a set of examinations at the end of an academic or professional course.

**finale** *n* the last part or item in a piece of music or other entertainment.

**finalist** *n* a contestant or team taking part in the final round of a competition.

**finality** *n* **1** the condition of being final. **2** a determined air or tone.

**finalize** *or* **-ise** *v* **1** to put into a final or finished form. **2** to give final approval to.

**finance**[1] *n* **1** the circulation and use of money in business and banking. **2** the management of large amounts of money. **3** (*in pl*) resources of money.

**finance**[2] *v* to raise or provide money for.

**financial** *adj* relating to money or finance. ➤ **financially** *adv.*

**financial year** *n* a fixed period of twelve months reckoned for tax and accounting purposes.

**financier** *n* a person who manages large-scale finance or investment.

**finch** *n* a songbird with a short conical beak.

**find**[1] *v* (*past tense and past part.* **found**) **1** to come upon or encounter accidentally or by searching. **2** to experience or be aware of. **3** to recognize (something) to be present in something or native to an area. **4** to seek or provide (money or time) for a purpose. **5** to discover or obtain by effort or experiment. **6** to seek or experience (a feeling). **7** to attain or reach (a level, etc). **8** to perceive (oneself) to be in a specified place or condition. **9** to discover (a person or thing) to have a specified quality, attribute, etc. **10** of a jury: to pronounce (a defendant) guilty or innocent after deliberation. * **find fault** (*often* + with) to criticize unfavourably. **find one's feet** to gain confidence with experience.

**find**[2] *n* a valuable object or talented person discovered.

**finding** *n* the result of an investigation or enquiry.

**find out** *v* **1** to learn or discover by study or inquiry. **2** to detect (a person) in a wrongdoing.

**fine**[1] *adj* **1** superior in quality. **2** satisfactory or acceptable. **3** of weather: dry and sunny. **4** in good health or spirits. **5** characterized by elegance or refinement. **6** performed with extreme care and accuracy. **7** narrow in gauge or width. **8** consisting of relatively small particles. **9** of a distinction: subtle or precise. * **cut it fine** to act at the last available moment. **go over with a fine-tooth comb** to search or examine in great detail. ➤ **finely** *adv.*

**fine**[2] *v* (*often* + down) to make finer in quality or size.

**fine**[3] *n* a sum payable as punishment for an offence.

**fine**[4] *v* to punish with a fine.

**fine art** *n* an aesthetic art such as painting or sculpture.

**fine print** *n* small print in which parts of some legal documents are printed.

**finery** *n* elaborate or special clothes or jewellery.

**finesse** *n* **1** refinement or delicacy of workmanship. **2** skilful and subtle handling of a situation.

**fine-tune** *v* to make small adjustments to.

**finger**[1] *n* **1** each of the five parts at the end of the hand, *esp* one other than the thumb. **2** something that resembles a finger in being long and narrow. **3** the breadth of a finger used as a measure of alcoholic drink. * **keep one's fingers crossed** to hope for the best. **not lift a finger** to make no effort to help. **put one's finger on** to identify a problem or cause.

**finger**[2] *v* to touch or handle.

**fingerboard** *n* the part of a stringed instrument against which the fingers press the strings to vary the pitch.

**fingering** *n* the use or position of the fingers in sounding notes on an instrument.

**fingernail** *n* the thin horny plate on the upper surface at the tip of a finger.

**fingerprint**[1] *n* an ink impression of the lines upon the fingertip taken for purposes of identification.

**fingerprint**[2] *v* to make an impression of the fingerprints of (somebody) for identification purposes.

**finial** *n* an ornament at the top of a spire, gable, etc, or on a piece of furniture.

**finicky** *adj* **1** having exacting taste or standards; fussy. **2** requiring delicate attention to detail.

**finish**[1] *v* **1** to reach or bring to an end. **2** to stop (doing something). **3** to eat, drink, use, or dispose of entirely. **4** to end a competition, etc in a specified place or order. **5** to complete or perfect (something). **6** to complete (something) by giving it an attractive surface or edge. **7** *informal* (*also* + off) to bring about the death or ruin of. **8** to exhaust utterly. **9** (*often* + up) to reach a specified place or state. * **finish with 1** to have no further need of. **2** to break off relations with. ➤ **finisher** *n.*

**finish**[2] *n* **1** the end or final stage. **2** the place where a race ends. **3** the final treatment or coating of a surface. **4** the final appearance of a manufactured article.

**finishing school** *n* a private school that trains girls in social refinement.

**finite** *adj* **1** having limits of size or extent. **2** subject to natural limitations.

**Finn** *n* a native or inhabitant of Finland.

**fiord** *n* see FJORD.

**fir** *n* an evergreen tree with flat needle-shaped leaves.

**fire**[1] *n* **1** the flames, heat, and light, produced when something burns. **2** a mass of burning fuel. **3** a destructive process of burning e.g. of a building or forest. **4** *Brit* a small domestic heater using gas or electricity. **5** intense energy or emotion. **6** the discharge of guns. **7** criticism or verbal attack. * **catch fire** to begin to burn. **hang fire** to hesitate or delay. **on fire** burning. **open/cease fire** to begin/stop shooting a weapon. **play with fire** to take foolhardy risks. **set fire to/set on fire** to start (something) burning, *esp* accidentally or maliciously. **under fire 1** being shot at. **2** being harshly criticized.

**fire**[2] *v* **1** to discharge a bullet or other projectile from (a gun or other weapon). **2** to direct (questions, commands, etc) in quick succession at somebody. **3** to dismiss (an employee). **4** to supply (a heating system) with fuel. **5** to set fire to (something). **6** to bake (pottery, ceramics, or bricks) in a kiln. **7** to kindle or stimulate (a person's imagination). **8** (*also* + up) to inspire or fill with enthusiasm. **9** of an internal-combustion engine: to become active on ignition of its fuel. * **in the firing line** most likely to be attacked or criticized.

**fire alarm** *n* a device that sounds to give warning of a fire.

**firearm** *n* a portable gun, *esp* a pistol or rifle.

**fireball** *n* **1** a ball of fire or flame. **2** *informal* a highly energetic person.

**firebomb**[1] *n* an incendiary bomb.

**firebomb**[2] *v* to attack or damage with a firebomb.

**firebrand** *n* **1** a piece of burning wood. **2** a person who creates unrest or strife.

**firebreak** *n* a strip of cleared land intended to check the spread of a fire.

**fire brigade** *n* an organization for controlling and putting out fires.

**firecracker** *n* a small firework that explodes with a series of bangs and jumps.

**fire door** *n* a fire-resistant door in a building.

**fire drill** *n* a practice of the emergency drill to be followed in the event of a fire.

**fire engine** *n* a vehicle that carries firefighting equipment and firefighters.

**fire escape** *n* a staircase or other means of escape from a burning building.

**fire-extinguisher** *n* an apparatus for putting out fires with chemicals.

**firefighter** *n* a person trained to fight and put out fires. ➤ **firefighting** *n.*

**firefly** *n* (*pl* **-ies**) a night-flying beetle that produces a bright intermittent light.

**fireguard** *n* a protective framework placed in front of an open fire.

**fire irons** *pl n* a set of tongs, poker, and shovel for tending a household fire.

**fireman** *n* (*pl* **firemen**) a male firefighter.

**fireplace** *n* an opening at the base of a chimney to hold a domestic fire.

**firepower** *n* the capacity to deliver effective fire on a target.

**fireproof** *adj* able to withstand fire or high temperatures.

**fire-raising** *n Brit* the act of deliberately setting fire to property. ➤ **fire-raiser** *n.*

**fire station** *n* a building where firefighting apparatus is kept and firefighters are on duty.

**firestorm** *n* a large fierce fire sustained by strong currents of air.

**firetrap** *n* a building that is difficult to escape from in case of fire.

**firewood** *n* wood used for fuel.

**firework** *n* **1** a device containing explosive material that goes off with dramatic light and sound effects when ignited. **2** (*in pl*) a display of temper or disagreement. **3** a sparkling display of brilliance.

**firing line** *n* **1** the troops stationed in the front line of battle. **2** the battle line from which fire is discharged against the enemy. * **in the firing line** in the forefront of an activity, *esp* one involving risk, difficulty, or criticism.

**firing squad** *n* a detachment of soldiers detailed to execute a condemned person.

**firm**[1] *adj* **1** solidly or securely fixed. **2** not yielding to pressure; solid and compact. **3** having a sustained strength. **4** of an opinion or principle: unchanging and steadfast. **5** having a strong relationship. **6** of a decision or arrangement: settled or definite. **7** resolute in dealing with people or situations. * **a firm hand** strong control or guidance. **hold/stand firm** to remain steadfast and unyielding. ➤ **firmly** *adv*, **firmness** *n.*

**firm**[2] *v* **1** to make firm. **2** (*also* + up) to settle or complete (an arrangement).

**firm**[3] *n* a business organization.
**firmament** *n* the heavens.
**first**[1] *adj* **1** having the position in a sequence corresponding to the number one. **2** preceding all the rest; earliest. **3** in the top or winning place. **4** most important. ✱ **first thing** early in the morning.
**first**[2] *adv* **1** before anybody or anything else. **2** to start with. **3** for the first time.
**first**[3] *n and pron* **1** a person, thing, or group, that is first. **2** a thing that has never happened before. **3** the lowest forward gear of a motor vehicle. **4** in Britain, a first-class honours degree. ✱ **at first** to start with; initially.
**first aid** *n* emergency treatment given to an ill or injured person. ➤ **first-aider** *n.*
**firstborn** *n* an eldest child.
**first class** *n* **1** the first or highest group in a system of classification. **2** the highest class of travel accommodation.
**first-degree** *adj* of a burn: mild and causing only a reddening of the skin.
**first-foot** *n esp* in Scotland, the first person to cross one's threshold in the New Year.
**first-footing** *n* the practice of visiting friends at New Year to be the first across the threshold in that year.
**first-hand** *adj* coming directly from the original source or personal experience. ✱ **at first hand** directly; without an intermediary.
**first lady** *n* the wife of a US president.
**first name** *n* a personal or given name.
**first person** *n* in grammar, the term used to refer to the speaker or speakers, represented by the pronouns *I* or *we*.
**first-rate** *adj* of the best class or quality; excellent.
**firth** *n* a sea inlet or estuary.
**fiscal** *adj* relating to income from taxation. ➤ **fiscally** *adv.*
**fish**[1] *n* (*pl* **fishes** *or* **fish**) **1** a cold-blooded animal that lives in water, with a long scaly body, fins, and gills. **2** the flesh of a fish used as food. **3** a person of a specified kind: *a strange fish.* ✱ **have other fish to fry** to have more important things to do.
**fish**[2] *v* **1** to try to catch fish. **2** to feel about looking for something. **3** (*often* + for) to try to obtain something by cunning or devious means.
**fisherman** *n* (*pl* **fishermen**) a person who catches fish as a living or for sport.
**fishery** *n* (*pl* **-ies**) a place or establishment for catching fish and other sea animals.
**fish-eye lens** *n* a wide-angle lens with a protruding front, covering an angle up to 180°.
**fishing rod** *n* a rod with a reel, used with a line and hook for catching fish.
**fishmonger** *n chiefly Brit* a person who sells fish for food.
**fishnet** *n* a coarse open-mesh fabric.
**fishwife** *n* (*pl* **fishwives**) a vulgar or loud-mouthed woman.
**fishy** *adj* (**-ier, -iest**) **1** resembling fish, *esp* in taste or smell. **2** *informal* causing doubt or suspicion.
**fissile** *adj* **1** of an atom or element: capable of undergoing nuclear fission. **2** of rock: easily split.
**fission** *n* **1** a splitting or breaking up into parts. **2** the splitting of an atomic nucleus with the release of large amounts of energy. **3** reproduction by division of cells into two or more parts which grow into new organisms.
**fissure** *n* a long narrow opening in rock.
**fist** *n* the hand clenched with the fingers doubled into the palm. ➤ **fistful** *n.*
**fisticuffs** *pl n* fighting with the fists.
**fit**[1] *adj* (**fitter, fittest**) **1** adapted or suited to a purpose. **2** in a suitable state. **3** strong and healthy. **4** acceptable or worthy. ✱ **see/think fit** to consider it proper or advisable. ➤ **fitness** *n.*
**fit**[2] *v* (**fitting,** *past tense and past part.* **fitted** *or NAmer* **fit**) **1** to be the right size or shape for. **2** to insert or adjust (something) so that it is correctly in position. **3** to install (a device or component). **4** to supply with equipment. **5** to match or correspond to. **6** to make (somebody) suitable for something. ➤ **fitter** *n.*
**fit**[3] *n* the manner in which something fits.
**fit**[4] *n* **1** a sudden violent attack of a disease accompanied by convulsions or unconsciousness. **2** an outburst of coughing, sneezing, etc. **3** a rapid burst of an activity. ✱ **by/in fits and starts** in an impulsive or irregular manner.
**fitful** *adj* spasmodic or intermittent. ➤ **fitfully** *adv.*
**fitment** *n* a fixed piece of equipment or furniture.
**fitted** *adj* **1** made to fit a space or shape closely. **2** (+ for/to) suitable or qualified for something.
**fitting**[1] *adj* appropriate to a situation. ➤ **fittingly** *adv.*
**fitting**[2] *n* **1** the trying on of clothes which are being made or altered. **2** a small standardized part. **3** (*in pl*) items in a property, e.g. carpets, curtains, etc, that the owner is entitled to remove if the property is sold. **4** the act of installing or securing something.
**five** *n* the number 5. ➤ **five** *adj.*
**fiver** *n informal Brit* a five-pound note.
**fix**[1] *v* **1** to position and attach firmly. **2** to make firm or stable or permanent. **3** to decide on (a date, price, etc). **4** to arrange (something) or make it possible. **5** to repair or mend (something). **6** to put right. **7** *chiefly NAmer* to prepare (food or drink). **8** to influence by illicit means. ➤ **fixer** *n.*
**fix**[2] *n informal* **1** a difficult or embarrassing situation. **2** a dose of a narcotic drug.

**fixate** *v* to focus one's eyes or attention on. * **be fixated on** to be obsessed with.

**fixation** *n* an excessive attachment to or preoccupation with somebody or something.

**fixative** *n* a substance used to protect or hold something.

**fixity** *n* the state of being fixed or stable.

**fixture** *n* **1** a piece of equipment or furniture that is fixed in position. **2** (*in pl*) items in a property, e.g. plumbing, cupboards, worktops, etc, that the owner leaves if the property is sold. **3** *chiefly Brit* a sporting event scheduled for a particular date.

**fix up** *v* **1** to organize or arrange. **2** *informal* to provide with something.

**fizz**[1] *v* **1** to make a hissing or sputtering sound. **2** of a liquid: to produce bubbles of gas.

**fizz**[2] *n* **1** the act or sound of fizzing. **2** spirit or liveliness.

**fizzle** *v* to make a weak fizzing sound.

**fizzle out** *v informal* to fail or end feebly or disappointingly.

**fizzy** *adj* (**-ier, -iest**) **1** of a drink: effervescent. **2** lively and exuberant.

**fjord** *or* **fiord** *n* a narrow inlet of the sea, *esp* in Norway.

**fl.** *abbr* fluid.

**flab** *n informal* soft loose body tissue.

**flabbergast** *v informal* to shock or astonish greatly.

**flabby** *adj* (**-ier, -iest**) of flesh: lacking resilience or firmness. ➤ **flabbiness** *n.*

**flaccid** /'flaksid, 'flasid/ *adj* **1** soft or limp. **2** lacking vigour or force. ➤ **flaccidity** *n.*

**flack** *n* see FLAK.

**flag**[1] *n* a piece of fabric of distinctive design used as an identifying symbol of a nation, or as a signalling device.

**flag**[2] *v* (**flagged, flagging**) **1** to mark for attention. **2** to direct by signalling with a flag.

**flag**[3] *v* (**flagged, flagging**) to become tired and lose energy.

**flag**[4] *or* **flagstone** *n* a slab of stone used for paving.

**flag**[5] *n* a plant with long bladelike leaves.

**flag down** *v* to signal to (a driver or vehicle) to stop.

**flagellate** *v* to whip (somebody) as a religious punishment or for sexual gratification. ➤ **flagellation** *n.*

**flagon** *n* a large squat jug or bottle for holding cider, wine, etc.

**flagpole** *or* **flagstaff** *n* a tall pole on which to hoist a flag.

**flagrant** *adj* conspicuous and outrageous. ➤ **flagrantly** *adv.*

**flagship** *n* **1** the ship that carries the commander of a fleet. **2** something considered the best thing produced by an organization.

**flail**[1] *n* a threshing implement consisting of a short swinging stick attached to a handle.

**flail**[2] *v* (*often* + about/around) to wave the arms and legs violently.

**flair** *n* **1** (+ for) a natural ability or talent. **2** style and originality.

**flak** *or* **flack** *n* **1** the fire from anti-aircraft guns. **2** *informal* heavy criticism.

**flake**[1] *n* **1** a small loose particle. **2** a thin flattened piece or layer.

**flake**[2] *v* **1** (+ off) to come away in flakes. **2** to separate into flakes. ➤ **flaky** *adj.*

**flambé**[1] *adj* of food: sprinkled with brandy, rum, etc and set alight.

**flambé**[2] *v* (**flambés, flambéed, flambéing**) to sprinkle (food) with brandy, rum, etc and set it alight.

**flamboyant** *adj* **1** lively and ostentatious. **2** colourful or exotic. ➤ **flamboyance** *n,* **flamboyantly** *adv.*

**flame**[1] *n* **1** a bright mass of burning gas coming from something that is on fire. **2** a brilliant reddish orange colour. **3** *informal* a former lover.

**flame**[2] *v* **1** to burn strongly. **2** to set alight. **3** of an emotion: to be felt or displayed with intensity. **4** to send an abusive email message to.

**flamenco** *n* (*pl* **-os**) a lively style of Spanish guitar music accompanied by singing and dancing.

**flamethrower** *n* a weapon that sends out a burning stream of liquid.

**flamingo** *n* (*pl* **-os** *or* **-oes**) a wading bird with long legs, curved beak, and rosy-white and pink plumage.

**flammable** *adj* easily set on fire.

**flan** *n* a dish of a pastry case baked with a sweet or savoury filling.

**flange** *n* a projecting rib or rim for strengthening or guiding something.

**flank**[1] *n* **1** the side of a person or animal between the ribs and the hip. **2** the side of something large, such as a mountain. **3** the right or left of a formation of troops or ships.

**flank**[2] *v* to be at the side of.

**flannel**[1] *n* **1** a loosely woven wool or worsted fabric with a slightly napped surface. **2** (*in pl*) trousers made of flannel. **3** *Brit* a small square of towelling used for washing. **4** *chiefly Brit, informal* vague or meaningless talk.

**flannel**[2] *v* (**flannelled, flannelling,** *NAmer* **flanneled, flanneling**) *chiefly Brit, informal* to speak or write in a vague or meaningless way.

**flannelette** *n* a cotton fabric resembling flannel.

**flap**[1] *n* **1** a flexible or hinged piece that hangs loose or covers an opening. **2** a movable surface on an aircraft wing for controlling its upward or downward movement. **3** a flapping movement. **4** *informal* a state of excitement or panic.

**flap**[2] *v* (**flapped, flapping**) **1** to move up and down or from side to side, creating a noise. **2** of a bird or bat: to move its wings in flight. **3** *informal* to be agitated or panic.

**flapjack** *n* **1** a soft biscuit made with oats and syrup. **2** *NAmer* a pancake.

**flapper** *n informal* a fashionable young woman of the 1920s.

**flare**[1] *v* **1** to shine or blaze with a sudden flame. **2** (*usu* + up) to become suddenly angry. **3** (*usu* + up) of violence, etc: to break out. **4** (*usu* + out) to get wider at one end. ➤ **flareup** *n.*

**flare**[2] *n* **1** a sudden glaring light or flame. **2** a device producing a very bright light used as a signal. **3** a sudden outburst of anger. **4** a gradual widening at one end. **5** (*in pl*) flared trousers.

**flash**[1] *v* **1** to shine with a bright light briefly or intermittently. **2** to move past at high speed. **3** to direct (a smile, look, etc) briefly. **4** to show quickly or briefly. **5** to display ostentatiously. **6** *informal* of a man: to show his genitals in public. ➤ **flasher** *n.*

**flash**[2] *n* **1** a sudden burst of light. **2** a sudden burst of perception or feeling. **3** a camera attachment that produces a flash of light for photography in poor light. **4** a fleeting glimpse. **5** an armband or patch worn on a uniform as a distinguishing symbol. ✱ **flash in the pan** a sudden brief success. **in a flash** very quickly.

**flash**[3] *adj informal* vulgarly ostentatious.

**flashback** *n* **1** a scene in a book, play, or film that shows events earlier than the time of the main action. **2** a sudden recollection of a past event.

**flash flood** *n* a sudden local flood caused by heavy rainfall.

**flashgun** *n* a device that produces a flash of bright artificial light, used for taking photographs in poor light.

**flashing** *n* a sheet of metal used in waterproofing a roof or the angle between a vertical surface and a roof.

**flashlight** *n* **1** a flashgun. **2** a powerful electric torch.

**flash point** *n* **1** the temperature at which vapour from a volatile substance ignites. **2** a point at which violence or anger erupts.

**flashy** *adj* (**-ier, -iest**) **1** tastelessly ostentatious or flamboyant. **2** superficially brilliant.

**flask** *n* **1** a glass container with a narrow neck. **2** a vacuum flask.

**flat**[1] *adj* (**flatter, flattest**) **1** of a surface: horizontal, not sloping. **2** smooth, without raised or hollow areas. **3** having a broad surface and little thickness. **4** clearly unmistakable; downright: *a flat refusal.* **5** of a charge: fixed. **6** dull or monotonous. **7** having lost effervescence or sparkle. **8** of a tyre: lacking air, deflated. **9** of a battery: completely or partially discharged. **10** of a musical note: lowered a semitone in pitch. **11** lower than the proper musical pitch. ✱ **that's flat** *informal* that's final. ➤ **flatly** *adv.*

**flat**[2] *n* **1** a flat part or surface. **2** (*in pl*) an area of level ground near water. **3** a musical note one semitone lower than a specified or particular note, or the character (♭) indicating this. **4** *informal* a flat tyre. **5** (*often* **the Flat**) the flat-racing season. ✱ **on the flat** on level ground.

**flat**[3] *adv* **1** on or against a flat surface. **2** so as to be spread out; at full length. **3** *informal* completely, utterly. ✱ **fall flat** to fail to achieve the intended effect. **flat out** as hard or fast as possible.

**flat**[4] *n* a self-contained set of rooms within a larger building used as a dwelling.

**flat feet** *pl n* a condition with the arches of the insteps flattened so that the soles rest entirely on the ground.

**flatfish** *n* (*pl* **flatfishes** *or* **flatfish**) a sea fish with both eyes on the upper surface of its flattened body.

**flat-footed** *adj* **1** affected with flat feet. **2** *informal* inept or clumsy.

**flatmate** *n Brit* someone who shares a flat with another person.

**flat race** *n* a race for horses on a course without jumps. ➤ **flat racing** *n.*

**flatten** *v* **1** (*also* + out) to make or become flat or flatter. **2** to press (oneself) flush against a surface. **3** to knock or raze to the ground.

**flatter** *v* **1** to praise insincerely out of self-interest. **2** (*usu in passive*) to make (somebody) feel valued or needed. **3** to display (a person or thing) to advantage. ➤ **flatterer** *n.*

**flattery** *n* insincere or excessive praise.

**flatulent** *adj* suffering from an accumulation of gas in the alimentary canal. ➤ **flatulence** *n.*

**flatworm** *n* a worm with a flattened body.

**flaunt** *v* to display ostentatiously or impudently.

***Usage Note:*** Do not confuse this word with *flout*, which means 'to treat with contemptuous disregard': *to flout the rules.*

**flautist** *n* a person who plays the flute.

**flavour**[1] (*NAmer* **flavor**) *n* **1** the particular taste of a substance in the mouth. **2** a characteristic quality. **3** a representative sample. ✱ **flavour of the month** a person or thing that is currently fashionable. ➤ **flavouring** *n,* **flavourless** *adj.*

**flavour**[2] (*NAmer* **flavor**) *v* to give or add flavour to. ➤ **flavoured** *adj.*

**flaw** *n* **1** a blemish or imperfection. **2** a hidden defect that can cause failure under stress. **3** a weakness or error. ➤ **flawless** *adj.*

**flawed** *adj* blemished or imperfect.

**flax** *n* **1** a slender blue-flowered plant cultivated for its strong woody fibre and seeds. **2** the fibre of the flax plant,

**flaxen** *adj* of hair: pale soft yellow.

**flay** *v* **1** to strip off the skin. **2** to whip savagely.

**flea** *n* a wingless jumping insect that feeds on the blood of animals. * **a flea in one's ear** a sharp reprimand.

**flea market** *n* an open-air market selling secondhand articles.

**fleapit** *n Brit, informal* a shabby cinema or theatre.

**fleck**[1] *n* **1** a small spot of colour or light. **2** a grain or particle.

**fleck**[2] *v* to cover with small spots or marks.

**fledged** *adj* of a young bird: having wing feathers developed enough for it to fly.

**fledgling** *or* **fledgeling** *n* a young bird that has just begun to fly.

**flee** *v* (**flees, fleeing,** *past tense and past part.* **fled**) to run away from danger or harm.

**fleece**[1] *n* **1** a sheep's coat of wool. **2** a soft warm fabric with a thick pile. **3** a jacket made of a synthetic fabric with a thick pile. ➤ **fleecy** *adj.*

**fleece**[2] *v informal* to overcharge or swindle.

**fleet**[1] *n* **1** a number of warships under a single command. **2** a group of vehicles operating together or owned by one management.

**fleet**[2] *adj* quick and nimble.

**fleeting** *adj* brief or transitory. ➤ **fleetingly** *adv.*

**flesh** *n* **1** the soft parts of the body. **2** an edible pulpy part of a plant or fruit. **3** the physical being of humans. **4** the physical or sensual aspect of human nature. * **in the flesh** in person.

**fleshly** *adj* (**-ier, -iest**) belonging or relating to the body; carnal or sensual.

**flesh out** *v* to add detail to (an idea or proposal).

**fleshpots** *pl n* places that offer exciting or sensual forms of entertainment.

**fleshy** *adj* (**-ier, -iest**) **1** plump. **2** succulent or pulpy.

**fleur-de-lis** *or* **fleur-de-lys** *n* (*pl* **fleurs-de-lis** *or* **fleurs-de-lys**) a stylized representation of three lily petals bound together at the base.

**flew** *v* past tense of FLY[1].

**flex**[1] *v* **1** to bend (a limb or joint). **2** to contract or tense (a muscle). **3** to bend and revert to an original position or shape.

**flex**[2] *n chiefly Brit* an electrical cable used to connect an appliance to a socket.

**flexible** *adj* **1** capable of being bent. **2** adaptable or versatile. ➤ **flexibility** *n,* **flexibly** *adv.*

**flexitime** (*NAmer* **flextime**) *n* a system by which employees can vary their working hours.

**flick**[1] *n* **1** a quick sharp movement with a hand. **2** *informal* a cinema film.

**flick**[2] *v* **1** to make a quick sharp movement of a hand. **2** to move with a flick. **3** to move lightly or jerkily. * **flick through** to look at or read cursorily.

**flicker**[1] *v* **1** to burn or shine unsteadily. **2** to move irregularly or unsteadily. **3** to appear irregularly or indistinctly.

**flicker**[2] *n* **1** an instance of flickering. **2** a momentary feeling or sensation.

**flick knife** *n* a knife with a blade that springs out from the handle when a button is pressed.

**flier** *n* see FLYER.

**flight** *n* **1** the act of flying. **2** a journey made in an aircraft or spacecraft. **3** the path of a struck ball or other object moving through the air. **4** escape from danger or captivity. **5** a group of birds or aircraft flying together. **6** a series of stairs leading from one floor to the next. * **flight of fancy** an imaginative idea. ➤ **flightless** *adj.*

**flight deck** *n* **1** the cockpit of a passenger aircraft. **2** the deck of an aircraft carrier.

**flight path** *n* the course taken by an aircraft or spacecraft.

**flighty** *adj* (**-ier, -iest**) irresponsible or flirtatious.

**flimsy** *adj* (**-ier, -iest**) **1** weak and insubstantial. **2** thin and light. **3** implausible or unconvincing. ➤ **flimsily** *adv.*

**flinch** *v* **1** to make a nervous shrinking movement in response to fear or pain. **2** (+ from) to avoid something from fear or nervousness.

**fling**[1] *v* (*past tense and past part.* **flung**) **1** to throw or hurl with force. **2** to send or put somewhere unceremoniously. **3** (+ into) to involve (oneself) energetically in an activity. **4** to move in a hasty or violent manner.

**fling**[2] *n* **1** a brief period of enjoyment. **2** *informal* a brief sexual relationship. **3** a vigorous Scottish reel or dance.

**flint** *n* **1** a hard quartz found in chalk or limestone. **2** a flaked piece of this used in antiquity to form a tool or weapon. **3** a metal alloy used for producing a spark in a cigarette lighter.

**flintlock** *n* an old type of gun with the charge ignited by sparks struck from a flint.

**flip**[1] *v* (**flipped, flipping**) **1** to turn over with a quick neat movement. **2** to propel with a flick of the fingers. **3** *informal* to lose self-control. * **flip one's lid** *informal* to become angry or lose self-control * **flip through** to read through quickly or casually.

**flip**[2] *n* **1** a flipping movement or action. **2** a somersault.

**flip**[3] *adj informal* flippant or impertinent.

**flip-flop** *n* a light sandal with two diagonal straps anchored between the big and second toes.

**flippant** *adj* not showing proper respect or seriousness. ➤ **flippancy** *n,* **flippantly** *adv.*

**flipper** *n* **1** a broad flat limb of seals and turtles, used for swimming. **2** a flat rubber paddle worn on each foot for underwater swimming.

**flip side** *n informal* **1** the less important side of a pop record. **2** the less familiar or more unwelcome side of a person or situation.

**flirt**[1] *v* to show playful sexual interest. * **flirt with 1** to show superficial or casual interest in. **2** to risk (danger or death) deliberately for excitement. ➤ **flirtation** *n*, **flirty** *adj.*

**flirt**[2] *n* a person who likes to flirt.

**flirtatious** *adj* liking to flirt. ➤ **flirtatiously** *adv.*

**flit**[1] *v* (**flitted, flitting**) to move or fly lightly and quickly.

**flit**[2] *n Brit* a hurried departure or escape.

**flitter** *v* to move about in a random or agitated way.

**float**[1] *n* **1** something that rests on the surface of a fluid without sinking. **2** a platform of a lorry supporting an exhibit in a parade. **3** an electrically powered delivery vehicle. **4** a sum of money available for giving change at a stall, in a shop, etc.

**float**[2] *v* **1** to rest on the surface of a fluid without sinking. **2** to drift on or through a liquid, or move gently in the air. **3** to wander aimlessly. **4** in sport, to send (a ball) on a high smooth flight. **5** to present (an idea) for consideration. **6** of a currency: to find its own level in the international exchange market. **7** to offer the shares of (a company) for the first time for sale on the stock market.

**floatation** *n* see FLOTATION.

**flock**[1] *n* **1** a group of birds or mammals in one place. **2** (*also in pl*) a large group. **3** a Christian congregation.

**flock**[2] *v* to gather or move in a crowd.

**flock**[3] *n* **1** a tuft of wool or cotton fibre. **2** woollen or cotton material used as stuffing. **3** short or pulverized fibre used to form a velvety pattern on cloth or paper. ➤ **flocky** *adj.*

**floe** *n* a sheet of floating ice.

**flog** *v* (**flogged, flogging**) **1** to beat with a stick or whip. **2** *Brit, informal* to sell. * **flog a dead horse** to waste time pursuing already settled issues.

**flood**[1] *n* **1** an overflowing of water onto dry land. **2** (**the Flood**) the biblical flooding of the earth caused by God as a punishment for human wickedness. **3** the inflow of water associated with a rising tide. **4** *literary* a body of water such as a river or the sea. **5** an overwhelming quantity or volume.

**flood**[2] *v* **1** to cover with or become submerged under water that has overflowed. **2** of a river: to rise and overflow its banks. **3** to arrive in a continuous stream or overwhelming quantities. **4** of sound, light, etc: to fill (a place).

**floodgate** *n* **1** a gate for shutting out or admitting water. **2** (*also in pl*) something that keeps back a potentially overwhelming flow.

**floodlight**[1] *n* a powerful lamp used for artificially illuminating a theatre stage or a sports ground.

**floodlight**[2] *v* (*past tense and past part.* **floodlit**) to illuminate with floodlights.

**floodplain** *n* a low-lying area beside a river that is subject to flooding.

**flood tide** *n* a tide while flowing in.

**floor**[1] *n* **1** the lower surface of a room or passage. **2** the bottom inside surface of a cave, the sea, etc. **3** a storey of a building. **4** (**the floor**) the part of a legislative or other assembly in which members sit and speak. **5** an area in a stock exchange where trading is done. **6** a lower limit. * **take the floor 1** to make a formal speech. **2** to begin dancing.

**floor**[2] *v* **1** to fit with a floor. **2** to knock to the floor or ground. **3** to confuse or disconcert.

**floorboard** *n* a long board or plank forming part of a wooden floor.

**floor show** *n* a cabaret or other entertainment at a nightclub.

**floozy** *or* **floozie** *or* **floosie** *n* (*pl* **-ies**) *informal* a disreputable or promiscuous woman or girl.

**flop**[1] *v* (**flopped, flopping**) **1** to swing or hang loosely and heavily. **2** to move or drop in a heavy or clumsy manner. **3** *informal* to fail completely.

**flop**[2] *n* **1** a flopping movement. **2** *informal* a complete failure.

**floppy** *adj* (**-ier, -iest**) limp and hanging loosely. ➤ **floppily** *adv.*

**floppy disk** *n* in computing, a flexible disc used for storing data.

**flora** *n* the plant life of a region or period.

**floral** *adj* relating to or composed of flowers.

**floret** *n* **1** each of the small flowers forming the head of a composite plant. **2** each of the flowering stems making up a cauliflower or broccoli head.

**florid** *adj* **1** tinged with red; ruddy. **2** excessively ornate in style.

**florin** *n* a former British coin worth two shillings.

**florist** *n* a person or shop that sells cut flowers.

**floss**[1] *n* **1** soft silk or cotton thread used in embroidery. **2** soft thread for cleaning between the teeth. **3** silky plant fibres on maize cobs or cotton bolls.

**floss**[2] *v* to clean the teeth with dental floss.

**flotation** *or* **floatation** *n* **1** the act or process of floating. **2** the launching of a company on the stock market by offering shares for the first time.

**flotilla** *n* a small fleet of ships or boats.

**flotsam** *n* floating wreckage of a ship or its cargo. * **flotsam and jetsam** odds and ends.

**flounce**[1] *v* (*often* + out/off/about/away) to move in an exaggerated or petulant manner.

**flounce**[2] *n* an instance of flouncing.

**flounce**[3] *n* a wide strip of fabric attached to the hem of a skirt or dress.

**flounder**[1] *n* (*pl* **flounders** *or* **flounder**) a small sea flatfish.

**flounder**[2] *v* **1** to stagger about in soft mud or water. **2** to behave or speak in a blundering or incompetent way.

**flour** *n* **1** finely ground meal, *esp* of wheat. **2** a fine soft powder. ➤ **floury** *adj.*

**flourish**[1] *v* **1** to grow or thrive. **2** to achieve success; to prosper. **3** to be in good health. **4** to wave or brandish with dramatic gestures.

**flourish**[2] *n* **1** a decorative embellishment in handwriting. **2** an ostentatious or dramatic gesture. **3** a fanfare on brass instruments.

**flout** *v* to disregard or ignore (a rule or custom).

***Usage Note:*** See note at FLAUNT.

**flow**[1] *v* **1** to move or pour steadily and continuously. **2** to hang or stream gracefully.

**flow**[2] *n* a continuous flowing or stream.

**flow chart** *n* a diagram showing the successive stages of a procedure or system.

**flower**[1] *n* **1** the part of a plant having bright petals, from which the seeds or fruit develop. **2** the finest part or example of something.

**flower**[2] *v* **1** to produce flowers. **2** to develop and flourish.

**flowerpot** *n* a container for growing plants.

**flowery** *adj* **1** patterned with flowers. **2** of language: highly ornate.

**flown** *v* past part. of FLY[1].

**flu** *n* influenza.

**fluctuate** *v* to rise and fall or change unpredictably. ➤ **fluctuation** *n.*

**flue** *n* a channel in a chimney for flame and smoke to escape.

**fluent** *adj* **1** able to speak, write, or read without difficulty. **2** effortlessly smooth and rapid. ➤ **fluency** *n,* **fluently** *adv.*

**fluff**[1] *n* **1** small loose bits of waste material gathered in sticking clumps. **2** soft light fur, down, etc. **3** *informal* a blunder in speaking or performing.

**fluff**[2] *v* **1** (+ out/up) to make fuller, plumper, or fluffier. **2** *informal* to do or say badly.

**fluffy** *adj* (**-ier, -iest**) **1** like or covered with fluff. **2** light and soft or airy. ➤ **fluffily** *adv.*

**flugelhorn** *n* a brass musical instrument resembling a cornet.

**fluid**[1] *n* **1** a liquid or gas. **2** a liquid in the body of an animal or plant.

**fluid**[2] *adj* **1** capable of flowing. **2** not fixed or firm. **3** of plans not yet definite. **4** effortlessly graceful. ➤ **fluidity** *n,* **fluidly** *adv.*

**fluid ounce** *n* a British unit of liquid capacity equal to one twentieth of a pint (about 28.4ml).

**fluke**[1] *n* a parasitic flatworm.

**fluke**[2] *n* a lucky success that happens by chance. ➤ **fluky** *adj.*

**flume** *n* **1** a sloping water channel. **2** a water chute at an amusement park or swimming pool.

**flummery** *n* (*pl* **-ies**) *informal* empty or pretentious talk.

**flummox** *v* to bewilder or confuse completely.

**flung** *v* past tense and past part. of FLING[1].

**flunk** *v chiefly NAmer, informal* to fail an examination or course.

**flunky** *or* **flunkey** *n* (*pl* **-ies** *or* **-eys**) **1** a person performing menial duties. **2** a liveried servant.

**fluoresce** *v* to glow brightly.

**fluorescent** *adj* **1** producing a bright light by emitting electromagnetic radiation. **2** brightly colourful. ➤ **fluorescence** *n.*

**fluoridate** *v* to add fluoride to (a water supply). ➤ **fluoridation** *n.*

**fluoride** *n* a compound of fluorine added to toothpaste or drinking water to reduce tooth decay.

**fluorine** *n* a pale yellowish toxic gas.

**fluorite** *n* = FLUORSPAR.

**fluorspar** *n* a mineral used in glass-making and as a flux in the manufacture of metals.

**flurry**[1] *n* (*pl* **-ies**) **1** a gust of wind. **2** a small mass of snow, rain, or leaves blown about by a light wind. **3** a state of nervous excitement. **4** a short burst of activity.

**flurry**[2] *v* (**-ies, -ied**) to make or become agitated and confused.

**flush**[1] *n* **1** a tinge of red in the cheeks. **2** an instance of flushing. **3** a fresh and vigorous state. **4** a transitory sensation of extreme heat. **5** a surge of emotion. **6** a sudden flow of water.

**flush**[2] *v* **1** to glow brightly with a rosy colour. **2** to blush. **3** to cleanse by causing liquid to flow over or through. **4** to dispose of (waste) by carrying it away on a stream of liquid. ✱ **be flushed with** to feel proud of and excited by.

**flush**[3] *adj* **1** level with a surface. **2** arranged edge to edge so as to fit snugly. **3** *informal* having plenty of money.

**flush**[4] *v* **1** to cause (a game bird) to take flight suddenly. **2** (*often* + out) to force (somebody) to leave a place of concealment.

**flush**[5] *n* in poker, a hand of playing cards of the same suit.

**fluster**[1] *v* to make or become agitated or confused. ➤ **flustered** *adj.*

**fluster**[2] *n* a state of agitated confusion.

**flute** *n* **1** a high-pitched woodwind instrument that consists of a cylindrical tube with finger holes stopped at one end, held horizontally and played by blowing air across a side hole. **2** a grooved pleat or frill. **3** a tall narrow wineglass.

**flutter**[1] *v* **1** to flap the wings rapidly. **2** to move or fall with quick wavering or flapping motions. **3** to beat or vibrate in irregular spasms. **4** to move about or behave in an agitated aimless manner. ➤ **flutterer** *n.*

**flutter**[2] *n* **1** a state of nervous confusion or excitement. **2** abnormal spasmodic fluttering of the heart. **3** *chiefly Brit* a small gamble or bet. ➤ **fluttery** *adj.*

**fluvial** *adj* relating to a stream or river.

**flux** *n* **1** a continuous flow. **2** continual change. **3** a substance used in soldering or brazing.

**fly**[1] *v* (**flies, flying, flew, flown**) **1** to move through the air by means of wings. **2** to float or wave in the air. **3** to operate (an aircraft or spacecraft) in flight. **4** to travel or transport in an aircraft. **5** to move or pass swiftly. **6** to pass suddenly and violently into a rage or other specified state. **7** *informal* to leave hurriedly. ✱ **fly at** to attack suddenly. **fly in the face of 1** to disobey. **2** to be contrary to. **fly off the handle** *informal* to become suddenly angry. **with flying colours** with great success or distinction.

**fly**[2] *n* (*pl* **flies**) **1** (*usu in pl*) an opening in the front of a pair of trousers, closed with buttons or a zip and covered by a fold of cloth. **2** (*in pl*) the space over a stage where scenery and equipment can be hung.

**fly**[3] *n* (*pl* **flies**) **1** a flying insect with two thin wings. **2** an artificial fly attached to a fishhook as bait. ✱ **fly in the ointment** a minor irritant or difficulty in a generally satisfactory situation. **fly on the wall** a hidden observer.

**fly**[4] *adj* (**flyer, flyest**) *chiefly Brit, informal* clever and knowing.

**flyaway** *adj esp* of the hair: tending not to stay in place.

**flyblown** *adj* contaminated by the eggs or young larvae of flies.

**fly-by-night** *adj* disreputable or untrustworthy.

**flycatcher** *n* a small bird that feeds on insects caught while flying.

**flyer** *or* **flier** *n* **1** a person or thing that flies or moves very fast. **2** a passenger on an aircraft. **3** a small leaflet or handbill. **4** *informal* a flying start in athletics.

**flying picket** *n* a person who travels to picket a place of work other than their own.

**flying saucer** *n* a round flying object supposed to come from outer space.

**flying squad** *n* a police unit ready to act swiftly in an emergency.

**flying start** *n* a successful beginning giving an advantage over competitors.

**flyleaf** *n* (*pl* **flyleaves**) a blank page at the beginning or end of a book and fastened to the cover.

**flyover** *n Brit* a crossing of two roads, railways, etc at different levels.

**flypaper** *n* a strip of sticky paper hung up to attract and kill flies.

**flypast** *n Brit* a ceremonial flight by aircraft over a gathering of people.

**flyposting** *n* the unauthorized posting of advertisements in public places.

**fly sheet** *n* **1** a protective sheet covering a tent or its entrance. **2** a small pamphlet or circular.

**flywheel** *n* a heavy wheel that revolves to make a machine or engine run smoothly.

**FM** *adj* frequency modulation (a broadcasting and receiving system).

**foal**[1] *n* a young animal of the horse family.

**foal**[2] *v* to give birth to a foal.

**foam**[1] *n* **1** a light frothy mass of fine bubbles formed on the surface of a liquid. **2** a substance in the form of a light frothy mass of bubbles. **3** a rubber or plastic material filled with small holes by the introduction of gas bubbles during manufacture. ➤ **foamy** *adj.*

**foam**[2] *v* to produce or form foam.

**fob** *n* **1** a tab on a key ring. **2** a short chain attached to a watch for carrying in a pocket.

**fob off** *v* (**fobbed, fobbing**) **1** (+ with) to put (somebody) off with a trick or excuse. **2** (+ on) to pass or offer (something spurious or inferior) as genuine or perfect.

**focal** *adj* of or located at a focus.

**focal length** *n* the distance between the optical centre of a lens or mirror and the focal point.

**focal point** *n* **1** the point or source at which rays of light converge or appear to converge. **2** a centre of activity or attention.

**fo'c'sle** *n* see FORECASTLE.

**focus**[1] *n* (*pl* **focuses** *or* **foci**) **1** a point at which rays of light or sound converge. **2** the point at which an object must be placed for an image formed by a lens or mirror to be sharp. **3** = FOCAL LENGTH. **4** adjustment of the eye to produce clear vision. **5** a centre of activity or attention. ✱ **in/out of focus** of an image: having or lacking sharpness of outline.

**focus**[2] *v* (**focused** *or* **focussed, focusing** *or* **focussing**) **1** to adjust (a camera or telescope) to obtain a sharp image. **2** to become able to see clearly. **3** to concentrate one's thoughts or attention on. **4** of rays: to converge on a point.

**focus group** *n* a group of people gathered together to discuss a new product or policy.

**fodder** *n* **1** food for cattle or other domestic animals. **2** something used to supply a constant demand.

**foe** *n literary* an enemy or adversary.

**foetid** *adj* see FETID.

**foetus** *or* **fetus** *n* (*pl* **foetuses** *or* **fetuses**) an unborn human baby or young of a mammal. ➤ **foetal** *adj.*

**fog**[1] *n* **1** fine particles of water suspended in the lower atmosphere causing a loss of visibility. **2** a state of confusion or bewilderment.

**fog**[2] *v* (**fogged, fogging**) **1** to cover or obscure with fog or condensation. **2** to make confused or confusing.

**fogey** *or* **fogy** *n* (*pl* **fogeys** *or* **fogies**) a person with old-fashioned ideas.

**foggy** *adj* (**-ier, -iest**) **1** thick with fog. **2** vague or confused.

**foghorn** *n* a deep horn sounded in a fog to give warning to ships.

**foible** *n* a minor weakness or shortcoming.

**foil**[1] *n* **1** metal in thin sheets. **2** a person or thing that serves as a contrast to another.
**foil**[2] *v* **1** to prevent (somebody) from doing something. **2** to frustrate or defeat (an attempt).
**foil**[3] *n* a light fencing sword with a blunted tip.
**foist** *v* (*usu* + on) to force acceptance of (something or somebody unwanted) on somebody.
**fold**[1] *v* **1** (*often* + over) to lay one part of (something) over another part. **2** (*often* + up) to reduce the length or bulk of (something) by doubling it over. **3** (*often* + up) to become folded or be capable of being folded. **4** to clasp (the arms) together. **5** to clasp closely. **6** to wrap or envelop. **7** (+ in/into) to gently incorporate (a food ingredient) into a mixture. **8** *informal* of a business: to stop operating. ➤ **foldable** *adj.*
**fold**[2] *n* **1** a part folded over. **2** a line or crease made by folding.
**fold**[3] *n* **1** an enclosure for sheep. **2** (**the fold**) a group of people adhering to a faith.
**folder** *n* a folded cover or envelope for holding loose papers.
**foliage** *n* the leaves of a plant or clump of plants.
**folic acid** *n* a vitamin found in green leafy vegetables and liver.
**folio** *n* (*pl* **-os**) **1** a sheet of paper folded once into four sides. **2** a book printed on pages of this size.
**folk** *n* **1** *informal* (*also* **folks**) people in general. **2** *informal* (**one's folks**) the members of one's own family or community. **3** = FOLK MUSIC.
**folk dance** *n* a traditional dance of a people or region.
**folklore** *n* the traditional customs and stories of a people.
**folk music** *n* the traditional music and songs of a people or region.
**folk song** *n* a traditional song of a people or region. ➤ **folksinger** *n.*
**folksy** *adj* (**-ier, -iest**) *informal* informal or familiar in manner or style.
**folk tale** *n* an anonymous traditional story that is transmitted orally.
**follicle** *n* a small cavity surrounding the root of a hair.
**follow** *v* **1** to go or come after. **2** to go after (somebody or something) to observe them or watch their movements. **3** to accept as a guide or leader. **4** to obey or act in accordance with (rules or instructions). **5** to copy or imitate. **6** to walk or proceed along (a path or route). **7** to engage in (an activity) as a calling or way of life. **8** to undertake (a course of action). **9** to come or take place after in time or order. **10** (+ with) to cause (something) to be followed by something else. **11** (*often* + from) to come into existence or take place as a result of. **12** to support or watch the progress of. **13** to understand the meaning or logic of. * **follow suit** to do as somebody else has done.
**follower** *n* **1** somebody who follows the opinions or teachings of another. **2** a fan or supporter.
**following**[1] *adj* **1** next after. **2** now to be mentioned.
**following**[2] *n* a group of followers or adherents.
**following**[3] *prep* subsequent to.
**follow on** *v* **1** to continue. **2** to come as a consequence.
**follow through** *v* to pursue or complete (an activity or process).
**follow up** *v* to continue or enquire into (something) further.
**folly** *n* (*pl* **-ies**) **1** a lack of good sense or prudence. **2** a foolish act or idea. **3** a fanciful building built for scenic effect.
**foment** *v* to incite (trouble, rebellion, etc).
**fond** *adj* **1** (+ of) having an affection or liking for. **2** affectionate; loving. **3** foolishly tender; indulgent. **4** foolish; naive. ➤ **fondly** *adv,* **fondness** *n.*
**fondant** *n* a soft creamy mixture of flavoured sugar and water, or a sweet made from this.
**fondle** *v* to handle or caress tenderly and lovingly or erotically.
**fondue** *n* a dish in which small pieces of food are dipped in a hot oil or a sauce.
**font**[1] *n* a receptacle in a church for the water used in baptism.
**font**[2] *n* = FOUNT[2].
**food** *n* material taken into the body of a living organism to provide energy and sustain life. * **food for thought** something that needs thinking about.
**food chain** *n* a sequence of organisms each of which uses the next as a food source.
**food poisoning** *n* a disorder caused by the toxic products of bacteria or by chemical residues in food.
**foodstuff** *n* a substance with food value.
**fool**[1] *n* **1** a person lacking in sense or understanding. **2** a jester employed by a royal or noble household. * **act/play the fool** to misbehave. **make a fool of oneself** to behave in an embarrassing way. ➤ **foolery** *n.*
**fool**[2] *v* **1** to trick or deceive. **2** to say or do something as a joke. **3** to behave in a silly or irresponsible way.
**fool**[3] *n chiefly Brit* a cold dessert made from fruit and whipped cream.
**fool about** *v* to behave in a silly or irresponsible way.
**foolhardy** *adj* (**-ier, -iest**) foolishly bold or rash.
**foolish** *adj* **1** unwise; silly. **2** absurd; ridiculous. ➤ **foolishly** *adv,* **foolishness** *n.*
**foolproof** *adj* extremely simple or reliable.
**foolscap** *n chiefly Brit* a size of paper usu 17 × 13½ in. (432 × 343mm).

**fool's gold** *n* a yellowish mineral that looks like gold.
**fool's paradise** *n* a state of illusory happiness.
**foot**[1] *n* (*pl* **feet**) **1** the end part of the leg on which an animal or person stands. **2** (*pl also* **foot**) a unit of length equal to 0.305m (12in.). **3** the lower edge or lowest part; the bottom. **4** the end of something that is opposite the head or top. **5** the basic unit of verse metre consisting of a group of syllables. * **feet of clay** a weakness in a generally admired person. **have/keep one's feet on the ground** to remain sensible and practical. **not put a foot wrong** to make no mistakes at all. **on/by foot** walking or running, as opposed to using transport. **put one's foot down** to take a firm stand. **put one's foot in it** to make an embarrassing blunder.
**foot**[2] *v* to pay (a bill).
**footage** *n* a length of cinema or television film.
**foot-and-mouth disease** *n* a disease of cattle, sheep, pigs, and goats, with ulcers in the mouth, round the hoofs, and on the udders.
**football** *n* **1** a team game that involves kicking a ball, *esp* Association Football in the UK or American football in the US. **2** the inflated round or oval ball used in a game of football. ➤ **footballer** *n.*
**footbridge** *n* a bridge for pedestrians.
**footfall** *n* the sound of a footstep.
**foothill** *n* a hill at the foot of a mountain.
**foothold** *n* **1** a place where the foot can be placed securely while climbing. **2** an established position or basis from which to progress.
**footing** *n* **1** a stable placing of the feet. **2** an established position from which progress can be made. **3** a position or rank in relation to others. **4** an enlargement at the lower end of a foundation, wall, or column.
**footlights** *pl n* a row of lights set across the front of a stage floor.
**footling** *adj* unimportant or trivial.
**footloose** *adj* free to go or do as one pleases.
**footman** *n* (*pl* **footmen**) a servant in livery who receives and attends to visitors.
**footnote** *n* an extra note or comment placed at the bottom of a printed page.
**footpad** *n archaic* a person who robbed passers-by on foot.
**footpath** *n* a path or pavement for people on foot.
**footprint** *n* an impression made by a foot or shoe.
**footsore** *adj* having sore feet from much walking.
**footstep** *n* a step or tread taken in walking.
**footstool** *n* a low stool used to support the feet when sitting.
**fop** *n* a man who is too concerned about his clothes and appearance. ➤ **foppish** *adj.*
**for**[1] *prep* **1** used to indicate purpose or reason. **2** used to indicate direction or intention. **3** because of. **4** in place of. **5** on behalf of. **6** in favour of. **7** considering: *tall for her age.* **8** with respect to: *a stickler for detail.* **9** used to indicate cost or payment: *work for nothing.*
**for**[2] *conj* because.
**forage**[1] *n* **1** food for animals, e.g. hay or straw. **2** a search.
**forage**[2] *v* **1** to search for food. **2** (*usu* + for) to rummage.
**foray**[1] *v* to make a raid or incursion.
**foray**[2] *n* **1** a sudden attack or raid into an enemy's territory. **2** a brief attempt in a new sphere.
**forbear**[1] *v* (**forbore, forborne**) to hold oneself back from (doing something), *esp* with difficulty.
**forbear**[2] *n* see FOREBEAR.
**forbearance** *n* patience or self-restraint.
**forbid** *v* (**forbidding,** *past tense* **forbade** *or* **forbad,** *past part.* **forbidden**) **1** to refuse to allow. **2** to refuse access to or use of. **3** to hinder or prevent.
**forbidding** *adj* looking threatening or unfriendly.
**force**[1] *n* **1** strength or energy exerted or brought to bear. **2** moral or mental strength. **3** capacity to persuade or convince. **4** violence or compulsion used to achieve something. **5** legal validity. **6** an organized body of soldiers or workers. **7** (*in pl*) the armed services of a nation or commander. * **in force 1** in great numbers. **2** valid or operative.
**force**[2] *v* **1** to compel (somebody) to do something. **2** to bring about by compulsion, violence, or great effort. **3** to press or drive (something) with a violent effort. **4** to break open (a door, lock, etc).
**force-feed** *v* (*past tense and past part.* **force-fed**) to feed (e.g. a person) against their will.
**forceful** *adj* powerful or effective. ➤ **forcefully** *adv.*
**forcemeat** *n* a savoury seasoned stuffing of breadcrumbs and meat.
**forceps** *n* (*pl* **forceps**) a pair of large pincers used in surgery.
**forcible** *adj* **1** effected by force. **2** powerful; forceful. ➤ **forcibly** *adv.*
**ford**[1] *n* a shallow part of a river or stream that can be crossed in a vehicle or on foot.
**ford**[2] *v* to cross (a river or stream, etc) at a ford. ➤ **fordable** *adj.*
**fore**[1] *adj and adv* situated in or towards the front.
**fore**[2] *n* a front part. * **to the fore** in a prominent position.
**forearm**[1] /'fawrahm/ *n* the human arm between the elbow and the wrist.
**forearm**[2] /faw'rahm/ *v* to prepare against attack or danger.
**forebear** *or* **forbear** *n* an ancestor or forefather.

**foreboding**[1] *n* a feeling of something bad about to happen.
**foreboding**[2] *adj* presaging something bad.
**forecast**[1] *v* (*past tense and past part.* **forecast** *or* **forecasted**) to estimate or predict (a future event or condition). ➤ **forecaster** *n.*
**forecast**[2] *n* a prediction of a future happening or condition.
**forecastle** *or* **fo'c'sle** *n* **1** a short raised deck at the bow of a ship. **2** a forward part of a merchant ship where the living quarters are situated.
**foreclose** *v* to cancel a mortgage and repossess a property because of nonpayment. ➤ **foreclosure** *n.*
**forecourt** *n* **1** an open or paved area in front of a building. **2** the part of a tennis court between the net and the service line.
**forefather** *n* an ancestor.
**forefinger** *n* the finger next to the thumb.
**forefoot** *n* (*pl* **forefeet**) each of the front feet of a four-footed animal.
**forefront** *n* the foremost part or place.
**forego** *v* see FORGO.
**foregoing** *adj* going before; immediately preceding.
**foreground** *n* **1** the part of a picture or view nearest to the viewer. **2** a prominent position.
**forehand** *n* a stroke in tennis, squash, etc made with the palm of the hand turned in the direction of movement.
**forehead** *n* the part of the face above the eyes.
**foreign** *adj* **1** born in or belonging to a country other than one's own. **2** relating to other nations. **3** occurring in an abnormal situation in the living body. **4** (*usu* + to) not characteristic of or relevant to.
**foreign body** *n* a piece of unwanted material that has entered something.
**foreigner** *n* **1** a person from a foreign country. **2** a stranger or outsider.
**foreign exchange** *n* currency of foreign countries.
**foreknowledge** *n* knowledge of an event before it happens.
**forelock** *n* a lock of hair growing just above the forehead.
**foreman** *n* (*pl* **foremen**) **1** a worker who supervises other workers. **2** the chairman and spokesman of a jury.
**foremast** *n* the mast nearest the bow of a ship.
**foremost**[1] *adj* **1** first in a series or progression. **2** of first rank or position; preeminent.
**foremost**[2] *adv* most importantly.
**forename** *n* a name that comes before a surname.
**forensic** *adj* **1** relating to the scientific investigation of crime. **2** belonging to courts of law.
**foreplay** *n* erotic stimulation preceding sexual intercourse.
**forerunner** *n* a person or thing that comes before a better known one exists.
**foresee** *v* (**foresaw, foreseen**) to be aware of (a development or event) beforehand. ➤ **foreseeable** *adj.*
**foreshadow** *v* to indicate or suggest beforehand.
**foreshore** *n* the part of a seashore between high-tide and low-tide marks.
**foreshorten** *v* (**foreshortened, foreshortening**) **1** to shorten (a detail in a drawing or painting) so as to create an illusion of depth. **2** to make more compact in scale or time.
**foresight** *n* the ability to foresee events, or the prudence arising from this.
**foreskin** *n* the fold of skin that covers the tip of the penis.
**forest**[1] *n* **1** a dense growth of trees covering a large area of land. **2** a large number of standing things.
**forest**[2] *v* to cover with trees or forest. ➤ **forestation** *n.*
**forestall** *v* to hinder or prevent by taking action in advance.
**forestry** *n* the scientific study or practice of managing forests.
**foretaste** *n* an advance indication or sampling.
**foretell** *v* (*past tense and past part.* **foretold**) to predict.
**forethought** *n* careful consideration of what is likely to happen or be needed.
**forever** *adv* **1** (*also* **for ever**) for all future time; indefinitely. **2** persistently; incessantly.
**forewarn** *v* to warn in advance. ➤ **forewarner** *n.*
**forewent** *v* past tense of FOREGO.
**foreword** *n* a preface to a book written by somebody other than the author of the text.
**forfeit**[1] *n* something lost, taken away, or imposed as a penalty.
**forfeit**[2] *v* (**forfeited, forfeiting**) to lose the right to (a privilege, etc) as a penalty. ➤ **forfeiture** *n.*
**forfeit**[3] *adj* lost as a forfeit.
**forge**[1] *n* an open furnace or workshop where metal is heated and worked.
**forge**[2] *v* **1** to shape (metal) by heating and hammering it. **2** to bring into being by an expenditure of effort. **3** to make a counterfeit copy of (a signature, document, or banknote). ➤ **forger** *n,* **forgery** *n.*
**forge**[3] *v* to move forwards slowly and steadily.
**forge ahead** *v* to make rapid progress.
**forget** *v* (**forgetting,** *past tense* **forgot,** *past part.* **forgotten,** *archaic or NAmer* **forgot**) **1** to be unable to remember. **2** to disregard or give no attention to. **3** to reject the possibility of. ✱ **forget oneself** to act unsuitably or unworthily. ➤ **forgettable** *adj.*

**forgetful** *adj* likely or apt to forget. ➤ **forgetfully** *adv*, **forgetfulness** *n*.
**forget-me-not** *n* a small low-growing plant with blue flowers.
**forgive** *v* (**forgave, forgiven**) **1** to stop feeling angry about (something) or resentful towards (somebody). **2** to pardon (somebody, an offence, etc). ➤ **forgivable** *adj*.
**forgiveness** *n* forgiving or being forgiven; pardon.
**forgo** *or* **forego** *v* (**forgoes** *or* **foregoes, forgoing** *or* **foregoing,** *past tense* **forwent** *or* **forewent,** *past part.* **forgone** *or* **foregone**) to abstain or refrain from (something desirable).
**fork**[1] *n* **1** an implement with two or more prongs for eating or serving food. **2** a similar larger tool for digging, carrying, etc. **3** either of two divided supports for a bicycle or motorcycle wheel. **4** a place where a road or river divides into two, or each of these divisions.
**fork**[2] *v* **1** to divide into two or more branches. **2** to make a turn into one of the branches of a fork. **3** to dig or work with a fork. **4** *informal* (+ out) to make a payment or contribution.
**forked** *adj* having one end divided into branches or points.
**forklift truck** *n* a vehicle for lifting heavy loads by means of two horizontal prongs at the front.
**forlorn** *adj* **1** miserably sad and lonely. **2** nearly hopeless. ➤ **forlornly** *adv*.
**form**[1] *n* **1** the shape and structure of something. **2** a kind or variety of something. **3** an established or correct method of proceeding or behaving. **4** a prescribed and set order of words. **5** a document with blank spaces for inserting information. **6** a long seat without a back. **7** *chiefly Brit* a school class organized for the work of a particular year. **8** the past performances of a competitor. **9** condition suitable for performing well. **10** *Brit, informal* a criminal record. ➤ **formless** *adj*.
**form**[2] *v* **1** to give shape or existence to. **2** to mould into a particular shape. **3** to come into existence; to take shape. **4** to serve to make up or constitute. **5** to arrange or be arranged in (a shape).
**formal** *adj* **1** characterized by dignity and the observance of correct procedure. **2** suitable for an important or ceremonial occasion. **3** done in accordance with established procedure. **4** arranged in a symmetrical or orderly pattern. ➤ **formally** *adv*.
**formaldehyde** *n* a pungent gas used chiefly as a disinfectant and preservative.
**formalin** *n* a clear solution of formaldehyde in water.
**formality** *n* (*pl* **-ies**) **1** the state of being formal. **2** observance of formal or conventional rules. **3** an established form or procedure. **4** something of little real significance that is required by rule or custom.
**formalize** *or* **-ise** *v* **1** to give formal status or approval to. **2** to give a definite shape to.
**format**[1] *n* **1** the general plan of organization or arrangement. **2** the shape, size, and general make-up of a book. **3** in computing, the structure by which data is held.
**format**[2] *v* (**formatted, formatting**) **1** to arrange in a particular format. **2** in computing, to prepare (a disk, etc) to receive data.
**formation** *n* **1** the giving or taking of form or shape. **2** the manner in which a thing is formed or arranged. **3** a group of people or things arranged in a special way.
**formative** *adj* having a significant influence on growth or development.
**former** *adj* **1** occurring in the past or having been previously. **2** (**the former**) denoting the first of two things mentioned or understood.
**formerly** *adv* at an earlier time; previously.
**Formica** *n trademark* a laminated plastic used to make heat-resistant surfaces for worktops, etc.
**formic acid** *n* a pungent corrosive liquid acid naturally produced by ants.
**formidable** *adj* **1** of a task, etc: difficult or challenging. **2** of a person: causing fear or respect. ➤ **formidably** *adv*.
**formula** *n* (*pl* **formulas** *or* **formulae**) **1** a mathematical rule or principle expressed in symbols. **2** a symbolic expression of the chemical composition of a substance. **3** a set form of words for use in a ceremony or ritual. **4** a set form or method of speaking or writing, often followed uncritically. **5** a recipe or the list of ingredients in it. **6** liquid baby food made from milk or soya. **7** a method or procedure for bringing something about. ➤ **formulaic** *adj*.
**formulate** *v* **1** to state as a formula or reduce to a formula. **2** to devise or develop (a plan, product, etc). ➤ **formulation** *n*.
**form up** *v* to arrange or be arranged in a particular formation.
**fornicate** *v formal* to have sexual relations with a person one is not married to. ➤ **fornication** *n*.
**forsake** *v* (**forsook, forsaken**) **1** to renounce. **2** to desert or abandon.
**forsooth** *adv archaic* indeed; actually.
**forswear** *v* (**forswore, forsworn**) **1** to renounce solemnly. **2** to perjure (oneself).
**forsythia** *n* a shrub with bright yellow flowers.
**fort** *n* a strongly fortified building maintained to resist attack. * **hold the fort** to take charge temporarily.
**forte** /'fawtay/ *n* something at which a person excels.
**forth** *adv archaic* **1** onwards in time, place, or order. **2** into notice or view. * **and so forth** and so on.

**forthcoming** *adj* **1** about to occur or appear. **2** made available. **3** willing to give information.
**forthright** *adj* unhesitatingly outspoken.
**forthwith** *adv* immediately.
**fortify** *v* (**-ies, -ied**) **1** to strengthen (a place) against attack. **2** to give strength or endurance to. **3** to add (alcohol to wine or vitamins to food) to strengthen or enrich it. ➤ **fortification** *n.*
**fortissimo** *adj and adv* of a piece of music: to be performed in a very loud manner.
**fortitude** *n* courage or endurance in the face of difficulty.
**fortnight** *n chiefly Brit* two weeks.
**fortnightly** *adj and adv* occurring or appearing once a fortnight.
**fortress** *n* a large fortified building or town.
**fortuitous** *adj* occurring by chance. ➤ **fortuitously** *adv.*
**fortunate** *adj* **1** unexpectedly bringing good luck; favourable. **2** lucky. ➤ **fortunately** *adv.*
**fortune** *n* **1** a large quantity of money or possessions. **2** luck or chance seen as a force affecting human affairs. **3** one's future destiny. **4** (*in pl*) a person's experiences.
**forty** *adj and n* (*pl* **-ies**) **1** the number 40. **2** (*in pl*) the numbers 40 to 49. ➤ **fortieth** *adj and n.*
**forty winks** *pl n informal* **a short sleep during the day**.
**forum** *n* (*pl* **forums** *or* **fora**) **1** a meeting place or gathering for exchanging opinions. **2** the marketplace or central public place of an ancient Roman city, used for public business.
**forward**[1] *adj* **1** directed or turned towards the front. **2** brash or assertive.
**forward**[2] *adv* **1** (*also* **forwards**) towards what is ahead or in front. **2** into the future. **3** to an earlier time. **4** into prominence or open view.
**forward**[3] *n* an attacking player in football, hockey, etc.
**forward**[4] *v* to send onwards to a further destination.
**forwent** *v* past tense of FORGO.
**fossil** *n* **1** the petrified remains of an animal or plant of a past geological age. **2** an outdated person or thing. ➤ **fossilize** *v.*
**fossil fuel** *n* a fuel, e.g. coal, that is derived from the remains of living things.
**foster**[1] *v* **1** to promote the growth or development of. **2** to give parental care to (a child not one's own by birth).
**foster**[2] *adj* providing or receiving care by fostering.
**fought** *v* past tense and past part. of FIGHT[1].
**foul**[1] *adj* **1** offensive to the smell or taste. **2** morally or spiritually evil. **3** particularly unpleasant or disagreeable. **4** obscene or abusive. **5** infringing the rules of a game or sport. **6** polluted. ✱ **fall/run foul of** to come into conflict with. ➤ **foully** *adv.*
**foul**[2] *n* an infringement of the rules in a game or sport.
**foul**[3] *v* **1** to make dirty; to pollute. **2** in sport, to commit a foul. **3** to obstruct or block. **4** to entangle or collide with.
**foulmouthed** *adj* using coarse or abusive language.
**foul play** *n* **1** murder or violence. **2** play that infringes the rules in a game or sport.
**foul up** *v* **1** to do badly. **2** to spoil or confuse by making mistakes. **3** to entangle or block. ➤ **foul-up** *n.*
**found**[1] *v* past tense and past part. of FIND[1].
**found**[2] *v* **1** to establish (an institution or organization). **2** (*often* + on/upon) to set or ground (e.g. a plan or system of thought) on something sure or solid.
**found**[3] *v* to melt (metal) and pour it into a mould to make an object.
**foundation** *n* **1** (*also in pl*) an underlying base or support, *esp* the part of the structure on which a building rests. **2** the basis or principle underlying something. **3** a reason or justification. **4** the act of establishing something. **5** an organization or institution established with provision for future maintenance. **6** a cream or lotion applied to the face as a base for other make-up.
**founder**[1] *n* a person who establishes an institution or organization.
**founder**[2] *v* **1** of a ship: to sink. **2** of a plan or project: to fail.
**foundling** *n* an infant abandoned by unknown parents and discovered and looked after by others.
**foundry** *n* (*pl* **-ies**) a place for casting metals.
**fount**[1] *n* **1** *literary* a fountain or spring. **2** a source of something pleasant or useful.
**fount**[2] *or* **font** *n* in printing: a complete set of characters for printing in one style.
**fountain** *n* **1** an ornamental structure that sends a jet of water into the air. **2** a spring of water issuing from the ground.
**fountainhead** *n* the main source of something.
**fountain pen** *n* a pen with a reservoir or cartridge of ink.
**four** *n* **1** the number 4. **2** a shot in cricket that crosses the boundary after having hit the ground and scores four runs. ➤ **four** *adj.*
**four-letter word** *n* a short vulgar or offensive word.
**four-poster** *n* a bed with corner posts supporting curtains or a canopy.
**foursome** *n* a group of four people or things.
**foursquare** *adj and adv* **1** solid; squarely based. **2** bold and resolute.
**fourteen** *adj and n* the number 14. ➤ **fourteenth** *adj and n.*
**fourth** *adj and n* **1** having the position in a sequence corresponding to the number four. **2**

one of four equal parts of something. ➤ **fourthly** *adv.*

**fowl** *n* (*pl* **fowls** *or* **fowl**) **1** a domestic bird such as a chicken, turkey, or duck. **2** = WILDFOWL.

**fox**[1] *n* **1** an animal of the dog family with a pointed muzzle, large erect ears, and a long bushy tail. **2** a clever or crafty person.

**fox**[2] *v* to outwit or baffle.

**foxglove** *n* a tall plant with white or purple tubular flowers.

**foxhole** *n* a pit dug as improvised cover against enemy fire.

**foxhound** *n* a hound of a breed developed to hunt foxes.

**foxtrot**[1] *n* a ballroom dance that includes slow walking and quick running steps.

**foxtrot**[2] *v* (**foxtrotted, foxtrotting**) to dance the foxtrot.

**foxy** *adj* (**-ier, -iest**) **1** clever or crafty. **2** like a fox.

**foyer** *n* an entrance hall or lobby in a theatre or large building.

**Fr** *abbr* the chemical symbol for francium.

**fracas** *n* (*pl* **fracas**) a noisy quarrel or brawl.

**fraction** *n* **1** a number that is not a whole number, and usu less than one, e.g., 0.75. **2** a small portion or amount. **3** in chemistry, a portion, e.g. of a distillate, separable by fractionation.

**fractional** *adj* **1** relating to or being a fraction. **2** relatively small. ➤ **fractionally** *adv.*

**fractious** *adj* irritable and hard to control.

***Usage Note:*** Do not confuse this word with *factious.*

**fracture**[1] *n* **1** a break in or the breaking of something, *esp* hard tissue such as bone. **2** a split or breach.

**fracture**[2] *v* **1** to cause a fracture in. **2** to undergo fracture. **3** to break into separate parts.

**fragile** *adj* **1** easily broken or shattered. **2** not secure. **3** of a person: weak or vulnerable. ➤ **fragility** *n.*

**fragment**[1] *n* a part that is incomplete or broken off something larger. ➤ **fragmentary** *adj.*

**fragment**[2] *v* to break or fall to pieces. ➤ **fragmentation** *n.*

**fragrance** *n* **1** a sweet or pleasant smell. **2** a perfume or aftershave.

**fragrant** *adj* smelling sweet or pleasant.

**frail** *adj* **1** weak and delicate. **2** easily broken.

**frailty** *n* (*pl* **-ies**) **1** being frail. **2** a moral or physical weakness.

**frame**[1] *n* **1** a structure that gives shape or strength to a building, opening, vehicle, etc. **2** a rigid surrounding structure for displaying a painting or photograph. **3** the physical structure of the human body. **4** (*in pl*) the outer structure holding the lenses of a pair of glasses. **5** a single picture of the series on a length of film. **6** one round of play in snooker or bowling.

**frame**[2] *v* **1** to put a frame round. **2** to plan or formulate. **3** to shape or construct. **4** to fit or adjust for a purpose. **5** *informal* to make up evidence against (an innocent person).

**frame of mind** *n* a particular mental or emotional state.

**framework** *n* **1** a supporting frame or structure. **2** a basic structure of ideas.

**franc** *n* the basic monetary unit of Switzerland, and formerly of France, Belgium, and Luxembourg (replaced by the euro in 2002).

**franchise**[1] *n* **1** (*usu* **the franchise**) the right to vote. **2** the right granted to an individual or group to market goods or services. **3** a business or service holding a franchise.

**franchise**[2] *v* to grant a franchise to.

**frank**[1] *adj* **1** honest and straightforward. **2** undisguised. ➤ **frankly** *adv,* **frankness** *n.*

**frank**[2] *v* to mark (a piece of mail) with an official stamp showing that postal charges have been paid.

**frankfurter** *n* a cured cooked sausage made from beef and pork.

**frankincense** *n* a fragrant gum resin which is burned as incense.

**frantic** *adj* **1** emotionally out of control. **2** marked by fast and nervous activity. ➤ **frantically** *adv.*

**fraternal** *adj* **1** relating to brothers; brotherly. **2** relating to a fraternity or society.

**fraternity** *n* (*pl* **-ies**) **1** a group of people organized for a common purpose or interest. **2** a club for male students in some US universities. **3** mutual friendly support.

**fraternize** *or* **-ise** *v* to be on friendly terms. ➤ **fraternization** *n.*

**fratricide** *n* **1** the act of killing one's brother or sister. **2** somebody who does this. ➤ **fratricidal** *adj.*

**fraud** *n* **1** deception for unlawful gain. **2** an act of deception; a trick. **3** a person who is not what they pretend to be; an impostor.

**fraudster** *n* somebody who commits a fraud.

**fraudulent** *adj* involving fraud. ➤ **fraudulently** *adv.*

**fraught** *adj* **1** (+ with) filled with (something unwelcome). **2** characterized by anxiety and tension.

**fray**[1] *v* **1** of fabric or rope: to become worn at the edges. **2** of a person's temper or nerves: to show strain.

**fray**[2] *n* **1** (**the fray**) a dispute or competition. **2** a brawl or fight.

**frazzle** *n informal* **1** a burnt state. **2** a state of exhaustion. ➤ **frazzled** *adj.*

**freak** *n* **1** a person, animal, or plant with a physical abnormality. **2** a highly unconventional person. **3** a highly unusual and unforeseeable event. **4** *informal* an obsessive enthusiast: *a sci-fi freak.* ➤ **freakish** *adj.*

**freak out** *v informal* to behave irrationally or wildly.

**freckle** *n* a small brown spot on the skin. ➤ **freckled** *adj*, **freckly** *adj*.

**free**[1] *adj* (**freer, freest**) **1** not subject to the control of another person. **2** not bound or detained by force. **3** (+ of/from) not subject to or affected by (something unwelcome). **4** having no obligations or commitments. **5** not obstructed or impeded; clear. **6** not being used or occupied. **7** not hampered or restricted. **8** not costing or charging anything. **9** (*usu* + with) lavish or unrestrained. **10** outspoken or familiar. **11** not determined by external influences. **12** voluntary or spontaneous. **13** of a translation: not literal or exact. * **free and easy** unrestrained or casual. **a free hand** freedom of action. ➤ **freely** *adv*.

**free**[2] *adv* **1** in a free manner. **2** without charge or cost.

**free**[3] *v* (**frees, freed, freeing**) **1** to cause to be free. **2** (*often* + up) to make available.

**freebie** *n informal* a gift or service offered free.

**freedom** *n* **1** the state of being free. **2** the right to speak or act as one wishes. **3** liberation from slavery or imprisonment. **4** (+ from) being exempt or released from something onerous. **5** (+ of) unrestricted use of something. **6** the rights and privileges of a citizen of a city, granted as an honour to a distinguished person.

**free enterprise** *n* an economic system that relies on private business operating competitively for profit.

**free fall** *n* unrestrained motion under gravity.

**free-for-all** *n* a disorganized contest or situation in which anyone may take part.

**free-form** *adj* not having a fixed structure; spontaneous.

**freehand** *adj and adv* drawn or written by hand without the aid of instruments.

**freehold** *n* ownership of land or property with an unconditional right to sell it. ➤ **freeholder** *n*.

**free house** *n* a public house that is entitled to sell products of more than one brewery.

**free kick** *n* in football or rugby, an unhindered kick awarded after a breach of the rules by the other side.

**freelance**[1] *n* a self-employed person who works for several companies. ➤ **freelance** *adj and adv*.

**freelance**[2] *v* to work as a freelance.

**freeload** *v informal* to take advantage of somebody else's generosity or hospitality. ➤ **freeloader** *n*.

**freeman** *n* (*pl* **freemen**) **1** somebody who has been granted the freedom of a city. **2** formerly, somebody who is no longer a slave.

**free market** *n* an economic market operating by free competition.

**Freemason** *n* a member of a secret fraternity who offer each other support and friendship. ➤ **Freemasonry** *n*.

**free-range** *adj* of farm animals: reared in the open air and allowed to move about.

**freesia** *n* a sweet-scented plant with red, white, yellow, or purple flowers.

**freestanding** *adj* standing alone; not supported by something else.

**freestyle** *n* a competition in which contestants use a style of their choice.

**freethinker** *n* a person who rejects or questions accepted opinions.

**free trade** *n* trade based on the unrestricted international exchange of goods.

**freeway** *n NAmer* a motorway or highway without tolls.

**freewheel** *v* to coast on a bicycle without using the pedals.

**free will** *n* the power of making one's own moral choices.

**freeze**[1] *v* (**froze, frozen**) **1** of a liquid: to turn solid from cold. **2** to convert (liquid) to a solid by cold. **3** to stick solidly by freezing. **4** to become or cause to become clogged with ice. **5** to become or make chilled with cold. **6** to preserve (food) by maintaining it at a temperature below 0°C. **7** to become fixed or motionless from fear or surprise. **8** of a computer screen: to stop responding to commands because of a fault. **9** to anaesthetize (a part of the body). **10** to cause to become fixed or unalterable.

**freeze**[2] *n* **1** freezing cold weather. **2** an act or period of freezing something.

**freeze-dry** *v* (**-ies, -ied**) to preserve (food) by dehydrating it while in a frozen state in a vacuum.

**freeze-frame** *n* the facility of a video camera or recorder to produce a static picture.

**freezer** *n* an insulated cabinet or room for freezing and storing food.

**freezing** *adj* **1** *informal* very cold. **2** below 0°C.

**freight**[1] *n* **1** goods transported commercially. **2** the commercial transport of goods.

**freight**[2] *v* to transport (goods) commercially.

**freighter** *n* a ship or aircraft used chiefly to carry freight.

**French**[1] *adj* relating to France, its people, or their language.

**French**[2] *n* **1** the language of France and parts of Belgium, Switzerland, Canada, and Africa. **2** (**the French**) the people of France.

**French cricket** *n* a game of cricket in which the legs of the player who is batting serve as a wicket.

**French dressing** *n* a salad dressing of oil, vinegar, and seasonings.

**french fries** *pl n chiefly NAmer* chips.

**French horn** *n* a brass instrument with a coiled tube that flares out at the end.

**French kiss** *n* a kiss with contact between tongues.
**French polish** *n* a solution of shellac used as a wood polish.
**French windows** *pl n Brit* a pair of glazed doors opening onto the exterior of a house.
**frenetic** *adj* frenzied or frantic. ➤ **frenetically** *adv.*
**frenzy** *n* (*pl* **-ies**) a state of extreme agitation or excitement. ➤ **frenzied** *adj.*
**frequency** *n* (*pl* **-ies**) **1** the rate at which something occurs over a period of time. **2** the state of occurring frequently. **3** the number of complete alternations per second of an alternating current of electricity. **4** the number of complete oscillations per second of an electromagnetic wave. **5** the number of sound waves per second produced by a sounding body.
**frequent**[1] *adj* **1** often repeated or occurring. **2** habitual or persistent. ➤ **frequently** *adv.*
**frequent**[2] *v* to visit (a place) often or habitually.
**fresco** *n* (*pl* **-oes** *or* **-os**) a painting done by applying watercolours to plaster before it is dry.
**fresh** *adj* **1** new or different. **2** newly come or arrived; inexperienced. **3** of food: newly made, not stale or preserved. **4** of water: not salty. **5** not worn or rumpled; clean. **6** of wind:cool and invigorating. **7** refreshed and alert. **8** of colours: clear and bright. **9** *informal* disrespectful or presumptuous. ➤ **freshly** *adv,* **freshness** *n.*
**freshen** *v* **1** to make or become fresh or fresher. **2** of wind: to increase in strength. **3** (**freshen up**) to wash and tidy oneself.
**fresher** *n chiefly Brit, informal* a first-year student at college or university.
**freshman** *n* (*pl* **freshmen**) a first-year student at university or (in the US) at high school.
**fret**[1] *v* (**fretted, fretting**) to be anxious and agitated.
**fret**[2] *n* each of a series of ridges fixed across the fingerboard of a guitar or other stringed instrument.
**fretful** *adj* anxious and nervous. ➤ **fretfully** *adv.*
**fretwork** *n* ornamental designs cut in thin wood.
**friable** *adj* easily crumbled.
**friar** *n* a member of a male religious order.
**friary** *n* (*pl* **-ies**) a building housing a community of friars.
**fricassee** *n* a dish of small pieces of stewed meat served in a white sauce.
**friction** *n* **1** the rubbing of one body against another. **2** resistance to relative motion between two bodies in contact. **3** disagreement between people or parties.
**Friday** *n* the day of the week following Thursday.
**fridge** *n chiefly Brit* a refrigerator.
**fried** *v* past tense and past part. of FRY[1].
**friend** *n* **1** a person one knows and likes. **2** somebody who supports a cause or institution. **3** (**Friend**) a Quaker. **make friends** to become friendly. ➤ **friendless** *adj,* **friendship** *n.*

***Usage Note:*** Note the spelling with *-ie-*.

**friendly**[1] *adj* (**-ier, -iest**) **1** like a friend; kind. **2** not hostile. **3** inclined to be favourable. **4** adapted to the needs of: *user-friendly* ➤ **friendliness** *n.*
**friendly**[2] *n* (*pl* **-ies**) *chiefly Brit* an informal match not played as part of a competition.
**frieze** *n* a sculptured or painted band on a building.
**frigate** *n Brit* a small warship.
**fright** *n* **1** fear excited by sudden danger or shock. **2** *informal* something unsightly or shocking.
**frighten** *v* **1** to make (somebody) afraid. **2** to force (somebody) by frightening them. ➤ **frightened** *adj,* **frightening** *adj.*
**frightful** *adj* **1** causing intense fear or shock. **2** *informal* unpleasant or difficult. ➤ **frightfully** *adv.*
**frigid** *adj* **1** intensely cold. **2** *formal* unenthusiastic or unfriendly. **3** *esp* of a woman: resistant to sexual contact. ➤ **frigidity** *n.*
**frill** *n* **1** a gathered or pleated fabric edging used on clothing or as ornament. **2** something decorative but not essential; a luxury. ➤ **frilly** *adj.*
**fringe**[1] *n* **1** an ornamental border of threads or tassels on a curtain or clothing. **2** a border. **3** *chiefly Brit* the hair that falls over the forehead. **4** something marginal or secondary. **5** (*treated as sing. or pl*) an unconventional or extreme group.
**fringe**[2] *v* **1** to provide or decorate with a fringe. **2** to serve as a fringe for.
**fringe benefit** *n* an extra benefit received by an employee in addition to wages.
**frippery** *n* (*pl* **-ies**) **1** showy ornamentation. **2** affected elegance or ostentation.
**Frisbee** *n trademark* a plastic disc thrown through the air with a flip of the wrist.
**frisk**[1] *v* **1** *informal* to search (a person) by running the hands over their clothing. **2** to leap or dance playfully.
**frisk**[2] *n* **1** *informal* an act of frisking somebody. **2** a playful leap or dance.
**frisky** *adj* (**-ier, -iest**) lively and energetic.
**frisson** *n* a shudder or thrill.
**fritillary** *n* (*pl* **-ies**) **1** a plant with bell-shaped flowers. **2** a butterfly with orange and black wings.
**fritter**[1] *n* a piece of food fried in batter.
**fritter**[2] *v* (*usu* + away) to waste (money or time) gradually.
**frivolous** *adj* **1** lacking value or purpose. **2** of a person: unconcerned and carefree. ➤ **frivolity** *n,* **frivolously** *adv.*
**frizz**[1] *v* of hair: to form a mass of tight curls.

**frizz**[2] *n* hair in a mass of tight curls.

**frock** *n* **1** *Brit* a woman's or girl's dress. **2** a loose garment, *esp* a monk's or friar's habit.

**frock coat** *n* a long jacket with knee-length skirts, formerly worn by men.

**frog** *n* a tailless leaping amphibian with a smooth skin and webbed feet. * **have a frog in one's throat** to be hoarse.

**frogman** *n* (*pl* **frogmen**) a diver equipped with a rubber suit, flippers, and an air supply for extended periods underwater.

**frogmarch** *v* to force (a person) to move forwards by holding their arms firmly from behind.

**frogspawn** *n* a gelatinous mass of frogs' eggs.

**frolic**[1] *v* (**frolicked, frolicking**) to play and run about happily.

**frolic**[2] *n* **1** a playful expression of high spirits. **2** a light-hearted game. ➤ **frolicsome** *adj.*

**from** *prep* **1** used to indicate a starting point of a journey or process. **2** used to indicate a starting point in measuring or reckoning. **3** used to indicate separation or removal. *take one from the shelf.* **4** used to indicate a source or cause: *suffering from the cold.*

**fromage frais** /ˌfromahzh ˈfray/ *n* a soft smooth cheese.

**frond** *n* a leaf of a palm or fern.

**front**[1] *n* **1** the part or surface of something that usually faces forward. **2** the part of the human body opposite to the back. **3** a line of battle. **4** a political coalition. **5** a particular situation or sphere of activity. **6** in meteorology, the boundary between two dissimilar air masses. **7** something that masks true identity or purpose. **8** demeanour or bearing in the face of a challenge or danger. * **in front of 1** directly ahead of. **2** in the presence of. **up front** as payment in advance.

**front**[2] *v* **1** to face towards. **2** to be in front of.

**front**[3] *adj* of or situated at the front.

**frontage** *n* **1** the front of a building. **2** the land between the front of a building and the street.

**frontal** *adj* situated at or showing the front. ➤ **frontally** *adv.*

**front bench** *n Brit* the benches in the House of Commons on which party leaders sit. ➤ **frontbencher** *n.*

**frontier** *n* **1** a border between two countries. **2** a region that forms the limit of settled territory. **3** (*also in pl*) the boundary between the known and the unknown.

**frontispiece** *n* an illustration facing the title page of a book or magazine.

**front line** *n* an army's position nearest the enemy.

**front man** *n* a person serving as a representative or figurehead.

**front-runner** *n* the leading contestant in a competition.

**frost**[1] *n* **1** a covering of ice crystals formed on a cold surface when the temperature falls below freezing. **2** a period of freezing weather.

**frost**[2] *v* to cover or be covered with frost.

**frostbite** *n* damage to the body caused by partial freezing.

**frosted** *adj* **1** covered with frost. **2** of glass: having a roughened translucent surface.

**frosting** *n* **1** a dull or roughened finish on metal or glass. **2** *chiefly NAmer* icing.

**frosty** *adj* (**-ier, -iest**) **1** marked by frost; freezing. **2** covered with frost; hoary. **3** cool and reserved in manner. ➤ **frostily** *adv.*

**froth**[1] *n* **1** a mass of bubbles formed on or in a liquid. **2** something insubstantial or of little value.

**froth**[2] *v* **1** (*often* + up) to cause (a liquid) to foam. **2** (*often* + up) to produce or emit froth. ➤ **frothy** *adj.*

**frown**[1] *v* **1** to contract the brow in anger, worry, or concentration. **2** (*often* + on) to show disapproval of.

**frown**[2] *n* a frowning expression.

**frowsty** *adj* (**-ier, -iest**) *chiefly Brit* lacking fresh air; stuffy.

**frowzy** *or* **frowsy** *adj* (**-ier, -iest**) having a slovenly or uncared-for appearance.

**froze** *v* past tense of FREEZE[1].

**frozen** *v* past part. of FREEZE[1].

**fructose** *n* a sweet sugar found in fruit and honey.

**frugal** *adj* economical in the use of resources. ➤ **frugality** *n,* **frugally** *adv.*

**fruit**[1] *n* **1** the usu edible reproductive body of a seed plant; *esp* one having a sweet pulp associated with the seed. **2** in botany, the ripened ovary of a flowering plant together with its contents. **3** the beneficial effect or consequence of an action. **4** *chiefly NAmer, informal, offensive* a male homosexual.

**fruit**[2] *v* to bear fruit.

**fruiterer** *n chiefly Brit* a person who sells fruit.

**fruitful** *adj* **1** yielding or producing fruit; fertile. **2** having beneficial results. ➤ **fruitfully** *adv.*

**fruition** *n* the realization or fulfilment of a project.

**fruitless** *adj* useless or unsuccessful. ➤ **fruitlessly** *adv.*

**fruit machine** *n Brit* a coin-operated gambling machine.

**fruity** *adj* (**-ier, -iest**) **1** resembling or having the flavour of fruit. **2** of a voice: deep and mellow. **3** *chiefly Brit, informal* sexually suggestive. ➤ **fruitiness** *n.*

**frump** *n* a dowdy unattractive girl or woman. ➤ **frumpy** *adj.*

**frustrate** *v* **1** to prevent (somebody) from carrying out a plan or intention. **2** to prevent (a plan) from being carried out or (a hope) from being realized. **3** to make (somebody) feel frustrated or vexed. ➤ **frustrating** *adj*, **frustration** *n*.

**fry**[1] *v* (**-ies, -ied**) **1** to cook in hot oil or fat over direct heat. **2** *informal* to feel very hot in the sun.

**fry**[2] *n* (*pl* **-ies**) **1** a dish of fried food. **2** (*in pl*) *chiefly NAmer* chips.

**fry**[3] *pl n* recently hatched fish.

**frying pan** *n* a shallow pan with a long handle, used for frying food. ✱ **out of the frying pan into the fire** free of one difficulty only to encounter a worse one.

**ft** *abbr* foot or feet.

**fuchsia** *n* a shrub with hanging deep red or purple flowers.

**fuddled** *adj* confused and dazed.

**fuddy-duddy** *n* (*pl* **-ies**) *informal* a person who is old-fashioned and pompous.

**fudge**[1] *n* **1** a soft creamy sweet made of sugar, milk, and butter. **2** a statement or decision that is intentionally vague and evades the central issues.

**fudge**[2] *v* to present (facts or figures) in a vague or misleading way.

**fuel**[1] *n* **1** a material used to produce heat or power when it is burned. **2** a material from which atomic energy can be produced in a nuclear reactor. **3** a source of strength or encouragement.

**fuel**[2] *v* (**fuelled, fuelling,** *NAmer* **fueled, fueling**) **1** to provide (a machine or vehicle) with fuel. **2** to stimulate (an emotion or activity).

**fuel cell** *n* a cell that continuously changes chemical energy to electrical energy.

**fuel injection** *n* the introduction of liquid fuel directly into the cylinders of an engine.

**fug** *n Brit, informal* a stuffy airless atmosphere. ➤ **fuggy** *adj*.

**fugitive**[1] *n* a person who flees or tries to escape.

**fugitive**[2] *adj* running away or trying to escape.

**fugue** *n* a musical composition in which a theme is repeated by successively entering voices, instruments, or parts.

**führer** *or* **fuehrer** *n* a tyrannnical leader, *esp* Hitler, leader of the Nazis in Germany.

**fulcrum** *n* (*pl* **fulcrums** *or* **fulcra**) the support about which a lever turns.

**fulfil** (*NAmer* **fulfill**) *v* (**fulfilled, fulfilling**) **1** to cause to happen as required or expected. **2** to put into effect; to carry out. **3** to satisfy (a requirement or condition). **4** to develop the full potential of. ➤ **fulfilment** *n*.

**full**[1] *adj* **1** containing as much or as many as possible or normal. **2** complete in detail, number, or duration: *the full story.* **3** (+ of) possessing or containing a great number or amount of. **4** at the highest or greatest degree; maximum. **5** of the face or figure: rounded in outline; plump. **6** of a garment: having much material. **7** rich and strong. ✱ **full of oneself** conceited. **full up** completely full. **in full swing** at a high level of activity. ➤ **fullness** *n*, **fulness** *n*.

**full**[2] *adv* **1** very. **2** exactly or squarely.

**full**[3] *n* (**the full**) the highest or fullest state, extent, or degree. ✱ **in full** completely or entirely.

**fullback** *n* in football, rugby, etc, a defensive player stationed close to the defended goal.

**full-blooded** *adj* forceful or vigorous; hearty.

**full-blown** *adj* fully developed or mature.

**full board** *n Brit* accommodation with all meals included.

**full-bodied** *adj* rich and full in flavour.

**fuller** *n* a person who cleanses and finishes woollen cloth.

**full-frontal** *adj* exposing the whole front of the body.

**full house** *n* **1** a full theatre or other venue. **2** in poker, a hand containing three of a kind and a pair. **3** a winning set of numbers at bingo.

**full moon** *n* the moon when its whole disc is illuminated.

**full-scale** *adj* **1** of a reproduction: identical in proportion and size to the original. **2** involving full use of resources.

**full time** *n* the end of a match or game.

**full-time** *adj and adv* working for all the available time.

**fully** *adv* **1** completely. **2** at least.

**fully-fledged** *adj* **1** of a bird: having all its feathers and able to fly. **2** completely developed.

**fulminate** *v* to protest or complain angrily. ➤ **fulmination** *n*.

**fulsome** *adj* **1** unnecessarily effusive or obsequious. **2** overabundant or copious. ➤ **fulsomely** *adv*.

**fumble**[1] *v* **1** to handle something clumsily or awkwardly. **2** to feel or handle (a ball) clumsily. **3** to deal with (something) awkwardly or clumsily.

**fumble**[2] *n* an act of fumbling.

**fume**[1] *n* a dirty and smelly effusion of smoke, vapour, or gas. ➤ **fumy** *adj*.

**fume**[2] *v* **1** to emit fumes. **2** to be very angry. ➤ **fuming** *adj*.

**fumigate** *v* to disinfect (a place) with chemical fumes. ➤ **fumigation** *n*.

**fun** *n* **1** amusement or enjoyment. **2** good humour. ✱ **in fun** not intended to be taken seriously. **make fun of** to make (somebody or something) an object of amusement or ridicule.

**function**[1] *n* **1** the purpose or primary use of a person or thing. **2** a large social gathering. **3** a mathematical relationship between each element of one set and at least one element of the same or another set.

**function**[2] *v* **1** to have a function; to serve. **2** to operate.

**functional** *adj* **1** designed for practical use. **2** relating to or performing a function. ➤ **functionality** *n,* **functionally** *adv.*

**functionary** *n* (*pl* **-ies**) an official.

**fund**[1] *n* **1** a sum of money set apart for a specific purpose. **2** (*in pl*) an available supply of money. **3** an available quantity of materials or resources.

**fund**[2] *v* to provide funds for.

**fundamental**[1] *adj* of central importance; principal. ➤ **fundamentally** *adv.*

**fundamental**[2] *n* a minimum constituent that characterizes something.

**fundamentalism** *n* a belief in the literal truth of a religious scripture or teaching. ➤ **fundamentalist** *n and adj.*

**funeral** *n* a formal ceremony at which a dead person is buried or cremated. ✱ **be somebody's funeral** *informal* to be somebody's own problem or fault.

**funeral director** *n* an undertaker.

**funerary** *adj* used for or associated with burial.

**funereal** *adj* gloomy or solemn.

**fun fair** *n chiefly Brit* an outdoor fair with amusements, sideshows, and rides.

**fungicide** *n* a substance used for destroying fungus. ➤ **fungicidal** *adj.*

**fungus** *n* (*pl* **fungi** *or* **funguses**) an organism, such as a mushroom or toadstool, that reproduces by means of spores. ➤ **fungal** *adj.*

**funicular railway** *n* a cable railway on a steep slope.

**funk**[1] *n informal* a state of paralysing fear or panic.

**funk**[2] *v informal* to lose the courage to do (something daunting).

**funk**[3] *n* dance music with a strong rhythm.

**funky** *adj* (**-ier, -iest**) *informal* **1** of dance music: having a strong rhythm. **2** *informal* original and stylish.

**funnel**[1] *n* **1** a utensil consisting of a hollow tapering cone with a tube at the smaller end, for pouring liquid or powder into a small opening. **2** a stack or flue for smoke or steam to escape.

**funnel**[2] *v* (**funnelled, funnelling,** *NAmer* **funneled, funneling**) to pass through a funnel or a narrow space.

**funny** *adj* (**-ier, -iest**) **1** causing amusement and laughter. **2** strange or odd. **3** involving deception or dishonesty. **4** unwilling to be helpful. **5** *informal* slightly unwell. ➤ **funnily** *adv.*

**funny bone** *n* the place at the elbow where a sensitive nerve rests against the bone.

**fur**[1] *n* **1** the soft thick hair of a mammal. **2** the dressed skin of an animal used for clothing. **3** an article of clothing made of or with fur. **4** a coating formed in kettles or pipes by the scale from hard water. ➤ **furred** *adj.*

**fur**[2] *v* (**furred, furring**) to become coated or clogged with scaly fur.

**furbelow** *n* **1** a flounce on women's clothing. **2** something showy or superfluous.

**furious** *adj* **1** extremely or violently angry. **2** having a stormy appearance. **3** intense or excited. ➤ **furiously** *adv.*

**furl** *v* to fold or roll tightly.

**furlong** *n* a unit of length equal to 220 yards (about 0.2km).

**furlough** *n* a leave of absence.

**furnace** *n* an enclosed apparatus in which intense heat is produced.

**furnish** *v* **1** to provide or supply. **2** to equip (a room or building) with furniture and fittings.

**furnishings** *pl n* articles of furniture and fittings used to make a room comfortable.

**furniture** *n* the movable articles that make an area suitable for living in or use.

**furore** (*NAmer* **furor**) *n* an outburst of general excitement or anger.

**furrier** *n* a fur dealer.

**furrow**[1] *n* **1** a trench in the earth made by a plough. **2** a deep wrinkle on the face.

**furrow**[2] *v* to make a furrow or line in.

**furry** *adj* (**-ier, -iest**) like or covered with fur.

**further**[1] *adv* **1** to a greater degree or extent. **2** moreover. **3** = FARTHER[1].

**further**[2] *adj* **1** extending beyond what exists or has happened; additional. **2** coming after the one referred to. **3** = FARTHER[2].

**further**[3] *v* to bring closer to completion. ➤ **furtherance** *n.*

**further education** *n Brit* education for people after leaving school.

**furthermore** *adv* in addition; moreover.

**furthest**[1] *adj* most distant in space or time.

**furthest**[2] *adv* **1** to or at the greatest distance in space, time, or degree. **2** by the greatest degree; most.

**furtive** *adj* using stealth; surreptitious or sly. ➤ **furtively** *adv.*

**fury** *n* (*pl* **-ies**) **1** intense or violent rage. **2** wild force or activity. **3** (**Fury**) each of three avenging deities who in Greek mythology punished crimes.

**furze** *n* = GORSE.

**fuse**[1] *n* **1** a length of combustible material for detonating an explosive charge. **2** the detonating device for setting off the charge in a bomb. **3** a wire or strip of metal that melts and interrupts an electrical circuit when the current exceeds a safe level.

**fuse**[2] *v* **1** to blend (two things) by melting them together. **2** to join to form a whole. **3** to become blended or combined. **4** to cause (an electrical appliance) to fail by fusing. **5** of an electrical appliance: to fail when a fuse melts. **6** to equip (a device) with an electrical fuse. **7** to fit a fuse to (a bomb or explosive).

**fuselage** *n* the central body of an aircraft.

**fusible** *adj* able to be fused or melted easily.

**fusilier** *n* a member of a British regiment formerly armed with fusils (light muskets).

**fusillade** *n* a number of shots fired simultaneously or in rapid succession.

**fusion** *n* **1** the process of joining things to form a whole. **2** the union of light atomic nuclei to form heavier nuclei, resulting in the release of large quantities of energy.

**fuss**[1] *n* **1** needless or useless bustle or excitement. **2** an objection or protest.

**fuss**[2] *v* **1** to pay undue attention to small details. **2** to become unnecessarily agitated or upset.

**fusspot** *n informal* a person who fusses a lot.

**fussy** *adj* (**-ier, -iest**) **1** showing too much concern over details. **2** fastidious. ➤ **fussily** *adv,* **fussiness** *n.*

**fusty** *adj* (**-ier, -iest**) **1** stale or musty. **2** old-fashioned.

**futile** *adj* ineffective or pointless. ➤ **futilely** *adv,* **futility** *n.*

**futon** *n* a padded quilt laid down to serve as a bed.

**future**[1] *n* **1** (**the future**) time that is to come. **2** a likelihood of success. **3** in grammar, the verb tense that expresses action or state in the future. * **in future** from now on.

**future**[2] *adj* **1** that is to be. **2** of or constituting the future tense.

**futuristic** *adj* **1** revolutionary or technologically advanced. **2** of a story: set in future time. ➤ **futuristically** *adv.*

**futurity** *n* time in the future.

**fuzz** *n* **1** fine light particles or fibres. **2** a distortion in vision or sound. **3** (**the fuzz**) *informal* the police.

**fuzzy** *adj* (**-ier, -iest**) **1** having the appearance or feel of fuzz. **2** blurred or indistinct. ➤ **fuzziness** *n.*

**G** *or* **g** *n* (*pl* **G's** *or* **Gs** *or* **g's**) the seventh letter of the English alphabet.

**g** *abbr* **1** gram(s). **2** gravity, or acceleration due to gravity.

**Ga** *abbr* the chemical symbol for gallium.

**gab** *v* (**gabbed, gabbing**) *informal* to chatter or blab.

**gabble**[1] *v* to talk rapidly or unintelligibly.

**gabble**[2] *n* rapid or unintelligible talk.

**gaberdine** *or* **gabardine** *n* a firm durable fabric used *esp* for making waterproof coats.

**gable** *n* the vertical triangular section of wall between two slopes of a pitched roof.

**gad** *v* (**gadded, gadding**) (+ about/around) to go about aimlessly, restlessly, or in search of pleasure.

**gadfly** *n* (*pl* **-ies**) **1** a fly that bites livestock. **2** a persistently annoying, provoking, or critical person.

**gadget** *n* a usu small and often novel mechanical or electronic device. ➤ **gadgetry** *n.*

**Gaelic** *n* the Celtic language of Ireland, the Isle of Man, and Scotland.

**gaff**[1] *n* a pole with a hook for landing heavy fish.

**gaff**[2] *n Brit, informal* a house or other dwelling place.

**gaffe** *n* a social or tactical blunder.

**gaffer** *n Brit, informal* **1** a boss or foreman. **2** an old man.

**gag**[1] *n* **1** something put over a person's mouth to stop them speaking. **2** a joke.

**gag**[2] *v* (**gagged, gagging**) **1** to put a gag over the mouth of. **2** to prevent (somebody) from having free speech. **3** to retch.

**gaga** *adj informal* **1** senile. **2** slightly mad.

**gage**[1] *n NAmer* see GAUGE[1].

**gage**[2] *v NAmer* see GAUGE[2].

**gaggle** *n* **1** a flock of geese. **2** *informal* a noisy or disorderly group of people.

**gaiety** *n* cheerfulness or merriment.

**gaily** *adv* **1** cheerfully or merrily. **2** with bright colours. **3** blithely; unthinkingly.

**gain**[1] *v* **1** to get possession of, win, or acquire. **2** (*often* + on) to start catching up with (somebody one is pursuing). **3** to arrive at (a place). **4** to increase in (e.g. speed, weight). **5** to get advantage; to profit. **6** of a watch or clock: to run fast.

**gain**[2] *n* **1** something acquired. **2** profit or a profit. **3** an increase in amount or degree.

**gainful** *adj* income-producing; profitable. ➤ **gainfully** *adv.*

**gainsay** *v* (**gainsays, gainsaid**) *formal* to deny or dispute (e.g. an allegation).

**gait** *n* a manner of walking.

**gaiter** *n usu in pl* a cloth or leather legging worn by men.

**gala** *n* **1** a festive gathering or entertainment. **2** *Brit* a special sports meeting.

**galactic** *adj* relating to a galaxy.

**galaxy** *n* (*pl* **-ies**) **1** a large star system. **2** (**the Galaxy**) the Milky Way.

**gale** *n* **1** a strong wind. **2** a noisy outburst of laughter.

**gall**[1] *n* **1** brazen and insolent audacity. **2** rancour or bitterness.

**gall**[2] *n* **1** exasperation. **2** a skin sore caused by rubbing.

**gall**[3] *v* to mortify and irritate. ➤ **galling** *adj.*

**gallant**[1] *adj* **1** nobly chivalrous and brave. **2** courteously attentive, *esp* to women. ➤ **gallantly** *adv.*

**gallant**[2] *n* a man who is particularly attentive to women.

**gallantry** *n* (*pl* **-ies**) **1** conspicuous bravery. **2** courteous attention to a lady.

**galleon** *n* a large sailing ship with several decks used for war or commerce.

**galley** *n* (*pl* **-eys**) **1** a large low single-decked ship propelled by oars and sails. **2** a narrow kitchen *esp* on a ship or aircraft.

**Gallic** *adj* of Gaul or France.

**gallivant** *v* to roam about looking for pleasure.

**gallon** *n* **1** a unit of liquid capacity equal to eight pints. **2** *informal* (*in pl*) large quantities.

**gallop**[1] *n* **1** the fastest natural gait of the horse. **2** a ride or run at a gallop.

**gallop**[2] *v* (**galloped, galloping**) **1** to go or ride at a gallop. **2** to read, talk, or proceed at great speed.

**gallows** *n* (*pl* **gallows** *or* **gallowses**) **1** a frame for hanging criminals. **2** (**the gallows**) hanging.

**gallows humour** *n* grim humour that makes fun of a very serious or terrifying situation.

**gallstone** *n* a rounded solid mass formed in the gall bladder or bile ducts.

**galore** *adj* (*used after a noun*) abundant or plentiful: *bargains galore.*
**galosh** *n* a rubber overshoe.
**galumph** *v informal* to bound along or around clumsily and exuberantly.
**galvanic** *adj* producing a direct current of electricity from chemical action.
**galvanize** *or* **-ise** *v* **1** to stimulate or shock into action. **2** to coat (iron or steel) with zinc as a protection from rust. ➤ **galvanized** *adj.*
**galvanometer** *n* an instrument for measuring a small electric current.
**gambit** *n* **1** a calculated move or remark. **2** a set of opening moves in chess.
**gamble**[1] *v* **1** to play a game of chance for money. **2** to take a risk with in the hope of gaining an advantage. **3** to risk (e.g. money) by gambling. ➤ **gambler** *n.*
**gamble**[2] *n* something involving an element of risk.
**gambol** *v* (**gambolled, gambolling,** *NAmer* **gamboled, gamboling**) to skip or leap about in play.
**game**[1] *n* **1** an activity engaged in for amusement. **2** a physical or mental competition conducted according to rules. **3** a sports match or similar contest. **4** a division of a larger contest, *esp* a tennis match. **5** (*in pl*) an organized event with contests in various types of sport. **6** a type of activity seen as competitive or governed by rules. **7** animals that are hunted; *esp* wild mammals, birds, and fish.
**game**[2] *v* to play for money; to gamble. ➤ **gaming** *adj.*
**game**[3] *adj* ready to take risks or try something new. ➤ **gamely** *adv.*
**game**[4] *adj* of somebody's leg: crippled or lame.
**gamekeeper** *n* somebody who breeds and protects game animals or birds on a private estate.
**gamesmanship** *n* the art of winning games by means other than superior skill without actually cheating.
**gamete** *n* a germ cell capable of fusing with another gamete of the other sex to form a zygote from which a new organism develops.
**gamine** *adj* of a girl or woman: having an impish, boyish appeal.
**gamma** *n* the third letter of the Greek alphabet (Γ, γ).
**gamma radiation** *n* radiation composed of gamma rays.
**gamma rays** *pl n* streams of high-energy electromagnetic radiation that have a shorter wavelength than X-rays.
**gammon** *n* **1** ham that has been smoked or cured. **2** the lower end of a side of bacon, including the hind leg.
**gammy** *adj* (**-ier, -iest**) *Brit, informal* of somebody's leg: injured or lame.
**gamut** *n* an entire range or series. ✱ **run the gamut** to go through the whole range of something.
**gander**[1] *n* an adult male goose.
**gander**[2] *n informal* a look or glance.
**gang**[1] *n* **1** a group of people associating for criminal or disreputable ends. **2** a group of people working together, e.g. as labourers. **3** a group of people who regularly spend time together.
**gang**[2] *v* (+ together) to move or act as a gang.
**gangling** *adj* tall, thin, and awkward.
**ganglion** *n* (*pl* **ganglia** *or* **ganglions**) **1** a small cyst on a joint or tendon. **2** a mass of nerve cells.
**gangplank** *n* a movable plank used to board a ship from a quay or another ship.
**gangrene** *n* the death of soft body tissues in a localized area, due to loss of blood supply. ➤ **gangrenous** *adj.*
**gangster** *n* a member of a criminal gang.
**gang up** *v* (*often* + on/against) to combine as a group, *esp* to attack somebody.
**gangway** *n* **1** a gangplank. **2** *Brit* a narrow passage, e.g. between sections of seats in a theatre.
**gannet** *n* **1** a large white fish-eating seabird. **2** *Brit, informal* a greedy person.
**gantry** *n* (*pl* **-ies**) a raised framework spanning something, which carries railway signals, a travelling crane, etc.
**gaol** *n and v Brit* see JAIL[1], JAIL[2].
**gap** *n* **1** a break in e.g. a wall or hedge. **2** an empty space between two objects. **3** an interval. **4** a disparity. ➤ **gappy** *adj.*
**gape**[1] *v* **1** to open or part widely. **2** to gaze openmouthed in surprise or wonder. ➤ **gaping** *adj.*
**gape**[2] *n* an act of gaping; *esp* an openmouthed stare.
**gap year** *n* a year's break between leaving school and starting further education.
**garage**[1] *n* **1** a building where motor vehicles are kept. **2** an establishment for providing essential services to motor vehicles, e.g. supplying fuel or carrying out repairs. **3** a style of house music with a soul influence.
**garage**[2] *v* to keep or put (a car) in a garage.
**garb**[1] *n* a style of clothing; dress.
**garb**[2] *v* to dress.
**garbage** *n* **1** *chiefly NAmer* rubbish or waste. **2** worthless writing or speech.
**garble** *v* to distort or confuse (a message, transmitted text).
**garden**[1] *n* **1** *Brit* a plot of ground, typically beside a house, where vegetables, flowers, etc are cultivated. **2** (*also in pl*) a public park. ✱ **lead somebody up the garden path** to mislead or deceive somebody.
**garden**[2] *v* to work in a garden. ➤ **gardener** *n.*
**gargantuan** *adj* gigantic.

**gargle**[1] *v* to cleanse one's mouth or throat by blowing through a liquid held in it.

**gargle**[2] *n* **1** a liquid used in gargling. **2** an act or the sound of gargling.

**gargoyle** *n* a rainwater spout in the form of a grotesque human or animal figure projecting from a roof gutter.

**garish** *adj* excessively and gaudily bright. ➤ **garishly** *adv.*

**garland**[1] *n* a wreath of flowers or leaves worn as an ornament or trophy.

**garland**[2] *v* to crown with a garland.

**garlic** *n* the pungent compound bulb of a plant of the lily family, used as a flavouring in cookery.

**garment** *n* an article of clothing.

**garner** *v* to collect (e.g. evidence or information).

**garnet** *n* a transparent deep red semiprecious stone.

**garnish**[1] *v* to decorate or embellish (*esp* food).

**garnish**[2] *n* an embellishment, *esp* a decorative addition to a dish.

**garret** *n* a small room just under the roof of a house.

**garrison**[1] *n* a body of troops stationed in a town or fortress to defend it.

**garrison**[2] *v* to station troops in (a place).

**garrotte**[1] (*NAmer* **garotte** *or* **garrote**) *n* a wire or cord used for strangling somebody.

**garrotte**[2] (*NAmer* **garotte** *or* **garrote**) *v* to kill with a garrotte.

**garrulous** *adj* excessively talkative. ➤ **garrulity** *n.*

**garter** *n* a band worn to hold up a stocking or sock. ➤ **gartered** *adj.*

**gas**[1] *n* (*pl* **gases** *or* **gasses**) **1** a fluid substance, e.g. air, that tends to expand indefinitely. **2** a gas or gaseous mixture used as a fuel, anaesthetic, etc. **3** *NAmer, informal* petrol. **4** *NAmer* flatulence.

**gas**[2] *v* (**gassed, gassing**) **1** to poison or affect adversely with gas. **2** *informal* to talk idly.

**gas chamber** *n* a chamber in which prisoners are executed or animals killed by poison gas.

**gaseous** *adj* having the form or nature of a gas.

**gash**[1] *v* to injure with a deep long cut.

**gash**[2] *n* a deep long cut.

**gasket** *n* a piece of sealing material for ensuring that a joint does not leak liquid or gas.

**gaslight** *n* light from a gas lamp. ➤ **gaslit** *adj.*

**gas mask** *n* a mask with a chemical air filter, used as a protection against harmful gases.

**gasoline** *or* **gasolene** *n NAmer* petrol.

**gasometer** *n* a large cylindrical storage container for gas.

**gasp**[1] *v* **1** to catch the breath suddenly and audibly, e.g. with shock. **2** to breathe laboriously. **3** (+ for) to crave.

**gasp**[2] *n* an audible catching of the breath.

**gassy** *adj* (**-ier, -iest**) **1** containing or like gas. **2** *informal* talkative.

**gastric** *adj* relating to the stomach.

**gastroenteritis** *n* inflammation of the lining of the stomach and the intestines.

**gastronomy** *n* the art or science of good eating. ➤ **gastronomic** *adj.*

**gasworks** *n* (*pl* **gasworks**) a place where gas is manufactured.

**gate** *n* **1** the usu hinged frame that closes an opening in a wall or fence. **2** a numbered exit from an airport building to the airfield. **3** either of a pair of barriers that let water in and out of a lock or close a road at a level crossing. **4** the number of spectators at a sporting event.

**gateau** *n* (*pl* **gateaux** *or* **gateaus**) a rich elaborate cream cake.

**gate-crash** *v* to attend (a party) without a ticket or invitation. ➤ **gate-crasher** *n.*

**gatefold** *n* a large folded page inserted in a book, journal, etc.

**gatehouse** *n* a lodge at the entrance to the grounds of a large house.

**gatekeeper** *n* somebody who guards a gate.

**gatepost** *n* the post on which a gate is hung or against which it closes.

**gateway** *n* **1** an opening for a gate. **2** a point of entry or access.

**gather**[1] *v* **1** to bring (things) together; to collect. **2** to come together in a body. **3** to pick or harvest (flowers, crops, etc). **4** to accumulate (speed). **5** to prepare (e.g. oneself) for an effort. **6** to clasp (somebody), e.g. to oneself, in an embrace. **7** to pull (fabric) together to create small tucks. **8** to reach a conclusion from hints or through inferences.

**gather**[2] *n* a tuck in cloth made by gathering.

**gathering** *n* an assembly or meeting.

**gauche** *adj* lacking social experience or grace.

**gaucho** *n* (*pl* **-os**) a cowboy of the pampas regions in S America.

**gaudy** *adj* (**-ier, -iest**) ostentatiously or tastelessly and brightly ornamented. ➤ **gaudily** *adv.*

**gauge**[1] (*NAmer* **gage**) *n* **1** an instrument for measuring or testing something, e.g. a dimension or quantity. **2** a measure of the thickness of a thin sheet of metal, plastic, etc, the diameter of wire, or the bore of a shotgun. **3** the distance between the rails of a railway, etc.

**gauge**[2] (*NAmer* **gage**) *v* **1** to measure exactly the size, dimensions, or capacity of. **2** to estimate or judge.

***Usage Note:*** Note the spelling with *-au-*.

**gaunt** *adj* **1** excessively thin and angular. **2** of a place: barren or desolate.

**gauntlet**[1] *n* **1** a strong protective glove with a wide extension above the wrist. **2** a glove formerly worn with medieval armour. ✱ **throw down the gauntlet** to issue a challenge.

**gauntlet**[2] *n* ✱ **run the gauntlet** to have to suffer criticism or a testing experience in order to achieve something.

**gauze** *n* **1** a thin often transparent fabric. **2** a fine mesh of metal or plastic. ➤ **gauzy** *adj.*

**gave** *v* past tense of GIVE[1].

**gavel** *n* a small mallet with which a chairman, judge, or auctioneer commands attention or confirms a vote, sale, etc.

**gavotte** *n* a popular 18th-cent. French dance.

**gawk** *v* to gawp.

**gawky** *adj* (**-ier, -iest**) awkward and lanky.

**gawp** *v Brit, informal* to gape or stare stupidly.

**gay**[1] *adj* **1** homosexual. **2** for or relating to homosexuals. **3** *dated* bright or attractive. **4** *dated* happily excited; carefree.

**gay**[2] *n* a homosexual; *esp* a man.

**gaze**[1] *v* to look steadily.

**gaze**[2] *n* a fixed intent look.

**gazebo** *n* (*pl* **-os** *or* **-oes**) a summerhouse, placed to command a view.

**gazelle** *n* (*pl* **gazelles** *or* **gazelle**) a small, graceful antelope.

**gazette** *n* a newspaper or journal, *esp* an official one.

**gazetteer** *n* a dictionary of place names.

**gazump** *v Brit* to thwart (a would-be house purchaser) by raising the price after agreeing to sell at a lower one. ➤ **gazumper** *n.*

**GB** *abbr* **1** (*also* **Gb**) gigabyte(s). **2** Great Britain.

**GBH** *abbr Brit* grievous bodily harm.

**GC** *abbr* George Cross.

**GCSE** *abbr Brit* General Certificate of Secondary Education.

**Gd** *abbr* the chemical symbol for gadolinium.

**Ge** *abbr* the chemical symbol for germanium.

**gear**[1] *n* **1** a set of interlocking wheels in the transmission system of a vehicle that determines the direction of travel or ratio of engine speed to vehicle speed. **2** a particular adjustment of the transmission system: *second gear.* **3** equipment. **4** *informal* clothing.

**gear**[2] *v* **1** to connect (machinery) by gears. **2** (+ to) to adjust so as to match, blend with, or satisfy.

**gearbox** *n* a set of vehicle gears or the protective casing enclosing them.

**gear lever** *n* a control rod on a gear-changing mechanism, *esp* a vehicle's gearbox.

**gear up** *v* to make ready for effective operation.

**gecko** *n* (*pl* **-os** *or* **-oes**) a small tropical lizard able to walk on vertical or overhanging surfaces.

**gee** *interj NAmer, informal* used as an exclamation of surprise or enthusiasm.

**geek** *n informal* **1** somebody unfashionable or socially awkward. **2** somebody obsessively interested in computers and technology. ➤ **geeky** *adj.*

**geese** *n* pl of GOOSE.

**gee up** *v informal* **1** to stir to greater activity. **2** to encourage (e.g. a horse) to go faster.

**geezer** *n informal* a man.

**Geiger counter** *n* an instrument for detecting and measuring radioactivity.

**geisha** /'gayshə/ *n* (*pl* **geisha** *or* **geishas**) a Japanese woman trained to provide entertaining and light-hearted company for men.

**gel**[1] *n* a jelly-like substance, e.g. a hair gel or shaving gel.

**gel**[2] *v* (**gelled, gelling**) **1** of a liquid: to set. **2** (*NAmer* **jell**) of an idea, plan, etc: to become definite. **3** (*NAmer* **jell**) of a group of people: to get on well together. **4** to put gel on (the hair).

**gelatin** *or* **gelatine** *n* a glutinous material obtained from animal tissues by boiling and used in food, e.g. to set jellies, and photography.

**geld** *v* to castrate (a male animal).

**gelding** *n* a castrated male horse.

**gelignite** *n* a type of dynamite.

**gem** *n* **1** a precious stone. **2** somebody or something highly prized.

**Gemini** *n* the third sign of the zodiac (the Twins).

**gemstone** *n* a mineral or petrified material used as a gem.

**gen** *n Brit, informal* information.

**gendarme** /'zhondahm/ *n* a member of an armed police force, *esp* in France.

**gender** *n* **1** in some languages, a grammatical class, , labelled as masculine, feminine, or neuter, that determines the agreement of *esp* nouns with other words. **2** the state of being male or female, *esp* as regards cultural and social differences. **3** the members of either sex.

**gene** *n* a unit of DNA that is carried on a chromosome and controls transmission of hereditary characteristics.

**genealogy** *n* (*pl* **-ies**) **1** the descent of a person, family, or group from an ancestor. **2** the study of family pedigrees. ➤ **genealogical** *adj,* **genealogist** *n.*

**genera** *n* pl of GENUS.

**general**[1] *adj* **1** involving, or applicable to, all or most members of a class, kind, or group. **2** concerned with the main or universal aspects of something rather than particular details. **3** taking precedence over others similarly titled: *the general manager.* ✱ **in general** usually; for the most part.

**general**[2] *n* **1** a commander of an army. **2** an officer in the British army ranking below a field marshal.

**general anaesthetic** *n* an anaesthetic that causes loss of consciousness and lack of sensation over the whole body.

**general election** *n* an election in which candidates are elected in all constituencies of a nation.

**generalist** *n* somebody whose skills, interests, etc extend to several different activities.

**generality** *n* (*pl* **-ies**) **1** a vague and unspecific statement. **2** the quality or state of being general.

**generalize** *or* **-ise** *v* **1** to make general or vague statements. **2** to make more general or widespread. ➤ **generalization** *n.*

**generally** *adv* **1** without regard to specific instances. **2** usually; as a rule. **3** as a whole.

**general practitioner** *n* a medical doctor who treats all types of disease for patients living in a particular area. ➤ **general practice** *n.*

**general-purpose** *adj* suitable for two or more basic purposes.

**generate** *v* **1** to create (e.g. energy) by a physical process. **2** to be the cause of (a situation, action, or state of mind).

**generation** *n* **1** a group of individuals born and living at the same time. **2** a group constituting a single step in the line of descent from an ancestor. **3** a class of objects developed from an earlier type. **4** the average time between the birth of parents and the birth of their offspring, usu about 30 years. **5** production or creation.

**generator** *n* a machine for producing electrical energy.

**generic** *adj* **1** characteristic of a whole group or class. **2** not having a trademark. **3** relating to a biological genus. ➤ **generically** *adv.*

**generous** *adj* **1** giving e.g. money or help freely and abundantly. **2** magnanimous and kindly. **3** marked by abundance or richness. ➤ **generosity** *n.*

**Genesis** *n* the first book of the Old Testament.

**genesis** *n* (*pl* **geneses**) the origin or coming into being of something.

**genetic** *adj* **1** relating to genetics. **2** relating to genes. ➤ **genetically** *adv.*

**genetically modified** *adj* of food: containing an ingredient that has had its genetic structure altered, e.g. to make it grow better.

**genetic engineering** *n* the artificial manipulation of the genetic material of living things for experimental or industrial purposes.

**genetic fingerprint** *n* a unique pattern of repeated DNA sequences in the genetic makeup of an individual that can be used to identify him or her. ➤ **genetic fingerprinting** *n.*

**genetics** *pl n* the branch of biology that deals with the ways in which hereditary characteristics are passed down. ➤ **geneticist** *n.*

**genial** *adj* cheerfully good-tempered. ➤ **geniality** *n,* **genially** *adv.*

**genie** *n* a spirit in Arabian folklore who can be summoned to grant wishes.

**genital** *adj* relating to or in the region of the genitalia.

**genitalia** *pl n* the external reproductive and sexual organs.

**genitals** *pl n* the genitalia.

**genitive** *adj* denoting a grammatical case expressing a relationship of possessor or source.

**genius** *n* (*pl* **geniuses**) **1** a person of a very high intelligence or skill. **2** extraordinary intellectual power.

**genocide** *n* the deliberate murder of a racial or cultural group. ➤ **genocidal** *adj.*

**genre** *n* a category of artistic, musical, or literary composition.

**gent** *n informal* a gentleman.

**genteel** *adj* showing, or trying to show, upper-class refinement or manners. ➤ **gentility** *n.*

**gentile**[1] *n* (*often* **Gentile**) a non-Jewish person.

**gentile**[2] *adj* (*often* **Gentile**) non-Jewish.

**gentle** *adj* **1** of a person: kind and mild. **2** soft or delicate. **3** of a breeze: moderate. **4** of a slope: gradual. ➤ **gentleness** *n,* **gently** *adv.*

**gentleman** *n* (*pl* **gentlemen**) **1** a man who is chivalrous and honourable. **2** a man belonging to the landed gentry or nobility. **3** in polite or formal use: a man. ➤ **gentlemanly** *adj.*

**gentleman's agreement** *n* an unwritten agreement secured only by the honour of the participants and not legally enforceable.

**gentry** *n* the upper class.

**genuflect** *v* to go down on one knee briefly, *esp* as a gesture of respect to sacred objects. ➤ **genuflection** *n.*

**genuine** *adj* **1** actually what it is claimed to be. **2** sincere. ➤ **genuinely** *adv.*

**gen up** *v* (**genned, genning**) *Brit, informal* (+ on) to find information or learn about something.

**genus** *n* (*pl* **genera**) a category in the classification of living things ranking between family and species.

**geodesic** *adj* relating to the plotting of straight lines on curved surfaces, or to a method of construction that uses light, straight structural elements to form a curved surface.

**geographical** *or* **geographic** *adj* to do with geography. ➤ **geographically** *adv.*

**geography** *n* **1** a science that deals with the earth, its physical features, and the distribution of plant, animal and human life over its surface. **2** the geographical features of an area. ➤ **geographer** *n.*

**geology** *n* **1** a science that deals with the structure and history of the earth, *esp* as recorded in rocks. **2** the geological features of an area. ➤ **geological** *adj,* **geologist** *n.*

**geometric** *adj* **1** relating to geometry. **2** using patterns formed from straight and curved lines. ➤ **geometrical** *adj,* **geometrically** *adv.*

**geometry** *n* (*pl* **-ies**) **1** a branch of mathematics that deals with the measurement, properties, and relationships of points, lines, angles, surfaces, and solids. **2** a surface shape, e.g. of a crystal.

**Geordie** *n Brit, informal* a native or inhabitant of Tyneside.

**Georgian** *adj* of the reigns of the first four King Georges of Britain (1714–1830).

**geranium** *n* a garden plant with red, pink or white flowers.

**gerbil** *n* a burrowing desert rodent with long hind legs.

**geriatric**[1] *adj* **1** relating to or for elderly people. **2** *informal, derog* aged or decrepit.

**geriatric**[2] *n* an elderly person.

**germ** *n* **1** a micro-organism, *esp* one that causes disease. **2** a small mass of cells capable of developing into an organism. **3** the rudimentary state from which something develops.

**German** *n* **1** a native or inhabitant of Germany. **2** the language of Germany, Austria, and parts of Switzerland. ➤ **German** *adj.*

**germane** *adj* relevant and appropriate.

**Germanic** *adj* **1** relating to a branch of the Indo-European language family containing English, German, Dutch, and the Scandinavian languages. **2** characteristic of the German people.

**German measles** *pl n* = RUBELLA.

**German shepherd** *n* = ALSATIAN.

**germicide** *n* a substance that kills germs. ➤ **germicidal** *adj.*

**germinal** *adj* **1** of or having the characteristics of a germ cell or early embryo. **2** in the earliest stage of development.

**germinate** *v* to begin to grow; to sprout. ➤ **germination** *n.*

**gerontology** *n* the study of ageing and the problems of old people.

**gerrymander** *v* to divide (an area) into election districts to give one political party an electoral advantage.

**gerund** *n* a noun ending in *-ing* that is formed from a verb and shows certain verbal features, e.g. *singing* in *He likes singing.*

**Gestapo** /gə'shtahpoh, gə'stahpoh/ *n* the secret police organization in Nazi Germany.

**gestation** *n* **1** the carrying or development of young in the uterus. **2** conception and development, *esp* in the mind.

**gesticulate** *v* to make expressive gestures, *esp* when speaking. ➤ **gesticulation** *n.*

**gesture**[1] *n* **1** a movement, usu of the body or limbs, that expresses an idea or attitude. **2** something said or done for its effect on the attitudes of others or to convey a feeling.

**gesture**[2] *v* to make a gesture.

**get** *v* (**getting,** *past tense* **got,** *past part.* **got** *or NAmer or archaic* **gotten**) **1** to gain possession of; to obtain or receive. **2** to fetch. **3** to capture. **4** to succeed in achieving. **5** to become affected by (an illness). **6** to suffer or undergo. **7** to cause (something or somebody) to come into a certain condition: *I must get my shoes mended.* **8** to persuade or induce. **9** to become: *to get drunk.* **10** to travel by (a form of public transport). **11** to succeed in coming or going: *Where did they get to?* **12** *informal* to hear or understand (something said). **13** *informal* to punish or harm (somebody). ✻ **get at 1** to reach. **2** *informal* to imply. **3** *informal* to criticize or tease. **4** *informal* to bribe.

**getaway** *n* a departure or escape.

**get away** *v* to escape. ✻ **get away with** to avoid punishment or blame for.

**get by** *v* to manage with difficulty or limited resources.

**get down** *v* to make dejected. ✻ **get down to** to start to give attention to (an activity).

**get off** *v* to escape punishment.

**get on** *v* **1** to be on friendly terms. **2** to succeed. ✻ **be getting on for** to be approaching (a specified age, time, distance, etc).

**get over** *v* **1** to overcome (a difficulty). **2** to recover from (something unpleasant). **3** to succeed in communicating (an idea, etc).

**get round** *v* to evade (a law or responsibility). ✻ **get round to** to make a start eventually on (a task, etc).

**get through** *v* **1** to reach the end of (an ordeal or difficulty). **2** to make contact by telephone. ✻ **get through to** to make oneself understood by.

**get-together** *n* an informal social gathering or meeting.

**get up** *v* to rise from a sitting or lying position, or from one's bed. ✻ **get up to** *Brit, informal* to be involved in (something wrong, mischievous, etc).

**get-up** *n informal* an outfit or costume.

**geyser** *n* a spring that intermittently throws out jets of heated water and steam.

**ghastly** *adj* (**-ier, -iest**) **1** terrifyingly horrible. **2** *informal* intensely unpleasant, disagreeable, or objectionable. **3** pale and wan. ➤ **ghastliness** *n.*

**gherkin** *n* a small pickled cucumber.

**ghetto** *n* (*pl* **-os** *or* **-oes**) **1** an area of a city in which a minority group live. **2** part of a city in which Jews formerly lived.

**ghetto blaster** *n informal* a large portable radio, usu incorporating a cassette or CD player.

**ghost**[1] *n* **1** a disembodied soul; *esp* the soul of a dead person haunting the living. **2** a faint shadowy trace.

**ghost**[2] *v* to ghostwrite (e.g. a book).

**ghostly** *adj* (**-ier, -iest**) of or like a ghost; spectral.

**ghost town** *n* a once-flourishing but now deserted town.

**ghostwrite** *v* (**ghostwrote, ghostwritten**) to write (e.g. a book) for another person, who is the presumed author. ➤ **ghostwriter** *n.*

**ghoul** *n* **1** an evil spirit or ghost. **2** a person with a morbid interest in fatal accidents, disasters, etc. ➤ **ghoulish** *adj.*

**GI** *n* (*pl* **GI's** *or* **GIs**) a member of the US army, *esp* a private.

**giant**[1] *n* **1** a legendary being, like a human in shape, but having great size and strength. **2** an extraordinarily large person, animal, or plant.

**giant**[2] *adj* extremely large.

**gibber** *v* to make rapid, inarticulate, and usu incomprehensible sounds.

**gibberish** *n* unintelligible or meaningless language.

**gibbet** *n* **1** a gallows. **2** an upright post with an arm, used formerly for displaying the bodies of executed criminals as a warning.

**gibbon** *n* a small tailless tree-dwelling ape of SE Asia.

**gibe** *v and n* see JIBE[1], JIBE[2].

**giblets** *pl n* a fowl's heart, liver, neck and other edible internal organs.

**giddy** *adj* (**-ier, -iest**) **1** feeling a sensation of unsteadiness and lack of balance as if everything is whirling round. **2** lightheartedly frivolous.

**gift**[1] *n* **1** something freely given by one person to another; a present or donation. **2** a natural capacity or talent. * **gift of the gab** *informal* the ability to talk persuasively.

**gift**[2] *v* to give as a gift.

**gifted** *adj* having great natural ability or intelligence.

**gig**[1] *n* a light two-wheeled carriage pulled by a horse.

**gig**[2] *n informal* a live performance by a singer, rock group, etc.

**gigabyte** *n* in computing, a quantity of data equal to one thousand million ($10^9$) bytes.

**gigantic** *adj* unusually great; enormous.

**giggle**[1] *v* to laugh in a silly or nervous manner.

**giggle**[2] *n* **1** an act of giggling. **2** *Brit, informal* something amusing. ➤ **giggly** *adj.*

**gigolo** *n* (*pl* **-os**) a man paid by a usu older woman for companionship or sex.

**gild** *v* (*past tense and past part.* **gilded** *or* **gilt**) **1** to overlay with a thin covering of gold. **2** to give an attractive but often deceptive appearance to.

**gill**[1] *n* **1** an organ, *esp* of a fish, for taking in oxygen dissolved in water. **2** a radiating plate on the undersurface of the cap of some fungi, e.g. mushrooms.

**gill**[2] *n* a unit of liquid capacity equal to a quarter of a pint.

**gilt**[1] *adj* covered with gold or gilt.

**gilt**[2] *n* gold leaf or gold paint laid on a surface.

**gilt-edged** *adj* of government securities: traded on the Stock Exchange and having a guaranteed fixed interest rate.

**gimlet** *n* a T-shaped tool for boring small holes in wood.

**gimmick** *n* a scheme or object devised to gain attention or publicity. ➤ **gimmickry** *n,* **gimmicky** *adj.*

**gin**[1] *n* a spirit made from distilled grain and flavoured with juniper berries.

**gin**[2] *n* **1** a machine for separating cotton fibre from seeds and waste material. **2** a machine for raising or moving heavy weights. **3** a snare for game.

**ginger** *n* **1** the rhizome of a tropical plant, which has a strong hot taste and is used in cooking or dried and ground to make a spice. **2** a reddish or yellowish brown colour.

**ginger ale** *n* a sweet carbonated non-alcoholic drink flavoured with ginger.

**ginger beer** *n* a weak fizzy alcoholic drink, made by fermenting ginger and syrup.

**gingerbread** *n* a thick cake made with treacle and flavoured with ginger.

**gingerly** *adv* very cautiously or carefully.

**gingham** *n* a lightweight cotton fabric with a checked pattern.

**gingivitis** *n* inflammation of the gums.

**ginormous** *adj Brit, informal* exceptionally large.

**ginseng** *n* the aromatic root of a Chinese or North American plant, widely valued as a tonic.

**gipsy** *n* see GYPSY.

**giraffe** *n* (*pl* **giraffes** *or* **giraffe**) a large African mammal with a very long neck.

**gird** *v* (*past tense and past part.* **girded** *or* **girt**) to encircle with a flexible band, e.g. a belt. * **gird (up) one's loins** to prepare for action.

**girder** *n* a strong horizontal metal beam.

**girdle**[1] *n* **1** a belt or cord encircling the body, usu at the waist. **2** a woman's tightly fitting undergarment that extends from the waist to below the hips.

**girdle**[2] *v* to encircle with , or as if with, a girdle.

**girl** *n* **1** a female child. **2** a young woman. **3** a girlfriend. ➤ **girlish** *adj.*

**girlfriend** *n* **1** a regular female companion with whom somebody is romantically or sexually involved. **2** a female friend.

**girn** *or* **gurn** *v Brit* to pull a grotesque face.

**giro** *n* (*pl* **-os**) **1** a computerized system of money transfer, comparable to a current account. **2** *informal* a giro cheque or payment, *esp* a social security benefit.

**girt** *v* past tense and past part. of GIRD.

**girth** *n* **1** a measurement round something, e.g. a tree trunk or somebody's waist. **2** a strap that passes under the body of a horse to fasten a saddle on its back.

**gist** *n* the main point of something said or written.

**give**[1] *v* (**gave, given**) **1** to transfer the possession or use of (something) to another person. **2** to offer (advice, a promise, etc). **3** to express or propose (a reason, argument, etc). **4** to provide or organize: *to give a party.* **5** to cause somebody to experience or suffer (something): *You gave me a fright.* **6** to utter (a sound). **7** to collapse or yield under physical pressure. ✱ **give or take** allowing for a specified margin of error. **give way 1** to allow someone to pass or go first. **2** to collapse under pressure. **give way to** to be replaced by. ➤ **giver** *n.*

**give**[2] *n* the capacity or tendency to yield to pressure.

**give-and-take** *n* the practice of making mutual concessions.

**giveaway** *n* **1** an unintentional revelation. **2** something given free or at a reduced price.

**give away** *v* **1** to make a present of. **2** to betray. **3** to reveal (a secret).

**give in** *v* to yield or surrender.

**given**[1] *v* past part. of GIVE[1].

**given**[2] *adj* **1** (+ to) prone; disposed. **2** fixed; specified.

**given**[3] *prep* in view of.

**given name** *n chiefly NAmer* = FORENAME.

**give off** *v* to emit (something unpleasant).

**give out** *v* **1** to distribute. **2** of a supply: to come to an end.

**give up** *v* **1** to abandon an activity and concede failure. **2** to discontinue (a habit). **3** to surrender (somebody or oneself) as a prisoner.

**gizmo** *or* **gismo** *n* (*pl* **-os**) *informal* a gadget.

**gizzard** *n* an enlargement of the digestive tract of birds, with thick muscular walls for breaking up and grinding food.

**glacé** *adj* of fruit: coated with a glaze; candied.

**glacial** *adj* **1** of or produced by glaciers. **2** extremely cold.

**glaciation** *n* the process of forming ice or glaciers.

**glacier** *n* a large body of ice moving slowly down a slope.

**glad** *adj* (**gladder, gladdest**) **1** expressing or experiencing joy or delight. **2** causing happiness. **3** (+ of) grateful for; pleased to have. ➤ **gladly** *adv.*

**gladden** *v* to make glad.

**glade** *n* an open space in a wood or forest.

**gladiator** *n* a man trained to fight another man or wild animals in a public arena in ancient Rome. ➤ **gladiatorial** *adj.*

**gladiolus** *n* (*pl* **gladioli** *or* **gladioluses**) a plant of the iris family with sword-shaped leaves and spikes of brilliantly coloured flowers.

**glad rags** *pl n informal* smart clothes worn for a party or special occasion.

**glamorize** *or* **-ise** *or* **glamourize** *or* **-ise** *v* **1** to make glamorous. **2** to romanticize. ➤ **glamorization** *n.*

**glamorous** *adj* romantically or excitingly attractive.

**glamour** (*NAmer* **glamor**) *n* a romantic, exciting, and often illusory attractiveness.

**glance**[1] *v* **1** (*usu* + at) to take a quick look. **2** (*often* + off) to strike a surface obliquely and go off at an angle.

**glance**[2] *n* a quick or cursory look.

**gland** *n* an organ of the body that secretes chemical substances.

**glandular** *adj* relating to or affecting a gland or glands.

**glandular fever** *n* an acute infectious disease, characterized by fever and swollen and painful lymph glands.

**glare**[1] *v* **1** to stare angrily or fiercely. **2** to shine with a harsh light.

**glare**[2] *n* **1** an angry or fierce stare. **2** a harsh uncomfortably bright light.

**glasnost** *n esp* in the former USSR, openness about government affairs and policy.

**glass** *n* **1** a hard brittle transparent substance formed by melting sand with metallic oxides. **2** a glass drinking vessel. **3** a mirror. **4** a barometer. ➤ **glassy** *adj.*

**glass-blowing** *n* the process of shaping a mass of semi-molten glass by blowing air into it through a tube.

**glass ceiling** *n* a hypothetical barrier to career advancement, *esp* one caused by sexism or racism.

**glasses** *pl n* a pair of glass lenses in a frame, worn in front of the eyes to correct defects of vision or for protection.

**glass fibre** *n* = FIBREGLASS.

**glasshouse** *n chiefly Brit* a greenhouse.

**glasspaper** *n* paper covered with a thin layer of powdered glass for use as an abrasive.

**glaucoma** *n* increased pressure within the eyeball causing damage to the retina and gradual impairment of vision.

**glaze**[1] *v* **1** to fit (e.g. a window frame) with glass. **2** to coat (e.g. food or pottery) with a glaze. **3** (*often* + over) to become dull or lifeless. ➤ **glazing** *n.*

**glaze**[2] *n* **1** a liquid preparation that hardens to give a glossy coating to food. **2** a vitreous coating used to seal or decorate pottery.

**glazier** *n* a person who fits glass, *esp* into windows and doors.

**gleam**[1] *n* **1** a short-lived appearance of reflected or subdued light. **2** a brief or faint indication of emotion, etc.

**gleam**[2] *v* to shine, *esp* with reflected light.

**glean** *v* **1** to gather grain left by reapers. **2** to gather (e.g. information) bit by bit.

**glee** *n* a feeling of joy or delight.

**gleeful** *adj* merry or triumphant. ➤ **gleefully** *adv.*

**glen** *n* a narrow valley, *esp* in Scotland or Ireland.

**glib** *adj* (**glibber, glibbest**) fluent in speaking or writing, often to the point of being superficial or dishonest. ➤ **glibly** *adv.*

**glide**[1] *v* **1** to move noiselessly in a smooth, continuous, and effortless manner. **2** of an aircraft: to fly without the use of engines.
**glide**[2] *n* an act of gliding.
**glider** *n* a light aircraft without an engine.
**glimmer**[1] *v* to shine faintly or unsteadily.
**glimmer**[2] *n* **1** a feeble or unsteady light. **2** a small sign or amount.
**glimpse**[1] *v* to see briefly or partially.
**glimpse**[2] *n* a brief look or partial view.
**glint**[1] *v* to shine with tiny bright flashes.
**glint**[2] *n* a tiny bright flash of usu reflected light.
**glisten** *v* to shine with the lustre of a wet or oily surface.
**glitch** *n informal* a temporary malfunction or setback.
**glitter**[1] *v* to shine by reflection in bright flashes.
**glitter**[2] *n* **1** bright shimmering reflected light. **2** small sparkling particles used for ornamentation. **3** a brilliantly attractive, but sometimes superficial quality. ➤ **glittery** *adj.*
**glitz** *n informal* superficial glamour.
**gloaming** *n* (**the gloaming**) *literary* twilight or dusk.
**gloat**[1] *v* (*often* + over) to talk about something, *esp* one's own achievements or another person's misfortunes, with great and often malicious satisfaction. ➤ **gloating** *adj.*
**gloat**[2] *n* the act of gloating.
**glob** *n chiefly informal* a blob, *esp* of a semiliquid substance.
**global** *adj* **1** involving the entire world. **2** general; comprehensive. ➤ **globally** *adv.*
**global village** *n* the world viewed as an integrated community linked by modern technology.
**global warming** *n* an increase in the average temperature of the earth's atmosphere believed to be caused by the greenhouse effect.
**globe** *n* **1** a spherical representation of the earth. **2** (**the globe**) the world; the earth. **3** something spherical or rounded, e.g. a glass bowl or light.
**globetrotter** *n informal* somebody who travels widely. ➤ **globetrotting** *n and adj.*
**globular** *adj* **1** spherical. **2** consisting of globules.
**glockenspiel** /'glokənspeel, -shpeel/ *n* a percussion instrument consisting of a series of graduated metal bars played with two hammers.
**gloom** *n* **1** partial or total darkness. **2** despondency.
**gloomy** *adj* (**-ier, -iest**) **1** dismally or depressingly dark. **2** feeling or causing despondency. ➤ **gloomily** *adv.*
**glorified** *adj* made to appear more special, important, etc than is really the case.
**glorify** *v* (**-ies, -ied**) **1** to make (something) appear admirable or splendid. **2** to give glory to (God), e.g. in worship. ➤ **glorification** *n.*
**glorious** *adj* **1** possessing or conferring glory. **2** marked by great beauty, splendour, or excellence. ➤ **gloriously** *adv.*
**glory**[1] *n* (*pl* **-ies**) **1** praise, honour, or renown. **2** worshipful praise and thanksgiving. **3** something that is splendid or brings renown. **4** splendour or magnificence.
**glory**[2] *v* (**-ies, -ied**) *informal* (*often* + in) to take great pride or pleasure.
**gloss**[1] *n* **1** surface lustre or sheen. **2** something that gives this: *lip gloss.* **3** a deceptively attractive outer appearance. **4** paint that gives a shiny finish.
**gloss**[2] *v* to give a gloss to.
**gloss**[3] *n* a brief explanation or translation of a difficult word or expression.
**gloss**[4] *v* to supply a gloss for (a word, text, etc).
**glossary** *n* (*pl* **-ies**) a list of terms, *esp* those used in a particular text or a specialized field, with their meanings.
**gloss over** *v* to try to hide (something undesirable) by rapid or superficial treatment.
**glossy**[1] *adj* (**-ier, -iest**) **1** having a lustre or sheen. **2** superficially attractive in a sophisticated manner.
**glossy**[2] *n* (*pl* **-ies**) *informal* a magazine expensively produced on glossy paper with many colour photographs.
**glottal** *adj* of or produced by the glottis.
**glottal stop** *n* a speech sound produced by closure and sudden reopening of the glottis, as between the two syllables in a Cockney pronunciation of *butter.*
**glottis** *n* (*pl* **glottises** *or* **glottides** /'glotideez/) *technical* the slit-like space between the two vocal cords in the larynx.
**glove** *n* **1** a close-fitting covering for the hand with separate sections for each of the fingers and the thumb. **2** a padded covering for the fist worn by a boxer.
**glove compartment** *n* a small storage compartment in a car's dashboard.
**glow**[1] *v* **1** to shine with a steady light. **2** of the complexion, etc: to have a strong, healthy, *esp* red, colour. **3** to show great pleasure or satisfaction.
**glow**[2] *n* a steady light.
**glower**[1] *v* to stare with sullen annoyance or anger.
**glower**[2] *n* a sullen or angry look.
**glowing** *adj* highly appreciative or commendatory.
**glow-worm** *n* a type of beetle that emits light from its abdomen.
**glucose** *n* a simple natural sugar that is the usual form in which carbohydrate is absorbed and used in the body by animals.
**glue**[1] *n* a substance used for sticking things together.
**glue**[2] *v* (**glues, glued, gluing** *or* **glueing**) **1** to cause to stick tightly with glue. **2** (**be glued to**)

to be unable to stop watching or listening to.

**glum** *adj* (**glummer, glummest**) sad; downcast. ➤ **glumly** *adv.*

**glut**[1] *n* an excessive supply of something.

**glut**[2] *v* (**glutted, glutting**) to fill or feed beyond capacity.

**gluten** *n* a protein substance, *esp* in wheat flour, that gives dough its cohesive and elastic properties.

**glutinous** *adj* resembling glue; sticky.

**glutton** *n* **1** a habitually greedy eater and drinker. **2** somebody who has a great liking for something. ➤ **gluttonous** *adj.*

**gluttony** *n* habitual greed in eating or drinking.

**glycerin** *or* **glycerine** *n* a sweet syrupy fluid obtained from fats and used as a solvent or in medicines.

**GM** *abbr* **1** genetically modified. **2** George Medal.

**gm** *abbr* gram.

**GMT** *abbr* Greenwich Mean Time.

**gnarled** *adj* **1** of a tree: covered with knots or lumps. **2** of hands, etc: rough and twisted, *esp* with age.

**gnash** *v* to grind (the teeth) together.

**gnat** *n* a small two-winged fly that bites.

**gnaw** *v* **1** to bite or chew on with the teeth, or wear away by persistent nibbling. **2** to cause continuous pain or anxiety.

**gnocchi** /'n(y)oki/ *pl n* small dumplings made from flour, semolina, or potatoes.

**gnome** *n* in folklore, a dwarf who lives under the earth and guards treasure.

**gnomic** /'nohmik, 'nomik/ *adj* mysterious or enigmatic.

**GNP** *abbr* gross national product.

**gnu** *n* (*pl* **gnus** *or* **gnu**) a large African antelope with an oxlike head and a short mane.

**GNVQ** *abbr Brit* General National Vocational Qualification.

**go**[1] *v* (**goes, going,** *past tense* **went,** *past part.* **gone**) **1** to proceed on a course; to travel. **2** to leave. **3** to make an expedition for a specified activity: *go fishing.* **4** to attend a specified institution habitually. **5** to extend. **6** to arrive at a specified state or condition. **7** to be consumed or spent. **8** to disappear. **9** to elapse. **10** to turn out in a specified manner. **11** to function *esp* in the proper way. **12** (+ an infinitive) to be about, intending, or destined: *Is it going to rain?* **13** (*often* + with) to be compatible or harmonize. **14** to be capable of passing, or of being contained or inserted. **15** to belong. **16** to be satisfactory or adequate. **17** to emit (a sound). **18** *Brit, informal* to say. ✱ **go about** to undertake or begin to tackle. **go ahead 1** to begin. **2** to continue or proceed. **go at** to undertake (e.g. a task) energetically. **go back on** to fail to keep (e.g. a promise). **go for 1** to try to gain. **2** to choose or accept. **3** to attack. **go into 1** of a number: to be contained in (another number). **2** to investigate or explain in depth. **go over** to examine, inspect, or check. **go through 1** to subject to examination, study, or discussion. **2** to experience (something difficult or unpleasant). **3** to spend or use up. **go without** to be deprived of. **leave/let go** to stop holding.

**go**[2] *n* (*pl* **goes**) **1** a turn in an activity, e.g. a game. **2** an attempt, a try. **3** energy; vigour. ✱ **have a go at** to attack, *esp* verbally. **on the go** *informal* constantly or restlessly active.

**goad**[1] *n* **1** a pointed rod used to urge on an animal. **2** something that stimulates somebody into action.

**goad**[2] *v* **1** to drive (e.g. cattle) with a goad. **2** to incite by nagging or persistent annoyance.

**go-ahead**[1] *adj* energetic and progressive.

**go-ahead**[2] *n* (**the go-ahead**) permission to proceed.

**goal** *n* **1** in sport, an area or object into which players must put a ball, etc to score. **2** an instance of putting a ball, etc into a goal. **3** an aim or objective. **4** the destination of a journey. ➤ **goalless** *adj.*

**goalkeeper** *n* a player who defends the goal in football, hockey, lacrosse, etc.

**go along** *v* to go as a companion. ✱ **go along with** to agree or cooperate with.

**goalpost** *n* either of two vertical posts forming part of the goal in football, rugby, etc. ✱ **move the goalposts** to change the rules, conditions, etc that apply to something.

**goat** *n* a mammal with backward-curving horns and a straight thick coat, living wild or farmed for milk.

**goatee** *n* a small beard covering only the bottom of the chin.

**goatherd** *n* somebody who tends goats.

**gob**[1] *n* a shapeless or sticky lump.

**gob**[2] *v* (**gobbed, gobbing**) *chiefly Brit, informal* to spit.

**gob**[3] *n Brit, informal* the mouth.

**gobbet** *n* a piece or portion.

**gobble**[1] *v* **1** to eat greedily or noisily. **2** (*often* + up) to take over or use up quickly.

**gobble**[2] *v* to make the guttural sound of a male turkey. ➤ **gobbler** *n.*

**gobbledygook** *or* **gobbledegook** *n* unintelligible jargon.

**go-between** *n* an intermediary or agent.

**goblet** *n* a drinking vessel with a rounded bowl, a foot, and a stem.

**goblin** *n* a grotesque mischievous elf.

**gobsmacked** *adj Brit, informal* utterly taken aback.

**gobstopper** *n* a large round hard sweet.

**goby** *n* (*pl* **gobies** *or* **goby**) a small spiny-finned sea fish.

**go-cart** *n* see GO-KART.

**god** *n* **1** (**God**) the being worshipped as creator and ruler of the universe. **2** a being or object

with supernatural attributes and powers.
**godchild** *n* (*pl* **godchildren**) somebody for whom another person becomes godparent.
**goddaughter** *n* a female godchild.
**goddess** *n* a female deity.
**godfather** *n* **1** a male godparent. **2** the leader of a criminal organization, *esp* the Mafia.
**God-fearing** *adj* devout.
**godforsaken** *adj* remote; desolate.
**godhead** *n* **1** divine nature or essence. **2** (**the Godhead**) God.
**godless** *adj* **1** not acknowledging a deity; atheistic. **2** wicked.
**godly** *adj* (**-ier, -iest**) pious; devout.
**godmother** *n* a female godparent.
**go down** *v* **1** to decrease. **2** to sink. **3** to be defeated. **4** of a computer system or program: to crash. **5** to be received in a specified way. **6** (*often* + with) to become ill.
**godparent** *n* somebody who undertakes responsibility for the religious education of another person at baptism.
**godsend** *n* something needed that comes at just the right time.
**godson** *n* a male godchild.
**goes** *v* third person present sing. of GO[1].
**goggle** *v* to stare with wide eyes.
**goggles** *pl n* protective glasses with a flexible, snugly fitting frame.
**go in** *v* to enter. ✱ **go in for 1** to engage in (an activity), *esp* for enjoyment. **2** to compete in (e.g. a test or race).
**going**[1] *n* **1** the condition of the ground, e.g. for horse racing. **2** the general conditions under which one tries to do something.
**going**[2] *adj* **1** living; existing: *the best novelist going*. **2** available; to be had. **3** current; prevailing.
**going concern** *n* a business that is operating and profitable.
**going-over** *n* (*pl* **goings-over**) **1** a thorough examination. **2** a severe beating.
**goings-on** *pl n* **1** actions or events. **2** dubious activities.
**goitre** (*NAmer* **goiter**) /'goytə/ *n* an abnormal enlargement of the thyroid gland visible as a swelling of the neck.
**go-kart** *or* **go-cart** *n* a small racing car used in karting.
**gold** *n* **1** a yellow precious metallic element, used *esp* in jewellery and as a currency reserve. **2** gold coins. **3** a deep metallic yellow colour.
**golden** *adj* **1** consisting of or containing gold. **2** of the colour of gold. **3** prosperous; flourishing. **4** favourable. **5** marking a 50th anniversary: *golden jubilee*.
**golden age** *n* **1** a period of great happiness, prosperity, or achievement. **2** a period when something, e.g. a particular art form, was flourishing.
**golden boy** *n* a man or boy who is very successful or popular.
**golden eagle** *n* a large eagle with brownish yellow tips on its head and neck feathers.
**golden girl** *n* a woman or girl who is very successful or popular.
**golden handshake** *n informal* a large sum of money given to an employee on leaving a company.
**golden rule** *n* a guiding principle.
**goldfinch** *n* a small red, black, yellow, and white European finch.
**goldfish** *n* (*pl* **goldfishes** *or* **goldfish**) a small orange-red fish related to the carps, kept in aquariums and ponds.
**gold leaf** *n* gold beaten into very thin sheets.
**gold medal** *n* a medal of gold awarded to the winner of a competition or race.
**gold rush** *n* a rush of people to a newly discovered goldfield in pursuit of riches.
**goldsmith** *n* somebody who makes articles of gold.
**gold standard** *n* a monetary system in which the basic unit of currency is defined by a stated quantity of gold.
**golf** *n* a game in which players using long-shafted clubs attempt to hit a small ball into each of the holes on a course. ➤ **golfer** *n*.
**golliwog** *n* a soft doll with a black face.
**gonad** /'gohnad/ *n* a primary sex gland in which egg or sperm cells are produced, e.g. the ovaries or testes.
**gondola** *n* a long narrow flat-bottomed boat used on the canals of Venice.
**gondolier** *n* somebody who propels a gondola.
**gone**[1] *v* past part. of GO[1].
**gone**[2] *adj* **1** past; ended. **2** used up.
**gone**[3] *adv Brit* later or older than: *It's gone three o'clock*.
**goner** *n informal* **1** an irreparable or irretrievable thing. **2** a dead person.
**gong** *n* **1** a metal disc that produces a resounding tone when struck. **2** *Brit, informal* a medal or decoration.
**gonorrhoea** (*NAmer* **gonorrhea**) /gonə'ri·ə/ *n* a sexually transmitted disease causing inflammation of the mucous membranes of the genital tracts.
**goo** *n informal* a sticky substance.
**good**[1] *adj* (**better, best**) **1** of a favourable or desirable character. **2** of a high standard. **3** agreeable; pleasant. **4** (+ for) beneficial to the health or character of. **5** morally commendable; virtuous. **6** well-behaved. **7** kind; benevolent. **8** (*often* + at) competent; skilful. **9** suitable; fit. **10** thorough; full. ✱ **as good as** virtually; in effect. **make good 1** to be successful in life. **2** *chiefly Brit* to repair. **3** to provide compensation for (a loss, expense, etc). **4** to fulfil (a promise, etc).

**good**[2] *n* **1** benefit; advantage. **2** (*usu in pl*) personal property. **3** (*usu in pl*) wares; merchandise. **4** *Brit* freight. * **for good** forever; permanently.

**goodbye**[1] *interj* used to express farewell.

**goodbye**[2] *n* (*pl* **goodbyes**) a concluding remark or gesture at parting.

**good faith** *n* honest or sincere intentions.

**good-for-nothing** *adj* of no value; worthless.

**Good Friday** *n* the Friday before Easter Sunday, observed in the Christian Church as the anniversary of the crucifixion of Christ.

**goodly** *adj* (**-ier, -iest**) significantly large; considerable.

**goodwill** *n* **1** a kindly feeling of approval and support. **2** the prestige of a business above and beyond its financial value.

**goody** *or* **goodie** *n* (*pl* **-ies**) *informal* **1** (*usu in pl*) something particularly attractive or desirable. **2** a good person or hero, *esp* in a film or book.

**goody-goody** *n* (*pl* **goody-goodies**) *informal* somebody who is affectedly or ingratiatingly virtuous.

**gooey** *adj* (**gooier, gooiest**) soft and sticky.

**goof**[1] *n chiefly NAmer, informal* **1** a ridiculous or stupid person. **2** a blunder.

**goof**[2] *v chiefly NAmer, informal* **1** (*often* + about/around) to fool around. **2** to make a foolish mistake.

**go off** *v* **1** to explode. **2** of food: to begin to decompose. **3** *informal* to stop liking or begin to dislike.

**goofy** *adj* (**-ier, -iest**) *informal* **1** *chiefly NAmer* silly; foolish. **2** *chiefly Brit* of teeth: protruding.

**goon** *n informal* **1** a silly or foolish person. **2** *chiefly NAmer* a bully or thug.

**go on** *v* **1** to continue. **2** to take place. **3** to talk, *esp* effusively.

**goose** *n* (*pl* **geese**) **1** a large water bird with a long neck and webbed feet. **2** the female of such a bird. **3** *informal* a foolish person.

**gooseberry** *n* (*pl* **-ies**) a small round edible green or yellow fruit with soft prickly skin.

**goose pimples** *pl n* small bumps on the skin caused by cold or fear.

**goose step** *n* a straight-legged marching step with the legs swung high.

**go out** *v* **1** to go to social events, entertainments, etc. **2** (+ with) to spend time regularly with somebody in a romantic relationship. **3** to be extinguished.

**gopher** *n* an American burrowing rodent with large cheek pouches.

**gore**[1] *n* thick or clotted blood, *esp* when shed as a result of violence.

**gore**[2] *v* of e.g. a bull: to wound with a horn or tusk.

**gore**[3] *n* a triangular piece of material used to give shape to e.g. a garment or sail.

**gorge**[1] *n* a narrow steep-walled valley.

**gorge**[2] *v* to eat hungrily or greedily.

**gorgeous** *adj* **1** splendidly beautiful. **2** *informal* very pleasant.

**gorgon** *n* **1** (**Gorgon**) any of three sisters in Greek mythology who had live snakes in place of hair and could turn anybody who looked at them to stone. **2** a repulsive or formidable woman.

**gorilla** *n* a large anthropoid ape of western equatorial Africa.

**gormless** *adj Brit, informal* slow to act or understand; stupid.

**gorse** *n* an evergreen shrub with yellow flowers and green spines.

**gory** *adj* (**-ier, -iest**) **1** full of violence and bloodshed. **2** covered with blood.

**gosling** /'gozling/ *n* a young goose.

**gospel** *n* **1** (*often* **Gospel**) the teachings of Jesus Christ. **2** (*usu* **Gospel**) any of the first four books of the New Testament relating these teachings. **3** something so authoritative as not to be questioned. **4** (*also* **gospel music**) a type of religious music rooted in black American culture.

**gossamer** *n* **1** a film of cobwebs floating in the air. **2** (*used before a noun*) light, delicate, or insubstantial.

**gossip**[1] *n* **1** a chatty talk. **2** talk or *esp* sensational allegations about other people. **3** somebody who habitually gossips. ➤ **gossipy** *adj.*

**gossip**[2] *v* (**gossiped, gossiping**) to engage in casual conversation or gossip.

**got** *v* past tense and past part. of GET.

**Gothic** *adj* **1** denoting a style of architecture of the 12th to the 16th centuries characterized by pointed arches. **2** (*often* **gothic** *or* **gothick**) of fiction: dealing with macabre or mysterious events.

**gotten** *v NAmer* past part. of GET.

**gouache** /goo'ahsh/ *n* **1** a method of painting using watercolours mixed with gum. **2** paint or a painting produced in this way.

**gouge**[1] /gowj/ *v* **1** to make (an uneven hole, dent, etc) in a surface. **2** (+ out) to force out roughly or violently.

**gouge**[2] *n* **1** a chisel with a concave blade. **2** a groove or cavity made by gouging.

**goujon** /'goohzhonh/ *n* a small strip of fish, chicken, etc, coated in batter or breadcrumbs and deep-fried.

**goulash** /'goohlash/ *n* a meat stew of Hungarian origin highly seasoned with paprika.

**go up** *v* **1** to increase. **2** to burst into flames.

**gourd** *n* the inedible fruit of a climbing plant, which has a hard rind used to make vessels and utensils.

**gourmand** *n* somebody who is excessively fond of food and drink.

**gourmet** /'gawmay, 'gooəmay/ *n* **1** a connoisseur of food and drink. **2** (*used before a noun*) suitable for a gourmet.

**gout** /gowt/ *n* a disorder that results in the joints, *esp* of the big toe, becoming painfully inflamed.

**govern** *v* **1** to control the making and administration of policy in (a state, organization, etc). **2** to be a deciding influence on. **3** to restrain.

**governance** *n formal* the action or manner of governing.

**governess** *n* a woman entrusted with the teaching of a child in a private household.

**government** *n* **1** the body of people that governs a state. **2** the act of governing. **3** the system by which a state, organization, etc is governed. ➤ **governmental** *adj.*

**governor** *n* **1** a ruler or chief executive of a political unit. **2** the most senior administrator of an institution, e.g. a prison. **3** a member of a body that controls an institution, e.g. a school.

**gown** *n* **1** a loose flowing robe worn *esp* by a professional or academic person when acting in an official capacity. **2** a woman's dress, *esp* an elegant or formal one. **3** a protective outer garment worn in an operating theatre.

**GP** *abbr* **1** general practitioner. **2** Grand Prix.

**gr.** *abbr* **1** grain. **2** gram. **3** gross.

**grab**[1] *v* (**grabbed, grabbing**) **1** to seize hastily or roughly. **2** to obtain unscrupulously or opportunistically. **3** *informal* to impress: *It doesn't really grab me.*

**grab**[2] *n* a sudden snatch. ✱ **up for grabs** *informal* available for anyone to take or win.

**grace**[1] *n* **1** ease and suppleness of movement. **2** a charming or attractive trait. **3** a temporary exemption; a reprieve. **4** (*also in pl*) approval; favour. **5** unmerited divine assistance given to human beings. **6** a short prayer at a meal giving thanks. **7** (**Her/His/Your Grace**) used as a title for a duke, duchess, or archbishop.

**grace**[2] *v* **1** (+ with) to confer honour on with one's presence. **2** to adorn or embellish.

**graceful** *adj* having or displaying grace or elegance. ➤ **gracefully** *adv.*

**graceless** *adj* devoid of elegance or charm.

**grace note** *n* a musical note added as an ornament.

**gracious** *adj* **1** marked by kindness and courtesy. **2** having qualities, e.g. comfort and elegance, made possible by wealth. **3** showing divine grace. ➤ **graciously** *adv.*

**gradation** *n* **1** a series of successive stages. **2** a step in such a series.

**grade**[1] *n* **1** a position in a scale of ranks or qualities. **2** a mark indicating a degree of accomplishment at school. ✱ **make the grade** to succeed.

**grade**[2] *v* **1** to sort according to quality. **2** to assign a grade to (e.g. a student's work). **3** to pass from one stage or level to another *esp* gradually.

**gradient** *n* **1** the degree of inclination of a slope. **2** a sloping road or railway.

**gradual** *adj* **1** happening by small degrees, usu over a long period. **2** of a slope: not steep. ➤ **gradually** *adv.*

**graduate**[1] *n* the holder of a first academic degree.

**graduate**[2] *v* **1** to mark (e.g. an instrument or vessel) with degrees of measurement. **2** to receive an academic degree. **3** (*often* + to) to move up to a higher stage of proficiency or prestige. ➤ **graduation** *n.*

**graffiti** *pl n* unauthorized drawings or writing painted on a wall in a public place.

**graft**[1] *v* **1** to cause (a plant cutting) to unite with a growing plant. **2** to attach or add. **3** to implant (living tissue) surgically. ➤ **grafter** *n.*

**graft**[2] *n* **1** a grafted plant cutting. **2** a surgical operation in which living tissue is grafted. **3** the living tissue implanted. **4** the improper use of one's position to one's own advantage.

**graft**[3] *v Brit, informal* to work hard.

**graft**[4] *n Brit, informal* hard work.

**Grail** *n* the cup or platter used, according to medieval legend, by Christ at the Last Supper.

**grain** *n* **1** cereals or similar food plants. **2** the edible seeds of cereal plants. **3** a small hard particle, e.g. of sand or salt. **4** the least amount possible. **5** the arrangement of the fibres, particles, etc in wood, rock, fabric, etc. **6** a unit of weight equal to approximately 0.065 gram. ✱ **against the grain** contrary to one's disposition or feeling. ➤ **grainy** *adj.*

**gram** *or* **gramme** *n* a metric unit of mass equal to one thousandth of a kilogram (about 0.04oz).

**grammar** *n* **1** the study of the functions of words and their relations in sentences. **2** the characteristic system of inflections and syntax of a language. **3** a grammar textbook.

**grammar school** *n Brit* a usu selective secondary school providing an academic type of education.

**grammatical** *adj* **1** relating to grammar. **2** conforming to the rules of grammar. ➤ **grammatically** *adv.*

**gramophone** *n Brit, dated* a record player.

**grampus** *n* **1** a marine animal resembling a dolphin but with a bulbous head. **2** a killer whale.

**gran** *n chiefly Brit, informal* one's grandmother.

**granary** *n* (*pl* **-ies**) a storehouse for threshed grain.

**granary bread** *n* brown bread containing malted wheat grains.

**grand**[1] *adj* **1** large and striking in size or conception. **2** characterized by magnificence or opulence. **3** extremely dignified and proud. **4** having more importance than others; principal. **5** *Brit, informal* very good; wonderful. ➤ **grandly** *adv.*

**grand**[2] *n informal* a thousand pounds or dollars.

**grandad** *or* **granddad** *n informal* one's grandfather.
**grandchild** *n* a child of one's son or daughter.
**granddaughter** *n* a daughter of one's son or daughter.
**grandee** *n* **1** a Spanish or Portuguese nobleman. **2** any senior or high-ranking man.
**grandeur** *n* **1** the quality of being large or impressive. **2** personal greatness, dignity, or power.
**grandfather** *n* the father of one's father or mother.
**grandiloquence** *n* high-sounding or pompously eloquent speech or writing. ➤ **grandiloquent** *adj.*
**grandiose** *adj* large-scale and intended to impress, but often overly ambitious or ostentatious.
**grandma** *n informal* one's grandmother.
**grandmother** *n* the mother of one's father or mother.
**grandpa** *n informal* one's grandfather.
**grandparent** *n* a parent of one's father or mother.
**grand piano** *n* a large piano with a horizontal frame and strings.
**Grand Prix** /ˌgronh 'pree/ *n* (*pl* **Grands Prix**) each of a series of world-championship motor races held in different countries.
**grand slam** *n* **1** the winning of all the major tournaments in a particular sport in a given year, or of all the games in a tournament. **2** in bridge, the winning of all 13 tricks by one player or side.
**grandson** *n* a son of one's son or daughter.
**grandstand** *n* the main stand at a racecourse or stadium, that gives the best view.
**grand total** *n* the final amount after lesser items have been added together.
**grange** *n* a large country house, often with many outbuildings.
**granite** *n* a very hard grey rock.
**granny** *or* **grannie** *n* (*pl* **-ies**) *informal* one's grandmother.
**granny flat** *n Brit* a part of a house converted into an independent dwelling to accommodate an elderly relative.
**granny knot** *n* a reef knot crossed the wrong way and therefore not secure.
**grant**[1] *v* **1** to consent to carry out (e.g. a wish or request). **2** to bestow or transfer (something, e.g. a title or property) formally. **3** to be willing to concede (something). ✱ **take for granted 1** to assume to be true, real, or certain to occur. **2** to value too lightly.
**grant**[2] *n* **1** an amount of money given by a government or other body for a particular purpose. **2** the act of granting.
**granted** *adv* admittedly.
**granulated** *adj* formed or crystallized into granules. ➤ **granulation** *n.*
**granule** *n* a small hard particle.
**grape** *n* a smooth-skinned juicy green or purple berry that grows in clusters on a grapevine, eaten as a fruit or fermented to produce wine.
**grapefruit** *n* a large round yellow citrus fruit with a somewhat acid juicy pulp.
**grapeshot** *n* ammunition for cannons, in the form of small iron balls shot in clusters.
**grapevine** *n* **1** a vine on which grapes grow. **2** (**the grapevine**) *informal* an unofficial means of circulating information or gossip.
**graph** *n* a diagram expressing a relation between quantities, typically a line joining points plotted relative to vertical and horizontal axes.
**graphic** *or* **graphical** *adj* **1** relating to drawing, pictures, or the pictorial arts. **2** marked by clear and vivid description; explicit. ➤ **graphically** *adv.*
**graphic design** *n* the art of combining text and illustration in the design of printed matter.
**graphics** *pl n* **1** designs (e.g. advertising posters) containing both typographical and pictorial elements. **2** the pictorial images on a computer screen. **3** the use of computers to create and manipulate images, e.g. in television and films.
**graphite** *n* a soft black form of carbon used in lead pencils, as a lubricant, and in lightweight sports equipment.
**graphology** *n* the study of handwriting, *esp* for character analysis. ➤ **graphologist** *n.*
**graph paper** *n* paper printed with small squares for drawing graphs and diagrams.
**grapple** *v* **1** (*often* + with) to engage in hand-to-hand fighting; to wrestle. **2** (+ with) to struggle to deal with.
**grappling iron** *or* **grappling hook** *n* a device like a small anchor with several radiating hooks, attached to a line and thrown to hook onto something.
**grasp**[1] *v* **1** to take hold of eagerly or firmly. **2** to take advantage of enthusiastically. **3** to succeed in understanding.
**grasp**[2] *n* **1** a firm hold. **2** the ability to seize or attain something. **3** ability to understand.
**grasping** *adj* eager for material possessions; greedy.
**grass**[1] *n* **1** vegetation in the form of low, spreading ground cover plants with slender green leaves. **2** an area covered in growing grass. **3** *slang* marijuana. **4** *Brit, slang* a police informer. ✱ **put/send out to grass** to cause to enter usu enforced retirement. ➤ **grassy** *adj.*
**grass**[2] *v* **1** to cover (an area) with grass. **2** *Brit, slang* (*often* + on/up) to inform on somebody to the police.
**grasshopper** *n* a plant-eating insect with hind legs that are adapted for leaping and produce a chirping noise when rubbed together.

**grass roots** *pl n* the ordinary members of society or an organization as opposed to the leadership.

**grate**[1] *n* **1** a frame of metal bars that holds the fuel in a fireplace or furnace. **2** = GRATING[1].

**grate**[2] *v* **1** to reduce (a hard food) to small particles by rubbing it on something rough. **2** to rub or rasp noisily. **3** to cause irritation; to jar.

**grateful** *adj* feeling or expressing thanks. ➤ **gratefully** *adv.*

**grater** *n* a tool with sharp-edged holes, used for grating food.

**gratify** *v* (**-ies, -ied**) **1** to give pleasure or satisfaction to. **2** to satisfy (an urge, whim, etc). ➤ **gratification** *n.*

**grating**[1] *n* a framework of parallel bars, e.g. covering a window.

**grating**[2] *adj* of sounds: annoyingly harsh; rasping.

**gratis** /'gratis, 'grah-/ *adv and adj* without charge; free.

**gratitude** *n* the state or feeling of being grateful; thankfulness.

**gratuitous** *adj* not called for by the circumstances; unwarranted. ➤ **gratuitously** *adv.*

**gratuity** *n* (*pl* **-ies**) a small sum of money given in return for a service; a tip.

**grave**[1] *n* **1** a pit excavated for the burial of a body. **2** (**the grave**) *literary* death.

**grave**[2] *adj* **1** serious; important. **2** causing concern. **3** solemn and dignified. ➤ **gravely** *adv.*

**grave**[3] *or* **grave accent** /grahv/ *n* a mark (ˋ) placed over a vowel in some languages to show that it is pronounced in a particular way.

**gravel** *n* loose fragments of rock or small stones, used to surface roads and paths.

**gravelly** *adj* **1** like or covered with gravel. **2** harsh-sounding; grating.

**graven image** *n* an idol carved from wood or stone.

**gravestone** *n* a usu inscribed stone over or at one end of a grave.

**graveyard** *n* an area of ground used for burials.

**gravitas** /'gravitas/ *n* a solemn and serious manner.

**gravitate** *v* to move gradually and steadily.

**gravitation** *n* movement caused by gravity. ➤ **gravitational** *adj.*

**gravity** *n* **1** the force that attracts objects towards the earth, or towards any body that has mass. **2** dignity or solemnity of bearing. **3** seriousness.

**gravy** *n* the fat and juices from cooked meat, thickened and seasoned and used as a sauce.

**gravy boat** *n* a small boat-shaped vessel used for pouring gravy.

**gray** *adj, n, and v NAmer* = GREY[1], GREY[2], and GREY[3].

**graze**[1] *v* **1** of animals: to feed on growing grass and other green plants. **2** *informal* to eat snacks frequently, instead of eating meals at regular times.

**graze**[2] *v* **1** to scrape or scratch (*esp* the skin), usu by glancing contact. **2** to touch lightly in passing.

**graze**[3] *n* an abrasion, *esp* of the skin, made by a scraping along a surface.

**grazing** *n* vegetation or land for animals to feed on.

**grease**[1] *n* **1** a thick oily substance, *esp* one used as a lubricant. **2** animal fat used or produced in cooking.

**grease**[2] *v* to smear or lubricate with grease. ✱ **grease somebody's palm** to bribe somebody.

**greasepaint** *n* theatrical make-up.

**greaseproof paper** *n* paper resistant to grease, oil, etc, used for wrapping food.

**greasy** *adj* (**-ier, -iest**) **1** smeared with or containing grease. **2** oily in texture. **3** insincerely polite or fawning.

**greasy spoon** *n informal* a café serving cheap, mainly fried food.

**great** *adj* **1** above the norm in size, number, amount or degree. **2** significant; momentous. **3** eminent or distinguished. **4** aristocratic or grand. **5** (*chiefly in combination*) one stage further removed in family relationship: *great-grandfather; great-aunt.* **6** remarkably skilled: *a great organizer.* **7** enthusiastic: *a great fan.* **8** *informal* used as a generalized term of approval. ➤ **greatness** *n.*

**greatcoat** *n* a heavy overcoat.

**Great Dane** *n* a very large, long-legged dog of a smooth-coated breed.

**greater** *adj* (*often* **Greater**) consisting of a central city together with adjacent, geographically or administratively connected areas.

**grebe** *n* a diving bird with lobed rather than webbed toes.

**Grecian** *adj* relating to ancient Greece.

**greed** *n* **1** excessive desire for food. **2** excessive desire to acquire or possess things.

**greedy** *adj* (**-ier, -iest**) having an excessive desire or need for something, *esp* food. ➤ **greedily** *adv.*

**Greek** *n* **1** a native or inhabitant of Greece. **2** the language of the people of ancient or modern Greece. ➤ **Greek** *adj.*

**green**[1] *adj* **1** of the colour of grass, between blue and yellow. **2** covered by grass or other vegetation. **3** of a person: inexperienced or naive. **4** beneficial to the natural environment. **5** (*often* Green) concerned about environmental issues.

**green**[2] *n* **1** a green colour. **2** (*in pl*) green vegetables. **3** an area of open grass for public use. **4** a smooth area of grass for a special purpose, *esp* bowling or putting. **5** (*often* **Green**) a member or supporter of an environmentalist party or group.

**green belt** *n* an area of parks, farmland, etc encircling an urban area and usu subject to restrictions on new building.
**green card** *n* a permit allowing a foreign person to settle permanently and work in the USA.
**greenery** *n* green foliage or plants.
**green-eyed monster** *n* jealousy.
**greenfield** *adj* consisting of land not previously built on.
**greenfinch** *n* a common European finch with green and yellow plumage.
**green fingers** *pl n* an unusual ability to make plants grow.
**greenfly** *n* (*pl* **greenflies** *or* **greenfly**) *Brit* a green aphid that is destructive to plants.
**greengage** *n* a small greenish cultivated plum.
**greengrocer** *n chiefly Brit* a retailer of fresh vegetables and fruit.
**greenhouse** *n* a building with walls and roof of glass, for the cultivation or protection of plants.
**greenhouse effect** *n* the warming of the atmosphere that occurs when solar radiation reflected from the earth cannot escape because of a build-up of carbon dioxide and other pollutants in the air.
**greenhouse gas** *n* a gas, *esp* carbon dioxide or methane, that contributes to the greenhouse effect.
**green light** *n* authority or permission to undertake a project.
**green pepper** *n* a green unripe fruit of the sweet pepper plant, eaten as a vegetable.
**greet** *v* **1** to acknowledge the presence or arrival of with gestures or words. **2** to react to in a specified manner.
**greeting** *n* **1** a phrase or gesture expressing welcome or recognition. **2** (*usu in pl*) an expression of good wishes; regards.
**gregarious** *adj* **1** of people: having a liking for companionship; sociable. **2** of animals: tending to associate with others of the same kind.
**Gregorian chant** *n* a type of unaccompanied liturgical chant developed in the early Middle Ages.
**gremlin** *n* a mischievous creature said to cause the unexplained malfunctioning of machinery or equipment.
**grenade** *n* a small bomb that is thrown by hand or fired from a launcher.
**grenadier** *n* **1** a soldier formerly specially trained in the use of grenades. **2** (*often* **Grenadier**) in Britain, a member of the Grenadier Guards, the first regiment of the royal household infantry.
**grew** *v* past tense of GROW.
**grey**[1] (*NAmer* **gray**) *adj* **1** of a colour between black and white, like that of ash or a rain cloud. **2** lacking sunshine or brightness; dull. **3** of hair: turning white with age. **4** without colour or character; nondescript.
**grey**[2] (*NAmer* **gray**) *n* **1** a grey colour. **2** a horse with white hair but dark skin.
**grey**[3] (*NAmer* **gray**) *v* to make or become grey.
**grey area** *n* a subject or situation that is imprecisely defined or difficult to categorize.
**greyhound** *n* a dog of a tall slender smooth-coated breed, used for racing.
**grey matter** *n informal* brains or intellect.
**grid** *n* **1** a framework of parallel or intersecting metal bars covering an opening; a grating. **2** a network of uniformly spaced intersecting horizontal and perpendicular lines, e.g. for locating points on a map. **3** a network of cables for the distribution of electricity.
**griddle** *n* a flat metal plate on which food is cooked by dry heat.
**gridiron** *n* a framework of metal bars on which food is placed to be cooked; a grill.
**gridlock** *n* a severe traffic jam affecting a whole area. ➤ **gridlocked** *adj.*
**grief** *n* **1** deep distress, *esp* caused by bereavement. **2** *informal* trouble of any kind. * **come to grief** to end badly; to fail.
**grievance** *n* a cause of dissatisfaction, constituting grounds for complaint.
**grieve** *v* **1** (*often* + for) to feel or express grief. **2** to cause to suffer grief; to distress.
**grievous** *adj* **1** causing severe pain or sorrow. **2** very serious. ➤ **grievously** *adv.*
**grievous bodily harm** *n* serious physical harm done to a person in a criminal attack.
**griffin** *or* **griffon** *or* **gryphon** *n* a mythical animal with the head and wings of an eagle and the body and tail of a lion.
**griffon** *n* **1** see GRIFFIN. **2** a large vulture with brown plumage. **3** a small wire-haired terrier.
**grill**[1] *n* **1** a cooking utensil consisting of a set of parallel bars on which food is exposed to heat. **2** *Brit* an apparatus on a cooker under which food is cooked or browned. **3** a dish of grilled food. **4** see GRILLE.
**grill**[2] *v* **1** to cook (food) on or under a grill. **2** *informal* to subject to intense questioning.
**grille** *or* **grill** *n* a grating forming a barrier or screen; *esp* an ornamental metal one at the front end of a motor vehicle.
**grim** *adj* (**grimmer, grimmest**) **1** forbidding in disposition or appearance. **2** unyielding. **3** *informal* unpleasant; nasty. ➤ **grimly** *adv.*
**grimace**[1] *n* a distorted facial expression, usu of disgust, anger, or pain.
**grimace**[2] *v* to express pain, disapproval, or disgust by twisting one's face.
**grime** *n* dirt, *esp* when sticking to a surface. ➤ **grimy** *adj.*
**grin**[1] *v* (**grinned, grinning**) to smile broadly, usu showing the teeth. * **grin and bear it** to put up with an unpleasant experience stoically.
**grin**[2] *n* a broad smile.

**grind**[1] *v* (*past tense and past part.* **ground**) **1** to reduce to powder or small fragments by crushing. **2** to polish, sharpen, or wear down by friction. **3** to rub, press, or twist harshly. **4** to move with friction, *esp* so as to make a grating noise. ➤ **grinder** *n.*

**grind**[2] *n* **1** dreary monotonous labour or routine. **2** an act of grinding.

**grind down** *v* to subject to domineering treatment.

**grind out** *v derog* to produce in a mechanical way.

**grindstone** *n* **1** a revolving stone or abrasive disc used for grinding, polishing, sharpening, etc. **2** a millstone.

**grip**[1] *v* (**gripped, gripping**) **1** to seize or hold firmly. **2** to attract and hold the interest of. **3** of an emotion: to take control of.

**grip**[2] *n* **1** a strong or tenacious grasp. **2** control, mastery, or power. **3** the ability to understand. **4** a part or device that grips. **5** a part by which something is grasped, *esp* a handle. **6** a travelling bag; a holdall. ✱ **come/get to grips with** to set about dealing with. **lose one's grip** to be unable any longer to deal with things effectively.

**gripe**[1] *v* **1** to cause to feel sharp intestinal pain. **2** *informal* to complain persistently.

**gripe**[2] *n* **1** (*usu in pl*) a stabbing spasmodic intestinal pain. **2** *informal* a grievance or complaint, *esp* a trivial or unjustified one.

**gripping** *adj* very exciting and absorbing.

**grisly** *adj* (**-ier, -iest**) inspiring horror, fear, or disgust. ➤ **grisliness** *n.*

**grist** *n* grain for grinding. ✱ **grist to the mill** something that can be put to use or profit.

**gristle** *n* tough cartilaginous matter in cooked meat. ➤ **gristly** *adj.*

**grit**[1] *n* **1** small hard particles of stone or coarse sand. **2** (*also* **gritstone**) coarse sandstone. **3** *informal* firmness of mind or spirit; determination.

**grit**[2] *v* (**gritted, gritting**) **1** to cover or spread (*esp* an icy road surface) with grit. **2** to clench (one's teeth) as a sign of determination.

**gritty** *adj* (**-ier, -iest**) **1** courageously determined. **2** not flinching from unpleasantness; uncompromising. **3** resembling or containing grit. ➤ **grittily** *adv.*

**grizzle** *v Brit, dated, informal* of a child: to cry quietly and fretfully.

**grizzled** *adj* streaked with grey.

**grizzly** *or* **grizzly bear** *n* (*pl* **-ies**) a very large bear that has brownish fur streaked with white.

**groan**[1] *v* to utter a deep moan.

**groan**[2] *n* a deep moaning sound.

**groat** *n* a former British coin worth four old pence.

**grocer** *n* a dealer in staple foodstuffs and household supplies.

**grocery** *n* a grocer's shop or business.

**grog** *n* an alcoholic spirit, usu rum, mixed with water.

**groggy** *adj* (**-ier, -iest**) weak and dazed.

**groin** *n* **1** the area of the body between the lower abdomen and the inner part of the thigh. **2** *euphem* the genitals. **3** *chiefly NAmer* = GROYNE.

**grommet** *n* **1** an eyelet to strengthen an opening. **2** a small plastic tube inserted in the ear to drain off fluid.

**groom**[1] *n* **1** somebody who takes care of horses. **2** a bridegroom.

**groom**[2] *v* **1** to clean and care for (e.g. a horse or dog), *esp* by brushing its coat. **2** to make (oneself or one's appearance) neat or attractive. **3** to get (somebody) ready for a specific role, e.g. by training.

**groove**[1] *n* **1** a long narrow channel cut into wood, stone, etc. **2** the continuous spiral track on a gramophone record. **3** a fixed routine.

**groove**[2] *v* **1** to make a groove in. **2** *dated, informal* to dance to or perform popular music.

**groovy** *adj* (**-ier, -iest**) *dated, informal* fashionably attractive or exciting.

**grope**[1] *v* **1** to search about blindly, *esp* with the hands. **2** to fondle for sexual pleasure.

**grope**[2] *n* an act of groping.

**gross**[1] *adj* **1** glaringly noticeable or objectionable; flagrant. **2** constituting an overall total before deductions (e.g. for taxes) are made. **3** of weight: including both the object in question and any incidentals, e.g. packaging or load. **4** coarse or vulgar. **5** *informal* disgustingly unpleasant; repulsive. **6** big or bulky, *esp* excessively overweight. ➤ **grossly** *adv.*

**gross**[2] *n* an overall total before deductions.

**gross**[3] *v* **1** to earn or bring in (an overall total) before deductions. **2** *informal* (+ out) to disgust or repel.

**gross**[4] *n* (*pl* **gross**) a group of twelve dozen (144) things.

**grotesque**[1] *adj* **1** amusingly or repellently ugly in appearance. **2** absurdly incongruous or inappropriate. ➤ **grotesquely** *adv.*

**grotesque**[2] *n* a grotesque person or thing.

**grotto** *n* (*pl* **-oes** *or* **-os**) a small natural or artificial cave.

**grotty** *adj* (**-ier, -iest**) *Brit, informal* **1** unpleasant. **2** of poor quality. **3** unwell.

**grouch** *n* **1** a bad-tempered complaint. **2** an irritable or complaining person. ➤ **grouchy** *adj.*

**ground**[1] *n* **1** the solid surface of the earth. **2** soil or earth. **3** an area of land used for a particular purpose. **4** (*in pl*) the area around and belonging to a large building. **5** (*also in pl*) a basis for belief, action, or argument. ✱ **gain ground** to become more widely accepted. **give ground** to retreat. **go to ground** to go into hiding. **off the ground** started and in progress.

**ground**[2] *v* **1** (*often* **be grounded in/on)** to provide a reason or justification for. **2** to forbid

(a pilot or aircraft) to fly. **3** *informal* to give (a child) the punishment of having to stay at home. **4** of a ship: to run aground.
**ground**[3] *v* past tense and past part. of GRIND[1].
**ground-breaking** *adj* introducing entirely new methods; pioneering.
**ground control** *n* the equipment and operators that control aircraft from the ground.
**ground floor** *n* the floor of a house on a level with the ground.
**ground frost** *n* a temperature below freezing on the ground.
**grounding** *n* fundamental training in a field of knowledge.
**groundless** *adj* having no basis in fact or reason; unjustified.
**groundnut** *n chiefly Brit* = PEANUT.
**ground rent** *n* the rent paid by the owner of a building to the owner of the land that it is built on.
**ground rule** *n* a basic rule of procedure.
**groundsel** *n* a common weed with small yellow flower heads.
**groundsheet** *n* a waterproof sheet placed on the ground (e.g. in a tent).
**groundsman** *n* (*pl* **groundsmen**) somebody who tends a playing field.
**groundswell** *n* **1** a heavy sea swell caused by an often distant gale or ground tremor. **2** a spontaneous build-up of public opinion.
**groundwork** *n* work done to provide a foundation or basis.
**group**[1] *n* **1** a number of people or things gathered together or forming a single unit. **2** a small band of musicians, *esp* playing pop music.
**group**[2] *v* to form or combine in a group.
**groupie** *n* an ardent fan, *esp* one who follows a famous person, e.g. a rock star, on tour.
**grouse**[1] *n* (*pl* **grouse**) a game bird with a plump body.
**grouse**[2] *v informal* to complain, *esp* annoyingly or without reason.
**grouse**[3] *n informal* a complaint.
**grout**[1] *n* (*also* **grouting**) a thin mortar used for filling spaces, *esp* the gaps between tiles.
**grout**[2] *v* to fill up the spaces between (tiles) with grout.
**grove** *n* a small wood or group of trees.
**grovel** *v* (**grovelled, grovelling,** *NAmer* **groveled, groveling**) **1** to lie or creep on the ground *esp* to show subservience. **2** to abase oneself in order to earn forgiveness or favour.
**grow** *v* (**grew, grown**) **1** of an organism: to increase in size and develop to maturity. **2** to increase or expand. **3** to become gradually. **4** to cause (a plant, fruit, or vegetables, etc) to grow; to cultivate. ➤ **grower** *n.*
**growl** *v* **1** to utter a deep sound in the throat that expresses hostility. **2** to speak in an angry or hostile way. **3** to make a continuous low sound. ➤ **growl** *n.*
**grown-up**[1] *adj* fully mature; adult.
**grown-up**[2] *n* an adult.
**grow on** *v* to become gradually more pleasing to.
**grow out of** *v* **1** to become too big to fit (a piece of clothing). **2** to become too mature to get enjoyment from.
**growth** *n* **1** the process of growing. **2** an increase or expansion. **3** something that grows or has grown. **4** a tumour.
**grow up** *v* of a person: to become mature.
**groyne** (*NAmer* **groin**) *n* a wall-like structure built out from a shore, *esp* to check erosion of the beach.
**grub**[1] *v* (**grubbed, grubbing**) **1** to dig in the ground. **2** (*usu* + up) to dig up or out.
**grub**[2] *n* **1** a wormlike larva of an insect. **2** *informal* food.
**grubby** *adj* (**-ier, -iest**) **1** dirty; grimy. **2** disreputable or sordid.
**grudge**[1] *v* **1** to be unwilling to give or admit. **2** to feel resentful towards (somebody) who has something one envies.
**grudge**[2] *n* a feeling of deep-seated resentment or ill will.
**grudging** *adj* offered or given only unwillingly. ➤ **grudgingly** *adv.*
**gruel** *n* thin porridge.
**gruelling** (*NAmer* **grueling**) *adj* extremely taxing or demanding.
**gruesome** *adj* inspiring horror or repulsion; ghastly.
**gruff** *adj* **1** brusque or stern in manner or speech. **2** deep and harsh. ➤ **gruffly** *adv.*
**grumble**[1] *v* **1** to mutter discontentedly or in complaint. **2** to rumble.
**grumble**[2] *n* a complaint or cause of complaint.
**grumpy** *adj* (**-ier, -iest**) moodily cross; surly. ➤ **grumpily** *adv.*
**grunge** *n* **1** *informal* dirt. **2** a style of rock music featuring markedly discordant guitar sound. ➤ **grungy** *adj.*
**grunt**[1] *v* **1** to utter the deep short guttural sound of a pig. **2** to utter a similar sound, e.g. in reluctant agreement or during strenuous exertion.
**grunt**[2] *n* a grunting sound.
**gryphon** *n* see GRIFFIN.
**G-string** *n* a small piece of cloth, leather, etc covering the genitals and held in place by thongs etc passed round the hips and between the buttocks.
**guano** *n* the excrement of seabirds used as a fertilizer.
**guarantee**[1] *n* **1** an assurance of the quality of a product, work, etc, accompanied by a promise of replacement or compensation if it proves defective. **2** (*also* **guaranty**) an agreement by which one person accepts responsibility for another's obligations, *esp* debts, in case of

default. **3** an assurance that something will happen.

**guarantee**[2] *v* (**guaranteed, guaranteeing**) **1** to provide a guarantee of replacement or repayment with respect to (a product, work, etc). **2** to give an assurance relating to. **3** to undertake to answer for the debt or default of.

***Usage Note:*** Note the spelling with *-ua-*.

**guarantor** *n* somebody who makes or gives a guarantee.

**guard**[1] *n* **1** the duty of protecting or defending or of preventing escape. **2** a person or group who performs this duty. **3** a protective or safety device, e.g. on a machine to prevent injury. **4** a state of readiness to deal with adverse events; vigilance: *They caught me off guard.* **5** *Brit* the person in charge of the carriages, passengers, etc in a railway train.

**guard**[2] *v* **1** to protect from danger. **2** to watch over so as to prevent escape, entry, etc. * **guard against** to attempt to prevent by taking precautions.

**guarded** *adj* marked by caution.

**guardian** *n* **1** somebody that guards or protects. **2** somebody entrusted by law with the care of a person who is of unsound mind, not of age, etc. ➤ **guardianship** *n.*

**guardian angel** *n* an angel who is thought to watch over a particular person.

**guava** /'gwahvə/ *n* a tropical fruit with pink aromatic flesh.

**gudgeon**[1] *n* **1** a pivot or spindle. **2** the socket into which the pins of a hinge fit. **3** a socket into which the rudder of a boat fits. **4** a pin that holds two blocks together.

**gudgeon**[2] *n* (*pl* **gudgeons** *or* **gudgeon**) a small European freshwater fish.

**guerrilla** *or* **guerilla** *n* a member of a small independent fighting force which engages in sabotage, unexpected assaults, etc.

**guess**[1] *v* **1** to estimate or judge without sufficient knowledge or information for an accurate assessment. **2** to arrive at a correct conclusion about by conjecture, chance, or intuition.

**guess**[2] *n* an opinion or estimate arrived at by guessing.

**guesswork** *n* the act of guessing, or a judgment based on a guess.

**guest** *n* **1** a person entertained in another's home or at another's expense. **2** a person who pays to stay at a hotel, etc. **3** somebody who is present or takes part, e.g. in a show, by invitation.

**guesthouse** *n* a private house used to accommodate paying guests.

**guffaw**[1] *n* a loud or boisterous laugh.

**guffaw**[2] *v* to laugh loudly or boisterously.

**guidance** *n* advice or instructions on how to do something.

**guide**[1] *n* **1** somebody who leads, directs, or advises others. **2** a book providing information about a place, activity, etc. **3** a principle that directs somebody's conduct. **4** a device or mark for directing the motion of something. **5** (**Guide**) *chiefly Brit* a member of a worldwide movement of girls founded with the aim of forming character and teaching good citizenship.

**guide**[2] *v* **1** to lead or direct along a route or to a place. **2** to control and direct the movement of, e.g. a missile. **3** to give advice or instructions to regarding behaviour, an appropriate course of action, etc.

**guidebook** *n* a book of information for travellers.

**guide dog** *n* a dog trained to lead a blind person.

**guideline** *n* a recommendation as to policy or conduct.

**guild** *n* **1** an association of people with similar interests or pursuits. **2** a medieval association of merchants or craftsmen.

**guilder** *n* (*pl* **guilders** *or* **guilder**) the basic monetary unit of the Netherlands before the euro.

**guildhall** *n* **1** a hall where a guild or corporation meets. **2** in some British towns, the town hall.

**guile** *n* deceitful cunning.

**guillemot** /'gilimot/ *n* (*pl* **guillemots** *or* **guillemot**) a sea bird with black-and-white plumage.

**guillotine**[1] /'giləteen/ *n* **1** a machine for beheading with a heavy blade that slides down between grooved posts. **2** an instrument (e.g. a paper cutter) that works like a guillotine.

**guillotine**[2] *v* to behead with a guillotine.

**guilt** *n* **1** the fact of having committed an offence, *esp* a crime. **2** a feeling of being at fault or to blame. ➤ **guiltless** *adj.*

**guilty** *adj* (**-ier, -iest**) **1** responsible for an offence or wrongdoing. **2** found to have committed a crime by a judge, jury, etc after a trial. **3** suggesting guilt. **4** feeling guilt. ➤ **guiltily** *adv.*

**guinea** *n* a former British gold coin worth 21 shillings.

**guinea fowl** *n* a large African game bird with white-speckled slate-coloured plumage.

**guinea pig** *n* **1** a tailless South American rodent often kept as a pet. **2** somebody or something used as a subject of research or experimentation.

**guise** *n* **1** assumed appearance. **2** external appearance.

**guitar** *n* a stringed musical instrument played by plucking. ➤ **guitarist** *n.*

**gulch** *n chiefly NAmer* a ravine.

**gulf** *n* **1** a partially landlocked part of the sea, usu larger than a bay. **2** a deep chasm. **3** an unbridgeable gap e.g. between the attitudes or opinions of different people.

**gull**[1] *n* a sea bird with long wings, webbed feet, and largely white, grey, or black plumage.
**gull**[2] *v dated* to trick or deceive.
**gull**[3] *n archaic* a person who is easily tricked or deceived.
**gullet** *n* the oesophagus or throat.
**gullible** *adj* easily tricked or deceived. ➤ **gullibility** *n.*
**gully** *or* **gulley** *n* (*pl* **-ies** *or* **-eys**) **1** a trench worn in the earth by running water. **2** a deep gutter or drain.
**gulp**[1] *v* **1** (*often* + down) to swallow hurriedly or greedily. **2** to make a sudden swallowing movement as if surprised or nervous.
**gulp**[2] *n* **1** a swallowing sound or action. **2** the amount swallowed in a gulp.
**gum**[1] *n* the tissue that surrounds the teeth.
**gum**[2] *n* **1** a plant substance that is sticky when moist but hardens on drying. **2** a soft glue used for sticking paper and other lightweight materials. **3** *informal* chewing gum.
**gum**[3] *v* (**gummed, gumming**) to stick with gum.
**gumboot** *n* a waterproof rubber boot reaching usu to the knee.
**gumdrop** *n* a hard jellylike sweet.
**gummy**[1] *adj* (**-ier, -iest**) viscous or sticky.
**gummy**[2] *adj* (**-ier, -iest**) with no teeth.
**gumption** *n* the intelligence and courage to take action; initiative.
**gun**[1] *n* **1** a weapon that discharges a bullet or shell through a metal tube. **2** a device that releases a controlled amount of something, e.g. grease or glue. ✱ **jump the gun** to move or act before the proper time. **stick to one's guns** to refuse to change one's intentions or opinion in spite of opposition.
**gun**[2] *v* (**gunned, gunning**) ✱ **be gunning for** to be intent on criticizing, punishing, or killing.
**gunboat** *n* a heavily armed ship of shallow draught.
**gundog** *n* a dog trained to locate or retrieve game for hunters.
**gun down** *v* to kill (somebody) by shooting them, usu in cold blood.
**gunge** *n Brit, informal* an unpleasant, dirty, or sticky substance.
**gung ho** *adj* excessively enthusiastic, *esp* for fighting or warfare.
**gunk** *n informal* any unpleasant, dirty, or sticky substance; gunge.
**gunman** *n* (*pl* **gunmen**) a man armed with a gun, *esp* a professional killer.
**gunmetal** *n* **1** a greyish form of bronze. **2** a bluish grey colour.
**gunnel** *n* see GUNWALE.
**gunner** *n* a soldier who operates a gun, *esp* a private in the Royal Artillery.
**gunnery** *n* the science of the effective use of guns.
**gunpoint** ✱ **at gunpoint** while threatening somebody, or being threatened, with a gun.
**gunpowder** *n* an explosive mixture of potassium nitrate, charcoal, and sulphur.
**gunrunner** *n* somebody who imports or deals in contraband arms and ammunition. ➤ **gunrunning** *n.*
**gunship** *n* a heavily armed helicopter.
**gunwale** *or* **gunnel** *n* the upper edge of a ship's or boat's side.
**guppy** *n* (*pl* **guppies** *or* **guppy**) a small fish native to the West Indies and South America.
**gurgle** *v* to make a low-pitched bubbling sound. ➤ **gurgle** *n.*
**Gurkha** *n* a soldier of Nepalese origin serving in the British or Indian army.
**gurn** *v* see GIRN.
**guru** *n* (*pl* **gurus**) **1** a Hindu or Sikh religious teacher and spiritual guide. **2** a mentor. **3** *informal* an acknowledged leader or expert in a field.
**gush**[1] *v* **1** to flow out or emit copiously or violently. **2** to make an effusive display of sentiment or enthusiasm. ➤ **gushing** *adj.*
**gush**[2] *n* a sudden outpouring.
**gushy** *adj* (**-ier, -iest**) marked by effusive often affected sentiment or enthusiasm.
**gusset** *n* a piece of material inserted in a seam (e.g. the crotch of an undergarment) to provide reinforcement or allow for movement.
**gust**[1] *n* **1** a sudden brief rush of wind. **2** a sudden outburst. ➤ **gusty** *adj.*
**gust**[2] *v* to blow in gusts.
**gusto** *n* enthusiastic and vigorous enjoyment or vitality.
**gut**[1] *n* **1** (*also in pl*) the belly or abdomen. **2** (*often in pl*) the intestine. **3** (*often used before a noun*) the part of a person that responds emotionally or instinctively: *a gut feeling*. **4** *informal* (*in pl*) the inner essential parts. **5** *informal* (*in pl*) courage or determination. ✱ **hate somebody's guts** *informal* to hate somebody with great intensity.
**gut**[2] *v* (**gutted, gutting**) **1** to remove the intestines of (*esp* an animal). **2** to destroy the inside of (*esp* a building).
**gutless** *adj informal* lacking courage; cowardly.
**gutsy** *adj* (**-ier, -iest**) *informal* courageous.
**gutted** *adj Brit, informal* deeply disappointed or disheartened.
**gutter**[1] *n* **1** a trough just below the eaves of a roof or at the side of a street to carry off water. **2** (**the gutter**) the lowest level or condition of human life.
**gutter**[2] *v* of a flame: to burn fitfully or feebly.
**guttering** *n* the gutters on the roof of a building.
**guttersnipe** *n dated* a deprived and ill-bred child living in poverty.
**guttural** *adj* of a sound: pronounced in the throat.

**guy**[1] *n* a rope, chain, etc used to secure something (e.g. a tent).

**guy**[2] *v* to secure with guys.

**guy**[3] *n* **1** *informal* a man. **2** *informal* (*in pl*) people of either sex. **3** a humorous effigy of a man burned in Britain on 5 November.

**guy**[4] *v dated* to make fun of; to ridicule.

**guzzle** *v* to consume greedily.

**gym** *n* **1** a gymnasium. **2** gymnastics.

**gymkhana** *n* a local sporting event featuring competitions and displays relating to horse riding.

**gymnasium** *n* (*pl* **gymnasiums** *or* **gymnasia**) a large room or separate building used for indoor sports and gymnastic activities.

**gymnast** *n* somebody trained in gymnastics.

**gymnastics** *pl n* (*treated as sing.*) physical exercises to develop bodily strength and coordination. ➤ **gymnastic** *adj.*

**gymslip** *n chiefly Brit* a girl's tunic or pinafore dress worn, *esp* formerly, as part of a school uniform.

**gynaecology** (*NAmer* **gynecology**) /gienə'koləji/ *n* a branch of medicine that deals with diseases and disorders of women, *esp* of the female reproductive system. ➤ **gynaecological** *adj,* **gynaecologist** *n.*

**gypsum** *n* hydrated calcium sulphate occurring as a mineral and used *esp* in plaster of Paris.

**gypsy** *or* **gipsy** *n* (*pl* **-ies**) a member of the Romany people, who retain an itinerant lifestyle in modern societies.

**gyrate** *v* **1** to move with a circular or spiral motion. **2** to dance wildly or erotically. ➤ **gyration** *n.*

**gyroscope** *n* a device containing a wheel that is mounted to spin rapidly about an axis and is free to turn in any direction so that it maintains the same orientation.

**H**[1] *or* **h** *n* (*pl* **H's** *or* **Hs** *or* **h's**) the eighth letter of the English alphabet.

**H**[2] *abbr* the chemical symbol for hydrogen.

**h** *abbr* hour.

**Ha** *abbr* the chemical symbol for hahnium.

**ha** *abbr* hectare.

**habeas corpus** /ˌhaybi·əs ˈkawpəs/ *n* a legal order requiring a detained person to be brought before a court.

**haberdashery** *n* (*pl* **-ies**) **1** articles used in sewing and dressmaking. **2** a shop selling these.

**habit** *n* **1** something a person does regularly. **2** an addiction to a drug. **3** a long dress-like garment worn by a monk or nun.

**habitable** *adj* suitable for living in.

**habitat** *n* the place where a plant or animal naturally grows or lives.

**habitation** *n* **1** the inhabiting of a place. **2** *formal* a residence or home.

**habitual** *adj* **1** done or doing something as a habit. **2** in accordance with habit; customary. ➤ **habitually** *adv.*

**habituate** *v* (+ to) to make or become used to something.

**habitué** /həˈbityooay/ *n* a person who frequents a place.

**hacienda** /hasiˈendə/ *n* in a Spanish-speaking country, a large house and estate.

**hack**[1] *v* **1** to cut with repeated rough blows. **2** to gain unauthorized access to a computer system. ✱ **hacking cough** a hard dry cough. ➤ **hacker** *n.*

**hack**[2] *n* a rough hacking blow.

**hack**[3] *n* **1** a journalist or other writer who turns out a lot of mediocre work. **2** a riding horse let out for hire.

**hack**[4] *adj* hackneyed or trite.

**hack**[5] *v* to ride a horse at an ordinary pace, *esp* over roads. ➤ **hacker** *n.*

**hackles** *pl n* the hairs along the neck and back of an animal, which rise when it is roused.

**hackney carriage** *n esp* a taxi.

**hackneyed** *adj* of a phrase: overused and lacking originality.

**hacksaw** *n* a fine-toothed saw for cutting metal.

**had** *v* past tense and past part. of HAVE.

**haddock** *n* (*pl* **haddocks** *or* **haddock**) a silver-grey sea fish used for food.

**hadn't** *contraction* had not.

**haematology** (*NAmer* **hematology**) *n* the study of diseases of the blood. ➤ **haematologist** *n.*

**haemoglobin** (*NAmer* **hemoglobin**) *n* a protein of red blood cells that carries oxygen from the lungs to the body tissues.

**haemophilia** (*NAmer* **hemophilia**) *n* a disorder involving delayed clotting of the blood, causing difficulty in controlling bleeding. ➤ **haemophiliac** *n and adj.*

**haemorrhage**[1] (*NAmer* **hemorrhage**) *n* a loss of blood from a burst blood vessel.

**haemorrhage**[2] (*NAmer* **hemorrhage**) *v* to undergo a haemorrhage.

**haemorrhoid** (*NAmer* **hemorrhoid**) *n* (*usu in pl*) a mass of swollen veins round the anus.

**haft** *n* the handle of a weapon or tool.

**hag** *n* an ugly or ill-natured old woman. ➤ **haggish** *adj.*

**haggard** *adj* having a worn or gaunt appearance, *esp* from tiredness.

**haggis** *n* (*pl* **haggis** *or* **haggises**) a Scottish dish of minced sheep's or calf's offal mixed with suet, oatmeal, and seasonings, and boiled in the stomach of the animal or in a substitute bag.

**haggle** *v* to bargain or wrangle. ➤ **haggler** *n.*

**hagiography** *n* (*pl* **-ies**) **1** biography of saints or venerated people. **2** an idealizing biography.

**ha-ha** *n* a fence sunk into a ditch, forming a boundary to grounds without uninterrupting the view.

**haiku** /ˈhiekooh/ *n* (*pl* **haiku** *or* **haikus**) a Japanese poem of three lines containing five, seven, and five syllables.

**hail**[1] *n* **1** a fall of small particles of clear ice or compacted snow. **2** a large number of things coming at once.

**hail**[2] *v* to fall as hail.

**hail**[3] *v* **1** to salute or greet. **2** to greet with approval; to acclaim. **3** to summon (a taxi) by calling. ✱ **hail from** to live in or come from (a place).

**hailstone** *n* a pellet of hail.

**hair** *n* **1** a slender threadlike strand growing from the skin of an animal. **2** a structure resembling a hair, e.g. on a plant. **3** a coating of hairs on the human head or an animal's body. ✱ **let one's hair down** to relax and enjoy oneself.

**not turn a hair** to remain completely unmoved. ➤ **hairless** *adj.*

**haircut** *n* **1** a cutting and shaping of the hair. **2** the style in which hair is cut.

**hairdo** *n* (*pl* **-os**) *informal* a person's hairstyle.

**hairdresser** *n* a person who cuts and styles people's hair. ➤ **hairdressing** *n.*

**hairdryer** *or* **hairdrier** *n* an electrical device for drying the hair with warm air.

**hairgrip** *n Brit* a flat hairpin.

**hairline** *n* **1** the line formed by the edge of a person's hair. **2** of a crack: very thin.

**hairnet** *n* a loosely woven net worn over the hair to keep it in place.

**hairpiece** *n* a piece of false hair worn to fill a gap in a person's natural hair.

**hairpin** *n* a two-pronged pin of thin wire for holding the hair in place.

**hairpin bend** *n* a sharp U-shaped bend in a road.

**hair-raising** *adj* causing great fear or alarm.

**hair shirt** *n* a shirt of coarse cloth formerly worn next to the skin as a penance.

**hairspray** *n* a substance sprayed on the hair to hold it in place.

**hairspring** *n* a slender spiral spring regulating the balance wheel of a watch.

**hairstyle** *n* a way in which the hair is cut or arranged. ➤ **hairstylist** *n.*

**hair trigger** *n* a trigger adjusted so that very slight pressure will release it.

**hairy** *adj* (**-ier, -iest**) **1** covered with hair or material like hair. **2** *informal* alarmingly difficult or dangerous.

**hake** *n* a large seafish related to the cod.

**halal** *or* **hallal** /hə'lahl/ *adj* of meat: prepared according to Islamic law.

**halberd** *n* a former weapon combining a spear and battle-axe. ➤ **halberdier** *n.*

**halcyon** *adj* denoting an idyllic past time.

**hale** *adj* of a person: sound and healthy.

**half**[1] *n* (*pl* **halves**) **1** either of two equal parts into which something can be divided. **2** *Brit, informal* half a pint of beer. **3** *informal* a half-price fare or ticket. ✱ **go halves** *informal* to pay half each.

**half**[2] *adj* amounting to half, or one of two equal parts.

**half**[3] *adv* **1** in an equal part or degree. **2** to the extent of a half. **3** incompletely or almost. ✱ **half a chance** *informal* the slightest opportunity. **half past** thirty minutes past (an hour). **not half** *informal* very much so.

**half-and-half** *adj and adv* half one thing and half another.

**halfback** *n* a player in rugby, football, hockey, etc positioned immediately behind the forward line.

**half-baked** *adj* badly thought out or planned.

**half-board** *n Brit* provision of bed, breakfast, and an evening meal.

**half brother** *n* a brother related through one parent only.

**half-caste** *n offensive* a person with parents of different races.

**half-cocked** *adj* lacking adequate preparation or forethought.

**half crown** *n* a former British coin worth two shillings and sixpence (12.5p).

**half-dozen** *or* **half a dozen** *n* a set of six.

**halfhearted** *adj* lacking enthusiasm or effort. ➤ **halfheartedly** *adv.*

**half hour** *n* a period of thirty minutes. ➤ **half-hourly** *adv and adj.*

**half-life** *n* the time required for half of the atoms of a radioactive substance to become disintegrated.

**half measures** *pl n* an inadequate line of action.

**half nelson** *n* a wrestling hold in which one arm is thrust under the arm of an opponent and the hand placed on the back of their neck.

**halfpenny** *or* **ha'penny** /'haypni/ *n* (*pl* **half-pennies** *or* **halfpence** *or* **ha'pennies**) a former British coin worth one half of an old penny.

**half sister** *n* a sister related through one parent only.

**half term** *n Brit* a short holiday halfway through a school term.

**half-timbered** *adj* built of a timber framework filled in with brickwork or plaster.

**halftime** *n* a pause between the two halves of a game or contest.

**halfway** *adj and adv* **1** midway between two points. **2** in the least; minimally.

**half-wit** *n informal* a foolish or stupid person. ➤ **half-witted** *adj.*

**halibut** *n* (*pl* **halibut**) a large flatfish used for food.

**halitosis** *n* abnormally bad-smelling breath.

**hall** *n* **1** the entrance room or passage of a building. **2** a large room for public assembly or entertainment. **3** (*also* **hall of residence**) a residential building for students of a college or university. **4** *Brit* the manor house of a landed proprietor.

**hallelujah** *or* **alleluia** *interj* used to express praise or joy.

**hallmark**[1] *n* **1** an official mark stamped on gold and silver articles to show their purity. **2** a distinguishing characteristic.

**hallmark**[2] *v* to stamp with a hallmark.

**hallo** *interj* = HELLO.

**hallowed** *adj* **1** made sacred. **2** greatly respected.

**Halloween** *or* **Hallowe'en** *n* 31 October, the eve of All Saints' Day.

**hallucinate** *v* to have hallucinations. ➤ **hallucinator** *n.*

**hallucination** *n* the perception of something apparently real but having no objective reality. ➤ **hallucinatory** *adj.*

**hallucinogen** *n* a substance that induces hallucinations. ➤ **hallucinogenic** *adj.*

**halo** *n* (*pl* **-oes** *or* **-os**) **1** in art, a circle of light surrounding the head of a holy person. **2** a circle of light round the sun or moon.

**halogen** *n* any of the elements fluorine, chlorine, bromine, iodine, and astatine.

**halt**[1] *v* to come or bring to a stop.

**halt**[2] *n* **1** a stop or interruption. **2** *Brit* a minor stopping place on a railway. ✻ **call a halt** to demand a stop to an activity.

**halter** *n* a rope or strap for leading or tying an animal.

**halter neck** *n* a neckline on a woman's dress formed by a strap passing from the front of it round the neck.

**halting** *adj* hesitant or faltering.

**halve** *v* **1** to divide into two equal parts. **2** to reduce (an amount) to a half.

**halyard** *or* **halliard** *n* a rope or tackle for hoisting or lowering a sail or flag.

**ham**[1] *n* **1** meat from the rear thigh of a pig, cured with salt. **2** (*usu in pl*) a buttock with its associated thigh.

**ham**[2] *n* **1** a showy or clumsy performer or actor. **2** an amateur radio operator.

**ham**[3] *v* (**hammed, hamming**) *informal* to overact.

**hamburger** *n* a round flat cake of minced beef, fried or grilled and usu served in a bread roll.

**ham-fisted** *adj informal* clumsy with the hands.

**hamlet** *n* a small village.

**hammer**[1] *n* **1** a hand tool with a heavy solid head, used for driving in nails. **2** a lever with a striking head for ringing a bell or striking a gong. **3** the part of the mechanism of a modern gun whose action ignites the cartridge. **4** an auctioneer's mallet. **5** a heavy metal ball attached by a flexible wire to a handle and thrown as an athletic contest. ✻ **hammer and tongs** with great energy.

**hammer**[2] *v* **1** to beat or drive with a hammer. **2** (+ into) to make (somebody) learn or remember something by repetition. **3** *informal* to defeat decisively.

**hammer away** *v* **1** to work hard and persistently. **2** (+ at) to go on repeating an opinion or attitude.

**hammerhead** *n* a shark with projections on each side of a flattened head.

**hammer out** *v* to produce or bring about through lengthy discussion.

**hammock** *n* a strip of netting or canvas suspended by cords at each end and used to lie on.

**hammy** *adj* (**-ier, -iest**) *informal* characterized by clumsy overacting.

**hamper**[1] *v* to restrict the movement or progress of.

**hamper**[2] *n* **1** a large basket with a cover for packing, storing, or transporting food, etc. **2** a selection of festive fare contained in a hamper, presented as a gift.

**hamster** *n* a small rodent with large cheek pouches.

**hamstring**[1] *n* any of the five tendons at the back of the knee.

**hamstring**[2] *v* (*past tense and past part.* **hamstrung**) **1** to cripple by cutting the leg tendons. **2** to restrict severely.

**hand**[1] *n* **1** the end of the arm beyond the wrist. **2** an indicator or pointer on a dial. **3** (*in pl*) possession. **4** (*in pl*) control or supervision. **5** a pledge of betrothal or marriage. **6** handwriting. **7** a unit of measure for a horse's height, equal to about 102mm (4in.). **8** a round of applause. **9** assistance or aid. **10** the cards or pieces held by a player in a game. **11** a person employed to work. ✻ **at hand** near in time or place. **by hand** with the hands, rather than mechanically. **give/lend a hand** to help. **go hand in hand** to be closely linked. **hand in glove** cooperating closely. **hand to mouth** satisfying one's immediate needs. **in hand** being done; in progress. **off hand** without checking or investigating. **on hand 1** ready to use. **2** present. **on one's hands** in one's possession or care. **out of hand 1** out of control. **2** without pause for consideration. **to hand** available and ready for use. **win hands down** *informal* to win with ease.

**hand**[2] *v* to give or pass (something) to somebody. ✻ **hand it to** to give credit to.

**handbag** *n Brit* a woman's bag for small personal articles and money.

**handball** *n* **1** a ball game played using the hands in a walled court. **2** the offence of handling the ball in football.

**handbill** *n* a small printed sheet of information handed out in the street.

**handbook** *n* a book giving information on a practical subject.

**hand brake** *n* a hand-operated brake used to hold a stationary motor vehicle.

**handcuff** *v* to put handcuffs on.

**handcuffs** *pl n* a pair of linked metal rings for locking round a prisoner's wrists.

**hand down** *v* **1** to pass on or bequeath. **2** to deliver (a judgment) in court.

**handful** *n* (*pl* **handfuls**) **1** an amount that can be held in the hand. **2** a small quantity or number. **3** *informal* a person who is difficult to control or deal with.

**hand grenade** *n* a grenade for throwing by hand.

**handgun** *n* a gun for holding and firing with one hand.

**handhold** *n* something to grasp for support in climbing.

**handicap**[1] *n* **1** a disability or disadvantage that makes a task unusually difficult. **2** an advantage or disadvantage given to contestants to even out the chances of winning. **3** the number of strokes by which a golfer on average exceeds par for a course. **4** the extra weight assigned to a racehorse as a handicap.

**handicap**[2] *v* (**handicapped, handicapping**) **1** to put at a disadvantage. **2** to assign handicaps to.

**handicapped** *adj* having a handicap or disadvantage.

**handicraft** *n* **1** a manual skill, or an occupation requiring it. **2** an article made by handicraft.

**handiwork** *n* **1** a person's own work or actions. **2** work done with the hands.

**handkerchief** *n* (*pl* **handkerchiefs** *or* **handkerchieves**) a small piece of cloth for wiping or blowing the nose.

**handle**[1] *n* **1** a part that is designed to be grasped by the hand. **2** *informal* a person's name or nickname. **3** *informal* a means of approaching or dealing with a situation.

**handle**[2] *v* **1** to touch or feel with the hands. **2** to deal with (a subject, idea, etc) in speech or writing, or as a work of art. **3** to manage or be in charge of. **4** to deal with (somebody or something). **5** to engage in buying, selling, or distributing (a commodity). **6** of a vehicle, etc: to respond to the controls in a specified way. ➤ **handler** *n.*

**handlebar** *n* (*also in pl*) a steering bar on a bicycle or motore cycle.

**handmade** *adj* made by hand rather than by machine.

**handmaid** *or* **handmaiden** *n archaic* a female servant.

**hand-me-down** *n* a piece of clothing that has been passed from an older to a younger member of a family.

**handout** *n* **1** an item of food, clothing, or money given free to people in need. **2** a sheet of information for free distribution.

**hand out** *v* to give (something) freely to a group of people.

**handover** *n* an act of transferring power or responsibility from one person or group to another.

**hand over** *v* to pass something officially to another person or organization.

**handpick** *v* to choose personally and carefully.

**handset** *n* **1** the part of a telephone that contains the mouthpiece and earpiece. **2** the remote-control device for a television set, video recorder, etc.

**handshake** *n* an act of shaking a person's hand in greeting or agreement.

**hands-off** *adj* keeping free of close involvement in an activity.

**handsome** *adj* **1** of a man: having a pleasing appearance; good-looking. **2** of a woman: attractive in a dignified way. **3** of a building, room, etc: well-proportioned; stately. **4** large or generous. ➤ **handsomely** *adv.*

**hands-on** *adj* taking a direct involvement in an activity.

**handspring** *n* a movement turning the body in a circle and landing first on the hands and then on the feet.

**handstand** *n* an act of balancing the body upside down on the hands with the legs in the air.

**hand-to-hand** *adj* involving physical contact; very close.

**handwriting** *n* **1** writing done with a pen or pencil. **2** a person's particular style of writing. ➤ **handwritten** *adj.*

**handy** *adj* (**-ier, -iest**) **1** convenient to use; useful. **2** conveniently near. **3** clever in practical ways. ➤ **handily** *adv.*

**handyman** *n* (*pl* **handymen**) a man who does various minor building and repair tasks.

**hang**[1] *v* (*past tense and past part.* **hung**) **1** to fasten or be fastened at the top so that the lower part is free. **2** (*past tense and past part.* **hanged**) to suspend (somebody) by the neck until dead, usu as a form of capital punishment. **3** to attach (a door, window, etc) to its frame so that it can be opened and closed freely. **4** to paste (wallpaper) to a wall. **5** to display (a picture). **6** to remain poised or stationary in the air. **7** to stay on; to persist. **8** (+ over) to be imminent or threatening. **9** (+ up) to depend on something.

**hang**[2] *n* the way in which something hangs. * **get the hang of** *informal* to learn how to use or deal with (something).

**hang about** *v Brit* to wait or stay without purpose or activity.

**hangar** *n* a shed; *esp* a large shed for housing aircraft.

**hangdog** *adj* ashamed or abject.

**hanger** *n* **1** a piece of shaped material with a hook, for hanging clothes on. **2** a person who hangs something.

**hanger-on** *n* (*pl* **hangers-on**) a fawning associate of a person or group.

**hang-glider** *n* a glider controlled by the movements of the person harnessed beneath it. ➤ **hang-gliding** *n.*

**hanging** *n* a tapestry or other decorative covering for a wall.

**hangman** *n* (*pl* **hangmen**) an executioner who hangs condemned prisoners.

**hangnail** *n* a piece of skin hanging loose at the side or root of a fingernail.

**hang on** *v* **1** to keep hold; to hold onto something. **2** *informal* to persist. **3** *informal* to wait for a short time.

**hang out** *v informal* to spend time in a leisurely or idle way.

**hangover** *n* **1** the unpleasant physical effects of heavy consumption of alcohol. **2** a custom that remains from the past.

**hang up** *v* to end a telephone conversation by replacing the receiver.
**hang-up** *n informal* a source of mental or emotional difficulty.
**hank** *n* a coil or loop of yarn, rope, wool, etc.
**hanker** *v* (+ after/for) to want something strongly or persistently. ➤ **hankering** *n.*
**hankie** *or* **hanky** *n* (*pl* **-ies**) *informal* a handkerchief.
**hanky-panky** *n informal* mildly improper behaviour.
**hansom** *n* a light two-wheeled covered carriage for two people.
**Hanukkah** *or* **Chanukah** *n* an eight-day Jewish festival in December.
**haphazard** *adj* lacking any method or order; aimless. ➤ **haphazardly** *adv.*
**hapless** *adj* unlucky or unfortunate.
**happen** *v* **1** to take place; to occur. **2** to occur by chance. ✱ **happen on** *literary* to encounter by chance. **happen to** to do or be the case by chance.
**happening**[1] *n* something that happens; an event.
**happening**[2] *adj informal* exciting and fashionable.
**happy** *adj* (**-ier, -iest**) **1** enjoying or expressing pleasure and contentment. **2** glad; pleased. **3** favoured by luck or fortune. **4** well adapted or fitting. **5** impulsively quick to do or use something: *trigger-happy.* ➤ **happily** *adv,* **happiness** *n.*
**happy-go-lucky** *adj* cheerfully unconcerned; carefree.
**happy hour** *n* a period of the day during which drinks are sold at a reduced price in a bar, pub, etc.
**hara-kiri** *n* suicide by ritual disembowelment with a sword, formerly practised by Japanese samurai when disgraced.
**harangue**[1] *n* a lengthy critical speech or piece of writing.
**harangue**[2] *v* to criticize (somebody) at tedious length.
**harass** *v* to annoy or worry persistently. ➤ **harassed** *n.*

***Usage Note:*** Note the spelling with *-r-* and *-ss.*

**harbinger** *n literary* a person or thing that signals a future event or change.
**harbour**[1] (*NAmer* **harbor**) *n* a port or coastal inlet providing safe anchorage for ships.
**harbour**[2] (*NAmer* **harbor**) *v* **1** to have or keep (thoughts or feelings) in the mind. **2** to give shelter or refuge to. **3** to be the habitat of (something unpleasant).
**hard**[1] *adj* **1** not easily penetrated or yielding to pressure; firm. **2** physically fit and tough. **3** revealing no weakness. **4** difficult to understand or explain. **5** demanding energy or stamina. **6** of currency: stable in value or soundly backed. **7** harsh or severe. **8** forceful or violent. **9** lacking consideration or compassion. **10** difficult to endure. **11** not speculative or conjectural; factual. **12** close or searching. **13** firm or definite. **14** of a drink: containing a high percentage of alcohol. **15** of water: containing salts that inhibit lathering. **16** of a drug: addictive and harmful. ✱ **hard feelings** offence or resentment. **hard going** arduous or difficult. **hard of hearing** rather deaf. ➤ **hardness** *n.*
**hard**[2] *adv* **1** with great effort or energy; strenuously. **2** in a firm manner; tightly. ✱ **be hard put to it** to have difficulty. **hard done by** harshly or unfairly treated.
**hardback** *n* a book bound in stiff covers.
**hard-bitten** *adj* steeled by difficult experience.
**hardboard** *n* board made by compressing shredded wood chips.
**hard-boiled** *adj* **1** of an egg: boiled until the yolk has solidified. **2** of a person: tough and insensitive.
**hard cash** *n* coins and bank notes as opposed to cheques or credit.
**hard copy** *n* a paper copy of data held on computer.
**hard core** *n* the most committed members of a group.
**hard-core** *adj* of pornography: extremely explicit.
**hard disk** *or* **hard drive** *n* a rigid high-capacity disk permanently installed in a computer.
**harden** *v* to make or become hard or harder.
**hardheaded** *adj* sober and realistic.
**hardhearted** *adj* severe and unsympathetic. ➤ **hardheartedly** *adv.*
**hard-line** *adj* strict and unyielding. ➤ **hard-liner** *n.*
**hardly** *adv* **1** not in the least. **2** used as a response: certainly not! **3** only just; barely.
**hard-nosed** *adj informal* sober and realistic.
**hardship** *n* suffering or privation.
**hard shoulder** *n Brit* a strip alongside a motorway, for use in an emergency.
**hard up** *adj informal* short of money.
**hardware** *n* **1** household tools and gardening equipment. **2** the physical components of a computer or other electronic device. **3** heavy military equipment such as tanks and missiles.
**hardwood** *n* **1** a broad-leaved as distinguished from a coniferous tree. **2** the wood of such a tree.
**hardy** *adj* (**-ier, -iest**) **1** inured to hardship; tough. **2** of a plant: capable of withstanding adverse conditions. ➤ **hardiness** *n.*
**hare**[1] *n* a mammal like a large rabbit with long ears and long hind legs.
**hare**[2] *v informal* to run fast.
**harebell** *n* a plant with blue bell-shaped flowers.

**harebrained** *adj* flighty or foolish.
**harelip** *n* a split in the upper lip occurring as a congenital deformity.
**harem** *n* **1** a secluded part of a house reserved for women in a Muslim household. **2** the women occupying a harem.
**haricot** *n* a type of French bean with white seeds.
**hark** *v literary* to listen. ✱ **hark at** used to draw attention to a foolish or pompous comment.
**harken** *v* see HEARKEN.
**Harlequin** *n* a mute pantomime character, wearing a mask and diamond-patterned costume.
**harlequin** *adj* of a pattern: brightly coloured.
**harlot** *n archaic* a prostitute.
**harm**[1] *n* **1** physical or mental damage or injury. **2** mischief or wrong. ➤ **harmful** *adj*, **harmfully** *adv*.
**harm**[2] *v* **1** to damage or injure. **2** to have a bad effect on.
**harmless** *adj* not likely to cause harm. ➤ **harmlessly** *adv*.
**harmonic**[1] *adj* **1** relating to musical harmony. **2** pleasing to the ear.
**harmonic**[2] *n* a flutelike overtone produced on a stringed instrument.
**harmonica** *n* a small rectangular wind instrument with a row of reeds recessed in air slots for blowing through to produce different notes.
**harmonious** *adj* **1** musically tuneful or pleasing. **2** having the parts arranged so as to produce a pleasing effect. **3** free from argument or conflict. ➤ **harmoniously** *adv*.
**harmonium** *n* a musical instrument of the reed organ family in which pedals operate a bellows that forces air through free reeds.
**harmonize** *or* **-ise** *v* **1** to play or sing in harmony. **2** (*often* + with) to be in harmony or keeping. **3** to provide (a tune) with harmony. **4** to make harmonious. ➤ **harmonization** *n*.
**harmony** *n* (*pl* **-ies**) **1** a pleasing combination of musical notes in a chord. **2** the structure of music with respect to the composition and progression of chords. **3** a pleasing arrangement of parts. **4** agreement or accord.
**harness**[1] *n* **1** a system of straps for attaching a horse or other draught animal to the thing it is pulling. **2** something that resembles a harness, e.g. in holding or fastening something. ✱ **in harness** in one's usual work or routine.
**harness**[2] *v* **1** to put a harness on. **2** to attach by means of a harness. **3** to make use of (a natural source of energy).
**harp**[1] *n* a musical instrument with strings stretched across an open triangular frame, plucked with the fingers. ➤ **harpist** *n*.
**harp**[2] *v* (+ on) to keep talking about something tediously or monotonously.
**harpoon**[1] *n* a barbed spear used in hunting large fish or whales.
**harpoon**[2] *v* to spear with a harpoon.
**harpsichord** *n* a keyboard instrument with a horizontal frame and strings that are plucked when keys are pressed. ➤ **harpsichordist** *n*.
**harpy** *n* (*pl* **-ies**) **1** (**Harpy**) a vicious creature of Greek mythology with the head of a woman and the body of a bird. **2** a cruel or spiteful woman.
**harridan** *n* a bad-tempered old woman.
**harrier** *n* **1** a hunting dog used for catching hares. **2** a slender hawk with long angled wings.
**harrow**[1] *n* a cultivating implement set with teeth or discs and drawn over the ground to break up or smooth the soil.
**harrow**[2] *v* to cultivate with a harrow.
**harrowing** *adj* causing distress.
**harry** *v* (**-ies, -ied**) **1** to attack (an enemy) repeatedly. **2** to harass or torment.
**harsh** *adj* **1** disagreeable or painful to the senses. **2** unduly exacting or severe. **3** of a climate or conditions: difficult to endure. ➤ **harshly** *adv*.
**hart** *n* an adult male red deer.
**harvest**[1] *n* **1** the gathering in of an agricultural crop. **2** a year's mature crop or yield.
**harvest**[2] *v* **1** to gather in (a crop). **2** to gather (a natural product) as if by harvesting. ➤ **harvester** *n*.
**has** *v* third person sing. present of HAVE.
**has-been** *n informal* a person or thing that is no longer important.
**hash**[1] *n* **1** a dish of reheated chopped food. **2** *informal* a muddle or jumble. ✱ **make a hash of something** *informal* to do something badly.
**hash**[2] *v* to chop (food) into small pieces.
**hash**[3] *n informal* hashish.
**hash**[4] *n* the symbol #.
**hashish** *n* cannabis.
**hasn't** *contraction* has not.
**hasp** *n* a hinged metal strip that fits over a metal loop and is secured by a pin or padlock as a fastening.
**hassle**[1] *n informal* **1** a difficult or trying situation. **2** harassment.
**hassle**[2] *v informal* to subject to persistent harassment.
**hassock** *n* a cushion for kneeling on in church.
**haste** *n* speedy or rash action.
**hasten** *v* **1** to make (something) happen more quickly. **2** to move or act quickly.
**hasty** *adj* (**-ier, -iest**) rash or hurried. ➤ **hastily** *adv*.
**hat** *n* a covering to fit the head. ➤ **hatless** *adj*.
**hatch**[1] *n* **1** a small door or opening. **2** an opening in the deck of a ship or in an aircraft.
**hatch**[2] *v* **1** of young: to emerge from an egg or pupa. **2** of an egg: to open and release young. **3** to incubate (an egg). **4** to devise (a plot or plan).
**hatch**[3] *v* to mark (a map or drawing) with fine closely spaced parallel lines. ➤ **hatching** *n*.

**hatchback** *n* a car with a large upward-opening door at the back.
**hatchet** *n* an axe with a short handle.
**hatchling** *n* a newly hatched animal.
**hate**[1] *v* to feel extreme dislike or hostility towards.
**hate**[2] *n* **1** intense dislike or hostility. **2** *informal* an object of hatred.
**hateful** *adj* deserving or arousing hate. ➤ **hatefully** *adv.*
**hatred** *n* intense dislike or hate.
**hat trick** *n* three successes by one person or side.
**haughty** *adj* (**-ier, -iest**) disdainfully proud or arrogant. ➤ **haughtily** *adv,* **haughtiness** *n.*
**haul**[1] *v* **1** to pull or drag with an effort. **2** to transport (goods) in a commercial vehicle.
**haul**[2] *n* **1** an amount gathered or acquired, *esp* illegally. **2** the fish taken in a single spell of fishing.
**haulage** *n* the act or process of hauling.
**haulier** *n* a person or establishment that transports goods commercially.
**haulm** *n* a plant stem.
**haunch** *n* **1** the human hip. **2** the hindquarters of a four-legged animal. **3** the back half of the side of a slaughtered animal.
**haunt**[1] *v* **1** of a ghost: to be present in (a place) regularly. **2** of a person: to visit (a place) often. **3** of a thought: to recur constantly and disturb (somebody).
**haunt**[2] *n* a place habitually frequented.
**haunted** *adj* **1** inhabited by a ghost. **2** worried or anguished.
**haunting** *adj* **1** of thoughts or memories: constantly recurring and evocative. **2** of music: poignant. ➤ **hauntingly** *adv.*
**haute couture** /ˌoht kooh'tyooə/ *n* the designing and making of fashionable clothes by leading fashion houses.
**haute cuisine** /kwi'zeen/ *n* cooking of a high standard and following French methods.
**have** *v* (*third person sing. present* **has,** *past tense and past part.* **had**) **1** to own or possess. **2** to display (a feeling or quality). **3** to experience or undergo (an illness). **4** to engage in (an activity). **5** to eat or drink. **6** to receive or be given. **7** to get (something) done or to get (somebody) to do something. **8** to accommodate or be the host of. **9** to arrange or organize. **10** used to form the perfect, pluperfect, and future perfect tenses of verbs. ✱ **have had it** *informal* to have failed or be useless. **have it out** *informal* to settle a disagreement. **have to** must.
**haven** *n* **1** a place of safety. **2** a harbour or port.
**haven't** *contraction* have not.
**have on** *v* **1** to be wearing. **2** to have planned or organized (an event). **3** *informal* to deceive or tease (somebody).
**haver** *v* **1** *Scot* to talk nonsense. **2** *chiefly Brit* to be indecisive.
**haversack** *n* a strong bag carried on the back.
**havoc** *n* **1** widespread destruction or devastation. **2** great confusion and disorder. ✱ **play havoc with** to disrupt.
**hawk**[1] *n* **1** a bird of prey with short rounded wings and a long tail. **2** a supporter of an aggressive policy. ➤ **hawkish** *adj.*
**hawk**[2] *v* to hunt game with a trained hawk.
**hawk**[3] *v* to offer (goods) for sale in the street. ➤ **hawker** *n.*
**hawk**[4] *v* **1** to clear the throat with a harsh noise. **2** to produce (phlegm) by hawking.
**hawser** *n* a large rope used on a ship.
**hawthorn** *n* a spiny shrub with white or pink flowers and small red fruits.
**hay** *n* grass that has been mown and dried for fodder.
**hay fever** *n* an allergy to pollen causing nasal catarrh and conjunctivitis.
**haystack** *n* a large pile of stacked hay.
**haywire** *adj informal* out of control; erratic.
**hazard**[1] *n* **1** a risk or peril. **2** a source of danger. **3** a bunker or other obstacle on a golf course.
**hazard**[2] *v* **1** to venture (an estimate or guess). **2** to expose to danger.
**hazardous** *adj* involving or causing danger.
**haze** *n* **1** a light mist caused by vapour, dust, etc in the air. **2** mental vagueness or confusion.
**hazel** *n* **1** a small tree bearing nuts in autumn and catkins in spring. **2** a yellowish brown colour.
**hazy** *adj* (**-ier, -iest**) **1** obscured or cloudy. **2** vague or indefinite. ➤ **hazily** *adv.*
**H-bomb** *n* a hydrogen bomb.
**He** *abbr* the chemical symbol for helium.
**he** *pron* **1** used to refer to a male person or animal previously mentioned. **2** used to refer to a person of either sex.
**head**[1] *n* **1** the upper or front part of the body containing the brain, mouth, and sense organs. **2** (*in pl*) the side of a coin bearing the head of a monarch or president. **3** a person or individual. **4** a specified number of livestock. **5** the end that is upper, higher, or opposite the foot. **6** the source of a stream, river, etc. **7** a director or leader. **8** a school principal. **9** a cluster of flowers or leaves. **10** the operational part of a weapon, tool, or device. **11** the flattened or rounded end of a nail or screw. **12** the pressure of a fluid. **13** the foam at the top of a glass of beer. ✱ **come to a head** to reach a crisis. **a head start** an initial advantage over competitors. **keep one's head** to retain one's composure. **lose one's head** to panic or behave irrationally. ➤ **headless** *adj.*
**head**[2] *adj* principal or chief.
**head**[3] *v* **1** to lead or be at the head of. **2** to put as the heading to. **3** to stand as the first item of. **4** to drive (a ball) with the head. **5** to move in a specified direction.

**headache** *n* **1** a prolonged pain in the head. **2** *informal* something that causes worry.
**headband** *n* a band of stretch fabric worn round the head.
**headboard** *n* an upright board at the head of a bed.
**headbutt**[1] *v* to hit (somebody) with the front of the head.
**headbutt**[2] *n* a blow with the head.
**headdress** *n* a decorative or ceremonial covering for the head.
**header** *n* **1** a shot or pass in football made with the head. **2** *informal* a headfirst fall or dive. **3** a raised water tank that maintains pressure in a system. **4** a line of text at the top of each page of a book or document.
**headfirst** *adv and adj* with the head foremost; headlong.
**headgear** *n* clothing for the head.
**headhunt** *v* to find and recruit personnel to fill business vacancies. ➤ **headhunter** *n.*
**heading** *n* **1** a title at the top of a letter, chapter, etc. **2** a compass direction. **3** the top edge of a curtain above the hooks.
**headland** *n* a point of high land jutting into the sea.
**headlight** *or* **headlamp** *n* a main light at the front of a motor vehicle.
**headline**[1] *n* **1** a title printed in large type above a newspaper story or article. **2** *Brit* (*in pl*) a summary at the beginning or end of a news broadcast.
**headline**[2] *v* **1** to provide (an article or story) with a headline. **2** to be a star performer in (a show).
**headlock** *n* a hold in which one arm is locked around a person's head.
**headlong** *adv and adj* **1** headfirst. **2** without pause or delay.
**headmaster** *or* **headmistress** *n chiefly Brit* a head teacher of a school.
**head off** *v* to stop and turn aside.
**head of state** *n* the official leader of a state.
**head-on** *adv and adj* **1** with the front making the initial contact. **2** in direct opposition.
**headphones** *pl n* a pair of earphones held over the ears by a band worn on the head.
**headquarters** *n* (*pl* **headquarters**) **1** a place from which a military commander directs operations. **2** the administrative centre of an enterprise.
**headset** *n* a set of earphones and microphone worn on the head.
**head start** *n* an initial advantage over competitors.
**headstone** *n* a memorial stone placed at the head of a grave.
**headstrong** *adj* wilful or obstinate.
**head teacher** *n chiefly Brit* the teacher in charge of a school.
**headway** *n* **1** advance or progress. **2** motion in a forward direction.
**headwind** *n* a wind blowing against the progress of a ship or aircraft.
**headword** *n* a word placed at the beginning of an encyclopedia or dictionary entry.
**heady** *adj* (**-ier, -iest**) **1** of alcoholic drinks: strong and intoxicating. **2** exciting or exhilarating.
**heal** *v* **1** to make healthy after an illness or injury. **2** to make (a wound) sound or whole. **3** to mend (a breach in relations).
**health** *n* **1** soundness of body or mind. **2** the general condition of the body.
**health farm** *n* a residential establishment providing treatment for people wishing to improve their health.
**health food** *n* organically grown food eaten for its health-giving properties.
**healthful** *adj* good for the health of body or mind.
**healthy** *adj* (**-ier, -iest**) **1** enjoying or enhancing good health. **2** prosperous or flourishing. **3** sufficient or substantial. ➤ **healthily** *adv.*
**heap**[1] *n* **1** a collection of things lying one on top of another. **2** *informal* (*in pl*) a large quantity. **3** *informal* a dilapidated vehicle or building.
**heap**[2] *v* **1** (*often* + up) to put or throw in a heap. **2** to form a heap. **3** (*often* + with) to supply with a lot of something. **4** to bestow (things) lavishly or in large quantities on somebody.
**hear** *v* (*past tense and past part.* **heard**) **1** to perceive (sound) with the ear. **2** to learn of by hearing. **3** (*also* + out) to listen to (somebody) with attention. **4** to give a legal or official hearing to (a case, complaint, etc). **5** (+ of/about) to gain information about; to learn. ✱ **hear from** to receive a communication from. **hear! hear!** an expression of agreement. **hear of** (*in negative contexts*) to entertain the idea of (something). ➤ **hearer** *n.*
**hearing** *n* **1** the faculty of perceiving sound. **2** earshot. **3** an opportunity to be heard. **4** a review of evidence in a court.
**hearing aid** *n* a device worn by a deaf person to enable them to hear better.
**hearken** *or* **harken** *v archaic* (*usu* + to) to listen.
**hearsay** *n* something heard from another person.
**hearse** *n* a vehicle for transporting a coffin at a funeral.
**heart** *n* **1** the organ that maintains the circulation of blood in the body. **2** the essential or most vital part of an organization or enterprise. **3** (*in pl*) the suit in a pack of cards that is marked with red figures in the shape of a heart. **4** tenderness or compassion. **5** love or affections. **6** courage or spirit. **7** one's innermost character or feelings. ✱ **by heart** from memory. **take**

**heart** to gain confidence. **take to heart** to be deeply affected by.

**heartache** *n* mental anguish or sorrow.

**heart attack** *n* a sudden failure of the heart.

**heartbeat** *n* **1** a single pulsation of the heart. **2** a driving impulse. **3** a brief moment.

**heartbreak** *n* intense grief or distress. ➤ **heartbreaking** *adj.*

**heartbroken** *adj* overcome by sorrow.

**heartburn** *n* indigestion in the form of a burning pain in the chest.

**hearten** *v* to cheer or encourage. ➤ **heartening** *adj.*

**heart failure** *n* a sudden failure of the heart to continue working.

**heartfelt** *adj* earnest or sincere.

**hearth** *n* the area in front of a fireplace.

**hearthrug** *n* a rug placed in front of a fireplace.

**heartily** *adv* **1** wholeheartedly or vigorously. **2** thoroughly.

**heartless** *adj* unfeeling or cruel.

**heart-rending** *adj* causing great sorrow.

**heart-searching** *n* close examination of one's motives or feelings.

**heart-throb** *n informal* a good-looking man.

**heart-to-heart** *adj* of talk: sincere and intimate.

**heart-warming** *adj* cheering or uplifting.

**hearty** *adj* (**-ier, -iest**) **1** vigorous or enthusiastic. **2** sincere or heartfelt. **3** robustly healthy. **4** of a meal: substantial or abundant.

**heat**[1] *n* **1** the state of being hot. **2** a form of energy associated with the motion of the molecules and atoms of matter. **3** intensity of feeling or reaction. **4** a preliminary round of a contest. **5** *informal* pressure or criticism. ✱ **on heat** of a female mammal: ready for mating.

**heat**[2] *v* **1** (*often* + up) to make or become hot. **2** (+ up) to make or become more exciting or intense.

**heater** *n* a device for heating air or water.

**heath** *n* an area of level uncultivated land, usu with heather and gorse.

**heathen** *n archaic* somebody who does not belong to any of the main religions. ➤ **heathen** *adj.*

**heather** *n* a shrub with purplish pink flowers.

**heating** *n* a system for supplying heat to a building.

**heatstroke** *n* a disorder caused by overheating of the body from prolonged exposure to high temperature.

**heat wave** *n* a prolonged period of unusually hot weather.

**heave**[1] *v* (*past tense and past part.* **heaved** *or* **hove**) **1** to lift or pull with great effort. **2** *informal* to throw (something heavy). **3** to utter (a loud sigh). **4** to rise and fall rhythmically. **5** to retch. ✱ **heave in sight/into view** to come into view.

**heave**[2] *n* an act of heaving.

**heaven** *n* **1** in some beliefs, the dwelling place of God or the gods, where good people go when they die. **2** (**the heavens**) *literary* the sky. **3** *informal* a place or state of complete happiness. ✱ **move heaven and earth** to do all one can.

**heavenly** *adj* **1** relating to heaven or the sky. **2** *informal* delightful.

**heavenly body** *n* a planet, star, or other body in space.

**heavy**[1] *adj* (**-ier, -iest**) **1** having great weight; difficult to carry, move, or lift. **2** large or heavy of its kind. **3** thick or solid. **4** of food: rich and difficult to digest. **5** of soil: full of clay and inclined to hold water. **6** not delicate. **7** slow or sluggish; clumsy. **8** falling with force; powerful. **9** loud and dull in sound. **10** of an unusually large amount, degree, or force: *heavy traffic.* **11** of rock music: loud and having a strong rhythm. **12** needing physical effort and strength. **13** needing considerable mental effort; serious or important. ✱ **heavy going** difficult to understand or deal with. ➤ **heavily** *adv,* **heaviness** *n.*

**heavy**[2] *n* (*pl* **-ies**) **1** *informal* a large intimidating man. **2** *informal* a powerful or important person.

**heavy-duty** *adj* designed to withstand unusual strain or wear.

**heavy industry** *n* production of large or heavy articles in large numbers.

**heavy metal** *n* **1** a metal with a high relative density or high relative atomic weight. **2** a type of highly amplified rock music.

**heavyweight** *n* **1** the heaviest weight in boxing and wrestling. **2** *informal* an important or influential person.

**Hebrew** *n* **1** a member of an ancient Semitic people. **2** the language of the Hebrews, or the modern form of it.

**heckle**[1] *v* to interrupt (a speaker) with shouts or jeers. ➤ **heckler** *n.*

**heckle**[2] *n* a heckling comment or jeer.

**hectare** *n* a metric unit of area equal to 10,000 square metres (2.471 acres).

**hectic** *adj* filled with excitement or feverish activity. ➤ **hectically** *adv.*

**hector** *v* to intimidate in a bullying way.

**he'd** *contraction* he had or he would.

**hedge**[1] *n* **1** a boundary formed by a dense row of shrubs or bushes. **2** a means of protection or defence. **3** an evasive use of language.

**hedge**[2] *v* **1** to enclose with a hedge. **2** to avoid saying anything definite. ✱ **hedge one's bets** to avoid committing oneself.

**hedgehog** *n* a small mammal covered in spines and able to roll into a ball when threatened.

**hedgerow** *n* a row of shrubs or trees surrounding a field.

**hedonism** *n* the pursuit of sensual pleasure. ➤ **hedonist** *n,* **hedonistic** *adj.*

**heebie-jeebies** *pl n* (**the heebie-jeebies**) *informal* a state of nervous anxiety.
**heed**[1] *v* to pay close attention to.
**heed**[2] *n* careful attention; notice. ✱ **pay/take heed** to take notice or care. ➤ **heedful** *adj.*
**heedless** *adj* thoughtless or reckless.
**heel**[1] *n* **1** the back of the foot below the ankle. **2** the part of the palm of the hand nearest the wrist. **3** the part of a shoe or boot that covers or supports the heel. ✱ **down at heel** run-down or shabby. **take to one's heels** to run away.
**heel**[2] *v* **1** to supply (a shoe) with a new heel. **2** of a dog: to walk close behind the person in charge of it.
**heel**[3] *v* of a ship: to tilt to one side.
**heft** *v* to hoist or to heave up.
**hefty** *adj* (**-ier, -iest**) large, heavy, or powerful.
**hegemony** *n* (*pl* **-ies**) domination or leadership of a nation or group.
**heifer** *n* a young cow.
**height** *n* **1** the distance from the top to the bottom. **2** the elevation above a level. **3** the quality of being tall or high. **4** a high point or position. **5** the most extreme or intense point.
**heighten** *v* **1** to increase the amount or degree of. **2** to deepen or intensify. **3** to make higher. **4** to become greater in extent or intensity.
**heinous** *adj* shockingly wicked. ➤ **heinously** *adv.*
**heir** *n* **1** a person who inherits property or rank. **2** a person who receives a position or role from a predecessor.
**heir apparent** *n* (*pl* **heirs apparent**) **1** an heir who cannot be displaced by the birth of another heir. **2** a person who seems most likely to succeed to the position of another.
**heiress** *n* a female heir.
**heirloom** *n* a piece of valuable property handed down within a family for generations.
**heist**[1] *n chiefly NAmer, informal* a robbery.
**heist**[2] *v chiefly NAmer, informal* to steal (something).
**held** *v* past tense and past part. of HOLD[1].
**helical** *adj* having the form of a helix; spiral.
**helicopter** *n* an aircraft which derives lift and power from a set of horizontally rotating rotors.
**helium** *n* a natural gas used *esp* for inflating large balloons.
**helix** *n* (*pl* **helices** *or* **helixes**) an object that is spiral in form.
**hell** *n* **1** in some beliefs, a place of torment and punishment for the dead. **2** a place or state of suffering or misery. ✱ **for the hell of it** *informal* just for fun. **give somebody hell** *informal* to scold them severely.
**he'll** *contraction* he shall or he will.
**hell-bent** *adj* stubbornly or recklessly determined.
**Hellenic** *adj* Greek.
**hellhole** *n* a place of extreme discomfort or squalor.
**hellish** *adj* **1** of or resembling hell; diabolical. **2** *informal* extremely difficult or unpleasant. ➤ **hellishly** *adv.*
**hello** *or* **hallo** *or* **hullo** *interj* **1** used as a greeting. **2** *Brit* used to express surprise or attract attention.
**hellraiser** *n* a person who acts in a wild or drunken manner.
**helm** *n* **1** a tiller or wheel for steering a ship. **2** (**the helm**) the position of control or leadership.
**helmet** *n* a protective head covering.
**helmsman** *n* (*pl* **helmsmen**) a person who steers a ship.
**help** *v* **1** to give assistance or support to. **2** to be of use or benefit to. **3** to promote or further the advancement of. **4** to refrain from (doing something). **5** to keep from occurring; to prevent. **6** to restrain (oneself) from taking action. **7** to remedy or improve (a situation). **8** to serve with food or drink. ✱ **help oneself** to take without permission or dishonestly. ➤ **helper** *n.*
**helpful** *adj* **1** ready to help. **2** useful. ➤ **helpfully** *adv.*
**helping** *n* a serving of food.
**helpless** *adj* **1** lacking protection or support. **2** powerless to act. **3** lacking control or restraint. ➤ **helplessly** *adv.*
**helpmate** *n* a companion and helper.
**helter-skelter**[1] *adj and adv* in a hurried and disorderly manner.
**helter-skelter**[2] *n Brit* a spiral slide at a fairground.
**hem** *n* the border of a cloth article when turned back and stitched down.
**hematology** *n NAmer* see HAEMATOLOGY.
**hemisphere** *n* **1** a half sphere. **2** the northern or southern half of the earth divided by the equator. ➤ **hemispherical** *adj.*
**hemline** *n* the line formed by the hem of a skirt or dress.
**hemlock** *n* a poison made from a plant with small white flowers.
**hemp** *n* **1** the fibre of an Asian plant, used for making rope and fabrics. **2** the drug cannabis.
**hen** *n* **1** a female bird, *esp* a domestic fowl. **2** (*in pl*) domestic fowls of both sexes.
**hence** *adv* **1** for this reason. **2** from this time.
**henceforth** *adv* from this time or point on.
**henchman** *n* (*pl* **henchmen**) a follower or supporter, *esp* an unscrupulous one.
**henna** *n* a reddish brown dye obtained from the leaves of a tropical shrub.
**hen night** *n Brit, informal* a party for women, held for a woman who is about to get married.
**henpecked** *adj* persistently nagged by a woman.

**hepatitis** *n* a disease marked by inflammation of the liver.

**heptagon** *n* a figure with seven angles and seven sides.

**heptathlon** *n* an athletic contest for women with seven events. ➤ **heptathlete** *n.*

**her**[1] *adj* belonging to or associated with a female person or animal already mentioned.

**her**[2] *pron* used as the objective case: she.

**herald**[1] *n* **1** formerly, an official crier or messenger. **2** somebody or something that is a sign of the arrival of something.

**herald**[2] *v* **1** to announce or give notice of. **2** to be a sign of the arrival of.

**heraldic** *adj* relating to heraldry.

**heraldry** *n* the system of designing and using coats of arms.

**herb** *n* **1** a plant used to flavour food or in medicine. **2** in botany, a plant that bears seeds and dies down at the end of a growing season. ➤ **herby** *adj.*

**herbaceous** *adj* relating to a herb (in the botanical sense).

**herbaceous border** *n* a permanent border of perennial flowering plants.

**herbage** *n* herbaceous plants used for grazing.

**herbalist** *n* somebody who grows or sells herbs for medicines. ➤ **herbalism** *n.*

**herbivore** *n* a plant-eating animal. ➤ **herbivorous** *adj.*

**Herculean** *adj* requiring or showing great effort or strength.

**herd**[1] *n* **1** a number of animals of one kind kept together or living as a group. **2** *derog* a large group of people.

**herd**[2] *v* **1** to keep or move (animals) together. **2** to assemble or move in a herd or group.

**here** *adv* in, at, or to this place or position. ✱ **neither here nor there** of no consequence.

**hereabouts** *or* **hereabout** *adv* in this vicinity.

**hereafter**[1] *adv formal* **1** after this. **2** in some future time or state. **3** after death.

**hereafter**[2] *n* (**the hereafter**) life after death.

**hereby** *adv formal* by this means.

**hereditary** *adj* **1** based on inheritance. **2** genetically transmitted from parent to offspring.

**heredity** *n* **1** the transmission of characteristics from one generation to the next. **2** the qualities genetically derived from ancestors.

**herein** *adv formal* in this document, matter, etc.

**hereof** *adv formal* of this document.

**heresy** *n* (*pl* **-ies**) **1** a belief or doctrine contrary to established doctrine. **2** a markedly unorthodox opinion.

**heretic** *n* a person who subscribes to a heresy. ➤ **heretical** *adj.*

**hereto** *adv formal* to this matter or document.

**heretofore** *adv formal* up to this time.

**herewith** *adv formal* with this.

**heritable** *adj* capable of being inherited.

**heritage** *n* **1** property that is inherited. **2** something valuable acquired from predecessors.

**hermaphrodite** *n* a person, animal, or plant having both male and female reproductive organs or characteristics.

**hermetic** *adj* **1** of a seal: airtight. **2** impervious to external influences. ➤ **hermetically** *adv.*

**hermit** *n* a person who lives in solitude, *esp* for religious reasons.

**hernia** *n* a protrusion of part of the intestine through the wall of its enclosing cavity.

**hero** *n* (*pl* **-oes**) **1** a person admired for special courage or achievements. **2** the principal male character in a literary or dramatic work.

**heroic** *adj* **1** showing great courage. **2** grand or impressive. ➤ **heroically** *adv.*

**heroin** *n* a strongly addictive narcotic drug made from morphine.

**heroine** *n* **1** a woman admired for special courage or great achievements. **2** the principal female character in a literary or dramatic work.

**heroism** *n* great courage.

**heron** *n* (*pl* **herons** *or* **heron**) a wading bird with a long neck, long legs, and a tapering bill.

**hero worship** *n* excessive admiration for somebody.

**herpes** *n* a viral disease of the skin, causing blisters.

**herring** *n* (*pl* **herrings** *or* **herring**) a silvery food fish common in the North Atlantic.

**herringbone** *n* a pattern made up of rows of parallel lines slanting in opposite directions on adjacent rows.

**hers** *pron* the one or ones that belong to or are associated with a female person or animal already mentioned.

***Usage Note:*** Note that there is no apostrophe in *hers.*

**herself** *pron* used reflexively or for emphasis to refer to a female person or animal that is the subject of the clause.

**hertz** *n* (*pl* **hertz**) the SI unit of frequency, equal to one cycle per second.

**he's** *contraction* he is or he has.

**hesitant** *adj* tending to hesitate; irresolute. ➤ **hesitancy** *n,* **hesitantly** *adv.*

**hesitate** *v* **1** to pause in doubt or indecision. **2** to be reluctant or unwilling to do something. ➤ **hesitation** *n.*

**hessian** *n* a coarse heavy fabric.

**heterogeneous** *adj* varied or disparate. ➤ **heterogeneity** *n.*

**heterosexual**[1] *adj* having a sexual preference for members of the opposite sex. ➤ **heterosexuality** *n.*

**heterosexual**[2] *n* a heterosexual person.

**het up** *adj informal* angry or upset.

**hew** *v* (*past part.* **hewed** *or* **hewn**) to chop or fell (wood) with a heavy cutting instrument.

**hex**[1] *v chiefly NAmer* to cast a spell on.

**hex**[2] *n chiefly NAmer* a magic spell or jinx.

**hexagon** *n* a figure with six angles and six sides. ➤ **hexagonal** *adj.*
**hexameter** *n* a line of verse consisting of six metrical feet.
**heyday** *n* the period of one's greatest vigour or prosperity.
**Hf** *abbr* the chemical symbol for hafnium.
**Hg** *abbr* the chemical symbol for mercury.
**HGV** *abbr Brit* heavy goods vehicle.
**hiatus** *n* (*pl* **hiatuses**) a break or gap in continuity.
**hibernate** *v* of an animal or plant: to pass the winter in a dormant or resting state. ➤ **hibernation** *n.*
**hibiscus** *n* a plant or shrub with large showy flowers.
**hiccup**[1] *or* **hiccough** *n* **1** an involuntary spasm in the glottis (opening between the throat and windpipe) accompanied by a sharp sound. **2** a brief interruption or setback.
**hiccup**[2] *or* **hiccough** *v* (**hiccuped** *or* **hiccupped, hiccuping** *or* **hiccupping**) to make the sound of a hiccup, or be affected with hiccups.
**hickory** *n* (*pl* **hickories** *or* **hickory**) a hardwood tree with sweet edible nuts and tough pale wood.
**hide**[1] *v* (**hid, hidden**) **1** to put out of sight; to conceal. **2** to conceal oneself. **3** to keep secret.
**hide**[2] *n* the skin of an animal.
**hide-and-seek** *n* a children's game in which a player hides and is sought by the others.
**hideaway** *n* a retreat or hideout.
**hidebound** *adj* narrow or inflexible in character or outlook.
**hideous** *adj* **1** extremely ugly or repulsive. **2** very unpleasant. ➤ **hideously** *adv.*
**hideout** *n* a hiding place used by a criminal.
**hiding**[1] *n* **1** a beating or thrashing. **2** *informal* a severe defeat. ✱ **on a hiding to nothing** *Brit* bound to fail.
**hiding**[2] *n* a state or place of concealment.
**hierarchy** *n* (*pl* **-ies**) **1** a system in which people or groups are ranked according to their status or authority. **2** a system in which things are ranked according to importance. ➤ **hierarchical** *adj.*
**hieroglyphic** *adj* relating to or using a system of writing in which pictures represent a word or sound. ➤ **hieroglyphics** *pl n.*
**hi-fi** *n* (*pl* **hi-fis**) *informal* a set of equipment for the high-fidelity reproduction of sound.
**higgledy-piggledy** *adv and adj* in confusion; disordered.
**high**[1] *adj* **1** extending upwards for a considerable distance. **2** situated at a considerable distance above the ground or above sea level. **3** having a specified elevation. **4** of greater degree, or amount than average. **5** foremost in rank, dignity, or standing. **6** near the upper end of a sound range. **7** forceful or strong. **8** of food: beginning to go bad. **9** *informal* elated or excited, *esp* as an effect of drugs or alcohol. ✱ **high time** time for something that should have happened already.
**high**[2] *adv* **1** at or to a high place or altitude. **2** highly. **3** of a sound: at or to a high pitch.
**high**[3] *n* **1** a high point or level. **2** a region of high atmospheric pressure. **3** *informal* a state of ecstasy or euphoria. ✱ **on high** in or to a high place.
**highbrow** *adj* refined in intellectual and cultural interests.
**High Church** *n* a movement or tendency in the Anglican Church that favours aspects of Roman Catholicism in liturgy and dogma.
**high commissioner** *n* an ambassador of one Commonwealth country stationed in another.
**high court** *n* a supreme judicial court.
**higher education** *n* education beyond the secondary level, at a college or university.
**high explosive** *n* a powerful explosive, e.g. TNT.
**highfalutin** *or* **highfaluting** *adj informal* pretentious or pompous.
**high fidelity** *n* sound reproduction that is close to the original.
**high-flier** *or* **high-flyer** *n* an ambitious or successful person.
**high-flown** *adj* **1** excessively ambitious or extravagant. **2** of language: pretentious.
**high gear** *n* a gear used for a high speed of travel.
**high-handed** *adj* overbearing or inconsiderate.
**high jinks** *pl n* high-spirited fun and games.
**high jump** *n* an athletic field event in which contestants jump over a high bar.
**highland** *n* **1** (*also in pl*) high or mountainous land. **2** (**the Highlands**) the mountainous northern part of Scotland. ➤ **highlander** *n.*
**highlight** *n* **1** an event or detail of special importance. **2** a light area in a painting or photograph. **3** (*usu in pl*) contrasting bright tints in the hair.
**highly** *adv* **1** to a high degree; extremely. **2** favourably.
**highly-strung** *adj Brit* extremely nervous or sensitive.
**high-minded** *adj* having elevated principles and feelings.
**Highness** *n* used as a title for a person of royal rank.
**high-rise** *adj* of a building: having a large number of storeys.
**high school** *n* a secondary school.
**high seas** *pl n* (**the high seas**) the part of a sea outside territorial waters.
**high-spirited** *adj* bold or lively.
**high tea** *n Brit* an early evening meal including a drink of tea.

**high-tech** *or* **hi-tech** *adj* using or requiring advanced technology.
**high technology** *n* advanced technological processes.
**high-tension** *adj* having or using a high voltage.
**high tide** *n* the time when the sea reaches its highest level.
**highway** *n* **1** a public road. **2** *chiefly NAmer* a main road.
**highwayman** *n* (*pl* **highwaymen**) formerly, a mounted robber of travellers on a road.
**hijack** *v* **1** to seize control of (a vehicle or aircraft) while it is in transit. **2** to steal or appropriate. ➤ **hijacker** *n.*
**hike**[1] *n* **1** a long walk in the country. **2** a big increase or rise.
**hike**[2] *v* **1** to go on a hike. **2** (*usu* + up) to pull or lift up. **3** (*usu* + up) to raise (prices, wages, etc). ➤ **hiker** *n.*
**hilarious** *adj* extremely funny. ➤ **hilariously** *adv,* **hilarity** *n.*
**hill** *n* a natural rise of land lower than a mountain. ✱ **over the hill** *informal* old and past one's prime. ➤ **hilly** *adj.*
**hillock** *n* a small hill.
**hilt** *n* the handle of a sword, dagger, or knife. ✱ **to the hilt** completely.
**him** *pron* used as the objective case: he.
**himself** *pron* used reflexively or for emphasis to refer to a male person or animal that is the subject of the clause.
**hind**[1] *adj* situated at the back or behind.
**hind**[2] *n* (*pl* **hinds** *or* **hind**) a female deer.
**hinder** *v* to retard or obstruct.
**Hindi** *n* the language of northern India.
**hindmost** *adj* furthest back.
**hindquarters** *pl n* the hind legs and adjoining parts of a four-legged animal.
**hindrance** *n* **1** the act of hindering. **2** an impediment or obstacle.
**hindsight** *n* understanding of a situation only after the event.
**Hindu** *n* an adherent of Hinduism.
**Hinduism** *n* a religion of the Indian subcontinent, including reincarnation and the worship of many gods.
**hinge**[1] *n* a device that enables a door, gate, lid, etc to turn.
**hinge**[2] *v* (**hingeing** *or* **hinging**) **1** to attach with a hinge. **2** (+ on) to depend on.
**hint**[1] *n* **1** a brief suggestion or piece of advice. **2** an indirect or veiled statement. **3** a slight indication or trace.
**hint**[2] *v* (*often* + at) to indicate indirectly or by allusion.
**hinterland** *n* **1** a region lying inland from a coast. **2** a region remote from a town or city.
**hip**[1] *n* the projecting part at each side of the body, formed by the pelvis and upper thigh.
**hip**[2] *n* the ripened fruit of a rose.
**hip**[3] *interj* used to begin a cheer.
**hip**[4] *adj* (**hipper, hippest**) *informal* fashionable.
**hip hop** *n* a style of popular music with spoken words and music having a regular heavy beat.
**hippie** *or* **hippy** *n* (*pl* **-ies**) a person who rejects established values and dresses unconventionally.
**hippo** *n* (*pl* **hippos** *or* **hippo**) *informal* a hippopotamus.
**hippopotamus** *n* (*pl* **hippopotamuses** *or* **hippopotami**) a large African mammal with an extremely large head and mouth, thick skin, and short legs, living partly in the water.
**hippy** *n* (*pl* **-ies**) see HIPPIE.
**hipsters** *pl n Brit* trousers that start at the hips rather than the waist.
**hire**[1] *v* **1** to pay to obtain the temporary use of. **2** (+ out) to allow (something) to be used for a time in return for payment. ➤ **hirer** *n.*
**hire**[2] *n* **1** payment for the temporary use of something. **2** hiring or being hired.
**hireling** *n derog* a person who is hired for dull or routine work.
**hire purchase** *n Brit* a system by which a customer pays for goods in instalments while having ownership of them.
**hirsute** *adj formal* hairy.
**his**[1] *adj* belonging to or associated with a male person or animal already known or mentioned.
**his**[2] *pron* the one or ones that belong to or are associated with a male person or animal already mentioned.
**Hispanic** *adj* relating to Spain or Spanish-speaking people.
**hiss**[1] *v* **1** to make a sharp sound like a prolonged *s*. **2** to utter angrily with a hiss.
**hiss**[2] *n* a hissing sound.
**histamine** *n* a chemical compound released in the body after injury or in the presence of an allergen.
**historian** *n* a student of or expert in history.
**historic** *adj* famous or important in history.
**historical** *adj* **1** relating to history and past events. **2** belonging to the past. ➤ **historically** *adv.*
**history** *n* (*pl* **-ies**) **1** the study of past events. **2** past events as a whole. **3** an account of past events. **4** a person's medical, sociological, etc background. **5** an unusual or interesting past.
**histrionic** *adj* deliberately affected or theatrical. ➤ **histrionics** *pl n.*
**hit**[1] *v* (**hitting,** *past tense and past part.* **hit**) **1** to aim a blow at with the hand or an implement. **2** to come or bring into violent contact with. **3** to propel (a ball, etc) with a blow. **4** to reach (a target). **5** to harm or have a bad effect on. **6** *informal* to arrive at (a place). ✱ **hit it off** *informal* to enjoy one another's company. **hit on** to arrive at (a solution) unexpectedly. **hit the roof** *informal* to become extremely angry.

**hit**[2] *n* **1** a blow, *esp* one that meets its target. **2** a popular or successful person or thing. **3** a successful match when a database is being searched. **4** *informal* a dose of a substance, e.g. a drug.

**hit-and-miss** *adj* = HIT-OR-MISS.

**hit-and-run** *adj* of a road accident: involving a driver who does not stop after causing damage or injury.

**hitch**[1] *v* **1** to move (something) by jerks. **2** to catch or fasten by a hook or knot. **3** *informal* to request and obtain (a free lift) in a passing vehicle. ✱ **get hitched** *informal* to get married.

**hitch**[2] *n* **1** a temporary setback. **2** a knot used for a temporary fastening. **3** *informal* an act of hitchhiking.

**hitchhike** *v* to travel by obtaining free lifts in passing vehicles. ➤ **hitchhiker** *n.*

**hither** *adv archaic* to or towards this place.

**hitherto** *adv* up to this time.

**hit list** *n* a list of criminal targets.

**hit-or-miss** *adj* inconsistent or haphazard.

**hit out** *v* to act or speak violently or aggressively.

**HIV** *abbr* human immunodeficiency virus, the virus that causes Aids.

**hive** *n* **1** a beehive. **2** a place full of busy people.

**hive off** *v chiefly Brit* to separate from a group or larger unit.

**hives** *pl n* an allergic rash on the skin.

**HM** *abbr* His/Her Majesty.

**HMS** *abbr* His/Her Majesty's Ship.

**HND** *abbr Brit* Higher National Diploma.

**Ho** *abbr* the chemical symbol for holmium.

**hoard**[1] *n* **1** a supply of money or food stored up for future use. **2** a store of useful information.

***Usage Note:*** Do not confuse this word with *horde*, which is a large disorganized group of people (*hordes of tourists*).

**hoard**[2] *v* to accumulate (a hoard). ➤ **hoarder** *n.*

**hoarding** *n Brit* **1** a large board for displaying advertisements. **2** a temporary fence put round a building site.

**hoarfrost** *n* a covering of minute ice crystals on the ground, trees, etc.

**hoarse** *adj* of a voice: rough or harsh in sound. ➤ **hoarsely** *adv.*

**hoary** *adj* (**-ier, -iest**) **1** grey or white with age. **2** having greyish or whitish hair. **3** venerably old. **4** hackneyed.

**hoax**[1] *n* a trick or practical joke.

**hoax**[2] *v* to deceive or trick. ➤ **hoaxer** *n.*

**hob** *n Brit* the top surface of a cooker, with hotplates for pans.

**hobble**[1] *v* **1** to walk unsteadily. **2** to fasten together the legs of (a horse) to prevent it from straying.

**hobble**[2] *n* **1** a hobbling movement. **2** a rope used to hobble a horse.

**hobby** *n* (*pl* **-ies**) a leisure activity or pastime.

**hobbyhorse** *n* **1** a toy consisting of an imitation horse's head attached to one end of a stick. **2** a favourite topic or preoccupation.

**hobgoblin** *n* a mischievous goblin.

**hobnail** *n* a short nail for studding the soles of shoes or boots. ➤ **hobnailed** *adj.*

**hobnob** *v* (**hobnobbed, hobnobbing**) *informal* to socialize or chat with.

**hobo** *n* (*pl* **-oes** *or* **-os**) *NAmer* a tramp or vagrant.

**Hobson's choice** *n* an apparently free choice that offers no real alternative.

**hock**[1] *n* **1** the middle joint of an animal's hind leg. **2** a knuckle of meat.

**hock**[2] *n Brit* a medium-dry white German wine.

**hock**[3] *v informal* to pawn.

**hock**[4] ✱ **in hock 1** having been pawned. **2** in debt.

**hockey** *n* a team game played with long hooked sticks and a small hard ball.

**hocus-pocus** *n* **1** nonsensical words uttered by a conjurer. **2** obscure or misleading nonsense.

**hod** *n* **1** a trough mounted on a pole handle for carrying mortar, bricks, etc. **2** a tall coal scuttle.

**hoe**[1] *n* an implement with a long handle and a flat blade, used for tilling, weeding, etc.

**hoe**[2] *v* **1** to weed or cultivate (land or a crop) with a hoe. **2** to remove (weeds) with a hoe.

**hoedown** *n NAmer* a lively square dance.

**hog**[1] *n* **1** a castrated male pig raised for slaughter. **2** *informal* a greedy person. ✱ **go the whole hog** *informal* to do something thoroughly.

**hog**[2] *v* (**hogged, hogging**) *informal* to take too much of (something); to monopolize. ➤ **hogger** *n.*

**Hogmanay** *n* in Scotland, New Year's Eve.

**hogshead** *n* a large cask or barrel.

**hogwash** *n informal* nonsensical talk.

**hoick** *v Brit, informal* to lift or pull abruptly.

**hoi polloi** *pl n* the common people.

**hoist**[1] *v* to raise into position by means of tackle.

**hoist**[2] *n* an apparatus for hoisting something.

**hoity-toity** *adj* haughty or self-important.

**hokey cokey** *n* a dance performed by a large group of people in a circle.

**hokum** *n informal* **1** nonsense. **2** the use of sentimentality to captivate the audience of a play, film, etc.

**hold**[1] *v* (*past tense and past part.* **held**) **1** to have or support something in the hands or arms. **2** to embrace. **3** to detain (somebody). **4** of a container: to contain or be able to contain. **5** to keep in a specified position. **6** to occupy (a position or job). **7** to maintain (a belief). **8** to consider (somebody) to be to blame for something. **9** to organize (a meeting, party, etc). **10** to take part in (a conversation). **11** to maintain a condition or position. **12** to keep a telephone connection. ✱ **hold forth** to speak at length. **hold one's own** to maintain one's position in the face of opposition. **hold somebody to something** to make somebody honour a commitment. **hold something against somebody** to have a grudge against somebody. **hold to** to remain faithful to (a principle). ➤ **holder** *n.*

**hold**[2] *n* **1** a manner of grasping something or somebody; a grip. **2** something for grasping as a support. **3** influence or control. **4** the cargo compartment of a ship or aircraft. ✱ **no holds barred** with no limits or restrictions. **on hold** postponed or temporarily suspended. **take hold 1** to grasp, or seize. **2** to take effect.

**holdall** *n Brit* a large bag for miscellaneous articles.

**hold back** *v* **1** to keep in check. **2** to hesitate.

**hold down** *v* to keep and manage well in (a job).

**holding** *n* **1** a piece of land held by a tenant. **2** (*in pl*) financial assets in the form of land or securities.

**hold off** *v* **1** to keep (an attacker or challenge) at a distance. **2** to delay (action). **3** of bad weather: not to occur.

**hold on** *v* **1** to persevere despite difficulties. **2** to wait. ✱ **hold on to** to keep possession of.

**hold out** *v* **1** to persevere despite difficulties. **2** to offer (hope). **3** to continue to be enough.

**hold over** *v* to postpone (an event).

**holdup** *n* **1** an armed robbery. **2** a delay.

**hold up** *v* **1** to delay (a person or activity). **2** to rob at gunpoint. **3** to retain force or value.

**hole**[1] *n* **1** a hollow in something solid. **2** a gap or opening through something. **3** in golf, a cylindrical cavity in a putting green into which the ball is played. **4** *informal* a small or unpleasant place. **5** *informal* an awkward situation. ✱ **make a hole in** to use up a lot of (a supply).

**hole**[2] *v* **1** to make a hole in. **2** in golf, to hit (the ball) into a hole.

**hole up** *v informal* (*usu* + in) to hide oneself in a confined place.

**holiday**[1] *n* **1** *Brit* an extended period taken as leave or a break from one's normal occupation. **2** an official day of leave from work.

**holiday**[2] *v* to take or spend a holiday.

**holidaymaker** *n* a person on holiday away form home.

**holiness** *n* **1** the quality of being holy. **2** (**His/Your Holiness**) a title for the Pope and other religious leaders.

**holistic** *adj* in alternative medicine, treating the whole person, not merely the symptoms. ➤ **holism** *n.*

**holler** *v NAmer* to shout loudly.

**hollow**[1] *adj* **1** having a recessed surface; curved inwards. **2** having a cavity within. **3** of a sound: echoing or muffled. **4** lacking in real value or significance. **5** insincere. ✱ **beat hollow** to defeat thoroughly. ➤ **hollowly** *adv.*

**hollow**[2] *v* (*usu* + out) to make hollow.

**hollow**[3] *n* **1** a small valley or basin. **2** an unfilled space or cavity.

**holly** *n* a shrub with thick glossy spiny-edged leaves and bright red berries.

**hollyhock** *n* a tall plant with large rounded leaves and tall spikes of showy flowers.

**holocaust** *n* **1** an instance of wholesale destruction or loss of life. **2** (**the Holocaust**) the persecution of European Jews by the Nazis during World War II.

**hologram** *n* a photograph that produces a three-dimensional image when illuminated. ➤ **holographic** *adj,* **holography** *n.*

**holster** *n* a holder for a pistol, usu worn on a belt.

**holy** *adj* (**-ier, -iest**) **1** set apart to the service of God or a god; sacred. **2** spiritually pure; godly.

**holy of holies** *n* a place considered sacred.

**Holy Spirit** *n* (**the Holy Spirit**) the third person of the Trinity.

**holy war** *n* a war undertaken in the name of religion.

**Holy Week** *n* the week before Easter.

**homage** *n* public honour or deference to a person.

**homburg** *n* a man's felt hat with a stiff curled brim and a high crown.

**home**[1] *n* **1** the place where one lives. **2** a place of origin. **3** an establishment providing residential care. **4** the finishing point in a race. ✱ **at home** relaxed and comfortable. ➤ **homeless** *adj,* **homeward** *adj and adv.*

**home**[2] *adv* **1** to or at one's home or family. **2** into place. ✱ **bring home to somebody** to make somebody aware of (a fact or circumstance). **home and dry** having reached one's objective.

**home**[3] *adj* **1** relating to one's home. **2** relating to one's own country. **3** denoting the headquarters or centre of operations. **4** of a match: played on a team's own ground.

**home**[4] *v* of a bird or animal: to return to its base by instinct. ✱ **home in on** to move towards or concentrate on.

**home economics** *pl n* the study of cookery and household management.

**home help** *n Brit* a person employed to carry out household chores.

**homeland** *n* one's native land.

**homely** *adj* (**-ier, -iest**) **1** commonplace or familiar. **2** simple and unpretentious. **3** affectionate and sympathetic. **4** *chiefly NAmer* plain or unattractive. ➤ **homeliness** *n.*

**homeopathy** *or* **homoeopathy** *n* a system of treating diseases by administering minute doses of substances that produce symptoms like those of the disease. ➤ **homeopathic** *adj.*

**home page** *n* the page of a website with general information, which is accessed first.
**home rule** *n* self-government by the people of a dependent political unit.
**home run** *n* in baseball, a hit that enables the batter to make a complete circuit of the bases and score a run.
**homesick** *adj* missing one's home while absent from it. ➤ **homesickness** *n.*
**homespun** *adj* lacking sophistication; simple.
**homestead** *n* a house with adjoining land.
**home truth** *n* (*also in pl*) an unpleasant fact about one's character or situation, heard from another person.
**homework** *n* **1** school work that a pupil is given to do at home. **2** preparatory reading or research.
**homicide** *n* murder. ➤ **homicidal** *adj.*
**homily** *n* (*pl* **-ies**) a talk on a religious or moral subject.
**homoeopathy** *n* see HOMEOPATHY.
**homogeneous** /homə'jeeni·əs/ *adj* **1** of the same or a similar kind. **2** of uniform structure or composition. ➤ **homogeneity** *n.*
**homogenize** *or* **-ise** *v* **1** to make or become uniform. **2** to break up the fat globules of (milk) so that the cream does not rise. ➤ **homogenized** *adj.*
**homonym** *n* a word that has the same spelling and pronunciation as another but a different meaning and origin, as with the noun and the verb *bear*.
**homophobia** *n* hostility to or fear of homosexuality and homosexuals. ➤ **homophobic** *adj.*
**homophone** *n* a word that is pronounced like another but has a different meaning, origin, or spelling, e.g. *to, too,* and *two*.
**Homo sapiens** *n* the species that includes humans.
**homosexual**[1] *adj* having a sexual preference for members of the same sex. ➤ **homosexuality** *n.*
**homosexual**[2] *n* a homosexual person.
**Hon.** *abbr* used as a title: Honourable.
**hone** *v* **1** to sharpen (a tool) with a stone. **2** to make keener or more effective.
**honest** *adj* **1** sincere and truthful. **2** earned fairly. **3** simple and unpretentious. ➤ **honestly** *adv.*
**honesty** *n* **1** sincerity and truthfulness. **2** upright and straightforward conduct.
**honey** *n* a sweet sticky golden liquid made by bees from the nectar of flowers and used as a food.
**honeybee** *n* a honey-producing bee.
**honeycomb** *n* **1** a mass of six-sided wax cells built by bees to contain their brood and stores of honey. **2** a cellular structure resembling this. ➤ **honeycombed** *adj.*
**honeydew** *n* a sweet deposit secreted on the leaves of plants by insects.
**honeyed** *or* **honied** *adj literary* of words: sweet and soothing.
**honeymoon** *n* **1** a holiday taken by a married couple immediately after their marriage. **2** a period of harmony and goodwill at the start of a new relationship.
**honeypot** *n* a place with attractions that draw many visitors.
**honeysuckle** *n* a climbing shrub with showy sweet-smelling flowers.
**honk**[1] *v* **1** to sound a car's horn. **2** to make the cry of a goose. ➤ **honker** *n.*
**honk**[2] *n* a honking sound.
**honky-tonk** *n* **1** ragtime piano playing. **2** *chiefly NAmer, informal* a cheap nightclub or dance hall.
**honorary** *adj* **1** of a title or award: conferred in recognition of achievement. **2** unpaid or voluntary.
**honorific** *adj* conferring or conveying honour.
**honour**[1] (*NAmer* **honor**) *n* **1** public recognition or fame. **2** a privilege. **3** a person who brings credit or recognition. **4** an award for achievement or excellence. **5** a sense of morality and justice. **6** a good name or reputation. **7** (*in pl*) the highest academic standard in a degree course or examination. **8** (**Your/His Honour**) used as a title for a judge in court. ✱ **in honour of** as a mark of respect for.
**honour**[2] (*NAmer* **honor**) *v* **1** to regard with deep respect. **2** to confer a mark of distinction on. **3** to fulfil (an obligation or commitment).
**honourable** (*NAmer* **honorable**) *adj* **1** characterized by a sense of honour. **2** worthy of respect. **3** (*often* **Honourable**) used as a title for Members of Parliament.
**hooch** *or* **hootch** *n NAmer, informal* a cheap or illicit alcoholic drink.
**hood**[1] *n* **1** a covering for the top and back of the head and neck. **2** a folding waterproof cover for an open car, pram, etc. **3** a cover or canopy. **4** *NAmer* the bonnet of a vehicle. ➤ **hooded** *adj.*
**hood**[2] *n NAmer, informal* a hoodlum or gangster.
**hoodlum** *n* a thug or gangster.
**hoodoo** *n* (*pl* **-os**) **1** voodoo. **2** a malign influence that haunts one.
**hoodwink** *v* to deceive or delude.
**hoof**[1] *n* (*pl* **hooves** *or* **hoofs**) a horny casing on the foot of a horse, cow, etc. ➤ **hoofed** *adj.*
**hoof**[2] *v informal* to kick (a ball, etc) firmly. ✱ **hoof it** *informal* to go on foot.
**hook**[1] *n* **1** a curved device for hanging things on or attaching things to. **2** a repeated melodic phrase in a song. **3** a sickle. **4** a short blow delivered with a circular motion while the elbow remains bent and rigid. ✱ **by hook or by crook** by any possible means. **hook, line, and**

**sinker** completely. **off the hook** *informal* freed from a difficulty.

**hook²** *v* **1** to attach with a hook. **2** (+ round/over) to crook or bend (an arm or leg) round something. **3** to get hold of with a hooked implement. ✱ **be hooked** *informal* to be addicted or infatuated.

**hookah** *n* an oriental tobacco pipe in which the smoke is drawn through a container of water by means of a flexible tube.

**hooker** *n* **1** in rugby, the player in the middle of the front row of the scrum. **2** *informal* a woman prostitute.

**hook up** *v* to link or be linked to (electronic equipment).

**hookworm** *n* a parasitic worm with strong mouth hooks for attaching to the host's intestinal lining.

**hooligan** *n* a violent young troublemaker. ➤ **hooliganism** *n.*

**hoop** *n* **1** a large circular strip of rigid material. **2** a circular figure or object. **3** an arch through which balls are hit in croquet. **4** a horizontal band of contrasting colour round a cap or sports shirt. ✱ **go through the hoops** to undergo difficult tests. ➤ **hooped** *adj.*

**hoop-la** *n* **1** *Brit* a fairground game in which rings are thrown over prizes to win them. **2** *NAmer* fuss or noise.

**hooray** *interj* = HURRAY.

**hoot¹** *v* **1** to make the cry of an owl. **2** to sound the horn of a vehicle. **3** to shout or laugh derisively.

**hoot²** *n* **1** a hooting sound. **2** *informal* a source of laughter or amusement.

**hooter** *n* **1** *chiefly Brit* a device for producing a loud hooting noise. **2** *informal* the nose.

**Hoover** *n trademark* a vacuum cleaner.

**hooves** *n* pl of HOOF¹.

**hop¹** *v* (**hopped, hopping**) **1** to jump repeatedly on one foot. **2** of an animal: to move with a quick springy leap. **3** of a bird: to jump with both feet. **4** to make a quick trip by air. **5** to jump over. ✱ **hop it!** *Brit, informal* go away! **hopping mad** *informal* extremely angry.

**hop²** *n* **1** a hopping leap or movement. **2** a short journey by air. **3** *informal* a dance. ✱ **on the hop** *informal* unprepared.

**hop³** *n* **1** a climbing plant with cone-shaped catkins. **2** (*in pl*) the ripe dried catkins of a hop used to give a bitter taste in brewing.

**hope¹** *v* **1** to desire or trust that something is or may be the case. **2** to desire and expect (to do something). **3** (+ for) to be eager for.

**hope²** *n* **1** (*also in pl*) the feeling that what one wants to happen can happen. **2** a chance that a desired thing may happen. **3** (*in pl*) the things one wants to happen. **4** a person or thing that one is depending on.

**hopeful¹** *adj* feeling or inspiring hope.

**hopeful²** *n* a person hoping or likely to succeed.

**hopefully** *adv* **1** in a hopeful manner. **2** *informal* it is hoped; I hope.

***Usage Note:*** The second meaning, as in *hopefully, I'll be home before dark*, is controversial.

**hopeless** *adj* **1** having no expectation of success. **2** unable to be dealt with or resolved. **3** incompetent or useless. ➤ **hopelessly** *adv,* **hopelessness** *n.*

**hopper** *n* a funnel-shaped receptacle for storing and dispensing grain, coal, etc.

**hopscotch** *n* a children's game in which players hop through a figure marked on the ground.

**horde** *n* a large disorganized group of people.

***Usage Note:*** Do not confuse this word with *hoard*, which is a supply of something (*a hoard of money*).

**horizon** *n* **1** the line in the distance where the land and the sky appear to meet. **2** (*also in pl*) one's range of perception, experience, or knowledge.

**horizontal** *adj* parallel to the earth's surface; level. ➤ **horizontally** *adv.*

**hormone** *n* **1** a substance produced in the body, creating a specific effect on the activity of cells. **2** a synthetic substance that imitates a natural hormone. ➤ **hormonal** *adj.*

**horn** *n* **1** a bony projection on the head of cattle, deer, and other animals. **2** the tough fibrous material forming the horns and hooves of animals. **3** a brass instrument with a coiled tube that flares out at the end. **4** a device on a vehicle, for making loud warning noises. ✱ **draw in one's horns** to reduce one's activities or spending. ➤ **horned** *adj.*

**hornblende** *n* a dark mineral consisting chiefly of silicates of calcium, magnesium, and iron.

**hornet** *n* a large wasp.

**hornpipe** *n* a lively sailors' dance.

**horny** *adj* (**-ier, -iest**) **1** made of or resembling horn. **2** *informal* sexually aroused.

**horology** *n* **1** the science of measuring time. **2** the art of making clocks and watches.

**horoscope** *n* a forecast of a person's future, based on the relative positions of planets and signs of the zodiac at the time of birth.

**horrendous** *adj* dreadful or horrible. ➤ **horrendously** *adv.*

**horrible** *adj* **1** causing horror. **2** *chiefly informal* extremely unpleasant. ➤ **horribly** *adv.*

**horrid** *adj* horrible or shocking.

**horrific** *adj* causing horror; horrifying. ➤ **horrifically** *adv.*

**horrify** *v* (**-ies, -ied**) to cause to feel horror.

**horror** *n* **1** intense fear or dread. **2** intense aversion or repugnance. **3** the quality of inspiring horror. **4** *informal* an unpleasant or ugly person or thing.

**hors d'oeuvre** /ˌaw 'duhv/ *n* (*pl* **hors d'oeuvres** *or* **hors d'oeuvre**) a savoury appetizer.

**horse**[1] *n* **1** a large four-footed mammal, used for riding or as a beast of burden. **2** (*treated as sing. or pl*) cavalry. **3** a wooden block for vaulting over in gymnastics. ✱ **from the horse's mouth** first-hand.

**horse**[2] *v informal* (*usu* + around/about) to fool about.

**horseback** *n* ✱ **on horseback** riding a horse.

**horsebox** *n* a lorry or trailer for transporting horses.

**horse chestnut** *n* **1** a large tree with five-lobed leaves and nuts enclosed in a spiny case. **2** a nut of this tree, a conker.

**horsefly** *n* (*pl* **-ies**) a large fly, the females of which suck blood.

**horse laugh** *n* a loud boisterous laugh.

**horseman** *n* (*pl* **horsemen**) a skilled rider on horseback. ➤ **horsemanship** *n.*

**horseplay** *n* rough or boisterous play.

**horsepower** *n* a unit of power equal to about 746 watts.

**horseradish** *n* a plant with a pungent root from which a sauce is made.

**horse sense** *n* ordinary common sense.

**horseshoe** *n* a U-shaped metal shoe for horses.

**horsewhip**[1] *n* a long whip used for controlling horses.

**horsewhip**[2] *v* (**horsewhipped, horsewhipping**) to beat with a horsewhip.

**horsewoman** *n* (*pl* **horsewomen**) a skilled female rider on horseback.

**hortative** *or* **hortatory** *adj formal* giving encouragement.

**horticulture** *n* the science of growing fruits, vegetables, and flowers. ➤ **horticultural** *adj.*

**hosanna** *interj and n* a cry of acclamation and adoration.

**hose**[1] *n* **1** a flexible tube for conveying fluids. **2** tights or stockings.

**hose**[2] *v* (*often* + down) to spray or water with a hose.

**hosepipe** *n* a length of hose for conveying water.

**hosiery** *n* socks, stockings, and tights.

**hospice** *n* a nursing home for terminally ill patients.

**hospitable** *adj* **1** offering a generous welcome to guests or strangers. **2** of an environment: pleasant and sustaining. ➤ **hospitably** *adv.*

**hospital** *n* a place where sick or injured people are given medical care.

**hospitality** *n* friendly treatment of guests and visitors.

**hospitalize** *or* **-ise** *v* to admit to a hospital as a patient. ➤ **hospitalization** *n.*

**host**[1] *n* **1** a person who receives or entertains guests socially. **2** an establishment that provides facilities for an event or function. **3** a compere on a radio or television programme. **4** a living animal or plant on or in which a parasite or smaller organism lives.

**host**[2] *v* to act as host at or of.

**host**[3] *n* **1** a very large number; a multitude. **2** *chiefly literary or archaic* an army.

**host**[4] *or* **Host** *n* the bread consecrated in the Christian Eucharist.

**hostage** *n* a person held captive to ensure that demands are met by another party. ✱ **hostage to fortune** a commitment that lays one open to the risk of failure or criticism.

**hostel** *n* an establishment providing accommodation for a particular group of people.

**hostelry** *n* (*pl* **-ies**) *archaic* an inn or hotel.

**hostess** *n* **1** a woman host. **2** a woman who welcomes male patrons at a bar or nightclub.

**hostile** *adj* **1** relating to an enemy. **2** aggressive and unfriendly.

**hostility** *n* (*pl* **-ies**) **1** hostile action or attitudes. **2** (*in pl*) overt acts of warfare.

**hot**[1] *adj* (**hotter, hottest**) **1** having a relatively high temperature. **2** uncomfortable from excessive heat. **3** of a taste: pungent or spicy. **4** interesting or exciting. **5** currently popular or retailing fast. **6** *informal* of goods: stolen and difficult to dispose. **7** (+ on) knowledgeable about. **8** (+ on) strict about rules, standards, etc. ✱ **hot under the collar** *informal* angry or irritated. **in hot water** in trouble. **not so hot** *informal* not very good.

**hot**[2] *v* (**hotted, hotting**) *informal* (+ up) to become more intense or exciting.

**hot air** *n informal* empty talk.

**hotbed** *n* a place of intense or exciting activity of a particular kind.

**hot-blooded** *adj* excitable or passionate.

**hotchpotch** (*NAmer* **hodgepodge**) *n* a random mixture or jumble.

**hot cross bun** *n* a spicy bun with a pastry cross on top, eaten on Good Friday.

**hot dog** *n* a hot sausage served in a bread roll.

**hotel** *n* an establishment that provides meals and accommodation for the public, in return for payment.

**hotelier** *n* the proprietor or manager of a hotel.

**hotfoot**[1] *adv* in haste.

**hotfoot**[2] ✱ **hotfoot it** *informal* to hurry.

**hothead** *n* an impetuous or hot-tempered person.

**hothouse** *n* a heated greenhouse.

**hotly** *adv* keenly or passionately.

**hot plate** *n* a metal plate on an electric cooker, for heating food.

**hot pot** *n Brit* a stew of meat and vegetables with sliced potatoes.

**hot rod** *n* a car modified for high speed.

**hotshot** *n informal* a showily successful or important person.

**hot spot** *n* a place of excitement or potential danger.

**hot-tempered** *adj* inclined to lose one's temper easily.
**hot-water bottle** *n* a rubber container filled with hot water and used to warm a bed.
**hot-wire** *v* to start (a vehicle) by bypassing the ignition switch.
**hound**[1] *n* a hunting dog.
**hound**[2] *v* to pursue or harass persistently.
**hour** *n* **1** the 24th part of a day; a period of 60 minutes. **2** a particular point in time. **3** a period of time set aside for a specified purpose. **4** (*in pl*) the period during which a business, etc is operational. ✱ **on the hour** at an exact hour. **till all hours** until very late at night.
**hourglass** *n* a device consisting of two glass bulbs joined by a narrow neck, with sand taking one hour to run from the top bulb to the lower.
**hourly** *adj and adv* **1** at or during every hour. **2** by the hour. **3** constant or constantly.
**house**[1] /hows/ *n* (*pl* **houses** /'howziz/) **1** a building for people to live in. **2** a building or establishment with a particular purpose: *an opera house; a boathouse.* **3** a specific type of business: *a publishing house.* **4** a legislative or deliberative assembly. **5** a division of pupils in a school. **6** an important or ancient family. **7** the area occupied by the audience in a theatre or cinema. ✱ **on the house** at the expense of the management. ➤ **houseful** *n.*
**house**[2] /howz/ *v* to provide with accommodation or storage.
**house arrest** *n* confinement in one's home instead of prison.
**houseboat** *n* a moored boat fitted out as a home.
**housebound** *adj* confined to one's house.
**housebreaking** *n* an act of breaking into a building with a criminal purpose. ➤ **housebreaker** *n.*
**household** *n* a dwelling and all the people who live in it.
**household name** *or* **household word** *n* a person or thing everyone has heard of.
**housekeeper** *n* a person employed to take charge of running a house.
**housemaid** *n* a female servant employed to do housework.
**housemaster** *or* **housemistress** *n* a teacher in charge of a house at a boarding school.
**house music** *n* dance music with a strong fast beat.
**House of Commons** *n* the lower house of the British Parliament.
**House of Lords** *n* the upper house of the British Parliament, including lords and bishops.
**house-proud** *adj* careful about the management and appearance of one's home.
**houseroom** ✱ **not give something houseroom** *Brit* to have no interest in something.
**housetrain** *v* to train (a pet) to defecate and urinate outdoors.
**housewarming** *n* a party to celebrate moving into a new house.
**housewife** *n* (*pl* **housewives**) a woman who runs her family's home.
**housework** *n* the work involved in running a home.
**housing** *n* **1** houses or living-places collectively. **2** a protective cover for machinery or instruments.
**hove** *v* past tense and past part. of HEAVE[1].
**hovel** *n* a small squalid dwelling.
**hover** *v* **1** to stay motionless in the air. **2** to linger or wait restlessly. **3** to be in a state of uncertainty or suspense. ➤ **hoverer** *n.*
**hovercraft** *n* (*pl* **hovercraft**) a vehicle supported on a cushion of air for travelling over land and water.
**how** *adv* **1** in what way or by what means. **2** in what state or condition. **3** to what extent or degree. **4** used in exclamations: *how odd!*
**howdah** *n* a seat for riding on the back of an elephant or camel.
**however** *adv* **1** be that as it may; nevertheless. **2** in whatever manner or way. **3** no matter how.
**howitzer** *n* a short cannon with a high trajectory.
**howl**[1] *v* **1** of a dog: to make a loud sustained cry. **2** to yell or cry loudly. **3** of wind: to make a sustained wailing sound.
**howl**[2] *n* a howling sound.
**howler** *n informal* a careless blunder.
**HP** *or* **hp** *abbr* **1** hire purchase. **2** horsepower.
**HQ** *abbr* headquarters.
**HRH** *abbr* His/Her Royal Highness.
**HTML** *abbr* hypertext markup language, a system for presenting computer text for use on a network.
**hub** *n* **1** the central part of a wheel, propeller, or fan. **2** the focal point of an activity.
**hubbub** *n* a noisy confusion or uproar.
**hubris** *n* excessive pride leading to retribution. ➤ **hubristic** *adj.*
**huckster** *n* **1** a hawker or pedlar. **2** a person who uses aggressive selling methods.
**huddle**[1] *v* **1** (*often* + together) to gather in a close group. **2** to curl up or crouch.
**huddle**[2] *n* **1** a crowded group. **2** a secretive meeting.
**hue** *n* **1** a colour or shade. **2** a complexion or aspect.
**hue and cry** *n* a loud public outcry.
**huff**[1] *v* **1** to emit loud puffs of breath. **2** to make empty threats.
**huff**[2] ✱ **in a huff** sulky and resentful. ➤ **huffy** *adj.*
**hug**[1] *v* (**hugged, hugging**) **1** to hold tightly in one's arms. **2** to keep close to.
**hug**[2] *n* an act of hugging.
**huge** *adj* very large. ➤ **hugely** *adv.*

**hugger-mugger** *adj and adv* confused or muddled.
**hula** *or* **hula-hula** /'hoohlə/ *n* a Polynesian dance involving swaying of the hips.
**hula hoop** *n* a large light hoop spun round the waist by movement of the body.
**hulk** *n* **1** the stripped hull of a disused ship. **2** a bulky or clumsy person or thing.
**hulking** *adj informal* bulky; massive.
**hull** *n* **1** the main body of a ship. **2** the outer covering of a fruit or seed. **3** the calyx that surrounds a strawberry or raspberry.
**hullabaloo** *n* (*pl* **-os**) *informal* a confused noise or uproar.
**hullo** *interj chiefly Brit* see HELLO.
**hum**[1] *v* (**hummed, humming**) **1** to utter a prolonged /m/ sound. **2** to make the droning noise of an insect in flight. **3** to sing with the lips closed. **4** *informal* to be lively or active. * **hum and haw** to be indecisive.
**hum**[2] *n* a humming sound.
**human**[1] *adj* **1** relating to people. **2** having the good attributes thought to be characteristic of people. ➤ **humanly** *adv.*
**human**[2] *n* a man, woman, or child.
**humane** *adj* marked by compassion or consideration for others. ➤ **humanely** *adv.*
**humanism** *n* a philosophy that asserts the intrinsic worth of human beings and rejects religious belief. ➤ **humanist** *n and adj*, **humanistic** *adj.*
**humanitarian**[1] *adj* relating to or promoting human welfare.
**humanitarian**[2] *n* a humanitarian person; a philanthropist.
**humanity** *n* (*pl* **-ies**) **1** human beings collectively. **2** the quality of being human or humane. **3** (*in pl*) the cultural branches of learning.
**humanize** *or* **-ise** *v* **1** to give (something) a human quality. **2** to make (a person) humane.
**humankind** *n* human beings collectively.
**humanoid**[1] *adj* having human form or characteristics.
**humanoid**[2] *n* a humanoid being.
**human rights** *pl n* the basic rights that all human beings are entitled to.
**humble**[1] *adj* **1** having a low opinion of oneself. **2** marked by deference or submission. **3** ranking low in a hierarchy or scale. **4** modest or unpretentious. ➤ **humbly** *adv.*
**humble**[2] *v* **1** to make humble in spirit or manner. **2** to destroy the power or importance of. **3** to sacrifice one's pride and abase (oneself).
**humbug** *n* **1** pretentious or deceptive talk. **2** an impostor or sham. **3** *Brit* a hard peppermint-flavoured striped sweet.
**humdrum** *adj* monotonous or dull.
**humerus** *n* (*pl* **humeri**) the bone of the upper arm, extending from the shoulder to the elbow.
**humid** *adj* of the atmosphere: warm and moist. ➤ **humidity** *n.*
**humiliate** *v* to make (somebody) feel foolish or unworthy. ➤ **humiliation** *n.*
**humility** *n* the quality of being humble.
**hummingbird** *n* a small brightly coloured bird with narrow wings that it beats rapidly making a humming sound.
**hummock** *n* a mound or hillock.
**hummus** *or* **hoummous** *n* a puree made from chick-peas and sesame seed paste.
**humorist** *n* a person noted for humour.
**humorous** *adj* characterized by or expressing humour. ➤ **humorously** *adv.*
**humour**[1] (*NAmer* **humor**) *n* **1** a comic or amusing quality. **2** a state of mind; temper. * **out of humour** in a bad temper. ➤ **humourless** *adj.*
**humour**[2] (*NAmer* **humor**) *v* to comply with the mood or wishes of.
**hump**[1] *n* **1** a humped or crooked back. **2** a fleshy lump on the back of a camel, bison, etc. **3** a mound or knoll. ➤ **humped** *adj.*
**hump**[2] *v* to carry with difficulty.
**humus** *n* an organic substance resulting from partial decomposition of plant or animal matter.
**hunch**[1] *v* **1** to assume a bent or crooked posture. **2** to arch (one's shoulders).
**hunch**[2] *n* a strong intuitive feeling.
**hunchback** *n offensive* a person with a humped back.
**hundred** *n* (*pl* **hundreds** *or* **hundred**) **1** (**a/one hundred**) the number 100. **2** (*in pl*) the numbers 100 to 999. **3** *informal* (*in pl*) a large number. ➤ **hundredth** *adj and n.*
**hundredweight** *n* (*pl* **hundredweights** *or* **hundredweight**) **1** a British unit of weight equal to 112lb (about 50.80kg). **2** *NAmer* a US unit of weight equal to 100lb (about 45.36kg).
**hung** *v* past tense and past part. of HANG[1]. * **hung up** *informal* emotionally anxious. **hung up on** *informal* obsessed with.
**hunger**[1] *n* **1** an unpleasant feeling caused by a need for food. **2** a strong desire or craving.
**hunger**[2] *v* (**hungered, hungering**) **1** to feel or suffer hunger. **2** (+ for/after) to have a strong desire for something.
**hunger strike** *n* refusal to eat, as an act of protest.
**hung over** *adj* suffering from a hangover.
**hung parliament** *n* a parliament in which no party holds an overall majority.
**hungry** *adj* (**-ier, -iest**) **1** feeling hunger. **2** eager or avid for something. ➤ **hungrily** *adv.*
**hunk** *n* **1** a large lump or piece of something. **2** *informal* an attractive muscular man. ➤ **hunky** *adj.*
**hunky-dory** *adj informal* pleasing or satisfactory.
**hunt**[1] *v* **1** to chase and kill (a wild animal) for food or enjoyment. **2** of an animal: to chase

and kill (prey). **3** to pursue (a suspect). **4** (+ for) to attempt to find something. **5** of a device, machine, etc: to run alternately fast and slowly. ➤ **hunter** *n.*

**hunt**[2] *n* **1** the act or an instance of hunting. **2** a group of mounted hunters and their hounds. **3** an area where people hunt.

**hunt down** *v* to pursue to capture or kill.

**huntsman** *n* (*pl* **huntsmen**) a person who hunts.

**hurdle**[1] *n* **1** a framework used for enclosing land or livestock. **2** a light barrier jumped by athletes or horses in a race. **3** an obstacle or testing experience.

**hurdle**[2] *v* to jump over (a barrier) while running. ➤ **hurdler** *n.*

**hurdy-gurdy** *n* (*pl* **-ies**) a musical instrument played by turning a handle.

**hurl** *v* **1** to throw forcefully. **2** to shout (abuse or insults) at somebody.

**hurling** *n* an Irish team game resembling hockey.

**hurly-burly** *n* an uproar or commotion.

**hurrah** *interj* = HURRAY.

**hurray** *or* **hooray** *interj* used as a cheer to express joy, approval, or encouragement.

**hurricane** *n* a cyclone with a wind speed greater than 117km/h (73mph).

**hurry**[1] *v* (**-ies, -ied**) **1** (*often* + up) to act or move quickly. **2** (*often* + up) to make (a person or process) go faster. ➤ **hurried** *adj,* **hurriedly** *adv.*

**hurry**[2] *n* haste or rush. ✱ **in a hurry** in haste; rushed.

**hurt**[1] *v* (*past tense and past part.* **hurt**) **1** to cause pain or injury to. **2** to be painful. **3** to offend or upset.

**hurt**[2] *adj* **1** injured. **2** upset or offended.

**hurt**[3] *n* emotional distress caused by being offended or upset.

**hurtful** *adj* unkind or likely to upset. ➤ **hurtfully** *adv.*

**hurtle** *v* to move rapidly or precipitately.

**husband**[1] *n* the man to whom a woman is married.

**husband**[2] *v* to make economical use of (a resource).

**husbandry** *n* **1** farming. **2** economical use of resources.

**hush**[1] *v* to quieten or become quiet. ➤ **hushed** *adj.*

**hush**[2] *n* a silence or calm.

**husk**[1] *n* the dry outer covering of a seed or fruit.

**husk**[2] *v* to strip the husk from.

**husky**[1] *adj* (**-ier, -iest**) **1** of a voice: hoarse and rough. **2** burly or hefty. ➤ **huskily** *adv.*

**husky**[2] *n* (*pl* **-ies**) a powerful sledge dog native to Greenland and Labrador.

**hussar** *n* a member of a cavalry regiment.

**hussy** *n* (*pl* **-ies**) *derog* an impudent or promiscuous woman or girl.

**hustings** *pl n* the speeches and campaigning of a political election.

**hustle**[1] *v* **1** to push or convey roughly or forcibly. **2** to force (somebody) into doing something. **3** *informal* to swindle or cheat (somebody) out of something. ➤ **hustler** *n.*

**hustle**[2] *n* the act of hustling.

**hut** *n* a small simple dwelling or shelter.

**hutch** *n* a pen or cage for a small animal.

**hyacinth** *n* a plant with blue, pink, or white flowers growing in spikes.

**hyaena** *n* see HYENA.

**hybrid** *n* **1** an offspring of two animals or plants of different breeds or varieties. **2** something formed from two or more different things.

**hydrangea** *n* a shrub with large clusters of white, pink, or pale blue flowers.

**hydrant** *n* a pipe with a valve and nozzle from which water may be drawn from a main.

**hydrate** *v* to cause (a substance) to absorb or combine with water. ➤ **hydration** *n.*

**hydraulic** *adj* operated by pressure in a liquid being forced through pipes, tubes, etc. ➤ **hydraulically** *adv.*

**hydraulics** *pl n* a branch of physics dealing with the uses of liquid in motion.

**hydrocarbon** *n* an organic compound containing only carbon and hydrogen.

**hydrocephalus** *or* **hydrocephaly** *n* an abnormal increase in fluid in the brain cavity.

**hydrochloric acid** *n* a solution of hydrogen and chlorine in water that is a strong corrosive acid.

**hydroelectric** *adj* relating to the production of electricity by water power. ➤ **hydroelectricity** *n.*

**hydrofoil** *n* a boat fitted with an aerofoil that lifts the hull out of the water at speed.

**hydrogen** *n* a flammable gas that is the simplest and lightest of the chemical elements.

**hydrogen bomb** *n* a bomb with enormous power due to the sudden release of atomic energy from the fusion of hydrogen nuclei.

**hydrogen sulphide** *n* an inflammable poisonous gas with a smell of rotten eggs.

**hydrophobia** *n* **1** abnormal dread of water. **2** rabies.

**hydroplane** *n* a speedboat that is raised out of the water when moving at speed.

**hydrous** *adj* containing water.

**hydroxide** *n* a compound of hydrogen and oxygen with an element or radical.

**hyena** *or* **hyaena** *n* a doglike nocturnal animal of Asia and Africa, with front legs longer than the rear legs.

**hygiene** *n* conditions and practices that encourage and maintain good health.

**hygienic** *adj* clean and conducive to good health. ➤ **hygienically** *adv.*

**hygienist** *n* a person who is trained in hygiene.

**hymen** *n* a membrane partly closing the opening of the vagina until it is broken, usu on the first occurrence of sexual intercourse.
**hymn**[1] *n* **1** a song of praise to God. **2** a song of praise or joy.
**hymn**[2] *v* to praise or worship with hymns.
**hymnal** *n* a book of hymns.
**hype**[1] *v informal* (*also* + up) to publicize or promote intensively or in an exaggerated way. * **be hyped up** to be stimulated or excited.
**hype**[2] *n informal* intensive or exaggerated advertising or publicity.
**hyper** *adj informal* over-excited; overwrought.
**hyperactive** *adj* excessively or abnormally active. ➤ **hyperactivity** *n.*
**hyperbola** *n* (*pl* **hyperbolas** *or* **hyperbolae**) a plane curve generated by a point moving so that the difference of its distances from two fixed points is a constant.
**hyperbole** *n* deliberate exaggeration for special effect, as in *It took me years to finish.* ➤ **hyperbolic** *adj.*
**hyperlink** *n* a link to another location from a hypertext document.
**hypermarket** *n* a very large supermarket.
**hypersensitive** *adj* abnormally sensitive. ➤ **hypersensitivity** *n.*
**hypersonic** *adj* **1** denoting a speed more than five times that of sound. **2** denoting sound frequencies above a thousand million hertz.
**hypertension** *n* abnormally high blood pressure. ➤ **hypertensive** *adj.*
**hypertext** *n* a type of computerized document that contains active links from one part to another.
**hyperventilate** *v* to breathe excessively fast and deeply. ➤ **hyperventilation** *n.*
**hyphen** *n* a punctuation mark (-) used to join words or to divide a word at the end of a line. ➤ **hyphened** *adj.*
**hyphenate** *v* to join or separate (words) with a hyphen. ➤ **hyphenation** *n.*
**hypnosis** *n* (*pl* **hypnoses**) a condition resembling sleep, in which a person is susceptible to suggestions made to them.
**hypnotherapy** *n* the treatment of disease using hypnosis.
**hypnotic** *adj* **1** relating to hypnosis. **2** tending to produce sleep. ➤ **hypnotically** *adv.*
**hypnotism** *n* the study or practice of hypnosis. ➤ **hypnotist** *n.*
**hypnotize** *or* **-ise** *v* **1** to induce hypnosis in. **2** to fascinate.
**hypoallergenic** *adj* of cosmetics: unlikely to cause an allergic reaction.
**hypochondria** *n* excessive concern about one's health.
**hypochondriac** *n* a person who is affected by hypochondria.
**hypocrisy** *n* (*pl* **-ies**) the advocacy to others of principles or qualities that one does not practise oneself.
**hypocrite** *n* a person given to hypocrisy. ➤ **hypocritical** *adj.*
**hypodermic**[1] *adj* of a syringe or needle: used to inject drugs beneath the skin.
**hypodermic**[2] *n* a hypodermic syringe or injection.
**hypotension** *n* abnormally low blood pressure. ➤ **hypotensive** *adj.*
**hypotenuse** *n* the longest side of a right-angled triangle, opposite the right angle.
**hypothermia** *n* abnormally low body temperature. ➤ **hypothermic** *adj.*
**hypothesis** *n* (*pl* **hypotheses**) a proposed explanation for a phenomenon, set of circumstances, etc, as a basis for argument.
**hypothesize** *or* **-ise** *v* to propose as a hypothesis.
**hypothetical** *adj* **1** involving hypothesis or a condition. **2** depending on supposition; conjectural. ➤ **hypothetically** *adv.*
**hysterectomy** *n* (*pl* **-ies**) surgical removal of the womb.
**hysteria** *n* **1** a mental disorder marked by extreme emotional excitability. **2** unmanageable emotional excess.
**hysterical** *adj* **1** relating to or affected by hysteria. **2** *informal* very funny.
**hysterics** *pl n* **1** a fit of hysteria. **2** *informal* uncontrollable laughter or crying.
**Hz** *abbr* hertz.

**I**[1] *or* **i** *n* (*pl* **I's** *or* **Is** *or* **i's**) **1** the ninth letter of the English alphabet. **2** the Roman numeral for one.

**I**[2] *pron* the word used by a speaker or writer to refer to himself or herself.

**I**[3] *abbr* the chemical symbol for iodine.

**iambic** *adj* in a poetic metre that consists of feet containing one unstressed syllable followed by one stressed syllable.

**ibex** *n* (*pl* **ibexes** *or* **ibices** *or* **ibex**) a wild mountain goat with large backward-curving horns.

**ibid.** *abbr* to be found in the same book, chapter, article, etc, as the quotation immediately preceding this one.

**ibis** *n* (*pl* **ibises** *or* **ibis**) a long-legged, long-necked wading bird with a slender downward-curving bill.

**ice**[1] *n* **1** frozen water. **2** *chiefly Brit* an ice cream. * **on ice** in abeyance; in reserve for later use. **on thin ice** in danger of getting into trouble.

**ice**[2] *v* **1** to cover (e.g. a cake) with icing. **2** to chill (e.g. a drink) with ice. **3** (*often* + over/up) to become covered with ice.

**ice age** *n* a period when much of the earth's surface was covered in ice.

**iceberg** *n* a large mass of ice floating in the sea. * **the tip of the iceberg** the small visible or known part of something much larger, *esp* of something potentially troublesome.

**icebox** *n* **1** *Brit* the freezing compartment of a refrigerator. **2** *NAmer* a refrigerator. **3** a container chilled by ice and used for keeping food and drink, etc cold.

**icebreaker** *n* a ship equipped to make a channel through ice.

**ice cap** *n* a permanent covering of ice, *esp* over a polar region of a planet.

**ice cream** *n* a sweet flavoured frozen food made from milk, cream, or custard.

**iced** *adj* **1** covered with icing. **2** cooled or mixed with ice.

**ice hockey** *n* a game resembling hockey played on an ice rink by two teams of six players.

**ice pack** *n* a bag of ice applied to part of the body to reduce swelling or lower temperature.

**ice skate** *n* a shoe with a metal runner attached for skating on ice.

**ichthyology** *n* the branch of zoology that deals with fish. ➤ **ichthyologist** *n.*

**icicle** *n* a hanging tapering mass of ice formed by the freezing of dripping water.

**icing** *n chiefly Brit* a sweet coating for cakes, biscuits, etc, usu made by mixing icing sugar with water, butter, or egg white. * **the icing on the cake** a final addition that perfects something already good.

**icing sugar** *n chiefly Brit* finely powdered sugar used in making icing.

**icon** *n* **1** (*also* **ikon**) a religious image, *esp* a small painting of Christ, the Virgin Mary, or a saint, used as an aid to devotion in the Eastern Orthodox churches. **2** an image or symbol. **3** a revered or idolized person, *esp* one regarded as symbolizing something. **4** in computing, a symbol displayed on a screen, representing and providing access to a program or facility. ➤ **iconic** *adj.*

**iconify** *v* (**-ies, -ied**) in computing, to reduce a screen window to an icon.

**iconoclast** *n* a person who attacks established beliefs or institutions. ➤ **iconoclasm** *n,* **iconoclastic** *adj.*

**iconography** *n* (*pl* **-ies**) **1** pictorial material relating to or illustrating a subject. **2** the use, or study, of imagery or symbolism in works of art. ➤ **iconographic** *adj.*

**icy** *adj* (**-ier, -iest**) **1** covered with or full of ice. **2** intensely cold. **3** extremely unwelcoming, unfriendly, or hostile. ➤ **icily** *adv.*

**ID**[1] *abbr* **1** identification. **2** identity.

**ID**[2] *v* (**IDs, IDed, IDing**) *informal* to identify or check the identity of.

**I'd** *contraction* **1** I had. **2** I should. **3** I would.

**id** *n* in psychoanalytic theory, the division of the mind that is completely unconscious and comprises a person's instinctual needs and drives.

**idea** *n* **1** a thought, concept, or image present in the mind. **2** an opinion or belief. **3** an indefinite or vague impression. **4** a plan of action. **5** (**the idea**) the central meaning or aim of a particular action. * **have no idea** not to know at all.

**ideal**[1] *n* **1** a principle or standard of excellence to be aspired to. **2** a person or thing that is regarded as perfect.

**ideal**[2] *adj* **1** perfect. **2** existing only in the mind. ➤ **ideally** *adv.*

**idealism** *n* **1** the practice of striving to live according to one's ideals. **2** the belief that ideals represent true reality. ➤ **idealist** *n,* **idealistic** *adj.*

**idealize** *or* **-ise** *v* to attribute excellence or perfection to, often unjustifiably. ➤ **idealization** *n.*

**identical** *adj* **1** the very same. **2** (*often* + to/with) exactly alike. **3** of twins, triplets, etc: derived from a single ovum and therefore very similar in appearance. ➤ **identically** *adv.*

**identification** *n* **1** the act of identifying. **2** evidence of identity.

**identify** *v* (**-ies, -ied**) **1** to establish the identity of. **2** to discover by observation or analysis. **3** (+ with) to equate or link (somebody, oneself, or something) with another person or thing. **4** (*usu* + with) to consider that one shares the same qualities or experiences as somebody else. ➤ **identifiable** *adj.*

**identity** *n* (*pl* **-ies**) **1** who or what somebody or something is. **2** the individual characteristics that define a person. **3** the condition of being exactly alike; sameness.

**identity parade** *n chiefly Brit* a line-up of people assembled by the police to see whether a witness can identify a suspect.

**ideology** *n* (*pl* **-ies**) **1** a systematic body of ideas underlying a social, political, or cultural programme. **2** a manner of thinking characteristic of an individual, group, or culture. ➤ **ideological** *adj.*

**idiocy** *n* (*pl* **-ies**) **1** foolishness. **2** something very stupid or foolish.

**idiom** *n* **1** an established expression in a language, which has a meaning that cannot be deduced from the meanings of its individual elements, e.g. *in hot water* meaning in serious trouble. **2** the words and expressions characteristically used by a particular group of people. **3** a characteristic style of artistic expression.

**idiomatic** *adj* **1** relating to idioms. **2** using a language in the way its native speakers naturally do.

**idiosyncrasy** *n* (*pl* **-ies**) **1** a characteristic of thought or behaviour peculiar to an individual; an eccentricity. **2** a characteristic peculiarity. ➤ **idiosyncratic** *adj.*

**idiot** *n* a silly or foolish person.

**idiotic** *adj* extremely foolish. ➤ **idiotically** *adv.*

**idle**[1] *adj* **1** lazy. **2** not occupied or employed. **3** not in use or operation. **4** having no purpose, effect, or foundation in reality. ➤ **idleness** *n,* **idly** *adv.*

**idle**[2] *v* **1** to spend time doing nothing. **2** *esp* of an engine: to run without being connected to the part that it drives. ➤ **idler** *n.*

**idol** *n* **1** an image of a god used as an object of worship. **2** a person who is the object of passionate or excessive devotion.

**idolatry** *n* **1** the worship of idols. **2** excessive attachment or devotion to somebody or something.

**idolize** *or* **-ise** *v* to love or admire to excess.

**idyll** *or* **idyl** *n* **1** a time or situation of peace and happiness. **2** a simple work in poetry or prose describing peaceful rustic life.

**idyllic** *adj* wonderfully happy, peaceful, or beautiful. ➤ **idyllically** *adv.*

**i.e.** *abbr* that is to say.

**if** *conj* **1** in the event that. **2** supposing. **3** on condition that. **4** whether. **5** although.

**igloo** *n* (*pl* **igloos**) an Inuit dwelling, usu made of snow blocks and in the shape of a dome.

**igneous** *adj* of rocks: formed by the solidification of molten rock from the earth's core.

**ignite** *v* **1** to set fire to, or to catch fire. **2** to arouse (an emotion). **3** to cause or start (e.g. a riot or protest).

**ignition** *n* **1** the act of igniting. **2** the process of igniting a fuel mixture, e.g. in an internal-combustion engine, or a device that does this.

**ignoble** *adj* base; dishonourable.

**ignominious** *adj* causing disgrace or discredit; humiliating. ➤ **ignominiously** *adv.*

**ignominy** *n* (*pl* **-ies**) deep humiliation and disgrace.

**ignoramus** *n* (*pl* **ignoramuses**) an ignorant or stupid person.

**ignorant** *adj* **1** having a general lack of knowledge or education. **2** (*often* + of) uninformed about or unaware of. **3** *chiefly informal* lacking social training; impolite. ➤ **ignorance** *n,* **ignorantly** *adv.*

**ignore** *v* to refuse or fail to take notice of.

**iguana** *n* a large tropical American lizard with a serrated crest on its back.

**ikon** *n* see ICON.

**ilk** *n* sort or kind.

**I'll** *contraction* I will or I shall.

**ill**[1] *adj* **1** not in good health. **2** nauseated. **3** causing discomfort or inconvenience; disagreeable: *ill effects.* **4** malevolent; hostile. **5** unlucky or disadvantageous. **6** harsh. ✱ **ill at ease** uneasy or uncomfortable.

**ill**[2] *adv* (**worse, worst**) **1** hardly; scarcely: *can ill afford.* **2** in a faulty, imperfect, or unpleasant manner.

**ill**[3] *n* **1** misfortune or trouble. **2** evil.

**ill-advised** *adj* **1** unwise. **2** showing lack of proper thought or planning.

**ill-bred** *adj* showing bad upbringing; impolite. ➤ **ill-breeding** *n.*

**ill-disposed** *adj* (*often* + to/towards) unfriendly; unsympathetic.

**illegal** *adj* not authorized by law. ➤ **illegality** *n,* **illegally** *adv.*

**illegible** *adj* unable to be read or deciphered. ➤ **illegibility** *n.*

**illegitimate** *adj* **1** not allowed by law or rules. **2** of a child: born to parents who are not lawfully married to each other. ➤ **illegitimacy** *n.*

**ill-fated** *adj* destined for misfortune; unlucky.

**ill-favoured** (*NAmer* **ill-favored**) *adj* unattractive in physical appearance.

**ill-gotten** *adj* acquired by illicit or improper means.

**illiberal** *adj* **1** not broad-minded; bigoted. **2** not generous; mean.

**illicit** *adj* not permitted by law, rules, or custom. ➤ **illicitly** *adv.*

**illiterate** *adj* **1** unable to read or write. **2** showing a lack of education, *esp* through poor grammar and spelling. **3** lacking knowledge in a particular field. ➤ **illiteracy** *n.*

**illness** *n* a disease or period of sickness.

**illogical** *adj* **1** contrary to logic. **2** not well reasoned; senseless. ➤ **illogicality** *n,* **illogically** *adv.*

**ill-starred** *adj* ill-fated; unlucky.

**ill-treat** *v* to treat cruelly or improperly. ➤ **ill-treatment** *n.*

**illuminate** *v* **1** to cast light on; to fill with light. **2** to elucidate or clarify. **3** to decorate (a manuscript) with elaborate and colourful initial letters or marginal designs. ➤ **illuminating** *adj.*

**illumination** *n* **1** the act of illuminating. **2** (*also in pl*) decorative lighting, e.g. on a building or street.

**illumine** *v literary* to illuminate.

**illusion** *n* **1** a false impression or belief. **2** something that deceives or misleads, either visually or intellectually. * **be under the illusion that** to have the mistaken belief that.

**illusionist** *n* a conjuror or magician.

**illusory** *or* **illusive** *adj* deceptive; unreal.

**illustrate** *v* **1** to provide (e.g. a book) with pictures. **2** to clarify, explain, or demonstrate, *esp* by using examples, analogy, etc. **3** to be an example of. ➤ **illustrative** *adj,* **illustrator** *n.*

**illustration** *n* **1** a picture or diagram illustrating the text of a book, magazine, etc. **2** an example that explains or clarifies something. **3** the act of illustrating.

**illustrious** *adj* **1** admired and well-known, *esp* for something done in the past. **2** of an action, etc: impressive and publicly acclaimed.

**ill will** *n* unfriendly feeling.

**I'm** *contraction* I am.

**image**[1] *n* **1** a picture or statue of a person or thing. **2** the optical counterpart of an object produced by a lens, mirror, etc, or on a screen, or in a photograph. **3** a mental picture of something not actually present. **4** a conception of the nature or character of a person or organization created in the minds of the general public. **5** a person who strikingly resembles another specified person. **6** a figure of speech, *esp* a metaphor or simile.

**image**[2] *v* to create or form an image of.

**imagery** *n* (*pl* **-ies**) **1** figurative language. **2** visual symbols.

**imaginary** *adj* existing only in imagination; lacking factual reality.

**imagination** *n* **1** the part of the mind that can form mental images of things not present to the senses or never before perceived in reality. **2** creative ability. **3** resourcefulness; inventiveness.

**imaginative** *adj* **1** having a lively imagination. **2** creative. **3** resourceful; inventive. ➤ **imaginatively** *adv.*

**imagine** *v* **1** to form a mental image of (something not present). **2** to suppose or think. **3** to believe (something) without sufficient basis.

**imam** *n* the person who leads the prayers in a mosque.

**imbalance** *n* a lack of proportion or balance.

**imbecile** *n informal* a fool or idiot. ➤ **imbecilic** *adj,* **imbecilically** *adv,* **imbecility** *n.*

**imbed** *v* see EMBED.

**imbibe** *v* **1** *chiefly formal or humorous.* **2** to drink (*esp* alcohol). **3** to receive (e.g. ideas) into the mind.

**imbroglio** *n* (*pl* **-os**) an intricate or complicated situation or misunderstanding.

**imbue** *v* (**imbues, imbued**) of a feeling, principle, etc: to be a pervasive presence in.

**imitate** *v* **1** to follow as a pattern, model, or example. **2** to mimic, *esp* for humorous effect. ➤ **imitator** *n.*

**imitation** *n* **1** the act of imitating. **2** a copy or counterfeit. **3** (*used before a noun*) not genuine; fake.

**imitative** *adj* imitating or copying something.

**immaculate** *adj* **1** spotlessly clean and very tidy. **2** free from flaw or error. ➤ **immaculately** *adv.*

**immanent** *adj* **1** existing within something; indwelling; inherent. **2** of God: always present in nature or the universe. ➤ **immanence** *n.*

**immaterial** *adj* **1** unimportant or not relevant. **2** not consisting of matter; incorporeal; spiritual.

**immature** *adj* **1** not yet full-grown or fully developed. **2** lacking the wisdom, good sense, etc, associated with adulthood. ➤ **immaturity** *n.*

**immeasurable** *adj* too vast to be measured. ➤ **immeasurably** *adv.*

**immediate** *adj* **1** occurring at once or likely to occur very shortly. **2** current; most in need of attention or action. **3** closest in space, time, or relationship. **4** acting without any intervening agency or factor; direct. ➤ **immediacy** *n.*

**immediately**[1] *adv* **1** at once; without delay. **2** in direct relation or proximity; directly.

**immediately**[2] *conj chiefly Brit* as soon as.

**immemorial** *adj* extending beyond the reach of memory, record, or tradition.

**immense** *adj* very great in size, degree, or extent. ➤ **immensely** *adv,* **immenseness** *n,* **immensity** *n.*
**immerse** *v* **1** to plunge completely into a fluid. **2** to engross (oneself) in something.
**immersion** *n* **1** the act of immersing. **2** intensive involvement in an activity or situation.
**immersion heater** *n* an electric water-heater fixed inside a domestic hot-water storage tank.
**immigrant** *n* a person who comes to a country to take up permanent residence.
**immigrate** *v* to come into a country of which one is not a native to take up permanent residence. ➤ **immigration** *n.*
**imminent** *adj* about to take place. ➤ **imminence** *n,* **imminently** *adv.*
**immiscible** *adj* of liquids: incapable of being mixed together.
**immobile** *adj* **1** incapable of being moved. **2** motionless. ➤ **immobility** *n.*
**immobilize** *or* **-ise** *v* **1** to prevent from moving freely or normally. **2** to prevent (somebody or a body part) from moving to encourage healing. ➤ **immobilization** *n.*
**immoderate** *adj* lacking moderation; excessive.
**immodest** *adj* **1** not conforming to accepted standards of sexual propriety. **2** bold; shameless.
**immolate** *v* to kill or offer as a sacrificial victim, *esp* by burning. ➤ **immolation** *n.*
**immoral** *adj* not conforming to accepted moral standards, e.g. in sexual matters or business: compare AMORAL. ➤ **immorality** *n.*
**immortal**[1] *adj* **1** living for ever. **2** enduring for ever; imperishable. ➤ **immortality** *n.*
**immortal**[2] *n* **1** a person or being that lives for ever, *esp* a classical god. **2** a person of lasting fame.
**immortalize** *or* **-ise** *v* to give everlasting existence or fame to.
**immovable** *or* **immoveable** *adj* **1** not able to be moved. **2** not able to be changed or persuaded. ➤ **immovably** *adv.*
**immune** *adj* **1** (*often* + to) not susceptible to something, *esp* having high resistance to a disease. **2** (*often* + to/from) not liable to be affected by something bad. **3** (*often* + from) free or exempt.
**immunity** *n* (*pl* **-ies**) **1** (*often* + from/to) the state of being immune. **2** (*often* + against/to) the ability to resist the effects of a disease-causing micro-organism.
**immunize** *or* **-ise** *v* to make immune, *esp* by inoculation. ➤ **immunization** *n.*
**immunology** *n* the branch of biology and medicine that deals with immunity to disease. ➤ **immunological** *adj,* **immunologist** *n.*
**immure** *v* to enclose within walls; to shut away or imprison.
**immutable** *adj* unchangeable or unchanging.
**imp** *n* **1** a small demon. **2** a mischievous child.
**impact**[1] /'impakt/ *n* **1** an *esp* violent contact or collision between one body and another. **2** a powerful effect or impression.
**impact**[2] /im'pakt/ *v* **1** to fix or press firmly. **2** to make contact, *esp* forcefully. **3** (*often* + on) to affect, *esp* strongly.
**impacted** *adj* of a tooth: unable to grow properly because of a lack of space in the jaw or obstruction by other teeth.
**impair** *v* to damage, spoil, or weaken. ➤ **impairment** *n.*
**impale** *v* to pierce with something pointed.
**impalpable** *adj* **1** incapable of being sensed by the touch. **2** not easily discerned by the mind.
**impart** *v* **1** to make known or disclose (information, etc). **2** to give or bestow.
**impartial** *adj* not showing any favouritism; unbiased. ➤ **impartiality** *n,* **impartially** *adv.*
**impassable** *adj* of a road, etc: blocked or unable to be travelled along.
**impasse** *n* a deadlock or stalemate.
**impassioned** *adj* showing great intensity of feeling.
**impassive** *adj* **1** incapable of emotion. **2** showing no emotion. ➤ **impassively** *adv.*
**impasto** *n* (*pl* **-os**) in art, the process of applying paint so thickly that it stands out from the canvas, etc.
**impatient** *adj* **1** lacking patience; quickly roused to anger or exasperation. **2** (+ of) intolerant. **3** (*often* + to/for) eagerly desirous; anxious. ➤ **impatience** *n,* **impatiently** *adv.*
**impeach** *v* **1** *Brit* to charge with a serious crime against the state. **2** *NAmer* to charge (a serving public official) with misconduct. ➤ **impeachment** *n.*
**impeccable** *adj* free from fault or blemish; flawless. ➤ **impeccably** *adv.*
**impecunious** *adj* having very little or no money.
**impedance** *n* the opposition in an electrical circuit to the flow of an alternating current.
**impede** *v* to interfere with or retard the progress of.
**impediment** *n* **1** (*often* + to) something that impedes. **2** a physiological speech defect, e.g. a stammer or lisp.
**impel** *v* (**impelled, impelling**) to urge forward or force into action.
**impending** *adj* about to happen.
**impenetrable** *adj* **1** incapable of being penetrated or pierced. **2** incapable of being understood. ➤ **impenetrability** *n.*
**impenitent** *adj* feeling or showing no regret or shame. ➤ **impenitence** *n.*
**imperative**[1] *adj* **1** very urgent or important. **2** commanding; showing authority. **3** denoting the grammatical mood that expresses command, e.g. the verb *stop* in *Stop that at once!*

**imperative**[2] *n* **1** a necessary or urgent act or duty. **2** the imperative mood or a verb form expressing this mood.

**imperceptible** *adj* too small, slight, or gradual to be perceived. ➤ **imperceptibly** *adv.*

**imperfect** *adj* **1** flawed, defective, or incomplete. **2** denoting a verb tense expressing a continuing state or an incomplete action in the past. ➤ **imperfection** *n,* **imperfectly** *adv.*

**imperial** *adj* **1** relating to an empire, emperor, or empress. **2** belonging to an official nonmetric British series of weights and measures such as the pound and the pint.

**imperialism** *n* the policy of extending the power and dominion of a nation over other nations, *esp* by territorial acquisition. ➤ **imperialist** *n and adj,* **imperialistic** *adj.*

**imperil** *v* (**imperilled, imperilling,** *NAmer* **imperiled, imperiling**) to put in danger or at risk of harm.

**imperious** *adj* marked by arrogant assurance; domineering. ➤ **imperiously** *adv.*

**impermanent** *adj* not permanent or lasting. ➤ **impermanence** *n.*

**impermeable** *adj* not permitting something, *esp* a fluid, to pass through.

**impersonal** *adj* **1** not influenced by or involving personal feelings or opinions; objective or unbiased. **2** cold, formal, or detached. **3** denoting a verb used with *it* because it has no identifiable subject, e.g. *rained* in *it rained.* **4** of a pronoun: not referring to a particular person, e.g. *it* in *it rained.* ➤ **impersonality** *n,* **impersonally** *adv.*

**impersonate** *v* to pretend to be (somebody), either for entertainment or as an act of deception. ➤ **impersonation** *n,* **impersonator** *n.*

**impertinent** *adj* rude; insolent. ➤ **impertinence** *n.*

**imperturbable** *adj* marked by great calm and composure.

**impervious** *adj* **1** (+ to) not capable of being affected or disturbed by something. **2** (*often* + to) not allowing a fluid to pass through.

**impetuous** *adj* acting or done hastily and without thinking things through. ➤ **impetuously** *adv.*

**impetus** *n* **1** a driving force. **2** an incentive or stimulus. **3** in physics, the energy possessed by a moving body.

**impinge** *v* **1** to encroach on something. **2** (+ on/upon) to make an impression.

**impious** *adj* lacking in reverence or proper respect, e.g. for God.

**implacable** *adj* **1** not capable of being appeased or pacified. **2** never stopping, weakening, or changing. ➤ **implacably** *adv.*

**implant**[1] *v* **1** to fix securely or deeply. **2** to set (e.g. an idea or principle) permanently in somebody's consciousness. **3** to insert (e.g. artificial tissue, a hormone, etc) in a living organism. ➤ **implantation** *n.*

**implant**[2] *n* something implanted *esp* in tissue.

**implausible** *adj* unlikely to be true. ➤ **implausibility** *n,* **implausibly** *adv.*

**implement**[1] *n* a utensil or tool, *esp* one with a specified purpose.

**implement**[2] *v* to put (plans, orders, etc) into effect. ➤ **implementation** *n.*

**implicate** *v* **1** (*often* + in) to show that (a person) is involved in a crime, wrongdoing, etc. **2** (**be implicated in**) to play a part in making something the way it is.

**implication** *n* **1** (*usu* + in) involvement *esp* in something incriminating. **2** a possible result or effect. **3** something implied. ➤ **implicative** *adj.*

**implicit** *adj* **1** implied rather than directly stated. **2** (+ in) present but underlying rather than explicit. **3** unquestioning; absolute. ➤ **implicitly** *adv.*

**implode** *v* to collapse inwards suddenly. ➤ **implosion** *n.*

**implore** *v* to beg (somebody) to do something. ➤ **imploring** *adj.*

**imply** *v* (**-ies, -ied**) **1** to express indirectly; to hint at. **2** to involve as a necessary or potential consequence.

**impolite** *adj* not having or showing good manners.

**impolitic** *adj* unwise or ill-advised.

**imponderable**[1] *adj* incapable of being precisely evaluated or assessed.

**imponderable**[2] *n* something whose effect is hard or impossible to calculate.

**import**[1] *v* **1** to bring in (*esp* goods) from a foreign or external source. **2** to transfer (a file, data, etc) from one computer or database into another. ➤ **importation** *n,* **importer** *n.*

**import**[2] *n* **1** something imported, *esp* goods from abroad. **2** the act of importing. **3** *formal* meaning or significance. **4** *formal* importance.

**important** *adj* **1** of considerable significance or consequence. **2** having great influence or responsibility, or high rank. ➤ **importance** *n,* **importantly** *adv.*

**importunate** *adj* **1** very persistent in making requests or demands. **2** made persistently.

**importune** *v* to make persistent demands of.

**impose** *v* **1** (*often* + on/upon) to make (a tax, fine, rule, etc) compulsory. **2** to force (oneself) into the company or on the attention of another. **3** (*often* + on/upon) to cause excessive trouble or inconvenience.

**imposing** *adj* large and impressive.

**imposition** *n* **1** the act of imposing. **2** a cause of excessive trouble or inconvenience.

**impossible** *adj* **1** incapable of existing or occurring. **2** extremely undesirable or difficult to deal with. ➤ **impossibility** *n,* **impossibly** *adv.*

**impostor** *or* **imposter** *n* a person who assumes a false identity for fraudulent purposes.

**imposture** *n* a fraud or deception.

**impotent** *adj* **1** lacking in efficacy or strength; powerless. **2** of a man: unable to have sexual intercourse through an inability to maintain an erection. ➤ **impotence** *n.*

**impound** *v* **1** to shut up (an animal) in a pound. **2** to take legal possession of (e.g. evidence from a crime scene or an illegally parked vehicle).

**impoverish** *v* **1** to make poor. **2** to deprive of strength, richness, or fertility. ➤ **impoverishment** *n.*

**impracticable** *adj* incapable of being carried out.

**impractical** *adj* **1** of a person: not good at doing practical tasks or dealing with everyday matters. **2** of an idea or plan: unrealistic. ➤ **impracticality** *n.*

**imprecation** *n* a curse.

**imprecise** *adj* vague or inaccurate. ➤ **imprecision** *n.*

**impregnable** *adj* **1** too strongly fortified to be taken by assault. **2** strong or unassailable.

**impregnate** *v* **1** to make (a female person or animal) pregnant. **2** (+ with) to soak or saturate with something. **3** of a quality, emotion, etc: to be a dominant presence in (speech or writing). ➤ **impregnation** *n.*

**impresario** *n* (*pl* **-os**) a person who organizes and finances a public entertainment, e.g. a concert.

**impress** *v* **1** (*often* + by/with) to produce a deep and usu favourable impression on. **2** (*usu* + on) to fix (e.g. an idea or thought) firmly in the mind or memory. **3** to apply (something) with pressure so as to imprint it on something.

**impression** *n* **1** an influence or effect on the mind or senses. **2** a thought or opinion. **3** a notion or recollection, *esp* one that is vague or subjective. **4** an imitation of a person, animal, etc; *esp* as a form of entertainment. **5** a mark produced by impressing something onto a surface. **6** all the copies of a book printed for issue at a single time.

**impressionable** *adj* easily influenced.

**impressionism** *n* (*often* **Impressionism**) a late 19th-cent. French art movement that aimed to reproduce images as they were actually seen by the artist at a particular moment.

**impressionist** *n* **1** (*often* **Impressionist**) a painter working in the style of impressionism. **2** an entertainer who does impressions.

**impressionistic** *adj* **1** based on subjective impression rather than knowledge or research. **2** (*usu* **Impressionistic**) relating to Impressionism.

**impressive** *adj* large, good, or skilful enough to arouse admiration. ➤ **impressively** *adv.*

**imprimatur** *n* sanction or approval.

**imprint[1]** *n* **1** a mark made by pressure. **2** a publisher's name or brand name under which a range of books is published.

**imprint[2]** *v* to make a mark on something by pressure.

**imprison** *v* to put in prison or confine as if in a prison. ➤ **imprisonment** *n.*

**improbable** *adj* unlikely to be true or to occur. ➤ **improbability** *n,* **improbably** *adv.*

**impromptu** *adj and adv* made or done on the spur of the moment.

**improper** *adj* **1** not in accordance with propriety; indecent. **2** inappropriate. **3** not in accordance with normal or correct procedure. ➤ **improperly** *adv.*

**impropriety** *n* (*pl* **-ies**) an absence of accepted standards of decency.

**improve** *v* **1** to make or become better. **2** (*usu* + on/upon) to produce something better than a previous version, result, etc. ➤ **improvement** *n.*

**improvident** *adj* not providing for the future; wasteful.

**improvise** *v* **1** to make or provide (something) using what is available. **2** to compose or perform (music, poetry, drama, etc) without a set script or musical score. ➤ **improvisation** *n.*

**imprudent** *adj* lacking discretion or caution.

**impudent** *adj* showing contemptuous disrespect. ➤ **impudence** *n,* **impudently** *adv.*

**impugn** *v* to dispute the validity or integrity of.

**impulse** *n* **1** a sudden spontaneous desire to do something. **2** a force that produces motion suddenly.

**impulsive** *adj* acting or done on the basis of a sudden whim or desire. ➤ **impulsively** *adv.*

**impunity** *n* freedom from punishment, harm, or retribution.

**impure** *adj* **1** not pure, *esp* as a result of contamination. **2** morally wrong.

**impurity** *n* (*pl* **-ies**) **1** the state of being impure. **2** something that makes something else impure.

**impute** *v* to attribute (*esp* something bad) to somebody, often unjustly. ➤ **imputation** *n.*

**In** *abbr* the chemical symbol for indium.

**in[1]** *prep* **1** used to indicate location within or inside an area or object. **2** used to indicate location in time. **3** = INTO. **4** used to indicate a means, instrument, or medium of expression: *in pencil.* **5** used to indicate a circumstance or condition: *in public; in pain.* **6** used to indicate the larger member of a ratio: *40p in the £.* * **in that** for the reason that; because.

**in[2]** *adv* **1** used to indicate movement towards the inside or centre. **2** used to indicate movement to or towards home, the shore, a destination, etc. **3** used to indicate presence at one's

home or business. * **be in for** to be certain to experience (usu something undesirable). **in on** having a share in or knowledge of something.
**in**[3] *adj* extremely fashionable.
**in.** *abbr* inch or inches.
**in-** *or* **il-** *or* **im-** *or* **ir-** *prefix* **1** not: *inaccurate.* **2** in, into, or towards: *influx.*
**inability** *n* lack of sufficient power, skill, intelligence, etc to do something.
**in absentia** *adv* in the absence of the specified person.
**inaccessible** *adj* **1** difficult or impossible to reach. **2** difficult or impossible to understand.
**inaccurate** *adj* faulty or imprecise. ➤ **inaccuracy** *n,* **inaccurately** *adv.*
**inaction** *n* lack of action or activity.
**inactive** *adj* **1** not moving or doing anything. **2** not functioning. ➤ **inactivity** *n.*
**inadequate** *adj* **1** not of the required quantity or quality. **2** unable to cope with people or situations. ➤ **inadequacy** *n,* **inadequately** *adv.*
**inadmissible** *adj esp* of evidence in a court: invalid. ➤ **inadmissibility** *n.*
**inadvertent** *adj* unintentional. ➤ **inadvertently** *adv.*
**inadvisable** *adj* likely to have unwanted consequences; unwise.
**inalienable** *adj* incapable of being removed or surrendered.
**inane** *adj* senseless or unintelligent. ➤ **inanely** *adv,* **inaneness** *n,* **inanity** *n.*
**inanimate** *adj* **1** not alive. **2** unconscious and apparently lifeless.
**inapplicable** *adj* not appropriate or relevant.
**inappropriate** *adj* not appropriate or suitable. ➤ **inappropriately** *adv.*
**inarticulate** *adj* **1** unable to express oneself coherently or effectively. **2** not coherently or effectively expressed. **3** not understandable as spoken words.
**inasmuch as** *conj* **1** = INSOFAR AS. **2** *formal* in view of the fact that.
**inattention** *n* failure to pay attention; disregard. ➤ **inattentive** *adj.*
**inaudible** *adj* unable to be heard. ➤ **inaudibly** *adv.*
**inaugural** *adj* **1** marking a beginning. **2** first in a series.
**inaugurate** *v* **1** to open (e.g. a new building) ceremonially. **2** to begin or introduce (a new system, project, etc). ➤ **inauguration** *n.*
**inauspicious** *adj* not promising future success.
**inauthentic** *adj* not genuine.
**inborn** *adj* **1** forming part of somebody's natural make-up. **2** existing from birth; congenital.
**inbred** *adj* **1** deeply ingrained in somebody's nature. **2** produced by inbreeding.
**inbreeding** *n* breeding involving closely related individuals.
**inbuilt** *adj* built-in; inherent or integral.
**Inc.** *abbr chiefly NAmer* incorporated.
**incalculable** *adj* **1** too great or numerous to be calculated. **2** unable to be predicted or estimated.
**incandescent** *adj* **1** glowing white with intense heat. **2** *informal* extremely angry.
**incantation** *n* a formula used in magic rituals. ➤ **incantatory** *adj.*
**incapable** *adj* **1** (*usu* + of) lacking the capacity, ability, etc to do something. **2** unfit, *esp* because of illness or the effects of alcohol or drugs. ➤ **incapability** *n.*
**incapacitate** *v* to prevent from functioning or operating properly. ➤ **incapacitation** *n.*
**incapacity** *n* (*pl* **-ies**) lack of ability or power.
**incarcerate** *v* to imprison. ➤ **incarceration** *n.*
**incarnate** *adj* invested with a human nature and form.
**incarnation** *n* **1** the human embodiment of a deity, spirit, or abstract quality. **2** (**Incarnation**) in Christian belief, the manifestation of Christ in human form.
**incautious** *adj* lacking care or caution; rash.
**incendiary**[1] *adj* **1** tending to inflame or stir up trouble. **2** *esp* of a bomb: designed to start fires.
**incendiary**[2] *n* (*pl* **-ies**) an incendiary bomb.
**incense**[1] *n* a substance that produces a fragrant smell when burned.
**incense**[2] *v* to make extremely angry or indignant.
**incentive** *n* something that motivates somebody.
**inception** *n* the beginning of a process or undertaking.
**incessant** *adj* continuing without interruption. ➤ **incessantly** *adv.*
**incest** *n* sexual intercourse between people so closely related that they are forbidden by law to marry.
**incestuous** *adj* **1** involving incest. **2** unhealthily close or shut off from outside influences. ➤ **incestuously** *adv.*
**inch**[1] *n* **1** a unit of length equal to one twelfth of a foot (about 2.54cm). **2** a small amount or distance.
**inch**[2] *v* to move slowly.
**incidence** *n* **1** the rate of occurrence of something. **2** the arrival of e.g. a projectile or a ray of light at a surface.
**incident** *n* **1** something that happens. **2** an occurrence that involves violence or is a cause of conflict.
**incidental** *adj* **1** occurring merely by chance. **2** (*often* + to) occurring as a minor consequence or accompaniment.
**incidentally** *adv* **1** by the way. **2** by chance.
**incidental music** *n* background music in a play, film, etc.
**incinerate** *v* to burn to ashes. ➤ **incineration** *n.*

**incinerator** *n* a furnace or container for incinerating waste.
**incipient** *adj* just beginning to emerge or develop.
**incise** *v* to carve letters, designs, etc into a surface.
**incision** *n* **1** a cut, *esp* one made in a surgical operation. **2** the act of cutting into something.
**incisive** *adj* **1** showing sharp intelligence. **2** impressively direct and decisive.
**incisor** *n* a cutting tooth at the front of the mouth.
**incite** *v* to encourage (violence, unlawful behaviour, etc), or encourage (somebody) to commit this. ➤ **incitement** *n.*
**incivility** *n* (*pl* **-ies**) discourtesy.
**inclement** *adj* of the weather: unpleasant, *esp* cold and wet. ➤ **inclemency** *n.*
**inclination** *n* **1** a particular, *esp* natural tendency or urge. **2** a liking. **3** a deviation from the vertical or horizontal.
**incline**[1] *v* **1** to influence (somebody) to a specified action or way of thinking. **2** to slope or slant. **3** to nod or bend (the head). ✱ **inclined to 1** having a tendency to (do or be something). **2** in favour of (doing something).
**incline**[2] *n* a slope.
**include** *v* **1** to take in, contain, or consider as a part of a larger whole. **2** to add or put in.
**including** *prep* with the inclusion of.
**inclusion** *n* **1** the act of including. **2** something or somebody that is included.
**inclusive** *adj* **1** including everything or the items specified. **2** including the stated limits. **3** broad in scope.
**incognito** *adv and adj* in disguise or under a false name.
**incoherent** *adj* **1** too confused and disordered to be clearly intelligible. **2** lacking logical connection. ➤ **incoherence** *n,* **incoherently** *adv.*
**incombustible** *adj* incapable of being burned.
**income** *n* money received from work, property, or investment.
**incomer** *n* a person who moves into an area.
**income tax** *n* a tax levied on personal income.
**incoming** *adj* **1** arriving or coming in. **2** about to take on a role or office.
**incommensurable** *adj* incapable of being compared.
**incommensurate** *adj* (*usu* + with) disproportionate to.
**incommode** *v formal* to inconvenience.
**incommunicado** *adv and adj* without means of communication with other people, e.g. while in solitary confinement.
**incomparable** *adj* incapable of being compared with anything else, *esp* because too good. ➤ **incomparably** *adv.*
**incompatible** *adj* **1** of people: unable to live or work together, because of opposing views, temperaments, etc. **2** unable to exist together. **3** unsuitable for use together. ➤ **incompatibility** *n.*
**incompetent** *adj* **1** lacking the skill, experience, etc needed for effective action. **2** not legally qualified. ➤ **incompetence** *n,* **incompetently** *adv.*
**incomplete** *adj* not complete. ➤ **incompletely** *adv.*
**incomprehensible** *adj* impossible to understand. ➤ **incomprehensibility** *n.*
**inconceivable** *adj* unimaginable or unbelievable. ➤ **inconceivably** *adv.*
**inconclusive** *adj* leading to no conclusion or definite result. ➤ **inconclusively** *adv.*
**incongruous** *adj* out of place. ➤ **incongruity** *n,* **incongruously** *adv.*
**inconsequential** *adj* **1** irrelevant. **2** unimportant. ➤ **inconsequentiality** *n.*
**inconsiderable** *adj* small in size, amount, etc.
**inconsiderate** *adj* showing a lack of care for others.
**inconsistent** *adj* **1** containing conflicting or contradictory elements. **2** (*often* + with) not in agreement. ➤ **inconsistency** *n.*
**inconsolable** *adj* incapable of being consoled; brokenhearted.
**inconspicuous** *adj* not readily noticeable. ➤ **inconspicuously** *adv.*
**inconstant** *adj* **1** likely to change without apparent reason. **2** *literary* unfaithful; unreliable.
**incontestable** *adj* indisputable. ➤ **incontestably** *adv.*
**incontinent** *adj* **1** unable to control urination or defecation. **2** lacking self-restraint, *esp* sexually. ➤ **incontinence** *n.*
**incontrovertible** *adj* not able to be denied or disputed. ➤ **incontrovertibly** *adv.*
**inconvenience**[1] *n* **1** the fact of being rather difficult or troublesome. **2** a cause of trouble or unnecessary effort to somebody. ➤ **inconvenient** *adj,* **inconveniently** *adv.*
**inconvenience**[2] *v* to cause inconvenience.
**incorporate** *v* to make (something) a usu indistinguishable part of a larger whole. ➤ **incorporation** *n.*
**incorporated** *adj* formed into a legal corporation.
**incorporeal** *adj* having no material body or form.
**incorrect** *adj* **1** inaccurate; factually wrong. **2** not in accordance with an established norm; improper. ➤ **incorrectly** *adv.*
**incorrigible** *adj* incapable of being corrected or improved, *esp* incurably bad.
**incorruptible** *adj* **1** incapable of being bribed or morally corrupted. **2** not subject to decay.
**increase**[1] *v* to make or become progressively greater in size, amount, number, or intensity. ➤ **increasing** *adj.*

**increase**[2] *n* an amount by which something increases.
**increasingly** *adv* to an ever greater extent.
**incredible** *adj* **1** too extraordinary and improbable to be believed. **2** *informal* excellent; outstanding. ➤ **incredibly** *adv.*
**incredulity** *n* unwillingness or inability to believe something.
**incredulous** *adj* unwilling or unable to believe something.
**increment** *n* an increase, *esp* a regular consecutive increase. ➤ **incremental** *adj.*
**incriminate** *v* to suggest or demonstrate that (somebody) is guilty of a crime. ➤ **incriminating** *adj.*
**incubate** *v* **1** of a bird: to sit on (eggs) to hatch them by the warmth of the body. **2** to keep (e.g. bacteria, cells) under conditions favourable for their development. **3** to develop (a disease) without any noticeable symptoms. ➤ **incubation** *n.*
**incubator** *n* **1** an apparatus in which a premature or sick baby is kept under controlled conditions. **2** an apparatus in which eggs are hatched artificially.
**inculcate** *v* to teach (something) by frequent repetition.
**incumbency** *n* the period of office of an incumbent.
**incumbent**[1] *n* the current holder of an office.
**incumbent**[2] *adj* **1** (+ on/upon) imposed as a duty on somebody. **2** currently holding a specified office.
**incur** *v* (**incurred, incurring**) to become liable or subject to (something unpleasant).
**incurable** *adj* not able to be cured. ➤ **incurably** *adv.*
**incurious** *adj* lacking curiosity; uninterested.
**incursion** *n* a sudden or brief invasion.
**indebted** *adj* **1** owing gratitude to somebody. **2** owing money. ➤ **indebtedness** *n.*
**indecent** *adj* **1** improper or unseemly. **2** morally offensive. ➤ **indecency** *n,* **indecently** *adv.*
**indecipherable** *adj* **1** illegible. **2** of a code: unable to be solved or understood.
**indecisive** *adj* **1** incapable of making quick or definite decisions. **2** giving an uncertain result. ➤ **indecision** *n,* **indecisively** *adv,* **indecisiveness** *n.*
**indeed** *adv* **1** used as an intensifier or for emphasis: *It has been very cold indeed.* **2** used to introduce additional information: actually.
**indefatigable** *adj* tireless or unflagging.
**indefensible** *adj* incapable of being justified or excused.
**indefinable** *adj* incapable of being precisely described or analysed.
**indefinite** *adj* **1** not precise; vague or unsettled. **2** lasting for an unspecified length of time. ➤ **indefinitely** *adv.*
**indefinite article** *n* the word *a* or *an.*
**indelible** *adj* **1** of a mark, stain, ink, etc: incapable of being removed or erased. **2** of a memory: not able to be forgotten. ➤ **indelibly** *adv.*
**indelicate** *adj* **1** almost indecent or offensive. **2** lacking in good manners or sensitivity.
**indemnify** *v* (**-ies, -ied**) **1** to exempt in advance from legal liability. **2** to compensate for harm or loss.
**indemnity** *n* (*pl* **-ies**) **1** exemption from incurred penalties or liabilities. **2** compensation for harm, loss, or damage.
**indent**[1] *v* **1** to set (a line of text, a paragraph, etc) in from the margin. **2** to notch the edge of (something).
**indent**[2] *n chiefly Brit* an official requisition or order.
**indentation** *n* **1** an angular cut in an edge. **2** a dent or depression. **3** the act of indenting.
**indenture** *n* **1** an official agreement or contract. **2** (*also in pl*) a contract binding an apprentice to work for an employer.
**independent**[1] *adj* **1** not connected with or relying on something else. **2** not controlled by others. **3** having or providing enough money to live on, *esp* without working. **4** of a country: self-governing. ➤ **independence** *n,* **independently** *adv.*
**independent**[2] *n* somebody who is independent.
**in-depth** *adj* comprehensively detailed and thorough.
**indescribable** *adj* unable to be put into words. ➤ **indescribably** *adv.*
**indestructible** *adj* impossible to destroy.
**indeterminate** *adj* not definitely or precisely fixed; vague.
**index**[1] *n* (*pl* **indexes** *or* **indices**) **1** an alphabetical list of names, topics, etc mentioned in a printed work. **2** a systematic guide or list to aid reference, e.g. a catalogue of publications. **3** an indicator of a fact or circumstance. **4** a number or scale used as an indicator or measure, e.g. of the cost of living.
**index**[2] *v* **1** to provide (e.g. a book) with an index. **2** to list (an item) in an index.
**index finger** *n* = FOREFINGER.
**index-linked** *adj* increasing or decreasing in proportion to a rise or fall in an index, *esp* the cost-of-living index.
**Indian** *n* **1** a native or inhabitant of India. **2** *dated, offensive* a member of an indigenous people of North, Central, or South America. ➤ **Indian** *adj.*
**Indian ink** *n Brit* an ink made from a solid black pigment and used in drawing and lettering.
**Indian summer** *n* a period of warm weather in late autumn or early winter.
**indicate** *v* **1** to point to or point out. **2** to be a sign or symptom of. **3** (**be indicated**) to be necessary or advisable. **4** to state briefly; to suggest. ➤ **indication** *n.*

**indicative** *adj* **1** (*usu* + of) serving to indicate. **2** in grammar, representing the act or state in question as an objective fact.

**indicator** *n* **1** a device that shows a measurement, level, etc, or gives information. **2** a flashing light on a vehicle, used to show that the driver intends to change direction.

**indict** *v* to charge with an offence, *esp* a serious crime. ➤ **indictable** *adj.*

**indictment** *n* **1** a formal written accusation by a prosecuting authority. **2** grounds for severe censure or condemnation of something.

**indifferent** *adj* **1** mediocre or poor. **2** (*often* + to) not interested or concerned. ➤ **indifference** *n,* **indifferently** *adv.*

**indigenous** *adj* growing or living naturally in a particular place.

**indigent** *adj* very needy or poor.

**indigestible** *adj* **1** difficult or impossible to digest. **2** difficult to understand, read, etc.

**indigestion** *n* pain or discomfort from difficulty in digesting something.

**indignant** *adj* filled with or marked by indignation. ➤ **indignantly** *adv.*

**indignation** *n* anger aroused by something unjust or mean.

**indignity** *n* (*pl* **-ies**) something that causes loss of dignity or self-respect.

**indigo** *n* a dark greyish blue colour or dye.

**indirect** *adj* **1** deviating from a direct line or course. **2** not going straight to the point. **3** not being a direct cause or consequence of something. ➤ **indirectly** *adv.*

**indirect question** *n* in grammar, a question in indirect speech, e.g. *He asked if I'd ever been to New York before.*

**indirect speech** *n* in grammar, the reporting of something previously said, e.g. *I told him I'd never been to New York.*

**indiscipline** *n* lack of discipline.

**indiscreet** *adj* not discreet, *esp* in revealing secret or private things. ➤ **indiscreetly** *adv.*

**indiscretion** *n* **1** lack of discretion. **2** an indiscreet act or remark.

**indiscriminate** *adj* **1** showing a lack of care in choosing or making distinctions. **2** random. ➤ **indiscriminately** *adv.*

**indispensable** *adj* not able to be done without.

**indisposed** *adj* **1** slightly ill. **2** (*usu* + to) unwilling to do something.

**indisposition** *n* a slight illness.

**indisputable** *adj* not able to be denied or called into question. ➤ **indisputably** *adv.*

**indissoluble** *adj* incapable of being dissolved or annulled.

**indistinct** *adj* not sharply outlined; not clearly visible, audible, etc. ➤ **indistinctly** *adv.*

**indistinguishable** *adj* (*usu* + from) incapable of being clearly identified as different; identical.

**individual**[1] *adj* **1** relating to or intended for a single person or thing. **2** existing as a distinct entity; separate. **3** having unusual or distinctive characteristics. ➤ **individually** *adv.*

**individual**[2] *n* **1** a particular person or thing, *esp* as distinguished from a group. **2** a person who has unusual or distinctive characteristics.

**individualism** *n* **1** independence and self-reliance. **2** a social theory stressing the political and economic independence of the individual. ➤ **individualist** *n and adj,* **individualistic** *adj.*

**individuality** *n* the quality of being distinctive or unique.

**individualize** *or* **-ise** *v* to make different or distinctive.

**indivisible** *adj* not able to be separated or divided.

**indoctrinate** *v* to teach (a person or group) to accept a view, ideology, etc uncritically. ➤ **indoctrination** *n.*

**Indo-European** *n* a family of languages containing those spoken in most of Europe and in Asia as far as North India. ➤ **Indo-European** *adj.*

**indolent** *adj* lazy. ➤ **indolence** *n.*

**indomitable** *adj* incapable of being subdued.

**indoor** *adj* done, situated, or belonging inside a building.

**indoors** *adv* inside or into a building.

**indubitable** *adj* too evident to be doubted or called into question. ➤ **indubitably** *adv.*

**induce** *v* **1** to persuade or influence to do something. **2** to cause or bring about. **3** to cause (labour) to begin, *esp* by the use of drugs.

**inducement** *n* **1** something that motivates or encourages somebody to do something. **2** *euphem* a bribe.

**induct** *v* to install formally into office or as a member of an organization.

**inductance** *n* a property of an electric circuit by which an electromotive force is induced in it by a variation of current.

**induction** *n* **1** the act of inducting, *esp* into office. **2** a method of reasoning that proceeds from particular premises to reach a general conclusion. **3** the act of inducing. **4** the production of an electric charge or magnetism in an object by its being close to, but not in contact with, a similarly energized body.

**indulge** *v* **1** to give free rein to (a taste, desire, etc). **2** (*often* + in) to allow oneself to do or have something pleasurable. **3** to treat with excessive leniency or generosity; to spoil.

**indulgence** *n* **1** the act of indulging. **2** something indulged in; a luxury. **3** leniency or tolerance.

**indulgent** *adj* characterized by indulgence. ➤ **indulgently** *adv.*

**industrial** *adj* relating to or used in industry. ➤ **industrially** *adv.*

**industrial action** *n* a strike, go-slow, work-to-rule, etc by a body of workers.
**industrial estate** *n chiefly Brit* an area designed for industries and businesses.
**industrialist** *n* somebody who is engaged in the management of an industry.
**industrialize** *or* **-ise** *v* to develop industries extensively in (a region). ➤ **industrialization** *n.*
**industrious** *adj* conscientious and hard-working. ➤ **industriously** *adv.*
**industry** *n* (*pl* **-ies**) **1** economic activity concerned with the manufacture of goods, the processing of raw materials, construction work, etc. **2** a specified branch of this. **3** hard work.
**inebriate** *v esp* of alcohol: to intoxicate. ➤ **inebriation** *n.*
**inedible** *adj* not fit to be eaten.
**ineffable** *adj* too great or intense to be expressed.
**ineffective** *adj* **1** not producing an effect or the intended effect. **2** not capable of performing efficiently or achieving results. ➤ **ineffectively** *adv.*
**ineffectual** *adj* **1** unable to get things done; weak in character. **2** ineffective. ➤ **ineffectually** *adv.*
**inefficient** *adj* failing to work, operate, etc in a capable or economical way. ➤ **inefficiency** *n,* **inefficiently** *adv.*
**inelegant** *adj* lacking in refinement, grace, or good taste. ➤ **inelegance** *n,* **inelegantly** *adv.*
**ineligible** *adj* not qualified to receive or do something.
**ineluctable** *adj formal* unavoidable; inescapable.
**inept** *adj* incompetent or clumsy. ➤ **ineptitude** *n,* **ineptly** *adv.*
**inequality** *n* (*pl* **-ies**) the state of being unequal.
**inequitable** *adj* unfair or unjust.
**inequity** *n* (*pl* **-ies**) injustice or unfairness.
**ineradicable** *adj* incapable of being eradicated.
**inert** *adj* **1** lacking the power to move. **2** lacking active chemical or biological properties. **3** inactive or indolent.
**inertia** *n* **1** a tendency to resist exertion or change. **2** in physics, a property of matter by which it remains at rest or in uniform motion in a straight line unless acted on by some external force.
**inescapable** *adj* incapable of being avoided, ignored, or denied.
**inessential**[1] *adj* not absolutely necessary.
**inessential**[2] *n* something that is not absolutely necessary.
**inestimable** *adj* too great, valuable, or excellent to be measured.
**inevitable** *adj* incapable of being avoided; bound to happen. ➤ **inevitability** *n,* **inevitably** *adv.*
**inexact** *adj* not precisely correct or true.
**inexcusable** *adj* too bad to be excused or justified.
**inexhaustible** *adj* **1** of a supply: incapable of being used up. **2** of a person: tireless.
**inexorable** *adj* **1** unable to be persuaded or moved by entreaty. **2** unable to be averted. ➤ **inexorably** *adv.*
**inexpensive** *adj* reasonable in price; cheap.
**inexperience** *n* lack of experience. ➤ **inexperienced** *adj.*
**inexpert** *adj* unskilled or lacking knowledge. ➤ **inexpertly** *adv.*
**inexplicable** *adj* incapable of being explained. ➤ **inexplicably** *adv.*
**inexpressive** *adj* lacking expression or meaning.
**in extremis** *adv* **1** in extremely difficult circumstances. **2** at the point of death.
**inextricable** *adj* incapable of being disentangled or separated. ➤ **inextricably** *adv.*
**infallible** *adj* **1** incapable of error. **2** known to be effective. ➤ **infallibility** *n.*
**infamous** *adj* **1** having a bad reputation; notorious. **2** disgraceful. ➤ **infamously** *adv,* **infamy** *n.*
**infancy** *n* (*pl* **-ies**) **1** early childhood. **2** an early period of existence or development.
**infant** *n* **1** a very young child. **2** *Brit* a schoolchild between the ages of five and seven.
**infanticide** *n* the act of killing a child.
**infantile** *adj* **1** relating to infants. **2** *derog* childish or immature.
**infantry** *n* soldiers trained and equipped to fight on foot.
**infatuate** *v* (**be infatuated with**), to have powerful but often superficial feelings of love for. ➤ **infatuation** *n.*
**infect** *v* **1** to contaminate (e.g. air or food) with an agent that causes disease. **2** to pass on a disease to.
**infection** *n* **1** an infectious disease. **2** the act of infecting.
**infectious** *adj* **1** of a disease: communicable to others. **2** capable of causing or spreading disease. **3** readily spread or communicated to others. ➤ **infectiously** *adv.*
**infer** *v* (**inferred, inferring**) to deduce (something) from available evidence or from what is suggested rather than explicitly stated.
**inference** *n* **1** the act of inferring. **2** a conclusion arrived at from the available evidence or from indirect hints.
**inferior**[1] *adj* of low or lower rank, quality, or importance. ➤ **inferiority** *n.*
**inferior**[2] *n* a person who is lower in rank, standing, ability, etc than another.

**infernal** *adj* **1** relating to hell. **2** *informal* dreadful; damned.
**inferno** *n* (*pl* **-os**) a raging fire.
**infertile** *adj* **1** not capable of producing offspring. **2** of land: not capable of sustaining vegetation, *esp* crops. ➤ **infertility** *n.*
**infest** *v* of insects or vermin, etc: to spread or swarm over causing damage or disease. ➤ **infestation** *n.*
**infidel** *n* **1** somebody who does not believe in a particular religion, *esp* Christianity or Islam. **2** an atheist.
**infidelity** *n* (*pl* **-ies**) unfaithfulness *esp* in marital or sexual matters.
**infighting** *n* dissension among members of a group or organization.
**infiltrate** *v* **1** to enter or become established in (e.g. an organization) gradually or unobtrusively, often to spy on it. **2** of a fluid: to filter or permeate into. ➤ **infiltration** *n,* **infiltrator** *n.*
**infinite** *adj* **1** having no limitations or boundaries in time, space, number, etc. **2** great, immense, or extreme. ➤ **infinitely** *adv.*
**infinitesimal** *adj* immeasurably or incalculably small. ➤ **infinitesimally** *adv.*
**infinitive** *n* the base form of a verb, without inflections, in English often preceded by *to* (e.g. *go* or *to go*).
**infinity** *n* (*pl* **-ies**) **1** unlimited time or space, etc. **2** an immeasurably distant point, e.g. where parallel lines are supposed to meet. **3** a very great number or amount.
**infirm** *adj* physically feeble, *esp* from age.
**infirmary** *n* (*pl* **-ies**) a hospital or sick room.
**infirmity** *n* (*pl* **-ies**) a disease or mental weakness.
**inflame** *v* **1** to arouse passion or strong feeling in. **2** to make (e.g. an emotion or dispute) more violent. **3** to cause inflammation in (body tissue).
**inflammable** *adj* easily set on fire; flammable.
**inflammation** *n* redness, heat, swelling, and pain in an area of body tissue as a result of injury or infection.
**inflammatory** *adj* **1** tending to arouse strong feeling, *esp* anger. **2** accompanied by or causing inflammation.
**inflatable**[1] *adj* capable of being inflated.
**inflatable**[2] *n* an inflatable boat, toy, etc.
**inflate** *v* **1** to swell (e.g. a balloon or tyre) by filling it with air or gas. **2** to increase abnormally or excessively. **3** to cause inflation in (e.g. prices or the economy).
**inflated** *adj* **1** exaggerated. **2** swollen or distended.
**inflation** *n* **1** a substantial and continuing rise in prices, e.g. caused by an increase in the supply of money and credit. **2** the act of inflating. ➤ **inflationary** *adj.*
**inflect** *v* **1** to change the form or ending of (a word). **2** to vary the pitch of (a voice).
**inflection** *or* **inflexion** *n* **1** in grammar, a change in the form of a word to show its case, gender, number, tense, etc. **2** variation in pitch or loudness of the voice.
**inflexible** *adj* **1** incapable of or resistant to change. **2** not variable to suit a particular circumstance. **3** not able to be bent.
**inflict** *v* (*usu* + on) to impose (something unpleasant or painful) on somebody. ➤ **infliction** *n.*
**influence**[1] *n* **1** the power or capacity to produce an effect on somebody or something, *esp* in indirect or intangible ways. **2** power resulting from wealth or position. **3** somebody or something that has or exerts influence. ✱ **under the influence** *informal* drunk.
**influence**[2] *v* to affect, *esp* by indirect or intangible means.
**influential** *adj* exerting or possessing influence.
**influenza** *n* a highly infectious viral disease characterized by fever, severe aches and pains, and catarrh.
**influx** *n* an arrival of people or things in large numbers.
**inform** *v* **1** to communicate knowledge or information to. **2** (*usu* + against/on) to give the police information about a criminal or crime.
**informal** *adj* **1** marked by an absence of formality or ceremony. **2** of clothes: suitable for a friendly and relaxed occasion. **3** of language: in a style appropriate to conversation rather than formal writing. ➤ **informality** *n,* **informally** *adv.*
**informant** *n* **1** a person who gives somebody information about something. **2** = INFORMER.
**information** *n* facts or data obtained from investigation, study, or instruction.
**information technology** *n* the use of computers, telecommunications, etc to store, retrieve, and send information.
**informative** *adj* conveying information; instructive.
**informed** *adj* **1** based on possession of information. **2** knowledgeable, *esp* about matters of contemporary interest.
**informer** *n* a person who gives information about a criminal or crime to the police.
**infraction** *n* an infringement, *esp* of a law or agreement.
**infra dig** *adj informal* beneath one's dignity.
**infrared** *adj* of electromagnetic radiation: lying outside the visible spectrum, with a wavelength between red light and microwaves.
**infrastructure** *n* the permanent features, e.g. road and rail networks, power supplies, etc, necessary for a country's economic well-being.
**infrequent** *adj* not occurring often. ➤ **infrequency** *n,* **infrequently** *adv.*

**infringe** *v* **1** to encroach on (a right or privilege). **2** to violate (a law, agreement, etc). ➤ **infringement** *n.*

**infuriate** *v* to make furious. ➤ **infuriating** *adj.*

**infuse** *v* **1** to steep (tea, herbs, etc) in liquid so as to extract the flavour, soluble properties, etc. **2** to imbue or pervade.

**infusion** *n* **1** the process of infusing. **2** an extract or drink obtained by infusing.

**ingenious** *adj* original, resourceful, and clever. ➤ **ingeniously** *adv.*

**ingenue** *or* **ingénue** /anzhay'nooh/ *n* a naive or artless young woman.

**ingenuity** *n* resourcefulness, cleverness, or inventiveness.

**ingenuous** *adj* showing innocent or childlike simplicity.

**ingest** *v* to take (food or drink) into the body.

**inglenook** *n* an alcove by a large open fireplace.

**inglorious** *adj* shameful; ignominious.

**ingoing** *adj* entering.

**ingot** *n* a mass of cast metal in the shape of a bar or brick.

**ingrained** *or* **engrained** *adj* **1** of a habit, moral value, etc: firmly and deeply implanted. **2** of dirt, stains, etc: thoroughly worked into something.

**ingratiate** *v* to gain favour for (e.g. oneself) by deliberate effort. ➤ **ingratiating** *adj.*

**ingratitude** *n* failure to appreciate kindness received.

**ingredient** *n* a component part of a compound or mixture, *esp* an edible substance combined in the preparation of food.

**ingress** *n* **1** the act of entering. **2** a way in; an entrance.

**ingrown** *or* **ingrowing** *adj esp* of a toenail: with the free end embedded in the flesh.

**inhabit** *v* (**inhabited, inhabiting**) to live in (a place). ➤ **inhabitable** *adj.*

**inhale** *v* to breathe in.

**inhaler** *n* a device used for inhaling a medication, e.g. to relieve asthma.

**inherent** *adj* forming an essential and indivisible part of something. ➤ **inherently** *adv.*

**inherit** *v* (**inherited, inheriting**) **1** to receive (property) from somebody at his or her death. **2** to receive (something, e.g. a physical attribute) by genetic transmission. **3** to come to possess (something) left by a predecessor.

**inheritance** *n* **1** the act of inheriting. **2** property that is inherited.

**inhibit** *v* (**inhibited, inhibiting**) **1** to discourage (somebody) from behaving freely or spontaneously. **2** to restrain (e.g. an impulse). ➤ **inhibited** *adj.*

**inhibition** *n* a psychological restraint on the way somebody thinks or behaves.

**inhospitable** *adj* **1** of a person: not friendly or welcoming. **2** of a place, climate, etc: hard to live in.

**in-house** *adj and adv* within a group or organization.

**inhuman** *adj* **1** extremely cruel; barbarous. **2** not human in nature or quality.

**inhumane** *adj* completely lacking in kindness or compassion.

**inhumanity** *n* (*pl* **-ies**) pitilessness or cruelty.

**inimical** *adj* adverse in influence or effects; harmful; hostile.

**inimitable** *adj* so good that no others can match it; unique. ➤ **inimitably** *adv.*

**iniquity** *n* (*pl* **-ies**) **1** wickedness. **2** a wicked act; a sin. ➤ **iniquitous** *adj.*

**initial**[1] *adj* **1** existing at the beginning. **2** placed at the beginning; first. ➤ **initially** *adv.*

**initial**[2] *n* the first letter of a name.

**initial**[3] *v* (**initialled, initialling,** *NAmer* **initialed, initialing**) to put one's initials on (something), usu to indicate ownership or authorization.

**initiate** *v* **1** to cause or allow to begin. **2** to introduce (somebody) to a new subject or activity, *esp* a complex one. **3** to grant (somebody) membership of an organization, traditionally by formal rites. ➤ **initiation** *n.*

**initiative** *n* **1** energy or resourcefulness displayed in acting without being prompted. **2** a new plan, strategy, or programme of action. **3** the opportunity to act first.

**inject** *v* **1** to force a fluid into the body using a syringe. **2** to introduce as an element or factor.

**injection** *n* **1** the act of injecting something, *esp* a medication, into a person's body. **2** the introduction of a new element or factor.

**in-joke** *n* a joke understood only by the members of a particular group.

**injudicious** *adj* showing a lack of judgment. ➤ **injudiciously** *adv,* **injudiciousness** *n.*

**injunction** *n* **1** a court order requiring somebody to do or refrain from doing a particular act. **2** a firm warning or an order.

**injure** *v* **1** to inflict bodily harm on. **2** to inflict damage or loss on.

**injurious** *adj* inflicting injury or harm.

**injury** *n* (*pl* **-ies**) **1** a physical hurt caused to somebody. **2** damage or loss.

**injustice** *n* **1** unfairness. **2** an unjust act or state of affairs.

**ink**[1] *n* **1** a coloured liquid used for writing and printing. **2** the black secretion of a squid, octopus, etc. ➤ **inky** *adj.*

**ink**[2] *v* to apply ink to.

**inkling** *n* **1** a slight knowledge or vague idea. **2** a hint.

**inland** *adj and adv* in or towards the interior part of a country.

**Inland Revenue** *n* the government department responsible for collecting taxes in Britain.

**in-law** *n informal* a relative by marriage.
**inlay**[1] *v* (*past tense and past part.* **inlaid**) **1** to set into a surface *esp* for decoration. **2** to decorate with inlaid material.
**inlay**[2] *n* a decorative inlaid pattern.
**inlet** *n* **1** a usu long and narrow recess in a shoreline. **2** a means of entry, *esp* for fluids.
**in loco parentis** *adv* having the responsibilities of a parent.
**inmate** *n* a resident of an institution, *esp* a prison or hospital.
**inn** *n* a pub.
**innards** *pl n informal* **1** the internal organs, *esp* the intestines. **2** the internal parts or mechanism.
**innate** *adj* belonging to an individual from birth. ➤ **innately** *adv.*
**inner** *adj* **1** situated inside something or near its centre. **2** relating to the mind or soul. **3** unexpressed; private.
**inner city** *n* the usu older and more densely populated central section of a city.
**innermost** *adj* **1** most inward or central. **2** most secret and private.
**inner tube** *n* an inflatable tube inside the casing of a tyre.
**innings** *n* (*pl* **innings**) in cricket, a division of a match during which one side bats and the other bowls.
**innkeeper** *n* the landlord or landlady of an inn.
**innocent**[1] *adj* **1** free from guilt or sin, *esp* not guilty of a crime. **2** harmless in effect or intention. **3** knowing little of life and human nature. ➤ **innocence** *n,* **innocently** *adv.*
**innocent**[2] *n* somebody who is innocent.
**innocuous** *adj* **1** having no harmful effects. **2** unlikely to offend.
**innovate** *v* to introduce new practices or ideas. ➤ **innovative** *adj,* **innovator** *n.*
**innovation** *n* **1** the act of innovating. **2** a change that introduces a new idea or practice.
**innuendo** *n* (*pl* **-os** *or* **-oes**) an obliquely worded comment, *esp* a suggestive or subtly disparaging one.
**innumerable** *adj* too many to be counted.
**innumerate** *adj Brit* not able to use numbers effectively or do basic arithmetic.
**inoculate** *v* to introduce a disease-causing organism into the body in order to induce immunity. ➤ **inoculation** *n.*
**inoffensive** *adj* not intended or intending to cause harm or offence.
**inoperable** *adj* **1** not suitable for treatment by surgery. **2** impracticable. **3** unable to be operated.
**inoperative** *adj* not functioning, or having no effect.
**inopportune** *adj* happening at an awkward time; inconvenient.
**inordinate** *adj* going beyond reasonable limits; excessive. ➤ **inordinately** *adv.*
**inorganic** *adj* **1** composed of or relating to matter that is not plant or animal. **2** not arising through natural growth.
**inpatient** *n* a patient who lives at a hospital while undergoing treatment.
**input**[1] *n* **1** something, e.g. energy, material, or data, supplied to a machine or system. **2** the entry point for an input into a system, machine, etc. **3** the act of putting something in. **4** work, suggestions, advice, etc that somebody contributes.
**input**[2] *v* (**inputting,** *past tense and past part.* **input** *or* **inputted**) to enter (data) into a computer.
**inquest** *n* **1** a judicial enquiry, *esp* by a coroner, into the cause of a death. **2** an investigation, *esp* into something that has failed.
**inquire** *v* see ENQUIRE.
**inquiry** *n* see ENQUIRY.
**inquisition** *n* a ruthless investigation or examination.
**inquisitive** *adj* **1** unduly curious about the affairs of others. **2** eager for knowledge or understanding. ➤ **inquisitively** *adv.*
**inquisitor** *n* somebody who conducts an inquisition.
**inroad** *n* * **make inroads into** to have made progress in dealing with or reducing.
**inrush** *n* a crowding or flooding in.
**insalubrious** *adj* unhealthy.
**ins and outs** *pl n* characteristic peculiarities and complexities; ramifications.
**insane** *adj* **1** *dated, offensive* suffering from a mental illness. **2** utterly absurd. ➤ **insanely** *adv,* **insanity** *n.*
**insanitary** *adj* unclean enough to endanger health.
**insatiable** *adj* incapable of being satisfied. ➤ **insatiably** *adv.*
**inscribe** *v* **1** to write, engrave, or print, *esp* on a hard surface. **2** to dedicate (*esp* a book) to somebody by a handwritten note.
**inscription** *n* any written or engraved form of words, e.g. on a statue or a coin or as a dedication in a book.
**inscrutable** *adj* hard to interpret or understand. ➤ **inscrutably** *adv.*
**insect** *n* a small invertebrate animal with three pairs of legs.
**insecticide** *n* a substance that destroys insects.
**insectivore** *n* an insect-eating plant or animal. ➤ **insectivorous** *adj.*
**insecure** *adj* **1** lacking in self-confidence. **2** not firmly fixed or supported. ➤ **insecurity** *n.*
**inseminate** *v* to introduce semen into (a woman or female animal). ➤ **insemination** *n.*
**insensate** *adj* **1** not capable of feeling. **2** lacking in human feeling; insensitive. **3** senseless; foolish. ➤ **insensately** *adv.*

**insensible** *adj* **1** unconscious. **2** numb. **3** *formal* (+ of) unaware or heedless.

**insensitive** *adj* **1** unsympathetic to the needs or feelings of others; callous; tactless. **2** (+ to) not physically or chemically sensitive. ➤ **insensitively** *adv,* **insensitiveness** *n,* **insensitivity** *n.*

**inseparable** *adj* **1** incapable of being separated. **2** always seen or found together. ➤ **inseparably** *adv.*

**insert**[1] *v* **1** to put in through an opening. **2** to introduce into the body of something, e.g. text. ➤ **insertion** *n.*

**insert**[2] *n* a piece of written or printed material placed between the pages of a book or magazine.

**inset**[1] *n* **1** a small illustration set within a larger one. **2** a piece of cloth set into a garment for decoration, shaping, etc.

**inset**[2] *v* (**insetting,** *past tense and past part.* **inset** *or* **insetted**) to insert.

**inshore** *adj and adv* **1** towards the shore. **2** at sea but near the shore.

**inside**[1] *n* **1** an inner side or surface. **2** an interior or internal part. **3** (*usu in pl*) the stomach or the intestines. * **inside out** with the inner surface on the outside.

**inside**[2] *adj* **1** of, on, near, or towards the inside. **2** carried out by somebody within an organization: *an inside job.*

**inside**[3] *prep* **1** in or into the interior of. **2** closer to the centre than. **3** in less than a particular period of time.

**inside**[4] *adv* **1** in or into the interior. **2** indoors. **3** within somebody's body or mind. **4** *chiefly Brit, informal* in or into prison.

**insider** *n* somebody accepted as a member of a group, *esp* somebody with access to confidential information.

**insidious** *adj* acting gradually but with very harmful consequences. ➤ **insidiously** *adv.*

**insight** *n* **1** the ability to discern the true nature of something. **2** an explanation that displays this ability.

**insignia** *n* (*pl* **insignia, insignias**) a badge of authority or honour.

**insignificant** *adj* **1** too unimportant to be worth consideration. **2** very small in size, amount, or number. ➤ **insignificance** *n,* **insignificantly** *adv.*

**insincere** *adj* not expressing feelings or opinions honestly. ➤ **insincerely** *adv,* **insincerity** *n.*

**insinuate** *v* **1** to suggest (something unpleasant) in a subtle or oblique manner. **2** (+ into) to gain acceptance for (e.g. oneself) by crafty means. **3** to squeeze in somewhere. ➤ **insinuating** *adj.*

**insinuation** *n* a sly and usu derogatory reference.

**insipid** *adj* **1** lacking flavour. **2** with no interesting or stimulating qualities.

**insist** *v* **1** to persist in maintaining that something is the case. **2** (*usu* + on/upon) to state wishes or requirements forcefully, accepting no refusal. **3** (+ on/upon) to refuse to stop doing something.

**insistent** *adj* **1** insisting forcefully or repeatedly. **2** demanding attention. ➤ **insistence** *n,* **insistently** *adv.*

**in situ** *adv and adj* in the natural or original position.

**insofar as** *conj* to the extent or degree that.

**insole** *n* **1** a shaped strip placed inside a shoe for e.g. a better fit. **2** a fixed inside sole of a shoe.

**insolent** *adj* showing disrespectful rudeness. ➤ **insolence** *n,* **insolently** *adv.*

**insoluble** *adj* **1** incapable of being dissolved in liquid. **2** impossible to solve or explain.

**insolvent** *adj* unable to pay one's debts. ➤ **insolvency** *n.*

**insomnia** *n* prolonged inability to sleep. ➤ **insomniac** *adj and n.*

**insomuch as** *conj* to the degree that.

**insouciance** *n* light-hearted unconcern; nonchalance. ➤ **insouciant** *adj.*

**inspect** *v* **1** to examine closely and critically. **2** to view or examine officially. ➤ **inspection** *n.*

**inspector** *n* **1** an official who assesses whether standards are being met or established rules followed. **2** a police officer ranking immediately above a sergeant.

**inspiration** *n* **1** the act of stimulating the intellect or emotions. **2** an inspiring agent or influence. **3** an inspired idea. ➤ **inspirational** *adj.*

**inspire** *v* **1** to have an animating or uplifting influence on. **2** to act as a stimulus for. **3** (+ with) to cause to feel a particular emotion. ➤ **inspiring** *adj.*

**inspired** *adj* **1** created by inspiration. **2** especially clever or effective.

**instability** *n* (*pl* **-ies**) lack of stability.

**install** (*NAmer* **instal**) *v* **1** to place in position for use. **2** to establish (somebody) in a specified place, office, or rank.

***Usage Note:*** Note the spelling with *-all.*

**installation** *n* **1** the act of installing. **2** a usu large piece of equipment installed to perform some specified function. **3** a military base or establishment. **4** a large-scale work of art assembled in the gallery where it is exhibited.

**instalment** (*NAmer* **installment**) *n* **1** a part into which a debt is divided for repayment. **2** each of a series of parts, e.g. of a publication or broadcast, presented at intervals.

**instance**[1] *n* an example or occurrence of something. * **for instance** as an example.

**instance**[2] *v* to put forward as a case or example.

**instant**[1] *n* **1** a very brief period of time; a second. **2** a precise point in time.

**instant**[2] *adj* **1** immediate. **2** of food: prepared for easy final preparation.

**instantaneous** *adj* occurring or acting instantly. ➤ **instantaneously** *adv.*

**instead** *adv* as a substitute or alternative.

**instep** *n* the arched middle portion of the human foot.

**instigate** *v* to initiate or bring about (a course of action or procedure). ➤ **instigation** *n.*

**instil** (*NAmer* **instill**) *v* (**instilled, instilling**) (+ in/into) to cause to become firmly fixed in someone's mind over time.

**instinct** *n* a natural or inherent way of acting or thinking. ➤ **instinctual** *adj.*

**instinctive** *adj* arising spontaneously and independent of judgment or will. ➤ **instinctively** *adv.*

**institute**[1] *n* an organization for research or education in a particular field.

**institute**[2] *v* to originate and establish.

**institution** *n* **1** an established organization or body, e.g. a university or hospital. **2** an established practice in a culture. **3** *dated* a psychiatric hospital or unit. ➤ **institutional** *adj.*

**institutionalize** *or* **-ise** *v* **1** to establish as a custom or regular practice. **2** to put or keep in an institution, *esp* a psychiatric hospital. **3** to cause to acquire personality traits typical of people in an institution, *esp* a lack of independent thought or action.

**instruct** *v* **1** to teach. **2** to command. **3** to engage (a lawyer) for a case. **4** to inform of something.

**instruction** *n* **1** (*usu in pl*) an order or command. **2** (*usu in pl*) a direction or piece of advice on how to do something. **3** teaching or training.

**instructive** *adj* giving useful information or advice. ➤ **instructively** *adv.*

**instructor** *n* a teacher.

**instrument** *n* **1** an implement, tool, or device *esp* for delicate work or measurement. **2** a device used to produce music. **3** a device used in navigating an aircraft or ship. **4** a formal legal document.

**instrumental**[1] *adj* **1** (+ in) serving as a means or agent. **2** composed for or performed on a musical instrument.

**instrumental**[2] *n* a musical composition for instruments but not voice.

**instrumentalist** *n* a player of a musical instrument.

**instrumentation** *n* **1** the instruments specified for the performance of a musical composition. **2** the navigation instruments on an aeroplane, ship, etc.

**insubordinate** *adj* disobedient. ➤ **insubordination** *n.*

**insubstantial** *adj* lacking firmness or solidity.

**insufferable** *adj* too bad, unpleasant, or annoying to put up with. ➤ **insufferably** *adv.*

**insufficient** *adj* not enough; inadequate. ➤ **insufficiency** *n,* **insufficiently** *adv.*

**insular** *adj* **1** relating to islands. **2** cut off from other people. **3** narrow-minded. ➤ **insularity** *n.*

**insulate** *v* **1** to separate from conducting bodies by means of nonconductors so as to prevent loss of electricity, heat, or sound. **2** to protect (somebody) from harsh realities. ➤ **insulator** *n.*

**insulation** *n* **1** material used in insulating. **2** the act of insulating.

**insulin** *n* a hormone that regulates the level of glucose in the blood.

**insult**[1] *v* to speak about or treat with insolence or contempt.

**insult**[2] *n* a remark, gesture, etc that insults.

**insuperable** *adj* incapable of being surmounted or overcome.

**insupportable** *adj* **1** unendurable. **2** incapable of being supported or sustained.

**insurance** *n* **1** a contract whereby one party undertakes to indemnify another against a particular type of loss, or the protection offered by such a contract. **2** the premium demanded under such a contract. **3** the sum for which something is insured. **4** the business of insuring people or property.

**insure** *v* **1** to procure insurance on (a property, etc) or for (an owner). **2** (+ against) to protect from something unpleasant. **3** *chiefly NAmer* to ensure.

---

***Usage Note:*** Do not confuse this word with *ensure*, which means 'to make sure'.

---

**insurgent**[1] *n* somebody who revolts against civil authority or an established government. ➤ **insurgency** *n.*

**insurgent**[2] *adj* rebellious.

**insurmountable** *adj* too great or difficult to overcome.

**insurrection** *n* a revolt against civil authority or established government.

**intact** *adj* not harmed or damaged.

**intake** *n* an amount or number taken in, *esp* the number of students entering a school or college in any one year.

**intangible** *adj* **1** not able to be perceived by touch. **2** not clear or definite. ➤ **intangibly** *adv.*

**integer** *n* a whole number.

**integral** *adj* **1** essential to completeness; constituent. **2** lacking nothing essential; whole.

**integrate** *v* **1** to form or blend (separate elements) into a whole. **2** (+ into) to incorporate into a larger unit.

**integrity** *n* **1** uncompromising adherence to a code of *esp* moral or artistic values. **2** the state of being complete or undivided. **3** *formal* an unimpaired condition; wholeness.

**intellect** *n* the capacity for intelligent thought.

**intellectual**[1] *adj* **1** of the intellect. **2** using or requiring the intellect for understanding, often in preference to emotion or experience. ➤ **intellectually** *adv.*

**intellectual**[2] *n* an intellectual person.

**intellectualize** *or* **-ise** *v* to consider in an intellectual way.

**intelligence** *n* **1** the ability to learn, apply knowledge, or think abstractly. **2** information concerning an enemy or competitor, or an organization with the task of gathering such information.

**intelligence quotient** *n* a number expressing the ratio of somebody's intelligence to the average for his or her age.

**intelligent** *adj* having or indicating the ability to learn and apply knowledge effectively. ➤ **intelligently** *adv.*

**intelligentsia** *n* intellectuals considered as a social or political class.

**intelligible** *adj* capable of being understood. ➤ **intelligibility** *n,* **intelligibly** *adv.*

**intemperate** *adj* going beyond the bounds of reasonable behaviour. ➤ **intemperance** *n.*

**intend** *v* **1** to have in mind as a purpose or goal. **2** to design for a specified use or destine for a particular future.

**intended**[1] *adj* planned; future.

**intended**[2] *n informal* somebody's future spouse.

**intense** *adj* **1** existing or occurring in an extreme degree. **2** feeling emotion deeply. ➤ **intensely** *adv,* **intensity** *n.*

**intensify** *v* (**-ies, -ied**) to make or become more intense.

**intensive** *adj* **1** very thorough and concentrated within a short time. **2** using a specified factor to a greater extent than others: *labour-intensive.* **3** designed to maximize productivity: *intensive farming.* ➤ **intensively** *adv.*

**intensive care** *n* continuous care and special treatment given to a seriously ill patient.

**intent**[1] *n* intention. ✱ **to all intents and purposes** in every practical or important respect.

**intent**[2] *adj* **1** (+ on/upon) having the mind or attention concentrated on. **2** (+ on/upon) determined to. **3** directed with strained or eager attention. ➤ **intently** *adv.*

**intention** *n* **1** what somebody intends to do; an aim. **2** a determination to act in a certain way. **3** (*in pl*) purpose with respect to proposal of marriage.

**intentional** *adj* deliberate. ➤ **intentionally** *adv.*

**inter** *v* (**interred, interring**) to place (a dead body) in the earth or a tomb.

**inter-** *prefix* **1** between; among: *intercity; interstellar.* **2** reciprocally: *interact.*

**interact** *v* to produce an effect upon each other. ➤ **interaction** *n.*

**interactive** *adj* **1** characterized by interaction. **2** involving the exchange of information between a computer and user while a program is being run.

**interbreed** *v* (*past tense and past part.* **interbred**) to crossbreed.

**intercede** *v* to plead with somebody on behalf of another person.

**intercept** *v* to stop (something or somebody) reaching the place they are going to. ➤ **interception** *n,* **interceptor** *n.*

**intercession** *n* the act of interceding, *esp* by prayer.

**interchange**[1] *v* **1** to put each of (two things) in the place of the other. **2** of two people: to give each other (a thing of the same kind). ➤ **interchangeability** *n,* **interchangeable** *adj.*

**interchange**[2] *n* **1** a junction of two or more roads at different levels. **2** the act of interchanging.

**intercity** *adj* existing or travelling between cities.

**intercom** *n* an internal communication system, e.g. in a building.

**interconnect** *v* to connect with one another.

**intercontinental** *adj* carried on, or capable of travelling, between continents.

**intercourse** *n* **1** = SEXUAL INTERCOURSE. **2** *formal* communication or dealings between people.

**intercut** *v* (**intercutting,** *past tense and past part.* **intercut**) to alternate shots from (one cinematic scene) with shots from a contrasting scene.

**interdependent** *adj* depending one on the other. ➤ **interdependence** *n.*

**interest**[1] *n* **1** readiness to be concerned with something. **2** a subject or activity that one is concerned with and enthusiastic about. **3** a quality in a thing that arouses interest. **4** a charge for borrowed money, generally a percentage of the amount borrowed. **5** benefit or advantage to somebody. **6** a right, title, or legal share in something, e.g. a business.

**interest**[2] *v* **1** to engage the attention or arouse the interest of. **2** (+ in) to persuade (somebody) to do or buy something. ➤ **interesting** *adj.*

**interested** *adj* **1** having the curiosity aroused or attention engaged. **2** involved; not impartial.

**interface**[1] *n* **1** the place at which independent systems meet and act on each other. **2** a piece of computer hardware or software that allows a user to communicate with a computer.

**interface**[2] *v* **1** to connect by means of an interface. **2** to interact.

**interfere** *v* **1** (+ with) to get in the way or be a hindrance. **2** (+ with) to handle or adjust without authorization. **3** (*often* + in) to take a part in matters that do not concern one. **4** *informal* (+ with) to carry out a sexual assault.

**interference** *n* **1** the act of interfering. **2** disturbance to received radio signals by other unwanted signals or noise.

**interferon** *n* a protein that inhibits the development of viruses.

**intergalactic** *adj* existing or operating between galaxies.

**interim**[1] *n* an intervening time.

**interim**[2] *adj* temporary or provisional.

**interior**[1] *adj* **1** lying or occurring inside something. **2** away from the border or shore. **3** relating to the domestic affairs of a country. **4** of the mind or soul.

**interior**[2] *n* **1** the internal or inner part of a thing. **2** the part of a country that lies away from the border or the shore. **3** the internal affairs of a country.

**interject** *v* to say something abruptly while something else is being said.

**interlace** *v* **1** to interweave. **2** to intersperse among other things.

**interleave** *v* **1** to intersperse (e.g. blank pages or protective sheets) between the pages of (a book). **2** to insert between layers.

**interlock** *v* to become firmly connected by parts designed to fit together.

**interlocutor** *n formal* somebody who takes part in dialogue or conversation.

**interloper** *n* somebody who interferes or encroaches.

**interlude** *n* **1** an intervening period or event, *esp* of a contrasting character. **2** a break between parts of a play or other performance. **3** a musical composition inserted between the parts of a longer composition.

**intermarry** *v* (**-ies, -ied**) to become connected by marriage with another group.

**intermediary** *n* (*pl* **-ies**) somebody acting as a mediator or go-between.

**intermediate** *adj* **1** existing or occurring in the middle or between two extremes. **2** involving a level of skill or knowledge greater than that of a beginner, but not yet considered advanced.

**interment** *n* the placing of a corpse in a grave.

**intermezzo** /intə'metsoh/ *n* (*pl* **intermezzi** *or* **intermezzos**) a movement that comes between the major sections of an extended musical work, e.g. an opera.

**interminable** *adj* seeming to have no end; wearisomely long. ➤ **interminably** *adv.*

**intermingle** *v* to mingle (things) together or combine (something) with something else.

**intermission** *n* **1** a break between the acts of a performance. **2** a pause or respite.

**intermittent** *adj* occurring at irregular intervals. ➤ **intermittently** *adv.*

**intern**[1] *v* to confine e.g. in prison or a concentration camp, *esp* during a war. ➤ **internment** *n.*

**intern**[2] *n chiefly NAmer* **1** a person receiving practical training in the workplace. **2** a junior doctor working under supervision in a hospital.

**internal** *adj* **1** existing or situated within the limits or surface of something. **2** present within the body. **3** operative within a state or an organization. **4** existing within the mind. ➤ **internally** *adv.*

**internal-combustion engine** *n* an engine in which the combustion that generates energy takes place inside, e.g. in a cylinder, as opposed to in a separate furnace.

**internalize** *or* **-ise** *v* to incorporate (e.g. learned values) within the self and use them as guiding principles.

**international**[1] *adj* **1** affecting or involving two or more nations. **2** known or recognized in more than one country. ➤ **internationally** *adv.*

**international**[2] *n* **1** a sporting or other contest between two national teams. **2** a player who has taken part in such a contest.

**internationalism** *n* support for cooperation among nations. ➤ **internationalist** *n.*

**internationalize** *or* **-ise** *v* to become or make international.

**internecine** *adj* involving conflict within a group.

**Internet** *n* (**the Internet**) the worldwide computer network for the exchange of information via telephone lines and satellite links.

**interpersonal** *adj* involving relations between people.

**interplanetary** *adj* existing or operating between planets.

**interplay** *n* the effect that two or more things have on each other; interaction.

**interpolate** *v* to insert (words) into a text or conversation. ➤ **interpolation** *n.*

**interpose** *v* **1** to place (something) between two things. **2** to interrupt with (words) during a conversation or argument.

**interpret** *v* (**interpreted, interpreting**) **1** to understand the meaning of (something), often in the light of one's beliefs or circumstances. **2** to explain the meaning of. **3** to give an oral translation of somebody's words. ➤ **interpretation** *n,* **interpreter** *n.*

**interracial** *adj* involving members of different races.

**interregnum** *n* (*pl* **interregnums** *or* **interregna**) the time during which a throne is vacant between reigns or normal government is suspended.

**interrelate** *v* to relate to one another. ➤ **interrelation** *n.*

**interrogate** *v* to question formally, exhaustively, or aggressively. ➤ **interrogation** *n,* **interrogator** *n.*

**interrogative**[1] *adj* **1** questioning. **2** used in a question. ➤ **interrogatively** *adv.*

**interrogative**[2] *n* a word, *esp* a pronoun, used in asking questions.

**interrupt** *v* **1** to break the flow of (a speaker or speech). **2** to break the uniformity or continuity of (something). ➤ **interruption** *n.*

**intersect** *v* **1** to divide (e.g. a line or area) by passing through or across it. **2** of lines, roads, etc: to meet and cross at a point.

**intersection** *n* a place where two or more things, e.g. streets, roads, etc, intersect.

**intersperse** *v* **1** to insert at intervals among other things. **2** (+ with) to vary with scattered things.

**interstate** *adj* between two or more states, *esp* of the USA or Australia.

**interstellar** *adj* existing or operating between the stars.

**interstice** *n formal* a small space between adjacent things.

**intertwine** *v* to twine together or join twisting round each other.

**interval** *n* **1** an intervening space, e.g. a time between events or states. **2** the difference in pitch between two notes. **3** *Brit* a break in the presentation of an entertainment, e.g. a play.

**intervene** *v* **1** to occur or come between two things. **2** to become involved so as to change a situation, e.g. to settle a dispute. ➤ **intervention** *n.*

**interview**[1] *n* **1** a formal consultation to evaluate e.g. a prospective student or employee. **2** a meeting at which information is obtained from somebody. ➤ **interviewee** *n,* **interviewer** *n.*

**interview**[2] *v* to invite or subject to an interview.

**interweave** *v* (**interwove, interwoven**) to weave together.

**intestate** *adj* having made no valid will.

**intestine** *n* (*also in pl*) the tubular organ connecting the stomach to the anus. ➤ **intestinal** *adj.*

**intimacy** *n* (*pl* **-ies**) **1** familiarity, *esp* close friendship. **2** an intimate remark.

**intimate**[1] *adj* **1** marked by a warm friendship developing through long association. **2** suggesting informal warmth or privacy. **3** of a very personal or private nature. **4** of knowledge: derived from a very close association or long familiarity. **5** *euphem* involved in a sexual relationship. ➤ **intimately** *adv.*

**intimate**[2] *v* **1** to make known, e.g. by a formal announcement. **2** to hint at or imply. ➤ **intimation** *n.*

**intimate**[3] *n* a close friend or confidant.

**intimidate** *v* **1** to frighten or unnerve. **2** to compel or deter with threats. ➤ **intimidation** *n.*

**into** *prep* **1** so as to be inside. **2** so as to become or find oneself in: *Don't get into trouble.* **3** used in division: *Divide 35 into 70.* **4** in the direction of. **5** *informal* involved with or keen on.

**intolerable** *adj* too bad or unpleasant to endure. ➤ **intolerably** *adv.*

**intolerant** *adj* **1** unwilling to accept others' views or allow others their own views, lifestyles, etc. **2** (+ of) unable to endure. ➤ **intolerance** *n.*

**intonation** *n* the rise and fall of the voice in speech.

**intone** *v* to recite or say in a monotonous tone.

**intoxicate** *v* **1** to excite or stupefy with alcohol or drugs, *esp* so that physical and mental control is markedly diminished. **2** to make very excited or elated. ➤ **intoxicating** *adj,* **intoxication** *n.*

**intra-** *prefix* inside; within: *intrauterine.*

**intractable** *adj* **1** not easily solved or dealt with. **2** stubborn.

**intranet** *n* an internal computer network that operates by using Internet protocols.

**intransigent** *adj* refusing to compromise or to abandon a position or attitude. ➤ **intransigence** *n.*

**intransitive** *adj* of a verb: not having a direct object.

**intrauterine** *adj* within the uterus.

**intravenous** *adj* in or by way of a vein. ➤ **intravenously** *adv.*

**intrepid** *adj* fearless and bold. ➤ **intrepidity** *n.*

**intricacy** *n* (*pl* **-ies**) **1** the quality of being intricate. **2** a detail or complexity.

**intricate** *adj* having many complexly interrelating parts. ➤ **intricately** *adv.*

**intrigue**[1] *v* **1** to arouse the interest or curiosity of. **2** to develop a secret or underhand scheme. ➤ **intriguer** *n,* **intriguing** *adj.*

**intrigue**[2] *n* **1** a secret scheme or plot. **2** the use of scheming or underhand plots in pursuit of an end. **3** a clandestine love affair.

**intrinsic** *adj* belonging to the essential nature of something. ➤ **intrinsically** *adv.*

**introduce** *v* **1** to bring into use or into play, *esp* for the first time. **2** to cause (somebody or oneself) to be acquainted with another person. **3** (+ to) to call somebody's attention to a subject for the first time. **4** to make preliminary remarks about (e.g. a speaker). **5** to occur at the beginning of. **6** to place or insert somewhere.

**introduction** *n* **1** the act of introducing or process of being introduced. **2** a formal presentation of one person to another. **3** a part of a book, lecture, etc that is preliminary to the main part. **4** a book or course of study that gives a basic grounding in a subject. **5** something introduced, e.g. a plant or animal new to an area.

**introductory** *adj* serving as an introduction; preliminary.

**introspection** *n* the examining of one's own mind or its contents. ➤ **introspective** *adj.*

**introvert** *n* a shy person whose attention is often directed to his or her own mental life: compare EXTROVERT. ➤ **introvert** *adj,* **introverted** *adj.*

**intrude** *v* **1** to thrust oneself into a situation or a place without invitation or welcome. **2** to force (something) in or on something, *esp* without permission.

**intruder** *n* **1** somebody who intrudes. **2** somebody who trespasses on or breaks into somebody's property.

**intrusion** *n* **1** the act of intruding. **2** something or somebody that intrudes.

**intrusive** *adj* constituting an intrusion; unwelcome.

**intuit** *v* (**intuited, intuiting**) to apprehend by intuition.

**intuition** *n* the power of attaining knowledge without evident rational thought.

**intuitive** *adj* **1** known or perceived by intuition. **2** possessing intuition or insight. ➤ **intuitively** *adv.*

**Inuit** *n* (*pl* **Inuits** *or* **Inuit**) **1** a member of the indigenous peoples inhabiting northern Canada, Alaska, and Greenland. **2** the language spoken by these peoples.

**inundate** *v* **1** to flood (an area). **2** to overwhelm with demands, offers, etc. ➤ **inundation** *n.*

**inure** *or* **enure** *v* (+ to) to accustom to something undesirable.

**invade** *v* **1** to enter (e.g. a country) for hostile purposes. **2** to encroach on. **3** to spread over or into (something) as if invading it. ➤ **invader** *n.*

**invalid**[1] *n* somebody who is unwell or disabled.

**invalid**[2] *adj* **1** without legal force. **2** logically inconsistent.

**invalid**[3] *v* (*usu* + out) to remove from active duty because of sickness or disability.

**invalidate** *v* to make invalid. ➤ **invalidation** *n.*

**invalidity** *n* **1** *Brit* the fact of being an invalid. **2** lack of validity.

**invaluable** *adj* very useful.

**invariable** *adj* not changing; constant.

**invariably** *adv* always.

**invasion** *n* **1** a hostile attack on a foreign territory by an army. **2** the incoming or spread of something harmful, e.g. a tumour.

**invasive** *adj* **1** involving an invasion or intrusion. **2** of medical treatment: involving the insertion of an instrument or other object into the body.

**invective** *n* abusive or insulting language.

**inveigh** *v* (+ against) to speak or protest bitterly or vehemently.

**inveigle** *v* (*usu* + into) to persuade to do something by ingenuity or flattery. * **inveigle oneself into** to gain access to (a place or situation) by ingenuity or trickery.

**invent** *v* **1** to produce (e.g. a device or machine) for the first time. **2** to think up, *esp* in order to deceive. ➤ **inventor** *n.*

**invention** *n* **1** something invented. **2** productive imagination; inventiveness. **3** the act of inventing.

**inventive** *adj* showing original thought or ingenuity; creative. ➤ **inventively** *adv.*

**inventory** *n* (*pl* **-ies**) **1** an itemized list, e.g. of the contents of a building or stock in a warehouse. **2** *NAmer* the quantity of goods in stock.

**inverse**[1] *adj* opposite in order, direction, nature, or effect. ➤ **inversely** *adv.*

**inverse**[2] *n* **1** a direct opposite. **2** in mathematics: a reciprocal quantity. ➤ **inversion** *n.*

**invert** *v* **1** to turn inside out or upside down. **2** to reverse the position, order, or relationship of.

**invertebrate** *n* an animal without spinal column, such as an insect, mollusc or worm.

**inverted comma** *n* = QUOTATION MARK.

**invest**[1] *v* **1** (*often* + in) to commit money to a particular use in order to earn a financial return. **2** (*often* + in) to devote (e.g. time or effort) to something for future advantages. **3** *informal* (+ in) to buy (*esp* something expensive). ➤ **investor** *n.*

**invest**[2] *v* **1** (+ in/with) to confer authority, office, or rank on. **2** (+ with) to endow with something.

**investigate** *v* **1** to make a systematic examination or study of. **2** to conduct an official enquiry into. ➤ **investigation** *n,* **investigative** *adj,* **investigator** *n.*

**investiture** *n* a formal ceremony conferring an office or honour on somebody.

**investment** *n* **1** a sum of money invested for income or profit. **2** an asset, e.g. property, purchased for its future usefulness or profitability. **3** the act of investing.

**inveterate** *adj* **1** firmly and persistently established. **2** confirmed in a habit; habitual.

**invidious** *adj* tending to cause discontent, ill will, or envy.

**invigilate** *v* *Brit* to supervise candidates at an examination. ➤ **invigilation** *n,* **invigilator** *n.*

**invigorate** *v* to give life and energy to. ➤ **invigorating** *adj.*

**invincible** *adj* incapable of being defeated or overcome. ➤ **invincibility** *n.*

**inviolable** *adj* that must not be violated or degraded.

**inviolate** *adj* not violated or profaned.

**invisible** *adj* **1** incapable of being seen, either by nature or because of concealment. **2** not included in statistics, financial statements, etc: *invisible earnings.* ➤ **invisibility** *n,* **invisibly** *adv.*

**invitation** *n* **1** the act of inviting. **2** a request to be present or participate. **3** something that induces somebody to behave in a particular way.

**invite**[1] *v* **1** to request (somebody) to be present at or take part in something. **2** to ask, *esp* formally, for (e.g. tenders, comments). **3** to increase the likelihood of.

**invite**[2] *n informal* an invitation.

**inviting** *adj* attractive or tempting. ➤ **invitingly** *adv.*

**in vitro** *adv and adj* outside the living body and in an artificial environment such as a test tube.

**invocation** *n* **1** the act of invoking. **2** a prayer asking a deity or spirit for help or support.

**invoice**[1] *n* a list of goods or services provided, together with a note of the sum owed.

**invoice**[2] *v* to submit an invoice to or for.

**invoke** *v* **1** to appeal to (an authority) for help, a judgment, etc. **2** to call forth (e.g. a spirit) by uttering a spell or magical formula. **3** to make an earnest request for.

**involuntary** *adj* **1** not subject to conscious control; reflex. **2** done against one's will. ➤ **involuntarily** *adv.*

**involve** *v* **1** to cause to be associated or take part. **2** to absorb (oneself) mentally or to commit (oneself) emotionally. **3** to require as a necessary accompaniment. ➤ **involvement** *n.*

**involved** *adj* **1** needlessly complex. **2** taking part. **3** connected with something, *esp* emotionally.

**invulnerable** *adj* incapable of being injured or harmed. ➤ **invulnerability** *n.*

**inwards** (*NAmer* **inward**) *adv* **1** towards the interior. **2** towards the mind or spirit.

**iodine** *n* **1** a blackish grey non-metallic chemical element. **2** a solution of iodine in alcohol, used as an antiseptic.

**ion** *n* an atom or group of atoms that carries a positive or negative electric charge through having lost or gained electrons.

**ionize** *or* **-ise** *v* to convert into ions. ➤ **ionization** *n.*

**ionizer** *n* a machine that emits ions into the air to improve air quality.

**ionosphere** *n* an upper layer of the earth's atmosphere extending from an altitude of about 60km to at least 480km.

**iota** *n* **1** the ninth letter of the Greek alphabet (Ι, ι). **2** an infinitesimal amount; a bit.

**IOU** *n* a written acknowledgment of a debt.

**ipso facto** *adv* by that very fact, or by the very nature of the case.

**IQ** *abbr* intelligence quotient.

**Ir** *abbr* the chemical symbol for iridium.

**IRA** *abbr* Irish Republican Army.

**irascible** *adj* easily provoked to anger; irritable.

**irate** *adj* extremely angry.

**ire** *n literary* anger.

**iridescent** *adj* displaying a shimmering shift of colours. ➤ **iridescence** *n.*

**iris** *n* **1** (*pl* **irises** *or* **irides**) the round coloured portion of the eye with the pupil in the centre. **2** (*pl* **irises** *or* **iris**) a plant with long straight leaves and large showy flowers.

**Irish**[1] *adj* of Ireland, its people, or the Irish language.

**Irish**[2] *n* **1** (**the Irish**) the people of Ireland. **2** (*also* **Irish Gaelic**) the Celtic language of the people of Ireland.

**irk** *v* to irritate or annoy.

**irksome** *adj* troublesome or annoying.

**iron**[1] *n* **1** a silver-white magnetic metal that is heavy and malleable, readily rusts in moist air. **2** a metal implement with a smooth flat heated base, used to smooth or press clothing. **3** (*usu in pl*) a device, *esp* fetters, used to bind or restrain. **4** a golf club with metal heads. **5** a tool, implement, or device made of iron.

**iron**[2] *adj* **1** made of iron. **2** resembling iron, e.g. in strength or durability.

**iron**[3] *v* to smooth (e.g. a garment) with a heated iron.

**Iron Age** *n* (**the Iron Age**) the period of human culture, dating from before 1000 BC, characterized by the widespread use of iron for making tools and weapons.

**Iron Curtain** *n* (**the Iron Curtain**) the political and ideological barrier formerly separating the Communist and non-Communist countries of Europe.

**ironic** *adj* **1** containing or constituting irony. **2** tending to use irony. ➤ **ironically** *adv.*

**ironmonger** *n Brit* a dealer in hardware. ➤ **ironmongery** *n.*

**ironwork** *n* **1** articles made of iron. **2** (*in pl*) a place where iron or steel is smelted or iron or steel products are made.

**irony** /ˈierəni/ *n* (*pl* **-ies**) **1** the *esp* humorous use of words to express a meaning opposite to their literal meaning. **2** incongruity between actual and the expected results of a particular event or course of action.

**irradiate** *v* **1** to expose (food) to radiation in order to kill bacteria and prolong its shelf life. **2** to cast rays of light on. ➤ **irradiation** *n.*

**irrational** *adj* not governed by or according to reason; illogical. ➤ **irrationality** *n,* **irrationally** *adv.*

**irreconcilable** *adj* **1** impossible to reconcile. **2** incompatible. ➤ **irreconcilably** *adv.*

**irrecoverable** *adj* not capable of being recovered or put right.

**irredeemable** *adj* too bad to be saved or improved. ➤ **irredeemably** *adv.*

**irreducible** *adj* impossible to reduce, *esp* to a simpler state.

**irrefutable** *adj* not able to be denied or disproved.
**irregular** *adj* **1** lacking continuity or occurring unpredictably. **2** lacking symmetry or evenness. **3** contrary to rules, customs, or moral principles. **4** of a word: not inflected in the normal manner. **5** of troops: not belonging to the regular army organization. ➤ **irregularity** *n.*
**irrelevant** *adj* not relevant; inapplicable. ➤ **irrelevance** *n,* **irrelevantly** *adv.*
**irreligious** *adj* hostile to or disrespectful of religion.
**irremediable** *adj* impossible to remedy; incurable.
**irreparable** *adj* not able to be repaired or set to rights. ➤ **irreparably** *adv.*
**irreplaceable** *adj* having no adequate substitute.
**irrepressible** *adj* impossible to restrain or control.
**irreproachable** *adj* beyond criticism or blame.
**irresistible** *adj* too attractive or powerful to resist. ➤ **irresistibly** *adv.*
**irresolute** *adj* lacking decisiveness or a firm purpose.
**irrespective** *adv* ✱ **irrespective of** without regard to.
**irresponsible** *adj* showing no regard for the consequences of one's actions. ➤ **irresponsibly** *adv.*
**irretrievable** *adj* not retrievable or recoverable. ➤ **irretrievably** *adv.*
**irreverence** *n* lack of respect. ➤ **irreverent** *adj,* **irreverently** *adv.*
**irreversible** *adj* unable to be changed back into a previous state. ➤ **irreversibly** *adv.*
**irrevocable** *adj* incapable of being revoked or altered. ➤ **irrevocably** *adv.*
**irrigate** *v* **1** to supply (land) with water by means of channels. **2** to flush (e.g. an eye or wound) with a stream of liquid. ➤ **irrigation** *n.*
**irritable** *adj* **1** easily angered or exasperated. **2** abnormally sensitive to stimuli. ➤ **irritability** *n,* **irritably** *adv.*
**irritant** *n* something that irritates.
**irritate** *v* **1** to make impatient or angry. **2** to cause (a part of the body) to become sore or inflamed. ➤ **irritating** *adj,* **irritatingly** *n.*
**is** *v* third person sing. present tense of BE.
**ISA** /ˈiesə/ *n* an individual savings account, a tax-free savings scheme.
**-ise** *suffix* see -IZE.
**-ish** *suffix* **1** denoting a particular quality: *childish.* **2** denoting nationality: *Finnish.* **3** slightly; somewhat: *biggish.* **4** approximately: *fortyish.*
**Islam** *n* **1** the religious faith of Muslims including belief in Allah as the sole deity and in Muhammad as his prophet. **2** the civilization based on Islam. ➤ **Islamic** *adj.*
**island** *n* **1** an area of land surrounded by water. **2** something that is isolated or surrounded. ➤ **islander** *n.*
**isle** *n* an island.
**islet** *n* a little island.
**-ism** *suffix* **1** denoting an act or practice: *cannibalism.* **2** denoting a state or a pathological condition: *magnetism; alcoholism.* **3** denoting a doctrine or cult: *Buddhism.* **4** denoting prejudice: *sexism.*
**isn't** *contraction* is not.
**isobar** *n* a line on a chart connecting places where the atmospheric pressure is the same.
**isolate** *v* **1** to set apart from others. **2** to separate out (a substance) in its pure form. ➤ **isolation** *n.*
**isolated** *adj* **1** cut off from others; remote; lonely. **2** single or exceptional.
**isolationism** *n* a policy of refraining from engaging in international relations. ➤ **isolationist** *n and adj.*
**isomer** *n* a chemical compound with the same chemical formula as another but a different arrangement of atoms.
**isometric** *adj* having equal dimensions or measurements.
**isosceles** /ieˈsosəleez/ *adj* of a triangle: having two equal sides.
**isotope** *n* any of two or more forms of a chemical element that have the same atomic number but differ in atomic mass and physical properties.
**Israeli** *n* (*pl* **Israelis**) a native or inhabitant of modern Israel. ➤ **Israeli** *adj.*
**Israelite** *n* a native or inhabitant of the ancient kingdom of Israel.
**issue**[1] *n* **1** a matter or topic, *esp* one that is in dispute. **2** any of a series of e.g. magazines regularly published under the same title. **3** the act of issuing something. ✱ **at issue** under discussion or in dispute. **take issue with** to disagree or argue with.
**issue**[2] *v* **1** to send (e.g. a newspaper) out for sale or circulation. **2** to give (e.g. a statement) out officially. **3** to go, come, or flow out.
**isthmus** *n* a narrow strip of land connecting two larger land areas.
**IT** *abbr* information technology.
**it** *pron* **1** that thing, animal, etc. **2** used as subject of an impersonal verb: *It's raining.* **3** used to refer to a state of affairs: *How's it going?* **4** the important or appropriate thing.
**Italian** *n* **1** a native or inhabitant of Italy. **2** the language of Italy. ➤ **Italian** *adj.*
**italic**[1] *n* a printed character that slants upwards to the right, like the labels *n, adj,* etc in this dictionary.
**italic**[2] *adj* of a printed character: in italic.

**itch**[1] *n* **1** an irritating sensation in the skin that makes one want to scratch. **2** *informal* a restless desire.
**itch**[2] *v* **1** to have or produce an itch. **2** *informal* to have a restless desire to do something.
**it'd** *contraction* **1** it had. **2** it would.
**item** *n* **1** a separate piece of news or information. **2** a separate article or unit in a series. **3** (**an item**) *informal* two people in a romantic relationship.
**itemize** *or* **-ise** *v* to set down in a list of individual elements.
**itinerant**[1] *adj* travelling from place to place.
**itinerant**[2] *n* somebody who moves from place to place.
**itinerary** *n* (*pl* **-ies**) the proposed route of a journey, usu including a list of stops on the way.
**it'll** *contraction* **1** it will. **2** it shall.
**its** *adj* belonging to or associated with a thing, animal, etc already mentioned.

***Usage Note:*** Do not confuse *its*, the possessive form of *it* with no apostrophe, and *it's*, a shortened form of *it is* or *it has*.

**it's** *contraction* **1** it is. **2** it has.
**itself** *pron* used reflexively or for emphasis to refer to a thing, animal, etc that is the subject of the clause.
**ITV** *abbr* Independent Television.
**IUD** *abbr* intrauterine device.
**I've** *contraction* I have.
**IVF** *abbr* in vitro fertilization.
**ivory** *n* (*pl* **-ies**) **1** the hard creamy-white substance of which the tusks of elephants are made. **2** a creamy white colour. **3** (**the ivories**) *informal* the keys of a piano.
**ivory tower** *n* a place or situation remote from everyday life or practical concerns.
**ivy** *n* a common climbing plant with evergreen leaves.
**-ize** *or* **-ise** *suffix* **1** to become or become like: *liquidize; Americanize.* **2** to subject to: *criticize.*

***Usage Note:*** Either spelling is correct, in British English, for most verbs: *criticize* or *criticise*; *organize* or *organise*; *privatise* or *privatize*. There are, however, a number of verbs which must end in *-ise*, e.g. *advertise, advise, chastise, comprise, compromise, despise, devise, enfranchise, excise, exercise, franchise, improvise, merchandise, revise, supervise, surmise, surprise*, and *televise*.

**J** *or* **j** *n* (*pl* **J's** *or* **Js** *or* **j's**) the tenth letter of the English alphabet.

**jab**[1] *v* (**jabbed, jabbing**) **1** to pierce or poke sharply. **2** to strike with a short straight blow.

**jab**[2] *n* **1** an act of jabbing. **2** *informal* an injection.

**jabber** *v* to talk rapidly and unintelligibly.

**jack**[1] *n* **1** a mechanism for lifting a vehicle on one side, e.g. to replace a tyre. **2** a playing card ranking below the queen. **3** an electrical connection. **4** a small target ball in the game of bowls. **5** a small national flag flown at the bow of a ship.

**jack**[2] *v* **1** (*usu* + up) to move or lift with a jack. **2** (+ up) to raise the level or quality of.

**jackal** *n* a wild dog that scavenges or hunts in packs.

**jackass** *n* **1** a male ass. **2** a stupid person.

**jackdaw** *n* a black and grey bird related to the crow.

**jacket**[1] *n* **1** an outer garment for the upper body opening down the front. **2** a protective or insulating covering. **3** the skin of a baked potato.

**jacket**[2] *v* (**jacketed, jacketing**) to enclose in a jacket.

**jacket potato** *n* (*pl* **-oes**) *Brit* a potato baked and served in its skin.

**jack-in-the-box** *n* a toy consisting of a small box out of which a figure springs when the lid is raised.

**jackknife**[1] *n* (*pl* **jackknives**) **1** a large pocket knife with a folding blade. **2** a dive in which the body is bent from the waist and then straightened before hitting the water.

**jackknife**[2] *v* **1** to double up like a jackknife. **2** to cause to jackknife. **3** of an articulated lorry: to form a V-shape in an uncontrolled skid.

**jack plug** *n* a single-pronged electrical plug.

**jackpot** *n* the largest prize in a lottery or on a fruit machine.

**Jacobean** *adj* of the reign of James I of England (1603–25).

**Jacobite** *n* a supporter of James II of England or of the Stuarts after 1688.

**jacquard** *n* **1** an apparatus for a loom holding punched cards that enable decorated and patterned fabrics to be woven. **2** a fabric made with this.

**Jacuzzi** /jə'koohzi/ *n trademark* a large bath with underwater jets that massage the body.

**jade** *n* a hard green mineral used as a stone.

**jaded** *adj* weary or bored by a surfeit of something.

**jagged** *adj* having a sharply indented or uneven edge or surface.

**jaguar** *n* a large wild cat having a brownish yellow coat with black spots.

**jail**[1] (*Brit* **gaol**) *or* **gaol** *n* a place where people are confined when accused or convicted of a crime.

**jail**[2] (*Brit* **gaol**) *or* **gaol** *v* to confine in a jail.

**jalopy** *n* (*pl* **-ies**) *informal* a dilapidated old car.

**jam**[1] *v* (**jammed, jamming**) **1** to squeeze or pack closely or tightly into a space. **2** to fill or overfill. **3** to fill (a street) so that passage along it is blocked. **4** to cause to become stuck so that it does not work or move. **5** to send out interfering signals to suppress (a radio signal). **6** (+ on) to apply (brakes) suddenly. **7** *informal* to take part in an improvised jazz session.

**jam**[2] *n* **1** a crowd or mass that impedes or blocks something. **2** the pressure or congestion of a crowd. **3** an instance of jamming. **4** *informal* a difficult or awkward situation. **5** an improvised jazz session.

**jam**[3] *n* a preserve made by boiling fruit and sugar.

**jamb** *n* a straight vertical post forming the side of a door or window opening.

**jamboree** *n* a large festive party or gathering.

**jammy** *adj* (**-ier, -iest**) **1** covered or filled with jam. **2** *Brit, informal* lucky.

**jam-packed** *adj* full to overflowing.

**jangle** *v* **1** to make or cause to make a harsh ringing noise. **2** of the nerves: to be tense. ➤ **jangly** *adj.*

**janitor** *n* a caretaker of a large building.

**January** *n* the first month of the year.

**Japanese** *n* (*pl* **Japanese**) **1** a native or inhabitant of Japan. **2** the language of Japan. ➤ **Japanese** *adj.*

**jape** *n* a jest or joke.

**jar**[1] *n* a cylindrical container made of glass.

**jar**[2] *v* (**jarred, jarring**) **1** to give (something or somebody) a shock or jolt. **2** to have a disagreeable or incongruous effect. **3** to make a harsh or discordant noise. **4** to jolt or vibrate.

**jar**[3] *n* **1** a sudden or unexpected jolt or shake. **2** an unsettling shock.

**jargon** *n* the terminology or idiom of a particular activity or group. ➤ **jargonistic** *adj.*
**jasmine** *n* a shrub or climbing plant with fragrant yellow or white flowers.
**jasper** *n* an opaque reddish brown quartz used as a gemstone.
**jaundice** *n* **1** an abnormal condition marked by yellowing of the skin. **2** a state of bitterness or resentment. ➤ **jaundiced** *adj.*
**jaunt** *n* a short journey for pleasure.
**jaunty** *adj* (**-ier, -iest**) having or showing lively self-confidence. ➤ **jauntily** *adv.*
**javelin** *n* a light spear thrown in an athletic field event or as a weapon.
**jaw**[1] *n* **1** each of two bony structures that form a framework above and below the mouth and in which the teeth are set. **2** (*in pl*) the two parts of a tool or machine that grips or crushes. **3** *informal* a long chat.
**jaw**[2] *v informal* to talk for a long time.
**jawbone** *n* the lower bone of a jaw.
**jay** *n* a bird of the crow family with strongly patterned plumage.
**jaywalk** *v* to cross a street carelessly without regard for traffic. ➤ **jaywalker** *n.*
**jazz** *n* music developed from ragtime and blues and characterized by syncopated rhythms and improvisation.
**jazz up** *v informal* to make more lively or interesting.
**jazzy** *adj* (**-ier, -iest**) **1** having the characteristics of jazz. **2** *informal* bright or showy. ➤ **jazzily** *adv.*
**jealous** *adj* **1** resentful and envious of an advantage enjoyed by somebody else. **2** apprehensive and suspicious of romantic or sexual rivalry. **3** vigilant in guarding a possession or right. ➤ **jealously** *adv,* **jealousy** *n.*
**jeans** *pl n* casual trousers made of denim.
**jeep** *n trademark* a small rugged motor vehicle with four-wheel drive.
**jeer**[1] *v* to speak or laugh mockingly or rudely.
**jeer**[2] *n* a jeering remark or taunt.
**Jehovah** *n* a Hebrew name for God.
**jejune** *adj* **1** lacking maturity; puerile. **2** lacking interest or significance.
**jell** *v chiefly NAmer* see GEL[2].
**jelly** *n* (*pl* **-ies**) **1** a soft fruit-flavoured transparent dessert set with gelatin. **2** a substance resembling jelly in consistency. ➤ **jellied** *adj.*
**jelly baby** *n* (*pl* **-ies**) a soft sweet made of gelatin in the shape of a baby.
**jellyfish** *n* (*pl* **jellyfishes** *or* **jellyfish**) a sea animal with a soft nearly transparent saucer-shaped body and stinging tentacles.
**jemmy**[1] *n* (*pl* **-ies**) a short crowbar.
**jemmy**[2] (*NAmer* **jimmy**) *v* (**-ies, -ied**) to force open with a jemmy.
**je ne sais quoi** /ˌzhə nə say 'kwah/ *n* a quality that cannot be readily described or expressed.
**jenny** *n* (*pl* **-ies**) a female donkey or ass.
**jeopardize** *or* **-ise** *v* to put in danger.
**jeopardy** *n* risk of death, loss, or harm.
**jerboa** *n* a desert rodent with long back legs adapted for jumping.
**jerk**[1] *v* to move with a short sudden movement.
**jerk**[2] *n* **1** a short sudden movement. **2** *chiefly NAmer, informal* a foolish or irritating person.
**jerkin** *n* a close-fitting sleeveless jacket.
**jerky** *adj* (**-ier, -iest**) marked by irregular or spasmodic movements. ➤ **jerkily** *adv.*
**jerry-built** *adj* built cheaply and flimsily.
**jerry can** *or* **jerrican** *n* a narrow flat-sided container for liquids.
**jersey** *n* **1** a knitted garment with sleeves. **2** a shirt worn by a footballer or other sports player. **3** a knitted fabric used for clothing. **4** (**Jersey**) a breed of cattle noted for rich milk.
**Jerusalem artichoke** *n* the edible sweet-tasting tubers of a sunflower.
**jest**[1] *n* a joke.
**jest**[2] *v* to make a joke or witty remark.
**jester** *n* a clown formerly employed in royal or noble households.
**Jesuit** /'jezyoo·it/ *n* a member of the Society of Jesus, a Roman Catholic order.
**jet**[1] *n* **1** a stream of liquid or gas forced out under pressure from a narrow opening or nozzle. **2** an aircraft powered by jet engines.
**jet**[2] *v* (**jetted, jetting**) **1** to spurt out. **2** to travel by jet aircraft.
**jet**[3] *n* **1** a hard black polished mineral used for jewellery. **2** (**jet black**) an intense black colour.
**jet engine** *n* an aircraft engine that produces motion by discharging hot gases produced by burning fuel.
**jet lag** *n* a temporary disruption of normal bodily rhythms after a long flight from one time zone to another. ➤ **jet-lagged** *adj.*
**jetsam** *n* goods thrown overboard from a ship and washed up on shore.
**jet set** *n* wealthy people who frequently travel by air. ➤ **jetsetter** *n.*
**jet-ski** *n* a small motorized vehicle ridden over water for sport.
**jettison** *v* **1** to discard or abandon. **2** to throw (goods) overboard to lighten the load of a ship or aircraft.
**jetty** *n* (*pl* **-ies**) a small landing pier for boats.
**Jew** *n* **1** a member of a Semitic people living in ancient Israel, or a modern descendant of this people. **2** a person whose religion is Judaism.
**jewel** *n* **1** a precious stone. **2** a piece of jewellery. **3** a highly valued person or thing. ➤ **jewelled** *adj.*
**jeweller** (*NAmer* **jeweler**) *n* a person who makes or deals in jewellery.
**jewellery** (*NAmer* **jewelry**) *n* personal ornaments such as rings and necklaces.
**Jewish** *adj* relating to Jews or Judaism.
**Jewry** *n* the Jewish people collectively.

**Jew's harp** *n* a small lyre-shaped instrument placed between the teeth and sounded by striking a metal tongue with the finger.
**Jezebel** *n* a shameless or immoral woman.
**jib**[1] *n* **1** a triangular sail at the front of a ship. **2** the projecting arm of a crane.
**jib**[2] *v* (**jibbed, jibbing**) of a horse: to refuse to go on. * **jib at** to take fright or balk at.
**jibe**[1] *or* **gibe** *v* to make jibes.
**jibe**[2] *or* **gibe** *n* a taunting or insulting remark.
**jiffy** *or* **jiff** *n informal* a moment or instant.
**jig**[1] *n* **1** a lively springy dance in triple time. **2** a device used to hold a piece of work in position and guide the tools working on it.
**jig**[2] *v* (**jigged, jigging**) **1** to dance a jig. **2** to move up and down in a rapid and jerky fashion.
**jiggle** *v informal* to move or cause to move with quick short jerks. ➤ **jiggle** *n,* **jiggly** *adj.*
**jigsaw** *n* **1** a puzzle consisting of small irregularly cut pieces of wood or card that are fitted together to form a picture. **2** a power-driven fretsaw.
**jihad** /ji'had/ *n* a holy war waged by Muslims against their enemies.
**jilt** *v* to break off a romantic relationship with (somebody) suddenly.
**jingle**[1] *v* to make or cause to make a light clinking or tinkling sound.
**jingle**[2] *n* **1** a light clinking or tinkling sound. **2** a short catchy song or tune. ➤ **jingly** *adj.*
**jingoism** *n* excessive patriotism; chauvinism. ➤ **jingoistic** *adj.*
**jink**[1] *n* a quick turn or sidestep while running.
**jink**[2] *v* to move quickly with sudden turns and shifts.
**jinx**[1] *n informal* somebody or something that brings bad luck.
**jinx**[2] *v* to bring bad luck to.
**jitterbug** *n* a lively swinging dance popular in the 1940s.
**jitters** *pl n* a feeling of extreme agitation. ➤ **jittery** *adj.*
**jive**[1] *n* a style of lively dancing popular in the 1940s and 1950s, performed to swing music and rock and roll.
**jive**[2] *v* to dance the jive.
**job**[1] *n* **1** a regular paid position of employment. **2** a piece of work. **3** a task. **4** a specific duty or function. **5** *informal* a crime. * **just the job** exactly what is needed. ➤ **jobless** *adj.*
**job**[2] *v* (**jobbed, jobbing**) to do occasional work. ➤ **jobber** *n.*
**jobcentre** *n* a government office where unemployed people can get information about jobs.
**job lot** *n* a miscellaneous collection of goods sold as one item.
**job share** *n* an arrangement by which two or more part-time employees share a single full-time job.
**jockey**[1] *n* (*pl* **-eys**) a professional rider in a horse race.
**jockey**[2] *v* (**-eys, -eyed**) to act deftly or deviously to get an advantage.
**jockstrap** *n* a support for a man's genitals.
**jocose** *adj formal* playfully humorous. ➤ **jocosity** *n.*
**jocular** *adj* jolly or joking. ➤ **jocularity** *n,* **jocularly** *adv.*
**jocund** *adj literary* cheerful and good-humoured.
**jodhpurs** *pl n* riding trousers made close-fitting below the knee.
**jog**[1] *v* (**jogged, jogging**) **1** to shake or push gently. **2** to prompt (the memory). **3** to run at a slow steady pace. **4** of a horse: to move at a slow trot. **5** (+ along) to progress slowly.
**jog**[2] *n* **1** a gentle shake or push. **2** a period of steady running. **3** a jogging pace.
**joggle** *v informal* to move or shake slightly.
**joie de vivre** /,zhwah də 'veevrə/ *n* keen enjoyment of life.
**join**[1] *v* **1** to put (two or more things) together to form a unit, or to come together in this way. **2** to connect, meet, or merge with. **3** to enter into the company of. **4** (*usu* + in) to associate oneself with (another or others) in an activity. **5** to become a member or employee of (a club, organization, etc). * **join forces** to form an alliance or combine efforts.
**join**[2] *n* a place where two parts are joined.
**joiner** *n* somebody who constructs or repairs wooden furniture or structures.
**joinery** *n* **1** the craft of a joiner. **2** woodwork done or made by a joiner.
**joint**[1] *n* **1** a place where two parts are joined. **2** a point of contact between two or more bones of the body. **3** a large piece of meat for roasting. **4** a point on a plant stem where a leaf or branch emerges. **5** *informal* a place of entertainment, café, etc. **6** *slang* a cannabis cigarette.
**joint**[2] *adj* **1** united or combined. **2** shared by or affecting two or more people. **3** sharing with another. ➤ **jointly** *adv.*
**joint**[3] *v* **1** to provide with a joint or joints. **2** to cut (meat) into joints.
**join up** *v* **1** to enlist in the armed forces. **2** to come together.
**joist** *n* a timber or beam that helps to support a floor or ceiling.
**jojoba** /hə'hohbə/ *n* a North American shrub with edible seeds that yield an oil used in cosmetics.
**joke**[1] *n* **1** a brief story told to provoke laughter. **2** a trick played on somebody for fun. **3** something or somebody that is ridiculously unsuitable or inadequate. ➤ **jokey** *adj,* **joky** *adj.*
**joke**[2] *v* to make jokes.
**joker** *n* **1** somebody who likes joking. **2** a playing card with a picture of a jester, used as a wild card. **3** *informal* a foolish or incompetent person.
**jollification** *n* merrymaking or a celebration.

**jollity** *n* the quality or state of being jolly; merriment.

**jolly**[1] *adj* (**-ier, -iest**) **1** cheerful and good-humoured. **2** lively and amusing. ➤ **jolliness** *n.*

**jolly**[2] *adv informal* very.

**jolly**[3] *v* (**-ies, -ied**) (+ along) to encourage (somebody) cheerfully.

**jolt**[1] *v* **1** to move with a jerky motion. **2** to give a sudden knock to. **3** to disconcert (somebody) abruptly.

**jolt**[2] *n* **1** an act of jolting. **2** a surprise or shock.

**josh** *v* to tease or make fun of.

**joss stick** *n* a thin stick of incense for burning.

**jostle** *v* **1** to push and shove roughly. **2** to vie with other people.

**jot**[1] *n* the least bit.

**jot**[2] *v* (**jotted, jotting**) (*usu* + down) to write briefly or hurriedly.

**jotter** *n* a small notebook or pad.

**joule** *n* the SI unit of work or energy.

**journal** *n* **1** a periodical dealing with a particular subject. **2** a daily record or diary.

**journalese** *n* a style of writing characteristic of newspapers.

**journalism** *n* the work of newspapers and journalists.

**journalist** *n* a person who writes about news and current affairs for a newspaper or broadcasting outlet. ➤ **journalistic** *adj.*

**journey**[1] *n* (*pl* **-eys**) **1** an act of travelling from one place to another. **2** the distance or time involved in travelling.

**journey**[2] *v* (**-eys, -eyed**) to travel.

**journeyman** *n* (*pl* **journeymen**) a reliable but not exceptional worker or performer.

**joust**[1] *n* a medieval combat on horseback between knights armed with lances.

**joust**[2] *v* **1** to fight in a joust or tournament. **2** (*often* + with) to engage in a contest or argument.

**jovial** *adj* good-humoured and cheerful. ➤ **joviality** *n,* **jovially** *adj.*

**jowl** *n* the lower jaw or cheek.

**joy** *n* **1** a feeling of great happiness or pleasure. **2** a cause of delight. **3** *Brit, informal* success or satisfaction. ➤ **joyless** *adj.*

**joyful** *adj* causing or feeling joy. ➤ **joyfully** *adv.*

**joyous** *adj literary* joyful. ➤ **joyously** *adv.*

**joyride** *n* a reckless ride in a stolen car. ➤ **joyrider** *n,* **joyriding** *n.*

**joystick** *n* **1** a lever used to control an aircraft. **2** a lever for controlling the position of an image on a computer screen.

**JP** *abbr* Justice of the Peace.

**jubilant** *adj* filled with or expressing great joy or triumph. ➤ **jubilantly** *adv.*

**jubilation** *n* great joy and satisfaction; rejoicing.

**jubilee** *n* a special anniversary of a major event such as a sovereign's accession.

**Judaism** *n* **1** the religious faith developed among the ancient Jews and characterized by belief in one God. **2** the cultural and social practices of the Jews. ➤ **Judaic** *adj.*

**Judas** *n* somebody who betrays a friend.

**judder**[1] *v chiefly Brit* to vibrate jerkily.

**judder**[2] *n* a sharp vibrating movement.

**judge**[1] *v* **1** to form or express an opinion about. **2** to give a legal verdict on. **3** to decide the result of (a competition).

**judge**[2] *n* **1** a public official who decides cases in a law court. **2** somebody appointed to decide the winner of a competition or contest. **3** somebody who is qualified to give an opinion.

**judgment** *or* **judgement** *n* **1** the capacity for forming good opinions or making wise decisions. **2** an opinion or evaluation. **3** a formal decision by a court or judge.

**judgmental** *or* **judgemental** *adj* **1** given to making moral judgments about other people. **2** relating to the use of judgment.

**Judgment Day** *n* in some beliefs, the day of judgment at the end of the world.

**judicature** *n* **1** the administration of justice. **2** judges collectively.

**judicial** *adj* relating to justice or a court of law. ➤ **judicially** *adv.*

**judiciary** *n* (*pl* **-ies**) judges collectively. ➤ **judiciary** *adj.*

**judicious** *adj* having or characterized by sound judgment. ➤ **judiciously** *adv.*

**judo** *n* a martial art using quick movement and leverage to throw an opponent.

**jug** *n* a rounded container with a handle and a lip, for holding and pouring liquids. ➤ **jugful** *n.*

**juggernaut** *n* **1** *chiefly Brit* a very large articulated transport vehicle. **2** an inexorable force or influence.

**juggle**[1] *v* **1** to keep several objects in motion in the air at the same time by alternately tossing and catching them. **2** to deal with (several activities) at the same time. **3** to manipulate (facts or figures). ➤ **juggler** *n.*

**juggle**[2] *n* an act of juggling.

**jugular** *adj* relating to the throat or neck.

**juice**[1] *n* **1** the liquid contained in a fruit or vegetable. **2** a drink made from fruit or vegetable juice. **3** (*in pl*) the natural fluids of an animal body. **4** *informal* an electric current.

**juice**[2] *v* to extract the juice from.

**juicy** *adj* (**-ier, -iest**) **1** succulent; full of juice. **2** *informal* titillatingly or scandalously interesting. **3** *informal* financially profitable.

**ju-jitsu** *or* **jiu-jitsu** /jooh'jitsooh/ *n* a Japanese martial art.

**jukebox** *n* a coin-operated machine that plays pop music.

**julep** *n* a drink made from a spirit and sugar poured over crushed ice.

**July** *n* the seventh month of the year.

**jumble**[1] *v* (*often* + up) to mix up in a confused manner.

**jumble**[2] *n* **1** a confused mass of things mingled together. **2** *Brit* articles for a jumble sale.

**jumble sale** *n Brit* a sale of secondhand articles to raise money for charity.

**jumbo** *n* (*pl* **-os**) **1** a very large example of its kind. **2** a jumbo jet. ➤ **jumbo** *adj.*

**jumbo jet** *n* a large jet passenger aircraft.

**jump**[1] *v* **1** to spring into the air using the feet and legs. **2** to pass over (an obstacle) by jumping. **3** to move quickly or energetically. **4** to move suddenly from shock or surprise. **5** to pass rapidly or abruptly from one point or state to another. **6** to undergo a sudden sharp increase. **7** (+ on) to make a sudden verbal or physical attack. **8** (**be jumping**) to bustle with activity. **9** to fail to stop at (a traffic light). * **jump at** to accept eagerly. **jump ship** of a sailor: to leave a ship without authority. **jump the queue** to move in front of others in a queue. **jump to it 1** to make an enthusiastic start. **2** to hurry.

**jump**[2] *n* **1** an act of jumping; a leap. **2** an obstacle to be jumped over. **3** a sudden involuntary movement. **4** a descent by parachute from an aircraft. **5** a sudden sharp increase.

**jumped-up** *adj derog* arrogantly displaying a rise in wealth or status.

**jumper** *n* **1** *Brit* a knitted garment worn on the upper body. **2** *NAmer* a pinafore dress.

**jump-jet** *n chiefly Brit* a jet aircraft able to take off and land vertically.

**jump leads** *pl n* a pair of thick cables used to start a vehicle's engine from another battery.

**jump-off** *n* an extra deciding round of a showjumping competition.

**jump seat** *n* a small folding seat in a vehicle or aircraft.

**jump-start** *v* to start (a motor vehicle) with jump leads. ➤ **jump start** *n.*

**jumpsuit** *n* a one-piece garment combining top and trousers.

**jumpy** *adj* (**-ier, -iest**) **1** nervous or jittery. **2** moving irregularly.

**junction** *n* **1** a place where things meet or join. **2** a place where roads or railway lines meet. **3** a point of contact or interface between dissimilar metals or semiconductor regions.

**juncture** *n* **1** a particular or signifcant point of time. **2** an instance or place of joining.

**June** *n* the sixth month of the year.

**jungle** *n* **1** a tropical area overgrown with trees and other vegetation. **2** a confused or complex mass. **3** a place of ruthless struggle for survival. **4** a type of fast electronic dance music.

**junior**[1] *n* **1** a person who is younger than another by a stated amount: *He is three years her junior.* **2** a person holding a lower or subordinate rank. **3** a member of a junior school, sports team, etc.

**junior**[2] *adj* **1** used after a name to distinguish a son with the same name as his father. **2** lower in standing or rank. **3** comprising younger pupils, players, etc. **4** of or for juniors.

**juniper** *n* an evergreen shrub with small purple cones resembling berries.

**junk**[1] *n* useless or discarded articles.

**junk**[2] *v informal* to get rid of (something) as worthless.

**junk**[3] *n* a flat-bottomed sailing ship in the Far East.

**junket** *n* **1** a dish of sweetened milk curdled with rennet. **2** *informal* an extravagant business trip or entertainment.

**junk food** *n* unhealthy processed food.

**junkie** *or* **junky** *n* (*pl* **-ies**) *informal* a drug addict.

**junk mail** *n* unsolicited advertising material received by post.

**junta** *n* (*treated as sing. or pl*) a group controlling a government after a revolution.

**jurisdiction** *n* **1** the power or authority to apply the law. **2** the limits within which authority may be exercised.

**jurisprudence** *n* the study of the law.

**jurist** *n* **1** an expert in law. **2** *NAmer* a lawyer or a judge. ➤ **juristic** *adj.*

**juror** *n* a member of a jury.

**jury** *n* (*pl* **-ies**) **1** a body of people who give a verdict based on evidence heard in court. **2** a committee judging a competition.

**just**[1] *adj* **1** conforming with what is morally upright. **2** being what is merited; appropriate. **3** legally correct. **4** of an opinion: well-founded. ➤ **justly** *adv.*

**just**[2] *adv* **1** exactly or precisely. **2** immediately or soon: *I'm just coming.* **3** by a very small margin. **4** only or simply. **5** *informal* very or completely. * **just about 1** almost. **2** not more than.

**justice** *n* **1** the quality or principle of being just. **2** the just administration of the law. **3** a judge or magistrate. * **do justice to** to appreciate or represent in the best light.

**justice of the peace** *n* a lay magistrate authorized to hear minor cases.

**justifiable** *adj* able to be justified; defensible. ➤ **justifiably** *adv.*

**justify** *v* (**-ies, -ied**) **1** to prove or show to be right or reasonable. **2** to space out (a line of printed text) so that it is flush with a margin. ➤ **justification** *n.*

**jut** *v* (**jutted, jutting**) (*often* + out) to extend beyond a normal line or limit; to project.

**jute** *n* the fibre of an Indian plant used for making rope or sacking.

**juvenile**[1] *adj* **1** relating to or suitable for young people. **2** physiologically immature or undeveloped.

**juvenile**[2] *n* **1** a young person, *esp* one under the age of 18. **2** a young bird or animal.

**juvenile delinquent** *n* a young person who has committed a criminal offence. ➤ **juvenile delinquency** *n.*

**juxtapose** *v* to place side by side. ➤ **juxtaposition** *n.*

**K**[1] *or* **k** *n* (*pl* **K's** *or* **Ks** *or* **k's**) the eleventh letter of the English alphabet.

**K**[2] *abbr informal* thousand.

**K**[3] *abbr* the chemical symbol for potassium.

**kaftan** *or* **caftan** *n* a long loose garment worn by men in Arab countries.

**kaiser** /'kiezə/ *n* a former German or Austrian emperor.

**kale** *or* **kail** *n* a cabbage with curled leaves.

**kaleidoscope** *n* **1** a tube with mirrors inside and pieces of coloured glass that form different patterns as the tube is rotated. **2** a pattern that is continually changing. ➤ **kaleidoscopic** *adj.*

**kamikaze**[1] /kami'kahzi/ *n* in World War II, a Japanese pilot who crashed an aircraft laden with explosives suicidally on a target.

**kamikaze**[2] *adj* reckless or self-destructive.

**kangaroo** *n* (*pl* **kangaroos**) an Australian animal that hops on its long powerful hind legs and has a long thick tail.

**kangaroo court** *n* an unofficial or irregular court in which justice is disregarded or perverted.

**kaolin** *n* a fine white clay used in ceramics and medicine.

**kapok** *n* a mass of silky fibres that surround the seeds of a tropical tree, used as a soft padding.

**kappa** *n* the tenth letter of the Greek alphabet (Κ, κ).

**kaput** *adj informal* broken or useless.

**karaoke** /karə'ohki/ *n* singing against a backing of recorded music from a machine.

**karate** /kə'rahti/ *n* a martial art using the hands and feet.

**karma** *n* in Hinduism and Buddhism, the force generated by a person's actions that is believed to influence their destiny.

**karst** *n* a limestone region with underground streams, caverns, and potholes.

**kart** *n* = GO-KART.

**karting** *n* racing in go-karts.

**kasbah** *or* **casbah** *n* the older Arab section of a North African city, or a market in this.

**kayak** /'kie(y)ak/ *n* a canoe made of a frame covered with a water-resistant covering.

**kazoo** *n* (*pl* **kazoos**) a musical instrument consisting of a tube that produces a humming sound when blown into.

**kebab** *n* **1** cubes of meat, vegetables, etc, grilled on a skewer. **2** = DONER KEBAB.

**kedgeree** *n* a dish of rice, flaked smoked fish, and chopped hard-boiled eggs.

**keel**[1] *n* a structure that runs along the bottom of a ship and improves its stability.

**keel**[2] *v* **1** (*usu* + over) to capsize or turn over. **2** *informal* (+ over) to fall over.

**keelhaul** *v* to drag (somebody) under the keel of a ship as punishment.

**keen**[1] *adj* **1** enthusiastic and eager. **2** of emotion or feeling: intense. **3** of a blade: sharp. **4** intellectually alert. **5** *Brit* of prices: competitively low. ✱ **keen on** attracted to or fond of. ➤ **keenly** *adv,* **keenness** *n.*

**keen**[2] *v* to wail loudly in lamentation for the dead.

**keep**[1] *v* (*past tense and past part.* **kept**) **1** to retain possession or control of. **2** to cause to remain in a specified place or condition. **3** to retain or store for future use. **4** to record (notes, accounts). **5** to defend or guard. **6** to support or provide for. **7** to obey or honour (a law, promise, etc). **8** to delay or detain (somebody). **9** to refrain from revealing (a secret). **10** to continue or persist in doing something. **11** to remain in a specified situation or condition: *keep calm.* **12** *esp* of food: to remain in good condition. ✱ **keep from** to refrain from (doing something). **keep to 1** to stay in or on (a place, path, etc). **2** not to deviate from (a commitment).

**keep**[2] *n* **1** the fortified tower of a castle. **2** food and other essentials of living. ✱ **for keeps** permanently.

**keeper** *n* **1** a protector or custodian. **2** somebody who looks after animals in a zoo. **3** a goalkeeper or wicketkeeper.

**keep fit** *n* physical exercises done for personal fitness.

**keeping** *n* **1** custody or care. **2** conforming or clashing with something implied or specified. ✱ **in keeping with** conforming to or consistent with.

**keepsake** *n* something kept as a memento of the giver.

**keep up** *v* **1** to persist in (an activity). **2** (*often* + with) to maintain an equal pace or rate of progress.

**keg** *n Brit* a small barrel.

**kelim** *n* see KILIM.

**kelp** *n* a large brown seaweed.

**kelvin** *n* an SI unit of temperature.

**ken**[1] *v* (**kenned** *or* **kent, kenning**) *chiefly Scot* to know or recognize.
**ken**[2] *n* range of perception or knowledge.
**kennel** *n* **1** a shelter for a dog. **2** (*also in pl*) an establishment for breeding or boarding dogs.
**kept** *v* past tense and past part. of KEEP[1].
**keratin** *n* a protein that forms the chemical basis of nails, claws, hooves, horns, feathers, and hair.
**kerb** (*NAmer* **curb**) *n* a stone edging to a pavement or path.
**kerb crawling** *n* driving slowly by a pavement looking for a prostitute.
**kerbstone** *n* a block of stone or concrete forming a kerb.
**kerchief** *n* (*pl* **kerchiefs** *or* **kerchieves**) a piece of cloth worn on the head.
**kerfuffle** *n Brit, informal* a fuss or commotion.
**kernel** *n* **1** the inner soft part of a seed, fruit stone, or nut. **2** a whole seed of a cereal. **3** a central or essential part of something.
**kerosene** *or* **kerosine** *n* = PARAFFIN.
**kestrel** *n* a small falcon that hovers in the air against the wind.
**ketch** *n* a small sailing vessel with two masts.
**ketchup** (*NAmer* **catchup**) *n* a sauce made from tomatoes, vinegar, and seasonings.
**kettle** *n* a vessel with a lid, handle, and spout, used for boiling water.
**kettledrum** *n* a large bowl-shaped drum with a covering stretched across it.
**key**[1] *n* **1** a metal instrument used to operate a lock. **2** a device used to wind a clock. **3** a small button on a panel or keyboard. **4** a lever of a musical instrument that is pressed to produce notes. **5** a small switch for opening or closing an electric circuit. **6** a means of gaining or preventing entrance or control. **7** an instrumental or deciding factor. **8** something that gives an explanation or solution. **9** in music, a system of seven notes based on their relationship to the first and lowest note. ➤ **keyed** *adj,* **keyless** *adj.*
**key**[2] *v* **1** (*often* + in) to enter (data) by means of a keyboard or keypad. **2** to roughen (a surface) to receive plaster or paint. **3** to bring into harmony or conformity. ✱ **be keyed into** to appreciate or sympathize with. **be keyed up** to be tense or excited.
**key**[3] *adj* of great importance.
**keyboard**[1] *n* **1** a set of keys on a piano or other musical instrument. **2** (*also in pl*) an electronic musical instrument having keys. **3** a set of keys for operating a computer or typewriter.
**keyboard**[2] *v* to enter (data) by means of a keyboard. ➤ **keyboarder** *n.*
**keyhole** *n* a hole in a lock into which the key is put.
**keyhole surgery** *n* surgery performed through a very small incision.
**keynote** *n* **1** a fundamental or central principle or idea. **2** of a speech: presenting the main theme of a conference. **3** the base note of a musical scale.
**keypad** *n* a small keyboard or set of buttons for operating a portable electronic device.
**keystone** *n* **1** the central locking piece at the top of an arch. **2** something on which associated things depend for support.
**keystroke** *n* a single act of pressing a key on a keyboard.
**kg** *abbr* kilogram.
**khaki** *n* **1** a dull yellowish brown colour. **2** cloth of this colour used for military uniforms.
**khan** /kahn/ *n* a medieval ruler over the Turkish, Tartar, and Mongol peoples.
**kHz** *abbr* kilohertz.
**kibble** *v* to grind (grain) coarsely.
**kibbutz** /ki'boots/ *n* a farm or settlement in Israel run as a cooperative.
**kibosh** *or* **kybosh** ✱ **put the kibosh on** to ruin or put an end to.
**kick**[1] *v* **1** to strike forcefully with the foot. **2** to strike out with the foot or feet. **3** *informal* to free oneself of (a habit). **4** to show opposition; to rebel. **5** of a gun: to recoil when fired. ✱ **kick oneself** to reprove oneself with hindsight. **kick one's heels** to be idle or kept waiting. **kick the bucket** *informal* to die. ➤ **kicker** *n.*
**kick**[2] *n* **1** an act of kicking. **2** a stimulating effect. **3** a pleasurable experience or feeling.
**kickback** *n* **1** a sharp violent reaction. **2** an illicit payment for help or favours given.
**kickboxing** *n* a martial art using gloved hands and the bare feet. ➤ **kickboxer** *n.*
**kick in** *v* to start functioning or taking effect.
**kickoff** *n* the start of a football game.
**kick off** *v* **1** in ball games, to start or resume play with a kickoff. **2** *informal* to begin proceedings.
**kick-start** *v* **1** to start (a motorcycle engine) by kicking down a lever. **2** to take swift action to resume (a process). ➤ **kick-start** *n.*
**kick up** *v informal* to stir up (a row or fuss).
**kid**[1] *n* **1** a young goat or related animal. **2** *informal* a child or young person. ✱ **with kid gloves** with great care.
**kid**[2] *v* (**kidded, kidding**) *informal* **1** to fool or deceive. **2** to tease playfully.
**kidnap** *v* (**kidnapped, kidnapping,** *NAmer* **kidnaped, kidnaping**) to seize and detain (a person) by force. ➤ **kidnap** *n,* **kidnapper** *n.*
**kidney** *n* (*pl* **-eys**) **1** either of a pair of organs that excrete urine. **2** the kidney of an animal eaten as food.
**kidney bean** *n* a dark red kidney-shaped bean.
**kidney machine** *n* a machine that purifies the blood when the kidneys do not function properly.
**kidney stone** *n* a hard stony mass formed abnormally in the kidney.

**kilim** *or* **kelim** *n* a pileless woven rug from Turkey or Iran.

**kill**[1] *v* **1** to deprive of life. **2** to put an end to. **3** to destroy or neutralize the effect of. **4** to pass (time). **5** *informal* to switch off or cause to stop. **6** *informal* to cause extreme pain to. **7** *informal* to exhaust or overwhelm.

**kill**[2] *n* **1** an act of killing. **2** something killed as game or prey.

**killer** *n* **1** a person or thing that kills. **2** *informal* something that is extremely arduous or exhausting.

**killer whale** *n* a flesh-eating black-and-white whale.

**killing**[1] *n* **1** an act of causing death. **2** *informal* a sudden huge gain or profit.

**killing**[2] *adj* **1** causing death. **2** *informal* extremely exhausting or difficult to endure. **3** *informal* highly amusing.

**killjoy** *n* somebody who spoils the pleasure of others.

**kiln** *n* an oven for burning, firing, or drying a substance, e.g. clay.

**kilo** /'keeloh/ *n* (*pl* **-os**) a kilogram.

**kilobyte** *n* in computing, a unit of memory or information equal to 1024 bytes.

**kilogram** *n* the basic metric SI unit of mass equal to the weight of one litre of water (about 2.205lb).

**kilometre** (*NAmer* **kilometer**) *n* a metric unit of length equal to 1000m (about 0.62mi).

**kiloton** *n* a unit of explosive force equivalent to 1000 tons of TNT.

**kilovolt** *n* 1000 volts.

**kilowatt** *n* 1000 watts.

**kilowatt-hour** *n* a unit of energy equal to that expended by one kilowatt in one hour.

**kilt** *n* a tartan pleated skirt worn as traditional dress by Scottish Highlanders.

**kilter** ✱ **out of kilter** not in proper working order or balance.

**kimono** *n* (*pl* **-os**) a loose Japanese robe with wide sleeves and a broad sash.

**kin** *n* one's relatives.

**kind**[1] *n* **1** fundamental nature or quality. **2** a group of people or things having common features. **3** a member of a category. ✱ **in kind** in goods or services as distinct from money.

**kind**[2] *adj* **1** considerate or compassionate. **2** helpful or generous.

**kindergarten** /'kindəgahtn/ *n* a school for young children.

**kindle** *v* **1** to cause to start burning. **2** to arouse (an emotion).

**kindling** *n* small sticks for lighting a fire.

**kindly**[1] *adj* (**-ier, -iest**) sympathetic or generous. ➤ **kindliness** *n.*

**kindly**[2] *adv* in a kind or appreciative manner.

**kindness** *n* **1** the quality of being kind. **2** a kind act.

**kindred**[1] *n* **1** one's relatives. **2** family relationship.

**kindred**[2] *adj* **1** similar in nature or character. **2** related.

**kindred spirit** *n* somebody with similar interests or opinions.

**kinetic** *adj* relating to motion. ➤ **kinetically** *adv.*

**king** *n* **1** the male ruler of a state. **2** the holder of a preeminent position within a particular sphere. **3** in chess, the principal piece on each side, which the opposing side tries to trap. **4** a playing card normally ranking below the ace. ➤ **kingly** *adv,* **kingship** *n.*

**kingdom** *n* **1** a country ruled by a king or queen. **2** a primary division in the classification of natural objects.

**kingfisher** *n* a brightly-coloured fish-eating bird with a large head and a long stout sharp bill.

**kingpin** *n* **1** the key person or thing in a group or undertaking. **2** a pin connecting two pivoting parts, e.g. on a hinge joint.

**king-size** *or* **king-sized** *adj* larger than the standard size.

**kink**[1] *n* **1** a short twist or curl. **2** an eccentricity or quirk. **3** an imperfection likely to cause difficulties.

**kink**[2] *v* to make or become twisted or curled.

**kinky** *adj* (**-ier, -iest**) **1** twisted or curled. **2** *informal* sexually deviant or unusual.

**kinsfolk** *pl n* one's relatives.

**kinship** *n* **1** blood relationship. **2** similarity.

**kinsman** *n* (*pl* **kinsmen**) a male relative.

**kinswoman** *n* (*pl* **kinswomen**) a female relative.

**kiosk** *n* **1** a small stall or stand for the sale of newspapers, cigarettes, and sweets. **2** *Brit* a public telephone box.

**kip**[1] *n chiefly Brit, informal* a short sleep.

**kip**[2] *v* (**kipped, kipping**) *chiefly Brit, informal* to sleep.

**kipper** *n* a fish, *esp* a herring that has been split open, salted, and smoked.

**kipper tie** *n* a very wide tie.

**kirk** *n chiefly Scot* a church.

**kismet** *n* fate or destiny.

**kiss**[1] *v* **1** to touch with the lips as a mark of affection or greeting. **2** to touch gently or lightly.

**kiss**[2] *n* an act of kissing.

**kiss-curl** *n* a small curl of hair falling on the forehead or cheek.

**kiss of life** *n* artificial respiration using mouth-to-mouth contact.

**kit**[1] *n* **1** a set of tools or implements. **2** a set of clothes or equipment for a particular activity.

**kit**[2] *v* (**kitted, kitting**) *chiefly Brit* (+ out/up) to provide with suitable clothes or equipment.

**kitbag** *n* a large cylindrical shoulder bag used by soldiers to carry their possessions.

**kitchen** *n* a room where food is prepared and cooked.
**kitchenette** *n* a small kitchen or part of a room containing cooking facilities.
**kitchen garden** *n* a garden in which vegetables and herbs are grown.
**kite** *n* **1** a light frame covered with thin material that is flown in the air at the end of a long string. **2** a hawk with long narrow wings and a forked tail. **3** a quadrilateral with two pairs of equal adjacent sides.
**kith** * **kith and kin** one's friends and relatives.
**kitsch** *n* sentimentally pretentious or inferior artistic or literary material. ➤ **kitschy** *adj.*
**kitten** *n* **1** a young cat. **2** the young of some other animals, e.g. the beaver. * **have kittens** *Brit, informal* to be extremely worried or upset.
**kittenish** *adj* coyly playful or flirtatious.
**kitty**[1] *n* (*pl* **-ies**) a cat or kitten.
**kitty**[2] *n* (*pl* **-ies**) **1** a jointly held fund of money. **2** a fund in a card game.
**kiwi** *n* (*pl* **kiwis**) **1** a flightless bird of New Zealand. **2** (**Kiwi**) *informal* a person from New Zealand.
**kiwi fruit** *n* the oval fruit of an Asian climbing plant with a brown hairy skin, green flesh, and black seeds.
**Klaxon** *n trademark* a powerful electrical horn or warning signal.
**kleptomania** *n* a recurrent desire to steal. ➤ **kleptomaniac** *n.*
**km** *abbr* kilometre.
**knack** *n* a special skill or aptitude.
**knacker**[1] *n Brit* somebody who buys and slaughters worn-out horses and other animals.
**knacker**[2] *v chiefly Brit, informal* to exhaust (somebody).
**knacker's yard** *n Brit* a slaughterhouse for old animals.
**knapsack** *n* a bag strapped on the back for carrying supplies or personal belongings.
**knave** *n* **1** *archaic* a wicked or unprincipled man. **2** a jack in a pack of playing cards. ➤ **knavish** *adj.*
**knead** *v* **1** to work and press (something soft) with the hands. **2** to manipulate as if by kneading.
**knee**[1] *n* **1** a joint in the leg between the thighbone and the shinbone. **2** the upper surface of a seated person's thigh.
**knee**[2] *v* to hit with the knee.
**kneecap**[1] *n* a thick flat bone that protects the front of the knee joint.
**kneecap**[2] *v* (**kneecapped, kneecapping**) to shoot the kneecap of (somebody) as a punishment.
**knee-deep** *adj* **1** immersed up to the knees. **2** deeply engaged or occupied.
**knee-jerk** *adj* occurring as a conditioned response; automatic.
**kneel** *v* (*past tense and past part.* **knelt** *or* **kneeled**) to be in a position supported by the knees.
**knees-up** *n Brit, informal* a lively celebration with dancing.
**knell**[1] *v* of a bell: to ring for a death, funeral, etc.
**knell**[2] *n* the sound of a bell rung slowly.
**knew** *v* past tense of KNOW[1].
**knickerbockers** *pl n* short baggy trousers gathered at the knee.
**knickers** *pl n Brit* women's or girls' underpants.
**knick-knack** *or* **nicknack** *n informal* a small trivial ornament or trinket.
**knife**[1] *n* (*pl* **knives**) a cutting implement consisting of a blade fixed in a handle.
**knife**[2] *v* to cut or stab with a knife.
**knife-edge** *n* an uncertain or precarious situation.
**knifepoint** *n* * **at knifepoint** under a threat of injury by being knifed.
**knight**[1] *n* **1** in medieval times, a mounted armed soldier serving a feudal superior. **2** in Britain, a man honoured by a sovereign for merit, bearing the title 'Sir'. **3** in chess, either of two pieces of each colour, usu in the shape of a horse's head, that move diagonally from one corner to another of a rectangle of three by two squares. ➤ **knighthood** *n.*
**knight**[2] *v* to make a knight of (somebody).
**knit**[1] *v* (**knitted** *or* **knit, knitting**) **1** to form (a fabric or garment) by working yarn into a series of interlocking loops using needles or a machine. **2** to make (stitches or rows) in this way. **3** to link or join together. **4** to contract (the brow) into wrinkles.
**knit**[2] *n* a fabric or garment made by knitting.
**knitwear** *n* knitted clothing.
**knob** *n* **1** a rounded protuberance or ornament. **2** a small rounded handle or control. **3** a small piece or lump.
**knobble** *n* a small knob or lump. ➤ **knobbly** *adj.*
**knock**[1] *v* **1** to strike (a surface) sharply with the knuckles or a hard object. **2** to strike a door to gain admission. **3** to drive, make, or remove by striking. **4** to collide or cause to collide. **5** *informal* to find fault with. **6** *informal* to have sexual intercourse with. **7** of an engine: to make a metallic rapping noise when faulty. * **knock spots off** *informal* to surpass or outdo with ease. **knock together** to make hurriedly.
**knock**[2] *n* **1** a sharp blow or collision. **2** the sound of knocking. **3** a setback or minor misfortune.
**knockabout** *adj* of comedy: characterized by boisterous antics.
**knocker** *n* a metal object hinged to a door for use in knocking.
**knock-knees** *pl n* a condition in which the legs curve inward at the knees. ➤ **knock-kneed** *adj.*

**knock off** *v* **1** to stop work. **2** to do or produce hurriedly. **3** to deduct (an amount). **4** *informal* to steal.

**knock-on effect** *n* an effect one action or situation has on the next in a series.

**knockout** *n* **1** knocking out or being knocked out. **2** in boxing, a blow that knocks an opponent down and ends the match. **3** a competition with successive rounds in which losing competitors are eliminated. **4** *informal* a striking person or thing.

**knock out** *v* **1** to make unconscious. **2** to eliminate from a knockout competition. **3** *informal* to impress or amaze greatly.

**knoll** *n* a small hill or mound.

**knot**[1] *n* **1** a looping of string, thread, etc pulled tight to form a fastening. **2** a tangled mass of hair or wool. **3** a sense of tight constriction in the stomach. **4** a lump or swelling in tissue. **5** the base of a woody branch enclosed in the stem from which it arises, or a hard mass this causes in timber. **6** a cluster of people or things. **7** a unit of speed equal to one nautical mile per hour. * **tie in knots** to confuse or bewilder. **tie the knot** to get married.

**knot**[2] *v* (**knotted, knotting**) **1** to tie with a knot. **2** to cause (hair or wool) to become tangled. **3** to cause (a muscle) to become tense or constricted.

**knotty** *adj* (**-ier, -iest**) **1** full of knots. **2** complicated or difficult to solve.

**know**[1] *v* (**knew, known**) **1** to be aware of or have information about. **2** to be convinced or certain of. **3** to have a practical understanding of. **4** to recognize or identify. **5** to be acquainted or familiar with. **6** to have experience of. * **be known as** to be called, e.g. as a nickname. **know the ropes** to be familiar with a routine or procedure. ➤ **knowable** *adj.*

**know**[2] * **in the know** having exclusive knowledge or information.

**know-all** *n* somebody who behaves as if they know everything.

**know-how** *n* expertise in a particular field.

**knowing** *adj* **1** implying knowledge of a secret. **2** shrewd or astute. **3** deliberate or conscious. ➤ **knowingly** *adv.*

**knowledge** *n* **1** information or understanding acquired through learning or experience. **2** the total of known facts about a subject.

**knowledgeable** *adj* having knowledge or intelligence; well-informed. ➤ **knowledgeably** *adv.*

**known**[1] *v* past part. of KNOW[1].

**known**[2] *adj* **1** generally recognized. **2** identified.

**knuckle** *n* **1** each of the joints between the hand and the fingers or between the bones of the fingers. **2** a cut of meat consisting of the lowest leg joint with the adjoining flesh. * **near the knuckle** almost improper or indecent.

**knuckle down** *v* to apply oneself earnestly.

**knuckle-duster** *n* a metal device worn over the knuckles as a weapon.

**knuckle under** *v* to give in or submit.

**koala** /koh'ahlə/ *n* an Australian tree-dwelling mammal with large ears and grey fur.

**kohl** *n* a black powder used to darken the eyelids.

**kohlrabi** /kohl'rahbi/ *n* (*pl* **kohlrabies**) a cabbage with a fleshy stem resembling a turnip.

**kookaburra** *n* a large Australian kingfisher with a call resembling loud laughter.

**Koran** /kaw'rahn, kə'rahn/ *or* **Qur'an** /koo'rahn/ *n* the sacred book of Islam, believed by Muslims to contain revelations made to Muhammad by Allah.

**kosher** /'kohshə/ *adj* **1** of food: prepared according to Jewish law. **2** *informal* proper or legitimate.

**kowtow**[1] *n* a former Chinese gesture of respect by kneeling and touching the ground with the forehead.

**kowtow**[2] *v* to show obsequious deference.

**Kr** *abbr* the chemical symbol for krypton.

**kraal** *n* **1** an enclosed village in southern Africa. **2** an enclosure for domestic animals.

**krill** *pl n* small sea animals that resemble shrimps and constitute the chief food of whales and other sea creatures.

**krona** *n* (*pl* **kronor**) the basic monetary unit of Sweden.

**krone** /'krohnə/ *n* (*pl* **kroner**) the basic monetary unit of Denmark and Norway.

**krypton** *n* a colourless gaseous element used in fluorescent lights.

**Ku** *abbr* the chemical symbol for kurchatovium.

**kudos** /'kyoohdos/ *n* renown and prestige resulting from achievement.

**kumquat** *or* **cumquat** *n* a small orange citrus fruit.

**kung fu** *n* a Chinese martial art resembling karate.

**Kurd** *n* a member of a pastoral people inhabiting adjoining parts of Turkey, Iran, and Iraq. ➤ **Kurdish** *adj.*

**kV** *abbr* kilovolt.

**kW** *abbr* kilowatt.

**L**[1] *or* **l** *n* (*pl* **L's** *or* **Ls** *or* **l's**) **1** the twelfth letter of the English alphabet. **2** the Roman numeral for 50.

**L**[2] *abbr Brit* learner driver.

**l** *abbr* **1** litre(s). **2** *archaic* pound(s).

**La** *abbr* the chemical symbol for lanthanum.

**lab** *n informal* a laboratory.

**label**[1] *n* **1** a slip, e.g. of paper or cloth, attached to something to give information about it. **2** a brand name, *esp* the name of a fashion house or a record company. **3** a descriptive or identifying word or phrase.

**label**[2] *v* (**labelled, labelling,** *NAmer* **labeled, labeling**) **1** to fasten a label to (an item). **2** to describe or categorize, *esp* unfairly or sweepingly.

**labia** *pl n* the outer and inner folds of the vulva.

**labor**[1] *n NAmer, Aus* see LABOUR[1].

**labor**[2] *v NAmer, Aus* see LABOUR[2].

**laboratory** *n* (*pl* **-ies**) **1** a place equipped for scientific experiment, testing, or analysis. **2** a place where chemicals and chemical products are developed.

**laborious** *adj* **1** requiring a lot of time or effort. **2** lacking grace and ease; laboured. ➤ **laboriously** *adv.*

**labour**[1] (*NAmer, Aus* **labor**) *n* **1** work, *esp* when difficult or done for wages. **2** workers collectively. **3** (**Labour**) the Labour Party. **4** the process of childbirth.

**labour**[2] (*NAmer, Aus* **labor**) *v* **1** to work hard. **2** to do unskilled manual work. **3** to struggle to do something difficult. **4** to move with difficulty. **5** (+ under) to be misled by (something). **6** to deal with or explain in laborious detail.

**labour camp** *n* a prison camp in which inmates are forced to work.

**laboured** (*NAmer* **labored**) *adj* showing signs of effort; lacking natural grace or easy fluency.

**labourer** (*NAmer* **laborer**) *n* a person who does unskilled manual work, *esp* outdoors.

**labour force** *n* people in work.

**labour-intensive** *adj* using many workers in the process of production.

**Labour Party** *n* in Britain, a political party founded to represent working people and based on socialist principles.

**Labrador** *n* a dog of a gold-coloured or black breed, often employed as a retriever or guide dog.

**laburnum** *n* a shrub or tree with bright yellow flowers that hang in clusters.

**labyrinth** *n* **1** a place that is a network of intricate passageways. **2** something perplexingly complex or tortuous. ➤ **labyrinthine** *adj.*

**lace**[1] *n* **1** a fine decorative fabric made by twisting or looping thread in symmetrical patterns. **2** a cord or string used for drawing together two edges, e.g. of a garment or shoe.

**lace**[2] *v* **1** to fasten (e.g. a shoe) by means of a lace. **2** to entwine or interlace (*esp* the fingers). **3** to add a dash of a stronger ingredient, *esp* an alcoholic drink, to (a drink or dish).

**lacerate** *v* to tear or cut (skin or flesh) roughly. ➤ **laceration** *n.*

**lachrymal** *or* **lacrimal** *adj* **1** *formal or literary* causing or marked by the shedding of tears. **2** (**lacrimal**) relating to the glands that produce tears.

**lachrymose** *adj formal or literary* **1** tearful. **2** mournful.

**lack**[1] *v* **1** to suffer from an absence or deficiency of. **2** (*often* + in/for) to be deficient in.

**lack**[2] *n* an absence or shortage of something.

**lackadaisical** *adj* **1** lacking enthusiasm or zest. **2** casual or negligent.

**lackey** *n* (*pl* **-eys**) **1** a servant, *esp* a liveried footman. **2** a servile follower.

**lacklustre** (*NAmer* **lackluster**) *adj* **1** lacking in vitality or enthusiasm; uninspired. **2** lacking in sheen or radiance.

**laconic** *adj* using a minimum of words. ➤ **laconically** *adv.*

**lacquer**[1] *n* **1** a clear or coloured varnish for wood. **2** decorative wooden articles that have been coated with lacquer. **3** *Brit* a substance sprayed onto the hair to fix it in place.

**lacquer**[2] *v* to coat or spray with lacquer.

**lacrimal** *adj* see LACHRYMAL.

**lacrosse** *n* an outdoor team game played with a long-handled stick with a loose mesh pouch for throwing and catching the ball.

**lactate** *v* of a female mammal: to produce milk. ➤ **lactation** *n.*
**lactic** *adj* relating to or obtained from milk.
**lactic acid** *n* an organic acid formed in the muscles during strenuous exercise and found in sour milk.
**lactose** *n* a sugar present in milk.
**lacuna** *n* (*pl* **lacunae** *or* **lacunas**) a blank space or missing part.
**lacy** *adj* (**-ier, -iest**) resembling, consisting of, or trimmed with lace.
**lad** *n* **1** *informal* a boy or young man. **2** *Brit, informal* a boisterous or macho man.
**ladder**[1] *n* **1** a structure for climbing up or down that has two long sidepieces joined at intervals by crosspieces on which one steps. **2** a hierarchical structure with stages allowing for promotion. **3** *Brit* a vertical line in hosiery or knitting caused by stitches becoming unravelled.
**ladder**[2] *v Brit* to cause a ladder to develop in (e.g. tights).
**laddish** *adj* irritatingly rowdy or macho.
**laden** *adj* carrying a heavy load.
**la-di-da** *or* **lah-di-dah** *adj informal* affectedly refined, *esp* in pronunciation.
**ladies** *n Brit* a public lavatory for women.
**ladle**[1] *n* a deep-bowled long-handled spoon.
**ladle**[2] *v* to serve with a ladle.
**lady** *n* (*pl* **-ies**) **1** a woman of refinement or superior social position. **2** in polite or formal use: a woman. **3** (**Lady**) a title given to a peeress or to the wife of a knight or peer. ✱ **my Lady** used as a form of address to women judges and noblewomen.
**ladybird** *n* a small beetle that has red wing cases with black spots.
**lady-in-waiting** *n* (*pl* **ladies-in-waiting**) a woman appointed to wait on a queen or princess.
**lady-killer** *n informal* a man who captivates women.
**ladylike** *adj* befitting a well-bred woman or girl; refined and dignified.
**lag**[1] *v* (**lagged, lagging**) (*often* + behind) to fall behind.
**lag**[2] *n* a delay between two events.
**lag**[3] *v* (**lagged, lagging**) to cover (e.g. pipes) with lagging.
**lager** *n* a light beer usu served chilled.
**laggard** *n* a person who lags or lingers.
**lagging** *n* material for thermal insulation, e.g. wrapped round pipes.
**lagoon** *n* a shallow saltwater pool separated from the sea by a sand bank, reef, etc.
**lah-di-dah** *adj* see LA-DI-DA.
**laid** *v* past tense and past part. of LAY[1].
**laid back** *adj informal* relaxed or casual.
**lain** *v* past part. of LIE[1].
**lair** *n* **1** the resting or living place of a wild animal. **2** a person's den.
**laird** *n Scot* a person who owns a large country estate.
**laissez-faire** /ˌlesay ˈfeə/ *n* **1** a doctrine opposing government interference in economic affairs. **2** deliberate non-interfererence in the freedom and choices of others.
**laity** *n* (**the laity**) lay people.
**lake** *n* a large inland body of water.
**lam** *v* (**lammed, lamming**) *informal* to hit hard.
**lama** *n* **1** a title given to a Tibetan Buddhist spiritual leader. **2** a Tibetan or Mongolian Buddhist monk.
**lamb**[1] *n* **1** a young sheep. **2** a meek or innocent person.
**lamb**[2] *v* **1** of a ewe: to give birth to lambs. **2** to tend (ewes) at lambing time.
**lambada** /lamˈbahdə/ *n* a fast ballroom dance of Brazilian origin.
**lambaste** *or* **lambast** *v* to criticize severely.
**lambda** *n* the eleventh letter of the Greek alphabet (Λ, λ).
**lambent** *adj literary* softly bright, radiant, or flickering.
**lame**[1] *adj* **1** having a leg or foot so disabled as to impair freedom of movement. **2** of a story or excuse: weak and unconvincing. ➤ **lamely** *adv,* **lameness** *n.*
**lamé** *n* a brocaded fabric interwoven with gold or silver threads.
**lame**[2] *v* to make (a person or animal) lame.
**lame duck** *n* a weak or incapable person or thing.
**lament**[1] *n* **1** an expression of grief. **2** a song or poem expressing grief.
**lament**[2] *v* **1** to feel or express grief for (a person's loss or death); to mourn. **2** to express regret or disappointment over something. ➤ **lamentation** *n.*
**lamentable** *adj* **1** woefully bad or inadequate. **2** regrettable. ➤ **lamentably** *adv.*
**laminate**[1] *v* **1** to overlay with a thin sheet of e.g. metal or plastic. **2** to make (e.g. a building material) by bonding superimposed layers of one or more materials. **3** to separate (a substance) into layers. **4** to roll (e.g. metal) into a thin plate. ➤ **lamination** *n.*
**laminate**[2] *n* a product made by laminating.
**lamp** *n* a device using electricity, oil, or gas to give out artificial light.
**lampoon**[1] *v* to satirize or ridicule.
**lampoon**[2] *n* a satirical attack on a person, literary work, etc.
**lamprey** *n* (*pl* **-eys**) an eel-like fish that has a large sucking mouth with no jaws.
**lance**[1] *n* a weapon with a long shaft and a sharp steel head, carried by horsemen.
**lance**[2] *v* to open (e.g. a boil) with a lancet or other sharp instrument.
**lance corporal** *n* a non-commissioned officer of the lowest rank in the British army.

**lancer** *n* a member of a regiment armed with lances.

**lancet** *n* a sharp-pointed, two-edged surgical instrument used to make small incisions.

**land**[1] *n* **1** the solid part of the earth's surface, as distinct from seas, lakes, rivers, etc. **2** ground owned as property or attached to a building. **3** (**the land**) ground used for agriculture. **4** a particular country or state.

**land**[2] *v* **1** to bring (e.g. an aircraft) to a surface from the air. **2** of an aircraft, bird, etc: to alight on a surface. **3** to set on shore, or go ashore, from a ship. **4** of a boat, ship, etc: to reach shore or a port. **5** *informal* to gain or secure. **6** to catch and bring in (a fish). **7** *informal* (+ in) to put (somebody) in a usu undesirable place or situation. **8** *informal* to cause (a blow) to hit somebody. **9** *informal* (+ with) to burden with something unwanted.

**landau** *n* a four-wheeled carriage with a folding top.

**landed** *adj* owning land.

**landfall** *n* an instance of sighting or reaching land after a voyage or flight.

**landfill** *n* **1** the disposal of rubbish by burying it in a pit. **2** rubbish disposed of in this way.

**landing** *n* **1** the act of coming or bringing to land. **2** a place for discharging and taking on passengers and cargo. **3** a level space at the top of a flight of stairs.

**landing craft** *n* a naval craft designed for putting troops and equipment ashore.

**landing gear** *n* the undercarriage of an aircraft.

**landlady** *n* (*pl* **-ies**) **1** a woman who owns and rents out land, buildings, or accommodation. **2** a woman who keeps a guesthouse or pub.

**landless** *adj* owning no land.

**landlocked** *adj* of e.g. a country: with no access to the sea; completely enclosed by land.

**landlord** *n* **1** a person, usu a man, who owns and rents out land, buildings, or accommodation. **2** a person, usu a man, who keeps a guesthouse or pub.

**landlubber** *n informal* a person unacquainted with the sea or seamanship.

**landmark** *n* **1** a conspicuous object that can be used to identify a locality. **2** an event that marks a turning point or new development.

**landmine** *n* an explosive mine hidden just below the surface of the ground.

**landscape**[1] *n* **1** an expanse of natural inland scenery. **2** a picture, drawing, etc of a landscape.

**landscape**[2] *v* to improve the look of (a garden, park, etc) by reshaping or adding natural features, planting trees, etc.

**landslide** *n* **1** a movement of a mass of rock, earth, etc down a slope. **2** an overwhelming victory in an election.

**land up** *v* to end up in a place or situation.

**lane** *n* **1** a narrow passageway or road. **2** a strip of road for a single line of vehicles. **3** any of several marked parallel courses for competitors in a running or swimming race. **4** a fixed route used by ships or aircraft.

**language** *n* **1** a means of communicating ideas or feelings by the use of sounds, gestures, or signs that have understood meanings. **2** the words, grammatical constructions, etc used and understood by a particular community or group. **3** a formal system of signs and symbols used in programming a computer. * **speak the same language** to have the same interests, ideas, etc.

**languid** *adj* **1** without energy; spiritless or apathetic. **2** weak or drooping from fatigue. ➤ **languidly** *adv.*

**languish** *v* **1** to be or become feeble. **2** to suffer hardship or neglect.

**languor** *n* a feeling of not unpleasant weariness or drowsiness. ➤ **languorous** *adj.*

**lank** *adj* of hair: straight and limp.

**lanky** *adj* (**-ier, -iest**) tall, thin, and ungraceful.

**lanolin** *or* **lanoline** *n* wool grease, *esp* when refined for use in ointments and cosmetics.

**lantern** *n* a light in a portable protective case with transparent windows.

**lanthanum** *n* a soft, silver-white metallic chemical element of the rare-earth group.

**lanyard** *or* **laniard** *n* **1** a piece of rope for fastening something on board ship. **2** a cord worn round the neck to hold something, e.g. a whistle.

**lap**[1] *n* the front part of the lower trunk and thighs of a seated person. * **in the lap of luxury** in an environment of great comfort and wealth. **in the lap of the gods** beyond human influence or control.

**lap**[2] *n* **1** one circuit round a course or track. **2** one stage of a journey. **3** a part of an object that overlaps another.

**lap**[3] *v* (**lapped, lapping**) to overtake (another contestant in a race) and lead them by a full circuit of a track.

**lap**[4] *v* (**lapped, lapping**) **1** of an animal: to take in (liquid) with the tongue. **2** of water: to splash against (something) in little waves.

**lapdog** *n* **1** a small, *esp* docile or pampered, pet dog. **2** somebody who is completely controlled by somebody else.

**lapel** *n* a fold of the top front edge of a coat or jacket.

**lapidary** *adj* **1** relating to the cutting, polishing, and engraving of stones and gems. **2** of a literary style: elegant and dignified.

**lapis lazuli** *n* a rich blue semiprecious stone, used in making jewellery.

**Lapp** *n* a member of a nomadic people of Lapland, a region of northern Scandinavia.

**lapse**[1] *n* **1** a slight error, e.g. of memory or in manners. **2** a decline in standards, *esp* of morality. **3** an elapsed period of time; an interval.

**lapse**[2] *v* **1** of e.g. a right: to become invalid, *esp* because it has not been exercised. **2** to abandon a religion or doctrine. **3** to decline from a higher to a lower level, e.g. of morals. **4** (+ into) to pass gradually into a particular state, way of behaving, etc.

**laptop** *n* a portable computer with an integral keyboard and a flat screen that folds down.

**lap up** *v* **1** to drink (a liquid). **2** to take in eagerly or uncritically.

**lapwing** *n* a crested plover with a shrill wailing cry.

**larboard** *n archaic* port.

**larceny** *n* (*pl* **-ies**) *dated* theft of personal property.

**larch** *n* a tree of the pine family with short deciduous needles.

**lard**[1] *n* soft white solid fat from a pig, used in cooking.

**lard**[2] *v* **1** to insert strips of fat or bacon into (meat) before cooking. **2** (+ with) to intersperse or embellish (speech or writing) with something.

**larder** *n* a room or cupboard where food is stored.

**large** *adj* **1** relatively great in size, quantity, extent, etc. **2** operating on an extensive scale, or having more than usual power or scope. * **at large 1** not imprisoned or restrained. **2** as a whole.

**largely** *adv* to a large extent; mostly.

**largesse** *or* **largess** *n* **1** generosity. **2** something, e.g. money, given generously.

**largo** *adj and adv* of a piece of music: performed in a very slow and broad manner.

**lariat** *n* a rope used as a lasso or for tethering animals.

**lark**[1] *n* a brown singing bird, e.g. a skylark.

**lark**[2] *n informal* **1** a prank or light-hearted adventure. **2** *Brit* an activity regarded as misguided or foolish.

**lark**[3] *v informal* (+ about/around) to have fun in a playful or mischievous way.

**larva** *n* (*pl* **larvae**) the immature, often worm-like form of an insect that hatches from an egg.

**laryngitis** *n* inflammation of the larynx.

**larynx** *n* (*pl* **larynges** *or* **larynxes**) the upper part of the throat, containing the vocal cords.

**lasagne** /lə'zanyə/ *n* **1** pasta in the form of broad flat sheets. **2** a baked dish of minced meat or vegetables layered with lasagne, white sauce, and cheese.

**lascivious** *adj* showing unseemly or offensive sexual interest. ➤ **lasciviously** *adv*, **lasciviousness** *n*.

**laser** *n* a device that generates an intense narrow beam of light.

**laserdisc** *n* a multimedia storage medium that looks like a large compact disc.

**lash**[1] *v* **1** to strike with a whip or similar object. **2** to beat hard against. **3** of an animal: to flick (the tail) quickly or sharply.

**lash**[2] *n* **1** a blow with a whip. **2** the flexible part of a whip. **3** an eyelash.

**lash**[3] *v* to bind or fasten with a cord, rope, etc.

**lashings** *pl n Brit, informal* (+ of) an abundance of something.

**lash out** *v* **1** to make a sudden physical attack. **2** *Brit, informal* to spend money freely.

**lass** *or* **lassie** *n chiefly Scot, N Eng* a girl or young woman.

**lassitude** *n* physical or mental fatigue.

**lasso**[1] *n* (*pl* **-os** *or* **-oes**) a rope with a running noose, used *esp* in North America for catching horses and cattle.

**lasso**[2] *v* (**lassoes** *or* **lassos, lassoed, lassoing**) to catch with a lasso.

**last**[1] *adj* **1** following all the rest in time, place, or order. **2** lowest in rank or importance. **3** most up-to-date; latest. **4** next before the present. **5** being the only remaining. **6 (the last)** least suitable or likely. * **on one's last legs** on the verge of failure, exhaustion, etc.

**last**[2] *adv* **1** on the most recent occasion. **2** after all others. **3** in conclusion.

**last**[3] *n and pron* (*pl* **last**) somebody or something that is last. * **at last/at long last** after a long time or much delay. **the last of** the remaining part, amount, etc of something.

**last**[4] *v* **1** to continue in time; to go on. **2** to remain in good or adequate condition. **3** to be enough for the needs of (somebody) during a particular length of time.

**last**[5] *n* a shoemaker's model of the human foot, on which a shoe is shaped or repaired.

**Last Judgment** *n* the final judgment of humankind before God at the end of the world.

**last rites** *pl n* rites performed by a Roman Catholic priest for somebody who is about to die.

**latch**[1] *n* **1** a fastener, e.g. for a gate, with a pivoted bar that falls into a notch. **2** a type of doorlock with a spring-loaded bolt that can only be opened from outside with a key.

**latch**[2] *v* to fasten (e.g. a door) with a latch.

**latchkey** *n* a key to an outside door, *esp* the front door of a house.

**latch on** *v* **1** to understand. **2** to attach oneself to somebody or something.

**late**[1] *adj* **1** occurring or arriving after the expected time. **2** happening far on in a particular period. **3** far on in the day or night. **4** (**the late**) recently deceased. **5** very recent. ➤ **lateness** *n*.

**late**[2] *adv* **1** after the usual or proper time. **2** at or near the end of a period of time or a process. **3** far on in the day or night. * **of late** recently.

**lately** *adv* recently.

**latent** *adj* present but not manifest or active. ➤ **latency** *n.*
**later** *adv* **1** afterwards. **2** at some time in the future.
**lateral** *adj* situated on, directed towards, or coming from the side. ➤ **laterally** *adv.*
**lateral thinking** *n chiefly Brit* thinking that concentrates on unexpected aspects of a problem to find a fresh approach to it.
**latest**[1] *adj* most recent; most up-to-date. * **at the latest** no later than the specified time.
**latest**[2] *n* (**the latest**) the most recent news.
**latex** *n* (*pl* **latices** *or* **latexes**) **1** a milky usu white fluid from various plants that is the source of rubber and chewing gum. **2** a water emulsion of a synthetic rubber or plastic, used e.g. in paints.
**lath** *n* a thin narrow strip of wood.
**lathe** *n* a machine for shaping wood or metal by rotating it against a fixed cutting tool.
**lather**[1] *n* **1** a foam or froth formed when a detergent, e.g. soap, is agitated in water. **2** foam or froth on a horse's skin from profuse sweating.
**lather**[2] *v* **1** to form or cover with a lather. **2** (+ with) to spread something with (a substance).
**Latin**[1] *n* the language of ancient Rome and the Roman Empire.
**Latin**[2] *adj* of or relating to Latin.
**Latin America** *n* the parts of the American continent where Spanish or Portuguese is spoken. ➤ **Latin American** *adj.*
**Latino** /la'teenoh/ *n* (*pl* **-os**) *NAmer* a person of Latin American or Spanish American descent.
**latitude** *n* **1** the angular distance of a place north or south of the equator. **2** (*in pl*) an area of the earth's surface between particular latitudes. **3** freedom of action or choice.
**latrine** *n* a small pit used as a toilet, *esp* in a military camp or barracks.
**latter** *adj* **1** near the end; later. **2** recent or present. **3** (**the latter**) denoting the second of two things mentioned or understood. ➤ **latterly** *adv.*
**latter-day** *adj* of present or recent times.
**lattice** *n* a framework of crossed wooden or metal strips with open spaces between.
**laud** *v formal* to praise enthusiastically.
**laudable** *adj* worthy of praise; commendable.
**laudanum** *n* a preparation of opium formerly used in medicine as a sedative.
**laudatory** *adj* expressing praise.
**laugh**[1] *v* **1** to make explosive vocal sounds expressing amusement. **2** (+ at) to ridicule; to make fun of. * **laugh on the other side of one's face** to be embarrassed after feeling confident or proud.
**laugh**[2] *n* an act of laughing. * **a laugh 1** *informal* a bit of fun. **2** *informal* a joke. **have the last laugh** to be proved right, successful, etc.
**laughable** *adj* ridiculous. ➤ **laughably** *adv.*
**laughing gas** *n* = NITROUS OXIDE.
**laughing stock** *n* an object of ridicule.
**laugh off** *v* to minimize or dismiss (something) by treating it as amusingly trivial.
**laughter** *n* the act or sound of laughing.
**launch**[1] *v* **1** to set (a boat or ship) afloat. **2** to send (e.g. a rocket) up into the air. **3** to initiate (something), or set (somebody) on e.g. a course or career. **4** to introduce (a new product) onto the market. **5** to throw (oneself) forward. **6** (+ into) to begin to do something energetically.
**launch**[2] *n* an act of launching something.
**launch**[3] *n* a large motorboat.
**launder** *v* **1** to wash and iron (dirty clothes, etc). **2** *informal* to pass (money obtained illegally) through a bank or legal business to disguise its origins.
**launderette** *or* **laundrette** *n* a self-service laundry providing coin-operated machines.
**laundry** *n* (*pl* **-ies**) **1** clothes and linen that have been, or are to be, washed and dried. **2** a place where laundering is done.
**laurel** *n* **1** an evergreen tree or shrub that has smooth shiny leaves. **2** (*in pl*) a crown of laurel awarded as a token of victory or preeminence. **3** distinction or honour. * **rest on one's laurels** to become complacent after previous successes or achievements.
**lava** *n* molten rock flowing from a volcano, or this same rock after it has cooled and solidified.
**lavatorial** *adj* **1** relating to lavatories. **2** of humour: characterized by excessive reference to bodily functions.
**lavatory** *n* (*pl* **-ies**) a toilet.
**lavender** *n* **1** a shrub with narrow aromatic leaves and spikes of lilac or purple flowers. **2** a pale purple colour.
**lavish**[1] *adj* **1** abundant or extravagant and sumptuous. **2** giving or spending in large quantities. ➤ **lavishly** *adv.*
**lavish**[2] *v* to spend or give in large quantities.
**law** *n* **1** a rule of conduct, recognized as binding or enforced by authority within a community. **2** the whole body of such rules. **3** a statement of scientific fact, e.g. describing the workings of a natural phenomenon. **4** a rule of procedure in a sport. **5** (**the law**) *informal* the police. * **be a law unto oneself** to be unconventional. **lay down the law** to give orders or express opinions forcefully.
**lawful** *adj* constituted or allowed by law; rightful or legal. ➤ **lawfully** *adv.*
**lawless** *adj* not regulated or restrained by law. ➤ **lawlessness** *n.*
**lawn**[1] *n* an area of ground covered with mown grass.
**lawn**[2] *n* a fine sheer linen or cotton fabric.
**lawn mower** *n* a machine for cutting grass on lawns.
**lawsuit** *n* a non-criminal case in a court of law.

**lawyer** *n* a person whose profession is to advise on legal matters and represent people in court.

**lax** *adj* **1** not strict or conscientious; negligent. **2** relaxed or slack. ➤ **laxity** *n.*

**laxative** *n* a medicinal preparation that relaxes the bowels to relieve constipation. ➤ **laxative** *adj.*

**lay**[1] *v* (*past tense and past part.* **laid**) **1** to put down on or spread over a surface. **2** to set in order or position for use: *to lay the table.* **3** to impose as a duty or burden. **4** to make (a charge or accusation). **5** to assign (blame, emphasis, etc). **6** of a bird: to produce (an egg). **7** to place (a bet). **8** *coarse slang* to have sexual intercourse with. ✻ **lay into** *informal* to attack or criticize fiercely. **lay to rest 1** to dispel (a fear or anxiety). **2** to bury (a body) in a grave.

**lay**[2] *v* past tense of LIE[1].

**lay**[3] *adj* **1** not belonging to the clergy. **2** not having expert or professional knowledge.

**lay**[4] *n* a simple poem intended to be sung.

**layabout** *n* a lazy shiftless person.

**lay-by** *n* (*pl* **lay-bys**) an area at the side of a road where vehicles can stop without obstructing traffic.

**lay down** *v* **1** to formulate (e.g. a rule). **2** to store (wine) in a cellar. **3** to sacrifice (one's life).

**layer**[1] *n* a single thickness of some substance lying over or under another.

**layer**[2] *v* to arrange in layers.

**layman** *n* (*pl* **laymen**) a male layperson.

**layoff** *n* **1** the laying off of an employee. **2** a period of unemployment or inactivity.

**lay off** *v* **1** to cease to employ (a worker) because of a shortage of work. **2** *informal* to give up: *lay off the beer.* **3** *informal* to leave (somebody) alone.

**layout** *n* the plan or arrangement of something laid out, e.g. rooms in a building or material to be printed.

**lay out** *v* **1** to arrange according to a plan. **2** *informal* to make unconscious. **3** *informal* to spend (an amount of money). **4** to prepare (a body) for burial.

**layperson** *n* (*pl* **laypeople**) **1** a person who is not a member of the clergy. **2** a person without special or professional knowledge of some field.

**lay up** *v* ✻ **be laid up** to be incapacitated by illness or injury.

**laze** *v* to act or rest lazily.

**lazy** *adj* (**-ier, -iest**) **1** disinclined or averse to activity. **2** not energetic or vigorous. ➤ **lazily** *adv,* **laziness** *n.*

**lazybones** *n* (*pl* **lazybones**) *informal* a lazy person.

**lb** *abbr* pound.

**lbw** *abbr* in cricket, leg before wicket.

**lea** *n chiefly literary* an area of grassland or pasture.

**leach** *v* to separate out from e.g. soil by the action of a liquid passing through it.

**lead**[1] *v* (*past tense and past part.* **led**) **1** to guide (a person or an animal) along a way, *esp* by going in front. **2** to go or be at the head of. **3** to be first or ahead, e.g. in a race. **4** to direct the operations or activities of. **5** to carry on (a specified kind of life or existence). **6** (*often* + to) to serve as an entrance or passage. **7** (*often* + to) to result in. **8** to influence (somebody) to do or believe something. ✻ **lead astray** to encourage somebody to behave badly. **lead on** to deceive (somebody). **lead up to** to be a preliminary to.

**lead**[2] *n* **1** a position at the front or ahead. **2** a position of advantage or superiority. **3** guidance or example. **4** an indication or clue. **5** a principal role in a play or film. **6** *Brit* a line or strap for leading or restraining a dog. **7** an insulated wire that conducts an electrical current.

**lead**[3] *n* **1** a bluish white metal that is heavy and soft. **2** a thin stick of graphite in a pencil.

**leaded** *adj* **1** of petrol: containing lead. **2** covered or framed with lead.

**leaden** *adj* **1** heavy, sluggish, or dull. **2** lacking spirit or animation; sluggish. **3** dull grey. ➤ **leadenly** *adv.*

**leader** *n* **1** somebody or something that guides, precedes, or holds an advantage over all others. **2** somebody who has commanding authority or influence. **3** the principal player among a group of musicians. **4** *Brit* a newspaper editorial. ➤ **leadership** *n.*

**leading** *adj* coming or ranking first; foremost.

**leading article** *n Brit* a newspaper editorial.

**leading light** *n* a prominent and influential person.

**leading question** *n* a question so phrased as to suggest the desired answer.

**leaf**[1] *n* (*pl* **leaves**) **1** a flat, usu green outgrowth from the stem of a plant. **2** the state of having foliage. **3** a sheet of paper, *esp* in a book, with a page on each side. **4** a part *esp* of a table that slides or is hinged. **5** metal, e.g. gold or silver, in very thin sheets. ✻ **take a leaf out of somebody's book** to copy somebody's behaviour. **turn over a new leaf** to make a change for the better, *esp* in one's way of living. ➤ **leafy** *adj.*

**leaf**[2] *v* ✻ **leaf through** to turn over the pages of (a book, magazine, etc) quickly while glancing at the contents.

**leaflet**[1] *n* **1** a single sheet of paper or small pamphlet containing advertisements or information. **2** a small leaf.

**leaflet**[2] *v* (**leafleted, leafleting**) to distribute leaflets to.

**league**[1] *n* **1** an association of nations, groups, or people for a common purpose. **2** an association of sports clubs that organizes a competition for an overall title. **3** a class or category. ✱ **in league** in alliance or conspiracy.

**league²** *n* a former unit of distance equal to about 3mi (5km).

**leak¹** *v* **1** of a liquid, gas, etc: to enter or escape through a crack or hole, usu accidentally. **2** of a container: to let something enter or escape in this way. **3** (*often* + out) of information: to become known despite efforts at concealment. **4** to give out (information) surreptitiously. ➤ **leakage** *n*, **leaky** *adj*.

**leak²** *n* **1** a crack or hole through which something leaks. **2** information that becomes known despite efforts at concealment.

**lean¹** *v* (*past tense and past part.* **leaned** *or* **leant**) **1** to incline from a vertical position. **2** (+ on/against) to rest for support against something. **3** (+ on/upon) to rely on for support. **4** (+ towards) to be inclined to favour a particular opinion, course of action, etc. **5** *informal* (+ on) to exert pressure on somebody to do something.

**lean²** *adj* **1** of a person or animal: deficient in flesh or bulk; thin. **2** of meat: containing little or no fat. **3** unproductive or unremunerative.

**leaning** *n* an attraction, tendency, or partiality.

**lean-to** *n* (*pl* **-os**) a small building with a roof that rests on the side of a larger building.

**leap¹** *v* (*past tense and past part.* **leaped** *or* **leapt**) **1** to jump in or through the air. **2** to pass over (something) by leaping. **3** to move abruptly from one state, topic, etc to another. **4** (+ at) to seize an opportunity, offer, etc eagerly.

**leap²** *n* **1** a jump. **2** a sudden transition or increase. ✱ **by/in leaps and bounds** very rapidly.

**leapfrog¹** *n* a game in which one player bends down and another leaps over them with legs apart.

**leapfrog²** *v* (**leapfrogged, leapfrogging**) **1** to leap over in leapfrog. **2** to progress rapidly by passing over (rivals, obstacles, etc).

**leap year** *n* a year with an extra day added, occurring every fourth year.

**learn** *v* (*past tense and past part.* **learned** *or* **learnt**) **1** to gain knowledge of or skill in. **2** to memorize. **3** to come to be able (to do something). **4** to come to realize or know. ➤ **learner** *n*.

**learned** *adj* having acquired great knowledge through study.

**learning** *n* knowledge or skills acquired by study.

**lease¹** *n* a contract putting the land or property of one party at the disposal of another, usu for a stated period and rent. ✱ **new lease of life** a renewed period of healthy activity or usefulness.

**lease²** *v* to grant or hold (property) by lease.

**leasehold** *n* tenure by lease.

**leash** *n* a lead for a dog.

**least¹** *adj* **1** smallest in quantity or extent. **2** lowest in or importance. ✱ **at least 1** as a minimum. **2** if nothing else. **3** anyway.

**least²** *adv* to the smallest degree or extent. ✱ **least of all** especially not. **not least** especially.

**leather¹** *n* tanned animal skin used in clothing, upholstery, etc.

**leather²** *v* (**leathered, leathering**) **1** to cover (something) with leather. **2** *informal* to beat (a person or animal) with a strap; to thrash (them).

**leathery** *adj* resembling leather; tough.

**leave¹** *v* (*past tense and past part.* **left**) **1** to go away from (a place, person, etc). **2** to desert or abandon (somebody). **3** to withdraw from (an organization, institution, etc). **4** to allow to remain in a specified place or condition: *She left her notes at home.* **5** (*also* + off/out) to fail to include. **6** to allow to do or continue something without interference. **7** to put or deposit (something) where it can be collected or dealt with. **8** to bequeath (property). **9** to have (a quantity) as a remainder: *Ten from twelve leaves two.* ✱ **leave alone/be** *informal* to refrain from interfering with, annoying, or disturbing. **leave off** to stop (doing something).

**leave²** *n* **1** authorized absence, e.g. from employment. **2** *formal* permission. ✱ **take one's leave** (*often* + of) to say farewell.

**leaven¹** *n* **1** a substance, e.g. yeast, used to lighten dough and make it rise. **2** something that modifies or enlivens something.

**leaven²** *v* to modify or enliven with an additional element.

**leaves** *n* pl of LEAF¹.

**lecher** *n* a lecherous man.

**lecherous** *adj* showing inordinate or offensive sexual desire. ➤ **lechery** *n*.

**lectern** *n* a tall stand with a sloping top designed to hold an open book, papers etc from which a person can read aloud, e.g. in church.

**lecture¹** *n* **1** a discourse on an educational subject read aloud to an audience. **2** a lengthy reprimand.

**lecture²** *v* **1** to deliver a lecture. **2** to reprimand at length or severely.

**led** *v* past tense and past part. of LEAD¹.

**ledge** *n* a narrow horizontal surface projecting from e.g. a wall or rock face.

**ledger** *n* a book recording financial accounts.

**lee** *n* the side, e.g. of a ship, that is sheltered from the wind.

**leech** *n* **1** a bloodsucking freshwater worm. **2** a person who tries to extract as much of another's wealth or resources from them as possible.

**leek** *n* a plant with a white cylindrical stalk and bulb, used as a vegetable.

**leer¹** *v* to give a lascivious or sly look.

**leer²** *n* a lascivious or sly look.

**leery** *adj* (**-ier, -iest**) (*often* + of) suspicious or wary.

**lees** *pl n* the sediment left in a barrel or bottle of wine.

**leeward** *adj and adv* in or facing the direction towards which the wind is blowing: compare WINDWARD.

**leeway** *n* an allowed margin of freedom or variation.

**left**[1] *adj* **1** on the side of somebody or something that is nearer the west when the front faces north. **2** (*often* **Left**) of the left wing in politics.

**left**[2] *adv* on or towards the left.

**left**[3] *n* **1** the part, direction, etc on the left side. **2** the left hand, or a blow struck with it. **3** *informal* a left turn. **4** (*often* **the Left**) those professing socialist or radical political views.

**left**[4] *v* past tense and past part. of LEAVE[1].

**left-field** *adj* unorthodox; not mainstream.

**leftover**[1] *n* (*also in pl*) something, *esp* food, that is left unused or unconsumed.

**leftover**[2] *adj* remaining unused or unconsumed.

**left wing** *n* **1** (*often* **Left Wing**) the more socialist or reformist division of a political party. **2** in sport, the left side of the field when facing towards the opposing team. ➤ **left-wing** *adj,* **left-winger** *n.*

**lefty** *n* (*pl* **-ies**) *informal* a left-wing person.

**leg** *n* **1** a limb of a person or animal used for supporting the body and walking. **2** an upright pole serving as a support, e.g. for a a table. **3** a portion of a trip or race; a stage. **4** a round of a competition, or one of two or more events constituting a round. ✱ **leg it** *informal* to run away. **not have a leg to stand on** to have no basis for one's position, *esp* in a controversy.

**legacy** *n* (*pl* **-ies**) **1** money or property received under a will. **2** something passed on by a predecessor or remaining from the past.

**legal** *adj* **1** relating to law. **2** permitted by law. ➤ **legally** *adv.*

**legal aid** *n* money from public funds to pay for legal advice for those who cannot afford it.

**legalize** *or* **-ise** *v* to make legal. ➤ **legalization** *n.*

**legal tender** *n* currency, usu coins and banknotes, acceptable as payment of a debt.

**legate** *n* a representative of the Pope.

**legation** *n* **1** a diplomatic mission headed by a minister rather than an ambassador. **2** the official residence of a diplomat.

**legato** /li'gahtoh/ *adj and adv* of a piece of music: performed in a smooth and connected manner.

**legend** *n* **1** a popular story coming down from the past that is not historically verifiable. **2** a very famous person, act, or thing. **3** an inscription on an object, e.g. a coin. **4** a caption. **5** the key to a map, chart, etc.

**legendary** *adj* **1** described in legends. **2** very famous.

**leggings** *pl n* **1** close-fitting stretchy trousers worn by women or children. **2** close-fitting protective garments for the legs.

**leggy** *adj* (**-ier, -iest**) **1** having long legs. **2** of a plant: having unnaturally long thin stems.

**legible** *adj* capable of being read or deciphered. ➤ **legibility** *n,* **legibly** *adv.*

**legion**[1] *n* **1** the principal unit of the ancient Roman army comprising 3000–6000 soldiers. **2** (*also in pl*) a very large number.

**legion**[2] *adj* many or numerous.

**legionnaire** *n* a member of a legion or ex-servicemen's association.

**legionnaire's disease** *n* a serious infectious disease resembling pneumonia.

**legislate** *v* **1** to make laws. **2** (+ for/against) to make preparations to deal with.

**legislation** *n* laws.

**legislative** *adj* **1** having the power to make laws. **2** relating to legislation.

**legislature** *n* a body of people with the power to make laws.

**legitimate**[1] *adj* **1** in accordance with law, or accepted rules and standards. **2** genuine. **3** of a child: born in wedlock. **4** in accordance with reason or logic. ➤ **legitimacy** *n,* **legitimately** *adv.*

**legitimate**[2] *v* = LEGITIMIZE.

**legitimize** *or* **-ise** *v* **1** to give legal status to. **2** to justify. ➤ **legitimization** *n.*

**legume** *n* a member of a large family of plants that have pods containing seeds, e.g. peas and beans. ➤ **leguminous** *adj.*

**leisure** *n* time free from work or duties. ✱ **at leisure** free; not working. **at one's leisure 1** at an unhurried pace. **2** at one's convenience.

**leisurely** *adj* unhurried; relaxed.

**lemming** *n* **1** a small furry Arctic rodent with a short tail, which periodically undertakes mass migrations resulting in the death of many through drowning in the sea. **2** a member of a group mindlessly risking self-destruction through their actions.

**lemon** *n* **1** an oval yellow citrus fruit with a thick rind and acid flesh. **2** a pale yellow colour. **3** *informal* a feeble or useless person or thing.

**lemonade** *n* a soft drink, often carbonated, flavoured with lemon.

**lemon curd** *n* a thick buttery lemon-flavoured conserve.

**lemur** *n* a tree-dwelling mammal of Madagascar with large eyes and a long furry tail.

**lend** *v* (*past tense and past part.* **lent**) **1** to give (something) to somebody for temporary use on condition that it is returned. **2** to give (money) to somebody on condition of repayment, usu with interest. **3** to add or contribute. **4** (**lend itself to**) to be suitable for. ➤ **lender** *n.*

**length** *n* **1** the quality of being long. **2** a measurement of how long something is. **3** the longest dimension of an object. **4** the extent from end to end, or from beginning to end. **5** duration or extent in time. **6** a piece of something long and narrow. * **at length 1** comprehensively. **2** for a long time. **3** at last. **go to great/ any lengths** to make a great/every effort or use any means.

**lengthen** *v* to become or make longer.

**lengthways** *or* **lengthwise** *adv and adj* in the direction of the length.

**lengthy** *adj* (**-ier, -iest**) long. ➤ **lengthily** *adv.*

**lenient** *adj* merciful or tolerant. ➤ **leniency** *n.*

**lens** *n* **1** a piece of transparent material with a curved surface, used to form an image by focusing rays of light, e.g. in a camera or microscope. **2** a transparent, nearly spherical body in the eye that focuses light rays on the retina.

**Lent** *n* the 40 weekdays preceding Easter Saturday, observed by Christians as a time of penitence and fasting.

**lent** *v* past tense and past part. of LEND.

**lentil** *n* a small flattish seed of a plant of the pea family, used as a vegetable.

**lento** *adj and adv* of a piece of music: performed slowly.

**Leo** *n* the fifth sign of the zodiac (the Lion).

**leonine** *adj* of or resembling a lion.

**leopard** *or* **leopardess** *n* a big cat of South Asia and Africa that has a tawny coat with black spots.

**leotard** *n* a close-fitting stretchy one-piece garment worn for dance, gymnastics, etc.

**leper** *n* **1** a person suffering from leprosy. **2** a person shunned for moral or social reasons.

**leprechaun** *n* a mischievous elf of Irish folklore.

**leprosy** *n* a contagious bacterial disease affecting the skin that can cause wasting of muscle and disfigurement.

**lesbian** *n* a homosexual woman. ➤ **lesbian** *adj,* **lesbianism** *n.*

**lesion** *n* an area of an organ, the skin, etc, structurally damaged by injury or disease.

**less**[1] *adj* **1** smaller in quantity or extent. **2** *informal* fewer.

***Usage Note:*** Strictly, *less* should be used only with a singular mass noun: *less tea. Fewer* should be used with a plural noun: *fewer teacups.*

**less**[2] *adv* to a smaller degree or extent.

**less**[3] *prep* minus.

**less**[4] *n* a smaller portion or quantity.

**-less** *suffix* **1** not having: *childless.* **2** free from: *painless.*

**lessee** *n* somebody who holds property under a lease.

**lessen** *v* to decrease in size, extent, etc.

**lesser** *adj and adv* less in size, quality, or significance.

**lesson** *n* **1** a period of instruction. **2** an instructive or warning example. **3** something learned by study or experience. **4** a passage from the Bible read during a church service.

**lessor** *n* somebody who lets property by lease.

**lest** *conj* **1** so that not; to avoid the possibility of. **2** used after an expression of fear, anxiety, etc: that.

**let**[1] *v* (**letting,** *past tense and past part.* **let**) **1** to allow. **2** used to introduce request or proposal: *Let's go now.* **3** to allow somebody the use of (accommodation) for rent or lease. * **let alone** and definitely not. **let alone/be** to leave alone. **let go 1** to stop holding. **2** to release (somebody captured). **let oneself go 1** to abandon self-restraint. **2** to allow one's appearance or habits to deteriorate.

**let**[2] *n Brit* a period for which premises are let.

**let**[3] *n* a serve or shot in tennis, squash, etc that does not count and must be replayed.

**letdown** *n informal* a disappointment or disillusionment.

**let down** *v* **1** to fail to support or assist (somebody). **2** to disappoint (somebody) by not keeping a promise, appointment, etc. **3** to deflate (e.g. a tyre).

**lethal** *adj* **1** capable of causing death. **2** seriously damaging or destructive. ➤ **lethally** *adv.*

**lethargic** *adj* slow moving, usu through lack of energy or interest. ➤ **lethargically** *adv.*

**lethargy** *n* **1** lack of energy or interest. **2** abnormal drowsiness.

**let off** *v* **1** to excuse from punishment or a responsibility. **2** to cause (a bomb or firework) to explode or (a gun) to fire.

**let's** *contraction* let us.

**letter**[1] *n* **1** a symbol representing a speech sound, forming part of an alphabet. **2** a written or printed message sent through the post. **3** *literary* (*in pl*) literature. **4** (**the letter**) the strict or literal meaning. * **to the letter** precisely or literally.

**letter**[2] *v* to mark with letters.

**letter bomb** *n* an explosive device concealed in an envelope or package.

**letter box** *n Brit* a hole in a door to receive material delivered by post.

**letterhead** *n* a printed heading on stationery showing the name, address, etc of a person or organization.

**lettering** *n* the letters used in an inscription.

**lettuce** *n* a common garden plant with edible leaves eaten raw in salads.

**letup** *n informal* a cessation or lessening of effort or intensity.

**let up** *v* to diminish or become less intense.

**leucocyte** (*NAmer* **leukocyte**) *n* a white blood cell.

**leukaemia** (*NAmer* **leukemia**) *n* a type of cancer characterized by an abnormal increase in white blood cells in the body tissues.
**levee** *n chiefly NAmer* an embankment constructed to prevent flooding.
**level**[1] *n* **1** a horizontal line, surface, or state. **2** height, *esp* in relation to the ground. **3** a layer in a vertical structure, e.g. a floor in a building. **4** a position in a scale or rank. * **on the level** *informal* honest; genuine.
**level**[2] *adj* **1** having no part higher than another. **2** (*often* + with) of or at the same height. **3** equal in quantity, position, or standing. * **a level playing field** a situation in which nobody has an unfair advantage. ➤ **levelly** *adv.*
**level**[3] *v* (**levelled, levelling,** *NAmer* **leveled, leveling**) **1** (*also* + off) to make (a line or surface) horizontal. **2** (*often* + at) to bring (a weapon) to a horizontal aiming position. **3** (+ at/against) to aim or direct (criticism, an accusation, etc). **4** to equalize. **5** to raze. **6** *informal* (+ with) to deal frankly and openly with somebody.
**level crossing** *n Brit* a place where a railway crosses a road on the same level.
**levelheaded** *adj* calm and sensible.
**lever**[1] *n* **1** a bar used for prising up or dislodging something. **2** a projecting part by which a mechanism is operated or adjusted.
**lever**[2] *v* to raise or move with a lever.
**leverage** *n* **1** the force exerted when using a lever. **2** power or influence.
**leveret** *n* a young hare.
**leviathan** *n* **1** (*often* **Leviathan**) a biblical sea monster. **2** something very large or powerful.
**levitate** *v* to rise or float in the air. ➤ **levitation** *n.*
**levity** *n* lack of seriousness or unseemly frivolity when dealing with a serious subject.
**levy**[1] *n* (*pl* **-ies**) **1** the imposing of a tax, fine, etc. **2** an amount levied. **3** *archaic* (*often pl*) troops enlisted for military service.
**levy**[2] *v* (**-ies, -ied**) **1** to impose (e.g. a tax) by legal authority. **2** *archaic* to enlist for military service.
**lewd** *adj* sexually coarse or suggestive.
**lexical** *adj* **1** relating to the words or the vocabulary of a language. **2** relating to dictionaries.
**lexicography** *n* the compiling of dictionaries. ➤ **lexicographer** *n.*
**lexicon** *n* **1** the vocabulary of a language, individual, or subject. **2** a dictionary.
**ley line** *n* a line linking ancient sites, supposed by some people to be a source of energy and connected with paranormal phenomena.
**liability** *n* (*pl* **-ies**) **1** the fact of being liable. **2** something for which one is liable, *esp* a debt. **3** a hindrance or drawback.
**liable** *adj* **1** legally responsible. **2** (+ to) subject to or punishable for something. **3** (+ to) likely to do something.
**liaise** *v* **1** (*often* + with) to establish a connection and cooperate. **2** to maintain communication and act as a go-between.
**liaison** *n* **1** communication and usu cooperation. **2** an illicit sexual relationship.

***Usage Note:*** Note the spelling with two *i*'s and one *a*.

**liana** *n* a climbing plant that attaches itself to trees *esp* in tropical rain forests.
**liar** *n* a person who tells lies.
**libation** *n* a drink poured out in sacrifice to a god.
**libel**[1] *n* **1** defamation of somebody by published writing as opposed to spoken words. **2** a false defamatory written statement. ➤ **libellous** *adj.*
**libel**[2] *v* (**libelled, libelling,** *NAmer* **libeled, libeling**) to publish a libel about.
**liberal**[1] *adj* **1** broad-minded or tolerant. **2** advocating individual rights and freedom and moderate reform. **3** (**Liberal**) in Britain, of, belonging to, or supporting the Liberal Democrats. **4** generous. **5** ample. **6** not strict or literal. ➤ **liberalism** *n,* **liberality** *n,* **liberally** *adv.*
**liberal**[2] *n* somebody with liberal views.
**liberalize** *or* **-ise** *v* to make less strict or restrictive. ➤ **liberalization** *n.*
**liberate** *v* **1** to set free. **2** to free from social conventions. ➤ **liberated** *adj,* **liberation** *n,* **liberator** *n.*
**libertine** *n* a person who leads a dissolute life.
**liberty** *n* (*pl* **-ies**) **1** the power to do as one pleases. **2** freedom from physical restraint or dictatorial control. **3** the power of choice. **4** a right or privilege. **5** *informal* (*also in pl*) a breach of etiquette or propriety. * **take liberties 1** to show disrespect or be overfamiliar. **2** to disregard requirements for strict accuracy.
**libidinous** *adj* marked by strong sexual desire.
**libido** *n* (*pl* **-os**) sexual drive.
**Libra** *n* the seventh sign of the zodiac (the Scales).
**librarian** *n* a person who manages or works in a library.
**library** *n* (*pl* **-ies**) **1** a room or building in which books, periodicals, etc are kept for reference or for borrowing by the public. **2** a person's collection of books.
**libretto** *n* (*pl* **libretti** *or* **librettos**) the text of an opera. ➤ **librettist** *n.*
**lice** *n* pl of LOUSE.
**licence** (*NAmer* **license**) *n* **1** an official document showing that the holder is authorized to do something. **2** freedom of action. **3** unrestrained and usu immoral behaviour.

***Usage Note:*** In British English the noun is spelled *-ence* and the verb *-ense*.

**license** *v* to give official permission to (somebody) to do something or for (something) to take place.

**licensee** *n* the holder of a licence, *esp* to sell alcoholic drink.

**license plate** *n NAmer* a numberplate.

**licentious** *adj* sexually unrestrained.

**lichen** *n* a plant that grows in flat, greyish patches on rocks and tree trunks.

**lich-gate** *n* see LYCHGATE.

**lick**[1] *v* **1** to pass the tongue over. **2** to touch lightly, *esp* with a darting movement. **3** *informal* to defeat, *esp* decisively. ✱ **lick into shape** to put into proper form or condition.

**lick**[2] *n* **1** an act of licking. **2** *informal* a small amount. ✱ **a lick and a promise** *informal* a quick wash. **at a lick** *informal* at a fast speed.

**licorice** *n NAmer* see LIQUORICE.

**lid** *n* **1** a hinged or detachable cover for a receptacle. **2** an eyelid.

**lido** *n* (*pl* **-os**) a public open-air swimming pool.

**lie**[1] *v* (**lying,** *past tense* **lay,** *past part.* **lain**) **1** to be or rest in a horizontal position. **2** (*often* + down) to assume a horizontal position. **3** to be in a specified state or condition: *The machinery was lying idle.* **4** to be located. ✱ **lie low** to stay in hiding or avoid notice. **the lie of the land 1** the contours and geographical features of an area. **2** the current nature of the situation.

**lie**[2] *n* an untrue statement, *esp* one made with intent to deceive.

**lie**[3] *v* (**lies, lied, lying**) to make an untrue statement or statements.

**lie detector** *n* an instrument that detects physical evidence, e.g. a change in pulse rate, of the mental tension that accompanies telling lies.

**liege**[1] *adj* **1** of a lord: entitled to feudal allegiance. **2** of a vassal: owing feudal allegiance.

**liege**[2] *n* **1** a feudal lord. **2** a feudal vassal.

**lieu** ✱ **in lieu of** instead of.

**lieutenant** *n* **1** a deputy or representative. **2** an officer in the Royal Navy ranking below a lieutenant commander. **3** an officer in the British army ranking below a captain.

**life** *n* (*pl* **lives**) **1** the quality that distinguishes living beings from dead or inanimate ones. **2** the period of existence of an individual. **3** a way or manner of living. **4** living beings, e.g. of a specified kind or environment: *forest life.* **5** the period of usefulness of e.g. a machine. **6** vitality or excitement. **7** *informal* a sentence of life imprisonment.

**life assurance** *n chiefly Brit* = LIFE INSURANCE.

**lifebelt** *n chiefly Brit* a buoyant ring for keeping a person afloat.

**lifeblood** *n* a vital or life-giving force.

**lifeboat** *n* **1** a shore-based boat for saving lives at sea. **2** a boat carried by a ship for use in an emergency.

**lifeguard** *n* a person employed to safeguard others at a swimming pool or beach.

**life insurance** *n* insurance providing for payment of a stipulated sum on the death of the insured person or at the end of a fixed period.

**life jacket** *n* an inflatable or buoyant jacket designed to keep a person afloat.

**lifeless** *adj* **1** dead. **2** inanimate. **3** having no living beings. **4** dull.

**lifelike** *adj* accurately representing or imitating real life.

**lifeline** *n* **1** a rope used to pull a person to safety from water. **2** something, *esp* a sole means of communication, indispensable for the protection of life. **3** a line on the palm of the hand, taken to be an indication of the length of a person's life.

**lifelong** *adj* lasting or continuing throughout life.

**life peer** *or* **life peeress** *n* a British peer whose title is not hereditary.

**life raft** *n* a usu inflatable raft for use in an emergency at sea.

**life span** *n* **1** the duration of existence of an individual. **2** the average length of life of a kind of organism or of a material object, *esp* in a particular environment or in specified circumstances.

**lifestyle** *n* an individual's way of life, or the activities, possessions, etc associated with this.

**lifetime** *n* the length of time for which a living being exists or a thing remains useful, valid, etc.

**lift**[1] *v* **1** to raise to a higher position. **2** to pick (something or somebody) up in order to move them. **3** to put an end to (e.g. a blockade). **4** to revoke (a restriction).

**lift**[2] *n* **1** *Brit* a device for conveying people or objects from one level to another, *esp* in a building. **2** a free ride as a passenger in a motor vehicle. **3** a feeling of cheerfulness or encouragement. **4** the upward force acting on an aircraft or wing that opposes the pull of gravity.

**ligament** *n* a tough band of tissue connecting two or more bones or cartilages or supporting an organ.

**ligature** *n* something that is used to bind; *esp* a thread used in surgery to tie off a severed artery.

**light**[1] *n* **1** natural radiation that makes vision possible by stimulating the sense of sight. **2** a source of light, e.g. a lamp or a candle. **3** daylight. **4** a flame lighting *esp* a cigarette. **5** (*also in pl*) a traffic light. **6** understanding or knowledge. **7** a particular aspect in which something is viewed. ✱ **bring to light** to disclose or reveal. **come to light** to be revealed or disclosed. **in the light of** with the insight provided by. **see the light 1** to understand suddenly. **2** to undergo conversion.

**light**[2] *adj* **1** having plenty of light; bright. **2** pale in colour. ➤ **lightness** *n.*

**light**[3] *v* (*past tense* **lit,** *past part.* **lit** *or* **lighted**) **1** to provide light in. **2** to catch fire. **3** to set fire to.

**light**[4] *adj* **1** having little weight; not heavy. **2** designed to carry a comparatively small load. **3** insufficient in weight. **4** not abundant or intense. **5** gentle or soft. **6** requiring little effort. **7** graceful, deft, or nimble. **8** intended chiefly to entertain: *light reading*. ➤ **lightly** *adv*, **lightness** *n*.

**light**[5] *v* (*past tense and past part.* **lit** *or* **lighted**) (+ on/upon) to find by chance.

**lighten**[1] *v* **1** to make or become lighter or less burdensome. **2** to make or become more cheerful.

**lighten**[2] *v* **1** to make (a colour, hair, etc) paler. **2** to brighten.

**lighter**[1] *n* a device for lighting a cigarette, cigar, etc.

**lighter**[2] *n* a large flat-bottomed barge used in unloading or loading ships.

**light-fingered** *adj* expert at or given to stealing.

**light-headed** *adj* faint or dizzy.

**light-hearted** *adj* **1** free from care or worry. **2** playful or amusing.

**lighthouse** *n* a tower equipped with a powerful light to warn or guide shipping.

**lighting** *n* **1** the apparatus providing a supply of light. **2** the arrangement of lights to produce a particular effect.

**lightning** *n* **1** the flash produced by a discharge of atmospheric electricity between two clouds or between a cloud and the earth. **2** (*used before a noun*) very quick, short, or sudden.

**lightning conductor** (*NAmer* **lightning rod**) *n* a metal rod fixed to the highest point of a building to carry lightning safely to earth.

**light pen** *n* **1** a pen-shaped photoelectric device moved over a VDU screen to communicate with a computer. **2** a pen-shaped device used to read bar codes.

**lights** *pl n* the lungs of a slaughtered sheep, pig, etc, used as food.

**light up** *v* **1** to illuminate or become illuminated. **2** to make or become more animated or cheerful. **3** to start smoking a cigarette, pipe, etc.

**lightweight**[1] *n* **1** a weight in boxing between welterweight and featherweight. **2** *informal* somebody of little ability or importance.

**lightweight**[2] *adj* **1** of less than average weight. **2** *informal* lacking in seriousness or profundity.

**light-year** *n* the distance that light travels in one year, approximately 9460 thousand million km (about 5878 thousand million mi).

**ligneous** *adj* of or resembling wood.

**likable** *or* **likeable** *adj* pleasant or agreeable.

**like**[1] *prep* **1** similar to. **2** typical of. **3** in the manner of. **4** such as.

**like**[2] *conj informal* **1** in the same way as. **2** as if.

**like**[3] *n* somebody or something that is similar. ✱ **the like** similar things.

**like**[4] *adj* similar in appearance, character, or quantity.

**like**[5] *v* **1** to find (something or somebody) agreeable or acceptable. **2** to wish or choose (to have, be, or do something).

**like**[6] *n* a liking or preference.

**likeable** *adj* see LIKABLE.

**likelihood** *n* probability.

**likely**[1] *adj* (**-ier, -iest**) **1** probable. **2** promising.

**likely**[2] *adv* probably.

**liken** *v* (+ to) to point out the resemblance of (a person or thing) to another.

**likeness** *n* **1** resemblance. **2** a portrait. **3** an appearance or semblance.

**likewise** *adv* **1** moreover; in addition. **2** similarly.

**liking** *n* **1** favourable regard. **2** taste or fondness.

**lilac** *n* **1** a shrub with heart-shaped leaves and large clusters of fragrant white or pale purple flowers. **2** a pale pinkish purple colour.

**Li-Lo** *n* (*pl* **-os**) *trademark* an airbed.

**lilt** *n* a rhythmic swing, flow, or rising and falling inflection in music or speech.

**lily** *n* (*pl* **-ies**) a plant that grows from bulbs and has showy trumpet-shaped flowers.

**lily-livered** *adj* cowardly.

**lily of the valley** *n* (*pl* **lilies of the valley**) a low-growing plant with fragrant bell-shaped white flowers.

**limb** *n* **1** a leg or arm of a human being. **2** a large branch of a tree. ✱ **out on a limb** in an exposed and unsupported position.

**limber up** *v* to prepare for physical action by gentle exercise.

**limbo**[1] *n* an intermediate or transitional state.

**limbo**[2] *n* (*pl* **-os**) an acrobatic West Indian dance that involves bending backwards to pass under a horizontal pole.

**lime**[1] *n* an alkaline substance used in building and in fertilizers.

**lime**[2] *n* a tree with heart-shaped leaves and clusters of yellow flowers.

**lime**[3] *n* **1** a small green citrus fruit with acid juicy pulp. **2** a bright greenish yellow colour.

**limelight** *n* (**the limelight**) the centre of public attention.

**limerick** *n* a humorous verse form of five lines with a rhyme scheme of aabba.

**limestone** *n* rock consisting mainly of calcium carbonate.

**limit**[1] *n* **1** a line or point that cannot or should not be passed. **2** the furthest point or extreme degree of something. **3** a prescribed maximum or minimum amount, quantity, or number. ➤ **limitless** *adj*.

**limit**[2] *v* (**limited, limiting**) to restrict to specific bounds or limits.

**limitation** *n* **1** a restriction. **2** a defect or weak point.
**limited** *adj* **1** restricted in size or scope. **2** lacking the ability to grow or do better. **3** (*often* **Limited**) *Brit* of a company: in which individual shareholders' responsibility for the company's debts is limited.
**limo** *n* (*pl* **-os**) *informal* = LIMOUSINE.
**limousine** *n* a large luxurious motor car.
**limp**[1] *v* **1** to walk with an uneven step, usu because of an injured leg. **2** to proceed slowly or with difficulty.
**limp**[2] *n* a limping gait.
**limp**[3] *adj* **1** lacking firmness and stiffness. **2** lacking energy. ➤ **limply** *adv.*
**limpet** *n* a shellfish with a large suction foot that enables it to cling very tightly to rock.
**limpid** *adj* transparent or clear.
**linchpin** *or* **lynchpin** *n* **1** a pin inserted crosswise through the end of an axle to hold a wheel in place. **2** somebody or something regarded as vital.
**linctus** *n* a syrupy usu medicated liquid used to relieve throat irritation and coughing.
**line**[1] *n* **1** a long narrow mark across a surface. **2** a narrow crease, e.g. on the face; a wrinkle. **3** a boundary, border, or defining outline. **4** a row or queue. **5** a horizontal row of written or printed characters. **6** (*in pl*) all of the text making up a particular role in a play. **7** *Brit* (*in pl*) a specified number of lines of writing to be copied as a school punishment. **8** a thread, string, cord, or rope. **9** a conducting wire or cable conveying electrical power or a telecommunications signal. **10** a telephone connection. **11** a railway track or route. **12** a related series of people or things coming one after the other in time. **13** a particular type of merchandise, product, or service. **14** a field of activity, interest, or business. **15** a linked series of trenches and fortifications, *esp* facing the enemy. ✱ **draw the line** to set a limit as to what is acceptable. **in line for** likely to get. **in line with** conforming to. **on the line** at risk. **out of line** *informal* behaving in an unacceptable fashion.
**line**[2] *v* **1** to form a line along. **2** to mark or cover with lines.
**line**[3] *v* to cover the inner surface of.
**lineage** *n* a line of descent from a common ancestor or source.
**lineal** *adj* **1** in a direct line of ancestry or descent. **2** arranged in lines. ➤ **lineally** *adv.*
**lineament** *n* (*also in pl*) a distinctive outline or feature, *esp* of the face.
**linear** *adj* **1** arranged in a straight line. **2** consisting of lines. **3** involving a single dimension. **4** showing a straightforward progression through a sequence of stages. ➤ **linearity** *n.*
**line dancing** *n* a type of dancing to country and western music, performed by people in rows executing a sequence of steps simultaneously.
**linen** *n* **1** cloth made from flax. **2** household articles, e.g. sheets and tablecloths, made, *esp* formerly, of linen.
**line-out** *n* in Rugby Union, a method of restarting play after the ball has crossed a touchline by throwing it in between two lines of opposing forwards.
**liner**[1] *n* **1** a large passenger ship. **2** something, e.g. a cosmetic, used to draw lines.
**liner**[2] *n* something used to line clothing or a container.
**linesman** *n* (*pl* **linesmen**) in sport: an official who assists the referee or umpire in determining if a ball or player is out of the playing area.
**line up** *v* **1** to arrange in or form a line. **2** to put into alignment. **3** to assemble or organize in readiness for something.
**line-up** *n* **1** an identity parade. **2** a group of people or items assembled for a particular purpose.
**ling**[1] *n* a long-bodied sea fish.
**ling**[2] *n* = HEATHER.
**linger** *v* **1** to delay going or be reluctant to leave. **2** to be slow in disappearing. **3** (+ over/on/upon) to spend a long time doing, dealing with, or looking at. ➤ **lingering** *adj.*
**lingerie** *n* women's underwear and nightclothes.
**lingo** *n* (*pl* **-oes** *or* **-os**) *informal* **1** a foreign language. **2** the special vocabulary of a particular subject; jargon.
**lingua franca** *n* (*pl* **lingua francas** *or* **linguae francae**) a language used as a common tongue among people not speaking the same native language.
**linguini** *or* **linguine** /ling'gweeni/ *pl n* pasta in the form of flat strands.
**linguist** *n* **1** somebody accomplished in languages. **2** somebody who studies linguistics.
**linguistic** *adj* relating to language or linguistics. ➤ **linguistically** *adv.*
**linguistics** *pl n* the scientific study of language.
**liniment** *n* a liquid medication applied to the skin, *esp* to relieve pain.
**lining** *n* a layer of a different material used to cover the inside of something, e.g. a garment.
**link**[1] *n* **1** a single ring of a chain. **2** a connection or relationship between people or things. **3** a system that enables people, machines, etc to communicate. **4** a means of transportation between one place and another.
**link**[2] *v* **1** (*often* + up) to join, connect, or to become connected. **2** to suggest that (people or things) are significantly associated.
**linkage** *n* **1** the act of linking. **2** a system of links.
**links** *pl n* a golf course, *esp* along the seashore.
**linnet** *n* a finch with a red breast and forehead.

**lino** *n* (*pl* **-os**) *chiefly Brit, informal* = LINOLEUM.
**linoleum** *n* a usu patterned floor covering made of hardened linseed oil and a filler, e.g. cork dust.
**linseed** *n* the seed of flax that is the source of linseed oil, which is used in paints, varnishes, linoleum, etc.
**lint** *n* **1** a soft absorbent material used chiefly for surgical dressings. **2** fluff or shreds of fibre from cloth.
**lintel** *n* a horizontal support above an opening, *esp* a door.
**lion** *or* **lioness** *n* **1** a flesh-eating African big cat with a tawny body and, in the male, a shaggy blackish mane. **2** a courageous or ferocious person. * **the lion's share** the largest portion or share.
**lionize** *or* **-ise** *v* to treat (somebody) as a celebrity.
**lip** *n* **1** either of the two fleshy folds that surround the mouth. **2** the edge of a hollow vessel or cavity. **3** *informal* impudent or insolent talk.
**liposuction** *n* a technique in plastic surgery for removing excess body fat by vacuum suction.
**lippy** *adj* (**-ier, -iest**) *informal* cheeky or impudent.
**lip-read** *v* (*past tense and past part.* **lip-read**) to understand speech by watching the movements of a person's lips.
**lipstick** *n* a stick of waxy solid cosmetic for colouring the lips.
**lip-synch** *or* **lip-sync** *v* to match one's lip movements to the words of a recorded speech or song.
**liquefy** *v* (**-ies, -ied**) to become or make liquid. ➤ **liquefaction** *n.*

***Usage Note:*** Note the spelling *-efy* not *-ify*.

**liqueur** *n* a strong usu sweet alcoholic drink.
**liquid**[1] *adj* **1** flowing freely like water. **2** shining and clear. **3** of sounds: flowing and free of harshness. **4** of assets: consisting of, or readily convertible into, cash.
**liquid**[2] *n* a substance that is liquid.
**liquidate** *v* **1** to settle (a debt). **2** to end the commercial activities of (a business) and use its assets to pay off its debts. **3** to convert (assets) into cash. **4** *informal* to kill. ➤ **liquidation** *n.*
**liquidity** *n* the liquid assets of a company.
**liquidize** *or* **-ise** *v* to mash (e.g. fruit or vegetables) into a liquid.
**liquor** *n* **1** alcoholic drink, *esp* spirits. **2** a liquid produced by cooking food or in which food has been cooked.
**liquorice** (*NAmer* **licorice**) *n* an extract from the black dried root of a plant of the pea family, used in sweets and as a laxative.
**lira** /'liərə/ *n* (*pl* **lire** *or* **liras**) the basic monetary unit of Turkey and formerly of Italy (replaced by the euro in 2002).
**lisp**[1] *n* a speech defect in which /s/ is pronounced as /th/.
**lisp**[2] *v* to speak with a lisp.
**lissom** *or* **lissome** *adj* slim, supple, and graceful.
**list**[1] *n* a series of words or numbers arranged in order usu down a page.
**list**[2] *v* **1** to make a list of. **2** to include on a list.
**list**[3] *v* of a ship: to lean to one side.
**listed** *adj* **1** *Brit* of a building: protected as being historically or architecturally important. **2** of a company: having its shares quoted on the main market of the London Stock Exchange.
**listen** *v* **1** to pay attention to sound. **2** (*often* + to) to hear and give thoughtful consideration to; to heed. **3** (*often* + out/for) to be alert to catch an expected sound. ➤ **listener** *n.*
**listeria** *n* a rod-shaped bacterium that causes sometimes fatal food poisoning.
**listing** *n* **1** an entry in a list. **2** a list or catalogue.
**listless** *adj* characterized by indifference and lack of energy. ➤ **listlessly** *adv.*
**list price** *n* the basic price of an item as published in a manufacturer's catalogue, etc.
**lit** *v* past tense and past part. of LIGHT[3], LIGHT[5].
**litany** *n* (*pl* **-ies**) **1** a prayer consisting of a series of petitions by the leader, each followed by a response from the congregation. **2** a repetitive recital.
**liter** *n NAmer* see LITRE.
**literacy** *n* **1** the ability to read and write. **2** knowledge of a particular subject: *computer literacy.*
**literal** *adj* **1** denoting the factual or primary meaning of a word or expression. **2** keeping strictly to the straightforward meaning of a written text. **3** reproduced or translated word for word.
**literally** *adv* **1** in the literal sense. **2** *informal* used to intensify a metaphorical expression.
**literary** *adj* **1** relating to literature. **2** of language: characteristic of literature; formal or picturesque.
**literate** *adj* **1** able to read and write. **2** possessing knowledge in a particular field of activity: *computer literate.*
**literati** /litə'rahtee/ *pl n* educated people with an interest in literature.
**literature** *n* **1** writings in prose or verse, *esp* those having artistic value. **2** the body of writings on a particular subject. **3** printed matter, e.g. leaflets or circulars.
**lithe** *adj* supple and athletic.
**lithium** *n* a light soft silver-white metallic element used in alloys.
**lithograph** /'lithəgrahf, -graf/ *n* a print made by lithography.
**lithography** *n* the process of printing from a metal surface treated so that the image to be printed is ink-receptive and the blank area ink-repellent.

**litigation** *n* the use of the courts or lawsuits to settle issues.
**litigious** *adj* inclined to take legal action frequently.
**litmus** *n* a colouring matter that turns red in acid solutions and blue in alkaline solutions.
**litmus paper** *n* paper coloured with litmus, used as an indicator of acidity or alkalinity.
**litmus test** *n* a sure test of something's worth.
**litre** (*NAmer* **liter**) *n* a metric unit of capacity equal to 1000 cubic centimetres (about 1.75 pints).
**litter**[1] *n* **1** scattered rubbish, *esp* in a public place. **2** an untidy accumulation of things. **3** a group of animal offspring born at one birth. **4** absorbent material placed in a location where a cat, urinates and defecates. **5** straw or similar material used as bedding for animals. **6** the uppermost slightly decayed layer of organic matter on a forest floor. **7** a covered and curtained couch carried by people or animals.
**litter**[2] *v* to strew (an area) with litter.
**little**[1] *adj* **1** small in size or extent. **2** of a person: young or younger. **3** not much. **4** short in duration or distance.
**little**[2] *adv* (**less, least**) **1** not much: *little-known.* **2** hardly or not at all.
**little**[3] *n* not much. ✻ **a little 1** to a small extent or degree. **2** a small amount or portion. **3** a short time or distance.
**liturgy** *n* (*pl* **-ies**) a prescribed form of public worship.
**live**[1] *v* **1** to be alive, or to be alive for or during a particular period of time. **2** to continue alive. **3** to have a particular way of life, aim in life, etc. **4** to maintain oneself or earn a living. **5** to have a home. ✻ **live it up** *informal* to live or celebrate lavishly. **live off** to rely on for subsistence. **live together** of two people: to share a home and have a sexual relationship without being married. **live up to** to achieve (an expected standard).
**live**[2] *adj* **1** having life. **2** connected to a source of electric power. **3** unexploded or unfired. **4** of continuing or current interest. **5** performed, performing, or recorded in the presence of an audience. **6** broadcast as it happens.
**live**[3] *adv* **1** in person and in front of an audience. **2** simultaneously as it happens.
**live down** *v* to overcome the shame or embarrassment caused by (a mistake or offence).
**livelihood** *n* something, *esp* a job, that provides a person with the means to support themselves.
**lively** *adj* (**-ier, -iest**) **1** active and energetic. **2** full of life, movement, or incident. ➤ **liveliness** *n.*
**liven** *v* (*often* + up) to make or become more lively.
**live out** *v* **1** to live to the end of (a period of time). **2** to carry out (something imagined) in real life.
**liver** *n* **1** a large glandular organ that secretes bile. **2** the liver of an animal eaten as food.
**liverish** *adj* **1** suffering from liver disorder; bilious. **2** peevish or irascible.
**livery** *n* (*pl* **-ies**) **1** a distinctive uniform worn by servants, employees, officials, etc. **2** a distinctive colour scheme, e.g. on a vehicle, distinguishing an organization. ➤ **liveried** *adj.*
**lives** *n* pl of LIFE.
**livestock** *n* farm animals.
**live wire** *n informal* a very dynamic or lively person.
**livid** *adj* **1** *informal* very angry. **2** discoloured by bruising.
**living**[1] *adj* **1** alive. **2** still in use, *esp* still spoken. ✻ **in living memory** in a time that people who are alive now can remember.
**living**[2] *n* **1** a means of subsistence; a livelihood. **2** the condition of being alive.
**living room** *n* a room in a home used for everyday activities.
**living wage** *n* a wage sufficient to provide an acceptable standard of living.
**lizard** *n* a small four-legged reptile with a long body and tail.
**llama** *n* a usu domesticated South American mammal with a woolly fleece.
**lo** *interj archaic* used to call attention or to express wonder.
**loach** *n* a small slender freshwater fish with spines round the mouth.
**load**[1] *n* **1** an amount, *esp* a large or heavy one, that is carried or supported. **2** a quantity carried at one time by a specified means. **3** a burden of responsibility, anxiety, etc. **4** *informal* (*also in pl*) a large quantity; a lot.
**load**[2] *v* **1** to put a load in or on e.g. a vehicle or ship. **2** to put ammunition into (a gun). **3** to insert (e.g. a film or tape) in a device or piece of equipment.
**loaded** *adj* **1** carrying a load. **2** of a question, argument, etc: biased, *esp* so as to produce a particular result. **3** having hidden implications. **4** of a dice: weighted so that it falls in a particular way. **5** *informal* having a large amount of money. **6** *informal* drunk.
**loaf**[1] *n* (*pl* **loaves**) a shaped mass of baked bread.
**loaf**[2] *v* to spend time in idleness.
**loafer** *n* **1** an idler or slacker. **2** *trademark* a low leather shoe with a broad flat heel.
**loam** *n* rich crumbly soil consisting of clay, silt, and sand.
**loan**[1] *n* **1** something lent, *esp* money lent at interest. **2** the act of lending. ✻ **on loan** being temporarily used by a borrower.
**loan**[2] *v* to lend.

**loan shark** *n informal* a person who lends money at exorbitant rates of interest.

**loath** *or* **loth** *adj* (*usu* + to) unwilling to do something; reluctant.

---

***Usage Note:*** Do not confuse this word with *loathe*, which is a verb.

---

**loathe** *v* to dislike intensely.

---

***Usage Note:*** Do not confuse this word with *loath*, which is an adjective.

---

**loathsome** *adj* hateful or disgusting.

**loaves** *n* pl of LOAF[1].

**lob[1]** *v* (**lobbed, lobbing**) to throw or hit (e.g. a ball) in a high arc.

**lob[2]** *n* in sports, a ball or shot that is lobbed.

**lobby[1]** *n* (*pl* **-ies**) **1** a porch or entrance hall. **2** an anteroom of a legislative chamber, *esp* one where Members of Parliament go to vote during a division or where they meet members of the public. **3** a group of people engaged in lobbying.

**lobby[2]** *v* (**-ies, -ied**) to try to influence members of a legislative body with respect to a particular issue. ➤ **lobbyist** *n.*

**lobe** *n* **1** a flat, curved projection, e.g. of the ear. **2** a rounded section of an organ, *esp* the brain.

**lobelia** *n* a plant with clusters of small blue, red, or white flowers.

**lobotomy** *n* (*pl* **-ies**) a brain operation in which nerve fibres in the cerebral cortex are cut, used formerly in the treatment of some mental disorders.

**lobster** *n* (*pl* **lobsters** *or* **lobster**) a large ten-legged shellfish with a pair of large claws.

**lobster pot** *n* a basket used as a trap for catching lobsters.

**local[1]** *adj* **1** relating to a particular place; not general or widespread. **2** serving the needs of a particular area. **3** affecting only a restricted part of a living organism. ➤ **locally** *adv.*

**local[2]** *n* **1** a local person or thing. **2** *Brit, informal* the neighbourhood pub.

**locale** /loh'kahl/ *n* a place, *esp* the setting for a particular event.

**locality** *n* (*pl* **-ies**) a particular area or neighbourhood.

**localize** *or* **-ise** *v* to restrict to a particular place. ➤ **localization** *n.*

**locate** *v* **1** to determine the position of. **2** to establish in a particular place. **3** (**be located**) to be sited or situated.

**location** *n* **1** a particular place or position. **2** a place outside a studio where a broadcast or film is made. **3** the act of locating.

**loch** /lokh/ *n* a lake or nearly landlocked arm of the sea in Scotland.

**loci** *n* pl of LOCUS.

**lock[1]** *n* **1** a fastening that can be opened only by means of a particular key or combination. **2** an enclosed section of a river or canal with gates at each end, in which the water level can be raised or lowered as boats pass through. **3** in wrestling, etc, a hold secured on a usu specified body part. **4** *chiefly Brit* the extent to which the front wheels of a vehicle are turned.

**lock[2]** *v* **1** to fasten with a lock. **2** to shut in or make inaccessible by locking a door, lid, etc. **3** become fixed or jammed immovably. ➤ **lockable** *adj.*

**lock[3]** *n* **1** a curl, tuft, etc of hair. **2** *literary* (*in pl*) the hair of the head.

**locker** *n* **1** a cupboard or compartment that can be locked. **2** a storage compartment on a boat or ship.

**locket** *n* a small gold or silver case with space for a memento, usu worn on a chain round the neck.

**lockjaw** *n* **1** an early symptom of tetanus characterized by an inability to open the jaws. **2** = TETANUS.

**lockout** *n* a temporary closing of a workplace by an employer in order to gain concessions from employees.

**locksmith** *n* somebody who makes or mends locks.

**lock, stock, and barrel** *adv* wholly or completely.

**lockup** *n* **1** a prison, *esp* a small or temporary one. **2** *Brit* a shop or garage that can be locked up.

**lock up** *v* **1** to lock all the doors of a building. **2** to put in prison.

**locomotion** *n* the act of moving from place to place.

**locomotive[1]** *n* a powered vehicle that pulls railway carriages and wagons.

**locomotive[2]** *adj* relating to movement from place to place.

**locum** *n informal* a doctor or cleric temporarily taking the place of another.

**locus** /'lohkəs, 'lokəs/ *n* (*pl* **loci** /'lohsie, 'lohkie/) a place or position.

**locust** *n* a large grasshopper that travels in vast swarms through tropical areas, stripping them of all vegetation.

**locution** *n* **1** a word or expression. **2** a style or manner of speaking.

**lode** *n* an ore deposit.

**lodestone** *n* a piece of magnetized mineral.

**lodge[1]** *n* **1** a house lived in during a particular season, e.g. the hunting season. **2** a small house at the gates or in the grounds of a country estate. **3** a porter's room, e.g. at the entrance to a college, block of flats, etc. **4** a branch of a fraternal organization such as the Freemasons. **5** a beaver's or otter's den. **6** a Native American tent or dwelling.

**lodge[2]** *v* **1** to reside temporarily as a lodger. **2** to fix or become fixed firmly in place. **3** to lay (e.g. a complaint) before an authority. **4** to deposit (e.g. money) for safekeeping.

**lodger** *n* somebody who occupies a rented room in somebody else's house.

**lodging** *n* **1** a temporary place to live. **2** (*in pl*) a rented room or rooms, usu in a private house.

**loft**[1] *n* **1** an attic. **2** a gallery in a church or hall. **3** an upper floor in a barn or warehouse used for storage. **4** a warehouse loft converted into an open-plan flat. **5** a shed or coop for pigeons.

**loft**[2] *v* to propel (e.g. a ball) high up into the air.

**lofty** *adj* (**-ier, -iest**) **1** impressively high. **2** showing high ideals or moral principles. **3** having a haughty overbearing manner. ➤ **loftily** *adv.*

**log**[1] *n* **1** a piece of unshaped timber ready for sawing or use as firewood. **2** the full record of a ship's voyage or an aircraft's flight. **3** an apparatus for measuring the speed of a ship.

**log**[2] *v* (**logged, logging**) **1** to enter in a log. **2** to attain (e.g. an indicated distance, speed, or time). **3** (*often* + up) to have to one's credit. **4** to cut down trees for timber. ➤ **logger** *n.*

**log**[3] *n* = LOGARITHM.

**loganberry** *n* (*pl* **-ies**) a sweet red edible berry, similar to a raspberry.

**logarithm** *n* a number expressed as the mathematical exponent of a base number. Adding and subtracting logarithms produces the same results respectively as multiplying and dividing ordinary numbers. ➤ **logarithmic** *adj.*

**logbook** *n* **1** a book recording the details of a ship's voyage or an aircraft's flight. **2** *Brit* an official document recording details of a motor vehicle and its ownership.

**loggerheads** *pl n* ✻ **at loggerheads** in quarrelsome disagreement.

**loggia** /ˈloj(i)ə/ *n* a roofed open gallery behind a colonnade or arcade.

**logic** *n* **1** a science that deals with the principles of reasoning. **2** rationality in thought or argument. **3** an inevitable progression of cause and effect. **4** the principles underlying the connection of circuit elements for performing operations in a computer. ➤ **logician** *n.*

**logical** *adj* **1** conforming with logic. **2** using or based on sound reasoning. **3** to be expected under the circumstances. ➤ **logically** *adv.*

**log in** *v* = LOG ON.

**logistics** *pl n* the work of planning and organizing a large and complex operation. ➤ **logistic** *adj.*

**logjam** *n* a deadlock or impasse.

**logo** *n* (*pl* **-os**) an identifying symbol used by a company.

**log off** *v* to end a session at a computer terminal.

**log on** *v* to begin a session at a computer terminal.

**log out** *v* = LOG OFF.

**-logy** *or* **-ology** *suffix* **1** denoting a doctrine, theory, or science: *archaeology.* **2** oral or written expression: *phraseology.* **3** writings of a specified kind: *trilogy.* ➤ **-logist** *suffix.*

**loin** *n* **1** the part of the body between the hipbone and the lower ribs. **2** a cut of meat comprising this part of a carcass. **3** (*in pl*) the genitals.

**loincloth** *n* a cloth worn round the hips and covering the genitals.

**loiter** *v* **1** to remain in an area for no obvious reason. **2** to dawdle. ➤ **loiterer** *n.*

**loll** *v* **1** to recline or move in a lazy manner. **2** to hang down loosely.

**lollipop** *n* a large round sweet of boiled sugar on the end of a stick.

**lollop** *v* (**lolloped, lolloping**) to move with an ungainly loping motion.

**lolly** *n* (*pl* **-ies**) **1** a lollipop. **2** (*also* **ice lolly**) a flavoured piece of ice or ice cream on a stick. **3** *Brit, informal* money.

**lone** *adj* **1** single or sole. **2** isolated.

**lonely** *adj* (**-ier, -iest**) **1** sad from being alone or without friends. **2** cut off from others; solitary. **3** not frequented by people. ➤ **loneliness** *n.*

**loner** *n* a person who prefers solitude.

**lonesome** *adj chiefly NAmer* = LONELY.

**lone wolf** *n* a person who prefers to work, act, or live alone.

**long**[1] *adj* **1** extending for a considerable distance. **2** having a specified length. **3** extending over a considerable or specified time. **4** containing a large or specified number of items: *a long list.* **5** of betting odds: greatly differing in the amounts wagered on each side and reflecting the unlikelihood of success. ✻ **be long** *informal* to take a long time. **in the long run** in the course of prolonged time, trial, or experience. **long in the tooth** old. **long on** *informal* having a large amount of. **not by a long chalk** see CHALK[1]. **the long and** (**the**) **short** the gist; the outline.

**long**[2] *adv* (**longer, longest**) **1** for a long time. **2** throughout a specified period: *all night long.* **3** far in the past. ✻ **no longer** not now, though usu previously. **so/as long as 1** during and up to the end of the time that; while. **2** on condition that. **so long** *informal* goodbye.

**long**[3] *v* (*often* + for) to feel a strong desire or craving.

**longboat** *n* the largest boat carried by a sailing vessel.

**longbow** *n* a medieval English bow of about 2m (6ft) in length.

**longevity** /lonˈjeviti, long-/ *n* great length of life.

**long face** *n* a sad facial expression.

**longhand** *n* handwriting.

**long haul** *n* **1** a lengthy period of time. **2** the transport of goods or passengers over long distances.

**longing** *n* a strong desire, *esp* for something difficult to attain. ➤ **longing** *adj,* **longingly** *adv.*

**longitude** *n* the angular distance of a place east or west of the Greenwich meridian.

**longitudinal** *adj* **1** extending lengthways. **2** relating to longitude. ➤ **longitudinally** *adv.*

**long johns** *pl n informal* underpants with legs extending to the ankles.

**long jump** *n* an athletic event consisting of a jump for distance from a running start.

**long-range** *adj* **1** fit for long distances. **2** involving a long period of time.

**longship** *n* a long open Viking warship propelled by oars and a sail.

**long shot** *n* a venture that involves considerable risk and has little chance of success.

**longsighted** *or* **long-sighted** *adj* unable to see things that are close to the eyes clearly.

**long-suffering** *adj* patiently enduring pain, difficulty, or provocation.

**longways** *adv* = LENGTHWAYS.

**long-winded** *adj* tediously long in speaking or writing.

**loo** *n Brit, informal* = TOILET.

**loofah** *n* a dried seed pod of a plant used as a bath sponge.

**look[1]** *v* **1** to direct one's sight in a specified direction. **2** to appear or seem. **3** to have a specified outlook. ✱ **look after** to take care of. **look back** to think about the past. **look down on** to regard as inferior. **look for** to try to find. **look into** to investigate.

**look[2]** *n* **1** an act of looking; a glance. **2** (*in pl*) physical appearance. **3** the general appearance of somebody or something. **4** a style or fashion.

**lookalike** *n* somebody or something that looks like another.

**looking glass** *n* = MIRROR[1].

**look on** *v* to be a spectator at an event.

**lookout** *n* **1** a place or structure affording a wide view for observation. **2** somebody engaged in keeping watch. **3** a careful watch.

**look out** *v* to remain alert in case of trouble.

**look up** *v* **1** to improve in prospects. **2** to search for in a source of reference. **3** *informal* to visit or make contact with. ✱ **look up to** to have great respect for.

**loom[1]** *n* a machine for weaving thread into cloth.

**loom[2]** *v* **1** to come into sight indistinctly, often in menacing form. **2** to be about to happen.

**loony[1]** *adj* (**-ier, -iest**) *informal* crazy or foolish.

**loony[2]** *n* (*pl* **-ies**) *informal* a crazy or foolish person.

**loop[1]** *n* **1** a shape formed when a line is drawn in an elongated circle and its ends are crossed. **2** a manoeuvre in which an aircraft flies in a vertical circle. **3** a piece of film or magnetic tape whose ends are spliced together so as to reproduce the same material continuously. **4** a closed electric circuit.

**loop[2]** *v* to form or move in a loop. ✱ **loop the loop** to perform a loop in an aircraft.

**loophole** *n* **1** an ambiguity or omission in a text through which its intent may be evaded. **2** a small opening through which missiles may be discharged.

**loopy** *adj* (**-ier, -iest**) *informal* slightly crazy or foolish.

**loose[1]** *adj* **1** not tightly fastened or securely attached. **2** not tight-fitting. **3** free from confinement or restraint. **4** not kept together in a bundle, container, etc. **5** not dense or compact in structure or arrangement. **6** not tightly drawn or stretched. **7** lacking in precision or exactness. **8** careless or irresponsible. **9** *dated* dissolute or promiscuous. ✱ **on the loose** free, *esp* having escaped. ➤ **loosely** *adv,* **looseness** *n.*

***Usage Note:*** Do not confuse this word with *lose,* which is a verb.

**loose[2]** *v* **1** to release. **2** to unfasten or detach. **3** (*often* + off) to fire (e.g. a bullet or a volley).

**loose cannon** *n* somebody who acts independently and disruptively in an organization.

**loose end** *n* an incomplete or unexplained detail. ✱ **at a loose end** bored or unoccupied.

**loose-leaf** *adj* of an album or book: bound so that individual leaves can be detached or inserted.

**loosen** *v* to make or become loose or looser.

**loosen up** *v* **1** to become more relaxed. **2** to warm up one's muscles before exercising.

**loot[1]** *n* **1** goods taken as plunder in war or illegally by force or deception. **2** *informal* money.

**loot[2]** *v* to steal goods from a place during a war or public disturbance. ➤ **looter** *n.*

**lop** *v* (**lopped, lopping**) **1** to cut off branches or twigs from a tree. **2** (+ off/away) to remove (something unnecessary or undesirable).

**lope[1]** *n* an easy bounding gait.

**lope[2]** *v* to move at a lope.

**lop-eared** *adj* of an animal: having ears that droop.

**lopsided** *adj* having one side heavier or lower than the other.

**loquacious** *adj formal* = TALKATIVE. ➤ **loquacity** *n.*

**Lord** *n* **1** God. **2** Jesus Christ. **3** (**the Lords**) the House of Lords. **4** used as the title of a lord or a prefix to some official titles. ✱ **my Lord** used as a form of address to judges, bishops, and noblemen.

**lord[1]** *n* **1** a nobleman. **2** a ruler or leader.

**lord[2]** *v* ✱ **lord it over** to behave domineeringly towards.

**Lord Chancellor** *n* a British officer of state who presides over the House of Lords and serves as head of the judiciary.

**Lord Chief Justice** *n* the president of the Queen's Bench Division of the High Court.

**lordly** *adj* (**-ier, -iest**) **1** dignified or noble. **2** disdainful and arrogant. ➤ **lordliness** *n.*

**Lord Mayor** *n* the mayor of the City of London and other large British cities.

**Lord's Day** *n* (*usu* **the Lord's Day**) = SUNDAY.

**Lordship** *n* used as a title for a bishop, a High Court Judge, or a peer.

**lore** *n* a specified body of knowledge or tradition.

**lorgnette** /law'nyet/ *n* (*also in pl*) a pair of glasses or opera glasses with a handle.

**lorry** *n* (*pl* **-ies**) *Brit* a large motor vehicle for carrying loads by road.

**lose** *v* (*past tense and past part.* **lost**) **1** to miss from one's possession and fail to find. **2** to cease to have or fail to keep. **3** to suffer loss through the death of. **4** to fail to win (a contest). **5** to fail to use (e.g. an opportunity). **6** *informal* to escape from(a pursuer). **7** to withdraw (oneself) from immediate reality. **8** (**be lost**) to be destroyed or killed. **9** to make less money from something than one has spent on it. ✱ **lose face** to lose one's dignity or reputation. **lose heart** to become dispirited. **lose it** *informal* to lose control of oneself. **lose one's way 1** to be unable to find the correct direction to go in. **2** to go astray intellectually or morally.

***Usage Note:*** Do not confuse this word with *loose*, which is an adjective.

**lose out** *v* **1** (*often* + on) to make a loss. **2** to be denied an opportunity, advantage, etc.

**loser** *n* **1** somebody who loses a contest. **2** somebody who loses consistently.

**loss** *n* **1** the act of losing possession of something. **2** the harm or privation resulting from loss. **3** a person, thing, or amount lost. **4** failure to gain or use something. **5** an amount by which cost exceeds revenue. ✱ **at a loss 1** uncertain or puzzled. **2** not making enough money to cover costs.

**loss leader** *n* an article sold at a loss to draw customers.

**lost**[1] *adj* **1** unable to find the way. **2** bewildered or helpless. **3** (*usu* + in) rapt or absorbed. ✱ **be lost for words** to be unable to think what to say, e.g. because of shock. **be lost on** to be unnoticed or unappreciated by. **get lost** *informal* to go away.

**lost**[2] *v* past tense and past part. of LOSE.

**lost cause** *n* a cause that has no prospect of success.

**lost generation** *n* a generation considered socially and emotionally disadvantaged.

**lot** *n* **1** (**a lot** *or* **lots**) *informal* a considerable amount or number. **2** (**the lot**) *chiefly Brit* the whole amount or number. **3** *informal* a number of associated people or things. **4** an article or a number of articles offered as one item in an auction sale. **5** one's fate. **6** *chiefly NAmer* a portion of land. ✱ **a lot 1** *informal* much or considerably. **2** *informal* often. **draw lots** to decide an issue by asking people to choose e.g. a slip of paper at random from among several such slips.

**loth** *adj* see LOATH.

**Lothario** /lə'thahrioh/ *n* (*pl* **-os**) a man whose chief interest is seducing women.

**lotion** *n* a medicinal or cosmetic liquid for external use.

**lottery** *n* (*pl* **-ies**) **1** a way of raising money by selling tickets bearing numbers, some of which are later randomly selected to entitle the holder to a prize. **2** an event whose outcome is decided by chance.

**lotus** *n* a water lily.

**lotus position** *n* a yoga position in which one sits with legs folded, the feet resting on the thighs.

**louche** /loohsh/ *adj* morally dubious; disreputable.

**loud** *adj* **1** producing a high volume of sound. **2** obtrusively or tastelessly bright in colour. ➤ **loudly** *adv,* **loudness** *n.*

**loud-hailer** *n chiefly Brit* = MEGAPHONE.

**loudmouth** *n informal* a person who talks in a loud offensive way. ➤ **loudmouthed** *adj.*

**loudspeaker** *n* a device that converts electrical energy into acoustic energy and that is used to reproduce sounds.

**lough** /lokh/ *n* a loch in Ireland.

**lounge**[1] *v* to sit, lie, or stand in a lazy or relaxed way.

**lounge**[2] *n* **1** a sitting room in a private house. **2** a room in a public building providing comfortable seating.

**lounge bar** *n Brit* a more comfortable and usu more expensive bar in a pub or hotel.

**lounger** *n* a comfortable extended chair for relaxing outdoors.

**lounge suit** *n Brit* a man's suit for wear during the day.

**lour** *or* **lower** /'lowə/ *v* **1** to scowl or look sullen. **2** of the sky or weather: to become dark and threatening.

**louse** *n* (*pl* **lice**) **1** a small wingless insect parasitic on animals, fish, or plants. **2** (*pl* **louses**) *informal* a contemptible person.

**louse up** *v informal* to spoil or make a mess of.

**lousy** *adj* (**-ier, -iest**) *informal* very bad, unpleasant, useless, etc.

**lout** *n* a rough ill-mannered man or boy. ➤ **loutish** *adj.*

**louvre** (*NAmer* **louver**) /'loohvə/ *n* a set of slanted strips fitted across an opening to allow air, light, or sound to enter while providing privacy.

**lovable** *or* **loveable** *adj* having qualities that inspire affection.
**lovage** *n* an aromatic plant cultivated as a herb.
**love**[1] *n* **1** a strong feeling of attachment, tenderness, and protectiveness for another person. **2** attraction or devotion based on sexual desire. **3** warm interest in and enjoyment of something. **4** an object of love. **5** a score of zero in tennis, squash, etc. * **make love** to have sexual intercourse. ➤ **loveless** *adj.*
**love**[2] *v* **1** to feel love for. **2** to have a great liking for. ➤ **lover** *n,* **loving** *adj,* **lovingly** *adv.*
**love affair** *n* **1** a sexual liaison or romantic attachment between people. **2** a lively enthusiasm.
**lovebird** *n* **1** a small usu grey or green parrot that shows great affection for its mate. **2** (*in pl*) an affectionate couple.
**love child** *n euphem* an illegitimate child.
**lovelorn** *adj* sad because of unrequited love.
**lovely** *adj* (**-ier, -iest**) **1** delightfully beautiful. **2** very pleasing; fine. ➤ **loveliness** *n.*
**lovesick** *adj* languishing with love.
**low**[1] *adj* **1** not high or tall. **2** situated or rising only a little above the ground. **3** of less than the usual degree, size, amount, or value. **4** considered comparatively unimportant. **5** of sound: soft or deep. **6** weak or depressed. **7** morally reprehensible or vulgar. **8** unfavourable. **9** humble in character or status.
**low**[2] *n* **1** a low point or level. **2** a region of low atmospheric pressure.
**low**[3] *adv* **1** at or to a low position. **2** softly or at a low pitch.
**low**[4] *v* to make the deep sound characteristic of a cow.
**lowbrow** *adj informal, derog* having unsophisticated or unintellectual tastes. ➤ **lowbrow** *n.*
**Low Church** *adj* tending to minimize emphasis on the priesthood, sacraments, and ceremonial in the Anglican Church.
**lowdown** *n* (**the lowdown**) *informal* useful information.
**lower**[1] *adj* **1** relatively low in position, rank, or order. **2** denoting the southern part of a specified area.
**lower**[2] *v* **1** to cause to descend. **2** to reduce in height, value, amount, pitch, etc. **3** to degrade.
**lower**[3] *v* see LOUR.
**lower case** *n* small letters, e.g. a, b, c rather than A, B, C. ➤ **lower-case** *adj.*
**lowest common denominator** *n* **1** the lowest number that two or more denominators can be exactly divided by. **2** *derog* something acceptable or comprehensible to the greatest possible number of people.
**low gear** *n* a gear designed for slow speed.
**low-key** *adj* of low intensity; restrained.
**lowland** *n* **1** (*also in pl*) low or level country. **2** (**the Lowlands**) the part of Scotland lying south and east of the Highlands. ➤ **lowlander** *n.*
**lowlife** *n* (*pl* **lowlifes**) *informal* a criminal or immoral person, or criminal and worthless people collectively.
**lowly** *adj* (**-ier, -iest**) low-ranking; humble. ➤ **lowliness** *n.*
**low tide** *n* the time when the sea reaches its lowest level.
**loyal** *adj* showing unswerving support for a person, country, or cause. ➤ **loyally** *adv.*
**loyalist** *n* **1** somebody loyal to a government or sovereign, *esp* in time of revolt. **2** (**Loyalist**) in Northern Ireland: a supporter of continued union with the United Kingdom.
**loyalty** *n* (*pl* **-ies**) **1** being loyal. **2** a feeling of allegiance or duty.
**loyalty card** *n Brit* a card issued by e.g. a supermarket to reward regular customers by giving them points towards discounts on future purchases.
**lozenge** *n* **1** a small medicated sweet. **2** a diamond or rhombus.
**LP** *n* a long-playing gramophone record.
**Lr** *abbr* the chemical symbol for lawrencium.
**LSD** *n* lysergic acid diethylamide, an illegal drug with a potent mind-altering effect.
**Ltd** *abbr Brit* Limited.
**Lu** *abbr* the chemical symbol for lutetium.
**lubricant** *n* a lubricating substance, e.g. grease or oil. ➤ **lubricant** *adj.*
**lubricate** *v* to apply a greasy substance to (something) to reduce friction and wear between its surfaces. ➤ **lubrication** *n.*
**lubricious** *adj formal* lecherous or salacious.
**lucid** *adj* **1** clear to the understanding; plain. **2** having full use of one's faculties; sane. ➤ **lucidity** *n,* **lucidly** *adv.*
**Lucifer** *n* the Devil.
**luck** *n* **1** whatever good or bad events happen to a person by chance. **2** good fortune. * **try one's luck** attempt to do something that may or may not succeed.
**luckless** *adj* unlucky or unfortunate.
**lucky** *adj* (**-ier, -iest**) having, resulting from, or bringing good luck.
**lucky dip** *n Brit* an attraction, e.g. at a fair, in which small prizes can be drawn unseen from a receptacle.
**lucrative** *adj* producing wealth; profitable.
**lucre** *n* money.
**Luddite** *n* **1** a member of a group of early 19th-cent. English workmen who destroyed labour-saving machinery to protect their jobs. **2** somebody opposed to technological progress.
**ludicrous** *adj* amusingly absurd. ➤ **ludicrously** *adv.*
**ludo** *n* a simple board game played with counters and dice.

**lug**[1] *v* (**lugged, lugging**) to drag or carry with great effort.
**lug**[2] *n* **1** something, e.g. a handle, that projects like an ear. **2** *Brit, dialect or humorous* an ear.
**luggage** *n* cases, bags, etc containing a traveller's belongings.
**lugubrious** *adj* mournful, *esp* exaggeratedly so.
**lukewarm** *adj* **1** moderately warm; tepid. **2** lacking enthusiasm.
**lull**[1] *v* **1** to calm with soothing sounds, motion, etc. **2** to cause to relax vigilance, *esp* by deception.
**lull**[2] *n* a temporary pause in activity.
**lullaby** *n* (*pl* **-ies**) a song used to lull children to sleep.
**lumbago** *n* muscular pain in the lower back.
**lumbar** *adj* relating to the region of the lower back.
**lumber**[1] *v* to move heavily or clumsily.
**lumber**[2] *n* **1** surplus or disused articles. **2** *NAmer* timber or logs.
**lumber**[3] *v Brit, informal* to encumber or saddle (somebody) with something.
**lumberjack** *n* a person engaged in logging.
**luminary** *n* (*pl* **-ies**) a brilliantly outstanding or important person.
**luminescence** *n* light produced at low temperatures e.g. by physiological processes or chemical action. ➤ **luminescent** *adj.*
**luminous** *adj* emitting or full of light; bright. ➤ **luminosity** *n.*
**lump**[1] *n* **1** a compact mass of indefinite size and shape. **2** an abnormal swelling. ➤ **lumpy** *adj.*
**lump**[2] *v* (*usu* + together) to group without discrimination. * **lump it** *informal* to put up with it.
**lumpen** *adj informal* stupid or unenlightened.
**lumpish** *adj* **1** dull or sluggish. **2** heavy or awkward.
**lump sum** *n* a large sum of money given in a single payment.
**lunacy** *n* **1** wild foolishness. **2** insanity.
**lunar** *adj* of the moon.
**lunar eclipse** *n* an eclipse in which the moon passes through the earth's shadow.
**lunar month** *n* the period of time, averaging 29½ days, between two successive new moons.
**lunatic** *n* **1** a mentally ill person. **2** a foolish or foolhardy person.
**lunch**[1] *n* a midday meal. * **out to lunch** *informal* crazy.
**lunch**[2] *v* to eat lunch.
**luncheon** *n formal* = LUNCH[1].
**lung** *n* either of the paired respiratory organs in the chest of air-breathing vertebrates.
**lunge**[1] *v* to make a sudden forward movement or thrust.
**lunge**[2] *n* a sudden forward movement or thrust.
**lupin** *or* **lupine** /'loohpin/ *n* a plant with long spikes of flowers.
**lupine** /'loohpien/ *adj* relating to or resembling a wolf.
**lurch**[1] *n* an abrupt, uncontrolled, and jerky movement.
**lurch**[2] *v* to move in an abrupt, uncontrolled, and jerky manner.
**lurch**[3] *n* * **in the lurch** in a vulnerable and unsupported position.
**lurcher** *n* a dog that is a cross between a greyhound and another breed, e.g. the collie or terrier.
**lure**[1] *n* **1** something used to entice or decoy. **2** the power to appeal or attract.
**lure**[2] *v* to attract with something that promises pleasure, food, or gain.
**Lurex** *n trademark* a type of thread that is partly coated to give a metallic appearance.
**lurid** *adj* **1** unnaturally or unattractively bright in colour. **2** sensational or shocking. ➤ **luridly** *adv.*
**lurk** *v* **1** to lie hidden in wait, *esp* with evil intent. **2** to be present but undetected.
**luscious** *adj* **1** having a delicious taste or smell. **2** *esp* of a woman: extremely attractive.
**lush**[1] *adj* **1** producing or covered by luxuriant growth. **2** opulent or sumptuous. ➤ **lushly** *adv,* **lushness** *n.*
**lush**[2] *n chiefly NAmer, informal* a heavy drinker.
**lust**[1] *n* **1** strong sexual desire. **2** an intense longing; a craving. ➤ **lustful** *adj.*
**lust**[2] *v* (*usu* + for/after) to have an intense *esp* sexual desire for.
**lustre** (*NAmer* **luster**) *n* **1** a glow of reflected light; a sheen. **2** glory or distinction. ➤ **lustrous** *adj.*
**lusty** *adj* (**-ier, -iest**) full of vitality; healthy and vigorous. ➤ **lustily** *adv.*
**lute** *n* a plucked stringed musical instrument with a large pear-shaped body and long neck.
**luxuriant** *adj* characterized by abundant growth. ➤ **luxuriance** *n,* **luxuriantly** *adv.*
**luxuriate** *v* (*often* + in) to enjoy the delights of something unrestrainedly.
**luxurious** *adj* extremely comfortable and usu expensive and elegant. ➤ **luxuriously** *adv.*
**luxury** *n* (*pl* **-ies**) **1** great ease or comfort based on the use of expensive items. **2** something desirable or expensive but not essential.
**-ly** *suffix* **1** having the characteristics of: *fatherly.* **2** recurring at intervals of: *hourly.* **3** in such a manner: *slowly.*
**lychee** *or* **litchi** *n* a small oval fruit with a scaly skin and soft white fragrant pulp.
**lychgate** *or* **lichgate** *n* a roofed gate at the entrance to a churchyard.
**Lycra** *n trademark* a synthetic stretchy yarn used chiefly in tight-fitting sportswear and swimwear.

**lye** *n* a strong alkaline solution, used e.g. in oven and drain cleaners.

**lying**[1] *v* present part. of LIE[1].

**lying**[2] *v* present part. of LIE[3].

**lymph** *n* a pale body fluid containing white blood cells.

**lymph node** *n* a rounded mass of tissue in which white blood cells are formed.

**lynch** *v* to put (an alleged offender) to death illegally by mob action.

**lynchpin** *n* see LINCHPIN.

**lynx** *n* (*pl* **lynxes** *or* **lynx**) a wildcat with a short tail, mottled coat, and tufted ears.

**lyre** *n* a stringed instrument of the harp family with a U-shaped frame, used by the ancient Greeks.

**lyric**[1] *n* **1** (*in pl*) the words of a popular song. **2** a lyric poem.

**lyric**[2] *adj* of poetry: expressing direct personal emotion.

**lyrical** *adj* **1** having a beautiful, songlike quality. **2** = LYRIC[2]. * **wax lyrical** talk with great admiration or enthusiasm about something. ➤ **lyrically** *adv.*

**lyricism** *n* **1** a pleasantly melodious and songlike quality, *esp* in music. **2** a directly personal style in art, literature, etc.

**lyricist** *n* a writer of song lyrics.

**M**[1] *or* **m** *n* (*pl* **M's** *or* **Ms** *or* **m's**) **1** the 13th letter of the English alphabet. **2** the Roman numeral for 1000.

**M**[2] *abbr* **1** Monsieur. **2** motorway.

**m** *abbr* **1** metre. **2** mile. **3** million. **4** minute.

**MA** *abbr* Master of Arts.

**ma'am** *n* madam.

**mac** *or* **mack** *n Brit, informal* a raincoat.

**macabre** /mə'kahb(r)ə/ *adj* gruesome in relating to or depicting unpleasant aspects of death.

**macadam** *n* broken stones compacted into a solid mass to make a road surface.

**macadamia** *n* the edible round nut of an Australian evergreen tree.

**macaroni** *pl n* pasta shaped in hollow tubes.

**macaroon** *n* a cake or biscuit made with ground almonds or coconut.

**macaw** *n* a large brightly coloured parrot of South and Central America.

**mace**[1] *n* **1** a heavy medieval spiked staff or club. **2** an ornamental staff used as a symbol of authority.

**mace**[2] *n* an aromatic spice made from the dried external covering of a nutmeg.

**macerate** *v* to make (food) soft by soaking it in liquid. ➤ **maceration** *n.*

**Mach** /mak, mahk/ *n* used to show a speed relative to the speed of sound: Mach1 is the speed of sound, Mach 2 is twice that, and so on.

**machete** /mə'sheti/ *n* a large heavy knife used for cutting vegetation or as a weapon.

**Machiavellian** *adj* cunning and opportunist.

**machination** *n* a scheming move or plot.

**machine**[1] *n* **1** a mechanical apparatus for performing a task. **2** an efficient and controlling person or organization.

**machine**[2] *v* to make or operate on with a machine. ➤ **machinability** *n.*

**machine gun** *n* an automatic gun for rapid continuous fire.

**machine-readable** *adj* in a form that can be processed by a computer.

**machinery** *n* **1** machines in general. **2** the working parts of a machine. **3** the system or organization controlling an activity or process.

**machinist** *n* a person who operates a machine or repairs machinery.

**machismo** /mə'kizmoh, mə'chizmoh/ *n* an assertion of masculinity.

**macho** /'machoh/ *adj* toughly or aggressively virile.

**mackerel** *n* (*pl* **mackerels** *or* **mackerel**) a food fish of the North Atlantic.

**mackintosh** *or* **macintosh** *n chiefly Brit* a raincoat.

**macramé** /mə'krahmi/ *n* the art of tying threads or cords in patterns to make decorative articles.

**macrobiotic** *adj* of a diet: consisting chiefly of whole grains and vegetables.

**macrocosm** *n* **1** the universe. **2** a complex that is a large-scale reproduction of one of its constituents.

**mad** *adj* (**madder, maddest**) **1** mentally disordered; insane. **2** utterly foolish. **3** very angry. **4** obsessively enthusiastic. **5** of a dog: affected with rabies. **6** distraught or frantic. ✱ **like mad** *informal* very hard, fast, loud, etc. ➤ **madly** *adv,* **madness** *n.*

**madam** *n* **1** a form of respectful address to a woman. **2** the female head of a brothel. **3** *Brit, informal* a conceited or petulant young girl.

**madame** /'madəm/ *n* (*pl* **mesdames** /'maydam, may'dam/) a title of or form of address to a French woman.

**madcap** *adj* impulsive or reckless.

**mad cow disease** *n informal* BSE (bovine spongiform encephalopathy).

**madden** *v* **1** to drive mad. **2** to exasperate or enrage. ➤ **maddening** *adj.*

**madder** *n* a red dye prepared from the root of a Eurasian plant.

**made** *v* past tense and past part. of MAKE[1].

**Madeira** *n* a fortified wine from Madeira.

**Madeira cake** *n Brit* a rich sponge cake.

**madeleine** *n* a small rich sponge cake baked in a mould.

**mademoiselle** /,madmwə'zel/ *n* (*pl* **mademoiselles** *or* **mesdemoiselles** /,maydmwə'zel/) a title of or form of address to an unmarried French woman.

**made-to-measure** *adj* of a garment: made according to an individual's measurements.

**made-up** *adj* **1** wearing make-up. **2** fictional or invented.

**Madonna** *n* (**the Madonna**) the Virgin Mary.

**madrigal** *n* **1** an unaccompanied secular song for several voices. **2** a short medieval love poem. ➤ **madrigalist** *n.*

**maelstrom** /'maylstrohm, 'maylstrəm/ *n* **1** a powerful whirlpool. **2** a turbulent or violent upheaval.

**maestro** /'miestroh/ *n* (*pl* **maestros** *or* **maestri** /'miestree/) a master in an art; *esp* an eminent musician.

**Mafia** *n* **1** (**the Mafia**) a secret international criminal organization originating in Sicily. **2** (**mafia**) an excessively influential coterie of a usu specified kind.

**mafioso** /mafi'ohsoh/ *n* (*pl* **mafiosi** /-see/) a member of the Mafia.

**magazine** *n* **1** an illustrated periodical containing miscellaneous pieces. **2** a holder from which cartridges can be fed into a gun chamber automatically. **3** a storeroom for arms, ammunition, or explosives.

**magenta** *n* a deep purplish red colour.

**maggot** *n* the soft-bodied larva of a fly. ➤ **maggoty** *adj.*

**magi** /'mayjie/ *n* the three wise men from the East who traditionally paid homage to the infant Jesus.

**magic**[1] *n* **1** the use of supernatural powers over natural forces. **2** the art of producing illusions by sleight of hand. **3** an extraordinary power or influence.

**magic**[2] *adj* **1** relating to magic. **2** having supernatural qualities. **3** *informal* very good or exciting. ➤ **magical** *adj,* **magically** *adv.*

**magic**[3] *v* (**magicked, magicking**) *informal* to create or affect by magic.

**magician** *n* **1** a person skilled in magic. **2** a conjurer.

**magisterial** *adj* **1** authoritative or masterly. **2** relating to the office of a magistrate.

**magistracy** *n* (*pl* **-ies**) **1** the office or power of a magistrate. **2** magistrates as a group.

**magistrate** *n* a local judicial officer who tries minor cases and holds preliminary hearings.

**magma** *n* molten rock material from within the earth.

**magnanimous** *adj* showing nobility of feeling and generosity of mind. ➤ **magnanimity** *n,* **magnanimously** *adv.*

**magnate** *n* a prominent and wealthy business person.

**magnesium** *n* a light silver-white metallic element which burns with an intense white light.

**magnet** *n* **1** a piece of iron or steel that has the property of attracting iron and producing a magnetic field outside itself. **2** a person or thing that attracts.

**magnetic** *adj* **1** relating to magnetism. **2** capable of being magnetized. **3** possessing an extraordinary ability to attract or charm. ➤ **magnetically** *adv.*

**magnetic pole** *n* either of two small regions in the North and South geographical polar areas of the earth towards which a magnetic needle points.

**magnetic storm** *n* a marked local disturbance of the earth's magnetic field.

**magnetic tape** *n* a ribbon of magnetizable tape used in recording sound or video signals.

**magnetism** *n* **1** the phenomenon by which magnets attract or repel metal objects. **2** an ability to attract or charm.

**magnetize** *or* **-ise** *v* to make magnetic. ➤ **magnetizable** *n.*

**magneto** /mag'neetoh/ *n* (*pl* **-os**) an alternator with permanent magnets formerly used to generate a high voltage for an engine's ignition.

**magnification** *n* **1** the process of magnifying. **2** the degree to which something is magnified.

**magnificent** *adj* **1** strikingly beautiful or impressive. **2** exceptionally fine. ➤ **magnificence** *n,* **magnificently** *adv.*

**magnify** *v* (**-ies, -ied**) **1** to enlarge in appearance by optical means. **2** to increase or exaggerate the significance of.

**magnifying glass** *n* a single lens for magnifying objects or print.

**magnitude** *n* **1** size or extent. **2** a numerical quantity or value. **3** importance or significance.

**magnolia** *n* **1** a shrub or tree with large white, yellow pink, or purple flowers. **2** a pale creamy white colour.

**magnum** *n* (*pl* **magnums**) a wine bottle holding twice the usual amount (about 1.5l).

**magpie** *n* **1** a large bird with a long tail and black-and-white plumage. **2** a person who collects objects randomly.

**maharajah** *or* **maharaja** *n* formerly, an Indian prince.

**mah-jong** *or* **mah-jongg** *n* a Chinese game played with small tiles.

**mahogany** *n* **1** the dark-coloured wood of a tropical tree. **2** a reddish brown colour.

**mahout** /mə'howt/ *n* a keeper and driver of an elephant.

**maid** *n* **1** a female servant. **2** *archaic* an unmarried girl or young woman.

**maiden**[1] *n* **1** *archaic or literary*. **2** an unmarried girl or young woman. **3** (*also* maiden over) in cricket, an over in which no runs are scored. ➤ **maidenhood** *n,* **maidenly** *adj.*

**maiden**[2] *adj* denoting the first instance of something: *a maiden voyage.*

**maidenhead** *n archaic* a woman's virginity.

**maiden name** *n* the surname of a woman before she is married.

**mail**[1] *n* **1** letters and parcels sent by post. **2** the postal system. **3** email.

**mail**[2] *v* **1** to send by post. **2** to contact by email.

**mail**[3] *n* armour made of interlocking metal rings or plates.

**mail order** *n* a system of ordering goods and receiving them by post.

**maim** *v* to injure or wound permanently.

**main**[1] *adj* chief or principal.

**main**[2] *n* **1** a principal pipe or cable carrying gas, electricity, or water. **2** (**the mains**) the central source of water, gas, or electricity supplied to an area. * **in the main** generally; on the whole.

**mainframe** *n* a large computer linked to a number of workstations.

**mainland** *n* the largest land area of a continent or country, considered apart from any offshore islands.

**mainly** *adv* in most cases or for the most part; chiefly.

**mainspring** *n* **1** the chief spring of a watch or clock. **2** the chief cause of or influence on something.

**mainstay** *n* **1** the chief support or main part of something. **2** a stretched rope or wire supporting the mainmast of a sailing ship.

**mainstream** *n* the prevailing influences, values, and activities of a group or society.

**maintain** *v* **1** to keep (something) in its normal state of operation or repair. **2** to sustain or defend. **3** to continue or keep up (something). **4** to support or provide for (e.g. dependants). **5** to assert.

**maintenance** *n* **1** the action of maintaining. **2** *chiefly Brit* payments for the support of one spouse by another after legal separation.

**maisonette** *n* a part of a house, usu on two floors, let or sold separately.

**maize** *n* a tall cereal grass bearing seeds on elongated ears.

**majestic** *adj* showing great grandeur or beauty. ➤ **majestically** *adv.*

**majesty** *n* (*pl* **-ies**) **1** impressive grandeur or beauty. **2** (**Majesty**) used in addressing or referring to a king or queen.

**major**[1] *adj* **1** notable in effect or scope; considerable. **2** greater in importance, size, rank, or degree. **3** of a musical scale: having semitones between the third and fourth and the seventh and eighth notes.

**major**[2] *n* **1** an army officer ranking below a lieutenant colonel. **2** *NAmer* a student specializing in a specified subject.

**major**[3] *v chiefly NAmer* (+ in) to take courses in a particular subject.

**major-domo** *n* (*pl* **major-domos**) the head steward of a large household.

**major general** *n* an army officer ranking below a lieutenant general.

**majority** *n* (*pl* **-ies**) **1** a number greater than half of a total. **2** the number by which the votes cast for the winning party in an election exceed those for its nearest rival or its rivals together. **3** the age, usu 18 or 21, at which full legal rights are acquired.

**make**[1] *v* (*past tense and past part.* **made**) **1** to form or put together from ingredients or parts. **2** to produce or bring about by work or effort. **3** to perform or carry out. **4** to cause to be in a particular state or act in a certain way. **5** (+ into) to change (something) so that it becomes something different. **6** to have as a possible function; to serve as. **7** to compel (somebody) to do something. **8** to earn (money) as income. **9** to achieve or reach. **10** to estimate as an amount or total. **11** to arrange (a bed) to be ready for use. **12** (+ for) to attempt to move in a particular direction. * **make away with** to take or steal. **make believe** to pretend. **make do** to manage with limited resources. **make something of 1** to attribute significance to. **2** to understand. **make way** to give room or allow somebody to pass. ➤ **maker** *n.*

**make**[2] *n* a manufacturer or brand. * **on the make** *informal* seeking a higher social or financial status.

**make-believe** *n* imagination or fantasy.

**make off** *v* to leave in haste. * **make off with** to take or steal.

**make out** *v* **1** to manage with difficulty to perceive or understand. **2** to claim or pretend. **3** to write out (a document). **4** *informal* to fare or manage.

**makeover** *n* **1** the refurbishing or renovation of a building, piece of clothing, etc. **2** the remodelling of a person's appearance.

**make over** *v* **1** to transfer the title of (property). **2** to refurbish or remodel.

**makeshift** *adj* crudely improvised.

**make up** *v* **1** to invent (a story or excuse). **2** to assemble or form (a whole). **3** to be reconciled. **4** (+ for) to compensate for a disadvantage or loss. **5** to apply cosmetics. * **make it up to** to compensate (somebody) for a disappointment or unfairness.

**make-up** *n* **1** cosmetics applied to the face. **2** the way in which the parts of something are put together.

**makeweight** *n* something added to bring a weight to the required value.

**malachite** *n* a green mineral used for ornaments.

**maladjusted** *adj* unable to cope with the normal conditions of life.

**maladroit** *adj* clumsy or inept.

**malady** *n* (*pl* **-ies**) a disease or disorder.

**malaise** *n* **1** a vague feeling of being unwell or dissatisfied. **2** social or economic disquiet.

**malapropism** *n* the wrong use of a word instead of another like it, as in 'polo bears'.

**malaria** *n* a disease caused by mosquito bites, with attacks of chills and fever. ➤ **malarial** *adj.*

**malarkey** *n informal* nonsense.

**malcontent** *n* an aggressively discontented person.

**male**[1] *adj* **1** relating to the sex that fertilizes or inseminates the female to produce offspring. **2** of a plant or flower: having stamens but no ovaries. **3** designed for fitting into a corresponding hollow part.

**male**[2] *n* a male person, animal, or plant.

**malediction** *n formal* a curse. ➤ **maledictory** *adj.*

**malefactor** *n formal* a person who commits a crime or does wrong.

**malevolent** *adj* intending to do harm to others. ➤ **malevolence** *n,* **malevolently** *adv.*

**malformation** *n* abnormal formation or structure. ➤ **malformed** *adj.*

**malfunction** *v* to fail to operate in the normal manner. ➤ **malfunction** *n.*

**malice** *n* a desire to do harm to others.

**malicious** *adj* intended to cause harm to others. ➤ **maliciously** *adv.*

**malign**[1] *adj* evil in nature or effect. ➤ **malignity** *n.*

**malign**[2] *v* to speak ill of.

**malignancy** *n* (*pl* **-ies**) **1** a malignant tumour. **2** being malevolent or malign.

**malignant** *adj* **1** harmful; malevolent. **2** of a tumour: tending to spread.

**malinger** *v* to pretend to be ill or injured to avoid work. ➤ **malingerer** *n.*

**mall** *n* **1** a large covered shopping precinct. **2** a public promenade.

**mallard** *n* a large wild duck with a shiny green head.

**malleable** *adj* **1** able to be beaten or rolled into shape. **2** easily influenced or persuaded. ➤ **malleability** *n.*

**mallet** *n* **1** a hammer with a large wooden head. **2** a long-handled implement with a wooden head for striking the ball in croquet or polo.

**mallow** *n* a plant with showy pink, purple, or white flowers.

**malnourished** *adj* suffering from malnutrition.

**malnutrition** *n* ill health caused by a faulty or inadequate diet.

**malodorous** *adj formal* smelling bad.

**malpractice** *n* failure to exercise due professional skill or care.

**malt** *n* softened and roasted grain used in brewing and distilling. ➤ **malted** *adj.*

**maltreat** *v* to treat cruelly or roughly. ➤ **maltreatment** *n.*

**mama** *or* **mamma** *n informal* one's mother.

**mamba** *n* a tropical African poisonous snake.

**mammal** *n* a warm-blooded animal that has mammary glands and nourishes the young with milk. ➤ **mammalian** *adj.*

**mammary** *adj* relating to the breasts or milk-producing organs.

**Mammon** *n* material wealth or possessions, considered as an evil.

**mammoth**[1] *n* an extinct hairy elephant with a long tail and long tusks.

**mammoth**[2] *adj* huge.

**man**[1] *n* (*pl* **men**) **1** an adult human male. **2** an individual or person. **3** the human race. **4** a piece in a board game.

**man**[2] *v* (**manned, manning**) to provide (a machine or a place) with the people needed to run it.

**manacle**[1] *n* (*usu in pl*) a shackle or handcuff.

**manacle**[2] *v* to confine with manacles.

**manage** *v* **1** to conduct the running of (an organization or group of people). **2** to use (money) economically. **3** to succeed in achieving (something difficult). **4** to be able to cope with a difficult situation. ➤ **manageable** *adj.*

**management** *n* **1** the activity of managing. **2** the people who manage an organization.

**manager** *n* **1** a person who manages an organization or group of people. **2** a person who manages a sports team or individual. ➤ **manageress** *n,* **managerial** *adj.*

**manatee** *n* a tropical plant-eating sea mammal with a broad tail.

**mandarin** *n* **1** (**Mandarin**) the official dialect of Chinese. **2** formerly, a senior Chinese official. **3** a person of position and influence. **4** a yellowish orange citrus fruit with a loose skin.

**mandate**[1] *n* **1** an authoritative command from a superior. **2** an authorization to act on behalf of another. **3** the authority granted by the electorate to the winner of an election to carry out a policy.

**mandate**[2] *v* to give a mandate to.

**mandatory** *adj* **1** constituting a command. **2** compulsory or obligatory.

**mandible** *n* **1** the lower jaw together with its surrounding soft parts. **2** the upper or lower part of a bird's bill. **3** an insect's mouth part for holding or biting food.

**mandolin** *or* **mandoline** *n* a musical instrument of the lute family with four pairs of strings and a fretted neck.

**mandrake** *n* a plant with a large forked root formerly used in medicine.

**mandrill** *n* a large baboon with red and blue striped cheeks and hindquarters.

**mane** *n* **1** a growth of thick hair growing on the neck of a horse, male lion, etc. **2** long thick hair on a person's head.

**maneuver** *n and v NAmer* see MANOEUVRE[1], MANOEUVRE[2].

**manful** *adj* showing courage and resolution. ➤ **manfully** *adv.*

**manganese** *n* a greyish white brittle metallic element.

**mange** *n* a contagious skin disease affecting domestic animals.

**mangel-wurzel** *n* a large type of beet grown as food for livestock.

**manger** *n* a trough or open box in a stable for holding feed.

**mangetout** /'monzhtooh/ *n* (*pl* **mangetouts** *or* **mangetout**) a variety of pea with thin flat edible pods.

**mangle**[1] *v* **1** to hack or crush. **2** to spoil by inept rendering.

**mangle**[2] *n* a machine with rollers for squeezing water from laundry.
**mangle**[3] *v* to squeeze (laundry) with a mangle.
**mango** *n* (*pl* **-oes** *or* **-os**) a yellowish red tropical fruit with a juicy pulp.
**mangrove** *n* a tropical tree or shrub with roots that form dense masses above ground.
**mangy** *or* **mangey** *adj* (**-ier, -iest**) **1** of an animal: suffering from mange. **2** badly worn or shabby. ➤ **manginess** *n.*
**manhandle** *v* **1** to move (a large or heavy object) by human force. **2** to handle (somebody or something) roughly.
**manhole** *n* a covered opening giving access to a sewer or other underground system.
**mania** *n* **1** abnormal excitement with hyperactivity and disorganization of behaviour. **2** an extreme enthusiasm or obsession.
**maniac** *n* **1** a person who behaves in a violent or uncontrolled way. **2** a person with an extreme enthusiasm for something.
**manic** *adj* of or affected by mania. ➤ **manically** *adv.*
**manic depression** *n* a mental disorder characterized by alternating periods of exhilaration and depression. ➤ **manic-depressive** *adj and n.*
**manicure**[1] *n* a treatment for the care of the hands and fingernails.
**manicure**[2] *v* to give a manicure to. ➤ **manicurist** *n.*
**manifest**[1] *adj* readily perceived; obvious. ➤ **manifestly** *adv.*
**manifest**[2] *v* **1** to show or display. **2** of a spirit, etc: to appear in visible form.
**manifest**[3] *n* a list of passengers and cargo on a ship.
**manifestation** *n* **1** something that provides evidence or proof. **2** a sign of the presence of a spirit.
**manifesto** *n* (*pl* **-os** *or* **-oes**) a public declaration of intentions by a political party before an election.
**manifold**[1] *adj* many and varied.
**manifold**[2] *n* a hollow fitting with several outlets or inlets for connecting one pipe with other pipes.
**manikin** *or* **mannikin** *n* **1** a little man. **2** an anatomical model of the body.
**manioc** *n* = CASSAVA.
**manipulate** *v* **1** to handle or operate skilfully. **2** to control or influence by artful or insidious means. ➤ **manipulation** *n,* **manipulative** *adj,* **manipulator** *n.*
**mankind** *n* the human race.
**manky** *adj* (**-ier, -iest**) *Brit, informal* nasty or dirty.
**manly** *adj* (**-ier, -iest**) having the qualities traditionally thought to befit a man, e.g. courage or strength. ➤ **manliness** *n.*
**man-made** *adj* made or produced by human beings rather than nature.
**manna** *n* in the Bible, food miraculously given to the Israelites on their journey through the wilderness.
**mannequin** *n* a model of the human figure used for displaying clothes in a shop.
**manner** *n* **1** the way in which something is done. **2** a characteristic or distinctive bearing or air. **3** (*in pl*) polite social behaviour.
**mannered** *adj* **1** having manners of the kind specified: *well-mannered.* **2** artificial or stilted.
**mannerism** *n* a characteristic gesture or idiosyncrasy.
**mannerly** *adj* having good manners; polite.
**mannish** *adj* of a woman: like a man in appearance or manner.
**manoeuvre**[1] (*NAmer* **maneuver**) *n* **1** a movement requiring skill and dexterity. **2** a deft or well-planned social or political action. **3** (*in pl*) a large-scale military training exercise.
**manoeuvre**[2] (*NAmer* **maneuver**) *v* **1** to perform a manoeuvre. **2** to use stratagems. **3** to guide carefully into position. ➤ **manoeuvrable** *adj.*
**man of letters** *n* **1** a scholar. **2** a distinguished male scholar or author.
**man of straw** *n* an unreliable or insignificant person.
**man of the cloth** *n* a clergyman.
**man-of-war** *or* **man-o'-war** *n* (*pl* **men-of-war** *or* **men-o'-war**) formerly, an armed sailing ship.
**manometer** *n* an instrument used for measuring the pressure of gases and vapours.
**manor** *n* a large country house with an estate. ➤ **manorial** *adj.*
**manpower** *n* the supply of people available for work.
**manse** *n* the house of a clergyman in Scotland.
**mansion** *n* a large imposing house.
**manslaughter** *n* the unlawful killing of somebody without malicious intent.
**mantel** *or* **mantle** *n* a mantelpiece or mantelshelf.
**mantelpiece** *or* **mantlepiece** *n* **1** an ornamental structure round a fireplace. **2** a mantelshelf.
**mantelshelf** *or* **mantleshelf** *n* a shelf forming the top of a mantelpiece.
**mantilla** *n* a light scarf worn over the head and shoulders by Spanish and Latin-American women.
**mantis** *n* (*pl* **mantises** *or* **mantes**) an insect that clasps its prey in forelimbs held as if in prayer.
**mantle**[1] *n* **1** a loose sleeveless cloak. **2** something that covers or conceals. **3** a role adopted or taken over from somebody else. **4** a sheath placed over the flame of a gas or oil lamp to increase the light given off. **5** the part of the

earth that lies between the crust and the central core.

**mantle**[2] *n* see MANTEL.

**mantra** *n* a word or sound used in meditation to focus the mind and help concentration.

**manual**[1] *adj* **1** of or involving the hands. **2** worked or done by hand rather than by machine. ➤ **manually** *adv.*

**manual**[2] *n* **1** a book of instructions or information. **2** a keyboard of an organ played with the hands.

**manufacture**[1] *n* **1** the large-scale making of products by machinery. **2** the act or process of producing something.

**manufacture**[2] *v* **1** to make (products) on a large scale by machinery. **2** to invent or fabricate. ➤ **manufacturer** *n.*

**manure** *n* animal dung used to fertilize land.

**manuscript** *n* a book or document written by hand or in a form prior to publication.

**Manx** *n* the Celtic language of the Isle of Man. ➤ **Manx** *adj.*

**Manx cat** *n* a cat of a short-haired breed with no tail.

**many**[1] *adj* (**more, most**) amounting to a large number.

**many**[2] *pron* a large number of people or things.

**many**[3] *n* (**the many**) *literary* the great majority.

**Maori** *n* (*pl* **Maoris** *or* **Maori**) **1** a member of the aboriginal people of New Zealand. **2** the language of this people.

**map**[1] *n* a reduced representation on a flat surface of part of the earth's surface, showing geographical features, towns, roads, etc.

**map**[2] *v* (**mapped, mapping**) **1** to make a map of. **2** (*often* + out) to plan in detail. ➤ **mapping** *n.*

**maple** *n* a tree having broad leaves with pointed lobes.

**maple syrup** *n* syrup made by concentrating the sap of sugar maple trees.

**map reference** *n* a pair of coordinates for finding a point on a map.

**mar** *v* (**marred, marring**) to spoil the perfection or wholeness of.

**maraca** /mə'rakə/ *n* each of a pair of rattles used as a percussion instrument.

**marathon** *n* **1** a long-distance running race, usu of 42.2km (about 26mi 385yd). **2** a lengthy or strenuous activity.

**maraud** *v* to roam about in search of plunder. ➤ **marauder** *n.*

**marble** *n* **1** a hard stone with a veined or mottled appearance that can be polished to a very smooth finish. **2** a small glass ball used in children's games. **3** *informal* (*in pl*) one's sanity or common sense. ➤ **marbly** *adj.*

**marbled** *adj* marked with a mottled or streaked pattern.

**March** *n* the third month of the year.

**march**[1] *v* **1** to move along with a steady pace. **2** to walk in a direct purposeful manner. **3** to make steady progress. **4** to take part in a protest march. **5** to make (somebody) march. ➤ **marcher** *n.*

**march**[2] *n* **1** the action of marching. **2** a regular step used in marching. **3** a musical composition suitable to accompany marching. **4** a procession organized as a demonstration of support or protest.

**march**[3] *n* (*often* **the Marches**) a border region between two countries.

**marchioness** *n* **1** the wife or widow of a marquess. **2** a woman having the rank of a marquess.

**Mardi Gras** /ˌmahdi'grah/ *n* a Shrove Tuesday carnival.

**mare**[1] *n* the female of a horse or other animal.

**mare**[2] /'mahray/ *n* (*pl* **maria** /'mahri·ə/) a large dark area on the surface of the moon or Mars.

**margarine** *n* a substitute for butter made from vegetable oils.

**margin** *n* **1** the edge or outside limit of an area. **2** a rim or border. **3** the part of a page outside the main area of text. **4** (*usu in pl*) the fringes of a movement, organization, etc. **5** an extreme limit of tolerance or practicability. **6** the difference between one amount and another. * **margin of error** an amount allowed for possible mistakes or miscalculation.

**marginal** *adj* **1** placed in the margin. **2** only just qualifying or acceptable. **3** denoting a parliamentary constituency where the MP has a small majority. ➤ **marginally** *adv.*

**marginalize** *or* **-ise** *v* to treat as peripheral or unimportant. ➤ **marginalization** *n.*

**marigold** *n* a plant of the daisy family with yellow or red flowers.

**marijuana** *or* **marihuana** /mari'(h)wahnə/ *n* a mild form of cannabis.

**marina** *n* a dock or basin providing moorings for yachts and small boats.

**marinade**[1] *n* a mixture in which food is soaked before cooking to enrich its flavour or make it tender.

**marinade**[2] *v* to soak in a marinade.

**marinate** *v* = MARINADE[2].

**marine**[1] *adj* **1** of the sea. **2** relating to the navigation or commerce of the sea.

**marine**[2] *n* a soldier able to serve at sea as well as on land.

**mariner** *n formal or literary* a sailor.

**marionette** *n* a small-scale figure operated by strings or wires.

**marital** *adj* relating to marriage or the relations between husband and wife.

**maritime** *adj* **1** relating to navigation or commerce on the sea. **2** associated with or found near the sea. **3** of a climate: having small variations in seasonal temperatures because of the influence of the sea.

**marjoram** *n* **1** a fragrant aromatic plant of the mint family with leaves used as a herb. **2** = OREGANO.

**mark**[1] *n* **1** a spot, scratch, etc on the surface of something. **2** a line, notch, etc designed to record position. **3** an identifying symbol. **4** a distinguishing characteristic. **5** a written or printed symbol. **6** a sign or token. **7** a point or level reached or achieved. **8** a symbol or figure indicating an assessment of merit. **9** a particular model of a vehicle, weapon, machine, etc. **10** a goal or target in a game. **11** the starting line or position in a track event. ✱ **make one's mark** to make a good impression. **near the mark** not far from the truth. **on your marks** used to instruct runners in a race to take starting positions. **quick off the mark** reacting promptly. **up to the mark** reaching the desired standard. **wide of the mark** not accurate or relevant.

**mark**[2] *v* **1** to make a mark on. **2** to evaluate or give a mark to (a piece of work). **3** to add appropriate symbols to (a text). **4** to indicate or identify by a mark or symbol. **5** to register or record. **6** to characterize or distinguish. **7** to be a sign of. **8** to be the occasion of (something notable). **9** (*usu* + off) to set apart or delineate. **10** to observe or take notice of. **11** in a team game, to stay close to (an opponent) to prevent them from getting or passing the ball. ✱ **mark time 1** to move the feet in march time without moving forward. **2** to pass time unproductively while waiting.

**mark**[3] *n* the former basic monetary unit of Germany (replaced by the euro in 2002).

**mark down** *v* to put a lower price on.

**marked** *adj* **1** having natural marks. **2** made identifiable by marking. **3** distinct and noticeable. **4** being an object of attack or suspicion. ➤ **markedly** /'mahkidli/ *adv.*

**marker** *n* **1** something used to mark a position, place, or direction. **2** a felt-tip pen with a broad tip. **3** a person who marks something. **4** in a team game, a player who marks an opponent.

**market**[1] *n* **1** a meeting of people for trading. **2** a place where provisions, livestock, etc are sold. **3** an opportunity for selling particular goods, or a section of the community offering this. **4** commercial activity or demand. ✱ **on the market** available for buying.

**market**[2] *v* (**marketed, marketing**) to sell or offer for sale. ➤ **marketable** *adj.*

**market garden** *n* a plot in which fruit and vegetables are grown for market. ➤ **market gardening** *n,* **market gardener** *n.*

**marketing** *n* the promotion and advertising of goods or services for sale.

**marketplace** *n* **1** an open place where markets are held. **2** an opportunity for selling.

**market research** *n* the collection information about consumer demand and preferences.

**market town** *n* a town that holds a regular public market.

**market value** *n* the value of something in a free market.

**marking** *n* **1** a mark or marks. **2** an arrangement or pattern of marks.

**marksman** *n* (*pl* **marksmen**) a person skilled in shooting. ➤ **marksmanship** *n.*

**markup** *n* an amount added to the price of something to guarantee the seller a profit.

**mark up** *v* to put a higher price on.

**marl** *n* a crumbly deposit of silt or clay, used as a fertilizer.

**marmalade** *n* a sweetened preserve made from oranges.

**marmoreal** *adj literary* made of or resembling marble.

**marmoset** *n* a small American monkey with a long tail and silky fur.

**marmot** *n* a burrowing rodent with short legs and coarse fur.

**maroon**[1] *v* to abandon (somebody) in a desolate place.

**maroon**[2] *n* a dark brownish red colour.

**marque** *n* a make of vehicle, as distinct from a particular model.

**marquee** *n* **1** a large tent for outdoor social events. **2** *NAmer* a canopy over an entrance to a large building.

**marquess** *n* a member of the British peerage ranking below a duke and above an earl.

**marquetry** *or* **marqueterie** *n* decorative work made from coloured pieces of wood, ivory, etc inlaid in the surface of furniture.

**marquis** *n* **1** a nobleman in Europe ranking above a count and below a duke. **2** a marquess.

**marquise** *n* a marchioness.

**marriage** *n* **1** the union of a man and woman in a special kind of social and legal dependence. **2** the state of being husband and wife. ➤ **marriageable** *adj.*

**married** *adj* joined in marriage.

**marrow** *n* **1** a fruit of a gourd, used as a vegetable. **2** a soft tissue inside bones, in which blood cells are produced.

**marrowbone** *n* a bone rich in marrow.

**marry** *v* (**-ies, -ied**) **1** to take as a husband or wife. **2** to join in marriage. **3** to bring (two or more things) together closely.

**marsh** *n* an area of soft continuously wet land. ➤ **marshy** *adj.*

**marshal**[1] *n* **1** an officer of the highest military rank. **2** a district law officer in the USA. **3** an official who organizes a public occasion.

**marshal**[2] *v* (**marshalled, marshalling,** *NAmer* **marshaled, marshaling**) **1** to place in proper rank or position. **2** to order (information) in an effective way. **3** to lead or usher (a group of people) ceremoniously.

**marshmallow** *n* **1** a pink-flowered marsh

plant. **2** a light spongy confection made from sugar, albumen, and gelatin.

**marsupial** *n* a mammal the females of which have a pouch on the abdomen for carrying young.

**mart** *n* a market or other place of trade.

**marten** *n* (*pl* **martens** *or* **marten**) a tree-dwelling mammal with a slender body.

**martial** *adj* relating to war.

**martial art** *n* an art of combat practised as a sport.

**martial law** *n* government by military forces in occupied territory or in an emergency.

**Martian**[1] *adj* relating to or coming from the planet Mars.

**Martian**[2] *n* a supposed inhabitant of Mars.

**martin** *n* a small swallow with a short tail.

**martinet** *n* a strict disciplinarian.

**martyr**[1] *n* **1** a person who is put to death because of their religious beliefs. **2** any person who suffers for any cause or set of beliefs. **3** a person who behaves in a deliberately self-sacrificing manner. ➤ **martyrdom** *n.*

**martyr**[2] *v* to put to death as a martyr.

**marvel**[1] *n* something or somebody amazing.

**marvel**[2] *v* (**marvelled, marvelling,** *NAmer* **marveled, marveling**) (+ at) to be filled with wonder or amazement.

**marvellous** (*NAmer* **marvelous**) *adj* **1** causing wonder. **2** extremely good. ➤ **marvellously** *adv.*

**Marxism** *n* the principles and policies of Karl Marx (d.1883), on which communism was based. ➤ **Marxist** *n and adj.*

**marzipan** *n* a paste made from ground almonds, sugar, and egg whites.

**mascara** *n* a cosmetic for darkening the eyelashes.

**mascot** *n* a person, animal, or object thought to bring good luck.

**masculine** *adj* **1** male. **2** characteristic of men. **3** of the gender that includes most words or grammatical forms referring to males. ➤ **masculinity** *n.*

**mash**[1] *n* **1** a soft pulpy mass produced by crushing a substance. **2** *Brit, informal* mashed potatoes.

**mash**[2] *v* to crush or pound to a soft pulpy state.

**mask**[1] *n* **1** a covering for all or part of the face, worn for disguise or protection. **2** a copy of a face made by sculpting or by means of a mould.

**mask**[2] *v* **1** to cover or conceal with a mask. **2** to disguise or conceal. **3** to make indistinct or imperceptible. **4** to cover for protection. ➤ **masked** *adj.*

**masochism** *n* the deriving of pleasure from being physically or mentally abused. ➤ **masochist** *n,* **masochistic** *adj.*

**mason** *n* **1** a skilled worker with stone. **2** (**Mason**) a Freemason.

**Masonic** *adj* relating to Freemasons.

**masonry** *n* stonework.

**masque** *n* a dramatic entertainment performed by masked actors.

**masquerade**[1] *n* **1** a social gathering of people wearing masks. **2** a show or pretence.

**masquerade**[2] *v* (+ as) to pretend to be something that one is not.

**mass**[1] *n* **1** (**Mass**) the Roman Catholic celebration of the Eucharist. **2** a musical setting for the fixed parts of the Mass.

**mass**[2] *n* **1** a quantity of matter irrespective of its shape. **2** in physics, the resistance of a body to a change in its speed or position, taken as a measure of the amount of material it contains. **3** the principal part or main body. **4** *informal* (*in pl*) a large quantity or amount. **5** a large body of people in a compact group. **6** (**the masses**) the ordinary people.

**mass**[3] *v* to assemble into a single mass.

**mass**[4] *adj* involving a lot of people.

**massacre**[1] *v* **1** to kill (a large number of people) brutally. **2** *informal* to defeat (an opponent) overwhelmingly.

**massacre**[2] *n* the brutal killing of large numbers of people.

**massage**[1] *n* the action of kneading and rubbing the body to relieve aches and give relaxation.

**massage**[2] *v* **1** to give a massage to. **2** (+ in/into) to rub a substance into (the skin or the scalp). **3** to adjust (data) to present a particular appearance.

**massage parlour** *n* **1** an establishment where professional massage is provided. **2** a brothel.

**masseur** /ma'suh/ *or* **masseuse** /ma'suhz/ *n* a person who provides professional massage.

**massif** /'maseef, ma'seef/ *n* a group of mountains with tall peaks.

**massive** *adj* **1** large and heavy. **2** unusually large or intense. ➤ **massively** *adv.*

**mass-market** *adj* of a product: intended for a wide range of people.

**mass-produce** *v* to produce (goods) in large quantities. ➤ **mass-produced** *adj.*

**mast**[1] *n* **1** a tall pole on a ship, for carrying sails. **2** a vertical pole or framework carrying a radio or television aerial.

**mast**[2] *n* nuts that have fallen on the forest floor and are eaten by animals.

**mastectomy** *n* (*pl* **-ies**) the amputation of a breast.

**master**[1] *n* **1** a person having control or authority over another. **2** the owner of a slave or animal. **3** a male teacher. **4** the head of a college. **5** a person holding an academic degree higher than a bachelor's but lower than a doctor's. **6** a skilled exponent of an art or activity. **7** an original film or recording from which copies can be made.

**master**[2] *v* **1** to acquire complete knowledge or skill in. **2** to gain control of.

**master³** *adj* principal or controlling.

**master class** *n* a class in which an eminent performer instructs advanced pupils.

**masterful** *adj* **1** inclined to take control and dominate. **2** having great artistic or intellectual skill. ➤ **masterfully** *adv.*

**master key** *n* a key designed to open several different locks.

**masterly** *adj* demonstrating exceptional expertise.

**mastermind¹** *n* a person who plans and implements a complex project.

**mastermind²** *v* to plan and implement (a complex project).

**master of ceremonies** *n* a person who directs the proceedings at a public entertainment or other event.

**masterpiece** *n* a work of exceptional skill.

**mastery** *n* **1** complete control or authority. **2** extensive skill or knowledge in a subject.

**masthead** *n* **1** the top of a ship's mast. **2** the name of a newspaper displayed on the top of the first page.

**mastic** *n* **1** an aromatic resin from an evergreen tree, used in varnishes. **2** a waterproof substance like putty used in building.

**masticate** *v* to grind or crush (food) before swallowing. ➤ **mastication** *n.*

**mastiff** *n* a large smooth-coated dog of a breed used as guard dogs.

**mastodon** *n* an extinct mammal similar to an elephant.

**mastoid** *or* **mastoid process** *n* a conical projecting part of the bone behind the ear.

**masturbate** *v* to stimulate one's genitals for sexual pleasure. ➤ **masturbation** *n,* **masturbatory** *adj.*

**mat¹** *n* **1** a piece of thick fabric used as a floor covering. **2** a flat piece of material used to protect a surface from heat, moisture, etc. **3** a thick pad used as a surface for wrestling and gymnastics. **4** a mass of intertwined or tangled strands.

**mat²** *v* (**matted, matting**) of fibres, hair, etc: to become tangled.

**matador** *n* a principal bullfighter.

**match¹** *n* **1** a contest between two or more teams or individuals. **2** a person or thing that is the equal of another. **3** one thing that corresponds exactly to another. **4** a pair of things that correspond exactly. **5** a prospective partner in marriage. **6** a marriage union.

**match²** *v* **1** to correspond or suit. **2** to be the exact counterpart of. **3** to be equal to. **4** to place (a person or thing) in competition with another.

**match³** *n* a short thin piece of wood or cardboard tipped with a mixture that ignites when rubbed against a rough surface.

**matchbox** *n* a small box that contains matches.

**matchless** *adj* having no equal.

**matchmaker** *n* a person who arranges marriages or romantic relationships.

**match point** *n* a point in tennis the winning of which also wins the match.

**matchstick** *n* the stem of a match.

**mate¹** *n* **1** a friend or companion. **2** an assistant to a more skilled worker. **3** an officer on a merchant ship ranking below captain. **4** a marriage partner. **5** either member of a breeding pair of animals.

**mate²** *v* of animals: to come together to breed.

**mate³** *v* in chess, to checkmate (an opponent).

**mate⁴** *n* in chess, checkmate.

**matelot** *n Brit, informal* a sailor.

**material¹** *n* **1** the substances of which something is made. **2** cloth or fabric. **3** (*in pl*) things needed for doing or making something.

**material²** *adj* **1** important or significant. **2** (+ to) relevant. **3** concerned with physical rather than spiritual things. ➤ **materially** *adv.*

**materialism** *n* **1** an interest in or emphasis on physical rather than spiritual things. **2** a theory that only physical matter is real. ➤ **materialist** *n and adj,* **materialistic** *adj.*

**materialize** *or* **-ise** *v* **1** to assume a bodily form. **2** to become reality.

**maternal** *adj* **1** relating to or characteristic of a mother. **2** related through one's mother. ➤ **maternally** *adv.*

**maternity** *n* motherhood.

**matey** *or* **maty** *adj* (**-ier, -iest**) *informal* friendly.

**mathematics** *pl n* the science of numbers and using them to make calculations and measurements. ➤ **mathematical** *adj,* **mathematically** *n.*

**maths** *pl n Brit* mathematics.

**matinée** *n* an afternoon performance in a theatre or cinema.

**matins** *pl n* a morning prayer service.

**matriarch** *n* a woman who is the head of her family.

**matriarchy** *n* (*pl* **-ies**) a system of social organization in which the female is the head of the family. ➤ **matriarchal** *adj.*

**matricide** *n* **1** the act of killing one's mother. **2** somebody who does this. ➤ **matricidal** *adj.*

**matriculate** *v* to admit be admitted as a member of a college or university. ➤ **matriculation** *n.*

**matrimony** *n* marriage. ➤ **matrimonial** *adj.*

**matrix** *n* (*pl* **matrices** *or* **matrixes**) **1** a substance, environment, etc within which something develops. **2** a mould in which something is cast. **3** a rectangular array of mathematical elements treated as a unit. **4** an arrangement of elements into rows and columns.

**matron** *n* **1** a woman in charge of living arrangements in a school or residential home. **2** *Brit* a woman in charge of the nursing in a

hospital. **3** a mature or dignifed married woman >. ➤ **matronly** *adj.*
**matron of honour** *n* a bride's principal married wedding attendant.
**matt** *or* **matte** *adj* lacking gloss; not shiny.
**matted** *adj* of fibres, hair, etc: tangled.
**matter**[1] *n* **1** the physical substance of an object. **2** a subject of interest or concern. **3** something to be considered or proved. **4** something written or printed. ✱ **for that matter** so far as that is concerned. **no matter 1** that is of no importance. **2** regardless of a certain thing.
**matter**[2] *v* to be important or relevant.
**matter-of-fact** *adj* practical and unimaginative.
**mattock** *n* a digging tool with a head like a pick and a blade like an axe.
**mattress** *n* a fabric case filled with resilient material or a setof springs, used on a bed.
**mature**[1] *adj* **1** fully grown. **2** physically, emotionally, or mentally advanced. **3** having completed natural growth; ripe. **4** sensible and well considered. ➤ **maturely** *adv.*
**mature**[2] *v* **1** to become mature. **2** of an insurance policy: to become due for payment.
**maturity** *n* **1** the quality or state of being mature. **2** the date when an insurance policy becomes due.
**maudlin** *adj* weakly sentimental.
**maul** *v* **1** of an animal: to attack and tear the flesh of. **2** to handle roughly.
**maunder** *v* **1** to act or wander idly. **2** to speak in a rambling or indistinct manner.
**mausoleum** *n* (*pl* **mausoleums**) a large elaborate tomb.
**mauve** *n* a pinkish purple colour.
**maverick** *n* an independent and nonconformist individual.
**maw** *n* the throat or jaws of a flesh-eating animal.
**mawkish** *adj* feebly sentimental.
**max.** *abbr* maximum.
**maxim** *n* a succinct expression of a general truth or principle.
**maximize** *or* **-ise** *v* **1** to make as large or numerous as possible. **2** to use to best advantage.
**maximum**[1] *n* (*pl* **maxima** *or* **maximums**) the greatest amount, number, or degree possible or recorded. ➤ **maximal** *adj.*
**maximum**[2] *adj* greatest in amount or number.
**May** *n* the fifth month of the year.
**may**[1] *v aux* (*third person sing. present tense* **may,** *past tense* **might**) **1** expressing permission. **2** expressing possibility. **3** expressing a wish or hope.
**may**[2] *n* hawthorn or hawthorn blossom.
**maybe** *adv* perhaps.
**Mayday** *n* an international radio distress signal.
**mayhem** *n* a state of great confusion or disorder.
**mayn't** *contraction* may not.
**mayonnaise** *n* a thick dressing made with egg yolks, vegetable oil, and vinegar or lemon juice.
**mayor** *n* the head of a city or borough council. ➤ **mayoral** *adj.*
**mayoralty** *n* (*pl* **-ies**) the term of office of a mayor.
**mayoress** *n* **1** the wife of a mayor. **2** a woman mayor.
**maypole** *n* a tall pole with ribbons hanging from the top, for dancing round on May Day.
**maze** *n* **1** a complex network of paths through which people have to find a way to the centre. **2** something very complicated.
**mazurka** *n* a Polish folk dance in moderate triple time.
**Mb** *abbr* megabyte(s).
**MBA** *abbr* Master of Business Administration.
**MBE** *abbr* Member of the Order of the British Empire.
**MC** *abbr* **1** Master of Ceremonies. **2** *Brit* Military Cross.
**MD** *abbr* **1** Doctor of Medicine. **2** *Brit* Managing Director.
**Md** *abbr* the chemical symbol for mendelevium.
**ME** *abbr* myalgic encephalomyelitis, a condition causing intense tiredness and aching joints.
**me** *pron* used as the objective case: I.
**mead**[1] *n* a fermented alcoholic drink made of water and honey.
**mead**[2] *n archaic* a meadow.
**meadow** *n* an area of level grassland.
**meagre** (*NAmer* **meager**) *adj* deficient in quality or quantity. ➤ **meagreness** *n.*
**meal**[1] *n* **1** the portion of food eaten at one time. **2** the time of eating a meal. ✱ **make a meal of** *informal* to deal laboriously with.
**meal**[2] *n* the ground seeds of a cereal grass or pulse.
**mealy** *adj* (**-ier, -iest**) **1** soft and crumbly. **2** containing meal. **3** pale.
**mealy-mouthed** *adj* unwilling to speak plainly or directly.
**mean**[1] *adj* **1** not generous; stingy. **2** unpleasant and spiteful. **3** inferior in quality or status. **4** merely ordinary. **5** *informal* excellent or impressive. ➤ **meanly** *adv,* **meanness** *n.*
**mean**[2] *v* (*past tense and past part.* **meant**) **1** to have in mind as a purpose. **2** of a word or statement: to have as its explanation or significance. **3** to intend for a particular use or purpose. **4** (*usu* + to) to have significance or importance.
**mean**[3] *n* **1** a middle point between extremes. **2** a value that is the average of a range of values.
**mean**[4] *adj* **1** midway between extremes. **2** average or intermediate.
**meander**[1] *v* **1** of a river or road: to follow a winding course. **2** to wander aimlessly.

**meander**[2] *n* **1** a turn or winding of a stream. **2** a winding path or pattern.

**meaning** *n* **1** what a word is intended to convey of signify. **2** sense or significance.

**meaningful** *adj* **1** having meaning. **2** having a special significance; expressive. **3** worthwhile. ➤ **meaningfully** *adv.*

**meaningless** *adj* having no meaning or purpose. ➤ **meaninglessly** *adv.*

**means** *pl n* **1** a method or way that enables a purpose to be achieved. **2** money or other resources available. * **by all means** of course; certainly. **by means of** with the help or use of. **by no means** not at all; in no way.

**means test** *n* an examination into somebody's financial state to determine their eligibility for public assistance.

**meant** *v* past tense and past part. of MEAN[2].

**meantime** *n* * **in the meantime** meanwhile.

**meanwhile** *adv* **1** during the intervening time. **2** during the same period.

**measles** *pl n* an infectious disease marked by a red rash and high fever.

**measly** *adj* (**-ier, -iest**) *informal* very small or few; worthless or insignificant.

**measure**[1] *v* **1** to find out the size, amount, or degree of in terms of a standard unit. **2** to have (a specified measurement). **3** (+ out) to take in measured amounts. **4** (+ up) to have the necessary ability or qualities. ➤ **measurable** *adj,* **measurably** *adv.*

**measure**[2] *n* **1** a step planned or taken to achieve an end. **2** a proposed legislative act or bill. **3** a standard or unit of measurement. **4** an instrument or utensil for measuring. **5** an appropriate or due portion. **6** a moderate extent, amount, or degree. **7** poetic rhythm or metre. **8** a metrical unit. * **for good measure** in addition to what is strictly necessary. **get the measure of** to understand the character or nature of.

**measured** *adj* **1** rhythmically slow and regular. **2** carefully thought out.

**measurement** *n* **1** the act of measuring. **2** a figure or amount obtained by measuring.

**meat** *n* animal flesh used as food.

**meatball** *n* a ball of minced meat for cooking.

**meaty** *adj* (**-ier, -iest**) **1** like meat. **2** fleshy or heavily built. **3** offering plenty to think about or discuss.

**Mecca** *n* a place that attracts a particular group of people.

**mechanic** *n* a skilled worker who repairs or maintains machinery.

**mechanical** *adj* **1** relating to or operated by machinery or machines. **2** done spontaneously or without thought. **3** in accordance with the principles of mechanics. ➤ **mechanically** *adv.*

**mechanics** *pl n* **1** the branch of science that deals with energy and forces and their effect on movement. **2** the working parts of something. **3** the functional details of something.

**mechanism** *n* **1** a set of moving parts designed to perform a function. **2** a process or technique for achieving a result.

**mechanize** *or* **-ise** *v* to equip with machines of mechanical equipment. ➤ **mechanization** *n.*

**medal** *n* a stamped metal disc commemorating a person or event or awarded for an achievement.

**medallion** *n* **1** a pendant in the shape of a medal. **2** a decorative tablet or panel bearing a figure or portrait in relief.

**medallist** (*NAmer* **medalist**) *n* a person who has been awarded a medal for a sporting achievement.

**meddle** *v* (*usu* + in/with) to interfere in the concerns of others. ➤ **meddler** *n.*

**meddlesome** *adj* interfering in other people's concerns.

**media** *n* **1** pl of MEDIUM[1]. **2** the press and television as a source of news and information for the public.

---

***Usage Note:*** The word *media* is plural, and should be followed by a plural verb: *The media have shown little interest in this event.*

---

**mediaeval** *adj* see MEDIEVAL.

**median**[1] *adj technical* positioned in the middle.

**median**[2] *n* **1** a statistical value midway in a range of values. **2** a line from a point where two sides of a triangle meet to the midpoint of the opposite side.

**mediate** *v* to intervene to settle a dispute. ➤ **mediation** *n,* **mediator** *n.*

**medic** *n informal* a medical doctor or student.

**medical**[1] *adj* relating to physicians or to medicine. ➤ **medically** *adv.*

**medical**[2] *n* an examination to determine a person's physical fitness.

**medicament** *n* a medicine.

**medicate** *v* **1** to treat with a medicine. **2** to impregnate with a medicinal substance.

**medication** *n* **1** a medicine or drug. **2** treatment with drugs.

**medicinal** *adj* **1** used to cure disease or relieve pain. **2** relating to medicines or drugs. ➤ **medicinally** *adv.*

**medicine** *n* **1** the science and practice of maintaining or restoring health and preventing disease. **2** a substance used in treating or preventing disease.

**medicine man** *n* a healer believed to have supernatural powers.

**medieval** *or* **mediaeval** *adj* dating from or typical of the Middle Ages.

**medievalist** *n* a specialist in medieval history or culture.

**mediocre** *adj* of ordinary or average quality.

**meditate** *v* **1** to fix the mind on one matter, as a religious or spiritual exercise. **2** (*often* + on) to consider or plan in the mind. ➤ **meditation** *n*, **meditative** *adj*.

**Mediterranean** *adj* of the Mediterranean Sea or the region round it.

***Usage Note:*** Note the spelling with *-t-* and *-rr-*.

**medium**[1] *n* (*pl* **media** *or* **mediums**) **1** a means of doing something. **2** a channel or means of large-scale communication. **3** a means of artistic expression. **4** (*pl* **mediums**) a person through whom others seek to communicate with the spirits of the dead. **5** a middle position or state.

**medium**[2] *adj* intermediate between extremes.

**medlar** *n* a small brown fruit like a crab apple.

**medley** *n* (*pl* **-eys**) **1** a varied or confused mixture. **2** a musical composition made up of short pieces.

**meek** *adj* timid or submissive. ➤ **meekly** *adv*.

**meerkat** *n* a small flesh-eating South African mammal related to the mongoose.

**meet**[1] *v* (*past tense and past part.* **met**) **1** to come into the presence of (somebody) by accident or design. **2** to become acquainted with (somebody). **3** (*often* + with) to encounter or experience. **4** to come into contact with. **5** to satisfy or conform to (a requirement).

**meet**[2] *n* a gathering or assembly of people.

**meeting** *n* **1** an assembly of people for formal discussion or business. **2** a coming together of two or more people.

**mega** *adj informal* very large or important.

**megabyte** *n* a unit of computer storage equal to one million bytes.

**megalith** *n* a large block of stone forming part or whole of a prehistoric monument. ➤ **megalithic** *adj*.

**megalomania** *n* an obsessive craving for or belief in power over others. ➤ **megalomaniac** *adj and n*.

**megaphone** *n* a funnel-shaped device for amplifying the voice.

**megaton** *n* an explosive force equivalent to one million tons of TNT.

**megawatt** *n* a unit of power equal to one million watts.

**melamine** *n* a hard plastic used for coatings.

**melancholia** *n* melancholy or depression.

**melancholy**[1] *n* deep sadness or depression. ➤ **melancholic** *adj*.

**melancholy**[2] *adj* **1** depressed or dejected. **2** causing sadness.

**melanin** *n* a dark pigment in the hair and skin, responsible for tanning when the skin is exposed to sunlight.

**melanoma** *n* (*pl* **melanomas** *or* **melanomata**) a tumour of the skin cells that produce melanin.

**meld** *v* to combine or blend.

**melee** *n* a confused or riotous fight or struggle.

**mellifluous** *adj* sounding sweet and smooth. ➤ **mellifluously** *adv*.

**mellow**[1] *adj* **1** rich and soft in colour or taste. **2** made gentle by age or experience. **3** relaxed and genial.

**mellow**[2] *v* to make or become mellow.

**melodic** *adj* **1** relating to or having melody. **2** melodious. ➤ **melodically** *adv*.

**melodious** *adj* having a pleasant sound or tune.

**melodrama** *n* **1** a film or play with an exciting plot and exaggerated emotions. **2** sensational or dramatic behaviour. ➤ **melodramatic** *adj*, **melodramatically** *adv*.

**melody** *n* (*pl* **-ies**) **1** a simple or basic tune. **2** the principal part in a harmonic composition.

**melon** *n* a large round fruit with sweet juicy flesh.

**melt** *v* **1** to change from a solid to a liquid state by heating. **2** to dissolve or disintegrate. **3** (+ away) to disappear gradually. **4** to become tender or gentle.

**meltdown** *n* **1** the overheating of the uranium fuel in the core of a nuclear reactor, so that it burns through its container. **2** a catastrophic collapse or failure.

**melting pot** *n* **1** a place where diverse peoples, traditions, etc influence each other. **2** an unstable situation.

**member** *n* **1** an individual or unit belonging to a group or organization. **2** *archaic* a limb or other part of the body. ➤ **membership** *n*.

**membrane** *n* **1** a thin layer covering, lining, or connecting organs or cells in animals and plants. **2** a thin pliable sheet of material. ➤ **membranous** *adj*.

**memento** *n* (*pl* **-os** *or* **-oes**) something kept as a reminder of the past.

**memo** *n* (*pl* **-os**) *informal* a brief note sent from one person to another in an organization.

**memoir** *n* **1** an account or narrative written from personal experience. **2** (*in pl*) the published reminiscences of a public figure.

**memorabilia** *pl n* objects valued because of their connection with people or events.

**memorable** *adj* **1** worth remembering; notable. **2** easy to remember. ➤ **memorably** *adv*.

**memorandum** *n* (*pl* **memorandums** *or* **memoranda**) **1** *formal* a memo. **2** a written reminder.

**memorial**[1] *n* a monument or occasion that commemorates a person or event.

**memorial**[2] *adj* serving to commemorate a person or event.

**memorize** *or* **-ise** *v* to commit (facts) to memory; to learn by heart.

**memory** *n* (*pl* **-ies**) **1** the ability of the mind to retain and recall facts and experiences. **2** the store of things learned and retained from an individual's experience. **3** an image or impression stored in the mind. **4** the time within which past events are remembered. **5** a computer's facility or capacity for storing data.

**men** *n* pl of MAN[1].

**menace[1]** *n* **1** a threatening or dangerous person or thing. **2** a threatening atmosphere or tone.

**menace[2]** *v* to threaten. ➤ **menacing** *adj.*

**ménage à trois** /me'nahzh ah 'trwah/ *n* a situation in which a third person lives with a married couple and shares their sexual life.

**menagerie** *n* a collection of animals for exhibition.

**mend[1]** *v* **1** to restore to good condition or working order. **2** to improve or rectify. **3** to improve in health.

**mend[2]** *n* a mended place or part. ✱ **on the mend** improving in health.

**mendacious** *adj* lying or untruthful. ➤ **mendacity** *n.*

**mendicant[1]** *n* **1** a friar living off alms. **2** a beggar.

**mendicant[2]** *adj* **1** dependent on alms or begging. **2** given to begging.

**menhir** *n* a prehistoric monument consisting of a single upright stone.

**menial[1]** *adj* of work: routine and involving little skill.

**menial[2]** *n* somebody with a menial job.

**meningitis** *n* a disease involving inflammation of the membranes enveloping the brain and spinal cord.

**meniscus** *n* (*pl* **menisci** *or* **meniscuses**) **1** the curved upper surface of a column of liquid. **2** a lens that is concave on one side and convex on the other.

**menopause** *n* the natural cessation of menstruation occurring between the ages of 45 and 50. ➤ **menopausal** *adj.*

**menorah** *n* a branched candelabrum, a symbol of Judaism.

**menstrual** *adj* relating to menstruation.

**menstruate** *v* of a woman: to discharge blood from the womb about once a month. ➤ **menstruation** *n.*

**-ment** *suffix* forming nouns: *development; encampment.*

**mental** *adj* **1** relating to or experienced by the mind. **2** relating to disorders of the mind. **3** *informal* mad. ➤ **mentally** *adv.*

**mentality** *n* (*pl* **-ies**) **1** a way of thinking. **2** mental power or capacity.

**menthol** *n* an alcohol that occurs in mint oils, with the properties of peppermint. ➤ **mentholated** *adj.*

**mention[1]** *n* **1** a brief reference to somebody or something. **2** a formal citation for outstanding achievement.

**mention[2]** *v* **1** to refer to briefly. **2** to cite for outstanding achievement.

**mentor** *n* a wise and trusted adviser or teacher.

**menu** *n* (*pl* **menus**) **1** a list of the dishes available in a restaurant. **2** the dishes to be served at a meal. **3** a list of available programs, functions, commands, etc, displayed on a computer screen.

**meow** *v* see MIAOW.

**MEP** *abbr* Member of the European Parliament.

**mercantile** *adj* relating to merchants or trading.

**mercenary[1]** *n* (*pl* **-ies**) a soldier who is hired to fight for a foreign country.

**mercenary[2]** *adj* acting primarily for financial reward.

**merchandise[1]** *n* goods for sale.

**merchandise[2]** *or* **-ize** *v* to promote the sale of.

**merchant** *n* **1** a wholesale trader. **2** *informal* a person who indulges in a specified unwelcome activity.

**merchantable** *adj* of a quality acceptable for sale.

**merchant bank** *n* a banking firm dealing with large corporations. ➤ **merchant banker** *n.*

**merchant navy** *n* the commercial shipping of a nation.

**merciful** *adj* **1** showing mercy. **2** affording relief from suffering. ➤ **mercifully** *adv.*

**merciless** *adj* showing no mercy; pitiless. ➤ **mercilessly** *adv.*

**mercurial** *adj* **1** having constant changes of mood. **2** of or containing mercury.

**mercury** *n* a heavy silver-white liquid metallic element used in thermometers and barometers.

**mercy** *n* (*pl* **-ies**) **1** compassion or forbearance shown to an offender or enemy. **2** a fortunate circumstance. ✱ **at the mercy of** wholly in the power of.

**mere[1]** *adj* **1** being what is specified and nothing else. **2** (**the merest**) the slightest.

**mere[2]** *n literary* a lake.

**merely** *adv* only; simply.

**meretricious** *adj* attractive in a showy or tawdry way.

**merge** *v* **1** to combine or unite. **2** to blend or come together gradually.

**merger** *n* a combining of two organizations to form one.

**meridian** *n* a circle on the earth's surface passing through both poles.

**meringue** *n* a mixture of stiffly beaten egg whites and sugar baked until crisp.

**merino** *n* (*pl* **-os**) **1** a sheep of a breed originating in Spain. **2** a soft wool obtained from this sheep.

**merit[1]** *n* **1** worth or excellence. **2** a good or praiseworthy quality.

**merit[2]** *v* (**merited, meriting**) to be worthy of.

**meritocracy** *n* (*pl* **-ies**) a society in which people hold power on the basis of their ability. ➤ **meritocratic** *adj.*

**meritorious** *adj* deserving reward or honour.

**mermaid** *n* a mythical sea creature having a woman's head and trunk and a fish's tail.
**merriment** *n* light-hearted fun.
**merry** *adj* (**-ier, -iest**) **1** cheerful and lively. **2** *Brit, informal* slightly drunk. ➤ **merrily** *adv.*
**merry-go-round** *n* a revolving fairground machine with model horses or vehicles that people ride on.
**merrymaking** *n* festive activity or fun.
**Mesdames** /may'dahm/ *n* pl of MRS.
**mesdemoiselles** /,maydəmwah'zel/ *n* pl of MADEMOISELLE.
**mesh**[1] *n* **1** the cords, wires, etc that make up a net. **2** an open space in a net or network. **3** an interlocking construction.
**mesh**[2] *v* **1** a gearwheel: to link with another gearwheel. **2** to become entangled. **3** to coordinate or harmonize.
**mesmeric** *adj* totally absorbing or hypnotic. ➤ **mesmerically** *adv.*
**mesmerism** *n* hypnotism.
**mesmerize** *or* **-ise** *v* to engross or fascinate totally.
**mess**[1] *n* **1** an untidy or dirty state or condition. **2** a state of confusion or disorder. **3** the excrement of a domestic animal. **4** a prepared dish of soft or liquid food. **5** a place where members of the armed forces eat their meals.
**mess**[2] *v* **1** to make untidy or dirty. **2** *informal* (+ with) to meddle with. **3** (+ about/around) to behave in a silly way.
**message** *n* **1** a written or spoken communication. **2** a central theme or idea. ✱ **get the message** *informal* to understand what somebody is saying.
**messenger** *n* a person who carries a message.
**messiah** *n* **1** (**the Messiah**) a name for Jesus Christ in Christianity. **2** a professed leader of a cause.
**messianic** *adj* associated with a messiah.
**messieurs** /me'syuh, mə'syuhz/ *n* pl of MONSIEUR.
**Messrs** *n* pl of MR.
**messy** *adj* (**-ier, -iest**) **1** untidy or dirty. **2** awkward or difficult to deal with. ➤ **messily** *adv,* **messiness** *n.*
**met** *v* past tense and past part. of MEET[1].
**metabolism** *n* the process in living cells by which energy is provided and new material is assimilated. ➤ **metabolic** *adj.*
**metabolize** *or* **-ise** *v* to process by metabolism.
**metal** *n* **1** a hard shiny substance capable of being melted and fused, and a good conductor of electricity and heat. **2** broken stones used in making roads.
**metalled** (*NAmer* **metaled**) *adj* of a road: covered with a hard surface.
**metallic** *adj* **1** containing or like metal. **2** of a sound: sharp and ringing.
**metallurgy** *n* the branch of science concerned with the properties of metals. ➤ **metallurgical** *adj,* **metallurgist** *n.*
**metamorphic** *adj* of rock: having undergone change resulting from heat and pressure.
**metamorphosis** *n* (*pl* **metamorphoses**) **1** a natural change in the form or structure of an insect or amphibian, e.g. the change from a tadpole to a frog. **2** a change of form, structure, or substance.
**metaphor** *n* a word or phrase literally denoting one kind of object or idea and applied to another to suggest an analogy, e.g. in *the ship ploughs the sea.* ➤ **metaphorical** *adj,* **metaphorically** *adv.*
**metaphysical** *adj* **1** relating to metaphysics. **2** beyond what is physical; supernatural. ➤ **metaphysically** *adv.*
**metaphysics** *pl n* the branch of philosophy concerned with ultimate causes and the underlying nature of things.
**mete** *v* (+ out) to allot or inflict (something unpleasant).
**meteor** *n* a small particle of matter from space that falls into the earth's atmosphere and is heated by friction so that it glows.
**meteoric** *adj* **1** associated with a meteor or meteorite. **2** rapidly and brilliantly successful.
**meteorite** *n* a rock from space that reaches the surface of the earth.
**meteorology** *n* the science of the atmosphere and its phenomena, *esp* the weather. ➤ **meteorological** *adj,* **meteorologist** *n.*
**meter**[1] *n* an instrument for measuring and recording the amount of something used.
**meter**[2] *v* to measure by means of a meter.
**meter**[3] *n NAmer* see METRE[1], METRE[2].
**methadone** *n* a synthetic drug used as a substitute narcotic in the treatment of heroin addiction and as a painkiller.
**methane** *n* a flammable gas that is a product of decomposition of plant or animal matter in marshes and mines, and is used as a fuel.
**methanol** *n* a flammable poisonous liquid alcohol that is added to ethyl alcohol to make it unfit to drink.
**methinks** *v* (*past tense* **methought**) *archaic* it seems to me.
**method** *n* **1** a systematic procedure for doing something. **2** an orderly arrangement or system. **3** the habitual practice of orderliness and regularity.
**methodical** *adj* done with method or order; systematic. ➤ **methodically** *adv.*
**Methodist** *n* a member of a Christian denomination having an evangelical character. ➤ **Methodism** *n.*
**methodology** *n* (*pl* **-ies**) a particular set of methods and rules. ➤ **methodological** *adj.*
**meths** *n Brit, informal* methylated spirits.
**methylated spirits** *or* **methylated spirit** *n* alcohol mixed with methanol to make it unfit for drinking.

**meticulous** *adj* marked by extreme care over detail. ➤ **meticulously** *adv.*

**métier** /'maytyay/ *n* a person's trade or special talent.

**metre**[1] (*NAmer* **meter**) *n* the basic metric SI unit of length equal to 100 centimetres (about 39.37in.).

**metre**[2] (*NAmer* **meter**) *n* the rhythm of verse.

**metric** *adj* using decimal units of measure.

**metrical** *adj* relating to or composed in poetic metre. ➤ **metrically** *adv.*

**metricate** *v* to change (measurements) to the metric system. ➤ **metrication** *n.*

**metric system** *n* a decimal system of weights and measures based on the metre, the litre, and the kilogram.

**metric ton** *or* **metric tonne** *n* a metric unit of weight equal to 1000 kilograms; a tonne.

**metro** *n* (*pl* **-os**) an underground railway system in a city.

**metronome** *n* a musicians' device marking the speed of a beat with a regular tick. ➤ **metronomic** *adj.*

**metropolis** *n* the chief city of a country or region.

**metropolitan** *adj* relating to a metropolis or a large urban area.

**mettle** *n* **1** strength of spirit or temperament. **2** stamina. ✱ **on one's mettle** ready to do one's best.

**mew** *v* to utter the high-pitched cry of a cat or gull.

**mewl** *v* **1** to cry weakly. **2** to mew.

**mews** *n* (*pl* **mews**) *Brit* a street or row of houses converted from former stables.

**mezzanine** *n* a storey situated between two main storeys of a building.

**mezzo** /'metsoh/ *or* **mezzo-soprano** *n* (*pl* **-os**) a female singer with a range between soprano and contralto.

**Mg** *abbr* the chemical symbol for magnesium.

**mg** *abbr* milligram(s).

**MHz** *abbr* megahertz.

**miaow** *or* **meow** *v* to make the cry of a cat. ➤ **miaow** *n.*

**miasma** *n* **1** a heavy or foul-smelling vapour. **2** an unhealthy or unpleasant influence or atmosphere.

**mica** *n* a silicate material occurring as crystals that separate into thin flexible leaves.

**mice** *n* pl of MOUSE.

**mickey** ✱ **take the mickey** *chiefly Brit, informal* to tease or ridicule somebody.

**microbe** *n* a bacterium or other micro-organism. ➤ **microbial** *adj.*

**microbiology** *n* the biology of viruses, bacteria and other microscopic organisms.

**microchip** *n* a miniature integrated circuit made with a thin piece of silicon.

**microclimate** *n* the climate of a small area or habitat.

**microcosm** *n* something regarded as having the characteristics of a larger whole.

**microfiche** *n* a sheet of microfilm containing rows of very small images of printed pages.

**microfilm** *n* a photographic film on which printed material can be recorded in miniature form.

**microlight** *n chiefly Brit* a very small light aircraft for one or two people.

**micrometer** *n* an instrument for measuring very small distances.

**micro-organism** *n* a bacterium or other organism of microscopic size.

**microphone** *n* a device that converts sounds into electrical signals, for transmission or recording.

**microprocessor** *n* an integrated circuit forming the central processing unit of a computer.

**microscope** *n* an optical instrument used to magnify minute objects.

**microscopic** *adj* needing a microscope to be visible or distinguishable. ➤ **microscopically** *adv.*

**microscopy** *n* the use of a microscope.

**microsurgery** *n* surgery done under a microscope with very small instruments.

**microwave**[1] *n* **1** a band of very short electromagnetic waves of between 0.001m and 0.3m in wavelength. **2** (*also* **microwave oven**) an oven in which food is heated by means of microwaves.

**microwave**[2] *v* to cook or heat in a microwave oven.

**mid**[1] *adj* **1** being in the middle. **2** occupying a middle position.

**mid**[2] *prep literary* amid.

**Midas touch** *n* a talent for producing wealth from any activity one takes on.

**midday** *n* the middle part of the day; noon.

**midden** *n* a pile of dung.

**middle**[1] *adj* **1** equally distant from the extremes of something; central. **2** intermediate in rank or quality.

**middle**[2] *n* **1** a middle point or position. **2** *informal* the waist and abdomen.

**middle age** *n* the period of life from about 40 to about 60. ➤ **middle-aged** *adj.*

**Middle Ages** *pl n* (*usu* **the Middle Ages**) the period of European history from about 1000 to 1500.

**middle class** *n* the social class consisting of business and professional people. ➤ **middle-class** *adj.*

**middle ear** *n* a cavity through which sound waves are transmitted from the eardrum to the inner ear.

**Middle East** *n* the countries of southwest Asia and northern Africa, including Libya, Egypt, Lebanon, Syria, Israel, Jordan, the states of the Arabian Peninsula, Iran, and Iraq. ➤ **Middle Eastern** *adj.*

**middleman** *n* (*pl* **middlemen**) a dealer intermediate between the producer of goods and the retailer or consumer.
**middling** *adj and adv* of middle or moderate size or degree.
**midfield** *n* the central part of a playing field between the goals. ➤ **midfielder** *n.*
**midge** *n* a small fly often found near water.
**midget** *n* **1** a very small person. **2** (*used before a noun*) smaller than usual.
**midland** *n* **1** the central region of a country. **2** (**the Midlands**) the central inland region of England.
**midnight** *n* twelve o'clock at night.
**midriff** *n* the middle part of the human torso.
**midship** *n* the middle section of a ship or boat.
**midshipman** *n* (*pl* **midshipmen**) a person training to become a naval officer in the Royal Navy.
**midships** *adv and adj* amidships.
**midst**[1] *n archaic* the inner or central part of something.
**midst**[2] *prep archaic* amid.
**midstream** *n* the part of a stream towards the middle. * **in midstream** in the middle of a process.
**midsummer** *n* **1** the period around the middle of summer. **2** the summer solstice.
**Midsummer Day** *or* **Midsummer's Day** *n* 24 June.
**midterm** *n* the period around the midpoint of an academic term, a term of office, or a pregnancy.
**midway** *adv and adj* halfway.
**midweek** *n* the middle of the week. ➤ **midweek** *adj and adv.*
**midwife** *n* (*pl* **midwives**) a nurse trained to assist women in childbirth. ➤ **midwifery** *n.*
**midwinter** *n* **1** the period around the middle of winter. **2** the winter solstice.
**mien** *n* a person's air or bearing.
**miff** *v informal* to annoy or upset slightly. ➤ **miffed** *adj.*
**might**[1] *v past tense of* MAY[1] **1** used to express permission or possibility. **2** used to express a polite question.
**might**[2] *n* great power or strength.
**mightn't** *contraction* might not.
**mighty** *adj* (**-ier, -iest**) very powerful or strong. ➤ **mightily** *adv,* **mightiness** *n.*
**migraine** *n* a recurrent severe headache usu associated with nausea and disturbances of vision.
**migrant** *n* **1** an animal that migrates. **2** a person who moves regularly to find seasonal work. ➤ **migrant** *adj.*
**migrate** *v* **1** of an animal: to pass seasonally from one region to another for feeding or breeding. **2** of a person: to move from one country or locality to another. ➤ **migration** *n,* **migratory** *adj.*
**mike** *n informal* a microphone.
**milch** *adj* of a domestic animal: bred or used for its milk.
**mild**[1] *adj* **1** gentle in nature or manner. **2** not severe. **3** not strong in flavour or effect. **4** not acutely felt or strongly expressed. **5** of the weather: quite warm. ➤ **mildly** *adv,* **mildness** *n.*
**mild**[2] *n Brit* a dark-coloured beer not flavoured with hops.
**mildew** *n* a whitish fungal growth on the surface of organic matter, e.g. paper or leather, ➤ **mildewed** *adj.*
**mile** *n* **1** (*also* **statute mile**) a unit of distance equal to 1760yd (about 1.61km). **2** = NAUTICAL MILE. **3** (*often in pl*) a large distance. * **be miles away** to be inattentive.
**mileage** *or* **milage** *n* **1** a distance covered in miles. **2** *informal* an advantage or benefit.
**mileometer** *or* **milometer** *n Brit* an instrument fitted in vehicle to record its mileage.
**miles** *adv informal* very much: *That's miles better.*
**milestone** *n* **1** a stone serving as a milepost. **2** a significant stage in development.
**milieu** /'meelyuh, meel'yuh/ *n* (*pl* **milieus** *or* **milieux**) a person's social environment.
**militant** *adj* forcefully or aggressively active in a cause. ➤ **militancy** *n,* **militant** *n,* **militantly** *adv.*
**militarism** *n* a policy of aggressive military preparedness. ➤ **militarist** *n,* **militaristic** *adj.*
**militarize** *or* **-ise** *v* to equip with military forces and defences.
**military**[1] *adj* relating to soldiers and warfare. ➤ **militarily** *adv.*
**military**[2] *n* (**the military**) a country's armed forces.
**militate** *v* (*usu* + against) to have a significant effect in preventing or counteracting.

***Usage Note:*** Do not confuse this word with *mitigate*, which means 'to make less harsh or intense'.

**militia** *n* a body of people who are not professional soldiers but are called on to fight in an emergency. ➤ **militiaman** *n.*
**milk**[1] *n* **1** a white liquid produced by female mammals to feed their young. **2** the milk of cows, goats, etc used as food for humans. **3** the juice of a plant or a coconut.
**milk**[2] *v* **1** to draw milk from (an animal). **2** to draw full advantage from (a situation or person). **3** to extract money from (somebody) over a period of time.
**milk chocolate** *n* solid chocolate made with added milk.
**milk float** *n Brit* a light electrically powered vehicle for carrying milk for domestic delivery.
**milkmaid** *n archaic* a girl or woman who works in a dairy.

**milkman** *n* (*pl* **milkmen**) a man who sells or delivers milk.
**milk round** *n Brit* a regular route for delivering milk.
**milk shake** *n* a drink made from milk blended or whisked with a flavouring syrup.
**milksop** *n* a weak and timid person.
**milk tooth** *n* a first tooth of a child, replaced when it is older.
**milky** *adj* (**-ier, -iest**) **1** containing milk. **2** resembling milk in colour or consistency. **3** cloudy or semi-opaque. ➤ **milkily** *adv*, **milkiness** *n*.
**Milky Way** *n* the galaxy of which the earth is a part, seen as a broad band of faint light stretching across the sky.
**mill**[1] *n* **1** a machine or building for grinding grain into flour. **2** a device for crushing or grinding coffee beans or peppercorns. **3** a building with machinery for manufacturing. ✱ **go/be put through the mill** to undergo a trying experience.
**mill**[2] *v* **1** to grind in a mill. **2** to shape or dress (metal) by means of a rotary cutter. **3** to give a raised rim or a ridged edge to (a coin). **4** (+ about/around) to move in a confused mass.
**millenary**[1] *n* (*pl* **-ies**) **1** a period of a thousand years. **2** a thousandth anniversary.
**millenary**[2] *adj* consisting of a thousand.
**millennium** *n* (*pl* **millennia** *or* **millenniums**) **1** a period of a thousand years. **2** a thousandth anniversary. **3** the date on which one period of a thousand years ends and another begins. ➤ **millennial** *adj*.

***Usage Note:*** *Millennium* is spelt with two *l*'s and two *n*'s.

**miller** *n* a person who owns or works a grain mill.
**millet** *n* a cereal cultivated for grain and used as food.
**millibar** *n* a unit of pressure equal to 1000th of a bar.
**milligram** *or* **milligramme** *n* one thousandth of a gram.
**millilitre** (*NAmer* **milliliter**) *n* one thousandth of a litre (0.002 pints).
**millimetre** (*NAmer* **millimeter**) *n* one thousandth of a metre (about 0.039in.).
**milliner** *n* a person who makes or sells women's hats. ➤ **millinery** *n*.
**million** *n* (*pl* **millions** *or* **million**) **1** the number 1,000,000 ($10^6$). **2** *informal* (*also in pl*) a very large number. ➤ **millionth** *adj and n*.
**millionaire** *or* **millionairess** *n* a person whose wealth is estimated at a million or more pounds or dollars.
**millipede** *n* an invertebrate animal with a segmented body and two pairs of legs on each segment.
**millisecond** *n* one thousandth of a second.
**millpond** *n* a pond produced by damming a stream to produce a head of water for operating a mill.
**millstone** *n* **1** each of a pair of circular stones that rotate against each other to grind grain. **2** a heavy responsibility.
**mill wheel** *n* a water-powered wheel that drives a mill.
**milometer** *n* see MILEOMETER
**mime**[1] *n* **1** the art of portraying a character or telling a story by gesture and body movement. **2** a performance of mime.
**mime**[2] *v* **1** to act a part with mime. **2** to pretend to sing or play a musical instrument against a recording.
**mimic**[1] *v* (**mimicked, mimicking**) **1** to imitate (a person or their mannerisms). **2** to ridicule by imitation. **3** to simulate (something). **4** in biology, to resemble (something) by mimicry.
**mimic**[2] *n* somebody or something that mimics others.
**mimosa** *n* an acacia tree with sweetly scented yellow flowers in compact globular clusters.
**minaret** *n* a slender tower attached to a mosque, with balconies from which Muslims are summoned to prayer.
**minatory** *adj formal* menacing; threatening.
**mince**[1] *v* **1** to cut or chop (meat) into very small pieces. **2** to walk with short steps in an affected manner. ✱ **not mince one's words** to speak honestly and frankly. ➤ **mincer** *n*.
**mince**[2] *n chiefly Brit* minced meat.
**mincemeat** *n* a mixture of dried fruit, suet, and spices, used as a pie filling.
**mind**[1] *n* **1** the conscious and unconscious mental processes of an organism that result in reasoning, thinking, perceiving, etc. **2** recollection or memory. **3** an intention or desire. **4** an opinion or view. ✱ **bear/keep in mind** to think of or remember (something). **change one's mind** to alter a decision or opinion. **on one's mind** occupying or troubling one. **out of one's mind** insane or overcome with worry.
**mind**[2] *v* **1** to be concerned or care about. **2** to give protective care to. **3** to object to. **4** to attend to (something) closely. **5** to pay attention to or follow (advice or orders). **6** to be careful or sure to do (something). **7** to be cautious about (something). **8** (*often* + out) to be attentive or wary.
**minded** *adj* inclined or disposed.
**minder** *n* **1** a person who looks after somebody or something. **2** *chiefly Brit, informal* a bodyguard.
**mindful** *adj* (*often* + of) keeping something in mind; aware of something.
**mindless** *adj* **1** involving no proper thought or concentration. **2** (+ of) inattentive to or heedless of something. ➤ **mindlessly** *adv*.

**mindset** *n* a habitual way of thinking about something.
**mine**[1] *pron* the one or ones that belong to or are associated with the speaker or writer.
**mine**[2] *n* **1** an excavation from which mineral substances are taken. **2** a rich source of something. **3** an encased explosive placed in the ground or sea and detonated by contact. **4** an underground passage beneath an enemy position.
**mine**[3] *v* **1** to obtain (ore, coal, etc) from a mine.**2** to dig into (the earth) for ore, coal, etc. **3** to place military mines in or on. ➤ **miner** *n.*
**minefield** *n* **1** an area where explosive mines have been laid. **2** a highly fraught or hazardous situation.
**miner** *n* a person who works in a mine.
**mineral** *n* **1** a solid inorganic substance. **2** any of various naturally occurring substances, e.g. stone, coal, or petroleum.
**mineralogy** *n* the scientific study of minerals. ➤ **mineralogical** *adj,* **mineralogist** *n.*
**mineral water** *n* water impregnated with mineral salts or gases.
**minestrone** /mini'strohni/ *n* a rich Italian soup containing vegetables and pasta.
**minesweeper** *n* a ship designed for removing or neutralizing explosive mines.
**mingle** *v* **1** to bring or mix together. **2** to go among a group of people.
**mingy** *adj* (**-ier, -iest**) *informal* mean or miserly.
**mini**[1] *n* (*pl* **minis**) a miniskirt.
**mini**[2] *adj* small of its kind; miniature.
**miniature**[1] *n* **1** a much smaller copy or representation. **2** something that is small of its kind. **3** a tiny portrait on ivory or metal. ➤ **miniaturist** *n.*
**miniature**[2] *adj* much smaller than the usual size.
**miniaturize** *or* **-ise** *v* **1** to design or construct as a small copy. **2** to reduce in scale.
**minibar** *n* a small refrigerator containing drinks in a hotel room.
**minibus** *n* a small bus for about ten passengers.
**minicab** *n* a taxi that can be hired by telephone but not hailed in the street.
**MiniDisc** *n trademark* a small CD for recording sound or data.
**minim** *n* a musical note with the time value of two crotchets.
**minimal** *adj* being a minimum; constituting the least possible. ➤ **minimally** *adv.*
**minimalism** *n* the use of minimal devices or resources in art, music, and design. ➤ **minimalist** *n and adj.*
**minimize** *or* **-ise** *v* **1** to reduce to a minimum. **2** to represent at less than true importance or value.
**minimum**[1] *n* (*pl* **minima** *or* **minimums**) the least possible quantity or value.
**minimum**[2] *adj* least in amount or number.
**minion** *n derog* a minor employee or official.
**miniskirt** *n* a very short skirt.
**minister**[1] *n* **1** a member of the clergy in a Protestant or nonconformist Church. **2** a head of a government department. **3** a diplomatic representative accredited to a foreign state. ➤ **ministerial** *adj.*
**minister**[2] *v* (+ to) to give assistance or care to.
**ministrations** *pl n* provision of assistance or care.
**ministry** *n* (*pl* **-ies**) **1** a government department headed by a minister. **2** the period of government of one Prime Minister. **3** the office or functions of a minister of religion.
**mink** *n* (*pl* **minks** *or* **mink**) a small mammal having a thick coat of soft fur.
**minnow** *n* (*pl* **minnows** *or* **minnow**) a small dark-coloured freshwater fish.
**minor**[1] *adj* **1** inferior in importance, size, or rank. **2** not serious or dangerous. **3** *esp* of a musical scale: having semitones between the second and third, fifth and sixth, or seventh and eighth notess.
**minor**[2] *n* a person who has not reached the age of legal responsibility.
**minority** *n* (*pl* **-ies**) **1** the smaller of two groups forming a whole. **2** a group of people sharing characteristics or interests that differ from those of the majority.
**minster** *n* a large or important church.
**minstrel** *n* a medieval singer, poet, or musician.
**mint**[1] *n* **1** a plant with a characteristic strong taste and smell, used as a flavouring. **2** the flavour of mint. **3** a sweet flavoured with peppermint. ➤ **minty** *adj.*
**mint**[2] *n* **1** a place where coins or medals are made. **2** *informal* a large sum of money. ✱ **in mint condition** new and unblemished.
**mint**[3] *v* to make (coins or medals) by stamping metal.
**minuet** *n* a slow graceful dance in triple time.
**minus**[1] *prep* **1** reduced or subtracted by. **2** *informal* without.
**minus**[2] *n* (*pl* **minuses**) **1** (*also* **minus sign**) the symbol (–) used to indicate subtraction or a negative quantity. **2** a deficiency or defect.
**minus**[3] *adj* **1** less than zero; negative. **2** involving a disadvantage. **3** falling lower than the specified grade. **4** of or having a negative electric charge.
**minuscule** *adj* very small.

***Usage Note:*** The spelling is *minuscule,* not *mini-.*

**minute**[1] *n* **1** a unit of time equal to one sixtieth of an hour. **2** a unit of angular measurement equal to one sixtieth of a degree. **3** *informal* a short space of time. **4** a short note or memorandum. **5** (*in pl*) the official record of the proceedings of a meeting.

**minute**[2] *v* **1** to make a summary of (a meeting). **2** to send a minute to.

**minute**[3] *adj* **1** extremely small. **2** painstaking and careful over details. ➤ **minutely** *adv.*

**minutiae** *pl n* small or precise details.

**minx** *n* a flirtatious or cheeky girl or young woman.

**miracle** *n* **1** an extraordinary event that is attributed to divine intervention. **2** a remarkable example or instance of something.

**miracle play** *n* a medieval drama based on episodes from the Bible.

**miraculous** *adj* **1** of the nature of a miracle. **2** evoking wonder; marvellous. ➤ **miraculously** *adv.*

**mirage** *n* **1** an optical illusion appearing *esp* as a pool of water or as the reflection of distant objects and caused by the reflection of rays of light by a layer of heated air. **2** something illusory and unattainable.

**mire**[1] *n* **1** a tract of soft waterlogged ground. **2** a situation of great difficulty or complexity. ➤ **miry** *adj.*

**mire**[2] *v* **1** to sink or stick fast in a mire. **2** to be in a difficult or complex situation.

**mirror**[1] *n* **1** a surface that forms images by reflection. **2** something that gives a true representation.

**mirror**[2] *v* **1** to reflect in a mirror. **2** to represent or correspond to exactly.

**mirror image** *n* something that has its parts arranged in reverse in comparison with an otherwise identical thing.

**mirth** *n* cheerful amusement. ➤ **mirthful** *adj.*

**mis-** *prefix* **1** bad or badly; wrong or wrongly: *misbehave*. **2** not: *misunderstand*.

**misadventure** *n* **1** a misfortune or mishap. **2** (*also* **death by misadventure**) in law, death due to an action not intended to cause harm.

**misalliance** *n* an unsuitable alliance or marriage.

**misanthrope** *or* **misanthropist** *n* a person who hates or distrusts other people. ➤ **misanthropic** *adj,* **misanthropy** *n.*

**misapprehend** *v* to misunderstand. ➤ **misapprehension** *n.*

**misappropriate** *v* to take (something) dishonestly. ➤ **misappropriation** *n.*

**misbegotten** *adj* not well thought out or planned.

**misbehave** *v* to behave badly. ➤ **misbehaviour** *n.*

**miscalculate** *v* to calculate or assess wrongly. ➤ **miscalculation** *n.*

**miscarriage** *n* the expulsion of a human foetus before it is able to survive outside the womb. * **miscarriage of justice** a failure to achieve justice in a law court.

**miscarry** *v* (**-ies, -ied**) **1** to have a miscarriage. **2** to fail or go wrong.

**miscast** *v* (*past tense and past part.* **miscast**) to cast (an actor) in an unsuitable role.

**miscellaneous** *adj* consisting of diverse items.

**miscellany** *n* (*pl* **-ies**) a collection of various things.

**mischance** *n* bad luck.

**mischief** *n* **1** playful or disruptive misbehaviour. **2** a person who misbehaves. **3** something that causes inconvenience or disruption.

**mischievous** *adj* **1** disruptively playful. **2** playfully provocative; arch. **3** able or tending to cause annoyance or minor injury. ➤ **mischievously** *adv.*

***Usage Note:*** Note the spelling with *-ie-*, and *-ous* not *-ious*.

**miscible** *adj* of liquids: capable of being mixed together.

**misconceive** *v* to fail to understand correctly.

**misconception** *n* a false or mistaken idea or understanding.

**misconduct** *n* bad or improper behaviour.

**misconstrue** *v* (**misconstrues, misconstrued, misconstruing**) to misinterpret or misunderstand. ➤ **misconstruction** *n.*

**miscreant** *n* a person who behaves badly or criminally.

**misdeed** *n* a wrong deed; an offence.

**misdemeanour** (*NAmer* **misdemeanor**) *n* a minor offence or wrongdoing that does not amount to a crime.

**misdiagnose** *v* to diagnose wrongly.

**misdirect** *v* to direct wrongly or inappropriately. ➤ **misdirection** *n.*

**miser** *n* a person who hoards money and lives meanly.

**miserable** *adj* **1** pitifully unhappy and distressed. **2** habitually gloomy or morose. **3** wretchedly inadequate or meagre. **4** causing great discomfort or unhappiness. **5** shameful or contemptible. ➤ **miserably** *adv.*

**misericord** *n* a ledge on the underside of the hinged seat of a choir stall to support the occupant in a standing position when the seat is turned up.

**miserly** *adj* **1** characteristic of a miser; mean. **2** of an amount: small and inadequate. ➤ **miserliness** *n.*

**misery** *n* (*pl* **-ies**) **1** great unhappiness or distress. **2** a cause of this. **3** *chiefly Brit, informal* a gloomy or morose person.

**misfire** *v* **1** of an engine: to fail to ignite the fuel at the proper time. **2** of a gun: to fail to fire. **3** to fail to have the intended effect.

**misfit** *n* **1** a person who is poorly adjusted to their environment. **2** something that fits badly.

**misfortune** *n* **1** bad luck. **2** an unfortunate incident or event.

**misgiving** *n* a feeling of doubt or suspicion.

**misguided** *adj* directed by mistaken ideas or motives.

**mishandle** *v* **1** to treat roughly; to maltreat. **2** to mismanage (a situation).
**mishap** *n* an unfortunate accident.
**mishear** *v* (*past tense and past part.* **misheard**) to hear wrongly.
**mishit** *v* (**mishitting,** *past tense and past part.* **mishit**) to hit or kick (a ball) badly.
**mishmash** *n informal* a hotchpotch or jumble.
**misinform** *v* to give untrue or misleading information to. ➤ **misinformation** *n.*
**misinterpret** *v* (**misinterpreted, misinterpreting**) to understand or explain wrongly. ➤ **misinterpretation** *n.*
**misjudge** *v* **1** to estimate wrongly. **2** to have an unjustly bad opinion of. ➤ **misjudgment** *n.*
**mislay** *v* (*past tense and past part.* **mislaid**) to put or leave (something) in a place that you later forget.
**mislead** *v* (*past tense and past part.* **misled**) to lead (somebody) into a mistaken action or belief. ➤ **misleading** *adj.*
**mismanage** *v* to manage wrongly or incompetently. ➤ **mismanagement** *n.*
**mismatch**[1] *v* to match (people or things) incorrectly or unsuitably, e.g. in marriage.
**mismatch**[2] *n* a poor or unsuitable match.
**misnomer** *n* **1** an incorrect or inappropriate name. **2** the wrong use of a name.
**misogynist** *n* a man who hates women. ➤ **misogynistic** *adj,* **misogyny** *n.*
**misplace** *v* to put in the wrong place.
**misplaced** *adj* **1** directed towards an unsuitable object or outcome. **2** wrong or inappropriate.
**misprint**[1] *n* a printing error.
**misprint**[2] *v* to print incorrectly.
**mispronounce** *v* to pronounce wrongly. ➤ **mispronunciation** *n.*
**misquote** *v* to quote or repeat incorrectly. ➤ **misquotation** *n.*
**misread** *v* (*past tense and past part.* **misread**) to read or interpret incorrectly.
**misrepresent** *v* to give an untrue or misleading account of. ➤ **misrepresentation** *n.*
**misrule**[1] *v* to rule (a nation, etc) incompetently; to misgovern.
**misrule**[2] *n* lack of government or of good government.
**miss**[1] *v* **1** to fail to hit, reach, meet, catch, or attain. **2** to feel the absence of. **3** to escape or avoid. **4** (*often* + out) to leave out; to omit. **5** to fail to understand. **6** to fail to attend or be present at. **7** to be too late to catch (a bus, train, etc). ✻ **miss out on** to fail to have or experience. **miss the boat** *informal* to fail to take advantage of an opportunity.
**miss**[2] *n* a failure to hit, catch, or achieve something.
**Miss** *n* **1** used as a form of address to a girl or unmarried woman. **2** used as a term of address to a female schoolteacher.
**missal** *n* a book containing the liturgy for the Roman Catholic mass for the year.
**misshapen** *adj* unnaturally shaped; deformed.
**missile** *n* **1** an object thrown or projected so as to hit something. **2** a self-propelled weapon that travels through the air.
**missing** *adj* **1** absent or lost. **2** not confirmed as alive or dead.
**mission** *n* **1** a specific task assigned to a person or group. **2** a group sent to a foreign country to negotiate or advise. **3** a permanent embassy or legation. **4** a military or scientific task or undertaking. **5** a religious ministry propagating its faith abroad. **6** a calling or vocation.
**missionary**[1] *n* (*pl* **-ies**) a person in charge of a religious mission.
**missionary**[2] *adj* relating to or engaged in a religious mission.
**missive** *n formal* a letter.
**misspell** *v* (*past tense* **misspelt,** *past part.* **misspelt** *or* **misspelled**) to spell incorrectly. ➤ **misspelling** *n.*
**misspend** *v* (*past tense and past part.* **misspent**) to spend (money or time) wrongly or unwisely.
**missus** *or* **missis** *n* **1** *informal* a person's wife. **2** *informal* a form of address to a married woman.
**mist**[1] *n* **1** water in the form of tiny particles in the atmosphere. **2** condensed water vapour on a surface.
**mist**[2] *v* to cover or be covered with mist.
**mistake**[1] *v* (**mistook, mistaken**) **1** to misunderstand the meaning or significance of. **2** to estimate wrongly. **3** to identify wrongly. **4** to confuse (somebody or something) with another.
**mistake**[2] *n* **1** an incorrect action, statement, or conclusion. **2** a misunderstanding of the meaning or significance of something.
**mistaken** *adj* **1** based on wrong thinking; incorrect. **2** of a person: wrong in opinion. ➤ **mistakenly** *adv.*
**mister** *n* **1** (**Mister**) = MR. **2** (*often* **Mister**) a generalized informal form of address to a man.
**mistime** *v* to do or say at a wrong or inappropriate time.
**mistletoe** *n* a shrub that grows as a parasite on trees and has thick leaves and waxy white berries.
**mistreat** *v* to treat badly or unkindly. ➤ **mistreatment** *n.*
**mistress** *n* **1** a woman in a position of power or authority. **2** a woman who has achieved mastery of a subject. **3** a woman with whom a married man has a sexual relationship outside marriage. **4** *chiefly Brit* a female schoolteacher.
**mistrial** *n* a trial declared void because of an error in the proceedings.
**mistrust**[1] *v* to have no trust in.
**mistrust**[2] *n* a lack of trust. ➤ **mistrustful** *adj.*
**misty** *adj* (**-ier, -iest**) **1** covered with or

obscured by mist. **2** consisting of or marked by mist. **3** indistinct or blurred.

**misunderstand** *v* (*past tense and past part.* **misunderstood**) to fail to understand correctly.

**misuse**[1] *v* **1** to use wrongly. **2** to abuse or maltreat.

**misuse**[2] *n* **1** incorrect or improper use. **2** abuse.

**mite** *n* **1** a minute invertebrate animal related to the spiders and ticks. **2** a small child or animal. **3** a very small amount. * **a mite** *informal* slightly, somewhat.

**mitigate** *v* to make less harsh or intense. ➤ **mitigation** *n.*

***Usage Note:*** Do not confuse this word with *militate*, which means 'to have a significant effect in preventing or counteracting'.

**mitre**[1] (*NAmer* **miter**) *n* **1** a tall pointed divided hat worn by bishops. **2** a joint made by cutting two pieces of wood to form a right angle when fitted together.

**mitre**[2] (*NAmer* **miter**) *v* **1** to cut (wood) to form a mitre. **2** to join in a mitre.

**mitt** *n* **1** a glove that leaves the ends of the fingers uncovered. **2** a mitten. **3** *informal* a person's hand.

**mitten** *n* a covering for the hand and wrist that has one section for all four fingers and another for the thumb.

**mix**[1] *v* **1** to combine or blend into one mass. **2** to combine (one ingredient) with others. **3** to prepare by mixing ingredients. **4** to control the balance of (various sounds) during a recording. **5** to enjoy a varied social life.

**mix**[2] *n* **1** a mixture or combination. **2** a commercially prepared mixture of food ingredients. **3** the proportion in which elements are mixed. **4** a version of a musical recording that has been mixed to produce a different type of sound from the original.

**mixed** *adj* **1** combining diverse elements. **2** involving people of different sexes or races. **3** including or accompanied by conflicting or dissimilar elements.

**mixed bag** *n* a miscellaneous assortment.

**mixer** *n* **1** a device or machine for mixing something. **2** a soft drink for mixing with an alcoholic one. **3** an electronic device for combining sound from several sources in a recording.

**mixture** *n* **1** the act or an instance of mixing. **2** a combination or blend produced by mixing. **3** a combination of components that retain their own properties. **4** the proportion of fuel to air supplied to an engine.

**mix up** *v* **1** to mistake or confuse (somebody or something) for another. **2** to make untidy or disordered. * **be/get mixed up in** to be involved in an illegal or suspect activity.

**mix-up** *n informal* a state or instance of confusion.

**mizzen** *or* **mizen** *n* the mast behind the mainmast in a sailing vessel.

**ml** *abbr* **1** mile(s). **2** millilitre.

**mm** *abbr* millimetre.

**MMR** *abbr* measles, mumps, and rubella (vaccination).

**Mn** *abbr* the chemical symbol for manganese.

**mnemonic**[1] *adj* helping to remember something.

**mnemonic**[2] *n* a word or code that helps to remember something.

**mnemonics** *pl n* a system for improving the memory.

**Mo** *abbr* the chemical symbol for molybdenum.

**moan**[1] *n* **1** a low prolonged sound of pain or grief. **2** a mournful sound made by the wind. **3** *informal* a minor complaint.

**moan**[2] *v* **1** to produce a moan. **2** *informal* to complain or grumble.

**moat** *n* a deep trench, usu filled with water, round a castle or fortified place.

**mob**[1] *n* **1** (*also before a noun*) a disorderly or riotous crowd. **2** *Brit, informal* a particular group of people. **3** (**the mob**) the ordinary populace. **4** (*usu* **the Mob**) *chiefly NAmer* the Mafia.

**mob**[2] *v* (**mobbed, mobbing**) **1** to attack in a large crowd or group. **2** to crowd round (somebody).

**mobile**[1] *adj* **1** capable of moving or being moved. **2** of a library, shop, etc: set up in a vehicle and able to move from place to place. **3** *informal* having the use of a vehicle for transport. **4** of people: able to move to a different location or job. **5** of features: readily expressing different moods. ➤ **mobility** *n.*

**mobile**[2] *n* **1** a decoration with suspended parts moved by air currents. **2** (*also* **mobile phone**) a portable telephone for use in a cellular radio system.

**mobilize** *or* **-ise** *v* **1** to prepare and assemble (troops) for active service. **2** to organize (people or resources) for action. ➤ **mobilization** *n.*

**mobster** *n informal* a member of a criminal gang.

**moccasin** *n* a soft leather shoe with the sole brought up the sides of the foot and joined to a U-shaped top piece.

**mocha** *n* **1** a coffee of fine quality. **2** a flavouring obtained from coffee or from coffee and chocolate.

**mock**[1] *v* **1** to ridicule or deride. **2** to copy or mimic in fun or derision.

**mock**[2] *n* (*also in pl*) a school examination used as practice for a public one.

**mock**[3] *adj* **1** not real; imitation. **2** of a battle, examination, etc: simulated for practice or training.

**mockery** *n* (*pl* **-ies**) **1** contemptuous words or ridicule. **2** an object of derision or ridicule. **3** a deceitful imitation; a travesty. ✱ **make a mockery of something** to make something look foolish or pointless.

**mockingbird** *n* an American songbird that imitates the calls of other birds.

**mock-up** *n* a full-sized model or representation for study or testing.

**modal** *adj* relating to form or structure, as opposed to substance or content.

**modal auxiliary verb** *n* in grammar, a verb that helps another verb to express what is possible or necessary, e.g. *will, shall, should, would, may, might*.

**mode** *n* **1** a way of doing something. **2** a prevailing fashion or style.

**model**[1] *n* **1** a three-dimensional replica of something. **2** an example used for reproducing or copying. **3** an outstanding example to be followed. **4** a person who poses for an artist or photographer. **5** a person who displays clothing by wearing it. **6** a type or design of an article or product.

**model**[2] *v* (**modelled, modelling,** *NAmer* **modeled, modeling**) **1** to shape in a mouldable material. **2** to produce a model of. **3** (*often* + on) to plan or construct(something) in imitation of something else. **4** to work as a fsahion model.

**modem** *n* a device that connects a computer to a telephone line.

**moderate**[1] *adj* **1** calm, mild, or temperate. **2** avoiding extreme political or social measures; not radical. **3** average in quality, amount, degree, or extent. ➤ **moderately** *adv.*

**moderate**[2] *v* **1** to decrease in violence or severity. **2** to ensure consistency of grading in (examination papers or results).

**moderate**[3] *n* a person who holds moderate views.

**moderation** *n* **1** the process of moderating. **2** the avoidance of extremes in behaviour and attitudes.

**moderator** *n* **1** a person who resolves disagreements. **2** a person who presides over an assembly or debate. **3** a person who moderates examination papers.

**modern** *adj* **1** relating to the present or immediate past. **2** involving recent techniques or ideas. ➤ **modernity** *n.*

**modernism** *n* **1** modern ideas practices, or styles. **2** a new direction in the arts or religion involving a break with the past. ➤ **modernist** *n and adj,* **modernistic** *adj.*

**modernize** *or* **-ise** *v* to adapt to modern ideas or practices. ➤ **modernization** *n.*

**modest** *adj* **1** showing a moderate estimate of one's abilities or worth. **2** small or limited in size, amount, or aim. **3** observant of proprieties; decent. ➤ **modestly** *adv,* **modesty** *n.*

**modicum** *n* a small or limited amount.

**modification** *n* **1** a small or limited change. **2** the making of a change.

**modifier** *n* **1** a word that qualifies the meaning of another, e.g. *horror* in *horror film*. **2** somebody or something that modifies.

**modify** *v* (**-ies, -ied**) to make minor changes in.

**modish** *adj* fashionable or stylish.

**modular** *adj* consisting of or made from separate parts.

**modulate** *v* **1** to vary (the voice) in tone, pitch, etc. **2** to keep in proper measure or proportion. **3** to vary the amplitude, frequency, or phase of (a wave) to match the variations of another. **4** in music, to pass from one key to another. ➤ **modulation** *n.*

**module** *n* **1** any of a set of standardized units that are combined to form a structure. **2** a unit of an educational course, treating a specific subject or topic. **3** an independent unit forming part of a space vehicle.

**moggie** *or* **moggy** *n* (*pl* **-ies**) *Brit, informal* a cat.

**mogul** *n informal* a wealthy or powerful person.

**mohair** *n* a fabric or yarn made from the hair of the Angora goat.

**Mohican** *n* a hairstyle in which the head is shaved except for a central strip of erect hair.

**moiety** *n* (*pl* **-ies**) a half.

**moist** *adj* slightly wet; damp. ➤ **moisten** *v.*

**moisture** *n* liquid diffused as vapour or condensed as tiny droplets.

**moisturize** *or* **-ise** *v* to add moisture to. ➤ **moisturizer** *n.*

**molar** *n* a grinding tooth towards the back of the jaw.

**molasses** *n* **1** a dark syrup left after refining raw sugar. **2** *NAmer* treacle or golden syrup.

**mold**[1] *n NAmer* see MOULD[1].

**mold**[2] *v NAmer* see MOULD[2].

**mold**[3] *n NAmer* see MOULD[3].

**mold**[4] *n NAmer* see MOULD[4].

**mole**[1] *n* **1** a small burrowing mammal with tiny eyes, concealed ears, and soft fur. **2** a spy operating from a well-established position of trust within an organization.

**mole**[2] *n* a dark spot on the skin.

**mole**[3] *n* **1** a solid structure laid in the sea as a pier or breakwater. **2** a harbour formed by a mole.

**mole**[4] *or* **mol** *n* the SI unit equal to the amount of a substance that contains the same number of atoms, molecules, ions, etc as there are atoms in 0.012kg of carbon.

**molecule** *n* the smallest unit of a substance, usu consisting of two or more bonded atoms.

**molehill** *n* a mound of earth thrown up by a burrowing mole.

**moleskin** *n* **1** the skin of a mole used as fur. **2** a heavy cotton fabric with a velvety nap on one side.

**molest** *v* **1** to pester unpleasantly. **2** to abuse sexually. ➤ **molestation** *n*, **molester** *n*.

**moll** *n informal* a gangster's female companion.

**mollify** *v* (**-ies, -ied**) **1** to lessen the anger or hostility of. **2** to reduce in intensity or severity. ➤ **mollification** *n*.

**mollusc** (*NAmer* **mollusk**) *n* an animal with a soft unsegmented body often enclosed in a shell, e.g. snails, shellfish, and squids.

**mollycoddle** *v* to treat with excessive indulgence or protection.

**molt** *v NAmer* see MOULT.

**molten** *adj* liquefied by heat; melted.

**molto** *adv* in music: very.

**molybdenum** *n* a hard silver-white metallic element.

**mom** *n NAmer, informal* = MUM[1].

**moment** *n* **1** a brief interval of time. **2** a specific point in time. **3** *formal* importance. **4** a tendency to produce rotational motion.

**momentarily** *adv* **1** for a short time. **2** *chiefly NAmer* very soon or immediately.

**momentary** *adj* lasting a short time; transitory.

**momentous** *adj* of great consequence or significance.

**momentum** *n* (*pl* **momenta**) the tendency to continue onwards possessed by a moving object.

**mommy** *n* (*pl* **-ies**) = MOM.

**monarch** *n* a person who reigns over a kingdom or empire. ➤ **monarchical** *adj*.

**monarchism** *n* the principle of monarchy, or support for it. ➤ **monarchist** *n and adj*.

**monarchy** *n* (*pl* **-ies**) **1** a state with a monarch as head of state. **2** the institution of a sovereign and royal family.

**monastery** *n* (*pl* **-ies**) a community of monks or the buildings they occupy.

**monastic** *adj* **1** relating to monks or nuns. **2** resembling life in a monastery. ➤ **monasticism** *n*.

**Monday** *n* the day of the week following Sunday.

**monetarism** *n* an economic theory that the best way of controlling the economy is by restricting the money supply. ➤ **monetarist** *n and adj*.

**monetary** *adj* relating to money.

**money** *n* (*pl* **-eys** *or* **-ies**) **1** coins or paper currency used as a means of payment. **2** payment. **3** wealth. **4** (*in pl*) a sum or sums of money.

**moneyed** *or* **monied** *adj* having a lot of money.

**money order** *n* a postal order issued by a bank.

**money spider** *n* a tiny spider supposedly bringing good fortune.

**Mongol** *n* a member of certain peoples of Mongolia, northern China, and central Asia.

**mongoose** *n* (*pl* **mongooses**) an African and Asian mammal with grey-brown fur, short legs, and a long tail.

**mongrel** *n* a dog of no recognized breed.

**moniker** *or* **monicker** *n informal* a name or nickname.

**monitor[1]** *n* **1** a pupil appointed to help a teacher. **2** a person or machine that monitors. **3** a receiver with a screen used to view data from a television or computer. **4** a large tropical lizard.

**monitor[2]** *v* to observe or record over a period of time.

**monk** *n* a male member of a religious order living under vows of poverty and chastity.

**monkey[1]** *n* **1** a primate with a long tail living in trees in tropical countries. **2** *informal* a mischievous child.

**monkey[2]** *v informal* **1** (*often* + about/around) to act in a silly or mischievous manner. **2** to meddle or tamper with.

**monkey business** *n informal* mischievous or underhand activity.

**monkey nut** *n Brit* a peanut.

**monkey-puzzle** *n* a South American evergreen tree with a network of branches covered with spirals of stiff sharp leaves.

**monkey wrench** *n* a large spanner with adjustable jaws.

**mono** *n* monophonic sound reproduction.

**monochrome** *adj* **1** reproduced in shades of black and white, or of a single colour. **2** lacking in variety or interest. ➤ **monochromatic** *adj*.

**monocle** *n* a single lens for one eye.

**monogamy** *n* the practice of being married to one person at any time. ➤ **monogamous** *adj*.

**monogram** *n* a design formed of the interwoven initials of a name. ➤ **monogrammed** *adj*.

**monograph** *n* a short book on a specialized subject.

**monolingual** *adj* knowing or using only one language.

**monolith** *n* **1** a single large block of stone. **2** a complex structure or organization.

**monolithic** *adj* **1** formed of a single large block of stone. **2** forming a large complex whole.

**monologue** *n* **1** a long speech by an actor alone on stage. **2** a long tedious speech that monopolizes a conversation.

**monomania** *n* an obsessive preoccupation with a single idea. ➤ **monomaniac** *n and adj*.

**monomer** *n* any of the identical units that combine to form a polymer. ➤ **monomeric** *adj*.

**monophonic** *adj* denoting a sound system using only one channel.

**monoplane** *n* an aeroplane with one main pair of wings.

**monopolize** *or* **-ise** *v* to assume exclusive control or use of.

**monopoly** *n* (*pl* **-ies**) **1** exclusive ownership or control of a commodity or market. **2** a person or group having a monopoly. **3** something controlled by a monopoly. **4** exclusive control or use of something.

**monorail** *n* a single rail serving as a track for a wheeled vehicle.

**monosyllabic** *adj* **1** consisting of one syllable. **2** of a person: using only short words. **3** brief or terse.

**monosyllable** *n* a word of one syllable.

**monotheism** *n* the belief that there is only one God. ➤ **monotheistic** *adj.*

**monotone** *n* **1** a single unvaried musical note. **2** a tedious sameness or repetition.

**monotonous** *adj* tediously uniform or repetitive. ➤ **monotonously** *adv,* **monotonousness** *n,* **monotony** *n.*

**monoxide** *n* an oxide containing one atom of oxygen.

**monsieur** /mə'syuh/ *n* (*pl* **messieurs** /mə'syuh, mə'syuhz/) a title of or form of address to a French man.

**monsignor** /mon'seenyə, monsee'nyaw/ *n* (*pl* **monsignori** /-'nyawree/) a title for certain high-ranking Roman Catholic priests.

**monsoon** *n* **1** a seasonal wind of southest Asia blowing from the southwest in summer and the northeast in winter. **2** the season of a monsoon, marked by heavy rains.

**monster** *n* **1** a terrifying imaginary creature. **2** something exceptionally large of its kind. **3** a wicked or cruel person.

**monstrosity** *n* (*pl* **-ies**) **1** something deviating wildly from the normal; a monster or freak. **2** an excessively bad or shocking example; a hideous thing.

**monstrous** *adj* **1** having the qualities or appearance of a monster. **2** extraordinarily large. **3** extraordinarily ugly or vicious. **4** outrageously wrong or ridiculous. **5** shocking; appalling. ➤ **monstrously** *adv,* **monstrousness** *n.*

**montage** /monh'tahzh/ *n* **1** a picture made by combining or overlapping several separate pictures. **2** a method of film editing in which the chronological sequence of events is interrupted by juxtaposed or rapidly succeeding shots. **3** a film sequence using montage.

**month** *n* **1** each of the twelve named periods into which the year is divided. **2** a period of four weeks. **3** the interval between the same date in successive months. ✱ **a month of Sundays** *informal* a very long period of time.

**monthly**[1] *adj* of or occurring every month.

**monthly**[2] *adv* every month.

**monthly**[3] *n* (*pl* **-ies**) a periodical published monthly.

**monument** *n* **1** a memorial stone, or sculpture erected to commemorate a person or event. **2** a structure or site of historical importance. **3** a lasting evidence or reminder of something important.

**monumental** *adj* **1** serving as a monument. **2** imposing or outstanding. ➤ **monumentally** *adv.*

**moo**[1] *v* to make the deep noise of a cow.

**moo**[2] *n* a mooing sound.

**mooch** *v informal* (+ around/about/along) to wander aimlessly or disconsolately.

**mood** *n* **1** a predominant emotion or frame of mind. **2** a bout of bad temper. **3** a form of a verb used to express a fact, possibility, wish, command, or question.

**moody** *adj* (**-ier, -iest**) **1** sullen or gloomy. **2** subject to changing moods; temperamental. ➤ **moodily** *adv,* **moodiness** *n.*

**moon**[1] *n* **1** (**the Moon**) the earth's natural satellite. **2** a satellite of any planet. **3** *literary* a month. ✱ **over the moon** *informal* delighted. ➤ **moonless** *adj.*

**moon**[2] *v* **1** *informal* (*often* + around/about) to behave or move about listlessly. **2** *informal* to expose one's buttocks to somebody as a joke or insult.

**moonlight**[1] *n* the light of the moon. ➤ **moonlit** *adj.*

**moonlight**[2] *v* (*past tense and past part.* **moonlighted**) *informal* to hold a second job in addition to one's regular work, without declaring it to the tax authorities. ➤ **moonlighter** *n.*

**moonscape** *n* the surface of the moon as a landscape.

**moonshine** *n* **1** empty talk; nonsense. **2** *NAmer, informal* illegally distilled or smuggled whisky.

**moonstone** *n* a milky-white translucent feldspar with a pearly lustre.

**moony** *adj* (**-ier, -iest**) *informal* inanely dreamy.

**Moor** *n* a member of an African Muslim people. ➤ **Moorish** *adj.*

**moor**[1] *n* an expanse of open land overgrown by heathers, grasses, etc.

**moor**[2] *v* to secure (a boat or buoy) in position.

**moorhen** *n* a blackish bird that nests near fresh water.

**mooring** *n* **1** (*also in pl*) a place where a ship or boat can be made fast. **2** (*usu in pl*) a rope or chain used to moor a vessel.

**moose** *n* (*pl* **moose**) a large North American deer related to the elk.

**moot**[1] *v* to put forward for discussion.

**moot**[2] *adj* open to question; debatable.

**mop**[1] *n* **1** a long handle with a head of absorbent material, used for cleaning floors. **2** a shock of untidy hair.

**mop**[2] *v* (**mopped, mopping**) **1** to clean or wipe with a mop. **2** (*often* + up) to soak up (water or other liquid) with a mop.

**mope** *v* to become listless or dejected. ➤ **mopy** *adj.*

**moped** *n* a low-powered motorcycle.

**moraine** *n* earth and stones deposited by a glacier.

**moral**[1] *adj* **1** relating to the principles of right and wrong in human behaviour. **2** conforming to a standard of right behaviour. ➤ **morally** *adv.*

**moral**[2] *n* **1** a moral or practical lesson to be learned from a story or experience. **2** (*in pl*) standards of behaviour.

**morale** *n* the degree or enthusiasm and loyalty shown by an individual or group.

**moralist** *n* a person who is srict about moral principles. ➤ **moralistic** *adj.*

**morality** *n* (*pl* **-ies**) **1** right behaviour or moral correctness. **2** degree of conformity to moral standards. **3** a system of moral values or principles.

**moralize** *or* **-ise** *v* to talk tediously or sanctimoniously about matters of morality.

**morass** *n* **1** a marsh or swamp. **2** a confused and disorganized situation.

**moratorium** *n* (*pl* **moratoriums** *or* **moratoria**) a temporary suspension of or ban on an activity or commitment.

**morbid** *adj* **1** having an unnatural interest in death or disease. **2** relating to disease. ➤ **morbidity** *n,* **morbidly** *adv.*

**mordant** *adj* caustic or sharply critical in manner or style.

**more**[1] *adj* **1** greater in amount or degree. **2** additional; further.

**more**[2] *adv* **1** as an additional amount. **2** to a greater degree, extent, or amount. **3** again: *once more.* **4** used with an adjective or adverb to form the comparative. ✱ **more or less** somewhat, approximately.

**more**[3] *n* a greater or additional amount or part.

**morello** *n* (*pl* **-os**) a sour cherry with a dark-red skin.

**moreover** *adv* in addition to what has been said.

**mores** *pl n* the customs of a particular group.

**morgue** *n* **1** a mortuary. **2** a collection of information used for writing obituaries in a newspaper office.

**moribund** *adj* **1** dying. **2** nearing the end of existence.

**Mormon** *n* a member of the Church of Jesus Christ of Latter-Day Saints. ➤ **Mormonism** *n.*

**morn** *n literary* morning.

**morning** *n* **1** the time from midnight to noon or sunrise to noon. **2** the dawn.

**morning sickness** *n* nausea and vomiting occurring during the earlier months of pregnancy.

**moron** *n informal* a stupid person. ➤ **moronic** *adj.*

**morose** *adj* gloomy and bad-tempered. ➤ **morosely** *adv.*

**morph** *v* in cinematography, to change gradually from one image to another.

**morphine** *n* a drug made from opium, used as a powerful painkiller.

**morris dance** *n* a traditional English dance performed by a group of people wearing costumes and carrying handkerchiefs or small sticks. ➤ **morris dancing** *n.*

**morrow** *n* (*usu* **the morrow**) *archaic or literary* the next day.

**Morse** *or* **Morse code** *n* a signalling code in which letters are represented by combinations of short and long sounds or flashes of light.

**morsel** *n* a small piece of food.

**mortal**[1] *adj* **1** subject to death. **2** of human existence. **3** causing death. **4** of an enemy: relentless until death. **5** intense or severe. ➤ **mortally** *adv.*

**mortal**[2] *n* a human being.

**mortality** *n* (*pl* **-ies**) **1** the state of being mortal. **2** the death people or animals in large numbers. **3** the number of deaths in a given time or place.

**mortal sin** *n* in Christian belief, a serious sin that can lead to damnation.

**mortar** *n* **1** a mixture of cement and lime with sand and water, used to join bricks, stones, etc or for plastering. **2** a bowl in which substances are ground with a pestle. **3** a light artillery gun used for firing shells at high angles.

**mortarboard** *n* **1** a square board with a handle underneath, used by bricklayers for holding mortar. **2** an academic cap consisting of a close-fitting crown with a stiff flat square on top.

**mortgage**[1] *n* **1** an agreement for borrowing money to buy a property, with the property as security. **2** a loan received by this agreement.

**mortgage**[2] *v* to assign the ownership of (property) to the lender in a mortgage. ➤ **mortgageable** *adj.*

**mortician** *n chiefly NAmer* an undertaker.

**mortify** *v* (**-ies, -ied**) **1** to subject to feelings of shame or embarrassment. **2** to subdue (bodily desires) by abstinence. ➤ **mortification** *n,* **mortifying** *adj.*

**mortise**[1] *or* **mortice** *n* a cavity cut into a piece of wood for receiving the end of another piece.

**mortise**[2] *or* **mortice** *v* **1** to join by a mortise joint. **2** to cut a mortise in.

**mortise lock** *n* a lock fitted into a mortise in the edge of a door.

**mortuary**[1] *n* (*pl* **-ies**) a room or building in which dead bodies are kept before burial or cremation.

**mortuary**[2] *adj* of death or the burial of the dead.

**mosaic** *n* a pattern or picture made from small pieces of glass or stone.

**mosey** *v* (**-eys, -eyed**) *informal* (*usu* + along/around/off) to go in a leisurely or aimless way.

**Moslem** *n* see MUSLIM.

**mosque** *n* a place of worship for Muslims.

**mosquito** *n* (*pl* **-oes** *or* **-os**) a small two-winged fly which can transmit diseases when sucking the blood of animals and humans.
**moss** *n* a mass or small green plants covering a surface. ➤ **mossy** *adj.*
**most**[1] *adj* greatest in amount or degree.
**most**[2] *adv* **1** (*often* **the most**) to the greatest degree or extent. **2** used with an adjective or adverb to form the superlative. **3** very.
**most**[3] *n* the greatest amount or part.
**mostly** *adv* **1** for the greatest part; mainly. **2** in most cases; usually.
**mote** *n* a particle of dust in the air.
**motel** *n* a roadside hotel for motorists.
**motet** *n* a choral composition on a sacred text.
**moth** *n* a flying insect similar to a butterfly, active at night.
**mothball**[1] *n* a ball of naphthalene or camphor, used to keep moths from stored clothing, linen, etc. ✱ **in mothballs** suspended or postponed.
**mothball**[2] *v* to set aside or postpone.
**moth-eaten** *adj* **1** damaged by moth larvae. **2** worn-out or shabby.
**mother**[1] *n* **1** a female parent. **2** a female acting as the parent of a child or offspring. **3** a woman considered as the originator or founder of something. **4** a source, origin, or producer of something. ➤ **motherhood** *n.*
**mother**[2] *v often derog* to care for or protect lovingly.
**mother-in-law** *n* (*pl* **mothers-in-law**) the mother of one's husband or wife.
**mother-of-pearl** *n* a hard pearly substance forming the inner layer of the shells of certain molluscs.
**mother tongue** *n* one's native language.
**motif** *n* **1** a recurring theme in a work of art, music, or literature. **2** a design or pattern.
**motion**[1] *n* **1** the act of changing position; a movement. **2** the way in which a person or thing moves. **3** a gesture. **4** a moving part or mechanism. **5** a formal proposal made for discussion at a meeting. **6** (*also in pl*) an evacuation of the bowels. ✱ **go through the motions** to carry out an activity half-heartedly or mechanically. ➤ **motionless** *adj.*
**motion**[2] *v* to direct by a gesture.
**motion picture** *n chiefly NAmer* a cinema film.
**motivate** *v* to provide with a motive to do something. ➤ **motivator** *n.*
**motivation** *n* **1** something that motivates. **2** enthusiasm or drive. ➤ **motivational** *adj.*
**motive**[1] *n* **1** a need or desire that causes somebody to act. **2** a motif.
**motive**[2] *adj* of or causing motion.
**motley**[1] *adj* (**-ier, -iest**) **1** composed of varied elements. **2** multicoloured.
**motley**[2] *n* **1** the characteristic clothing of mixed colours worn by a jester. **2** a haphazard mixture.
**motocross** *n* cross-country motorcycle racing.
**motor**[1] *n* **1** any of various machines or devices that transform energy into motion. **2** *chiefly Brit* a car. **3** (*used before a noun*) conveying motion or impulses.
**motor**[2] *v* **1** to travel by car. **2** *informal* to make rapid progress.
**motor bike** *n informal* a motorcycle.
**motorboat** *or* **motor boat** *n* a small boat propelled by a motor.
**motorcade** *n* a procession of motor vehicles.
**motorcycle** *n* a two-wheeled motor vehicle. ➤ **motorcyclist** *n.*
**motorist** *n* somebody who drives a car.
**motor vehicle** *n* a road vehicle powered by a motor.
**motorway** *n Brit* a major road for high-speed traffic, having separate carriageways each with several lanes.
**mottled** *adj* marked with spots or patches of a different colour.
**motto** *n* (*pl* **-oes** *or* **-os**) **1** a short expression of a principle or belief. **2** a humorous or sentimental saying.
**mould**[1] (*NAmer* **mold**) *n* **1** a dish for shaping an object from hot liquid poured into it. **2** a fixed pattern or form. **3** distinctive character or type.
**mould**[2] (*NAmer* **mold**) *v* **1** to give shape to. **2** to form in a mould. **3** to exert a steady formative influence on.
**mould**[3] (*NAmer* **mold**) *n* a growth of minute fungi that forms on the surface of damp or decaying organic matter.
**mould**[4] (*NAmer* **mold**) *n* crumbling soft soil rich in humus.
**moulder** (*NAmer* **molder**) *v* (*often* + away) to decay or crumble.
**moulding** (*NAmer* **molding**) *n* a band or strip with moulded designs used for decoration in a building.
**moult** (*NAmer* **molt**) *v* of birds or animals: to shed (hair, feathers, or skin) periodically.
**mount**[1] *v* **1** to go up or climb. **2** to seat oneself on a horse or bicycle to ride it. **3** (*often* + up) to increase in amount or degree. **4** to attach to a support or backing. **5** to organize (a plan or activity).
**mount**[2] *or* **mounting** *n* **1** something on which a picture or other object is mounted for display or use. **2** a horse for riding.
**mount**[3] *n* **1** *literary* a hill. **2** a hill or mountain.
**mountain** *n* **1** a tall landmass that is higher than a hill. **2** (*also in pl*) a vast amount or quantity.
**mountaineer** *n* a person who climbs mountains.
**mountaineering** *n* the pastime or technique of climbing mountains.
**mountainous** *adj* **1** containing many mountains. **2** huge.
**mountebank** *n* a swindler or charlatan.

**mourn** *v* to feel or express great sorrow at the death of. ➤ **mourner** *n.*

**mournful** *adj* expressing great sorrow; gloomy or sad. ➤ **mournfully** *adv.*

**mourning** *n* **1** the expression of great sorrow for somebody who has died. **2** black clothes worn while formally mourning.

**mouse** *n* (*pl* **mice**) **1** a small rodent with a pointed snout and a long thin tail. **2** (*pl also* **mouses**) in computing, a small device operated by hand to direct the cursor on a VDU screen and execute commands by clicking buttons. **3** a shy or timid person.

**moussaka** *or* **mousaka** *n* a Greek dish of minced lamb with aubergines, tomatoes, and a cheese topping.

**mousse** *n* **1** a sweet or savoury dish made with whipped egg whites. **2** a frothy cosmetic applied to the hair to hold it in position.

**moustache** (*NAmer* **mustache**) *n* a band of hair growing on a man's upper lip.

**mousy** *or* **mousey** *adj* (**-ier, -iest**) **1** quiet or stealthy. **2** timid. **3** light greyish brown.

**mouth**[1] *n* (*pl* **mouths**) **1** the opening on the face in which food is put and from which sounds are made. **2** an opening or entrance. **3** the place where a river enters a sea or lake.

**mouth**[2] *v* **1** to say insincerely or pompously. **2** to form (words) soundlessly.

**mouthful** *n* (*pl* **mouthfuls**) **1** an amount of food or drink put into the mouth. **2** a long or difficult word or phrase.

**mouth organ** *n* a harmonica.

**mouthpiece** *n* **1** a part of a musical instrument or a telephone that is put into or next to the mouth. **2** somebody who speaks on another's behalf.

**mouthwash** *n* a preparation for cleansing the mouth.

**mouth-watering** *adj* **1** appetizing. **2** extremely attractive.

**mouthy** *adj* (**-ier, -iest**) inclined to talk impudently or boastfully.

**movable** *or* **moveable** *adj* **1** capable of being moved. **2** of a church festival: changing date from year to year.

**move**[1] *v* **1** to go or move in a particular direction. **2** to change position or shape. **3** to change one's home or place of work. **4** to change to a new activity, topic, etc. **5** to take action or prompt (somebody) to take action. **6** to spend one's time in a particular social environment. **7** to affect emotionally. **8** to propose formally for discussion or consideration. **9** of the bowels: to discharge faeces. ➤ **mover** *n.*

**move**[2] *n* **1** an act of moving; a movement. **2** a step taken to achieve something. **3** a change of home or work. **4** the act of moving a piece in a game. ✱ **get a move on** to hurry up.

**movement** *n* **1** the act or process of moving. **2** a particular manner of moving. **3** (*in pl*) the activities of a person during a specified time. **4** an organization for achieving a particular objective. **5** a trend or change. **6** the moving parts of a mechanism. **7** a distinct section of a musical composition. **8** an act of emptying the bowels.

**move on** *v* to change to a new location, job, etc.

**move out** *v* to leave one's home or place of work.

**movie** *n* a cinema film.

**moving** *adj* causing a strong emotional response. ➤ **movingly** *adv.*

**mow** *v* (*past tense* **mowed,** *past part.* **mowed** *or* **mown**) **1** to cut or trim (grass, hay, etc). **2** to cut down the growth in (a field). ➤ **mower** *n.*

**mow down** *v* to kill or knock down in large numbers.

**mozzarella** *n* a moist white Italian curd cheese.

**MP** *abbr* Member of Parliament.

**Mr** *n* a title used before a man's name.

**MRI** *abbr* magnetic resonance imaging, a process for scanning an image of a part of the body.

**Mrs** *n* a title used before a married woman's name.

**MS** *abbr* **1** manuscript. **2** multiple sclerosis.

**Ms** *n* a title used before the name of a woman regardless of her marital status.

**MSc** *abbr* Master of Science.

**MSP** *abbr* Member of the Scottish Parliament.

**Mt**[1] *abbr* Mount.

**Mt**[2] *abbr* the chemical symbol for meitnerium.

**mu** *n* the twelfth letter of the Greek alphabet (M, μ).

**much**[1] *adj and n* **1** a large amount or or extent. **2** used in questions about quantity or extent: *how much?* ✱ **a bit much** *informal* rather excessive or unreasonable. **not up to much** not very good.

**much**[2] *adv* to a great degree or extent.

**muck** *n* **1** moist dirt or filth. **2** soft moist manure. ➤ **mucky** *adj.*

**muck about** *or* **muck around** *v Brit, informal* **1** to waste time or act in a silly way. **2** (+ with) to interfere with or spoil.

**muck in** *v Brit, informal* to share a task or accommodation.

**muck out** *v* to remove manure or filth from an animal's quarters.

**muck up** *v informal* to bungle or spoil.

**mucous** *adj* of or covered with mucus.

**mucous membrane** *n* a membrane that secretes mucus, lining the nose and other body passages.

**mucus** *n* a thick slimy secretion produced by the mucous membranes.

**mud** *n* soft wet or sticky earth. ✱ **sling/throw mud at** to be abusive about.

**muddle**[1] *v* **1** to confuse. **2** (*often* + up) to confuse (two or more people or things) in one's mind. **3** (*often* + up) to get (things) confused or

out of order. **4** (+ along/through) to manage with difficulty. ➤ **muddled** *adj*, **muddly** *adj*.
**muddle²** *n* a state of confusion.
**muddleheaded** *adj* mentally confused.
**muddy¹** *adj* (**-ier, -iest**) **1** covered with mud. **2** obscure or unclear.
**muddy²** *v* (**-ies, -ied**) to make muddy or confused.
**mudflap** *n* a flap hung behind the wheel of a vehicle to prevent mud and splashes being thrown up.
**mudflat** *n* a muddy area of ground exposed at low tide.
**mudguard** *n* a guard over a vehicle wheel to deflect or catch mud.
**muesli** *n* (*pl* **mueslis**) a breakfast dish of rolled oats, dried fruit, and nuts.
**muezzin** *n* a mosque official who calls Muslims to prayer.
**muff¹** *n* a warm cylindrical wrap in which both hands are placed.
**muff²** *v* to handle clumsily; to bungle.
**muffin** *n* **1** a light round bun, eaten toasted and buttered. **2** *NAmer* a small round cake.
**muffle** *v* **1** (*often* + up) to wrap up so as to conceal or keep warm. **2** to deaden the sound of.
**muffler** *n* **1** a scarf worn round the neck. **2** a device for deadening sound.
**mufti¹** *n* (*pl* **muftis**) a professional Muslim jurist.
**mufti²** *n* civilian clothes worn by somebody who is normally in uniform.
**mug¹** *n* **1** a large cylindrical drinking cup with a handle. **2** *informal* the face or mouth. **3** *Brit, informal* a foolish or gullible person.
**mug²** *v* (**mugged, mugging**) to assault and rob in a public place. ➤ **mugger** *n*.
**muggins** *n informal* oneself, regarded as foolish or gullible.
**muggy** *adj* (**-ier, -iest**) of the weather: warm and close.
**mug shot** *n informal* a police photograph of a person's face.
**mug up** *v Brit, informal* to study something intensively, e.g. for an exam.
**mulatto** *n* (*pl* **-oes** *or* **-os**) a person who has one black and one white parent.
**mulberry** *n* (*pl* **-ies**) **1** an edible red, purple, or white fruit resembling a raspberry. **2** a dark purple colour.
**mulch¹** *n* a covering of leaves and compost spread on the ground to enrich the soil.
**mulch²** *v* to cover or treat with mulch.
**mule¹** *n* the offspring of female horse and a male donkey.
**mule²** *n* a backless shoe or slipper.
**mulish** *adj* obstinate.
**mull¹** *v* to sweeten and flavour (warmed wine or beer) with spices.
**mull²** *n* crumbly soil humus forming a layer on top of mineral soil.
**mullah** *n* a Muslim trained in traditional Islamic law and doctrine.
**mullet** *n* (*pl* **mullets** *or* **mullet**) a food fish with barbels on the chin.
**mulligatawny** *n* a rich Indian meat soup seasoned with curry.
**mullion** *n* a slender vertical bar between panes of a window. ➤ **mullioned** *adj*.
**mull over** *v* to consider at length.
**multicoloured** (*NAmer* **multicolored**) *adj* having many colours.
**multicultural** *adj* relating to or composed of several cultural groups. ➤ **multiculturalism** *n*.
**multifaceted** *adj* having several facets or aspects.
**multifarious** *adj* diverse.
**multilateral** *adj* **1** involving more than two participants. **2** having many sides. ➤ **multilaterally** *adv*.
**multilingual** *adj* using or speaking several languages.
**multimillionaire** *n* a person whose wealth is estimated at several million pounds or dollars.
**multinational¹** *adj* involving more than two countries.
**multinational²** *n* a company operating in several countries.
**multiple¹** *adj* **1** involving more than one part or element. **2** many and varied. **3** of a disease: affecting several parts of the body.
**multiple²** *n* a number that can be divided exactly by a given number.
**multiple-choice** *adj* of an examination question: giving several choices from which the correct answer had to be chosen.
**multiple sclerosis** *n* a chronic condition with progressive paralysis resulting from the formation of hardened tissue in nerves of the brain and spinal cord.
**multiplex** *n* **1** a cinema with several auditoriums. **2** a multiplex communications system.
**multiplication** *n* the process of multiplying.
**multiplication sign** *n* the symbol (×) denoting quantities to be multiplied together.
**multiplicity** *n* (*pl* **-ies**) a great number or variety.
**multiply** *v* (**-ies, -ied**) **1** to increase in number. **2** to add a number to itself a specified number of times to produce a larger number. **3** to breed or propagate.
**multiracial** *adj* involving several racial groups.
**multistorey¹** *adj* of a building: having several storeys.
**multistorey²** *n* (*pl* **-eys**) a multistorey car park.
**multitude** *n* **1** a great number or crowd. **2** (**the multitude**) the ordinary people.
**multitudinous** *adj formal* very numerous.
**mum¹** *n Brit, informal* one's mother.

**mum**[2] *adj* not divulging information.
**mumble**[1] *v* to speak or say in a low indistinct voice.
**mumble**[2] *n* words said in a low indistinct voice.
**mumbo jumbo** *n* elaborate but meaningless language.
**mummify** *v* (**-ies, -ied**) to embalm and dry (a dead body). ➤ **mummification** *n.*
**mummy**[1] *n* (*pl* **-ies**) *informal* one's mother.
**mummy**[2] *n* (*pl* **-ies**) a body embalmed and wrapped for burial in the manner of the ancient Egyptians.
**mumps** *pl n* a disease marked by swelling of the glands in the sides of the face.
**munch** *v* to eat ponderously and noisily.
**mundane** *adj* dully practical or ordinary. ➤ **mundanity** *n.*
**municipal** *adj* of a municipality.
**municipality** *n* (*pl* **-ies**) a a town, city, or district having some self-government.
**munificent** *adj formal* generous. ➤ **munificence** *n,* **munificently** *adv.*
**munitions** *pl n* military weapons, ammunition, and equipment.
**mural**[1] *n* painting done directly on a wall.
**mural**[2] *adj* relating to a wall or walls.
**murder**[1] *n* **1** the crime of intentionally killing a person. **2** *informal* something very difficult or dangerous.
**murder**[2] *v* to kill unlawfully and intentionally. ➤ **murderer** *n,* **murderess** *n.*
**murderous** *adj* **1** capable of murder. **2** causing murder or bloodshed. **3** *informal* extremely difficult or dangerous.
**murk** *or* **mirk** *n* **1** gloom or darkness. **2** fog.
**murky** *adj* (**-ier, -iest**) **1** dark and gloomy. **2** of water: cloudy or dirty. **3** obscure or unknown.
**murmur**[1] *n* **1** a low indistinct sound or utterance. **2** a half-suppressed complaint. **3** an unusual heartbeat indicating an abnormality.
**murmur**[2] *v* **1** to say in a murmur. **2** to make a murmur.
**muscle** *n* **1** a tissue of cells that contract and relax when stimulated to produce motion. **2** an organ consisting of this tissue that moves a part of the body. **3** muscular strength. **4** power or force. ➤ **muscly** *adj.*
**muscular** *adj* **1** of or affecting the muscles. **2** having well-developed muscles.
**muscular dystrophy** *n* a hereditary disease with progressive wasting of the muscles.
**musculature** *n* the system of muscles in the body.
**muse**[1] *v* **1** to become absorbed in thought. **2** to think or say reflectively.
**muse**[2] *n* **1** (**Muse**) each of the nine goddesses in Greek mythology who were the patrons of the arts and sciences. **2** a woman who is a source of inspiration to a creative artist.
**museum** *n* an institution displaying objects of historical or cultural interest.
**mush** *n* **1** a soft mass of semiliquid material. **2** mawkish sentimentality. ➤ **mushy** *adj.*
**mushroom**[1] *n* a fungus consisting of a stem bearing a flattened or domed cap.
**mushroom**[2] *v* to grow or multiply rapidly.
**mushroom cloud** *n* a mushroom-shaped cloud of dust that forms above a nuclear explosion.
**music** *n* **1** the sounds of voices and instruments made to have rhythm, melody, or harmony. **2** the art of writing music. **3** a musical accompaniment. **4** the score of a musical composition set down on paper.
**musical**[1] *adj* **1** relating to music or musicians. **2** having the harmonious qualities of music. **3** having a talent for music. **4** accompanied by music. ➤ **musically** *adv.*
**musical**[2] *n* a film or play with songs and dances.
**music hall** *n* **1** formerly, entertainment consisting of a comedy acts, singing, and dancing. **2** a theatre where this was performed.
**musician** *n* a composer or performer of music. ➤ **musicianship** *n.*
**musicology** *n* the study of musical theory and history. ➤ **musicologist** *n.*
**musk** *n* a strong-smelling substance obtained from a gland of the male musk deer and used in perfume. ➤ **musky** *adj.*
**musk deer** *n* a small hornless deer of central Asia.
**musket** *n* a long-barrelled gun fired from the shoulder.
**musketeer** *n* formerly, a soldier armed with a musket.
**musk ox** *n* a wild ox of Greenland and North America.
**muskrat** *n* (*pl* **muskrats** *or* **muskrat**) a rodent of North America with glands at the base of its tail.
**Muslim** *or* **Moslem** *n* a follower of Islam.
**muslin** *n* a delicate plain-woven cotton fabric.
**musquash** *n archaic* = MUSKRAT.
**mussel** *n* a mollusc with a dark elongated shell.
**must**[1] *v aux* (*third person sing. present tense* **must,** *past tense in reported speech* **must**) **1** to have to; to be obliged to. **2** to be required or necessary. **3** to be supposed or likely. **4** used to express insistence.
**must**[2] *n* an essential or prerequisite.
**must**[3] *n* grape juice before fermentation.
**mustache** *n* see MOUSTACHE.
**mustang** *n* a small wild horse of the western plains of the USA.
**mustard** *n* **1** a pungent yellow or brown paste made from the seeds of a plant of the cabbage family. **2** a brownish yellow colour.
**mustard gas** *n* an irritant oily liquid used as a poison gas.
**muster**[1] *v* **1** to assemble (troops) for fighting.

**2** of people: to come together. **3** (*often* + up) to summon (courage) to meet a need.

**muster**[2] *n* an assembling of troops for fighting. * **pass muster** to be acceptable or satisfactory.

**mustn't** *contraction* must not.

**musty** *adj* (**-ier, -iest**) **1** affected by mould or damp. **2** tasting or smelling of damp and decay.

**mutable** *adj* capable of or liable to change. ➤ **mutability** *n.*

**mutant**[1] *n* an animal or organism that has undergone mutation.

**mutant**[2] *adj* relating to or affected by mutation.

**mutate** *v* to undergo mutation.

**mutation** *n* **1** the act or an instance of changing. **2** a relatively permanent change in an organism's hereditary material. **3** an individual or strain resulting from such a change.

**mute**[1] *adj* **1** not speaking. **2** unable to speak. **3** felt but not expressed. **4** in law, refusing to plead. **5** of a letter: used in the spelling of a word but not pronounced. ➤ **mutely** *adv.*

**mute**[2] *n* **1** a person who cannot speak. **2** a device attached to a musical instrument to soften its tone.

**mute**[3] *v* **1** to muffle or reduce the sound of. **2** to reduce the strength of (a colour).

**mutilate** *v* to injure or damage severely. ➤ **mutilation** *n.*

**mutineer** *n* somebody who mutinies.

**mutinous** *adj* tending to mutiny; rebellious.

**mutiny**[1] *n* (*pl* **-ies**) open resistance to authority, *esp* an organized revolt of soldiers or sailors against their commanders.

**mutiny**[2] *v* (**-ies, -ied**) to take part in a mutiny; to rebel.

**mutt** *n informal* **1** a mongrel dog. **2** a dull or foolish person.

**mutter**[1] *v* **1** to utter sounds in a low indistinct voice. **2** to utter muffled complaints.

**mutter**[2] *n* muttered sounds or words.

**mutton** *n* the flesh of a mature sheep used as food.

**mutual** *adj* **1** directed by two people or groups towards the other. **2** having the same specified feeling for each other. **3** shared by two or more people or groups. **4** of a building society: owned by its members. ➤ **mutuality** *n,* **mutually** *adv.*

**muzzle**[1] *n* **1** the jaws and nose of an animal. **2** a covering for the mouth of an animal. **3** the discharging end of a gun barrel.

**muzzle**[2] *v* **1** to put a muzzle on (an animal). **2** to restrain from free expression.

**muzzy** *adj* (**-ier, -iest**) **1** mentally confused; befuddled. **2** blurred or unclear. ➤ **muzziness** *n.*

**my** *adj* belonging to or associated with the person speaking or writing.

**myalgia** *n* pain in the muscles. ➤ **myalgic** *adj.*

**mycology** *n* the scientific study of fungi. ➤ **mycologist** *n.*

**mynah** *or* **myna** *or* **mina** *n* an Asian bird that can imitate sounds of human speech.

**myopia** *n* shortsightedness. ➤ **myopic** *adj.*

**myriad**[1] *n* (*also in pl*) an indefinitely large number.

**myriad**[2] *adj* innumerable; countless.

**myrrh** *n* an aromatic gum resin obtained from various African and Asian trees, used in perfumes and incense.

**myrtle** *n* an evergreen shrub with fragrant white or rosy flowers and black berries.

**myself** *pron* used reflexively or for emphasis to refer to the person speaking or writing.

**mysterious** *adj* difficult to understand or explain. ➤ **mysteriously** *adv.*

**mystery** *n* (*pl* **-ies**) **1** something or somebody not easily understood or explained. **2** a secretive quality or character. **3** a fictional work dealing with the solution of a mysterious crime. **4** a religious truth disclosed by revelation alone.

**mystery play** *n* a medieval drama based on biblical episodes or the lives of the saints.

**mystic**[1] *n* a person who believes that God or ultimate reality can be apprehended by direct personal experience.

**mystic**[2] *adj* = MYSTICAL.

**mystical** *adj* **1** having a sacred or spiritual meaning not understood by normal thought. **2** relating to mysticism. **3** mysterious or esoteric. **4** arousing awe and wonder. ➤ **mystically** *adv.*

**mysticism** *n* **1** the belief that direct knowledge of God or ultimate reality can be attained through prayer and meditation. **2** a vague belief without sound basis.

**mystify** *v* (**-ies, -ied**) **1** to perplex or bewilder. **2** to make mysterious or obscure. ➤ **mystifying** *adj.*

**mystique** *n* **1** a reverential quality associated with a person or thing. **2** an aura of secrecy and special skill surrounding an activity.

**myth** *n* **1** a traditional story, often involving gods and heroes, that embodies popular beliefs or explains a natural phenomenon. **2** = MYTHOLOGY. **3** a fictitious person or thing. **4** a widely believed but false notion.

**mythical** *adj* **1** based on or described in a myth. **2** invented or imagined.

**mythology** *n* (*pl* **-ies**) **1** a body of myths. **2** a set of attractive and widely held but essentially false beliefs. ➤ **mythological** *adj,* **mythologist** *n.*

**myxomatosis** *n* a severe and usu fatal viral disease of rabbits.

**N**[1] *or* **n** *n* (*pl* **N's** *or* **Ns** *or* **n's**) the 14th letter of the English alphabet.
**N**[2] *abbr* **1** north. **2** northern.
**N**[3] *abbr* the chemical symbol for nitrogen.
**Na** *abbr* the chemical symbol for sodium.
**n/a** *abbr* **1** not applicable. **2** not available.
**naan** *n* see NAN[2].
**nab** *v* (**nabbed, nabbing**) *informal* **1** to arrest. **2** to catch hold of.
**nacho** *n* (*pl* **-os**) a piece of tortilla covered with melted cheese, chopped peppers, etc.
**nadir** *n* **1** in astronomy, the point of the celestial sphere directly opposite the ZENITH and vertically downward from the observer. **2** the lowest or worst point.
**naff** *adj Brit, informal* lacking sophistication, coolness, or style.
**nag**[1] *n* a horse, *esp* an old or inferior one.
**nag**[2] *v* (**nagged, nagging**) **1** to subject to constant scolding or urging. **2** to be a persistent source of annoyance or discomfort.
**nag**[3] *n* **1** a person who nags habitually. **2** a nagging feeling.
**naiad** *n* (*pl* **naiads** *or* **naiades**) (*often* **Naiad**) a water nymph in classical mythology.
**nail**[1] *n* **1** a slender pointed and headed spike designed to be hammered into a surface. **2** a horny sheath protecting the upper end of each finger and toe. * **hit the nail on the head** to describe or explain the situation exactly. **on the nail** of payment: immediate.
**nail**[2] *v* **1** (*often* + down/together) to fasten with nails. **2** *informal* to detect or arrest (a criminal, etc). **3** *informal* to expose (a lie or liar).
**nail-biting** *adj informal* characterized by or causing emotional tension.
**naive** *or* **naïve** *adj* lacking in worldly wisdom or sophistication; ➤ **naively** *adv.*
**naivety** *or* **naïvety** *or* **naiveté** *n* naive behaviour; lack of sophistication or worldliness.
**naked** *adj* **1** having no clothes on. **2** of a plant, animal, or object: without its usual covering. **3** of a light: not shaded. **4** of a feeling: open and undisguised. * **the naked eye** eyesight unaided by a magnifying glass, telescope, etc. ➤ **nakedness** *n.*
**namby-pamby** *adj* weak, cowardly, and soft.
**name**[1] *n* **1** a word or phrase by which a person, place, or thing is known and referred to. **2** a famous or important person. **3** one's reputation. * **call somebody names** to insult somebody verbally. **in name only** officially, but not in reality. **in the name of 1** reserved, intended, etc, for (somebody). **2** for the sake of (a cause, etc). **the name of the game** *informal* the main feature or purpose of some activity.
**name**[2] *v* **1** to give a name to. **2** to identify or mention by name. **3** to appoint. **4** to specify (a sum, date, etc). * **name after** (*NAmer* **name for**) to give (somebody or something) the same name as somebody or something else.
**name-dropping** *n* the practice of trying to impress others by mentioning prominent people as if they were one's acquaintances or contacts.
**nameless** *adj* **1** without a name. **2** not named, e.g. to avoid embarrassment. **3** too vague or too terrible to describe.
**namely** *adv* that is to say.
**namesake** *n* somebody or something with the same name as the person or thing in question.
**nan**[1] *n Brit, informal* used by children: one's grandmother.
**nan**[2] *or* **naan** *n* a traditional Indian type of bread, usu formed into flat leaf-shaped pieces.
**nanny** *or* **nannie** *n* (*pl* **-ies**) *chiefly Brit* a woman employed to look after children in their own home.
**nanny goat** *n informal* a female domestic goat.
**nanosecond** *n* one thousand-millionth of a second.
**nap**[1] *v* (**napped, napping**) to take a short sleep, *esp* during the day. * **catch somebody napping** to catch somebody unprepared.
**nap**[2] *n* a short sleep, *esp* during the day.
**nap**[3] *n* a hairy or downy surface on a woven fabric.
**napalm** *n* jellied petrol used in incendiary bombs and flamethrowers.
**nape** *n* the back of the neck.
**naphtha** *n* a liquid hydrocarbon mixture extracted from petroleum, coal, etc, used chiefly as a solvent.
**napkin** *n* **1** a square piece of material, e.g. linen or paper, used at table to wipe the lips or fingers and protect the clothes. **2** *chiefly Brit, formal* a baby's nappy. **3** *chiefly NAmer* a sanitary towel.
**nappy** *n* (*pl* **-ies**) *chiefly Brit* a shaped pad or a

square piece of towelling worn by babies to absorb urine and faeces.

**narcissism** *n* abnormal interest in oneself or one's appearance. ➤ **narcissist** *n and adj*, **narcissistic** *adj*.

**narcissus** *n* (*pl* **narcissi** *or* **narcissuses**) a daffodil with pale outer petals and an orange or bright yellow centre.

**narcotic**[1] *n* **1** a drug that induces drowsiness or unconsciousness, and relieves pain. **2** any drug, *esp* an illegal or addictive one, that affects mood and behaviour.

**narcotic**[2] *adj* relating to narcotics.

**nark**[1] *n informal Brit, Aus, NZ* a police informer.

**nark**[2] *v informal* to annoy or offend.

**narrate** *v* **1** to tell (a story). **2** to give a spoken commentary for (a film, etc). ➤ **narration** *n*, **narrator** *n*.

**narrative**[1] *n* something that is narrated; a story.

**narrative**[2] *adj* relating to narration.

**narrow**[1] *adj* **1** of little width, *esp* in comparison with height or length. **2** limited in size or scope. **3** only just sufficient or successful. ➤ **narrowly** *adv*, **narrowness** *n*.

**narrow**[2] *n* (*in pl*) a narrow sea passage; = STRAIT 1.

**narrow**[3] *v* **1** to make or become narrower. **2** (*often* + down) to restrict the scope of (research, an enquiry, etc).

**narrowboat** *n* a canal barge with a width of 2.1m (7ft) or less.

**narrow-minded** *adj* lacking tolerance of, or openness to, others and their views. ➤ **narrow-mindedness** *n*.

**NASA** *abbr NAmer* National Aeronautics and Space Administration.

**nasal** *adj* **1** relating to the nose. **2** of somebody's speech: characterized by resonance produced through the nose. ➤ **nasally** *adv*.

**nascent** *adj formal* in the process of being born; just beginning to develop.

**nasturtium** *n* a common garden plant with circular leaves and bright orange, red, or yellow flowers.

**nasty** *adj* (**-ier, -iest**) **1** unpleasant, repugnant, or disgusting. **2** of people or their behaviour: spiteful, bad-tempered, or vicious. **3** harmful or dangerous. ➤ **nastily** *adv*, **nastiness** *n*.

**natal** *adj* associated with one's birth.

**nation** *n* **1** a people with a common origin, tradition, and language. **2** a community of people possessing a defined territory and government.

**national**[1] *adj* **1** relating or belonging to a nation. **2** of an industry, etc: run by the central government. ➤ **nationally** *adv*.

**national**[2] *n* a citizen of a specified nation.

**national curriculum** *n* a curriculum designed to operate throughout the state-maintained school system in England and Wales.

**national debt** *n* the amount of money owed by the government of a country.

**national grid** *n* **1** in Britain, a country-wide network of high-voltage cables between major power stations. **2** in Britain, the system of coordinates used for map reference by the Ordnance Survey.

**National Insurance** *n Brit* a compulsory social-security scheme, funded by employers, employees, and the government, which insures individuals against sickness, retirement, and unemployment.

**nationalism** *n* **1** excessive devotion to and admiration for one's nation. **2** the pursuit of political independence for one's nation. ➤ **nationalist** *n and adj*, **nationalistic** *adj*.

**nationality** *n* (*pl* **-ies**) **1** the status of belonging to a particular nation. **2** an ethnic group.

**nationalize** *or* **-ise** *v* to transfer control or ownership of (an industry) to the state government. ➤ **nationalization** *n*.

**national park** *n* an area of countryside, maintained by the government for public enjoyment or the preservation of wildlife, etc.

**national service** *n* a period of compulsory service in one's country's armed forces.

**nationwide** *adj and adv* throughout the whole country.

**native**[1] *adj* **1** relating to the place of one's birth. **2** belonging to a particular place by birth. **3** of a plant, etc: living or growing naturally in a particular region. **4** characteristic of a particular locality or its indigenous population. **5** inborn; innate.

**native**[2] *n* **1** a person born or reared in a particular place. **2** *dated, offensive* an original or indigenous inhabitant, *esp* of a country colonized by Europeans. **3** a plant, animal, etc living or growing in a particular locality. **4** *chiefly humorous* a local resident.

**Native American** *n* a member of any of the indigenous races of North, South, or Central America.

**native speaker** *n* a person who speaks the language in question as their native language.

**nativity** *n* (*pl* **-ies**) **1** one's birth. **2** (**the Nativity**) the birth of Jesus Christ.

**NATO** *or* **Nato** *abbr* North Atlantic Treaty Organization.

**natter**[1] *v chiefly Brit, informal* to chatter or gossip.

**natter**[2] *n chiefly Brit, informal* a chat.

**natterjack** *n* a common brownish yellow toad that runs rather than hops.

**natty** *adj* (**-ier, -iest**) *informal* of clothes or their wearer: neat and stylish.

**natural**[1] *adj* **1** existing in or produced by nature without human intervention. **2** happening in accordance with the ordinary course of nature. **3** normal; to be expected. **4** innate; inherent. **5** not affected or forced; easy and relaxed. **6** related by blood rather than adoption. **7** of musical notes: neither sharp nor flat. ➤ **naturally** *adv.*

**natural**[2] *n* **1** *informal* a person having natural skills, talents, or abilities. **2** an off-white or creamy beige colour. **3** in music, a natural note, or a sign (♮) indicating that a note is not sharp or flat.

**natural childbirth** *n* the management of labour by the mother, through special breathing and relaxation techniques, so that the use of drugs is kept to a minimum.

**natural gas** *n* gas occurring naturally underground and used chiefly as a fuel.

**natural history** *n* the study of plants and animals.

**naturalism** *n* extreme realism in art or literature, without concealment of the ugly and distasteful.

**naturalist** *n* a person who studies animals and plants.

**naturalistic** *adj* **1** very true to life. **2** in accordance with the principles of naturalism in art or literature. ➤ **naturalistically** *adv.*

**naturalize** *or* **-ise** *v* **1** to make (a foreigner) a citizen of a country. **2** to establish (a plant or animal) in an area where it is not indigenous.

**natural selection** *n* a natural process of evolution that tends to result in the survival of organisms best adapted to their environment.

**nature** *n* **1** the physical world of landscape, plants, and animals, as distinct from human creations. **2** the inherent character of a person or thing. **3** a kind or class of thing.

**nature reserve** *n* an officially protected area of great botanical or zoological interest.

**naturism** *n* = NUDISM. ➤ **naturist** *adj and n.*

**naught** *n archaic or literary* nothing.

**naughty** *adj* (**-ier, -iest**) **1** of a child: badly behaved; disobedient. **2** *euphem or humorous* slightly improper. ➤ **naughtiness** *n.*

**nausea** *n* **1** a feeling of discomfort in the stomach and an urge to vomit. **2** extreme disgust.

**nauseate** *v* to affect with nausea or disgust. ➤ **nauseating** *adj,* **nauseatingly** *adv.*

**nauseous** *adj* **1** feeling nausea or disgust. **2** disgusting.

**nautical** *adj* relating to sailors, navigation, or ships.

**nautical mile** *n* a unit of distance used for sea and air navigation, equal to 1852m (about 6076.17ft).

**naval** *adj* relating to a navy.

**nave** *n* the main long central space of a church.

**navel** *n* the depression in the middle of the abdomen marking the point where the umbilical cord was attached.

**navel orange** *n* a seedless orange with a pit at the top.

**navigable** *adj* **1** suitable for ships to pass through or along. **2** of e.g. a website: containing hypertext links for access to other information.

**navigate** *v* **1** to plan or direct the course of a ship or aircraft. **2** in computing, to explore (the Internet) using hypertext links. **3** of a car passenger: to advise the driver about the route.

**navigation** *n* **1** the science of determining the position, course, etc of a ship or aircraft. **2** traffic on any stretch of water. ➤ **navigational** *adj.*

**navvy** *n* (*pl* **-ies**) *Brit* an unskilled labourer.

**navy** *n* (*pl* **-ies**) **1** (*often* **Navy**) the branch of a country's armed services supplying crews and supporting personnel for warships. **2** = NAVY BLUE.

**navy blue** *n* a deep dark blue colour. ➤ **navy blue** *adj.*

**nay** *adv archaic* no.

**Nazi** /'nahtsi/ *n* (*pl* **Nazis**) a member of the National Socialist German Workers' Party, which controlled Germany from 1933 to 1945. ➤ **Nazi** *adj,* **Nazism** *n.*

**NB** *abbr* (Latin) nota bene: note well.

**Nb** *abbr* the chemical symbol for niobium.

**Nd** *abbr* the chemical symbol for neodymium.

**NE** *abbr* **1** northeast. **2** northeastern.

**Ne** *abbr* the chemical symbol for neon.

**Neanderthal** *n* an extinct species of human that inhabited Europe between 120,000 and 35,000 years ago.

**neap tide** *n* a tide at the time when the difference between high and low tide is at its smallest.

**near**[1] *adv* **1** (*often* + to) at or to only a short distance away. **2** almost: *with near-disastrous results.*

**near**[2] *prep* a short distance or time from.

**near**[3] *adj* **1** close in place or time. **2** almost but not quite a particular thing: *a near disaster.* **3** closely related. ➤ **nearness** *n.*

**near**[4] *v* to approach (a place or point).

**nearby** *adv and adj* close at hand.

**Near East** *n* the countries of Southwest Asia between the Mediterranean coast and India.

**nearly** *adv* **1** almost but not quite. **2** closely.

**nearside** *n Brit* the side of a vehicle nearest the kerb.

**nearsighted** *adj* able to see near things more clearly than distant ones.

**neat** *adj* **1** tidy or orderly. **2** well-defined or precise. **3** *NAmer, informal* excellent. **4** of spirits: without addition or dilution. ➤ **neatly** *adv,* **neatness** *n.*

**neaten** *v* to make neat.

**nebula** *n* (*pl* **nebulas** *or* **nebulae**) an immense body of highly rarefied gas or dust in interstellar space.

**nebulous** *adj* of ideas, etc: indistinct or vague.

**necessarily** *adv* as a necessary consequence; inevitably.

**necessary**[1] *adj* **1** essential; indispensable. **2** inevitable; inescapable.

**necessary**[2] *n* (*pl* **-ies**) an indispensable item. * **the necessary 1** *informal* the action required. **2** *Brit, informal* money.

**necessitate** *v* to make necessary or unavoidable.

**necessity** *n* (*pl* **-ies**) **1** the quality of being necessary. **2** pressing need or desire. **3** something indispensable. * **of necessity** necessarily.

**neck**[1] *n* **1** the part of a person or animal that connects the head with the body. **2** the constricted end of a bottle. **3** the part of a stringed musical instrument extending from the body and supporting the fingerboard and strings. **4** *Brit, informal* insolent boldness; cheek. * **catch/get it in the neck** *informal* to be severely rebuked or punished. **neck and neck** keeping abreast in a race. **neck of the woods** *usu humorous* a district or locality. **up to one's neck in** deeply involved in (some business).

**neck**[2] *v informal* to kiss and caress in sexual play.

**neckerchief** *n* a square of fabric folded and worn round the neck.

**necklace** *n* a string of jewels, beads, etc worn round the neck as an ornament.

**necklet** *n* a rigid, close-fitting ornament for wearing round the neck.

**neckline** *n* the upper edge of a garment that forms the opening for the neck and head.

**necromancy** *n* **1** the conjuring up of the spirits of the dead in order to predict the future. **2** magic or sorcery generally. ➤ **necromancer** *n.*

**necrophilia** *n* obsession with, erotic interest in, or sexual intercourse with corpses. ➤ **necrophiliac** *adj and n.*

**necropolis** *n* a cemetery, *esp* a large and elaborate one.

**necrosis** *n* (*pl* **necroses**) the death of living tissue through disease, injury, or interruption of the blood supply.

**nectar** *n* **1** a sweet liquid secreted by plants and made into honey by bees. **2** in classical mythology, the drink of the gods.

**nectarine** *n* a type of peach with a smooth thin skin.

**née** *or* **nee** /nay/ *adj* used to identify a married woman by her maiden name: born as: *Mary Thomson, née Wilkinson.*

**need**[1] *v* **1** to have to have (something or somebody) in order to function, be complete, be happy, etc. **2** to be in a position where it is essential to do something: *We need to discuss this urgently.* **3** to be compelled or obliged to do something: *She need not decide straight away.*

**need**[2] *n* **1** obligation. **2** sufficient reason. **3** (*also in pl*) something one requires. **4** poverty; want.

**needful** *adj* necessary.

**needle**[1] *n* **1** a small slender pointed instrument with an eye for thread at one end, used for sewing. **2** a thin rod used in crocheting or knitting. **3** the hollow pointed end of a hypodermic syringe. **4** a slender pointed indicator on a dial or compass. **5** a stylus for playing records. **6** a needle-shaped leaf, *esp* of a conifer.

**needle**[2] *v informal* to provoke by persistent teasing or gibes.

**needlecord** *n* a fine corduroy with close ribs.

**needlepoint** *n* embroidery worked on canvas usu in a simple even stitch.

**needless** *adj* not needed; unnecessary. * **needless to say** naturally; of course. ➤ **needlessly** *adv.*

**needlework** *n* sewing or embroidery.

**needn't** *contraction* need not.

**needy** *adj* (**-ier, -iest**) in want; impoverished. ➤ **neediness** *n.*

**ne'er** *adv literary* never.

**ne'er-do-well** *n* an idle worthless person.

**nefarious** *adj* highly suspect or criminal.

**negate** *v* **1** to make ineffective or invalid. **2** to deny the existence or truth of. ➤ **negation** *n.*

**negative**[1] *adj* **1** expressing denial, prohibition, or refusal. **2** denoting the absence of something. **3** having a critical, unfavourable, or discouraging attitude or qualities. **4** of a number: less than zero. **5** having lower electric potential and constituting the part towards which the current flows from the external circuit. **6** of a photographic image: having the light and dark parts or the colours of the subject reversed. ➤ **negatively** *adv,* **negativity** *n.*

**negative**[2] *n* **1** in grammar, etc, a word, e.g. *no, not,* or *never,* or a statement that negates something. **2** a negative photographic image used for printing positive pictures.

**neglect**[1] *v* **1** to fail to give (a person, animal, or thing) proper care and attention. **2** to fail (to do something required of one).

**neglect**[2] *n* **1** lack of proper care and attention. **2** the act of neglecting something.

**neglectful** *adj* (*often* + of) careless, heedless, or forgetful.

**negligee** *or* **negligé** /'neglizhay/ *n* a woman's light decorative dressing gown.

**negligence** *n* **1** carelessness or forgetfulness. **2** in law, the offence of failing to take due care, so that damage or harm results. ➤ **negligent** *adj.*

**negligible** *adj* so slight or insignificant as to be not worth considering.

**negotiable** *adj* **1** transferable to another person. **2** of a road, route, etc: capable of being passed along. **3** capable of being dealt with through discussion.

**negotiate** *v* **1** to confer with others with the aim of reaching agreement over a disputed issue. **2** to achieve (a settlement, etc) by discussion with others. **3** to succeed in passing (an obstacle en route). **4** to transfer (a cheque or bill of exchange) to somebody else's legal possession. ➤ **negotiator** *n*, **negotiation** *n*.

**Negro** *n* (*pl* **-oes**) *offensive* a black person. ➤ **Negro** *adj*.

**neigh** *v* to make the characteristic cry of a horse. ➤ **neigh** *n*.

**neighbour** (*NAmer* **neighbor**) *n* a person who lives next door, or very close, to one. ➤ **neighbourly** *adj*.

**neighbourhood** (*NAmer* **neighborhood**) *n* **1** the area surrounding one's own home. **2** the area around the person or thing specified. **3** a particular area of a town.

**neighbouring** (*NAmer* **neighboring**) *adj* adjoining, or situated near to, a place.

**neither**[1] *adj and pron* not the one or the other of two.

**neither**[2] *conj* used used before the first of two or more alternatives that are part of the same negative statement: *Neither Janet nor her sister is coming.*

**neither**[3] *adv* similarly not; also not: *'I can't understand it.' 'Neither can I'.*

**nemesis** *n* (*pl* **nemeses**) a person or thing that brings deserved retribution to somebody.

**neoclassical** *adj* relating to a revival of classical forms in the arts. ➤ **neoclassicism** *n*, **neoclassicist** *n and adj*.

**Neolithic** *adj* of the last period of the Stone Age.

**neologism** *n* a new word or expression.

**neon** *n* a gaseous chemical element that glows when electricity passes through it, used in fluorescent signs and lighting.

**neonate** *n technical* a newborn child less than a month old. ➤ **neonatal** *adj*.

**neophyte** *n* **1** a beginner in a subject, skill, etc. **2** a recently ordained priest or a novice in a religious order.

**nephew** *n* the son of one's brother or sister.

**nephritis** *n* inflammation of the kidneys.

**nepotism** *n* favouritism shown to a relative.

**nerd** *or* **nurd** *n informal* a person who is obsessed with a technical subject, *esp* computing, and is often boring or socially inept.

**nerve**[1] *n* **1** a threadlike band of fibrous tissue that conducts the impulses that transmit sensations and messages to the brain and other organs. **2** a combination of courage, self-discipline, and tenacity. **3** *informal* cheek; audacity. **4** (*in pl*) feelings of acute nervousness or anxiety. ✱ **get on somebody's nerves** to annoy somebody.

**nerve**[2] *v* (*also* + up/for) to prepare (oneself) psychologically for a challenge.

**nerve cell** *n* = NEURON.

**nerve gas** *n* a deadly gas that interferes with nerve transmission and disrupts the vital functions.

**nerveless** *adj* **1** lacking strength or vigour. **2** not agitated or afraid.

**nerve-racking** *or* **nerve-wracking** *adj* causing great tension and anxiety.

**nervous** *adj* **1** relating to the nerves. **2** anxious or apprehensive. **3** constitutionally anxious or easily upset. ➤ **nervously** *adv*, **nervousness** *n*.

**nervous breakdown** *n* a mental and emotional disorder in which depression, severe tiredness, etc prevent one from coping with one's responsibilities.

**nervous system** *n* the brain, spinal cord, and nerves together forming a system for interpreting stimuli from the sense organs and transmitting impulses to muscles, glands, etc.

**nervy** *adj* (**-ier, -iest**) *chiefly Brit* suffering from nervousness or anxiety.

**-ness** *suffix* **1** denoting a state or quality: *goodness*. **2** happiness.

**nest**[1] *n* **1** a structure built by a bird to lay eggs in and shelter its young. **2** a structure where other creatures, e.g. insects, breed or shelter. **3** a set of things in a range of sizes, that fit one inside the other.

**nest**[2] *v* **1** of birds: to construct or occupy a nest. **2** to fit (a set of tables, etc) one inside the other.

**nest egg** *n* an amount of money saved up as a reserve.

**nestle** *v* **1** to settle snugly or comfortably. **2** of a place: to lie in a sheltered position.

**nestling** *n* a young bird that has not abandoned the nest.

**net**[1] *n* **1** a fabric made of threads, etc, twisted, knotted, or woven together at regular intervals to leave square spaces in between. **2** a device made of net for catching fish, birds, or insects. **3** a net barricade which divides a tennis, badminton, etc court in half. **4** a football, hockey, etc goal. **5** (**the Net**) the Internet.

**net**[2] *v* (**netted, netting**) **1** to catch (a fish, etc) in a net. **2** to hit or kick (a ball or puck) into the goal in hockey, football, etc.

**net**[3] *or Brit* **nett** *adj* **1** remaining after all deductions, e.g. for taxes, outlay, or loss. **2** excluding the weight of the packaging or container. **3** final; overall.

**net**[4] *or Brit* **nett** *v* (**netted, netting**) to make (a sum) as clear profit.

**netball** *n* a game played between teams of seven players who try to score goals by tossing an inflated ball through a high horizontal ring on a post.

**nether** *adj formal* lower or under.

**nettle**[1] *n* a plant with jagged leaves covered with stinging hairs. ✱ **grasp the nettle** to tackle a problem with bold determination.

**nettle**[2] *v* of a remark, etc: to goad or annoy.
**network**[1] *n* **1** a structure of crisscrossing horizontal and vertical lines, cords, wires, etc. **2** a system of interconnected railways, roads, etc. **3** a group of broadcasting stations linked together for a simultaneous broadcast. **4** a set of interconnected computers or terminals. **5** a group of people who maintain contact with each other and exchange information.
**network**[2] *v* to create useful contacts for oneself by talking and interacting with others. ➤ **networker** *n.*
**neural** *adj* relating to a nerve or the nervous system. ➤ **neurally** *adv.*
**neuralgia** *n* intense pain radiating along a nerve, *esp* in the head or face. ➤ **neuralgic** *adj.*
**neurology** *n* the study of the nervous system, its structure, and function. ➤ **neurological** *adj*, **neurologist** *n.*
**neuron** *or* **neurone** *n* a specialized type of cell that transmits impulses through the nervous system.
**neurosis** *n* (*pl* **neuroses**) a nervous disorder in which phobias, compulsions, anxiety, and obsessions make normal life difficult.
**neurotic** *adj* **1** relating to or caused by a neurosis. **2** hypersensitive or obsessive about something. **3** *informal* unduly anxious. ➤ **neurotic** *n*, **neurotically** *adv.*
**neuter**[1] *adj* **1** of nouns: neither masculine nor feminine. **2** lacking sexual or reproductive organs.
**neuter**[2] *v* to spay or castrate (a domestic animal).
**neutral**[1] *adj* **1** of a country or a person: not engaged on either side of a war, dispute, etc. **2** impartial or unbiased. **3** having no strongly distinctive characteristics. **4** denoting a colour that is any shade of beige or grey. **5** denoting chemical substances having a pH value of about 7, so neither acid nor alkaline. **6** not electrically charged. ➤ **neutrality** *n*, **neutrally** *adv.*
**neutral**[2] *n* **1** a neutral person or state. **2** the gear position in which no gear is engaged.
**neutralize** *or* **-ise** *v* **1** to counteract or nullify by having the opposite effect. **2** to make neutral. ➤ **neutralization** *n.*
**neutrino** *n* (*pl* **-os**) an uncharged elementary particle that is created in the process of particle decay and is believed to be massless.
**neutron** *n* an uncharged elementary particle with a mass about that of the proton.
**never** *adv* **1** not ever; at no time. **2** used emphatically for *not.*
**nevermore** *adv literary* never again.
**never-never** *or* **the never-never** *n Brit, informal* = HIRE PURCHASE.
**nevertheless** *adv* in spite of that; however.
**new**[1] *adj* **1** recently bought, made, built, invented, etc. **2** fresh; unused. **3** doing something for the first time. **4** replacing the previous one. **5** fresh; unfamiliar; different. **6** refreshed; regenerated. ➤ **newness** *n.*
**new**[2] *adv* newly or recently.
**New Age** *n* a cultural movement of the late 1980s, characterized by enthusiasm for alternative beliefs, environmentalism, and holistic medicine.
**newborn** *adj* just born.
**newcomer** *n* **1** a recent arrival. **2** a beginner or novice.
**newel** *n* an upright post supporting either end of a staircase handrail.
**newfangled** *adj derog* modern and unnecessarily complicated or gimmicky.
**newly** *adv* **1** lately; recently. **2** anew.
**newlywed** *n* a recently married person.
**new moon** *n* the phase of the moon when its dark side is towards the earth or it reappears as a thin crescent.
**news** *n* **1** information about something that has recently happened. **2** (**the news**) a broadcast report of recent events.
**newsagent** *n chiefly Brit* a retailer of newspapers and magazines.
**newscast** *n* a broadcast news report. ➤ **newscaster** *n.*
**newsflash** *n* a brief broadcast reporting an important item of news, *esp* one that interrupts a programme.
**newsgroup** *n* a forum of Internet users who exchange news and views about topics of mutual interest.
**newsletter** *n* a publication containing news relevant to a particular group, association, etc, for circulation to its members.
**newspaper** *n* a printed daily or weekly publication containing news reports and articles.
**newsprint** *n* cheap paper used mostly for newspapers.
**newsreader** *n* a broadcaster who reads the news.
**newsreel** *n* a short film dealing with current events.
**newsroom** *n* a place, e.g. an office, where news is prepared for publication or broadcast.
**newsworthy** *adj* (**-ier, -iest**) sufficiently interesting to warrant reporting.
**newt** *n* a small amphibian with a long slender body and tail and short legs.
**New Testament** *n* the second part of the Christian Bible, comprising the Gospels and Epistles, the books of Acts, and the book of Revelation.
**newton** *n* the SI unit of force.
**New World** *n* (**the New World**) North and South America.
**New Year** *n* **1** the first day or days of a calendar year. **2** the festive period around 31 December and 1 January.

**next**[1] *adj* immediately adjacent or following, in place, time, or order.

***Usage Note:*** When used of days of the week, *next* usually refers to the relevant day in the following week, so that on Monday 1st *next Wednesday* more often means Wednesday 10th than Wednesday 3rd.

**next**[2] *adv* **1** in the time, place, or position immediately following. **2** on the following occasion.
**next**[3] *n* a person or thing that is next.
**next door** *adv* in or to the next building, room, etc.
**next-door** *adj* situated or living in the next building, room, etc.
**next of kin** *n* (*pl* **next of kin**) the person most closely related to oneself.
**nexus** *n* (*pl* **nexuses** *or* **nexus**) **1** a connection. **2** a connected group or series.
**NHS** *abbr Brit* National Health Service.
**Ni** *abbr* the chemical symbol for nickel.
**nib** *n* the pointed end of a pen, from which the ink is distributed.
**nibble**[1] *v* **1** to bite cautiously, gently, or playfully. **2** to eat or chew in small bites.
**nibble**[2] *n* **1** an act of nibbling. **2** a very small amount, e.g. of food. **3** *informal* (*in pl*) savoury snacks served at a reception, etc.
**nice** *adj* **1** pleasant or agreeable. **2** of a person: kind, considerate, or accommodating. **3** socially respectable. **4** satisfactorily performed. **5** subtle. ➤ **nicely** *adv*, **niceness** *n.*
**nicety** *n* (*pl* **-ies**) **1** a fine point or distinction. **2** subtlety or precision.
**niche** *n* **1** a recess in a wall. **2** a place or activity for which a person is best suited.
**nick**[1] *n* **1** a small cut or notch. **2** (**the nick**) *Brit, informal* a prison or police station. ✱ **in good/bad nick** *Brit, informal* in good or bad condition. **in the nick of time** just before it would be too late.
**nick**[2] *v* **1** to make a nick in. **2** *Brit, informal* to steal. **3** *Brit, informal* to arrest.
**nickel** *n* **1** a silver-white metallic element, used in coins and in alloys. **2** a US coin worth five cents.
**nickname**[1] *n* a familiar or humorous name used in place of a proper name.
**nickname**[2] *v* to give (a person or thing) a nickname.
**nicotine** *n* a poisonous chemical compound that occurs in tobacco.
**niece** *n* the daughter of one's brother or sister.

***Usage Note:*** Note the spelling with *-ie-*.

**niff**[1] *n Brit, informal* an unpleasant smell.
**niff**[2] *v Brit, informal* to smell unpleasant.
**nifty** *adj* (**-ier, -iest**) *informal* **1** very good or effective. **2** quick or deft.
**niggardly** *adj* grudgingly mean; miserly.
**nigger** *n offensive or derog* a black person.
**niggle**[1] *v* **1** to cause minor but persistent discomfort or anxiety. **2** to find fault constantly in a petty way.
**niggle**[2] *n* **1** a petty criticism. **2** a minor cause of anxiety.
**nigh** *adv, adj, and prep archaic* near.
**night** *n* **1** the period of darkness from dusk to dawn. **2** an evening characterized by a specified event or activity.
**nightcap** *n* **1** formerly, a cloth cap worn in bed. **2** a drink taken at bedtime.
**nightclub** *n* a place of entertainment open at night, usu with a disco and a bar.
**nightdress** *n* a woman's or girl's nightgown.
**nightfall** *n* dusk.
**nightgown** *n* a loose garment for sleeping in.
**nightie** *or* **nighty** *n* (*pl* **-ies**) *informal* a nightdress.
**nightingale** *n* a small thrush with brown plumage, noted for its sweet song, typically heard at night.
**nightjar** *n* an insect-eating bird with large eyes and greyish brown plumage that is active at night.
**nightlife** *n* late-evening entertainment or social life.
**nightly** *adj and adv* happening every night.
**nightmare** *n* **1** a frightening or distressing dream. **2** a very unpleasant or terrifying experience or situation. ➤ **nightmarish** *adj.*
**night owl** *n informal* somebody who tends to be most active at night.
**nightshade** *n* a poisonous rambling plant with purple flowers and black (*deadly nightshade*) or red (*woody nightshade*) berries.
**nightshirt** *n* a long loose shirt for sleeping in.
**nightspot** *n informal* a nightclub.
**nihilism** *n* a view that rejects all values and beliefs as meaningless or unfounded. ➤ **nihilist** *n*, **nihilistic** *adj.*
**nil** *n* nothing; zero.
**nimble** *adj* **1** quick and light in movement. **2** quick and clever in thinking and understanding. ➤ **nimbly** *adv.*
**nimbus** *n* (*pl* **nimbi** *or* **nimbuses**) a heavy grey rain-bearing cloud.
**Nimby** *n* (*pl* **Nimbys** *or* **Nimbies**) a person who is not against something in principle, but objects when it happens in their immediate vicinity.
**nincompoop** *n* a silly or foolish person.
**nine** *n* the number 9. ✱ **dressed to/up to the nines** *informal* dressed very smartly or elaborately. ➤ **nine** *adj.*
**nineteen** *adj and n* the number 19. ✱ **talk nineteen to the dozen** *informal* to talk or converse volubly. ➤ **nineteenth** *adj and n.*
**ninety** *adj and n* (*pl* **-ies**) **1** the number 90. **2** (*in pl*) the numbers 90 to 99. ➤ **ninetieth** *adj and n.*
**ninny** *n* (*pl* **-ies**) *informal* a silly or weak person.

**ninth** *adj and n* **1** having the position in a sequence corresponding to the number nine. **2** one of nine equal parts of something. ➤ **ninthly** *adv.*

**nip**[1] *v* (**nipped, nipping**) **1** to bite, squeeze, or pinch sharply. **2** *chiefly Brit, informal* to go quickly or briefly; to hurry. ✻ **nip something in the bud** to prevent the growth or development of something at an early stage.

**nip**[2] *n* **1** a sharp chill in the air. **2** a sharp squeeze, pinch, or bite.

**nip**[3] *n* a small measure or drink of spirits.

**nipper** *n* **1** (*in pl*) pincers or pliers. **2** *chiefly Brit, informal* a child.

**nipple** *n* the small protuberance of a mammary gland, e.g. a breast, from which milk is drawn.

**nippy** *adj* (**-ier, -iest**) **1** nimble and lively. **2** of the weather: chilly.

**nirvana** /nuh'vahnə/ *n* (*often* **Nirvana**) a Hindu and Buddhist state of final bliss and freedom from the cycle of rebirth.

**nit**[1] *n* the egg of a louse.

**nit**[2] *n chiefly Brit, informal* a nitwit.

**nit-picking** *n* petty and often unjustified criticism.

**nitrate** *n* a salt or ester of nitric acid.

**nitric acid** *n* a corrosive liquid acid.

**nitrite** *n* a salt or ester of nitrous acid.

**nitrogen** *n* a gas that constitutes about 78% of the atmosphere.

**nitroglycerine** *or* **nitroglycerin** *n* an oily explosive liquid used in making dynamite.

**nitrous oxide** *n* a gas used as a general anaesthetic.

**nitty-gritty** *n informal* the important basic realities.

**nitwit** *n informal* a scatterbrained or stupid person.

**No** *abbr* the chemical symbol for nobelium.

**no**[1] *interj* used in answers expressing negation, dissent, denial, or refusal.

**no**[2] *adv* not in any respect or degree.

**no**[3] *adj* **1** not any. **2** not a: *He's no expert.* ✻ **no way** *informal* certainly not!

**no**[4] *n* (*pl* **noes** *or* **nos**) a negative reply or vote.

**no.** *abbr* number.

**nob** *n chiefly Brit, informal* a wealthy or influential person.

**no-ball** *n and interj* an illegal delivery of the ball in cricket that counts one run to the batsman's side.

**nobble** *v informal* **1** to incapacitate (a racehorse), *esp* by drugging. **2** to win over to one's side, *esp* by dishonest means.

**nobility** *n* (*pl* **-ies**) **1** the quality of being noble. **2** the class of people who have aristocratic rank and titles.

**noble**[1] *adj* **1** having a title such as duke, earl, etc. **2** imposing; stately. **3** having or showing a magnanimous character or high ideals. ➤ **nobly** *adv.*

**noble**[2] *n* a person of noble rank or birth.

**nobleman** *n* (*pl* **noblemen**) a man of noble rank.

**noblewoman** *n* (*pl* **noblewomen**) a woman of noble rank.

**nobody**[1] *pron* no person.

**nobody**[2] *n* (*pl* **-ies**) a person of no influence or consequence.

**no-claims bonus** *n Brit* a discount allowed in an insurance premium when no claim has been made in previous years.

**nocturnal** *adj* occurring or active at night.

**nocturne** *n* a work of art dealing with evening or night, *esp* a dreamy pensive composition for the piano.

**nod**[1] *v* (**nodded, nodding**) **1** to make a short downward movement of the head, e.g. in assent, understanding, or greeting. **2** to make repeated down-and-up movements with the head. **3** to become drowsy or sleepy.

**nod**[2] *n* an act of nodding.

**node** *n* **1** in anatomy, any normal or abnormal knot, thickness, or swelling. **2** in a plant, the point on a stem at which one or more leaves are attached. **3** a point in a network where lines cross or branch.

**nod off** *v* to fall asleep, *esp* unintentionally while in a sitting position.

**nodule** *n* any small hardish rounded mass, e.g. of cells in the body. ➤ **nodular** *adj.*

**Noel** *or* **Noël** *n* Christmas.

**noggin** *n* a small measure of spirits, usu 0.142 litres (¼pt).

**Noh** *n* classic Japanese dance-drama.

**noise** *n* **1** loud confused or discordant sound. **2** a sound, *esp* if sudden or harsh. **3** unwanted signals or fluctuations in an electrical circuit. ➤ **noiseless** *adj.*

**noisome** *adj literary* repellent; offensive.

**noisy** *adj* (**-ier, -iest**) **1** making a lot of noise. **2** full of noise. ➤ **noisily** *adv,* **noisiness** *n.*

**nomad** *n* **1** a member of a people that wanders from place to place, e.g. to find grazing for its animals. **2** a person who has an unsettled or wandering lifestyle. ➤ **nomadic** *adj.*

**nom de plume** /ˌnom də 'ploohm/ *n* (*pl* **noms de plume**) a pseudonym under which an author writes.

**nomenclature** *n* a system of terms used in a particular science, discipline, or art.

**nominal** *adj* **1** in name only. **2** of a sum of money: very small. ➤ **nominally** *adv.*

**nominate** *v* **1** to recommend for an appointment, award, etc. **2** *literary* to designate or specify by name. ➤ **nomination** *n,* **nominee** *n.*

**nominative** *n* the case used for the subject of a verb.

**non-** *prefix* **1** not of the class or category specified: *non-alcoholic.* **2** the reverse or absence of the thing specified: *nonconformity.*

**nonagenarian** *n* a person between 90 and 99 years old.

**nonchalant** *adj* giving an impression of easy unconcern or indifference. ➤ **nonchalance** *n,* **nonchalantly** *adv.*

**non-commissioned officer** *n* a subordinate officer, e.g. a sergeant, in the armed forces who does not hold a commission.

**non-committal** *adj* giving no clear indication of attitude or feeling. ➤ **non-committally** *adv.*

**non compos mentis** *adj* not of sound mind; insane.

**nonconformist** *n* **1** a person who does not conform to a generally accepted pattern of thought or behaviour. **2** (*often* **Nonconformist**) a member of a Protestant Church separated from the Church of England. ➤ **Nonconformism** *n,* **nonconformity** *n.*

**nondescript** *adj* lacking distinctive or interesting qualities; dull.

**none**[1] *pron* **1** not any. **2** *literary* nobody.

**none**[2] *adv* not in the least; not at all.

**nonentity** *n* (*pl* **-ies**) **1** somebody or something of little importance or interest. **2** nonexistence.

**nonetheless** *or* **none the less** *adv* nevertheless.

**non-event** *n* an event that turns out to be much duller or less important than expected.

**non-existent** *adj* **1** not real. **2** totally absent.

**no-nonsense** *adj* serious, businesslike, or straightforward.

**nonplus** *v* (**nonplussed, nonplussing,** *NAmer* **nonplused, nonplusing**) to perplex or disconcert.

**non-profitmaking** *adj* not run with the intention of making a profit.

**non-proliferation** *n* action to stop something, *esp* nuclear weapons, becoming more widespread.

**nonsense** *n* **1** meaningless words or language. **2** frivolous or insolent behaviour. ➤ **nonsensical** *adj.*

**non sequitur** *n* a statement that does not follow logically from anything previously said.

**non-starter** *n* **1** somebody or something that is sure to fail. **2** a competitor, racehorse, etc that fails to take part in a race.

**non-stick** *adj* of a pan: having a surface treated so that food does not stick to it during cooking.

**non-stop** *adj* **1** continuous. **2** of a journey: with no intermediate stops. ➤ **non-stop** *adv.*

**noodle** *n* (*usu in pl*) a narrow flat ribbon of pasta made with egg.

**nook** *n* a small secluded or sheltered place; a corner or recess. ✻ **every nook and cranny** everywhere possible.

**noon** *n* twelve o'clock in the day; midday.

**noonday** *adj literary* occurring in the middle of the day.

**no one** *or* **no-one** *pron* nobody.

**noose** *n* a loop with a running knot that tightens as the rope is pulled.

**nor** *adv and conj* and not; neither.

**Nordic** *adj* characteristic of Scandinavia, Finland, and Iceland and their peoples.

**norm** *n* **1** (**the norm**) the average or usual level or situation. **2** an authoritative standard; a model.

**normal**[1] *adj* conforming to ordinary expectations; usual or typical. ➤ **normality** *n,* **normally** *adv.*

**normal**[2] *n* the normal condition or state of affairs.

**normalize** *or* **-ise** *v* to make (something abnormal or irregular) normal. ➤ **normalization** *n.*

**Norman**[1] *n* a member of a people of mixed Frankish and Scandinavian stock who settled in Normandy in the tenth century and conquered England in 1066.

**Norman**[2] *adj* relating to the Normans or Normandy.

**normative** *adj* serving as or prescribing a norm.

**Norse**[1] *n* = OLD NORSE.

**Norse**[2] *adj* of ancient or medieval Scandinavia or Norway.

**north**[1] *n* **1** the direction in which a compass needle normally points, 90° anticlockwise from east. **2** regions or countries lying to the north. ➤ **northbound** *adj and adv.*

**north**[2] *adj and adv* **1** at or towards the north. **2** of the wind: blowing from the north.

**northeast**[1] *n* **1** the direction midway between north and east. **2** regions lying to the northeast. ➤ **northeastern** *adj.*

**northeast**[2] *adj and adv* **1** at or towards the northeast. **2** of the wind: blowing from the northeast.

**northeasterly** *adj and adv* **1** in a northeastern position or direction. **2** of the wind: blowing from the northeast.

**northerly** *adj and adv* **1** in a northern position or direction. **2** of the wind: blowing from the north.

**northern** *adj* in or towards the north.

**Northerner** *n* a person from the northern part of a country.

**northern lights** *pl n* = AURORA BOREALIS.

**northward** *adj and adv* towards the north; in a direction going north. ➤ **northwards** *adv.*

**northwest**[1] *n* **1** the direction midway between north and west. **2** regions lying to the northwest. ➤ **northwestern** *adj.*

**northwest**[2] *adj and adv* **1** at or towards the northwest. **2** of the wind: blowing from the northwest.

**northwesterly** *adj and adv* **1** in a northwestern position or direction. **2** of the wind: blowing from the northwest.

**nose**[1] *n* **1** the projecting part of the face above the mouth, containing the nostrils and used for breathing and smelling. **2** the front end of a vehicle. **3** the aroma or bouquet of wine. **4** an instinct for detecting a certain thing. * **get up somebody's nose** *informal* to annoy somebody. **keep one's nose clean** *informal* to stay out of trouble. **keep one's nose out of** *informal* to refrain from interfering in (e.g. somebody else's business). **look down one's nose at** *informal* to show or express disdain for. **nose to tail** of vehicles: in a long slowly-moving queue. **pay through the nose** *informal* to pay exorbitantly. **turn one's nose up at** *informal* to show or express disdain for (a person or thing).

**nose**[2] *v* **1** of an animal: to push its nose into or against. **2** (*often* + about/around) to pry. **3** of a vehicle or driver: to move slowly forward.

**nose bag** *n* a bag for feeding a horse or other animal that covers its muzzle.

**nosebleed** *n* an attack of bleeding from the nose.

**nose dive** *n* **1** a downward nose-first plunge of an aircraft. **2** a sudden dramatic drop.

**nose-dive** *v* to make a nose dive.

**nosegay** *n* a small bunch of flowers.

**nosh**[1] *n informal* food; a meal.

**nosh**[2] *v informal* to eat.

**nostalgia** *n* a wistful yearning for something past or irrecoverable. ➤ **nostalgic** *adj.*

**nostril** *n* either of the two external openings of the nose.

**nostrum** *n* (*pl* **nostrums**) a medicine or remedy favoured by somebody, which is often of questionable effectiveness.

**nosy** *or* **nosey** *adj* (**-ier, -iest**) *informal* inquisitive; prying.

**not** *adv* **1** used to express a negative. **2** less than (a surprisingly small amount).

**notable**[1] *adj* worthy of note; remarkable or distinguished. ➤ **notably** *adv.*

**notable**[2] *n* a prominent person.

**notary** *n* (*pl* **-ies**) a legal official appointed to administer oaths and draw up and authenticate documents.

**notation** *n* a system of marks, signs, symbols, etc used in e.g. mathematics, music, or choreography.

**notch**[1] *n* **1** a V-shaped indentation or cut. **2** a degree or point on a scale.

**notch**[2] *v* **1** to make a notch in. **2** (+ up) to score or achieve (e.g. a success).

**note**[1] *n* **1** (*also in pl*) a short written record. **2** a brief comment or explanation. **3** a short informal letter. **4** a piece of paper money. **5** a sound having a definite pitch and length, made by a musical instrument or the human voice. **6** a written symbol used to indicate such a sound. **7** a feeling or element of something. * **of note 1** distinguished. **2** significant. **take note** (*often* + of) to pay attention.

**note**[2] *v* **1** to pay due attention to. **2** (*often* + down) to record (information) in writing.

**notebook** *n* **1** a book for notes or memoranda. **2** a small portable computer.

**noted** *adj* well-known; famous.

**notepaper** *n* paper for letter-writing.

**noteworthy** *adj* worthy of or attracting attention.

**nothing** *pron and noun* **1** not anything. **2** a thing of no consequence or significance. **3** nought. * **for nothing 1** without pay or without paying. **2** to no purpose. **nothing but** only. **sweet nothings** *humorous* affectionate exchanges between lovers.

**nothingness** *n* **1** nonexistence. **2** a void; emptiness.

**notice**[1] *n* **1** attention or observation. **2** advance warning. **3** formal notification of one's intention to terminate an agreement, typically relating to employment or tenancy. **4** a placard or poster displaying information. **5** a brief announcement in a newspaper, etc. **6** a short critical review of a play, etc. * **at short notice** with little or no warning. **take no notice of** to disregard or pay no heed to.

**notice**[2] *v* to become aware of.

**noticeable** *adj* capable of being noticed; perceptible. ➤ **noticeably** *adv.*

**notifiable** *adj* of a disease: required by law to be reported to the health authorities.

**notify** *v* (**-ies, -ied**) (*also* + of) to let (somebody) know about something, *esp* formally or officially. ➤ **notification** *n.*

**notion** *n* **1** a broad general concept. **2** an idea or belief, *esp* a fanciful one.

**notional** *adj* theoretical, speculative, or imaginary. ➤ **notionally** *adv.*

**notoriety** *n* the fact of being notorious.

**notorious** *adj* well-known for something bad or unfavourable. ➤ **notoriously** *adv.*

**notwithstanding**[1] *prep* in spite of.

**notwithstanding**[2] *adv* nevertheless.

**nougat** *n* a sweet consisting of nuts or fruit pieces in a semisolid sugar paste.

**nought** *n and pron* **1** the arithmetical symbol 0; zero. **2** nothing.

**noun** *n* a word that is a name or term identifying a person, thing, animal, quality, or state.

**nourish** *v* **1** to provide (a person, animal, or plant) with the substances needed for healthy growth and development. **2** to cherish or entertain (an idea, feeling, etc). ➤ **nourishing** *adj.*

**nourishment** *n* food or nutriment.

**nous** *n chiefly Brit* practical common sense.

**nouveau riche** /ˌnoohvoh ˈreesh/ *n* (*pl* **nouveaux riches**) a person who has recently become rich.

**nouvelle cuisine** /noohˈvel kwiˈzeen/ *n* a style of cooking that emphasizes the natural flavours and textures of the food and attractive presentation.

**nova** *n* (*pl* **novas** *or* **novae**) a double star system that becomes suddenly much brighter as a result of a thermonuclear explosion and then fades away.
**novel**[1] *n* an invented prose narrative of book length.
**novel**[2] *adj* new and unlike anything previously known.
**novelist** *n* a writer of novels.
**novella** *n* (*pl* **novellas** *or* **novelle**) a short novel or substantial short story.
**novelty** *n* (*pl* **-ies**) **1** something new and unusual. **2** the quality of being novel. **3** a small ornament or toy.
**November** *n* the eleventh month of the year.
**novice** *n* **1** a new or inexperienced person in a job, etc; a beginner. **2** a person admitted to probationary membership of a religious community.
**novitiate** *or* **noviciate** *n* **1** the period of being a novice in a religious order. **2** a house where novices are trained.
**now**[1] *adv* **1** at the present time. **2** immediately. **3** in the light of recent developments. ✱ **now and again/then** occasionally.
**now**[2] *conj* (*often* + that) as a result of the circumstance that; since.
**nowadays** *adv* in these modern times, in contrast to the past.
**nowhere** *adv and pron* not anywhere.
**noxious** *adj* harmful to living things.
**nozzle** *n* a projecting part with a usu adjustable outlet for liquid or gas.
**Np** *abbr* the chemical symbol for neptunium.
**nu** *n* the 13th letter of the Greek alphabet (N, ν).
**nuance** *n* a subtle but distinct gradation in colour, meaning, or tone.
**nub** *n* **1** a knob, lump, or protuberance. **2** (**the nub**) the crux of a matter.
**nubile** *adj* **1** of a girl: **2** of marriageable age. **3** young and sexually attractive.
**nuclear** *adj* **1** relating to a nucleus. **2** relating to or using the energy released when atomic nuclei are split or fused. **3** possessing nuclear weapons.
**nuclear family** *n* a family unit that consists of husband, wife, and children.
**nuclear physics** *n* the branch of physics concerned with atomic nuclei and their interactions, *esp* as a source of energy.
**nucleic acid** *n* a complex organic substance such as DNA or RNA, present in living cells.
**nucleus** *n* (*pl* **nuclei** *or* **nucleuses**) **1** the central and main part of *esp* a group. **2** a specialized structure within a cell containing the chromosomes and surrounded by a membrane. **3** the positively charged central part of an atom.
**nude**[1] *adj* without clothing; naked. ➤ **nudity** *n.*
**nude**[2] *n* a painting or sculpture of a nude human figure.
**nudge**[1] *v* **1** to poke (somebody) gently with one's elbow, *esp* to draw their attention to something. **2** to push or move gently in a certain direction.
**nudge**[2] *n* **1** the act of nudging. **2** a gentle hint or reminder.
**nudism** *n* the cult or practice of going nude as much as possible. ➤ **nudist** *n.*
**nugatory** *adj formal* trifling; inconsequential.
**nugget** *n* a solid lump of a precious metal in its natural state.
**nuisance** *n* a person or thing that is a source of annoyance or inconvenience.
**nuke**[1] *n informal* a nuclear weapon.
**nuke**[2] *v informal* to attack with nuclear weapons.
**null** *adj* having no force in law; invalid.
**nullify** *v* (**-ies, -ied**) **1** to make legally null and void. **2** to render ineffective or cancel out. ➤ **nullification** *n.*
**nullity** *n* (*pl* **-ies**) **1** in law, something that is legally null and void. **2** the state of being legally null and void.
**numb**[1] *adj* **1** devoid of sensation, *esp* as a result of cold or anaesthesia. **2** unable to feel emotion or react. ➤ **numbly** *adv,* **numbness** *n.*
**numb**[2] *v* **1** to make (a person or a body part) numb. **2** to reduce the sharpness of (a pain).
**number**[1] *n* **1** a word, numeral, or other symbol used in counting or calculating quantities. **2** a numeral or set of digits used to identify something. **3** a quantity or total. **4** (**a number of**) several. **5** a single issue of a periodical. **6** a song or a piece of pop or jazz music. ✱ **somebody's number is up** *informal* somebody is doomed. ➤ **numberless** *adj.*
**number**[2] *v* **1** to amount to (a certain total). **2** to assign numbers to (things in a series). **3** (*usu* + among) to regard (a person or thing) as being included in a certain group.
**numberplate** *n chiefly Brit* a rectangular plate on a vehicle showing its registration number.
**numbskull** *n* see NUMSKULL.
**numeral** *n* a symbol that represents a number or zero.
**numerate** *adj* understanding basic mathematics; able to use numbers in calculation. ➤ **numeracy** *n.*
**numeration** *n* **1** counting. **2** designating by a number.
**numerator** *n* the part of a fraction that is above the line.
**numerical** *adj* relating to, expressed in, or involving numbers. ➤ **numerically** *adv.*
**numerous** *adj* **1** many. **2** consisting of many units or individuals. ➤ **numerously** *adv.*
**numinous** *adj* awe-inspiring or mysterious; suggesting the presence of a god.
**numismatics** *pl n* the study or collection of coins or medals. ➤ **numismatic** *adj,* **numismatist** *n.*

**numskull** *or* **numbskull** *n* a stupid person.
**nun** *n* a female member of a religious order living in a convent under vows of chastity, poverty, and obedience.
**nuncio** *n* (*pl* **-os**) a papal ambassador to a civil government.
**nunnery** *n* (*pl* **-ies**) a convent of nuns.
**nuptial**[1] *adj* relating to marriage.
**nuptial**[2] *n* (*usu in pl*) a wedding.
**nurse**[1] *n* a person trained to care for the sick or injured.
**nurse**[2] *v* **1** to tend (e.g. a sick person). **2** to suckle (a baby). **3** to hold or handle carefully. **4** to harbour (a feeling) in one's mind.
**nursemaid** *n* a girl or woman employed to look after children.
**nursery** *n* (*pl* **-ies**) **1** a child's bedroom or playroom. **2** = NURSERY SCHOOL. **3** an area where plants, trees, etc are grown for sale or transplanting.
**nursery rhyme** *n* a short traditional story in rhyme for children.
**nursery school** *n* a school for children aged usu from three to five.
**nursing home** *n* a usu private hospital or home, where care is provided for the aged, chronically ill, etc.
**nurture**[1] *n* the provision of food, care, and the means for growth and development.
**nurture**[2] *v* **1** to provide with food, care and the means for growth and development. **2** to encourage and develop (an interest, talent, etc). **3** to cherish (a hope, ambition, etc).
**nut** *n* **1** a dry fruit or seed consisting of a hard separable rind or shell and an often edible kernel. **2** the kernel of such a fruit. **3** a small metal block with a threaded central hole, which can be screwed onto something, *esp* a bolt. **4** *informal* a person's head. **5** *informal*. **6** an insane or wildly eccentric person. **7** an ardent enthusiast. ➤ **nutty** *adj.*
**nutcase** *n informal* a mad person.
**nutcracker** *n* (*also in pl*) an implement for cracking nuts.
**nutmeg** *n* the round hard seed of an Indonesian tree, used as a spice.
**nutrient** *n* something that provides nourishment.
**nutriment** *n* something that nourishes or promotes growth.
**nutrition** *n* the processes by which an organism takes in and uses food. ➤ **nutritional** *adj,* **nutritionist** *n.*
**nutritious** *adj* nourishing.
**nutritive** *adj* **1** relating to nutrition. **2** nourishing.
**nuts** *adj informal* crazy; mad.
**nuts and bolts** *n informal* **1** the basic practical issues. **2** the practical workings (e.g. of a business or enterprise).
**nutshell** *n* the hard outside covering of a nut. * **in a nutshell** in brief; in essence.
**nutter** *n chiefly Brit, informal* a crazy fool.
**nuzzle** *v* to rub (something or somebody) affectionately with the nose or face.
**NVQ** *abbr Brit* National Vocational Qualification.
**NW** *abbr* **1** northwest. **2** northwestern.
**nylon** *n* **1** a strong light synthetic material, used *esp* in textiles and plastics. **2** (*in pl*) stockings made of nylon.
**nymph** *n* **1** a minor female spirit of nature in classical mythology. **2** an immature insect; *esp* a larva of a dragonfly.
**nymphet** *or* **nymphette** *n* a sexually desirable girl in early adolescence.
**nymphomania** *n* excessive sexual desire in a female. ➤ **nymphomaniac** *n.*

**O**[1] *or* **o** *n* (*pl* **O's** *or* **Os** *or* **o's**) **1** the 15th letter of the English alphabet. **2** a representation in speech of zero.

**O**[2] *abbr* the chemical symbol for oxygen.

**oaf** *n* a clumsy, slow-witted, or boorish person. ➤ **oafish** *adj.*

**oak** *n* a tree with a tough hard wood and lobed leaves, which produces acorns.

**oaken** *adj* made of oak wood.

**OAP** *abbr Brit* old age pensioner.

**oar** *n* a long usu wooden shaft with a broad blade at one end, used for propelling a boat.

**oarsman** *or* **oarswoman** *n* (*pl* **oarsmen** *or* **oarswomen**) somebody who rows a boat.

**oasis** *n* (*pl* **oases**) **1** a fertile area in a desert or other dry region. **2** a place or time affording relaxation or relief.

**oast house** *n* a usu circular building housing a kiln for drying hops.

**oat** *n* (*usu in pl*) a cereal grass with a loosely branched flower head, producing grain used mainly to feed livestock. ✱ **sow one's wild oats** to enjoy a wild youth.

**oatcake** *n* a savoury biscuit made of oatmeal.

**oath** *n* (*pl* **oaths**) **1** a form of words by which one solemnly swears to do something *esp* to tell the truth. **2** a swearword. ✱ **on/under oath** bound by a solemn promise to tell the truth.

**oatmeal** *n* meal made from oats, used *esp* in porridge and oatcakes.

**obdurate** *adj* stubbornly refusing to change opinions, decisions, etc. ➤ **obduracy** *n.*

**OBE** *abbr* Officer of the Order of the British Empire.

**obedient** *adj* willingly carrying out the commands of another person. ➤ **obedience** *n,* **obediently** *adv.*

**obeisance** /oh'bay(i)səns/ *n* **1** a gesture made as a sign of respect or submission. **2** deference or homage.

**obelisk** *n* an upright four-sided pillar that tapers towards the top.

**obese** *adj* very overweight. ➤ **obesity** *n.*

**obey** *v* **1** to submit to the commands or authority of. **2** to comply with (instructions, the law, etc).

**obfuscate** *v* to make difficult to understand. ➤ **obfuscation** *n.*

**obituary** *n* (*pl* **-ies**) a short biography of a recently dead person, printed in a newspaper, etc.

**object**[1] *n* **1** something that can be seen and touched. **2** something that is being considered or examined. **3** something or somebody that arouses an emotion or provokes a reaction. **4** a goal or purpose. **5** a noun following a preposition or representing the recipient of the action of a verb.

**object**[2] *v* (*often* + to) to feel or express dislike or disapproval. ➤ **objector** *n.*

**objectify** *v* (**-ies, -ied**) **1** to represent (something abstract) as a concrete thing. **2** to reduce to the status of a mere object.

**objection** *n* a feeling or statement of dislike, disapproval, or opposition.

**objectionable** *adj* unpleasant or offensive.

**objective**[1] *adj* **1** dealing with facts without distortion by personal feelings or prejudices. **2** existing independently of the mind; belonging to the external world and observable or verifiable. ➤ **objectively** *adv,* **objectivity** *n.*

**objective**[2] *n* a goal or aim.

**objet d'art** /ˌobzhay 'dah/ *n* (*pl* **objets d'art** /ˌobzhay/) a usu small article of some artistic value.

**oblate** *adj* of a spheroid: flattened at the poles.

**oblation** *n* an offering made for religious purposes.

**obligate** *v* to compel legally or morally.

**obligation** *n* **1** something one is bound to do; a duty. **2** indebtedness for a service or favour.

**obligatory** *adj* compulsory.

**oblige** *v* **1** to compel by force, law, or circumstance. **2** to do a favour for. **3** (**be obliged**) to be grateful or indebted.

**obliging** *adj* eager to help; accommodating. ➤ **obligingly** *adv.*

**oblique** *adj* **1** sloping. **2** not straightforward or explicit; indirect. ➤ **obliquely** *adv.*

**obliterate** *v* **1** to destroy all trace of. **2** to make illegible. ➤ **obliteration** *n.*

**oblivion** *n* **1** the state of being oblivious. **2** the state of being forgotten or no longer existing.

**oblivious** *adj* (+ of/to) completely unaware.

**oblong**[1] *adj* rectangular with adjacent sides of unequal length.

**oblong**[2] *n* something that is oblong in shape.

**obloquy** *n* (*pl* **-ies**) **1** strongly worded condemnation. **2** discredit or disgrace.
**obnoxious** *adj* highly offensive or repugnant.
**oboe** *n* a woodwind musical instrument with a double reed. ➤ **oboist** *n.*
**obscene** *adj* **1** offending standards of sexual propriety or decency. **2** morally repugnant. ➤ **obscenely** *adv.*
**obscenity** *n* (*pl* **-ies**) **1** the state of being obscene. **2** an obscene act or utterance.
**obscure**[1] *adj* **1** hard to understand. **2** not well-known. **3** difficult to see or identify. ➤ **obscurely** *adv.*
**obscure**[2] *v* **1** to prevent from being seen, identified, or discovered. **2** to make indistinct or unintelligible.
**obscurity** *n* **1** the state of being little known. **2** the state of being difficult to understand.
**obsequies** /'obsikwiz/ *pl n formal* funeral rites.
**obsequious** *adj* excessively respectful and eager to oblige or admire; fawning. ➤ **obsequiously** *adv,* **obsequiousness** *n.*
**observance** *n* **1** (*usu in pl*) a customary *esp* religious rite or ceremony. **2** compliance with a custom, rule, or law.
**observant** *adj* **1** quick to notice. **2** paying close attention; watchful.
**observation** *n* **1** the act of observing, or the condition of being observed. **2** the gathering of information by noting facts or occurrences. **3** a remark or comment.
**observatory** *n* (*pl* **-ies**) a building containing a telescope for the observation of astronomical phenomena.
**observe** *v* **1** to perceive or take note of. **2** to keep a close watch on. **3** to act in conformity with (e.g. a law). **4** to celebrate or follow the traditional procedures for (e.g. a ceremony or festival). **5** to remark or comment. ➤ **observable** *adj,* **observer** *n.*
**obsess** *v* to preoccupy intensely or abnormally. ➤ **obsessed** *adj.*
**obsession** *n* **1** a persistent and usu excessive preoccupation with something or somebody. **2** something that preoccupies somebody. ➤ **obsessional** *adj.*
**obsessive** *adj* **1** suffering from an obsession. **2** excessive to the point of abnormality. ➤ **obsessively** *adv,* **obsessiveness** *n.*
**obsessive-compulsive** *adj* denoting a psychiatric disorder in which a particular type of behaviour is frequently repeated as a means of keeping fears or other unwelcome thoughts at bay.
**obsidian** *n* a usu black volcanic glass-like rock.
**obsolescent** *adj* becoming obsolete. ➤ **obsolescence** *n.*
**obsolete** *adj* **1** no longer in use. **2** outmoded.
**obstacle** *n* something that hinders or obstructs.
**obstetrician** *n* a doctor who specializes in obstetrics.
**obstetrics** *pl n* a branch of medicine dealing with the treatment of women during childbirth. ➤ **obstetric** *adj.*
**obstinate** *adj* **1** clinging stubbornly to an opinion, decision, or course of action. **2** not easily remedied or removed. ➤ **obstinacy** *n,* **obstinately** *adv.*
**obstreperous** *adj* noisy and unruly.
**obstruct** *v* **1** to block or close with an obstacle. **2** to impede the progress of; to hinder.
**obstruction** *n* **1** something that obstructs. **2** the act of deliberately hindering or delaying somebody or something.
**obstructive** *adj* deliberately hindering or delaying somebody or something.
**obtain** *v* **1** to gain by effort or request. **2** *formal* to be generally accepted or practised. ➤ **obtainable** *adj.*
**obtrude** *v* to thrust oneself or itself forward with unwelcome assertiveness. ➤ **obtrusion** *n.*
**obtrusive** *adj* unduly or irritatingly noticeable.
**obtuse** *adj* **1** lacking sensitivity or mental alertness. **2** of an angle: greater than 90° but less than 180°. **3** not pointed or sharp.
**obverse** *n* **1** the side of a coin, medal, etc that bears the principal design and lettering. **2** a counterpart or opposite.
**obviate** *v* to anticipate and dispose of (a difficulty, etc) in advance.
**obvious** *adj* **1** very easily perceived by the senses or understanding; clear. **2** lacking subtlety. ➤ **obviously** *adv.*
**ocarina** *n* a simple egg-shaped wind instrument with finger holes in its body.
**occasion**[1] *n* **1** a time at which something occurs. **2** a suitable opportunity. **3** *formal* a reason or grounds. **4** a special event or ceremony. ✱ **on occasion** from time to time. **rise to the occasion** to perform well when a situation demands it.
**occasion**[2] *v formal* to cause.
**occasional** *adj* **1** occurring at irregular or infrequent intervals. **2** acting in a specified capacity from time to time. ➤ **occasionally** *adv.*
**occidental** *or* **Occidental** *adj* of or situated in the countries of the West.
**occlude** *v* to stop up or block (a passage or opening).
**occult**[1] *n* (**the occult**) matters involving the action or influence of supernatural agencies or some secret knowledge of them. ➤ **occultism** *n,* **occultist** *n.*
**occult**[2] *adj* **1** involving supernatural powers. **2** known only to the initiated few; esoteric.
**occupancy** *n* (*pl* **-ies**) **1** the act of occupying land, a property, etc. **2** the proportion of a building, e.g. a hotel, that is occupied.

**occupant** *n* somebody who occupies a particular building.
**occupation** *n* **1** an activity by which one earns a living. **2** an activity in which one engages. **3** the act of taking possession or control of a place, *esp* by a foreign military force.
**occupational** *adj* of or resulting from a particular job or profession.
**occupational therapy** *n* creative activity used as therapy for promoting recovery or rehabilitation.
**occupy** *v* (**-ies, -ied**) **1** to engage the attention or energies of. **2** to fill up (a portion of space or time). **3** to take or maintain possession of (e.g. land). **4** to reside in or use (a building) as owner or tenant. ➤ **occupier** *n.*
**occur** *v* (**occurred, occurring**) **1** to happen. **2** to be found; to exist. **3** (+ to) to come to mind.
**occurrence** *n* **1** something that takes place; an event. **2** the act of occurring.
**ocean** *n* **1** any or all of the large expanses of salt water that cover much of the earth's surface. **2** *informal* (*in pl*) a huge amount.
**oceanic** /ohshi'anik/ *adj* relating to the oceans.
**oceanography** *n* the science dealing with oceans and their biology and resources. ➤ **oceanographer** *n.*
**ocelot** *n* a medium-sized wildcat of Central and South America with a dotted and striped coat.
**ochre** (*NAmer* **ocher**) *n* an earthy usu red or yellow pigment.
**o'clock** *adv* used in specifying the exact hour when telling the time.
**octagon** *n* a polygon with eight angles and eight sides. ➤ **octagonal** *adj.*
**octahedron** *n* (*pl* **octahedrons** *or* **octahedra**) a polyhedron with eight faces.
**octane** *n* a colourless liquid chemical compound occurring *esp* in petroleum.
**octave** *n* **1** a musical interval of eight notes on the diatonic scale. **2** the whole series of notes within this interval.
**octavo** /ok'tayvoh/ *n* (*pl* **-os**) a size of book page that is created when a standard sheet is folded into 8 leaves or 16 pages.
**octet** *n* **1** a group of eight instruments, voices, or performers. **2** a musical composition for an octet.
**October** *n* the tenth month of the year.
**octogenarian** *n* a person between 80 and 89 years old.
**octopus** *n* (*pl* **octopuses** *or* **octopi**) a sea creature with eight muscular arms equipped with suckers.
**ocular** *adj* of the eye.
**oculist** *n* an ophthalmologist or optician.
**OD** *v* (**OD's, OD'd, OD'ing**) to take an overdose of a drug.
**odalisque** *n* a female slave or concubine in a harem.
**odd** *adj* **1** different from the usual or conventional; strange. **2** left over when others are paired or grouped. **3** not matching. **4** of a number: not divisible by two without leaving a remainder. **5** occasional; spare: *at odd moments.* **6** somewhat more than the specified number: *300-odd pages.* ➤ **oddly** *adv,* **oddness** *n.*
**oddball** *n informal* an eccentric or peculiar person.
**oddity** *n* (*pl* **-ies**) **1** an odd person, thing, or event. **2** strangeness.
**odd man out** *n* somebody or something that differs from all the others in a group.
**oddment** *n* **1** something left over; a remnant. **2** (*in pl*) miscellaneous things.
**odds** *pl n* **1** the ratio between the amount to be paid for a winning bet and the amount of the bet. **2** (**the odds**) the probability, often expressed as a ratio, that one thing will happen rather than another. **3** (**the odds**) a difference in terms of advantage or disadvantage. ✻ **at odds** in disagreement or at variance.
**odds and ends** *pl n* miscellaneous items or remnants.
**odds-on** *adj* **1** viewed as having a better than even chance to win. **2** likely to succeed, happen, etc.
**ode** *n* a poem of medium length, often addressed to a particular person or thing or celebrating an event, and usu marked by an exalted tone.
**odious** *adj* arousing hatred or revulsion.
**odium** *n formal* general condemnation or disgrace.
**odoriferous** *adj* giving off an odour.
**odour** (*NAmer* **odor**) *n* a scent or smell. ➤ **odorous** *adj,* **odourless** *adj.*
**odyssey** *n* (*pl* **-eys**) a long and wandering journey or quest.
**OED** *abbr* Oxford English Dictionary.
**oedema** (*NAmer* **edema**) *n* abnormal swelling caused by an accumulation of liquid between tissue cells.
**oesophagus** (*NAmer* **esophagus**) /ee'sofəgəs/ *n* (*pl* **oesophagi** /-gie/) the muscular tube leading from the back of the mouth to the stomach; the gullet.
**oestrogen** (*NAmer* **estrogen**) *n* a steroid hormone that stimulates the development of secondary sex characteristics in females.
**oeuvre** /'uhvrə/ *n* all the works produced by a writer, artist, or composer, considered as a body.
**of** *prep* **1** used to indicate origin or derivation. **2** composed or made from. **3** containing. **4** from among. **5** belonging or related to. **6** possessing or characterized by. **7** connected with.
**of course** *adv* **1** as might be expected. **2** used in reply to express agreement or permission.
**off**[1] *adv* **1** from a place or position. **2** away in space or ahead in time. **3** away from a course or

direction. **4** so as not to be in contact or attached. **5** to or in a state of non-operation or suspension. **6** away from work. **7** into sleep or unconsciousness.

**off**[2] *prep* **1** used to indicate physical separation or distance from. **2** lying or turning aside from. **3** so as to become detached from. **4** not occupied in. **5** no longer interested in or using. **6** below the usual standard or level of.

**off**[3] *adj* **1** started on a journey or race. **2** cancelled. **3** not busy; slack. **4** no longer fresh; beginning to decay. **5** provided: *How are you off for socks?* **6** *informal* of behaviour: not what one has a right to expect.

**off**[4] *n* the start or outset.

**offal** *n* the inner organs, e.g. liver, kidney, etc, of an animal used as food.

**offbeat** *adj informal* unusual or unconventional.

**off chance** *n* a remote possibility. ✱ **on the off chance** just in case.

**off-colour** *adj* unwell.

**offcut** *n* a piece of e.g. fabric or wood left after the required amount has been cut.

**offence** (*NAmer* **offense**) *n* **1** a breach of a law, rule, etc; a crime. **2** a feeling of displeasure or resentment.

**offend** *v* **1** to cause pain or displeasure to; to hurt or insult. **2** to cause to feel indignation or disgust. **3** to commit a crime or wrongdoing. ➤ **offender** *n.*

**offensive**[1] *adj* **1** causing indignation, outrage, or disgust. **2** of or designed for attack. ➤ **offensively** *adv.*

**offensive**[2] *n* **1** an attacking attitude or position. **2** a large-scale military attack or non-military campaign.

**offer**[1] *v* **1** to present for acceptance, rejection, or consideration. **2** to make available; to provide. **3** to declare one's willingness (to do something).

**offer**[2] *n* **1** an undertaking to do or give something. **2** a price named by a prospective buyer. **3** an article on sale at a reduced price. ✱ **on offer 1** available. **2** for sale at a reduced price.

**offering** *n* something offered or presented, e.g. a sacrifice or donation.

**offertory** *n* (*pl* **-ies**) **1** the offering of the Communion bread and wine to God before consecration. **2** the collection of money from the congregation at public worship.

**offhand**[1] *or* **offhanded** *adj* **1** without proper courtesy or warmth. **2** informal or casual.

**offhand**[2] *adv* without forethought or preparation.

**office** *n* **1** a room in which administrative or clerical work is done. **2** a building where the business of a particular organization is carried out. **3** a position giving authority or having special responsibilities. **4** *formal* (*in pl*) services carried out for other people.

**officer** *n* **1** somebody who holds a position of authority in the armed forces. **2** a member of a police force. **3** somebody who holds a position with special duties or responsibilities, e.g. in a government or business.

**official**[1] *adj* **1** sanctioned or carried out by people in authority. **2** holding a position of authority. **3** suitable for or characteristic of people in authority. ➤ **officially** *adv.*

**official**[2] *n* somebody who holds a position of authority, *esp* in a public organization or institution. ➤ **officialdom** *n.*

**officiate** *v* **1** to perform an *esp* religious ceremony. **2** to act as an official.

**officious** *adj* overzealous in exercising authority, and tending to interfere in other people's affairs.

**offing** *n* ✱ **in the offing** likely to happen in the near future.

**off-licence** *n Brit* a shop licensed to sell alcoholic drinks to be consumed off the premises.

**off-line** *adv and adj* not connected to or controlled by a computer.

**off-load** *v* **1** to unload (cargo). **2** to get rid of (something unwanted).

**off-peak** *adj and adv* at a time of relatively light demand or activity.

**off-putting** *adj chiefly Brit, informal* disagreeable or disconcerting.

**offset** *v* (**offsetting,** *past tense and past part.* **offset**) to balance or compensate for.

**offshoot** *n* something that develops out of something else.

**offshore** *adj and adv* **1** away from the shore. **2** at a distance from the shore. **3** located or operating abroad.

**offside** *adv and adj* illegally in advance of the ball or puck in a team game.

**offspring** *n* (*pl* **offspring**) the progeny of a person, animal, or plant.

**offstage** *adv and adj* not visible to the audience in a theatre.

**off-white** *adj* of a yellowish or greyish white colour. ➤ **off-white** *n.*

**often** *adv* **1** at many times. **2** in many cases.

**ogle** *v* to stare at with sexual interest, *esp* offensively.

**ogre** *or* **ogress** *n* **1** a hideous giant of folklore believed to feed on human beings. **2** a dreaded person or thing.

**ohm** *n* the SI unit of electrical resistance.

**oik** *n slang* a vulgar, loud, or otherwise obnoxious person.

**oil**[1] *n* **1** a smooth greasy liquid substance, obtained from plants or animals, that is not soluble in water. **2** = PETROLEUM. **3** a substance derived from petroleum, used for fuel, lubrication, etc. **4** (*also in pl*) = OIL PAINT.

**oil**[2] *v* to apply oil to, *esp* for lubrication.

**oilfield** *n* a region rich in petroleum deposits.

**oil paint** *n* artist's paint consisting of ground pigment mixed with oil. ➤ **oil painting** *n.*

**oilskin** *n* **1** an oiled waterproof cloth. **2** an outer garment made of oilskin or other waterproof material.

**oily** *adj* (**-ier, -iest**) **1** resembling, containing, or covered with oil. **2** too eager to please or flatter. ➤ **oiliness** *n.*

**oink** *v* of a pig: to make a characteristic grunting noise. ➤ **oink** *n.*

**ointment** *n* a soothing or healing oily cream applied to the skin.

**OK**[1] *or* **okay** *interj* an expression of agreement or permission.

**OK**[2] *or* **okay** *adj* **1** quite good, but not outstanding. **2** permissible; acceptable. **3** unharmed or in good health.

**OK**[3] *adv* quite well; adequately or satisfactorily.

**OK**[4] *or* **okay** *v* (**OK's, OK'd, OK'ing** *or* **okays, okayed, okaying**) to give approval or authorization to.

**OK**[5] *or* **okay** *n* (*pl* **OK's** *or* **okays**) an approval or endorsement.

**okapi** /oh'kahpi/ *n* (*pl* **okapis** *or* **okapi**) an African mammal closely related to the giraffe but with a shorter neck and ring marks on the upper legs.

**okra** *n* the long green pods of a tropical plant, used as a vegetable.

**old** *adj* **1** having lived or existed for many years. **2** having lived or existed for a specified period of time. **3** dating from the past, *esp* the remote past. **4** persisting from an earlier time. **5** of long standing. **6** former.

**old age** *n* the final stage of the normal life span.

**old boy** *n chiefly Brit* **1** a former pupil of a particular school. **2** *informal* an old man.

**olden** *adj literary* of a bygone era.

**Old English** *n* the earliest form of the English language, dating from around the seventh to the eleventh centuries; Anglo-Saxon.

**old-fashioned** *adj* belonging to a past era; outdated.

**old girl** *n chiefly Brit* **1** a former pupil of a particular school. **2** *informal* an old woman.

**old guard** *n* the conservative members of a group.

**old hand** *n* somebody with a great deal of experience.

**old hat** *adj* tediously familiar or old-fashioned.

**old maid** *n derog* a single woman of advanced age.

**old master** *n* **1** a distinguished European painter of the 16th to early 18th cents. **2** a painting produced by an old master.

**Old Nick** *n informal* the devil.

**Old Norse** *n* the ancient or medieval language of Scandinavia and Iceland.

**Old Testament** *n* a collection of writings forming the Jewish canon of Scripture and the first part of the Christian Bible.

**old wives' tale** *n* a traditional superstitious notion.

**Old World** *n* (**the Old World**) Europe, Asia, and Africa.

**oleaginous** *adj* **1** oily. **2** obsequious or unctuous in manner.

**O level** *n* a former secondary school examination in England and Wales, replaced by the GCSE.

**olfactory** *adj* relating to the sense of smell.

**oligarch** *n* a member of the ruling group in an oligarchy.

**oligarchy** *n* (*pl* **-ies**) **1** a state or organization in which a small group exercises control. **2** a small group governing or exercising control. ➤ **oligarchic** *adj.*

**olive** *n* **1** a small green or purplish black fruit with a stone, used as a food and a source of oil. **2** the small evergreen tree that bears this fruit. **3** (*also* **olive green**) a dull greyish green colour. ➤ **olive** *adj.*

**olive branch** *n* an offer or gesture of conciliation.

**olive oil** *n* oil obtained from ripe olives, used in cooking and salad dressings.

**Olympiad** *n* a holding of the Olympic Games.

**Olympian**[1] *adj* **1** of or dwelling on Mount Olympus. **2** of the Olympic Games.

**Olympian**[2] *n* **1** any of the ancient Greek deities dwelling on Olympus. **2** a participant in the Olympic Games.

**Olympic** *adj* relating to the Olympic Games.

**Olympic Games** *pl n* **1** an international sports meeting held once every four years in a different host country. **2** an ancient Greek festival held every four years with athletic, literary, and musical contests.

**Olympics** *pl n* (**the Olympics**) the modern Olympic Games.

**ombudsman** *n* (*pl* **ombudsmen**) a government official appointed to investigate complaints made by individuals against government or public bodies.

**omega** *n* the 24th and last letter of the Greek alphabet (Ω, ω).

**omelette** (*NAmer* **omelet**) *n* a mixture of beaten eggs cooked in a shallow pan until set.

**omen** *n* an event believed to be a sign of some future occurrence.

**omicron** *n* the 15th letter of the Greek alphabet (Ο, ο).

**ominous** *adj* suggesting future disaster or evil. ➤ **ominously** *adv.*

**omission** *n* **1** the act of omitting. **2** something omitted. **3** failure to do something.

**omit** *v* (**omitted, omitting**) **1** to leave out or unmentioned. **2** to fail to do.

**omni-** *comb. form* all or universally: *omniscient.*

**omnibus** *n* **1** a book containing reprints of a number of works originally published separately. **2** a television or radio programme consisting of two or more episodes of a series, originally broadcast separately. **3** *formal, dated* a bus.

**omnipotent** *adj* having unlimited or very great power. ➤ **omnipotence** *n.*

**omnipresent** *adj* **1** present in all places at all times. **2** very widespread or frequently encountered. ➤ **omnipresence** *n.*

**omniscient** *adj* knowing everything. ➤ **omniscience** *n.*

**omnivorous** *adj* **1** feeding on both animal and vegetable substances. **2** avidly taking in, *esp* reading, everything.

**on**[1] *prep* **1** in contact with or supported from below by. **2** attached or fastened to. **3** carried on the person of. **4** positioned at or towards. **5** with regard to; concerning. **6** belonging to (e.g. a team). **7** paid for by. **8** in the specified state, process, manner, etc: *on fire.* **9** using by way of transport. **10** regularly taking (a drug). **11** indicating a time, *esp* a day of the week, when something happens. **12** in the course of. **13** broadcast by or recorded with.

**on**[2] *adv* **1** so as to be supported from below. **2** so as to be worn. **3** so as to be attached. **4** ahead or forwards in space or time. **5** with the specified part forward. **6** without interruption. **7** in or into operation.

**on**[3] *adj* **1** taking place. **2** performing or broadcasting. **3** operating. **4** *chiefly Brit* possible or practicable.

**onanism** *n* masturbation.

**once**[1] *adv* **1** one time and no more. **2** at some indefinite time in the past; formerly. ✱ **at once** **1** immediately. **2** simultaneously. **once again/more** **1** now again as before. **2** for one more time. **once in a while** occasionally. **once or twice** a few times. **once upon a time** used as a traditional formula to begin a children's story: at some time in the past.

**once**[2] *conj* from the moment when; as soon as.

**once-over** *n informal* a swift appraising glance.

**oncoming** *adj* approaching from the front.

**one**[1] *adj* **1** being a single unit or thing. **2** being a particular but unspecified instance. **3** the same; identical. **4** in a state of agreement; united. **5** being some unspecified future time. **6** being a particular object or person.

**one**[2] *pron* (*pl* **ones**) **1** an indefinitely indicated person; anybody at all. **2** used to refer to a noun or noun phrase previously mentioned or understood.

**one**[3] *n* **1** the number 1. **2** the first in a set or series. **3** a particular example or instance. ✱ **at one** in agreement or harmony. **one after another/the other** in succession. **one by one** singly or successively. **one or other** either; any. **one or two** a few.

**one-armed bandit** *n* a fruit machine that is operated by a lever on one side.

**one-liner** *n* a short funny remark.

**oneness** *n* the state of being whole, identical, or in agreement.

**one-off**[1] *adj chiefly Brit* intended as a single and unrepeated item or occurrence.

**one-off**[2] *n* a unique person or thing.

**onerous** *adj* representing or involving a burden. ➤ **onerousness** *n.*

**oneself** *pron* used reflexively or for emphasis to refer to an indefinitely indicated person or to people in general.

**one-upmanship** *n* the art of gaining a psychological advantage over others.

**ongoing** *adj* **1** actually in progress. **2** growing or developing.

**onion** *n* a pungent smelling, strong tasting edible bulb that is used as a vegetable.

**on-line** *adv and adj* connected to or controlled by a computer or network.

**onlooker** *n* a passive spectator.

**only**[1] *adj* **1** alone in its class or kind; sole. **2** without a brother or sister.

**only**[2] *adv* **1** nothing more than; merely. **2** solely or exclusively. **3** with nevertheless the final result. **4** no earlier than.

**only**[3] *conj informal* **1** but or however. **2** were it not for the fact that.

**onomatopoeia** *n* the use of words intended to be a vocal imitation of the sound associated with the thing or action designated, e.g. *buzz.* ➤ **onomatopoeic** *adj.*

**onrush** *n* a forceful rushing forwards.

**onset** *n* a time or point at which something begins.

**onshore** *adj and adv* **1** towards the shore. **2** on or near the shore.

**onside** *adv and adj* **1** in a position permitted by the rules of the game; not offside. **2** in a position of agreement or support.

**onslaught** *n* a fierce attack.

**onstage** *adj and adv* on or onto the stage; in view of the audience.

**onto** *or* **on to** *prep* **1** to a position on. **2** in or into a state of awareness about. **3** *chiefly Brit* in or into contact with.

**ontology** *n* a branch of philosophy concerned with the nature of being. ➤ **ontological** *adj.*

**onus** *n* a duty or responsibility.

**onward**[1] *adj* directed or moving forwards.

**onward**[2] *adv* = ONWARDS.

**onwards** *adv* towards a point lying ahead in space or time.

**onyx** *n* a translucent semiprecious stone with layers of different colours.

**oodles** *pl n informal* a great quantity; a lot.

**oomph** *n informal* vitality or enthusiasm.

**ooze**[1] *v* **1** of a liquid: to move or be emitted slowly. **2** to display (a quality) in abundance.

**ooze**[2] *n* the act of oozing.

**op** *n informal* a military or surgical operation.
**opacity** *n* the quality of being opaque.
**opal** *n* a semitransparent iridescent mineral used as a gem.
**opalescent** *adj* reflecting a milky iridescent light.
**opaque** *adj* **1** not able to be seen through. **2** hard to understand; unintelligible.
**op. cit.** *abbr* (Latin) opere citato = in the work cited.
**open**[1] *adj* **1** allowing access or passage; not shut or locked. **2** not fastened or sealed. **3** not covered or protected. **4** not enclosed, blocked, or restricted. **5** having the parts or surfaces spread out or unfolded. **6** in operation, *esp* ready for business or use. **7** not disguised, concealed, or kept secret. **8** (+ to) liable to undergo (e.g. attack or criticism). **9** (*often* + to) available or remaining available. **10** not finally decided or settled. **11** (+ to) willing to receive and consider. **12** candid or frank. **13** unprejudiced: *an open mind.* ➤ **opener** *n*, **openly** *adv*, **openness** *n.*
**open**[2] *v* **1** to make or become open. **2** to unfold or spread out. **3** to start operating for business. **4** to begin an activity. **5** to declare to be available for use, especially in a ceremony. **6** (+ into/onto) to give access.
**open**[3] *n* **1** (**the open**) a large outdoor space, *esp* in the countryside. **2** (*often* **Open**) a contest in which anybody can compete.
**open air** *n* (**the open air**) a large outdoor space; outdoors. ➤ **open-air** *adj.*
**open-and-shut** *adj* easily settled.
**opencast** *adj* of a mine or mining: worked from or carried out on the earth's surface by removing material covering the mineral.
**open-heart surgery** *n* surgery in which the heart is actually exposed.
**open house** ✱ **keep open house** to be ready to receive visitors at all times.
**opening**[1] *n* **1** a space through which something can pass; a gap. **2** a beginning or first part. **3** a ceremony marking the first time a building, exhibition, etc can be visited by the public. **4** a first performance. **5** a favourable opportunity; a chance. **6** an opportunity for employment; a vacancy.
**opening**[2] *adj* coming at or marking the beginning of something.
**open letter** *n* a letter addressed to an individual but published so that it can be read by the general public.
**open market** *n* a market based on free competition and an unrestricted flow of goods.
**open-minded** *adj* receptive to new arguments or ideas. ➤ **open-mindedness** *n.*
**open-plan** *adj* having no or few internal dividing walls.
**open verdict** *n* a verdict at an inquest that does not state the cause of death.
**opera**[1] *n* a drama set to music and made up of vocal pieces and orchestral music.
**opera**[2] *n* pl of OPUS.
**operable** *adj* **1** suitable for surgical treatment. **2** fit or possible to use.
**opera glasses** *pl n* small binoculars suitable for use at the opera or theatre.
**operate** *v* **1** to function or cause (e.g. a machine) to function. **2** to act or produce a desired effect. **3** to be in effect. **4** to carry out trade or business. **5** to carry on a military or naval action. **6** (*often* + on) to perform surgery.
**operatic** *adj* **1** of opera. **2** overtly theatrical in behaviour. ➤ **operatically** *adv.*
**operation** *n* **1** the act of operating. **2** the state of being functional or operative. **3** an action or manoeuvre, *esp* an organized or complex one, e.g. by the military. **4** a surgical procedure carried out on a living body with special instruments. **5** a single step performed by a computer in executing a program. **6** a business organization.
**operational** *adj* **1** relating to or involved in the operations of an organization. **2** currently functioning or able to function. ➤ **operationally** *adv.*
**operative**[1] *adj* **1** in force or operation. **2** significant or relevant. **3** of or using a surgical operation.
**operative**[2] *n* a worker.
**operator** *n* **1** somebody who operates a machine or device. **2** somebody who owns or runs a business, organization, etc. **3** somebody who works at a telephone switchboard. **4** *informal* somebody who manipulates people or situations shrewdly.
**operetta** *n* a less formal or serious opera, usu on a romantic or humorous theme.
**ophthalmic** *adj* relating to the eye and diseases of the eye.
**ophthalmology** *n* the branch of medical science dealing with the structure, functions, and diseases of the eye. ➤ **ophthalmologist** *n.*
**opiate** *n* a preparation or derivative of opium.
**opine** *v formal* to state as an opinion.
**opinion** *n* **1** a view or judgment formed about a particular matter. **2** a belief that is not supported by positive knowledge. **3** a generally held view. **4** a formal expression by an expert of his or her professional judgment or advice. ✱ **matter of opinion** something that cannot be decided objectively or proved conclusively.
**opinionated** *adj* having strong opinions and always ready to express them.
**opinion poll** *n* a survey conducted by questioning a selected number of people to establish public opinion on some matter.
**opium** *n* an addictive drug derived from the juice of poppy seeds.

**opossum** *n* (*pl* **opossums** *or* **opossum**) **1** an American tree-dwelling marsupial with a prehensile tail. **2** = POSSUM.

**opponent** *n* **1** somebody who takes the opposite side in a contest, conflict, etc. **2** somebody who opposes something, e.g. a plan or proposal.

**opportune** *adj* **1** suitable for a particular occurrence or action. **2** occurring at an appropriate time.

**opportunist** *n* somebody who takes advantage of opportunities with little regard for principles or consequences. ➤ **opportunist** *adj*, **opportunistic** *adj*.

**opportunity** *n* (*pl* **-ies**) **1** a favourable set of circumstances. **2** a chance for advancement or progress.

**oppose** *v* **1** to be hostile to; to resist. **2** to fight or compete with. **3** to place opposite or against something else, e.g. as a contrast or counterbalance. * **as opposed to** in contrast to. ➤ **opposing** *adj*.

**opposite**[1] *adj* **1** positioned at a distance from and facing somebody or something else, often on the other side of something. **2** diametrically different; contrary. **3** being the other of a matching or contrasting pair: *the opposite sex*.

**opposite**[2] *prep* **1** across from and usu facing. **2** in a role in a play or film complementary to that of.

**opposite**[3] *adv* on or to an opposite side.

**opposite**[4] *n* an opposite person or thing.

**opposition** *n* **1** hostility or resistance. **2** the state of being opposed or opposite. **3** a body of people opposing something. **4** (*often* **Opposition**) the main political party opposing the party in power. ➤ **oppositional** *adj*.

**oppress** *v* **1** to treat in a harsh or authoritarian manner. **2** to be a heavy burden on the mind or spirit of. ➤ **oppression** *n*, **oppressor** *n*.

**oppressive** *adj* **1** unreasonably harsh or severe. **2** causing a sense of being mentally weighed down. **3** of the weather: stiflingly warm and windless; close. ➤ **oppressively** *adv*.

**opprobrious** *adj formal* sharply critical, scornful, or abusive.

**opprobrium** *n formal* **1** scornful criticism. **2** the public disgrace that results from shameful behaviour.

**opt** *v* to make a choice.

**optic**[1] *adj* of vision or the eye.

**optic**[2] *n Brit* a device fitted to the neck of an inverted bottle to deliver a measure of alcoholic spirit.

**optical** *adj* relating to optics, vision, or light.

**optical fibre** *n* a very thin glass fibre used to transmit light.

**optical illusion** *n* something that makes observers believe they are seeing something that they are not.

**optician** *n* somebody who examines eyes and prescribes correctional lenses for eye defects.

**optics** *pl n* the science of the nature, properties, and uses of light.

**optimal** *adj* most satisfactory. ➤ **optimally** *adv*.

**optimism** *n* a tendency to emphasize favourable aspects of situations or events or to expect the best possible outcome. ➤ **optimist** *n*.

**optimistic** *adj* emphasizing favourable aspects or expecting a successful outcome. ➤ **optimistically** *adv*.

**optimize** *or* **-ise** *v* to make as effective or advantageous as possible. ➤ **optimization** *n*.

**optimum**[1] *adj* most favourable or desirable.

**optimum**[2] *n* (*pl* **optima** *or* **optimums**) the most favourable or desirable condition.

**option** *n* **1** an alternative course of action; a choice. **2** the right to choose. **3** a right to buy or sell something at a specified price during a stipulated period.

**optional** *adj* available as a choice; not compulsory. ➤ **optionally** *adv*.

**optometry** *n* the profession of examining the eye for defects and prescribing correctional lenses or exercises. ➤ **optometrist** *n*.

**opt out** *v* to choose not to participate in something.

**opulent** *adj* rich or luxurious. ➤ **opulence** *n*, **opulently** *adv*.

**opus** *n* (*pl* **opera** *or* **opuses**) **1** a musical composition or set of compositions. **2** an artistic work of any kind.

**or** *conj* **1** used to join two or more alternatives. **2** used to introduce a word or phrase that defines or explains a preceding word or phrase. **3** otherwise.

**-or** *suffix* denoting somebody or something that performs an action: *vendor*.

**oracle** *n* a priest or priestess of ancient Greece or Rome who delivered answers, purporting to come from a god and often cryptically worded, to questions regarding the future.

**oracular** *adj* resembling an oracle in authority or obscurity of expression.

**oral**[1] *adj* **1** involving speech rather than writing. **2** of, taken through, or affecting the mouth. ➤ **orally** *adv*.

**oral**[2] *n* an oral examination.

**orange** *n* **1** a spherical fruit with a reddish yellow rind and sweet juicy edible pulp. **2** the colour of oranges, between red and yellow in the spectrum.

**orangeade** *n* sweetened orange juice mixed with carbonated water.

**orang-utan** *or* **orang-utang** *n* a tree-dwelling anthropoid ape with orange-brown skin and hair and very long arms.

**oration** *n* a formal speech.

**orator** *n* a skilled public speaker.

**oratorio** *n* (*pl* **-os**) a large-scale choral work usu with orchestral accompaniment and based on a religious subject.

**oratory[1]** *n* (*pl* **-ies**) a place of prayer, *esp* a private or institutional chapel.

**oratory[2]** *n* **1** the art of public speaking. **2** impressive or eloquent speech. ➤ **oratorical** *adj.*

**orb** *n* **1** a golden globe surmounted by a cross, symbolizing royal power. **2** a spherical object.

**orbit[1]** *n* **1** a path followed regularly by a moon, spacecraft or satellite round a celestial body. **2** a sphere of activity or influence.

**orbit[2]** *v* (**orbited, orbiting**) to revolve in an orbit round (e.g. a celestial body).

**orbital** *adj* **1** relating to an orbit in space. **2** of a road: bypassing and circling a major city.

**orca** *n* = KILLER WHALE.

**orchard** *n* a usu enclosed area in which fruit trees are planted.

**orchestra** *n* **1** a large group of musicians, *esp* one comprising string, woodwind, brass, and percussion sections. **2** = ORCHESTRA PIT. ➤ **orchestral** *adj.*

**orchestra pit** *n* in a theatre, the space in front of the stage where the members of the orchestra sit.

**orchestrate** *v* **1** to arrange (music) for an orchestra. **2** to arrange cleverly to achieve the desired outcome. ➤ **orchestration** *n.*

**orchid** *n* a plant having colourful flowers with an enlarged liplike middle petal.

**ordain** *v* **1** to invest with the authority of a priest or minister. **2** to order by decree or law.

**ordeal** *n* a severe or testing experience.

**order[1]** *n* **1** a command. **2** a request for goods to be supplied, food to be served, work to be done, etc. **3** regular, correct, or harmonious arrangement. **4** an arrangement of objects, people, etc according to sequence in space, time, value or importance. **5** a proper, orderly, or functioning condition. **6** the rule of law or proper authority. **7** the customary procedure, e.g. for a debate or a religious service. **8** a category or kind. **9** a rank or group in a community. **10** a category in the classification of living things ranking above the family and below the class. **11** a religious body or community living under a specific rule. **12** (*in pl*) the office of a person in the Christian ministry. **13** a group of people who have been awarded a specific type of honour, *esp* a knighthood: *the Order of the Bath.* ✱ **in/of the order of** approximately. **out of order 1** not in the correct sequence. **2** not in working condition. **3** *informal* not acceptable or appropriate.

**order[2]** *v* **1** to put in order; to arrange. **2** to give a command to or for. **3** to place an order for (e.g. goods).

**orderly[1]** *adj* **1** arranged or carried out in a neat and methodical way. **2** well behaved or peaceful. ➤ **orderliness** *n.*

**orderly[2]** *n* (*pl* **-ies**) **1** a soldier assigned to carry messages, relay orders, etc for a superior officer. **2** a hospital attendant who does routine or heavy work.

**ordinal** *adj* of a specified order or rank in a series.

**ordinal number** *n* a number, e.g. first, second, or third, designating the place occupied by an item in a series.

**ordinance** *n* **1** an authoritative order or regulation. **2** a prescribed practice or ceremony.

**ordinary** *adj* **1** routine or usual. **2** not exceptional; commonplace. ✱ **out of the ordinary** not usual or customary. ➤ **ordinarily** *adv,* **ordinariness** *n.*

**Ordinary level** *n* = O LEVEL.

**ordination** *n* the act of ordaining somebody as a priest or minister.

**ordnance** *n* **1** military supplies. **2** heavy artillery.

**ordure** *n formal* excrement.

**ore** *n* a mineral containing a metal or other valuable constituent.

**oregano** /ori'gahnoh, ə'regənoh/ *n* a bushy plant whose leaves are used as a herb in cooking.

**organ** *n* **1** a musical instrument with a keyboard and sets of pipes activated by compressed air. **2** an electronic keyboard instrument producing a similar sound. **3** a specialized biological structure, e.g. the heart or a leaf, performing some specific function in an organism. **4** *formal* a newspaper or periodical. ➤ **organist** *n.*

**organic** *adj* **1** of or derived from living organisms. **2** of food, farming, etc: produced or carried out without the aid of chemical fertilizers, pesticides, etc. **3** of or arising in a bodily organ. **4** of e.g. development: proceeding in a natural and usu gradual and unforced manner. **5** containing, or dealing with materials containing, carbon compounds. ➤ **organically** *adv.*

**organism** *n* **1** an individual member of a biological species; a being. **2** a complex structure of interdependent elements.

**organization** *or* **-isation** *n* **1** the act of organizing. **2** the state of being arranged or proceeding in an orderly manner. **3** an association of people undertaking a particular activity, e.g. a business or a political party. ➤ **organizational** *adj.*

**organize** *or* **-ise** *v* **1** to arrange in an orderly way or so as to form a functioning whole. **2** to plan and make the necessary preparations for (an event). ➤ **organizer** *n.*

**orgasm** *n* the climax of sexual excitement. ➤ **orgasmic** *adj.*

**orgy** *n* (*pl* **-ies**) **1** a wild party characterized by sexual promiscuity, drunken revelry, etc. **2** an excessive indulgence in a specified activity. ➤ **orgiastic** *adj.*

**oriel window** *n* a bay window projecting from an upper storey.

**orient**[1] *n* (**the Orient**) *dated* the countries of eastern Asia, *esp* China, Japan, and their neighbours.

**orient**[2] *v* = ORIENTATE.

**oriental** *adj* (*often* **Oriental**) from or characteristic of the Orient.

**orientate** *v chiefly Brit* **1** to set in position in relation to the points of the compass. **2** to adjust to a particular environment or situation. * **orientate oneself** to ascertain one's position in unfamiliar surroundings.

**orientation** *n* **1** the act of orientating. **2** an arrangement, alignment, or relative position. **3** a lasting tendency of thought, inclination, or interest.

**orienteering** *n* a sport in which contestants have to cross unfamiliar country on foot using a map and compass.

**orifice** *n* an opening.

**origami** /ori'gahmi/ *n* the Japanese art of folding paper into complex shapes.

**origin** *n* **1** a source or starting-point. **2** ancestry or parentage.

**original**[1] *adj* **1** initial or earliest. **2** not secondary, derivative, or imitative. **3** inventive or creative. ➤ **originality** *n*, **originally** *adv.*

**original**[2] *n* something from which a copy, reproduction, or translation is made.

**original sin** *n* in Christianity, the innate sinfulness of all human beings that resulted from Adam's disobedience to God.

**originate** *v* **1** to begin or come into existence. **2** to bring into existence. ➤ **origination** *n*, **originator** *n.*

**ormolu** *n* gilded brass or bronze used to decorate furniture, ornaments, etc.

**ornament**[1] *n* **1** something that adds beauty to a person or thing. **2** a small decorative object. **3** decoration or embellishment. ➤ **ornamental** *adj.*

**ornament**[2] *v* to decorate or embellish. ➤ **ornamentation** *n.*

**ornate** *adj* elaborately or excessively decorated. ➤ **ornately** *adv.*

**ornithology** *n* a branch of zoology dealing with birds. ➤ **ornithological** *adj*, **ornithologist** *n.*

**orphan**[1] *n* a child whose parents are dead.

**orphan**[2] *v* to make (somebody) an orphan.

**orphanage** *n* an institution for the care of orphans.

**orthodontics** *pl n* a branch of dentistry dealing with the correction of irregularities of the teeth. ➤ **orthodontic** *adj*, **orthodontist** *n.*

**orthodox** *adj* **1** conforming to established or official doctrine or practice. **2** conventional or normal. **3** (**Orthodox**) of or denoting any of the Eastern Churches, e.g. in Greece or Russia, headed by the patriarch of Constantinople.

**orthodoxy** *n* (*pl* **-ies**) **1** being orthodox. **2** an orthodox belief or practice.

**orthography** *n* (*pl* **-ies**) the spelling system of a language. ➤ **orthographic** *adj.*

**orthopaedics** (*NAmer* **orthopedics**) *pl n* a branch of medicine dealing with the correction of skeletal and muscular deformities. ➤ **orthopaedic** *adj.*

**Os** *abbr* the chemical symbol for osmium.

**Oscar** *n* a gold statuette awarded for outstanding achievement in the cinema.

**oscillate** *v* **1** to swing backward and forward like a pendulum. **2** to vary between opposing beliefs, feelings, courses of action, etc. ➤ **oscillation** *n*, **oscillator** *n.*

**osier** *n* a willow with pliable twigs that are used for furniture and basketry.

**osmium** *n* a hard brittle blue-grey metallic element.

**osmosis** *n* **1** movement of a solvent through a membrane into a solution of higher concentration. **2** a process of gradual assimilation, e.g. of knowledge. ➤ **osmotic** *adj*, **osmotically** *adv.*

**osprey** *n* (*pl* **-eys**) a large fish-eating hawk with dark brown and white plumage.

**osseous** *adj technical* consisting of bone.

**ossify** *v* (**-ies, -ied**) **1** to change into bone. **2** to become inflexible in habit or attitude. ➤ **ossification** *n.*

**ostensible** *adj* seeming to be so, but not necessarily true or real. ➤ **ostensibly** *adv.*

**ostentation** *n* unnecessary display of wealth, knowledge, etc designed to attract attention.

**ostentatious** *adj* designed to impress or attract attention. ➤ **ostentatiously** *adv.*

**osteoarthritis** *n* a degenerative form of arthritis usu associated with increasing age. ➤ **osteoarthritic** *adj.*

**osteopathy** *n* a system of treatment of disease based on the manipulation of bones or other parts of the body. ➤ **osteopath** *n.*

**osteoporosis** *n* a disease that causes the bones to become thin, brittle, and porous.

**ostinato** *n* (*pl* **-os**) a musical figure repeated persistently throughout a composition.

**ostler** (*NAmer* **hostler**) *n* formerly, a groom or stableman at an inn.

**ostracize** *or* **-ise** *v* to exclude from a group or society over a period of time and have nothing to do with. ➤ **ostracism** *n.*

**ostrich** *n* a large flightless African bird that has dark plumage, a long neck, and long legs.

**other**[1] *adj* **1** distinct from that or those previously mentioned. **2** not the same; different. **3** additional or further. **4** second; alternate: *every other Tuesday.* **5** far or opposite. **6** recently past: *the other day.*

**other**[2] *pron* **1** the remaining or opposite one. **2** a different or additional one.

**otherness** *n* the state of being other or different.

**otherwise** *adv* **1** in different circumstances. **2** in other respects. **3** in a different way. **4** if not; or else.

**otherworldly** *adj* **1** suggestive of a spiritual or non-terrestrial realm of existence. **2** concerned with spiritual or intellectual matters and ignoring practical realities.

**otiose** *adj formal* futile or pointless.

**OTT** *abbr* over the top.

**otter** *n* (*pl* **otters** *or* **otter**) an aquatic fish-eating mammal with webbed feet and a long streamlined body.

**ottoman** *n* (*pl* **ottomans**) a low upholstered seat without a back or arms.

**oubliette** /oohbli'et/ *n* a dungeon with an opening only at the top.

**ought** *v aux* (*third person sing. present tense* **ought,** *past tense in reported speech* **ought**) **1** used to express moral obligation. **2** used to express what is advisable or recommended. **3** used to express probability or expectation.

**oughtn't** *contraction* ought not.

**Ouija board** /'weejə, 'weeji/ *n trademark* a board with letters around the edge and a moving pointer, used to produce messages in spiritualistic seances.

**ounce** *n* **1** a unit of weight equal to one sixteenth of a pound (about 28.35g). **2** the least amount.

**our** *adj* **1** belonging to or associated with me and one or more other people. **2** belonging to or associated with people in general.

**ours** *pron* the one or ones that belong to or are associated with us.

***Usage Note:*** Note that there is no apostrophe in *ours.*

**ourselves** *pron* used reflexively or for emphasis to refer to the people speaking or to a person speaking and associated people.

**-ous** *suffix* full of or characterized by: *envious.* ➤ **-ously** *suffix.*

**oust** *v* to remove *esp* from a position of authority, or supplant.

**out**[1] *adv* **1** away from the inside or centre. **2** away from a place. **3** away from one's home or business. **4** clearly in or into view or public knowledge. **5** inaccurate in reckoning. **6** no longer in vogue or fashion. **7** to the fullest extent or degree; completely. **8** aloud. **9** so as to be eliminated, *esp* from a game. **10** in or into a state of unconsciousness. ✱ **have it out** *informal* to settle a matter of contention by discussion or a fight. **out of 1** from within to the outside of. **2** beyond the range or limits of. **3** away from. **4** used to indicate a position or state that is not correct or desirable: *out of alignment.* **5** used to indicate origin or cause. **6** using the specified material. **7** used to indicate exclusion from or deprivation of. **8** from among.

**out**[2] *v informal* to reveal that (somebody) is homosexual.

**out**[3] *adj* **1** directed outwards. **2** not permissible, possible, or worth considering. **3** in cricket, baseball, etc, not allowed to continue batting. **4** of a ball, shot, etc: landing outside the prescribed area. **5** *informal* open about one's homosexuality.

**out**[4] *prep non-standard or NAmer* out of.

**outback** *n* (**the outback**) remote rural areas, *esp* in Australia.

**outbid** *v* (**outbidding,** *past tense and past part.* **outbid**) to make a higher bid than.

**outboard**[1] *adv and adj* on or towards the outside of a ship or an aircraft.

**outboard**[2] *n* an outboard motor.

**outboard motor** *n* a motor, propeller, and rudder attached as a unit to the stern of a small boat.

**outbreak** *n* a sudden or violent occurrence of something.

**outbuilding** *n* a smaller building separate from but belonging to a main building.

**outburst** *n* **1** a violent expression of feeling. **2** a surge of activity or growth.

**outcast** *n* a person who is rejected by society.

**outclass** *v* to far surpass in quality, skill, etc.

**outcome** *n* a result.

**outcrop** *n* the part of a rock formation that appears at the surface of the ground.

**outcry** *n* (*pl* **-ies**) a public expression of anger or disapproval.

**outdated** *adj* old-fashioned or obsolete.

**outdistance** *v* to go far ahead of (somebody), e.g. in a race.

**outdo** *v* (**outdoes,** *past tense* **outdid,** *past part.* **outdone**) to surpass in action or performance.

**outdoor** *adj* **1** situated, performed, or used outdoors. **2** fond of open-air activities.

**outdoors**[1] *adv* in or into the open air.

**outdoors**[2] *n* a place or the whole area outside buildings; the open air.

**outer** *adj* **1** external. **2** situated farther out.

**outermost** *adj* farthest from the centre.

**outface** *v* to cause (somebody) to waver or submit by confronting them unflinchingly.

**outfall** *n* the outlet for a river, lake, drain, sewer, etc.

**outfit**[1] *n* **1** a set of garments worn together. **2** *informal* a group that works as a team.

**outfit**[2] *v* (**outfitted, outfitting**) to provide with an outfit. ➤ **outfitter** *n.*

**outflank** *v* **1** to outmanoeuvre (an opposing force) by going round their flank. **2** to gain an advantage over (somebody) by doing something unexpected.

**outfox** *v* to get the better of by cunning.

**outgoing** *adj* **1** about to give up a position or office. **2** going away; departing. **3** friendly or sociable.

**outgoings** *pl n* expenditure.

**outgrow** *v* (**outgrew, outgrown**) **1** to grow too large for (e.g. clothes). **2** to lose (e.g. a habit) as one grows older.
**outhouse** *n* an outbuilding.
**outing** *n* a short pleasure trip.
**outlandish** *adj* strikingly unusual; bizarre.
**outlast** *v* to last longer than.
**outlaw**[1] *n* a fugitive from the law.
**outlaw**[2] *v* to make illegal; to ban.
**outlay** *n* expenditure or a payment.
**outlet** *n* **1** a place or opening through which something, *esp* a liquid or gas, is let out. **2** a means of release or expression for e.g. an emotion or talent. **3** a shop or other agency through which a product is sold.
**outline**[1] *n* **1** a line around the outer edge of something, indicating its shape. **2** a drawing showing the outline of something with no shading or detail. **3** a plan, draft, summary showing the main features only.
**outline**[2] *v* **1** to draw the outline of. **2** to summarize, or indicate the principal features of.
**outlive** *v* to live longer than.
**outlook** *n* **1** a view from a particular place. **2** an attitude or point of view. **3** a prospect for the future.
**outlying** *adj* remote from a centre or main point.
**outmanoeuvre** (*NAmer* **outmaneuver**) *v* to defeat by more skilful manoeuvring.
**outmoded** *adj* no longer in fashion; obsolete.
**outnumber** *v* to exceed in number.
**out of bounds** *adv* outside the prescribed boundaries or limits.
**out-of-date** *adj* **1** old-fashioned or obsolete. **2** no longer valid or usable.
**outpace** *v* to surpass in speed, growth, development, etc.
**outpatient** *n* a patient who visits a hospital for treatment but does not stay there overnight.
**outperform** *v* to perform better than.
**outplay** *v* to play better than.
**outpost** *n* **1** a post established at a distance from a main body of troops. **2** an outlying or frontier settlement.
**outpouring** *n* **1** an outburst of powerful emotion. **2** something that pours out.
**output**[1] *n* **1** something produced, or the amount produced, by somebody or something. **2** the process of producing. **3** power or energy produced by a machine or system. **4** the terminal for the output on an electrical device.
**output**[2] *v* (**outputting,** *past tense and past part.* **output**) to produce as output.
**outrage**[1] *n* **1** anger and resentment aroused by injury or insult. **2** an act of shocking violence, criminality, or immorality.
**outrage**[2] *v* to arouse intense anger or resentment in.
**outrageous** *adj* **1** shocking or offensive. **2** not conventional or moderate; extravagant. ➤ **outrageously** *adv.*
**outran** *v* past tense of OUTRUN.
**outrank** *v* to rank higher than.
**outré** /'oohtray/ *adj* rather shockingly unconventional or bizarre.
**outreach** *n* involvement with and education of people in the community.
**outrider** *n* a mounted attendant or motorcyclist escorting a carriage or car.
**outrigger** *n* a projecting framework, often with a float, attached to the side of a boat.
**outright**[1] *adv* **1** completely; altogether. **2** instantaneously; on the spot. **3** without reservation or restrictions.
**outright**[2] *adj* **1** utter; complete. **2** without reservation or restrictions.
**outrun** *v* (**outrunning,** *past tense* **outran,** *past part.* **outrun**) to run or travel faster than.
**outsell** *v* (*past tense and past part.* **outsold**) to exceed in numbers sold.
**outset** *n* (**the outset**) the beginning or start.
**outshine** *v* (*past tense and past part.* **outshone**) **1** to shine brighter than. **2** to outdo or surpass.
**outside**[1] *n* **1** the outer side or surface of something. **2** the outward appearance of something or somebody. **3** the part surrounding or beyond the boundaries of something. **4** the side of a curve or bend that has the longer edge. ✻ **at the outside** at the most.
**outside**[2] *adj* **1** of, on, or near the outside. **2** originating elsewhere. **3** not belonging to one's regular occupation or duties. **4** maximum. **5** barely possible; remote: *an outside chance.*
**outside**[3] *adv* **1** on or to the outside. **2** outdoors.
**outside**[4] *prep* **1** on or to the outside of. **2** beyond the limits of.
**outsider** *n* **1** somebody who does not belong to a particular group. **2** a competitor who has only a remote chance of winning.
**outsize** *adj* of an exceptionally large size.
**outskirts** *pl n* the parts of a town or city that are farthest from the centre.
**outsmart** *v* to get the better of by superior cleverness.
**outsold** *v* past tense and past part. of OUTSELL.
**outspoken** *adj* direct and open in speech or expression; frank.
**outstanding** *adj* **1** conspicuously good; excellent. **2** conspicuous. **3** unpaid. **4** continuing or unresolved. ➤ **outstandingly** *adv.*
**outstay** *v* to stay beyond the time or limits of.
**outstrip** *v* (**outstripped, outstripping**) **1** to go faster or farther than. **2** to do better than.
**out-take** *n* a section of film, recording, etc that is cut out during editing.
**outvote** *v* to defeat by a majority of votes.
**outward** *adj* **1** situated on or directed towards the outside. **2** being or going away from a place.

**3** relating to external appearances. ➤ **outwardly** *adv.*
**outwards** *or* **outward** *adv* towards the outside; away from the centre.
**outweigh** *v* to exceed in weight, value, or importance.
**outwit** *v* (**outwitted, outwitting**) to get the better of by superior cleverness.
**ouzo** /'oohzoh/ *n* an unsweetened Greek spirit flavoured with aniseed.
**ova** *n* pl of OVUM.
**oval**[1] *adj* having the shape of an egg or ellipse.
**oval**[2] *n* an oval figure or object.
**ovary** *n* (*pl* **-ies**) **1** a female reproductive organ that produces eggs and female sex hormones. **2** the base of the female reproductive organ of a flowering plant. ➤ **ovarian** *adj.*
**ovation** *n* a burst of sustained and enthusiastic applause.
**oven** *n* an enclosed compartment or chamber used for baking, heating, or drying, *esp* one used in a kitchen for cooking food.
**ovenproof** *adj* sufficiently heat-resistant for use in an oven.
**ovenware** *n* heat-resistant dishes for cooking food in an oven.
**over**[1] *adv* **1** across a barrier or intervening space. **2** to a particular place. **3** downwards from an upright position. **4** so as to be inverted or reversed. **5** beyond some quantity or limit. **6** in excess; remaining. **7** so as to cover the whole surface. **8** at an end. **9** used to show repetition.
**over**[2] *prep* **1** higher than. **2** vertically above but not touching. **3** across. **4** so as to cover. **5** used to indicate authority, power, or preference. **6** more than. **7** by means of (a medium or channel of communication). **8** during. **9** used to indicate an object of care, reference, occupation, or activity. ✱ **over and above** besides; in addition to.
**over**[3] *n* in cricket, a series of six balls bowled by one bowler from the same end of the pitch.
**over-** *prefix* **1** outer or covering: *overcoat.* **2** excessive or excessively: *overactive.* **3** above: *overarching.*
**overact** *v* to speak and gesture in an exaggerated way while acting.
**overactive** *adj* too active, *esp* restless or uncontrollable.
**overall**[1] *n chiefly Brit* a usu loose-fitting protective coat or suit worn over other clothing.
**overall**[2] *adj and adv* including or considering everything.
**overarching** *adj* **1** forming an arch overhead. **2** dominating or embracing everything else.
**overarm** *adj and adv* with the hand and arm brought forward and down from above shoulder level.
**overawe** *v* to make nervous or silent with respect or fear.
**overbalance** *v* **1** to lose balance and fall. **2** to cause to overbalance.
**overbearing** *adj* harshly masterful or domineering.
**overblown** *adj* inflated or pretentious.
**overboard** *adv* over the side of a ship or boat into the water. ✱ **go overboard 1** to be very enthusiastic. **2** to go to extremes.
**overcast** *adj* cloudy.
**overcharge** *v* to charge (a customer) too much.
**overcoat** *n* **1** a warm coat for wearing outdoors over other clothing. **2** a protective coat of paint or varnish.
**overcome** *v* (**overcame, overcome**) **1** to deal with (a problem, handicap, etc) successfully. **2** to overpower or overwhelm.
**overcommit** ✱ **overcommit oneself** to take on more work or responsibilities than one can handle.
**overcompensate** *v* to try to make up for a weakness or failing by exaggerating some other trait.
**overcrowded** *adj* containing too many people or things for the available space.
**overdo** *v* (**overdoes,** *past tense* **overdid,** *past part.* **overdone**) **1** to do or use to excess. **2** to exaggerate. **3** to cook (food) too much. ✱ **overdo it** to exhaust oneself, *esp* through overwork.
**overdose**[1] *n* a dangerously excessive dose of drugs, medicine, etc.
**overdose**[2] *v* to take an overdose.
**overdraft** *n* **1** permission from a bank to take more money out of one's account than has been credited to it. **2** the amount by which an account is overdrawn.
**overdrawn** *adj* **1** of a bank account: in deficit. **2** of a person: having an overdrawn account.
**overdress** *v* to dress too elaborately or formally.
**overdrive** *n* a gear in a motor vehicle that provides a higher ratio than top gear. ✱ **go into/be in overdrive** to be extremely active.
**overdue** *adj* **1** unpaid when due. **2** delayed beyond the proper or appointed time.
**overestimate** *v* **1** to estimate as being more than the actual amount or size. **2** to overrate. ➤ **overestimate** *n.*
**overexpose** *v* **1** to expose (photographic film) to too much light. **2** (**be overexposed**) to receive too much attention from the media. ➤ **overexposed** *adj,* **overexposure** *n.*
**overflow**[1] *v* **1** to flow over or beyond a brim or edge. **2** to be too numerous, large, etc to be contained in. **3** to be filled with an emotion.
**overflow**[2] *n* **1** an excess of people, things, etc that cannot be accommodated. **2** an outlet for surplus liquid.
**overground** *adj and adv* on the surface; not underground.

**overgrown** *adj* **1** covered or choked with vegetation. **2** grown too large.
**overhang**[1] *v* (*past tense and past part.* **overhung**) to project over or beyond.
**overhang**[2] *n* something that overhangs.
**overhaul** *v* **1** to examine (e.g. a machine) thoroughly and carry out any necessary repairs. **2** to overtake. ➤ **overhaul** *n.*
**overhead** *adv and adj* above one's head.
**overheads** *pl n* business expenses, e.g. rent, insurance, or heating, that are not chargeable to a particular part of the work or product.
**overhear** *v* (*past tense and past part.* **overheard**) to hear without the speaker's knowledge or intention.
**overheat** *v* to make or become excessively hot.
**overindulge** *v* **1** to indulge in something to an excessive degree. **2** to indulge (somebody) to an excessive degree. ➤ **overindulgence** *n.*
**overjoyed** *adj* extremely pleased.
**overkill** *n* an amount or effort beyond what is required for a particular purpose.
**overland** *adv and adj* by land rather than sea or air.
**overlap**[1] *v* (**overlapped, overlapping**) **1** to extend over and cover a part of. **2** to coincide partly; to have something in common.
**overlap**[2] *n* a part or amount that overlaps.
**overlay**[1] *v* (*past tense and past part.* **overlaid**) **1** (+ with) to cover or decorate (a surface) with something laid over it. **2** to superimpose another feeling, quality, etc on.
**overlay**[2] *n* something laid or spread over something else.
**overleaf** *adv* on the other side of the page.
**overload** *v* to load to excess. ➤ **overload** *n.*
**overlook** *v* **1** to fail to notice. **2** to ignore or excuse. **3** to have or provide a view of from above.
**overlord** *n* an absolute or supreme ruler.
**overly** *adv* to an excessive degree.
**overmuch** *adj and adv and n* too much.
**overnight**[1] *adv* **1** during or throughout the night. **2** for a single night. **3** suddenly.
**overnight**[2] *adj* **1** occurring, operating, or used during the night. **2** lasting for a single night. **3** sudden.
**overpass** *n* = FLYOVER.
**overplay** *v* to give too much emphasis to.
**overpower** *v* **1** to defeat by superior force. **2** to be so strong or intense as to overwhelm. ➤ **overpowering** *adj.*
**overprice** *v* to price too high.
**overqualified** *adj* having more education, training, or experience than a job calls for.
**overrate** *v* to consider (something or somebody) to be better than they actually are.
**overreach** *v* ✱ **overreach oneself** to fail by trying to do or gain too much.
**overreact** *v* to show an excessive or exaggerated reaction. ➤ **overreaction** *n.*
**override**[1] *v* (**overrode, overridden**) **1** to be more important than. **2** to use one's superior authority to set aside or annul (e.g. a decision by somebody else). **3** to take manual control of (e.g. an automatic control).
**override**[2] *n* a device or system used to override a control.
**overrule** *v* **1** to use one's superior authority to reject or disallow (a decision, judgment, objection, etc). **2** to overrule the decision, argument, objection, etc of (somebody).
**overrun** *v* (**overrunning,** *past tense* **overran,** *past part.* **overrun**) **1** to invade and occupy (a place) in large numbers. **2** to go beyond or past. **3** to exceed (e.g. an allowed cost or time). ➤ **overrun** *n.*
**overseas** *adv and adj* beyond or across the sea; abroad; foreign.
**oversee** *v* (**oversaw, overseen**) to watch and supervise (a task, operation, etc). ➤ **overseer** *n.*
**oversexed** *adj* having an abnormally strong sexual drive.
**overshadow** *v* **1** to cast a shadow over. **2** to exceed in importance. **3** to cause (an occasion) to be less happy than it should have been.
**overshoot** *v* (*past tense and past part.* **overshot**) **1** to pass over or beyond (e.g. a target) and miss it. **2** of an aircraft: to fly or taxi beyond the end of a runway. ➤ **overshoot** *n.*
**oversight** *n* an inadvertent omission or error.
**oversimplify** *v* (**-ies, -ied**) to simplify to such an extent as to cause distortion, misunderstanding, or error. ➤ **oversimplification** *n.*
**oversized** *or* **oversize** *adj* of above average or normal size.
**oversleep** *v* (*past tense and past part.* **overslept**) to sleep beyond the intended time for waking.
**overspend**[1] *v* (*past tense and past part.* **overspent**) to spend too much.
**overspend**[2] *n* an amount spent that exceeds the available budget.
**overspill** *n chiefly Brit* the movement of excess urban population into less crowded areas, e.g. new towns, or the excess population itself.
**overstate** *v* to state in too strong terms; to exaggerate. ➤ **overstatement** *n.*
**overstay** *v* to stay beyond the time or limits of.
**overstep** *v* (**overstepped, overstepping**) to go beyond (a limit). ✱ **overstep the mark** to go beyond what is acceptable.
**overstretch** *v* to make too many demands on (e.g. resources).
**oversubscribed** *adj* having more applicants than there are e.g. places or shares available.
**overt** *adj* not concealed or disguised. ➤ **overtly** *adv.*
**overtake** *v* (**overtook, overtaken**) **1** to catch up with and move past (e.g. a vehicle going in

the same direction). **2** to catch up with and do better than. **3** to happen to (somebody) suddenly.

**overthrow**[1] *v* (**overthrew, overthrown**) to remove from power.

**overthrow**[2] *n* **1** removal from power. **2** in cricket, a run scored when a fielder returns the ball inaccurately.

**overtime** *n* working time in excess of a standard working day or week.

**overtone** *n* (*also in pl*) a secondary effect, quality, or meaning.

**overture** *n* **1** the orchestral introduction to a musical dramatic work. **2** an orchestral concert piece written as a single movement. **3** (*also in pl*). **4** an initiative towards an agreement, negotiation, or relationship.

**overturn** *v* **1** to upset, capsize, or invert, or become upset or inverted. **2** to cancel or reverse (e.g. a decision).

**overuse**[1] *n* excessive use.

**overuse**[2] *v* to use excessively.

**overview** *n* a usu brief general survey.

**overweening** *adj* arrogant or presumptuous.

**overweight** *adj* exceeding the expected, normal, or proper weight.

**overwhelm** *v* **1** to defeat by superior force or numbers. **2** to affect with intense emotion. **3** to cover over completely; to submerge. ➤ **overwhelming** *adj.*

**overwork** *v* **1** to work or cause to work too hard or too long. **2** to make excessive use of. ➤ **overwork** *n.*

**overwrite** *v* (**overwrote, overwritten**) **1** to write on top of (existing writing). **2** to destroy (existing data) in a computer file by replacing it with new data. **3** to write in an inflated or pretentious style.

**overwrought** *adj* **1** extremely excited or agitated. **2** too elaborate in construction or design.

**ovulate** *v* to produce eggs or discharge them from an ovary. ➤ **ovulation** *n.*

**ovum** *n* (*pl* **ova**) a female reproductive cell in animals that when fertilized can develop into a new individual.

**owe** *v* **1** to be under obligation to pay (money) to somebody. **2** to be under obligation to give or show (an explanation, respect, etc) to somebody. **3** (*usu* + to) to have as a result of the action or existence of something or somebody else: *He owes his success to luck.*

**owing** *adj* unpaid; due. ✱ **owing to** because of.

**owl** *n* a nocturnal bird of prey with large eyes and a short hooked bill.

**owlish** *adj* having a round face or a wide-eyed stare.

**own**[1] *adj* used after a possessive: belonging to, relating to, or done by oneself or itself.

**own**[2] *v* **1** to possess. **2** *literary* to acknowledge or admit.

**own**[3] *pron* used after a possessive: one or ones belonging to oneself or itself. ✱ **come into one's own** to begin to be fully effective. **get one's own back** to have revenge. **on one's own 1** in solitude; alone. **2** without assistance or control.

**owner** *n* the person who owns something. ➤ **ownership** *n.*

**own up** *v* to confess to a fault or wrongdoing.

**ox** *n* (*pl* **oxen** *or* **ox**) **1** a domestic bovine mammal. **2** an castrated bull.

**Oxbridge** *n* the universities of Oxford and Cambridge.

**oxidation** *n* **1** the process of oxidizing. **2** the state of being oxidized.

**oxide** *n* a compound of oxygen with a chemical element or group.

**oxidize** *or* **-ise** *v* to combine with oxygen.

**oxtail** *n* the tail of an ox, used *esp* in making soup.

**oxygen** *n* a colourless odourless gas that forms about 21% of the atmosphere and is essential for the life of most organisms.

**oxygenate** *v* to combine or supply (e.g. blood) with oxygen.

**oxymoron** *n* a combination of contradictory or incongruous words, e.g. *cruel kindness*.

**oyster** *n* **1** an edible marine invertebrate animal with a rough irregular hinged shell. **2** a pinkish or greyish white colour.

**oz** *abbr* ounce.

**ozone** *n* **1** a poisonous form of oxygen with three atoms in each molecule, which has a pungent smell. **2** *informal* pure and refreshing air.

**ozone layer** *n* an atmospheric layer at heights of approximately 30–50km (20–30mi) that has a high ozone content and protects the earth by absorbing ultraviolet radiation from the sun.

**P**[1] *or* **p** *n* (*pl* **P's** *or* **Ps** *or* **p's**) the 16th letter of the English alphabet.

**P**[2] *abbr* **1** parking. **2** the chemical symbol for phosphorus.

**PA** *abbr* **1** personal assistant. **2** public address.

**Pa** *abbr* **1** pascal. **2** the chemical symbol for protactinium.

**p.a.** *abbr* per annum (= every year).

**pace**[1] *n* **1** a step taken in walking. **2** the rate or speed of moving, working, or developing. * **keep pace with** to progress at the same speed as. **put somebody through their paces** to test somebody by making them demonstrate their abilities.

**pace**[2] *v* **1** to walk with a steady tread. **2** (*often* + out/off) to measure (a distance) by pacing. **3** to set (oneself) a steady rate of working or doing something.

**pacemaker** *n* **1** a person who sets the pace or leads by example. **2** an electronic device implanted in the body to stimulate or steady the heartbeat.

**pachyderm** *n* an elephant, rhinoceros, or other animal with a thick skin.

**pacific** *adj* **1** tending to bring about peace. **2** (**Pacific**) of or found near the Pacific Ocean.

**pacifism** *n* opposition to war and violence as means of settling disputes. ➤ **pacifist** *n and adj.*

**pacify** *v* (**-ies, -ied**) **1** to make less angry or agitated. **2** to restore (a country) to a peaceful state.

**pack**[1] *n* **1** a light paper or cardboard container for goods. **2** a knapsack or rucksack. **3** a set of playing cards. **4** a number of animals kept or grouping together for hunting. **5** an organized group of Cub Scouts or Brownie Guides. **6** the forwards in a rugby team. **7** the main group of competitors running close together in a race behind the leaders. **8** a concentrated mass of snow or ice. **9** an absorbent pad for applying to the body for therapeutic purposes.

**pack**[2] *v* **1** to place in a container for transportation or storage. **2** to cover or surround with packing material for protection. **3** (*often* + away) to be collapsible for storage or transport. **4** (*often* + with) to fill with a large quantity of material or things. **5** (+ in/into) to fit (a large number of people) into a small space. **6** *informal* (+ in) to attract a large number of (people). **7** to influence the composition of (a jury) so as to influence the verdict. * **pack a punch 1** to be capable of hitting hard. **2** to be very strong or effective. **send packing** *informal* to dismiss (somebody) abruptly. ➤ **packable** *adj,* **packer** *n.*

**package**[1] *n* **1** an object or number of objects wrapped or packed up together. **2** a group of proposals or terms offered together.

**package**[2] *v* **1** to enclose in a package or covering. **2** to group (various items) together for sale as a whole. **3** to present in an appealing way.

**package deal** *n* an offer or agreement which has to be accepted in its entirety.

**package holiday** *n* a holiday organized by an agent who is responsible for all aspects of travel and accommodation.

**packed** *adj* full or crowded.

**packet** *n* **1** a paper or cardboard container. **2** a parcel. **3** *Brit, informal* a large sum of money.

**packhorse** *n* a horse used to carry loads.

**pack ice** *n* a large mass of ice floating in the sea.

**pack in** *informal* to end (an activity).

**pack off** *v informal* to send (somebody) away abruptly or unceremoniously.

**pack up** *v informal* to break down.

**pact** *n* an agreement or treaty.

**pacy** *or* **pacey** *adj* (**-ier, -iest**) *Brit* fast or speedy.

**pad**[1] *n* **1** a thick piece of soft or absorbent material. **2** a piece of padding used to shield parts of the body against impact. **3** the thickened underside of an animal's foot. **4** a number of sheets of paper fastened together at one edge. **5** a flat surface for a helicopter to land on or for launching a rocket. **6** *informal* the place where a person lives.

**pad**[2] *v* (**padded, padding**) **1** to provide with a pad or padding. **2** (*often* + out) to fill out (speech or writing) with superfluous matter. **3** to walk with a muffled step.

**padding** *n* material with which something is padded.

**paddle**[1] *n* **1** a wooden implement like a small oar, used to propel a boat. **2** an implement with a broad flat blade used for stirring and mixing. **3** a flattened limb or flipper of a swimming bird or mammal. **4** a spell of paddling in water.

**paddle**[2] *v* **1** to propel (a boat) with a paddle.

2 to swim with short strokes like an animal. **3** to walk or wade in shallow water. ➤ **paddler** *n.*

**paddle steamer** *n* a boat driven by steam-powered paddle wheels.

**paddle wheel** *n* a power-driven wheel with paddles round its circumference, used to propel a boat.

**paddock** *n* **1** a small enclosed field for horses. **2** an area where racehorses or racing cars are paraded before a race.

**paddy**[1] *n* (*pl* **-ies**) (*also* **paddyfield**) a field of wet ground for growing rice.

**paddy**[2] *n* (*pl* **-ies**) *Brit, informal* a temper tantrum.

**padlock**[1] *n* a detachable lock with a shackle that can be passed through a link and secured.

**padlock**[2] *v* to secure using a padlock.

**paean** *n* a song of praise or tribute.

**paediatrician** *n* a specialist in paediatrics.

**paediatrics** (*NAmer* **pediatrics**) *pl n* the branch of medicine dealing with the diseases of children. ➤ **paediatric** *adj.*

**paedophile** (*NAmer* **pedophile**) *n* a person who is sexually attracted to children. ➤ **paedophilia** *n.*

**paella** /pie'ela/ *n* a Spanish dish of rice, meat, seafood, and vegetables.

**pagan** *n* a follower of a religion that is not one of the main religions. ➤ **pagan** *adj,* **paganism** *n.*

**page**[1] *n* **1** a leaf of a book or periodical, or a single side of a leaf. **2** an Internet document.

**page**[2] *v* (*often* + through) to turn pages in a haphazard manner.

**page**[3] *n* **1** a boy attending the bride at a wedding. **2** a young man or boy employed to deliver messages or run errands. **3** formerly, a boy being trained for the rank of knight.

**page**[4] *v* to summon over a public-address system or with a pager.

**pageant** *n* **1** an entertainment with dramatic presentations or a procession. **2** an ostentatious display.

**pageantry** *n* colourful or elaborate display.

**pager** *n* a small electronic device that emits an audible tone or receives a text message, as a means of communication or alert.

**paginate** *v* to number the pages of (a book or periodical). ➤ **pagination** *n.*

**pagoda** *n* a Buddhist temple with upturned projecting roofs at the division of each storey.

**paid** *v* past and past part. of PAY[1]. * **put paid to** to bring to an abrupt end.

**pail** *n* a bucket.

**pain**[1] *n* **1** an unpleasant bodily sensation induced by injury or illness. **2** mental or emotional distress. **3** *informal* an annoyance or nuisance. **4** (*in pl*) trouble or care taken. * **on pain of** subject to penalty of.

**pain**[2] *v* to cause pain or distress to.

**painful** *adj* **1** causing or feeling pain or distress. **2** proceeding with great effort. **3** *informal* very bad. ➤ **painfully** *adv.*

**painkiller** *n* a drug that relieves pain.

**painless** *adj* **1** not causing any pain. **2** easy or effortless. ➤ **painlessly** *adv.*

**painstaking** *adj* showing diligence and effort. ➤ **painstakingly** *adv.*

**paint**[1] *v* **1** to apply paint or cosmetics to. **2** to apply with a movement resembling that used in painting. **3** to represent on a surface by applying paint. **4** to describe vividly.

**paint**[2] *n* a mixture of a pigment and liquid which forms a coloured coating on a surface.

**painter**[1] *n* **1** an artist who paints pictures. **2** somebody who applies paint to buildings.

**painter**[2] *n* a line used for securing or towing a boat.

**painting** *n* **1** a painted work of art. **2** the art or occupation of painting.

**paintwork** *n* a painted surface of a building or vehicle.

**pair**[1] *n* **1** two corresponding things used or considered together. **2** an implement of piece of clothing made up of two connected pieces. **3** two people in a marriage or partnership. **4** two mated animals.

**pair**[2] *v* (*often* + up) to arrange in pairs.

**pair off** *v* to form a couple or a group of two.

**paisley** *n* a pattern of colourful abstract curved figures.

**pajamas** *pl n NAmer* = PYJAMAS.

**pakora** *n* an Indian savoury snack of diced vegetables or meat fried in batter.

**pal** *n informal* a friend.

**palace** *n* **1** a large stately house or public building. **2** the official residence of a sovereign or bishop.

**Palaeolithic** *adj* (*NAmer* **Paleolithic**) of the earliest period of the Stone Age.

**palaeontology** (*NAmer* **paleontology**) *n* the study of geological periods as discovered from fossil remains. ➤ **palaeontologist** *n.*

**palatable** *adj* **1** pleasant to the taste. **2** acceptable.

**palate** *n* **1** the roof of the mouth. **2** the sense of taste. **3** an intellectual taste or liking.

**palatial** *adj* grand and spacious. ➤ **palatially** *adv.*

**palaver** *n* a fuss or bother.

**pale**[1] *adj* **1** lacking intensity of colour. **2** not bright or brilliant. **3** feeble or faint. **4** of a colour: light in shade. ➤ **palish** *adj.*

**pale**[2] *v* **1** to become pale. **2** to seem less important by comparison.

**pale**[3] *n* **1** an upright post forming part of a fence. **2** formerly, a district within a boundary. * **beyond the pale** not socially acceptable.

**palette** *n* **1** a thin board on which a painter mixes pigments. **2** a particular range or use of colour.

**palette knife** *n* a knife with a blunt flexible blade, used for mixing paints.

**palimpsest** *n* a parchment or tablet, reused over earlier writing.

**palindrome** *n* a word or phrase that reads the same backwards or forwards, e.g. *radar*.

**paling** *n* **1** a fence made of stakes. **2** a stake used in such a fence.

**palisade** *n* a fence of stakes for defence.

**pall**[1] *n* **1** a heavy cloud of smoke or dust that covers or conceals. **2** a heavy cloth draped over a coffin or tomb.

**pall**[2] *v* to cease to be interesting or attractive.

**palladium** *n* a silver-white metallic element.

**pallbearer** *n* a person who helps to carry the coffin at a funeral.

**pallet**[1] *n* **1** a portable platform for storing or moving materials. **2** a tool with a flat blade for shaping clay.

**pallet**[2] *n* **1** a straw-filled mattress. **2** a makeshift bed.

**palliate** *v* **1** to lessen the bad effects of (a disease). **2** to moderate the intensity or gravity of. ➤ **palliative** *n and adj.*

**pallid** *adj* **1** pale or lacking colour. **2** lacking liveliness.

**pallor** *n* paleness in the face.

**pally** *adj* (**-ier, -iest**) *informal* friendly.

**palm**[1] *n* **1** a tropical or subtropical tree with a crown of large leaves. **2** a palm leaf representing distinction.

**palm**[2] *n* the inside of the human hand between the fingers and the wrist.

**palm**[3] *v* (*often* + off ) to get rid of (something unwanted), or persuade (somebody) to take something awkward or unwanted.

**palmistry** *n* the activity of reading a person's character or future from markings on the palms. ➤ **palmist** *n.*

**palmtop** *n* a small computer that can be held in the hand.

**palmy** *adj* (**-ier, -iest**) prosperous or flourishing.

**palomino** *n* (*pl* **-os**) a light tan horse with slender legs.

**palpable** *adj* **1** capable of being touched or felt. **2** easily perceptible; obvious. ➤ **palpably** *adv.*

**palpate** *v* to examine (a part of the body) medically by touching it. ➤ **palpation** *n.*

**palpitate** *v* **1** of the heart: to beat rapidly and strongly. **2** to tremble or flutter. ➤ **palpitation** *n.*

**palsy** *n* (*pl* **-ies**) *dated* uncontrollable tremor of the body. ➤ **palsied** *adj.*

**paltry** *adj* (**-ier, -iest**) **1** very small or insignificant. **2** mean and petty. ➤ **paltriness** *n.*

**pampas** *n* an extensive area of grassy plains in South America.

**pamper** *v* to treat with excessive care and attention.

**pamphlet**[1] *n* a small printed publication with a paper cover.

**pamphlet**[2] *v* (**pamphleted, pamphleting**) to hand out pamphlets to.

**pan**[1] *n* **1** a metal container with a long handle, used for cooking food. **2** any shallow open receptacle for various uses. **3** each of the receptacles in a pair of scales. **4** *Brit* the bowl of a toilet. **5** a hollow in land.

**pan**[2] *v* (**panned, panning**) **1** to wash earth or gravel in a pan in search of gold. **2** *informal* to criticize harshly.

**pan**[3] *v* (**panned, panning**) to rotate (a film or television camera) horizontally so as to keep a moving object in view or for a panoramic effect.

**pan-** *comb. form* all or completely: *Pan-American.*

**panacea** *n* a remedy for all diseases or difficulties.

**panache** *n* dash or flamboyance in style and action.

**panama** *n* a lightweight hat of plaited straw.

**panatella** *n* a long slender cigar.

**pancake** *n* a thin flat cake of batter fried in an open pan.

**pancake landing** *n* an emergency landing by an aircraft descending level with the undercarriage retracted.

**pancreas** *n* a large gland that secretes digestive enzymes into the intestines. ➤ **pancreatic** *adj.*

**panda** *n* **1** (*also* **giant panda**) a large black-and-white mammal of China resembling a bear but related to the raccoons. **2** (*also* **red panda**) a long-tailed Himalayan mammal resembling the American raccoon and having long chestnut fur.

**pandemic**[1] *adj* of a disease: affecting a high proportion of the population.

**pandemic**[2] *n* an outbreak of a pandemic disease.

**pandemonium** *n* a scene of confusion or uproar.

**pander** *v* (+ to) to provide gratification for the desires of.

**pane** *n* a framed sheet of glass in a window or door.

**panegyric** *n* a speech or piece of writing in praise of somebody or something.

**panel** *n* **1** a flat section of a door or other surface. **2** a mounting for a set of controls or instruments. **3** a group of people brought together to consider a matter or take part in a broadcast game or quiz. **4** a list of people summoned for jury service. ➤ **panelled** *adj,* **panellist** *n.*

**pang** *n* a brief spasm of pain or fear.

**panic**[1] *n* a sudden frenzied feeling of fear or anxiety. ➤ **panicky** *adj.*

**panic**[2] *v* (**panicked, panicking**) to feel or cause to feel panic.

**pannier** *n* each of a pair of baskets or boxes carried on both sides of an animal, bicycle, or motorcycle.
**panoply** *n* a magnificent or impressive array of things.
**panorama** *n* **1** an open view of a landscape or area. **2** a comprehensive survey of a topic or series of events. ➤ **panoramic** *adj.*
**pan out** *v* to turn out in a particular way
**panpipes** *pl n* a wind instrument consisting of a row of vertical pipes varying in length.
**pansy** *n* (*pl* **-ies**) **1** a garden plant with flowers having rounded velvety petals. **2** *informal, derog* an effeminate or homosexual man.
**pant** *v* to breathe quickly or in a laboured manner. ➤ **pant** *n.*
**pantaloons** *pl n* **1** women's loose-fitting trousers gathered at the ankles. **2** formerly, men's tight-fitting trousers fastened with straps under the feet.
**pantechnicon** *n Brit* a large van for transporting furniture.
**pantheism** *n* a belief that God exists in nature. ➤ **pantheist** *n,* **pantheistic** *adj.*
**pantheon** *n* **1** the gods of a people collectively. **2** a building containing memorials to famous dead. **3** a group of famous people.
**panther** *n* **1** a black leopard. **2** *NAmer*a puma.
**panties** *pl n* short underpants for women or girls.
**pantile** *n* a roofing tile with an S-shape that fits over the tile next to it.
**panto** *n* (*pl* **-os**) *Brit, informal* a pantomime.
**pantomime** *n Brit* a slapstick musical entertainment based on a nursery story.
**pantry** *n* (*pl* **-ies**) a room or cupboard for storing food.
**pants** *pl n* **1** *Brit* underpants or knickers. **2** *NAmer* trousers.
**pantyhose** *or* **pantihose** *pl n NAmer* women's tights.
**pap** *n* **1** soft food for babies or invalids. **2** feeble fiction or drama.
**papa** *n informal* one's father.
**papacy** *n* (*pl* **-ies**) the office of pope.
**papal** *adj* relating to a pope or the papacy.
**paparazzo** *n* (*pl* **paparazzi**) a news photographer who seeks out celebrities to photograph.
**papaya** *n* a large oval tropical fruit with a yellow skin, orange flesh, and round black seeds.
**paper**[1] *n* **1** a material for writing, printing on, etc made from compacted vegetable fibres in the form of thin sheets. **2** (*also in pl*) a written or printed document. **3** (*in pl*) an individual's personal documents and records, diaries, etc. **4** a newspaper. **5** a written composition designed for publication or to be read aloud. **6** a government report or discussion document. **7** a set of questions to be answered in an examination. ✱ **on paper 1** in writing. **2** in theory.
**paper**[2] *v* to cover (a wall) with wallpaper.
**paperback** *n* a book with a flexible paper binding.
**paper clip** *n* a small clip made from two loops of wire, used for holding sheets of paper together.
**paperknife** *n* (*pl* **paperknives**) a blunt knife for slitting envelopes open.
**paper over** *v* to conceal or suppress (differences or weaknesses) for the sake of appearances.
**paper round** *n* a round of delivering newspapers to people's houses.
**paper tiger** *n* a person or power that appears threatening, but is actually ineffectual.
**paperweight** *n* a small heavy object used to hold down loose papers.
**paperwork** *n* routine clerical or work.
**papery** *adj* thin and light like paper.
**papier-mâché** *n* a light strong moulding material made of paper pulped with glue.
**papist** *or* **Papist** *n deroga* Roman Catholic.
**paprika** *n* a powdered red spice made from sweet peppers.
**papyrus** *n* (*pl* **papyri**) a writing material made in antiquity from the pith of a sedge plant of the Nile valley.
**par** *n* **1** in golf, the standard score of a good player for each hole of a course. **2** an amount taken as an average or norm. **3** a usual standard of physical condition or health. ✱ **on a par with** equal to. **par for the course** what is to be expected in a particular situation.
**parable** *n* a short story illustrating a moral or religious principle.
**parabola** *n* a symmetrical curve of the kind generated when a cone is intersected by a plane parallel to its side.
**paracetamol** *n* a chemical compound used as a painkiller.
**parachute**[1] *n* a folding expanse of light fabric attached by lines to a harness, that opens out into an umbrella shape to slow the descent of a person or thing dropped from a great height. ➤ **parachutist** *n.*
**parachute**[2] *v* to drop by means of a parachute.
**parade**[1] *n* **1** a public procession. **2** a formal assembly or march past by a troops. **3** a succession of things or people on display. **4** an ostentatious display. **5** *chiefly Brit* a row of shops. **6** a place for walking along.
**parade**[2] *v* **1** to march in a procession. **2** to walk up and down. **3** to display ostentatiously.
**paradigm** *n* **1** a clear or typical example of something. **2** a model used in science as a framework for ideas. ➤ **paradigmatic** *adj.*
**paradise** *n* **1** (*often* **Paradise**) heaven. **2** (*often* **Paradise**) the Garden of Eden. **3** an idyllic place or state.
**paradox** *n* **1** a true statement that seems contradictory or absurd. **2** a person or thing with

seemingly contradictory features. ➤ **paradoxical** *adj*, **paradoxically** *adv*.

**paraffin** *n* **1** a waxy mixture of hydrocarbons obtained from coal, petroleum, etc and used in candles, chemical synthesis, and cosmetics. **2** *Brit* an inflammable liquid hydrocarbon obtained from petroleum and used as a fuel.

**paragliding** *n* the sport of travelling through the air with a rectangular parachute after being released at a height. ➤ **paraglider** *n*.

**paragon** *n* a model of excellence or of a particular quality.

**paragraph** *n* a division of a piece of writing, starting on a new line.

**parakeet** *or* **parrakeet** *n* a small slender parrot with a long tail.

**parallax** *n* the apparent difference in position or direction of an object as seen from different points not on the same straight line.

**parallel**[1] *adj* **1** extending in the same direction at a constant distance apart. **2** occurring simultaneously. **3** analogous or comparable.

**parallel**[2] *n* **1** somebody or something equal or similar to another. **2** a comparison that shows a resemblance. **3** a line representing any of the imaginary circles on the surface of the earth parallel to the equator.

**parallel**[3] *v* (**paralleled, paralleling**) **1** to run parallel to. **2** to equal or match. **3** to correspond to.

***Usage Note:*** Note the spelling with *-ll-* followed by *-l*.

**parallel bars** *pl n* a pair of horizontal bars supported on a base, used in gymnastics.

**parallelogram** *n* a four-sided figure with opposite sides parallel and equal.

**paralyse** (*NAmer* **paralyze**) *v* **1** to affect with paralysis. **2** to make powerless or ineffective. **3** to make immobile.

**paralysis** *n* (*pl* **paralyses**) **1** total or partial loss of movement or sensation in a part of the body. **2** loss of the ability to move or to act.

**paralytic** *adj* **1** of paralysis. **2** *informal* very drunk.

**paramedic** *n* a member of a medical team who is not a qualified doctor. ➤ **paramedical** *adj*.

**parameter** *n* **1** a property whose value determines the characteristics or behaviour of something. **2** *informal* a limiting factor or characteristic.

**paramilitary**[1] *adj* organized on military principles.

**paramilitary**[2] *n* (*pl* **-ies**) a member of a paramilitary organization.

**paramount** *adj* superior to or more powerful than all others.

**paramour** *n archaic* a lover.

**paranoia** *n* a mental disorder characterized by delusions of persecution. ➤ **paranoiac** *adj and n*, **paranoid** *adj and n*.

**paranormal** *adj* not scientifically explainable; supernatural.

**parapet** *n* **1** a wall, rampart, or mound of earth to protect soldiers. **2** a low wall along the edge of a platform, roof, or bridge.

**paraphernalia** *n* the things needed for a particular pursuit or production.

**paraphrase**[1] *n* a restatement of a text or statement giving the meaning in another form.

**paraphrase**[2] *v* to make a paraphrase of.

**paraplegia** *n* paralysis of the lower half of the body. ➤ **paraplegic** *adj and n*.

**paraquat** *n* a poisonous weedkiller.

**parasite** *n* **1** an organism living in or on another organism and drawing its nourishment from it. **2** a person who depends on somebody else without making a useful return. ➤ **parasitic** *adj*, **parasitical** *adj*, **parasitism** *n*.

**parasol** *n* a lightweight umbrella used for protection from the sun.

**paratroops** *pl n* troops equipped to parachute from aircraft. ➤ **paratrooper** *n*.

**parboil** *v* to boil (vegetables) until partly cooked.

**parcel**[1] *n* **1** an object wrapped in paper for sending by post. **2** a plot of land. **3** a collection or group of people or things.

**parcel**[2] *v* (**parcelled, parcelling,** *NAmer* **parceled, parceling**) **1** (*often* + up) to make up into a parcel. **2** (+ out) to divide or distribute.

**parch** *v* to make or become dry or scorched.

**parched** *adj* **1** of land: dry from lack of rain. **2** *informal* of a person: extremely thirsty.

**parchment** *n* **1** the skin of a sheep or goat formerly used as writing material. **2** strong paper resembling parchment.

**pardon**[1] *n* **1** forgiveness for a fault or offence. **2** a release from legal penalties.

**pardon**[2] *v* **1** to absolve from the consequences of a fault or crime. **2** to allow (an offence) to pass without punishment. ➤ **pardonable** *adj*.

**pare** *v* **1** to cut or shave off the outer surface or edges of. **2** (*often* + down/away) to diminish gradually. ➤ **parer** *n*.

**parent**[1] *n* **1** a father or mother. **2** an animal or plant regarded in relation to its offspring. **3** the material or source from which something is derived. ➤ **parental** *adj*, **parenthood** *n*.

**parent**[2] *v* to be or act as the parent of.

**parentage** *n* descent from parents or ancestors.

**parenthesis** *n* (*pl* **parentheses**) **1** an extra or explanatory word or phrase inserted in a passage and set off, in writing, by punctuation. **2** either or both of the curved marks ( or ) used in writing and printing to enclose a parenthesis. ➤ **parenthetic** *adj*, **parenthetical** *adj*.

**par excellence** *adj* (*used after a noun*) the best of its kind: *a poet par excellence*.

**pariah** *n* a rejected person or outcast.

**paring** *n* a thin piece cut off from a surface.

**parish** *n* **1** a district of a diocese served by a single church or clergyman. **2** a unit of local government in rural England.
**parishioner** *n* a member or inhabitant of a church parish.
**parity** *n* the state of being equal or equivalent.
**park**[1] *n* **1** an area of land for recreation in a city or town. **2** an area maintained in its natural state as a public property. **3** an enclosed area of lawns, woodland, etc attached to a country house. **4** a site for a number of buildings housing establishments of a similar type. **5** an area for parking vehicles.
**park**[2] *v* **1** to leave (a vehicle) for a time. **2** *informal* to leave (somebody or something) temporarily.
**parka** *n* a weatherproof jacket with a hood.
**Parkinson's disease** *or* **Parkinsonism** *n* a progressive nervous disease, marked by tremor and weakness of the muscles.
**parky** *adj* (**-ier, -iest**) *Brit, informal* chilly.
**parlance** *n* a manner of speaking.
**parley**[1] *v* to discuss terms with an enemy.
**parley**[2] *n* (*pl* **-eys**) a meeting under truce to discuss terms with an enemy.
**parliament** *n* **1** the supreme legislative body of the UK, consisting of the House of Commons and the House of Lords and summoned and dissolved by the sovereign. **2** a similar body in other countries.➤ **parliamentary** *adj.*

***Usage Note:*** Note the spelling with an *-a-* in the middle.

**parliamentarian** *n* a member of a parliament.
**parlour** (*NAmer* **parlor**) *n* **1** *dated* a sitting room in a private house. **2** a shop or business specializing in a special line.
**parlous** *adj formal* giving cause for concern or alarm.
**Parma ham** *n* Italian cured ham in thin slices.
**Parmesan** *n* a hard strongly flavoured Italian cheese.
**parochial** *adj* **1** relating to a church parish. **2** limited or provincial in outlook. ➤ **parochialism** *n.*
**parody**[1] *n* (*pl* **-ies**) **1** a literary or musical work in which a particular style is imitated for comic effect. **2** a feeble or ridiculous imitation.
**parody**[2] *v* (**-ies, -ied**) to imitate for comic effect.
**parole**[1] *n* the early release of a prisoner on condition of good behaviour.
**parole**[2] *v* to release (a prisoner) on parole.
**paroxysm** *n* **1** a sudden attack of pain or convulsions. **2** a sudden violent emotion. ➤ **paroxysmal** *adj.*
**parquet** *n* a floor or flooring made of wood blocks arranged in patterns.
**parricide** *n* **1** the act of murdering one's father or mother. **2** a person who commits parricide. ➤ **parricidal** *adj.*
**parrot**[1] *n* a large tropical bird with brightly coloured plumage and a hooked beak, some of which can mimic human speech.
**parrot**[2] *v* (**parroted, parroting**) to repeat or imitate without understanding or thought.
**parrot-fashion** *adv* repeated without regard for meaning.
**parry**[1] *v* (**-ies, -ied**) **1** to ward off (a blow). **2** to avoid answering (a question or accusation) directly.
**parry**[2] *n* (*pl* **-ies**) **1** an act of parrying a blow. **2** an evasive reply.
**parse** *v* to explain (a sentence) in terms of its grammatical parts.
**parsimony** *n* a tendency to be careful with money. ➤ **parsimonious** *adj.*
**parsley** *n* a plant of the carrot family with leaves used in cooking.
**parsnip** *n* a plant of the carrot family used as a vegetable.
**parson** *n* a clergyman in charge of an Anglican parish.
**parsonage** *n* a house provided for a parson.
**parson's nose** *n* a fatty extension of the rump of a cooked fowl.
**part**[1] *n* **1** a piece or section which along with others forms the whole of something. **2** a certain amount of something but not the whole. **3** a separable piece in a machine. **4** an organ or member of a plant or animal body. **5** the music for a particular voice or instrument in a group. **6** an actor's role in a play. **7** somebody's contribution to an action or event. **8** (*in pl*) an unspecified territorial area. * **in part** partially. **on the part of** by or on behalf of. **take part** (*often* + in) to join in.
**part**[2] *v* **1** to separate from somebody. **2** to separate into parts or sections. **3** (+ with) to relinquish possession of. * **part company** to leave in different directions.
**partake** *v* (**partook, partaken**) *formal* (+ in/of) to participate in. ➤ **partaker** *n.*
**partial** *adj* **1** not whole or total. **2** inclined to favour one side over another. **3** (+ to) markedly fond of. ➤ **partiality** *n,* **partially** *adv.*
**participate** *v* to join with others in doing something. ➤ **participant** *n,* **participation** *n,* **participator** *n,* **participatory** *adj.*
**participle** *n* a verbal form, e.g. *singing* or *sung*, that has the function of an adjective and can also be used in compound verb forms. ➤ **participial** *adj.*
**particle** *n* **1** a minute quantity or fragment of something. **2** a minute subdivision of matter, *esp* at subatomic level, e.g. an electron or proton.
**particular**[1] *adj* **1** relating to a single person or thing. **2** worthy of notice; special, unusual. **3** detailed or exact. **4** meticulous or exacting.

**particular²** *n* an individual fact, point, or detail. ✱ **in particular** specifically or especially.
**particularly** *adv* **1** to an unusual degree. **2** in detail; specifically.
**parting** *n* **1** the act of parting from somebody. **2** *Brit* the line where the hair is parted.
**partisan** *n* **1** a firm adherent to a party or cause, or person. **2** a member of a guerrilla band operating behind enemy lines. ➤ **partisan** *adj.*
**partition¹** *n* **1** division into parts. **2** a part or section of a whole. **3** a light interior dividing wall. ➤ **partitioner** *n,* **partitionist** *n.*
**partition²** *v* **1** to divide (a country or region) into parts. **2** to divide (a room) with a partition.
**partly** *adv* not completely; to some extent or degree.
**partner¹** *n* **1** a member of a partnership. **2** an associate in a joint venture. **3** each of two people in a joint activity. **4** a spouse or lover.
**partner²** *v* to act as a partner to.
**part of speech** *n* a class of words having a particular type of meaning and grammatical function, e.g. noun, verb, and adjective.
**partook** *v* past of PARTAKE.
**partridge** *n* (*pl* **partridges** *or* **partridge**) a game bird with variegated plumage.
**part song** *n* an unaccompanied song consisting of two or more voice parts.
**part-time** *adj and adv* involving less than the normal working hours. ➤ **part-timer** *n.*
**parturition** *n formal* childbirth.
**party¹** *n* (*pl* **-ies**) **1** an informal social gathering with food and drink. **2** a political group representing a particular standpoint and putting up candidates for election. **3** a group of people carrying out an activity together. **4** a person or group taking one side of a dispute or contest. ✱ **be party to** to be involved in (an activity, decision, etc).
**party²** *v* (**-ies, -ied**) *informal* to celebrate with a party.
**party line** *n* the official principles of a political party.
**party wall** *n* a wall dividing two adjoining properties.
**parvenu** *n* a person of low social position who has recently acquired wealth or power.
**pascal** *n* the SI unit of pressure.
**pass¹** *v* **1** to move or proceed past or in a specified direction. **2** to transfer or be transferred to another person. **3** to go past (another vehicle) in the same direction. **4** of time: to elapse. **5** of a situation or event: to complete its course. **6** to spend (time). **7** to go from one quality or state to another. **8** to be successful in (an examination or test). **9** to declare to be successful or satisfactory. **10** to approve or enact (a law or proposal). **11** in a team game, to hit, throw, or kick (the ball) to another player. **12** to pronounce (a judgment or sentence). **13** to utter (a remark). **14** to decline an opportunity or offer. ✱ **pass as/for** resemble or qualify as.
**pass²** *n* **1** the act of passing. **2** a written permission for somebody to go somewhere or to go on leave. **3** a ticket allowing free travel or admission. **4** the passing of an examination. **5** *informal* a sexual approach. **6** a single complete operation in a process. **7** an act of passing a ball to a teammate.
**pass³** *n* a narrow route through a mountain range.
**passable** *adj* **1** barely acceptable; tolerable. **2** capable of being travelled on. ➤ **passably** *adv.*
**passage** *n* **1** the action or process of passing from one place or condition to another. **2** a way through or along which one can move. **3** a corridor or lobby. **4** an act of travelling by sea or air. **5** a right or permission to pass. **6** a brief portion of a text or musical composition.
**passageway** *n* a narrow passage or corridor between rooms or buildings.
**pass away** *v* to die.
**passé** *adj* no longer fashionable.
**passenger** *n* **1** somebody, other than the driver or crew, who travels in a vehicle. **2** a member of a group who contributes little to its functioning.
**passer-by** *n* (*pl* **passers-by**) a person who happens to pass by a particular place.
**passim** *adv* occurring at various points throughout the text.
**passing¹** *adj* **1** having a brief duration. **2** carried out quickly or casually.
**passing²** *n* a person's death.
**passion** *n* **1** intense or uncontrollable feeling. **2** an outbreak of anger. **3** ardent affection; love. **4** a strong liking or interest. **5** strong sexual desire. **6** (*usu* **Passion**) the sufferings and death of Christ.
**passionate** *adj* **1** expressing intense love, hatred, or anger. **2** extremely enthusiastic. ➤ **passionately** *adv.*
**passionflower** *n* a tropical plant with showy flowers.
**passionfruit** *n* a fruit from a passionflower.
**passion play** *n* a dramatic representation of Christ's Passion and crucifixion.
**passive¹** *adj* **1** lacking in energy or initiative. **2** offering no resistance; submissive. **3** acted on by external forces or impressions. **4** in grammar, of a verb: having as the subject the person or thing affected by the action, e.g. *was hit* in *the ball was hit.* ➤ **passively** *adv,* **passiveness** *n,* **passivity** *n.*
**passive²** *n* a passive verb form or voice.
**passive resistance** *n* nonviolent forms of resistance.
**passive smoking** *n* the inhalation of tobacco smoke from other people's cigarettes.

**pass off** *v* **1** (+ off) to represent falsely in order to deceive. **2** to take place successfully.
**pass out** *v* to lose consciousness.
**Passover** *n* the Jewish festival celebrating the liberation of the Israelites from slavery in Egypt.
**passport** *n* an official document issued by a government as proof of identity and nationality to its citizens for use when leaving or reentering the country.
**pass up** *v* to decline or reject (an opportunity).
**password** *n* a word or phrase to be uttered or entered before being admitted.
**past**[1] *adj* **1** just gone or elapsed. **2** having gone by; earlier. **3** finished or ended. **4** of the verb tense that expresses action or state in time gone by. **5** preceding or former.
**past**[2] *prep* **1** beyond the age of or for. **2** subsequent to. **3** at the farther side of. **4** up to and then beyond. **5** beyond the capacity or scope of. * **past it** *informal* no longer in one's prime.
**past**[3] *n* **1** time gone by. **2** a verb form expressing past events. **3** a person's earlier life.
**past**[4] *adv* so as to pass by the speaker.
**pasta** *n* dough formed into various shapes and boiled in water.
**paste**[1] *n* **1** an adhesive made from starch and water. **2** a clay mixture used in making pottery or porcelain. **3** a soft smooth substance. **4** a brilliant glass used in making imitation gems.
**paste**[2] *v* **1** to cover or stick with paste. **2** in computing, to insert (a piece of text) into a document.
**pastel**[1] *n* **1** a crayon made from a paste of powdered pigment mixed with gum. **2** a drawing in pastels. **3** a pale colour.
**pastel**[2] *adj* pale in colour.
**pasteurize** *or* **-ise** *v* to sterilize (milk) by heating and cooling it. ➤ **pasteurization** *n.*
**pastiche** *n* an artistic or musical work that imitates the style of a previous work.
**pastille** *or* **pastil** *n* an aromatic or medicated lozenge.
**pastime** *n* a hobby or game undertaken for enjoyment.
**past master** *n* an expert in a particular activity.
**pastor** *n* the minister in charge of a church congregation. ➤ **pastorate** *n.*
**pastoral**[1] *adj* **1** used for livestock rearing. **2** of or relating to the countryside. **3** peaceful and innocent; idyllic. **4** providing spiritual care or guidance for a church congregation. **5** providing personal guidance for students. ➤ **pastoralism** *n,* **pastorally** *adv.*
**pastoral**[2] *n* a pastoral description, portrayal, or piece of music.
**past participle** *n* a participle, e.g. *taken,* used to form the pefect tense and passive voice.
**pastrami** *n* a highly seasoned smoked beef.
**pastry** *n* (*pl* **-ies**) **1** a fatty dough used to make pies, flans, and tarts. **2** a sweet tart or small cake.
**pasture**[1] *n* land used for grazing cattle or sheep.
**pasture**[2] *v* to feed (animals) on pasture.
**pasty**[1] *n* (*pl* **-ies**) a small savoury pastry case with a filling.
**pasty**[2] *adj* (**-ier, -iest**) **1** pallid and unhealthy in appearance. **2** having the consistency of paste.
**pat**[1] *n* **1** a light tap with the hand or a flat instrument. **2** a light tapping sound. **3** a small mass of butter. * **a pat on the back** an informal compliment.
**pat**[2] *v* (**patted, patting**) **1** to strike lightly with the open hand. **2** to put into place or shape with light blows.
**pat**[3] *adj* **1** prompt or immediate. **2** suspiciously appropriate or contrived.
**pat**[4] *adv* aptly or promptly. * **have something off pat** to have memorized something so that one can say it without hesitation.
**patch**[1] *n* **1** a piece of material used to mend a hole or reinforce a weak spot. **2** a shield worn over an injured eye. **3** a small area distinct from its surroundings. **4** a small piece of land used for growing. **5** a piece of medicated adhesive plaster worn on the skin to allow the drug to be absorbed. **6** a small file supplied to correct a fault in a computer program. **7** *Brit, informal* an area for which a particular person or group has responsibility. * **not a patch on** *Brit, informal* not nearly as good as.
**patch**[2] *v* **1** to mend with a patch. **2** to mend hastily or temporarily. **3** *informal* (+ up) to end (a quarrel or disagreement).
**patchwork** *n* **1** pieces of coloured cloth sewn together. **2** something made of incongruous parts.
**patchy** *adj* (**-ier, -iest**) **1** uneven in quality. **2** occurring in some areas and not others. ➤ **patchily** *adv.*
**pate** *n archaic or humorous* the head.
**pâté** *n* a rich savoury paste of spiced meat, fish, etc.
**patella** *n* (*pl* **patellae**) the kneecap.
**patent**[1] *n* an official licence allowing somebody the exclusive right to make, use, or sell an invention for a specified period.
**patent**[2] *adj* **1** readily visible or intelligible. **2** protected by or made under a patent. ➤ **patently** *adv.*
**patent**[3] *v* to obtain a patent for.
**patent leather** *n* leather with a hard glossy surface.
**paterfamilias** *n* the male head of a household.
**paternal** *adj* **1** typical of or characteristic of a father. **2** related through one's father. ➤ **paternally** *adv.*

**paternalism** *n* a system of dealing with subjects or employees in an authoritarian but protective way. ➤ **paternalistic** *adj.*
**paternity** *n* fatherhood.
**paternoster** *n* the Latin form of the Lord's Prayer.
**path** *n* **1** a track made for walking on or worn by walking. **2** a course or route. **3** in computing, the sequence of directories giving the location of a file.
**pathetic** *adj* **1** arousing pity; pitiful. **2** *informal* feeble or inadequate. ➤ **pathetically** *adv.*
**pathological** (*NAmer* **pathologic**) *adj* **1** involving or caused by disease. **2** *informal* irrationally habitual. ➤ **pathologically** *adv.*
**pathology** *n* **1** the study of the causes and nature of diseases. **2** the processes that characterize a particular disease. ➤ **pathologist** *n.*
**pathos** *n* a quality evoking pity or compassion.
**pathway** *n* a path or course.
**patience** *n* **1** the capacity to bear pains or trials without complaint. **2** *Brit* a card game played by one person.
**patient**[1] *adj* having or showing patience. ➤ **patiently** *adv.*
**patient**[2] *n* a person awaiting or receiving medical care.
**patina** *n* **1** a green or brown film formed by weathering on copper and bronze. **2** a surface shine developed on old polished wood.
**patio** *n* (*pl* **-os**) a paved area adjoining a house.
**patisserie** *n* an establishment where pastries and cakes are sold.
**patois** *n* (*pl* **patois**) **1** the local dialect of a region. **2** the jargon of a particular group.
**patriarch** *n* **1** a man who is head of a family or social group. **2** any of the biblical fathers of the human race. **3** a venerable old man. **4** a bishop in Orthodox and Eastern churches. ➤ **patriarchal** *adj.*
**patriarchy** *n* (*pl* **-ies**) a system of social organization with the father as head of the family and descent through the male line.
**patrician** *n* a person of high birth; an aristocrat. ➤ **patrician** *adj.*
**patricide** *n* **1** the act of killing one's father. **2** somebody who does this. ➤ **patricidal** *adj.*
**patrimony** *n* (*pl* **-ies**) property inherited from one's father or male ancestor.
**patriot** *n* a person who strongly supports their country. ➤ **patriotic** *adj*, **patriotism** *n.*
**patrol**[1] *n* a person or group sent to monitor or observe and area.
**patrol**[2] *v* (**patrolled, patrolling**) to carry out a patrol of (an area). ➤ **patroller** *n.*
**patron** *n* **1** a person who gives financial support to an individual or institution. **2** a regular customer of a hotel, restaurant, etc.
**patronage** *n* **1** support given by a patron. **2** the power to control political appointments. **3** custom provided by patrons of an establishment.
**patronize** *or* **-ise** *v* **1** to adopt an air of condescension towards. **2** to be a regular customer of. ➤ **patronizing** *adj.*
**patron saint** *n* a saint regarded as protecting a particular person, group, etc.
**patter**[1] *v* **1** to strike lightly and rapidly. **2** to run with quick light steps.
**patter**[2] *n* a quick succession of taps or pats.
**patter**[3] *n* rapid glib talk or jargon.
**pattern**[1] *n* **1** a repeated decorative design. **2** a regular arrangement or sequence. **3** a design, model, or set of instructions for making something. **4** an example or model for imitation.
**pattern**[2] *v* **1** to decorate with a pattern. **2** (+ on/after) to make according to a pattern.
**patty** *n* (*pl* **-ies**) a small pie or pasty.
**paucity** *n* smallness of number or quantity.
**paunch** *n* a large or protruding stomach. ➤ **paunchy** *adj.*
**pauper** *n* a very poor person.
**pause**[1] *n* a temporary stop in a process or activity.
**pause**[2] *v* to stop talking or doing something briefly.
**pave** *v* to cover (a piece of ground) with a flat surface of stones or concrete. ➤ **paving** *n.*
**pavement** *n* **1** *Brit* a raised walk for pedestrians at the side of a road. **2** *NAmer* the covered surface of a road. **3** a level area of bare rock.
**pavilion** *n* **1** *Brit* a building on a sports ground containing changing rooms, etc. **2** a light ornamental structure in a garden or park. **3** a temporary structure for an individual exhibitor at an exhibition.
**pavlova** *n* a dessert made of meringue topped with cream and fruit.
**paw**[1] *n* the clawed foot of an animal.
**paw**[2] *v* **1** to touch or scrape with a paw or hoof. **2** *informal* to touch (somebody) clumsily or indecently.
**pawn**[1] *n* **1** each of eight chess pieces of each colour of least value. **2** somebody who is exploited for another's purpose.
**pawn**[2] *v* to deposit (something) with a pawnbroker as security.
**pawn**[3] *n* the state of being pledged.
**pawnbroker** *n* a person who lends money on the security of personal property pledged, which can be sold if the money is not repaid.
**pawnshop** *n* a pawnbroker's shop.
**pawpaw** *or* **papaw** *n* a papaya.
**pay**[1] *v* (*past and past part.* **paid**) **1** to give money to in return for goods or services. **2** to give (money required or owed). **3** to discharge a debt on (a bill or account). **4** to give or forfeit (something) in reparation or retribution. **5** to give or offer (attention, one's respects, etc). **6** to make (a visit). **7** to make amends or be punished. ➤ **payable** *adj.*
**pay**[2] *n* money paid as a salary or wage.

**pay back** *v* **1** to repay (money owed). **2** to get revenge on.
**PAYE** *abbr Brit* pay as you earn, a system by which an employer deducts income tax from pay.
**payee** *n* a person receiving payment.
**paymaster** *n* an official whose duty it is to pay salaries or wages.
**payment** *n* **1** the act of paying. **2** a sum of money paid.
**payoff** *n informal* **1** a profit or reward. **2** a decisive factor resolving a situation.
**payola** *n chiefly NAmer* an undercover payment for unofficial promotion of a commercial product.
**payroll** *n* a list of employees of a company and of the amounts due to them in pay.
**Pb** *abbr* the chemical symbol for lead.
**PC** *abbr* **1** personal computer. **2** police constable. **3** political correct or correctness.
**Pd** *abbr* the chemical symbol for palladium.
**PE** *abbr* physical education.
**pea** *n* the rounded green seed of a climbing plant used as a vegetable.
**peace** *n* **1** a state of tranquillity or quiet. **2** freedom from anxiety. **3** public order and security. **4** freedom from hostility between countries. **5** an agreement to end hostilities.
**peaceable** *adj* **1** wanting to avoid hostility or conflict. **2** free from strife or disorder. ➤ **peaceably** *adv.*
**peaceful** *adj* **1** untroubled by noise or conflict; tranquil. **2** not involving violence or force. **3** not inclined to dispute or quarrel. ➤ **peacefully** *adv.*
**peach** *n* **1** a fruit with downy skin and sweet yellow flesh. **2** a light yellowish pink colour. **3** *informal* a fine or beautiful person or thing.
**peacock** *n* a large bird with a small head and brightly coloured tail feathers that can be spread in a fan.
**peahen** *n* a female bird of the peacock.
**peak**[1] *n* **1** a mountain or its pointed top. **2** a projecting part on the front of a cap. **3** a high point in a course of development. **4** the highest level or greatest degree. ➤ **peaked** *adj.*
**peak**[2] *v* to reach a maximum or high point.
**peal**[1] *n* **1** the loud ringing of bells. **2** a set of tuned bells. **3** a loud prolonged sound, e.g. of thunder or laughter.
**peal**[2] *v* to ring or sound loudly.
**peanut** *n* **1** a small oval seed that grows in a pod. **2** *informal* (*in pl*) a trifling amount of money.
**peanut butter** *n* a spread made from ground peanuts.
**pear** *n* a yellowish brown fruit, with a rounded shape narrowing towards the stalk.
**pearl** *n* **1** a hard round milky-white ball that forms in the shell of some molluscs and is used as a gem. **2** something very rare or precious. ➤ **pearly** *adj.*
**pearl barley** *n* barley that has been ground into medium-sized grains.
**pearlescent** *adj* having a shiny finish like a pearl.
**peasant** *n* **1** a member of a class of poor farm labourers or owners of smallholdings, having low social status. **2** *informal* an uneducated or rude person. ➤ **peasantry** *n.*
**pease pudding** *n* a puree of boiled split peas.
**peat** *n* partially carbonized vegetable tissue formed by partial decomposition in water of plants found in large bogs. ➤ **peaty** *adj.*
**pebble** *n* **1** a small rounded stone. **2** *informal* (*used before a noun*) very thick. ➤ **pebbly** *adj.*
**pebbledash** *n chiefly Brit* small pebbles embedded in a stucco base, used to coat exterior walls.
**pecan** *n* a smooth oblong edible nut.
**peccadillo** *n* (*pl* **-oes** *or* **-os**) a slight or trifling offence.
**peck**[1] *v* **1** of a bird: to strike or pierce with its beak. **2** to kiss (somebody) gently. **3** *informal* to eat reluctantly in small bites.
**peck**[2] *n* **1** an act of pecking. **2** a quick sharp stroke. **3** a light kiss.
**peck**[3] *n* a unit of volume or capacity equal to 2 gallons (9.092l).
**pecker** *n* ✱ **keep one's pecker up** *Brit, informal* to stay cheerful despite difficulty.
**pecking order** *n* a hierarchy of importance in a group of animals or people.
**peckish** *adj chiefly Brit, informal* slightly hungry.
**pectin** *n* a substance in fruit that acts as a setting agent in jams and jellies. ➤ **pectic** *adj.*
**pectoral**[1] *adj* relating to the chest.
**pectoral**[2] *n* each of the muscles connecting the front walls of the chest with the bones of the upper arm and shoulder.
**peculiar** *adj* **1** different from the usual; strange. **2** (+ to) belonging exclusively to. ➤ **peculiarly** *adv.*
**peculiarity** *n* (*pl* **-ies**) **1** a distinguishing characteristic. **2** the state of being peculiar.
**pecuniary** *adj formal* relating to money.
**pedagogue** *n formal* a teacher. ➤ **pedagogy** *n.*
**pedal**[1] *n* a lever operated by the foot, e.g. on a bicycle or in a motor vehicle, or one pressed in playing a musical instrument.
**pedal**[2] *v* (**pedalled, pedalling,** *NAmer* **pedaled, pedaling**) to work the pedals of (a bicycle).
**pedalo** *n* (*pl* **-os** *or* **-oes**) *Brit* a small pleasure boat with paddles turned by pedals.
**pedant** *n* a person who is excessively concerned with detail. ➤ **pedantic** *adj,* **pedantry** *n.*

**peddle** *v* **1** to sell (goods) as a pedlar. **2** to sell (illegal drugs). **3** *derog* to seek to disseminate (ideas or opinions).
**peddler** *n* **1** a person who peddles something. **2** *NAmer* see PEDLAR.
**pederast** *or* **paederast** *n* a man who has sexual intercourse with a boy. ➤ **pederasty** *n.*
**pedestal** *n* **1** a base supporting a column or statue. **2** a supporting column of a washbasin or a toilet.
**pedestrian**[1] *n* a person going on foot.
**pedestrian**[2] *adj* dull or commonplace.
**pedicure** *n* a treatment for the care of the feet and toenails.
**pedigree** *n* **1** the record of an animal's line of descent. **2** the distinguished ancestral line of a person. **3** the origin and history of something.
**pediment** *n* in a classical building, the triangular piece of wall in the angle formed by the two slopes of the roof.
**pedlar** (*NAmer* **peddler**) *n* a person who travels about offering small wares for sale.
**pedometer** *n* an instrument that records the distance a walker covers by responding to body motion at each step.
**pee**[1] *v informal* to urinate.
**pee**[2] *n informal* **1** an act of urinating. **2** urine.
**peek**[1] *v* **1** to take a brief look. **2** to be just visible behind something else.
**peek**[2] *n* a brief look.
**peel**[1] *v* **1** to strip the skin or rind off (a fruit or vegetable). **2** to remove (something) by stripping it. **3** to lose an outer layer.
**peel**[2] *n* the skin or rind of a fruit or vegetable.
**peep**[1] *v* **1** to look cautiously or slyly. **2** (*often* + out) to begin to emerge from concealment.
**peep**[2] *n* **1** a brief or furtive look. **2** the first faint appearance of something.
**peep**[3] *v* to make a short shrill sound. ➤ **peep** *n.*
**peephole** *n* a hole in a door through which callers can be observed.
**peeping Tom** *n* a voyeur.
**peep show** *n* a sequence of pictures viewed through a small hole.
**peer**[1] *v* **1** to look curiously or searchingly at something. **2** to be partially visible.
**peer**[2] *n* **1** a member of the British nobility. **2** a person of the same age or social group as another.
**peerage** *n* **1** the rank or title of a peer. **2** (**the peerage**) the body of peers.
**peeress** *n* **1** a woman having the rank of a peer. **2** the wife or widow of a peer.
**peer group** *n* a group of people of approximately the same age or status.
**peerless** *adj* matchless or incomparable.
**peeve**[1] *v informal* to annoy.
**peeve**[2] *n informal* a grievance or grudge.
**peevish** *adj* querulous or fretful. ➤ **peevishly** *adv.*
**peewit** *or* **pewit** *n Brit* a lapwing.
**peg**[1] *n* **1** a small pointed or tapered piece of hard material used to hang things on or hold things down. **2** a clip for holding washing on a line for drying. ✱ **off the peg** *chiefly Brit* of clothes: ready-made.
**peg**[2] *v* (**pegged, pegging**) **1** to fix or mark with pegs. **2** to hold (prices, etc) at a certain level.
**peg out** *v chiefly Brit, informal* to die.
**peignoir** *n* a woman's loose negligee.
**pejorative** *adj* expressing criticism; disparaging. ➤ **pejoratively** *adv.*
**Pekinese** *n* a small dog with a snub nose and a thick soft coat.
**pelican** *n* a bird with a pouch hanging from its bill for catching and keeping fish.
**pelican crossing** *n* a pedestrian crossing controlled by traffic lights.
**pellagra** *n* a disease associated with a deficiency in the diet, marked by inflammation of the skin, diarrhoea, and disorders of the central nervous system.
**pellet** *n* **1** a small rounded mass of a substance. **2** a piece of small shot.
**pell-mell** *adv and adj* in confusion or disorder.
**pellucid** *adj* **1** clear or transparent. **2** easy to understand.
**pelmet** *n* a length of board or fabric placed above a window to conceal curtain fixtures.
**pelt**[1] *v* **1** to throw things at. **2** of rain: to fall heavily. **3** to run fast.
**pelt**[2] *n* ✱ **at full pelt** with great speed.
**pelt**[3] *n* an undressed animal skin with its hair, wool, or fur.
**pelvis** *n* a basin-shaped structure at the base of the spine. ➤ **pelvic** *adj.*
**pen**[1] *n* an implement for writing or drawing with ink.
**pen**[2] *v* (**penned, penning**) to write.
**pen**[3] *n* a small enclosure for farm animals.
**pen**[4] *v* (**penned, penning**) to shut in a pen.
**pen**[5] *n* a female swan.
**penal** *adj* **1** relating to or prescribing punishment. **2** of an offence: liable to punishment. **3** harsh.
**penalize** *or* **-ise** *v* **1** to inflict a penalty on. **2** to put at a disadvantage.
**penalty** *n* (*pl* **-ies**) **1** a punishment imposed for doing wrong or breaking a rule. **2** a penalty kick. **3** disadvantage, loss, or suffering due to some action.
**penalty area** *n* a rectangular area in front of each goal on a football pitch.
**penalty kick** *n* in football, a free kick at goal in football or rugby.
**penance** *n* **1** a penalty or personal sacrifice undertaken to show repentance for sin. **2** a sacramental rite of some Churches involving confession and performance of a penance.
**pence** *n* pl of PENNY.
**penchant** *n* a strong liking.

**pencil**[1] *n* an implement for writing or drawing consisting of a slender strip of graphite in a wooden case.

**pencil**[2] *v* (**pencilled, pencilling,** *NAmer* **penciled, penciling**) to draw or write with a pencil. ✱ **pencil in** to record a provisional appointment.

**pencil skirt** *n* a narrow straight skirt.

**pendant** *n* **1** an ornament hanging from a chain worn round the neck. **2** an electric light fitting suspended from the ceiling.

**pending**[1] *prep* while awaiting; until.

**pending**[2] *adj* **1** not yet decided or dealt with. **2** about to happen.

**pendulous** *adj* hanging down.

**pendulum** *n* a weight suspended from a fixed point so as to swing freely, used to regulate the mechanism of a clock.

**penetrate** *v* **1** to pass into or through. **2** to enter (an organization or a market) by overcoming resistance. **3** to insert the penis into the vagina or anus of (a sexual partner). **4** to see into or through. **5** to discover the inner contents or meaning of. **6** to diffuse through or into. **7** to be understood. ➤ **penetration** *n.*

**pen-friend** *n* a person with whom a friendship is made by exchanging letters.

**penguin** *n* a flightless sea bird of the southern hemisphere, with a dark back and white belly, wings resembling flippers, and webbed feet.

**penicillin** *n* an antibiotic originally obtained from moulds.

**penile** *adj* relating to the penis.

**peninsula** *n* a narrow strip of land almost surrounded by water. ➤ **peninsular** *adj.*

**penis** *n* (*pl* **penises** *or* **penes**) the male organ used for sexual intercourse and urination.

**penitent**[1] *adj* feeling sorrow for sins or offences. ➤ **penitence** *n,* **penitential** *adj.*

**penitent**[2] *n* somebody who repents of sin.

**penitentiary** *n* (*pl* **-ies**) *NAmer* a prison for people convicted of serious crimes.

**penknife** *n* (*pl* **penknives**) a small knife with a blade that folds into the handle.

**pennant** *n* a flag that tapers to a point or divides into two points.

**penne** *pl n* pasta in short tubes with diagonally cut ends.

**penniless** *adj* having no money.

**penny** *n* (*pl* **pennies** *or* **pence**) **1** a unit of currency worth 100th of a pound. **2** formerly in Britain, a bronze coin worth 240th of a pound.

**penny-farthing** *n Brit* an early type of bicycle with a small rear wheel and a large front wheel.

**penny-pinching** *adj* mean or stingy. ➤ **penny-pincher** *n.*

**penny whistle** *n* a simple whistle with finger holes.

**pension**[1] *n* a fixed sum paid regularly to a retired person.

**pension**[2] *v* to pay a pension to. ➤ **pensionable** *adj.*

**pension**[3] /'ponhsyonh/ *n* a hotel or boarding house in a European country.

**pensioner** *n* a person who receives a retirement pension.

**pension off** *v* to retire (somebody) from service with a pension.

**pensive** *adj* deeply thoughtful. ➤ **pensively** *adv.*

**pentacle** *n* a pentagram.

**pentagon** *n* a figure with five angles and five sides. ➤ **pentagonal** *adj.*

**pentagram** *n* a five-pointed star used as a magical symbol.

**pentameter** *n* a line of verse consisting of five metrical feet.

**pentathlon** *n* an athletic contest consisting of five events.

**Pentecost** *n* a Christian festival commemorating the descent of the Holy Spirit on the apostles, observed on the seventh Sunday after Easter.

**Pentecostal** *adj* **1** of evangelical Christian bodies that lay emphasis on the gifts of the Holy Spirit, e.g. healing the sick. **2** relating to Pentecost. ➤ **Pentecostalism** *n.*

**penthouse** *n* an apartment on the roof or top floor of a building.

**penultimate** *adj* last but one.

**penumbra** *n* **1** a region of partial darkness in a shadow surrounding the umbra. **2** a less dark region surrounding the dark centre of a sunspot. ➤ **penumbral** *adj.*

**penurious** *adj formal* very poor.

**penury** *n* severe poverty.

**peony** *or* **paeony** *n* (*pl* **-ies**) a plant with large showy flowers.

**people**[1] *pl n* **1** human beings in general. **2** one's family. **3** (**the people**) the inhabitants or citizens of a state. **4** a body of persons forming a politically organized group.

**people**[2] *v* **1** to fill (a place) with people. **2** to dwell in or inhabit (a place).

**pep**[1] *n informal* energy or high spirits.

**pep**[2] *v* (**pepped, pepping**) (*usu* + up) to fill with energy or enthusiasm.

**pepper**[1] *n* **1** a hot-tasting ground black or white powder obtained from peppercorns, used for flavouring. **2** any of various fruits of tropical plants. ➤ **peppery** *adj.*

**pepper**[2] *v* **1** to season with pepper. **2** to cover extensively with many instances of a thing. **3** to shower (somebody or something) with shot or other missiles.

**peppercorn** *n* a dried berry of a plant, used as a spice or ground as powder.

**peppercorn rent** *n Brit* a very low or nominal rent.

**peppermint** *n* **1** a mint plant with dark green tapering leaves and whorls of small pink flowers. **2** an aromatic essential oil obtained from this. **3** a sweet flavoured with peppermint oil.
**pepperoni** *or* **peperoni** *n* a spicy Italian beef and pork sausage.
**pep talk** *n informal* a talk designed to encourage morale.
**peptic** *adj* of or promoting digestion.
**peptic ulcer** *n* an ulcer in the mucous membranes of the digestive tract.
**per** *prep* **1** for each. **2** by the means of.
**perambulate** *v formal* to travel on foot. ➤ **perambulation** *n.*
**perambulator** *n formal* a pram.
**per annum** *adv* for each year.
**per capita** *adv and adj* for each person.
**perceive** *v* **1** to become aware of (something) through the senses. **2** to regard in the specified way. ➤ **perceivable** *adj.*

***Usage Note:*** Note the spelling with *-ei-*.

**per cent**[1] *adv* for each hundred.
**per cent**[2] *n* (*pl* **per cent**) **1** one part in a hundred. **2** a percentage.
**percentage** *n* **1** a proportion expressed as per cent of a whole. **2** a share or proportion of a whole.
**percentile** *n* each of the 100 groups of individuals comprising a part of a population for statistical purposes.
**perceptible** *adj* able to be perceived by the senses. ➤ **perceptibly** *adv.*
**perception** *n* **1** an awareness of one's surroundings produced by the senses. **2** a result of perceiving; an observation. **3** intuitive discernment; insight.
**perceptive** *adj* showing keen perception; observant or discerning. ➤ **perceptively** *adv.*
**perceptual** *adj* relating to perception or sensory experience. ➤ **perceptually** *adv.*
**perch**[1] *n* **1** a roost for a bird. **2** a seat or resting place.
**perch**[2] *v* **1** to settle briefly or precariously. **2** to place in a high or precarious spot.
**perch**[3] *n* (*pl* **perches** *or* **perch**) a freshwater fish with vertical stripes and spiny fins.
**perchance** *adv archaic* perhaps or possibly.
**percipient** *adj* perceptive or discerning. ➤ **percipience** *n.*
**percolate** *v* **1** of a liquid or gas: to pass through a porous substance. **2** of information: to spread gradually through a group or area. **3** to prepare (coffee) in a percolator. **4** of coffee: to be prepared in a percolator. ➤ **percolation** *n.*
**percolator** *n* a coffee pot in which boiling water passes through a perforated basket containing ground coffee beans.
**percussion** *n* musical instruments played by striking or shaking them. ➤ **percussionist** *n.*
**perdition** *n* in Christianity, eternal damnation.
**peregrination** *n archaic* a long and wandering journey.
**peregrine** *n* a falcon with dark grey wings and back.
**peremptory** *adj* aggressively or unreasonably insistent. ➤ **peremptorily** *adv.*
**perennial**[1] *adj* **1** lasting throughout the year or for several years. **2** of a plant: living for several years with new growth each year. ➤ **perennially** *adv.*
**perennial**[2] *n* a perennial plant.
**perestroika** *n* the political and social reform of the communist system of the former Soviet Union.
**perfect**[1] *adj* **1** entirely without fault or defect; flawless or entirely satisfactory. **2** lacking in no essential detail; complete. **3** absolute or utter. **4** of the verb tense that expresses an action or state completed at the time of speaking or at a time spoken of. ➤ **perfectly** *adv.*
**perfect**[2] *v* to make perfect. ➤ **perfectible** *adj.*
**perfection** *n* **1** making or being perfect. **2** something or somebody that is pefect.
**perfectionism** *n* a wish for everything one does to be perfect. ➤ **perfectionist** *adj and n.*
**perfect pitch** *n* the ability to sing or identify a note of a given pitch.
**perfidious** *adj* treacherously disloyal.
**perfidy** *n literary* faithlessness or disloyalty.
**perforate** *v* to make a hole or holes in. ➤ **perforation** *n.*
**perforce** *adv formal* by necessity.
**perform** *v* **1** to do or carry out. **2** to give a rendering of (a dramatic or musical piece). ➤ **performer** *n.*
**performance** *n* **1** the act or an instance of performing. **2** a presentation to an audience of a play, piece of music, dance, etc. **3** the ability of a machine to operate. **4** *informal* a tedious process or piece of behaviour.
**performing arts** *pl n* arts that are performed to an audience, e.g. music, dance, and drama.
**perfume**[1] *n* **1** a pleasant-smelling liquid preparation applied to the skin. **2** a sweet or pleasant smell. ➤ **perfumery** *n.*
**perfume**[2] *v* **1** to give a sweet smell to. **2** to apply perfume to.
**perfunctory** *adj* mechanical or cursory. ➤ **perfunctorily** *adv.*
**pergola** *n* an arched framework for training plants over.
**perhaps** *adv* possibly but not certainly; maybe.
**peril** *n* exposure to the risk of being injured or lost. ➤ **perilous** *adj,* **perilously** *adv.*
**perimeter** *n* **1** the boundary of a closed plane figure. **2** an outer edge or limit. ➤ **perimetric** *adj.*
**period** *n* **1** a portion of time. **2** a stage of history. **3** (*used before a noun*) of a particular

historical time: *period costume.* **4** any of the divisions of the school day. **5** an occurrence of menstruation. **6** *chiefly NAmer* a full stop.

**periodic** *adj* recurring at regular intervals.

**periodical[1]** *adj* **1** recurring at regular intervals.**2** of a magazine or journal: published at fixed intervals. ➤ **periodically** *adv.*

**periodical[2]** *n* a periodical publication.

**periodic table** *n* a listing of the chemical elements by their atomic numbers.

**period piece** *n* a piece of furniture or work of art that evokes a historical period.

**peripatetic** *adj* travelling or itinerant.

**peripheral[1]** *adj* **1** of or forming an outer limit or boundary. **2** of relatively minor significance. **3** auxiliary or supplementary. ➤ **peripherally** *adv.*

**peripheral[2]** *n* a printer or other device connected to a computer.

**periphery** *n* (*pl* **-ies**) **1** the outer limits or edge of something. **2** a less important or central position.

**periscope** *n* a tubular optical instrument containing mirrors or prisms for seeing objects not in the direct line of sight.

**perish** *v* **1** to die. **2** to be ruined or destroyed. **3** to deteriorate or rot. **4** of cold or exposure: to weaken or numb (somebody). * **perish the thought** *informal* used to express horror at an idea.

**perishable** *adj* of food: liable to rot or decay.

**peristalsis** *n* successive waves of involuntary contraction passing along the walls of the intestine and forcing the contents onward.

**peritoneum** *n* (*pl* **peritoneums** *or* **peritonea**) a smooth transparent membrane lining the cavity of the abdomen. ➤ **peritoneal** *adj.*

**peritonitis** *n* inflammation of the peritoneum.

**periwinkle** *n* **1** a trailing evergreen plant with blue or white flowers. **2** a marine snail with a spiral shell.

**perjure** *v* to make (oneself) guilty of perjury.

**perjury** *n* (*pl* **-ies**) the deliberate violation of an oath in a court of law.

**perk** *n informal* an extra privilege or benefit.

**perk up** *v* to become more lively or cheerful.

**perky** *adj* (**-ier, -iest**) lively and cheerful.

**perm[1]** *n* a long-lasting arrangement of the hair by using chemicals.

**perm[2]** *v* to give a perm to (the hair).

**perm[3]** *n Brit, informal* a permutation of the teams in a football pool.

**permafrost** *n* a layer of permanently frozen ground in cold regions.

**permanent** *adj* lasting or stable. ➤ **permanence** *n,* **permanently** *adv.*

**permeable** *adj* having pores or openings that permit liquids or gases to pass through.

**permeate** *v* to spread throughout.

**permissible** *adj* allowed.

**permission** *n* formal consent or authorization to do something.

**permissive** *adj* tolerant with regard to social or sexual morality. ➤ **permissiveness** *n.*

**permit[1]** *v* (**permitted, permitting**) **1** to give authorization to do something. **2** to consent to. **3** *formal* (+ of) to make possible.

**permit[2]** *n* an official document allowing somebody to do or keep something.

**permutation** *n* each of various possible arrangements of things.

**pernicious** *adj* highly injurious or destructive.

**pernickety** *adj* **1** fussy about details. **2** requiring precision and care.

**peroration** *n* the concluding part of a speech.

**peroxide** *n* **1** an oxide containing a high proportion of oxygen. **2** a chemical used in bleaching hair.

**perpendicular[1]** *adj* at right angles to the plane of the horizon or a given line or plane.

**perpendicular[2]** *n* a perpendicular line, plane, or surface.

**perpetrate** *v* to be guilty of (something wrong). ➤ **perpetration** *n,* **perpetrator** *n.*

**perpetual** *adj* **1** continuing for all time. **2** repeated or constant. ➤ **perpetually** *adv.*

**perpetuate** *v* to cause to last indefinitely. ➤ **perpetuation** *n.*

**perpetuity** *n* (*pl* **-ies**) the state of being perpetual.

**perplex** *v* to puzzle or confuse. ➤ **perplexity** *n.*

**perquisite** *n formal* an extra privilege or benefit.

**per se** *adv* in itself.

**persecute** *v* **1** to harass or harm (somebody) because of their religion, political beliefs, etc. **2** to annoy or pester. ➤ **persecution** *n,* **persecutor** *n.*

**persevere** *v* (*often* + in/with) to persist in an undertaking in spite of difficulties. ➤ **perseverance** *n.*

**Persian** *n* **1** a native or inhabitant of ancient Persia or modern Iran. **2** the language of ancient Persia and modern Iran. **3** a short-nosed cat with a long silky coat. ➤ **Persian** *adj.*

**persimmon** *n* a round fruit with flesh that is sweet when ripe.

**persist** *v* **1** (*often* + in/with) to continue resolutely in spite of difficulty. **2** to continue to exist.

**persistent** *adj* **1** persisting in a course of action. **2** continuing or recurring. ➤ **persistence** *n,* **persistently** *adv.*

**person** *n* (*pl* **people** *or formal* **persons**) **1** a distinct human being. **2** a living human body. **3** any of three forms of a verb or pronoun that indicate reference to the speaker, to somebody or something spoken to, or to somebody or something spoken of: compare FIRST PERSON, SECOND PERSON, THIRD PERSON. ✱ **in person** physically present oneself.

**persona** *n* (*pl* **personas** *or* **personae**) a role or character adopted by a person.

**personable** *adj* pleasing in person; attractive. ➤ **personably** *adv.*

**personage** *n* a person of rank or distinction.

**personal** *adj* **1** affecting a particular person; private. **2** done in person without the intervention of another. **3** carried on between individuals directly. **4** of the person or body. **5** relating to the private affairs of an individual. **6** referring offensively to the character, appearance, or private affairs of an individual.

**personal column** *n* a section of a newspaper containing personal messages and advertisements.

**personality** *n* (*pl* **-ies**) **1** the behavioural and emotional tendencies that an individual person has. **2** distinction or excellence of personal and social traits. **3** an important or celebrated person.

**personalize** *or* **-ise** *v* **1** to mark (something) as the property of a particular person. **2** to design or make (something) to fit in with a person's wishes or needs. **3** to focus (an argument, etc) on personalities rather than issues.

**personal pronoun** *n* a pronoun, e.g. *I, you, he, she*, or *they*, that relates to the speaker, the person addressed, or a person or people reffered to.

**personal stereo** *n* a small cassette player or CD player used with earphones or headphones.

**persona non grata** /puh,sohnə non 'grahtə/ *n* a person who is unwelcome at a particular place.

**personify** *v* (**-ies, -ied**) **1** to conceive of or represent (something not human) as having human qualities or human form. **2** to be the embodiment of (a quality) in human form. ➤ **personification** *n.*

**personnel** *n* a body of people employed by an organization.

**perspective** *n* **1** the relationship of solid objects to each other in space as they appear to the eye, or the technique of showing this on a flat surface. **2** the aspect of an object of thought from a particular standpoint. **3** the capacity to understand the true relationship or relative importance of things. **4** a picture showing a vista.

**Perspex** *n trademark* a transparent acrylic plastic.

**perspicacious** *adj* having acute mental vision or discernment. ➤ **perspicacity** *n.*

**perspicuous** *adj* clear and precise and easy to understand. ➤ **perspicuity** *n.*

**perspiration** *n* **1** the process of sweating. **2** sweat.

**perspire** *v* to sweat.

**persuade** *v* to make (somebody) believe or do something by argument, reasoning, or entreaty. ➤ **persuadable** *adj.*

**persuasion** *n* **1** the process of persuading or being persuaded. **2** a particular belief or system of beliefs.

**persuasive** *adj* tending or able to persuade. ➤ **persuasively** *adv.*

**pert** *adj* **1** impudent and forward; saucy. **2** trim and chic; jaunty.

**pertain** *v* to belong to or be appropriate to.

**pertinacious** *adj formal* clinging resolutely to an opinion or purpose. ➤ **pertinacity** *n.*

**pertinent** *adj* relevant to the matter in hand. ➤ **pertinence** *n*, **pertinently** *adv.*

**perturb** *v* to disturb greatly in the mind; to trouble. ➤ **perturbation** *n.*

**peruse** *v formal* to read or examine in detail. ➤ **perusal** *n.*

**pervade** *v* to become diffused through every part of. ➤ **pervasive** *adj.*

**perverse** *adj* **1** obstinate in opposing what is reasonable or accepted. **2** arising from stubbornness or obstinacy. **3** uncooperative or contrary. ➤ **perversely** *adv*, **perverseness** *n*, **perversity** *n.*

**perversion** *n* **1** the act of perverting. **2** abnormal sexual behaviour.

**pervert**[1] *v* **1** to cause (somebody) to turn away from what is true or morally right. **2** to divert to a wrong use or purpose. **3** to twist the meaning or sense of.

**pervert**[2] *n* a person who enjoys abnormal sexual behaviour.

**perverted** *adj* sexually abnormal.

**pervious** *adj* allowing liquid to pass through.

**peseta** /pə'saytə/ *n* the former basic monetary unit of Spain (replaced by the euro in 2002).

**pesky** *adj* (**-ier, -iest**) *informal* troublesome or annoying.

**pessary** *n* (*pl* **-ies**) a device worn in the vagina to support the uterus or prevent conception.

**pessimism** *n* a tendency to stress the worst aspects of something to expect the worst outcome. ➤ **pessimist** *n*, **pessimistic** *adj*, **pessimistically** *adv.*

**pest** *n* **1** a nuisance. **2** an animal or insect that causes damage or carries disease.

**pester** *v* to harass or annoy with petty irritations and demands.

**pesticide** *n* a chemical used to destroy insects and other pests.

**pestilence** *n* a virulent epidemic disease.

**pestilential** *adj* **1** destructive of life; deadly. **2** morally harmful; pernicious. **3** *informal* annoying or irritating.

**pestle** *n* an implement with a rounded tip for pounding substances in a mortar.

**pesto** *n* a paste made from crushed basil leaves, garlic, pine nuts, olive oil, and Parmesan cheese.

**pet**[1] *n* **1** an animal, bird, etc kept for pleasure. **2** somebody who is treated with special favour.

**pet**[2] *adj* **1** favourite. **2** special or strongest.

**pet**[3] *v* (**petted, petting**) **1** to stroke (an animal) in a gentle or loving manner. **2** to engage in amorous caressing.

**pet**[4] *n* a fit of sulkiness or anger.

**petal** *n* any of the outer parts that form a flower.

**peter out** *v* to diminish gradually and come to an end.

**petite** *adj* of a woman: having a small trim figure.

**petit four** /ˌpeti ˈfaw/ *n* (*pl* **petits fours** *or* **petit fours** /ˌpeti ˈfawz/) a small fancy cake or biscuit.

**petition**[1] *n* **1** a formal written request made to somebody in authority by a large number of people. **2** an earnest request.

**petition**[2] *v* to present a petition to. ➤ **petitioner** *n.*

**petit point** /ˌpeti ˈpoynt/ *n* embroidery on canvas across single threads in tent stitch.

**pet name** *n* an informal name used for endearment.

**petrel** *n* a sea bird that comes inland to breed.

**petri dish** *or* **Petri dish** *n* a small shallow glass or plastic dish with a loose cover, used in laboratories.

**petrify** *v* (**-ies, -ied**) **1** to paralyse with fear or amazement. **2** to convert into stone or a hard or stony substance.

**petrochemical**[1] *n* a chemical obtained from petroleum or natural gas.

**petrochemical**[2] *adj* relating to petrochemicals or the properties of petroleum and natural gas.

**petrol** *n chiefly Brit* a mixture refined from petroleum and used as a fuel for internal-combustion engines.

**petroleum** *n* an inflammable liquid composed of a mixture of hydrocarbons, refined for use as petrol, naphtha, etc.

**petticoat** *n* a woman's light undergarment hanging from the waist or shoulders.

**pettifogging** *adj archaic* quibbling or trivial.

**pettish** *adj* peevish or petulant. ➤ **pettishly** *adv.*

**petty** *adj* (**-ier, -iest**) **1** trivial. **2** having little importance. **3** small-minded. **4** of a crime: minor. ➤ **pettiness** *n.*

**petty cash** *n* an amount of cash kept for payment of minor items.

**petty officer** *n* a rank of non-commissioned naval officer.

**petulant** *adj* childishly bad-tempered or peevish. ➤ **petulance** *n,* **petulantly** *adv.*

**petunia** *n* a plant with large brightly coloured funnel-shaped flowers.

**pew** *n* **1** a bench fixed in a row for the use of the congregation in a church. **2** *Brit, informal* a seat.

**pewter** *n* an alloy of tin and lead or one containing copper and antimony.

**pfennig** /ˈ(p)fenig, ˈ(p)fenikh/ *n* a former unit of currency in Germany, worth 100th of a mark (replaced by the euro in 2002).

**PFI** *abbr* Private Finance Initiative.

**PG** *adj* in Britain, a classification of cinema films for which parental guidance is recommended.

**pH** *n* a figure used to show how acid or alkaline a solution is.

**phalanx** *n* **1** a close arrangement of people, animals, or things. **2** a body of troops in close array behind a wall of shields.

**phallic** *adj* of or resembling a phallus.

**phallus** *n* (*pl* **phalli** *or* **phalluses**) a representation of an erect penis.

**phantasm** *n literary* **1** an illusion or figment. **2** a ghost or spectre.

**phantasmagoria** *n* a confused succession of things imagined in a dream or feverish state.

**phantom**[1] *n* **1** a ghost. **2** something existing only in the imagination.

**phantom**[2] *adj* non-existent.

**pharaoh** *n* a ruler of ancient Egypt. ➤ **pharaonic** *adj.*

---
***Usage Note:*** Note the spelling *-aoh* not *-oah.*

---

**pharisee** *n* a member of a Jewish party that interpreted religious law strictly.

**pharmaceutical**[1] *adj* relating to medicinal substances.

**pharmaceutical**[2] *n* a medicinal drug.

**pharmacology** *n* the science of drugs and their effect on living things. ➤ **pharmacological** *adj,* **pharmacologist** *n.*

**pharmacy** *n* (*pl* **-ies**) **1** a place where medicines are prepared and dispensed. **2** a chemist's shop. **3** the preparation and dispensing of medicinal drugs. ➤ **pharmacist** *n.*

**pharynx** *n* (*pl* **pharynges** *or* **pharynxes**) the part of the alimentary canal between the mouth cavity and the throat.

**phase**[1] *n* a distinct part or stage in a process or activity.

**phase**[2] *v* to carry out (an activity) in planned phases.

**phase in** *v* to introduce in gradual stages.

**phase out** *v* to discontinue in gradual stages.

**PhD** *abbr* Doctor of Philosophy.

**pheasant** *n* (*pl* **pheasants** *or* **pheasant**) a large long-tailed game bird.

**phenomenal** *adj* extraordinary or remarkable. ➤ **phenomenally** *adv.*

**phenomenon** *n* (*pl* **phenomena**) **1** an observable fact or event. **2** an exceptional or unusual person, thing, or event.

---
***Usage Note:*** *Phenomenon* is a singular noun, and *phenomena* is the plural.

---

**pheromone** *n* a chemical substance produced by an animal that stimulates responses in the same species.

**phi** *n* the 21st letter of the Greek alphabet (Φ, ϕ).

**phial** *n* a small bottle for holding liquid medicine.

**philander** *v* of a man: to have many casual love affairs. ➤ **philanderer** *n.*

**philanthropy** *n* active effort to promote the welfare of others. ➤ **philanthropic** *adj,* **philanthropist** *n.*

**philately** *n* the study and collection of postage stamps. ➤ **philatelist** *n.*

**philharmonic** *adj* used *esp* in the names of choirs and orchestras: devoted to music.

**philippic** *n literary* an attacking speech or declamation.

**philistine** *n* **1** (**Philistine**) a member of a people of ancient Palestine. **2** a person who has no interest in intellectual or aesthetic values. ➤ **philistinism** *n.*

**philology** *n* the study of the development and structure of languages. ➤ **philological** *adj,* **philologist** *n.*

**philosopher** *n* **1** somebody who studies philosophy. **2** a scholar or thinker.

**philosophical** *adj* **1** of philosophers or philosophy. **2** calm in the face of trouble. ➤ **philosophically** *adv.*

**philosophize** *or* **-ise** *v* to engage in philosophical reasoning.

**philosophy** *n* (*pl* **-ies**) **1** the study of the nature of knowledge and existence. **2** a specific set of philosophical principles.

**phlegm** *n* thick mucus in the nose and throat.

**phlegmatic** *adj* having a calm temperament. ➤ **phlegmatically** *adv.*

**phobia** *n* an irrational fear of something. ➤ **phobic** *adj and n.*

**phoenix** (*NAmer* **phenix**) *n* a mythical bird believed to burn itself on a pyre and rise alive from the ashes.

**phone**[1] *n* a telephone.

**phone**[2] *v* to make a telephone call.

**phonecard** *n* a plastic card used to make telephone calls from a public telephone.

**phonetic** *adj* **1** of spoken language or speech sounds. **2** representing speech sounds by symbols that each have one value only. ➤ **phonetically** *adv.*

**phonetics** *pl n* the study and classification of speech sounds.

**phoney**[1] *or* **phony** *adj* (**-ier, -iest**) *informal* not genuine or real.

**phoney**[2] *or* **phony** *n* (*pl* **-eys** *or* **-ies**) a phoney person or thing.

**phonic** *adj* **1** of or producing sound; acoustic. **2** relating to speech sounds. ➤ **phonically** *adv.*

**phonics** *pl n* a system of teaching reading through the phonetic value of syllables.

**phonograph** *n* **1** an early device for recording and reproducing sound. **2** *NAmer* a record player.

**phosphate** *n* a salt or ester of a phosphoric acid.

**phosphorescence** *n* **1** light emission caused by the absorption of radiation and continuing after the radiation has stopped. **2** lasting emission of light without noticeable heat. ➤ **phosphorescent** *adj.*

**phosphoric acid** *n* an acid used in preparing phosphates, used in fertilizers and as a flavouring.

**phosphorus** *n* a non-metallic element that occurs as phosphates. ➤ **phosphorous** *adj.*

**photo** *n* (*pl* **-os**) a photograph.

**photocall** *n* a session at which a famous person is photographed publicity.

**photocopy**[1] *n* (*pl* **-ies**) a reproduction of written or printed text, photographs, etc by a process involving photography.

**photocopy**[2] *v* (**-ies, -ied**) to make a photocopy of. ➤ **photocopiable** *adj,* **photocopier** *n.*

**photoelectric** *adj* involving electrical effects caused by the interaction of radiation with matter.

**photo finish** *n* a close finish to a race with the winner decided from a photograph.

**photofit** *n* a likeness of a person's face constructed from photographs.

**photogenic** *adj* looking attractive in photographs.

**photograph**[1] *n* a picture or likeness obtained by photography.

**photograph**[2] *v* to take a photograph of. ➤ **photographer** *n,* **photographic** *adj.*

**photography** *n* the process of producing images on a sensitized surface by the action of light.

**photogravure** *n* a process for making prints from an engraving produced from photographic negatives, or a picture produced in this way.

**photometer** *n* an instrument for measuring light intensity or brightness. ➤ **photometric** *adj,* **photometry** *n.*

**photon** *n* a very small quantity of electromagnetic radiation.

**photosensitive** *adj* sensitive to light.

**Photostat** *n* **1** *trademark* a device for making a photographic copy of documents. **2** (**photostat**) a copy made in this way.

**photostat** *v* (**photostatted, photostatting**) to copy on a Photostat or similar device.

**photosynthesis** *n* the process by which plants synthesize organic chemical compounds from carbon dioxide using light. ➤ **photosynthetic** *adj.*

**phrase**[1] *n* **1** a group of words that go together in a sentence but do not form a clause. **2** in music, a group of notes forming a unit of melody. ➤ **phrasal** *adj.*

**phrase**[2] *v* to express in a particular form of words.

**phrase book** *n* a book containing words and phrases in a foreign language with their translation.

**phraseology** *n* (*pl* **-ies**) a manner of putting words and phrases together.

**phrenology** *n* the former study of the shape of the skull as a supposed indicator of mental faculties and character. ➤ **phrenologist** *n.*

**phylum** *n* (*pl* **phyla**) a major group of related species in the classification of plants and animals.

**physical**[1] *adj* **1** having material existence; perceptible through the senses. **2** relating to material things. **3** relating to the body: *a physical examination.* **4** concerned or preoccupied with the body and its needs, as opposed to spiritual matters. **5** involving bodily contact. **6** relating to sciences such as physics, chemistry, and astronomy. ➤ **physicality** *n,* **physically** *adv.*

**physical**[2] *n* a medical examination to determine a person's health and fitness.

**physical education** *n* instruction in sports, athletics, and gymnastics.

**physician** *n* a person skilled in medicine.

**physics** *pl n* the branch of science that deals with matter and energy and their properties. ➤ **physicist** *n.*

**physiognomy** *n* (*pl* **-ies**) a person's face and facial features.

**physiology** *n* the branch of biology that deals with the functions and activities of life or of living matter. ➤ **physiological** *adj,* **physiologist** *n.*

**physiotherapy** *n* the treatment of disease or injury by massage and regulated exercise. ➤ **physiotherapist** *n.*

**physique** *n* the form or structure of a person's body.

**pi** *n* **1** the 16th letter of the Greek alphabet (Π, π). **2** the ratio of the circumference of a circle to its diameter with a value of 3.14159265.

**pianissimo** *adj and adv* of a piece of music: performed very softly.

**piano**[1] *n* (*pl* **-os**) a standing keyboard instrument with strings stretched across a frame and struck by hammers when keys are pressed. ➤ **pianist** *n.*

**piano**[2] *adj and adv* of a piece of music: performed in softly or quietly.

**pianoforte** /pi,anoh'fawti/ *n formal* a piano.

**piazza** /pi'atsə/ *n* an open square in a town.

**picador** *n* (*pl* **picadors** *or* **picadores**) in bullfighting, a horseman who prods the bull with a lance to weaken its neck and shoulder muscles.

**picaresque** *adj* of a type of fiction narrating the adventures of a likeable rogue.

**piccalilli** *n* (*pl* **piccalillies** *or* **piccalillis**) a hot relish of chopped vegetables, mustard, and spices.

**piccaninny** (*NAmer* **picaninny** *or* **pickaninny**) *n* (*pl* **-ies**) *offensive* a small black child.

**piccolo** *n* (*pl* **-os**) a small flute with a range an octave higher than an ordinary flute.

**pick**[1] *v* **1** to choose from a number of choices or possibilities. **2** to remove (a fruit or flower) by pulling it from a tree or plant. **3** to remove (unwanted matter) with a finger or pointed instrument. **4** to steal from (a person's pocket). **5** to provoke (a quarrel or fight). **6** to unlock (a lock) with a wire or other device other than the key. * **pick at** to eat (food) sparingly and with little appetite. **pick holes in** to find fault or weaknesses in. **pick on** to single out for unpleasant treatment. **pick one's way** to go forward carefully or with difficulty. **pick somebody's brains** to get ideas from them. **pick through/over** to sort (a number of items). ➤ **picker** *n.*

**pick**[2] *n* **1** the act of choosing; a choice. **2** the best or choicest.

**pick**[3] *or* **pickaxe** *n* a heavy iron or steel tool with a long wooden handle and a head that is pointed at one or both ends.

**picket**[1] *n* **1** a person or group of people posted at a place of work affected by a strike to try to persuade workers not to work. **2** a pointed stake or post.

**picket**[2] *v* (**picketed, picketing**) to be a picket outside (a place of work).

**pickings** *pl n* **1** eatable fragments or scraps. **2** gains or rewards obtained by dubious means.

**pickle**[1] *n* **1** a brine or vinegar solution in which foods are preserved. **2** a mixture of chopped vegetables preserved in a brine or vinegar solution. **3** *informal* a difficult or confused situation.

**pickle**[2] *v* to preserve in pickle.

**pick off** *v* to shoot at (a target in a group).

**pick out** *v* **1** to select (one person or thing) in a group. **2** to play the notes of (a tune) by ear.

**pickpocket** *n* a person who steals from pockets or bags.

**pickup** *n* **1** the act or an instance of picking up. **2** a light motor truck having an open body with low sides and tailboard. **3** the device on a record player that holds the stylus. **4** a device on a guitar that converts the vibrations of the strings into electrical signals.

**pick up** *v* **1** to take hold of and lift. **2** to collect or take in a vehicle. **3** to acquire or learn casually. **4** to begin a casual relationship with. **5** to receive (a radio signal). **6** to become aware of (another person's feeling, etc). **7** to recover or improve. * **pick up on** to criticize (a previous speaker).

**picky** *adj* (**-ier, -iest**) fussy or choosy.

**picnic**[1] *n* an informal meal eaten in the open. * **no picnic** *informal* something by no means straightforward or pleasant.

**picnic**[2] *v* (**picnicked, picnicking**) to have or go on a picnic. ➤ **picnicker** *n.*

**Pict** *n* a member of a Celtic people of northern Britain in Roman times.

**pictograph** *n* **1** an ancient or prehistoric drawing or painting, often on a rock wall. **2** a small picture used as a symbol in some writing systems. ➤ **pictographic** *adj.*

**pictorial** *adj* consisting of or illustrated by pictures. ➤ **pictorially** *adv.*

**picture**[1] *n* **1** a design or representation made by painting, drawing, or photography. **2** a vivid description. **3** an image on a television screen. **4** a cinema film. **5** *chiefly Brit, informal* (*in pl*) the cinema. * **in the picture** *informal* fully informed.

**picture**[2] *v* **1** to depict or represent in a picture. **2** to form a mental image of.

**picturesque** *adj* quaintly or charmingly attractive.

**picture window** *n* a large single-paned window.

**piddle** *v informal* **1** (*usu* + about/around) to act in an idle or trifling manner. **2** to urinate.

**piddling** *adj informal* trivial or paltry.

**pidgin** *n* a language based on two or more languages and used between people with different native languages.

**pie** *n* a baked dish with a sweet or savoury filling covered by pastry. * **pie in the sky** *informal* an illusory hope or prospect.

**piebald** *adj* of a horse: spotted with different colours.

**piece**[1] *n* **1** a part detached from a whole, or forming one element of it. **2** a distinct separate bit or item of something. **3** a literary or musical work. **4** a coin of a specified value. **5** a small object used in playing a board game. * **go to pieces** to lose control of oneself.

**piece**[2] *v* (*often* + together) to join into a whole.

**pièce de résistance** /ˌpyes də rəˈzistanhs/ *n* (*pl* **pièces de résistance**) the most outstanding item.

**piecemeal** *adj and adv* **1** done gradually or one piece at a time. **2** in pieces or fragments.

**piecework** *n* work that is paid for at a set rate per unit.

**pie chart** *n* a chart in which each component of a whole is represented by a sector of a circle.

**pied** *adj* having patches of two or more colours.

**pied-à-terre** /ˌpyay dah ˈteə/ *n* (*pl* **pieds-à-terre**) a second lodging kept for occasional use.

**pie-eyed** *adj informal* drunk.

**pier** *n* **1** a structure extending into a sea or lake and used as a landing place or promenade. **2** a support for a bridge or wall.

**pierce** *v* **1** to make a hole in or through. **2** to force or make a way into or through.

**piercing** *adj* **1** very loud or shrill. **2** penetratingly cold.

**piety** *n* (*pl* **-ies**) the quality of being pious or religious.

**piffle** *n informal* trivial nonsense.

**piffling** *adj informal* trivial or derisory.

**pig**[1] *n* **1** an animal with a thick bristly skin and a long snout. **2** *informal* a dirty, greedy, or disagreeable person. **3** a shaped mass of cast crude metal. ➤ **piggish** *adj,* **piglet** *n.*

**pig**[2] *v* (**pigged, pigging**) *informal* **1** to eat (food) greedily. **2** to overindulge (oneself).

**pigeon** *n* a bird with a stout body and smooth plumage.

**pigeonhole**[1] *n* **1** a small open compartment for letters or documents. **2** a convenient but often oversimplified category. **3** a hole for a pigeon to nest in.

**pigeonhole**[2] *v* to assign to a particular category.

**pigeon-toed** *adj* having the toes turned in.

**piggery** *n* (*pl* **-ies**) a place where pigs are kept.

**piggy**[1] *n* (*pl* **-ies**) used by or to children: a pig.

**piggy**[2] *adj* (**-ier, -iest**) resembling a pig.

**piggyback** *n* a ride on somebody's back and shoulders.

**piggy bank** *n* a money box in the shape of a pig.

**pigheaded** *adj* obstinate or stubborn.

**pig iron** *n* crude iron from a blast furnace, before refining.

**pigment**[1] *n* **1** a powdered substance mixed with a liquid to colour paints, inks, plastics, etc. **2** any of various colouring matters in animals and plants. ➤ **pigmentation** *n.*

**pigment**[2] *v* to colour with pigment.

**pigskin** *n* leather made from the skin of a pig.

**pigsty** *n* (*pl* **-ies**) **1** an enclosure for pigs. **2** a dirty or untidy place.

**pigswill** *n* waste food fed to pigs.

**pigtail** *n* a tight plait of hair worn at the back of the head. ➤ **pigtailed** *adj.*

**pike**[1] *n* (*pl* **pikes** *or* **pike**) a long bony food fish.

**pike**[2] *n* a long wooden shaft with a pointed steel head, formerly used by foot soldiers.

**pikestaff** *n* the staff of a foot soldier's pike. * **plain as a pikestaff** very plain or obvious.

**pilaster** *n* a shallow pier or column projecting slightly from a wall.

**pilchard** *n* a food fish of the herring family.

**pile**[1] *n* **1** a quantity of things heaped together. **2** *informal* a large quantity or amount. **3** *informal* a large building.

**pile**[2] *v* **1** (*often* + up) to lay or place (things) in a pile. **2** to put or heap (things) in large quantities. **3** (+ into/out of) to get into or out of a vehicle in a confused rush. * **pile into** of a vehicle: to crash into.

**pile**[3] *n* a soft raised surface on a fabric or carpet, consisting of cut threads or loops.

**pile**[4] *n* a beam driven into the ground to carry a vertical load.

**pile-driver** *n* a machine for driving piles into the ground.
**piles** *pl n* haemorrhoids.
**pile up** *v* to accumulate.
**pile-up** *n informal* a collision involving several vehicles.
**pilfer** *v* to steal (items of little value).
**pilgrim** *n* **1** a person making a pilgrimage. **2** *archaic or literary* a traveller.
**pilgrimage** *n* a journey to a shrine or sacred place as an act of devotion.
**pill** *n* **1** a small solid mass of medicine to be swallowed whole. **2** (**the Pill**) an oral contraceptive.
**pillage**[1] *n* the act of looting or plundering.
**pillage**[2] *v* to plunder or loot (a place).
**pillar** *n* **1** a firm upright support for a structure. **2** a supportive and helpful person. * **from pillar to post** hurriedly from one place or one situation to another.
**pillar box** *n* a red pillar-shaped public postbox.
**pillbox** *n* **1** a small box for pills. **2** a small low concrete weapon emplacement. **3** a small round brimless hat with a flat crown and straight sides.
**pillion** *n* a seat for a passenger on a motorcycle.
**pillory**[1] *n* (*pl* **-ies**) a device for publicly punishing offenders, consisting of a wooden frame with holes to hold the head and hands.
**pillory**[2] *v* (**-ies, -ied**) **1** to put in a pillory. **2** to expose to public ridicule.
**pillow** *n* a cloth container filled with soft material to support the head when lying down.
**pillowcase** *n* a removable cover for a pillow.
**pillow talk** *n* intimate conversation between two people in bed.
**pilot**[1] *n* **1** a person who flies an aircraft or spacecraft. **2** a person qualified to conduct a ship into and out of a port. **3** a trial of a project or broadcast programme, e.g. to test public opinion.
**pilot**[2] *v* (**piloted, piloting**) **1** to act as a pilot of (an aircraft or ship). **2** to test (a product, programme, etc) by means of a pilot.
**pilot light** *n* a small permanent flame used to ignite gas in a cooker or boiler.
**pimento** *or* **pimiento** *n* (*pl* **-os**) a mild sweet pepper.
**pimp**[1] *n* a man who solicits clients for prostitutes and takes some of their earnings.
**pimp**[2] *v* to act as a pimp.
**pimple** *n* a small solid inflamed elevation of the skin. ➤ **pimply** *adj*.
**PIN** *or* **PIN number** *abbr* personal identification number, a four-digit security code used with a bank card.
**pin**[1] *n* **1** a small thin pointed piece of metal with a head used for fastening cloth, paper, etc. **2** an ornament or badge fastened with a pin. **3** a slender piece of wood or metal, used for fastening, as a safety catch, or as a support. **4** a skittle or other target. **5** a projecting metal bar on an electrical plug. **6** *informal* (*usu in pl*) a leg.
**pin**[2] *v* (**pinned, pinning**) **1** to fasten or attach with a pin or pins. **2** to hold (somebody) so they cannot move. * **pin something on somebody** to blame them for it.
**pinafore** *n Brit* **1** an apron with a bib. **2** a sleeveless dress worn over a blouse or sweater.
**pinball** *n* a game in which balls are shot across a sloping surface at pins and score points if they hit them.
**pince-nez** /'pans nay, 'pins/ *n* glasses clipped to the nose by a spring.
**pincer** *n* **1** (*in pl*) a tool with two strong jaws for gripping things. **2** the front claw of a lobster, crab, etc. **3** each part of a two-pronged attack.
**pinch**[1] *v* **1** to squeeze tightly between the finger and thumb or between the jaws of an instrument. **2** to squeeze or compress painfully. **3** *informal* to steal. **4** to cause physical or mental pain to.
**pinch**[2] *n* **1** an act of pinching; a squeeze. **2** as much as may be held between the finger and thumb. * **at a pinch** in an emergency. **feel the pinch** to be short of money.
**pinched** *adj* of the face: thin or shrunken from cold or illness.
**pincushion** *n* a small cushion in which pins are stuck ready for use.
**pin down** *v* **1** to force (somebody) to be decisive or explicit about their intentions. **2** to trap (an enemy or fugitive) by surrounding them or firing on them.
**pine**[1] *n* an evergreen tree with cones and long slender needles.
**pine**[2] *v* **1** to lose vigour or health. **2** (+ for) to yearn intensely for somebody or something.
**pineapple** *n* a large oval prickly fruit with succulent yellow flesh.
**pine nut** *n* the edible seed of a pine tree.
**ping** *v* to make a sharp ringing sound. ➤ **ping** *n*, **pinger** *n*.
**Ping-Pong** *n trademark* table tennis.
**pinion**[1] *n* the section of a bird's wing where the flight feathers grow.
**pinion**[2] *v* **1** to restrain (somebody) by holding their arms. **2** to restrain (a bird) from flight by cutting off the pinion of a wing.
**pinion**[3] *n* a gear with a small number of teeth designed to mesh with a larger gear wheel or rack.
**pink**[1] *adj* of a colour midway between red and white.
**pink**[2] *n* a colour midway between red and white. * **in the pink** flourishing or in good health.
**pink**[3] *n* a plant with scented pink or white flowers.
**pink**[4] *v* to cut a zigzag pattern on the edge of (fabric) to prevent fraying.

**pink**[5] *v* of an engine: to make rattling noises when the mixture of fuel and air is faulty.
**pinkie** *or* **pinky** *n* (*pl* **-ies**) *informal* the little finger.
**pinking shears** *pl n* scissors with a saw-toothed inner edge on the blades, used for pinking cloth.
**pin money** *n* money for casual spending.
**pinnacle** *n* **1** the most successful point in an activity. **2** a mountain peak or similar structure. **3** an ornament like a small spire crowning a buttress.
**pinpoint**[1] *v* to locate precisely.
**pinpoint**[2] *adj* extremely precise.
**pinpoint**[3] *n* a very small point or area.
**pinprick** *n* a small puncture made by a pin.
**pins and needles** *pl n* a pricking tingling sensation in a part of the body recovering from numbness.
**pinstripe** *n* **1** a very thin stripe on a fabric. **2** (*usu in pl*) a suit or trousers with pinstripes. ➤ **pinstriped** *adj.*
**pint** *n* **1** a unit of capacity equal to one eighth of a gallon (0.568l in Britain). **2** *Brit, informal* a pint of beer.
**pint-sized** *adj informal* small.
**pin tuck** *n* a very narrow tuck in a garment.
**pin-up** *n* a picture or poster of a sexually attractive person.
**pinwheel** *n* a type of cogwheel with pins projecting from its rim.
**pioneer**[1] *n* **1** any of the first people to settle in a territory. **2** a person or group that helps open up a new line of thought or activity.
**pioneer**[2] *v* to originate or take part in the development of.
**pious** *adj* **1** devout; deeply religious. **2** dutiful; reverential. **3** marked by sham or hypocritical virtue; sanctimonious. ➤ **piously** *adv.*
**pip**[1] *n* a small fruit seed of a fruit.
**pip**[2] *n* (*usu in pl*) a short high-pitched tone given as a radio or telephone signal.
**pip**[3] *n* a symbol or dot indicating value on a playing card or domino.
**pip**[4] *v* (**pipped, pipping**) *informal* to beat by a narrow margin. ✱ **pip at the post** to beat at the very last minute.
**pipe**[1] *n* **1** a long tube through which a liquid or gas can flow. **2** a tube of wood or clay with a mouthpiece at one end and a small bowl at the other, for smoking tobacco. **3** a simple wind instrument consisting of a tube with holes in it, the holes being covered by the fingers to produce different notes. **4** (**the pipes**) bagpipes. **5** each of several cylindrical tubes that produce sound on an organ.
**pipe**[2] *v* **1** to convey (a liquid or gas) along a pipe. **2** to transmit (a broadcast, music, or an electrical signal) along wires or cables. **3** to put (a decoration) on a cake in icing or cream using a bag with a nozzle. **4** to trim with decorative cord. **5** to say or sing in a shrill voice. **6** to play (a tune) on a pipe.
**pipe cleaner** *n* a piece of wire covered with tufted fabric, used to clean a tobacco pipe.
**piped music** *n* recorded music played through loudspeakers in public places.
**pipe down** *v informal* to stop talking or making noise.
**pipe dream** *n* an unattainable plan or hope.
**pipeline** *n* a line of pipe for conveying a liquid or gas over a long distance. ✱ **in the pipeline** in the process of being developed or received.
**piper** *n* somebody who plays a pipe or bagpipes.
**pipette** (*NAmer* **pipet**) *n* a narrow tube into which a liquid is drawn by suction for measuring or transferring small quantities.
**pipe up** *v* to begin to speak suddenly.
**piping** *n* **1** a quantity or system of pipes. **2** a narrow cord trimming. **3** a thin line of icing or cream used to decorate cakes.
**piping hot** *adj* of food: hot and ready to eat.
**pipistrelle** *n* a small insect-eating bat.
**pipit** *n* a small songbird with brown streaked plumage.
**pippin** *n* an eating apple with a yellow skin flushed with red.
**pipsqueak** *n informal* a small or insignificant person.
**piquant** *adj* having an agreeably sharp taste. ➤ **piquancy** *n,* **piquantly** *adv.*
**pique**[1] *n* resentment or bad temper resulting from wounded pride.
**pique**[2] *v* (**piques, piqued, piquing**) **1** to arouse anger or resentment in (somebody). **2** to arouse (curiosity or interest).
**piracy** *n* **1** the act of committing robbery at sea. **2** the infringement of copyright on published books or recordings.
**piranha** /pi'rahn(y)ə/ *n* a small freshwater fish with strong jaws and sharp teeth.
**pirate**[1] *n* **1** somebody who commits robbery at sea. **2** (*used before a noun*) violating copyright: *pirate videos.* ➤ **piratic** *adj.*
**pirate**[2] *v* to reproduce (copyright material) without authorization.
**pirouette**[1] *n* in ballet, a fast spin of the body on one foot.
**pirouette**[2] *v* to perform a pirouette.
**piscatorial** *adj* relating to fishing.
**Pisces** *n* the twelfth sign of the zodiac (the Fish).
**piss**[1] *v coarse slang* to urinate.
**piss**[2] *n coarse slang* **1** urine. **2** an act of urinating.
**pissed** *adj* **1** *Brit, coarse slang* drunk. **2** *NAmer, slang* angry or upset.
**pistachio** *n* (*pl* **-os**) a pale green nut.
**piste** /peest/ *n* a prepared slope for skiing.
**pistil** *n* the female parts of a flowering plant, comprising the ovary, style, and stigma.
**pistol** *n* a small gun for firing with one hand.
**piston** *n* a sliding disc or cylinder fitted closely

in a tube in which it moves up and down in an internal-combustion engine.

**pit[1]** *n* **1** a hole or shaft in the ground. **2** a mine where coal or minerals are excavated. **3** an area at the side of a motor-racing track for servicing and refuelling during a race. **4** a natural hollow in the surface of the body. **5** the hollow of the stomach. **6** a sunken area in a garage or workshop where mechanics can work on the underside of vehicles. **7** the area in front of a theatre stage where the orchestra plays. **8** (**the pits**) *informal* the worst imaginable.

**pit[2]** *v* (**pitted, pitting**) **1** to make small holes in the surface of. **2** (+ against) to set (a person or oneself) in competition with another person.

**pit-a-pat** *or* **pitapat** *n* a series of light tapping sounds.

**pit bull terrier** *n* a breed of short-haired terrier with a stocky muscular body.

**pitch[1]** *n* **1** *Brit* a piece of ground marked out for playing a team sport. **2** the distinctive quality that a sound has according to the frequency of the vibrations that produce it. **3** the slope of a roof. **4** a level or degree, *esp* an advanced or extreme one. **5** *informal* a way of speaking or arguing. **6** *Brit* a place regularly used by a a street vendor or performer. **7** the up-and-down movement of a ship or aircraft.

**pitch[2]** *v* **1** to throw in a rough or casual way. **2** to move or fall heavily forwards or downwards. **3** of a ship or aircraft: to move with a rocking motion. **4** to express or adapt (speech or writing) for a particular audience. **5** to set at a specified level. **6** to erect (a tent) temporarily.

**pitch[3]** *n* a black or dark viscous substance made from tar.

**pitch-black** *adj* completely black or dark.

**pitched** *adj* of a roof: sloping.

**pitched battle** *n* a battle between armies fought on previously chosen ground.

**pitcher** *n* a large jug.

**pitchfork** *n* a long-handled fork with two long curved prongs used for lifting hay.

**piteous** *adj* causing or deserving pity. ➤ **piteously** *adv.*

**pitfall** *n* a hidden danger or difficulty.

**pith** *n* **1** a white tissue directly below the skin of a citrus fruit. **2** spongy cellular tissue in the stems of some plants. **3** the essential part or susbstance of something.

**pithead** *n* the top of a mining pit and the ground around it.

**pith helmet** *n* a hat made from the pith of swamp plants and worn in tropical regions as protection from the sun.

**pithy** *adj* (**-ier, -iest**) **1** of language: full of meaning concisely expressed. **2** of a plant fruit: having a lot of pith. ➤ **pithily** *adv.*

**pitiable** *adj* **1** deserving or arousing pity. **2** contemptibly inadequate.

**pitiful** *adj* **1** deserving or arousing pity. **2** very small or inadequate. ➤ **pitifully** *adv.*

**pitiless** *adj* showing no pity. ➤ **pitilessly** *adv.*

**piton** *n* a spike or peg driven into a rock or ice surface as a support in mountaineering.

**pitta** (*NAmer* **pita**) *n* slightly leavened bread that can be split open to hold a filling.

**pittance** *n* a small amount or allowance of money.

**pitter-patter** *n* a rapid succession of light tapping sounds.

**pituitary gland** *n* an organ attached to the brain which secretes hormones controlling growth and metabolism.

**pity[1]** *n* (*pl* **-ies**) **1** sympathetic sorrow for the suffering of others. **2** a cause of regret or disappointment.

**pity[2]** *v* (**-ies, -ied**) to feel pity for.

**pivot[1]** *n* a shaft or pin on which a mechanism turns.

**pivot[2]** *v* (**pivoted, pivoting**) **1** to turn on a pivot, or as if on a pivot. **2** (*usu* + on) to depend on.

**pivotal** *adj* vitally important.

**pixel** *n* each of thousands of tiny spots on a computer screen that together form an image.

**pixie** *or* **pixy** *n* (*pl* **-ies**) a little person depicted in folklore as a small human with pointed ears.

**pizza** *n* a round base of baked dough spread with tomatoes, cheese, herbs, etc.

**pizzeria** /peetsə'riə/ *n* a restaurant providing pizzas.

**pizzicato** /pitsi'kahtoh/ *adj and adv* of a piece of music for strings: performed by plucking instead of bowing. ➤ **pizzicato** *n.*

**placard** *n* a sign or notice for display, placed on a wall or carried in a demonstration.

**placate** *v* to soothe or mollify by making concessions. ➤ **placatory** *adj.*

**place[1]** *n* **1** a position or point in space. **2** a city, town, or other geographical location. **3** a right or duty. **4** an appropriate occasion for something. **5** a position in a sequence, e.g. of winners in a competition or race. **6** a short residential street or square. ✱ **in place of** as a substitute for. **take place** to happen.

**place[2]** *v* **1** to put in a specified position or condition. **2** to cause to be in a specified position or condition. **3** to assert or assign a role to (a quality, etc). **4** to remember or identify. **5** to find employment or a home for. **6** to submit or confirm (a bet, order, etc).

**placebo** *n* (*pl* **-os**) a medication that has no physiological effect and is prescribed for the patient's psychological benefit.

**placement** *n* **1** the act or result of putting somebody or something in a specified place. **2** a temporary spell of work offered for practical experience.

**placenta** *n* (*pl* **placentas** *or* **placentae**) an organ that develops in the womb during pregnancy and provides the foetus with oxygen and nourishment.

**placid** *adj* not easily upset or excited. ➤ **placidly** *adv.*

**placket** *n* a flap of fabric covering a slit in a piece of clothing.

**plagiarize** *or* **-ise** *v* to appropriate and pass off (the ideas or words of another) as one's own. ➤ **plagiarism** *n,* **plagiarist** *n.*

**plague**[1] *n* **1** an epidemic disease caused by a bacterium carried by rat fleas and transmitted to humans via their bite. **2** a large destructive influx of insects or animals causing widespread damage.

**plague**[2] *v* (**plagues, plagued, plaguing**) **1** to annoy or harass continually. **2** to infest or afflict with disease or calamity.

**plaice** *n* (*pl* **plaice**) a large flatfish with a brown skin flecked with orange.

**plaid** *n* a woollen fabric with a tartan pattern.

**plain**[1] *adj* **1** simple, ordinary, or without decoration. **2** without a pattern. **3** consisting of a single colour. **4** obvious; easy to understand. **5** of speech: candid. **6** of a person: unattractive. **7** utter; absolute. ➤ **plainly** *adv,* **plainness** *n.*

**plain**[2] *n* a large area of level country with few trees.

**plain**[3] *adv* totally; utterly.

**plain chocolate** *n Brit* dark chocolate with no added milk.

**plain clothes** *pl n* ordinary civilian dress as opposed to uniform.

**plain sailing** *n* easy or steady progress.

**plainsong** *n* unaccompanied vocal music of the medieval church.

**plaintiff** *n* somebody who brings a civil legal action against another in a court of law.

**plait**[1] *n* a length of interwoven strands of hair or rope.

**plait**[2] *v* to form into a plait or plaits.

**plan**[1] *n* **1** a detailed proposal of how something can be done. **2** (*also in pl*) a proposed course of action. **3** a financial arrangement designed to give security in the future. **4** a detailed diagram or map.

**plan**[2] *v* (**planned, planning**) **1** to arrange in advance. **2** (+ to/on) to intend to do something. **3** to design. ➤ **planner** *n.*

**plane**[1] *n* **1** a flat or level physical surface. **2** a level of existence or development. **3** *informal* an aeroplane.

**plane**[2] *adj* **1** having no elevations or depressions; flat. **2** of or dealing with geometric planes. **3** lying in a plane.

**plane**[3] *v* **1** of a bird: to fly with the wings still. **2** to skim across the surface of water.

**plane**[4] *n* a cutting tool for smoothing a wooden surface by removing thin shavings.

**plane**[5] *v* to smooth (a surface) with a plane.

**plane**[6] *n* a large tree with lobed leaves and thin bark that is shed in flakes.

**planet** *n* a large celestial body that orbits a star. ➤ **planetary** *adj.*

**planetarium** *n* (*pl* **planetariums** *or* **planetaria**) a building or room with a domed ceiling for showing images of stars and planets.

**plangent** *adj literary* of a sound: having an expressive plaintive quality.

**plank** *n* a long flat piece of sawn timber. ✱ **walk the plank** formerly, to be made to walk off the end of a plank jutting out from a ship.

**plankton** *n* minute animals and plants that float near the surface of seas and lakes.

**plant**[1] *n* **1** a living organism such as a tree or flower, with root systems for absorbing water and leaves that manufacture nutrients. **2** a place where large-scale manufacturing or processing takes place. **3** machinery used in manufacturing or processing. **4** a person placed in an organization as a spy. **5** something placed surreptitiously in a person's belongings in order to incriminate them.

**plant**[2] *v* **1** to put (a seed, plant, bulb, etc) in the ground for it to grow. **2** to put or settle firmly in a specified place. **3** to place (somebody) as a spy in an organization. **4** to place or hide (an explosive device). **5** to establish (an idea, etc) in somebody's mind. **6** to put (something incriminating) surreptitiously in somebody's belongings. ➤ **planter** *n.*

**Plantagenet** *n* a member of the English royal house that ruled from 1154 to 1485.

**plantain**[1] *n* a short-stemmed plant with dense spikes of flowers and a rosette of oval or sword-shaped leaves.

**plantain**[2] *n* a green-skinned fruit resembling a banana.

**plantation** *n* **1** a large estate where commercial crops, such as coffee, tea, tobacco, and rubber, are grown. **2** an area where trees are grown.

**plaque** *n* **1** an inscribed tablet fixed to a wall. **2** a film of mucus on teeth where bacteria multiply.

**plasma** *n* **1** the fluid part of blood, lymph, or milk in which corpuscles, fat globules, and other cells are suspended. **2** a highly ionized gas containing approximately equal numbers of positive ions and electrons.

**plaster**[1] *n* **1** a mixture of lime, water, and sand that hardens on drying and is used to form a surface on walls and ceilings. **2** an adhesive strip used for covering and protecting small cuts. **3** a rigid dressing made from plaster of Paris and used for setting a broken bone.

**plaster**[2] *v* **1** to coat (a surface) with plaster. **2** to coat or cover thickly. **3** to cause to lie flat or stick to another surface. ➤ **plasterer** *n.*

**plasterboard** *n* a board with a plaster core used as a lining for interior walls.

**plaster of Paris** *n* a white powder made from gypsum and forming a quick-hardening paste when mixed with water, used in setting bones and in sculpture.

**plastic**[1] *n* **1** a synthetic substance that can be moulded while soft and set to have a rigid or slightly elastic form. **2** *informal* credit cards.

**plastic**[2] *adj* **1** made of plastic. **2** soft and pliable. **3** *derog* artificial. ➤ **plasticity** *n.*

**Plasticine** *n trademark* a soft substance used for modelling.

**plastic surgery** *n* surgery done to repair or restore parts of the body.

**plate**[1] *n* **1** a flat dish from which food is eaten or served. **2** a thin flat sheet or strip of metal used to coat another metal. **3** metal or metal objects coated in this. **4** tableware and other household articles made of gold or silver. **5** a thin piece of metal or plastic bearing an inscription. **6** any of the rigid but mobile blocks that together form the earth's crust. **7** a full-page illustration in a book. * **on a plate** without having to make any great effort. **on one's plate** to be dealt with.

**plate**[2] *v* to coat (a metal) with a thin layer of rolled or hammered gold, silver, or steel.

**plateau**[1] *n* (*pl* **plateaus** *or* **plateaux**) **1** a flat area of high ground. **2** a state of stability after a period of activity.

**plateau**[2] *v* (**plateaus, plateaued, plateauing**) to reach a stable stage after a period of activity.

**plate glass** *n* thick sheet glass used for shop and office windows.

**platelet** *n* any of the minute discs in the blood of vertebrates that assist in blood clotting.

**platen** *n* **1** a flat plate in a printing press that holds the paper against the type. **2** the roller of a typewriter against which the paper is held.

**platform** *n* **1** a raised area where a speaker or performer can be seen by the audience. **2** a level horizontal surface that is raised above the area around it. **3** a raised area by the track at a railway station where passengers stand. **4** a raised structure housing the equipment used for drilling for oil and gas. **5** a declared political policy that distinguishes one party or group from others. **6** an opportunity or place for expressing opinions. **7** (*usu in pl*) a shoe with a built-up sole.

**platinum** *n* a greyish white precious metallic element.

**platitude** *n* a trite remark stating the self-evident. ➤ **platitudinous** *adj.*

**platonic** *adj* **1** (**Platonic**) relating to the Greek philosopher Plato (d.349 BC). **2** of friendship or love: close but not sexual. ➤ **platonically** *adv.*

**platoon** *n* (*treated as sing. or pl*) a subdivision of a military company.

**platter** *n* a large plate for serving food.

**platypus** *n* (*pl* **platypuses**) a small aquatic egg-laying mammal with a bill like a duck's, webbed feet, and a broad flattened tail.

**plaudit** *n* (*usu in pl*) an expression of approval.

**plausible** *adj* **1** apparently fair or reasonable. **2** of a person: persuasive or believable. ➤ **plausibility** *n,* **plausibly** *adv.*

**play**[1] *v* **1** to take part in activities for enjoyment or recreation. **2** (+ with) to use something for amusement or fun. **3** to take part in (a sport or game). **4** to compete with (an opponent) in a game. **5** to make use of (a card or piece) at one's turn in a game. **6** to perform music on a musical instrument. **7** to make (a radio, etc) produce music or sounds. **8** to perform (a role) in a drama or film. **9** (+ on) to take advantage of (a weakness or opportunity). * **play ball** *informal* to cooperate. **play the game** to behave fairly. **play with** to treat frivolously or unfairly.

**play**[2] *n* **1** activity that is done for recreation or amusement. **2** a piece of dramatic literature for acting on stage or broadcast on television or radio. **3** taking part in sports or games. **4** in a sport or game, a move or the action. **5** ease of movement of a machine part. **6** freedom or scope. * **make a play for** to try to obtain.

**play about** *v* **1** to behave irresponsibly. **2** *informal* to have a sexual affair.

**play-act** *v* **1** to pretend or make believe. **2** to behave in a misleading or insincere manner.

**play along** *v* to pretend to cooperate.

**playboy** *n* a wealthy man who devotes himself to enjoyment.

**play down** *v* to minimize the importance of.

**player** *n* **1** a person who takes part in a sport or game. **2** a person who plays a musical instrument. **3** a device for playing music, videos, etc. **4** a person or group taking part in some activity.

**playful** *adj* **1** full of fun; high-spirited. **2** humorously light-hearted or good-natured. ➤ **playfully** *adv.*

**playground** *n* a piece of land for children to play on.

**playgroup** *n chiefly Brit* a supervised play activity for children below school age.

**playhouse** *n* **1** a theatre. **2** a toy house for children to play in.

**playing card** *n* each of a set of small cards with numbers and symbols on them, used in playing games.

**playmate** *n* a friend with whom a child regularly plays.

**play off** *v* **1** to bring (other people) into conflict for one's own advantage. **2** of two teams or players: to take part in a play-off.

**play-off** *n* a final contest or an extra match played to determine a winner.

**playpen** *n* a portable enclosure in which a baby or young child can play safely.

**plaything** *n* **1** a toy. **2** a person regarded or treated dismissively.

**play up** *v* **1** to emphasize the importance of. **2** *Brit, informal.* **3** to cause distress to. **4** to be troublesome or mischievous. **5** to be not working properly. * **play up to** to flatter.
**playwright** *n* a writer of plays.
**plaza** *n* **1** a public square in a city or town. **2** *NAmer* a shopping complex.
**plc** *abbr* (*also* **PLC**) public limited company.
**plea** *n* **1** an earnest or emotional request or appeal. **2** an accused person's answer to an indictment.
**plead** *v* (*past tense and past part.* **pleaded** *or* **plead** *or NAmer, Scot* **pled**) **1** to make an impassioned request or appeal. **2** to give or offer (a specified condition) as an excuse or reason. **3** of an accused person in a court of law: to answer an accusation in a specified way. **4** to argue (a case) or put forward (a point of law).
**pleasant** *adj* **1** having qualities that tend to give pleasure. **2** likable and friendly. ➤ **pleasantly** *adv.*
**pleasantry** *n* (*pl* **-ies**) a polite but trivial remark.
**please**[1] *v* **1** to give a feeling of satisfaction or pleasure to. **2** *formal* to be the wish or will of (somebody or something). * **please oneself** to do as one likes. ➤ **pleasing** *adj.*
**please**[2] *adv* used in a polite request or an urgent appeal.
**pleased** *adj* **1** satisfied or contented. **2** glad or willing (to do something).
**pleasurable** *adj* pleasant or enjoyable. ➤ **pleasurably** *adv.*
**pleasure** *n* **1** a feeling of satisfaction or contentment. **2** a source of enjoyment. **3** enjoyment or recreation. **4** sensual gratification or indulgence.
**pleat**[1] *n* a fold in cloth made by doubling material over on itself and stitching or pressing it in place.
**pleat**[2] *v* to make pleats in.
**pleb** *n chiefly Brit, informal, derog* a member of the ordinary people. ➤ **plebby** *adj.*
**plebeian**[1] *n* a member of the ordinary people.
**plebeian**[2] *adj* **1** of plebeians. **2** ordinary or common.
**plebiscite** *n* a vote by the people of a country for or against an important proposal.
**plectrum** *n* (*pl* **plectra** *or* **plectrums**) a thin flat piece of plastic, metal, etc used to pluck the strings of a guitar.
**pled** *v NAmer, Scot* past tense and past part. of PLEAD.
**pledge**[1] *n* **1** a solemn promise or undertaking. **2** something given as a token of love or remembrance. **3** something handed over to an authority as security.
**pledge**[2] *v* **1** to promise solemnly. **2** to deposit as security.
**plenary** *adj* **1** absolute; unqualified. **2** of a meeting: attended by all entitled to be present.
**plenipotentiary**[1] *n* (*pl* **-ies**) a diplomat invested with full power to transact business.
**plenipotentiary**[2] *adj* having full power to act.
**plenitude** *n formal* **1** an abundance. **2** the condition of being full or complete.
**plenteous** *adj literary* plentiful.
**plentiful** *adj* producing or existing in large quantities. ➤ **plentifully** *adv.*
**plenty**[1] *n* (*pl* **-ies**) **1** a full or more than adequate amount or supply. **2** a large number or amount. **3** ample supplies.
**plenty**[2] *adv informal* quite or abundantly.
**plenum** *n* (*pl* **plenums**) an assembly or meeting at which all the people eligible to attend are present.
**plethora** *n* a large or excessive quantity.
**pleurisy** *n* inflammation of the membranes that line the chest, causing fever and painful breathing.
**plexus** *n* (*pl* **plexus** *or* **plexuses**) a network of parts or elements in a structure or system.
**pliable** *adj* **1** easily bent. **2** yielding readily to others. ➤ **pliability** *n.*
**pliant** *adj* pliable.
**pliers** *pl n* pincers with flattened jaws for gripping small objects or for bending and cutting wire.
**plight**[1] *n* a condition of extreme hardship or danger.
**plight**[2] *v archaic* to promise solemnly.
**plimsoll** *n Brit* a sports shoe with a rubber sole and canvas top.
**plink** *v* to make a quick sharp tinkling noise. ➤ **plink** *n.*
**plinth** *n* a square block serving as a base for a column or statue.
**PLO** *abbr* Palestine Liberation Organization.
**plod**[1] *v* (**plodded, plodding**) **1** to walk heavily or slowly. **2** to work laboriously and monotonously.
**plod**[2] *n* a slow heavy walk.
**plonk**[1] *v* to put (something) down heavily or carelessly.
**plonk**[2] *n Brit, informal* cheap or inferior wine.
**plonker** *n informal* a foolish or useless person.
**plop** *v* (**plopped, plopping**) to drop suddenly with a sound like something dropping into water. ➤ **plop** *n.*
**plot**[1] *n* **1** a secret plan to do something illegal or harmful. **2** the main sequence of events of a literary work, film, etc. **3** a small piece of landmakred out for a specific purpose.
**plot**[2] *v* (**plotted, plotting**) **1** to plan a plot to do (something illegal or harmful). **2** to mark or note on a map or chart. ➤ **plotter** *n.*
**plough**[1] (*NAmer* **plow**) *n* **1** a device used to cut, lift, and turn over soil in preparation for sowing. **2** (**the Plough**) a formation of seven stars in the northern sky.
**plough**[2] (*NAmer* **plow**) *v* **1** to turn or work (earth or land) with a plough. **2** (*often* + into) to

force a way violently. **3** (*often* + through) to proceed steadily and laboriously. **4** (*often* + in/into) to invest (money or resources).

**plough back** *v* to reinvest (profits) in an industry.

**ploughman's lunch** *n Brit* a lunch of bread, cheese, and pickle.

**plover** *n* (*pl* **plovers** *or* **plover**) a stout wading bird with a short beak.

**ploy** *n* a cunningly devised plan or act.

**pluck**[1] *v* **1** to take a firm hold of (something) and remove it. **2** to pick (a flower, fruit, etc). **3** to pull out (hairs or feathers). **4** to remove the feathers from (a bird's carcass). **5** to produce sounds from (a stringed instrument) using the fingers or a plectrum.

**pluck**[2] *n* courage.

**pluck up** *v* to find (the necessary courage) to do something difficult or frightening.

**plucky** *adj* (**-ier, -iest**) showing spirited courage and determination. ➤ **pluckily** *adv.*

**plug**[1] *n* **1** a piece of solid material used to seal a hole. **2** an insulated device with metal prongs that connects an appliance to an electricity supply at a socket. **3** *informal* a publicity boost.

**plug**[2] *v* (**plugged, plugging**) **1** to block or close (a hole or gap) with a plug. **2** *informal* to publicize (a book, film, etc). **3** *informal* to shoot (somebody or something). **4** (*usu* + away) to work doggedly and persistently. ➤ **plugger** *n.*

**plughole** *n Brit* a hole in a sink or bath through which the water drains away.

**plug in** *v* to connect (an electrical appliance) to a power point.

**plum** *n* **1** an oval fruit with yellow, purple, red, or green skin and an oblong seed. **2** a dark reddish purple colour. **3** *informal* (*used before a noun*) excellent or desirable: *a plum job.*

**plumage** *n* a bird's feathers.

**plumb**[1] *n* a lead weight attached to a cord to gauge the depth of water or to establish a vertical line.

**plumb**[2] *adv informal* exactly.

**plumb**[3] *v* **1** to measure (the depth of water) with a plumb. **2** to examine minutely and critically. **3** to test (a surface) for being vertial with a plumb line.

**plumb**[4] *adj* exactly vertical or true.

**plumber** *n* a person who installs and repairs water piping and fittings.

**plumbing** *n* **1** a plumber's occupation or trade. **2** the system of pipes, tanks, and fixtures installed for a water supply and heating in a building.

**plumb line** *n* a line with a weight at one end, used to determine whether a surface is vertical.

**plume** *n* **1** a long attractive and brightly coloured feather or group of feathers. **2** a cloud of smoke or vapour reaching high into the sky. ➤ **plumed** *adj.*

**plummet**[1] *v* (**plummeted, plummeting**) to fall sharply and rapidly.

**plummet**[2] *n* a rapid fall or drop.

**plummy** *adj* (**-ier, -iest**) of a voice: resembling that associated with the English upper classes.

**plump**[1] *adj* having a full rounded form; slightly fat.

**plump**[2] *v* (*also* + up) to make or become rounder or fatter.

**plump**[3] *v* **1** (*usu* + down/into) to drop or sink suddenly or heavily. **2** (+ for) to make a choice of.

**plunder**[1] *v* **1** to pillage or sack (a place). **2** to take (goods) by force.

**plunder**[2] *n* **1** goods taken by plundering. **2** the act of plundering.

**plunge**[1] *v* **1** to fall or move rapidly or unexpectedly. **2** (*usu* + into) to jump or dive in water. **3** to cause (a place) to be in an unwelcome condition. **4** to immerse in a liquid.

**plunge**[2] *n* **1** an act of plunging. **2** a sudden decline in value. * **take the plunge** *informal* to decide to do something after some consideration.

**plunge pool** *n* a small deep pool of cold water, for use after a sauna.

**plunger** *n* **1** a device that acts with a plunging or thrusting motion. **2** a rubber suction cup on a handle used for clearing blocked pipes or drains.

**plunk** *v* to play (a keyboard instrument) so as to produce a hollow metallic sound.

**pluperfect** *n* of the verb tense, usually formed with *had*, that expresses an action or state completed before a past time spoken of.

**plural**[1] *adj* **1** consisting of more than one. **2** in grammar, of a word or word form: denoting more than one. ➤ **plurally** *adv.*

**plural**[2] *n* in grammar, a plural number or word.

**pluralism** *n* **1** the existence in a society of diverse social groups with their own cultures or special interests. **2** the holding of two or more offices at the same time. ➤ **pluralist** *adj and n.*

**plurality** *n* (*pl* **-ies**) **1** the state of being plural or numerous. **2** a large number or quantity.

**plus**[1] *prep* **1** increased by; with the addition of. **2** and also.

**plus**[2] *n* (*pl* **pluses** *or* **plusses**) **1** a positive factor, quantity, or quality. **2** (*also* **plus sign**) a sign (+) denoting addition or a positive value

**plus**[3] *adj* **1** of a number: having a positive value. **2** having a positive electric charge. **3** additional and welcome: *a plus factor.* **4** of a grade: slightly higher than that specified: *B plus.*

**plus**[4] *conj* and moreover.

**plus fours** *pl n* loose wide trousers gathered on a band and finishing just below the knee.

**plush**[1] *n* a fabric with a soft even pile.

**plush**[2] *adj* luxurious or lavish.

**plutocracy** *n* (*pl* **-ies**) **1** government by the

wealthy. **2** a state that is governed by wealthy people. ➤ **plutocratic** *adj.*

**plutocrat** *n* a person whose power is based on wealth.

**plutonium** *n* a radioactive metallic element used in weapons and as a fuel for atomic reactors.

**ply**[1] *n* (*pl* **-ies**) **1** a strand in a yarn, wool, etc. **2** a layer of a material forming a whole with others.

**ply**[2] *v* (**-ies, -ied**) **1** to use (a tool) carefully. **2** to perform (a job) steadily and diligently. **3** to keep supplying something to (somebody). **4** to keep asking (somebody) questions. **5** to go over (a specified route) regularly.

**plywood** *n* a a board made from thin sheets of wood glued together with the grains arranged crosswise.

**Pm** *abbr* the chemical symbol for promethium.

**p.m.** *abbr* post meridiem, after midday.

**PMT** *abbr* premenstrual tension.

**pneumatic** *adj* operated by or containing gas or air under pressure. ➤ **pneumatically** *adv.*

**pneumonia** *n* an infection causing inflammation of the lungs.

**Po** *abbr* the chemical symbol for polonium.

**poach**[1] *v* to cook in a simmering liquid.

**poach**[2] *v* **1** to take (game or fish) illegally by hunting or fishing without permission. **2** to entice (employees, customers, etc) away from their present loyalties. ➤ **poacher** *n.*

**pock** *n* a pockmark. ➤ **pocked** *adj.*

**pocket**[1] *n* **1** a small bag sewn in clothing and open at the top or side. **2** financial resources. **3** a pouchlike compartment for storage. **4** an opening at the corner or side of a billiard or snooker table into which balls are struck. **5** a small isolated area or group. * **in pocket** having made a profit. **out of pocket** having lost money. ➤ **pocketful** *n.*

**pocket**[2] *v* **1** to put in one's pocket. **2** to steal or appropriate.

**pocket money** *n* **1** money regularly given to a child by its parents. **2** money for small personal expenses.

**pockmark** *n* a mark or pit in the skin left by smallpox, chickenpox, etc. ➤ **pockmarked** *adj.*

**pod**[1] *n* **1** a long seed case of a pea or bean. **2** a detachable compartment on a spacecraft or aircraft.

**pod**[2] *v* (**podded, podding**) **1** of a plant: to produce pods. **2** to remove (peas or beans) from their pods.

**pod**[3] *n* a small group of whales, seals, or other sea mammals.

**podgy** *adj* (**-ier, -iest**) short and plump.

**podium** *n* (*pl* **podiums** *or* **podia**) a small raised platform for giving a speech or conducting an orchestra.

**poem** *n* a literary composition in verse.

**poesy** *n archaic or literary* poetry.

**poet** *n* **1** a person who writes poetry. **2** a very imaginative or sensitive person with considerable powers of expression.

**poetic** *adj* **1** relating to poets or poetry. **2** having qualities associated with poetry. ➤ **poetically** *adv.*

**poetic justice** *n* an outcome of appropriate punishment and reward.

**poetic licence** *n* freedom to depart from the normal rules of language or accuracy for a particular literary effect.

**Poet Laureate** *n* (*pl* **Poets Laureate**) in Britain, a poet appointed for life to write poetry to celebrate important events.

**poetry** *n* **1** literary writing in the form of poems. **2** a quality of beauty and grace.

**po-faced** *adj Brit, informal* looking affectedly serious or disapproving.

**pogo stick** *n* a toy consisting of a pole on a spring for jumping about on.

**pogrom** *n* an organized massacre of people from an ethnic group, *esp* of Jews in eastern Europe and Russia.

**poignant** *adj* of memories etc: causing distress or pity; painfully sad. ➤ **poignancy** *n,* **poignantly** *adv.*

**point**[1] *n* **1** the sharp, tapering, or narrow and rounded end of something; a tip. **2** a very small mark; a dot. **3** a full stop. **4** a decimal point. **5** a precisely indicated position. **6** an exact moment. **7** an end or object to be achieved; a purpose. **8** (*often* **the point**) the most important element of a discussion or matter. **9** an individual detail; an item. **10** a unit of counting, e.g. in scoring a game. **11** each of 32 compass directions. **12** a projecting piece of land. **13** *Brit* (*in pl*) a device with movable rails that joins two railway lines. **14** *Brit* an electric socket. **15** a contact in the distributor of a motor vehicle. * **beside the point** irrelevant. **make a point of** to take particular care to. **on the point of** just about to. **to the point** relevant. **up to a point** to a certain extent.

**point**[2] *v* **1** to indicate the position or direction of something, *esp* by directing a finger. **2** to cause to be turned in a particular direction. **3** to face a particular direction. **4** (+ to) to indicate the fact or probability of. **5** to fill the joints of (brickwork) with mortar.

**pointed** *adj* **1** having a point. **2** *esp* of a remark: aimed at a particular person or group. **3** conspicuous.

**pointer** *n* **1** a needle indicating a reading on a dial or scale. **2** a useful suggestion or hint. **3** a large strong gundog of a smooth-haired breed that indicates the presence of game by pointing its head and body towards it.

**pointless** *adj* devoid of meaning or purpose. ➤ **pointlessly** *adv.*

**point of order** *n* (*pl* **points of order**) a question of procedure in an official meeting.

**point of view** *n* (*pl* **points of view**) a particular opinion or attitude.
**point out** *v* to direct somebody's attention to.
**point-to-point** *n* a cross-country race for riders on hunting horses.
**point up** *v* to emphasize or show the importance of.
**poise**[1] *n* **1** easy self-possessed assurance of manner. **2** a graceful manner of carrying oneself.
**poise**[2] *v* **1** to hold or carry in equilibrium. **2** to hold (something) supported or suspended in a steady position. **3** to be poised.
**poison**[1] *n* **1** a substance that through its chemical action kills or harms a living organism. **2** something that destroys or corrupts.
**poison**[2] *v* **1** to harm or kill with poison. **2** to contaminate with poison. **3** to have a harmful influence on. ➤ **poisoner** *n.*
**poisonous** *adj* **1** having the properties or effects of poison. **2** malicious or spiteful.
**poke**[1] *v* **1** to strike or prod with a fingertip or something sharp. **2** to protrude or cause to protrude. **3** (+ about/around) to look about or through something.
**poke**[2] *n* **1** a prod or jab. **2** *informal* a punch.
**poke**[3] *n NAmer, Scot* a bag or sack.
**poker**[1] *n* a metal rod for poking a fire.
**poker**[2] *n* a card game in which players bet on the value of their hands.
**poker face** *n* an inscrutable face that conceals thoughts or feelings. ➤ **poker-faced** *adj.*
**poky** *or* **pokey** *adj* (**-ier, -iest**) *informal* of a space: small and cramped.
**polar** *adj* **1** in the region near a geographical pole. **2** of the poles of a magnet. **3** in chemistry, having groups with opposing properties at opposite ends. **4** completely opposite in nature or action.
**polar bear** *n* a large white Arctic bear.
**polarity** *n* (*pl* **-ies**) **1** the condition of having properties or powers in opposite directions. **2** magnetic attraction in a specific direction. **3** the state of having a positive or negative electrical charge.
**polarize** *or* **-ise** *v* **1** to cause (light waves) to vibrate in a definite pattern or direction. **2** to give (something) electrical or magnetic polarity. **3** to divide (people or their opinions) into two opposing groups. ➤ **polarization** *n.*
**Polaroid** *n* **1** *trademark.* **2** a material used in sunglasses to polarize the light and prevent glare. **3** a camera that produces a finished print after each exposure.
**Pole** *n* a native or inhabitant of Poland. ➤ **Polish** *adj.*
**pole**[1] *n* a long thin cylindrical piece of wood, metal, etc, used as a support.
**pole**[2] *n* **1** either of the two points at the northern and southern extremities of the earth's axis. **2** either of the terminals of an electric cell or battery. **3** any of two or more regions in a magnetized body at which the magnetism is concentrated. ✱ **be poles apart** to have no connection or similarity.
**poleaxe**[1] (*NAmer* **poleax**) *n* an axe with a short handle and a large head.
**poleaxe**[2] (*NAmer* **poleax**) *v* **1** to attack or knock down with a heavy blow. **2** *informal* to give (somebody) a great shock.
**polecat** *n* **1** a animal like a weasel with dark brown fur, noted for its unpleasant smell. **2** *NAmer* a skunk.
**polemic** *n* **1** an aggressive attack on or refutation of somebody's opinions or principles. **2** (*in pl*) the art of discussion or argument. ➤ **polemic** *adj,* **polemical** *adj,* **polemicist** *n.*
**pole vault** *n* an athletic event consisting of a jump over a high bar using a long flexible pole. ➤ **pole-vault** *v.*
**police**[1] *n* a body of trained people entrusted with maintaining public order and enforcing the law.
**police**[2] *v* to enforce law and order in (an area, event, etc).
**policeman** *or* **policewoman** *n* (*pl* **policemen** *or* **policewomen**) a man or woman police officer.
**police officer** *n* a member of the police.
**police state** *n* a country or state with repressive governmental control of political and and social life, enforced by secret police.
**police station** *n* the headquarters of a local police force.
**policy**[1] *n* (*pl* **-ies**) **1** a definite course of action proposed or adopted. **2** an overall plan for guiding and determining decisions. **3** wise or sensible procedure.
**policy**[2] *n* (*pl* **-ies**) a contract of insurance.
**polio** *or* **poliomyelitis** *n* an infectious disease with inflammation of the nerve cells of the spinal cord, causing paralysis.
**Polish** *n* the Slavonic language of Poland. ➤ **Polish** *adj.*
**polish**[1] *v* **1** to make smooth and glossy by rubbing. **2** to make more refined. **3** (*often* + up) to bring (knowledge or a skill) to a more highly developed level. ➤ **polisher** *n.*
**polish**[2] *n* **1** a special cream or liquid rubbed on a surface to give it a shine. **2** the act of polishing. **3** a smooth glossy surface. **4** refinement or social grace.
**polish off** *v* to consume or dispose of rapidly.
**polite** *adj* **1** considerate and respectful in speech or manner. **2** showing correct social usage; refined. ➤ **politely** *adv,* **politeness** *n.*
**politic** *adj* **1** wise or expedient. **2** shrewd in dealing with people and situations.
**political** *adj* **1** relating to government or public affairs. **2** relating to politics. ➤ **politically** *adv.*
**political correctness** *n* the practice of avoiding offence to particular groups of people by

choice of language or behaviour. ➤ **politically correct** *adj.*
**political prisoner** *n* a person imprisoned for their political beliefs.
**politician** *n* **1** a person who is engaged in politics, *esp* as an elected representative. **2** *NAmer, derog* somebody who uses underhand methods for personal advancement.
**politicize** *or* **-ise** *v* **1** to give a political character to. **2** to make politically aware or active. **3** to discuss or engage in politics. ➤ **politicization** *n.*
**politics** *pl n* **1** the art or practice of government. **2** the activities associated with government; political affairs. **3** political life as a profession. **4** a person's political sympathies. **5** the relations and use of power between individuals within an organization or group.
**polity** *n* (*pl* **-ies**) **1** a state regarded as a political unit. **2** a form of government or social organization.
**polka** *n* a lively dance with two beats to the bar.
**polka dot** *n* each of a pattern of distributed dots in a design.
**poll**[1] *n* **1** the casting or recording of votes. **2** the number of votes recorded. **3** a survey of people questioned at random or by quota.
**poll**[2] *v* **1** to receive (a specified number of votes). **2** to record the votes of (a constituency or an electorate). **3** to question (people) in a poll.
**pollard**[1] *n* a tree cut back to the main stem to promote growth of foliage.
**pollard**[2] *v* to make a pollard of (a tree).
**pollen** *n* a fine dust of granules discharged from the male reproductive organ of a flower to fertilize the ovules.
**pollen count** *n* a measure of the amount of pollen in the air.
**pollinate** *v* to place pollen on the female reproductive organ of (a flower or plant) and so fertilize it. ➤ **pollination** *n.*
**pollster** *n* somebody who conducts opinion polls.
**poll tax** *n* a fixed tax levied on every adult.
**pollute** *v* **1** to contaminate with toxic substances. **2** to corrupt or defile. ➤ **pollutant** *n,* **polluter** *n.*
**pollution** *n* **1** the act of polluting or the state of being polluted. **2** material that pollutes.
**polo** *n* a team game played on horseback using long mallets to drive a wooden ball into the opponents' goal.
**polo neck** *n chiefly Brit* a high folded over collar on a jumper.
**polo shirt** *n* a casual cotton shirt with a soft collar and buttons at the neck.
**poltergeist** *n* a ghost said to make loud noises and throw objects about.
**poly-** *comb. form* many or much: *polyphonic.*
**polychrome** *adj* having several colours. ➤ **polychromatic** *adj.*
**polyester** *n* **1** a polymer used in making fibres or plastics. **2** a synthetic fibre made from polyester.
**polygamy** *n* the practice of being married to more than one person at a time. ➤ **polygamist** *n,* **polygamous** *adj.*
**polyglot** *adj* speaking several languages.
**polygon** *n* a two-dimensional figure with three or more straight sides. ➤ **polygonal** *adj.*
**polygraph** *n* an instrument recording the pulse rate, used as a lie detector.
**polyhedron** *n* (*pl* **polyhedrons** *or* **polyhedra**) a solid figure with four or more faces.
**polymath** *n* somebody who has a wide range of knowledge.
**polymer** *n* a chemical compound consisting of repeating structural units and formed by chemical combination of many molecules. ➤ **polymeric** *adj,* **polymerize** *v.*
**polymorphic** *adj* having various forms.
**polyp** *n* **1** a sea organism with a hollow cylindrical body that is attached at one end and has a central mouth surrounded by tentacles at the other. **2** a small abnormal growth projecting from a mucous membrane.
**polyphony** *n* in music, the harmonic combination of different parts played simultaneously. ➤ **polyphonic** *adj.*
**polystyrene** *n* a rigid light transparent material made from a polymer.
**polysyllabic** *adj* having two or more syllables.
**polytheism** *n* the worship of more than one god. ➤ **polytheistic** *adj.*
**polythene** *n* a tough lightweight plastic.
**polyunsaturated** *adj* of a fat or oil: having a chemical structure that is thought to be less conducive to the formation of cholesterol.
**polyurethane** *n* any of various polymers used in foams, paints, and resins.
**pomade** *n* a perfumed ointment for the hair or scalp.
**pomander** *n* a bag of aromatic substances used to scent clothes or perfume a room.
**pomegranate** *n* a thick-skinned reddish fruit containing many seeds and a crimson pulp.
**pommel** *n* **1** the raised part at the front and top of a saddle. **2** a knob on the hilt of a sword.
**Pommy** *or* **Pommie** *n* (*pl* **-ies**) *Aus, NZ, informal, chiefly derog* a British person.
**pomp** *n* **1** a stately or ceremonial display; splendour. **2** ostentatious boastful display.
**pompom** *n* an ornamental ball or tuft used on clothing.
**pompous** *adj* **1** affectedly self-important and opinionated. **2** excessively elevated or ornate. ➤ **pomposity** *n,* **pompously** *adv.*
**ponce**[1] *n Brit, informal* **1** a pimp for a prostitute. **2** *derog* an effeminate man. ➤ **poncey** *adj,* **poncy** *adj.*

**ponce²** *v Brit, informal* (+ around/about) to act in a silly or effeminate manner.
**poncho** *n* (*pl* **ponchos**) a cloak resembling a blanket with a slit in the middle for the head.
**pond** *n* a small body of fresh water.
**ponder** *v* to think about carefully.
**ponderous** *adj* **1** heavy and unwieldy. **2** oppressively dull. ➤ **ponderously** *adv.*
**pondweed** *n* a water plant with spikes of greenish flowers.
**pong¹** *v Brit, informal* to emit a strong unpleasant smell.
**pong²** *n* a strong unpleasant smell.
**pontiff** *n* the Pope.
**pontifical** *adj* of the pope; papal.
**pontificate¹** *v* to express opinions in a pompous or dogmatic way.
**pontificate²** *n* the office or term of office of a pope.
**pontoon¹** *n* **1** a flat-bottomed boat or portable float used in building a temporary bridge or in salvage work. **2** a floating landing stage, e.g. in a marina.
**pontoon²** *n* a card game in which players try to achieve a score as close as possible to 21.
**pony** *n* (*pl* **-ies**) a small horse, *esp* of a breed under 14.2 hands in height.
**ponytail** *n* a hairstyle in which the hair is drawn back tightly and tied at the back of the head.
**poo¹** *n informal* faeces.
**poo²** *v* (**poos, pooed, pooing**) *informal* to defecate.
**pooch** *n informal* a dog.
**poodle** *n* **1** a dog of a breed with a thick curly coat that is often clipped and shaved. **2** a servile person.
**poof** *or* **pouf** *n Brit, informal, offensive* an effeminate or homosexual man.
**pooh** *interj* used to express contempt or disgust.
**pooh-pooh** *v* to disparage or belittle.
**pool¹** *n* **1** a small body of standing water. **2** a small deep body of still water in a stream or river. **3** = SWIMMING POOL.
**pool²** *n* **1** players' combined stakes in a gambling game. **2** (*in pl*) a form of organized gambling based on forecasting football results. **3** a game similar to billiards. **4** an amount of money, vehicles, etc for general use.
**pool³** *v* to combine (resources or effort) for a common purpose.
**poop** *n* a raised deck at the back of a ship.
**poor** *adj* **1** not having much money. **2** inferior or inadequate. **3** (+ in) lacking in something specified. **4** inspiring pity.
**poorhouse** *n* a workhouse.
**poorly¹** *adv* in a poor or inferior manner.
**poorly²** *adj* unwell.
**pootle** *v Brit, informal* to go in a leisurely fashion.
**pop¹** *v* (**popped, popping**) **1** to make a sharp explosive sound. **2** to cause to burst open. **3** *informal* to go or come suddenly or quickly. **4** *informal* to put quickly or for a short time. **5** of the eyes: to appear to stick out, e.g. in amazement. ✱ **pop the question** *informal* to propose marriage.
**pop²** *n* **1** a popping sound. **2** a flavoured fizzy soft drink.
**pop³** *n chiefly NAmer, informal* an affectionate name for one's father.
**pop⁴** *adj* **1** of pop music. **2** popularized by the media.
**pop⁵** *n* (*also* **pop music**) a modern popular music having a strong beat.
**pop art** *n* art incorporating items from popular culture and the mass media.
**popcorn** *n* maize kernels that swell and burst when heated to form a white starchy mass.
**pope** *n* (*often* **Pope**) the bishop of Rome as head of the Roman Catholic Church.
**popery** *n derog* Roman Catholicism. ➤ **popish** *adj.*
**pop-eyed** *adj* having staring or bulging eyes.
**popinjay** *n archaic* a conceited or supercilious person.
**poplar** *n* a tall slender tree of the willow family.
**poplin** *n* a plain cotton fabric with fine crosswise ribs.
**poppadom** *or* **poppadum** *n* in Indian cookery, a crisp wafer-thin pancake of deep-fried dough.
**popper** *n Brit, informal* a press-stud.
**poppet** *n chiefly Brit, informal* a lovable or enchanting person.
**poppy** *n* (*pl* **-ies**) a plant with bright flowers and a large seed case.
**poppycock** *n informal* nonsense.
**populace** *n* the general public.
**popular** *adj* **1** generally liked or admired. **2** liked or favoured by a particular person or group. **3** suited to the needs or tastes of ordinary people. **4** of or used by the general public. ➤ **popularity** *n,* **popularly** *adv.*
**popularize** *or* **-ise** *v* **1** to make popular. **2** to present in a generally understandable or interesting form. ➤ **popularization** *n.*
**populate** *v* **1** to occupy or inhabit (a place). **2** to provide (a place) with inhabitants.
**population** *n* the people living in a place, or their total number.
**populist** *n* somebody who aims to represent or appeal to ordinary people. ➤ **populism** *n,* **populist** *adj.*
**populous** *adj* having many inhabitants.
**porcelain** *n* a hard translucent white ceramic material.
**porch** *n* **1** a covered entrance to a building. **2** *NAmer* a veranda.
**porcine** *adj* like a pig or pigs.

**porcupine** *n* a rodent with stiff protective bristles.

**pore**[1] *n* each of many minute openings in the skin or other surface.

**pore**[2] *v* (+ over/through) to study closely or attentively.

***Usage Note:*** Do not confuse this word with the verb *pour*.

**pork** *n* the flesh of a pig used as food.

**porker** *n* a young pig fattened for food.

**porn** *n informal* pornography.

**pornography** *n* books, photographs, and films intended to cause sexual excitement. ➤ **pornographic** *adj.*

**porous** *adj* allowing liquids and gases to pass through. ➤ **porosity** *n.*

**porpoise** *n* (*pl* **porpoises** *or* **porpoise**) a small whale with a blunt snout.

**porridge** *n* a soft food made by boiling oatmeal in milk or water.

**port**[1] *n* a town or city with a harbour for ships.

**port**[2] *n* the left side of a ship or aircraft looking forward.

**port**[3] *n* a fortified sweet wine made in Portugal.

**port**[4] *n* **1** an opening in machinery, allowing liquid or gas to pass. **2** a socket in a computer for connecting a device to it. **3** an opening in a ship's side for loading and unloading cargo. **4** an opening in an armoured vehicle or fortification through which guns can be fired.

**portable**[1] *adj* small and light enough to be carried about. ➤ **portability** *n.*

**portable**[2] *n* a portable device.

**portal** *n* a grand door or gateway.

**portcullis** *n* a heavy grating that can be lowered to prevent passage through a gateway.

**portend** *v* to be a warning or sign of (something unpleasant or momentous).

**portent** *n* a sign or warning of something unpleasant or momentous.

**portentous** *adj* **1** being a portent; ominous. **2** self-consciously solemn. ➤ **portentously** *adv.*

**porter**[1] *n chiefly Brit* an official who regulates entry at the entrance to a large building.

**porter**[2] *n* **1** somebody employed to carry luggage. **2** somebody employed to move patients or equipment in a hospital. **3** a heavy dark brown beer.

**portfolio** *n* (*pl* **-os**) **1** a flexible case for carrying loose papers, pictures, etc. **2** a set of drawings, photographs, etc presented as evidence of creative talent. **3** the office or responsibilities of a government minister. **4** the securities held by an investor.

**porthole** *n* a small window in the side of a ship or aircraft.

**portico** *n* (*pl* **-oes** *or* **-os**) a roof supported by columns at the entrance to a building.

**portion**[1] *n* **1** a part or share of something. **2** a helping of food.

**portion**[2] *v* to share out in portions.

**portly** *adj* (**-ier, -iest**) rather fat.

**portmanteau** *n* (*pl* **portmanteaus** *or* **portmanteaux**) a large bag that opens into two parts.

**port of call** *n* **1** a port where ships call during a voyage. **2** a stop in an itinerary.

**portrait** *n* **1** a painting or drawing of a person. **2** a description of a person in a novel, film, etc. ➤ **portraiture** *n.*

**portray** *v* **1** to make a picture of. **2** to describe in words. **3** to represent in a particular way. ➤ **portrayal** *n.*

**Portuguese** *n* (*pl* **Portuguese**) **1** a native or inhabitant of Portugal. **2** the language of Portugal and Brazil. ➤ **Portuguese** *adj.*

***Usage Note:*** Note the spelling with a second *u* after the *g*.

**pose**[1] *v* **1** to assume a certain position to be painted or photographed. **2** to constitute (a problem or threat). **3** to present (a question) for attention. **4** (+ as) to pretend to be. **5** *Brit, informal* to behave in an affectedly stylish way to impress others.

**pose**[2] *n* **1** a position adopted to be painted or photographed. **2** an affected manner intended to impress others.

**poser** *n* **1** a puzzling or baffling question. **2** somebody who poses to impress others.

**poseur** *n* somebody who is insincere or affects a style of behaviour to impress others.

**posh** *adj informal* exclusive or luxurious.

**posit** *v* (**posited, positing**) to put forward as fact or basis for argument.

**position**[1] *n* **1** the place occupied by somebody or something. **2** the proper place for something. **3** the way in which somebody or something is disposed or arranged. **4** a condition or situation. **5** social or official rank or status. **6** *formal* a post or job. ➤ **positional** *adj.*

**position**[2] *v* to put in a proper or specified position.

**positive**[1] *adj* **1** concentrating on what is good or beneficial; optimistic. **2** capable of being constructively applied; helpful. **3** indicating acceptance or approval. **4** showing the presence of something. **5** confident or certain. **6** utter, complete. **7** greater than zero. **8** of a photographic image: having the light and dark parts corresponding to those of the original subject. **9** having higher electric potential and constituting the part from which the current flows to the external circuit. ➤ **positively** *adv.*

**positive**[2] *n* **1** a positive state or quality. **2** a positive photograph or a print.

**positive discrimination** *n* a bias in favour of members of a group that is discriminated against or inadequately represented.

**positive vetting** *n* thorough investigation into the character of a candidate for the civil service.

**positivism** *n* a theory of knowledge based on the scientific observation of natural phenomena. ➤ **positivist** *adj and n.*

**positron** *n* a positively charged elementary particle that has the same mass and magnitude of electrical charge as the electron.

**posse** *n* **1** formerly, a body of men summoned by a sheriff to assist in enforcing the law. **2** a large group of people.

**possess** *v* **1** to have as property; to own. **2** to have as an attribute or skill. **3** to influence or dominate (somebody). ➤ **possessor** *n.*

**possession** *n* **1** the state of having or owning something. **2** something owned.

**possessive**[1] *adj* **1** demanding undivided love or attention. **2** reluctant to share or give up possessions. **3** in grammar, denoting ownership or a similar relation. ➤ **possessively** *adv.*

**possessive**[2] *n* the possessive case or a word in this case.

**possibility** *n* (*pl* **-ies**) **1** the condition or fact of being possible. **2** something possible. **3** a person or thing worth considering. **4** (*usu in pl*) potential or prospective value.

**possible**[1] *adj* **1** within the limits of ability or realization. **2** that may or may not occur.

**possible**[2] *n* **1** something possible. **2** somebody or something that may be chosen.

**possibly** *adv* **1** it is possible that; maybe. **2** used as an intensifier with *can* or *could.*

**possum** *n* **1** an opossum. **2** an Australian tree-dwelling marsupial animal. ✱ **play possum** *informal* to pretend to be asleep or unaware.

**post**[1] *n* **1** a fixed upright piece of timber or metal forming a stay or support. **2** a pole marking the start or finish of a race.

**post**[2] *v* **1** to display (a notice) in a public place. **2** to announce or advertise.

**post**[3] *n chiefly Brit* **1** the dispatch and delivery of letters, parcels, etc. **2** a single collection or delivery of post. **3** letters and parcels dispatched or received.

**post**[4] *v* **1** to send by post. **2** to enter (an item) in a ledger. ✱ **keep posted** to provide with any news or information.

**post**[5] *n* **1** the place at which somebody is stationed. **2** an office to which a person is appointed.

**post**[6] *v* **1** to station (a sentry or police officer) somewhere. **2** *chiefly Brit* to send (somebody) to work in a different unit or location.

**post-** *prefix* after or later (than): *postdate; postscript.*

**postage** *n* the charge for sending something by post.

**postal** *adj* relating to the sending of things by post. ➤ **postally** *adv.*

**postal order** *n Brit* an order issued by a post office and sent to another person who can exchange it for money.

**postbox** *n* a box for the posting of mail.

**postcard** *n* a card for sending a message by post without an envelope.

**postcode** *n* a combination of letters and numbers that identifies a postal address.

**postcode lottery** *n Brit* disparities in medical treatment or social care in different parts of the country.

**postdate** *v* **1** to put a future date on (a cheque). **2** to follow (something) in time.

**poster** *n* a large picture or sign put up for advertisement or decoration.

**poste restante** /ˌpohst ˈrestont/ *n chiefly Brit* a service by which mail is kept for collection by the recipient at a post office.

**posterior**[1] *adj* **1** later in time or order. **2** situated towards the back.

**posterior**[2] *n informal* the buttocks.

**posterity** *n* future generations.

**postgraduate** *n* a student continuing higher education after completing a first degree.

**posthaste** *adv* with all possible speed.

**posthumous** *adj* occurring or published after a person's death. ➤ **posthumously** *adv.*

**posting** *n* an appointment to a position abroad.

**postman** *n* (*pl* **postmen**) a man who delivers the post.

**postmark**[1] *n* a cancellation mark showing the date and place of posting of a piece of mail.

**postmark**[2] *v* to stamp with a postmark.

**postmaster** *or* **postmistress** *n* a person in charge of a post office.

**postmodernism** *n* an artistic movement advocating a reinterpretation of classical ideas and forms. ➤ **postmodern** *adj,* **postmodernist** *n and adj.*

**postmortem** *n* an examination of a dead body to determine the cause of death.

**postnatal** *adj* relating to the period after childbirth.

**post office** *n* **1** a national organization that runs a postal system. **2** a local branch of a national post office.

**postpone** *v* to move to a later time; to defer. ➤ **postponement** *n.*

**postscript** *n* a note added at the end of a letter.

**postulant** *n* a person seeking admission to a religious order.

**postulate** *v* to assume (something) to be true for the purposes of argument.

**posture**[1] *n* **1** a position in which the body is held. **2** an attitude or frame of mind. ➤ **postural** *adj.*

**posture**[2] *v* to assume an affected posture designed to impress others.

**posy** *n* (*pl* **-ies**) a small bouquet of flowers.

**pot**[1] *n* **1** a rounded container for holding liquids or solids. **2** a flowerpot. **3** the total of the bets taken in a gambling game. ✱ **go to pot** *informal* to deteriorate or collapse. ➤ **potful** *n.*
**pot**[2] *v* (**potted, potting**) **1** to preserve (food) in a sealed pot or jar. **2** to plant in a flowerpot. **3** to shoot or kill (an animal or person). **4** in billiards or snooker, to send (a ball) into a pocket.
**pot**[3] *n informal* cannabis.
**potable** *adj* of water: suitable for drinking.
**potash** *n* potassium or a potassium compound, *esp* as used in agriculture or industry.
**potassium** *n* a silver-white metallic element.
**potato** *n* (*pl* **-oes**) a starchy edible tuber used as a vegetable.
**potbelly** *n* (*pl* **-ies**) a protruding abdomen. ➤ **potbellied** *adj.*
**potent** *adj* **1** strong and powerful. **2** of a man: able to achieve an erection. ➤ **potency** *n.*
**potentate** *n* a ruler or monarch.
**potential**[1] *adj* capable of coming into being or developing further. ➤ **potentiality** *n,* **potentially** *adv.*
**potential**[2] *n* **1** capacity to develop in a particular way. **2** qualities that indicate future achievements or benefits.
**pothole**[1] *n* **1** a hole in a road surface. **2** a deep hole in the ground or in the floor of a cave. ➤ **potholed** *adj.*
**pothole**[2] *v* to explore underground pothole systems as a leisure activity. ➤ **potholer** *n,* **potholing** *n.*
**potion** *n* a dose of medicine, poison, etc in liquid form.
**pot-luck** *n* whatever happens to be available.
**potpourri** *n* **1** a mixture of dried flowers, herbs, and spices, kept for their fragrance. **2** a miscellaneous collection.
**potshot** *n* a casual shot at an easy target.
**pottage** *n* a thick soup or stew.
**potted** *adj* **1** planted or grown in a flowerpot. **2** preserved in a sealed pot. **3** *chiefly Brit* abridged or summarized.
**potter**[1] *n* somebody who makes pottery.
**potter**[2] *v* **1** (*often* + around/about) to spend time aimlessly. **2** to move in a random fashion.
**pottery** *n* (*pl* **-ies**) **1** articles made of baked clay. **2** the craft of making pottery. **3** a place where pottery is made.
**potting shed** *n* a garden shed for potting plants and storing tools.
**potty**[1] *adj* (**-ier, -iest**) *Brit, informal* **1** slightly crazy. **2** foolish or silly. **3** (*usu* + about) having a great liking for something or somebody.
**potty**[2] *n* (*pl* **-ies**) a bowl-shaped receptacle used as a toilet by a small child.
**pouch** *n* **1** a small bag made of flexible material. **2** a pocket of skin in the abdomen of marsupials for carrying their young.
**pouf** *n* see POOF.
**pouffe** *or* **pouf** *n* a large firmly stuffed cushion used to sit on or rest the feet on.
**poulterer** *n* somebody who deals in poultry or game.
**poultice** *n* a soft moist mass of clay, bread, mustard, etc spread on cloth and applied to inflamed or injured parts of the body.
**poultry** *n* chickens, ducks, and other domestic fowl kept for eggs or meat.
**pounce**[1] *v* **1** to spring forward down to seize something. **2** (*often* + on) to react swiftly to criticize a mistake.
**pounce**[2] *n* the act of pouncing.
**pound**[1] *n* (*pl* **pounds** *or* **pound**) **1** a unit of weight equal to 16oz (about 0.454kg) avoirdupois or 12oz (about 0.373kg) troy. **2** the basic monetary unit of the UK.
**pound**[2] *v* **1** to reduce to powder or pulp by beating or crushing. **2** to strike heavily or repeatedly. **3** to move along with heavy steps. **4** to beat or throb with a heavy rhythm.
**pound**[3] *n* an enclosure for stray animals or lost property.
**pour** *v* **1** to flow or cause to flow in a stream. **2** to dispense (a drink) into a container. **3** to supply or produce freely or copiously. **4** to move or go with a continuous flow and in large quantities. **5** (*often* + down) to rain hard. **6** (+ out) to express (feelings) at length. ✱ **pour cold water on** to be unenthusiastic about.

***Usage Note:*** Do not confuse this word with the verb *pore*, which means 'to study closely'.

**pout**[1] *v* to thrust out the lips to show displeasure or in a sexually provocative way. ➤ **pouty** *adj.*
**pout**[2] *n* an act of pouting.
**poverty** *n* **1** the state of being poor. **2** a deficiency.
**powder**[1] *n* **1** a mass of dry loose particles. **2** a cosmetic or medicine produced as fine particles. ➤ **powdery** *adj.*
**powder**[2] *v* **1** to sprinkle or cover with powder. **2** to reduce to powder.
**powder blue** *n* pale blue.
**power**[1] *n* **1** the ability to do something. **2** legal authority or right. **3** the possession of control over others. **4** somebody or something that possesses authority or influence. **5** a sovereign state having military strength and international influence. **6** physical strength. **7** mental or moral effectiveness. **8** electricity or another form of energy. **9** the energy or driving force generated by a motor or a similar machine. **10** in physics, the amount of work done or energy emitted or transferred per unit of time. **11** the number of times a given number is to be multiplied by itself.
**power**[2] *v* **1** to supply with power. **2** (*often* +

down/up) to switch an electrical device off or on. **3** to move in a forceful manner.

**powerboat** *n* a powerful motorboat.

**power cut** *n* a failure in the supply of electric power to an area.

**power dressing** *n* a formal style of dressing as an expression of status by professional women.

**powerful** *adj* **1** having great power or influence. **2** very strong or forceful. **3** extremely effective. ➤ **powerfully** *adv.*

**powerhouse** *n informal* a person or thing having great energy and force.

**powerless** *adj* lacking the authority or capacity to act.

**power station** *n* an electricity generating station.

**power steering** *n* steering reinforced by power from the engine.

**powwow**[1] *n* **1** a traditional Native American ceremony with feasting and dancing. **2** *informal* a meeting for discussion.

**powwow**[2] *v* to hold a powwow.

**pox** *n* **1** a disease causing the formation of spots on the skin that may leave pockmarks after healing. **2** *informal* syphilis.

**poxy** *adj* (**-ier, -iest**) *chiefly Brit, informal* of poor quality or value.

**pp** *abbr* **1** pages. **2** Latin *per procurationem*: used to indicate that a person is signing on behalf of somebody else.

**PPS** *abbr* **1** Parliamentary Private Secretary. **2** Latin *post postscriptum*: used to introduce a second or further postscript.

**PR** *abbr* **1** proportional representation. **2** public relations.

**Pr** *abbr* the chemical symbol for praseodymium.

**practicable** *adj* capable of being done. ➤ **practicability** *n*, **practicably** *adv.*

**practical**[1] *adj* **1** relating to actual performance and experience rather than theory. **2** suitable for real situations. **3** adapted or suitable for a particular use. **4** realistic in dealing with problems or situations. **5** good at carrying out ordinary tasks. **6** very nearly as described: *a practical certainty.*

**practical**[2] *n* an examination or lesson that tests or teaches the ability to put theory into practice.

**practicality** *n* (*pl* **-ies**) **1** the practical nature of something or somebody. **2** (*in pl*) the practical aspects of a situation or question.

**practical joke** *n* a trick played on somebody to make them appear foolish.

**practically** *adv* **1** almost; nearly. **2** in a practical manner.

**practice** *n* **1** regular or repeated exercise to acquire skill. **2** the actual carrying out of tasks as opposed to theory. **3** a habit. **4** the usual way something is done. **5** work in a profession, e.g. law or medicine. **6** the business or premises of a professional person. ✱ **in practice** in real situations.

***Usage Note:*** In British English *practice* is the correct spelling for the noun and *practise* for the verb.

**practise** (*NAmer* **practice**) *v* **1** to perform (an activity) repeatedly so as to become skilled in it. **2** to carry out or apply (something) in fact or in real situations. **3** to be a member of (a particular religion). **4** to be professionally engaged in (a particular type of work).

**practitioner** *n* somebody who practises a profession or art.

**pragmatic** *adj* concerned with practicalities rather than theory; realistic. ➤ **pragmatically** *adv.*

**pragmatism** *n* a practical approach to problems and affairs. ➤ **pragmatist** *n.*

**prairie** *n* an extensive area of treeless grassland in North America.

**praise**[1] *v* **1** to express approval or admiration of. **2** to glorify or extol (God or a god).

**praise**[2] *n* words expressing admiration and approval.

**praiseworthy** *adj* deserving praise; commendable.

**praline** *n* a sweet substance made from nuts heated in boiling sugar.

**pram** *n Brit* a four-wheeled carriage for a baby, pushed by a person on foot.

**prance** *v* to walk in a silly and affected manner.

**prang**[1] *v Brit, informal* to crash (a vehicle or aircraft).

**prang**[2] *n Brit, informal* a crash involving a vehicle or aircraft.

**prank** *n* a mischievous act or trick.

**prankster** *n* somebody who plays pranks.

**prat** *n Brit, informal* a foolish person.

**prate** *v* (*often* + about) to talk foolishly and excessively; to chatter.

**prattle** *v* to chatter in silly or inconsequential manner.

**prawn** *n* a crustacean like a large shrimp.

**pray**[1] *v* **1** to say a prayer. **2** (*usu* + for) to wish or hope fervently.

**pray**[2] *adv formal* please.

**prayer** *n* **1** a personal request or expression of praise or thanksgiving addressed to God or a god. **2** (*in pl*) a religious service consisting chiefly of prayers. **3** an earnest request or devout wish.

**praying mantis** *n* = MANTIS.

**pre-** *prefix* before or earlier (than): *prehistoric.*

**preach** *v* **1** to deliver a sermon. **2** (*often* + at) to give advice or warnings in a tiresome or highly moral manner. **3** to advocate (something) earnestly. ➤ **preacher** *n.*

**preamble** *n* an introductory statement.

**prearrange** *v* to arrange beforehand.

**precarious** *adj* **1** likely to fall or collapse. **2** dependent on chance. ➤ **precariously** *adv.*

**precaution** *n* **1** a measure taken to avoid undesirable consequences. **2** *informal* (*in pl*) contraceptive measures. ➤ **precautionary** *adj.*
**precede** *v* to go or happen before something or somebody else.
**precedence** *n* greater importance or priority in status or treatment.
**precedent** *n* an earlier similar occurrence of something under consideration, *esp* a judicial decision that serves as a rule for similar cases.
**precept** *n* a principle serving as a general rule of conduct.
**precinct** *n* **1** (*in pl*) the region immediately surrounding a place. **2** an enclosure surrounded by buildings. **3** an area of a town closed to traffic. **4** *NAmer* an administrative district.
**precious** *adj* **1** of great value or high price. **2** highly esteemed or cherished. **3** excessively refined; affected. **4** used as an ironic intensifier: *Precious help you were!*
**precious metal** *n* a valuable metal, e.g. gold, silver, or platinum.
**precious stone** *n* a valuable stone used as a jewel, e.g. a diamond, ruby, or emerald.
**precipice** *n* a sheer rockface or cliff.
**precipitate**[1] *v* **1** to hurl or throw violently. **2** to bring about (an event or action) suddenly or unexpectedly. **3** to separate out, or cause (a substance) to separate out, from a solution or suspension. **4** to cause (vapour) to condense and fall as rain, snow, etc.
**precipitate**[2] *n* a substance separated from a solution by chemical or physical change.
**precipitate**[3] *adj* acting or carried out suddenly or with undue haste. ➤ **precipitately** *adv.*
**precipitation** *n* **1** rain, snow, etc falling in the atmosphere. **2** the process of precipitating something.
**precipitous** *adj* **1** dangerously steep or high. **2** extremely sudden and severe in effect.
**precis**[1] /'praysee/ *n* (*pl* **precis**) a concise summary.
**precis**[2] *v* (**precising, precised**) to make a precis of.
**precise** *adj* **1** specific or detailed. **2** carried out with attention to accuracy. **3** taking great care to be accurate; punctilious. **4** particular; very. ➤ **precisely** *adv.*
**precision** *n* the quality of being precise and careful.
**preclude** *v* to make impossible in advance. ➤ **preclusion** *n.*
**precocious** *adj* showing mature qualities at an unusually early age. ➤ **precociously** *adv,* **precocity** *n.*
**precognition** *n* the apparent ability to foresee future events.
**preconceived** *adj* of an opinion: reached without actual knowledge or experience.
**preconception** *n* **1** a preconceived idea. **2** a prejudice.
**precondition** *n* something that must happen or exist to enable something else to happen or exist.
**precursor** *n* somebody or something that precedes and prepares the way for somebody or something similar.
**predate** *v* to exist or occur earlier than.
**predator** *n* an animal that lives by hunting and killing other animals.
**predatory** *adj* **1** of an animal: hunting and killing other animals. **2** taking advantage of other people.
**predecease** *v* to die before (another person).
**predecessor** *n* **1** the previous occupant of a job or position. **2** a person or thing that has been replaced or superseded by something else.
**predestination** *n* the religious doctrine that God has decided all events in advance, including matters of salvation.
**predestined** *adj* decided by God or by fate in advance.
**predetermine** *v* to decide on or arrange beforehand.
**predeterminer** *n* in grammar, an adjective or adverb that can occur before a determiner, e.g. *both* in *both her hands.*
**predicament** *n* a difficult or trying situation.
**predicate**[1] *n* the part of a sentence or clause that contains the verb and says something about the subject.
**predicate**[2] *v formal* to base or found on something else.
**predicative** *adj* contained in the predicate of a sentence, e.g. *red* in *the dress is red.* ➤ **predicatively** *adv.*
**predict** *v* to assert in advance the likelihood of (something happening). ➤ **predictor** *n.*
**predictable** *adj* **1** capable of being predicted. **2** always behaving in an expected way. ➤ **predictability** *n,* **predictably** *adv.*
**prediction** *n* **1** a statement of what will happen. **2** the act of predicting. ➤ **predictive** *adj.*
**predilection** *n* a liking or preference.
**predispose** *v* **1** to make more likely or willing to do something. **2** (+ to) to make susceptible to something. ➤ **predisposition** *n.*
**predominant** *adj* **1** constituting the largest part of something. **2** having greater strength or influence. ➤ **predominance** *n,* **predominantly** *adv.*
**predominate** *v* **1** to be the main part of. **2** to exert a controlling power. ➤ **predomination** *n.*
**preeminent** *adj* superior to all others. ➤ **preeminence** *n,* **preeminently** *adv.*
**preempt** *v* **1** to take action to prevent. **2** to take (something) over, *esp* to prevent others having it. ➤ **preemption** *n,* **preemptive** *adj.*

**preen** *v* **1** of a bird: to clean and smooth its feathers with its beak. **2** to make oneself look attractive. **3** *usu derog* to pride or congratulate (oneself) on something.

**preexist** *v* to exist at a previous time. ➤ **preexistence** *n.*

**prefab** *n* a prefabricated structure or building.

**prefabricated** *adj* of a building: manufactured in parts ready for assembly on site.

**preface**[1] *n* an introduction to a book.

**preface**[2] *v* (*usu* + by/with) to say or write by way of introduction to.

**prefect** *n* **1** *Brit* a senior pupil in a secondary school with some authority over other pupils. **2** the chief administrative officer of a region in some countries.

**prefecture** *n* a district governed by a prefect.

**prefer** *v* (**preferred, preferring**) **1** (*often* + to) to like better than. **2** *formal* to bring (a charge) against somebody. **3** *archaic* to give promotion or advancement to.

**preferable** *adj* more desirable or suitable. ➤ **preferably** *adv.*

**preference** *n* **1** (*usu* + for) greater liking for one thing over another. **2** a person or thing preferred. **3** special favour or consideration.

**preferential** *adj* showing special or undue favour. ➤ **preferentially** *adv.*

**preferment** *n* promotion to a higher rank or office.

**prefigure** *v* to represent or suggest in advance.

**prefix**[1] *n* **1** a group of letters placed at the beginning of a word and affecting its meaning, e.g. *un-* in *unhappy*. **2** a title used before a person's name.

**prefix**[2] *v* to add a prefix to.

**pregnancy** *n* (*pl* **-ies**) the state or period of being pregnant.

**pregnant** *adj* **1** of a woman: having an unborn child in the womb. **2** rich in meaning.

**prehensile** *adj* of a tail: adapted for seizing or grasping.

**prehistoric** *adj* dating from the period of time before written records.

**prehistory** *n* the time before the existence of written records.

**preindustrial** *adj* prior to the development of large-scale industry.

**prejudge** *v* to pass judgment on prematurely.

**prejudice**[1] *n* **1** an opinion formed without sufficient reason or knowledge. **2** preconceived or biased judgments generally. **3** irrational hostility against an individual or group.

**prejudice**[2] *v* **1** to cause to have a prejudice. **2** to cause harm to or put at a disadvantage. ➤ **prejudiced** *adj.*

**prejudicial** *adj* **1** harmful or disadvantageous. **2** leading to prejudiced judgments.

**prelate** *n* a bishop or other clergyman of high rank.

**preliminary**[1] *n* (*pl* **-ies**) something that is preparatory to something else.

**preliminary**[2] *adj* preparing for what is to follow.

**prelude** *n* **1** an introductory performance, action, or event. **2** an introductory piece of music. ➤ **preludial** *adj.*

**premarital** *adj* occurring before marriage.

**premature** *adj* **1** happening or done before the proper time. **2** of a baby: born before the end of the normal gestation period. ➤ **prematurely** *adv.*

**premeditated** *adj* considered and planned beforehand. ➤ **premeditation** *n.*

**premenstrual** *adj* occurring in the period before menstruation.

**premier**[1] *adj* first in position, rank, or importance.

**premier**[2] *n* a head of government. ➤ **premiership** *n.*

**premiere**[1] *n* a first public performance of a play, film, etc.

**premiere**[2] *v* to give the premiere of.

**premise** *or* **premiss** *n* a proposition used as a basis of argument.

**premises** *pl n* a piece of land with the buildings on it.

**premium** *n* **1** a sum paid to obtain insurance. **2** an extra sum added to a standard price. **3** a high value. **4** (*used before a noun*) of exceptional quality or amount. ✱ **at a premium** valuable because rare or difficult to obtain.

**premonition** *n* a strong feeling that something is going to happen. ➤ **premonitory** *adj.*

**prenatal** *adj* before birth.

**preoccupation** *n* **1** complete mental absorption or obsession. **2** something that absorbs one's attention.

**preoccupy** *v* (**-ies, -ied**) to engage all the attention of.

**preordain** *v* to decree or decide in advance.

**prep** *n Brit* school work done outside ordinary lessons.

**prepaid** *v* paid for in advance.

**preparation** *n* **1** the activity of preparing for something. **2** (*usu in pl*) a preparatory act or measure. **3** a medicine or other prepared substance.

**preparatory** *adj* **1** intended to prepare for something. **2** (+ to) in preparation for something.

**preparatory school** *n Brit* a private school for pupils from the age of seven.

**prepare** *v* **1** to make ready for some purpose or activity. **2** to put into a suitable frame of mind. **3** to work out the details of. **4** to put together from various ingredients. ✱ **to be prepared to** to be willing to do something.

**preparedness** *n* a state of readiness to act.

**preponderant** *adj* **1** occurring in greater number or quantity. **2** having superior force or influence. ➤ **preponderance** *n*, **preponderantly** *adv*.

**preposition** *n* a word used to link a noun, pronoun, etc to another part of the sentence, e.g. *in*, *by*. ➤ **prepositional** *adj*.

**prepossessing** *adj* attractive or appealing.

**preposterous** *adj* ridiculous and absurd. ➤ **preposterously** *adv*.

**prep school** *n* a preparatory school.

**prepubescent** *adj* in the period before puberty.

**prerequisite** *n* a requirement that must be satisfied in advance.

**prerogative** *n* **1** an exclusive right or privilege. **2** a discretionary power.

**presage** *v* to be an omen or warning of.

**Presbyterian**[1] *adj* denoting a Christian Church governed by elected representative bodies. ➤ **Presbyterianism** *n*.

**Presbyterian**[2] *n* a member of a Presbyterian Church.

**presbytery** *n* (*pl* **-ies**) **1** a local ruling body in Presbyterian Churches. **2** the house of a Roman Catholic parish priest. **3** the part of a church reserved for the clergy.

**prescience** *n* foreknowledge of events. ➤ **prescient** *adj*.

**prescribe** *v* **1** of a doctor: to order or recommend (a medicine or treatment) as a remedy. **2** to recommend as beneficial. **3** to give specific instructions regarding.

**prescription** *n* **1** a written direction for the preparation and use of a medicine. **2** an authoritative ruling.

**prescriptive** *adj* giving instructions or laying down rules.

**presence** *n* **1** the fact or condition of being present. **2** the immediate proximity of a person. **3** something non-physical that is felt to be present. **4** a body of people playing an influential role. **5** impressive personal distinction or magnetism. **6** a dignified bearing or appearance. ✱ **presence of mind** composure in difficult circumstances.

**present**[1] *n* something presented; a gift.

**present**[2] *v* **1** to give formally or ceremonially. **2** (+ with) to allow (somebody) to gain something without effort. **3** to introduce (somebody) formally. **4** to bring before the public. **5** to introduce (a television or radio programme). **6** to offer (a particular type of appearance) to the view of others; to show or exhibit. **7** to submit for approval or consideration. **8** to describe or explain (a plan, idea, etc) in a particular way. **9** to constitute or pose (a problem or difficulty). ✱ **present oneself** to be present; to attend. ➤ **presenter** *n*.

**present**[3] *adj* **1** in or at a place. **2** existing in something mentioned or understood. **3** now existing or in progress. **4** currently doing something or being considered. **5** of the verb tense that expresses present time or the time of speaking.

**present**[4] *n* (**the present**) the time now in progress. ✱ **at present** now. **for the present** for the time being.

**presentable** *adj* **1** fit to be seen or inspected. **2** smart enough to appear in company.

**presentation** *n* **1** the manner in which something is presented. **2** the act or process of presenting something. **3** an informative talk or lecture.

**presentiment** *n* a feeling that something is about to happen.

**presently** *adv* **1** before long; soon. **2** now.

**present participle** *n* a participle, e.g. *dancing*, *being*, expressing a current event or state.

**preservative** *n* a substance that helps to preserve food.

**preserve**[1] *v* **1** to keep in its original condition. **2** to keep in existence. **3** to maintain (an appearance or type of behaviour) in spite of adverse circumstances or provocation. **4** to keep safe from injury or harm. **5** to treat and store (food) for future use. ➤ **preservation** *n*.

**preserve**[2] *n* **1** a jam, jelly, or other food preserved by cooking with sugar. **2** an area restricted for the preservation of natural resources. **3** a sphere of activity reserved for certain people.

**preset** *v* (**presetting**, *past tense and past part*. **preset**) to set the controls on (a device) so that it operates in a certain way.

**preside** *v* **1** to have charge of a meeting or court. **2** (+ over) to exercise guidance or control.

**presidency** *n* (*pl* **-ies**) **1** the office of president. **2** the period during which a president holds office.

**president** *n* **1** the elected head of state in a republic. **2** the chief officer of a business. ➤ **presidential** *adj*.

**presidium** *or* **praesidium** *n* (*pl* **presidia** *or* **presidiums**) a permanent executive committee in a communist country.

**press**[1] *v* **1** to push firmly and steadily against (something). **2** to move (something) in this way. **3** to flatten or mould to a particular shape by pressing. **4** to iron (clothes). **5** to squeeze. **6** to squeeze the juice from (a fruit). **7** to try to persuade (somebody) to do something. **8** (+ for) to make vigorous efforts to obtain or bring about. **9** to put forward (e.g. a claim) forcefully. **10** (*often* + ahead/forward) to make one's way determinedly. ✱ **be pressed for time** to have little time available. **be pressed to do** to have difficulty in doing.

**press**[2] *n* **1** a device for shaping material, extracting liquid, or compressing something. **2** a printing press. **3** a publishing house or printing firm. **4** (**the press**) newspapers and magazines collectively. **5** a crowd of people.

**press**[3] *v* formerly, to force into military service. ✻ **press into service** to use (something) temporarily for a makeshift purpose.

**press conference** *n* an interview given by a public figure to journalists.

**press gang** *n* a body of men who forced people into military service.

**press-gang** *v* to force (somebody) to do something unwillingly.

**pressing**[1] *adj* **1** needing immediate action or attention. **2** earnest or insistent.

**pressing**[2] *n* an object produced from a mould or matrix.

**press on** *v* to continue or proceed resolutely.

**press release** *n* a prepared statement released to the news media.

**press-stud** *n Brit* a fastener consisting of two parts joined by pressing.

**press-up** *n* an exercise performed in a prone position by raising and lowering the body with the arms while supporting it only on the hands and toes.

**pressure**[1] *n* **1** the application of force to something by something else in direct contact with it. **2** influence or compulsion directed towards achieving a particular end. **3** demands needing a quick response or a sustained effort. **4** distress or difficulty resulting from domestic, social, or economic factors. **5** in physics, the force or thrust exerted over a surface divided by its area.

**pressure**[2] *v* to try to persuade (somebody) to do something.

**pressure cooker** *n* an airtight saucepan used to cook food quickly in steam heated under pressure. ➤ **pressure-cook** *v.*

**pressure group** *n* a group organized to influence government policy or public opinion.

**pressurize** *or* **-ise** *v* **1** to maintain near-normal atmospheric pressure in (an aircraft cabin). **2** to subject to strong persuasion or coercion.

**prestige** *n* high standing based on achievement or success.

**prestigious** *adj* enjoying or bringing prestige.

**presto** *adj and adv* of a piece of music: performed at a fast tempo.

**prestressed** *adj* of a beam: having internal stresses introduced in it to counteract external stresses in use.

**presumably** *adv* as one may reasonably assume.

**presume** *v* **1** to suppose or assume with some degree of certainty. **2** to take for granted. **3** to undertake (to do something) without justification. **4** (+ on/upon) to take advantage unfairly. ➤ **presumable** *adj,* **presumer** *n.*

**presumption** *n* **1** overconfident or forward conduct. **2** an attitude or belief based on reasonable grounds. **3** a ground or reason for presuming something.

**presumptuous** *adj* overconfident or forward. ➤ **presumptuously** *adv.*

**presuppose** *v* **1** to suppose beforehand, usu without proof or justification. **2** to require (something) to exist or be the case in order that something else may exist or be true or valid. ➤ **presupposition** *n.*

**pretence** (*NAmer* **pretense**) *n* **1** an act of pretending. **2** (+ to) a claim made or implied, when not supported by fact.

**pretend** *v* **1** to act as if something were the case that is not. **2** to make it appear that one has a particular feeling. **3** (+ to) to claim to have something.

**pretender** *n* somebody who lays claim to a title or position.

**pretension** *n* **1** an unjustified claim to a status or quality. **2** an ambition or aspiration. **3** vanity; pretentiousness.

**pretentious** *adj* trying to impress by a false display of importance or some other quality. ➤ **pretentiousness** *n.*

**preternatural** *adj* **1** beyond what is natural. **2** extraordinary. ➤ **preternaturally** *adv.*

**pretext** *n* a false reason or excuse.

**prettify** *v* (**-ies, -ied**) to make pretty or depict prettily.

**pretty**[1] *adj* (**-ier, -iest**) attractive or aesthetically pleasing. ➤ **prettily** *adv,* **prettiness** *n.*

**pretty**[2] *adv* **1** to some degree; moderately. **2** very. ✻ **be sitting pretty** to be in an advantageous position. **pretty much/nearly/well** *informal* almost; very nearly.

**pretty**[3] *v* (**-ies, -ied**) *informal* (*usu* + up) to make pretty.

**pretzel** *n* a brittle glazed and salted biscuit in the shape of a knot.

**prevail** *v* **1** (*often* + against/over) to defeat or subdue from superior strength. **2** (+ on/upon/with) to persuade somebody successfully. **3** to be frequent or widespread.

**prevalent** *adj* widely occurring or existing; widespread. ➤ **prevalence** *n.*

**prevaricate** *v* to speak or act evasively. ➤ **prevarication** *n.*

**prevent** *v* **1** to stop from happening or existing. **2** (*often* + from) to stop (somebody) from doing something. ➤ **preventable** *adj,* **prevention** *n.*

**preventive** *or* **preventative** *adj* intended to prevent something.

**preview**[1] *v* **1** to view or show (a film or exhibition) before its public presentation. **2** to report on (events, films, programmes, etc) that are to be presented in the near future.

**preview**[2] *n* **1** an advance showing of a film or exhibition. **2** a description of coming events or entertainments.

**previous** *adj* **1** going before in time or order. **2** *informal* acting too soon; premature. ✻ **previous to** before; prior to. ➤ **previously** *adv.*

**prey**[1] *n* **1** an animal killed by another animal

for food. **2** somebody or something that is unable to resist attack; a victim.

**prey**[2] *v* **1** (*often* + on/upon) to seize and devour prey. **2** (*often* + on/upon) to live by deception or taking advantage. **3** (+ on/upon) to preoccupy (one's mind). ➤ **preyer** *n.*

**price**[1] *n* **1** the amount of money for which something is bought or sold. **2** something unpleasant suffered in order to achieve something. **3** the odds in betting. ✱ **at any price** whatever the cost or sacrifice.

**price**[2] *v* to set a price for.

**priceless** *adj* **1** so valuable it cannot be priced. **2** *informal* highly amusing.

**pricey** *or* **pricy** *adj* (**-ier, -iest**) *informal* expensive.

**prick**[1] *v* **1** to pierce slightly with a sharp point. **2** to make a small hole in by piercing. **3** to feel or cause discomfort as if from being pricked. **4** (*often* + up). **5** (*usu* + out) to transplant (seedlings). ✱ **prick up one's ears 1** of an animal: to raise its ears when alert. **2** to start to listen intently.

**prick**[2] *n* **1** the act of pricking or the sensation of being pricked. **2** a hole made by pricking. **3** *coarse slang* the penis. **4** *coarse slang* a disagreeable person.

**prickle**[1] *n* **1** a small sharp pointed spike on a plant or animal. **2** a pricking or tingling sensation.

**prickle**[2] *v* to feel a pricking or tingling sensation.

**prickly** *adj* (**-ier, -iest**) **1** full of or covered with prickles. **2** causing a prickling sensation. **3** easily irritated.

**prickly pear** *n* a cactus that produces a prickly oval fruit.

**pride**[1] *n* **1** a feeling of satisfaction arising from some action, achievement or possession. **2** a consciousness of one's own worth and dignity; self-respect. **3** an excessive sense of one's own importance; conceit. **4** a source of pride. **5** the best in a group or class. **6** a group of lions. ✱ **pride of place** the most prominent position.

**pride**[2] *v* ✱ **pride oneself on** to be particularly proud of.

**priest** *n* **1** a person authorized to perform the sacred rites of a religion. **2** a Christian clergyman ranking below a bishop and above a deacon. ➤ **priesthood** *n,* **priestly** *adj.*

**prig** *n* somebody who is excessively self-righteous. ➤ **priggish** *adj.*

**prim** *adj* (**primmer, primmest**) **1** stiffly formal and proper. **2** prudish. ➤ **primly** *adv.*

**prima ballerina** *n* (*pl* **prima ballerinas**) the principal female dancer in a ballet company.

**primacy** *n formal* the state of being first or most important.

**prima donna** *n* (*pl* **prima donnas**) **1** the principal female singer in an opera company. **2** an extremely temperamental person.

**primaeval** *adj* see PRIMEVAL.

**prima facie** *adj and adv* valid from a first impression until disproved.

**primal** *adj* **1** original or primitive. **2** first in importance; fundamental.

**primarily** *adv* **1** for the most part; chiefly. **2** in the first place; originally.

**primary**[1] *adj* **1** first in importance or value. **2** basic or fundamental. **3** first in order of time or development. **4** preparatory to something else. **5** relating to the education of children from fiveto eleven.

**primary**[2] *n* (*pl* **-ies**) in the USA, an election to choose a candidate for political office or to select delegates for a party convention.

**primary care** *n* the first level of health care provided by general practitioners and clinics.

**primary colour** *n* each of the three coloured pigments red, yellow, and blue that are mixed to produce other pigments.

**primate** *n* **1** any of an order of mammals, including human beings, apes, and monkeys. **2** a bishop who has precedence in a province or nation.

**prime**[1] *n* the most active stage of one's life.

**prime**[2] *adj* **1** first in importance. **2** first-rate or excellent. **3** of the highest grade or quality. **4** not deriving from something else; primary. **5** of a number: that can only be divided by itself and 1. ➤ **primely** *adv,* **primeness** *n.*

**prime**[3] *v* **1** to make ready for use or action. **2** to give (somebody) information or instructions beforehand. **3** to put (primer) on a surface.

**prime minister** *n* the chief minister of a government.

**primer** *n* **1** a book with basic information on a subject. **2** a type of paint used as a first coat on some surfaces.

**prime time** *n* the time when a television or radio audience is at its highest.

**primeval** *or* **primaeval** *adj* relating to the earliest times.

**primitive** *adj* **1** characteristic of an early stage of development; crude or rudimentary. **2** characteristic of a relatively simple people or culture. **3** of accommodation or facilities: of a low or basic standard. **4** of behaviour: lacking in good manners or sophistication. ➤ **primitively** *adv.*

**primordial** *adj* existing from the beginning of time.

**primp** *v chiefly NAmer* to arrange (one's appearance) fastidiously.

**primrose** *n* a plant with pale yellow flowers.

**primula** *n* any of a genus of plants that includes the primrose and cowslip.

**Primus** *n trademark* a portable oil-burning stove.

**prince** *n* **1** the son or grandson of a monarch. **2** a sovereign ruler of a principality.

**prince consort** *n* the husband of a reigning queen.

**princeling** *n* a petty or insignificant prince.

**princely** *adj* **1** relating to or befitting a prince. **2** lavish or generous.

**princess** *n* **1** a daughter or granddaughter of a sovereign. **2** the wife or widow of a prince.

**princess royal** *n* the eldest daughter of a reigning king or queen.

**principal**[1] *adj* most important or influential; chief. ➤ **principally** *adv.*

***Usage Note:*** Do not confuse this word with *principle*, which is a noun only.

**principal**[2] *n* **1** the person in charge of an organization. **2** the head of an educational institution. **3** *NAmer* a headteacher. **4** the peron for whom somebody acts. **5** a leading performer in a group. **6** a capital sum earning interest or due as a debt. ➤ **principalship** *n.*

**principal boy** *n* the role of the hero in British pantomime, played by a woman.

**principality** *n* (*pl* **-ies**) the office or territory of a prince.

**principle** *n* **1** a rule or law on which action or behaviour is based. **2** a rule or code of conduct. **3** devotion to the rules of right morality. **4** the basic idea behind something. **5** a law or fact of nature underlying the working of a natural phenomenon. **6** a chemical that imparts a characteristic quality. * **in principle** in theory. **on principle** on the basis of one's beliefs or moral code.

***Usage Note:*** Do not confuse this word with *principal*.

**principled** *adj* based on moral principles.

**print**[1] *n* **1** printed words or text. **2** a copy made by printing. **3** an impression or mark made by pressure. * **in/out of print** of a book: obtainable (or no longer obtainable) from the publisher.

**print**[2] *v* **1** to stamp or impress with a mark, design, etc. **2** to make a copy of by transferring ink to paper automatically. **3** to publish (e.g. a book or newspaper). **4** to make (a positive image) from a negative or transparency. **5** to write with each letter produced separately. ➤ **printable** *adj.*

**printing** *n* **1** reproduction in printed form. **2** handwriting with unjoined letters.

**printing press** *n* a machine that produces printed matter by pressing paper against an inked surface.

**printout** *n* a printed record produced by a computer.

**prion** *n* a protein particle thought to be responsible for brain diseases such as BSE and CJD.

**prior**[1] *adj* **1** earlier in time or order. **2** taking precedence. * **prior to** before in time.

**prior**[2] *n* **1** the deputy head of a monastery, ranking below abbot. **2** the head of a religious house.

**prioritize** *or* **-ise** *v* **1** to give priority to. **2** to arrange in order of priority. ➤ **prioritization** *n.*

**priority** *n* (*pl* **-ies**) **1** the fact of being considered more important. **2** the right to go first. **3** something meriting prior attention. **4** (*in pl*) the relative importance attached to various things.

**prise** *or* **prize** *v* **1** to press or force open or apart. **2** to remove with difficulty.

**prism** *n* **1** a three-dimensional figure with ends that are equal and parallel and sides that are parallelograms. **2** a piece of glass having this form with triangular ends, used to deflect or disperse light.

**prison** *n* a building in which people are confined while awaiting trial or for punishment after conviction.

**prisoner** *n* **1** somebody kept in enforced confinement. **2** somebody who is trapped by circumstances.

**prisoner of conscience** *n* a person imprisoned for political or religious beliefs.

**prisoner of war** *n* somebody captured in war.

**prissy** *adj* (**-ier, -iest**) prim and prudish in a fussy way. ➤ **prissily** *adv,* **prissiness** *n.*

**pristine** *adj* **1** in its original unspoilt state. **2** fresh and clean as if new.

**privacy** *n* **1** a state of being apart from other people. **2** freedom from undesirable intrusions.

**private**[1] *adj* **1** restricted to the use of a particular person or group. **2** owned or run by an independent individual or company. **3** not intended to be known by others. **4** not wishing for the company of others. **5** of a person: not holding public office or employment. **6** of a place: where one is likely to be alone or undisturbed. **7** of a soldier: having the rank of private.

**private**[2] *n* a soldier of the lowest rank in the army.

**private company** *n* a company whose shares cannot be offered for sale to the general public.

**private detective** *n* a detective who acts privately and is not a member of a police force.

**private enterprise** *n* business undertaken by privately owned companies.

**privateer** *n* formerly, a privately owned warship commissioned by a government in wartime.

**private eye** *n informal* a private detective.

**private means** *n* incomce derived from investments or inheritance rather than earnings.

**private member** *n* a Member of Parliament who does not hold a government appointment.

**private parts** *pl n euphem* a person's genitalia.

**private practice** *n* medical practice outside a state system.
**private school** *n Brit* a school supported by payment of fees.
**private secretary** *n* **1** a secretary employed to assist with a person's confidential business matters. **2** a civil servant who advises a senior government official.
**private sector** *n* the part of the economy that is not controlled by the state.
**privation** *n* lack of the basic necessities of life.
**privatize** *or* **-ise** *v* to transfer (a business or industry) to private ownership. ➤ **privatization** *n.*
**privet** *n* an ornamental shrub with small white flowers, used in hedges.
**privilege** *n* **1** a special right or advantage granted to a particular person or group. **2** the possession of privileges conferred by rank or wealth. **3** immunity from normal legal sanctions.
**privileged** *adj* **1** having one or more privileges. **2** of information: not subject to public disclosure.
**privy**[1] *adj* (+ to) sharing in the knowledge of something secret.
**privy**[2] *n* (*pl* **-ies**) a toilet in a small outside building.
**Privy Council** *n* an advisory council to the monarch.
**prize**[1] *n* **1** something offered as a reward for success or achievement. **2** something exceptionally desirable or precious.
**prize**[2] *v* to value highly.
**prize**[3] *v* see PRISE.
**pro**[1] *n* (*pl* **pros**) ✱ **pros and cons** the arguments for and against something.
**pro**[2] *prep* for; in favour of.
**pro**[3] *n* (*pl* **pros**) *informal* a professional.
**pro**[4] *adj* professional.
**pro-** *prefix* **1** before in time or order: *prologue.* **2** favouring; supporting: *pro-European.*
**proactive** *adj* taking the initiative rather than just reacting.
**probability** *n* (*pl* **-ies**) **1** the state of being probable. **2** something that is probable.
**probable** *adj* **1** supported by strong evidence but not certain. **2** likely to be or occur. ➤ **probably** *adv.*
**probate** *n* the judicial process of declaring a will to be valid.
**probation** *n* **1** a method of dealing with offenders by which sentence is suspended subject to good behaviour under supervision. **2** a period of testing of a new recruit to a job. ➤ **probationary** *adj,* **probationer** *n.*
**probe**[1] *n* **1** a surgical instrument used to examine a cavity. **2** a device inserted in something to be monitored or measured. **3** an unmanned spacecraft used for exploring. **4** a penetrating or critical investigation.
**probe**[2] *v* **1** to examine with a probe. **2** to investigate thoroughly. ➤ **probing** *adj.*
**probity** *n formal* honesty and integrity.
**problem** *n* **1** a situation or question that is difficult to understand or resolve. **2** something or somebody that is difficult to deal with.
**problematic** *or* **problematical** *adj* presenting a problem.
**proboscis** /prəˈbosis/ *n* (*pl* **proboscises** /-seez/ *or* **proboscides** /-deez/) **1** an animal's long flexible snout, e.g. the trunk of an elephant. **2** an elongated sucking tube extending from the mouth of some insects.
**procedure** *n* **1** a particular or established way of doing something. **2** a series of ordered steps. ➤ **procedural** *adj.*
**proceed** *v* **1** to begin and carry on an action. **2** to move along a course. **3** to continue after a pause or interruption. **4** to arise from a source.
**proceedings** *pl n* **1** the events involved in an established procedure. **2** legal action. **3** an official record of things said or done.
**proceeds** *pl n* money earned or obtained.
**process**[1] *n* **1** a series of actions or operations designed to achieve an end. **2** a natural series of changes: *the growth process.*
**process**[2] *v* **1** to subject to a special process or treatment. **2** to take appropriate action on. ➤ **processor** *n.*
**process**[3] *v chiefly Brit* to move in a procession.
**procession** *n* **1** a group of people, vehicles, etc, moving in an orderly way. **2** the action of moving along. **3** a succession or sequence.
**proclaim** *v* **1** to declare publicly and officially. **2** to show clearly. ➤ **proclamation** *n.*
**proclivity** *n* (*pl* **-ies**) an inclination to do something undesirable.
**procrastinate** *v formal* to delay until a later time. ➤ **procrastination** *n.*
**procreate** *v formal* to conceive or produce offspring. ➤ **procreation** *n.*
**proctor** *n* an officer in charge of student discipline at certain universities.
**procurator** *n* an agent or attorney.
**procurator fiscal** *n* a local coroner and public prosecutor in Scotland.
**procure** *v* to obtain by special care and effort. ➤ **procurement** *n.*
**prod**[1] *v* (**prodded, prodding**) **1** to poke or jab with a finger or pointed instrument. **2** to incite to action.
**prod**[2] *n* **1** a prodding action or jab. **2** a pointed instrument. **3** an incitement to act.
**prodigal**[1] *adj* **1** recklessly extravagant or wasteful. **2** lavish. ➤ **prodigally** *adv.*
**prodigal**[2] *n* **1** an extravagant or wasteful person. **2** a repentant sinner or reformed spendthrift.
**prodigious** *adj* remarkable in size or achievement. ➤ **prodigiously** *adv.*

**prodigy** *n* (*pl* **-ies**) an exceptionally talented child.

**produce**[1] *v* **1** to give being, form, or shape to; to make or manufacture. **2** to make happen or exist. **3** to offer to view or notice. **4** to supervise the making of (a film, play, piece of recorded music, etc). ➤ **producer** *n.*

**produce**[2] *n* **1** agricultural products, *esp* fresh fruit and vegetables. **2** a product or products.

**product** *n* **1** a commodity made available for sale. **2** something produced by a process. **3** a result of a combination of causes. **4** the result of multiplying numbers together.

**production** *n* **1** the act of producing something. **2** the total output of a commodity or an industry. **3** something produced; a product. **4** a theatrical or broadcast work.

**production line** *n* an assembly line.

**productive** *adj* **1** producing large quantities of something. **2** yielding significant results or benefits. ➤ **productively** *adv.*

**productivity** *n* **1** the quality of being productive. **2** the effectiveness of labour in terms of industrial output.

**profane**[1] *adj* **1** not concerned with religion or religious purposes. **2** debasing or defiling what is holy.

**profane**[2] *v* to treat irreverence or contempt. ➤ **profanation** *n.*

**profanity** *n* (*pl* **-ies**) **1** profane language. **2** a swear word.

**profess** *v* **1** to declare openly or freely. **2** to claim or pretend. **3** to declare one's allegiance to (a religion).

**profession** *n* **1** an occupation requiring special training and qualifications. **2** the people engaged in such an occupation. **3** an act of declaring a faith, opinion, etc. **4** a declaration or claim.

**professional**[1] *adj* **1** relating or belonging to a profession. **2** conforming to the standards associated with a profession. **3** of a person: taking part in an activity as a paid occupation. ➤ **professionally** *adv.*

**professional**[2] *n* **1** a professional person. **2** a person having the qualifications of a profession.

**professionalism** *n* the knowledge and standards associated with professional people.

**professor** *n* **1** an acaedmic of the highest academic rank at a university. **2** *NAmer* a university teacher. ➤ **professorial** *adj,* **professorship** *n.*

**proffer** *v* to present for acceptance.

**proficient** *adj* competent or skilled. ➤ **proficiency** *n.*

**profile**[1] *n* **1** a side view of the human face. **2** an outline seen in sharp relief. **3** a concise biographical or descriptive outline. **4** the extent to which somebody attracts public attention. * **keep a low profile** to avoid attracting attention.

**profile**[2] *v* to produce a profile of.

**profit**[1] *n* **1** the excess of income over expenditure. **2** a gain or benefit. ➤ **profitless** *adj.*

**profit**[2] *v* (**profited, profiting**) **1** (*often* + from/by) to derive benefit; to gain. **2** to be of service to.

**profitable** *adj* producing a profit. ➤ **profitability** *n,* **profitably** *adv.*

**profiteer** *v* to make an excessive or unreasonable profit. ➤ **profiteering** *n.*

**profiterole** *n* a small ball of choux pastry filled with cream and covered with a chocolate sauce.

**profit margin** *n* the difference between the selling price of a product and its cost price.

**profligate**[1] *adj* **1** utterly dissolute; immoral. **2** wildly extravagant; prodigal. ➤ **profligacy** *n.*

**profligate**[2] *n* a profligate person.

**profound** *adj* **1** having intellectual depth and insight. **2** difficult to fathom or understand. **3** extending far below a surface. **4** of a feeling: strongly felt. ➤ **profoundly** *adv,* **profundity** *n.*

**profuse** *adj* **1** extravagant. **2** abundant. ➤ **profusely** *adv,* **profusion** *n.*

**progenitor** *n* **1** a parent or direct ancestor. **2** a precursor or originator.

**progeny** *n* descendants or children.

**progesterone** *n* a steroid hormone that causes changes in the uterus in preparation for pregnancy.

**prognosis** *n* (*pl* **prognoses**) **1** an assessment of how an illness is likely to develop. **2** a forecast or prediction.

**programmatic** *adj* resembling or having a programme.

**programme**[1] (*NAmer* **program**) *n* **1** a systematic plan of action. **2** a radio or television broadcast. **3** a list of features to be presented in a public performance. **4** (**program**) a sequence of coded instructions for a computer to follow to perform a function.

**programme**[2] (*NAmer* **program**) *v* (**programmed, programming,** *NAmer* **programed, programing**) **1** to arrange or provide a programme for. **2** to enter in a programme. **3** to condition (something or somebody). **4** (**program**) to provide (a computer) with a program. ➤ **programmable** *adj,* **programmer** *n.*

**progress**[1] *n* **1** forward movement towards a destination or objective. **2** development towards a better or more complete state.

**progress**[2] *v* **1** to move forward. **2** to develop or improve.

**progression** *n* **1** the act of progressing; an advance. **2** a continuous and connected series.

**progressive**[1] *adj* **1** characterized by progress or progression. **2** making use of or interested in new ideas or opportunities. **3** moving forward in stages. **4** of a disease: increasing in severity. ➤ **progressively** *adv.*

**progressive**[2] *n* somebody who advocates progressive political or social ideas.

**prohibit** *v* (**prohibited, prohibiting**) **1** to forbid formally. **2** to prevent (something) from happening.

**prohibition** *n* **1** the act of prohibiting something. **2** an order that forbids something.

**prohibitive** *adj* **1** tending to prohibit or restrain. **2** of a cost: unreasonably high. ➤ **prohibitively** *adv.*

**project**[1] *n* **1** a specific plan or design; a scheme. **2** a piece of research with a definite plan. **3** a task or problem engaged in usu by a group of pupils.

**project**[2] *v* **1** to devise in the mind; to design. **2** to calculate or estimate on the basis of known data or trends. **3** to cause (light or an image) to fall on a surface. **4** to protrude or cause to protrude. **5** to cause (the voice) to be heard at a distance. **6** to present or express (oneself) in a manner that wins approval.

**projectile** *n* a missile or other object fired at a target.

**projector** *n* an apparatus for projecting films or slides onto a surface.

**prolapse** *n* a condition in which a body part has slipped from its usual position.

**proletarian** *n* a member of the proletariat. ➤ **proletarian** *adj.*

**proletariat** *n* the working people of a community.

**proliferate** *v* **1** to grow or reproduce rapidly. **2** to increase rapidly in number or quantity. ➤ **proliferation** *n.*

**prolific** *adj* **1** producing offspring, fruit, etc freely. **2** highly inventive or productive. ➤ **prolifically** *adv.*

**prolix** *adj* tediously prolonged or repetitious. ➤ **prolixity** *n.*

**prologue** (*NAmer* **prolog**) *n* **1** the introductory part of a literary or musical work. **2** an introductory event or development.

**prolong** *v* to lengthen in time or space. ➤ **prolongation** *n*, **prolonged** *adj.*

**prom** *n* **1** a promenade concert. **2** a promenade for walking. **3** *NAmer* a formal dance at a high school or college.

**promenade**[1] *n* a paved walk by the sea.

**promenade**[2] *v* to take a leisurely walk.

**promenade concert** *n* a concert of classical music at which some of the audience stand.

**prominence** *n* **1** the state or quality of being prominent. **2** something that sticks out.

**prominent** *adj* **1** famous and eminent. **2** readily noticeable. **3** projecting beyond a surface or line. ➤ **prominently** *adv.*

**promiscuous** *adj* having many casual sexual relationships. ➤ **promiscuity** *n.*

**promise**[1] *n* **1** a declaration that one will or will not do something. **2** grounds for expecting success or excellence.

**promise**[2] *v* **1** to make a promise. **2** to give grounds for expectating something.

**promising** *adj* showing signs of success. ➤ **promisingly** *adv.*

**promissory note** *n* a written promise to pay a specified sum of money.

**promo** *n* (*pl* **-os**) *informal* an advertising video or film.

**promontory** *n* (*pl* **-ies**) a high point of land projecting into the sea.

**promote** *v* **1** to contribute to the start or development of. **2** to advertise or publicize. **3** to contribute to in a beneficial way. **4** to give (somebody) a higher position or rank. ➤ **promoter** *n.*

**promotion** *n* **1** being raised in position or rank. **2** the advertising and marketing of a product. **3** a concession intended to promote a product or increase sales. ➤ **promotional** *adj.*

**prompt**[1] *v* **1** to move (somebody) to action; to incite. **2** to serve as the cause of; to urge. **3** to remind (an actor) of the next words to be spoken.

**prompt**[2] *adj* **1** done readily or immediately. **2** ready and quick to act. **3** happening or arriving on time. ➤ **promptly** *adv*, **promptness** *n.*

**prompt**[3] *n* **1** an instance of prompting. **2** somebody or something that prompts. **3** a symbol on a VDU screen marking the place where a command will take effect.

**prompt**[4] *adv informal* exactly; punctually: *six o'clock prompt.*

**promulgate** *v* **1** to make known openly. **2** to put (a law, decree, etc) into force. **3** to promote publicly. ➤ **promulgation** *n.*

**prone** *adj* **1** (+ to) having a tendency or inclination to something. **2** lying flat or face downward.

**prong**[1] *n* **1** each of the sharp-pointed parts of a fork. **2** a distinct part of an attack.

**prong**[2] *v* to pierce with a prong.

**pronominal** *adj* of a pronoun.

**pronoun** *n* a word used as a substitute for a noun already mentioned, e.g. *I, he, these.*

**pronounce** *v* **1** to utter the sound or sounds of (a word). **2** to declare officially. ➤ **pronounceable** *adj*, **pronouncement** *n.*

**pronounced** *adj* strongly marked or conspicuous.

**pronto** *adv informal* without delay.

**pronunciation** *n* the act or manner of pronouncing a word.

---

***Usage Note:*** Note the spelling *-nunc-* not *-nounc-*.

---

**proof**[1] *n* **1** evidence that establishes a truth or fact. **2** the process of establishing the truth or validity of something. **3** an operation designed to establish a fact or the truth. **4** a sample printing of a piece of text for correction. **5** a test of the quality of an article or substance. **6** the alcoholic content of a drink.

**proof**[2] *adj* resisting or repelling: *soundproof.*

**prop**[1] *n* **1** a rigid vertical support, e.g. a pole. **2** a source of strength or support.

**prop**[2] *v* (**propped, propping**) **1** to support with a prop. **2** to place against a vertical surface for support.

**prop**[3] *n* an object used in a play or film other than painted scenery or costumes.

**prop**[4] *n informal* a propeller.

**propaganda** *n* the systematic spreading of ideas and information to promote an institution or point of view. ➤ **propagandist** *n.*

**propagate** *v* **1** to cause (a plant) to reproduce or multiply. **2** to publicize (information). ➤ **propagation** *n.*

**propane** *n* a gas found in crude petroleum and natural gas and used as a fuel.

**propel** *v* (**propelled, propelling**) **1** to drive (something) forward. **2** to urge (somebody) on.

**propellant** *n* a gas that releases the contents from a pressurized container.

**propeller** *n* a device with radiating twisted blades, used to propel a ship or aircraft.

**propensity** *n* (*pl* **-ies**) *formal* a natural inclination or tendency.

**proper** *adj* **1** suitable; appropriate. **2** strictly accurate; correct. **3** decorous or genteel. **4** being strictly so-called: *the city proper.* **5** (+ to) belonging characteristically to.

**proper fraction** *n* a fraction in which the number above the line is less than the number below the line.

**proper noun** *n* a noun with a capital initial that denotes a particular person, place, or thing.

**property** *n* (*pl* **-ies**) **1** something owned or possessed. **2** a piece of land and the buildings on it. **3** a quality or attribute.

**prophecy** *n* (*pl* **-ies**) a prediction of what will happen.

**prophesy** *v* (**-ies, -ied**) to predict that something will happen at a certain time.

**prophet** *or* **prophetess** *n* **1** a person who claims to utter divinely inspired revelations. **2** somebody who foretells future events.

**prophetic** *adj* **1** characteristic of a prophet or prophecy. **2** foretelling events.

**prophylactic**[1] *adj* protecting from or preventing disease.

**prophylactic**[2] *n* a prophylactic drug.

**propinquity** *n* nearness in place or time.

**propitiate** *v* to gain or regain the favour of. ➤ **propitiation** *n*, **propitiatory** *adj.*

**propitious** *adj* **1** boding well. **2** opportune.

**proponent** *n* somebody who argues in favour of something.

**proportion** *n* **1** the relation of one part to another or to the whole. **2** harmonious relation of parts. **3** a relationship of constant ratio. **4** a proper or equal share. **5** a fraction or percentage. **6** (*in pl*) size or dimensions. ✱ **sense of proportion** an ability to assess the relative importance of things.

**proportional** *or* **proportionate** *adj* corresponding in size, shape, etc. ➤ **proportionally** *adv.*

**proportional representation** *n* an electoral system in which political groups gain seats in proportion to the number of votes they receive.

**proposal** *n* **1** a proposed idea or plan of action. **2** an offer of marriage. **3** the act of putting something forward for consideration.

**propose** *v* **1** to present for consideration or adoption. **2** to establish as an aim or intention. **3** to recommend or nominate. **4** to announce (a toast). **5** to make an offer of marriage. ➤ **proposer** *n.*

**proposition**[1] *n* **1** something offered for consideration. **2** a formal mathematical statement to be proved. **3** somebody or something to be dealt with. ➤ **propositional** *adj.*

**proposition**[2] *v* to propose sexual intercourse to (somebody).

**propound** *v formal* to offer for consideration.

**proprietary** *adj* **1** characteristic of a proprietor. **2** made and marketed under a patent or trademark. **3** privately owned and managed.

**proprietor** *or* **proprietress** *n* a person with a legal right or exclusive title to something. ➤ **proprietorial** *adj.*

**propriety** *n* (*pl* **-ies**) **1** the quality or state of being proper. **2** correctness of behaviour. **3** (*in pl*) the conventions and manners of polite society.

**propulsion** *n* the action or process of propelling. ➤ **propulsive** *adj.*

**prop up** *v* to give support to.

**pro rata** /ˌproh ˈrahtə/ *adj and adv* proportional or proportionally.

**prosaic** *adj* **1** characteristic of prose. **2** dull or commonplace. ➤ **prosaically** *adv.*

**proscenium** *n* (*pl* **proscenia** *or* **prosceniums**) the part of a theatre stage in front of the curtain.

**proscenium arch** *n* the arch in a conventional theatre through which the spectator sees the stage.

**proscribe** *v* **1** to condemn or forbid something harmful); to prohibit. **2** to outlaw or exile. ➤ **proscription** *n.*

**prose** *n* ordinary language as spoken or written.

**prosecute** *v* **1** to pursue criminal proceedings against. **2** *formal* to follow (something) through, to pursue. ➤ **prosecutor** *n.*

**prosecution** *n* **1** the formal institution of a criminal charge. **2** the party that institutes criminal proceedings.

**proselyte** *n* a person who has been newly converted to a religion or cause.

**proselytize** *or* **-ise** *v* to convert to a new religion or cause.

**prosody** *n* **1** the patterns of rhythm and metre used in poetry. **2** the study of verse structure.

**prospect**[1] *n* **1** a mental picture of something to come. **2** the expectation or possibility of something happening. **3** (*in pl*) financial and social expectations. **4** (*in pl*) chances, *esp* of success. **5** a potential client, candidate, etc.

**prospect**[2] *v* to explore (an area) for mineral deposits. ➤ **prospector** *n.*

**prospective** *adj* likely to be or happen. ➤ **prospectively** *adv.*

**prospectus** *n* (*pl* **prospectuses**) a printed brochure describing an organization or enterprise.

**prosper** *v* to succeed or thrive.

**prosperous** *adj* financially successful. ➤ **prosperity** *n.*

**prostate** *n* in male mammals, a gland situated round the neck of the bladder and secreting most of the volume of semen.

**prostitute**[1] *n* a person who engages in sexual activities for money.

**prostitute**[2] *v* **1** to make a prostitute of. **2** to devote (something) to unworthy purposes. ➤ **prostitution** *n.*

**prostrate**[1] *adj* **1** lying full-length face downwards. **2** overcome with exhaustion.

**prostrate**[2] *v* **1** to put into a prostrate position. **2** to humble (oneself). **3** to reduce to submission or helplessness. ➤ **prostration** *n.*

**protagonist** *n* **1** the leading part in a drama or film. **2** a notable supporter of a cause.

**protean** *adj* able to change or adapt readily.

**protect** *v* **1** to cover or shield from injury or destruction. **2** to guard or defend against attack or harm. ➤ **protector** *n.*

**protection** *n* **1** the act of protecting. **2** something that protects. **3** immunity from threatened violence, in exchange for payment.

**protectionism** *n* the shielding of the producers of a country from foreign competition by import tariffs. ➤ **protectionist** *adj and n.*

**protective** *adj* providing or able to provide protection.

**protectorate** *n* a state that is partly controlled by and dependent on the protection of another.

**protégé** *or* **protégée** /'protizhay/ *n* somebody under the protection and guidance of a more experienced person.

**protein** *n* a naturally occurring chemical compound that is an important part of the human diet.

***Usage Note:*** Note the spelling with *-ei-*.

**protest**[1] *v* **1** to express strong disagreement or objection. **2** to take part in a public demonstration of disapproval. **3** to declare formally: *He protested his innocence.* ➤ **protester** *n,* **protestor** *n.*

**protest**[2] *n* **1** a formal declaration of disapproval or objection. **2** a public demonstration of disapproval.

**Protestant** *n* a member of any of the Western Christian Churches that are separate from the Roman Catholic Church. ➤ **Protestant** *n.*

**protestation** *n* **1** the act or an instance of protesting. **2** a solemn declaration or avowal.

**protocol** *n* **1** a code or system of conduct on official occasions. **2** the correct way to behave in a particular situation. **3** a signed record of agreement made at a diplomatic conference.

**proton** *n* an elementary particle that carries a single positive electrical charge.

**prototype** *n* an original model from which later versions are developed.

**protozoan** *or* **protozoon** *n* a minute single-celled animal.

**protract** *v* to prolong in time or space. ➤ **protracted** *adj.*

**protractor** *n* a flat semicircular instrument marked with degrees, used for measuring angles.

**protrude** *v* to project from or extend beyond a surface. ➤ **protrusion** *n.*

**protuberance** *n* something that projects from a surrounding or adjacent surface. ➤ **protuberant** *adj.*

**proud** *adj* **1** pleased or satisfied with an achievement or possession. **2** having excessive self-esteem. **3** having proper self-respect. **4** stately or magnificent. **5** giving reason for pride. **6** projecting slightly from a surface. ✱ **do somebody proud 1** to treat somebody very well. **2** to give somebody cause for pride. ➤ **proudly** *adv.*

**prove** *v* (*past part.* **proved** *or* **proven**) **1** to establish the truth or validity of by evidence or demonstration. **2** to show (oneself) to have the required qualities. **3** to turn out to be. ➤ **provable** *adj.*

**proven** *adj* known from experience to be sound or reliable.

**provenance** *n* the place of origin of a work of art or other object.

**provender** *n* dry food for domestic animals.

**proverb** *n* a brief pithy saying embodying a truth or belief.

**proverbial** *adj* **1** of or resembling a proverb. **2** characteristic or well-known. ➤ **proverbially** *adv.*

**provide** *v* **1** to give or make available. **2** (+ with) to supply (somebody) with. **3** (+ for) to supply what is needed for sustenance. **4** (+ for) to take action in relation to a possible event.

**provided** *or* **providing** *conj* on condition that.

**providence** *n* **1** (**Providence**) God or nature as the power guiding human destiny. **2** adequate preparation for the future.

**provident** *adj* careful in providing for the future.
**providential** *adj* happening by good fortune; lucky. ➤ **providentially** *adv.*
**province** *n* **1** an administrative district or division of a country. **2** (**the provinces**) all of a country outside the capital. **3** a field of knowledge or activity.
**provincial**[1] *adj* **1** of a province or the provinces. **2** limited in outlook; narrow-minded. ➤ **provincialism** *n.*
**provincial**[2] *n* somebody living in the provinces.
**provision**[1] *n* **1** the act of providing something. **2** a preparation or precaution. **3** (*in pl*) a stock of food or other supplies. **4** a proviso or stipulation in a legal document.
**provision**[2] *v* to supply with provisions.
**provisional** *adj* serving for the time being and requiring later confirmation. ➤ **provisionally** *adv.*
**proviso** *n* (*pl* **-os** *or* **-oes**) a condition in an agreement.
**provocation** *n* **1** the act of provoking. **2** something that angers or irritates.
**provocative** *adj* **1** tending to provoke or make indignant. **2** sexually stimulating. ➤ **provocatively** *adv.*
**provoke** *v* **1** to incite to anger; to incense. **2** to cause to behave in a specified way. **3** to stir up or evoke. **4** to provide the needed stimulus for.
**provost** *n* **1** the head of certain university colleges and public schools. **2** the head of certain Scottish district councils. **3** the head of the assembly of canons in a cathedral or other church.
**prow** *n* the bow of a ship or boat.
**prowess** *n* **1** outstanding ability. **2** military valour.
**prowl**[1] *v* to move about in a stealthy or predatory manner. ➤ **prowler** *n.*
**prowl**[2] *n* the act of prowling.
**proximity** *n* nearness in space, time, or association.
**proxy** *n* (*pl* **-ies**) **1** a deputy authorized to act for another. **2** authority to act or vote for another.
**prude** *n* a person who affects extreme modesty or propriety in sexual matters. ➤ **prudish** *adj.*
**prudent** *adj* acting with good sense and caution. ➤ **prudence** *n.*
**prudential** *adj* exercising prudence in business matters.
**prune**[1] *n* a dried plum.
**prune**[2] *v* **1** to remove unwanted parts of (a plant or shrub). **2** to remove as superfluous.
**prurient** *adj* having or arousing an excessive interest in sexual matters. ➤ **prurience** *n.*
**pry** *v* (**-ies, -ied**) (*usu* + into) to show an excessively eager interest in.
**PS** *abbr* postscript.
**psalm** *n* a sacred song or poem used in worship.
**Psalter** *n* a book of biblical psalms.
**pseudo** *adj* **1** apparent rather than actual. **2** *informal* false; pretentious.
**pseudonym** *n* a fictitious name used by an author.
**psi** /sie, psie/ *n* the 23rd letter of the Greek alphabet (Ψ, ψ).
**psoriasis** *n* a skin condition with red patches covered by white scales.
**psych** *or* **psyche** *v informal* **1** (+ out) to intimidate psychologically. **2** (+ up) to prepare (oneself) mentally.
**psyche** *n* the soul, mind, or spirit.
**psychedelia** *n* art, music, etc, associated with psychedelic drugs.
**psychedelic** *adj* **1** of drugs: producing hallucinations. **2** having strong colours and a swirling pattern. ➤ **psychedelically** *adv.*
**psychiatry** *n* a branch of medicine that deals with mental disorders. ➤ **psychiatric** *adj,* **psychiatrist** *n.*
**psychic** *adj* **1** lying outside the sphere of physical science or knowledge. **2** sensitive to supernatural forces or influences. **3** of or originating in the mind. ➤ **psychical** *adj,* **psychically** *adv.*
**psycho** *n* (*pl* **-os**) *informal* a psychopath.
**psychoanalyse** (*NAmer* **psychoanalyze**) *v* to treat by means of psychoanalysis.
**psychoanalysis** *n* a method of analysing unconscious mental processes to treat mental disorders. ➤ **psychoanalyst** *n,* **psychoanalytic** *adj.*
**psychological** *adj* **1** relating to psychology. **2** of the mind. ➤ **psychologically** *adv.*
**psychology** *n* **1** the study of the mind. **2** a person's mental or behavioural characteristics. ➤ **psychologist** *n.*
**psychopath** *n* a person suffering from a disorder with violent antisocial tendencies. ➤ **psychopathic** *adj.*
**psychosis** *n* (*pl* **psychoses**) a mental disorder leading to loss of contact with reality.
**psychosomatic** *adj* resulting from the interaction of psychological and physical factors. ➤ **psychosomatically** *adv.*
**psychotherapy** *n* treatment of mental disorders by psychological methods. ➤ **psychotherapist** *n.*
**psychotic** *adj* relating to or suffering from a psychosis.
**PT** *abbr* physical training.
**Pt** *abbr* the chemical symbol for platinum.
**pt** *abbr* **1** pint. **2** point.
**PTA** *abbr* Parent-Teacher Association.
**Pte** *abbr* Private.
**pterodactyl** *n* a flying dinosaur with toothed jaws and a long neck.
**PTO** *abbr* please turn over.
**pub** *n Brit* an establishment where alcoholic beverages are sold and consumed.

**puberty** *n* the period during which adolescents become sexually mature.
**pubes** *n* the lower front part of the abdomen.
**pubescence** *n* the beginning of puberty. ➤ **pubescent** *adj.*
**pubic** *adj* in the region of the pubis or pubes.
**pubis** *n* (*pl* **pubes**) the bottom front of the three principal bones that form either half of the pelvis.
**public**[1] *adj* **1** of or affecting all the people. **2** of or being in the service of the community. **3** general or popular. **4** of national or community concerns. **5** accessible to all members of the community. **6** exposed to general view; open. ➤ **publicly** *adv.*
**public**[2] *n* (**the public**) people as a whole. ✱ **in public** in the presence of strangers.
**public-address system** *n* an apparatus including a microphone and loudspeakers used to address a large audience.
**publican** *n chiefly Brit* a person who owns or runs as pub.
**publication** *n* **1** the act or process of publishing. **2** a published work.
**public company** *n* a company whose shares can be traded on the stock exchange.
**public house** *n Brit* an establishment where alcoholic beverages are sold and consumed.
**publicist** *n* a person whose job is to publicize a product or organization.
**publicity** *n* **1** information issued as a means of gaining public attention or support. **2** public attention or acclaim.
**publicize** *or* **-ise** *v* to give publicity to.
**public limited company** *n* a company whose shareholders have only a limited liability for any debts or losses created by the company.
**public prosecutor** *n* an official who conducts criminal prosecutions on behalf of the state.
**public relations** *pl n* the business of informing the public about an organization so as to secure their goodwill.
**public school** *n* in Britain, an independent fee-paying school.
**public sector** *n* the part of the economy owned or controlled by the state.
**publish** *v* **1** to produce (a book, newspaper, etc) for sale. **2** to print (information) in a book, newspaper, etc. **3** to announce publicly. ➤ **publisher** *n.*
**puce** *n* a brownish purple colour.
**puck** *n* a hard rubber disc used in ice hockey.
**pucker**[1] *v* to become wrinkled or creased.
**pucker**[2] *n* a crease or wrinkle.
**pudding** *n* **1** a sweet dish eaten at the end of a meal. **2** a sweet or savoury dish made from flour, suet, etc.
**puddle** *n* a small pool of liquid, *esp* of rainwater on the ground.
**pudgy** *adj* (**-ier, -iest**) short and plump.
**puerile** *adj* childish or silly.
**puff**[1] *v* **1** to exhale or blow forcibly. **2** to breathe hard and quickly. **3** to emit small whiffs of smoke or steam. **4** to move while emitting puffs of smoke. **5** (*usu* + out/up) to become distended; to swell. **6** (*usu* + out/up) to inflate. **7** to smoke (a pipe, cigarette, etc).
**puff**[2] *n* **1** the act of puffing. **2** a slight explosive sound accompanying a puff. **3** a small cloud of smoke emitted in a puff. **4** a draw on a pipe or cigarette. **5** a light round hollow pastry made of puff pastry. **6** *chiefly Brit, informal* one's breath.
**puffball** *n* a fungus that discharges a cloud of ripe spores when pressed or struck.
**puffin** *n* a seabird with a short neck and a deep brightly coloured bill.
**puff pastry** *n* a type of light flaky pastry made with a rich dough.
**puffy** *adj* (**-ier, -iest**) *esp* of the eyes or cheeks: swollen.
**pug** *n* a dog of a breed with a small sturdy compact body and a broad wrinkled face.
**pugilism** *n formal* boxing. ➤ **pugilist** *n,* **pugilistic** *adj.*
**pugnacious** *adj* inclined to fight or quarrel; belligerent. ➤ **pugnacity** *n.*
**puke**[1] *v informal* (*often* + up) to vomit.
**puke**[2] *n informal* vomit.
**pukka** *adj* **1** *informal.* **2** genuine or authentic. **3** first-class or excellent.
**pulchritude** *n formal* physical beauty.
**pull**[1] *v* **1** to exert a force on (somebody or something) so as to make it move towards oneself. **2** to move (something) in this way. **3** to make something come apart by force. **4** to remove or detach by pulling. **5** to strain (a muscle, tendon, etc). **6** to move steadily. **7** *informal* to attract (somebody) sexually. ✱ **pull a face** to grimace. **pull oneself together** to regain one's self-control. **pull one's punches** to be more restrained than one might. **pull one's weight** to do one's full share of work. **pull somebody's leg** to deceive or tease somebody. **pull strings** to use one's influence to achieve something.
**pull**[2] *n* **1** the act of pulling. **2** a force that attracts or influences. **3** a deep draught of liquid. **4** an inhalation of smoke.
**pull apart** *v* **1** to separate into pieces. **2** to criticize harshly.
**pull back** *v* to withdraw or retreat.
**pull down** *v* to demolish or destroy.
**pullet** *n* a young female domestic fowl.
**pulley** *n* (*pl* **-eys**) a wheel round which a rope or chain passes to lift heavy loads.
**pull in** *v* of a vehicle: to stop by the side of the road.
**pull off** *v* to achieve (something difficult).
**pull out** *v* **1** of a vehicle: to move out into a stream of traffic. **2** to withdraw from an undertaking.

**pullover** *n* a sweater put on by being pulled over the head.
**pull up** *v* to come to a stop.
**pulmonary** *adj* in the region of the lungs.
**pulp**[1] *n* **1** the soft fleshy part of a fruit or vegetable. **2** a soft mass of vegetable matter. **3** a soft shapeless mass produced by crushing or beating. **4** (*used before a noun*) cheap and sensational: *pulp fiction.* ➤ **pulpy** *adj.*
**pulp**[2] *v* to reduce to pulp.
**pulpit** *n* a raised platform in a church, from which sermons are preached.
**pulsar** *n* a celestial source of frequent intermittent bursts of radio waves.
**pulsate** *v* **1** to beat with a pulse. **2** to throb or move rhythmically; to vibrate. **3** in physics and astronomy, to vary in brightness, magnitude, etc. ➤ **pulsation** *n.*
**pulse**[1] *n* **1** a regular throbbing caused in the arteries by the contractions of the heart. **2** rhythmical vibrating or sounding. **3** a single beat or throb. **4** a short-lived variation of electrical current, voltage, etc whose value is normally constant. **5** an electromagnetic wave or sound wave of brief duration.
**pulse**[2] *v* to pulsate or throb.
**pulse**[3] *n* the edible seeds of various crops, e.g. peas, beans, or lentils.
**pulverize** *or* **-ise** *v* **1** to reduce to very small particles. **2** *informal* to defeat utterly.
**puma** *n* (*pl* **pumas** *or* **puma**) a large American wild cat with a tawny coat.
**pumice** *n* a light volcanic rock used as an abrasive.
**pummel** *v* (**pummelled, pummelling,** *NAmer* **pummeled, pummeling**) to pound or strike repeatedly with the fists.
**pump**[1] *n* a device that moves liquids or gases by suction and pressure.
**pump**[2] *v* **1** to move (air, water, etc) with a pump. **2** to raise (water, etc) with a pump. **3** (*often* + out) to draw a gas or liquid out of (a container) with a pump. **4** (*usu* + up) to inflate (a tyre, etc) with a pump. **5** to move rapidly up and down. **6** *informal* to question persistently.
**pump**[3] *n* a light flat shoe.
**pumpkin** *n* the large round fruit of the gourd family, used as a vegetable.
**pun**[1] *n* a humorous use of a word with more than one meaning.
**pun**[2] *v* (**punned, punning**) to make puns. ➤ **punster** *n.*
**punch**[1] *v* **1** to hit with a hard thrust of the fist. **2** to push (a button or key).
**punch**[2] *n* **1** a blow with the fist. **2** *informal* energy or forcefulness.
**punch**[3] *n* **1** a tool for perforating, embossing, cutting, or driving the heads of nails below a surface. **2** a device for cutting holes in paper.
**punch**[4] *v* to make a hole in or a pattern on.
**punch**[5] *n* a drink made from wine or spirits mixed with fruit, spices, and water.
**punchbag** *n* an inflated or stuffed bag punched with the fists as a form of exercise.
**punch bowl** *n* **1** a large bowl for mixing and serving punch. **2** *Brit* a bowl-shaped hollow among hills.
**punch-drunk** *adj* **1** suffering brain damage as a result of repeated blows to the head. **2** confused or dazed.
**punch line** *n* a sentence or phrase that forms the climax to a joke or story.
**punchy** *adj* (**-ier, -iest**) effective or forceful.
**punctilious** *adj* **1** strict or precise in observing codes of behaviour. **2** paying careful attention to detail. ➤ **punctiliously** *adv.*
**punctual** *adj* arriving or happening at the exact or agreed time. ➤ **punctuality** *n,* **punctually** *adv.*
**punctuate** *v* **1** to mark with punctuation marks. **2** to interrupt at intervals.
**punctuation** *n* **1** the use of marks such as commas, colons, and full stops, to clarify a piece of writing. **2** the marks used in punctuation.
**puncture**[1] *n* a hole made by piercing with a pointed object.
**puncture**[2] *v* to pierce with a pointed object.
**pundit** *n* a person who gives opinions in an authoritative manner.
**pungent** *adj* **1** having a strong sharp smell or taste. **2** of remarks: to the point, highly expressive. ➤ **pungency** *n.*
**punish** *v* **1** to impose a penalty on. **2** to impose a penalty for (an offence). **3** *informal* to treat roughly or damagingly. ➤ **punishable** *adj.*
**punishment** *n* **1** the act of punishing. **2** something done in order to punish. **3** *informal* rough or damaging treatment.
**punitive** *adj* inflicting or intended to inflict punishment.
**punk** *n* **1** (*also* **punk rock**) a loud aggressive style of rock music. **2** somebody who listens to or plays punk rock. **3** *NAmer, informal* a worthless person.
**punnet** *n Brit* a small basket for soft fruit or vegetables.
**punt**[1] *n* a long narrow flat-bottomed boat propelled with a pole.
**punt**[2] *v* to travel in a punt.
**punt**[3] *v Brit, informal* to bet or gamble.
**punt**[4] *n Brit, informal* a bet.
**punt**[5] *v* to kick (a ball) after dropping it onto the foot.
**punt**[6] *n* the act of punting a ball.
**punt**[7] /poont/ *n* the former basic monetary unit of the Republic of Ireland (replaced by the euro in 2002).
**punter** *n informal* **1** a person who gambles. **2** *Brit* a client or customer.

**puny** *adj* (**-ier, -iest**) **1** small and weak. **2** insignificant.

**pup**[1] *n* **1** a young dog. **2** a young seal, rat, or other animal.

**pup**[2] *v* (**pupped, pupping**) to give birth to a pup or pups.

**pupa** *n* (*pl* **pupae**) an insect at the stage between larva and adult. ➤ **pupal** *adj.*

**pupate** *v* of an insect: to become a pupa. ➤ **pupation** *n.*

**pupil**[1] *n* a child or young person who is being taught.

**pupil**[2] *n* the round dark opening in the centre of the iris of the eye.

**puppet** *n* **1** a toy figure that is moved by strings, wires, or rods, or by movements of the hand and fingers inside the body. **2** a person controlled by somebody else. ➤ **puppeteer** *n,* **puppetry** *n.*

**puppy** *n* (*pl* **-ies**) a young dog. ➤ **puppyish** *adj.*

**puppy fat** *n* temporary plumpness in children.

**puppy love** *n* short-lived love between adolescents.

**purblind** *adj* **1** partly blind. **2** lacking in vision or insight.

**purchase**[1] *v* to buy. ➤ **purchaser** *n.*

**purchase**[2] *n* **1** something bought. **2** the act of buying. **3** a firm grip or contact.

**purdah** *n* the seclusion of women from public view among some Muslims and Hindus.

**pure** *adj* **1** not mixed with any other matter. **2** free from anything that spoils or weakens. **3** free from contamination. **4** free from moral fault; innocent. **5** sheer or unmitigated: *pure folly.* **6** abstract or theoretical: *pure mathematics.* **7** of a sound: in tune and free from harshness. ➤ **purely** *adv.*

**puree**[1] *or* **purée** /'pyooəray/ *n* a thick pulp of fruit or vegetables produced by blending or crushing.

**puree**[2] *or* **purée** *v* (**purees** *or* **purées, pureed** *or* **puréed, pureeing** *or* **puréeing**) to make into a puree.

**purgative**[1] *adj* causing evacuation of the bowels.

**purgative**[2] *n* a purgative substance or medicine.

**purgatory** *n* (*pl* **-ies**) in Roman Catholic doctrine, a place of punishment in which the souls of sinners may make amends for past sins and so become fit for heaven.

**purge**[1] *v* **1** to rid of impurities. **2** to rid (a nation, party, etc) of unwanted or undesirable members. **3** to get rid of (undesirable people) by means of a purge. **4** to cause evacuation of faeces from (the bowels).

**purge**[2] *n* an instance of purging.

**purify** *v* (**-ies, -ied**) to make pure. ➤ **purification** *n.*

**purist** *n* a person who keeps strictly to established or traditional usage, *esp* in language. ➤ **purism** *n.*

**puritan** *n* **1** (**Puritan**) a member of a 16th- and 17th-cent. Protestant group that wished to purify the Church of England of all elaborate forms of worship. **2** a person who preaches a rigorous or severe moral code. ➤ **Puritan** *adj,* **puritan** *adj,* **puritanical** *adj.*

**purity** *n* the state of being pure.

**purl**[1] *n* a basic knitting stitch made by inserting the needle into the back of a stitch that produces a raised pattern on the back of the work.

**purl**[2] *v* to knit (a stitch) in purl.

**purlieu** *n* (*pl* **purlieus**) (*in pl*) the environs or neighbourhood of a place.

**purloin** *v formal* to steal.

**purple** *n* **1** the colour between red and blue. **2** the red robes of a cardinal.

**purple patch** *n* **1** a piece of obtrusively ornate writing. **2** *informal* a period of good luck or success.

**purport**[1] *n formal* **1** professed or implied meaning. **2** purpose or intention.

**purport**[2] *v* to seem or claim to be. ➤ **purportedly** *adv.*

**purpose**[1] *n* **1** the object for which something exists or is done. **2** resolution or determination. **3** use or value. ✱ **on purpose** intentionally. ➤ **purposeless** *adj.*

**purpose**[2] *v formal* to have as a purpose.

**purposeful** *adj* **1** full of determination. **2** having a purpose or aim. ➤ **purposefully** *adv.*

**purposely** *adv* with a deliberate or express purpose.

**purposive** *adj formal* **1** serving or effecting a useful. **2** having or tending to fulfil a conscious purpose.

**purr** *v* **1** of a cat: to make a low vibratory murmur. **2** of an engine: to run smoothly. ➤ **purr** *n.*

**purse**[1] *n* **1** a small bag for holding money. **2** *NAmer* a handbag. **3** resources or funds. **4** a sum of money offered as a prize or present.

**purse**[2] *v* to pucker or knit (the lips).

**purser** *n* an officer on a ship who has charge of documents and accounts.

**purse strings** *pl n* control over expenditure.

**pursuance** *n formal* the act of carrying out a plan or order.

**pursuant to** *prep formal* in accordance with.

**pursue** *v* (**pursues, pursued, pursuing**) **1** to follow in order to overtake or capture. **2** to try to accomplish (a goal). **3** to engage in (an activity). **4** to follow up (an argument). ➤ **pursuer** *n.*

**pursuit** *n* **1** the act of pursuing. **2** an activity engaged in as a pastime.

**purulent** *adj* of or containing pus. ➤ **purulence** *n.*

**purvey** *v* to supply (provisions, etc) by way of business. ➤ **purveyor** *n.*

**purview** *n formal* **1** the range or limit of authority or concern. **2** the range of vision or understanding.

**pus** *n* thick yellowish or greenish fluid matter formed in an abscess or other infected part of the body.

**push**[1] *v* **1** to exert a force on (somebody or something) so as to make it move away from oneself. **2** to move (something) in this way. **3** to urge (somebody or oneself) to do something. **4** to develop or promote (an idea or argument). **5** to make strong efforts to sell (a product). **6** *informal* to engage in the illicit sale of (drugs). **7** to approach in age or number. **8** to press forward energetically. * **be pushed** *informal* have too little time. **push for** to demand strenuously. **push one's luck** *informal* to risk having continuing luck after initial success. ➤ **pusher** *n.*

**push**[2] *n* **1** the act of pushing. **2** a vigorous effort. * **at a push** *Brit, informal* if really necessary.

**push-bike** *n Brit, informal* a pedal cycle.

**pushchair** *n Brit* a light folding chair on wheels in which a young child can be pushed.

**push in** *v* to force one's way into a queue.

**push off** *v Brit, informal* to leave hastily.

**pushover** *n informal* **1** a person who is easily defeated or persuaded. **2** something accomplished easily.

**push through** *v* to force acceptance of (a proposal).

**pushy** *adj* (**-ier, -iest**) very self-assertive. ➤ **pushiness** *n.*

**pusillanimous** *adj* lacking courage or resolution. ➤ **pusillanimity** *n.*

**pussy** *n* (*pl* **-ies**) *informal* a cat.

**pussyfoot** *v* to move or act warily or stealthily.

**pussy willow** *n* a willow having grey silky catkins.

**pustule** *n* a small raised spot on the skin containing pus. ➤ **pustular** *adj.*

**put**[1] *v* (**putting,** *past tense and past part.* **put**) **1** to place in or move to a specified position. **2** to bring into a specified condition: *He tried to put us right.* **3** to devote or apply to some purpose. **4** to assign to do something. **5** to estimate or set a value on. **6** to present (an idea or proposal) for consideration. **7** to throw (a shot or weight) in athletics. **8** of a ship: to take a specified course.

**put**[2] *n* the act of putting the shot.

**putative** *adj formal* commonly accepted or supposed.

**put by** *v* to save (money) for future use.

**put down** *v* **1** to suppress or bring to an end. **2** to kill (a sick or injured animal) painlessly. **3** to pay (a sum of money) as a deposit. **4** *informal* to disparage publicly.

**put off** *v* **1** to disconcert or discourage. **2** to postpone.

**put on** *v* **1** to assume (an attitude or feeling). **2** to increase in weight by a specified amount. **3** to present (a performance).

**put out** *v* **1** to annoy or irritate. **2** to inconvenience. **3** of a ship: to set out from shore.

**putrefy** *v* (**-ies, -ied**) to become rotten or putrid. ➤ **putrefaction** *n.*

**putrid** *adj* decaying or rotten and foul-smelling.

**putsch** /pooch/ *n* a secret plot to overthrow a government.

**putt**[1] *n* a gentle golf stroke.

**putt**[2] *v* to hit (a golf ball) gently towards or into the hole.

**putter**[1] *n* a golf club used for putting.

**putter**[2] *n* a rapidly repeated popping sound made by a small motor.

**putter**[3] *v* of a motor: to make a rapidly repeated popping sound.

**putting green** *n* an area of smooth grass round each hole on a golf course.

**putty** *n* (*pl* **-ies**) a soft building paste used for fixing glass in windows and filling gaps in woodwork.

**put up** *v* **1** to build or erect. **2** to accommodate for a short time. **3** to offer or present. * **put up to** to encourage (somebody) to do something wrong or unwise. **put up with** to tolerate.

**puzzle**[1] *v* **1** to confuse or perplex with a problem or difficulty that is hard to understand. **2** to make (oneself) think hard about something. **3** (*usu* + about/over) to be uncertain about an action or choice. ➤ **puzzlement** *n,* **puzzling** *adj.*

**puzzle**[2] *n* **1** somebody or something that is difficult to understand. **2** a problem, toy, etc designed to test one's ingenuity. ➤ **puzzler** *n.*

**PVC** *abbr* polyvinyl chloride, a plastic vinyl.

**pygmy** *or* **pigmy** *n* (*pl* **-ies**) **1** (**Pygmy**) a member of an African people short in height. **2** a very small person or thing. **3** (*used before a noun*) being a small variety of something.

**pyjamas** (*NAmer* **pajamas**) *pl n* a loose jacket and trousers for sleeping in.

**pylon** *n* a tower for supporting electricity power cables.

**pyramid** *n* a massive stone structure with walls in the form of four triangles that meet in a point at the top. ➤ **pyramidal** *adj.*

**pyre** *n* a heap of combustible materialfor ritually burning a dead body.

**pyrites** *n* (*pl* **pyrites**) a metallic-looking sulphide mineral that is a compound of iron and sulphur.

**pyromania** *n* a compulsive urge to start fires. ➤ **pyromaniac** *n.*

**pyrotechnics** *pl n* **1** a display of fireworks. **2** the art of making fireworks. ➤ **pyrotechnic** *adj.*

**Pyrrhic victory** *n* a victory won at so great a cost as to be worthless.

**python** *n* a large snake that kills its prey by crushing it.

**Q**[1] *or* **q** *n* (*pl* **Q's** *or* **Qs** *or* **q's**) the 17th letter of the English alphabet.
**Q**[2] *abbr* question.
**QC** *abbr* Queen's Counsel.
**QED** *abbr* (Latin) quod erat demonstrandum = which was to be demonstrated, used at the conclusion of a proof.
**qt** *abbr* quart.
**qua** *prep* in the capacity or character of.
**quack**[1] *v* to make the cry of a duck.
**quack**[2] *n* **1** somebody who pretends to have medical skills or qualifications. **2** *informal* a doctor. ➤ **quackery** *n.*
**quad** *n* **1** a quadrangle. **2** a quadruplet.
**quad bike** *n* an off-road vehicle, resembling a motorcycle, with four large wheels.
**quadrangle** *n* **1** = QUADRILATERAL[1]. **2** a courtyard, with buildings on all four sides. ➤ **quadrangular** *adj.*
**quadrant** *n* **1** a quarter of the circumference or area of a circle. **2** formerly, a navigational or astronomical instrument for measuring angles.
**quadraphonic** *or* **quadrophonic** *adj* recording or reproducing sound using four channels.
**quadrate** *adj* square or approximately square.
**quadratic** *adj* in mathematics, relating to the power of two, but no higher power.
**quadrennial** *adj* occurring every four years.
**quadriceps** *n* (*pl* **quadriceps**) the large muscle at the front of the thigh that straightens the leg.
**quadrilateral**[1] *n* a polygon having four sides.
**quadrilateral**[2] *adj* having four straight sides.
**quadrille** *n* a square dance for four couples.
**quadriplegia** *n* paralysis of both arms and both legs. ➤ **quadriplegic** *adj and n.*
**quadruped** *n* an animal that walks on four legs.
**quadruple**[1] *adj* **1** having four parts. **2** being four times as great or as many.
**quadruple**[2] *v* to become or make four times as great or as many.
**quadruplet** *n* any of four offspring born at one birth.
**quaff** *v* to drink, *esp* in long draughts.
**quagmire** *n* **1** an area of soft boggy land. **2** a predicament from which it is difficult to extricate oneself.
**quail**[1] *n* (*pl* **quails** *or* **quail**) a small game bird with a rounded body and short tail.
**quail**[2] *v* to shrink back in fear.
**quaint** *adj* pleasingly old-fashioned or unusual. ➤ **quaintly** *adv.*
**quake**[1] *v* **1** to shake or vibrate. **2** to tremble or shudder, *esp* from fear.
**quake**[2] *n informal* an earthquake.
**Quaker** *n* a member of a pacifist Christian sect, the Society of Friends, that rejects sacraments and a formal ministry. ➤ **Quakerism** *n.*
**qualification** *n* **1** an official record that a person has completed a course or passed an examination. **2** a quality or skill that makes a person suitable for a particular task or appointment. **3** a restriction in meaning or application. **4** the act of qualifying.
**qualifier** *n* **1** a contestant or team that qualifies in e.g. a tournament. **2** a preliminary heat or contest; a qualifying round. **3** in grammar, a word that restricts the meaning of another.
**qualify** *v* (**-ies, -ied**) **1** to be, or to make (somebody), fit for or entitled to something, e.g. a job or position. **2** to obtain a qualification or reach an accredited level of competence in a profession. **3** to become eligible for the higher rounds of a contest by succeeding in a preliminary round. **4** to restrict the meaning or application of (a statement). **5** (*often* + as) to characterize or describe.
**qualitative** *adj* relating to, or involving the assessment of, quality. ➤ **qualitatively** *adv.*
**quality** *n* (*pl* **-ies**) **1** degree of excellence in comparison to others of the kind. **2** superior nature or standard. **3** a distinguishing attribute; a characteristic. **4** peculiar and essential character; nature.
**qualm** *n* a scruple or feeling of uneasiness.
**quandary** *n* (*pl* **-ies**) a state of perplexity or doubt.
**quango** *n* (*pl* **-os**) *Brit* an autonomous body set up by the government and having statutory powers in a specific field.
**quantify** *v* (**-ies, -ied**) to express or measure the quantity of. ➤ **quantifiable** *adj.*
**quantitative** *adj* relating to, or involving the measurement of, quantity. ➤ **quantitatively** *adv.*
**quantity** *n* (*pl* **-ies**) **1** a specified or unspecified amount or number. **2** (*also in pl*) a considerable amount or number. **3** the aspect in which

something is measurable in terms of magnitude.

**quantity surveyor** *n* somebody who estimates quantities of materials and labour needed for a building project.

**quantum** *n* (*pl* **quanta**) in physics, the smallest discrete unit of quantity into which energy can be subdivided or by which it can increase or decrease.

**quantum leap** *n* a sudden large increase or major advance.

**quantum mechanics** *pl n* a branch of mechanics that deals with the physical behaviour of atoms and particles of matter, for which the laws of classical mechanics are inapplicable.

**quarantine**[1] *n* a state or period of isolation for people or animals, designed to prevent the spread of disease.

**quarantine**[2] *v* to put into quarantine.

**quark** *n* in physics, a hypothetical particle that carries a fractional electric charge and is held to be a constituent of known elementary particles, e.g. the proton or neutron.

**quarrel**[1] *n* **1** a usu verbal conflict between people; an argument. **2** a reason for dispute or complaint.

**quarrel**[2] *v* (**quarrelled, quarrelling,** *NAmer* **quarreled, quarreling**) **1** to have a quarrel. **2** (+ with) to find fault with.

**quarrelsome** *adj* inclined or quick to quarrel.

**quarry**[1] *n* (*pl* **-ies**) an open excavation from which building materials are obtained.

**quarry**[2] *v* (**-ies, -ied**) to obtain (e.g. stone) from a quarry.

**quarry**[3] *n* (*pl* **-ies**) **1** the prey of a predator or hunter. **2** somebody or something pursued.

**quart** *n* a unit of liquid capacity equal to 2 pints (about 1.136l in Britain), (about 0.946l in the USA).

**quarter**[1] *n* **1** any of four equal parts into which something can be divided. **2** a quarter of a pound or hundredweight. **3** any of four three-month divisions of a year. **4** a point of time 15 minutes before or after the hour. **5** a coin worth a quarter of a US or Canadian dollar. **6** a person, group, direction, or place not specifically identified: *We had financial help from many quarters.* **7** a district of a town or city. **8** (*in pl*) living accommodation or lodgings. **9** mercy for a defeated enemy.

**quarter**[2] *v* **1** to divide into four equal parts. **2** to provide (somebody) with lodgings or shelter. **3** formerly, to divide (a criminal's body) into four parts after execution by hanging.

**quarterdeck** *n* the stern area of a ship's upper deck.

**quarterfinal** *n* any of four matches in the round that is second from last in a knockout competition.

**quarterly**[1] *adv and adj* at three-monthly intervals.

**quarterly**[2] *n* (*pl* **-ies**) a periodical published at three-monthly intervals.

**quartermaster** *n* an army officer who provides supplies and quarters for a body of troops.

**quarter tone** *n* in music, an interval of half a semitone.

**quartet** *or* **quartette** *n* **1** a group of four instruments, voices, or performers. **2** a musical composition for a quartet.

**quarto** *n* (*pl* **-os**) a size of book page that is created when a standard sheet is folded into 4 leaves or 8 pages.

**quartz** *n* a crystalline mineral consisting of silicon dioxide, found in many rocks, e.g. granite and sandstone.

**quasar** *n* a very distant and very compact celestial object that emits enormous amounts of energy and is thought to be a supermassive black hole in the centre of a galaxy.

**quash** *v* **1** to annul (e.g. a law or judgment). **2** to suppress or crush (e.g. a rumour or rebellion).

**quasi-** *prefix* **1** to some degree; partly: *quasi-officially.* **2** seemingly: *quasi-stellar object.*

**quatrain** *n* a stanza of four lines.

**quaver**[1] *v esp* of the voice: to tremble or shake. ➤ **quavery** *adj.*

**quaver**[2] *n* **1** a musical note with the time value of half a crotchet. **2** a tremulous sound.

**quay** *n* a landing place for loading and unloading ships.

**quayside** *n* a quay or the land bordering a quay.

**queasy** *adj* (**-ier, -iest**) suffering from nausea. ➤ **queasiness** *n.*

**queen** *n* **1** a female monarch. **2** the wife or widow of a king. **3** a woman who is preeminent in a specified sphere. **4** in chess, the most powerful piece of each colour, which has the power to move any number of squares in any direction. **5** a playing card marked with a picture of a queen and ranking below the king. **6** the fertile fully developed female in a colony of bees, wasps, ants, or termites. **7** *informal* an effeminate male homosexual. ➤ **queenly** *adj.*

**queen mother** *n* a woman who is the widow of a king and the mother of the reigning sovereign.

**Queensberry rules** *pl n* the basic rules of boxing.

**queer**[1] *adj* **1** odd or strange. **2** *informal* slightly unwell; faint or queasy. **3** *informal, derog* homosexual.

**queer**[2] *v informal* to spoil or thwart. * **queer somebody's pitch** to prejudice or ruin somebody's chances in advance.

**queer**[3] *n informal, derog* a male homosexual.

**quell** *v* **1** to overwhelm (e.g. a rebellion) thoroughly; to suppress or subdue. **2** to overcome or alleviate (e.g. a feeling).

**quench** *v* **1** to relieve or satisfy (thirst) with liquid. **2** to bring to an end, *esp* by satisfying, damping, or decreasing. **3** to put out (e.g. a fire).
**querulous** *adj* complaining, *esp* habitually. ➤ **querulously** *adv.*
**query**[1] *n* (*pl* **-ies**) a question, *esp* one expressing doubt or uncertainty.
**query**[2] *v* (**-ies, -ied**) **1** to question the accuracy of (e.g. a statement). **2** to express doubt or uncertainty about.
**quest**[1] *n* a search, *esp* a long or arduous one, or one involving a journey.
**quest**[2] *v literary* to search for something.
**question**[1] *n* **1** a word, phrase, or sentence used to elicit information or test knowledge. **2** a subject that is in dispute or at issue. **3** a thing on which the outcome of a situation depends: *It's simply a question of availability.* **4** a problem to be resolved. **5** doubt or objection. **6** chance or possibility. * **in question** under discussion. **out of the question** preposterous or impossible.
**question**[2] *v* **1** to ask (somebody) a question or a series of questions. **2** to doubt or dispute (something). ➤ **questioner** *n.*
**questionable** *adj* **1** open to doubt or challenge. **2** of doubtful morality or propriety. ➤ **questionably** *adv.*
**question mark** *n* a punctuation mark (?) used at the end of a sentence to indicate a direct question.
**questionnaire** *n* a set of questions, usu on a form, used to obtain statistically useful information.
**queue**[1] *n* a line of *esp* people or vehicles waiting.
**queue**[2] *v* (**queues, queued, queuing** *or* **queueing**) to line up or wait in a queue.
**queue-jump** *v* to join a queue at a point in front of those already waiting.
**quibble**[1] *n* a minor objection or criticism.
**quibble**[2] *v* to make minor or trivial objections.
**quiche** *n* a pastry shell filled with a rich savoury egg and cream custard and other ingredients.
**quick**[1] *adj* **1** fast in development or occurrence. **2** marked by speed, readiness, or promptness of physical movement. **3** lasting a short time. **4** inclined to hastiness, e.g. in action or response: *quick to find fault.* **5** fast in understanding, thinking, or learning. **6** of e.g. temper: aroused immediately and intensely. ➤ **quickly** *adv.*
**quick**[2] *adv informal* fast; soon.
**quick**[3] *n* **1** painfully sensitive flesh, *esp* under a fingernail or toenail. **2** somebody's emotional centre or most sensitive feelings.
**quicken** *v* **1** to become or make more rapid. **2** to enliven or stimulate. **3** of a foetus: to begin to show signs of life.
**quicklime** *n* = LIME[1].
**quicksand** *n* a deep mass of loose wet sand into which heavy objects easily sink.
**quicksilver**[1] *n* liquid mercury.
**quicksilver**[2] *adj* changeable in mood or rapid in movement.
**quickstep** *n* a ballroom dance with short rapid steps.
**quick-tempered** *adj* easily angered.
**quick-witted** *adj* quick in understanding or response.
**quid** *n* (*pl* **quid**) *Brit, informal* a pound sterling. * **quids in** *Brit, informal* having made a profit.
**quid pro quo** *n* (*pl* **quid pro quos**) something given or received in exchange for something else.
**quiescent** *adj* at rest; inactive. ➤ **quiescence** *n.*
**quiet**[1] *adj* (**quieter, quietest**) **1** making little or no noise. **2** free from noise, activity, or excitement; peaceful. **3** gentle or reserved. **4** private or discreet: *a quiet word.* **5** informal and usu involving small numbers of people: *a quiet wedding.* ➤ **quietly** *adv,* **quietness** *n.*
**quiet**[2] *n* tranquillity or silence. * **on the quiet** without telling anyone.
**quiet**[3] *adv* in a quiet manner.
**quieten** (*NAmer* **quiet**) *v* to become or make quiet.
**quietude** *n formal* being quiet; repose.
**quiff** *n Brit* a lock of hair brushed so that it stands up over the forehead.
**quill** *n* **1** the hollow horny barrel of a feather. **2** any of the large stiff feathers of a bird's wing or tail. **3** any of the hollow sharp spines of a porcupine, hedgehog, etc. **4** a bird's feather made into a writing pen.
**quilt**[1] *n* a thick warm top cover for a bed consisting of padding held in place between two layers of cloth by lines of stitching.
**quilt**[2] *v* to stitch or sew (fabric) together in layers with padding in between. ➤ **quilted** *adj,* **quilter** *n.*
**quin** *n Brit* a quintuplet.
**quince** *n* a yellow round or pear-shaped fruit, used for making marmalade, jelly, and preserves.
**quinine** *n* a bitter-tasting chemical compound obtained from cinchona bark, formerly used to treat malaria.
**quintessence** *n* **1** the pure and concentrated essence. **2** the most typical example or perfect embodiment.
**quintessential** *adj* representing a perfect example or embodiment. ➤ **quintessentially** *adv.*
**quintet** *n* **1** a group of five instruments, voices, or performers. **2** a musical composition for a quintet.
**quintuple**[1] *adj* **1** having five parts. **2** being five times as great or as many.

**quintuple**[2] *v* to become or make five times as great or as many.
**quintuplet** *n* any of five offspring born at one birth.
**quip**[1] *n* a clever, witty, or sarcastic remark.
**quip**[2] *v* (**quipped, quipping**) to make a quip.
**quire** *n* **1** 24 or 25 sheets of paper; one twentieth of a ream. **2** four sheets of paper folded to form eight leaves or sixteen pages.
**quirk** *n* **1** an odd or peculiar trait. **2** an accident or vagary. ➤ **quirky** *adj.*
**quisling** *n* a traitor who collaborates with invaders.
**quit** *v* (**quitting,** *past tense and past part.* **quitted** *or* **quit**) **1** to leave (a person or place). **2** to give up (e.g. an activity or employment). **3** *informal* to admit defeat. ➤ **quitter** *n.*
**quite**[1] *adv* **1** wholly or completely. **2** certainly: *It's quite the best I've seen.* **3** more than usually; rather: *It took quite a while.* **4** *chiefly Brit* to only a moderate degree.
**quite**[2] *interj* used to express agreement.
**quits** *adj* on even terms as a result of repaying a debt or retaliating for an injury.
**quiver**[1] *n* a case for carrying or holding arrows.
**quiver**[2] *v* to shake with a slight rapid trembling motion.
**quiver**[3] *n* the act of quivering; a tremor.
**quixotic** *adj* idealistic in a rash or impractical way. ➤ **quixotically** *adv.*
**quiz**[1] *n* (*pl* **quizzes**) a test of knowledge, *esp* as a form of entertainment.
**quiz**[2] *v* (**quizzes, quizzed, quizzing**) to question closely.
**quizzical** *adj* indicating a state of puzzlement; questioning. ➤ **quizzically** *adv.*
**quoin** *n* **1** a solid exterior corner of a building. **2** a block used to form a quoin.
**quoit** *n* **1** a ring used in a throwing game. **2** (*in pl*) a game in which quoits are thrown at an upright pin.
**quorate** *adj formal* having a quorum.
**quorum** *n* (*pl* **quorums**) the minimum number of members of a body that must be assembled for proceedings to be constitutionally valid.
**quota** *n* **1** the share or proportion to be either contributed or received by an individual. **2** a numerical limit set on a particular kind of people or things.
**quotation** *n* **1** something quoted. **2** the act of quoting. **3** a statement of the expected cost of a service or commodity.
**quotation mark** *n* (*usu in pl*) either of a pair of punctuation marks (" " or ' ') used to indicate the beginning and end of a direct quotation or to enclose a word or phrase, e.g. a title or definition.
**quote**[1] *v* **1** to repeat (something previously said or written, *esp* by somebody else) in writing or speech. **2** to give a quotation for a service or commodity. **3** to name the current buying or selling price of (a commodity, stock, share, etc). **4** to quote the shares of (a company) on a stock exchange.
**quote**[2] *n informal* **1** = QUOTATION 1, 3. **2** = QUOTATION MARK.
**quoth** *v archaic* said.
**quotidian** *adj* **1** occurring every day. **2** commonplace or ordinary.
**quotient** *n* the result of dividing one number by another.
**q.v.** *abbr* (Latin) quod vide = which see, used to indicate a cross-reference.
**qwerty** *adj* of computer and typewriter keyboards: having the conventional arrangement of keys for English, with *q,w,e,r,t,y* on the left side of the top row of letters.

**R**[1] *or* **r** *n* (*pl* **R's** *or* **Rs** *or* **r's**) the eighteenth letter of the alphabet.

**R**[2] *abbr* **1** (Latin) Regina = Queen. **2** (Latin) Rex = King. **3** river.

**Ra** *abbr* the chemical symbol for radium.

**rabbi** *n* (*pl* **rabbis**) **1** a Jewish scholar qualified to teach Jewish law. **2** the official leader of a Jewish congregation.

**rabbit**[1] *n* (*pl* **rabbits** *or* **rabbit**) a small long-eared short-tailed mammal that lives in a burrow.

**rabbit**[2] *v* (**rabbited, rabbiting**) *Brit, informal* (*often* + on) to talk aimlessly or inconsequentially.

**rabbit punch** *n* a short chopping blow to the back of the neck.

**rabble** *n* **1** a disorderly crowd of people. **2** (**the rabble**) the lowest class of society.

**rabid** *adj* **1** unreasoning or fanatical. **2** affected with rabies. ➤ **rabidly** *adv.*

**rabies** *n* a usu fatal viral disease of mammals, transmitted through the bite of an affected animal and characterized by convulsions and extreme fear of water.

**raccoon** *or* **racoon** *n* (*pl* **raccoons** *or* **racoons** *or* **raccoon** *or* **racoon**) a small North American mammal that has a bushy ringed tail and lives in trees.

**race**[1] *n* **1** a contest of speed, e.g. in running or riding. **2** a contest for a prize or position. **3** a strong or rapid current of water. **4** a swift-flowing watercourse used industrially, e.g. to turn a mill wheel. ➤ **racer** *n.*

**race**[2] *v* **1** to compete in a race. **2** to have a race with. **3** to go or move at top speed. **4** of a motor, engine, etc: to run at a very high speed.

**race**[3] *n* **1** a division of humankind having physical characteristics that are transmissible by descent, e.g. skin colour. **2** an ethnic group. **3** a subspecies of plants or animals.

**racecourse** *n* a place or track where races, *esp* horse races, are held.

**racehorse** *n* a horse bred or kept for racing.

**raceme** *n* a simple stalk of flowers in which the flowers are borne on short side-stalks along a tall main stem.

**race relations** *pl n* relations between members of a country's different racial communities.

**racetrack** *n* a track on which races, e.g. between cars or runners, are held.

**racial** *adj* **1** relating to race or based on distinctions of race. **2** existing between people of different races. ➤ **racially** *adv.*

**racialism** *n* = RACISM. ➤ **racialist** *n and adj.*

**racism** *n* **1** the belief that race is the main source of human traits and abilities. **2** hostility towards or discrimination against people of races other than one's own. ➤ **racist** *n and adj.*

**rack**[1] *n* **1** a framework or stand on which articles are placed. **2** (**the rack**) an instrument of torture formerly used to stretch the victim's body. **3** a triangular frame for arranging pool balls at the beginning of a game. **4** the front rib section of lamb used for chops or as a roast. ✱ **rack/wrack and ruin** a state of destruction or extreme neglect.

**rack**[2] *v* **1** (*also* **wrack**) to cause to suffer torture, pain, or anguish. **2** to place (an object) in a rack. ✱ **rack/wrack one's brains** to make a great mental effort.

**racket**[1] *or* **racquet** *n* **1** a lightweight bat with netting stretched across an open frame, used in tennis, squash, badminton, etc. **2** (*in pl*) a game similar to squash, played on a four-walled court.

**racket**[2] *n* **1** a loud and confused noise. **2** *informal* a fraudulent scheme engaged in profit.

**racketeer** *n* a person who makes money through fraudulent schemes. ➤ **racketeering** *n.*

**raconteur** *n* a person who is good at telling anecdotes.

**racoon** *n* see RACCOON.

**racy** *adj* (**-ier, -iest**) **1** slightly indecent; risqué. **2** full of zest or vigour. ➤ **racily** *adv,* **raciness** *n.*

**radar** *n* an electronic system that detects nearby ships, aircraft, etc by generating high-frequency radio waves and analysing those reflected back from objects they strike.

**raddled** *adj* haggard with age or the effects of a dissipated lifestyle.

**radial** *adj* **1** arranged like rays emerging from a central point or axis. **2** of a tyre: having the cords of its fabric running at right angles to the circumference of the tyre. ➤ **radially** *adv.*

**radian** *n* a unit equal to the angle at the centre of a circle formed by a part of the circumference equal in length to the radius, 57.3°.

**radiant** *adj* **1** vividly bright and shining. **2** expressing love or happiness, health, etc. **3** transmitted by radiation. ➤ **radiance** *n*, **radiantly** *adv*.

**radiate** *v* **1** to send (energy) out, or to be given out, in rays or waves. **2** to show or display (a quality, feeling, etc) clearly. **3** to proceed outwards in straight lines from a central point.

**radiation** *n* **1** the process of radiating. **2** energy radiated in the form of waves or particles.

**radiator** *n* **1** a room heater with a large surface area, *esp* one through which hot water circulates as part of a central heating system. **2** a device for cooling an internal-combustion engine.

**radical**[1] *adj* **1** involving the basic nature or composition of something; fundamental. **2** marked by a considerable departure from the usual or traditional. **3** favouring or making extreme changes in existing conditions or institutions. **4** of surgery: designed to remove the root of a disease or all diseased tissue. **5** of a mathematical root. ➤ **radicalism** *n*, **radically** *adj*.

**radical**[2] *n* **1** a person who who holds radical views. **2** in chemistry, a group of atoms that is capable of remaining unchanged during a series of reactions.

**radii** *n* pl of RADIUS.

**radio**[1] *n* (*pl* **-os**) **1** the transmission and reception of sound signals by means of electromagnetic waves. **2** a device designed to receive sound broadcasts. **3** the radio broadcasting industry.

**radio**[2] *v* (**radios, radioed, radioing**) to send a message to somebody by radio.

**radioactive** *adj* emitting harmful rays or particles.

**radioactivity** *n* the spontaneous emission of harmful rays or particles by the disintegration of the atomic nuclei of some elements, e.g. uranium.

**radiocarbon** *n* a radioactive isotope of carbon, used in carbon dating.

**radiography** *n* the production of images by a form of radiation other than light, *esp* X-rays. ➤ **radiographer** *n*.

**radioisotope** *n* a radioactive isotope.

**radiology** *n* the study and use of radioactive substances and X-rays in the diagnosis and treatment of disease. ➤ **radiologist** *n*.

**radiotherapy** *n* the treatment of disease, e.g. cancer, by means of X-rays.

**radish** *n* the dark red root of a plant of the mustard family, eaten as a salad vegetable.

**radium** *n* an intensely radioactive metallic element.

**radius** *n* (*pl* **radii** *or* **radiuses**) **1** a straight line extending from the centre of a circle or sphere to the circumference or surface. **2** the circular area defined by a stated radius. **3** the bone on the thumb side of the human forearm.

**radon** *n* a radioactive gas.

**RAF** *abbr Brit* Royal Air Force.

**raffia** *n* fibre from the leaves of a Madagascan palm tree used for making baskets, etc.

**raffish** *adj* not entirely respectable or honest, but not unattractive.

**raffle**[1] *n* a lottery in which the prizes are usually goods.

**raffle**[2] *v* to offer as a prize in a raffle.

**raft**[1] *n* **1** a flat usu wooden floating structure used as a platform or vessel. **2** an inflatable boat or mat.

**raft**[2] *v* to travel or transport by raft. ➤ **rafting** *n*.

**raft**[3] *n* a large collection or quantity.

**rafter** *n* any of the parallel beams that form the framework of a roof.

**rag**[1] *n* **1** a piece of old worn cloth. **2** (*in pl*) clothes that are in poor or ragged condition. **3** *informal* a newspaper, *esp* one that is sensational or poorly written. ✱ **lose one's rag** *informal* to lose one's temper.

**rag**[2] *n* a series of processions and stunts organized by students to raise money for charity.

**rag**[3] *v* (**ragging, ragged**) *Brit* to tease.

**rag**[4] *n* ragtime music, or a ragtime tune.

**ragamuffin** *n* a ragged often disreputable person, *esp* a child.

**ragbag** *n* a miscellaneous collection.

**rage**[1] *n* **1** violent and uncontrolled anger. **2** a fashionable and temporary enthusiasm, or the object of it.

**rage**[2] *v* **1** to be in a rage. **2** to be unchecked in violence or effect.

**ragged** /'ragid/ *adj* **1** of clothes: torn or worn to tatters. **2** wearing tattered clothes. **3** having an irregular edge or outline; jagged. **4** performed in an irregular, faulty, or uneven manner. ➤ **raggedly** *adv*.

**ragout** /ra'gooh/ *n* a thick well-seasoned stew of meat and vegetables.

**ragtag** *adj* consisting of a varied or odd mixture.

**ragtime** *n* music with a strongly syncopated rhythm, developed in America in about 1900 and usu played on the piano.

**rag trade** *n informal* the clothing trade.

**ragwort** *n* a yellow-flowered plant with deeply cut leaves.

**raid**[1] *n* **1** a surprise attack or incursion by a small force, often to seize somebody or something. **2** a sudden invasion by the police, e.g. in search of criminals or stolen goods. **3** an act of robbery.

**raid**[2] *v* **1** to make a raid on. **2** to take or steal something from (a place). ➤ **raider** *n*.

**rail**[1] *n* **1** a fixed horizontal bar, serving as a barrier or from which something may be hung. **2** either of a pair of lengths of steel forming the running surface for trains or other wheeled vehicles. **3** the railway. ✱ **go off the rails 1** *informal* to behave strangely or become mentally unbalanced. **2** *informal* to be misguided or mistaken.

**rail**[2] *v* (*often* + off) to enclose or separate (an area) with a rail or rails.

**rail**[3] *v* (*often* + against/at) to utter angry complaints or abuse.

**railhead** *n* the farthest point reached by a railway.

**railing** *n* a fence or similar barrier made of rails.

**raillery** *n* good-humoured teasing.

**railroad**[1] *n NAmer* a railway.

**railroad**[2] *v informal* to hustle into taking action or making a decision.

**railway** *n chiefly Brit* **1** a track usu having two parallel rails on which trains run. **2** a railway network or the organization that runs it.

**raiment** *n archaic or literary* clothing.

**rain**[1] *n* **1** water falling in drops condensed from vapour in the atmosphere. **2** rainy weather. **3** (*in pl*) the rainy season. **4** a dense flow or fall of something.

**rain**[2] *v* **1** of rain: to fall in drops from the clouds. **2** to fall or bestow in profusion. ✱ **rain cats and dogs** to rain heavily.

**rainbow** *n* a multicoloured arch in the sky formed by the refraction of the sun's rays in raindrops, spray, etc.

**raincoat** *n* a coat made from waterproof material.

**rainfall** *n* the amount of rain that has fallen.

**rainforest** *n* a dense tropical woodland with a heavy annual rainfall.

**rain off** *v* (*usu* **be rained off**) to be prevented or interrupted by rain.

**rainy** *adj* (**-ier, -iest**) characterized by heavy rainfall.

**rainy day** *n* a future time when money or other things may be in short supply.

**raise**[1] *v* **1** to lift to a higher position. **2** to bring to an upright position. **3** to increase the amount, level, strength, intensity, etc of. **4** to bring up (a subject) for consideration or debate. **5** to express (*esp* a doubt or objection). **6** to collect (e.g. money). **7** to cause to occur or appear. **8** to rear (a child or an animal). **9** to grow or cultivate (crops or other plants). **10** to multiply (a quantity) by itself a number of times so as to produce a specified power. **11** *Brit, informal* to establish radio or telephone communication with (a person or place). ✱ **raise hell 1** *informal* to create a disturbance. **2** *informal* to complain angrily about something. **raise the roof** *informal* to make a loud noise, *esp* by cheering.

**raise**[2] *n chiefly NAmer* an increase in salary; a rise.

**raisin** *n* a dried grape.

**raison d'être** /ˌrayzon(h) ˈdetrə/ *n* (*pl* **raisons d'être** /ˌrayzon(h) ˈdetrə/) the main reason that something or somebody exists.

**Raj** *n* (**the Raj**) British rule in India before 1947.

**rajah** *or* **raja** *n* an Indian or Malayan prince or chief.

**rake**[1] *n* a long-handled implement with a row of prongs on the head for gathering grass, leaves etc or for loosening or levelling the ground.

**rake**[2] *v* **1** to gather or level with a rake. **2** to scrape, e.g. in passing. **3** to sweep the length of, e.g. with gunfire. **4** (+ through) to search through.

**rake**[3] *n* inclination from the perpendicular; a sloping angle.

**rake**[4] *v* to set at an angle from the perpendicular.

**rake**[5] *n* a dissolute man, *esp* in fashionable society.

**rake in** *v informal* to earn or gain (money) rapidly or in abundance.

**rake up** *v* to revive (something long and often best forgotten).

**rakish** *adj* **1** of a car, boat, etc: smart, stylish, and suggestive of speed. **2** suggestive of a lively or rather disreputable personality.

**rally**[1] *v* (**-ies, -ied**) **1** to bring or come together for a common cause. **2** to come or bring together again to renew an effort. **3** to recover from illness, a state of depression, etc. **4** of e.g. shares: to recover value after a fall. **5** to drive in a rally. ✱ **rally round** to give practical or emotional support.

**rally**[2] *n* (*pl* **-ies**) **1** a mass meeting of people supporting a common cause. **2** a motor race over public roads or countryside tracks, designed to test driving and navigational skills. **3** a recovery of strength, courage, value, etc. **4** a series of strokes interchanged between players, e.g. in tennis.

**ram**[1] *n* **1** an uncastrated male sheep. **2** a battering ram. **3** the weight that strikes the blow in a pile driver.

**ram**[2] *v* (**rammed, ramming**) **1** to force down or in by driving, pressing, or pushing. **2** to strike against (something) violently and usu head-on. ✱ **ram something down somebody's throat** to force somebody to accept or listen to something.

**Ramadan** *n* the ninth month of the Muslim year, during which Muslims fast daily from dawn to sunset.

**ramble**[1] *v* **1** to walk for pleasure in the countryside. **2** to talk or write in a disconnected long-winded fashion. ➤ **rambler** *n*, **rambling** *adj and n*.

**ramble**[2] *n* a leisurely walk taken for pleasure in the countryside.

**ramekin** *or* **ramequin** *n* an individual baking and serving dish.

**ramification** *n* (*usu in pl*) a wide-reaching and complex consequence.

**ramp** *n* **1** a slope leading from one level to another. **2** a stairway for entering or leaving an aircraft. **3** *Brit* a point where roadworks cause a rise or fall in the level of the road.

**rampage[1]** *v* to rush about wildly or violently.

**rampage[2]** *n* * **on the rampage** behaving in a wild or violent way.

**rampant** *adj* **1** spreading or growing unchecked. **2** of a heraldic animal: rearing up on one hind leg with forelegs extended.

**rampart** *n* a broad embankment or wall built as a fortification.

**ram raid** *n* a robbery in which entrance is gained to a building by driving a vehicle through the front window. ➤ **ram-raider** *n.*

**ramrod** *n* a rod for ramming home the charge in a muzzle-loading firearm.

**ramshackle** *adj* badly constructed or needing repair.

**ran** *v* past tense of RUN[1].

**ranch** *n* a large farm for raising livestock, *esp* in North America. ➤ **rancher** *n.*

**rancid** *adj* of food: smelling or tasting unpleasantly sour.

**rancour** (*NAmer* **rancor**) *n* bitter and deep-seated ill will or hatred. ➤ **rancorous** *adj.*

**rand** *n* (*pl* **rand**) the basic monetary unit of South Africa.

**R & B** *abbr* rhythm and blues.

**random** *adj* lacking a definite plan, purpose, or pattern; occurring or selected by chance. * **at random** without a definite aim, rule, or method; unpredictably. ➤ **randomly** *adv,* **randomness** *n.*

**randy** *adj* (**-ier, -iest**) *chiefly Brit, informal* sexually aroused; lustful.

**rang** *v* past tense of RING[3].

**range[1]** *n* **1** a sequence or series between limits. **2** a number of individual people or objects forming a distinct class or series. **3** the distance or extent covered or within which something functions. **4** the distance between a weapon and target, a camera and subject, etc. **5** a large connected group of mountains. **6** an open region over which livestock may roam and feed, *esp* in North America. **7** a place where something, *esp* shooting, is practised. **8** a large cooking stove with one or more ovens and a flat metal top for heating pans.

**range[2]** *v* **1** to change or differ within limits. **2** to travel or roam at large or freely. **3** to include a large number of topics. **4** to set in a particular order or position. * **be ranged against** to oppose.

**ranger** *n* a keeper of a park or forest.

**rangy** *adj* (**-ier, -iest**) **1** of a person: tall and slender. **2** of an animal: long-limbed and long-bodied.

**rank[1]** *n* **1** a degree or position in a hierarchy or order, *esp* in the armed forces. **2** high social position. **3** a row or series of people or things, *esp* a line of soldiers standing side by side. **4** (**the ranks**) the ordinary members of an armed force as distinguished from the officers. * **close ranks** to unite to resist a threat. **pull rank** to make use of one's senior position to compel somebody to do something.

**rank[2]** *v* **1** to have a position in relation to others. **2** to arrange in lines. **3** to determine the relative position of; to rate.

**rank[3]** *adj* **1** offensive in odour or flavour. **2** of vegetation: excessively vigorous in growth. **3** absolute or complete.

**rank and file** *n* the ordinary members of an organization, etc as distinguished from the leaders.

**rankle** *v* to cause continuing anger, irritation, or bitterness.

**ransack** *v* **1** to go through (a place) stealing things and causing general chaos. **2** to search thoroughly.

**ransom[1]** *n* a price paid or demanded for the release of a captured or kidnapped person. * **hold to ransom 1** to kidnap (somebody) and demand money for their release. **2** to try to make somebody do something by threatening to cause harm.

**ransom[2]** *v* to free from captivity by paying a ransom.

**rant** *v* to talk in a wild or declamatory manner.

**rap[1]** *n* **1** a sharp blow or knock, or the sound made by it. **2** a sharp rebuke or criticism. **3** (**the rap**) *informal* the responsibility for or adverse consequences of an action. **4** *chiefly NAmer, informal* a criminal charge. * **a rap on/over the knuckles** *informal* a scolding.

**rap[2]** *v* (**rapped, rapping**) **1** to strike with a sharp blow. **2** to strike against something hard. **3** (+ out) to utter (e.g. a command) abruptly and forcibly. **4** *informal* to criticize sharply.

**rap[3]** *n* a type of pop music characterized by rapidly chanted lyrics accompanied by electronic music with a heavy beat. ➤ **rapper** *n.*

**rapacious** *adj* ferociously grasping or covetous. ➤ **rapaciously** *adv,* **rapacity** *n.*

**rape[1]** *n* **1** the crime of forcing somebody to have sexual intercourse against their will. **2** the act of despoiling: *the rape of the countryside.*

**rape[2]** *v* **1** of a man: to commit rape on. **2** to treat in a violent or destructive way.

**rape[3]** *n* a plant with bright yellow flowers grown for its oil-rich seeds.

**rapid[1]** *adj* moving, acting, or occurring with speed. ➤ **rapidity** *n,* **rapidly** *adv.*

**rapid[2]** *n* (*usu in pl*) a part of a river where the water flows swiftly over a rocky slope.

**rapier** *n* a straight sword with a narrow pointed blade.

**rapist** *n* a man who commits rape.

**rapport** /ra'paw/ *n* a sympathetic or harmonious relationship.
**rapprochement** /ra'proshmonh/ *n* the re-establishment of cordial relations.
**rapscallion** *n archaic* a rascal.
**rapt** *adj* completely engrossed.
**rapture** *n* **1** great joy; ecstasy. **2** (*usu in pl*) an expression of extreme happiness or enthusiasm.
**rapturous** *adj* feeling or expressing great joy or pleasure. ➤ **rapturously** *adv.*
**rare**[1] *adj* **1** seldom occurring or found. **2** marked by unusual quality or appeal. ➤ **rareness** *n.*
**rare**[2] *adj* of red meat: cooked lightly so that the inside is still red.
**rarebit** *n* = WELSH RAREBIT.
**rare earth** *n* any of a series of metallic elements with atomic numbers from 58 to 71, e.g. lanthanum.
**rarefied** *adj* **1** of air or the atmosphere: of a density that is lower than normal; thin. **2** distant from ordinary reality and practical concerns; esoteric or abstruse.
**raring** *adj informal* full of enthusiasm or eagerness to do something.
**rarity** *n* (*pl* **-ies**) **1** the state of being rare. **2** a rare person or thing.
**rascal** *n* **1** a mischievous person. **2** an unprincipled or dishonest person. ➤ **rascally** *adj.*
**rash**[1] *adj* acting with or resulting from undue haste or impetuosity. ➤ **rashly** *adv,* **rashness** *n.*
**rash**[2] *n* **1** an outbreak of red spots or patches on the body. **2** a large number of instances of something during a short period.
**rasher** *n* a thin slice of bacon.
**rasp**[1] *v* **1** to file with a rasp. **2** to utter in a harsh tone. **3** to make a grating sound.
**rasp**[2] *n* **1** a coarse file. **2** a grating sound.
**raspberry** *n* (*pl* **-ies**) **1** a reddish pink edible berry. **2** *informal* a rude sound made by sticking the tongue out and blowing noisily.
**Rasta** *n and adj informal* = RASTAFARIAN.
**Rastafarian** *n* a member of a religious and political movement among black West Indians that takes the former Emperor of Ethiopia, Haile Selassie, to be God. ➤ **Rastafarianism** *n.*
**rat**[1] *n* **1** a rodent resembling but considerably larger than a mouse. **2** *informal* a contemptible person, *esp* somebody who betrays or deserts friends or associates.
**rat**[2] *v* (**ratted, ratting**) **1** to catch or hunt rats. **2** *informal* to desert one's party or cause. **3** *informal* (+ on) to betray or inform on one's associates. **4** *informal* (+ on) to default on an agreement. ➤ **ratting** *n.*
**ratatouille** /ratə'tooh·i/ *n* a vegetable stew typically containing tomatoes, onions, aubergines, courgettes, and peppers.
**ratchet** *n* a mechanism that consists of a bar or wheel with angled teeth into which a cog, etc drops so that motion is allowed in one direction only.
**rate**[1] *n* **1** a quantity or frequency of something measured per unit of something else. **2** a fixed charge, payment, or price. **3** speed of movement, change, development, etc. **4** (*usu in pl*) a tax based on property values, levied by a British local authority formerly on domestic and business premises, now only on businesses. ✻ **at any rate** in any case; anyway.
**rate**[2] *v* **1** to assign a relative rank or class to. **2** to consider to be of a particular standard. **3** to be worthy of. **4** *informal* to think highly of.
**rate**[3] *v archaic* to scold angrily; to berate.
**rateable** *or* **ratable** *adj* capable of being rated or estimated.
**rather** *adv* **1** more readily or willingly; sooner: *I'd rather not go.* **2** to some degree; somewhat. **3** more properly, reasonably, or truly. **4** on the contrary; instead.
**ratify** *v* (**-ies, -ied**) to approve or confirm (e.g. a treaty) formally, so that it can come into force. ➤ **ratification** *n.*
**rating** *n* **1** a classification according to grade. **2** (*in pl*) an index that lists television programmes, etc in order of popularity. **3** *Brit* a noncommissioned sailor, *esp* an ordinary seaman.
**ratio** *n* (*pl* **-os**) the relationship in quantity or degree between one thing and another; proportion.
**ratiocinate** *v formal* to reason logically. ➤ **ratiocination** *n.*
**ration**[1] *n* **1** a share or amount, e.g. of food in short supply, that somebody is allowed. **2** (*in pl*) regular supplies of food given to troops.
**ration**[2] *v* **1** to limit (a person or commodity) to a fixed ration. **2** to use sparingly.
**rational** *adj* **1** based on or compatible with reason; reasonable. **2** endowed with the ability to think logically. ➤ **rationality** *n,* **rationally** *adv.*
**rationale** /rashə'nahl/ *n* a logical basis for or explanation of beliefs, actions, or phenomena.
**rationalism** *n* the belief that reason, not emotion, intuition, religion, etc, should govern the actions that people take. ➤ **rationalist** *adj and n,* **rationalistic** *adj.*
**rationalize** *or* **-ise** *v* **1** to attribute (e.g. one's actions) to rational and creditable motives in order to justify conduct. **2** to increase the efficiency of (e.g. an industry) by more effective organization. ➤ **rationalization** *n.*
**rat race** *n informal* a fiercely competitive struggle, e.g. to progress in a career or survive the pressures of modern life.
**rat run** *n Brit, informal* a minor road used by drivers to avoid congestion.

**rattan** *n* a tropical climbing palm tree with long tough stems used for furniture and wickerwork.

**rattle**[1] *v* **1** to make a succession of short sharp knocking or jangling sounds when shaken. **2** *informal* to upset or make anxious. **3** (+ off) to say or perform in a brisk lively fashion. **4** (*often* + on) to chatter incessantly and aimlessly.

**rattle**[2] *n* **1** a rattling sound. **2** a device or toy that produces a rattling sound.

**rattlesnake** *n* an American poisonous snake with horny joints at the end of its tail that rattle when shaken.

**ratty** *adj* (**-ier, -iest**) **1** *Brit, informal* irritable. **2** *informal* dilapidated or shabby.

**raucous** *adj* disagreeably harsh or strident. ➤ **raucously** *adv.*

**raunchy** *adj* (**-ier, -iest**) *informal* sexually suggestive.

**ravage**[1] *v* to wreak havoc on; to devastate.

**ravage**[2] *n* (*usu in pl*) damage resulting from ravaging.

**rave**[1] *v* **1** to talk irrationally, *esp* in delirium. **2** to talk or write with passionate enthusiasm.

**rave**[2] *n chiefly Brit, informal* a very large organized party with dancing to loud electronic music.

**raven**[1] *n* a very large black bird of the crow family.

**raven**[2] *adj* of a glossy black colour.

**ravening** *adj literary* fiercely greedy or predatory.

**ravenous** *adj* extremely hungry. ➤ **ravenously** *adv.*

**raver** *n informal* an uninhibited person who enjoys a wild social life.

**rave-up** *n Brit, informal* a wild party.

**ravine** *n* a narrow steep-sided valley.

**raving**[1] *n* (*usu in pl*) a burst of irrational or incoherent speech.

**raving**[2] *adj and adv informal* used as an intensifier: great or greatly.

**ravioli** /raviˈohli/ *pl n* pasta in the form of little cases containing meat, cheese, etc.

**ravish** *v archaic or literary* **1** to fill with joy, delight, etc. **2** to rape.

**ravishing** *adj* extremely beautiful.

**raw**[1] *adj* **1** not cooked. **2** not processed or purified; still in its natural state. **3** of data: not analysed or modified. **4** having the surface abraded or chafed. **5** sensitive. **6** of emotion: not refined or disguised in the least; crude. **7** lacking experience, training, etc. **8** disagreeably damp or cold. ➤ **rawness** *n.*

**raw**[2] *n* (**the raw**) a sensitive place or state.

**rawboned** *adj* lean and having prominent bones.

**ray**[1] *n* **1** a narrow beam of radiant energy, e.g. light or X-rays. **2** a slight manifestation or trace: *a ray of hope.*

**ray**[2] *n* a fish with a flat body, winglike pectoral fins, and a long narrow tail.

**rayon** *n* a fabric made from cellulose fibre.

**raze** *or* **rase** *v* to destroy (e.g. a town or building) completely.

**razor** *n* a sharp-edged cutting implement for shaving hair.

**razzle** ✱ **on the razzle** *informal* enjoying a spell of partying or drinking.

**razzmatazz** *or* **razzamatazz** *n informal* a noisy, colourful, and showy atmosphere or activity.

**Rb** *abbr* the chemical symbol for rubidium.

**RC** *abbr* Roman Catholic.

**Re** *abbr* the chemical symbol for rhenium.

**re** *prep* with regard to.

**re-** *prefix* **1** again or anew: *reprint.* **2** back or to a previous state: *recede; restore.*

**reach**[1] *v* **1** to make a stretch with one's hand. **2** to touch or grasp by extending a part of the body. **3** to extend to. **4** to achieve or arrive at. **5** to contact or communicate with. ➤ **reachable** *adj.*

**reach**[2] *n* **1** the extent of somebody's ability to reach. **2** range, e.g. of somebody's comprehension. **3** (*often in pl*) a continuous stretch or expanse, *esp* a straight portion of a river.

**react** *v* **1** to respond to something in a particular way. **2** to undergo chemical reaction or physical change.

**reaction** *n* **1** a mental or emotional response to circumstances. **2** a bodily response to a stimulus. **3** tendency towards a former and usu outmoded political or social order. **4** a chemical transformation, *esp* interaction between atoms, molecules, etc to form new substances. **5** in physics, the equal and opposing force exerted by something subjected to the action of a force.

**reactionary**[1] *adj* opposing social or political change.

**reactionary**[2] *n* (*pl* **-ies**) a reactionary person.

**reactivate** *v* to make active again. ➤ **reactivation** *n.*

**reactor** *n* an apparatus in which a controlled chain reaction takes place, *esp* for the production of nuclear power.

**read**[1] *v* (*past tense and past part.* **read**) **1** to look at and understand (e.g. words). **2** to utter aloud (printed or written words). **3** to be worded or phrased in a particular way. **4** to understand the nature of by observing outward expression or signs. **5** (*often* + into) to attribute a sometimes non-existent meaning to; to interpret. **6** to look at the measurement shown on (e.g. a dial or gauge). **7** to indicate (a specified measurement). **8** *chiefly Brit* to study (a subject), *esp* for a degree. ✱ **read between the lines** to work out the implicit meaning of something, rather than what is actually written. **take**

**something as read** to accept something as agreed. ➤ **reader** *n.*

**read**² *n informal* something to read considered in terms of the interest, enjoyment, etc it provides.

**readership** *n* the readers of a particular publication or author.

**readily** *adv* **1** without hesitating; willingly. **2** easily.

**reading** *n* **1** an event at which something is read to an audience. **2** material read or intended for reading. **3** a particular interpretation. **4** the value indicated by an instrument.

**readjust** *v* **1** to adapt to new or changing circumstances. **2** to adjust (e.g. a control) to a new setting. ➤ **readjustment** *n.*

**ready**¹ *adj* (**-ier, -iest**) **1** prepared for an experience or action. **2** prepared or available for immediate use. **3** willing. **4** likely or about to do the specified thing. **5** spontaneously prompt. ➤ **readiness** *n.*

**ready**² *v* (**-ies, -ied**) to prepare.

**ready**³ *n* (*pl* **-ies**) (**readies** *or* **the ready**) *Brit, informal* available money. ✱ **at the ready** available for immediate use.

**reagent** *n* a substance that takes part in or brings about a particular chemical reaction.

**real**¹ *adj* **1** actual, genuine, or authentic. **2** significant. **3** used chiefly for emphasis: complete or great: *Her visit was a real surprise.*

**real**² *adv chiefly NAmer, Scot, informal* very.

**real estate** *n chiefly NAmer* property in the form of buildings and land.

**realign** *v* **1** to align again or in a different way. **2** to become part of a different *esp* political grouping. ➤ **realignment** *n.*

**realism** *n* **1** concern for fact or reality and rejection of the impractical or visionary. **2** representation of things in art and literature in a way that is true to nature. ➤ **realist** *adj and n.*

**realistic** *adj* **1** basing aims or opinions on known facts or reasonable expectations. **2** depicting things in a way that seems real. ➤ **realistically** *adv.*

**reality** *n* (*pl* **-ies**) **1** the state of being real. **2** a real entity or state of affairs. **3** the totality of real things and events.

**reality TV** *or* **reality television** *n* television programmes whose entertainment value is based on the spontaneous reactions of a group of real people placed in a particular situation.

**realize** *or* **-ise** *v* **1** to be or become fully aware of. **2** to cause to become a reality; to accomplish. **3** to convert (property, assets, etc) into actual money. **4** to earn (money) by sale, investment, or effort. ➤ **realization** *n.*

**really**¹ *adv* **1** in reality; actually. **2** without question; thoroughly.

**really**² *interj* used as an expression of surprise or indignation.

**realm** *n* **1** a kingdom. **2** (*also in pl*) a domain or sphere.

**real tennis** *n* an early form of tennis, played with a racket and a solid ball in an irregularly-shaped indoor court.

**ream** *n* **1** a quantity of paper equal to 500 sheets. **2** (*usu in pl*) a great amount, e.g. of something written or printed.

**reap** *v* **1** to cut or harvest (a crop). **2** to obtain or win, *esp* as the reward for effort.

**reaper** *n* a person or machine that harvests crops. ✱ **the reaper/grim reaper** death, *esp* personified as a skeleton wielding a scythe.

**rear**¹ *n* **1** the back part of something. **2** *informal* the buttocks. ✱ **bring up the rear** to be the last in a group, series, etc.

**rear**² *adj* at the back.

**rear**³ *v* **1** to breed (an animal) for use or sale. **2** to bring up (a child). **3** (*often* + up) *esp* of a horse: to rise up on the hind legs. **4** (+ up) to react with anger, indignation, or resentment. **5** *literary* (*usu* + up/over) to rise to a height.

**rear admiral** *n* a naval officer ranking below a vice admiral.

**rear guard** *n* a military detachment for guarding the rear of a main force.

**rearm** *v* to arm (e.g. a nation or military force) again, *esp* with new or better weapons. ➤ **rearmament** *n.*

**rearrange** *v* to arrange differently. ➤ **rearrangement** *n.*

**reason**¹ *n* **1** an explanation or justification. **2** a rational ground or motive. **3** a cause. **4** the power of thinking, *esp* in an orderly rational way. **5** sanity. **6** sensible or logical thinking. ✱ **it stands to reason** it is obvious or reasonable. **listen to reason** to be willing to accept advice to act sensibly. **within reason** within reasonable limits.

**reason**² *v* **1** to use the faculty of reason to arrive at conclusions. **2** (+ with) to talk or argue with another person so as to influence or persuade them. ➤ **reasoning** *n.*

**reasonable** *adj* **1** moderate or fair; not extreme or excessive. **2** in accord with reason; logical. **3** sensible. ➤ **reasonably** *adv.*

**reassure** *v* to restore confidence to; to calm. ➤ **reassurance** *n*, **reassuring** *adj.*

**rebarbative** *adj formal* repellent or unattractive.

**rebate** *n* **1** a return of part of a payment. **2** a deduction from a sum before payment.

**rebel**¹ *n* somebody who rebels against a government, authority, convention, etc.

**rebel**² *v* (**rebelled, rebelling**) **1** to oppose or disobey authority or control. **2** to carry out armed resistance to a government. **3** to feel or show opposition or revulsion.

**rebellion** *n* **1** opposition to authority or dominance. **2** a campaign of open armed resistance to an established government.

**rebellious** *adj* given to or engaged in rebellion. ➤ **rebelliously** *adv.*
**rebirth** *n* a renaissance or revival.
**reborn** *adj* **1** brought back to life. **2** regenerated or spiritually renewed.
**rebound**[1] *v* **1** to spring back on collision or impact with another body. **2** to return to an original strong or healthy state after a setback, illness, etc. **3** (*often* + on) to have unexpected adverse effects.
**rebound**[2] *n* a shot or ball that rebounds. * **on the rebound** while in an unsettled or emotional state resulting from a setback, the end of a relationship, etc.
**rebuff**[1] *v* to reject or refuse sharply.
**rebuff**[2] *n* a curt rejection or refusal.
**rebuild** *v* (*past tense and past part.* **rebuilt**) **1** to build again, *esp* after damage or destruction. **2** to make extensive changes to.
**rebuke**[1] *v* to criticize severely; to reprimand.
**rebuke**[2] *n* a reprimand.
**rebus** *n* a representation of words or syllables by pictures that suggest the same sound.
**rebut** *v* (**rebutted, rebutting**) to disprove or expose the falsity of (e.g. a claim). ➤ **rebuttal** *n.*
**recalcitrant** *adj* defiant of authority or restraint; uncooperative. ➤ **recalcitrance** *n.*
**recall**[1] *v* **1** to remember. **2** to make somebody think of. **3** to summon (somebody) back officially. **4** to request the return of (a faulty product) to the manufacturer.
**recall**[2] *n* **1** a summons to return or a request to return something. **2** remembrance or ability to remember.
**recant** *v* to withdraw or renounce (a statement or belief). ➤ **recantation** *n.*
**recap** *v* (**recapped, recapping**) *informal* = RECAPITULATE.
**recapitulate** *v* to repeat the principal points of (an argument, discourse, etc); to sum up.
**recapture** *v* **1** to capture again. **2** to recreate or experience again. ➤ **recapture** *n.*
**recast** *v* (*past tense and past part.* **recast**) to remodel or refashion.
**recce** *n chiefly Brit, informal* a reconnaissance.
**recede** *v* **1** to move back or away. **2** to slant backwards: *a receding chin.* **3** of hair or a hairline: to stop growing around the temples and above the forehead. **4** to diminish.
**receipt** *n* **1** a written acknowledgment of having received goods or money. **2** the act of receiving. **3** (*usu in pl*) something, *esp* money, received.
**receive** *v* **1** to acquire or be given. **2** to take delivery of. **3** *chiefly Brit, informal* to buy and sell (stolen goods). **4** to convert (an incoming signal, *esp* radio waves) into a form suitable for human perception. **5** to act in response to. **6** to elicit (a particular response). **7** to suffer or be forced to experience. **8** to admit, greet, or entertain formally.
**received** *adj* accepted as authoritative or true: *received wisdom.*
**Received Pronunciation** *n* the form of British English pronunciation used by many educated people in southeastern England and widely regarded as standard.
**receiver** *n* **1** a radio, television, or other part of a communications system that receives the signal. **2** the part of a telephone that contains the mouthpiece and earpiece. **3** a person appointed to administer the affairs of a business that is being wound up. **4** somebody who or something that receives. ➤ **receivership** *n.*
**recent** *adj* **1** of a time not long past. **2** having lately come into existence. ➤ **recently** *adv.*
**receptacle** *n* an object that receives and contains something.
**reception** *n* **1** the act of receiving. **2** a formal social gathering during which guests are received. **3** an office or desk where visitors or clients are received on arrival. **4** a response or reaction. **5** the quality of the radio or television signal received.
**receptionist** *n* a person employed to greet and assist callers or clients, e.g. at an office or hotel.
**receptive** *adj* able or inclined to receive, *esp* open and responsive to ideas, impressions, or suggestions. ➤ **receptivity** *n.*
**receptor** *n* a cell or group of cells in the body that receives stimuli from the environment, e.g. light, sound, etc, which are then transmitted as nerve impulses.
**recess**[1] *n* **1** an alcove or niche. **2** (*in pl*) hidden, secret, or secluded places. **3** a suspension of business or activity, e.g. of a legislative body or law court, usu for a period of rest.
**recess**[2] *v* to make a recess in (e.g. a wall).
**recession** *n* a period of reduced economic activity and prosperity.
**recessive** *adj* of a gene or inherited characteristic: suppressed if the contrasting dominant gene or characteristic is present.
**recharge** *v* to charge (*esp* a battery) again. ➤ **rechargeable** *adj.*
**recherché** /rə'sheəshay/ *adj* **1** obscure or rare. **2** pretentious or affected.
**recidivist** *n* somebody who relapses, *esp* into criminal behaviour. ➤ **recidivism** *n.*
**recipe** /'resipi/ *n* **1** a list of ingredients and instructions for making a food dish. **2** a procedure likely to result in the specified thing: *a recipe for success.*
**recipient** *n* somebody who receives something.
**reciprocal** *adj* **1** felt or shown by both sides; mutual. **2** given or done in return. ➤ **reciprocally** *adv.*

**reciprocate** *v* to return (a thing, feeling, treatment, etc of the same kind as has been previously given or shown to one). ➤ **reciprocation** *n.*

**reciprocity** *n* a situation in which help, privileges, etc are mutually exchanged.

**recital** *n* **1** a concert given by a musician or a small group of musicians. **2** a detailed account.

**recite** *v* **1** to repeat from memory or read aloud. **2** to relate in detail; to enumerate. ➤ **recitation** *n.*

**reckless** *adj* marked by lack of proper caution; careless of consequences. ➤ **recklessly** *adv,* **recklessness** *n.*

**reckon** *v* **1** to estimate or calculate. **2** to consider or think of in a specified way. **3** *informal* to suppose or think. **4** (+ on) to expect or rely on. ✱ **reckon with** to take into account. **reckon without** to fail to take into account. **to be reckoned with** of considerable power or importance.

**reckoning** *n* **1** the act of calculating or estimating. **2** *archaic* an account or bill. **3** events regarded as retribution for earlier behaviour. ✱ **into/out of the reckoning** included among/omitted from the things or people to be considered.

**reclaim** *v* **1** to get back; to recover. **2** to make (e.g. submerged or waste land) available for human use. **3** to obtain (a useful substance) from a waste product. ➤ **reclamation** *n.*

**recline** *v* **1** to lean backwards. **2** to be in a relaxed position.

**recluse** *n* somebody who deliberately avoids company and leads a solitary life. ➤ **reclusive** *adj.*

**recognition** *n* **1** the act of recognizing. **2** acknowledgment or reward for one's efforts, talents, etc.

**recognize** *or* **-ise** *v* **1** to perceive to be something or somebody previously known or encountered. **2** to acknowledge the status, validity, independence, etc of. **3** to show appreciation of, e.g. by praise or reward. ➤ **recognizable** *adj.*

**recoil**[1] *v* **1** to shrink back physically or emotionally, e.g. in horror, fear, or disgust. **2** of a firearm: to move backwards sharply when fired. **3** (+ on/upon) to have unexpected adverse effects on the doer.

**recoil**[2] *n* the act of recoiling.

**recollect** *v* **1** to remember. **2** to bring (oneself) back to a state of composure or concentration. ➤ **recollection** *n.*

**recommend** *v* **1** to declare to be suitable, competent, etc or worth trying. **2** to advise (a course of action). **3** to make acceptable or desirable: *The school has other things to recommend it.* ➤ **recommendation** *n.*

**recompense**[1] *v* **1** to pay or reward , e.g. for a service rendered. **2** to compensate for damage incurred.

**recompense**[2] *n* a return for something done, suffered, or given.

**reconcile** *v* **1** to restore (e.g. opposing factions) to friendship or harmony. **2** to settle or resolve (e.g. differences of opinion). **3** (+ with) to make (something) consistent or compatible with something else. **4** (+ to) to persuade (somebody) to submit to or accept something.

**reconciliation** *n* **1** a return to friendly relations after conflict. **2** the act of reconciling e.g. differences of opinion or opposing ideas.

**recondite** *adj* known only by a few people; obscure.

**recondition** *v Brit* to restore to good working condition, e.g. by replacing parts.

**reconnaissance** /ri'konəs(ə)ns/ *n* an exploratory military survey of enemy territory or positions.

**reconnoitre** (*NAmer* **reconnoiter**) /rekə'noytə/ *v* (**reconnoitres, reconnoitred, reconnoitring,** *NAmer* **reconnoiters, reconnoitered, reconnoitering**) to make a reconnaissance of (e.g. an enemy position or a region of land).

**reconsider** *v* to consider again, *esp* with a view to changing the original decision. ➤ **reconsideration** *n.*

**reconstitute** *v* **1** to reestablish or thoroughly reorganize. **2** to restore (dried food, etc) to its natural state by adding water. ➤ **reconstitution** *n.*

**reconstruct** *v* **1** to rebuild. **2** to reorganize or reestablish. **3** to build up a mental image of or reenact (e.g. a crime or a battle) on the basis of available evidence. ➤ **reconstruction** *n.*

**record**[1] *v* **1** to commit (something) to writing, film, etc so as to supply evidence of it. **2** to register by mechanical or other means. **3** to indicate (a measurement on a scale). **4** to give evidence of; to show. **5** to convert (e.g. sound) into a permanent form for reproduction.

**record**[2] *n* **1** a permanent account of something that serves as evidence of it. **2** a body of known or recorded facts regarding something or somebody. **3** a list of previous criminal convictions. **4** a performance, occurrence, etc that goes beyond all others of its kind; *esp* the best recorded performance in a competitive sport. **5** a flat plastic disc with a spiral groove encoding musical or other sounds for reproduction. ✱ **for the record** to be reported as official. **off the record** not for publication. **put/set the record straight** to correct a mistake or misapprehension.

**recorder** *n* **1** something that records. **2** a person who keeps official records. **3** a simple woodwind instrument consisting of a tube with usu eight finger holes and a mouthpiece.

**recording** *n* something, e.g. sound or a television programme, that has been recorded.
**record player** *n* an apparatus for playing records.
**recount**[1] *v* to relate in detail.
**recount**[2] *v* to count again.
**recount**[3] *n* a second or fresh counting, *esp* of votes.
**recoup** *v* to regain or make up for (something lost).
**recourse** *n* **1** a source of help or strength. **2** (+ to) the use of somebody or something for help or protection.
**recover** *v* **1** to regain possession or use of. **2** to regain a normal or stable condition, *esp* of health. **3** to make up for (e.g. losses). ➤ **recoverable** *adj.*
**recovery** *n* (*pl* **-ies**) **1** a return to normal health. **2** a regaining of balance or control, e.g. after a stumble or mistake. **3** an economic upturn, e.g. after a depression. **4** the act of recovering something.
**recreate** *v* to reproduce exactly.
**recreation** *n* pleasurable activity engaged in for relaxation or enjoyment. ➤ **recreational** *adj.*
**recrimination** *n* (*usu in pl*) an accusation of wrongdoing made against somebody who has made a similar accusation.
**recrudescence** *n formal* a new outbreak or recurrence.
**recruit**[1] *n* a newcomer to an occupation or activity, *esp* a newly enlisted member of the armed forces.
**recruit**[2] *v* to enlist (a person) as a new member of the armed forces or a workforce. ➤ **recruitment** *n.*
**rectal** *adj* relating to the rectum.
**rectangle** *n* a polygon with four right angles and four sides, *esp* one with adjacent sides of different lengths. ➤ **rectangular** *adj.*
**rectify** *v* (**-ies, -ied**) **1** to put right; to remedy or correct. **2** to convert (alternating current) to direct current. ➤ **rectification** *n.*
**rectilinear** *adj* **1** moving in a straight line. **2** characterized by straight lines.
**rectitude** *n formal* moral integrity.
**recto** *n* (*pl* **-os**) a right-hand page.
**rector** *n* **1** a priest in charge of a parish. **2** the head of a university or college.
**rectory** *n* (*pl* **-ies**) a rector's residence.
**rectum** *n* (*pl* **rectums** *or* **recta**) the last part of the intestine, ending at the anus.
**recumbent** *adj* lying down or reclining.
**recuperate** *v* **1** to regain a former healthy state or condition. **2** to regain (something lost). ➤ **recuperation** *n.*
**recur** *v* (**recurred, recurring**) to occur again, *esp* repeatedly or after an interval. ➤ **recurrence** *n.*
**recurrent** *adj* happening repeatedly or periodically.
**recycle** *v* **1** to convert (sewage, waste paper, glass, etc) back into a useful product. **2** to reuse. ➤ **recyclable** *adj.*
**red**[1] *adj* (**redder, reddest**) **1** of the colour of blood or a ruby. **2** of hair or fur: of a colour between orange and brown. **3** of the face: flushed, *esp* with anger or embarrassment. **4** of wine: made from dark grapes and coloured by their skins. **5** *informal, derog* communist or socialist. ➤ **reddish** *adj.*
**red**[2] *n* **1** a red colour. **2** *informal, derog* a communist or socialist. ✱ **in the red** not in credit; insolvent. **see red** *informal* to become angry suddenly.
**red-blooded** *adj* full of vigour; virile.
**red card** *n* a red card held up by a football referee to indicate the sending-off of a player.
**red carpet** *n* a long piece of red carpet for an important guest to walk on.
**redcurrant** *n* a small red edible berry.
**redden** *v* to make or become red.
**redeem** *v* **1** to offset the bad effect of. **2** to atone for (a mistake, error of judgment, etc). **3** to release from blame or debt. **4** to free from the consequences of sin or evil. **5** to make up for an earlier poor performance or wrongdoing by (oneself). **6** to get or buy back, e.g. by repaying a loan or debt. **7** to convert (trading stamps, tokens, etc) into money or goods. **8** to fulfil (e.g. a promise).
**Redeemer** *n* **1** (**the Redeemer**) Jesus Christ. **2** (**redeemer**) a person who redeems somebody or something.
**redemption** *n* the act of redeeming or the fact of being redeemed.
**redeploy** *v* to transfer (e.g. troops or workers) from one area or activity to another. ➤ **redeployment** *n.*
**red-faced** *adj* flushed with embarrassment.
**red-handed** *adj* in the act of committing a crime or misdeed.
**redhead** *n* a person with red hair.
**red herring** *n* something irrelevant that distracts attention from the real issue.
**red-hot** *adj* **1** glowing red with heat. **2** very intense, exciting, or popular.
**Red Indian** *n dated, offensive* a Native American.
**red-letter day** *n* a day of special significance, *esp* a particularly happy occasion.
**red-light district** *n* a district that has many brothels.
**redneck** *n NAmer, informal, derog* **1** a white rural working-class person from the southern USA. **2** a bigoted reactionary.
**redolent** *adj* **1** (+ of/with) suggestive; evocative. **2** (+ of/with) having a specified smell. ➤ **redolence** *n.*

**redouble** *v* to make or become greater or more intense.
**redoubt** *n* a small usu temporary fortified structure.
**redoubtable** *adj* arousing fear or respect; formidable.
**redound** *v formal* (+ to) to lead or contribute to something.
**redress**[1] *v* **1** to set right. **2** to adjust and make equal again.
**redress**[2] *n* action or payment to compensate for wrong or loss.
**redskin** *n dated, offensive* a Native American.
**red tape** *n* excessively complex bureaucratic routines that result in delay.
**reduce** *v* **1** to make or become less. **2** to lower the price of. **3** (+ to) to bring or force to a specified state or condition. **4** (+ to) to change to a simpler or more basic form. **5** to make more concentrated, e.g. by boiling. ➤ **reducible** *adj.*
**reduction** *n* **1** the act of reducing. **2** the amount by which something is reduced.
**reductive** *adj* expressing complex data or phenomena in simplified or oversimplified terms.
**redundant** *adj* **1** no longer useful or necessary. **2** excessive, *esp* excessively wordy. **3** *chiefly Brit* no longer required for a job. ➤ **redundancy** *n.*
**redwood** *n* a very tall American pine tree with reddish wood.
**reed** *n* **1** a tall grass that grows in wet or marshy areas. **2** a thin piece of cane, metal, or plastic, fastened over an air opening in e.g. an oboe or clarinet, which produces a sound by vibration.
**reedy** *adj* (**-ier, -iest**) **1** full of of reeds. **2** of a voice: thin and high.
**reef**[1] *n* a ridge of rocks, sand, or coral at or near the surface of water.
**reef**[2] *n* a part of a sail taken in or let out to regulate the area exposed to the wind.
**reef**[3] *v* to reduce the area of (a sail) by taking in a portion.
**reefer** *n informal* a cannabis cigarette.
**reefer jacket** *n* a close-fitting double-breasted jacket of thick cloth.
**reef knot** *n* a secure symmetrical knot.
**reek**[1] *v* **1** to have a strong or offensive smell. **2** (+ of/with) to give a strong impression of some undesirable quality or feature.
**reek**[2] *n* a strong or disagreeable smell.
**reel**[1] *n* **1** a spool for thread, film, tape, cable, etc. **2** a quantity of something wound on a reel.
**reel**[2] *v* (+ in) to draw (something) towards one by turning a reel.
**reel**[3] *v* **1** to be giddy or bewildered. **2** to walk or move unsteadily.
**reel**[4] *n* a lively Scottish or Irish dance.
**reel off** *v* to recite or repeat readily and without pause.
**re-entry** *n* (*pl* **-ies**) **1** the return to the earth's atmosphere by a space vehicle. **2** a second or new entry, e.g. to a country.
**refectory** *n* (*pl* **-ies**) a dining hall in an institution, e.g. a monastery or college.
**refer** *v* (**referred, referring**) **1** (+ to) to direct attention to something by mentioning it. **2** (+ to) to describe or relate to. **3** (+ to) to have recourse to something, e.g. for information. **4** (*often* + to) to send (somebody) for treatment, aid, information, etc.
**referee**[1] *n* **1** an official who supervises the play and enforces the rules in a sport, e.g. football or boxing. **2** a person who reviews an academic paper before publication. **3** a person who gives a professional or character reference to a candidate's prospective employer.
**referee**[2] *v* (**referees, refereed, refereeing**) to act as a referee for.
**reference** *n* **1** the act of referring to or consulting something or somebody. **2** bearing on or connection with a matter. **3** an allusion or mention. **4** a source of information to which somebody is referred. **5** a statement of the character, ability, or qualifications of a person seeking employment. **6** a standard for measuring, evaluating, etc.
**referendum** *n* (*pl* **referendums** *or* **referenda**) a vote by the whole electorate on a single question or measure.
**referral** *n* the act of referring somebody to another person, *esp* a medical specialist.
**refine** *v* **1** to free (a raw material) from impurities. **2** to improve or perfect (e.g. a method) by making small adjustments.
**refined** *adj* **1** without crudeness or vulgarity; elegant or cultivated. **2** subtle and sophisticated. **3** processed industrially to remove impurities.
**refinement** *n* **1** the act of refining or the state of being refined. **2** a subtle feature or improvement.
**refinery** *n* (*pl* **-ies**) a plant where raw materials, e.g. oil or sugar, are refined.
**refit**[1] *v* (**refitted, refitting**) to fit out (e.g. a ship) again with new fixtures and equipment.
**refit**[2] *n* a repair or replacement of parts, fittings, etc.
**reflect** *v* **1** to send (light, sound, etc) back from a surface. **2** to show the image or likeness of. **3** to make manifest or apparent. **4** (*often* + on) to think quietly and calmly. **5** (+ on) to give people a specified impression of something: *The results reflect unfavourably on the department.*
**reflection** *n* **1** the reflecting of light, sound, etc. **2** an image given back by a reflecting surface. **3** an effect produced by a particular state of affairs. **4** (*usu* + on) an indirect criticism. **5** thought or consideration.
**reflective** *adj* **1** capable of reflecting light, etc. **2** thoughtful. ➤ **reflectively** *adv.*
**reflector** *n* something intended to reflect light, etc.

**reflex**[1] *n* an action that takes place automatically in response to a stimulus and involves no conscious thought.
**reflex**[2] *adj* **1** produced without intervention of consciousness. **2** of an angle: greater than 180° but less than 360°.
**reflexive** *adj* referring back to the subject of a clause or sentence, e.g. *herself* in *she blames herself*.
**reflexology** *n* a therapy that involves massaging nerve endings in the feet to relieve tension or to treat disorders. ➤ **reflexologist** *n.*
**refocus** *v* (**refocused** *or* **refocussed, refocusing** *or* **refocussing**) **1** to focus (a lens or the eyes) again. **2** to change the emphasis or direction of.
**reform**[1] *v* **1** to change for the better. **2** to cause (somebody) to adopt a more virtuous, healthier, etc way of life.
**reform**[2] *n* the act of reforming.
**reformation** *n* **1** the act of reforming. **2** (**the Reformation**) a 16th-century religious movement marked ultimately by the rejection of papal authority and the establishment of the Protestant Churches.
**reformism** *n* a doctrine, policy, or movement of reform. ➤ **reformist** *n and adj.*
**refract** *v* to deflect (e.g. light) from a straight path when it enters another medium at an angle.
**refractory** *adj* **1** *formal* resisting control or authority. **2** resistant to treatment or cure.
**refrain**[1] *v* (+ from) to keep oneself from doing, feeling, or indulging in something.
**refrain**[2] *n* a regularly recurring phrase, *esp* at the end of each verse of a poem or song.
**refresh** *v* **1** to restore strength, vigour, or freshness to. **2** to arouse or stimulate (e.g. the memory). **3** in computing, to update the data in (a file, web page, etc).
**refresher** *n* a course of instruction designed to keep one abreast of developments in one's field.
**refreshing** *adj* **1** cooling and restorative. **2** agreeably stimulating because of freshness or newness. ➤ **refreshingly** *adv.*
**refreshment** *n* **1** the act of refreshing. **2** something, e.g. food or drink, that refreshes. **3** (*in pl*) assorted food and drink, *esp* for a light snack.
**refrigerant** *n* a substance used in refrigeration.
**refrigerate** *v* to make or keep cold or cool, *esp* to freeze or chill (e.g. food) for preservation. ➤ **refrigeration** *n.*
**refrigerator** *n* an insulated appliance for keeping food, drink, etc cool.
**refuel** *v* (**refuelled, refuelling,** *NAmer* **refueled, refueling**) to provide with or take on additional fuel.
**refuge** *n* **1** a place that provides protection. **2** a person, thing, or course of action that is resorted to in difficulties.
**refugee** *n* somebody who flees to a foreign country to escape danger or persecution.
**refund**[1] *v* **1** to return (money) to somebody. **2** to pay (somebody) back. ➤ **refundable** *adj.*
**refund**[2] *n* **1** the act of refunding. **2** a sum refunded.
**refurbish** *v* to repair, redecorate, and usu re-equip (e.g. a house). ➤ **refurbishment** *n.*
**refuse**[1] *v* **1** to show unwillingness to accept or do (something). **2** to be unwilling to allow or grant (something) to (somebody).
**refuse**[2] *n* rubbish.
**refusenik** *n* **1** formerly, a Soviet Jew who was refused permission to emigrate, *esp* to Israel. **2** somebody who refuses to accept a situation or proposal.
**refute** *v* to prove wrong by argument or evidence. ➤ **refutation** *n.*

***Usage Note:*** To *refute* statements, accusations, or people is to prove them wrong, not merely to assert that they are wrong.

**regain** *v* **1** to recover possession of. **2** to reach (a place) again.
**regal** *adj* **1** of a king or queen. **2** stately or splendid. ➤ **regally** *adv.*
**regale** *v* **1** to entertain sumptuously. **2** to give pleasure or amusement to.
**regalia** *pl n* **1** the ceremonial emblems of royalty. **2** special dress, *esp* official finery.
**regard**[1] *n* **1** attention or consideration. **2** a protective interest; care. **3** esteem. **4** (*in pl*) friendly greetings. **5** an aspect or respect: *We were fortunate in that regard.* **6** a gaze or look. ✱ **in/with regard to** concerning.
**regard**[2] *v* **1** (*usu* + as/with) to think of or feel about in a specified way. **2** to look steadily at. ✱ **as regards** in so far as it concerns.
**regarding** *prep* about; on the subject of.
**regardless**[1] *adj* (+ of) heedless or careless.
**regardless**[2] *adv* despite everything.
**regatta** *n* a sports event consisting of a series of boat races.
**regency** *n* (*pl* **-ies**) **1** the period of rule of a regent. **2** (**Regency**) the period (1811–1820) when George, Prince of Wales (later George IV) was regent of Great Britain.
**regenerate** *v* **1** to replace (a body part or tissue) by new growth. **2** to change radically and for the better. ➤ **regeneration** *n.*
**regent** *n* somebody who governs a kingdom in the minority, absence, or disability of the sovereign.
**reggae** /'regay/ *n* popular music of West Indian origin, combining elements of rock, soul, and calypso.
**regicide** *n* **1** the act of murdering a king. **2** a person who commits regicide.

**regime** /ray'zheem/ *n* **1** a form of management or government. **2** a government in power. **3** = REGIMEN.

**regimen** *n* a systematic plan, e.g. of diet, exercise, or medical treatment.

**regiment**[1] *n* **1** a permanent military unit. **2** a large number or group. ➤ **regimental** *adj.*

**regiment**[2] *v* to subject (people or things) to strict organization or control. ➤ **regimentation** *n,* **regimented** *adj.*

**Regina** /ri'jienə/ *n* **1** a title given to a reigning queen. **2** used in legal cases, when the British monarch is a queen, to denote the Crown as a party to the action.

**region** *n* **1** an indefinite area of the world or universe. **2** a broadly uniform geographical or ecological area. **3** an administrative area. **4** an indefinite area surrounding a specified body part. * **in the region of** approximately. ➤ **regional** *adj,* **regionally** *adv.*

**register**[1] *n* **1** an official written record of items, names, transactions, etc. **2** a part of the range of a human voice or musical instrument. **3** the language style and vocabulary appropriate to particular circumstances.

**register**[2] *v* **1** to enter (information) officially in a register. **2** to put one's name in a register. **3** to record automatically; to indicate. **4** to show (an emotion) through facial expression or body language. **5** to become aware of. **6** to make or convey an impression.

**register office** *n Brit* a place where births, marriages, and deaths are recorded and civil marriages are conducted.

**registrar** *n* **1** an official keeper of records. **2** a senior administrative officer of a university. **3** *Brit* a senior hospital doctor ranking below a consultant.

**registration** *n* **1** the act of registering. **2** (*also* **registration number**) the identifying set of letters and numbers on a vehicle's number-plate.

**registry** *n* (*pl* **-ies**) **1** a place where registers are kept. **2** registration.

**registry office** *n* = REGISTER OFFICE.

**regress** *v* to revert to an earlier or less advanced state. ➤ **regression** *n.*

**regressive** *adj* **1** characterized by regression. **2** of a tax: decreasing in rate as the amount taxed increases.

**regret**[1] *v* (**regretted, regretting**) to be very sorry about.

**regret**[2] *n* **1** grief or sorrow tinged with disappointment, longing, or remorse. **2** (*in pl*) a conventional expression of disappointment or apology. ➤ **regretful** *n.*

**regrettable** *adj* not as one would wish; unwelcome.

**regular**[1] *adj* **1** done or recurring at fixed or uniform intervals. **2** following or arranged according to a discernible pattern. **3** steady or uniform in practice or occurrence; habitual, usual, or constant. **4** done in conformity with established or prescribed usages, rules, etc. **5** in grammar, of a word, *esp* a verb: conforming to the normal pattern of inflection. **6** of a polygon: having sides of equal length and angles of equal size. **7** belonging to a permanent standing army. ➤ **regularity** *n,* **regularly** *adv.*

**regular**[2] *n* somebody who is usu present or participating, *esp* a habitual customer.

**regularize** *or* **-ise** *v* to make regular. ➤ **regularization** *n.*

**regulate** *v* **1** to control or direct according to rules. **2** to fix or adjust the amount, degree, or rate of. ➤ **regulator** *n,* **regulatory** *adj.*

**regulation**[1] *n* **1** the act of regulating. **2** an authoritative rule dealing with details or procedure.

**regulation**[2] *adj* **1** official. **2** *informal* standard; usual.

**regurgitate** *v* **1** to bring (incompletely digested food) back from the stomach to the mouth. **2** to reproduce (information) with little or no alteration. ➤ **regurgitation** *n.*

**rehabilitate** *v* **1** to restore to a condition of health or useful activity, e.g. after illness or imprisonment. **2** to reestablish the good name of. ➤ **rehabilitation** *n.*

**rehash**[1] *v* to present or use again without substantial change or improvement.

**rehash**[2] *n* something rehashed.

**rehearsal** *n* a practice session, *esp* of a play, concert, etc preparatory to a public performance.

**rehearse** *v* **1** to hold a rehearsal of (a play, piece of music, etc). **2** to recount or repeat (something) in order, *esp* tediously.

**rehydrate** *v* to restore fluid to (something dehydrated).

**Reich** /riekh/ *n* the German empire.

**reign**[1] *n* the time during which somebody or something reigns.

**reign**[2] *v* **1** to exercise sovereign power; to rule. **2** to be predominant or prevalent. **3** to be the current holder of a trophy or title: *the reigning champion.*

**reimburse** *v* to pay back (money) to (somebody). ➤ **reimbursement** *n.*

**rein**[1] *n* **1** (*usu in pl*) a long strap by which a rider or driver controls an animal. **2** (*in pl*) controlling or guiding power. * **give free rein to** to allow to proceed or function freely.

**rein**[2] *v* **1** (*often* + in) to check or stop (a horse) by pulling on the reins. **2** (*often* + in) to restrain or stop.

**reincarnate** *v* (**be reincarnated**) to be reborn in another body after death. ➤ **reincarnation** *n.*

**reindeer** *n* (*pl* **reindeers** *or* **reindeer**) a deer with large antlers that inhabits cold northern regions.

**reinforce** *v* **1** to strengthen with additional material or support. **2** to strengthen (e.g. an army) with additional forces.

**reinforcement** *n* **1** the act of reinforcing. **2** (*in pl*) additional military personnel sent to strengthen an existing force.

**reinstate** *v* to restore to a former position or status. ➤ **reinstatement** *n.*

**reiterate** *v* to say or do again or repeatedly. ➤ **reiteration** *n.*

**reject**[1] *v* **1** to refuse to accept, consider, or submit to. **2** to refuse love or care to (somebody). **3** to fail to accept (e.g. a skin graft or transplanted organ). ➤ **rejection** *n.*

**reject**[2] *n* a rejected person or thing.

**rejig** *v* (**rejigged, rejigging**) to rearrange or reorganize.

**rejoice** *v* **1** to feel or express joy or great delight. **2** (+ in) to have or enjoy (something noteworthy).

**rejoin**[1] *v* to say in response, *esp* in a sharp or critical way.

**rejoin**[2] *v* **1** to return to. **2** to join (two things) together again.

**rejoinder** *n* a reply, *esp* a sharp or critical answer.

**rejuvenate** *v* **1** to make young or youthful again. **2** to restore to a more vigorous state. ➤ **rejuvenation** *n.*

**rekindle** *v* **1** to arouse (e.g. an emotion) again. **2** to light (a fire) again.

**relapse**[1] *n* a recurrence of symptoms of a disease after a period of improvement.

**relapse**[2] *v* to slip or fall back into a former worse state.

**relate** *v* **1** to give an account of. **2** to show a logical or causal connection between (two or more things). **3** (*often* + to) to have reference or connection. **4** (+ to) to sympathize with or respond to. **5** (**be related to**) to have a relationship by blood or marriage with.

**relation** *n* **1** a person connected by blood, marriage, or adoption. **2** relationship by blood, marriage, or adoption. **3** (*in pl*) the attitude or behaviour which people or groups show towards one another. **4** *euphem* (*in pl*) sexual intercourse. **5** an aspect or quality that connects two or more things. ✱ **in/with relation to** with regard to; concerning.

**relationship** *n* **1** the way in which people or things are related. **2** the relations or dealings that exist between people, groups, organizations, etc. **3** a close friendship or love affair.

**relative**[1] *n* = RELATION (1).

**relative**[2] *adj* **1** considered in comparison with something else; not absolute. **2** existing only in connection with, or measurable only by reference to, something else. **3** of a pronoun, adverb, etc: introducing a subordinate clause qualifying a preceding word. **4** of a clause: introduced in this way. ✱ **relative to** with regard to.

**relatively** *adv* **1** in comparison with other things. **2** quite; fairly.

**relativism** *n* a theory that knowledge and moral principles are relative and have no objective standard. ➤ **relativist** *n.*

**relativity** *n* **1** the state of being dependent on or determined by a relation to something else. **2** in physics: a theory, formulated by Albert Einstein, that asserts that mass, dimension, and time will change with increased velocity.

**relax** *v* **1** to make or become less tense or rigid. **2** to refrain from work or rest and enjoy leisure. **3** to make (e.g. a rule) less severe or stringent. ➤ **relaxation** *n.*

**relay**[1] *n* **1** a number of people or animals that relieve others in some work. **2** a race between teams in which each team member covers a set portion of the course and then is replaced by another. **3** a device set in operation by variation in an electric circuit and operating other devices in turn. **4** a device that receives and retransmits a signal.

**relay**[2] *v* **1** to pass (e.g. information) along by relay. **2** to broadcast (a radio or television signal) by means of a relay.

**release**[1] *v* **1** to set free from restraint or confinement. **2** to free from an obligation or responsibility. **3** to give permission for the publication, performance, or sale of. **4** to publish or issue. **5** to move (e.g. a handle or catch) in order to allow a mechanism free movement.

**release**[2] *n* **1** the act of releasing. **2** relief from sorrow, suffering, or trouble. **3** a newly issued film, CD, etc.

**relegate** *v* **1** to remove to an inferior or insignificant status. **2** *Brit* to demote (a team) to a lower division of a sporting competition. ➤ **relegation** *n.*

**relent** *v* **1** to become less severe, harsh, or strict. **2** to become less intense or violent.

**relentless** *adj* **1** of a person: showing no sign of stopping or becoming less determined. **2** remaining constant at the same demanding level. ➤ **relentlessly** *adv.*

**relevant** *adj* having a significant bearing on the matter at hand. ➤ **relevance** *n.*

**reliable** *adj* able to be relied on. ➤ **reliability** *n,* **reliably** *adv.*

**reliance** *n* the act of relying; dependence or trust. ➤ **reliant** *adj.*

**relic** *n* **1** an object left behind after something has decayed or disappeared. **2** an outmoded custom, belief, or practice. **3** an object, e.g. part of the body of a saint, preserved as an object of religious reverence.

**relief** *n* **1** the removal or lightening of something oppressive, painful, or distressing. **2** a feeling of happiness or comfort brought about by the removal of a burden. **3** a means of breaking monotony or boredom. **4** aid in the form of money or necessities. **5** somebody who takes over from somebody else who has been on duty. **6** the liberation of a besieged city, castle, etc. **7** a method of sculpture in which forms stand out from a flat surface.

**relief map** *n* a map showing the differences in height of a land surface by shading, etc.

**relieve** *v* **1** (*often* + of) to free from a burden, obligation, or restriction. **2** to remove or alleviate (e.g. pain). **3** (**be relieved**) to stop feeling anxious or distressed. **4** to release (somebody) from a post or duty by taking their place. **5** to lessen the monotony of. * **relieve oneself** to urinate or defecate.

***Usage Note:*** Note the spelling with *-ie-*.

**religion** *n* **1** the organized belief in and worship of a god or gods. **2** a particular system of religious beliefs.

**religious** *adj* **1** relating to religion. **2** pious or devout. **3** scrupulously and conscientiously faithful. ➤ **religiously** *adv.*

**relinquish** *v* to renounce or abandon; to give up. ➤ **relinquishment** *n.*

**reliquary** *n* (*pl* **-ies**) a container in which sacred relics are kept.

**relish**[1] *n* **1** enjoyment of or delight in something. **2** a highly seasoned sauce, e.g. of pickles or mustard, eaten with plainer food.

**relish**[2] *v* **1** to enjoy greatly. **2** to anticipate with pleasure.

**relive** *v* to experience again in the imagination.

**reload** *v* to load (*esp* a firearm) again.

**relocate** *v* to establish one's home or business in a new place. ➤ **relocation** *n.*

**reluctant** *adj* not eager to do something; unwilling. ➤ **reluctance** *n,* **reluctantly** *adv.*

**rely** *v* (**-ies, -ied**) **1** (+ on/upon) to have confidence in; to trust. **2** (+ on/upon) to be dependent.

**remain** *v* **1** to stay in the same place. **2** to continue to be. **3** to survive unchanged. **4** to be left over.

**remainder** *n* **1** a group, part, number, etc that is left over or yet to appear. **2** the final undivided part left after division.

**remains** *pl n* **1** a remaining part or trace. **2** a dead body.

**remand**[1] *v* to place (a defendant or prisoner) in custody or on bail until they appear again in court.

**remand**[2] *n* * **on remand** in custody awaiting trial.

**remark**[1] *v* **1** to express as an observation or comment. **2** *formal* to notice.

**remark**[2] *n* an expression of an opinion or judgment.

**remarkable** *adj* striking or extraordinary. ➤ **remarkably** *adv.*

**rematch** *n* a second match between the same contestants or teams.

**remedial** *adj* **1** intended as a remedy. **2** designed to help people with learning difficulties.

**remedy**[1] *n* (*pl* **-ies**) **1** a medicine or treatment that relieves or cures a disease. **2** something that counteracts an evil or deficiency.

**remedy**[2] *v* (**-ies, -ied**) to provide or serve as a remedy for.

**remember** *v* **1** to bring to mind or think of again. **2** to retain in the memory. **3** to not forget or fail to do something. **4** to convey greetings from (somebody) to somebody.

**remembrance** *n* **1** the act of remembering. **2** an important memory. **3** a commemoration.

**remind** *v* **1** to cause (somebody) to remember something. **2** (+ of) to appear to (somebody) to be like somebody or something else.

**reminder** *n* a thing that helps somebody to remember something.

**reminisce** *v* to talk or write about events or people from one's past.

**reminiscence** *n* **1** the process of reminiscing. **2** (*usu in pl*) an account of a memorable experience.

**reminiscent** *adj* tending to remind one of something seen or known before.

**remiss** *adj* negligent in the performance of work or duty.

**remission** *n* **1** the act of remitting. **2** a period during which something, e.g. a disease, is remitted. **3** *Brit* reduction of a prison sentence.

**remit**[1] *v* (**remitted, remitting**) **1** to refrain from inflicting or exacting (e.g. a debt or punishment). **2** to pardon (a sin). **3** to send (money) in payment. **4** to refer (something) for consideration or judgment.

**remit**[2] *n* the area of responsibility or concern assigned to a person or organization.

**remittance** *n* **1** a sum of money remitted. **2** the act of remitting money.

**remix**[1] *v* to change the balance of sounds of (a recording).

**remix**[2] *n* a remixed recording.

**remnant** *n* a usu small part or trace remaining.

**remonstrate** *v* (*usu* + with) to make one's objections or opposition to somebody's conduct, opinions, etc known forcefully. ➤ **remonstration** *n.*

**remorse** *n* deep distress arising from a sense of guilt for past wrongdoing. ➤ **remorseful** *adj,* **remorsefully** *adv.*

**remorseless** *adj* **1** having no remorse; merciless. **2** continuing without letup. ➤ **remorselessly** *adv.*

**remote** *adj* **1** far removed in space or time. **2** situated far away from the main centres of activity or population. **3** not belonging to one's close family. **4** controlling something, or being controlled, from a distance, *esp* by an infrared or radio signal. **5** small in degree; slight. **6** distant in manner; aloof. ➤ **remotely** *adv,* **remoteness** *n.*

**remote control** *n* **1** control over e.g. a machine or weapon exercised from a distance, usu by means of an electrical circuit or radio waves. **2** a device by which this is carried out. ➤ **remote-controlled** *adj.*

**removal** *n* **1** the act of removing. **2** *Brit* the moving of household goods from one residence to another.

**remove**[1] *v* **1** to move by lifting, pushing aside, or taking away or off. **2** to get rid of. **3** to dismiss from office. ➤ **removable** *adj,* **remover** *n.*

**remove**[2] *n* a degree or stage of separation.

**removed** *adj* **1** separated by a specified degree of relationship: *my first cousin once removed.* **2** very different in character.

**remunerate** *v* to pay (somebody) for work done. ➤ **remuneration** *n.*

**remunerative** *adj* profitable or well-paid.

**renaissance** *n* **1** (**Renaissance**) the revival of classical influence in Europe from the 14th to the 17th century. **2** a rebirth or revival.

**renal** *adj* relating to or in the region of the kidneys.

**rename** *v* to give a different name to.

**renascence** *n* a rebirth or revival.

**rend** *v* (*past tense and past part.* **rent**) **1** to pull or tear apart or in pieces. **2** to cause mental or emotional pain to.

**render** *v* **1** to cause to be or become. **2** to submit (e.g. an opinion) for consideration, approval, etc. **3** to do (a service) for or give (assistance) to somebody. **4** to reproduce by artistic or verbal means. **5** to give a performance of (e.g. a piece of music). **6** to translate. **7** to melt down (fat). **8** to apply a coat of plaster or cement directly to (brickwork, stone, etc). ➤ **rendering** *n.*

**rendezvous**[1] /'rondayvooh/ *n* (*pl* **rendezvous** /-vooh/) **1** a meeting at an appointed place and time. **2** a place appointed for meeting.

**rendezvous**[2] *v* (**rendezvouses** /-voohz/, **rendezvoused** /-voohd/, **rendezvousing** /-vooh·ing/) to come together at a rendezvous.

**rendition** *n* a performance or interpretation.

**renegade** *n* a deserter from one faith, cause, or allegiance to another.

**renege** *v* (+ on) to go back on a commitment.

**renew** *v* **1** to begin (something) again. **2** to restore to freshness, vigour, or perfection. **3** to grant or obtain an extension of (e.g. a subscription or licence). **4** to replace or replenish. ➤ **renewal** *n.*

**rennet** *n* a preparation containing an extract from the stomach lining of a young calf, used in cheese-making.

**renounce** *v* **1** to state, usu by formal declaration, that one is giving up (something that one formerly possessed, believed, practised, etc). **2** to break off, usu formally, one's connection with or allegiance to (somebody).

**renovate** *v* to restore to a better state, e.g. by cleaning, repairing, or rebuilding. ➤ **renovation** *n.*

**renown** *n* the state of being widely known and admired; fame.

**renowned** *adj* celebrated or famous.

**rent**[1] *n* **1** a periodical payment made by a tenant of property to the owner. **2** a similar payment for the use of goods, equipment, etc.

**rent**[2] *v* **1** to take and use (e.g. property or equipment) under an agreement to pay rent. **2** to grant the use of (e.g. property or equipment) for rent.

**rent**[3] *n* a split or tear.

**rent**[4] *v* past tense and past part. of REND.

**rental** *n* **1** an amount paid or collected as rent. **2** the act of renting.

**rent boy** *n Brit, informal* a young male prostitute.

**renunciation** *n* the act of renouncing.

**reorganize** *or* **-ise** *v* to organize again or in a different way. ➤ **reorganization** *n.*

**rep**[1] *n informal* a sales representative.

**rep**[2] *n informal* a repertory theatre or company.

**repaid** *v* past tense and past part. of REPAY.

**repair**[1] *v* to restore (something damaged or worn) to a sound or working condition. ➤ **repairable** *adj,* **repairer** *n.*

**repair**[2] *n* **1** the act of repairing. **2** an instance or result of repairing. **3** the condition of something with respect to its soundness or need of repair: *in good repair.*

**repair**[3] *v formal* to go.

**reparable** *adj* capable of being repaired.

**reparation** *n* **1** the act of making amends for a wrong or injury. **2** (*usu in pl*) compensation payable by a defeated nation for war damages.

**repartee** *n* the exchange of amusing and witty remarks.

**repast** *n formal* a meal.

**repatriate** *v* to send (somebody or something) back to their country of origin. ➤ **repatriation** *n.*

**repay** *v* (*past tense and past part.* **repaid**) **1** to pay back. **2** to do something in return for (a previous kindness or injury). **3** to reward or be worthy of (e.g. investigation). ➤ **repayment** *n.*

**repeal**[1] *v* to revoke (a law).

**repeal**[2] *n* the act of repealing.

**repeat**[1] *v* **1** to say or state again. **2** to make, do, experience, etc again. **3** to express (oneself) again in the same words. **4** to present (itself) again in the same form. ➤ **repeated** *adj,* **repeatedly** *adv.*

**repeat**[2] *n* **1** the act of repeating. **2** something repeated, e.g. a television or radio programme that has previously been broadcast at least once.

**repel** *v* (**repelled, repelling**) **1** to drive back or away. **2** to disgust. **3** to be incapable of sticking to, mixing with, etc. **4** of a magnetic pole: to tend to force (e.g. another magnet) away.

**repellent**[1] *or* **repellant** *adj* **1** serving to repel something. **2** repulsive. ➤ **repellently** *adv.*

**repellent**[2] *or* **repellant** *n* something that repels, e.g. a substance used to prevent insect attacks.

**repent** *v* to feel regret or contrition. ➤ **repentance** *n,* **repentant** *adj.*

**repercussion** *n* a widespread, indirect, or unforeseen effect of an action or event.

**repertoire** *n* **1** a list of works or parts that a company or person is prepared to perform. **2** a range of skills, techniques, etc.

**repertory** *n* (*pl* **-ies**) **1** the presentation of several different plays, in alternation or for short periods, in one season at a theatre. **2** = REPERTOIRE.

**repetition** *n* **1** the act of repeating. **2** a repeat or copy.

**repetitious** *adj* characterized by *esp* tedious repetition. ➤ **repetitiously** *adv.*

**repetitive** *adj* **1** done, uttered, etc repeatedly. **2** = REPETITIOUS. ➤ **repetitively** *adv.*

**rephrase** *v* to put in different words.

**repine** *v formal or literary* to feel dejection or discontent.

**replace** *v* **1** to restore to a former place or position. **2** to take the place of. **3** (*often* + with) to put something new in the place of (something). ➤ **replaceable** *adj.*

**replacement** *n* **1** the process of replacing or being replaced. **2** something or somebody that replaces something or somebody else.

**replay**[1] *v* to play (something) again.

**replay**[2] *n* **1** the act of replaying. **2** the playing of a tape, e.g. a videotape. **3** a repetition or reenactment. **4** a match played to resolve a tie in an earlier match.

**replenish** *v* to stock or fill up again. ➤ **replenishment** *n.*

**replete** *adj* **1** (+ with) abundantly provided or filled. **2** full with food. ➤ **repletion** *n.*

**replica** *n* an accurate reproduction, copy, or model.

**replicate** *v* **1** to duplicate or repeat. **2** to make an exact copy of. ➤ **replication** *n.*

**reply**[1] *v* (**-ies, -ied**) **1** to respond in words or writing. **2** to do something in response.

**reply**[2] *n* (*pl* **-ies**) something said, written, or done in answer.

**report**[1] *n* **1** a usu detailed account or statement. **2** *Brit* a statement of a pupil's performance at school. **3** a loud explosive noise.

**report**[2] *v* **1** (*often* + on) to make or submit a report. **2** (*often* + on) to give news of or information about. **3** to make a formal complaint about, *esp* to the authorities. **4** to present oneself, *esp* on arrival somewhere. **5** *chiefly Brit* ( + to) to be responsible to somebody superior.

**reportage** *n* writing intended to give a usu factual account of events.

**reporter** *n* a journalist who reports news for the press, radio, or television.

**repose**[1] *n* the state of resting after exertion or strain.

**repose**[2] *v* **1** to lie resting. **2** *formal* (+ in) to place (e.g. confidence or trust) in someone or something.

**repository** *n* (*pl* **-ies**) **1** a place or container where something is stored. **2** somebody or something that contains something, e.g. knowledge or secrets, *esp* in large quantities.

**repossess** *v* to resume possession of (goods) when the due payments are not made. ➤ **repossession** *n.*

**reprehensible** *adj* deserving censure; culpable.

**represent** *v* **1** to act for or in the place of. **2** to serve as the elected member of a legislative body for (a particular constituency or electorate). **3** to serve as a specimen, example, or instance of. **4** to serve as a sign or symbol of. **5** to have the nature or effect of; to constitute. **6** to portray in art. **7** to attribute a specified character or identity to, *esp* falsely.

**representation** *n* **1** a likeness or image. **2** the act of representing. **3** (*in pl*) statements made to influence opinion or express a protest.

**representational** *adj* **1** relating to representation. **2** in the graphic or plastic arts, involving realistic depiction of physical objects or appearances.

**representative**[1] *adj* **1** serving as a typical or characteristic example. **2** containing typical examples. **3** acting on behalf of somebody else. **4** based on representation of the people in government or lawmaking. **5** serving to represent.

**representative**[2] *n* **1** somebody who represents another person or a group; an agent or delegate. **2** somebody who represents a business organization, *esp* a sales representative. **3** a typical example of a group, class, or quality.

**repress** *v* **1** to subdue by force. **2** to prevent the natural or normal expression of (e.g. an emotion). **3** to prevent the normal activity or development of. ➤ **repressed** *adj,* **repression** *n.*

**repressive** *adj* unjustly or unduly restricting people's freedom.

**reprieve**[1] *v* **1** to delay or cancel the punishment of (e.g. a condemned prisoner). **2** to remove the threat of an unpleasant fate, e.g. demolition, closure, etc, from.

**reprieve**[2] *n* **1** a suspension or cancellation of a punishment. **2** a temporary removal of a threat.

**reprimand**[1] *n* a formal expression of disapproval.

**reprimand**[2] *v* to criticize formally, usu from a position of authority.

**reprint**[1] *n* **1** the act of reprinting (e.g. a book). **2** a reprinted copy of something.

**reprint**[2] *v* to print again.

**reprisal** *n* a retaliatory act.

**reproach**[1] *v* to express disappointment and displeasure with (somebody) for blameworthy conduct.

**reproach**[2] *n* an expression of rebuke or disapproval. ➤ **reproachful** *adj*, **reproachfully** *adv*.

**reprobate**[1] *n* somebody who is morally dissolute or unprincipled.

**reprobate**[2] *adj* morally dissolute; unprincipled.

**reproduce** *v* **1** to repeat, copy, or emulate. **2** to make an image or copy of. **3** to produce offspring.

**reproduction** *n* **1** the sexual or asexual process by which plants and animals give rise to offspring. **2** a copy, *esp* of a work of art. ➤ **reproductive** *adj*.

**reproof** *n* criticism for a fault.

**reprove** *v* to express disapproval of. ➤ **reproving** *adj*.

**reptile** *n* a cold-blooded vertebrate of a class that includes crocodiles, lizards, snakes, turtles, and extinct related forms, e.g. dinosaurs. ➤ **reptilian** *adj*.

**republic** *n* a state whose head is not a monarch and in which supreme power resides in the people and is exercised by their elected representatives.

**republican**[1] *adj* **1** relating to or belonging to a republic. **2** advocating a republic. **3** (**Republican**) denoting a political party in the USA favouring a restricted governmental role in social and economic life. ➤ **republicanism** *n*.

**republican**[2] *n* **1** somebody who favours republican government. **2** (**Republican**) a member of the US Republican party. **3** (**Republican**) a supporter of the union of Northern Ireland with the Irish Republic.

**repudiate** *v* **1** to refuse to have anything to do with; to disown. **2** to reject as unauthorized or invalid or as untrue or unjust. ➤ **repudiation** *n*.

**repugnance** *n* strong dislike or antipathy; disgust.

**repugnant** *adj* arousing strong dislike.

**repulse**[1] *v* **1** to drive (attackers) back. **2** to reject or rebuff. **3** to cause repulsion in.

**repulse**[2] *n* the act of repelling.

**repulsion** *n* **1** a feeling of strong aversion. **2** in physics, a force, e.g. between like magnetic poles, tending to produce separation.

**repulsive** *adj* arousing strong aversion or disgust. ➤ **repulsively** *adv*.

**reputable** *adj* held in good repute; well regarded.

**reputation** *n* overall quality or character as seen or judged by others.

**repute**[1] *n* **1** the character or status commonly ascribed to somebody or something. **2** the state of being favourably known or spoken of.

**repute**[2] *v* (*usu* **be reputed**) to be believed or considered to be as specified.

**request**[1] *n* **1** an instance of asking for something, *esp* politely or formally. **2** something asked for.

**request**[2] *v* **1** to make a request to (somebody). **2** to ask for (something), *esp* politely or formally.

**requiem** *n* **1** a mass for the dead. **2** (*often* **Requiem**) a musical setting of the mass for the dead.

**require** *v* **1** to have to have (something) because it is necessary or essential. **2** to call for as suitable or appropriate. **3** to impose an obligation on.

**requirement** *n* **1** something wanted or needed. **2** a necessary precondition for something.

**requisite**[1] *adj* necessary or required.

**requisite**[2] *n* **1** something that is required or necessary. **2** an article of the specified sort.

**requisition**[1] *n* **1** the act of compulsorily taking over goods or property for official use. **2** an authoritative written demand or application.

**requisition**[2] *v* to demand the use or supply of officially.

**rerun** *v* (**rerunning,** *past tense* **reran,** *past part.* **rerun**) **1** to run (something, e.g. a race) again. **2** to show (e.g. a film or television programme) again. ➤ **rerun** *n*.

**resat** *v* past tense and past part. of RESIT.

**reschedule** *v* **1** to change the time that (an event) is to take place. **2** to set a new timetable for the repayment of (a debt).

**rescind** *v* to cancel (e.g. an order).

**rescue**[1] *v* to free from confinement, danger, or difficulty; to save. ➤ **rescuer** *n*.

**rescue**[2] *n* the act of rescuing somebody or something.

**research**[1] *n* study, investigations, experiments, etc aimed at making discoveries, establishing facts, or enabling new conclusions.

**research**[2] *v* to engage in research on (a subject) or for (e.g. a book or television programme). ➤ **researcher** *n*.

**resemblance** *n* **1** the state of resembling somebody or something else. **2** a point on which two people or things are similar.

**resemble** *v* to be similar to, *esp* in appearance.

**resent** *v* to harbour or express ill will at (something considered wrong or unfair). ➤ **resentful** *adj*, **resentfully** *adv*.

**resentment** *n* a feeling of bitterness caused by something considered wrong or unfair.

**reservation** *n* **1** the act of reserving something, e.g. a seat or hotel room, or a record of this. **2** (*usu in pl*) a doubt or objection with regard to something. **3** an area of land set aside, *esp* one designated for the use of Native Americans.

**reserve**[1] *v* **1** to retain for future use. **2** to arrange that (a seat, hotel room, etc) be kept for one's own or another's use at a specified future time. **3** to hold over (*esp* a judgment) until later. **4** to retain (e.g. a right).

**reserve**[2] *n* **1** a supply of something retained for future use or need. **2** *chiefly Brit* an area of land set apart for the conservation of natural resources or rare plants and animals. **3** = RESERVATION 3. **4** caution or lack of openness in one's words and actions; reticence. **5** a qualification or doubt. **6** (*usu in pl*) a military force available as a support for regular forces when needed. **7** in sport, a player who has been selected to substitute for another if the need should arise. **8** (**the reserves**) a team made up of players who do not currently form part of the first team. **9** (*also in pl*) money, gold, foreign exchange, etc kept in hand usu to meet liabilities. * **in reserve** held back ready for use if needed.

**reserved** *adj* restrained in speech and behaviour.

**reservist** *n* a member of a military reserve.

**reservoir** *n* **1** a natural or artificial lake where water is collected for use by a community. **2** a place or part in which fluid gathers or is stored. **3** an available extra source or supply.

**reshuffle** *v* **1** to rearrange (something) by altering the relative positions of its elements. **2** to reorganize (a group *esp* of government ministers) by a redistribution of roles. ➤ **reshuffle** *n.*

**reside** *v* **1** to occupy a place as one's permanent home. **2** (+ in) to lie in, or be associated with, a certain thing. **3** (+ in) to be vested as a right in a certain personage, etc.

**residence** *n* **1** the fact of living in a place. **2** a dwelling, *esp* a large and impressive house or a dignitary's official home. * **in residence** of a writer, artist, etc: working in e.g. a college or gallery, and available to give instruction, advice, etc.

**residency** *n* (*pl* **-ies**) **1** = RESIDENCE 1. **2** a period of time spent as a writer or artist in residence.

**resident**[1] *adj* **1** living in a place, *esp* for some length of time. **2** serving in a regular or full-time capacity.

**resident**[2] *n* **1** somebody who lives in a place. **2** a guest staying at a hotel.

**residential** *adj* **1** used as a residence or by residents. **2** relating to or involving residence. **3** given over to private housing as distinct from industry or commerce.

**residual** *adj* remaining as a residue.

**residue** *n* something that remains after a part, *esp* the greater part, has been taken away or used up.

**resign** *v* **1** to give up one's job or position. **2** (+ to) to reconcile (oneself) to an unpleasant fact, circumstance, etc.

**resignation** *n* **1** the act of resigning. **2** a formal notification of resigning. **3** the state of being resigned to something.

**resilient** *adj* **1** able to withstand shocks or return to shape after bending, stretching, etc. **2** *esp* of a person: able to recover from or adjust to misfortune or change. ➤ **resilience** *n.*

**resin** *n* **1** a sticky plant secretion that is used *esp* in varnishes, inks, and plastics. **2** a synthetic substance that has the qualities of natural resin.

**resist** *v* **1** to withstand the force or effect of. **2** to strive against or oppose. **3** to refrain from (something tempting).

**resistance** *n* **1** the act of resisting. **2** the ability to resist e.g. infection or the effects of drugs, etc. **3** an opposing or retarding force. **4** in physics, the opposition offered to the passage of a steady electric current through a body, circuit, etc. **5** (*often* **Resistance**) an underground organization operating against occupying forces in a country or those in power. ➤ **resistant** *adj.*

**resistor** *n* a component included in an electrical circuit to provide resistance.

**resit** *v* (**resitting**, *past tense and past part.* **resat** ) *Brit* to take (an examination) again after failing.

**resolute** *adj* firmly resolved. ➤ **resolutely** *adv.*

**resolution** *n* **1** the process of resolving, e.g. a problem or dispute. **2** courageous firmness of purpose. **3** a formal expression of opinion or intent by a body or group. **4** the capability, e.g. of a television or computer screen, to produce a clear and detailed image, or the degree of clarity produced.

**resolve**[1] *v* **1** to find a solution to (a problem). **2** to reach a firm decision to do something. **3** to decide by a formal resolution and vote. **4** to break up or separate into constituent parts.

**resolve**[2] *n* **1** the state of being determined or decided. **2** a firm decision.

**resonant** *adj* **1** of a sound: rich or echoing. **2** of a space, object, etc: tending to intensify and enrich sound. **3** suggesting meanings or associations other than those that are immediately present. ➤ **resonance** *n.*

**resonate** *v* to resound or reverberate.

**resort**[1] *n* **1** a frequently visited place providing accommodation and recreation, *esp* for holidaymakers. **2** somebody or something turned to for help or protection. **3** recourse.

**resort**[2] *v* **1** (+ to) to turn to somebody or something in order to achieve an end. **2** *formal* to go.

**resound** *v* **1** to become filled with sound. **2** to produce a sonorous or echoing sound.

**resounding** *adj* clear; unqualified.

**resource**[1] *n* **1** (*usu in pl*) an available means of support or provision. **2** (*usu in pl*) a source of wealth or revenue, e.g. minerals. **3** a source of information or expertise. **4** (*usu in pl*) the ability to deal with a difficult situation.

**resource²** *v* to supply with resources.

**resourceful** *adj* good at devising ways of dealing with difficult situations. ➤ **resourcefully** *adv*, **resourcefulness** *n*.

**respect¹** *n* **1** high or special regard; esteem. **2** politeness or deference. **3** (*in pl*) expressions of respect or politeness. **4** an aspect or detail. ✱ **with respect to** in relation to; concerning.

**respect²** *v* **1** to consider worthy of respect. **2** to refrain from violating or interfering with. **3** to recognize and abide by (e.g. a decision).

**respectable** *adj* **1** decent or conventional in character or conduct. **2** acceptable in size or quantity. ➤ **respectability** *n*, **respectably** *adv*.

**respectful** *adj* showing respect or deference. ➤ **respectfully** *adv*.

**respecting** *prep* with regard to; concerning.

**respective** *adj* belonging or relating to each.

**respectively** *adv* separately and in the order given.

**respiration** *n* **1** the act of breathing. **2** a single breath.

**respirator** *n* **1** a device worn over the mouth or nose to prevent the breathing of poisonous gases, etc. **2** a device for maintaining artificial respiration.

**respiratory** *adj* relating to breathing.

**respire** *v formal* to breathe.

**respite** *n* a period of rest or relief.

**resplendent** *adj* shining brilliantly; splendid.

**respond** *v* to write, speak, or act in reply.

**respondent** *n* **1** a defendant, *esp* in an appeal or divorce case. **2** a person who replies to a survey, advertisement, etc.

**response** *n* a reply or reaction.

**responsibility** *n* (*pl* **-ies**) **1** the state of being responsible. **2** something or somebody for which one is responsible. **3** the opportunity to act, take decisions, etc independently.

**responsible** *adj* **1** liable to be called to account as the person who did something. **2** constituting the reason or cause of something. **3** (*usu* + for) having control or care of. **4** involving important duties, decision-making, accountability, etc. **5** trustworthy, reliable,or sensible. **6** (+ to) required to answer to the specified person or body. ➤ **responsibly** *adv*.

**responsive** *adj* quick to respond appropriately or sympathetically.

**rest¹** *n* **1** freedom or a break from activity or work. **2** a state of motionlessness or inactivity. **3** repose, relaxation, or sleep. **4** in music, a silence of a specified duration. **5** something used for support.

**rest²** *v* **1** to relax the body or mind, e.g. by lying down or sleeping. **2** to stop working or exerting oneself. **3** to lie supported. **4** to place on a support. **5** (+ on) to be based or founded. **6** (+ with) to depend for action or accomplishment. **7** to remain as specified. ✱ **rest on one's laurels** see LAUREL.

**rest³** *n* **1** (**the rest**) the part, amount, or number that remains. **2** (**the rest**) the other people or things.

**restaurant** *n* a place where meals are sold, usu to be eaten on the premises.

**restaurateur** *n* the manager or proprietor of a restaurant.

**restful** *adj* quiet, peaceful, or soothing.

**restitution** *n* **1** the returning of something, e.g. property, to its rightful owner. **2** compensation given for an injury or wrong.

**restive** *adj* **1** resisting authority or control. **2** restless and uneasy.

**restless** *adj* **1** unable to rest, *esp* due to mental agitation. **2** giving no rest. **3** continuously moving or active. ➤ **restlessly** *adv*.

**restorative** *adj* capable of restoring health or vigour. ➤ **restorative** *n*.

**restore** *v* **1** to bring back to a former or original state, e.g. by repairing damage. **2** to bring back into existence, force, or use. **3** *formal* to give back. **4** *formal* to put (somebody) in possession of something again. ➤ **restoration** *n*, **restorer** *n*.

**restrain** *v* **1** to keep under control. **2** to hold onto and physically prevent (a person or animal) from moving.

**restrained** *adj* characterized by restraint, *esp* not extravagant or emotional.

**restraint** *n* **1** moderation of one's behaviour. **2** the absence of extravagance or indulgence. **3** the act of restraining. **4** a restraining force or influence. **5** a device that prevents freedom of movement.

**restrict** *v* **1** to prevent from moving or acting freely. **2** to limit.

**restricted** *adj* **1** not general; limited. **2** available only to particular groups or for a particular purpose. **3** narrow or confined.

**restriction** *n* **1** a regulation that restricts or restrains. **2** the act of restricting.

**restrictive** *adj* limiting freedom of action or movement.

**restrictive practice** *n* **1** an anti-competitive trading agreement between companies. **2** a practice by a trade union that limits the freedom of action of other workers or management.

**rest room** *n NAmer* public toilet facilities in a building.

**result¹** *v* **1** to proceed or arise as an effect or conclusion. **2** (+ in) to have the specified outcome.

**result²** *n* **1** a consequence, effect, or conclusion. **2** something obtained by calculation, experiment, or investigation. **3** the outcome or final score, mark, etc of a contest or examination. **4** *informal* a win in a sporting contest or successful conclusion to an operation.

**resultant** *adj* resulting from something else.

**resume** *v* **1** to take or occupy (e.g. a position) again. **2** to continue or begin again after an interruption. ➤ **resumption** *n.*

**résumé** *n* **1** a summary. **2** *NAmer* = CURRICULUM VITAE.

**resurgence** *n* a rising again into life, activity, or influence. ➤ **resurgent** *adj.*

**resurrect** *v* **1** to bring back to life from the dead. **2** to bring back into use.

**resurrection** *n* **1** (**the Resurrection**) the rising of Christ from the dead. **2** a resurgence, revival, or restoration.

**resuscitate** *v* **1** to revive from unconsciousness or apparent death. **2** to revitalize. ➤ **resuscitation** *n.*

**retail**[1] *v* **1** to sell (goods) to final consumers who will not resell them. **2** (*often* + at/for) to be sold , *esp* at a specified price. ➤ **retailer** *n.*

**retail**[2] *n* the sale of goods in small quantities to final consumers who will not resell them.

**retain** *v* **1** to continue to have or hold. **2** to keep in one's mind or memory. **3** to have the ability to hold or contain. **4** to hold in place.

**retainer** *n* **1** a fee paid to a lawyer for access to their services whenever required. **2** an old and trusted domestic servant.

**retake**[1] *v* (**retook, retaken**) **1** to recapture. **2** to sit (a test or examination) again.

**retake**[2] *n* a retaken test or examination.

**retaliate** *v* to take action that repays somebody for some wrong they have done. ➤ **retaliation** *n.*

**retard**[1] *v* to hinder the progress, development, or accomplishment of something. ➤ **retardation** *n.*

**retard**[2] *n* *offensive* a person with learning difficulties.

**retarded** *adj* slow in intellectual or emotional development.

**retch** *v* to experience a vomiting spasm without actually vomiting anything. ➤ **retch** *n.*

**retention** *n* the act of retaining.

**retentive** *adj* able to retain something, *esp* knowledge.

**rethink** *v* (*past tense and past part.* **rethought**) to reconsider (a plan, attitude, etc) with a view to changing it. ➤ **rethink** *n.*

**reticent** *adj* inclined to be uncommunicative or reluctant to speak openly. ➤ **reticence** *n.*

**retina** *n* (*pl* **retinas** *or* **retinae**) the light-sensitive membrane at the back of the eye that is connected with the brain by the optic nerve.

**retinue** *n* a group of attendants accompanying an important person.

**retire** *v* **1** to give up one's position or occupation permanently, *esp* at the end of one's working life. **2** to cause or force to retire from a position or occupation. **3** *formal* to withdraw from a place. **4** *formal* to go to bed. **5** of troops: to fall back or retreat. **6** to withdraw from a sporting contest. **7** of a jury: to leave the court to consider their verdict. ➤ **retired** *adj.*

**retirement** *n* **1** permanent withdrawal from active working life. **2** the age at which one normally retires from work. **3** the state or period of being retired. **4** *literary* seclusion.

**retiring** *adj* tending to avoid contact with other people; shy.

**retook** *v* past tense of RETAKE[1].

**retort**[1] *v* to answer back sharply or tersely.

**retort**[2] *n* a witty, angry, or cutting reply.

**retouch** *v* to restore or improve the appearance of with small additions or changes.

**retrace** *v* **1** to go over (e.g. footsteps or a route) again, often in the opposite direction. **2** to go back over (something) e.g. for purposes of clarification.

**retract** *v* **1** to draw back or in. **2** to withdraw (something said or written). **3** to refuse to abide by (e.g. a promise or agreement). ➤ **retractable** *adj,* **retraction** *n.*

**retreat**[1] *n* **1** the forced withdrawal of troops *esp* after losing a battle. **2** the act of withdrawing, *esp* from something difficult or dangerous. **3** a place of peace, privacy, or safety. **4** a period of withdrawal for prayer, meditation, and study.

**retreat**[2] *v* to make a retreat.

**retrench** *v* **1** to reduce (*esp* costs or expenses). **2** to economize. ➤ **retrenchment** *n.*

**retrial** *n* a second or subsequent legal trial.

**retribution** *n* punishment or retaliation for an insult or injury.

**retrieve** *v* **1** to get back again. **2** to rescue or save. **3** of a dog: to find and bring in (killed or wounded game). **4** to recover (e.g. data) from a computer memory. ➤ **retrieval** *n.*

**retriever** *n* a dog of a breed used to retrieve game.

**retrograde** *adj* **1** resulting in a worse or less advanced state. **2** moving or directed backward.

**retrogress** *v* to return to an earlier usu worse state. ➤ **retrogression** *n,* **retrogressive** *adj.*

**retrorocket** *n* a rocket used to slow down an aircraft, spacecraft, etc by producing thrust in a direction opposite to its motion.

**retrospect** *n* ✱ **in retrospect** when considering the past or a past event, *esp* in the light of present knowledge or experience.

**retrospective**[1] *adj* **1** relating to or affecting things in the past. **2** of an art exhibition: showing the evolution of an artist's work over a period. ➤ **retrospectively** *adv.*

**retrospective**[2] *n* a retrospective exhibition.

**retroussé** /rə'troohsay/ *adj* of a nose: turned up at the end.

**retsina** *n* a white Greek wine flavoured with resin.

**return**[1] *v* **1** to go back or come back. **2** (+ to) to go back to something in thought, conversation, or practice. **3** to put back in a former place or state. **4** to give or send back, *esp* to its owner. **5** to elect (a candidate). **6** to state or present (a verdict). **7** to bring in (e.g. a profit). **8** to repay (e.g. a compliment or favour). **9** in sport, to play (a ball) hit by an opponent.

**return**[2] *n* **1** the act of returning. **2** *Brit* a ticket bought for a trip to a place and back again: compare. **3** (*also in pl*) the profit from work, investment, or business. ✱ **in return** in compensation or repayment.

**reunify** *v* (**-ies, -ied**) to restore the unity of (e.g. a previously divided country). ➤ **reunification** *n.*

**reunion** *n* **1** a gathering of people after a period of separation. **2** the act of reuniting.

**reunite** *v* to come or bring together again.

**reuse** *v* to use again. ➤ **reusable** *adj,* **reuse** *n,* **reuser** *n.*

**Rev.** *abbr* Reverend.

**rev**[1] *n informal* (*usu in pl*) a revolution per minute of an engine.

**rev**[2] *v* (**revved, revving**) *informal* (*often* + up) to increase the number of revolutions per minute of (an engine).

**revamp**[1] *v* to change and improve the appearance or structure of.

**revamp**[2] *n* a modified or improved version.

**reveal** *v* **1** to make known (something secret or hidden). **2** to open (something) up to view.

**revealing** *adj* **1** exposing something, *esp* part of the body, usu concealed from view. **2** providing significant or interesting information.

**reveille** *n* a signal, *esp* a military bugle call, to get up in the morning.

**revel**[1] *v* (**revelled, revelling,** *NAmer* **reveled, reveling**) **1** (+ in) to derive intense satisfaction from. **2** to enjoy oneself in a noisy and exuberant way. ➤ **reveller** *n,* **revelry** *n.*

**revel**[2] *n* (*also in pl*) a riotous party or celebration.

**revelation** *n* **1** the act of revealing something. **2** something revealed, *esp* a sudden and illuminating disclosure.

**revelatory** *adj* serving to reveal something.

**revenge**[1] *n* **1** the act of retaliating in order to get even for a wrong or injury. **2** a desire to retaliate in this way.

**revenge**[2] *v* **1** to retaliate for (an insult, injury, etc). **2** to take revenge on behalf of (oneself or somebody else).

**revenue** *n* the total income produced by a given source or received by a business, government, etc.

**reverberate** *v* **1** of a sound: to continue in a series of echoes. **2** to have a continuing and powerful effect. ➤ **reverberation** *n.*

**revere** *v* to regard with deep and devoted respect.

**reverence** *n* profound respect, *esp* accorded to something sacred.

**Reverend** *adj* used as a title for a member of the clergy.

**reverend** *n informal* a member of the clergy.

**reverent** *adj* characterized by reverence. ➤ **reverently** *adv.*

**reverie** *n* a daydream.

**reversal** *n* the act of reversing, *esp* a change to an opposite direction, position, policy, etc.

**reverse**[1] *adj* **1** contrary to a previous or usual condition or direction. **2** causing backward movement.

**reverse**[2] *v* **1** to go or drive backward. **2** to change to an opposite position or direction. **3** to turn upside down or inside out. **4** to annul (a legal judgment). **5** to change (e.g. a decision or policy) to the contrary. ✱ **reverse the charges** *Brit* to arrange for the recipient of a telephone call to pay for it. ➤ **reversible** *adj.*

**reverse**[3] *n* **1** the opposite of something. **2** the side of a coin, medal, etc that does not bear the principal design and lettering. **3** a gear that causes backward motion. **4** a change for the worse; a setback. ✱ **in reverse 1** backward. **2** in the opposite direction.

**reversion** *n* a return to an earlier inferior state.

**revert** *v* to return to a former state, practice, belief, etc.

**review**[1] *n* **1** an act of inspecting or examining something, *esp* in order to decide if changes need to be made. **2** a critical evaluation of a book, play, etc. **3** a magazine or newspaper, or part of one, devoted chiefly to critical articles. **4** a general survey, e.g. of current affairs. **5** a formal military or naval inspection. **6** = REVUE.

**review**[2] *v* **1** to make, write, etc a review of. **2** to examine or study again. ➤ **reviewer** *n.*

**revile** *v* to criticize very harshly or abusively.

**revise** *v* **1** to make an amended version of (a text). **2** *Brit* to refresh one's knowledge of (a subject), *esp* before an examination. **3** to change (e.g. an opinion), *esp* in the light of further consideration or new information. ➤ **revision** *n.*

**revisionism** *n chiefly derog* a movement in Marxist socialism favouring an evolutionary rather than a revolutionary transition to socialism. ➤ **revisionist** *adj and n.*

**revitalize** *or* **-ise** *v* to give new life or vigour to. ➤ **revitalization** *n.*

**revival** *n* **1** a return or bringing back to life, vigour, popularity, etc. **2** a new presentation or production, e.g. of a play. **3** a period of renewed religious fervour.

**revivalism** *n* efforts to bring about a return to religious faith. ➤ **revivalist** *n and adj.*

**revive** *v* **1** to return to a state of consciousness, health, or strength. **2** to bring back into an active state or current use.

**revivify** *v* (**-ies, -ied**) to revitalize.

**revoke** *v* to declare to be no longer valid or operative. ➤ **revocation** *n.*
**revolt**[1] *v* **1** to rebel. **2** to cause to feel disgust or loathing.
**revolt**[2] *n* a rebellion, *esp* a determined and armed one.
**revolting** *adj* extremely offensive; nauseating.
**revolution** *n* **1** the overthrow of one government and the substitution of another. **2** a sudden or far-reaching change. **3** one complete turn of an object round a central point or axis.
**revolutionary**[1] *adj* **1** completely new and different. **2** promoting or engaging in revolution.
**revolutionary**[2] *n* (*pl* **-ies**) somebody who advocates or is engaged in a revolution.
**revolutionize** *or* **-ise** *v* to change fundamentally or completely.
**revolve** *v* **1** to move in a circular course or round a central point or axis. **2** (+ around) to be centred on a specified theme or main point. ➤ **revolving** *adj.*
**revolver** *n* a handgun with revolving chambers each holding one cartridge.
**revue** *n* a theatrical production consisting typically of brief often satirical sketches, songs, and dances.
**revulsion** *n* a feeling of utter distaste or repugnance.
**reward**[1] *n* **1** something offered or given for service, effort, or achievement. **2** a sum of money offered for the capture of a criminal or the recovery of lost or stolen property.
**reward**[2] *v* to give a reward to (somebody) or for (something).
**rewarding** *adj* personally satisfying.
**rewind** *v* (*past tense and past part.* **rewound**) to wind (film, tape, etc) back to the beginning or to an earlier point.
**rewire** *v* to provide (e.g. a house) with new electric wiring.
**rework** *v* to revise, alter, or make suitable for a different purpose.
**Rf** *abbr* the chemical symbol for rutherfordium.
**Rh**[1] *abbr* rhesus (factor).
**Rh**[2] *abbr* the chemical symbol for rhodium.
**rhapsodize** *or* **-ise** *v* to speak or write with ardent enthusiasm.
**rhapsody** *n* (*pl* **-ies**) **1** an expression of ardent enthusiasm. **2** a musical composition in one continuous movement. ➤ **rhapsodic** *adj.*
**rheostat** *n* a device that regulates an electric current by varying resistance.
**rhesus baby** *n* a baby born with a blood disease because the rhesus factor of its mother's blood is incompatible with that of its own blood.
**rhesus factor** *n* a substance present in red blood cells that defines blood groups and can provoke intense allergic reactions when incompatible blood types are mixed.
**rhesus monkey** *n* a small pale brown monkey of southern Asia.
**rhetoric** *n* **1** the art of effective public speaking. **2** impressive language that may be insincere or exaggerated.
**rhetorical** *adj* **1** relating to or involving rhetoric. **2** of language: impressive or used merely to impress. ➤ **rhetorically** *adv.*
**rhetorical question** *n* a question to which no answer is expected, used to make a statement with dramatic effect.
**rheumatic** *adj* relating to or suffering from rheumatism.
**rheumatism** *n* a condition characterized by inflammation and pain in muscles, joints, or fibrous tissue.
**rhinestone** *n* an imitation diamond.
**rhino** *n* (*pl* **rhinos** *or* **rhino**) *informal* a rhinoceros.
**rhinoceros** *n* (*pl* **rhinoceroses** *or* **rhinoceros**) a large plant-eating mammal of Africa and Asia with a very thick skin and either one or two horns on its snout.
**rhizome** *n* a horizontal underground plant stem that produces both roots and buds.
**rho** *n* the 17th letter of the Greek alphabet (Ρ, ρ).
**rhododendron** *n* a shrub with clusters of showy red, pink, purple, or white flowers and leathery evergreen leaves.
**rhombus** *n* (*pl* **rhombuses** *or* **rhombi**) a parallelogram with equal sides but unequal angles; a diamond-shaped figure.
**rhubarb** *n* a plant with large fleshy leaves and edible stalks that are cooked and eaten as a dessert.
**rhumba** *n* see RUMBA.
**rhyme**[1] *n* **1** correspondence in the sound of words or their final syllables, *esp* those at the ends of lines of verse. **2** a word that corresponds with another in this way. **3** rhyming verse or a rhyming poem. ✱ **rhyme or reason** reasonableness or logic.
**rhyme**[2] *v* **1** of a word: (*often* + with) to correspond in sound. **2** of verse: to have lines ending with a rhyming word or syllable.
**rhyming slang** *n* slang in which a word is replaced by a rhyming phrase often subsequently reduced to the first element, e.g. *head* becomes *loaf of bread* and then *loaf*.
**rhythm** *n* **1** a repeated pattern in the flow of sound, e.g. in music or poetry. **2** movement or fluctuation marked by a regular recurrence of particular elements.
**rhythm and blues** *n* a type of popular music with elements of blues and jazz.
**rhythmic** *adj* **1** of or involving rhythm. **2** regularly recurring. ➤ **rhythmically** *adv.*
**rib**[1] *n* **1** any of the paired curved rods of bone that stiffen the body walls of most vertebrate animals and protect the heart, lungs, etc. **2** a structural member in the framework of a ship or the wing of an aircraft. **3** a rod supporting the fabric of an umbrella. **4** an arched support in

architectural vaulting. **5** a vein of a leaf. **6** a narrow ridge in a knitted or woven fabric.

**rib**[2] *v* (**ribbed, ribbing**) *informal* to tease (somebody). ➤ **ribbing** *n.*

**ribald** *adj* crudely or obscenely humorous. ➤ **ribaldry** *n.*

**riband** *n* a ribbon.

**ribbon** *n* **1** a narrow band of fabric used for decorative effect or as a fastening. **2** a long narrow strip. **3** a strip of inked material used in a typewriter or computer printer. **4** (*in pl*) tatters or shreds.

**ribcage** *n* the enclosing wall of the chest consisting chiefly of the ribs and their connective tissue.

**riboflavin** *n* a yellow chemical compound of the vitamin B complex occurring *esp* in green vegetables, milk, eggs, and liver.

**rice** *n* **1** a cereal grass widely cultivated in warm climates. **2** the grains of this plant used as food.

**rice paper** *n* a very thin edible material resembling paper, usu made from plant pith and used in baking and for oriental painting.

**rich** *adj* **1** having a great deal of money and possessions. **2** of a country or area: having abundant natural resources, successful industries, a strong economy, etc. **3** having high worth, value, or quality. **4** (*often* + in) well supplied or endowed. **5** vivid and deep in colour. **6** full and mellow in tone or quality. **7** of soil: having abundant plant nutrients. **8** of food: highly seasoned, fatty, oily, or sweet.

**riches** *pl n* great wealth.

**richly** *adv* **1** in a rich manner. **2** in full measure; amply.

**Richter scale** *n* a scale for expressing the magnitude of earthquakes.

**rick**[1] *n* a stack of hay, corn, etc in the open air.

**rick**[2] *v chiefly Brit* to wrench or sprain (e.g. one's neck).

**rickets** *pl n* a disease, *esp* of children, characterized by softening and deformation of bones.

**rickety** *adj* likely to collapse, *esp* because badly made or old and worn.

**rickshaw** *or* **ricksha** *n* a small covered two-wheeled vehicle pulled by one or more people, used *esp* in Southeast Asia.

**ricochet**[1] *n* **1** the rebound of a projectile (e.g. a bullet) that strikes a hard or flat surface at an angle. **2** something that ricochets.

**ricochet**[2] *v* (**ricocheted, ricocheting**) of e.g. a bullet: to rebound off a surface.

**rictus** *n* an unnatural gaping grin or grimace.

**rid** *v* (**ridding,** *past tense and past part.* **rid** *or* **ridded**) to relieve of something unwanted. ✱ **get rid of** to free oneself of (something unwanted).

**riddance** *n* ✱ **good riddance** an expression of relief at becoming free of something or somebody unwanted.

**-ridden** *comb. form* **1** afflicted or excessively concerned with: *guilt-ridden.* **2** excessively full of: *priest-ridden.*

**riddle**[1] *n* **1** a short and *esp* humorous verbal puzzle. **2** something or somebody difficult to understand.

**riddle**[2] *n* a large coarse sieve.

**riddle**[3] *v* **1** to pierce with many holes. **2** (**be riddled with**) to have (something undesirable) spread throughout itself.

**ride**[1] *v* (**rode, ridden**) **1** to travel mounted on and controlling an animal, bicycle, etc. **2** to travel in a vehicle. **3** to be borne up or supported by. **4** (*usu* + out) to survive (e.g. a storm) without great damage or loss. **5** (*usu* + up) of clothing: to work its way up the body as one moves. ✱ **be riding for a fall** to act in such a way as to make disaster seem inevitable. **ride high** to experience success. **ride on** to be dependent on.

**ride**[2] *n* **1** an outing or journey by horseback or by vehicle. **2** any of various mechanical devices, e.g. at a funfair, for riding on. **3** a path used for riding. ✱ **take for a ride** *informal* to deceive or trick (somebody).

**rider** *n* **1** somebody who rides a horse, a bicycle, or a motorcycle. **2** a clause appended to a legal document.

**ridge** *n* **1** a long narrow stretch of elevated land or mountain range. **2** the top of a roof at the point where the two sloping sides meet. **3** an elongated part raised above a surrounding surface. ➤ **ridged** *adj.*

**ridicule**[1] *n* scornful or contemptuous words or actions.

**ridicule**[2] *v* to mock.

**ridiculous** *adj* deserving ridicule; absurd. ➤ **ridiculously** *adv.*

**riding** *n* (*often* **Riding**) any of three former administrative jurisdictions of Yorkshire.

**rife** *adj* **1** occurring everywhere or to a great degree. **2** (+ with) full of.

**riff** *n* a constantly repeated phrase in jazz or rock music.

**riffle** *v* **1** to leaf through (something) rapidly. **2** to search through (something) rapidly.

**riffraff** *n* disreputable or worthless people.

**rifle**[1] *n* a firearm with a long barrel with spiral grooves cut inside it.

**rifle**[2] *v* **1** to cut spiral grooves inside the barrel of (a rifle, cannon, etc). **2** to propel (e.g. a ball) with great force or speed.

**rifle**[3] *v* to search through (e.g. a drawer or safe) in order to find and steal something.

**rift** *n* **1** a fissure or crack. **2** a disruption of friendly relations.

**rig**[1] *v* (**rigged, rigging**) **1** to fit out (e.g. a ship) with rigging, sails, etc. **2** (*usu* + out) to clothe or dress. **3** (*often* + out) to supply with equipment for a particular use. **4** (*often* + up) to assemble or erect. **5** to manipulate or control for dishonest purposes.

**rig**[2] *n* **1** an outfit of clothing worn for a particular activity. **2** equipment or machinery fitted for a usu specified purpose, e.g. for extracting oil or gas.

**rigging** *n* the ropes and chains used aboard a ship for controlling sails and supporting masts.

**right**[1] *adj* **1** in accordance with what is morally good, just, or proper. **2** conforming to facts or truth. **3** suitable or appropriate. **4** in a correct, proper, or healthy state. **5** on the side of somebody or something that is nearer the east when the front faces north. **6** (*often* **Right**) of the right wing in politics. **7** *chiefly Brit, informal* real or utter. * **on the right side of 1** in favour with. **2** less than the specified age. ➤ **rightly** *adv.*

**right**[2] *n* **1** qualities that together merit moral approval. **2** a power, privilege, etc to which one has a just claim. **3** (*in pl*) entitlement to publish, perform, film, etc a work. **4** the part, direction, etc on the right side. **5** the right hand, or a blow struck with it. **6** *informal* a right turn. **7** (*often* **the Right**) those professing conservative or reactionary political views. * **by rights** with reason or justice; properly. **in one's own right** by virtue of one's own qualifications or attributes. **in the right** correct in what one says or does. **to rights** into proper order.

**right**[3] *adv* **1** on or towards the right. **2** in a proper or correct manner. **3** exactly. **4** in a direct line; straight. **5** all the way; completely.

**right**[4] *v* **1** to correct. **2** to restore (e.g. a boat) to an upright position. **3** to compensate for or avenge (a wrong, an injustice, etc).

**right angle** *n* an angle of 90°, e.g. at the corner of a square. ➤ **right-angled** *adj.*

**righteous** *adj* morally right or justified. ➤ **righteously** *adv,* **righteousness** *n.*

**rightful** *adj* **1** having a just claim; legitimate. **2** held by right; legal. **3** fitting or proper. ➤ **rightfully** *adv.*

**right of way** *n* (*pl* **rights of way**) **1** a legal right to pass over another person's property. **2** a public path along which a right of way exists. **3** precedence accorded to one vehicle, vessel, etc over another.

**right wing** *n* **1** (*often* **Right Wing**) the more conservative division of a political party. **2** in sport, the right side of the field when facing towards the opposing team. ➤ **right-wing** *adj,* **right-winger** *n.*

**rigid** *adj* **1** unable to bend or be bent; stiff. **2** inflexibly set in opinions or habits. **3** unable to be changed. ➤ **rigidity** *n,* **rigidly** *adv.*

**rigmarole** *n* **1** an absurdly long and complex procedure. **2** a nonsensical account or explanation.

**rigor mortis** *n* the temporary rigidity of muscles that occurs after death.

**rigorous** *adj* **1** very strict. **2** harsh or severe. **3** scrupulously accurate; precise. ➤ **rigorously** *adv.*

**rigour** (*NAmer* **rigor**) *n* **1** strictness. **2** (*in pl*) conditions that make life difficult or unpleasant.

**rile** *v* to make angry or resentful.

**rill** *n* a small brook.

**rim**[1] *n* **1** an outer edge of something circular. **2** an outer edge or boundary.

**rim**[2] *v* (**rimmed, rimming**) to serve as a rim for; to border.

**rime** *n* a thin coating of frost.

**rind** *n* a tough outer layer of fruit, cheese, bacon, etc.

**ring**[1] *n* **1** a circular band usu of precious metal, worn on the finger. **2** a circular line, figure, arrangement, or object. **3** a circular electric element or gas burner set into the top of a cooker. **4** a space, often a circular one, for shows, competitions, or *esp* a circus. **5** a square enclosure in which boxing or wrestling matches are held. **6** an exclusive association of people, often for a corrupt purpose. * **hold the ring** to act as a neutral umpire in a dispute. **run rings round somebody** *informal* to outdo or outwit somebody completely.

**ring**[2] *v* (*past tense and past part.* **ringed**) to place, form, draw, etc a ring round; to encircle. ➤ **ringed** *adj.*

**ring**[3] *v* (**rang, rung**) **1** to make, or cause to make, a resonant sound like that of a bell. **2** (+ for) to sound a bell as a summons. **3** (*often* + with) to be filled with resonant sound. **4** of one's ears: to have the sensation of a continuous humming sound. **5** *chiefly Brit* (*often* + up) to telephone. * **ring a bell** to sound familiar. **ring the changes** to vary the manner of doing or arranging something. **ring true** to appear to be true or authentic.

**ring**[4] *n* **1** a clear resonant sound as made by vibrating metal. **2** the act of ringing. **3** *Brit, informal* a telephone call. **4** a sound or character suggestive of a particular quality or feeling: *This story has a familiar ring to it.*

**ring binder** *n* a loose-leaf binder with split metal rings to hold the paper.

**ringing** *adj* **1** resounding. **2** unequivocal.

**ringleader** *n* a leader of a group engaged in illegal or objectionable activities.

**ringlet** *n* a lock of hair curled in a spiral.

**ringmaster** *n* the person in charge of a circus performance.

**ring off** *v Brit* to end a telephone conversation.

**ring out** *v* to sound resonantly.

**ring-pull** *n* a built-in ring-shaped device for opening a tin.

**ring road** *n* a road round a town or town centre designed to relieve traffic congestion.

**ring up** *v* **1** to record (a sale) by means of a cash register. **2** to telephone.

**ringworm** *n* a contagious fungal disease in which itchy ring-shaped patches form on the skin.

**rink** *n* **1** a surface of ice for ice-skating, ice hockey, or curling. **2** an enclosure for roller-skating. **3** part of a bowling green being used for a match.

**rinse**[1] *v* **1** (*often* + out) to remove soap from (washed clothing) with clean water. **2** (*often* + out) to remove (dirt, impurities, or unwanted matter) by washing lightly.

**rinse**[2] *n* **1** an act of rinsing. **2** liquid used for rinsing. **3** a solution that temporarily tints the hair.

**riot**[1] *n* **1** a violent public disturbance caused by a large crowd of people. **2** a profuse and random display. **3** *informal* somebody or something wildly funny. ✱ **run riot** to act wildly or without restraint.

**riot**[2] *v* (**rioted, rioting**) to participate in a riot. ➤ **rioter** *n.*

**riotous** *adj* **1** wild and disorderly; constituting a riot. **2** profuse and brightly coloured.

**RIP** *abbr* rest in peace.

**rip**[1] *v* (**ripped, ripping**) **1** to tear or become torn. **2** (+ out/off) to remove by force. ✱ **let rip** *informal* to do something without restraint.

**rip**[2] *n* a tear or torn split.

**rip**[3] *n* a body of rough water formed by the meeting of opposing currents, winds, etc.

**riparian** *adj* of or occurring on the bank of a river.

**ripcord** *n* a cord for releasing a parachute from its pack.

**ripe** *adj* **1** of fruit or grain: fully developed and ready for harvesting or eating. **2** of a cheese or wine: aged to full flavour. **3** (+ for) fully prepared or ready for. ✱ **a ripe old age** a very great age. ➤ **ripely** *adv,* **ripeness** *n.*

**ripen** *v* to make or become ripe.

**rip off** *v informal* **1** to rob or defraud. **2** to steal.

**rip-off** *n informal* **1** an instance of financial exploitation, *esp* overcharging. **2** an act of stealing.

**riposte** *n* a quick-witted reply or retort.

**ripple**[1] *n* **1** a small wave or a succession of small waves. **2** a sound like that of rippling water. **3** a feeling or emotion that spreads through a person, place, etc. **4** ice cream with coloured and flavoured bands of syrup running through it.

**ripple**[2] *v* **1** to stir up small waves on (water). **2** to flow in small waves. **3** to spread irregularly outwards, *esp* from a central point.

**rip-roaring** *adj* noisily excited or exciting; exuberant.

**riptide** *n* **1** = RIP[3]. **2** a strong surface current flowing outwards from a shore.

**rise**[1] *v* (**rose, risen**) **1** to move upwards. **2** to slope upwards. **3** to assume an upright position, *esp* from lying, kneeling, or sitting. **4** to get up from sleep or from one's bed. **5** of the sun, moon, etc: to appear above the horizon. **6** to increase in amount, number, volume, or intensity. **7** to attain a higher office or rank. **8** (+ to) to show oneself equal to (a challenge). **9** (*often* + up) to rebel; to take up arms. **10** of a river: to have its source. ✱ **rise above** to overcome or not be affected by (difficulties, unworthy feelings, etc).

**rise**[2] *n* **1** a movement upwards. **2** an upward slope. **3** an increase. **4** *Brit* an increase in pay. ✱ **give rise to** to be the origin or cause of.

**riser** *n* **1** somebody who rises in a specified manner: *an early riser.* **2** the upright part between two consecutive stair treads.

**risible** *adj* arousing laughter; ridiculous. ➤ **risibility** *n.*

**rising**[1] *adj* **1** approaching a specified age. **2** achieving a higher rank or greater influence.

**rising**[2] *n* an insurrection or uprising.

**rising damp** *n Brit* moisture that has entered the floor of a building and moved up a wall.

**risk**[1] *n* **1** a dangerous element or factor. **2** a possibility of loss, injury, or damage. **3** somebody or something that is a hazard. ✱ **at risk** (*often* + of) in danger. **at somebody's (own)** risk with the person concerned accepting responsibility for any possible harm or loss to themselves.

**risk**[2] *v* **1** to expose (e.g. one's life) to danger. **2** to incur the possibility of (something unpleasant happening).

**risky** *adj* (**-ier, -iest**) involving danger or the possibility of loss or failure. ➤ **riskily** *adv,* **riskiness** *n.*

**risotto** *n* (*pl* **-os**) an Italian dish of rice flavoured with vegetables, shellfish, etc.

**risqué** *adj* verging on impropriety or indecency.

**rissole** *n* a small fried cake of cooked minced food, *esp* meat.

**rite** *n* a ceremonial, *esp* religious act or procedure.

**rite of passage** *n* a ritual associated with a change of status, e.g. assuming adult responsibilities.

**ritual**[1] *n* **1** a solemn or religious ceremony involving a series of actions carried out in a set order. **2** an action habitually carried out in a set order.

**ritual**[2] *adj* relating to rituals; ceremonial. ➤ **ritually** *adv.*

**ritzy** *adj* (**-ier, -iest**) *informal* ostentatiously smart.

**rival**[1] *n* **1** any of two or more people competing for a single goal. **2** somebody or something that equals another in desirable qualities. ➤ **rivalry** *n.*

**rival**[2] *v* (**rivalled, rivalling,** *NAmer* **rivaled, rivaling**) to possess qualities that approach or equal (those of another).

**rive** *v* (*past part.* **riven**) (*usu* **be riven**) to be torn apart.
**river** *n* **1** a natural stream of water of considerable volume. **2** (*often in pl*) a copious or overwhelming quantity.
**rivet**[1] *n* a headed metal pin used to join two metal plates.
**rivet**[2] *v* (**riveted, riveting**) **1** to fasten with rivets. **2** to attract and hold (the attention, etc) completely.
**riveting** *adj* holding the attention; fascinating.
**riviera** *n* (*also* **Riviera**) a coastal region, usu with a mild climate, frequented as a resort.
**rivulet** *n* a small stream.
**RN** *abbr Brit* Royal Navy.
**Rn** *abbr* the chemical symbol for radon.
**RNA** *n* a nucleic acid similar to DNA that is associated with the control of cellular chemical activities.
**roach**[1] *n* (*pl* **roaches** *or* **roach**) a silver-white European freshwater fish of the carp family.
**roach**[2] *n chiefly NAmer, informal* a cockroach.
**road** *n* **1** an open, usu paved way for the passage of vehicles, people, and animals. **2** a route or path: *the road to ruin.*
**roadblock** *n* a road barricade set up by an army, the police, etc.
**roadholding** *n* the ability of a moving vehicle to remain stable, *esp* when cornering.
**roadie** *n informal* a person who looks after the transport and setting up of equipment of a rock group.
**road map** *n* **1** a map showing the roads of an area. **2** a plan of action for achieving a particular result.
**road rage** *n* violent and aggressive behaviour by a motorist towards another road user.
**road show** *n* **1** a public-relations or government information unit that travels from place to place to give displays. **2** a radio or television programme broadcast from different locations.
**roadster** *n* an open sports car.
**road test** *n* a test of a vehicle, or other piece of equipment, under practical operating conditions. ➤ **road-test** *v.*
**roadway** *n* the part of a road used by vehicles.
**roadworks** *pl n Brit* the repair or construction of roads.
**roadworthy** *adj* of a vehicle: in a fit condition to be used on the roads.
**roam** *v* **1** to wander. **2** to wander over (an area).
**roan** *adj* of horses and cattle: having a reddish brown coat lightened by some white hairs.
**roar**[1] *n* **1** the deep prolonged cry of a wild animal, e.g. a lion. **2** a loud cry of pain, anger, or laughter. **3** a loud continuous confused sound.
**roar**[2] *v* **1** to give a roar. **2** to laugh loudly. **3** of a fire: to burn fiercely and noisily. **4** to happen or progress rapidly.
**roaring** *adj informal* marked by energetic or successful activity: *a roaring trade.*
**roast**[1] *v* **1** to cook (*esp* meat) by exposing it to dry heat, e.g. in an oven. **2** to be excessively hot.
**roast**[2] *n* a piece of meat roasted or suitable for roasting.
**roast**[3] *adj* of food, *esp* meat: roasted.
**roasting**[1] *adj informal* extremely hot.
**roasting**[2] *n informal* a severe scolding.
**rob** *v* (**robbed, robbing**) **1** to steal something from (a person or place), *esp* by violence or threat. **2** (+ of) to deprive of. **3** *informal* to overcharge. ➤ **robber** *n.*
**robbery** *n* (*pl* **-ies**) the act of robbing.
**robe**[1] *n* **1** a long flowing outer garment, esp one used for ceremonial occasions or as a symbol of office. **2** *NAmer* a dressing gown.
**robe**[2] *v* to clothe or cover with a robe.
**robin** *n* a small brownish bird with an orange-red throat and breast.
**robot** *n* **1** a machine programmed to carry out a sequence of actions automatically. **2** *esp* in science fiction, a machine that carries out human functions.
**robotic** *adj* **1** relating to robots. **2** stiff and mechanical; lacking human warmth.
**robotics** *pl n* the study of the construction and behaviour of robots.
**robust** *adj* **1** exhibiting vigorous health or stamina. **2** strongly formed or constructed. **3** forceful and determined. ➤ **robustly** *adv.*
**rock**[1] *n* **1** hard solid mineral matter forming the earth's crust. **2** a particular form of this, e.g. granite or limestone. **3** a large mass of rock forming an outcrop, cliff, etc. **4** a boulder. **5** *NAmer* a stone. **6** *Brit* a sweet in the form of a hard and brittle cylindrical stick. **7** *informal* a gem, *esp* a diamond. ✱ **on the rocks 1** *informal* in difficulties. **2** of a drink: served over ice cubes.
**rock**[2] *v* **1** to move gently back and forth or from side to side. **2** to sway or cause to sway rapidly or violently. **3** to disturb or upset. **4** to dance to or play rock music. ✱ **rock the boat** to cause problems for one's colleagues, etc.
**rock**[3] *n* a style of popular music played on electronically amplified instruments and with a persistent, heavily accented beat.
**rock and roll** *n* see ROCK 'N' ROLL.
**rock bottom** *n* the lowest level.
**rocker** *n* **1** a rock musician or fan. **2** a curved piece of wood or metal on which an object, e.g. a cradle, rocks. ✱ **off one's rocker** *informal* crazy.
**rockery** *n* (*pl* **-ies**) a bank of rocks and earth where rock plants are grown.
**rocket**[1] *n* **1** a firework with a guiding stick that shoots high into the air before bursting. **2** a spacecraft, missile, etc propelled by a jet engine that operates independently of the oxygen in the air. **3** *Brit, informal* a sharp reprimand.

**rocket**$^2$ *v* (**rocketed, rocketing**) **1** of prices, etc: to increase rapidly or spectacularly. **2** to travel with the speed of a rocket.

**rocket**$^3$ *n* a Mediterranean plant of the cabbage family, used in salad.

**rocking chair** *n* a chair mounted on rockers.

**rocking horse** *n* a toy horse mounted on rockers.

**rock music** *n* = ROCK$^3$.

**rock 'n' roll** *or* **rock and roll** *n* a style of popular music, originating in the 1950s, characterized by a heavy beat, simple melodies, and often country, folk, and blues elements.

**rock salt** *n* common salt occurring as a solid mineral.

**rock solid** *adj* **1** completely firm, fixed, or stable. **2** completely reliable or committed.

**rocky**$^1$ *adj* (**-ier, -iest**) **1** full of or consisting of rocks. **2** filled with obstacles; difficult.

**rocky**$^2$ *adj* (**-ier, -iest**) unsteady; tottering.

**rococo** *adj* of an 18th-century style of architecture and decoration characterized by elaborate curved forms and shell motifs.

**rod** *n* **1** a slender bar, e.g. of wood or metal. **2** a pole with a line for fishing.

**rode** *v* past tense of RIDE$^1$.

**rodent** *n* any of an order of gnawing mammals including the mice, rats, squirrels, and beavers.

**rodeo** *n* (*pl* **-os**) a public performance featuring the riding skills of cowboys.

**roe** *n* the eggs or sperm of a fish.

**roebuck** *n* (*pl* **roebucks** *or* **roebuck**) a male roe deer.

**roe deer** *n* a small graceful deer with erect cylindrical antlers.

**roentgen** *n* see RÖNTGEN.

**roger** *interj* used in radio communications to indicate that a message has been received and understood.

**rogue** *n* **1** a wilfully dishonest or corrupt person. **2** a mischievous person. **3** an animal roaming alone and vicious and destructive.

**roguish** *adj* mischievous.

**roister** *v archaic* to engage in noisy revelry.

**role** *or* **rôle** *n* **1** a part played by an actor. **2** the function or expected contribution to a job, situation, etc of a person or thing.

**role model** *n* somebody who serves as an example to others of how to behave.

**role playing** *n* behaving in a way typical of another person or of a stereotype.

**roll**$^1$ *v* **1** to move along by turning over and over. **2** of a vehicle: to move on wheels. **3** to rotate (the eyes) in their sockets. **4** to move steadily onward or pass in succession. **5** of a ship, aircraft, etc: to rock from side to side as it moves forward. **6** to begin operating, or to cause (a machine) to begin operating. **7** (*often* + up) to wrap (something) round itself to form a cylinder or ball. **8** (*often* + up) to curl or wind itself into a cylindrical shape. **9** to shape or flatten by rolling. **10** of thunder: to make a long reverberating sound. ✱ **be rolling in it/in money** *informal* to be very wealthy.

**roll**$^2$ *n* **1** something rolled up to resemble a cylinder. **2** a small round or cylindrical loaf of bread. **3** an official list of people's names.

**roll**$^3$ *n* **1** a rolling or swaying movement. **2** a gymnastic manoeuvre in which the body is tucked up and rolled completely over forwards or backwards. **3** a sound produced by rapid strokes on a drum. **4** a prolonged reverberating sound of thunder. ✱ **on a roll** *informal* having a period of success.

**roll call** *n* the calling out of a list of names, e.g. for checking attendance.

**roller** *n* **1** a revolving cylinder used to move, press, shape, or apply something. **2** a hair curler. **3** a long heavy wave.

**Rollerblade** *n trademark* (*usu in pl*) a roller skate with a single central line of wheels.

**roller coaster** *n* **1** an elevated railway in a funfair, constructed with steep curves and inclines. **2** a situation in which one experiences highs and lows.

**roller skate** *n* a boot with four small wheels attached to the sole that allow the wearer to glide over hard surfaces. ➤ **roller-skate** *v*, **roller skater** *n*, **roller skating** *n*.

**rollicking**$^1$ *adj* boisterously carefree.

**rollicking**$^2$ *n Brit, informal* a severe scolding.

**rolling pin** *n* a long cylinder for rolling out dough.

**rolling stock** *n* the vehicles owned and used by a railway.

**rollmop** *n* a herring fillet rolled up and pickled.

**roll neck** *n* a loose high collar, *esp* on a jumper, worn rolled over.

**roll-on** *adj* of e.g. deodorant: applied to the skin by means of a rolling ball.

**roll up** *v* **1** to roll into a cylinder. **2** *informal* to arrive.

**roly-poly**$^1$ *n* (*pl* **-ies**) a pudding consisting of suet pastry spread with jam, rolled, and baked or steamed.

**roly-poly**$^2$ *adj informal* short and plump.

**Roman**$^1$ *adj* **1** of Rome or the Romans. **2** (**roman**) of type: not slanted; perpendicular.

**Roman**$^2$ *n* **1** a native or inhabitant of ancient or modern Rome. **2** (**roman**) roman letters or type.

**Roman alphabet** *n* the alphabet used for writing most European languages, including English.

**Roman candle** *n* a cylindrical firework that discharges balls of fire at intervals.

**Roman Catholic**$^1$ *n* a member of the Roman Catholic Church. ➤ **Roman Catholicism** *n*.

**Roman Catholic**$^2$ *adj* relating or belonging to the Roman Catholic Church.

**Roman Catholic Church** *n* a Christian episcopal church headed by the pope and having a form of service centred on the Mass.

**Romance** *n* the family of languages developed from Latin that includes e.g. French, Spanish, and Italian.

**romance**[1] *n* **1** romantic love, or the feelings and behaviour usually associated with it. **2** a love affair. **3** a story or film about romantic love. **4** an emotional aura attaching to an enthralling era, adventure, or pursuit.

**romance**[2] *v* to court (somebody).

**Romanesque** *n* a style of architecture developed in western Europe between c.AD 900 and 1200 and characterized by the use of round arches. ➤ **Romanesque** *adj.*

**Roman numeral** *n* a numeral in the ancient Roman system of numbering using the symbols I, V, X, L, C, D, and M.

**romantic**[1] *adj* **1** involving sexual attraction accompanied by tender, loving feelings and elaborate courtship. **2** associated with or conducive to love. **3** impractical or overly idealistic. **4** (*often* **Romantic**) of or having the characteristics of romanticism. ➤ **romantically** *adv.*

**romantic**[2] *n* **1** a romantic person. **2** (**Romantic**) a Romantic writer, artist, or composer.

**romanticism** *n* (*also* **Romanticism**) a late 18th- and early 19th-century literary and artistic movement that emphasized individual aspirations, nature, and the emotions.

**romanticize** *or* **-ise** *v* to present (a person or incident) in a misleadingly romantic way.

**Romany** *n* (*pl* **-ies**) **1** the Indic language of the gypsies. **2** a gypsy.

**Romeo** *n* (*pl* **-os**) a romantic male lover.

**romp**[1] *v* **1** to play in a boisterous manner. **2** *informal* to engage in light-hearted sexual activity. * **romp home** *informal* to win easily. **romp through** to accomplish very easily.

**romp**[2] *n* **1** boisterous or bawdy entertainment or play. **2** *informal* a period of light-hearted sexual activity.

**rompers** *pl n* a one-piece child's garment.

**rondo** *n* (*pl* **-os**) an instrumental composition with an opening section that recurs in the form ABACADA.

**röntgen** *or* **roentgen** *n* a unit of ionizing radiation.

**rood screen** *n* a large crucifix on a screen at the entrance to the chancel of a church.

**roof**[1] *n* (*pl* **roofs**) **1** the upper rigid cover of a building, vehicle, etc. **2** the vaulted or covering part of the mouth, skull, etc. **3** a ceiling. * **go through the roof 1** of e.g. prices: to reach extraordinarily high levels. **2** hit the roof (see HIT[1]).

**roof**[2] *v* to cover with a roof. ➤ **roofed** *adj,* **roofer** *n,* **roofing** *n.*

**roofer** *n* a person who builds or repairs roofs.

**roof rack** *n chiefly Brit* a metal carrying frame fixed on top of a car.

**rook**[1] *n* a common bird with black plumage, similar to a crow but nesting in colonies and having a bare grey face.

**rook**[2] *v informal* to defraud, cheat, or overcharge.

**rook**[3] *n* in chess, a castle-shaped piece that can move in a straight line across any number of squares.

**rookery** *n* (*pl* **-ies**) **1** the nests, usu built in the upper branches of trees, of a colony of rooks. **2** a breeding ground of a colony of penguins, seals, etc.

**rookie** *n informal* a new recruit.

**room**[1] *n* **1** a partitioned part of the inside of a building. **2** (*also in pl*) a set of rooms used as a separate lodging. **3** an extent of space sufficient or available for something.

**room**[2] *v NAmer* (*often* + with) to share lodgings.

**roomy** *adj* (**-ier, -iest**) having ample room; spacious.

**roost**[1] *n* a support or place where birds roost.

**roost**[2] *v* of a bird: to settle down for rest or sleep.

**rooster** *n* = COCK[1].

**root**[1] *n* **1** the underground part of a flowering plant that anchors it and absorbs food. **2** the part of a tooth, hair, the tongue, etc by which it is attached to the body. **3** an underlying cause or basis. **4** (*in pl*) family background or origin, or a feeling of belonging established through familiarity with a particular place. **5** a number which produces a given number when multiplied by itself an indicated number of times. * **take root 1** of a plant: to become rooted. **2** to become fixed or established.

**root**[2] *v* **1** to enable (a plant) to develop roots. **2** to fix or implant as if by roots. **3** (**be rooted in**) to originate or have developed from. ➤ **rooted** *adj.*

**root**[3] *v* **1** of a pig: to dig with the snout. **2** (+ about/in) to search unsystematically.

**root**[4] *v informal* (+ for) to lend vociferous or enthusiastic support to.

**rootless** *adj* having no established home or attachment to a particular place.

**root out** *v* to get rid of or destroy completely.

**rootstock** *n* **1** an underground plant part formed from several stems. **2** a plant onto which a scion is grafted.

**rope**[1] *n* **1** a strong thick cord composed of strands of fibres or wire twisted together. **2** a row or string of things. **3** (**the ropes**) the sides of a boxing ring. **4** (**the ropes**) the methods or procedures used in a job or activity. * **on the ropes** close to defeat.

**rope**[2] *v* **1** to fasten or tie with a rope. **2** (*usu* + off) to enclose or separate off with a rope.

**rope in** *v* to persuade (somebody) to join in or help with an activity.

**rope ladder** *n* a ladder having rope sides.

**ropy** *or* **ropey** *adj* (**-ier, -iest**) *Brit, informal* **1** of poor quality; shoddy. **2** somewhat unwell.

**rosary** *n* (*pl* **-ies**) a string of beads used in counting prayers while they are being recited.

**rose**[1] *n* **1** a prickly shrub with showy fragrant flowers. **2** a flower of this shrub. **3** a perforated outlet for water, e.g. from a shower or watering can. **4** a circular fitting that anchors the flex of a light bulb to a ceiling. **5** a pale to dark pinkish colour.

**rosé** *n* a light pink table wine.

**rose**[2] *v* past tense of RISE[1].

**rosehip** *n* see HIP[2].

**rosemary** *n* a shrubby plant with fragrant leaves that are used as a cooking herb.

**rosette** *n* **1** an ornament made of material gathered to resemble a rose and worn as a badge, trophy, or trimming. **2** a stylized carved or moulded rose used as a decorative motif in architecture.

**rosewood** *n* the valuable dark red or purplish wood of a tropical tree.

**Rosh Hashanah** *or* **Rosh Hashana** *n* the Jewish New Year.

**rosin** *n* a translucent resin used for rubbing on violin bows.

**roster**[1] *n* **1** a list giving the order in which personnel are to perform a duty, go on leave, etc. **2** a list of people available for a particular task or duty.

**roster**[2] *v* to place on a roster.

**rostrum** *n* (*pl* **rostra** *or* **rostrums**) a raised platform, *esp* for making a speech.

**rosy** *adj* (**-ier, -iest**) **1** rose-pink. **2** characterized by or encouraging optimism.

**rot**[1] *v* (**rotted, rotting**) to decompose, *esp* by the action of bacteria or fungi.

**rot**[2] *n* **1** the state of being rotten. **2** *informal* nonsense or rubbish.

**rota** *n chiefly Brit* a list specifying a fixed order of rotation, e.g. of people or duties.

**rotary** *adj* **1** characterized by rotation. **2** having a principal part that turns on an axis.

**rotate** *v* **1** to turn about an axis or a centre. **2** to take turns at performing an act or operation. **3** to cause (a crop or crops) to grow in rotation. **4** to exchange (individuals or units) with others. ➤ **rotatory** *adj.*

**rotation** *n* **1** movement on or around an axis. **2** one complete turn. **3** recurrence in a regular series. **4** the growing of different crops in succession in one field.

**rote** *n* the mechanical repetition of something to implant it in the memory.

**rotisserie** *n* a rotating spit on which meat is cooked.

**rotor** *n* **1** a part that revolves, *esp* in an electrical machine. **2** the system of a hub and horizontal blades that enables a helicopter to fly.

**rotten** *adj* **1** having rotted. **2** morally corrupt. **3** *informal* extremely unpleasant. **4** *informal* unhappy; ashamed. **5** *informal* inferior; useless.

**rotter** *n informal, dated* an objectionable or unprincipled person.

**Rottweiler** *n* a tall strongly-built black-and-tan dog with short hair.

**rotund** *adj* **1** markedly plump. **2** rounded.

**rouble** *or* **ruble** *n* the basic monetary unit of Russia.

**roué** *n* a debauched man.

**rouge** *n* a red cosmetic, *esp* for the cheeks or lips.

**rough**[1] *adj* **1** having an irregular or uneven surface; not smooth. **2** not gentle; harsh or violent. **3** of the sea: moving violently, with large waves. **4** of the weather: unpleasant; stormy. **5** lacking finish or refinement. **6** crudely or hastily made. **7** not thoroughly worked out; approximate. **8** of a voice: harsh-sounding. **9** *informal* difficult or unpleasant.

**rough**[2] *n* **1** *chiefly Brit, informal* a hooligan or ruffian. **2** (**the rough**) uneven ground covered with high grass, brush, and stones bordering a golf fairway. **3** a quick preliminary drawing or layout.

**rough**[3] *adv Brit* in want of material comforts; without proper lodging.

**rough**[4] *v* ✱ **rough it** *informal* to live in uncomfortable or primitive conditions.

**roughage** *n* coarse bulky food, e.g. bran, that is relatively high in fibre.

**rough diamond** *n* **1** an uncut diamond. **2** a person without social graces but of an upright or amiable nature.

**roughen** *v* to make or become rough.

**rough justice** *n* harsh or unfair treatment.

**roughly** *adv* **1** with insolence or violence. **2** crudely. **3** approximately.

**roughneck** *n* **1** *informal* a tough. **2** a worker who handles heavy drilling equipment on an oil rig.

**rough out** *v* to shape or plan in a preliminary way.

**roughshod** ✱ **ride roughshod over** to treat (a person or their rights) without justice or consideration.

**rough up** *v informal* to beat up.

**roulette** *n* a gambling game in which players bet on which compartment of a revolving wheel a small ball will come to rest in.

**round**[1] *adj* **1** circular. **2** cylindrical. **3** spherical. **4** shaped in a smooth curve. **5** of a voice: richly resonant in tone. **6** of a number: approximately correct; expressed as the nearest large unit. ➤ **roundness** *n.*

**round**[2] *adv chiefly Brit* **1** in a circular or curved path. **2** with revolving or rotating motion. **3** in circumference. **4** in an encircling position. **5** in or to the other or a specified direction. **6** in the specified order or relationship: *the right way round.* **7** to a particular person or place: *invite somebody round.* **8** back to consciousness or awareness. **9** from beginning to end: *all year* *round.* ✱ **round about 1** approximately; more or less. **2** in a ring round; on all sides of.

**round³** *prep chiefly Brit* **1** so as to revolve or progress about (a centre). **2** so as to encircle or enclose. **3** so as to avoid or get past. **4** in a position on the other side of: *round the corner.* **5** near to: *somewhere round here.*

**round⁴** *n* **1** a circular piece or spherical mass. **2** a route regularly travelled, e.g. by a person making deliveries. **3** a recurring sequence of events or tasks: *the weekly round.* **4** an event or series of events constituting a single stage in a larger process, *esp* in sport. **5** a division of a boxing or wrestling match. **6** in music, an unaccompanied song for three or more voices in which each sings the same tune starting one after the other. **7** a set of drinks served at one time to each person in a group. **8** a unit of ammunition enabling a gun to fire one shot. **9** *Brit* a sandwich made with two whole slices of bread.

**round⁵** *v* **1** to go round (a bend or corner). **2** (*often* + off/up/down) to express (a figure) as a round number. **3** (*often* + off) to make round or rounded. **4** (*often* + off/out) to bring to completion or perfection.

**roundabout¹** *n* **1** a road junction with a central island about which traffic moves in one direction only. **2** *Brit* a merry-go-round. **3** *Brit* a rotatable platform that is an amusement in a children's playground.

**roundabout²** *adj* circuitous; indirect.

**rounded** *adj* **1** smoothly curved. **2** fully developed in all respects.

**roundel** *n* **1** a circular panel, window, etc. **2** a circular mark identifying the nationality of a warplane.

**rounders** *n* a team game with bat and ball, where players try to score by running round all four bases before the ball is fielded.

**Roundhead** *n* an adherent of Parliament in the English Civil War.

**roundly** *adv* **1** in a blunt or severe manner. **2** thoroughly.

**round on** *v* to attack or scold (somebody) suddenly.

**round robin** *n* **1** a tournament in which every contestant plays every other contestant in turn. **2** a written petition or protest.

**round-the-clock** *adj* lasting or continuing 24 hours a day; constant.

**round trip** *n* a trip to a place and back.

**round up** *v* to gather in or bring together (people or things) from various quarters.

**roundworm** *n* a round-bodied parasitic worm that infests the intestines of people and animals.

**rouse** *v* **1** to wake up. **2** to make active. **3** to stimulate or excite (e.g. one's curiosity).

**rousing** *adj* stirring.

**rout¹** *n* **1** a confused retreat. **2** a disastrous defeat.

**rout²** *v* to defeat (an army, team, etc) decisively or disastrously.

**route¹** *n* a course planned or taken to get from a starting point to a destination.

**route²** *v* (**routeing** *or* **routing**) to send by a selected route.

**routine¹** *n* **1** a sequence of actions performed regularly or habitually in the same order. **2** a fixed piece of entertainment often repeated. **3** a sequence of computer instructions for carrying out a given task.

**routine²** *adj* **1** in accordance with established procedure. **2** commonplace or repetitious in character. ➤ **routinely** *adv.*

**roux** /rooh/ *n* (*pl* **roux**) a cooked mixture of fat and flour used as a thickening agent in a sauce.

**rove** *v* **1** to wander aimlessly or idly. **2** of the eyes: to look around at one object after the other. ➤ **rover** *n.*

**row¹** /roh/ *n* a number of objects or people arranged in a straight line. ✱ **in a row** *informal* one after another.

**row²** /roh/ *v* to propel a boat by means of oars. ➤ **rower** *n.*

**row³** /row/ *n informal* **1** *chiefly Brit* a noisy quarrel. **2** *chiefly Brit* excessive or unpleasant noise.

**row⁴** /row/ *v chiefly Brit, informal* to quarrel.

**rowan** *n* a small tree with white flowers and red berries.

**rowdy¹** *adj* (**-ier, -iest**) rough or boisterous.

**rowdy²** *n* (*pl* **-ies**) a rowdy person.

**rowlock** *n* a device on the side of a boat for holding an oar in place.

**royal¹** *adj* **1** relating, related, or belonging to a monarch. **2** suitable for royalty; regal or magnificent. **3** of superior size or quality. ➤ **royally** *adv.*

**royal²** *n informal* a member of a royal family.

**royal blue** *n* rich purplish blue.

**royalist** *n* (*also* **Royalist**) a supporter of a king or queen or of monarchical government, e.g. a Cavalier. ➤ **royalist** *adj.*

**royal jelly** *n* a highly nutritious secretion of the honeybee fed to larvae that will develop into queens.

**royalty** *n* (*pl* **-ies**) **1** people of royal blood. **2** regal character or bearing. **3** a payment made to an author or composer each time a work of theirs is performed or a copy of it is sold.

**RSPCA** *abbr Brit* Royal Society for the Prevention of Cruelty to Animals.

**RSVP** *abbr* (French) répondez s'il vous plaît = please reply.

**Rt Hon.** *abbr Brit* Right Honourable.

**Ru** *abbr* the chemical symbol for ruthenium.

**rub¹** *v* (**rubbed, rubbing**) **1** to move over the surface of (something), *esp* with a back-and-forth motion, while pressing down on it. **2** to move along a surface while pressing against it. **3** to apply (a substance) to a surface by rubbing.

✱ **rub shoulders** to mix socially. **rub up the wrong way** to irritate or displease.

**rub**[2] *n* **1** an act of rubbing. **2** a cream or ointment for rubbing on a painful body part. **3** (**the rub**) an obstacle or difficulty.

**rub along** *v Brit, informal* **1** to continue coping in a difficult situation. **2** to remain on friendly terms.

**rubber**[1] *n* **1** an elastic substance obtained by coagulating the juice of a tropical tree and used in car tyres, waterproof materials, etc. **2** *Brit* a small piece of rubber or plastic used for rubbing out pencil marks. **3** *NAmer, informal* a condom. ➤ **rubbery** *adj.*

**rubber**[2] *n* in bridge or whist, a unit of play consisting of three or five games.

**rubber band** *n* a loop of rubber used for holding small objects together.

**rubberneck** *v informal* **1** to show exaggerated curiosity. **2** to engage in sightseeing.

**rubber plant** *n* a plant of the fig family with glossy leathery leaves, grown as a houseplant.

**rubber stamp** *n* **1** a stamp of rubber for making imprints. **2** a routine endorsement or approval.

**rubber-stamp** *v* to approve (a plan, etc) as a matter of routine or at the dictate of somebody else.

**rubbing** *n* an image of a raised surface obtained by placing paper over it and rubbing the paper with charcoal, chalk, etc.

**rubbish**[1] *n* **1** *chiefly Brit* worthless or rejected articles. **2** nonsense. ➤ **rubbishy** *adj.*

**rubbish**[2] *v Brit, informal* to condemn as rubbish.

**rubble** *n* broken fragments of building material, e.g. brick or stone.

**rub down** *v* to clean, smooth, or dry by rubbing. ➤ **rubdown** *n.*

**rubella** *n* a virus disease, similar to but milder than measles.

**rubicund** *adj* ruddy.

**ruble** *n* see ROUBLE.

**rub off** *v* **1** to remove by rubbing, or disappear through rubbing. **2** (*often* + on) to be transferred to somebody through contact or example.

**rub out** *v* to remove or be removable with a rubber.

**rubric** *n* **1** a heading, e.g. in a book or manuscript. **2** an authoritative rule, *esp* for the conduct of church ceremonial.

**ruby** *n* (*pl* **-ies**) **1** a red precious stone. **2** the dark red colour of the ruby. **3** (*used before a noun*) marking a 40th anniversary.

**RUC** *abbr* Royal Ulster Constabulary.

**ruche** *n* a pleated or gathered strip of fabric used for trimming. ➤ **ruched** *adj.*

**ruck**[1] *n* **1** in rugby, a loose scrum formed round the ball when it is on the ground. **2** an indistinguishable mass of people or things. **3** *Brit, informal* a fight.

**ruck**[2] *v* in rugby, to be part of a ruck.

**ruck**[3] *v* (*often* + up) to wrinkle or crease.

**ruck**[4] *n* a wrinkle or crease.

**rucksack** *n* a lightweight bag carried on the back by shoulder straps.

**ruckus** *n* a row or disturbance.

**ruction** *n informal* **1** (*in pl*) a violent dispute. **2** a disturbance or uproar.

**rudder** *n* **1** a flat hinged piece attached vertically to a ship's stern and used for steering. **2** a movable piece attached to the tailfin of an aircraft to enable it to turn horizontally.

**ruddy** *adj* (**-ier, -iest**) **1** said of a complexion: having a healthy reddish colour. **2** red; reddish. **3** *Brit, euphem* = BLOODY 4.

**rude** *adj* **1** discourteous. **2** vulgar; indecent. **3** sudden and unpleasant; abrupt. **4** robust; vigorous. ➤ **rudely** *adv,* **rudeness** *n.*

**rudiment** *n* **1** (*usu in pl*) a basic principle or element, or a fundamental skill. **2** (*usu in pl*) something in its earliest stage of development.

**rudimentary** *adj* **1** basic and simple. **2** undeveloped or only partly developed.

**rue** *v* to feel bitter regret for (e.g. a past deed).

**rueful** *adj* expressing regret, often mixed with self-deprecating humour. ➤ **ruefully** *adv.*

**ruff** *n* **1** a broad starched collar of fluted linen or muslin. **2** a fringe of long hairs or feathers growing round the neck of a bird or animal.

**ruffian** *n* a brutal and lawless person.

**ruffle**[1] *v* **1** to disturb the smoothness of. **2** to trouble or vex. **3** to make (fabric) into a ruffle. ➤ **ruffled** *adj.*

**ruffle**[2] *n* a strip of fabric gathered or pleated on one edge.

**rug** *n* **1** a small carpet. **2** *chiefly Brit* a woollen blanket used as a wrap.

**rugby** *or* **Rugby** *n* a team game played with an oval ball, which features kicking, hand-to-hand passing, and tackling.

**rugged** *adj* **1** of terrain: having a rough uneven surface or outline. **2** strongly built or constituted; sturdy. **3** of a man: having attractively strong masculine features. ➤ **ruggedly** *adv,* **ruggedness** *n.*

**rugger** *n Brit, informal* rugby.

**ruin**[1] *n* **1** destruction or spoiling. **2** (*often in pl*) the remains of something dilapidated or destroyed. **3** a person's downfall, or the cause of it. **4** the total loss of one's money and other assets.

**ruin**[2] *v* **1** to damage irreparably. **2** to reduce to financial ruin. **3** to make thoroughly unpleasant or unenjoyable; to spoil.

**ruination** *n* the act of ruining, or a cause of ruin.

**ruinous** *adj* **1** causing ruin or the likelihood of ruin. **2** ruined. ➤ **ruinously** *adv.*

**rule**[1] *n* **1** a statement of what constitutes right conduct that people are expected to obey. **2** the exercise of sovereign authority, or the period during which a particular ruler or government exercises it. **3** (**the rule**) what happens normally or customarily. **4** = RULER 2. **5** a printed or written line or dash. ✱ **as a rule** generally; for the most part.
**rule**[2] *v* **1** to have sovereign power over (a nation or people). **2** to exercise control over. **3** to keep under control; to restrain. **4** to make a judicial decision. **5** to draw (a line) with a ruler. **6** to mark (paper) with parallel lines.
**rule in** *v* to consider as a possibility.
**rule of thumb** *n* a rough practical or common-sense method.
**rule out** *v* **1** to exclude. **2** to deny the possibility of. **3** to make impossible.
**ruler** *n* **1** somebody who rules. **2** a smooth-edged strip of wood, plastic, etc that is marked off in units, e.g. centimetres, and is used for drawing straight lines or measuring.
**ruling** *n* an official or authoritative decision.
**rum**[1] *n* an alcoholic spirit made by distilling molasses.
**rum**[2] *adj* (**rummer, rummest**) *Brit, informal, dated* peculiar; strange.
**rumba** *or* **rhumba** *n* a ballroom dance of Cuban origin marked by pronounced hip movements.
**rumble**[1] *v* **1** to make a low heavy rolling sound. **2** *Brit, informal* to discover the true character of.
**rumble**[2] *n* **1** a rumbling sound. **2** *NAmer, informal* a street fight, *esp* between gangs.
**rumbustious** *adj chiefly Brit, informal* irrepressibly exuberant.
**ruminant** *n* a mammal, e.g. a cow, sheep, or camel, that chews the cud.
**ruminate** *v* **1** to engage in deep thought. **2** of a ruminant: to chew the cud.
**rummage**[1] *v* to engage in a haphazard search.
**rummage**[2] *n* **1** a search, *esp* among a jumbled assortment of objects. **2** *chiefly NAmer* = JUMBLE[2].
**rummy** *n* a card game in which each player tries to assemble combinations of related cards.
**rumour**[1] (*NAmer* **rumor**) *n* a statement circulated without confirmation of its truth.
**rumour**[2] (*NAmer* **rumor**) *v* (**be rumoured**) to be said, according to rumour, to be.
**rump** *n* **1** the rear part of a mammal, bird, etc. **2** *humorous* a person's buttocks. **3** a small or inferior remnant of a larger group.
**rumple** *v* to make or become wrinkled, crumpled, or dishevelled. ➤ **rumpled** *adj.*
**rumpus** *n* a noisy commotion.
**run**[1] *v* (**running,** *past tense* **ran,** *past part.* **run**) **1** to go at a speed faster than a walk, with only one foot on the ground at any time. **2** to hasten or move quickly. **3** to cause to move lightly or freely: *She ran a comb through her hair.* **4** of a bus or train: to operate on a regular route. **5** to convey (somebody) a short distance in a vehicle. **6** to take part in a race. **7** to be a candidate in an election. **8** to manage or carry on (a business, enterprise, etc). **9** to operate (a vehicle, machine, etc). **10** of a machine: to function. **11** of an agreement etc: to continue in force. **12** to continue or extend over a specified period or length. **13** (+ in) of a characteristic: to be prevalent. **14** to cause (water, etc) to flow. **15** of a liquid: to flow. **16** of a colour: to spread or dissolve when wet. **17** to be at a specified level: *Inflation is running at 4 per cent.* **18** to publish (a story in a newspaper, etc). **19** to smuggle (e.g. guns or drugs). **20** (+ by/past) to outline (an idea, plan, etc) to somebody in order to ascertain their opinion of it. ✱ **run across** to meet with or discover by chance. **run after** to pursue or chase. **run into 1** to encounter (somebody) by chance. **2** to collide with. **run short of** to have little left of (a supply).
**run**[2] *n* **1** an act of running. **2** a journey or excursion in a car. **3** a regularly travelled course or route. **4** an inclined course, e.g. for skiing. **5** a continuous period or sequence: *a run of bad luck.* **6** (**the run of**) free access to every part of a place. **7** general tendency or direction. **8** the average or prevailing kind or class: *the general run of students.* **9** an enclosure for domestic animals. **10** a unit of scoring in cricket or baseball. **11** a ladder in tights or a stocking. ✱ **give somebody a run for their money** to present a serious challenge to somebody. **on the run 1** without pausing. **2** trying to avoid arrest or capture, *esp* after escaping from custody.
**run along** *v informal* to leave.
**runaround** *n* (**the runaround**) *informal* delaying action, *esp* in response to a request: *When I phoned to complain, they just gave me the runaround.*
**runaway**[1] *n* a fugitive.
**runaway**[2] *adj* **1** running out of control. **2** of a victory, success, etc: decisive.
**run away** *v* **1** to flee or escape. **2** to avoid responsibilities. ✱ **run away with 1** to go beyond the control of. **2** to believe too easily.
**rundown** *n* an itemized report or summary.
**run down** *v* **1** to knock down with a vehicle. **2** to criticize or disparage. **3** to reduce or be reduced in size or strength. **4** to deteriorate.
**run-down** *adj* **1** in a state of disrepair. **2** in poor health.
**rune** *n* **1** a character from an ancient Germanic alphabet. **2** a magical or cryptic utterance or inscription. ➤ **runic** *adj.*
**rung**[1] *n* **1** any of the crosspieces of a ladder. **2** a level or stage in something.
**rung**[2] *v* past part. of RING[3].
**run in** *v* **1** to use (a vehicle) carefully when it is new. **2** *informal* to arrest (somebody).
**runnel** *n* **1** a small stream; a brook. **2** a gutter.

**runner** *n* **1** a person who runs in a race or for exercise. **2** an entrant for a race that actually competes in it. **3** a messenger. **4** somebody who smuggles illicit or contraband goods. **5** a groove or bar on which something, e.g. a drawer, a sledge, or an ice skate, slides. **6** a horizontal stem from the base of a plant that buds to produce new plants. **7** a long narrow carpet. ✱ **do a runner** *Brit, informal* to leave in haste or escape.

**runner bean** *n chiefly Brit* the long green pod of a climbing bean, used as a vegetable.

**runner-up** *n* (*pl* **runners-up**) a competitor or team that comes second in a contest.

**running**[1] *n* **1** the act of running. **2** management; operation. ✱ **in/out of the running** having a good/poor chance of winning. **make the running** to set the pace.

**running**[2] *adj* **1** of water: flowing in a stream, etc or available through pipes. **2** of e.g. a sore: producing pus. **3** having stages that follow in rapid succession. **4** made during the course of a process or activity: *a running commentary.*

**running**[3] *adv* in succession.

**running board** *n* a footboard along the side of a car.

**runny** *adj* (**-ier, -iest**) **1** of a thinner or more liquid consistency than usual. **2** of the nose: continuously producing mucus.

**run off** *v* **1** to compose or produce quickly. **2** to decide a competition with an extra contest.

**run-of-the-mill** *adj* average; commonplace.

**run out** *v* **1** to become used up. **2** to come to an end; to expire. **3** in cricket: to dismiss a batsman by breaking the wicket while the batsman is making a run. ✱ **run out of** to finish the available supply of. **run out on** *informal* to desert (somebody).

**run over** *v* **1** to injure or kill with a motor vehicle. **2** to read through quickly.

**runt** *n* an unusually small animal, *esp* the smallest of a litter.

**run through** *v* **1** to pierce with a weapon. **2** to read through quickly.

**run up** *v* **1** to accumulate (debts). **2** to make or erect quickly. ✱ **run up against** to experience (an unexpected difficulty).

**run-up** *n* **1** a period that immediately precedes an action or event. **2** an approach run to provide momentum, e.g. for a jump or throw.

**runway** *n* an strip of ground on which aircraft land and take off.

**rupee** /rooh'pee/ *n* the basic monetary unit of India, Pakistan, and Sri Lanka.

**rupture**[1] *n* **1** the act of breaking apart or bursting. **2** a hernia.

**rupture**[2] *v* **1** to break or burst. **2** to cause a hernia in (oneself or a body part).

**rural** *adj* relating to the country, country people, or country life. ➤ **rurally** *adv.*

**ruse** *n* a wily scheme or trick.

**rush**[1] *v* **1** to move forward, progress, or act quickly or eagerly or without preparation. **2** to perform or finish in a short time or at high speed. **3** to urge (somebody) to an excessive speed. **4** to attack with a sudden charge.

**rush**[2] *n* **1** a rapid and violent forward motion. **2** a sudden onset of emotion. **3** a surge of busy or hurried activity. **4** a sudden demand for something. **5** a great movement of people, *esp* in search of wealth. **6** (*in pl*) the unedited print of a film scene processed directly after shooting. **7** an immediate brief pleasurable feeling after taking a drug such as heroin.

**rush**[3] *n* a tufted marsh plant with leaves used to make the seats of chairs, mats, etc.

**rush hour** *n* a period of the day when traffic is at a peak.

**rusk** *n* a dry and crisp piece of twice-baked bread, or a light dry biscuit.

**russet** *n* **1** a reddish to yellowish brown colour. **2** a russet-coloured eating apple.

**Russian roulette** *n* an act of bravado consisting of spinning the cylinder of a revolver loaded with one cartridge, pointing the muzzle at one's own head, and pulling the trigger.

**rust**[1] *n* **1** brittle reddish coating formed on iron by contact with moist air. **2** a destructive fungal disease of plants. **3** a reddish brown to orange colour.

**rust**[2] *v* to form rust.

**rustic**[1] *adj* characteristic of the countryside, *esp* in being simple or unsophisticated. ➤ **rusticity** *n.*

**rustic**[2] *n often derog* an unsophisticated rural person.

**rustle**[1] *n* a quick succession of faint crackling sounds.

**rustle**[2] *v* **1** to make or cause a rustle. **2** to steal cattle or horses. ➤ **rustler** *n.*

**rustle up** *v informal* to produce (food, etc) at short notice.

**rusty** *adj* (**-ier, -iest**) **1** affected by rust. **2** of the colour of rust. **3** slow or inexpert through lack of practice.

**rut**[1] *n* **1** a groove in a track worn by a wheel. **2** a tedious routine. ➤ **rutted** *adj.*

**rut**[2] *n* **1** an annually recurrent state of readiness to copulate, in the male deer or other mammals. **2** (*often* **the rut**) the period during which rut normally occurs.

**rut**[3] *v* (**rutted, rutting**) to be in a state of rut.

**ruthless** *adj* showing no pity or compassion. ➤ **ruthlessly** *adv,* **ruthlessness** *n.*

**rye** *n* **1** a hardy grass widely grown for grain. **2** whisky made from rye.

**ryegrass** *n* a type of grass used *esp* for pasture and lawns.

**S**[1] *or* **s** *n* (*pl* **S's** *or* **Ss** *or* **s's**) the 19th letter of the English alphabet.

**S**[2] *abbr* **1** South. **2** Southern.

**S**[3] *abbr* the chemical symbol for sulphur.

**sabbath** *n* (*usu* **the Sabbath**) a day observed for rest and worship.

**sabbatical** *n* a period of paid leave granted to academics for study or travel.

**sable**[1] *n* (*pl* **sables** *or* **sable**) a mammal like a marten, found in the forests of northern Asia and having a valuable dark brown fur.

**sable**[2] *adj* **1** (*often used after a noun*) in heraldry, black. **2** *literary* black, dark, or gloomy.

**sabotage**[1] *n* **1** deliberate damage done to military or industrial installations. **2** deliberate subversion of a plan or project.

**sabotage**[2] *v* to destroy or subvert by sabotage.

**saboteur** *n* somebody who commits sabotage.

**sabre** (*NAmer* **saber**) *n* **1** a heavy sword with a curved blade. **2** a light fencing sword with an arched guard and a tapering blade.

**sabre-toothed tiger** *n* an extinct wild cat with long curved upper canine teeth.

**sac** *n* a pouch, often filled with fluid, in an animal or plant.

**saccharin** *n* a sweet-tasting compound that is used as a substitute for sugar.

**saccharine** *adj* sentimental or mawkish.

**sacerdotal** *adj* of priests or the priesthood.

**sachet** *n* a small sealed bag or packet containing a small amount of something.

**sack**[1] *n* **1** a large bag of plastic or thick material. **2** (**the sack**) *informal* dismissal from employment. **3** (**the sack**) *informal* bed. ✱ **hit the sack** *informal* to go to bed.

**sack**[2] *v* *informal* to dismiss (somebody) from employment. ➤ **sackable** *adj.*

**sack**[3] *n* the destruction of a place captured in war.

**sack**[4] *v* to plunder and destroy (a place) after capturing it.

**sackcloth** *n* a coarse fabric used as sacking.

**sacra** *n* pl of SACRUM.

**sacrament** *n* **1** a formal religious act regarded as conferring divine grace on the recipient. **2** (**the Sacrament**) the bread and wine used in the Eucharist. **3** something considered to have sacred or religious significance.

**sacred** *adj* **1** dedicated or set apart for the worship of a god or gods. **2** dedicated as a memorial. **3** worthy of religious veneration; holy. **4** commanding reverence and respect. **5** relating to or used in religion.

**sacred cow** *n* something regarded as beyond criticism.

**sacrifice**[1] *n* **1** the killing of a victim on an altar as an offering to a deity. **2** a person or animal offered in sacrifice. **3** the losing of one thing for the sake of a greater. **4** something forgone or done without.

**sacrifice**[2] *v* **1** to offer as a sacrifice. **2** to give up (something) for the sake of an ideal or end. ➤ **sacrificial** *adj.*

**sacrilege** *n* an improper use of or attitude to something sacred. ➤ **sacrilegious** *adj.*

**sacristan** *or* **sacrist** *n* an official in charge of the sacristy of a church.

**sacristy** *n* (*pl* **-ies**) a room in a church where the clergy put on their vestments.

**sacrosanct** *adj* accorded the highest reverence and respect.

**sacrum** *n* (*pl* **sacra**) the part of the spinal column that is directly connected with or forms part of the pelvis.

**sad** *adj* (**sadder, saddest**) **1** affected with or expressing unhappiness. **2** causing unhappiness. **3** *informal* pathetic or contemptible. ➤ **sadly** *adv,* **sadness** *n.*

**sadden** *v* to make sad.

**saddle**[1] *n* **1** a padded seat secured to the back of a horse for the rider to sit on. **2** a seat on a bicycle or motorcycle. **3** a ridge connecting two peaks. **4** a cut of meat from the back of an animal.

**saddle**[2] *v* **1** to put a saddle on (a horse). **2** to burden with a task or responsibility.

**saddlebag** *n* a bag attached to the back of a saddle.

**saddler** *n* somebody who makes and sells saddles and other equipment for horses.

**saddlery** *n* (*pl* **-ies**) **1** saddles, bridles, etc, used for riding a horse. **2** the making, repair, or sale of saddlery. **3** a saddler's place of work or trade.

**sadism** *n* the act of obtaining sexual gratification by inflicting physical pain and humiliation on another person. ➤ **sadist** *n,* **sadistic** *adj.*

**sadomasochism** *n* the act obtaining sexual gratification through sadism and masochism. ➤ **sadomasochist** *n,* **sadomasochistic** *adj.*

**safari** *n* (*pl* **safaris**) an expedition to observe wild animals in their natural habitat.

**safari park** *n* a large area of land where wild animals are kept for visitors to observe as they drive through.

**safe**[1] *adj* **1** secure from threat of danger or loss. **2** no longer in danger. **3** providing protection from danger. **4** not threatening or involving danger. **5** unlikely to cause controversy. **6** not liable to take risks. **7** trustworthy; reliable. ➤ **safely** *adv.*

**safe**[2] *n* a reinforced room or cabinet, often with a complex lock, for keeping money and valuables.

**safeguard**[1] *n* a precautionary measure or stipulation.

**safeguard**[2] *v* to provide a safeguard for.

**safe house** *n* a place of concealment and safety for people threatened with violence.

**safekeeping** *n* protection or the state of being kept safe.

**safe sex** *n* sexual activity in which precautions are taken to prevent the transmission of diseases.

**safety** *n* (*pl* **-ies**) the condition of being safe.

**safety belt** *n* a seat belt in a vehicle.

**safety net** *n* **1** a net designed to protect acrobats by catching them if they fall. **2** a protective measure.

**safety pin** *n* a pin in the form of a clasp with a guard covering its point when fastened.

**saffron** *n* a yellow spice made from the dried stigmas of a type of crocus, used to colour and flavour food.

**sag** *v* (**sagged**, **sagging**) **1** to drop or sink from weight or pressure. **2** to lose strength.

**saga** *n* **1** a medieval narrative dealing with historic or legendary figures and events. **2** a long detailed account of successive events.

**sagacious** *adj* having sound judgment. ➤ **sagacity** *n.*

**sage**[1] *n* a person renowned for great wisdom.

**sage**[2] *adj* having or showing great wisdom. ➤ **sagely** *adv.*

**sage**[3] *n* a plant of the mint family with aromatic leaves used as a herb.

**Sagittarius** *n* the ninth sign of the zodiac (the Archer).

**sago** *n* a dry powdered starch made from the pith of a palm and used as a food.

**sahib** *n* a respectful term of address to a man, used in India.

**said**[1] *v* past tense and past part. of SAY[1].

**said**[2] *adj* mentioned previously.

**sail**[1] *n* **1** an expanse of fabric spread to catch the wind as a means of propelling a ship or boat. **2** a flat board forming an arm of a windmill. **3** a voyage by ship or boat.

**sail**[2] *v* **1** to travel in a boat or ship. **2** to handle a sailing boat as a sport. **3** to travel on water by the action of wind on sails. **4** to move in a stately manner. **5** to begin a journey by water. **6** to direct the movement of (a ship or boat). ✱ **sail close to the wind** to take risks. **sail through** to succeed in (something) with ease.

**sailboard** *n* a flat board with a mast and a sail, used in windsurfing.

**sailcloth** *n* **1** a heavy canvas used for making sails. **2** a lightweight canvas used for clothing.

**sailing boat** *n* a boat propelled by sails.

**sailor** *n* **1** somebody who sails a ship or boat. **2** a member of a ship's crew. **3** somebody who sails for sport. **4** a person considered in terms of their likelihood to be seasick.

**saint**[1] *n* **1** a person officially recognized by the Christian Church as being holy and worthy of veneration. **2** any of the spirits of the dead in heaven. **3** a person of outstanding piety or virtue. ➤ **sainthood** *n,* **saintly** *adj.*

**saint**[2] *v* to recognize or designate as a saint.

**Saint Elmo's fire** *n* an electrical discharge seen as flame in stormy weather at prominent points.

**Saint George's Cross** *n* a red cross on a white background, *esp* on the national flag of England.

**Saint John's wort** *n* a preparation made from a plant and used to relieve depression.

**saint's day** *n* in the Christian Church, a day on which a particular saint is commemorated each year.

**sake**[1] *n* benefit, purpose, or interest. ✱ **for goodness sake** used as an exclamation of protest or impatience. **for the sake of 1** for the benefit of. **2** in the interest of.

**sake**[2] *or* **saki** /'sahki/ *n* a Japanese alcoholic drink made from fermented rice.

**salaam**[1] *n* a ceremonial greeting performed in Muslim countries by bowing low and placing the right palm on the forehead.

**salaam**[2] *v* to make a salaam.

**salacious** *adj* **1** arousing sexual desire. **2** lecherous or lustful.

**salad** *n* a dish of mixed raw vegetables.

**salad days** *pl n* a time of youthful inexperience.

**salamander** *n* **1** an amphibian resembling a lizard but covered with a soft moist skin. **2** a mythical animal that can withstand the effects of fire.

**salami** /sə'lahmi/ *n* (*pl* **salamis**) a highly seasoned sliced sausage.

**salary** *n* (*pl* **-ies**) a fixed monthly payment made to an employee. ➤ **salaried** *adj.*

**sale** *n* **1** the act or an instance of selling. **2** an event at which goods are sold or auctioned. **3** a period in which goods are sold at reduced prices. ✱ **for sale** available to be bought. ➤ **saleable** *adj.*

**saleroom** *n chiefly Brit* a place where goods are displayed for sale, *esp* by auction.

**salesman** *or* **saleswoman** *n* (*pl* **salesmen** *or* **saleswomen**) a man or woman employed to sell goods. ➤ **salesmanship** *n.*

**salesperson** *n* (*pl* **salespersons** *or* **salespeople**) a person employed to sell goods.

**salient**[1] *adj* most noticeable or important. ➤ **salience** *n.*

**salient**[2] *n* a piece of land or part of a fortification that projects from its surroundings.

**saline** *adj* **1** containing salt. **2** *esp* of a laxative: containing salts of potassium, sodium, or magnesium. ➤ **salinity** *n.*

**saliva** *n* a mixture of water, protein, salts, and enzymes that is secreted into the mouth by glands, to help with chewing and digesting food. ➤ **salivary** *adj.*

**salivate** *v* to have a flow of saliva in the mouth. ➤ **salivation** *n.*

**sallow** *adj* of a sickly yellowish colour.

**sally**[1] *n* (*pl* **-ies**) **1** a sortie of troops from a besieged position. **2** a witty remark or retort.

**sally**[2] *v* (**-ies, -ied**) (*usu* + forth) to set out with determination.

**salmon** *n* (*pl* **salmons** *or* **salmon**) a large food fish of the North Atlantic that is highly valued for its pink flesh.

**salmonella** *n* (*pl* **salmonellae**) a bacterium that causes food poisoning.

**salon** *n* **1** an establishment where hairdressers, beauticians, couturiers, etc work. **2** an elegant reception room or living room. **3** formerly, a gathering of writers and artists in a fashionable home.

**saloon** *n* **1** *Brit* a more comfortable bar in a pub. **2** *NAmer* a bar. **3** *Brit* an enclosed car with a separate boot. **4** a well-appointed railway carriage.

**salopettes** *pl n* high-waisted padded or quilted trousers with shoulder straps, worn for skiing.

**salsa** *n* **1** a lively and rhythmic type of Latin American popular music. **2** a spicy Mexican sauce.

**salt**[1] *n* **1** sodium chloride occurring naturally, and used in the form of white powder or crystals for seasoning or preserving food. **2** a chemical compound resulting from replacement of all or part of the hydrogen atoms of an acid by a metal atom or other chemical group. ✻ **the salt of the earth** a person noted for goodness, kindness, honesty, etc. **take something with a pinch/grain of salt** to have doubts or reservations about it.

**salt**[2] *v* **1** to season or preserve with salt. **2** to sprinkle salt on (a road or path) to melt ice or snow.

**salt**[3] *adj* **1** containing salt. **2** growing in salt water.

**saltcellar** *n* a small open dish or shaker for salt.

**saltings** *pl n* a marshy coastal area flooded regularly by tides.

**saltpetre** (*NAmer* **saltpeter**) *n* a white powder (potassium nitrate) used in making gunpowder.

**salty** *adj* (**-ier, -iest**) **1** seasoned with or containing salt. **2** piquant or witty. **3** earthy or coarse. ➤ **saltiness** *n.*

**salubrious** *adj* **1** promoting health or wellbeing. **2** of a place: pleasant and respectable.

**salutary** *adj* of a bad experience: offering an opportunity to learn or improve.

**salutation** *n* an expression of greeting.

**salute**[1] *v* **1** to address (somebody) with expressions of greeting or respect. **2** to show recognition to (a superior) by raising the hand to the side of the head. **3** to honour (somebody) by the firing of a guns into the air. **4** to praise or admire. ➤ **saluter** *n.*

**salute**[2] *n* **1** a greeting or salutation. **2** a sign or ceremony expressing goodwill or respect. **3** an act of saluting somebody. **4** a ceremonial firing of guns into the air.

**salvage**[1] *n* **1** the act of rescuing a ship or its cargo from loss at sea. **2** property saved or rescued from a wreck or fire.

**salvage**[2] *v* **1** to rescue (a ship or its cargo) from loss at sea. **2** to extract or preserve (something of use or value) from destruction or failure. ➤ **salvageable** *adj.*

**salvation** *n* **1** deliverance from danger or destruction. **2** somebody or something that brings about salvation. **3** in Christian theology, deliverance from sin brought about by faith.

**salve**[1] *n* **1** an ointment for soothing wounds or sores. **2** a soothing influence or agency.

**salve**[2] *v* to soothe or assuage.

**salver** *n* an ornamental tray.

**salvo** *n* (*pl* **-os** *or* **-oes**) **1** a simultaneous discharge of guns. **2** a sudden or emphatic burst of criticism or applause.

**Samaritan** *n* **1** a native or inhabitant of Samaria in ancient Palestine. **2** somebody who gives aid to those in distress.

**samba**[1] *n* a Brazilian dance of African origin.

**samba**[2] *v* (**sambas, sambaed, sambaing**) to dance the samba.

**same**[1] *adj* **1** being one single thing, person, or group. **2** identical in appearance, quantity, type, etc.

**same**[2] *pron* **1** the same thing, person, or group. **2** something previously mentioned. ✻ **all/just the same** nevertheless.

**same**[3] *adv* (*usu* **the same**) in the same manner: *two words spelt the same.*

**samey** *adj* (**samier, samiest**) *Brit, informal* lacking in individuality or originality.

**samovar** *n* a Russian tea urn with a tap at its base and an interior heating tube.

**sample**[1] *n* **1** a part or item serving to show the character or quality of a larger whole or group. **2** a selection of individuals used as a basis for statistical analysis. **3** a specimen taken for scientific testing or analysis.

**sample²** *v* **1** to take a sample of. **2** to experience or get a taste of. **3** to take an extract from (a recording) and mix it into a new recording.

**sampler** *n* **1** a piece of needlework embroidered in various stitches as an example of skill. **2** a piece of equipment used for sampling a recording.

**samurai** /'sam(y)oorie/ *n* (*pl* **samurai**) a member of the warrior class of feudal Japan.

**sanatorium** *n* (*pl* **sanatoriums** *or* **sanatoria**) **1** a medical establishment for treating people with long-term illnesses. **2** *Brit* a room in a boarding school where sick pupils are looked after.

**sanctify** *v* (**-ies, -ied**) **1** to set apart for a sacred purpose. **2** to give moral, social, or religious sanction to. ➤ **sanctification** *n*, **sanctifier** *n*.

**sanctimonious** *adj* making a show or pretence of piety.

**sanction¹** *n* **1** official permission or authoritative ratification. **2** a penalty attached to an offence. **3** (*in pl*) economic or military measures adopted to force a nation to comply with a requirement.

**sanction²** *v* **1** to give approval or consent to. **2** to make valid or binding.

**sanctity** *n* (*pl* **-ies**) the quality or state of being holy.

**sanctuary** *n* (*pl* **-ies**) **1** a consecrated place. **2** a place of refuge and protection. **3** a wildlife refuge. **4** a refuge for animals that have been injured or ill-treated. **5** immunity from the law formerly extended to somebody taking refuge in a church.

**sanctum** *n* (*pl* **sanctums** *or* **sancta**) **1** a sacred place. **2** a private or secluded place.

**sand¹** *n* **1** loose granular particles formed from the disintegration of rock, forming the main constituent of beaches and the beds of seas and rivers. **2** (*usu in pl*) an area of sand.

**sand²** *v* to smooth or prepare (a surface) by rubbing with sandpaper.

**sandal** *n* a light shoe consisting of a sole held on the foot by straps.

**sandalwood** *n* the fragrant yellowish wood of an Asian tree.

**sandbag¹** *n* a bag filled with sand and used as ballast or to form a barrier.

**sandbag²** *v* (**sandbagged, sandbagging**) to support or protect with sandbags.

**sandbank** *n* a large deposit of sand that becomes visible at low tide.

**sandbar** *n* a ridge of sand built up by currents in a river or sea.

**sandblast** *v* to clean (stone or glass) with a high-speed jet of sand.

**sandcastle** *n* a model of a castle made from sand.

**sander** *n* a power tool used for smoothing a surface.

**sandpaper¹** *n* paper with a thin layer of sand glued to it, used for smoothing wood.

**sandpaper²** *v* to rub or smooth (a surface) with sandpaper.

**sandpit** *n* an enclosure containing sand for children to play in.

**sandstone** *n* a rock consisting of compressed sand grains.

**sandstorm** *n* a strong wind driving clouds of sand in a desert.

**sandwich¹** *n* **1** two slices of bread with a filling between. **2** a sponge cake with jam or cream between its layers.

**sandwich²** *v* **1** (+ between) to insert (something) between two things of a different kind. **2** (+ together) to put together in layers.

**sandwich board** *n* a pair of boards hung in front of and behind the body of a walking person, used for advertising.

**sandwich course** *n* *Brit* a vocational course including periods of practical experience.

**sandy** *adj* (**-ier, -iest**) **1** consisting of or sprinkled with sand. **2** yellowish brown.

**sane** *adj* **1** mentally sound. **2** sensible or rational.

**sang** *v* past tense of SING.

**sangfroid** /song'frwah/ *n* self-possession or coolness under strain.

**sanguinary** *adj formal* bloodthirsty or murderous.

**sanguine** *adj* cheerfully confident and optimistic.

**sanitarium** *n* (*pl* **sanitariums** *or* **sanitaria**) *NAmer* = SANATORIUM.

**sanitary** *adj* **1** of or promoting health. **2** hygienic.

**sanitary towel** *n* a pad worn by a woman during menstruation to absorb the flow of blood.

**sanitation** *n* facilities and measures involved in the promotion of hygiene and prevention of disease, e.g. the disposal of sewage and collection of rubbish.

**sanitize** *or* **-ise** *v* **1** to make hygienic. **2** to make (something unpleasant) more acceptable. ➤ **sanitization** *n*.

**sanity** *n* **1** the state of being sane. **2** rational behaviour or judgment.

**sank** *v* past tense of SINK¹.

**Sanskrit** *n* an ancient language of the people of India.

**Santa Claus** *or* **Santa** *n* Father Christmas.

**sap¹** *n* **1** a watery solution that circulates through a plant bringing nourishment. **2** vitality or vigour.

**sap²** *v* (**sapped, sapping**) to drain of vitality.

**sapling** *n* a young tree.

**sapper** *n* a soldier who digs trenches, lays mines, and does other engineering work.

**sapphic** *adj* relating to lesbians.
**sapphire** *n* **1** a transparent blue gem. **2** a brilliant blue colour.
**saprophyte** *n* a plant or fungus that lives on dead or decaying plant and animal tissues. ➤ **saprophytic** *adj.*
**Saracen** *n* a Muslim at the time of the Crusades.
**sarcasm** *n* the use of caustic and ironic language to express contempt or bitterness.
**sarcastic** *adj* using sarcasm. ➤ **sarcastically** *adv.*
**sarcophagus** *n* (*pl* **sarcophagi**) a large decorated stone coffin.
**sardine** *n* (*pl* **sardines** *or* **sardine**) a small fish of the herring family.
**sardonic** *adj* derisively mocking. ➤ **sardonically** *adv.*
**sari** *or* **saree** /'sahri/ *n* (*pl* **saris** *or* **sarees**) a length of cloth draped over the body, worn by women from the Indian subcontinent.
**sarky** *adj* (**-ier, -iest**) *Brit, informal* sarcastic. ➤ **sarkily** *adv.*
**sarnie** *n Brit, informal* a sandwich.
**sarong** *n* a long strip of cloth wrapped round the body, worn in parts of SE Asia.
**sartorial** *adj* relating to tailoring or clothing. ➤ **sartorially** *adv.*
**sash**[1] *n* a band of cloth worn round the waist or over one shoulder.
**sash**[2] *n* a frame holding a pane of glass in a window.
**sashay** /'sashay/ *v informal* to walk with exaggerated swaying movements of the hips and shoulders.
**sash window** *n* a window having two sashes that slide up and down.
**Sassenach** *n Scot, Irish, derog* an English person.
**sassy** *adj informal* cheeky or impudent.
**SAT** *abbr* standard assessment task.
**sat** *v* past tense and past part. of SIT[1].
**Satan** *n* the Devil.
**satanic** *adj* of Satan or satanism.
**satanism** *n* the worship of Satan. ➤ **satanist** *n and adj.*
**satchel** *n* a bag with a shoulder strap.
**sated** *adj* having as much as, or more than, one wants.
**satellite** *n* **1** a celestial body orbiting another of larger size. **2** an artificial device that orbits the earth or another planet, used for collecting scientific information or in communications. **3** somebody or something that is dependent on and controlled by another.
**satellite dish** *n* a dish-shaped aerial used to transmit and receive signals in satellite communications.
**satellite television** *n* television broadcasting using satellites to transmit and receive signals.
**satiate** *v* to give as much as or more than somebody wants. ➤ **satiation** *n.*
**satiety** *n* the state of being sufficiently or excessively fed or gratified.
**satin** *n* a smooth silky fabric. ➤ **satiny** *adj.*
**satire** *n* **1** the use of wit, irony, or sarcasm to expose foolishness or vice. **2** a literary work that uses satire. ➤ **satirist** *n.*
**satirical** *or* **satiric** *adj* involving the use of satire. ➤ **satirically** *adv.*
**satirize** *or* **-ise** *v* to censure or ridicule with satire.
**satisfaction** *n* **1** the fulfilment of something that is necessary or the good feeling arising from this. **2** compensation for a loss or injury. **3** the discharge of a legal obligation.
**satisfactory** *adj* fulfilling a need; acceptable. ➤ **satisfactorily** *adv.*
**satisfy** *v* (**-ies, -ied**) **1** to fulfil the needs or expectations of. **2** to meet or comply with (requirements). **3** to provide with reassurance.
**satsuma** *n* a sweet type of tangerine with a loose skin.
**saturate** /'sachoorayt/ *v* **1** to provide or fill (a substance) with another substance to the point where no more of it can be absorbed. **2** to cause (two or more substances) to combine chemically until there is no further ability or tendency to combine. **3** to make thoroughly wet. **4** to supply (a market) with all the goods it will absorb. **5** to overwhelm (an area) with military forces or firepower. ➤ **saturation** *n.*
**saturated** *adj* **1** of a solution: not capable of absorbing any more of the substance it contains. **2** of a chemical compound: unable to form products by chemical addition or by uniting directly with another compound. **3** of a colour: bright and rich.
**Saturday** *n* the day of the week following Friday.
**saturnine** *adj* **1** of a person or their temperament: gloomy or sullen. **2** dark and brooding.
**satyr** *n* (*also* **Satyr**) in classical mythology, a lustful woodland god represented as a man with the ears, legs, and tail of a horse or goat.
**sauce** *n* **1** a thick liquid used as a relish to food. **2** *informal* cheek or impudence.
**sauce boat** *n* a shallow jug for serving sauce, gravy, etc.
**saucepan** *n* a deep cooking pan with a long handle and a lid.
**saucer** *n* a small shallow dish on which a cup is placed.
**saucy** *adj* (**-ier, -iest**) *informal* **1** cheeky. **2** mildly titillating or sexually suggestive. ➤ **saucily** *adv.*
**sauerkraut** /'sowəkrowt/ *n* finely chopped pickled cabbage.
**sauna** *n* a small room for invigorating the body in hot dry air or steam.
**saunter**[1] *v* to walk about in an idle or casual manner.
**saunter**[2] *n* a casual stroll.

**sausage** *n* **1** a food consisting of a tubular skin filled with finely chopped meat, eaten grilled or fried. **2** a food made from cooked or cured meat and spices, eaten cold in thin slices. ✻ **not a sausage** *Brit, informal* nothing at all.
**sausage dog** *n Brit, informal* a dachsund.
**sausage meat** *n* seasoned minced meat used in sausages or as a stuffing.
**sausage roll** *n* a piece of sausage meat wrapped in pastry.
**sauté**[1] /'sawtay, 'sohtay/ *v* (**sautés, sautéed** *or* **sautéd, sautéing**) to fry (potatoes) in oil or fat.
**sauté**[2] *adj* fried quickly in shallow oil or fat.
**savage**[1] *adj* **1** not domesticated; untamed. **2** very severe. **3** brutal or cruel and violent. ➤ **savagely** *adv*, **savagery** *n.*
**savage**[2] *n* **1** a member of a people regarded as lacking a developed culture. **2** a brutal person.
**savage**[3] *v* **1** to attack or treat brutally or ferociously. **2** to criticize ruthlessly.
**savanna** *or* **savannah** *n* a tropical grassland with scattered trees.
**savant** *or* **savante** /'sav(ə)nt/ *n* a person with exceptional knowledge.
**save**[1] *v* **1** to rescue or deliver from danger or harm. **2** to prevent (somebody) from dying. **3** to preserve or guard from injury or loss. **4** in Christianity, to preserve (a soul) from damnation. **5** to put aside for future use. **6** in computing, to preserve (data) by storing it in the computer's memory. **7** to conserve or avoid use of (a resource). **8** to prevent an opponent from scoring or winning (a goal or point). ✻ **save face** to avoid being humiliated. **save the day** to find a solution against expectation.
**save**[2] *n* in sport, an act of preventing an opponent from scoring.
**save**[3] *prep and conj* except or other than.
**saveloy** *n Brit* a smoked pork sausage.
**saving**[1] *n* **1** an economy or reduction in money or time. **2** (*in pl*) money that has been put aside for future use.
**saving**[2] *prep* except.
**saving grace** *n* a redeeming or compensatory quality.
**saviour** (*NAmer* **savior**) *n* **1** a person who saves somebody or something from danger or harm. **2** (**Saviour**) in Christianity, Jesus Christ or God.
**savoir faire** /,savwah 'feə/ *n* the ability to behave appropriately in social situations.
**savour**[1] (*NAmer* **savor**) *v* **1** to appreciate (food or drink) with relish. **2** to enjoy and appreciate to the full.
**savour**[2] (*NAmer* **savor**) *n* a characteristic taste or smell.
**savoury**[1] (*NAmer* **savory**) *adj* **1** of food: having a salty or spicy flavour. **2** morally wholesome or respectable.
**savoury**[2] (*NAmer* **savory**) *n* (*pl* **-ies**) *Brit* a savoury snack or dish.
**savvy**[1] *v* (**-ies, -ied**) *informal* to know or understand.
**savvy**[2] *n informal* practical knowledge or judgment.
**savvy**[3] *adj* (**-ier, -iest**) *informal* shrewd or knowledgeable.
**saw**[1] *v* past tense of SEE[1].
**saw**[2] *n* a tool with a long toothed blade, used for cutting wood by passing it back and forth.
**saw**[3] *v* (*past part.* **sawn,** *NAmer* **sawed**) **1** to cut with a saw. **2** to cut through or off with a saw.
**saw**[4] *n* a maxim or proverb.
**sawdust** *n* wood powder produced in sawing.
**sawmill** *n* a factory where wood is cut into logs or planks.
**sawtooth** *or* **sawtoothed** *adj* shaped or arranged like the teeth of a saw.
**sawyer** *n* a person who saws timber.
**sax** *n informal* a saxophone.
**Saxon** *n* **1** a member of a Germanic people that settled in southern England in the fifth and sixth cents. **2** the language of the ancient Saxons. ➤ **Saxon** *adj.*
**saxophone** *n* a brass instrument with a single reed like a clarinet and a conical bore like an oboe. ➤ **saxophonist** *n.*
**say**[1] *v* (*third person sing. present tense* **says,** *past tense and past part.* **said**) **1** to state in spoken words. **2** to utter or pronounce (a sound, word, sentence, etc). **3** to recite or repeat. **4** of a clock or watch: to indicate or show. **5** (usu in passive) to report or allege. **6** to assume for the purposes of discussion.
**say**[2] *n* a chance to speak or give one's opinion.
**saying** *n* a maxim or proverb.
**Sc** *abbr* the chemical symbol for scandium.
**scab**[1] *n* **1** a crust of hardened blood that forms over a wound. **2** *informal, offensive* a person who declines to take part in a strike. ➤ **scabby** *adj.*
**scab**[2] *v* (**scabbed, scabbing**) to become covered with a scab.
**scabbard** *n* a sheath for a sword or dagger.
**scabies** *n* a skin disease with intense itching and inflammation.
**scabrous** *adj* **1** covered with scabs. **2** indecent or salacious.
**scaffold** *n* **1** a raised platform formerly used for executions. **2** a structure made from scaffolding.
**scaffolding** *n* **1** a temporary structure of poles and planks, erected on the outside of a building that is being built or repaired. **2** the poles and planks used for this.
**scald**[1] *v* **1** to injure or burn with hot liquid or steam. **2** to bring (a liquid) almost to boiling point. **3** to dip briefly in boiling water.
**scald**[2] *n* an injury or burn caused by scalding.
**scale**[1] *n* **1** each of the overlapping plates that cover and protect the skin of fish and reptiles. **2** a dry flake of dead skin. **3** a white deposit of

lime formed on the inside of a kettle or pipe caused by hard water. **4** a hard deposit on the teeth.

**scale**[2] *v* **1** to remove the scales from. **2** to come off in scales or flakes.

**scale**[3] *n* **1** (*usu in pl*) an instrument for weighing. **2** either pan or tray of a balance. * **tip the scales** to be a deciding factor.

**scale**[4] *n* **1** a graduated range of values used in measuring. **2** a measuring instrument marked with a range of values. **3** the relative size or extent of something. **4** the ratio of the size of an object to a representation of it. **5** in music, a series of regularly rising or falling notes. * **to scale** reduced or enlarged by a constant factor.

**scale**[5] *v* **1** to climb up or over (something high). **2** to make a model or representation of (something) using a uniform size ratio. **3** to regulate or estimate according to a rate or standard. **4** (+ down/up) to decrease or increase in size or amount.

**scallion** *n* an onion with a small bulb, e.g. a spring onion or shallot.

**scallop**[1] *n* **1** an edible mollusc with a shell consisting of two fan-shaped halves having wavy edges. **2** each of a series of rounded projections forming a decorative border.

**scallop**[2] *v* (**scalloped, scalloping**) to shape or finish with decorative scallops.

**scallywag** (*NAmer* **scalawag**) *n informal* a mischievous but likable person.

**scalp**[1] *n* **1** the skin at the top and back of the human head. **2** a part of this with the hair attached, formerly cut from an enemy as a battle trophy by Native American warriors.

**scalp**[2] *v* to remove the scalp of (an enemy).

**scalpel** *n* a small sharp knife with a thin blade, used in surgery.

**scaly** *adj* (**-ier, -iest**) **1** covered with scales. **2** dry and flaky.

**scam** *n informal* a dishonest scheme for obtaining money.

**scamp** *n* a mischievous child.

**scamper**[1] *v* to run nimbly and lightly.

**scamper**[2] *n* a dash or scurry.

**scampi** *n* (*treated as sing. or pl*) large prawns prepared and cooked.

**scan**[1] *v* (**scanned, scanning**) **1** to glance at (something) hastily or in search of a particular item. **2** to examine the whole of (an object) with a sensing device. **3** to make a detailed examination of (part or all of the body) using ultrasonic waves, X-rays, etc. **4** to change (an image) into an electrical signal by moving an electron beam across it according to a predetermined pattern for television transmission. **5** to convert (data) into a digital format for electronic purposes. **6** to examine or search (an object or region) using a radar scanner. **7** to read or mark (a piece of verse) in order to show metrical structure. **8** of verse: to conform to a metrical pattern. ➤ **scannable** *adj.*

**scan**[2] *n* **1** the act of scanning. **2** a medical examination using a scanner. **3** an image produced by a scanner.

**scandal** *n* **1** an act or event that causes great public indignation. **2** rumour or that arises from this.

**scandalize** *or* **-ise** *v* to shock or offend by immoral or disgraceful behaviour.

**scandalous** *adj* **1** causing public indignation. **2** offensive to propriety. ➤ **scandalously** *adv.*

**scanner** *n* **1** a device used to scan the human body with X-rays, ultrasonic waves, etc. **2** a device that converts data into a digital format for electronic purposes.

**scansion** *n* **1** the analysis of verse to show its metre. **2** the rhythm of a particular piece of verse.

**scant** *adj* barely sufficient; inadequate.

**scanty** *adj* (**-ier, -iest**) small or insufficient in quantity. ➤ **scantily** *adv.*

**scapegoat**[1] *n* a person who is blamed for the wrongdoing of another.

**scapegoat**[2] *v* to make a scapegoat of.

**scapula** *n* (*pl* **scapulae** *or* **scapulas**) the shoulder blade.

**scar**[1] *n* **1** a mark left on the skin or body tissue by a healed injury. **2** a mark left on a plant stem where a leaf formerly grew. **3** a psychological ill effect caused by trauma.

**scar**[2] *v* (**scarred, scarring**) to form or mark with a scar.

**scar**[3] *n* a steep rocky cliff or outcrop.

**scarab** *n* **1** a large dung beetle held sacred by the ancient Egyptians. **2** a gemstone representation of this.

**scarce** *adj* **1** not plentiful or sufficient to meet demand. **2** few in number. ➤ **scarcity** *n.*

**scarcely** *adv* **1** only just. **2** almost not. **3** certainly or probably not.

**scare**[1] *v* **1** to frighten suddenly. **2** (+ off/away) to drive (a person or animal) away by frightening them. **3** to become afraid.

**scare**[2] *n* **1** a sudden fright. **2** a widespread state of alarm.

**scarecrow** *n* an object made to look like a person set up to frighten birds away from crops.

**scarf** *n* (*pl* **scarves** *or* **scarfs**) a strip or square of cloth worn round the neck or head.

**scarify** *v* (**-ies, -ied**) **1** to scrape (a lawn) to remove moss, dead leaves, and other debris. **2** to break up and loosen the surface of (soil). **3** to make scratches or small cuts in (the skin). **4** to criticize hurtfully.

**scarlatina** *n* scarlet fever.

**scarlet** *n* a vivid red colour.

**scarlet fever** *n* an infectious disease with a fever and a red rash.

**scarp** *n* a steep slope.

**scarper** *v Brit, informal* to run away.

**scarves** *n* pl of SCARF.

**scary** *adj* (**-ier, -iest**) *informal* causing fear or alarm. ➤ **scarily** *adv.*

**scat**[1] *v* (**scatted, scatting**) *informal* to leave hurriedly.

**scat**[2] *n* jazz singing with improvised vocals sounding like an instrument.

**scathing** *adj* bitterly severe; scornful. ➤ **scathingly** *adv.*

**scatology** *n* an obsession with excrement or excretion. ➤ **scatological** *adj.*

**scatter** *v* **1** to cause to separate widely. **2** to throw in all directions or at random. **3** to separate and go in various directions.

**scattered** *adj* found in various places over an area.

**scatty** *adj* (**-ier, -iest**) *Brit, informal* forgetful and disorganized.

**scavenge** *v* **1** to search for (something useful) among discarded items. **2** of animals: to search for and feed on (carrion or refuse).

**scenario** *n* (*pl* **-os**) **1** an outline of a dramatic work, novel, or film. **2** an account of a projected course of action.

**scene** *n* **1** a setting in which something real or imaginary happens. **2** a landscape or view. **3** an episode or sequence in a play, film, etc. **4** a stage setting. **5** a public display of strong feeling. **6** a sphere of activity or interest. **7** *informal* something in which a person is particularly interested. ✱ **behind the scenes** out of public view.

**scenery** *n* **1** the natural features of a landscape. **2** the painted scenes or hangings used on a theatre stage or film set.

**scenic** *adj* having attractive natural scenery. ➤ **scenically** *adv.*

**scent**[1] *n* **1** a pleasant characteristic smell. **2** a light perfume worn on the skin. **3** a smell left by an animal, by which it can be traced.

**scent**[2] *v* **1** to give a pleasant smell to. **2** to perceive by smell. **3** to get an inkling of. ➤ **scented** *adj.*

**sceptic** (*NAmer* **skeptic**) *n* a person who doubts accepted opinions or beliefs. ➤ **scepticism** *n.*

**sceptical** (*NAmer* **skeptical**) *adj* doubtful about accepted opinions or beliefs.

**sceptre** (*NAmer* **scepter**) *n* a staff carried by a ruler as a symbol of sovereignty. ➤ **sceptred** *adj.*

**schedule**[1] *n* **1** a plan of things to be done and the order in which to do them. **2** a timetable. ✱ **on schedule** as planned or on time.

**schedule**[2] *v* **1** to plan for (something) to occur at a fixed time. **2** to include in a schedule.

**scheduled** *adj* of a flight: operating as part of a regular timetable, not chartered.

**schema** *n* (*pl* **schemata** *or* **schemas**) an outline or diagram of a plan or theory.

**schematic** *adj* **1** representing something in a simplified way. **2** of understanding or an idea: unsophisticated or formulaic. ➤ **schematically** *adv.*

**scheme**[1] *n* **1** a systematic plan for putting something into effect. **2** a systematic arrangement or design. **3** a secret or dishonest plan.

**scheme**[2] *v* to make a dishonest plan. ➤ **schemer** *n.*

**scherzo** /'skeətsoh/ *n* (*pl* **scherzos** *or* **scherzi**) a lively instrumental piece of music.

**schism** *n* a fundamental disagreement or split between parts of an institution or organization.

**schist** *n* a metamorphic rock made of thin layers of different minerals.

**schizoid** *adj* **1** of a person: extremely shy and unable to cope in social situations. **2** *informal* suffering from schizophrenia.

**schizophrenia** *n* a mental disorder characterized by loss of contact with reality and disintegration of personality. ➤ **schizophrenic** *adj and n.*

**schmaltz** *or* **schmalz** *n* excessive sentimentality. ➤ **schmaltzy** *adj.*

**schnapps** /shnaps/ *n* (*pl* **schnapps**) a strong alcoholic drink resembling gin.

**scholar** *n* **1** a person who specializes in a particular academic subject. **2** a student holding a scholarship.

**scholarly** *adj* characteristic of or suitable for advanced academic study.

**scholarship** *n* **1** academic learning and work. **2** a grant of money awarded to a student to pay for education and upkeep.

**scholastic** *adj* relating to education or schools.

**school**[1] *n* **1** a building or organization for educating children. **2** an establishment that teaches a specific subject or skill. **3** a department or faculty in a university. **4** *NAmer, informal* a university. **5** a group of philosophers, artists, etc, who share the same approach to a subject or follow the same principles.

**school**[2] *v* **1** *NAmer or formal* to educate. **2** to train in a specific subject or skill.

**school**[3] *n* a large number of fish or sea animals swimming together.

**schooling** *n* education received in school.

**schooner** *n* **1** a sailing ship with two or more masts. **2** *Brit* a large sherry glass.

**sciatic** *adj* relating to the hip or the nerves that run from the lower spine down the back of each thigh.

**sciatica** *n* pain in the back of the thigh and lower back caused by pressure on the sciatic nerve.

**science** *n* **1** the study of the nature and behaviour of phenomena in the physical and natural world. **2** a branch of knowledge and study.

**science fiction** *n* fiction involving the imaginative use of science, set in the future.

**science park** *n* an area where businesses involved in scientific and technological research and manufacturing are based.

**scientific** *adj* **1** relating to or based on science. **2** systematic. ➤ **scientifically** *adv.*
**scientist** *n* a person who studies or is an expert in one of the natural or physical sciences.
**sci-fi** *n informal* science fiction.
**scimitar** *n* a short sword with a curved blade.
**scintillating** *adj* **1** shining or sparkling. **2** lively or witty.
**scion** *n* **1** a detached living part of a plant. **2** a descendant of a notable family.
**scissors** *pl n* a cutting instrument with two blades pivoted so that their cutting edges slide past each other.
**sclerosis** *n* **1** abnormal hardening of body tissue. **2** a disease involving this, *esp* multiple sclerosis.
**scoff**[1] *v* (*often* + at) to speak contemptuously about something.
**scoff**[2] *v chiefly Brit, informal* to eat greedily or rapidly.
**scold** *v* to reprove angrily.
**sconce** *n* a wall bracket for holding a candle or light.
**scone** *n* a small lightly sweetened cake made from a dough or batter.
**scoop**[1] *n* **1** a large ladle with a deep bowl. **2** a utensil for spooning out ice cream. **3** a deep bucket forming part of a mechanical digger. **4** *informal* a news item published by a newspaper ahead of its competitors.
**scoop**[2] *v* **1** to take out or up with a scoop. **2** (*often* + out) to make (a hollow). **3** to pick up as if with a scoop. **4** *informal* to report a news item in advance of (a competitor). **5** *informal* to obtain (something, *esp* money) by swift action or sudden good fortune.
**scoot** *v informal* to go or move suddenly and swiftly.
**scooter** *n* **1** a child's toy consisting of a narrow board with a wheel at each end and an upright steering handle, propelled by pressing one foot against the ground. **2** a light motorcycle.
**scope** *n* **1** space or opportunity for action, thought, or development. **2** extent of treatment, activity, or responsibility.
**scorch**[1] *v* **1** to burn or become burned in a way that causes a change in colour. **2** to cause (land or vegetation) to become dried up from the effects of heat. **3** *informal* to move or travel at great speed.
**scorch**[2] *n* a mark resulting from scorching.
**scorcher** *n informal* a very hot day or period.
**score**[1] *n* **1** the number of points, goals, etc a team or individual makes in a game. **2** (*pl* **score**) a group of twenty people or things. **3** an unspecified large quantity. **4** (**the score**) *informal* the present state of affairs. **5** the written or printed music of a composition. **6** a scratch or incision. ✱ **settle the score** to take revenge.
**score**[2] *v* **1** to gain (points, etc) in a game. **2** to keep score in a game or contest. **3** to mark (a surface) with lines or scratches. **4** (+ out/through) to delete or cancel something written or printed. **5** to arrange (music) for an orchestra. ➤ **scorer** *n.*
**scoreline** *n* the result of a game or match.
**scorn**[1] *n* strong contempt or disdain.
**scorn**[2] *v* **1** to treat with angry contempt. **2** to refuse or reject contemptuously.
**scornful** *adj* feeling or expressing scorn. ➤ **scornfully** *adv.*
**Scorpio** *n* the eighth sign of the zodiac (the Scorpion).
**scorpion** *n* an arachnid with an elongated body and a narrow tail bearing a poisonous sting at the tip.
**Scot** *n* a native or inhabitant of Scotland.
**Scotch** *n* (*also* **Scotch whisky**) whisky distilled in Scotland.
**scotch** *v* **1** to put an end to. **2** *archaic* to temporarily disable or make harmless.
**Scotch egg** *n* a hard-boiled egg covered with sausage meat.
**scot-free** *adj* without any penalty or injury.
**Scots**[1] *adj* Scottish.
**Scots**[2] *n* the form of English used in Scotland.
**Scottish** *adj* relating to Scotland.
**scoundrel** *n* an unscrupulous or dishonest person.
**scour**[1] *v* **1** to clean by vigorous rubbing with abrasive material. **2** of running water or a glacier: to create an eroded channel in.
**scour**[2] *v* to search thoroughly.
**scourge**[1] *n* **1** a cause of trouble or distress. **2** a whip.
**scourge**[2] *v* **1** to whip. **2** to cause great distress to.
**Scouse** *n Brit, informal* **1** the dialect or accent of Liverpool. **2** (*also* **Scouser**) a native or inhabitant of Liverpool. ➤ **Scouse** *adj.*
**scout**[1] *n* **1** a person sent forward to survey land or assess an enemy's position or strength. **2** (**Scout**) a member of the Scout Association, a worldwide movement for young people. **3** a talent scout.
**scout**[2] *v* **1** to make an advance survey to obtain information. **2** to look for something. **3** to explore (a place) to obtain information.
**scowl**[1] *v* to frown in an angry or displeased way.
**scowl**[2] *n* an angry frown.
**scrabble** *v* **1** to scratch or scrape about to find or catch hold of something. **2** to scramble or clamber.
**scraggy** *adj* (**-ier, -iest**) lean and lanky.
**scram** *v* (**scrammed, scramming**) *informal* to leave hurriedly.
**scramble**[1] *v* **1** to move or climb using the hands and feet. **2** to compete chaotically for something. **3** to make or become muddled. **4** *esp* of a fighter aircraft: to take off quickly in response to an alert. **5** to cook (eggs) beaten in a

pan. **6** to put (a message) into a form that needs decoding by the recipient.

**scramble**[2] *n* **1** the act of scrambling. **2** *Brit* a motorcycle race over rough ground. **3** a muddle or jumble.

**scrap**[1] *n* **1** a small detached fragment of something. **2** (*in pl*) discarded or leftover food. **3** discarded metal suitable for reprocessing.

**scrap**[2] *v* (**scrapped, scrapping**) **1** to discard or get rid of. **2** to convert into scrap.

**scrap**[3] *v* (**scrapped, scrapping**) *informal* to fight or quarrel.

**scrap**[4] *n informal* a fight or quarrel.

**scrapbook** *n* a blank book for pasting pictures or cuttings.

**scrape**[1] *v* **1** to grate harshly over or against. **2** to damage or injure by contact with a rough surface. **3** to draw roughly over a surface. **4** to remove (matter) from a surface with an edged instrument. **5** to achieve (an exam grade or a pass) by a narrow margin.

**scrape**[2] *n* **1** an act or sound of scraping. **2** an injury or mark caused by scraping. **3** *informal* an awkward predicament.

**scrappy** *adj* (**-ier, -iest**) disjointed or incomplete. ➤ **scrappily** *adv.*

**scrapyard** *n Brit* a yard where scrap metal is collected.

**scratch**[1] *v* **1** to mark or cut the surface of (something) with a sharp object. **2** to make a superficial wound on. **3** to scrape or rub (a body part) to relieve itching. **4** to cancel or erase with or as if with a line. **5** to withdraw from a competition. **6** to abandon or cancel (an event or project).

**scratch**[2] *n* **1** a mark or injury produced by scratching. **2** *informal* a slight wound. **3** an act or sound of scratching. * **from scratch** from the very beginning. **up to scratch** satisfactory or adequate.

**scratch**[3] *adj* put together haphazardly or hastily.

**scratchcard** *n* a small card with a coated section to be scratched off to reveal whether a prize has been won.

**scrawl**[1] *v* to write or draw awkwardly or hastily.

**scrawl**[2] *n* an untidy piece of writing or drawing.

**scrawny** *adj* (**-ier, -iest**) thin and bony.

**scream**[1] *v* **1** to make a loud piercing cry in fear or pain. **2** to move with great speed.

**scream**[2] *n* **1** a loud shrill cry or noise. **2** *informal* a highly amusing person or thing.

**scree** *n* loose stones or rocky debris on a hillside or mountain slope.

**screech**[1] *v* to make a shrill piercing cry or sound.

**screech**[2] *n* a shrill sound or cry.

**screed** *n* **1** a long speech or piece of writing. **2** a mixture applied to a floor to give it a level surface.

**screen**[1] *n* **1** the part of a television set or computer monitor on which images or data are displayed. **2** a blank surface for projecting photographs or films. **3** the medium of films or television. **4** a partition or curtain used to divide a room or provide privacy. **5** something that protects or conceals.

**screen**[2] *v* **1** to shelter or protect with a screen. **2** to guard from injury or danger. **3** (*also* + off) to separate or enclose with a screen. **4** to show or broadcast (a film or broadcast) on a screen. **5** to carry out a test on (somebody) for the presence of disease.

**screenplay** *n* the script of a film with stage directions.

**screen saver** *n* a computer program that generates a blank screen or moving screen images after a period of inactivity.

**screen test** *n* an audition to assess an actor's suitability for a film role.

**screenwriter** *n* a writer of screenplays. ➤ **screenwriting** *n.*

**screw**[1] *n* **1** a metal pin with a spiral thread running round it and a slotted head turned by a screwdriver to fasten parts together. **2** the propeller of a ship or aircraft. **3** *informal* a prison warder. **4** *coarse slang* an act of sexual intercourse. * **have a screw loose** *informal* to be eccentric.

**screw**[2] *v* **1** to fasten, close, or tighten with a screw. **2** to join or assemble (parts) by means of a screw. **3** to cause to rotate spirally about an axis. **4** *informal* to cheat or defraud. **5** *coarse slang* to have sexual intercourse with.

**screwdriver** *n* a tool with a tip that fits into the head of a screw to turn it.

**screw up** *v* **1** to crush or crumple. **2** *informal* to make emotionally disturbed. **3** *informal* to bungle or cause to go wrong.

**screwy** *adj informal* odd or eccentric.

**scribble**[1] *v* to write or draw hurriedly or carelessly.

**scribble**[2] *n* a scribbled drawing or piece of writing.

**scribe** *n* formerly, a person who copied manuscripts. ➤ **scribal** *adj.*

**scrimmage** *n* a disorderly struggle or fight.

**scrimp** *v* (*often* + on) to be frugal or sparing; to skimp.

**script**[1] *n* **1** the written text of a stage play, film, or broadcast. **2** written characters; handwriting.

**script**[2] *v* to write a script for.

**scripture** *n* **1** (*also in pl*) the sacred writings of Christianity as contained in the Bible. **2** the sacred writings of another religion. ➤ **scriptural** *adj.*

**scrofula** *n* a former name for tuberculosis of the lymph glands. ➤ **scrofulous** *adj.*

**scroll**[1] *n* **1** a roll of parchment with writing or

drawing on it. **2** a stylized ornamental design imitating the spiral curves of a scroll.
**scroll**[2] *v* to move (text on a computer screen) up and down to view different parts of it.
**Scrooge** *n* a mean or miserly person.
**scrotum** *n* (*pl* **scrota** *or* **scrotums**) the pouch of skin that contains the testicles.
**scrounge** *v informal* to try to get or be given (something) for nothing. ➤ **scrounger** *n.*
**scrub**[1] *v* (**scrubbed, scrubbing**) **1** to clean by hard rubbing. **2** *informal* to cancel or abandon.
**scrub**[2] *n* an act of scrubbing.
**scrub**[3] *n* **1** vegetation consisting chiefly of stunted trees or shrubs. **2** an area covered with such vegetation. ➤ **scrubby** *adj.*
**scruff**[1] *n* the back of the neck.
**scruff**[2] *n Brit, informal* an untidy or grubby person.
**scruffy** *adj* (**-ier, -iest**) slovenly and untidy in personal appearance. ➤ **scruffily** *adv.*
**scrum** *n* **1** in rugby, a set piece in which the forwards of each side crouch in a tight formation and push against each other as the ball is put into play between them. **2** *Brit, informal* a disorderly crowd.
**scrummy** *adj* (**-ier, -iest**) *informal* delicious.
**scrump** *v Brit, informal* to steal (fruit) from an orchard or garden.
**scrumptious** *adj informal* delicious or delightful.
**scrumpy** *n Brit* dry rough cider brewed in the English West Country.
**scrunch** *v* to crunch or crush.
**scruple**[1] *n* a feeling of doubt about the morality of an action.
**scruple**[2] *v* to hesitate on grounds of conscience.
**scrupulous** *adj* **1** painstakingly exact. **2** eager to avoid doing anything wrong or immoral. ➤ **scrupulously** *adv.*
**scrutinize** *or* **-ise** *v* to examine in detail.
**scrutiny** *n* (*pl* **-ies**) a searching study or inspection.
**scuba-dive** *v* to swim underwater with an aqualung. ➤ **scuba-diving** *n.*
**scud** *v* (**scudded, scudding**) to move or run swiftly.
**scuff**[1] *v* **1** to scrape or damage the surface of (a shoe or other object). **2** to drag or shuffle (the feet) while walking.
**scuff**[2] *n* a mark or damage caused by scuffing.
**scuffle**[1] *n* a brief confused fight.
**scuffle**[2] *v* to engage in a scuffle.
**scull**[1] *n* **1** either of a pair of light oars used by a single rower. **2** a narrow light racing boat propelled by a scull or sculls.
**scull**[2] *v* to propel a boat with sculls.
**scullery** *n* (*pl* **-ies**) a small kitchen used mainly for washing dishes.
**sculpt** *v* to create by sculpture.
**sculptor** *n* an artist who makes sculptures.
**sculpture**[1] *n* **1** the art of making three-dimensional works of art by carving or modelling. **2** a piece of work produced in this way. ➤ **sculptural** *adj.*
**sculpture**[2] *v* **1** to make (a work of art) by sculpture. **2** to form (wood or stone) into a work of art. **3** to shape by carving or moulding.
**scum** *n* **1** impurities that have collected on the surface of a liquid. **2** *informal* a despicable person or group of people. ➤ **scummy** *adj.*
**scupper** *v* **1** *Brit, informal* to prevent (something) from working, happening, etc. **2** to sink (a ship) deliberately.
**scurf** *n* thin dry flakes of skin. ➤ **scurfy** *adj.*
**scurrilous** *adj* offensive and defamatory.
**scurry** *v* (**-ies, -ied**) to move with short hurried steps.
**scurvy** *n* a disease caused by a lack of vitamin C.
**scut** *n* the short erect tail of a rabbit, hare, or deer.
**scuttle**[1] *n* a container used for carrying or storing coal indoors.
**scuttle**[2] *v* to run hurriedly or furtively.
**scuttle**[3] *v* **1** to sink (one's own ship) deliberately. **2** to destroy or wreck.
**scythe**[1] *n* a tool with a long curving blade for cutting grass or corn.
**scythe**[2] *v* to cut with a scythe.
**SE** *abbr* **1** Southeast. **2** Southeastern.
**Se** *abbr* the chemical symbol for selenium.
**sea** *n* **1** the salt water that covers much of the earth. **2** a large body of salt water. **3** something vast or overwhelming. ✱ **at sea** lost or confused.
**sea anemone** *n* a brightly coloured sea creature with a cluster of tentacles resembling a flower.
**seabird** *n* a bird that lives on the sea or coast.
**seaboard** *n* an area beside or near the sea.
**sea change** *n* a complete transformation.
**sea cow** *n* a manatee or other plant-eating sea animal.
**seafaring** *n* travel by sea. ➤ **seafarer** *n.*
**seafood** *n* edible sea fish, shellfish, etc.
**seafront** *n* the part of a seaside town facing the sea.
**seagoing** *adj* designed for travel on the sea.
**sea gull** *n* a gull.
**sea horse** *n* a small upright fish with a head like that of a horse.
**seal**[1] *n* **1** a closure that has to be broken in order to give access. **2** a tight closure preventing the passage of air, water, etc. **3** a guarantee or assurance. **4** an emblem or word stamped in wax on a document as a mark of authenticity.
**seal**[2] *v* **1** to fasten or close tightly. **2** to close (a container) in a way that prevents unauthorized opening. **3** to cover (a porous surface) with a coating of a nonporous substance. **4** to confirm (an arrangement) or make it secure. **5** to set or

affix an authenticating seal to (e.g. a document). **6** to authenticate or ratify. **7** to mark with a stamp or seal.

**seal³** *n* (*pl* **seals** *or* **seal**) a sea animal with webbed flippers for swimming.

**sealant** *n* a sealing agent for making something watertight or airtight.

**sea legs** *pl n* the ability to walk steadily and avoid being seasick when on a ship at sea.

**sea level** *n* the mean level of the sea's surface midway between high and low tides.

**sealing wax** *n* a wax that becomes soft when heated, used for sealing letters, parcels, etc.

**sea lion** *n* a large seal with short coarse fur and large flippers.

**seal off** *v* to close an area to prevent movement in or out.

**seam¹** *n* **1** a line of stitching joining two pieces of fabric. **2** a line or ridge formed at the meeting of two edges. **3** a layer of coal or rock.

**seam²** *v* to join with a seam.

**seaman** *n* (*pl* **seamen**) a sailor or mariner. ➤ **seamanship** *n.*

**sea mile** *n* a nautical mile.

**seamless** *adj* **1** without seams. **2** without breaks or gaps; continuous.

**seamy** *adj* (**-ier, -iest**) unpleasant or sordid.

**séance** *or* **seance** /'sayons, 'sayonhs/ *n* a meeting at which people attempt to communicate with the dead.

**seaplane** *n* an aeroplane designed to take off from and land on the water.

**seaport** *n* a port or town accessible to seagoing ships.

**sear** *v* **1** to burn or scorch with a sudden intense heat. **2** of heat or pain: to be felt as a burning sensation.

**search¹** *v* **1** (*usu* + for) to look or enquire carefully or thoroughly. **2** (*often* + for) to look through thoroughly to find or discover something. **3** to examine (a person) for concealed articles. **4** to investigate (a computer file, database, etc) to find information. ➤ **searcher** *n.*

**search²** *n* the act of searching.

**searching** *adj* seeking to obtain detailed or personal information.

**searchlight** *n* an apparatus for projecting a movable beam of light.

**search party** *n* a group of people organized to search for a missing person.

**search warrant** *n* a warrant authorizing police to search premises.

**seascape** *n* a picture representing a view of the sea.

**seashell** *n* the empty shell of a sea mollusc.

**seashore** *n* sandy or stony land next to the sea.

**seasick** *adj* suffering from sickness caused by the motion of a ship. ➤ **seasickness** *n.*

**seaside** *n* land bordering the sea, *esp* a holiday resort or beach.

**season¹** *n* **1** each of the four parts into which the year is divided (spring, summer, autumn, and winter). **2** a period characterized by a particular kind of weather or activity: *the dry season; the holiday season.* ✱ **in season 1** of food: readily available for eating. **2** of a female animal: ready to mate.

**season²** *v* **1** to add spices or flavouring to (food). **2** to enliven or make more interesting. **3** to treat or expose (timber) to prepare it for use.

**seasonable** *adj* **1** suitable to the season or circumstances. **2** *archaic* occurring in good or proper time.

**seasonal** *adj* **1** occurring or produced at a particular season. **2** determined by seasonal need or availability. ➤ **seasonally** *adv.*

**seasoned** *adj* fit or expert from experience.

**seasoning** *n* salt, pepper, or spices added to food to give it flavour.

**season ticket** *n* a ticket allowing repeated travel or admission over a period.

**seat¹** *n* **1** a piece of furniture for sitting on. **2** the part of something on which one rests when sitting. **3** the buttocks. **4** a place for sitting, e.g. in a vehicle, or the right to this. **5** a right of sitting in parliament or on an elected committee. **6** *Brit* a parliamentary constituency. **7** a place where something is established or practised: *a seat of learning.* **8** a large country mansion.

**seat²** *v* **1** to provide a seat or seats for. **2** to have sitting accommodation for. ➤ **seating** *n.*

**seat belt** *n* a belt for securing a person in a seat in a vehicle or aircraft.

**sea urchin** *n* a sea creature with a thin shell covered with movable spines.

**seaweed** *n* thick slimy plants growing in the sea.

**seaworthy** *adj* of a ship: fit or safe for travel at sea. ➤ **seaworthiness** *n.*

**sebaceous** *adj* secreting fatty material.

**secateurs** *pl n chiefly Brit* small pruning shears.

**secede** *v* to withdraw from an organization or federation.

**secession** *n* the act of seceding.

**secluded** *adj* screened or hidden from view.

**seclusion** *n* the condition of being private or secluded.

**second¹** *adj* **1** having the position in a sequence corresponding to the number two. **2** next to the first in value, quality, or degree. **3** (+ to) inferior or subordinate. **4** next below the top in authority or importance. **5** alternate: *every second year.* ➤ **secondly** *adv.*

**second²** *n* **1** somebody or something that is second. **2** an assistant to someone boxing or fighting a duel. **3** a slightly flawed or inferior article for sale. **4** *informal* (*in pl*) a second helping of food.

**second³** *n* **1** a 60th part of a minute. **2** a brief moment.

**second**[4] *v* **1** to give support or encouragement to. **2** to endorse (a motion or nomination). ➤ **seconder** *n.*

**second**[5] *v chiefly Brit* to release (an employee) for temporary duty elsewhere. ➤ **secondment** *n.*

**secondary** *adj* **1** of second or lesser rank or importance. **2** of a level of education following primary. ➤ **secondarily** *adv.*

**second best** *n* not quite the best in quality or worth.

**second class** *n* the second and next to highest group in a classification.

**second-class** *adj* **1** of a second class. **2** inferior or mediocre.

**second cousin** *n* a child of a first cousin of either of one's parents.

**second-degree** *adj* of a burn: causing blisters and surface damage to the skin.

**second fiddle** *n* a secondary or subordinate role or function.

**second-guess** *v* to try to guess the actions of.

**secondhand** *adj* **1** acquired after being owned by another. **2** dealing in secondhand goods. **3** received from an intermediary.

**second-in-command** *n* an officer immediately below a commander.

**second nature** *n* an action or ability that has become instinctive.

**second person** *n* in grammar, the term used to refer to a person or thing addressed, represented by the pronoun *you.*

**second-rate** *adj* of inferior quality.

**second sight** *n* the ability to see future events.

**second thoughts** *pl n* a reconsideration of a previous decision.

**second wind** *n* renewed energy after a period of exertion.

**secret**[1] *adj* **1** kept or hidden from knowledge or view. **2** secretive. ➤ **secrecy** *n,* **secretly** *adv.*

**secret**[2] *n* **1** something kept hidden or unexplained. **2** a special and not commonly known way of achieving something.

**secret agent** *n* a spy.

**secretariat** *n* a government administrative department or its staff.

**secretary** *n* (*pl* **-ies**) **1** a person who is employed to handle correspondence and manage routine administrative work. **2** an official of an organization responsible for its records and correspondence. **3** in Britain, a senior civil servant. ➤ **secretarial** *adj.*

**secretary of state** *n* **1** in Britain, a government minister who is the head of a department. **2** in the USA, the government official responsible for foreign affairs.

**secrete**[1] *v* to form and give off (a substance). ➤ **secretion** *n.*

**secrete**[2] *v* to put in a secret place.

**secretive** *adj* inclined to say little and hide one's feelings. ➤ **secretively** *adv.*

**secret police** *n* a police organization operating secretly for the political purposes of a government.

**secret service** *n* a government agency concerned with national security and intelligence.

**sect** *n* a small group within a religious or political organization that differs in its beliefs from the main body.

**sectarian** *adj* of or characteristic of a sect. ➤ **sectarianism** *n.*

**section**[1] *n* **1** a distinct part or division of something. **2** a distinct part of a community or group of people. **3** the action of cutting or separating by cutting in surgery. **4** a shape or figure resulting from cutting through a solid form.

**section**[2] *v* to cut or separate into sections.

**sector** *n* **1** a distinct part or division. **2** a part of a circle between two lines joining the centre to the circumference.

**secular** *adj* **1** of this world rather than the heavenly or spiritual. **2** not overtly or specifically religious. ➤ **secularism** *n.*

**secure**[1] *adj* **1** free from danger or risk of loss. **2** firmly fixed or fastened. **3** calm in mind. **4** assured or certain. ➤ **securely** *adv.*

**secure**[2] *v* **1** to fix or fasten firmly. **2** to make safe from risk or danger. **3** to obtain by effort.

**security** *n* (*pl* **-ies**) **1** freedom from danger, fear, or anxiety. **2** the safety of a state or organization against attack or subversion. **3** something pledged to guarantee the fulfilment of an obligation.

**sedan** *n* **1** *NAmer* a saloon car. **2** a portable enclosed chair carried on poles by two people.

**sedate**[1] *adj* calm and even in temper or pace. ➤ **sedately** *adv.*

**sedate**[2] *v* to give a sedative to.

**sedation** *n* the act of sedating somebody, or the condition of being sedated.

**sedative**[1] *adj* tending to calm or to tranquillize somebody.

**sedative**[2] *n* a sedative drug.

**sedentary** *adj* **1** doing or involving much sitting. **2** of birds: that do not migrate. **3** of animals: permanently attached to a surface.

**sedge** *n* a marsh plant having a solid stem.

**sediment** *n* **1** matter that settles at the bottom of a liquid. **2** material deposited by water, wind, or glaciers. ➤ **sedimentary** *adj.*

**sedition** *n* incitement to defy or rise up against the government. ➤ **seditious** *adj.*

**seduce** *v* **1** to persuade (somebody) to have sexual intercourse. **2** to incite to wrongdoing or disloyalty. ➤ **seduction** *n.*

**seductive** *adj* tending to seduce; alluring or attractive. ➤ **seductively** *adv.*

**sedulous** *adj formal* diligent and careful. ➤ **sedulously** *adv.*

**see**[1] *v* (**saw, seen**) **1** to perceive with the eyes. **2** to perceive or deduce by thinking. **3** to imagine or envisage. **4** to determine or decide. **5** to make sure of. **6** to call on or visit. **7** to consult professionally. **8** to keep company with. **9** to escort (somebody) to a specified place. ✱ **see about** to deal with or consider. **see the back of** to be rid of. **see through 1** to undergo or endure to the end. **2** to be aware of (a deception). **see to** to attend to or take care of.

**see²** *n* the area over which a bishop has authority.

**seed¹** *n* (*pl* **seeds** *or* **seed**) **1** the fertilized ovule of a flowering plant or conifer that contains an embryo and can produce a new plant. **2** the grains or fertilized ovules of plants used for sowing. **3** a source of development or growth. **4** a competitor who has been seeded in a tournament. **5** something that resembles a seed in shape or size. **6** *archaic* semen. **7** *archaic* offspring. ➤ **seedless** *adj.*

**seed²** *v* **1** of a plant: to produce or shed seeds. **2** to plant seeds in (a field, plot, etc). **3** to extract the seeds from. **4** to schedule (tournament players or teams) so that strong ones will not meet each other in early rounds.

**seedling** *n* a plant grown from seed.

**seedy** *adj* (**-ier, -iest**) **1** shabby or grubby. **2** disreputable or run-down. ➤ **seediness** *n.*

**seeing** *conj* (*often* + that) because; since.

**seek** *v* (*past tense and past part.* **sought**) **1** (*often* + out) to go in search of. **2** to try to discover. **3** to ask for (advice, etc). **4** to try to acquire or gain. **5** to make an effort (to do something). ➤ **seeker** *n.*

**seem** *v* to give the impression of being or doing something. ✱ **not seem** used for 'seem not': *He doesn't seem to understand.*

**seeming** *adj* apparent rather than real.

**seemly** *adj* (**-ier, -iest**) in accord with good taste or propriety. ➤ **seemliness** *n.*

**seen** *v* past part. of SEE¹.

**see off** *v* **1** to accompany (somebody) to the place where they are leaving. **2** *informal* to chase away.

**see out** *v* **1** to escort out of a room or building. **2** to last until the end of.

**seep** *v* to pass slowly through fine pores or small openings. ➤ **seepage** *n.*

**seer** *n* a person who predicts future events.

**seersucker** *n* a light slightly puckered fabric.

**seesaw¹** *n* a plank balanced in the middle so that one end goes up as the other goes down, used for amusement.

**seesaw²** *v* **1** to move backward and forward or up and down. **2** to alternate or vacillate.

**seethe** *v* **1** to feel suppressed anger. **2** to be in a state of agitated movement.

**see-through** *adj esp* of clothing: transparent or nearly so.

**segment¹** *n* each of the parts into which something is divided or marked off. ➤ **segmental** *adj.*

**segment²** *v* to separate or divide into segments.

**segregate** *v* **1** to keep separate from others; to set apart. **2** to cause or force the separation of (racial groups, religions, or sexes) from the rest of a community. ➤ **segregation** *n.*

**segue** /ˈsegway, ˈsaygway/ *v* (**segues, segued, segueing**) to pass directly from one musical number or theme to another.

**seine** *n* a large fishing net with floats at one end that hangs vertically in the water.

**seismic** *adj* **1** of or caused by an earthquake. **2** very great in importance or effect.

**seismology** *n* the study of earthquakes. ➤ **seismological** *adj,* **seismologist** *n.*

**seize** *v* **1** to take hold of abruptly or forcefully. **2** to confiscate by legal authority. **3** (+ on) to use or take advantage of eagerly. **4** (*often* + up) of machinery: to become locked and fail to work.

---

Usage Note: Note the spelling with *-ei-*

---

**seizure** *n* **1** the act of seizing. **2** a sudden attack of a fit or other illness.

**seldom** *adv* rarely or infrequently.

**select¹** *adj* **1** picked out in preference to others. **2** of special value or quality. **3** socially exclusive.

**select²** *v* to pick out or choose carefully.

**select committee** *n* a committee appointed by a legislative body to examine a particular matter.

**selection** *n* **1** the act of selecting. **2** somebody or something selected. **3** a collection of selected items. **4** a range of things from which to choose.

**selective** *adj* **1** using or involving selection. **2** tending to choose carefully. **3** affecting only some in a group. ➤ **selectively** *adv,* **selectivity** *n.*

**selenium** *n* a grey chemical element used in electronic devices.

**self** *n* (*pl* **selves**) **1** the entire being of an individual. **2** a person's individual character. **3** the physical and emotional elements that make up the particular identity of a person.

**self-absorbed** *adj* preoccupied with one's own thoughts or activities. ➤ **self-absorption** *n.*

**self-abuse** *n* masturbation.

**self-addressed** *adj* addressed for return to the sender.

**self-appointed** *adj* assuming a position of authority not approved by others.

**self-assessment** *n* **1** assessment of one's own performance. **2** a system of calculating one's own liability for income tax.

**self-assurance** *n* confidence in oneself. ➤ **self-assured** *adj.*

**self-catering** *adj* of holiday accommodation: including kitchen facilities.

**self-centred** *adj* preoccupied with one's own wishes or needs.
**self-certification** *n* in Britain, a system by which an employee who has been absent from work for a short period can declare the reason in writing without needing a doctor's certificate.
**self-confessed** *adj* openly acknowledged.
**self-confidence** *n* confidence in oneself and one's abilities. ➤ **self-confident** *adj.*
**self-congratulation** *n* a complacent acknowledgment of one's own superiority or achievements. ➤ **self-congratulatory** *adj.*
**self-conscious** *adj* uncomfortably conscious of oneself as an object of attention. ➤ **self-consciously** *adv.*
**self-contained** *adj* complete in itself.
**self-control** *n* the ability to control one's own impulses or emotions. ➤ **self-controlled** *adj.*
**self-defeating** *adj* of a plan or action: preventing its own success.
**self-defence** *n* the act of defending or justifying oneself.
**self-denial** *n* the limitation of one's desires or their gratification.
**self-deprecating** *adj* critical of oneself. ➤ **self-deprecation** *n.*
**self-destruct** *v* to destroy itself automatically. ➤ **self-destructive** *adj.*
**self-determination** *n* the right of a person or country to manage their affairs without interference.
**self-discipline** *n* the ability to control one's thoughts and actions. ➤ **self-disciplined** *adj.*
**self-doubt** *n* a lack of confidence in oneself.
**self-effacement** *n* the act of avoiding attention. ➤ **self-effacing** *adj.*
**self-employed** *adj* working for oneself and not an employer. ➤ **self-employment** *n.*
**self-esteem** *n* confidence and satisfaction in oneself.
**self-evident** *adj* requiring no proof; obvious. ➤ **self-evidently** *adv.*
**self-explanatory** *adj* capable of being understood without explanation.
**self-expression** *n* the expression of one's own thoughts and feelings, e.g. by painting or poetry.
**self-fulfilling** *adj* of a prediction: bound to come true because it causes people to behave in a way that causes this.
**self-help** *n* dependence on one's own efforts.
**self-importance** *n* an exaggerated sense of one's own importance. ➤ **self-important** *adj.*
**self-indulgence** *n* excessive gratification of one's own appetites or desires. ➤ **self-indulgent** *adj.*
**self-interest** *n* a concern for one's own advantage and well-being. ➤ **self-interested** *adj.*
**selfish** *adj* concerned chiefly with one's own advantage or needs. ➤ **selfishly** *adv,* **selfishness** *n.*
**selfless** *adj* having more concern for others than for oneself.
**self-made** *adj* having achieved success by one's own efforts.
**self-pity** *n* a self-indulgent dwelling on one's own misfortunes. ➤ **self-pitying** *adj.*
**self-portrait** *n* a portrait in which the artist is the subject.
**self-possessed** *adj* composed in mind or manner; calm. ➤ **self-possession** *n.*
**self-preservation** *n* an instinctive tendency to protect oneself.
**self-raising flour** (*NAmer* **self-rising flour**) *n* a form of flour with its own raising agent.
**self-regard** *n* **1** concern or consideration for oneself. **2** self-respect. ➤ **self-regarding** *adj.*
**self-reliance** *n* reliance on one's own efforts and resources. ➤ **self-reliant** *adj.*
**self-respect** *n* confidence in and respect for oneself. ➤ **self-respecting** *adj.*
**self-restraint** *n* restraint imposed on oneself and one's feelings.
**self-righteous** *adj* sure that one is right or morally superior.
**self-sacrifice** *n* sacrifice of oneself or one's well-being for the sake of others. ➤ **self-sacrificing** *adj.*
**selfsame** *adj* precisely the same.
**self-satisfied** *adj* smugly satisfied with oneself or one's achievements. ➤ **self-satisfaction** *n.*
**self-seeking** *adj* seeking only to safeguard one's own interests. ➤ **self-seeker** *n.*
**self-service** *adj* of a shop, cafeteria, etc: where customers serve themselves.
**self-styled** *adj* called by oneself, *esp* without justification: *a self-styled expert.*
**self-sufficient** *adj* able to provide for one's own needs without outside help. ➤ **self-sufficiency** *n.*
**self-worth** *n* self-esteem.
**sell** *v* (*past tense and past part.* **sold**) **1** to give (goods or property) in exchange for money. **2** to achieve a sale of (a certain number). **3** to be sold or achieve sales. **4** to persuade somebody of the worth of (an idea, etc). ✱ **sell short** to belittle or disparage. ➤ **seller** *n.*
**selling point** *n* a particularly good feature that makes something desirable.
**sell off** *v* to sell all of (something) quickly and cheaply. ➤ **sell-off** *n.*
**Sellotape** *n trademark* a transparent adhesive tape.
**sell out** *v* **1** to sell all of (something). **2** to be sold entirely. **3** to betray or be unfaithful to.
**sell-out** *n* **1** an event for which all tickets or seats are sold. **2** *informal* a betrayal.
**selvage** *or* **selvedge** *n* the edge on a woven fabric, finished to prevent unravelling.

**selves** *n* pl of SELF.

**semantic** *adj* relating to meaning in language. ➤ **semantically** *adv.*

**semantics** *pl n* **1** the branch of linguistics concerned with meaning. **2** the meaning of a sentence, word, etc. ➤ **semanticist** *n.*

**semaphore** *n* a system of visual signalling with the arms or a pair of flags held one in each hand.

**semblance** *n* the way something seems or appears.

**semen** *n* a fluid containing sperm, produced by the male reproductive glands.

**semester** *n* an academic term lasting half a year.

**semi** *n* (*pl* **semis**) *informal* **1** *Brit* a semidetached house. **2** a semifinal.

**semiautomatic** *adj* of a gun: equipped to load each cartridge in turn, but needing manual release of the trigger for each shot.

**semibreve** *n* a musical note with the time value of two minims or four crotchets.

**semicircle** *n* a half circle. ➤ **semicircular** *adj.*

**semicolon** *n* a punctuation mark (;) used to indicate a break or pause that is more marked than one indicated by a comma.

**semiconductor** *n* a substance that conducts electricity in proportion to temperature or the presence of certain impurities.

**semidetached** *adj* of a house: joined to another house by a common wall.

**semifinal** *n* a match or round that is next to the last in a knockout competition. ➤ **semifinalist** *n.*

**seminal** *adj* **1** originating and influencing future development. **2** relating to seed or semen.

**seminar** *n* **1** a meeting of university students with a teacher for discussion. **2** a meeting for exchanging and discussing information.

**seminary** *n* (*pl* **-ies**) an institution for the training of the clergy.

**semiotics** *pl n* the study of signs and symbols as a feature of language. ➤ **semiotic** *adj.*

**semiprecious** *adj* of a gemstone: of less value than a precious stone.

**semiquaver** *n* a musical note with the time value of half a quaver.

**semiskimmed** *adj* of milk: with some of its cream removed.

**semitone** *n* a musical interval equal to half a tone.

**semolina** *n* the purified hard parts left after milling of wheat, used to make pasta and puddings.

**senate** *n* (*treated as sing. or pl*) **1** the upper chamber in some legislatures. **2** the supreme council of ancient Rome. **3** the governing body of some universities.

**senator** *n* a member of a senate. ➤ **senatorial** *adj.*

**send** *v* (*past tense and past part.* **sent**) **1** to cause or direct to go to a place. **2** to cause to move quickly or violently. **3** (*often* + out) to emit or discharge. **4** to cause (somebody) to be in a specified state. **5** (*usu* + for) to summon or order somebody or something. ➤ **sender** *n.*

**send down** *v* **1** *Brit* to suspend or expel (a student) from a university. **2** *informal* to sentence (somebody) to a term in prison.

**send off** *v* of a referee: to order (a player) to leave the field.

**send-off** *n* a gathering of people to say goodbye to somebody starting a journey.

**send up** *v chiefly Brit* to imitiate mockingly.

**senile** *adj* losing mental or physical faculties through old age. ➤ **senility** *n.*

**senior**[1] *adj* **1** higher in standing or rank. **2** older. **3** relating to old age and older people. **4** *Brit* relating to students in the upper years of secondary school. **5** *NAmer* relating to students in the final year of higher education. **6** used to distinguish a father with the same name as his son; elder. ➤ **seniority** *n.*

**senior**[2] *n* **1** a person who is older than another person by a specified amount. **2** in sporting competitions, an adult or more advanced competitor. **3** *Brit* a student in the upper years of secondary school. **4** *NAmer* a student in the final year of higher education.

**senior citizen** *n* an old age pensioner.

**senna** *n* the dried pods of certain plants, used as a laxative.

**sensation** *n* **1** a mental process resulting from stimulation of a sense organ. **2** a general state of awareness of something external. **3** a surge of interest or excitement, or the cause of this.

**sensational** *adj* **1** arousing great general interest or excitement. **2** *informal* exceptionally fine or impressive. ➤ **sensationally** *adv.*

**sensationalize** *or* **-ise** *v* to report (a story, etc) in sensationalist terms.

**sense**[1] *n* **1** any of the faculties of perceiving things by touching, hearing, seeing, smelling, or tasting. **2** an ability to use the senses for a specified purpose: *a sense of balance.* **3** a vague awareness or impression. **4** an awareness that motivates action or judgment: *a sense of justice.* **5** a capacity for appreciating something: *a sense of humour.* **6** (*usu in pl, but treated as sing.*) soundness of mind or judgment. **7** the use of practical intelligence. **8** a meaning conveyed by a word or expression. ✱ **make sense** to be understandable or reasonable.

**sense**[2] *v* **1** to perceive by the senses. **2** to become vaguely aware of. **3** to grasp or comprehend. **4** to detect automatically.

**senseless** *adj* **1** unconscious. **2** foolish or stupid. **3** having no meaning or purpose.

**sensibility** *n* (*pl* **-ies**) **1** (*usu in pl*) the degree of being sensitive to feelings and tastes. **2** the ability to discern or appreciate emotion in others.

**sensible** *adj* **1** having or showing good sense or sound reason. **2** plain and practical. **3** (+ of/to) capable of feeling something: *sensible to pain.* ➤ **sensibly** *adv.*

**sensitive** *adj* **1** (+ to) capable of being stimulated by external agents such as light, gravity, or contact. **2** (*often* + to) easily affected emotionally. **3** (*often* + to) finely aware of the feelings of others. **4** controversial and needing tactful handling. **5** of information: secret or classified. ➤ **sensitively** *adv,* **sensitivity** *n.*

**sensitize** *or* **-ise** *v* to make sensitive to or aware of something.

**sensor** *n* a device that responds to heat, light, sound, or other physical attributes.

**sensory** *adj* of sensation or the senses.

**sensual** *adj* relating to the gratification of the physical senses. ➤ **sensuality** *n,* **sensually** *adv.*

**sensuous** *adj* **1** relating or appealing to the senses rather than the intellect. **2** producing rich imagery or sense impressions. ➤ **sensuously** *adv.*

**sent** *v* past tense and past part. of SEND.

**sentence**[1] *n* **1** a group of words that is grammatically complete and expresses a statement, question, command, wish, or exclamation. **2** a punishment pronounced by a lawcourt.

**sentence**[2] *v* (*often* + to) to impose a judicial sentence on.

**sententious** *adj* given to pompous moralizing.

**sentient** *adj* capable of perceiving through the senses.

**sentiment** *n* **1** strong or exaggerated emotion or feeling. **2** a specific view or opinion. **3** a feeling or attitude.

**sentimental** *adj* **1** appealing to or resulting from feeling rather than reason. **2** having an excess of superficial sentiment. ➤ **sentimentality** *n,* **sentimentally** *adv.*

**sentinel** *n* somebody that keeps guard; a sentry.

**sentry** *n* (*pl* **-ies**) a soldier standing guard at a gate, door, etc.

**sepal** *n* any of the modified leaves forming the green outer part of a flower.

**separable** *adj* capable of being separated or dissociated. ➤ **separability** *n.*

**separate**[1] *v* **1** to move or come apart. **2** to stop living together as spouses or partners. **3** to divide or stand between (two or more people or things). **4** (*often* + from) to make a distinction between. **5** to detach from a larger group. **6** (*often* + out) to divide into constituent parts or types. ➤ **separative** *adj.*

**separate**[2] *adj* **1** set or kept apart; detached or separated. **2** not shared with another. **3** existing independently. **4** different in kind; distinct. ➤ **separately** *adv.*

***Usage Note:*** Note the spelling with *-ar-*.

**separation** *n* **1** the act of separating. **2** the living apart of a husband and wife while still married.

**separatism** *n* a belief or movement advocating separation from a main group. ➤ **separatist** *n and adj.*

**sepia** *n* a rich dark brown.

**sepoy** *n* an Indian soldier serving with the British army.

**sepsis** *n* (*pl* **sepses**) the spread of bacteria from a focus of infection.

**September** *n* the ninth month of the year.

**septet** *n* **1** a group of seven instruments, voices, or performers. **2** a musical composition for a septet.

**septic** *adj* infected with bacteria. ➤ **septically** *adv,* **septicity** *n.*

**septicaemia** (*NAmer* **septicemia**) *n* blood poisoning caused by micro-organisms.

**septic tank** *n* an underground tank in which sewage is disintegrated by bacteria.

**septuagenarian** *n* a person between 70 and 79 years old.

**septum** *n* (*pl* **septa**) a membrane between bodily spaces or masses of soft tissue.

**septuple** *adj* **1** having seven parts. **2** being seven times as great or as many.

**septuplet** *n* any of seven offspring born at one birth.

**sepulchral** *adj* **1** having to do with a tomb or burial. **2** sombre or dismal. ➤ **sepulchrally** *adv.*

**sepulchre** (*NAmer* **sepulcher**) *n* a tomb or place of burial.

**sequel** *n* **1** a play, film, or literary work continuing the story of a previous one. **2** a subsequent development or course of events.

**sequence**[1] *n* **1** a continuous or connected series. **2** a continuous progression. **3** the order of succession of things, events, etc.

**sequence**[2] *v* to place in a sequence.

**sequential** *adj* **1** of or arranged in a sequence. **2** following in sequence. ➤ **sequentially** *adv.*

**sequester** *v* **1** to segregate from the company of others. **2** in law, to seize (property) until a debt is paid.

**sequestrate** *v* in law, to sequester (property). ➤ **sequestration** *n,* **sequestrator** *n.*

**sequin** *n* a small shining disc used on clothing for ornamentation.

**sequoia** *n* a tall coniferous Californian tree.

**seraglio** /se'rahlioh, -lyoh/ *n* (*pl* **-os**) **1** a harem. **2** the women's apartments in a sultan's palace.

**seraph** *n* (*pl* **seraphim** *or* **seraphs**) any of the six-winged angels standing in the presence of God. ➤ **seraphic** *adj.*

**serenade**[1] *n* a piece of music played outdoors at night by a man for a woman he is courting.

**serenade**[2] *v* to perform a serenade for.

**serendipity** *n* the discovery of pleasing or interesting things by chance. ➤ **serendipitous** *adj.*

**serene** *adj* calm and tranquil. ➤ **serenely** *adv,* **serenity** *n.*

**serf** *n* an agricultural labourer in a feudal society, bound in service to a lord. ➤ **serfdom** *n.*

**serge** *n* a durable woollen fabric.

**sergeant** *or* **serjeant** *n* **1** a British police officer ranking below an inspector. **2** a non-commissioned officer in the army, ranking above a corporal.

**sergeant major** *n* (*pl* **sergeant majors**) a non-commissioned officer in the British army or Royal Marines.

**serial**[1] *n* a story published or broadcast in parts at intervals.

**serial**[2] *adj* **1** of or constituting a series, rank, or row. **2** appearing in successive instalments. **3** repeating the same offence several times: *a serial rapist.* ➤ **serially** *adv.*

**serialism** *n* music based on a series of notes in an arbitrary but fixed order without traditional tonality.

**serialize** *or* **-ise** *v* to publish or broadcast in serial form. ➤ **serialization** *n.*

**serial number** *n* a number used as a means of identifying an object.

**series** *n* (*pl* **series**) **1** a number of things or events of the same kind following one another. **2** a number of radio or television programmes of the same type or on the same theme. **3** a mathematical sequence whose terms are to be added together.

**serious** *adj* **1** grave or thoughtful in appearance or manner. **2** sincere and in earnest. **3** deeply interested or committed. **4** severe or dangerous. **5** requiring careful attention. ➤ **seriously** *adv,* **seriousness** *n.*

**sermon** *n* a religious talk given as a part of a church service.

**serpent** *n literary* a large snake.

**serpentine** *adj* winding or twisting.

**serrated** *adj* having projections like the teeth of a saw.

**serration** *n* each of the points of a serrated edge.

**serried** *adj* of rows or ranks: crowded or pressed together.

**serum** *n* (*pl* **serums** *or* **sera**) the protein-rich fluid constituent of blood.

**servant** *n* a person employed to perform personal or domestic duties.

**serve**[1] *v* **1** to perform duties or obligations for. **2** to be a member of the armed forces of (a country). **3** to be imprisoned for (a period of time). **4** to attend to (a customer) in a shop, bar, etc. **5** to provide with (food or drinks). **6** to fulfil a particular purpose; to help or benefit. **7** to be adequate or satisfactory. **8** in tennis and other games, to begin a period of play by hitting the ball or shuttlecock. ✱ **serve somebody right** to be their just deserts.

**serve**[2] *n* the act of serving in tennis, badminton, etc.

**server** *n* **1** the player who serves, e.g. in tennis. **2** a person or thing that serves. **3** a computer or program that connects users in a network to a centralized store of data.

**service**[1] *n* **1** work or duty carried out for a person, organization, country, etc. **2** a system or facility designed to meet a public need. **3** the work of attending to customers in a shop, bar, etc. **4** a helpful action or favour. **5** a religious ceremony in a Christian church. **6** a routine inspection and repair of a machine or motor vehicle. **7** a set of matching tableware for serving food. **8** (*usu in pl*) any of a nation's military forces. **9** *Brit* (*in pl*) facilities provided for the users of a motorway. **10** (*in pl*) gas, water, and other utilities connected to a building. **11** a serve in tennis, badminton, etc. ✱ **in service** working as a domestic servant. **out of service** not currently being used or operated.

**service**[2] *v* **1** to provide a service or services for. **2** to carry out routine repairs and maintenance on. **3** to meet interest payments on (a debt).

**serviceable** *adj* **1** in good working order. **2** reliable and durable.

**service industry** *n* an industry that provides a service and does not produce goods.

**serviceman** *or* **servicewoman** *n* (*pl* **servicemen** *or* **servicewomen**) a member of the armed forces.

**service station** *n* a roadside garage selling petrol, oil, etc.

**serviette** *n chiefly Brit* a table napkin.

**servile** *adj* **1** slavishly willing to please or satisfy others. **2** characteristic of a slave or menial. ➤ **servility** *n.*

**serving** *n* a single portion of food.

**servitude** *n* the state of being a slave or completely subject to somebody.

**servo** *n* (*pl* **-os**) a device that converts a low power input into a much larger power output.

**sesame** *n* a tropical plant with seeds used as a source of oil and as a flavouring.

**session** *n* **1** a period devoted to a particular activity. **2** a meeting or series of meetings of a court or council.

**set**[1] *v* (**setting,** *past tense and past part.* **set**) **1** to put in a particular place or position. **2** to put in a specified condition. **3** to decide on and fix (an amount, etc). **4** to give somebody (a task) to perform. **5** to prepare or adjust (a device) for use. **6** to prepare (a table) for use at a meal. **7** to describe (an event, story, etc) as taking place at a particular place and time. **8** to provide music for (a text). **9** to arrange (type) for printing. **10** to fix (wet hair) in the right style after washing.

11 to put (a dislocated or fractured bone or limb) into its normal position for healing. **12** to fix (a gem) in a border of metal. **13** to become solid or thickened. **14** of the sun, moon, etc: to go down below the horizon. * **set on** to attack suddenly and violently. **set sail** to begin a voyage by sea. **set to work** to start to do something.

**set**[2] *adj* **1** arranged or fixed in advance. **2** (*usu* + on) resolutely determined. **3** unchanging and immovable. **4** prepared and ready.

**set**[3] *n* **1** a number of things of the same kind belonging or used together. **2** a radio or television apparatus. **3** in tennis and similar sports, a number of games forming a unit for scoring. **4** the artificial scenery used for a play. **5** bearing or posture.

**set about** *v* **1** to start doing something. **2** to attack.

**set aside** *v* **1** to discard or put to one side. **2** to override (a decision).

**setback** *n* a problem or difficulty that causes a delay or interruption.

**set forth** *v* **1** to start on a journey. **2** to give an account of.

**set off** *v* **1** to start on a journey. **2** to cause (a bomb) to explode.

**set out** *v* **1** to start on a journey. **2** to have as an intention. **3** to state or describe in detail.

**set square** *n chiefly Brit* a flat triangular instrument with a right angle, used to mark out angles.

**sett** *n* the burrow of a badger.

**settee** *n* a long upholstered seat for more than one person.

**setting** *n* **1** the physical or historical background for an object or event. **2** the way in which something is set. **3** the music composed for a text. **4** a set of cutlery, glasses, etc for one person at a meal. **5** the frame in which a gem is mounted.

**settle**[1] *v* **1** to find an acceptable answer or solution to. **2** (*often* + down) to make or become calm or orderly. **3** (*usu* + down) to adopt an ordered or stable lifestyle. **4** to place or arrange firmly or comfortably. **5** to become established in a particular place or position. **6** to establish a home or a colony. **7** to come to rest. **8** to pay (a debt). **9** (+ on) to make a decision or choice. **10** (+ for) to accept something less than one hoped for. * **settle down to** to begin (an activity) in a purposeful way.

**settle**[2] *n* a wooden bench with arms and a high back.

**settle in** *v* to become comfortably established in a new environment.

**settlement** *n* **1** the process of settling. **2** an agreement resolving differences. **3** a place where a new community has been established. **4** the act of leaving property or money to somebody in a will.

**set-to** *n* (*pl* **-os**) *informal* a brief and vigorous conflict.

**set up** *v* **1** to raise into position. **2** to establish or found.

**seven** *n* the number 7. ➤ **seven** *adj.*

**seventeen** *adj and n* the number 17. ➤ **seventeenth** *adj and n.*

**seventh** *adj and n* **1** having the position in a sequence corresponding to the number seven. **2** one of seven equal parts of something.

**seventy** *adj and n* (*pl* **-ies**) **1** the number 70. **2** (*in pl*) the numbers 70 to 79. ➤ **seventieth** *adj and n.*

**sever** *v* **1** to divide by cutting. **2** to put or keep apart. **3** to terminate. ➤ **severable** *adj.*

**several** *adj and n* **1** more than two but not many. **2** *formal* separate or distinct.

**severance** *n* **1** the act of separating by cutting. **2** the state of being separated. **3** the ending of a relationship.

**severe** *adj* **1** stern or austere. **2** strict or stringent. **3** restrained in decoration or manner. **4** of something difficult or unwelcome: great or extreme. ➤ **severely** *adv,* **severity** *n.*

**sew** *v* (*past tense* **sewed,** *past part.* **sewn** *or* **sewed**) **1** to join or attach by stitches made with a needle and thread. **2** to make or mend by sewing.

**sewage** *n* waste matter carried off by sewers.

**sewer** *n* an underground channel or pipe used to carry off waste matter from drains. ➤ **sewerage** *n.*

**sewing machine** *n* a machine for sewing, with a motor or handle that moves the needle.

**sex** *n* **1** either of two categories, male or female, into which organisms are divided. **2** the characteristics that distinguish males and females. **3** sexual intercourse or activity.

**sexagenarian** *n* a person between 60 and 69 years old.

**sex appeal** *n* the quality of being sexual attractive.

**sexism** *n* discrimination or prejudice, *esp* against women, on the basis of a person's sex. ➤ **sexist** *adj and n.*

**sexless** *adj* **1** lacking sex appeal or the sexual urge. **2** not male or female.

**sex symbol** *n* a famous person noted for sex appeal.

**sextant** *n* an instrument for measuring angles and distances in surveying and navigation.

**sextet** *n* **1** a group of six instruments, voices, or performers. **2** a musical composition for a sextet.

**sexton** *n* an official in charge of church property.

**sextuple** *adj* **1** having six parts. **2** being six times as much or as many.

**sextuplet** *n* any of six offspring born at one birth.

**sexual** *adj* **1** relating to sex and to physical attraction and contact between individuals. **2** relating to male and female or to relations between the two sexes. **3** of reproduction: involving the fusion of male and female reproductive cells. ➤ **sexually** *adv.*

**sexual harassment** *n* repeated unwelcome physical contact or sexual suggestions directed at somebody, *esp* in the workplace.

**sexual intercourse** *n* sexual activity with penetration of the vagina by the erect penis.

**sexuality** *n* (*pl* **-ies**) **1** the condition of experiencing sexual desires. **2** a person's sexual orientation or preference.

**sexy** *adj* (**-ier, -iest**) **1** sexually attractive or stimulating. **2** sexually aroused. **3** *informal* interesting or fashionable. ➤ **sexily** *adv,* **sexiness** *n.*

**shabby** *adj* (**-ier, -iest**) **1** worn or threadbare. **2** shameful or despicable. ➤ **shabbily** *adv.*

**shack** *n* a small crudely built hut or shelter.

**shackle**[1] *n* **1** a pair of metal rings joined by a chain used to fasten a prisoner's hands or legs. **2** (*usu in pl*) something that restricts or prevents free action.

**shackle**[2] *v* **1** to chain or fasten with shackles. **2** to restrain or handicap.

**shack up** *v informal* (*usu* + together/with) to live with as a sexual partner.

**shad** *n* (*pl* **shads** *or* **shad**) a fish of the herring family.

**shade**[1] *n* **1** partial darkness caused when sunlight is obstructed. **2** a place sheltered from the rays of the sun. **3** a lampshade. **4** *informal* (*in pl*) sunglasses. **5** a particular variety of a colour. **6** a small amount. **7** a ghost. ✱ **a shade** slightly; somewhat. **shades of** reminiscent of.

**shade**[2] *v* **1** to shelter or screen from light or heat. **2** to cover or darken with a shade. **3** to mark (a picture or drawing) with shading or darker colour. **4** to change gradually. **5** (+ into) to pass imperceptibly into a different state. ➤ **shaded** *adj.*

**shading** *n* lines, dots, or colour used to represent degrees of light and dark.

**shadow**[1] *n* **1** a dark shape made on a surface by an object that is between it and a source of light. **2** partial darkness caused when light is interrupted. **3** the slightest trace trace: *not a shadow of doubt.* **4** a much reduced and weakened form of a person or thing. **5** a source of gloom or disquiet. **6** a person who accompanies or follows somebody else. **7** (*used before a noun*) denoting a member of the opposition who speaks on matters for which the corresponding government minister is responsible. ➤ **shadowy** *adj.*

**shadow**[2] *v* **1** to cast a shadow over. **2** to follow or keep under surveillance.

**shadow-box** *v* to box with an imaginary opponent as a form of training.

**shady** *adj* (**-ier, -iest**) **1** producing or giving shade. **2** sheltered from the sun. **3** *informal* of questionable legality or integrity.

**shaft**[1] *n* **1** the long narrow body of a spear or arrow or handle of a tool. **2** a rotating cylindrical bar used to transmit power or motion in a machine. **3** an opening to a mine, well, etc. **4** a vertical passage through the floors of a building. **5** a beam of light shining from an opening. **6** either of two poles between which a horse is hitched to a vehicle.

**shaft**[2] *v informal* to treat unfairly or harshly.

**shag**[1] *n* **1** long coarse or matted fibre. **2** a strong coarse tobacco. **3** a bird similar to a cormorant but smaller.

**shag**[2] *v* (**shagged, shagging**) *Brit, coarse slang* to have sexual intercourse with.

**shag**[3] *n Brit, coarse slang* an act of sexual intercourse.

**shaggy** *adj* (**-ier, -iest**) **1** having long, coarse, or matted hair. **2** unkempt.

**shah** *n* formerly, a sovereign of Iran.

**shake**[1] *v* (**shook, shaken**) **1** to move back and forth or up and down with short rapid movements. **2** to tremble. **3** to shock or upset. **4** to weaken (somebody's confidence). ✱ **shake a leg** *informal* to hurry up. **shake hands** to clasp hands in greeting or agreement. **shake on it** to shake hands as a sign of agreement. **shake one's head** to move one's head from side to side to express refusal or disagreement.

**shake**[2] *n* **1** an act of shaking. **2** a milk shake.

**Shakespearean** *or* **Shakespearian** *adj* relating to the English dramatist and poet William Shakespeare (d.1616).

**shake up** *v* **1** to rouse from inactivity or complacency. **2** *informal* to reorganize drastically.

**shaky** *adj* (**-ier, -iest**) **1** not firm or stable; unsteady. **2** precarious or uncertain. ➤ **shakily** *adv.*

**shale** *n* a finely stratified or laminated rock formed by the consolidation of clay, mud, or silt.

**shall** *v aux* (*third person sing. present tense* **shall,** *past tense* **should**) **1** used in the first person to express a future action or state: *We shall try to be there.* **2** used to express determination or insistence: *They shall not stop us.* **3** used to express a polite request or suggestion: *Shall I leave?*

**shallot** *n* an edible bulb like a small onion.

**shallow** *adj* **1** having little depth. **2** superficial in knowledge or thought. ➤ **shallowly** *adv.*

**shallows** *pl n* a shallow area in a body of water.

**sham**[1] *n* **1** something that is not genuine or what it seems to be. **2** a person who pretends or makes false claims.

**sham**[2] *adj* **1** not genuine; imitation. **2** pretended or feigned.

**sham**[3] *v* (**shammed, shamming**) to pretend.

**shaman** *n* (*pl* **shamans**) a priest believed to exercise magic powers of healing and divination. ➤ **shamanism** *n.*

**shamble** *v* to walk awkwardly with dragging feet.

**shambles** *n* (*pl* **shambles**) a state of complete chaos or confusion.

**shambolic** *adj Brit, informal* completely chaotic or confused.

**shame**[1] *n* **1** an unpleasant feeling caused by awareness of having done something wrong or foolish. **2** humiliating disgrace or ignominy. **3** a cause of disgrace. **4** a cause of regret. * **put to shame** to show obvious superiority over.

**shame**[2] *v* to cause to feel shame.

**shamefaced** *adj* showing shame. ➤ **shamefacedly** *adv.*

**shameful** *adj* **1** bringing disgrace or ignominy. **2** causing a feeling of shame. ➤ **shamefully** *adv.*

**shameless** *adj* not feeling any shame. ➤ **shamelessly** *adv.*

**shammy** *n* (*pl* **-ies**) *informal* a chamois leather.

**shampoo**[1] *n* (*pl* **shampoos**) **1** a liquid soap for washing the hair. **2** a similar cleaning agent used on a carpet, car, etc. **3** an act of washing with shampoo.

**shampoo**[2] *v* (**shampoos, shampooed, shampooing**) to wash or clean with shampoo.

**shamrock** *n* a clover with three-part leaves, the national emblem of Ireland.

**shandy** *n* (*pl* **-ies**) beer mixed with lemonade or ginger beer.

**shanghai** *v* (**shanghais, shanghaied, shanghaiing**) *informal* to trick or force (somebody) into doing something.

**shank** *n* **1** the leg between the knee and the ankle. **2** a straight narrow part of an object.

**shanks's pony** *n* one's own legs as a means of transport.

**shan't** *contraction* shall not.

**shantung** *n* a silk fabric in plain weave with a slightly irregular surface.

**shanty**[1] *n* (*pl* **-ies**) a small crudely built hut or shelter.

**shanty**[2] *n* (*pl* **-ies**) a song sung by sailors in rhythm with their work.

**shantytown** *n* a poor area of a town consisting mainly of shanties.

**shape**[1] *v* **1** to give a particular shape to. **2** to determine the nature or course of. **3** (*often* + up) to develop or proceed. ➤ **shaper** *n.*

**shape**[2] *n* **1** the form of something determined by its outline and outer surface. **2** a circle, square, or other standard geometrical form. **3** a piece of paper or material cut into a particular form. **4** definite physical or mental form. **5** the condition of a person or thing at a particular time. * **in shape** in good physical condition. **take shape** to take on a definite form.

**shapeless** *adj* having no definite shape.

**shapely** *adj* (**-ier, -iest**) having a pleasing shape.

**shape up** *v* **1** to develop in a particular way. **2** of a person: to become physically fit.

**shard** *n* a piece of broken glass or earthenware.

**share**[1] *n* **1** a portion belonging to or contributed by an individual. **2** the part belonging to any member of a group owning property together. **3** any of the equal portions into which the invested capital of a company is divided.

**share**[2] *v* **1** to use or experience (something) with others. **2** (+ out) to divide and distribute in shares. ➤ **sharer** *n.*

**shareholder** *n* an owner of shares in a company. ➤ **shareholding** *n.*

**shark**[1] *n* a large sea fish with a tall fin on its back and its mouth on the under part of its body.

**shark**[2] *n* a person who extorts money dishonestly from others.

**sharp**[1] *adj* **1** having a thin edge or fine point for cutting or piercing. **2** characterized by hard lines and angles. **3** involving an abrupt change in direction. **4** clear or distinct. **5** sudden and forceful. **6** capable of reacting quickly. **7** able to perceive clearly or understand quickly. **8** causing sudden strong anguish. **9** pungent, tart, or acid in flavour. **10** of a sound: shrill or piercing. **11** intensely cold. **12** of a musical note: raised one semitone in pitch. **13** slightly higher than the true or desired pitch. ➤ **sharply** *adv,* **sharpness** *n.*

**sharp**[2] *adv* **1** in an abrupt manner. **2** exactly or precisely.

**sharp**[3] *n* **1** a musical note one semitone higher than the note at that position on the staff. **2** the character (#) that indicates such a note.

**sharpen** *v* to make or become sharp. ➤ **sharpener** *n.*

**sharpish** *adv Brit, informal* promptly; without delay.

**sharpshooter** *n* a person skilled in shooting.

**shatter** *v* **1** to break apart suddenly and violently. **2** to break (something) into pieces, e.g. by a sudden blow. **3** to cause (something) to break down; to impair or destroy. **4** to have a forceful effect on the feelings of. **5** *informal* to make exhausted. ➤ **shattered** *adj.*

**shave**[1] *v* (*past part.* **shaved** *or* **shaven**) **1** to cut off hair close to the skin with a razor. **2** to cut or trim closely. **3** (*often* + off) to remove in thin layers or slices. **4** to reduce (e.g. a price) by a small amount. **5** to brush against in passing.

**shave**[2] *n* the process of shaving.

**shaven** *v* past part. of SHAVE[1].

**shaver** *n* an electric razor.

**shaving** *n* a thin layer or shred shaved off.

**shawl** *n* a piece of fabric worn to cover the head or shoulders.

**she** *pron* **1** used to refer to a female person or animal previously mentioned. **2** used to refer to something regarded as female, e.g. a vehicle or ship.

**sheaf** *n* (*pl* **sheaves**) **1** a bundle of stalks and ears of a cut cereal grass. **2** a collection of papers.

**shear** *v* (*past part.* **sheared** *or* **shorn**) **1** to cut off the wool from (a sheep). **2** to cut with shears. **3** (*often* + off) to cut or break (something) off something else. * **be shorn of** to be deprived of. ➤ **shearer** *n.*

**shears** *pl n* a cutting implement like a large pair of scissors.

**sheath** *n* (*pl* **sheaths**) **1** a cover for the blade of a knife or sword. **2** a close-fitting casing or covering. **3** a condom.

**sheathe** *v* **1** to insert (a knife or sword) into a sheath. **2** to enclose in a protective covering.

**shebang** *n informal* an affair or business.

**shed**[1] *v* (**shedding,** *past tense and past part.* **shed**) **1** to cast off or let fall (leaves, hair, skin, etc). **2** to take off (an item of clothing). **3** to get rid of. **4** to allow to flow or spill. **5** to cast or spread (light). **6** to drop (a load) accidentally. * **shed tears** to cry.

**shed**[2] *n* **1** a simple garden building for storage. **2** a large building for storing or repairing vehicles, machinery, etc.

**she'd** *contraction* **1** she had. **2** she would.

**sheen** *n* **1** brightness or lustre. **2** a subdued surface shine.

**sheep** *n* (*pl* **sheep**) an animal with a thick woolly coat, kept for its flesh and wool.

**sheep-dip** *n* a liquid in which sheep are dipped to destroy parasites.

**sheepdog** *n* a breed of dog used for guarding and driving sheep.

**sheepish** *adj* embarrassed by shame or shyness. ➤ **sheepishly** *adv.*

**sheepskin** *n* **1** the skin of a sheep with the wool on. **2** the skin of a sheep or leather made from it.

**sheer**[1] *adj* **1** absolute or utter. **2** forming a vertical or almost vertical surface from a great height. **3** of fabric: transparently fine. ➤ **sheerly** *adv.*

**sheer**[2] *adv* **1** altogether or completely. **2** straight up or down.

**sheer**[3] *v* to change or move from a course.

**sheet**[1] *n* **1** a broad piece of cotton or other fabric used on a bed. **2** a rectangular piece of paper. **3** a piece of thin flat material such as glass or metal. **4** a broad flat expanse. **5** a suspended or moving mass of flame, water, etc.

**sheet**[2] *n* a rope controlling the angle at which a sail is set in relation to the wind.

**sheet music** *n* music printed on sheets of paper.

**sheikh** *or* **sheik** /shayk, sheek/ *n* an Arab or Muslim leader. ➤ **sheikhdom** *n.*

**shekel** /'shekl/ *n* the basic monetary unit of Israel.

**shelf** *n* (*pl* **shelves**) **1** a flat long piece of a solid material fastened horizontally to hold objects. **2** a partially submerged sandbank or ledge of rocks. **3** a flat projecting layer of rock. * **off the shelf** available from stock. **on the shelf** of a woman: unlikely or too old to marry.

**shelf-life** *n* the length of time for which an item for sale can be kept in a shop.

**shell**[1] *n* **1** a hard rigid covering of an animal, e.g. a turtle or beetle. **2** the hard outer covering of an egg, nut, or seed. **3** a seashell. **4** a framework or exterior structure. **5** a projectile filled with an explosive charge for firing from a large gun. **6** a hollow metal or paper case. ➤ **shelly** *adj.*

**shell**[2] *v* **1** to take (something) out of its shell. **2** to fire shells at.

**she'll** *contraction* **1** she will. **2** she shall.

**shellfish** *n* a water animal with a shell, *esp* an edible mollusc or crustacean.

**shell shock** *n* a mental disorder resulting from the stress of continued wartime combat.

**shell suit** *n* a lightweight top and trousers with a soft lining and a shiny covering.

**shelter**[1] *n* **1** a structure providing cover or protection. **2** the state of being protected.

**shelter**[2] *v* **1** to serve as a shelter for. **2** to keep concealed or protected. **3** to take cover or find refuge.

**sheltered** *adj* **1** protected from hardship or unpleasantness. **2** of accommodation: designed for elderly or disabled people to live in, and having a resident warden.

**shelve** *v* **1** to provide with shelves. **2** to place on a shelf. **3** to postpone or discontinue for a time. **4** of ground: to slope gently.

**shelves** *n* pl of SHELF.

**shenanigans** *pl n* **1** deliberate deception or trickery. **2** lively mischief.

**shepherd**[1] *n* somebody who tends sheep. ➤ **shepherdess** *n.*

**shepherd**[2] *v* **1** to tend (sheep) as a shepherd. **2** to guide or conduct.

**shepherd's pie** *n* a dish of minced meat covered with mashed potato.

**sherbet** *n* **1** a sweet effervescent powder, eaten dry or used to make fizzy drinks. **2** a Middle Eastern cold drink of sweetened diluted fruit juice.

**sheriff** *n* **1** the chief executive officer in an English or Welsh county, with mainly judicial and ceremonial duties. **2** the chief judge of a Scottish county or district. **3** a county law enforcement officer in the USA.

**Sherpa** *n* (*pl* **Sherpa** *or* **Sherpas**) a member of a Tibetan people living on the southern slopes of the Himalayas.

**sherry** *n* (*pl* **-ies**) a blended fortified wine from southern Spain.

**she's** *contraction* **1** she is. **2** she has.

**Shetland pony** *n* a small shaggy pony originating in the Shetland Islands.

**shiatsu** *n* a medical treatment involving the application of pressure with the hands to particular points of the body.
**shibboleth** *n* a custom or belief that characterizes the members of a particular group.
**shied** *v* past tense and past part. of SHY[2], SHY[3].
**shield[1]** *n* **1** a piece of armour carried as protection against blows. **2** somebody or something that protects or defends. **3** a guard or device protecting people from injury from moving parts of machinery. **4** an armoured screen protecting an otherwise exposed gun. **5** a defined area on which heraldic arms are displayed. **6** a sports trophy in the form of a small mounted shield. **7** a decorative or identifying emblem.
**shield[2]** *v* to protect or conceal.
**shift[1]** *v* **1** to change or move from a place, position, or direction. **2** *Brit, informal* to move fast. **3** *Brit* to remove (e.g. a stain) by hard cleaning. **4** *informal* to sell or dispose of.
**shift[2]** *n* **1** a change in place, position, or direction. **2** a change in emphasis, judgment, or attitude. **3** a group who work together in alternation with other groups, or the period of their work. **4** a key on a computer keyboard that changes the characters entered from small to capital letters, and changes other functions. **5** a loose dress or slip.
**shiftless** *adj* lacking ambition; lazy.
**shifty** *adj* (**-ier, -iest**) appearing to be dishonest or untrustworthy. ➤ **shiftily** *adv.*
**Shiite** /'shee·iet/ *n* an adherent of the branch of Islam tracing its authority to Muhammad's son-in-law Ali.
**shilling** *n* **1** a former British monetary unit, worth one 20th of a pound or twelve old pence. **2** the basic monetary unit of Kenya, Somalia, Tanzania, and Uganda.
**shilly-shally** *v* (**-ies, -ied**) to be indecisive.
**shimmer[1]** *v* to shine with a softly wavering light.
**shimmer[2]** *n* a shimmering light. ➤ **shimmery** *adj.*
**shimmy** *v* (**-ies, -ied**) **1** to dance a body-shaking jazz dance. **2** to shake or tremble.
**shin[1]** *n* the front part of the leg below the knee.
**shin[2]** *v* (**shinned, shinning**) (*usu* + up/down) to climb by gripping with the arms and the legs and moving oneself up or down.
**shindig** *n informal* a lively social gathering.
**shine[1]** *v* (*past tense and past part.* **shone**) **1** to give out or reflect light. **2** to be outstanding or distinguished. **3** to have a radiant or lively appearance. **4** to direct the light of (a lamp or torch). **5** (*past tense and past part.* **shined)** to polish.
**shine[2]** *n* **1** brightness from light. **2** brilliance or splendour. **3** an act of polishing. ✱ **take a shine to** *informal* to like immediately.
**shiner** *n informal* a black eye.
**shingle[1]** *n* a wooden tile laid in overlapping rows as a roof or wall covering.
**shingle[2]** *n* a mass of small rounded pebbles on the seashore. ➤ **shingly** *adj.*
**shingles** *pl n* a disease affecting the nerve endings, caused by a virus and involving a rash of painful blisters.
**shin pad** *n* a pad worn to protect the shin in ball games.
**shiny** *adj* (**-ier, -iest**) **1** bright or glossy in appearance. **2** reflecting light.
**ship[1]** *n* a large floating vessel for travelling by sea.
**ship[2]** *v* (**shipped, shipping**) **1** to transport (goods) by ship or by other means. **2** of a boat or ship: to take in (water) over the side.
**-ship** *suffix* forming nouns: *friendship; scholarship; membership.*
**shipbuilder** *n* a person or company that designs or builds ships. ➤ **shipbuilding** *n.*
**shipment** *n* **1** the process of transporting goods. **2** a quantity of goods transported.
**shipping** *n* **1** the ships of a particular country or route. **2** the business of transporting goods.
**shipshape** *adj* neat and tidy.
**shipwreck[1]** *n* **1** the destruction or loss of a ship at sea. **2** a wrecked ship or its remains.
**shipwreck[2]** *v* to cause to undergo shipwreck.
**shipyard** *n* a place where ships are built or repaired.
**shire** *n* **1** an English county. **2** (*usu* **the Shires**) conservative rural areas of England.
**shire horse** *n* a large powerful draught horse.
**shirk** *v* to evade (a duty or responsibility). ➤ **shirker** *n.*
**shirt** *n* a piece of clothing for the upper body, with sleeves and a collar, and buttons down the front. ✱ **keep one's shirt on** *informal* to remain calm.
**shirtsleeves** *pl n* ✱ **in shirtsleeves** wearing a shirt without a jacket.
**shirty** *adj* (**-ier, -iest**) *informal* bad-tempered.
**shish kebab** *n* a kebab cooked on a skewer.
**shiver[1]** *v* to shake or tremble with cold or fever.
**shiver[2]** *n* an act of shivering or trembling. ➤ **shivery** *adj.*
**shiver[3]** *n* a small piece of something shattered.
**shoal[1]** *n* **1** an underwater sandbank exposed at low tide. **2** an area of shallow water.
**shoal[2]** *v* of water: to become shallow or less deep.
**shoal[3]** *n* a large group of fish.
**shock[1]** *n* **1** a sudden disturbance of a person's thoughts or emotions. **2** something that disturbs or upsets in this way. **3** a state in which bodily functions temporarily cease to operate as normal, caused usu by severe injury or trauma. **4** sudden stimulation of the nerves and convulsive contraction of the muscles caused by electricity passing through the body. **5** a

violent impact or collision. **6** a violent shaking or jarring.
**shock**[2] *v* **1** to cause to feel sudden surprise, alarm, or offence. **2** to cause to undergo a physical or nervous shock. ➤ **shockproof** *adj.*
**shock**[3] *n* a thick bushy mass of hair.
**shock absorber** *n* a device on a vehicle for absorbing sudden jolts or shocks.
**shocking** *adj* **1** causing shock or indignation. **2** *Brit, informal* very bad. ➤ **shockingly** *adv.*
**shock troops** *pl n* troops trained and selected for sudden assault.
**shock wave** *n* a high-pressure wave formed by an explosion or by a body exceeding the speed of sound.
**shod** *v* past tense and past part. of SHOE[2].
**shoddy** *adj* (**-ier, -iest**) **1** hastily or poorly done; inferior. **2** discreditable or despicable. ➤ **shoddily** *adv.*
**shoe**[1] *n* **1** an outer covering for the foot, having a stiff sole. **2** a horseshoe. **3** the part of a vehicle's brake that presses on the drum. ✱ **be in somebody's shoes** to be in their position.
**shoe**[2] *v* (**shoes, shoed, shoeing,** *past tense and past part.* **shod**) **1** to fit (a horse) with a shoe. **2** (*usu in passive*) to equip with shoes.
**shoehorn**[1] *n* a curved piece of metal or plastic used to ease the heel into the back of a shoe.
**shoehorn**[2] *v* to force into a tight space.
**shoelace** *n* a lace or string for fastening a shoe.
**shoestring** *n NAmer* a shoelace. ✱ **on a shoestring** *informal* with very little money available
**shogun** /'shohgən/ *n* formerly, a Japanese military governor.
**shone** *v* past tense and past part. of SHINE[1].
**shook** *v* past tense of SHAKE[1].
**shoot**[1] *v* (*past tense and past part.* **shot**) **1** to wound or kill (a person or animal) with a bullet, arrow, or similar missile. **2** to fire (a gun) or release an arrow from (a bow). **3** to move suddenly or rapidly. **4** to drive (a ball or puck) towards a goal or hole. **5** to direct (a sudden glance or question) at somebody. **6** to photograph or film (a person or scene). **7** to push or slide (a bolt) into or out of a fastening. **8** of a boat: to pass swiftly over (rapids). **9** to produce a piercing sensation through part of the body. **10** of a plant: to put out shoots.
**shoot**[2] *n* **1** a new stem or branch of a plant. **2** a shooting trip or party. **3** a session of photography or filming.
**shooter** *n* **1** somebody who uses a gun. **2** *informal* a gun.
**shooting star** *n* a meteor appearing as a temporary streak of light in the sky.
**shooting stick** *n* a spiked stick with a handle that opens into a seat.
**shop**[1] *n* **1** a building or room for the sale of goods. **2** a place where things are manufactured or repaired. ✱ **talk shop** to talk about one's work outside working hours.
**shop**[2] *v* (**shopped, shopping**) **1** to visit a shop to buy goods. **2** *informal* to inform on. ➤ **shopper** *n,* **shopping** *n.*
**shop around** *v* to look around for the best price for something.
**shopfloor** *n* **1** *Brit* the area of a factory where machinery or workbenches are located. **2** workers as distinct from management.
**shopkeeper** *n* somebody who runs a retail shop.
**shoplift** *v* to steal from a shop. ➤ **shoplifter** *n,* **shoplifting** *n.*
**shopping** *n* **1** the buying of goods from a shop. **2** things bought from a shop.
**shopping centre** *n* a group of shops in one place.
**shopsoiled** *adj chiefly Brit* dirty or worn from handling or display in a shop.
**shop steward** *n* a union member elected to represent workers in dealings with the management.
**shore**[1] *n* **1** the land bordering the sea or another body of water. **2** land as distinguished from the sea.
**shore**[2] *v* (*often* + up) to support with a beam or prop to prevent sinking or sagging.
**shoreline** *n* the line where a body of water and the shore meet.
**shorn** *v* past part. of SHEAR.
**short**[1] *adj* **1** having little or insufficient length or height. **2** not extended in time; brief. **3** limited in distance. **4** not meeting a requirement: *in short supply.* **5** not reaching far enough. **6** (*often* + of/on) insufficiently supplied with. **7** (*often* + for) abbreviated from. **8** abrupt or curt. **9** of betting odds: almost even. **10** of pastry: crisp and crumbly from containing a high proportion of fat. ✱ **in the short run** for the immediate future. ➤ **shortness** *n.*
**short**[2] *adv* **1** abruptly or suddenly. **2** not as far as intended or required. ✱ **be taken/caught short** *Brit, informal* to need suddenly to defecate or urinate. **bring/pull somebody up short** to make somebody stop or pause suddenly.
**short**[3] *n* **1** *Brit, informal* a drink of spirits. **2** a brief film or documentary. **3** a short circuit. ✱ **for short** as an abbreviation. **in short** briefly.
**short**[4] *v* to short-circuit.
**shortage** *n* a lack or deficit.
**shortbread** *or* **shortcake** *n* a thick crumbly biscuit made from flour, sugar, and fat.
**shortchange** *v* to give less than the due change or amount to.
**short circuit** *n* the joining of two parts of an electric circuit, allowing an excessive current to flow.
**short-circuit** *v* (**short-circuited, short-circuiting**) to cause a short circuit in.
**shortcoming** *n* a deficiency or defect.

**shortcrust pastry** *n* a pastry used for pies and tarts, made with half as much fat as flour.

**shortcut** *n* a route or procedure that is more direct than the usual one.

**shorten** *v* to make or become shorter.

**shortening** *n* fat used in making pastry.

**shortfall** *n* a state of not being enough; a deficit.

**shorthand** *n* a method of rapidly writing down what somebody is saying by use of special symbols and abbreviations.

**shorthanded** *adj* not having enough staff or help.

**short list** *n Brit* a list of selected candidates from which a final choice is made.

**short-list** *v Brit* to place on a short list.

**short-lived** *adj* not living or lasting long.

**shortly** *adv* **1** in a short time; soon. **2** abruptly or curtly.

**shorts** *pl n* knee-length or thigh-length trousers.

**short shrift** *n* summary or inconsiderate treatment.

**short-sighted** *adj* **1** unable to see distant objects clearly. **2** not taking likely consequences into account.

**short-staffed** *adj* not having enough staff.

**short-tempered** *adj* quickly or easily made angry.

**shot**[1] *n* **1** the act of firing a gun or other weapon. **2** somebody who shoots, *esp* with regard to their ability. **3** a stroke, throw, or kick in a game when attempting to score. **4** *informal* an attempt or try. **5** a wild guess. **6** (*pl* **shot**) a small pellet fired from a shotgun. **7** a heavy metal ball thrown as an athletic field event. **8** a single photographic exposure. **9** a single sequence of a film taken by one camera. **10** an injection of a drug or vaccine. **11** *informal* a single drink of spirits. **12** the launch of a rocket into space. * **a shot in the dark** a wild guess. **a shot in the arm** *informal* a stimulus or boost. **like a shot** *informal* very rapidly.

**shot**[2] *adj* (+ with) permeated with a quality or element. * **be/get shot of** *Brit, informal* to be or get rid of.

**shot**[3] *v* past tense and past part. of SHOOT[1].

**shotgun** *n* a gun for firing metal shot at short range.

**shotgun wedding** *n informal* a wedding that is forced by the bride's pregnancy.

**shot put** *n* an athletic field event involving the throwing of a heavy metal ball. ➤ **shot-putter** *n.*

**should** *v aux* past tense of SHALL, used: **1** with *if* to introduce a possibility: *I should be surprised if he came.* **2** to express obligation or recommendation: *You should apologize.* **3** to express probability: *They should be here soon.* **4** to express a polite form of direct statement: *I should try if I were you.*

**shoulder**[1] *n* the joint linking the upper arm to the trunk. * **shoulder to shoulder** side by side or united.

**shoulder**[2] *v* **1** to carry on one's shoulders. **2** to assume the burden or responsibility of. **3** to push or thrust with one's shoulder.

**shoulder blade** *n* each of two flat triangular bones at the top of the back.

**shouldn't** *contraction* should not.

**shout**[1] *v* **1** to utter a sudden loud cry. **2** to utter in a loud voice.

**shout**[2] *n* **1** a loud cry or call. **2** *Brit, informal* a person's turn to buy a round of drinks.

**shove**[1] *v* **1** to push along steadily or forcefully. **2** to put roughly or carelessly.

**shove**[2] *n* a hard push.

**shovel**[1] *n* an implement like a spade with a broad dished blade, used to lift and throw loose material.

**shovel**[2] *v* (**shovelled, shovelling,** *NAmer* **shoveled, shoveling**) **1** to dig or clear with a shovel. **2** to convey clumsily or in a mass.

**show**[1] *v* (*past part.* **shown** *or* **showed**) **1** to cause or permit to be seen. **2** to be visible. **3** to exhibit or put on display. **4** to present (a film or broadcast) for people to watch. **5** to display (a feeling or reaction). **6** to indicate or point out. **7** to explain. **8** to establish or prove. **9** to conduct to a specified place. **10** *informal* to arrive as expected. * **show one's face** to let oneself be seen. **show somebody the door** to ask somebody to leave.

**show**[2] *n* **1** a presentation or entertainment in a theatre. **2** a light radio or television programme. **3** a large display or exhibition. **4** a competitive exhibition of animals, plants, etc. **5** a demonstration of something; a sign or display. **6** a false appearance; a pretence. * **for show** just to impress or attract attention. **on show** being displayed.

**show biz** *n informal* = SHOW BUSINESS.

**show business** *n* the entertainment industry, including the theatre, films, pop music, and broadcasting.

**showcase** *n* **1** a case with a glass front or top used for displaying articles. **2** a setting for exhibiting something to best advantage.

**showdown** *n* a final confrontation to settle a disagreement.

**shower**[1] *n* **1** a brief fall of rain, snow, etc. **2** a large number of things arriving or presented together. **3** an apparatus that sprays water over the body for washing. **4** an act of washing oneself in this way. ➤ **showery** *adj.*

**shower**[2] *v* **1** to fall or cause to fall in a shower. **2** to wash in a shower. **3** to present (somebody) with a lot of of things at once.

**showgirl** *n* a young woman who dances or sings in a musical show.

**showing** *n* **1** a display or presentation. **2** a performance in competing.

**showjumping** *n* the competitive sport of riding horses over a course of obstacles.
**shown** *v* past part. of SHOW[1].
**show off** *v* **1** to behave boastfully or ostentatiously. **2** to display proudly.
**show-off** *n* somebody who shows off; an exhibitionist.
**showpiece** *n* an outstanding example used for exhibition.
**showroom** *n* a room where goods for sale are displayed.
**show trial** *n* a trial conducted by a state to make an impression rather than to see justice done.
**show up** *v* **1** to be evident or conspicuous. **2** *informal* to arrive. **3** to reveal the shortcomings of (something) by comparison. **4** *informal* to embarrass.
**showy** *adj* (**-ier, -iest**) **1** making an attractive show. **2** bright and colourful.
**shrank** *v* past tense of SHRINK[1].
**shrapnel** *n* fragments of metal thrown out in the explosion of a bomb or shell.
**shred**[1] *n* **1** a narrow strip cut or torn off. **2** a fragment or scrap.
**shred**[2] *v* (**shredded, shredding**) to cut or tear into shreds. ➤ **shredder** *n.*
**shrew** *n* **1** a small mammal with a long pointed snout and small eyes. **2** a bad-tempered nagging woman.
**shrewd** *adj* marked by keen discernment and judgment. ➤ **shrewdly** *adv,* **shrewdness** *n.*
**shrewish** *adj* of a woman: bad-tempered and nagging.
**shriek** *v* to make a shrill piercing cry. ➤ **shriek** *n.*
**shrike** *n* a grey or brownish songbird that impales its prey on thorns.
**shrill**[1] *adj* making a high-pitched sound; piercing. ➤ **shrilly** *adv.*
**shrill**[2] *v* to make a shrill sound.
**shrimp**[1] *n* (*pl* **shrimps** *or* **shrimp**) **1** a small edible crustacean with a long slender body. **2** *informal* a very small person.
**shrimp**[2] *v* to fish for shrimps.
**shrine** *n* **1** a place where people pray to a saint or deity. **2** a place for sacred images or relics.
**shrink**[1] *v* (**shrank, shrunk** *or* **shrunken**) **1** to make or become smaller or shorter. **2** to draw back or cower away in fear or revulsion. **3** (*usu* + from) to be reluctant to accept or do something.
**shrink**[2] *n informal* a psychiatrist.
**shrinkage** *n* the process or degree of shrinking.
**shrinking violet** *n informal* a meek or shy person.
**shrink wrap** *n* tough plastic film used as a tight-fitting wrapping. ➤ **shrink-wrap** *v.*
**shrivel** *v* (**shrivelled, shrivelling,** *NAmer* **shriveled, shriveling**) to shrink and become wrinkled through loss of moisture.
**shroud**[1] *n* **1** a piece of cloth for wrapping a corpse for burial. **2** something that covers or conceals. **3** any of the ropes supporting a ship's mast.
**shroud**[2] *v* **1** to conceal or disguise. **2** to wrap (a corpse) in a shroud.
**shrub** *n* a woody plant with several stems. ➤ **shrubby** *adj.*
**shrubbery** *n* (*pl* **-ies**) a planting or growth of shrubs.
**shrug**[1] *v* (**shrugged, shrugging**) to lift and contract (the shoulders) to express uncertainty or lack of concern.
**shrug**[2] *n* a shrugging of the shoulders.
**shrug off** *v* to disregard or belittle.
**shudder** *v* to tremble with a sudden convulsive movement. ➤ **shudder** *n.*
**shuffle**[1] *v* **1** to walk by moving the feet without lifting them. **2** to fidget restlessly. **3** to rearrange (playing cards) to produce a random order. **4** to rearrange in different positions or locations. **5** (*usu* + off) to avoid or get rid of.
**shuffle**[2] *n* **1** a shuffling, e.g. of cards. **2** an act of shuffling. **3** a dragging movement of the feet.
**shun** *v* (**shunned, shunning**) to avoid deliberately.
**shunt** *v* **1** *Brit* to move (railway vehicles) to different positions on the same or another track. **2** to move (something or somebody) to a less important position. **3** to travel back and forth. ➤ **shunter** *n.*
**shut**[1] *v* (**shutting,** *past tense and past part.* **shut**) **1** to move into a position to close an opening. **2** to fasten with a lock or bolt. **3** to close by bringing parts together. **4** (+ out) to prevent entrance to (a building or street). **5** (+ in) to confine in a space. **6** to suspend operation, or cause to do this.
**shut**[2] *adj* **1** in the closed position. **2** not open for business.
**shutdown** *n* the stopping of work or other activity.
**shut down** *v* to stop work or cease business.
**shut off** *v* to stop (something) flowing or working.
**shutter**[1] *n* **1** each of a pair of hinged outside covers for a window. **2** a device that opens and closes the lens aperture of a camera.
**shutter**[2] *v* to provide or close with shutters.
**shuttle**[1] *n* **1** a device in weaving that passes the thread of the weft between the threads of the warp. **2** a public-transport vehicle that travels back and forth over a regular route. **3** a space vehicle that travels from and back to earth.
**shuttle**[2] *v* **1** to travel back and forth on a regular route. **2** to transport in a shuttle.
**shuttlecock** *n* a rounded cork or plastic piece with projecting feathers, struck with rackets in badminton.
**shut up** *v* **1** to lock and prevent access to. **2** to imprison or confine. **3** *informal* to stop talking.

**shy**[1] *adj* (**-er, -est**) **1** easily alarmed; timid. **2** reserved or retiring. **3** (*often* + of) circumspect or reluctant. ➤ **shyly** *adv*, **shyness** *n.*

**shy**[2] *v* (**-ies, -ied**) **1** *esp* of a horse: to start in fright. **2** (*usu* + away/from) to avoid through nervousness.

**shy**[3] *v* (**-ies, -ied**) *dated* to throw with a jerking movement.

**shy**[4] *n* (*pl* **-ies**) a toss or throw.

**shyster** *n informal* a dishonest lawyer or other professional person.

**SI** *n abbr* Système International (d'Unités), an international system of units for measurement.

**Si** *abbr* the chemical symbol for silicon.

**Siamese** *n* (*pl* **Siamese**) **1** *dated* a native or inhabitant of Siam (now Thailand). **2** *dated* the Thai language. ➤ **Siamese** *adj.*

**Siamese cat** *n* a cat of a breed having blue eyes and short pale fur with a darker face.

**Siamese twin** *n* each of a pair of twins joined at birth.

**sibilant**[1] *adj* producing a hissing sound. ➤ **sibilance** *n.*

**sibilant**[2] *n* in phonetics, a sibilant speech sound.

**sibling** *n* a brother or sister.

**sibyl** *n* an ancient Greek or Roman female prophet. ➤ **sibylline** *adj.*

**sic** *adv* actually so written: used when copying a piece of text that is apparently misspelt or inappropriate.

**sick**[1] *adj* **1** affected by a disease; ill. **2** likely or about to vomit. **3** (+ of) having had too much of. **4** disgusted. **5** *informal* disappointed or upset. **6** mentally or emotionally disturbed. **7** of humour: macabre or morbid. ✻ **be sick 1** to be ill. **2** *Brit* to vomit.

**sick**[2] *n Brit, informal* vomit.

**sick**[3] *v Brit, informal* (*usu* + up) to vomit.

**sickbay** *n* a room where sick people are treated.

**sickbed** *n* the bed on which somebody lies sick.

**sicken** *v* **1** to become ill. **2** to cause to feel disgust or loathing.

**sickle** *n* an implement with a curved blade, for cutting plants or hedges.

**sick leave** *n* absence from work because of illness.

**sickly** *adj* (**-ier, -iest**) **1** often unwell. **2** feeble or weak. **3** producing sickness or disease. **4** tending to produce nausea. **5** mawkish or sentimental.

**sickness** *n* **1** ill health. **2** a particular illness. **3** nausea or vomiting.

**side**[1] *n* **1** a surface forming a face of an object, usually not the front, back, top, or bottom. **2** either surface of a thin object. **3** a boundary line of a geometrical figure. **4** a position to the right or left of a person, object, or point. **5** a region or direction considered in relation to a centre or line of division. **6** the right or left part of the body. **7** a sports team. **8** a person or group in competition or dispute with another. **9** the opinion or point of view of such a person or group. **10** an aspect or part of something or somebody. **11** *Brit, informal* a television channel. ✻ **on the side** in addition to a principal occupation. **take sides** to support one of the people or parties in a dispute.

**side**[2] *adj* additional or subordinate.

**side**[3] *v* (+ with/against) to support or oppose in a dispute.

**side**[4] *n Brit, informal* a self-important manner.

**sideboard** *n* **1** a piece of furniture with cupboards and drawers for storing crockery, cutlery, etc. **2** *Brit* (*in pl*) sideburns.

**sideburns** *pl n* a strip of hair on each side of a man's face in front of the ears.

**sidecar** *n* a small vehicle with a single wheel, attached to the side of a motorcycle to carry passengers.

**side effect** *n* a secondary effect of a drug.

**sidekick** *n informal* a person's helper or assistant.

**sidelight** *n* a small extra light beside the headlight on a motor vehicle.

**sideline**[1] *n* **1** a business or activity additional to a main occupation. **2** a line marking a side of a court or playing field. **3** (**the sidelines**) the standpoint of people not directly involved in something.

**sideline**[2] *v* to remove (somebody) from action or participation.

**sidelong** *adj and adv* directed to or from one side.

**sidereal** /sieˈdiəri·əl/ *adj* of, or expressed in relation to, stars or constellations.

**sidesaddle** *adj and adv* of a woman: riding a horse with both legs on the same side.

**sideshow** *n* a small show or stall at a circus or fairground.

**sidestep** *v* (**sidestepped, sidestepping**) **1** to avoid by stepping to one side. **2** to evade (an issue or question).

**side street** *or* **side road** *n* a minor street or road branching off a main road.

**sideswipe** *n* an incidental critical remark.

**sidetrack**[1] *v* to divert from a course or purpose.

**sidetrack**[2] *n* an unimportant line of thought.

**sidewalk** *n NAmer* a pavement.

**sideways** *adv and adj* **1** to or from the side. **2** with one side forward.

**siding** *n* a short length of railway track connected with a main track.

**sidle** *v* to walk timidly or furtively.

**siege** *n* **1** a military operation in which a place is surrounded and blockaded to compel it to surrender. **2** a similar operation by police to force somebody to surrender.

***Usage Note:*** Note the spelling with *-ie-*.

**sienna** *n* an earthy substance used as a brownish yellow or reddish brown pigment.

**siesta** *n* an afternoon nap or rest.

**sieve**[1] *n* a device with a mesh for straining liquids or separating coarse from fine solids.

**sieve**[2] *v* to filter with a sieve.

**sift** *v* **1** to put through a sieve. **2** (*often* + out) to separate or remove from a mixture using a sieve. **3** to study or examine thoroughly.

**sigh**[1] *v* to take a deep audible breath in relief, weariness, or grief.

**sigh**[2] *n* an act or sound of sighing.

**sight**[1] *n* **1** the process or power of seeing. **2** the perception of an object by the eye. **3** the distance or area one can see. **4** something interesting to be seen. **5** (*in pl*) the things regarded as worth seeing in a particular place. **6** *informal* something ridiculous or displeasing in appearance. **7** an aiming device on a gun. **8** an observation to determine direction or position. **9** *informal* a great deal; a lot. ✱ **a sight for sore eyes** *informal* somebody or something one is delighted to see. **at first sight** when first considered. **out of sight** hidden or not visible. **raise/lower one's sights** to become more (or less) ambitious. **set one's sights on** to aim to have or achieve.

**sight**[2] *v* to see or have a glimpse of.

**sighted** *adj* **1** able to see. **2** having sight of a specified kind: *short-sighted.*

**sightless** *adj* unable to see; blind.

**sight-read** *v* (*past tense and past part.* **sight-read**) to read and perform (music) without previous study.

**sightsee** *v* to make a tour of interesting sights. ➤ **sightseeing** *n*, **sightseer** *n*.

**sigma** *n* the 18th letter of the Greek alphabet (Σ, σ, or at the end of a word ς).

**sign**[1] *n* **1** something that indicates the presence or existence of something. **2** a presage or portent. **3** a board or notice giving information, direction, etc. **4** a motion or gesture by which a thought or wish is made known. **5** a mark with a conventional meaning, e.g. in music or mathematics. **6** any of the twelve divisions of the zodiac.

**sign**[2] *v* **1** to put a signature to (a letter, cheque, etc). **2** to write (one's name). **3** (*often* + over) to assign formally. **4** to engage or hire with a contract of employment. **5** to indicate or express by a sign. **6** to make a sign or signal. **7** to use sign language. ➤ **signer** *n*.

**signal**[1] *n* **1** an action, gesture, or word with an agreed meaning. **2** anything that prompts a particular action or event to take place. **3** a conventional sign, sound, etc that conveys information or gives a warning. **4** a set of coloured lights that regulates the flow of road or rail traffic. **5** the sound or image conveyed by telephone, radio, radar, or television.

**signal**[2] *v* (**signalled, signalling,** *NAmer* **signaled, signaling**) **1** to make or send a signal. **2** to warn or order (somebody) to do something by a signal. **3** to communicate (something) by signals. **4** to be a sign of. ➤ **signaller** *n*.

**signal**[3] *adj* conspicuous or outstanding. ➤ **signally** *adv*.

**signal box** *n Brit* a building by a railway line from which signals and points are worked.

**signatory** *n* (*pl* **-ies**) somebody who has signed a document.

**signature** *n* **1** the name of a person written distinctively to serve as identification or authorization. **2** the act of signing one's name. **3** a distinguishing or identifying mark, feature, or quality.

**signature tune** *n* an identifying tune used at the beginning of a television or radio programme.

**signet** *n* an official seal formerly used instead of a signature.

**signet ring** *n* a ring engraved with a seal or monogram.

**significance** *n* **1** something conveyed as a meaning. **2** importance or consequence.

**significant** *adj* **1** having meaning or importance. **2** suggesting or containing a veiled or special meaning. **3** having or likely to have influence or effect; important. ➤ **significantly** *adv*.

**signify** *v* (**-ies, -ied**) **1** to mean or denote. **2** to be an indication of or imply. **3** to show by a word, signal, or gesture. **4** to be important. ➤ **signification** *n*.

**signing** *n* **1** somebody who has recently signed a contract with a sports team. **2** sign language. **3** an event at which copies of a book are signed by the author for publicity.

**sign language** *n* a system of hand gestures and other signs used by deaf people.

**sign off** *v* **1** to end a letter, message, or broadcast. **2** of a doctor: to declare (somebody) unfit for work.

**sign on** *v* **1** to commit oneself to a job by signature or agreement. **2** to give a job to. **3** *Brit* to register as unemployed.

**sign out** *v* **1** to indicate departure by signing a register. **2** to record the release or withdrawal of.

**signpost**[1] *n* a post by the road with signs on it to direct travellers.

**signpost**[2] *v* **1** to give information about (a road or place) with a signpost. **2** to indicate or mark.

**sign up** *v* to join an organization or accept an obligation by signing a contract.

**Sikh** /seek/ *n* an adherent of a religion of India combining aspects of Hinduism and Islam. ➤ **Sikhism** *n*.

**silage** *n* fodder stored in a silo and converted into feed for livestock.

**silence**[1] *n* **1** absence of sound or noise. **2** a state of being unable or unwilling to speak.

**silence**[2] *v* **1** to make silent or much quieter. **2** to prevent from speaking or expressing an opinion.

**silencer** *n* a device for muffling the noise made by a gun or vehicle exhaust.

**silent** *adj* **1** free from sound or noise. **2** saying nothing. **3** not talkative. **4** of a letter: not pronounced, e.g. the *b* in *doubt.* **5** of a film: without spoken dialogue. ➤ **silently** *adv.*

**silhouette**[1] *n* the shape of somebody or something as it appears against a lighter background.

**silhouette**[2] *v* to show in silhouette.

**silica** *n* silicon dioxide occurring in many rocks and minerals, e.g. quartz, opal, and sand.

**silicon** *n* a non-metallic element that is used in alloys, as a semiconductor, and in the manufacture of glass.

**silicone** *n* an organic silicon compound used for lubricants, varnishes, electrical insulators, etc.

**silk** *n* **1** a tough shiny fibre produced by silkworms and used for textiles. **2** thread or fabric made from silk filaments. **3** *Brit, informal* a King's or Queen's Counsel. ✱ **take silk** *Brit* to become a King's or Queen's Counsel.

**silken** *adj* **1** made of silk. **2** silky.

**silkworm** *n* the larva of a silk moth, which spins strong silk in making its cocoon.

**silky** *adj* (**-ier, -iest**) **1** resembling silk in softness or shine. **2** consisting of silk.

**sill** *n* a narrow shelf projecting from the base of a window frame or doorway.

**silly** *adj* (**-ier, -iest**) **1** showing a lack of common sense or sound judgment. **2** trifling or frivolous. ➤ **silliness** *n.*

**silo** *n* (*pl* **-os**) **1** a sealed trench, pit, or tower used for making and storing silage. **2** an underground structure for housing a guided missile.

**silt**[1] *n* a deposit of sediment at the bottom of a river. ➤ **silty** *adj.*

**silt**[2] *v* (*often* + up) to make or become choked or obstructed with silt.

**silver**[1] *n* **1** a soft white metal used in jewellery, ornaments, etc. **2** coins made of silver or a silver-like metal. **3** tableware made of or plated with silver. **4** a shiny whitish grey colour. ➤ **silvery** *adj.*

**silver**[2] *adj* **1** resembling silver in colour or sheen. **2** marking a 25th anniversary: *silver jubilee.*

**silver**[3] *v* to cover or coat with silver.

**silver birch** *n* a birch tree with silvery peeling bark.

**silverfish** *n* (*pl* **silverfishes** *or* **silverfish**) a small silvery wingless insect found in houses.

**silver medal** *n* a medal of silver awarded for second place in a competition or race.

**silver plate** *n* **1** a coating of silver on another metal. **2** tableware and cutlery of silver or coated with silver.

**silverside** *n Brit* a cut of beef from the outer part of the top of the leg.

**silversmith** *n* somebody who makes objects of silver.

**simian**[1] *adj* of or resembling a monkey or ape.

**simian**[2] *n* a monkey or ape.

**similar** *adj* having a general resemblance but not identical. ➤ **similarity** *n,* **similarly** *adv.*

**simile** /'simili/ *n* a figure of speech comparing two different things, e.g. *bold as brass.*

**simmer** *v* **1** of a liquid: to bubble gently just below boiling point. **2** to cook in a simmering liquid. **3** to be agitated by suppressed emotion. ➤ **simmer** *n.*

**simmer down** *v* to become calm or less excited.

**simper**[1] *v* to smile in a foolish self-conscious manner.

**simper**[2] *n* a foolish self-conscious smile.

**simple** *adj* **1** easily understood or done. **2** basic or plain. **3** free from showiness; unpretentious. **4** lacking intelligence. **5** of humble birth or position. **6** not compound or subdivided.

**simple fracture** *n* a bone fracture in which the skin and tissue are undamaged.

**simpleton** *n* somebody who lacks common sense or intelligence.

**simplicity** *n* the state or quality of being simple.

**simplify** *v* (**-ies, -ied**) to make simple or simpler. ➤ **simplification** *n.*

**simplistic** *adj* presenting a complex matter as if it were simple; oversimplified. ➤ **simplistically** *adv.*

**simply** *adv* **1** without ambiguity; clearly. **2** without ornamentation or show. **3** solely or merely. **4** without any question.

**simulacrum** /simyoo'laykrəm/ *n* (*pl* **simulacra** *or* **simulacrums**) *formal* **1** an image or representation. **2** a vague or superficial likeness.

**simulate** *v* **1** to assume the outward qualities or appearance of. **2** to make a functioning model of (a system or device). ➤ **simulation** *n,* **simulator** *n.*

**simultaneous** *adj* existing or happening at the same time. ➤ **simultaneously** *adv.*

**sin**[1] *n* **1** an offence against moral or religious law. **2** an action considered to be wrong.

**sin**[2] *v* (**sinned, sinning**) to commit a sin.

**since**[1] *adv* **1** continuously or at a point between a time in the past and now. **2** before now; ago.

**since**[2] *prep* in the period between a time in the past and now.

**since**[3] *conj* **1** in or during the time after. **2** because.

**sincere** *adj* free from deceit or hypocrisy; honest or genuine. ➤ **sincerely** *adv,* **sincerity** *n.*

**sine** *n* in mathematics, the ratio in a right-angled triangle between the side opposite a particular angle and the hypotenuse.

**sinecure** /ˈsinikyooə, ˈsie-/ *n* a paid job that involves little or no work.
**sine qua non** /ˌsini kwah ˈnon/ *n* an absolutely essential thing.
**sinew** *n* tissue that connects a muscle with a bone. ➤ **sinewy** *adj.*
**sinful** *adj* being a sin; wicked. ➤ **sinfully** *adv,* **sinfulness** *n.*
**sing** *v* (**sang, sung**) **1** to produce musical sounds with the voice. **2** to perform (a song) by singing. **1** to make a shrill whistling sound. **2** *esp* of a bird: to produce melodious sounds. **3** (*usu* + out) to make a loud clear utterance. **4** to express enthusiastically. ➤ **singer** *n.*
**singalong** *n* an informal gathering for singing.
**singe[1]** *v* (**singed, singeing**) to burn superficially or slightly.
**singe[2]** *n* a superficial burn.
**single[1]** *adj* **1** not accompanied by others. **2** individual or distinct: *every single one.* **3** suitable for or involving only one person. **4** consisting of or having only one part. **5** having only one aspect; uniform. **6** not married. **7** *Brit* of a ticket: valid for a journey to a place but not back again. ➤ **singly** *adv.*
**single[2]** *n* **1** a CD or record with one short track or a small amount of music. **2** a single thing or amount.
**single[3]** *v* (+ out) to select specially from a number or group.
**single-breasted** *adj* of a coat, jacket, etc: having a centre fastening with one row of buttons.
**single cream** *n* light thin cream suitable for pouring.
**single file** *n* a line of people moving one behind the other.
**single-handed** *adj* done by one person alone or without help. ➤ **single-handedly** *adv.*
**single-minded** *adj* having a single overriding purpose. ➤ **single-mindedly** *adv.*
**single parent** *n* a person bringing up a child without a partner.
**singlet** *n chiefly Brit* a vest or a similar garment without sleeves.
**singleton** *n* an individual as opposed to a pair or group.
**singsong** *n* **1** a monotonous way of speaking like the rhythm of song. **2** *Brit* an informal gathering for singing.
**singular[1]** *adj* **1** superior; exceptional. **2** very unusual or strange. **3** in grammar, of a word or word form: denoting more one person or thing. ➤ **singularity** *n,* **singularly** *adv.*
**singular[2]** *n* in grammar, a singular number or word.
**sinister** *adj* **1** darkly or frighteningly evil. **2** threatening evil or ill fortune. ➤ **sinisterly** *adv.*
**sink[1]** *v* (**sank, sunk**) **1** to go down below the surface of liquid. **2** of a ship: to fall or cause to fall to the bottom of the sea. **3** (*usu* + in/into) to penetrate or cause to penetrate the surface of something soft. **4** to dig or bore (a well or shaft) in the earth. **5** to fall or drop to a lower place or level. **6** to disappear below the horizon. **7** to pass into a specified state. **8** to worsen or deteriorate. **9** to invest (money or energy) in something.
**sink[2]** *n* a basin connected to a drain and a water supply.
**sinker** *n* a weight for sinking a fishing line.
**sink hole** *n* a hollow through which surface water disappears into an underground area.
**sink in** *v* of information etc: to be understood.
**sinner** *n* a person who commits sins.
**sinuous** *adj* **1** having a wavy form; winding. **2** lithe or supple. **3** intricate or tortuous. ➤ **sinuously** *adv.*
**sinus** *n* a cavity in the bones of the skull that connects with the nostrils.
**sinusitis** *n* inflammation of a nasal sinus.
**sip[1]** *v* (**sipped, sipping**) to drink delicately or a little at a time.
**sip[2]** *n* a small amount of a drink taken by sipping.
**siphon[1]** *or* **syphon** *n* a tube for transferring liquid up over the side of a container and down to a lower level by atmospheric pressure.
**siphon[2]** *or* **syphon** *v* **1** to draw off (liquid) with a siphon. **2** (+ off) to take (money) in small amounts.
**sir** *n* **1** a form of respectful address to a man. **2** (**Sir**) used as a title of a knight or baronet.
**sire[1]** *n* **1** the male parent of an animal. **2** a father or male ancestor. **3** *archaic* a form of address to a king.
**sire[2]** *v esp* of a male animal: to beget (offspring).
**siren** *n* **1** a device that makes a loud wailing sound as a warning. **2** (**Siren**) in Greek mythology, each of a group of winged women who lured sailors to destruction by their singing. **3** a dangerously seductive woman.
**sirloin** *n* a cut of beef from the upper part of the hind loin.
**sisal** *n* a strong fibre obtained from the leaves of a Mexican plant, used for ropes, matting, etc.
**sissy** *n* (*pl* **-ies**) *informal* an effeminate or effete man.
**sister** *n* **1** a woman or girl having the same parents as another person. **2** a female colleague. **3** a female member of a religious order. **4** *Brit* a senior female nurse. ➤ **sisterly** *adj.*
**sisterhood** *n* **1** the state of being sisters. **2** a community of women bound by religious vows. **3** a group of women bound by a common interest.
**sister-in-law** *n* (*pl* **sisters-in-law**) **1** the sister of one's husband or wife. **2** the wife of one's brother.
**sit[1]** *v* (**sitting,** *past tense and past part.* **sat**) **1** to rest in a position supported by the buttocks and with the back upright. **2** of an animal: to rest

with its body close to the ground. **3** to be a member of an official body. **4** of a political body, etc: to be in session for official business. **5** to lie or stand in a particular position. **6** of a bird: to cover eggs for hatching. **7** to pose as a model for an artist or photographer. **8** *Brit* to be a candidate in (an examination). **9** to have enough seats for. * **sit tight** *informal* to maintain one's position.

**sit²** *n* a period of sitting.

**sitar** *n* an Indian lute with a long neck. ➤ **sitarist** *n.*

**sitcom** *n informal* a situation comedy.

**site¹** *n* **1** an area of ground occupied by a building, town, etc. **2** a scene of a specified activity. **3** a website.

**site²** *v* to place or build in a particular position.

**sit in** *v* **1** to be present as a visitor or observer. **2** to be a substitute.

**sit-in** *n* the occupation of a building by a body of people as a protest.

**sitter** *n* **1** a person who sits as an artist's model. **2** a babysitter.

**sitting** *n* **1** a period of posing for a portrait. **2** a period when a group of people are served a meal. **3** a session of an official body.

**sitting duck** *n informal* an easy target for attack or criticism.

**sitting room** *n chiefly Brit* a room for sitting and relaxing.

**sitting tenant** *n Brit* a tenant who is occupying a property with the legal right to remain.

**situate** *v* to place in a particular location or situation.

**situation** *n* **1** the way in which something is placed in relation to its surroundings. **2** the conditions and circumstances at a particular time or place. **3** a job or post. ➤ **situational** *adj.*

**situation comedy** *n* a broadcast comedy series involving characters in successive episodes.

**six** *n* **1** the number 6. **2** a shot in cricket that crosses the boundary before it bounces and scores six runs. * **at sixes and sevens** in confusion or disorder. **knock for six** *Brit, informal* to overwhelm or astonish. ➤ **six** *adj.*

**sixpence** *n* a former silver-coloured coin worth six old pence (2.5p).

**sixteen** *adj and n* the number 16. ➤ **sixteenth** *adj and n.*

**sixth** *adj and n* **1** having the position in a sequence corresponding to the number six. **2** one of six equal parts of something.

**sixth-form college** *n Brit* a state school for pupils above GCSE level.

**sixth sense** *n* a keen intuitive power independent of the five physical senses.

**sixty** *adj and n* (*pl* **-ies**) **1** the number 60. **2** (*in pl*) the numbers 60 to 69. ➤ **sixtieth** *adj and n.*

**sizable** *or* **sizeable** *adj* fairly large.

**size¹** *n* **1** the overall dimensions or measurement of something. **2** each of a series of graduated measurements in which items of clothing are made. * **the size of it** *informal* the actual state of affairs.

**size²** *v* to arrange or grade according to size.

**size³** *n* a thick sticky material used for preparing surfaces of paper or plaster in decorating.

**size⁴** *v* to treat with size.

**sizeable** *adj* see SIZABLE.

**size up** *v* **1** to form an opinion or estimate of. **2** to alter the size of according to requirements.

**sizzle¹** *v* **1** to make the hissing sound of frying food. **2** *informal* to be very hot. ➤ **sizzling** *adj.*

**sizzle²** *n* a sizzling sound.

**skate¹** *n* an ice skate or a roller skate. * **get/put one's skates on** *informal* to hurry.

**skate²** *v* to glide along on skates. * **skate over/round** to avoid dealing with (something difficult or awkward). ➤ **skater** *n.*

**skate³** *n* (*pl* **skates** *or* **skate**) a food fish of the ray family.

**skateboard¹** *n* a narrow board mounted on small wheels for riding on.

**skateboard²** *v* to ride on a skateboard. ➤ **skateboarder** *n.*

**skedaddle** *v informal* to leave hurriedly.

**skein** *n* a loosely coiled length of yarn or thread.

**skeletal** *adj* **1** attached to or resembling a skeleton. **2** of an idea: existing only in outline.

**skeleton** *n* **1** a framework of an organism, *esp* the bones of a vertebrate animal. **2** something reduced to its bare essentials. **3** an emaciated person or animal. **4** a basic framework. **5** (*used before a noun*) reduced to a minimum: *a skeleton staff.* * **skeleton in the cupboard** a secret cause of shame.

**skeleton key** *n* a key that is able to open several locks.

**skeptic** *n NAmer* see SCEPTIC.

**sketch¹** *n* **1** a rough drawing. **2** a brief description or outline. **3** a short comic act.

**sketch²** *v* **1** to make a sketch of. **2** (*often* + out) to describe briefly.

**sketchbook** *n* a pad of plain paper for sketching.

**sketchy** *adj* (**-ier, -iest**) lacking detail; superficial or scanty. ➤ **sketchily** *adv.*

**skew¹** *adj* placed or running obliquely.

**skew²** *n* **1** obliqueness or slant. **2** distortion or bias.

**skew³** *v* **1** to take an oblique course; to twist or swerve. **2** to distort or give a bias to.

**skewbald** *adj* of a horse: marked with patches of white and brown.

**skewer¹** *n* a long wooden or metal pin for holding food together while cooking.

**skewer²** *v* to hold or pierce with a skewer.

**ski¹** *n* (*pl* **skis**) each of a pair of long narrow strips of wood, metal, or plastic attached to the feet for gliding over snow.

**ski²** *v* (**skis, skied, skiing**) to travel on skis. ➤ **skier** *n.*

**skid¹** *v* (**skidded, skidding**) **1** of a vehicle: to slide sideways out ofcontrol. **2** to slip or slide.

**skid²** *n* **1** an act of skidding. **2** a runner used as part of the landing gear of an aircraft.

**skiff** *n* a light rowing or sailing boat.

**ski jump** *n* a steep ramp overhanging a slope, used for jumping on skis. ➤ **ski-jump** *v.*

**skilful** (*NAmer* **skillful**) *adj* having or showing skill; expert. ➤ **skilfully** *adv.*

***Usage Note:*** Note the spelling with one *l* and then *-ful*.

**ski lift** *n* a series of seats suspended from an overhead cable, used for transporting skiers up and down a mountainside.

**skill** *n* **1** special ability in a particular field. **2** a task or technique requiring skill.

**skilled** *adj* **1** having skill. **2** requiring trained workers.

**skillet** *n* a small frying pan.

**skim** *v* (**skimmed, skimming**) **1** to clear (a liquid) of floating matter. **2** to remove (fat or scum) from the surface of a liquid. **3** to pass swiftly or lightly over. **4** to read over quickly. **5** (*usu* + through/over) to consider briefly.

**skimmed milk** *n* milk with the cream removed.

**skimp** *v* (*usu* + on) to devote too little time, money, or effort to.

**skimpy** *adj* (**-ier, -iest**) inadequate in quality, size, etc; scanty. ➤ **skimpily** *adv.*

**skin¹** *n* **1** the external covering of the body. **2** an outer covering, e.g. the peel or rind of a fruit or vegetable or the casing of a sausage. **3** the external covering of an animal, prepared and used e.g. for clothing. **4** a film that forms on the surface of a liquid. * **by the skin of one's teeth** only just; barely. **get under somebody's skin** *informal* to irritate or interest somebody intensely. **no skin off somebody's nose** *informal* no disadvantage to somebody. **skin and bone** thin and emaciated.

**skin²** *v* (**skinned, skinning**) **1** to remove the skin of. **2** to scrape or graze (part of the body).

**skin-deep** *adj* transitory or superficial.

**skin diving** *n* swimming under water with flippers and an aqualung.

**skinflint** *n informal* a mean or niggardly person.

**skinhead** *n* a member of a group of young people with extremely short hair.

**skinny** *adj* (**-ier, -iest**) *informal* very thin. ➤ **skinniness** *n.*

**skint** *adj Brit, informal* having no money.

**skintight** *adj* of a piece of clothing: fitting close to the body.

**skip¹** *v* (**skipped, skipping**) **1** to move with light leaps, or by hopping on alternate feet. **2** to jump repeatedly over a rope swung over the head and under the feet. **3** to pass over or omit. **4** (+ through) to deal with hastily or cursorily. **5** to fail to attend.

**skip²** *n* a skipping movement.

**skip³** *n* a large open container for waste or rubble, removed when full.

**skipper¹** *n informal* the captain of a ship, aircraft, or sports team.

**skipper²** *v* to be captain of.

**skipper³** *n* **1** somebody or something that skips. **2** a small butterfly with a stout hairy body and a darting flight.

**skirl** *v* to emit the high shrill sound of bagpipes. ➤ **skirl** *n.*

**skirmish¹** *n* a brief clash or fight.

**skirmish²** *v* to engage in a skirmish.

**skirt¹** *n* a women's and girls' piece of clothing that hangs from the waist.

**skirt²** *v* **1** to extend along the edge of. **2** (*also* + round) to avoid through difficulty or danger.

**skirting** *or* **skirting board** *n* a strip of board fixed along the base of an interior wall.

**skit** *n* a humorous sketch or story.

**skitter** *v* to move lightly or swiftly.

**skittish** *adj* **1** of an animal: nervous and easily frightened. **2** lively or frisky. ➤ **skittishly** *adv.*

**skittle** *n* **1** (*in pl*) a game played by rolling a wooden ball at a group of pins in order to knock them over. **2** a pin used in skittles.

**skive** *v Brit, informal* (*often* + off) to avoid work or duty. ➤ **skiver** *n.*

**skivvy** *n* (*pl* **-ies**) *Brit, informal* a female domestic servant.

**skua** *n* a large dark-coloured seabird.

**skulduggery** *or* **skullduggery** *n* underhand or unscrupulous behaviour.

**skulk** *v* to move stealthily or furtively.

**skull** *n* a bony case forming the skeleton of the head and enclosing the brain.

**skull and crossbones** *n* a representation of a human skull over two crossed thigh bones, used as a warning of danger and formerly shown on pirate flags.

**skullcap** *n* a close-fitting cap without a peak.

**skunk** *n* an American mammal that can eject a foul-smelling liquid in self-defence.

**sky** *n* (*pl* **-ies**) the upper atmosphere seen from the earth.

**sky blue** *n* a light blue colour.

**skydiving** *n* the sport of jumping from an aircraft and executing body manoeuvres in the air before opening a parachute. ➤ **skydiver** *n.*

**skylark¹** *n* a lark that sings in flight.

**skylark²** *v* to behave in a high-spirited or mischievous manner.

**skylight** *n* a window in a roof or ceiling.

**skyline** *n* an outline of buildings or landscape seen against the the sky.

**skyrocket¹** *n* a rocket fired high into the air as a flare or firework.

**skyrocket²** *v* (**skyrocketed, skyrocketing**) to increase rapidly or suddenly.

**skyscraper** *n* a very tall building with many storeys.

**slab** *n* **1** a large thick flat piece of stone. **2** a thick slice of cheese, cake, etc.

**slack**[1] *adj* **1** not taut; loose. **2** lazy or sluggish. **3** negligent or lax. **4** lacking in activity; not busy. ➤ **slackly** *adv*, **slackness** *n*.

**slack**[2] *n* **1** the part of a rope or string that is not held taut. **2** (*in pl*) casual trousers. **3** *informal* a lull in activity.

**slack**[3] *v* **1** to work sluggishly or carelessly. **2** (*often* + off) to release tension in; to loosen. **3** to lessen or moderate. **4** (+ off/up) to be or become slack. ➤ **slacker** *n*.

**slack**[4] *n* coal in very small pieces.

**slacken** *v* **1** to make or become less taut. **2** to make or become less active, rapid, or intense.

**slag**[1] *n* **1** waste matter from the smelting of metal ores. **2** *Brit* waste material from coal mining. **3** *Brit, informal, derog* a promiscuous woman or girl.

**slag**[2] *v* (**slagged, slagging**) *Brit, informal* (*also* + off) to criticize abusively.

**slagheap** *n Brit* a mound of waste material from a mine.

**slain** *v* past part. of SLAY.

**slake** *v* to satisfy or quench (a thirst or desire).

**slalom** *n* a skiing or canoeing race on winding course between obstacles.

**slam**[1] *v* (**slammed, slamming**) **1** to shut forcibly and noisily. **2** to put or throw down noisily. **3** (*usu* + into) to crash into violently. **4** *informal* to criticize harshly. **5** *informal* to defeat easily.

**slam**[2] *n* a banging noise as made by a door in closing.

**slam**[3] *n* in bridge, the winning of all tricks or all tricks but one.

**slander**[1] *n* **1** the crime ofsaying untrue things that damage a person's reputation. **2** something said that is untrue and defamatory. ➤ **slanderous** *adj*.

**slander**[2] *v* to utter slander about. ➤ **slanderer** *n*.

**slang** *n* informal spoken words and phrases, often of a kind associated with a particular group of people. ➤ **slangy** *adj*.

**slanging match** *n chiefly Brit, informal* an angry and abusive argument between two or more people.

**slant**[1] *v* **1** to lean or slope. **2** to interpret or present (information) from a particular point of view.

**slant**[2] *n* **1** a slanting direction, line, or plane. **2** a particular point of view. ➤ **slantwise** *adv and adj*.

**slap**[1] *n* **1** a sharp blow with the open hand. **2** a noise that suggests a slap. ✱ **slap in the face** a rebuff or insult.

**slap**[2] *v* (**slapped, slapping**) **1** to hit with the open hand or a flat object. **2** to hit with the sound of a slap. **3** (*usu* + on) to apply hastily or carelessly.

**slap**[3] *adv informal* directly or with force.

**slap-bang** *adv informal* **1** in an abrupt or forceful manner. **2** precisely.

**slapdash** *adj and adv* done in a haphazard or slipshod manner.

**slap down** *v* to criticize or reprimand abruptly.

**slapstick** *n* comedy characterized by farce and horseplay.

**slap-up** *adj chiefly Brit, informal* of a meal: lavish or extravagant.

**slash**[1] *v* **1** to cut with violent sweeping strokes. **2** to cut slits in. **3** *informal* to reduce (a price) drastically.

**slash**[2] *n* **1** a cut or stroke made by slashing. **2** a stroke (/) used to show alternatives or elements of a fraction.

**slat** *n* a thin narrow flat strip of wood or metal forming an overlapping series. ➤ **slatted** *adj*.

**slate**[1] *n* **1** a fine-grained rock that is easily split into thin layers. **2** a piece of this used as roofing material. **3** a tablet of slate or similar material for writing on. ➤ **slaty** *adj*.

**slate**[2] *v* to cover with slates. ➤ **slater** *n*.

**slate**[3] *v chiefly Brit, informal* to criticize severely.

**slattern** *n dated* an untidy slovenly woman. ➤ **slatternly** *adj*.

**slaughter**[1] *n* **1** the killing of livestock for food. **2** the violent killing of many people.

**slaughter**[2] *v* **1** to kill (animals) for food. **2** to kill (people) violently or in large numbers.

**slaughterhouse** *n* a place where animals are killed for food.

**Slav** *n* a member of a group of peoples of eastern Europe who speak a Slavonic language.

**slave**[1] *n* **1** a person held as the property of another and bound to obey them. **2** a person who is dominated by a specified thing: *a slave to fashion*.

**slave**[2] *v* to work very hard.

**slave driver** *n informal* a harsh taskmaster.

**slave labour** *n* hard work for little reward.

**slaver**[1] /'slavə/ *v* to drool or slobber.

**slaver**[2] *n* saliva dribbling from the mouth.

**slavery** *n* **1** the state of being a slave. **2** the practice of owning slaves.

**slavish** *adj* **1** imitative; having no originality. **2** excessively servile. ➤ **slavishly** *adv*.

**Slavonic** *adj* of a group of lanuages including Bulgarian, Czech, Polish, Russian, and Serbo-Croatian.

**slay** *v* (**slew, slain**) **1** *archaic* to kill violently or with great bloodshed. **2** *NAmer* to murder.

**sleaze** *n informal* corrupt or immoral behaviour.

**sleazy** *adj* (**-ier, -iest**) **1** of a place: squalid and disreputable. **2** of behaviour: corrupt or immoral.

**sled**[1] *n NAmer* = SLEDGE[1].

**sled**[2] *v* (**sledded, sledding**) *NAmer* = SLEDGE[2].

**sledge**[1] *n* **1** a vehicle with runners for travelling over snow or ice, often pulled by dogs. **2** *Brit* a toboggan.

**sledge**[2] *v* to ride or carry on a sledge.

**sledgehammer** *n* a large heavy hammer.

**sleek**[1] *adj* **1** smooth and glossy. **2** smart and well-groomed. **3** looking prosperous. ➤ **sleekly** *adv.*

**sleek**[2] *v* to make (the hair) sleek or smooth.

**sleep**[1] *n* **1** a natural state of unconsciousness with the eyes closed and the body relaxed. **2** a period spent sleeping. ✱ **go to sleep 1** to fall asleep. **2** to become numb. **put to sleep** to kill (an animal) humanely. ➤ **sleepless** *adj.*

**sleep**[2] *v* (*past tense and past part.* **slept**) **1** to rest in a state of sleep. **2** *informal* (+ with/together) to have sexual relations with. **3** to provide sleeping accommodation for (a specified number of people).

**sleep around** *v* to be sexually promiscuous.

**sleeper** *n* **1** a sleeping car. **2** *Brit* a ring or stud worn in a pierced ear to keep the hole open. **3** each of a series of wooden or concrete supports on which railway rails are laid.

**sleeping bag** *n* a padded bag for sleeping in when camping.

**sleeping car** *n* a railway carriage having berths for sleeping.

**sleeping partner** *n* a partner who takes no active part in the running of a business.

**sleeping pill** *n* a tablet or capsule taken to induce sleep.

**sleeping policeman** *n* a hump in a road designed to slow traffic down.

**sleeping sickness** *n* a tropical disease marked by prolonged lethargy.

**sleepwalk** *v* to walk in one's sleep. ➤ **sleepwalker** *n.*

**sleepy** *adj* (**-ier, -iest**) **1** ready to fall asleep. **2** sluggish or lethargic. **3** of a place: quiet and inactive. ➤ **sleepily** *adv,* **sleepiness** *n.*

**sleet**[1] *n* partly frozen falling rain, or snow and rain falling together.

**sleet**[2] *v* to fall as sleet.

**sleeve** *n* **1** the part of a garment covering the arm or upper arm. **2** a covering for a record. **3** a tubular machine part designed to fit over another part. ✱ **up one's sleeve** kept hidden for future use. ➤ **sleeveless** *adj.*

**sleigh** *n* a large sledge pulled by horses or reindeer.

**sleight** *n literary* deceitful craftiness.

**sleight of hand** *n* **1** skilful use of the hands in conjuring or juggling. **2** shrewd deception.

**slender** *adj* **1** gracefully slim. **2** flimsy or meagre.

**slept** *v* past tense and past part. of SLEEP[2].

**sleuth**[1] *n informal* a detective.

**sleuth**[2] *v informal* to act as a detective.

**slew**[1] *v* to slide or swing about out of control.

**slew**[2] *v* past tense of SLAY.

**slice**[1] *n* **1** a thin broad flat piece cut from a larger whole. **2** a portion or share. **3** an implement with a broad blade for lifting food. **4** in sports, the flight of a ball that deviates from a straight course.

**slice**[2] *v* **1** to cut with a knife. **2** to cut into slices. **3** to hit (a ball) so that it deviates from a straight course. **4** to move rapidly or effortlessly.

**slick**[1] *adj* **1** deft or skilful. **2** superficially plausible or impressive; glib. **3** smooth or slippery. ➤ **slickly** *adv.*

**slick**[2] *n* a film of oil floating on water.

**slick**[3] *v* to make (hair) sleek or smooth.

**slide**[1] *v* (*past tense and past part.* **slid**) **1** to move over a smooth surface in continuous contact with it. **2** to glide over a slippery surface. **3** to pass quietly and unobtrusively. **4** to move smoothly and easily. **5** to pass gradually to a lower level or worse state.

**slide**[2] *n* **1** a structure with a sloping smooth surface down which children slide in play. **2** the act of sliding. **3** a sliding part or mechanism. **4** a flat piece of glass for mounting an object to be examined under a microscope. **5** a photographic transparency viewed with a projector.

**slide rule** *n* a ruler with a central sliding strip for making calculations.

**sliding scale** *n* a scale of fees or payments that changes according to the variation in some other factor.

**slight**[1] *adj* **1** small in amount or degree. **2** having a slim or frail build. **3** lacking strength or bulk; flimsy. **4** unimportant; trivial. **5** not serious; minor. ➤ **slightly** *adv.*

**slight**[2] *v* to treat with disdain or indifference; to snub.

**slight**[3] *n* a humiliating affront.

**slim**[1] *adj* (**slimmer, slimmest**) **1** attractively thin. **2** small in width in relation to length or height. **3** scanty or slight: *a slim chance.*

**slim**[2] *v* (**slimmed, slimming**) **1** to make or become thinner. **2** (*often* + down) to reduce the number of. ➤ **slimmer** *n.*

**slime** *n* an unpleasantly thick and slippery substance.

**slimy** *adj* (**-ier, -iest**) **1** resembling or covered with slime. **2** *informal* obsequious or ingratiating in a repellent way.

**sling**[1] *n* **1** a looped line used to raise or support something. **2** a bandage suspended from the neck to support an injured arm. **3** a short strap used as a simple weapon for throwing stones.

**sling**[2] *v* (*past tense and past part.* **slung**) **1** to throw carelessly. **2** to throw (a stone) with a sling. **3** to raise or carry in a sling. **4** *Brit, informal* (+ out) to expel unceremoniously.

**slingback** *n* a shoe held on by a strap passing round the ankle.

**slingshot** *n NAmer* a catapult.

**slink** *v* (*past tense and past part.* **slunk**) to move gracefully or stealthily.

**slinky** *adj* (**-ier, -iest**) *informal* sleek and flowing in movement or outline.

**slip**[1] *v* (**slipped, slipping**) **1** to slide out of place or away from one's grasp. **2** to slide on a slippery surface. **3** to decline from a standard or accustomed level by degrees. **4** to move or cause to move smoothly. **5** to move quietly and cautiously. **6** to pass imperceptibly from one state into another. **7** of time: to elapse. **8** to free oneself from (a restraint). **9** (+ on/off) to put on or take off (clothing) quickly or easily. **10** to place or pass quietly or secretly. **11** to leave (the clutch of a vehicle) partially engaged. * **let slip** **1** to say casually or accidentally. **2** to fail to take (a chance). **slip one's mind** to be forgotten or overlooked. ➤ **slippage** *n.*

**slip**[2] *n* **1** an instance of slipping. **2** a minor mistake. **3** a woman's short undergarment. **4** in cricket, a fielding position close to the batsman. * **give somebody the slip** *informal* to elude or evade somebody.

**slip**[3] *n* **1** a small piece of paper. **2** a small young person: *a slip of a girl.* **3** a shoot cut for planting or grafting.

**slipknot** *n* a knot that can be untied by pulling or that slides along the line it is tied to.

**slip-on** *adj esp* of shoes: having no fastenings.

**slipped disc** *n* a displaced disc in the spine, producing pressure on the nerves and causing pain.

**slipper** *n* a flat comfortable shoe for wearing indoors.

**slippery** *adj* (**-ier, -iest**) **1** tending to cause sliding from being icy, greasy, wet, or polished. **2** tending to slip from the grasp. **3** of a person: not to be trusted.

**slippy** *adj* (**-ier, -iest**) *informal* slippery.

**slip road** *n Brit* a road providing access to or exit from a major road or motorway.

**slipshod** *adj* careless or slovenly.

**slipstream** *n* **1** a stream of air or water driven backward by a propeller. **2** an area of reduced air pressure immediately behind a moving vehicle.

**slip up** *v* to make a careless mistake.

**slip-up** *n informal* a mistake or oversight.

**slipway** *n* a ramp sloping down into water, for launching or landing ships or boats.

**slit**[1] *v* (**slitting,** *past tense and past part.* **slit**) to make a narrow cut in.

**slit**[2] *n* a long narrow cut or opening.

**slither** *v* **1** to move smoothly with a sliding or twisting motion. **2** to slide unsteadily on a slippery surface. ➤ **slither** *n,* **slithery** *adj.*

**sliver**[1] *n* a small slender piece cut or broken off something.

**sliver**[2] *v* to cut or break into slivers.

**slob** *n informal* a lazy slovenly person.

**slobber**[1] *v* **1** to let saliva dribble from the mouth. **2** (*often* + over) to express excessive emotion about.

**slobber**[2] *n* saliva dribbled from the mouth. ➤ **slobbery** *adj.*

**sloe** *n* the small blue-black fruit of the blackthorn.

**slog**[1] *v* (**slogged, slogging**) **1** to move slowly and laboriously. **2** to work laboriously. **3** to hit hard and wildly. * **slog it out** to compete fiercely.

**slog**[2] *n* **1** a spell of hard work. **2** an arduous march. **3** a hard blow.

**slogan** *n* a brief catchy phrase used in advertising or to characterize a particular point of view.

**sloop** *n* a sailing boat with one mast.

**slop** *v* (**slopped, slopping**) **1** of a liquid: to spill over the side of a container. **2** to serve or apply messily.

**slope**[1] *v* **1** to lie at a slant; to incline. **2** to cause to incline or slant. ➤ **sloping** *adj.*

**slope**[2] *n* **1** a strip or area that is lower at one end than the other. **2** (*usu in pl*) the side of a mountain or hill.

**slop out** *v* to empty the contents of a chamber pot.

**sloppy** *adj* (**-ier, -iest**) **1** wet so as to splash. **2** disagreeably wet or watery. **3** slovenly or careless. **4** excessively sentimental. ➤ **sloppily** *adv,* **sloppiness** *n.*

**slops** *pl n* **1** waste food or thin gruel fed to animals. **2** liquid household refuse. **3** tasteless drink or liquid food.

**slosh**[1] *n* **1** the sound of splashing liquid. **2** *Brit, informal* a heavy blow. ➤ **sloshy** *adj.*

**slosh**[2] *v* **1** of liquid: to move with a splashing motion or sound. **2** to flounder or splash through water, mud, etc. **3** to move or splash about in liquid. **4** *Brit, informal* to hit heavily. ➤ **sloshy** *adj.*

**sloshed** *adj informal* drunk.

**slot**[1] *n* **1** a narrow opening for inserting something. **2** a place in an organization or scheme.

**slot**[2] *v* (**slotted, slotting**) (*often* + in/into) to fit or place in a slot or position.

**sloth** *n* **1** laziness. **2** a slow-moving mammal that hangs from the branches of trees. ➤ **slothful** *adj.*

**slot machine** *n* **1** *Brit* = VENDING MACHINE. **2** a machine operated by inserting a coin in a slot.

**slouch**[1] *v* to sit, stand, or walk limply or lazily.

**slouch**[2] *n* a limp or drooping gait or posture. * **no slouch** *informal* able or competent.

**slough**[1] /slow/ *n* **1** a swamp. **2** a state of dejection or hopelessness.

**slough**[2] /sluf/ *v* of an animal: to cast off a skin or shell.

**slovenly** *adj* **1** untidy or dirty, *esp* in personal appearance. **2** lazy and careless. ➤ **slovenliness** *n.*

**slow**[1] *adj* **1** moving or only able to move at a low speed. **2** marked by lack of speed or haste. **3** requiring or taking a long time. **4** of a clock or watch: showing a time earlier than the actual time. **5** not quickly learning or understanding. **6** lacking in activity. **7** of an oven: set at a low temperature. ➤ **slowly** *adv*, **slowness** *n*.

**slow**[2] *adv* slowly.

**slow**[3] *v* (*often* + down/up) to make or become slow or slower.

**slowcoach** *n Brit, informal* a person who moves or acts slowly.

**slow motion** *n* the playing back of a video recording at less than the standard speed.

**slow puncture** *n* a puncture that causes a tyre to deflate gradually.

**slowworm** *n* a small lizard with a snakelike body.

**sludge** *n* soft wet mud or slimy substance. ➤ **sludgy** *adj*.

**slug**[1] *n* a small slimy animal like a snail with no shell.

**slug**[2] *n* **1** a quantity of alcoholic drink swallowed in one gulp. **2** a bullet.

**slug**[3] *v* (**slugged, slugging**) to swallow in one gulp.

**slug**[4] *v* (**slugged, slugging**) *informal* to hit hard. ✱ **slug it out** to compete fiercely.

**sluggard** *n* a lazy person.

**sluggish** *adj* **1** slow in movement or action. **2** lacking energy or activity. ➤ **sluggishly** *adv*.

**sluice**[1] *n* **1** (*also* **sluice gate**) a gate or other device for controlling the flow of water. **2** a channel for draining or carrying off surplus water.

**sluice**[2] *v* **1** to wash in running water. **2** to drench or flush.

**slum**[1] *n* **1** a poor run-down area in a city. **2** a squalid place to live. ➤ **slummy** *adj*.

**slum**[2] *v* (**slummed, slumming**) to live in squalor or poverty. ✱ **slum it** *informal* to live temporarily in poor conditions.

**slumber**[1] *v literary* to sleep.

**slumber**[2] *n literary* sleep.

**slump**[1] *v* **1** to sit or drop down heavily. **2** to decline rapidly.

**slump**[2] *n* **1** an instance of slumping. **2** a marked decline.

**slung** *v* past tense and past part. of SLING[2].

**slunk** *v* past tense and past part. of SLINK.

**slur**[1] *v* (**slurred, slurring**) **1** to pronounce (words or sounds) unclearly. **2** (+ over) to pass over without due mention or consideration. **3** in music, to perform (successive notes of different pitch) in a smooth or connected manner.

**slur**[2] *n* **1** a slurred utterance or manner of speech. **2** in music, a curved line connecting notes to be slurred.

**slur**[3] *v* (**slurred, slurring**) to insult or disparage.

**slur**[4] *n* an insulting remark.

**slurp**[1] *v* to eat or drink with a loud sucking sound.

**slurp**[2] *n* a slurping sound.

**slurry** *n* (*pl* **-ies**) a watery mixture of mud, manure, or lime.

**slush** *n* **1** partly melted or watery snow. **2** liquid mud. **3** *informal* excessively sentimental language. ➤ **slushy** *adj*.

**slush fund** *n* a fund for dishonest uses.

**slut** *n* a promiscuous or slovenly woman. ➤ **sluttish** *adj*.

**sly** *adj* (**-er, -est**) **1** cunning and furtive. **2** humorously mischievous; roguish. ✱ **on the sly** secretly. ➤ **slyly** *adv*.

**smack**[1] *n* **1** a sharp blow with the open hand. **2** the sound of such a blow. **3** a loud kiss. ✱ **smack in the eye** *informal* a setback or rebuff.

**smack**[2] *v* **1** to hit with the open hand. **2** to strike or collide with sharply. **3** to put down forcefully or noisily. **4** to open (the lips) with a sudden sharp sound.

**smack**[3] *adv informal* squarely or directly.

**smack**[4] *v* **1** (+ of) to taste or smell of. **2** (+ of) to have a trace of (something unwelcome).

**smack**[5] *n* a small fishing vessel.

**smack**[6] *n slang* heroin.

**smacker** *n informal* **1** a loud kiss. **2** *Brit* a pound sterling.

**small**[1] *adj* **1** of less than normal size. **2** young or immature. **3** not great in quantity, value, importance, etc. **4** operating on a limited scale. **5** mean or petty. **6** humiliated. ➤ **smallness** *n*.

**small**[2] *n* **1** the narrowest part of the back. **2** *Brit, informal* (*in pl*) small articles of underwear.

**small arms** *pl n* (*usu in pl*) guns that can be carried about.

**small beer** *n chiefly Brit* unimportant matters.

**small change** *n* **1** coins of low denomination. **2** something unimportant.

**small fry** *pl n* **1** small fish. **2** young or insignificant people or things.

**smallholding** *n Brit* a small farm. ➤ **smallholder** *n*.

**small hours** *pl n* (**the small hours**) the hours after midnight.

**smallpox** *n* an infectious disease with fever and pustules that form scabs, usually leaving permanent scars.

**small print** *n* a part of a document with unattractive conditions, often printed in small type.

**small talk** *n* light or casual conversation.

**small-time** *adj informal* insignificant or petty.

**smarmy** *adj* (**-ier, -iest**) *informal* obsequiously friendly or polite.

**smart**[1] *adj* **1** neat or elegant in dress or appearance. **2** of a place: frequented by fashionable society. **3** *informal* mentally alert; clever. ➤ **smartly** *adv*, **smartness** *n*.

**smart**[2] *v* **1** to have or give a sharp stinging pain. **2** to feel upset or angry.

**smart card** *n* a plastic card with a memory chip that holds information.
**smarten** *v* (*often* + up) to make or become smarter.
**smartish** *adv chiefly Brit, informal* promptly and quickly.
**smash**[1] *v* **1** to break violently into pieces. **2** to drive, throw, or hit violently. **3** in sports, to hit (a ball) downward forcefully. **4** to destroy or defeat. **5** (+ into) to collide with.
**smash**[2] *n* **1** the action or sound of smashing. **2** a violent blow or collision. **3** *informal* a smash hit.
**smash hit** *n informal* a very successful song, show, etc.
**smashing** *adj Brit, informal* excellent.
**smattering** *n* **1** a small amount. **2** a slight knowledge of a subject.
**smear**[1] *v* **1** to spread or mark with a sticky or greasy substance. **2** to obscure or blur. **3** to blacken the reputation of. ➤ **smeary** *adj.*
**smear**[2] *n* **1** a sticky or greasy mark. **2** an unsupported accusation. **3** material smeared on a slide for examination under a microscope.
**smear test** *n* a test for cervical cancer.
**smell**[1] *v* (*past tense and past part.* **smelt** *or* **smelled**) **1** to perceive the odour of. **2** to sniff (something) in order to perceive its odour. **3** to detect or become aware of by instinct. **4** to have a specified smell. **5** (+ of) to be suggestive of. **6** to have an unpleasant smell. ✻ **smell a rat** *informal* to suspect that something is wrong.
**smell**[2] *n* **1** the sense by which odours are perceived through sensitive areas in the nose. **2** the quality of something as perceived by this sense; an odour. **3** an unpleasant odour. **4** a pervading quality or aura. **5** the act of smelling.
**smelling salts** *pl n* a preparation sniffed as a stimulant to relieve faintness.
**smelly** *adj* (**-ier, -iest**) having a strong unpleasant smell.
**smelt**[1] *n* (*pl* **smelts** *or* **smelt**) a small fish with a delicate oily flesh.
**smelt**[2] *v* **1** to melt (ore) to separate the metal. **2** to separate (metal) by smelting ore. ➤ **smelter** *n.*
**smelt**[3] *v* past part. of SMELL[1].
**smidgin** *or* **smidgen** *n informal* a small amount; a bit.
**smile**[1] *v* to form the face into an expression in which the corners of the mouth curve upwards to express amusement, friendliness, pleasure, etc.
**smile**[2] *n* an act of smiling.
**smirk**[1] *v* to smile in a fatuous or smug manner.
**smirk**[2] *n* an act of smirking.
**smite** *v* (**smote, smitten**) *archaic* **1** to strike sharply or heavily. **2** to kill, injure, or damage. ✻ **be smitten by/with** to be attracted or emotionally affected by.
**smith** *n* a person who works in metal, *esp* a blacksmith.
**smithereens** *pl n* small fragments.
**smithy** *n* (*pl* **-ies**) a blacksmith's forge.
**smock** *n* **1** a protective garment worn over clothes. **2** a garment like a long loose shirt or dress gathered into a yoke and decorated with smocking.
**smocking** *n* a decorative effect made by gathering cloth in regularly spaced tucks held in place with ornamental stitching.
**smog** *n* a fog made heavier and darker by smoke and fumes. ➤ **smoggy** *adj.*
**smoke**[1] *n* **1** the visible gaseous products of burning. **2** an act or spell of smoking tobacco. **3** *informal* something, e.g. a cigarette, that is smoked. ✻ **go up in smoke** to come to nothing.
**smoke**[2] *v* **1** to emit smoke. **2** to inhale and exhale the smoke of (a cigarette, pipe, etc). **3** to smoke cigarettes, cigars, a pipe, etc, *esp* habitually. **4** to cure (meat or fish) by exposure to smoke. **5** to colour or darken (glass). ➤ **smoked** *adj,* **smoker** *n.*
**smokeless** *adj* producing little or no smoke.
**smoke out** *v* to drive out or away with smoke.
**smoke screen** *n* **1** a screen of smoke produced to conceal a military position or activity. **2** something said or done to conceal or confuse.
**smokestack** *n* a chimney or funnel through which smoke and gases are discharged, e.g. from a ship or factory.
**smoking jacket** *n* a man's loosely fitting jacket formerly worn while smoking after a meal.
**smoky** *adj* (**-ier, -iest**) **1** filled with or producing a lot of smoke. **2** like smoke in form or appearance.
**smolder** *v NAmer* see SMOULDER.
**smooch** *v informal* to kiss and cuddle. ➤ **smoochy** *adj.*
**smooth**[1] *adj* **1** having a continuous even surface. **2** of liquid: free from lumps. **3** free from difficulties or obstructions. **4** even and uninterrupted in movement or flow. **5** urbane and courteous. **6** excessively suave or ingratiating. **7** of a flavour: not sharp or acid. ➤ **smoothly** *adv,* **smoothness** *n.*
**smooth**[2] *v* **1** to make or become smooth. **2** (*often* + out) to press flat. **3** (*often* + down) to cause to lie evenly. **4** to free from obstruction or difficulty.
**smoothie** *or* **smoothy** *n* (*pl* **-ies**) *informal* a suave or ingratiating person.
**smooth-talking** *adj* ingratiating and persuasive in speech. ➤ **smooth-talk** *v.*
**smorgasbord** *n* a variety of foods and dishes, e.g. hors d'oeuvres, hot and cold meat or fish, cheeses, salads, etc.
**smote** *v* past tense of SMITE.

**smother** *v* **1** to suffocate by covering the nose and mouth. **2** to extinguish (a fire) by excluding oxygen. **3** to prevent the growth or development of. **4** to cause to feel overwhelmed or oppressed. **5** to cover thickly.

**smoulder** (*NAmer* **smolder**) *v* **1** to burn with smoke but no flame. **2** to show suppressed anger, hate, jealousy, etc.

**smudge**[1] *v* **1** to smear or daub. **2** to make indistinct; to blur.

**smudge**[2] *n* a blurry mark or streak. ➤ **smudgy** *adj.*

**smug** *adj* (**smugger, smuggest**) excessively pleased with oneself; self-satisfied. ➤ **smugly** *adv,* **smugness** *n.*

**smuggle** *v* **1** to import or export (goods) illegally without paying duties. **2** to convey secretly. ➤ **smuggler** *n.*

**smut** *n* **1** a particle of soot or dirt. **2** indecent language, writing, or pictures. ➤ **smutty** *adj.*

**Sn** *abbr* the chemical symbol for tin.

**snack**[1] *n* a light meal eaten between regular meals.

**snack**[2] *v* to eat a snack.

**snaffle**[1] *n* a simple jointed bit for a bridle.

**snaffle**[2] *v informal* to take secretly.

**snag**[1] *n* **1** a hidden or unexpected difficulty. **2** a sharp or jagged projecting part. **3** an irregular tear or flaw.

**snag**[2] *v* (**snagged, snagging**) to catch or tear on a snag.

**snaggle-toothed** *adj* having irregular or broken teeth.

**snail** *n* a small slow-moving animal with a soft body and a hard shell that it can contract into.

**snake**[1] *n* **1** a reptile with a long tapering body and no legs. **2** a sly treacherous person. * **snake in the grass** a secretly treacherous friend or associate. ➤ **snaky** *adj.*

**snake**[2] *v* to move silently with a twisting motion.

**snakes and ladders** *pl n* a board game in which players move counters along squares, advancing up a ladder or going back down a snake.

**snap**[1] *v* (**snapped, snapping**) **1** to break with a sharp cracking sound. **2** to bite or close the jaws with force. **3** to close or fit in place with a sharp sound. **4** to reply irritably. **5** to lose self-control suddenly. **6** (+ up) to acquire (something) suddenly or eagerly. **7** to take a snapshot of. * **snap out of** *informal* to free oneself from a mood, habit, etc with an effort.

**snap**[2] *n* **1** the act or sound of snapping. **2** a sudden spell of harsh weather. **3** a thin brittle biscuit. **4** a snapshot. **5** a card game in which players try to be the first to shout '*snap*' when two cards of identical value are laid successively.

**snap**[3] *adj* done suddenly or unexpectedly.

**snapdragon** *n* a plant with bright white, red, or yellow two-lipped flowers.

**snapper** *n* (*pl* **snappers** *or* **snapper**) a flesh-eating sea fish.

**snappy** *adj* (**-ier, -iest**) **1** curt and irritable. **2** stylish or smart. * **make it snappy** *informal* be quick. ➤ **snappily** *adv.*

**snapshot** *n* a casual photograph taken quickly.

**snare**[1] *n* **1** a trap for catching small animals, consisting of a noose that is pulled tight. **2** something likely to trap or deceive. **3** a string or metal spiral placed over the skin of a snare drum to produce a rattling sound.

**snare**[2] *v* to catch in a snare.

**snare drum** *n* a small double-headed drum with snares stretched across its lower head.

**snarl**[1] *v* (*often* + up) to make or become tangled or confused.

**snarl**[2] *v* **1** to growl with bared teeth. **2** to speak in an aggressive or bad-tempered manner.

**snarl-up** *n informal* a traffic jam.

**snatch**[1] *v* **1** to seize or grab suddenly and forcibly. **2** to take or grasp abruptly or hastily. **3** (*often* + at) to attempt to seize something suddenly.

**snatch**[2] *n* **1** an act of snatching. **2** a brief period of time or activity. **3** a fragment of music or conversation.

**snazzy** *adj* (**-ier, -iest**) *informal* attractive and stylish.

**sneak**[1] *v* (*past tense and past part.* **sneaked** *or NAmer informal* **snuck**) **1** to go stealthily or furtively. **2** *Brit, informal* to tell somebody in authority of another's wrongdoing. **3** to put, bring, or take in a furtive or devious manner.

**sneak**[2] *n* **1** somebody who acts in a stealthy or furtive manner. **2** *Brit, informal* somebody who informs on others. **3** (*used before a noun*) done secretly or unofficially: *a sneak preview.*

**sneaker** *n chiefly NAmer* (*usu in pl*) a soft casual or sports shoe.

**sneaking** *adj* **1** not openly expressed; secret. **2** of a feeling: instinctively felt but unconfirmed.

**sneaky** *adj* unpleasantly furtive or secretive. ➤ **sneakily** *adv.*

**sneer**[1] *v* to smile or speak in a scornfully jeering manner.

**sneer**[2] *n* a sneering expression or remark.

**sneeze**[1] *v* to expel air suddenly from the nose and mouth, as a reflex caused by irritation in the nasal passages. * **not to be sneezed at** not to be underestimated.

**sneeze**[2] *n* an act or sound of sneezing.

**snick**[1] *v* to cut slightly; to nick.

**snick**[2] *n* a small cut or nick.

**snicker**[1] *v* **1** to snigger. **2** of a horse: to whinny.

**snicker**[2] *n* a snigger or whinny.

**snide** *adj* slyly disparaging or insinuating.

**sniff**[1] *v* **1** to draw air audibly up the nose. **2** to smell (something). **3** (+ out) to detect or seek.

✱ **sniff at** to regard with contempt or disdain. ➤ **sniffer** *n.*

**sniff**[2] *n* **1** an act or sound of sniffing. **2** *informal* a trace or hint.

**sniffle**[1] *v* to sniff repeatedly, e.g. when crying. ➤ **sniffler** *n.*

**sniffle**[2] *n* **1** an act or sound of sniffling. **2** a slight cold. ➤ **sniffly** *adj.*

**sniffy** *adj* (**-ier, -iest**) *informal* haughty or supercilious. ➤ **sniffily** *adv.*

**snifter** *n informal* a small drink of spirits.

**snigger**[1] *v* to laugh in a partly suppressed or derisive manner.

**snigger**[2] *n* an act or sound of sniggering.

**snip**[1] *n* **1** a small piece, *esp* one snipped off. **2** a cut made by snipping. **3** an act or sound of snipping. **4** *Brit, informal* a bargain. **5** *Brit, informal* something easy to do; a cinch. **6** (*in pl*) shears used *esp* for cutting sheet metal by hand.

**snip**[2] *v* (**snipped, snipping**) to cut with shears or scissors with short rapid strokes.

**snipe**[1] *n* (*pl* **snipes** *or* **snipe**) a wading bird with a long straight bill.

**snipe**[2] *v* **1** (*often* + at) to shoot at people from a hiding place at long range. **2** (*usu* + at) to criticize in a sly or bad-tempered manner. ➤ **sniper** *n.*

**snippet** *n* a small piece from writing or conversation.

**snitch**[1] *v* **1** *informal* to inform on somebody. **2** *informal* to steal.

**snitch**[2] *n informal* an informer.

**snivel** *v* (**snivelled, snivelling,** *NAmer* **sniveled, sniveling**) **1** to have a runny nose. **2** to complain in a whining way. ➤ **snivel** *n.*

**snob** *n* **1** somebody who looks down on social inferiors. **2** somebody with an air of superiority in matters of knowledge or taste. ➤ **snobbery** *n,* **snobbish** *adj,* **snobby** *adj.*

**snog**[1] *v* (**snogged, snogging**) *Brit, informal* to kiss and cuddle.

**snog**[2] *n informal* an act or spell of snogging.

**snood** *n* **1** a net worn at the back of a woman's head to hold the hair. **2** a knitted garment worn as a hood or scarf.

**snooker**[1] *n* **1** a game played on a billiard table with cues, a white ball, and 21 coloured balls. **2** a position of the balls in snooker in which a legal direct shot cannot be made.

**snooker**[2] *v* **1** to position the cue ball in snooker to prevent (an opponent) from making a direct shot. **2** *informal* to present an obstacle or difficulty to.

**snoop**[1] *v* to look or pry in an interfering manner. ➤ **snooper** *n.*

**snoop**[2] *n* **1** somebody who snoops. **2** an act of snooping.

**snooty** *adj* (**-ier, -iest**) *informal* snobbish or supercilious.

**snooze**[1] *v informal* to sleep lightly for a short time.

**snooze**[2] *n informal* a short light sleep.

**snore**[1] *v* to breathe with a hoarse noise during sleep.

**snore**[2] *n* an act or sound of snoring.

**snorkel** *n* a tube allowing a swimmer to breathe while under water. ➤ **snorkelling** *n.*

**snort**[1] *v* **1** to force air through the nose with a rough harsh sound. **2** *informal* to inhale (a drug).

**snort**[2] *n* **1** an act or sound of snorting. **2** *informal* a small drink of spirits. **3** *informal* an amount of a drug for inhaling.

**snot** *n informal* mucus from the nose.

**snotty** *adj* (**-ier, -iest**) *informal* **1** covered with nasal mucus. **2** arrogantly unpleasant.

**snout** *n* **1** the projecting nose of a pig or other animal. **2** *informal* a cigarette or tobacco. **3** *informal* an informer.

**snow**[1] *n* **1** ice crystals formed in the atmosphere and falling as light white flakes. **2** (*in pl*) falls of snow.

**snow**[2] *v* **1** to fall as snow. **2** (+ in/up) to shut in or block with snow. ✱ **be snowed under** to have a lot of work to do.

**snowball**[1] *n* a round mass of compressed snow.

**snowball**[2] *v* to increase or expand rapidly.

**snowboard** *n* a board resembling a short wide ski, used to slide down over snow. ➤ **snowboarder** *n,* **snowboarding** *n.*

**snowbound** *adj* confined or surrounded by snow.

**snowdrift** *n* a deep bank of snow formed by the wind.

**snowdrop** *n* a plant that bears white flowers in late winter.

**snowfall** *n* the amount of snow falling at one time or in a given period.

**snowflake** *n* a flake or crystal of snow.

**snow line** *n* the height above which land is permanently covered in snow.

**snowman** *n* (*pl* **snowmen**) a pile of snow shaped to resemble a human figure.

**snowplough** (*NAmer* **snowplow**) *n* a vehicle or device for clearing snow.

**snowshoe** *n* a flat frame attached to a boot or shoe for walking over soft snow.

**snowstorm** *n* a storm with snow driven by the wind.

**snowy** *adj* (**-ier, -iest**) **1** covered with snow. **2** white like snow.

**snub**[1] *v* (**snubbed, snubbing**) to ignore or reject (somebody) ostentatiously.

**snub**[2] *n* an act of snubbing.

**snub nose** *n* a short and slightly turned-up nose.

**snuck** *v NAmer, informal* past tense and past part. of SNEAK[1].

**snuff**[1] *v* **1** to extinguish (a flame or candle). **2** (+ out) to put a sudden end to. ✱ **snuff it** *informal* to die.

**snuff**[2] *n* powdered tobacco inhaled through the nostrils. * **up to snuff** *informal* good enough.
**snuff**[3] *v* to inhale or sniff at.
**snuffle**[1] *v* **1** to sniff audibly and repeatedly. **2** to breathe noisily through a partially blocked nose.
**snuffle**[2] *n* **1** an act or sound of snuffling. **2** (**the snuffles**) a cold in the nose. ➤ **snuffly** *adj.*
**snug**[1] *adj* (**snugger, snuggest**) **1** warm and comfortable. **2** fitting closely. ➤ **snugly** *adv.*
**snug**[2] *n Brit* a small comfortable bar in a pub.
**snuggle** *v* **1** to curl up comfortably. **2** to draw close for comfort or in affection.
**so**[1] *adv* **1** in this or the same way. **2** used as a substitute for a word or phrase: *Do you think so?* **3** correspondingly. **4** to such an extreme degree. **5** very. **6** to a limited degree: *We can only do so much.* **7** most certainly; indeed. **8** therefore; consequently. * **and so forth/and so on** and more or further. **or so** approximately. **so as to/so that** having as a purpose or result.
**so**[2] *conj* **1** with the result that. **2** in order that. **3** for that reason.
**soak**[1] *v* **1** to immerse or lie immersed in liquid. **2** to make thoroughly wet. **3** of a liquid: to spread over or pass through (something) completely. **4** (*often* + up) to absorb (a liquid, information, etc). **5** to immerse the mind and feelings of.
**soak**[2] *n* **1** an act or period of soaking. **2** *informal* a person who drinks a lot of alcohol.
**so-and-so** *n* (*pl* **so-and-sos**) **1** an unnamed or unspecified person or thing. **2** a disliked or unpleasant person.
**soap**[1] *n* **1** a substance used with water to produce a lather for washing or cleaning. **2** a soap opera. ➤ **soapy** *adj.*
**soap**[2] *v* to wash with soap.
**soapbox** *n* an improvised platform used for standing on by a speaker outdoors.
**soap opera** *n* a radio or television serial dealing with the lives of a group of characters.
**soapstone** *n* a soft stone having a soapy feel.
**soar** *v* **1** to fly or rise high into the air. **2** to increase rapidly.
**sob**[1] *v* (**sobbed, sobbing**) **1** to cry convulsively. **2** to express or utter with sobs.
**sob**[2] *n* an act or sound of sobbing.
**sober**[1] *adj* **1** not drunk. **2** serious. **3** subdued in tone or colour. ➤ **soberly** *adv.*
**sober**[2] *v* (*usu* + up) to make or become sober or serious.
**sobriety** *n* the state of being sober.
**sobriquet** /'sohbrikay/ *or* **soubriquet** /'sooh-, 'soh-/ *n* a nickname.
**so-called** *adj* commonly or wrongly named.
**soccer** *n* a football game with a round ball that must not be handled during play except by the goalkeepers.
**sociable** *adj* **1** eager to seek or enjoy companionship. **2** encouraging friendliness and good social relations. ➤ **sociability** *n,* **sociably** *adv.*
**social**[1] *adj* **1** relating to human society. **2** of or based on status in a particular society. **3** involving or promoting friendly interaction with others. **4** seeking the company of others; gregarious. **5** of animals: living and breeding in organized communities. ➤ **socially** *adv.*
**social**[2] *n* a social gathering or party.
**socialism** *n* a political theory advocating state ownership of the means of production and distribution of goods. ➤ **socialist** *adj and n.*
**socialite** *n* somebody who is active in fashionable society.
**socialize** *or* **-ise** *v* **1** to mix socially with other people. **2** to make (somebody) fit for life in society.
**social science** *n* **1** the study of human society and relationships. **2** a subject dealing with a particular aspect of this. ➤ **social scientist** *n.*
**social security** *n* a system of financial benefits provided by the state for those in need.
**social services** *pl n* public services provided by the state, e.g. education, housing, and health care.
**social worker** *n* a state employee concerned with supporting the poor, elderly, disadvantaged, etc. ➤ **social work** *n.*
**society** *n* (*pl* **-ies**) **1** the human race as a structure of social institutions. **2** a community of people with common traditions, institutions, and interests. **3** wealthy or privileged people regarded as arbiters of fashion or manners. **4** an organized group working or meeting together because of common interests, beliefs, etc. **5** companionship or association with others. ➤ **societal** *adj.*
**sociology** *n* the study of social institutions and relations. ➤ **sociological** *adj,* **sociologist** *n.*
**sock**[1] *n* a knitted covering for the foot extending above the ankle. * **pull one's socks up** *informal* to make an effort to do better.
**sock**[2] *v informal* to hit forcefully. * **sock it to** *informal* to impress with an achievement.
**sock**[3] *n informal* a forceful blow or punch.
**socket** *n* **1** an opening or hollow into which something fits. **2** an electrical device into which a plug, bulb, etc can be fitted.
**sod**[1] *n* **1** a clump of grass together with roots and soil. **2** *literary* grass-covered ground.
**sod**[2] *n Brit, informal* **1** an objectionable person. **2** a person of a specified kind: *a lucky sod.* * **sod all** *Brit, informal* nothing at all.
**soda** *n* **1** a chemical compound containing sodium. **2** soda water. **3** *chiefly NAmer* a sweet fizzy drink.
**soda water** *n* water made fizzy with carbon dioxide.

**sodden** *adj* **1** full of moisture; saturated. **2** having drunk too much alcohol: *whisky-sodden.*
**sodium** *n* a soft silver-white metallic element.
**sodium bicarbonate** *n* a white chemical compound used in baking powder and medicine.
**sodium chloride** *n* salt as a chemical compound.
**sodium hydroxide** *n* a white caustic chemical compound used in making soap, rayon, and paper.
**sod off** *v Brit, slang* to go away.
**sodomite** *n* somebody who practises sodomy.
**sodomy** *n* anal intercourse.
**sofa** *n* a long upholstered seat with a back and arms or raised ends.
**soft** *adj* **1** yielding to physical pressure. **2** easily shaped, spread, or cut. **3** smooth or delicate in texture. **4** of light or colour: not bright or glaring. **5** quiet in pitch or volume. **6** of a drink: non-alcoholic. **7** of water: free from chemical compounds that prevent lathering. **8** of a drug: not of the most addictive or harmful kind. **9** gentle or mild. **10** kind or lenient. **11** *informal* silly or foolish. **12** *informal* demanding little effort; easy. **13** of a target: not well protected; vulnerable. **14** not sharply outlined: *soft focus.* * **have a soft spot for** to be sentimentally fond of. **soft on** amorously attracted to. ➤ **softly** *adv,* **softness** *n.*
**softball** *n* a game similar to baseball played with a larger softer ball.
**soft-core** *adj* of pornography: mildly titillating and not highly explicit.
**soften** *v* **1** to make or become soft or softer. **2** (*often* + up) to reduce the strength or resistance of.
**soft-hearted** *adj* kind and understanding.
**softly-softly** *adj Brit* patient and cautious.
**soft sell** *n* the use of gentle persuasion in selling.
**soft-soap** *v informal* to persuade with flattery or guile.
**soft-top** *n* a car with a top that can be folded back.
**soft touch** *n informal* a person who is easily imposed on or taken advantage of.
**software** *n* the programs and procedures used by a computer.
**softwood** *n* the wood of a coniferous tree.
**soggy** *adj* (**-ier, -iest**) **1** soaked or waterlogged. **2** heavy and damp.
**soil**[1] *n* **1** the upper layer of the surface of the earth, in which plants grow. **2** a nation's territory or land. **3** (**the soil**) agriculture.
**soil**[2] *v* **1** to make or become dirty. **2** to blacken or tarnish (a reputation).
**soiree** *or* **soirée** /'swahray/ *n* (*pl* **soirees** *or* **soirées**) an evening party or reception.
**sojourn**[1] *n formal* a temporary stay.
**sojourn**[2] *v formal* to stay temporarily.
**solace**[1] *n* consolation or comfort in grief or difficulty.
**solace**[2] *v* to give comfort to.
**solar** *adj* relating to the sun or its light or heat.
**solar cell** *n* a device that converts sunlight into electrical energy.
**solar eclipse** *n* an eclipse in which the moon wholly or partially obscures the sun.
**solarium** *n* (*pl* **solaria** *or* **solariums**) a room equipped with sunbeds, sunlamps, etc.
**solar panel** *n* a collection of solar cells providing energy.
**solar plexus** *n* a network of nerves in the abdomen behind the stomach.
**solar system** *n* the sun together with the planets and other bodies that revolve round it.
**sold** *v* past tense and past part. of SELL.
**solder**[1] *n* a soft alloy used to join metal surfaces.
**solder**[2] *v* to join with solder.
**soldering iron** *n* an electrical device for melting and applying solder.
**soldier**[1] *n* **1** a person who is serving in an army. **2** an enlisted man or woman. ➤ **soldierly** *adj.*
**soldier**[2] *v* **1** to serve as a soldier. **2** (+ on) to persevere.
**soldier of fortune** *n* a mercenary.
**soldiery** *n* (*pl* **-ies**) a body of soldiers.
**sole**[1] *n* the underside of the foot, or of a shoe or boot.
**sole**[2] *v* to provide (a shoe) with a sole.
**sole**[3] *n* (*pl* **soles** *or* **sole**) a sea flatfish used for food.
**sole**[4] *adj* **1** being the only one; only. **2** belonging or relating to one individual or group only. ➤ **solely** *adv.*
**solecism** /'solisiz(ə)m/ *n* **1** a minor grammatical error. **2** a breach of etiquette.
**solemn** *adj* **1** said or done formally. **2** marked by established form or ceremony. **3** serious. **4** sombre or gloomy. ➤ **solemnly** *adv.*
**solemnity** *n* (*pl* **-ies**) **1** the state of being solemn. **2** formal or ceremonious observance. **3** a solemn event or occasion.
**solemnize** *or* **-ise** *v* **1** to observe with solemnity. **2** to perform (a marriage) with ceremony. **3** to make solemn or serious.
**solenoid** /'solənoyd/ *n* a coil of wire that produces a magnetic field when an electric current passes through it. ➤ **solenoidal** *adj.*
**solicit** *v* (**solicited, soliciting**) **1** to make a formal request to. **2** to try to obtain by formal request. **3** to approach (somebody) to be a prostitute's client. ➤ **solicitation** *n.*
**solicitor** *n* a qualified lawyer who advises clients, represents them in the lower courts, and prepares cases for barristers to try in the higher courts.
**solicitous** *adj* showing care or concern about somebody. ➤ **solicitously** *adv.*
**solicitude** *n* care or concern.

**solid**[1] *adj* **1** without an internal cavity. **2** having no opening or division. **3** having a single substance or character. **4** three-dimensional. **5** retaining shape without needing external support. **6** hard, dense, or compact. **7** without break or interruption. **8** reliable or sound; of good quality. **9** united or unanimous. ➤ **solidity** *n*, **solidly** *adv.*

**solid**[2] *n* **1** a solid substance. **2** (*in pl*) solid food. **3** a three-dimensional figure.

**solidarity** *n* unity based on shared interests, objectives, and standards.

**solidify** *v* (**-ies, -ied**) to make or become solid. ➤ **solidification** *n.*

**solid-state** *adj* **1** relating to semiconductors. **2** using the electric or magnetic properties of solid materials and not thermionic valves.

**soliloquy** *n* (*pl* **-ies**) a speech expressing thoughts aloud while alone, especially on stage.

**solipsism** *n* the belief that the self is the only thing that can be known to exist. ➤ **solipsist** *n*, **solipsistic** *adj.*

**solitaire** *n* **1** a game for one person in which pieces are removed from a board by jumping one over another until only one piece remains. **2** *NAmer* = PATIENCE 2. **3** a single gem set alone in a ring.

**solitary** *adj* **1** liking to be alone. **2** lonely. **3** done or used by itself. **4** single; sole. **5** of a place: unfrequented or remote.

**solitary confinement** *n* the isolation of a prisoner as a punishment.

**solitude** *n* the state of being alone.

**solo**[1] *n* (*pl* **solos** *or* **soli**) **1** a musical composition, song, or dance for one performer. **2** a flight by one person alone in an aircraft. ➤ **soloist** *n.*

**solo**[2] *adj and adv* done or performed by one person.

**solo**[3] *v* (**soloes, soloed, soloing**) to perform or fly solo.

**so long** *interj informal* goodbye.

**solstice** *n* each of two occasions each year when the sun is furthest from the celestial equator and highest or lowest in the sky at noon.

**soluble** *adj* **1** of a substance: able to be dissolved in liquid. **2** capable of being solved. ➤ **solubility** *n.*

**solution** *n* **1** an answer to a problem. **2** the means or process of solving a problem. **3** a mixture formed when a substance is distributed in a solvent.

**solve** *v* to find an answer to or explanation for (a problem, mystery, etc).

**solvent**[1] *adj* **1** having enough money to pay all debts. **2** of a substance: able to dissolve other substances. ➤ **solvency** *n.*

**solvent**[2] *n* a liquid that is capable of dissolving other substances.

**sombre** (*NAmer* **somber**) *adj* **1** dark and gloomy. **2** of a dull or dark colour. **3** serious or grave. ➤ **sombrely** *adv.*

**sombrero** *n* (*pl* **-os**) a felt or straw hat with a wide brim.

**some**[1] *adj* **1** unspecified in amount or number. **2** unknown or unspecified. **3** being an unspecified member of a class. **4** appreciable or considerable. **5** *chiefly informal* striking or excellent.

**some**[2] *pron* some part, amount, or number but not all.

**some**[3] *adv* approximately; about.

**somebody** *pron* some person.

**some day** *adv* at some future time.

**somehow** *adv* **1** by some unknown means. **2** no matter how. **3** for some unknown reason.

**someone** *pron* some person.

**someplace** *adv NAmer* somewhere.

**somersault**[1] *n* a movement in which a person turns forward or backward in a complete revolution bringing the feet over the head.

**somersault**[2] *v* to perform a somersault.

**something**[1] *pron* **1** some unspecified or unknown thing. **2** a certain amount.

**something**[2] *adv* in some degree; somewhat.

**sometime**[1] *adv* at some unknown or unspecified time.

**sometime**[2] *adj* having been formerly.

**sometimes** *adv* at intervals; occasionally.

**somewhat** *adv* to some degree.

**somewhere**[1] *adv* **1** in or to some unknown or unspecified place. **2** at an unspecified point.

**somewhere**[2] *n* an unspecified place.

**somnambulist** *n* somebody who walks in their sleep. ➤ **somnambulism** *n.*

**somnolent** *adj* **1** sleepy; drowsy. **2** tending to induce sleep. ➤ **somnolence** *n.*

**son** *n* **1** a boy or man having the relation of child to parent. **2** a male descendant. **3** (**Son** *or* **the Son**) the second person of the Trinity.

**sonar** *n* a system for detecting an object under water by means of reflected sound waves.

**sonata** *n* a musical composition for one instrument, often with piano accompaniment.

**son et lumière** *n* an entertainment held in the dark at a noteworthy site, with lighting and recorded sound to describe its history.

**song** *n* **1** a set of words sung to a musical tune. **2** the act of singing. **3** the melodious sounds made by birds and some other animals. **4** *literary* poetry or a poem. ✱ **for a song** for very little money. **on song** *Brit, informal* performing well.

**song and dance** *n Brit, informal* a fuss or commotion.

**songbird** *n* a bird that utters musical tones.

**songster** *n* a skilled singer or writer of songs.

**sonic** *adj* using or relating to sound waves. ➤ **sonically** *adv.*

**sonic boom** *n* an explosive sound produced by an aircraft travelling at supersonic speed.

**son-in-law** *n* (*pl* **sons-in-law**) the husband of one's daughter.

**sonnet** *n* a poem of 14 lines having a fixed rhyme scheme.

**sonorous** *adj* **1** pleasantly rich or deep in sound. **2** impressive in effect or style. ➤ **sonority** *n*, **sonorously** *adv*.

**soon** *adv* **1** after a short time. **2** promptly. **3** in comparisons: rather: *I'd sooner stay here.* ✱ **sooner or later** eventually.

**soot** *n* a fine black powder formed by the incomplete burning of coal or other organic matter. ➤ **sooty** *adj*.

**soothe** *v* **1** to calm (somebody) by comforting. **2** to relieve (pain). ➤ **soothing** *adj*.

**soothsayer** *n* somebody who predicts the future.

**sop**[1] *n* something offered or done as a concession or appeasement.

**sop**[2] *v* (**sopped, sopping**) (*usu* + up) to mop up (liquid).

**sophism** *n* a false or deceptive argument.

**sophist** *n* a person who uses false or deceptive reasoning. ➤ **sophistic** *adj*.

**sophisticate** *n* a sophisticated person.

**sophisticated** *adj* **1** highly developed or complex. **2** having refined tastes; cultured. **3** intellectually subtle or refined. ➤ **sophistication** *n*.

**sophistry** *n* (*pl* **-ies**) plausible but unsound reasoning.

**sophomore** *n NAmer* a second-year student at university or high school.

**soporific** *adj* tending to cause sleep.

**sopping** *adj* wet through; soaking.

**soppy** *adj* (**-ier, -iest**) *informal* **1** weakly sentimental; mawkish. **2** *chiefly Brit, informal* feeble or silly. ➤ **soppily** *adv*, **soppiness** *n*.

**soprano** *n* (*pl* **-os**) a female singer with the highest singing voice.

**sorbet** *n* a water ice.

**sorcerer** *or* **sorceress** *n* a man or woman who uses magic. ➤ **sorcery** *n*.

**sordid** *adj* **1** dirty or squalid. **2** base or immoral. ➤ **sordidly** *adv*.

**sore**[1] *adj* **1** causing or suffering pain. **2** painful or tender. **3** severe; urgent. **4** *chiefly NAmer* angry or upset. ➤ **soreness** *n*.

**sore**[2] *n* a painful area on the body.

**sore**[3] *adv archaic* greatly or extremely.

**sorely** *adv* much; extremely.

**sore point** *n* a cause of irritation or distress.

**sorghum** *n* a tropical grass similar to maize.

**sorority** *n* (*pl* **-ies**) a club for female students at some US universities.

**sorrel** *n* **1** a plant with bitter-flavoured leaves eaten in salads. **2** a brownish orange to light brown colour.

**sorrow**[1] *n* **1** deep distress caused by a loss or failure. **2** a cause of sorrow.

**sorrow**[2] *v* to feel or express sorrow.

**sorry** *adj* (**-ier, -iest**) **1** full of regret or pity. **2** inspiring sorrow, pity, or scorn. **3** bad or regrettable.

**sort**[1] *n* **1** a group having some common characteristic; a class or kind. **2** *informal* a person: *a cheerful sort.* **3** a process of arranging in a certain order. ✱ **out of sorts** slightly unwell or disgruntled. **sort of** *informal* somewhat; in a way.

**sort**[2] *v* to arrange in order or in groups. ➤ **sortable** *adj*, **sorter** *n*.

**sorted** *adj Brit, informal* **1** organized or ready. **2** emotionally well-adjusted.

**sortie** *n* **1** a sudden attack by troops from a defensive position. **2** a mission or attack by one aircraft. **3** a brief trip to an unfamiliar place.

**sort out** *v* **1** to deal with (a difficulty) effectively. **2** to separate from a mass or group. **3** to clear up or tidy.

**SOS** *n* **1** an internationally recognized signal of distress. **2** a call for help.

**so-so** *adj* neither very good nor very bad.

**sot** *n* a habitual drunkard. ➤ **sottish** *adj*.

**sotto voce** *adv and adj* in a quiet voice.

**soubriquet** *n* see SOBRIQUET.

**soufflé** *n* a light fluffy baked dish made by folding egg yolks into stiffly beaten whites.

**sought** *v* past tense and past part. of SEEK.

**sought-after** *adj* much in demand.

**souk** *n* an open-air market in an Arab country.

**soul** *n* **1** the spiritual part of a human being, believed by some to be immortal. **2** the essential character of a person, group, or thing. **3** emotional sensitivity or depth. **4** a person: *a dear old soul.* **5** exemplification or personification: *the soul of tact.* **6** a kind of music originating in black American gospel singing, characterized by intensity of feeling.

**soul-destroying** *adj esp* of a task, job, etc: very dull and uninteresting.

**soulful** *adj* expressing intense feeling. ➤ **soulfully** *adv*.

**soulless** *adj* **1** lacking sensitivity or compassion. **2** bleak or uninviting.

**soul mate** *n* a person with whom one has a close affinity.

**soul-searching** *n* close scrutiny of one's feelings and motives.

**sound**[1] *n* **1** the sensation perceived by the sense of hearing, caused by vibrations travelling through the air. **2** something heard; a noise or tone. **3** an impression conveyed by being heard. **4** recorded sounds or radio broadcasting. ➤ **soundless** *adj*.

**sound**[2] *v* **1** to make or cause to make a sound. **2** to give a specified impression; to seem. **3** to test the condition of (the chest or lungs) by tapping.

**sound**[3] *adj* **1** healthy or in good condition. **2** free from error or fallacy. **3** having good knowledge and judgment. **4** financially secure. **5** of sleep: deep and undisturbed. **6** thorough or severe. ➤ **soundly** *adv,* **soundness** *n.*

**sound**[4] *n* a long passage of water connecting two larger bodies or separating a mainland and an island.

**sound**[5] *v* **1** to measure the depth of (water). **2** to explore (a body cavity) with a probe.

**sound barrier** *n* the point at which an aircraft nears the speed of sound.

**sound bite** *n* a short pithy or apt excerpt from a speech or statement.

**sound effect** *n* a sound other than speech or music used to create an effect in a play, film, etc.

**sounding** *n* **1** the act of measuring the depth of water. **2** a measurement taken by sounding. **3** (*also in pl*) a test or sampling of opinion.

**sounding board** *n* someone whose reaction serves as a test for new ideas.

**sound off** *v informal* to voice opinions freely and vigorously.

**sound out** *v* to seek the views or intentions of.

**soundproof**[1] *adj* preventing or minimizing the penetration of sound.

**soundproof**[2] *v* to make soundproof.

**sound track** *n* the dialogue and sounds accompanying a film.

**sound wave** *n* a wave by which sound is transmitted.

**soup** *n* a liquid food made from stock and often containing pieces of solid food. * **in the soup** *informal* in an awkward predicament.

**soupçon** /'soohpson, 'soohpsonh/ *n* a very small amount of something.

**soup kitchen** *n* a place where free food is provided for the poor or homeless.

**soup up** *v informal* to increase the power of (an engine or car).

**sour**[1] *adj* **1** having an acid taste like vinegar or lemons. **2** rancid or rotten. **3** disenchanted or embittered. ➤ **sourly** *adv,* **sourness** *n.*

**sour**[2] *v* to make or become sour.

**source**[1] *n* **1** a place, person, or thing from which something is obtained. **2** an origin or cause. **3** the point of origin of a river or stream. **4** a person, publication, etc that supplies information.

**source**[2] *v* **1** to obtain (materials or components) for a manufacturing process. **2** to trace to a source.

**sour cream** *n* cream made sour with added bacteria.

**sour grapes** *pl n* an attitude of disparagement towards something one is unable to have or achieve oneself.

**sourpuss** *n informal* a bitter or bad-tempered person.

**souse** *v* **1** to pickle. **2** to plunge in liquid. **3** to drench or saturate.

**south**[1] *n* **1** the direction 90° clockwise from east. **2** regions or countries lying to the south. ➤ **southbound** *adj and adv.*

**south**[2] *adj and adv* **1** at or towards the south. **2** of the wind: blowing from the south.

**southeast**[1] *n* **1** the direction between south and east. **2** regions lying to the southeast. ➤ **southeastern** *adj.*

**southeast**[2] *adj and adv* **1** at or towards the southeast. **2** of the wind: blowing from the southeast.

**southeasterly** *adj and adv* **1** in a southeastern position or direction. **2** of a wind: blowing from the southeast.

**southerly** *adj and adv* **1** in a southern position or direction. **2** of a wind: blowing from the south.

**southern** *adj* in or towards the south.

**Southerner** *n* (*also* **southerner**) a person from the southern part of a country.

**southpaw** *n* **1** a left-handed boxer who leads with the right hand and guards with the left. **2** *chiefly NAmer* a left-handed person.

**southward** *adj and adv* towards the south; in a direction going south. ➤ **southwards** *adv.*

**southwest**[1] *n* **1** the direction between south and west. **2** regions lying to the southwest. ➤ **southwestern** *adj.*

**southwest**[2] *adj and adv* **1** at or towards the southwest. **2** of the wind: blowing from the southwest.

**southwesterly** *adj and adv* **1** in a southwestern position or direction. **2** of a wind: blowing from the southwest.

**souvenir** *n* something one keeps as a reminder of a person, place, or event.

**sou'wester** *n* a waterproof hat with a brim extended at the back.

**sovereign**[1] *n* **1** somebody possessing supreme power, *esp* a king or queen. **2** a former British gold coin worth one pound.

**sovereign**[2] *adj* **1** possessing supreme power. **2** of a country: politically independent.

**sovereignty** *n* (*pl* **-ies**) **1** supreme power over a politically organized body. **2** freedom from external influence or control. **3** an autonomous state.

**soviet** *n* **1** an elected council in the former USSR. **2** (**Soviets**) the people of the former USSR. ➤ **Soviet** *adj.*

**sow**[1] /sow/ *n* an adult female pig.

**sow**[2] /soh/ *v* (*past part.* **sown** *or* **sowed**) **1** to put (seed) in the ground to grow into plants. **2** to plant (an area) with seed. **3** to implant or initiate (something unwelcome). ➤ **sower** *n.*

**soya bean** (*NAmer* **soybean**) *n* a bean high in protein, obtained from an Asian plant.

**soy sauce** *n* a sauce made from fermented soya beans.

**sozzled** *adj informal* very drunk.

**spa** *n* **1** a spring of mineral water. **2** a resort with mineral springs.

**space**[1] *n* **1** the three-dimensional extent in which objects and events occur and have position. **2** the region beyond the earth's atmosphere. **3** a continuous unoccupied area or volume. **4** an amount of room set apart or available for something. **5** freedom for personal development and fulfilment. **6** a period of time. **7** a blank area separating words or lines on a page.

**space**[2] *v* (*often* + out) to place (two or more things) at intervals or with space between them.

**spacecraft** *n* (*pl* **spacecraft**) a vehicle for travelling beyond the earth's atmosphere.

**spaced out** *adj informal* dazed or stupefied.

**spaceman** *or* **spacewoman** *n* (*pl* **spacemen** *or* **spacewomen**) a man or woman who travels in space.

**spaceship** *n* a manned spacecraft.

**space shuttle** *n* a vehicle for making repeated journeys into space and back to earth.

**space station** *n* a manned artificial satellite serving as a base for manned travel in space.

**space suit** *n* a suit equipped to make life in space possible for an astronaut.

**spacial** *adj* see SPATIAL.

**spacious** *adj* containing ample space; roomy.

**spade** *n* a digging implement with a flat metal blade and a long handle. ✱ **call a spade a spade** to speak frankly and plainly. **in spades** *informal* in the extreme.

**spades** *pl n* the suit in a pack of playing cards that is marked with black heart-shaped figures.

**spadework** *n* hard or routine preparatory work.

**spaghetti** *pl n* pasta in thin solid strings.

**spake** *v archaic* past tense of SPEAK.

**Spam** *n trademark* tinned meat made from pork and ham.

**spam** *n* unsolicited email messages sent to multiple addresses.

**span**[1] *n* **1** an extent or distance from one side to the other. **2** a length of time. **3** the full reach or extent. **4** a part of a bridge between supports. **5** the distance from the end of the thumb to the end of the little finger of a spread hand.

**span**[2] *v* (**spanned, spanning**) to extend across.

**spangle** *n* **1** a sequin. **2** a small glittering object or particle. ➤ **spangly** *adj.*

**Spaniard** *n* a native or inhabitant of Spain.

**spaniel** *n* a dog of a breed with short legs, long wavy hair, and large drooping ears.

**Spanish** *n* the chief language of Spain and many Central and South American countries. ➤ **Spanish** *adj.*

**spank**[1] *v* to slap on the buttocks with the open hand or something flat.

**spank**[2] *n* a slap or a series of slaps.

**spanking**[1] *adj* **1** vigorous or brisk. **2** remarkable or striking.

**spanking**[2] *n* a series of spanks.

**spanner** *n Brit* a tool shaped for turning nuts or bolts. ✱ **spanner in the works** *informal* an obstruction or hindrance to a plan or operation.

**spar**[1] *n* **1** a stout pole. **2** a thick bar or pole used to support the sail of a ship.

**spar**[2] *v* (**sparred, sparring**) **1** to box without putting full force into the blows. **2** to argue or wrangle.

**spar**[3] *n* a sparring match or session.

**spare**[1] *adj* **1** not in use. **2** in excess of what is required; surplus. **3** plain and unelaborate. **4** healthily lean or thin. ✱ **go spare** *Brit, informal* to become extremely angry.

**spare**[2] *v* **1** to make available for use by others. **2** to refrain from killing or harming. **3** to refrain from using. **4** to relieve of the need to experience something unpleasant. ✱ **spare no expense** to pay whatever is needed.

**spare**[3] *n* **1** a spare or duplicate item or part, e.g. for a machine or vehicle. **2** a spare tyre.

**sparerib** *n* a pork rib with most of the meat removed for bacon.

**spare tyre** *n* **1** an extra tyre carried by a motor vehicle. **2** *informal* a roll of fat at the waist.

**sparing** *adj* not wasteful; frugal. ➤ **sparingly** *adv.*

**spark**[1] *n* **1** a small burning particle thrown out by something on fire or left among its ashes. **2** a luminous electrical discharge of short duration. **3** a sparkle or flash. **4** something that starts an event or development. **5** a trace that may develop.

**spark**[2] *v* **1** to produce or give off sparks. **2** (+ off) to prompt or precipitate (something).

**sparking plug** *n* = SPARK PLUG.

**sparkle**[1] *v* **1** to give off or reflect glittering points of light. **2** to show brilliance or animation.

**sparkle**[2] *n* **1** a little spark or flash of light. **2** liveliness and fun. ➤ **sparkly** *adj.*

**sparkler** *n* a hand-held firework that gives out sparks.

**spark plug** *n* a device that produces the electric spark to ignite the fuel in an internal-combustion engine.

**sparrow** *n* a small dull-coloured songbird.

**sparrow hawk** *n* a small hawk that preys on smaller birds.

**sparse** *adj* few and scattered; not thickly grown or settled. ➤ **sparsely** *adv,* **sparseness** *n.*

**spartan** *adj* not comfortable or pleasant; austere.

**spasm** *n* **1** an involuntary muscular contraction. **2** a sudden strong effort or emotion.

**spasmodic** *adj* occurring unpredictably at intervals. ➤ **spasmodically** *adv.*

**spastic**[1] *adj* **1** of or characterized by spasm. **2** *dated, offensive* affected by cerebral palsy. ➤ **spasticity** *n.*

**spastic**[2] *n dated, offensive* somebody who has cerebral palsy.

**spat**[1] *v* past tense and past part. of SPIT[1].

**spat**[2] *n* a cloth or leather gaiter covering the instep and ankle.

**spat**[3] *n informal* a petty quarrel or disagreement.

**spat**[4] *v* (**spatted, spatting**) to quarrel pettily.

**spate** *n* **1** a large number or amount in a short space of time. **2** a state of flood.

**spathe** *n* a sheath enclosing the cluster of flowers on some plants.

**spatial** *or* **spacial** *adj* relating to or occurring in space. ➤ **spatially** *adv.*

**spatter**[1] *v* (**spattered, spattering**) **1** to splash or sprinkle with drops of liquid. **2** to scatter by splashing or sprinkling. **3** to spurt out in scattered drops.

**spatter**[2] *n* the act or sound of spattering.

**spatula** *n* an implement with a thin flat blade, used for spreading, mixing, etc.

**spawn**[1] *v* **1** of a water animal: to produce or deposit (eggs). **2** to produce abundantly.

**spawn**[2] *n* eggs produced by frogs, oysters, fish, etc.

**spay** *v* to remove the ovaries of (a female animal).

**speak** *v* **1** to utter words with the voice. **2** to make a speech. **3** to use or be able to use (a language) for oral communication. **4** to be indicative or suggestive of. ✱ **speak one's mind** to say frankly what one thinks. **speak volumes** to communicate or reveal a great deal.

**speakeasy** *n* (*pl* **-ies**) *informal* a place where alcoholic drinks were illegally sold during Prohibition in the USA.

**speaker** *n* **1** somebody who speaks, *esp* in public. **2** somebody who speaks a specified language. **3** the presiding officer of a legislative assembly. **4** a loudspeaker.

**speak out** *v* to speak loudly or boldly; to state one's opinion frankly.

**speak up** *v* **1** to speak more loudly. **2** to state one's opinion frankly. **3** (+ for) to speak in defence of.

**spear**[1] *n* a weapon with a long shaft and pointed head, for thrusting or throwing.

**spear**[2] *v* to pierce or strike with a spear.

**spear**[3] *n* a young blade or sprout of asparagus or broccoli.

**spearhead**[1] *n* a leading element or force in a development or course of action.

**spearhead**[2] *v* to lead (an attack or initiative).

**spearmint** *n* a common mint grown for its aromatic oil.

**spec**[1] *n* ✱ **on spec** *informal* in the hope of finding or obtaining something wanted.

**spec**[2] *n informal* a specification or description.

**special**[1] *adj* **1** superior or distinguished in some way from others. **2** held in particular esteem. **3** other than or in addition to the usual. **4** meant for particular purpose or need.

**special**[2] *n* **1** a special person or thing. **2** a dish in a restaurant that is not on the regular menu. **3** a special offer in a shop.

**Special Branch** *n* in Britain, the branch of the police force concerned with political security.

**special constable** *n Brit* somebody trained as an extra policeman for particular circumstances.

**special effects** *pl n* unusual visual or sound effects introduced into a film or television recording by special processing.

**specialist** *n* somebody who specializes in a special field or branch of knowledge. ➤ **specialism** *n.*

**speciality** (*NAmer* **specialty**) *n* (*pl* **-ies**) **1** a special aptitude or skill. **2** a particular occupation or branch of knowledge. **3** a product, service, etc that a person or place specializes in.

**specialize** *or* **-ise** *v* **1** (*often* + in) to concentrate on a special activity or field. **2** to adapt to a particular mode of life or environment. ➤ **specialization** *n.*

**specialized** *or* **-ised** *adj* designed for a specific purpose or occupation.

**specially** *adv* **1** for a particular purpose. **2** in a special way.

**special pleading** *n* an argument that ignores the damaging or unfavourable aspects of a case.

**species** *n* (*pl* **species**) **1** a class of organisms having common attributes and designated by a common name. **2** a kind or sort.

**specific** *adj* **1** clearly and individually identified. **2** free from ambiguity; explicit or particular. **3** (*usu* + to) confined to a particular individual, group, or circumstance. **4** having a particular rather than a general influence. ➤ **specifically** *adv.*

**specification** *n* **1** the act of specifying. **2** a detailed description of the structure and design of something. **3** a standard required in the workmanship and materials used in making something.

**specifics** *pl n* the exact particulars.

**specify** *v* (**-ies, -ied**) **1** to identify clearly and individually. **2** to state explicitly or in detail.

**specimen** *n* **1** an item or part typical of a group or whole. **2** a sample taken for medical examination. **3** an individual typical of a particular category. **4** *informal* a person of a partiuclar kind: *an unfortunate specimen.*

**specious** *adj* **1** seeming to be persuasive or sound but in fact wrong. **2** having a deceptive attraction or fascination.

**speck**[1] *n* **1** a small spot or blemish. **2** a small particle.

**speck**[2] *v* to mark with specks.

**speckle**[1] *n* a little speck of colour.

**speckle**[2] *v* to mark with speckles. ➤ **speckled** *adj.*

**specs** *pl n informal* spectacles.
**spectacle** *n* a striking or dramatic public display or show.
**spectacles** *pl n* a pair of glasses.
**spectacular**[1] *adj* extremely impressive or exciting. ➤ **spectacularly** *adv.*
**spectacular**[2] *n* a spectacular display or show.
**spectate** *v* to be a spectator.
**spectator** *n* **1** somebody who attends a show or sports event. **2** an onlooker.
**spectral** *adj* **1** of or suggesting a spectre. **2** of or made by a spectrum.
**spectre** (*NAmer* **specter**) *n* **1** a visible ghost. **2** something that haunts the mind.
**spectrum** *n* (*pl* **spectra**) **1** the series of colours produced when a beam of white light is dispersed by a prism or in a rainbow. **2** the range of light in the order of wavelengths. **3** the entire range of wavelengths or frequencies of electromagnetic radiation or of any particular type of it. **4** an interrelated sequence or range.
**speculate** *v* **1** to form an opinion or theory without definite evidence. **2** to assume a business risk in the hope of gain. ➤ **speculation** *n,* **speculator** *n.*
**speculative** *adj* **1** involving speculation rather than firm evidence. **2** questioning or enquiring. ➤ **speculatively** *adv.*
**speech** *n* **1** the expression of thoughts in spoken words. **2** a public discourse or address. **3** a group of lines to be spoken by a character in a play.
**speechify** *v* (**-ies, -ied**) to make a speech in a pompous manner.
**speechless** *adj* unable to speak, from anger or revulsion.
**speech therapy** *n* therapy for people who have problems with speaking. ➤ **speech therapist** *n.*
**speed**[1] *n* **1** the act or state of moving swiftly. **2** rate at which something moves. **3** rate of performance or execution. **4** the sensitivity to light of a photographic film. **5** each of the gear ratios of a bicycle. **6** *slang* an amphetamine drug. ✱ **at speed** while moving fast.
**speed**[2] *v* (*past tense and past part.* **sped** *or* **speeded**) **1** to move or go quickly. **2** to travel at excessive or illegal speed. **3** *archaic* to meet with success or prosperity.
**speedboat** *n* a fast motorboat.
**speed dating** *n* a dating system in which people gather together to spend a few minutes with each of many potential partners before choosing one or more dates.
**speedometer** *n* an instrument for indicating a vehicle's speed.
**speed up** *v* to move or work more quickly.
**speedway** *n* **1** an oval racecourse for motorcycles. **2** the sport of racing motorcycles.
**speedy** *adj* (**-ier, -iest**) swift or quick. ➤ **speedily** *adv,* **speediness** *n.*
**spell**[1] *n* **1** a spoken word or form of words held to have magic power. **2** a state of enchantment. **3** a compelling influence or attraction.
**spell**[2] *v* (*past tense and past part.* **spelt** *or* **spelled**) **1** to name or write the letters of (a word) in order. **2** of letters: to form (a word). **3** to amount to or mean (something).
**spell**[3] *n* a short period or phase.
**spellbind** *v* (*past tense and past part.* **spellbound**) to hold the entire attention of. ➤ **spellbinding** *adj.*
**spellchecker** *n* a computer program that checks the spelling of words in a document.
**spelling** *n* **1** the forming of words from letters. **2** the sequence of letters that make up a word.
**spell out** *v* to explain clearly and in detail.
**spend**[1] *v* (*past tense and past part.* **spent**) **1** to use or pay out (money). **2** to wear out; to exhaust. **3** to cause or permit (time) to elapse. ✱ **spend a penny** *Brit, informal, euphem* to urinate. ➤ **spender** *n.*
**spend**[2] *n informal* an amount of money spent.
**spendthrift** *n* somebody who spends carelessly or wastefully.
**sperm** *n* (*pl* **sperms** *or* **sperm**) **1** the male fertilizing fluid. **2** a spermatozoon.
**spermatozoon** /ˌspuhmətəˈzoh·ən/ *n* (*pl* **spermatozoa**) a male gamete, which fertilizes a female egg.
**spermicide** *n* a contraceptive that kills sperm. ➤ **spermicidal** *adj.*
**sperm whale** *n* a large toothed whale with a blunt head.
**spew**[1] *v* **1** to vomit. **2** to eject or be ejected in great quantity.
**spew**[2] *n* vomit.
**sphagnum** *n* a moss that grows in wet acid areas, e.g. bogs.
**sphere** *n* **1** a space or solid enclosed by a surface, all points of which are the same distance from the centre. **2** an area of knowledge or interest.
**spherical** *adj* having the form of a sphere. ➤ **spherically** *adv.*
**sphincter** *n* a muscular ring surrounding a bodily opening.
**sphinx** *n* (*pl* **sphinxes** *or* **sphinges**) an ancient Egyptian image in the form of a lion with a human head.
**spice**[1] *n* **1** a vegetable product, e.g. pepper, ginger, or nutmeg, used to season or flavour foods. **2** something that adds excitement or enjoyment.
**spice**[2] *v* **1** to season with spice. **2** (*often* + up) to add zest or relish to.
**spick-and-span** *or* **spic-and-span** *adj* spotlessly clean and tidy.
**spicy** *adj* (**-ier, -iest**) **1** having the strong flavour of spice. **2** strongly seasoned with spices. **3** somewhat indecent. ➤ **spicily** *adv,* **spiciness** *n.*

**spider** *n* a small invertebrate animal with eight legs, which makes webs for trapping its prey.

**spiel** *n informal* a glib line of talk designed to influence or persuade.

**spiffing** *adj Brit, informal, dated* extremely good; excellent.

**spigot** *n* **1** a small plug or tap to stop up a cask. **2** a projection on the end of a piece of piping that fits into the next piece.

**spike**[1] *n* **1** a thin pointed object or projection. **2** a metal projection set in the sole and heel of a running shoe to improve its grip. ➤ **spiky** *adj.*

**spike**[2] *v* **1** to pierce with a spike. **2** to add spirits or a drug secretly to (drink or food).

**spike**[3] *n* **1** a cluster of flowers growing directly from a single stem. **2** an ear of grain.

**spill**[1] *v* (*past tense and past part.* **spilt** *or* **spilled**) **1** to flow or cause to flow out of a container so as to be lost or wasted. **2** to cause (blood) to be shed. **3** to flow or empty out of something. **4** to spread beyond a limit; to overflow. **5** *informal* to divulge (information). ✻ **spill the beans** *informal* to divulge information indiscreetly. ➤ **spillage** *n.*

**spill**[2] *n* **1** a quantity of liquid spilt. **2** a fall from a horse or vehicle.

**spill**[3] *n* a thin strip of paper or wood for lighting a fire.

**spin**[1] *v* (**spinning,** *past tense and past part.* **spun**) **1** to revolve rapidly; to whirl. **2** of wheels: to revolve rapidly without gripping. **3** of a ball: to revolve in the air and deviate from a straight line on bouncing. **4** to feel dizzy or faint. **5** to draw out and twist fibre into yarn or thread. **6** of a spider, silkworm,etc: to form (a web or silk) by sending out a sticky liquid in threads. **7** to dry (clothes) in a spin-drier. **8** to tell (a long involved tale). **9** *informal* to present (information, news, etc) in a way that creates a favourable impression.

**spin**[2] *n* **1** the act of spinning. **2** *informal* a particular interpretation or slant given to a piece of information. **3** *informal* a short excursion. ✻ **in a spin** *informal* in a state of mental confusion.

**spina bifida** *n* a congenital defect in the formation of the spine, allowing part of it to be exposed.

**spinach** *n* a plant with large dark green leaves used as a vegetable.

**spinal** *adj* in the region of the backbone.

**spinal column** *n* the elongated structure of bone running from the head to the lower back and enclosing the spinal cord.

**spinal cord** *n* the cord of nervous tissue enclosed in the spinal column.

**spindle** *n* **1** a round stick with tapered ends used to form and twist the yarn in hand spinning. **2** a pin or axis round which something turns.

**spindly** *adj* (**-ier, -iest**) unnaturally tall or slender in appearance.

**spin doctor** *n informal* an official employed by a political party or individual to present information in the most favourable light.

**spin-drier** *or* **spin-dryer** *n* a machine that dries clothes by spinning them in a drum.

**spindrift** *n* sea spray.

**spine** *n* **1** the spinal column. **2** something forming a central axis or chief support. **3** the back of a book, holding the pages together. **4** a stiff pointed part of a plant or animal. ➤ **spiny** *adj.*

**spine-chiller** *n* a book, film, etc with a sinister terrifying theme.

**spine-chilling** *adj* exciting and terrifying.

**spineless** *adj* **1** having no spinal column. **2** lacking strength of character. **3** free from spines.

**spinet** *n* a small harpsichord.

**spinnaker** *n* a large triangular sail set forward of a yacht's mast and used when running before the wind.

**spinney** *n* (*pl* **-eys**) *Brit* a small wood with undergrowth.

**spinning wheel** *n* a machine for spinning yarn or thread by means of a spindle driven by a hand- or foot-operated wheel.

**spin-off** *n* **1** a by-product. **2** something which is a further development of some idea or product.

**spin out** *v* **1** to cause to last longer. **2** to extend or prolong.

**spinster** *n* an unmarried woman past the usual age for marriage. ➤ **spinsterhood** *n.*

**spiral**[1] *adj* winding round a centre or pole in a continuous curve. ➤ **spirally** *adv.*

**spiral**[2] *n* **1** a spiral curve, object, or pattern. **2** a continuous increase or decrease in prices or incomes.

**spiral**[3] *v* (**spiralled, spiralling,** *NAmer* **spiraled, spiraling**) **1** to follow a spiral course. **2** to increase or decrease continuously or uncontrollably.

**spire** *n* a tall pointed structure on top of a church tower.

**spirit**[1] *n* **1** the non-physical conscious part of a person. **2** the soul. **3** a supernatural being. **4** (*in pl*) temper or state of mind. **5** liveliness, energy, or courage. **6** the prevailing character, attitude, or feeling in somebody or something. **7** the true meaning of something as distinct from the literal. **8** (*also in pl*) strong alcoholic drink, e.g. whisky or gin. **9** (*also in pl*) a readily vaporizing liquid obtained by distillation.

**spirit**[2] *v* (**spirited, spiriting**) (*often* + away) to carry off secretly or mysteriously.

**spirited** *adj* full of energy and determination. ➤ **spiritedly** *adv.*

**spirit level** *n* a device that uses the position of a bubble in a transparent tube of liquid to indicate whether a surface is level.

**spiritual**[1] *adj* **1** relating to the spirit as distinct from body. **2** relating to religious matters. **3** based on sympathy of thought or feeling. ➤ **spirituality** *n*, **spiritually** *adv*.
**spiritual**[2] *n* an emotional religious song of a kind developed among black Christians in the southern USA.
**spiritualism** *n* a belief that spirits of the dead can communicate with the living through a medium. ➤ **spiritualist** *n*.
**spirogyra** *n* a type of algae with cells containing spiral chlorophyll bands.
**spit**[1] *v* (**spitting**, *past tense and past part.* **spat** *or* **spit**) **1** to eject saliva, liquid, or food forcibly from the mouth. **2** to rain lightly. **3** to sputter. **4** (*often* + out) to utter (words) or express (feelings) vehemently. * **spit it out** to say what is on one's mind.
**spit**[2] *n* **1** spittle or saliva. **2** the act of spitting.
**spit**[3] *n* **1** a slender pointed rod for holding and turning meat over a source of heat. **2** an elongated strip of sand or shingle extending into the sea.
**spite**[1] *n* petty ill will or malice. * **in spite of** regardless of.
**spite**[2] *v* to annoy or hinder out of spite.
**spiteful** *adj* deliberately malicious. ➤ **spitefully** *adv*.
**spitfire** *n* a quick-tempered person.
**spitting image** *n* (**the spitting image**) the exact likeness.
**spittle** *n* saliva ejected from the mouth.
**spittoon** *n* a receptacle for spitting into.
**spiv** *n Brit, informal* a slick individual who lives by sharp practice or petty fraud. ➤ **spivvy** *adj*.
**splash**[1] *v* **1** to fall into or move through a liquid causing it to fly up and scatter in drops. **2** of a liquid: to be scattered in large quantities. **3** to make wet with scattered drops of liquid. **4** to display or print (something) in a conspicuous position. **5** *chiefly Brit* (*usu* + out) to spend money liberally.
**splash**[2] *n* **1** the action or sound of splashing. **2** a spot or daub from splashed liquid. **3** a vivid patch of colour. **4** a small amount of liquid added to a drink. **5** *informal* a conspicuous news item. * **make a splash** to make a vivid impression. ➤ **splashy** *adj*.
**splash down** *v* of a spacecraft: to land in the sea. ➤ **splashdown** *n*.
**splat** *n* a splattering sound.
**splatter**[1] *v* to fall in or splash with heavy drops.
**splatter**[2] *n* a splash of liquid in heavy drops.
**splay** *v* to spread or open out.
**spleen** *n* **1** an organ concerned in the destruction of blood cells, storage of blood, and production of lymphocytes. **2** bad temper.
**splendid** *adj* **1** magnificent or sumptuous. **2** excellent. ➤ **splendidly** *adv*.
**splendour** (*NAmer* **splendor**) *n* **1** magnificent appearance or impression. **2** grandeur or pomp.
**splenetic** *adj* bad tempered or spiteful.
**splice**[1] *v* **1** to join (ropes) by interweaving the strands. **2** to join (lengths of film, magnetic tape, or timber) at their ends. * **get spliced** *Brit, informal* **to get married**.
**splice**[2] *n* a joint made by splicing.
**spliff** *n informal* a marijuana cigarette.
**splint** *n* a support for an injured body part, e.g. a broken arm.
**splinter**[1] *n* a sharp thin piece of wood or glass, split or broken off lengthways.
**splinter**[2] *v* to split into splinters; to shatter.
**splinter group** *n* a small group that has broken away from the main part of an organization.
**split**[1] *v* (**splitting**, *past tense and past part.* **split**) **1** to divide or separate lengthways. **2** to separate (parts) by putting something between. **3** to break or burst apart. **4** to divide or share between people. **5** to divide (a political party) into opposing groups. **6** (*often* + up) to end a relationship or connection. * **split hairs** to make trivial distinctions. ➤ **splitter** *n*.
**split**[2] *n* **1** a narrow break made by splitting. **2** the act of splitting. **3** a division into opposing groups. **4** (**the splits**) a jump or position with the legs extended at right angles to the trunk.
**split infinitive** *n* an infinitive with a word, usu an adverb, between *to* and the verb, as in *to fully agree*.
**split-level** *adj* of a room, house, etc: divided into two main levels.
**split second** *n* a very short moment. ➤ **split-second** *adj*.
**splitting** *adj* of a headache: intense and piercing.
**splodge**[1] *n Brit, informal* a large spot, smear, or blot.
**splodge**[2] *v Brit, informal* to mark with a large smear.
**splosh**[1] *v informal* to make a splashing sound.
**splosh**[2] *n informal* a splashing sound.
**splurge**[1] *n informal* **1** an extravagantly large amount of something. **2** an ostentatious display. **3** an extravagant spending spree.
**splurge**[2] *v informal* (*often* + on) to spend money extravagantly.
**splutter**[1] *v* **1** to make a series of noisy spitting sounds. **2** to speak hastily and confusedly.
**splutter**[2] *n* a spluttering sound.
**spoil** *v* (*past tense and past part.* **spoilt** *or* **spoiled**) **1** to damage or ruin. **2** to impair the enjoyment of. **3** to fill in (a voting paper) wrongly so as to render invalid. **4** to impair the character of (a child) by excessive lenience. **5** to treat indulgently. **6** to become unfit for use or consumption. * **spoiling for a fight** very eager to fight.

**spoiler** *n* **1** a long strip on an aircraft wing that can be raised for reducing lift and increasing drag. **2** a strip across the front or rear of a car, for increasing stability at high speeds.

**spoils** *pl n* plunder taken in war or a robbery.

**spoilsport** *n* somebody who spoils the enjoyment of others.

**spoke**[1] *v* past tense of SPEAK.

**spoke**[2] *n* each of the radiating bars connecting the hub of a wheel with the rim.

**spoken**[1] *adj* speaking in a specified manner: *soft-spoken.*

**spoken**[2] *v* past part. of SPEAK.

**spokesman** *or* **spokeswoman** *n* (*pl* **spokesmen** *or* **spokeswomen**) a person who speaks on behalf of a group.

**spokesperson** *n* (*pl* **spokespersons** *or* **spokespeople**) a spokesman or spokeswoman.

**sponge**[1] *n* **1** a type of soft sea creature without a backbone, able to absorb water when wet. **2** a piece of sponge or similar material for cleaning. **3** a light type of cake or pudding. ➤ **spongy** *adj.*

**sponge**[2] *v* **1** to clean or wipe with a sponge. **2** *informal* to obtain money by exploiting people's natural generosity. ➤ **sponger** *n.*

**sponge bag** *n Brit* a small bag for holding toilet articles.

**sponsor**[1] *n* **1** a person or organization that pays towards the cost of a cultural or sporting event. **2** somebody who contributes to a charity by giving money for a participant's efforts in a fund-raising event. **3** somebody who introduces a bill in parliament. ➤ **sponsorship** *n.*

**sponsor**[2] *v* to be sponsor for.

**spontaneous** *adj* **1** done from a natural feeling or sudden impulse. **2** unconstrained or uninhibited by nature. **3** developing without apparent external influence. ➤ **spontaneity** *n,* **spontaneously** *adv.*

**spoof** *n informal* **1** a humorous parody. **2** a hoax or deception.

**spook**[1] *n* **1** *informal* a ghost. **2** *chiefly NAmer* a spy.

**spook**[2] *v* to frighten or startle.

**spooky** *adj* (**-ier, -iest**) *informal* sinister and frightening. ➤ **spookily** *adv.*

**spool**[1] *n* a cylindrical device on which thread, wire, tape, etc is wound.

**spool**[2] *v* to wind onto a spool.

**spoon**[1] *n* an implement consisting of a small shallow bowl with a handle, used for eating or serving food. ➤ **spoonful** *n* (*pl* **spoonfuls**).

**spoon**[2] *v* to pick up or transfer with a spoon.

**spoonbill** *n* a wading bird with a long bill flattened at the tip.

**spoonerism** *n* a transposition of the initial sounds or letters of two or more words, e.g. in *tons of soil* for *sons of toil.*

**spoon-feed** *v* **1** to feed with a spoon. **2** to give help or information to (somebody) in a way that avoids the need for further thought.

**sporadic** *adj* occurring occasionally or in scattered instances. ➤ **sporadically** *adv.*

**spore** *n* a primitive reproductive body produced by plants, algae, etc.

**sporran** *n* a leather pouch worn in front of the kilt in traditional Highland dress.

**sport**[1] *n* **1** a competitive activity or game requiring physical skill and having a set of rules. **2** these activities collectively. **3** a person who is generous-minded and accepts defeat graciously.

**sport**[2] *v* **1** to wear (something distinctive). **2** *literary* to play about happily.

**sporting** *adj* **1** concerned with or fond of sport. **2** generous-minded. ✱ **a sporting chance** a reasonable chance of success.

**sportive** *adj literary* cheerful and playful.

**sports car** *n* a small fast car.

**sports jacket** *n* a man's jacket for informal wear.

**sportsman** *or* **sportswoman** *n* (*pl* **sportsmen** *or* **sportswomen**) **1** a man or woman who engages in sports. **2** a fair and generous-minded person. ➤ **sportsmanship** *n.*

**sporty** *adj* (**-ier, -iest**) **1** fond of or skilled at sport. **2** of clothes: suitable for sporting activities or casual wear. **3** of a car: small and fast.

**spot**[1] *n* **1** a small round area different in colour or texture from the surrounding surface. **2** a dirty mark or stain. **3** a pimple or small blemish on the skin. **4** *Brit, informal* a small amount. **5** a place or area. ✱ **in a spot/in a tight spot** *informal* in difficulties. **on the spot 1** immediately. **2** at the place of action.

**spot**[2] *v* (**spotted, spotting**) **1** to notice or detect. **2** to single out or identify. **3** to mark with spots. **4** *Brit* (*with 'it' as subject*) to fall lightly in scattered drops. ➤ **spotted** *adj,* **spotter** *n,* **spotty** *adj.*

**spot check** *n* a random check made to test quality, accuracy, etc.

**spot-check** *v* to submit to a spot check.

**spotless** *adj* **1** free from dirt or stains. **2** pure or unblemished. ➤ **spotlessly** *adv.*

**spotlight**[1] *n* **1** a lamp projecting a narrow intense beam of light focused on a person or place. **2** (**the spotlight**) full public attention.

**spotlight**[2] *v* (**spotlighting,** *past tense and past part.* **spotlighted** *or* **spotlit**) **1** to illuminate with a spotlight. **2** to direct attention towards.

**spot-on** *adj Brit, informal* absolutely correct or accurate.

**spouse** *n* a husband or wife.

**spout**[1] *v* **1** to eject (liquid, etc) or flow in a copious stream. **2** to express in a strident or pompous manner. **3** to declaim or recite.

**spout**[2] *n* **1** a projecting tube for pouring liquid from a kettle, pot, etc. **2** a downpipe carrying water from a roof gutter. **3** a forceful jet of liquid. ✱ **up the spout** *informal* ruined or useless.

**sprain**[1] *v* to wrench or twist (a joint) violently so as to stretch or tear the ligaments and cause swelling and bruising.

**sprain**[2] *n* **1** an instance of spraining. **2** a sprained joint.

**sprang** *v* past tense of SPRING[1].

**sprat** *n* a small sea fish of the herring family.

**sprawl**[1] *v* **1** to lie or sit with arms and legs spread out carelessly. **2** to spread over a landscape, etc.

**sprawl**[2] *n* **1** a sprawling position. **2** an irregular spreading mass or group.

**spray**[1] *v* **1** to discharge or apply (a fluid) as a spray. **2** to direct a spray of something onto (a surface) or throughout (a place). **3** of a male cat: to mark out its territory by urinating throughout (an area). ➤ **sprayer** *n.*

**spray**[2] *n* **1** fine drops of water blown or falling through the air. **2** a jet of vapour or finely divided liquid. **3** an aerosol or other device by which liquid is sent out in a spray. **4** a substance for spraying.

**spray**[3] *n* **1** a flowering branch or shoot of a plant. **2** a small bouquet of cut flowers.

**spread**[1] *v* (**spreading,** *past tense and past part.* **spread**) **1** to open or extend (something contracted or folded). **2** to distribute or be distributed over an area or period of time. **3** to cover (a surface) with an even layer of something. **4** to communicate to an increasing group. ➤ **spreader** *n.*

**spread**[2] *n* **1** the distribution or expansion of something. **2** a gap or span between two points. **3** a range of things. **4** the two facing pages forming an opening in a newspaper or magazine. **5** a food product designed to be spread. **6** *informal* a sumptuous meal.

**spread-eagled** *adj* stretched out with the arms and legs at an angle to the trunk.

**spreadsheet** *n* a computer progran in which numerical data can be displayed in rows and columns, and rapid calculations made.

**spree** *n* a bout of unrestrained activity: *a spending spree.*

**sprig** *n* a small shoot or twig.

**sprightly** *adj* (**-ier, -iest**) usu of an elderly person: full of vitality and liveliness. ➤ **sprightliness** *n.*

**spring**[1] *v* (**sprang, sprung**) **1** to move suddenly with a jumping action. **2** to move by the release of a spring. **3** (*often* + up) of plants or buildings: to appear suddenly. **4** (*usu* + from) to appear suddenly or unexpectedly. **5** (*usu* + from) to originate or arise. **6** ( + on) to cause (something) to happen, be revealed, or be entrusted to somebody suddenly.

**spring**[2] *n* **1** the season of new growth between winter and summer. **2** a piece of bent or coiled metal that recovers its original shape when released after being compressed or stretched. **3** capacity for springing; resilience or bounce. **4** a jump or bound. **5** a source of water issuing from the ground.

**springboard** *n* **1** a flexible board on which a diver or gymnast springs to gain extra height. **2** something that provides an initial stimulus or impetus.

**springbok** *n* (*pl* **springboks** *or* **springbok**) a graceful southern African gazelle noted for its habit of springing suddenly into the air.

**spring-clean** *v* to give a thorough cleaning to (a house or furnishings). ➤ **spring-clean** *n.*

**springer spaniel** *n* a small spaniel of a breed once used chiefly for flushing small game.

**spring-loaded** *adj* operated by means of spring tension or compression.

**spring onion** *n chiefly Brit* an onion with a small mild-flavoured bulb and long green shoots that is chiefly eaten raw in salads.

**springy** *adj* (**-ier, -iest**) having an elastic or bouncy quality.

**sprinkle**[1] *v* **1** to scatter in fine drops or fine particles. **2** to scatter fine drops or particles over (a surface). **3** to dot here and there.

**sprinkle**[2] *n* = SPRINKLING.

**sprinkler** *n* **1** a nozzle installed in a ceiling as part of an automatic fire-extinguishing system. **2** an apparatus for watering a lawn by spraying.

**sprinkling** *n* a small quantity or number, *esp* scattered in drops or particles or distributed randomly.

**sprint**[1] *v* to run at top speed, *esp* over a short distance. ➤ **sprinter** *n.*

**sprint**[2] *n* **1** a running race of no more than 400m. **2** a short fast swimming or cycling race. **3** a burst of speed.

**sprite** *n* a fairy or elf, *esp* one associated with water.

**spritzer** *n* a drink of wine diluted with soda water or lemonade.

**sprocket** *n* a tooth or projection on the rim of a wheel, shaped so as to engage the links of a chain or the perforations on the edge of a film.

**sprout**[1] *v* **1** of a plant: to send out shoots or new growth. **2** to develop or grow (something).

**sprout**[2] *n* **1** a shoot, e.g. from a seed or root. **2** = BRUSSELS SPROUT.

**spruce**[1] *n* an evergreen coniferous tree with a conical head of dense foliage.

**spruce**[2] *adj* neat or smart in dress or appearance.

**spruce**[3] *v* (+ up) to make (oneself or another person) spruce.

**sprung**[1] *v* past part. of SPRING[1].

**sprung**[2] *adj* fitted with springs, or possessed of springiness.

**spry** *adj* (**sprier** *or* **spryer, spriest** *or* **spryest**) *esp* of an old person: vigorously active; nimble.

**spud** *n informal* a potato.

**spume** *n literary* froth or foam.
**spun** *v* past tense and past part. of SPIN[1].
**spunk** *n* **1** *informal* spirit; pluck. **2** *Brit, coarse slang* semen. ➤ **spunky** *adj.*
**spur[1]** *n* **1** a pointed or wheel-shaped metal device on the heel of a rider's boot, used to urge the horse on. **2** a goad to action; an incentive. **3** a fruit-bearing side shoot. **4** a ridge that extends sideways from a mountain. **5** a short road or length of railway connecting with a major route. **6** * **on the spur of the moment** suddenly; on impulse.
**spur[2]** *v* (**spurred, spurring**) **1** to urge (a horse) on with spurs. **2** (*often* + on) to encourage to make a greater effort.
**spurious** *adj* **1** false; fake; invented. **2** of argument or reasoning: apparently sound but containing flaws.
**spurn** *v* to reject with disdain.
**spurt[1]** *or* **spirt** *v* **1** to gush out in a jet. **2** to put on speed or increase effort.
**spurt[2]** *or* **spirt** *n* **1** a sudden forceful gush. **2** a sudden increase in effort or speed.
**sputter[1]** *v* to make, or to speak with, explosive popping sounds.
**sputter[2]** *n* the act or sound of sputtering.
**sputum** *n* (*pl* **sputa**) mucus and saliva that is coughed up.
**spy[1]** *v* (**-ies, -ied**) **1** to work for a government or other organization by secretly gathering data about enemies or rivals. **2** (+ on) to watch somebody secretly. **3** to catch sight of or spot.
**spy[2]** *n* (*pl* **-ies**) a person who keeps secret watch on somebody or something or collects information secretly.
**spyglass** *n* a small telescope.
**spyhole** *n Brit* = PEEPHOLE.
**sq.** *abbr* square.
**squab** *n* **1** a fledgling bird, *esp* a pigeon. **2** *Brit* a thick upholstery cushion for a chair, car seat, etc.
**squabble[1]** *v* to quarrel noisily, *esp* over trifles.
**squabble[2]** *n* a noisy quarrel.
**squad** *n* **1** a small group of military personnel assembled for a purpose. **2** a small group working as a team. **3** a group of players from whom a sports team is selected.
**squaddy** *or* **squaddie** *n* (*pl* **-ies**) *Brit, informal* a private in the armed forces.
**squadron** *n* **1** a unit of an air force consisting usu of between 10 and 18 aircraft. **2** a naval unit consisting of a number of warships on a particular operation.
**squalid** *adj* **1** filthy and degraded from neglect or poverty. **2** sordid; disreputable. ➤ **squalidly** *adv.*
**squall[1]** *v* of a baby: to cry noisily.
**squall[2]** *n* a noisy cry.
**squall[3]** *n* a sudden violent wind, often with rain or snow. ➤ **squally** *adj.*
**squalor** *n* the state of being squalid.
**squander** *v* to waste, dissipate, or misuse (e.g. money, time, or talents).
**square[1]** *n* **1** a plane figure with all four sides equal and four right angles. **2** an open usu four-sided space in a town. **3** a woman's headscarf. **4** a quadrilateral space marked out on a board, used for playing games. **5** a T-shaped or L-shaped instrument used to draw or test right angles. **6** the product of a number multiplied by itself. **7** *informal, dated* a person who is excessively conventional or conservative. * **back to/at square one** back where one started.
**square[2]** *adj* **1** having four equal sides and four right angles. **2** forming a right angle. **3** at right angles. **4** level or parallel. **5** of a shape or build suggesting strength and solidity. **6** denoting an area equal to that of a square whose sides are of the specified unit: *ten square feet.* **7** placed after a length measurement: denoting the area of a square expanse or object whose sides are of the specified measurement: *ten foot square.* **8** (*often* **all square**) even or equal, e.g. as regards a score or the settlement of accounts. **9** *informal, dated* excessively conservative; dully conventional. * **square peg in a round hole** a person in an environment incompatible with their personality or abilities. ➤ **squarely** *adv.*
**square[3]** *v* **1** (*often* + off) to make square or rectangular. **2** (*often* + off) to mark off (a surface) into squares or rectangles. **3** to multiply (a number) by itself. **4** (+ with) to be in, or bring into, agreement with. **5** to balance or settle (an account). **6** to even the score of (a contest).
**square[4]** *adv* **1** directly; precisely. **2** transversely across a cricket pitch or football field.
**square dance** *n* a dance for four couples who form a hollow square.
**square deal** *n* an honest and fair arrangement or transaction.
**square leg** *n* in cricket, a fielding position halfway to the boundary on the leg side, level with the batsman.
**square meal** *n* a nutritionally balanced and satisfying meal.
**square up** *v* **1** to settle a bill or debt. **2** (+ to) to face a challenge.
**squash[1]** *v* **1** to press or crush into a flat mass. **2** to squeeze or press into a space. **3** to suppress (e.g. a rebellion or rumour) forcefully. **4** to humiliate or silence, e.g. with a cutting remark. ➤ **squashy** *adj.*
**squash[2]** *n* **1** the situation where one is squashed, e.g. in a crowd. **2** an indoor game played by two people in a four-walled court with rackets and a small rubber ball that can be hit against any wall. **3** *Brit* a soft drink made by diluting sweetened and concentrated fruit juice.
**squash[3]** *n* (*pl* **squashes** *or* **squash**) a gourd whose flesh is cooked and eaten as a vegetable.

**squat**[1] *v* (**squatted, squatting**) **1** (*also* + down) to assume a position in which the knees are bent and the haunches rest on the heels. **2** to occupy property as a squatter.

**squat**[2] *n* **1** a squatting posture. **2** an empty building occupied by squatters. **3** the act of squatting in an uninhabited building.

**squat**[3] *adj* (**squatter, squattest**) short or low and broad.

**squatter** *n* a person who occupies otherwise empty property without rights of ownership or payment of rent.

**squaw** *n offensive* a Native North American woman or wife.

**squawk**[1] *v* **1** to utter a harsh abrupt scream. **2** *informal* to make a loud or vehement protest.

**squawk**[2] *n* an act of squawking.

**squeak**[1] *n* a short shrill cry or noise. * **a narrow/near squeak** an escape barely managed. ➤ **squeaky** *adj.*

**squeak**[2] *v* **1** to make a squeak or utter in a squeak. **2** (+ through) to pass an examination or otherwise succeed, by the narrowest of margins.

**squeaky-clean** *adj informal* **1** absolutely clean. **2** morally unassailable; goody-goody.

**squeal**[1] *n* a shrill sharp cry or noise: *squeals of delight.*

**squeal**[2] *v* **1** to utter or make a squeal. **2** *informal* to turn informer. **3** *informal* to complain or protest.

**squeamish** *adj* **1** easily made to feel faint or nauseous. **2** easily shocked or offended.

**squeegee** *n* (*pl* **squeegees**) a tool with a rubber blade used for removing liquid from a surface, e.g. when cleaning a window.

**squeeze**[1] *v* **1** to compress by applying physical pressure to the sides. **2** to extract (liquid, etc) from something by pressure. **3** to force or cram into or through a restricted space. **4** (+ in/into) to fit (a person or task) into a tight schedule. **5** (+ out) to force (somebody) out of their job, area of activity, etc.

**squeeze**[2] *n* **1** an act of squeezing. **2** a quick hug or embrace. **3** a quantity squeezed out from something. **4** *informal* a condition of being crowded together. **5** financial pressure caused by restricting credit.

**squeezy** *adj* (**-ier, -iest**) of a plastic container: flexible, so as to dispense its contents when squeezed.

**squelch**[1] *v* **1** to make the sucking sound typical of somebody walking through mud. **2** *informal* to crush or suppress (opposition, etc).

**squelch**[2] *n* a squelching sound.

**squib** *n* a small firework that burns with a fizz.

**squid** *n* (*pl* **squids** *or* **squid**) a mollusc with eight arms, two long tentacles, and a long tapered body.

**squiffy** *or* **squiffed** *adj* (**-ier, -iest**) *chiefly Brit, informal* slightly drunk; tipsy.

**squiggle** *n* a short wavy twist or line, *esp* in handwriting or drawing. ➤ **squiggly** *adj.*

**squint**[1] *v* **1** to have a squint in the eye. **2** to look or peer with eyes partly closed.

**squint**[2] *n* **1** abnormal alignment of an eye, so that it turns permanently towards or away from the nose. **2** *informal* a quick glance.

**squire**[1] *n* **1** formerly, a young nobleman acting as a knight's attendant and training for knighthood. **2** the principal landowner of a district.

**squire**[2] *v* to escort (a woman).

**squirm** *v* **1** to twist about like a worm; to wriggle. **2** to feel acutely embarrassed or ashamed. ➤ **squirm** *n.*

**squirrel**[1] *n* a tree-dwelling rodent with a long bushy tail.

**squirrel**[2] *v* (**squirrelled, squirrelling,** *NAmer* **squirreled, squirreling**) (*usu* + away) to secrete somewhere or hoard for future use.

**squirt**[1] *v* **1** to issue, or squeeze out, in a jet from a narrow opening. **2** to direct a jet or stream of liquid at.

**squirt**[2] *n* **1** a small rapid stream of liquid. **2** *informal* a small, insignificant, or impudent person.

**squish**[1] *v* **1** to make a slight squelching or sucking sound. **2** *informal* to squash.

**squish**[2] *n* the sound of squishing.

**Sr**[1] *abbr* **1** senior. **2** Sister.

**Sr**[2] *abbr* the chemical symbol for strontium.

**SS**[1] *n* Adolf Hitler's bodyguard and special police force.

**SS**[2] *abbr* **1** saints. **2** steamship.

**St** *abbr* **1** Saint. **2** street.

**stab**[1] *n* **1** a thrust with a pointed weapon. **2** a sharp spasm of pain or emotion. * **a stab in the back** an act of treachery. **have/make a stab at** *informal* to make an attempt at.

**stab**[2] *v* (**stabbed, stabbing**) **1** to pierce or wound with a pointed weapon. **2** to thrust or jab (a pointed object) somewhere. **3** to cause a sharp pain.

**stability** *n* the quality of being stable.

**stabilize** *or* **-ise** *v* to make or become stable. ➤ **stabilization** *n.*

**stable**[1] *n* **1** (*also in pl*) a building in which horses are kept. **2** (*also in pl*) an establishment where racehorses are kept and trained. **3** a group of people working as a team or under one person's management.

**stable**[2] *v* to put or keep (a horse) in a stable.

**stable**[3] *adj* **1** not likely to collapse, overturn, etc. **2** securely established so as to endure and be dependable. **3** not subject to change or fluctuation. **4** of a patient or their condition: not likely to deteriorate suddenly. **5** not subject to mental or emotional insecurity.

**stablemate** *n* another horse stabled with the one in question.

**staccato** *adj and adv* **1** of a piece of music: performed with each note produced in an abrupt, detached style. **2** of speech: with a jerky delivery.

**stack**[1] *n* **1** a pile, *esp* an orderly one. **2** a cone-shaped, rectangular, or cylindrical pile of hay or straw. **3** a number of aircraft circling an airport waiting their turn to land. **4** a chimney. **5** *informal* (*also in pl*) a large quantity or number.

**stack**[2] *v* **1** to pile (things) into a stack. **2** to fill with stacks of things. **3** to assign (an aircraft) to a particular altitude and position within a stack. **4** to shuffle (a pack of cards) in such a way as to enable one to cheat. * **be stacked against/in favour of** to be highly likely to produce an unfavourable/favourable result for.

**stadium** *n* (*pl* **stadiums** *or* **stadia**) a sports ground surrounded by tiers of seats for spectators.

**staff**[1] *n* **1** the people who work for an institution, business, etc. **2** the teachers at a school or university. **3** a group of officers appointed to assist a commanding officer. **4** (*pl* **staves**) a long stick carried for support when walking or as a weapon. **5** a rod carried as a symbol of office or authority. **6** (*pl* **staves**) in music, the STAVE[1] 3.

**staff**[2] *v* to supply (an organization, etc) with a staff.

**staff nurse** *n Brit* a qualified hospital nurse ranking below a sister or charge nurse.

**stag** *n* an adult male deer.

**stage**[1] *n* **1** a raised platform. **2** the raised platform or other area in a theatre where actors perform. **3** (**the stage**) the acting profession. **4** a distinguishable period or step in the development of something. **5** a section of journey, race, or rally. **6** = STAGECOACH. * **set the stage for** to provide the necessary conditions for the arrival, appearance, or occurrence of.

**stage**[2] *v* **1** to produce and perform (a theatrical work). **2** to organize (a public event).

**stagecoach** *n* formerly, a horse-drawn passenger and mail coach that ran a regular scheduled route.

**stage fright** *n* nervousness felt at appearing before an audience.

**stagehand** *n* a theatre worker who handles scenery, props, or lights.

**stage-manage** *v* **1** to be the stage manager of (a play, etc). **2** to arrange (an event, etc) so as to achieve a desired result. ➤ **stage management** *n*.

**stage manager** *n* a person who is in overall charge of the stage, cast, and technical staff during performances of a play.

**stage whisper** *n* a loud whisper by an actor, audible to the audience, but supposedly inaudible to others on stage.

**stagger**[1] *v* **1** to move unsteadily or jerkily as if in danger of falling over. **2** to dumbfound or astonish. **3** to arrange (a set of things) so that they are not in line, start at different times, or partially overlap.

**stagger**[2] *n* **1** a staggered arrangement. **2** a lurching movement.

**staggering** *adj* astonishing or overwhelming. ➤ **staggeringly** *adv*.

**staging post** *n* a regular stopping place for vehicles.

**stagnant** *adj* **1** of water: not flowing and usu overgrown or foul. **2** dull or inactive.

**stagnate** *v* to become or remain stagnant. ➤ **stagnation** *n*.

**stag night** *n* a party for men on the night before one of them is married.

**stagy** *or* **stagey** *adj* (**-ier, -iest**) artificially dramatic; consciously theatrical.

**staid** *adj* unadventurous and usu old-fashioned in attitude.

**stain**[1] *v* **1** to mark, discolour, or soil. **2** *literary* to dishonour (a person or their character, reputation, etc). **3** to colour (wood or a biological specimen) by using chemicals or dyes.

**stain**[2] *n* **1** a soiled or discoloured spot. **2** a moral taint or blemish. **3** a preparation, e.g. of dye or pigment, used in staining.

**stained glass** *n* glass coloured or stained, usu for use in leaded windows.

**stainless** *adj* **1** free from stain or stigma. **2** rust-resistant.

**stainless steel** *n* steel containing chromium and highly resistant to rusting and corrosion.

**stair** *n* **1** (*usu in pl*) a flight of steps for passing from one level to another. **2** any step of a stairway.

**staircase** *n* a flight of stairs with the supporting framework, casing, and balusters.

**stairway** *n* one or more flights of stairs, usu with intermediate landings.

**stairwell** *n* a vertical shaft in which stairs are located.

**stake**[1] *n* **1** a pointed wooden or iron post used for driving into the ground as a marker or support. **2** (**the stake**) a post to which a person was formerly bound for execution by burning.

**stake**[2] *v* **1** (*often* + off/out) to mark out (an area) with stakes. **2** to support (a plant) with a stake. * **stake one's claim** to assert one's ownership of, or right to, something.

**stake**[3] *v* **1** to bet (a sum of money, one's reputation, etc). **2** *chiefly NAmer* to back (a person or business concern) financially.

**stake**[4] *n* **1** something, *esp* a sum of money, that is staked. **2** an interest or share in an undertaking. **3** (*in pl*) what is to be won or lost in a contest or competitive situation. **4** (*in pl*) used after a noun to denote that an aspect of life is thought of as a competion between people: *not doing terribly well in the promotion stakes*. * **at stake 1** to be won or lost. **2** at risk.

**stake out** *v informal* to conduct a surveillance of (a suspected area, person, etc). ➤ **stakeout** *n.*
**stalactite** *n* an icicle-like deposit of calcium carbonate hanging from the roof or sides of a cave.
**stalagmite** *n* a spike-like deposit of calcium carbonate growing upward from the floor of a cave.
**stale** *adj* **1** *esp* of food: no longer fresh; unpalatable or musty. **2** of news: no longer interesting. **3** lacking vigour or effectiveness through overexertion or repetition. ➤ **staleness** *n.*
**stalemate** *n* **1** a position in chess representing a draw, where the king, although not in check, can move only into check. **2** a deadlock.
**stalk**[1] *v* **1** to pursue (a prey or quarry) stealthily. **2** to follow and watch (a person with whom one has become obsessed), to the point of persecution. **3** to walk in a stiff haughty fashion. ➤ **stalker** *n.*
**stalk**[2] *n* **1** the main stem of a plant. **2** the stem of a leaf or fruit.
**stall**[1] *n* **1** a compartment for a domestic animal in a stable or barn. **2** (*usu in pl*) a compartment in a mechanically operated device from which horses are simultaneously released to start a race. **3** any small compartment, e.g. one of a row of toilets. **4** a stand or counter at which articles are offered for sale, e.g. in a market. **5** *Brit* (*in pl*) the seats on the main floor of an auditorium, e.g. in a theatre. **6** a seat in the chancel of a church. **7** the cutting-out of a vehicle engine. **8** the condition of an aircraft when it loses lift, e.g. from moving forward too slowly.
**stall**[2] *v* **1** of a vehicle, engine, driver, aircraft, or pilot: to suffer a stall. **2** (*usu* **be stalled**) to be unable to progress. **3** to play for time; to delay. **4** to divert or delay (somebody), usu to give oneself more time.
**stallion** *n* an uncastrated male horse.
**stalwart**[1] *adj* **1** strong. **2** dependable; staunch.
**stalwart**[2] *n* a staunch supporter.
**stamen** *n* the organ of a flower that produces the male reproductive cell.
**stamina** *n* the capacity for sustained mental and physical effort.
**stammer**[1] *v* to speak or utter with involuntary stops and repetitions, *esp* of initial consonants.
**stammer**[2] *n* a tendency to stammer.
**stamp**[1] *v* **1** to bring down (one's foot) forcibly. **2** to walk with loud heavy steps. **3** to impress or imprint (words, etc) on something. **4** to leave (a permanent or indelible image) in someone's mind, etc. **5** of a quality, etc: to characterize (something). **6** to attach a postage stamp to (an envelope, etc).
**stamp**[2] *n* **1** a printed adhesive piece of paper used to indicate that postage has been paid. **2** an instrument for stamping a mark, etc on a surface. **3** the impression or mark made by stamping. **4** a characteristic quality. **5** the act or sound of stamping the foot.
**stamp duty** *n* a tax levied for legal recognition of certain documents.
**stampede**[1] *n* **1** a wild headlong rush of frightened animals. **2** a sudden mass movement of people.
**stampede**[2] *v* to run away or rush in panic, or to cause (people or animals) to do this.
**stamping ground** *n* one's favourite or habitual haunt.
**stamp out** *v* to eradicate or destroy.
**stance** *n* **1** a way of standing. **2** an intellectual or emotional attitude.
**stanch** *v NAmer* see STAUNCH[1].
**stanchion** *n* an upright bar, post, or support.
**stand**[1] *v* (*past tense and past part.* **stood**) **1** to support oneself on one's feet in an upright position. **2** to rise to this position. **3** to rest upright on the ground or other surface. **4** to occupy a position or location. **5** to remain stationary. **6** to have a particular attitude or opinion. **7** to remain valid. **8** ( + to) to be likely to receive or experience something. **9** to tolerate or like: *I can't stand her husband.* **10** to withstand. **11** to treat (somebody) to a meal or drink. **12** *Brit* to be a candidate in an election. * **leave standing** to surpass spectacularly. **stand by 1** to wait in readiness. **2** to do nothing while something is happening. **3** to support or remain loyal to. **stand for 1** to represent. **2** to permit or tolerate. **stand on one's own feet/two feet** to be self-reliant.
**stand**[2] *n* **1** a definite attitude taken towards something. **2** a determined effort to fight for or resist something. **3** (*also in pl*) a structure of tiered seats for spectators of a sport or spectacle. **4** a raised platform for a band, speaker, etc. **5** a small outdoor stall selling food, etc. **6** a frame or rack on or in which to place things. **7** (**the stand**) *NAmer* the witness-box.
**standard**[1] *n* **1** a level of quality or achievement. **2** a norm used for comparison. **3** (*in pl*) principles of acceptable behaviour. **4** a flag or banner.
**standard**[2] *adj* **1** regularly and widely used; accepted as a norm. **2** of language: used in the speech and writing of educated people and considered as the norm.
**standard-bearer** *n* **1** a person who carries a banner. **2** a conspicuous figure at the forefront of an organization, etc.
**standardize** *or* **-ise** *v* to make (things) conform to a standard. ➤ **standardization** *n.*
**standard lamp** *n* a lamp with a tall support that stands on the floor.
**standard of living** *n* a measure of the prosperity of an individual or community, shown *esp* by their level of consumption.

**standby**[1] *n* (*pl* **standbys**) **1** a person or thing held in reserve in case of necessity. **2** a state of readiness for duty or use.

**standby**[2] *adj* **1** held in reserve and ready for use or duty. **2** of tickets: unreserved and available for sale shortly before e.g. a performance.

**stand down** *v Brit* to relinquish an office or position.

**stand in** *v* to act as substitute for somebody.

**standing**[1] *adj* permanently existing, in force, or available.

**standing**[2] *n* **1** status, position, or reputation. **2** length of existence or duration.

**standing joke** *n* something that is a regular source of amusement or target of derision.

**standing order** *n Brit* **1** an order to a bank to pay a specified sum of money to another named account at specified times. **2** an instruction, e.g. to a supplier, in force until specifically changed.

**standing ovation** *n* a prolonged burst of applause during which the audience rise to their feet.

**standoff** *n* a state of deadlock between opponents.

**standoffish** *adj derog* reserved; aloof.

**stand out** *v* to be especially visible, noteworthy, or good. * **stand out for** to be stubborn in insisting on.

**standpoint** *n* **1** the position from which one views something. **2** one's point of view with regard to some issue.

**standstill** *n* a stationary state; a stop or impasse.

**stand up** *v* **1** to rise to a standing position. **2** to bear close scrutiny: *That argument won't stand up*. **3** *informal* to fail to keep an appointment with (somebody). * **stand up and be counted** to make one's views known. **stand up for** to defend against criticism. **stand up to 1** to confront or prepare to resist. **2** to withstand (wear, etc).

**stank** *v* past tense of STINK[1].

**stanza** *n* a number of lines forming a basic division of a poem.

**staple**[1] *n* **1** a small wire clip that can be driven through sheets of paper to secure them together. **2** a sharp-ended U-shaped metal loop, driven into a surface to secure something to it.

**staple**[2] *v* to fasten or attach with staples. ➤ **stapler** *n.*

**staple**[3] *n* **1** the main element or constituent of something. **2** the main trading commodity or raw material of a region.

**staple**[4] *adj* **1** depended on as basic. **2** main.

**star**[1] *n* **1** a gaseous body that radiates energy and is visible as a point of light in the night sky. **2** a stylized figure with five or more points that represents a star. **3** a famous entertainer, performer, or sports personality. **4** the leading or outstanding performer in a group. **5** *informal* a kind or generous person. ➤ **stardom** *n.*

**star**[2] *v* (**starred, starring**) **1** of a film, play, etc: to feature (a certain star) in a leading role. **2** to play a leading role in a production. **3** to mark with a star or asterisk.

**starboard** *n* the right side of a ship or aircraft looking forward.

**starch**[1] *n* **1** a carbohydrate that is an important foodstuff, obtained chiefly from cereals and potatoes. **2** a powder or spray used to stiffen fabric.

**starch**[2] *v* to stiffen (clothes or fabric) with starch.

**starchy** *adj* (**-ier, -iest**) **1** of foods or other substances: containing a lot of starch. **2** of somebody's manner, etc: stiff and formal.

**stare**[1] *v* to look fixedly, often with wide-open eyes. * **stare somebody in the face** of a solution, etc: to be only too obvious.

**stare**[2] *n* a staring look or expression.

**starfish** *n* (*pl* **starfishes** *or* **starfish**) a sea creature with a body consisting of a central disc surrounded by five equally spaced arms.

**stark** *adj* **1** of a landscape, surroundings, etc: bleak or bare; desolate. **2** harshly clear or plain. **3** sheer; utter. ➤ **starkly** *adv.*

**starkers** *adj Brit, informal* completely naked.

**stark-naked** *adj* completely naked.

**starlet** *n* a young film actress being coached for starring roles.

**starling** *n* a gregarious bird with glossy greenish black plumage.

**starry** *adj* (**-ier, -iest**) **1** of the sky: studded with stars. **2** *informal* relating to the stars of the entertainment world.

**starry-eyed** *adj* naively idealistic or over-optimistic.

**starship** *n* in science fiction, a large spaceship for interstellar journeys.

**start**[1] *v* **1** to come into operation or existence. **2** to begin functioning or moving, or to make (something) do this. **3** to begin (an activity or undertaking). **4** to cause (somebody) to do something. **5** to range from a specified amount: *Prices start from £300*. **6** to move suddenly or violently, *esp* as a result of shock or surprise. * **to start with** as the first thing to be considered.

**start**[2] *n* **1** the beginning of a movement, activity, journey, etc. **2** a starting place, e.g. for a race. **3** a lead conceded to a competitor at the start of a race. **4** a sudden involuntary bodily movement, e.g. from surprise or alarm. * **for a start** in the first place.

**starter** *n* **1** the person who gives the signal to start a race. **2** an automatic device that activates machinery, *esp* a vehicle engine. **3** *chiefly Brit* (*also in pl*) the first course of a meal. * **for starters** *chiefly Brit, informal* in the first place.

**startle** *v* to cause (somebody) to start in alarm, etc. ➤ **startled** *adj*, **startling** *adj*.
**start off** *v* to begin talking, operating, etc, or to cause (somebody or something) to do this.
**start out** *v* to begin a journey or undertaking.
**start up** *v* **1** to begin to operate, or cause (e.g. an engine) to begin to operate. **2** to begin a commercial undertaking. ➤ **start-up** *n and adj*.
**starve** *v* **1** to suffer severely or die from hunger. **2** to cause (a person or animal) to suffer from or to die of hunger. **3** *informal* to be ravenous. **4** (+ of) to deprive of. ➤ **starvation** *n*.
**stash**[1] *v informal* (*often* + away) to store in a secret place for future use.
**stash**[2] *n informal* a secret store of drugs, weapons, etc.
**stasis** *n* (*pl* **stases**) a state of static balance without activity or change; stagnation.
**state**[1] *n* **1** the condition or situation of somebody or something. **2** a politically organized community usu occupying a definite territory. **3** the operations or concerns of the central government of a country. **4** a constituent unit of a nation having a federal government. **5** (**the States**) the United States of America. **6** (**a state**) *informal* an upset, confused, or dirty condition. ✱ **state of affairs** (*also* **state of things**) a situation. **state of emergency** a situation involving national danger or extreme disaster, during which the government assumes special powers. **state of play 1** *Brit* the current score in a cricket or football match. **2** *Brit* the current situation.
**state**[2] *v* to declare formally.
**stately** *adj* (**-ier, -iest**) imposing; dignified.
**stately home** *n Brit* a large country residence, usu of historical or architectural interest and open to the public.
**statement** *n* **1** a declaration or account of something given orally or in writing. **2** a summary of a financial account. **3** an account of events given to the police or in court.
**state-of-the-art** *adj* using the most advanced technology available.
**statesman** *or* **stateswoman** *n* (*pl* **statesmen** *or* **stateswomen**) an experienced and respected political leader.
**static**[1] *adj* characterized by a lack of movement, animation, or change. ➤ **statically** *adv*.
**static**[2] *n* **1** electrical disturbances causing unwanted signals in a radio or television system; atmospherics. **2** = STATIC ELECTRICITY.
**static electricity** *n* an electrical charge built up, e.g. by friction, in a material from which it cannot be conducted away.
**station**[1] *n* **1** a regular or major stopping place for trains. **2** the place or position in which something or somebody stands or is placed. **3** standing; rank. **4** a place established to provide a public service. **5** an establishment equipped for radio or television transmission or reception. **6** a radio or television channel.
**station**[2] *v* to assign to a post or station.
**stationary** *adj* **1** having a fixed position; immobile. **2** neither progressing nor deteriorating.

***Usage Note:*** Do not confuse this word with *stationery*.

**stationer** *n* a shopkeeper who deals in stationery.
**stationery** *n* paper, envelopes, and other materials used for writing, typing, etc.

***Usage Note:*** Do not confuse this word with *stationary*.

**stationmaster** *n* an official in charge of a railway station.
**station wagon** *n NAmer* an estate car.
**statistic** *n* a single term or quantity from a collection of statistics.
**statistical** *adj* relating to or produced from statistics. ➤ **statistically** *adv*.
**statistics** *pl n* **1** a branch of mathematics dealing with the collection and analysis of masses of numerical data. **2** (*treated as pl*) a collection of numerical data relating to a subject. ➤ **statistician** *n*.
**statuary** *n* statues collectively.
**statue** *n* a likeness, e.g. of a person or animal, sculptured or modelled in a solid material.
**statuesque** *adj* tall, well-proportioned, and stately.
**statuette** *n* a small statue.
**stature** *n* **1** the natural height of a person when standing upright. **2** standing or reputation.
**status** *n* **1** the legal condition or standing of a person, territory, etc. **2** position in relation to others in a hierarchy or social structure. **3** prestige. **4** the state of affairs.
**status quo** *n* the existing state of affairs.
**status symbol** *n* a possession recognized as indicating high social status or wealth.
**statute** *n* **1** a law passed by a legislative body. **2** any of the permanent rules of an organization.
**statutory** *adj* **1** established, regulated, or imposed by statute. **2** *informal* standard; usual or expected. ➤ **statutorily** *adv*.
**staunch**[1] (*NAmer* **stanch**) *v* to stop the flow of (blood, etc).
**staunch**[2] *adj* steadfast in loyalty or principle. ➤ **staunchly** *n*.
**stave**[1] *n* **1** an iron pole or wooden stick. **2** any of the narrow strips of wood placed edge to edge to form a barrel, bucket, etc. **3** a set of five horizontal spaced lines on which music is written.
**stave**[2] *v* (*past tense and past part.* **staved** *or* **stove**) (+ in) to crush or break (a hard casing, etc) inward.

**stave off** v (*past tense and past part.* **staved off**) to ward or fend off (a threatening danger), *esp* temporarily.

**stay**[1] v **1** to remain in a place and not move. **2** to remain in a particular state and not change. **3** to reside temporarily somewhere. **4** to delay or prevent (a judicial procedure, such as an execution). * **stay put** to stay where placed or left.

**stay**[2] n **1** a period of residing at a place. **2** the suspension of a judicial procedure.

**stay**[3] n **1** *literary* somebody or something that serves as a prop or support. **2** (*in pl*) formerly, a corset stiffened with bones.

**staying power** n *informal* stamina.

**stead** n * **in somebody's or something's stead** in place of somebody or something else. **stand somebody in good stead** to be an advantage to somebody.

**steadfast** *adj* loyal or unwavering. ➤ **steadfastly** *adv.*

**steady**[1] *adj* (**-ier, -iest**) **1** firmly positioned or balanced; not shaking, rocking, etc. **2** showing, or continuing with, little variation or fluctuation. **3** not easily moved or upset. **4** constant and dependable; consistent, not erratic. ➤ **steadily** *adv,* **steadiness** *n.*

**steady**[2] v (**-ies, -ied**) to become or make steady.

**steady**[3] *adv* * **go steady** *informal* to have a long-term relationship with a boyfriend or girlfriend. **steady on!** used to tell somebody to calm down.

**steak** n **1** a lean high-quality slice of meat, *esp* beef, suitable for grilling or frying. **2** poorer-quality beef suitable for braising or stewing. **3** a cross-sectional slice of a large fish.

**steal**[1] v (**stole, stolen**) **1** to take (something) without permission or illegally, with no intention of returning it. **2** to take (a look, etc) surreptitiously. **3** to come or go stealthily or unobtrusively. * **steal a march on** to gain an advantage over (somebody) by stealthy or underhand means. **steal the show** to make a bigger impression than other ostensibly more prominent participants.

**steal**[2] n *informal* a bargain.

**stealth**[1] n caution and surreptitiousness in movement or activity.

**stealth**[2] *adj* denoting *esp* aircraft designed to be able to avoid radar detection.

**stealthy** *adj* (**-ier, -iest**) characterized by stealth. ➤ **stealthily** *adv.*

**steam**[1] n **1** the vapour into which water is converted when boiled. **2** the mist formed when water vapour condenses. **3** energy or power generated by steam under pressure. * **let off/blow off steam** *informal* to release one's pent-up energy, emotional tension, etc. **under one's own steam** independently.

**steam**[2] v **1** to give off steam. **2** to move by means of steam power. **3** *informal* to move or progress quickly. **4** (+ up) to become covered with steam. **5** to cook (food) in steam from boiling water. **6** to clean or press using steam. * **get steamed up** *informal* to get angry or agitated.

**steamboat** n a boat propelled by steam power.

**steam engine** n a stationary or locomotive engine driven by steam.

**steamroll** v – STEAMROLLER[2].

**steamroller**[1] n a machine equipped with wide heavy rollers for compacting newly laid road surfaces, etc.

**steamroller**[2] v (**steamrollered, steamrollering**) **1** to force acceptance of (a law, etc) by crushing opposition or curtailing discussion. **2** to force (somebody) into doing something.

**steamy** *adj* (**-ier, -iest**) **1** full of steam. **2** hot and humid. **3** *informal* portraying sexual activity.

**steed** n *archaic or literary* a horse.

**steel**[1] n **1** an alloy of iron with carbon, notable for its strength and hardness. **2** cold hardness or unyielding strength.

**steel**[2] v to nerve (oneself) to do something.

**steel band** n a band that plays instruments made from empty oil drums.

**steel wool** n steel fibres used for scouring and burnishing.

**steelworks** *pl n* a factory where steel is made.

**steely** *adj* (**-ier, -iest**) **1** resembling steel. **2** unyielding; relentless.

**steep**[1] *adj* **1** sloping sharply, or nearly vertical. **2** of a rise or fall in an amount, level, etc: substantial and rapid. **3** *informal* of a price: unreasonably high. **4** *informal* excessive. ➤ **steeply** *adv.*

**steep**[2] v **1** to soak or be soaked in a liquid. **2** (*usu* **be steeped in**) to be thoroughly imbued with.

**steepen** v to become or make steeper.

**steeple** n a church tower with a spire.

**steeplechase** n **1** a horse race over a racecourse with hedges and ditches for jumping. **2** a middle-distance running race over obstacles. ➤ **steeplechaser** *n,* **steeplechasing** *n.*

**steeplejack** n a person who climbs chimneys, towers, etc to paint or repair them.

**steer**[1] v **1** to guide or control the course of (a vehicle or ship). **2** to guide (somebody or something) in a certain direction. * **steer clear of** to keep well away from. ➤ **steering** *n.*

**steer**[2] n a bullock.

**steerage** n formerly, the section of a passenger ship for passengers paying the lowest fares.

**steering wheel** n a wheel that is turned by a driver or helmsman to steer a motor vehicle, ship, etc.

**steersman** n (*pl* **steersmen**) a helmsman.

**stegosaurus** /stegə'sawrəs/ n a large dinosaur with projecting bony plates along its back.

**stellar** *adj* relating to a star or stars.

**stem** *n* **1** the main stalk or trunk of a plant or shrub. **2** the slender stalk of a flower, leaf, or fruit. **3** the main unchanging part of a word. **4** a vertical stroke of a letter or musical note. **5** the tube of a tobacco pipe. **6** the slender support between the base and bowl of a wineglass. * **from stem to stern** of a ship: from end to end.

**stench** *n* a stink.

**stencil**[1] *n* a sheet of e.g. paper or metal, perforated with a design or lettering through which ink or paint is forced onto the surface below.

**stencil**[2] *v* (**stencilled, stencilling,** *NAmer* **stenciled, stenciling**) **1** to produce (a design, etc) by means of a stencil. **2** to decorate (a surface) with a stencil.

**stenography** *n* the writing and transcription of shorthand. ➤ **stenographer** *n*, **stenographic** *adj.*

**stentorian** *adj* of a person's voice: extremely loud.

**step**[1] *n* **1** a movement made by raising one foot and bringing it down in front of the other in walking. **2** the space passed over in one step. **3** a short distance. **4** a flat supporting surface for the foot in ascending or descending. **5** (*in pl*) a stepladder. **6** a level or grade in a scale. **7** a stage in the progress of something. **8** an action, proceeding, or measure.

**step**[2] *v* (**stepped, stepping**) to move by raising one foot and bringing it down in front of the other, or in another position. * **step aside 1** to stand clear of something. **2** to resign from a position. **step back** to distance oneself from a situation in order to assess it more objectively. **step forward** to volunteer one's services. **step on it/the gas** *informal* to drive or move faster; to hurry up. **step out of line** to fail to conform.

**stepbrother** *n* a son of one's stepparent by a former marriage.

**stepchild** *n* (*pl* **stepchildren**) a child of one's wife or husband by a former marriage.

**stepdaughter** *n* a daughter of one's wife or husband by a former marriage.

**step down** *v* to retire or resign.

**stepfather** *n* the husband of one's mother by a subsequent marriage.

**step in** *v* **1** to intervene. **2** to take somebody's place for a time.

**stepladder** *n* a hinged ladder with flat rungs and often a platform.

**stepmother** *n* the wife of one's father by a subsequent marriage.

**stepparent** *n* the husband or wife of one's parent by a subsequent marriage.

**steppe** *n* a vast grassy treeless plain, *esp* in southeastern Europe or Asia.

**stepping stone** *n* **1** a stone on which to step when crossing a stream. **2** something regarded as a means of progress or advancement.

**stepsister** *n* a daughter of one's stepparent by a former marriage.

**stepson** *n* a son of one's wife or husband by a former marriage.

**step up** *v* to increase the amount, speed, or intensity of.

**stereo**[1] *n* (*pl* **-os**) **1** stereophonic sound. **2** a stereophonic record-player, etc.

**stereo**[2] *adj* stereophonic.

**stereophonic** *adj* denoting a sound system using two different channels to give spatial effect.

**stereotype**[1] *n* a standardized simplistic image of a person or thing. ➤ **stereotypical** *adj.*

**stereotype**[2] *v* to represent (a person or thing) as a stereotype.

**sterile** *adj* **1** unable to produce young, seeds, or crops. **2** deficient in ideas or originality. **3** free from living organisms, *esp* micro-organisms. ➤ **sterility** *n.*

**sterilize** *or* **-ise** *v* to make sterile. ➤ **sterilization** *n.*

**sterling**[1] *n* British money.

**sterling**[2] *adj* **1** of a person's character or efforts: of genuine worth or quality. **2** of silver: at least 92.25% pure.

**stern**[1] *adj* **1** harsh, strict, or severe. **2** firm; uncompromising. ➤ **sternly** *adv.*

**stern**[2] *n* the rear end of a ship.

**sternum** *n* (*pl* **sternums** *or* **sterna**) the breastbone.

**steroid** *n* **1** a chemical compound of a class characterized by a ring of carbon atoms and including various hormones. **2** an anabolic steroid.

**stertorous** *adj* of breathing: characterized by a harsh snoring or gasping sound.

**stethoscope** *n* an instrument used to detect and study sounds produced in the body, *esp* by the heart and lungs.

**Stetson** *n NAmer trademark* a broad-brimmed high-crowned felt hat.

**stevedore** *n* a person employed to load and unload ships.

**stew**[1] *n* **1** a dish of meat, vegetables, or both, cooked in liquid in a closed pan. **2** *informal* an agitated state.

**stew**[2] *v* **1** to cook (meat, fruit, etc) in liquid in a closed vessel. **2** of tea: to become strong and bitter from prolonged brewing. **3** *informal* to be in a state of agitation. * **stew in one's own juice** *informal* to suffer the consequences of one's own stupidity.

**steward** *n* **1** a person who attends to the needs of passengers on an airliner, ship, etc. **2** a person who supervises the provision of food and drink in a club, college, etc. **3** an official in charge of arrangements or crowd-control at a large public event. **4** a person employed to manage a large house or estate. ➤ **stewardship** *n.*

**stewardess** *n* a woman who attends to the needs of passengers on an airliner, ship, etc.

**stick**[1] *n* **1** a twig or slender branch from a tree or shrub. **2** a club or staff used as a weapon; a stave. **3** a walking stick. **4** an implement used for striking or propelling a ball or other object in a game. **5** something prepared in a long, slender, often cylindrical form. **6** the threat of punishment as a means of obtaining compliance. **7** *informal* critical disapproving comment. **8** (**the sticks**) *informal, derog* remote or backward rural areas.

**stick**[2] *v* (*past tense and past part.* **stuck**) **1** (*often* + into) of something sharp or pointed: to be fixed in something. **2** to thrust (a sharp or pointed object) into or through something. **3** *informal* to poke (something) somewhere. **4** *informal* to put somewhere, *esp* temporarily. **5** to attach (one thing) to another with adhesive. **6** (*often* + to) to adhere or become fixed or attached to a surface, etc. **7** to become fixed or unable to move. **8** *chiefly Brit, informal* to bear or stand (a person or thing). **9** to protrude or project. **10** (+ at) to persist at a task, etc. **11** (+ with) to persevere with something. **12** (+ to) not to deviate from something. * **be stuck 1** to be unable to move. **2** to be unable to solve a problem, finish a task, etc. **be stuck for** to lack or need. **be stuck on** *informal* to be infatuated with. **be stuck with** *informal* to be unable to escape from. **get stuck in/into** *informal* to involve oneself wholeheartedly in a task, etc. **stick by 1** to continue to support (somebody). **2** to honour (a promise, etc). **stick one's neck out** *informal* to take an initiative or risk that leaves one vulnerable. **stick together** to continue to support each other; to remain united.

**stick around** *v informal* to linger somewhere.

**sticker** *n* an adhesive label or notice.

**stick insect** *n* an insect with a long thin body resembling a stick.

**stickleback** *n* a small fish with spines on its back.

**stickler** *n* a person who insists on things being done exactly right.

**stick out** *v* **1** to jut out; to project. **2** to be prominent or conspicuous. * **stick it out** *informal* to endure something to the end. **stick out for** to insist on or persist in demanding.

**stick up** *v* to stand upright or on end; to protrude. * **stick up for** to defend against attack or criticism.

**sticky** *adj* (**-ier, -iest**) **1** adhesive. **2** viscous; gluey. **3** coated with a sticky substance. **4** of the weather: humid or muggy. **5** sweaty or clammy. **6** difficult; problematic. * **come to a sticky end** *informal* to meet with ruin, disaster, a nasty death, etc.

**stiff**[1] *adj* **1** not easily bent. **2** of a handle, lock, etc: hard to operate or turn. **3** of the body or a part of it: not moving freely, or painful to move as a result e.g. of intensive exercise. **4** of a mixture: thick. **5** of social relations: not relaxed and friendly. **6** lacking in ease or grace. **7** of an alcoholic drink: strong. **8** of a punishment: harsh or severe. * **a stiff upper lip** a stoical, dry-eyed self-control. ➤ **stiffly** *adv,* **stiffness** *n.*

**stiff**[2] *n informal* a corpse.

**stiffen** *v* to make or become stiff. ➤ **stiffener** *n.*

**stifle** *v* **1** to prevent (a person or animal) from breathing freely or suffocate (them). **2** to suppress (a yawn, a giggle, etc). **3** to curb or repress.

**stifling** *adj* uncomfortably hot and stuffy. ➤ **stiflingly** *adv.*

**stigma** *n* (*pl* **stigmas** *or* **stigmata**) **1** a connotation of disgrace associated with certain things. **2** (*pl* **stigmata**) (*in pl*) in Christianity, marks on a person resembling those left on Christ's body by the Crucifixion. **3** the part of a flower that receives the pollen.

**stigmatize** *or* **-ise** *v* (*often* + as) to describe or categorize in disapproving terms. ➤ **stigmatization** *n.*

**stile** *n* a step or set of steps for climbing over a fence or wall.

**stiletto** *n* (*pl* **-os** *or* **-oes**) **1** a slender rodlike dagger. **2** *Brit* an extremely narrow tapering high heel on a woman's shoe.

**still**[1] *adj* **1** not moving. **2** calm or tranquil. **3** of drinks: not fizzy. ➤ **stillness** *n.*

**still**[2] *v* to make calm or quiet.

**still**[3] *adv* **1** as before: *Drink it while it's still hot.* **2** in spite of that; nevertheless. **3** even; yet.

**still**[4] *n* **1** a still photograph, *esp* a single frame from a cinema film. **2** quiet; silence.

**still**[5] *n* an apparatus used in distillation, *esp* of spirits.

**stillborn** *adj* of a baby: dead at birth.

**still life** *n* (*pl* **still lifes**) a picture showing an arrangement of inanimate objects, e.g. fruit or flowers.

**stilt** *n* **1** either of two poles with a footrest, which enable the user to walk along above the ground. **2** any of a set of posts that support a building above ground or water level.

**stilted** *adj* of writing or speech: stiffly formal and unnatural.

**Stilton** *n* a strong variety of cheese, either white or with blue veins.

**stimulant** *n* something, e.g. a drug, that stimulates.

**stimulate** *v* **1** to cause (a physiological process) to take place, or increase the activity of (an organ). **2** to provoke increased activity or interest in (somebody). ➤ **stimulation** *n.*

**stimulus** *n* (*pl* **stimuli**) **1** something, e.g. an environmental change, that directly influences the activity of living organisms, e.g. by exciting a sensory organ. **2** an incentive or inducement.

**sting**[1] *v* (*past tense and past part.* **stung**) **1** *esp* of a plant or insect: to give an irritating or poisonous wound to. **2** of a part of the body: to smart. **3** to cause a pang of bitterness or pain in.

**sting**[2] *n* **1** a sharp organ in certain plants or insects that can wound by piercing and injecting a poisonous secretion. **2** a wound or pain caused by stinging. * **a sting in the tail** a telling and unexpected climax to a story, etc.

**stingray** *n* a ray with a whiplike tail bearing a long poisonous spine.

**stingy** *adj* (**-ier, -iest**) *informal* mean or ungenerous.

**stink**[1] *v* (*past tense* **stank** *or* **stunk,** *past part.* **stunk**) **1** to give off a strong offensive smell. **2** *informal* to be highly suspect or very bad. ➤ **stinker** *n.*

**stink**[2] *n* **1** a strong offensive smell. **2** *informal* a row or scandal.

**stinking**[1] *adj informal* **1** severe and unpleasant. **2** having a strong offensive smell.

**stinking**[2] *adv informal* extremely: *stinking rich.*

**stint**[1] *v* **1** to restrict (somebody) to a small share. **2** (*often* + on) to be sparing or frugal.

**stint**[2] *n* one's quota or round of duty or work.

**stipend** *n* a fixed sum of money paid periodically as a salary or to meet expenses.

**stipendiary** *adj* receiving a stipend, as distinct from working voluntarily.

**stipple** *v* **1** to dapple, speckle, or fleck. **2** to texture or roughen (a painted or cemented surface).

**stipulate** *v* to specify as a condition of an agreement or offer. ➤ **stipulation** *n.*

**stir**[1] *v* (**stirred, stirring**) **1** to move (a liquid or semiliquid) around by repeated circular movement with a spoon, etc, usu in order to blend the ingredients. **2** to make a slight movement. **3** to wake and begin to move. **4** (*often* + up) to rouse (somebody) to activity. **5** *Brit, informal* to create trouble or ill-feeling between people by gossip, tale-bearing, etc. ➤ **stirrer** *n.*

**stir**[2] *n* **1** the act or an instance of stirring. **2** a sensation or commotion.

**stir**[3] *n informal* prison.

**stir-fry** *v* (**-ies, -ied**) to cook (small pieces of food) by stirring them together while frying them rapidly.

**stirring** *adj* rousing; inspiring. ➤ **stirringly** *adv.*

**stirrup** *n* either of a pair of D-shaped metal frames attached to a saddle in which a horse-rider's feet are placed.

**stitch**[1] *n* **1** a loop of thread or yarn left in material by a single in-and-out movement of the needle in sewing, embroidery, knitting, or crochet. **2** a method of stitching. **3** a sharp and sudden pain in the side brought on by running or exercise. * **in stitches** laughing uncontrollably.

**stitch**[2] *v* to sew (fabric, a garment, etc).

**stitch up** *v informal* to incriminate maliciously.

**stoa** *n* (*pl* **stoas** *or* **stoae**) in classical Greek architecture, a portico, roofed colonnade, or colonnaded walk.

**stoat** *n* (*pl* **stoats** *or* **stoat**) a European weasel with a brown coat that turns white in winter in northern regions.

**stock**[1] *n* **1** a store or supply of raw materials or finished goods. **2** (*also in pl*) one's store or supply of anything. **3** farm animals. **4** the capital raised by a company through selling shares. **5** (*in pl*) the shares of a particular company or type of company. **6** the liquid in which meat, fish, or vegetables have been simmered. **7** the trunk or main stem of a plant. **8** a plant grown for its sweet-scented flowers. **9** a person's line of descent. **10** a breed or variety of a plant or animal. **11** (*in pl*) formerly, a wooden frame with holes in which an offender's feet could be locked as a public punishment. * **in stock** in the shop or warehouse and available for delivery. **out of stock** sold out; having none available for delivery. **take stock** to review a situation.

**stock**[2] *v* **1** to supply (a place) with a stock of something. **2** to start or keep a stock of (something). * **stock up** (*often* + on) to lay in a supply of something.

**stock**[3] *adj informal* commonly used; standard.

**stockade** *n* a line of stout posts set vertically to form an enclosure or a defensive barrier.

**stockbroker** *n* a broker who buys and sells securities. ➤ **stockbroking** *n.*

**stock car** *n* a strengthened assembly-line car used in races where drivers try to force each other off the track.

**stock exchange** *n* a stock market or the building housing it.

**stocking** *n* **1** a woman's closely fitting garment for the foot and leg. **2** *NAmer or archaic* a man's long sock. **3** (*also* **Christmas stocking**) an ornamental stocking hung up by children on Christmas Eve, to be filled with presents. ➤ **stockinged** *adj.*

**stock-in-trade** *n* **1** the equipment used in a trade or business. **2** the range of skills habitually used by an individual in an activity.

**stockist** *n Brit* a retailer who stocks goods of a particular kind.

**stock market** *n* a market where brokers buy and sell stocks and shares, or the transactions made there.

**stockpile**[1] *n* a reserve supply of something essential for use during a shortage.

**stockpile**[2] *v* to accumulate a stockpile of (an essential commodity, etc).

**stock-still** *adv* completely motionless.

**stocktaking** *n* the process of taking an inventory of goods or supplies held e.g. in a shop.

**stocky** *adj* (**-ier, -iest**) *esp* of a person: short and sturdy.

**stodge** *n chiefly Brit, informal* heavy filling starchy food, such as steamed pudding. ➤ **stodgy** *adj.*

**stoic** *n* a stoical person.

**stoical** *adj* bearing pain, hardship, and sorrow without complaining. ➤ **stoically** *adv.*

**stoke** *v* **1** to supply (a fire or furnace) with fuel. **2** to feed or encourage (an emotion). ➤ **stoker** *n.*

**stole**[1] *v* past tense of STEAL[1].

**stole**[2] *n* a large rectangular scarf or shawl worn by women across the shoulders.

**stolen** *v* past part. of STEAL[1].

**stolid** *adj* difficult to arouse emotionally or mentally. ➤ **stolidity** *n,* **stolidly** *adv.*

**stomach**[1] *n* **1** a saclike internal organ in which the first stages of digestion occur. **2** the part of the body that contains the stomach; the belly or abdomen. **3** appetite or inclination.

**stomach**[2] *v* **1** to find (food) palatable or digestible. **2** to bear (something irksome) without protest.

**stomp** *v informal* to walk or dance with a heavy step.

**stone**[1] *n* **1** the hard mineral matter of which rock is composed. **2** a piece of rock; a pebble. **3** a gem. **4** a piece of stone adapted to a particular function, e.g. a gravestone. **5** the hard seed in a peach, cherry, plum, etc. **6** (*pl usu* **stone**) *Brit* a unit of weight equal to 14 pounds (about 6.35 kilograms). ✱ **a stone's throw** no very great distance. **leave no stone unturned** to make every possible effort to find or obtain something.

**stone**[2] *v* **1** to hurl stones at. **2** to remove the stones or seeds of (a fruit).

**stone**[3] *adv* completely: *stone deaf.*

**Stone Age** *n* (**the Stone Age**) the first known period of prehistoric human culture characterized by the use of stone tools.

**stoned** *adj informal* intoxicated by a drug, e.g. marijuana, or alcohol.

**stonewall** *v* **1** to be evasive or obstructive. **2** *chiefly Brit* to bat very defensively in cricket.

**stony** *adj* (**-ier, -iest**) **1** full of stones. **2** resembling stone. **3** cold or unresponsive. ➤ **stonily** *adv.*

**stood** *v* past tense and past part. of STAND[1].

**stooge** *n* **1** a person being used by somebody more powerful to do distasteful jobs. **2** the member of a comedy duo who is the butt of the other's jokes.

**stool** *n* **1** a seat usu without back or arms. **2** *esp* in medicine, a discharge of faecal matter. ✱ **fall between two stools** to fail to fit into either of two categories or avail oneself of either of two possibilities.

**stool pigeon** *n chiefly NAmer* a police informer.

**stoop**[1] *v* **1** to bend the body forward and downward. **2** to lower oneself morally.

**stoop**[2] *n* a stooping position or posture.

**stop**[1] *v* (**stopped, stopping**) **1** to come or bring to an end. **2** to discontinue moving. **3** of a bus or train: to call at a place to take on or let off passengers. **4** to prevent from doing or continuing something. **5** to prevent from happening. **6** to cease or discontinue (an activity). **7** to block or plug (a leak, opening, etc). ✱ **stop at nothing** to be unscrupulous in achieving one's ends. **stop dead** to come to a sudden halt.

**stop**[2] *n* **1** the act of stopping. **2** a place where a train or bus halts to let passengers on or off. **3** a device or mechanism that prevents movement. **4** a knob on an organ that brings a particular set of pipes into play. ✱ **pull out all the stops** to do everything possible to achieve something. **put a stop to something** to prevent something from continuing.

**stopcock** *n* a valve for stopping or regulating flow, e.g. of fluid through a pipe.

**stopgap** *n* a temporary expedient; a makeshift.

**stop off** *or* **stop over** *v* to break one's journey somewhere, *esp* overnight.

**stoppage** *n* **1** an act of stopping. **2** a blockage. **3** a cessation of work by a group of employees as a form of industrial action. **4** *Brit* a deduction from pay for National Insurance, etc.

**stopper**[1] *n* a plug or bung.

**stopper**[2] *v* to close or secure with a stopper.

**stop press** *n* late news added to a newspaper after printing has begun.

**stop up** *v* **1** to block (a hole, passage, etc). **2** *Brit, informal* to delay going to bed until late.

**stopwatch** *n* a watch that can be started and stopped at will for exact timing of races, etc.

**storage** *n* **1** the act of storing. **2** space available for storing things.

**storage heater** *n Brit* an electric device that stores heat at night, when electricity is cheap, and radiates it during the daytime.

**store**[1] *v* **1** (*often* + up/away) to keep or accumulate as a reserve supply. **2** to place (property, furniture, etc) in a warehouse, etc for later use or disposal. **3** to enter (data) in a computer memory, on a diskette, etc, for future access.

**store**[2] *n* **1** a quantity of things kept for future use. **2** (*in pl*) in the armed forces, etc, a supply of food, equipment, ammunition, etc. **3** a collection or accumulation. **4** storage. **5** (*also* **department store**) a large shop selling a variety of goods. **6** *NAmer* a shop. ✱ **in store** awaiting one in the future. **set store by something** to regard something as important and worthwhile.

**storey** (*NAmer* **story**) *n* (*pl* **-eys** *or NAmer* **-ies**) a horizontal division or level of a building.

**stork** *n* a large wading bird with a long stout bill and black and white plumage.

**storm**[1] *n* **1** a violent disturbance of the weather marked by high winds and usu by rain, thunder and lightning, etc. **2** a tumultuous outburst.

* **storm in a teacup** a disproportionate fuss about something relatively minor.

**storm**[2] *v* **1** to shout angrily; to rage. **2** to rush furiously. **3** of troops: to make a sudden violent attack on (a place) to capture it.

**storm troops** *pl n* = SHOCK TROOPS.

**stormy** *adj* (**-ier, -iest**) **1** wild, windy, or characterized by storms. **2** full of turmoil or fury.

**story**[1] *n* (*pl* **-ies**) **1** an account of real or imaginary events. **2** the plot of a literary or dramatic work. **3** a rumour. **4** a lie. **5** a news article or broadcast.

**story**[2] *n* (*pl* **-ies**) *NAmer* see STOREY.

**stoup** *n* a basin for holy water at the entrance of a church.

**stout**[1] *adj* **1** heavily built; fat. **2** strong and thick. **3** bold and brave. ➤ **stoutly** *adv.*

**stout**[2] *n* a dark sweet heavy-bodied beer.

**stove**[1] *n* **1** an enclosed appliance that burns fuel for heating. **2** a cooker.

**stove**[2] *v* a past tense and past part. of STAVE[2].

**stow** *v* to pack away in an orderly fashion in an enclosed space.

**stowaway** *n* a person who stows away, *esp* on a ship.

**stow away** *v* to hide on board *esp* a ship, as a means of travelling without payment or undetected.

**straddle** *v* **1** to stand, sit, or be astride. **2** to be on land on either side of.

**strafe** *v* to attack (ground troops, etc) with fire from low-flying aircraft.

**straggle** *v* **1** to lag behind or stray away from a body of people going somewhere together. **2** to grow or spread untidily. ➤ **straggler** *n,* **straggly** *adj.*

**straight**[1] *adj* **1** extending in one direction without bends or curves. **2** level, upright, or symmetrically positioned; not skew. **3** in a proper or tidy state. **4** honest or fair. **5** clear, simple, or logical. **6** candid; frank; not evasive. **7** of successes: following consecutively or uninterruptedly. **8** of an alcoholic drink: unmixed; neat. **9** *informal* conventional in appearance, habits, opinions, etc. **10** *informal* heterosexual. * **keep a straight face** to refrain from laughing.

**straight**[2] *adv* **1** directly; in a straight line. **2** without delay or hesitation. * **go straight** to leave one's life of crime and live honestly. **straight off/out** without hesitation.

**straight**[3] *n* a straight part or piece of something, *esp* a racetrack.

**straightaway** *or* **straight away** *adv* immediately.

**straighten** *v* to make or become straight.

**straightforward** *adj* **1** truthful and direct. **2** presenting no hidden difficulties. ➤ **straightforwardly** *adv.*

**straightjacket** *n* see STRAITJACKET.

**straightlaced** *adj* see STRAITLACED.

**strain**[1] *v* **1** to exert (a part of one's body) to the maximum. **2** to wrench or sprain (a part of one's body) through over-exertion. **3** to make great or excessive demands on. **4** to pass (a liquid) through a sieve or filter.

**strain**[2] *n* **1** a pulling or stretching force exerted on something. **2** a great demand on one's strength, resources, etc. **3** mental or emotional stress. **4** an injury caused by excessive tension, effort, or use. **5** (*also in pl*) a tune or passage of music.

**strain**[3] *n* **1** a breed or variety of an animal or plant. **2** an inherited but not dominant characteristic, quality, or disposition.

**strained** *adj* **1** done or produced with excessive effort; not spontaneous. **2** tense; uneasy. **3** showing the effects of strain.

**strainer** *n* a device, e.g. a sieve, to retain solid pieces while a liquid passes through.

**strait** *n* **1** (*also in pl*) a narrow channel connecting two large bodies of water. **2** (*in pl*) a situation of difficulty or distress.

**straitened** *adj* poverty-stricken or necessitating severe economies.

**straitjacket** *or* **straightjacket** *n* **1** an outer garment of strong material used to bind the arms of a violent prisoner or psychiatric patient. **2** something very restrictive or confining.

**straitlaced** *or* **straightlaced** *adj* excessively strict in manners or morals.

**strand**[1] *v* **1** to cause (a ship or whale) to run aground on a shore. **2** to leave (a person) in a strange place without the means to leave it.

**strand**[2] *n literary* a shore or beach.

**strand**[3] *n* **1** any of the threads, strings, or wires twisted to make a cord, rope, etc. **2** any of the elements interwoven in a complex whole.

**strange** *adj* **1** not known, heard, seen, or visited before. **2** exciting wonder or surprise. ➤ **strangely** *adv.*

**stranger** *n* **1** a person with whom one is unacquainted. **2** a person unfamiliar in the place in question.

**strangle** *v* **1** to choke (a person or animal), *esp* to death, by compressing their throat. **2** to hinder the development of (something). ➤ **strangler** *n.*

**stranglehold** *n* **1** a grip round the neck that can lead to strangulation. **2** a total control or monopoly of something.

**strangulation** *n* the act of strangling.

**strap**[1] *n* **1** a strip of flexible material used for fastening, securing, holding together, or carrying. **2** (**the strap**) punishment by beating with a leather strap. ➤ **strapless** *adj,* **strappy** *adj.*

**strap**[2] *v* (**strapped, strapping**) to secure with or attach by a strap.

**strapping** *adj* of a person: big, strong, and sturdy.

**stratagem** *n* a scheme for deceiving and outwitting an opponent.

**strategic** *adj* **1** relating to the long-term pursuit of objectives. **2** relating to military effectiveness. **3** of weapons, missiles, etc: designed to attack the enemy homeland, rather than for use on the battlefield. ➤ **strategically** *adv.*

**strategy** *n* (*pl* **-ies**) **1** military planning on a broad scale for the conduct of a campaign or battle: compare TACTICS. **2** long-term planning in the pursuit of objectives. **3** a plan or method devised to achieve a long-term objective. ➤ **strategist** *n.*

**stratify** *v* (**-ies, -ied**) to form, deposit, or arrange (material, etc) in strata. ➤ **stratification** *n.*

**stratosphere** *n* **1** the layer of the earth's atmosphere above the troposphere at a height of 10–50 km. **2** *informal* the highest levels of something. ➤ **stratospheric** *adj.*

**stratum** *n* (*pl* **strata**) **1** a horizontal layer or series of layers of rock. **2** a socioeconomic level of society.

**straw** *n* **1** dry stalks of grain, used for bedding, thatching, fodder, etc. **2** a single stalk of grain. **3** a tube of paper, plastic, etc for sucking up a drink. **4** a pale yellow colour. * **catch/clutch/grasp at straws** to turn in desperation to any means of saving the situation. **draw the short straw** to be the person chosen to do something unpleasant. **the last straw** the last of a series of misfortunes, which makes a situation unbearable.

**strawberry** *n* (*pl* **-ies**) a small sweet red fruit covered with seeds.

**strawberry blonde** *n* a reddish blonde hair colour.

**straw poll** *n* an unofficial test of opinion.

**stray**[1] *v* **1** to wander away from the main group, or from the proper place or route. **2** of an eye or hand: to move apparently casually in some direction.

**stray**[2] *adj* **1** of a domestic animal: having strayed; lost. **2** not in the proper place. **3** occurring at random or sporadically.

**streak**[1] *n* **1** a line or band of a different colour from the background. **2** an inherent quality, *esp* in somebody's character: *a mean streak.* **3** a series of successes, failures, etc.

**streak**[2] *v* **1** to make streaks on or in. **2** to move swiftly. **3** *informal* to run naked through a public place. ➤ **streaked** *n,* **streaking** *n.*

**streaky** *adj* (**-ier, -iest**) **1** marked with streaks. **2** of bacon: having lines of fat and lean.

**stream**[1] *n* **1** a body of running water, smaller and narrower than a river. **2** an unbroken flow, procession, or succession, e.g. of gas, traffic, or people. **3** *Brit* a group to which schoolchildren of the same age are assigned according to their general academic ability. * **on/off stream** operational or available/not so.

**stream**[2] *v* **1** to flow in a stream, or in large quantities. **2** to trail or extend in a trail. **3** to run profusely with liquid. **4** *Brit* to divide (a school or an age group of pupils) into streams.

**streamer** *n* **1** a coiled strip of coloured paper for throwing at a party. **2** a pennant.

**streamline** *v* **1** to design (a vehicle, etc) so as to minimize resistance to motion, e.g. through air. **2** to make (an organization) simpler or more efficient.

**street** *n* a public road in a city, town, or village. * **on the streets** earning one's living as a prostitute. **streets ahead/better** *informal* immeasurably better. **up/down one's street** suited to one's abilities or tastes.

**streetcar** *n NAmer* a tram.

**streetwalker** *n* a prostitute who solicits in the streets.

**streetwise** *adj informal* resourceful at surviving and prospering in modern urban conditions.

**strength** *n* **1** the physical power one has in one's body. **2** in a material object: ability to withstand pressure, prolonged use, etc. **3** the intensity of something. **4** the number of people who belong to or are needed for a particular type of group. **5** a good point. * **go from strength to strength** to become ever more successful. **on the strength of** on the basis of (something).

**strengthen** *v* to make or become stronger.

**strenuous** *adj* **1** vigorous and wholehearted. **2** requiring effort or stamina. ➤ **strenuously** *adv.*

**stress**[1] *n* **1** pressure exerted on a physical object. **2** mental or emotional tension. **3** emphasis given to a syllable, word, etc. **4** relative importance attached to an idea, fact, etc.

**stress**[2] *v* **1** to emphasize (a point, etc). **2** to accent or emphasize (a word, syllable, etc). **3** (*usu in passive, also* + out) to subject to emotional or mental stress.

**stressful** *adj* causing mental or emotional tension.

**stretch**[1] *v* **1** to pull or extend (material) till it becomes taut. **2** of material, garments, etc: to have an elastic quality. **3** of materials, garments, etc: to become permanently enlarged. **4** to extend one's body or limbs to full length. **5** (+ out) to lie at full length. **6** to extend in space or time. **7** to provide an adequate challenge for (a person or their mind). **8** to strain (some resource, etc). ➤ **stretchy** *adj.*

**stretch**[2] *n* **1** an act of stretching. **2** elasticity. **3** an extent or area. **4** a period of time. **5** *informal* a period in prison. * **not by any stretch of the imagination** not conceivably.

**stretcher**[1] *n* a light portable bed for carrying a sick, injured, or dead person, typically a sheet of canvas stretched between two poles.

**stretcher**[2] *v* to carry (an injured or sick person) on a stretcher.

**strew** *v* (*past part.* **strewn**) **1** to spread by scattering. **2** (+ with) to cover (a place) with something scattered.

**striated** *adj* marked with grooves, ridges, or streaks.

**stricken**[1] *adj* **1** horrified or distressed. **2** badly hurt or affected by illness, calamity, emotion, etc: *panic-stricken.*

**stricken**[2] *v NAmer* past part. of STRIKE[1].

**strict** *adj* **1** determined to enforce discipline and observance of rules. **2** rigorously conforming to rules or standards. **3** exact or precise. ➤ **strictly** *n.*

**stricture** *n* **1** a restraint or restriction. **2** a censure.

**stride**[1] *v* (**strode, stridden**) to walk with long steps.

**stride**[2] *n* **1** a long step. **2** a state of maximum competence or capability: *get into one's stride.* ✱ **make strides** to make good progress. **take something in one's stride** to deal with something difficult or unpleasant calmly.

**strident** *adj* **1** loud and obtrusive. **2** expressing opinions, demands, etc loudly or urgently. ➤ **stridency** *n,* **stridently** *adv.*

**strife** *n* bitter conflict or dissension.

**strike**[1] *v* (*past tense* **struck,** *past part.* **struck** *or NAmer* **stricken**) **1** to hit with one's hand, a weapon, a bat, etc. **2** to collide with. **3** to carry out an attack. **4** to make a mental impact on. **5** to occur suddenly to. **6** to make and ratify (a bargain). **7** to indicate (the time) by sounding. **8** to create (a particular mood, atmosphere, etc): *The speech struck a gloomy note.* **9** to put (somebody) suddenly in a particular state: *The blow struck him unconscious.* **10** (*often* + out) to delete or cancel. **11** to cause (a match) to ignite. **12** to discover (something, *esp* minerals). **13** (+ off/out) to embark on a journey, *esp* in a particular direction. **14** to withdraw one's labour in protest against an employer.

**strike**[2] *n* **1** a stoppage of work by employees. **2** a discovery of a valuable mineral deposit. **3** a military attack, *esp* an air attack.

**strike off** *v* to forbid (*esp* a doctor) to continue in professional practice.

**striker** *n* **1** a football player whose main role is to score goals. **2** a worker on strike.

**strike up** *v* **1** to begin to sing or play. **2** to cause (e.g. a friendship or conversation) to begin.

**striking** *adj* attracting attention; unusual or impressive. ➤ **strikingly** *adv.*

**string**[1] *n* **1** a narrow cord used *esp* to tie or fasten things. **2** a length of gut, wire, etc used to produce notes in certain musical instruments, e.g. the violin and piano. **3** (*in pl*) the stringed instruments of an orchestra. **4** a group of objects threaded on a string. **5** a succession or sequence. **6** (*in pl*) conditions or obligations attached to something: *a relationship with no strings attached.*

**string**[2] *v* (*past tense and past part.* **strung**) **1** to equip with strings. **2** to thread (things) on a string. **3** to tie, hang, or fasten with string. **4** (*often* + out) to extend, stretch, or prolong. ➤ **stringed** *adj.*

**string along** *v informal* to deceive or fool.

**string bean** *n* a bean with stringy fibres between the sides of the pods, e.g. a runner bean.

**stringent** *adj* rigorous or strict. ➤ **stringency** *n,* **stringently** *adv.*

**string quartet** *n* a group of four musicians playing stringed instruments, usu comprising two violins, a viola, and a cello.

**stringy** *adj* (**-ier, -iest**) resembling string; in long thin pieces or fibrous in texture.

**strip**[1] *v* (**stripped, stripping**) **1** to remove clothing, covering, or surface material from. **2** to remove one's clothes. **3** to remove (wallpaper, paint, etc) from a surface. **4** (+ of) to deprive of possessions, privileges, or rank. **5** to remove furniture, equipment, or accessories from (e.g. a house or ship). **6** (*often* + down) to dismantle (e.g. an engine).

**strip**[2] *n* the act of undressing, *esp* a striptease.

**strip**[3] *n* **1** a long narrow piece of material. **2** a long narrow area of land. **3** *Brit* the distinctive clothes worn by a sports team.

**strip cartoon** *n* a series of drawings forming a usu humorous narrative.

**stripe**[1] *n* a narrow band differing in colour or texture from adjacent parts. ➤ **stripey** *adj,* **stripy** *adj.*

**stripe**[2] *v* to mark stripes on. ➤ **striped** *adj.*

**strip light** *n* a long tubular fluorescent lamp.

**stripling** *n archaic or humorous* an adolescent boy.

**stripper** *n* **1** somebody who performs a striptease. **2** a tool or solvent for removing something, *esp* paint.

**striptease** *n* an entertainment in which a performer undresses gradually in an erotic manner.

**strive** *v* (*past tense* **strove** *or* **strived,** *past part.* **striven** *or* **strived**) **1** to try hard. **2** (+ against) to struggle against.

**strobe** *n* a bright intermittently flashing light, e.g. at a disco.

**strode** *v* past tense of STRIDE[1].

**stroke**[1] *v* to pass the hand over gently.

**stroke**[2] *n* an act of stroking.

**stroke**[3] *n* **1** an act of striking. **2** a striking of the ball in a game, *esp* one that constitutes the scoring unit in golf. **3** an unexpected occurrence: *a stroke of luck.* **4** a sudden disabling attack caused by rupture or obstruction of an artery of the brain. **5** a technique for propelling the body or a boat through water. **6** a repeated movement e.g. of a mechanical part such as a piston rod. **7** the sound of a striking clock. **8** a mark made by a single movement of a pen, brush, etc. **9** *Brit* a punctuation mark (/) used e.g. to separate alternatives. ✻ **at a stroke** by a single action. **off one's stroke** performing below one's usual standard.

**stroll**[1] *v* to walk in a leisurely manner.

**stroll**[2] *n* a leisurely walk.

**strong** *adj* **1** having or marked by great physical power or resistance. **2** having moral or intellectual power. **3** having great resources of wealth, talent, etc. **4** striking or superior of its kind. **5** effective or efficient, *esp* in a specified area. **6** forceful or cogent. **7** rich in some active agent, e.g. a flavour or extract; concentrated. **8** of a colour: intense. **9** full of passion or enthusiasm. **10** of a specified number: *an army ten thousand strong.* ✻ **(still) going strong** *informal* continuing to be active, effective, successful, etc. ➤ **strongly** *adv.*

**strongarm** *adj* using or involving undue force.

**strongbox** *n* a strongly made chest for money or valuables.

**stronghold** *n* **1** a fortified place. **2** a place dominated by a specified group.

**strong room** *n* a fireproof and burglarproof room in which money and valuables are stored.

**strontium** *n* a silver-white metallic element.

**strop**[1] *n* a leather band used for sharpening a razor.

**strop**[2] *n Brit, informal* an angry mood.

**stroppy** *adj* (**-ier, -iest**) *Brit, informal* quarrelsome or angrily uncooperative.

**strove** *v* past tense of STRIVE.

**struck** *v* past tense and past part. of STRIKE[1].

**structural** *adj* relating to or forming part of a structure. ➤ **structurally** *adv.*

**structure**[1] *n* **1** something constructed, e.g. a building. **2** the way in which something is constructed or organized.

**structure**[2] *v* to construct or organize in a particular way.

**strudel** *n* a dessert made from a thin sheet of dough rolled up with filling and baked.

**struggle**[1] *v* **1** to proceed with difficulty or great effort. **2** to make violent or strenuous efforts against opposition or confinement. **3** to make strenuous efforts to do something. ➤ **struggler** *n.*

**struggle**[2] *n* **1** a violent effort or exertion. **2** a determined attempt in adverse circumstances. **3** a difficult task.

**strum** *v* (**strummed, strumming**) to play (e.g. a guitar) by brushing the thumb, the fingertips, or a plectrum over the strings.

**strumpet** *n archaic or humorous* a prostitute or promiscuous woman.

**strung** *v* past tense and past part. of STRING[1].

**strut**[1] *v* (**strutted, strutting**) to walk with a proud or erect gait. ✻ **strut one's stuff** to show off one's skills or talents.

**strut**[2] *n* **1** a structural piece designed to support or strengthen a framework. **2** a strutting step or walk.

**strychnine** *n* a bitter poisonous chemical compound obtained from an Asian plant.

**Stuart** *adj* relating to the royal house that ruled Scotland from 1371 to 1603 and Britain from 1603 to 1649 and from 1660 to 1714.

**stub**[1] *n* **1** a small part of a chequebook page, ticket, etc left as a record of the contents of the part torn away. **2** a short remaining part of a pencil, cigarette, etc left after the larger part has been used up.

**stub**[2] *v* (**stubbed, stubbing**) **1** to strike (one's foot or toe) against a hard object or surface accidentally. **2** (+ out) to extinguish (e.g. a cigarette) by crushing the end.

**stubble** *n* **1** the stalky remnants of crops left in the soil after harvest. **2** a rough growth of short bristly hairs on a man's face. ➤ **stubbly** *adj.*

**stubborn** *adj* **1** determined, *esp* unreasonably determined, not to change or give way. **2** difficult to get rid of. ➤ **stubbornly** *adv,* **stubbornness** *n.*

**stucco** *n* (*pl* **-os** *or* **-oes**) a fine plaster used to coat or decorate ceilings and walls. ➤ **stuccoed** *adj.*

**stuck** *v* past tense and past part. of STICK[1].

**stuck-up** *adj informal* self-important or conceited.

**stud**[1] *n* **1** a solid button with a shank on the back inserted through an eyelet in a garment as a fastener or ornament. **2** a rivet or nail with a large head used for ornament or protection. **3** a small piece of jewellery for a pierced ear, etc. **4** a projecting piece, e.g. on a boot or tyre, to increase grip.

**stud**[2] *v* (**studded, studding**) **1** to decorate, cover, or protect with studs. **2** to set thickly with prominent objects.

**stud**[3] *n* **1** an animal, esp a stallion, or group of animals kept primarily for breeding. **2** a place, e.g. a farm, where such animals are kept. **3** *informal* a sexually active man.

**student** *n* **1** somebody who studies something, *esp* at a college or university. **2** a pupil at *esp* a secondary school.

**studied** *adj* carefully considered or prepared.

**studio** *n* (*pl* **-os**) **1** the workroom of a painter, sculptor, or photographer. **2** a place for the study of an art, e.g. dancing, singing, or acting. **3** a place where films are made. **4** a room equipped for the production of radio or television programmes.

**studio flat** *n* a small flat with one main room.

**studious** *adj* **1** pursuing studies seriously and with commitment. **2** deliberate and meticulous. ➤ **studiously** *adv.*

**study**[1] *n* (*pl* **-ies**) **1** the application of the mind to acquiring knowledge, *esp* by reading. **2** a careful examination or analysis of a subject. **3** a room devoted to study, writing, reading, etc. **4** a literary or artistic work intended as preliminary or experimental.

**study²** *v* (**-ies, -ied**) **1** to engage in study. **2** to engage in the study of (a subject). **3** to read, observe, or consider attentively or in detail.

**stuff¹** *n* **1** materials, supplies, or equipment used in various activities. **2** personal property; possessions. **3** an unspecified material substance. **4** a group of miscellaneous objects. **5** subject matter or expertise. **6** the essence of a usu abstract thing.

**stuff²** *v* **1** to fill by packing things or stuffing inside. **2** to gorge (oneself) with food. **3** to fill out the skin of (an animal) for mounting. **4** to force or thrust into a confined space. **5** (*usu* + up) to block up (the nasal passages). **6** *Brit, informal* to defeat or thwart.

**stuffing** *n* **1** material used to stuff e.g. upholstered furniture, soft toys, etc. **2** a seasoned mixture of ingredients used to stuff meat, vegetables, etc.

**stuffy** *adj* (**-ier, -iest**) **1** badly ventilated; close. **2** of the nose: blocked or congested. **3** narrowly conventional in behaviour.

**stultify** *v* (**-ies, -ied**) to bore (somebody) by being tedious or repetitive. ➤ **stultifying** *adj*.

**stumble¹** *v* **1** to trip in walking or running. **2** to walk unsteadily or clumsily. **3** to speak in a hesitant manner. **4** (+ upon/on/across) to find or discover unexpectedly or by chance.

**stumble²** *n* an act of stumbling.

**stumbling block** *n* an obstacle.

**stump¹** *n* **1** the part of a tree remaining in the ground after the tree has been felled. **2** a remaining part. **3** in cricket, any of the three upright wooden rods that, with the bails, form the wicket. ✱ **on the stump** *informal* making a political speech as part of a campaign.

**stump²** *v* **1** *informal* to baffle or bewilder. **2** to walk heavily or noisily.

**stumpy** *adj* (**-ier, -iest**) short and thick; stubby.

**stun** *v* (**stunned, stunning**) **1** to make dazed or briefly unconscious, e.g. by a blow. **2** to overcome with astonishment or disbelief.

**stung** *v* past tense and past part. of STING¹.

**stunk** *v* past tense and past part. of STINK¹.

**stunner** *n informal* an unusually attractive or impressive person or thing.

**stunning** *adj informal* strikingly attractive or impressive. ➤ **stunningly** *adv*.

**stunt¹** *v* to hinder the growth or development of.

**stunt²** *n* **1** a difficult feat displaying physical or acrobatic prowess. **2** something done purely as a way of attracting attention or publicity.

**stuntman** *or* **stuntwoman** *n* (*pl* **stuntmen** *or* **stuntwomen**) a man or woman employed as a substitute for an actor in scenes involving dangerous feats.

**stupefy** *v* (**-ies, -ied**) **1** to make groggy or insensible. **2** to astonish. ➤ **stupefaction** *n*.

**stupendous** *adj* marvellous. ➤ **stupendously** *adv*.

**stupid** *adj* **1** lacking common sense or intelligence. **2** dulled in feeling or perception. ➤ **stupidity** *n*, **stupidly** *adv*.

**stupor** *n* a stupefied condition.

**sturdy** *adj* (**-ier, -iest**) **1** strongly built or constructed. **2** showing determination or firmness of purpose. ➤ **sturdily** *n*.

**sturgeon** *n* a large edible fish whose roe is made into caviar.

**stutter¹** *v* **1** to speak with involuntary hesitations, repetitions, or prolongations of sounds. **2** to make a series of abrupt sounds or movements. ➤ **stutterer** *n*.

**stutter²** *n* **1** the act of stuttering. **2** a speech disorder that produces stuttering.

**sty¹** *n* (*pl* **-ies**) = PIGSTY.

**sty²** *or* **stye** *n* (*pl* **sties** *or* **styes**) an inflamed swelling at the edge of an eyelid.

**Stygian** *adj literary* extremely dark or gloomy.

**style¹** *n* **1** a distinctive or characteristic manner of doing something. **2** a particular design or arrangement of something, e.g. hair. **3** a manner of expression in writing, painting, music, etc, characteristic of an individual, period, etc. **4** elegance or sophistication in dress, social behaviour, etc. **5** a prolongation of a plant ovary with a stigma at the top. ✱ **in style** with much elegance or extravagance.

**style²** *v* **1** to design or arrange in a particular style. **2** to designate by an identifying term.

**styli** *n* pl of STYLUS.

**stylish** *adj* **1** fashionably elegant. **2** characterized by elegance and skill. ➤ **stylishly** *n*.

**stylist** *n* **1** a hairdresser. **2** an artist, designer, etc who is an expert in matters of style.

**stylistic** *adj* relating to style. ➤ **stylistically** *adv*.

**stylize** *or* **-ise** *v* to represent or design with an artistically simplified, streamlined, etc shape rather than according to nature. ➤ **stylized** *adj*.

**stylus** *n* (*pl* **styli** *or* **styluses**) **1** a tiny piece of material, e.g. diamond, used in a gramophone to follow the groove on a record and transmit the sound. **2** a pointed instrument used in ancient times for writing on clay or waxed tablets.

**stymie** *v* (**stymies, stymied, stymying** *or* **stymieing**) to thwart.

**styptic** *adj* tending to contract tissues, *esp* to check bleeding.

**suave** *adj* **1** smoothly charming and polite. **2** *esp* of men: elegant and sophisticated. ➤ **suavely** *n*.

**sub¹** *n informal* **1** a submarine. **2** a subscription. **3** a substitute, *esp* in a sport.

**sub**[2] *v* (**subbed, subbing**) *informal* to act as a substitute.

**sub-** *prefix* **1** under, beneath, or below: *submarine.* **2** lower or next below in rank. **3** a further or secondary instance of a specified action or process: *sublet.* **4** having an incomplete or partial resemblance to: *subhuman.*

**subaltern** *n* a commissioned officer in the British Army ranking below a captain.

**subatomic** *adj* **1** occurring within an atom. **2** smaller than an atom.

**subconscious**[1] *adj* existing in the mind but not admitted to consciousness. ➤ **subconsciously** *adv.*

**subconscious**[2] *n* (**the subconscious**) the part of the mind in which mental activity takes place below the threshold of consciousness.

**subcontinent** *n* a distinct, large subdivision of a continent.

**subcontract** *v* to engage a third party to perform all or part of (work included in an original contract). ➤ **subcontractor** *n.*

**subculture** *n* a sector of society whose members share a pattern of behaviour and values distinguishable from the mainstream culture.

**subcutaneous** *adj* situated or applied under the skin.

**subdivide** *v* to divide (a part of something already divided) into more and smaller parts. ➤ **subdivision** *n.*

**subdue** *v* (**subdues, subdued, subduing**) **1** to bring under control; to curb. **2** to conquer and bring (e.g. a people) into subjection.

**subdued** *adj* **1** lacking normal cheerfulness or liveliness; low-spirited. **2** reduced in force, intensity, or strength.

**subedit** *v* (**subedited, subediting**) *chiefly Brit* to edit (e.g. a newspaper article) in preparation for printing. ➤ **subeditor** *n.*

**subhuman** *adj* below the level expected of normal human beings.

**subject**[1] *n* **1** a branch of knowledge or learning, *esp* one taught or studied. **2** the person or thing that is being discussed, written about, studied, represented, etc. **3** in grammar, the word or phrase in a sentence or clause denoting the person or thing that performs the action of a verb. **4** somebody owing obedience or allegiance to a ruler.

**subject**[2] *adj* **1** (*often* + to) owing obedience or allegiance to. **2** (+ to) dependent or conditional on something. **3** (+ to) liable or exposed to something. **4** (+ to) prone to.

**subject**[3] *v* **1** (+ to) to cause to undergo something. **2** (*often* + to) to bring (e.g. a people) under control or rule. ➤ **subjection** *n.*

**subjective** *adj* determined or affected by a particular individual's views and feelings. ➤ **subjectively** *adv,* **subjectivity** *n.*

**sub judice** /'joohdisi/ *adv* currently being considered by a court and therefore not open to discussion.

**subjugate** *v* to bring under the control of another authority. ➤ **subjugation** *n.*

**subjunctive**[1] *adj* in grammar, denoting a verb mood that represents an act or state not as a fact but as a possibility or wish.

**subjunctive**[2] *n* a verb form expressing the subjunctive mood.

**sublet** *v* (**subletting**, *past tense and past part.* **sublet**) of a tenant: to lease or rent (all or part of a rented property).

**sublimate** *v* **1** in psychology, to divert the expression of (an instinctual impulse) into a socially or culturally acceptable form. **2** = SUBLIME[2]. ➤ **sublimation** *n.*

**sublime**[1] *adj* **1** of the highest moral or spiritual worth; exalted. **2** astoundingly beautiful or grand. **3** outstanding or extreme. ➤ **sublimely** *adv.*

**sublime**[2] *v* in chemistry, to pass directly from the solid to the vapour state when heated, without liquefying.

**subliminal** *adj* existing or functioning below the level of conscious awareness. ➤ **subliminally** *adv.*

**submachine gun** *n* a portable rapid-firing gun.

**submarine**[1] *n* a vessel, *esp* a warship, designed for undersea operations. ➤ **submariner** *n.*

**submarine**[2] *adj* situated, occurring, or growing under the sea.

**submerge** *v* **1** to go or put under water. **2** to cover with water; to flood. **3** to cover or suppress completely.

**submerse** *v technical* to submerge. ➤ **submersion** *n.*

**submersible**[1] *adj* capable of going or operating under water.

**submersible**[2] *n* a vessel used for undersea exploration and construction work.

**submicroscopic** *adj* too small to be seen using an ordinary microscope.

**submission** *n* **1** the act of submitting. **2** something submitted for consideration, inspection, etc.

**submissive** *adj* willing or tending to submit to others. ➤ **submissively** *adv.*

**submit** *v* (**submitted, submitting**) **1** to yield to the authority or will of another. **2** (+ to) to allow oneself to be subjected to something. **3** (+ to) to subject to a process or practice. **4** to send (something) to another person or authority for consideration, inspection, judgment, etc. **5** to put forward as an opinion; to suggest.

**subordinate**[1] *adj* **1** occupying a lower class, rank, or position. **2** of secondary importance.

**subordinate**[2] *n* a person of lower rank.

**subordinate**[3] *v* (*often* + to) to treat as less important than. ➤ **subordination** *n.*

**subplot** *n* a subordinate plot in fiction or drama.
**subpoena**[1] *n* a writ commanding somebody to appear in court.
**subpoena**[2] *v* (**subpoenas, subpoenaed, subpoenaing**) to serve with a subpoena.
**subscribe** *v* **1** (+ to) to pay regularly in order to receive a periodical or service. **2** (+ to) to feel favourably disposed to something; to agree with it. **3** to give a written pledge to contribute (an amount of money). ➤ **subscriber** *n.*
**subscript** *adj* of a letter, number, etc: written or printed below another character.
**subscription** *n* **1** the act of subscribing to something. **2** a sum of money subscribed. **3** *Brit* membership fees paid regularly.
**subsection** *n* a subdivision of a section.
**subsequent** *adj* following in time or order; succeeding. ➤ **subsequently** *adv.*
**subservient** *adj* **1** obsequiously submissive. **2** subordinate. ➤ **subservience** *n.*
**subside** *v* **1** to become less forceful or intense. **2** to fall to a lower level or return to a normal level. **3** of ground: to cave in. **4** of a building: to sink into the ground.
**subsidence** *n* the slow sinking of an area of land.
**subsidiary**[1] *adj* **1** supplementary or auxiliary. **2** of secondary importance.
**subsidiary**[2] *n* (*pl* **-ies**) a company that is wholly controlled by another.
**subsidize** *or* **-ise** *v* **1** to provide with a subsidy. **2** to pay part of the cost of (a product or service), making it cheaper for those who buy or use it. ➤ **subsidization** *n.*
**subsidy** *n* (*pl* **-ies**) a grant or gift of money, e.g. by a government to assist an enterprise deemed advantageous to the public.
**subsist** *v* to have only the basic necessities of life.
**subsistence** *n* the minimum, e.g. of food and shelter, necessary to support life.
**subsoil** *n* the layer of weathered material that lies under the surface soil.
**subsonic** *adj* travelling at a speed less than that of sound in air.
**substance** *n* **1** a physical material. **2** the fundamental or essential part or meaning. **3** correspondence with reality. **4** material of real value or importance.
**substandard** *adj* of lesser quality than expected or prescribed.
**substantial** *adj* **1** significantly large. **2** ample to satisfy and nourish. **3** firmly constructed; solid. **4** relating to the essence of something.
**substantially** *adv* **1** for the most part; basically. **2** by a large amount; greatly.
**substantiate** *v* to establish (e.g. a statement or claim) by proof or evidence.
**substantive** *adj* having substance or significance. ➤ **substantively** *adv.*
**substitute**[1] *n* somebody or something that takes the place of another.
**substitute**[2] *v* (*usu* + for) to put (one thing) in the place of another. ➤ **substitution** *n.*
**subsume** *v* to include as a member of a group; to incorporate.
**subterfuge** *n* **1** deception or trickery used as a means of concealment or evasion. **2** a trick or ruse.
**subterranean** *adj* existing or occurring under the surface of the earth.
**subtext** *n* the underlying meaning or theme of a text.
**subtitle**[1] *n* **1** a printed text, e.g. a translation, that appears at the bottom of the screen during a film or television broadcast. **2** a secondary or explanatory title.
**subtitle**[2] *v* to provide a subtitle or subtitles for.
**subtle** *adj* **1** pleasantly or tastefully delicate; understated. **2** difficult to understand, analyse, or distinguish. **3** showing keen insight and perception. **4** cleverly contrived; ingenious. ➤ **subtlety** *n,* **subtly** *adv.*
**subtotal** *n* the sum of part of a series of figures.
**subtract** *v* to take (one number) away from another in calculating the difference between them. ➤ **subtraction** *n.*
**suburb** *n* an outlying part of a city or large town, *esp* a residential district.
**suburbia** *n* the suburbs of a city, or their inhabitants.
**subversive**[1] *adj* tending to undermine the established system, e.g. of government.
**subversive**[2] *n* a person engaged in subversive activities.
**subvert** *v* to overthrow or undermine the power of (e.g. a government or institution). ➤ **subversion** *n.*
**subway** *n* **1** *Brit* a passage under a street for pedestrians. **2** *NAmer* an underground railway.
**succeed** *v* **1** to achieve a desired object or end. **2** to attain wealth or fame. **3** (+ to) to inherit something, *esp* sovereignty, rank, or title. **4** to follow after another in order.
**success** *n* **1** the achievement of a desired object or end. **2** the attainment of wealth or fame. **3** somebody or something that succeeds.
**successful** *adj* **1** resulting in success. **2** having succeeded. **3** having gained wealth, fame, etc. ➤ **successfully** *adv.*
**succession** *n* **1** a number of people or things that follow each other in sequence. **2** the process of becoming entitled to a another person's property or title. ✱ **in succession** following one another without interruption.
**successive** *adj* following one after the other. ➤ **successively** *adv.*
**successor** *n* a person who succeeds another in a title, office, etc.
**succinct** *adj* clearly expressed in few words. ➤ **succinctly** *adv.*

**succour**[1] (*NAmer* **succor**) *n* assistance in time of difficulty.
**succour**[2] (*NAmer* **succor**) *v* to go to the aid of.
**succulent**[1] *adj* **1** of food: full of juice and flavour. **2** of a plant: having juicy fleshy tissues. ➤ **succulence** *n.*
**succulent**[2] *n* a succulent plant, e.g. a cactus.
**succumb** *v* **1** (+ to) to give in to something or somebody with superior strength or overpowering appeal. **2** to die from disease or injury.
**such**[1] *adj and adv* **1** of the kind, quality, or extent. **2** of that or the same sort: *There's no such place.* **3** of so extreme a degree or extraordinary a nature: *in such a hurry.* ✻ **such as 1** for example: *reptiles, such as lizards.* **2** the same kind as; like: *women such as my sister.*
**such**[2] *pron* (*pl* **such**) (*in pl*) similar people or things: *tin and glass and such.* ✻ **as such** in himself, herself, itself, or themselves; intrinsically.
**such and such** *adj informal* not named or specified.
**suchlike**[1] *adj* of the kind mentioned; similar.
**suchlike**[2] *pron* (*pl* **suchlike**) a similar person or thing.
**suck**[1] *v* **1** to draw (e.g. liquid) into the mouth by creating a partial vacuum with the lips and tongue. **2** to draw liquid from (something) in this way. **3** to eat (e.g. a sweet) by means of sucking movements of the lips and tongue. **4** to draw in or up by suction. **5** (+ in/into) to draw (somebody) by irresistible force.
**suck**[2] *n* an act of sucking.
**sucker** *n* **1** a cup-shaped device, *esp* of rubber, that can cling to a surface by suction. **2** a mouth or other animal organ adapted for sucking or clinging to a surface. **3** a shoot from the roots or stem of a plant that can grow into an independent plant. **4** *informal* a gullible person. **5** *informal* a person irresistibly attracted by something specified.
**suckle** *v* **1** to give milk to (a baby or young animal) from the breast or udder. **2** of a baby or young animal: to take milk from the breast or udder.
**suckling** *n* an unweaned baby or young animal.
**suck up** *v informal* (*often* + to) to act in an obsequious manner.
**sucralose** *n* an artificial sweetener about 600 times sweeter than sugar.
**sucrose** *n* the form of sugar obtained from sugarcane and sugar beet and occurring in most plants.
**suction** *n* a force that draws something in or causes it to adhere, produced by a partial vacuum over part of its surface.
**sudden** *adj* **1** happening or coming unexpectedly. **2** marked by haste; abrupt. ➤ **suddenly** *adv,* **suddenness** *n.*
**suds** *pl n* the lather on soapy water.
**sue** *v* **1** to bring a legal action against (a person, institution, etc). **2** (*usu* + for) to make a formal request for.
**suede** *n* leather with a velvety surface produced by rubbing the flesh side.
**suet** *n* the hard fat round the kidneys and loins in cattle or sheep, used in cooking.
**suffer** *v* **1** (*often* + from) to be affected by or be subject to (an illness or condition). **2** to experience (something unpleasant). **3** to sustain loss or damage. **4** *archaic* to tolerate. ➤ **sufferer** *n.*
**sufferance** *n* tolerance implying a lack of objection rather than actual approval.
**suffice** *v* **1** to be enough. **2** to be enough for (somebody or something).
**sufficiency** *n* (*pl* **-ies**) **1** a sufficient amount. **2** adequacy.
**sufficient** *adj* enough; adequate. ➤ **sufficiently** *adv.*
**suffix** *n* a group of letters placed at the end of a word and affecting its meaning, e.g. *-ness* in *happiness.*
**suffocate** *v* to die or cause to die from being unable to breathe. ➤ **suffocation** *n.*
**suffrage** *n* the right to vote in political elections.
**suffragette** *n* a woman campaigning for the right to vote to be extended to women in Britain in the early 20th cent.
**suffuse** *v* to spread over or through.
**Sufi** *n* (*pl* **Sufis**) a Muslim mystic. ➤ **Sufism** *n.*
**sugar**[1] *n* **1** a sweet crystalline substance obtained from sugarcane or sugar beet. **2** a sweet water-soluble carbohydrate found in plant and animal tissue.
**sugar**[2] *v* to sprinkle, coat, or sweeten with sugar.
**sugar beet** *n* a variety of beet grown for the sugar in its roots.
**sugarcane** *n* a tall tropical grass with stout stems grown as a source of sugar.
**sugar daddy** *n informal* an elderly man who lavishes gifts and money on a young woman in return for sex or companionship.
**suggest** *v* **1** to put forward as a possibility or for consideration. **2** to call to mind by thought or association. **3** to express indirectly; to imply.
**suggestible** *adj* easily influenced by suggestion.
**suggestion** *n* **1** something, *esp* an idea or plan, suggested. **2** the impressing of an idea, attitude, etc on the mind of another person. **3** a slight indication; a trace.
**suggestive** *adj* **1** (*often* + of) tending to suggest; indicative or evocative. **2** risqué. ➤ **suggestively** *adv.*
**suicide** *n* **1** the act of killing oneself intentionally. **2** the ruining of one's own interests. **3** somebody who commits suicide. ➤ **suicidal** *adj,* **suicidally** *adv.*

**suit**[1] *n* **1** an outer costume of two or more matching articles of clothing, *esp* a jacket and trousers or a skirt. **2** a costume worn for a specified purpose. **3** all the playing cards in a pack bearing the same symbol, i.e. hearts, clubs, diamonds, or spades. **4** a lawsuit.

**suit**[2] *v* **1** to please or be convenient or good for. **2** to be becoming to or look right with. **3** to adapt (something) to a particular situation, circumstance, etc. * **suit oneself** to do as one likes. **suit somebody down to the ground** to suit somebody extremely well.

**suitable** *adj* appropriate for a particular person, situation, etc. ➤ **suitability** *n*, **suitably** *adv.*

**suitcase** *n* a rectangular case with a hinged lid and a handle, used for carrying clothes, etc when travelling.

**suite** *n* **1** a group of rooms occupied as a unit. **2** a set of matching furniture. **3** an instrumental musical form consisting of a series of pieces.

**suitor** *n dated* somebody who courts a woman with a view to marriage.

**Sukkoth** *or* **Succoth** *n* a Jewish harvest festival celebrated in September or October.

**sulfur** *n NAmer* see SULPHUR.

**sulk**[1] *v* to be moodily silent through resentment or disappointment.

**sulk**[2] *n* (*usu in pl*) a fit of sulking.

**sulky** *adj* (**-ier, -iest**) sulking or given to fits of sulking. ➤ **sulkily** *adv.*

**sullen** *adj* silently gloomy or resentful. ➤ **sullenly** *adv.*

**sully** *v* (**-ies, -ied**) to defile or tarnish.

**sulphur** (*NAmer* **sulfur**) *n* a non-metallic combustible chemical element that occurs naturally as yellow crystals.

**sulphuric** (*NAmer* **sulfuric**) *adj* containing sulphur.

**sulphuric acid** *n* a corrosive oily acid.

**sulphurous** (*NAmer* **sulfurous**) *adj* containing or derived from sulphur.

**sultan** *n* a sovereign of a Muslim state.

**sultana** *n* **1** a light brown seedless raisin. **2** a sultan's wife.

**sultry** *adj* (**-ier, -iest**) **1** oppressively hot and humid. **2** exciting strong sexual desire; sensual.

**sum** *n* **1** an amount of money. **2** the result of adding numbers. **3** a simple arithmetical problem involving addition, subtraction, multiplication, or division.

**summarize** *or* **-ise** *v* to reduce to a summary; to express concisely.

**summary**[1] *n* (*pl* **-ies**) a brief account covering the main points of something.

**summary**[2] *adj* **1** done quickly without delay or formality. **2** tried or triable in a magistrates' court. ➤ **summarily** *adv.*

**summation** *n* **1** the process of adding numbers. **2** the act of summing up. **3** a summary.

**summer**[1] *n* the season between spring and autumn. ➤ **summery** *adj.*

**summer**[2] *v* (+ in) to spend the summer in a particular place.

**summerhouse** *n* a small building in a garden designed to provide a shady place in summer.

**summit** *n* **1** the highest point of a hill or mountain. **2** the topmost level attainable. **3** a conference of heads of government.

**summon** *v* **1** to order to come. **2** to call people to attend (a meeting). **3** (*often* + up) to cause (a particular quality, e.g. courage) to show itself in oneself or others.

**summons** *n* (*pl* **summonses**) **1** a written notification ordering somebody to appear in court. **2** an order to come to a particular place, person, etc.

**sumo** *n* a Japanese form of wrestling.

**sump** *n chiefly Brit* a reservoir for lubricating oil underneath an internal-combustion engine.

**sumptuous** *adj* lavishly rich, costly, or luxurious. ➤ **sumptuously** *adv.*

**sum total** *n* the whole amount.

**sum up** *v* **1** to summarize. **2** to appraise concisely.

**sun**[1] *n* **1** (*often* **Sun**) the star round which the earth and other planets revolve. **2** a star. **3** the heat or light radiated from the sun.

**sun**[2] *v* (**sunned, sunning**) to expose (oneself) to the rays of the sun.

**sunbathe** *v* to lie or sit in the sun in order to get a suntan. ➤ **sunbather** *n.*

**sunbeam** *n* a ray of light from the sun.

**sunbed** *n* **1** a bed or reclining chair used for sunbathing. **2** a unit consisting of a couch and an array of sunlamps.

**sunblock** *n* a cream that protects exposed skin from the ultraviolet rays in sunlight.

**sunburn** *n* inflammation of the skin caused by overexposure to sunlight. ➤ **sunburnt** *or* **sunburned** *adj.*

**sundae** *n* a dish of ice cream served with a topping of fruit, nuts, syrup, etc.

**Sunday** *n* the day of the week following Saturday, the traditional day of worship for Christians.

**Sunday school** *n* a class of religious instruction for children, held on Sundays.

**sunder** *v literary* to break apart or in two.

**sundial** *n* an instrument that shows the time of day by the shadow cast by a pointer.

**sundries** *pl n* miscellaneous small articles or items.

**sundry** *adj* of various kinds; miscellaneous.

**sunflower** *n* a tall plant with large yellow-rayed flowers.

**sung** *v* past part. of SING.

**sunglasses** *pl n* tinted glasses worn to protect the eyes from the sun.

**sunk** *v* past part. of SINK[1].

**sunken** *adj* **1** submerged, *esp* lying at the bottom of the sea. **2** lying below the surrounding level.

**sunlamp** *n* an electric lamp that emits ultraviolet light, used *esp* for tanning the skin.

**sunlight** *n* light emitted by the sun; sunshine.

**Sunni** *n* (*pl* **Sunni** *or* **Sunnis**) **1** the major branch of Islam that acknowledges the first four caliphs as rightful successors of Muhammad. **2** a follower of Sunni.

**sunny** *adj* (**-ier, -iest**) **1** bright with sunshine. **2** cheerful, optimistic. **3** exposed to or warmed by the sun.

**sunrise** *n* the rising of the sun above the horizon or the time when this happens.

**sunroof** *n* an opening or removable panel in the roof of a car.

**sunscreen** *n* a substance or preparation that protects the skin from excessive ultraviolet radiation.

**sunset** *n* the descent of the sun below the horizon or the time when this happens.

**sunshade** *n* **1** a parasol. **2** an awning.

**sunshine** *n* the sun's light or direct rays.

**sunspot** *n* a transient dark marking on the visible surface of the sun caused by a relatively cooler area.

**sunstroke** *n* heatstroke caused by direct exposure to the sun.

**suntan** *n* a browning of the skin from exposure to the sun. ➤ **suntanned** *adj.*

**sup**[1] *v* (**supped, supping**) *chiefly dialect* to drink (liquid) in small mouthfuls.

**sup**[2] *n chiefly dialect* a sip.

**sup**[3] *v* (**supped, supping**) *dated* to eat one's evening meal.

**super** *adj informal* a general term of approval.

**super-** *prefix* **1** higher in quantity, quality, or degree than: *superhuman.* **2** extra: *supertax.* **3** to an excessive degree: *superabundant.* **4** surpassing others of its kind in size or power: *supertanker.* **5** placed above something: *superscript.*

**superannuated** *adj* **1** retired on a pension. **2** obsolete.

**superannuation** *n* the regular contribution made by employees to their pension scheme, deducted from wages or salary.

**superb** *adj* **1** of excellent quality. **2** grand or magnificent. ➤ **superbly** *adv.*

**supercharger** *n* a device supplying fuel and air to an internal-combustion engine at a pressure higher than normal for greater efficiency. ➤ **supercharged** *adj.*

**supercilious** *adj* coolly disdainful; haughty.

**superficial** *adj* **1** lying on or affecting only the surface. **2** apparent rather than real. **3** of a person: not capable of serious thought; shallow. **4** not careful, thorough, or deep. ➤ **superficiality** *n,* **superficially** *adv.*

**superfluous** *adj* exceeding what is necessary.

**superglue** *n* a very strong, quick-setting adhesive.

**supergrass** *n Brit, informal* a police informer who gives information about a large number of criminals.

**superhero** *n* (*pl* **-oes**) a character in a cartoon, film, etc with extraordinary powers that they use to fight crime, etc.

**superhuman** *adj* exceeding normal human power or capability.

**superimpose** *v* to place (one thing) over or above something else. ➤ **superimposition** *n.*

**superintend** *v* to be in charge of.

**superintendent** *n* **1** a person who supervises or manages something. **2** a British police officer ranking above a chief inspector.

**superior**[1] *adj* **1** of higher rank, quality, or importance. **2** excellent of its kind. **3** greater in quantity or number. **4** in printing, superscript. **5** conceited or supercilious. ➤ **superiority** *n.*

**superior**[2] *n* a person who is above another in rank or office.

**superlative**[1] *adj* **1** of the highest degree or quality. **2** in grammar, denoting the degree of comparison expressing an extreme or unsurpassed level, e.g. *smallest.*

**superlative**[2] *n* an exaggerated expression of praise.

**superman** *n* (*pl* **supermen**) *informal* a man of extraordinary power or achievements.

**supermarket** *n* a large self-service retail shop selling foods and household merchandise.

**supermodel** *n* a very successful fashion model who has become a celebrity.

**supernatural**[1] *adj* transcending the laws of nature, *esp* involving a god, spirit, devil, ghost, etc.

**supernatural**[2] *n* (**the supernatural**) supernatural forces or beings.

**supernova** *n* (*pl* **supernovae** *or* **supernovas**) a star that explodes, becoming immensely brighter for a few weeks or months.

**supernumerary** *adj* **1** exceeding the usual or stated number. **2** not listed among the regular members of a group.

**superpower** *n* any of a very few dominant nations in the world.

**superscript** *adj* of a letter, number, etc: written or printed above another character.

**supersede** *v* to take the place of (*esp* something inferior or outmoded).

---

***Usage Note:*** Note the spelling with *-sede* not *-cede* or *-ceed.*

---

**supersonic** *adj* moving at a speed above the speed of sound in air.

**superstar** *n* an extremely popular or successful entertainer or sportsperson.

**superstition** *n* **1** irrational belief in the influence of the supernatural on human affairs. **2** a superstitious belief.

**superstitious** *adj* believing or suggesting, on no rational basis, that certain actions have supernatural repercussions and bring good or bad luck. ➤ **superstitiously** *adv.*

**superstore** *n* a very large supermarket, often on the outskirts of a town.

**superstructure** *n* **1** the structural part of a ship above the main deck. **2** the part of a structure built on top of a lower or more fundamental part.

**supervene** *v* to happen in a way that interrupts some plan or process.

**supervise** *v* to oversee (a task or workers). ➤ **supervision** *n,* **supervisor** *n,* **supervisory** *adj.*

**supine** *adj* **1** lying on the back. **2** weak and inactive.

**supper** *n* an evening meal or snack.

**supplant** *v* to oust or supersede.

**supple** *adj* able to perform bending or twisting movements with ease and grace. ➤ **suppleness** *n.*

**supplement**[1] *n* **1** something that completes or makes a useful addition. **2** a part issued to extend a book or periodical. **3** an extra charge payable for something.

**supplement**[2] *v* to add a supplement to. ➤ **supplemental** *adj.*

**supplementary** *adj* added as a supplement; additional.

**suppliant**[1] *adj* humbly imploring or entreating.

**suppliant**[2] *n* a person who supplicates.

**supplicate** *v* to ask humbly and earnestly for something. ➤ **supplicant** *n and adj,* **supplication** *n.*

**supply**[1] *v* (**-ies, -ied**) **1** to provide somebody with (something). **2** to provide for or satisfy (a need, etc). ➤ **supplier** *n.*

**supply**[2] *n* (*pl* **-ies**) **1** the quantity of a commodity needed or available. **2** (*usu in pl*) provisions or stores. **3** the act of supplying something. **4** a teacher who fills temporary vacancies in schools.

**support**[1] *v* **1** to serve as a foundation or prop for. **2** to help, e.g. by giving money. **3** to approve of, encourage, or defend. **4** to substantiate or corroborate. **5** to be an enthusiastic or loyal follower of (e.g. a football team). **6** to provide with a home and the means of subsistence. **7** to enable (e.g. life) to exist. ➤ **supporter** *n.*

**support**[2] *n* **1** the act of supporting. **2** something that holds something up or serves as a prop. **3** somebody who offers help and encouragement.

**supportive** *adj* providing help and encouragement.

**suppose** *v* **1** to believe or think probable, usu without proof. **2** to assume or presuppose. * **be supposed to do something** to be expected or required to do something.

**supposed** *adj* believed or imagined to be such. ➤ **supposedly** *adv.*

**supposition** *n* something that is believed or thought likely, but is unproven.

**suppository** *n* (*pl* **-ies**) a cone or cylinder of medicated material intended to melt after insertion into the rectum or vagina.

**suppress** *v* **1** to put an end to by force. **2** to stop the publication or revelation of. **3** to restrain or inhibit (e.g. a feeling). ➤ **suppression** *n,* **suppressive** *adj.*

**suppurate** *v* to form or discharge pus. ➤ **suppuration** *n.*

**supremacist** *n* an advocate of group supremacy, e.g. of the superiority of one race over another.

**supremacy** *n* supreme authority, power, or position.

**supreme** *adj* **1** highest in rank or authority. **2** greatest, strongest, or most important. ➤ **supremely** *adv.*

**Supreme Court** *n* the highest judicial tribunal in a state.

**supremo** *n* (*pl* **-os**) *Brit, informal* a leader, or the person in charge of something.

**surcharge** *n* an additional charge, tax, or cost.

**surd** *n* in mathematics, a root, e.g. the square root of 2, that cannot be expressed exactly by dividing one integer by another.

**sure**[1] *adj* **1** marked by feelings of confident certainty. **2** (+ of) confident that something is true, will happen, etc. **3** certain; bound: *She is sure to win.* **4** true and reliable. * **for sure** as a certainty. **to be sure** admittedly. ➤ **sureness** *n.*

**sure**[2] *adv chiefly NAmer, informal* certainly.

**sure-fire** *adj informal* certain to succeed.

**surely** *adv* **1** it is to be hoped or expected that. **2** without doubt; certainly.

**surety** *n* (*pl* **-ies**) **1** a person who assumes legal liability for the debt or failure in duty of somebody else. **2** a pledge given for the fulfilment of an undertaking; a guarantee.

**surf**[1] *n* the foam and swell of waves breaking on the shore.

**surf**[2] *v* **1** to stand or lie on a surfboard and ride on the waves towards the shore. **2** to browse through (the Internet or TV channels) randomly. ➤ **surfer** *n,* **surfing** *n.*

**surface**[1] *n* **1** the exterior or upper boundary or layer of something. **2** the uppermost level of a body of liquid. **3** the superficial aspect of something. * **on the surface** to all outward appearances.

**surface**[2] *v* **1** to come or bring to the surface, *esp* of water. **2** to become apparent. **3** to give a surface to (e.g. a road).

**surfboard** *n* a long narrow buoyant board used in surfing.

**surfeit** *n* an excessive amount.
**surge**[1] *n* **1** a powerful rising or onrushing movement. **2** a sudden increase. **3** a sudden experience of an intense emotion.
**surge**[2] *v* **1** to move with a surge. **2** to increase suddenly.
**surgeon** *n* **1** a medical specialist who practises surgery. **2** a medical officer in the navy.
**surgery** *n* (*pl* **-ies**) **1** the branch of medicine that deals with disorders by cutting open the body to repair or remove damaged parts. **2** a surgical operation. **3** *Brit* a place where a doctor or dentist treats patients. **4** *Brit* a session at which a lawyer, MP, etc is available for consultation.
**surgical** *adj* **1** relating to or used in surgery. **2** providing support for a body part or correcting a deformity. **3** involving precision bombing. ➤ **surgically** *adv.*
**surgical spirit** *n Brit* a mixture consisting mainly of methylated spirits and used *esp* as a skin disinfectant.
**surly** *adj* (**-ier, -iest**) irritably sullen and bad-tempered.
**surmise**[1] *v* to imagine or infer on scanty evidence.
**surmise**[2] *n* a conjecture or guess.
**surmount** *v* **1** to overcome (a difficulty or obstacle). **2** to stand or lie on the top of.
**surname** *n* the name shared by members of a family.
**surpass** *v* to go beyond in quality, degree, or performance.
**surplice** *n* a loose white outer ecclesiastical vestment.
**surplus**[1] *n* **1** a surplus amount. **2** an excess of income over expenditure.
**surplus**[2] *adj* remaining over and above what is needed.
**surprise**[1] *n* **1** the feeling caused by an unexpected event; astonishment. **2** something unexpected or surprising. ✱ **take somebody by surprise 1** to come upon somebody without warning. **2** to astonish somebody.
**surprise**[2] *v* **1** to fill with wonder or amazement. **2** to take unawares. **3** to attack or capture unexpectedly. ➤ **surprised** *adj.*
**surreal** *adj* having a strange dreamlike irrational quality.
**surrealism** *n* an artistic movement that used the incongruous images formed by the unconscious in its work. ➤ **surrealist** *n and adj.*
**surrender**[1] *v* **1** to admit defeat and submit to an opponent. **2** to hand over to the control or possession of somebody else. **3** *formal* to give up or hand in (e.g. a ticket). **4** (+ to) to allow (oneself) to be controlled by an emotion, influence, etc.
**surrender**[2] *n* the act of surrendering.
**surreptitious** *adj* done by stealth. ➤ **surreptitiously** *adv.*
**surrogate** *n* a substitute. ➤ **surrogacy** *n.*
**surrogate mother** *n* a woman who carries and bears a child for a couple who cannot have children.
**surround**[1] *v* **1** to encircle, or enclose on all sides. **2** to be associated with.
**surround**[2] *n* **1** a border or edging. **2** (*in pl*) surroundings.
**surroundings** *pl n* the area or circumstances by which one is surrounded.
**surtax** *n* a tax on an item charged in addition to an existing tax.
**surtitle** *n* a translation of the dialogue of an opera or play that is projected onto a screen above the stage.
**surveillance** *n* close watch kept over somebody, e.g. by a detective.
**survey**[1] *v* **1** to examine closely. **2** to contemplate as a whole. **3** to determine the form and features of (an area of land), prior to e.g. making a map of it. **4** *Brit* to examine and report on the condition of (a building, e.g. a house for sale). **5** to conduct a statistical survey on (a group of people). ➤ **surveyor** *n.*
**survey**[2] *n* **1** a statistical enquiry into the opinions or preferences of a group of people. **2** an act of surveying, e.g. an examination of a building to determine its condition. **3** a report drawn up by a surveyor.
**survival** *n* **1** the fact of continuing to live or exist. **2** something that survives, *esp* after others of its kind have disappeared.
**survive** *v* **1** to continue to exist or live. **2** to escape alive from (an accident or disaster). **3** to remain alive after the death of (somebody). ➤ **survivor** *n.*
**susceptibility** *n* (*pl* **-ies**) **1** the fact of being susceptible. **2** (*in pl*) feelings or sensibilities.
**susceptible** *adj* **1** open or vulnerable to some influence or agency. **2** easily moved or emotionally affected.
**sushi** *n* a Japanese dish of balls of cold boiled rice garnished with raw fish or other ingredients.
**suspect**[1] *v* **1** to imagine (something) to be true or probable. **2** to believe (somebody) to be guilty without conclusive proof. **3** to distrust (something).
**suspect**[2] *n* somebody who is suspected, e.g. of a crime.
**suspect**[3] *adj* likely to be false or dangerous.
**suspend** *v* **1** to hang (something), *esp* so that it is unsupported except at the top. **2** to cause to stop temporarily. **3** to defer (a prison sentence) on particular conditions. **4** to defer or delay (e.g. judgment) awaiting fuller information. **5** to debar temporarily from office, employment, or attendance at school.
**suspended animation** *n* temporary suspension of the vital body functions, e.g. in people nearly drowned.

**suspender** *n* **1** *Brit* a strap with a fastening device, attached to a belt or corset to hold up a woman's stocking. **2** *NAmer* (*in pl*) = BRACES.

**suspense** *n* a state of excited or anxious uncertainty as to a decision or outcome.

**suspension** *n* **1** the act of suspending, or the state of being suspended. **2** the system of devices, e.g. springs, supporting the upper part of a vehicle on the axles. **3** a state in which particles are mixed with but undissolved in a liquid.

**suspension bridge** *n* a type of bridge that has its roadway suspended from cables.

**suspicion** *n* **1** an unsubstantiated idea or feeling that something is the case, *esp* that somebody has done something wrong. **2** a feeling of mistrust. **3** a slight trace. * **above suspicion** too honest or virtuous to be suspected of having done something wrong. **under suspicion** suspected of having done something wrong.

**suspicious** *adj* **1** tending to arouse suspicion. **2** inclined to suspect; distrustful. ➤ **suspiciously** *adv.*

**suss** *v Brit, informal* **1** (*often* + out) to uncover the truth about. **2** (*often* + out) to work out; to realize.

**sustain** *v* **1** to support the weight of. **2** to give support, sustenance, or relief to. **3** to cause to continue; to prolong. **4** to suffer or undergo. ➤ **sustained** *adj.*

**sustainable** *adj* **1** able to be sustained. **2** of energy, development, etc: not exhausting natural resources or damaging the environment. ➤ **sustainability** *n.*

**sustenance** *n* **1** food or provisions; nourishment. **2** the act of sustaining.

**suture**[1] *n* **1** a fibre used in the sewing together of parts of the living body. **2** a stitch made with a suture.

**suture**[2] *v* to close or secure with sutures.

**suzerainty** *n* control by one state of the foreign relations of another internally autonomous state.

**svelte** *adj* slender in an elegant and attractive way.

**SW** *abbr* **1** Southwest. **2** Southwestern.

**swab**[1] *or* **swob** *n* **1** a wad of absorbent material used for applying medication, cleaning wounds, taking specimens, etc. **2** a specimen taken with a swab.

**swab**[2] *or* **swob** *v* (**swabbed** *or* **swobbed, swabbing** *or* **swobbing**) **1** to clean (a wound) with a swab. **2** (*often* + down) to clean (a surface) by washing, *esp* with a mop.

**swaddle** *v* to swathe or envelop.

**swaddling clothes** *pl n* narrow strips of cloth formerly wrapped round a baby to restrict its movement.

**swag** *n* **1** an arrangement of fabric, plaster decorations, etc in a drooping curve. **2** *informal* goods acquired by unlawful means; loot.

**swagger**[1] *v* to walk with an air of overbearing self-confidence or self-satisfaction. ➤ **swaggering** *adj.*

**swagger**[2] *n* a self-confident or arrogant gait or manner.

**swain** *n literary* a male admirer or suitor.

**swallow**[1] *n* a small migrant bird with long wings and a forked tail.

**swallow**[2] *v* **1** to cause (food or drink) to pass from the mouth through the oesophagus into the stomach. **2** (*often* + up) to envelop or engulf. **3** to accept or believe without question.

**swallow**[3] *n* an act of swallowing.

**swam** *v* past tense of SWIM[1].

**swamp**[1] *n* an area of wet spongy land; a marsh. ➤ **swampy** *adj.*

**swamp**[2] *v* **1** to submerge. **2** to fill (a boat) with water until it sinks. **3** to overwhelm with too much of something.

**swan**[1] *n* a large long-necked mostly pure white aquatic bird. ➤ **swanlike** *adj.*

**swan**[2] *v* (**swanned, swanning**) *Brit, informal* to go around in a leisurely, aimless or ostentatious fashion.

**swank**[1] *v informal* to show off.

**swank**[2] *n informal* ostentation or boasting.

**swanky** *adj* (**-ier, -iest**) *informal* **1** fashionably smart and expensive. **2** inclined to show off.

**swan song** *n* a farewell appearance or performance, or a final work.

**swap**[1] *or* **swop** *v* (**swapped** *or* **swopped, swapping** *or* **swopping**) **1** to exchange (things), usu with another person. **2** to exchange or substitute.

**swap**[2] *or* **swop** *n* an act of exchanging things.

**sward** *n* a surface of short grass.

**swarm**[1] *n* **1** a large mass of flying insects. **2** a large number of honeybees, *esp* when emigrating from a hive with a queen bee to start a new colony elsewhere. **3** a group of people or things massing together.

**swarm**[2] *v* **1** to move or assemble in a crowd. **2** (+ with) to teem with something. **3** (+ up) to climb rapidly by gripping with the hands and feet.

**swarthy** *adj* (**-ier, -iest**) of a dark complexion.

**swashbuckler** *n* a swaggering adventurer or daredevil. ➤ **swashbuckling** *adj.*

**swastika** *n* **1** an ancient symbol in the shape of a cross with the ends of the arms bent at right angles. **2** this symbol used as the emblem of the German Nazi Party.

**swat**[1] *v* (**swatted, swatting**) to hit (an insect) with a sharp slapping blow. ➤ **swatter** *n.*

**swat**[2] *n* **1** a quick crushing blow. **2** a swatter.

**swatch** *n* a sample piece of fabric or other material.

**swath** *n chiefly NAmer* = SWATHE[1].

**swathe**[1] *n* **1** a row of cut grain or grass left by a scythe or mowing machine. **2** a long broad strip.

**swathe**[2] *v* **1** to wrap with a bandage or strip of material. **2** to envelop.

**swathe**[3] *n* something that swathes or envelops.

**sway**[1] *v* **1** to move slowly and rhythmically back and forth or from side to side. **2** to change the opinions of.

**sway**[2] *n* **1** a swaying movement. **2** controlling influence or power. * **hold sway** to have influence or power.

**swear** *v* (**swore, sworn**) **1** to use profane or obscene language. **2** to utter or take (an oath) solemnly. **3** to promise emphatically or earnestly. * **swear by** to place great confidence in. **swear to** to express certainty about.

**swear in** *v* to induct into office by administration of an oath.

**swearword** *n* a profane or obscene word.

**sweat**[1] *n* **1** fluid excreted through the pores from the glands under the skin, when one is hot, etc. **2** *informal* a state of anxiety or impatience. **3** *informal* hard work; drudgery. * **no sweat** *informal* not a problem. ➤ **sweaty** *adj.*

**sweat**[2] *v* (*past tense and past part.* **sweated** *or NAmer* **sweat**) **1** to excrete sweat. **2** to emit moisture. **3** to work hard. **4** to feel tense or anxious. **5** to cook (vegetables) gently.

**sweatband** *n* a band of material worn round the head or wrist to absorb sweat.

**sweater** *n* a usu long-sleeved pullover.

**sweatshirt** *n* a loose collarless pullover of heavy cotton.

**sweatshop** *n* a place of work in which people are employed for long hours at low wages and under poor conditions.

**Swede** *n* a native or inhabitant of Sweden.

**swede** *n* a plant with a bulbous yellow-fleshed root used as a vegetable.

**sweep**[1] *v* (*past tense and past part.* **swept**) **1** to clean by brushing. **2** to remove with a single forceful action. **3** to move or carry along with irresistible force. **4** (+ away) to abolish or destroy completely. **5** to search (an area) systematically. * **sweep somebody off their feet** to cause somebody to fall in love with one. **sweep something under the carpet** to conceal hoping that it will be ignored. **sweep the board** to win everything in a contest.

**sweep**[2] *n* **1** an act of sweeping. **2** (*also* **chimney sweep**) a person who cleans chimneys. **3** a curving course or line. **4** a broad extent. **5** scope. **6** *informal* a sweepstake. ➤ **sweeper** *n.*

**sweeping** *adj* **1** extending in a wide curve or over a wide area. **2** extensive; wide-ranging. **3** of a statement: marked by wholesale and indiscriminate inclusion.

**sweepstake** *n* (*also in pl*) a lottery or other form of gambling, e.g. on a horse race, in which the stakes form the prize or prizes.

**sweet**[1] *adj* **1** inducing a taste similar to that of sugar. **2** having a pleasant smell or taste. **3** of air or water: fresh and pure. **4** delightful or charming. **5** marked by gentle good humour or kindliness. **6** pleasing to the ear or eye. **7** satisfying. * **sweet on somebody** *informal, dated* in love with somebody. ➤ **sweetly** *adv,* **sweetness** *n.*

**sweet**[2] *n* **1** *Brit* a small piece of confectionery prepared with sugar or chocolate. **2** *Brit* a dessert.

**sweet-and-sour** *adj* seasoned with a sauce containing sugar and vinegar or lemon juice.

**sweetbread** *n* the pancreas or thymus of a young animal used for food.

**sweet corn** *n* maize with kernels that contain a high percentage of sugar, used as a vegetable.

**sweeten** *v* **1** to make or become sweet. **2** to make less painful or trying.

**sweetener** *n* **1** a substance added to food or drink to sweeten it, *esp* one used instead of sugar. **2** *chiefly Brit, informal* a bribe.

**sweetheart** *n* a person that one loves.

**sweetmeat** *n archaic* a sweet or delicacy rich in sugar.

**sweet pea** *n* a climbing plant of the pea family with colourful fragrant flowers.

**sweet potato** *n* a plant with large sweet tubers used as a vegetable.

**sweet talk** *n informal* flattery.

**sweet-talk** *v informal* to persuade (somebody) to do something by flattering them.

**sweet tooth** *n* a fondness for sweet food.

**swell**[1] *v* (*past tense* **swelled,** *past part.* **swollen** *or* **swelled**) **1** to expand, *esp* to curve outwards or upwards. **2** to increase the number, volume, or intensity of.

**swell**[2] *n* **1** a rounded protuberance or bulge. **2** a gradual increase. **3** a surging or undulating movement of water.

**swell**[3] *adj NAmer, informal, dated* excellent.

**swelling** *n* an abnormal bodily protuberance or enlargement.

**swelter** *v* to suffer from heat.

**sweltering** *adj* oppressively hot.

**swept** *v* past tense and past part. of SWEEP[1].

**swerve**[1] *v* to turn aside abruptly from a straight course.

**swerve**[2] *n* an instance of swerving.

**swift**[1] *adj* **1** moving or capable of moving at great speed. **2** occurring suddenly or lasting a very short time. ➤ **swiftly** *adv,* **swiftness** *n.*

**swift**[2] *n* a dark-coloured bird noted for its fast darting flight.

**swig**[1] *n* a quantity drunk in one swallow.

**swig**[2] *v* (**swigged, swigging**) to drink in long draughts.

**swill**[1] *v* **1** *Brit* (*often* + out) to wash, *esp* by flushing with water. **2** *Brit, informal* to drink or eat greedily.

**swill**[2] *n* food for pigs, composed of edible refuse mixed with water or milk.

**swim**[1] *v* (**swimming,** *past tense* **swam,** *past part.* **swum**) **1** to propel the body in water by bodily movements. **2** to be immersed in or flooded with a liquid. **3** to have a floating, whirling, or dizzy sensation. ➤ **swimmer** *n.*

**swim**[2] *n* a period of swimming.

**swimming bath** *n Brit* (*also in pl*) an indoor swimming pool.

**swimming costume** *n Brit* a close-fitting garment worn for swimming.

**swimmingly** *adv informal* very well; splendidly.

**swimming pool** *n* an artificial pool for people to swim in.

**swimsuit** *n* = SWIMMING COSTUME.

**swindle**[1] *v* to take money or property from by fraud or deceit. ➤ **swindler** *n.*

**swindle**[2] *n* an act of fraud or deceit.

**swine** *n* **1** (*pl* **swine**) *formal* a pig. **2** (*pl* **swine** *or* **swines**) *informal* a contemptible person. ➤ **swinish** *adj.*

**swing**[1] *v* (*past tense and past part.* **swung**) **1** to move freely to and fro when suspended. **2** to move in in a circle or arc. **3** to move into a new position by grasping a fixed support. **4** to throw (a punch) with a sweeping arm movement. **5** to fluctuate from one condition, position, or object of attention to another. **6** to influence decisively. **7** *informal* to succeed in doing or having (something).

**swing**[2] *n* **1** a suspended seat on which a person can swing to and fro. **2** a swinging movement. **3** a stroke or blow delivered with a sweeping movement. **4** a change in public opinion or political preference. **5** jazz played with a steady lively rhythm and simple harmony. ✱ **get into the swing of things** *informal* to accustom oneself to a situation or undertaking. **go with a swing** *informal* to be enjoyable and successful. **in full swing** at the height of activity. **swings and roundabouts** *Brit, informal* a situation in which a loss or disadvantage is balanced by a gain or advantage of another kind.

**swingeing** *adj chiefly Brit* severe or drastic.

**swinging** *adj informal* **1** lively and exciting. **2** sexually liberated.

**swipe**[1] *v* **1** *informal* to strike or hit out with a sweeping motion. **2** *informal* to steal. **3** *informal* to pass (a card) through a machine that can read its magnetic strip.

**swipe**[2] *n informal* **1** a strong sweeping blow. **2** an unexpected criticism.

**swipe card** *n* a plastic card containing a magnetic strip encoded with information that can be read when the card is passed through a special machine.

**swirl**[1] *n* **1** a whirling mass or motion. **2** a twisting shape or pattern. ➤ **swirly** *adj.*

**swirl**[2] *v* to move in eddies or whirls.

**swish**[1] *n* a hissing or brushing sound, or a movement causing it.

**swish**[2] *v* to move with a swish.

**swish**[3] *adj Brit, informal* smart and fashionable.

**Swiss** *n* (*pl* **Swiss**) a native or inhabitant of Switzerland. ➤ **Swiss** *adj.*

**Swiss roll** *n Brit* a thin sheet of sponge cake spread with jam, cream, etc and rolled up.

**switch**[1] *n* **1** a device for making or breaking a connection in an electrical circuit. **2** a sudden shift or change. **3** a slender flexible twig or rod.

**switch**[2] *v* **1** to make a sudden change in. **2** to exchange (things).

**switchback** *n Brit* something, e.g. a road or rollercoaster, with alternating steep ascents and descents.

**switchblade** *n chiefly NAmer* a flick knife.

**switchboard** *n* a panel with switching devices that enable telephone calls to be directed manually to particular numbers.

**switch off** *v* **1** to turn off (e.g. a light or machine) by operating an electrical switch. **2** *informal* to lose interest.

**switch on** *v* to turn on (e.g. a light or machine) by operating an electrical switch.

**swivel**[1] *n* a device joining two parts so that one part can pivot freely.

**swivel**[2] *v* (**swivelled, swivelling,** *NAmer* **swiveled, swiveling**) to turn on a swivel; to turn rapidly and smoothly.

**swiz** *or* **swizz** *n* (*pl* **swizzes**) *Brit, informal* something that does not live up to one's hopes or expectations.

**swob**[1] *n* see SWAB[1].

**swob**[2] *v* see SWAB[2].

**swollen** *v* past part. of SWELL[1].

**swoon**[1] *v* to faint.

**swoon**[2] *n* a loss of consciousness.

**swoop**[1] *v* **1** *esp* of a bird: to descend steeply through the air, e.g. to seize prey. **2** to make a sudden attack or raid.

**swoop**[2] *n* an act of swooping. ✱ **at one fell swoop** see FELL[4].

**swop**[1] *v* see SWAP[1].

**swop**[2] *n* see SWAP[2].

**sword** *n* a cutting or thrusting weapon with a long sharp-pointed and sharp-edged blade. ✱ **cross swords** to fight or argue.

**swordfish** *n* (*pl* **swordfishes** *or* **swordfish**) a large oceanic food fish with a sword-like beak.

**swore** *v* past tense of SWEAR.

**sworn**[1] *v* past part. of SWEAR.

**sworn**[2] *adj* **1** made under oath. **2** determined to remain as specified: *sworn enemies.*

**swot**[1] *n Brit, informal* a person who studies excessively.

**swot**[2] *v* (**swotted, swotting**) *Brit, informal* to study hard.

**swum** *v* past part. of SWIM[1].

**swung** *v* past tense and past part. of SWING[1].

**sybarite** *n* somebody who likes to indulge in sensual pleasures. ➤ **sybaritic** *adj.*

**sycamore** *n* **1** a Eurasian maple tree. **2** *NAmer* a plane tree.

**sycophant** *n* a self-seeking flatterer; a toady. ➤ **sycophancy** *n,* **sycophantic** *adj.*

**syllable** *n* a unit of spoken language that usu consists of one vowel sound with or without an accompanying consonant sound.

**syllabus** *n* (*pl* **syllabi** *or* **syllabuses**) a summary of a course of study or of examination requirements.

**syllogism** *n* a pattern of deductive reasoning consisting of two premises and a conclusion.

**sylph** *n* **1** a slender graceful woman or girl. **2** an imaginary being inhabiting the air. ➤ **sylph-like** *adj.*

**sylvan** *or* **silvan** *adj* **1** located in or characteristic of woods. **2** full of trees.

**symbiosis** *n* (*pl* **symbioses**) the living together of two dissimilar organisms in intimate association, usu to the benefit of both. ➤ **symbiotic** *adj.*

**symbol** *n* **1** something or somebody that stands for or suggests something else by association or convention, *esp* a visible sign of something abstract. **2** a special sign used in writing or printing to represent something.

**symbolic** *adj* using or constituting a symbol or symbols. ➤ **symbolically** *adv.*

**symbolism** *n* the use of symbols to represent other things.

**symbolize** *or* **-ise** *v* **1** to serve as a symbol of. **2** to represent by means of symbols.

**symmetrical** *or* **symmetric** *adj* having the same proportions, shape, etc on both sides. ➤ **symmetrically** *adv.*

**symmetry** *n* (*pl* **-ies**) **1** the property of being symmetrical. **2** beauty of form arising from balanced proportions.

**sympathetic** *adj* **1** showing compassion and sensitivity to others' feelings. **2** favourably inclined. **3** congenial. ➤ **sympathetically** *adv.*

**sympathize** *or* **-ise** *v* **1** to share in distress or suffering. **2** to agree with somebody or something. ➤ **sympathizer** *n.*

**sympathy** *n* (*pl* **-ies**) **1** the act or capacity of sharing the feelings or interests of another. **2** inclination to think or feel alike. **3** (*also in pl*) a feeling of loyalty.

**symphonic** *adj* relating to, or having the form of, a symphony.

**symphony** *n* (*pl* **-ies**) an extended piece for orchestra, typically in four contrasting movements.

**symposium** *n* (*pl* **symposia** *or* **symposiums**) a formal meeting at which several specialists deliver short addresses on a topic.

**symptom** *n* **1** something giving indication of a disease or other physical disorder. **2** something that indicates the existence of *esp* something undesirable.

**synagogue** *n* the house of worship and communal centre of a Jewish congregation.

**synapse** *n* the point between two nerves across which a nervous impulse is transmitted. ➤ **synaptic** *adj.*

**sync** *or* **synch** *n informal* synchronization. ✱ **in/out of sync** in/not in harmony or agreement.

**synchromesh** *n* a system designed to synchronize the speeds of the different moving parts involved in a gear change.

**synchronize** *or* **-ise** *v* to cause to happen at the same time. ➤ **synchronization** *n,* **synchronizer** *n.*

**synchronous** *adj* happening or arising at precisely the same time. ➤ **synchronously** *adv.*

**syncopate** *v* to modify or affect (musical rhythm) by stressing a weak beat or omitting a strong beat. ➤ **syncopation** *n.*

**syndicate**[1] *n* a group of people or organizations who combine to carry out a particular transaction or to promote a common interest.

**syndicate**[2] *v* **1** to sell (e.g. a cartoon) to a syndicate for simultaneous publication in many newspapers or periodicals. **2** to manage by a syndicate. ➤ **syndication** *n.*

**syndrome** *n* a group of symptoms that occur together and characterize a particular medical disorder.

**synergy** *n* cooperation between two organizations or things that achieves more than both would achieve if they worked separately.

**synod** *n* **1** the governing assembly of an Anglican province, diocese, or deanery. **2** a formal meeting to decide ecclesiastical matters.

**synonym** *n* any of two or more words in a language that are used with the same meaning.

**synonymous** *adj* **1** having the same meaning. **2** closely associated.

**synopsis** *n* (*pl* **synopses**) a condensed statement or outline.

**syntax** *n* the way in which words are put together to form phrases, clauses, or sentences.

**synthesis** *n* (*pl* **syntheses**) **1** the combination of separate or diverse elements into a coherent whole. **2** the artificial production of a substance by chemical reaction.

**synthesize** *or* **-ise** *v* **1** to produce by synthesis. **2** to combine (things) to form a whole. **3** to produce (sound) electronically.

**synthesizer** *n* an electronic keyboard musical instrument that produces a sound that can be altered, e.g. to mimic other instruments.

**synthetic**[1] *adj* **1** produced by chemical synthesis, *esp* as an imitation of something natural. **2** not genuine or sincere. ➤ **synthetically** *adv.*

**synthetic**[2] *n* a synthetic textile fibre.

**syphilis** *n* a serious sexually transmitted bacterial disease. ➤ **syphilitic** *adj and n.*

**syphon**[1] *n* see SIPHON[1].

**syphon**[2] *v* see SIPHON[2].

**syrup** (*NAmer* **sirup**) *n* **1** a thick sticky solution of sugar and water, often flavoured or mixed with medicinal substances. **2** the concentrated juice of a fruit or plant.

**syrupy** *adj* **1** like syrup. **2** cloyingly sweet or sentimental.

**system** *n* **1** a regularly interacting or interdependent group of items forming a unified whole. **2** a form of social, economic, or political organization. **3** an organized or established procedure or method. **4** order. **5** the body considered as a functional unit. **6** (**the system**) society or its rules regarded as stultifying or restrictive. * **get something out of one's system** *informal* to stop thinking about something.

**systematic** *adj* methodical in procedure or plan; thorough. ➤ **systematically** *adv.*

**systematize** *or* **-ise** *v* to arrange according to a system.

**systemic** *adj* involving a system, e.g. affecting the body generally.

**T**[1] *or* **t** *n* (*pl* **T's** *or* **Ts** *or* **t's**) the twentieth letter of the English alphabet. ✱ **to a T** to perfection; exactly.

**T**[2] *abbr* the chemical symbol for tritium.

**TA** *abbr* Territorial Army.

**Ta** *abbr* the chemical symbol for tantalum.

**ta** *interj Brit, informal* thanks.

**tab**[1] *n* **1** a projecting flap, loop, or strip of material by which something can be held or lifted. **2** *chiefly NAmer* a bill, *esp* for a meal or drinks. ✱ **keep tabs on** *informal* to keep under close surveillance. **pick up the tab** *informal* to pay a bill, e.g. in a restaurant.

**tab**[2] *n* = TABULATOR.

**tab**[3] *n informal* a tablet, *esp* one containing an illegal drug.

**tabby** *n* (*pl* **-ies**) a domestic cat with a brownish or grey coat striped with darker shades.

**tabernacle** *n* **1** (*often* **Tabernacle**) a tent sanctuary used by the Israelites during the Exodus. **2** the meeting place or church of Nonconformists or Mormons.

**table**[1] *n* **1** a piece of furniture consisting of a smooth flat slab of wood, etc fixed on legs or some other support. **2** a systematically arranged list of figures, information, etc. **3** (*also* **multiplication table**) a list of the results of multiplying a number by various other numbers. ✱ **on the table** *chiefly Brit* put forward for discussion. **turn the tables** to reverse the relative fortunes of two contending parties.

**table**[2] *v Brit* to place (a matter) on the agenda.

**tableau** *n* (*pl* **tableaux** *or* **tableaus**) a depiction of a scene by silent and motionless costumed participants.

**tablecloth** *n* a cloth that is spread over a dining table.

**table d'hôte** *n* (*pl* **tables d'hôte** *or* **table d'hôtes**) a meal consisting of a fixed number of courses with a limited choice, provided at a fixed price: compare À LA CARTE.

**tablespoon** *n* a large spoon used for serving.

**tablet** *n* **1** a small solid shaped mass or capsule of medicinal material. **2** a flat slab suitable for an inscription.

**table tennis** *n* a game, based on tennis, played with round wooden bats and a small hollow plastic ball on an indoor table.

**tabloid** *n* a newspaper having a relatively small page size and usu containing news stories written in a relatively simple style.

**taboo**[1] *or* **tabu** *adj* forbidden on grounds of morality, tradition, or social usage.

**taboo**[2] *or* **tabu** *n* (*pl* **taboos** *or* **tabus**) a prohibition imposed by social custom.

**tabular** *adj* of data or statistics: arranged in a table.

**tabulate** *v* to arrange (data) in tabular form. ➤ **tabulation** *n.*

**tabulator** *n* an attachment to a typewriter or a word-processing function used for arranging data in columns.

**tachograph** *n* a device for automatically recording the speed of a vehicle, *esp* a lorry.

**tachometer** *n* a device for indicating speed of rotation, e.g. of a vehicle engine.

**tachycardia** *n* relatively rapid heart rate, often indicative of disease.

**tacit** *adj* implied or understood but not actually expressed. ➤ **tacitly** *adv.*

**taciturn** *adj* not communicative or talkative. ➤ **taciturnity** *n.*

**tack**[1] *n* **1** a small nail with a broad flat head. **2** a long loose stitch used to hold layers of fabric together temporarily. **3** the direction of a sailing vessel with respect to the direction of the wind. **4** a change of course from one tack to another. **5** a course of action.

**tack**[2] *v* **1** to fasten or attach with tacks. **2** to sew together with tacks. **3** (*often* + on) to add as a supplement. **4** to change the course of (a sailing vessel) by turning the bow towards the wind. **5** to follow a zigzag course.

**tack**[3] *n* equipment used in horse riding.

**tack**[4] *n* cheap or worthless things or material.

**tackle**[1] *n* **1** a set of equipment used in a particular activity. **2** an assembly of ropes and pulleys arranged for hoisting and pulling. **3** an instance of tackling in sport.

**tackle**[2] *v* **1** to attempt to take the ball from (an opposing player) in hockey or football. **2** to set about dealing with (a problem, etc). **3** to speak to (somebody) about a difficult matter. ➤ **tackler** *n.*

**tacky**[1] *adj* (**-ier, -iest**) slightly sticky to the touch.

**tacky**[2] *adj* (**-ier, -iest**) *informal* in poor taste; vulgar.

**tact** *n* a keen sense of how to handle people or affairs so as to avoid giving offence.

**tactful** *adj* showing tact. ➤ **tactfully** *adv.*
**tactic** *n* a method for achieving an end.
**tactical** *adj* **1** carried out with only a limited or immediate end in view. **2** of voting: in favour of the candidate most likely to defeat the candidate one least wants to win rather than in favour of one's preferred candidate. **3** of nuclear weapons: of or designed for air attack in close support of ground forces. ➤ **tactically** *adv.*
**tactics** *pl n* **1** military planning concerned with the disposition and manoeuvres of forces in combat: compare STRATEGY. **2** the skill of employing available means to accomplish an end.
**tactile** *adj* **1** relating to the sense of touch. **2** of a person: in the habit of touching people in a friendly way.
**tactless** *adj* insensitive or likely to cause offence. ➤ **tactlessly** *adv.*
**tad** *n informal* a small amount. * **a tad** somewhat, rather.
**tadpole** *n* the larva of an amphibian, such as a frog or toad, that lives in water and has a rounded body, long tail, no legs, and external gills.
**taffeta** *n* a crisp lustrous fabric.
**tag**[1] *n* **1** a flap or loop on a garment by which to hang it up, or that carries information such as washing instructions. **2** an electronic monitoring device worn around the wrist or ankle by people convicted of a crime but not held in custody. **3** a trite quotation or saying. **4** an identifying word or phrase accompanying or replacing a name. **5** a rigid binding on an end of a shoelace.
**tag**[2] *v* (**tagged, tagging**) **1** to supply with an identifying marker, price label, etc. **2** to fit with an electronic tag. **3** (*often* + on) to attach as an addition. **4** (*usu* + along/on) to go with somebody.
**tag**[3] *n* a children's game in which one player chases the others.
**tagliatelle** *pl n* pasta in the form of narrow ribbons.
**tail**[1] *n* **1** a flexible extension of the rear end of the body of an animal or bird. **2** the rear part of an aircraft consisting of horizontal and vertical stabilizing and control surfaces. **3** the luminous trail behind a comet. **4** the lower or inferior part of something. **5** (*in pl*) = TAILCOAT. **6** (*in pl*) the reverse of a coin. **7** *informal* a person who follows or keeps watch on somebody. * **turn tail** *informal* to run away.
**tail**[2] *v* **1** *informal* to follow (somebody) for purposes of surveillance. **2** (*often* + back) to form a long queue. **3** (+ off/away) to diminish gradually in strength, volume, etc.
**tailback** *n* a long queue of stationary motor vehicles.
**tailcoat** *n* a man's formal evening coat with two long tapering skirts at the back.
**tailgate** *n* **1** a hinged board at the rear of a vehicle. **2** a door at the rear of a car, *esp* one that opens upwards.
**tailor**[1] *n* somebody whose occupation is making or altering clothes.
**tailor**[2] *v* **1** to make (a garment) for a particular customer. **2** (+ for/to) to adapt to suit a special need or purpose.
**tailored** *adj* cut so as to fit the figure well.
**tailplane** *n* the horizontal projection of an aircraft's tail.
**tailspin** *n* **1** a spiralling dive by an aircraft. **2** *informal* a state of chaos or panic.
**tailwind** *n* a wind blowing from behind a vehicle, aircraft, or ship.
**taint**[1] *v* **1** to spoil or contaminate. **2** to corrupt morally.
**taint**[2] *n* a slight trace of contamination or of something undesirable.
**take**[1] *v* (**took, taken**) **1** to reach for and hold. **2** to get into one's possession or control. **3** to remove. **4** to proceed to occupy. **5** to subtract (a number). **6** to choose. **7** to lead or carry to another place. **8** to use as a route or means of transport. **9** to bring to a particular state: *Her ability should take her far.* **10** to affect in a specified way: *The remark took us by surprise.* **11** to consume (food, drink, medicine, etc). **12** to adopt or advance (a particular view). **13** to be taught (a subject of study). **14** to hold or accommodate. **15** to need or call for. **16** to submit to or undergo. **17** to tolerate or endure. **18** to accept in payment. **19** to accept or make use of (a risk, opportunity, etc). **20** to regard in a particular way. * **take after** to resemble (an older relative) in appearance or character. **take against** *chiefly Brit* to come to dislike. **take apart 1** to dismantle. **2** *informal* to criticize or treat severely. **take it** to infer or assume. **take to 1** to form a liking for. **2** to begin to do (something). **what it takes** the qualities or resources needed.
**take**[2] *n* **1** the uninterrupted recording, filming, or televising of something. **2** proceeds or takings. **3** *chiefly NAmer, informal* interpretation or slant. * **on the take** *informal* taking bribes.
**takeaway** *n Brit* **1** a cooked meal eaten away from the premises from which it was bought. **2** a shop or restaurant that sells takeaways.
**take away** *v* **1** to remove. **2** to subtract. * **take away from** to detract from.
**take back** *v* **1** to retract (a statement). **2** to return (unsatisfactory goods) to the place where they were bought.
**take down** *v* **1** to remove or dismantle. **2** to write down on paper.
**take-home pay** *n* the part of gross salary or wages remaining after deductions, e.g. for income tax, insurance, etc.

**take in** *v* **1** to offer accommodation or shelter to. **2** *informal* to deceive or trick. **3** to make (a garment) smaller by alteration. **4** to include. **5** to understand.

**takeoff** *n* **1** a caricature or impersonation. **2** the launching of an aircraft or rocket.

**take off** *v* **1** to remove (clothing). **2** to deduct (an amount). **3** to mimic (somebody). **4** of an aircraft: to become airborne. **5** *informal* to leave abruptly. **6** *informal* to be quickly successful.

**take on** *v* **1** to agree to (a task or undertaking). **2** to engage (staff, etc). **3** to assume (an appearance or quality). **4** *informal* to become emotional or distraught.

**takeout** *n NAmer* = TAKEAWAY.

**take out** *v* **1** to extract or remove. **2** to obtain (authorization, insurance, etc). **3** to escort on a social occasion. * **take it out of** to fatigue or exhaust. **take it out on** to vent one's anger or frustration on.

**takeover** *n* an act of taking over, *esp* of gaining control of a business company by buying a majority of the shares.

**take over** *v* to assume control or possession of.

**take up** *v* **1** to pick up or lift. **2** to become engaged or interested in (an activity). **3** to occupy or require (space or time). **4** to shorten (a garment). **5** to discuss or pursue (a matter) further. * **take somebody up on 1** to accept (an offer) from somebody. **2** to venture to disagree about (something). **take up with** to begin to associate with.

**takings** *pl n* the amount of money earned by a business during a specified period.

**talc** *n* **1** = TALCUM POWDER. **2** a soft mineral with a greasy feel.

**talcum powder** *n* finely powdered talc, often perfumed, used for dusting the body.

**tale** *n* **1** a story. **2** a lie.

**talent** *n* **1** a special creative or artistic aptitude. **2** general ability or intelligence. **3** talented people. **4** *informal* people considered in terms of their sexual attractiveness. **5** an ancient unit of weight or money.

**talented** *adj* having a special natural aptitude or skill.

**talisman** *n* (*pl* **talismans**) an object believed to bring good fortune or produce magical effects.

**talk¹** *v* **1** to convey information or communicate in speech. **2** (+ about/of) to make the subject of conversation. **3** (+ over/through) to discuss (something) at length. **4** to be able to speak. **5** to reveal secret or confidential information. **6** (+ into/out of) to persuade (somebody) by talking.

**talk²** *n* **1** a conversation. **2** (*also in pl*) a formal discussion or exchange of views. **3** an address or lecture. **4** rumour; gossip.

**talkative** *adj* given to talking a lot.

**talk back** *v* to answer impertinently.

**talk down** *v* (+ to) to speak in a condescending fashion to.

**talking-to** *n* (*pl* **talking-tos**) *informal* a reprimand or scolding.

**talk round** *v* to persuade or convince.

**tall** *adj* **1** of above average height. **2** of a specified height. **3** highly exaggerated; incredible: *a tall story*. * **a tall order** an unreasonably difficult task or requirement.

**tallow** *n* the solid white rendered fat of cattle and sheep, used in soap and candles.

**tall ship** *n* a sailing ship with tall masts.

**tally¹** *n* (*pl* **-ies**) **1** a record of items, amounts, or a score. **2** the current number of things achieved by somebody.

**tally²** *v* (**-ies, -ied**) **1** to correspond or match. **2** to make a count of.

**tally-ho** *n* (*pl* **-os**) a call given by a huntsman to the hounds on sighting a fox.

**Talmud** *n* the authoritative body of Jewish tradition.

**talon** *n* a curved claw, *esp* of a bird of prey.

**tamarind** *n* a pod-like fruit with sticky brown pulp.

**tamarisk** *n* a shrub with tiny narrow leaves and masses of minute flowers.

**tambourine** *n* a shallow one-headed drum with loose metallic discs at the sides, played by shaking or striking.

**tame¹** *adj* **1** of an animal: not afraid of or dangerous to human beings. **2** of a person: docile and submissive. **3** lacking zest or interest. ➤ **tamely** *adv*.

**tame²** *v* to make tame.

**tamp** *v* (*often* + down) to pack (something) in or down by a succession of blows.

**tamper** *v* (+ with) to interfere or meddle without permission.

**tampon** *n* an absorbent plug put into the vagina to absorb menstrual bleeding.

**tan¹** *v* (**tanned, tanning**) **1** to convert (animal skin) into leather. **2** to make or become light brown by exposure to the sun. * **tan somebody's hide** *informal* to beat somebody severely.

**tan²** *n* **1** a brown colour given to the skin by exposure to sun. **2** a light yellowish brown.

**tandem¹** *n* a bicycle having two seats one behind the other. * **in tandem 1** in partnership or conjunction. **2** arranged one behind the other.

**tandem²** *adv* one behind the other.

**tandoori** *n* a North Indian method of cooking meat in a clay oven.

**tang** *n* **1** a sharp distinctive flavour or smell. **2** a projecting shank on a blade that connects with a handle.

**tangent** *n* **1** in mathematics, the ratio in a right-angled triangle between the sides opposite and adjacent to an acute angle. **2** a straight line touching a curve or surface at only one point. * **fly/go off at a tangent** to change suddenly from one subject or course of action to another.

**tangential** *adj* **1** acting along or lying in a tangent. **2** incidental; barely relevant.

**tangerine** *n* a small loose-skinned citrus fruit with deep orange skin and pulp.

**tangible** *adj* **1** capable of being perceived by touch. **2** real; material. ➤ **tangibility** *n*, **tangibly** *adv*.

**tangle**[1] *v* **1** to intertwine in a disordered mass. **2** *informal* (*often* + with) to engage in conflict or argument. ➤ **tangled** *adj*.

**tangle**[2] *n* **1** a confused twisted mass. **2** a complicated state.

**tango**[1] *n* (*pl* **-os**) a Latin-American ballroom dance, characterized by long pauses and stylized body positions.

**tango**[2] *v* (**-oes, -oed**) to dance the tango.

**tank** *n* **1** a large receptacle for liquids or gas. **2** a container for fuel in a motor vehicle. **3** a clear-sided container in which to keep fish. **4** an enclosed heavily armoured combat vehicle that moves on caterpillar tracks.

**tankard** *n* a silver or pewter beer mug sometimes with a hinged lid.

**tank engine** *n* a steam locomotive that carries its own water and coal and does not have a tender.

**tanker** *n* a ship, aircraft, or road or rail vehicle designed to carry liquid in bulk.

**tank top** *n* a sleeveless pullover usu worn over a shirt or jumper.

**tannin** *n* a soluble astringent substance used in tanning and dyeing, and present in tea.

**Tannoy** *n trademark* a public address system that can broadcast throughout a large building.

**tantalize** *or* **-ise** *v* to tease by presenting something desirable that is just out of reach or promising something and then withholding it. ➤ **tantalizing** *adj*.

**tantamount** *adj* (+ to) equivalent in significance or effect to.

**tantrum** *n* (*pl* **tantrums**) a fit of childish bad temper.

**Taoiseach** *n* the prime minister of the Republic of Ireland.

**tap**[1] *n* **1** a device with a spout and valve attached to a pipe or container to control the flow of a liquid or gas. **2** a device that can be attached to a telephone to allow somebody to listen secretly to conversations. * **on tap 1** of beer, etc: on draught. **2** readily available.

**tap**[2] *v* (**tapped, tapping**) **1** to pierce (a container, tree, etc) so as to let out or draw off a fluid. **2** to draw from (a source or supply). **3** to connect a listening device to (a telephone wire) in order to acquire secret information. **4** *informal* (*usu* + for) to ask for money or information from (somebody).

**tap**[3] *n* **1** a light blow, or the sound it makes. **2** tap dancing.

**tap**[4] *v* (**tapped, tapping**) **1** to strike lightly with a slight sound. **2** to give a light blow with (something).

**tapas** *pl n* light savoury Spanish snacks eaten with an alcoholic drink.

**tap dancing** *n* a style of dancing in which the steps are tapped out audibly by small pieces of metal fitted to the dancer's shoes.

**tape**[1] *n* **1** a narrow band of woven fabric. **2** the string stretched above the finishing line of a race. **3** adhesive tape, insulating tape, or masking tape. **4** = MAGNETIC TAPE. **5** a tape recording. **6** a cassette of audio tape or videotape.

**tape**[2] *v* **1** to fasten or bind with tape. **2** to record on magnetic tape. * **have something taped** to be confident of one's ability to deal with something.

**tape measure** *n* a narrow strip of tape marked off in units for measuring.

**taper** *v* **1** to decrease gradually in thickness, diameter, or width towards one end. **2** (*often* + off) to diminish gradually. ➤ **tapering** *adj*.

**tape recorder** *n* a device for recording sounds on magnetic tape and reproducing them. ➤ **tape recording** *n*.

**tapestry** *n* (*pl* **-ies**) a piece of heavy fabric decorated with woven or embroidered designs.

**tapeworm** *n* a parasitic worm with a long, ribbon-like body that lives in the intestine of human beings.

**tapioca** *n* grains of cassava starch used *esp* in puddings.

**tapir** *n* (*pl* **tapirs** *or* **tapir**) a hoofed mammal with an elongated flexible snout.

**tappet** *n* a lever or projection moved by or moving some other piece, such as a cam.

**tar**[1] *n* **1** a dark viscous liquid obtained by distilling wood, coal, peat, etc. **2** a brown residue present in tobacco smoke.

**tar**[2] *v* (**tarred, tarring**) to cover or smear with tar. * **tarred with the same brush** of two or more people: having the same faults.

**tar**[3] *n informal, dated* a sailor.

**taramasalata** *n* a pinkish paste made from fish roe, olive oil, and seasoning, usu eaten as a starter.

**tarantula** *n* (*pl* **tarantulas** *or* **tarantulae**) **1** a large hairy spider of tropical and subtropical America. **2** a large southern European spider.

**tardy** *adj* (**-ier, -iest**) **1** delayed; late. **2** sluggish. ➤ **tardily** *adv*, **tardiness** *n*.

**tare** *n* the weight of an unloaded goods vehicle without its fuel.

**target**[1] *n* **1** an object to fire at in practice or competition, consisting of a series of concentric circles with a bull's-eye at the centre. **2** a person or object that is selected to be fired at, attacked, criticized, etc. **3** a goal or objective.

**target**[2] *v* (**targeted, targeting**) **1** to make

(somebody or something) a target. **2** (+ at/on) to aim (e.g. a missile) at.

**tariff** *n* **1** a duty imposed by a government on imported or exported goods. **2** the rates charged by a business, e.g. a hotel, or a list of these rates.

**tarmac**[1] *n* **1** a mixture of tar and aggregates used for surfacing roads. **2** a runway or other area surfaced with tarmac.

**tarmac**[2] *v* (**tarmacked, tarmacking**) to apply tarmac to (a road or path).

**tarn** *n* a small mountain lake.

**tarnish**[1] *v* **1** to dull the lustre of (something) by dirt, air, etc. **2** to bring discredit on.

**tarnish**[2] *n* a film of chemically altered material on the surface of a metal or mineral.

**tarot** *n* a set of 22 pictorial playing cards used for fortune-telling.

**tarpaulin** *n* a sheet of heavy waterproof tarred canvas.

**tarragon** *n* a herb with aromatic leaves.

**tarry** *v* (**-ies, -ied**) *archaic or literary* **1** to stay in or at a place. **2** to delay.

**tarsus** *n* (*pl* **tarsi**) the group of small bones in the ankle, heel, and upper part of the foot.

**tart**[1] *adj* **1** sharp or acid to the taste. **2** sarcastic or hurtful. ➤ **tartly** *adv.*

**tart**[2] *n* a pastry shell containing a sweet or savoury filling.

**tart**[3] *n informal* **1** a female prostitute. **2** a sexually promiscuous woman. ➤ **tarty** *adj.*

**tartan** *n* **1** a textile design of Scottish origin consisting of checks and stripes of varying colour, usu patterned to designate a particular clan. **2** a fabric with a tartan design.

**tartar**[1] *n informal* a formidable or irascible person.

**tartar**[2] *n* **1** a substance formed during fermentation that is deposited in wine casks as a reddish sediment. **2** an incrustation on the teeth consisting of calcium salts.

**tartare sauce** *n* mayonnaise with chopped pickles, olives, capers, and parsley, served *esp* with fish.

**tart up** *v* **1** to dress (oneself) up, put on make-up, etc. **2** to decorate or refurbish (a place) *esp* cheaply or gaudily.

**task** *n* an assigned piece of work; a duty. ✱ **take to task** to rebuke for a failure or mistake.

**task force** *n* **1** a temporary military grouping assembled to accomplish a particular objective. **2** a group of people that has been assigned a specific task.

**taskmaster** *or* **taskmistress** *n* a person who assigns tasks.

**tassel** *n* a bunch of cords or threads of even length fastened at one end, used as an ornament.

**taste**[1] *v* **1** to take a little (food, drink, etc) into the mouth to test its flavour. **2** to recognize (a substance, flavour, etc) by tasting. **3** (*often* + of) to have a specified flavour. **4** to experience or undergo. ➤ **taster** *n.*

**taste**[2] *n* **1** the faculty of perceiving the flavours of substances through the taste buds and distinguishing them as sweet, bitter, sour, or salt. **2** the flavour of a substance as perceived by this sense. **3** an instance of tasting. **4** a small amount tasted. **5** an experience of something. **6** an individual preference. **7** discernment in aesthetic or social matters.

**taste bud** *n* any of the small organs on the surface of the tongue that transmit the sensation of taste.

**tasteful** *adj* conforming to good judgment or acceptable behaviour. ➤ **tastefully** *adv.*

**tasteless** *adj* **1** lacking flavour. **2** not conforming to good judgment or acceptable behaviour. ➤ **tastelessly** *adv.*

**tasty** *adj* (**-ier, -iest**) **1** having an appetizing flavour. **2** *informal* arousing interest. **3** *Brit, informal* sexually appealing.

**tat** *n Brit, informal* low-quality or tasteless goods.

**tatter** *n* an irregular torn shred of material. ✱ **in tatters 1** torn to pieces; ragged. **2** in a state of ruin or disarray.

**tattered** *adj* old and torn.

**tattle**[1] *v* to chatter or gossip.

**tattle**[2] *n* chatter; gossip.

**tattoo**[1] *n* (*pl* **-os**) an indelible mark or design on the skin made by tattooing.

**tattoo**[2] *v* (**tattooed, tattooing**) to mark (the body) by inserting pigments under the skin. ➤ **tattooist** *n.*

**tattoo**[3] *n* (*pl* **tattoos**) **1** an outdoor military display of marching, music, etc. **2** a rapid rhythmic beating or tapping.

**tatty** *adj* (**-ier, -iest**) *chiefly Brit, informal* shabby; dilapidated.

**tau** *n* the 19th letter of the Greek alphabet (Τ, τ).

**taught** *v* past tense and past part. of TEACH.

**taunt**[1] *v* to provoke or jeer at (somebody) in a mocking way.

**taunt**[2] *n* a sarcastic provocation or insult.

**Taurus** *n* the second sign of the zodiac (the Bull).

**taut** *adj* **1** stretched or pulled tight. **2** tense; stressed. ➤ **tauten** *v,* **tautly** *adv.*

**tautology** *n* (*pl* **-ies**) the needless repetition of an idea, statement, or word. ➤ **tautological** *adj,* **tautologous** *adj.*

**tavern** *n Brit, humorous or archaic* a pub or inn.

**tawdry** *adj* (**-ier, -iest**) **1** cheap and tastelessly ornate. **2** sordid or sleazy. ➤ **tawdriness** *n.*

**tawny** *adj* (**-ier, -iest**) of a warm sandy or brownish orange colour.

**tax**[1] *n* a charge imposed by a government on individuals, organizations, or property, *esp* to raise revenue.

**tax**[2] *v* **1** to levy a tax on (income, a person, etc). **2** to pay tax on (a vehicle). **3** to make strenuous demands on. **4** (+ with) to charge (somebody) with a fault, or blame them for it. ➤ **taxable** *adj.*

**taxation** *n* **1** the imposition of taxes. **2** revenue obtained from taxes.

**tax-deductible** *adj* legally permitted to be deducted from income or capital before tax is paid on it.

**tax exile** *n* a person who lives abroad in order to avoid paying high taxes in their home country.

**tax haven** *n* a country with a relatively low level of taxation.

**taxi**[1] *n* (*pl* **taxis**) a motor car that may be hired, together with its driver, to carry passengers.

**taxi**[2] *v* (**taxis** *or* **taxies, taxied, taxiing** *or* **taxying**) of an aircraft: to move at low speed along a runway before takeoff or after landing.

**taxicab** *n* = TAXI[1].

**taxidermy** *n* the art of preparing, stuffing, and mounting the skins of animals to give a lifelike appearance. ➤ **taxidermist** *n.*

**taxing** *adj* physically, mentally, or emotionally demanding.

**taxi rank** *n* a place where taxis park to wait for customers.

**taxonomy** *n* (*pl* **-ies**) **1** classification, *esp* of plants and animals according to their presumed natural relationships. **2** the scientific study of classification. ➤ **taxonomic** *adj.*

**tax return** *n* a form on which a person states their income and allowable deductions for tax assessment purposes.

**tax year** *n* the year that is taken as the basis for calculations of tax (in Britain generally from 6 April to 5 April).

**TB** *n* = TUBERCULOSIS.

**Tb** *abbr* the chemical symbol for terbium.

**tbs** *or* **tbsp** *abbr* (*pl* **tbs** *or* **tbsp** *or* **tbsps**) tablespoonful.

**Tc** *abbr* the chemical symbol for technetium.

**Te** *abbr* the chemical symbol for tellurium.

**tea** *n* **1** the leaves and leaf buds of an evergreen Asian shrub prepared and cured. **2** a drink prepared by steeping tea leaves in boiling water. **3** a drink made from the leaves, flowers, or fruit of various other plants. **4** refreshments, usu including tea with sandwiches, cakes, or biscuits, served in the late afternoon. **5** a late-afternoon or early-evening meal.

**tea bag** *n* a cloth or paper bag holding enough tea for an individual drink.

**tea cake** *n* a round sweet bun often containing currants, usu eaten toasted with butter.

**teach** *v* (*past tense and past part.* **taught**) **1** to cause (somebody or something) to know something or how to do something. **2** to impart the knowledge of (a subject, skill, etc). **3** to cause (somebody) to understand something by experience. **4** to advocate. ➤ **teaching** *n.*

**teacher** *n* a person whose occupation is teaching, *esp* in a school.

**tea cloth** *n* = TEA TOWEL.

**teacup** *n* a small cup used for tea.

**teak** *n* the hard yellowish brown wood of a tall tree native to India and Southeast Asia.

**teal** *n* (*pl* **teals** *or* **teal**) a small freshwater duck.

**team**[1] *n* **1** a group of players forming one side in a sporting contest, game, etc. **2** a group of two or more people who work together. **3** two or more draught animals harnessed together.

**team**[2] *v* **1** (*often* + up) to come together as a team. **2** (+ with) to combine (e.g. an item of clothing) with another for a particular effect.

**teammate** *n* a fellow member of a team.

**team spirit** *n* willing and enthusiastic cooperation to achieve group objectives.

**teamwork** *n* mutual cooperation in a group enterprise.

**teapot** *n* a usu round pot with a lid, spout, and handle in which tea is brewed.

**tear**[1] *n* a drop of clear salty fluid secreted into the eye and often released as a result of grief or other emotion. ✱ **in tears** crying; weeping.

**tear**[2] *v* (**tore, torn**) **1** to rip or pull apart by force; to damage in this way. **2** to wound (e.g. a muscle or ligament) by tearing. **3** (*often* + from/off) to remove by force. **4** (**be torn**) be unable to decide between two alternatives. **5** to move with great speed or haste. ✱ **tear a strip off** *informal* to rebuke (somebody) angrily. **tear into** to attack (somebody) physically or verbally without restraint.

**tear**[3] *n* a hole or rip made by tearing.

**tearaway** *n Brit, informal* an unruly and reckless young person.

**tear down** *v* to demolish.

**teardrop** *n* a single tear.

**tearful** *adj* **1** causing tears. **2** crying or inclined to cry. ➤ **tearfully** *adv.*

**tear gas** *n* a gas that causes the eyes to stream with tears and is used chiefly in dispersing crowds.

**tearjerker** *n informal* a very sad or sentimental play, film, etc.

**tearoom** *n* a restaurant where light refreshments are served.

**tear up** *v* to tear into pieces.

**tease**[1] *v* **1** to try, usu playfully, to irritate or embarrass (somebody) by making fun of them. **2** to arouse (somebody) sexually with no intention of permitting sexual fulfilment. **3** to disentangle and straighten (wool) by combing it.

**tease**[2] *n informal* somebody or something that teases.

**teasel** *or* **teazel** *or* **teazle** *n* a tall plant with flower heads that are covered with stiff hooked bracts.

**tease out** *v* to gain (information, the truth, etc) with difficulty, e.g. by working through a mass of data.

**teaspoon** *n* **1** a small spoon used for adding sugar, etc to hot drinks and stirring them. **2** = TEASPOONFUL.

**teaspoonful** *n* (*pl* **teaspoonfuls**) as much as a teaspoon will hold (about 5ml).

**teat** *n* **1** a nipple of the mammary gland of a female animal. **2** a rubber or plastic mouthpiece attached to the top of a baby's feeding bottle.

**tea towel** *n* a cloth for drying dishes after they have been washed.

**technical** *adj* **1** involving special and usu practical knowledge, *esp* of mechanical, industrial, or scientific subjects. **2** relating to or used in a particular subject: *technical terms.* **3** complicated or difficult to understand. **4** marked by a strict legal interpretation or rigid application of the rules. **5** relating to technique. ➤ **technically** *adv.*

**technical college** *n* a further education college that offers courses in practical subjects.

**technicality** *n* (*pl* **-ies**) **1** a detail meaningful only to a specialist. **2** a detail arising from a strict or literal interpretation of a rule or law.

**technician** *n* **1** a specialist in the technical details of a subject or occupation. **2** somebody employed to do practical work, e.g. in a laboratory.

**Technicolor** *n trademark* a process of colour photography in the cinema.

**technique** *n* **1** the manner in which an artist, performer, or athlete displays their skill. **2** a method of accomplishing a desired aim.

**techno** *n* a form of fast electronically produced modern dance music.

**technology** *n* (*pl* **-ies**) **1** the application of science for practical purposes *esp* in commerce and industry. **2** the study of applied scientific methods. ➤ **technological** *adj,* **technologically** *n.*

**tectonic** *adj* relating to the earth's crust.

**teddy** *n* (*pl* **-ies**) = TEDDY BEAR.

**teddy bear** *n* a stuffed toy bear.

**Teddy boy** *n* a male member of a British youth cult of the 1950s, characterized by supposedly Edwardian-style clothing, hair styled in swept-up quiffs, and enthusiasm for rock 'n' roll.

**tedious** *adj* dull, boring, and apparently interminable. ➤ **tediously** *adv.*

**tedium** *n* the state of being tedious.

**tee**[1] *n* a mark aimed at in various games, e.g. curling or quoits.

**tee**[2] *n* **1** the area from which a golf ball is struck at the beginning of play on a hole. **2** a peg used to raise a golf ball into position for striking at the beginning of play on a hole.

**tee**[3] *v* (*often* + up) to place (a golf ball) on a tee.

**teem** *v* **1** (+ with) to be filled with large numbers of moving and active beings. **2** *Brit* (*also* + down) to rain hard.

**teen**[1] *adj informal* = TEENAGE.

**teen**[2] *n informal* = TEENAGER.

**teenage** *adj* relating to or suitable for teenagers. ➤ **teenaged** *adj.*

**teenager** *n* a person who is aged between 13 and 19.

**teens** *pl n* the years 13 to 19 in a lifetime.

**teeny** *or* **teensy** *adj* (**-ier, -iest**) *informal* tiny.

**tee off** *v* to drive a golf ball from a tee.

**teepee** *n* see TEPEE.

**tee shirt** *n* see T-SHIRT.

**teeter** *v* to wobble or move unsteadily.

**teeth** *n* pl of TOOTH.

**teethe** *v* to cut one's milk teeth.

**teetotal** *adj* practising complete abstinence from alcoholic drinks. ➤ **teetotalism** *n,* **teetotaller** *n.*

**telecommunications** *pl n* the science and technology of communication at a distance, e.g. by telegraph, telephone, television, etc.

**teleconferencing** *n* the process of holding a meeting involving people in different places who are linked by telephone or video.

**telegram** *n* a message sent by telegraph and delivered as a written or typed note.

**telegraph**[1] *n* an apparatus or system for sending messages along a wire.

**telegraph**[2] *v* to send a message to (somebody) by telegraph.

**telegraphic** *adj* **1** of the telegraph. **2** concise; terse.

**telekinesis** *n* the supposed ability to move distant objects without physically touching them, *esp* just by concentrating the mind on them. ➤ **telekinetic** *adj.*

**telepathy** *n* communication that supposedly occurs directly from one mind to another without use of the known senses. ➤ **telepathic** *adj.*

**telephone**[1] *n* **1** a device for converting sounds into electrical impulses for transmission by wire or radio to a particular receiver. **2** the system of communications that uses telephones. ➤ **telephonic** *adj.*

**telephone**[2] *v* to speak to (somebody) by telephone.

**telephone box** *n* a booth containing a public telephone.

**telephone directory** *n* a book giving the telephone numbers of subscribers.

**telephonist** *n Brit* a telephone switchboard operator.

**telephony** *n* the use of telephones for communication, or the technology of telephones.

**telephoto lens** *n* a camera lens that produces a magnified image of a distant object.

**teleprinter** *n* a machine with a typewriter keyboard and printing device that transmits, and receives and prints, telegraphic signals.

**telesales** *pl n* sales or selling transacted by telephone.
**telescope**[1] *n* a usu tubular optical instrument for viewing distant objects in magnified form by means of a lens or a concave mirror. ➤ **telescopic** *adj.*
**telescope**[2] *v* **1** to slide one part within anotherlike the cylindrical sections of a hand telescope. **2** to condense or shorten.
**Teletext** *n trademark* an information service provided by a television network.
**telethon** *n* a long television programme designed to raise money for charity.
**televise** *v* to broadcast (a programme, event, etc) by television.
**television** *n* **1** an electronic system for transmitting images together with sound as electrical signals along a wire or through space to a receiving device that then reproduces them. **2** a device with a screen and sound system for receiving and displaying television signals. **3** the television broadcasting industry. ➤ **televisual** *adj.*
**teleworking** *n* the practice of carrying on an occupation or business from home using a computer, modem, e-mail, etc to communicate with employers or clients. ➤ **teleworker** *n.*
**telex**[1] *n* **1** a communications service involving teleprinters connected by wire through automatic exchanges. **2** a message sent by telex. **3** a telex machine.
**telex**[2] *v* to send (a message) by telex.
**tell** *v* (*past tense and past part.* **told**) **1** to make known the incidents, characters, etc involved in (a story) to. **2** to give information to. **3** to order or instruct (somebody) to do something. **4** to distinguish. **5** (*often* + on) to have an effect: *The strain was beginning to tell.* ✻ **tell on** *informal* to inform on. **tell tales 1** to be untruthful. **2** to reveal secrets or spread gossip. **tell the time** to read the information on a clock or watch.
**teller** *n* **1** somebody who tells e.g. a story. **2** somebody appointed to count votes. **3** a member of a bank's staff who deals directly with customers' transactions.
**telling** *adj* producing a marked effect; significant. ➤ **tellingly** *adv.*
**telling-off** *n* (*pl* **tellings-off** *or* **telling-offs**) *informal* a harsh or severe reprimand.
**tell off** *v informal* to scold or reprimand.
**telltale**[1] *n* somebody who informs on somebody or their actions.
**telltale**[2] *adj* revealing, betraying, or indicating something.
**telly** *n* (*pl* **-ies**) *chiefly Brit, informal* = TELEVISION.
**temerity** *n* excessive boldness.
**temp**[1] *n informal* a person, e.g. an office worker, employed temporarily.
**temp**[2] *v informal* to work as a temp.
**temper**[1] *n* **1** an uncontrolled and often disproportionate rage. **2** proneness to displays of rage. **3** a characteristic cast of mind or state of feeling. **4** the degree of hardness or resilience given to steel by tempering. ✻ **keep one's temper** to keep one's anger under control. **lose one's temper** to show one's anger.
**temper**[2] *v* **1** to moderate (something harsh). **2** to bring (*esp* steel) to the right degree of hardness by reheating and cooling it.
**tempera** *n* a method of painting using pigment mixed with egg yolk and water.
**temperament** *n* a person's own particular mental and emotional character, *esp* with regard to its effect on behaviour.
**temperamental** *adj* **1** easily upset or irritated. **2** unpredictable in behaviour or operation. **3** arising from an individual's character or constitution. ➤ **temperamentally** *adv.*
**temperance** *n* abstinence from alcohol.
**temperate** *adj* **1** moderate in the indulgence of appetites or desires. **2** having a moderate climate. ➤ **temperately** *adv.*
**temperature** *n* **1** degree of hotness or coldness as measured on a scale, e.g. in degrees Celsius. **2** *informal* an abnormally high body heat, usu indicative of illness.
**tempest** *n* a violent storm.
**tempestuous** *adj* **1** characterized by passion, violence, and emotional turbulence. **2** characterized by storms and bad weather.
**template** *or* **templet** *n* **1** a pattern, mould, or stencil used as a guide when making, drawing, cutting out, or drilling something. **2** a thing that serves as a model.
**temple**[1] *n* a building dedicated to religious worship *esp* in non-Christian religions.
**temple**[2] *n* the flattened space on either side of the forehead.
**tempo** *n* (*pl* **tempi** *or* **tempos**) **1** the speed of a musical piece or passage. **2** the rate of motion or activity.
**temporal** *adj* **1** relating to time as opposed to eternity or space. **2** relating to lay or secular matters.
**temporary** *adj* lasting only for a limited time. ➤ **temporarily** *adv.*
**temporize** *or* **-ise** *v* to avoid making a decision or commitment.
**tempt** *v* **1** to make (somebody) feel strongly inclined to do something. **2** to attract or appeal to. **3** to try to persuade (somebody) to do something wicked, immoral, or unwise, by the promise of pleasure or gain. ✻ **tempt fate** to do or say something that suggests overconfidence and might bring disaster. ➤ **tempter** *n,* **tempting** *adj.*
**temptation** *n* **1** an urge to do, take, or enjoy something, *esp* something forbidden or unwise. **2** the state of being tempted. **3** something tempting.

**temptress** *n* a woman with very strong and obvious sex appeal.
**ten** *n* the number 10. ➤ **ten** *adj.*
**tenable** *adj* **1** capable of being defended or justified. **2** (*usu* + for) of a position, award, etc: to be held for a specified period.
**tenacious** *adj* **1** holding on very firmly. **2** unwilling to desist or to give up on something. ➤ **tenaciously** *adv,* **tenacity** *n.*
**tenancy** *n* (*pl* **-ies**) temporary occupancy of land, a house, etc under a lease or rental agreement.
**tenant**[1] *n* somebody who rents or leases a house or flat from a landlord.
**tenant**[2] *v* to live in (a property) as a tenant.
**tench** *n* (*pl* **tenches** *or* **tench**) a freshwater fish of the carp family with a greenish or blackish skin.
**Ten Commandments** *pl n* the commandments given by God to Moses, recorded in Exodus 20:1–17.
**tend**[1] *v* **1** to be likely or inclined to do something, or to have the habit of doing something. **2** to move in a specified direction.
**tend**[2] *v* **1** to be in charge and take care of. **2** to provide care and treatment for.
**tendency** *n* (*pl* **-ies**) **1** an inclination or predisposition to do something. **2** a general trend or movement.
**tendentious** *adj* presenting a biased view.
**tender**[1] *adj* **1** showing great gentleness and kindness. **2** showing love or affection. **3** of meat: easy to cut and chew. **4** sensitive or sore. **5** young and vulnerable. **6** demanding careful and sensitive handling. ✱ **tender mercies** unkind treatment. ➤ **tenderly** *adv,* **tenderness** *n.*
**tender**[2] *n* **1** a boat that carries supplies, passengers, etc to and from ships. **2** a vehicle attached to a steam locomotive for carrying a supply of fuel and water. **3** a road vehicle that carries tools, equipment, or personnel, e.g. for the fire service.
**tender**[3] *v* **1** to present formally for acceptance. **2** to offer (money) in payment. **3** (*often* + for) to present a bid in the hope of gaining a contract.
**tender**[4] *n* a formal offer or bid.
**tendon** *n* a cord or band of fibrous tissue that connects a muscle with a bone.
**tendril** *n* a slender coiling outgrowth that attaches a climbing plant to its support.
**tenebrous** *adj literary* dark; murky.
**tenement** *n* a large building divided up into separate dwellings.
**tenet** *n* a principle, belief, or doctrine.
**tenner** *n Brit, informal* a ten-pound note.
**tennis** *n* a game for two or four players that is played with rackets and a ball on a flat court divided by a low net.
**tennis elbow** *n* inflammation and pain of the elbow, usu resulting from overuse of the hand and forearm.
**tenon** *n* a projecting piece of wood specially shaped to fit into a matching slot.
**tenor** *n* **1** a male singer having a high voice but below the range of an alto. **2** the general meaning of something spoken or written.
**tenpin bowling** *n* an indoor bowling game using ten bottle-shaped pins and a large ball.
**tense**[1] *adj* **1** feeling or showing nervousness and anxiety. **2** marked by strain or suspense. **3** stretched tight; taut. ➤ **tensely** *adv.*
**tense**[2] *v* (*often* + up) to become or make tense.
**tense**[3] *n* a set of inflectional forms of a verb that express action taking place at a particular time.
**tensile** *adj* **1** able to be stretched or drawn out. **2** relating to tension.
**tension** *n* **1** the condition of being stretched tight. **2** the strain caused by two forces pulling in opposite directions. **3** mental or emotional unease; stress. **4** a feeling of nervous and excited anticipation or suspense. **5** a state of latent hostility between individuals or groups. **6** voltage or electrical potential.
**tent** *n* a collapsible shelter made of canvas or similar material supported by poles. ➤ **tented** *adj.*
**tentacle** *n* an elongated flexible animal part, usu around the mouth, used for feeling, grasping, etc.
**tentative** *adj* **1** not fully worked out or developed; provisional. **2** hesitant or uncertain. ➤ **tentatively** *adv.*
**tenterhook** *n* ✱ **on tenterhooks** in a state of suspense or nervous anticipation.
**tenth** *adj and n* **1** having the position in a sequence corresponding to the number ten. **2** one of ten equal parts of something.
**tenuous** *adj* **1** weak or flimsy. **2** not thick; fine. ➤ **tenuously** *adv.*
**tenure** *n* **1** the holding of a position or an office. **2** the conditions under which a property is held or occupied. **3** *NAmer* a secure employment status *esp* for teaching staff.
**tenured** *adj NAmer* providing secure employment status.
**tepee** *or* **teepee** *n* a Native American conical tent, usu made of skins.
**tepid** *adj* **1** moderately warm. **2** not enthusiastic.
**tequila** /tə'keelə/ *n* a strong Mexican alcoholic drink.
**tercentenary** *n* (*pl* **-ies**) a 300th anniversary.
**term**[1] *n* **1** a word or expression with a precise meaning. **2** (*in pl*) provisions relating to an agreement. **3** the time for which something lasts. **4** any of the usu three periods of instruction into which an academic year is divided. **5** the time at which a pregnancy of normal length ends. **6** a mathematical expression that

forms part of a fraction, equation, ratio, etc. * **be on good/bad terms with** to have a friendly/unfriendly relationship with (somebody). **come to terms** (+ with) to accept or resign oneself to something sad or unpleasant. ➤ **termly** *adj and adv.*

**term**[2] *v* to apply a particular term to.

**termagant** *n* an overbearing or nagging woman.

**terminal**[1] *adj* **1** forming an end, boundary, or terminus. **2** relating to or suffering from a disease that is certain to cause death. **3** *informal* extreme or irreversible. ➤ **terminally** *adv.*

**terminal**[2] *n* **1** the end of a transport route, with its associated buildings and facilities. **2** a building at an airport with facilities for arriving and departing passengers. **3** a point where a wire or cable can be connected to an electrical apparatus. **4** a device through which a user can communicate with a computer.

**terminate** *v* **1** to bring or come to an end. **2** to take action to end (a pregnancy) prematurely. **3** to reach a terminus. ➤ **terminator** *n.*

**termination** *n* the ending, *esp* of a pregnancy.

**terminology** *n* (*pl* **-ies**) the technical terms used in a particular subject. ➤ **terminological** *adj.*

**terminus** *n* (*pl* **termini** *or* **terminuses**) the end of a transport line or travel route.

**termite** *n* an insect with a pale-coloured soft body that lives in colonies and feeds on wood.

**tern** *n* a white seabird with a black cap and a forked tail.

**ternary** *adj* made up of three parts.

**terpsichorean** *adj literary or humorous* relating to dancing.

**terrace**[1] *n* **1** a level paved or planted area adjoining a building. **2** a horizontal ridge cut into a hillside and used for farming. **3** *chiefly Brit* a row of similar houses joined by common dividing walls. **4** *Brit* a series of shallow steps providing standing accommodation for spectators.

**terrace**[2] *v* to make (an area of ground) into a terrace or terraces.

**terracotta** *n* unglazed brownish red earthenware.

**terra firma** *n* dry land; solid ground.

**terrain** *n* an area of land, *esp* with respect to its physical features.

**terrapin** *n* a water reptile like a small tortoise.

**terrestrial** *adj* **1** relating to the planet earth or its inhabitants. **2** relating to land as distinct from air or water. **3** of organisms: living on or in land or soil. **4** of a television system: not transmitting programmes via a satellite.

**terrible** *adj* **1** *informal* of very poor quality. **2** *informal* highly unpleasant. **3** *informal* extreme or very great. **4** *informal* very unwell, upset, or guilty. **5** terrifying.

**terribly** *adv informal* **1** very. **2** very badly.

**terrier** *n* a usu small dog of various breeds, orig used to hunt out game from underground.

**terrific** *adj* **1** *informal* extraordinarily large or intense. **2** *informal* excellent or highly enjoyable. **3** arousing fear or awe. ➤ **terrifically** *adv.*

**terrify** *v* (**-ies, -ied**) to fill with terror. ➤ **terrifying** *adj.*

**terrine** *n* **1** an earthenware baking dish. **2** a food, *esp* pâté, cooked in a terrine.

**territorial** *adj* **1** relating to territory or land. **2** of an animal or bird: marking out and defending its own territory.

**Territorial Army** *n* in Britain, a voluntary force providing a trained army reserve for emergencies.

**territory** *n* (*pl* **-ies**) **1** a geographical area under the jurisdiction of a government. **2** an administrative subdivision of a country. **3** an assigned area; *esp* one in which an agent, sales representative, or distributor operates. **4** an area occupied and defended by an animal or group of animals.

**terror** *n* **1** a state of intense fear. **2** somebody or something that inspires fear. **3** acts of terrorism. **4** *informal* an annoying or appalling person.

**terrorism** *n* the systematic use of terror, violence, and intimidation for political ends. ➤ **terrorist** *adj and n.*

**terrorize** *or* **-ise** *v* to fill with terror or anxiety.

**terry** *n* (*pl* **-ies**) an absorbent fabric used *esp* for towels.

**terse** *adj* using few words. ➤ **tersely** *adv.*

**tertiary** *adj* **1** of third rank, importance, or value. **2** *Brit* relating to higher education.

**tessellated** *adj* paved or decorated with stones arranged in a pattern. ➤ **tessellation** *n.*

**test**[1] *n* **1** a means of assessing the quality, capabilities, reliability, etc of somebody or something. **2** a series of questions or exercises for measuring the knowledge, intelligence, ability, etc of an individual or group. **3** a real-life situation that subjects something or somebody to stress, difficulties, etc. **4** an *esp* chemical procedure, used to identify the presence of a substance. **5** = TEST MATCH.

**test**[2] *v* **1** to subject to a test. **2** to subject to severe strain. **3** (*usu* + for) to produce a specified result in a medical or chemical test: *She tested negative for HIV.* ➤ **tester** *n.*

**testament** *n* **1** (**Testament**) either of the two main divisions of the Bible. **2** a proof of or tribute to something. **3** a will. ➤ **testamentary** *adj.*

**testate** *adj* having made a valid will.

**test card** *n* a picture broadcast by a television transmitting station to facilitate the testing or adjustment of receivers.

**test case** *n* in law, a representative case whose outcome is likely to serve as a precedent.

**testicle** *n* either of the two oval sperm-producing organs of a male mammal, usu with its enclosing structures. ➤ **testicular** *adj.*

**testify** *v* (**-ies, -ied**) **1** to give evidence under oath as a witness in a court. **2** (*usu* + to) to serve as evidence or proof.

**testimonial** *n* **1** a letter of recommendation. **2** a public expression of appreciation or esteem.

**testimony** *n* (*pl* **-ies**) **1** a sworn statement or the evidence given by a witness in a court. **2** an outward sign; evidence.

**test match** *n* an international cricket or rugby match.

**testosterone** *n* a hormone that produces and maintains male secondary sex characteristics.

**test tube** *n* a thin glass tube closed at one end and used in chemistry, biology, etc.

**test-tube baby** *n* a baby conceived by fertilization of an ovum outside the mother's body.

**testy** *adj* (**-ier, -iest**) easily annoyed. ➤ **testily** *adv.*

**tetanus** *n* an infectious disease characterized by muscle spasms, *esp* in the jaw.

**tetchy** *adj* (**-ier, -iest**) irritably or peevishly sensitive. ➤ **tetchily** *adv.*

**tête-à-tête**[1] /ˌtet ah ˈtet, ˌtayt ah ˈtayt/ *adv and adj* in private; private and intimate.

**tête-à-tête**[2] *n* a private conversation between two people.

**tether**[1] *n* a rope, chain, etc by which an animal is fastened.

**tether**[2] *v* to fasten or restrain (an animal or person) by a tether.

**tetrahedron** *n* (*pl* **tetrahedrons** *or* **tetrahedra**) a polyhedron with four faces.

**TETRA mast** *n* a telecommunications mast erected as part of mobile phone communication system (Terrestrial Trunked Radio) being set up for use by the police.

**Teutonic** *adj* supposedly characteristic of the Germans.

**text**[1] *n* **1** printed or written words. **2** the main body of printed matter on a page or in a book, as opposed to illustrations, notes, etc. **3** a literary or other work selected for special study. **4** a passage of Scripture chosen *esp* for the subject of a sermon. **5** = TEXT MESSAGE. ➤ **textual** *adj.*

**text**[2] *v* to send a text message to. ➤ **texting** *n.*

**textbook**[1] *n* a book used in the study of a subject.

**textbook**[2] *adj* exemplary or typical.

**textile** *n* cloth, *esp* a woven or knitted cloth.

**text message** *n* a written message sent from one mobile phone to another. ➤ **text-messaging** *n.*

**texture**[1] *n* the visual or tactile surface characteristics of something, *esp* fabric. ➤ **textural** *adj.*

**texture**[2] *v* to give a particular texture to.

**Th** *abbr* the chemical symbol for thorium.

**Thai** /tie/ *n* (*pl* **Thai** *or* **Thais**) **1** a native or inhabitant of Thailand. **2** the national language of Thailand.

**thalidomide** *n* a sedative and hypnotic drug found to cause foetal malformation when used during pregnancy.

**than** *conj* **1** used to introduce the second element in a comparison: *She is older than I am.* **2** used to introduce an alternative or a contrast: *They would starve rather than beg.* **3** used after expressions such as *no sooner* to introduce what happened next.

**thane** *n* **1** an Anglo-Saxon nobleman holding lands in exchange for military service. **2** a Scottish feudal lord.

**thank** *v* **1** to express gratitude to. **2** (*usu* + for) to hold responsible; to blame. ✱ **thank you** used as a conventional and polite formula for expressing gratitude.

**thankful** *adj* **1** grateful. **2** expressing thanks. **3** pleased or glad. ➤ **thankfulness** *n.*

**thankfully** *adv* **1** in a thankful manner. **2** it is a relief that.

**thankless** *adj* **1** bringing neither profit nor appreciation. **2** not expressing or feeling gratitude.

**thanks** *pl n* **1** an expression of gratitude. **2** thank you. ✱ **thanks to 1** with the help of. **2** because of or owing to.

**thanksgiving** *n* **1** an expression of gratefulness, *esp* to God. **2** (**Thanksgiving**) a public holiday occurring in November in the USA and in October in Canada.

**that**[1] *pron* (*pl* **those**) **1** the thing or idea just mentioned. **2** a relatively distant person or thing introduced for observation or discussion. **3** (*in pl*) people. ✱ **and (all) that** *informal* and everything connected with it. **that is (to say)** in other words. **that's that** that concludes the matter.

**that**[2] *adj* (*pl* **those**) **1** denoting the person, thing, or idea specified, mentioned, or understood. **2** denoting the one farther away or less immediately under consideration.

**that**[3] *conj* used to introduce a noun clause or a subordinate clause expressing purpose, reason, or result.

**that**[4] *pron* used to introduce a restrictive relative clause identifying or characterizing a particular person, thing, or group: *The book that you want is on the table.*

**that**[5] *adv* **1** to the extent indicated or understood: *a nail about that long.* **2** very; extremely: *It's not that expensive.*

**thatch**[1] *n* plant material such as straw or reeds used as a roof covering.

**thatch**[2] *v* to roof (a building) with thatch. ➤ **thatcher** *n.*

**thaw**[1] *v* **1** to go or cause to go from a frozen to a liquid state. **2** (*often* + out) to become less numb or stiff from cold. **3** of the weather: to be warm enough to melt ice and snow. **4** to make or become less hostile or reserved.

**thaw²** *n* **1** a period of weather warm enough to thaw ice. **2** a lessening of hostility or aloofness.

**the** *definite article* **1** used before nouns when the object or person in question has been previously referred to or is obvious from the circumstances. **2** used to refer to somebody or something unique or universally recognized: *the pope*. **3** used before a singular noun to indicate generic use: *a history of the novel*.

**theatre** (*NAmer* **theater**) *n* **1** a building specially constructed for the presentation of dramatic performances. **2** dramatic literature or performances. **3** (**the theatre**) the world of actors, acting, and drama generally. **4** a place where significant events or actions take place. **5** (*also* **operating theatre**) *Brit* a room where surgical operations are carried out.

**theatrical** *adj* relating to the theatre or the presentation of plays. ➤ **theatricality** *n*, **theatrically** *adv*.

**theatricals** *or* **theatrics** *pl n* **1** the art of performing plays, or theatrical performances. **2** theatrical behaviour.

**thee** *pron archaic or dialect* used as the objective case: thou.

**theft** *n* the act or crime of stealing.

**their** *adj* **1** belonging to or associated with them. **2** belonging to or associated with an indefinite singular person.

***Usage Note:*** Do not confuse this word with *there* or *they're*.

**theirs** *pron* the one or ones that belong to or are associated with them.

***Usage Note:*** Note that there is no apostrophe in *theirs*.

**them** *pron* used as the objective case: they.

**thematic** *adj* **1** relating to or constituting a theme. **2** classified according to subject. ➤ **thematically** *adv*.

**theme** *n* **1** a subject or topic dealt with in a discursive or artistic work and usu forming a unifying thread running through it. **2** a unifying concept in the planning or design of something. **3** a group of notes or melody forming the basis of a musical composition.

**theme music** *n* a signature tune.

**theme park** *n* an amusement park based on a specific theme.

**theme song** *n* a recurring melody in a musical play or film that characterizes the production or one of its characters.

**theme tune** *n* a signature tune.

**themself** *pron* = THEMSELVES 2.

**themselves** *pron* **1** used reflexively or for emphasis to refer to the people, animals, or things that are the subject of the clause. **2** used reflexively to refer to an indefinite singular person that is the subject of the clause.

**then** *adv* **1** at that time. **2** soon after that; next. **3** besides or in addition. **4** in that case. ✱ **then and there** at once.

**thence** *adv* **1** from there. **2** *formal* consequently.

**thenceforth** *adv archaic or formal* from that time or point on.

**theocracy** *n* (*pl* **-ies**) government by priests. ➤ **theocratic** *adj*.

**theodolite** *n* a surveyor's instrument for measuring horizontal and vertical angles.

**theologian** *n* a specialist in theology.

**theology** *n* (*pl* **-ies**) **1** the study of God and the teachings of an organized religion. **2** a system of religious beliefs. ➤ **theological** *adj*, **theologist** *n*.

**theorem** *n* a proposition in mathematics or logic deducible from other more basic propositions.

**theoretical** *adj* **1** relating to or having the character of theory; abstract. **2** confined to theory, *esp* not involving practical experience. **3** hypothetical. ➤ **theoretically** *adv*.

**theoretician** *n* somebody who specializes in the theoretical aspects of a subject.

**theorist** *n* = THEORETICIAN.

**theorize** *or* **-ise** *v* to form a theory; to speculate.

**theory** *n* (*pl* **-ies**) **1** an idea or set of ideas put forward to explain why something happens. **2** the general or abstract principles of a subject. ✱ **in theory** on the basis of abstract principles or under ideal circumstances, but not necessarily in practice or reality.

**therapeutic** *adj* **1** relating to the treatment of disease or disorders. **2** having a beneficial effect on a person's health. ➤ **therapeutically** *adv*.

**therapy** *n* (*pl* **-ies**) treatment of physical or mental disorders, or a specific type of treatment. ➤ **therapist** *n*.

**there** *adv* **1** in, at, or to that place. **2** on that point or in that particular respect. **3** used to draw attention to something. ✱ **there is/are** used to introduce a sentence or clause stating that something exists or is true.

***Usage Note:*** Do not confuse this word with *their* or *they're*.

**thereabouts** *adv* **1** near that place. **2** near that time, quantity, etc.

**thereafter** *adv formal* after that.

**thereby** *adv* by that means; as a result of which.

**therefore** *adv* because of that.

**therein** *adv formal* in that; *esp* in that respect.

**thereof** *adv formal* of that or it.

**there's** *contraction* **1** there is. **2** there has.

**thereupon** *adv formal* immediately after that.

**therewith** *adv* **1** *formal* with that or it. **2** *archaic* thereupon.

**thermal¹** *adj* **1** relating to heat. **2** designed to prevent body heat from escaping. ➤ **thermally** *adv*.

**thermal**[2] *n* **1** a rising current of warm air. **2** (*in pl*) thermal underwear or clothing.
**thermionic** *adj* **1** relating to the emission of electrons from incandescent substances. **2** of e.g. a valve: using thermionic electrons as charge carriers.
**thermodynamics** *pl n* the branch ofphysics dealing with the relations between heat and other forms of energy. ➤ **thermodynamic** *adj.*
**thermometer** *n* an instrument that measures and indicates temperature, *esp* a glass tube containing a liquid, e.g. mercury, that rises and falls with changes of temperature.
**thermonuclear** *adj* relating to or making use of transformations occurring in atomic nuclei at very high temperatures.
**Thermos** *n trademark* a vacuum flask.
**thermostat** *n* an automatic device for regulating temperature. ➤ **thermostatic** *adj,* **thermostatically** *adv.*
**thesaurus** *n* (*pl* **thesauri** *or* **thesauruses**) a book listing words and their synonyms.
**these** *pron* pl of THIS[1].
**thesis** *n* (*pl* **theses**) **1** a proposition that a person offers to substantiate by argument. **2** a dissertation embodying the results of original research, *esp* one submitted for a doctorate.
**thespian**[1] *adj* relating to acting, drama, or the theatre.
**thespian**[2] *n formal or humorous* an actor.
**theta** *n* the eighth letter of the Greek alphabet (Θ, θ).
**they** *pron* **1** used to refer to a previously mentioned group of people or things. **2** used to refer to a single person of either sex previously mentioned. **3** people in general. **4** the authorities.
**they'd** *contraction* **1** they had. **2** they would.
**they'll** *contraction* **1** they will. **2** they shall.
**they're** *contraction* they are.

***Usage Note:*** Do not confuse this word with *their* or *there.*

**they've** *contraction* they have.
**thiamine** *or* **thiamin** *n* vitamin $B_1$, found *esp* in cereals and beans.
**thick**[1] *adj* **1** having a relatively great distance between opposite surfaces. **2** of large diameter in relation to length. **3** containing closely-packed objects or material. **4** (+ with) covered with a thick layer of. **5** not flowing or pouring easily. **6** of fog, etc: not easy to see through; dense. **7** of speech: imperfectly articulated. **8** of an accent: marked. **9** *informal* stupid. **10** *informal* on close terms; intimate. ✱ **a bit thick** *Brit, informal* unreasonable or unfair. **be as thick as thieves** *informal* to be very friendly or intimate with each other. **give somebody/get a thick ear** *Brit, informal* to give somebody/receive a blow on the ear as punishment. **lay it on thick 1** to overstate or exaggerate something. **2** to flatter somebody excessively. **thick and fast** in very quick succession. ➤ **thickly** *adv.*
**thick**[2] *n* the most crowded or active part. ✱ **through thick and thin** in good times and bad times.
**thicken** *v* to make or become thick or thicker.
**thicket** *n* a dense growth of shrubbery or small trees.
**thickhead** *n informal* a stupid person. ➤ **thick-headed** *adj.*
**thickness** *n* **1** the distance through an object as opposed to its length or height. **2** a layer or ply.
**thickset** *adj* heavily built; burly.
**thief** *n* (*pl* **thieves**) somebody who steals. ➤ **thievery** *n,* **thievish** *adj.*
**thieve** *v* to be a thief.
**thigh** *n* the part of the leg that extends from the hip to the knee.
**thimble** *n* a metal or plastic cap worn to protect the finger and to push the needle in sewing.
**thin**[1] *adj* (**thinner, thinnest**) **1** having little depth between opposite surfaces. **2** of narrow diameter in relation to length. **3** without much flesh or fat on the body. **4** not dense or closely-packed. **5** more rarefied than normal. **6** few in number. **7** of a liquid: very diluted; lacking substance or strength. **8** flimsy or unconvincing. **9** of a voice or sound: somewhat feeble and lacking in resonance. **10** *informal* disappointingly poor or hard. ➤ **thinly** *adv,* **thinness** *n.*
**thin**[2] *v* (**thinned, thinning**) **1** to make or become thin or thinner. **2** (+ out) to reduce the thickness or density of.
**thine** *pron* (*pl* **thine**) *archaic* the one or ones that belong to or are associated with thee.
**thing** *n* **1** an inanimate object as distinguished from a living being. **2** an object or entity not able to be precisely named. **3** a matter, affair, or concern. **4** an event or circumstance. **5** (*in pl*) personal possessions, clothes, equipment, etc. **6** used with an adjective expressing pity, envy, etc: a person or animal: *Poor thing!* **7** (**the thing**) what is required or to be striven for. ✱ **one's (own) thing** *informal* something that one finds especially interesting or enjoyable.
**think**[1] *v* (*past tense and past part.* **thought**) **1** to produce or work on ideas in the mind. **2** to have a particular belief or opinion. **3** (+ of/about) to have in one's mind as the object of consideration or reflection. **4** (+ of) to remember or call to mind. **5** to expect or suspect. ✱ **think better of** to decide on reflection to abandon (a plan). **think nothing of 1** to be entirely unconcerned about. **2** to disregard. **think twice** to consider very carefully. ➤ **thinker** *n.*
**think**[2] *n informal* an act of thinking.
**think over** *v* to consider.
**think tank** *n* a group of people who evolve new ideas and offer expert advice.
**thinner** *n* a solvent used to thin e.g. paint or varnish.
**third** *adj and n* **1** having the position in a sequence corresponding to the number three.

**2** one of three equal parts of something. **3** the third forward gear of a motor vehicle. **4** in Britain, a third-class honours degree. ➤ **thirdly** *adv.*

**third degree** *n* (**the third degree**) harsh interrogation or treatment to obtain information from a prisoner.

**third-degree burn** *n* a very serious burn characterized by destruction of the skin and the underlying tissues.

**third party** *n* somebody other than the people principally involved in an action.

**third-party** *adj* of insurance: covering loss or damage sustained by somebody other than the insured.

**third person** *n* in grammar, the term used to refer to a person or thing other than the speaker or the person addressed, represented by the pronouns *he, she, it,* or *they.*

**third way** *n* a political programme that is neither of the right nor left, but aimed at reaching a consensus in the centre.

**Third World** *n* the less industrialized nations of the world.

**thirst**[1] *n* **1** a desire or need to drink. **2** an ardent desire; a craving.

**thirst**[2] *v* **1** to feel thirsty. **2** (*often* + for/after) to crave eagerly.

**thirsty** *adj* (**-ier, -iest**) **1** feeling thirst. **2** causing thirst. **3** of a machine or engine: consuming large quantities of fuel. **4** having a strong desire. ➤ **thirstily** *adv.*

**thirteen** *adj and n* the number 13. ➤ **thirteenth** *adj and n.*

**thirty** *adj and n* (*pl* **-ies**) **1** the number 30. **2** (*in pl*) the numbers 30 to 39. ➤ **thirtieth** *adj and n.*

**this**[1] *pron* (*pl* **these**) **1** the thing or idea that has just been mentioned. **2** a nearby person or thing introduced for observation or discussion.

**this**[2] *adj* (*pl* **these**) denoting the person or thing that is nearer at hand or more immediately under consideration.

**this**[3] *adv* to the extent indicated or specified.

**thistle** *n* a prickly plant with dense heads of usu purple flowers.

**thistledown** *n* the fluffy hairs from the ripe flower head of a thistle.

**thither** *adv formal* to or towards that place.

**tho'** *or* **tho** *adv or conj informal or literary* though.

**thong** *n* **1** a narrow strip, *esp* of leather. **2** a skimpy bathing costume or piece of underwear resembling a G-string.

**thorax** *n* (*pl* **thoraxes** *or* **thoraces**) **1** the part of a mammal's body between the neck and the abdomen, or the cavity inside it. **2** the central section of the body of an insect, spider, etc carrying the legs and wings. ➤ **thoracic** *adj.*

**thorn** *n* **1** a short projecting plant part with a sharp point. **2** a woody plant, shrub, or tree with branches covered in thorns. ✱ **a thorn in somebody's flesh/side** a cause of great irritation.

**thorny** *adj* (**-ier, -iest**) **1** covered in thorns. **2** full of difficulties or controversial points.

**thorough** *adj* **1** carried out with or showing great care and attention to detail. **2** complete; utter. ➤ **thoroughly** *adv,* **thoroughness** *n.*

**thoroughbred**[1] *adj* bred from the best members of the same breed, strain, etc over many generations.

**thoroughbred**[2] *n* a thoroughbred animal.

**thoroughfare** *n* a public way, e.g. a road, street, or path.

**thoroughgoing** *adj* **1** extremely thorough. **2** absolute or utter.

**those** *pron and adj* pl of THAT[1] and THAT[2].

**thou** *pron archaic or dialect* the one being addressed; you.

**though**[1] *adv* however.

**though**[2] *conj* **1** in spite of the fact that. **2** and yet; but.

**thought**[1] *v* past tense and past part. of THINK[1].

**thought**[2] *n* **1** the act or process of thinking. **2** serious consideration. **3** an idea, opinion, concept, or intention. **4** reasoning or conceptual power. **5** the views of a period, place, group, or individual. **6** (+ of) hope or expectation.

**thoughtful** *adj* **1** absorbed in thought. **2** showing careful reasoned thinking. **3** showing concern for others. ➤ **thoughtfully** *adv.*

**thoughtless** *adj* **1** rash. **2** lacking concern for others. ➤ **thoughtlessly** *adv.*

**thousand** *n* (*pl* **thousands** *or* **thousand**) **1** the number 1000. **2** (*also in pl*) an indefinitely large number. ➤ **thousandth** *adj and n.*

**thrall** *n* a state of complete absorption or enslavement.

**thrash** *v* **1** to beat soundly, *esp* with a stick or whip. **2** to defeat heavily or decisively. **3** (+ around/about) to move or toss about violently.

**thread**[1] *n* **1** a thin continuous strand formed by spinning and twisting together short textile fibres. **2** a projecting spiral ridge, e.g. on a bolt or pipe, by which parts can be screwed together. **3** a pervasive recurring element.

**thread**[2] *v* **1** to pass a thread through the eye of (a needle). **2** to pass something into or through. **3** to string (things) together on a thread. **4** to make one's way cautiously. ➤ **threader** *n.*

**threadbare** *adj* worn or shabby.

**threat** *n* **1** an indication of something unpleasant to come. **2** an expression of an intention to inflict punishment, injury, or damage. **3** something that is a source of danger or harm.

**threaten** *v* **1** to utter threats against. **2** to giveominous signs of. **3** to be a potential source of harm or danger to. ➤ **threatening** *adj.*

**three** *n* the number 3. ➤ **three** *adj.*

**three-dimensional** *adj* **1** having, or giving

the illusion of having, length, breadth, and height. **2** of a fictional character: lifelike.

**threepence** *n* the sum three old pence (1.25p). ➤ **threepenny** *adj.*

**threesome** *n* a group of three people or things.

**threnody** *n* (*pl* **-ies**) a song of lamentation, *esp* for the dead.

**thresh** *v* **1** to separate the grain from (harvested corn) by beating it with a machine or flail. **2** to move or toss about violently. ➤ **thresher** *n.*

**threshold** *n* **1** the plank, stone, etc that lies under a door. **2** a doorway. **3** the point or level at which something begins.

***Usage Note:*** Note that there is only one *h* in the second half of the word.

**threw** *v* past tense of THROW[1].

**thrice** *adv archaic or literary* three times.

**thrift** *n* careful management, *esp* of money; frugality. ➤ **thrifty** *adj.*

**thrill**[1] *n* **1** a sudden feeling of pleasurable excitement. **2** something that causes such a feeling. **3** a sudden tremor of nervousness or emotion.

**thrill**[2] *v* **1** to cause to experience a thrill of excitement or emotion. **2** (+ at/to) to be pleasurably excited by.

**thriller** *n* a novel, film, or drama characterized by a high degree of suspense.

**thrilling** *adj* intensely exciting. ➤ **thrillingly** *adv.*

**thrive** *v* (*past tense* **throve** *or* **thrived,** *past part.* **thriven** *or* **thrived**) **1** to grow vigorously. **2** to prosper. **3** (+ on) to enjoy or be stimulated by something. ➤ **thriving** *adj.*

**throat** *n* **1** the passage through the neck to the stomach and lungs. **2** the front part of the neck. * **at each other's throats** quarrelling violently.

**throaty** *adj* (**-ier, -iest**) hoarse or guttural. ➤ **throatily** *adv.*

**throb**[1] *v* (**throbbed, throbbing**) **1** to pulsate with unusual force or rapidity. **2** of a pain: to come in rhythmic waves.

**throb**[2] *n* a beat or pulse.

**throe** *n* (*usu in pl*) a pang or spasm. * **in the throes of** undergoing the difficult process of.

**thrombosis** *n* (*pl* **thromboses**) the formation or presence of a blood clot within a blood vessel.

**throne** *n* **1** the ceremonial chair of a sovereign or bishop. **2** (**the throne**) sovereignty.

**throng**[1] *n* a large crowd.

**throng**[2] *v* to crowd into (a place).

**throttle**[1] *n* a valve for regulating the supply of a fluid, e.g. fuel, to an engine.

**throttle**[2] *v* **1** to strangle or choke. **2** (*usu* + back/down) to regulate, *esp* reduce the speed of (an engine).

**through**[1] (*NAmer* **thru**) *prep* **1** into at one side or point and out at the other. **2** (*usu* + all) during the entire period of. **3** over the whole area or extent of. **4** by means of. **5** because of.

**through**[2] (*NAmer* **thru**) *adv* **1** from one end or side to the other. **2** from beginning to end. **3** to the core; completely. **4** *chiefly Brit* connected by telephone. * **through and through** thoroughly; completely.

**through**[3] (*NAmer* **thru**) *adj* **1** allowing a continuous journey from point of origin to destination. **2** starting before and continuing beyond a particular place: *through traffic.* **3** having qualified for the next round of a competition. **4** finished.

**throughout** *adv and prep* **1** in or to every part. **2** from beginning to end.

**throughput** *n* the amount of material processed during an operation.

**throve** *v* past tense of THRIVE.

**throw**[1] *v* (**threw, thrown**) **1** to send through the air by a forward motion of the hand and arm. **2** to cause to move violently into or against something. **3** to force (somebody) to fall to the ground. **4** of a horse: to unseat (its rider). **5** to put (somebody) in a specified position or condition, *esp* suddenly. **6** (+ on/off) to put (clothing) on or off hurriedly. **7** to direct (light, a look, etc) in a certain direction. **8** to move (a lever or switch). **9** to shape (a pot, etc) by hand on a potter's wheel. **10** to give (a party). **11** to have (a tantrum or fit). **12** *informal* to confuse or disconcert. * **be thrown back on** to have to rely on (something) when no other resources are available. **throw oneself into** to devote one's energy to (an activity). **throw one's weight about/around** *informal* to behave in a bullying or domineering manner.

**throw**[2] *n* **1** an act of throwing. **2** a light cover, e.g. for a bed. **3** *informal* a chance, try, turn, etc.

**throwaway** *adj* **1** designed to be discarded after use. **2** of a remark: made with deliberate casualness.

**throw away** *v* **1** to get rid of as worthless or unwanted. **2** to use in a foolish or wasteful manner. **3** to fail to take advantage of (an opportunity, etc).

**throwback** *n* an individual exhibiting the characteristics of earlier genetic type or phase.

**throw in** *v* **1** to add as a free item with other goods or services. **2** to introduce or interject (a remark, etc). * **throw in the sponge/towel** to abandon a struggle or contest.

**throw-in** *n* in football, a throw made from the touchline to put the ball back in play.

**throw out** *v* **1** to get rid of as worthless or unwanted. **2** to expel abruptly from a room or building. **3** to dismiss or reject (a plan, proposal, etc).

**throw up** *v informal* to vomit.

**thrum**[1] *v* (**thrummed, thrumming**) to make a monotonous hum.

**thrum**[2] *n* a thrumming sound.

**thrush**[1] *n* a light-brown bird with a spotted breast, noted for its singing ability.

**thrush**[2] *n* a whitish irritating fungal growth occurring *esp* in the mouth or vagina.

**thrust**[1] *v* (*past tense and past part.* **thrust**) **1** to push or drive with force. **2** (+ on/upon) to force or impose the acceptance of (something or somebody) on.

**thrust**[2] *n* **1** a push or lunge with a pointed weapon. **2** a concerted military attack. **3** the essential meaning. **4** the force exerted by a propeller, jet engine, etc to give forward motion.

**thrusting** *adj* aggressive or pushy.

**thud** *v* (**thudded, thudding**) to make a dull heavy sound. ➤ **thud** *n.*

**thug** *n* a violent person, *esp* a violent criminal. ➤ **thuggery** *n,* **thuggish** *adj.*

**thumb**[1] *n* the short thick digit of the hand that is separate from the other fingers. ✱ **under somebody's thumb** under somebody's control.

**thumb**[2] *v* **1** to leaf through (pages) with the thumb. **2** to request (a lift) in a passing vehicle by signalling with the thumb.

**thumb index** *n* a series of notches cut in the unbound edge of a book for ease of reference.

**thumbnail** *n* the nail of the thumb.

**thumbnail sketch** *n* a brief, concise description.

**thumbscrew** *n* an instrument of torture for squeezing the thumb.

**thumbs-down** *n informal* rejection or disapproval.

**thumbs-up** *n informal* approval.

**thump**[1] *v* **1** to thrash or beat. **2** to strike or knock with a thump. **3** of the heart: to beat rapidly. **4** to make a thumping sound.

**thump**[2] *n* a blow with something blunt or heavy, or the sound of this.

**thumping** *adj* **1** *Brit, informal* impressively large or excellent. **2** throbbing.

**thunder**[1] *n* **1** the low loud sound that follows a flash of lightning and is caused by sudden expansion of the air. **2** a loud reverberating noise. ➤ **thundery** *adj.*

**thunder**[2] *v* **1** to make thunder or a sound like thunder. **2** to roar or shout. **3** to move fast and noisily.

**thunderbolt** *n* a single discharge of lightning with the accompanying thunder.

**thunderclap** *n* a sudden loud sound of thunder.

**thundercloud** *n* a cloud charged with electricity and producing lightning and thunder.

**thunderous** *adj* **1** making a noise like thunder. **2** angry and threatening. ➤ **thunderously** *adv.*

**thunderstorm** *n* a storm accompanied by lightning and thunder.

**thunderstruck** *adj* extremely surprised; astonished.

**Thursday** *n* the day of the week following Wednesday.

**thus** *adv formal* **1** because of this preceding fact or premise; consequently. **2** in this way. **3** to this degree or extent.

**thwack**[1] *v* to whack.

**thwack**[2] *n* a sharp blow; a whack.

**thwart** *v* to prevent somebody from carrying out (a plan, etc).

**thy** *adj archaic or dialect* of thee or thyself.

**thyme** *n* a garden plant with small aromatic leaves used in cooking.

**thymus** *n* (*pl* **thymi**) a gland in the lower neck region that functions in the development of the body's immune system.

**thyroid** *n* (*also* **thyroid gland**) a large endocrine gland at the base of the neck that produces hormones that influence growth and development.

**Ti** *abbr* the chemical symbol for titanium.

**tiara** *n* a decorative jewelled band worn on the head by women.

**tibia** *n* (*pl* **tibiae** *or* **tibias**) the inner and usu larger of the two bones between the knee and ankle.

**tic** *n* a habitual spasmodic motion of particular muscles, *esp* of the face.

**tick**[1] *n* **1** a mark (✓) used to label something as correct, to check off an item on a list, etc. **2** a light audible tap or beat, or a series of such sounds. **3** *Brit, informal* a moment or second.

**tick**[2] *v* **1** to mark with a written tick. **2** (*often* + off) to label or count with ticks. **3** to make the sound of a tick. **4** (+ away/by) of seconds, minutes, etc: to pass, bringing the end of something closer.

**tick**[3] *n* a bloodsucking arachnid that often transmits infectious diseases.

**tick**[4] *n* ✱ **on tick** *informal* on credit.

**ticker** *n* **1** *informal* a watch. **2** *informal* the heart. **3** *NAmer* a telegraphic receiving instrument that automatically prints out information on paper tape.

**ticker tape** *n* the paper tape on which a ticker prints out its information.

**ticket** *n* **1** a printed card or piece of paper entitling its holder to certain services, *esp* showing that a fare or admission has been paid. **2** a tag or label. **3** an official notification issued to somebody who has violated a traffic regulation.

**ticking** *n* a strong linen or cotton fabric used to cover a mattress or pillow.

**tickle**[1] *v* **1** to touch (a person or a body part) lightly and repeatedly so as to cause uneasiness, laughter, or spasmodic movements. **2** to provoke to laughter. **3** to amuse or delight. ➤ **tickly** *adj.*

**tickle**[2] *n* **1** a tickling sensation. **2** the act of tickling.
**ticklish** *adj* **1** sensitive to tickling. **2** of a cough: causing irritation in the throat. **3** requiring delicate handling.
**tick off** *v Brit, informal* to scold or rebuke.
**tick over** *v* of an engine: to be turned on and running slowly with the transmission disengaged.
**tidal** *adj* of, caused by, or having tides. ➤ **tidally** *adv.*
**tidal wave** *n* **1** an unusually high sea wave. **2** an unexpected, intense, and often widespread reaction.
**tidbit** *n NAmer* see TITBIT.
**tiddler** *n Brit, informal* somebody or something small, *esp* a small fish.
**tiddly** *adj* (**-ier, -iest**) *informal* **1** *chiefly Brit* slightly drunk. **2** *Brit* very small.
**tiddlywinks** *pl n* a game in which the object is to flick small discs into a container.
**tide** *n* **1** the periodic rise and fall of the surface of the sea caused by the gravitational attraction of the sun and moon. **2** a general trend in events. **3** a powerful surge of feeling.
**tidings** *pl n* a piece of news.
**tidy**[1] *adj* (**-ier, -iest**) **1** neat and orderly in appearance or habits. **2** *informal* large or substantial: *a tidy sum.* ➤ **tidily** *adv,* **tidiness** *n.*
**tidy**[2] *v* (**-ies, -ied**) to put in order; to make neat or tidy.
**tidy**[3] *n* (*pl* **-ies**) **1** an act of tidying. **2** a receptacle for odds and ends.
**tie**[1] *v* (**ties, tied, tying**) **1** to fasten or attach with cord, string, etc. **2** to form a knot or bow in. **3** to make a bond or connection between. **4** (*often* + down) to restrict the range of activity of. **5** to achieve an equal score in a game or contest.
**tie**[2] *n* **1** something that serves as a connecting link. **2** a narrow length of material designed to be worn round the neck and tied in a knot in the front. **3** *Brit* a match or game between two teams, players, etc. **4** a draw or dead heat in a contest.
**tie break** *or* **tie breaker** *n* a contest or game used to select a winner from among contestants with tied scores.
**tied** *adj* **1** *Brit* of a house: owned by an employer and reserved for occupancy by an employee. **2** of a public house: bound to sell only the products of the brewery that owns it.
**tie-dye** *v* to produce patterns in textiles by tying portions of the fabric or yarn so that they will not absorb dye.
**tie in** *v* **1** (*usu* + with) to bring into harmony with. **2** (*usu* + with) to correspond with.
**tie-in** *n* a related product issued to coincide with a film or television production.
**tiepin** *n* a decorative pin used to hold a tie in place.
**tier** *n* **1** any of several rows or levels of e.g. seating arranged one above and behind the other. **2** any of a series of levels, e.g. in an administration. ➤ **tiered** *adj.*
**tie up** *v* **1** to attach or fasten securely. **2** to bind a person's arms or legs to prevent them moving or escaping. **3** to conclude (a matter) satisfactorily. **4** to make unavailable for other activities or uses. **5** (+ with) to relate to something.
**tiff** *n informal* a petty quarrel.
**tiger** *n* a very large Asian cat with a tawny coat striped with black.
**tight**[1] *adj* **1** fixed very firmly in place. **2** stretched taut. **3** of clothing: fitting closely or too closely. **4** impermeable to e.g. liquid or gas. **5** of e.g. control: characterized by firmness and strictness. **6** set or packed close together. **7** of a space: difficult to move or manoeuvre in. **8** characterized by scarcity. **9** *informal* stingy or miserly. **10** *informal* intoxicated; drunk. ➤ **tightly** *adv,* **tightness** *n.*
**tight**[2] *adv* **1** firmly or securely. **2** very close together.
**tighten** *v* to make or become tight or tighter.
**tightfisted** *adj informal* reluctant to part with money.
**tight-knit** *adj* of a group of people: closely linked because of shared interests or affection.
**tight-lipped** *adj* **1** having the lips compressed, e.g. in determination. **2** reluctant to speak.
**tightrope** *n* a rope or wire stretched taut for acrobats to perform on.
**tights** *pl n* a skintight garment covering each leg and foot and reaching to the waist.
**tigress** *n* a female tiger.
**tilde** /ˈtildə/ *n* a mark (˜) placed over the letter *n* in Spanish or over vowels in Portuguese to indicate nasal pronunciation.
**tile**[1] *n* a thin slab of fired clay, stone, concrete, cork, etc used to surface roofs, floors, walls, etc.
**tile**[2] *v* **1** to cover (a surface) with tiles. **2** to arrange (windows) on a computer screen without overlapping. ➤ **tiler** *n,* **tiling** *n.*
**till**[1] *prep and conj* until.
**till**[2] *n* a cash register or drawer in which money is kept.
**till**[3] *v* to work (land) by ploughing, sowing, and raising crops.
**tiller** *n* a lever used to turn the rudder of a boat.
**tilt**[1] *v* **1** to cause to slope or sit at an angle. **2** formerly, to point or thrust (a lance) in a joust.
**tilt**[2] *n* **1** the act of tilting. **2** a sloping position. **3** formerly, a joust. ✱ **full tilt/at full tilt** with maximum speed.
**tilth** *n* the condition of tilled land.
**timber** *n* wood suitable for carpentry or woodwork.
**timbre** *n* the quality of tone distinctive of a particular singing voice or musical instrument.
**time**[1] *n* **1** the continuum of past, present, and future in which events succeed one another. **2**

the point or period when something occurs. **3** a moment, hour, day, or year as measured or indicated by a clock or calendar. **4** the period required or taken for an action. **5** an appointed, fixed, or customary moment for something to happen, begin, or end. **6** any of a series of recurring instances or repeated actions. **7** (*also in pl*) a historical period. **8** *informal* a term of imprisonment. **9** in music, a tempo. **10** a person's specified experience, *esp* on a particular occasion: *We had a good time.* ✱ **behind the times** old-fashioned. **for the time being** for the present. **have no time for** to be unable or reluctant to spend time on. **in no time** very soon; very quickly. **in time 1** sufficiently early. **2** eventually. **make time** to find enough time to do something. **on time** at the appointed time. **time off** time spent away from work or relaxing. **time out** a break or rest.

**time**[2] *v* **1** to measure the time, duration, or speed of. **2** to arrange the time of. **3** to regulate the moment or duration of, *esp* to achieve the desired effect.

**time bomb** *n* a bomb equipped with device that makes it explode at a predetermined time.

**time capsule** *n* a sealed capsule containing contemporary articles that is buried for people to dig up and open in future years.

**time-honoured** *adj* sanctioned by custom or tradition.

**timekeeper** *n* **1** somebody who records the time worked by employees, elapsed in a race, etc. **2** an employee considered with regard to their punctuality. ➤ **timekeeping** *n.*

**timeless** *adj* not affected by time; eternal.

**timely** *adj* occurring or done at an appropriate time.

**timepiece** *n* a clock, watch, etc.

**timer** *n* **1** a device that gives an indication when an interval of time has passed, or that starts or stops a device at predetermined times. **2** a stopwatch for timing races.

**time scale** *n* the amount of time allotted for the completion of something.

**timeserver** *n* **1** somebody who fits their behaviour and ideas to prevailing opinions or their superiors' views. **2** somebody who makes little effort at work because they are soon to retire or leave.

**timeshare** *n* **1** = TIME-SHARING. **2** a share in a property under a time-sharing scheme.

**time-sharing** *n* an arrangement whereby people buy a share of a lease on a holiday property, entitling them to spend a proportionate amount of time there each year.

**time signature** *n* a sign on a musical staff showing the number of beats in a bar.

**timetable**[1] *n* a schedule showing a planned order of events.

**timetable**[2] *v* to arrange or provide for in a timetable.

**timid** *adj* lacking in courage, boldness, or self-confidence. ➤ **timidity** *n,* **timidly** *adv.*

**timorous** *adj* timid or nervous.

**timpani** *or* **tympani** *pl n* a set of two or three kettledrums played by one performer in an orchestra. ➤ **timpanist** *n.*

**tin**[1] *n* **1** a silvery metallic element used for plating and in alloys. **2** *chiefly Brit* a hermetically sealed tinplate or aluminium container for preserving foods. **3** a container in which food is cooked.

**tin**[2] *v* (**tinned, tinning**) *chiefly Brit* to can (food). ➤ **tinned** *adj.*

**tincture** *n* **1** a solution of a substance in alcohol for medicinal use. **2** a slight addition; a trace.

**tinder** *n* a combustible substance used for kindling a fire.

**tinderbox** *n* formerly, a metal box for holding tinder and usu a flint and steel for striking a spark.

**tine** *n* a prong, e.g. of a fork.

**tinfoil** *n* a thin metal sheeting of tin, aluminium, or a tin alloy.

**tinge**[1] *v* (**tingeing** *or* **tinging**) **1** to colour with a slight shade. **2** to impart a slight smell, taste, or other quality to.

**tinge**[2] *n* a slight modifying quality, *esp* a trace of a colour.

**tingle**[1] *v* to feel a stinging, prickling, or thrilling sensation. ➤ **tingly** *adj.*

**tingle**[2] *n* a tingling sensation.

**tinker**[1] *n* **1** a travelling mender of pots and pans. **2** an act of tinkering.

**tinker**[2] *v* (+ with) to repair, adjust, or work with something in an unskilled or experimental manner.

**tinkle**[1] *v* to make or cause to make a short light ringing sound.

**tinkle**[2] *n* **1** a tinkling sound. **2** *Brit, informal* a telephone call.

**tinnitus** *n* a ringing or roaring sensation in the ears.

**tinny** *adj* (**-ier, -iest**) **1** having a thin metallic sound. **2** not solid or durable; shoddy.

**tinplate** *n* thin sheet iron or steel coated with tin.

**tinpot** *adj informal* paltry or inferior.

**tinsel** *n* strips of metal threaded on a string, used to produce a glittering effect, *esp* in Christmas decorations.

**tint**[1] *n* **1** a lighter or darker shade of a colour. **2** a hair dye.

**tint**[2] *v* **1** to apply a tint to. **2** to dye (the hair).

**tintinnabulation** *n formal* a ringing sound, *esp* made by bells.

**tin whistle** *n* = PENNY WHISTLE.

**tiny** *adj* (**-ier, -iest**) very small.

**tip**[1] *n* **1** the pointed end of something. **2** a small part serving as an end or cap of something.

✱ **on the tip of one's tongue 1** about to be uttered. **2** not quite remembered.

**tip**[2] *v* (**tipped, tipping**) **1** to supply with a tip. **2** to cover the tip of. ➤ **tipped** *adj.*

**tip**[3] *v* (**tipped, tipping**) **1** (*often* + over) to overturn or upset. **2** to tilt. **3** *Brit* to deposit (rubbish, etc) by tilting a container.

**tip**[4] *n* **1** *Brit* a place for tipping something, e.g. rubbish. **2** *informal* a messy place.

**tip**[5] *n* an extra sum of money given in appreciation of a service performed.

**tip**[6] *v* (**tipped, tipping**) to give (somebody) a tip.

**tip**[7] *n* **1** a piece of useful advice. **2** a piece of inside information which may bring financial gain, e.g. from betting or investment.

**tip**[8] *v* (**tipped, tipping**) *Brit* to mention as a prospective winner, success, or profitable investment.

**tip off** *v* to give a tip-off to.

**tip-off** *n informal* a tip given usu as a warning.

**tipple**[1] *v* to drink alcohol, *esp* continuously in small amounts. ➤ **tippler** *n.*

**tipple**[2] *n informal* an alcoholic drink.

**tipster** *n* somebody who gives tips, *esp* as regards the likely winners of horseraces.

**tipsy** *adj* (**-ier, -iest**) slightly drunk. ➤ **tipsily** *adv.*

**tiptoe**[1] *v* to walk silently or stealthily with one's heels off the ground.

**tiptoe**[2] *n* ✱ **on tiptoe** *or* **tiptoes** balancing on the toes or the balls of the feet.

**tip-top** *adj* excellent or first-rate.

**tirade** *n* a long vehement speech or denunciation.

**tire**[1] *v* **1** to become or make tired. **2** (+ of) to become bored with.

**tire**[2] *n NAmer* see TYRE.

**tired** *adj* **1** needing sleep or rest. **2** (+ of) bored or exasperated with. **3** trite; hackneyed. **4** lacking freshness. ➤ **tiredness** *n.*

**tireless** *adj* continuing without rest or loss of vigour. ➤ **tirelessly** *adv.*

**tiresome** *adj* wearisome; tedious. ➤ **tiresomely** *adv.*

**'tis** *contraction* it is.

**tissue** *n* **1** any of the structural materials of a plant or animal. **2** = TISSUE PAPER. **3** a paper handkerchief. **4** a web or network.

**tissue paper** *n* a thin gauzy paper.

**tit**[1] *n* a small tree-dwelling bird that lives on insects.

**tit**[2] *n* **1** *coarse slang* a woman's breast. **2** *Brit, informal* a stupid person.

**titan** *n* **1** (**Titan**) a giant god in Greek mythology. **2** somebody who is very strong, powerful, or notable for outstanding achievement.

**titanic** *adj* colossal or gigantic.

**titanium** *n* a grey metallic element that is light and strong and used mainly in alloys.

**titbit** (*NAmer* **tidbit**) *n* **1** a tasty piece of food. **2** an interesting piece of information.

**titchy** *adj* (**-ier, -iest**) *Brit, informal* small or short. ➤ **titch** *n.*

**tit for tat** *n* the act of retaliating by making the other person suffer an equivalent injury, loss etc.

**tithe** *n* a contribution of a tenth part of something, e.g. income, for the support of a religious establishment or other charitable work.

**titillate** *v* to excite pleasurably or sexually. ➤ **titillating** *n.*

**titivate** *v informal* to make smarter. ➤ **titivation** *n.*

**title**[1] *n* **1** the distinguishing name of e.g. a book, film, or musical composition. **2** a word indicating a person's job, status, etc. **3** a hereditary or acquired appellation given to a person or family as a mark of rank. **4** designation as champion. **5** legal ownership. **6** (*usu in pl*) written material introduced into a film or television programme to represent credits, dialogue, or fragments of narrative.

**title**[2] *v* (*usu in passive*) **1** to provide a title for. **2** to designate or call by a title.

**titled** *adj* having an aristocratic title such as *Lord* or *Lady*.

**title deed** *n* the deed constituting evidence of ownership of property.

**title music** *n* music played while the titles are shown at the beginning or end of a film or television programme.

**title role** *n* the role in a film, play, etc whose name is used as the title of the work.

**titration** *n* a method of determining the amount of a substance in a solution by adding measured quantities of a reagent until a reaction occurs.

**titter**[1] *v* to giggle or snigger.

**titter**[2] *n* a giggle or snigger.

**tittle** *n* a very small part.

**tittle-tattle**[1] *n* gossip.

**tittle-tattle**[2] *v* to gossip.

**titular** *adj* **1** of or constituting a title. **2** in title only; nominal.

**tizzy** *or* **tizz** *n* (*pl* **tizzies** *or* **tizzes**) *informal* a highly excited and confused state of mind.

**Tl** *abbr* the chemical symbol for thallium.

**Tm** *abbr* the chemical symbol for thulium.

**TNT** *n* trinitrotoluene, a high explosive.

**to**[1] *prep* **1** used to indicate a terminal point or destination. **2** before the hour mentioned: *five minutes to five.* **3** used to indicate the the person or thing affected by an action. **4** used to indicate addition, connection, or possession. **5** used to indicate relationship or conformity. **6** used to introduce an infinitive form of a verb. **7** used to denote purpose: *He did it to annoy them.*

**to**[2] *adv* of a door or window: into contact, *esp* with the frame; shut. ✱ **to and fro** from one place to another; back and forth.

**toad** *n* a tailless leaping amphibian with a short squat body.

**toadstool** *n* a poisonous or inedible umbrella-shaped fungus.

**toady**[1] *n* (*pl* **-ies**) a sycophant.

**toady**[2] *v* (**-ies, -ied**) to be obsequious.

**to-and-fro** *v* (**toing-and-froing**) to move to and fro; to come and go.

**toast**[1] *n* **1** sliced bread browned on both sides by heat. **2** the act of drinking in honour of somebody or something. **3** a highly popular or admired person.

**toast**[2] *v* **1** to make (bread, etc) crisp, hot, and brown by heat. **2** to drink a toast to.

**toaster** *n* an electrical appliance for toasting bread.

**tobacco** *n* (*pl* **-os**) the leaves of an American plant, prepared for use in smoking or chewing or as snuff.

**tobacconist** *n chiefly Brit* a person who sells tobacco.

**toboggan** *n* a light sledge, used for gliding downhill over snow.

**toccata** /tə'kahtə/ *n* a musical composition, usu for a keyboard instrument, characterized by rapid runs and intended to show off the performer's technique.

**tod** ✱ **on one's tod** *Brit, informal* alone.

**today**[1] *adv* **1** on this day. **2** at the present time or age.

**today**[2] *n* **1** this day. **2** the present time or age.

**toddle** *v* **1** of a very young child: to walk unsteadily. **2** *informal* to take a stroll. ➤ **toddle** *n.*

**toddler** *n* a very young child who is just learning to walk.

**toddy** *n* (*pl* **-ies**) a hot drink of spirits mixed with water, sugar, and spices.

**to-do** *n informal* bustle or fuss.

**toe**[1] *n* **1** any of the digits of a human's or animal's foot. **2** the lower end or part. ✱ **on one's toes** alert; ready to act.

**toe**[2] *v* to touch, reach, or drive with the toe. ✱ **toe the line** to conform rigorously to a rule or standard.

**toe cap** *n* a piece of steel or leather attached to the toe of a shoe or boot.

**toehold** *n* a place of support for the toes, e.g. in climbing.

**toenail** *n* the nail of a toe.

**toff** *n chiefly Brit, derog* a rich or upper-class person.

**toffee** *n* a sweet with a texture ranging from chewy to brittle, made by boiling sugar and butter.

**toffee-apple** *n* a toffee-covered apple held on a stick.

**toffee-nosed** *adj chiefly Brit, informal* stuck-up.

**tofu** *n* a soft cheeselike food prepared from soya-bean milk.

**tog**[1] *v* (**togged, togging**) *informal* (+ up/out) to dress up.

**tog**[2] *n Brit* a unit used to measure the insulating properties of a quilt, a garment, etc.

**toga** *n* a loose outer garment worn in public by citizens of ancient Rome.

**together**[1] *adv* **1** in or into one place, mass, collection, or group. **2** in collaboration; as a group. **3** in or into contact. **4** in or into association, relationship, or harmony. **5** at one time; simultaneously. **6** to or with each other. ✱ **together with** as well as. ➤ **togetherness** *n.*

**together**[2] *adj informal* self-possessed and emotionally stable.

**toggle** *n* a crosspiece attached to a loop in a cord, chain, etc, to serve as a fastening.

**togs** *pl n informal* clothes.

**toil**[1] *n* tiring work.

**toil**[2] *v* **1** to work hard and long. **2** to proceed with laborious effort.

**toilet** *n* **1** a fixture for receiving and disposing of faeces and urine. **2** a room or compartment containing a toilet and sometimes a washbasin. **3** *archaic or literary* the act of dressing and grooming oneself.

**toiletry** *n* (*pl* **-ies**) (*usu in pl*) an article or preparation used in washing, grooming, etc.

**toilet training** *n* the process of training a young child to use the toilet. ➤ **toilet-train** *v.*

**toilet water** *n* a light perfume.

**token**[1] *n* **1** an outward sign or expression, e.g. of an emotion. **2** a souvenir or keepsake. **3** a coinlike disc for use in place of money, e.g. for a bus fare. **4** a voucher for a specified form of merchandise. ✱ **by the same token** furthermore and for the same reason.

**token**[2] *adj* done or given without enthusiasm merely for show or to fulfil an obligation.

**told** *v* past tense and past part. of TELL.

**tolerable** *adj* **1** capable of being borne or endured. **2** moderately good or agreeable. ➤ **tolerably** *adv.*

**tolerance** *n* **1** allowance or acceptance of beliefs or practices differing from one's own. **2** the physiological ability to endure the effects of a drug, virus, radiation, etc. **3** an allowable variation from a standard dimension.

**tolerant** *adj* **1** marked by forbearance or endurance. **2** exhibiting tolerance, e.g. to a drug or environmental condition. ➤ **tolerantly** *adv.*

**tolerate** *v* **1** to allow or accept (e.g. other people or their views) without prohibition, hindrance, or contradiction. **2** to endure the action of (a drug, etc) without grave or lasting injury. ➤ **toleration** *n.*

**toll**[1] *n* **1** a fee paid for some right or privilege, e.g. of passing over a highway or bridge. **2** an amount of loss or damage suffered, e.g. the number of casualties caused by an accident or disaster.

**toll²** *v* **1** to sound (a bell) by pulling the rope. **2** to announce by means of a tolled bell. **3** of a bell: to sound with slow measured strokes.

**toll³** *n* the sound of a tolling bell.

**tom** *n* a tomcat.

**tomahawk** *n* a light axe used by Native Americans as a throwing or hand weapon.

**tomato** *n* (*pl* **-oes**) a rounded usu red pulpy fruit used as a vegetable, *esp* in salads.

**tomb** *n* a chamber or vault for the dead, built either above or below ground and usu serving as a memorial.

**tombola** *n Brit* a lottery in which the tickets that entitle people to prizes are drawn from a revolving drum.

**tomboy** *n* a girl who behaves in a manner thought of as typical of a boy. ➤ **tomboyish** *adj.*

**tombstone** *n* = GRAVESTONE.

**tomcat** *n* a male cat.

**tome** *n formal* a book, *esp* a large scholarly one.

**tomfoolery** *n* foolish behaviour.

**tomography** *n* a diagnostic technique using X-rays or ultrasound to produce an image of a cross-section of the body. ➤ **tomographic** *adj.*

**tomorrow¹** *adv* on the day after today.

**tomorrow²** *n* **1** the day after today. **2** the future.

**tomtit** *n Brit* a blue tit or other bird of the tit family.

**tom-tom** *n* a long narrow drum beaten with the hands.

**ton** *n* **1** (*also* **long ton**) a unit of weight equal to 2240lb (about 1016kg). **2** (*also* **short ton**) *NAmer* a unit of weight equal to 2000lb (about 907kg). **3** a metric ton. **4** a unit approximately equal to the volume of one long ton of seawater, used in reckoning the displacement of ships, and equal to 0.99 cubic m (35 cubic ft). **5** *informal* (*also in pl*) a great quantity. **6** *chiefly Brit, informal* a score or speed of 100.

**tonal** *adj* **1** relating to tone. **2** of music: based on one of the traditional keys. ➤ **tonality** *n*, **tonally** *adv.*

**tone¹** *n* **1** a vocal or musical sound. **2** an inflection of the voice expressive of a mood or emotion. **3** style or manner of verbal expression. **4** prevailing character, quality, or trend, e.g. of morals. **5** a musical interval comprising two semitones. **6** colour quality or value. **7** of muscles: normal tension or responsiveness to stimuli.

**tone²** *v* (*often* + up) to impart strength and firmness to (part of the body).

**tone-deaf** *adj* relatively insensitive to musical pitch.

**tone down** *v* to soften or reduce in colour, intensity, force, etc.

**toner** *n* **1** a cosmetic preparation applied to the skin to reduce oiliness. **2** powdered or liquid ink used in a photocopier, laser printer, etc.

**tongs** *pl n* a grasping device consisting of two pieces joined at one end by a pivot or hinged like scissors.

**tongue¹** *n* **1** a fleshy muscular organ in the mouth used in tasting and swallowing food and as a speech organ. **2** manner or quality of utterance. **3** a language. **4** a long narrow strip of land projecting into a body of water. **5** the flap under the lacing or buckles on the front of a shoe. ✱ **hold one's tongue** to say nothing.

**tongue²** *v* (**tongues, tongued, tonguing**) to articulate (notes) on a wind instrument by interrupting the stream of air with the tongue.

**tongue and groove** *n* a joint in which a projection fits into a groove.

**tongue-in-cheek** *adj* characterized by irony or whimsical exaggeration.

**tongue-tied** *adj* unable to speak freely, e.g. because of shyness.

**tongue twister** *n* a word or phrase that is difficult to articulate.

**tonic** *n* **1** something that invigorates, refreshes, or stimulates, *esp* an invigorating medicine. **2** (*also* **tonic water**) carbonated, slightly bitter mineral water, often drunk with gin.

**tonight¹** *adv* on this night or the night following today.

**tonight²** *n* this night or the night following today.

**tonnage** *n* **1** total weight in tons shipped, carried, or produced. **2** the size or carrying capacity of a ship in tons.

**tonne** *n* a metric unit of weight equal to 1000kg.

**tonsil** *n* either of a pair of small oval masses of tissue that lie one on each side of the throat.

**tonsillectomy** *n* (*pl* **-ies**) the surgical removal of the tonsils.

**tonsillitis** *n* inflammation of the tonsils.

**tonsure** *n* the shaved patch on a monk's or other cleric's head.

**too** *adv* **1** to a greater degree than is necessary, desirable, permissible, etc; excessively. **2** *informal* very. **3** also; in addition.

**took** *v* past tense of TAKE¹.

**tool¹** *n* **1** an implement, e.g. a hammer or knife, used to carry out work of a mechanical nature. **2** something that is useful in performing an operation or necessary for one's work; an aid. **3** somebody who is used or manipulated by somebody else.

**tool²** *v* **1** to work, shape, or finish (something) with a tool, *esp* to letter or ornament (leather, etc) by means of hand tools. **2** (*often* + up) to equip (a plant or industry) with tools, machines, and instruments for production.

**toot** *v* to produce a short blast on a horn, etc. ➤ **toot** *n.*

**tooth** *n* (*pl* **teeth**) **1** any of the hard bony structures in the jaws used for biting and chewing food. **2** any of the regular projections on the rim of a cogwheel, a comb, or the blade of a saw, etc. ✱ **get one's teeth into something** *informal* to begin to make progress in tackling or understanding something. **in the teeth of** in direct opposition to. **tooth and nail** with every available means. ➤ **toothed** *adj*, **toothless** *adj*.

**toothache** *n* pain in a tooth.

**toothbrush** *n* a brush for cleaning the teeth.

**toothcomb** ✱ **with a fine toothcomb** *Brit* thoroughly.

**toothpaste** *n* a paste for cleaning the teeth.

**toothpick** *n* a pointed instrument for removing food particles lodged between the teeth.

**toothsome** *adj* **1** of food: delicious. **2** *informal* sexually attractive.

**toothy** *adj* (**-ier, -iest**) having prominent teeth.

**tootle** *v* **1** to toot gently or continuously. **2** *informal* to go along in a leisurely manner. ➤ **tootle** *n*.

**top**[1] *n* **1** the highest or uppermost point, level, or part of something. **2** a garment worn on the upper body. **3** a part serving as an upper piece, lid, or covering. **4** (**the top**) the highest position, e.g. in rank or achievement. **5** the highest degree or pitch. ✱ **off the top of one's head** without taking time to think about or research the matter; impromptu. **on top 1** resting on the highest point or surface of something. **2** in a dominant position. **on top of 1** placed on or above the highest part of. **2** in control of. **3** in sudden and unexpected proximity to. **4** in addition to. **on top of the world** in high spirits. **over the top** exaggerated; *esp* excessively dramatic.

**top**[2] *v* (**topped, topping**) **1** to be or become higher than. **2** to exceed, surpass, or be superior to. **3** to cover with a top or topping. **4** to rise to, reach, or be at the top of. **5** *informal* to kill.

**top**[3] *adj* **1** of or at the top. **2** foremost or leading. **3** of the highest quality, amount, or degree.

**top**[4] *n* a child's toy that has a tapering point on which it is made to spin.

**topaz** *n* a transparent or yellow gemstone.

**topcoat** *n* **1** a lightweight overcoat. **2** a final coat of paint.

**top dog** *n informal* a person in a position of superiority.

**top-flight** *adj* of the highest rank or quality.

**top hat** *n* a man's tall-crowned hat with a flat top and vertical sides.

**top-heavy** *adj* unstable or out of proportion because the top part is too heavy for the lower part.

**topiary** *n* (*pl* **-ies**) **1** the art of training and trimming trees or shrubs into ornamental shapes. **2** trees or shrubs cut in this way.

**topic** *n* a subject for discussion or consideration.

**topical** *adj* **1** concerned with events and matters of current interest. **2** relating to or arranged by topics. ➤ **topicality** *n*, **topically** *adv*.

**topknot** *n* an arrangement of hair on the top of the head.

**topless** *adj and adv* having the breasts exposed.

**topography** *n* **1** the configuration of a land surface, including its relief and the position of its natural and man-made features. **2** the practice of making detailed maps of a region. ➤ **topographic** *adj*, **topographical** *adj*.

**topple** *v* **1** to fall down or over, *esp* through being top-heavy. **2** to cause to topple.

**topsoil** *n* surface soil, *esp* the organic layer in which plants grow.

**topspin** *n* spin that causes a ball to rotate forwards in the direction of its travel.

**topsy-turvy** *adj and adv* **1** upside down. **2** in utter confusion or disorder.

**top up** *v* **1** to make up to the full quantity or capacity. **2** to increase (a sum of money). **3** to replenish (a drink).

**top-up fees** *pl n* additional fees to be charged by universities to bridge the gap between the basic tuition fees they receive and actual tuition costs.

**tor** *n* a mound, hill, or rocky peak.

**torch**[1] *n* **1** *Brit* a small portable electric lamp powered by batteries. **2** formerly, a stick of wood coated or wrapped with inflammable material and burned to give light.

**torch**[2] *v informal* to set fire to.

**tore** *v* past tense of TEAR[1].

**toreador** /'tori·ədaw/ *n* a bullfighter, *esp* one on horseback.

**torment**[1] *n* **1** extreme pain or anguish. **2** a source of torment.

**torment**[2] *v* **1** to cause severe usu persistent distress of body or mind to. **2** to tease unkindly. ➤ **tormentor** *n*.

**torn** *v* past part. of TEAR[1].

**tornado** *n* (*pl* **-oes** *or* **-os**) a violent or destructive whirlwind.

**torpedo**[1] *n* (*pl* **-oes**) a self-propelling cigar-shaped underwater explosive projectile used to attack ships.

**torpedo**[2] *v* (**torpedoes, torpedoed, torpedoing**) **1** to hit or destroy (e.g. a ship) by torpedo. **2** to destroy or nullify (e.g. a plan).

**torpid** *adj* inactive and lacking energy or vigour. ➤ **torpidity** *n*.

**torpor** *n* a state of sleepy inactivity or sluggishness.

**torque** *n* a force that produces rotation.

**torrent** *n* **1** a violent stream of water, lava, etc. **2** a violent outpouring.

**torrential** *adj* of rain: falling fast and in large quantities.

**torrid** *adj* **1** extremely hot and dry. **2** involving passionate sex. **3** very uncomfortable or unpleasant.

**torsion** *n* the process of twisting or the state of being twisted.

**torso** *n* (*pl* **torsos** *or* **torsi**) the human trunk.

**tort** *n* in law, a wrongful act for which a civil action for damages may be brought.

**tortilla** /taw'teeyə/ *n* **1** in Mexican cooking, a thin maize pancake, usu eaten hot with a filling. **2** in Spanish cooking, a thick omelette containing potato.

**tortoise** *n* a reptile with a bony shell into which the head, limbs, and tail may be withdrawn.

**tortoiseshell** *n* **1** the mottled brown-and-yellow horny shell of some marine turtles used in making various ornamental articles. **2** a butterfly with striking orange, yellow, brown, and black coloration. **3** a cat of a breed with black, brown, and yellow markings.

**tortuous** *adj* **1** marked by repeated twists and turns. **2** circuitous or involved. ➤ **tortuously** *adv.*

**torture**[1] *n* **1** the infliction of intense physical or mental suffering as a means of punishment, coercion, or sadistic gratification. **2** anguish of body or mind. ➤ **torturous** *adj.*

**torture**[2] *v* to subject (a person or animal) to torture. ➤ **torturer** *n.*

**Tory** *n* (*pl* **-ies**) a supporter of the British Conservative Party.

**toss**[1] *v* **1** to throw with a quick, light, or careless motion. **2** to throw up in the air. **3** to move repeatedly to and fro or up and down. **4** to jerk (one's head, hair, mane, etc) backwards. **5** to move and turn (food) lightly in a liquid, flour, etc until well coated. **6** to flip (a coin) to decide an issue according to which face lands uppermost.

**toss**[2] *n* an act or instance of tossing. ✱ **not give/care a toss** *Brit, informal* not to care at all.

**toss off** *v* **1** to produce or write quickly or easily. **2** *Brit, coarse slang* to masturbate.

**toss-up** *n* **1** the tossing of a coin. **2** *informal* an even chance or choice.

**tot**[1] *n* **1** a small child; a toddler. **2** a small amount of spirits.

**tot**[2] *v* (**totted, totting**) **1** *chiefly Brit* (*usu* + up) to add (figures or amounts) together. **2** *chiefly Brit* (+ up) to increase by additions.

**total**[1] *adj* **1** comprising or constituting a whole; entire. **2** complete or absolute. ➤ **totally** *adv.*

**total**[2] *n* the end product of adding two or more smaller amounts together.

**total**[3] *v* (**totalled, totalling,** *NAmer* **totaled, totaling**) **1** to amount to (a figure). **2** to add (something) up. **3** *informal* to demolish completely.

**totalitarian** *adj* of a political regime: based on strict control over all aspects of the life and productive capacity of the nation. ➤ **totalitarianism** *n.*

**totalizator** *or* **totalisator** *n* **1** a machine for registering bets and calculating winnings in the tote betting system. **2** = TOTE[2].

**tote**[1] *v informal* to carry.

**tote**[2] *n* (**the tote**) *informal* a betting system, using a totalizator, in which winners are paid a proportion of the total amount staked, based on the size of their stake.

**totem** *n* a natural object or animal revered by and serving as the emblem of a family or clan. ➤ **totemic** *adj.*

**totem pole** *n* a pole carved and painted with totemic symbols erected by some Native American peoples.

**totter**[1] *v* **1** to tremble or rock as if about to fall. **2** to move unsteadily.

**totter**[2] *n* an unsteady gait.

**toucan** *n* a bird of tropical America with brilliant colouring and a very large beak.

**touch**[1] *v* **1** to bring the hand or other part of the body in contact with. **2** to grasp or move in any way or degree. **3** to meet or adjoin without overlapping or penetrating. **4** to harm. **5** to use, consume, or accept. **6** to concern or affect. **7** to move to sympathetic feeling. **8** *informal* to rival in ability or value. **9** (+ on/upon) to treat a topic in a brief or casual manner. ✱ **touch wood** with luck.

**touch**[2] *n* **1** an act of touching. **2** the sense of feeling derived from physical contact *esp* with the hands. **3** a distinctive style or skill in dealing with something. **4** an effective and appropriate detail. **5** a small amount. **6** (a touch) a bit; a little. **7** in sport, the area outside the touchlines. ✱ **in touch** having up-to-date information or contact. **out of touch** lacking up-to-date information or contact.

**touch-and-go** *adj* highly uncertain or precarious.

**touch down** *v* **1** in rugby, to score by placing (the ball) on the ground over an opponent's goal line. **2** of an aircraft or spacecraft: to reach the ground in landing. ➤ **touchdown** *n.*

**touché** /tooh'shay/ *interj* used to acknowledge a hit in fencing or the success of an argument or witty point.

**touching** *adj* capable of arousing tenderness or compassion. ➤ **touchingly** *adv.*

**touchline** *n* in rugby and football, either of the lines that bound the sides of the field of play.

**touch off** *v* to cause or ignite.

**touchstone** *n* a test or criterion for determining the genuineness of something.

**touch-type** *v* to type without looking at the keyboard.

**touch up** *v* **1** to improve or perfect by small alterations. **2** *Brit, informal* to make unwelcome physical or sexual contact with.

**touchy** *adj* (**-ier, -iest**) **1** ready to take offence on slight provocation. **2** calling for tact, care, or caution.

**tough**[1] *adj* **1** strong and flexible; hard-wearing. **2** of food: not easily chewed. **3** characterized by severity or uncompromising determination. **4** capable of enduring great hardship or exertion. **5** aggressive or threatening in behaviour. **6** extremely difficult or testing. **7** *informal* unfortunate or unpleasant. ➤ **toughness** *n.*

**tough**[2] *n informal* somebody who is aggressive and violent.

**toughen** *v* to become or make tough.

**toupee** *n* a wig or hairpiece worn to cover a bald spot.

**tour**[1] *n* **1** a journey, e.g. for business or pleasure, in which one visits several places. **2** a visit, e.g. to a historic site or factory, for pleasure or information. **3** a series of professional engagements involving travel.

**tour**[2] *v* to make a tour of.

**tour de force** /ˌtooə dəˈfaws/ *n* (*pl* **tours de force**) an extremely impressive feat, performance, piece of work, etc.

**tourism** *n* **1** the activity of visiting places, *esp* in foreign countries, for pleasure. **2** the organizing by commercial companies of travel, accommodation, etc for tourists.

**tourist** *n* **1** somebody who takes a holiday abroad. **2** a member of a sports team that is visiting another country. ➤ **touristy** *adj.*

**tournament** *n* **1** a series of games or contests for a championship. **2** a contest between two parties of mounted medieval knights armed with usu blunted lances or swords.

**tourney** *n* (*pl* **-eys**) a tournament in the Middle Ages.

**tourniquet** *n* a bandage or other device tied tightly around a limb to stop the blood flow.

**tousle** *v* to make (something, *esp* somebody's hair) untidy.

**tout**[1] *v* **1** to try to sell. **2** *Brit* to sell (tickets in great demand) at exploitative prices. **3** to praise or publicize extravagantly.

**tout**[2] *n* (*also* **ticket tout**) *Brit* somebody who offers tickets for an event at vastly inflated prices.

**tow**[1] *v* to draw or pull along behind.

**tow**[2] *n* the act of towing. ✱ **in tow 1** being towed. **2** in the position of a companion or follower.

**towards** *or* **toward** *prep* **1** moving or situated in the direction of. **2** along a course leading to. **3** in relation to. **4** turned in the direction of. **5** not long before. **6** for the partial financing of.

**towel**[1] *n* an absorbent cloth or piece of paper for wiping or drying.

**towel**[2] *v* (**towelled, towelling,** *NAmer* **toweled, toweling**) to rub or dry with a towel.

**towelling** (*NAmer* **toweling**) *n* absorbent fabric used for making towels.

**tower**[1] *n* **1** a tall and narrow building or structure, standing alone or attached to a larger structure. **2** a tall unit for storage.

**tower**[2] *v* to reach or rise to a great height.

**tower block** *n Brit* a tall multi-storey building, usu containing flats or offices.

**towering** *adj* **1** impressively high or great. **2** reaching a high point of intensity.

**town** *n* **1** a compactly settled area, *esp* one larger than a village but smaller than a city. **2** the business centre of a large town or city. **3** the townspeople. ✱ **go to town** to deal with or exploit something enthusiastically. **on the town** in pursuit of entertainment or amusement.

**town crier** *n* somebody employed to make public proclamations.

**town hall** *n* the chief administrative building of a town.

**town planning** *n* the arrangement of the various components of the urban environment for best results. ➤ **town planner** *n.*

**townscape** *n* the overall visual aspect of a town.

**township** *n* **1** *esp* formerly, an urban area inhabited by non-white citizens in South Africa. **2** in the USA and Canada, a subdivision of a county.

**towpath** *n* a path, e.g. along a canal, for use in towing boats.

**toxic** *adj* **1** = POISONOUS. **2** relating to or caused by a poison. ➤ **toxicity** *n.*

**toxicology** *n* a branch of biology that deals with poisons and their effects. ➤ **toxicologist** *n.*

**toxin** *n* an often extremely poisonous protein produced by a living organism, e.g. a bacterium.

**toy**[1] *n* **1** something for a child to play with. **2** something designed for amusement or diversion rather than practical use.

**toy**[2] *adj* **1** used as a toy. **2** denoting an animal of a breed of exceptionally small size.

**toy**[3] *v* **1** (+ with) to touch or handle in an absent-minded or nonchalant way. **2** (+ with) to consider as a possibility but without committing oneself.

**toy boy** *n Brit, informal* a young man taken as lover by an older woman.

**trace**[1] *n* **1** a mark or line left by something that has passed. **2** a sign or evidence of some past thing. **3** a minute or barely detectable amount or indication. **4** the graphic record made by a recording instrument.

**trace**[2] *v* **1** to find by using signs, evidence, or remains. **2** to study in detail or step by step, *esp* working back towards the source or origin of something. **3** to follow the course or trail of. **4** to copy (e.g. a drawing) by following the lines or letters as seen through a semitransparent superimposed sheet. **5** to delineate or sketch. ➤ **traceable** *adj.*

**trace element** *n* a chemical element present in minute quantities.

**tracer** *n* **1** ammunition that is chemically treated to mark its trajectory by a trail of smokeor fire. **2** a substance used to trace the course of a chemical or biological process.

**tracery** *n* (*pl* **-ies**) **1** an ornamental pattern of stonework and spaces in architecture. **2** a decorative interlacing of lines.

**trachea** *n* (*pl* **tracheae** *or* **tracheas**) the tube by which air passes to and from the lungs.

**tracheotomy** *n* (*pl* **-ies**) the surgical operation of cutting into the trachea usu to relieve suffocation by inhaled matter.

**track**[1] *n* **1** a roughly made path or road. **2** detectable evidence, e.g. a line of footprints or a wheel rut, that something has passed. **3** a specially laid-out course, *esp* for racing. **4** the parallel rails of a railway. **5** a rail or length of railing along which something, *esp* a curtain, moves. **6** the course along which something, e.g. a missile, moves. **7** a single song or piece of music on a compact disc, record, or cassette. * **keep/lose track of** to remain aware/no longer be aware of the development or whereabouts of. **make tracks** *informal* to leave. **on the right/wrong track** attempting to do something in way that is likely/unlikely to be successful.

**track**[2] *v* **1** to follow the tracks or traces of. **2** to observe or plot the course of (e.g. a spacecraft or missile) instrumentally. **3** to move a film or television camera towards, beside, or away from a subject while shooting a scene. ➤ **tracker** *n.*

**track down** *v* to search for until found.

**track event** *n* an athletic event that takes place on a track; a race.

**track record** *n* a record of the past achievements of an individual, organization, team, etc.

**tracksuit** *n* a warm loose-fitting suit worn *esp* by athletes when training.

**tract**[1] *n* a pamphlet on a religious subject.

**tract**[2] *n* **1** a region or area of land of indefinite extent. **2** a system of connected body parts or organs.

**tractable** *adj* **1** of a person or animal: easily taught or controlled. **2** of a problem: easy to deal with.

**traction** *n* **1** the act of pulling, or the force exerted in pulling. **2** in medicine, a pulling force exerted on part of the body to treat fractures, cure deformities, etc. **3** the adhesive friction of a moving body on a surface, e.g. a tyre on a road.

**traction engine** *n* a large steam- or diesel-powered vehicle used to pull heavy loads.

**tractor** *n* **1** a vehicle used for pulling farm machinery. **2** a truck with a short chassis and a driver's cab, used to haul a large trailer.

**trad** *adj informal* = TRADITIONAL.

**trade**[1] *n* **1** the business of buying and selling or bartering commodities. **2** the business or work in which one engages regularly. **3** an occupation requiring manual or mechanical skill; a craft. **4** the people or firms engaged in a particular business or industry.

**trade**[2] *v* **1** to engage in the exchange, purchase, or sale of goods. **2** to exchange. **3** (+ on) to exploit or take advantage of. ➤ **trader** *n.*

**trademark** *n* **1** a legally registered name or distinctive symbol attached to goods produced by a particular firm. **2** a distinguishing feature firmly associated with somebody or something.

**trade off** *v* to sacrifice (something) for something else.

**tradesman** *n* (*pl* **tradesmen**) **1** a shopkeeper. **2** a worker in a skilled trade.

**trade union** (*Brit also* **trades union**) *n* an organization of workers formed for the purpose of advancing its members' interests. ➤ **trade unionism** *n,* **trade unionist** *n.*

**tradition** *n* **1** the handing down of information, beliefs, and customs from one generation to another. **2** a belief, custom, or practice inherited from previous generations.

**traditional** *adj* relating to or handed down by tradition. ➤ **traditionally** *adv.*

**traditionalism** *n* adherence to traditional methods, usu in preference to newer ones. ➤ **traditionalist** *n and adj.*

**traduce** *v formal* to defame.

**traffic**[1] *n* **1** the movement, e.g. of vehicles or pedestrians, through an area or along a route. **2** the vehicles, pedestrians, ships, or aircraft moving along a route. **3** the information or signals transmitted over a communications system. **4** the business of transporting passengers or freight. **5** trade, *esp* in illegal merchandise.

**traffic**[2] *v* (**trafficked, trafficking**) to trade in something illegal or disreputable. ➤ **trafficker** *n.*

**traffic island** *n* a paved or planted area in the middle of a road designed to guide the flow of traffic and provide refuge for pedestrians.

**traffic jam** *n* a line of vehicles that cannot move normally because of an obstruction.

**traffic light** *n* (*usu in pl*) an automatically operated signal with coloured lights for controlling traffic.

**traffic warden** *n Brit* an official who enforces parking regulations.

**tragedian** *n* **1** an actor who plays tragic roles. **2** a writer of tragedies.

**tragedy** *n* (*pl* **-ies**) **1** a disastrous or very sad event. **2** a serious drama in which the main characters meet an unhappy fate.

**tragic** *adj* **1** very sad, deplorable, or disastrous. **2** relating to literary tragedy. ➤ **tragically** *adv.*

**tragicomedy** *n* (*pl* **-ies**) a literary work in which tragic and comic elements are mixed. ➤ **tragicomic** *adj.*

**trail**[1] *n* **1** a trace or mark left by somebody or something that has passed. **2** a marked path through a forest or mountainous region. **3** a route followed or to be followed for a particularpurpose. **4** something that follows or moves along as if being drawn behind something.

**trail**[2] *v* **1** to follow the trail of. **2** to draw (something) along behind one. **3** to hang down so as to sweep the ground. **4** (*usu* + along) to walk or proceed heavily or wearily. **5** to do poorly in relation to others. **6** (*usu* + off/away) to become quieter or weaker; to dwindle.

**trailblazer** *n* **1** somebody who finds a new route through wild country. **2** a pioneer; an innovator. ➤ **trailblazing** *adj.*

**trailer** *n* **1** a wheeled vehicle designed to be towed. **2** *NAmer* = CARAVAN. **3** the rear part of an articulated lorry. **4** a set of short excerpts from a film shown in advance for publicity purposes.

**train**[1] *n* **1** a connected line of railway carriages or wagons pulled by a locomotive. **2** a moving file of people, vehicles, or animals. **3** a connected series of ideas, actions, or events. **4** a part of a gown that trails behind the wearer.

**train**[2] *v* **1** to teach (a person or animal) to do something. **2** to undergo training. **3** to make oneself fit by exercise, e.g. in preparation for a race or contest. **4** to direct the growth of (a plant) by bending, pruning, and tying. **5** (*usu* + **on**) to aim (something) at an object. ➤ **training** *n.*

**trainee** *n* somebody who is being trained for a job.

**trainer** *n* **1** a person who trains people or animals. **2** *Brit* a sports shoe designed for running, jogging, etc.

**trainspotter** *n Brit* somebody whose hobby is to collect the numbers of railway locomotives. ➤ **trainspotting** *n.*

**traipse**[1] *v* to walk or trudge about, often to little purpose.

**traipse**[2] *n* a long or unpleasant walk.

**trait** *n* a distinguishing quality or characteristic.

**traitor** *n* **1** somebody who betrays another's trust. **2** somebody who commits treason. ➤ **traitorous** *adj.*

**trajectory** *n* (*pl* **-ies**) the curve that a moving object follows through space.

**tram** *or* **tramcar** *n chiefly Brit* a passenger vehicle running on rails and typically operating on urban streets.

**tramline** *n* **1** *Brit* a track on which trams run. **2** (*in pl*) either of the two pairs of sidelines on a tennis or badminton court marking the area used in doubles.

**trammel**[1] *n* **1** a net with three layers. **2** *literary* (*in pl*) something that impedes freedom of action.

**trammel**[2] *v* (**trammelled, trammelling,** *NAmer* **trammeled, trammeling**) to restrain or confine.

**tramp**[1] *v* **1** to walk or tread heavily. **2** to travel about on foot.

**tramp**[2] *n* **1** a homeless person who travels around and survives by taking occasional jobs or by begging. **2** a usu long and tiring walk. **3** the heavy rhythmic tread of feet. **4** *NAmer* a promiscuous woman.

**trample** *v* **1** to press down, crush, or injure by treading. **2** (*usu* + on/over) to treat ruthlessly or with contempt.

**trampoline** *n* a resilient sheet supported by springs in a frame, used for bouncing up and down on and performing gymnastic tricks in the air. ➤ **trampolining** *n.*

**trance** *n* **1** a state of semiconsciousness or unconsciousness with diminished sensitivity to external stimuli. **2** a state of altered consciousness or ecstasy in which religious or mystical visions may be experienced.

**tranche** *n* a portion.

**tranquil** *adj* calm, quiet, or peaceful. ➤ **tranquillity** *n,* **tranquilly** *adv.*

**tranquillize** *or* **-ise** (*NAmer* **tranquilize**) *v* to make calm, *esp* with drugs.

**tranquillizer** *or* **tranquilliser** (*NAmer* **tranquilizer**) *n* a drug used to tranquillize.

**transact** *v* to conduct (business).

**transaction** *n* **1** an instance of buying and selling or a business deal. **2** the act of conducting business.

**transatlantic** *adj* **1** crossing the Atlantic Ocean. **2** relating to people or places situated beyond the Atlantic Ocean.

**transcend** *v* **1** to go beyond the limits of. **2** to surpass.

**transcendent** *adj* **1** extraordinarily great, good, etc. **2** beyond the limits of ordinary experience. **3** of God: existing outside the material universe. ➤ **transcendence** *n.*

**transcendental** *adj* extending beyond ordinary experience, *esp* into the mystical realm. ➤ **transcendentally** *adv.*

**transcontinental** *adj* crossing a continent.

**transcribe** *v* **1** to make a written copy or version of. **2** to write (something) in a different medium; to transliterate. **3** to make a musical transcription of.

**transcript** *n* a written, printed, or typed copy *esp* of dictated or spoken material or shorthand notes.

**transcription** *n* **1** the act of transcribing. **2** a transcript. **3** an arrangement of a musical composition for some instrument or voice other than the original.

**transept** *n* either of the projecting arms of a cross-shaped church extending at right angles to the nave.

**transfer**[1] *v* (**transferred, transferring**) **1** to carry or take from one person, place, or situation to another. **2** to move to another location, job, etc. **3** to make over the possession or control of (e.g. property). **4** to change from one vehicle or transport system to another. ➤ **transferable** *n.*

**transfer**[2] *n* **1** an act of transferring. **2** *Brit* a graphic image transferred by contact from one surface to another. ➤ **transference** *n.*

**transfiguration** *n* **1** a change in form or appearance, *esp* to something more beautiful or exalted. **2** (**Transfiguration**) a festival of the Christian Church commemorating the transfiguration of Christ (Matthew 17:2 and Mark 9:2–3).

**transfigure** *v* to transform outwardly, *esp* to make more beautiful.

**transfix** *v* **1** to hold (a person or animal) motionless, *esp* with horror or shock. **2** to pierce through, e.g. with a pointed weapon.

**transform** *v* to change radically in structure, appearance, or character. ➤ **transformation** *n.*

**transformer** *n* a device that changes an electric current, usu from high voltage to low, or from alternating to direct.

**transfusion** *n* a medical procure to transfer a quantity of another person's blood into the body of a patient.

**transgress** *v* to do wrong, *esp* by violating a law, rule, command, etc. ➤ **transgression** *n,* **transgressor** *n.*

**transient**[1] *adj* **1** transitory. **2** staying or working in a place for only a short time. ➤ **transience** *n,* **transiently** *adv.*

**transient**[2] *n* a transient guest or worker.

**transistor** *n* **1** a semiconductor device that makes use of a small current to control a larger one. **2** (*also* **transistor radio**) a small portable radio using transistors in its circuits.

**transit** *n* **1** the act of passing through or over. **2** *NAmer* transportation.

**transition** *n* the process of passing from one state, stage, form, topic, etc to another. ➤ **transitional** *adj.*

**transitive** *adj* of a verb: having a direct object. ➤ **transitivity** *n.*

**transitory** *adj* of brief duration; not lasting.

**translate** *v* **1** to reproduce the meaning of (a word, text, etc) in another language. **2** to explain or interpret (something difficult to understand). **3** (*usu* + into) to convert or be converted into another medium.

**translation** *n* **1** the act of rendering from one language into another. **2** a version thus produced.

**translator** *n* somebody who translates from one language into another.

**transliterate** *v* to represent or spell (a letter or word) in the characters of another alphabet. ➤ **transliteration** *n.*

**translucent** *adj* allowing some light to pass through, but not enough for objects beyond to be seen clearly; semitransparent. ➤ **translucence** *n.*

**transmission** *n* **1** the act of transmitting. **2** something, e.g. a message or television programme, that is transmitted. **3** an assembly of parts by which power is transmitted from a motor vehicle engine to an axle.

**transmit** *v* (**transmitted, transmitting**) **1** to send or pass from one person or place to another. **2** to cause (e.g. force or energy) to be conveyed through a medium. **3** to send out (a signal) either by radio waves or over a wire.

**transmitter** *n* a device that sends out e.g. radio or television signals in the form of electromagnetic waves.

**transmogrify** *v* (**-ies, -ied**) to transform, often with grotesque or humorous effect. ➤ **transmogrification** *n.*

**transmute** *v* to change in form, substance, or characteristics. ➤ **transmutation** *n.*

**transom** *n* **1** the planking forming the stern of a square-ended boat. **2** a horizontal crossbar used to strengthen a structure.

**transparency** *n* (*pl* **-ies**) **1** the quality of being transparent. **2** a photographic slide.

**transparent** *adj* **1** transmitting light without appreciable scattering so that bodies lying beyond are entirely visible. **2** free from pretence or deceit. **3** easily detected or seen through. **4** readily understood. ➤ **transparently** *adv.*

**transpire** *v* **1** to become known. **2** to occur. **3** of plants: to give off water vapour from the surfaces of leaves. ➤ **transpiration** *n.*

**transplant**[1] *v* **1** to lift and reset (a plant) in another soil or place. **2** to remove (something) from one place and settle or introduce it elsewhere. **3** to transfer (an organ or tissue) from one part or individual to another. ➤ **transplantation** *n.*

**transplant**[2] *n* **1** the act of transplanting, *esp* a surgical operation to transplant an organ. **2** something transplanted.

**transport**[1] *v* **1** to transfer or convey from one place to another. **2** to delight or enrapture. **3** formerly, to send (a convict) to a penal colony overseas. ➤ **transportation** *n,* **transporter** *n.*

**transport**[2] *n* **1** the conveying of goods or people from one place to another. **2** a means of travelling or of conveying passengers or goods. **3** a ship or aircraft for carrying soldiers or military equipment. **4** an experience of strong and usu pleasurable emotion.

**transpose** *v* **1** to change the relative position of (two or more things). **2** to transfer from one place or period to another. **3** to write or perform (music) in a different key. ➤ **transposition** *n.*

**transsexual** *or* **transexual** *n* somebody physically of one sex with an urge to belong to or resemble the opposite sex.

**transubstantiation** *n* the miraculous change by which, according to Roman Catholic and Eastern Orthodox dogma, the bread and wine used at communion become the body and blood of Christ when consecrated.

**transverse** *adj* lying or set crosswise. ➤ **transversely** *adv.*

**transvestite** *n* somebody who adopts the dress of the opposite sex. ➤ **transvestism** *n.*

**trap**[1] *n* **1** a device for catching animals. **2** a plan or trick designed to catch a person unawares and put them at a disadvantage. **3** a situation from which it is difficult or impossible to escape. **4** a light carriage with springs, pulled by a horse or pony. **5** *informal* the mouth.

**trap**[2] *v* (**trapped, trapping**) **1** to catch in a trap. **2** to place in a position from which it is difficult to escape. **3** to stop or retain.

**trapdoor** *n* a lifting or sliding door covering an opening in a floor, ceiling, etc.

**trapeze** *n* an apparatus consisting of a short horizontal bar suspended by two parallel ropes, used *esp* by circus acrobats.

**trapezium** *n* (*pl* **trapeziums** *or* **trapezia**) *Brit* a quadrilateral that has only two sides parallel.

**trapper** *n* a person who traps wild animals.

**trappings** *pl n* **1** outward signs and accessories. **2** ornamental coverings and harness for a horse.

**Trappist** *n* a member of a monastic order noted for its vow of silence.

**trash**[1] *n chiefly NAmer* **1** junk or rubbish. **2** inferior or worthless literary or artistic work. **3** a worthless person or worthless people.

**trash**[2] *v chiefly NAmer, informal* to destroy or vandalize.

**trash can** *n NAmer* a dustbin.

**trashy** *adj* (**-ier, -iest**) of poor quality.

**trauma** *n* (*pl* **traumas**) **1** a disordered mental or behavioural state resulting from emotional stress or shock. **2** a deeply shocking or distressing experience. **3** in medicine, an injury, e.g. a wound. ➤ **traumatic** *adj.*

**traumatize** *or* **-ise** *v* to cause to suffer emotional trauma.

**travail** *n literary* (*also in pl*) painful or laborious effort.

**travel**[1] *v* (**travelled, travelling,** *NAmer* **traveled, traveling**) **1** to go on a journey or tour. **2** to journey along (a road) or through (an area). **3** to move or be transmitted from one place to another.

**travel**[2] *n* **1** the act of travelling. **2** (*in pl*) journeys, *esp* to distant or unfamiliar places.

**travel agency** *n* an agency that gives information on and arranges travel. ➤ **travel agent** *n.*

**traveller** (*NAmer* **traveler**) *n* **1** somebody who is on a journey or who travels frequently. **2** a gypsy, or a person who has an itinerant alternative lifestyle.

**traveller's cheque** (*NAmer* **traveler's check**) *n* a cheque purchased from a bank or travel agency that may be exchanged abroad for foreign currency.

**travelogue** (*NAmer* **travelog**) *n* a film, book, illustrated talk, etc on travel, usu to some exotic or remote place.

**traverse** *v* to travel or extend across, over, or through.

**travesty** *n* (*pl* **-ies**) a distorted or grossly inferior imitation.

**trawl**[1] *v* **1** to fish with a trawl. **2** to search through a large number of things.

**trawl**[2] *n* **1** a large conical fishing net dragged along the sea bottom. **2** an act of trawling.

**trawler** *n* a boat used in trawling.

**tray** *n* an open receptacle with a flat bottom and a low rim for holding or carrying articles.

**treacherous** *adj* **1** involving a betrayal of trust. **2** providing insecure footing or support. **3** marked by hidden dangers or hazards. ➤ **treacherously** *adv,* **treachery** *n.*

**treacle** *n* **1** *chiefly Brit* molasses. **2** golden syrup. ➤ **treacly** *adj.*

**tread**[1] *v* (*past tense* **trod,** *past part.* **trodden** *or* **trod**) **1** to walk or step. **2** to step or walk along, on, or over. **3** to press down with the feet; to trample. ✱ **tread on somebody's toes/corns** to give offence to somebody, *esp* by encroaching on their rights. **tread water 1** to keep the body nearly upright in water by a treading motion of the feet. **2** to stay in the same position without making progress.

**tread**[2] *n* **1** the sound or manner of stepping or treading. **2** the upper horizontal part of a step. **3** the part of a tyre that makes contact with the road. **4** the part of a sole that touches the ground.

**treadle** *n* a lever pressed by the foot to drive e.g. a sewing machine.

**treadmill** *n* **1** a wide wheel with a horizontal axis turned by people or animals treading on steps inside it, formerly used to drive machinery or punish prisoners. **2** an exercise machine that has a continuous moving belt on which to run or walk. **3** a wearisome or monotonous routine.

**treason** *n* (*also* **high treason**) the offence of violating the duty of allegiance owed to one's sovereign or government. ➤ **treasonable** *adj.*

**treasure**[1] *n* **1** coins, jewels, and other valuable objects. **2** something of great worth or value. **3** *informal* somebody highly valued or prized.

**treasure**[2] *v* to treat as precious; to look after carefully, cherish, or prize.

**treasure hunt** *n* a game in which each player tries to be first to find an object that has been hidden.

**treasurer** *n* the person in charge of the finances of e.g. a society.

**treasure trove** *n* under English law until 1996, hidden valuables of unknown ownership that become the property of the Crown when found.

**treasury** *n* (*pl* **-ies**) **1** a depository where the collected funds or revenues of a state, organization, or individual are kept. **2** (*often* **Treasury**) the government department in charge of finance and the economy. **3** a collection of valuable or pleasing things.

**treat**[1] *v* **1** to behave towards or deal with in a certain way. **2** to care for or attend to medically or surgically. **3** to present and discuss (a subject). **4** to apply a process or substance to. **5** (+ to) to provide (somebody) with food, drink, or entertainment at one's own expense. **6** (+ to) to provide (oneself) with enjoyment or gratification. ➤ **treatable** *adj.*

**treat**[2] *n* something that gives great pleasure. ✱ **a treat** *Brit, informal* very well or successfully: *The speech went down a treat.*

**treatise** *n* a formal written report on a subject.

**treatment** *n* **1** behaviour towards somebody or something, or the way in which somebody or something is dealt with. **2** the medicine, therapy, surgery, etc involved in dealing with a patient, injury, or illness. **3** the discussion or presentation of a subject, theme, etc. **4** the use of a chemical substance to preserve, purify etc something.

**treaty** *n* (*pl* **-ies**) a formal agreement made by negotiation, *esp* between states.

**treble**[1] *adj* **1** having three parts. **2** being three times as great or as much. **3** relating to the range or part of a treble. **4** high-pitched or shrill.

**treble**[2] *n* **1** a boy singer with a high-pitched voice. **2** the higher portion of the audio frequency range.

**treble**[3] *v* to increase to three times as much or as many.

**treble clef** *n* in music, a clef placing the G above middle C on the second lowest line of the stave.

**tree** *n* **1** a woody plant with a single tall and erect main stem and, generally, few or no branches on its lower part. **2** a tree diagram. ✱ **be barking up the wrong tree** *informal* to be acting misguidedly.

**tree diagram** *n* a diagram in the form of branching lines.

**tree house** *n* a structure built in the branches of a tree for children to play in.

**tree line** *n* the upper limit of tree growth on a mountain.

**treen** *n* small domestic articles made of wood.

**trefoil** *n* **1** a wild plant with three-lobed leaves. **2** a stylized ornament, *esp* in architecture, in the form of a three-lobed leaf or flower.

**trek**[1] *n* a journey, *esp* a long or arduous one made on foot.

**trek**[2] *v* (**trekked, trekking**) to go on a trek. ➤ **trekker** *n.*

**trellis** *n* a frame of latticework used *esp* as a support for climbing plants.

**tremble**[1] *v* **1** to shake involuntarily, *esp* with fear or cold. **2** to quiver or vibrate. **3** to feel fear or apprehension.

**tremble**[2] *n* a fit or spell of involuntary shaking or quivering.

**tremendous** *adj* **1** very great in size, degree, amount, intensity, etc. **2** *informal* highly impressive, unusual, or exciting. ➤ **tremendously** *adv.*

**tremolo** *n* (*pl* **-os**) in music, a trembling effect produced by very rapid repetition of notes.

**tremor** *n* **1** an involuntary trembling or shaking, e.g. because of a nervous disorder. **2** a distinct small movement of the earth that precedes or follows an earthquake. **3** a sudden thrill of fear or excitement.

**tremulous** *adj* **1** shaking or quivering. **2** uncertain, timid, or fearful.

**trench** *n* **1** a long narrow excavation in the ground. **2** a deep ditch dug to provide cover for troops from enemy fire. **3** a long, narrow, and usu steep-sided depression in the ocean floor.

**trenchant** *adj* incisive and penetrating. ➤ **trenchancy** *n.*

**trench coat** *n* a double-breasted raincoat with a belt.

**trencher** *n* a wooden platter formerly used for serving food.

**trend** *n* **1** a general or prevailing direction or tendency, *esp* in the way things develop or change. **2** a current style, fashion, or taste.

**trendsetter** *n* somebody who popularizes a new fashion, idea, theory, etc. ➤ **trendsetting** *adj.*

**trendy** *adj* (**-ier, -iest**) *informal* very fashionable or up-to-date.

**trepan**[1] *n* formerly, a surgical instrument for removing circular pieces of tissue or bone, *esp* from the skull.

**trepan**[2] *v* (**trepanned, trepanning**) to remove a circular piece of bone using a trepan.

**trepidation** *n* a feeling of nervous agitation or fear.

**trespass**[1] *v* **1** to enter somebody's land or property unlawfully or without permission. **2** (+ on/upon) to make an unwarranted or uninvited intrusion on. **3** *archaic* (+ against) to commit an offence against. ➤ **trespasser** *n.*

**trespass**[2] *n* **1** to the act of trespassing on somebody's land or property. **2** *archaic* a sin.

**tress** *n* (*also in pl*) a long lock of hair.

**trestle** *n* a framework consisting typically of a horizontal bar held at each end by a pair of sloping legs, designed as a support *esp* for a table top.

**triad** *n* **1** a group of three related people or things. **2** (*often* **Triad**) a Chinese secret society engaged in organized crime.

**trial**[1] *n* **1** a formal examination of the evidence in a court case to determine an accused person's guilt or innocence. **2** a test or period of probation to ascertain whether something or somebody performs adequately or is suitable. **3** (*in pl*) a competition in which the individual skills of a person or an animal are tested. **4** a test of faith, patience, or stamina. ✱ **on trial 1** undergoing trial in a court of law. **2** undergoing testing.

**trial**[2] *v* (**trialled, trialling,** *NAmer* **trialed, trialing**) to test (something) in order to assess its quality, durability, performance, etc.

**trial and error** *n* a process of trying out a number of methods to find which achieves a desired result.

**triangle** *n* **1** a polygon with three angles and three sides. **2** a percussion instrument consisting of a steel rod bent into a triangle and sounded with a small metal rod. **3** a romantic or sexual relationship involving three people. ➤ **triangular** *adj.*

**triangulation** *n* the measurement of the angles and one side of a triangle to find an unknown position, distance, etc, *esp* in surveying.

**triathlon** *n* an athletic contest involving three events, typically long-distance running, swimming, and cycling. ➤ **triathlete** *n.*

**tribalism** *n* loyalty to one's tribe.

**tribe** *n* **1** in traditional societies, a group of people, families, or clans with usu a common culture, dialect, religion, and ancestry, led by a chief. **2** *informal* (*also in pl*) a large number of people or things. ➤ **tribal** *adj.*

**tribesman** *or* **tribeswoman** *n* (*pl* **tribesmen** *or* **tribeswomen**) a person who is a member of a tribe.

**tribulation** *n* a state or cause of great distress or suffering.

**tribunal** *n* **1** *Brit* a board appointed to decide disputes. **2** a court of justice.

**tribune** *n* an official of ancient Rome elected by the common people to protect their interests.

**tributary** *n* (*pl* **-ies**) a stream or river feeding a larger river or a lake.

**tribute** *n* **1** something, *esp* a gift or a formal statement, given or made as a demonstration of respect, gratitude, or affection. **2** evidence of the worth or effectiveness of something. **3** a payment formerly made by one ruler or nation to another more powerful one.

**trice** *n* ✱ **in a trice** very soon or immediately.

**tricentenary** *n* (*pl* **-ies**) = TERCENTENARY.

**triceps** *n* (*pl* **tricepses** *or* **triceps**) the large muscle along the back of the upper arm.

**triceratops** *n* a large plant-eating dinosaur with three horns.

**trichology** *n* the scientific study of hair and the scalp. ➤ **trichologist** *n.*

**trick**[1] *n* **1** a crafty action or plan intended to deceive, defraud, or outwit somebody. **2** a dexterous or ingenious feat designed to puzzle or amuse. **3** an illusion. **4** a mannerism. **5** a single round of a card game. ✱ **do the trick** *informal* to produce the desired result. **tricks of the trade** the techniques that are used by experts in a particular profession or craft. ➤ **trickery** *n.*

**trick**[2] *v* to deceive, defraud, cheat, or outwit.

**trickle**[1] *v* **1** to flow in drops or a thin slow stream. **2** to go gradually or one by one.

**trickle**[2] *n* a thin slow stream or movement.

**trickster** *n* a person who defrauds others by trickery.

**tricksy** *adj* (**-ier, -iest**) full of tricks; mischievous.

**tricky** *adj* (**-ier, -iest**) **1** of a task, problem etc: requiring great skill, care, or tact. **2** full of difficulties, hazards, or problems. **3** inclined to be sly or deceitful.

**tricolour** (*NAmer* **tricolor**) *n* a flag with three bands of different colours, *esp* the French national flag.

**tricycle** *n* a three-wheeled pedal-driven vehicle.

**trident** *n* a three-pronged spear.

**tried** *v* past tense and past part. of TRY[1].

**triennial** *adj* **1** lasting for three years. **2** occurring every three years.

**trier** *n* somebody who perseveres with something.

**trifle**[1] *n* **1** *Brit* a type of cold dessert made from sponge cake, fruit, jelly, custard, and whipped cream. **2** something of little value or importance. **3** an insignificant amount.

**trifle**[2] *v* (*often* + with) to behave frivolously, thoughtlessly, or disrespectfully towards.

**trifling** *adj* unimportant or frivolous.

**trigger**[1] *n* **1** a small lever that activates a mechanism, *esp* that makes a gun fire. **2** something that causes an event or reaction.

**trigger**[2] *v* **1** to activate (a mechanism). **2** (*often* + off) to initiate, bring about, or set off.

**trigger-happy** *adj* inclined to resort to violence or guns too quickly.

**trigonometry** *n* the branch of mathematics concerned with the relations between the sides and angles of triangles.

**trilby** *n* (*pl* **-ies**) *chiefly Brit* a soft felt hat with an indented crown.

**trill**[1] *n* **1** in music, a rapid alternation of a main note and one above it. **2** a high-pitched warbling sound.

**trill**[2] *v* to produce a warbling sound. ➤ **triller** *n.*

**trillion** *n* (*pl* **trillions** *or* **trillion**) **1** a million million ($10^{12}$). **2** *Brit, dated* a million million million ($10^{18}$). ➤ **trillionth** *adj and n.*

**trilobite** *n* an extinct sea creature with a three-lobed body.

**trilogy** *n* (*pl* **-ies**) a group of three closely related literary or cinematic works.

**trim**[1] *v* (**trimmed, trimming**) **1** to make neater, shorter, or smaller by cutting or clipping. **2** to reduce the size of (e.g. expenditure). **3** to decorate with ribbons, lace, ornaments, etc. **4** to adjust (a sail) to take advantage of the wind direction.

**trim**[2] *n* **1** an act of trimming. **2** material used for decoration or trimming. **3** the upholstery, interior, and decorative accessories of a motor vehicle. ✱ **in trim 1** fit and healthy. **2** well-maintained.

**trim**[3] *adj* (**trimmer, trimmest**) in good order; neat and smart.

**trimaran** *n* a yacht with three parallel hulls.

**trimming** *n* **1** (*in pl*) pieces cut off in trimming something. **2** a decoration added to clothing, upholstery, linen, etc. **3** *informal* (*in pl*) the traditional garnishes accompanying a dish or meal.

**trinity** *n* (*pl* **-ies**) **1** (**the Trinity**) according to Christian theology, the unity of Father, Son, and Holy Spirit as three persons in one Godhead. **2** a group of three people or things.

**trinket** *n* a small inexpensive ornament or piece of jewellery.

**trio** *n* (*pl* **-os**) **1** a group or set of three. **2** a group of three musicians or singers. **3** a musical composition for a trio.

**trip**[1] *v* (**tripped, tripping**) **1** (*also* + on/up/over) to catch the foot against something and stumble or fall. **2** (+ up) to make a mistake. **3** to dance, skip, or walk with light quick steps. **4** to cause (a device or mechanism) to start or stop operating. **5** *informal* to experience the effects of a psychedelic drug. ✱ **trip the light fantastic** to dance.

**trip**[2] *n* **1** a journey or outing. **2** the act of stumbling or falling. **3** *informal* a hallucinogenic experience induced by a psychedelic drug. **4** *informal* an obsessive, self-indulgent, or self-serving course of action. **5** a device that activates a mechanism.

**tripartite** *adj* **1** composed of three parts. **2** involving three parties.

**tripe** *n* **1** the stomach tissue of a cow or sheep used as food. **2** *informal* rubbish or nonsense.

**triplane** *n* an aircraft with three pairs of wings arranged one above the other.

**triple**[1] *adj* **1** consisting of three things or parts. **2** three times as much or as many.

**triple**[2] *v* to become or make three times as much or as many.

**triple jump** *n* an athletic field event in which a competitor takes a running start and then performs a hop, a step, and a jump in succession.

**triplet** *n* **1** one of three children or animals born at one birth. **2** a group of three musical notes performed in the time of two or four.

**triplicate**[1] *adj* existing in three identical parts or copies.

**triplicate**[2] *v* **1** to make three copies of. **2** to multiply by three.

**tripod** *n* a three-legged stand for supporting a camera, etc.

**tripper** *n Brit, informal* somebody who goes on a journey or outing for pleasure.

**triptych** *n* a picture or carving covering three panels.

**trip wire** *n* a concealed wire placed near the ground that is used to trip up an intruder or to activate an explosive or warning device.

**trite** *adj* of a remark, idea, etc: lacking originality; overused.

**triumph**[1] *n* **1** a notable success, victory, or achievement. **2** the feeling of happiness or satisfaction brought by success. **3** a highly successful or spectacular example of something. **4** in ancient Rome, a ceremonial procession for a victorious general. ➤ **triumphal** *adj.*

**triumph**[2] *v* **1** (*often* + over) to obtain victory. **2** to celebrate victory or success, *esp* boastfully.

**triumphant** *adj* **1** victorious. **2** jubilant. ➤ **triumphantly** *adv.*

**triumvirate** *n* a group of three rulers or powerful people.

**trivet** *n* a three-legged stand to support a cooking pot or kettle.

**trivia** *pl n* unimportant matters, details, or facts.

**trivial** *adj* of little worth or importance; insignificant. ➤ **triviality** *n*, **trivially** *adv.*

**trivialize** *or* **-ise** *v* to treat (something) as being unimportant or less important than it is. ➤ **trivialization** *n.*

**trod** *v* past tense and past part. of TREAD[1].

**trodden** *v* past part. of TREAD[1].

**troglodyte** *n* a person who lives in a cave.

**troika** *n* **1** a Russian vehicle pulled by three horses abreast. **2** a group of three people working as a team.

**Trojan** *n* a native or inhabitant of ancient Troy in Asia Minor. ✱ **work like a Trojan** to work very hard.

**Trojan Horse** *n* somebody or something that undermines an organization from within.

**troll**[1] *n* in Scandinavian folklore, an ugly dwarf or giant.

**troll**[2] *v* to fish with a hook and line drawn through the water behind a moving boat.

**trolley** *n* (*pl* **-eys**) *Brit* **1** a large basket or a small cart on wheels, used for carrying e.g. shopping or luggage. **2** a shelved stand on wheels used for conveying food or drinks. **3** a hospital stretcher on wheels used for transporting patients. * **off one's trolley** *Brit, informal* crazy or stupid.

**trolleybus** *n* an electrically propelled bus running on a road and drawing power from overhead wires.

**trollop** *n* a promiscuous woman.

**trombone** *n* a brass musical instrument with a movable slide to extend its length and thus vary the pitch. ➤ **trombonist** *n.*

**troop**[1] *n* **1** (*in pl*) soldiers or the army. **2** a subdivision of a cavalry or tank regiment. **3** an artillery unit smaller than a battery. **4** a group of similar people, animals, etc.

**troop**[2] *v* of a group of people: to move together.

**trooper** *n* **1** a private in a cavalry or tank regiment. **2** *NAmer* a state police officer.

**trophy** *n* (*pl* **-ies**) **1** a cup, medal, plate, etc awarded to a person or team as a symbol of victory in a contest. **2** a memento of a successful achievement.

**tropic** *n* **1** (**tropic of Cancer**) a line of latitude 23½° north of the equator. **2** (**tropic of Capricorn**) a line of latitude 23½° south of the equator. **3** (**the tropics**) the region between these two lines of latitude.

**tropical** *adj* **1** relating to the tropics. **2** of the weather or a climate: very hot and usu humid. ➤ **tropically** *adv.*

**trot**[1] *v* (**trotted, trotting**) **1** to progress or ride at a trot. **2** to run at a moderately fast pace.

**trot**[2] *n* **1** a moderately fast pace of a horse in which the legs move in diagonal pairs. **2** a period of trotting. * **on the trot** *Brit, informal* in succession.

**troth** *n* * **pledge/plight one's troth** to make a solemn promise to be faithful or loyal, *esp* in marriage.

**trot out** *v informal* to say or produce with tedious regularity.

**trotter** *n* the foot of a pig, used as food.

**troubadour** *n* a medieval poet musician.

**trouble**[1] *n* **1** difficulty, problems, or danger. **2** a cause or source of difficulty, etc. **3** a problem, snag, or drawback. **4** public unrest or demonstrations of dissatisfaction. **5** effort taken over something. * **ask for trouble** *informal* to do or say something that may lead to problems or punishment. **in trouble** liable to be punished or suffer something unpleasant.

**trouble**[2] *v* **1** to cause distress, anxiety, or inconvenience to. **2** (*often* + to) to make an effort or take the time to do or say something.

**troubled** *adj* **1** worried or anxious. **2** characterized by or experiencing trouble.

**troublemaker** *n* somebody who deliberately and habitually causes trouble.

**troubleshoot** *v* to identify the causes of faults, problems, or disputes and try to remedy them. ➤ **troubleshooter** *n.*

**troublesome** *adj* causing difficulty or problems.

**trough** *n* **1** a long shallow receptacle for the food or drinking water of domestic animals. **2** an intervening lower area, e.g. between waves or ridges. **3** in meteorology, an elongated area of low atmospheric pressure. **4** a notably low point, e.g. in a trade cycle or on a statistical graph.

**trounce** *v* to defeat decisively.

**troupe** *n* a touring group of actors or other performers.

**trouper** *n* **1** a veteran actor or entertainer. **2** a loyal or dependable person.

**trousers** *pl n* an outer garment extending from the waist to the ankles, with tube-like parts that cover each leg separately. * **wear the trousers** *informal* to be the dominant person in a relationship.

**trousseau** /'troohsoh/ *n* (*pl* **trousseaux** *or* **trousseaus**) the clothes, linen, and other items that a woman collects for her marriage.

**trout** *n* (*pl* **trouts** *or* **trout**) a fish related to the salmon, with distinctive spotted markings.

**trove** *n* a store of valuable things.

**trowel** *n* **1** a small hand tool with a flat blade used to apply, mix, and spread plaster, cement, etc. **2** a small hand tool with a scoop-shaped blade used for lifting small plants, turning earth, etc.

**troy** *n* a system of weights, used mainly for precious metals and gemstones, in which there are 12oz to the pound.

**truant**[1] *n* a pupil who stays away from school without good reason or permission. * **play truant** to truant. ➤ **truancy** *n.*

**truant**[2] *v* to stay away from school without good reason or permission.

**truant**[3] *adj* straying or wandering.

**truce** *n* an agreement between enemies to stop fighting, often for a set period of time.

**truck**[1] *n* **1** a lorry. **2** *Brit* a wagon for carrying goods by rail.

**truck**[2] *n* * **have no truck with** to refuse to have anything to do with.

**truculent** *adj* aggressively defiant, sullen, or antagonistic. ➤ **truculence** *n,* **truculently** *adv.*

**trudge**[1] *v* to walk with slow, weary, or laborious steps.

**trudge**[2] *n* a long tiring walk.

**true** *adj* (**truer, truest**) **1** in accordance with fact or reality. **2** genuine or real. **3** properly or strictly so called. **4** accurate. **5** correctly adjusted or aligned, *esp* upright or level. **6** steadfast, loyal, or trusted. **7** (*usu* + to) consistent with what is expected of. * **come true** to happen; to become real. **true to form/type** behaving as expected. **true to life 1** accurately reflecting what goes on in real life. **2** realistic or lifelike. ➤ **truly** *adv.*

**truffle** *n* **1** a fungus that grows underground and is considered a great delicacy. **2** a rich chocolate sweet.

**trug** *n Brit* a shallow wooden basket used for carrying fruit, flowers, and vegetables.

**truism** *n* a truth that is too obvious or unimportant to be mentioned.

**trump**[1] *n* **1** (*in pl*) in various card games, the suit of cards that has been chosen to have a higher value than the other three suits. **2** a card of the suit that is trumps. **3** (*also* **trump card**) something that can be used to gain an advantage. ✱ **come/turn up trumps** *chiefly Brit, informal* to do what is needed or desirable, *esp* at the last moment.

**trump**[2] *v* **1** to play a trump on (a card of another suit). **2** to surpass by doing or saying something better.

**trumpery** *adj* **1** worthless or useless. **2** cheap or tawdry.

**trumpet**[1] *n* **1** the highest-pitched brass musical instrument, with a a flared bell and three valves. **2** the loud penetrating cry of an elephant. ✱ **blow one's (own) trumpet** to boast about one's own abilities, achievements, etc.

**trumpet**[2] *v* (**trumpeted, trumpeting**) **1** to play a trumpet. **2** to make the characteristic sound of an elephant. **3** to proclaim (something) loudly or widely. ➤ **trumpeter** *n.*

**truncate** *v* to shorten by cutting off the top or end part. ➤ **truncation** *n.*

**truncheon** *n chiefly Brit* a short thick stick carried as a weapon by police officers.

**trundle** *v* to move slowly on wheels.

**trunk** *n* **1** the main stem of a tree. **2** a person's or animal's body apart from the head, limbs, and other appendages. **3** the long flexible muscular nose of an elephant. **4** a large rigid box with a hinged lid, used for storing or transporting personal articles. **5** *NAmer* the boot of a motor vehicle.

**trunk call** *n Brit, dated* a long-distance telephone call.

**trunk road** *n* a main road connecting major cities.

**trunks** *pl n* men's tight-fitting shorts worn swimming or boxing.

**truss**[1] *n* **1** a rigid framework supporting a roof or bridge. **2** a padded belt used as a support for a hernia.

**truss**[2] *v* **1** to tie up the wings or legs of (a chicken, turkey, etc) in preparation for cooking. **2** (*often* + up) to secure or bind tightly.

**trust**[1] *n* **1** confident belief in or reliance on the character, ability, honesty, truth etc of somebody or something. **2** responsibility for something or somebody. **3** an arrangement whereby money or other property is held by one person for the benefit of another. **4** something managed by trustees.

**trust**[2] *v* **1** to rely on or believe in the truthfulness, accuracy, ability, etc of. **2** to be confident about allowing (somebody) to do, have, or look after something. **3** (*often* + to/in) to place one's confidence in or rely on somebody or something. **4** (*often* + to) to place (somebody or something) in somebody's care or keeping. **5** to hope or assume: *I trust you are well.* ➤ **trusted** *adj.*

**trustee** *n* a person appointed to administer money or other property for a beneficiary.

**trustful** *adj* trusting. ➤ **trustfully** *adv.*

**trust fund** *n* property, money, shares, or other assets held in trust.

**trusting** *adj* showing great trust, often to the extent of risking being exploited or hurt. ➤ **trustingly** *adv.*

**trustworthy** *adj* known to be honest, truthful, and reliable. ➤ **trustworthiness** *n.*

**trusty** *adj* (**-ier, -iest**) *archaic or humorous* reliable; trustworthy.

**truth** *n* **1** the state or quality of being true. **2** (**the truth**) the facts regarding something. **3** something that is true or is believed to be true.

**truthful** *adj* **1** telling the truth. **2** of a portrait, sculpture, etc: realistic. ➤ **truthfully** *n.*

**try**[1] *v* (**-ies, -ied**) **1** to make an attempt (to do something). **2** (*often* + out) to test or operate (something) to see if it is working or effective. **3** to conduct the trial of (an accused person). **4** to make severe demands on. ✱ **tried and tested** known to be reliable.

**try**[2] *n* (*pl* **-ies**) **1** an attempt. **2** an experimental trial. **3** in rugby, a score made by touching down the ball behind the opponent's goal line.

**trying** *adj* annoying, unpleasant, or tiring.

**try on** *v* to put on (a piece of clothing) to see if it is suitable.

**tryst** *n literary* a secret agreement for a romantic meeting.

**tsar** *or* **czar** *or* **tzar** /zah, tsah/ *n* an emperor of Russia before 1917. ➤ **tsarist** *n and adj.*

**tsetse** /'tetsi, 'tsetsi/ *n* a two-winged bloodsucking African fly that transmits sleeping sickness.

**T-shirt** *or* **tee-shirt** *n* a short-sleeved casual top.

**T square** *n* a T-shaped ruler for drawing right angles and parallel lines.

**tsp** *abbr* teaspoonful.

**tsunami** /tsoo'nahmi/ *n* (*pl* **tsunami** *or* **tsunamis**) a huge sea wave that is produced by an underwater earthquake or volcanic eruption.

**tub** *n* **1** a low wide lidless container used for holding water, growing plants, etc. **2** a small plastic or cardboard container for food. **3** *informal* an old or slow boat, *esp* one that is awkward to sail.

**tuba** *n* the largest and lowest-pitched of the brass musical instruments.

**tubby** *adj* (**-ier, -iest**) *informal* podgy or fat.

**tuber** *n* a short fleshy usu underground stem, e.g. of a potato, bearing buds that may develop into new plants.
**tubercular** *adj* relating to or affected with tuberculosis.
**tuberculosis** *n* a serious infectious disease characterized by fever and the formation of abnormal lumps in the lungs.
**tub-thumping** *adj informal* of a person, speech, etc: expressing opinions in an impassioned or overzealous way.
**tubular** *adj* **1** cylindrical and hollow, like a tube. **2** made of or fitted with tubes.
**TUC** *abbr Brit* Trades Union Congress.
**tuck**[1] *v* **1** to push or fold into a confined space or between two surfaces. **2** to push (something loose) into a more secure or tidy position. **3** (+ in/up) to settle (somebody or oneself) comfortably in bed with the bedclothes firmly in place. **4** (*often* + up) to draw or gather (*esp* one's legs) into a folded position. * **tuck in/into** to start eating (food) with enjoyment.
**tuck**[2] *n* **1** a fold stitched into fabric or a garment. **2** *Brit, dated, informal* food eaten as a snack by schoolchildren.
**tuck away** *v* to store or hide in a place that is difficult to find.
**tucker** *n Aus, NZ* food.
**Tudor** *adj* relating to the royal house that ruled England from 1485 until 1603.
**Tuesday** *n* the day of the week following Monday.
**tufa** *n* a porous rock formed as a deposit by mineral springs.
**tuffet** *n* **1** a tuft or clump, *esp* of grass. **2** a low seat or footstool.
**tuft** *n* a small cluster of long hairs, feathers, grasses, etc attached together at the base. ➤ **tufted** *adj*, **tufty** *adj*.
**tug**[1] *v* (**tugged, tugging**) to pull hard or suddenly.
**tug**[2] *n* **1** a hard sudden pull or jerk. **2** (*also* **tugboat**) a small powerful boat used for towing larger boats and ships.
**tuition** *n* teaching or instruction.
**tulip** *n* a plant with a single richly coloured cup-shaped flower.
**tulle** *n* a sheer, often silk, net fabric used chiefly for veils and dresses.
**tumble**[1] *v* **1** to fall suddenly, helplessly, or awkwardly. **2** to roll over and over or to and fro. **3** to move hurriedly and confusedly. **4** of prices, etc: to decline suddenly and sharply. **5** *informal* (+ to) to realize, understand, or become aware of suddenly.
**tumble**[2] *n* **1** an unexpected fall or drop. **2** a confused heap or an untidy state.
**tumbledown** *adj* of a building, etc: in a state of disrepair.
**tumble-dryer** *or* **tumble-drier** *n* an electric machine that dries laundry by rotating it in hot air inside a metal drum. ➤ **tumble-dry** *v*.
**tumbler** *n* **1** a large drinking glass without a handle. **2** an acrobat. **3** a movable part of a lock that must be adjusted to a particular position before the lock can be opened.
**tumbrel** *or* **tumbril** *n* **1** an open-ended farm cart. **2** a cart of this kind used for carrying political prisoners to the guillotine during the French Revolution.
**tumescent** *adj* swollen or distended, or in the process of becoming so.
**tumid** *adj esp* of a body part or tissue: swollen.
**tummy** *n* (*pl* **-ies**) *informal* a person's stomach or the area around it.
**tumour** (*NAmer* **tumor**) *n* an abnormal growth of tissue that may be benign or malignant.
**tumult** *n* **1** a loud confused noise. **2** a state of violent mental or emotional agitation.
**tumultuous** *adj* **1** characterized by great enthusiasm, loud cheering, etc. **2** marked by turbulence or upheaval.
**tumulus** *n* (*pl* **tumuli**) an artificial mound over a grave.
**tun** *n* a large cask, *esp* for beer or wine.
**tuna** *n* (*pl* **tunas** *or* **tuna**) a large food fish of warm seas.
**tundra** *n* a vast treeless plain characteristic of arctic and subarctic regions, with a permanently frozen subsoil.
**tune**[1] *n* a succession of musical notes; a melody. * **call the tune** see CALL[1]. **change one's tune** *informal* to adopt a noticeably different attitude or point of view. **in/out of tune 1** of a musician, singer, musical instrument, etc: having or not having the correct musical pitch. **2** of people: in or not in harmony or agreement. **to the tune of** *informal* to the amount of (a specified sum of money).
**tune**[2] *v* **1** to bring (a musical instrument) to a standard pitch. **2** (*often* + up) to adjust (the engine of a motor vehicle) for optimum performance. **3** (*often* + in) to adjust (a radio or television receiver) to respond to waves of a particular frequency. **4** (+ in to) to become aware of. ➤ **tuning** *n*.
**tuneful** *adj* having a pleasant tune. ➤ **tunefully** *adv*.
**tuneless** *adj* not pleasant to listen to. ➤ **tunelessly** *adv*.
**tuner** *n* **1** a person who tunes musical instruments, *esp* pianos. **2** the part of a stereo system that receives radio signals.
**tungsten** *n* a hard grey–white metallic element with a high melting point, used *esp* for the filaments in light bulbs.
**tunic** *n* **1** a simple loose sleeveless thigh-length or knee-length garment. **2** a close-fitting hip-length jacket worn as part of a uniform.
**tuning fork** *n* a two-pronged metal implement that gives a fixed tone when struck.

**tunnel**[1] *n* **1** an underground passage that allows people, vehicles, etc to pass under an obstruction such as a hill, river, or building. **2** a small underground passage excavated by a burrowing animal.

**tunnel**[2] *v* (**tunnelled, tunnelling,** *NAmer* **tunneled, tunneling**) to construct a tunnel.

**tunnel vision** *n* **1** an eye condition in which only objects straight ahead can be seen distinctly. **2** *informal* extreme narrowness of viewpoint.

**tunny** *n* (*pl* **tunnies** *or* **tunny**) a tuna.

**tuppence** *n Brit* see TWOPENCE. ➤ **tuppenny** *adj.*

**turban** *n* a headdress worn *esp* by Muslim and Sikh men, consisting of a long cloth wound either round a cap or directly round the head. ➤ **turbaned** *adj,* **turbanned** *adj.*

**turbid** *adj* of a liquid: cloudy, thick, or opaque.

**turbine** *n* a power-generating machine with a wheel or rotor driven by the pressure of water, steam, exhaust gases, etc.

**turbo** *n* (*pl* **-os**) **1** a turbine. **2** a turbocharger.

**turbocharger** *n* a supercharger powered by a turbine driven by the exhaust gases from an internal-combustion engine. ➤ **turbocharged** *adj.*

**turbofan** *n* a jet engine with a turbine-driven fan to increase thrust.

**turbojet** *n* a jet engine with a turbine-powered compressor that supplies compressed air to the combustion chamber.

**turboprop** *n* a jet engine with a turbine-driven propeller.

**turbot** *n* (*pl* **turbots** *or* **turbot**) a large edible flatfish.

**turbulence** *n* **1** agitation, tumult, or disorderliness. **2** irregular atmospheric motion characterized by strong currents of rising and falling air.

**turbulent** *adj* **1** characterized by agitation or tumult; stormy. **2** *technical* denoting a disturbed flow in a gas or liquid. ➤ **turbulently** *adv.*

**turd** *n coarse slang* a piece of excrement.

**tureen** *n* a deep bowl for serving soup.

**turf**[1] *n* (*pl* **turfs** *or* **turves**) **1** grass and the soil that is bound to its roots, forming a thick mat. **2** a piece of this cut from the ground. **3** (**the turf**) the sport or business of horse racing. **4** *informal.* **5** an area regarded as the domain of a particular person or group.

**turf**[2] *v* to cover (an area) with turf.

**turf out** *v* **1** to force to leave. **2** to get rid of.

**turgid** *adj* **1** swollen or distended. **2** of language, etc: pompous or bombastic.

**turkey** *n* **1** a large domesticated game bird with a heavy rounded body and a bald head. **2** *chiefly NAmer, informal* a flop.

**Turkish** *n* the national language of the people of Turkey. ➤ **Turkish** *adj.*

**Turkish bath** *n* a therapeutic or relaxing treatment that involves sitting in hot steam followed by a rubdown, massage, and cold shower.

**Turkish delight** *n* a jellylike sweet, cut in cubes and dusted with icing sugar.

**turmeric** *n* **1** an Asian plant of the ginger family with a large rhizome. **2** a bright yellow aromatic powder obtained from this plant.

**turmoil** *n* an extremely confused or agitated state.

**turn**[1] *v* **1** to move round on an axis. **2** to move round so as to be facing in a different or the opposite direction. **3** to go round (*esp* a corner). **4** to make or become something: *The weather has turned cold.* **5** to sprain (an ankle). **6** to make or form using a lathe. **7** of milk: to become sour. ✱ **turn against** to become hostile towards. **turn to** to have recourse to (somebody) for help or support.

**turn**[2] *n* **1** an act of turning. **2** a bend or curve in a path, road, river, etc. **3** a place where a road divides; a turning. **4** a point at the beginning or end of a century or other period. **5** an opportunity or obligation to do something: *It's your turn to drive.* **6** an attack of illness, faintness, dizziness, etc. **7** a short act or performance, e.g. in a variety show. **8** a short walk or drive taken for pleasure. ✱ **by turns** alternately or successively. **do somebody a good turn** to do a favour for somebody. **in/out of turn** in/not in the correct order of succession. **take turns/ take it in turns** to do something alternately or successively. **to a turn** to the required degree.

**turn away** *v* **1** to reject or dismiss. **2** to start to leave or change direction.

**turn back** *v* **1** to return or go in the opposite direction. **2** to prevent from advancing.

**turncoat** *n* a person who switches support from one party or cause to an opposing one.

**turn down** *v* **1** to reduce the strength or intensity of (volume level, etc). **2** to decline to accept.

**turn in** *v* **1** to hand (somebody) over to the authorities. **2** *informal* to go to bed for the night.

**turning** *n* **1** a road, path, etc, that branches off another. **2** a road junction.

**turnip** *n* a large white edible root, used as a vegetable and livestock fodder.

**turnkey** *n* (*pl* **turnkeys**) *archaic* a jailer.

**turn off** *v* **1** to stop from working or flowing by operating a switch or tap. **2** to cause (somebody) to lose interest. **3** to leave one road and join another.

**turn-off** *n* **1** a turning. **2** *informal* somebody or something that a person finds repulsive or boring.

**turn on** *v* **1** to cause to start working or flowing by operating a switch or tap. **2** to attack (somebody) suddenly. **3** to make (somebody) interested or excited, *esp* sexually.

**turn-on** *n informal* somebody or something that a person finds attractive, exciting, or sexually stimulating.

**turnout** *n* the number of people attending or taking part in an event.

**turn out** *v* **1** to turn off (an electric light). **2** to empty (a room, pocket, etc). **3** to produce (work, etc). **4** to prove ultimately to be: *The play turned out to be a success.* **5** to make the effort to attend an event. **6** (**be turned out**) to be dressed.

**turnover** *n* **1** the amount of money taken by a business in a particular period. **2** the rate at which a business loses and replaces its staff. **3** the rate at which a shop sells and replaces stock. **4** an individual pie made by folding a circle of pastry in half to enclose a filling.

**turn over** *v* **1** to put or be put the other way up. **2** of an engine: to revolve at low speed. **3** to think about (a matter, problem, etc). **4** to search roughly through (a place). **5** to deliver to the proper authority.

**turnpike** *n* in the USA or formerly in Britain, a major road on which a toll is payable.

**turn round** *v* **1** to complete the handling or processing of (goods or work) in a specified time. **2** to reform (a failing concern) so that it becomes successful.

**turnstile** *n* a gate with pivoting arms that turns to admit one person at a time.

**turntable** *n* a circular rotating platform, esp one on which a gramophone record is placed while being played.

**turn up** *v* **1** to appear unexpectedly, *esp* after being lost. **2** to arrive or occur. **3** to find or discover. **4** to increase the strength or intensity of (volume level, etc).

**turn-up** *n Brit* **1** a hem on a pair of trousers that is folded up over itself on the outside. **2** *informal* an unexpected or surprising event or outcome.

**turpentine** *n* a liquid distilled from the resin of conifer trees, used *esp* as a solvent for paints and varnishes.

**turpitude** *n formal* baseness, depravity, or wickedness.

**turps** *n informal* turpentine.

**turquoise** *n* **1** a blue, bluish green, or greenish gemstone. **2** a light greenish blue colour.

**turret** *n* **1** a little tower, often at the corner of a larger building. **2** an armoured, usu revolving structure on warships, tanks, aircraft, etc in which guns are mounted. ➤ **turreted** *adj.*

**turtle** *n* a reptile with a bony or leathery shell, resembling a tortoise, but with limbs adapted for swimming. ✱ **turn turtle** *esp* of a boat: to capsize or overturn.

**turtledove** *n* a small wild dove with a distinctive soft cooing call.

**turtleneck** *n* **1** *Brit* a high close-fitting neck on a garment. **2** *NAmer* = POLO NECK.

**turves** *n* pl of TURF[1].

**tusk** *n* a very long tapering tooth, e.g. of an elephant, walrus, boar, etc, that is visible when the animal's mouth is closed.

**tussle**[1] *v* to struggle or fight roughly.

**tussle**[2] *n* a rough fight.

**tussock** *n* a compact tuft of grass, sedge, etc.

**tutelage** *n formal* **1** guardianship. **2** tuition.

**tutelary** *adj formal* acting as a guardian to somebody or something.

**tutor**[1] *n* **1** a person employed as a private teacher, *esp* one who teaches individuals or small groups. **2** *Brit* a university or college teacher who teaches a small group and often has responsibility for students' welfare.

**tutor**[2] *v* to act as a tutor to.

**tutorial**[1] *n* a session of tuition given by a university or college tutor.

**tutorial**[2] *adj* relating to a tutor or the work of a tutor.

**tutu** *n* a very short projecting stiff skirt worn by a ballerina.

**tuxedo** *n* (*pl* **-os** *or* **-oes**) *chiefly NAmer* a man's dinner jacket.

**TV** *n* television.

**twaddle** *n informal* trivial or nonsensical speech or writing; drivel.

**twain** *n archaic* two.

**twang**[1] *n* **1** a strong quick ringing sound like that of the string of a musical instrument being plucked. **2** a distinctive nasal quality in the speech of a person or region. ➤ **twangy** *adj.*

**twang**[2] *v* to make a twang.

**tweak**[1] *v* **1** to give a sudden slight jerk or twist to. **2** *informal* to make fine adjustments to.

**tweak**[2] *n* an act of tweaking.

**twee** *adj* (**tweer, tweest**) *Brit* excessively or affectedly sentimental, pretty, cute, or coy.

**tweed** *n* a rough woollen fabric, often brownish or greenish and flecked with other colours, used *esp* for suits and coats.

**tweet**[1] *v* to make the characteristic chirping sound of a small bird.

**tweet**[2] *n* a tweeting sound.

**tweeter** *n* a small loudspeaker that mainly reproduces higher frequencies.

**tweezers** *pl n* (*also* **pair of tweezers**) a small pincer-like device used for plucking out hairs and handling small objects.

**twelfth** *adj and n* **1** having the position in a sequence corresponding to the number twelve. **2** one of twelve equal parts of something.

**twelve** *n* the number 12. ➤ **twelve** *adj.*

**twenty** *adj and n* (*pl* **-ies**) **1** the number 20. **2** (*in pl*) the numbers 20 to 29. ➤ **twentieth** *adj and n.*

**twerp** *or* **twirp** *n informal* a stupid person.

**twice** *adv* **1** on two occasions. **2** in double the quantity or degree.

**twiddle**[1] *v* **1** (*often* + with) to fiddle with. **2** to rotate or twist lightly or idly. * **twiddle one's thumbs** to have nothing to do.

**twiddle**[2] *n* an act of twiddling. ➤ **twiddly** *adj.*

**twig**[1] *n* a small woody shoot or branch of a tree or bush.

**twig**[2] *v* (**twigged, twigging**) *Brit, informal* to realize or understand something.

**twilight** *n* **1** the soft shadowy or glowing light between sunset and full darkness. **2** the period between sunset and full night. **3** a period of decline.

**twill** *n* a fabric with slightly raised parallel diagonal lines.

**twin**[1] *n* **1** either of two offspring born to the same mother at the same birth. **2** either of two people or things closely resembling each other.

**twin**[2] *v* (**twinned, twinning**) **1** (+ with) to link or pair (one thing) with another. **2** *Brit* (+ with) to associate (a town in one country) officially with a town in another.

**twin**[3] *adj* denoting either of two children who are twins, or either of two objects that function as a pair.

**twine**[1] *n* strong string made from two or more strands twisted together.

**twine**[2] *v* (*usu* + round/around) to coil or twist around something.

**twinge** *n* **1** a sudden sharp stab of pain. **2** a moral or emotional pang.

**twinkle**[1] *v* **1** of a star, light, etc: to shine with a flickering or sparkling effect. **2** of a person's eyes: to have a bright sparkle, *esp* as a sign of amusement, mischief, etc.

**twinkle**[2] *n* a flickering or sparkling effect.

**twinkling** *n* * **in a twinkling (of an eye)** immediately or very quickly.

**twin set** *n chiefly Brit* a woman's jumper and cardigan designed to be worn together.

**twirl**[1] *v* to spin round rapidly.

**twirl**[2] *n* an act of twirling. ➤ **twirly** *adj.*

**twist**[1] *v* **1** to cause to move with a rotating motion. **2** (*often* + round) to turn to face in a different direction. **3** to twine or coil. **4** to bend in a specified direction, *esp* out of true. **5** to follow a winding course. **6** to join (two or more things or parts) together by winding. **7** to wrench (a joint) painfully. **8** to distort the meaning of. **9** to dance the twist. * **twist somebody's arm** *informal* to persuade or force a person to do something.

**twist**[2] *n* **1** an act of twisting. **2** something with a spiral shape or made by twisting e.g. paper. **3** (**the twist**) a dance, popular in the 1960s, featuring exaggerated twisting movements of the hips and legs. **4** an unexpected turn or development. * **round the twist** *Brit, informal* completely mad.

**twister** *n* **1** *Brit, informal* a dishonest person; a cheat or swindler. **2** *chiefly NAmer* a tornado.

**twit**[1] *n chiefly Brit, informal* a silly or stupid person.

**twit**[2] *v* (**twitted, twitting**) *informal* to tease or ridicule, *esp* light-heartedly.

**twitch**[1] *v* to move with a sudden jerky motion.

**twitch**[2] *n* a twitching movement.

**twitchy** *adj* (**-ier, -iest**) *informal* nervous or anxious.

**twitter**[1] *v* **1** of a bird: to make a series of quick chirping sounds. **2** to talk quickly, *esp* in a nervous or giggling way.

**twitter**[2] *n* a twittering sound. * **all of/in a twitter** *informal* in a state of nervous agitation; quivering.

**two** *n* the number 2. * **put two and two together** to use the available evidence or information to draw a conclusion. ➤ **two** *adj.*

**two-dimensional** *adj* **1** having two dimensions, *esp* length and breadth but no depth. **2** of a fictional character, etc: lacking depth; superficial.

**two-faced** *adj* insincere, double-dealing, or hypocritical.

**twopence** *or* **tuppence** /ˈtup(ə)ns/ *n Brit* the sum of two pence, *esp* before decimalization in 1971. ➤ **twopenny** *adj.*

**twosome** *n* a group of two people or things.

**two-time** *v informal* **1** to be unfaithful to (a partner or lover) by having a relationship with somebody else. **2** to cheat or double-cross.

**tycoon** *n* a person in business or industry who has exceptional wealth and power.

**tying** *v* present part. of TIE[1].

**tyke** *or* **tike** *n informal* a cheeky or mischievous small child.

**tympani** *n* see TIMPANI.

**tympanum** *n* (*pl* **tympana** *or* **tympanums**) the eardrum.

**type**[1] *n* **1** a class or group of people, animals, or things that share similar characteristics. **2** a person or thing considered to be representative of a class or group. **3** *informal* a person who has a specified characteristic, nature, etc: *He's the quiet type.* **4** printed characters, words, etc, or the blocks used to print them.

**type**[2] *v* to write using a typewriter or computer. ➤ **typing** *n.*

**typecast** *v* (*past tense and past part.* **typecast**) (*usu* **be typecast**) of an actor: to be repeatedly given the same kind of role.

**typeface** *n* in printing, a particular style of type.

**typescript** *n* a typed copy of a text.

**typeset** *v* (**typesetting,** *past tense and past part.* **typeset**) to arrange the printing type for (a text). ➤ **typesetter** *n.*

**typewriter** *n* a machine with a keyboard for writing in characters resembling printed type.

**typhoid** *n* a serious infectious bacterial disease characterized by fever, spots, diarrhoea, headache, and intestinal inflammation.

**typhoon** *n* a violent tropical storm.

**typhus** *n* an infectious disease marked by high fever, delirium, intense headache, and a dark red rash.

**typical** *adj* **1** exhibiting the essential characteristics of a type. **2** characteristic of somebody or something. ➤ **typically** *adv.*

**typify** *v* (**-ies, -ied**) to be typical of.

**typist** *n* a person who uses a typewriter.

**typo** *n* (*pl* **typos**) *informal* a printing error.

**typography** *n* the style, arrangement, or appearance of printed matter. ➤ **typographer** *n,* **typographic** *adj,* **typographical** *adj.*

**tyrannical** *adj* characterized by oppressive, unjust, or arbitrary use of power. ➤ **tyrannically** *adv.*

**tyrannize** *or* **-ise** *v* to treat cruelly or oppressively.

**tyrannosaurus** *or* **tyrannosaurus rex** *n* a very large flesh-eating dinosaur that walked on its hind legs.

**tyranny** *n* (*pl* **-ies**) rule or government that is cruel or oppressive. ➤ **tyrannous** *adj.*

**tyrant** *n* **1** a cruel or oppressive ruler. **2** any person who exerts cruel or oppressive power.

**tyre** (*NAmer* **tire**) *n* a solid or inflated hollow rubber cushion fitted round a wheel.

**tyro** *or* **tiro** *n* (*pl* **tyros** *or* **tiros**) a beginner or novice.

**tzar** *n* see TSAR.

**tzatziki** *n* a Greek dip or side dish, made from yoghurt, cucumber, and garlic.

**U**[1] *or* **u** *n* (*pl* **U's** *or* **Us** *or* **u's**) the 21st letter of the English alphabet.
**U**[2] *abbr* the chemical symbol for uranium.
**U**[3] *n* in Britain, a classification of cinema films suitable for all age groups.
**ubiquitous** *adj* existing or seeming to be everywhere. ➤ **ubiquitously** *adv*, **ubiquity** *n*.
**U-boat** *n* a German submarine, *esp* as used in World Wars I and II.
**UCAS** *abbr Brit* Universities and Colleges Admissions Service.
**udder** *n* a bag-like organ producing milk in female cattle.
**UFO** *n* (*pl* **UFO's** *or* **UFOs**) an unidentified flying object, *esp* one popularly believed to be of extraterrestrial origin.
**ugly** *adj* (**-ier, -iest**) **1** offensive or displeasing to see or hear. **2** ominous or threatening. ➤ **ugliness** *n*.
**ugly duckling** *n* somebody or something that appears unattractive or unpromising but turns out to be admirable or successful.
**UK** *abbr* United Kingdom.
**ukulele** *n* a small four-stringed guitar.
**ulcer** *n* an open sore on the skin or a mucous membrane. ➤ **ulcerated** *adj*, **ulceration** *n*, **ulcerous** *adj*.
**ulna** *n* (*pl* **ulnae** *or* **ulnas**) the bone of the human forearm on the side of the little finger.
**ulterior** *adj* of a motive: underlying but not expressed.
**ultimate**[1] *adj* **1** last in a progression or series. **2** eventual. **3** fundamental; basic. **4** best or greatest. ➤ **ultimately** *adv*.
**ultimate**[2] *n* (**the ultimate**) the most extreme or important of its kind.
**ultimatum** *n* (*pl* **ultimatums** *or* **ultimata**) a final demand before resorting to direct action or retaliation.
**ultramarine** *n* a vivid deep blue pigment or colour.
**ultramicroscopic** *adj* too small to be seen with an ordinary microscope.
**ultrasonic** *adj* of sound waves: having a frequency above the range of the human ear. ➤ **ultrasonically** *adv*.
**ultraviolet** *adj* of electromagnetic radiation: having a wavelength between the violet end of the visible spectrum and X-rays.
**ululate** *v* to howl or wail in grief. ➤ **ululation** *n*.
**umber** *n* a dark or yellowish brown colour.
**umbilical** *adj* relating to the navel or the umbilical cord.
**umbilical cord** *n* a ropelike tube that connects a foetus with the placenta.
**umbilicus** *n technical* the navel.
**umbra** *n* (*pl* **umbras** *or* **umbrae**) a region of total shadow in an eclipse.
**umbrage** *n* a feeling of pique or resentment.
**umbrella** *n* **1** a collapsible circular shade for protection against rain. **2** something that provides protection or cover. **3** (*used before a noun*) including a wide range of elements or factors.
**umlaut** *n* a mark (¨) placed over a vowel to show a change of sound.
**umpire**[1] *n* a referee in some sports.
**umpire**[2] *v* to act as umpire of.
**umpteen** *adj and n informal* very many. ➤ **umpteenth** *adj*.
**UN** *abbr* United Nations.
**un-** *prefix* **1** forming words denoting a lack or opposite: *unskilled; unrest.* **2** forming verbs denoting the reverse of an action: *undress*.
**unabashed** *adj* not embarrassed or ashamed.
**unabated** *adj* at full strength or force.
**unable** *adj* not able; incapable.
**unacceptable** *adj* **1** not satisfactory. **2** not permissible. ➤ **unacceptably** *adv*.
**unaccountable** *adj* **1** inexplicable. **2** not responsible. ➤ **unaccountably** *adv*.
**unaccustomed** *adj* **1** not usual or common. **2** (+ to) not used to.
**unacquainted** *adj* **1** (+ with) lacking experience of or familiarity with. **2** never having met.
**unadulterated** *adj* **1** not mixed with anything inferior. **2** complete; utter.
**unaffected** *adj* **1** not influenced by something. **2** free from affectation; genuine.
**unaffordable** *adj* too expensive for most people.
**unaided** *adj* done without help.
**unalloyed** *adj* **1** not mixed with another metal. **2** complete and perfect.
**unalterable** *adj* not capable of being altered; permanent. ➤ **unalterably** *adv*.
**unambiguous** *adj* not ambiguous; clear or precise. ➤ **unambiguously** *adv*.

**unanimous** *adj* **1** all of one mind. **2** having the agreement of all. ➤ **unanimity** *n,* **unanimously** *adv.*
**unannounced** *adj* **1** happening without warning. **2** not publicized.
**unanswerable** *adj* **1** having no answer. **2** irrefutable. ➤ **unanswerably** *adv.*
**unappealing** *adj* not appealing; unattractive.
**unappetizing** *or* **unappetising** *adj* not appetizing; unattractive.
**unapproachable** *adj* aloof or unfriendly.
**unarmed** *adj* having no weapons.
**unashamed** *adj* without shame or embarrassment. ➤ **unashamedly** *adv.*
**unassailable** *adj* **1** not open to question. **2** not able to be attacked or challenged.
**unassisted** *adj* acting or done without help.
**unassuming** *adj* modest.
**unattached** *adj* **1** not involved in a romantic or sexual relationship. **2** not joined or united.
**unattended** *adj* not cared for or looked after.
**unauthorized** *or* **unauthorised** *adj* not having official approval.
**unavailable** *adj* not capable of being obtained, contacted, etc. ➤ **unavailability** *n.*
**unavailing** *adj* futile; useless.
**unavoidable** *adj* not avoidable; inevitable. ➤ **unavoidably** *adv.*
**unaware** *adj* (*often* + of) not aware; ignorant or lacking knowledge.
**unawares** *adv* **1** without noticing or intending. **2** suddenly; unexpectedly.
**unbalanced** *adj* **1** mentally disordered or deranged. **2** biased or partial.
**unbearable** *adj* not endurable; intolerable. ➤ **unbearably** *adv.*
**unbeatable** *adj* not able to be defeated or surpassed.
**unbecoming** *adj* **1** not attractive or flattering. **2** improper.
**unbeknown** *adj* (+ to) without the knowledge of.
**unbelievable** *adj* **1** too improbable to believe. **2** extraordinary. ➤ **unbelievably** *adv.*
**unbeliever** *n* somebody with no religious belief.
**unbend** *v* (*past tense and past part.* **unbent**) **1** to return to a straight position. **2** to become more relaxed.
**unbending** *adj* aloof or unsociable.
**unbiased** *or* **unbiassed** *adj* free from prejudice; impartial.
**unbidden** *adj* **1** unasked or uninvited. **2** spontaneous.
**unborn** *adj* not yet born.
**unbounded** *adj* having no limits.
**unbowed** *adj* not defeated or subdued.
**unbridgeable** *adj* of a difference in opinions etc: extreme and unlikely to be resolved.
**unbridled** *adj* uncontrolled.
**unbroken** *adj* **1** not broken; intact. **2** not beaten or surpassed. **3** uninterrupted.
**unburden** *v* (**unburdened, unburdening**) **1** to free from a burden. **2** to relieve (oneself) of fears, worries, etc, by confiding in somebody else.
**uncalled-for** *adj* unnecessary and unwelcome.
**uncanny** *adj* (**-ier, -iest**) strange or mysterious. ➤ **uncannily** *adv.*
**unceasing** *adj* continuous or incessant. ➤ **unceasingly** *adv.*
**unceremonious** *adj* abrupt or rude. ➤ **unceremoniously** *adv.*
**uncertain** *adj* **1** not definitely known. **2** not confident or sure. **3** not reliable or trustworthy. * **in no uncertain terms** forcefully and clearly. ➤ **uncertainly** *adv,* **uncertainty** *n.*
**uncharitable** *adj* harsh or unkind in treating others. ➤ **uncharitably** *adv.*
**uncharted** *adj* of an area of land or sea: not recorded or plotted on a map.
**unchecked** *adj* allowed to develop without restraint.
**unchristian** *adj* **1** contrary to the teachings of Christianity. **2** uncharitable.
**unclassified** *adj* **1** not placed in a class. **2** of information: not subject to a security restriction.
**uncle** *n* the brother of one's father or mother, or the husband of one's aunt.
**unclean** *adj* **1** dirty. **2** morally or spiritually impure.
**Uncle Sam** *n* the US nation, people, or government.
**uncomfortable** *adj* causing or feeling discomfort. ➤ **uncomfortably** *adv.*
**uncommon** *adj* **1** not normally encountered; unusual. **2** remarkable; exceptional. ➤ **uncommonly** *adv.*
**uncommunicative** *adj* not inclined to speak much; reserved.
**uncomprehending** *adj* not able to understand something. ➤ **uncomprehendingly** *adv.*
**uncompromising** *adj* not wanting to compromise; inflexible. ➤ **uncompromisingly** *adv.*
**unconcern** *n* a lack of interest; indifference. ➤ **unconcerned** *adj.*
**unconditional** *adj* not having any conditions attached. ➤ **unconditionally** *adv.*
**unconfined** *adj* **1** not confined or limited. **2** of an emotion: without restraint.
**unconfirmed** *adj* not confirmed as true.
**uncongenial** *adj* **1** not compatible or suitable. **2** disagreeable; unpleasant.
**unconscionable** *adj* **1** unscrupulous; unprincipled. **2** excessive; unreasonable. ➤ **unconscionably** *adv.*

**unconscious**[1] *adj* **1** not knowing or perceiving. **2** having lost consciousness. **3** not resulting from conscious thought or sensation. **4** not intentional or deliberate. ➤ **unconsciously** *adv*, **unconsciousness** *n*.

**unconscious**[2] *n* the part of the mind that one is not normally aware of but influences behaviour and feelings.

**unconstitutional** *adj* not in accordance with the constitution of a nation, organization, etc. ➤ **unconstitutionally** *adv*.

**uncontrollable** *adj* incapable of being controlled. ➤ **uncontrollably** *adv*.

**unconventional** *adj* not conforming with generally accepted behaviour or ideas. ➤ **unconventionally** *adv*.

**unconvincing** *adj* not convincing; implausible. ➤ **unconvincingly** *adv*.

**uncooperative** *adj* not willing to cooperate with others.

**uncoordinated** *adj* **1** lacking in bodily coordination. **2** badly organized.

**uncouth** *adj* uncultivated in speech or behaviour.

**uncover** *v* **1** to remove the cover from. **2** to reveal or discover.

**uncritical** *adj* not expressing criticism or using discrimination. ➤ **uncritically** *adv*.

**unction** *n* **1** the act of anointing as a rite of consecration. **2** exaggerated earnestness.

**unctuous** *adj* falsely sincere or courteous. ➤ **unctuously** *adv*.

**uncut** *adj* **1** not cut or cut off. **2** not abridged.

**undaunted** *adj* not discouraged by danger or difficulty.

**undecided** *adj* **1** not having decided. **2** without a result.

**undemonstrative** *adj* not showing one's feelings.

**undeniable** *adj* plainly true; incontestable. ➤ **undeniably** *adv*.

**under**[1] *adv* **1** in a position below or beneath something. **2** in a condition of subjection or unconsciousness.

**under**[2] *prep* **1** lower than. **2** vertically below but not touching. **3** covered or protected by. **4** subject to the authority or control of, or during the rule of. **5** inferior in rank to. **6** undergoing the action or effect of. **7** within the group or category of: *under this heading*. **8** less than.

**under-** *prefix* **1** situated below: *underground*. **2** lower in rank: *undersecretary*. **3** less than normal: *undernourished*.

**underachieve** *v* to achieve less than is expected. ➤ **underachievement** *n*.

**under-age** *adj* below the legal age.

**underarm** *adj and adv* made with the hand below shoulder level.

**underbelly** *n* (*pl* **-ies**) **1** the underside of an animal. **2** a vulnerable area.

**undercarriage** *n* the part of an aircraft's structure that supports it on the ground.

**underclass** *n* the lowest class of people, *esp* the very poor.

**underclothes** *pl n* underwear.

**undercoat** *n* a coat of paint applied as a base for another coat.

**undercover** *adj and adv* seeking information secretly.

**undercurrent** *n* a hidden or underlying feeling or tendency.

**undercut** *v* (**undercutting**, *past tense and past part.* **undercut**) to charge less than (a competitor).

**underdeveloped** *adj* of a region: lacking modern industries.

**underdog** *n* a competitor who is expected to lose in a struggle or contest.

**underdone** *adj* not fully cooked.

**underdressed** *adj* dressed less formally than is appropriate.

**underestimate**[1] *v* **1** to estimate as being less than the actual size, quantity, etc. **2** to regard (somebody) as less capable or powerful than they actually are. ➤ **underestimation** *n*.

**underestimate**[2] *n* an estimate that is too low.

**underfoot** *adv* **1** against the ground. **2** in the way.

**undergarment** *n* an item of underwear.

**undergo** *v* (**undergoes, underwent, undergone**) **1** to experience. **2** to be subjected to (something unpleasant).

**undergraduate** *n* a student at a college or university studying for a first degree.

**underground**[1] *adj and adv* **1** below the surface of the ground. **2** in hiding or in secret.

**underground**[2] *n* **1** a secret movement or group resisting a government or occupying enemy. **2** *Brit* an underground railway.

**undergrowth** *n* vegetation growing on the ground in a wood.

**underhand** *adj* done secretly or by deception.

**underlay**[1] *v* (*past tense and past part.* **underlaid**) to raise or support by laying something underneath.

**underlay**[2] *n* thick foam or felt laid under a carpet.

**underlie** *v* (**underlying, underlay, underlain**) **1** to lie or be situated under. **2** to be the basis or cause of.

**underline** *v* **1** to mark with a line underneath. **2** to emphasize.

**underling** *n* a subordinate or inferior.

**undermine** *v* **1** to weaken or destroy gradually. **2** to wear away the base or foundations of.

**underneath**[1] *prep and adv* **1** directly below. **2** so as to be hidden by. **3** on the lower side.

**underneath**[2] *n* the bottom part or surface.

**underpants** *pl n* an undergarment covering the hips, crotch, and upper thighs.

**underpart** *n* a part lying on the lower side.

**underpass** *n* a tunnel or road under another road or a railway.
**underpin** *v* (**underpinned, underpinning**) **1** to strengthen the foundation of (a structure). **2** to support or substantiate.
**underplay** *v* to represent as being less significant than is the case.
**underprivileged** *adj* lacking the normal social or economic conditions of a civilized society.
**underrate** *v* to undervalue or underestimate.
**underscore** *v* to underline.
**undersea** *adj* situated under the surface of the sea.
**undersecretary** *n* (*pl* **-ies**) **1** in Britain, a junior minister. **2** a civil servant subordinate to a principal secretary.
**undersell** *v* (*past tense and past part.* **undersold**) **1** to sell at a lower price than. **2** to make little of the merits of.
**underside** *n* the side or surface lying underneath.
**undersigned** *n* (**the undersigned**) the person or people whose names are signed at the end of a document.
**undersized** *adj* of less than normal size.
**understaffed** *adj* not having enough staff.
**understand** *v* (*past tense and past part.* **understood**) **1** to grasp the meaning of. **2** to have a thorough knowledge of or expertise in. **3** to assume or suppose. **4** to interpret in a particular way. **5** to supply mentally (something implied though not expressed). **6** to show sympathy or tolerance.
**understandable** *adj* **1** normal and reasonable. **2** capable of being understood. ➤ **understandably** *adv.*
**understanding**[1] *n* **1** a mental grasp or comprehension. **2** the power of comprehending. **3** a particular meaning or interpretation. **4** a friendly or harmonious relationship. **5** an informal mutual agreement. **6** tolerance or sympathy.
**understanding**[2] *adj* tolerant or sympathetic.
**understate** *v* to represent as being less significant than is the case. ➤ **understatement** *n.*
**understudy**[1] *v* (**-ies, -ied**) to study another actor's part in order to be able to take it over in an emergency.
**understudy**[2] *n* (*pl* **-ies**) an actor who learns another actor's part and takes it over if needed.
**undertake** *v* (**undertook, undertaken**) **1** to take on oneself as a task or responsibility. **2** to guarantee or promise to do something.
**undertaker** *n* somebody who prepares dead bodies for burial or cremation and organizes funerals.
**undertaking** *n* **1** an enterprise. **2** a pledge or guarantee. **3** the business of an undertaker.
**undertone** *n* **1** a low or subdued tone. **2** a quality or feeling underlying a statement or action.
**undertow** *n* an underwater current that flows in a different direction from the surface current.
**underwater** *adj and adv* situated or used below the surface of the water.
**underwear** *n* clothing worn under other clothing next to the skin.
**underweight** *adj* weighing less than the normal or suitable weight.
**underwhelm** *v humorous* to fail to impress.
**underworld** *n* **1** the world of organized crime. **2** in mythology, the place beneath the surface of the earth where the souls of the dead live.
**underwrite** *v* (**underwrote, underwritten**) **1** to assume liability for payment on (an insurance policy). **2** to guarantee financial support of. ➤ **underwriter** *n.*
**undesirable**[1] *adj* unwanted or objectionable. ➤ **undesirability** *n,* **undesirably** *adv.*
**undesirable**[2] *n* an undesirable or unpleasant person or thing.
**undeterred** *adj* not deterred by setbacks.
**undies** *pl n informal* items of underwear.
**undisputed** *adj* not questioned or challenged.
**undistinguished** *adj* lacking in distinction; not exceptional.
**undivided** *adj* **1** not split into separate parts. **2** complete; total.
**undo** *v* (**undid, undone**) **1** to open or loosen by releasing a fastening. **2** to reverse or cancel the effects of. **3** to destroy the standing or reputation of.
**undoing** *n* **1** ruin. **2** a cause of ruin or downfall.
**undoubted** *adj* not disputed; certain or genuine. ➤ **undoubtedly** *adv.*
**undreamed** *or* **undreamt** *adj* (*usu* + of) not unimagined or regarded as possible.
**undress**[1] *v* **1** to remove the clothes from (somebody). **2** to take off one's clothes.
**undress**[2] *n* a state of having little or no clothing on.
**undue** *adj* excessive or immoderate.
**undulate** *v* **1** to rise and fall in waves; to fluctuate. **2** to have a wavy form or appearance. ➤ **undulation** *n.*
**unduly** *adv* excessively.
**undying** *adj* eternal; perpetual.
**unearned** *adj* of income: not gained from employment.
**unearth** *v* **1** to dig up out of the ground. **2** to find or discover after searching.
**unearthly** *adj* **1** weird or mysterious. **2** *informal* unreasonable or preposterous: *at an unearthly hour.*
**unease** *n* a feeling of disquiet or awkwardness.
**uneasy** *adj* (**-ier, -iest**) **1** apprehensive or worried. **2** uncomfortable or awkward. **3** precarious or unstable. ➤ **uneasily** *adv,* **uneasiness** *n.*

**unedifying** *adj* unpleasant.
**uneducated** *adj* not well educated; ignorant.
**unemployable** *adj* not acceptable or fitted for any form of employment.
**unemployed** *adj* not having a paid job.
**unemployment** *n* **1** the state of being unemployed. **2** the number or percentage of unemployed people.
**unending** *adj* never ending; seeming to go on indefinitely. ➤ **unendingly** *adv.*
**unenviable** *adj* unpleasant or undesirable. ➤ **unenviably** *adv.*
**unequal** *adj* **1** not equal. **2** not fairly or evenly applied. **3** badly balanced or matched. **4** (+ to) not capable of taking on (a task). ➤ **unequally** *adv.*
**unequalled** (*NAmer* **unequaled**) *adj* better than all others.
**unequivocal** *adj* clear and unambiguous. ➤ **unequivocally** *adv.*
**unerring** *adj* faultless or unfailing. ➤ **unerringly** *adv.*
**UNESCO** *abbr* United Nations Educational, Scientific, and Cultural Organization.
**uneven** *adj* **1** not level or smooth. **2** irregular or inconsistent. **3** varying in quality. ➤ **unevenly** *adv,* **unevenness** *n.*
**uneventful** *adj* without anything important or interesting happening. ➤ **uneventfully** *adv.*
**unexceptionable** *adj* beyond reproach or criticism. ➤ **unexceptionably** *adv.*
**unexceptional** *adj* commonplace or ordinary. ➤ **unexceptionally** *adv.*
**unexpected** *adj* not expected or foreseen. ➤ **unexpectedly** *adv.*
**unexpurgated** *adj* not abridged or censored.
**unfailing** *adj* **1** able to be relied on; constant or sure. **2** continuous. ➤ **unfailingly** *adv.*
**unfair** *adj* not fair or just. ➤ **unfairly** *adv,* **unfairness** *n.*
**unfaithful** *adj* **1** not faithful; disloyal. **2** having sexual relations with a person other than one's spouse or partner. **3** inaccurate. ➤ **unfaithfully** *adv.*
**unfasten** *v* to loosen or untie.
**unfathomable** *adj* impossible to understand fully.
**unfavourable** (*NAmer* **unfavorable**) *adj* **1** expressing disapproval. **2** disadvantageous; adverse. ➤ **unfavourably** *adv.*
**unfazed** *adj informal* not disconcerted or daunted.
**unfit** *adj* **1** unsuitable or inappropriate. **2** in poor physical or mental condition. ➤ **unfitly** *adv,* **unfitness** *n.*
**unflagging** *adj* never flagging; tireless.
**unflappable** *adj informal* remaining calm and composed; imperturbable. ➤ **unflappably** *adv.*
**unflinching** *adj* not flinching or shrinking; steadfast. ➤ **unflinchingly** *adv.*
**unfold** *v* **1** to open and spread or straighten out (something folded). **2** to reveal or be revealed gradually.
**unforeseen** *adj* not predicted or expected. ➤ **unforeseeable** *adj.*
**unforgettable** *adj* memorable or exciting. ➤ **unforgettably** *adv.*
**unforgivable** *adj* too bad to be forgiven or excused. ➤ **unforgivably** *adv.*
**unfortunate**[1] *adj* **1** unsuccessful or unlucky. **2** resulting in misfortune. **3** unsuitable; inappropriate. ➤ **unfortunately** *adv.*
**unfortunate**[2] *n* an unlucky person.
**unfounded** *adj* lacking a sound basis; groundless.
**unfrequented** *adj* not often visited.
**unfunny** *adj* serious; not funny.
**unfurl** *v* to open out or unroll.
**ungainly** *adj* (**-ier, -iest**) clumsy or awkward. ➤ **ungainliness** *n.*
**ungenerous** *adj* not generous; mean or petty. ➤ **ungenerously** *adv.*
**ungetatable** *adj informal* inaccessible; unapproachable.
**ungodly** *adj* (**-ier, -iest**) **1** irreligious or impious. **2** wicked or immoral. **3** *informal* unreasonable or inconvenient. ➤ **ungodliness** *n.*
**ungovernable** *adj* not capable of being controlled or restrained.
**ungracious** *adj* **1** rude or impolite. **2** not pleasing; disagreeable. ➤ **ungraciously** *adv.*
**ungrateful** *adj* showing no gratitude. ➤ **ungratefully** *adv.*
**unguarded** *adj* **1** of a remark: hasty or careless. **2** without a guard or screen.
**unguent** *n* a soothing or healing ointment.
**ungulate** *n* a hoofed animal.
**unhappy** *adj* (**-ier, -iest**) **1** not happy; sad. **2** unfortunate; unlucky. **3** unsuitable. ➤ **unhappily** *adv,* **unhappiness** *n.*
**unharmed** *adj* not harmed.
**unhealthy** *adj* (**-ier, -iest**) **1** not in good health. **2** not conducive to good health. ➤ **unhealthily** *adv.*
**unheard** *adj* **1** not perceived by the ear. **2** disregarded.
**unheard-of** *adj* previously unknown.
**unhelpful** *adj* not helpful; uncooperative. ➤ **unhelpfully** *adv.*
**unheralded** *adj* not previously announced.
**unhesitating** *adj* prompt; without hesitation.
**unhinged** *adj* mentally unbalanced.
**unholy** *adj* (**-ier, -iest**) **1** wicked or immoral. **2** unnatural or harmful. **3** *informal* terrible; awful.
**unhurried** *adj* not hurried; leisurely. ➤ **unhurriedly** *adv.*
**unhurt** *adj* not hurt or harmed.
**unhygienic** *adj* not hygienic.

**unicameral** *adj* of a parliament: having a single legislative chamber.
**UNICEF** *abbr* United Nations Children's Fund.
**unicorn** *n* a mythical white horse with a horn on its forehead.
**unicycle** *n* a cycle with a single wheel. ➤ **unicyclist** *n.*
**unidentified** *adj* not known or identified.
**unification** *n* the process of unifying or the state of being unified.
**uniform**[1] *adj* not varying in character or appearance. ➤ **uniformity** *n,* **uniformly** *adv.*
**uniform**[2] *n* clothing of a distinctive design worn by members of a particular institution or group.
**unify** *v* (**-ies, -ied**) to make or become a unit or whole.
**unilateral** *adj* done or undertaken by only one person or group. ➤ **unilaterally** *adv.*
**unimaginative** *adj* **1** not given to creative thought. **2** not interesting or innovative. ➤ **unimaginatively** *adv.*
**unimpeachable** *adj* not to be doubted or blamed. ➤ **unimpeachably** *adv.*
**unimportant** *adj* having little or no importance. ➤ **unimportance** *n.*
**uninhabited** *adj* having no inhabitants.
**uninhibited** *adj* acting or speaking without regard for what others might think.
**uninitiated** *adj* lacking special knowledge or experience of something.
**uninspiring** *adj* not arousing interest or enthusiasm.
**unintelligible** *adj* impossible to understand. ➤ **unintelligibility** *n,* **unintelligibly** *adv.*
**unintentional** *adj* not done deliberately. ➤ **unintentionally** *adv.*
**uninterested** *adj* not interested or concerned.

***Usage Note:*** Do not confuse *uninterested* with *disinterested,* which means 'impartial'.

**uninterrupted** *adj* **1** not interrupted; continuous. **2** not obstructed.
**union** *n* **1** the act of joining two or more things into one. **2** a unified condition. **3** a marriage. **4** a club or association. **5** an organization run by students. **6** a trade union. **7** (*also* **Union**) a political unit made up from previously independent units. **8** (**the Union**) the northern states during the American Civil War.
**unionist** *n* **1** a member or supporter of a trade union. **2** (**Unionist**) a member of a political party in Northern Ireland that favours union with Great Britain. ➤ **unionism** *n.*
**unionize** *or* **-ise** *v* to join or cause to join a trade union. ➤ **unionization** *n.*
**Union Jack** *n* the national flag of the United Kingdom.
**unique** *adj* **1** being the only one; sole. **2** without a like or equal. **3** (+ to) belonging to or occurring in only one person, place, etc. ➤ **uniquely** *adv.*
**unisex** *adj* suitable or designed for either sex.
**unison** *n* the performing of several parts in a musical passage in harmony at the same time.
**unit** *n* **1** a single thing, person, or group that can form part of a larger whole. **2** a part of an organization that has a specific function. **3** a distinct military force forming part of a larger force. **4** an apparatus or device serving one particular function. **5** a building or group of buildings having a specified purpose. **6** an agreed quantity used as a standard of measurement.
**Unitarian** *n* a member of a Christian denomination that rejects the doctrine of the Trinity and believes that God is a single being. ➤ **Unitarian** *n.*
**unitary** *adj* **1** of or relating to a unit or units. **2** undivided; whole. ➤ **unitarily** *adv.*
**unite** *v* **1** to join together to form a single unit. **2** to form, or cause to form, an alliance or association. ➤ **united** *adj,* **unitive** *adj.*
**unit trust** *n* a company that invests in a range of shares on behalf of investors who can buy units of shares.
**unity** *n* (*pl* **-ies**) **1** the state of being one or united. **2** agreement or concord. **3** a whole made up of related parts. **4** the number one.
**universal** *adj* **1** including or concerning all in the world or in a particular area or group. **2** present or occurring everywhere or under all conditions. **3** adjustable to meet any requirements. ➤ **universality** *n,* **universally** *adv.*
**universe** *n* **1** all things that exist. **2** a sphere of activity.
**university** *n* (*pl* **-ies**) an institution of higher education that undertakes academic research and teaches degree courses.
**unjust** *adj* not just or fair. ➤ **unjustly** *adv.*
**unjustified** *adj* not justified; unfair or inappropriate.
**unkempt** *adj* untidy or dishevelled.
**unkind** *adj* not kind or sympathetic. ➤ **unkindly** *adv,* **unkindness** *n.*
**unknowable** *adj* that cannot be known or understood.
**unknowing** *adj* not knowing; unaware. ➤ **unknowingly** *adv.*
**unknown**[1] *adj* **1** not known. **2** not famous or familiar.
**unknown**[2] *n* somebody or something that is little known.
**unknown quantity** *n* (*pl* **-ies**) an unpredictable or idiosyncratic person or thing.
**Unknown Soldier** *n* an unidentified soldier whose body is buried in a national memorial as a representative of all the armed forces who died in a war.
**unladylike** *adj* of a woman: not showing good manners.

**unlawful** *adj* against the law or the rules. ➤ **unlawfully** *adv.*

**unleaded** *adj esp* of petrol: not treated with lead or lead compounds.

**unleash** *v* to loose from restraint or control.

**unleavened** *adj* of bread: containing no yeast or other raising agent.

**unless** *conj* if not; except when.

**unlicensed** *adj* not having a licence to sell alcoholic drinks.

**unlike**[1] *prep* **1** different from. **2** not characteristic of. **3** in contrast to.

**unlike**[2] *adj* dissimilar; different.

**unlikely** *adj* (**-ier, -iest**) **1** not likely to exist or occur. **2** not expected or believable. ➤ **unlikelihood** *n.*

**unlimited** *adj* **1** lacking any controls or restrictions. **2** boundless; infinite.

**unload** *v* **1** to remove cargo from a vehicle, ship, or aircraft. **2** to get rid of (something unwanted).

**unlock** *v* to unfasten the lock of (a door or container).

**unlooked-for** *adj* not foreseen or expected.

**unloose** *v* to release from restraints.

**unlovely** *adj* disagreeable or unpleasant.

**unlucky** *adj* (**-ier, -iest**) experiencing or causing bad luck or misfortune. ➤ **unluckily** *adv.*

**unmade** *adj Brit* of a road: not having a finished surface.

**unmanageable** *adj* difficult or impossible to handle or control. ➤ **unmanageably** *adv.*

**unmanly** *adj* weak or cowardly.

**unmanned** *adj* not having or needing a human crew.

**unmarried** *adj* not married; single.

**unmask** *v* to reveal the true character or nature of.

**unmatched** *adj* not matched or equalled.

**unmentionable** *adj* not fit to be mentioned; unspeakable.

**unmerciful** *adj* showing no mercy. ➤ **unmercifully** *adv.*

**unmindful** *adj* (+ of) not conscious of or considering.

**unmissable** *adj* too easy or too good to miss.

**unmistakable** or **unmistakeable** *adj* not capable of being mistaken; clear or obvious. ➤ **unmistakably** *adv.*

**unmitigated** *adj* **1** not diminished in intensity. **2** complete; downright.

**unmoved** *adj* not affected by emotion.

**unnatural** *adj* **1** not in accordance with nature or what is normal. **2** artificial or contrived. ➤ **unnaturally** *adv.*

**unnecessary** *adj* not necessary. ➤ **unnecessarily** *adv.*

**unnerve** *v* to cause to feel discouraged or uncertain.

**unnoticed** *adj* not seen or noticed.

**unobtainable** *adj* impossible to obtain.

**unobtrusive** *adj* not easily seen or noticed. ➤ **unobtrusively** *adv.*

**unoccupied** *adj* **1** not lived in. **2** not busy.

**unofficial** *adj* not authorized or official. ➤ **unofficially** *adv.*

**unopposed** *adj* not challenged or opposed.

**unorthodox** *adj* not conventional in behaviour, beliefs, etc.

**unpack** *v* to remove the contents of (a bag, suitcase, package, etc).

**unpaid** *adj* **1** not yet paid. **2** not paying a wage or fee. **3** not receiving payment.

**unpalatable** *adj* **1** not pleasing to the taste. **2** unpleasant or disagreeable. ➤ **unpalatably** *adv.*

**unparalleled** *adj* having no equal; unique.

**unpardonable** *adj* that cannot be forgiven. ➤ **unpardonably** *adv.*

**unperturbed** *adj* not disturbed or concerned.

**unpick** *v* **1** to undo (sewing) by taking out stitches. **2** to analyse (an argument, theory, etc) in detail.

**unpleasant** *adj* not pleasant or agreeable. ➤ **unpleasantly** *adv,* **unpleasantness** *n.*

**unplug** *v* (**unplugged, unplugging**) **1** to disconnect (an electrical appliance) by removing its plug from the socket. **2** to remove an obstruction from.

**unplumbed** *adj* not known or explored.

**unpopular** *adj* not generally liked or approved of. ➤ **unpopularity** *n.*

**unprecedented** *adj* having no precedent; not previously done.

**unpredictable** *adj* not predictable; changeable or erratic. ➤ **unpredictability** *n,* **unpredictably** *adv.*

**unprejudiced** *adj* impartial; fair.

**unpremeditated** *adj* not planned or intended.

**unprepared** *adj* not ready or made ready.

**unprepossessing** *adj* not attractive or pleasing.

**unpretentious** *adj* not pretentious or ostentatious. ➤ **unpretentiously** *adv.*

**unprincipled** *adj* lacking moral principles.

**unprintable** *adj* too controversial or offensive to be printed.

**unproductive** *adj* not producing much or having much use.

**unprofessional** *adj* not conforming to the standards of a profession. ➤ **unprofessionally** *adv.*

**unprofitable** *adj* **1** not yielding profit. **2** useless; vain. ➤ **unprofitably** *adv.*

**unpromising** *adj* seeming unlikely to succeed or be worthwhile.

**unpronounceable** *adj* too difficult to pronounce.

**unprovoked** *adj* done or happening without provocation.

**unqualified** *adj* **1** not having the necessary qualifications. **2** complete; utter.
**unquestionable** *adj* not able to be doubted or challenged. ➤ **unquestionably** *adv.*
**unquestioned** *adj* not doubted or challenged.
**unravel** *v* (**unravelled, unravelling,** *NAmer* **unraveled, unraveling**) **1** to separate the threads of (something knitted, woven, or tangled), or to become separated. **2** to solve (a problem or mystery). **3** to begin to fail.
**unreadable** *adj* **1** not legible. **2** too difficult or tedious to read.
**unready** *adj* not ready or prepared.
**unreal** *adj* **1** lacking in reality or substance. **2** strange or illusory. ➤ **unreality** *n.*
**unrealistic** *adj* not in accordance with reality or practicality. ➤ **unrealistically** *adv.*
**unreasonable** *adj* **1** not based on or according with reason. **2** excessive or immoderate. ➤ **unreasonably** *adv.*
**unrecognizable** *or* **unrecognisable** *adj* not able to be recognized.
**unrelenting** *adj* **1** not weakening in determination or severity. **2** continuing to show vigour. ➤ **unrelentingly** *adv.*
**unreliable** *adj* not able to be relied on. ➤ **unreliability** *n,* **unreliably** *adv.*
**unrelieved** *adj* unchanging or uninterrupted.
**unremitting** *adj* constant; incessant; never lessening.
**unrepeatable** *adj* **1** incapable of being repeated. **2** too shocking or offensive to be repeated.
**unrepentant** *adj* showing no shame or regret for wrongdoing.
**unrequited** *adj* of love: not returned.
**unreserved** *adj* **1** unqualified; without any reservation. **2** frank and open in manner. **3** not booked or set aside. ➤ **unreservedly** *adv.*
**unrest** *n* agitation or turmoil, *esp* caused by rebellion or dissatisfaction.
**unrivalled** (*NAmer* **unrivaled**) *adj* unequalled; better than all others.
**unroll** *v* to open out; to uncoil or unwind.
**unruffled** *adj* **1** poised and serene in the face of difficulty. **2** smooth; calm.
**unruly** *adj* (**-ier, -iest**) difficult to control or manage. ➤ **unruliness** *n.*
**unsafe** *adj* **1** not safe; dangerous. **2** of a legal verdict: based on unreliable or inadequate evidence.
**unsatisfactory** *adj* not acceptable or adequate. ➤ **unsatisfactorily** *adv.*
**unsaturated** *adj* **1** able to form products by chemical addition, esp containing double or triple bonds between carbon atoms. **2** of a fat: containing a high proportion of fatty acids with double bonds and less likely to result in higher cholesterol levels.
**unsavoury** (*NAmer* **unsavory**) *adj* **1** disagreeable or distasteful. **2** unpleasant to taste or smell.
**unscathed** *adj* entirely unharmed or uninjured.
**unschooled** *adj* untaught; untrained.
**unscientific** *adj* not in accordance with scientific principles. ➤ **unscientifically** *adv.*
**unscrew** *v* to unfasten or remove by twisting or by taking out screws.
**unscrupulous** *adj* without moral scruples; unprincipled. ➤ **unscrupulously** *adv.*
**unseasonable** *adj* **1** untimely. **2** not normal for the season of the year.
**unseasonal** *adj* not normal for the season of the year.
**unseat** *v* **1** to cause to fall from a seat or saddle. **2** to remove from a position of power.
**unseeing** *adj* not noticing anything.
**unseemly** *adj* not conforming to established standards of behaviour or taste.
**unseen** *adj* **1** not observed or perceived. **2** of a passage for translation: not previously seen by those for whom it is set.
**unselfish** *adj* not selfish; generous. ➤ **unselfishly** *adv.*
**unserviceable** *adj* not working or fit for use.
**unsettle** *v* to perturb or agitate.
**unsettled** *adj* **1** anxious or uneasy. **2** variable; changeable. **3** not resolved or worked out.
**unshakable** *or* **unshakeable** *adj* of a belief: incapable of being changed or set aside. ➤ **unshakably** *adv.*
**unshaven** *adj* not having shaved.
**unsightly** *adj* (**-ier, -iest**) not pleasing to the eye; ugly.
**unskilled** *adj* not having or needing a special skill.
**unsociable** *adj* not enjoying social activity. ➤ **unsociably** *adv.*
**unsocial** *adj* **1** unsociable. **2** of working hours: falling outside the normal working day. ➤ **unsocially** *adv.*
**unsolicited** *adj* not ordered or asked for.
**unsophisticated** *adj* **1** not socially or culturally sophisticated. **2** simple and straightforward.
**unsound** *adj* **1** not healthy or whole. **2** not firmly made or fixed. **3** not valid or true.
**unsparing** *adj* **1** hard or ruthless. **2** liberal; generous. ➤ **unsparingly** *adv.*
**unspeakable** *adj* too bad or shocking to be spoken. ➤ **unspeakably** *adv.*
**unspoilt** *adj* of a place: not spoilt by modern developments.
**unstable** *adj* **1** likely to fall; not firmly fixed. **2** unsteady or irregular. **3** given to changes of mood or an inability to control the emotions.
**unsteady** *adj* (**-ier, -iest**) **1** not firm or stable; likely to fall. **2** not uniform or even. ➤ **unsteadily** *adv.*
**unstick** *v* (*past tense and past part.* **unstuck**) to release from being stuck or fixed. * **come unstuck** to go wrong.

**unstinting** *adj* done or given generously.
**unsuccessful** *adj* not successful. ➤ **unsuccessfully** *adv.*
**unsuitable** *adj* not suitable or appropriate. ➤ **unsuitability** *n,* **unsuitably** *adv.*
**unsung** *adj* not celebrated or praised.
**unsure** *adj* not certain or confident.
**unsurpassed** *adj* better than all others.
**unsuspecting** *adj* unaware of something dangerous or undesirable.
**unsustainable** *adj* not able to be maintained or supported.
**unswerving** *adj* not turning aside; constant.
**unsympathetic** *adj* not sympathetic or understanding.
**unsystematic** *adj* not systematic.
**untangle** *v* **1** to unravel or free from tangles. **2** to make less confusing.
**untapped** *adj* of a resource: not yet exploited.
**untaught** *adj* not educated; ignorant.
**untenable** *adj* of an argument, theory, etc: not able to be defended.
**unthinkable** *adj* impossible to contemplate; out of the question.
**unthinking** *adj* **1** without thinking; heedless. **2** inconsiderate. ➤ **unthinkingly** *adv.*
**untidy** *adj* (**-ier, -iest**) not neat; slovenly or disorderly. ➤ **untidily** *adv,* **untidiness** *n.*
**untie** *v* (**unties, untied, untying**) to undo or unfasten.
**until** *prep and conj* up to as late or as far as (a specified time or event).
**untimely** *adj* **1** occurring before the natural or proper time. **2** happening at an unsuitable time.
**untitled** *adj* not having a title.
**unto** *prep archaic* to (a place or person).
**untold** *adj* **1** too many to be listed. **2** not told or revealed.
**untouchable**[1] *adj* **1** not able to be touched. **2** unable to be criticized or equalled.
**untouchable**[2] *n* a member of the lowest and formerly segregated Hindu caste.
**untouched** *adj* **1** not touched or handled. **2** not influenced; unaffected.
**untoward** *adj* unexpected and unwelcome.
**untrue** *adj* **1** false. **2** not faithful; disloyal.
**untrustworthy** *adj* unable to be trusted.
**unusable** *adj* not fit for use.
**unused** *adj* **1** /un'yoohzd/ not used; fresh or new. **2** /un'yoohst/ (+ to) unaccustomed to.
**unusual** *adj* **1** uncommon; rare. **2** exceptional. ➤ **unusually** *adv.*
**unutterable** *adj* too bad or unpleasant to describe. ➤ **unutterably** *adv.*
**unvarnished** *adj* **1** not varnished. **2** of facts: plainly expressed.
**unveil** *v* **1** to remove a veil or covering from. **2** to make public (something new).
**unwaged** *adj* not in paid employment.
**unwanted** *adj* not wanted or needed.
**unwarrantable** *adj* not justifiable; inexcusable. ➤ **unwarrantably** *adv.*
**unwarranted** *adj* not justified.
**unwary** *adj* not alert or cautious. ➤ **unwarily** *adv.*
**unwavering** *adj* fixed; steadfast.
**unwelcome** *adj* not welcome or wanted.
**unwell** *adj* ill.
**unwholesome** *adj* **1** having a harmful effect on health. **2** unpleasant in appearance.
**unwieldy** *adj* (**-ier, -iest**) awkward in shape or size for moving or handling.

***Usage Note:*** Note the spelling with *-ie-* and only one *l*.

**unwilling** *adj* not willing; reluctant. ➤ **unwillingly** *adv,* **unwillingness** *n.*
**unwind** *v* (*past tense and past part.* **unwound**) **1** to undo (something wound up). **2** to relax after effort or stress.
**unwitting** *adj* **1** not intended; inadvertent. **2** ignorant or unaware. ➤ **unwittingly** *adv.*
**unwonted** *adj* not usual or characteristic.
**unworkable** *adj* not practicable or feasible.
**unworldly** *adj* **1** naive or unsophisticated. **2** not interested in wealth or personal gain. **3** not of this world; spiritual. ➤ **unworldliness** *n.*
**unworn** *adj* not worn or damaged by use.
**unworthy** *adj* not worthy.
**unwrap** *v* (**unwrapped, unwrapping**) to remove the wrapping from.
**unwritten** *adj* of a law or rule: based on custom and precedent, and not codified.
**unyielding** *adj* **1** hard and inflexible. **2** stubborn or uncompromising.
**unzip** *v* (**unzipped, unzipping**) **1** to undo the zip of. **2** to decompress (a computer file).
**up**[1] *adv* **1** at or towards a relatively high level. **2** in or to a raised or upright position. **3** out of bed. **4** to the top; so as to be full. **5** in or into a relatively better condition. **6** above a normal or former level. **7** towards a higher number, degree, or rate. **8** in or into existence or prominence. * **up against 1** touching. **2** faced with; confronting. **up to 1** as far as; until. **2** equal to or good enough for. **3** being the responsibility or choice of.
**up**[2] *adj* **1** moving or directed upwards. **2** going on or taking place. **3** at an end. **4** of a road: being repaired.
**up**[3] *v* (**upped, upping**) *informal* to increase or raise.
**up**[4] *prep* **1** at or to a higher position on. **2** at the top of.
**up-and-coming** *adj* likely to succeed.
**upbeat** *adj informal* optimistic and cheerful.
**upbraid** *v* to scold or reproach.
**upbringing** *n* a particular way of educating and rearing a child.
**upcoming** *adj* about to happen; forthcoming.
**upcountry** *adj and adv* characteristic of an inland or outlying region.

**update**[1] *v* to bring up-to-date.
**update**[2] *n* **1** an act of updating. **2** something that has been updated.
**upend** *v* to cause to stand on end.
**up-front**[1] *adj* **1** paid or done in advance. **2** honest and candid.
**up-front**[2] *adv* in advance or at the beginning.
**upgrade**[1] *v* to improve the standard or performance of.
**upgrade**[2] *n* **1** the act or an instance of upgrading. **2** an upgraded version of something.
**upheaval** *n* a great disturbance or change.
**uphill**[1] *adv* upwards on a hill or incline.
**uphill**[2] *adj* **1** going up; ascending. **2** difficult or laborious: *an uphill task.*
**uphold** *v* (*past tense and past part.* **upheld**) **1** to give support to or maintain. **2** to support or defend against opposition or challenge.
**upholster** *v* to provide (e.g. a chair or sofa) with upholstery. ➤ **upholsterer** *n.*
**upholstery** *n* **1** the fabric, padding, and springs used to make a soft covering for furniture. **2** the art of upholstering furniture.
**upkeep** *n* the process or cost of maintaining something in good condition.
**upland** *n* (*also in pl*) an area of high land.
**uplift**[1] *v* **1** to raise or elevate. **2** to make (somebody) feel more hopeful or optimistic. ➤ **uplifting** *adj.*
**uplift**[2] *n* **1** the act or result of uplifting something. **2** support for the breasts provided by a bra, etc. **3** a quality or effect that produces hope or optimism.
**up-market** *adj* designed to appeal to more prosperous or sophisticated customers.
**upon** *prep formal* on or on top of.
**upper**[1] *adj* higher in physical position, rank, or order. * **have/get the upper hand** to have or gain a position of control or advantage.
**upper**[2] *n* the parts of a shoe or boot above the sole. * **on one's uppers** having no money.
**upper**[3] *n informal* a stimulant drug, *esp* an amphetamine.
**upper case** *n* capital letters, e.g. A, B, C rather than a, b, c. ➤ **upper-case** *adj.*
**upper class** *n* the class occupying the highest position in a society. ➤ **upper-class** *adj.*
**uppercut** *n* a swinging blow directed upwards with a bent arm.
**upper house** *n* in Britain, the House of Lords.
**uppermost** *adj and adv* in or into the highest or most prominent position.
**uppity** *adj informal* behaving in a superior or supercilious manner.
**upright**[1] *adj* **1** perpendicular; vertical. **2** having a greater height than width. **3** honest or honourable.
**upright**[2] *adv* in or into an upright position.
**upright**[3] *n* **1** a vertical support. **2** a piano with a vertical frame and strings.
**uprising** *n* a localized rebellion.
**upriver** *adv and adj* upstream.
**uproar** *n* **1** a noisy commotion or violent disturbance. **2** a noisy or violent protest.
**uproarious** *adj* **1** noisy and boisterous. **2** extremely funny. ➤ **uproariously** *adv.*
**uproot** *v* **1** to pull up by the roots. **2** to move (somebody) away from their home or country.
**upscale** *adj and adv chiefly NAmer* up-market.
**upset**[1] *v* (**upsetting,** *past tense and past part.* **upset**) **1** to make (somebody) unhappy, disappointed, or anxious. **2** to knock over or overturn. **3** to throw into disorder; to disrupt. **4** to make (somebody) slightly ill.
**upset**[2] *n* **1** an unexpected defeat or setback. **2** a slight illness. **3** an emotional disturbance.
**upset**[3] *adj* **1** unhappy, disappointed, or anxious. **2** physically disturbed or disordered.
**upshot** *n* the eventual result or outcome.
**upside** *n* the favourable aspect of something.
**upside down** *adv and adj* **1** with the upper and the lower parts reversed. **2** in disorder or confusion.
**upsilon** *n* the 20th letter of the Greek alphabet (Υ, υ).
**upstage**[1] *adv and adj* at or towards the back of a theatre stage.
**upstage**[2] *v* to steal attention from (somebody else) by doing something better or more exciting.
**upstairs** *adv and adj* on or to a higher floor.
**upstanding** *adj* honest and respectable.
**upstart** *n* somebody who behaves arrogantly when given authority.
**upstate** *adv and adj* to or in the part of a US state away from city areas.
**upstream** *adv and adj* in the direction opposite to the flow of a stream or river.
**upsurge** *n* a rapid or sudden rise.
**uptake** *n* the act of accepting or starting to use something. * **quick/slow on the uptake** *informal* quick or slow to understand.
**uptight** *adj informal* **1** tense or nervous. **2** angry or indignant.
**up-to-date** *adj* **1** knowing or including the latest information or developments. **2** abreast of the times; modern.
**up-to-the-minute** *adj* completely up-to-date.
**upturn**[1] *v* to turn up or upside down.
**upturn**[2] *n* a change towards better conditions.
**upward** *adj* moving or extending upwards; ascending.
**upwards** *adv* from a lower to a higher place or level.
**upwind** *adv and adj* in the direction from which the wind is blowing.
**uranium** *n* a radioactive metallic element used as fuel in nuclear reactors.
**urban** *adj* relating to or part of a city or town.
**urbane** *adj* **1** courteous and suave in manner. **2** elegant or sophisticated. ➤ **urbanity** *n.*
**urchin** *n* a poor and dishevelled young child.

**Urdu** *n* the language of Pakistan, Bangladesh, and parts of India.

**ureter** *n* a duct that carries urine from the kidney to the bladder.

**urethra** *n* (*pl* **urethras** *or* **urethrae**) the canal that carries urine from the bladder out of the body, and in the male also conveys semen. ➤ **urethral** *adj.*

**urge**[1] *v* **1** to encourage or try hard to persuade. **2** to advocate or demand.

**urge**[2] *n* a strong impulse or desire.

**urgent** *adj* **1** calling for immediate attention. **2** persistent or demanding. ➤ **urgency** *n,* **urgently** *adv.*

**urinal** *n* a fixture attached to a wall in a public toilet, for men to urinate into.

**urinate** *v* to pass urine out of the body. ➤ **urination** *n.*

**urine** *n* liquid waste material secreted by the kidney and stored in the bladder until passed out of the body. ➤ **urinary** *adj.*

**URL** *abbr* uniform resource locator: the address of a page on the World Wide Web.

**urn** *n* **1** a container for the ashes of a dead person. **2** a large closed container with a tap, for making and serving tea or coffee.

**ursine** *adj* of or resembling a bear.

**US** *abbr* United States.

**us** *pron* used as the objective case: we.

**USA** *abbr* United States of America.

**usable** *or* **useable** *adj* capable of being used. ➤ **usability** *n.*

**usage** *n* **1** established practice or procedure. **2** the action or manner of using something.

**use**[1] /yoohs/ *n* **1** the action or manner of using something. **2** the right or benefit of using something. **3** the ability or power to use a part of the body. **4** a purpose or end. **5** practical worth or application. * **make use of** to use or take advantage of.

**use**[2] /yoohz/ *v* **1** to put into action or service. **2** to employ for a specified purpose. **3** to expend or consume. **4** to consume or take regularly. **5** to exploit (somebody) as a means to one's own ends. **6** to treat (somebody or something) in a specified manner.

**used** *adj* **1** /yoohzd/ secondhand. **2** /yoohst/ accustomed; habituated. * **be used to** to be familiar with or accustomed to. **used to** expressing a habitual action or state in the past: *I used to play golf.*

**useful** *adj* having a practical worth or application. ➤ **usefully** *adv,* **usefulness** *n.*

**useless** *adj* **1** having no use or purpose. **2** *informal* lacking skill or aptitude. ➤ **uselessly** *adv.*

**user** *n* somebody who uses something.

**user-friendly** *adj* easy to operate or understand.

**use up** *v* to consume completely.

**usher**[1] *n* **1** somebody who shows people to their seats in a theatre, cinema, or church. **2** an official who performs routine tasks in a court of law.

**usher**[2] *v* **1** to guide or escort to a place. **2** (*usu* + in) to introduce.

**usherette** *n* a woman who shows people to their seats in a theatre or cinema.

**USSR** *abbr* formerly, Union of Soviet Socialist Republics.

**usual** *adj* commonly or ordinarily done or used. ➤ **usually** *adv.*

**usurer** *n* somebody who lends money at an exorbitant rate of interest. ➤ **usury** *n.*

**usurp** *v* to seize authority wrongfully from. ➤ **usurpation** *n,* **usurper** *n.*

**utensil** *n* a tool or container used in the household.

**uterus** *n* (*pl* **uteri**) the female organ that contains and nourishes the young before birth; the womb. ➤ **uterine** *adj.*

**utilitarian** *adj* practical and useful rather than attractive.

**utilitarianism** *n* the theory that what matters is the greatest happiness of the greatest number.

**utility** *n* (*pl* **-ies**) **1** fitness to be used for some purpose. **2** an organization performing a public service, e.g. providing gas, electricity, or water.

**utility room** *n* a room containing a washing machine and other domestic equipment.

**utilize** *or* **-ise** *v* to make practical use of. ➤ **utilization** *n.*

**utmost**[1] *adj* farthest, greatest, or most extreme.

**utmost**[2] *n* the highest point or degree.

**utopia** *or* **Utopia** *n* an imagined place or state of perfection.

**utopian** *or* **Utopian** *adj* impossibly ideal. ➤ **utopianism** *n.*

**utter**[1] *adj* absolute; total. ➤ **utterly** *adv.*

**utter**[2] *v* to emit as sound or language.

**utterance** *n* **1** a sound or statement made. **2** the act of speaking.

**uttermost** *adj and n* = UTMOST[1], UTMOST[2].

**U-turn** *n* **1** the forward turning of a vehicle to face the opposite direction. **2** a total reversal of policy.

**uvula** *n* (*pl* **uvulas** *or* **uvulae**) the fleshy lobe hanging from the back of the soft palate. ➤ **uvular** *adj.*

**uxorious** *adj formal* excessively fond of one's wife.

**V**[1] *or* **v** *n* (*pl* **V's** *or* **Vs** *or* **v's**) **1** the 22nd letter of the English alphabet. **2** the Roman numeral for five.

**V**[2] *abbr* volt.

**V**[3] *abbr* the chemical symbol for vanadium.

**v** *abbr* versus.

**vacancy** *n* (*pl* **-ies**) **1** an unfilled job or position. **2** an unoccupied room in a hotel or guest house. **3** empty space.

**vacant** *adj* **1** of a job or position: awaiting an appointment. **2** of a room or building: not occupied or lived in. **3** of the face: showing no expression. ➤ **vacantly** *adv.*

**vacate** *v* **1** to give up the possession or occupancy of (a room or building). **2** to leave (a job or position). ➤ **vacatable** *adj.*

**vacation**[1] *n* **1** a period during which the activity of an institution, e.g. a university or law court, is suspended. **2** the act of vacating a place. **3** *NAmer* a holiday.

**vacation**[2] *v NAmer* to take a holiday.

**vaccinate** *v* to inject with a vaccine. ➤ **vaccination** *n.*

**vaccine** *n* a substance prepared from organisms that cause a disease, injected into the body to increase immunity.

**vacillate** *v* **1** to hesitate or waver about something. **2** to fluctuate. ➤ **vacillation** *n.*

**vacuous** *adj* **1** stupid; inane. **2** idle; aimless. ➤ **vacuity** *n.*

**vacuum**[1] *n* (*pl* **vacuums** *or* **vacua**) **1** a space containing no matter or from which air or other matter has been removed. **2** a state in which an important person or thing is missing and has not been replaced.

**vacuum**[2] *v informal* to clean using a vacuum cleaner.

**vacuum cleaner** *n* an electrical appliance for removing dust and dirt by means of suction.

**vacuum flask** *n Brit* a container with a vacuum between an inner and an outer wall used to keep liquids hot or cold.

**vagabond** *n* a wanderer or tramp.

**vagary** *n* (*pl* **-ies**) an erratic or unpredictable action, change, etc.

**vagina** *n* (*pl* **vaginas**) a canal in a female mammal that leads from the womb to an external opening. ➤ **vaginal** *adj.*

**vagrant**[1] *n* a person who has no home or means of support.

**vagrant**[2] *adj* living as a vagrant. ➤ **vagrancy** *n.*

**vague** *adj* **1** not precise in meaning or clearly expressed. **2** not thinking or expressing one's thoughts clearly or precisely. **3** not sharply outlined; hazy. ➤ **vaguely** *adv,* **vagueness** *n.*

**vain** *adj* **1** having or showing excessive pride in one's appearance or abilities. **2** of an attempt: unsuccessful or ineffectual. ✱ **in vain** without success or result. ➤ **vainly** *adv.*

**vainglorious** *adj literary* excessively proud or boastful.

**valance** *or* **valence** *n* **1** a piece of drapery hung as a border along the edge of a bed, canopy, or shelf. **2** a pelmet.

**vale** *n literary* a valley.

**valediction** *n formal* **1** an act of saying farewell. **2** a statement of farewell.

**valedictory** *adj formal* expressing a farewell.

**valency** (*NAmer* **valence**) *n* (*pl* **-ies**) the degree of combining power of an element as shown by the number of atomic weights of hydrogen with which the atomic weight of the element will combine or for which it can be substituted.

**valentine** *n* **1** a lover or sweetheart chosen on St Valentine's Day, 14 February. **2** a greeting card sent or given to such a person.

**valerian** *n* **1** a perennial plant, some types of which have medicinal properties. **2** a sedative drug made from the roots of valerian.

**valet**[1] *n* an employee who attends to day-to-day needs for a man, the guests at a hotel, etc.

**valet**[2] *v* (**valeted, valeting**) **1** to serve (somebody) as a valet. **2** to clean (a car) as a service.

**valetudinarian** *n formal* a weak or sickly person, *esp* a hypochondriac.

**valiant** *adj* showing valour or courage. ➤ **valiantly** *adv.*

**valid** *adj* **1** well-grounded or justifiable. **2** of an argument: logically sound. **3** having legal force or value. ➤ **validity** *n.*

**validate** *v* **1** to make legally valid. **2** to corroborate or authenticate. ➤ **validation** *n.*

**valise** *n* a small travelling bag or case.

**Valium** *n trademark* a tranquillizing drug used to treat anxiety.

**valley** *n* (*pl* **-eys**) a low-lying area between hills or mountains.

**valour** (*NAmer* **valor**) *n* personal bravery in the face of danger. ➤ **valorous** *adj.*

**valuable** *adj* **1** having high money value. **2** of great use or worth. ➤ **valuably** *adv.*
**valuables** *pl n* personal possessions having a high money value.
**valuation** *n* **1** the process of valuing property or valuables. **2** the estimated value of something.
**value**[1] *n* **1** the worth in money or commodities of something. **2** relative worth, usefulness, or importance. **3** (*usu in pl*) a moral principle or standard of behaviour. **4** a numerical quantity assigned or computed. **5** the magnitude of a physical quantity. **6** the relative duration of a musical note.
**value**[2] *v* (**values, valued, valuing**) **1** (*often* + at) to estimate the money worth of. **2** to rate in terms of usefulness or importance. **3** to consider or rate highly. ➤ **valuer** *n.*
**value-added tax** *n* a tax levied on goods and services based on the increase of value at each stage of their development.
**valve** *n* **1** a structure in the heart or a vein that restricts the flow of blood to one direction only. **2** a mechanical device for controlling the flow of liquid, gas, or loose material. **3** a device in a brass musical instrument for varying the tube length to change the note.
**vamp**[1] *n informal* a woman who uses her charm to seduce men. ➤ **vampish** *adj.*
**vamp**[2] *v informal* (+ up) to rework (something old) with new material or in a new way.
**vampire** *n* **1** a dead person believed to come from the grave at night and suck the blood of sleeping people. **2** (*also* **vampire bat**) a South American bat that feeds on blood. ➤ **vampirism** *n.*
**van**[1] *n* **1** a motor vehicle used for transporting goods. **2** *Brit* an enclosed railway goods wagon.
**van**[2] *n* the leading people in a group or movement.
**vanadium** *n* a grey chemical element used in alloys.
**vandal** *n* a person who deliberately destroys or damages property. ➤ **vandalism** *n.*
**vandalize** *or* **-ise** *v* to destroy or damage (property) deliberately.
**vane** *n* a thin flat or curved blade that is moved about an axis by wind or water.
**vanguard** *n* **1** the troops moving at the head of an army. **2** the leading people in an action or movement.
**vanilla** *n* a flavouring obtained from the pod of a tropical American climbing orchid.
**vanish** *v* **1** to pass quickly from sight; to disappear. **2** to cease to exist.
**vanity** *n* (*pl* **-ies**) **1** excessive pride in oneself; conceit. **2** the quality of being vain or futile.
**vanity case** *n* a women's small case for carrying toilet articles and cosmetics.
**vanquish** *v literary* to defeat or overcome.
**vantage** *n* a position giving a strategic advantage.
**vantage point** *n* a place or position that affords a clear view over an area.
**vapid** *adj* lacking liveliness or interest. ➤ **vapidity** *n.*
**vaporize** *or* **-ise** *v* to convert (liquid) into vapour. ➤ **vaporization** *n,* **vaporizer** *n.*
**vapour** (*NAmer* **vapor**) *n* **1** smoke, fog, etc suspended in the air. **2** a substance in the gaseous state that is liquid under normal conditions. ➤ **vaporous** *adj.*
**variable**[1] *adj* **1** able to vary or be varied. **2** of behaviour, etc: fickle or inconstant. ➤ **variability** *n,* **variably** *adv.*
**variable**[2] *n* **1** something that varies or that can be varied. **2** a quantity that may assume any of a set of values. **3** a symbol representing a variable quantity or entity. **4** a variable wind. **5** (*in pl*) a region where variable winds occur.
**variance** *n* **1** the fact or quality of being variable or variant. **2** the state of disagreeing or disputing. * **at variance with** not agreeing with.
**variant** *n* something that shows variation from a type or norm.
**variation** *n* **1** the act or extent of varying. **2** something showing variation. **3** a varied version of a musical idea.
**varicose** *adj* of a vein: abnormally swollen or dilated.
**varied** *adj* **1** having different forms or types. **2** having a variety of contents or parts.
**variegated** *adj* marked with patches of different colours. ➤ **variegation** *n.*
**variety** *n* (*pl* **-ies**) **1** the state of varying; diversity. **2** an assortment of differing things of the same general kind. **3** something differing from others of the same general kind. **4** a group of plants or animals ranking below a species. **5** theatrical entertainment consisting of songs, sketches, acrobatics, etc.
**various** *adj* **1** of differing kinds or forms. **2** more than one; several. ➤ **variously** *adv.*
**varnish**[1] *n* a liquid coating that forms a hard shiny surface when it dries.
**varnish**[2] *v* to apply varnish to.
**vary** *v* (**-ies, -ied**) **1** to show or undergo change. **2** (*usu* + from) to deviate. **3** to make a change in. **4** to ensure variety in.
**vascular** *adj* relating to the system of channels conducting blood, sap, etc in a plant or animal.
**vas deferens** /ˌvaz ˈdefərenz, ˌvas/ *n* (*pl* **vasa deferentia**) the duct that carries sperm from the testis to the penis.
**vase** *n* an ornamental vessel used for holding flowers.
**vasectomy** *n* (*pl* **-ies**) surgical cutting out of a section of the vas deferens as a means of sterilization.

**Vaseline** *n trademark* a type of petroleum jelly.

**vassal** *n* in a feudal society, a man who vowed loyalty to a lord in return for protection and land.

**vast** *adj* very great in amount, degree, or intensity. ➤ **vastly** *adv*, **vastness** *n*.

**VAT** *n Brit* value-added tax.

**Vatican** *n* (**the Vatican**) the official residence of the pope in Rome.

**vaudeville** *n* a light theatrical entertainment combining pantomime, dancing, and song.

**vault**[1] *n* **1** an arched structure forming a ceiling or roof. **2** a cellar or room with an arched ceiling. **3** an underground room or store. **4** a strongroom or compartment for valuables. **5** a burial chamber beneath a church or in a cemetery. ➤ **vaulted** *adj*.

**vault**[2] *v* to leap over something using the hands or a pole. ➤ **vaulter** *n*.

**vault**[3] *n* the act of vaulting.

**vaunt** *v* to call attention to (one's achievements), proudly or boastfully. ➤ **vaunted** *adj*.

**VC** *abbr* Victoria Cross.

**VCR** *abbr* videocassette recorder.

**VDU** *n* a visual display unit.

**veal** *n* the meat of a calf.

**vector** *n* **1** a quantity, e.g. velocity or force, that has magnitude and direction. **2** an organism that transmits a disease-causing agent.

**Veda** /'veedə, 'vaydə/ *n* a collection of Hindu sacred writings.

**veer** *v* **1** to change direction. **2** of the wind: to shift in a clockwise direction.

**vegan** *n* a strict vegetarian who avoids products derived from animals.

**vegetable** *n* **1** a plant grown for food. **2** *derog* a person with impaired mental capability caused by brain damage.

**vegetal** *adj formal* relating to plants.

**vegetarian** *n* a person who does not eat meat. ➤ **vegetarianism** *n*.

**vegetate** *v* to lead a dull inactive existence.

**vegetation** *n* plant life.

**vegetative** *adj* **1** relating to nutrition and growth. **2** involving propagation by nonsexual processes. **3** relating to involuntary bodily functions. **4** inactive.

**vehement** *adj* intensely felt or expressed; impassioned. ➤ **vehemence** *n*, **vehemently** *adv*.

**vehicle** *n* **1** an object with wheels and an engine used to carry people or goods, e.g. a car, bus, or lorry. **2** a medium through which something is expressed or communicated. ➤ **vehicular** *adj*.

**veil**[1] *n* **1** a length of cloth worn by women as a covering for the head or face. **2** something that hides or obscures. **3** a disguise or pretext. **4** the outer covering of a nun's headdress. ✻ **draw a veil over** to avoid mentioning (something unwelcome).

**veil**[2] *v* to cover with a veil.

**veiled** *adj* **1** thinly disguised. **2** indistinct or muffled.

**vein** *n* **1** any of the tubes that carry blood towards the heart. **2** a blood vessel. **3** a streak of a different colour in wood, marble, cheese, etc. **4** any of the ribs forming the framework of a leaf. **5** any of the thickened ribs that stiffen the wings of an insect. **6** a deposit of ore, coal, etc in rock. **7** a distinctive element or quality. **8** a mood or frame of mind. ➤ **veined** *adj*.

**Velcro** *n trademark* a fastening device consisting of two strips of fabric that stick to each other.

**veld** *or* **veldt** /velt, felt/ *n* open grassland in southern Africa.

**vellum** *n* a fine parchment for writing on.

**velociraptor** *n* a ferocious dinosaur that walked on two legs.

**velocity** *n* (*pl* **-ies**) speed in a given direction.

**velour** *or* **velours** *n* (*pl* **velours**) a fabric with a pile or surface resembling velvet.

**velvet** *n* a fabric with a short soft pile. ➤ **velvety** *adj*.

**velveteen** *n* a fabric with a short pile like velvet.

**venal** *adj* open to bribery. ➤ **venality** *n*.

**vend** *v* to sell (goods) in a small way.

**vendetta** *n* a blood feud arising from the murder of a member of one family by a member of another.

**vending machine** *n* a coin-operated machine for selling small items.

**vendor** *or* **vender** *n* **1** a seller of small items. **2** in law, the seller of a property.

**veneer** *n* **1** a thin layer of wood, plastic, etc forming the surface of a cheaper material. **2** a superficially or deceptively attractive appearance. ➤ **veneered** *adj*.

**venerable** *adj* commanding respect through age, character, and achievements.

**venerate** *v* to respect or regard with honour. ➤ **veneration** *n*.

**venereal disease** *n* a disease contracted from sexual contact.

**Venetian** *n* a native or inhabitant of Venice. ➤ **Venetian** *adj*.

**venetian blind** *n* a window blind made of horizontal slats that can be adjusted to vary the amount of light admitted.

**vengeance** *n* punishment inflicted on somebody in retaliation for an injury received or offence felt. ✻ **with a vengeance** with great force or intensity.

**vengeful** *adj* wanting or seeking revenge. ➤ **vengefully** *adv*.

**venial** *adj* of a wrongdoing: minor and pardonable.

**venison** *n* the meat of a deer.

**Venn diagram** *n* a graph that uses circles to represent sets, the circles overlapping to show common elements.

**venom** *n* **1** poison secreted by the bites of snakes, scorpions, etc. **2** strong hatred or malevolence.
**venomous** *adj* **1** poisonous. **2** spiteful or malevolent. ➤ **venomously** *adv.*
**venous** *adj* relating to a vein or the veins.
**vent**[1] *n* an opening for the escape of a gas or liquid or for the relief of pressure. ✱ **give vent to** to express (feelings) forcefully.
**vent**[2] *v* **1** to release (gas, etc) through a vent. **2** to express (feelings) forcefully.
**vent**[3] *n* a slit in a garment.
**ventilate** *v* to cause air to circulate through (a room or building). ➤ **ventilation** *n.*
**ventilator** *n* **1** an apparatus or opening for circulating fresh air. **2** an apparatus for providing artificial respiration for a patient who cannot breathe normally.
**ventral** *adj* relating to the front, lower, or inner surface of something.
**ventricle** *n* a chamber of the heart that receives blood from a corresponding atrium and from which blood is pumped into the arteries.
**ventriloquism** *n* the technique of projecting the voice so that it seems to come from a source other than the speaker, used to make a dummy appear to speak, as entertainment. ➤ **ventriloquist** *n.*
**venture**[1] *v* **1** (*often* + out/forth) to proceed despite danger or difficulty. **2** to offer (a controversial opinion).
**venture**[2] *n* **1** an undertaking involving risk or danger. **2** money or property at risk in a speculative venture.
**venturesome** *adj* ready to take risks; daring.
**venue** *n* the place where a gathering or event takes place.
**Venus flytrap** *or* **Venus's-flytrap** *n* a plant with leaves that snap together to trap and digest insects.
**veracious** *adj formal* truthful; honest. ➤ **veracity** *n.*
**veranda** *or* **verandah** *n* a roofed open gallery or portico along the outside of a building.
**verb** *n* a word that expresses an action or state, e.g. *run, give, be.*
**verbal** *adj* **1** involving or expressed in words. **2** spoken rather than written. **3** of or formed from a verb. ➤ **verbally** *adv.*
**verbalize** *or* **-ise** *v* to express in words.
**verbatim** /vuh'baytim, və-/ *adv and adj* in the exact words used.
**verbiage** *n* use of an unnecessary number of words.
**verbose** *adj* using more words than necessary. ➤ **verbosity** *n.*
**verdant** *adj* green with growing plants.
**verdict** *n* **1** the decision of a jury about the guilt or innocence of an accused. **2** an opinion or judgment.
**verdigris** *n* a green or bluish deposit formed on copper, brass, or bronze surfaces.
**verdure** *n* growing green vegetation.
**verge**[1] *n* **1** something that forms a border or limit. **2** *Brit* a planted strip of land at the side of a road. **3** the brink or threshold of something.
**verge**[2] *v* ✱ **verge on** to resemble or come near to.
**verger** *n* a church official who acts as an usher and caretaker.
**verify** *v* (**-ies, -ied**) **1** to establish the truth, accuracy, or reality of. **2** to confirm or fulfil. ➤ **verifiable** *adj,* **verification** *n.*
**verily** *adv archaic* certainly; truly.
**verisimilitude** *n formal* the quality of appearing to be true.
**veritable** *adj* actual; not false or imaginary. ➤ **veritably** *adv.*
**verity** *n* (*pl* **-ies**) **1** the quality being true or real. **2** a true statement.
**vermicelli** /vuhmi'cheli/ *pl n* **1** pasta in the form of long thin threads. **2** tiny strands of sugar or chocolate used as a decoration on cakes.
**vermilion** *or* **vermillion** *n* a brilliant red colour or pigment.
**vermin** *pl n* **1** lice, rats, or other common harmful animals. **2** birds and mammals that prey on game. ➤ **verminous** *adj.*
**vermouth** *n* a dry or sweet wine flavoured with aromatic herbs.
**vernacular** *n* **1** the language spoken by the ordinary people of a region. **2** *informal* the mode of expression of a group or class.
**vernal** *adj* of or occurring in the spring.
**verruca** *n* (*pl* **verrucas**) a wart on the underside of the foot.
**versatile** *adj* able to turn to or be turned to a variety of activities or uses. ➤ **versatility** *n.*
**verse** *n* **1** writing having a fixed rhythm and metre. **2** a distinct short section of a poem, song, or hymn. **3** each of the short divisions of a chapter of the Bible.
**versed** *adj* (+ in) having knowledge of or skill in something.
**versify** *v* (**-ies, -ied**) to write verses, or turn (words) into verse. ➤ **versification** *n.*
**version** *n* **1** an account or description of something told from a particular point of view. **2** a form or variant of a type or original. **3** an adaptation or arrangement of a work of art or piece of music.
**verso** *n* (*pl* **-os**) a left-hand page.
**versus** *prep* **1** against. **2** in contrast to.
**vertebra** *n* (*pl* **vertebrae** *or* **vertebras**) each of the bony segments forming the spinal column. ➤ **vertebral** *adj.*
**vertebrate** *n* an animal that has a backbone, e.g. a mammal, bird, reptile, amphibian, or fish.
**vertex** *n* (*pl* **vertices** *or* **vertexes**) **1** the highest

point. **2** in mathematics, the point where lines or curves meet or cross each other.

**vertical**[1] *adj* going up or down at right angles to a horizontal line or surface. ➤ **verticality** *n*, **vertically** *adv*.

**vertical**[2] *n* **1** verticality. **2** a vertical line or surface.

**vertiginous** *adj* very high or steep and likely to cause vertigo.

**vertigo** *n* a state of imbalance and dizziness caused by looking down from a high position.

**verve** *n* energy or vitality.

**very**[1] *adv* **1** to a high degree; exceedingly. **2** used for emphasis: *the very best*.

**very**[2] *adj* **1** actual; same: *the very man*. **2** mere: *the very thought of it*.

**Vesak** *n* a Buddhist festival held in May.

**vespers** *n* a service of evening worship.

**vessel** *n* **1** a large structure designed to travel on water; a ship or large boat. **2** a container for liquid, e.g. a jug, cup, or bowl. **3** a tube or canal in which fluid is carried in the body or in a plant.

**vest**[1] *n* **1** *Brit* a sleeveless undergarment for the upper body. **2** *NAmer* a waistcoat.

**vest**[2] *v* to give a legal right or title to.

**vested interest** *n* **1** a personal interest in the outcome of a situation or action, *esp* when bringing financial benefit. **2** an interest carrying a legal right.

**vestibule** *n* a lobby or chamber between the outer door and the interior of a building.

**vestige** *n* **1** a trace left by something that has disappeared. **2** a minute amount. ➤ **vestigial** *adj*.

**vestment** *n* a ceremonial garment worn by members of the clergy or of a church choir.

**vestry** *n* (*pl* **-ies**) a room in a church where the clergy put on vestments.

**vet**[1] *n* a veterinary surgeon.

**vet**[2] *v* (**vetted, vetting**) to subject (somebody) to thorough investigation or appraisal before giving them a job or responsibility.

**vetch** *n* a plant of the pea family, used for fodder and improving the soil.

**veteran** *n* **1** a person who has had long experience of an occupation or skill. **2** *NAmer* a former member of the armed forces.

**veterinarian** *n NAmer* a veterinary surgeon.

**veterinary** *adj* relating to the medical care of animals.

**veterinary surgeon** *n* a person who is qualified to treat diseases and injuries of animals.

**veto**[1] *n* (*pl* **-oes**) **1** the right to forbid or reject a decision or proposal. **2** the process of exercising this right.

**veto**[2] *v* (**vetoes, vetoed, vetoing**) to use a veto against (a decision or proposal).

**vex** *v* to cause annoyance or distress to. ➤ **vexation** *n*, **vexatious** *adj*.

**vexed** *adj* **1** annoyed or distressed. **2** of a question or issue: controversial and having no satisfactory solution.

**VHF** *abbr* very high frequency.

**VHS** *abbr trademark* video home system.

**via** *prep* **1** passing through or calling at (a place) on the way. **2** through the medium of; by means of.

**viable** *adj* **1** capable of working; practicable. **2** of a foetus: developed enough to be capable of living. **3** capable of growing or developing. ➤ **viability** *n*.

**viaduct** *n* a long bridge carrying a road or railway over a deep valley.

**vial** *n* = PHIAL.

**viands** *pl n archaic* food.

**vibes** *pl n informal* the emotional atmosphere of a place.

**vibrant** *adj* **1** oscillating or pulsating rapidly. **2** full of life and vigour. **3** of sound: strong and resonant. **4** of colour: vivid. ➤ **vibrancy** *n*, **vibrantly** *adv*.

**vibraphone** *n* an electric percussion instrument producing a vibrato.

**vibrate** *v* **1** to move to and fro rapidly. **2** of a sound: to resonate.

**vibration** *n* **1** the action of vibrating. **2** *informal* (*in pl*) the characteristic emotional atmosphere of a place.

**vibrato** /vi'brahtoh/ *n* an expressive musical effect produced by rapid slight variations in pitch.

**vibrator** *n* a vibrating electrical apparatus used in massage or for sexual stimulation.

**vicar** *n* in the Church of England, a member of the clergy in charge of a parish.

**vicarage** *n* a vicar's house.

**vicarious** *adj* **1** experienced through imaginative sharing of another's experience. **2** delegated. ➤ **vicariously** *adv*.

**vice**[1] *n* **1** immoral or corrupt behaviour. **2** criminal trade in prostitution and drugs. **3** a grave moral fault. **4** a habitual minor fault or shortcoming.

**vice**[2] (*NAmer* **vise**) *n* a tool with adjustable jaws that hold an object tightly to be worked on.

**vice-** *comb. form* next in rank to; deputy: *vice-president*.

**viceroy** *n* an official sent by a sovereign to govern a subject territory.

**vice versa** /ˌvies 'vuhsə, ˌviesi/ *adv* with the order changed or reversed; conversely.

**vicinity** *n* (*pl* **-ies**) a surrounding area or district.

**vicious** *adj* **1** cruel and violent. **2** fierce and dangerous. ➤ **viciously** *adv*, **viciousness** *n*.

**vicious circle** *n* a situation in which dealing with one difficulty creates a new difficulty that makes the original difficulty worse.

**vicissitudes** *pl n* unpredictable changes in human fortunes.

**victim** *n* **1** a person who is killed, injured, deceived, or mistreated. **2** a living animal or person offered as a sacrifice in a religious rite.

**victimize** *or* **-ise** *v* **1** to punish or mistreat selectively. **2** to make a victim of. ➤ **victimization** *n.*

**victor** *n* a person, country, etc that defeats an enemy or opponent.

**Victorian** *adj* relating to the reign of Queen Victoria (1837–1901).

**victorious** *adj* having won a victory or success. ➤ **victoriously** *adv.*

**victory** *n* (*pl* **-ies**) the act of overcoming an enemy or opponent.

**victuals** *pl n archaic* food.

**video**[1] *n* (*pl* **-os**) **1** pictures and sound recorded on a magnetic tape or disc. **2** a tape or cassette of recorded material. **3** a machine for recording and playing this material.

**video**[2] *v* (**videoes, videoed, videoing**) to make a video recording of.

**videodisc** *n* a disc on which digital information is stored.

**video game** *n* a computer game played on a VDU screen.

**videophone** *n* an electronic device for transmitting sound and pictures down a telephone line.

**videorecorder** *n* a machine for recording on and playing videotapes.

**videotape**[1] *n* **1** magnetic tape used for recording visual images. **2** a cassette of this magnetic tape.

**videotape**[2] *v* to record on videotape.

**vie** *v* (**vies, vied, vying**) to compete with others for something.

**view**[1] *n* **1** a scene or scenery seen from a particular position, e.g. a window. **2** the ability to see something; sight. **3** a picture or photograph of a place. **4** an attitude or opinion. ✱ **in view of** because of; considering. **with a view to** intending to.

**view**[2] *v* **1** to see or watch. **2** to regard in a specified way. **3** to inspect. **4** to consider.

**viewer** *n* **1** a person who watches television. **2** an optical device.

**viewfinder** *n* a device on a camera showing an image of what will appear in the photograph.

**viewpoint** *n* **1** a standpoint; a point of view. **2** a place from which something can be viewed.

**vigil** *n* a period of staying awake in the night, to keep watch or to pray.

**vigilant** *adj* alert to spot trouble or danger. ➤ **vigilance** *n,* **vigilantly** *adv.*

**vigilante** /viji'lanti/ *n* a member of a group of self-appointed guardians of law and order. ➤ **vigilantism** *n.*

**vignette** *n* **1** an engraving or photograph that shades off gradually into the surrounding background. **2** a short descriptive literary sketch. **3** a brief attractive incident or scene in a play or film.

**vigorous** *adj* **1** full of strength and energy. **2** done with vigour. ➤ **vigorously** *adv.*

**vigour** (*NAmer* **vigor**) *n* **1** active physical strength or force. **2** intensity of action or effect.

**Viking** *n* a Norse trader and warrior of the eighth to tenth cents.

**vile** *adj* **1** morally despicable or abhorrent. **2** unpleasant or repulsive. ➤ **vilely** *adv.*

**vilify** *v* (**-ies, -ied**) to speak slanderously or abusively about. ➤ **vilification** *n.*

**villa** *n* **1** *Brit* a detached or semidetached suburban house. **2** a holiday house abroad. **3** a large house of an ancient Roman.

**village** *n* a small group of streets and houses in the country. ➤ **villager** *n.*

**villain** *n* **1** a scoundrel or criminal. **2** a bad character in a story or play. ➤ **villainous** *n.*

**villein** *n* formerly, a peasant working for a feudal lord in exchange for land.

**vim** *n informal* energy and enthusiasm.

**vinaigrette** *n* a salad dressing of oil and vinegar flavoured with salt, pepper, mustard, and herbs.

**vindicate** *v* **1** to absolve from blame. **2** to provide justification for. ➤ **vindication** *n.*

**vindictive** *adj* **1** eager to seek revenge. **2** intended as revenge. ➤ **vindictively** *adv,* **vindictiveness** *n.*

**vine** *n* a climbing plant, *esp* one that bears grapes.

**vinegar** *n* a sour liquid obtained from wine, cider, etc and used as a seasoning or preservative. ➤ **vinegary** *adj.*

**vineyard** *n* a plantation of grapevines used in making wine.

**vintage**[1] *n* **1** a season's yield of grapes or wine from a vineyard. **2** a superior wine of a particular type, region, and year. **3** the act or time of harvesting grapes or making wine. **4** a period of origin or manufacture.

**vintage**[2] *adj* **1** denoting superior wine of a particular year. **2** of enduring value; classic.

**vintner** *n* a wine merchant.

**vinyl** *n* a strong tough plastic that is derived from ethylene.

**viol** *n* an early stringed instrument having six strings and frets.

**viola**[1] *n* a stringed instrument of the violin family, intermediate in size and range between the violin and cello.

**viola**[2] *n* a cultivated violet with flowers resembling pansies.

**violate** *v* **1** to fail to comply with (a rule or law). **2** to assault sexually. **3** to fail to respect (something sacred). ➤ **violation** *n,* **violator** *n.*

**violence** *n* **1** exertion of physical force so as to kill or injure or to cause harm to property. **2** intense or turbulent action or force. **3** vehement feeling or expression.

**violent** *adj* **1** using or marked by violence. **2** powerfully intense or furious. ➤ **violently** *adv.*
**violet** *n* **1** a plant with sweet-scented purple or blue flowers. **2** a bluish purple colour.
**violin** *n* a musical instrument having four strings, played with a bow and with one end held under the chin. ➤ **violinist** *n.*
**violoncello** /ˌvie·ələnˈcheloh/ *n* (*pl* **-os**) *formal* = CELLO.

***Usage Note:*** Note the spelling *violon-* not *violin-*.

**VIP** *n* a very important person.
**viper** *n* a poisonous snake of the adder family.
**virago** *n* (*pl* **-oes** *or* **-os**) a loud domineering woman.
**viral** *adj* relating to or caused by a virus or viruses.
**virgin**[1] *n* **1** a person who has not had sexual intercourse. **2** (**the Virgin**) the Virgin Mary. ➤ **virginal** *adj*, **virginity** *n.*
**virgin**[2] *adj* **1** not having had sexual intercourse. **2** not altered by human activity. **3** of olive oil: obtained from the first pressing of olives.
**Virgo** *n* in astrology, the sixth sign of the zodiac (the Virgin).
**virile** *adj* **1** having the nature or qualities typical of a man. **2** of a man: having a strong sexual appetite. ➤ **virility** *n.*
**virtual** *adj* **1** essentially or nearly as described though not definitely or actually such. **2** in computing, simulating reality or the appearance of reality. ➤ **virtuality** *n*, **virtually** *adv.*
**virtual reality** *n* a computer environment in which images are produced that have the appearance of reality and can be manipulated electronically as if they were real.
**virtue** *n* **1** thought and behaviour conforming to a high moral standard. **2** a good moral quality. **3** *archaic* chastity, *esp* in a woman. ✱ **by virtue of** because of.
**virtuoso** /vuhtyoohˈohsoh, -zoh/ *n* (*pl* **virtuosos** *or* **virtuosi**) a person who excels in musical or artistic technique. ➤ **virtuosity** *n.*
**virtuous** *adj* **1** having virtue; morally good. **2** *archaic* chaste. ➤ **virtuously** *adv.*
**virulent** *adj* **1** of a disease: severe and developing rapidly. **2** full of malice; malignant. **3** objectionably harsh or strong. ➤ **virulence** *n*, **virulently** *adv.*
**virus** *n* **1** a parasitic micro-organism that can cause disease. **2** *informal* a disease caused by a virus. **3** a piece of computer code maliciously introduced into a system to destroy programs and data.
**visa** *n* an endorsement made on a passport allowing entry into or exit from a country.
**visage** *n literary* a face or countenance.
**vis-à-vis** /ˌvee zah ˈvee/ *prep* in relation to.
**viscera** /ˈvisərə/ *pl n* the heart, liver, intestines, and other internal organs.
**visceral** *adj* **1** relating to the viscera. **2** felt or known instinctively rather than by reasoning. **3** deeply or intensely felt. ➤ **viscerally** *adv.*
**viscose** *n* a solution made from cellulose and used in making rayon and other fabrics.
**viscosity** *n* (*pl* **-ies**) **1** the state or extent of being viscous. **2** the property of a liquid or gas that enables it to resist flowing.
**viscount** *n* a member of the British peerage ranking below an earl.
**viscous** *adj* **1** sticky or glutinous. **2** having high viscosity.
**vise** *n NAmer* see VICE[2].
**visibility** *n* **1** the state of being visible. **2** the clearness of the atmosphere as revealed by the greatest distance at which prominent objects can be identified visually with the naked eye. **3** this distance. **4** capability of affording an unobstructed view.
**visible** *adj* able to be seen or perceived. ➤ **visibly** *adv.*
**vision** *n* **1** the power of seeing. **2** something seen. **3** a beautiful person or sight. **4** imaginative thinking about the future. **5** the picture on a television screen, or its clarity. **6** something imagined or seen in a dream or trance.
**visionary**[1] *adj* **1** showing foresight or imagination. **2** able or likely to see visions. **3** of the nature of a vision.
**visionary**[2] *n* (*pl* **-ies**) a visionary person.
**visit**[1] *v* (**visited, visiting**) **1** to go to be with (a person) or stay at (a place) for a time. **2** to inflict (something unpleasant) on a person or place. ➤ **visitor** *n.*
**visit**[2] *n* an act of visiting.
**visitation** *n* **1** an official visit, e.g. for inspection. **2** an appearance by a supernatural being. **3** a punishment regarded as coming from God. **4** a severe trial or affliction.
**visor** *or* **vizor** *n* **1** a movable part of a helmet that covers the face. **2** a flat sunshade attached at the top of a vehicle windscreen.
**vista** *n* a pleasing view into the distance.
**visual**[1] *adj* relating to or produced by vision. ➤ **visually** *adv.*
**visual**[2] *n* a photograph, graph, chart, etc used for illustration or information.
**visual display unit** *n Brit* a device that displays computer data on a screen.
**visualize** *or* **-ise** *v* to form a mental image of. ➤ **visualization** *n.*
**vital** *adj* **1** of the utmost importance; essential. **2** necessary to maintaining life. **3** full of life and vigour. ➤ **vitally** *adv.*
**vitality** *n* physical or mental liveliness.
**vitalize** *or* **-ise** *v* to give vitality to; to animate.
**vital statistics** *pl n informal* the measurements of a woman's bust, waist, and hips.
**vitamin** *n* any of various organic substances naturally present in foods and essential for the maintenance of health and growth.

**vitiate** *v* **1** to make faulty or defective. **2** to invalidate.
**viticulture** *n* the process of cultivating grapevines.
**vitreous** *adj* consisting of or resembling glass.
**vitreous humour** *n* the colourless transparent jelly that fills the eyeball behind the lens.
**vitrify** *v* (**-ies, -ied**) to convert into glass or a glassy substance by heat and fusion.
**vitriol** *n* **1** virulent speech or feeling. **2** concentrated sulphuric acid. ➤ **vitriolic** *adj.*
**vituperation** *n* harsh or abusive language. ➤ **vituperative** *adj.*
**viva**[1] /'veevə/ *interj* an expression of goodwill.
**viva**[2] /'vievə/ *or* **viva voce**/ˌvievə 'vohchi/ *n* an oral examination for an academic degree.
**vivacious** *adj* pleasantly lively. ➤ **vivaciously** *adv,* **vivacity** *n.*
**vivarium** *n* (*pl* **vivaria**) an enclosure for keeping and observing plants or animals indoors.
**vivid** *adj* **1** of a light or colour: clear and bright. **2** producing strong feelings or mental pictures. ➤ **vividly** *adv,* **vividness** *n.*
**vivify** *v* (**-ies, -ied**) to give vitality or interest to.
**viviparous** *adj* of an animal: producing living young rather than eggs.
**vivisection** *n* the practice of operating on living animals for scientific investigation.
**vixen** *n* **1** a female fox. **2** a scolding ill-tempered woman.
**viz.** *abbr* (Latin) videlicet = namely; in other words.
**vizor** *n* see VISOR.
**V neck** *n* a V-shaped neckline on a piece of clothing.
**vocabulary** *n* (*pl* **-ies**) **1** the words used in a language or activity or by an individual or group. **2** a list of words with definitions or translations.
**vocal**[1] *adj* **1** relating to the voice or speech. **2** having or exercising the power of producing voice, speech, or sound. **3** expressing opinions frankly; outspoken. **4** of music: written for or including parts for the human voice. ➤ **vocally** *adv.*
**vocal**[2] *n* (*usu in pl*) a sung part in a piece of music.
**vocal cords** *pl n* each of a pair of membranes in the throat that vibrate to produce sound.
**vocalist** *n* a singer.
**vocalize** *or* **-ise** *v* to speak or utter (sounds or words).
**vocation** *n* **1** a strong inner feeling that one should follow a particular activity or course of action, *esp* a divine call to the religious life. **2** a person's work or career. ➤ **vocational** *adj.*
**vocative** *adj* of a grammatical case expressing a person or thing addressed.
**vociferous** *adj* loud and insistent. ➤ **vociferously** *adv.*
**vodka** *n* a clear alcoholic spirit made by distilling a mash of rye or wheat.
**vogue** *n* the prevailing fashion. ➤ **voguish** *adj.*
**voice**[1] *n* **1** sound, in the form of speech or song, produced by forcing air from the lungs through the larynx. **2** the ability to speak. **3** the power or ability to sing. **4** a melodic part in a piece of music. **5** the use of the voice in singing or acting. **6** the expressed wish or opinion. **7** in grammar, distinction between active and passive use of a verb to indicate the relation of the subject of the verb to the action. ➤ **voiceless** *adj.*
**voice**[2] *v* to express in words.
**voice box** *n* the larynx.
**voice mail** *n* a system for storing telephone messages in digitalized form.
**voice-over** *n* the voice of an unseen narrator in a film or television programme.
**void**[1] *adj* **1** having no legal force. **2** empty or unoccupied. **3** vain or useless. **4** (+ of) devoid of or lacking.
**void**[2] *n* an empty space.
**void**[3] *v* **1** to nullify or annul (a contract, transaction, etc). **2** to discharge or emit (urine, excrement, etc).
**voile** *n* a fine soft sheer fabric.
**volatile** *adj* **1** readily vaporized at a low temperature. **2** unstable or explosive. **3** characterized by rapid change. ➤ **volatility** *n.*
**vol-au-vent** /'vol oh vonh/ *n* a round case of puff pastry filled with meat or vegetables in a sauce.
**volcanic** *adj* **1** of or produced by a volcano. **2** explosively violent.
**volcano** *n* (*pl* **-oes** *or* **-os**) a hill or mountain with an outlet at the top from which molten rock and lava may erupt from the earth's crust.
**vole** *n* a small rodent with a blunt nose and short ears.
**volition** *n* the act or power of choosing or deciding for oneself.
**volley**[1] *n* (*pl* **-eys**) **1** a flight of arrows, bullets, or other missiles, or the simultaneous firing of these. **2** a rapid sequence of questions or criticisms. **3** in ball games, a return of the ball before it touches the ground.
**volley**[2] *v* (**-eys, -eyed**) to hit (a ball) before it touches the ground.
**volleyball** *n* a team game in which players volley a ball over a high net using their hands.
**volt** *n* the SI unit of electrical potential.
**voltage** *n* an electric force measured in volts.
**volte-face** /ˌvolt 'fas/ *n* (*pl* **volte-face** *or* **volte-faces**) a sudden reversal of attitude or policy.
**voluble** *adj* talking readily and at length. ➤ **volubility** *n,* **volubly** *adv.*
**volume** *n* **1** a book, *esp* one forming part of a large work. **2** space occupied as measured in

cubic units. **3** the amount of something occupying a space. **4** the degree of loudness of a sound.

**voluminous** *adj* **1** containing a large quantity; very large. **2** of clothing: having a lot of material. **3** writing much or at great length.

**voluntary**[1] *adj* **1** resulting from free choice or consent. **2** acting or done without payment. ➤ **voluntarily** *adv.*

**voluntary**[2] *n* (*pl* **-ies**) an organ piece played before or after a religious service.

**volunteer**[1] *n* **1** a person who undertakes a service by free choice. **2** a person who offers to enter military service.

**volunteer**[2] *v* **1** to offer freely to do something. **2** to express (a remark or opinion) spontaneously.

**voluptuary** *n* (*pl* **-ies**) a person who enjoys luxury and sensual pleasure.

**voluptuous** *adj* **1** involving luxury and sensual gratification. **2** shapely and sexually attractive. ➤ **voluptuously** *adv.*

**vomit**[1] *v* (**vomited, vomiting**) **1** to eject the contents of the stomach through the mouth. **2** to eject violently or abundantly.

**vomit**[2] *n* vomited matter.

**voodoo** *n* (*pl* **voodoos**) a set of beliefs and rituals practised chiefly in the Caribbean and involving trance-induced contact with spirits. ➤ **voodooism** *n.*

**voracious** *adj* **1** having a huge appetite; ravenous. **2** excessively eager; insatiable. ➤ **voraciously** *adv,* **voracity** *n.*

**vortex** *n* (*pl* **vortices** *or* **vortexes**) a mass of whirling water or air.

**votary** *n* (*pl* **-ies**) **1** a devoted admirer or follower. **2** a person who has taken religious vows.

**vote**[1] *n* **1** the formal process of making a choice between several candidates for office or courses of action. **2** (*usu* **the vote**) the right to take part in an election.

**vote**[2] *v* to cast one's vote in an election. ➤ **voter** *n.*

**votive** *adj* offered to a deity in fulfilment of a vow.

**vouch** *v* (+ for) to affirm that something is true or that somebody is genuine or trustworthy.

**voucher** *n* a ticket that can be exchanged for specific goods or services.

**vouchsafe** *v* **1** to grant in a gracious or condescending manner. **2** to condescend or deign (to do something).

**vow**[1] *n* a solemn promise or assertion.

**vow**[2] *v* to promise something solemnly.

**vowel** *n* **1** any of a class of speech sounds, e.g. /ee/ or /i/, characterized by lack of closure in the breath channel or lack of audible friction. **2** a letter or character representing such a sound.

**voyage**[1] *n* a long journey by sea or air.

**voyage**[2] *v* to make a voyage. ➤ **voyager** *n.*

**voyeur** /vwah'yuh/ *n* **1** a person who gets sexual gratification from watching other people's sexual activities. **2** a person who enjoys seeing other people's suffering or distress. ➤ **voyeurism** *n,* **voyeuristic** *adj.*

**vs.** *abbr* versus.

**V sign** *n* a contemptuous gesture made by raising the index and middle fingers outwards in a V.

**vulcanize** *or* **-ise** *v* to treat (rubber or similar material) chemically to give it elasticity or strength.

**vulgar** *adj* **1** lacking in cultivation or taste. **2** ostentatious in one's behaviour or lifestyle. **3** lewd or indecent. ➤ **vulgarity** *n,* **vulgarly** *adv.*

**vulgar fraction** *n Brit* a fraction expressed by numbers above and below a line.

**vulgarize** *or* **-ise** *v* to make vulgar or less refined.

**vulnerable** *adj* open to being attacked or harmed. ➤ **vulnerability** *n,* **vulnerably** *adv.*

**vulpine** *adj* of or resembling a fox.

**vulture** *n* **1** a large bird of prey that feeds on carrion. **2** a predatory person.

**vulva** *n* the external parts of the female genital organs.

**vying** *v* present part. of VIE.

**W**[1] *or* **w** *n* (*pl* **W's** *or* **Ws** *or* **w's**) the 23rd letter of the English alphabet.

**W**[2] *abbr* **1** watt(s). **2** West. **3** Western.

**W**[3] *abbr* the chemical symbol for tungsten.

**wacky** *or* **whacky** *adj* (**-ier, -iest**) *informal* absurdly or amusingly eccentric or irrational.

**wad**[1] *n* **1** a mass or bundle of soft material used e.g. to stop an aperture or pad a garment. **2** a roll of paper, *esp* paper money.

**wad**[2] *v* (**wadded, wadding**) **1** to form (material) into a wad. **2** to stuff, pad, or line with some soft substance.

**waddle**[1] *v* to walk with short steps, swinging the body from side to side.

**waddle**[2] *n* an awkward clumsy swaying gait.

**wade** *v* **1** to walk through water or mud. **2** (+ through) to read something lengthy and tedious. **3** *informal* (+ in/into) to attack with determination or vigour.

**wader** *n* **1** (*usu in pl*) a high waterproof boot. **2** a long-legged bird, e.g. a sandpiper or snipe, that wades in water in search of food.

**wafer** *n* **1** a thin crisp biscuit. **2** a round thin piece of unleavened bread used in the Eucharist.

**waffle**[1] *n* a baked cake of batter that has a crisp dimpled surface.

**waffle**[2] *v chiefly Brit, informal* to talk or write inconsequentially and usu at length.

**waffle**[3] *n chiefly Brit, informal* empty or pretentious words.

**waft**[1] *v* to be conveyed lightly *esp* through the air.

**waft**[2] *n* **1** a slight breeze; a puff. **2** something, e.g. a smell, that is wafted.

**wag**[1] *v* (**wagged, wagging**) to move to and fro rapidly.

**wag**[2] *n informal* a wit or joker. ➤ **waggish** *adj.*

**wage**[1] *n* (*often in pl*) a regular payment for *esp* manual work. ➤ **waged** *adj.*

**wage**[2] *v* to engage in or carry on (a war, conflict, etc).

**wager**[1] *n* a bet.

**wager**[2] *v* (*often* + on) to bet.

**waggle**[1] *v* to move repeatedly from side to side or up and down.

**waggle**[2] *n* the act of waggling

**wagon** *or* **waggon** *n* **1** a usu four-wheeled vehicle for transporting bulky or heavy loads, usu drawn by animals. **2** *Brit* a railway goods vehicle. ✱ **on the wagon** *informal* abstaining from alcoholic drink.

**wagtail** *n* a bird with a very long tail that it habitually jerks up and down.

**waif** *n* a stray helpless person or animal, *esp* a homeless child.

**wail**[1] *n* **1** a loud prolonged high-pitched cry expressing grief or pain. **2** a sound suggestive of wailing.

**wail**[2] *v* to utter a wail.

**wain** *n archaic* a wagon or cart.

**wainscot** *n* a usu panelled wooden lining of the lower part of an interior wall.

**waist** *n* **1** the part of the body between the chest and hips. **2** a narrow part resembling the human waist.

**waistband** *n* a band, e.g. on trousers or a skirt, fitting round the waist.

**waistcoat** *n Brit* a sleeveless upper garment that fastens down the centre front, often worn as part of a man's suit.

**waistline** *n* the body circumference at the waist.

**wait**[1] *v* **1** (*often* + for) to remain stationary or refrain from beginning an activity for a period until something happens. **2** (*often* + for) to pause for somebody to catch up. **3** to be delayed or postponed. **4** to act as a waiter. ✱ **wait on/upon** to act as an attendant to.

**wait**[2] *n* the act or a period of waiting. ✱ **in wait** in a hidden position, *esp* in readiness to attack.

**waiter** *or* **waitress** *n* somebody who serves diners, e.g. in a restaurant.

**waive** *v* to refrain from demanding or enforcing (e.g. a right).

**waiver** *n* **1** the relinquishing of a right. **2** a document giving proof of this.

**wake**[1] *v* (*past tense* **woke** *or NAmer* **waked,** *past part.* **woken** *or NAmer* **waked**) **1** (*often* + up) to stop sleeping, or to rouse (somebody) from sleep. **2** (+ up) to pay more attention to what is happening or what one is doing. **3** (+ up to) to become aware of.

**wake**[2] *n* **1** a watch held over the body of a dead person. **2** festivities after a funeral.

**wake**[3] *n* the track left by a moving body, e.g. a ship, in a fluid, e.g. water. ✱ **in the wake of** following and as a result of.

**wakeful** *adj* **1** not sleeping or able to sleep. **2** spent without sleep. **3** alert. ➤ **wakefulness** *n.*
**waken** *v* (*often* + up) = WAKE[1].
**walk[1]** *v* **1** to move along on foot, with at least one foot always in contact with the ground. **2** to pass on foot through, along, or over (e.g. a route). **3** to take (an animal) for a walk. **4** to accompany (somebody) on foot. ✱ **walk away/off with** *informal* **1** to steal. **2** to win (a prize, trophy, etc). **walk it** *informal* to win easily. ➤ **walker** *n.*
**walk[2]** *n* **1** a journey or outing on foot. **2** a manner of walking. **3** a route or path for walking. **4** a relatively slow rate of motion or progress, as of a person or horse walking. ✱ **walk of life** a person's occupation or position in society.
**walking stick** *n* a stick used as an aid to walking.
**Walkman** *n* (*pl* **Walkmen** *or* **Walkmans**) *trademark* a small portable cassette or CD player with earphones.
**walk-on** *n* (*also* **walk-on part**) a small usu nonspeaking part in a play.
**walkout** *n* **1** a strike by workers. **2** the act of leaving a meeting or organization as an expression of protest.
**walk out** *v* **1** to go on strike. **2** to depart suddenly, often as an expression of protest. ✱ **walk out on** to abandon.
**walkover** *n* an easily won contest.
**walkway** *n* a passage, path, or platform for walking.
**wall[1]** *n* **1** an upright and solid structure of stone, brick, concrete, etc serving *esp* as the side of a room or building or to divide an area of land. **2** in anatomy, a lining or membrane enclosing a cavity or structure. **3** something that acts as a barrier or defence. ✱ **go to the wall** *informal* to go bankrupt or out of business. **off the wall** *NAmer* unconventional. **up the wall** into a state of exasperation or unreasoning fury.
**wall[2]** *v* **1** (*usu* + in) to protect or surround with a wall. **2** (+ off) to separate or shut out by a wall. **3** (+ up) to close (an opening) with a wall.
**wallaby** *n* (*pl* **wallabies** *or* **wallaby**) a small or medium-sized mammal closely related to the kangaroo.
**wall bars** *pl n* horizontal parallel bars that are attached to a wall and used for gymnastic exercises.
**wallet** *n* a flat folding holder for paper money and credit and similar cards.
**walleye** *n* an eye that turns outwards, showing more than a normal amount of white. ➤ **wall-eyed** *adj.*
**wallflower** *n* **1** a plant that bears clusters of sweet-scented flowers in early spring. **2** *informal* a woman who fails to get partners at a dance.
**wallop[1]** *v* (**walloped, walloping**) *informal* **1** to hit forcefully. **2** to beat (an opponent) by a wide margin.
**wallop[2]** *n informal* a powerful blow.
**wallow[1]** *v* **1** to roll or lie around lazily or luxuriously. **2** (+ in) to indulge oneself immoderately. **3** of a ship: to struggle laboriously in or through rough water.
**wallow[2]** *n* **1** an act of wallowing. **2** a muddy or dusty area used by animals for wallowing.
**wallpaper[1]** *n* **1** decorative paper for the walls of a room. **2** in computing, a decorative background on a monitor.
**wallpaper[2]** *v* to apply wallpaper to (the walls of a room).
**wally** *n* (*pl* **-ies**) *Brit, informal* a silly or useless person.
**walnut** *n* an edible two-lobed nut with wrinkled surface.
**walrus** *n* (*pl* **walruses** *or* **walrus**) a large northern sea mammal, related to the seal, with ivory tusks.
**waltz[1]** *n* a ballroom dance in triple time.
**waltz[2]** *v* **1** to dance a waltz. **2** to move in a casually confident or overconfident manner.
**waltzer** *n* a revolving fairground ride that moves its cars up and down as it revolves.
**wan** *adj* (**wanner, wannest**) **1** suggestive of poor health; pallid. **2** lacking vitality; feeble. **3** of light: dim or faint. ➤ **wanly** *adv.*
**wand** *n* **1** a slender rod used by conjurers and magicians. **2** a slender staff carried as a sign of office.
**wander[1]** *v* **1** to go or travel without a fixed route or destination. **2** to deviate from a course, or from what one is supposed to be saying, thinking about, etc. ➤ **wanderer** *n.*
**wander[2]** *n* a walk or journey without a fixed route or destination.
**wanderlust** *n* eagerness to go travelling.
**wane[1]** *v* **1** of the moon: to diminish in apparent size or intensity. **2** to decrease or decline.
**wane[2]** *n* ✱ **on the wane** in a state of decline.
**wangle** *v* to bring about or get by devious means.
**wank[1]** *v Brit, coarse slang* to masturbate.
**wank[2]** *n Brit, coarse slang* an act of masturbating.
**wanker** *n Brit, coarse slang* a foolish or unpleasant person.
**want[1]** *v* **1** to have a wish or desire for. **2** to wish or demand the presence of (somebody). **3** to feel sexual desire for. **4** (**be wanted**) to be sought by the police. **5** *chiefly Brit, informal* to require: *This room wants decorating.* **6** (*often* + for) to lack; to be in need of.
**want[2]** *n* **1** lack. **2** grave and extreme poverty. **3** a need or desire.
**wanting** *adj* **1** not present or available. **2** not up to the required standard. **3** lacking or deficient in.

**wanton** *adj* **1** sexually promiscuous. **2** gratuitously brutal or violent. ➤ **wantonly** *adv.*

**WAP** *abbr* Wireless Application Protocol, the technology that allows mobile phone users to send e-mails and connect to the Internet.

**wapiti** *n* (*pl* **wapitis** *or* **wapiti**) a large North American deer.

**war**[1] *n* **1** a state or period of armed hostile conflict *esp* between states or nations. **2** a struggle between opposing forces or for a particular end.

**war**[2] *v* (**warred, warring**) to engage in warfare.

**warble** *v* to sing in a pure tone with many turns and variations.

**warbler** *n* any of a family of small insect-eating birds, many of which are noted singers.

**war crime** *n* a crime committed during or in connection with war.

**war cry** *n* a cry or slogan used to rally warriors in battle or people to a cause.

**ward** *n* **1** a room in a hospital for one or usu a number of patients. **2** a division of a city, town, or other area for electoral or administrative purposes. **3** somebody under the care or control of a legal guardian. **4** a projecting ridge of metal in a lock allowing only a key with a corresponding notch to operate.

**war dance** *n* a dance performed as preparation for battle or in celebration of victory.

**warden** *n* **1** an official charged with special supervisory duties or with the enforcement of specified laws or regulations. **2** *Brit* the title of the head of some colleges or schools. **3** *NAmer* a prison governor.

**warder** *n chiefly Brit* a prison guard.

**wardrobe** *n* **1** a large cupboard where clothes are kept. **2** a collection of clothes, e.g. belonging to one person. **3** a collection of stage costumes and accessories.

**wardroom** *n* a dining or common room in a warship for commissioned officers.

**ware** *n* **1** manufactured articles or products of art or craft: *tinware.* **2** (*in pl*) goods for sale. **3** a specified make of pottery or china.

**warehouse** *n* **1** a building or room for the storage of merchandise or commodities. **2** *chiefly Brit* a large retail outlet.

**warfare** *n* hostilities or war.

**warhead** *n* the section of a missile containing the explosive charge.

**warhorse** *n* **1** a powerful horse used in battle. **2** *informal* a veteran soldier or public figure.

**warlike** *adj* **1** military; useful in war. **2** threatening; hostile.

**warlock** *n* a man practising black magic.

**warlord** *n* a military leader, *esp* a regional commander operating outside government control.

**warm**[1] *adj* **1** having, experiencing, or giving out moderate heat. **2** serving to maintain or preserve heat. **3** enthusiastic or cordial. **4** affectionate and outgoing in temperament. **5** of a colour: in the range yellow through orange to red. **6** in children's games: near to a goal, object, or solution sought. ➤ **warmly** *adv.*

**warm**[2] *v* to make or become warm. ✱ **warm to/towards** to begin to like. ➤ **warmer** *n.*

**warm**[3] *n* (**the warm**) a warm place or state.

**warm-blooded** *adj* having a relatively high and constant body temperature more or less independent of the environment.

**warmonger** *n* somebody who attempts to stir up war.

**warmth** *n* the quality of being warm in temperature or in feeling.

**warm up** *v* **1** to do gentle exercises before more strenuous physical activity. **2** of an engine or machine: to come to the necessary temperature for efficient working. **3** to put (an audience) into a receptive mood, e.g. before a comedy show.

**warn** *v* **1** to give notice to beforehand, *esp* of danger. **2** to inform (somebody) of the likely adverse consequences for them of a course of action. **3** (+ off) to order to go or stay away.

**warning** *n* **1** notification or a sign of a possible threat or danger. **2** a statement cautioning somebody whose actions are likely to have adverse consequences. **3** advance notice.

**warp**[1] *v* **1** to twist or bend (*esp* something flat or straight) out of shape. **2** to distort, *esp* by making odd or abnormal.

**warp**[2] *n* **1** a twist or curve that has developed in something originally flat or straight. **2** a series of yarns extended lengthways in a loom and crossed by the weft.

**warrant**[1] *n* **1** a commission or document giving authority, e.g. a document authorizing a police officer to make an arrest, a search, etc. **2** a document authorizing somebody to receive money, goods, etc. **3** a ground or justification; proof.

**warrant**[2] *v* **1** to serve as adequate ground or reason for. **2** to guarantee. ➤ **warrantable** *adj.*

**warrant officer** *n* an officer in the armed forces holding a rank below commissioned officers but above non-commissioned officers.

**warranty** *n* (*pl* **-ies**) a usu written guarantee of the soundness of a product and of the maker's responsibility for repair or replacement.

**warren** *n* **1** a network of burrows where rabbits live and breed. **2** a crowded district usu with a maze of narrow passageways.

**warrior** *n* a person engaged or experienced in warfare.

**warship** *n* an armed ship for use in warfare.

**wart** *n* a lumpy projection on the skin. ✱ **warts and all** *informal* not disguising any blemishes. ➤ **warty** *adj.*

**warthog** *n* an African wild pig with two pairs of rough warty lumps on its face and tusks.

**wary** *adj* (**-ier, -iest**) cautious and watchful so as to detect and escape danger. ➤ **warily** *adv,* **wariness** *n.*

**was** *v* first person and third person sing. past tense of BE.

**wash**[1] *v* **1** to make clean by using water and soap or detergent. **2** of water: to flow along, dash against, or overflow. **3** to carry away or deposit (something) by the force of water in motion. **4** to cover lightly with an application of a thin liquid, e.g. whitewash or watercolour. **5** *informal* to be convincing: *The story didn't wash with me.* ✱ **wash one's dirty linen in public** *informal* to reveal one's private affairs openly. **wash one's hands of** to disclaim interest in or responsibility for. ➤ **washable** *adj.*

**wash**[2] *n* **1** an act of washing. **2** articles, *esp* clothes, that have been or are to be washed. **3** a thin liquid used for coating or painting a surface. **4** an antiseptic or soothing lotion. **5** a disturbance in water or the air produced by the movement of a boat or an aircraft.

**wash bag** *n Brit* a small waterproof bag for toiletries.

**washbasin** *n* a basin or sink for washing the hands and face.

**washboard** *n* a board with a corrugated rectangular metal surface set into a wooden frame, used for scrubbing clothes when washing.

**washed-out** *adj* **1** faded in colour. **2** listless or exhausted.

**washed-up** *adj informal* no longer successful or useful.

**washer** *n* **1** somebody or something that washes. **2** a thin flat ring often fitted round the shank of a bolt to protect a surface when the bolt is screwed into it.

**washing** *n* articles, *esp* clothes, that have been or are to be washed.

**washing machine** *n* a machine for washing clothes and household linen.

**washing powder** *n* powdered detergent for use in a washing machine.

**washing-up** *n Brit* dishes and utensils to be washed.

**washout** *n informal* a failure or fiasco.

**wash out** *v* (**be washed out**) **1** to be cancelled because of rain. **2** *informal* to be pale and exhausted.

**washroom** *n NAmer, euphem* a toilet.

**washstand** *n* formerly, a piece of furniture used to hold a basin, jug, etc needed for washing one's face and hands.

**wash up** *v Brit* to wash the dishes and utensils after a meal.

**wasn't** *contraction* was not.

**wasp** *n* a slender insect with black and yellow stripes and an extremely painful sting.

**waspish** *adj* irritable or spiteful. ➤ **waspishly** *adv.*

**wasp waist** *n* a very narrow waist. ➤ **wasp-waisted** *adj.*

**wassail**[1] *n archaic* revelry; carousing.

**wassail**[2] *v* **1** *archaic* to carouse. **2** *Brit, dialect or archaic* to sing carols from house to house at Christmas.

**wastage** *n* **1** the wasteful or avoidable loss of something. **2** an amount wasted. **3** reduction in workforce numbers usu caused by individuals leaving or retiring voluntarily.

**waste**[1] *n* **1** the act of wasting. **2** damaged, defective, or superfluous material. **3** a sparsely settled, barren, or devastated region; a desert. ✱ **go to waste** to be squandered or wasted. **lay waste to** to destroy (a place) completely.

**waste**[2] *v* **1** to spend or use carelessly or inefficiently. **2** to fail to use (e.g. an opportunity). **3** (*often* + away) to lose weight, strength, substance, or vitality. **4** (**be wasted on**) to fail to be understood or appreciated by.

**waste**[3] *adj* **1** discarded as refuse. **2** of land: not cultivated or used; not productive.

**wasted** *adj informal* drunk or affected by illegal drugs.

**wasteful** *adj* given to or marked by careless and inefficient use of resources. ➤ **wastefully** *adv.*

**wasteland** *n* an area of barren, uncultivated, or uninhabited land.

**wastrel** *n* somebody who spends or consumes wastefully.

**watch**[1] *v* **1** to look at attentively. **2** to take an interest in the progress of. **3** to keep under surveillance or protective guard. **4** to be careful or cautious about. **5** (+ for) to be attentive or vigilant. ✱ **watch one's step** to proceed with care; to act or talk warily. ➤ **watchable** *adj,* **watcher** *n.*

**watch**[2] *n* **1** a small timepiece worn on the wrist or carried in the pocket. **2** close observation; surveillance. **3** a period of time during which a part of a ship's company is on duty while another part rests. **4** a body of firefighters or police officers working a particular shift. ✱ **keep watch** to be on duty or on guard looking out for possible danger.

**watchdog** *n* **1** a dog kept to guard property. **2** a person or group that guards against inefficiency, undesirable practices, etc.

**watchful** *adj* carefully observant or attentive. ➤ **watchfully** *adv,* **watchfulness** *n.*

**watchman** *n* (*pl* **watchmen**) a guard whose job is to protect a building, *esp* at night.

**watch out** *v* to be careful or vigilant.

**watchtower** *n* a tower from which a lookout can keep watch.

**watchword** *n* a motto that embodies a guiding principle; a slogan.

**water**[1] *n* **1** the colourless odourless liquid that falls as rain and forms rivers, lakes, and seas. **2** (*in pl*) a stretch of sea under the control of a specified sovereignty. **3** a watery liquid, *esp* urine. **4** (*usu in pl*) the amniotic fluid surrounding a foetus in the womb and discharged shortly before birth. * **hold water** to stand up under criticism or analysis. **water under the bridge** past events that it is futile to try to alter. ➤ **waterless** *adj*, **watery** *adj*.

**water²** *v* **1** to moisten, sprinkle, or soak (e.g. plants or ground) with water. **2** to supply (e.g. a horse) with water to drink. **3** to be a source of water for (an area). **4** (*often* + down) to dilute. **5** (*often* + down) to make less forceful, controversial, etc. **6** to secrete tears or saliva.

**water bed** *n* a bed with a water-filled plastic or rubber mattress.

**water boatman** *n* an aquatic bug that swims on its back moving its long hind legs like oars.

**water buffalo** *n* an often domesticated Asian buffalo with large horns.

**water cannon** *n* a device for shooting out a jet of water with great force, e.g. to disperse a crowd.

**water closet** *n dated* a flush toilet.

**watercolour** (*NAmer* **watercolor**) *n* **1** a paint made from pigment mixed with water. **2** a picture painted with watercolours.

**watercourse** *n* a natural or artificial channel through which water flows.

**watercress** *n* a cress that grows in wet places.

**waterfall** *n* a vertical or steep descent of the water of a river or stream.

**waterfowl** *n* (*pl* **waterfowls** *or* **waterfowl**) a bird, *esp* a duck, that frequents water.

**waterfront** *n* a section of a town bordering on a body of water.

**water hole** *n* a natural hollow in which water collects, used by animals as a drinking place.

**water ice** *n* a frozen dessert of water, sugar, and flavouring.

**watering can** *n* a vessel with a handle and a long spout, used for watering plants.

**watering hole** *n* **1** a pool where animals come to drink. **2** *informal* a pub, hotel, etc used for convivial drinking.

**water lily** *n* an aquatic plant with floating leaves and usu showy colourful flowers.

**waterline** *n* the level on the hull of a vessel to which the water comes when it is afloat.

**waterlogged** *adj* filled or soaked with water.

**watermark** *n* a marking in paper visible when the paper is held up to the light.

**water meadow** *n* a meadow that is regularly flooded by a bordering river.

**watermelon** *n* a large melon with a hard green rind and sweet watery red pulp.

**water mill** *n* a mill whose machinery is moved by water.

**water on the brain** *n informal* hydrocephalus.

**water polo** *n* a game played in water by teams of swimmers who try to get an inflated ball into the opposing side's goal.

**waterproof¹** *adj* impervious to water.

**waterproof²** *n Brit* a waterproof garment.

**waterproof³** *v* to make waterproof.

**watershed** *n* **1** a dividing ridge separating streams, rivers etc that flow into different seas. **2** a crucial turning point. **3** *Brit* the time of day before which material considered unsuitable for children should not be shown on television.

**water ski** *n* a board used singly or in pairs for standing on while being towed over water at speed.

**water-ski** *v* (**water-skis, water-skied** *or* **water-ski'd, water-skiing**) to use water skis. ➤ **water-skier** *n*, **water-skiing** *n*.

**waterspout** *n* a funnel-shaped column of rotating wind and spray extending from the underside of a cloud to the surface of a sea, lake, etc.

**water table** *n* the level below which the ground is wholly saturated with water.

**watertight** *adj* **1** so closely sealed that water cannot pass through. **2** of an argument: impossible to disprove.

**water tower** *n* a tower supporting a raised water tank to provide the necessary steady pressure to distribute water.

**waterway** *n* a navigable route or body of water.

**waterwheel** *n* **1** a wheel made to rotate by direct action of water, and used *esp* to drive machinery. **2** a wheel for raising water.

**waterworks** *n* (*pl* **waterworks**) the reservoirs, buildings, and equipment used to supply water e.g. to a city.

**watt** *n* the SI unit of power, *esp* electrical power.

**wattage** *n* an amount of electrical power expressed in watts.

**wattle** *n* **1** a framework of poles interwoven with branches or reeds and used, *esp* formerly, in building. **2** a fleshy protuberance on the head or neck of a bird.

**wattle and daub** *n* wattle covered with clay, used, *esp* formerly, in building construction.

**wave¹** *v* **1** to move the hand or something held in the hand to and fro in greeting, as a signal, etc. **2** to sway, flutter, or swing loosely to and fro. **3** to give a curving or undulating shape to (e.g. hair).

**wave²** *n* **1** a moving ridge on the surface of a body of water, e.g. the sea. **2** a shape or outline that has successive curves, e.g. in the hair. **3** a surge of sensation or emotion. **4** a sudden increase or wide occurrence of a phenomenon or activity. **5** an act of waving, *esp* as a signal or greeting. **6** in physics, a periodic disturbance or variation of a physical quantity by which energy is transferred progressively from point to point. * **make waves 1** *informal* to cause trouble. **2** *informal* to create a considerable, usu good, impression.

**wave band** *n* a band of radio frequency waves.

**wavelength** *n* the distance from the peak of one electromagnetic wave to the peak of the next. * **be on somebody's/the same wavelength** to have the same outlook, views, etc as somebody else.

**wavelet** *n* a little wave.

**waver** *v* **1** to vacillate between choices. **2** to sway unsteadily to and fro; to flicker. **3** to hesitate as if about to give way; to falter. ➤ **waverer** *n.*

**wavy** *adj* (**-ier, -iest**) having a wavelike form or outline.

**wax**[1] *n* **1** = BEESWAX. **2** a malleable substance that is similar to, but harder and less greasy than, a fat, used in making candles, polishes, etc. ➤ **waxen** *adj,* **waxy** *adj.*

**wax**[2] *v* **1** to treat or rub with wax. **2** to remove hair from (a part of the body) using melted wax.

**wax**[3] *v* **1** of the moon: to have an increasing area of the illuminated surface visible. **2** to show the emotional quality specified, *esp* when speaking or writing: *wax lyrical.* **3** *literary* to increase.

**waxwork** *n* **1** an effigy in wax, usu of a person. **2** (*in pl*) an exhibition of wax effigies.

**way**[1] *n* **1** a method or manner of doing something. **2** a characteristic manner of behaving or happening. **3** a feature or respect. **4** a course leading in a direction or towards an objective. **5** a road or path. **6** an opening one can pass through: *the way in.* **7** space or room, *esp* for forward movement. **8** the length of a course; a distance. **9** a direction or side: *a one-way street.* **10** (*in pl*) used to denote a specified number of participants: *They split the money four ways.* **11** motion or speed of a ship or boat through the water. * **by the way** incidentally. **by way of 1** via. **2** in the form of. **get/have one's own way** to get what one wants. **have a way with** to be good at dealing with (people, animals, etc). **in a way** to some extent. **in the way** obstructing movement. **no way** *informal* under no circumstances. **on the way 1** while moving along a course. **2** coming or approaching. **out of the way 1** secluded or remote. **2** done or completed. **under way** in progress; started.

**way**[2] *adv informal* considerably; far. * **way back** long ago.

**waybill** *n* a document giving details of the nature, destination, etc of the goods carried on a vehicle.

**wayfarer** *n literary* a traveller, *esp* on foot.

**waylay** *v* (*past tense and past part.* **waylaid**) **1** to ambush and attack. **2** to accost and detain.

**way-out** *adj informal* out of the ordinary, *esp* in being daring or experimental.

**wayside** *n* the side of a road.

**wayward** *adj* unpredictable and difficult to control.

**WC** *abbr Brit* water closet.

**we** *pron* referring to the speaker and others associated with the speaker.

**weak** *adj* **1** deficient in physical strength and vigour. **2** not able to exert or sustain much weight, pressure, or strain. **3** not having or exerting authority or political power. **4** unable to withstand temptation or persuasion. **5** (*often* + in) lacking skill or proficiency. **6** deficient in strength or flavour; diluted. ➤ **weakly** *adv.*

**weaken** *v* to make or become weak.

**weakling** *n* a weak person or animal.

**weakness** *n* **1** the quality of being weak. **2** a fault or defect. **3** (+ for) a special desire or fondness. **4** something one is especially fond of.

**weal** *or* **wheal** *n* a raised mark on the surface of the body.

**wealth** *n* **1** abundance of money and valuable material possessions. **2** the state of being rich. **3** an abundant supply.

**wealthy** *adj* (**-ier, -iest**) having wealth; rich.

**wean** *v* **1** to accustom (a child or other young mammal) to take food other than the mother's milk. **2** (*usu* + off/from) to cause to abandon a usu unwholesome dependence on something. **3** (**be weaned on**) to have been acquainted with something from an early age.

**weapon** *n* **1** an instrument of attack or defence, *esp* in combat. **2** a means used to further one's cause in conflict. ➤ **weaponry** *n.*

**wear**[1] *v* (**wore, worn**) **1** to have (e.g. a garment) on the body as clothing or adornment. **2** to have or show (a specified expression) on the face. **3** to damage or diminish, or be damaged or diminished, by use. **4** to endure use: *The carpet is wearing well.* **5** (*often* + on) of time: to go by slowly or tediously. * **wear the trousers** to have the controlling authority in a household. **wear thin** to become weakened or exhausted. ➤ **wearer** *n.*

**wear**[2] *n* **1** wearing or being worn. **2** clothing, usu of a specified kind or for a specified occasion: *swimwear.* **3** minor damage or deterioration through use.

**wear down** *v* to overcome by persistence.

**wearing** *adj* causing fatigue; tiring.

**wearisome** *adj* causing weariness; tiresome.

**wear off** *v* to lose effectiveness gradually.

**wear out** *v* **1** to make or become useless by long or excessive wear. **2** to tire or exhaust.

**weary**[1] *adj* (**-ier, -iest**) **1** exhausted or tired. **2** expressing or causing weariness. **3** (+ of) no longer able to endure or enjoy. ➤ **wearily** *adv,* **weariness** *n.*

**weary**[2] *v* (**-ies, -ied**) **1** to make weary. **2** (+ of) to become fed up with.

**weasel** *n* (*pl* **weasels** *or* **weasel**) a small slender flesh-eating mammal with a mostly reddish brown coat.

**weather**[1] *n* the prevailing atmospheric conditions with regard to heat or cold, wetness or dryness, etc. * **keep a weather eye on** to remain alert to. **make heavy weather of** *informal* to have unnecessary difficulty in doing or completing. **under the weather** *informal* mildly ill or depressed.

**weather**[2] *v* **1** to come safely through (e.g. a storm). **2** to undergo, or be resistant to, change caused by exposure to wind, rain, sun, etc.

**weatherboard** *n* **1** any of a series of overlapping horizontal boards forming a protective outdoor wall covering. **2** a sloping board fixed to the bottom of a door for excluding rain, snow, etc. ➤ **weatherboarding** *n.*

**weathercock** *n* a weather vane, *esp* one in the figure of a cockerel.

**weatherman** *or* **weatherwoman** *n* (*pl* **weathermen** *or* **weatherwomen**) a person, *esp* a meteorologist, who reports and forecasts the weather, usu on the radio or television.

**weather vane** *n* a revolving pointer attached to an elevated structure in order to show the direction of the wind.

**weave**[1] *v* (*past tense* **wove,** *past part.* **wove** *or* **woven**) **1** to form cloth by interlacing warp and weft threads. **2** to produce by elaborately combining elements into a coherent whole. **3** (*usu* + in/into) to introduce as an appropriate element.

**weave**[2] *n* a pattern or method for interlacing the threads of woven fabrics.

**weave**[3] *v* to move in a zigzag course, *esp* to avoid obstacles.

**web** *n* **1** the netlike structure spun by most spiders as a trap for prey. **2** an intricate structure or network. **3** (**the Web**) the World Wide Web. **4** the tissue uniting the toes of a bird or animal that lives in water.

**webbed** *adj* having toes joined by a web.

**webbing** *n* a strong narrow tape used for straps, upholstery, or harnesses.

**webcam** /'webkam/ *n* a camera, connected to a computer, that produces images for display on a web page.

**web page** *n* a hypertext document that can be accessed via the World Wide Web.

**website** *n* a group of related web pages giving information about a particular subject, company, institution, etc.

**wed** *v* (**wedding,** *past tense and past part.* **wedded** *or* **wed**) **1** to marry. **2** to unite (two things).

**we'd** *contraction* **1** we had. **2** we would. **3** we should.

**wedded** *adj* **1** of marriage; conjugal. **2** (+ to) committed to.

**wedding** *n* **1** a marriage ceremony, usu with its accompanying festivities. **2** a wedding anniversary or its celebration.

**wedge**[1] *n* **1** a piece of wood, metal, etc that tapers to a thin edge. **2** a shoe with a wedge-shaped sole. **3** an iron golf club with a broad face angled for maximum loft. * **thin end of the wedge** something apparently insignificant that is the forerunner of a more important development.

**wedge**[2] *v* **1** to secure with or as if with a wedge. **2** (+ in/into) to force into a narrow space.

**wedlock** *n* the state of being married; marriage.

**Wednesday** *n* the day of the week following Tuesday.

**wee**[1] *adj* (**weer, weest**) *chiefly Scot* very small.

**wee**[2] *n chiefly Brit, informal* urine or an act of passing urine.

**wee**[3] *v* (**wees, weed, weeing**) *chiefly Brit, informal* to urinate.

**weed**[1] *n* **1** a wild plant that grows where it is not wanted. **2** *informal* a weak or unattractively thin person. **3** (**the weed**) *informal* tobacco. **4** *informal* cannabis.

**weed**[2] *v* **1** to remove weeds. **2** (+ out) to remove (harmful or undesirable people or things).

**weedkiller** *n* a substance used for killing weeds.

**weedy** *adj* (**-ier, -iest**) **1** covered with or consisting of weeds. **2** *informal* weak, thin, and ineffectual.

**week**[1] *n* **1** a period of seven consecutive days. **2** the working days, usu Monday to Friday, during each seven-day period.

**week**[2] *adv chiefly Brit* at a time that is seven days after a specified day: *Tuesday week.*

**weekday** *n* any day of the week except Saturday and Sunday.

**weekend**[1] *n* Saturday and Sunday.

**weekend**[2] *v informal* to spend the weekend.

**weekly** *adv and adj* **1** every week. **2** once a week. **3** by the week.

**weeny** *adj* (**-ier, -iest**) *informal* tiny.

**weep**[1] *v* (*past tense and past part.* **wept**) **1** to express grief or other emotion by shedding tears. **2** *esp* of a wound: to exude a liquid, pus, etc slowly.

**weep**[2] *n* a period of weeping.

**weepy** *adj* (**-ier, -iest**) **1** *informal* tearful. **2** sentimental.

**weevil** *n* a small beetle that is harmful to grain, fruit, and plants.

**weft** *n* the crosswise yarn that interlaces the warp in a fabric.

**weigh** *v* **1** to ascertain the heaviness of. **2** to have a specified weight. **3** (*often* + out) to measure (a definite quantity of something) on scales. **4** (*often* + up) to consider carefully in order to reach a conclusion. **5** (+ down) to be a burden to. **6** to be considered important; to count. **7** (*often* + on/upon) to be oppressive or a cause of worry to. * **weigh anchor** to pull up an anchor preparatory to sailing.

**weighbridge** *n* a large scale used for weighing vehicles.

**weigh in** *v* **1** of a jockey, boxer, etc: to be weighed before or after a race or match. **2**

*informal* to make a contribution. ➤ **weigh-in** *n.*

**weight[1]** *n* **1** the amount that something or somebody weighs. **2** a system of units of weight or mass. **3** any of the units used in such a system. **4** a piece of metal of known weight for use in weighing articles. **5** something heavy. **6** a heavy object used to hold or press something down. **7** a heavy object lifted as an athletic exercise or contest. **8** a burden or pressure. **9** relative importance, authority, or influence. ➤ **weightless** *adj.*

**weight[2]** *v* **1** to make heavy or hold down with a weight. **2** to arrange in such a way as to create a bias.

**weighting** *n* **1** an allowance made to compensate for something that has a distorting effect. **2** *Brit* an additional sum paid on top of wages or salary, *esp* to offset the higher cost of living in a particular area.

**weightlifting** *n* a sport that involves competitors lifting progressively heavier weights. ➤ **weightlifter** *n.*

**weighty** *adj* (**-ier, -iest**) **1** having importance, influence, or consequence. **2** heavy.

**weir** *n* a low dam in a watercourse to control its flow.

**weird** *adj* **1** suggestive of or caused by the supernatural. **2** *informal* very strange or bizarre. ➤ **weirdly** *adv,* **weirdness** *n.*

**weirdo** *n* (*pl* **-os**) *informal* somebody who is very strange or eccentric.

**welch** *v* see WELSH.

**welcome[1]** *n* a greeting or reception on arrival or first appearance.

**welcome[2]** *adj* **1** received gladly into one's presence or companionship. **2** received gratefully, *esp* because fulfilling a need. **3** (+ to) willingly permitted to do or have something. ✱ **you're welcome** used as a reply to an expression of thanks.

**welcome[3]** *v* **1** to greet (somebody) hospitably and with courtesy. **2** to receive or accept (something) with pleasure.

**weld[1]** *v* **1** to fuse (metallic parts) together by heating and/or hammering. **2** to unite closely or inseparably. ➤ **welder** *n.*

**weld[2]** *n* a welded joint.

**welfare** *n* **1** well-being. **2** aid in the form of money or necessities for those not able to provide for themselves.

**welfare state** *n* a social system in which the state assumes responsibility for the provision of pensions, benefits, health care, etc to its citizens.

**well[1]** *adv* (**better, best**) **1** in a good or proper manner. **2** with skill. **3** in a kind or friendly manner. **4** in a prosperous or affluent manner. **5** thoroughly or fully. **6** with good reason. **7** much or considerably. **8** in all likelihood; indeed. ✱ **as well 1** also; in addition. **2** with an effect that is the same or preferable. **well out of** *informal* lucky to be free from or not involved in. **well up on** *informal* very knowledgeable about.

***Usage Note:*** Adjectives such as *well-known, well-mannered,* etc should always be spelt with a hyphen when used before a noun: *a well-known story.* The hyphen is not usually necessary when the adjective is used after a verb: *As is probably well known to most of you…*

**well[2]** *adj* (**better, best**) **1** healthy, *esp* cured or recovered. **2** satisfactory or pleasing. **3** advisable or desirable. ➤ **wellness** *n.*

**well[3]** *interj* **1** used to express surprise, indignation, or resignation. **2** used to indicate a pause in talking or to introduce a remark.

**well[4]** *n* **1** a pit, shaft, or hole sunk in the earth to reach a supply of water or a natural deposit, e.g. oil or gas. **2** a space or hole made to contain liquid. **3** a source from which something springs. **4** an open space extending vertically through the floors of a structure, e.g. for stairs or a lift.

**well[5]** *v* **1** (*often* + up) of liquid: to rise to the surface. **2** (*often* + up) of emotion: to arise within one.

**we'll** *contraction* **1** we will. **2** we shall.

**well-advised** *adj* acting with or showing wisdom; prudent.

**well-appointed** *adj* having good and complete facilities, furniture, etc.

**well-behaved** *adj* showing proper manners or conduct.

**well-being** *n* the state of being happy, healthy, or prosperous.

**well-disposed** *adj* having a favourable or sympathetic attitude.

**well done** *interj* used to express congratulations.

**well-done** *adj* of food, *esp* meat: cooked thoroughly.

**well-heeled** *adj informal* wealthy.

**wellington** *or* **wellington boot** *n Brit* a waterproof rubber boot usu reaching to the knee.

**well-nigh** *adv literary* almost or nearly.

**well-off** *adj* **1** prosperous or rich. **2** in a favourable situation. **3** (*usu* + for) well provided.

**well-spoken** *adj* speaking clearly, courteously, and usu with a refined accent.

**well-to-do** *adj* rich; prosperous.

**well-wisher** *n* somebody who feels or expresses goodwill towards a person, cause, etc.

**welly** *or* **wellie** *n Brit, informal* **1** = WELLINGTON. **2** power or effort.

**Welsh** *n* **1** (**the Welsh**) (*in pl*) the people of Wales. **2** the Celtic language spoken in Wales. ➤ **Welsh** *adj.*

**welsh** *or* **welch** *v* (*usu* + on) to evade an obligation, *esp* payment of a debt.

**Welsh rarebit** *n* a snack of melted cheese, mixed with seasonings, on toast.

**welt** *n* **1** a strip, usu of leather, fastening the sole of a shoe to the upper. **2** a weal.

**welter** *n* a chaotic mass or jumble.

**welterweight** *n* a weight in boxing and wrestling between lightweight and middleweight.

**wench** *n archaic or humorous* a young woman.

**wend** *v* to proceed on (one's way), often at a leisurely pace.

**wendy house** *n* (*often* **Wendy house**) *chiefly Brit* a toy house for children to play in.

**went** *v* past tense of GO[1].

**wept** *v* past tense and past part. of WEEP[1].

**were** *v* second person sing. past, plural past, and past subjunctive of BE.

**we're** *contraction* we are.

**weren't** *contraction* were not.

**werewolf** /ˈweəwoolf, ˈwiəwoolf/ *n* (*pl* **werewolves**) in folklore, a person who periodically transforms into a wolf.

**west**[1] *n* **1** the direction of sunset, 180° from east. **2** regions or countries lying to the west. **3** (*usu* **the West**) Europe and North America. ➤ ***westbound*** *adj and adv.*

**west**[2] *adj and adv* **1** at or towards the west. **2** of the wind: blowing from the west.

**westerly** *adj and adv* **1** in a western position or direction. **2** of a wind: blowing from the west.

**western**[1] *adj* **1** in or towards the west. **2** (*often* **Western**) of Europe or North America.

**western**[2] *n* a novel, film, etc dealing with cowboys, frontier life, etc in the western USA.

**Westerner** *n* a person from the western part of a country or from Europe or North America.

**westernize** *or* **-ise** *v* to cause to adopt the culture, economics, politics, etc of North America or Europe.

**westward** *adv and adj* towards the west; in a direction going west. ➤ **westwards** *adv.*

**wet**[1] *adj* (**wetter, wettest**) **1** covered or soaked with liquid, e.g. water. **2** of weather: rainy. **3** of paint, cement, etc: not yet dry or set. **4** *Brit, informal* of a person: feeble, ineffectual, or dull. ✻ **wet behind the ears** *informal* immature or inexperienced. ➤ **wetly** *adv,* **wetness** *n.*

**wet**[2] *n* **1** moisture or wetness. **2** (**the wet**) rainy weather. **3** *Brit, informal* a feeble, ineffectual, or dull person.

**wet**[3] *v* (**wetting,** *past tense and past part.* **wet** *or* **wetted**) **1** to make wet. **2** to urinate in or on.

**wet blanket** *n informal* a person who spoils other people's fun, e.g. by a lack of enthusiasm.

**wether** *n* a castrated male sheep.

**wet nurse** *n* a woman who breastfeeds a child she did not give birth to.

**wet suit** *n* a close-fitting rubber suit that retains body heat so as to insulate its wearer in cold water.

**we've** *contraction* we have.

**whack**[1] *v informal* **1** to strike with a sharp or resounding blow. **2** to defeat. **3** to place or insert roughly, casually, or quickly.

**whack**[2] *n informal* **1** a sharp resounding blow. **2** *Brit* a portion or share. ✻ **top/full whack** *chiefly Brit* the maximum amount.

**whacked** *adj informal* exhausted.

**whacking** *adj Brit, informal* enormous.

**whacky** *adj* see WACKY.

**whale** *n* (*pl* **whales** *or* **whale**) a very large sea mammal with a tail modified as a paddle. ✻ **have a whale of a time** to have an exceptionally enjoyable time.

**whalebone** *n* a horny substance found in two rows of plates along the upper jaw of some whales.

**whaler** *n* a person or ship engaged in whaling.

**whaling** *n* the occupation of catching whales for oil, food, etc.

**whammy** *n* (*pl* **-ies**) *informal* something that has a bad effect.

**wharf** *n* (*pl* **wharves** *or* **wharfs**) a structure built along the shore of navigable water so that ships may load and unload.

**what**[1] *pron and adj* (*pl* **what**) **1** used to ask about the identity, nature, purpose, occupation, etc of something or somebody. **2** used to ask for repetition of something not properly heard or understood. **3** used to express surprise or excitement. **4** whatever. ✻ **what about** used to make suggestions. **what if** what will or would be the result if. **what of it** what does it matter. **what's his/her/its name** used to replace a forgotten name. **what's what** the true state of things.

**what**[2] *adv* in what respect?; how much?

**whatever**[1] *pron* **1** anything or everything that. **2** no matter what. **3** *informal* used for emphasis in place of the interrogative adverb *what.*

**whatever**[2] *adj* **1** no matter what. **2** of any kind at all.

**whatnot** *n informal* other usu related goods, objects, etc.

**whatsoever** *pron and adj* whatever.

**wheat** *n* a cereal grass whose grain yields a fine white flour.

**wheatear** *n* a small white-rumped bird related to the thrush.

**wheat germ** *n* the central part of the wheat kernel used *esp* as a source of vitamins.

**wheatmeal** *n* brown flour made from wheat with some bran and germ taken out.

**wheedle** *v* **1** to use soft words or flattery. **2** to influence, persuade, or entice by wheedling. ➤ **wheedler** *n.*

**wheel**[1] *n* **1** a solid circular disc, or a circular frame joined to a central hub by spokes, that is capable of turning on an axle. **2** (**the wheel**) the wheel that controls the steering of a ship or vehicle. **3** a curving or circular movement.

**wheel**[2] *v* **1** to move in a circle or curve. **2** to turn round to face in the opposite direction. **3** to push (a wheeled vehicle). **4** to convey or move in a wheeled vehicle. * **wheel and deal** to pursue one's own commercial interests, *esp* in a shrewd or unscrupulous manner.

**wheelbarrow** *n* a load-carrying device consisting of a shallow box supported at one end by a wheel and at the other by legs.

**wheelbase** *n* the distance between the front and rear axles of a vehicle.

**wheelchair** *n* a chair mounted on wheels for disabled people or invalids.

**wheeler-dealer** *n* a shrewd operator, *esp* in business or politics.

**wheel out** *v informal* to resort to with tedious regularity.

**wheeze**[1] *v* **1** to breathe with difficulty, usu with a whistling sound. **2** to make a sound like that of wheezing.

**wheeze**[2] *n* **1** a sound of wheezing. **2** *Brit, informal* a clever scheme. ➤ **wheezy** *adj.*

**whelk** *n* a large usu edible sea snail.

**whelp**[1] *n* **1** a young dog. **2** a disagreeable or impudent young man.

**whelp**[2] *v* to give birth to (e.g. a puppy).

**when**[1] *adv* **1** at what time? **2** at or during which time.

**when**[2] *conj* **1** at or during the time that. **2** as soon as. **3** whenever. **4** in the event that; if. **5** considering that. **6** although.

**whence** *adv and conj formal* **1** from which place, source, or cause. **2** to the place from which.

**whenever**[1] *or* **whensoever** *conj* **1** at every or whatever time. **2** in any circumstance.

**whenever**[2] *adv informal* used for emphasis in place of the interrogative adverb *when.*

**where**[1] *adv* **1** at, in, or to what place? **2** at, in, or to what situation, direction, or respect? **3** at, in, or to which.

**where**[2] *conj* **1** at, in, or to the place at which. **2** wherever. **3** in a case, situation, or respect in which. **4** whereas.

**whereabouts**[1] *adv and conj* in what vicinity.

**whereabouts**[2] *pl n* the place or general locality where a person or thing is.

**whereas** *conj* **1** while on the contrary. **2** in view of the fact that; since.

**whereby** *conj formal* by which means.

**wherefore** *adv formal* **1** why. **2** therefore.

**wherein** *adv formal* **1** in what respect. **2** in which.

**whereof** *conj, pron, and adv formal* of what, which, or whom.

**whereupon** *adv and conj* closely following which.

**wherever**[1] *adv* used for emphasis in place of the interrogative adverb *where.*

**wherever**[2] *or* **wheresoever** *conj* at, in, or to every or whatever place.

**wherewithal** *n* means or resources, *esp* money.

**wherry** *n* (*pl* **-ies**) a light rowing boat or barge.

**whet** *v* (**whetted, whetting**) **1** to sharpen (a blade). **2** to stimulate.

**whether** *conj* **1** used to indicate an indirect question involving alternatives. **2** used to indicate a choice between two alternatives. **3** used to indicate indifference between alternatives.

**whetstone** *n* a stone for sharpening an edge, e.g. of a chisel.

**whey** *n* the watery part of milk separated from the curd.

**which**[1] *adj* **1** used to ask for identification of one or ones out of a known or limited group. **2** whichever.

**which**[2] *pron* (*pl* **which**) **1** which thing, person, etc. **2** whichever. **3** used to introduce a non-restrictive clause, *esp* in reference to an animal, thing, or idea.

**whichever** *pron and adj* (*pl* **whichever**) **1** any one or ones out of a group. **2** no matter which.

**whiff**[1] *n* **1** a slight or passing odour. **2** *Brit, informal* an unpleasant smell. **3** a quick puff or slight gust. **4** a slight trace.

**whiff**[2] *v Brit, informal* to smell unpleasant.

**Whig** *n* a member of a British political party of the 18th and early 19th centuries seeking to limit royal authority and increase parliamentary power.

**while**[1] *n* a period of time. * **a while** for some time. **worth one's while** worth the time and effort used.

**while**[2] *conj* **1** during the time that. **2** providing that; as long as. **3** when on the other hand; whereas. **4** although.

**while away** *v* to pass (time) in a leisurely and usu pleasant manner.

**whilst** *conj chiefly Brit* while.

**whim** *n* a sudden, capricious, or eccentric idea or impulse.

**whimper** *v* to make a low plaintive whining sound. ➤ **whimper** *n.*

**whimsical** *adj* **1** resulting from or suggesting whimsy. **2** full of whims; capricious. ➤ **whimsically** *adv.*

**whimsy** *or* **whimsey** *n* (*pl* **-ies** *or* **-eys**) **1** an amusingly or quaintly fanciful quality, *esp* in writing or art. **2** a whim or caprice.

**whin** *n* = GORSE.

**whine**[1] *v* **1** to utter a prolonged high-pitched cry, usu expressive of distress or pain, or make a sound resembling such a cry. **2** to complain querulously or peevishly.

**whine**[2] *n* a whining sound. ➤ **whiny** *adj.*

**whinge**[1] *v* (**whinges, whingeing, whinged**) *Brit, informal* to complain or moan. ➤ **whinger** *n.*

**whinge**[2] *n Brit, informal* a complaint.

**whinny** *v* (**-ies, -ied**) to utter a low gentle neigh or similar sound. ➤ **whinny** *n.*

**whip**[1] *n* **1** an instrument consisting of a flexible leather strip or cord attached to a handle, used for driving animals and for punishment. **2** somebody appointed by a political party to enforce party discipline and secure the attendance of party members for important votes. **3** *Brit* an instruction from a whip to be in attendance for voting. **4** a dessert made by whipping some of the ingredients. * **the whip hand** the advantage.

**whip**[2] *v* (**whipped, whipping**) **1** to strike (a person or animal) with a whip. **2** to beat (e.g. eggs or cream) into a froth. **3** to thrash about flexibly like a whiplash. **4** to take, pull, or move very quickly and forcefully. **5** *Brit, informal* to steal. ➤ **whipping** *n.*

**whiplash** *n* **1** the flexible part of a whip. **2** injury to the neck resulting from a sudden sharp movement, e.g. in a car collision.

**whippersnapper** *n informal* an insignificant but impudent person, *esp* a child.

**whippet** *n* a dog of a small slender short-haired breed related to the greyhound.

**whipping boy** *n* a person who is blamed or punished for the mistakes, incompetence, etc of others.

**whippoorwill** /'wipəwil/ *n* a North American nightjar.

**whip-round** *n Brit, informal* a collection of money made usu for a benevolent purpose.

**whip up** *v* **1** to stir up or stimulate. **2** to produce in a hurry.

**whirl**[1] *v* **1** to turn abruptly or rapidly round on an axis. **2** of the head: to become giddy or dizzy.

**whirl**[2] *n* **1** a rapid rotating or circling movement. **2** a rapid succession of events, engagements, etc. **3** a confused or disturbed state. **4** *informal* a try.

**whirligig** *n* **1** a child's toy, e.g. a top, that whirls. **2** a merry-go-round.

**whirlpool** *n* **1** a circular eddy of rapidly moving water. **2** a bath equipped with a device to produce whirling currents of hot water.

**whirlwind**[1] *n* **1** a small rapidly rotating windstorm. **2** a confused rush; a whirl.

**whirlwind**[2] *adj* happening with great speed or suddenness: *a whirlwind romance.*

**whirr**[1] *or* **whir** *v* (**whirred, whirring**) to revolve or move with a continuous buzzing sound.

**whirr**[2] *or* **whir** *n* a whirring sound.

**whisk**[1] *n* **1** a small usu hand-held kitchen utensil used for beating food until frothy. **2** a small bunch of flexible strands, e.g. twigs or feathers, attached to a handle for use as a brush.

**whisk**[2] *v* **1** to mix or beat (e.g. egg whites) with a whisk. **2** to convey or remove briskly. **3** to flick.

**whisker** *n* **1** a long projecting hair or bristle growing near the mouth of an animal. **2** (*in pl*) the hair of a man's beard or moustache. **3** (**a whisker**) *informal* a very small amount or narrow margin. ➤ **whiskery** *adj.*

**whisky** (*NAmer and Irish* **whiskey**) *n* (*pl* **-ies**) a spirit made by distilling barley or other grain.

**whisper**[1] *v* **1** to speak softly. **2** to make a hissing or rustling sound.

**whisper**[2] *n* **1** a very soft speaking voice or something spoken very softly. **2** a hissing or rustling sound. **3** a rumour. **4** a hint or trace.

**whist** *n* a card game scored by winning tricks.

**whistle**[1] *n* **1** a device with a slit through which air, steam, the breath, etc is forced to produce a loud high-pitched sound. **2** a shrill clear sound produced by forcing air through pursed lips or by a whistle. * **blow the whistle on** *informal* to report (a person acting wrongly or a wrong act) to an authority.

**whistle**[2] *v* **1** to make a shrill clear sound by blowing or drawing air through the puckered lips. **2** to make a whistling sound by rapid movement. **3** to blow a whistle.

**whistle-blower** *n informal* somebody who reveals or reports wrongdoing.

**whistle-stop** *adj* consisting of brief stops in several places.

**Whit** *n* Whitsuntide.

**whit** *n* * **not a whit** not in the smallest degree; not a bit.

**white**[1] *adj* **1** of the colour of new snow or milk. **2** very pale. **3** of wine: having a light yellow or amber colour. **4** *Brit* of coffee or tea: containing milk or cream. **5** of flour, sugar, etc: refined and white in colour. **6** relating to people having pale skin colour. **7** free from moral impurity. **8** of a wedding: in which the bride wears a white dress. * **bleed white** to deprive eventually of all money or resources. ➤ **whiteness** *n.*

**white**[2] *n* **1** a white colour or fabric. **2** the mass of albumin-containing material surrounding the yolk of an egg. **3** the white part of the ball of the eye. **4** a person belonging to a light-skinned people.

**whitebait** *n* the young of a herring or sprat eaten whole.

**white-collar** *adj* relating to non-manual employees, *esp* those who work in offices.

**white elephant** *n* a possession that is troublesome to maintain or no longer of value to its owner.

**white feather** *n* a symbol of cowardice.

**white flag** *n* a flag of plain white used to request a truce or as a token of surrender.

**white goods** *pl n* **1** major articles of household equipment, e.g. cookers and refrigerators. **2** household linen.

**white-hot** *adj* glowing white with heat.

**white lie** *n* a harmless or unimportant lie, e.g. told to avoid hurting somebody's feelings.

**white magic** *n* magic used for good purposes.

**whiten** *v* to become or make white. ➤ **whitener** *n.*

**white noise** *n* low-volume sound that has many continuous frequencies of equal intensity.

**White Paper** *n* a British government report containing information about or proposals on a particular issue.

**white sauce** *n* a sauce made with flour, butter, and milk or a chicken or fish stock.

**white spirit** *n* a flammable liquid distilled from petroleum and used as a solvent and thinner for paints.

**whitewash**[1] *n* **1** a liquid mixture, e.g. of lime and water, for whitening *esp* exterior walls. **2** a deliberate concealment of a mistake or fault.

**whitewash**[2] *v* **1** to apply whitewash to (e.g. a wall). **2** to gloss over or cover up (e.g. a mistake or fault).

**whither** *adv and conj formal or archaic* **1** to or towards what place? **2** to the place at, in, or to which. **3** what does the future hold for?

**whiting** *n* (*pl* **whiting**) a seafish related to the cod.

**Whitsun** *n* Whitsuntide.

**Whit Sunday** *n* a Christian feast commemorating the descent of the Holy Spirit at Pentecost, observed on the seventh Sunday after Easter.

**Whitsuntide** *n* the week beginning with Whit Sunday.

**whittle** *v* **1** to shape (wood) by cutting off chips from its surface. **2** (+ down/away) to reduce, remove, or destroy gradually.

**whizz**[1] *or* **whiz** *v* **1** to speed through the air with a buzzing, whirring, or hissing sound. **2** *informal* to move or go swiftly.

**whizz**[2] *or* **whiz** *n* **1** a whizzing sound. **2** (*also* **wiz**) *informal* somebody who is very clever or skilful.

**whizz kid** *or* **whiz kid** *n* a person who is unusually clever or successful, *esp* at an early age.

**WHO** *abbr* World Health Organization.

**who** *pron* (*pl* **who**) **1** what or which person? **2** used to introduce a restrictive or non-restrictive clause in reference to a person or people.

**whoa** /'woh·ə, woh/ *interj* used as a command, e.g. to a horse, to stand still.

**who'd** *contraction* **1** who would. **2** who had.

**whodunit** *or* **whodunnit** *n* a play, film, or story dealing with the detection of crime or criminals.

**whoever** *or* **whosoever** *pron* **1** whatever person. **2** no matter who. **3** *informal* used for emphasis in place of the interrogative pronoun *who*.

**whole**[1] *adj* **1** each or all of; total or entire. **2** having all its proper constituents: *whole milk*. **3** unhurt or intact. ➤ **wholeness** *n*.

**whole**[2] *n* something that is complete in itself or that results from putting all the required component parts together. ✱ **as a whole** considered all together or in general. **on the whole 1** all things considered. **2** in most instances.

**whole**[3] *adv* in an undivided piece or state.

**wholefood** *n* (*also in pl*) food in a simple and natural form that has undergone minimal processing and refining.

**wholehearted** *adj* earnestly committed or devoted. ➤ **wholeheartedly** *adv.*

**wholemeal** *adj* of bread or flour: produced from ground entire wheat kernels.

**wholesale**[1] *n* the sale of commodities in large quantities usu for resale by a retailer.

**wholesale**[2] *adj and adv* **1** selling or sold by wholesale. **2** on a large scale, *esp* without discrimination.

**wholesale**[3] *v* to sell (commodities) by wholesale. ➤ **wholesaler** *n.*

**wholesome** *adj* promoting health of body or mind.

**wholly** *adv* **1** completely. **2** solely.

***Usage Note:*** Note that the spelling is *wholly* and not *wholely*.

**whom** *pron* used in place of *who*, as the object of a verb or preposition.

**whoop**[1] /woohp/ *n* a loud yell of eagerness or jubilation.

**whoop**[2] *v* to utter or make a whoop. ✱ **whoop it up** *informal* to celebrate riotously.

**whoopee**[1] *interj informal* used to express exuberance.

**whoopee**[2] *n* ✱ **make whoopee 1** *informal* to celebrate noisily. **2** *informal* to have sexual intercourse.

**whooper swan** /'hoohpə/ *n* a European swan with a loud ringing call.

**whooping cough** /'hoohping/ *n* an infectious bacterial disease, *esp* of children, marked by a convulsive spasmodic cough followed by a crowing intake of breath.

**whoops** *interj* used to express dismay or apology, *esp* on being clumsy or making a silly mistake.

**whoosh** *or* **woosh** *v* to move quickly with a rushing sound. ➤ **whoosh** *n.*

**whopper** *n informal* **1** something unusually large or extreme of its kind. **2** a blatant lie.

**whopping** *adj informal* extremely big.

**whore** /haw/ *n* a prostitute or a promiscuous woman. ➤ **whorish** *adj.*

**whorehouse** *n informal* a brothel.

**whorl** /wuhl, wawl/ *n* **1** an arrangement of similar parts, e.g. leaves, in a circle round a stem. **2** something spiral in form or movement. **3** a single turn of a spiral.

**who's** *contraction* **1** who is. **2** who has.

***Usage Note:*** Do not confuse this word with *whose*.

**whose** *adj and pron* of whom or which, *esp* as possessor or object of an action.

**why**[1] *adv* for what cause, reason, or purpose? ✱ **why not** used in making a suggestion.

**why**[2] *conj* **1** the cause, reason, or purpose for which. **2** on which grounds.

**why**[3] *interj* used to express mild surprise, approval, disapproval, or anger.

**wick** *n* a cord or strip of material through which a liquid, e.g. paraffin, oil, or melted wax, is drawn up for burning in a candle, lamp, etc. ✱ **get on somebody's wick** *Brit, informal* to annoy or irritate somebody.

**wicked** *adj* **1** morally bad; evil. **2** disposed to mischief. **3** very unpleasant, vicious, or dangerous. **4** *informal* extremely stylish or skilful; good. ➤ **wickedly** *adv,* **wickedness** *n.*

**wicker** *n* interlaced twigs, canes, or rods used to make baskets, furniture, etc. ➤ **wickerwork** *n.*

**wicket** *n* **1** in cricket, either of the two sets of stumps at which the ball is bowled. **2** a small gate or door.

**wicketkeeper** *n* in cricket, the fielder who is stationed behind the wicket.

**wide**[1] *adj* **1** having great horizontal extent; broad; vast. **2** having a specified width. **3** fully opened. **4** embracing much; comprehensive. **5** extending over a considerable range. **6** deviating from a target or from something specified. ➤ **widely** *adv.*

**wide**[2] *adv* **1** over a great horizontal distance or extent. **2** to the fullest extent. **3** so as to leave much space or distance between. **4** so as to miss by a considerable distance.

**wide-awake** *adj* **1** fully awake. **2** alert and watchful.

**wide boy** *n Brit, informal* a man who is involved in petty crime.

**wide-eyed** *adj* **1** amazed or astonished. **2** naive.

**widen** *v* to become or make wider.

**widespread** *adj* widely distributed or prevalent.

**widgeon** *n* see WIGEON.

**widget** *n informal* a small usu mechanical device whose name is unknown or irrelevant.

**widow**[1] *n* a woman whose husband has died and who has not remarried.

**widow**[2] *v* (**be widowed**) to become a widow or widower.

**widower** *n* a man whose wife has died and who has not remarried.

**width** *n* **1** the measurement taken at right angles to the length. **2** largeness of extent or scope.

**widthways** *adv* in the direction of the width; crosswise.

**wield** *v* **1** to handle (a tool or weapon) effectively. **2** to exert or exercise (power or influence).

***Usage Note:*** Note the spelling with *-ie-*.

**wife** *n* (*pl* **wives**) a married woman, *esp* in relation to her husband. ➤ **wifely** *adj.*

**wig** *n* a manufactured covering of natural or synthetic hair for the head.

**wigeon** *or* **widgeon** *n* (*pl* **wigeons** *or* **wigeon**) a freshwater dabbling duck, the male of which has a chestnut head.

**wiggle**[1] *v* to move or cause to move from side to side or up and down with short jerky movements.

**wiggle**[2] *n* a wiggling movement. ➤ **wiggly** *adj.*

**wigwam** *n* a conical or dome-shaped framework of poles covered with bark, rush mats, or hides, used formerly by Native Americans as a dwelling.

**wild**[1] *adj* **1** living or growing in a natural state. **2** of land: not inhabited or cultivated. **3** uncontrolled or unruly. **4** *informal* (*usu* + about) passionately eager or enthusiastic. **5** *informal* very angry; infuriated. **6** not sensible or well-founded. ➤ **wildly** *adv,* **wildness** *n.*

**wild**[2] *n* **1** (**the wild**) a wild, free, or natural state. **2** (**the wilds**) remote country.

**wild card** *n* **1** a playing card able to represent any card designated by the holder. **2** an irregular or unpredictable person or thing. **3** in computing, a character that can be used, e.g. in searching, to represent any character or string of characters.

**wildcat** *n* (*pl* **wildcats** *or* **wildcat**) a cat living in the wild that resembles but is heavier than the domestic cat.

**wildcat strike** *n* a strike initiated suddenly by a group of workers without union approval.

**wildebeest** /ˈwildəbeest, ˈvil-/ *n* (*pl* **wildebeests** *or* **wildebeest**) = GNU.

**wilderness** *n* **1** a region or area that is uncultivated and uninhabited by human beings. **2** the state of exclusion from office or power.

**wildfire** *n* ✱ **spread like wildfire** to spread very rapidly.

**wildfowl** *n* (*pl* **wildfowl**) a game bird, *esp* a waterfowl.

**wild goose chase** *n* a hopeless pursuit after something unattainable.

**wildlife** *n* the wild animals, birds, and insects of an area collectively.

**wile** *n* (*usu in pl*) a deceitful trick or stratagem.

**wilful** (*NAmer* **willful**) *adj* **1** deliberate. **2** obstinately and often perversely insisting on having one's own way. ➤ **wilfully** *adv,* **wilfulness** *n.*

**will**[1] *v* (*third person sing. present tense* **will,** *past tense* **would**) **1** used to express an action or state in the future. **2** used to express intention or determination. **3** used to express willingness or consent. **4** used to express a request or invitation. **5** used to express capability. **6** *formal, literary* to wish or desire.

**will**[2] *n* **1** a mental power by which one controls one's wishes, choices, intentions, etc or initiates action. **2** a desire, wish, or intention. **3** willpower; self-control. **4** a legal declaration of the manner in which somebody wishes to have their property disposed of after their death. * **at will** as one wishes. **with the best will in the world** no matter how good one's intentions are.

**will**[3] *v* **1** (+ to) to bequeath (property) to somebody. **2** to decree or ordain. **3** to cause or attempt to cause by exercise of the will. ➤ **willer** *n.*

**willies** *pl n* (**the willies**) *informal* a feeling of nervousness or fear.

**willing** *adj* **1** consenting, ready, or eager to do something. **2** done or given without reluctance. ➤ **willingly** *adv.*

**will-o'-the-wisp** *n* **1** a phosphorescent light sometimes seen at night over marshy ground and often caused by the combustion of gas from decomposed organic matter. **2** an enticing but elusive goal.

**willow** *n* a tree with pliant branches bearing catkins of flowers with no petals.

**willowy** *adj* of a person: gracefully tall and slender.

**willpower** *n* self-control and resoluteness.

**willy** *or* **willie** *n* (*pl* **-ies**) *Brit, informal* a penis.

**willy-nilly** *adv* **1** whether one wants to or not. **2** in a haphazard or random manner.

**wilt**[1] *v* **1** of a plant: to lose freshness and become limp. **2** of a person: to grow weak, tired, or faint.

**wilt**[2] *n* a disease of plants marked by wilting.

**wily** *adj* (**-ier, -iest**) crafty.

**wimp** *n informal* a weak, ineffectual, or cowardly person. ➤ **wimpish** *adj,* **wimpy** *adj.*

**wimple** *n* a cloth covering worn over the head and round the neck and chin by women in the late medieval period and by some nuns.

**win**[1] *v* (**winning,** *past tense and past part.* **won**) **1** to gain the victory in a battle, contest, or dispute. **2** to gain (a prize) in a contest. **3** to get possession of. **4** (+ over/round) to gain the approval of or persuade somebody. ➤ **winnable** *adj.*

**win**[2] *n* a victory or success in a game or sporting contest.

**wince** *v* to shrink back or grimace involuntarily, e.g. in pain. ➤ **wince** *n.*

**winceyette** *n Brit* a lightweight cotton fabric with a nap.

**winch**[1] *n* a machine for hoisting or pulling by means of a rope or chain wound round a rotating drum.

**winch**[2] *v* to hoist or pull with a winch.

**wind**[1] *n* **1** a natural horizontal movement of air. **2** breath or the ability to breathe. **3** *Brit* gas generated in the stomach or the intestines. **4** musical wind instruments collectively. * **get wind of** to hear a rumour of. **in the wind** about to happen. **put the wind up somebody** *Brit, informal* to scare or frighten somebody. **take the wind out of somebody's sails 1** to frustrate somebody by anticipating or forestalling them. **2** to make somebody less confident or self-important. ➤ **windy** *adj.*

**wind**[2] *v* **1** to make short of breath. **2** *Brit* to help (a baby) to bring up wind after feeding.

**wind**[3] *v* (*past tense and past part.* **wound**) **1** to have a twisting or spiralling course. **2** to pass round an object or central core so as to encircle it, *esp* repeatedly. **3** to tighten the spring of (a clock, watch, etc), e.g. by turning a key, to make it operate. **4** to put into the specified state or position by winding: *Wind the video back to the beginning.* ➤ **winding** *adj.*

**windbag** *n informal* an excessively talkative person.

**windbreak** *n* something, e.g. a line of trees or a screen, that gives protection from the force of the wind.

**windcheater** *n chiefly Brit* a windproof coat or jacket, fitting closely at the neck, waist, and cuffs.

**wind down** *v* **1** *informal* to become gradually more relaxed. **2** of a clockwork mechanism: to become slower because of decreasing tension in the spring. **3** to bring to an end gradually.

**windfall** *n* **1** a fruit blown down by the wind. **2** an unexpected gain or advantage.

**wind instrument** *n* a musical instrument, e.g. a trumpet or clarinet, sounded by the player's breath.

**windlass** *n* a winch used on a ship, e.g. to raise the anchor.

**windmill** *n* **1** a mill operated by vanes that are turned by the wind. **2** a similar structure using wind power to generate electricity, pump water, etc.

**window** *n* **1** an opening in the wall of a building, side of a vehicle, etc to let in light and air, usu fitted with glass. **2** a transparent panel in an envelope. **3** in computing, a rectangular area on the screen within which a separate file can be displayed. **4** a brief time available for something.

**window dressing** *n* **1** the act of arranging a display of merchandise in a shop window. **2** the act of presenting or emphasizing the more attractive features of something in order to gain acceptance for it.

**windowpane** *n* a panel of glass forming part of a window.

**window-shop** *v* to look at the displays in shop windows without intending to buy anything. ➤ **window-shopper** *n,* **window-shopping** *n.*

**windowsill** *n* the shelf at the bottom of a window.

**windpipe** *n* = TRACHEA.

**windscreen** *n Brit* a transparent screen at the front of a motor vehicle.
**windshield** *n NAmer* = WINDSCREEN.
**windsock** *n* a cloth cone mounted on a pole, used to indicate the direction of the wind, *esp* at an airfield.
**windsurfing** *n* the sport of riding across water on a sailboard. ➤ **windsurfer** *n.*
**windswept** *adj* exposed to strong winds.
**wind tunnel** *n* a tunnel-like apparatus through which air is blown to test the aerodynamic properties of an object placed inside it.
**wind up** *v* **1** to bring to a conclusion. **2** to bring (a business) to an end by liquidation. **3** *Brit, informal* to deceive playfully; to tease. **4** *informal* to arrive in a place, situation, or condition at the end of a course of action.
**windward** *adj and adv* facing the direction from which the wind is blowing: compare LEEWARD.
**wine**[1] *n* an alcoholic drink made from fermented grape juice.
**wine**[2] *v* ✻ **wine and dine** to entertain with good food and wine.
**wine bar** *n* an establishment serving wine and usu food for consumption on the premises.
**wine cellar** *n* **1** a room for storing wines. **2** a stock of wines.
**winery** *n* (*pl* **-ies**) a wine-making establishment.
**wing**[1] *n* **1** one of a pair of movable feathered or membranous appendages that enable a bird, bat, or insect to fly. **2** either of the horizontal structures projecting from the sides of an aircraft, which provide lift and stability. **3** a part of a building projecting from the main or central part. **4** a group or faction within an organized body, e.g. a political party. **5** (*in pl*) the area at the sides of a theatre stage out of sight of the audience. **6** the section near the sideline on the left or right of a playing field. **7** *Brit* a part of the body of a motor vehicle above the wheels. **8** a unit of the Royal Air Force larger than a squadron. ✻ **in the wings** in the background. **on the wing** of a bird: in flight. **under one's wing** under one's protection; in one's care. ➤ **winged** *adj.*
**wing**[2] *v* **1** to wound (a bird) in the wing. **2** to wound (somebody), e.g. with a bullet, without killing them. **3** to go with or as if with wings; to fly. ✻ **wing it** *informal* to perform or speak without rehearsal; to improvise.
**winger** *n* a player positioned on the wing in football, hockey, etc.
**wing nut** *n* a nut with projecting flanges so that it may be turned by finger and thumb.
**wingspan** *n* the distance between the tips of the two wings of a bird or aircraft.
**wink**[1] *v* **1** to shut one eye briefly as a signal or in teasing. **2** to gleam or flash intermittently.
**wink**[2] *n* **1** an act of winking. **2** a brief period, *esp* of sleep. ✻ **tip somebody the wink** *informal* to give somebody a useful piece of information, *esp* covertly.
**winkle** *n* an edible sea snail with a spiral shell.
**winkle out** *v chiefly Brit* **1** to extract from a snug or embedded position. **2** to extract (information) from somebody who is reluctant to give it.
**winkle-picker** *n Brit, informal* a shoe with a very pointed toe.
**winning** *adj* **1** endearing. **2** that wins or has won. **3** that results in victory. ➤ **winningly** *adv.*
**winnings** *pl n* money won, *esp* in gambling.
**winnow** *v* to remove waste matter from grain by exposure to a current of air.
**wino** *n* (*pl* **-os**) *informal* an alcoholic, *esp* one who drinks cheap wine.
**win out** *v* = WIN THROUGH.
**winsome** *adj* pleasing and engaging.
**winter**[1] *n* the season between autumn and spring.
**winter**[2] *v* to pass or survive the winter.
**win through** *v* to reach a desired or satisfactory end, *esp* after overcoming difficulties.
**wintry** *adj* (**-ier, -iest**) **1** of the weather: characteristic of winter; cold. **2** chilling or cheerless.
**wipe**[1] *v* **1** to clean or dry by rubbing lightly or quickly. **2** to remove by wiping. **3** to erase (e.g. data or a recording) completely. ✻ **wipe the floor with** *informal* to defeat decisively. ➤ **wiper** *n.*
**wipe**[2] *n* **1** an act of wiping. **2** a disposable moist cloth.
**wipe out** *v informal* **1** to destroy completely; to annihilate. **2** to obliterate or cancel.
**wire**[1] *n* **1** metal in the form of a flexible thread. **2** a line of wire, usu insulated, for conducting electrical current. **3** a telephone or telegraph wire or system. **4** *informal, dated* a telegram. **5** a microphone and transmitter concealed under somebody's clothes.
**wire**[2] *v* **1** to provide with wiring. **2** to connect or fasten with wire. **3** *chiefly NAmer, informal, dated* to send a message to (somebody) by telegraph.
**wireless** *n chiefly Brit, dated* a radio.
**wiretapping** *n* the act of tapping a telephone or telegraph wire, e.g. to monitor conversations to obtain information.
**wiring** *n* a system of wires carrying electric current in a device, building, etc.
**wiry** *adj* (**-ier, -iest**) **1** resembling wire. **2** lean and vigorous.
**wisdom** *n* **1** good sense; judgment. **2** accumulated learning, knowledge, and experience.
**wisdom tooth** *n* any of the four molar teeth at the back of the jaws in human beings that are the last to erupt.

**wise**[1] *adj* **1** characterized by deep understanding and sound judgment. **2** judicious or prudent. **3** *informal* (+ to) aware of. ➤ **wisely** *adv.*

**wise**[2] *n archaic* manner or way.

**wisecrack**[1] *n informal* a flippant remark or witticism.

**wisecrack**[2] *v informal* to make wisecracks.

**wish**[1] *v* **1** to feel or express a desire for; to want. **2** to express the hope that somebody will have or attain (something). ✱ **wish on** to hope that (somebody) will suffer (e.g. an unpleasant situation).

**wish**[2] *n* **1** an instance of wanting or hoping for something; a desire. **2** an object of desire. ✱ **best/good wishes** a conventional greeting or sentiment wishing people health, happiness, etc.

**wishbone** *n* a forked bone in front of the breastbone of a bird.

**wishful** *adj* **1** having a wish; desirous. **2** in accordance with wishes rather than reality: *wishful thinking.* ➤ **wishfully** *adv.*

**wishy-washy** *adj informal* **1** lacking in strength or intensity; watery. **2** lacking in character or determination; ineffectual.

**wisp** *n* a thin insubstantial strand, streak, or fragment. ➤ **wispy** *adj.*

**wisteria** *or* **wistaria** *n* a climbing plant with showy blue, white, purple, or rose flowers.

**wistful** *adj* **1** full of unfulfilled desire; yearning. **2** musingly sad. ➤ **wistfully** *adv,* **wistfulness** *n.*

**wit** *n* **1** (*also in pl*) reasoning power; intelligence. **2** (*also in pl*) sanity. **3** the ability to use words or ideas to create a humorous effect. **4** a person with this ability. ✱ **be at one's wits' end** to be so harassed or worried that one does not know what to do. **have/keep one's wits about one** to be alert. **live by one's wits** to make one's living by cleverness or cunning rather than honest work.

**witch** *n* a woman who is credited with supernatural powers or who practises magic for evil ends.

**witchcraft** *n* the use of sorcery or magic.

**witch doctor** *n* a professional sorcerer, *esp* in a tribal society, who is credited with healing and other powers.

**witch hazel** *n* a shrub whose bark and leaves are used to make a soothing astringent lotion.

**witch-hunt** *n* the searching out and harassment of those with unpopular or unorthodox views.

**witching hour** *n* (**the witching hour**) *humorous* midnight.

**with** *prep* **1** used to indicate accompaniment or association. **2** used to indicate reciprocal action or communication. **3** in the direction of. **4** in possession of; having or bearing. **5** in addition to. **6** by means of; using. **7** used to indicate manner of action. **8** in opposition to; against. **9** in relation to. **10** able to follow the reasoning of. **11** on the side of (a person or group); for. **12** employed by (a company, institution, etc).

**withdraw** *v* (**withdrew, withdrawn**) **1** to draw (something) back, away, or aside; to remove. **2** to remove (money) from a place of deposit, e.g. a bank account. **3** to retract (e.g. an offer or statement). **4** to leave a place, *esp* to retreat. **5** to retire from participation. **6** to become socially or emotionally detached.

**withdrawal** *n* **1** the act of withdrawing. **2** the discontinuance of use of a drug, often accompanied by unpleasant side effects.

**withdrawn** *adj* shy and unresponsive.

**wither** *v* **1** to become dry and shrivelled, e.g. from age or disease. **2** to lose vitality, force, or freshness. **3** to cause to wither.

**withering** *adj* scornful and humiliating. ➤ **witheringly** *adv.*

**withers** *pl n* the ridge between the shoulder bones of a horse.

**withhold** *v* (*past tense and past part.* **withheld**) **1** to refrain from granting or giving. **2** to check or restrain.

***Usage Note:*** Note the spelling with *-hh-* in the middle.

**within**[1] *prep* **1** inside. **2** in the range of. **3** not further than a specified distance. **4** during or before the end of (a period of time).

**within**[2] *adv* **1** inside. **2** inside one's body or mind.

**with it** *adj informal* **1** up-to-date; fashionable. **2** mentally quick or alert.

**without** *prep* **1** used to indicate the absence or lack of something. **2** used to indicate that something does not happen.

**withstand** *v* (*past tense and past part.* **withstood**) **1** to be unharmed by. **2** to resist with determination.

**witless** *adj* foolish.

**witness**[1] *n* **1** a person who sees an event take place. **2** a person who gives evidence, *esp* in a court of law. **3** a person who watches another sign a document and adds their own signature as an indication of authenticity. **4** something that serves as evidence.

**witness**[2] *v* **1** to observe (an event) personally or directly. **2** to be the scene or time of (an event). **3** to act as legal witness of (e.g. the signing of a document). **4** (+ to) to testify to something.

**witter** *v Brit, informal* to talk in a long-winded fashion about inconsequential matters.

**witticism** *n* a witty remark.

**witty** *adj* (**-ier, -iest**) showing wit; cleverly humorous. ➤ **wittily** *adv.*

**wives** *n* pl of WIFE.

**wizard** *n* **1** a man with supernatural or magical powers. **2** a person who is very clever or skilful. **3** a computer program providing a step-by-step guide to a particular task. ➤ **wizardry** *n.*

**wizened** *adj* dry, shrunken, and wrinkled as a result of ageing.
**woad** *n* a plant formerly grown for the blue dye obtained from its leaves.
**wobble** *v* **1** to rock unsteadily from side to side. **2** of the voice: to tremble or quaver. ➤ **wobbly** *adj.*
**woe** *n* **1** *literary* great sorrow or suffering. **2** (*usu in pl*) a trouble or affliction. * **woe betide somebody** somebody will suffer or be punished if they do the specified thing.
**woebegone** *adj* looking very sorrowful.
**woeful** *adj* **1** feeling or expressing woe. **2** pitifully bad. ➤ **woefully** *adv.*
**wok** *n* a large bowl-shaped cooking utensil used *esp* for stir-frying in Chinese cookery.
**woke** *v* past tense of WAKE[1].
**woken** *v* past part. of WAKE[1].
**wold** *n* an upland area of open country.
**wolf[1]** *n* (*pl* **wolves** *or* **wolf**) a large predatory mammal of the dog family that hunts in packs. * **cry wolf** to raise a false alarm and risk the possibility that a future real need will not be taken seriously. **wolf in sheep's clothing** a person who hides hostile intentions behind a friendly manner. ➤ **wolfish** *adj.*
**wolf[2]** *v* (*often* + down) to eat (food) greedily.
**wolfhound** *n* a dog of a large breed formerly used in hunting wolves.
**wolfram** *n* = TUNGSTEN.
**wolf whistle** *n* a distinctive whistle sounded to express sexual admiration, *esp* by a man for a woman. ➤ **wolf-whistle** *v.*
**wolverine** /'woolvəreen/ *n* a fierce flesh-eating mammal of northern forests that is related to the weasel and has blackish fur.
**woman** *n* (*pl* **women**) an adult human female.
**womanize** *or* **-ise** *v* of a man: to seek to have casual sexual relations with many women. ➤ **womanizer** *n,* **womanizing** *n and adj.*
**womankind** *n* women as a whole, *esp* as distinguished from men.
**womb** *n* the hollow organ in a woman's body in which a baby develops before birth.
**wombat** *n* a plant-eating Australian marsupial resembling a small bear.
**won** *v* past tense and past part. of WIN[1].
**wonder[1]** *n* **1** rapt attention, admiration, or astonishment at something unexpected, strange, beautiful, etc. **2** a cause of wonder. * **no wonder** it is no surprise. **work/do wonders** to have a positive effect.
**wonder[2]** *v* **1** to feel curiosity or doubt. **2** (*often* + at) to marvel.
**wonderful** *adj* unusually good; admirable or excellent. ➤ **wonderfully** *adv.*
**wonderland** *n* a place where strange or magical things happen.
**wondrous** *adj literary* wonderful.
**wonky** *adj* (**-ier, -iest**) *informal* **1** awry or crooked. **2** shaky or unsteady.
**wont** *n formal* customary practice: *as was his wont.*
**won't** *contraction* will not.
**wonted** *adj literary* customary or habitual.
**woo** *v* (**woos, wooed, wooing**) **1** to try to win the love of (somebody, *esp* a woman). **2** to try to win the support or favour of. ➤ **wooer** *n.*
**wood** *n* **1** a hard fibrous plant tissue that makes up the greater part of the stems and branches of trees or shrubs. **2** (*also in pl*) a dense growth of trees, usu smaller than a forest. **3** a golf club with a wooden head. **4** a wooden bowling ball. * **not see the wood for the trees** to fail to have overall understanding of a subject, situation, etc as a result of concentration on details. **out of the wood/woods** escaped from danger or difficulty. ➤ **woody** *adj.*
**woodcut** *n* a print taken from a wooden block with a design cut on it in relief.
**woodcutter** *n* a person who cuts down trees or chops wood.
**wooded** *adj* of land: covered with growing trees.
**wooden** *adj* **1** made of wood. **2** awkwardly stiff. ➤ **woodenly** *adv.*
**woodland** *n* (*also in pl*) land covered with trees.
**woodlouse** *n* (*pl* **woodlice**) a small ground-living animal with a grey segmented body.
**woodpecker** *n* a bird with a very hard bill used to drill holes in trees to find insects for food.
**woodshed** *n* a shed for storing firewood.
**woodsman** *n* (*pl* **woodsmen**) a man who lives in, frequents, or works in the woods.
**woodturning** *n* the art of producing wooden articles on a lathe. ➤ **woodturner** *n.*
**woodwind** *n* **1** any of a group of orchestral wind instruments including the clarinet, flute, oboe, and bassoon. **2** the woodwind section of an orchestra.
**woodworm** *n* the larva of a beetle that bores in dead wood.
**woof[1]** *n* the low gruff sound characteristic of a dog.
**woof[2]** *v* to utter a woof.
**woof[3]** /woohf/ *n* = WEFT.
**woofer** /'woohfə/ *n* a loudspeaker that responds mainly to low frequencies.
**wool** *n* **1** the soft fibre forming the coat of sheep. **2** yarn made from wool by spinning. * **pull the wool over somebody's eyes** to blind somebody to the true situation; to hoodwink them.
**woollen[1]** (*NAmer* **woolen**) *adj* **1** made of wool. **2** relating to the manufacture or sale of woollen products.
**woollen[2]** (*NAmer* **woolen**) *n* (*in pl*) woollen garments.
**woolly[1]** (*NAmer* **wooly**) *adj* (**-ier, -iest**) **1** made of or resembling wool. **2** of an animal or plant: covered with wool or with soft hairs

resembling wool. **3** marked by vagueness or confusion. ➤ **woolliness** *n.*

**woolly**[2] (*NAmer* **wooly**) *n* (*pl* **-ies**) *chiefly Brit* a woollen jumper or cardigan.

**woozy** *adj* (**-ier, -iest**) *informal* dizzy or slightly nauseous. ➤ **woozily** *adv.*

**word**[1] *n* **1** a meaningful unit of language that is usu set off by spaces on either side in writing or printing. **2** a short remark, statement, or conversation. **3** (*in pl*) the text of a vocal musical composition. **4** (*in pl*) an angry conversation. **5** (**the word**) an order, command, or verbal signal. **6** (**one's word**) a promise. **7** (**one's word**) what one says or claims about something. **8** news or information. ✱ **be as good as one's word** to keep a promise. **from the word go** from the beginning. **in other words** expressing the same thing in a different and usu more straightforward way. **in so many words** in exactly those terms. **take somebody at their word** to believe somebody literally. **take the words out of somebody's mouth** to say the very thing that somebody else was about to say.

**word**[2] *v* to express in particular words; to phrase.

**word class** *n* a group of grammatically similar words; a part of speech.

**word-for-word** *adj* in or following the exact words used.

**wording** *n* the words used in a text or to express something.

**word of honour** *n* a promise pledging one's honour.

**word of mouth** *n* oral communication.

**word processor** *n* a computer or program that enables text to be written, stored, and printed. ➤ **word processing** *n.*

**wordy** *adj* (**-ier, -iest**) using or containing too many words. ➤ **wordily** *n.*

**wore** *v* past tense of WEAR[1].

**work**[1] *n* **1** activity in which one exerts physical strength or mental faculties to do or produce something. **2** the activities that provide one's accustomed means of livelihood. **3** a specific task, duty, function, or assignment. **4** something produced in a specified way, by a specified person or thing, or from a specified material. **5** (*in pl*) a place where industrial activity is carried out; a factory. **6** (*in pl*) the working or moving parts of a mechanism. ✱ **have one's work cut out** to have a difficult task. **out of work** unemployed.

**work**[2] *v* (*past tense and past part.* **worked**) **1** to do work to achieve a result or earn one's living. **2** to cause (a person or animal) to do work. **3** of a machine: to operate or function. **4** of a person: to operate (e.g. a machine). **5** to produce a desired effect; to succeed. **6** to prepare or form into a desired state by kneading, hammering, etc. **7** to get into a specified condition by slow or imperceptible movements: *The knot worked loose.* **8** to carry on an operation, e.g. farming or mining, in. **9** to bring about (an effect or result). **10** (+ on) to strive to influence or persuade somebody.

**workable** *adj* **1** capable of being worked. **2** of a plan: practicable or feasible.

**workaday** *adj* ordinary.

**workbench** *n* a bench on which *esp* mechanical or carpentry work is performed.

**worked up** *adj* emotionally aroused; angry or upset.

**worker** *n* **1** a person who works. **2** a member of the working class. **3** any of the usu sterile members of a colony of ants, bees, etc that perform most of the labour.

**workforce** *n* **1** the workers employed by a particular company or engaged in a specific activity. **2** the people potentially available for work.

**workhouse** *n* formerly in Britain, an institution maintained at public expense to house needy people.

**working**[1] *adj* **1** that functions or performs work. **2** engaged in paid work. **3** during which one works. **4** suitable for or used in work. **5** serving as a basis for further activity, discussion, etc.

**working**[2] *n* **1** (*usu in pl*) a mine, quarry, or similar excavation. **2** (*usu in pl*) the act or manner of functioning or operating.

**working class** *n* the class of people who work, *esp* manually, for wages. ➤ **working-class** *adj.*

**working party** *n Brit* a committee set up to investigate and report on a particular problem.

**work load** *n* the amount of work that somebody has to do.

**workman** *n* (*pl* **workmen**) **1** a manual worker. **2** a person considered with regard to their skill at their trade.

**workmanlike** *adj* skilful or competent.

**workmanship** *n* **1** the relative skill of a workman. **2** the quality or finish exhibited by a product.

**workout** *n* a period of usu vigorous physical exercise.

**work out** *v* **1** to solve (a question, problem, etc) by calculation or reasoning. **2** to elaborate (a plan, etc) in detail. **3** to prove effective or successful. **4** (*often* + at/to) to amount to (a total or calculated figure). **5** to engage in physical exercise.

**work permit** *n* a document authorizing a foreigner to do paid work in a country.

**workshop** *n* **1** a place in which manufacturing or repair work is carried out. **2** a brief intensive session of study, training, or discussion with an emphasis on active participation.

**workstation** *n* a self-contained unit, e.g. a VDU and keyboard, linked to a computer network in an office.

**worktop** *n Brit* a flat surface on a kitchen unit that is suitable for working on.

**work-to-rule** *n chiefly Brit* a form of industrial action designed to reduce output or efficiency by deliberately keeping very rigidly to rules and regulations.

**work up** *v* **1** (**get worked up**) to become agitated or angry. **2** (+ to) to approach something through a series of increasingly more intense or demanding preparatory steps.

**world** *n* **1** (**the world**) the earth with everybody and everything on it. **2** (**the world**) secular affairs as distinguished from religious or spiritual matters. **3** a distinctive class of people or their sphere of interest. **4** the personal environment of one's life or work. **5** an indefinite or very great number or amount. **6** a planet. * **best of both worlds** the advantages of two alternatives, *esp* without their disadvantages. **bring/come into the world** to give birth to/be born. **out of this world** *informal* of extraordinary excellence. **think the world of** to have great love or admiration for.

**worldly** *adj* (**-ier, -iest**) **1** of this world and its pursuits rather than religion or spiritual affairs. **2** = WORLDLY-WISE.

**worldly-wise** *adj* possessing a shrewd understanding of human affairs; sophisticated.

**world music** *n* a type of popular music that incorporates elements of traditional music from various countries.

**world power** *n* a state powerful enough to affect the entire world by its actions.

**world-shaking** *adj* having tremendous importance.

**world war** *n* a war engaged in by most of the principal nations of the world.

**world-weary** *adj* bored with life and the material pleasures of the world.

**worldwide** *adj and adv* throughout or involving the entire world.

**World Wide Web** *n* a vast information system composed of interconnected sites and files to which individuals have access through the Internet.

**worm**[1] *n* **1** a relatively small elongated limbless invertebrate animal with a soft body, e.g. an earthworm. **2** (*in pl*) infestation with or disease caused by parasitic worms.

**worm**[2] *v* **1** to proceed by winding or wriggling. **2** to make (one's way) insidiously or deviously. **3** (+ out of) to extract (information) from somebody by artful or persistent questioning. **4** to rid (an animal) of parasitic worms.

**wormcast** *n* a small heap of earth or sand excreted by a worm on the surface.

**wormwood** *n* a plant that yields a bitter aromatic oil used to flavour absinthe and vermouth.

**worn** *v* past part. of WEAR[1].

**worn-out** *adj* **1** exhausted. **2** made useless by wear.

**worried** *adj* feeling or showing anxiety or concern. ➤ **worriedly** *adv.*

**worrisome** *adj chiefly NAmer* **1** causing distress or worry. **2** inclined to worry or fret.

**worry**[1] *v* (**-ies, -ied**) **1** to feel or cause to feel concern or anxiety, *esp* about unpleasant things that have happened or may happen. **2** to bother or disturb (somebody). **3** of a dog: to chase and harass (e.g. a sheep). **4** (+ at) of a dog: to bite, pick up, and shake (something) repeatedly. ➤ **worrier** *n*, **worrying** *adj.*

**worry**[2] *n* (*pl* **-ies**) **1** mental distress or agitation. **2** a cause of worry; a trouble or difficulty.

**worse**[1] *adj* **1** of a lower quality. **2** in poorer health. **3** more serious or severe. * **the worse for** harmed by. **worse off** suffering worse circumstances, *esp* financially.

**worse**[2] *adv* **1** less well. **2** more seriously or severely.

**worse**[3] *n* something worse.

**worsen** *v* to make or become worse.

**worship**[1] *n* **1** praise, prayer, and thanksgiving offered to a divine being. **2** religious practices and rituals. **3** extravagant admiration or devotion. **4** (**Your/His/Her Worship**) *chiefly Brit* used as a title for various officials, e.g. mayors.

**worship**[2] *v* (**worshipped, worshipping,** *NAmer* **worshiped, worshiping**) **1** to offer prayer and praise to (a deity). **2** to regard with great or excessive admiration or devotion. ➤ **worshipper** *n.*

**worshipful** *adj* **1** rendering worship or veneration. **2** (**Worshipful**) *chiefly Brit* used as a title for various people or groups of rank or distinction.

**worst**[1] *adj* **1** of the lowest quality. **2** least appropriate or advisable. **3** most severe or serious.

**worst**[2] *adv* **1** least well. **2** most seriously or severely.

**worst**[3] *n* (*pl* **worst**) **1** the worst state or part. **2** (**the worst**) what is least desirable. * **at worst/at the worst** under the worst circumstances. **do one's worst** to do the utmost harm of which one is capable. **if the worst comes to the worst** if the very worst thing happens.

**worsted** /'woostid/ *n* a high-quality fabric with no nap made from smooth compact yarn.

**worth**[1] *adj and prep* **1** equal in value to. **2** having money or property equal to (a sum). **3** deserving of. * **for all one is worth** *informal* with all one's energy or enthusiasm. **worth it** worth the time or effort spent.

**worth**[2] *n* **1** value, *esp* financial value. **2** the equivalent of a specified amount or figure: *twenty pounds' worth of petrol.* **3** moral or personal merit.

**worthless** *adj* **1** valueless. **2** useless. **3** contemptible or despicable.

**worthwhile** *adj* worth the time or effort spent.
**worthy**[1] *adj* (**-ier, -iest**) **1** (+ of) good or important enough for; deserving. **2** deserving respect, support, etc, or deserving the position, title, etc attained. **3** commendable but dull. ➤ **worthily** *adv*, **worthiness** *n*.
**worthy**[2] *n* (*pl* **-ies**) *often humorous* a worthy or prominent person.
**would** *v aux* **1** the past tense of WILL[1]. **2** used to introduce a possibility or presumption. **3** used after a verb expressing a wish or request. **4** used to express a polite request or invitation. **5** used in reported speech to express an action or state in the future. **6** used to express a preference. **7** *literary* used to express a wish or desire.
**would-be** *adj* wishing or aspiring to be.
**wouldn't** *contraction* would not.
**wound**[1] *n* **1** an injury, e.g. from violence, accident, or surgery, that involves tearing, cutting, or breaking the skin. **2** a mental or emotional hurt.
**wound**[2] *v* to inflict a wound on. ➤ **wounded** *adj*, **wounding** *adj*.
**wound**[3] *v* past tense and past part. of WIND[1].
**wove** *v* past tense of WEAVE[1].
**woven** *v* past part. of WEAVE[1].
**wow**[1] *interj informal* used to express pleasure, admiration, or surprise.
**wow**[2] *n informal* a striking success.
**wow**[3] *v informal* to excite (e.g. an audience) to enthusiastic admiration or approval.
**WPC** *abbr Brit* Woman Police Constable.
**wrack**[1] *v* = RACK[2] (1).
**wrack**[2] *n* a brown seaweed, *esp* kelp.
**wraith** *n* an apparition of a living person seen shortly before or after death.
**wrangle**[1] *n* an angry or prolonged dispute or quarrel.
**wrangle**[2] *v* to quarrel angrily or at length.
**wrap**[1] *v* (**wrapped, wrapping**) **1** to cover, pack, or enfold in something flexible, e.g. paper or fabric. **2** to fold or wind (something flexible) round somebody or something.
**wrap**[2] *n* **1** a shawl. **2** material used for wrapping. * **under wraps** secret.
**wrapper** *n* a covering for an article.
**wrap up** *v* **1** to dress in warm outer garments. **2** to complete or end. **3** (**be wrapped up in**) to be completely engrossed in.
**wrasse** *n* (*pl* **wrasses** *or* **wrasse**) a brilliantly coloured seafish with spiny fins, thick lips, and strong teeth.
**wrath** *n* strong vengeful anger. ➤ **wrathful** *adj*.
**wreak** *v* **1** to inflict (e.g. revenge). **2** to cause or create (havoc or destruction).
**wreath** *n* (*pl* **wreaths**) **1** flowers or leaves intertwined into a circular shape. **2** a curl, ring, or coil.
**wreathe** *v* **1** (**be wreathed in**) to be surrounded by a cloud, coils, etc of something. **2** to twist or move in coils.
**wreck**[1] *n* **1** a shipwreck. **2** destruction. **3** the broken remains of something, e.g. a building or vehicle, wrecked or ruined. **4** a person in very poor health or spirits.
**wreck**[2] *v* **1** (*usu* **be wrecked**) of a vessel: to sink, break up, or be destroyed. **2** to ruin or destroy by violent action or accident. **3** to bring disaster or ruin to (e.g. plans or a marriage).
**wreckage** *n* broken parts or material from a wrecked structure.
**wren** *n* a very small bird with a short erect tail.
**wrench**[1] *v* **1** to pull or twist violently. **2** to injure (a part of the body) by a violent twisting or straining. **3** to snatch forcibly.
**wrench**[2] *n* **1** a violent twisting or a sideways pull. **2** acute emotional distress caused by e.g. a parting. **3** a spanner, *esp* an adjustable spanner.
**wrest** *v* **1** to take by violent pulling or twisting. **2** to obtain with difficulty by force or determination.
**wrestle**[1] *v* **1** to take part in wrestling. **2** to engage in a violent or determined struggle. **3** to push, pull, or manhandle by force. ➤ **wrestler** *n*, **wrestling** *n*.
**wrestle**[2] *n* an act of wrestling, *esp* a wrestling bout.
**wretch** *n* **1** a profoundly unhappy or unfortunate person. **2** *informal* a despicable person.
**wretched** *adj* **1** deeply afflicted or unfortunate. **2** deplorably bad. **3** mean, squalid, or contemptible. ➤ **wretchedly** *adv*.
**wriggle**[1] *v* **1** to move to and fro with short writhing movements. **2** to move by twisting and turning. **3** (*usu* + out of) to extricate oneself by manoeuvring, equivocation, etc. ➤ **wriggler** *n*.
**wriggle**[2] *n* a wriggling movement. ➤ **wriggly** *adj*.
**wring** *v* (*past tense and past part.* **wrung**) **1** to twist or compress, *esp* so as to extract liquid. **2** (*often* + from/out of) to extort by coercion or with difficulty. **3** to twist (an animal's neck), *esp* so as to break it. **4** to twist (one's hands) together as a sign of anguish. **5** to shake (somebody's hand) vigorously in greeting.
**wringer** *n* = MANGLE[2].
**wringing** *adj* of clothes, etc: so wet that liquid is dripping out.
**wrinkle**[1] *n* a small ridge or crease formed in the skin, in fabric, etc.
**wrinkle**[2] *v* **1** to contract into wrinkles. **2** to become marked with wrinkles.
**wrinkly**[1] *adj* (**-ier, -iest**) having many wrinkles.
**wrinkly**[2] *n* (*pl* **-ies**) *Brit, derog* an elderly person.
**wrist** *n* the joint between the hand and the arm.
**wristwatch** *n* a watch attached to a strap and worn round the wrist.

**writ** *n* a formal document issued in the name of a court commanding or forbidding a specified act.

**write** *v* (**wrote, written**) **1** to form (legible words, symbols, etc) on a surface, *esp* with a pen, pencil, etc. **2** to be the author or composer of (a piece of writing, music, etc). **3** to compose and send (a letter). **4** to complete or fill in (e.g. a cheque) by writing.

**write down** *v* to record (information) in written form.

**write off** *v* **1** to deem to be irreparably lost or useless. **2** to cancel the record of (bad debt). **3** to damage (a motor vehicle) beyond repair.

**write-off** *n* something or somebody written off.

**write up** *v* **1** to write an account of. **2** to put into finished written form.

**write-up** *n* a written account or review.

**writhe** *v* to twist or squirm in pain or embarrassment.

**writing** *n* **1** the act or occupation of literary composition. **2** written letters or words, *esp* handwriting. **3** (*usu in pl*) a written composition. ✱ **the writing on the wall** an omen of impending disaster or ruin.

**wrong**[1] *adj* **1** not according to truth or facts; incorrect. **2** in error; mistaken. **3** wicked, immoral, unjust, or unfair. **4** not satisfactory, e.g. in condition. ✱ **get (hold of) the wrong end of the stick** to misunderstand. **on the wrong side of 1** out of favour with. **2** more than the specified age. ➤ **wrongly** *adv.*

**wrong**[2] *adv* **1** without accuracy; incorrectly. **2** without regard for what is right or proper. **3** out of proper working order.

**wrong**[3] *n* an injurious or unfair act. ✱ **in the wrong 1** mistaken or incorrect. **2** being or appearing to be guilty.

**wrong**[4] *v* to treat unjustly or unfairly.

**wrongdoer** *n* a person who behaves immorally or illegally. ➤ **wrongdoing** *n.*

**wrong-foot** *v* **1** *Brit* to make (an opponent) move in the wrong direction, e.g. in tennis or football. **2** to put at a disadvantage by a sudden change of approach.

**wrongful** *adj* wrong, unjust, or unlawful. ➤ **wrongfully** *n.*

**wrongheaded** *adj* perverse.

**wrote** *v* past tense of WRITE.

**wrought** *adj* **1** of metals: beaten into shape by tools. **2** formed by artistry or effort. **3** (+ up) deeply stirred.

**wrought iron** *n* a tough pure form of iron that is easily worked.

**wrung** *v* past tense and past part. of WRING.

**wry** *adj* (**wryer** *or* **wrier, wryest** *or* **wriest**) **1** ironically or grimly humorous. **2** bent or twisted, *esp* to one side. **3** contorted into an expression of distaste, disapproval, etc. ➤ **wryly** *adv.*

**wunderkind** /ˈvoondəkint/ *n* (*pl* **wunderkinds** *or* **wunderkinder** /-kində/) a person who succeeds in a competitive field at an early age.

**WWF** *abbr* World Wide Fund for Nature.

**WWI** *abbr* World War I.

**WWII** *abbr* World War II.

**WWW** *abbr* World Wide Web.

**wych elm** *or* **witch elm** *n* a hardy elm that grows in northern Europe and Asia.

**WYSIWYG** /ˈwiziwig/ *adj* denoting a computer system in which all text and graphics displayed on screen can be reproduced in exactly the same form on printout (*what you see is what you get*).

**wyvern** *n* a mythical and heraldic animal represented as a two-legged winged creature resembling a dragon.

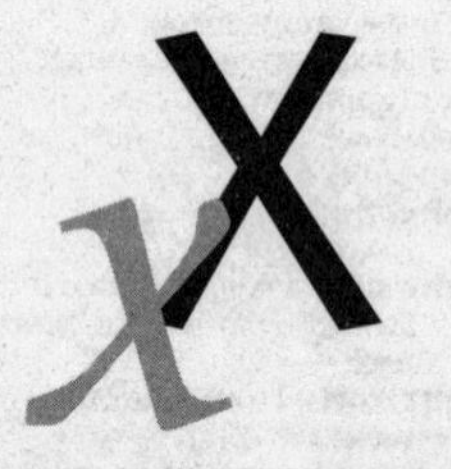

**X** *or* **x** *n* (*pl* **X's** *or* **Xs** *or* **x's**) **1** the 24th letter of the English alphabet. **2** the Roman numeral for ten. **3** somebody or something whose identity is unknown or withheld. **4** used as a symbol to mark something as incorrect. **5** used as a symbol for a kiss.

**X certificate** *n* formerly, a classification of a film as suitable for adults only.

**X chromosome** *n* a sex chromosome that is usu paired with another X chromosome in a female cell and with a Y chromosome in a male cell.

**Xe** *abbr* the chemical symbol for xenon.

**xenon** *n* a heavy colourless odourless gas.

**xenophobia** *n* intense fear or dislike of foreigners or strangers. ➤ **xenophobe** *n,* **xenophobic** *adj.*

**Xerox** *n trademark* a photocopier or photocopy.

**Xmas** *n informal* Christmas.

**X-rated** *adj* involving pornography, indecency, or extreme violence.

**X-ray**[1] *n* an electromagnetic radiation of very short wavelength that can penetrate various solids and act like light to expose photographic films or plates.

**X-ray**[2] *v* to examine, treat, or photograph using X-rays.

**xylophone** *n* a percussion instrument consisting of a series of wooden bars that are struck with two small hammers.

**Y**[1] *or* **y** *n* (*pl* **Y's** *or* **Ys** *or* **y's**) the 25th letter of the English alphabet.

**Y**[2] *abbr* the chemical symbol for yttrium.

**yacht** /yot/ *n* a relatively small sailing or powered vessel used for pleasure cruising or racing. ➤ **yachting** *n.*

**yahoo** *n* (*pl* **yahoos**) *informal* an uncouth or rowdy person.

**yak**[1] *n* (*pl* **yaks** *or* **yak**) a large long-haired wild or domesticated ox of Tibet.

**yak**[2] *or* **yack** *v* (**yakked** *or* **yacked, yakking** *or* **yacking**) *informal* to talk persistently; to chatter.

**yam** *n* an edible starchy tuberous root used as a vegetable.

**yang** *n* in Chinese philosophy, the masculine active principle in nature.

**Yank** *n informal, often derog* an American.

**yank** *v informal* to pull or extract with a quick vigorous movement. ➤ **yank** *n.*

**Yankee** *n* **1** *informal* an American. **2** *NAmer, informal* somebody from New England or the northern USA. **3** *NAmer, informal* a Federal soldier in the Civil War.

**yap** *v* (**yapped, yapping**) to bark in a high-pitched or snappish way. ➤ **yap** *n,* **yappy** *adj.*

**yard**[1] *n* **1** a unit of length equal to three feet (about 0.914m). **2** a unit of volume equal to one cubic yard (about 0.765$m^3$). **3** a long spar tapered towards the ends to support and spread a sail.

**yard**[2] *n* **1** *chiefly Brit* a small usu walled and often paved area open to the sky and adjacent to a building. **2** an area with buildings and facilities set aside for a specified business or activity. **3** *NAmer* a garden of a house.

**yardarm** *n* either end of the yard of a square-rigged ship.

**Yardie** *n informal* a member of a West Indian criminal gang.

**yardstick** *n* a standard used for comparison.

**yarmulke** *or* **yarmulka** *n* a skullcap worn by Jewish males.

**yarn** *n* **1** thread prepared and used for weaving, knitting, and sewing. **2** *informal* a narrative of adventures, *esp* a tall tale.

**yashmak** *n* a veil worn over the face by Muslim women, so that only the eyes remain exposed.

**yaw** *v* of a ship, aircraft, or spacecraft: to deviate from a straight course, *esp* by side-to-side movement. ➤ **yaw** *n.*

**yawn**[1] *v* **1** to open the mouth wide and inhale, usu in fatigue or boredom. **2** to be menacingly wide, deep, and open.

**yawn**[2] *n* **1** a deep usu involuntary intake of breath through the wide open mouth. **2** *informal* a boring thing or person.

**Yb** *abbr* the chemical symbol for ytterbium.

**Y chromosome** *n* a sex chromosome that usu occurs paired with a dissimilar chromosome in the male sex and does not occur in the female sex.

**yd** *abbr* yard.

**ye**[1] *pron archaic or dialect* you.

**ye**[2] *definite article archaic* the.

**yea** /yay/ *adv archaic* yes.

**yeah** *adv informal* yes.

**year** *n* **1** the period of about 365¼ solar days required for one revolution of the earth round the sun. **2** a cycle of 365 or 366 days divided into twelve months beginning on 1 January and ending on 31 December. **3** a period of time equal to this but beginning at a different time. **4** a period of time during which something, e.g. a school, is in session. **5** the body of students who enter a school, university, etc in one academic year. **6** *informal* (*in pl*) a very long time. **7** (*in pl*) age.

**yearling** *n* an animal one year old or in its second year.

**yearly** *adj* done or occurring once every year; annual. ➤ **yearly** *adv.*

**yearn** *v* to long persistently or sadly. ➤ **yearning** *n and adj.*

**yeast** *n* **1** a minute fungus that is able to ferment sugars and other carbohydrates. **2** a commercial product containing yeast, used for the fermentation of alcohol or for raising bread.

**yell**[1] *v* to utter a sharp loud cry, scream, or shout.

**yell**[2] *n* a sharp loud scream or shout.

**yellow**[1] *adj* **1** of the colour of egg yolk or lemons. **2** *informal* cowardly. ➤ **yellowish** *adj.*

**yellow**[2] *n* a yellow colour. ➤ **yellowy** *adj.*

**yellow**[3] *v* to make or become yellow.

**yellow card** *n* a yellow card held up by a football referee to indicate the taking of a player's name for committing an offence.

**yellow fever** *n* an often fatal infectious disease of warm regions, marked by fever, jaundice, and often bleeding.

**yellowhammer** *n* a common bunting, the male of which is largely yellow with a reddish brown back.

**Yellow Pages** *pl n trademark* a telephone directory that lists organizations and services alphabetically within sections classified according to the nature of their business.

**yelp** *v* to utter a quick shrill cry or bark. ➤ **yelp** *n.*

**yen**[1] *n* (*pl* **yen**) the basic monetary unit of Japan.

**yen**[2] *n informal* a strong desire or inclination.

**yeoman** *n* (*pl* **yeomen**) formerly, a small farmer who cultivated his own land.

**Yeoman of the Guard** *n* a member of a military corps who serve as ceremonial attendants of the sovereign and warders of the Tower of London.

**yes**[1] *interj* **1** used in answers expressing affirmation, agreement, or willingness. **2** used to indicate polite interest or attentiveness. **3** used to express great satisfaction or delight.

**yes**[2] *n* (*pl* **yeses** *or* **yesses**) an affirmative reply or vote.

**yes-man** *n* (*pl* **yes-men**) *informal* an obsequious supporter of superiors.

**yesterday**[1] *adv* on the day before today.

**yesterday**[2] *n* **1** the day before today. **2** time not long past.

**yesteryear** *n literary* **1** the years of the fairly recent past. **2** last year.

**yet**[1] *adv* **1** up to this or that time. **2** only having done so much or got so far. **3** as of now; still. **4** at some future time and despite present appearances. **5** in addition. **6** used to indicate a still greater degree; even. **7** nevertheless.

**yet**[2] *conj* but nevertheless.

**yeti** *n* = ABOMINABLE SNOWMAN.

**yew** *n* an evergreen coniferous tree with poisonous red fruits.

**Y-fronts** *pl n Brit, trademark* men's underpants in which the front seams take the form of an inverted Y.

**Yiddish** *n* a language closely related to German spoken by Jews chiefly in or from Eastern Europe. ➤ **Yiddish** *adj.*

**yield**[1] *v* **1** to bring forth as a natural product. **2** to produce as a result of expended effort. **3** to produce (money or its equivalent) as revenue. **4** (*often* + up) to give up possession of (e.g. a position of advantage or point of superiority). **5** (*often* + to) to give way to pressure or influence. **6** to give way under physical force. **7** to surrender or submit. ➤ **yielder** *n,* **yielding** *adj.*

**yield**[2] *n* something yielded, or the amount of it.

***Usage Note:*** Note the spelling with *-ie-*.

**yin** *n* in Chinese philosophy, the feminine passive principle in nature.

**YMCA** *abbr* Young Men's Christian Association.

**yob** *n Brit, slang* a loutish young man. ➤ **yobbish** *adj.*

**yobbo** *n* (*pl* **-os** *or* **-oes**) *Brit, slang* = YOB.

**yodel**[1] *v* (**yodelled, yodelling,** *NAmer* **yodeled, yodeling**) to sing or call by suddenly changing from a natural voice to a falsetto and back. ➤ **yodeller** *n.*

**yodel**[2] *n* a yodelled song or call.

**yoga** *n* **1** (**Yoga**) a Hindu philosophy teaching control of all activity of body, mind, and will so that the self may attain liberation. **2** a system of exercises for attaining bodily or mental control and well-being. ➤ **yogic** *adj.*

**yoghourt** *or* **yoghurt** *n* see YOGURT.

**yogi** *n* (*pl* **yogis**) somebody who practises or is a master of yoga.

**yogurt** *or* **yoghurt** *or* **yoghourt** *n* a slightly acid semisolid food made of milk fermented by bacteria.

**yoke**[1] *n* **1** a bar or frame by which two draught animals, e.g. oxen, are joined at the necks for working together. **2** two animals yoked together. **3** a frame fitted to somebody's shoulders to carry a divided load, e.g. two buckets or baskets. **4** a fitted or shaped piece at the top of a garment from which the rest hangs. **5** something that is felt to be oppressive or burdensome.

**yoke**[2] *v* **1** to put a yoke on (e.g. a pair of oxen). **2** to connect or couple (two things).

**yokel** *n* a naive or gullible country person.

**yolk** *n* the usu yellow round mass that forms the inner portion of an egg.

**Yom Kippur** /ˌyom kiˈpooə, ˈkipə/ *n* a Jewish festival observed with fasting and prayer on the tenth day of the Jewish year.

**yon** *adj and adv literary or dialect* = YONDER.

**yonder** *adj and adv archaic or dialect* over there.

**yonks** *n Brit, informal* a long time; ages.

**yore** *n* ✱ **of yore** *literary* long ago.

**you** *pron* (*pl* **you**) **1** used as subject or object: the person or people being addressed. **2** a person; one.

**you'd** *contraction* **1** you had. **2** you would.

**you'll** *contraction* **1** you will. **2** you shall.

**young**[1] *adj* (**younger, youngest**) **1** in the first or an early stage of life, growth, or development. **2** suitable for or characteristic of young people.

**young**[2] *pl n* **1** offspring, *esp* of an animal. **2** (**the young**) young people.

**youngster** *n* a young person or creature.

**your** *adj* **1** belonging to or associated with the person or people being addressed. **2** belonging to or associated with people in general.

**you're** *contraction* you are.

**yours** *pron* (*pl* **yours**) the one or ones that belong to or are associated with you.

***Usage Note:*** Note that there is no apostrophe in *yours.*

**yourself** *pron* (*pl* **yourselves**) **1** used reflexively or for emphasis to refer to the person or people being addressed. **2** = ONESELF.

**youth** *n* **1** the time of life when one is young, *esp* adolescence. **2** a young male adolescent. **3** young people. **4** the quality or state of being youthful.

**youth club** *n* a local organization providing leisure activities for young people.

**youthful** *adj* **1** relating to or characteristic of youth. **2** not yet mature or old; young. ➤ **youthfully** *adv*, **youthfulness** *n.*

**youth hostel** *n* a place providing inexpensive bed and breakfast accommodation, *esp* for young travellers or hikers. ➤ **youth-hosteller** *n*, **youth-hostelling** *n.*

**you've** *contraction* you have.

**yowl** *v* to utter a loud long wail of pain or distress. ➤ **yowl** *n.*

**yo-yo**[1] *n* (*pl* **yo-yos**) *trademark* a toy consisting of two joined discs that is made to fall and rise when held by a string attached and wound between the discs.

**yo-yo**[2] *v* (**yo-yoes** *or* **yo-yos, yo-yoed, yo-yoing**) to fluctuate.

**yucca** *n* a plant with long often rigid leaves and a large cluster of white flowers.

**yuck** *or* **yuk** *interj informal* used to express a sense of disgust and revulsion. ➤ **yucky** *adj*, **yukky** *adj.*

**Yule** *or* **Yuletide** *n archaic* Christmas.

**yummy** *adj* (**-ier, -iest**) *informal* delicious.

**yuppie** *or* **yuppy** *n* (*pl* **-ies**) *informal, derog* a young person in a professional job with a high income and a fashionable lifestyle.

**YWCA** *abbr* Young Women's Christian Association.

**Z** *or* **z** *n* (*pl* **Z's** *or* **Zs** *or* **z's**) the 26th letter of the English alphabet.

**zany** *adj* (**-ier, -iest**) fantastically or absurdly comical.

**zap** *v* (**zapped, zapping**) *informal* **1** to destroy or kill. **2** to move with speed or force. **3** to switch swiftly from channel to channel on a television set by means of a remote control. ➤ **zapper** *n.*

**zeal** *n* eagerness to accomplish something.

**zealot** *n* a zealous person; *esp* a fanatical partisan of a religious or political movement. ➤ **zealotry** *n.*

**zealous** *adj* filled with or characterized by zeal. ➤ **zealously** *adv.*

**zebra** *n* (*pl* **zebras** *or* **zebra**) a black and white striped fast-running African mammal related to the horse.

**zebra crossing** *n Brit* a road crossing marked by a series of broad white stripes to indicate that pedestrians have the right of way.

**zebu** *n* an Asian ox of a domesticated breed with a large fleshy hump over the shoulders.

**zeitgeist** /'tsietgiest/ *n* the general intellectual and moral character of an era.

**Zen** *n* a Japanese Buddhist sect that aims at enlightenment by direct intuition through meditation.

**zenith** *n* **1** the point of the celestial sphere that is directly opposite the nadir and vertically above the observer. **2** the highest point reached in the heavens by a celestial body. **3** the highest or most successful point.

**zephyr** *n literary* a gentle breeze, *esp* from the west.

**zeppelin** *n* (*also* **Zeppelin**) a large German airship of the early 20th cent.

**zero[1]** *n* (*pl* **-os** *or* **-oes**) **1** the arithmetical symbol 0; nought. **2** the point from which the graduation of a scale, e.g. of a thermometer, begins. **3** a temperature of 0° Celsius (32° Fahrenheit), the freezing point of water.

**zero[2]** *v* (**zeroes** *or* **zeros, zeroed, zeroing**) to return (a counter) to zero.

**zero hour** *n* the time at which an event, *esp* a military attack, is scheduled to begin.

**zero in** *v* **1** (+ on) to adjust one's aim so as to hit. **2** (+ on) to focus attention on.

**zero tolerance** *n* a policy of total strictness in law enforcement in which not even the most minor offences are overlooked.

**zest** *n* **1** enthusiastic enjoyment; gusto. **2** an exciting or stimulating quality. **3** the outer peel of a citrus fruit used as flavouring. ➤ **zestful** *adj.*

**zeta** *n* the sixth letter of the Greek alphabet (Z, ζ).

**zigzag[1]** *n* a line or course consisting of a series of alternate sharp turns in opposite directions.

**zigzag[2]** *adj and adv* forming or going in a zigzag.

**zigzag[3]** *v* (**zigzagged, zigzagging**) to proceed along a zigzag course.

**zilch** *n informal* zero.

**zillion** *n* (*pl* **zillions** *or* **zillion**) *informal* (*also in pl*) an indefinitely large number. ➤ **zillionth** *adj and n.*

**Zimmer frame** *n trademark* a tubular frame with four legs, designed to help people who have difficulty in walking.

**zinc** *n* a bluish white metallic element, used *esp* as a protective coating for iron and steel.

**zing[1]** *n informal* energy or vim.

**zing[2]** *v informal* to move briskly.

**Zionism** *n* a movement initially for setting up a Jewish homeland in Palestine, now for furthering the interests of the state of Israel. ➤ **Zionist** *adj and n.*

**zip[1]** *n* **1** *chiefly Brit* a fastener that joins two edges by means of two flexible rows of teeth brought together by a sliding clip. **2** *informal* energy or liveliness. **3** *NAmer, informal* nothing; zero.

**zip[2]** *v* (**zipped, zipping**) **1** (*often* + up) to close or open with a zip. **2** in computing, to compress (a file). **3** *informal* to move with speed and vigour.

**zip code** *n* (*also* **ZIP code**) a number used as a postcode in the USA.

**zipper** *n chiefly NAmer* a zip.

**zippy** *adj* (**-ier, -iest**) **1** *informal* lively or energetic. **2** fast; having good acceleration.

**zircon** *n* a brownish or semitransparent mineral used as a gem.

**zirconium** *n* a steel-grey metallic element that is corrosion-resistant.

**zit** *n chiefly NAmer, informal* a pimple on the skin, *esp* of the face.

**zither** *n* a musical instrument having usu 30 to 40 strings over a shallow horizontal soundboard and played with plectrum and fingers.

**Zn** *abbr* the chemical symbol for zinc.

**zodiac** *n* a band in the sky, through which the apparent paths of the sun, moon, and all the principal planets except Pluto pass and which is divided into twelve signs for astrological purposes. ➤ **zodiacal** *adj.*

**zombie** *n* **1** in voodooism, a human being who is believed to have died and been reanimated. **2** *informal* a person resembling the walking dead, *esp* a shambling automaton.

**zone**[1] *n* **1** an area distinct from adjoining parts. **2** any of the sections into which an area is divided e.g. for planning purposes. **3** (*also* **time zone**) an area where a common standard time applies. ➤ **zonal** *adj.*

**zone**[2] *v* to arrange in, mark off, or partition into zones.

**zonk** *v informal* to strike (somebody or something) hard.

**zonked** *adj* **1** *informal* completely exhausted. **2** *slang* (*often* + out) highly intoxicated by alcohol or drugs.

**zoo** *n* (*pl* **zoos**) a place where a collection of living animals is kept and usu exhibited to the public.

**zoology** *n* **1** the branch of biology that deals with animals and animal life. **2** the animals found in a particular area. ➤ **zoological** *adj,* **zoologist** *n.*

**zoom**[1] *v* **1** to move quickly. **2** to operate the zoom lens of a camera.

**zoom**[2] *n* **1** the action of zooming. **2** a zoom lens.

**zoom lens** *n* a camera lens allowing progressive change from long to short shot.

**Zr** *abbr* the chemical symbol for zirconium.

**zucchini** /zoo'keeni/ *n* (*pl* **zucchinis** *or* **zucchini**) *chiefly NAmer* a courgette.

**zygote** *n* a cell formed by the union of two gametes. ➤ **zygotic** *adj.*

THE PENGUIN SPELLING DICTIONARY

*The Penguin*

# SPELLING DICTIONARY

*Market House Books*

SECOND EDITION

PENGUIN BOOKS

PENGUIN BOOKS

Published by the Penguin Group
Penguin Books Ltd, 80 Strand, London WC2R 0RL, England
Penguin Group (USA) Inc., 375 Hudson Street, New York, New York 10014, USA
Penguin Group (Canada), 90 Eglinton Avenue East, Suite 700, Toronto, Ontario, Canada M4P 2Y3 (a division of Pearson Penguin Canada Inc.)
Penguin Ireland, 25 St Stephen's Green, Dublin 2, Ireland (a division of Penguin Books Ltd)
Penguin Group (Australia), 250 Camberwell Road, Camberwell, Victoria 3124, Australia (a division of Pearson Australia Group Pty Ltd)
Penguin Books India Pvt Ltd, 11 Community Centre, Panchsheel Park, New Delhi – 110 017, India
Penguin Group (NZ), 67 Apollo Drive, Rosedale, North Shore 0632, New Zealand (a division of Pearson New Zealand Ltd)
Penguin Books (South Africa) (Pty) Ltd, 24 Sturdee Avenue, Rosebank, Johannesburg 2196, South Africa

Penguin Books Ltd, Registered Offices: 80 Strand, London WC2R 0RL, England

www.penguin.com

First published 1990
8



Typeset in 7.5/10.5 pt Linotype Stone
Typeset by Market House Books Ltd
Printed in England by Clays Ltd, St Ives plc



ISBN: 978-0-140-51425-4

# CONTENTS

# PREFACE TO THE FIRST EDITION

English is a difficult language to spell correctly – and not only for the foreigner. Native speakers, too, find it hard. The problem is that modern English is such a rich and resourceful language, derived from so many sources, that its spelling does not obey simple rules. Although much of the language *is* regular, in the sense that it does obey rules, there are very large numbers of exceptions to the common patterns. While the only safe way to be sure of a spelling is to look it up in this dictionary, the basic rules are given on the following pages.

*The Penguin Spelling Dictionary* is divided into three sections: the main spelling list; a list of first names; and a list of biographical names.

*Spelling list*

This, the largest section, contains normal vocabulary words, place names, some trademarks, and biblical and mythological names not included in the names lists (see below). Unhyphenated two-word compounds (e.g. phrasal verbs and nouns) are usually not listed, as each element will have its own entry. Exceptions include compounds with irregular inflections (see below) and some eponymous terms (terms derived from the name of a person), in which both elements are included as an aid to the sense.

Centred dots within a word indicate the points at which it can be hyphenated. These divisions are phonetic, rather than etymological, and correspond to syllabification breaks; note, however, that when syllabification breaks are not acceptable as hyphenation points they are not shown. Monosyllabic words should never be hyphenated, nor – if possible – should people's names.

Inflections (changes in the form of a word to indicate changes in grammatical function) are included if they are irregular. In general, regular inflections are not included. For rules on the formation of regular and irregular inflections, see under **The Rules of Spelling** on the following pages.

US spellings and British variant spellings are included after the preferred spelling of the word; they also have their own entries, with an appropriate gloss, if they are widely separated alphabetically from the preferred spelling.

Short glosses are provided for unfamiliar words and to avoid confusion between similarly spelt or pronounced words. Most of the proper names in this section are also glossed.

A few common misspellings are included in the list. These words are bracketed and the correct spelling indicated.

*First names*

This section comprises a comprehensive list of English first names, together with their spelling variants. It does not include the more obscure biblical and mythological names (many of which are listed in the main section of the dictionary) or the names of monarchs and other rulers that are unfamiliar or foreign (many of these are listed under the biographical names).

*Biographical names*

This section includes the names of people from all countries, past and present, who have achieved fame in some sphere of human activity. Monarchs are generally not included if their names appear in the first names list. Biographical names are listed in alphabetical order of the surname, followed by first names and any titles; the less familiar names of a subject are bracketed. Variant spellings and pseudonyms are also listed, and similar names are glossed to avoid confusion.

# PREFACE TO THE SECOND EDITION

The response to the first edition of *The Penguin Spelling Dictionary*, published in 1990, has been so encouraging that the publishers have decided to produce a revised edition.

Although most standard spellings have not changed over the past ten years, geographical references have been updated to account for such events as the collapse of the Soviet Union, the renaming of Zaïre, and local government reorganization in the UK. We have added a number of new words, reflecting changes in areas as diverse as politics, popular culture, and medicine. We have also included terms that have become more widespread, such as database and organophosphate.

The biographical appendix has been expanded to include major figures who have risen to prominence during the past decade.

Our aim has been to ensure that *The Penguin Spelling Dictionary* continues to be an up-to-date, useful, and comprehensive book.

# THE RULES OF SPELLING

## Nouns

### *Regular inflections*

Regular plurals are formed by adding *-s*; for nouns ending in *-s*, *-x*, *-z*, *-ch*, or *-sh*, add *-es*.

### *Irregular inflections*

1. Nouns of Latin origin ending in *-a*, especially in scientific or technical usage, usually have the plural ending *-ae* (e.g. **alga/algae**; **nebula/nebulae**).

   Such nouns ending in *-ma* usually have the plural ending *-mata* (e.g. **stoma/stomata**).
2. Nouns ending in *-f* either form regular plurals (e.g. **chief/chiefs**) or have the plural ending *-ves* (e.g. **calf/calves**).

   Most nouns ending in *-fe* form regular plurals (e.g. **safe/safes**) but a few have the plural ending *-ves* (e.g. **wife/wives**).
3. Nouns ending in *-i* usually form regular plurals but a few have the plural ending *-ies* (e.g. **chilli/chillies**).
4. Nouns ending in *-is* either form regular plurals (e.g. **iris/irises**) or have the plural ending *-es* (e.g. **basis/bases**). Some scientific and technical nouns have the plural ending *-ides* (e.g. **apsis/apsides**).
5. Most nouns ending in *-o* either form regular plurals (e.g. **albino/albinos**) or have the plural ending *-oes* (e.g. **tomato/tomatoes**). Nouns of Italian origin have the plural form *-i*, either as the only plural or as an alternative (e.g. **graffito/graffiti**; **virtuoso/virtuosos** *or* **virtuosi**).
6. Some nouns of Greek origin ending in *-on* have the plural ending *-a* (e.g. **criterion/criteria**).
7. Nouns of Latin origin ending in *-um*, especially in scientific or technical usage, have the plural ending *-a* (e.g. **bacterium/bacteria**; **stratum/strata**).
8. Many nouns of Latin origin ending in *-us*, especially in scientific or technical usage, have the preferred or alternative plural ending *-i* (e.g. **fungus/fungi**; **stylus/styli** *or* **styluses**). A few such nouns have the plural ending *-era* or *-ora* (e.g. **genus/genera**; **corpus/corpora**).
9. Most nouns ending in *-x* form regular plurals (e.g. **tax/taxes**) but a few, usually in scientific or technical usage, have the plural ending *-ces* (e.g. **appendix/appendices**).

   Such nouns ending in *-ex* have the plural ending *-ices* (e.g. **index/indices**).

Such nouns ending in *-nx* have the plural ending *-nges* (e.g. **meninx/meninges**).

10. Nouns ending in *-y* preceded by a vowel form regular plurals (e.g. **donkey/donkeys**). Nouns ending in *-y* preceded by a consonant or *-qu-* have the plural ending *-ies* (e.g. **family/families; colloquy/colloquies**). Note that proper names ending *-y* form regular plurals, irrespective of the preceding letter (e.g. **Sally/Sallys**).
11. In phrasal nouns and most other hyphenated nouns, the final element is pluralized (e.g. **lay-by/lay-bys**), but in some hyphenated and multiword nouns the noun element may be pluralized irrespective of its position (e.g. **looker-on/lookers-on; court martial/court martials** *or* **courts martial**).

    Note, however, that this does not apply to nouns ending in *-ful* (e.g. **spoonful/spoonfuls;** *not* **spoonsful**).
12. Some nouns, especially animals, have the same singular and plural forms (e.g. **sheep/sheep; fish/fish** *or* **fishes**).
13. Abbreviations and numerals usually have the plural ending *-s* (e.g. **MPs; 1920s**).

*Suffixes*

Many nouns are formed by adding suffixes to the corresponding verb or adjective. A few general rules apply.

1. *-ation*

   For words ending in *-l* preceded by a single vowel, the *-l* is doubled (e.g. **cancel/cancellation**).
2. *-er* and *-or*

   Either of these suffixes may be added to form nouns meaning the 'doer' of the corresponding verb, but the *-er* forms greatly outnumber the *-or* forms. For some verbs, both forms exist; in these cases the following rules may apply:

   (a) the *-or* form is used for objects and the *-er* form for people (e.g. **resister**, person who resists; **resistor**, electrical component).

   (b) the *-or* form is preferred in legal or scientific contexts (e.g. **bailer**, one who bails; **bailor**, transferrer of goods by bailment).
3. *-ment*

(a) For words ending in *-dge*, the preferred form is to drop the *-e* (e.g. **judge/judgment**).

(b) For words ending in *-ll*, the terminal *-l* is dropped (e.g. **install/instalment**).

(c) For words of more than one syllable ending in *-y* preceded by a consonant, the *-y* is changed to *-i* (e.g. **merry/merriment**).

4. *-ness*

   For words of more than one syllable preceded by a consonant, the *-y* is changed to *-i* (e.g. **happy/happiness**).

## Adjectives

### Regular Inflections

Regular comparatives and superlatives, for adjectives of one or two syllables, are formed by adding *-er* and *-est*, respectively.

For adjectives ending in *-e*, the *-e* is dropped before adding *-er* or *-est* (e.g. **nice/nicer, nicest; free/freer, freest**).

Adjectives of three or more syllables are preceded by *more* and *most* to form the comparative and superlative respectively.

### Irregular Inflections

1. For adjectives ending in *-y* preceded by a consonant, the comparative and superlative are formed by dropping the *-y* and adding *-ier* and *-iest* respectively (e.g. **tidy/tidier, tidiest**).
2. For monosyllabic adjectives ending in a consonant preceded by a single vowel, the comparative and superlative are formed by doubling the terminal consonant before adding *-er* and *-est* respectively (e.g. **hot/hotter, hottest**).

### Suffixes

*-able* and *-ible*

The great majority of these adjectives have the ending *-able*; they are derived from native English verbs and nouns. Certain verbs and nouns of Latin origin, however, take the suffix *-ible*; some common examples are **accessible, comprehensible, convertible, divisible, eligible, perceptible, permissible, tangible**. Some can end in either *-able* or *-ible* (e.g. **collectable/collectible, discussible/discussable**).

For adjectives ending in *-able*, the following rules generally apply, although there are exceptions:

(a) For verbs and nouns ending in *-e*, the *-e* is dropped before adding *-able* unless it is preceded by *-c-* or *-g-* (e.g. **noticeable, changeable**) or when its retention aids pronunciation (e.g. **blameable, saleable**).

(b) For words ending in *-y* preceded by a consonant, the *-y* is changed to *-i* before adding *-able* (e.g. **justifiable**).

(c) For verbs ending in *-l* preceded by a single vowel, the *-l* is doubled before adding *-able* (e.g. **distil/distillable**).

## Verbs

### Regular Inflections

1. The third person singular is formed by adding *-s* or, for verbs ending in *-s*, *-x*, *-z*, *-ch*, or *-sh*, by adding *-es*.
2. The present participle is formed by adding *-ing*.
3. The past tense and past participle are formed by adding *-ed*.

4. For verbs ending in *-e* preceded by a consonant, the *-e* is dropped before adding *-ing* or *-ed* (compare **Irregular inflections** 3 and 4).

*Irregular Inflections*

1. For verbs ending in *-y* preceded by a consonant, the past tense and past participle are formed by dropping the *-y* and adding *-ied* (e.g. **marry/married**).
2. In monosyllabic verbs ending in a consonant preceded by a single vowel, the terminal consonant is doubled when inflecting (e.g. **pat/patting, patted**).

   With some exceptions, this rule also applies to verbs of more than one syllable, notably when:

   (a) the terminal consonant is *-l* (e.g. **marvel/marvelling, marvelled**); note that in American English the *-l* is not doubled.

   (b) the stress is on the last syllable (e.g. **refer/referring, referred**).
3. For verbs ending in *-e* preceded by a vowel, the *-e* is dropped before adding *-ed* but retained before *-ing* (e.g. **hoe/hoeing, hoed**).
4. For a few verbs ending in *-e* preceded by a consonant, the *-e* is dropped before adding *-ed* but retained before *-ing*, usually to avoid confusion with very similar words (e.g. **singe/singeing, singed**).
5. For verbs ending in *-ac-* or *-ic*, the present participle is formed by adding *-king* and the past tense and participle by adding *-ked* (e.g. **traffic/trafficking, trafficked**).

*Suffixes*

1. *-ize* and *-ise*

   Most of these verbs have the preferred ending *-ize*, with *-ise* as an acceptable variant in British English (but not in American English); the same applies to the derived nouns (e.g. **specialize/specialization**). Exceptions include **advertise, compromise, improvise, supervise**; for these verbs *-ise* is the only acceptable ending in British and American English.
2. *-yse* and *-yze*

   *-yse* is the only acceptable form in British English; *-yze* is the US spelling (e.g. **catalyse**/*US* **catalyze**; **paralyse**/*US* **paralyze**).

## Adverbs

Many adverbs are formed by adding *-ly* to the corresponding adjectives or nouns. Note:

1. For adjectives or nouns ending in *-e*, the *-e* is usually, but not always, retained (e.g. **pale/palely; rude/rudely**). Exceptions include **true/truly, whole/wholly**.
2. For adjectives or nouns ending in *-l*, the *-l* is retained (e.g. **eventual/eventually**).
3. For adjectives ending in *-ll*, the penultimate *-l* is dropped before adding *-ly* (e.g. **full/fully**).
4. For adjectives or nouns ending in *-y*, the adverb is formed by dropping the *-y* and adding *-ily* (e.g. **merry/merrily**).

## *Common spelling problems*

1. *-cede* or *-ceed*

    There is no general rule here: the usual ending is *-cede* (e.g. **concede, precede**); the only verbs ending in *-ceed* are **exceed, proceed,** and **succeed.** Note particularly the spelling of **supersede.**

2. *-ei-* or *-ie-*

    The rule 'i before e except after c' works fairly well when the sound is pronounced 'ee' (e.g. **niece, siege**; but **receipt, receive**). Exceptions include **seize, weir, weird.**

    When the sound is pronounced 'ai' (as in paid), the spelling is *-ei-* (e.g. **deign, neighbour, weigh**).

3. *Difficult words*

    A few words cause many people problems because they follow no rules:

| accommodate | exaggerate | phenomenon |
|---|---|---|
| anomalous | forty | pursue |
| business | gauge | surprise |
| commemorate | harass | threshold |
| desiccate | inoculate | withhold |
| ecstasy | necessary | |
| embarrass | parallel | |

# A

**aa** rock
**Aachen** German city
**Aal•borg** (*or* **Ål•**) Danish port
**aalii** shrub
**aard•vark**
**aard•wolf** (*plural* **•wolves**)
**Aar•gau** Swiss canton
**Aar•hus** (*or* **År•**) Danish port
**aba•ca** fibre
**aback**
**ab•ac•ti•nal** zoology term
**aba•cus** (*plural* **•ci** *or* **•cuses**)
**Aba•dan** Iranian port
**Abad•don** the devil
**abaft** nautical term
**aba•lo•ne** mollusc
**ab•am•pere** electrical unit
**aban•don**
**aban•doned**
**aban•doned•ly**
**aban•donee** legal term
**aban•don•ment**
**abase**
**abase•ment**
**abash**
**abash•ed•ly**
**abat•able**
**abate**
**abate•ment**
**aba•tis** (*or* **ab•at•tis**) fortifications term
**aba•tor** legal term
**ab•at•toir**
**ab•ax•ial** away from the axis; *compare* **adaxial**
**ab•ba•cy** (*plural* **•cies**)
**Abbasid** dynasty of caliphs
**ab•ba•tial**
**abbé** *French* abbott
**ab•bess**
**Abbe•vill•ian** archaeological period
**ab•bey**
**ab•bot**
**ab•bre•vi•ate**
**ab•bre•via•tion**
**ab•bre•via•tor**
(**abcess**) *incorrect spelling of* abscess
**ab•cou•lomb** electrical unit
**ab•di•cable**
**ab•di•cate**
**ab•di•ca•tion**
**ab•dica•tive**
**ab•di•ca•tor**
**ab•do•men**
**ab•domi•nal**
**ab•domi•nal•ly**
**ab•du•cens** nerve
**ab•du•cent** anatomy term
**ab•duct**
**ab•duc•tion**
**abeam** nautical term
**abece•dar•ian** learner
**abed**
**abele** poplar
**Abelian** maths term
**abel•mosk** plant
**Ab•eo•ku•ta** Nigerian town
**Ab•er•dare** Welsh town
**Ab•er•deen**
**Ab•er•do•nian**
**ab•er•nethy** biscuit
**ab•er•rance** (*or* **•ran•cy**)
**ab•er•rant**
**ab•er•ra•tion**
**Ab•er•yst•wyth**
**abet** (**abet•ting, abet•ted**)
**abet•ment**
**abet•ter** (*or esp. in legal contexts* **•tor**)
**abey•ance**
**abey•ant**
**ab•far•ad** electrical unit
**ab•hen•ry** (*plural* **•ries**) electrical unit
**ab•hor** (**•hor•ring, •horred**)
**ab•hor•rence**
**ab•hor•rent**
**ab•hor•rer**
**abid•ance**
**abide** (**abid•ing, abode** *or* **abid•ed**)
**abid•er**
**abid•ing**
**abid•ing•ly**
**Abid•jan** Côte d'Ivoire port
**abi•et•ic acid**
**abi•gail** maid
**Abi•lene** Texan city
**abil•ity** (*plural* **•ities**)
**Ab•ing•don**
**ab ini•tio** *Latin* from the start
**abio•gen•esis** biological theory
**abio•genet•ic**
**abiog•enist**
**abio•sis** absence of life
**abiot•ic**
**ab•ir•ri•tant** relieving irritation
**ab•ir•ri•tate**
**ab•ject**
**ab•jec•tion**
**ab•ju•ra•tion**
**ab•jure** renounce; *compare* **adjure**
**ab•jur•er**
**Ab•khaz** (*plural* **•khaz**) Georgian people
**Ab•kha•zia** Georgian republic
**ab•late**
**ab•la•tion**
**ab•la•tive** grammar term
**ab•la•tor** heat shield
**ab•laut** linguistics term
**ablaze**
**able**
**able-bodied**
**abloom**
**ab•lu•tion**
**ab•lu•tion•ary**
**ably**
**ab•ne•gate**
**ab•ne•ga•tion**
**ab•ne•ga•tor**
**ab•nor•mal**
**ab•nor•mal•ity** (*plural* **•ities**)
**ab•nor•mal•ly**
**aboard**
**abode**
**ab•ohm** electrical unit
**aboi•deau** (*plural* **•deaus** *or* **•deaux**) Canadian dyke
**abol•ish**
**abol•ish•er**
**abol•ish•ment**
**abo•li•tion**
**abo•li•tion•ary**
**abo•li•tion•ism**

**abo•li•tion•ist**
**abo•ma•sum** ruminant's stomach
**abomi•nable**
**abomi•nably**
**abomi•nate**
**abomi•na•tion**
**abomi•na•tor**
**ab•oral** zoology term
**Abo•rigi•nal**
**abo•rigi•nal**
**Abo•rigi•ne** native Australian
**abo•rigi•ne** an original inhabitant
**abort**
**abor•ti•cide**
**abor•ti•fa•cient** inducing abortion
**abor•tion**
**abor•tion•al**
**abor•tion•ist**
**abor•tive**
**Abou•kir** battle site
**abou•lia** *variant spelling of* **abulia**
**abound**
**about**
**about-turn** (*or esp. US* **about-face)**
**above**
**ab•ra•ca•dab•ra**
**abra•dant**
**abrade**
**abrad•er**
**abran•chi•ate** (*or* **•chial)** zoology term
**abra•sion**
**abra•sive**
**abrax•as** magic charm
**ab•re•act** psychology term
**ab•re•ac•tion**
**ab•re•ac•tive**
**abreast**
**abridg•able** (*or* **abridge•)**
**abridge**
**abridg•er**
**abridg•ment** (*or* **abridge•)**
**abroad**
**ab•ro•gate**
**ab•ro•ga•tion**
**ab•ro•ga•tor**
**ab•rupt**
**ab•rup•tion** breaking off
**ab•rupt•ness**
**Abruz•zi** Italian region
**ab•scess**
**ab•scise** to separate
**ab•scis•sa** (*plural* **•sas** *or* **•sae)** maths term
**ab•scis•sion** shedding of plant parts
**ab•scond**
**ab•scond•er**
**ab•seil** mountaineering term
**ab•sence**
**ab•sent**
**ab•sen•tee**
**ab•sen•tee•ism**
**ab•sent•er**
**ab•sen•te reo** *Latin* the defendant being absent
**absent-minded**
**absent-minded•ness**
**ab•sinthe** (*or* **•sinth)**
**ab•sit omen** *Latin* may the foreboding not be realized
**ab•so•lute**
**ab•so•lute•ly**
**ab•so•lu•tion**
**ab•so•lut•ism**
**ab•solu•tory**
**ab•solv•able**
**ab•solve**
**ab•solv•er**
**ab•sorb** take into or permeate; *compare* **adsorb**
**ab•sorb•abil•ity**
**ab•sorb•able**
**ab•sorb•ance** physics term
**ab•sorb•ed•ly**
**ab•sor•be•fa•cient** inducing absorption
**ab•sorb•en•cy**
**ab•sorb•ent**
**ab•sorb•er**
**ab•sorb•ing**
**ab•sorb•ing•ly**
**ab•sorp•tance** physics term
**ab•sorp•tion**
**ab•sorp•tive**
**ab•sorp•tiv•ity** physics term
**ab•squatu•late** decamp
**ab•stain**
**ab•stain•er**
**ab•ste•mi•ous**
**ab•sten•tion**
**ab•sten•tious**
**ab•ster•gent** cleansing
**ab•sti•nence**
**ab•sti•nent**
**ab•stract**
**ab•stract•ed•ly**
**ab•stract•ed•ness**
**ab•strac•tion**
**ab•strac•tion•ism** theory of abstract art
**ab•strac•tive**
**ab•stric•tion** biology term
**ab•struse**
**ab•struse•ness**
**ab•surd**
**ab•surd•ity** (*or* **•ness;** *plural* **•ities** *or* **•nesses)**
**Abu Dha•bi** sheikdom
**Abu•ja** Nigerian capital
**abu•lia** (*or* **abou•)** loss of willpower
**abu•lic**
**abun•dance**
**abun•dant**
**abuse**
**abus•er**
**Abu Sim•bel** Egyptian temple
**abu•sive**
**abu•sive•ness**
**abut (abut•ting, abut•ted)**
**abu•ti•lon** shrub
**abut•ment** (*or* **abut•tal)**
**abut•tals** legal term
**abut•ter** owner of adjoining property
**abuzz**
**ab•volt** electrical unit
**ab•watt** electrical unit
**Aby•dos** ancient Egyptian town
**abysm** *Archaic* abyss
**abys•mal** immeasurable; very bad
**abys•mal•ly**
**abyss**
**abys•sal** of ocean depths
**Ab•ys•sinia** *former name of* **Ethiopia**
**Ab•ys•sin•ian**
**aca•cia**
**aca•deme**
**aca•demia**
**aca•dem•ic**
**aca•dem•ical•ly**
**aca•dem•icals** academic dress
**acad•emi•cian**

**aca•demi•cism** (*or* **acad•emism)** conventionalism
**acad•emy** (*plural* **•emies)**
**Aca•dia** Canadian region; *compare* **Arcadia**
**Aca•dian** of Acadia; *compare* **Accadian**
**aca•jou** mahogany
**ac•an•tha•ceous** botany term
**acan•thine**
**acan•tho•cepha•lan** wormlike animal
**acan•thoid** spiny
**ac•an•thop•ter•yg•ian** fish
**acan•thous** thornlike
**acan•thus** (*plural* **•thuses** *or* **•thi)** plant; architectural ornament
**a cap•pel•la** musical term
**Aca•pul•co** Mexican port
**aca•ria•sis** tick or mite infestation
**aca•rid** (*or* **acari•dan)** tick or mite
**aca•roid**
**aca•rol•ogy**
**acar•pel•lous** lacking carpels
**acar•pous** producing no fruit
**aca•rus** mite
**acata•lec•tic** verse form
**acau•dal** (*or* **•date)** having no tail
**acau•les•cent** having no stem
**Ac•cad** *variant spelling of* **Akkad**
**Ac•cad•ian** *variant spelling of* **Akkadian**; *compare* **Acadian**
**ac•cede**
**ac•ced•ence**
**ac•ced•er**
**ac•cel•era•able**
**ac•cel•er•an•do** (*plural* **•dos)** musical term
**ac•cel•er•ant**
**ac•cel•er•ate**
**ac•cel•era•tion**
**ac•cel•era•tive** (*or* **•tory)**
**ac•cel•era•tor**
**ac•cel•er•om•eter**
**ac•cent**
**ac•cen•tor** bird
**ac•cen•tual** rhythmical
**ac•cen•tu•ate**
**ac•cen•tua•tion**
**ac•cept**
**ac•cept•abil•ity** (*or* **•able•ness)**
**ac•cept•able**
**ac•cept•ably**
**ac•cept•ance**
**ac•cept•ant**
**ac•cep•ta•tion**
**ac•cept•ed•ly**
**ac•cep•ter** (*or esp. in legal contexts, chemistry, and electronics* **•tor)**
**ac•cess**
**ac•ces•sa•ry** (*plural* **•ries)** *variant spelling of* **accessory**
**ac•ces•sibil•ity**
**ac•ces•sible**
**ac•ces•sibly**
**ac•ces•sion**
**ac•ces•sion•al**
**ac•ces•so•rial**
**ac•ces•so•ri•ly**
**ac•ces•so•ri•ness**
**ac•ces•so•ry** (*or in legal contexts* **•sa•ry**; *plural* **•ries)**
**ac•ciac•ca•tu•ra** (*plural* **•ras** *or* **•re)** musical term
**ac•ci•dence** linguistics term
**ac•ci•dent**
**ac•ci•den•tal**
**ac•ci•den•tal•ly**
**ac•ci•die** apathy
**ac•cipi•ter** hawk
**ac•cipi•tral** (*or* **•trine)**
**ac•claim**
**ac•cla•ma•tion**
**ac•clama•tory**
**ac•cli•ma•tiz•able** (*or* **•ma•tis•able, •mat•able)**
**ac•cli•ma•ti•za•tion** (*or* **•ma•ti•sa•tion, •ma•tion)**
**ac•cli•ma•tize** (*or* **•ma•tise, •mate)**
**ac•cli•ma•tiz•er** (*or* **•tis•er)**
**ac•clivi•tous** (*or* **•cli•vous)**
**ac•cliv•ity** (*plural* **•ities)** upward slope
**ac•co•lade**
**ac•com•mo•date**
**ac•com•mo•dat•ing**
**ac•com•mo•dat•ing•ly**
**ac•com•mo•da•tion**
**ac•com•mo•da•tive**
**(accomodate)** *incorrect spelling of* **accommodate**
**ac•com•pa•ni•er**
**ac•com•pa•ni•ment**
**ac•com•pa•nist** (*or esp. US* **•pa•ny•ist)**
**ac•com•pa•ny** (**•nies, •ny•ing, •nied)**
**ac•com•plice**
**ac•com•plish**
**ac•com•plish•able**
**ac•com•plish•er**
**ac•com•plish•ment**
**ac•cord**
**ac•cord•able**
**ac•cord•ance**
**ac•cord•ant**
**ac•cord•er**
**ac•cord•ing**
**ac•cord•ing•ly**
**ac•cor•di•on**
**ac•cor•di•on•ist**
**ac•cost**
**ac•cost•able**
**ac•count**
**ac•count•abil•ity**
**ac•count•able**
**ac•count•ably**
**ac•count•an•cy**
**ac•count•ant**
**ac•count•ing**
**ac•cou•ple•ment** supporting beam
**ac•cou•tre** (*US* **•ter)**
**ac•cou•tre•ment** (*US* **•ter•)**
**Ac•cra** Ghanaian capital
**ac•cred•it**
**ac•credi•ta•tion**
**ac•cres•cent** botany term
**ac•crete**
**ac•cre•tion**
**ac•cre•tive** (*or* **ac•cre•tion•ary)**
**Ac•cring•ton**
**ac•cru•al** (*or* **•ment)**
**ac•crue** (**•cru•ing, •crued)**
**ac•cul•tur•ate**
**ac•cul•tura•tion**
**ac•cum•ben•cy**
**ac•cum•bent** botany term
**ac•cu•mu•lable**
**ac•cu•mu•late**
**ac•cu•mu•la•tion**

**ac•cu•mu•la•tive**
**ac•cu•mu•la•tor**
**ac•cu•ra•cy** (*plural* **•cies**)
**ac•cu•rate**
**ac•cu•rate•ly**
**ac•curs•ed**
**ac•cus•al**
**ac•cu•sa•tion**
**ac•cu•sa•ti•val**
**ac•cu•sa•tive** grammar term
**ac•cu•sa•to•rial** (*or* **•tory**)
**ac•cuse**
**ac•cused**
**ac•cus•er**
**ac•cus•ing•ly**
**ac•cus•tom**
**ac•cus•tomed**
**Ac•cu•tron** (*Trademark*) watch
**ace**
**acedia** apathy
**acel•lu•lar**
**acen•tric**
**acepha•lous** headless
**ac•er•ate** *variant of* **acerose**
**ac•er•bate** embitter
**acer•bic**
**acer•bity** (*plural* **•bities**)
**ac•er•ose** (*or* **•ous, •ate**) needle-shaped
**acer•vate** growing in clusters
**aces•cence** (*or* **•cen•cy**)
**aces•cent** turning sour
**ac•etabu•lum** (*plural* **•la**) cavity in hipbone
**ac•etal** chemical compound
**ac•et•al•de•hyde**
**ac•et•am•ide** (*or* **•id**)
**ac•et•ani•lide** (*or* **•lid**)
**ac•etate**
**acetic acid**
**aceti•fi•ca•tion**
**aceti•fi•er**
**aceti•fy** (**•fies, •fy•ing, •fied**) convert into vinegar
**ac•etom•eter**
**ac•etone**
**ac•etous** (*or* **•etose**) resembling vinegar
**acetum** vinegar
**ac•etyl**
**acety•late**
**acety•la•tion**
**acetyl•cho•line** biochemical compound
**acety•lene**
**acety•len•ic**
**acety•lide**
**ac•etyl•sali•cyl•ic acid** *chemical name for* **aspirin**
**acey-deucy** backgammon
**Achaea** (*or* **Achaia**) region of Greece
**Achae•an** (*or* **Achaian**)
**Achaemenid** member of Persian dynasty
**Acha•tes** loyal friend
**ache**
**ach•ing•ly**
**achene** (*or* **akene**) botany term
**achenial** (*or* **akenial**)
**Acher•nar** star
**Ach•er•on** mythological river
**Acheu•lian** (*or* **•lean**) archaeological period
**achiev•able**
**achieve**
**achieve•ment**
**achiev•er**
**Ach•il•lean**
**Achilles**
**ach•la•myd•eous** lacking petals and sepals
**achlor•hy•dria** lacking stomach acid
**achon•drite** meteorite
**achon•drit•ic**
**achon•dro•pla•sia** skeletal disorder
**achon•dro•plas•tic**
**ach•ro•mat** type of lens
**ach•ro•mat•ic**
**ach•ro•mati•cal•ly**
**achro•ma•tin** part of cell nucleus
**achro•ma•tism** (*or* **•tic•ity**)
**achro•ma•ti•za•tion** (*or* **•sa•tion**)
**achro•ma•tize** (*or* **•tise**) remove colour from
**achro•ma•tous**
**a•chro•mic** (*or* **achro•mous**) colourless
**ach-y-fi** Welsh expression of disgust
**acicu•la** (*plural* **•lae**) needle-shaped structure
**acicu•lar**
**acicu•late** (*or* **•lat•ed**)
**acicu•lum** (*plural* **•lums** *or* **•la**) zoology term
**acid**
**acid-fast**
**acid-forming**
**acid•ic**
**acidi•fi•able**
**acidi•fi•ca•tion**
**acidi•fi•er**
**acidi•fy** (**•fies, •fy•ing, •fied**)
**aci•dim•eter**
**acidi•met•ric** (*or* **•ri•cal**)
**aci•di•met•ri•cal•ly**
**aci•dim•etry**
**acid•ity** (*plural* **•ities**)
**acid•ness**
**aci•dom•eter** hydrometer for acids
**aci•do•phil** (*or* **•phile**) biology term
**aci•do•phil•ic** (*or* **•dophi•lous**)
**aci•dophi•lus** bacterium
**aci•do•sis** medical condition
**aci•dot•ic**
**acidu•late** make acid
**acidu•la•tion**
**acidu•lous** (*or* **•lent**)
**aci•er•ate** change into steel
**aci•era•tion**
**aci•naci•form** botany term
**acin•ic** (*or* **aci•nous, aci•nose**)
**acini•form**
**aci•nus** (*plural* **•ni**) biology term
**Acis** mythological character
**ack-ack** anti-aircraft fire
**ackee** (*or* **akee**) fruit
**ac•knowl•edge**
**ac•knowl•edge•able**
**ac•knowl•edg•er**
**ac•knowl•edg•ment** (*or* **•edge•**)
**aclin•ic line** magnetic equator
**acme** peak
**acne** skin disease
**ac•no•dal**
**ac•node** maths term
**Acol** bridge term

**aco•lyte**
**aco•nite** (*or* **•ni•tum)**
**aco•nit•ic**
**acorn**
**acoty•ledon** botany term
**acoty•ledon•ous**
**acou•chi** (*or* **•chy)** rodent
**acous•tic** (*or* **•ti•cal)**
**acous•ti•cal•ly**
**acous•ti•cian**
**acous•tics**
**ac•quaint**
**ac•quaint•ance**
**ac•quaint•ance•ship**
**ac•quaint•ed**
**ac•qui•esce**
**ac•qui•es•cence**
**ac•qui•es•cent**
**ac•quir•able**
**ac•quire**
**ac•quire•ment**
**ac•quir•er**
**ac•qui•si•tion**
**ac•quisi•tive**
**ac•quisi•tive•ness**
**ac•quit (•quit•ting, •quit•ted)**
**ac•quit•tal**
**ac•quit•tance**
**ac•quit•ter**
**acre**
**acre•age**
**acred** having acres of land
**acre-foot** (*plural* **-feet)**
**acre-inch**
**ac•rid**
**ac•ri•dine** chemical compound
**acrid•ity** (*or* **•ness)**
**ac•ri•fla•vine** antiseptic
**Ac•ri•lan** (*Trademark*)
**ac•ri•mo•ni•ous**
**ac•ri•mo•ny** (*plural* **•nies)**
**ac•ro•bat**
**ac•ro•bat•ic**
**ac•ro•bati•cal•ly**
**ac•ro•bat•ics**
**ac•ro•car•pous** botany term
**ac•ro•dont** zoology term
**ac•ro•drome** botany term
**ac•ro•gen** botany term
**ac•ro•gen•ic** (*or* **acrog•enous)**
**acro•lein** chemical compound
**ac•ro•lith** type of sculpture
**ac•ro•me•gal•ic**
**ac•ro•mega•ly** hormonal disease
**acro•mi•on** (*plural* **•mia)** part of shoulder blade
**acrony•chal** (*or* **•cal)** occurring at sunset
**ac•ro•nym**
**ac•ro•nym•ic** (*or* **acrony•mous)**
**acrop•etal** botany term
**ac•ro•pho•bia** fear of heights
**ac•ro•pho•bic**
**Acropo•lis**
**ac•ro•spire** botany term
**across**
**acros•tic**
**acros•ti•cal•ly**
**acro•ter** architectural term
**acryl•ic**
**ac•ry•lo•ni•trile**
**ac•ry•lyl**
**act**
**act•abil•ity**
**act•able**
**ac•tin** protein
**ac•ti•nal** zoology term
**act•ing**
**ac•tinia** (*plural* **•tiniae** *or* **•tinias)** sea anemone
**ac•tin•ic** type of radiation
**ac•tini•cal•ly**
**ac•ti•nide** (*or* **•non)**
**ac•tini•form** (*or* **ac•ti•noid)** star-shaped
**ac•tin•ism**
**ac•tin•ium** radioactive element
**ac•ti•noid** *variant of* **actiniform**
**ac•tino•lite** mineral
**ac•ti•no•mere** biology term
**ac•ti•nom•eter** radiation measurer
**ac•ti•no•met•ric** (*or* **•ri•cal)**
**ac•ti•nom•etry**
**ac•ti•no•mor•phic** (*or* **•phous)** botany term
**ac•ti•no•my•cete** bacterium
**ac•ti•no•my•cin** antibiotic
**ac•ti•no•my•co•sis** bacterial infection
**ac•ti•no•my•cot•ic**
**ac•ti•non** *variant of* **actinide**
**ac•tino•pod** protozoan
**ac•ti•no•thera•py** radiotherapy
**ac•ti•no•ura•nium** isotope of uranium
**ac•ti•no•zo•an** marine organism
**ac•tion**
**ac•tion•able**
**ac•tion•ably**
**action-packed**
**Ac•ti•um** ancient Greek town
**ac•ti•vate**
**ac•ti•va•tion**
**ac•ti•va•tor**
**ac•tive**
**ac•tive•ly**
**ac•tive•ness**
**ac•tiv•ism**
**ac•tiv•ist**
**ac•tiv•ity** (*plural* **•ities)**
**ac•to•myo•sin** protein
**Ac•ton** London district
**ac•tor**
**ac•tress**
**ac•tual**
**ac•tu•al•ity** (*plural* **•ities)**
**ac•tu•ali•za•tion** (*or* **•sa•tion)**
**ac•tu•al•ize** (*or* **•ise)**
**ac•tu•al•ly**
**ac•tu•ari•al**
**ac•tu•ary** (*plural* **•aries)**
**ac•tu•ate**
**ac•tua•tion**
**ac•tua•tor**
**acu•ity**
**acu•leate** (*or* **•leat•ed)** pointed
**acu•leus** (*plural* **•lei)** prickle
**acu•men**
**acu•mi•nate** pointed
**acu•mi•na•tion**
**acu•mi•nous**
**acu•punc•ture**
**acut•ance** photography term
**acute**
**acute•ly**
**acute•ness**
**acy•clic** chemistry term
**acyl**
**ad** *Slang* advertisement

**adac•ty•lous** without fingers or toes
**ad•age**
**ada•gio** (*plural* **•gios**) musical term
**ada•mant**
**ada•man•tine** very hard
**Ada•ma•wa** language group
**Ad•am•ite** nudist
**Ad•ams** US mountain
**ad•ams•ite** tear gas
**Ada•na** Turkish city
**adapt**
**adapt•abil•ity** (*or* **•able•ness**)
**adapt•able**
**adapt•ably**
**ad•ap•ta•tion**
**adapt•er** one who adapts; *compare* **adaptor**
**adap•tive**
**adapt•or** electrical device; *compare* **adapter**
**ad•ax•ial** towards the axis; *compare* **abaxial**
**add**
**ad•dax** antelope
**ad•dend** number added to
**ad•den•dum** (*plural* **•da**)
**ad•der** snake
**add•er** calculator
**ad•dict**
**ad•dic•tion**
**ad•dic•tive**
**Ad•dis Aba•ba** Ethiopian capital
**ad•di•tion**
**ad•di•tion•al**
**ad•di•tion•al•ly**
**ad•di•tive**
**ad•dle**
**ad•dress**
**ad•dressee**
**ad•dress•er** (*or* **•dres•sor**)
**Ad•dres•so•graph** (*Trademark*)
**ad•duce**
**ad•duce•able** (*or* **•duc•ible**)
**ad•du•cent**
**ad•duct** pull towards
**ad•duc•tion**
**ad•duc•tor** muscle
**Ad•elaide** Australian city
**ademp•tion** legal term
**Aden** Yemeni city
**ad•enec•to•my** (*plural* **•mies**) removal of gland
**ad•enine** biochemical compound
**ad•eni•tis** inflammation of a gland
**ad•eno•car•ci•no•ma** (*plural* **•mas** *or* **•ma•ta**) tumour
**ad•eno•hy•phophy•sis** part of pituitary gland
**ad•enoid** resembling a gland
**ad•enoi•dal** affected by enlarged adenoids
**ad•enoid•ec•to•my** (*plural* **•mies**)
**ad•enoids** tonsil tissue
**ad•eno•ma** (*plural* **•mas** *or* **•ma•ta**) glandular tumour
**adeno•sine** biochemical compound
**ad•eno•vi•rus**
**adept**
**ad•equa•cy**
**ad•equate**
**à deux** *French* of or for two persons
**ad•here**
**ad•her•ence**
**ad•her•ent** (*noun, adj*)
**ad•he•sion**
**ad•he•sive**
**ad•he•sive•ness**
**ad hoc** *Latin* for a particular purpose
**ad ho•mi•nem** *Latin* to the man
**adia•bat•ic** physics term
**adi•aph•or•ism** theological term
**adi•apho•rist**
**adi•apho•ris•tic**
**adi•apho•rous** medical term
**adieu** (*plural* **adieus** *or* **adieux**) goodbye
**ad in•fi•ni•tum** *Latin* without end
**ad in•ter•im** *Latin* for the meantime
**adi•os** *Spanish* goodbye
**adi•po•cere** waxy substance
**adi•poc•er•ous**
**adi•pose** fatty
**adi•pos•ity**
**Adi•ron•dacks** US mountains
**adit** mine shaft
**Adi•va•si** Indian people
**ad•ja•cen•cy**
**ad•ja•cent**
**ad•jec•ti•val**
**ad•jec•tive**
**ad•join**
**ad•join•ing**
**ad•joint** maths term
**ad•journ**
**ad•journ•ment**
**ad•judge**
**ad•ju•di•cate**
**ad•ju•di•ca•tion**
**ad•ju•di•ca•tive**
**ad•ju•di•ca•tor**
**ad•junct**
**ad•junc•tive**
**ad•ju•ra•tion**
**ad•jura•tory**
**ad•jure** appeal to solemnly; *compare* **abjure**
**ad•jur•er** (*or* **•ju•ror**)
**ad•just**
**ad•just•able**
**ad•just•ment**
**ad•ju•tan•cy**
**ad•ju•tant**
**ad•ju•vant** helping; auxiliary
**ad lib** spontaneously; freely
**ad-lib** (**-libbing, -libbed**) improvise
**ad-libber**
**ad•man** (*plural* **•men**)
**ad•mass** people susceptible to advertising
**ad•meas•ure**
**ad•meas•ure•ment**
**Admetus** mythological king
**ad•min** *short for* **administration**
**ad•mini•cle** legal term
**ad•min•is•ter**
**ad•min•is•trable**
**ad•min•is•trate**
**ad•min•is•tra•tion**
**ad•min•is•tra•tive**
**ad•min•is•tra•tor** (*fem* **•trix** *in legal contexts*)
**ad•mi•rable**
**ad•mi•rably**
**ad•mi•ral**
**ad•mi•ral•ty** (*plural* **•ties**)
**ad•mi•ra•tion**

**ad•mire**
**ad•mirer**
**ad•mir•ing•ly**
**ad•mis•sibil•ity** (*or* **•sible•ness**)
**ad•mis•sible**
**ad•mis•sion**
**ad•mis•sive**
**ad•mit** (**•mit•ting, •mit•ted**)
**ad•mit•tance**
**ad•mit•ted•ly**
**ad•mix**
**ad•mix•ture**
**ad•mon•ish**
**ad•mon•ish•er** (*or* **•moni•tor**)
**ad•mo•ni•tion**
**ad•moni•tory**
**ad•nate** botany term
**ad nau•seam** *Latin* to a disgusting extent
**ad•nomi•nal** word modifying a noun
**ad•noun** adjective used as noun
**ado**
**ado•be** building term
**ado•les•cence**
**ado•les•cent**
**Adon•ic** type of verse line
**Adonis** mythological character
**adopt**
**adopt•able**
**adopt•ed**
**adop•tee**
**adopt•er**
**adop•tion**
**adop•tion•ism** (*or* **•tian•**)
**adop•tion•ist** (*or* **•tian•**)
**adop•tive**
**ador•able**
**ador•ably**
**ado•ra•tion**
**adore**
**ador•er**
**adorn**
**adorn•ment**
**ad rem** *Latin* to the point
**ad•re•nal gland**
**adrena•line** hormone
**ad•ren•er•gic** biology term
**adre•no•cor•ti•co•troph•ic** (*US* **•trop•ic**) stimulating adrenal cortex
**Adri•at•ic**
**adrift**
**adroit**
**adroit•ness**
**ad•sci•ti•tious** additional
**ad•sorb** accumulate on a surface; *compare* **absorb**
**ad•sorb•abil•ity**
**ad•sorb•able**
**ad•sorb•ate**
**ad•sor•bent**
**ad•sorp•tion**
**adu•laria** mineral
**adu•late**
**adu•la•tion**
**adu•la•tor**
**adu•la•tory**
**adult**
**adul•ter•ant**
**adul•ter•ate**
**adul•tera•tion**
**adul•ter•ator**
**adul•ter•er** (*fem* **•ess**)
**adul•ter•ine** fake
**adul•ter•ous**
**adul•tery** (*plural* **•teries**)
**adult•hood**
**ad•um•bral** shadowy
**ad•um•brate**
**ad•um•bra•tion**
**ad•um•bra•tive**
**Adu•wa** Ethiopian town
**ad va•lo•rem** *Latin* according to value
**ad•vance**
**ad•vanced**
**ad•vance•ment**
**ad•vanc•er**
**ad•vanc•ing•ly**
**ad•van•tage**
**ad•van•ta•geous**
**ad•van•ta•geous•ness**
**ad•vec•tion**
**Ad•vent** coming of Christ
**ad•vent** arrival
**Ad•ven•tist**
**ad•ven•ti•tia** anatomy term
**ad•ven•ti•tious** happening by chance; growing in abnormal position
**ad•ven•tive**
**ad•ven•ture**
**ad•ven•tur•er** (*fem* **•ess**)
**ad•ven•tur•ism**
**ad•ven•tur•ist**
**ad•ven•tur•ous**
**ad•verb**
**ad•ver•bial**
**ad•ver•sary** (*plural* **•saries**)
**ad•ver•sa•tive** linguistics term
**ad•verse**
**ad•ver•sity** (*plural* **•sities**)
**ad•vert** refer to; *Slang* advertisement
**ad•vert•ence** (*or* **•en•cy**)
**ad•vert•ent•ly**
**ad•ver•tise**
**ad•ver•tise•ment**
**ad•ver•tis•er**
**ad•ver•tis•ing**
**(advertize)** *incorrect spelling of* **advertise**
**ad•vice**
**ad•vis•abil•ity**
**ad•vis•able**
**ad•vise**
**ad•vised**
**ad•vis•ed•ly**
**ad•vise•ment** *US* careful consideration
**ad•vis•er** (*or* **•vi•sor**)
**ad•vi•so•ry**
**ad•vo•caat**
**ad•vo•ca•cy** (*plural* **•cies**)
**ad•vo•cate**
**ad•vo•ca•tion**
**ad•vo•ca•tory**
**Ady•gei** (*plural* **•gei** *or* **•geis**) Russian people
**ady•na•mia** weakness
**ady•nam•ic**
**adze** (*US* **adz**) tool
**Adzhar**
**Adzha•ria** Georgian republic
**ad•zuki** (*or* **•su•ki**) bean
**aecio•spore**
**aecium** (*or* **aecid•ium**; *plural* **aecia** *or* **•ia**) fungal structure
**aedes** mosquito
**aedile** (*US also* **edile**) Roman magistrate
**Aeëtes** mythological king
**Aegean**
**Aegi•na** Greek island
**Aegir** Norse god
**aegis** (*US also* **egis**)
**aegro•tat** university degree
**Aegyptus** mythological king

**Aeneas** mythological prince
**Aene•id** epic poem
**Aeo•lian**
**aeo•lian harp**
**Aeol•ic** ancient Greek dialect
**aeoli•pile** model steam turbine
**Aeo•lis** Greek god
**aeon** (*US* **eon**)
**aeo•nian** (*or* **eo•**) everlasting
**aepy•or•nis** extinct bird
**aer•ate**
**aera•tion**
**aera•tor**
**aer•en•chy•ma** plant tissue
**aer•ial** relating to air; radio or TV device; *compare* **ariel**
**aeri•al•ist** trapeze artist
**aerie** *variant spelling of* **eyrie**
**aeri•fi•ca•tion**
**aeri•form** gaseous
**aeri•fy** (**•fies, •fy•ing, •fied**)
**aero•bal•lis•tics**
**aero•bat•ics**
**aer•obe** (*or* **aero•bium;** *plural* **•obes** *or* **•bia**)
**aero•bic** requiring oxygen
**aero•bics** exercises
**aero•bio•sis**
**aero•bio•tic**
**aero•bium** *variant of* **aerobe**
**aero•do•net•ics** study of gliding flight
**aero•drome**
**aero•dy•nam•ic**
**aero•dy•nami•cal•ly**
**aero•dy•nam•ics**
**aero•dyne** heavier-than-air machine
**aero•em•bo•lism** nitrogen in the blood
**aero-engine**
**aero•foil**
**aero•gel** solid foam
**aero•gram** (*or* **•gramme**)
**aer•og•ra•phy**
**aero•lite** meteorite
**aero•lo•gic** (*or* **•logi•cal**)
**aer•olo•gist**
**aer•ol•ogy** study of the atmosphere
**aero•mechan•ic**
**aero•mechani•cal**
**aero•mechan•ics**
**aer•om•eter**
**aero•met•ric**
**aer•om•etry** branch of physics
**aero•naut**
**aero•nau•ti•cal** (*or* **aero•nau•tic**)
**aero•naut•ics**
**aero•neu•ro•sis**
**aero•pause** region of upper atmosphere
**aero•pha•gia** swallowing of air
**aero•pho•bia**
**aero•pho•bic** afraid of draughts
**aero•plane**
**aero•sol**
**aero•space**
**aero•sphere** earth's atmosphere
**aero•stat** lighter-than-air craft
**aero•stat•ic** (*or* **•stati•cal**)
**aero•stat•ics**
**aero•sta•tion**
**aero•ther•mo•dy•nam•ic**
**aero•ther•mo•dy•nam•ics**
**aeru•go** verdigris
**aeru•gin•ous**
**aery** *variant spelling of* **eyrie**; *poetic* airy; insubstantial
**Aes•cu•la•pian**
**Aesculapius** Roman god
**Aesir** Norse gods
**aes•the•sia** (*US* **es•**) normal sensitivity
**aes•thete** (*US also* **es•**)
**aes•thet•ic** (*or* **•theti•cal;** *US also* **es•**)
**aes•theti•cal•ly** (*US also* **es•**)
**aes•the•ti•cian** (*US also* **es•**)
**aes•theti•cism** (*US also* **es•**)
**aes•thet•ics** (*US also* **es•**)
**aes•ti•val** (*US* **es•**) occurring in the summer
**aes•ti•vate** (*US* **es•**)
**aes•ti•va•tion** (*US* **es•**) biology term
**aes•ti•va•tor** (*US* **es•**)
**aether** *former spelling of* **ether** (anaesthetic); *variant spelling of* **ether** (hypothetical medium)
**aethe•real** *rare spelling of* **ethereal**
**aethe•real•ity** *rare spelling of* **ethereality**
**aetio•logi•cal** (*US* **etio•**)
**aeti•olo•gist** (*US* **eti•**)
**aeti•ol•ogy** (*US* **eti•**) study of causes
**Aeto•lia** Greek region
**afar**
**afebrile** without fever
**af•fabil•ity**
**af•fable**
**af•fably**
**af•fair**
**af•faire** *French* love affair
**af•fect** have an effect on; *compare* **effect** (*verb*)
**af•fec•ta•tion**
**af•fect•ed**
**af•fect•ed•ly**
**af•fect•ed•ness**
**af•fect•ing**
**af•fect•ing•ly**
**af•fec•tion**
**af•fec•tion•al**
**af•fec•tion•ate**
**af•fec•tive** arousing emotions
**af•fec•tiv•ity** (*or* **•tive•ness**)
**af•fen•pin•scher** dog
**af•fer•ent** conducting inwards; *compare* **efferent**
**af•fet•tuo•so** musical term
**af•fi•ance** betroth
**af•fi•ant** *US* person who makes an affidavit
**af•fi•da•vit**
**af•fili•ate**
**af•filia•tion**
**af•fine** maths term
**af•fined** closely related
**af•fini•tive**
**af•fin•ity** (*plural* **•ities**)
**af•firm**
**af•firm•able**
**af•fir•ma•tion**
**af•firma•tive**
**af•firm•er** (*or* **•ant**)
**af•fix**
**af•fix•ture**
**af•fla•tus** creative power
**af•flict**
**af•flic•tion**
**af•flic•tive**

**af•flu•ence**
**af•flu•ent**
**af•flux** flowing towards
**af•ford**
**af•for•est**
**af•for•esta•tion**
**af•fran•chise** release from obligation
**af•fran•chise•ment**
**af•fray**
**af•freight•ment**
**af•fri•cate**
**af•frica•tive** phonetics term
**af•fright**
**af•front**
**af•fu•sion** baptism
**Af•ghan** hound
**Af•ghan** (*or* **•ghani**) people
**af•ghan** shawl
**af•ghani** Afghan currency
**Af•ghani•stan**
**afi•cio•na•do** (*plural* **•dos**) supporter
**afield**
**afire**
**aflame**
**af•la•tox•in**
**afloat**
**aflut•ter**
**afoot**
**afore**
**afore•men•tioned**
**afore•said**
**afore•thought**
**a for•tio•ri** *Latin* for a stronger reason
**afoul**
**afraid**
**af•reet** Arabian demon
**afresh**
**Af•ri•ca**
**Af•ri•can**
**Af•ri•can•ism**
**Af•ri•kaans** language of Afrikaners
**Af•ri•kan•der** (*or* **•can•**) cattle
**Af•ri•ka•ner** White South African
**Af•ri•ka•ner•dom**
**Afro** (*plural* **Afros**) hairstyle
**Afro-American**
**Afro-Asian**
**Afro-Asiatic**
**af•ror•mo•sia** wood
**aft**
**af•ter**
**after•birth**
**after•body** (*plural* **•bodies**) discarded part of rocket
**after•brain**
**after•burner**
**after•burning**
**after•care**
**after•damp** gas in mines
**after•deck**
**after•effect**
**after•glow**
**after•heat**
**after•image**
**after•life**
**after•math**
**after•noon**
**after•pains**
**after•piece** brief additional comic play
**af•ters** *Slang* dessert
**after•sensation**
**after•shaft** type of feather
**after•shave**
**after•shock**
**after•taste**
**after•thought**
**after•wards** (*or esp. US* **•ward**)
**after•word** postscript
**after•world**
**aga** (*or* **agha**) Turkish title
**Aga•dir** Moroccan port
**again**
**against**
**agal•loch** tree
**aga•ma** lizard
**Agamemnon** mythological king
**agam•ete** biology term
**agam•ic** biology term
**agami•cal•ly**
**aga•mo•gen•esis** biology term
**aga•mo•genet•ic**
**aga•mo•geneti•cal•ly**
**aga•pan•thus** lily
**Agape** Christian love
**agape** gaping
**agar** seaweed product
**aga•ric** mushroom
**agari•ca•ceous**
**Agar•ta•la** Indian city
**ag•ate**
**agate•ware**
**aga•ve** plant
**age** (**age•ing** *or esp. US* **ag•ing, aged**)
**aged** (*adj, noun*)
**agee** *Scot* awry
**age•ing** (*or esp. US* **ag•ing**)
**age•less**
**agen•cy** (*plural* **•cies**)
**agen•da** (*or* **•dum**; *plural* **•das** *or* **•dums**)
**agen•esis** imperfect development
**agenet•ic**
**agent**
**agen•tial**
**agen•tive** (*or* **•tial**) linguistics term
**agent pro•vo•ca•teur** (*plural* **agents pro•vo•ca•teurs**)
**ag•era•tum** plant
**ag•ger** Roman earthwork
**ag•gior•na•men•to** (*plural* **•ti**) updating Catholic church
**ag•glom•er•ate**
**ag•glom•era•tion**
**ag•glom•era•tive**
**ag•glu•ti•nabil•ity**
**ag•glu•ti•nable**
**ag•glu•ti•nant**
**ag•glu•ti•nate**
**ag•glu•ti•na•tion**
**ag•glu•ti•na•tive**
**ag•glu•ti•nin** antibody
**ag•glu•tino•gen**
**ag•grada•tion**
**ag•grade** geology term
**ag•gran•dize** (*or* **•dise**)
**ag•gran•dize•ment** (*or* **•dise•ment**)
**ag•gran•diz•er** (*or* **•dis•er**)
**ag•gra•vate**
**ag•gra•va•tion**
**ag•gre•gate**
**ag•gre•ga•tion**
**ag•gress**
**ag•gres•sion**
**ag•gres•sive**
**ag•gres•sor**
**ag•grieve**
**ag•griev•ed•ly**
**ag•gro** *Slang* aggression
**aghast**
**ag•ile**

**agil•ity**
**Ag•in•court**
**ag•ing** *variant spelling* (*esp. US*) *of* **ageing**
**agio•tage** business of currency exchange
**agist** legal term
**agi•tate**
**agi•ta•tion**
**agi•ta•to** musical term
**agi•ta•tor**
**agit•prop** communist propaganda
**Aglaia** Greek goddess
**agleam**
**ag•let** (*or* **aiglet**) shoelace tag
**agley** *Scot* awry
**aglit•ter**
**aglow**
**agma** phonetic symbol
**ag•mi•nate** gathered together
**ag•nate** having common male ancestor
**ag•no•men** (*plural* **•nomi•na**) ancient Roman's fourth name
**ag•nomi•nal**
**ag•nos•tic**
**ag•nos•ti•cism**
**Ag•nus Dei** liturgical chant
**ago**
**agog**
**à gogo** *French* as much as one likes
**agon** (*plural* **ago•nes**) ancient Greek festival
**agon•ic** forming no angle
**ago•nist**
**ago•nis•tic**
**ago•nize** (*or* **•nise**)
**ago•niz•ing•ly** (*or* **•nis•**)
**ago•ny** (*plural* **•nies**)
**ago•ra** (*plural* **•rae** *or* **•ras**) Greek marketplace
**ago•ra** (*plural* **•rot**) Israeli coin
**ago•ra•pho•bia**
**ago•ra•pho•bic**
**agou•ti** (*plural* **•tis** *or* **•ties**) rodent
**Agra** Indian city
**agraffe** fastening
**agran•ulo•cy•tosis** blood disorder
**ag•ra•pha** sayings of Christ
**agraphia** inability to write
**agrar•ian**
**agrari•an•ism**
**agree** (**agree•ing, agreed**)
**agree•able**
**agree•able•ness**
**agree•ably**
**agreed**
**agree•ment**
**agres•tal** growing as a weed
**agres•tic** rural
**ag•ri•busi•ness**
**ag•ri•cul•tur•al**
**ag•ri•cul•ture**
**ag•ri•cul•tur•ist** (*or* **•tur•al•ist**)
**ag•ri•mo•ny** (*plural* **•nies**) plant
**ag•ro•bio•logi•cal**
**ag•ro•bi•olo•gist**
**ag•ro•bi•ol•ogy**
**ag•ro•logi•cal**
**agrol•ogy** study of soils
**ag•ro•nom•ic** (*or* **•nomi•cal**)
**ag•ro•nom•ics** land economics
**agrono•mist**
**agrono•my** science of cultivation
**ag•ros•tol•ogy** study of grasses
**aground**
**ag•ryp•not•ic** of insomnia
**Aguas•ca•lien•tes** Mexican state
**ague** malaria
**ague•weed**
**Agul•has** South African headland
**ah**
**aha**
**ahead**
**ahem**
**Ah•meda•bad** (*or* **•mada•**) Indian city
**Ah•med•na•gar** (*or* **•mad•**) Indian city
**ahoy**
**Ah•waz** (*or* **•vaz**) Iranian town
**ai** (*plural* **ais**) animal
**aid** help
**aide** assistant
**aide-de-camp** (*plural* **aides-**)
**aide-mémoire** (*plural* **aides-**)
**aid•er**
**AIDS** (*or* **Aids**)
**aigrette** (*or* **aigret**) feather on hat
**aiguille** mountain peak
**aiguil•lette** military ornament
**aikido** self-defence
**ail**
**ailan•thus** (*plural* **•thuses**) tree
**ailer•on**
**ail•ing**
**ail•ment**
**ailu•ro•phile** cat lover
**ailu•ro•philia**
**ailu•ro•phobe** fearer of cats
**ailu•ro•phobia**
**aim**
**aim•less**
**aim•less•ness**
**ain** *Scot* own
**ain't** *Nonstandard* am not, is not, has not, have not, are not
**Ainu** (*plural* **Ainus** *or* **Ainu**) Japanese people
**aïoli** garlic mayonnaise
**Aïr** Saharan region
**air**
**air•borne**
**air•brick**
**air•brush**
**air•burst**
**air•bus**
**air-conditioned**
**air-conditioner**
**air-conditioning**
**air-cool**
**air•craft** (*plural* **•craft**)
**air•craft•man** (*or* **•crafts•**; *plural* **•men**)
**air•craft•woman** (*or* **•crafts•**; *plural* **•women**)
**air•crew**
**Air•drie** Scottish town
**air•drop** (**•drop•ping, •dropped**) delivery by parachute
**air-dry** (**-dries, -dry•ing, -dried**)

**Aire•dale** Yorkshire district; terrier
**air•field**
**air•flow**
**air•foil**
**air•frame** part of aircraft
**air•glow**
**air•head** military term
**airi•ly**
**airi•ness**
**air•ing**
**air-intake**
**air•less**
**air•less•ness**
**air•lift**
**air•line**
**air•lin•er**
**air•lock**
**air•man** (*plural* **•men**)
**air•plane** *US* aeroplane
**air•port**
**air•screw** propeller
**air•ship**
**air•sick**
**air•sick•ness**
**air•space**
**air•speed**
**air•stream**
**air•strip**
**air•tight**
**air•waves**
**air•way**
**air•woman** (*plural* **•women**)
**air•worthi•ness**
**air•worthy**
**airy** (**airi•er, airi•est**)
**airy-fairy**
**aisle**
**Aisne** French river
**ait** *Dialect* islet
**aitch** letter H
**aitch•bone** cut of beef
**Aix-en-Provence** French city
**Ajac•cio** Corsican port
**ajar**
**Ajax** mythological character
**Aj•mer** Indian city
**Ake•la** cub-scout leader
**akha•ra** Indian gymnasium
**akim•bo**
**akin**
**Ak•kad** (*or* **Ac•cad**) Babylonian city
**Ak•ka•dian** (*or* **Ac•ca•**)
**Ak•mo•la** *former name of* **Astana**
**Ak•tyu•binsk** Kazakh city
**à la** *French* in the style of
**ala** (*plural* **alae**) winglike structure
**Ala•bama**
**Ala•bam•ian**
**ala•bas•ter**
**à la carte**
**alack**
**alacka•day**
**alac•ri•tous**
**alac•rity**
**Aladdin**
**Ala•go•as** Brazilian state
**Alai** Central Asian mountain range
**ala•meda** *US* tree-lined promenade
**Ala•mo**
**à la mode** fashionable
**ala•mode** silk
**ala•nine** amino acid
**alan•nah** Irish term of endearment
**alap** Indian music
**alar** of wings
**alarm**
**alarmed**
**alarm•ing**
**alarm•ing•ly**
**alarm•ism**
**alarm•ist**
**alar•um** *Archaic* alarm
**alary** of wings
**alas**
**Alas•ka**
**Alas•kan**
**alate** winged
**al•ba•core** fish
**Alba Lon•ga** ancient city
**Al•ba•nia**
**Al•ba•nian**
**Al•ba•ny** US city; Canadian river; Australian port
**al•ba•ta** alloy
**al•ba•tross**
**al•be•do** (*plural* **•dos**) physics term
**al•be•it**
**Al•bert** lake in Uganda and the Democratic Republic of Congo
**Al•ber•ta** Canadian province
**al•bert•ite** variety of bitumen
**al•bes•cence**
**al•bes•cent** becoming white
**Al•bi•gen•ses** medieval heretics
**Al•bi•gen•sian**
**al•bin•ic** (*or* **•bin•is•tic**)
**al•bi•nism**
**al•bi•no** (*plural* **•nos**)
**Al•bi•on** *Archaic* Britain
**al•bite** mineral
**al•bit•ic**
**Ål•borg** *variant spelling of* **Aalborg**
**al•bum**
**al•bu•men** white of egg; *compare* **albumin**
**al•bu•menize** (*or* **•menise**)
**al•bu•min** a protein; *compare* **albumen**
**al•bu•mi•nate**
**al•bu•mi•noid**
**al•bu•mi•nous**
**al•bu•mi•nu•ria** urine containing albumin
**Al•bu•quer•que** US city
**al•bur•num** sapwood
**Al•bu•ry** Australian city
**Al•ca•ic** verse form
**al•caide** Spanish commander
**al•cal•de** Spanish mayor
**Al•ca•traz** US island
**al•ca•zar** Moorish palace
**Alcestis** mythological queen
**al•chem•ic** (*or* **•chemi•cal, •chem•is•tic**)
**al•che•mist**
**al•che•mize** (*or* **•mise**)
**al•che•my** (*plural* **•mies**)
**al•che•rin•ga** Aboriginal golden age
**Al•chevsk** Ukrainian city
**al•ci•dine** ornithology term
**al•co•hol**
**al•co•hol•ic**
**al•co•hol•ic•ity**
**al•co•hol•ism**
**al•co•holi•za•tion** (*or* **•sa•tion**)
**al•co•hol•ize** (*or* **•ise**)
**al•co•hol•om•eter**
**al•co•pop**
**Al•co•ran** Koran

**al•cove**
**Alcyone** (*or* **Halcyone)** mythological character
**Al•dab•ra** Indian Ocean islands
**Al•deba•ran** star
**al•de•hyde**
**al den•te** *Italian* cooked until still firm
**al•der**
**al•der•man** (*plural* **•men)**
**al•der•man•ic**
**Al•der•mas•ton**
**Al•der•ney** Channel Island
**Al•der•shot**
**al•dol** chemical compound
**al•dose** sugar
**al•dos•terone** hormone
**ald•ox•ime** chemical compound
**al•drin** insecticide
**ale**
**alea•to•ry** dependent on chance
**ale•cost** plant
**alee** nautical term
**al•egar** malt vinegar
**ale•house**
**Ale•man•ni** Germanic people
**Al•eman•nic**
**alem•bic**
**alem•bi•cat•ed** excessively refined
**aleph** Hebrew letter
**aleph-null** (*or* -zero) maths term
**Alep•po** Syrian city
**alert**
**alert•ness**
**Ales•san•dria** Italian town
**alethic** logic term
**aleu•rone** (*or* **•ron)** plant protein
**al•evin** young fish
**ale•wife** fish
**al•ex•an•ders** plant
**Al•ex•an•dria** Egyptian port
**Al•ex•an•drian**
**Al•ex•an•drine** type of verse
**al•ex•an•drite** gemstone
**alexia** word blindness
**alex•in** immunology term
**al•fal•fa**
**al•fila•ria** (*or* **•fil•eria)** plant
**al•fres•co**
**al•gae** (*sing.* **alga)**
**al•gal**
**al•gar•ro•ba** (*or* **•ga•ro•ba)** tree
**al•ge•bra**
**al•ge•bra•ic** (*or* **•brai•cal)**
**al•ge•brai•cal•ly**
**al•ge•bra•ist**
**Al•ge•ci•ras** Spanish port
**Al•ge•ria**
**Al•ge•rian** (*or* **•rine)**
**al•gerine** fabric
**al•gi•cide**
**al•gid** chilly
**Al•giers** Algerian capital
**al•gin** biochemical compound
**al•gi•nate**
**al•gin•ic acid**
**al•goid** resembling algae
**Al•gol** star; computer language
**al•go•lag•nia** sexual perversion
**al•go•lag•nic**
**al•go•lag•nist**
**al•golo•gist**
**al•gol•ogy** study of algae
**al•gom•eter**
**al•gom•etry**
**Al•gon•quian** (*or* **•kian)**
**Al•gon•quin** (*or* **•kin**; *plural* **•quins, •quin** *or* **•kins, •kin)** American Indian
**al•go•pho•bia** fear of pain
**al•gor** chill
**al•go•rism** counting system
**al•go•ris•mic**
**al•go•rithm** maths term
**al•go•rith•mic**
**al•go•rith•mi•cal•ly**
**Al•ham•bra** Spanish citadel
**Al•ham•bresque**
**Al Hasa** Saudi Arabian province
**Al Hu•fuf** (*or* **Ho•fuf)** Saudi Arabian town
**ali•as** (*plural* **•ases)**
**Ali Baba**
**ali•bi** (*plural* **•bis)**
**Ali•can•te** Spanish town
**ali•cy•clic** chemistry term
**ali•dade** (*or* **•dad)** surveying instrument
**al•ien**
**al•ien•abil•ity**
**al•ien•able**
**al•ien•age**
**al•ien•ate**
**al•iena•tion**
**al•iena•tor**
**al•ienee** legal term
**al•ien•ism**
**al•ien•ist** *US* psychiatrist
**al•ien•or** legal term
**ali•form** wing-shaped
**Ali•garh** Indian city
**alight (alight•ing, alight•ed** *or* **alit)**
**align**
**align•ment**
**alike**
**ali•ment**
**ali•men•ta•ry**
**ali•men•ta•tion**
**ali•men•ta•tive**
**ali•mo•ny**
**aline** *rare spelling of* **align**
**ali•ped** having winglike limbs
**ali•phat•ic** chemistry term
**ali•quant** maths term
**ali•quot** maths term
**aliun•de** from another source
**alive**
**aliza•rin** dye
**al•ka•hest** (*or* **•ca•)** alchemical solvent
**al•ka•li** (*plural* **•lis** *or* **•lies)**
**al•kal•ic**
**al•ka•li•fy (•fies, •fy•ing, •fied)**
**al•ka•lim•eter**
**al•ka•li•met•ric**
**al•ka•lim•etry**
**al•ka•line**
**al•ka•lin•ity**
**al•ka•liz•able** (*or* **•lis•able)**
**al•ka•lize** (*or* **•lise)**
**al•ka•loid** plant compound
**al•ka•lo•sis** medical condition
**al•kane** chemistry term
**al•ka•net** plant
**al•kene** chemistry term
**al•kyd**
**al•kyl**
**al•kyla•tion** chemistry term

**al•kyne** chemistry term
**all**
**Allah**
**Al•laha•bad** Indian city
**al•lan•ite** mineral
**al•lan•to•ic**
**al•lan•toid**
**al•lan•toi•dal**
**al•lan•to•is** (*plural* **•ides)** embryology term
**al•lar•gan•do** musical term
**al•lay**
**(alledge)** *incorrect spelling of* **allege**
**al•le•ga•tion**
**al•lege**
**al•leged**
**al•leg•ed•ly**
**al•le•giance**
**al•le•gori•cal** (*or* **•gor•ic)**
**al•le•gori•cal•ly**
**al•le•go•rist**
**al•le•gori•za•tion** (*or* **•sa•tion)**
**al•le•go•rize** (*or* **•rise)**
**al•le•go•ry** (*plural* **•ries)**
**al•le•gret•to** (*plural* **•tos)** musical term
**al•le•gro** (*plural* **•gros)**
**al•lele** (*or* **al•le•lo•morph)** genetics term
**al•lel•ic**
**al•lel•ism**
**al•le•luia** (*or* **hal•le•lu•jah;** *note Handel's* **Hallelujah Chorus)**
**alle•mande** musical term
**Al•len** Irish bog
**Al•len•town** US city
**Al•lep•pey** Indian port
**al•ler•gen** allergy-causing substance
**al•ler•gen•ic**
**al•ler•gic**
**al•ler•gist** allergy specialist
**al•ler•gy** (*plural* **•gies)**
**al•le•thrin** insecticide
**al•le•vi•ate**
**al•le•via•tion**
**al•le•via•tive**
**al•le•via•tor**
**al•ley** narrow lane; *compare* **ally**
**alley•way**
**All•hal•lows**
**All•hal•low•tide**
**all•heal** plant
**al•lia•ceous** of allium
**al•li•ance**
**al•lied**
**Al•lier** French river
**Al•lies** in World War II
**al•lies** *plural of* **ally**
**al•li•ga•tor**
**all-important**
**all-inclusive**
**al•lit•er•ate**
**al•lit•era•tion**
**al•lit•era•tive**
**al•lium** onion genus
**Al•loa** Scottish town
**al•lo•cate**
**al•lo•ca•tion**
**al•loch•tho•nous** geology term
**al•lo•cu•tion** formal speech
**al•lo•dial**
**al•lo•dium** (*or* **al•lod;** *plural* **•dia** *or* **•lods)** legal term
**al•loga•mous**
**al•loga•my** biology term
**al•lo•graph** signature written for another
**al•lo•graph•ic**
**al•lom•er•ism** chemistry term
**al•lom•er•ous**
**al•lo•met•ric**
**al•lom•etry** biology term
**al•lo•morph**
**al•lo•mor•phic**
**al•lo•mor•phism** chemistry term
**al•lo•nym** assumed name
**al•lo•path** (*or* **•lopa•thist)** medical practitioner
**al•lo•path•ic**
**al•lo•pathi•cal•ly**
**al•lopa•thy**
**al•lo•pat•ric** biology term
**al•lo•pat•ri•cal•ly**
**al•lo•phane** mineral
**al•lo•phone** linguistics term
**al•lo•phon•ic**
**al•lo•plasm** biology term
**al•lo•plas•mic**
**al•lo•pu•ri•nol** anti-gout drug
**al•lot** **(•lot•ting, •lot•ted)**
**al•lot•ment**
**al•lo•trope** chemistry term
**al•lo•trop•ic**
**al•lo•tropi•cal•ly**
**al•lot•ro•py** (*or* **•pism)**
**al•lot•tee**
**al•low**
**al•low•able**
**al•low•ance**
**Al•lo•way** Scottish village
**al•low•ed•ly**
**al•loy**
**all-round**
**all•rounder**
**all•seed** plant
**all•spice**
**all-star** (*adj*)
**all-time** (*adj*)
**al•lude** refer; *compare* **elude; illude**
**al•lure**
**al•lure•ment**
**al•lur•er**
**al•lur•ing**
**al•lu•sion** reference; *compare* **illusion**
**al•lu•sive**
**al•lu•sive•ness**
**al•lu•vial**
**al•lu•vion** overflow
**al•lu•vium** (*plural* **•viums** *or* **•via)** soil; *compare* **eluvium**
**ally** (*verb* **allies, ally•ing, allied;** *noun, plural* **allies)** friend; *compare* **alley**
**al•lyl**
**Alma-Ata** Kazakh city
**Al•ma•da** Portuguese city
**Al•ma•gest** astronomy treatise
**alma ma•ter** *Latin* one's school or university
**al•ma•nac**
**al•ma•nack** almanac; *Archaic except in proper names, as* **Whitaker's Almanack**
**al•man•dine** gemstone
**Al Marj** Libyan town
**al•me•mar** platform in synagogue
**Al•mería** Spanish port
**al•mighti•ly**
**al•mighti•ness**
**Al•mighty** God

**al•mighty**
**Al•mo•hades** Muslim group
**al•mond**
**al•mon•er**
**al•mon•ry**
**Al•mo•ra•vides** Muslim group
**al•most**
**alms**
**alms•house**
**al•mu•can•tar** astronomy term
**al•muce** monk's cape
**Al•ni•co** (*Trademark*)
**aloe** (*plural* **aloes**) plant
**aloes** purgative drug
**alo•etic**
**aloe ve•ra**
**aloft**
**alo•ha** Hawaiian greeting
**alo•in** chemical compound
**alone**
**along**
**along•shore**
**along•side**
**aloof**
**aloof•ness**
**alo•pecia**
**aloud**
**alow** nautical term
**alp**
**al•paca**
**alpen•glow**
**alpen•horn** *variant of* **alphorn**
**alpen•stock**
**Alpes-de-Haute-Pro•vence** French department
**Alpes Ma•ri•times** French department
**al•pes•trine**
**al•pha**
**al•pha•bet**
**al•pha•beti•cal** (*or* **•bet•ic**)
**al•pha•beti•cal•ly**
**al•pha•beti•za•tion** (*or* **•sa•tion**)
**al•pha•bet•ize** (*or* **•ise**)
**al•pha•bet•iz•er** (*or* **•is•er**)
**Al•pha Cen•tau•ri** constellation
**al•pha•nu•mer•ic** (*or* **al•pha•mer•ic**)
**al•pha•nu•meri•cal•ly** (*or* **al•pha•meri•cal•ly**)
**alp•horn** (*or* **alpen•horn**)
**al•pho•sis** absence of skin pigmentation
**Al•pine** of the Alps
**al•pine** of mountains
**al•pin•ism**
**al•pin•ist**
**Alps**
**al•ready**
**al•right** *variant spelling of* **all right**, *regarded by some as nonstandard*
**Al•sace** French region
**Alsace-Lorraine** French region
**Al•sa•tia** *ancient name of* Alsace
**Al•sa•tian**
**al•sike** plant
**also**
**also-ran**
**alt** high in pitch
**Al•tai** Asian mountains
**Al•ta•ic** language group
**Al•tair** star
**al•tar** table in church; *compare* **alter**
**altar•piece**
**alt•azi•muth** astronomical instrument
**al•ter** to change; *compare* **altar**
**al•ter•abil•ity**
**al•ter•able**
**al•tera•tion**
**al•tera•tive** therapeutic drug
**al•ter•cate**
**al•ter•ca•tion**
**al•ter ego**
**al•ter•nant**
**al•ter•nate**
**al•ter•nate•ly**
**al•ter•na•tion**
**al•ter•na•tive**
**al•ter•na•tive•ly**
**al•ter•na•tor**
**al•thaea** (*US* **•thea**) plant
**Al•thing** Icelandic parliament
**alt•horn** brass instrument
**al•though**
**al•time•ter**
**al•ti•met•ri•cal**
**al•tim•etry**
**Al•ti•pla•no** Andean plateau
**al•tis•si•mo** musical term
**al•ti•tude**
**al•ti•tu•di•nal**
**alto** (*plural* **altos**)
**alto•cu•mu•lus** (*plural* **•li**) cloud
**al•to•geth•er** entirely; *note* **all together** all at the same time
**Al•to•na** German port
**al•to re•lie•vo** (*or* **ri•**; *plural* **•vos**) sculpture term
**al•to•stra•tus** (*plural* **•ti**) cloud
**al•tri•cial** ornithology term
**Al•trin•cham** English town
**al•tru•ism**
**al•tru•ist**
**al•tru•is•tic**
**al•tru•is•ti•cal•ly**
**alu•del** chemical vessel
**alu•la** (*plural* **•lae**) tuft of feathers
**alum**
**alu•mi•na** aluminium oxide
**alu•mi•nate**
**alu•mi•nif•er•ous**
**alu•min•ium** (*US* **•min•um**)
**alu•mi•nize** (*or* **•nise**)
**alu•mi•nos•ity**
**alu•mi•no•ther•my** chemical process
**alu•mi•nous** resembling aluminium
**alu•mi•num** *US spelling of* **aluminium**
**alum•nus** (*fem* **•na**; *plural* **•ni**, *fem* **•nae**) *US* former student
**alum•root**
**Alun•dum** (*Trademark*)
**alu•nite** mineral
**al•veo•lar**
**al•veo•late**
**al•veo•la•tion**
**al•veo•lus** (*plural* **•li**) anatomy term
**al•vine** anatomy term
**al•ways**
**alys•sum** plant
**Alzheimer's dis•ease**
**am**
**ama•da•vat** *variant of* **avadavat**
**ama•dou** fungal substance

**Ama•ga•sa•ki** Japanese city
**amah** Eastern nurse
**amal•gam**
**amal•gam•ate**
**amal•gama•tion**
**(amalgum)** *incorrect spelling of* amalgam
**ama•ni•ta** fungus
**amanu•en•sis** (*plural* **•ses**)
**ama•ranth** plant
**ama•ran•tha•ceous**
**ama•ran•thine**
**ama•relle** cherry
**Ama•ril•lo** US city
**ama•ryl•li•da•ceous**
**Ama•ryl•lis** *Poetic* shepherdess
**ama•ryl•lis** plant
**amass**
**amass•er**
**ama•teur**
**ama•teur•ish**
**ama•teur•ish•ness**
**ama•teur•ism**
**Amati** violin
**ama•tol** explosive substance
**ama•tory** (*or* **•to•rial**)
**amau•ro•sis** blindness
**amau•rot•ic**
**amaut** Eskimo woman's hood
**amaze**
**amaze•ment**
**amaz•ing**
**amaz•ing•ly**
**Ama•zon** South American river; female warrior
**ama•zon** aggressive female
**Ama•zo•nas** Brazilian state
**Ama•zo•nian**
**ama•zon•ite** gemstone
**Am•ba•la** Indian city
**am•ba•ry** (*or* **•ri**; *plural* **•ries** *or* **•ris**) plant; fibre
**am•bas•sa•dor**
**am•bas•sa•dor•ial**
**am•bas•sa•dor•ship**
**am•bas•sa•dress**
**am•ber**
**amber•gris** substance from sperm whale
**amber•jack** fish
**am•ber•oid** (*or* **am•broid**) synthetic amber
**am•bi•dex•ter•ity** (*or* **•dex•trous•ness**)
**am•bi•dex•trous**
**am•bi•ence** (*or* **•ance**)
**am•bi•ent**
**am•bi•gu•ity** (*plural* **•ities**)
**am•bigu•ous**
**am•bigu•ous•ness**
**am•bit**
**am•bi•tion**
**am•bi•tious**
**am•biva•lence** (*or* **•len•cy**)
**am•biva•lent**
**am•bi•ver•sion**
**am•bi•vert** psychology term
**am•ble**
**am•bler**
**am•blygo•nite** mineral
**am•blyo•pia** impaired vision
**am•bly•op•ic**
**ambo** (*plural* **ambos**) pulpit
**am•bo•cep•tor** immune substance
**Am•boi•na** Indonesian island
**am•boy•na** (*or* **•boi•**) wood
**am•bro•sia**
**am•bro•sial** (*or* **•sian**)
**am•bro•type** photography term
**am•bry** (*or* **aum•**; *plural* **•bries**) cupboard
**ambs•ace** lowest throw at dice
**am•bu•lac•ral**
**am•bu•lac•rum** (*plural* **•ra**) band on starfish
**am•bu•lance**
**am•bu•lant**
**am•bu•late**
**am•bu•la•tion**
**am•bu•la•tory** (*plural* **•tories**)
**am•bus•cade** ambush
**am•bush**
**ameba** *US spelling of* amoeba
**ame•lio•rant**
**ame•lio•rate**
**ame•lio•ra•tion**
**ame•lio•ra•tive**
**ame•lio•ra•tor**
**amen**
**ame•nabil•ity** (*or* **•nable•ness**)
**ame•nable**
**ame•nably**
**amend** change; *compare* emend
**amend•able**
**amenda•tory** *US* corrective
**amend•er**
**amend•ment**
**amends**
**amen•ity** (*plural* **•ities**)
**amen•or•rhoea** (*US* **•rhea**)
**Amen-Ra** Egyptian god
**ament** mentally deficient person
**am•ent** (*or* **am•en•tum**; *plural* **•ents** *or* **•ta**) catkin
**amen•tia** mental deficiency
**Ameri•ca**
**Ameri•can**
**Ameri•ca•na**
**Ameri•can•ism**
**Ameri•cani•za•tion** (*or* **•sa•tion**)
**Ameri•can•ize** (*or* **•ise**)
**Ameri•can•iz•er** (*or* **•is•er**)
**am•eri•cium** radioactive element
**Am•er•in•dian** North American Indian
**Am•er•in•dic**
**am•ethyst**
**am•ethys•tine**
**am•etro•pia** eye disorder
**Am•ha•ra** Ethiopian province
**Am•har•ic** Ethiopian language
**ami•abil•ity** (*or* **•able•ness**)
**ami•able**
**ami•ably**
**ami•an•thine** (*or* **•thoid, •thoid•al**)
**ami•an•thus** variety of asbestos
**ami•cabil•ity** (*or* **•cable•ness**)
**ami•cable**
**ami•cably**
**am•ice** part of priest's vestment
**ami•cus cu•riae** *Latin* friend of the court
**amid**

**am•ide** chemical compound
**amid•ic**
**Ami•dol** (*Trademark*) photographic developer
**amid•ships**
**amidst**
**Ami•ens** French city
**ami•go** (*plural* **•gos**)
**amine** organic base; *compare* **ammine**
**ami•no acid**
**ami•no•ben•zo•ic acid**
**ami•no•phenol**
**ami•no•py•rine**
**amir** Afghan ruler
**amiss**
**ami•to•sis** form of cell division
**ami•tot•ic**
**ami•toti•cal•ly**
**am•ity** (*plural* **•ities**)
**Am•man** Jordanian capital
**am•meter**
**am•mine** ammonia compound; *compare* **amine**
**ammo** *short for* **ammunition**
**am•mo•coete** zoology term
**am•mo•nal** explosive compound
**am•mo•nate**
**am•mo•nia**
**am•mo•ni•ac** gum resin
**am•mo•nia•cal**
**am•mo•ni•ate**
**am•mo•nia•tion**
**am•mon•ic**
**am•moni•cal**
**am•moni•fi•ca•tion**
**am•moni•fy** (**•fies, •fy•ing, •fied**)
**am•mo•nite** fossil
**am•mo•nit•ic**
**am•mo•nium**
**am•mu•ni•tion**
**am•ne•sia**
**am•ne•si•ac** (*or* **am•ne•sic**)
**am•nes•ty** (*noun, plural* **•ties**; *verb* **•ties, •ty•ing, •tied**)
**am•nio•cen•tesis**
**am•ni•on** (*plural* **•ni•ons** *or* **•nia**) fetal membrane
**am•ni•ot•ic**
**amoe•ba** (*US* **ame•**; *plural* **•bae** *or* **•bas**)
**am•oebaean** (*or* **•oebean**; *US* **am•ebean**) verse form
**am•oebia•sis** (*US* **am•ebia•**; *plural* **•ses**) parasitic infection
**amoe•bic** (*US* **ame•**)
**amoe•bo•cyte** (*US* **ame•**)
**amoe•boid** (*US* **ame•**)
**amok** (*or* **amuck**)
**among** (*or* **amongst**)
**amon•til•la•do** (*plural* **•dos**) sherry
**amor•al** morally neutral; *compare* **immoral**
**amo•ral•ity**
**amor•al•ly**
**amo•ret•to** (*or* **•ri•no**; *plural* **•ret•ti** *or* **•ri•ni**) cupid
**amo•rist**
**amo•ro•so** musical term
**amo•rous**
**amo•rous•ness**
**amor pa•triae** *Latin* love of one's country
**amor•phism**
**amor•phous**
**amor•tiz•able** (*or* **•tis•able**)
**amor•ti•za•tion** (*or* **•sa•tion**)
**amor•tize** (*or* **•tise**)
**amor•tize•ment** (*or* **•tise•ment**)
**amount**
**amour** love affair
**amour-propre** self-respect
**Amoy** Chinese port
**amp**
**am•pe•lop•sis** vine
**am•per•age**
**am•pere**
**ampere-hour**
**ampere-turn**
**am•per•sand** the character &
**am•pheta•mine**
**am•phi•ar•thro•sis** (*plural* **•ses**) anatomy term
**am•phi•as•ter** biology term
**am•phib•ian**
**am•phi•bi•ot•ic** zoology term
**am•phibi•ous**
**am•phi•blas•tu•la** sponge larva
**am•phi•bole** mineral
**am•phi•bol•ic** (*or* **•phibo•lous**)
**am•phibo•lite** rock
**am•phibo•logi•cal**
**am•phi•bol•ogy** (*or* **am•phibo•ly**; *plural* **•ogies** *or* **•lies**) ambiguity
**am•phi•brach** metrical foot
**am•phi•brach•ic**
**am•phi•chro•ic** (*or* **am•phi•chro•mat•ic**) producing two colours
**am•phi•coe•lous** zoology term
**am•phic•ty•on** ancient Greek religious councillor
**am•phic•ty•on•ic**
**am•phic•tyo•ny** (*plural* **•nies**)
**am•phi•dip•loid** biology term
**am•phi•gor•ic**
**am•phi•go•ry** (*or* **•gou•ri**; *plural* **•ries** *or* **•ris**) nonsense writing
**am•phima•cer** metrical foot
**am•phi•mix•is** (*plural* **•mixes**) sexual reproduction
**am•phi•ox•us** (*plural* **•oxi** *or* **•ox•uses**) aquatic organism
**am•phi•pod** aquatic organism
**am•phip•ro•sty•lar**
**am•phip•ro•style** architectural term
**am•phis•bae•na** (*plural* **•nae** *or* **•nas**) worm lizard
**am•phis•bae•nic**
**am•phi•sty•lar** architectural term
**am•phi•thea•tre** (*US* **•ter**)
**am•phi•thecium** (*plural* **•thecia**) botany term
**am•phit•ri•cha** bacteria
**am•phit•ri•chous**
**Amphitrite** Greek goddess
**am•phit•ro•pous** botany term
**Amphitryon** mythological character
**am•pho•ra** (*plural* **•rae** *or* **•ras**)
**am•pho•ter•ic** chemistry term

**am•ple**
**am•plexi•caul** botany term
**am•pli•fi•able**
**am•pli•fi•ca•tion**
**am•pli•fi•er**
**am•pli•fy** (**•fies, •fy•ing, •fied**)
**am•pli•tude**
**am•ply**
**am•poule** (*or esp. US* **•pule**) container for injectable liquids
**am•pul•la** (*plural* **•lae**) flask
**am•pul•la•ceous** (*or* **•ceal**)
**am•pul•lar** (*or* **•lary**)
**am•pu•tate**
**am•pu•ta•tion**
**am•pu•tee**
**Am•ra•va•ti** Indian town
**am•ri•ta** (*or* **•ree•**) Hindu concept
**Am•rit•sar** Indian city
**Am•ster•dam**
**amuck** *variant spelling of* **amok**
**amu•let**
**Amur** Asian river
**amuse**
**amuse•ment**
**amus•ing**
**amus•ing•ly**
**amyg•da•la** (*plural* **•lae**) anatomy term
**amyg•da•late** of almonds
**amyg•dale** geology term
**amyg•da•lin** almond extract
**amyg•da•line** relating to tonsils or almonds
**amyg•da•loid** rock
**amyg•da•loi•dal**
**amyl**
**amy•la•ceous** starchy
**am•yl•ase** enzyme
**am•yl•ene** chemical compound
**amy•loid** starchlike protein
**amy•loly•sis** biology term
**amy•lo•pec•tin** component of starch
**amy•lop•sin** enzyme
**am•yl•ose** component of starch
**amy•lum** starch
**Amy•tal** (*Trademark*) drug
**an**
**ana•bae•na** plant
**ana•ban•tid** fish
**Ana•bap•tist** Protestant sect
**ana•bas** fish
**anaba•sis** (*plural* **•ses**) military expedition
**ana•bat•ic**
**ana•bio•sis** resuscitation
**ana•bleps** (*plural* **•bleps**) fish
**ana•bol•ic**
**anabo•lism**
**anabo•lite**
**anabo•lit•ic**
**ana•branch**
**ana•car•dia•ceous** botany term
**anacho•rism** geographical misplacement
**ana•chron•ic** out of date order
**anach•ro•nism**
**anach•ro•nis•tic**
**anach•ro•nis•ti•cal•ly**
**ana•cli•nal** geology term
**ana•cli•sis**
**ana•clit•ic** psychology term
**ana•co•lu•thia** lack of grammatical sequence
**ana•co•lu•thic**
**ana•co•lu•thon** (*plural* **•tha**)
**ana•con•da**
**ana•cous•tic** soundless
**ana•cru•sis** (*plural* **•ses**) linguistics term
**ana•crus•tic**
**ana•dem** garland
**ana•di•plo•sis** rhetorical term
**anad•ro•mous** migrating up river; *compare* **catadromous**
**anaemia** (*US* **anemia**)
**anaemic** (*US* **anemic**)
**an•aer•obe** (*or* **•aero•bium**; *plural* **•aer•obes** *or* **•aero•bia**)
**an•aero•bic** not requiring oxygen
**an•aero•bi•cal•ly**
**an•aes•the•sia** (*US* **•es•**)
**an•aes•thet•ic** (*US* **•es•**)
**an•aes•thet•ics** (*US* **an•es•the•si•ology**)
**anaes•the•tist** (*US* **an•es•the•si•olo•gist**) doctor specializing in anaesthetics; *compare* **anesthetist**
**anaes•the•ti•za•tion** (*or* **•sa•tion**; *US* **anes•the•ti•za•tion**)
**anaes•the•tize** (*or* **•tise**; *US* **anes•the•tize**)
**ana•glyph** stereoscopic picture
**ana•glyph•ic** (*or* **•glyphi•cal, •glyp•tic, •glyp•ti•cal**)
**Ana•glyp•ta** (*Trademark*) wallpaper
**ana•go•ge** (*or* **•gy**) allegorical interpretation
**ana•gog•ic** (*or* **•gogi•cal**)
**ana•gogi•cal•ly**
**ana•gram**
**ana•gram•mat•ic** (*or* **•mati•cal**)
**ana•gram•mati•cal•ly**
**ana•gram•ma•tism**
**ana•gram•ma•tist**
**ana•gram•ma•tize** (*or* **•tise**)
**Ana•heim** Californian city
**anal**
**(analagous)** *incorrect spelling of* **analogous**
**anal•cite** (*or* **•cine**) mineral
**ana•lec•tic**
**ana•lects** (*or* **•lec•ta**)
**ana•lem•ma** (*plural* **•mas** *or* **•ma•ta**) type of sundial
**ana•lem•mat•ic**
**ana•lep•tic** restorative drug
**an•al•gesia** (*or* **•gia**)
**an•alge•sic**
**ana•log** *US variant spelling of* **analogue**
**ana•logi•cal** (*or* **•log•ic**)
**analo•gist**
**analo•gize** (*or* **•gise**) draw comparisons
**analo•gous**
**ana•logue** (*US also* **analog**; *in the UK the US spelling is often used in computer science and in electronics*)
**anal•ogy** (*plural* **•ogies**)
**an•al•pha•bet•ic**
**an•al•pha•beti•cal•ly**
**ana•lys•able**

**analy•sand** person undergoing psychoanalysis
**ana•ly•sa•tion**
**ana•lyse** (*US* **•lyze**)
**ana•lys•er** (*US* **•lyz•**)
**analy•sis** (*plural* **•ses**)
**ana•lyst** analyser; *compare* **annalist**
**ana•lyt•ic** (*or* **•lyti•cal**)
**ana•lyti•cal•ly**
**Anam•bra** Nigerian state
**an•am•ne•sis** (*plural* **•ses**) recollection
**an•am•nes•tic**
**an•am•nes•ti•cal•ly**
**ana•mor•phic**
**ana•mor•phism** geology term
**ana•mor•pho•scope** optical device
**ana•mor•pho•sis** (*plural* **•ses**) distorted image
**an•an•drous** botany term
**Ananias** biblical character
**an•an•thous** flowerless
**ana•pest** (*or* **•paest**) metrical foot
**ana•pes•tic** (*or* **•paes•**)
**ana•phase** biology term
**anapho•ra** rhetorical device
**anapho•ral** (*or* **ana•phor•ic**)
**ana•phori•cal•ly**
**an•aph•ro•disia**
**an•aph•ro•dis•iac**
**ana•phy•lac•tic**
**ana•phy•lac•ti•cal•ly**
**ana•phy•lax•is** type of allergy
**ana•pla•sia** biology term
**ana•plas•tic**
**ana•plas•ty** plastic surgery
**an•ap•tyc•tic**
**an•ap•tyx•is** (*plural* **•tyxes**) linguistics term
**an•ar•chic** (*or* **•chi•cal**)
**an•ar•chi•cal•ly**
**an•ar•chism**
**an•ar•chist**
**an•ar•chis•tic**
**an•ar•chy**
**an•ar•thria** loss of speech
**an•ar•throus**
**ana•sar•ca** medical term
**ana•sar•cous**
**an•as•tig•mat** type of lens
**an•as•tig•mat•ic**
**anas•to•mose**
**anas•to•mo•sis** (*plural* **•ses**)
**anas•to•mot•ic**
**anas•tro•phe** rhetorical device
**ana•tase** mineral
**anath•ema** (*plural* **•emas**)
**anath•ema•ti•za•tion** (*or* **•sa•tion**)
**anath•ema•tize** (*or* **•tise**)
**Ana•to•lia** part of Turkey
**Ana•to•lian**
**ana•tomi•cal**
**ana•tomi•cal•ly**
**anato•mist**
**anato•mi•za•tion** (*or* **•sa•tion**)
**anato•mize** (*or* **•mise**)
**anato•miz•er** (*or* **•mis•er**)
**anato•my** (*plural* **•mies**)
**anat•ro•pous** botany term
**an•bury** (*plural* **•buries**) animal tumour
**an•ces•tor**
**an•ces•tral**
**an•ces•tral•ly**
**an•ces•tress**
**an•ces•try** (*plural* **•tries**)
**Anchises** mythological prince
**an•chor**
**An•chor•age** Alaskan city
**an•chor•age**
**an•cho•rite** (*fem* **•ress**) recluse; *compare* **ankerite**
**an•cho•veta** fish
**an•cho•vy** (*plural* **•vies** *or* **•vy**)
**an•chu•sa** plant
**an•cien ré•gime** (*plural* **an•ciens ré•gimes**) *French* pre-Revolutionary France
**an•cient**
**an•cient•ness**
**an•cil•lary** (*plural* **•laries**)
**an•cipi•tal** (*or* **•tous**) biology term
**an•con** (*or* **•cone**; *plural* **•cones**) architectural term
**An•co•na** Italian port
**an•co•nal** (*or* **•neal**)
**an•cy•los•to•mia•sis** (*or* **an•ky•, an•chy•**) hookworm disease
**and**
**An•da•lu•sia** Spanish region
**an•da•lu•site** mineral
**an•dan•te** musical term
**an•dan•ti•no** (*plural* **•nos**) musical term
**An•dean**
**An•der•lecht** Belgian town
**An•der•son** Canadian river
**An•des**
**an•desine** mineral
**an•desite** rock
**An•dhra Pra•desh** Indian state
**and•iron**
**An•di•zhan** Uzbek city
**An•dor•ra**
**An•dor•ra La Vel•la** capital of Andorra
**An•dor•ran**
**And•over**
**an•dra•dite** gemstone
**Androcles** legendary character
**an•dro•clin•ium** botany term
**an•droe•cial**
**an•droe•cium** (*plural* **•cia**) stamens of flower
**an•dro•gen** hormone
**an•dro•gen•ic**
**an•drog•enous** producing only male offspring; *compare* **androgynous**
**an•dro•gyne**
**an•drogy•nous** having male and female characteristics; *compare* **androgenous**
**an•droid**
**Andromache** mythological character
**An•drom•eda** constellation
**An•dros** Greek island
**an•dro•sphinx** (*plural* **•sphinxes** *or* **•sphinges**)
**an•dros•ter•one** hormone
**Andvari** mythological character
**ane** *Scot* one
**an•ec•dot•age**
**an•ec•do•tal**
**an•ec•dote**
**an•ec•dot•ic**
**an•ec•dot•ist**
**an•echo•ic**

**anemia** *US spelling of* anaemia
**anemic** *US spelling of* anaemic
**anemo•chore** botany term
**anemo•graph**
**anemo•graph•ic**
**anemo•graphi•cal•ly**
**an•emog•ra•phy** recording wind measurements
**an•emol•ogy**
**an•emom•eter**
**an•emo•met•ric**
**an•emo•met•ri•cal**
**an•emom•etry**
**anemo•ne**
**an•emophi•lous** wind-pollinated
**an•emophi•ly**
**anemo•scope**
**anent** *Scot* concerning
**aner•gic** lacking energy
**an•er•gy**
**an•er•oid**
**an•es•the•sia** *US spelling of* **anaesthesia**
**an•es•thesi•olo•gist** *US* anaesthetist
**an•es•thesi•ology** *US* anaesthetics
**an•es•the•tist** *US* person qualified to administer anaesthetics, not necessarily a doctor; *compare* **anaesthetist**
**an•es•trus** *US spelling of* **anoestrus**
**an•ethole** organic compound
**an•eu•ploid** biology term
**aneu•rin** vitamin
**aneu•rysm** (*or* **•rism**) blood-vessel defect
**aneu•rys•mal** (*or* **•ris•mal, •rys•mat•ic, •ris•mat•ic**)
**anew**
**an•frac•tu•os•ity** (*plural* **•ities**)
**an•frac•tu•ous** convoluted
**An•garsk** Russian city
**an•ga•ry** legal term
**an•gel**
**An•ge•leno** (*plural* **•nos**) inhabitant of Los Angeles
**angel•fish** (*plural* **•fish** *or* **•fishes**)
**an•gel•ic**
**an•gel•ica**
**an•geli•cal**
**an•gel•ol•ogy**
**An•ge•lus** Roman Catholic prayers
**an•ger**
**An•gers** French town
**An•ge•vin** inhabitant of Anjou
**an•gi•na**
**an•gi•nal**
**an•gi•na pec•to•ris**
**an•gi•nose** (*or* **•nous**)
**an•gi•ol•ogy** branch of medicine
**an•gio•ma** (*plural* **•mas** *or* **•ma•ta**) tumour
**an•gi•oma•tous**
**an•gio•sperm** botany term
**an•gio•sper•mous**
**Ang•kor** Cambodian region
**An•gle** ancient German invader
**an•gle**
**an•gler**
**An•gle•sey**
**an•gle•site** mineral
**angle•worm**
**An•glian** of Angles or East Anglia
**An•gli•can** of Church of England
**An•gli•can•ism**
**An•gli•cism** English idiom
**An•gli•cist**
**an•gli•ci•za•tion** (*or* **•sa•tion**)
**an•gli•cize** (*or* **•cise**)
**an•gli•fy** (**•fies, •fy•ing, •fied**)
**an•gling**
**Anglo-American**
**Anglo-Catholic**
**Anglo-Catholicism**
**Anglo-Irish**
**An•glo•ma•nia**
**An•glo•phile** (*or* **•phil**)
**An•glo•philia**
**An•glo•phili•ac** (*or* **•phil•ic**)
**An•glo•phobe**
**An•glo•pho•bia**
**An•glo•phone** native English speaker
**Anglo-Saxon**
**An•go•la**
**An•go•lan**
**an•go•ra**
**an•gos•tu•ra** bitter-tasting bark
**An•gos•tu•ra Bit•ters** (*Trademark*)
**an•gri•ly**
**an•gry** (**•gri•er, •gri•est**)
**angst** anxiety
**ang•strom** unit of length
**An•guil•la** West Indian island
**an•guil•li•form** eel-shaped
**an•guine** snakelike
**an•guish**
**an•gu•lar**
**an•gu•lar•ity** (*plural* **•ities**)
**an•gu•late**
**an•gu•la•tion**
**An•gus** Scottish council area
**ang•wan•ti•bo** (*plural* **•bos**) animal
**An•halt** German region
**an•he•dral**
**an•hin•ga** bird
**An•hwei** Chinese province
**an•hy•dride**
**an•hy•drite**
**an•hy•drous**
**ani** (*plural* **anis**) bird
**Ani•ak•chak** Alaskan volcano
**an•icon•ic**
**anil** shrub
**an•ile** like an old woman
**ani•line** organic compound
**anil•ity**
**ani•ma**
**ani•mad•ver•sion**
**ani•mad•vert**
**ani•mal**
**ani•mal•cu•lar**
**ani•mal•cule** (*or* **•cu•lum**; *plural* **•cules** *or* **•cu•la**) microscopic animal
**ani•mal•ism**
**ani•mal•ist**
**ani•mal•ity**
**ani•mali•za•tion** (*or* **•sa•tion**)
**ani•mal•ize** (*or* **•ise**)

**ani•mate**
**ani•ma•tion**
**ani•ma•tism**
**ani•ma•to** music term
**ani•ma•tor** (*or* **•mat•er**)
**ani•mé** resin
**ani•mism**
**ani•mist**
**ani•mis•tic**
**ani•mos•ity** (*plural* **•ities**)
**ani•mus**
**an•ion** chemistry term
**ani•on•ic**
**an•ise** plant
**ani•seed**
**an•isei•ko•nia** visual defect
**an•isei•kon•ic**
**ani•sette** liqueur
**ani•so•dac•tyl** zoology term
**ani•so•dac•ty•lous**
**ani•soga•mous**
**ani•soga•my** type of sexual reproduction
**ani•sole** chemical compound
**an•isom•er•ous** botany term
**an•iso•met•ric**
**an•iso•metro•pia** visual disorder
**an•iso•trop•ic**
**an•isot•ro•py**
**An•jou** French province
**An•ka•ra** Turkish city
**an•ker•ite** mineral; *compare* **anchorite**
**ankh** Egyptian cross
**An•king** Chinese city
**an•kle**
**ankle•bone**
**an•klet**
**an•ky•lo•saur** dinosaur
**an•ky•lose** (*or* **•chy•**)
**an•ky•lo•sis** (*or* **•chy•**) immobility of joint
**an•ky•lot•ic** (*or* **•chy•**)
**an•lace** medieval dagger
**an•la•ge** (*plural* **•gen** *or* **•ges**) biology term
**An•na•ba** Algerian port
**an•na•berg•ite** mineral
**an•nal**
**an•nal•ist** compiler of annals; *compare* **analyst**
**an•nal•is•tic**
**an•nals**
**An•nam** (*or* **Anam**) part of Vietnam
**An•napo•lis** US city
**An•na•pur•na** (*or* **Ana•**) Nepalese mountains
**an•nates** pope's revenue
**an•nat•to** (*or* **anat•**; *plural* **•tos**) tree
**an•neal**
**an•neal•er**
**Anne•cy** French lake
**an•nelid** worm
**an•neli•dan**
**an•nex** take over or add on; *compare* **annexe**
**an•nexa•tion**
**an•nexa•tion•al**
**an•nexa•tion•ism**
**an•nexa•tion•ist**
**an•nexe** addition to building; *compare* **annex**
**an•ni•hil•able**
**an•ni•hi•late**
**an•ni•hi•la•tion**
**an•ni•hi•la•tive**
**an•ni•hi•la•tor**
**an•ni•ver•sa•ry** (*plural* **•saries**)
**anno Domi•ni** *Latin* year of our Lord
**an•no•tate**
**an•no•ta•tion**
**an•no•ta•tive**
**an•no•ta•tor**
**an•nounce**
**an•nounce•ment**
**an•nounc•er**
**an•noy**
**an•noy•ance**
**an•nual**
**an•nual•ly**
**an•nui•tant**
**an•nu•ity** (*plural* **•ities**)
**an•nul** (**•nul•ling**, **•nulled**)
**an•nu•lar**
**an•nu•late** ringed
**an•nu•la•tion**
**an•nu•let** architectural moulding
**an•nul•lable**
**an•nul•ment**
**an•nu•lose** segmented
**an•nu•lus** (*plural* **•li** *or* **•luses**)
**an•nun•ci•ate** announce; *compare* **enunciate**
**An•nun•cia•tion** Christian feast
**an•nun•cia•tion** announcement
**an•nun•cia•tive** (*or* **•tory**)
**an•nun•cia•tor**
**anoa** cattle
**an•ode**
**an•od•ic**
**ano•dize** (*or* **•dise**)
**ano•dyne** painkiller
**an•oes•trus** (*US* **•es•**)
**anoint**
**anoint•er**
**anoint•ment**
**anole** lizard
**anoma•lis•tic**
**anoma•lis•ti•cal•ly**
**anoma•lous**
**anoma•ly** (*plural* **•lies**)
**anom•ic**
**an•omie** (*or* **•omy**) lack of social standards
**anon** *Archaic* soon
**ano•nym** pseudonym
**ano•nym•ity**
**anony•mous**
**anophe•les** (*plural* **•les**) mosquito
**ano•rak**
**ano•rexia ner•vo•sa**
**ano•rex•ic**
**an•or•thite** mineral
**an•or•thit•ic**
**an•or•tho•site** rock
**an•os•mat•ic** (*or* **an•os•mic**)
**an•os•mia** inability to smell
**an•oth•er**
**an•ox•aemia** (*US* **•emia**) oxygen deficiency in blood
**an•ox•aemic** (*US* **•emic**)
**an•oxia** lack of oxygen
**an•ox•ic**
**an•sate** having a handle
**An•schluss** union of Austria with Germany
**an•ser•ine** (*or* **•ous**) of geese
**An•shan** Chinese city
**an•swer**
**an•swer•abil•ity** (*or* **•able•ness**)
**an•swer•able**
**ant**

**anta** architectural term
**An•ta•buse** (*Trademark*)
**ant•acid**
**an•tago•nism**
**an•tago•nist**
**an•tago•nis•tic**
**an•tago•nis•ti•cal•ly**
**an•tago•niz•able** (*or* **•nis•able**)
**an•tago•ni•za•tion** (*or* **•sa•tion**)
**an•tago•nize** (*or* **•nise**)
**ant•al•ka•li** (*plural* **•lis** *or* **•lies**)
**ant•al•ka•line**
**An•ta•na•na•ri•vo** Madagascan capital
**Ant•arc•tic**
**Ant•arc•ti•ca**
**An•tar•es** star
**ante** stake in poker; advance payment; *compare* **anti**
**ant•eater**
**ante•bel•lum**
**ante•cede**
**ante•ced•ence**
**ante•ced•ent**
**an•te•ced•ents**
**ante•choir** part of church
**ante•date**
**ante•di•lu•vian**
**ante•fix** (*plural* **•fixes** *or* **•fixa**) roof ornament
**ante•fix•al**
**ante•lope**
**ante•me•rid•ian** (*adj*)
**ante me•ridi•em** *Latin* before noon
**ante-mortem** (*adj*) before death
**ante•na•tal**
**an•ten•na** (*plural* **•nae**) insect feelers
**an•ten•na** (*plural* **•nas**) aerial
**an•ten•nule**
**ante•pen•dium** (*plural* **•dia**) altar covering
**ante•penult**
**ante•penul•ti•mate**
**ante•ri•or**
**ante•room**
**ante•type** earlier form
**ante•ver•sion**
**ante•vert** tilt forwards
**ant•he•li•on** (*plural* **•lia**) meteorology term
**ant•he•lix** (*or* **anti•**; *plural* **•heli•ces** *or* **•he•lixes**) ear cartilage
**an•thel•min•tic** (*or* **•thic**) vermifuge
**an•them**
**an•themi•on** (*plural* **•mia**) Greek design
**an•ther**
**an•ther•idial**
**an•ther•id•ium** (*plural* **•ia**) botany term
**an•thero•zo•id** botany term
**an•thesis** flowering
**an•tho•cya•nin** (*or* **•cy•an**) pigment
**an•tho•dium** (*plural* **•dia**) botany term
**an•tho•logi•cal**
**an•tholo•gist**
**an•tholo•gize** (*or* **•gise**)
**an•thol•ogy** (*plural* **•ogies**)
**an•tho•phore** botany term
**an•tho•taxy** botany term
**an•tho•zo•an** marine organism
**an•thra•cene** chemical compound
**an•thra•cite** coal
**an•thra•cit•ic**
**an•thrac•nose** fungal disease
**an•thra•coid**
**an•thra•qui•none** chemical compound
**an•thrax** (*plural* **•thra•ces**)
**an•thro•po•cen•tric**
**an•thro•po•cen•trism**
**an•thro•po•gen•esis** (*or* **•geny**) study of man's origin
**an•thro•po•genet•ic** (*or* **•gen•ic**)
**an•thro•poid**
**an•thro•poi•dal**
**an•thro•po•logi•cal**
**an•thro•polo•gist**
**an•thro•pol•ogy**
**an•thro•po•met•ric** (*or* **•ri•cal**)
**an•thro•po•met•ri•cal•ly**
**an•thro•pome•trist**
**an•thro•pom•etry**
**an•thro•po•mor•phic**
**an•thro•po•mor•phism**
**an•thro•po•mor•phist**
**an•thro•po•mor•phize** (*or* **•phise**)
**an•thro•po•mor•pho•sis**
**an•thro•po•mor•phous**
**an•thro•po•path•ic**
**an•thro•popa•thy** (*or* **•thism**) attribution of human passions to a deity
**an•thro•popha•gi** (*sing.* **•gus**) cannibals
**an•thro•po•phag•ic**
**an•thro•popha•gite**
**an•thro•popha•gy** cannibalism
**an•thro•po•soph•ic**
**an•thro•poso•phy**
**an•thu•rium** plant
**anti** *Slang* opposed to; *compare* **ante**
**anti-aircraft**
**an•ti•ar** tree
**anti•bary•on** physics term
**An•tibes** French port
**anti•bio•sis**
**anti•bi•ot•ic**
**anti•body** (*plural* **•bodies**)
**an•tic**
**anti•cata•lyst**
**anti•cath•ode**
**anti•chlor**
**anti•chlo•ris•tic**
**anti•cho•lin•er•gic** physiology term
**anti•cho•lin•es•ter•ase** enzyme
**Anti•christ**
**an•tici•pant**
**an•tici•pate**
**an•tici•pa•tion**
**an•tici•pa•tive**
**an•tici•pa•tor**
**an•tici•pa•to•ri•ly**
**an•tici•pa•tory**
**anti•clas•tic** maths term
**anti•cleri•cal**
**anti•cli•mac•tic**
**anti•cli•mac•ti•cal•ly**
**anti•cli•max**
**anti•cli•nal**
**anti•cline** geology term
**anti•cli•no•rium** (*plural* **•ria**) geology term

**anti•clock•wise**
**anti•co•agu•lant**
**anti•con•vul•sant**
**An•ti•cos•ti** Canadian island
**anti•cy•clone**
**anti•cy•clon•ic**
**anti•de•pres•sant**
**anti•dote**
**anti•drom•ic** biology term
**An•tie•tam** US battle site
**anti•febrile**
**anti•fer•ro•mag•ne•tism**
**anti•foul•ing** protective paint
**anti•freeze**
**anti•gen**
**anti•gen•ic**
**anti•geni•cal•ly**
**Antigone** mythological character
**An•ti•gua** West Indian island
**anti•ha•la•tion** photography term
**anti•he•ro** (*plural* **•roes**)
**anti•his•ta•mine**
**anti-icer**
**anti-imperi•al•ism**
**anti-imperi•al•ist**
**anti•knock** petrol additive
**anti•lep•ton** physics term
**An•til•les** West Indian islands
**anti•log**
**anti•loga•rithm**
**anti•loga•rith•mic**
**an•tilo•gism** philosophy term
**an•til•ogy** (*plural* **•ogies**) contradiction in terms
**anti•ma•cas•sar**
**anti•mag•net•ic**
**anti•ma•lar•ial**
**anti•masque** grotesque dance
**anti•mat•ter**
**anti•mere** biology term
**anti•mer•ic**
**an•tim•er•ism**
**anti•mis•sile**
**anti•mo•nar•chic**
**anti•mo•nar•chist**
**anti•mo•nial**
**anti•mo•nic**
**anti•mo•nous**
**anti•mo•ny** chemical element; *compare* antinomy
**anti•mo•nyl**
**anti•na•tion•al•ist**
**anti•na•tion•al•is•tic**
**anti•neu•tri•no** (*plural* **•nos**)
**anti•neu•tron**
**anti•nod•al**
**anti•node** physics term
**anti•nom•ic**
**anti•nomi•cal•ly**
**an•tino•my** (*plural* **•mies**) paradox; *compare* antimony
**anti•nu•cleon**
**An•ti•och** Turkish city
**anti•oxi•dant**
**anti•par•al•lel**
**anti•par•ticle**
**anti•pas•to** (*plural* **•ti**) Italian hors d'oeuvres
**anti•pa•thet•ic** (*or* **•ical**)
**anti•pa•theti•cal•ly**
**an•tipa•thy** (*plural* **•thies**)
**anti•peri•od•ic**
**anti•peri•stal•sis** physiology term
**anti•per•son•nel**
**anti•per•spi•rant**
**anti•phlo•gis•tic**
**anti•phon**
**an•tipho•nal**
**an•tipho•nal•ly**
**an•tipho•nary** (*plural* **•naries**) collection of biblical passages
**an•tipho•ny** (*plural* **•nies**) type of choral singing
**an•tiph•ra•sis** rhetorical device
**an•tipo•dal**
**anti•pode**
**an•tipo•dean**
**An•tipo•des** Australia and New Zealand
**an•tipo•des** points diametrically opposite on Earth
**anti•pope**
**anti•prag•mat•ic**
**anti•prag•ma•tism**
**anti•pro•ton**
**anti•psy•chia•try**
**anti•psy•chot•ic**
**anti•py•resis**
**anti•py•ret•ic**
**anti•py•rine**
**anti•quar•ian**
**anti•quary** (*plural* **•quaries**)
**anti•quate**
**anti•quat•ed**
**anti•qua•ted•ness**
**an•tique**
**an•tiq•uity** (*plural* **•uities**)
**anti•ra•chit•ic** preventing rickets
**anti•racism**
**anti•racist**
**anti•repub•li•can**
**anti•revo•lu•tion•ary**
**an•tir•rhi•num**
**anti•scor•bu•tic** preventing scurvy
**anti-Semite**
**anti-Semitic**
**anti-Semitism**
**anti•sep•sis**
**anti•sep•tic**
**anti•sep•ti•cal•ly**
**anti•serum** (*plural* **•serums** *or* **•sera**)
**anti•slav•ery**
**anti•so•cial**
**anti•spas•mod•ic**
**anti•stat•ic**
**an•tis•tro•phe**
**anti•stroph•ic**
**anti•sub•ma•rine**
**anti•tank**
**an•tith•esis** (*plural* **•ses**)
**anti•theti•cal** (*or* **•thet•ic**)
**anti•theti•cal•ly**
**anti•tox•ic**
**anti•tox•in**
**anti•trades** winds
**an•tit•ra•gus** (*plural* **•gi**) part of ear
**anti•tus•sive** alleviating coughing
**anti•type**
**anti•ven•in**
**anti•vi•ral**
**anti•vivi•sec•tion**
**anti•vivi•sec•tion•ist**
**anti•world** world composed of antimatter
**ant•ler**
**ant•lered**
**Ant•lia** constellation

**ant•like**
**ant•li•on** insect
**An•to•fa•gas•ta** Chilean port
**an•to•no•ma•sia** figure of speech
**an•to•no•mas•tic**
**an•to•no•mas•ti•cal•ly**
**an•to•nym**
**an•tony•mous**
**an•tre** cavern
**An•trim**
**an•trorse** directed upwards
**an•trum** (*plural* **•tra**) anatomy term
**An•tung** Chinese port
**Ant•werp**
**Anubis** Egyptian god
**anu•ran** tailless amphibian
**anu•resis** inability to urinate
**anu•ria** inability to form urine
**anu•rous** tailless
**anus**
**an•vil**
**anxi•ety** (*plural* **•eties**)
**anx•ious**
**anx•ious•ness**
**any**
**An•yang** Chinese town
**any•body**
**any•how**
**any•one**
**any•thing**
**any•way**
**any•where**
**any•wise**
**An•zac** Australian and New Zealand Army Corps
**An•zio** Italian port
**aorist** linguistics term
**aoris•tic**
**aoris•ti•cal•ly**
**aor•ta** (*plural* **•tas** *or* **•tae**)
**aor•tic** (*or* **•tal**)
**aou•dad** sheep
**apace**
**Apache** (*plural* **Apaches** *or* **Apache**) American Indian
**apache** gangster
**apa•go•ge** logic term
**apa•gog•ic** (*or* **•gogi•cal**)
**apa•gogi•cal•ly**
**ap•an•age** *variant spelling of* **appanage**
**Apar•ri** Philippine port
**apart**
**apart•heid**
**apart•ment**
**apa•tet•ic** of animal coloration
**apa•thet•ic**
**apa•theti•cal•ly**
**apa•thy**
**apa•tite** mineral
**ape**
**apeak**
**Apel•doorn** Dutch town
**ape•like**
**ape•man** (*plural* **•men**)
**Ap•en•nines**
**aper•çu** *French* outline or insight
**aperi•ent**
**aperi•od•ic** at irregular intervals
**aperi•odi•cal•ly**
**aperio•dic•ity**
**apé•ri•tif** drink before meal; *compare* **aperitive**
**ape•ri•tive** laxative; *compare* **apéritif**
**ap•er•ture**
**ap•ery** (*plural* **•eries**) imitative behaviour
**apet•al•ous** petal-less
**apet•aly**
**apex** (*plural* **apexes** *or* **api•ces**)
**aphaer•esis** (*or* **apher•**; *plural* **•ses**) linguistics term
**apha•gia** inability to swallow
**apha•nite** rock
**apha•sia** language disorder
**apha•sic**
**ap•he•lian**
**ap•he•li•on** (*plural* **•lia**) point in planet's orbit
**ap•he•lio•trop•ic** botany term
**apher•esis** *variant spelling of* **aphaeresis**
**aph•esis** linguistics term
**aphet•ic**
**apheti•cal•ly**
**aphid**
**aphidi•ous**
**aphis** (*plural* **aphi•des**)
**apho•nia** (*or* **•ny**) loss of voice
**aphon•ic**
**apho•rism**
**apho•rist**
**apho•ris•tic**
**apho•rize** (*or* **•rise**)
**apho•tic** without light
**aph•ro•di•sia**
**aph•ro•disi•ac**
**Aphrodite** Greek goddess
**aph•tha** (*plural* **•thae**) ulcer
**aphyl•lous** leafless
**aphyl•ly**
**apian** of bees
**api•ar•ian** of beekeeping
**apia•rist**
**api•ary** (*plural* **•aries**) beehive; *compare* **aviary**
**api•cal**
**api•cal•ly**
**api•ces** *plural of* **apex**
**apicu•late**
**api•cul•tur•al**
**api•cul•ture**
**api•cul•tur•ist**
**apiece**
**à pied** *French* on foot
**Api•ezon** (*Trademark*)
**Apis** sacred bull
**ap•ish**
**ap•ish•ness**
**apiv•or•ous** bee-eating
**apla•cen•tal**
**ap•la•nat•ic** physics term
**ap•la•nati•cal•ly**
**aplano•sphere**
**aplano•spore**
**apla•sia** congenital absence of organ
**aplas•tic**
**aplen•ty**
**ap•lite** (*or* **hap•**) rock
**ap•lit•ic** (*or* **hap•**)
**aplomb**
**ap•noea** (*US* **•nea**) inability to breath
**Apo** Philippine mountain
**apoca•lypse**
**apoca•lyp•tic**
**apoca•lyp•ti•cal•ly**
**apo•carp**
**apo•car•pous** botany term
**apo•chro•mat**
**apo•chro•mat•ic** physics term
**apo•chro•ma•tism**

**apoco•pate**
**apoco•pa•tion**
**apoco•pe** linguistics term
**apo•crine** physiology term
**Apoc•ry•pha** Old Testament appendix
**apoc•ry•phal** of doubtful authenticity
**apoc•ry•phal•ly**
**apocy•na•ceous** botany term
**apo•cyn•thi•on** astronomy term
**apo•dal** without feet
**apo•dic•tic** (*or* **•deic•**) unquestionably true
**apo•dic•ti•cal•ly** (*or* **•deic•**)
**apodo•sis** (*plural* **•ses**) grammar term
**apo•en•zyme**
**apo•gam•ic**
**apoga•mous**
**apoga•my** type of plant reproduction
**apo•gee**
**apo•geo•trop•ic** botany term
**apo•geot•ro•pism**
**apo•liti•cal**
**apo•liti•cal•ly**
**Apol•li•naris** mineral water
**Apollo** Greek god
**Apol•lo** spacecraft
**Ap•ol•lo•nian**
**Apollyon** the Devil
**apolo•get•ic**
**apolo•geti•cal•ly**
**apolo•get•ics** branch of theology
**apo•lo•gia**
**apolo•gist**
**apolo•gize** (*or* **•gise**)
**apolo•giz•er** (*or* **•gis•er**)
**apo•logue** moral fable
**apol•ogy** (*plural* **•ogies**)
**apo•lune** astronomy term
**apo•mict**
**apo•mic•tic**
**apo•mixis** (*plural* **•mixes**) asexual reproduction
**apo•mor•phine** alkaloid
**apo•neu•ro•sis** (*plural* **•ses**) anatomy term
**apo•neu•rot•ic**
**apopha•sis** rhetorical device
**apo•phthegm** (*or* **apo•thegm**) cryptic remark; *compare* **apothem**
**apophy•ge** architectural term
**apophyl•lite** mineral
**apophy•sate**
**apophy•sial**
**apophy•sis** (*plural* **•ses**) outgrowth
**apo•plec•tic**
**apo•plexy**
**aport** nautical term
**apo•semat•ic** zoology term
**apo•sio•pe•sis** (*plural* **•ses**) rhetorical device
**apo•sio•pet•ic**
**apo•spory** botany term
**apos•ta•sy** (*plural* **•sies**)
**apos•tate**
**apos•ta•tize** (*or* **•tise**)
**a pos•terio•ri** *Latin* from effect to cause; *compare* **a priori**
**apos•til** marginal note
**apos•tle**
**apos•to•late**
**ap•os•tol•ic**
**apos•tro•phe**
**apo•stroph•ic**
**apos•tro•phize** (*or* **•phise**)
**apoth•ecary** (*plural* **•ecaries**)
**apo•the•cial**
**apo•the•cium** (*plural* **•cia**)
**apo•thegm** *variant spelling of* **apophthegm**
**apo•them** geometry term; *compare* **apophthegm**
**apoth•eo•sis** (*plural* **•ses**)
**apoth•eo•size** (*or* **•sise**) glorify
**apo•tro•pa•ic** preventing evil
**ap•pal** (*US* **•pall**; **•pal•ling, •palled**)
**Ap•pa•la•chia** US region
**Appa•la•chian**
**ap•pal•ling**
**ap•pal•ling•ly**
**Ap•pa•loo•sa** horse
**ap•pa•nage** (*or* **apa•nage**) perquisite
**ap•pa•rat•us** (*plural* **•rat•us** *or* **•rat•uses**)
**ap•par•el** (**•el•ling, •elled;** *US* **•el•ing, •eled**)
**ap•par•ent**
**ap•par•ent•ness**
**ap•pa•ri•tion**
**ap•pari•tor** ecclesiastical court officer
**ap•pas•sio•na•to** musical term
**ap•peal**
**ap•peal•able**
**ap•peal•er**
**ap•peal•ing•ly**
**ap•pear**
**ap•pear•ance**
**ap•peas•able**
**ap•pease**
**ap•peas•er**
**ap•pease•ment**
**ap•pel** fencing term
**ap•pel•lant**
**ap•pel•late**
**ap•pel•la•tion**
**ap•pel•la•tive**
**ap•pel•lee**
**ap•pend**
**ap•pend•age**
**ap•pen•dant**
**ap•pen•di•cec•to•my** (*or esp. US* **ap•pen•dec•to•my;** *plural* **•mies**)
**ap•pen•di•ci•tis**
**ap•pen•di•cle** small appendage
**ap•pen•dicu•lar**
**ap•pen•dix** (*plural* **•dixes** *or* **•di•ces**)
**Ap•pen•zell** Swiss canton
**ap•per•ceive**
**ap•per•cep•tion** psychology term
**ap•per•cep•tive**
**ap•per•tain**
**ap•pes•tat** hunger control centre in brain
**ap•pe•tence** (*or* **•ten•cy;** *plural* **•tences** *or* **•ten•cies**)
**ap•pe•tite**
**ap•pe•tiz•er** (*or* **•tis•er**)
**ap•pe•tiz•ing** (*or* **•tis•ing**)
**ap•plaud**
**ap•plaud•er**
**ap•plaud•ing•ly**
**ap•plause**
**ap•ple**

**apple•cart**
**apple•jack**
**apple•snits** Canadian apple dish
**ap•pli•ance**
**ap•plic•abil•ity**
**ap•pli•cable**
**ap•pli•cably**
**ap•pli•cant**
**ap•pli•ca•tion**
**ap•plica•tive**
**ap•pli•ca•tor**
**ap•pli•ca•tory**
**ap•plied**
**ap•pli•er**
**ap•pli•qué** (**•qué•ing, •quéd**)
**ap•ply** (**•plies, •ply•ing, •plied**)
**ap•pog•gia•tu•ra** (*plural* **•ras** *or* **•re**) musical term
**ap•point**
**ap•poin•tee**
**ap•point•er**
**ap•point•ment**
**ap•poin•tor** legal term
**Ap•po•mat•tox** US battle site
**ap•por•tion**
**ap•por•tion•able**
**ap•por•tion•er**
**ap•por•tion•ment**
**ap•pose**
**ap•po•site** apt; *compare* **opposite**
**ap•po•si•tion**
**ap•posi•tive** linguistics term
**ap•prais•able**
**ap•prais•al** (*or* **•praise•ment**)
**ap•praise** assess; *compare* **apprise**
**ap•prais•er**
**ap•prais•ing•ly**
**ap•prais•ive**
**ap•pre•ci•able**
**ap•pre•ci•ate**
**ap•pre•cia•tion**
**ap•pre•cia•tive** (*or* **•tory**)
**ap•pre•cia•tive•ness**
**ap•pre•hend**
**ap•pre•hen•sibil•ity**
**ap•pre•hen•sible**
**ap•pre•hen•sion**
**ap•pre•hen•sive**
**ap•pre•hen•sive•ness**
**ap•pren•tice**
**ap•pren•tice•ship**
**ap•pressed** pressed closely against
**ap•prise** (*or* **•prize**) inform; *compare* **appraise**
**ap•proach**
**ap•proach•abil•ity** (*or* **•able•ness**)
**ap•proach•able**
**ap•pro•bate** Scottish legal term; *US* approve
**ap•pro•ba•tion**
**ap•pro•ba•tive** (*or* **•tory**)
**ap•pro•pri•able**
**ap•pro•pri•ate**
**ap•pro•pri•ate•ness**
**ap•pro•pria•tion**
**ap•pro•pria•tor**
**ap•prov•al**
**ap•prove**
**ap•proved**
**ap•proxi•mal** situated side by side
**ap•proxi•mate**
**ap•proxi•mate•ly**
**ap•proxi•ma•tion**
**ap•proxi•ma•tive**
**ap•pulse** astronomy term
**ap•pul•sive**
**ap•pur•te•nance**
**ap•pur•te•nant**
**apraxia** disorder of nervous system
**aprax•ic** (*or* **aprac•tic**)
**après-ski**
**apri•cot**
**April**
**a prio•ri** *Latin* from cause to effect; *compare* **a posteriori**
**apri•or•ism**
**apri•or•ity**
**apron**
**ap•ro•pos**
**apse** recess in church
**ap•si•dal**
**ap•sis** (*plural* **•si•des**) point in planet's orbit
**apt**
**ap•ter•al** architectural term
**ap•ter•ous** wingless
**ap•ter•yg•ial** lacking fins or wings
**ap•ter•yx** kiwi
**ap•ti•tude**
**apt•ness**
**Apu•lia** Italian region
**Apu•ri•mac** Peruvian river
**apy•re•tic**
**Aqa•ba** (*or* **Aka•ba**) Jordanian port
**aqua** (*plural* **aquae** *or* **aquas**)
**aqua•cul•ture** cultivation of marine organisms; *compare* **aquiculture**
**aqua•lung**
**aqua•marine**
**aqua•naut**
**aqua•pho•bia**
**aqua•plane**
**aqua re•gia** strong acid
**aqua•relle**
**aqua•rel•list** water-colour painter
**aqua•rist** aquarium curator
**aquar•ium** (*plural* **aquar•iums** *or* **aquaria**)
**Aquar•ius**
**aquat•ic**
**aquat•ics**
**aqua•tint**
**aqua•vit** aromatic spirit
**aqua vi•tae** *Archaic* brandy
**aque•duct**
**aque•ous**
**aqui•cul•tur•al**
**aqui•cul•ture** hydroponics; *compare* **aquaculture**
**aqui•cul•tur•ist**
**aqui•fer** water-containing rock
**Aqui•la** constellation
**aqui•legia**
**aqui•line**
**Aqui•taine** French region
**Ara** constellation
**Arab**
**ara•besque**
**Ara•bia**
**Ara•bian**
**Ara•bic** language
**arabi•nose** sugar
**Ar•ab•ist**
**ar•able**
**Ara•by** *Archaic* Arabia
**Ara•ca•jú** Brazilian port
**Arachne** mythological character
**arach•nid** spider

**arach•ni•dan**
**arach•noid** membrane covering brain
**Arad** Romanian city
**Ara•gon** Spanish region
**Ara•go•nese**
**arago•nite** mineral
**Ara•guaia** Brazilian river
**Arak** Iranian town
**arak** *variant spelling of* **arrack**
**Aral•dite** (*Trademark*)
**ara•lia•ceous** botany term
**Ara•ma•ic** language
**Aran** Irish islands; type of sweater; *compare* **Arran**
**ara•neid** spider
**Arapa•ho** (*plural* **•hos** *or* **•ho**) American Indian
**ara•pai•ma** fish
**Ara•rat** Turkish mountain
**ara•ro•ba** tree; medicinal substance
**Aras** Asian river
**Arau•ca•nia** Chilean region
**Arau•ca•nian**
**arau•ca•ria** tree
**Ara•wak•an** American Indian language
**ar•ba•lest** crossbow
**ar•bi•ter**
**ar•bi•trable**
**ar•bi•trage** financial term
**ar•bi•tral**
**ar•bit•ra•ment**
**ar•bi•trari•ly**
**ar•bi•trari•ness**
**ar•bi•trary**
**ar•bi•trate**
**ar•bi•tra•tion**
**ar•bi•tra•tor**
**ar•bi•tress**
**ar•bor** rotating shaft; *US spelling of* **arbour**
**ar•bora•ceous**
**ar•bor•eal**
**ar•bo•reous**
**ar•bo•res•cence**
**ar•bo•res•cent**
**ar•bo•retum** (*plural* **•ta** *or* **•tums**)
**ar•bori•cul•ture**
**ar•bor•ist**
**ar•bori•za•tion** (*or* **•sa•tion**)
**ar•bor vi•tae** tree
**ar•bour** (*US* **•bor**) tree-lined shelter; *compare* **arbor**
**Ar•broath** Scottish port
**ar•bu•tus** (*plural* **•tuses**) shrub
**arc** part of curve; *compare* **ark**
**ar•cade**
**Ar•ca•dia** department of Greece; *compare* **Acadia**
**Ar•ca•dian**
**Ar•ca•dy** (*or* **•dia**) rustic paradise
**ar•ca•na** tarot cards
**ar•cane**
**ar•ca•num** (*plural* **•na**)
**ar•ca•ture** small arcade
**arch**
**Ar•chaean** (*or esp. US* **•chean**) geology term
**ar•chaeo•logi•cal** (*US also* **•cheo•**)
**ar•chaeo•logi•cal•ly** (*US also* **•cheo•**)
**ar•chae•olo•gist** (*US also* **•che•**)
**ar•chae•ol•ogy** (*US also* **•che•**)
**ar•chaeo•mag•net•ism** (*US also* **•cheo•**)
**ar•chae•op•ter•yx**
**ar•chae•or•nis** extinct bird
**Ar•chaeo•zo•ic** (*US also* **•cheo•**)
**ar•cha•ic**
**ar•chai•cal•ly**
**ar•cha•ism**
**ar•cha•ist**
**ar•cha•is•tic**
**ar•cha•is•ti•cal•ly**
**ar•cha•ize** (*or* **•ise**)
**ar•cha•iz•er** (*or* **•is•er**)
**Arch•an•gel** Russian port
**arch•angel**
**arch•angelic**
**arch•bishop**
**arch•bishop•ric**
**arch•deacon**
**arch•deacon•ry** (*plural* **•ries**)
**arch•dioc•esan**
**arch•dio•cese**
**arch•ducal**
**arch•duchess**
**arch•duchy** (*plural* **•duchies**)
**arch•duke**
**arched**
**ar•che•go•nium** (*plural* **•nia**) botany term
**arch•en•emy** (*plural* **•emies**)
**ar•chen•ter•ic**
**ar•chen•ter•on** embryology term
**ar•che•ol•ogy** *US variant spelling of* **archaeology**
**arch•er**
**archer•fish** (*plural* **•fish** *or* **•fishes**)
**ar•chery**
**ar•che•spore** (*or* **•spo•rium**; *plural* **•spores** *or* **•spo•ria**) spore-making cell
**ar•che•spo•rial**
**ar•che•typ•al** (*or* **•typi•cal**)
**ar•che•typ•al•ly** (*or* **•typi•cal•ly**)
**ar•che•type**
**arch•fiend**
**archi•carp** fungal structure
**archi•di•aco•nal**
**archi•di•aco•nate**
**archi•epis•co•pal**
**archi•epis•co•pate** (*or* **•co•pa•cy**)
**ar•chil** *variant spelling of* **orchil**
**archi•mage** great magician
**archi•man•drite** head of Orthodox monastery
**Archi•medean**
**archi•pelag•ic** (*or* **•pe•lagian**)
**archi•pela•go** (*plural* **•gos** *or* **•goes**)
**archi•tect**
**archi•tec•ton•ic**
**archi•tec•toni•cal•ly**
**archi•tec•ton•ics**
**archi•tec•tur•al**
**archi•tec•tur•al•ly**
**archi•tec•ture**
**archi•trave** moulding
**ar•chiv•al**
**ar•chive**
**archi•vist**
**archi•volt** moulding around arch
**arch•ness**
**ar•cho•plasm** (*or* **archi•**) type of protoplasm

**ar•cho•plas•mic**
**arch•priest**
**arch•way**
**arco•graph** geometric instrument
**Arc•tic** North Pole region
**arc•tic** very cold
**Arc•to•gaea** (*US* **•gea**) zoogeographical area
**Arc•to•gaean** (*US* **•gean**)
**Arc•tu•rian**
**Arc•tu•rus** star
**ar•cu•ate** arc-shaped
**ar•cua•tion**
**ar•deb** unit of measure
**Ar•dèche** French department
**Arden (Forest of)**
**ar•den•cy**
**Ar•dennes** W European hills
**ar•dent**
**ar•dour** (*US* **•dor**)
**ar•du•ous**
**ar•du•ous•ness**
**are**
**area**
**areal**
**area•way** passageway
**ar•eca** palm tree
**arena**
**ar•ena•ceous** geology term
**ar•enico•lous** living in sandy places
**ar•enite** sandstone
**ar•enit•ic**
**aren't** are not
**ar•eog•ra•phy** description of Mars
**areo•la** (*plural* **•lae** *or* **•las**)
**areo•lar** (*or* **•late**)
**areo•la•tion**
**Arequi•pa** Peruvian city
**Ares** Greek god
**arête** mountain ridge
**ar•ethu•sa** plant
**Arez•zo** Italian city
**ar•ga•li** (*or* **ar•gal**; *plural* **•ga•li** *or* **•gals**) wild sheep
**ar•gent** silver
**Ar•gen•teuil** Parisian suburb
**ar•gen•tic**
**ar•gen•tif•er•ous**
**Ar•gen•ti•na**
**Ar•gen•tine** of Argentina
**ar•gen•tine** of silver
**Ar•gen•tin•ean**
**ar•gen•tite** mineral
**ar•gen•tous**
**ar•gil** potter's clay
**ar•gil•la•ceous**
**ar•gil•lif•er•ous**
**ar•gil•lite** rock
**ar•gil•lit•ic**
**ar•gi•nine** amino acid
**Argo** Jason's ship; constellation
**ar•gol** deposit in wine vats
**Ar•go•lis** region of ancient Greece
**ar•gon** chemical element
**Ar•go•naut**
**Ar•gonne** French region
**ar•go•non** gas
**Ar•gos** ancient Greek city
**ar•go•sy** (*plural* **•sies**) large merchant ship
**ar•got**
**ar•got•ic**
**ar•gu•able**
**ar•gu•ably**
**ar•gue** (**•gu•ing, •gued**)
**ar•gu•er**
**ar•gu•fy** (**•fies, •fy•ing, •fied**)
**ar•gu•ment**
**ar•gu•men•ta•tion**
**ar•gu•men•ta•tive**
**ar•gu•men•ta•tive•ness**
**ar•gu•men•tum** (*plural* **•ta**) *Latin* argument
**Argus** mythological giant
**argy-bargy** (*plural* **-bargies**)
**ar•gyle** fabric
**Ar•gyll** (*or* **•gyll•shire**) former Scottish county
**År•hus** *variant spelling of* **Aarhus**
**aria**
**Arian** follower of Arianism; *compare* **Aryan**
**Ari•an•ism** heretical doctrine
**arid**
**arid•ity** (*or* **ar•id•ness**)
**Ariège** French department
**Ari•el** satellite of Uranus
**ari•el** gazelle; *compare* **aerial**
**Aries** constellation; sign of the zodiac
**ari•et•ta** (*plural* **•et•tas, •et•te** *or* **•ettes**) short aria
**aright**
**aril** botany term
**ar•il•late**
**ar•il•lode**
**Ari•ma•thea** Palestinian town
**ario•so** musical term
**arise** (**aris•ing, arose, aris•en**)
**aris•ta** (*plural* **•tae**) bristle
**Ar•is•tar•chus** moon crater
**aris•tate**
**ar•is•toc•ra•cy** (*plural* **•cies**)
**aris•to•crat**
**aris•to•crat•ic**
**aris•to•crati•cal•ly**
**Ar•is•to•telian**
**arith•me•tic** (*noun*)
**arith•met•ic** (*or* **•meti•cal**; *adj*)
**arith•meti•cal•ly**
**arith•meti•cian**
**Ari•zo•na**
**ark** Noah's boat; *compare* **arc**
**Ar•kan•sas**
**ar•kose** sandstone
**Ar•ling•ton** US county
**arm**
**ar•ma•da**
**ar•ma•dil•lo** (*plural* **•los**)
**Ar•ma•ged•don**
**Ar•magh**
**Ar•ma•gnac** French brandy
**ar•ma•ment**
**ar•ma•men•tar•ium** (*plural* **•tar•iums** *or* **•taria**) doctor's equipment
**ar•ma•ture** moving electrical part
**arm•band**
**arm•chair**
**Arm•co** (*Trademark*) safety barrier
**armed**
**Ar•me•nia**
**Ar•me•nian**
**Ar•men•tières** French town
**ar•met** medieval helmet
**arm•ful**
**arm•hole**
**ar•mi•ger** heraldic term
**ar•mil•lary** of bracelets
**arm•ing**

**Ar•mini•an**
**Ar•mini•an•ism** Protestant doctrine
**ar•mipo•tence**
**ar•mipo•tent** strong in battle
**ar•mi•stice**
**arm•less**
**arm•let**
**ar•moire** cabinet
**ar•mo•ri•al**
**ar•mour** (*US* **•mor**)
**ar•moured** (*US* **•mored**)
**ar•mour•er** (*US* **•mor•**)
**ar•moury** (*US* **•mory**; *plural* **•mouries**, *US* **•mories**)
**arm•pit**
**arm•rest**
**arms**
**ar•mure** fabric
**army** (*plural* **armies**)
**Arn•hem** Dutch city
**ar•ni•ca** plant
**Arno** Italian river
**ar•oid** botany term
**aro•ma**
**aro•mat•ic**
**aro•mati•cal•ly**
**aro•ma•tic•ity**
**aro•ma•ti•za•tion** (*or* **•sa•tion**)
**aro•ma•tize** (*or* **•tise**)
**arose**
**around**
**arous•al**
**arouse**
**arous•er**
**ar•peg•gio** (*plural* **•gios**)
**ar•que•bus** (*or* **har•**) early musket
**ar•rack** (*or* **arak**) alcoholic spirit
**ar•raign**
**ar•raign•er**
**ar•raign•ment** legal term
**Ar•ran** Scottish island; *compare* **Aran**
**ar•range**
**ar•range•able**
**ar•range•ment**
**ar•rang•er**
**ar•rant**
**Ar•ras** French town
**ar•ras** hanging tapestry; *compare* **arris**
**ar•ray**
**ar•ray•al**
**ar•rears**
**ar•rest**
**ar•rest•able**
**ar•rest•er**
**ar•rest•ing**
**ar•rest•ing•ly**
**ar•rhyth•mia** abnormal heartbeat
**arrière-pensée** (*plural* **arrière-pensées**) *French* mental reservation
**Ar Ri•mal** Arabian desert
**ar•ris** (*plural* **•ris** *or* **•rises**) sharp edge; *compare* **arras**
**ar•ri•val**
**ar•rive**
**ar•riv•er**
**ar•ri•viste** ambitious person
**ar•ro•ba** unit of weight
**ar•ro•gance**
**ar•ro•gant**
**ar•ro•gate** claim without justification
**ar•ro•ga•tion**
**ar•roga•tive**
**ar•ro•ga•tor**
**ar•ron•disse•ment** French district
**ar•row**
**arrow•head**
**arrow•root**
**arrow•wood**
**arrow•worm**
**arro•yo** *US* gully
**ars antiqua** 13th-century music style; *compare* **ars nova**
**arse**
**ar•senal**
**ar•senate**
**ar•senic**
**ar•seni•cal**
**ar•senide**
**ar•seni•ous** (*or* **•sen•ous**)
**ar•senite**
**ar•seno•py•rite** mineral
**ar•sine** chemical compound
**ar•sis** (*plural* **•ses**) prosody term
**ars nova** 14th-century music style; *compare* **ars antiqua**
**ar•son**
**ars•phena•mine** drug
**arsy-versy** *Slang* backwards
**art**
**Art Deco** 1920–40 art style; *compare* **Art Nouveau**
**ar•te•fact** (*or* **•ti•**)
**ar•tel** cooperative in the former Soviet Union
**Artemis** Greek goddess
**ar•te•mi•sia** plant
**ar•te•rial**
**ar•te•ri•ali•za•tion** (*or* **•sa•tion**)
**ar•te•ri•al•ize** (*or* **•ise**)
**ar•te•ri•ole** subdivision of artery
**ar•te•rio•sclero•sis**
**ar•te•rio•sclerot•ic**
**ar•te•rio•venous**
**ar•te•ri•tis**
**ar•tery** (*plural* **•teries**)
**ar•te•sian**
**art•ful**
**art•ful•ly**
**art•ful•ness**
**ar•thral•gia** joint pain
**ar•thral•gic**
**ar•thrit•ic**
**ar•thri•tis**
**arthro•mere** zoology term
**arthro•mer•ic**
**arthro•pod**
**ar•thropo•dous** (*or* **•dal**)
**arthro•spore**
**ar•thro•spor•ic** (*or* **•ous**)
**Ar•thu•rian**
**ar•ti•choke**
**ar•ti•cle**
**ar•ticu•lar**
**ar•ticu•late**
**ar•ticu•late•ness** (*or* **•la•cy**)
**ar•ticu•la•tion**
**ar•ticu•la•tor**
**ar•ticu•la•tory**
**ar•ti•fact** *variant spelling of* **artefact**
**ar•ti•fice**
**ar•tifi•cer**
**ar•ti•fi•cial**
**ar•ti•fi•ci•al•ity**
**ar•til•lery**
**ar•tillery•man** (*plural* **•men**)
**arti•ness**
**ar•tio•dac•tyl** zoology term
**ar•tio•dac•ty•lous**

**ar•ti•san**
**art•ist** person skilled in art, etc.
**ar•tiste** entertainer
**ar•tis•tic**
**ar•tis•ti•cal•ly**
**art•ist•ry**
**art•less**
**art•less•ness**
**Art Nouveau** 1890–1910 art style; *compare* **Art Deco**
**Ar•tois** former French province
**art•work**
**arty** (**arti•er, arti•est**)
**Aru•ba** West Indian island
**arum**
**Aru•na•chal Pra•desh** Indian state
**Ar•un•del**
**arun•di•na•ceous** resembling a reed
**Aru•wi•mi** river in the Democratic Republic of Congo
**Aryan** (*or* **Arian**) non-Jewish Caucasian; *compare* **Arian**
**Ary•an•ize** (*or* **•ise**)
**aryl** chemistry term
**ary•te•noid** (*or* **•tae•**) anatomy term
**ary•te•noid•al**
**as**
**asa•foeti•da** (*or esp. US* **•feti•**) resin
**Asan•te•he•ne** Ghanaian ruler
**asa•ra•bac•ca** plant
**asa•rum** dried ginger root
**as•bes•tos** (*US also* **•tus**)
**as•bes•to•sis**
**as•ca•ria•sis**
**as•ca•rid** parasitic worm
**as•cend**
**as•cend•ancy** (*or* **•ency, •ance, •ence**)
**as•cend•ant** (*or* **•ent**)
**as•cend•er**
**As•cen•sion** Christian feast; S Atlantic island
**as•cen•sion**
**as•cen•sion•al**
**As•cen•sion•tide**
**as•cent** upward movement; *compare* **assent**
**as•cer•tain**
**as•cer•tain•able**
**as•cer•tain•ment**
**as•cesis** (*plural* **•ceses**) self-discipline
**as•cet•ic**
**as•ceti•cal•ly**
**as•ceti•cism**
**asci** *plural of* **ascus**
**Ascii** computer language
**as•cid•ian** marine animal
**as•cid•ium** (*plural* **•cidia**) botany term
**as•ci•tes** medical term
**as•cit•ic**
**as•cle•pia•da•ceous** botany term
**Asclepius** Greek god
**as•co•carp** part of a fungus
**as•co•go•nium** (*plural* **•nia**) fungal reproductive body
**as•co•my•cete** fungus
**as•co•my•cetous**
**ascor•bic acid**
**as•co•spore**
**As•cot** Berkshire town; racecourse
**as•cot** cravat
**as•crib•able**
**as•cribe**
**as•crip•tion** (*or* **ad•scrip•**)
**as•cus** (*plural* **asci**) fungal part
**as•dic** echo sounder
**ase•ity** philosophy term
**asep•al•ous**
**asep•sis**
**asep•tic**
**asexu•al**
**asexu•al•ity**
**asexu•al•ly**
**As•gard** home of Norse gods
**ash**
**ashamed**
**asham•ed•ly**
**Ashan•ti** Ghanaian region
**ash•en**
**Ashes** cricket trophy
**ashet** *Dialect* dish
**Ash•ga•bat** *variant spelling of* **Ashkhabad**
**Ash•ke•na•zi** (*plural* **•zim**) Jew of E European descent
**ash•key**
**Ash•kha•bad** capital of Turkmenistan
**ash•lar** (*or* **•ler**)
**ash•lar•ing** building material
**ashore**
**(ashphalt)** *incorrect spelling of* **asphalt**
**ash•plant**
**ash•ram** Hindu religious retreat
**Ashtoreth** biblical character
**ash•tray**
**ashy** (**ashi•er, ashi•est**)
**Asia**
**Asian**
**Asi•at•ic**
**aside**
**asi•nine**
**asi•nin•ity**
**Asir** Saudi Arabian region
**ask**
**askance** (*or* **askant**)
**ask•er**
**askew**
**aslant**
**asleep**
**As•ma•ra** capital of Eritrea
**Asmodeus** Jewish demon
**As•nières** Parisian suburb
**aso•cial**
**aso•cial•ly**
**asp**
**as•para•gine** amino acid
**as•para•gus**
**as•par•tic acid**
**as•pect**
**as•pec•tual** linguistics term
**as•pen**
**as•per** Turkish coin
**as•per•gil•lo•sis** (*plural* **•ses**)
**as•per•gil•lus** (*plural* **•li**) fungus
**as•per•ity** (*plural* **•ities**)
**as•perse**
**as•pers•er**
**as•per•sion**
**as•per•sive**
**as•per•so•rium** (*plural* **•ria**) basin for holy water
**as•phalt**
**as•phal•tic**
**as•phal•tite**
**as•phal•tum**
**as•pho•del** plant

**as•phyxia**
**as•phyx•ial**
**as•phyxi•ant**
**as•phyxi•ate**
**as•phyxia•tion**
**as•phyxia•tor**
**as•pic**
**as•pi•dis•tra**
**as•pir•ant**
**as•pi•rate**
**as•pi•ra•tion**
**as•pi•ra•tor**
**as•pira•tory**
**as•pire**
**as•pir•er**
**as•pi•rin** (*plural* **•rin** *or* **•rins**)
**as•pir•ing**
**(asprin)** *incorrect spelling of* **aspirin**
**asquint**
**ass**
**as•sai** musical term; palm tree
**as•sail**
**assail•able**
**as•sail•ant**
**as•sail•er**
**assail•ment**
**As•sam** Indian state
**As•sa•mese** (*plural* **•mese**)
**as•sas•sin**
**as•sas•si•nate**
**as•sas•si•na•tion**
**as•sault**
**as•sault•er**
**as•say** test; *compare* **essay**
**as•say•able**
**as•say•er**
**as•se•gai** (*or* **•sa•**; *plural* **•gais**) spear
**as•sem•blage**
**as•sem•ble**
**as•sem•bler**
**as•sem•bly** (*plural* **•blies**)
**as•sembly•man** (*plural* **•men**)
**as•sent** consent; *compare* **ascent**
**as•sen•ta•tion** servile agreement
**as•sen•tient** approving
**as•sen•tor**
**as•sert**
**as•sert•er** (*or* **•ser•tor**)
**as•sert•ible**
**as•ser•tion**
**as•ser•tive**
**as•ser•tive•ness**
**as•sess**
**as•sess•able**
**as•sess•ment**
**as•ses•sor**
**as•ses•so•rial**
**as•set**
**asset-stripper**
**asset-stripping**
**as•sev•er•ate** declare emphatically
**as•sev•era•tion**
**as•sibi•late** phonetics term
**as•sibi•la•tion**
**as•si•du•ity** (*plural* **•ities**)
**as•sidu•ous**
**as•sidu•ous•ness**
**as•sign**
**as•sign•abil•ity**
**as•sign•able**
**as•sig•nat** former French currency
**as•sig•na•tion**
**as•signee** legal term
**as•sign•er**
**as•sign•ment**
**as•sign•or** legal term
**as•simi•lable**
**as•simi•late**
**as•simi•la•tion**
**as•simi•la•tive** (*or* **•tory**)
**As•sini•boine** Canadian river
**as•sist**
**as•sis•tance**
**as•sis•tant**
**as•sist•er**
**as•size**
**as•sizes**
**as•so•ci•able**
**as•so•ci•ate**
**as•so•cia•tion**
**as•so•cia•tion•ism** psychology term
**as•so•cia•tive**
**as•so•nance** grammar term
**as•so•nant**
**as•so•nan•tal**
**as•sort**
**as•sorta•tive** (*or* **•sort•ive**)
**as•sort•ed**
**as•sort•er**
**as•sort•ment**
**as•suage**
**as•suage•ment**
**as•suag•er**
**as•sua•sive**
**as•sum•able**
**as•sume**
**as•sumed**
**as•sum•er**
**as•sum•ing**
**As•sump•tion** Christian feast
**as•sump•tion**
**as•sump•tive**
**Assur** Assyrian god
**as•sur•able**
**as•sur•ance** *note* **life assurance**; *compare* **insurance**
**as•sure**
**as•sured**
**as•sur•ed•ly**
**as•sur•ed•ness**
**as•sur•er**
**as•sur•gent** curving upwards
**(assymetric)** *incorrect spelling of* **asymmetric**
**(assymptote)** *incorrect spelling of* **asymptote**
**As•syria**
**As•syr•ian**
**As•syri•olo•gist**
**As•syri•ol•ogy**
**As•ta•na** Kazakh capital
**Astarte** Phoenician goddess
**astat•ic** unstable
**astati•cal•ly**
**astati•cism**
**as•ta•tine** chemical element
**as•ter**
**as•te•ri•at•ed** crystallography term
**as•ter•isk**
**as•ter•ism**
**astern**
**aster•nal** anatomy term
**as•ter•oid**
**as•teroi•dal**
**as•the•nia** (*or* **•ny**)
**as•then•ic** weak
**as•the•no•pia** eyestrain
**as•the•nop•ic**
**as•theno•sphere** layer of atmosphere
**asth•ma**
**asth•mat•ic**

**asthmati•cal•ly**
**Asti** Italian town
**as•tig•mat•ic**
**as•tig•mati•cal•ly**
**astig•ma•tism** (*or* **astig•mia**)
**astil•be** plant
**astir**
**Asti Spumante** wine
**As•to•lat** Arthurian town
**astoma•tous** biology term
**aston•ish**
**aston•ish•ing**
**aston•ish•ing•ly**
**aston•ish•ment**
**As•to•ria** US port
**astound**
**astound•ed**
**astound•ing**
**astound•ing•ly**
**astrad•dle**
**as•tra•gal** architectural moulding
**astraga•lus** anklebone
**As•tra•khan** Russian city
**as•tra•khan** fur
**as•tral**
**as•tra•pho•bia** (*or* **•tro•**) fear of thunderstorms
**as•tra•pho•bic** (*or* **•tro•**)
**astray**
**astride**
**as•trin•gen•cy** (*or* **•gence**)
**as•trin•gent**
**as•tro•bi•ol•ogy**
**as•tro•bota•ny**
**as•tro•com•pass**
**as•tro•cyte** cytology term
**as•tro•dome**
**as•tro•dy•nam•ics**
**as•tro•geol•ogy**
**as•troid** maths term
**as•tro•labe** astronomers' instrument
**as•trolo•ger** (*or* **•gist**)
**as•tro•logi•cal**
**as•tro•logi•cal•ly**
**as•trol•ogy**
**as•tro•met•ric** (*or* **•ri•cal**)
**as•trom•etry** branch of astronomy
**as•tro•naut**
**as•tro•nau•tic** (*or* **•ti•cal**)
**as•tro•nau•ti•cal•ly**
**as•tro•nau•tics**
**as•tro•navi•ga•tion**
**as•tro•navi•ga•tor**
**as•trono•mer**
**as•tro•nomi•cal** (*or* **•nom•ic**)
**as•tro•nomi•cal•ly**
**as•trono•my**
**as•tro•photo•graph•ic**
**as•tro•pho•tog•ra•phy**
**as•tro•physi•cal**
**as•tro•physi•cist**
**as•tro•phys•ics**
**as•tro•sphere** cytology term
**As•tu•ri•as** former Spanish kingdom
**as•tute**
**as•tute•ness**
**Astyanax** mythological character
**asty•lar** architectural term
**Asun•ción** Paraguayan capital
**asun•der**
**As•wan** Egyptian city
**aswarm**
**asyl•lab•ic**
**asy•lum**
**asym•met•ric** (*or* **•ri•cal**)
**asym•met•ri•cal•ly**
**asym•me•try**
**asymp•to•mat•ic**
**asymp•to•mati•cal•ly**
**as•ymp•tote** geometry term
**as•ymp•tot•ic** (*or* **•toti•cal**)
**as•ymp•toti•cal•ly**
**asyn•chro•nism**
**asyn•chro•nous**
**as•yn•det•ic**
**as•yn•deti•cal•ly**
**asyn•de•ton** (*plural* **•deta**) grammar term
**Asyut** (*or* **As•siut**) Egyptian city
**at**
**atac•tic** chemistry term
**Atalanta** mythological character; *compare* **Atlanta**
**ata•man** (*plural* **•mans**) Cossack leader
**ata•rac•tic** (*or* **•rax•ic**)
**ata•raxia** (*or* **•raxy**) peace of mind
**ata•vism**
**ata•vist**
**ata•vis•tic** (*or* **•vic**)
**ata•vis•ti•cal•ly**
**ataxia** (*or* **ataxy**) lack of muscular coordination
**atax•ic** (*or* **atac•tic**)
**At•ba•ra** Sudanese town
**Ate** Greek goddess
**ate**
**at•elec•ta•sis** lung collapse
**at•el•ier** *French* workshop
**Atha•bas•ka** Canadian lake
**athe•ism**
**athe•ist**
**athe•is•tic** (*or* **•ti•cal**)
**athe•is•ti•cal•ly**
**ath•el•ing** Anglo-Saxon prince
**ath•emat•ic** musical term
**Athena** Greek goddess
**Ath•enaeum**
**ath•enaeum** (*US also* **ath•eneum**) institution of learning
**Athe•nian**
**Ath•ens**
**ather•man•cy**
**ather•ma•nous** opaque to radiant heat
**ath•ero•ma** (*plural* **•mas** *or* **•ma•ta**)
**ath•er•oma•tous**
**ath•ero•scle•ro•sis** (*plural* **•ses**)
**ath•ero•scle•rot•ic**
**athirst**
**ath•lete**
**ath•let•ic**
**ath•leti•cal•ly**
**ath•leti•cism**
**ath•let•ics**
**atho•dyd** ramjet
**at-home** social gathering
**athwart**
**athwart•ships**
**atilt**
**At•lan•ta** US city; *compare* **Atalanta**
**At•lan•tean**
**at•lan•tes** architectural term
**At•lan•tic**
**At•lan•tis** legendary continent
**At•las** mountain range
**at•las**
**Atli** legendary king
**at•man** Hindu self
**at•moly•sis** (*plural* **•ses**)

**at•mom•eter**
**at•mom•etry**
**at•mos•phere**
**at•mos•pher•ic** (*or* **•pheri•cal**)
**at•mos•pheri•cal•ly**
**at•mos•pher•ics**
**at•oll**
**atom**
**atom•ic**
**atomi•cal•ly**
**ato•mic•ity**
**at•om•ism**
**at•om•ist**
**at•om•is•tic** (*or* **•ti•cal**)
**at•om•is•ti•cal•ly**
**at•omi•za•tion** (*or* **•sa•tion**)
**at•om•ize** (*or* **•ise**)
**at•om•iz•er** (*or* **•is•er**)
**aton•able** (*or* **atone•**)
**aton•al** musical term
**aton•al•ism**
**ato•nal•ity**
**ato•nal•ly**
**atone**
**atone•able** *variant spelling of* atonable
**atone•ment**
**aton•er**
**aton•ic**
**ato•nic•ity**
**ato•ny**
**atop**
**atrial**
**atrio•ven•tricu•lar**
**atrip** nautical term
**atrium** (*plural* **atria**)
**atro•cious**
**atro•cious•ness**
**atroc•ity** (*plural* **•ities**)
**atroph•ic**
**at•ro•phy** (*noun, plural* **•phies**; *verb* **•phies, •phy•ing, •phied**)
**at•ro•pine** (*or* **•pin**) alkaloid
**atta•boy**
**at•tach**
**at•tach•able**
**at•ta•ché** diplomat
**at•tach•er**
**at•tach•ment**
**at•tack**
**at•tack•er**
**at•tain**
**at•tain•abil•ity** (*or* **•able•ness**)
**at•tain•able**
**at•tain•der** legal term
**at•tain•ment**
**at•taint**
**at•tar** (*or* **ot•**) essential oil
**(attatchment)** *incorrect spelling of* **attachment**
**at•tempt**
**at•tempt•able**
**at•tempt•er**
**at•tend**
**at•tend•ance**
**at•tend•ant**
**at•tend•er**
**at•ten•tion**
**at•ten•tive**
**at•ten•tive•ness**
**at•tenu•ant**
**at•tenu•ate**
**at•tenua•tion**
**at•tenua•tor** physics term
**at•test**
**at•test•able**
**at•test•ant** (*or* **•test•er**)
**at•tes•ta•tion**
**at•test•or** (*or* **•test•ta•tor**) legal term
**At•tic** of Attica
**at•tic**
**At•ti•ca** Greek region
**at•ti•cism** clear expression
**at•tire**
**at•ti•tude**
**at•ti•tu•di•nal**
**at•ti•tu•di•nize** (*or* **•nise**)
**at•ti•tu•di•niz•er** (*or* **•nis•er**)
**at•torn**
**at•tor•ney**
**at•torn•ment**
**at•tract**
**at•tract•able**
**at•tract•ant**
**at•trac•tion**
**at•trac•tive**
**at•trac•tive•ness**
**at•trac•tor** (*or* **•tract•er**)
**at•trib•ut•able**
**at•trib•ute**
**at•trib•ut•er** (*or* **•tribu•tor**)
**at•tribu•tion**
**at•tribu•tive**
**at•tri•tion**
**at•tri•tion•al**
**at•tri•tive**
**Attu** island off Alaska
**at•tune**
**atypi•cal**
**atypi•cal•ly**
**aubade** ode
**Aube** French river
**auberge** *French* inn
**auber•gine**
**Auber•vil•liers** Parisian suburb
**aubrie•tia** (*or* **aubre•**) plant
**au•burn**
**Aubus•son** French town
**Auck•land** New Zealand city; S Pacific islands
**au cou•rant** *French* up-to-date
**auc•tion**
**auc•tion•eer**
**auc•to•rial** of an author
**auda•cious**
**auda•cious•ness**
**audac•ity** (*plural* **•ities**)
**Aude** French department
**audibil•ity** (*or* **audible•ness**)
**audible**
**audi•ence**
**audile** psychology term
**audio**
**audio•gen•ic**
**audio•logi•cal**
**audi•olo•gist**
**audi•ol•ogy**
**audi•om•eter**
**audio•met•ric**
**audio•met•ri•cal•ly**
**audi•om•etrist**
**audi•om•etry**
**audio•phile** hi-fi enthusiast
**audio•typ•ing**
**audio•typist**
**audio•visual**
**audi•phone** hearing aid
**audit**
**audi•tion**
**audi•tor**
**audi•to•rium** (*plural* **•riums** *or* **•ria**)
**audi•tory**
**au fait** *French* well-informed
**au fond** *French* fundamentally
**auf Wie•der•seh•en** *German* goodbye

**Augean** mythological stables; very dirty
**augend** number added
**auger** boring tool; *compare* **augur**
**aught** (*or* **ought**) *Archaic* anything; zero; *compare* **ought**
**augite** mineral
**au•git•ic**
**aug•ment**
**aug•ment•able**
**aug•men•ta•tion**
**aug•menta•tive**
**aug•men•tor** (*or* **•ment•er**)
**Augs•burg** German city
**augur** predict; *compare* **auger**
**augur•al**
**augu•ry** (*plural* **•ries**)
**August** month
**august** imposing
**Au•gus•ta** Sicilian port
**Augus•tan** of Emperor Augustus; literary period
**Augus•tin•ian** of St Augustine
**auk**
**auk•let**
**au lait** *French* with milk
**auld lang syne** *Scot* old times; *compare* **langsyne**
**aulic** of a royal court
**Aulis** ancient Greek town
**aum•bry** *variant spelling of* **ambry**
**au na•tu•rel** *French* nude or raw
**aunt**
**auntie** (*or* **aunty**; *plural* **aunties**)
**au pair**
**aura** (*plural* **auras** *or* **aurae**)
**aural** of the ear; *compare* **oral**
**aural•ly**
**aure•ate** gilded
**aure•ole** (*or* **aureo•la**) halo
**Aureo•my•cin** (*Trademark*) antibiotic
**aure•us** (*plural* **aurei**) Roman coin
**au re•voir**
**auric** chemistry term
**auri•cle** anatomical part
**auricu•la** (*plural* **•lae** *or* **•las**) primrose
**auricu•lar**
**auricu•late** (*or* **•lat•ed**) having ears
**aurif•er•ous**
**Auri•ga** constellation
**Aurig•na•cian** Palaeolithic culture
**aurist** ear specialist
**aurochs** extinct cattle
**Aurora** Roman goddess
**auro•ra** (*plural* **•ras** *or* **•rae**)
**auro•ra aus•tra•lis**
**auro•ra bo•real•is**
**auro•ral**
**aur•ous**
**aurum** gold
**Ausch•witz**
**aus•cul•tate**
**aus•cul•ta•tion**
**aus•cul•ta•tor**
**aus•form•ing** steel heat treatment
**aus•pex** (*plural* **•pices**) Roman soothsayer
**aus•pice** (*plural* **•pices**) omen; guidance
**aus•pi•cious**
**aus•pi•cious•ness**
**aus•ten•ite** metallurgy term
**aus•ten•it•ic**
**aus•tere**
**aus•tere•ness**
**aus•ter•ity** (*plural* **•ities**)
**Aus•ter•litz** battle site
**aus•tral** of the south
**Aus•tral•asia**
**Aus•tral•asian**
**Aus•tralia**
**Aus•tral•ian**
**Aus•tral•ia•na**
**Aus•trali•an•ism**
**Aus•trali•an•ize** (*or* **•ise**)
**Aus•tra•loid**
**aus•tra•lo•pithe•cine** fossil man
**Aus•tra•lo•pithe•cus** genus of fossil men
**Aus•tral•orp** domestic fowl
**Aus•tria**
**Aus•trian**
**Austro-Asiatic**
**Aus•tro•nesia** S Pacific islands
**Aus•tro•nesian**
**auta•coid** body secretion
**autar•chic** (*or* **•chi•cal**)
**autar•chy** (*plural* **•chies**) unrestricted rule; *compare* **autarky**
**autar•kic** (*or* **•ki•cal**, **•chic**, **•chi•cal**)
**autar•ky** (*or* **•chy**; *plural* **•kies** *or* **•chies**) economic self-sufficiency; *compare* **autarchy**
**aut•eco•logi•cal**
**aut•ecol•ogy**
**auteur** film director
**authen•tic**
**authen•ti•cal•ly**
**authen•ti•cate**
**authen•ti•ca•tion**
**au•then•ti•ca•tor**
**au•then•tic•ity**
**author**
**author•ess**
**autho•rial**
**authori•tar•ian**
**authori•tari•an•ism**
**authori•ta•tive**
**authori•ta•tive•ness**
**author•ity** (*plural* **•ities**)
**authori•za•tion** (*or* **•sa•tion**)
**author•ize** (*or* **•ise**)
**author•iz•er** (*or* **•is•er**)
**author•ship**
**autism**
**autis•tic**
**auto** (*plural* **autos**) *Slang* motor car
**auto•anti•body** (*plural* **•bodies**)
**auto•bahn**
**auto•bi•og•ra•pher**
**auto•bio•graphi•cal**
**auto•bi•og•ra•phy** (*plural* **•phies**)
**auto•cade** *US* motorcade
**auto•ca•taly•sis** (*plural* **•ses**) chemistry term
**auto•chang•er** record-changing device
**autoch•thon** (*plural* **•thons** *or* **•tho•nes**) earliest known inhabitant
**autoch•thon•ism** (*or* **•tho•ny**)

**autoch•tho•nous** (*or* **•tho•nal)**
**auto•clave**
**auto•cor•re•la•tion**
**autoc•ra•cy** (*plural* **•cies)**
**auto•crat**
**auto•crat•ic**
**auto•crati•cal•ly**
**auto•cross**
**auto•cue**
**auto-da-fé** (*plural* **autos-da-fé)** ceremony of Spanish Inquisition
**auto•di•dact** self-taught person
**autoe•cious** botany term
**autoe•cism**
**autoga•mous** (*or* **auto•gam•ic)**
**autoga•my** biology term
**auto•gen•esis** (*or* **autog•eny)**
**auto•genet•ic**
**autog•enous**
**auto•gi•ro** (*or* **•gy•**; *plural* **•ros)**
**auto•graft**
**auto•graph**
**auto•graph•ic**
**auto•graphi•cal•ly**
**autog•ra•phy**
**auto•hyp•no•sis**
**auto•hyp•not•ic**
**auto•hyp•noti•cal•ly**
**autoi•cous** botany term
**auto•im•mune**
**auto•im•mun•ity**
**auto•ioni•za•tion** (*or* **•sa•tion)**
**auto•ki•net•ic**
**Autoly•cus** moon crater
**Autolycus** mythological character
**auto•lyse** (*US* **•lyze)**
**auto•ly•sin**
**autoly•sis** self-destruction of cells
**auto•lyt•ic**
**auto•mat**
**automa•ta** *plural of* **automaton**
**auto•mate**
**auto•mat•ic**
**auto•mati•cal•ly**
**auto•ma•tion**
**automa•tism**
**automa•tist**
**automa•tize** (*or* **•tise)**
**automa•ton** (*plural* **•tons** *or* **•ta)**
**automa•tous**
**auto•mo•bile**
**auto•mo•bil•ist**
**auto•mo•tive**
**auto•nom•ic**
**auto•nomi•cal•ly**
**autono•mist**
**autono•mous**
**autono•my** (*plural* **•mies)**
**auto•phyte** botany term
**auto•phyt•ic**
**auto•phyti•cal•ly**
**auto•pi•lot**
**auto•pis•ta** Spanish motorway
**auto•plas•tic**
**auto•plas•ty** transplantation from own body
**autop•sy** (*plural* **•sies)**
**auto•put** Yugoslav motorway
**auto•radio•graph**
**auto•radio•graph•ic**
**auto•ra•di•og•ra•phy**
**auto•ro•ta•tion**
**auto•so•mal**
**auto•some** type of chromosome
**auto•sta•bil•ity**
**auto•stra•da** Italian motorway
**auto•sug•ges•tion**
**auto•sug•ges•tive**
**auto•tim•er**
**auto•tom•ic**
**autoto•mize** (*or* **•mise)**
**autoto•my** (*plural* **•mies)** shedding of body part
**auto•tox•ic**
**auto•tox•in**
**auto•trans•form•er**
**auto•troph•ic** biology term
**auto•type**
**auto•typ•ic**
**auto•typy**
**autoxi•da•tion** chemistry term
**autumn**
**autum•nal**
**autun•ite** mineral
**Auvergne** French region
**auxa•nom•eter**
**aux•esis** biology term
**aux•ilia•ry** (*plural* **•ries)**
**aux•in** hormone
**auxo•chrome** chemistry term
**ava•da•vat** (*or* **ama•)** bird
**avail**
**avail•abil•ity**
**avail•able**
**avail•ably**
**ava•lanche**
**Ava•lon** Arthurian paradise
**avant-garde**
**Avar** former European people
**ava•rice**
**ava•ri•cious**
**avast** nautical interjection
**ava•tar** manifestation of Hindu deity
**ave** *Latin* welcome; farewell
**Ave•bury** Wiltshire village; Neolithic stone circle
**Ave•lla•ne•da** Argentine city
**avenge**
**aveng•er**
**av•ens** (*plural* **•ens)** plant
**Av•en•tine** Roman hill
**aven•tu•rine** (*or* **aven•tu•rin, avan•tu•rine)** dark glass
**av•enue**
**aver** **(aver•ring, averred)**
**av•er•age**
**aver•ment**
**averse**
**aver•sion**
**aver•sive**
**avert**
**avert•ible** (*or* **•able)**
**Aves•ta** Zoroastrian scriptures
**Aves•tan**
**Avey•ron** French department
**avian** of birds
**aviary** (*plural* **aviaries)** place for keeping birds; *compare* **apiary**
**avi•ate**
**avia•tion**
**avia•tor**
**avia•trix** (*or* **•tress)**
**avi•cul•ture** bird-rearing

**avi•cul•tur•ist**
**avid**
**avi•din** a protein
**avid•ity**
**avid•ness**
**Avie•more** Scottish resort
**avi•fau•na**
**avi•fau•nal**
**Avi•gnon** French city
**avi•on•ic**
**avi•on•ics**
**aviru•lent**
**avita•mino•sis** (*plural* **•ses**)
**avi•zan•dum** Scottish legal term
**avo•ca•do** (*plural* **•dos**)
**avo•cet** (*or* **•set**) bird
**avoid**
**avoid•able**
**avoid•ance**
**avoid•er**
**av•oir•du•pois** system of weights
**Avon** English river and former county
**avow**
**avow•able**
**avow•al**
**avowed**
**avow•er**
**avul•sion**
**avun•cu•lar**
**avun•cu•late**
**await**
**awake** (**awak•ing, awoke** *or* **awaked, awok•en** *or* **awaked**)
**awak•en**
**award**
**award•able**
**awardee**
**award•er**
**aware**
**aware•ness**
**awash**
**away**
**awe**
**aweath•er** nautical term
**aweigh**
**awe-inspiring**
**awe•some**
**awe•some•ness**
**awe-stricken** (*or* **awe-struck**)
**aw•ful**
**aw•ful•ly**
**aw•ful•ness**
**awhile**
**awk•ward**
**awk•ward•ness**
**awl**
**awl•wort** plant
**awn** plant bristle
**awn•ing**
**awoke**
**awry**
**axe** (*US* **ax**)
**axel** ice-skating jump; *compare* **axil; axle**
**axen•ic** uncontaminated
**ax•ial**
**axil** angle between leaf and stem; *compare* **axel; axle**
**ax•ile** attached to an axis
**ax•il•la** (*plural* **•lae**) armpit
**ax•il•lary** (*plural* **•laries**) of armpit; feather
**axio•logi•cal**
**axi•olo•gist**
**axi•ol•ogy** study of values
**axi•om**
**axio•mat•ic** (*or* **•mati•cal**)
**axio•mati•cal•ly**
**Axis** Nazi alliance
**axis** (*plural* **axes**)
**axle** mechanical part; *compare* **axel; axil**
**axle•tree** carriage axle
**Ax•min•ster** Devon town; carpet
**axo•lotl** salamander
**axon** part of nerve cell
**ax•seed** plant
**ay** (*or* **aye**) *Archaic* always; *compare* **aye**
**ayah** maid
**aya•huas•ca** plant
**ayatollah**
**Ay•cliffe** English town
**aye** (*or* **ay**) *Archaic or dialect* yes; *compare* **ay**
**aye aye** animal
**Ayles•bury**
**Ay•ma•ra** (*plural* **•ras** *or* **•ra**) South American Indian
**Ayr** Scottish port
**Ayr•shire** cattle
**Ayur•veda** Hindu medical treatise
**Ayut•tha•ya** Thai city
**azalea**
**azan** Islamic call to prayer
**aza•thio•prine** drug
**Az•bine** Saharan region
**azeda•rach** medicinal bark
**azeo•trope** chemistry term
**azeo•trop•ic**
**Azer•bai•jan** Central Asian country; region of Iran
**Azer•bai•ja•ni** (*plural* **•ni** *or* **•nis**)
**az•ide**
**azi•muth** astronomy term
**azi•muth•al**
**az•ine**
**azo•ben•zene**
**azo•ic** without life
**az•ole** chemical compound
**Azores** Atlantic islands
**az•ote** *Obsolete* nitrogen
**azo•tae•mia** (*US* **•te•**) uraemia
**azo•tae•mic** (*US* **•te•**)
**az•oth** mercury
**azot•ic** of nitrogen
**azo•to•bac•ter** bacterium
**Az•tec**
**az•ure**
**az•ur•ite** mineral
**azy•gous**

# B

**Ba** soul in Egyptian mythology
**baa** (**baa•ing, baaed**)
**Baal** Semitic god
**Baal•bek** Lebanese town
**baba** cake
**ba•bas•su** palm tree
**bab•bitt** line with alloy
**Bab•bitt met•al**

**bab•ble**
**bab•bler**
**babe**
**Ba•bel** biblical tower
**ba•biche** rawhide thongs
**babi•ru•sa** wild pig
**ba•boon**
(**babtize**) *incorrect spelling of* **baptize**
**ba•bul** acacia tree
**baby** (*noun, plural* **babies**; *verb* **babies, ba•by•ing, ba•bied**)
**ba•by•hood**
**ba•by•ish**
**Baby•lon** city
**Baby•lo•nia** kingdom
**Baby•lo•nian**
**baby's-breath** (*or* **babies'-**) plant
**baby-sit** (**-sitting, -sat**)
**baby-sitter**
**baby-snatch•er**
**bac•ca•lau•re•ate**
**bac•ca•rat**
**bac•cate** berry-like
**Bac•chae** priestesses of Bacchus
**bac•cha•nal**
**bac•cha•na•lia**
**bac•cha•na•lian**
**bac•chant** (*fem* **•chan•te**; *plural* **•chants** *or* **•chan•tes**, *fem* **•chan•tes**) drunken reveller
**Bac•chic**
**bac•chius** (*plural* **•chii**) metrical foot
**Bacchus** god of wine
**bac•cif•er•ous**
**bac•ci•form**
**bac•civ•or•ous**
**bac•cy** *Slang* tobacco
**bach•elor**
**bachelor's-buttons** plant
**ba•cil•lary** (*or* **•lar**)
**ba•cil•li•form**
**ba•cil•lus** (*plural* **•li**) rod-shaped bacterium
**baci•tra•cin** antibiotic
**back**
**back•ache**
**back•bencher**
**back•bend**
**back•bite** (**•bit•ing, bit, bit•ten** *or* **bit**)
**back•board**
**back•bone**
**back•breaker**
**back•breaking**
**back•chat**
**back•cloth** (*or* **•drop**)
**back•comb**
**back•cross** genetics term
**back•date**
**back•door**
**back•er**
**back•fill** archaeology term
**back•fire**
**back•gam•mon**
**back•ground**
**back•hand**
**back•hand•ed**
**back•handed•ly**
**back•handed•ness**
**back•hand•er**
**back•ing**
**back•lash**
**back•less**
**back•list**
**back•log**
**back•most**
**back-pedal** (**-pedalling, -pedalled**; *US* **-pedaling, -pedaled**)
**back•saw**
**Backs** Cambridge college grounds
**back•scratch•er**
**back•side**
**back•sight**
**back-slapping**
**back•slide** (**•slid•ing, •slid, •slid** *or* **•slid•den**)
**back•slid•er**
**back•space**
**back•spin**
**back•stage**
**back•stairs**
**back•stay** nautical term
**back•stitch**
**back•stop**
**back•street**
**back•stroke**
**back•swept**
**back•track**
**back•up** (*noun*)
**back•veld** South African rural area
**back•ward** (*adj*)
**back•warda•tion** stock exchange term
**back•ward•ness**
**back•wards** (*US* **•ward**; *adv*)
**back•wash**
**back•water**
**back•woods•man** (*plural* **•men**)
**Ba•co•lod** Philippine town
**ba•con**
**ba•con•er** pig
**bac•te•rae•mia** (*US* **•re•**) bacteria in the blood
**bac•te•ria** *plural of* **bacterium**
**bac•te•rial**
**bac•te•ri•cid•al**
**bac•te•ri•cide**
**bac•te•rin** vaccine
**bac•te•rio•logi•cal**
**bac•te•ri•olo•gist**
**bac•te•ri•ol•ogy**
**bac•te•ri•oly•sis** disintegration of bacteria
**bac•te•rio•lyt•ic**
**bac•te•rio•phage** virus that destroys bacteria
**bac•te•rio•phag•ic**
**bac•te•ri•opha•gous**
**bac•te•rio•sta•sis**
**bac•te•rio•stat•ic**
**bac•te•rio•stati•cal•ly**
**bac•te•rium** (*plural* **•ria**)
**bac•ter•oid**
**Bac•tria** ancient Asian country
**Bac•trian**
**ba•cu•li•form** rod-shaped
**bacu•lum** (*plural* **•la** *or* **•lums**)
**bad** (**worse, worst**)
**Ba•da•joz** Spanish city
**Ba•da•lo•na** Spanish port
**bad•der•locks** seaweed
**bad•dy** (*or* **•die**; *plural* **•dies**)
**bade**
**Ba•den** former German state; Swiss spa
**Baden-Baden** German spa
**Baden-Wurttem•berg** German state
**badge**
**badg•er**
**badi•nage**

**bad•lands**
**bad•ly**
**bad•man** (*plural* **•men)**
**bad•min•ton**
**bad•mouth**
**bad•ness**
**Bae•de•ker** travel guidebook
**bael** tree
**Baf•fin** Canadian island and bay
**baf•fle**
**baf•fle•ment**
**baf•fler**
**bag (bag•ging, bagged)**
**Ba•gan•da** (*plural* **•da** *or* **•das)** African people
**ba•gasse** sugar-cane pulp
**baga•telle**
**ba•gel** (*or* **bei•**) bread roll
**bag•gage**
**bag•gi•ly**
**bag•gi•ness**
**bag•ging**
**bag•gy (•gier, •gi•est)**
**bagh** Indian garden
**Bagh•dad** (*or* **Bag•dad)**
**bag•man** (*plural* **•men)**
**bag•pipe**
**ba•guette** (*or* **•guet)**
**bag•wig** 18th-century wig
**bag•worm**
**Ba•hai**
**Ba•ha•ism** religion
**Ba•ha•ist**
**Ba•ha•mas**
**Ba•ha•mian**
**Ba•hia** Brazilian town
**Ba•hía Blan•ca** Argentine port
**Bah•rain** (*or* **•rein)**
**Bah•rai•ni** (*or* **•rei•)**
**baht** Thai currency
**ba•hu•vri•hi** linguistics term
**Bai•kal** Russian lake
**bail** (*noun*) security for prisoner; part of wicket; *compare* **bale**
**bail** (*or* **bale**; *verb*) remove water from boat
**bail•able**
**bailee** legal term
**bail•er** (*or* **bal•**) one who bails water
**bai•ley** castle wall
**Bailey bridge**
**bailie** *Scot* magistrate
**bail•iff**
**baili•wick** legal term
**bail•ment** legal term
**bail•or** legal term
**bails•man** (*plural* **•men)** one who stands bail
**bain•ite** component of steel
**bain-marie** (*plural* **bains-marie)** cooking utensil
**Bai•ram** Muslim festival
**Bai•riki** capital of Kiribati
**bairn**
**bait** enticement; to torment; *compare* **bate**
**baize**
**bake**
**bake•house**
**Ba•ke•lite** (*Trademark*)
**bak•er**
**bak•ery** (*plural* **•eries)**
**Bake•well** English town; tart
**bak•la•va** cake
**bak•sheesh**
**Baku** capital of Azerbaijan
**Bala** Welsh lake
**Balaam** biblical character
**Bala•cla•va** helmet
**Bala•kla•va** (*or* **•cla•**) Ukrainian port
**bala•lai•ka**
**bal•ance**
**bal•ance•able**
**bal•anc•er**
**bal•as** gemstone
**bala•ta** tree
**Ba•la•ton** Hungarian lake
**Bal•boa** Panamanian port
**bal•boa** Panamanian currency
**bal•brig•gan** fabric
**bal•co•nied**
**bal•co•ny** (*plural* **•nies)**
**bald**
**bal•da•chin** brocade
**Balder** Norse god
**bal•der•dash**
**bald•headed**
**bald•ing**
**bald•money** plant
**bald•ness**
**bald•pate**
**bal•dric** sash for sword
**bale** (*noun*) block of hay; *compare* **bail**
**bale** (*verb*) make bales; jump from aircraft; *variant spelling of* **bail**
**Bal•ear•ic Is•lands**
**ba•leen** whalebone
**bale•ful**
**bale•ful•ly**
**bale•ful•ness**
**bal•er** agricultural machine; *variant spelling of* **bailer**
**Bali** Indonesian island
**bali•bun•tal** straw hat
**Ba•lik•pa•pan** Indonesian city
**Ba•li•nese** (*plural* **•nese)**
**balk** (*or* **baulk**) stop short; avoid; timber beam; *compare* **baulk**
**Bal•kan**
**Bal•kani•za•tion** (*or* **•sa•tion)**
**balk•er** (*or* **baulk•)**
**balky** (*or* **baulky; balki•er** *or* **baulki•er, balki•est** *or* **baulki•est)**
**ball**
**bal•lad**
**bal•lade** verse form
**bal•lad•eer**
**bal•lad•ry**
**Bal•la•rat** Australian town
**bal•last**
**bal•le•ri•na**
**bal•let**
**bal•let•ic**
**bal•leto•mane**
**bal•leto•ma•nia**
**ball•flower** architectural ornament
**bal•lis•ta** (*plural* **•tae)** ancient catapult
**bal•lis•tic**
**bal•lis•ti•cal•ly**
**bal•lis•tics**
**bal•locks** *variant spelling of* **bollocks**
**bal•lo•net** gas compartment in balloon
**bal•loon**
**bal•loon•ist**
**bal•lot (•lot•ing, •lot•ed)**
**bal•lotte•ment** medical term

**ball•park**
**ball•point**
**ball•room**
**bal•ly** slang term
**bal•ly•hoo**
**balm**
**bal•ma•caan** overcoat
**balmi•ly**
**balmi•ness**
**Bal•mor•al** Scottish castle; flat cap
**balmy (balmi•er, balmi•est)** soft and soothing; *variant spelling* (*esp. US*) *of* **barmy**
**bal•ne•al**
**bal•neo•logi•cal**
**bal•ne•olo•gist**
**bal•ne•ol•ogy** study of therapeutic baths
**ba•lo•ney** (*or* **bo•**)
**bal•sa** wood
**bal•sam**
**bal•sam•ic**
**bal•sam•if•er•ous**
**bal•sa•mi•na•ceous**
**Balt** person from Baltic States
**Bal•tic**
**Bal•ti•more**
**Ba•lu•chi** (*or* **•lo•**; *plural* **•chis** *or* **•chi**) Muslim people
**Ba•lu•chi•stan** region of Asia
**bal•us•ter**
**bal•us•trade**
**Ba•ma•ko** capital of Mali
**Bam•ba•ra** (*plural* **•ra** *or* **•ras**) African people
**Bam•berg** German town
**bam•bi•no** (*plural* **•nos** *or* **•ni**)
**bam•boo** (*plural* **•boos**)
**bam•boo•zle**
**bam•boo•zle•ment**
**bam•boo•zler**
**ban (ban•ning, banned)**
**ba•nal**
**ba•nal•ity**
**ba•na•na**
**Ban•at** plain in E Europe
**ba•nau•sic** utilitarian
**Ban•bury**
**banc** legal term
**band**
**band•age**
**ban•dan•na** (*or* **ban•dana**)
**Ban•dar Seri Beg•a•wan** capital of Brunei
**band•box**
**ban•deau** (*plural* **•deaux**) headband
**ban•de•ril•la** bullfighter's dart
**ban•de•ril•lero** (*plural* **•leros**) bullfighter's assistant
**ban•de•role** (*or* **•de•rol, •ne•rol**) flag
**ban•di•coot**
**ban•dit** (*plural* **•dits** *or* **•dit•ti**)
**ban•dit•ry**
**Band•jar•ma•sin** (*or* **Ban•jer•ma•sin**) Indonesian port
**band•master**
**ban•do•leer** (*or* **•lier**) shoulder belt
**ban•do•line** hairdressing substance
**ban•dora** (*or* **pan•**) musical instrument
**bands•man** (*plural* **•men**)
**band•spreading** radio tuning control
**band•stand**
**Ban•dung** Indonesian city
**band•wagon**
**band•width**
**ban•dy** (*adj* **•di•er, •di•est**; *verb* **•dies, •dy•ing, •died**)
**bandy-bandy** (*plural* **-bandies**) snake
**bane**
**bane•berry** (*plural* **•berries**)
**bane•ful**
**Banff** former Scottish county; Canadian town
**bang**
**Ban•ga•lore** Indian city
**bang•er**
**Bang•ka** Indonesian island
**Bang•kok**
**Bang•la•desh**
**Bang•la•deshi**
**ban•gle**
**Bangor** Welsh or Northern Irish town
**Ban•gui** capital of Central African Republic
**ban•ish**
**ban•ish•ment**
**ban•is•ter**
**ban•jo** (*plural* **•jos** *or* **•joes**)
**ban•jo•ist**
**Ban•jul** Gambian capital
**bank**
**bank•able**
**bank•book**
**bank•er**
**bank•et** gold-bearing rock
**bank•ing**
**bank•roll**
**bank•rupt**
**bank•rupt•cy** (*plural* **•cies**)
**bank•sia** shrub
**banned**
**ban•ner**
**ban•ner•ette**
**ban•ning**
**(bannister)** *incorect spelling of* **banister**
**ban•nock** Scottish cake
**Ban•nock•burn** Scottish battle site
**banns** (*or* **bans**) of marriage
**ban•quet** feast
**ban•quette** seat
**ban•shee**
**bant** *Dialect* string
**ban•tam**
**bantam•weight**
**ban•ter**
**ban•ter•er**
**Ban•toid** language
**Ban•tu** (*plural* **•tu** *or* **•tus**)
**Ban•tu•stan** former South African Bantu homeland
**ban•yan** (*or* **•ian**) tree
**ban•zai** Japanese salutation
**bao•bab** tree
**bap**
**bap•tism**
**bap•tis•mal**
**Bap•tist** member of Christian sect
**bap•tist•ry** (*or* **•tis•tery**; *plural* **•ries** *or* **•teries**)
**bap•tize** (*or* **•tise**)
**bar (bar•ring, barred)**
**Barabbas** biblical character
**bara•thea** fabric
**barb**

**Bar•ba•dian**
**Bar•ba•dos**
**bar•bar•ian**
**bar•bar•ian•ism**
**bar•bar•ic**
**bar•bari•cal•ly**
**bar•bar•ism**
**bar•bar•ity** (*plural* **•ities**)
**bar•ba•rize** (*or* **•rise**)
**bar•ba•rous**
**bar•ba•rous•ness**
**Bar•ba•ry** N African region
**bar•bate**
**bar•becue** (**•becu•ing, •becued**)
**bar•bel** fish; bristle
**bar•bell** weight
**bar•bel•late** covered with bristles
**bar•ber**
**bar•ber•ry** (*plural* **•ries**)
**barber•shop**
**bar•bet** bird
**bar•bette** gun platform
**Bar•bi•can** area of London
**bar•bi•can** fortified place
**bar•bi•cel**
**bar•bi•tone** (*US* **•tal**)
**bar•bi•tu•rate**
**Bar•bour** overcoat
**Bar•bu•da** West Indian island
**bar•bule**
**bar•ca•role** (*or* **•rolle**)
**Bar•ce•lo•na**
**bar•chan** (*or* **•khan, •chane, •kan**) sand dune
**bard**
**bard•ic**
**bar•dola•try**
**bare** uncovered; naked; expose; *compare* **bear**
**bare•back** (*or* **•backed**)
**bare•faced**
**bare•fac•ed•ness**
**bare•foot** (*or* **•footed**)
**bare•handed**
**bare•headed**
**Ba•reil•ly** Indian city
**bare•ly**
**bare•ness**
**Bar•ents** Arctic sea
**bar•gain**
**barge**
**bar•gee**
**barge•pole**
**Bari** Italian port
**bar•ic** of atmospheric pressure
**ba•ril•la** plant extract
**bari•tone**
**bar•ium**
**bark** dog's cry; outer layer of tree; *compare* **barque**
**bark•er**
**Bark•ing and Dag•en•ham** London borough
**bar•ley**
**barley•corn**
**barm** *Dialect* yeast
**bar•maid**
**bar•man** (*plural* **•men**)
**Bar•mecide** (*or* **•mecid•al**) illusory
**bar mitz•vah**
**bar•my** (*or esp. US* **balmy; •mi•er, •mi•est**) *Slang* crazy; *compare* **balmy**
**barn**
**bar•na•cle**
**Bar•na•ul** Russian city
**barn-brack** *Dialect* fruit muffin
**Bar•net** London borough
**bar•ney** *Slang* argument
**barn•storm**
**barn•yard**
**Ba•ro•da** Indian city
**baro•gram**
**baro•graph**
**baro•graphic**
**ba•rom•eter**
**baro•met•ric**
**baro•met•ri•cal•ly**
**bar•on**
**bar•on•age**
**bar•on•ess**
**bar•on•et**
**bar•on•et•age**
**bar•on•et•cy** (*plural* **•cies**)
**ba•rong** Philippine knife
**ba•ro•nial**
**baro•ny** (*plural* **•nies**)
**ba•roque**
**baro•recep•tor**
**baro•scope**
**baro•stat**
**Ba•rot•se** (*plural* **•se** *or* **•ses**) African people
**Ba•rot•se•land** Zambian region
**ba•rouche** horse-drawn carriage
**barque** (*US also* **bark**) boat; *compare* **bark**
**bar•quen•tine** (*or* **•quan•**)
**Bar•qui•si•me•to** Venezuelan city
**bar•rack** (*verb*)
**bar•racks**
**bar•ra•cou•ta** fish
**bar•ra•cu•da** (*plural* **•da** *or* **•das**) fish
**bar•rage**
**bar•ra•mun•da** (*or* **•di**; *plural* **•das, •da**; *or* **•dis, •dies, di**) fish
**bar•ran•ca** *US* ravine
**Bar•ran•quil•la** Colombian port
**bar•ra•tor**
**bar•ra•trous** (*or* **bar•retrous**)
**bar•ra•try** (*or* **bar•retry**) legal term
**bar•ré** music term
**barred**
**bar•rel** (**•rel•ling, •relled**; *US* **•rel•ing, •reled**)
**bar•ren**
**bar•ren•ness**
**bar•rens** *US* barren land
**barren•wort** plant
**bar•ret** cap
**bar•rette** hair clasp
**bar•ri•cade**
**bar•ri•cad•er**
**bar•ri•er**
**bar•ring**
**bar•ris•ter**
**bar•room**
**bar•row**
**Bar•ry** Welsh port
**Bar•sac** wine
**bar•tender**
**bar•ter**
**bar•ter•er**
**bar•ti•zan** small turret
**Bart•lett** pear
**bary•cen•tre** centre of mass
**bar•ye** unit
**bary•on** physics term
**bary•sphere**
**ba•ry•tes** mineral
**bary•ton** bass viol

**ba•sal**
**bas•alt**
**basalt•ware**
**bas•cule** bridge
**base**
**base•ball**
**base•board**
**base•born**
**Ba•sel** (*or* **Basle**) Swiss city
**base•less**
**base•line**
**base•man** (*plural* **•men**) baseball fielder
**base•ment**
**base•ness**
**Ba•sen•ji** dog
**ba•ses** *plural of* **base** *or* **basis**
**bash**
**Ba•shan** biblical region
**bash•ful**
**bash•ful•ly**
**bash•ful•ness**
**bashi•ba•zouk** Turkish soldier
**Bash•kir** (*plural* **•kir** *or* **•kirs**) Mongoloid people
**ba•sic**
**ba•si•cal•ly**
**ba•sic•ity** chemistry term
**ba•sid•ial**
**ba•sidio•my•cete** fungus
**ba•sidio•my•cet•ous**
**ba•sidio•spore**
**ba•sidio•spor•ous**
**ba•sid•ium** (*plural* **•ia**) fungal structure
**basi•fixed** botany term
**basi•fy** (**•fies, •fy•ing, •fied**) make basic
**bas•il** herb
**basi•lar** anatomy term
**basi•lary**
**Ba•sil•don** Essex town
**Ba•sil•ian** Eastern monk
**ba•sil•ic** vein
**ba•sili•ca** Roman building
**ba•sil•i•can** (*or* **•sil•ic**)
**Ba•si•li•ca•ta** Italian region
**basi•lisk** lizard
**ba•sin**
**basi•net** medieval helmet; *compare* **bassinet**
**ba•sin•ful**
**Ba•sing•stoke** Hampshire town
**ba•sion** anatomy term
**ba•sip•etal** botany term
**ba•sis** (*plural* **•ses**)
**bask**
**Baskerville** style of type
**bas•ket**
**basket•ball**
**bas•ket•ry**
**basket-star** starfish
**basket•work**
**Basle** *variant spelling of* **Basel**
**ba•so•phil** (*or* **•phile, •phil•ic**) stained by basic dyes
**Ba•so•tho** (*plural* **•tho** *or* **•thos**) African people
**Basque** Pyrenean people and language
**Bas•ra** (*or* **Bas•rah, Bus•ra, Bus•rah**) Iraqi port
**bas-relief** (*or* **bas•relief**)
**Bas-Rhin** French department
**bass** voice; singer
**bass** (*plural* **bass** *or* **basses**) fish
**Bas•sein** Burmese city
**Bas•sen•thwaite**
**bas•set**
**Basse-Terre** West Indian island
**bas•si•net** cradle; *compare* **basinet**
**bass•ist** double bass player
**bas•so** (*plural* **•sos** *or* **•si**) bass singer
**bas•soon**
**bas•soon•ist**
**bass•wood**
**bast** plant tissue
**bas•tard**
**bas•tardi•za•tion** (*or* **•sa•tion**)
**bas•tard•ize** (*or* **•ise**)
**bas•tard•ry** *Austral* malicious behaviour
**bas•tardy** illegitimacy
**baste**
**Bas•tille** fortress
**bas•ti•na•do** (*noun, plural* **•does**; *verb* **•does, •do•ing, •doed**) torture
**bast•ing**
**bas•ti•on**
**bast•naes•ite** (*or* **•nas•ite**) mineral
**Ba•su•to•land** *former name of* **Lesotho**
**bat** (**bat•ting, bat•ted**)
**Ba•tan•gas** Philippine port
**batch**
**(batchelor)** *incorrect spelling of* **bachelor**
**bate** restrain; *Slang* rage; *compare* **bait**
**ba•teau** boat
**bat•ed**
**bat•fish** (*plural* **•fish** *or* **•fishes**)
**Bath** English city; order of knighthood
**bath** container; wash in bath
**bathe** swim; wash wound, etc.
**bath•er**
**ba•thet•ic**
**bath•house**
**bath•ing**
**batho•lith** (*or* **•lite**) granite mass
**batho•lith•ic** (*or* **•lit•ic**)
**ba•thom•eter**
**batho•met•ric**
**batho•met•ri•cal•ly**
**ba•thom•etry**
**ba•thos**
**bath•robe**
**bath•room**
**bath•tub**
**Bath•urst** Australian city; *former name of* **Banjul**
**bathy•al** of ocean depths
**bathy•met•ric**
**bathy•met•ri•cal•ly**
**ba•thym•etry**
**bathy•scaph** (*or* **•scaphe, •scape**)
**bathy•sphere**
**ba•tik** (*or* **bat•tik**) fabric-printing process
**ba•tiste** fabric
**Bat•ley** West Yorkshire town
**bat•man** (*plural* **•men**)
**ba•ton**
**Bat•on Rouge** US city
**ba•tra•chi•an** amphibian
**bats•man** (*plural* **•men**)
**bats•man•ship**

**batt** quilt wadding
**bat•tal•ion**
**bat•ted**
**bat•ten**
**Bat•ten•burg** cake
**bat•ter**
**bat•ter•er**
**bat•tery** (*plural* **•teries**)
**bat•ting**
**bat•tle**
**battle-axe**
**bat•tle•dore** racket game
**battle•field**
**bat•tle•ment**
**battle•piece**
**bat•tler**
**battle-scarred**
**battle•ship**
**bat•tue** hunting term
**bat•ty** (**•ti•er, •ti•est**)
**Ba•tum** (*or* **Ba•tu•mi**) Georgian city
**bat•wing**
**bat•woman** (*plural* **•women**)
**bau•ble**
**Bau•chi** Nigerian state
**baud** unit of speed; *compare* **bawd**
**Bau•haus** school of arts
**bau•hinia** plant
**baulk** billiards term (*US* **balk**); *variant spelling of* **balk**
**Bau•tzen** German city
**baux•ite**
**Ba•varia**
**Ba•var•ian**
**baw•bee** former Scottish coin
**bawd** brothel keeper; *compare* **baud**
**bawdi•ly**
**bawdi•ness**
**bawd•ry**
**bawdy** (**bawdi•er, bawdi•est**)
**bawdy•house**
**bawl**
**bawl•er**
**bay**
**ba•ya•dere** Hindu dancing girl
**Ba•ya•mon** Puerto Rican city
**bay•berry** (*plural* **•berries**)
**Ba•yeux** French town
**bayo•net** (**•net•ing, •net•ed** *or* **•net•ting, •net•ted**)
**bayou** marshy stream
**bay•wood**
**ba•zaar** (*or* **•zar**)
**ba•zoo** *US* mouth
**ba•zoo•ka**
**bdel•lium** tree
**be**
**beach** shore; *compare* **beech**
**beach•comber**
**beach•head**
**Beach-la-Mar** Pacific language
**bea•con**
**Bea•cons•field** English town
**bead**
**beadi•ly**
**beadi•ness**
**bead•ing**
**bea•dle**
**beady** (**beadi•er, beadi•est**)
**bea•gle**
**beak**
**beaked**
**beak•er**
**beaky**
**beam**
**beam-ends**
**beamy**
**bean**
**bean•bag**
**bean•ery** (*plural* **•eries**) *US* cheap restaurant
**bean•feast**
**beanie** *US* close-fitting hat
**beano** (*plural* **beanos**) *Slang* party
**bean•pole**
**beanstalk**
**bear** (**bear•ing, bore, borne**) support; convey; endure; *compare* **bare**
**bear** (**bear•ing, bore, born**) give birth to
**bear** (*plural* **bears** *or* **bear**) animal
**bear•able**
**bear•ably**
**bear•berry** (*plural* **•berries**)
**beard**
**beard•ed**
**beard•less**
**bear•er**
**bear•ish**
**Bé•ar•naise** sauce
**bear's-breech** (*or* **-breeches**) plant
**bear's-foot** plant
**bear•skin**
**beast**
**beast•ings** *US spelling of* **beestings**
**beast•li•ness**
**beast•ly** (**•lier, •liest**)
**beat** (**beat•ing, beat, beat•en** *or* **beat**)
**beat•able**
**beat•er**
**bea•tif•ic**
**bea•tifi•cal•ly**
**be•ati•fi•ca•tion**
**be•ati•fy** (**•fies, •fy•ing, •fied**)
**be•ati•tude**
**beat•nik**
**beau** (*plural* **beaus** *or* **beaux**)
**Beau•fort** meteorological scale
**beau•jo•lais** (*or* **Beau•**) wine
**beau monde** fashionable society
**Beau•mont** Texan city
**Beaune** French city; wine
**beaut** *Slang* good
**beau•te•ous**
**beau•ti•cian**
**beau•ti•fi•ca•tion**
**beau•ti•ful**
**beau•ti•ful•ly**
**beau•ti•fy** (**•fies, •fy•ing, •fied**)
**beau•ty** (*plural* **•ties**)
**Beau•vais** French town
**beaux-arts** fine art
**bea•ver**
**Beaver•board** (*Trademark*)
**be•bee•rine** alkaloid
**Beb•ing•ton** English town
**be•bop** jazz
**be•calmed**
**be•came**
**be•cause**
**bec•ca•fi•co** (*plural* **•cos**) bird
**bé•cha•mel** sauce
**bêche-de-mer** marine organism

**Bechua•na•land** *former name of* **Botswana**
**beck**
**beck•et** nautical term
**beck•on**
**beck•on•er**
**be•cloud**
**be•come** (**•com•ing, •came, •come**)
**be•com•ing•ly**
**bed** (**bed•ding, bed•ded**)
**be•daub**
**be•daz•zle**
**be•daz•zle•ment**
**bed•bug**
**bed•dable**
**bed•ded**
**bed•der**
**bed•ding**
**be•deck**
**be•dev•il** (**•il•ling, •illed;** *US* **•il•ing, •iled**)
**be•dev•il•ment**
**be•dew**
**bed•fellow**
**Bed•ford**
**Bed•ford•shire**
**be•dim** (**•dim•ming, •dimmed**)
**bed•lam**
**Bed•ling•ton** terrier
**Bedou•in** (*or* **Bedu•in;** *plural* **•ins** *or* **•in**)
**bed•pan**
**bed•plate**
**bed•post**
**be•drag•gle**
**bed•rail**
**bed•rid•den**
**bed•rock**
**bed•roll**
**bed•room**
**bed•side**
**bed•sitter** (*or* **•sit**)
**bed•sore**
**bed•spread**
**bed•stead**
**bed•straw** plant
**bed•time**
**bed•warmer**
**bee**
**bee•bread**
**beech** tree; *compare* **beach**
**beech•nut**
**bee-eater**
**beef** (*plural* **beeves**) cattle
**beef** (*plural* **beefs**) cut of meat; complaint
**beef•bur•ger**
**beef•cake**
**beef•eater**
**beefi•ness**
**beef•steak**
**beef•wood**
**beefy** (**beefi•er, beefi•est**)
**bee•hive**
**bee•keeper**
**bee•line**
**Beelzebub** the Devil
**been**
**beep**
**beep•er**
**beer**
**beeri•ness**
**Beer•she•ba** Israeli town
**beery** (**beeri•er, beeri•est**)
**beest•ings** (*or* **biest•ings;** *US also* **beast•ings**) cow's first milk
**bees•wax**
**bees•wing** crust in port
**beet**
**beet•fly** (*plural* **•flies**)
**bee•tle**
**beet•root**
**bee•zer** *Slang* fellow
**be•fall** (**•fal•ling, •fell, •fall•en**)
**be•fit** (**•fit•ting, •fit•ted**)
**be•fit•ting•ly**
**be•fog** (**•fog•ging, •fogged**)
**be•fool**
**be•fore**
**before•hand**
**be•foul**
**be•foul•er**
**be•foul•ment**
**be•friend**
**be•fud•dle**
**beg** (**beg•ging, begged**)
**be•gan**
**be•get** (**•get•ting, •got** *or* **•gat, •got•ten** *or* **•got**)
**be•get•ter**
**beg•gar**
**beg•gar•li•ness**
**beg•gar•ly**
**beggar•weed**
**beg•gary**
**begged**
**beg•ging**
**be•gin** (**gin•ning, •gan, •gun**)
**be•gin•ner**
**be•gird** surround
**be•gone**
**be•gonia**
**be•gor•ra** Irish exclamation
**be•got**
**be•got•ten**
**be•grime**
**be•grudge**
**be•grudg•ing•ly**
**be•guile** (**•guil•ing, •guiled**)
**be•guile•ment**
**be•guil•er**
**be•guil•ing•ly**
**be•guine** dance
**be•gum** (*or* **•gam**) Muslim woman ruler
**be•gun**
**be•half**
**be•have**
**be•hav•iour** (*US* **•ior**)
**be•hav•iour•al** (*US* **•ior•**)
**be•hav•iour•ism** (*US* **•ior•**)
**be•hav•iour•ist** (*US* **•ior•**)
**be•hav•iour•is•tic** (*US* **•ior•**)
**be•head**
**be•held**
**be•he•moth** biblical monster
**be•hest**
**be•hind**
**behind•hand**
**be•hold** (**•hold•ing, •held**)
**be•hold•en**
**be•hold•er**
**be•hove** (*US* **•hoove**)
**beige**
**bei•gel** *variant spelling of* **bagel**
**Bei•jing** capital of China
**be•ing**
**Bei•ra** Mozambique port
**Bei•rut** (*or* **Bey•routh**) Lebanese capital
**be•jew•el** (**•el•ling, •elled;** *US* **•el•ing, •eled**)
**bel** unit of power
**be•la•bour** (*US* **•bor**)
**be•lah** tree
**Be•la•rus** E European country

**Be•la•rus•sia** *variant spelling of* **Belorussia**
**be•lat•ed**
**be•lat•ed•ness**
**Be•lau** Pacific Ocean country
**be•lay** **(•lay•ing, •layed)** make secure
**belch**
**belch•er**
**be•lea•guer**
**Be•lém** Brazilian port
**be•lem•nite** fossil
**Bel•fast**
**Bel•fort** French department
**bel•fry** **(*plural* •fries)**
**Bel•gae** Celtic people
**Bel•gian**
**Bel•gium**
**Bel•grade** Yugoslav capital
**Bel•gra•via** London district
**Belial** demon
**be•lie** **(•ly•ing, •lied)**
**be•lief**
**be•li•er**
**be•liev•able**
**be•lieve**
**be•liev•er**
**Belisha** traffic beacon
**be•lit•tle**
**be•lit•tle•ment**
**be•lit•tler**
**be•lit•tling•ly**
**Be•lize** Central American state
**bell**
**bel•la•don•na**
**bel•lar•mine** jar
**Bel•la•trix** star
**bell•bird**
**bell•boy**
**belle** beautiful woman
**belle époque** *French* period before World War I
**Bel•leek** porcelain
**Bellerophon** mythological hero
**belles-lettres** *French* literary works
**bel•let•rist**
**bel•let•ris•tic**
**bell•hop**
**bel•li•cose**
**bel•li•cos•ity**
**bel•lig•er•ence**
**bel•lig•er•en•cy**
**bel•lig•er•ent**
**Bellona** Roman goddess
**bel•low**
**bel•low•er**
**bel•lows**
**bell•pull**
**bell•push**
**bell-ringer**
**bell-ringing**
**bell•wether** flock leader
**bell•wort** plant
**bel•ly** **(*noun, plural* •lies; *verb* •lies, •ly•ing, •lied)**
**belly•band** part of harness
**belly•button**
**belly-flop** **(-flopping, -flopped)**
**bel•ly•ful**
**Bel•mo•pan** Belize capital
**Belo Ho•ri•zon•te** Brazilian city
**be•long**
**be•long•ings**
**Be•lo•rus•sia** **(*or* Bye•)** *another name for* **Belarus**
**Be•lo•rus•sian** **(*or* Bye•)**
**be•lov•ed**
**Be•lo•vo** **(*or* Bye•)** Russian city
**be•low**
**Bel Pa•ese** cheese
**Bel•sen** concentration camp
**Belshazzar** biblical character
**belt**
**Bel•tane** Celtic festival
**belt•way** *US* ring road
**be•lu•ga** sturgeon
**bel•vedere** building with view
**bema** Athenian speaker's platform
**Bem•ba** **(*plural* •ba *or* •bas)** African people
**be•mire**
**be•moan**
**be•muse**
**be•mused**
**ben** *Scot* mountain peak
**Bena•dryl** **(*Trademark*)**
**Be•na•res** Indian city
**bench**
**bench•er** a judge
**bend** **(bend•ing, bent)**
**bend•er**
**Ben•di•go** Australian city
**bends** decompression sickness
**bendy** **(bendi•er, bendi•est)**
**be•neath**
**Ben•edi•ci•te** canticle
**ben•edi•ci•te** blessing
**Ben•edic•tine** order of monks; liqueur
**ben•edic•tion**
**ben•edic•tory**
**Ben•edic•tus** canticle
**ben•efac•tion**
**ben•efac•tor**
**ben•efac•tress**
**be•nef•ic** *rare variant of* **beneficient**
**ben•efice**
**be•nefi•cence**
**be•nefi•cent**
**ben•efi•cial**
**ben•efi•cial•ly**
**bene•fi•ciary** **(*plural* •ciaries)**
**ben•efit**
**Bene•lux**
**Be•ne•ven•to** Italian city
**be•nevo•lence**
**be•nevo•lent**
**Ben•gal**
**Ben•ga•lese**
**Ben•ga•li**
**ben•ga•line** fabric
**Ben•gha•zi** **(*or* •ga•si)** Libyan port
**be•night•ed**
**be•nign**
**be•nig•nan•cy**
**be•nig•nant**
**be•nig•nity** **(*plural* •nities)**
**Be•nin** African republic
**beni•son**
**ben•ne** plant
**Ben Ne•vis**
**ben•ny** *Slang* amphetamine tablet
**Be•no•ni** South African city
**bent**
**ben•thic**
**ben•thos** **(*or* •thon)** biology term
**ben•ton•ite** clay
**bent•wood**
**Be•nue** Nigerian state
**be•numb**

**ben•zal•de•hyde**
**Ben•ze•drine** (*Trademark*)
**ben•zene** chemical compound; *compare* **benzine**
**ben•zi•dine**
**ben•zine** (*or* **•zin**) petrol; *compare* **benzene**
**ben•zo•ate**
**ben•zo•caine** anaesthetic
**Ben•zo•drine** (*Trademark*)
**ben•zo•fu•ran**
**ben•zo•ic**
**ben•zo•in** gum resin
**ben•zol** (*or* **•zole**)
**ben•zo•phe•none**
**ben•zo•qui•none**
**ben•zo•yl**
**ben•zyl**
**Beo•wulf** epic poem
**be•queath**
**be•queath•er**
**be•quest**
**Be•rar** Indian region
**be•rate**
**Ber•ber** Caucasoid Muslim
**Ber•bera** Somalian port
**ber•beri•da•ceous** botany term
**ber•ber•ine** alkaloid
**ber•ber•is** shrub
**ber•ceuse** lullaby
**Berch•tes•ga•den** German town
**be•reave**
**be•reave•ment**
**be•reft**
**be•ret**
**Be•rez•ni•ki** Russian city
**berg** iceberg; mountain; *compare* **burg; burgh**
**Ber•ga•mo** Italian city
**ber•ga•mot** tree; oil
**Ber•gen** Norwegian port
**berg•schrund** crevasse in glacier
**beri•beri** disease
**Bering** Arctic sea and strait
**berk** *variant spelling of* **burk**
**Berkeley** Californian city
**ber•kelium** radioactive element
**Berk•shire**
**Ber•lin** German capital
**berm** narrow ledge
**Ber•mu•da**
**Bern** (*or* Berne) Swiss capital
**Ber•nese**
**ber•ry** (*noun, plural* **•ries**; *verb* **•ries, •ry•ing, •ried**)
**ber•sa•gliere** Italian soldier
**ber•seem** plant
**ber•serk**
**berth**
**Ber•wick** former Scottish county
**Berwick-upon-Tweed** English town
**ber•yl** mineral
**ber•yl•ine**
**be•ryl•lium** chemical element
**Bes** Egyptian god
**Be•san•çon** French city
**be•seech** (**•seech•ing, •sought**)
**be•set** (**•set•ting, •set**)
**be•side**
**be•sides**
**be•siege**
**be•sieg•er**
**be•smear**
**be•smirch**
**be•som**
**be•sot•ted**
**be•span•gle**
**be•spat•ter**
**be•speak** (**•speak•ing, •spoke, spo•ken** *or* **•spoke**)
**be•spec•ta•cled**
**be•spoke**
**be•spread**
**be•sprent** sprinkled over
**be•sprin•kle**
**Bes•sa•ra•bia** E European region
**best**
**bes•tial**
**bes•ti•al•ity** (*plural* **•ities**)
**bes•ti•al•ize** (*or* **•ise**)
**bes•tial•ly**
**bes•ti•ary** (*plural* **•aries**)
**be•stir** (**•stir•ring, •stirred**)
**be•stow**
**be•stow•al** (*or* **•ment**)
**be•stow•er**
**be•strew** (**•strew•ing, •strewed, •strewn** *or* **•strewed**)
**be•stride** (**•strid•ing, •strode** *or* **•strid, •strid•den** *or* **•strid**)
**bet** (**bet•ting, bet** *or* **bet•ted**)
**beta**
**be•ta•ine** alkaloid
**be•take** (**•tak•ing, •took, •tak•en**)
**be•ta•tron** particle accelerator
**be•tel** plant
**Be•tel•geuse** (*or* **•geux**) star
**bête noire** (*plural* **bêtes noires**) pet hate
**beth** Hebrew letter
**Betha•ny** biblical village
**Beth•el** biblical town
**Beth•le•hem**
**be•tide**
**bê•tise** folly
**be•to•ken**
**beto•ny** (*plural* **•nies**) plant
**be•took**
**be•tray**
**be•tray•al**
**be•tray•er**
**be•troth**
**be•troth•al**
**be•trothed**
**bet•ta** fish
**bet•ter** improved
**bett•er** one who bets
**bet•ter•ment**
**betu•la•ceous** botany term
**be•tween**
**be•tween•times**
**be•twixt**
**Beu•lah** biblical place
**beva•tron** synchrotron
**bev•el** (**•el•ling, •elled**; *US* **•el•ing, •eled**)
**bev•er•age**
**Bev•er•ly Hills** Californian city
**bev•vy** (*plural* **•vies**) *Dialect* alcoholic drink
**bevy** (*plural* **bevies**) flock
**be•wail**
**be•wail•er**
**be•ware**
**be•wil•der**
**be•wil•der•ing•ly**
**be•wil•der•ment**
**be•witch**
**be•witch•ing•ly**

**bey** Turkish title
**Bey•og•lu** district of Istanbul
**be•yond**
**bez•ant** gold coin
**bez•el** face of tool or gem
**be•zique** card game
**be•zoar** hairball
**Bha•gal•pur** Indian city
**Bha•ga•vad-Gita** Hindu text
**bhang** narcotic
**Bha•rat** *Hindi* India
**Bha•ra•ti•ya** Indian
**Bhat•pa•ra** Indian city
**bha•van** house
**Bhav•na•gar** Indian port
**bhin•di** vegetable
**Bho•pal** Indian port
**Bhu•ba•nes•war** Indian city
**Bhu•tan** Asian kingdom
**Bhu•tan•ese**
**Bi•afra** Nigerian region
**Bia•ły•stok** Polish city
**bi•an•nual** twice a year; *compare* **biennial**
**bi•an•nual•ly**
**bi•an•nu•late** zoology term
**Biar•ritz** French town
**bias** (**•as•ing, •ased** *or* **•as•sing, •assed**)
**bi•ath•lon** sport
**bi•auricu•late** (*or* **•lar**)
**bi•ax•ial**
**bib** (**bib•bing, bibbed**)
**bib•ber**
**bib•cock** tap with nozzle
**bi•belot** trinket
**Bi•ble**
**bib•li•cal**
**Bib•li•cist**
**bib•lio•graph•er** (*or* **•graph**)
**bib•lio•graph•ic** (*or* **•graphi•cal**)
**bib•li•og•ra•phy** (*plural* **•phies**)
**bib•li•ola•try**
**bib•lio•man•cy**
**bib•lio•ma•nia**
**bib•lio•ma•ni•ac**
**bib•lio•phile** (*or* **•phil**)
**bib•li•ophi•lis•tic**
**bib•li•oph•ism**
**bib•lio•pole** (*or* **•li•opo•list**) dealer in rare books
**bib•lio•the•ca** (*plural* **•cas** *or* **•cae**) library
**bibu•lous**
**bi•cam•er•al**
**bi•cap•su•lar**
**bicarb**
**bi•car•bo•nate**
**bice** blue colour
**bi•cen•tenary** (*plural* **•tenaries**)
**bi•cepha•lous** two-headed
**bi•ceps** (*plural* **•ceps** *or* **•cepses**)
**bi•chlo•ride**
**bi•cip•i•tal** of the biceps
**bick•er**
**bick•er•er**
**bi•col•lat•er•al**
**bi•col•our** (*or* **•oured;** *US* **•or** *or* **•ored**)
**bi•con•cave**
**bi•con•cav•ity**
**bi•con•vex**
**bi•corn** (*or* **•cor•nate, •cor•nu•ate**)
**bi•cus•pid**
**bi•cus•pi•date**
**bi•cy•cle**
**bi•cy•clic** (*or* **•cli•cal**)
**bi•cy•clist** (*or* **•cler**)
**bid** (**bid•ding; bad, bade,** *or* **bid; bid•den** *or* **bid**)
**bi•dar•ka** (*or* **•kee**) Eskimo canoe
**bid•dable**
**bid•der**
**bid•dy** (*plural* **•dies**)
**bide** (**bid•ing, bid•ed** *or* **bode, bid•ed**)
**bi•den•tate**
**bi•det**
**Bie•der•mei•er** furniture and art style
(**biege**) *incorrect spelling of* **beige**
**Biel** Swiss town
**bield** *Dialect* refuge
**Bie•le•feld** German city
**Biel•sko-Bia•ła** Polish town
**bi•en•nial** every two years; *compare* **biannual**
**bi•en•nial•ly**
**bier** coffin support; *compare* **byre**
**bier•kel•ler**
**bi•fa•cial**
**bi•fari•ous** botany term
**biff**
**bif•fin** apple
**bi•fid** divided into two lobes
**bi•fid•ity**
**bi•fi•lar** having two parallel threads
**bi•flag•el•late** biology term
**bi•fo•cal**
**bi•fo•cals**
**bi•fo•li•ate** having two leaves
**bi•fo•lio•late** having two leaflets
**bi•fo•rate** having two openings
**bi•form**
**Bif•rost** Norse mythological rainbow
**bi•fur•cate** forked
**bi•fur•ca•tion**
**big** (**big•ger, big•gest**)
**biga•mist**
**biga•mous**
**biga•my** (*plural* **•mies**)
**big•ar•reau** cherry
**bi•gen•er** hybrid organism
**bi•gener•ic**
**big•eye** fish
**big•ger**
**big•gest**
**big•gin** close-fitting cap
**big•gish**
**big•head**
**big•headed**
**big•headed•ness**
**big•horn** (*plural* **•horns** *or* **•horn**)
**bight** bay; bend in rope; *compare* **bite; byte**
**big•mouth**
**big•no•nia** shrub
**big•no•nia•ceous**
**big•ot**
**big•ot•ed**
**big•ot•ry** (*plural* **•ries**)
**bi•gua•nide** biochemical compound
**big•wig**
**Bi•har** Indian state
**Bi•ha•ri**
**Bi•ja•pur** Indian city
**bi•jec•tion** maths term
**bi•jec•tive**

**bi•jou** (*plural* **•joux)**
**bi•jou•terie** jewellery
**bi•ju•gate** (*or* **•gous)** botany term
**Bi•ka•ner** Indian city
**bike**
**bi•ki•ni**
**bi•la•bial**
**bi•la•bi•ate**
**bil•an•der** cargo ship
**bi•lat•er•al**
**bi•lat•er•al•ly**
**Bil•bao** Spanish port
**bil•berry** (*plural* **•berries)**
**bil•boes** ankle shackles
**bile**
**bile•stone**
**bilge**
**bil•har•zia** parasite
**bil•har•zia•sis**
**bili•ary**
**bi•lin•ear**
**bi•lin•gual**
**bi•lin•gual•ism**
**bili•ous**
**bil•ious•ness**
**bili•ru•bin** bile pigment
**bili•ver•din** bile pigment
**bilk** thwart
**bilk•er**
**bill**
**bil•la•bong**
**bill•board**
**bil•let**
**billet-doux** (*plural* **billets-doux)** love letter
**bill•fish** (*plural* **•fish** *or* **•fishes)**
**bill•fold**
**bill•hook**
**bil•liard**
**bill•ing**
**Bil•lings•gate**
**bil•lion** (*plural* **•lions** *or* **•lion)**
**bil•lion•aire**
**bil•lionth**
**bil•lon** alloy
**bil•low**
**bil•lowi•ness**
**bil•lowy**
**bill•poster**
**bil•ly** (*plural* **•lies)**
**bil•ly•can**
**bill•yo** slang term
**bi•lo•bate** (*or* **•lobed)**
**bi•locu•lar** (*or* **•late)**
**Bim** native of Barbados
**bima•nous** two-handed
**bim•bo** (*plural* **•bos** *or* **•boes)**
**bi•mes•trial** lasting two months
**bi•me•tal•lic**
**bi•met•al•lism** economic doctrine
**bi•mo•lec•u•lar**
**bi•month•ly** (*plural* **•lies)**
**bi•morph** electronics term
**bin (bin•ning, binned)**
**bi•nal** twofold
**bi•na•ry** (*plural* **•ries)**
**bi•nate** occurring in pairs
**bin•aural**
**bind (bind•ing, bound)**
**bind•er**
**bind•ery** (*plural* **•eries)**
**bindi-eye** plant
**bind•weed**
**bine** botany term
**binge**
**bin•gey** *Austral* stomach
**bin•gle** *Austral* minor crash
**bin•go**
**bin•na•cle**
**binned**
**bin•ning**
**bin•ocu•lar** (*adj*)
**bin•ocu•lars**
**bi•no•mial**
**bi•nomi•nal** biology term
**bint** *Slang* girl
**bin•tu•rong** animal
**bi•nu•cle•ar**
**bi•nu•cle•ate**
**bio•assay**
**bio•as•tro•nau•tics**
**bio•cata•lyst**
**bio•cata•lyt•ic**
**bi•oc•el•late** biology term
**bio•cenol•ogy** branch of ecology
**bio•chemi•cal**
**bio•chemi•cal•ly**
**bio•chem•ist**
**bio•chem•is•try**
**bio•cid•al**
**bio•cide**
**bio•cli•ma•tol•ogy**
**bio•cy•cle** ecological region
**bio•degrad•able**
**bio•deg•ra•da•tion**
**bio•di•ver•sity**
**bio•dy•nam•ic** (*or* **•nami•cal)**
**bio•dy•nam•ics**
**bio•en•er•get•ics**
**bio•en•gi•neer**
**bio•en•gi•neer•ing**
**bio•feed•back**
**bio•fla•vo•noid** vitamin
**bio•gen** hypothetical protein
**bio•gen•esis**
**bio•genet•ic** (*or* **bio•geneti•cal, biog•enous)**
**bio•geneti•cal•ly**
**bio•geo•graphi•cal**
**bio•geog•ra•phy**
**bi•og•ra•pher**
**bio•graphi•cal**
**bi•og•ra•phy** (*plural* **•phies)**
**bio•herm** organic rock
**bio•logi•cal** (*or* **•log•ic)**
**bio•logi•cal•ly**
**bi•olo•gist**
**bi•ol•ogy**
**bio•lu•mi•nes•cence**
**bio•lu•mi•nes•cent**
**bi•oly•sis**
**bio•lyt•ic**
**bio•mass** ecology term
**bi•ome** ecology term
**bio•met•ric**
**bio•met•ri•cal•ly**
**bi•om•etry** (*or* **bio•met•rics)**
**bi•on•ic**
**bi•on•ics**
**bio•nom•ic**
**bio•nomi•cal•ly**
**bio•nom•ics** ecology
**bi•ono•mist**
**bio•physi•cal**
**bio•physi•cist**
**bio•phys•ics**
**bio•plasm**
**bio•plas•mic**
**bio•poi•esis** biology term
**bi•op•sy** (*plural* **•sies)**
**bi•op•tic**
**bio•rhythm**
**bio•scope**
**bi•os•co•py** (*plural* **•pies)**
**bio•sphere** ecology term
**bio•stat•ic**

**bio•stati•cal•ly**
**bio•stat•ics**
**bio•strome** fossil-rich rock
**bio•syn•the•sis**
**bio•syn•thet•ic**
**bio•syn•theti•cal•ly**
**bio•ta** biology term
**bio•tech•no•logi•cal**
**bio•tech•nolo•gist**
**bio•tech•nol•ogy**
**bi•ot•ic**
**bio•tin** vitamin
**bio•tite** mineral
**bio•tit•ic**
**bio•tope** ecological area
**bio•type** biology term
**bio•typ•ic**
**bi•pa•ri•etal**
**bip•ar•ous**
**bi•par•ti•san** (*or* **•zan**)
**bi•par•ti•san•ship** (*or* **•zan•**)
**bi•par•tite**
**bi•par•ti•tion**
**bi•ped**
**bi•ped•al**
**bi•pet•al•ous**
**bi•phen•yl**
**bi•pin•nate** botany term
**bi•plane**
**bi•pod**
**bi•po•lar**
**bi•pro•pel•lant**
**bi•quad•rate** maths term
**bi•quad•rat•ic**
**bi•quar•ter•ly**
**bi•ra•cial**
**bi•ra•dial**
**bi•ra•mous** divided into two parts
**birch**
**bird**
**bird•bath**
**bird-brained**
**bird•cage**
**bird•house**
**birdie**
**bird•like**
**bird•lime**
**bird•man** (*plural* **•men**)
**bird•seed**
**bird's-eye** (*adj*)
**bird's-foot** (*or* **bird-**; *plural* **-foots**) plant
**bird-watcher**
**bird-watching**
**bi•refrin•gence**
**bi•refrin•gent**
**bi•reme** ship
**bi•ret•ta** (*or* **ber•ret•ta**) clerical cap
**bi•ria•ni** Indian food
**Bir•ken•head**
**Bir•ming•ham**
**Biro** (*Trademark; plural* **Biros**)
**Bi•ro•bi•dzhan** Russian city
**birr** make whirring sound; *compare* **bur; burr**
**birth**
**birth•day**
**birth•mark**
**birth•place**
**birth•right**
**birth•root** plant
**birth•stone**
**birth•wort** plant
**Bis•cay** (**Bay of**)
**bis•cuit**
**bise** wind
**bi•sect**
**bi•sec•tion**
**bi•sec•tor**
**bi•sec•trix** (*plural* **•tri•ces**) maths term
**bi•ser•rate** botany term
**bi•sex•ual**
**bi•sexu•al•ism** (*or* **•ity**)
**bish** *Slang* mistake
**Bish•kek** capital of Kyrgyzstan
**bish•op**
**bishop•bird**
**bish•op•ric**
**Bis•kra** Algerian town
**Bis•marck** US city
**bis•muth**
**bis•muth•al**
**bis•mu•thic**
**bis•muth•in•ite** mineral
**bis•muth•ous**
**bi•son** (*plural* **•son**)
**bisque** colour; soup; sports term
**Bis•sau** (*or* **•sao**) capital of Guinea-Bissau
**bis•sex•tile** of a leap year
**bis•ter** *US spelling of* **bistre**
**bis•tort** plant
**bis•tou•ry** (*plural* **•ries**) surgical knife
**bis•tre** (*US* **•ter**) drawing pigment
**bis•tro** (*plural* **•tros**) restaurant
**bi•sul•cate** cleft
**bi•sul•phate** (*US* **•fate**)
**bi•sul•phide** (*US* **•fide**)
**bi•sul•phite** (*US* **•fite**)
**bi•sym•met•ric** (*or* **•ri•cal**)
**bi•sym•met•ri•cal•ly**
**bi•sym•met•ry**
**bit**
**bi•tar•trate**
**bitch**
**bitchi•ly**
**bitchy** (**bitchi•er, bitchi•est**)
**bite** (**bit•ing, bit, bit•ten**) grip with teeth; *compare* **bight; byte**
**Bi•thynia** ancient Asian country
**bit•ing•ly**
**bit•ing•ness**
**bit•ser** *Austral* mongrel dog
**bit•stock**
**bitt** mooring post
**bit•ten**
**bit•ter**
**Bit•ter Lakes**
**bit•ter•ling** fish
**bit•tern** bird
**bit•ter•ness**
**bitter•nut**
**bit•ters** drink
**bitter•sweet**
**bitter•weed**
**bitter•wood**
**bit•ty** (**•ti•er, •ti•est**)
**bi•tu•men**
**bi•tu•mi•ni•za•tion** (*or* **•sa•tion**)
**bi•tu•mi•nize** (*or* **•nise**)
**bi•tu•mi•nous**
**bi•va•len•cy**
**bi•va•lent**
**bi•valve**
**bi•val•vu•lar**
**bivou•ac** (**•ack•ing, •acked**)
**biv•vy** (*plural* **•vies**) *Slang* tent
**bi•week•ly** (*plural* **•lies**)
**bi•year•ly**
**Biysk** (*or* **Biisk, Bisk**) Russian town

**bi•zarre**
**Bi•zer•te** (*or* **•ta**) Tunisian port
**blab** **(blab•bing, blabbed)**
**blab•ber**
**blabber•mouth**
**black**
**black•ball**
**black•berry** (*plural* **•berries**)
**black•bird**
**black•board**
**black•buck** antelope
**Black•burn**
**black•butt** tree
**black•cap** bird
**black•cock** male grouse
**black•cur•rant**
**black•damp**
**black•en**
**black•fish** (*plural* **•fish** *or* **•fishes**)
**black•fly** (*plural* **•flies**)
**Black•foot** (*plural* **•feet** *or* **•foot**) American Indian
**black•guard**
**black•guard•ism**
**black•guard•ly**
**black•head**
**black•heart** plant disease
**black-hearted**
**black•ing**
**black•ish**
**black•jack**
**black•leg** **(•leg•ging, •legged)**
**black•list**
**black•mail**
**black•mail•er**
**black-market** (*verb*)
**black•ness**
**black•out**
**black•poll** bird
**Black•pool**
**Black•shirt** fascist
**black•smith**
**black•snake**
**black•tail** deer
**black•thorn**
**black•top** *US* paving material
**Black•wood** bridge term
**black•wood** Australian tree
**blad•der**
**blad•der ket•mia** plant
**bladder•nose** seal
**bladder•nut**
**bladder•wort**
**bladder•wrack**
**blade**
**blah** silly talk
**blain** blister
**Blair•ite** follower of Tony Blair
**blam•able** (*or* **blame•**)
**blame**
**blame•ful**
**blame•ful•ness**
**blame•less**
**blame•less•ness**
**blame•worthi•ness**
**blame•worthy**
**blanch** make white; *compare* blench
**blanc•mange**
**bland**
**blan•dish**
**blan•dish•ment**
**bland•ness**
**blank**
**blan•ket**
**blank•ly**
**Blan•tyre-Limbe** Malawian city
**blare**
**blar•ney**
**bla•sé** indifferent
**blas•pheme**
**blas•phem•er**
**blas•phe•mous**
**blas•phe•my** (*plural* **•mies**)
**blast**
**blasted**
**blas•te•ma** (*plural* **•mas** *or* **•ma•ta**) biology term
**blas•tem•ic**
**blast•ing**
**blas•to•coel** (*or* **•coele**) embryology term
**blas•to•cyst**
**blas•to•derm** (*or* **•disc**) embryology term
**blas•to•derm•ic**
**blast•off**
**blas•to•gen•esis**
**blas•to•gen•ic** (*or* **•genet•ic**)
**blas•to•mere** embryology term
**blas•to•mer•ic**
**blas•to•pore** embryology term
**blas•to•por•ic** (*or* **•al**)
**blas•to•sphere**
**blas•tu•la** (*plural* **•las** *or* **•lae**) embryology term
**blas•tu•lar**
**blat** *US* bleat
**bla•tan•cy**
**bla•tant**
**blath•er** (*or* **bleth•**)
**blather•skite** talkative person
**blau•bok** (*plural* **•bok** *or* **•boks**) antelope
**Blay•don** English town
**blaze**
**blaz•er**
**bla•zon**
**bla•zon•ry** (*plural* **•ries**)
**bleach**
**bleach•able**
**bleach•er**
**bleak**
**bleak•ness**
**blear**
**bleari•ness**
**bleary** **(bleari•er, bleari•est)**
**bleat**
**bleat•er**
**bleat•ing•ly**
**bleb** blister
**bleed** **(bleed•ing, bled)**
**bleed•er**
**bleep**
**bleep•er**
**blem•ish**
**blem•ish•er**
**blench** shy away; *compare* blanch
**blench•er**
**blench•ing•ly**
**blend** combine
**blende** type of ore
**blend•er**
**Blen•heim** German village
**blen•ni•oid** fish
**blen•ny** (*plural* **•nies**)
**blepha•ri•tic**
**blepha•ri•tis** inflammation of eyelids
**bles•bok** (*or* **•buck**; *plural* **•boks**, **•bok** *or* **•bucks**, **•buck**) antelope
**bless** **(bless•ing, blessed** *or* **blest)**
**bless•ed** (*adj*)

**bless•ed•ness**
**blest**
**blet** fruit decay
**blew**
**blew•its** edible fungus; *compare* **bluet**
**Bli•da** Algerian city
**blight**
**blight•er**
**Blighty** *Slang* England
**bli•mey**
**blimp**
**blimp•ish**
**blind**
**blind•age** military screen
**blind•er**
**blind•fish** (*plural* **•fish** *or* **•fishes)**
**blind•fold**
**blind•ing**
**blind•ly**
**blind•ness**
**blind•storey** (*or* **•story)**
**blind•worm**
**blini** (*or* **blin•is)** pancake
**blink**
**blink•er**
**blink•ers**
**blink•ing**
**blintz** (*or* **blintze)** filled pancake
**blip (blip•ping, blipped)**
**bliss**
**bliss•ful**
**bliss•ful•ly**
**bliss•ful•ness**
**blis•ter**
**blis•ter•ing•ly**
**blithe**
**blithe•ness**
**blith•er•ing**
**blithe•some**
**blitz**
**blitz•krieg**
**bliz•zard**
**bloat**
**bloated**
**bloat•er**
**blob (blob•bing, blobbed)**
**bloc** group of nations
**block**
**block•ade**
**block•ad•er**
**block•age**
**block•board**
**block•bust•er**
**block•bust•ing**
**block•er**
**block•head**
**block•house**
**Bloem•fon•tein** South African city
**bloke**
**blond** (*fem* **blonde)**
**blond•ness** (*fem* **blonde•ness)**
**blood**
**blood•curdling**
**blood•ed**
**blood•fin**
**blood•hound**
**bloodi•ly**
**bloodi•ness**
**blood•less**
**blood-letting**
**blood•root**
**blood•shed**
**blood•shot**
**blood•stain**
**blood•stained**
**blood•stock**
**blood•stone**
**blood•sucker**
**blood•thirsti•ly**
**blood•thirsti•ness**
**blood•thirsty (•thirsti•er, •thirsti•est)**
**blood•worm**
**bloody** (*adj* **bloodi•er, bloodi•est;** *verb* **blood•ies, bloody•ing, blood•ied)**
**bloody-minded**
**bloom**
**bloom•er**
**bloom•ers**
**bloom•ery** (*plural* **•eries)** ironworks
**bloom•ing**
**Blooms•bury**
**bloop•er** *US* blunder
**blos•som**
**blot (blot•ting, blot•ted)**
**blotch**
**blotchi•ly**
**blotchi•ness**
**blotchy (blotchi•er, blotchi•est)**
**blot•ter**
**blot•to** *Slang* drunkenly unconscious
**blouse**
**blou•son**
**blow (blow•ing, blew, blown)**
**blow-dry (-dries, -dry•ing, -dried)**
**blow•er**
**blow•fish** (*plural* **•fish** *or* **•fishes)**
**blow•fly** (*plural* **•flies)**
**blow•hard** boastful person
**blow•hole**
**blow•lamp**
**blown**
**blow•out** (*noun*)
**blow•pipe**
**blow•torch**
**blow-wave**
**blowy (blowi•er, blowi•est)**
**blowzi•ly** (*or* **blowsi•)**
**blowzi•ness** (*or* **blowsi•ness)**
**blowzy** (*or* **blowsy; blowzi•er, blowzi•ier** *or* **blowsi•er, blowsi•est)**
**blub (blub•bing, blubbed)**
**blub•ber**
**blub•bery**
**bludge** *Austral* scrounge
**bludg•eon**
**bludg•eon•er**
**blue** (*adj* **blu•er, blu•est;** *verb* **blue•ing** *or* **blu•ing, blued)**
**Blue•beard**
**blue•bell**
**blue•berry** (*plural* **•berries)**
**blue•bill**
**blue•bird**
**blue-blooded**
**blue•bonnet** Scottish hat
**blue•book** government publication
**blue•bottle**
**blue•fish** (*plural* **•fish** *or* **•fishes)**
**blue•gill** fish
**blue•grass**
**blue•ing** (*or* **blu•ing)**
**blue•jacket**
**blue•ness**
**blue•nose** *US* puritanical person
**blue•print**
**blues**

**blue•stocking**
**blue•stone**
**bluet** plant; *compare* **blewits**
**blue•throat** bird
**blue•tit**
**blue•tongue** lizard
**blu•ey** *Austral* blanket
**bluff**
**bluff•er**
**bluff•ness**
**blu•ing** *variant spelling of* **blueing**
**blu•ish** (*or* **blue•ish**)
**blun•der**
**blun•der•buss**
**blun•der•er**
**blun•der•ing•ly**
**blunge** ceramics term
**blung•er**
**blunt**
**blunt•ness**
**blur** (**blur•ring, blurred**)
**blurb**
**blur•red•ly**
**blur•red•ness**
**blur•ry**
**blurt**
**blush**
**blush•er**
**blush•ing•ly**
**blus•ter**
**blus•ter•er**
**blus•ter•ing•ly** (*or* **•ous•ly**)
**blus•tery** (*or* **•ter•ous**)
**Blyth** English port
**B'nai B'rith** Jewish society
**boa**
**boar** male pig; *compare* **boor; bore**
**board**
**board•er**
**board•ing**
**board•room**
**board•walk** *US* wooden promenade
**boar•fish** (*plural* **•fish** *or* **•fishes**)
**boar•hound**
**boar•ish** coarse; sensual; *compare* **boorish**
**boar•ish•ness**
**boast**
**boast•er**
**boast•ful**
**boast•ful•ly**
**boast•ful•ness**
**boast•ing•ly**
**boat**
**boat•el** waterside hotel
**boat•er**
**boat•hook**
**boat•house**
**boat•ing**
**boat•load**
**boat•man** (*plural* **•men**)
**boat•swain** (*or* **bo•sun**)
**bob** (**bob•bing, bobbed**)
**bob•bery** (*plural* **•beries**) pack of dogs
**bob•bin**
**bob•bi•net** fabric
**bob•ble**
**bob•by** (*plural* **•bies**)
**bob•cat**
**bob•float** fishing float
**bob•let** bobsleigh
**bobo•link** bird
**bo•bo•tie** curried dish
**bob•owler** *Dialect* moth
**bob•sleigh** (*or esp. US* **•sled**)
**bob•stay**
**bob•tail**
**bob•white** bird
**bo•cage** wooded country
**boc•cia** bowls game
**Boche** *Slang* German
**Bo•chum** German city
**bock** beer
**bod** *Slang* person
**bode**
**bo•dega** wine shop
**bodge**
**bodg•er**
**bodgie** *Austral* unruly man
**Bo•dhi•satt•va** Buddhist divine
**bod•ice**
**bodi•less**
**bodi•ly**
**bod•kin**
**Bod•lei•an** Oxford library
**Bod•min**
**Bo•do•ni** style of type
**body** (*noun, plural* **bodies**; *verb* **bodies, body•ing, bod•ied**)
**body-centred**
**body•check**
**body•guard**
**body-snatcher**
**body•work**
**boehm•ite** mineral
**Boeo•tia** region of ancient Greece
**Boeo•tian**
**Boer** Dutch South African
**boeuf Bour•gui•gnon** beef casserole
**bof•fin**
**bog** (**bog•ging, bogged**)
**bo•gan** *Canadian* side stream
**bo•gey** golf term; *compare* **bogie**
**bo•gey** (*or* **bogy**; *plural* **•geys** *or* **bogies**) evil spirit; *compare* **bogie**
**bogey•man** (*plural* **•men**)
**bog•gart** *Dialect* poltergeist
**bog•gi•ness**
**bog•gle**
**bog•gy** (**•gi•er, •gi•est**)
**bo•gie** wheeled undercarriage; *compare* **bogey**
**bo•gle** *Dialect* bogey
**Bog•nor Re•gis**
**bo•gong** moth
**Bo•gor** Indonesian city
**Bo•go•tá** Colombian capital
**bo•gus**
**bog•wood**
**bogy** *variant spelling of* **bogey**
**bo•hea** China tea
**Bo•he•mia**
**Bo•he•mian**
**Bo•hol** Philippine island
**boil**
**boil•able**
**boil•er**
**boiler•maker**
**boiler•plate**
**boiler•suit**
**boil•ing•ly**
**Bois de Bou•logne** Parisian park
**Boi•se** US city
**bois•ter•ous**
**bois•ter•ous•ness**
**bok•ma•kie•rie** bird
**bola** weapon
**Bo•land** South African region
**bold**

**bold•face** (*adj*)
**bold•ness**
**bole** tree trunk; *compare* bowl
**bo•lec•tion** architectural term
**bo•lero** (*plural* **•ros**)
**bo•letus** (*plural* **•letuses** *or* **•leti**) fungus
**bo•lide** meteor
**boli•var** (*plural* **•vars** *or* **•vares**) Venezuelan currency
**Bo•livia**
**Bo•liv•ian**
**boll**
**bol•lard**
**bol•locks** (*or* **bal•locks**)
**boll•worm**
**bolo** (*plural* **bolos**) knife
**Bo•lo•gna** Italian city
**Bo•lo•gnese**
**bo•lom•eter**
**bo•lo•met•ric**
**bo•lo•met•ri•cal•ly**
**bo•lo•ney** *variant spelling of* baloney
**Bol•she•vik** (*plural* **•viks** *or* **•vi•ki**)
**Bol•she•vism**
**Bol•she•vist**
**Bol•shie** (*or* **•shy**)
**bol•son** US desert valley
**bol•ster**
**bol•ster•er**
**bol•ster•ing•ly**
**bolt**
**bolt•er**
**Bol•ton**
**bol•to•nia** plant
**bolt•rope** rope on a sail
**bo•lus** (*plural* **•luses**) chewed food
**Bol•za•no** Italian city
**bomb**
**bom•ba•ca•ceous** botany term
**bom•bard**
**bom•bar•dier**
**bom•bard•ment**
**bom•bar•don** musical instrument
**bom•bast**
**bom•bas•tic**
**bom•bas•ti•cal•ly**
**Bom•bay**
**bom•ba•zine**
**bom•be** dessert
**bom•bé** furniture style
**bomb•er**
**bom•bora** submerged reef
**bomb•shell**
**bomb•sight** bomb-aiming device
**bomb site** bomb-destroyed area
**bom•by•cid** moth
**bona fide** genuine
**bona fides** good faith
**Bon•aire** West Indian island
**bo•nan•za**
**Bo•na•part•ism**
**bona va•can•tia** unclaimed goods
**bon•bon**
**bonce** *Slang* head
**bond**
**bond•age**
**bond•ed**
**bond•holder**
**bond•maid**
**bond•servant**
**bonds•man** (*plural* **•men**)
**bone**
**bone•black**
**bone•fish** (*plural* **•fish** *or* **•fishes**)
**bone•head**
**bone•less**
**bon•er** *Slang* blunder
**bone•set** plant
**bone•set•ter**
**bone•shaker**
**bone•yard**
**bon•fire**
**bong**
**bon•go** (*plural* **•gos** *or* **•goes**) drum
**bon•go** (*plural* **•go** *or* **•gos**) antelope
**bon•ho•mie**
**boni•ness**
**bon•ism**
**bo•ni•to** (*plural* **•tos** *or* **•toes**) fish
**bonk•ers**
**bon mot** (*plural* **bons mots**) fitting remark
**Bonn** former West German capital
**bon•net**
**bon•ny** (**•ni•er, •ni•est**)
**bon•sai** (*plural* **•sai**)
**bon•sela** African gift
**bon•spiel** curling match
**bon•te•bok** (*plural* **•boks** *or* **•bok**) antelope
**bo•nus**
**bony** (**boni•er, boni•est**)
**bonze** Buddhist priest
**boo** (**boo•ing, booed**)
**boob**
**boo•bi•al•la** shrub
**boo•book** owl
**boo•by** (*plural* **•bies**)
**booby-trap** (*verb*; **-trap•ping, -trapped**)
**boo•dle**
**booed**
**boo•gie**
**boogie-woogie**
**boo•hoo** (**•hoo•ing, •hooed**)
**boo•ing**
**book**
**book•binder**
**book•bindery** (*plural* **•binderies**)
**book•bind•ing**
**book•case**
**bookie**
**book•ing**
**book•ish**
**book•ish•ness**
**book-keeper**
**book-keeping**
**book-learning**
**book•let**
**book•louse** insect
**book•maker**
**book•making**
**book•mark** (*or* **•marker**)
**book•plate**
**book•rack**
**book•sell•er**
**book•shelf** (*plural* **•shelves**)
**book•shop**
**book•stall**
**book•stand**
**book•worm**
**Bool•ean** type of algebra
**boom**
**boom•er**
**boom•er•ang**
**boom•slang** snake
**boon**

**boon•docks** *US* wild country
**boon•dog•gle** *US* do futile work
**boor** unpleasant person; *compare* **boar; bore**
**boor•ish** ill-mannered; insensitive; *compare* **boarish**
**boor•ish•ness**
**boost**
**boost•er**
**boot**
**boot•black**
**boot•ed**
**bootee**
**Boö•tes** constellation
**booth**
**boot•lace**
**Boo•tle**
**boot•leg (•leg•ging, •legged)**
**boot•leg•ger**
**boot•less**
**boot•lick**
**boot•lick•er**
**boot•loader**
**boot•strap**
**boo•ty** (*plural* **•ties)**
**booze**
**booz•er**
**boozi•ness**
**boozy (boozi•er, boozi•est)**
**bop (bop•ping, bopped)**
**bora** north wind
**Bora Bora** Pacific island
**bo•ra•cic**
**bo•ra•cite** mineral
**bor•age** plant
**bo•ragi•na•ceous**
**bo•rak** *Austral* nonsense
**bo•rane** chemical compound
**bo•rate**
**bo•rax** (*plural* **•raxes** *or* **•ra•ces)**
**bo•ra•zon** chemical compound
**bor•bo•ryg•mus** (*plural* **•mi)** stomach rumbling
**Bor•deaux** French port; wine
**Bor•delaise** sauce
**bor•del•lo** (*plural* **•los)**
**bor•der**
**bor•dereau** (*plural* **•dereaux)** insurance invoice
**bor•der•er**
**border•land**
**border•line**
**Bor•ders** Scottish region
**bor•dure** heraldry term
**bore** dull person; drill hole; *compare* **boar; boor**
**bo•real** of the north
**Boreas** Greek god
**bore•dom**
**boree** tree
**bor•er**
**bo•ric**
**bo•ride** chemical compound
**bor•ing**
**born** given birth to
**borne** carried
**Bor•neo** Malaysian island
**bor•neol** chemical compound
**born•ite** mineral
**Bor•no** Nigerian state
**Bo•ro•di•no** battle site
**bo•ron** chemical element
**bo•ro•nia** shrub
**bo•ro•sili•cate**
**bor•ough**
**bor•row**
**bor•row•er**
**bor•stal**
**bort** (*or* **boart, bortz)** inferior diamond
**bor•zoi** (*plural* **•zois)**
**bos•cage** (*or* **•kage)** thicket
**bosch•vark** wild pig
**bosh**
**bosk** small wood
**bos•ket** (*or* **•quet)** thicket
**Bos•kop** prehistoric African race
**bosky (boski•er, boski•est)**
**Bos•nia-Her•cego•vi•na** (*or* **•zego•)** S European country
**Bos•nian**
**bos•om**
**bos•omy**
**bos•on** physics term
**Bos•po•rus** (*or* **Bos•pho•rus)** Turkish strait
**boss**
**bos•sa nova** dance
**bossi•ly**
**bossi•ness**
**bossy (bossi•er, bossi•est)**
**Bos•ton**
**bo•sun** *variant spelling of* **boatswain**
**Bos•worth** battle site
**bot** (*or* **bott)** botfly larva
**bo•tani•cal** (*or* **•tan•ic)**
**bota•nist**
**bota•nize** (*or* **•nise)**
**bota•ny** (*plural* **•nies)**
**bo•tar•go** (*plural* **•goes)** fish roe
**botch**
**botch•er**
**botchi•ly**
**botchiness**
**botchy (botchi•er, botchi•est)**
**bot•fly** (*plural* **•flies)**
**both**
**both•er**
**both•era•tion**
**both•er•some**
**bothy** (*plural* **bothies)** *Scot* small shelter
**bot•ryoi•dal** (*or* **•ry•ose)**
**bots** horse disease
**Bot•swa•na**
**bot•tle**
**bottle•brush** shrub
**bottle•neck**
**bottle•nose** dolphin
**bot•tom**
**bot•tom•less**
**bottom•most**
**bot•tom•ry** (*plural* **•ries)** legal term
**Bot•trop** German city
**botu•lin** toxin
**botu•li•nus** (*plural* **•nuses)** bacterium
**botu•lism**
**Boua•ké** Côte d'Ivoire town
**bou•chée** vol-au-vent
**Bouches-du-Rhone** French department
**bou•clé** knobbly yarn
**bou•clée** support for billiard cue
**bou•doir**
**bouf•fant**
**Bou•gain•ville** Pacific island
**bou•gain•vil•lea** (*or* **•laea)** plant
**bough**
**bought**

**bought•en** *Dialect* bought
**bou•gie** catheter
**bouil•la•baisse** fish soup
**bouil•lon** broth
**boul•der**
**boule** gem; *compare* **boulle**
**boule•vard**
**boule•var•di•er** fashionable man
**boule•verse•ment** *French* upheaval
**boulle** (*or* **boule, buhl**) marquetry; *compare* **boule**
**Bou•logne**
**bounce**
**bounc•er**
**bounci•ly**
**bounci•ness**
**bounc•ing**
**bouncy** (**bounci•er, bounci•est**)
**bound**
**bounda•ry** (*plural* **•ries**)
**bound•en**
**bound•er**
**bound•less**
**bound•less•ness**
**bounds**
**boun•te•ous**
**boun•te•ous•ness**
**boun•ti•ful**
**boun•ti•ful•ness**
**boun•ty** (*plural* **•ties**)
**bou•quet**
**bou•quet gar•ni** (*plural* **bou•quets gar•nis**)
**bour•bon** US whiskey
**bour•don** organ stop
**bourg** French market town
**bour•geois** (*fem* **•geoise**)
**bour•geoi•sie**
**bourn** stream
**bourne** (*or* **bourn**) destination; boundary
**Bourne•mouth**
**bour•rée** dance
**Bourse** French stock exchange
**bouse** (*or* **bowse**) nautical term
**bou•stro•phedon** alternately ordered word lines
**bout**
**bou•tique**
**bou•ton•ni•ere** buttonhole flower
**bou•zouki**
**bo•vid**
**bo•vine**
**Bov•ril** (*Trademark*)
**bov•ver** *Slang* rowdiness
**bow**
**bowd•lcr•ism**
**bowd•leri•za•tion** (*or* **•sa•tion**)
**bowd•ler•ize** (*or* **•ise**)
**bow•el**
**bow•er**
**bower•bird**
**Bow•ery** New York street and area
**bow•fin** fish
**bow•head** whale
**bow•ing**
**bow•knot**
**bowl** basin; wooden ball; *compare* **bole**
**bow-legged**
**bowl•er**
**bowl•ful**
**bow•line**
**bowl•ing**
**bowls**
**bow•man** (*plural* **•men**)
**bow•saw**
**bowse** *variant spelling of* **bouse**
**bow•ser** fuel tanker
**bow•shot**
**bow•sprit**
**bow•string**
**bow-wow**
**bow•yer** maker of archery bows
**box**
**box•berry** (*plural* **•berries**)
**box•board**
**box•car** *US* closed railway van
**box•er**
**box•ing**
**box•room**
**box•wood**
**boy**
**boy•ar**
**boy•cott**
**boy•friend**
**boy•hood**
**boy•ish**
**boy•ish•ness**
**boy•la** Aboriginal witch doctor
**Boyne** Irish river
**boysen•berry** (*plural* **•berries**)
**bra**
**Bra•bant** Belgian province
**brace**
**brace•let**
**brac•er**
**bra•chial** of the arm
**bra•chi•ate**
**bra•chia•tion**
**bra•chio•pod** marine invertebrate
**bra•chio•saur•us**
**bra•chium** (*plural* **•chia**) armlike part
**brachy•cephal•ic** (*or* **•cepha•lous**) broad-headed
**brachy•cepha•ly** (*or* **•lism**)
**brachy•dac•tylia** (*or* **•tyl•ism**)
**brachy•dac•tyl•ic**
**bra•chylo•gous**
**bra•chyl•ogy** (*plural* **•ogies**) concise style
**bra•chyp•ter•ous** short-winged
**brachy•ur•an** crustacean
**brac•ing**
**brac•ing•ly**
**brack•en**
**brack•et**
**brack•ish**
**brack•ish•ness**
**Brack•nell** English town
**bract**
**bract•eal**
**brac•te•ate**
**brac•teo•late**
**brac•te•ole**
**brad** small nail
**brad•awl**
**Brad•ford**
**Bradshaw** railway timetable
**brady•car•dia** abnormally slow heartbeat
**brady•car•di•ac**
**brady•kin•in** blood protein
**brae** *Scot* hill
**brag** (**brag•ging, bragged**)
**Bra•ga** Portuguese city

**brag•ga•do•cio** (*plural* **•cios**) boasting
**brag•gart**
**brag•ger**
**brag•ging•ly**
**Brah•ma** Hindu god
**Brah•man** (*or* **•min**; *plural* **•mans, •min,** *or* **•mins)** Hindu caste
**Brah•ma•na** Hindu treatise
**Brah•ma•ni** (*plural* **•nis)** woman Brahman
**Brah•man•ic** (*or* **•min•ic)**
**Brah•man•ism** (*or* **•min•ism)**
**Brah•ma•pu•tra** Asian river
**Brah•min** *variant spelling of* **Brahman**
**Bra•hui** Pakistani language
**braid**
**braid•ed**
**braid•er**
**braid•ing**
**brail** nautical term
**Braille** writing for blind
**brain**
**brain•child** (*plural* **•children)**
**braini•ness**
**brain•less**
**brain•less•ness**
**brain•pan**
**brain•sick**
**brain•stem**
**brain•storm**
**brain•storm•er**
**brain•storm•ing**
**brain•wash**
**brain•wash•er**
**brain•wash•ing**
**brain•wave**
**brainy (braini•er, braini•est)**
**braise** cook; *compare* **braze**
**brake**
**brakes•man** (*plural* **•men)**
**bram•ble**
**bram•bling** bird
**Bram•ley** apple
**bran**
**branch**
**bran•chia** (*plural* **•chiae)** animal's gill
**bran•chial**
**bran•chi•ate**
**branch•ing**
**bran•chio•pod** crustacean
**brand**
**Bran•den•burg** German city
**bran•dish**
**bran•dish•er**
**brand•ling** earthworm
**brand-new**
**bran•dy** (*plural* **•dies)**
**bran•le** dance
**brash**
**brashi•ness** state of being brashy
**brash•ly**
**brash•ness**
**brashy (brashi•er, brashi•est)** fragmented
**Bra•sília** Brazilian capital
**Bra•şou** Romanian city
**brass**
**bras•sard** (*or* **•sart)** armband
**brass•bound**
**bras•se•rie**
**bras•si•ca** vegetable
**bras•si•ca•ceous**
**brassie** (*or* **brassy**; *plural* **brassies)** golf club
**bras•siere**
**brassi•ly**
**brassi•ness**
**brassy (brassi•er, brassi•est)**
**brat**
**Bra•ti•sla•va** capital of Slovakia
**brat•tice** mining term
**brat•tish•ing** architectural term
**brat•wurst** sausage
**braun•ite** mineral
**bra•va•do** (*plural* **•does** *or* **•dos)**
**brave**
**brave•ness**
**brav•ery** (*plural* **•eries)**
**bra•vo** (*plural* **•voes** *or* **•vos)**
**bra•vu•ra**
**braw** *Scot* excellent
**brawl**
**brawl•er**
**brawn**
**brawni•ly**
**brawni•ness**
**brawny (brawni•er, brawni•est)**
**braxy** sheep disease
**bray**
**bray•er**
**braze** solder metal; *compare* **braise**
**bra•zen**
**bra•zen•ness**
**braz•er** one who brazes
**bra•zi•er** brass worker; charcoal-burning pot
**Bra•zil**
**bra•zil•ein** (*or* **•sil•ein)** red dye
**Bra•zil•ian**
**brazi•lin** (*or* **brasi•lin)** yellow dye
**Braz•za•ville** capital of Congo
**breach** break; gap; *compare* **breech**
**bread**
**bread•board**
**bread•crumb**
**bread•fruit** (*plural* **•fruits** *or* **•fruit)**
**bread•line**
**bread•nut**
**bread•root** plant
**breadth**
**bread•winner**
**break (break•ing, broke, brok•en)**
**break•able**
**break•age**
**break•away**
**break•down**
**break•er**
**break•fast**
**break•front**
**break-in** (*noun*)
**break•neck**
**break-out** (*noun*)
**break•point**
**break•through** (*noun*)
**break-up** (*noun*)
**break•water**
**bream** (*plural* **bream)**
**breast**
**breast•bone**
**breast-feed (-feed•ing, -fed)**
**breast•pin**
**breast•plate**
**breast•stroke**
**breast•work** fortification
**breath**
**breatha•lyse**

**Breatha•lyz•er** (*or* **•lys•er**) (*Trademark*)
**breathe**
**breath•er**
**breathi•ly**
**breathi•ness**
**breath•ing**
**breath•less**
**breath•less•ness**
**breath•taking**
**breathy** (**breathi•er, breathi•est**)
**brec•cia** rock
**brec•ci•at•ed**
**Brec•on** (*or* **Breck•nock**) Welsh town
**Brec•on•shire** (*or* **Breck•nock•shire**) former Welsh county
**bred**
**Bre•da** Dutch city
**bree** *Scot* thin soup
**breech** part of gun; buttocks (*note* **breech birth**); *compare* **breach**
**breech•block**
**breech•clout** loincloth
**breeches**
**breech•ing** harness strap
**breech•loader**
**breech-loading**
**breed** (**breed•ing, bred**)
**breed•er**
**breeze**
**breezi•ly**
**breezi•ness**
**breezy** (**breezi•er, breezi•est**)
**breg•ma** (*plural* **•ma•ta**) part of skull
**Bre•men** German city
**Brem•er•ha•ven** German port
**brems•strah•lung** physics term
**Bren gun**
**Bren•ner Pass**
**Brent** London borough
**brent** (*plural* **brents** *or* **brent**) goose
**br'er** *US dialect* brother
**Bre•scia** Italian city
**Brest** French port
**breth•ren**
**Bret•on** of Brittany
**breve** accent; musical note
**bre•vet** (**•vet•ting, •vet•ted** *or* **•vet•ing, •vet•ed**) military term
**brev•et•cy**
**brevia•ry** (*plural* **•ries**)
**bre•vier** size of type
**brevi•ros•trate** ornithology term
**brev•ity** (*plural* **•ities**)
**brew**
**brew•age**
**brew•er**
**brew•ery** (*plural* **•eries**)
**brew•ing**
**brew•is** *Dialect* gravy-soaked bread
**bri•ar** (*or* **•er**) tobacco pipe; *variant spelling of* **brier**
**Briareus** Greek giant
**briar•root** (*or* **brier•**)
**brib•able** (*or* **bribe•able**)
**bribe**
**brib•er**
**brib•ery** (*plural* **•eries**)
**bric-a-brac**
**brick**
**brick•bat**
**brickie** *Slang* bricklayer
**brick•layer**
**brick•laying**
**brick•le** *Dialect* brittle
**brick•work**
**brick•yard**
**bri•cole** billiards term
**brid•al**
**bride**
**bride•groom**
**brides•maid**
**bride•well** jail
**bridge**
**bridge•able**
**bridge•board**
**bridge•head**
**Bridge•port** US port
**Bridge•town** capital of Barbados
**bridge•work**
**bridg•ing**
**Bridg•wa•ter** English town
**bri•die** *Scot* meat pie
**bri•dle**
**bri•dler**
**bri•doon** horse's bit
**Brie** cheese
**brief**
**brief•case**
**brief•ing**
**brief•ly**
**bri•er** (*or* **•ar**) thorny shrub; *compare* **briar**
**bri•ery** (*or* **•ary**)
**brig**
**bri•gade**
**briga•dier**
**briga•low** tree
**brig•and**
**brig•an•dine** armour
**brig•an•tine** ship
**bright**
**bright•en**
**bright•en•er**
**bright•ness**
**Bright•on**
**brights** *US* headlights
**bright•work** metal car trimmings
**brill** (*plural* **brill** *or* **brills**)
**bril•liance** (*or* **•lian•cy**)
**bril•liant**
**bril•lian•tine**
**brim** (**brim•ming, brimmed**)
**brim•ful** (*or* **•full**)
**brim•mer**
**brim•stone**
**brin•dle**
**brin•dled**
**brine**
**bring** (**bring•ing, brought**)
**brini•ness**
**brink**
**brink•man•ship**
**brin•ny** (*plural* **•nies**) *Austral* a stone
**briny** (**brini•er, brini•est**)
**bri•oche**
**brio•lette** jewel
**bri•quette**
**bri•sance** power of explosion
**Bris•bane**
**brise-soleil** window protection
**brisk**
**bris•ket**
**bris•ling** fish
**bris•tle**
**bristle-grass**
**bristle•tail** insect

**bris•tly**
**Bris•tol**
**bris•tols** *Slang* breasts
**Brit** *Slang* Briton
**brit** young herring
**Brit•ain**
**Bri•tan•nia**
**Bri•tan•nic**
**Briti•cism**
**Brit•ish**
**Brit•ish•er**
**Brit•ish•ism**
**Brit•on**
**Brit•ta•ny**
**brit•tle**
**brit•tle•ness**
**brittle•star** starfish
**Brno** Czech city
**broach** raise topic; tap container; *compare* **brooch**
**broach•er**
**broad**
**broad•bill** bird
**broad•brim** hat
**broad•cast** (**cast•ing, •cast** *or* **•cast•ed**)
**broad•cast•er**
**broad•cloth**
**broad•en**
**broad•leaf** (*plural* **•leaves**) tobacco plant
**broad-leaved** denoting nonconiferous trees
**broad•loom**
**broad•ly**
**broad-minded**
**broad-minded•ness**
**Broad•moor**
**Broads** East Anglian lakes
**broad•sheet**
**broad•side**
**broad•sword**
**broad•tail** Persian lamb
**Broad•way**
**Brob•ding•nag**
**bro•cade**
**broca•telle** brocade
**broc•co•li**
**broch** Scottish tower
**bro•ché** woven with raised design
**bro•chette** skewer
**bro•chure**
**brock** badger
**brock•et** deer
**brod•dle** *Dialect* poke
**bro•de•rie an•glaise**
**Broeder•bond** South African Afrikaner society
**bro•gan** boot
**brogue**
**broil**
**broil•er**
**broke**
**bro•ken**
**broken-down**
**broken•hearted**
**bro•ker**
**bro•ker•age**
**brol•ga** bird
**brol•ly** (*plural* **•lies**)
**bro•mal** sedative
**bro•mate**
**brome** grass
**bro•melia•ceous**
**bro•meli•ad** botany term
**brom•eo•sin** dye
**bro•mic**
**bro•mide**
**bro•mid•ic** dull
**bro•min•ate** chemistry term
**bro•mina•tion**
**bro•mine** chemical element
**bro•mism** (*or* **bro•min•ism**) bromine poisoning
**bro•mo•form** chemical compound
**Broms•grove** English town
**bron•chi** *plural of* **bronchus**
**bron•chia** bronchial tubes
**bron•chial**
**bron•chi•ec•ta•sis** bronchial disease
**bron•chio•lar**
**bron•chi•ole**
**bron•chit•ic**
**bron•chi•tis**
**bron•cho•pneu•mo•nia**
**bron•cho•scope**
**bron•cho•scop•ic**
**bron•chos•co•pist**
**bron•chos•co•py**
**bron•chus** (*plural* **•chi**)
**bron•co** (*or* **•cho;** *plural* **•cos** *or* **•chos**) wild pony
**bronco•buster**
**bron•to•sau•rus** (*or* **•to•saur**)
**Bronx** New York borough
**bronze**
**bronzy**
**brooch** piece of jewellery; *compare* **broach**
**brood**
**brood•er**
**broodi•ness**
**broody** (**broodi•er, broodi•est**)
**brook**
**brook•able**
**brook•ite** mineral
**brook•let**
**brook•lime** trailing plant
**Brook•lyn** New York borough
**brook•weed**
**broom**
**broom•corn** sorghum
**broom•rape** plant
**broom•stick**
**brose** *Scot* porridge
**broth**
**broth•el**
**broth•er**
**brother•hood**
**brother-in-law** (*plural* **brothers-**)
**broth•er•li•ness**
**broth•er•ly**
**brough•am** carriage
**brought**
**brou•ha•ha**
**brow**
**brow•band** part of bridle
**brow•beat** (**•beat•ing, •beat, •beat•en**)
**brown**
**browned-off**
**Brownie** junior Guide
**brownie** chocolate cake
**brown•ing**
**brown•ish**
**brown•out** *US* power reduction
**browse**
**brows•er**
**bru•cel•lo•sis**
**bruc•ine** alkaloid
**Bruges** Belgian city
**bru•in**
**bruise**
**bruised**
**bruis•er**
**bruis•ing**
**bruit** *Archaic* report
**bru•mal** wintry

**brume** mist
**Brum•ma•gem** *Slang* Birmingham
**Brum•mie** *Slang* Birmingham native
**brum•ous**
**brunch**
**Bru•nei** Malaysian state
**bru•nette**
**Brunhild** (*or* **Brünnhilde**) legendary queen
**Bruns•wick** German city
**brunt**
**brush**
**brush•er**
**brush•off** (*noun*)
**brush-up** (*noun*)
**brush•wood**
**brush•work**
**brusque**
**brusque•ness**
**Brus•sels**
**brut** denoting dry champagne
**bru•tal**
**bru•tal•ity** (*plural* **•ities**)
**bru•tali•za•tion** (*or* **•sa•tion**)
**bru•tal•ize** (*or* **•ise**)
**bru•tal•ly**
**brute**
**bru•ti•fy** (**•fies, •fy•ing, •fied**) brutalize
**brut•ish**
**brut•ish•ness**
**Bry•ansk** Russian city
**bryo•logi•cal**
**bry•olo•gist**
**bry•ol•ogy** study of mosses
**bryo•ny** (*or* **brio•**; *plural* **•nies**)
**bryo•phyte** botany term
**bryo•phyt•ic**
**bryo•zoan** invertebrate animal
**Bry•thon•ic** language group
**bu•bal** (*or* **bu•ba•lis**) antelope
**bu•ba•line**
**bub•ble**
**bub•bler**
**bub•bly** (**•bli•er, •bli•est**)
**bubo** (*plural* **buboes**) swelling
**bu•bon•ic**
**bu•bono•cele** medical term
**Bu•ca•ra•man•ga** Colombian city
**buc•cal** of the cheek
**buc•ca•neer**
**buc•ci•na•tor** muscle
**bu•cen•taur** Venetian barge
**Bu•cha•rest** Romanian capital
**Buch•en•wald** concentration camp
**bu•chu** shrub
**buck**
**bucka•roo** *US* cowboy
**buck•bean**
**buck•board** carriage
**buck•et**
**buck•et•ful** (*plural* **•fuls**)
**buck•eye** tree
**buck•horn**
**buck•hound**
**Buck•ing•ham**
**Buck•ing•ham•shire**
**buck•jump•er** *Austral* untamed horse
**buck•le**
**buckler-fern**
**buck•ling** bloater
**bucko** *Irish* young fellow
**buck•ram** (**ram•ing, •ramed**)
**buck•saw**
**buck•shee**
**buck•shot**
**buck•skin**
**buck•thorn**
**buck•tooth** (*plural* **•teeth**)
**buck•wheat**
**bu•col•ic**
**bu•coli•cal•ly**
**bud** (**bud•ding, bud•ded**)
**Bu•da•pest** Hungarian capital
**Bud•dhism**
**Bud•dhist**
**bud•ding**
**bud•dle** trough
**bud•dleia**
**bud•dy** (*plural* **•dies**)
**budge**
**budg•eri•gar**
**budg•et**
**budgie**
**Bue•na•ven•tu•ra** Colombian port
**Bue•nos Aires** Argentinian capital
**buff**
**Buf•fa•lo** port in New York State
**buf•fa•lo** (*plural* **•loes, •los,** *or* **•lo**)
**buff•er**
**buf•fet** restaurant; sideboard
**buf•fet** (**•fet•ing, •fet•ed**) to batter; a blow
**buf•fet•er**
**buffle•head** duck
**buf•foon**
**buf•foon•ery**
**bug** (**bug•ging, bugged**)
**buga•boo** source of fear
**Bu•gan•da** Ugandan state
**bug•bane** plant
**bug•bear**
**bugged**
**bug•ger**
**bug•gery**
**bug•ging**
**bug•gy** (*noun, plural* **•gies**; *adj* **•gi•er, •gi•est**)
**bu•gle**
**bu•gler**
**bugle•weed**
**bu•gloss**
**buhl** *variant spelling of* **boulle**
**buhr•stone** (*or* **bur•** *or* **burr•**)
**build** (**build•ing, built**)
**build•er**
**build•ing**
**build-up** (*noun*)
**built**
**built-in**
**built-up**
(**buisness**) *incorrect spelling of* **business**
**Bu•jum•bu•ra** capital of Burundi
**Bu•kha•ra** (*or* **Bo•**) Uzbek city
**Bu•ko•vi•na** (*or* **•co•**) E European region
**Bu•la•wa•yo** Zimbabwean city
**bul•ba•ceous**
**bulb•ar**
**bulb•if•er•ous**
**bul•bil** (*or* **•bel**) small bulb

**bulb•ous**
**bul•bul** bird
**Bul•garia**
**Bul•gar•ian**
**bulge**
**bulgi•ness**
**bulg•ing•ly**
**bulgy**
**bu•limia** insatiable hunger
**bulk**
**bulk•head**
**bulki•ly**
**bulki•ness**
**bulky (bulki•er, bulki•est)**
**bull**
**bul•la** (*plural* **•lae**) seal on papal bull; blister
**bul•lace** damson
**bul•late** blistered
**bull•bat** bird
**bull•dog**
**bull•doze**
**bull•doz•er**
**bul•let**
**bul•letin**
**bullet•proof**
**bull•fight**
**bull•fighter**
**bull•fighting**
**bull•finch**
**bull•frog**
**bull•head** fish
**bul•lion**
**bull•ish**
**bull-necked**
**bull•ock**
**bull•pen**
**bull•ring**
**bull's-eye**
**bull•shit**
**bull•whip**
**bul•ly** (*noun*, *plural* **•lies**; *verb* **•lies, •ly•ing, •lied)**
**bully•rag (•rag•ging, •ragged)**
**bul•rush**
**bul•wark**
**bum (bum•ming, bummed)**
**bum•bailiff**
**bum•ble**
**bumble•bee**
**bum•bler**
**bum•boat**
**bum•ma•lo** (*plural* **•lo)** Bombay duck
**bum•mer**
**bump**
**bump•er**
**bumph** (*or* **bumf)** *Slang* documents
**bumpi•ly**
**bumpi•ness**
**bump•kin**
**bump•tious**
**bump•tious•ness**
**bumpy (bumpi•er, bumpi•est)**
**bun**
**Buna** (*Trademark*) rubber
**bunch**
**bunchi•ness**
**bunchy (bunchi•er, bunchi•est)**
**bun•combe** *US variant spelling of* **bunkum**
**Bund** (*plural* **Bunds** *or* **Bün•de)** federation
**bund** embankment
**Bun•da•berg** Australian city
**Bun•del•khand** Indian region
**Bun•des•rat** German federal council
**Bun•des•tag** German legislative assembly
**bundh** Indian strike
**bun•dle**
**bun•dler**
**bun•du** *S African* wild region
**bung**
**bun•ga•low**
**bung•hole**
**bun•gle**
**bun•gler**
**bun•gling**
**bun•ion**
**bunk**
**bun•ker**
**bun•kum** (*US also* **•combe)**
**bun•ny** (*plural* **•nies)**
**bun•raku** Japanese puppet theatre
**Bun•sen burn•er**
**bunt**
**bunt•al** straw
**bunt•ing**
**bunt•line**
**bunya-bunya** tree
**bun•yip** Australian monster
**buoy**
**buoy•age**
**buoy•an•cy**
**buoy•ant**
**bu•pres•tid** beetle
**bur (bur•ring, burred)** seed vessel; *compare* **birr; burr**
**bu•ran** blizzard
**Bu•ray•dah** (*or* **•rai•da)** Saudi Arabian town
**Bur•ber•ry** (*Trademark*; *plural* **•ries)**
**bur•ble**
**bur•bler**
**bur•bot** (*plural* **•bots** *or* **•bot)** fish
**bur•den**
**bur•den•some**
**bur•dock**
**bu•reau** (*plural* **•reaus** *or* **•reaux)**
**bu•reau•cra•cy** (*plural* **•cies)**
**bu•reau•crat**
**bu•reau•crat•ic**
**bu•reau•crati•cal•ly**
**bu•reau•crat•ism**
**bu•reau•cra•tize** (*or* **•tise)**
**bu•rette** (*or esp. US* **•ret)**
**burg** fortified town; *compare* **berg; burgh**
**Bur•gas** Bulgarian port
**bur•gee** ship's flag
**Bur•gen•land** Austrian province
**bur•geon** (*or* **bour•geon)**
**burg•er** hamburger
**bur•gess** citizen of borough
**burgh** Scottish town; *compare* **berg; burg**
**burgh•al**
**burgh•er** citizen
**bur•glar**
**bur•glar•ize** *US* burgle
**bur•gla•ry** (*plural* **•ries)**
**bur•gle**
**bur•go•mas•ter**
**bur•go•net** helmet
**bur•grave** German governor
**Bur•gun•dian**
**Bur•gun•dy**
**bur•ial**
**buri•er**
**bu•rin** chisel
**burk** (*or* **berk)** *Slang* fool

**bur•ka** Muslim garment
**burke** suffocate
**Bur•kina Faso** African country
**burl** small lump
**bur•lap** fabric
**burl•er**
**bur•lesque** (*or* **•lesk; •lesqu•ing, •lesqued** *or* **•lesk•ing, •lesked)**
**bur•les•quer** (*or* **•lesk•er)**
**bur•ley** tobacco
**bur•li•ness**
**Bur•ling•ton** Canadian and US cities
**bur•ly (•li•er, •li•est)**
**Bur•ma**
**Bur•mese**
**burn (burn•ing, burnt** *or* **burned)**
**burn•er**
**bur•net** plant
**burn•ing**
**burn•ing•ly**
**bur•nish**
**burn•ish•able**
**burn•ish•er**
**Burn•ley** Lancashire town
**bur•noose** (*or* **bur•nous** *or* **bur•nouse)** Arab hood
**burn•sides** *US* side-whiskers
**burnt**
**bu•roo** *Dialect* dole
**burp**
**burr** rough edge; small drill; dialect characteristic; *compare* **birr; bur**
**bur•ra•wang** plant
**burred**
**bur•ring**
**bur•ro** (*plural* **•ros)** donkey
**bur•row**
**bur•row•er**
**bur•ry (•ri•er, •ri•est)** prickly
**Bur•sa** Turkish city
**bur•sa** (*plural* **•sae** *or* **•sas)** medical term; *compare* **bursar**
**bur•sal**
**bur•sar** financial official; *compare* **bursa**
**bur•sar•ial**
**bur•sa•ry** (*plural* **•ries)**
**burse** *Scot* student allowance
**bur•ser•aceous** botany term
**bur•si•form**
**bur•si•tis**
**burst (burst•ing, burst)**
**burst•er**
**bur•ton** hoisting tackle
**Burton-upon-Trent**
**Bu•run•di** African republic
**bur•weed**
**Bury** town in Greater Manchester
**bury (buries, bury•ing, bur•ied)**
**Bur•yat** Mongoloid people
**Bury St Ed•munds**
**bus** (*noun, plural* **buses** *or* **busses;** *verb* **bus•ing** *or* **bus•sing, bused** *or* **bussed)**
**bus•bar** electrical conductor
**bus•by** (*plural* **•bies)**
**bu•sera** Ugandan drink
**bush**
**bush•baby** (*plural* **•babies)**
**bush•buck** (*or* **bosch•bok;** *plural* **•bucks, •buck** *or* **•boks, •bok)** antelope
**bush•el (•el•ing, •elled;** *US* **•el•ing, •eled)** unit; *US* mend garment
**bush•el•ler** (*US* **•el•er)**
**bush•hammer**
**Bu•shi•do** samurai code
**bushi•ness**
**bush•ing**
**Bu•shire** Iranian port
**Bush•man** (*plural* **•man** *or* **•men)** S African people
**bush•man** (*plural* **•men)** bush dweller
**bush•master** snake
**bush•pig**
**bush•ranger**
**bush•tit** bird
**Bush•veld**
**bush•whack**
**bush•whacker**
**bushy (bushi•er, bushi•est)**
**busi•ly**
**busi•ness** trade, etc.; *compare* **busyness**
**business•like**
**business•man** (*plural* **•men)**
**business•woman** (*plural* **•women)**
**bus•ing** (*or* **bus•sing)**
**busk**
**busk•er**
**bus•kin** boot
**bust**
**bus•tard**
**bust•er**
**bus•tle**
**bus•tler**
**busty (busti•er, busti•est)**
**bu•suu•ti** garment
**busy** (*adj* **busi•er, busi•est;** *verb* **busies, busy•ing bus•ied)**
**busy•body** (*plural* **•bodies)**
**busy Liz•zie** plant
**busy•ness** state of being busy; *compare* **business**
**but**
**bu•ta•di•ene**
**bu•tane**
**bu•ta•nol**
**bu•ta•none**
**butch**
**butch•er**
**butcher•bird**
**butcher's-broom** shrub
**butch•ery** (*plural* **•eries)**
**bu•tene**
**but•ler**
**but•lery** (*plural* **•leries)**
**butt**
**butte** steep-sided hill
**but•ter** food
**butt•er** one that butts
**but•ter•bur** plant
**butter•cup**
**butter•fat**
**butter•fingered**
**butter•fingers**
**butter•fish** (*plural* **•fish** *or* **•fishes)**
**butter•fly** (*plural* **•flies)**
**but•ter•ine** artificial butter
**But•ter•mere** lake
**butter•milk**
**butter•nut**
**butter•scotch**
**butter•wort** plant
**but•tery** (*plural* **•teries)**
**but•tock**
**but•ton**
**button•hole**
**button•hook**
**button•mould** (*US* **•mold)**
**but•ton•wood**
**but•tress**

**but•ty** (*plural* **•ties)** *Dialect* sandwich
**bu•tyl**
**bu•tyra•ceous**
**bu•tyr•al•de•hyde**
**bu•tyr•ate**
**bu•tyr•ic acid**
**bu•tyr•in**
**bux•om**
**bux•om•ness**
**Bux•ton** Derbyshire town
**buy (buys, buy•ing, bought)**
**buy•er**
**buzz**
**buz•zard**
**buzz•er**
**bwa•na**
**by**
**by-bidder**
**by-blow**
**Byd•goszcz** Polish city
**bye** sports term; something incidental
**by-election** (*or* **bye-election)**
**Bye•lo•rus•sia** *variant spelling of* **Belorussia**
**Bye•lo•rus•sian** *variant spelling of* **Belorussian**
**Bye•lo•vo** *variant spelling of* **Belovo**
**by•gone**
**by•law** (*or* **bye-law)**
**by-line**
**by•pass (•pass•ing, •passed** *or* **•past)**
**by•path**
**by-product**
**byre** cowshed; *compare* **bier**
**byr•nie** armour
**by•road**
**By•ron•ic**
**bys•si•no•sis** lung disease
**bys•sus** (*plural* **•suses** *or* **•si)** zoology term
**by•stander**
**by•street**
**byte** computer term; *compare* **bight; bite**
**By•tom** Polish city
**by•way**
**by•word**
**Byz•an•tine**
**By•zan•tium**

# C

**cab**
**ca•bal (•bal•ling, •balled)** secret group
**ca•bal•le•ro** (*plural* **•ros)**
**ca•ba•na** tent
**Ca•ba•na•tuan** Philippine city
**caba•ret**
**cab•bage**
**cabbage•town** city slum
**cab•ba•la** (*or* **ca•ba•la, kab•ba•la, ka•ba•la)** Jewish teaching
**cab•ba•lism** (*or* **caba•, kab•ba•, kaba•)**
**cab•ba•list** (*or* **caba•, kab•ba•, kaba•)**
**cab•ba•lis•tic** (*or* **caba•, kab•ba•, kaba•)**
**cab•by** (*or* **cab•bie;** *plural* **•bies)**
**ca•ber**
**cab•ezon** (*or* **•ezone)** fish
**Ca•bi•mas** Venezuelan town
**cab•in**
**Cabi•net** government
**cabi•net** furniture
**cabinet-maker**
**cabinet•work**
**ca•ble**
**ca•ble•gram**
**cable-laid**
**ca•blet** small cable
**cable•way**
**cab•man** (*plural* **•men)**
**cabo•chon** polished gem
**ca•boo•dle**
**ca•boose**
**Ca•bo•ra Bas•sa** African dam
**cabo•tage** coastal navigation
**ca•bret•ta** leather
**ca•bril•la** fish
**cab•ri•ole** furniture leg
**cab•rio•let** horse-drawn carriage
**ca•cao** cocoa tree
**cac•cia•to•re** (*or* **•ra)** cookery term
**cacha•lot** whale
**cache**
**ca•chec•tic** weakened
**cache•pot** flowerpot container
**ca•chet**
**ca•chexia** (*or* **•chexy)** weakness
**cach•in•nate** laugh loudly
**cach•in•na•tion**
**ca•chou** lozenge; *variant of* **catechu;** *compare* **cashew**
**ca•chu•cha** dance
**ca•cique** American Indian chief
**cack-handed**
**cack•le**
**cack•ler**
**caco•demon**
**caco•dyl** chemical compound
**caco•epy** bad pronunciation
**caco•ethes** uncontrollable urge
**caco•eth•ic**
**caco•gen•ics**
**caco•graph•ic**
**ca•cog•ra•phy** bad handwriting
**ca•col•ogy** bad speech
**caco•mis•tle** (*or* **•mix•le)** animalcab
**cacophonic**
**caco•phon•ic**
**ca•copho•nous**
**ca•copho•ny** (*plural* **•nies)**
**cac•ta•ceous**
**cac•tus** (*plural* **•tuses** *or* **•ti)**
**ca•cu•mi•nal** phonetics term
**cad**
**ca•das•ter** (*or* **•tre)** property register
**ca•dav•er**

**ca•dav•er•ic**
**ca•dav•er•ine** chemical compound
**ca•dav•er•ous**
**ca•dav•er•ous•ness**
**cad•die** (*or* **•dy**; *noun, plural* **•dies**; *verb* **•dies, •dy•ing, •died**) golf term; *compare* **caddy**
**cad•dis** fly
**cad•dis** (*or* **•dice**) textile
**cad•dish**
**Cad•do•an** language group
**cad•dy** (*plural* **•dies**) tea container; *compare* **caddie**
**cade** tree
**ca•delle** beetle
**ca•dence**
**ca•den•cy** (*plural* **•cies**) heraldic term
**ca•dent**
**ca•den•za**
**ca•det**
**cadge**
**cadg•er**
**cadi** Muslim judge
**Cadillac** (*Trademark*)
**Cá•diz** Spanish port
**cad•mium**
**ca•dre** trained personnel
**ca•du•ceus** (*plural* **•cei**) medical emblem
**ca•du•city** senility
**ca•du•cous** biology term
**cae•cal** (*US* **ce•**)
**cae•cil•ian** amphibian
**cae•cum** (*US* **ce•**; *plural* **•ca**) part of intestine
**Cae•lian** Roman hill
**Cae•lum** constellation
**Caen** French city
**cae•no•gen•esis** (*or* **cai•, kai•**; *US* **ce•** *or* **ke•**) biology term
**cae•no•genet•ic** (*or* **cai•, kai•**; *US* **ce•** *or* **ke•**)
**caeo•ma** botany term
**Caer•leon** Welsh town
**Caer•nar•von** (*or* **•fon**)
**Caer•nar•von•shire** (*or* **•fon•shire**) former Welsh county
**Caer•phil•ly**
**caes•al•pinia•ceous** botany term
**Caesa•rea** Israeli port
**Cae•sar•ean** (*or* **•ian**) of Caesar
**Cae•sar•ean sec•tion** (*or* **cae•**; *US* **ce•sar•ean sec•tion**)
**Cae•sar•ism** autocratic government
**cae•sium** (*US* **ce•**)
**caes•pi•tose** (*US* **ces•**) growing in tufts
**cae•su•ra** (*plural* **•ras** *or* **•rae**)
**café**
**caf•eteria**
**caf•feine** (*or* **•fein**)
**caf•tan** *variant spelling of* **kaftan**
**cage**
**cage•ling**
**cag•ey** (*or* **cagy; cagi•er, cagi•est**)
**cagi•ly**
**cagi•ness**
**Ca•glia•ri** Sardinian port
**cag•mag** *Dialect* chat
**ca•goule**
**ca•hier** *French* notebook
**ca•hoots**
**Caiaphas** biblical character
**Cai•cos** West Indian islands
**Cain** biblical character
**Cai•no•zo•ic** *variant spelling of* **Cenozoic**
**caïque** boat
**cairn**
**cairn•gorm** quartz
**Cairngorm** Scottish mountains
**Cai•ro**
**cais•son** watertight structure
**Caith•ness**
**cai•tiff** cowardly person
**ca•jole**
**ca•jol•ery** (*plural* **•eries**)
**Ca•jun** Acadian descendant
**caju•put** (*or* **caj•eput**) shrub
**cake**
**cake•walk**
**Cala•bar** Nigerian port
**cala•bash** tree
**Ca•lab•ria** Italian region
**ca•la•dium** plant
**Cal•ais**
**cala•lu** Caribbean leaves
**cala•man•co** fabric
**cala•man•der** wood
**cala•mine** lotion
**cala•mint** plant
**cala•mite** plant
**ca•lami•tous**
**ca•lam•ity** (*plural* **•ities**)
**cala•mon•din** fruit
**cala•mus** (*plural* **•mi**) plant; cane
**cal•an•dria** heat-exchanger vessel
**ca•lash** (*or* **•leche**) carriage
**cala•thus** (*plural* **•thi**) Greek symbol
**ca•lav•er•ite** mineral
**cal•ca•neal** (*or* **•nean**)
**cal•ca•neus** (*or* **•neum**; *plural* **•nei**) heel bone
**cal•car** (*plural* **•caria**) spur
**cal•car•eous** containing lime
**cal•ca•rif•er•ous**
**cal•cei•form** (*or* **•ceo•late**) botany term
**cal•ceo•lar•ia** plant
**cal•ces** (*plural of* **calx**)
**cal•cic** containing calcium
**cal•ci•cole** lime-loving plant
**cal•cico•lous**
**cal•cif•er•ol** vitamin
**cal•cif•er•ous**
**cal•cif•ic**
**cal•ci•fi•ca•tion**
**cal•ci•fu•gal**
**cal•ci•fuge** acid-loving plant
**cal•cifu•gous**
**cal•ci•fy** (**•fies, •fy•ing, •fied**)
**cal•ci•mine** (*or* **kal•so•mine**) wash for walls
**cal•ci•na•tion**
**cal•cine** chemistry term
**cal•cite** mineral
**cal•cit•ic**
**cal•ci•ton•in** hormone
**cal•cium**
**calc•sinter** rock
**cal•cu•la•bil•ity** (*plural* **•ities**)
**cal•cu•lable**
**cal•cu•late**
**cal•cu•la•tion**
**cal•cu•la•tive**
**cal•cu•la•tor**

**cal•cu•lous**
**cal•cu•lus** (*plural* **•luses**) maths term
**cal•cu•lus** (*plural* **•li**) stone in body
**Cal•cut•ta**
**cal•dar•ium** Roman bathroom
**cal•de•ra** volcanic crater
**cal•dron** *variant spelling of* **cauldron**
**Cal•edo•nia**
**Cal•edo•nian**
**cal•efa•cient**
**cal•efac•tion**
**cal•efac•tory** (*plural* **•tories**)
**cal•en•dar** dates; *compare* **colander**
**cal•en•der** smoothing machine; *compare* **colander**
**cal•ends** (*or* **kal•ends**)
**ca•len•du•la** plant
**cal•en•ture** fever
**calf** (*plural* **calves**)
**calf•skin**
**Cal•ga•ry** Canadian city
**Cali** Colombian city
**cali•brate**
**cali•bra•tion**
**cali•bra•tor** (*or* **•brat•er**)
**cali•bre** (*US* **•ber**)
**cali•bred** (*US* **•bered**)
**cali•ces** *plural of* **calix**
**ca•li•che** geology term
**cali•co** (*plural* **•coes** *or* **•cos**)
**Cali•cut** Indian port
**Cali•for•nia**
**cali•for•nium** radioactive element
**cali•pash** (*or* **cal•li•pash**) turtle meat
**cali•pee** turtle meat
**cali•per** *US spelling of* **calliper**
**ca•liph** (*or* **ca•lif, ka•lif, kha•lif**)
**ca•li•phate** (*or* **ca•li•fate, ka•li•fate**)
**cali•sa•ya** cinchona bark
**cal•is•then•ic** *variant spelling of* **callisthenic**
**ca•lix** (*plural* **cali•ces**) chalice; *compare* **calyx**
**calk** *variant spelling of* **caulk**
**calk** (*or* **cal•kin**) spike on shoe
**call**
**cal•la** plant
**call•able**
**cal•lais** ornamental stone
**cal•lant** (*or* **•lan**) youth
**Ca•llao** Peruvian port
**call•boy**
**call•er** one who calls
**cal•ler** *Scot* fresh food
**cal•lig•ra•pher** (*or* **•phist**)
**cal•li•graph•ic**
**cal•li•graphi•cal•ly**
**cal•lig•ra•phy**
**call•ing**
**cal•lio•pe** *US* steam organ
**cal•li•pash** *variant spelling of* **calipash**
**cal•li•per** (*US* **cali•per**)
**cal•li•pyg•ian** (*or* **•py•gous**) having shapely buttocks
**cal•lis•then•ic** (*or* **cal•is•**)
**cal•lis•then•ics** (*or* **cal•is•**)
**Cal•lis•to** satellite of Jupiter
**cal•los•ity** (*plural* **•ities**)
**cal•lous** (*adj*)
**cal•lous•ness**
**cal•low**
**cal•low•ness**
**cal•lus** (*noun; plural* **•luses**)
**calm**
**cal•ma•tive**
**calm•ness**
**calo•mel** purgative
**Cal•or** (*Trademark*)
**ca•lor•ic**
**calo•ric•ity** (*plural* **•ities**)
**Calo•rie** kilocalorie
**calo•rie**
**calo•rif•ic**
**calo•rifi•cal•ly**
**calo•rim•eter**
**calo•ri•met•ric** (*or* **•ri•cal**)
**calo•ri•met•ri•cal•ly**
**calo•rim•etry**
**ca•lotte** priest's skullcap
**calo•yer** Greek Orthodox monk
**cal•pac** (*or* **cal•pack, kal•pak**) brimless hat
**calque** (**calqu•ing, calqued**) linguistics term
**cal•trop** (*or* **•trap, •throp**) plant
**calu•met** peace pipe
**ca•lum•ni•ate**
**ca•lum•nia•tion**
**ca•lum•ni•ous** (*or* **•nia•tory**)
**cal•um•ny** (*plural* **•nies**)
**calu•tron** physics term
**Cal•va•dos** French department; brandy
**cal•varia** top of skull
**Cal•va•ry** Crucifixion site
**cal•va•ry** (*plural* **•ries**) suffering
**calve** (*verb*)
**calves** *plural of* **calf**
**Cal•vin•ism**
**Cal•vin•ist**
**Cal•vin•is•tic**
**cal•vi•ti•es** baldness
**calx** (*plural* **calxes** *or* **cal•ces**) oxide
**caly•cate** having a calyx
**caly•cine** (*or* **ca•lyci•nal**) of a calyx
**caly•cle** (*or* **ca•lycu•lus**; *plural* **•cles** *or* **•li**) biology term
**Calypso** mythological character
**ca•lyp•so** (*plural* **•sos**) song
**ca•lyp•tra** botany term
**ca•lyp•trate**
**ca•lyp•tro•gen**
**ca•lyx** (*plural* **ca•lyxes** *or* **caly•ces**) sepals of plant; *compare* **calix**
**Cam** river
**cam** machinery
**Ca•ma•güey** Cuban city
**ca•mail** armour
**ca•ma•ra•derie**
**cama•ril•la** Spanish cabal
**cam•ass** (*or* **•as**) plant
**cam•ber**
**Cam•ber•well**
**cam•bial** of cambium
**cam•bist** foreign-exchange dealer
**cam•bist•ry** (*plural* **•ries**)
**cam•bium** (*plural* **•biums** *or* **•bia**) plant tissue
**Cam•bo•dia**
**Cam•bo•dian**
**cam•bo•gia** gum resin
**cam•boose** lumberjack's cabin

**Cam•brai** French town
**Cam•bria** *Latin* Wales
**Cam•brian** geological period
**cam•bric** fabric
**Cam•bridge**
**Cam•bridge•shire**
**Cam•den** London borough
**came**
**cam•el**
**cam•el•eer**
**ca•mel•lia**
**ca•melo•pard** giraffe
**Ca•melo•par•dus** (*or* **•da•lis**) constellation
**Cam•elot**
**Cam•em•bert** cheese
**cameo** (*noun, plural* **cameos**; *verb* **cameos, cameo•ing, cam•eoed**)
**cam•era**
**cam•er•al**
**cam•era lu•ci•da**
**camera•man** (*plural* **•men**)
**cam•era ob•scu•ra**
**camera-ready**
**cam•er•len•go** (*or* **•lin•go**; *plural* **•gos**) papal treasurer
**Cam•eroon**
**cami•knick•ers**
**cami•on** lorry
**ca•mise** smock
**cami•sole**
**cam•let** cloth
**camo•mile** (*or* **chamo•**)
**ca•moo•di** snake
**Ca•mor•ra** secret society
**camou•flage**
**camp**
**Cam•pa•gna** Italian plain
**cam•paign**
**cam•paign•er**
**Cam•pa•nia** Italian region
**cam•pa•ni•le** bell tower
**cam•pa•nolo•gist**
**cam•pa•nol•ogy**
**cam•panu•la** flower
**cam•panu•la•ceous**
**cam•panu•late** bell-shaped
**Cam•peche** Mexican state
**camp•er**
**cam•pes•tral** of fields
**cam•phene**
**cam•phire** henna
**cam•phor**
**cam•pho•rate**
**cam•phor•ic**
**Cam•pi•nas** Brazilian city
**camp•ing**
**cam•pi•on**
**cam•po** Brazilian savanna
**campo•ree** Scout meeting
**Cam•pos** Brazilian city
**cam•pus** (*plural* **•puses**)
**cam•shaft**
**cam•wood**
**can** (**can•ning, canned**)
**Cana** biblical town
**Ca•naan** biblical region
**Ca•naan•ite**
**Cana•da**
**Ca•na•dian**
**Ca•na•di•an•ism**
**ca•nai•gre** plant
**ca•naille** *French* mob
**ca•nal** (**•nal•ling, •nalled**; *US* **•nal•ing, •naled**)
**cana•licu•lar**
**cana•licu•lus** (*plural* **•li**) small channel
**cana•li•za•tion** (*or* **•sa•tion**)
**cana•lize** (*or* **•lise**)
**cana•pé**
**ca•nard** rumour
**ca•nary** (*plural* **•naries**)
**Ca•nary Is•lands** (*or* **Ca•naries**)
**ca•nas•ta** card game
**can•as•ter** tobacco
**Ca•nav•er•al** US cape
**Can•ber•ra**
**can•can**
**can•cel** (**•cel•ling, •celled**; *US* **•cel•ing, •celed**)
**can•cel•late** (*or* **•lous, •lat•ed**) medical term
**can•cel•la•tion**
**can•cel•ler** (*US* **•cel•er**)
**Can•cer** sign of zodiac
**can•cer** disease
**can•cer•ous**
**can•croid**
**can•de•la** unit
**can•de•la•brum** (*or* **•bra**; *plural* **•bra, •brums**, *or* **•bras**)
**can•did**
**can•di•da•cy** (*or* **•da•ture**)
**can•di•date**
**can•did•ness**
**can•died**
**Can•di•ot** Cretan
**can•dle**
**candle•berry** (*plural* **•berries**)
**candle•fish** (*plural* **•fish** *or* **•fishes**)
**candle•light**
**Candle•mas**
**candle•nut**
**candle•pins** bowling game
**candle•power**
**can•dler**
**candle•stick**
**candle•wick**
**candle•wood**
**can•dour** (*US* **•dor**)
**can•dy** (*noun, plural* **•dies**; *verb* **•dies, •dy•ing, •died**)
**candy•floss**
**candy-striped**
**candy•tuft**
**cane**
**cane•brake** US thicket
**ca•nel•la** spice
**can•er**
**ca•nes•cent** hoary
**can•field** card game
**cangue** wooden collar
**Ca•nicu•la** the star Sirius
**ca•nicu•lar** of Sirius
**ca•nine**
**can•ing**
**can•is•ter**
**can•ker**
**can•ker•ous**
**canker•worm**
**can•na** plant
**can•na•bic**
**can•na•bin**
**can•na•bis**
**Can•nae** battle site
**canned**
**can•nel** coal
**can•nel•lo•ni** (*or* **•ne•lo•ni**)
**can•ne•lure** groove
**can•ner**
**can•nery** (*plural* **•neries**)
**Cannes** French town
**can•ni•bal**
**can•ni•bal•ism**
**can•ni•bal•is•tic**
**can•ni•bali•za•tion** (*or* **•sa•tion**)
**can•ni•bal•ize** (*or* **•ise**)

**can•ni•kin** (*or* **cana•kin,** **cani•kin**) small can
**can•ni•ly**
**can•ni•ness**
**can•ning**
**Can•nock** Staffordshire town
**can•non** (*plural* **•nons** *or* **•non**) artillery; *compare* **canon**
**can•non•ade**
**cannon•ball**
**can•non•eer**
**can•non•ry** (*plural* **•ries**) artillery; *compare* **canonry**
**can•not**
**can•nu•la** (*or* **canu•la;** *plural* **•las** *or* **•lae**) surgical tube
**can•nu•late** (*or* **canu•late**)
**can•ny** (**•ni•er, •ni•est**)
**ca•noe** (**•noes, •noe•ing, •noed**)
**ca•noe•ist**
**can•on** priest; decree; *compare* **cannon**
**can•on•ess**
**ca•noni•cal**
**ca•noni•cate** office of canon
**can•on•ic•ity**
**can•on•ist**
**can•oni•za•tion** (*or* **•sa•tion**)
**can•on•ize** (*or* **•ise**)
**can•on•ry** (*plural* **•ries**) office of canon; *compare* **cannonry**
**ca•noo•dle**
**Ca•no•pus** Egyptian port
**cano•py** (*noun, plural* **•pies;** *verb* **•pies, •py•ing, •pied**)
**Ca•nos•sa** Italian castle
**cans** *Slang* headphones
**cant** platitudes; slope
**can't** cannot
**can•ta•bi•le** musical term
**Can•ta•brian** Spanish mountains
**Can•ta•brig•ian** of Cambridge
**Can•tal** French department; cheese
**can•ta•la** plant
**can•ta•loupe** (*or* **•loup**)
**can•tan•ker•ous**
**can•ta•ta**
**can•ta•trice** singer
**can•teen**
**can•ter**
**Can•ter•bury**
**can•thari•des** (*sing.* **•tha•ris**) medicine
**can•thus** (*plural* **•thi**) corner of eye
**cant•ic**
**can•ti•cle**
**can•ti•lena** musical term
**can•ti•lever**
**can•til•late**
**can•til•la•tion**
**can•ti•na** Spanish bar
**cant•ing**
**can•tle** saddle part
**can•to** (*plural* **•tos**)
**Can•ton** Chinese port
**can•ton** division of Switzerland
**can•ton•al**
**Can•ton•ese** (*plural* **•ese**)
**can•ton•ment**
**can•tor** religious singer
**can•tor•is** musical term
**can•trip** magic spell
**can•tus** (*plural* **•tus**) medieval church singing
**canty** *Dialect* lively
**can•vas** cloth
**canvas•back** (*plural* **•backs** *or* **•back**) duck
**can•vass** solicit
**can•vass•er**
**can•yon**
**can•zo•na** musical term
**can•zo•ne** (*plural* **•ni**) song
**can•zo•net** song
**caou•tchouc** rubber
**cap** (**cap•ping, capped**)
**ca•pa•bil•ity** (*plural* **•ities**)
**ca•pable**
**ca•pably**
**ca•pa•cious**
**ca•paci•tance** physics term
**ca•paci•tate**
**ca•paci•ta•tion**
**ca•paci•tive**
**ca•paci•tor**
**ca•pac•ity** (*plural* **•ities**)
**cap-a-pie** from head to foot
**ca•pari•son**
**cape**
**cap•elin** (*or* **cap•lin**) fish
**Ca•pel•la** star
**ca•per**
**cap•er•cail•lie** (*or* **•cail•zie**)
**Ca•per•na•um** Israeli town
**Cape Roca** Portuguese cape
**cape•skin**
**Capet** French dynasty
**Ca•petian**
**Cape Verde** island country
**ca•pi•as** legal term
**cap•il•la•ceous** hairy
**cap•il•lar•ity** surface tension
**ca•pil•lary** (*plural* **•laries**)
**capi•tal**
**capi•tal•ism**
**capi•tal•ist**
**capi•tal•is•tic**
**capi•tali•za•tion** (*or* **•sa•tion**)
**capi•tal•ize** (*or* **•ise**)
**capi•tal•ly**
**capi•tate** headlike
**capi•ta•tion**
**capi•ta•tive**
**Capi•tol** US Congress building
**Capi•to•line** Roman hill
**ca•pitu•lar**
**ca•pitu•lary** (*plural* **•laries**)
**ca•pitu•late**
**ca•pitu•la•tion**
**ca•pitu•la•tor**
**ca•pitu•lum** (*plural* **•la**) biology term
**capo** (*plural* **capos**) guitar attachment
**ca•pon**
**ca•pon•ize** (*or* **•ise**)
**capo•ral** tobacco; *compare* **corporal**
**ca•pote** cloak
**Cap•pa•do•cia** ancient Asian region
**cap•pa•ri•da•ceous** botany term
**capped**
**cap•per**
**cap•pie** *Scot* ice-cream cone
**cap•ping**
**cap•puc•ci•no** (*plural* **•nos**)
**cap•reo•late** botany term
**Ca•pri**
**ca•pric•cio** (*plural* **•cios** *or* **•ci**) musical work
**ca•pric•cio•so** musical term
**ca•price**

**ca•pri•cious**
**ca•pri•cious•ness**
**Cap•ri•corn** sign of zodiac
**Cap•ri•cor•nus** (*plural* **•ni**) constellation
**cap•ri•fi•ca•tion**
**cap•ri•fig** wild fig
**cap•ri•fo•lia•ceous** botany term
**cap•rine** of goats
**cap•ri•ole**
**cap•sai•cin** alkaloid
**cap•si•cum**
**cap•sid** plant bug
**cap•size**
**cap•stan**
**cap•stone** (*or* **cope•**)
**cap•su•lar**
**cap•su•late** (*or* **•lat•ed**)
**cap•su•la•tion**
**cap•sule**
**cap•sul•ize** (*or* **•ise**)
**cap•tain**
**cap•tain•cy** (*or* **•tain•ship**; *plural* **•cies** *or* **•ships**)
**cap•tion**
**cap•tious**
**cap•ti•vate**
**cap•ti•va•tion**
**cap•ti•va•tor**
**cap•tive**
**cap•tiv•ity** (*plural* **•ities**)
**cap•tor**
**cap•ture**
**Capua** Italian town
**ca•puche** friar's hood
**Capu•chin** friar
**capu•chin** monkey
**ca•put** (*plural* **capi•ta**) head; *compare* **kaput**
**capy•ba•ra** rodent
**car**
**cara•bao** water buffalo
**cara•bid** beetle
**cara•bi•neer** (*or* **•nier**) *variants of* **carbineer**
**ca•ra•bi•nie•re** (*plural* **•ri**) Italian policeman
**cara•cal** lynx
**ca•ra•ca•ra** bird
**Ca•ra•cas** Venezuelan capital
**cara•cole** (*or* **•col**) dressage term
**cara•cul** fur; *variant spelling of* **karakul**
**ca•rafe**
**cara•geen** *variant spelling of* **carrageen**
**ca•ram•ba** (*or* **•bo•la**) tree; fruit
**cara•mel**
**cara•mel•ize** (*or* **•ise**)
**ca•ran•gid** (*or* **•goid**) fish
**cara•pace**
**car•at** weight; *compare* **caret**
**cara•van** (**•van•ning**, **•vanned**)
**cara•van•se•rai** (*or* **•sa•ry**; *plural* **•rais** *or* **•ries**)
**cara•vel** (*or* **car•vel**) ship
**cara•way**
**car•ba•mate**
**car•bami•dine**
**car•ban•ion** chemistry term
**car•ba•zole**
**car•bene** chemistry term
**car•bide**
**car•bine** rifle
**car•bi•neer** (*or* **cara•bi•neer**, **cara•bi•nier**) soldier
**car•bo•hy•drate**
**car•bo•lat•ed**
**car•bol•ic**
**car•bo•lize** (*or* **•lise**)
**car•bon**
**car•bo•na•ceous**
**car•bo•nade** beef stew
**car•bo•na•do** (*noun, plural* **•does** *or* **•dos**; *verb* **•do•ing**, **•doed**) grilled meat; industrial diamond
**Car•bo•na•ri** political society
**car•bon•ate**
**car•bona•tion**
**car•bon•ic**
**car•bon•if•er•ous**
**car•boni•za•tion** (*or* **•sa•tion**)
**car•bon•ize** (*or* **•ise**)
**car•bon•ous**
**car•bon•yl**
**Car•bo•run•dum** (*Trademark*)
**car•box•yl**
**car•box•yl•ase** enzyme
**car•box•yl•ate**
**car•box•yl•ic**
**car•boy** large bottle
**car•bun•cle**
**car•bun•cu•lar**
**car•bu•ra•tion**
**car•bu•ret** (**•ret•ting**, **•ret•ted**; *US* **•ret•ing**, **•ret•ed**)
**car•bu•ret•tor** (*or* **•ter**; *US* **•retor**)
**car•bu•ri•za•tion** (*or* **•sa•tion**)
**car•bu•rize** (*or* **•rise**)
**car•byla•mine**
**car•cass** (*or* **•case**)
**Car•chem•ish** ancient Syrian city
**car•cino•gen**
**car•cino•gen•ic**
**car•ci•no•ma** (*plural* **•mas** *or* **•ma•ta**)
**car•ci•no•ma•toid** (*or* **•tous**)
**car•ci•no•ma•to•sis**
**card**
**car•da•mom** (*or* **•mum**, **•mon**) spice
**card•board**
**card-carrying**
**car•di•ac**
**car•di•al•gia** heart pain
**car•di•al•gic**
**Car•diff**
**Car•di•gan** Welsh bay
**car•di•gan**
**car•di•nal**
**car•di•nal•ate** (*or* **•ship**)
**car•di•nal•ly**
**card•ing**
**car•dio•gram** record
**car•dio•graph** instrument
**car•di•og•ra•pher**
**car•dio•graph•ic** (*or* **•graphi•cal**)
**car•di•og•ra•phy**
**car•di•oid**
**car•dio•logi•cal**
**car•di•olo•gist**
**car•di•ol•ogy**
**car•dio•mega•ly** heart enlargement
**car•dio•vas•cu•lar**
**car•di•tis**
**car•doon** plant
**card•sharp** (*or* **•sharper**)
**car•dua•ceous** botany term
**care**

**ca•reen** nautical term
**ca•reer**
**ca•reer•ist**
**care•free**
**care•ful**
**care•ful•ly**
**care•ful•ness**
**care•less**
**care•less•ness**
**ca•ress**
**ca•ress•er**
**ca•ress•ing•ly**
**car•et** printing symbol; *compare* **carat**
**care•taker**
**care•worn**
**car•fare** *US* bus fare
**car•fax** crossroads
**car•go** (*plural* **•goes** *or* **•gos**)
**car•hop**
**Caria** ancient Asian region
**Car•ib** (*plural* **•ibs** *or* **•ib**) American Indian
**Car•ib•bean**
**Car•ib•bees** West Indian islands
**cari•bou** (*plural* **•bous** *or* **•bou**)
**cari•ca•ture**
**cari•ca•tur•ist**
**cari•es** (*plural* **cari•es**) tooth decay
**ca•ril•lon** (**•lon•ning, •lonned**)
**ca•ril•lon•neur**
**Ca•ri•na** constellation
**ca•ri•na** (*plural* **•nae** *or* **•nas**) keel-shaped part
**cari•nate** (*or* **•nat•ed**)
**Ca•rin•thia** Austrian province
**cario•ca** dance
**cario•gen•ic** producing tooth decay
**cari•ole** (*or* **car•ri•ole**) cart
**cari•os•ity** (*or* **cari•ous•ness**)
**cari•ous**
**car•line** plant
**car•ling** (*or* **•line**) ship's beam
**Car•lisle** Cumbrian city
**Car•low** Irish county
**Carl•ton** English town
**car•ma•gnole** French costume
**car•man** (*plural* **•men**)
**Car•mar•then**
**Car•mar•then•shire** Welsh county
**Car•mel** Israeli mountain
**Car•mel•ite** friar or nun
**car•mina•tive**
**car•mine**
**car•nage**
**car•nal**
**car•nal•ist**
**car•nal•ity**
**car•nall•ite** mineral
**car•nal•ly**
**car•nas•sial** tooth
**Car•nat•ic** Indian region
**car•na•tion**
**car•nau•ba** wax
**car•nel•ian** *variant spelling of* **cornelian**
**car•net** travel document; customs licence
**car•ni•fi•ca•tion**
**car•ni•fy** (**•fies, •fy•ing, •fied**) medical term
**Car•nio•la** Slovenian region
**car•ni•val**
**car•ni•vore**
**car•nivo•rous**
**car•no•tite**
**car•ny** (*or* **•ney; •nies, •ny•ing, •nied** *or* **•neys, •ney•ing, •neyed**) coax
**car•ob**
**ca•roche** carriage
**car•ol** (**•ol•ling, •olled**; *US* **•ol•ing, •oled**)
**car•ol•er**
**Caro•li•na**
**Caro•line** (*or* **Caro•lean**) of King Charles
**Caro•lin•gian** Frankish dynasty
**Caro•lin•ian** of Carolina
**caro•lus** (*plural* **•luses** *or* **•li**) coin
**car•om** billiards term
**caro•tene** (*or* **•tin**) orange pigment
**ca•rot•enoid**
**ca•rot•id** artery
**ca•rot•id•al**
**ca•rous•al** drinking party; *compare* **carousel**
**ca•rouse**
**carou•sel** *US* merry-go-round; *compare* **carousal**
**ca•rous•er**
**carp**
**car•pal** of the wrist; *compare* **carpel**
**Car•pa•thian Moun•tains**
**car•pel** flower part; *compare* **carpal**
**car•pel•lary**
**car•pel•late**
**Car•pen•ta•ria** Australian gulf
**car•pen•ter**
**car•pen•try**
**car•pet**
**carpet•bag**
**carpet•bag•ger**
**car•phol•ogy** medical term; *compare* **carpology**
**car•po•go•nial**
**car•po•go•nium** (*plural* **•nia**) botany term
**car•po•logi•cal**
**car•polo•gist**
**car•pol•ogy** branch of botany; *compare* **carphology**
**car•po•meta•car•pus** bird bone
**car•popha•gous** feeding on fruit
**car•po•phore** botany term
**car•port**
**car•po•spore**
**car•pus** (*plural* **•pi**) wrist
**car•rack** galleon
**car•ra•geen** (*or* **•gheen, cara•geen**) seaweed
**Car•ra•ra** Italian town
**car•re•four** crossroads
**car•rel** (*or* **•rell**) library cubicle
**car•riage**
**carriage•way**
**car•rick**
**car•ri•er**
**car•ri•on**
**car•ron•ade** cannon
**car•rot**
**car•roty**
**car•ry** (**•ries, •ry•ing, •ried**)
**carry•all**
**carry•cot**

**carse** *Scot* low-lying land
**car•sey** *variant spelling of* **carzey**
**car•sick**
**car•sick•ness**
**cart**
**cart•age**
**Car•ta•gena** Colombian port
**carte blanche** (*plural* **cartes blanches**)
**car•tel**
**car•tel•ize**
**car•teli•za•tion**
**Car•tesian** of Descartes
**cart•ful**
**Car•thage**
**Car•tha•gin•ian**
**cart•horse**
**Car•thu•sian** monk
**car•ti•lage**
**car•ti•lagi•nous**
**cart•load**
**car•to•gram** map
**car•tog•ra•pher**
**car•to•graph•ic**
**car•to•graphi•cal**
**car•tog•ra•phy**
**carto•man•cy** fortune-telling
**car•ton**
**car•toon**
**car•toon•ist**
**car•touche** (*or* **•touch**)
**car•tridge**
**car•tu•lary** (*or* **char•**; *plural* **•laries**) legal records
**cart•wheel**
**car•un•cle** fleshy outgrowth
**car•un•cu•lar** (*or* **•lous**)
**car•un•cu•late** (*or* **•lat•ed**)
**carve**
**car•vel** *variant of* **caravel**
**carvel-built**
**carv•er**
**carv•ery** (*plural* **•eries**)
**carv•ing**
**cary•at•id** (*plural* **•ids** *or* **•ati•des**)
**cary•ati•dal** (*or* **•dean, cary•at•ic, cary•atid•ic**)
**caryo•phyl•la•ceous** botany term
**cary•op•sis** (*plural* **•ses** *or* **•si•des**) botany term
**car•zey** (*or* **•sey**) *Slang* lavatory
**ca•sa•ba** (*or* **cas•sa•ba**) melon
**Casa•blan•ca**
**cas•bah** *variant spelling of* **kasbah**
**cas•cade**
**cas•ca•ra**
**cas•ca•ril•la** shrub
**case**
**ca•sease** enzyme
**ca•seate** medical term
**ca•sea•tion**
**case•bound**
**ca•sefy** (**•sefies, •sefy•ing, •sefied**) become cheesy
**case-harden**
**ca•sein** protein
**ca•seino•gen** protein
**case•mate** part of ship
**case•ment**
**ca•seose** biochemical compound
**ca•seous** cheeselike
**ca•sern** (*or* **•serne**) soldier's billet
**Ca•ser•ta** Italian town
**case•work**
**cash**
**cash•able**
**cash-and-carry**
**cash-book**
**cash•ew** nut; *compare* **cachou**
**cash•ier**
**cash•mere**
**cas•ing**
**ca•si•no** (*plural* **•nos**) gaming house; *compare* **cassino**
**cask**
**cas•ket**
**Cas•lon** style of type
**Cas•pian Sea**
**casque** helmet
**casqued**
**cas•sa•reep** cassava juice
**cas•sa•ta** ice cream
**cas•sa•tion** legal term
**cas•sa•va** plant
**Cas•se•grain•ian** telescope
**cas•se•role**
**cas•sette**
**cas•sia** plant
**cas•si•mere** (*or* **casi•mere**) cloth
**cas•si•no** (*or* **ca•si•no**) card game; *compare* **casino**
**Cas•sio•peia** constellation
**cas•sis** liqueur
**cas•sit•er•ite** mineral
**cas•sock** priest's garment; *compare* **hassock**
**cas•socked**
**cas•sou•let** French stew
**cas•so•wary** (*plural* **•waries**) bird
**cast** (**•ing, cast**)
**cas•ta•net**
**cast•away**
**caste** Hindu class
**cas•tel•lan** keeper of castle
**cas•tel•lat•ed**
**cas•tel•la•tion**
**cast•er** one who casts; *compare* **castor**
**cas•ter** (*or* **•tor**) sugar dispenser; wheel on furniture; *compare* **castor**
**cas•ti•gate**
**cas•ti•ga•tion**
**cas•ti•ga•tor**
**Cas•tile** (*or* **Cas•til•la**)
**Cas•til•ian**
**cast•ing**
**cas•tle**
**cas•tled**
**cast-off** (*adj*)
**cast•off** (*noun*)
**Cas•tor** star; mythological character
**cas•tor** plant oil; beaver secretion; *compare* **caster**
**cas•trate**
**cas•tra•tion**
**cas•tra•to** (*plural* **•ti** *or* **•tos**)
**cas•tra•tor**
**Cas•tries** capital of St Lucia
**cas•ual**
**casu•al•ly**
**casu•al•ty** (*plural* **•ties**)
**casua•ri•na** tree
**casu•ist**
**casu•is•tic** (*or* **•ti•cal**)
**casu•is•ti•cal•ly**
**casu•ist•ry** (*plural* **•ries**)
**ca•sus bel•li** *Latin* occasion of war
**cat**

**ca•taba•sis** (*plural* **•ses**) descent
**cata•bat•ic**
**cata•bol•ic** (*or* **kata•**)
**cata•boli•cal•ly** (*or* **kata•**)
**ca•tabo•lism** (*or* **ka•**)
**ca•tabo•lite**
**cata•caus•tic** physics term
**cata•chre•sis** incorrect use of words
**cata•chres•tic** (*or* **•ti•cal**)
**cata•cla•sis** (*plural* **•ses**) geology term
**cata•clas•tic**
**cata•cli•nal** geology term
**cata•clysm**
**cata•clys•mic** (*or* **•mal**)
**cata•comb**
**ca•tad•ro•mous** migrating down river; *compare* **anadromous**
**cata•falque**
**Cata•lan** language or inhabitant of Catalonia
**cata•lase** enzyme
**cata•lec•tic** prosody term
**cata•lep•sy** medical term
**cata•lep•tic**
**cata•logue** (*US* **•log**)
**cata•logu•er** (*or* **•logu•ist**; *US* **•log•**)
**Cata•lo•nia** Spanish region
**ca•tal•pa** tree
**cata•lyse** (*US* **•lyze**)
**cata•lys•er** (*US* **•lyz•**)
**ca•taly•sis** (*plural* **•ses**)
**cata•lyst**
**cata•lyt•ic**
**cata•ma•ran**
**cata•menia** menstruation
**cata•menial**
**cata•mite** homosexual boy
**cata•mount** (*or* **•mount•ain**) animal
**Ca•ta•nia** Sicilian port
**cata•pho•resis** chemistry term
**cata•phyll** leaf
**cata•pla•sia** pathology term
**cata•plasm** poultice
**cata•plas•tic**
**cata•plexy** paralysis
**cata•pult**
**cata•ract**
**ca•tarrh**
**ca•tarrh•al** (*or* **•ous**)
**cat•arrh•ine** zoology term
**ca•tas•tro•phe**
**cata•stroph•ic**
**cata•strophi•cal•ly**
**ca•tas•tro•phism** geological theory
**ca•tas•tro•phist**
**cata•to•nia** schizophrenia
**cata•ton•ic**
**Ca•taw•ba** (*plural* **•bas** *or* **•ba**) American Indian people
**cat•bird**
**cat•boat**
**cat•call**
**catch** (**catch•ing, caught**)
**catch•er**
**catch•fly** (*plural* **•flies**) plant
**catchi•ness**
**catch•ing**
**catch•ment**
**catch•penny** (*plural* **•pennies**)
**catch•pole** sheriff's officer
**catch•up** *US variant of* **ketchup**
**catch•weight**
**catch•word**
**catchy** (**catchi•er, catchi•est**)
**cate•cheti•cal** (*or* **cat•echet•ic**) teaching method
**cat•echeti•cal•ly**
**cat•echin** chemical compound
**cat•echism**
**cat•echis•mal**
**cat•echist** (*or* **cate•chiz•er, cate•chis•er**)
**cat•echis•tic** (*or* **•ti•cal**)
**cat•echi•za•tion** (*or* **•sa•tion**)
**cat•echize** (*or* **•ise**)
**cat•echol** chemical compound
**cat•echola•mine**
**cat•echu** (*or* **ca•chou, cutch**) resin
**cat•echu•men** convert
**cat•ego•rial**
**cat•egori•cal** (*or* **•egor•ic**)
**cat•egori•cal•ly**
**cat•ego•ri•za•tion** (*or* **•sa•tion**)
**cat•ego•rize** (*or* **•rise**)
**cat•ego•ry** (*plural* **•ries**)
**ca•tena** (*plural* **•tenae**) biblical comments
**cat•enane** chemistry term
**cat•enar•ian**
**ca•tena•ry** (*plural* **•ries**) geometric curve
**cat•enate** biology term
**cat•ena•tion**
**cat•enoid** geometric surface
**ca•tenu•late** botany term
**ca•ter**
**cat•er•an** brigand
**ca•ter•er**
**ca•ter•ing**
**cat•er•pil•lar**
**cat•er•waul**
**cat•fall** nautical term
**cat•fish** (*plural* **•fish** *or* **•fishes**)
**cat•gut**
**Cath•ar** (*plural* **•ars** *or* **•ari**) heretical Christian
**Cath•ar•ism**
**ca•thar•sis**
**ca•thar•tic** purgative
**ca•thar•ti•cal•ly**
**Ca•thay** *Archaic* China
**cat•head** nautical term
**ca•thec•tic** psychology term
**ca•thedra** (*plural* **•thedrae**) bishop's throne
**ca•thedral**
**ca•thep•sin** enzyme
**Cathe•rine wheel** firework
**cath•eter**
**cath•eteri•za•tion** (*or* **•sa•tion**)
**cath•eter•ize** (*or* **•ise**)
**ca•thex•is** (*plural* **•thexes**) psychiatry term
**ca•thod•al**
**cath•ode**
**ca•thod•ic** (*or* **•thodi•cal**)
**Catholic** religion
**catho•lic** universal
**Ca•tholi•cism**
**catho•lic•ity**
**ca•tholi•ci•za•tion** (*or* **•sa•tion**)
**ca•tholi•cize** (*or* **•cise**)

**ca•tholi•con** universal remedy
**cati•on** positive ion
**cati•on•ic**
**cat•kin**
**cat•like**
**cat•ling** surgical knife
**cat•mint** (*or esp. US* **•nip**)
**cat•nap** (*verb* **•nap•ping, •napped**)
**cat-o'-nine-tails** (*plural* **-tails**)
**ca•top•tric** (*or* **•tri•cal**)
**ca•top•trics** branch of optics
**cat's-ear** plant
**cat's-eye**
**cat's-foot** (*plural* **-feet**) plant
**cat's-paw**
**cat•sup** *US variant of* ketchup
**cat•ta•lo** (*or* **cata•lo**; *plural* **•loes** *or* **•los**) cattle
**cat•tery** (*plural* **•teries**)
**cat•ti•ly**
**cat•ti•ness**
**cat•tish**
**cat•tle**
**cattle•man** (*plural* **•men**)
**catt•leya** orchid
**cat•ty** (**•ti•er, •ti•est**)
**cat•walk**
**Cau•ca•sia**
**Cau•ca•sian**
**Cau•ca•soid**
**Cau•ca•sus** mountain range
**cau•cus** (*plural* **•cuses**)
**cau•dad** towards the tail
**cau•dal** of the tail
**cau•dal•ly**
**cau•date** (*or* **•dat•ed**)
**cau•da•tion**
**cau•dex** (*plural* **•di•ces** *or* **•dexes**) stem
**cau•dil•lo** (*plural* **•los**) Spanish leader
**cau•dle** spiced wine
**caught**
**caul**
**caul•dron** (*or* **cal•dron**)
**cau•les•cent**
**cau•li•cle** plant stalk
**cau•li•flow•er**
**cau•line**
**caulk** (*or* **calk**) fill cracks
**caulk•er** (*or* **calk•er**)
**caus•abil•ity**
**caus•able**
**caus•al**
**cau•sal•gia** pathology term
**cau•sal•ity** (*plural* **•ities**)
**cau•sal•ly**
**cau•sa•tion**
**causa•tive**
**cause cé•lè•bre** (*plural* **causes cé•lè•bres**)
**caus•er**
**cau•serie** informal talk
**cause•way**
**caus•tic**
**caus•ti•cal•ly**
**caus•tic•ness** (*or* **•tic•ity**)
**cau•ter•ant** caustic
**cau•teri•za•tion** (*or* **•sa•tion**)
**cau•ter•ize** (*or* **•ise**)
**cau•tery** (*plural* **•teries**)
**cau•tion**
**cau•tion•ary**
**cau•tious**
**cau•tious•ness**
**cav•al•cade**
**cava•lier**
**cava•lier•ism**
**ca•val•la** (*or* **•ly**; *plural* **•la, •las,** *or* **•lies**) fish
**cav•al•ry** (*plural* **•ries**)
**cav•al•ry•man** (*plural* **•men**)
**Cav•an** Irish county
**cava•ti•na** (*plural* **•ne**) musical work
**cave**
**ca•veat** warning
**ca•veat emp•tor** *Latin* let the buyer beware
**ca•vea•tor** legal term
**cave•fish** (*plural* **•fish** *or* **•fishes**)
**cave•man** (*plural* **•men**)
**cav•en•dish** tobacco
**cav•er**
**cav•ern**
**cav•ern•ous**
**cav•es•son** horse's noseband
**ca•vet•to** (*plural* **•ti**) architectural moulding
**cavi•ar** (*or* **•are**)
**cavi•corn** hollow-horned
**ca•vie** *Scot* hen coop
**cav•il** (**•il•ling, •illed**; *US* **•il•ing, •iled**)
**cav•il•ler**
**cav•ing**
**cavi•ta•tion**
**Ca•vi•te** Philippine port
**cav•ity** (*plural* **•ities**)
**cavo-relievo** (*or* **-rilievo**; *plural* **cavo-relievos** *or* **cavi-rilievi**) architectural term
**ca•vort**
**cavy** (*plural* **cavies**) rodent
**caw**
**Cawn•pore** Indian city
**Cax•ton** style of type
**cay** low island or bank
**cay•enne**
**cay•man** (*or* **cai•man**; *plural* **•mans**) crocodile
**Cay•man Is•lands**
**cay•use** *US* small pony
**cea•no•thus** shrub
**Cea•ra** Brazilian state
**cease**
**cease•fire**
**cease•less**
**ce•cal** *US spelling of* **caecal**
**ce•ci•ty** blindness
**Cecrops** mythological character
**ce•cum** *US spelling of* **caecum**
**ce•dar** tree; *compare* **ceder**
**cede**
**ced•er** one who cedes; *compare* **cedar**
**cedi** Ghanaian currency
**ce•dil•la**
**cei•ba** tree
**cei•lidh** Gaelic party
**ceil•ing**
**ceil•om•eter**
**cela•don** porcelain
**cel•an•dine**
**Ce•la•ya** Mexican city
**Cel•ebes** Indonesian island
**cel•ebrant**
**cel•ebrate**
**cel•ebra•tion**
**cel•ebra•tive**
**cel•ebra•tor**
**cel•ebra•tory**
**ce•leb•rity** (*plural* **•rities**)
**ce•leri•ac** vegetable
**ce•ler•ity** speed
**cel•ery**

**ce•les•ta** (*or* **•leste**) musical instrument
**ce•les•tial**
**ce•les•tial•ly**
**cel•es•tite** (*or* **•tine**) mineral
**ce•li•ac** *US spelling of* **coeliac**
**celi•ba•cy** (*plural* **•cies**)
**celi•bate**
**cell**
**cel•la** (*plural* **•lae**) room in temple
**cel•lar**
**cel•lar•age**
**cel•lar•er** monastic official
**cel•lar•et** bottle stand
**Cel•le** German city
**cel•list**
**cel•lo** (*plural* **•los**)
**cel•lo•bi•ose** (*or* **cel•lose**) biochemical compound
**cel•loi•din** chemical compound
**cel•lo•phane**
**cel•lu•lar**
**cel•lu•lase** enzyme
**cel•lule**
**cel•lu•li•tis**
**Cel•lu•loid** (*Trademark*)
**cel•lu•lose**
**cel•lu•lo•sic**
**ce•lom** *US spelling of* **coelom**
**ce•lo•mate** *US spelling of* **coelomate**
**Celsius** temperature scale
**celt** axe
**Celt** (*or* **Kelt**) people
**Celt•ic** (*or* **Kelt•ic**)
**Celti•cist** (*or* **Celt•ist, Kelti•cist, Kelt•ist**)
**cem•ba•lo** (*plural* **•los**) harpsichord
**ce•ment**
**ce•men•ta•tion**
**ce•ment•er**
**ce•ment•ite** chemical compound
**ce•men•tum** tooth substance
**cem•etery** (*plural* **•eteries**)
**cena•cle** (*or* **coena•cle**) supper room
**ce•nes•the•sia** *variant spelling of* **coenesthesia**
**ce•no•bite** *variant spelling of* **coenobite**
**ce•no•gen•esis** *US spelling of* **caenogenesis**
**ce•no•genet•ic** *US spelling of* **caenogenetic**
**ce•no•spe•cies** (*plural* **•spe•cies**) biology term
**ceno•taph**
**ceno•taph•ic**
**ce•no•te** well
**Ce•no•zo•ic** (*or* **Cai•**) geological era
**cense** burn incense
**cen•ser** incense container
**cen•sor** suppressor; to ban; *compare* **sensor**
**cen•sor•able**
**cen•so•rial**
**cen•so•ri•ous**
**cen•so•ri•ous•ness**
**cen•sor•ship**
**cen•sual** of a census; *compare* **sensual**
**cen•sur•able**
**cen•sure**
**cen•sus** (*plural* **•suses**)
**cent**
**cen•tal** unit
**cen•taur**
**Cen•tau•rus** constellation
**cen•tau•ry** (*plural* **•ries**) plant
**cen•te•nar•ian**
**cen•te•nary** (*plural* **•naries**)
**cen•ten•nial**
**cen•ter** *US spelling of* **centre**
**cen•tesi•mal** hundredth
**cen•tesi•mo** (*plural* **•mos**) monetary unit
**cen•ti•are** (*or* **cen•tare**) unit
**cen•ti•grade**
**cen•ti•gram** (*or* **•gramme**)
**cen•ti•li•tre** (*US* **•ter**)
**cen•til•lion** (*plural* **•lions** *or* **•lion**) $10^{600}$
**cen•time**
**cen•ti•me•tre** (*US* **•ter**)
**cen•ti•pede**
**centi•poise** unit
**cent•ner**
**cen•to** (*plural* **•tos**) type of poem
**cen•tral**
**cen•tral•ism**
**cen•tral•ity** (*plural* **•ities**)
**cen•trali•za•tion** (*or* **•sa•tion**)
**cen•tral•ize** (*or* **•ise**)
**cen•tral•ly**
**cen•tre** (*US* **•ter**)
**centre•board** (*US* **center-**) keel
**centre-fire** (*US* **center-**)
**centre•fold** (*US* **center•**)
**centre•piece** (*US* **center•**)
**cen•tric** (*or* **•tri•cal**)
**cen•tric•ity**
**cen•trifu•gal**
**cen•trifu•gal•ly**
**cen•trifu•ga•tion**
**cen•tri•fuge**
**cen•tring** (*US* **•tering**)
**cen•tri•ole** biology term
**cen•trip•etal**
**cen•trip•etal•ly**
**cen•trist** moderate
**cen•tro•bar•ic**
**cen•tro•cli•nal** geology term
**cen•troid**
**cen•tro•mere** chromosome part
**cen•tro•mer•ic**
**cen•tro•some** cell part
**cen•tro•som•ic**
**cen•tro•sphere**
**cen•trum** (*plural* **•trums** *or* **•tra**) part of vertebra
**cen•tum** linguistics term
**cen•tu•pli•cate**
**cen•tu•rial**
**cen•tu•ri•on**
**cen•tu•ry** (*plural* **•ries**)
**cep** fungus
**cepha•lad** towards the head
**cepha•lal•gia** headache
**ce•phal•ic**
**cepha•lin** (*or* **kepha•**) biochemical compound
**cepha•li•za•tion** (*or* **•sa•tion**)
**cepha•lo•chor•date** zoology term
**cepha•lom•eter**
**cepha•lo•met•ric**
**cepha•lom•etry**
**Cepha•lo•nia** Greek island
**cepha•lo•pod** mollusc
**cepha•lopo•dan**
**cepha•lo•pod•ic** (*or* **•lopo•dous**)

**cepha•lo•tho•rac•ic**
**cepha•lo•tho•rax** (*plural* **•raxes** *or* **•races**)
**Ce•pheus** constellation
**ce•ra•ceous** waxy
**Ce•ram** Indonesian island
**ce•ram•ic**
**ce•ram•ics**
**cera•mist** (*or* **ce•rami•cist**)
**ce•rar•gy•rite** mineral
**ce•ras•tes** (*plural* **•tes**) snake
**ce•rate** ointment
**ce•rat•ed** ornithology term
**ce•rato•dus** (*plural* **•duses**) extinct fish
**Cerberus** mythological dog
**cer•cal** zoology term
**cer•caria** (*plural* **•cariae**) larva
**cer•car•ial** (*or* **•ian**)
**cer•cis** plant
**cer•co•pi•thecoid** monkey
**cer•cus** (*plural* **•ci**) zoology term
**cere** swelling on bird's beak; *compare* **sere**
**ce•real** crop; *compare* **serial**
**cer•ebel•lar**
**cer•ebel•lum** (*plural* **•lums** *or* **•la**)
**cer•ebral**
**cer•ebral•ly**
**cer•ebrate**
**cer•ebra•tion**
**cer•ebric**
**cer•ebroid**
**cer•ebro•side** biochemical compound
**cer•ebro•spi•nal**
**cer•ebro•vas•cu•lar**
**cer•ebrum** (*plural* **•ebrums** *or* **•ebra**)
**cere•cloth** waxed cloth
**Ce•re•di•gi•on** Welsh county
**cere•ment** burial clothes
**cer•emo•nial**
**cer•emo•ni•al•ism**
**cer•emo•ni•al•ist**
**cer•emo•nial•ly**
**cer•emo•ni•ous**
**cer•emo•ny** (*plural* **•nies**)
**Ce•res** asteroid
**Ceres** Roman goddess
**cer•esin** wax
**ce•reus** cactus
**ce•ria** chemical compound
**ce•ric**
**ce•rise**
**ce•rium** chemical element
**cer•met** metal–ceramic material
**cer•nu•ous** drooping
**cero** (*plural* **cero** *or* **ceros**) fish
**ce•ro•graph•ic** (*or* **•graphi•cal**)
**ce•rog•ra•phist**
**ce•rog•ra•phy** engraving on wax
**ce•ro•plas•tic**
**ce•ro•plas•tics**
**ce•ro•type** printing process
**ce•rous**
**cert** *Slang* certainty
**cer•tain**
**cer•tain•ly**
**cer•tain•ty** (*plural* **•ties**)
**cer•ti•fi•able**
**cer•ti•fi•ably**
**cer•tifi•cate**
**cer•ti•fi•ca•tion**
**cer•tifi•ca•tory**
**cer•ti•fy** (**•fies, •fy•ing, •fied**)
**cer•tio•ra•ri** legal term
**cer•ti•tude**
**ce•ru•lean** deep blue
**ce•ru•men** earwax
**ce•ru•mi•nous**
**ce•ruse** white lead
**ce•rus•site** (*or* **•ru•site**) mineral
**cer•ve•lat** sausage
**cer•vi•cal**
**cer•vi•ci•tis**
**cer•vid** zoology term
**cer•vine** of deer
**cer•vix** (*plural* **•vixes** *or* **•vi•ces**)
**ce•sar•ean sec•tion** *US spelling of* **Caesarean section**
**ce•sium** *US spelling of* **caesium**
**ces•pi•tose** *US spelling of* **caespitose**
**cess**
**ces•sa•tion**
**ces•ser** legal term
**ces•sion** act of ceding; *compare* **session**
**ces•sion•ary** (*plural* **•aries**) legal term
**cess•pool** (*or* **•pit**)
**ces•tode** tapeworm
**ces•toid** ribbon-shaped
**ce•ta•cean** whale
**ce•ta•ceous**
**ce•tane** chemical compound
**cete** group of badgers
**ce•teris pa•ri•bus** *Latin* other things being equal
**ce•to•logi•cal**
**ce•tolo•gist**
**ce•tol•ogy** study of whales
**Ce•tus** constellation
**Ce•vennes** mountain range
**Cey•lon**
**Cey•lon•ese**
**chaba•zite** mineral
**chab•lis** wine
**cha-cha** (*or* **cha-cha-cha**)
**chac•ma** baboon
**cha•conne** musical term
**Chad** African republic; lake
**Chad•ean**
**Chad•ic** language group
**chae•ta** (*plural* **•tae**) bristle on worm
**chae•tog•nath** wormlike animal
**chae•to•pod** worm
**chafe**
**chaf•er** beetle
**chaff**
**chaff•er** (*noun*)
**chaf•fer** (*verb*) haggle
**chaf•finch**
**chaffy**
**chaf•ing**
**Cha•gas' dis•ease**
**cha•grin**
**chain**
**chain•man** (*plural* **•men**)
**chain•plate**
**chain-react**
**chain-smoke**
**chain-stitch**
**chain-store**
**chair**
**chair•borne**
**chair•man** (*plural* **•men**)
**chair•man•ship**
**chair•person**

**chair•woman** (*plural* **•women**)
**chaise** carriage
**chaise longue** (*plural* **chaise longues** *or* **chaises longues**)
**cha•la•za** (*plural* **•zas** *or* **•zae**) biology term
**cha•la•zal**
**chal•can•lite** mineral
**chal•cedon•ic**
**chal•cedo•ny** (*plural* **•nies**)
**chal•cid** insect
**Chal•cidi•ce** Greek peninsula
**Chal•cis** Greek city
**chal•co•cite** mineral
**chal•cog•ra•pher** (*or* **•phist**)
**chal•co•graph•ic** (*or* **•graphi•cal**)
**chal•cog•ra•phy** engraving
**chal•co•lith•ic** archaeology term
**chal•co•py•rite** mineral
**Chal•dea** (*or* **•daea**) Babylonian region
**Chal•dean** (*or* **•daean**)
**Chal•dee** language
**chal•dron** unit
**cha•let**
**chal•ice** goblet; *compare* **challis**
**chali•co•there** extinct mammal
**chalk**
**chalk•board** *US* blackboard
**chalki•ness**
**chalk•pit**
**chalky** (**chalki•er, chalki•est**)
**chal•lah** (*or* **hal•lah**; *plural* **•lahs** *or* **•loth**) Jewish bread
**chal•lenge**
**chal•lenge•able**
**chal•leng•er**
**chal•lis** (*or* **•lie**) fabric; *compare* **chalice**
**chal•one** internal secretion
**cha•lyb•eate** containing iron
**cha•made** military signal
**cham•ber**
**cham•ber•lain**
**chamber•maid**
**cham•bray** cloth
**cha•me•le•on**
**cha•meleon•ic**
**cham•fer**
**cham•fer•er**
**cham•ois** (*plural* **•ois**)
**Cha•mo•nix** French town
**champ**
**cham•pac** (*or* **•pak**) tree
**Cham•pagne** French region
**cham•pagne** wine
**cham•paign** open country
**cham•pers** *Slang* champagne
**cham•per•tous**
**cham•per•ty** (*plural* **•ties**) legal term
**cham•pi•gnon** mushroom
**cham•pi•on**
**cham•pion•ship**
**champ•le•vé** enamelling process
**Champs Ély•sées**
**chance**
**chan•cel**
**chan•cel•lery** (*or* **•lo•ry**; *plural* **•leries** *or* **•lo•ries**)
**chan•cel•lor**
**chan•cel•lor•ship**
**chan•cery** (*plural* **•ceries**)
**chanci•ly**
**chan•cre** pathology term
**chan•croid** ulcer
**chan•croi•dal**
**chan•crous**
**chancy** (**chanci•er, chanci•est**)
**chan•de•lier**
**chan•delle** aeronautics term
**Chan•der•na•gore** Indian port
**Chan•di•garh** Indian city
**chan•dler**
**chan•dlery** (*plural* **•dleries**)
**Chang•chia•kow** (*or* **•k'ou**) Chinese city
**Chang•chow** (*or* **Ch'ang-chou**) Chinese city
**Chang•chun** (*or* **Ch'ang Ch'un**) Chinese city
**change**
**change•abil•ity** (*or* **•able•ness**)
**change•able**
**change•ably**
**change•ful**
**change•less**
**change•less•ness**
**change•ling**
**change•over**
**chang•er**
**change-ringing**
**Chang•sha** (*or* **Ch'ang-sha**) Chinese port
**Chang•teh** (*or* **Ch'ang-te**) Chinese port
**chan•nel** (**•nel•ling, •nelled**; *US* **•nel•ing, •neled**)
**chan•nel•ize** (*or* **•ise**)
**chan•nel•ler** (*US* **•nel•er**)
**chan•son** *French* song
**chant**
**chant•er**
**chan•te•relle** mushroom
**chan•teuse**
**chan•tey** *US spelling of* **shanty**
**chan•ti•cleer** (*or* **•cler**) cock
**Chan•til•ly** French town
**chan•try** (*plural* **•tries**)
**chan•ty** *variant spelling of* **shanty**
**Chao•an** Chinese city
**cha•os**
**cha•ot•ic**
**cha•oti•cal•ly**
**chap** (**chap•ping, chapped**)
**chapa•rejos** cowboy's overalls
**chap•ar•ral** wooded area
**cha•pat•ti** (*or* **•pa•ti**; *plural* **•ti** *or* **•tis**) bread
**chap•book**
**chape** scabbard mounting
**cha•peau** (*plural* **•peaux** *or* **•peaus**) hat
**chap•el**
**chap•er•on** (*or* **•one**)
**chap•er•on•age**
**chap•fallen** (*or* **chop•**) dejected
**chapi•ter** architectural term
**chap•lain**
**chap•lain•cy** (*plural* **•cies**)
**chap•let** strung beads
**chap•let•ed**
**chap•pal** sandal
**chapped**
**chap•pie** *Slang* fellow

**chap•ping**
**chaps** *short for* **chaparejos**
**chap•stick** *US* lip salve
**chap•ter**
**chap•ter•house**
**char** (**char•ring, charred**)
**char** (*or* **charr**; *plural* **char, chars** *or* **charr, charrs**) fish
**chara•banc**
**chara•cin** (*or* **•cid**) fish
**char•ac•ter**
**char•ac•ter•ful**
**char•ac•ter•is•tic**
**char•ac•ter•is•ti•cal•ly**
**char•ac•teri•za•tion** (*or* **•sa•tion**)
**char•ac•ter•ize** (*or* **•ise**)
**char•ac•ter•less**
**cha•rade**
**char•as** hashish
**char•coal**
**char•cu•te•rie** delicatessen
**chard**
**Cha•rente** French river
**Charente-Maritime** French department
**charge**
**charge•abil•ity**
**charge•able**
**char•gé d'af•faires** (*plural* **char•gés d'af•faires**)
**charg•er**
**Cha•ri** African river
**chari•ly**
**chari•ness**
**Char•ing Cross**
**Chari-Nile** language group
**chari•ot**
**chari•ot•eer**
**cha•ris•ma** (*or* **char•ism**)
**char•is•mat•ic**
**char•is•mati•cal•ly**
**chari•table**
**chari•table•ness**
**chari•tably**
**char•ity** (*plural* **•ities**)
**cha•ri•va•ri** (*or* **shiva•ree**) mock serenade
**char•kha** (*or* **•ka**) spinning wheel
**char•lady** (*plural* **•ladies**)
**char•la•tan**
**char•la•tan•ism** (*or* **•ry**)
**char•la•tan•is•tic**
**Charles•ton** US city
**charles•ton** dance
**char•lie** *Slang* fool
**char•lock** plant
**Char•lotte** US city
**char•lotte** pudding
**Charlotte Ama•lie** capital of US Virgin Islands
**charm**
**charm•er**
**Char•meuse** (*Trademark*) fabric
**Char•mi•nar** Indian monument
**charm•ing**
**char•nel** sepulchral
**Char•ol•lais** cattle
**Charon** mythological character
**char•poy** (*or* **•pai**) bedstead
**char•qui** dried meat
**char•quid**
**chart**
**chart•able**
**char•ter**
**char•tered**
**Char•ter•house** Carthusian monastery
**Chart•ism** reform movement
**Chart•ist**
**chart•ist** share analyst
**Char•tres** French city
**char•treuse** liqueur
**char•woman** *plural* **•women**
**chary** (**chari•er, chari•est**)
**Cha•ryb•dis** mythological monster
**chase**
**chas•er**
**chasm**
**chas•mal** (*or* **•mic**)
**chas•sé** ballet step
**chas•seur** French huntsman
**chas•sis** (*plural* **•sis**)
**chaste**
**chas•ten**
**chas•ten•er**
**chas•tis•able**
**chas•tise**
**chas•tise•ment**
**chas•tity**
**chasu•ble**
**chat** (**chat•ting, chat•ted**)
**cha•teau** (*or* **châ•**; *plural* **•teaux** *or* **•teaus**)
**chat•elain** (*fem* **•elaine**) castle keeper
**Chat•ham** Kent town; Pacific islands
**cha•toy•an•cy**
**cha•toy•ant** changing in lustre
**Chat•ta•noo•ga** US city
**chat•tel**
**chat•ter**
**chatter•box**
**chat•ter•er**
**chat•ti•ly**
**chat•ty** (**•ti•er, •ti•est**)
**Chau•cerian**
**chaud•froid** sauce
**chauf•fer** (*or* **chau•fer**) heater
**chauf•feur** (*fem* **•feuse**)
**chaul•moo•gra** tree
**chausses** medieval garment
**chau•vin•ism**
**chau•vin•ist**
**chau•vin•is•tic**
**chau•vin•is•ti•cal•ly**
**chaw** *Dialect* chew tobacco
**cha•yo•te** plant
**cheap** inexpensive; *compare* **cheep**
**cheap•en**
**cheap•ness**
**cheap•skate**
**cheat**
**cheat•er**
**Che•bo•ksa•ry** Russian port
**Che•chen** (*plural* **•chens** *or* **•chen**) Russian people
**Che•che•nia** (*or* **Chechnya**) Russian republic
**Chech•nya** *variant spelling of* **Chechenia**
**check** pause; pattern; etc.; *US spelling of* **cheque**
**check•able**
**check•book** *US spelling of* **chequebook**
**check•er** one who checks; *US spelling of* **chequer**
**check•ered** *US spelling of* **chequered**
**checker•berry** (*plural* **•berries**)
**checker•bloom** plant
**checker•board** *US* draughtboard

**check•ers** *US* draughts
**check-in** (*noun*)
**check•mate**
**check•out** (*noun*)
**check•point**
**check•up** (*noun*)
**checky** heraldic term
**Ched•dar**
**chedd•ite** explosive
**cheek**
**cheek•bone**
**cheeki•ly**
**cheeki•ness**
**cheek•piece**
**cheeky** (**cheeki•er, cheeki•est**)
**cheep** chirp; *compare* **cheap**
**cheep•er**
**cheer**
**cheer•ful**
**cheer•ful•ly**
**cheer•ful•ness**
**cheeri•ly**
**cheeri•ness**
**cheerio**
**cheer•leader**
**cheer•less**
**cheer•less•ness**
**cheers**
**cheery** (**cheeri•er, cheeri•est**)
**cheese**
**cheese•board**
**cheese•burg•er**
**cheese•cake**
**cheese•cloth**
**cheese•mon•ger**
**cheese•paring**
**cheesi•ness**
**cheesy** (**cheesi•er, cheesi•est**)
**chee•tah** (*or* **che•tah**)
**chef**
**chef-d'oeuvre** (*plural* **chefs-d'oeuvre**) *French* masterpiece
**Che•kiang** Chinese province
**che•la** (*plural* **•lae**) claws
**che•la** (*plural* **•las**) Hindu disciple
**che•la•ship**
**che•late** chemistry term
**che•la•tion**
**che•lic•era** (*plural* **•erae**) spider's claw
**che•lic•er•al**
**che•lic•er•ate**
**che•lif•er•ous**
**che•li•form**
**Chelms•ford**
**che•loid** *variant spelling of* **keloid**
**che•lo•nian** tortoise or turtle
**chelp** *Dialect* chatter
**Chel•sea**
**Chel•ten•ham**
**Chel•ya•binsk** Russian city
**chemi•cal**
**chemi•cal•ly**
**chemi•lu•mi•nes•cence**
**chemi•lu•mi•nes•cent**
**che•min de fer** gambling game
**che•mise**
**chemi•sette** underbodice
**chemi•sorb** (*or* **chemo•**)
**chemi•sorp•tion**
**chem•ist**
**chem•is•try** (*plural* **•tries**)
**Chem•nitz** German city
**chemo•pro•phy•lac•tic**
**chemo•pro•phy•lax•is**
**chemo•recep•tor** (*or* **chemo•cep•tor**)
**chem•os•mo•sis**
**chem•os•mot•ic**
**chemo•sphere** layer of atmosphere
**chemo•spher•ic**
**che•mo•stat**
**chemo•syn•thesis**
**chemo•syn•thet•ic**
**chemo•syn•theti•cal•ly**
**chemo•tac•tic**
**chemo•tac•ti•cal•ly**
**chemo•tax•is** biology term
**chemo•thera•pist**
**chemo•thera•py**
**chemo•trop•ic**
**chemo•tropi•cal•ly**
**che•mot•ro•pism** botany term
**chem•pa•duk** tree
**chem•ur•gic** (*or* **•gi•cal**)
**chem•ur•gy** branch of chemistry
**Che•nab** Himalayan river
**Cheng•chow** (*or* **Cheng-chou**) Chinese city
**Cheng•teh** Chinese city
**Cheng•tu** (*or* **Ch'eng-tu**) Chinese city
**che•nille**
**Chen•nai** *Indian name of* **Madras**
**che•no•pod** plant
**che•no•po•dia•ceous**
**cheong•sam** Chinese dress
**cheque** (*US* **check**)
**cheque•book** (*US* **check•**)
**cheq•uer** (*US* **check•**) pattern of squares; *compare* **checker**
**chequer•board** (*US* **checker•**)
**cheq•uered** (*US* **check•ered**)
**Cheq•uers** premier's country house
**cheq•uers** *US* draughts game
**Cher** French river
**Cher•bourg** French port
**Che•rem•kho•vo** Russian city
**cher•ish**
**cher•ish•able**
**cher•ish•er**
**Cher•nov•tsy** Ukrainian city
**cher•no•zem** (*or* **tscher•no•sem**) black soil
**Chero•kee** (*plural* **•kees** *or* **•kee**)
**che•root**
**cher•ry** (*plural* **•ries**)
**cher•so•nese** peninsula
**chert** quartz
**Chert•sey** Surrey town
**cherty**
**cher•ub** (*plural* **•ubs** *or* **cheru•bim**)
**che•ru•bic**
**che•ru•bi•cal**
**cher•vil**
**cher•vo•nets** former Soviet coin
**Chesa•peake** US bay
**Chesh•ire**
**chess**
**chess•board**
**ches•sel** cheese mould
**chess•man** (*plural* **•men**)
**chest**

**chest•ed**
**Ches•ter**
**Ches•ter•field** Derbyshire town
**ches•ter•field** sofa
**chesti•ly**
**chesti•ness**
**chest•nut**
**chesty (chesti•er, chesti•est)**
**cheval-de-frise** barrier of spikes
**cheva•lier**
**che•vet** part of church
**Che•vi•ot** hills; sheep
**che•vi•ot** fabric
**chev•rette** goat skin
**chev•ron**
**chev•ro•tain** animal
**chew**
**chew•able**
**chew•er**
**chewy (chewi•er, chewi•est)**
**Chey•enne** American Indian; US city
**chez** *French* at the home of
**chi** Greek letter
**chi•ack** *Austral* to tease
**chi•an•ti**
**Chi•apas** Mexican state
**chia•ro•scur•ism**
**chia•ro•scu•rist**
**chia•ro•scu•ro** (*plural* **•ros**) art term
**chi•as•ma** (*or* **chi•asm**; *plural* **•mas, •ma•ta,** *or* **•asms**) biology term
**chi•as•mal**
**chi•as•mic**
**chi•as•mus** (*plural* **•mi**) rhetoric term
**chi•as•tic**
**chi•as•to•lite** mineral
**Chi•ba** Japanese city
**chi•bouk** (*or* **•bouque**) Turkish pipe
**chic**
**Chi•ca•go**
**chi•ca•lo•te** poppy
**chi•cane**
**chi•can•er**
**chi•can•ery** (*plural* **•eries**)
**Chich•es•ter**
**chi•chi**
**Chi•chi•haerh** (*or* **Ch'i-ch'i-haerh**) Chinese city
**chick**
**chicka•bid•dy**
**chicka•dee** bird
**chicka•ree** squirrel
**Chicka•saw** (*plural* **•saws** *or* **•saw**) American Indian
**chick•en**
**chicken-hearted** (*or* **-livered**)
**chicken•pox**
**chick•pea**
**chick•weed**
**Chi•cla•yo** Peruvian city
**chic•le** gum
**chi•co** shrub
**chico•ry** (*or* **chic•co•ry;** *plural* **•ries**)
**chide (chid•ing; chid•ed** *or* **chid; chid•ed, chid,** *or* **chid•den)**
**chid•er**
**chief**
**chief•ly**
**chief•tain**
**chiff•chaff** bird
**chif•fon**
**chif•fo•nier** (*or* **•fon•nier**) furniture
**chig•etai** wild ass
**chig•ger** larva
**chi•gnon**
**chigoe** flea
**Chi•hua•hua** Mexican state; dog
**chil•blain**
**child** (*plural* **chil•dren**)
**child•bed**
**child•birth**
**child•hood**
**child•ish**
**child•ish•ness**
**child•less**
**child•less•ness**
**child•like**
**chil•dren** *plural of* **child**
**Chile**
**Chil•ean**
**chili•ad** group of one thousand
**chili•ad•al** (*or* **•ad•ic**)
**chili•asm** theology term
**chili•ast**
**chili•as•tic**
**chill**
**chil•li** (*plural* **•lies**)
**chil•li con car•ne**
**chil•li•ness**
**Chil•lon** Swiss castle
**chil•lum** clay pipe
**chil•ly** (**•li•er, •li•est**)
**chi•lo•pod** invertebrate
**Chil•tern** Hills; Hundreds
**Chi•lung** (*or* **Chi-lung**) Taiwanese port
**chi•maera** fish; *compare* **chimera**
**Chim•bo•te** Peruvian port
**chime**
**chi•mera** (*or* **•maera**) monster; biology term; *compare* **chimaera**
**chi•mere** (*or* **chim•er, chim•ar**) bishop's gown
**chi•meri•cal** (*or* **•mer•ic**) fanciful
**Chim•kent** Kazakh city
**chim•ney**
**chimney•piece**
**chimney•pot**
**chimp**
**chim•pan•zee**
**chin**
**Chi•na** country
**chi•na** porcelain
**china•berry** (*plural* **•berries**)
**China•graph** (*Trademark*)
**China•man** (*plural* **•men**)
**China•town**
**china•ware**
**chinch** *US* bedbug
**chin•che•rin•chee** plant
**chin•chil•la**
**Chin-Chou** (*or* **Chin•chow**) Chinese city
**Chin•dit**
**Chin•dwin** Burmese river
**chine**
**chi•né** mottled
**Chi•nee** *Slang* Chinaman
**Chi•nese** (*plural* **•nese**)
**Ching** (*or* **Ch'ing**) Chinese dynasty
**chink**
**Chin•kiang** (*or* **Cheng-chiang**) Chinese port
**chin•less**

**chino** (*plural* **chinos**) cloth
**chi•noi•serie**
**Chi•nook** (*plural* **•nook** *or* **•nooks**) American Indian
**chi•nook** wind
**Chi•nook•an**
**chin•qua•pin** (*or* **•ca•pin, •ka•pin**) tree
**chintz**
**chintzy** (**chintzi•er, chintzi•est**)
**chin•wag** (**•wag•ging, •wagged**)
**chi•ono•doxa** plant
**Chios** Greek island
**chip** (**chip•ping, chipped**)
**chip•board**
**chip•munk**
**chipo•la•ta**
**chip•per**
**chip•ping**
**chip•py** (*noun, plural* **•pies**; *adj* **•pi•er, •pi•est**)
**chir•al** chemistry term
**chi•ral•ity**
**chirm** chirp
**chi•rog•ra•pher**
**chi•ro•graph•ic** (*or* **•graphi•cal**)
**chi•rog•ra•phy** calligraphy
**chi•ro•man•cy** palmistry
**Chiron** centaur
**chi•ropo•dist**
**chi•ropo•dy**
**chi•ro•prac•tic**
**chi•ro•prac•tor**
**chi•rop•ter** bat
**chi•rop•ter•an**
**chirp**
**chirp•er**
**chirpi•ly**
**chirpi•ness**
**chirpy** (**chirpi•er, chirpi•est**)
**chirr** (*or* **chirre, churr**) make shrill sound
**chir•rup**
**chir•rup•er**
**chir•rupy**
**chis•el** (**•el•ling, •elled**; *US* **•el•ing, •eled**)
**chis•el•ler** (*US* **•el•er**)
**Chi•şi•nău** capital of Moldova
**chi-square** statistics term
**chit**
**Chi•ta** Russian city
**chi•tal** deer
**chi•tar•ro•ne** (*plural* **•ni**) lute
**chit•chat** (**•chat•ting, •chat•ted**)
**chi•tin** biochemical compound
**chi•tin•oid**
**chi•tin•ous**
**chi•ton** Greek tunic
**Chit•ta•gong** Bangladeshi port
**chit•ter** *US* twitter
**chit•ter•lings** (*or* **chit•lins, chit•lings**) pig intestines
**chiv** *Slang* knife
**chiv•al•ric**
**chiv•al•rous**
**chiv•al•ry** (*plural* **•ries**)
**chive** (*or* **chives**)
**chivy** (*or* **chiv•vy; chivies, chivy•ing, chiv•ied** *or* **chiv•vies, •vy•ing, •vied**)
**chlamy•date** zoology term
**chla•myd•eous** botany term
**chla•mydo•spore**
**chlor•acne** skin disease
**chlo•ral** chemical compound
**chlo•ram•bu•cil** drug
**chlo•ra•mine** chemical compound
**chlo•ram•pheni•col** antibiotic
**chlo•rate**
**chlor•dane** (*or* **•dan**) insecticide
**chlo•rel•la** alga
**chlo•ren•chy•ma** plant tissue
**chlo•ric**
**chlo•ride**
**chlo•rid•ic**
**chlo•rin•ate**
**chlo•rina•tion**
**chlo•rina•tor**
**chlo•rine** (*or* **•rin**)
**chlo•rite** mineral
**chlo•rit•ic**
**chlo•ro•ben•zene**
**chlo•ro•form**
**chlo•ro•hy•drin**
**Chlo•ro•my•ce•tin** (*Trademark*)
**chlo•ro•phyll** (*or* **•phyl**)
**chlo•ro•phyl•loid**
**chlo•ro•phyl•lous**
**chlo•ro•pic•rin** (*or* **chlor•pic•rin**) pesticide
**chlo•ro•plast**
**chlo•ro•plast•ic**
**chlo•ro•prene** chemical compound
**chlo•ro•quine** drug
**chlo•ro•sis** disease
**chlo•ro•thia•zide**
**chlo•rot•ic**
**chlo•rous** of chlorine
**chlor•proma•zine** drug
**chlor•pro•pa•mide** drug
**cho•ano•cyte** zoology term
**choc-ice**
**chock**
**chock-a-block**
**chock•er** *Slang* fed up
**chock-full**
**choco•late**
**choco•laty**
**Choc•taw** (*plural* **•taws** *or* **•taw**) American Indian
**Chog•yal** Indian ruler
**choice**
**choice•ly**
**choice•ness**
**choir** choral group; *compare* **quire**
**choir•boy**
**choir•master**
**Choi•seul** Pacific island
**choke**
**choke•able**
**choke•berry** (*plural* **•berries**)
**choke•bore** shotgun
**choke•cherry** (*plural* **•cherries**)
**chok•er**
**choky** (*or* **•ey**)
**cho•lecal•cif•er•ol** vitamin
**chol•an•gi•og•raphy** bile-duct examination
**chol•ecys•tec•to•my** (*plural* **•mies**) removal of gall bladder
**chol•ecys•tog•raphy** gall-bladder examination
**chol•er** anger
**chol•era**

**chol•er•ic**
**chol•eroid**
**cho•les•ter•ol** (*or* **•ter•in**)
**cho•li** bodice
**cho•line** biochemical compound
**cho•lin•er•gic** biology term
**cho•lin•es•ter•ase** enzyme
**chol•la** cactus
**Cho•lon** Vietnamese city
**chomp**
**chon** Korean coin
**chon•dri•fi•ca•tion**
**chon•dri•fy** (**•fies, •fy•ing, •fied**) change into cartilage
**chon•drio•so•mal**
**chon•drio•some** biology term
**chon•drite** meteorite
**chon•drit•ic**
**chon•dro•ma** (*plural* **•mas** *or* **•ma•ta**) tumour
**chon•dro•ma•tous**
**chon•drule** meteorology term
**Chong•jin** (*or* **Chung•**) Korean port
**Chon•ju** Korean city
**choose** (**choos•ing, chose, cho•sen**)
**choos•er**
**choosi•ly**
**choosi•ness**
**choosy** (**choosi•er, choosi•est**)
**chop** (**chop•ping, chopped**)
**cho•pine** shoe
**chop•logic**
**chop•per**
**chop•pi•ly**
**chop•pi•ness**
**chop•py** (**•pi•er, •pi•est**)
**chop•stick**
**cho•ra•gus** Greek chorus leader
**cho•ral** (*adj*)
**cho•rale** (*noun*)
**cho•ral•ly**
**chord** maths and music senses; *compare* **cord**
**chord•al**
**chor•date** animal with notochord; *compare* **cordate**
**chord•ing** musical term
**chordo•phone** musical instrument
**chore**
**cho•rea** neurological disorder
**cho•real** (*or* **cho•re•ic**)
**cho•reo•dra•ma**
**cho•reo•graph**
**cho•reog•ra•pher** (*or* **•reg•ra•pher**)
**cho•reo•graph•ic** (*or* **•regraph•ic**)
**cho•reo•graphi•cal•ly** (*or* **•regraphi•**)
**cho•reog•ra•phy** (*or* **•reg•ra•phy**)
**cho•ri•amb** (*or* **•am•bus**; *plural* **•ambs** *or* **•am•bi**) prosody term
**cho•ri•am•bic**
**cho•ric** of a chorus
**cho•ri•on** embryonic membrane
**cho•ri•on•ic** (*or* **cho•rial**)
**chor•is•ter**
**Chor•ley** Lancashire town
**cho•rog•ra•pher**
**cho•ro•graph•ic** (*or* **•graphi•cal**)
**cho•ro•graphi•cal•ly**
**cho•rog•ra•phy** mapping regions
**cho•roid** membrane of eyeball
**cho•rol•ogy** geography term
**chor•tle**
**cho•rus** (*plural* **•ruses**)
**Chor•zow** Polish city
**chose**
**cho•sen**
**Cho•ta Nag•pur** Indian plateau
**Chou** Chinese dynasty
**chou** (*plural* **choux**) cabbage; *compare* **choux**
**chough** bird
**choux** pastry; *plural of* **chou**
**chow**
**chow-chow**
**chow•der** soup
**chow mein** Chinese food
**chre•ma•tis•tic** of money-making
**chres•ard** biology term
**chrism** (*or* **chris•om**) anointing oil; *compare* **chrisom**
**chris•mal**
**chris•ma•tory** (*plural* **•tories**) receptacle for consecrated oil
**chris•om** baptismal robe; *compare* **chrism**
**Christ**
**Chris•ta•del•phian**
**Christ•church** New Zealand city; Dorset town
**chris•ten**
**Chris•ten•dom**
**chris•ten•er**
**chris•ten•ing**
**Chris•tian**
**Chris•tia•nia** *former name of* **Oslo**
**Chris•ti•an•ity**
**Chris•tiani•za•tion** (*or* **•sa•tion**)
**Chris•tian•ize** (*or* **•ise**)
**Chris•tian•iz•er** (*or* **•is•er**)
**Chris•tian•ly**
**Christ•like**
**Christ•mas**
**Christ•mas•sy**
**Christmas•tide**
**Chris•to•logi•cal**
**Chris•tol•ogist**
**Chris•tol•ogy**
**Christ's-thorn** plant
**chro•ma** physics term
**chro•mate**
**chro•mat•ic**
**chro•mati•cal•ly**
**chro•mati•cism**
**chro•ma•tic•ity** physics term
**chro•mat•ic•ness** physics term
**chro•mat•ics** (*or* **chro•ma•tol•ogy**) science of colour
**chro•ma•tid** chromosome part
**chro•ma•tin** substance of chromosomes
**chro•ma•tin•ic**
**chro•ma•tist** (*or* **chro•ma•tolo•gist**)
**chro•ma•to•gram**
**chro•ma•tog•ra•pher**

**chro•ma•to•graph•ic**
**chro•ma•to•graphi•cal•ly**
**chro•ma•tog•ra•phy** chemical analysis
**chro•ma•tol•ogy** *variant of* **chromatics**
**chro•ma•toly•sis** cytology term
**chro•ma•to•phore** zoology term
**chro•ma•to•phor•ic**
**chro•ma•toph•or•ous**
**chrome**
**chro•mic**
**chro•mi•nance** physics term
**chro•mite** mineral
**chro•mium**
**chro•mo•gen**
**chro•mo•gen•ic** colour-producing
**chro•mo•litho•graph**
**chro•mo•li•thog•ra•pher**
**chro•mo•litho•graph•ic**
**chro•mo•li•thog•ra•phy**
**chro•mo•mere** cytology term
**chro•mo•nema** (*plural* **•nema•ta**) biology term
**chro•mo•nemal** (*or* **•nemat•ic, •nemic**)
**chro•mo•phore** chemistry term
**chro•mo•phor•ic** (*or* **•ous**)
**chro•mo•plast** part of cell
**chro•mo•pro•tein**
**chro•mo•so•mal**
**chro•mo•some**
**chro•mo•sphere** layer of sun
**chro•mo•spher•ic**
**chro•mous**
**chro•myl**
**chro•naxie** (*or* **•naxy**) physiology term
**chron•ic**
**chroni•cal•ly**
**chro•nic•ity**
**chroni•cle**
**chroni•cler**
**Chroni•cles** Old Testament book
**chrono•bi•ol•ogy**
**chrono•gram**
**chrono•gram•mat•ic** (*or* **•mati•cal**)
**chrono•graph** time recorder
**chro•nog•ra•pher**
**chrono•graph•ic**
**chrono•logi•cal**
**chrono•logi•cal•ly**
**chro•nolo•gist**
**chro•nol•ogy** (*plural* **•ogies**)
**chro•nom•eter** timepiece
**chrono•met•ric** (*or* **•ri•cal**)
**chrono•metri•cal•ly**
**chro•nom•etry**
**chro•non** unit
**chrono•scope**
**chrono•scop•ic**
**chrysa•lis** (*plural* **•lises, •lids,** *or* **chry•sali•des**)
**chry•san•themum**
**chrysa•ro•bin** drug
**chrys•el•ephan•tine** statuary term
**chryso•ber•yl**
**chryso•lite** gemstone
**chryso•lit•ic**
**chryso•prase** gemstone
**chryso•tile** mineral
**chtho•nian** (*or* **•nic**) of the underworld
**chub** (*plural* **chub** *or* **chubs**)
**Chubb** (*Trademark*) lock
**chub•bi•ness**
**chub•by** (**•bi•er, •bi•est**)
**chuck**
**chuck•le**
**chuck•ler**
**chuck•wal•la** lizard
**chuck-will's-widow** bird
**chud•dar** Indian shawl
**chu•fa** sedge
**chuff**
**chuffed**
**chuf•fy** *Scot* chubby
**chug** (**chug•ging, chugged**)
**chu•kar** partridge
**Chuk•chi** Siberian peninsula
**chuk•ker** (*or* **•ka**) polo term
**chum** (**chum•ming, chummed**)
**chum•mi•ly**
**chum•mi•ness**
**chum•my** (**•mi•er, •mi•est**)
**chump**
**chump•ing** *Dialect* collecting wood
**chun•der**
**chun•der•ous** *Austral* nauseating
**Chung•king** (*or* **Ch'ung-ch'ing**) Chinese port
**chunk**
**chunki•ly**
**chunki•ness**
**chunky** (**chunki•er, chunki•est**)
**Chun•nel** Channel tunnel
**chun•ter**
**church**
**church•goer**
**church•going**
**Church•ill** Canadian river
**church•man** (*plural* **•men**)
**church•warden**
**church•woman** (*plural* **•women**)
**church•yard**
**chu•ri•dars** Indian trousers
**chu•rin•ga** Aboriginal amulet
**churl**
**churl•ish**
**churn**
**churr** *variant spelling of* **chirr**
**chute**
**chut•ney** (*or* **•nee**)
**chut•tie** *Austral* chewing gum
**Chu•vash** (*plural* **•vash** *or* **•vashes**) Russian people
**chy•la•ceous** (*or* **chy•lous**)
**chyle** intestinal fluid
**chyme** digested food
**chy•mo•sin** rennin
**chy•mo•tryp•sin** enzyme
**chy•mo•tryp•sino•gen** enzyme precursor
**chy•mous**
**cia•bat•ta** Italian bread
**ciao** Italian greeting
**ci•bo•rium** (*plural* **•ria**) communion vessel
**ci•ca•da** (*or* **ci•ca•la**; *plural* **•das, •dae** *or* **•las, •le**)
**cica•tri•cial**
**cica•tric•le** biology term
**ci•cat•ri•cose**
**cica•trix** (*plural* **•tri•ces**) scar
**cica•tri•zant** (*or* **•sant**)
**cica•tri•za•tion** (*or* **•sa•tion**)
**cica•trize** (*or* **•trise**) heal

**cica•triz•er** (*or* **•tris•er**)
**cic•ely** plant
**cic•ero** (*plural* **•eros**) unit
**cic•ero•ne** (*plural* **•nes** *or* **•ni**) tourist guide
**Cic•ero•nian** eloquent
**cich•lid** fish
**cich•loid**
**ci•der**
**ci•gar**
**ciga•rette**
**ciga•ril•lo** (*plural* **•los**) cigar
**cig•gy** (*plural* **•gies**) *Slang* cigarette
**cilia** *plural of* **cilium**
**cili•ary**
**cili•ate**
**cili•at•ed**
**cili•ation**
**cil•ice** haircloth
**cilio•late**
**cil•ium** (*plural* **cilia**) minute hair
**cim•ba•lom** dulcimer
**Cim•bri** Germanic people
**Cim•brian**
**Cim•bric**
**ci•mex** (*plural* **cimi•ces**) bedbug
**Cim•me•rian** very dark
**cinch**
**cin•cho•na** tree bark
**cin•choni•dine** alkaloid
**cin•cho•nine** alkaloid
**cin•chon•ism** poisoning
**cin•cho•ni•za•tion** (*or* **•sa•tion**)
**cin•cho•nize** (*or* **•nise**)
**Cin•cin•nati**
**cinc•ture** surround
**cin•der**
**cin•dery**
**cine** film
**cin•easte** film enthusiast
**cin•ema**
**Cin•ema•scope** (*Trademark*)
**cin•ema•theque** small cinema
**cin•emat•ic**
**cin•emati•cal•ly**
**cin•emato•graph**
**cin•ema•tog•ra•pher**
**cin•emato•graph•ic**
**cin•ema•tog•ra•phy**
**cin•eol** (*or* **•eole**) eucalyptol
**Cin•era•ma** (*Trademark*)
**cin•eraria** plant
**cin•erar•ium** (*plural* **•eraria**) place for cremation ashes
**cin•erary** (*adj*)
**cin•era•tor** cremation furnace
**ci•ner•eous** (*or* **cin•eri•tious**) greyish
**cin•erin** chemical compound
**cin•gu•late** (*or* **•lat•ed**)
**cin•gu•lum** (*plural* **•la**) anatomical part
**cin•na•bar** mineral
**cin•na•mon**
**cin•na•mon•ic** (*or* **ci•nam•ic**)
**cin•quain** poem
**cinque** five
**cinque•foil** plant
**Cinque Ports**
**Cin•za•no** (*Trademark*)
**ci•pher** (*or* **cy•pher**) secret writing; *compare* **sypher**
**cipo•lin** marble
**cir•ca**
**cir•ca•dian** daily
**Cir•cas•sia** Russian region
**Cir•cas•sian**
**Circe** mythological character
**cir•ci•nate** botany term
**Cir•ci•nus** constellation
**cir•cle**
**cir•cler**
**cir•clet**
**cir•cuit**
**cir•cuit•al** of a circuit
**cir•cui•tous** indirect
**cir•cui•tous•ly**
**cir•cuit•ry** circuit system
**cir•cu•ity** (*plural* **•ities**)
**cir•cu•lar**
**cir•cu•lar•ity** (*or* **•ness**)
**cir•cu•lari•za•tion** (*or* **•sa•tion**)
**cir•cu•lar•ize** (*or* **•ise**)
**cir•cu•lar•iz•er** (*or* **•is•er**)
**cir•cu•late**
**cir•cu•la•tion**
**cir•cu•la•tive**
**cir•cu•la•tor**
**cir•cu•la•tory**
**cir•cum•am•bi•ence** (*or* **•en•cy**)
**cir•cum•am•bi•ent**
**cir•cum•am•bu•late**
**cir•cum•am•bu•la•tion**
**cir•cum•am•bu•la•tor**
**cir•cum•am•bu•la•tory**
**cir•cum•ben•di•bus** circumlocution
**cir•cum•cise**
**cir•cum•ci•sion**
**cir•cum•fer•ence**
**cir•cum•fer•en•tial**
**cir•cum•flex**
**cir•cum•flex•ion**
**cir•cum•flu•ous** surrounded by water
**cir•cum•fuse**
**cir•cum•fu•sion**
**cir•cum•lo•cu•tion**
**cir•cum•locu•tory**
**cir•cum•lu•nar**
**cir•cum•navi•gable**
**cir•cum•navi•gate**
**cir•cum•navi•ga•tion**
**cir•cum•navi•ga•tor**
**cir•cum•nu•tate** botany term
**cir•cum•nu•ta•tion**
**cir•cum•po•lar**
**cir•cum•scis•sile** botany term
**cir•cum•scribe**
**cir•cum•scrip•tion**
**cir•cum•spect**
**cir•cum•spec•tion**
**cir•cum•spec•tive**
**cir•cum•stance**
**cir•cum•stan•tial**
**cir•cum•stan•ti•ality** (*plural* **•alities**)
**cir•cum•stan•tial•ly**
**cir•cum•stan•ti•ate**
**cir•cum•stan•tia•tion**
**cir•cum•val•late** surround with fortification
**cir•cum•val•la•tion**
**cir•cum•vent**
**cir•cum•vent•er** (*or* **ven•tor**)
**cir•cum•ven•tion**
**cir•cum•vo•lu•tion**
**cir•cum•vo•lu•tory**
**cir•cus** (*plural* **•cuses**)
**ciré** waxed
**Ci•ren•ces•ter**

**cirque** mountain feature
**cir•rate** (*or* **cir•rose, cir•rous**) biology term
**cir•rhosed**
**cir•rho•sis**
**cir•rhot•ic**
**cir•ri•pede** (*or* **•ped**) marine animal
**cir•ro•cu•mu•lus** (*plural* **•li**)
**cir•rose** (*or* **•rous**)
**cir•ro•stra•tus** (*plural* **•ti**)
**cir•rus** (*plural* **•ri**) cloud; tentacle; *compare* **schirrhus**
**cir•soid** medical term
**cis•al•pine**
**cis•co** (*plural* **•coes** *or* **•cos**) fish
**cis•lu•nar** between earth and moon
**cis•mon•tane**
**cis•soid** curve
**cist** box; *compare* **cyst**
**cis•ta•ceous** botany term
**Cis•ter•cian** monk
**cis•tern**
**cis•ter•na** (*plural* **•nae**) anatomy term
**cis•tron** genetics term
**cit•able** (*or* **cite•able**)
**cita•del**
**ci•ta•tion**
**cite**
**citha•ra** (*or* **kitha•ra**) musical instrument
**citi•fy** (*or* **city•fy; •fies, •fy•ing, •fied**)
**citi•zen**
**citi•zen•ry** (*plural* **•ries**)
**citi•zen•ship**
**Ci•tlal•té•petl** Mexican volcano
**cit•ral** plant oil
**cit•rate**
**cit•re•ous** greenish-yellow
**cit•ric**
**cit•ri•cul•ture**
**cit•rin** vitamin
**cit•rine** gemstone
**cit•ron** fruit
**cit•ron•el•la** grass
**cit•ron•el•lal** plant oil
**cit•rul•line** amino acid
**cit•rus** (*plural* **•ruses**)
**cit•tern** musical instrument
**City** London's commercial area
**city** (*plural* **cities**)
**civ•et**
**civ•ic**
**civi•cal•ly**
**civ•ics**
**civ•il**
**ci•vil•ian**
**ci•vil•ity** (*plural* **•ities**)
**civi•li•za•tion** (*or* **•sa•tion**)
**civi•lize** (*or* **•lise**)
**civi•liz•er** (*or* **•lis•er**)
**civ•il•ly**
**civ•vy** (*plural* **•vies**) *Slang* civilian
**clack**
**Clack•man•nan•shire** Scottish county
**Clac•ton** Essex town
**Clac•to•nian** Palaeolithic culture
**clad** (**clad•ding, clad**)
**clade**
**cla•dis•tic**
**cla•dis•tics**
**cla•doc•er•an** animal
**clad•ode** (*or* **clado•phyll**) plant stem
**claim**
**claim•able**
**claim•ant**
**claim•er**
**clair•audi•ence** psychology term
**clair-obscure** art term
**clair•voy•ance**
**clair•voy•ant**
**clam** (**clam•ming, clammed**)
**cla•mant** noisy
**clama•to•rial** ornithology term
**clam•bake**
**clam•ber**
**clam•mi•ly**
**clam•mi•ness**
**clam•my** (**•mi•er, •mi•est**)
**clam•or•ous**
**clam•our** (*US* **•or**)
**clamp**
**clamp•er** shoe spike
**clan**
**clan•des•tine**
**clang**
**clang•er** that which clangs; mistake
**clang•or** (*or* **•our**) loud noise
**clang•or•ous** (*or* **•our•ous**)
**clank**
**clan•nish**
**clans•man** (*plural* **•men**)
**clans•woman** (*plural* **•women**)
**clap** (**clap•ping, clapped**)
**clap•board**
**Clap•ham**
**clap•per**
**clapper•board**
**clap•trap**
**claque** hired applauders
**clara•bel•la** (*or* **clari•**) organ stop
**clar•ence** carriage
**Clar•en•don** village near Salisbury
**clar•en•don** typeface
**clar•et**
**clari•fi•ca•tion**
**clari•fier**
**clari•fy** (**•fies, •fy•ing, •fied**)
**clari•net**
**clari•net•ist** (*or* **•net•tist**)
**cla•rino** musical term
**clari•on**
**clario•net** *Obsolete* **clarinet**
**clar•ity**
**clarkia** plant
**cla•ro** cigar
**clarts** *Dialect* lumps of mud
**clary** (*plural* **claries**) plant
**clash**
**clash•er**
**clasp**
**clasp•er**
**class**
**class-conscious**
**class-conscious•ness**
**clas•sic**
**clas•si•cal**
**clas•si•cal•ism**
**clas•si•cal•ity**
**clas•si•cal•ly**
**clas•si•cism** (*or* **clas•si•cal•ism**)
**clas•si•cist** (*or* **clas•si•cal•ist**)
**clas•si•cis•tic**
**clas•sics**
**clas•si•fi•able**
**clas•si•fi•ca•tion**

**clas•si•fi•ca•tion•al**
**clas•si•fi•ca•tory**
**clas•si•fi•er**
**clas•si•fy** (**•fies, •fy•ing, •fied**)
**classi•ly**
**classi•ness**
**clas•sis** (*plural* **•ses**) church elders
**class•less**
**class•less•ness**
**class•mate**
**class•room**
**classy** (**classi•er, classi•est**)
**clas•tic** geology term
**clath•rate** netlike
**clat•ter**
**clat•tery**
**clau•di•ca•tion** lameness
**claus•al**
**clause**
**claus•tral** *variant spelling of* **cloistral**
**claus•tro•phobe**
**claus•tro•pho•bia**
**claus•tro•pho•bic**
**claus•tro•pho•bi•cal•ly**
**cla•vate** (*or* **clavi•form**) club-shaped
**clav•er** *Scot* gossip
**clavi•chord**
**clavi•chord•ist**
**clavi•cle**
**clavi•corn** beetle
**cla•vicu•lar**
**cla•vier** musical instrument
**Cla•vi•us** moon crater
**claw**
**claw•er**
**clay**
**clay•bank** *US* brown colour
**clay•ey**
**clay•like**
**clay•more** sword
**clay•pan** clay layer
**clay•stone**
**clay•to•nia** plant
**clean**
**clean•able**
**clean-cut**
**clean•er**
**clean-limbed**
**clean•li•ness**
**clean•ly** (**•li•er, •li•est**)
**clean•ness**
**cleans•able**
**cleanse**
**cleans•er**
**clean-shaven**
**clear**
**clear•ance**
**clear•cole** wall whiting
**clear-cut**
**clear-eyed**
**clear-headed**
**clear-headed•ness**
**clear•ing**
**clear•ness**
**clear-sighted**
**clear•way**
**clear•wing** moth
**cleat**
**cleav•able**
**cleav•age**
**cleave** (**cleav•ing; cleaved** *or* **clove; cleft, cleaved**, *or* **clo•ven**)
**cleav•er**
**cleav•ers** goosegrass
**cleck** *Dialect* gossip
**cleek** golf club
**Clee•thorpes** English resort
**clef**
**cleft**
**cleg** horsefly
**cleis•toga•mous** (*or* **•to•gam•ic**)
**cleis•toga•my** botany term
**clem** (**clem•ming, clemmed**) *Dialect* be hungry
**clema•tis**
**clem•en•cy** (*plural* **•cies**)
**clem•ent**
**clem•en•tine**
**clench**
**cleo•me** plant
**clep•to•ma•nia** *variant spelling of* **kleptomania**
**clere•storied** (*or* **clear•storied**)
**clere•story** (*or* **clear•**; *plural* **•stories**) church windows
**cler•gy** (*plural* **•gies**)
**clergy•man** (*plural* **•men**)
**cler•ic**
**cleri•cal**
**cleri•cal•ism**
**cleri•cal•ly**
**cleri•hew** verse
**clerk**
**clerk•dom**
**clerk•ly**
**clerk•ship**
**Clermont-Ferrand** French city
**cle•ru•chy** Athenian colony
**cleve•ite** mineral
**Cleve•land**
**clev•er**
**clev•er•ly**
**clev•er•ness**
**clev•is** coupling device
**clew** yarn; *compare* **clue**
**cli•ché**
**cli•ché'd** (*or* **•chéd**)
**Cli•chy** Parisian suburb
**click**
**click•er**
**cli•ent**
**cli•en•tal** of a client
**cli•en•tele** customers
**cliff**
**cliff•hanger**
**cliff•hanging**
**cli•mac•ter•ic** critical period
**cli•mac•teri•cal**
**cli•mac•tic** (*or* **•ti•cal**) of a climax
**cli•mate**
**cli•mat•ic** (*or* **•mati•cal** *or* **•mat•al**)
**cli•ma•to•log•ic** (*or* **•logi•cal**)
**cli•ma•tolo•gist**
**cli•ma•tol•ogy**
**cli•max**
**climb**
**climb•er**
**clime** climate
**clin•al** of a cline
**cli•nan•drium** (*plural* **•dria**) botany term
**clinch**
**clinch•er**
**cline** ecology term
**cling** (**cling•ing, clung**)
**cling•er**
**cling•fish** (*plural* **•fish** *or* **•fishes**)
**clingi•ness** (*or* **cling•ing•ness**)
**cling•stone** peach
**clingy**
**clin•ic**

**clini•cal**
**cli•ni•cian**
**clink**
**clink•er**
**clinker-built** (*or* **clincher-**)
**clink•stone**
**cli•nom•eter** surveying instrument
**cli•no•met•ric** (*or* **•ri•cal**)
**cli•nom•etry**
**cli•no•stat** botany term
**clin•quant** tinsel
**clin•to•nia** plant
**clip** (**clip•ping, clipped**)
**clip•board**
**clip-clop**
**clip•per**
**clip•pers**
**clip•pie** *Slang* bus conductress
**clip•ping**
**clique**
**cli•quey** (*or* **•quy**)
**cli•quish**
**clish•ma•clav•er** *Scot* gossip
**cli•tel•lum** (*plural* **•la**) part of worm
**clit•ic** unstressed
**clito•ral**
**clito•ris**
**cloa•ca** (*plural* **•cae**) zoology term
**cloa•cal**
**cloak**
**cloak•room**
**clob•ber**
**cloche**
**clock**
**clock•maker**
**clock•wise**
**clock•work**
**clod**
**clod•dish**
**clod•dy**
**clod•hop•per**
**clod•hop•ping**
**clog** (**clog•ging, clogged**)
**clog•gi•ness**
**clog•gy** (**•gi•er, •gi•est**)
**cloi•son•né** enamel work
**clois•ter**
**clois•tered**
**clois•tral** (*or* **claus•tral**)
**clomp**
**clon•al**
**clone** (*or* **clon**)
**clon•ic** medical term
**clo•nic•ity**
**clonk**
**clo•nus** convulsion
**clop** (**clop•ping, clopped**)
**close**
**close-down** (*noun*)
**close-fisted**
**close-grained**
**close-hauled** sailing term
**close-knit**
**close•ly**
**close•ness**
**clos•er**
**close-stool**
**clos•et**
**close-up** (*noun*)
**clos•ing**
**clos•trid•ial** (*or* **•ian**)
**clos•trid•ium** (*plural* **•iums** *or* **•ia**) bacterium
**clo•sure**
**clot** (**clot•ting, clot•ted**)
**cloth**
**cloth•bound**
**clothe** (**cloth•ing, clothed** *or* **clad**)
**clothes**
**clothes•horse**
**clothes•line**
**clothes-press**
**clo•thi•er**
**cloth•ing**
**clo•ture** *US* closure
**cloud**
**cloud•berry** (*plural* **•berries**)
**cloud•burst**
**cloud-cuckoo-land**
**cloudi•ly**
**cloudi•ness**
**cloud•less**
**cloud•let**
**cloud•scape**
**cloudy** (**cloudi•er, cloudi•est**)
**clough** *Dialect* gorge
**clout**
**clove**
**clo•ven**
**clo•ver**
**clover•leaf** (*plural* **•leaves**)
**clown**
**clown•ery**
**clown•ish**
**cloy**
**cloy•ed•ness**
**cloy•ing•ly**
**cloy•ing•ness**
**club** (**club•bing, clubbed**)
**club•bable** (*or* **•able**)
**club•by** (**•bi•er, •bi•est**)
**club-footed**
**club•haul** nautical term
**club•house**
**club•land**
**club•man** (*plural* **•men**)
**cluck**
**clucky** *Austral* pregnant
**clue** (**clu•ing, clued**) evidence; *compare* **clew**
**clue•less**
**Cluj** Romanian city
**clum•ber** spaniel
**clump**
**clump•ish** (*or* **clump•like**)
**clumpy**
**clum•si•ly**
**clum•si•ness**
**clum•sy** (**•si•er, •si•est**)
**clung**
**Clu•ni•ac** of Cluny
**clunk**
**Clu•ny** French town
**clu•peid** fish
**clu•peoid**
**clus•ter**
**clus•tery**
**clutch**
**clut•ter**
**Clw•yd** former Welsh county
**Clyde** Scottish river
**Clyde•bank** Scottish town
**Clydes•dale** horse
**clype** *Scot* tell tales
**clyp•eal** (*or* **clype•ate**)
**clyp•eus** (*plural* **clypei**) part of insect's head
**clys•ter** enema
**cni•dar•ian** zoology term
**cnido•blast** zoology term
**Cni•dus** ancient Greek city
**Cnos•sus** *variant spelling of* **Knossos**
**co•ac•er•vate** chemistry term
**co•ac•er•va•tion**
**coach**
**coach•er**

**coach•ing**
**coach•man** (*plural* **•men)**
**coach•work**
**co•ac•tion**
**co•ac•tive**
**co•ac•tiv•ity**
**co•ad•ju•tant**
**co•ad•ju•tor** bishop's assistant
**co•adu•nate** biology term
**co•adu•na•tion**
**co•adu•na•tive**
**co•agu•lable**
**co•agu•lant** (*or* **co•agu•la•tor)**
**co•agu•lase** enzyme
**co•agu•late**
**co•agu•la•tion**
**co•agu•la•tive**
**co•agu•lum** (*plural* **•la)** coagulated mass
**Coa•hui•la** Mexican state
**coal**
**coal•er** coal transporter
**coa•lesce**
**coa•les•cence**
**coa•les•cent**
**coal•face**
**coal•field**
**coal•fish** (*plural* **•fish** *or* **•fishes)**
**coa•li•tion**
**coa•li•tion•al**
**coa•li•tion•ist** (*or* **•er)**
**coal•man** (*plural* **•men)**
**Coal•port** china
**coaly**
**coam•ing** nautical term
**co•ap•ta•tion** joining two surfaces
**co•arc•tate** zoology term
**co•arc•ta•tion**
**coarse** rough; *compare* **corse; course**
**coarse•ly**
**coars•en**
**coarse•ness**
**coast**
**coast•al**
**coast•er**
**coast•guard**
**coast•line**
**coat**
**coat•ed**
**coatee** small coat
**coa•ti** (*or* **coati-mundi)** animal
**coat•ing**
**coat•less**
**coat-tail**
**co•author**
**coax**
**coax•er**
**co•ax•ial** (*or* **•ax•al)**
**cob**
**co•balt**
**co•bal•tic**
**co•bal•tite** (*or* **•tine)** mineral
**co•bal•tous**
**cob•ber** *Austral* friend
**cob•ble**
**cob•bler**
**cobble•stone**
**co•bel•lig•er•ent**
**co•bia** fish
**co•ble** *Scot* fishing boat
**Co•blenz** *variant spelling of* **Koblenz**
**cob•nut**
**Cobol** computer language
**co•bra**
**Co•burg** German city
**co•burg** loaf
**cob•web**
**cob•webbed**
**cob•web•by**
**coca** shrub
**Coca-Cola** (*Trademark*)
**co•caine** (*or* **•cain)**
**co•cain•ism**
**co•caini•za•tion** (*or* **•sa•tion)**
**co•cain•ize** (*or* **•ise)**
**coc•cal**
**coc•ci** *plural of* **coccus**
**coc•cid** insect
**coc•cidi•oi•do•my•co•sis** fungal disease
**coc•cidio•sis** (*plural* **•ses)** animal disease
**coc•cif•er•ous**
**coc•coid**
**coc•co•lith** geology term
**coc•cous** (*adj*)
**coc•cus** (*plural* **•ci)** bacterium
**coc•cyg•eal**
**coc•cyx** (*plural* **•cy•ges)**
**Co•cha•bam•ba** Bolivian city
**Co•chin** Indian region and port
**cochi•neal**
**coch•lea** (*plural* **•leae)** ear part
**coch•lear**
**coch•leate** shell-shaped
**cock**
**cock•ade**
**cock-a-doodle-doo**
**cock-a-hoop**
**Cock•aigne** imaginary land
**cock-a-leekie** soup
**cocka•lo•rum** self-important person
**cocka•tiel** (*or* **•teel)** parrot
**cocka•too** (*plural* **•toos)** parrot
**cocka•trice** monster
**cock•chafer** beetle
**cock•crow**
**cock•er**
**cock•er•el**
**cock•eye**
**cock•eyed**
**cock•fight**
**cock•horse**
**cocki•ly**
**cocki•ness**
**cock•le**
**cockle•bur** weed
**cockle•shell**
**cock•loft** garret
**cock•ney**
**cock•ney•fi•ca•tion** (*or* **•ni•)**
**cock•ney•fy** (*or* **•ni•; •fies, •fy•ing, •fied)**
**cock•ney•ism**
**cock•pit**
**cock•roach**
**cocks•comb** (*or* **cox•comb)**
**cocks•foot** (*plural* **•foots)** grass
**cock•shy** throw
**cock•spur** grass
**cock•sure**
**cock•swain** *variant spelling of* **coxswain**
**cock•tail**
**cock•up**
**cocky** **(cocki•er, cocki•est)**
**coco** (*plural* **cocos)** *short for* **coconut**
**co•coa**
**coco de mer** tree

**coco•nut**
**co•coon**
**co•co•pan** mining wagon
**co•cotte**
**co•co•yam** vegetable
**cod** (*noun, plural* **cod** *or* **cods**; *verb* **cod•ding, cod•ded**)
**coda**
**cod•dle**
**cod•dler**
**code**
**co•dec•li•na•tion**
**co•deine**
**cod•er**
**co•dex** (*plural* **co•di•ces**)
**cod•fish** (*plural* **•fish** *or* **•fishes**)
**codg•er**
**codi•cil**
**codi•cil•la•ry**
**co•di•col•ogy**
**codi•fi•ca•tion**
**codi•fi•er**
**codi•fy** (**•fies, •fy•ing, •fied**)
**cod•ling** (*or* **•lin**) apple
**co•do•main** maths term
**co•don** genetics term
**cod•piece**
**co-driver**
**cods•wallop**
**co-ed**
**co•edit**
**co•edi•tion**
**co•edi•tor**
**co•edu•ca•tion**
**co•edu•ca•tion•al**
**co•edu•ca•tion•al•ly**
**co•ef•fi•cient**
**coe•la•canth** primitive fish
**coe•len•ter•ate** animal
**coe•len•ter•ic**
**coe•len•ter•on** (*plural* **•tera**) zoology term
**coe•li•ac** (*US* **ce•**) of the abdomen
**coe•lom** (*US* **ce•**) body cavity
**coe•lo•mate** (*US* **ce•**)
**coe•lo•stat** astronomical instrument
**coe•nes•the•sia** (*or* **•sis, ce•**)
**coe•nes•thet•ic** (*or* **ce•**)
**coe•no•bite** (*or* **ce•**) member of religious order
**coe•no•cyte** botany term
**coe•no•cyt•ic**
**coe•no•sarc** zoology term
**coe•nu•rus** larva
**co•en•zyme**
**co•equal**
**co•equali•ty**
**co•equal•ly**
**co•erce**
**co•er•cible**
**co•er•cion**
**co•er•cion•ary**
**co•er•cion•ist**
**co•er•cive**
**co•er•cive•ness**
**co•er•civ•ity** physics term
**co•es•sen•tial**
**co•es•sen•tial•ity** (*or* **•ness**)
**co•eter•nity**
**co•eval** contemporary
**co•eval•ity**
**co•eval•ly**
**co•ex•ist**
**co•ex•ist•ence**
**co•ex•ist•ent**
**co•ex•tend**
**co•ex•ten•sion**
**co•ex•ten•sive**
**coff** *Scot* buy
**cof•fee**
**coffee•pot**
**cof•fer**
**coffer•dam** underwater chamber
**cof•fin**
**cof•fle** chained slaves
**cog** (**cog•ging, cogged**)
**co•gen•cy**
**co•gent**
**cogi•tate**
**cogi•ta•tion**
**cogi•ta•tive**
**cogi•ta•tor**
**Cog•nac** French town; brandy
**cog•nate**
**cog•na•tion** relatedness
**cog•ni•tion** perception
**cog•ni•tive**
**cog•ni•zable** (*or* **•sable**)
**cog•ni•zance** (*or* **•sance**)
**cog•ni•zant** (*or* **•sant**)
**cog•nize** (*or* **•nise**) perceive
**cog•no•men** Roman family name
**co•gno•scen•ti** (*or* **cono•scen•ti**; *sing.* **•te**)
**co•gon** grass
**cog•wheel**
**co•hab•it**
**co•hab•it•ant** (*or* **•it•er**)
**co•habi•ta•tion**
**co•heir**
**co•here**
**co•her•ence** (*or* **•en•cy**)
**co•her•ent**
**co•her•er**
**co•he•sion**
**co•he•sive**
**coho** (*plural* **coho** *or* **cohos**) fish
**co•ho•bate** redistil
**co•hort**
**co•hosh** plant
**co•hune** palm tree
**coif** cap
**coif•feur** (*fem* **•feuse**) hairdresser
**coif•fure** hair style
**coign** (*or* **coigne**) *variant spellings of* **quoin**; *compare* coin
**coil**
**coil•er**
**Co•im•ba•tore** Indian city
**Coim•bra** Portuguese city
**coin** currency; *compare* **quoin**
**coin•age**
**co•in•cide**
**co•in•ci•dence**
**co•in•ci•dent**
**co•in•ci•dent•al**
**co•in•ci•dent•al•ly**
**coin•er**
**coin-op**
**co•in•sur•ance**
**co•in•sure**
**Coin•treau** (*Trademark*)
**coir** coconut fibre
**coit** *Austral* buttocks
**coi•tal**
**coi•tus** (*or* **•tion**)
**Coke** (*Trademark*) Coca-Cola
**coke**
**coku•lo•ris** film term
**col**
**cola** (*or* **kola**) tree; nut
**col•an•der** sieve; *compare* **calendar; calender**

**co•lati•tude**
**col•can•non** cabbage dish
**Col•ches•ter**
**col•chi•cine** alkaloid
**col•chi•cum** plant
**Col•chis** ancient Asian country
**col•co•thar** rouge
**cold**
**cold-blooded**
**cold-blooded•ness**
**cold-drawn** metallurgy term
**cold-hearted**
**cold•ish**
**cold•ness**
**cold-weld**
**cole** cabbage
**co•lec•to•my** (*plural* **•mies**)
**cole•man•ite** mineral
**col•eop•ter•an** (*plural* **•ter•ans** *or* **•tera**) beetle
**col•eop•ter•ist**
**col•eop•ter•ous**
**col•eop•tile** botany term
**col•eo•rhi•za** (*plural* **•zae**) botany term
**cole•slaw**
**co•leus** (*plural* **•uses**) plant
**col•ey** fish; *compare* **coly**
**col•ic**
**col•icky**
**colic•root**
**colic•weed**
**Co•li•ma** Mexican state and city
**coli•seum** (*or* **col•os•seum**)
**co•li•tic**
**co•li•tis** (*or* **colo•ni•tis**)
**col•labo•rate**
**col•labo•ra•tion**
**col•labo•ra•tive**
**col•labo•ra•tor**
**col•lage**
**col•la•gen** protein
**col•la•gen•ic** (*or* **•gen•ous**)
**col•lag•ist**
**col•lap•sar** black hole
**col•lapse**
**col•laps•ibil•ity**
**col•laps•ible** (*or* **•able**)
**col•lar**
**collar•bone**
**col•lard** cabbage
**col•lar•ette**
**col•late**
**col•lat•er•al**
**col•lat•er•al•ly**
**col•la•tion**
**col•la•tive**
**col•la•tor**
**col•league**
**col•lect**
**col•lect•able** (*or* **•ible**)
**col•lec•ta•nea** miscellany
**col•lec•tion**
**col•lec•tive**
**col•lec•tiv•ism**
**col•lec•tiv•ist**
**col•lec•tiv•is•tic**
**col•lec•tiv•ity** (*plural* **•ities**)
**col•lec•tivi•za•tion** (*or* **•sa•tion**)
**col•lec•ti•vize** (*or* **•vise**)
**col•lec•tor**
**col•lec•to•rate**
**col•leen** *Irish* girl
**col•lege**
**col•le•gial**
**col•legian**
**col•legi•ate**
**col•legium** (*plural* **•legiums** *or* **•legia**)
**col•lem•bo•lan** insect
**col•len•chy•ma** plant tissue
**Colles' frac•ture**
**col•let** jewellery setting
**col•lide**
**col•lie**
**col•li•er**
**col•liery** (*plural* **•lieries**)
**col•li•gate** join
**col•li•ga•tion**
**col•li•ga•tive**
**col•li•mate**
**col•li•ma•tion**
**col•li•ma•tor** optical device
**col•lin•ear**
**col•lin•ear•ity**
**col•lin•sia** plant
**col•li•sion**
**col•lo•cate**
**col•lo•ca•tion**
**col•lo•cu•tor**
**col•lo•di•on** (*or* **•dium**) liquid
**col•logue** (**•lo•guing, •logued**) conspire
**col•loid**
**col•loi•dal**
**col•loi•dal•ity**
**col•lop** *Dialect* meat slice
**col•lo•quial**
**col•lo•qui•al•ism**
**col•lo•qui•al•ly**
**col•lo•quium** (*plural* **•quiums** *or* **•quia**)
**col•lo•quy** (*plural* **•quies**)
(**collossus**) *incorrect spelling of* **colossus**
**col•lo•type** printing process
**col•lo•typ•ic**
**col•lude**
**col•lu•sion**
**col•lu•sive**
**col•lu•vial**
**col•lu•vium** (*plural* **•via** *or* **•viums**) rock fragments
**col•ly** *Dialect* soot
**col•lyr•ium** (*plural* **•lyria** *or* **•lyr•iums**) eye lotion
**col•ly•wob•bles**
**colo•bus** monkey
**colo•cynth** plant
**co•loga•rithm**
**co•logne** perfume
**Co•logne** German city
**Co•lom•bia** South American republic; *compare* **Columbia**
**Co•lom•bian**
**Co•lom•bo** Sri Lankan capital
**co•lon**
**Co•lón** Panamanian port
**colo•nel**
**colo•nel•cy** (*or* **colo•nel•ship**)
**co•lo•nial**
**co•lo•ni•al•ism**
**co•lo•ni•al•ist**
**co•lo•ni•al•ly**
**co•lon•ic**
**colo•nist**
**colo•ni•tis** *variant of* **colitis**
**colo•niz•able** (*or* **•nis•able**)
**colo•ni•za•tion** (*or* **•sa•tion**)
**colo•nize** (*or* **•nise**)
**colo•niz•er** (*or* **•nis•er**)
**col•on•nade**
**col•on•nad•ed**
**Col•on•say** Hebridean island
**colo•ny** (*plural* **•nies**)
**colo•phon** emblem
**co•lopho•ny** rosin

**col•or** *US spelling of* **colour**
**Colo•ra•do**
**col•or•ant**
**col•ora•tion**
**colo•ra•tu•ra** (*or* **col•ora•ture**) musical term
**col•or•if•ic**
**col•or•im•eter**
**col•ori•met•ric** (*or* **•ri•cal**)
**col•or•im•etry**
**co•los•sal**
**co•los•sal•ly**
**Col•os•seum** Roman amphitheatre
**col•os•seum** *variant spelling of* **coliseum**
**co•los•sus** (*plural* **•si** *or* **•suses**)
**co•los•to•my** (*plural* **•mies**) artificial colon opening
**co•los•tral**
**co•los•trum** first breast milk
**co•loto•my** (*plural* **•mies**)
**col•our** (*US* **col•or**)
**col•our•able** (*US* **•or•**)
**col•our•ant** (*US* **•or•**)
**(colouration)** *incorrect spelling of* **coloration**
**colour-blind** (*US* **color-**)
**col•oured** (*US* **•ored**)
**colour•fast** (*US* **color•**)
**col•our•ful** (*US* **•or•**)
**col•our•ful•ly** (*US* **•or•**)
**col•our•ing** (*US* **•or•**)
**col•our•ist** (*US* **•or•**)
**col•our•is•tic** (*US* **•or•**)
**col•our•ize** (**•ise**; *US* **col•or•ize**)
**col•our•less** (*US* **•or•**)
**colour•man** (*US* **color•**; *plural* **•men**) paint dealer
**col•oury** (*or* **•ory**)
**col•pi•tis** medical term
**col•por•teur** book pedlar
**Colt** (*Trademark*) revolver
**colt**
**col•ter** *US spelling of* **coulter**
**colt•ish**
**colts•foot** (*plural* **•foots**) plant
**colu•brid** snake
**colu•brine** of snakes
**co•lu•go** lemur
**Co•lum•ba** constellation
**col•um•bar•ium** (*plural* **•ia**) dovecote
**Co•lum•bia** US river and city; *compare* **Colombia**
**Co•lum•bian**
**co•lum•bic**
**Col•um•bine** pantomime character
**col•um•bine** plant
**co•lum•bite** mineral
**co•lum•bium** chemical element
**Co•lum•bus** US city
**colu•mel•la** (*plural* **•lae**) biology term
**colu•mel•lar**
**col•umn**
**co•lum•nar**
**col•umned** (*or* **•um•nat•ed**)
**co•lum•nia•tion**
**col•umn•ist**
**co•lure** circle on sphere
**Col•wyn Bay**
**coly** (*plural* **colies**) bird; *compare* **coley**
**col•za** rape plant
**coma** (*plural* **comas**) unconsciousness
**coma** (*plural* **comae**) cloud round comet
**com•al**
**Co•man•che** (*plural* **•ches** *or* **•che**)
**Co•man•chean**
**co•mate** hairy
**co•ma•tose**
**co•matu•lid** (*or* **•matu•la**; *plural* **•lids** *or* **•lae**) marine animal
**comb**
**com•bat**
**com•bat•able**
**com•bat•ant**
**com•bat•er**
**com•bat•ive**
**combe** *variant spelling of* **coomb**
**comb•er**
**com•bin•able**
**com•bi•na•tion**
**com•bi•na•tive** (*or* **•to•rial**, **•tory**)
**com•bine**
**com•bin•er**
**comb•ing**
**com•bo** (*plural* **•bos**) jazz band
**com•bust**
**com•bus•tibil•ity** (*or* **•tible•ness**)
**com•bus•tible**
**com•bus•tion**
**com•bus•tor** engine part
**come** (**com•ing, came**)
**come•back**
**Com•econ** former Communist economic association
**co•median**
**co•medic**
**co•medi•enne**
**com•edo** (*plural* **•edos** *or* **•edo•nes**) blackhead
**come•down**
**com•edy** (*plural* **•edies**)
**come•ly** (**•li•er, •li•est**)
**come-on** (*noun*)
**com•er**
**co•mes•tible**
**com•et**
**come•up•pance**
**com•fit** sweet
**com•fort**
**com•fort•able**
**com•fort•ably**
**com•fort•er**
**com•fort•ing**
**com•fort•less**
**com•frey** plant
**com•fy** (**•fi•er, •fi•est**)
**com•ic**
**comi•cal**
**comi•cal•ly**
**Com•in•form** former Communist Information Bureau
**com•ing**
**Com•in•tern** former international Communist organization
**co•mi•tia** Roman assembly
**com•ity** (*plural* **•ities**) courtesy
**com•ma**
**com•mand**
**com•man•dant**
**com•man•deer**
**com•mand•er**
**com•mand•er•ship**
**com•mand•ing**

**com•mand•ment**
**com•man•do** (*plural* **•dos** *or* **•does**)
**com•mea•sure**
**com•media dell'arte** Italian comic theatre
**comme il faut** *French* as it should be
**com•memo•rate**
**com•memo•ra•tion**
**com•memo•ra•tive** (*or* **•tory**)
**com•memo•ra•tor**
**com•mence**
**com•mence•ment**
**com•mend**
**com•mend•able**
**com•mend•ably**
**com•men•dam** Church office
**com•men•da•tion**
**com•menda•tory**
**com•men•sal** biology term
**com•men•sal•ism** (*or* **•sal•ity**)
**com•men•su•rable**
**com•men•su•rate**
**com•men•su•ra•tion**
**com•ment**
**com•men•tar•ial**
**com•men•tary** (*plural* **•taries**)
**com•men•tate**
**com•men•ta•tor**
**com•ment•er**
**com•merce**
**com•mer•cial**
**com•mer•cial•ism**
**com•mer•cial•ist**
**com•mer•cial•is•tic**
**com•mer•ci•al•ity**
**com•mer•ciali•za•tion** (*or* **•sa•tion**)
**com•mer•cial•ize** (*or* **•ise**)
**com•mer•cial•ly**
**com•mère** female compere
**com•mi•na•tion** threatening vengeance
**com•mina•tory**
**com•min•gle**
**com•mi•nute** reduce to fragments
**com•mi•nu•tion**
**com•mis** agent
**com•mis•er•ate**
**com•mis•era•tion**
**com•mis•era•tive**
**com•mis•era•tor**
**com•mis•sar**
**com•mis•sar•ial**
**com•mis•sari•at**
**com•mis•sary** (*plural* **•saries**)
**com•mis•sion**
**com•mis•sion•aire**
**com•mis•sion•al** (*or* **•ary**)
**com•mis•sion•er**
**com•mis•su•ral**
**com•mis•sure** anatomy term
**com•mit** (**•mit•ting, •mit•ted**)
**com•mit•ment**
**com•mit•tal**
**com•mit•tee**
**committee•man** (*plural* **•men**)
**com•mit•ter**
(committment) *incorrect spelling of* **commitment**
**com•mode**
**com•mo•di•ous**
**com•mod•ity** (*plural* **•ities**)
**com•mo•dore**
**com•mon**
**com•mon•able** legal term
**com•mon•age** legal term
**com•mon•al•ity** commonness
**com•mon•al•ty** (*or* **•ity**) ordinary people
**com•mon•er**
**com•mon•ly**
**com•mon•ness**
**common•place**
**Com•mons** (**House of**)
**common•weal** *Archaic* common goods; commonwealth
**Common•wealth** of Nations; republican England
**common•wealth** independent community
**com•mo•tion**
**com•mo•tion•al**
**com•mu•nal**
**com•mu•nal•ism**
**com•mu•nal•ist**
**com•mu•nal•is•tic**
**com•mu•nal•ity**
**commu•nali•za•tion** (*or* **•sa•tion**)
**com•mu•nal•ize** (*or* **•ise**)
**Com•mu•nade** supporter of Paris Commune
**com•mu•nard** member of a commune
**Com•mune** Paris Revolutionary government
**com•mune**
**com•mu•ni•cabil•ity** (*or* **•cable•ness**)
**com•mu•ni•cable**
**com•mu•ni•cant**
**com•mu•ni•cate**
**com•mu•ni•ca•tion**
**com•mu•ni•ca•tive**
**com•mu•ni•ca•tor**
**com•mu•ni•ca•tory**
**Com•mun•ion** Eucharist
**com•mun•ion**
**com•mun•ion•al**
**com•mun•ion•ist**
**com•mu•ni•qué**
**com•mun•ism**
**Com•mun•ist** political party
**com•mun•ist** supporter of communism
**com•mu•nis•tic**
**com•mu•ni•tar•ian**
**com•mu•nity** (*plural* **•nities**)
**com•mu•ni•za•tion** (*or* **•sa•tion**)
**com•mu•nize** (*or* **•nise**) nationalize
**com•mut•able** exchangeable
**com•mu•tate**
**com•mu•ta•tion**
**com•mu•ta•tive** involving substitution
**com•mu•ta•tor** electrical device
**com•mute**
**com•mut•er**
**Como** Italian city and lake
**Como•ros** island country
**co•mose** hairy
**comp** *Slang* compositor
**com•pact**
**com•pact•er**
**com•pact•ness**
**com•pan•der** sound transmission

**com•pan•ion**
**com•pan•ion•able**
**com•pan•ion•ably**
**com•pan•ion•able**
**com•pan•ion•ate**
**com•pan•ion•ship**
**com•pan•ion•way** stairway on ship
**com•pa•ny** (*plural* **•nies**)
**com•pa•rabil•ity**
**com•pa•rable**
**com•pa•rably**
**com•para•tive**
**com•para•tive•ly**
**com•para•tor**
**com•pare**
**com•par•er**
**com•pari•son**
**com•part•ment**
**com•part•men•tal**
**com•part•men•tali•za•tion** (*or* **•sa•tion**)
**com•part•men•tal•ize** (*or* **•ise**)
**com•part•men•ted**
**com•pass**
**com•pass•able**
**com•pas•sion**
**com•pas•sion•ate**
**com•pat•ibil•ity**
**com•pat•ible**
**com•pat•ibly**
**com•pat•ri•ot**
**com•pat•ri•ot•ic**
**com•pat•ri•ot•ism**
**com•peer** equal status
**com•pel** (**•pel•ling, •pelled**)
**com•pel•ler**
**com•pen•di•ous**
**com•pen•dium** (*plural* **•diums** *or* **•dia**)
**com•pen•sate**
**com•pen•sa•tion**
**com•pen•sa•tive**
**com•pen•sa•tor**
**com•pen•sa•tory**
**com•pere**
**com•pete**
**com•pe•tence**
**com•pe•ten•cy** (*plural* **•cies**) legal term
**com•pe•tent**
**com•pe•ti•tion**
**com•peti•tive**
**com•peti•tor**
**com•pi•la•tion**
**com•pile**
**com•pil•er**
**com•pla•cen•cy** (*or* **com•pla•cence;** *plural* **•cencies** *or* **•cences**) self-satisfaction; *compare* **complaisance**
**com•pla•cent**
**com•plain**
**com•plain•ant**
**com•plain•er**
**com•plaint**
**com•plai•sance** willingness to comply; *compare* **complacency**
**com•plai•sant**
**com•ple•ment** complete; that which completes; *compare* **compliment**
**com•ple•men•tary** (*or* **•tal**)
**com•ple•men•tiz•er** grammar term
**com•plete**
**com•plete•ness**
**com•plet•er**
**com•ple•tion**
**com•ple•tive**
**com•plex**
**com•plex•ion**
**com•plex•ity** (*plural* **•ities**)
**com•pli•ance** (*or* **•an•cy**)
**com•pli•ant** (*or* **•able**)
**com•pli•cate**
**com•pli•cat•ed**
**com•pli•ca•tion**
**com•plic•ity** (*plural* **•ities**)
**com•pli•er**
**com•pli•ment** praise; *compare* **complement**
**com•pli•men•tary**
**com•pline** (*or* **•plin**) canonical hour
**com•ply** (**•plies, •ply•ing, •plied**)
**com•po** (*plural* **•pos**) mixture; *Austral* compensation
**com•po•nent**
**com•po•nen•tial**
**com•po•ny** (*or* **•ne**) heraldic term
**com•port**
**com•port•ment**
**com•pose**
**com•pos•er**
**com•po•site**
**com•po•si•tion**
**com•po•si•tion•al**
**com•posi•tor**
**com•pos men•tis** *Latin* sane
**com•post**
**com•po•sure**
**com•pote**
**com•pound**
**com•pound•er**
**com•pra•dor** foreign agent
**com•pre•hend**
**com•pre•hen•sibil•ity** (*or* **•sible•ness**)
**com•pre•hen•sible** (*or* **•hend•ible**)
**com•pre•hen•sibly**
**com•pre•hen•sion**
**com•pre•hen•sive**
**com•press**
**com•press•ibil•ity** (*or* **•ible•ness**)
**com•press•ible**
**com•pres•sion**
**com•pres•sion•al**
**com•pres•sive**
**com•pres•sor**
**com•pris•able**
**com•pris•al**
**com•prise**
**com•pro•mise**
**com•pro•mis•er**
**Comp•tom•eter** (*Trademark*)
**comp•trol•ler**
**com•pul•sion**
**com•pul•sive**
**com•pul•so•ry**
**com•pul•so•ri•ly**
**com•punc•tion**
**com•punc•tious**
**com•put•abil•ity**
**com•put•able**
**com•pu•ta•tion**
**com•pu•ta•tion•al**
**com•pute**
**com•put•er**
**com•put•eri•za•tion** (*or* **•sa•tion**)
**com•put•er•ize** (*or* **•ise**)
**com•rade**
**com•rade•ship**
**com•sat** *short for* communications satellite

**com•stock•ery** *US* excessive censorship
**Comus** Roman god
**con** (**con•ning, conned**)
**con amo•re** musical term
**Con•akry** capital of Guinea
**co•na•tion** psychology term
**cona•tive** linguistics term
**co•na•tus** (*plural* **•tus**) striving
**con brio** musical term
**con•cat•enate**
**con•cat•ena•tion** series of events
**con•cave**
**con•cav•ity** (*plural* **•ities**)
**concavo-concave**
**concavo-convex**
**con•ceal**
**con•ceal•ment**
**con•cede**
**con•ced•er**
**con•ceit**
**con•ceit•ed**
**con•ceiv•able**
**con•ceiv•ably**
**con•ceive**
**con•cel•ebrate**
**con•cel•ebra•tion**
(**concensus**) *incorrect spelling of* **consensus**
**con•cen•trate**
**con•cen•tra•tion**
**con•cen•tra•tive**
**con•cen•tra•tor**
**con•cen•tre** to concentrate
**con•cen•tric** (*or* **•tri•cal**)
**con•cen•tri•cal•ly**
**con•cen•tric•ity**
**Con•cep•ción** Chilean city
**con•cept**
**con•cep•ta•cle** botany term
**con•cep•tion**
**con•cep•tion•al**
**con•cep•tive**
**con•cep•tual**
**con•cep•tu•al•ism**
**con•cep•tu•al•ist**
**con•cep•tu•al•is•tic**
**con•cep•tu•ali•za•tion** (*or* **•sa•tion**)
**con•cep•tu•al•ize** (*or* **•ise**)
**con•cern**
**con•cerned**
**con•cern•ed•ly**
**con•cern•ing**
**con•cert**
**con•cer•tan•te** musical work
**con•cert•ed**
**con•cert•go•er**
**con•cer•ti•na** (**•nas, •na•ing, •naed**)
**con•cer•ti•no** (*plural* **•ni**) musical work
**con•cer•tize**
**con•cer•to** (*plural* **•tos** *or* **•ti**)
**con•cer•to gros•so** (*plural* **•ti gros•si**)
**con•ces•sible**
**con•ces•sion**
**con•ces•sion•aire** (*or* **•er, •ary**; *plural* **•aires, •ers,** *or* **•aries**)
**con•ces•sion•ary**
**con•ces•sive**
**conch** (*plural* **conchs** *or* **conches**) mollusc
**con•cha** (*plural* **•chae**) shell-shaped part
**con•chal**
**con•chif•er•ous**
**con•chio•lin** protein
**con•choid** geometric curve
**con•choi•dal** geology term
**con•cho•logi•cal**
**con•cholo•gist**
**con•chol•ogy** study of shells
**con•chy** (*plural* **•chies**) *Slang* conscientious objector
**con•ci•erge**
**con•cili•ar** of ecclesiastical councils
**con•cili•ate**
**con•cili•ation**
**con•cilia•tive**
**con•cili•ator**
**con•cilia•tory** (*or* **•tive**)
**con•cin•nity** (*plural* **•nities**) harmonious arrangement
**con•cin•nous**
**con•cise**
**con•ci•sion**
**con•clave**
**con•clav•ist**
**con•clude**
**con•clu•sion**
**con•clu•sive**
**con•coct**
**con•coct•er** (*or* **•coc•tor**)
**con•coc•tion**
**con•coc•tive**
**con•comi•tance**
**con•comi•tant**
**Con•cord** US and Australian cities; *compare* **Concorde**
**con•cord** agreement
**con•cord•ance**
**con•cord•ant**
**con•cor•dat** treaty
**Con•corde** airliner; *compare* **Concord**
**con•course**
**con•cres•cence** biology term
**con•crete**
**con•cre•tion**
**con•cre•tion•ary**
**con•cre•tive**
**con•creti•za•tion** (*or* **•sa•tion**)
**con•cre•tize** (*or* **•tise**)
**con•cu•bi•nage**
**con•cu•bine**
**con•cu•pis•cence**
**con•cu•pis•cent**
**con•cur** (**•cur•ring, •curred**)
**con•cur•rence**
**con•cur•rent**
**con•cuss**
**con•cus•sion**
**con•cus•sive**
**con•demn**
**con•demn•able**
**con•dem•na•tion**
**con•dem•na•tory**
**con•demn•er**
**con•den•sabil•ity** (*or* **•sibil•ity**)
**con•den•sable** (*or* **•sible**)
**con•den•sate**
**con•den•sa•tion**
**con•dense**
**con•dens•er**
**con•de•scend**
**con•de•scend•ence** legal term
**con•de•scend•ing**
**con•de•scen•sion**
**con•dign** well-deserved
**con•di•ment**
**con•di•tion**
**con•di•tion•al**
**con•di•tion•al•ity**
**con•di•tion•al•ly**
**con•di•tioned**
**con•di•tion•er**

**con•di•tion•ing**
**con•do•la•tory**
**con•dole**
**con•do•lence** (*or* **•dole•ment**)
**con•dol•er**
**con•dom**
**con•do•min•ium** (*plural* **•iums**)
**con•do•na•tion**
**con•done**
**con•don•er**
**con•dor** vulture
**con•dot•tiere** (*plural* **•tieri**) mercenary
**con•duce**
**con•duc•er**
**con•duc•ible**
**con•du•cive**
**con•duct**
**con•duct•ance** physics term
**con•duct•ible**
**con•duc•tion**
**con•duc•tive**
**con•duc•tiv•ity** (*plural* **•ities**)
**con•duc•tor** (*fem* **•tress**)
**con•duit**
**con•du•pli•cate** botany term
**con•du•pli•ca•tion**
**con•dy•lar**
**con•dyle** bone projection
**con•dy•loid**
**con•dy•lo•ma** (*plural* **•mas** *or* **•ma•ta**) tumour
**con•dy•loma•tous**
**cone**
**cone•flower**
**co•ney** *variant spelling of* **cony**
**Co•ney Is•land** US resort
**con•fab** *Slang* chat
**con•fabu•late**
**con•fabu•la•tion**
**con•fabu•la•tor**
**con•fabu•la•tory**
**con•fect** combine ingredients
**con•fec•tion**
**con•fec•tion•ary** (*plural* **•aries**) place where confections are made
**con•fec•tion•er**
**con•fec•tion•ery** (*plural* **•eries**) sweets
**Con•fed•era•cy** seceding US states
**con•fed•era•cy** (*plural* **•cies**)
**Con•fed•er•ate**
**con•fed•er•ate**
**Con•fed•era•tion** original US states
**con•fed•era•tion**
**con•fed•era•tion•ism**
**con•fed•era•tion•ist**
**con•fer** (**•fer•ring, •ferred**)
**con•feree** (*or* **•fer•ree**)
**con•fer•ence**
**con•fer•en•tial**
**con•fer•ment** (*or* **•fer•ral**)
**con•fer•rable**
**con•fer•rer**
**con•fer•va** (*plural* **•vae** *or* **•vas**) alga
**con•fer•val**
**con•fer•void**
**con•fess**
**confessant**
**con•fess•ed•ly**
**con•fes•sion**
**con•fes•sion•al**
**con•fes•sion•ary**
**con•fes•sor**
**con•fet•ti**
**con•fi•dant** (*fem* **•dante**) person in whom one confides
**con•fide**
**con•fi•dence**
**con•fi•dent** self-assured
**con•fi•den•tial**
**con•fi•den•ti•al•ity** (*or* **•tial•ness**)
**con•fi•den•tial•ly**
**con•fid•er**
**con•fid•ing**
**con•figu•ra•tion**
**con•figu•ra•tion•al** (*or* **•ra•tive**)
**con•figu•ra•tion•ism** Gestalt psychology
**con•figu•ra•tion•ist**
**con•fin•able** (*or* **•fine•able**)
**con•fine**
**con•fine•ment**
**con•firm**
**con•firm•and** candidate for confirmation
**con•fir•ma•tion**
**con•firma•tory** (*or* **•tive**)
**con•fis•cable**
**con•fis•cate**
**con•fis•ca•tor**
**con•fis•ca•tory**
**Con•fit•eor** prayer
**con•fi•ture** confection
**con•fla•gra•tion**
**con•fla•gra•tive**
**con•flate** combine
**con•fla•tion**
**con•flict**
**con•flic•tion**
**con•flic•tive** (*or* **•tory**)
**con•flu•ence** (*or* **con•flux**)
**con•flu•ent**
**con•fo•cal**
**con•form**
**con•form•abil•ity** (*or* **•able•ness**)
**con•form•able**
**con•form•ably**
**con•for•mal** maths term
**con•for•ma•tion**
**con•form•er**
**con•form•ist**
**con•form•ity** (*or* **•ance**; *plural* **•ities** *or* **•ances**)
**con•found**
**con•found•er**
**con•fra•ter•nal**
**con•fra•ter•nity** (*plural* **•nities**)
**con•frère** fellow member
**con•front**
**con•fron•ta•tion** (*or* **con•front•ment**)
**con•front•er**
**Con•fu•cian**
**Con•fu•cian•ism**
**Con•fu•cian•ist**
**con fuo•co** musical term
**con•fus•able**
**con•fuse**
**con•fus•ed•ly**
**con•fus•ing**
**con•fus•ing•ly**
**con•fu•sion**
**con•fu•ta•tion**
**con•fu•ta•tive**
**con•fute**
**con•fut•er**
**con•ga** (**•ga•ing, •gaed**) dance; *compare* **conger**

**con•gé** dismissal
**con•geal**
**con•geal•ment**
**con•ge•la•tion**
**con•ge•ner** member of group
**con•ge•ner•ic**
**con•gen•ial**
**con•ge•ni•al•ity** (*or* **con•gen•ial•ness**)
**con•gen•ial•ly**
**con•geni•tal** present from birth
**con•geni•tal•ly**
**con•ger** eel; *compare* **conga**
**con•ge•ries** collection
**con•gest**
**con•gest•ible**
**con•ges•tion**
**con•ges•tive**
**con•gi•us** (*plural* **•gii**) unit
**con•glo•bate** form into ball
**con•glo•ba•tion**
**con•glom•er•ate**
**con•glom•er•at•ic** (*or* **•it•ic**)
**con•glom•era•tion**
**con•glu•ti•nant**
**con•glu•ti•nate** heal together
**con•glu•ti•na•tive**
**Con•go** African republic
**con•go eel**
**Con•go•lese**
**con•gou** (*or* **•go**) China tea
**con•grats**
**con•gratu•late**
**con•gratu•la•tion**
**con•gratu•la•tor**
**con•gratu•la•tory**
**con•gre•gant**
**con•gre•gate**
**con•gre•ga•tion**
**Con•gre•ga•tion•al** evangelical church
**con•gre•ga•tion•al**
**Con•gre•ga•tion•al•ism**
**Con•gre•ga•tion•al•ist**
**con•gre•ga•tive**
**con•gre•ga•tor** (*or* **•gre•gant**)
**Con•gress** US legislature
**con•gress**
**Con•gres•sion•al**
**con•gres•sion•al**
**Con•gres•sion•al•ist**
**con•gres•sion•al•ist**
**Congress•man** (*plural* **•men**)
**Congress•woman** (*plural* **•women**)
**con•gru•ence** (*or* **•en•cy**; *plural* **•ences** *or* **•cies**)
**con•gru•ent**
**con•gru•ity** (*plural* **•ities**)
**con•gru•ous**
**con•ic** (*or* **coni•cal**)
**con•ics**
**co•nid•ial** (*or* **•ian**)
**co•nidio•phore**
**co•nid•ium** (*plural* **•nidia**) fungal spore
**co•ni•fer**
**co•nif•er•ous**
**co•ni•ine** (*or* **co•nin, co•nine**) alkaloid
**Con•is•ton** lake
**co•nium** hemlock
**con•jec•tur•al**
**con•jec•ture**
**con•jec•tur•er**
**con•join**
**con•join•ed•ly**
**con•join•er**
**con•joint**
**con•ju•gable**
**con•ju•gal**
**con•ju•gal•ly**
**con•ju•gal•ity**
**con•ju•gant**
**con•ju•gate**
**con•ju•ga•tion**
**con•ju•ga•tion•al**
**con•ju•ga•tive**
**con•ju•ga•tor**
**con•junct**
**con•junc•tion**
**con•junc•tion•al**
**con•junc•ti•va** (*plural* **•vas** *or* **•vae**) eyeball membrane
**con•junc•ti•val**
**con•junc•tive**
**con•junc•ti•vi•tis**
**con•junc•tur•al**
**con•junc•ture**
**con•jura•tion**
**con•jure**
**con•jur•er** (*or* **•or**)
**conk**
**conk•er**
**con moto** musical term
**Con•nacht** Northern Irish province
**con•nate**
**con•natu•ral**
**Con•naught** *former name of* Connacht
**con•nect**
**con•nect•ible** (*or* **•able**)
**Con•necti•cut**
**con•nec•tion** (*or* **•nex•ion**)
**con•nec•tion•al** (*or* **•nex•ion•al**)
**con•nec•tive**
**con•nect•or** (*or* **•er**)
**conned**
**Con•ne•ma•ra**
**con•ning**
**con•nip•tion** *US* rage
**con•niv•ance** (*or* **•ence**)
**con•nive**
**con•niv•ent**
**con•niv•er**
**con•nois•seur**
**con•no•ta•tion**
**con•no•ta•tive** (*or* **con•no•tive**)
**con•note**
**con•nu•bial**
**con•nu•bi•al•ity**
**con•nu•bi•al•ly**
**co•no•dont** fossil tooth
**co•noid** geometry term
**co•noi•dal**
**con•quer**
**con•quer•or**
**con•quest**
**con•quis•ta•dor** (*plural* **•dors** *or* **•do•res**)
**con•san•guin•eous** (*or* **•guine**)
**con•san•guin•ity**
**con•science**
**conscience-stricken**
**con•sci•en•tious**
**con•sci•en•tious•ness**
**con•scion•able**
**con•scious**
**con•scious•ness**
**con•script**
**con•scrip•tion**
**con•scrip•tion•al**
**con•scrip•tion•ist**
**con•se•crate**
**con•se•cra•tion**
**con•se•cra•tor**

**con•se•cra•tory** (*or* **•tive**)
**con•se•cu•tion** sequence of events
**con•secu•tive**
**con•sen•sual**
**con•sen•sus**
**con•sent**
**con•sent•er**
**con•sen•tience**
**con•sen•tient** in agreement
**con•se•quence**
**con•se•quent**
**con•se•quen•tial**
**con•se•quen•tial•ly**
**con•se•quen•ti•al•ity** (*or* **•tial•ness**)
**con•se•quent•ly**
**con•serv•able**
**con•serv•an•cy** (*plural* **•cies**)
**con•ser•va•tion**
**con•ser•va•tion•al**
**con•ser•va•tion•ist**
**con•serva•tism**
**Con•serva•tive** political party
**con•serva•tive** opposed to change
**con•serva•toire** musical institution
**con•ser•va•tor** custodian
**con•serva•tory** (*plural* **•tories**)
**con•serve**
**con•serv•er**
**Con•sett** Durham town
**con•sid•er**
**con•sid•er•able**
**con•sid•er•ably**
**con•sid•er•ate**
**con•sid•era•tion**
**con•sid•er•er**
**con•sign**
**con•sign•able**
**con•signa•tion**
**con•signee**
**con•sign•ment**
**con•sign•or** (*or* **•er**)
**con•sist**
**con•sist•en•cy** (*or* **•ence**; *plural* **•cies** *or* **•ences**)
**con•sist•ent**
**con•sis•to•rial** (*or* **•rian**)
**con•sis•tory** (*plural* **•tories**) diocesan court
**con•so•ci•ate**
**con•so•cia•tion**
**con•so•cies** (*plural* **•cies**) ecology term
**con•sol•able**
**con•so•la•tion**
**con•sola•tory**
**con•sole**
**con•sol•er**
**con•soli•date**
**con•soli•da•tion**
**con•soli•da•tor**
**con•sols** government securities
**con•so•lute** chemistry term
**con•som•mé**
**con•so•nance** (*or* **•nan•cy**; *plural* **•nances** *or* **•cies**) agreement
**con•so•nant**
**con•so•nan•tal**
**con•sort**
**con•sort•er**
**con•sor•tial**
**con•sor•tium** (*plural* **•tia**)
**con•spe•cif•ic**
**con•spec•tus** overall view
**con•spicu•ous**
**con•spicu•ous•ness**
**con•spira•cy** (*plural* **•cies**)
**con•spira•tor**
**con•spira•to•rial** (*or* **con•spira•tory**)
**con•spira•to•rial•ly**
**con•spira•tress**
**con•spire**
**con•sta•ble**
**con•stabu•lary** (*plural* **•laries**)
**Con•stance** European lake
**Con•stance** (*or* **Kon•stanz**) German city
**con•stan•cy**
**con•stant**
**Con•stan•ţa** Romanian port
**con•stant•an** alloy
**Con•stan•tine** Algerian city
**Con•stan•ti•no•ple**
**con•sta•ta•tion** establishing truth
**con•stel•late** form clusters
**con•stel•la•tion**
**con•stel•la•tory**
**con•ster•nate**
**con•ster•na•tion**
**con•sti•pate**
**con•sti•pat•ed**
**con•sti•pa•tion**
**con•stitu•en•cy** (*plural* **•cies**)
**con•stitu•ent**
**con•sti•tute**
**con•sti•tut•er** (*or* **•tu•tor**)
**con•sti•tu•tion**
**con•sti•tu•tion•al**
**con•sti•tu•tion•al•ism**
**con•sti•tu•tion•al•ist**
**con•sti•tu•tion•al•ity**
**con•sti•tu•tion•al•ly**
**con•sti•tu•tive**
**con•strain**
**con•strain•er**
**con•straint**
**con•strict**
**con•stric•tion**
**con•stric•tive**
**con•stric•tor**
**con•struct**
**con•struct•ible**
**con•struc•tion**
**con•struc•tion•al**
**con•struc•tive**
**con•struc•tiv•ism** art movement
**con•struc•tiv•ist**
**con•struc•tor** (*or* **•ter**)
**con•strue** (**•stru•ing, •strued**)
**con•stru•er**
**con•sub•stan•tia•tion** Christian doctrine
**con•suetude** custom
**con•suetu•di•nary**
**con•sul**
**con•su•lar**
**con•su•late**
**con•sult**
**con•sul•tan•cy** (*plural* **•cies**)
**con•sult•ant**
**con•sul•ta•tion**
**con•sul•ta•tive** (*or* **ta•tory, con•sul•tive**)
**con•sult•er** (*or* **•sul•tor**)
**con•sum•able**
**con•sume**
**con•sum•er**
**con•sum•er•ism**
**con•sum•mate**
**con•sum•ma•tion**
**con•sum•ma•tive** (*or* **•tory**)
**con•sum•ma•tor**
**con•sump•tion**

**con•sump•tive**
**con•tact**
**con•tac•tor**
**con•tac•tual**
**con•ta•gion**
**con•ta•gious**
**con•ta•gious•ness**
**con•ta•gium** (*plural* **•gia**) transmission of disease
**con•tain**
**con•tain•er**
**con•tain•eri•za•tion** (*or* **•sa•tion**)
**con•tain•er•ize** (*or* **•ise**)
**con•tain•ment**
**con•tami•nant**
**con•tami•nate**
**con•tami•na•tion**
**con•tami•na•tor**
**con•tan•go** (*noun, plural* **•gos**; *verb* **•goes, •go•ing, •goed**) stock-exchange term
**conte** *French* short story
**con•té** crayon
**con•temn** scorn
**con•temn•er** (*or* **•tem•nor**)
**con•tem•nible**
**con•tem•plate**
**con•tem•pla•tion**
**con•tem•pla•tive**
**con•tem•pla•tor**
**con•tem•po•ra•neity**
**con•tem•po•ra•neous**
**con•tem•po•rari•ly**
**con•tem•po•rary** (*plural* **•raries**)
**con•tem•po•rize** (*or* **•rise**) synchronize
**con•tempt**
**con•tempt•ibil•ity** (*or* **•ible•ness**)
**con•tempt•ible**
**con•temp•tu•ous**
**con•tend**
**con•tend•er**
**con•tent**
**con•tent•ed**
**con•ten•tion**
**con•ten•tion•al**
**con•ten•tious**
**con•tent•ment**
**con•ter•mi•nous**
**con•test**
**con•test•able**
**con•test•ant**
**con•tes•ta•tion**
**con•test•er**
**con•text**
**con•tex•tual**
**con•tex•tu•al•ize** (*or* **•ise**)
**con•tex•tual•ly**
**con•tex•tur•al**
**con•tex•ture** weaving
**con•ti•gu•ity**
**con•tigu•ous**
**con•ti•nence** (*or* **con•ti•nen•cy**)
**Con•ti•nent** mainland Europe
**con•ti•nent** large landmass
**Con•ti•nen•tal**
**con•ti•nen•tal**
**Con•ti•nen•tal•ism**
**Con•ti•nen•ta•list**
**con•ti•nen•tal•ity**
**con•tin•gence**
**con•tin•gen•cy** (*plural* **•cies**)
**con•tin•gent**
**con•tinu•able**
**con•tin•ual**
**con•tinu•al•ity** (*or* **•al•ness**)
**con•tin•ual•ly**
**con•tinu•ance**
**con•tinu•ant**
**con•tinu•ation**
**con•tinu•ative** linguistics term
**con•tinu•ator**
**con•tinue**
**con•tinu•er**
**con•tinu•ing•ly**
**con•ti•nu•ity** (*plural* **•ities**)
**con•tinuo** (*plural* **•tinuos**) musical term
**con•tinu•ous**
**con•tin•uum** (*plural* **•tinua** *or* **•tin•uums**)
**con•to** (*plural* **•tos**) Portuguese currency
**con•tort**
**con•tor•tion**
**con•tor•tion•al**
**con•tor•tion•ist**
**con•tor•tion•is•tic**
**con•tour**
**contra•band**
**contra•band•ist**
**contra•bass** musical instrument
**contra•bass•ist**
**contra•bas•soon**
**contra•bas•soon•ist**
**contra•cep•tion**
**contra•cep•tive**
**con•tract**
**con•tract•able** able to enter contract
**con•tract•ibil•ity** (*or* **•ible•ness**)
**con•tract•ible** able to be shortened
**con•trac•tile**
**con•trac•til•ity**
**con•trac•tion**
**con•trac•tion•al**
**con•trac•tive**
**con•trac•tor**
**con•trac•tual**
**con•trac•tual•ly**
**con•trac•ture** muscle disorder
**contra•dict**
**contra•dict•able**
**contra•dict•er** (*or* **•dic•tor**)
**contra•dic•tion**
**contra•dic•tive** (*or* **•tious**)
**contra•dic•tory**
**contra•dis•tinc•tion**
**contra•dis•tinc•tive**
**contra•dis•tin•guish**
**con•trail** aircraft vapour trail
**contra•in•di•cant**
**contra•in•di•cate**
**contra•in•di•ca•tion**
**con•tral•to** (*plural* **•tos** *or* **•ti**)
**contra•po•si•tion**
**con•trap•tion**
**contra•pun•tal**
**contra•pun•tal•ly**
**contra•pun•tist** (*or* **•tal•ist**)
**contra•ri•ety** (*plural* **•eties**)
**con•tra•ri•ly**
**con•tra•ri•ness**
**con•tra•ri•wise**
**con•tra•ry** (*plural* **•ries**)
**con•trast**
**con•tras•tive**
**con•trasty**
**contra•val•la•tion** fortifications
**contra•vene**
**contra•ven•er**
**contra•ven•tion**

**contra•yer•va** plant root
**con•tre•danse** dance
**con•tre•temps** (*plural* **•temps**)
**con•trib•ute**
**con•tri•bu•tion**
**con•tribu•tive**
**con•tribu•tor**
**con•tribu•to•rial**
**con•tribu•tory**
**con•trite**
**con•tri•tion**
**con•triv•ance**
**con•trive**
**con•trol** (**•trol•ling, •trolled**)
**con•trol•lable**
**con•trol•lably**
**con•trol•ler**
**con•tro•ver•sial**
**contro•ver•sial•ism**
**contro•ver•sial•ist**
**con•tro•ver•sial•ly**
**con•tro•ver•sy** (*plural* **•sies**)
**con•tro•vert** deny
**contro•vert•er**
**contro•vert•ible**
**con•tu•ma•cious** obstinate
**con•tu•ma•cy** (*plural* **•cies**)
**con•tu•meli•ous** insolent
**con•tu•mely** (*plural* **•melies**)
**con•tuse** bruise
**con•tu•sion**
**con•tu•sioned**
**con•tu•sive**
**co•nun•drum**
**con•ur•ba•tion**
**con•ure** parrot
**con•va•lesce**
**con•va•les•cence**
**con•va•les•cent**
**con•vec•tion**
**con•vec•tion•al**
**con•vec•tive**
**con•vec•tor**
**con•ven•able**
**con•ve•nance** *French* propriety
**con•vene**
**con•ven•er**
**con•veni•ence**
**con•veni•ent**
**con•vent**
**con•ven•ti•cle** secret assembly
**con•ven•tion**
**con•ven•tion•al**
**con•ven•tion•al•ism**
**con•ven•tion•al•ist**
**con•ven•tion•al•ity** (*plural* **•ities**)
**con•ven•tion•ali•za•tion** (*or* **•sa•tion**)
**con•ven•tion•al•ize** (*or* **•ise**)
**con•ven•tion•al•ly**
**con•ven•tual** of a convent
**con•verge**
**con•ver•gence**
**con•ver•gen•cy**
**con•ver•gent**
**con•vers•able**
**con•ver•sance** (*or* **•san•cy**)
**con•ver•sant**
**con•ver•sa•tion**
**con•ver•sa•tion•al**
**con•ver•sa•tion•al•ist** (*or* **•tion•ist**)
**con•ver•sa•tion•al•ly**
**con•ver•sa•zio•ne** (*plural* **•zio•ni** *or* **•zio•nes**) *Italian* artistic discussion
**con•verse**
**con•vers•er**
**con•ver•sion**
**con•ver•sion•al** (*or* **•ary**)
**con•vert**
**con•vert•er** (*or* **•ver•tor**)
**con•vert•ibil•ity** (*or* **•ible•ness**)
**con•vert•ible**
**con•verti•plane** (*or* **•verta•, •verto•**)
**con•vex**
**con•vex•ity** (*plural* **•ities**)
**convexo-concave**
**convexo-convex**
**con•vey**
**con•vey•able**
**con•vey•ance**
**con•vey•anc•er**
**con•vey•anc•ing**
**con•vey•or** (*or* **•er**)
**con•vict**
**con•vict•able** (*or* **•ible**)
**con•vic•tion**
**con•vic•tive** convincing
**con•vince**
**con•vinc•er**
**con•vinc•ible**
**con•vinc•ing**
**con•viv•ial**
**con•vivi•al•ity**
**con•viv•ial•ly**
**con•vo•ca•tion** legislative assembly
**con•vo•ca•tion•al**
**con•voca•tive**
**con•vo•ca•tor**
**con•voke** summon
**con•vok•er**
**con•vo•lute**
**con•vo•lut•ed**
**con•vo•lu•tion**
**con•volve** coil
**con•vol•vu•la•ceous**
**con•vol•vu•lus** (*plural* **•luses** *or* **•li**) plant
**con•voy**
**con•vul•sant**
**con•vulse**
**con•vul•sion**
**con•vul•sive**
**cony** (*or* **co•ney**; *plural* **conies** *or* **•neys**)
**coo** (**coo•ing, cooed**)
**Cooch Be•har** Indian city
**cooee** (*or* **coo•ey**)
**cook**
**cook•able**
**cook•book**
**cook•er**
**cook•ery**
**cook•house**
**cookie**
**cook•ing**
**cook•out** *US* barbecue
**cool**
**coo•la•bah** (*or* **•li•**) tree
**cool•ant**
**cool•er**
**coolie** (*or* **cooly**; *plural* **coolies**)
**cool•ly** (*adv*)
**cool•ness**
**coomb** (*or* **combe, coombe**) valley
**coon**
**coon•can** card game
**coon•skin**
**coon•tie** plant
**coop**
**co-op**
**coop•er** barrel-maker
**coop•er•age**
**co•oper•ate** (*or* **co-operate**)

**co•opera•tion** (*or* **co-operation**)
**co•opera•tive** (*or* **co-operative**)
**co•opera•tor** (*or* **co-operator**)
**coop•ery**
**co•opt** (*or* **co-opt**)
**co•opta•tion** (*or* **co-optation**)
**co•opta•tive** (*or* **co-optative**)
**co•option** (*or* **co-option**)
**co•or•di•nal** (*or* **co-ordinal**) biology term
**co•or•di•nate** (*or* **co-ordinate**)
**co•or•di•na•tion** (*or* **co-ordina•tion**)
**co•or•di•na•tor** (*or* **co-ordina•tor**)
**Coorg** former Indian province
**coot**
**cootch** hiding place
**cootie** *US* louse
**cop** (**cop•ping, copped**)
**co•pai•ba** (*or* **•va**) resin
**co•pal** resin
**co•palm** resin
**co•par•cenary** (*or* **•ceny**) joint ownership
**co•par•cener**
**co•part•ner**
**cope**
**Co•pen•ha•gen**
**co•pepod** plankton constituent
**co•per** horse dealer
**Co•per•ni•can**
**cope•stone**
**copi•er**
**co•pilot**
**cop•ing**
**co•pi•ous**
**co•pla•nar**
**co•pla•nar•ity**
**co•poly•mer** chemistry term
**co•poly•meri•za•tion** (*or* **•sa•tion**)
**co•poly•mer•ize** (*or* **•ise**)
**cop•per**
**cop•per•as** chemical compound
**copper•head** snake
**copper•plate**
**copper•smith**
**cop•pery**
**cop•pice** *variant of* **copse**
**cop•ra** coconut kernel
**cop•ro•la•lia** obscene language
**cop•ro•lite** fossilized faeces
**cop•ro•lit•ic**
**cop•ropha•gous**
**cop•ropha•gy**
**cop•ro•philia** abnormal interest in faeces
**co•prophi•lous** growing on dung
**copse** (*or* **cop•pice**)
**Copt**
**cop•ter** *short for* helicopter
**Cop•tic** language; Church
**copu•la** (*plural* **•las** *or* **•lae**) linking verb; *compare* **cupola**
**copu•lar**
**copu•late**
**copu•la•tion**
**copu•la•tive**
**copy** (*noun, plural* **copies**; *verb* **copies, copy•ing, copied**)
**copy•book**
**copy-edit**
**copy-editor**
**copy•hold**
**copy•holder**
**copy•ist**
**copy•read** *US* subedit
**copy•right**
**copy•writer**
**copy•writing**
**coq au vin** chicken dish
**coque•li•cot** corn poppy
**co•quet** (**•quet•ting, •quet•ted**) to flirt
**co•quet•ry** (*plural* **•ries**)
**co•quette**
**co•quet•tish**
**co•quille** seafood
**co•qui•na** limestone
**co•qui•to** (*plural* **•tos**) tree
**cora•cii•form** ornithology term
**cora•cle**
**cora•coid** zoology term
**cor•al** animal; jewellery; *compare* **corral**
**cor•al•line** (*or* **•loid**)
**cor•al•lite** fossil coral
**coral•root**
**cor an•glais** (*plural* **cors an•glais**) musical instrument
**cor•ban** biblical gift
**cor•beil** (*or* **•beille**) architectural ornament
**cor•bel** (**•bel•ling, •belled**) bracket on building
**cor•bicu•la** (*plural* **•lae**) pollen basket
**cor bli•mey**
**cord** string; anatomical senses; *compare* **chord**
**cord•age**
**cor•date** heart-shaped; *compare* **chordate**
**cord•ed**
**Cor•delier** Franciscan friar
**Cor•deliers** French political club
**cor•dial**
**cor•di•al•ity** (*plural* **•ities**)
**cor•di•al•ly**
**cor•di•er•ite** mineral
**cor•di•form** heart-shaped
**cor•dil•lera** mountain range
**Cor•dil•leras** American mountain range
**cord•ite** explosive
**cord•less**
**Cór•do•ba** Argentinian and Spanish cities
**cor•do•ba** Nicaraguan currency
**cor•don**
**cor•don bleu**
**cor•do•van** leather
**cords** corduroy trousers
**cor•du•roy**
**cord•wood**
**core**
**co•reli•gion•ist**
**co•reop•sis** plant
**corer**
**co-respon•den•cy**
**co-respond•ent** adulterer; *compare* **correspondent**
**corf** (*plural* **corves**) wagon
**Cor•fam** (*Trademark*)
**Cor•fu**
**cor•gi** (*plural* **•gis**)
**co•ria•ceous** of leather

**co•ri•an•der**
**Cor•inth** Greek port; region of ancient Greece
**Co•rin•thian**
**Co•rin•thians** New Testament book
**co•rium** (*plural* **•ria**) layer beneath skin
**Cork**
**cork**
**cork•age**
**cork•board**
**corked**
**cork•er**
**cork•ing**
**cork•screw**
**cork•wood**
**corky**
**corm**
**cor•mel** new corm
**cor•mo•phyte** botany term
**cor•mo•phyt•ic**
**cor•mo•rant**
**cor•mous**
**corn**
**cor•na•ceous** botany term
**corn•cob**
**corn•cockle** plant
**corn•crake** bird
**corn•crib** *US* maize store
**cor•nea** (*plural* **•neas** *or* **•neae**) eye layer
**cor•neal**
**corned**
**cor•nel** plant
**cor•nel•ian** of cornel
**cor•nel•ian** (*or* **car•**) gemstone
**cor•neous** horny
**cor•ner**
**corner•stone**
**cor•net**
**cor•net•ist** (*or* **•net•tist**)
**cor•nett** (*or* **•net**) old woodwind instrument
**corn•field**
**corn•flakes**
**corn•flour** cooking ingredient
**corn•flower** plant
**corn•husk**
**cor•nice** architectural embellishment
**cor•niche** coastal road
**cor•nicu•late** horned
**Cor•nish**
**corn•stalk** *Austral* native Australian
**corn•starch** *US* cornflour
**cor•nu** (*plural* **•nua**) anatomical part
**cor•nual**
**cor•nu•co•pia**
**cor•nute** (*or* **•nut•ed**) hornlike
**Corn•wall**
**corny** (**corni•er, corni•est**)
**co•rol•la** flower petals
**cor•ol•la•ceous**
**cor•ol•lary** (*plural* **•laries**)
**co•ro•na** (*plural* **•nas** *or* **•nae**)
**Co•ro•na Aus•tra•lis** constellation
**Co•ro•na Bo•real•is** constellation
**co•ro•nach** *Scot* dirge
**co•ro•na•graph** (*or* **•no•**) optical instrument
**coro•nal**
**coro•nary** (*plural* **•naries**) artery; thrombosis
**coro•na•tion**
**coro•ner**
**coro•ner•ship**
**coro•net**
**coro•net•ed**
**cor•po•ra** *plural of* **corpus**
**cor•po•ral** army officer; of the body; *compare* **corporeal; caporal**
**cor•po•ra•le** altar cloth
**cor•po•ral•ity**
**cor•po•ral•ship**
**cor•po•rate**
**cor•po•ra•tion**
**cor•po•ra•tive**
**cor•po•ra•tor** member of corporation
**cor•po•real** physical; *compare* **corporal**
**cor•po•real•ly**
**cor•po•real•ity** (*or* **•ness**)
**cor•po•reity** bodily nature
**cor•po•sant** atmospheric phenomenon
**corps** (*plural* **corps**) group of people
**corpse** dead body
**cor•pu•lence** (*or* **•len•cy**)
**cor•pu•lent**
**cor•pus** (*plural* **•po•ra**)
**Cor•pus Chris•ti** Christian festival
**cor•pus•cle**
**cor•pus•cu•lar**
**cor•pus de•lic•ti** legal term
**cor•pus lu•teum** (*plural* **cor•po•ra lu•tea**) tissue in ovary
**cor•pus stria•tum** (*plural* **cor•po•ra stria•ta**) brain part
**cor•pus vile** (*plural* **cor•po•ra vilia**) *Latin* worthless body
**cor•rade** geology term
**cor•ral** (**•ral•ling, •ralled**) animal enclosure; *compare* **coral**
**cor•ra•sion** geology term; *compare* **corrosion**
**cor•ra•sive**
**cor•rect**
**cor•rect•able** (*or* **•ible**)
**cor•rec•tion**
**cor•recti•tude**
**cor•rec•tive**
**cor•rect•ness**
**cor•rec•tor**
**Cor•regi•dor** Philippine island
**cor•re•late**
**cor•re•la•tion**
**cor•rela•tive** mutually related
**cor•rela•tive•ness** (*or* **•tiv•ity**)
**cor•re•spond**
**cor•re•spond•ence**
**cor•re•spond•ent** one who corresponds; *compare* **co-respondent**
**Cor•rèze** French region
**cor•ri•da** *Spanish* bullfight
**cor•ri•dor**
**cor•rie** hollow in hill
**Cor•rie•dale** sheep
**Cor•ri•en•tes** Argentine port
**cor•ri•gen•dum** (*plural* **•da**)
**cor•ri•gibil•ity**
**cor•ri•gible**
**cor•robo•rant**
**cor•robo•rate**
**cor•robo•ra•tion**

**cor•robo•ra•tive**
**cor•robo•ra•tor**
**cor•robo•ree** *Austral* noisy gathering
**cor•rod•ant** (*or* **•ent**)
**cor•rode**
**cor•rod•er**
**cor•rod•ibil•ity**
**cor•rod•ible**
**cor•ro•sion** wearing away; *compare* **corrasion**
**cor•ro•sive**
**cor•ru•gate**
**cor•ru•gat•ed**
**cor•ru•ga•tion**
**cor•ru•ga•tor** muscle
**cor•rupt**
**cor•rupt•er** (*or* **•rup•tor**)
**cor•rupt•ibil•ity** (*or* **•ible•ness**)
**cor•rup•tible**
**cor•rup•tion**
**cor•rup•tion•ist**
**cor•rup•tive**
**cor•sac** fox
**cor•sage**
**cor•sair**
**corse** *Archaic* corpse; *compare* **coarse; course**
**corse•let** (*or* **cors•let**)
**cor•set**
**cor•setière** (*masc* **•setier**)
**cor•set•ry**
**Cor•si•ca**
**Cor•si•can**
**cor•tege** (*or* **•tège**)
**Cor•tes** Spanish parliament
**cor•tex** (*plural* **•ti•ces**)
**cor•ti•cal**
**cor•ti•cate** (*or* **•cat•ed**) having rind or bark
**cor•ti•ca•tion**
**cor•ti•co•ster•oid** (*or* **cor•ti•coid**) hormone
**cor•ti•co•ster•one**
**cor•ti•co•tro•phic** (*US* **•pic**)
**cor•ti•co•tro•phin** (*US* **•pin**) hormone
**cor•ti•sol** hormone
**cor•ti•sone**
**co•run•dum** mineral
**Co•run•na** *variant of* **La Coruña**
**co•rus•cate** sparkle
**cor•us•ca•tion**
**cor•vée** feudal labour
**corves** *plural of* **corf**
**cor•vette**
**cor•vine** of crows
**co•ryda•lis** plant
**cor•ymb** botany term
**co•rym•bose** (*or* **•bous**)
**cory•phaeus** (*plural* **•phaei**) chorus leader
**cory•phée** ballet dancer
**co•ry•za** head cold
**cos** lettuce; *short for* **cosine**
**co•sec** *short for* **cosecant**
**co•secant** geometry term
**co•sech** geometry term
**co•seis•mal** (*or* **•mic**)
**Co•sen•za** Italian city
**cosh**
**cosh•er**
**co•sig•na•tory**
**co•si•ly** (*US* **•zi•**)
**co•sine** geometry term
**co•si•ness**
**cos•met•ic**
**cos•meti•cal•ly**
**cos•me•ti•cian**
**cos•mic** (*or* **•mi•cal**)
**cos•mine** (*or* **•min**) zoology term
**cos•mo•drome** zoology term
**cos•mogo•nal**
**cos•mo•gon•ic** (*or* **•goni•cal**)
**cos•mogo•nist**
**cos•mogo•ny** (*plural* **•nies**) origin of universe
**cos•mog•ra•phy** mapping of universe
**cos•moid** fish scale
**cos•mo•logi•cal** (*or* **•log•ic**)
**cos•molo•gist**
**cos•mol•ogy** study of universe
**cos•mo•naut**
**cos•mopo•lis** international city
**cos•mo•poli•tan**
**cos•mo•poli•tan•ism**
**cos•mopo•lite** cosmopolitan plant or animal
**cos•mopo•lit•ism**
**cos•mos**
**Cos•mo•tron** particle accelerator
**coss** Indian unit
**Cos•sack**
**cos•set**
**cost** (**cost•ing, cost**)
**cos•ta** (*plural* **•tae**) rib
**Cos•ta Bra•va**
**cos•tal** of ribs
**co-star** (**-star•ring, -starred**)
**cos•tard** apple
**Cos•ta Rica**
**Cos•ta Ri•can**
**cos•tate**
**cost-effective**
**cos•ter•mon•ger**
**cost•ing**
**cos•tive** constipated
**cost•li•ness**
**cost•ly** (**•li•er, •li•est**)
**cost•mary** (*plural* **•maries**) plant
**cos•toto•my** (*plural* **•mies**)
**cost-plus**
**cos•tume**
**cos•tumi•er** (*or* **•tum•er**)
**cosy** (*US* **cozy**; *noun, plural* **cosies**, *US* **cozies**; *adj* **cosi•er, cosi•est**, *US* **coz•ier, cozi•est**)
**cot**
**co•tan•gent** geometry term
**cote** shelter for doves
**Côte d'Azur**
**Côte d'Ivoire** African country
**Côte-d'Or** French department
**co•ten•an•cy**
**co•ten•ant**
**co•terie**
**co•ter•mi•nous**
**Côtes-du-Nord** French department
**co•tid•al**
**co•til•lion** dance
**co•tin•ga** bird
**co•to•neas•ter** shrub
**Coto•paxi** volcano in Ecuador
**Cots•wold** sheep
**Cots•wolds** hills
**cot•ta** surplice; *compare* **cotter**
**cot•tage**
**cot•tag•er**
**cot•ter** securing pin; peasant farmer; *compare* **cotta**

**cot•tier** Irish smallholder
**cot•ton**
**cot•ton•ade** fabric
**cotton•seed** (*plural* **•seeds** *or* **•seed)**
**cotton•tail** US rabbit
**cotton•weed**
**cotton•wood**
**cot•tony**
**coty•ledon** seed leaf
**coty•ledo•nal**
**coty•ledo•na•ry**
**coty•ledo•nous** (*or* **•noid)**
**coty•loid** (*or* **•oi•dal)** cup-shaped
**cou•cal** bird
**couch**
**cou•chant** heraldic term
**couch•er**
**cou•chette**
**couch•ing** embroidery; eye surgery
**cou•dé** telescope
**cou•gar**
**cough**
**could**
**couldn't**
**cou•lee** lava
**cou•lisse** timber
**cou•loir** gully
**cou•lomb** unit
**cou•lom•eter** (*or* **•lomb•meter)**
**coul•ter** (*US* **col•)** plough blade
**cou•ma•ric** (*or* **cu•)**
**cou•ma•rin** (*or* **cu•)**
**cou•ma•rone**
**coun•cil** assembly
**coun•cil•lor** (*US* **•ci•lor)** council member
**coun•cil•lor•ship** (*US* **•ci•lor•)**
**coun•sel** (**•sel•ling, •selled;** *US* **•sel•ing, •seled)** advice; advise
**coun•sel•lor** (*US* **•sel•or)** advisor
**count**
**count•down**
**coun•te•nance**
**count•er**
**counter•act**
**counter•ac•tion**
**counter•ac•tive**
**counter•at•tack**
**counter•bal•ance**
**counter•blast**
**counter•change**
**counter•charge**
**counter•check**
**counter•claim**
**counter•claim•ant**
**counter•clockwise** *US* anticlockwise
**counter•culture**
**counter•es•pio•nage**
**counter•feit**
**counter•feit•er**
**counter•foil**
**counter•glow** glow in sky
**counter•in•sur•gen•cy**
**counter•in•tel•li•gence**
**counter•ir•ri•tant**
**counter•ir•ri•ta•tion**
**counter•mand**
**counter•march**
**counter•meas•ure**
**counter•mine**
**counter•move**
**counter•of•fen•sive**
**counter•pane**
**counter•part**
**counter•plot** (**•plot•ting, •plot•ted)**
**counter•point**
**counter•poise**
**counter•pro•duc•tive**
**counter•proof** printing term
**counter•pro•pos•al**
**Counter-Reformation** religious movement
**counter-revolu•tion**
**counter-revo•lu•tion•ary**
**counter•scarp** fortification
**counter•shad•ing**
**counter•shaft**
**counter•sign**
**counter•sink** (**•sink•ing, •sank, •sunk)**
**counter•spy** (*plural* **•spies)**
**counter•ten•or**
**counter•type**
**counter•vail**
**counter•weigh**
**counter•weight**
**counter•word**
**counter•work**
**coun•tess**
**count•less**
**coun•tri•fy** (*or* **•try•fy; •fies, •fy•ing, •fied)**
**coun•try** (*plural* **•tries)**
**country•man** (*plural* **•men)**
**country•side**
**country•woman** (*plural* **•women)**
**coun•ty** (*plural* **•ties)**
**coup**
**coup de grâce** (*plural* **coups de grâce)**
**coup d'état** (*plural* **coups d'état)**
**coupe** dish; ice-cream
**cou•pé** car; carriage
**cou•ple**
**cou•pler**
**cou•plet**
**cou•pling**
**cou•pon**
**cour•age**
**cou•ra•geous**
**cou•rante** musical work
**cour•gette**
**cou•ri•er** messenger; *compare* **currier**
**cour•lan** bird
**Cour•land** (*or* **Kur•land)** Latvian region
**course** direction, etc.; *compare* **coarse; corse**
**cours•er**
**cours•ing** hunting
**court**
**Cour•telle** (*Trademark*)
**cour•teous**
**cour•tesan** (*or* **•tezan)**
**cour•tesy** (*plural* **•tesies)**
**court•house**
**cour•ti•er**
**court•ing**
**court•ly** (**•li•er, •li•est)**
**court mar•tial** (*noun, plural* **court mar•tials** *or* **courts mar•tial)**
**court-martial** (*verb* **-martial•ling, -martialled;** *US* **-martial•ing, -martialed)**
**court•room**
**court•ship**
**court•yard**
**cous•cous** spicy dish; *compare* **cuscus**

**cous•in** relation; *compare* cozen
**cou•teau** knife
**couth** refined
**couthie** *Scot* friendly
**cou•ture**
**cou•tu•ri•er** (*fem* **•ère**)
**cou•vade** primitive custom
**co•va•len•cy** (*US* **•va•lence**) chemistry term
**co•va•lent**
**co•vari•ance**
**cove**
**cov•en**
**cov•enant**
**cov•enan•tal**
**cov•enan•tee**
**Cov•enant•er** Scottish Presbyterian
**cov•enan•tee**
**cov•enant•er** (*or* **•enan•tor**)
**Cov•en•try**
**cov•er**
**cov•er•age**
**cov•er•er**
**cov•er•ing**
**cov•er•less**
**cov•er•let**
**co•vers** maths term
**cov•ert**
**cov•er•ture** legal term
**cover-up**
**cov•et**
**cov•et•er**
**cov•et•ous**
**cov•et•ous•ness**
**cov•ey** flock
**cov•in** conspiracy
**cow**
**cow•age** (*or* **•hage**) plant
**cow•ard**
**cow•ard•ice**
**cow•ard•li•ness**
**cow•ard•ly**
**cow•bane** plant
**cow•bell**
**cow•berry** (*plural* **•berries**)
**cow•bind** plant
**cow•bird**
**cow•boy**
**cow•er**
**Cowes**
**cow•fish** (*plural* **•fish** *or* **•fishes**)
**cow•girl**
**cow•hand**
**cow•herb**
**cow•herd**
**cow•hide**
**cow•itch** plant
**cowl**
**cow•lick**
**cowl•ing**
**cow•man** (*plural* **•men**)
**co-worker**
**cow•pat**
**cow•pea** plant
**cow•pox**
**cow•ry** (*or* **•rie**; *plural* **•ries**) mollusc
**cow•shed**
**cow•slip**
**cox**
**coxa** (*plural* **coxae**) hip joint
**cox•al**
**cox•al•gia**
**cox•al•gic**
**cox•comb**
**cox•comb•ry** (*plural* **•ries**)
**cox•swain** (*or* **cock•**)
**coy**
**coy•ness**
**coy•ote** (*plural* **•otes** *or* **•ote**)
**co•yo•til•lo** (*plural* **•los**) shrub
**coy•pu** (*plural* **•pus** *or* **•pu**)
**co•zen** to trick; *compare* cousin
**coz•en•age**
**coz•en•er**
**cozy** *US spelling of* **cosy**
**crab** (**crab•bing, crabbed**)
**crab-apple**
**crab•ber** fisherman
**crab•by** (**•bi•er, •bi•est**)
**crab•stick**
**crab•wise**
**crack**
**crack•brain**
**crack•brained**
**cracked**
**crack•er**
**cracker•jack**
**crack•et** *Dialect* stool
**crack•ing**
**crack•jaw**
**crack•le**
**crack•ling**
**crack•nel**
**crack•pot**
**Cra•cow** Polish city
**cra•dle**
**cradle-snatch•er**
**cradle•song**
**craft** skill; *compare* **kraft**
**crafti•ly**
**crafti•ness**
**crafts•man** (*plural* **•men**)
**crafts•man•ship**
**crafty** (**crafti•er, crafti•est**)
**crag**
**crag•ged** *US* craggy
**crag•gy** (**•gi•er, •gi•est**)
**Cra•iova** Romanian city
**crake** bird
**cram** (**cram•ming, crammed**)
**cram•bo** (*plural* **•boes**) word game
**cram•mer**
**cramoi•sy** crimson
**cramp**
**cram•pon** (*or* **•poon**)
**cran** herring measure
**cran•age**
**cran•berry** (*plural* **•berries**)
**crane**
**cranes•bill**
**cra•nial**
**cra•ni•ate** having a skull
**cra•nio•logi•cal**
**cra•ni•olo•gist**
**cra•ni•ol•ogy**
**cra•ni•om•eter**
**cra•nio•met•ric** (*or* **•ri•cal**)
**cra•ni•om•etry**
**cra•ni•oto•my** (*plural* **•mies**)
**cra•nium** (*plural* **•niums** *or* **•nia**)
**crank**
**crank•case**
**cranki•ly**
**cranki•ness**
**crank•pin**
**crank•shaft**
**cranky** (**cranki•er, cranki•est**)
**cran•nied**
**cran•ny** (*plural* **•nies**)
**crap** (**crap•ping, crapped**)
**crape** *variant spelling of* **crepe**
**crap•pie** (*plural* **•pies**) fish
**crap•py** *Slang* worthless
**craps** US dice game

**crap•shooter**
**crapu•lence**
**crapu•lous** (*or* **•lent**) drunken
**cra•que•lure** cracks on paintings
**crash**
**crash•ing**
**crash-land**
**crash-landing**
**cra•sis** (*plural* **•ses**) linguistics term
**crass**
**crass•ness** (*or* **cras•si•tude**)
**cras•su•la•ceous** botany term
**cratch** fodder rack
**crate**
**cra•ter**
**cra•ter•ous**
**craunch** *Dialect* crunch
**cra•vat**
**crave**
**cra•ven**
**crav•ing**
**craw** animal stomach
**craw•fish** *variant spelling of* crayfish
**crawl**
**crawl•er**
**Craw•ley** Sussex town
**cray** *Austral* crayfish
**cray•fish** (*or* **craw•**; *plural* **•fish** *or* **•fishes**)
**cray•on**
**cray•on•ist**
**craze**
**crazed**
**cra•zi•ly**
**cra•zi•ness**
**cra•zy** (**•zi•er**, **•zi•est**)
**creak** noise; *compare* **creek**
**creaki•ness**
**creaky** (**creaki•er**, **creaki•est**)
**cream**
**cream•cups** flower
**cream•er**
**cream•ery** (*plural* **•eries**)
**cream•laid** (*or* **•woven**) type of paper
**creamy** (**creami•er**, **creami•est**)
**crease**
**crease•less**
**cre•ate**
**crea•tine** (*or* **•tin**) biochemical compound
**cre•ati•nine** biochemical compound
**crea•tion**
**crea•tion•al**
**crea•tion•ism** theological belief
**crea•tive**
**crea•tive•ly**
**crea•tiv•ity**
**crea•tor**
**crea•tur•al** (*or* **•ture•ly**)
**crea•ture**
**crèche**
**Cré•cy** battlefield
**cred•al** *variant spelling of* creedal
**cre•dence**
**cre•den•dum** (*plural* **•da**) article of faith
**cre•dent** *Archaic* believing
**cre•den•tial**
**cre•den•za** sideboard
**cred•ibil•ity** (*or* **•ible•ness**)
**cred•ible**
**cred•ibly**
**cred•it**
**cred•it•able**
**cred•it•able•ness** (*or* **•abil•ity**)
**cred•it•ably**
**credi•tor**
**cre•do** (*plural* **•dos**)
**cre•du•lity**
**credu•lous**
**Cree** American Indian
**creed**
**creed•al** (*or* **cred•al**)
**creek** inlet; *compare* **creak**
**creel** basket
**creep** (**creep•ing**, **crept**)
**creep•er**
**creepie** *Scot* stool
**creepi•ly**
**creepi•ness**
**creeps** (*noun*)
**creepy** (**creepi•er**, **creepi•est**)
**creepy-crawly** (*plural* **-crawlies**)
**cre•mate**
**cre•ma•tion**
**cre•ma•tion•ism**
**cre•ma•tion•ist**
**cre•ma•tor**
**crema•to•rium** (*plural* **•riums** *or* **•ria**)
**crema•tory** (*adj*)
**crème** *French* cream
**crème cara•mel**
**crème de menthe** liqueur
**Cre•mo•na** Italian city
**cre•nate** (*or* **•nat•ed**) scalloped
**cre•na•tion** (*or* **crena•ture**)
**cren•el** (*or* **•nelle**)
**cren•el•late** (*US* **•el•ate**) supply with battlements; indent
**cren•el•la•tion** (*US* **•ela•tion**)
**crenu•late** (*or* **•lat•ed**) notched
**crenu•la•tion**
**creo•dont** extinct mammal
**Cre•ole** people
**cre•ole** language
**creo•lized** (*or* **•lised**)
**Creon** legendary king
**cre•opha•gous** flesh-eating
**cre•opha•gy**
**creo•sol** constituent of creosote; *compare* **cresol**
**creo•sote**
**creo•sot•ic**
**crepe** (*or* **crape**) fabric
**crêpe** pancake
**crepe de Chine** fabric
**crêpe su•zette** (*plural* **crêpes su•zettes**) orange pancake
**crepi•tant**
**crepi•tate** crackle
**crepi•ta•tion**
**crepi•tus** medical term
**crept**
**cre•pus•cu•lar** active at dusk
**cre•scen•do** (*plural* **•dos**)
**cres•cent**
**cres•cen•tic**
**cre•sol** disinfectant; *compare* **creosol**
**cress**
**cres•set**
**crest**
**crest•ed**
**crest•fallen**
**crest•ing**
**cre•syl•ic**

**Cre•ta•ceous** geological period
**cre•ta•ceous** of chalk
**Cre•tan**
**Crete**
**cre•tic** metrical foot
**cret•in**
**cret•in•ism**
**cret•in•oid**
**cret•in•ous**
**cre•tonne** fabric
**Creuse** French region
**cre•vasse** glacier crack
**crev•ice** cleft
**crew**
**Crewe** Cheshire town
**crew•el** yarn; *compare* **cruel**
**crew•el•ist**
**crewel•work**
**crew-neck** (*or* **-necked**)
**crib** (**crib•bing, cribbed**)
**crib•bage**
**cri•bel•lum** spider's organ
**crib•ri•form** (*or* **crib•rous**) sievelike
**crib•work** timber framework
**crick**
**crick•et**
**crick•et•er**
**cri•coid** anatomy term
**cried**
**cri•er**
**cri•key**
**crim** *Austral* criminal
**crime**
**Cri•mea**
**Cri•mean**
**crime pas•sio•nel** (*plural* **crimes pas•sio•nel**)
**crimi•nal**
**crimi•nal•ity** (*plural* **•ities**)
**crimi•nal•ly**
**crimi•no•logi•cal** (*or* **•log•ic**)
**crimi•nolo•gist**
**crimi•nol•ogy**
**crimp**
**crimp•er**
**crim•ple** crumple
**Crimp•lene** (*Trademark*)
**crim•son**
**cringe**
**crin•gle** nautical term
**cri•nite** having hairs
**crin•kle**
**crinkle•root** plant
**crin•kly**
**crinkum-crankum** twisted object
**cri•noid** marine organism
**crino•line**
**cri•num** plant
**cri•ol•lo** (*plural* **•los**) cocoa
**cripes** slang expression
**crip•ple**
**crip•pling**
**cri•sis** (*plural* **•ses**)
**crisp**
**cris•pate** (*or* **•pat•ed**) curled
**cris•pa•tion**
**crisp•bread**
**crisp•er**
**crisp•ness**
**crispy** (**crispi•er, crispi•est**)
**cris•sal** of a crissum
**criss•cross**
**cris•sum** (*plural* **•sa**) ornithology term
**cris•ta** (*plural* **•tae**) biology term
**cris•tate** (*or* **•tat•ed**) crested
**cri•teri•on** (*plural* **•teria** *or* **•terions**)
**crit•ic**
**criti•cal**
**criti•cal•ly**
**criti•cism**
**criti•cize** (*or* **•cise**)
**criti•cizer** (*or* **•ciser**)
**cri•tique**
**crit•ter** *US* creature
**croak**
**croak•er**
**croaki•ly**
**croaki•ness**
**croaky**
**Cro•at**
**Croa•tia** S European country
**Croa•tian**
**cro•cein** dye
**cro•chet** (**•chet•ing, •cheted**) knitting; *compare* **crotchet**
**cro•chet•er**
**cro•cido•lite** asbestos
**crock**
**crock•ery**
**crock•et** architectural ornament
**Crock•ford** clergy directory
**croco•dile**
**croco•dil•ian**
**cro•co•ite** (*or* **•coi•site**) mineral
**cro•cus** (*plural* **•cuses**)
**croft**
**croft•er**
**crois•sant**
**Cro-Magnon** prehistoric man
**crom•bec** bird
**crom•lech** prehistoric structure
**Crom•wel•lian**
**crone**
**cronk** *Austral* unsound
**Cronus** Titan
**cro•ny** (*plural* **•nies**)
**cro•ny•ism**
**crook**
**crook•ed**
**crook•ed•ness**
**croon**
**croon•er**
**crop** (**crop•ping, cropped**)
**crop-eared**
**crop•per**
**cro•quet** (**•quet•ing, •queted**) game
**cro•quette** savoury cake
**cro•sier** (*or* **•zier**) bishop's crook
**cross**
**cross•bar**
**cross•beam**
**cross•bill**
**cross•bones**
**cross•bow**
**cross•breed** (**•breed•ing, •bred**)
**cross•check**
**cross-country**
**cross•current**
**cross•cut** (**•cut•ting, cut**)
**crosse** lacrosse stick
**cross-examina•tion**
**cross-examine**
**cross-examiner**
**cross-eye**
**cross-eyed**
**cross-fertili•za•tion** (*or* **•sa•tion**)
**cross-fertilize** (*or* **-fertilise**)
**cross•fire**
**cross-garnet** hinge

**cross-grained**
**cross•hatch**
**cross•head**
**cross-index**
**cross•ing**
**cross•jack** sail
**cross-legged**
**cross•let** heraldry term
**cross-link**
**cros•sop•te•ryg•ian** primitive fish
**cross•over**
**cross•patch**
**cross•piece**
**cross-ply** (*adj*)
**cross-pollinate**
**cross-pollina•tion**
**cross-purposes**
**cross-question**
**cross-question•ing**
**cross-refer**
**cross-reference**
**cross•road** (*or* **•roads**)
**cross•ruff** bridge term
**cross-section•al**
**cross-slide**
**cross-stitch**
**cross•talk**
**cross•tree** nautical term
**cross•walk** *US* pedestrian crossing
**cross•wind**
**cross•wise** (*or* **•ways**)
**cross•word**
**cross•wort** plant
**crotch**
**crotch•et** musical note; *compare* **crochet**
**crotch•ety** *Slang* irritable
**cro•ton** shrub
**crouch**
**croup** disease
**croup** (*or* **croupe**) horse's hindquarters
**crou•pi•er**
**croup•ous** (*or* **croupy**)
**crouse** *Dialect* saucy
**croute** toast
**crou•ton** cookery garnish
**crow** (**crow•ing, crowed** *or* **crew**)
**crow•bar**
**crow•berry** (*plural* **•berries**)
**crow•boot** Eskimo boot
**crowd**
**crowd•ed**
**crow•er**
**crow•foot** (*plural* **•foots**) plant
**crown**
**crown•piece** bridle part
**crown•work**
**crow's-foot** (*plural* **-feet**)
**crow's-nest**
**Croy•don**
**croze** barrel recess
**cro•zier** *variant spelling of* **crosier**
**cru** vineyard
**cru•ces** *plural of* **crux**
**cru•cial** important
**cru•cial•ly**
**cru•cian** fish
**cru•ci•ate**
**cru•ci•ble**
**cru•ci•fer** plant
**cru•cif•er•ous**
**cru•ci•fier**
**cru•ci•fix**
**cru•ci•fix•ion**
**cru•ci•form**
**cru•ci•fy** (**•fies, •fy•ing, •fied**)
**cruck** roof timber
**crud** *Slang* rubbish
**crude**
**crud•ity** (*or* **crude•ness**; *plural* **•ities** *or* **•nesses**)
**cru•el** (**•el•ler, •el•lest**) unkind; *compare* **crewel**
**cru•el•ly**
**cru•el•ty** (*plural* **•ties**)
**cru•et**
**cruise** sea trip; *compare* **cruse**
**cruis•er**
**cruiser•weight**
**cruise•way**
**crul•ler** cake
**crumb**
**crum•ble**
**crum•bly** (**•bli•er, •bli•est**)
**crumby** (**crumbi•er, crumbi•est**) full of crumbs; *compare* **crummy**
**crum•horn** musical instrument
**crum•my** (**•mi•er, •mi•est**) *Slang* inferior; *compare* **crumby**
**crump** to thud
**crum•pet**
**crum•ple**
**crum•ply**
**crunch**
**crunchi•ly**
**crunchi•ness**
**crunchy** (**crunchi•er, crunchi•est**)
**cru•node** maths term
**crup•per** saddle strap
**cru•ra** *plural of* **crus**
**cru•ral**
**crus** (*plural* **cru•ra**) lower leg
**cru•sade**
**cru•sad•er**
**cruse** small pot; *compare* **cruise**
**crush**
**crush•er**
**crust**
**crus•ta•cean**
**crus•ta•ceous**
**crus•tal**
**crust•ed**
**crusti•ly**
**crusti•ness**
**crusty** (**crusti•er, crusti•est**)
**crutch**
**crux** (*plural* **cruxes** *or* **cru•ces**)
**crux an•sa•ta** ankh
**cru•zei•ro** (*plural* **•ros**) Brazilian currency
**crwth** musical instrument
**cry** (*noun, plural* **cries**; *verb* **cries, cry•ing, cried**)
**cry•baby** (*plural* **•babies**)
**cryo•bi•olo•gist**
**cryo•bi•ol•ogy**
**cryo•gen** freezing mixture
**cryo•gen•ics**
**cryo•hy•drate**
**cryo•lite** mineral
**cry•om•eter**
**cry•om•etry**
**cry•on•ics**
**cryo•phil•ic**
**cryo•phyte** plant growing on snow
**cryo•plank•ton**
**cryo•scope**
**cryo•scop•ic**
**cry•os•co•py**
**cryo•stat**

**cryo•sur•gery**
**cryo•thera•py** (*or* **cry•mo•thera•py)**
**cryo•tron** electronic device
**crypt**
**cryp•taes•thesia** (*US* **•tes•**) extrasensory perception
**crypt•al** of crypts; *compare* **cryptic**
**crypt•analy•sis** study of codes
**crypt•ana•lyst**
**crypt•ana•lyt•ic**
**cryp•tic** (*or* **•ti•cal**) obscure; *compare* **cryptal**
**cryp•ti•cal•ly**
**cryp•to•clas•tic** geology term
**cryp•to•crys•tal•line**
**cryp•to•gam** plant
**cryp•to•gam•ic** (*or* **•toga•mous**)
**cryp•to•gen•ic** of unknown origin
**cryp•to•gram**
**cryp•to•graph**
**cryp•tog•ra•pher** (*or* **•phist**)
**cryp•to•graph•ic** (*or* **•graphi•cal**)
**cryp•tog•ra•phy** (*or* **•tol•ogy**) study of codes
**cryp•tolo•gist**
**cryp•to•meria** tree
**cryp•to•zo•ic** living in dark places
**cryp•to•zo•ite** malarial parasite
**crys•tal**
**crys•tal•line**
**crys•tal•lin•ity**
**crys•tal•lite**
**crys•tal•lit•ic**
**crys•tal•lize** (*or* **•tal•ize, •tal•lise, •tal•ise**)
**crys•tal•log•ra•pher**
**crys•tal•lo•graph•ic**
**crys•tal•log•ra•phy**
**crys•tal•loid**
**cte•nid•ium** (*plural* **•ia**) mollusc's gill
**cte•noid** comblike
**cte•nopho•ran**
**cteno•phore** invertebrate
**cub (cub•bing, cubbed)**
**Cuba**
**cub•age**
**Cu•ban**
**cub•ane** chemical compound
**cu•ba•ture** cubic contents
**cubbed**
**cub•bing**
**cubby•hole**
**cube**
**cu•beb** plant
**cu•bic**
**cu•bi•cal** (*adj*) of volume
**cu•bi•cle** (*noun*) small room
**cu•bicu•lum** burial chamber
**cu•bi•form**
**cub•ism**
**cub•ist**
**cu•bis•tic**
**cu•bit** unit
**cu•bi•tal** of the forearm
**cu•boid**
**Cu-bop** jazz music
**cuck•old**
**cuck•old•ry**
**cuckoo** (*plural* **cuckoos**)
**cuckoo•pint**
**cu•cu•li•form** ornithology term
**cu•cul•late** hood-shaped
**cu•cum•ber**
**cu•cur•bit** plant
**cu•cur•bi•ta•ceous**
**Cú•cu•ta** Colombian city
**cud**
**cud•bear** lichen
**cud•dle**
**cud•dle•some**
**cud•dly (•dli•er, •dli•est)**
**cud•dy** (*plural* **•dies**) cabin
**cudg•el (•el•ling, •elled;** *US* **•el•ing, •eled)**
**cudg•el•ler** (*US* **•el•er**)
**cudg•erie** tree
**cud•weed**
**cue (cu•ing, cued)** signal; billiard shaft; *compare* **queue**
**Cuer•na•va•ca** Mexican city
**cues•ta** ridge
**cuff**
**Cuia•bá** (*or* **Cu•ya•bá**) Brazilian port and river
**cu•ing**
**cui•rass** armour
**cui•ras•sier**
**cuir-bouilli** leather
**cui•sine**
**cuisse** armour
**culch** (*or* **cultch**) oyster bed
**cul-de-sac** (*plural* **culs-de-sac** *or* **cul-de-sacs**)
**cu•let** armour
**cu•lex** (*plural* **•li•ces**) mosquito
**Cu•lia•cán** Mexican city
**cu•lic•id** mosquito
**culi•nary**
**cull**
**cull•er**
**cul•let** waste glass
**cul•lis** gutter
**Cul•lod•en** battlefield
**cul•ly** (*plural* **•lies**) *Slang* pal
**culm** stem
**cul•mif•er•ous**
**cul•mi•nant**
**cul•mi•nate**
**cul•mi•na•tion**
**cu•lottes** women's trousers
**cul•pa** (*plural* **•pae**) fault
**cul•pabil•ity**
**cul•pable**
**cul•pably**
**cul•prit**
**cult**
**cul•tic**
**cul•ti•gen** plant
**cult•ism**
**cult•ist**
**cul•ti•vable** (*or* **cul•ti•vat•able)**
**cul•ti•var** plant
**cul•ti•vate**
**cul•ti•vat•ed**
**cul•ti•va•tion**
**cul•ti•va•tor**
**cul•trate** (*or* **•trat•ed**) knife-shaped
**cul•tur•al**
**cul•tur•al•ly**
**cul•ture**
**cul•tured**
**cul•tur•ist**
**cul•ver** *Archaic* dove
**cul•ver•in** cannon
**cul•vert**
**Cu•ma•ná** Venezuelan city
**cum•ber**
**Cum•ber•land** former English county

**Cum•ber•nauld** Scottish town
**cum•ber•some**
**cum•brance**
**Cum•bria**
**Cum•brian**
**cum•in** (*or* **cum•min**) herb
**cum•mer•bund** (*or* **kum•**)
**cum•shaw** tip; gift
**cu•mu•late**
**cu•mu•la•tion**
**cu•mu•la•tive**
**cu•mul•et** pigeon
**cu•mu•li•form** cloud-shaped
**cu•mu•lo•nim•bus** (*plural* **•bi** *or* **•buses**) cloud
**cu•mu•lo•stra•tus** (*plural* **•ti**)
**cu•mu•lous** (*adj*)
**cu•mu•lus** (*noun*; *plural* **•li**)
**cu•neal**
**cu•neate**
**cu•nei•form** writing
**cun•jevoi** plant
**cun•ni•lin•gus**
**cun•ning**
**cunt**
**cup** (**cup•ping, cupped**)
**cup•bearer**
**cup•board**
**cup•cake**
**cu•pel** (**•pel•ling, •pelled**; *US* **•pel•ing, •peled**)
**cu•pel•la•tion** metallurgical process
**cup•ful** (*plural* **•fuls**)
**Cupid**
**cu•pid•ity**
**cu•po•la** dome; *compare* **copula**
**cu•po•lat•ed**
**cup•pa** (*or* **•per**) *Slang* cup of tea
**cupped**
**cup•ping**
**cu•pre•ous**
**cu•pric**
**cu•prif•er•ous**
**cu•prite** mineral
**cu•pro•nick•el**
**cu•prous**
**cu•pu•late** (*or* **•lar**) cup-shaped
**cu•pule**
**cur**
**cur•abil•ity**
**cur•able**
**Cu•ra•çao** Carribean island; liqueur
**cu•ra•cy** (*plural* **•cies**)
**cu•ra•re** (*or* **•ri**) poison
**cu•ra•rine** muscle relaxant
**cu•ra•ri•za•tion** (*or* **•sa•tion**)
**cu•ra•rize** (*or* **•rise**)
**cu•ras•sow** bird
**cu•rate**
**cu•ra•tive**
**cu•ra•tor** museum keeper
**cu•ra•to•rial**
**curb** restrain; *US spelling of* **kerb**
**curch** woman's cap
**cur•cu•lio** (*plural* **•lios**) weevil
**cur•cu•ma** plant
**curd**
**curdi•ness**
**cur•dle**
**cur•dler**
**curdy**
**cur•able**
**cure**
**cure-all**
**cu•rette** (*or* **•ret; •ret•ting, •ret•ted**) surgical instrument
**cu•ret•tage** (*or* **•rette•ment**)
**cur•few**
**cu•ria** (*plural* **•riae**) papal court
**Cu•ria Re•gis** Norman king's court
**cu•rie** unit
**cu•rio** (*plural* **•rios**) collector's item
**cu•rio•sa** curiosities
**cu•ri•os•ity** (*plural* **•ities**)
**cu•ri•ous**
**cu•ri•ous•ness**
**Cu•ri•ti•ba** Brazilian city
**cu•rium** radioactive element
**curl**
**curl•er**
**cur•lew**
**cur•li•cue** (*or* **•ly•**)
**curli•ness**
**curl•ing**
**curl•paper**
**curly** (**curli•er, curli•est**)
**cur•mudg•eon**
**cur•mudg•eon•ly**
**cur•rant** fruit; *compare* **current**
**cur•ra•jong** *variant spelling of* **kurrajong**
**cur•ra•wong** bird
**cur•ren•cy** (*plural* **•cies**)
**cur•rent** flow; up-to-date; *compare* **currant**
**cur•ri•cle** carriage
**cur•ricu•lar**
**cur•ricu•lum** (*plural* **•la** *or* **•lums**)
**cur•ricu•lum vi•tae** (*plural* **•la vi•tae**)
**cur•ri•er** leather worker; *compare* **courier**
**cur•ri•ery** (*plural* **•eries**)
**cur•rish** rude
**cur•ry** (*noun, plural* **•ries**; *verb* **•ries, •ry•ing, •ried**)
**curry•comb**
**curse**
**curs•ed** (*or* **curst**)
**cur•sive** printing term
**cur•sor** VDU device
**cur•so•rial** adapted for running
**cur•sori•ly**
**cur•sory** hasty
**curt**
**cur•tail**
**cur•tail•ment**
**cur•tain**
**curtain-raiser**
**cur•ta•na** sword
**cur•ti•lage** enclosed land
**curt•ness**
**curt•sy** (*or* **•sey**; *noun, plural* **•sies** *or* **•seys**; *verb* **•sies, •sy•ing, •sied** *or* **•seys, •sey•ing, •seyed**)
**cur•va•ceous**
**cur•va•ture**
**curve**
**cur•vet** (**•vet•ting** *or* **•vet•ing, •vet•ted** *or* **•vet•ed**) dressage term
**cur•vi•lin•ear** (*or* **•eal**)
**cur•vi•lin•ear•ity**
**curvy** (**curvi•er, curvi•est**)
**cus•cus** marsupial; *compare* **couscous**
**cu•sec** unit
**Cush** biblical character
**cush•ion**

**cush•iony**
**Cush•it•ic** language
**cushy** *Slang* easy
**cus•pate** (*or* **•pat•ed, cusped)**
**cus•pid**
**cus•pi•date** (*or* **•dat•ed, •pidal)**
**cus•pi•da•tion** architectural term
**cus•pi•dor** spittoon
**cuss**
**cuss•ed**
**cuss•ed•ness**
**cus•tard**
**cus•to•dial**
**cus•to•dian**
**cus•to•dy** (*plural* **•dies)**
**cus•tom**
**cus•tom•ari•ly**
**cus•tom•ary**
**custom-built**
**cus•tom•er**
**cus•tom•ize** (*or* **•ise)**
**cus•tos** (*plural* **cus•to•des)** Franciscan
**cus•tu•mal** customary
**cut (cut•ting, cut)**
**cu•ta•neous**
**cut•away**
**cut•back**
**Cutch** *variant spelling of* **Kutch**
**cutch** *variant of* **catechou**
**cute**
**cute•ness**
**cu•ti•cle**
**cu•ticu•la** (*plural* **•lae)** cuticle
**cu•ticu•lar** (*adj*)
**cutie**
**cu•tin** plant substance
**cu•tin•ize** (*or* **•ise)**
**cu•tis** (*plural* **•tes** *or* **•tises)** skin
**cut•lass**
**cut•ler**
**cut•lery**
**cut•let**
**cut-price**
**cut•purse** pickpocket
**Cut•tack** Indian city
**cut•ter**
**cut•throat**
**cut•ting**
**cut•tle**
**cuttle•bone**
**cuttle•fish** (*plural* **•fish** *or* **•fishes)**
**cut•ty** *Dialect* short
**cut•water**
**cut•work** embroidery
**cut•worm** caterpillar
**cu•vette** dish
**Cux•ha•ven** German port
**Cuz•co** (*or* **Cus•co)** Peruvian city
**cwm** valley
**Cwm•bran** Welsh town
**cyan** blue colour
**cy•ana•mide** (*or* **•mid)**
**cya•nate**
**cy•an•ic**
**cya•ni•da•tion**
**cya•nide**
**cya•nine** (*or* **•nin)** dye
**cya•nite** mineral
**cya•nit•ic**
**cya•no•co•bala•min** vitamin
**cy•ano•gen** poisonous gas
**cya•no•hy•drin**
**cya•no•sis** blueness of skin
**cya•not•ic**
**cy•ano•type** blueprint
**Cybele** Phrygian goddess
**cy•ber•café**
**cy•ber•nate**
**cy•ber•na•tion**
**cy•ber•net•ic**
**cy•ber•neti•cist**
**cy•ber•net•ics**
**cy•ber•space**
**cy•cad** plant
**cyca•da•ceous**
**Cyc•la•des** Aegean islands
**cy•cla•mate**
**cyc•la•men**
**cy•cle**
**cy•clic** (*or* **•cli•cal)**
**cy•cli•cal•ly**
**cy•clist**
**cy•clo•al•kane**
**cy•clo•hex•ane**
**cy•cloid**
**cy•cloi•dal**
**cy•clom•eter**
**cy•clom•etry**
**cy•clone**
**cy•clon•ic** (*or* **•cloni•cal, •clo•nal)**
**cy•clo•nite** explosive
**Cy•clo•pean**
**cy•clo•pedia** (*or* **•pae•dia)**
**cy•clo•pedic** (*or* **•pae•dic)**
**cy•clo•pen•tane**
**cy•clo•plegia** medical term
**cy•clo•pro•pane**
**Cy•clops** one-eyed giant
**cy•clops** crustacean
**cy•clo•rama**
**cy•clo•ram•ic**
**cy•clo•sis** (*plural* **•ses)** biological process
**cy•clos•to•mate** (*or* **•clo•stoma•tous)**
**cy•clo•stome** primitive vertebrate
**cy•clo•style**
**cy•clo•thy•mia** mood swings
**cy•clo•thy•mic** (*or* **•mi•ac)**
**cy•clo•tron** physics term
**cyg•net** young swan; *compare* **signet**
**Cyg•nus** constellation
**cyl•in•der**
**cy•lin•dri•cal** (*or* **•dric)**
**cy•lin•dri•cal•ly**
**cyl•in•droid**
**cyma** (*plural* **cymae** *or* **cymas)** architectural moulding
**cy•mar** woman's jacket
**cy•ma•tium** architectural moulding
**cym•bal** musical instrument; *compare* **symbol**
**cym•bal•er** (*or* **•eer, •bal•ist)**
**cym•ba•lo** (*plural* **•los)** dulcimer
**cyme** botany term
**cy•mene** chemical compound
**cy•mif•er•ous**
**cy•mo•gene** *US* petroleum distillate
**cy•mo•graph** *variant spelling of* **kymograph**
**cy•moid** like a cyma
**cy•mo•phane** mineral
**cy•mose** of a cyme

**Cym•ric** (*or* **Kym•**) Welsh language
**Cym•ry** (*or* **Kym•**) Welsh people
**cyn•ic**
**cyni•cal**
**cyni•cal•ly**
**cyni•cism**
**cy•no•sure**
**cy•pher** *variant spelling of* **cipher**
**cy•pera•ceous** botany term
**cy pres** legal term
**cy•press** tree; *compare* **Cyprus**
**Cyp•rian**
**cy•pri•nid** fish
**cy•prino•dont** fish
**cy•pri•noid** carplike
**Cyp•ri•ot** (*or* **•ote**)
**cyp•ri•pedium** orchid
**Cy•prus** country; *compare* **cypress**
**cyp•sela** (*plural* **•selae**) botany term
**Cyr•enai•ca** (*or* **Cir•**) Libyan region
**Cy•ril•lic** Slavonic alphabet
**cyst** lump; sac; *compare* **cist**
**cys•tec•to•my** (*plural* **•mies**) removal of bladder
**cys•teine** amino acid
**cys•tein•ic**
**cyst•ic**
**cys•ti•cer•coid** larva
**cys•ti•cer•cus** (*plural* **•ci**) larva
**cys•tine** amino acid
**cys•ti•tis** bladder inflammation
**cys•to•carp** botany term
**cys•to•carp•ic**
**cys•to•cele**
**cys•toid**
**cys•to•lith** bladder stone
**cys•to•scope** medical term
**cys•to•scop•ic**
**cys•tos•co•py** (*plural* **•pies**)
**cys•toto•my** (*plural* **•mies**)
**cy•tas•ter** cytology term
**Cyth•era** Greek island
**cyti•dine** biochemical compound
**cy•to•chemi•cal**
**cy•to•chem•is•try**
**cy•to•chrome** biochemical compound
**cy•to•gen•esis** (*or* **•tog•eny**) origin of cells
**cy•to•genet•ics**
**cy•to•ki•nesis**
**cy•to•logi•cal**
**cy•tolo•gist**
**cy•tol•ogy** study of cells
**cy•toly•sin**
**cy•toly•sis**
**cy•ton** nerve-cell body
**cy•to•plasm**
**cy•to•plasm•ic**
**cy•to•plast**
**cy•to•sine** biochemical compound
**cy•to•taxo•nom•ic**
**cy•to•tax•ono•mist**
**cy•to•tax•on•omy**
**Cyzi•cus** ancient Greek colony
**czar** *variant spelling of* **tsar**
**czar•das** dance
**Czech**
**Czecho•slo•vak**
**Czecho•slo•va•kia**
**Czecho•slo•va•kian**
**Czę•sto•cho•wa** Polish city

# D

**dab** (**dab•bing, dabbed**)
**dab•ber**
**dab•ble**
**dab•bler**
**dab•chick**
**da capo** musical term
**Dac•ca** *variant of* **Dhaka**
**dace**
**da•cha** (*or* **•tcha**) Russian country house
**dachs•hund**
**da•coit** armed robber
**da•coity**
**Da•cron** (*Trademark*)
**dac•tyl** metrical foot; finger
**dac•tyl•ic**
**dac•tyli•cal•ly**
**dac•tylo•gram** *US* fingerprint
**dac•tyl•og•ra•phy**
**dac•ty•lol•ogy** (*plural* **•ogies**) sign language
**dad**
**Dada** artistic movement
**Da•da•ism**
**Da•da•ist**
**Da•da•is•tic**
**Da•da•is•ti•cal•ly**
**dad•dy** (*plural* **•dies**)
**dado** (*plural* **da•does** *or* **da•dos**) lower part of wall
**Daedalus** mythological character
**dae•mon** (*or* **dai•**) spirit; demigod; *compare* **demon**
**dae•mon•ic** (*or* **dai•**)
**daff** *Scot* to frolic; *Slang* daffodil
**daf•fo•dil**
**daffy** (**daffi•er, daffi•est**) *Slang* daft
**daft**
**Da•gan** Babylonian god
**Dag•en•ham**
**Da•ge•stan** (*or* **Da•ghe•stan**) Russian republic
**dag•ga** narcotic
**dag•ger**
**dagger•board**
**dag•lock** encrusted wool
**da•go** (*plural* **•gos** *or* **•goes**)
**da•go•ba** Buddhist shrine
**da•guerreo•type**
**da•guerreo•typ•er** (*or* **•ist**)
**da•guerreo•typy**
**dah** Morse code sound
**dahl•ia**
**Dah•na** Arabian desert
**Da•ho•man** (*or* **Da•ho•mean**)
**Da•ho•mey** *former name of* **Benin**

**Dáil Ei•reann** Irish parliament
**dai•ly** (*plural* **•lies**)
**dai•mon** *variant spelling of* **daemon**
**dain•ti•ly**
**dain•ti•ness**
**dain•ty** (*noun, plural* **•ties**; *adj* **•ti•er, •ti•est**)
**dai•qui•ri** (*plural* **•ris**) drink
**dairy** (*plural* **dairies**)
**dairy•ing**
**dairy•man** (*plural* **•men**)
**dais** platform
**dai•sy** (*plural* **•sies**)
**daisy•cutter** cricket
**Da•kar** Senegalese capital
**Da•ko•ta**
**Da•ko•tan**
**dal** Indian food
**Dalai Lama** Tibetan leader
**da•la•si** Gambian currency
**dale**
**Dales** Yorkshire region
**dales•man** (*plural* **•men**)
**Dal•las** US city
**dal•li•ance**
**dal•ly** (**•lies, •ly•ing, •lied**)
**Dal•ma•tia** Croatian region
**Dal•ma•tian**
**dal•mat•ic** tunic
**dal•ton** unit
**dal•ton•ic**
**dal•ton•ism** colour blindness
**dam** (**dam•ming, dammed**) river barrier; female parent; *compare* **damn**
**dam•age**
**dam•age•abil•ity**
**dam•age•able**
**dam•ag•er**
**dam•ages**
**Da•man** Indian region
**Da•man•hûr** Egyptian city
**Da•ma•ra** (*plural* **•ras** *or* **•ra**) African people
**Dama•scene** of Damascus
**dama•scene** decorate metal
**Da•mas•cus** Syrian capital
**dam•ask**
**dame**
**Dami•et•ta** Egyptian town
**dam•mar** (*or* **da•mar, dam•mer**) resin
**dammed** obstructed; *compare* **damned**
**dam•ming**
**damn** condemn; *compare* **dam**
**dam•nabil•ity**
**dam•nable**
**dam•nably**
**dam•na•tion**
**dam•na•tory**
**damned** condemned; *compare* **dammed**
**damned•est**
**dam•ni•fi•ca•tion**
**dam•ni•fy** (**•fies, •fy•ing, •fied**) injure
**Damocles** mythological character
**damp**
**damp•course**
**damp•en**
**damp•en•er**
**damp•er**
**damp•ly**
**damp•ness**
**dam•sel**
**damsel•fish** (*plural* **•fish** *or* **•fishes**)
**damsel•fly** (*plural* **•flies**)
**dam•son**
**dan** buoy; judo grade
**Danaë** mythological character
**dance**
**danc•er**
**danc•ing**
**dan•de•lion**
**dan•der**
**Dan•die Din•mont** terrier
**dan•di•fi•ca•tion**
**dan•di•fy** (**•fies, •fy•ing, •fied**)
**dan•di•prat** coin
**dan•dle** fondle
**dan•dler**
**dan•druff** (*or* **•driff**)
**dan•druffy** (*or* **•driffy**)
**dan•dy** (*plural* **•dies**)
**dandy•ish**
**dandy•ism**
**Dane**
**Dane•geld** (*or* **•gelt**) Anglo-Saxon tax
**Dane•law** (*or* **•lagh**) England under Danish law
**dane•wort** shrub
**dang** damn
**dan•ger**
**dan•ger•ous**
**dan•ger•ous•ness**
**dan•gle**
**dan•gler**
**danio** (*plural* **danios**) fish
**Dan•ish**
**dank**
**dank•ness**
**dan•seur** (*fem* **•seuse**) *French* dancer
**Dan•ube**
**Danu•bian**
**Dan•zig** Gdańsk; pigeon
**dap** (**dap•ping, dapped**)
**daphne** shrub
**daph•nia** flea
**Daph•nis** mythological character
**dap•per**
**dap•ple**
**dapple-grey** (*US* **-gray**)
**dar•af** unit
**dar•bies** *Slang* handcuffs
**Dar•dan** (*or* **•da•nian**) Trojan
**Dar•da•nelles**
**Dar•da•nus** mythological character
**Dar•dic** language group
**dare**
**dare•devil**
**dare•devil•ry** (*or* **•try**)
**dar•er**
**Dar es Sa•laam** Tanzanian capital
**Dar•fur** Sudanese province
**darg** *Dialect* day's work
**dar•ic** coin
**Dari•en** part of Panama
**dar•ing**
**dari•ole** cookery mould
**Dar•jee•ling** Indian town; tea
**dark**
**dark•en**
**dark•en•er**
**dar•kle** darken
**dark•ly**
**dark•ness**
**dark•room**
**dark•some**

**darky** (*or* **darkie, dark•ey;** *plural* **darkies** *or* **•eys)**
**Dar•ling** Australian river
**dar•ling**
**Dar•ling•ton** Durham town
**Darm•stadt** German city
**darn**
**darned**
**dar•nel** grass
**darn•er**
**darn•ing**
**dart**
**dart•board**
**dart•er**
**Dart•ford** Kent town
**Dart•moor**
**Dart•mouth** Devon port
**darts**
**Dar•win** Australian port
**Dar•win•ian**
**Dar•win•ism**
**Dar•win•ist**
**dash**
**dash•board**
**da•sheen** plant
**dash•er**
**da•shi•ki** garment
**dash•ing**
**dash•pot** vibration damper
**Dasht-i-Lut** (*or* -e-) Iranian desert
**das•sie** animal
**das•tard**
**das•tard•li•ness**
**das•tard•ly**
**dasy•ure** marsupial
**da•ta** information; *plural of* **datum**
**data•base**
**dat•able** (*or* **date•)**
**dat•able•ness** (*or* **date•)**
**da•ta•ry** (*plural* **•ries)** Catholic official
**date**
**dat•ed**
**dat•ed•ness**
**date•less**
**date•line**
**dat•er**
**dat•ing**
**da•ti•val**
**da•tive**
**dato** Philippine chief
**da•to•lite** mineral
**da•tum** (*plural* **•ta)** fact; *compare* **data**
**da•tu•ra** plant
**daub** smear
**daube** stew
**daub•er**
**daub•ery** (*or* **•ry)**
**dauby**
**Dau•gav•pils** Latvian city
**daugh•ter**
**daughter-in-law** (*plural* **daughters-)**
**daugh•ter•li•ness**
**daugh•ter•ly**
**daunt**
**daunt•er**
**daunt•ing**
**daunt•less**
**dau•phin** heir to French throne
**Dau•phi•né** former French province
**dau•phine** (*or* **•phin•ess)** wife of dauphin
**dav•en•port** desk
**dav•it**
**daw** jackdaw
**daw•dle**
**daw•dler**
**dawn**
**Daw•son** Canadian town
**day**
**day•book**
**day•boy**
**day•break**
**day•dream**
**day•dream•er**
**day•dream•ing**
**day•dreamy**
**day•flower**
**day•light**
**day•long**
**day-neutral** botany term
**day•star** sun
**day•time**
**day-to-day**
**Day•ton** US city
**Day•to•na Beach** US city
**day-tripper**
**daze**
**daz•zle**
**dea•con**
**dea•con•ess**
**dea•con•ry** (*plural* **•ries)**
**dea•con•ship**
**de•ac•tiv•ate**
**de•ac•ti•va•tion**
**de•ac•ti•va•tor**
**dead**
**dead•beat**
**dead•en**
**dead•en•er**
**dead•eye** nautical term
**dead•fall** trap
**dead•head**
**dead•light** nautical term
**dead•line**
**dead•li•ness**
**dead•lock**
**dead•ly** **(•li•er, •li•est)**
**dead•ness**
**dead-nettle**
**dead•pan**
**dead•wood**
**deaf**
**deaf-and-dumb**
**deaf•en**
**deaf-mute**
**deaf-muteness** (*or* **-mutism)**
**deaf•ness**
**deal** **(deal•ing, dealt)** take action, etc.; *compare* **dele**
**dea•late** (*or* **•lat•ed)** wingless
**dea•la•tion**
**deal•er**
**deal•fish** (*plural* **•fish** *or* **•fishes)**
**deal•ing**
**dealt**
**de•ami•nate** (*or* **•am•in•ize, •am•in•ise)** biochemistry term
**de•ami•na•tion** (*or* **•ami•ni•za•tion, •ami•ni•sa•tion)**
**dean** university official, etc.; *compare* **dene**
**dean•ery** (*plural* **•eries)**
**dean•ship**
**dear**
**dear•ly**
**dear•ness**
**dearth**
**deary** (*or* **dearie;** *plural* **dearies)**
**death**
**death•bed**
**death•blow**
**death•less**
**death•li•ness**

**death•ly**
**death's-head**
**death•trap**
**death•watch**
**Deau•ville** French resort
**deb** *short for* **debutante**
**de•ba•cle**
**de•bag** (**•bag•ging, •bagged**)
**de•bar** (**•bar•ring, •barred**)
**de•bark** disembark
**de•bar•ka•tion**
**de•bar•ment**
**de•base**
**de•bas•ed•ness**
**de•base•ment**
**de•bas•er**
**de•bat•able** (*or* **•bate•able**)
**de•bat•ably**
**de•bate**
**de•bat•er**
**de•bauch**
**debau•chee**
**de•bauch•er**
**de•bauch•ery** (*or* **•ment**)
**de•ben•ture** bond
**de•bili•tate**
**de•bili•ta•tion**
**de•bili•ta•tive**
**de•bil•ity** (*plural* **•ities**)
**deb•it**
**debo•nair** (*or* **deb•on•naire**)
**de•bouch** move into larger space
**de•bouch•ment** (*or* **•bou•chure**)
**De•bre•cen** Hungarian city
**dé•bride•ment** surgical term
**de•brief**
**de•bris** (*or* **dé•**)
**debt**
**debt•or**
**de•bug** (**•bug•ging, •bugged**)
**de•bunk**
**de•bunk•er**
**de•bus** (**•bus•ing, •bused** *or* **•bus•sing, •bussed**) unload; alight
**de•but**
**debu•tante**
**de•ca•dal**
**dec•ade**
**deca•dence** (*or* **•den•cy**)
**deca•dent**
**de•caf•fein•ate**
**deca•gon**
**de•cago•nal**
**deca•he•dral**
**deca•he•dron**
**de•cal** transferred design
**de•cal•ci•fi•ca•tion**
**de•cal•ci•fi•er**
**de•cal•ci•fy** (**•fies, •fy•ing, •fied**)
**de•cal•co•ma•nia** transferring designs
**de•ca•les•cence** physics term
**de•ca•les•cent**
**Deca•logue** Ten Commandments
**de•camp**
**de•camp•ment**
**de•ca•nal** of a dean
**dec•ane** chemical compound
**dec•ane•dio•ic acid**
**de•ca•ni** musical term
**deca•no•ic acid**
**de•cant**
**de•cant•er**
**de•capi•tate**
**de•capi•ta•tion**
**de•capi•ta•tor**
**deca•pod** crustacean
**de•capo•dal** (*or* **•dan, •dous**)
**de•car•bon•ate**
**de•car•boni•za•tion** (*or* **•sa•tion**)
**de•car•bon•ize** (*or* **•ise**)
**de•car•bon•iz•er** (*or* **•is•er**)
**de•car•boxy•la•tion**
**dec•are** unit
**deca•style** architectural term
**deca•syl•lab•ic**
**deca•syl•lable**
**de•cath•lete**
**de•cath•lon**
**de•cay**
**Dec•can** Indian plateau
**de•cease**
**de•ceased**
**de•cedent** deceased
**de•ceit**
**de•ceit•ful**
**de•ceit•ful•ly**
**de•ceiv•able**
**de•ceiv•able•ness** (*or* **•abil•ity**)
**de•ceive**
**de•ceiv•er**
**de•cel•er•ate**
**de•cel•era•tion**
**de•cel•era•tor**
**de•cel•erom•eter**
**De•cem•ber**
**De•cem•brist** Russian revolutionary
**de•cena•ry** (*or* **de•cen•na•ry**) of tithing
**de•cen•cy** (*plural* **•cies**)
**de•cen•nial**
**de•cen•nium** (*or* **de•cen•na•ry**; *plural* **•niums, •nia,** *or* **•naries**) decade
**de•cent**
**de•cen•tral•ist**
**de•cen•trali•za•tion** (*or* **•sa•tion**)
**de•cen•tral•ize** (*or* **•ise**)
**de•cep•tion**
**de•cep•tive**
**de•ce•rebrate** remove brain
**de•ce•rebra•tion**
**de•cern** legal term
**deci•are** unit
**deci•bel**
**de•cid•able**
**de•cide**
**de•cid•ed**
**de•cid•ed•ly**
**de•cid•er**
**de•cidua** (*plural* **•cid•uas** *or* **•ciduae**) anatomy term
**de•cid•ual** (*or* **•cidu•ate**)
**de•cidu•ous**
**dec•ile** statistics term
**de•cil•lion** $10^{60}$
**de•cil•lionth**
**deci•mal**
**deci•mali•za•tion** (*or* **•sa•tion**)
**deci•mal•ize** (*or* **•ise**)
**deci•mate**
**deci•ma•tion**
**deci•ma•tor**
**deci•metre** (*US* **•meter**)
**de•ci•pher**
**de•ci•pher•abil•ity**
**de•ci•pher•able**
**de•ci•pher•er**
**de•ci•pher•ment**
**de•ci•sion**

**de•ci•sion•al**
**de•ci•sive**
**de•ci•sive•ness**
**deck**
**deck•house**
**deck•le** (*or* **•el**) frame
**deckle-edged**
**de•claim**
**de•claim•er**
**dec•la•ma•tion**
**de•clama•to•ri•ly**
**de•clama•tory**
**de•clar•able**
**de•clar•ant**
**dec•la•ra•tion**
**de•clara•tive**
**de•clara•tor** legal term
**de•clara•to•ri•ly**
**de•clara•tory**
**de•clare**
**de•clar•er**
**de•class**
**dé•clas•sé** (*fem* **•sée**) *French* having lost status
**de•clas•si•fi•able**
**de•clas•si•fi•ca•tion**
**de•clas•si•fy** (**•fies, •fy•ing, •fied**)
**de•clen•sion**
**de•clen•sion•al**
**de•clen•sion•al•ly**
**de•clin•able**
**dec•li•nate** drooping
**dec•li•na•tion**
**de•cli•na•tory**
**de•cline**
**de•clin•er**
**dec•li•nom•eter**
**de•clivi•tous**
**de•cliv•ity** (*plural* **•ities**) downward slope
**de•clutch**
**de•coct**
**de•coc•tion**
**de•code**
**de•cod•er**
**de•coke**
**de•col•late** separate
**de•col•la•tion**
**de•col•la•tor**
**dé•colle•tage** low neckline
**dé•colle•té**
**de•colo•nize** (*or* **•nise**)
**de•col•or•ant**
**de•col•ori•za•tion** (*or* **•sa•tion, de•col•ora•tion**)
**de•col•or•ize** (*or* **•ise, de•col•our**)
**de•com•mis•sion**
**de•com•pos•abil•ity**
**de•com•pos•able**
**de•com•pose**
**de•com•pos•er**
**de•com•po•si•tion**
**de•com•pound** type of leaf
**de•com•press**
**de•com•pres•sion**
**de•com•pres•sive**
**de•com•pres•sor**
**de•con•gest•ant**
**de•con•secrate**
**de•con•tami•nant**
**de•con•tami•nate**
**de•con•tami•na•tion**
**de•con•tami•na•tive**
**de•con•tami•na•tor**
**de•con•trol** (**•trol•ling, •trolled**)
**dé•cor** (*or* **de•**)
**deco•rate**
**deco•ra•tion**
**deco•ra•tive**
**deco•ra•tor**
**deco•rous**
**de•cor•ti•cate** remove shell
**de•cor•ti•ca•tion**
**de•cor•ti•ca•tor**
**de•co•rum**
**de•cou•page** decoration
**de•cou•pling** electronics term
**de•coy**
**de•coy•er**
**de•crease**
**de•creas•ing•ly**
**de•cree** (**•cree•ing, •creed**)
**de•cree•able**
**de•cree nisi**
**de•cre•er**
**dec•re•ment** diminution
**de•crep•it**
**de•crepi•tate** crackle on heating
**de•crepi•ta•tion**
**de•crepi•tude**
**de•cres•cence**
**de•cres•cent** decreasing
**de•cre•tal** papal edict
**de•cre•tal•ist**
**de•cre•tive**
**dec•re•tory**
**de•cri•al**
**de•cri•er**
**de•cry** (**•cries, •cry•ing, •cried**)
**de•crypt** decode
**de•cum•bence** (*or* **•ben•cy**)
**de•cum•bent** lying flat
**de•cu•ple** increase tenfold
**de•cu•ri•on** Roman councillor
**de•cur•rent** botany term
**de•curved** bent downwards
**decu•ry** (*plural* **•ries**) ten Roman soldiers
**de•cus•sate** intersect
**de•cus•sa•tion**
**De•dé•ag•ach** Greek port
**dedi•cate**
**dedi•cat•ed**
**dedi•ca•tee**
**dedi•ca•tion**
**dedi•ca•tor**
**dedi•ca•tory** (*or* **•tive**)
**de•dif•fer•en•tia•tion**
**de•duce**
**de•duc•ibil•ity** (*or* **•ible•ness**)
**de•duc•ible**
**de•duct**
**de•duct•ibil•ity**
**de•duct•ible**
**de•duc•tion**
**de•duc•tive**
**Dee** river
**deed**
**deek** *Dialect* look at
**deem** consider; *compare* deme
**deem•ster** (*or* **demp•**) Manx magistrate
**deep**
**deep•en**
**deep•en•er**
**deep•freeze** (*noun*)
**deep-freeze** (*verb*; **-freez•ing, -froze** *or* **-freezed, -frozen** *or* **-freezed**)
**deep-fry** (**-fries, -fry•ing, -fried**)
**deep-laid**
**deep•ness**
**deep-rooted** (*or* **-seated**)

**deer** (*plural* **deer** *or* **deers**)
**deer•grass**
**deer•hound**
**deer•skin**
**deer•stalker**
**de-escalate**
**de-escala•tion**
**de•face**
**de•face•able**
**de•face•ment**
**de•fac•er**
**de fac•to**
**(defaecate)** *incorrect spelling of* **defecate**
**de•fal•cate** legal term
**de•fal•ca•tion**
**de•fal•ca•tor**
**defa•ma•tion**
**de•fama•to•ri•ly**
**de•fama•tory**
**de•fame**
**de•fam•er**
**de•fault**
**de•fault•er**
**de•fea•sance** annulment
**de•fea•sible**
**de•feat**
**de•feat•er**
**de•feat•ism**
**de•feat•ist**
**def•ecate**
**def•eca•tion**
**def•eca•tor**
**de•fect**
**de•fec•tion**
**de•fec•tive**
**de•fec•tor**
**de•fence** (*US* **•fense**)
**de•fence•less** (*US* **•fense•**)
**de•fence•less•ness** (*US* **•fense•**)
**de•fend**
**de•fend•able**
**de•fend•ant**
**de•fend•er**
**de•fen•es•tra•tion** throwing from window
**de•fen•sibil•ity** (*or* **•sible•ness**)
**de•fen•sible**
**de•fen•sibly**
**de•fen•sive**
**de•fer** (**•fer•ring, •ferred**)
**def•er•ence**
**def•er•ent**
**def•er•en•tial**
**def•er•en•tial•ly**
**de•fer•ment** (*or* **•fer•ral**)
**de•fer•rable** (*or* **•fer•able**)
**de•fer•ral**
**de•ferred**
**de•fer•rer**
**de•fi•cient**
**defi•cit**
**de•fi•er**
**defi•lade** military term
**de•file**
**de•file•ment**
**de•fil•er**
**de•fin•able**
**de•fine**
**de•fin•er**
**de•fini•en•dum** (*plural* **•da**) thing defined
**de•fini•ens** (*plural* **•en•tia**) definition
**defi•nite**
**defi•nite•ly**
**defi•nite•ness**
**defi•ni•tion**
**defi•ni•tion•al**
**de•fini•tive**
**de•fini•tive•ly**
**de•fini•tude**
**def•la•grate** burn
**def•la•gra•tion**
**de•flate**
**de•fla•tion**
**de•fla•tion•ary**
**de•fla•tion•ist**
**de•fla•tor**
**de•flect**
**de•flec•tion** (*or* **•flex•ion**)
**de•flec•tive**
**de•flec•tor**
**de•flexed**
**de•floc•cu•late** disperse
**de•floc•cu•la•tion**
**de•flo•ra•tion**
**de•flow•er**
**de•flow•er•er**
**de•fo•li•ant**
**de•fo•li•ate**
**de•fo•lia•tion**
**de•fo•lia•tor**
**de•force** withhold
**de•force•ment**
**de•for•ciant** legal term
**de•for•est**
**de•for•esta•tion**
**de•for•est•er**
**de•form**
**de•form•able**
**de•for•ma•tion**
**de•formed**
**de•form•ed•ness**
**de•form•er**
**de•form•ity** (*plural* **•ities**)
**de•fraud**
**de•frau•da•tion**
**de•fraud•er**
**de•fraud•ment**
**de•fray**
**de•fray•able**
**de•fray•al** (*or* **•ment**)
**de•fray•er**
**de•frock**
**de•frost**
**de•frost•er**
**deft**
**deft•ness**
**de•funct**
**de•func•tive**
**de•fuse**
**defy** (**•fies, •fy•ing, •fied**)
**dé•ga•gé** *French* casual
**de•gas** (**•gas•ses** *or* **•gases, •gas•sing, •gassed**)
**de•gas•ser**
**de•gauss** demagnetize
**de•gen•era•cy** (*plural* **•cies**)
**de•gen•er•ate**
**de•gen•er•ate•ness**
**de•gen•era•tion**
**de•gen•era•tive**
**de•glu•ti•nate** extract gluten
**de•glu•ti•na•tion**
**de•glu•ti•tion** swallowing
**de•gra•dable**
**deg•ra•da•tion**
**de•grade**
**de•grad•ed**
**de•grad•er**
**de•grad•ing**
**de•grease**
**de•gree**
**degree-day** unit
**de•gres•sion** decrease
**de•hisce** burst open
**de•his•cence**
**de•his•cent**
**de•horn**
**Deh•ra Dun** Indian city
**de•hu•mani•za•tion** (*or* **•sa•tion**)

**de•hu•man•ize** (*or* **•ise**)
**de•hu•midi•fi•ca•tion**
**de•hu•midi•fi•er**
**de•hu•midi•fy** (**•fies, •fy•ing, •fied**)
**de•hy•drate**
**de•hy•dra•tion**
**de•hy•dra•tor**
**de•hydro•gen•ase** enzyme
**de•hydro•gen•ate** (*or* **•ize, •ise**) remove hydrogen
**de•hydro•gena•tion**
**de•hydro•geni•za•tion** (*or* **•sa•tion**)
**de•hyp•no•tize** (*or* **•ise**)
**de-ice**
**de-icer**
**dei•ci•dal**
**dei•cide** killing a god
**deic•tic** logic term
**deic•ti•cal•ly**
**de•ific** godlike
**dei•fi•ca•tion**
**dei•fi•er**
**dei•form**
**dei•fy** (**•fies, •fy•ing, •fied**)
**deign**
**deil** *Scot* devil
**de•in•dus•tri•ali•za•tion** (*or* **•sa•tion**)
**de•in•dus•tri•al•ize** (*or* **•ise**)
**de•ism**
**de•ist**
**de•ist•ic** (*or* **•is•ti•cal**)
**de•ity** (*plural* **•ities**)
**deix•is** linguistics term
**déjà vu**
**de•ject**
**de•jec•ta** body waste
**de•ject•ed**
**de•ject•ed•ness**
**de•jec•tion**
**de jure** *Latin* according to law
**dek•ko** (*plural* **•kos**) *Slang* look
**de•laine** fabric
**de•lami•nate** divide into layers
**de•lami•na•tion**
(**delapidate**) *incorrect spelling of* **dilapidate**
**de•late** denounce
**Dela•ware** US state
**Dela•war•ean**
**de•lay**
**de•lay•er**
**dele** (**de•leing, de•led**) symbol for deletion; *compare* **deal**
**de•lec•table**
**de•lec•table•ness** (*or* **•tabil•ity**)
**de•lec•tably**
**de•lec•ta•tion**
**del•egable**
**del•ega•cy** (*plural* **•cies**) committee
**del•egate**
**del•ega•tion**
**de•lete**
**del•eteri•ous**
**de•letion**
**Delft** Dutch town; earthenware
**Del•hi** Indian capital
**deli** *short for* **delicatessen**
**De•lian** of Delos
**de•lib•er•ate**
**de•lib•er•ate•ness**
**de•lib•era•tion**
**de•lib•era•tive**
**de•lib•era•tor**
**deli•ca•cy** (*plural* **•cies**)
**deli•cate**
**deli•ca•tes•sen**
**de•li•cious**
**de•lict** civil wrong
**de•light**
**de•light•ed**
**de•light•er**
**de•light•ful**
**de•light•ful•ly**
**de•light•ful•ness**
**de•lim•it** (*or* **•limi•tate**)
**de•limi•ta•tion**
**de•limi•ta•tive**
**de•lin•eable**
**de•lin•eate**
**de•lin•ea•tion**
**de•lin•ea•tive**
**de•lin•ea•tor** tailor's pattern
**de•lin•quen•cy** (*plural* **•cies**)
**de•lin•quent**
**deli•quesce** chemistry term
**deli•ques•cence**
**deli•ques•cent**
**de•liri•ant**
**de•liri•ous**
**de•liri•ous•ness**
**de•lir•ium** (*plural* **•lir•iums** *or* **•liria**)
**de•lir•ium tre•mens**
**deli•tes•cence** medical term
**deli•tes•cent**
**de•liv•er**
**de•liv•er•able**
**de•liv•er•ance**
**de•liv•er•er**
**de•liv•ery** (*plural* **•eries**)
**dell**
**Del•mar•va** US peninsula
**de•lo•cali•za•tion** (*or* **•sa•tion**)
**de•lo•cal•ize** (*or* **•ise**)
**De•los** Greek island
**de•louse**
**Del•phi** Greek oracle
**Del•phian**
**Del•phic**
**del•phin•ium** (*plural* **•phin•iums** *or* **•phinia**)
**Del•phi•nus** constellation
**del•ta**
**del•ta•ic** (*or* **del•tic**)
**del•ti•olo•gist**
**del•ti•ol•ogy** collecting postcards
**del•toid** muscle
**de•lude**
**de•lud•er**
**del•uge**
**de•lu•sion**
**de•lu•sion•al**
**de•lu•sive**
**de•lu•so•ry**
**de luxe**
**delve**
**delv•er**
**de•mag•neti•za•tion** (*or* **•sa•tion**)
**de•mag•net•ize** (*or* **•ise**)
**de•mag•net•iz•er** (*or* **•is•er**)
**dema•gog•ic** (*or* **•gogi•cal**)
**dema•gogi•cal•ly**
**dema•gogue** (*US also* **•gog**)
**dema•gogu•ery** (*or* **•ism**)
**dema•gogy** (*plural* **•gogies**)
**de•mand**
**de•mand•able**
**de•mand•ant**
**de•mand•er**
**de•mand•ing**
**de•man•toid** gemstone
**de•mar•cate**

**de•mar•ca•tion** (*or* **•ka•tion**)
**de•mar•ca•tor**
**dé•marche** *French* diplomatic manoeuvre
**de•ma•teri•al•ize** (*or* **•ise**)
**Dema•vend** Iranian volcano
**deme** biology term; ancient local-government unit; *compare* **deem**
**de•mean**
**de•mean•ing**
**de•mean•our** (*US* **•or**)
**de•ment**
**de•ment•ed**
**de•ment•ed•ness**
**de•men•tia**
**Dem•erara** Guyanese river
**dem•erara** sugar
**de•mer•it**
**de•meri•to•ri•ous**
**de•mer•sal** living in deep water
**de•mesne** land
**Demeter** Greek goddess
**demi•bas•ti•on** fortification
**demi•can•ton**
**demi•god** (*fem* **•god•dess**)
**demi•john** bottle
**de•mili•ta•ri•za•tion** (*or* **•sa•tion**)
**de•mili•ta•rize** (*or* **•rise**)
**demi•lune** crescent shape
**demi•mon•daine** unrespectable woman
**demi•monde**
**de•min•er•al•ize** (*or* **•ise**)
**demi•relief**
**de•mis•able**
**de•mise**
**demi•semi•qua•ver**
**de•mis•sion** giving up office
**de•mist**
**de•mist•er**
**demi•tasse** small coffee cup
**demi•urge** philosophy term
**demi•vierge** *French* promiscuous virgin
**demi•volt** (*or* **•volte**)
**demo** (*plural* **demos**) *Slang* demonstration
**de•mob** (**•mob•bing, •mobbed**)
**de•mo•bi•li•za•tion** (*or* **•sa•tion**)
**de•mo•bi•lize** (*or* **•lise**)
**de•moc•ra•cy** (*plural* **•cies**)
**Demo•crat** political party member
**demo•crat**
**Demo•crat•ic**
**demo•crat•ic**
**demo•crati•cal•ly**
**de•moc•ra•ti•za•tion** (*or* **•sa•tion**)
**de•moc•ra•tize** (*or* **•tise**)
**dé•mo•dé** *French* out of fashion
**de•modu•late**
**de•modu•la•tion** electronics term
**de•modu•la•tor**
**De•mo•gor•gon** underworld god
**de•mog•ra•pher** (*or* **•phist**)
**de•mo•graph•ic** (*or* **•graphi•cal**)
**de•mo•graphi•cal•ly**
**de•mog•ra•phy**
**demoi•selle** damsel; bird
**de•mol•ish**
**de•mol•ish•er**
**de•mol•ish•ment**
**demo•li•tion**
**demo•li•tion•ist**
**de•mon** devil; *compare* **daemon**
**de•mon•eti•za•tion** (*or* **•sa•tion**)
**de•mon•etize** (*or* **•etise**)
**de•mo•ni•ac** (*or* **•nia•cal**)
**de•mo•nia•cal•ly**
**de•mon•ic**
**de•moni•cal•ly**
**de•mon•ism**
**de•mon•ist**
**de•mon•ize** (*or* **•ise**)
**de•mon•ola•ter** demon worshipper
**de•mon•ola•try**
**de•mono•logi•cal**
**de•mon•olo•gist**
**de•mon•ol•ogy**
**de•mon•strabil•ity** (*or* **•strable•ness**)
**de•mon•strable**
**de•mon•strably**
**dem•on•strate**
**dem•on•stra•tion**
**de•mon•stra•tion•al**
**de•mon•stra•tion•ist**
**de•mon•stra•tive**
**de•mon•stra•tor**
**de•mor•ali•za•tion** (*or* **•sa•tion**)
**de•mor•al•ize** (*or* **•ise**)
**de•mor•al•iz•er** (*or* **•is•er**)
**de•mos** nation
**de•mote**
**de•mot•ic** of the people
**de•mo•tion**
**de•mot•ist**
**de•mount**
**de•mount•able**
**demp•ster** *variant of* **deemster**
**de•mul•cent** soothing
**de•mul•si•fi•ca•tion**
**de•mul•si•fi•er**
**de•mul•si•fy** (**•fies, •fy•ing, •fied**)
**de•mur** (**•mur•ring, •murred**)
**de•mure**
**de•mure•ness**
**de•mur•rable**
**de•mur•rage**
**de•mur•ral**
**de•mur•rer** objection
**de•mu•tu•al•ize**
**demy** paper size
**de•mys•ti•fi•ca•tion**
**de•mys•ti•fy** (**•fies, •fy•ing, •fied**)
**de•my•tholo•gize** (*or* **•gise**)
**den** (**den•ning, denned**)
**de•nar•ius** (*plural* **•narii**) coin
**de•nary** based on ten
**de•na•tion•ali•za•tion** (*or* **•sa•tion**)
**de•na•tion•al•ize** (*or* **•ise**)
**de•natu•rali•za•tion** (*or* **•sa•tion**)
**de•natu•ral•ize** (*or* **•ise**)
**de•na•tur•ant**
**de•na•tura•tion**
**de•na•ture** (*or* **•tur•ize, •tur•ise**)
**de•na•zi•fy** (**•fies, •fy•ing, •fied**)
**Den•bigh•shire** Welsh county
**den•dri•form** branching
**den•drite** part of nerve cell
**den•drit•ic** (*or* **•driti•cal**)

**den•driti•cal•ly**
**den•dro•chrono•logi•cal**
**den•dro•chro•nolo•gist**
**den•dro•chro•nol•ogy** study of tree rings
**den•droid** (*or* **•droi•dal**) treelike
**den•dro•logi•cal** (*or* **•log•ic, •drolo•gous**)
**den•drolo•gist**
**den•drol•ogy**
**dene** wooded valley; *compare* **dean**
**Den•eb** star
**de•nega•tion**
**den•gue** viral disease
**de•ni•able**
**de•ni•al**
**de•nico•tin•ize** (*or* **•ise**)
**de•ni•er** one who denies
**den•ier** unit of weight
**deni•grate**
**deni•gra•tion**
**deni•gra•tor**
**den•im**
**de•ni•trate** chemistry term
**de•ni•tra•tion**
**de•ni•tri•fi•ca•tion**
**de•ni•tri•fy** (**•fies, •fy•ing, •fied**)
**deni•zen**
**Den•mark**
**denned**
**den•ning**
**de•nomi•nable**
**de•nomi•nate**
**de•nomi•na•tion**
**de•nomi•na•tion•al**
**de•nomi•na•tion•al•ism**
**de•nomi•na•tion•al•ist**
**de•nomi•na•tive** naming
**de•nomi•na•tor**
**de•not•able**
**de•no•ta•tion**
**de•no•ta•tive**
**de•note**
**de•note•ment**
**de•noue•ment**
**de•nounce**
**de•nounce•ment**
**de•nounc•er**
**dense**
**dense•ness**
**den•sim•eter**
**den•si•met•ric**
**den•sim•etry**
**den•si•tom•eter**
**den•si•to•met•ric**
**den•si•tom•etry**
**den•sity** (*plural* **•sities**)
**dent**
**den•tal**
**den•ta•lium** (*plural* **•liums** *or* **•lia**) mollusc
**den•tate**
**den•ta•tion** state of having teeth; *compare* **dentition**
**den•tex** fish
**den•ti•cle** small tooth
**den•ticu•late**
**den•ticu•la•tion**
**den•ti•form**
**den•ti•frice**
**den•til** architectural term
**den•ti•la•bial**
**den•ti•lin•gual** phonetics term
**den•tin•al**
**den•tine** (*or* **•tin**) tooth tissue
**den•tist**
**den•tis•try**
**den•ti•tion** set of teeth; *compare* **dentation**
**den•toid**
**Den•ton** Lancashire town
**den•ture**
**de•nu•cleari•za•tion** (*or* **•sa•tion**)
**de•nu•clear•ize** (*or* **•ise**)
**denu•date**
**denu•da•tion**
**de•nude**
**de•nud•er**
**de•nu•mer•able**
**de•nun•ci•ate**
**de•nun•cia•tion**
**de•nun•cia•tor**
**de•nun•cia•tory**
**Den•ver** US city
**deny** (**de•nies, de•ny•ing, de•nied**)
**deo•dand** legal term
**deo•dar** tree
**de•odor•ant**
**de•odori•za•tion** (*or* **•sa•tion**)
**de•odor•ize** (*or* **•ise**)
**de•odor•iz•er** (*or* **•is•er**)
**de•on•tic** logic term
**de•on•to•logi•cal**
**de•on•tolo•gist**
**de•on•tol•ogy** branch of ethics
**de•oxi•di•za•tion** (*or* **•sa•tion**)
**de•oxi•dize** (*or* **•dise**)
**de•oxi•diz•er** (*or* **•dis•er**)
**de•oxy•cor•ti•co•ster•one** (*or* **de•oxy•cor•tone**) hormone
**de•oxy•gen•ate** (*or* **•ize, •ise**)
**de•oxy•gena•tion**
**de•oxy•ri•bo•nu•cle•ic acid** (*or* **des•**)
**de•oxy•ri•bose** (*or* **des•**) a sugar
**de•part**
**de•part•ment**
**de•part•men•tal**
**de•part•men•tal•ism**
**de•part•men•tali•za•tion** (*or* **•sa•tion**)
**de•part•ment•al•ize** (*or* **•ise**)
**de•part•men•tal•ly**
**de•par•ture**
**de•pas•ture**
**de•pend**
**de•pend•abil•ity** (*or* **•able•ness**)
**de•pend•able**
**de•pend•ably**
**de•pend•ant** (*noun*)
**de•pend•ence** (*US also* **•ance**)
**de•pend•en•cy** (*US also* **•an•cy**; *plural* **•cies**)
**de•pend•ent** (*US also* **•ant**; *adj*)
**de•per•son•ali•za•tion** (*or* **•sa•tion**)
**de•per•son•al•ize** (*or* **•ise**)
**de•pict**
**de•pict•er** (*or* **•pic•tor**)
**de•pic•tion**
**de•pic•tive**
**de•pic•ture**
**depi•late**
**depi•la•tion**
**depi•la•tor**
**de•pila•tory** (*plural* **•tories**)
**de•plane**
**de•plet•able**
**de•plete**
**de•ple•tion**

**de•ple•tive** (*or* **•tory**)
**de•plor•able**
**de•plor•able•ness** (*or* **•abil•ity**)
**de•plor•ably**
**de•plore**
**de•plor•er**
**de•plor•ing•ly**
**de•ploy**
**de•ploy•ment**
**de•plu•ma•tion**
**de•plume** deprive of feathers
**de•po•lari•za•tion** (*or* **•sa•tion**)
**de•po•lar•ize** (*or* **•ise**)
**de•po•lar•iz•er** (*or* **•is•er**)
**de•po•liti•cize** (*or* **•cise**)
**de•pone** *Scot* testify
**de•po•nent** linguistics term; deposition maker
**de•popu•late**
**de•popu•la•tion**
**de•port**
**de•port•able**
**de•por•ta•tion**
**de•por•tee**
**de•port•ment**
**de•pos•able**
**de•pos•al**
**de•pose**
**de•pos•er**
**de•pos•it**
**de•posi•tary** (*plural* **•taries**) person; *compare* **depository**
**depo•si•tion**
**de•posi•tor**
**de•posi•tory** (*plural* **•tories**) warehouse; *compare* **depositary**
**de•pot**
**dep•ra•va•tion** corruption; *compare* **deprivation**
**de•prave**
**de•praved**
**de•praved•ness**
**de•prav•er**
**de•prav•ity** (*plural* **•ities**)
**dep•re•cate** protest against; *compare* **depreciate**
**dep•re•ca•tion**
**dep•re•ca•tive**
**dep•re•ca•tor**
**dep•re•ca•to•ri•ly**
**dep•re•ca•tory**
**de•pre•ciable**
**de•pre•ci•ate** lose value; *compare* **deprecate**
**de•pre•cia•tion**
**de•pre•cia•tor**
**de•pre•cia•tory** (*or* **•tive**)
**dep•re•date** plunder
**dep•re•da•tion**
**de•press**
**de•pres•sant**
**de•pressed**
**de•press•ible**
**de•press•ing**
**de•pres•sion**
**de•pres•sive**
**de•pres•so•mo•tor** physiology term
**de•pres•sor**
**de•pres•suri•za•tion** (*or* **•sa•tion**)
**de•pres•sur•ize**
**de•priv•able**
**dep•ri•va•tion** (*or* **de•priv•al**) loss; *compare* **depravation**
**de•prive**
**de•prived**
**de•priv•er**
**dep•side** chemistry term
**depth**
**depu•rate** purify
**depu•ra•tion**
**depu•ra•tive** purifying
**depu•ra•tor**
**depu•ta•tion**
**de•pute**
**depu•tize** (*or* **•tise**)
**depu•ty** (*plural* **•ties**)
**de•rac•in•ate** uproot
**de•raci•na•tion**
**de•rail**
**de•rail•leur** bicycle gear
**de•rail•ment**
**de•range**
**de•range•ment**
**de•ra•tion**
**Der•by**
**Der•by•shire**
**de•reg•is•ter**
**der•elict**
**der•elic•tion**
**de•re•strict**
**de•re•strict•ed**
**de•re•stric•tion**
**de•ride**
**de•rid•er**
**de ri•gueur**
**de•ris•ible**
**de•ri•sion**
**de•ri•sive** (*or* **•sory**)
**de•ri•sive•ness**
**de•riv•able**
**deri•va•tion**
**deri•va•tion•al**
**de•riva•tive**
**de•rive**
**de•riv•er**
**der•ma** skin
**der•mal**
**der•ma•ti•tis**
**der•mato•gen** plant tissue
**derma•to•glyph•ics** skin pattern
**der•ma•toid**
**der•ma•to•logi•cal**
**der•ma•tolo•gist**
**der•ma•tol•ogy**
**der•ma•tome** surgical instrument
**der•ma•tom•ic**
**der•ma•to•phyte** parasitic fungus
**der•ma•to•phyt•ic**
**der•ma•to•phy•to•sis**
**der•ma•to•plas•tic**
**der•ma•to•plas•ty** skin grafting
**der•ma•to•sis** (*plural* **•ses**) skin disease
**der•mic**
**der•mis** skin layer
**der•moid**
**dero•gate** disparage
**dero•gation**
**de•roga•tive**
**de•roga•to•ri•ly**
**de•roga•to•ri•ness**
**de•roga•tory**
**der•rick**
**der•rière** buttocks
**derring-do** bold action
**der•rin•ger** (*or* **der•in•ger**) pistol
**der•ris** plant
**Der•ry** Londonderry
**der•ry** *Austral* grudge
**derv** diesel oil
**der•vish**
**Der•went** river

**Derwent•water** lake
**de•sali•nate** (*or* **•nize, •nise**)
**de•sali•na•tion** (*or* **•ni•za•tion, •ni•sa•tion**)
**de•scale**
**des•cant**
**des•cant•er**
**de•scend**
**des•cend•able**
**de•scend•ant** (*noun*)
**de•scend•ent** (*adj*)
**de•scend•er**
**de•scend•ible** (*or* **•able**)
**de•scent**
**de•school**
**de•scrib•able**
**de•scribe**
**de•scrib•er**
**de•scri•er**
**de•scrip•tion**
**de•scrip•tive**
**de•scrip•ti•vism**
**de•scry** (**•scries, •scry•ing, •scried**)
**des•ecrate**
**des•ecra•tion**
**des•ecra•tor** (*or* **•ter**)
**de•seg•re•gate**
**de•seg•re•ga•tion**
**de•seg•re•ga•tion•ist**
**de•sen•si•ti•za•tion** (*or* **•sa•tion**)
**de•sen•si•tize** (*or* **•tise**)
**de•sen•si•tiz•er** (*or* **•tis•er**)
**des•ert** plantless region; *compare* **dessert**
**de•sert** abandon; merit; *compare* **dessert**
**de•sert•ed**
**de•sert•er**
**des•ert•ifi•ca•tion**
**de•ser•tion**
**de•serve**
**de•serv•ed•ly**
**de•serv•ed•ness**
**de•serv•er**
**de•serv•ing**
**de•sexu•ali•za•tion** (*or* **•sa•tion**)
**de•sexu•al•ize** (*or* **•ise**)
**des•ha•bille** *variant spelling of* **dishabille**
**des•ic•cant**
**des•ic•cate**
**des•ic•ca•ted**
**des•ic•ca•tion**
**des•ic•ca•tive**
**des•ic•ca•tor**
**de•sid•er•ate** long for
**de•sid•era•tion**
**de•sid•era•tive**
**de•sid•era•tum** (*plural* **•ta**) something wanted
**de•sign**
**de•sign•able**
**des•ig•nate**
**des•ig•na•tion**
**des•ig•na•tive** (*or* **•tory**)
**des•ig•na•tor**
**de•sign•ed•ly**
**de•sign•er**
**de•sign•ing**
**desi•nence** word ending
**desi•nent** (*or* **•nen•tial**)
**de•sir•abil•ity** (*or* **•sirable•ness**)
**de•sir•able**
**de•sire**
**de•sir•er**
**de•sir•ous**
**de•sist**
**de•sist•ance** (*or* **•ence**)
**desk**
**des•man** (*plural* **•mans**) animal
**des•mid** alga
**des•mid•ian**
**des•moid** tumour
**Des Moines** US city
**deso•late**
**deso•lat•er** (*or* **•or**)
**deso•la•tion**
**de•sorb** chemistry term
**de•sorp•tion**
**des•pair**
**des•patch** *variant spelling of* **dispatch**
**des•pe•ra•do** (*plural* **•does** *or* **•dos**)
**des•per•ate**
**des•pera•tion**
**des•pi•cabil•ity** (*or* **•cable•ness**)
**des•pic•able**
**des•pic•ably**
**des•pise**
**de•spis•er**
**de•spite**
**de•spoil**
**de•spoil•er**
**de•spoil•ment**
**de•spo•lia•tion**
**de•spond**
**de•spond•en•cy** (*or* **•ence**)
**de•spond•ent**
**des•pot**
**des•pot•ic** (*or* **•poti•cal**)
**des•poti•cal•ly**
**des•pot•ism**
**des•pu•mate** clarify
**des•pu•ma•tion**
**des•qua•mate**
**des•qua•ma•tion**
**Des•sau** German city
**des•sert** sweet; *compare* **desert**
**dessert•spoon**
**des•sia•tine** Russian unit
(dessicate) *incorrect spelling of* **desiccate**
**des•ti•na•tion**
**des•tine**
**des•tined**
**des•ti•ny** (*plural* **•nies**)
**des•ti•tute**
**des•ti•tu•tion**
**de•stroy**
**de•stroy•able**
**de•stroy•er**
**de•struct**
**de•struc•tibil•ity**
**de•struct•ible**
**de•struc•tion**
**de•struc•tion•ist**
**de•struc•tive**
**de•struc•tive•ness** (*or* **•tiv•ity**)
**de•struc•tor** furnace
**desue•tude** state of disuse
**des•ul•to•ri•ly**
**des•ul•to•ri•ness**
**des•ul•tory**
**de•tach**
**de•tach•abil•ity**
**de•tach•able**
**de•tached**
**de•tach•er**
**de•tach•ment**
**de•tail**
**de•tailed**
**de•tain**
**de•tain•able**
**de•tainee**
**de•tain•er**
**de•tain•ment**

**de•tect**
**de•tect•able** (*or* **•ible**)
**de•tec•tion**
**de•tec•tive**
**de•tec•tor**
**de•tent** locking device
**dé•tente** easement
**de•ten•tion**
**de•ter** (**•ter•ring, •terred**)
**de•terge** cleanse
**de•ter•gen•cy** (*or* **•gence**)
**de•ter•gent**
**de•terio•rate**
**de•terio•ra•tion**
**de•terio•ra•tive**
**de•ter•ment**
**de•ter•mi•nable**
**de•ter•mi•nant**
**de•ter•mi•nate**
**de•ter•mi•na•tion**
**de•ter•mi•na•tive**
**de•ter•mine**
**de•ter•mined**
**de•ter•mined•ly**
**de•ter•mined•ness**
**de•ter•min•er**
**de•ter•min•ism**
**de•ter•min•ist**
**de•ter•min•is•tic**
**de•ter•rence**
**de•ter•rent**
**de•ter•sive**
**de•test**
**de•test•abil•ity** (*or* **•able•ness**)
**de•test•able**
**de•tes•ta•tion**
**de•test•er**
**de•throne**
**de•throne•ment**
**de•thron•er**
**deti•nue** legal term
**Det•mold** German city
**deto•nate**
**deto•na•tion**
**deto•na•tive**
**deto•na•tor**
**de•tour**
**de•toxi•cant**
**de•toxi•cate**
**de•toxi•ca•tion**
**de•toxi•fi•ca•tion**
**de•toxi•fy** (**•fies, •fy•ing, •fied**)
**de•tract**
**de•trac•tion**
**de•trac•tive** (*or* **•tory**)
**de•trac•tor**
**de•train**
**de•train•ment**
**de•trib•ali•za•tion** (*or* **•sa•tion**)
**de•trib•al•ize** (*or* **•ise**)
**det•ri•ment**
**det•ri•men•tal**
**det•ri•men•tal•ly**
**de•tri•tal**
**de•tri•tion** wearing away
**de•tri•tus** debris
**De•troit** US city
**de trop** *French* superfluous
**de•trude** thrust out
**de•trun•cate**
**de•trun•ca•tion**
**de•tru•sion**
**de•tu•mes•cence**
**Deucalion** mythological character
**deuce**
**deu•ced**
**deus ex machi•na** *Latin* providential resolver
**deu•ter•ago•nist** drama term
**deu•tera•nope**
**deu•tera•no•pia** green blindness
**deu•ter•an•op•ic**
**deu•ter•ide** chemistry term
**deu•ter•ium** hydrogen isotope
**deu•tero•ca•noni•cal**
**deu•ter•oga•mist**
**deu•ter•oga•my**
**deu•ter•on** deuterium nucleus
**Deu•ter•ono•my** biblical book
**deu•to•plasm** (*or* **deu•tero•**) egg yolk
**deu•to•plas•mic** (*or* **•tic**)
**Deut•sche Mark**
**deut•zia** shrub
**Deux-Sèvres** French city
**deva** oriental god; *compare* **diva**
**de•valua•tion**
**de•value** (*or* **•valu•ate; •valu•ing, •val•ued** *or* **•at•ing, •ated**)
**De•va•na•ga•ri** Indian script
**dev•as•tate**
**dev•as•ta•tion**
**dev•as•ta•tive**
**dev•as•ta•tor**
**de•vel•op**
**de•vel•op•able**
**de•vel•op•er**
**de•vel•op•ment**
**de•vel•op•men•tal**
**de•vel•op•men•tal•ly**
**de•vi•ance**
**de•vi•ant**
**de•vi•ate**
**de•via•tion**
**de•via•tion•ism**
**de•via•tion•ist**
**de•via•tor**
**de•via•tory**
**de•vice** contrivance; plan; *compare* **devise**
**dev•il** (**•il•ling, •illed;** *US* **•il•ing, •iled**)
**devil•fish** (*plural* **•fish** *or* **•fishes**)
**dev•il•ish**
**dev•il•ish•ness**
**dev•il•ment**
**dev•il•ry** (*plural* **•ries**)
**de•vi•ous**
**de•vi•ous•ness**
**de•vis•able**
**de•vis•al** act of devising
**de•vise** to plan; leave by will; a gift by will; *compare* **device**
**de•vi•see** inheritor
**de•vis•er** (*or in legal contexts* **•vi•sor**) one who devises; *compare* **divisor**
**de•vi•tali•za•tion** (*or* **•sa•tion**)
**de•vi•tal•ize** (*or* **•ise**)
**de•vit•ri•fi•ca•tion**
**de•vit•ri•fy** (**•fies, •fy•ing, •fied**) chemistry term
**de•vo•cal•ize** (*or* **•ise**)
**de•voice** phonetics term
**de•void**
**de•voirs** (*plural*) *French* compliments
**de•vo•lu•tion**
**de•vo•lu•tion•ary**
**de•vo•lu•tion•ist**
**de•volve**

de•volve•ment
Dev•on
De•vo•nian
Dev•on•shire
de•vote
de•vot•ed
de•vot•ed•ness
devo•tee
de•vote•ment
de•vo•tion
de•vo•tion•al
de•vo•tion•al•ity (*or* •ness)
de•vour
de•vour•er
de•vour•ing•ly
de•vout
de•vout•ness
dew
de•wan Indian minister
dew•berry (*plural* •berries)
dew•claw
dew•drop
dewi•ly
dewi•ness
dew•lap
Dews•bury Yorkshire town
dewy (dewi•er, dew•iest)
dewy-eyed
Dex•edrine (*Trademark*)
dex•ter
dex•ter•ity
dex•ter•ous (*or* dex•trous)
dex•ter•ous•ness (*or* dex•trous•ness)
dex•tral
dex•tral•ity
dex•tral•ly
dex•tran biochemical compound
dex•trin (*or* •trine) adhesive gum
dextro•am•pheta•mine
dextro•glu•cose
dextro•gy•rate (*or* •gyre)
dextro•ro•ta•tion
dextro•ro•ta•tory (*or* dextro•ro•ta•ry)
dex•trorse (*or* •tror•sal) spiralling left to right
dex•trose form of glucose
dex•trous
dey Algerian ruler
Dhah•ran Saudi Arabian town
dhak tree
Dhaka (*or* Dac•ca) Bangladeshi capital
dhal vegetable
dhar•ma Hindu custom
dhar•na Indian sit-in
Dhau•la•gi•ri Nepalese mountain
dho•bi Indian washerman
dhole animal
dho•ti (*or* dhoo•ti, dhoo•tie, dhu•ti) loincloth
dhow boat
dia•base rock
dia•ba•sic
dia•be•tes
dia•bet•ic
dia•ble•rie devilry
dia•bol•ic
dia•boli•cal
dia•boli•cal•ly
dia•boli•cal•ness
diabo•lism
di•abo•list
di•abo•lize (*or* •lise)
di•abo•lo (*plural* •los) game
dia•caus•tic physics term
di•ac•etyl•mor•phine
dia•chron•ic linguistics term
di•acid
dia•cid•ic
di•aco•nal of a deacon
di•aco•nate
dia•crit•ic phonetic symbol
dia•criti•cal
di•ac•tin•ic physics term
di•ac•tin•ism
dia•del•phous botany term
dia•dem
di•ad•ro•mous fan-shaped
di•aer•esis *variant spelling of* dieresis
di•aeret•ic *variant spelling of* dieretic
dia•gen•esis chemistry term
dia•geo•trop•ic
dia•geot•ro•pism response to gravity
di•ag•nos•able
di•ag•nose
di•ag•no•sis (*plural* •ses)
di•ag•nos•tic
di•ag•nos•ti•cal•ly
di•ag•nos•ti•cian
di•ag•nos•tics
di•ago•nal
di•ago•nal•ly
dia•gram (•gram•ming, •grammed; *US* •gram•ing, •gramed)
dia•gram•mat•ic
dia•gram•mati•cal•ly
dia•graph drawing instrument
dia•ki•nesis biology term
dial (dial•ling, dialled; *US* dial•ing, dialed)
dia•lect
dia•lec•tal
dia•lec•tic
dia•lec•ti•cal
dia•lec•ti•cal•ly
dia•lec•tics branch of logic
dia•lec•to•logi•cal
dia•lec•tolo•gist
dia•lec•tol•ogy
di•al•lage mineral
dial•ler
di•alo•gism philosophy term
di•alo•gist
dia•lo•gis•tic (*or* •ti•cal)
di•alo•gize (*or* •gise)
dia•logue (*US also* •log)
dia•logu•er
dia•lys•abil•ity
dia•lys•able
dia•ly•sa•tion
dia•lyse (*US* •lyze)
dia•lys•er (*US* •lyz•)
di•aly•sis (*plural* •ses)
dia•lyt•ic
dia•lyti•cal•ly
dia•mag•net
dia•mag•net•ic
dia•mag•neti•cal•ly
dia•mag•net•ism
dia•man•té decorated with sequins
dia•man•tine of diamonds
di•am•eter
di•am•etral
dia•met•ric (*or* •ri•cal)
dia•met•ri•cal•ly
dia•mine chemistry term
dia•mond
diamond•back terrapin
di•an•drous botany term
dia•no•et•ic of thought

**dia•noia** philosophy term
**di•an•thus** (*plural* **•thuses**) plant
**dia•pa•son** organ stop
**dia•pa•son•al** (*or* **•son•ic**)
**dia•pause** suspended growth
**dia•pede•sis** medical term
**dia•pedet•ic**
**dia•per**
**di•apha•nous**
**di•apha•nous•ness** (*or* **•nei•ty**)
**dia•phone** linguistics term
**dia•phon•ic**
**di•apho•ny** musical term
**dia•pho•resis**
**dia•pho•ret•ic** causing perspiration
**dia•pho•to•trop•ic** biology term
**dia•photo•trop•ism**
**dia•phragm**
**dia•phrag•mat•ic**
**dia•phrag•mati•cal•ly**
**dia•phys•ial**
**di•aphy•sis** bone shaft
**dia•pir** geological fold
**di•apo•phys•ial**
**dia•pophy•sis** (*plural* **•ses**) anatomy term
**dia•posi•tive** positive transparency
**di•arch** botany term
**di•ar•chic** (*or* **di•ar•chi•cal, di•ar•chal, dy•**)
**di•ar•chy** (*or* **dy•**; *plural* **•chies**) two-state government
**dia•rist**
**di•ar•rhoea** (*US* **•rhea**)
**di•ar•rhoeal** (*or* **•rhoe•ic**; *US* **•rheal** *or* **•rhe•ic**)
**di•ar•thro•dial**
**di•ar•thro•sis** (*plural* **•ses**) movable joint
**dia•ry** (*plural* **•ries**)
**dia•scope** projector
**Di•as•po•ra** Jews' dispersion
**dia•spore** mineral
**dia•stal•sis** (*plural* **•ses**) physiology term
**dia•stal•tic**
**dia•stase** enzyme
**dia•sta•sic**
**dia•sta•sis** (*plural* **•ses**) separation
**dia•stat•ic**
**dia•ste•ma** (*plural* **•ma•ta**) fissure
**di•as•ter** biology term
**di•as•to•le** dilation of heart
**di•as•tol•ic**
**di•as•tral** biology term
**dia•stroph•ic**
**di•as•tro•phism** movement of earth's crust
**dia•style** architectural term
**dia•tes•sa•ron** musical term
**dia•ther•man•cy** (*plural* **•cies**) heat transmission
**dia•ther•man•ous**
**dia•ther•mic**
**dia•ther•my** (*or* **•mia**) medical term
**diath•esis** (*plural* **•eses**) susceptibility to disease
**dia•thet•ic**
**dia•tom** alga
**dia•to•ma•ceous**
**dia•tom•ic**
**di•ato•mic•ity**
**di•ato•mite** rock
**dia•ton•ic** musical term
**dia•toni•cal•ly**
**dia•toni•cism**
**dia•tribe**
**dia•trop•ic**
**di•at•ro•pism** biology term
**dia•zine** (*or* **•zin**) chemistry term
**di•azo** (*plural* **•azos** *or* **•azoes**) chemistry term
**dia•zole**
**di•azo•methane**
**dia•zo•nium**
**dia•zo•ti•za•tion** (*or* **•sa•tion**)
**dia•zo•tize** (*or* **•tise**)
**dib** (**dib•bing, dibbed**)
**di•ba•sic**
**di•ba•sic•ity**
**dib•ber**
**dib•ble** garden tool
**dib•bler**
**di•bran•chi•ate** zoology term
**di•bro•mide**
**di•car•box•yl•ic acid**
**dic•ast** Athenian juror
**dice**
**di•cen•tra** plant
**di•cepha•lism**
**di•cepha•lous** two-headed
**di•cer**
**dicey** (**dici•er, dici•est**)
**di•cha•sial**
**di•cha•sium** (*plural* **•sia**) botany term
**di•chla•myd•eous** botany term
**di•chlo•ride**
**di•chloro•di•fluoro-methane**
**di•chloro•di•phenyl•tri-chloro•ethane** DDT
**di•choga•mous** (*or* **•cho•gam•ic**)
**di•choga•my** botany term
**di•choto•mist**
**di•choto•mi•za•tion** (*or* **•sa•tion**)
**di•choto•mize** (*or* **•mise**)
**di•choto•mous** (*or* **•cho•tom•ic**)
**di•choto•my** (*plural* **•mies**)
**di•chro•ic** (*or* **di•chro•it•ic**)
**di•chro•ism** crystallography term
**di•chro•ite**
**di•chro•mate** chemistry term
**di•chro•mat•ic** having two colours
**di•chro•mati•cism** crystallography term
**di•chro•ma•tism**
**di•chro•mic** involving two colours
**di•chro•scope** (*or* **•chroi•scope, •chroo•scope**) optical instrument
**di•chro•scop•ic** (*or* **•chroi•scop•ic, •chroo•scop•ic**)
**dick•ens** slang term
**Dick•en•sian**
**dick•er** *US* barter
**dicky** (*or* **dick•ey**; *noun, plural* **dickies** *or* **dick•eys**; *adj* **dicki•er, dicki•est**)
**di•cli•nism**
**di•cli•nous** botany term
**di•cli•ny**

**di•coty•ledon** botany term
**di•coty•ledon•ous**
**di•crot•ic** (*or* **•cro•tal**) having a double pulse
**di•cro•tism**
**dic•ta** *plural of* **dictum**
**Dic•ta•phone** (*Trademark*)
**dic•tate**
**dic•ta•tion**
**dic•ta•tion•al**
**dic•ta•tor**
**dic•ta•tor•ial**
**dic•ta•tor•ial•ly**
**dic•ta•tor•ship**
**dic•ta•tress** (*or* **•trix**)
**dic•tion**
**dic•tion•ary** (*plural* **•aries**)
**Dic•to•graph** (*Trademark*)
**dic•tum** (*plural* **•tums** *or* **•ta**)
**di•cyno•dont** extinct reptile
**did**
**Dida•che** treatise
**di•dac•tic**
**di•dac•ti•cal•ly**
**di•dac•ti•cism**
**di•dac•tics** teaching
**did•dle**
**did•geri•doo** musical instrument
**didi•coy** (*or* **did•di•coy, dida•kai**; *plural* **•coys** *or* **•kais**) gypsy
**didn't**
**Dido** mythological character
**didst**
**di•dym•ium** chemistry term
**didy•mous** in pairs
**di•dyna•mous** botany term
**die** (*verb*; **dy•ing, died**) expire; *compare* **dye**
**die** (*noun*) tool; *Archaic* dice; *compare* **dye**
**die•back** tree disease
**die-cast** (**-casting, -cast**)
**di•ecious** *variant spelling* (*esp. US*) *of* **dioecious**
**die-hard**
**die-hardism**
**diel•drin** insecticide
**di•elec•tric**
**di•elec•tri•cal•ly**
**Dien Bien Phu** Vietnamese battle site
**di•en•cephal•ic**
**di•en•cepha•lon** brain part
**Di•eppe** French port
**di•er•esis** (*or* **•aer•**; *plural* **•eses**) phonetics symbol; *compare* **diuresis**
**di•eret•ic** (*or* **•aeret•**) of dieresis; *compare* **diuretic**
**die•sel**
**diesel-electric**
**diesel-hydrau•lic**
**di•esis** (*plural* **•eses**) printing term
**die•stock** tool
**di•estrus** *US spelling of* **dioestrus**
**diet**
**di•etary**
**di•et•er**
**di•etet•ic** (*or* **•eteti•cal**)
**di•eteti•cal•ly**
**di•etet•ics**
**di•ethyl•stil•boes•trol** (*US* **•bes•**)
**di•eti•tian** (*or* **•cian**)
**dif•fer**
**dif•fer•ence**
**dif•fer•ent**
**dif•fer•en•tia** (*plural* **•tiae**) logic term
**dif•fer•en•ti•abil•ity**
**dif•fer•en•ti•able**
**dif•fer•en•tial**
**dif•fer•en•ti•ate**
**dif•fer•en•tia•tion**
**dif•fer•en•tia•tor**
**dif•fi•cult**
**dif•fi•cul•ty** (*plural* **•ties**)
**dif•fi•dence**
**dif•fi•dent**
**dif•fract**
**dif•frac•tion**
**dif•frac•tive**
**dif•frac•tom•eter**
**dif•fuse**
**dif•fuse•ness**
**dif•fus•er** (*or* **•fu•sor**)
**dif•fus•ibil•ity** (*or* **•ible•ness**)
**dif•fus•ible**
**dif•fu•sion**
**dif•fu•sive**
**dif•fu•siv•ity**
**dig** (**dig•ging, dug**)
**diga•mist**
**di•gam•ma** obsolete Greek letter
**diga•mous**
**diga•my** (*plural* **•mies**) second marriage
**di•gas•tric** jaw muscle
**di•gen•esis** zoology term
**di•genet•ic**
**di•gest**
**di•gest•ant**
**di•gest•er**
**di•gest•ibil•ity** (*or* **•ible•ness**)
**di•gest•ible**
**di•ges•tif** *French* digestive drink
**di•ges•tion**
**di•ges•tion•al**
**di•ges•tive** (*or* **•tant**)
**dig•ger**
**dig•ging**
**dig•it**
**digi•tal**
**digi•tal•in** chemical compound
**digi•tal•is**
**digi•tal•ism**
**digi•tali•za•tion** (*or* **•sa•tion**)
**digi•tal•ize** (*or* **•ise**)
**digi•tal•ly**
**digi•tate** (*or* **•tat•ed**)
**digi•ta•tion**
**digi•ti•form**
**digi•ti•grade** walking on toes
**dig•iti•za•tion** (*or* **•sa•tion**)
**dig•it•ize** (*or* **•ise**)
**digi•tox•in** chemical compound
**digi•tron** electronics term
**di•glot** bilingual
**di•glot•tic**
**dig•ni•fy** (**•fies, •fy•ing, •fied**)
**dig•ni•tary** (*plural* **•taries**)
**dig•nity** (*plural* **•nities**)
**di•graph** two-letter sound
**di•graph•ic**
**di•gress**
**di•gress•er**
**di•gres•sion**
**di•gres•sion•al**
**di•gres•sive**
**di•he•dral**
**di•he•dron**
**di•hy•brid**

**di•hy•brid•ism**
**Di•jon** French city
**dik-dik** antelope
**dike** *variant spelling of* **dyke**
**dik•tat** decree
**di•lapi•date**
**di•lapi•da•ted**
**di•lapi•da•tion**
**di•lapi•da•tor**
**di•lat•abil•ity** (*or* **•able•ness**)
**di•lat•able**
**di•la•tan•cy** physics term
**di•la•tant**
**di•la•ta•tion**
**dila•ta•tion•al**
**di•late**
**di•la•tion**
**di•la•tive**
**dila•tom•eter**
**dila•to•met•ric**
**dila•to•met•ri•cal•ly**
**dila•tom•etry**
**di•la•tor** (*or* **•lat•er, di•la•ta•tor**)
**dila•to•ri•ness**
**di•la•tory**
**dil•do** (*or* **•doe**; *plural* **•dos** *or* **•does**) artificial penis
**di•lem•ma**
**dil•em•mat•ic** (*or* **dil•em•mic**)
**dil•et•tante** (*plural* **•tan•tes** *or* **•tan•ti**)
**dil•et•tan•tish** (*or* **•teish**)
**dil•et•tan•tism** (*or* **•teism**)
**dili•gence**
**dili•gent**
**dill**
**dil•ly** *Slang* remarkable person
**dilly-dally** (**-dallies, -dally•ing, -dallied**)
**dilu•ent**
**di•lute**
**di•lu•tee**
**di•lut•er**
**di•lu•tion**
**di•lu•vial** (*or* **•vian**)
**di•lu•vium** (*plural* **•via**) geology term
**dim** (*adj* **dim•mer, dim•mest**; *verb* **dim•ming, dimmed**)
**dime**
**di•men•hy•dri•nate** drug
**di•men•sion**
**di•men•sion•al**
**di•men•sion•al•ity**
**di•men•sion•less**
**di•mer** chemistry term
**di•mer•cap•rol** drug
**di•mer•ic**
**dim•er•ism**
**dim•er•ous** divided into two
**dim•eter** verse line
**di•methyl•sulph•ox•ide**
**di•met•ric** crystallography term
**di•midi•ate** halve; divided in halves
**di•midi•ation**
**di•min•ish**
**di•min•ish•able**
**di•min•ish•ment**
**di•minu•en•do** (*plural* **•dos**)
**dimi•nu•tion**
**di•minu•tive**
**dim•is•sory** permission to depart
**dim•ity** (*plural* **•ities**) fabric
**dim•ly**
**dimmed**
**dim•mer**
**dim•mest**
**dim•ming**
**dim•ness**
**di•morph**
**di•mor•phism**
**di•mor•phous** (*or* **•phic**) chemistry term
**dim•ple**
**dim•ply**
**dim•wit**
**dim-witted**
**dim-witted•ness**
**din** (**din•ning, dinned**)
**di•nar** currency
**dine**
**din•er**
**di•ner•ic** chemistry term
**di•nette**
**ding**
**ding•bat** *US* unnamed object
**ding•bats** *Austral* delirium tremens
**ding-dong**
**dinge**
**din•ghy** (*or* **•gy, •gey**; *plural* **•ghies, •gies,** *or* **•geys**)
**din•gi•ly**
**din•gi•ness**
**din•gle** dell
**din•go** (*plural* **•goes**)
**din•gy** (**•gi•er, •gi•est**)
**di•ni•tro•ben•zene**
**dink** *Scot* neat
**Din•ka** (*plural* **•kas** *or* **•ka**) Sudanese people
**din•kum**
**dinky** (**dinki•er, dinki•est**)
**dinned**
**din•ner**
**din•ning**
**di•noc•er•as** extinct mammal
**di•no•flag•el•late** unicellular organism
**di•no•saur**
**di•no•saur•ian**
**di•no•there** extinct mammal
**dint**
**di•oc•esan**
**dio•cese**
**di•ode**
**di•oecious** (*or esp. US* **•ecious, •oicious**) botany term
**di•oestrus** (*US* **•estrus**) biology term
**Diomedes** mythological king
**Dio•ny•sia** ancient Greek festivals
**Dio•nysi•ac**
**Dio•ny•sian**
**Dionysus** Greek god
**di•op•side** mineral
**di•op•tase** mineral
**di•op•tom•eter**
**di•op•tom•etry**
**di•op•tral**
**di•op•tre** (*US* **•ter**) unit
**di•op•tric** (*or* **•tri•cal**)
**di•op•tri•cal•ly**
**di•op•trics**
**dio•ra•ma** display
**dio•ram•ic**
**dio•rite** rock
**dio•rit•ic**
**di•ox•an** (*or* **•ane**) chemical compound

**di•ox•ide**
**dip (dip•ping, dipped)**
**di•pep•tide**
**di•pet•al•ous** having two petals
**di•phase** (*or* **•phas•ic)** physics term
**di•phenyl** biphenyl
**di•phenyl•amine**
**di•phos•gene**
**diph•theria**
**diph•therial** (*or* **•therit•ic, •ther•ic)**
**diph•theroid**
**diph•thong**
**diph•thon•gal**
**diph•thongi•za•tion** (*or* **•sa•tion)**
**diph•thong•ize** (*or* **•ise)**
**di•phy•cer•cal** zoology term
**di•phy•let•ic** descent from two ancestors
**di•phyl•lous** having two leaves
**diphy•odont** dentition
**di•plegia** paralysis
**di•plegic**
**di•plex** electronics term
**di•plex•er**
**dip•lo•blas•tic** zoology term
**dip•lo•car•di•ac** zoology term
**dip•lo•coc•cal** (*or* **•cic)**
**dip•lo•coc•cus** (*plural* **•coc•ci)** bacterium
**dip•lo•do•cus** (*plural* **•cuses)** dinosaur
**dip•loë** bone
**dip•loid** biology term
**dip•loi•dic**
**dip•loidy**
**di•plo•ma**
**di•plo•ma•cy** (*plural* **•cies)**
**dip•lo•mat**
**dip•lo•mate**
**dip•lo•mat•ic** (*or* **•mati•cal)**
**dip•lo•mati•cal•ly**
**dip•lo•mat•ics** study of historical documents
**di•plo•ma•tist**
**dip•lont** biology term
**di•plo•pia** double vision
**di•plop•ic**
**dip•lo•pod** invertebrate
**di•plo•sis** biology term
**dip•lo•ste•mo•nous** botany term
**dip•lo•tene** genetics term
**dip•noan** lungfish
**dipo•dy** (*plural* **•dies)** metrical unit
**di•po•lar**
**di•pole** physics term
**dipped**
**dip•per**
**dip•ping**
**dip•py** *Slang* crazy
**di•pro•pel•lant**
**di•proto•dont** marsupial
**dip•so•ma•nia**
**dip•so•ma•ni•ac**
**dip•so•ma•nia•cal**
**dip•stick**
**dip•ter•al** architectural term
**dip•ter•an** (*or* **•on)** two-winged insect
**dip•tero•car•pa•ceous** botany term
**dip•ter•ous** two-winged
**(diptheria)** *incorrect spelling of* **diphtheria**
**(dipthong)** *incorrect spelling of* **diphthong**
**dip•tych**
**dire**
**di•rect**
**di•rec•tion**
**di•rec•tion•al**
**di•rec•tion•al•ity**
**di•rec•tion•al•ly**
**di•rec•tive**
**di•rect•ly**
**di•rect•ness**
**Di•rec•toire** French Revolutionary government
**di•rec•tor**
**di•rec•to•rate**
**di•rec•to•rial**
**di•rec•tor•ship**
**di•rec•tory** (*plural* **•tories)**
**di•rec•tress**
**di•rect•rix** (*plural* **•rixes** *or* **•rices)** geometry term
**dire•ful**
**dirge**
**dir•ham** Moroccan currency
**diri•gibil•ity**
**di•rig•ible** steerable
**di•ri•ment** invalidating
**dirk**
**dirndl** dress or skirt
**dirt**
**dirti•ly**
**dirti•ness**
**dirty** (*adj* **dirti•er, dirti•est;** *verb* **dirties, dirty•ing, dirt•ied)**
**Dis** Roman god
**dis•abil•ity** (*plural* **•ities)**
**dis•able**
**dis•able•ment**
**dis•abus•al**
**dis•abuse**
**di•sac•cha•ride** (*or* **•rid)**
**dis•ac•cord**
**dis•ac•cred•it**
**dis•ac•cus•tom**
**dis•ad•vant•age**
**dis•ad•van•taged**
**dis•ad•van•ta•geous**
**dis•af•fect**
**dis•af•fect•ed•ly**
**dis•af•fec•tion**
**dis•af•fili•ate**
**dis•af•fili•ation**
**dis•af•firm**
**dis•af•fir•mance** (*or* **•ma•tion)**
**dis•af•for•est** legal term
**dis•af•for•es•ta•tion** (*or* **dis•af•for•est•ment)**
**dis•agree (•agree•ing, •agreed)**
**dis•agree•able**
**dis•agree•able•ness** (*or* **•abil•ity)**
**dis•agree•ably**
**dis•agree•ment**
**dis•al•low**
**dis•al•low•able**
**dis•al•low•ance**
**dis•am•bigu•ate**
**dis•an•nul (•nul•ling, •nulled)**
**dis•an•nul•ment**
**dis•ap•pear**
**dis•ap•pear•ance**
**dis•ap•point**
**dis•ap•point•ed**
**dis•ap•point•er**
**dis•ap•point•ing**
**dis•ap•point•ment**
**dis•ap•pro•ba•tion**
**dis•ap•prov•al**
**dis•ap•prove**

**dis•ap•prov•er**
**dis•arm**
**dis•arma•ment**
**dis•arm•er**
**dis•arm•ing**
**dis•ar•range**
**dis•ar•range•ment**
**dis•ar•ray**
**dis•ar•ticu•late**
**dis•ar•ticu•la•tion**
**dis•ar•ticu•la•tor**
**dis•as•sem•ble**
**dis•as•sem•bly**
**dis•as•so•ci•ate**
**dis•as•so•cia•tion**
**dis•as•ter**
**dis•as•trous**
**dis•avow**
**dis•avow•al**
**dis•avow•ed•ly**
**dis•avow•er**
**dis•band**
**dis•band•ment**
**dis•bar** (**•bar•ring, •barred**)
**dis•bar•ment**
**dis•be•lief**
**dis•be•lieve**
**dis•be•liev•er**
**dis•be•liev•ing•ly**
**dis•branch**
**dis•bud** (**•bud•ding, •bud•ded**)
**dis•bur•den**
**dis•bur•den•ment**
**dis•burs•able**
**dis•burse**
**dis•burse•ment** (*or* **•burs•al**)
**dis•burs•er**
**disc** (*US* **disk**) circular plate; record; *compare* **disk**
**dis•calced** barefooted
**dis•card**
**dis•card•er**
**dis•cern**
**dis•cern•er**
**dis•cern•ible** (*or* **•able**)
**dis•cern•ing**
**dis•cern•ment**
**dis•charge**
**dis•charge•able**
**dis•charg•er**
**dis•ci•ple**
**dis•ci•ple•ship**
**dis•ci•plin•able**
**dis•ci•pli•nal**
**dis•ci•pli•nant** member of Catholic sect
**dis•ci•pli•nar•ian**
**dis•ci•pli•nary**
**dis•ci•pline**
**dis•ci•plin•er**
**dis•cipu•lar** of disciples
**dis•claim**
**dis•claim•er**
**dis•cla•ma•tion**
**dis•cli•max** ecology term
**dis•close**
**dis•clos•er**
**dis•clo•sure**
**dis•co** (*plural* **•cos**)
**dis•cobo•lus** (*or* **•los**; *plural* **•li**) discus thrower
**dis•cog•ra•pher**
**dis•cog•ra•phy** (*plural* **•phies**) record catalogue
**dis•coid**
**dis•coi•dal**
**dis•col•ora•tion**
**dis•col•our** (*US* **•or**)
**dis•col•our•ment** (*US* **•or•**)
**dis•com•bobu•late** confuse
**dis•com•fit** disconcert
**dis•com•fit•er**
**dis•com•fi•ture**
**dis•com•fort**
**dis•com•mend**
**dis•com•mode**
**dis•com•mo•di•ous**
**dis•com•mod•ity** (*plural* **•ities**) economics term
**dis•com•mon** legal term
**dis•com•pose**
**dis•com•pos•ed•ly**
**dis•com•pos•ing•ly**
**dis•com•po•sure**
**dis•con•cert**
**dis•con•cert•ed**
**dis•con•cert•ing•ly**
**dis•con•cer•tion** (*or* **•cert•ment**)
**dis•con•form•ity** (*plural* **•ities**)
**dis•con•nect**
**dis•con•nect•ed**
**dis•con•nect•er**
**dis•con•nec•tion** (*or* **•nex•ion**)
**dis•con•nec•tive**
**dis•con•so•late**
**dis•con•so•la•tion** (*or* **•late•ness**)
**dis•con•tent**
**dis•con•tent•ed**
**dis•con•tent•ed•ness**
**dis•con•tent•ment**
**dis•con•tinu•ance**
**dis•con•tinua•tion**
**dis•con•tinue** (**•tinu•ing, •tinued**)
**dis•con•ti•nu•ity** (*plural* **•ities**)
**dis•con•tinu•ous**
**dis•co•phile** (*or* **•phil**) record collector
**dis•cord**
**dis•cord•ance** (*or* **•an•cy**)
**dis•cord•ant**
**dis•co•theque**
**dis•count**
**dis•count•able**
**dis•coun•tenance**
**dis•count•er**
**dis•cour•age**
**dis•cour•age•ment**
**dis•cour•ag•er**
**dis•cour•ag•ing•ly**
**dis•course**
**dis•cours•er**
**dis•cour•teous**
**dis•cour•tesy** (*plural* **•tesies**)
**dis•cov•er**
**dis•cov•er•able**
**dis•cov•er•er**
**dis•cov•ert** legal term
**dis•cov•er•ture**
**dis•cov•ery** (*plural* **•eries**)
**dis•cred•it**
**dis•cred•it•able**
**dis•cred•it•ably**
**dis•creet** tactful; *compare* discrete
**dis•creet•ness**
**dis•crep•an•cy** (*plural* **•cies**)
**dis•crep•ant**
**dis•crete** distinct; separate; *compare* **discreet**
**dis•crete•ness**
**dis•cre•tion**
**dis•cre•tion•ari•ly** (*or* **•tion•al•ly**)
**dis•cre•tion•ary** (*or* **•al**)
**dis•cri•mi•nant**
**dis•crimi•nate**
**dis•crimi•nat•ing**

**dis•crimi•na•tion**
**dis•crimi•na•tion•al**
**dis•crimi•na•tor**
**dis•crimi•na•to•ri•ly** (*or* **dis•crimi•na•tive•ly**)
**dis•crimi•na•tory** (*or* **•tive**)
**dis•cur•sive**
**dis•cus** (*plural* **•cuses** *or* **•ci**) disc
**dis•cuss** debate
**dis•cus•sant** (*or* **•cuss•er**)
**dis•cuss•ible** (*or* **•able**)
**dis•cus•sion**
**dis•cus•sion•al**
**dis•dain**
**dis•dain•ful**
**dis•dain•ful•ly**
**dis•ease**
**dis•eased**
**dis•em•bark**
**dis•em•bar•ka•tion** (*or* **•bark•ment**)
**dis•em•bar•rass**
**dis•em•bar•rass•ment**
**dis•em•bod•ied**
**dis•em•bodi•ment**
**dis•em•body** (**•bodies, •body•ing, •bod•ied**)
**dis•em•bogue** (**•bogu•ing, •bogued**) discharge
**dis•em•bogue•ment**
**dis•em•bow•el** (**•el•ling, •elled;** *US* **•el•ing, •eled**)
**dis•em•bow•el•ment**
**dis•em•broil**
**dis•en•able**
**dis•en•able•ment**
**dis•en•chant**
**dis•en•chant•er**
**dis•en•chant•ment**
**dis•en•cum•ber**
**dis•en•cum•ber•ment**
**dis•en•dow**
**dis•en•dow•er**
**dis•en•dow•ment**
**dis•en•fran•chise**
**dis•en•fran•chise•ment**
**dis•en•gage**
**dis•en•gage•ment**
**dis•en•tail**
**dis•en•tail•ment**
**dis•en•tan•gle**
**dis•en•tan•gle•ment**
**dis•en•thral** (*or* **•thrall; •thral•ling, •thralled**)
**dis•en•thral•ment** (*or* **•thrall•**)
**dis•en•ti•tle**
**dis•en•tomb**
**dis•en•twine**
**di•sepa•lous** botany term
**dis•equi•lib•rium**
**dis•es•tab•lish**
**dis•es•tab•lish•ment**
**dis•es•teem**
**di•seur** (*fem* **•seuse**) *French* monologue performer
**dis•fa•vour** (*US* **•vor**)
**dis•fea•ture**
**dis•fea•ture•ment**
**dis•fig•ure**
**dis•fig•ure•ment** (*or* **•ura•tion**)
**dis•fig•ur•er**
**dis•fran•chise**
**dis•fran•chise•ment**
**dis•gorge**
**dis•gorge•ment**
**dis•gorg•er**
**dis•grace**
**dis•grace•ful**
**dis•grace•ful•ly**
**dis•grac•er**
**dis•grun•tle**
**dis•grun•tled**
**dis•grun•tle•ment**
**dis•guis•able**
**dis•guise**
**dis•guis•er**
**dis•gust**
**dis•gust•ed•ly**
**dis•gust•ing**
**dish**
**dis•ha•bille** (*or* **des•**) half-dressed
**dis•har•mo•ni•ous**
**dis•har•mo•ny** (*plural* **•nies**)
**dish•cloth**
**dis•heart•en**
**dis•heart•en•ment**
**dished**
**di•shev•el** (**•el•ling, •elled;** *US* **•el•ing, •eled**)
**di•shev•el•ment**
**dis•hon•est**
**dis•hon•es•ty** (*plural* **•ties**)
**dis•hon•our** (*US* **•or**)
**dis•hon•our•able** (*US* **•or•**)
**dis•hon•our•ably** (*US* **•or•**)
**dis•hon•our•er** (*US* **•or•**)
**dish•washer**
**dish•water**
**dishy** (**dishi•er, dishi•est**)
**dis•il•lu•sion**
**dis•il•lu•sion•ment**
**dis•il•lu•sive**
**dis•in•cen•tive**
**dis•in•cli•na•tion**
**dis•in•cline**
**dis•in•fect**
**dis•in•fect•ant**
**dis•in•fec•tion**
**dis•in•fec•tor**
**dis•in•fest**
**dis•in•fes•ta•tion**
**dis•in•fla•tion**
**dis•in•genu•ous**
**dis•in•genu•ous•ness**
**dis•in•her•it**
**dis•in•heri•tance**
**dis•in•te•grable**
**dis•in•te•grate**
**dis•in•te•gra•tion**
**dis•in•te•gra•tive**
**dis•in•te•gra•tor**
**dis•in•ter** (**•ter•ring, •terred**)
**dis•in•ter•est**
**dis•in•ter•est•ed** impartial; *compare* **uninterested**
**dis•in•ter•ment**
**dis•ject** break apart
**dis•join** separate
**dis•join•able**
**dis•joint** dislocate
**dis•joint•ed**
**dis•junct**
**dis•junc•tion** (*or* **•ture**)
**dis•junc•tive**
**disk** computer device; *US spelling of* **disc**
**dis•lik•able** (*or* **•like•**)
**dis•like**
**dis•limn** efface
**dis•lo•cate**
**dis•lo•ca•tion**
**dis•lodge**
**dis•lodg•ment** (*or* **•lodge•**)
**dis•loy•al**
**dis•loy•al•ty** (*plural* **•ties**)
**dis•mal**
**dis•mal•ly**
**dis•mal•ness**
**dis•man•tle**
**dis•man•tle•ment**
**dis•man•tler**

**dis•mast**
**dis•mast•ment**
**dis•may**
**dis•mem•ber**
**dis•mem•ber•er**
**dis•mem•ber•ment**
**dis•miss**
**dis•mis•sal**
**dis•miss•ible**
**dis•miss•ive**
**dis•mount**
**dis•mount•able**
**Dis•ney•land**
**dis•obedi•ence**
**dis•obedi•ent**
**dis•obey**
**dis•obey•er**
**dis•oblige**
**dis•oblig•ing**
**dis•op•era•tion** ecology term
**dis•or•der**
**dis•or•der•li•ness**
**dis•or•der•ly**
**dis•or•gani•za•tion** (*or* **•sa•tion)**
**dis•or•gan•ize** (*or* **•ise)**
**dis•or•gan•iz•er** (*or* **•is•er)**
**dis•ori•en•tate** (*or* **dis•ori•ent)**
**dis•ori•en•ta•tion**
**dis•own**
**dis•own•er**
**dis•own•ment**
**dis•par•age**
**dis•par•age•ment**
**dis•par•ag•er**
**dis•par•ate**
**dis•par•ity** (*plural* **•ities)**
**dis•pas•sion** detachment
**dis•pas•sion•ate**
**dis•pas•sion•ate•ness**
**dis•patch** (*or* **des•)**
**dis•patcher** (*or* **des•)**
**dis•pel** (**•pel•ling, •pelled)**
**dis•pel•ler**
**dis•pen•sabil•ity** (*or* **•sable•ness)**
**dis•pen•sable**
**dis•pen•sa•ry** (*plural* **•ries)**
**dis•pen•sa•tion**
**dis•pen•sa•tion•al**
**dis•pen•sa•tory** (*plural* **•tories)** drug catalogue
**dis•pense**
**dis•pens•er**
**di•sper•mous** botany term
**dis•per•sal**
**dis•per•sant**
**dis•perse**
**dis•pers•er**
**dis•per•sion**
**dis•per•sive**
**dis•per•soid** chemistry term
**dis•pir•it**
**dis•pir•it•ed**
**dis•pir•it•ing**
**dis•place**
**dis•place•able**
**dis•place•ment**
**dis•plac•er**
**dis•play**
**dis•play•er**
**dis•please**
**dis•pleas•ure**
**dis•port**
**dis•pos•abil•ity** (*or* **•able•ness)**
**dis•pos•able**
**dis•pos•al**
**dis•pose**
**dis•posed**
**dis•pos•er**
**dis•po•si•tion**
**dis•po•si•tion•al**
**dis•pos•sess**
**dis•pos•ses•sion**
**dis•pos•ses•sor**
**dis•pos•ses•so•ry**
**dis•praise**
**dis•prais•er**
**dis•proof**
**dis•pro•por•tion**
**dis•pro•por•tion•able**
**dis•pro•por•tion•ate**
**dis•pro•por•tiona•tion**
**dis•prov•able**
**dis•prov•al**
**dis•prove**
**dis•put•abil•ity** (*or* **•able•ness)**
**dis•put•able**
**dis•put•ably**
**dis•pu•tant**
**dis•pu•ta•tion**
**dis•pu•ta•tious** (*or* **•tive)**
**dis•pute**
**dis•put•er**
**dis•quali•fi•able**
**dis•quali•fi•ca•tion**
**dis•quali•fi•er**
**dis•quali•fy** (**•fies, •fy•ing, •fied)**
**dis•qui•et**
**dis•qui•et•ed•ly** (*or* **dis•qui•et•ly)**
**dis•qui•et•ed•ness** (*or* **dis•qui•et•ness)**
**dis•qui•et•ing**
**dis•qui•etude**
**dis•qui•si•tion** formal discourse
**dis•rate** reduce to lower rank
**dis•re•gard**
**dis•re•gard•er**
**dis•re•gard•ful**
**dis•rel•ish**
**dis•re•pair**
**dis•repu•tabil•ity** (*or* **•table•ness)**
**dis•repu•table**
**dis•repu•tably**
**dis•re•pute**
**dis•re•spect**
**dis•re•spect•abil•ity**
**dis•re•spect•able**
**dis•re•spect•ful**
**dis•re•spect•ful•ly**
**dis•robe**
**dis•robe•ment**
**dis•rob•er**
**dis•rupt**
**dis•rupt•er** (*or* **•rup•tor)**
**dis•rup•tion**
**dis•rup•tive**
**dis•sat•is•fac•tion**
**dis•sat•is•fac•tory**
**dis•sat•is•fy** (**•fies, •fy•ing, •fied)**
**dis•sect**
**dis•sec•tible**
**dis•sec•tion**
**dis•sec•tor**
**dis•seise** (*or* **•seize)** legal term
**dis•sei•sin** (*or* **•zin)**
**dis•sei•sor** (*or* **•zor)**
**dis•sem•blance**
**dis•sem•ble**
**dis•sem•bler**
**dis•semi•nate**
**dis•semi•na•tion**
**dis•semi•na•tive**
**dis•semi•na•tor**

**dis•semi•nule** botany term
**dis•sen•sion**
**dis•sent**
**dis•sent•er**
**dis•sen•tience** (*or* **•tien•cy**)
**dis•sen•tient** dissenting
**dis•sen•tious** argumentative
**dis•sepi•ment** dividing membrane
**dis•sepi•men•tal**
**dis•ser•tate**
**dis•ser•ta•tion**
**dis•ser•ta•tion•al**
**dis•ser•ta•tion•ist**
**dis•ser•vice**
**dis•ser•vice•able**
**dis•sev•er** break off
**dis•sev•er•ance** (*or* **•er•ment, •era•tion**)
**dis•si•dence**
**dis•si•dent**
**dis•simi•lar**
**dis•simi•lar•ity** (*plural* **•ities**)
**dis•simi•late** phonetics term; *compare* **dissimulate**
**dis•simi•la•tion**
**dis•simi•la•tive**
**dis•simi•la•tory**
**dis•si•mili•tude**
**dis•simu•late** pretend; *compare* **dissimilate**
**dis•simu•la•tion**
**dis•simu•la•tive**
**dis•simu•la•tor**
**dis•si•pate**
**dis•si•pat•ed**
**dis•si•pat•er** (*or* **•pa•tor**)
**dis•si•pa•tion**
**dis•si•pa•tive**
**dis•so•ci•abil•ity** (*or* **•able•ness**)
**dis•so•ci•able**
**dis•so•ci•ate**
**dis•so•cia•tion**
**dis•so•cia•tive**
**dis•sol•ubil•ity** (*or* **•uble•ness**)
**dis•sol•uble**
**dis•so•lute**
**dis•so•lute•ness**
**dis•so•lu•tion**
**dis•so•lu•tive**
**dis•solv•abil•ity** (*or* **•able•ness**)
**dis•solv•able**
**dis•solve**
**dis•sol•vent**
**dis•solv•er**
**dis•so•nance** (*or* **•nan•cy**)
**dis•so•nant**
**dis•suad•able**
**dis•suade**
**dis•suad•er**
**dis•sua•sion**
**dis•sua•sive**
**dis•sua•sive•ness**
**dis•syl•lab•ic** (*or* **di•syl•**)
**dis•syl•la•ble** (*or* **di•syl•**)
**dis•sym•met•ric** (*or* **•ri•cal**)
**dis•sym•me•try** (*plural* **•tries**)
**dis•taff**
**dis•tal** anatomy term
**dis•tal•ly**
**dis•tance**
**dis•tant**
**dis•taste**
**dis•taste•ful**
**dis•taste•ful•ly**
**dis•tem•per**
**dis•tend**
**dis•tend•er**
**dis•ten•si•bil•ity**
**dis•ten•sible**
**dis•ten•sion** (*or* **•tion**)
**dis•tich** poem
**dis•ti•chal**
**dis•ti•chous** in two rows
**dis•til** (*US* **dis•till; •til•ling, •tilled**)
**dis•till•able**
**dis•til•late**
**dis•til•la•tion** (*or* **dis•till•ment**)
**dis•til•la•tory**
**dis•till•er**
**dis•till•ery** (*plural* **•eries**)
**dis•tinct**
**dis•tinc•tion**
**dis•tinc•tive**
**dis•tinc•tive•ness**
**dis•tinct•ness**
**dis•tin•gué** (*fem* **•guée**) *French* distinguished
**dis•tin•guish**
**dis•tin•guish•able**
**dis•tin•guish•ably**
**dis•tin•guished**
**dis•tin•guish•er**
**dis•tort**
**dis•tort•ed**
**dis•tort•er**
**dis•tor•tion**
**dis•tor•tion•al**
**dis•tor•tive**
**dis•tract**
**dis•tract•ed**
**dis•tract•er**
**dis•tract•ibil•ity**
**dis•tract•ible**
**dis•trac•ting**
**dis•trac•tion**
**dis•trac•tive**
**dis•train**
**dis•train•able**
**dis•trainee** legal term
**dis•train•ment**
**dis•trai•nor** (*or* **•train•er**)
**dis•traint** legal term
**dis•trait** absent-minded
**dis•traught**
**dis•tress**
**dis•tressed**
**dis•tress•ful**
**dis•tress•ful•ly**
**dis•tress•ing**
**dis•trib•ut•able**
**dis•tribu•tary** (*plural* **•taries**) stream
**dis•trib•ute**
**dis•tribu•tee** legal term
**dis•tri•bu•tion**
**dis•tri•bu•tion•al**
**dis•tribu•tive**
**dis•tribu•tor** (*or* **•tribut•er**)
**dis•trict**
**dis•trin•gas** legal term
**dis•trust**
**dis•trust•er**
**dis•trust•ful**
**dis•trust•ful•ly**
**dis•turb**
**dis•turb•ance**
**dis•turbed**
**dis•turb•er**
**di•sul•fi•ram** drug
**di•sul•phate** (*US* **•fate**)
**di•sul•phide** (*US* **•fide**)
**di•sul•phu•ric** (*US* **•fu•**)
**dis•un•ion**
**dis•unite**
**dis•unity** (*plural* **•unities**)
**dis•use**
**dis•used**
**dis•util•ity**

**dit** Morse code sound
**dita** shrub
**ditch**
**ditch•er**
**di•theism**
**di•theist**
**di•theis•tic**
**dith•er**
**dith•er•er**
**di•thio•nite** chemical compound
**dithy•ramb** ancient Greek hymn
**dithy•ram•bic**
**dithy•ram•bi•cal•ly**
**dit•tan•der** plant
**dit•ta•ny** (*plural* **•nies**) plant
**dit•to** (*noun, plural* **•tos**; *verb* **•tos, •to•ing, •toed**)
**dit•to•graph•ic**
**dit•tog•ra•phy** (*plural* **•phies**) repetition
**dit•ty** (*plural* **•ties**)
**di•uresis** increased urination; *compare* **dieresis**
**di•uret•ic** increasing urination; *compare* **dieretic**
**di•ureti•cal•ly**
**di•ur•nal** of the day
**di•ur•nal•ly**
**div** *Slang* stupid person
**diva** (*plural* **divas** *or* **dive**) prima donna; *compare* **deva**
**di•va•lency**
**di•va•lent**
**di•van**
**di•vari•cate** branching
**di•vari•ca•tion**
**di•vari•ca•tor** zoology term
**dive** (**div•ing, dived** (*US* **dove**))
**dive-bomb**
**div•er**
**di•verge**
**di•ver•gence** (*or* **•gen•cy**; *plural* **•gences** *or* **•cies**)
**di•ver•gent**
**di•vers** *Archaic* several
**di•verse** varied
**di•ver•si•fi•abil•ity**
**di•ver•si•fi•able**
**di•ver•si•fi•ca•tion**
**di•ver•si•fi•er**
**di•ver•si•form**
**di•ver•si•fy** (**•fies, •fy•ing, •fied**)
**di•ver•sion**
**di•ver•sion•al** (*or* **•ary**)
**di•ver•sity**
**di•vert**
**di•vert•ed•ly**
**di•vert•er**
**di•vert•ible**
**di•ver•ticu•lar**
**di•ver•ticu•li•tis**
**di•ver•ticu•lo•sis**
**di•ver•ticu•lum** (*plural* **•la**) anatomical pouch
**di•ver•ti•men•to** (*plural* **•ti**) musical work
**di•vert•ing•ly**
**di•ver•tisse•ment** brief entertainment
**di•ver•tive**
**Dives** biblical character
**di•vest**
**di•vest•ible**
**di•vesti•ture** (*or* **•ves•ture, •vest•ment**)
**di•vid•able**
**di•vide**
**divi•dend**
**di•vid•er**
**di•vid•ers** measuring compass
**divi-divi** (*plural* **-divis** *or* **-divi**) tree
**di•vin•able**
**divi•na•tion**
**di•vina•tory**
**di•vine**
**di•vin•er**
**div•ing**
**di•vin•ing**
**di•vin•ity** (*plural* **•ities**)
**divi•ni•za•tion** (*or* **•sa•tion**)
**divi•nize** (*or* **•nise**) deify
**di•vis•ibil•ity**
**di•vi•sible**
**di•vi•sion**
**di•vi•sion•al** (*or* **•ary**)
**di•vi•sion•ism**
**di•vi•sion•ist**
**di•vi•sive**
**di•vi•sor** maths term; *compare* **deviser**
**di•vorce**
**di•vor•cé** (*fem* **•cée**) divorced person
**di•vorce•able**
**di•vorce•ment**
**di•vorc•er**
**di•vor•cive**
**div•ot** turf
**di•vulge**
**di•vul•gence** (*or* **•vulge•ment**)
**di•vulg•er**
**di•vul•sion** tearing apart
**di•vul•sive**
**div•vy** (*plural* **•vies**) *Slang* dividend
**Dixie** southern states of USA
**dixie** metal pot
**Dixie•land** jazz
**Di•yar•ba•kir** (*or* **•bekir**) Turkish city
**diz•zi•ly**
**diz•zi•ness**
**diz•zy** (*adj* **•zi•er, •zi•est**; *verb* **•zies, •zy•ing, •zied**)
**Dja•ja** *variant spelling of* **Jaya**
**Dja•ja•pu•ra** *variant spelling of* **Jajapura**
**Dja•kar•ta** (*or* **Ja•**) *variant spelling of* **Jakarta**
**Djam•bi** (*or* **Jam•**) *variant spelling of* **Jambi**
**Djer•ba** Tunisian island
**Dji•bou•ti** (*or* **Ji•**) African republic
**djin•ni** (*or* **•ny**) *variant spellings of* **jinni**
**Djok•ja•kar•ta** *variant spelling of* **Jogjakarta**
**Dne•pro•dzer•zhinsk** Ukrainian city
**Dne•pro•pe•trovsk** Ukrainian city
**Dnie•per** (*or* **Dnepr**) E European river
**Dnie•ster** (*or* **Dnestr**) E European river
**do** (*verb* **does, do•ing, did, done**; *noun, plural* **dos** *or* **do's**)
**doab** land between rivers
**do•able**
**dob•bin**
**dob•by** (*plural* **•bies**) loom attachment
**Do•ber•man pin•scher** dog
**do•bla** coin

**Do•bro** (*Trademark; plural* **•bros**) guitar
**Do•bru•ja** E European region
**dobson•fly** (*plural* **•flies**)
**doc** *Slang* doctor
**do•cent** US lecturer
**do•cent•ship**
**Do•cetism** heresy
**doc•ile**
**do•cil•ity**
**dock**
**dock•age** dock charge
**dock•er**
**dock•et**
**dock•land**
**dock•yard**
**doc•tor**
**doc•tor•al** (*or* **•to•rial**)
**doc•tor•ate**
**doc•tri•naire**
**doc•tri•nair•ism** (*or* **•nar•ism**)
**doc•tri•nal**
**doc•tri•nal•ity**
**doc•tri•nar•ian**
**doc•trine**
**doc•trin•ism**
**docu•ment**
**docu•men•ta•ri•ly**
**docu•men•tary** (*plural* **•taries**)
**docu•men•ta•tion**
**dod•der** totter, tremble (*verb*); plant (*noun*)
**dod•der•er**
**dod•der•ing**
**dod•dery**
**dod•dle**
**do•deca•gon** 12-sided figure
**do•de•cago•nal**
**do•deca•he•dral**
**do•deca•he•dron** 12-faced solid
**Do•deca•nese** Aegean islands
**do•deca•phon•ic** musical term
**do•deca•phon•ism**
**do•deca•phon•ist**
**do•deca•phony**
**dodge**
**Dodg•em** (*Trademark*)
**dodg•er**
**dodgy** (**dodgi•er, dodgi•est**)
**dodo** (*plural* **dodos** *or* **dodoes**)
**dodo•ism**
**Do•do•ma** Tanzanian town
**Do•do•na** Greek town
**doe** (*plural* **does** *or* **doe**)
**doek** African headscarf
**doer**
**does** (*present tense of* **do**; *plural of* **doe**)
**doe•skin**
**doff**
**doff•er**
**dog** (**dog•ging, dogged**)
**dog•bane** plant
**dog•berry** (*plural* **•berries**) shrub
**dog•berry•ism** officialdom
**dog•cart**
**doge** Venetian magistrate
**dog-ear**
**dog-eared**
**dog•fight**
**dog•fish** (*plural* **•fish** *or* **•fishes**)
**dog•ged** (*adj*)
**dog•ged•ness**
**Dog•ger** North Sea sandbank
**dog•ger** fishing vessel
**dog•ger•el** (*or* **dog•rel**)
**dog•gery** (*plural* **•geries**) surly behaviour
**dog•gish**
**dog•go** *Slang* in hiding
**dog•gone** US slang term
**dog•gy** (*adj*; **•gi•er, •gi •est**)
**dog•gy** (*or* **•gie**; *noun; plural* **•gies**)
**dog•house**
**do•gie** *US* motherless calf
**dog•leg** (**•leg•ging, •legged**) bend sharply
**dog•leg•ged** (*adj*)
**dog•ma** (*plural* **•mas** *or* **•ma•ta**)
**dog•man** (*plural* **•men**) *Austral* crane-driver's assistant
**dog•mat•ic** (*or* **•mati•cal**)
**dog•mati•cal•ly**
**dog•mat•ics**
**dog•ma•tism**
**dog•ma•tist**
**dog•ma•ti•za•tion** (*or* **•sa•tion**)
**dog•ma•tize** (*or* **•tise**)
**dog•ma•tiz•er** (*or* **•tis•er**)
**do-gooder**
**dogs•body** (*plural* **•bodies**)
**dog's-tail** grass
**dog-tired**
**dog•tooth** (*plural* **•teeth**)
**dog•trot**
**dog•vane** wind vane
**dog•watch** nautical term
**dog•wood**
**doh** musical note
**Doha** capital of Qatar
**doi•ly** (*or* **doy•ley, doy•ly**; *plural* **•lies** *or* **•leys**)
**do•ing**
**doit** coin
**do-it-yourself**
**dol** unit of pain
**do•lab•ri•form** (*or* **•rate**) hatchet-shaped
**Dol•by** (*Trademark*) recording system
**dol•ce** musical term
**dol•ce vita** *Italian* luxurious life
**dol•drums**
**dole**
**dole•ful**
**dole•ful•ly**
**dole•ful•ness**
**dol•er•ite** rock
**dol•er•it•ic**
**doli•cho•cephal•ic** (*or* **cepha•lous**) long-headed
**doli•cho•cepha•lism** (*or* **•ly**)
**do•li•na** (*or* **•ne**) ground depression
**doll**
**dol•lar**
**dollar•bird**
**dollar•fish** (*plural* **•fish** *or* **•fishes**)
**doll•ish**
**dol•lop**
**dol•ly** (*noun, plural* **•lies**; *verb* **•ly•ing, •lied**)
**dol•man** (*plural* **•mans**) robe
**dol•mas** (*or* **•ma**) stuffed vine leaves
**dol•men** tomb
**do•lo•mite** mineral

**Do•lo•mites** mountain range
**dolo•mit•ic**
**dol•or•im•etry** pain measurement
**do•lo•ro•so** musical term
**dol•or•ous**
**dol•our** (*US* **•or**) grief
**dol•phin**
**dol•phin•ar•ium**
**dolt**
**dolt•ish**
**dom** monk's title
**do•main**
**dome**
**dome•like**
**domes•day** *variant spelling of* **doomsday**
**Domes•day Book** (*or* **Dooms•**)
**do•mes•tic**
**do•mes•ti•cable**
**do•mes•ti•cal•ly**
**do•mes•ti•cate**
**do•mes•ti•ca•tion**
**do•mes•ti•ca•tive**
**do•mes•ti•ca•tor**
**do•mes•ti•city** (*plural* **•cities**)
**domi•cal** (*or* **do•mic**) of a dome
**domi•cile**
**domi•cili•ary**
**domi•cili•ate**
**domi•nance**
**domi•nant**
**domi•nate**
**domi•na•tion**
**domi•na•tive**
**domi•na•tor**
**do•mi•nee** Afrikaner clergyman
**domi•neer**
**Domi•ni•ca** West Indian country
**do•mini•cal** relating to the Lord
**Do•mini•can** Republic; friar
**domi•nie** *Scot* schoolmaster
**do•min•ion**
**do•min•ium** (*or* **•ion**) legal term
**domi•no** (*plural* **•noes**)
**Don** Spanish title; Russian river
**don** (**don•ning, donned**)
**Doña** Spanish woman's title
**Donar** Germanic god
**do•nate**
**do•na•tion**
**dona•tive** gift
**do•na•tor**
**Don•bass** (*or* **•bas**) Ukrainian industrial region
**Don•cas•ter**
**done**
**do•nee** receiver of gift
**Don•egal** Irish county
**Do•nets** Ukrainian river
**Do•netsk** Ukrainian city
**dong**
**don•jon** castle keep
**Don Juan** legendary seducer
**don•key**
**Don•na** Italian woman's title
**donned**
**don•nert** *Scot* stunned
**don•ning**
**don•nish**
**donny•brook** rowdy brawl
**do•nor**
**do•nor•ship**
**don't** do not
**do•nut** *variant spelling* (*esp. US*) *of* **doughnut**
**doo•dah**
**doo•dle**
**doodle•bug**
**doo•dler**
**doom**
**dooms•day** (*or* **domes•**)
**door**
**door•bell**
**do-or-die**
**door•frame**
**door•jamb**
**door•keeper**
**door•man** (*plural* **•men**)
**door•mat**
**door•nail**
**door•post**
**door•sill**
**door•step**
**door•stop**
**door•way**
**door•yard** *US* outside yard
**do•pant** chemistry term
**dope**
**dopey** (*or* **dopy; dopi•er, dopi•est**)
**dopi•ness**
**Dop•pel•gäng•er** ghost
**Dop•per** Afrikaner churchgoer
**dor** beetle
**Do•ra•do** constellation
**Dor•ches•ter**
**Dor•dogne** French region and river
**Dor•drecht** Dutch port
**Do•rian** ancient Greek
**Dor•ic** architectural term
**Do•ris** region of ancient Greece
**Dor•king**
**dorm** *Slang* dormitory
**dor•man•cy**
**dor•mant**
**dor•mer**
**dor•mie** (*or* **•my**) golf term
**dor•mi•tory** (*plural* **•tories**)
**Dor•mo•bile** (*Trademark*)
**dor•mouse** (*plural* **•mice**)
**dor•nick** (*or* **•neck**) cloth
**do•roni•cum** plant
**dorp** South African village
**dor•sad** towards the back
**dor•sal** of the back
**dor•sal•ly**
**Dor•set**
**dor•si•grade** walking on backs of toes
**dor•si•ven•tral** having upper and lower surfaces
**dor•si•ven•tral•ity**
**dor•so•ven•tral** from back to belly
**dor•so•ven•tral•ly**
**dor•sum** (*plural* **•sa**) the back
**Dort•mund** German city
**dorty** *Scot* sullen
**dory** (*plural* **dories**) fish; boat
**dos•age**
**dose**
**dos•er**
**do-si-do** dance figure
**do•sim•eter** (*or* **dose•meter**)
**do•si•met•ric**
**do•si•metri•cian** (*or* **do•sim•etrist**)
**do•sim•etry**

**doss**
**dos•sal** (*or* **•sel**) church hanging
**dos•ser** *Slang* tramp; dosshouse
**doss•house**
**dos•si•er**
**dot** (**dot•ting, dot•ted**)
**dot•age**
**do•tard**
**do•ta•tion** endowment
**dote**
**dot•er**
**dotted**
**dot•ted**
**dot•ter**
**dot•ter•el** (*or* **•trel**)
**dot•ti•ly**
**dot•ti•ness**
**dot•ting**
**dot•tle** (*or* **•tel**) tobacco in pipe
**dot•ty** (**•ti•er, •ti•est**)
**Douai** French city
**Doua•la** (*or* **Dua•la**) Cameroon port
**Dou•ay** bible
**dou•ble**
**double-acting**
**double-barrelled** (*US* **-barreled**)
**double-bass** (*adj*)
**double-blind**
**double-breasted**
**double-check**
**double-cross**
**double-dealing**
**double-decker**
**double-dotted** musical term
**double-edged**
**dou•ble en•ten•dre**
**double-faced**
**double-glazing**
**double-header**
**double-hung**
**double-jointed**
**double-park**
**double-quick**
**dou•bler**
**double-reed**
**dou•bles** tennis
**double-space**
**double-stop** (**-stopping, -stopped**)
**dou•blet**
**double•think**
**dou•ble•ton** bridge term
**double-tongue** (**-tonguing, •tongued**) musical term
**double•tree** horizontal bar on vehicle
**dou•bloon** (*or* **do•blon**) coin
**dou•blure** lining inside book
**dou•bly**
**Doubs** French river
**doubt**
**doubt•able**
**doubt•er**
**doubt•ful**
**doubt•ful•ly**
**doubt•ful•ness**
**doubt•less**
**douc** monkey
**douce** *Scot* sedate
**dou•ceur** bribe
**douche**
**dough**
**dough•boy** *Slang* dumpling
**dough•nut** (*or esp. US* **do•nut**)
**doughti•ly**
**dough•ty** (**•ti•er, •ti•est**) hardy
**doughy** (**doughi•er, doughi•est**)
**Doug•las** Manx town
**Dou•kho•bors** Russian sect
**doum** (*or* **doom**) palm tree
**dour** sullen; *compare* **dower**
**dou•rine** horse disease
**dour•ness**
**Dou•ro** Spanish–Portuguese river
**dou•rou•cou•li** monkey
**douse** (*or* **dowse**) drench; *compare* **dowse**
**dous•er** (*or* **dows•**)
**dove** bird; *US past tense of* **dive**
**dove•cote** (*or* **•cot**)
**dove•kie** (*or* **•key**) bird
**Do•ver**
**dove•tail**
**dov•ish**
**dow•able** legal term
**dowa•ger**
**dow•di•ly**
**dow•di•ness**
**dow•dy** (*noun, plural* **•dies**; *adj* **•di•er, •di•est**)
**dow•el**
**dow•er** widow's inheritance; *compare* **dour**
(**dowery**) *incorrect spelling of* **dowry**
**dow•itch•er** bird
**Dow-Jones av•er•age** US stock exchange index
**down**
**down•beat**
**down-bow**
**down•cast**
**down•com•er** (*or* **•come**) plumbing term
**down•fall**
**down•fallen**
**down•grade**
**down•haul** nautical term
**down•hearted**
**down•hearted•ness**
**down•hill**
**downi•ness**
**Down•ing Street**
**down-market**
**Down•pat•rick** Irish town
**down•pipe**
**down•pour**
**down•range**
**down•right**
**Downs** Sussex hills
**downs** chalk uplands
**down•side**
**down•size**
**down•spout** *US* drainpipe
**Down's syn•drome**
**down•stage**
**down•stairs**
**down•state** *US* S part of state
**down•stream**
**down•swing**
**down•throw**
**down-to-earth**
**down•town**
**down•trod•den** (*or* **•trod**)
**down•turn**
**down•ward** (*adj*)
**down•wards** (*adv*)
**down•wash**
**down•wind**
**downy** (**downi•er, downi•est**)
**dow•ry** (*plural* **•ries**)

**dowse** to divine water; *variant spelling of* **douse**
**dows•er**
**dows•ing**
**dox•as•tic** logic term
**doxo•logi•cal**
**dox•ol•ogy** (*plural* **•ogies**)
**doxy** (*plural* **doxies**)
**doy•en** (*fem* **•enne**)
**doze**
**doz•en**
**doz•enth**
**doz•er**
**dozy** (**dozi•er, dozi•est**)
**drab** (**drab•ber, drab•best**)
**drab•bet** fabric
**drab•ble** make wet
**drab•ly**
**drab•ness**
**dra•cae•na** plant
**drachm** fluid dram
**drach•ma** (*plural* **•mas** *or* **•mae**) Greek currency
**Dra•co** constellation
**dra•cone** container towed by ship
**Dra•co•nian** (*or* **•con•ic**) harsh
**Dra•co•ni•an•ism**
**dra•con•ic** dragon-like
**dra•coni•cal•ly**
**draff** husks
**draffy**
**draft** sketch; military selection; money order; *US spelling of* **draught**
**draftee**
**draft•er**
**drafts•man** (*plural* **•men**) document drafter; *compare* **draughtsman**
**drag** (**drag•ging, dragged**)
**dra•gée** sweet
**drag•gle** trail
**drag•hound**
**drag•line**
**drag•net**
**dra•go•man** (*plural* **•mans** *or* **•men**) interpreter
**drag•on**
**drag•on•ess**
**drag•on•et** fish
**dragon•fly** (*plural* **•flies**)
**dragon•head** (*or* **dragon's-head**) plant
**drag•on•ish**
**drag•on•nade** persecution by dragoons
**dragon•root**
**dra•goon**
**dra•goon•age**
**drag•rope**
**drail** weighted hook
**drain**
**drain•able**
**drain•age**
**drain•er**
**drain•pipe**
**drake**
**Dra•kens•berg** African mountain
**dram** 1/16 ounce; tot; *compare* **drachm**
**dra•ma**
**Dra•ma•mine** (*Trademark*)
**dra•mat•ic**
**dra•mati•cal•ly**
**dra•mat•ics**
**dra•ma•tis per•so•nae** characters in a play
**drama•tist**
**drama•tiz•able** (*or* **•tis•able**)
**drama•ti•za•tion** (*or* **•sa•tion**)
**drama•tize** (*or* **•tise**)
**drama•tiz•er** (*or* **•tis•er**)
**drama•turge** (*or* **•tur•gist**) dramatist
**drama•tur•gic** (*or* **•gi•cal**)
**drama•tur•gy**
**Drambuie** (*Trademark*)
**drank**
**drap•able** (*or* **drape•able**)
**drape**
**drap•er**
**dra•per•ied**
**dra•pery** (*plural* **•peries**)
**drapes** *US* curtains
**dras•tic**
**dras•ti•cal•ly**
**drat**
**drat•ted**
**draught** (*US* **draft**) air current; drink; load pulling; *compare* **draft**
**draught•board** (*or* **draughts•**)
**draught•er** (*US* **draft•**)
**draughti•ness** (*US* **drafti•**)
**draughts** game
**draughts•man** (*US* **drafts•**; *plural* **•men**) plan drafter; *compare* **draftsman**
**draughts•man•ship** (*US* **drafts•**)
**draughty** (*US* **drafty**; **draughti•er, draughti•est**; *US* **drafti•er, drafti•est**)
**Dra•va** European river
**Dra•vid•ian** language group
**draw** (**draw•ing, drew, drawn**)
**draw•able**
**draw•back**
**draw•bar**
**draw•bridge**
**drawee**
**draw•er**
**drawer•ful**
**drawers** undergarment
**draw•ing**
**draw•knife** (*or* **•shave**; *plural* **•knives** *or* **•shaves**) woodcutting tool
**drawl**
**drawl•er**
**drawly**
**drawn**
**draw•plate** extrusion plate
**draw•string**
**draw•tube**
**dray** cart; *compare* **drey**
**dray•horse**
**dread**
**dread•ful**
**dread•fully**
**dread•ful•ness**
**dread•nought** (*or* **•naught**) battleship
**dream** (**dream•ing, dreamt** *or* **dreamed**)
**dream•er**
**dreami•ly**
**dreami•ness**
**dream•ing•ly**
**dream•less**
**dream•like**
**dreamy** (**dreami•er, dreami•est**)
**dreari•ly**
**dreari•ness**
**dreary** (**dreari•er, dreari•est**)
**dredge**
**dredg•er**

**dree** *Scot* endure
**dreg**
**dreg•gy** (**•gi•er, •gi•est**)
**drench**
**drench•er**
**Dren•the** Dutch region
**Dres•den** German city
**dress**
**dres•sage**
**dressed**
**dress•er**
**dressi•ly**
**dressi•ness**
**dress•ing**
**dress•maker**
**dress•making**
**dressy** (**dressi•er, dressi•est**)
**drew**
**drey** squirrel's nest; *compare* **dray**
**drib•ble**
**drib•bler**
**drib•let** (*or* **•blet**) small amount
**dried**
**dri•er** (*adj*)
**dri•est**
**drift**
**drift•age**
**drift•er**
**drift•wood**
**drifty**
**drill**
**drill•able**
**drill•er**
**drill•ing**
**drill•master**
**drill•stock** tool part
**dri•ly**
**drink** (**drink•ing, drank, drunk**)
**drink•able**
**drink•er**
**drip** (**drip•ping, dripped**)
**drip-dry** (**-dries, -dry•ing, -dried**)
**drip•ping**
**drip•py** (**•pi•er, •pi•est**)
**drip•stone**
**driv•able** (*or* **drive•**)
**drive** (**driv•ing, drove, driv•en**)
**drive-in**
**driv•el** (**•el•ling, •elled**; *US* **•el•ing, •eled**)
**driv•el•ler** (*US* **•el•er**)
**driv•en**
**driv•er**
**driv•er•less**
**drive•way**
**driv•ing**
**driz•zle**
**driz•zly**
**drogue**
**droit** right
**droll**
**droll•ery** (*plural* **•eries**)
**droll•ness**
**Drôme** French department
**drom•edary** (*plural* **•edaries**) camel
**drom•ond** sailing vessel
**drone**
**dron•go** (*plural* **•gos**) bird
**dron•ish**
**drool**
**droop** sag; *compare* **drupe**
**droopi•ly**
**droopi•ness**
**droopy** (**droopi•er, droopi•est**)
**drop** (**drop•ping, dropped**)
**drop•let**
**drop•light**
**drop•out**
**drop•per**
**drop•pings**
**drop•si•cal**
**drop•sied**
**drop•sonde** meteorological device
**drop•sy** fluid in body
**drop•wort** plant
**drosh•ky** (*or* **dros•ky**; *plural* **•kies**) carriage
**dro•sophi•la** (*plural* **•las** *or* **•lae**) fruit fly
**dross**
**drossi•ness**
**drossy** (**drossi•er, drossi•est**)
**drought** (*or* **drouth**)
**droughty**
**drove**
**drov•er**
**drown**
**drown•er**
**drowse**
**drowsi•ly**
**drowsi•ness**
**drowsy** (**drowsi•er, drowsi•est**)
**drub** (**drub•bing, drubbed**) beat
**drub•ber**
**drudge**
**drudg•er**
**drudg•ery** (*plural* **•eries**)
**druf•fen** *Dialect* drunk
**drug** (**drug•ging, drugged**)
**drug•get** fabric
**drug•gist**
**drug•store**
**dru•id** (*fem* **•id•ess**)
**dru•id•ic** (*or* **•idi•cal**)
**dru•id•ism**
**drum** (**drum•ming, drummed**)
**drum•beat**
**drum•fire**
**drum•fish** (*plural* **•fish** *or* **•fishes**)
**drum•head**
**drum•lin** landform
**drum•mer**
**drum•stick**
**drunk**
**drunk•ard**
**drunk•en**
**drunk•en•ness**
**dru•pa•ceous**
**drupe** fruit; *compare* **droop**
**drupe•let** (*or* **dru•pel**) small fruit
**Dru•ry Lane**
**Druse** (*or* **Druze**) religious sect
**druse** crystals lining cavity
**dry** (*adj* **dri•er, dri•est**; *verb* **dries, dry•ing, dried**)
**dry•able**
**dry•ad** (*plural* **•ads** *or* **•ades**) wood nymph
**dry•ad•ic**
**dry-clean**
**dry-cleaner**
**dry-cleaning**
**dry•er** (*noun*)
**dry•ness**
**dryo•pith•ecine** extinct ape
**dry-salt** preserve by salting
**dry-stone** wall
**dual** two; *compare* **duel**
**Du•ala** (*plural* **•ala** *or* **•alas**) African people

**dual•ism**
**dual•ist**
**dual•is•tic**
**dual•is•ti•cal•ly**
**dual•ity** (*plural* **•ities)**
**dual-purpose**
**dub (dub•bing, dubbed)**
**Du•bai** sheikdom
**dub•bin** (*or* **dub•bing)** leather grease
**du•bi•ety** (*or* **du•bi•os•ity;** *plural* **•ties)**
**du•bi•ous**
**du•bi•ous•ness**
**du•bi•table**
**du•bi•ta•tion** doubt
**Dub•lin**
**Du•bon•net** (*Trademark*)
**Du•brov•nik** Croatian port
**du•cal**
**duc•at** coin
**duce** *Italian* leader
**duch•ess**
**duchy** (*plural* **duchies)**
**duck**
**duck•board**
**duck•er**
**duck•ling**
**ducks** trousers
**duck•weed**
**ducky** (*or* **duckie;** *plural* **duckies)**
**duct**
**duc•tile**
**duc•til•ity** (*or* **•tile•ness)**
**dud**
**dude**
**du•deen** clay pipe
**dudg•eon** anger
**Dud•ley** English town
**due**
**duel (duel•ling, duelled;** *US* **duel•ing, dueled)** fight; *compare* **dual**
**duel•ler** (*or* **•list;** *US* **•er** *or* **•ist)**
**du•el•lo** (*plural* **•los)** duelling
**du•en•na** chaperon
**duet** (*or* **du•ette)**
**duet•tist**
**duff**
**duf•fel** (*or* **•fle)**
**duf•fer**
**dug**
**du•gong** animal
**dug•out**
**dui•ker** (*plural* **•kers** *or* **•ker)** antelope
**Duis•burg** German city
**duke**
**duke•dom**
**dul•cet**
**dul•ci•ana** organ stop
**dul•ci•fy (•fies, •fying, •fied)** sweeten
**dul•ci•mer** musical instrument
**du•lia** veneration for saints
**dull**
**dull•ard**
**dull•ness** (*or* **dul•ness)**
**dulls•ville** boredom
**dul•ly** in a dull way
**du•lo•sis** zoology term
**dulse** seaweed
**Du•luth** US port
**duly** appropriately
**dumb**
**Dum•bar•ton** Scottish town
**dumb•bell**
**dumb-cane** plant
**dumb•found** (*or* **dum•)**
**dumb•found•er** (*or* **dum•)**
**dumb•ness**
**dumb•struck** (*or* **•stricken)**
**dumb•waiter** stand for dishes
**dum•dum** bullet
**Dum•fries**
**dum•my** (*noun, plural* **•mies;** *verb* **•mies, •my•ing, •mied)**
**du•mor•ti•erite** mineral
**dump**
**dump•er**
**dumpi•ness**
**dump•ling**
**dumpy (dumpi•er, dumpi•est)**
**Dum•yat** Egyptian town
**dun** (*verb* **dun•ning, dunned;** *adj* **dun•ner, dun•nest)**
**Dun•bar** Scottish port
**dunce**
**Dun•dalk** Irish town
**Dun•dee**
**dunder•head**
**dune**
**Dun•edin** New Zealand port
**Dun•ferm•line**
**dung**
**dun•ga•ree** fabric
**dun•ga•rees** overalls
**Dun•ge•ness** Kent headland
**dun•geon**
**dung•hill**
**dungy**
**dun•ite** rock
**dunk**
**dunk•er**
**Dun•kirk** French port
**Dun Laoghaire** Irish port
**dun•lin** bird
**dun•nage** cargo-packing material
**dun•na•kin** *Dialect* lavatory
**dunned**
**dun•ner**
**dun•nest**
**dun•ning**
**dun•nite** explosive
**dun•nock** bird
**dun•ny** *Scot* cellar
**Du•noon** Scottish town
**Dun•si•nane** Scottish hill
**Dun•sta•ble**
**dunt** *Dialect* a blow
**duo** (*plural* **duos** *or* **dui)**
**duo•deci•mal** of 12
**duo•deci•mo** (*plural* **•mos)** book size
**duo•denal**
**duo•dena•ry**
**duo•deni•tis**
**duo•denum** (*plural* **•dena** *or* **•denums)**
**duo•logue**
**duo•mo** (*plural* **•mos)** cathedral
**duo•tone** printing process
**dup** *Dialect* open
**dup•abil•ity**
**dup•able**
**dupe**
**dup•er**
**dup•ery**
**du•ple** musical term
**du•plet** chemistry term
**du•plex**
**du•plex•ity**
**du•pli•cabil•ity**
**du•pli•cable**
**du•pli•cate**

**du•pli•ca•tion**
**du•pli•ca•tive**
**du•pli•ca•tor**
**du•plic•ity** (*plural* **•ities**)
**du•pon•dius** coin
**du•rabil•ity** (*or* **•rable•ness**)
**du•rable**
**Du•ralu•min** (*Trademark*) aluminium alloy
**dura ma•ter** membrane round brain
**du•ra•men** wood
**du•rance** imprisonment
**Du•ran•go** Mexican state
**du•ra•tion**
**du•ra•tion•al**
**du•ra•tive** linguistics term
**Dur•ban** South African port
**dur•bar** African court
**du•ress**
**Du•rex** (*Trademark*) condom
**Dur•ham**
**du•rian** (*or* **•ri•on**) fruit
**dur•ing**
**dur•mast** tree
**duro** (*plural* **duros**) coin
**Du•roc** US pig
**dur•ra** (*or* **dou•ra, dou•rah**) grass
**durst** *past tense of* **dare**
**du•rum** wheat
**Du•shan•be** Tadzhik capital
**dusk**
**duski•ness**
**dusky** (**duski•er, duski•est**)
**Düs•sel•dorf** German city
**dust**
**dust•bin**
**dust•cart**
**dust•er**
**dusti•ly**
**dusti•ness**
**dust•man** (*plural* **•men**)
**dust•pan**
**dust•sheet**
**dust-up** *Slang* fight
**dusty** (**dusti•er, dusti•est**)
**Dutch**
**Dutch•man** (*plural* **•men**)
**du•teous** *Archaic* dutiful
**du•ti•abil•ity**
**du•ti•able**
**du•ti•ful**
**du•ti•ful•ly**
**du•ti•ful•ness**
**duty** (*plural* **duties**)
**duty-free**
**du•vet**
**du•vetyn** (*or* **•vetine, •vetyne**) fabric
**dux** *Scot* best pupil
**dvan•dva** compound word
**dwale** deadly nightshade
**dwarf** (*plural* **dwarfs** *or* **dwarves**)
**dwarf•ish**
**dwarf•ish•ness**
**dwarf•ism**
**dwell** (**dwell•ing, dwelt** *or* **dwelled**)
**dwell•er**
**dwell•ing**
**dwin•dle**
**dy•able** (*or* **dye•able**)
**dyad** maths term
**dy•ad•ic** twofold
**Dyak** (*plural* **Dyaks** *or* **Dyak**) Malaysian people
**dy•ar•chic** (*or* **•chi•cal, •chal**) *variant spelling of* **diarchic**
**dy•ar•chy** (*plural* **•chies**) *variant spelling of* **diarchy**
**dyb•buk** (*plural* **•buks** *or* **•buk•kim**) Hebrew spirit
**dye** (**dye•ing, dyed**) colour; *compare* **die**
**dye•ing** colouring; *compare* **dying**
**dye•line** blueprint
**dy•er**
**dyer's-greenweed**
**dyer's-weed**
**dye•stuff**
**dye•wood**
**Dyf•ed** former Welsh county
**dy•ing** expiring; *compare* **dyeing**
**dyke** (*or* **dike**)
**dy•nam•eter**
**dy•nam•ic**
**dy•nami•cal•ly**
**dy•nam•ics**
**dy•na•mism** philosophical theory
**dy•na•mist**
**dy•na•mis•tic**
**dy•na•mite**
**dy•na•mit•er** (*or* **•mit•ist**)
**dy•na•mit•ic**
**dy•na•mo** (*plural* **•mos**)
**dy•na•mo•elec•tric** (*or* **•tri•cal**)
**dy•na•mom•eter**
**dy•na•mo•met•ric** (*or* **•ri•cal**)
**dy•na•mom•etry**
**dy•na•mo•tor**
**dyn•ast** ruler
**dy•nas•tic** (*or* **•ti•cal**)
**dyn•as•ty** (*plural* **•ties**)
**dy•na•tron** type of oscillator
**dyne** unit
**dy•node** electrode
**dys•en•ter•ic**
**dys•en•tery**
**dys•func•tion**
**dys•gen•ic**
**dys•gen•ics** reducing quality of race
**dys•graphia** impaired writing ability
**dys•lexia** impaired reading ability
**dys•lex•ic** (*or* **•lec•tic**)
**dys•men•or•rhoea** (*US* **•rhea**)
**dys•men•or•rhoeal** (*US* **•rheal**)
**dys•pep•sia** (*or* **•sy**) indigestion
**dys•pep•tic** (*or* **•ti•cal**)
**dys•pha•gia** difficulty in swallowing
**dys•phag•ic**
**dys•pha•sia** impaired speech
**dys•pha•sic**
**dys•phe•mism** substitution of offensive word
**dys•pho•nia** impaired speech
**dys•phon•ic**
**dys•pho•ria** uneasy feeling
**dys•phor•ic**
**dys•pla•sia** abnormal organ development
**dys•plas•tic**
**dysp•noea** (*US* **•nea**) difficulty in breathing
**dysp•noeal** (*or* **•noe•ic**; *US* **•neal** *or* **•ne•ic**)

**dys•pro•sium** chemical element
**dys•tel•eol•ogy** philosophy term
**dys•thy•mia** neurotic condition
**dys•thy•mic**
**dys•to•pia** worst possible place
**dys•troph•ic**
**dys•tro•phy** (*or* **•phia**) wasting of tissues
**dys•uria** painful urination
**dys•uric**
**dy•tis•cid** beetle
**Dyu•la** (*plural* **•la** *or* **•las**) African people
**Dzer•zhinsk** Russian city
**Dzong•ka** Asian language
**Dzun•ga•ria** (*or* **Zun•**) Chinese region

# E

**each**
**eager** keen; *compare* **eagre**
**eager•ness**
**eagle**
**eagle-eyed**
**eagle•stone**
**eaglet**
**eagle•wood**
**eagre** (*or* **eager**) tidal bore; *compare* **eager**
**eal•dor•man** Anglo-Saxon official
**Ealing**
**ear**
**ear•ache**
**ear•bash** *Austral* talk
**ear•drop**
**ear•drum**
**eared**
**ear•flap**
**ear•ful**
**ear•ing** nautical term
**earl**
**ear•lap**
**earl•dom**
**ear•li•ness**
**ear•ly** (**•li•er, •li•est**)
**Ear•ly Bird** satellite
**ear•mark**
**ear•muff**
**earn**
**earn•er**
**ear•nest**
**ear•nest•ness**
**earn•ings**
**ear•phone**
**ear•piece**
**ear•plug**
**ear•ring**
**ear•shot**
**ear•splitting**
**earth**
**earth•born**
**earth•bound**
**earth•en**
**earthen•ware**
**earthi•ly**
**earthi•ness**
**earth•light** *variant of* **earthshine**
**earth•li•ness**
**earth•ling**
**earth•ly** (**•li•er, •li•est**)
**earth•nut**
**earth•quake**
**earth•rise**
**earth•shaking**
**earth•shine** (*or* **•light**) earth's reflected light
**earth•star** fungus
**earth•wards** (*or esp. US* **•ward**)
**earth•work**
**earth•worm**
**earthy** (**earthi•er, earthi•est**)
**ear•wax**
**ear•wig**
**ease**
**ease•ful**
**ease•ful•ness**
**easel**
**ease•ment**
**eas•er**
**easi•ly**
**easi•ness**
**east**
**East An•glia**
**East An•glian**
**East Ber•lin**
**East Ber•lin•er**
**east•bound**
**East•bourne**
**East•er**
**Easter-ledges** plant
**east•er•ly** (*plural* **•lies**)
**east•ern**
**east•ern•er**
**east•ern•most**
**East•er•tide**
**East Ger•man**
**East Ger•ma•ny**
**East In•dian**
**East In•dies**
**east•ing** nautical term
**East Kil•bride** Scottish town
**East•leigh** Hampshire town
**east-northeast**
**east-southeast**
**east•ward** (*adj*)
**east•ward•ly**
**east•wards** (*adv*)
**easy** (**easi•er, easi•est**)
**easy-going**
**eat** (**eat•ing, ate, eat•en**)
**eat•able**
**eat•age** *Dialect* grazing rights
**eat•en**
**eat•er**
**eau de Co•logne**
**eau de Ja•velle** bleaching solution
**eau de nil** greenish colour
**eau de vie** brandy
**eaves**
**eaves•drop** (**•drop•ping, •dropped**)
**eaves•drop•per**
**ebb**
**Ebbw Vale**
**ebon** ebony
**eb•on•ite** rubber
**eb•on•ize** (*or* **•ise**)
**eb•ony** (*plural* **•onies**)
**Ebora•cum** *Latin* York

**ebrac•te•ate**
**ebul•lience** (*or* **•lien•cy)**
**ebul•lient**
**ebul•li•os•co•py** chemistry term
**ebul•li•tion** boiling
**ebur•na•tion** bone condition
**ecad** ecology term
**écar•té** card game
**Ec•bata•na** Iranian city
**ec•bol•ic** medi term
**ec•cen•tric**
**ec•cen•tri•cal•ly**
**ec•cen•tri•city** (*plural* **•cities)**
**ec•chy•mo•sis** (*plural* **•ses)** skin condition
**Ec•cles** English town; cake
**ec•cle•sia** (*plural* **•siae)** church congregation
**ec•cle•si•arch** sacristan
**Ec•cle•si•as•tes** Old Testament book
**ec•cle•si•as•tic**
**ec•cle•si•as•ti•cal**
**ec•cle•si•as•ti•cal.ly**
**ec•cle•si•as•ti•cism**
**Ec•cle•si•as•ti•cus** book of Apocrypha
**ec•cle•si•ola•ter**
**ec•cle•si•ola•try** ecclesiastical obsession
**ec•cle•sio•logi•cal** (*or* **•log•ic)**
**ec•cle•si•olo•gist**
**ec•cle•si•ol•ogy** study of Church
**ec•crine**
**ec•crin•ol•ogy** study of glands
**ec•dys•ial**
**ec•dysi•ast** striptease artist
**ec•dy•sis** (*plural* **•ses)** moulting
**ec•dy•sone** hormone
**ecesis** ecology term
**ec•hard** biology term
**eche•lon**
**ech•eve•ria** plant
**echid•na** (*plural* **•nas** *or* **•nae)** spiny anteater
**echi•nate** (*or* **•nat•ed)** having bristles
**echi•no•coc•cus** tapeworm
**echi•no•derm** marine animal
**echi•no•der•mal** (*or* **•ma•tous)**
**echi•noid** marine animal
**echi•nus** (*plural* **•ni)** sea urchin
**echo** (*noun, plural* **echoes;** *verb* **echoes, echo•ing, ech•oed)**
**echo•ic**
**echo•ism** linguistics term
**echo•la•lia** psychiatric term
**echo•la•lic**
**echo•location**
**echo•prac•tic**
**echo•praxia** (*or* **•prax•is)** psychiatric term
**echo•virus**
**éclair**
**ec•lamp•sia** pregnancy condition
**ec•lamp•tic**
**éclat** acclaim
**ec•lec•tic** selecting the best
**ec•lec•ti•cism**
**eclipse**
**eclips•er**
**eclip•sis** linguistics term
**eclip•tic** astronomy term
**eclip•ti•cal•ly**
**ec•lo•gite** rock
**ec•logue** poem
**eclo•sion** emergence of insect
**eco•cide** environmental destruction
**eco•friend•ly**
**eco•logi•cal** (*or* **•log•ic)**
**eco•logi•cal•ly**
**ecolo•gist**
**ecol•ogy**
**econo•met•ric** (*or* **•ri•cal)**
**econo•me•tri•cian** (*or* **•met•rist)**
**econo•met•rics** economics
**eco•nom•ic**
**eco•nomi•cal**
**eco•nomi•cal•ly**
**eco•nom•ics**
**econo•mist**
**econo•mi•za•tion** (*or* **•sa•tion)**
**econo•mize** (*or* **•mise)**
**econo•miz•er** (*or* **•mis•er)**
**econo•my** (*plural* **•mies)**
**écor•ché** anatomical figure
**eco•spe•cies**
**eco•spe•cif•ic**
**eco•sphere**
**écoss•aise** dance
**eco•sys•tem**
**eco•ter•ror•ism**
**eco•ter•ror•ist**
**eco•ton•al**
**eco•tone** ecology term
**eco•type**
**eco•typ•ic**
**eco•typi•cal•ly**
**écra•seur** surgical device
**ecru** yellowish colour
**ec•sta•sy** (*plural* **•sies)**
**ec•stat•ic**
**ec•stati•cal•ly**
**ec•stat•ics**
**ec•thy•ma** skin condition
**ec•to•blast** biology term
**ec•to•blas•tic**
**ec•to•derm** (*or* **exo•derm)** embryo part
**ec•to•der•mal** (*or* **•mic)**
**ec•to•en•zyme**
**ec•to•gen•esis**
**ec•tog•enous** (*or* **•to•gen•ic)** biology term
**ec•to•mere** embryology term
**ec•to•mer•ic**
**ec•to•morph**
**ec•to•mor•phic** thin
**ec•to•morphy**
**ec•to•para•site**
**ec•to•para•sit•ic**
**ec•to•phyte** parasitic plant
**ec•to•pia** congenital displacement
**ec•top•ic** in abnormal position; *compare* **entopic**
**ec•to•plasm**
**ecto•plas•mic**
**ec•to•proct** animal
**ec•to•sarc** amoeba ectoplasm
**ecto•sar•cous**
**ec•ty•pal**
**ec•type** copy
**Ecua•dor**
**Ecua•do•rian** (*or* **•ran)**
**ecu•men•ic**
**ecu•meni•cal** (*or* **oecu•)**

**ecu·meni·cal·ism** (*or* **·cism**) Christian unity
**ecu·meni·cal·ly**
**écu·rie** motor-racing team
**ec·ze·ma**
**ec·zema·tous**
**eda·cious** greedy
**eda·cious·ness**
**edac·ity**
**Edam**
**edaph·ic** of soil
**edaphi·cal·ly**
**Edda** Norse poems
**eddo** plant
**eddy** (*noun, plural* **eddies**; *verb* **eddies, eddy·ing, eddied**)
**Ed·dy·stone** rocks; lighthouse
**Ede** Dutch city
**edel·weiss**
**ede·ma** *US spelling of* **oedema**
**edema·tous** *US spelling of* **oedematous**
**Eden** biblical garden
**eden·tate** zoology term
**eden·tu·lous** (*or* **·late**) toothless
**edge**
**Edge·hill** English battle site
**edg·er**
**edge·ways**
**edgi·ly**
**edgi·ness**
**edg·ing**
**edgy** (**edgi·er, edgi·est**)
**edh** runic character
**ed·ibil·ity** (*or* **·ible·ness**)
**ed·ible**
**edict**
**edic·tal**
**edi·fi·ca·tion**
**edifi·ca·tory**
**edi·fice**
**edi·fi·cial**
**edi·fi·er**
**edi·fy** (**·fies, ·fy·ing, ·fied**)
**edi·fy·ing·ly**
**edile** *US variant spelling of* **oedile**
**Ed·in·burgh**
**edit**
**edi·tion**
**edi·tio prin·ceps** (*plural* **edi·tio·nes prin·ci·pes**) *Latin* first edition
**edi·tor**
**edi·to·rial**
**edi·to·ri·al·ist**
**edi·to·ri·ali·za·tion** (*or* **·sa·tion**)
**edi·to·ri·al·ize** (*or* **·ise**)
**edi·to·ri·al·iz·er** (*or* **·is·er**)
**edi·to·ri·al·ly**
**edi·tor·ship**
**Ed·mon·ton** Canadian city
**Edom** biblical people
**edu·cabil·ity** (*or* **educat·abil·ity**)
**edu·cable** (*or* **·cat·able**)
**edu·cate**
**edu·cat·ed**
**edu·ca·tion**
**edu·ca·tion·al**
**edu·ca·tion·al·ist** (*or* **·tion·ist**)
**edu·ca·tion·al·ly**
**edu·ca·tive**
**edu·ca·tor**
**edu·ca·tory**
**educe** logic term
**educ·ible**
**educt** chemistry term
**educ·tion**
**educ·tive**
**edul·co·rate** wash
**edul·co·ra·tion**
**Ed·ward·ian**
**eel**
**eel·grass**
**eel-like**
**eel·pout** fish
**eel·worm**
**e'er** ever; *compare* **ere**
**eerie** (**eeri·er, eeri·est**) weird; *compare* **eyrie**
**eeri·ly**
**eeri·ness**
**eff**
**ef·fable** expressible
**ef·face**
**ef·face·able**
**ef·face·ment**
**ef·fac·er**
**ef·fect** (*noun*) result; (*verb*) cause; *compare* **affect**
**ef·fect·er**
**ef·fect·ible**
**ef·fec·tive**
**ef·fec·tive·ly**
**ef·fec·tive·ness**
**ef·fec·tor** physiology term
**ef·fects**
**ef·fec·tual**
**ef·fec·tu·al·ity** (*or* **·al·ness**)
**ef·fec·tu·al·ly**
**ef·fec·tu·ate** bring about
**ef·fec·tu·ation**
**ef·femi·na·cy** (*or* **·nate·ness**)
**ef·femi·nate**
**ef·fen·di** (*plural* **·dis**) Turkish title
**ef·fer·ence**
**ef·fer·ent** conducting outwards; *compare* **afferent**
**ef·fer·vesce**
**ef·fer·ves·cence**
**ef·fer·ves·cent**
**ef·fer·ves·cible**
**ef·fer·ves·cing·ly**
**ef·fete** weak
**ef·fi·ca·cious**
**ef·fi·ca·cy** (*or* **·cious·ness**)
**ef·fi·cien·cy** (*plural* **·cies**)
**ef·fi·cient**
**ef·fig·ial**
**ef·fi·gy** (*plural* **·gies**)
**ef·flo·resce**
**ef·flo·res·cence**
**ef·flo·res·cent**
**ef·flu·ence** (*or* **ef·flux**)
**ef·flu·ent**
**ef·flu·vial**
**ef·flu·vium** (*plural* **·via** *or* **·viums**) bad smell
**ef·flux** *variant of* **effluence**
**ef·fort**
**ef·fort·ful**
**ef·fort·less**
**ef·fort·less·ness**
**ef·fron·tery** (*plural* **·teries**)
**ef·ful·gence**
**ef·ful·gent** radiant
**ef·fuse** spread out
**ef·fu·si·om·eter** physics apparatus
**ef·fu·sion**
**ef·fu·sive**
**ef·fu·sive·ness**
**Efik** (*plural* **Efik** *or* **Efiks**) African people
**eft** newt

**egad**
**egali•tar•ian**
**egali•tari•an•ism**
**Egeria** female adviser
**egest** excrete
**eges•ta**
**eges•tion**
**eges•tive**
**egg**
**egg•beater**
**eg•ger** (*or* **•gar**) moth
**egg•head**
**egg•nog** (*or* **egg-noggin**)
**egg•plant** *US* aubergine
**egg•shell**
**eggy**
**Eg•ham** Surrey town
**egis** *US variant spelling of* **aegis**
**eg•lan•tine** plant
**Eg•mont** extinct volcano
**ego** (*plural* **egos**)
**ego•cen•tric**
**ego•cen•tric•ity**
**ego•cen•trism**
**ego•ism** self-interest; *compare* **egotism**
**ego•ist**
**ego•is•tic** (*or* **•ti•cal**)
**ego•ma•nia**
**ego•ma•ni•ac**
**ego•ma•nia•cal**
**ego•tism** self-centredness; *compare* **egoism**
**ego•tist**
**ego•tis•tic** (*or* **•ti•cal**)
**ego•tis•ti•cal•ly**
**egre•gious** bad
**egre•gious•ness**
**egress**
**egres•sion**
**egret** bird
**Egypt**
**Egyp•tian**
**Egyp•to•logi•cal**
**Egyp•tolo•gist**
**Egyp•tol•ogy**
**eh**
**eider**
**eider•down**
**eidet•ic** psychology term
**eideti•cal•ly**
**eido•lon** (*plural* **•la** *or* **•lons**) apparition
**Eiffel Tower**
**eigen•func•tion** physics term
**Eiger** Swiss mountain
**eight**
**eight•een**
**eight•een•mo** (*plural* **•mos**)
**eight•eenth**
**eight•fold**
**eighth**
**eighti•eth**
**eight•some**
**eight•vo** (*plural* **•vos**)
**eighty** (*plural* **eighties**)
**Eilat** Israeli port
**Eind•ho•ven** Dutch city
**ein•korn** wheat
**Ein•stein•ian**
**ein•stein•ium** radioactive element
**Eire**
**eireni•con** (*or* **ireni•**) philosophy term
**eise•gesis** (*plural* **•geses**) text interpretation
**Eisen•ach** German city
**eistedd•fod** (*plural* **•fods** *or* **•fodau**)
**eistedd•fod•ic**
**ei•ther**
**ejacu•late**
**ejacu•la•tion**
**ejacu•la•tive**
**ejacu•la•tor**
**ejacu•la•tory**
**eject**
**ejec•ta** volcanic material
**ejec•tion**
**ejec•tive** phonetics term
**ejec•tor**
**eke**
**ekis•ti•cal** (*or* **•tic**)
**ekis•tics** human settlements
**elabo•rate**
**elabo•rate•ness**
**elabo•ra•tion**
**elabo•ra•tive**
**elabo•ra•tor**
**el•aeop•tene** *variant spelling of* **eleoptene**
**El Ala•mein** Egyptian battle site
**Elam** ancient kingdom
**Elam•ite** (*or* **•it•ic**)
**élan** style
**eland** antelope
**élan vital** philosophy term
**ela•pid** snake
**elapse**
**elas•mo•branch** fish
**elas•mo•saur** reptile
**elas•tance** physics term
**elas•tic**
**elas•ti•cal•ly**
**elas•ti•cate**
**elas•ti•ca•tion**
**elas•tici•ty**
**elas•ti•cize** (*or* **•cise**)
**elas•tin** protein
**elas•to•mer** rubbery material
**elas•to•mer•ic**
**Elas•to•plast** (*Trademark*)
**elate**
**elat•ed**
**elat•ed•ness**
**ela•ter** biology term
**elat•er•id** beetle
**elat•er•in** purgative
**elat•er•ite** bitumen
**ela•terium** purgative
**ela•tion**
**ela•tive** linguistics term
**Elba** Italian island
**Elbe** European river
**el•bow**
**elbow•room**
**El•brus** Russian mountain
**el•der**
**elder•berry** (*plural* **•berries**)
**el•der•li•ness**
**el•der•ly**
**el•der•ship**
**eld•est**
**El Do•ra•do** legendary city
**el•dritch** (*or* **•drich**) unearthly
**Ele•at•ic**
**Ele•ati•cism** philosophy term
**ele•cam•pane** plant
**elect**
**elect•able**
**elec•tion**
**elec•tion•eer**
**elec•tion•eer•er**
**elec•tion•eer•ing**
**elec•tive**
**elec•tiv•ity** (*or* **•tive•ness**)
**elec•tor**
**elec•tor•al**

**elec•tor•ate**
**elec•tor•ship**
**Electra** mythological character
**elec•tret** physics term
**elec•tric**
**elec•tri•cal**
**elec•tri•cal•ly**
**elec•tri•cian**
**elec•tric•ity**
**elec•tri•fi•able**
**elec•tri•fi•ca•tion**
**elec•tri•fi•er**
**elec•tri•fy (•fies, •fy•ing, •fied)**
**elec•tro** (*plural* **•tros)**
**elec•tro•acous•tic** (*or* **•ti•cal)**
**elec•tro•acous•tics**
**elec•tro•analy•sis**
**elec•tro•ana•lytic** (*or* **•lyti•cal)**
**elec•tro•car•dio•gram**
**elec•tro•car•dio•graph**
**elec•tro•car•dio•graph•ic** (*or* **•graphi•cal)**
**elec•tro•car•di•og•ra•phy**
**elec•tro•chemi•cal**
**elec•tro•chem•ist**
**elec•tro•chem•is•try**
**elec•tro•con•vul•sive**
**elec•tro•cor•ti•co•gram** record of brainwaves
**elec•tro•cute**
**elec•tro•cu•tion**
**elec•trode**
**elec•tro•de•pos•it**
**elec•tro•depo•si•tion** chemistry term
**elec•tro•di•aly•sis**
**elec•tro•dy•nam•ic** (*or* **•nami•cal)**
**elec•tro•dy•nam•ics**
**elec•tro•dy•na•mom•eter**
**elec•tro•en•cepha•lo•gram**
**elec•tro•en•cepha•lo•graph**
**elec•tro•en•cepha•lo•graph•ic**
**elec•tro•en•cepha•lo•graphi•cal•ly**
**elec•tro•en•cepha•log•ra•phy**
**elec•tro•form** form by electrolysis
**elec•tro•graph** printing term
**elec•tro•graph•ic**
**elec•tro•graphi•cal•ly**
**elec•trog•ra•phy**
**elec•tro•jet** physics term
**elec•tro•ki•net•ic**
**elec•tro•ki•net•ics**
**elec•tro•lu•mi•nes•cence**
**elec•tro•lu•mi•nes•cent**
**elec•tro•ly•sa•tion** (*US* **•za•tion)**
**elec•tro•lyse** (*US* **•lyze)**
**elec•tro•lys•er** (*US* **•lyz•er)**
**elec•troly•sis**
**elec•tro•lyte**
**elec•tro•lyt•ic** (*or* **•lyti•cal)**
**elec•tro•mag•net**
**elec•tro•mag•net•ic**
**elec•tro•mag•neti•cal•ly**
**elec•tro•mag•ne•tism**
**elec•tro•me•chani•cal**
**elec•tro•mer•ism** chemistry term
**elec•tro•met•al•lur•gi•cal**
**elec•tro•me•tal•lur•gist**
**elec•tro•met•al•lur•gy**
**elec•trom•eter**
**elec•tro•met•ric** (*or* **•ri•cal)**
**elec•trom•etry**
**elec•tro•mo•tive** current-producing
**elec•tron**
**elec•tro•nega•tive**
**elec•tro•nega•tiv•ity**
**elec•tron•ic**
**elec•troni•cal•ly**
**elec•tron•ics**
**elec•tron•volt** unit
**elec•tro•phil•ic** chemistry term
**elec•tro•phone** musical term
**elec•tro•phon•ic**
**elec•tro•pho•resis** physics term
**elec•tro•pho•ret•ic**
**elec•tropho•rus** physics apparatus
**elec•tro•physio•logi•cal**
**elec•tro•physi•olo•gist**
**elec•tro•physi•ol•ogy**
**elec•tro•plate**
**elec•tro•plat•er**
**elec•tro•po•si•tive**
**elec•tro•scope**
**elec•tro•scop•ic**
**elec•tro•stat•ic**
**elec•tro•stati•cal•ly**
**elec•tro•stat•ics**
**elec•tro•stric•tion** physics term
**elec•tro•sur•gery**
**elec•tro•sur•gi•cal**
**elec•tro•thera•peu•tic** (*or* **•ti•cal)**
**elec•tro•thera•peu•tics**
**elec•tro•thera•pist**
**elec•tro•thera•py**
**elec•tro•ther•mal**
**elec•tro•ton•ic**
**elec•troto•nus** physiology term
**elec•tro•type** printing term
**elec•tro•typ•er**
**elec•tro•va•len•cy** (*or* **•lence)** chemistry term
**elec•tro•va•lent**
**elec•trum** alloy
**elec•tu•ary** (*plural* **•aries)** medical term
**el•eemosy•nary** dependent on charity
**el•egance** (*or* **el•egan•cy;** *plural* **•egances** *or* **•cies)**
**el•egant**
**el•egi•ac**
**el•egist**
**el•egize** (*or* **•egise)**
**el•egy** (*plural* **•egies)**
**el•ement**
**el•ement•al**
**el•emen•ta•ri•ness**
**el•emen•ta•ry**
**el•emi** (*plural* **•emis)** resin
**elen•chus** (*plural* **•chi)** logic term
**elenc•tic**
**el•eop•tene** (*or* **•aeop•)** chemistry term
**el•ephant** (*plural* **•ephants** *or* **•ephant)**
**el•ephan•ti•as•ic**
**el•ephan•tia•sis** disease
**el•ephan•tine**
**el•ephan•toid**
**elephant's-ear** plant
**elephant's-foot** (*or* **elephant-)** plant
**Eleu•sin•ian**
**Eleu•sis** Greek town
**el•evate**

**el•evat•ed**
**el•eva•tion**
**el•eva•tor**
**elev•en**
**eleven-plus**
**elev•en•ses**
**elev•enth**
**el•evon** aircraft control surface
**elf** (*plural* **elves**)
**El Fai•yum** (*or* **Al Fai•yum**) Egyptian city
**elfin**
**elf•ish** (*or* **elv•**)
**elf•lock**
**Elgin** Scottish town; marbles
**El Giza** Egyptian city
**Elia** Greek department
**elic•it** evoke; *compare* **illicit**
**elic•it•able**
**elici•ta•tion**
**elici•tor**
**elide** linguistics term
**elid•ible**
**eli•gibil•ity**
**eli•gible**
**eli•gibly**
**elimi•nable**
**elimi•nant**
**elimi•nate**
**elimi•na•tion**
**elimi•na•tive** (*or* **•tory**)
**elimi•na•tor**
**Elis** ancient Olympic Games site
**eli•sion** linguistics term
**elite** (*or* **élite**)
**elit•ism**
**elit•ist**
**elix•ir**
**Eliza•bethan**
**elk**
**elk•hound**
**ell** unit of length
**Elles•mere** Canadian Island
**el•lipse** flattened circle
**el•lip•sis** (*plural* **•ses**) missing words
**el•lip•soid**
**el•lip•soi•dal**
**el•lip•tic**
**el•lip•ti•cal**
**el•lip•ti•cal•ly**
**el•lip•ti•cal•ness**
**el•lip•ti•city**
**elm**
**El Man•su•ra** (*or* **Al Man•su•rah**) Egyptian city
**El Min•ya** Egyptian port
**El Mis•ti** Peruvian volcano
**El Obeid** Sudanese city
**elo•cu•tion**
**elo•cu•tion•ary**
**elo•cu•tion•ist**
**elon•gate**
**elon•ga•tion**
**elon•ga•tive**
**elope**
**elope•ment**
**elop•er**
**elo•quence**
**elo•quent**
**elo•quent•ness**
**El Paso** Texan city
**El Sal•va•dor**
**else•where**
**El•si•nore**
**elu•ant** *variant spelling of* **eluent**
**elu•ci•date**
**elu•ci•da•tion**
**elu•ci•da•tive** (*or* **•da•tory**)
**elu•ci•da•tor**
**elude** escape from; *compare* **allude; illude**
**elud•er**
**elu•ate** chemistry term
**elu•ent** (*or* **•ant**)
**elu•sion**
**elu•sive** evasive; *compare* **illusive**
**elu•sive•ness**
**elute** chemistry term
**elu•tri•ant**
**elu•tri•ate**
**elu•tria•tion**
**elu•tria•tor**
**elu•vial**
**elu•via•tion**
**elu•vium** (*plural* **•via**) rock particles; *compare* **alluvium**
**el•ver** eel
**elves** *plural of* **elf**
**elv•ish** *variant spelling of* **elfish**
**Ely**
**Ély•sée** Parisian palace
**Ely•sian**
**Ely•sium** mythological heaven
**ely•troid** (*or* **•trous**)
**ely•tron** (*or* **•trum**; *plural* **•tra**) beetle's wing
**em** printer's measure; *compare* **en**
**ema•ci•ate**
**ema•cia•ted**
**ema•cia•tion**
**ema•nate**
**ema•na•tion**
**ema•na•tion•al**
**ema•na•tive**
**ema•na•tor**
**ema•na•tory**
**eman•ci•pate**
**eman•ci•pa•tion**
**eman•ci•pa•tion•ist**
**eman•ci•pa•tive**
**eman•ci•pa•tor**
**eman•ci•pa•tory**
**emar•gi•nate** (*or* **•nat•ed**) notched
**emar•gi•na•tion**
**emas•cu•late**
**emas•cu•la•tion**
**emas•cu•la•tive** (*or* **•tory**)
**emas•cu•la•tor**
**em•balm**
**em•balm•er**
**em•balm•ment**
**em•bank**
**em•bank•ment**
**(embarass)** *incorrect spelling of* **embarrass**
**em•bar•go** (*noun, plural* **•goes**; *verb* **•goes, •go•ing, •goed**)
**em•bark**
**em•bar•ka•tion**
**em•bark•ment**
**em•bar•rass**
**em•bar•rass•ing**
**em•bar•rass•ment**
**em•bas•sy** (*plural* **•sies**)
**em•bat•tle**
**em•bay**
**em•bay•ment** bay-shaped
**em•bed** (**•bed•ding, •bed•ded**)
**em•bed•ment**
**em•bel•lish**
**em•bel•lish•er**
**em•bel•lish•ment**

**em•ber**
**em•bez•zle**
**em•bez•zle•ment**
**em•bez•zler**
**em•bit•ter**
**em•bit•ter•er**
**em•bit•ter•ment**
**em•bla•zon**
**em•bla•zon•ment**
**em•bla•zon•ry**
**em•blem**
**em•blem•at•ic** (*or* **•ati•cal**)
**em•blem•ati•cal•ly**
**em•blema•tize** (*or* **•tise, •blem•ize, •blem•ise**)
**em•ble•ments** legal term
**em•bodi•ment** (*or* **im•**)
**em•body** (**•bod•ies, •body•ing, •bod•ied**)
**em•bold•en**
**em•bo•lec•to•my** (*plural* **•mies**)
**em•bol•ic**
**em•bo•lism**
**em•bo•lis•mic**
**em•bo•lus** (*plural* **•li**) material blocking blood vessel
**em•bo•ly** (*plural* **•lies**) embryology term
**em•bon•point** *French* plumpness
**em•boss**
**em•boss•er**
**em•boss•ment**
**em•bou•chure** (*plural* **•chures**)
**em•bow** architecture term
**em•bow•el**
**em•bow•er**
**em•bow•ment**
**em•brace**
**em•brace•able**
**em•brace•ment**
**em•brac•er**
**em•brac•ery** *Obsolete* jury bribing
**em•branch•ment**
**em•bra•sure** fortification
**em•bra•sured**
**em•brec•to•my** (*plural* **•mies**)
**em•bro•cate**
**em•bro•ca•tion**
**em•broi•der**
**em•broi•der•er**
**em•broi•dery** (*plural* **•deries**)
**em•broil**
**em•broil•er**
**em•broil•ment**
**em•bry•ec•to•my** (*plural* **•mies**)
**em•bruc** *variant spelling of* **imbrue**
**em•bryo** (*plural* **•bryos**)
**em•bryo•gen•ic**
**em•bry•og•eny** development of embryo
**em•bry•oid**
**em•bryo•logi•cal** (*or* **•log•ic**)
**em•bry•olo•gist**
**em•bry•ol•ogy**
**em•bry•on•ic** (*or* **•bryo•nal**)
**em•bry•oni•cal•ly**
**em•bus** (**•bus•ing, •bused** *or* **•bus•sing, •bussed**)
**emend** improve text; *compare* **amend**
**emend•able**
**emen•da•tion**
**emen•da•tor**
**emen•da•tory**
**em•er•ald**
**emerge**
**emer•gence**
**emer•gen•cy** (*plural* **•cies**)
**emer•gent**
**emeri•tus**
**emersed** botany term
**emer•sion** emerging; *compare* **immersion**
**em•ery** mineral
**em•esis** vomiting
**emet•ic**
**emeti•cal•ly**
**em•etine** (*or* **•etin**) alkaloid
**emi•grant**
**emi•grate** leave country; *compare* **immigrate**
**emi•gra•tion**
**emi•gra•tion•al**
**emi•gra•tive**
**émi•gré** *French* emigrant
**Emilia-Romagna** Italian region
**Emi•nence** (*or* **•nen•cy**; *plural* **•nences** *or* **•nen•cies**) cardinal's title
**emi•nence** (*or* **•nen•cy**; *plural* **•nences** *or* **•nen•cies**) superiority
**émi•nence grise** (*plural* **emi•nences grises**) *French* powerful person
**emi•nent** distinguished; *compare* **immanent; imminent**
**emir** (*or* **emeer**) Islamic ruler
**emir•ate** (*or* **emeer•**)
**em•is•sary** (*plural* **•saries**)
**emis•sion**
**emis•sive**
**emis•siv•ity** physics term
**emit** (**emit•ting, emit•ted**)
**emit•ter**
**Em•men** Dutch city
**em•mena•gog•ic**
**em•mena•gogue** medical term
**Em•men•thal** (*or* **•tal, •thal•er, •tal•er**) cheese
**em•mer** wheat
**em•met** *Dialect* ant
**em•me•tro•pia** perfect vision
**em•me•trop•ic**
**Emmy** television award
**emol•lience**
**emol•lient** soothing
**emolu•ment** salary
**emote**
**emot•er**
**emo•tion**
**emo•tion•al**
**emo•tion•al•ism**
**emo•tion•al•ist**
**emo•tion•al•is•tic**
**emo•tion•al•ity**
**emo•tion•ali•za•tion** (*or* **•sa•tion**)
**emo•tion•al•ize** (*or* **•ise**)
**emo•tion•al•ly**
**emo•tive**
**emo•tive•ness** (*or* **•tiv•ity**)
**emo•ti•vism**
**em•pale** *less common spelling of* **impale**
**em•pan•el** (*US* **im•**; **•el•ling, •elled**, *US* **•el•ing, •eled**)
**em•pan•el•ment** (*US* **im•**)
**em•path•ic** (*or* **•pa•thet•ic**)

**em•pathi•cal•ly** (*or* **•pa•theti•cal•ly)**
**em•pa•thize** (*or* **•thise)**
**em•pa•thy**
**em•pen•nage** aircraft tail
**em•per•or**
**em•per•or•ship**
**em•pery** power
**em•pha•sis** (*plural* **•ses)**
**em•pha•size** (*or* **•sise)**
**em•phat•ic**
**em•phati•cal•ly**
**em•phati•cal•ness**
**em•phy•sema** lung condition
**em•phy•sema•tous**
**em•pire**
**em•pir•ic**
**em•piri•cal**
**em•piri•cal•ly**
**em•piri•cal•ness**
**em•piri•cism**
**em•piri•cist**
**em•place**
**em•place•ment**
**em•plane**
**em•ploy**
**em•ploy•abil•ity**
**em•ploy•able**
**em•ployee**
**em•ploy•er**
**em•ploy•ment**
**em•poi•son**
**em•po•rium** (*plural* **•riums** *or* **•ria)**
**em•pov•er•ish** *less common spelling of* **impoverish**
**em•pow•er**
**em•pow•er•ment**
**em•press**
**empt** *Dialect* empty
**emp•ti•able**
**emp•ti•ly**
**emp•ti•ness**
**emp•ty** (*adj* **•ti•er, •ti•est;** *verb* **•ties, •ty•ing, •tied)**
**empty-handed**
**empty-headed**
**em•py•ema** pus accumulation
**em•py•emic**
**em•py•real**
**em•py•rean** heavens
**em•py•reu•ma** burning smell
**emu**
**emu•late**
**emu•la•tion**
**emu•la•tive**
**emu•la•tor**
**emu•lous** competitive
**emu•lous•ness**
**emul•si•fi•able** (*or* **emul•sible)**
**emul•si•fi•ca•tion**
**emul•si•fi•er**
**emul•si•fy** (**•fies, •fy•ing, •fied)**
**emul•sion**
**emul•sive**
**emul•soid** chemistry term
**emunc•tory** (*plural* **•tories)** excretory organ
**en** half an em; *compare* **em**
**en•able**
**en•abler**
**en•act**
**en•ac•tion**
**en•ac•tive**
**en•act•ment**
**en•ac•tor**
**en•ac•tory**
**enam•el** (**•el•ling, •elled;** *US* **•el•ing, •eled)**
**enam•el•ler** (*US* **•el•er)**
**enam•el•list** (*US* **•el•ist)**
**enam•el•work**
**en•am•our** (*US* **•or)**
**en•am•oured** (*US* **•ored)**
**en•antio•morph** crystal form
**en•antio•mor•phic**
**en•antio•morph•ism**
**en•ar•thro•dial**
**en•ar•thro•sis** (*plural* **•ses)** ball-and-socket joint
**enate** of the mother
**enat•ic**
**en bloc** *French* in a block
**en•cae•nia** festival
**en•cage**
**en•camp**
**en•camp•ment**
**en•cap•su•late**
**en•cap•su•la•tion**
**en•case** (*or* **in•)**
**en•case•ment** (*or* **in•)**
**en•cash**
**en•cash•able**
**en•cash•ment**
**en•caus•tic** ceramics term
**en•caus•ti•cal•ly**
**en•ceinte** pregnant
**Enceladus** mythological giant
**en•cephal•ic** of the brain
**en•cepha•lin** (*or* **•kepha•)** brain chemical
**en•cepha•li•tic**
**en•cepha•li•tis**
**en•cepha•lo•gram**
**en•cepha•lo•graph**
**en•cepha•lo•graphi•cal**
**en•cepha•log•ra•phy**
**en•cepha•lo•ma** (*plural* **•mas** *or* **•ma•ta)** tumour
**en•cepha•lo•my•eli•tic**
**en•cepha•lo•my•eli•tis**
**en•cepha•lon** (*plural* **•la)** brain
**en•cepha•lous**
**en•chain**
**en•chain•ment**
**en•chant**
**en•chant•er**
**en•chant•ing**
**en•chant•ment**
**en•chant•ress**
**en•chase** engrave
**en•chi•la•da** Mexican food
**en•chon•dro•ma** (*plural* **•mas** *or* **•ma•ta)** tumour
**en•chon•droma•tous**
**en•cho•rial** (*or* **•ric)** of a particular country
**en•ci•pher**
**en•ci•pher•er**
**en•ci•pher•ment**
**en•cir•cle**
**en•cir•cle•ment**
**en•clasp**
**en•clave**
**en•clit•ic** linguistics term
**en•cliti•cal•ly**
**en•clos•able** (*or* **in•)**
**en•close**
**en•clos•er**
**en•clo•sure**
**en•code**
**en•code•ment**
**en•cod•er**
**en•co•mi•ast** writer of eulogies
**en•co•mi•as•tic** (*or* **•ti•cal)**
**en•co•mi•as•ti•cal•ly**

**en•co•mium** (*plural* **•miums** *or* **•mia)**
**en•com•pass**
**en•com•pass•ment**
**en•core**
**en•coun•ter**
**en•coun•ter•er**
**en•cour•age**
**en•cour•age•ment**
**en•cour•ag•er**
**en•cour•ag•ing•ly**
**en•cri•nite** fossil
**en•croach**
**en•croach•er**
**en•croach•ing•ly**
**en•croach•ment**
**en•crust** (*or* **in•**)
**en•crust•ant** (*or* **in•**)
**en•crus•ta•tion** (*or* **in•**)
**en•cul•tu•ra•tion**
**en•cul•tu•ra•tive**
**en•cum•ber** (*or* **in•**)
**en•cum•ber•ing•ly** (*or* **in•**)
**en•cum•brance** (*or* **in•**)
**en•cum•branc•er** legal term
**en•cyc•lic**
**en•cyc•li•cal** letter from pope
**en•cy•clo•pedia** (*or* **•pae•dia)**
**en•cy•clo•pedic** (*or* **•pae•dic)**
**en•cy•clo•pedi•cal•ly** (*or* **•pae•di•)**
**en•cy•clo•pedism** (*or* **•pae•dism)**
**en•cy•clo•pedist** (*or* **•pae•dist)**
**en•cyst** biology term
**en•cyst•ment** (*or* **•ta•tion)**
**end**
**en•dam•age**
**en•dam•age•ment**
**en•da•moeba** (*US* **•meba;** *plural* **•moebae** *or* **•moebas,** *US* **•mebas)**
**en•dan•ger**
**en•dan•ger•ment**
**end•arch** botany term
**end-blown** music term
**end•brain**
**en•dear**
**en•dear•ing**
**en•dear•ing•ly**
**en•dear•ment**
**en•deav•our** (*US* **•or)**
**en•deav•our•er** (*US* **•or•)**
**en•dem•ic** (*noun*) localized disease; *compare* **epidemic**
**en•dem•ic** (*or* **•demi•al, •demi•cal;** *adj*)
**en•demi•cal•ly**
**en•de•mism** (*or* **•mic•ity)**
**end•er**
**en•der•mic** absorbed through skin
**end•game**
**end•ing**
**en•dive**
**end•less**
**end•less•ness**
**end•long**
**end•most**
**endo•blast** embryology term
**endo•blas•tic**
**endo•car•dial** (*or* **•di•ac)**
**endo•car•di•tic**
**endo•car•di•tis**
**endo•car•dium** (*plural* **•dia)** heart membrane
**endo•carp** part of fruit
**endo•car•pal** (*or* **•pic)**
**endo•cen•tric** linguistics term
**endo•cra•nium** (*plural* **•nia)** anatomy term
**endo•crin•al**
**endo•crine** ductless; *compare* **exocrine**
**endo•crin•ic**
**endo•crino•log•ic** (*or* **•ic•al)**
**endo•cri•nolo•gist**
**endo•cri•nol•ogy** study of hormones
**en•doc•ri•nous**
**endo•derm** (*or* **ento•**) part of embryo
**endo•der•mal** (*or* **ento•**)
**endo•der•mic** (*or* **ento•**)
**endo•derm•is** botany term
**endo•don•tia**
**endo•don•tic**
**endo•don•tics** dentistry term
**endo•don•tist**
**endo•don•tol•ogy**
**endo•en•zyme**
**endo•er•gic** energy-absorbing; *compare* **exoergic**
**en•doga•mous** (*or* **endo•gam•ic)**
**en•doga•my**
**en•dog•enous** developing in an organism
**en•dog•eny**
**endo•lymph** fluid in ear
**endo•lym•phat•ic**
**endo•metrial**
**endo•metrio•sis**
**endo•metrium** (*plural* **•metria)** womb lining
**endo•morph**
**endo•mor•phic** heavily built
**endo•mor•phism** geology term
**endo•mor•phy**
**endo•neu•rium** anatomy term
**endo•para•site**
**endo•para•sit•ic**
**endo•pep•ti•dase** enzyme
**endo•phyte** (*or* **ento•**) parasitic plant
**endo•phyt•ic** (*or* **ento•**)
**endo•plasm** biology term
**endo•plas•mic**
**en•dor•phin** brain chemical
**en•dors•able** (*or* **in•**)
**en•dorse** (*or* **in•**)
**en•dor•see** (*or* **in•**)
**en•dorse•ment** (*or* **in•**)
**en•dors•er** (*or* **•dor•sor, in•)**
**endo•scope** medical instrument
**endo•scop•ic**
**en•dos•co•pist**
**en•dos•co•py**
**endo•skel•etal**
**endo•skel•eton**
**en•dos•mo•sis** biology term
**en•dos•mot•ic**
**en•dos•moti•cal•ly**
**endo•some** cell nucleus part
**endo•sperm** seed tissue
**endo•sper•mic**
**endo•spore**
**en•dos•por•ous**
**en•dos•teal**
**en•dos•teum** (*plural* **•tea)** anatomy term
**en•dos•to•sis** (*plural* **•ses)** physiology term
**endo•thecial**

**endo•thecium** (*plural* **•thecia**) botany term
**endo•thelial**
**endo•theli•oid**
**endo•thelio•ma** (*plural* **•mata**) tumour
**endo•thelium** (*plural* **•thelia**) anatomy term
**endo•ther•mic** (*or* **•mal**) heat-absorbing; *compare* **exothermic**
**endo•ther•mi•cal•ly**
**endo•ther•mism**
**endo•tox•ic**
**endo•tox•in**
**en•dow**
**en•dow•er**
**en•dow•ment**
**end•paper** part of book
**end•plate**
**end•play** bridge term
**en•due** (*or* **in•**; **•dues, •du•ing, •dued**) endow
**en•dur•abil•ity** (*or* **•dur•able•ness**)
**en•dur•able**
**en•dur•ance**
**en•dure**
**en•dur•ing**
**en•dur•ing•ly**
**end•ways**
**Endymion** mythological character
**en•ema** (*plural* **•emas** *or* **•ema•ta**)
**en•emy** (*plural* **•emies**)
**en•er•get•ic**
**en•er•geti•cal•ly**
**en•er•geti•cist**
**en•er•get•ics**
**en•er•gid** biology term
**en•er•gize** (*or* **•gise**)
**en•er•giz•er** (*or* **•gis•er**)
**en•er•gu•men** possessed person
**en•er•gy** (*plural* **•gies**)
**en•er•vate** weaken; *compare* **innervate; innovate**
**en•er•va•tion**
**en•er•va•tive**
**en•er•va•tor**
**en•face**
**en face** *French* facing forwards
**en•face•ment**
**en fa•mille** *French* informally
**en•fant ter•ri•ble** (*plural* **en•fants ter•ri•bles**) *French* indiscreet person
**en•fee•ble**
**en•fee•ble•ment**
**en•fee•bler**
**en•feoff** legal term
**en•feoff•ment**
**En•field** London borough; rifle
**en•fi•lade** military term
**en•fleu•rage** *French* perfume-making
**en•fold** (*or* **in•**)
**en•fold•er** (*or* **in•**)
**en•fold•ment** (*or* **in•**)
**en•force**
**en•force•abil•ity**
**en•force•able**
**en•forc•ed•ly**
**en•force•ment**
**en•forc•er**
**en•fran•chise**
**en•fran•chise•ment**
**en•fran•chis•er**
**En•ga•dine** Swiss region
**en•gage**
**en•gagé** *French* committed
**en•gaged**
**en•gage•ment**
**en•gag•er**
**en•gag•ing**
**en•gag•ing•ly**
**en•gag•ing•ness**
**en garde** *French* on guard
**en•gen•der**
**en•gen•der•er**
**en•gen•der•ment**
**en•gine**
**en•gi•neer**
**en•gi•neer•ing**
**en•gine•ry** (*plural* **•ries**)
**en•gla•cial**
**Eng•land**
**Eng•lish**
**Eng•lish•ism**
**English•man** (*plural* **•men**)
**English•woman** (*plural* **•women**)
**en•glut** devour
**en•gorge**
**en•gorge•ment**
**en•graft** (*or* **in•**)
**en•graf•ta•tion** (*or* **en•graft•ment, in•**)
**en•grail** indent coin
**en•grail•ment**
**en•grain** *variant spelling of* **ingrain**
**en•grained** *variant spelling of* **ingrained**
**en•gram** psychology term
**en•gram•mic** (*or* **•gram•at•ic**)
**en•grave**
**en•grav•er**
**en•grav•ing**
**en•gross**
**en•gross•ed•ly**
**en•gross•er**
**en•gross•ing•ly**
**en•gross•ment**
**en•gulf** (*or* **in•**)
**en•gulf•ment**
**en•hance**
**en•hance•ment**
**en•hanc•er**
**en•hanc•ive**
**en•har•mon•ic**
**en•har•moni•cal•ly**
**enig•ma**
**en•ig•mat•ic** (*or* **•mati•cal**)
**en•ig•mati•cal•ly**
**Eni•we•tok** Pacific atoll
**en•jamb•ment** (*or* **•jambe•**) poetry term
**en•join**
**en•join•er**
**en•join•ment**
**en•joy**
**en•joy•able**
**en•joy•ably**
**en•joy•er**
**en•joy•ment**
**en•kepha•lin** *variant spelling of* **encephalin**
**en•kin•dle**
**en•kin•dler**
**en•lace**
**en•lace•ment**
**en•large**
**en•large•able**
**en•large•ment**
**en•larg•er**
**en•light•en**
**en•light•en•er**
**en•light•en•ing•ly**

**En•light•en•ment** 18th-century movement
**en•light•en•ment**
**en•list**
**en•list•er**
**en•list•ment**
**en•liv•en**
**en•liv•en•er**
**en•liv•en•ing•ly**
**en•liv•en•ment**
**en masse** *French* in a mass
**en•mesh** (*or* **in•, im•**)
**en•mity** (*plural* **•mities**)
**en•nage** printing term
**en•nead** group of nine
**en•nead•ic**
**en•nea•gon**
**en•nea•he•dral**
**en•nea•he•dron** (*plural* **•drons** *or* **•dra**)
**En•nis** Irish town
**En•nis•kil•len** (*or* **In•nis•kil•ling**) Northern Irish town
**en•no•ble**
**en•no•ble•ment**
**en•no•bler**
**en•no•bling•ly**
**en•nui** apathy
**enol** chemistry term
**enol•ogy** *US spelling of* **aenology**
**enor•mity** (*plural* **•mities**)
**enor•mous**
**eno•sis** union of Greece and Cyprus
**enough**
**enounce** enunciate
**en pas•sant** *French* in passing
**en•phy•tot•ic** botany term
**en•plane**
**en•quire** (*or esp. US* **in•**) ask; *compare* **inquire**
**en•quir•er** (*or esp. US* **in•**)
**en•quiry** (*or esp. US* **in•**; *plural* **•quiries**)
**en•rage**
**en•rag•ed•ly**
**en•rage•ment**
**en rap•port** *French* in sympathy
**en•rap•ture**
**en•rich**
**en•rich•er**
**en•rich•ment**
**en•robe**
**en•rob•er**
**en•rol** (*US* **•roll; •rol•ling, •rolled**)
**en•rol•lee**
**en•rol•ler**
**en•rol•ment** (*US* **•roll•**)
**en•root**
**en route** *French* on the way
**ens** metaphysics term
**en•san•guine** stain with blood
**En•schede** Dutch city
**en•sconce**
**en•sem•ble**
**en•shrine** (*or* **in•**)
**en•shrine•ment**
**en•shroud**
**en•si•form** sword-shaped
**en•sign**
**en•sign•ship** (*or* **•cy**; *plural* **•ships** *or* **•cies**)
**en•si•labil•ity**
**en•si•lage**
**en•sile** store in silo
**en•slave**
**en•slave•ment**
**en•slav•er**
**en•snare** (*or* **in•**)
**en•snare•ment**
**en•snar•er**
**en•soul** (*or* **in•**)
**en•sphere** (*or* **in•**)
**en•sta•tite** mineral
**en•sue** (**•su•ing, •sued**)
**en•su•ing•ly**
**en suite** forming a unit
**en•sure** make sure; *compare* insure
**en•sur•er**
**en•swathe**
**en•tab•la•ture**
**en•ta•ble•ment** platform
**en•tail**
**en•tail•er**
**en•tail•ment**
**en•ta•moeba** (*or* **en•da•**; *US* **•meba**; *plural* **•moebae** *or* **•moebas**, *US* **•mebas**) amoeba
**en•tan•gle**
**en•tan•gle•ment**
**en•tan•gler**
**en•ta•sia**
**en•ta•sis** (*plural* **•ses**) architectural term
**En•teb•be** Ugandan town
**en•tel•echy** (*plural* **•echies**) philosophy term
**en•tel•lus** monkey
**en•tente cor•diale** *French* friendly relations
**en•ter**
**en•ter•able**
**en•ter•al•ly**
**en•ter•er**
**en•ter•ic** (*or* **•al**) intestinal
**en•teri•tis**
**en•tero•gas•trone** hormone
**en•tero•ki•nase** enzyme
**en•ter•on** (*plural* **•tera**) digestive tract
**en•ter•os•to•my** (*plural* **•mies**)
**en•ter•ot•omy** (*plural* **•omies**)
**en•tero•vi•rus** (*plural* **•ruses**)
**en•ter•prise**
**en•ter•pris•er**
**en•ter•pris•ing**
**en•ter•tain**
**en•ter•tain•er**
**en•ter•tain•ing**
**en•ter•tain•ing•ly**
**en•ter•tain•ment**
**en•thal•py** physics term
**en•thet•ic** medical term
**en•thral** (*US* **•thrall; •thral•ling, •thralled**)
**en•thrall•er**
**en•thral•ling•ly**
**en•thral•ment** (*US* **•thrall•**)
**en•throne**
**en•throne•ment**
**en•thuse**
**en•thu•si•asm**
**en•thu•si•ast**
**en•thu•si•as•tic**
**en•thu•si•as•ti•cal•ly**
**en•thy•memat•ic** (*or* **•ical**)
**en•thy•meme** logic term
**en•tice**
**en•tice•ment**
**en•tic•er**
**en•tic•ing•ly**
**en•tic•ing•ness**
**en•tire**
**en•tire•ly**
**en•tire•ness**

**en•tirety** (*plural* **•tireties**)
**en•ti•tle**
**en•ti•tle•ment**
**en•tity** (*plural* **•tities**)
**ento•blast** embryology term
**ento•blas•tic**
**ento•derm** *variant of* **endoderm**
**ento•der•mal** (*or* **•mic**)
**en•tomb**
**en•tomb•ment**
**en•tom•ic** of insects
**ento•mo•logi•cal** (*or* **•log•ic**)
**ento•molo•gist**
**ento•mo•lo•gize** (*or* **•gise**)
**ento•mol•ogy** study of insects; *compare* **etymology**
**ento•mopha•gous**
**ento•mophi•lous** insect-pollinated
**ento•mophi•ly**
**ento•mos•tra•can** crustacean
**ento•mos•tra•cous**
**ento•phyte** *variant of* **endophyte**
**ento•phyt•ic** *variant of* **endophytic**
**en•top•ic** in normal position; *compare* **ectopic**
**en•tou•rage**
**ento•zo•ic** living inside an animal
**ento•zo•on** (*or* **•an**; *plural* **•zoa**)
**en•tr'acte** *French* interval between acts
**en•trails**
**en•train** board a train
**en•train•ment**
**en•tram•mel** (**•mel•ling, •melled**; *US* **•mel•ing, •meled**) obstruct
**en•trance**
**en•trance•ment**
**en•tranc•ing•ly**
**en•trant**
**en•trap** (**•trap•ping, •trapped**)
**en•trap•ment**
**en•trap•per**
**en•treat**
**en•treat•ing•ly**
**en•treat•ment**
**en•treaty** (*plural* **•treaties**)
**en•tre•chat** ballet movement
**en•tre•côte**
**en•trée**
**en•tre•mets** (*plural* **•mets**) dessert
**en•trench**
**en•trench•er**
**en•trench•ment**
**en•tre nous** *French* between ourselves
**en•tre•pôt** trading centre
**en•tre•pre•neur**
**en•tre•pre•neur•ial**
**en•tre•pre•neur•ship**
**en•tre•sol** *French* between floors
**en•tro•py** (*plural* **•pies**) physics term
**en•trust**
**en•trust•ment**
**en•try** (*plural* **•tries**)
**en•twine**
**en•twine•ment**
**enu•cleate** remove nucleus
**enu•clea•tion**
**enu•clea•tor**
**Enu•gu** Nigerian city
**enu•mer•able** countable; *compare* **innumerable**
**enu•mer•ate**
**enu•mera•tion**
**enu•mera•tive**
**enu•mera•tor**
**enun•ci•abil•ity**
**enun•ci•able**
**enun•ci•ate** articulate; *compare* **annunciate**
**enun•cia•tion**
**enun•cia•tive** (*or* **•tory**)
**enun•cia•tor**
**en•ure** *variant spelling of* **inure**
**enu•resis** bedwetting
**enu•ret•ic**
**en•vel•op** (*verb*)
**en•velope** (*noun*)
**en•vel•op•ment**
**en•ven•om**
**en•ven•omed**
**en•vi•able**
**en•vi•able•ness**
**en•vi•ably**
**en•vi•er**
**en•vi•ous**
**en•vi•ous•ness**
**en•vi•ron** (*verb*) encircle
**en•vi•ron•ment**
**en•vi•ron•men•tal**
**en•vi•ron•men•tal•ism**
**en•vi•ron•men•tal•ist**
**en•vi•ron•men•tal•ly**
**en•vi•rons** (*noun*) vicinity
**en•vis•age**
**en•vis•age•ment**
**en•vi•sion**
**en•voy**
**en•vy** (*noun, plural* **•vies**; *verb* **•vies, •vy•ing, •vied**)
**en•vy•ing•ly**
**en•wind** (**•wind•ing, •wound**)
**en•womb**
**en•wrap** (*or* **•in**; **•wrap•ping, •wrapped**)
**en•wreath**
**en•zo•ot•ic** veterinary term
**en•zo•oti•cal•ly**
**en•zy•mat•ic** (*or* **•zy•mic**)
**en•zyme** catalyst
**en•zy•mo•logi•cal**
**en•zy•molo•gist**
**en•zy•mol•ogy**
**en•zy•moly•sis** (*or* **•mo•sis**)
**en•zy•mo•lyt•ic**
**eobi•ont** biology term
**Eocene** geological period
**Eogene** geological period
**eohip•pus** fossil horse
**eolith** stone tool
**Eolith•ic** Stone Age period
**eon** *US spelling of* **aeon**
**eonism** psychiatry term
**Eos** Greek goddess
**eosin** (*or* **eosine**) dye
**eosin•ic**
**eosino•phil** blood cell
**eosino•phil•ic** (*or* **eosi•nophi•lous**)
**Eozo•ic** geological period
**epact** astronomy term
**ep•arch** Eastern bishop
**ep•ar•chial**
**ep•ar•chy** (*or* **•chate**; *plural* **•chies** *or* **•chates**)
**ep•aulet** (*or* **•aulette**)
**épée** sword
**épée•ist**

**epei•ric** (*or* **epei•ro•gen•ic, epei•ro•genet•ic**) of continental drift
**ep•ei•rog•eny** (*or* **epi•rog•eny, ep•ei•ro•gen•esis**)
**ep•en•cephal•ic**
**ep•en•cepha•lon** (*plural* **•la**) part of brain
**epen•thesis** (*plural* **•theses**) linguistics term
**ep•en•thet•ic**
**epergne** table ornament
**ep•ex•egesis** (*plural* **•egeses**) linguistics term
**ep•ex•eget•ic** (*or* **•egeti•cal**)
**ep•ex•egeti•cal•ly**
**ephah** Hebrew unit
**ephebe** Greek youth
**ephed•rine** (*or* **•rin**) alkaloid
**ephem•era** (*plural* **•eras** *or* **•erae**) short-lived insect; *compare* **emphemeron**
**ephem•er•al**
**ephem•er•al•ity** (*or* **•al•ness**)
**ephem•er•id** mayfly
**ephem•er•is** (*plural* **eph•emer•ides**) astronomical table
**ephem•er•on** (*plural* **•era** *or* **•er•ons**) transitory thing; *compare* **ephemera**
**Ephesian**
**Eph•esus** ancient Greek city
**ephod** vestment
**eph•or** Greek magistrate
**epi•blast** embryology term
**epi•blas•tic**
**epi•bol•ic**
**epibo•ly** (*plural* **•lies**) embryology term
**epic**
**epi•ca•lyx** (*plural* **•lyxes** *or* **•ly•ces**) botany term
**epi•can•thus** (*plural* **•thi**) anatomy term
**epi•car•di•ac** (*or* **•dial**)
**epi•car•dium** (*plural* **•dia**) anatomy term
**epi•carp** (*or* **exo•**) botany term
**epi•cene**
**epi•cen•ism**
**epi•cen•tral**
**epi•cen•tre** (*US* **•ter**)
**epi•clesis** theology term
**epi•con•ti•nen•tal**
**epi•cot•yl** botany term
**epi•cri•sis** medical term
**epi•crit•ic** anatomy term
**epi•cure**
**Epi•cu•rean** of Epicurus
**epi•cu•rean** devoted to pleasure
**Epi•cu•rean•ism**
**epi•cur•ism** (*or* **•cu•rean•ism**)
**epi•cy•cle**
**epi•cy•clic** (*or* **•cli•cal**)
**epi•cy•cloid** geometric curve
**epi•cy•cloid•al**
**Epi•daur•us** Greek port
**epi•deic•tic** (*or* **•dic•tic**) rhetorical term
**epi•dem•ic** widespread disease; *compare* **endemic**
**epi•demi•cal**
**epi•demio•logi•cal**
**epi•demi•olo•gist**
**epi•demi•ol•ogy**
**epi•der•mal** (*or* **•mic, •moid**)
**epi•der•mis**
**epi•dia•scope** projector
**epi•didy•mal**
**epi•di•dy•mis** (*plural* **•dymi•des**) anatomy term
**epi•dote** mineral
**epi•dot•ic**
**epi•dur•al** anaesthetic
**epi•fo•cal** geology term
**epi•gas•tric** (*or* **•trial**)
**epi•gas•trium** (*plural* **•tria**) abdominal part
**epi•geal** (*or* **•gean, •geous**) botany term
**epi•gene** formed at earth's surface
**epi•gen•esis** biology theory
**epi•gen•esist** (*or* **epig•enist**)
**epi•genet•ic**
**epi•geneti•cal•ly**
**epig•enous**
**epi•glot•tal** (*or* **•tic**)
**epi•glot•tis** (*plural* **•tises** *or* **•ti•des**) anatomy term
**epi•gone** (*or* **•gon**) imitator
**epi•gram** saying
**epi•gram•mat•ic**
**epi•gram•mati•cal•ly**
**epi•gram•ma•tism**
**epi•gram•ma•tist**
**epi•gram•ma•tize** (*or* **•tise**)
**epi•graph** inscription
**epig•ra•pher**
**epi•graph•ic** (*or* **•graphi•cal**)
**epi•graphi•cal•ly**
**epig•ra•phist**
**epig•ra•phy**
**epigy•nous** botany term
**epigy•ny**
**epi•lep•sy**
**epi•lep•tic**
**epi•lep•ti•cal•ly**
**epi•lep•toid** (*or* **•lep•ti•form**)
**epi•lim•ni•on** lake water
**epilo•gist**
**epi•logue**
**epi•mere** embryology term
**epi•mor•phic**
**epi•mor•pho•sis** zoology term
**epi•my•sium** (*plural* **•sia**) anatomy term
**epi•nas•tic**
**epi•nas•ty** (*plural* **•ties**) botany term
**epi•neph•rine** *US* adrenaline
**epi•neu•rial**
**epi•neu•rium** anatomy term
**epi•phan•ic**
**Epipha•ny** Christian festival
**epipha•ny** (*plural* **•nies**) manifestation
**epi•phenom•enal**
**epi•phenom•enal•ism** philosophy term
**epi•phenom•enal•ist**
**epi•phenom•enon** (*plural* **•ena**)
**epi•phragm** shell
**epi•phys•eal** (*or* **•ial**)
**epiphy•sis** (*plural* **•ses**) anatomy term
**epi•phyte** botany term
**epi•phyt•ic** (*or* **•phyti•cal**)
**epi•phyti•cal•ly**
**epi•phy•tot•ic**
**epi•ro•gen•ic** (*or* **•genet•ic**) *variants of* **epeirogenic**
**epi•rog•eny** *variant spelling of* **epeirogeny**

**Epi•rus** Greek region
**epis•co•pa•cy** (*plural* **•cies**) church government
**epis•co•pal**
**epis•co•pa•lian**
**epis•co•pa•lian•ism**
**epis•co•pal•ism**
**epis•co•pal•ly**
**epis•co•pate**
**epi•scope** projector
**epi•semat•ic** zoology term
**epi•si•oto•my** (*plural* **•mies**) medical term
**epi•sode**
**epi•sod•ic** (*or* **•sodi•cal**)
**epi•sodi•cal•ly**
**epi•some**
**epi•spas•tic** producing a blister
**epi•sta•sis** medical term
**epi•stat•ic**
**epi•stax•is** nosebleed
**ep•is•tem•ic** relating to knowledge
**epis•temo•logi•cal**
**epis•temolo•gist**
**epis•temol•ogy**
**epi•ster•num** (*plural* **•na**) breastbone part
**epis•tle**
**epis•tler** (*or* **•to•ler, •to•list**)
**epis•to•lary** (*or* **epi•stol•ic, epis•to•la•tory**)
**epis•to•ler**
**epis•tro•phe** rhetorical term
**epi•style** architectural term
**epi•taph** inscription
**epi•taph•ic**
**epi•taph•ist**
**epita•sis** drama term
**epi•tax•ial**
**epi•taxy** (*or* **•tax•is**) crystal growth
**epi•tha•lam•ic**
**epi•tha•la•mium** (*or* **•mi•on**; *plural* **•mia**) nuptial ode
**epi•thelial** (*or* **•theli•oid**)
**epi•thelio•ma** (*plural* **•mas** *or* **•ma•ta**) tumour
**epi•theli•oma•tous**
**epi•thelium** (*plural* **•thelia**) tissue
**epi•thet**
**epi•thet•ic** (*or* **theti•cal**)
**epito•me** typical example
**epi•tom•ic** (*or* **•tomi•cal**)
**epito•mist**
**epito•mi•za•tion** (*or* **•sa•tion**)
**epito•mize** (*or* **•mise**)
**epito•miz•er** (*or* **•mis•er**)
**epi•zo•ic** zoology term
**epi•zo•ism**
**epi•zo•ite**
**epi•zo•on** (*plural* **•zoa**) animal parasite
**epi•zo•ot•ic** veterinary term
**epi•zo•oti•cal•ly**
**ep•och**
**ep•och•al**
**epoch-making**
**ep•ode** prosody term
**epo•nym** something named after a person
**epony•mous** (*or* **epo•nym•ic**)
**epony•my**
**épo•pée** (*or* **epo•poeia**) poem
**epos** body of poetry
**epox•ide**
**epoxy**
**Ep•ping**
**Ep•si•lon** astronomy term
**ep•si•lon** Greek letter
**Ep•som**
**epyl•li•on** (*plural* **•lia**) poem
**eq•uabil•ity** (*or* **•uable•ness**)
**eq•uable**
**eq•uably**
**equal** (**equal•ling, equalled**; *US* **equal•ing, equaled**)
**equal-area** cartography term
**equali•tar•ian**
**equali•tari•an•ism**
**equali•ty** (*plural* **•ties**)
**equali•za•tion** (*or* **•sa•tion**)
**equal•ize** (*or* **•ise**)
**equal•iz•er** (*or* **•is•er**)
**equal•ly**
**equa•nim•ity**
**equani•mous**
**equat•abil•ity**
**equat•able**
**equate**
**equa•tion**
**equa•tion•al**
**equa•tor**
**equa•to•rial**
**Equa•to•rial Guinea** African republic
**eq•uer•ry** (*plural* **•ries**)
**eques•trian**
**eques•tri•an•ism**
**eques•tri•enne**
**equi•an•gu•lar**
**equi•dis•tance**
**equi•dis•tant**
**equi•lat•eral**
**equili•brant**
**equili•brate**
**equi•li•bra•tion**
**equi•li•bra•tor**
**equili•brist**
**equili•bris•tic**
**equi•lib•rium** (*plural* **•riums** *or* **•ria**)
**equi•mo•lecu•lar**
**equine**
**equin•ity**
**equi•noc•tial**
**equi•nox**
**equip** (**equip•ping, equipped**)
**equi•page** carriage
**equi•par•ti•tion** physics term
**equip•ment**
**equi•poise** equilibrium
**equi•pol•lence** (*or* **•len•cy**)
**equi•pol•lent** equal in effect
**equi•pon•der•ance** (*or* **•ancy**)
**equi•pon•der•ant**
**equi•pon•der•ate** counterbalance
**equi•po•tent**
**equi•po•ten•tial** physics term
**equi•po•ten•ti•al•ity**
**equip•per**
**equi•setum** (*plural* **•setums** *or* **•seta**) plant
**equi•table**
**equi•table•ness**
**equi•tably**
**equi•tant** botany term
**equi•ta•tion** horsemanship
**equi•tes** Roman cavalry
**equi•ty** (*plural* **•ties**)
**equiva•lence**
**equi•va•len•cy** (*or* **•va•lence**) chemistry term

**equiva•lent**
**equivo•cal**
**equivo•cal•ity** (*or* **•ca•cy**)
**equivo•cal•ly**
**equivo•cate**
**equivo•cat•ing•ly**
**equivo•ca•tion**
**equivo•ca•tory**
**equi•voque** (*or* **•voke**) pun
**Equul•eus** constellation
**era**
**era•di•ate** radiate
**era•dia•tion**
**eradi•cable**
**eradi•cant**
**eradi•cate**
**eradi•ca•tion**
**eradi•ca•tive**
**eradi•ca•tor**
**eras•able**
**erase**
**eras•er**
**era•sion**
**Eras•ti•an•ism** state supremacy over church
**eras•ure**
**Er•bil** (*or* **Ir•bil, Ar•bil**) Iraqi city
**er•bium** chemical element
**ere** *Poetic* before; *compare* **e'er**
**Erebus** Greek god
**Erech•theum** (*or* **•thei•on**) Athenian temple
**erect**
**erect•able**
**erect•er** (*or* **erec•tor**)
**erec•tile**
**erec•til•ity**
**erec•tion**
**erect•ness**
**erec•tor** (*or* **•ter**)
**er•emite** hermit
**er•emit•ic** (*or* **•emiti•cal**)
**er•emit•ism**
**erep•sin** enzyme
**er•ethism** medical term
**er•ethis•mic** (*or* **•ethis•tic, •ethit•ic**)
**Er•furt** German city
**erg** unit
**er•ga•toc•ra•cy** (*plural* **•cies**) government by workers
**ergo** *Latin* therefore
**er•go•graph** muscle-measuring instrument
**er•gom•eter** dynamometer
**er•go•nom•ic**
**er•go•nom•ics**
**er•gono•mist**
**er•gos•terol** biochemical compound
**er•got** crop disease
**er•got•ism** human disease
**eri•ca** shrub
**eri•ca•ceous**
**Erida•nus** constellation
**Erie** Canadian lake
**erig•er•on** plant
**Erin** *Archaic* Ireland
**eri•na•ceous** of hedgehogs
**Eris** Greek goddess
**er•is•tic** logic term
**er•is•ti•cal**
**Eri•trea**
**Eri•trean**
**erk** *Slang* aircraftsman
**Er•lang** unit
**erl•king** malevolent spirit
**er•mine** (*plural* **•mines** *or* **•mine**)
**erne** eagle
**Er•nie** computer lottery
**erode**
**erod•ent**
**ero•genei•ty**
**erog•enous** (*or* **ero•gen•ic**)
**Eros**
**erose** uneven
**ero•sion**
**ero•sion•al**
**ero•sive**
**ero•sive•ness**
**ero•tema** (*or* **•teme, •tesis**) rhetorical question
**ero•temat•ic** (*or* **•tet•ic**)
**erot•ic** (*or* **eroti•cal**)
**eroti•ca**
**eroti•cal•ly**
**eroti•cism** (*or* **ero•tism**)
**ero•to•gen•ic** *variant of* erogenous
**erot•ol•ogy**
**ero•to•ma•nia**
**ero•to•ma•ni•ac**
**err**
**er•ran•cy** (*plural* **•cies**)
**er•rand**
**er•rant**
**er•rant•ry** (*plural* **•tries**)
**er•ra•ta** *plural of* **erratum**
**er•rat•ic**
**er•rati•cal•ly**
**er•rati•cism**
**er•ra•tum** (*plural* **•ta**) printing error
**er•rhine** causing nasal secretion
**Er Rif** Moroccan region
**er•ro•neous**
**er•ro•neous•ness**
**er•ror**
**er•satz** artificial
**Erse** Gaelic
**erst•while**
**eru•bes•cence** redness
**eru•bes•cent**
**eruct** (*or* **eruc•tate**) belch
**eruc•ta•tion**
**eruc•ta•tive**
**eru•dite**
**eru•di•tion** (*or* **eru•dite•ness**)
**erum•pent** bursting out
**erupt** break out; *compare* **irrupt**
**erupt•ible**
**erup•tion**
**erup•tion•al**
**erup•tive**
**erup•tiv•ity** (*or* **•tive•ness**)
**Ery•man•thus** Greek mountain
**eryn•go** (*or* **erin•**; *plural* **•goes** *or* **•gos**) plant
**ery•sip•elas** skin disease
**ery•si•pela•tous**
**ery•sip•eloid**
**ery•thema** skin redness
**ery•themat•ic** (*or* **•thema•tous, •themic**)
**eryth•rism** abnormal redness
**ery•thris•mal**
**eryth•rite** mineral
**eryth•ri•tol** (*or* **•rite**) drug
**eryth•ro•blast** marrow cell
**eryth•ro•blas•tic**
**eryth•ro•blas•to•sis** blood disease
**eryth•ro•cyte** blood cell
**eryth•ro•cyt•ic**
**eryth•ro•cy•tom•eter**

**eryth•ro•cy•tom•etry**
**eryth•ro•my•cin** antibiotic
**eryth•ro•poi•esis** red blood cell formation
**eryth•ro•poi•et•ic**
**Er•zu•rum** Turkish city
**Es•bjerg** Danish port
**es•ca•drille** aircraft squadron; *compare* **espadrille**
**es•ca•lade** scaling walls
**es•ca•lad•er**
**es•ca•late**
**es•ca•la•tion**
**es•ca•la•tor**
**es•cal•lo•nia** shrub
**es•cal•lope** scallop
**es•ca•lope** veal slice
**es•cap•able**
**es•ca•pade**
**es•cape**
**es•capee**
**es•cape•ment**
**es•cap•er**
**es•cap•ism**
**es•cap•ist**
**es•ca•polo•gist**
**es•ca•pol•ogy**
**es•carp** fortification
**es•carp•ment** steep slope
**escha•lot** shallot
**es•char** scab
**es•cha•rot•ic**
**es•cha•to•logi•cal**
**es•cha•tolo•gist**
**es•cha•tol•ogy** theology
**es•cheat** legal term
**es•chew** avoid
**es•chew•al**
**es•chew•er**
**es•co•lar** (*plural* **•lars** *or* **•lar**) fish
**Es•co•rial** Spanish village
**es•cort**
**es•cri•toire**
**es•crow** legal term
**es•cu•do** (*plural* **•dos**) Portuguese currency
**es•cu•lent** edible
**es•cutch•eon** heraldry term
**es•cutch•eoned**
**Es•dra•elon** Israeli plain
**es•em•plas•tic** unifying
**es•er•ine** alkaloid
**Es•fa•han** *variant spelling of* **Isfahan**
**Esher**
**es•ker** (*or* **•kar**) glacial deposit
**Eskil•stu•na** Swedish city
**Es•ki•mo** (*plural* **•mos** *or* **•mo**)
**Es•ki•moan**
**Es•ki•moid**
**Es•ki•sehir** Turkish city
**esopha•gus** *US spelling of* **oesophagus**
**eso•ter•ic** abstruse; *compare* **exoteric**
**eso•teri•cal•ly**
**eso•teri•cism**
**es•pa•drille** canvas shoe; *compare* **escadrille**
**es•pal•ier** wall-trained tree
**es•par•to** (*plural* **•tos**) grass
**es•pe•cial**
**es•pe•cial•ly**
**Es•pe•ran•to** artificial language
**es•pial**
**espi•er**
**es•pio•nage**
**Es•pí•ri•to San•to** Brazilian state
**Es•pí•ri•tu San•to** Pacific island
**es•pla•nade**
**es•pous•al**
**es•pouse**
**es•pous•er**
**es•pres•so** (*plural* **•sos**) coffee
**es•prit** liveliness
**es•prit de corps** group pride
**espy** (**espies, espy•ing, espied**)
**es•quire**
**es•say** composition; attempt; *compare* **assay**
**es•say•ist**
**Es•sen** German city
**es•sence**
**Es•sene** Jewish sect
**es•sen•tial**
**es•sen•tial•ism** philosophical doctrine
**es•sen•tial•ist**
**es•sen•tial•ity** (*or* **•ness**)
**es•sen•tial•ly**
**Es•sequi•bo** South American river
**Es•sex**
**Es•sonne** French department
**es•tab•lish**
**es•tab•lish•er**
**es•tab•lish•ment**
**es•tab•lish•men•tar•ian**
**es•tab•lish•men•tar•ian•ism**
**es•ta•mi•net** French café
**es•tan•cia** ranch
**es•tate**
**es•teem**
**es•ter** chemistry term
**es•ter•ase** enzyme
**es•teri•fi•ca•tion**
**es•teri•fy** (**•fies, •fy•ing, •fied**)
**es•ti•mable**
**es•ti•mable•ness**
**es•ti•mate**
**es•ti•ma•tion**
**es•ti•ma•tive**
**es•ti•ma•tor**
**estipu•late** (*or* **ex•stipu•**) botany term
**es•thete** *US variant spelling of* **aesthete**
**es•thetic** *US variant spelling of* **aesthetic**
**es•ti•val** *US spelling of* **aestival**
**es•ti•vate** *US spelling of* **aestivate**
**Es•to•nia**
**Es•to•nian**
**es•top** (**•top•ping, •topped**) legal term
**es•top•page**
**es•top•pel**
**es•to•vers** legal term
**es•trade** dais
**es•tra•di•ol** *US spelling of* **oestradiol**
**es•tra•gon** tarragon
**es•trange**
**es•tranged**
**es•trange•ment**
**es•trang•er**
**es•tray**
**es•treat** legal term
**Es•tre•ma•du•ra** Spanish region

**es•tri•ol** *US spelling of* **oestriol**
**es•tro•gen** *US spelling of* **oestrogen**
**es•trone** *US spelling of* **oestrone**
**es•trous** *US spelling of* **oestrous**
**es•trus** *US spelling of* **oestrus**
**es•tu•ar•ial**
**es•tua•rine**
**es•tu•ary** (*plural* **•aries**)
**esu•ri•ence** (*or* **•en•cy**)
**esu•ri•ent** greedy
**eta** Greek letter
**etae•rio** (*plural* **•rios**) botany term
**éta•gère** *French* ornament stand
**eta•lon** physics device
**eta•mine** (*or* **•min**) fabric
**et cet•era** and so on
**et•cet•eras** (*plural noun*) extra things
**etch**
**etch•ant** etching acid
**etch•er**
**etch•ing**
**eter•nal**
**eter•nal•ity** (*or* **•ness**)
**eter•nali•za•tion** (*or* **eter•ni•, •sa•tion**)
**eter•nal•ize** (*or* **eter•nize, •ise**)
**eter•nal•ly**
**eter•nity** (*plural* **•nities**)
**ete•sian** meteorology term
**ethane**
**ethane•di•ol**
**etha•nol**
**eth•ene** *variant of* **ethylene**
**ether** anaesthetic
**ether** (*or* **aether**) hypothetical medium
**ethe•real**
**ethe•real•ity** (*or* **•ness**)
**ethe•reali•za•tion** (*or* **•sa•tion**)
**ethe•real•ize** (*or* **•ise**)
**ethe•real•ly**
**ether•ic**
**etheri•fi•ca•tion**
**etheri•fy** (**•fies, •fy•ing, •fied**)
**etheri•za•tion** (*or* **•sa•tion**)
**ether•ize** (*or* **•ise**)
**ether•iz•er** (*or* **•is•er**)
**eth•ic**
**ethi•cal**
**ethi•cal•ly**
**ethi•cal•ness** (*or* **•cali•ty**)
**ethi•cist**
**ethi•cize** (*or* **•cise**)
**eth•ics**
**Ethio•pia**
**Ethio•pian**
**Ethio•pic**
**eth•moid** facial bone
**eth•moi•dal**
**eth•narch** Roman ruler
**eth•nar•chy** (*plural* **•chies**)
**eth•nic** (*or* **•ni•cal**)
**eth•ni•cal•ly**
**eth•no•bota•ny** botanical folklore
**eth•no•cen•tric**
**eth•no•cen•tri•cal•ly**
**eth•no•cen•tric•ity**
**eth•no•cen•trism** belief in group's superiority
**eth•no•gen•ic**
**eth•nog•enist**
**eth•nog•eny** origin of races
**eth•nog•ra•pher**
**eth•no•graph•ic** (*or* **•graphi•cal**)
**eth•no•graphi•cal•ly**
**eth•nog•ra•phy** anthropology term
**eth•no•log•ic** (*or* **•logi•cal**)
**eth•nolo•gist**
**eth•nol•ogy** study of races; *compare* **ethology**
**etho•log•ic** (*or* **•logi•cal**)
**etho•logi•cal•ly**
**etholo•gist**
**ethol•ogy** study of animal behaviour; *compare* **ethnology**
**etho•none** chemical compound
**ethos**
**eth•ox•ide**
**eth•oxy•ethane**
**ethyl**
**eth•yl•ate**
**eth•yla•tion**
**eth•yl•ene** (*or* **eth•ene**)
**eth•yl•enic**
**ethyl•ic**
**ethyne** chemical compound
**etio•late**
**etio•la•tion**
**eti•ol•ogy** *US spelling of* **aetiology**
**eti•quette**
**Etna**
**Eton**
**Eto•nian**
**Etru•ria** ancient Italian country
**Etrus•can** (*or* **Etru•rian**)
**étude** musical composition
**étui** needle case
**ety•mo•logi•cal** (*or* **•log•ic**)
**ety•molo•gist**
**ety•mol•ogy** (*plural* **•ogies**) study of words; *compare* **entomology**
**ety•mon** (*plural* **•mons** *or* **•ma**) original word form
**Etzel** legendary king
**eubac•te•ria** (*sing.* **•rium**)
**Euboea** Greek island
**Euboean**
**eucaine** anaesthetic
**euca•lyp•tol** (*or* **•tole**) essential oil
**euca•lyp•tus** (*or* **•lypt**; *plural* **•tuses, •ti** *or* **•lypts**)
**eucha•ris** plant
**Eucha•rist** sacrament
**Eucha•ris•tic** (*or* **•ti•cal**)
**Eucha•ris•ti•cal•ly**
**euchlo•rine** (*or* **•rin**) explosive gas
**euchre** US card game
**euchro•mat•ic**
**euchro•ma•tin** chromosome part
**Euclid•ean** (*or* **•ian**)
**eudemon** benevolent spirit
**eudemo•nia** (*or* **eudaemo•**) happiness
**eudemon•ic** (*or* **eudaemon•**)
**eudemon•ics** (*or* **eudaemon•**)
**eudemon•ism** (*or* **eudaemon•**)
**eudemon•is•ti•cal•ly** (*or* **eudaemon•**)
**eudi•om•eter** chemistry term
**eudio•met•ric** (*or* **•ri•cal**)

**eudio•met•ri•cal•ly**
**eudi•om•etry**
**eugen•ic** (*or* **eugeni•cal**)
**eugeni•cal•ly**
**eugeni•cist**
**eugen•ics**
**eugenol** essential oil
**euglena** protozoan
**euhe•mer•ism** study of myths
**euhe•mer•ist**
**euhe•mer•is•tic**
**euhe•mer•is•ti•cal•ly**
**euhe•mer•ize** (*or* **•ise**)
**eula•chon** (*or* **•chan**; *plural* **•chons, •chon** *or* **•chans, •chan**) fish
**eulo•gia** holy bread
**eulo•gist** (*or* **•giz•er, •gis•er**)
**eulo•gis•tic** (*or* **•ti•cal**)
**eulo•gis•ti•cal•ly**
**eulo•gize** (*or* **•gise**)
**eulogy** (*plural* **eulogies**)
**Eumeni•des** Greek Furies
**eunuch**
**euony•mus** (*or* **evony•**) tree
**eupa•to•rium** plant
**eupat•rid** Greek landowner
**eupep•sia** (*or* **•sy**) good digestion
**eupep•tic**
**euphau•si•id** crustacean
**euphemism** inoffensive word; *compare* **euphuism**
**euphemist**
**euphemis•tic** (*or* **•ti•cal**)
**euphemis•ti•cal•ly**
**euphemize** (*or* **euphemise**)
**euphemiz•er** (*or* **euphemis•er**)
**euphon•ic** (*or* **euphoni•cal**)
**euphoni•cal•ly**
**eupho•ni•ous**
**eupho•ni•ous•ly**
**eupho•ni•ous•ness**
**eupho•nium** musical instrument
**eupho•nize** (*or* **•nise**)
**eupho•ny** (*plural* **•nies**) pleasing sound
**euphor•bia** plant
**euphor•bia•ceous**
**eupho•ria** elation
**eupho•ri•ant**
**euphor•ic**
**euphori•cal•ly**
**eupho•tic** ecology term
**euphra•sy** (*plural* **•sies**) plant
**Euphra•tes** Asian river
**euphroe** (*or* **uphroe**) nautical term
**Euphrosyne** Greek goddess
**euphuism** prose style; *compare* **euphemism**
**euphu•ist**
**euphu•is•tic** (*or* **•ti•cal**)
**euphu•is•ti•cal•ly**
**euplas•tic** healing quickly
**euploid** biology term
**eup•noea** (*US* **•nea**) normal breathing
**eup•noe•ic** (*US* **•ne•**)
**Eura•sia**
**Eura•sian**
**Eur•at•om** European Atomic Energy Commission
**Eure** French department
**Eure-et-Loir** French department
**eureka**
**eurhyth•mic** (*or* **•mi•cal**)
**eurhyth•mics**
**eurhyth•my**
**euri•pus** (*plural* **•pi**) channel
**euro** currency unit
**Euroc•ly•don** biblical wind
**Euro•com•mun•ism**
**Euro•crat** EU administrator
**Euro•dol•lar**
**Euro•mar•ket** (*or* **•mart**)
**Eu•ro•pa** satellite of Jupiter
**Europa** mythological character
**Europe**
**Euro•pean**
**Euro•pean•ism**
**Euro•peani•za•tion** (*or* **•sa•tion**)
**Euro•pean•ize** (*or* **•ise**)
**Euro•phile**
**euro•pium** chemical element
**Euro•poort** Dutch port
**Euro•scep•tic**
**Euro•vis•ion** broadcasting network
**Eurus** mythological wind
**Eurydice** dryad
**euryp•ter•id** extinct animal
**eury•ther•mal** (*or* **•mic, •mous**) ecology term
**eury•trop•ic** ecology term
**euspo•ran•gi•ate** botany term
**Eusta•chian tube** anatomy term
**eusta•sy**
**eustat•ic** geology term
**eustati•cal•ly**
**eutec•tic** (*or* **•toid**) physics term
**Euterpe** Greek Muse
**eutha•na•sia**
**euthen•ics** environmental study
**euthen•ist**
**euthe•rian** zoology term
**eutroph•ic** ecology term
**eutrophi•ca•tion**
**eux•enite** mineral
**evacu•ant**
**evacu•ate**
**evacu•ation**
**evacu•ative**
**evacu•ator**
**evac•uee**
**evad•able** (*or* **•ible**)
**evade**
**evad•er**
**evad•ing•ly**
**evagi•nate** turn inside out
**evagi•na•tion**
**evalu•ate**
**evalu•ation**
**evalu•ative**
**evalu•ator**
**eva•nesce** fade gradually
**eva•nes•cence**
**eva•nes•cent**
**evan•gel** gospel
**evan•geli•cal**
**evan•geli•cal•ism**
**evan•geli•cal•ly**
**evan•gelism**
**evan•gelist**
**evan•gelis•tic**
**evan•gelis•ti•cal•ly**
**evan•geli•za•tion** (*or* **•sa•tion**)
**evan•gelize** (*or* **•gelise**)
**evan•geliz•er** (*or* **•gelis•er**)
**Ev•ans•ville** US city
**evapo•rabil•ity**
**evapo•rable**

**evapo•rate**
**evapo•ra•tion**
**evapo•ra•tive**
**evapo•ra•tor**
**evapo•rim•eter** (*or* **•rom•**)
**evapo•rite** rock
**evapo•tran•spi•ra•tion**
**eva•sion**
**eva•sive**
**eva•sive•ness**
**eve**
**evec•tion** astronomy term
**evec•tion•al**
**even**
**even-handed**
**even-handed•ness**
**eve•ning**
**even•ness**
**evens** betting term
**even•song**
**event**
**even-tempered**
**event•ful**
**event•ful•ly**
**event•ful•ness**
**even•tide**
**even•tual**
**even•tu•al•ity** (*plural* **•ities**)
**even•tu•al•ly**
**even•tu•ate** result in
**even•tua•tion**
**ever**
**Ev•er•est**
**Ever•glades** Florida region
**ever•green**
**ever•lasting**
**ever•lasting•ness**
**ever•more**
**ever•sible**
**ever•sion**
**evert** turn inside out
**evert•or** muscle
**every**
**every•body**
**every•day**
**Every•man** medieval play
**every•one**
**every•thing**
**every•where**
**Eve•sham**
**evict**
**evic•tion**
**evic•tor**
**evi•dence**
**evi•dent**
**evi•den•tial**
**evi•den•tial•ly**
**evi•dent•ly**
**evil**
**evil•doer**
**evil•doing**
**evil•ly**
**evil-minded**
**evil-minded•ness**
**evil•ness**
**evince**
**evin•cible**
**evin•cive**
**evis•cer•ate** disembowel
**evis•cera•tion**
**evis•cera•tor**
**evo•cable**
**evo•ca•tion**
**evoca•tive**
**evoca•tive•ness**
**evo•ca•tor** biology term
**evoke**
**evok•er**
**evo•lute** geometry term
**evo•lu•tion**
**evo•lu•tion•ary** (*or* **•al**)
**evo•lu•tion•ism**
**evo•lu•tion•ist**
**evo•lu•tion•is•tic**
**evolv•able**
**evolve**
**evolve•ment**
**evolv•er**
**evony•mus** *variant spelling of* **euonymus**
**ev•zone** Greek soldier
**ewe**
**ewe-neck**
**ewer**
**ex**
**ex•ac•er•bate** aggravate
**ex•ac•er•bat•ing•ly**
**ex•ac•er•ba•tion**
**ex•act**
**ex•act•able**
**ex•act•ing**
**ex•act•ing•ness**
**ex•ac•tion**
**ex•acti•tude**
**ex•act•ly**
**ex•act•ness**
**ex•ac•tor** (*or* **•ter**)
**ex•ag•ger•ate**
**ex•ag•ger•at•ed**
**ex•ag•ger•at•ed•ly**
**ex•ag•ger•at•ing•ly**
**ex•ag•gera•tion**
**ex•ag•gera•tive** (*or* **•tory**)
**ex•ag•gera•tor**
**ex•alt**
**ex•al•ta•tion**
**ex•alt•ed**
**ex•alt•ed•ly**
**ex•alt•ed•ness**
**ex•alt•er**
**exam**
**exa•men** examination of conscience
**ex•am•in•able**
**ex•ami•na•tion**
**ex•ami•na•tion•al**
**ex•am•ine**
**ex•ami•nee**
**ex•am•in•er**
**ex•am•ple**
**ex•ani•mate**
**ex•ani•ma•tion**
**ex•an•thema** (*or* **•them**; *plural* **•thema•ta**, **•themas**, *or* **•thems**) rash
**ex•an•thema•tous** (*or* **•themat•ic**)
**exa•rate** entomology term
**ex•arch** Eastern bishop; botany term
**ex•arch•al**
**ex•arch•ate** (*or* **•ar•chy**; *plural* **•ates** *or* **•chies**)
**ex•as•per•ate**
**ex•as•per•at•ed•ly**
**ex•as•per•at•er**
**ex•as•per•at•ing•ly**
**ex•as•pera•tion**
**Ex•cali•bur** magic sword
**ex ca•thedra** *Latin* with authority
**ex•cau•date** tailless
**ex•ca•vate**
**ex•ca•va•tion**
**ex•ca•va•tor**
**ex•ceed**
**ex•ceed•able**
**ex•ceed•er**
**ex•ceed•ing•ly**
**ex•cel** (**•cel•ling**, **•celled**)
**ex•cel•lence**
**Ex•cel•len•cy** (*or* **•lence**; *plural* **•cies** *or* **•lences**) title
**ex•cel•lent**
**ex•cel•si•or**

**ex•cept**
**ex•cept•able**
**ex•cept•ing**
**ex•cep•tion**
**ex•cep•tion•able** objectionable
**ex•cep•tion•able•ness**
**ex•cep•tion•al** very good
**ex•cep•tion•al•ity**
**excep•tion•al•ly**
**ex•cep•tion•al•ness**
**ex•cep•tive**
**ex•cerpt** book extract; *compare* **exert; exsert**
**ex•cerpt•er** (*or* **•cerp•tor**)
**ex•cerpt•ible**
**ex•cerp•tion**
**ex•cess**
**ex•ces•sive**
**ex•ces•sive•ly**
**ex•ces•sive•ness**
**ex•change**
**ex•change•abil•ity**
**ex•change•able**
**ex•chang•er**
**Ex•cheq•uer** Treasury
**ex•cipi•ent** medical term
**ex•cis•able**
**ex•cise**
**ex•cise•man** (*plural* **•men**)
**ex•ci•sion**
**ex•cit•abil•ity** (*or* **•able•ness**)
**ex•cit•able**
**ex•cit•ant**
**ex•ci•ta•tion**
**ex•cita•tive** (*or* **•tory**)
**ex•cite**
**ex•cit•ed**
**ex•cit•ed•ly**
**ex•cit•ed•ness**
**ex•cite•ment**
**ex•cit•er** oscillator
**ex•cit•ing**
**ex•cit•ing•ly**
**ex•ci•ton** chemistry term
**ex•ci•tor** nerve
**ex•claim**
**ex•claim•er**
**ex•cla•ma•tion**
**ex•cla•ma•tion•al**
**ex•clama•to•ri•ly**
**ex•clama•tory**
**ex•claus•tra•tion** release of nun or monk
**ex•clave**
**ex•clo•sure**
**ex•clud•abil•ity**
**ex•clud•able** (*or* **•ible**)
**ex•clude**
**ex•clud•er**
**ex•clu•sion**
**ex•clu•sion•ary**
**ex•clu•sion•ist**
**ex•clu•sive**
**ex•clu•sive•ness** (*or* **•sivi•ty**)
**ex•cogi•tate** devise
**ex•cog•ita•tion**
**ex•cogi•ta•tive**
**ex•cogi•ta•tor**
**ex•com•muni•cable**
**ex•com•muni•cate**
**ex•com•mu•ni•ca•tion**
**ex•com•mu•ni•ca•tive** (*or* **•tory**)
**ex•com•mu•ni•ca•tor**
**ex•co•ri•ate**
**ex•co•ria•tion**
**ex•cre•ment**
**ex•cre•men•tal** (*or* **•ti•tious**)
**ex•cres•cence**
**ex•cres•cen•cy** (*plural* **•cies**)
**ex•cres•cent**
**ex•cre•ta**
**ex•cre•tal**
**ex•crete**
**ex•cret•er**
**ex•cre•tion**
**ex•cre•tive**
**ex•cre•tory**
**ex•cru•ci•ate**
**ex•cru•ci•at•ing**
**ex•cru•ci•at•ing•ly**
**ex•cru•cia•tion**
**ex•cul•pable**
**ex•cul•pate** vindicate
**ex•cul•pa•tion**
**ex•cul•pa•tory**
**ex•cur•rent** flowing outwards
**ex•cur•sion**
**ex•cur•sion•ist**
**ex•cur•sive**
**ex•cur•sive•ness**
**ex•cur•sus** (*plural* **•suses** *or* **•sus**) digression
**ex•cus•able**
**ex•cus•able•ness**
**ex•cus•ably**
**ex•cusa•tory**
**ex•cuse**
**ex-directory** (*adj*)
**ex•eat** leave of absence
**ex•ecrable**
**ex•ecrable•ness**
**ex•ecrate** loathe
**ex•ecra•tion**
**ex•ecra•tive** (*or* **•tory**)
**ex•ecut•able**
**ex•ecu•tant**
**ex•ecute**
**ex•ecut•er** one who executes something; *compare* **executor**
**ex•ecu•tion**
**ex•ecu•tion•er**
**ex•ecu•tive**
**ex•ecu•tor** trustee of will; *compare* **executer**
**ex•ecu•to•rial**
**ex•ecu•tor•ship**
**ex•ecu•tory** legal term
**ex•ecu•trix** (*plural* **•tri•ces** *or* **•trixes**) female executor
**ex•edra** continuous bench
**ex•egesis** (*plural* **•egeses**) Bible interpretation
**ex•egete** (*or* **•egetist**)
**ex•eget•ic** (*or* **•egeti•cal**)
**ex•egeti•cal•ly**
**ex•eget•ics**
**ex•em•plar**
**ex•em•pla•ri•ly**
**ex•em•pla•ri•ness**
**ex•em•pla•ry**
**ex•em•pli•fi•able**
**ex•em•pli•fi•ca•tion**
**ex•em•pli•fi•ca•tive**
**ex•em•pli•fi•er**
**ex•em•pli•fy** (**•fies, •fy•ing, •fied**)
**ex•em•pli gra•tia** *Latin* for the sake of example
**ex•em•plum** (*plural* **•pla**) example
**ex•empt**
**ex•empt•ible**
**ex•emp•tion**
**ex•en•ter•ate** remove surgically
**ex•en•tera•tion**
**ex•equa•tur** official authorization
**ex•equies** funeral rites
**ex•er•cis•able**

**ex•er•cise** train; use; *compare* exorcise
**ex•er•cis•er**
**ex•ergual**
**ex•ergue** date on coin
**ex•ert** make effort; *compare* excerpt; exsert
**ex•er•tion**
**ex•er•tive**
**Ex•eter**
**ex•eunt** *Latin* they leave
**ex•fo•li•ate**
**ex•fo•lia•tion**
**ex•fo•lia•tive**
**ex gra•tia** *Latin* gratuitous
**ex•hal•able**
**ex•hal•ant**
**ex•ha•la•tion**
**ex•hale**
**ex•haust**
**ex•haust•er**
**ex•haust•ibil•ity**
**ex•haust•ible**
**ex•haus•tion**
**ex•haus•tive**
**ex•haust•ive•ness**
**ex•hib•it**
**ex•hi•bi•tion**
**ex•hi•bi•tion•er** scholarship student
**ex•hi•bi•tion•ism**
**ex•hi•bi•tion•ist**
**ex•hi•bi•tion•is•tic**
**ex•hibi•tive** illustrative
**ex•hibi•tor** (*or* **•hib•it•er)**
**ex•hibi•tory**
**ex•hil•ar•ant**
**ex•hila•rate**
**ex•hil•arat•ing•ly**
**ex•hila•ra•tion**
**ex•hila•ra•tive** (*or* **•tory)**
**ex•hila•ra•tor**
**ex•hort**
**ex•hor•ta•tion**
**ex•hor•ta•tive** (*or* **•tory)**
**ex•hort•er**
**ex•hu•ma•tion**
**ex•hume**
**ex•hum•er**
**exi•gen•cy** (*or* **exi•gence;** *plural* **•cies** *or* **•gences)**
**exi•gent** urgent
**exi•gible** required
**exi•gu•ity** (*or* **ex•igu•ous•ness)**
**ex•igu•ous** meagre
**ex•ile**
**ex•il•ic** (*or* **•ian)**
**ex•ist**
**ex•ist•ence**
**ex•ist•ent**
**ex•is•ten•tial**
**ex•is•ten•tial•ism**
**ex•is•ten•tial•ist**
**ex•is•ten•tial•ly**
**exit**
**exi•tance** physics term
**ex li•bris** *Latin* from the library of
**Ex•moor**
**exo•bi•olo•gist**
**exo•bi•ol•ogy** astrobiology
**exo•cen•tric** linguistics term
**exo•crine** having a duct; *compare* **endocrine**
**exo•derm** *variant of* **ectoderm**
**exo•don•tics** dentistry
**exo•don•tist**
**Exo•dus** Old Testament book
**exo•dus**
**exo•en•zyme**
**exo•er•gic** energy-emitting; *compare* **endoergic**
**ex of•fi•cio** *Latin* by right of office
**ex•oga•mous** (*or* **exo•gam•ic)**
**ex•oga•my** marrying into another tribe
**ex•og•enous**
**ex•on•er•ate**
**ex•on•era•tion**
**ex•on•era•tive**
**ex•on•era•tor**
**exo•nym** foreigner's version of placename
**exo•pep•ti•dase** enzyme
**ex•oph•thal•mic**
**ex•oph•thal•mos** (*or* **•mus, •mia)** protrusion of eyeball
**exo•rabil•ity**
**exo•rable** moved by pleading
**ex•or•bi•tance**
**ex•or•bi•tant**
**ex•or•cise** (*or* **•cize)** expel evil spirit; *compare* **exercise**
**ex•or•cis•er** (*or* **•ciz•er)**
**ex•or•cism**
**ex•or•cist**
**ex•or•dial**
**ex•or•dium** (*plural* **•diums** *or* **•dia)** beginning of speech
**exo•skel•etal**
**exo•skel•eton**
**ex•os•mo•sis** biology term
**ex•os•mot•ic** (*or* **ex•os•mic)**
**exo•sphere** atmospheric layer
**exo•spore** botany term
**exo•spor•ous**
**ex•os•to•sis** (*plural* **•ses)** outgrowth from bone
**exo•ter•ic** comprehensible; *compare* **esoteric**
**exo•teri•cal•ly**
**exo•teri•cism**
**exo•ther•mic** (*or* **•mal)** heat-emitting; *compare* **endothermic**
**exo•ther•mi•cal•ly** (*or* **•ther•mal•ly)**
**ex•ot•ic**
**ex•oti•ca**
**ex•oti•cal•ly**
**ex•oti•cism**
**ex•ot•ic•ness**
**exo•tox•ic**
**exo•tox•in**
**ex•pand**
**ex•pand•able** (*or* **•ible)**
**ex•pand•er**
**ex•panse**
**ex•pan•sibil•ity**
**ex•pan•sible**
**ex•pan•sile**
**ex•pan•sion**
**ex•pan•sion•ary**
**ex•pan•sion•ism**
**ex•pan•sion•ist**
**ex•pan•sion•is•tic**
**ex•pan•sive**
**ex•pan•sive•ness**
**ex par•te** legal term
**ex•pa•ti•ate** enlarge upon; *compare* **expiate**
**ex•pa•tia•tion**
**ex•pa•tia•tor**
**ex•pat•ri•ate**
**ex•pat•ria•tion**
**ex•pect**

**ex•pect•able**
**ex•pec•tan•cy** (*or* **•tance**; *plural* **•cies** *or* **•tances)**
**ex•pec•tant**
**ex•pec•ta•tion**
**ex•pec•ta•tive**
**ex•pec•to•rant**
**ex•pec•to•rate**
**ex•pec•to•ra•tion** spitting
**ex•pec•to•ra•tor**
**ex•pedi•en•cy** (*or* **•ence**; *plural* **•cies** *or* **•ences)**
**ex•pedi•ent**
**ex•pedi•en•tial**
**ex•pedite**
**ex•pedit•er** (*or* **•pedi•tor)**
**ex•pedi•tion**
**ex•pedi•tion•ary**
**ex•pedi•tious**
**ex•pedi•tious•ness**
**ex•pel** (**•pel•ling, •pelled)**
**ex•pel•lable**
**ex•pel•lant** (*or* **•lent)**
**ex•pel•lee**
**ex•pel•ler**
**ex•pend**
**ex•pend•abil•ity**
**ex•pend•able**
**ex•pend•er**
**ex•pendi•ture**
**ex•pense**
**ex•pen•sive**
**ex•pen•sive•ness**
**ex•peri•ence**
**ex•peri•en•tial**
**ex•peri•ment**
**ex•peri•men•tal**
**ex•peri•men•tal•ism**
**ex•peri•men•tal•ist**
**ex•peri•men•tal•ly**
**ex•peri•men•ta•tion**
**ex•peri•ment•er**
**ex•pert**
**ex•per•tise**
**ex•pert•ness**
**ex•pi•able**
**ex•pi•ate** atone; *compare* expatiate
**ex•pia•tion**
**ex•pia•tor**
**ex•pia•tory**
**ex•pi•ra•tion**
**ex•pira•tory** of exhalation
**ex•pire**
**ex•pir•er**
**ex•pi•ry** (*plural* **•ries)**
**ex•plain**
**ex•plain•able**
**ex•plain•er**
**ex•pla•na•tion**
**ex•plana•to•ri•ly**
**ex•plana•tory** (*or* **•tive)**
**ex•plant** biology term
**ex•plan•ta•tion**
**ex•pletive** swear word
**ex•pli•cable**
**ex•pli•cate** explain
**ex•pli•ca•tion**
**ex•pli•ca•tive** (*or* **•tory)**
**ex•pli•ca•tor**
**ex•plic•it**
**ex•plic•it•ness**
**ex•plode**
**ex•plod•er**
**ex•ploit**
**ex•ploit•able** (*or* **•ploita•tive)**
**ex•ploi•ta•tion**
**ex•plo•ra•tion**
**ex•plora•tory** (*or* **•tive)**
**ex•plore**
**ex•plor•er**
**ex•plo•sion**
**ex•plo•sive**
**ex•plo•sive•ness**
**ex•po•nent**
**ex•po•nen•tial** maths term
**ex•po•nen•tial•ly**
**ex•pon•ible** needing explanation
**ex•port**
**ex•port•abil•ity**
**ex•port•able**
**ex•por•ta•tion**
**ex•port•er**
**ex•pos•able**
**ex•pos•al**
**ex•pose**
**ex•po•sé** exposure of scandal
**ex•posed**
**ex•pos•ed•ness**
**ex•pos•er**
**ex•po•si•tion**
**ex•po•si•tion•al**
**ex•posi•tor** expounder
**ex•posi•to•ri•ly** (*or* **•tive•ly)**
**ex•posi•tory** (*or* **•tive)**
**ex post fac•to** *Latin* retrospective
**ex•pos•tu•late** dissuade
**ex•pos•tu•lat•ing•ly**
**ex•pos•tu•la•tion**
**ex•pos•tu•la•tor**
**ex•pos•tu•la•tory** (*or* **•tive)**
**ex•po•sure**
**ex•pound**
**ex•pound•er**
**ex•press**
**ex•press•age** conveyance by express
**ex•press•er**
**ex•press•ible**
**ex•pres•sion**
**ex•pres•sion•al**
**ex•pres•sion•ism**
**ex•pres•sion•ist**
**ex•pres•sion•is•tic**
**ex•pres•sion•less**
**ex•pres•sive**
**ex•pres•sive•ness**
**ex•pres•siv•ity**
**(expresso)** *incorrect spelling of* espresso
**ex•press•way** US motorway
**ex•pro•pri•able**
**ex•pro•pri•ate**
**ex•pro•pria•tion**
**ex•pro•pria•tor**
**ex•pul•sion**
**ex•pul•sive**
**ex•punc•tion**
**ex•punge**
**ex•pung•er**
**ex•pur•gate**
**ex•pur•ga•tion**
**ex•pur•ga•tor**
**ex•pur•ga•tory** (*or* **•to•rial)**
**ex•quis•ite**
**ex•quis•ite•ness**
**ex•san•gui•nate** drain blood from
**ex•san•guin•ation**
**ex•san•guine** (*or* **•gui•nous)**
**ex•san•guin•ity**
**ex•scind** (*or* **•sect)** cut off
**ex•sect** cut out
**ex•sec•tion**
**ex•sert** protrude; *compare* excerpt; exert
**ex•ser•tile**
**ex•ser•tion**
**ex•sic•cate** dry
**ex•sic•ca•tion**
**ex•sic•ca•tive**

**ex•sic•ca•tor**
**ex•stipu•late** (*or* **es•tipu•late**) botany term
(extasy) *incorrect spelling of* ecstasy
**ex•stro•phy** medical term
**ex•tant** surviving
**ex•tem•po•ra•neous** (*or* **•po•rary**)
**ex•tem•po•ra•neous•ness**
**ex•tem•po•rari•ly**
**ex•tem•po•rari•ness**
**ex•tem•po•re** impromptu
**ex•tem•po•ri•za•tion** (*or* **•sa•tion**)
**ex•tem•po•rize** (*or* **•rise**)
**ex•tem•po•riz•er** (*or* **•ris•er**)
**ex•tend**
**ex•tend•ed•ness**
**ex•tend•er**
**ex•tend•ibil•ity** (*or* **•abil•ity**)
**ex•tend•ible** (*or* **•able**)
**ex•ten•sibil•ity** (*or* **•sible•ness**)
**ex•ten•sible** (*or* **•sile**)
**ex•ten•sion**
**ex•ten•sion•al**
**ex•ten•sion•al•ity** (*or* **•ism**)
**ex•ten•sity** psychology term
**ex•ten•sive**
**ex•ten•sive•ness**
**ex•ten•som•eter** (*or* **•sim•**) physics term
**ex•ten•sor** muscle
**ex•tent**
**ex•tenu•ate**
**ex•tenu•at•ing•ly**
**ex•tenu•ation**
**ex•tenu•ator**
**ex•tenu•atory**
**ex•te•ri•or**
**ex•te•ri•ori•za•tion** (*or* **•sa•tion**)
**ex•te•ri•or•ize** (*or* **•ise**) medical term
**ex•ter•mi•nable**
**ex•ter•mi•nate**
**ex•ter•mi•na•tion**
**ex•ter•mi•na•tive** (*or* **•tory**)
**ex•ter•mi•na•tor**
**ex•tern** (*or* **•terne**) *US* nonresident hospital doctor
**ex•ter•nal**
**ex•ter•nal•ism**
**ex•ter•nal•ist**
**ex•ter•nal•ity** (*plural* **•ities**)
**ex•ter•nali•za•tion** (*or* **•sa•tion**)
**ex•ter•nal•ize** (*or* **•ise**)
**ex•ter•nal•ly**
**ex•tero•cep•tive**
**ex•tero•cep•tor** biology term
**ex•ter•ri•to•rial**
**ex•ter•ri•to•ri•al•ity**
**ex•tinct**
**ex•tinc•tion**
**ex•tinc•tive**
**ex•tine** (*or* **•ine**) botany term
**ex•tin•guish**
**ex•tin•guish•able**
**ex•tin•guish•ant**
**ex•tin•guish•er**
**ex•tin•guish•ment**
**ex•tir•pate** destroy
**ex•tir•pa•tion**
**ex•tir•pa•tive**
**ex•tir•pa•tor**
**ex•tol** (*US* **•toll**; **•tol•ling**, **•tolled**)
**ex•tol•ler**
**ex•tol•ling•ly**
**ex•tol•ment**
**ex•tort**
**ex•tort•er**
**ex•tor•tion**
**ex•tor•tion•able**
**ex•tor•tion•ary**
**ex•tor•tion•ate**
**ex•tor•tion•ist** (*or* **•er**)
**ex•tor•tive**
**ex•tra**
**extra•ca•noni•cal** outside scripture
**extra•cel•lu•lar**
**ex•tract**
**ex•tract•abil•ity** (*or* **•ibil•ity**)
**ex•tract•able** (*or* **•ible**)
**ex•trac•tion**
**ex•trac•tive**
**ex•trac•tor**
**extra•cur•ricu•lar**
**extra•dit•able**
**extra•dite**
**extra•di•tion**
**extra•dos** (*plural* **•dos** *or* **•doses**) architecture term
**extra•ga•lac•tic**
**extra•ju•di•cial**
**extra•mari•tal**
**extra•mun•dane** outside the world
**extra•mu•ral**
**extra•neous**
**extra•neous•ness**
**extra•nu•clear**
**extraor•di•nari•ly**
**extraor•di•nari•ness**
**ex•traor•di•nary**
**ex•trapo•late**
**ex•trapo•la•tion**
**ex•trapo•la•tive** (*or* **•tory**)
**ex•trapo•la•tor**
**extra•po•si•tion**
**extra•sen•so•ry**
**extra•ter•res•trial**
**extra•ter•ri•to•rial** (*or* **ex•ter•**)
**extra•ter•ri•to•ri•al•ity**
**extra•uter•ine**
**ex•trava•gance**
**ex•trava•gant**
**ex•trava•gan•za**
**ex•trava•gate** *Archaic* roam
**ex•trava•ga•tion**
**ex•trava•sate** exude
**ex•trava•sa•tion**
**extra•vas•cu•lar**
**extra•vehicu•lar** outside a spacecraft
**extra•vert** *variant spelling of* **extrovert**
**ex•treme**
**ex•treme•ly**
**ex•treme•ness**
**ex•trem•ism**
**ex•trem•ist**
**ex•trem•ity** (*plural* **•ities**)
**ex•tri•cable**
**ex•tri•cate**
**ex•tri•ca•tion**
**ex•trin•sic** not contained within; *compare* **intrinsic**
**ex•trin•si•cal•ly**
(extrordinary) *incorrect spelling of* **extraordinary**
**ex•trorse** (*or* **•tror•sal**) turned outwards
**extro•ver•sion** (*or* **extra•**)
**extro•ver•sive** (*or* **extra•**)

**extro•vert** (*or* **extra•**)
**extro•vert•ed** (*or* **extra•**)
**ex•trude**
**ex•tru•sion**
**ex•tru•sive**
**exu•ber•ance** (*or* **•ancy**)
**exu•ber•ant**
**exu•ber•ate**
**exu•da•tion**
**exu•da•tive**
**ex•ude**
**ex•ult**
**ex•ult•ant**
**ex•ul•ta•tion**
**ex•ult•ing•ly**
**ex•ur•bia** *US* outside suburbs
**exu•viae** shed skin
**exu•vial**
**exu•vi•ate**
**exu•via•tion**
**ex-works** excluding delivery cost
**eyas** nestling hawk
**eye** (**eye•ing** *or* **ey•ing, eyed**)
**eye•ball**
**eye•bath**
**eye•bolt**
**eye•bright** plant
**eye•brow**
**eye-catcher**
**eye-catching**
**eye•cup**
**eyed**
**eye•dropper**
**eye•ful**
**eye•glass**
**eye•glasses** *US* spectacles
**eye•hole**
**eye•ing** (*or* **ey•ing**)
**eye•lash**
**eye•less**
**eye•let**
**eye•let•eer**
**eye•lid**
**eye•liner**
**eye-opener**
**eye•piece**
**eye•shade**
**eye•shot**
**eye•sight**
**eye•sore**
**eye•spot**
**eye•stalk**
**eye•strain**
**eye•tooth** (*plural* **•teeth**)
**eye•wash**
**eye•witness**
**eyra** animal
**Eyre** Canadian lake; Australian peninsula
**ey•rie** (*or* **aerie, aery**; *plural* **ey•ries** *or* **aeries**) eagle's nest; *compare* **eerie**
**ey•rir** (*plural* **aurar**) Icelandic coin

# F

**fa** (*or* **fah**) musical note
**fab**
**fa•ba•ceous** botany term
**Fa•bian**
**Fa•bi•an•ism**
**fa•ble**
**fa•bled**
**fa•bler**
**fab•ric**
**fab•ri•cate**
**fab•ri•ca•tion**
**fab•ri•ca•tive**
**fab•ri•ca•tor**
**Fab•ri•koid** (*Trademark*) waterproof fabric
**fabu•list** teller of fables
**fabu•lous**
**fabu•lous•ness**
**fa•çade** (*or* **•cade**)
**face**
**face•able**
**face•bar** wrestling hold
**face-centred** (*US* **-centered**) crystallography term
**face-harden** metallurgy term
**face•less**
**face•less•ness**
**face-lift**
**face-off** ice hockey term
**face•plate** lathe part
**fac•er**
**face-saving**
**fac•et** (*verb* **•et•ing, •et•ed** *or* **•et•ting, •et•ted**)
**fa•cetiae** witty sayings
**fa•cetious**
**fa•cetious•ness**
**fa•cia** *variant spelling of* **fascia**
**fa•cial**
**fa•cial•ly**
**fa•cies** (*plural* **•cies**) appearance; *compare* **fasces; fascia**
**fac•ile**
**fac•ile•ly**
**fac•ile•ness**
**fa•cili•tate**
**fa•cili•ta•tion**
**fa•cili•ta•tive**
**fa•cili•ta•tor**
**fa•cil•ity** (*plural* **•ities**)
**fac•ing**
**fac•simi•le** (**•le•ing, •led**)
**fact**
**fact•ful**
**fac•tice** rubbery material
**fac•tion**
**fac•tion•al**
**fac•tion•al•ism**
**fac•tion•al•ist**
**fac•tious** factional; *compare* **factitious**
**fac•tious•ness**
**fac•ti•tious** contrived; *compare* **factious; fictitious**
**fac•ti•tious•ness**
**fac•ti•tive** linguistics term
**fac•tor**
**fac•tor•abil•ity**
**fac•tor•able**
**fac•tor•age** commission paid to factor
**fac•torial**
**fac•to•ri•al•ly**
**fac•tor•ing** business term
**fac•tori•za•tion** (*or* **•sa•tion**)
**fac•tor•ize** (*or* **•ise**)
**fac•tor•ship**
**fac•to•ry** (*plural* **•ries**)
**fac•to•tum**
**fac•tual**
**fac•tu•al•ism**

**fac•tu•al•ist**
**fac•tu•al•is•tic**
**fac•tu•al•ly**
**fac•tu•al•ness** (*or* **•ity**)
**facu•la** (*plural* **•lae**) sun spot
**facu•lar**
**fac•ul•ta•tive** optional
**fac•ul•ty** (*plural* **•ties**)
**fad**
**fad•able**
**fad•di•ness**
**fad•dish**
**fad•dism**
**fad•dist**
**fad•dy** (**•di•er, •di•est**)
**fade**
**fad•ed**
**fad•ed•ness**
**fade-in**
**fade•less**
**fade-out**
**fad•er**
**fadge** *Dialect* agree
**fad•ing**
**fae•cal** (*US* **fe•**)
**fae•ces** (*US* **fe•**)
**Fa•en•za** Italian city
**fae•rie** (*or* **•ry;** *plural* **•ries**) *Archaic* fairyland
**Fae•roes** (*or* **Fa•roes**) North Atlantic islands
**Faero•ese** (*or* **Faro•;** *plural* **•ese**)
**faff** *Slang* fuss
**fag** (**fag•ging, fagged**)
**fa•ga•ceous** botany term
**fagged**
**fag•ging**
**fag•got** (*or esp. US* **fag•ot**)
**fag•got•ing** (*or esp. US* **fag•ot•**) needlework term
**fah** *variant spelling of* **fa**
**fahl•band** rock
**Fahr•en•heit** temperature scale
**faï•ence** (*or* **fai•**) pottery
**fail**
**fail•ing**
**faille** fabric
**fail-safe**
**fail•ure**
**fain**
**fai•ne•ance** (*or* **•an•cy**)
**fai•né•ant** (*or* **•ne•**) idle
**faint** pale; collapse; *compare* **feint**
**faint•er**
**faint•ing**
**faint•ing•ly**
**faint•ish**
**faint•ly**
**faint•ness**
**faints** *variant spelling of* **feints**
**fair** just; not dark; event; *compare* **fare**
**Fair•banks** Alaskan city
**fair•ground**
**fair•ing**
**fair•ish**
**fair•lead** (*or* **•leader**) nautical term
**fair•ly**
**fair-minded**
**fair-minded•ness**
**fair•ness**
**fair-spoken**
**fair•way**
**fair-weather** (*adj*)
**fairy** (*plural* **fairies**)
**fairy•land**
**fairy-like**
**fait ac•com•pli** (*plural* **faits accomplis**) *French* something done
**faith**
**faith•ful**
**faith•ful•ly**
**faith•ful•ness**
**faith•less**
**faith•less•ness**
**Faiza•bad** Afghan city; *variant spelling of* **Fyzabad**
**fake**
**fak•er** one who fakes
**fa•kir** (*or* **•qir, •keer**) holy man
**fa-la** refrain
**Fa•lange** Spanish Fascist movement
**Fa•lang•ism**
**Fa•lan•gist**
**fal•ba•la** gathered frill
**fal•cate** (*or* **•ci•form**) sickle-shaped
**fal•chion** sword
**fal•con**
**fal•con•er**
**fal•con•et** small falcon
**fal•coni•form**
**fal•con•ry**
**fal•deral** (*or* **fal•derol, fol•derol**) trifle
**fald•stool** bishop's seat
**Fa•lerii** ancient Italian city
**Fa•lis•can** language
**Fal•kirk** Scottish town
**Falk•land Is•lands**
**fall** (**fall•ing, fell, fall•en**)
**fal•la•cious**
**fal•la•cious•ness**
**fal•la•cy** (*plural* **•cies**)
**fal•lal** ornament
**fal•lal•ery**
**fall•en**
**fall•er**
**fall•fish** (*plural* **•fish, •fishes**)
**fal•libil•ity** (*or* **•lible•ness**)
**fal•lible**
**fal•li•bly**
**Fal•lo•pian tube** anatomy term
**fall•out**
**fal•low**
**fal•low•ness**
**Fal•mouth** Cornish port
**false**
**false-card** bridge term
**false•hood**
**false•ly**
**false•ness**
**fal•set•to** (*plural* **•tos**)
**false•work** framework
**fal•sies** false breasts
**fal•si•fi•able**
**fal•si•fi•ca•tion**
**fal•si•fi•er**
**fal•si•fy** (**•fies, •fy•ing, •fied**)
**fal•sity** (*plural* **•sities**)
**falt•boat** collapsible boat
**fal•ter**
**fal•ter•er**
**fal•ter•ing•ly**
**Fa•lun** Swedish city
**Fa•ma•gu•sta** Cypriot port
**fame**
**fa•mil•ial**
**fa•mili•ar**
**fa•mili•ar•ity** (*plural* **•ities**)
**fa•mil•iari•za•tion** (*or* **•sa•tion**)
**fa•mil•iar•ize** (*or* **•ise**)
**fa•mil•iar•iz•er** (*or* **•is•er**)
**fa•mili•ar•ness**

**Fami•list** member of sect
**fa•mille** Chinese porcelain
**fami•ly** (*plural* **•lies**)
**fam•ine**
**fam•ish**
**fam•ish•ment**
**fa•mous**
**fa•mous•ness**
**famu•lus** (*plural* **•li**) sorcerer's attendant
**fan** (**fan•ning, fanned**)
**Fana•ga•lo** (*or* **•ka•lo**) African language
**fa•nat•ic**
**fa•nati•cal**
**fa•nati•cal•ly**
**fa•nati•cism**
**fa•nati•cize** (*or* **•cise**)
**fan•cied**
**fan•ci•er**
**fan•ci•ful**
**fan•ci•ful•ly**
**fan•ci•ful•ness**
**fan•ci•ly**
**fan•ci•ness**
**fan•cy** (*adj* **•ci•er, •ci•est**; *noun, plural* **•cies**; *verb* **•cies, •cy•ing, •cied**)
**fancy-free**
**fancy•work**
**fan•dan•gle** ornament
**fan•dan•go** (*plural* **•gos**) dance
**fan•fare**
**fang**
**fanged**
**fan•go** mud from thermal springs
**fan•ion** surveyor's flag
**fan•jet** jet engine
**fan•kle** *Scot* entangle
**fan•light**
**fanned**
**fan•ner**
**fan•ning**
**fan•ny** (*plural* **•nies**) *Slang* female genitals
**fan•on** vestment
**fan•tail**
**fan-tailed**
**fan-tan** game
**fan•ta•sia**
**fan•ta•size** (*or* **•sise**)
**fan•tast** visionary
**fan•tas•tic** (*or* **•ti•cal**)
**fan•ta•sy** (*or* **phan•**; *noun, plural* **•sies**; *verb* **•sies, •sy•ing, •sied**)
**Fan•ti** (*plural* **•tis** *or* **•ti**) Ghanaian people
**fan•toc•ci•ni** marionettes
**far** (**far•ther** *or* **fur•ther, far•thest** *or* **fur•thest**)
**far•ad** unit
**fara•day** unit
**fa•rad•ic** physics term
**fara•dism** medical use of electricity
**fara•di•za•tion** (*or* **•sa•tion**)
**fara•dize** (*or* **•dise**)
**fara•diz•er** (*or* **•dis•er**)
**far•an•dole** dance
**far•away**
**farce**
**far•ceur** (*fem* **•ceuse**) farce writer
**far•ci** stuffed
**far•ci•cal**
**far•ci•cal•ity** (*or* **•ness**)
**far•ci•cal•ly**
**far•cy** (*plural* **•cies**) animal disease
**far•del** bundle
**fare** payment; food; to manage; *compare* **fair**
**Fare•ham** Hampshire town
**far•er**
**fare•well**
**far-fetched**
**far-flung**
**fa•ri•na** flour
**fari•na•ceous** containing starch
**fari•nose** flourlike
**farl** (*or* **farle**) cake
**farm**
**farm•able**
**farm•er**
**farm•house**
**farm•ing**
**farm•land**
**farm•stead**
**farm•yard**
**Farn•bor•ough** Hampshire town
**far•nesol** chemical compound
**far•ness**
**Farn•ham** Surrey town
**faro** card game
**Fa•roes** *variant spelling of* **Faeroes**
**Faro•ese** *variant spelling of* **Faeroese**
**far-off**
**fa•rouche** sullen
**far•ragi•nous**
**far•ra•go** (*plural* **•goes**) hotchpotch
**far-reaching**
**far•ri•er**
**far•ri•ery** (*plural* **•eries**)
**far•row**
**far-seeing**
**far-sighted**
**far-sighted•ly**
**far-sighted•ness**
**fart**
**far•ther** (*or* **fur•**) more distant; *compare* **further**
**farther•most**
**far•thest** (*or* **fur•**)
**far•thing**
**far•thin•gale** hoop under skirt
**fart•lek** sports term
**fas•ces** (*plural noun; sing.* **•cies**) Roman insignia; *compare* **facies**
**fas•cia** (*or* **fa•cia**; *plural* **•ciae**) flat surface; fibrous tissue; *compare* **facies**
**fas•cial** (*or* **fa•cial**)
**fas•ci•ate** (*or* **•at•ed**)
**fas•cia•tion** botany term
**fas•ci•cle** bundle
**fas•ci•cled**
**fas•cicu•lar** (*or* **•late**)
**fas•cicu•la•tion**
**fas•ci•cule** instalment
**fas•ci•cu•lus** (*plural* **•li**)
**fas•ci•nate**
**fas•ci•nat•ed•ly**
**fas•ci•nat•ing**
**fas•ci•na•tion**
**fas•ci•na•tive**
**fas•cine** bundle of sticks
**fas•cism**
**fas•cist**
**fa•scis•tic**
**fa•scis•ti•cal•ly**
**fash** *Scot* worry
**fash•ion**
**fash•ion•able**
**fash•ion•ably**

**fash•ion•able•ness**
**fash•ion•er**
**Fa•sho•da** Sudanese town
**fast**
**fast•back** car
**fast-breeder** nuclear reactor
**fas•ten**
**fas•ten•er**
**fas•ten•ing**
**fast•er**
**fas•tidi•ous**
**fas•tidi•ous•ness**
**fas•tigi•ate** (*or* **•at•ed)** biology term
**fast•ness**
**fat (fat•ter, fat•test)**
**fa•tal**
**fa•tal•ism**
**fa•tal•ist**
**fa•tal•is•tic**
**fa•tal•is•ti•cal•ly**
**fa•tal•ity** (*plural* **•ities)**
**fa•tal•ly**
**fat•back** pork fat
**fate**
**fat•ed**
**fate•ful**
**fate•ful•ly**
**fate•ful•ness**
**Fates** Greek goddesses
**fat•head**
**fa•ther**
**father•hood**
**father-in-law** (*plural* **fathers-)**
**father•land**
**fa•ther•less**
**father-like**
**fa•ther•li•ness**
**fa•ther•ly**
**fath•om**
**fath•om•able**
**fath•om•er**
**Fa•thom•eter** (*Trademark*)
**fath•om•less**
**fa•tid•ic** (*or* **•tidi•cal)** prophetic
**fati•gabil•ity (•gable•ness)**
**fa•tig•able**
**fa•tigue (•tigu•ing, •tigued)**
**fat•ling** fattened young animal
**fat•ness**
**Fat•shan** Chinese city
**fat•so** (*plural* **•sos** or **•soes)**
**fat-soluble**
**fat•ted**
**fat•ten**
**fat•ten•able**
**fat•ten•er**
**fat•ti•ly**
**fat•ti•ness**
**fat•tish**
**fat•ty** (*adj* **•ti•cr, •ti•est;** *noun, plural* **•ties)**
**fa•tui•tous** fatuous; *compare* **fortuitous**
**fa•tu•ity** (*plural* **•ities)**
**fatu•ous**
**fatu•ous•ness**
**fau•bourg** French suburb
**fau•cal** (*or* **•cial)**
**fau•ces** (*plural* **•ces)** anatomy term
**fau•cet** *US* tap
**faugh** exclamation
**fault**
**fault-finder**
**fault-finding**
**faulti•ly**
**faulti•ness**
**fault•less**
**fault•less•ness**
**faulty (faulti•er, faulti•est)**
**faun** Roman deity; *compare* **fawn**
**fau•na** (*plural* **•nas** *or* **•nae)** animals
**fau•nal**
**Faust** (*or* **Faustus)** legendary magician
**Faust•ian**
**faute de mieux** *French* lacking better
**fau•teuil** armchair
**Fauv•ism** art movement
**Fauv•ist**
**faux pas** (*plural* **faux pas)**
**fa•veo•late** honeycombed
**fa•vo•nian** of the west wind
**fa•vour** (*US* **•vor)**
**fa•vour•able** (*US* **•vor)**
**fa•vour•ably** (*US* **•vor•)**
**fa•vour•able•ness** (*US* **•vor•)**
**fa•vour•er** (*US* **•vor•)**
**fa•vour•ing•ly** (*US* **•vor•)**
**fa•vour•ite** (*US* **•vor•)**
**fa•vour•it•ism** (*US* **•vor•)**
**Fav•rile glass**
**fa•vus** skin disease
**fawn** animal; colour; cringe; *compare* **faun**
**fawn•er**
**fawn•ing•ly**
**fax** facsimile transmission
**fay** fairy; *compare* **fey**
**fay•al•ite** mineral
**faze** *US* disconcert
**fe•al•ty** (*plural* **•ties)** feudal loyalty
**fear**
**fear•er**
**fear•ful**
**fear•ful•ly**
**fear•ful•ness**
**fear•less**
**fear•less•ness**
**fear•nought** (*or* **•naught)** fabric
**fear•some**
**fear•some•ly**
**fear•some•ness**
**fea•sibil•ity** (*or* **•sible•ness)**
**fea•sible**
**fea•sibly**
**feast**
**feast•er**
**feat** exploit; *compare* **feet**
**feath•er**
**feather•bed (•bedding, •bedded)**
**feather•bedding** overmanning
**feather•brain**
**feather•brained**
**feather•edge**
**feath•er•ing**
**feather•stitch**
**feather-veined**
**feather•weight**
**feath•ery**
**fea•ture**
**feature-length** (*adj*)
**fea•ture•less**
**fea•ture•less•ness**
**feaze** nautical term
**fe•bric•ity**
**feb•ri•fa•cient**
**fe•brif•ic** (*or* **•brif•er•ous)**
**fe•brifu•gal**
**feb•ri•fuge** fever-reducing drug
**fe•brile** feverish
**fe•bril•ity**
**Feb•ru•ary** (*plural* **•aries)**

**fe•cal** *US spelling of* **faecal**
**fe•ces** *US spelling of* **faeces**
**fe•cit** *Latin* made it
**feck•less**
**feck•less•ness**
**fecu•la** (*plural* **•lae**) starch
**fecu•lence**
**fecu•lent** filthy
**fe•cund** fertile
**fe•cun•date**
**fe•cun•da•tion**
**fe•cun•da•tor**
**fe•cun•da•tory**
**fe•cun•dity**
**fed**
**fe•da•yee** (*plural* **•yeen**) Arab commando
**fed•er•al**
**fed•er•al•ly**
**fed•er•al•ism**
**fed•er•al•ist**
**fed•er•al•is•tic**
**fed•er•ali•za•tion** (*or* **•sa•tion**)
**fed•er•al•ize** (*or* **•ise**)
**fed•er•ate**
**fed•era•tion**
**fed•era•tive**
**fe•do•ra** hat
**fee** (**fee•ing, feed**)
**fee•ble**
**feeble-minded**
**feeble-minded•ly**
**feeble-minded•ness**
**fee•ble•ness**
**feed** (**feed•ing, fed**)
**feed•able**
**feed•back**
**feed•bag**
**feed•er**
**feed•lot**
**feel** (**feel•ing, felt**)
**feel•er**
**feel•ing**
**feet** *plural of* **foot**; *compare* **feat**
**feeze** *Dialect* beat
**feign**
**feign•er**
**feign•ing•ly**
**feint** mock action; printing term; *compare* **faint**
**feints** (*or* **faints**) whisky residue
**feis•ty**
**feld•spar** (*or* **fel•spar**) mineral
**feld•spath•ic** (*or* **fel•**)
**feld•spath•ose** (*or* **fel•**)
**fe•li•cif•ic** making happy
**fe•lici•tate**
**fe•lici•ta•tion**
**fe•lici•ta•tor**
**fe•lici•tous** apt
**fe•lici•tous•ness**
**fe•lic•ity** (*plural* **•ities**)
**fe•lid** animal
**fe•line**
**fe•lin•ity** (*or* **•line•ness**)
**fell**
**fell•able**
**fel•lah** (*plural* **•lahs, •la•hin,** *or* **•la•heen**) Arab peasant
**fel•la•tio** oral sex
**fell•er**
**fell•monger** animal skin dealer
**fel•loe** (*or* **•ly**; *plural* **•loes** *or* **•lies**) wheel segment
**fel•low**
**fel•low•ship**
**felo de se** (*plural* **fe•lo•nes de se** *or* **fe•los de se**) suicide
**fel•on**
**fe•lo•ni•ous**
**fe•lo•ni•ous•ness**
**fel•on•ry** (*plural* **•ries**)
**felo•ny** (*plural* **•nies**)
**fel•site** (*or* **•stone**) rock
**fel•sit•ic**
**felt**
**felt•ing**
**fe•luc•ca** boat
**fel•wort** plant
**fe•male**
**fe•male•ness**
**feme** woman (*in legal contexts*)
**femi•nine**
**femi•nine•ly**
**femi•nin•ity**
**femi•nism**
**femi•nist**
**femi•ni•za•tion** (*or* **•sa•tion**)
**femi•nize** (*or* **•nise**)
**femme de cham•bre** (*plural* **femmes de cham•bre**) chambermaid
**femme fa•tale** (*plural* **femmes fa•tales**) seductive woman
**femo•ral** of the thigh
**fe•mur** (*plural* **•murs** *or* **femo•ra**) thigh bone
**fen**
**fence**
**fenc•er**
**fenc•ing**
**fend**
**fend•er**
**fend•ered**
**fen•es•tel•la** (*plural* **•lae**) wall niche
**fe•nes•tra** (*plural* **•trae**) biology term
**fe•nes•tral**
**fe•nes•trat•ed** (*or* **•trate**) having windows
**fen•es•tra•tion**
**Fe•nian** Irish revolutionary
**fen•nec** fox
**fen•nel**
**fennel•flower**
**fen•ny** marshy
**Fenrir** (*or* **Fenris, Fenriswolf**) mythological wolf
**Fens**
**fenu•greek** plant
**feoff** *variant spelling of* **fief**
**fe•ral** (*or* **•rine**) wild
**fer•bam** fungicide
**fer-de-lance** snake
**fer•etory** (*plural* **•etories**) shrine
**Fer•ga•na** Asian region
**fe•ria** (*plural* **•rias** *or* **•riae**) weekday
**fe•rial**
**fe•rine** *variant of* **feral**
**fer•ity** wildness
**Fer•man•agh** Northern Irish county
**fer•ma•ta** (*plural* **•tas** *or* **•te**) musical term
**fer•ment** undergo fermentation; *compare* **foment**
**fer•ment•abil•ity**
**fer•ment•able**
**fer•men•ta•tion**
**fer•menta•tive**
**fer•menta•tive•ness**

**fer•ment•er**
**fer•mi** unit
**fer•mi•on** particle
**fer•mium** radioactive element
**fern**
**fern•ery** (*plural* **•eries**)
**ferny**
**fe•ro•cious**
**fe•roc•ity** (*or* **•ro•cious•ness**)
**Fer•ra•ra** Italian city
**fer•rate** chemistry term
**fer•reous** containing iron
**fer•ret**
**fer•ret•ing** silk tape
**fer•ret•er**
**fer•rety**
**fer•ri•age**
**fer•ric** chemistry term
**fer•ri•cy•an•ic acid**
**fer•ri•cya•nide**
**fer•rif•er•ous** producing iron
**fer•ri•mag•net•ic**
**fer•ri•mag•net•ism**
**Ferris wheel** fairground wheel
**fer•rite** ceramic
**fer•ri•tin** protein
**fer•ro•cene** chemical compound
**fer•ro•chro•mium** (*or* **fer•ro•chrome**)
**fer•ro•con•crete**
**fer•ro•cy•an•ic acid**
**fer•ro•cya•nide**
**fer•ro•elec•tric**
**fer•ro•elec•tri•cal•ly**
**fer•ro•elec•tric•ity**
**fer•ro•mag•ne•sian**
**fer•ro•mag•net•ic**
**fer•ro•mag•net•ism**
**fer•ro•man•ga•nese**
**fer•ro•sili•con**
**fer•ro•type** photography term
**fer•rous**
**fer•ru•gi•nous** containing iron
**fer•rule** (*or* **fer•ule**) metal cap; *compare* **ferule**
**fer•ry** (*noun, plural* **•ries**; *verb* **•ries, •ry•ing, •ried**)
**fer•tile**
**fer•til•ity** (*or* **•tile•ness**)
**fer•ti•liz•able** (*or* **•lis•able**)
**fer•ti•li•za•tion** (*or* **•sa•tion**)
**fer•ti•lize** (*or* **•lise**)
**fer•ti•liz•er** (*or* **•lis•er**)
**feru•la** (*plural* **•las** *or* **•lae**) plant
**feru•la•ceous**
**fer•ule** flat cane; *compare* **ferrule**
**fer•ven•cy**
**fer•vent** (*or* **•vid**)
**fer•vent•ly** (*or* **•vid•ly**)
**fer•vid** *variant of* **fervent**
**fer•vour** (*US* **•vor**)
**fes•cue** grass
**fesse** (*or* **fess**) heraldry term
**fes•tal** festive
**fes•ter**
**fes•ti•na•tion** quickening of gait
**fes•ti•val**
**fes•tive**
**fes•tive•ly**
**fes•tive•ness**
**fes•tiv•ity** (*plural* **•ities**)
**fes•toon**
**fes•toon•ery**
**fest•schrift** (*plural* **•schrift•en** *or* **•schrifts**) commemorative writings
**feta** cheese
**fe•tal** (*or* **foe•**)
**fe•ta•tion** (*or* **foe•**) pregnancy
**fetch**
**fetch•er**
**fetch•ing**
**fête** (*or* **fete**)
**fe•tial** (*plural* **fe•tia•les**) Roman herald
**fet•ich** *variant spelling of* **fetish**
**fe•ti•cid•al** (*or* **foe•**)
**fe•ti•cide** (*or* **foe•**) destruction of fetus
**fet•id** (*or* **foet•**) foul-smelling
**fe•tipa•rous** (*or* **foe•**) of marsupial birth
**fet•ish** (*or* **•ich**)
**fet•ish•ism** (*or* **•ich•**)
**fet•ish•ist** (*or* **•ich•**)
**fet•lock** (*or* **fetter•**) part of horse's leg
**fe•tor** (*or* **foe•**) stench
**fet•ter**
**fet•ter•er**
**fet•ter•less**
**fet•tle**
**fet•tling** refractory material
**fet•tu•ci•ne** (*or* **•tuc•ci•, tu•ci•ni**) pasta
**fe•tus** (*or* **foe•**; *plural* **•tuses**)
**feud**
**feu•dal**
**feu•dal•ism**
**feu•dal•ist**
**feu•dal•is•tic**
**feu•dal•ity** (*plural* **•ities**)
**feu•dali•za•tion** (*or* **•sa•tion**)
**feu•dal•ize** (*or* **•ise**)
**feu•da•tory**
**feud•ist**
**feuil•le•ton** review section of paper
**feuil•le•ton•ism**
**feuil•le•ton•ist**
**feuil•le•ton•is•tic**
**fe•ver**
**fe•vered**
**fe•ver•few** plant
**fe•ver•ish** (*or* **•ous**)
**fe•ver•ish•ness**
**fever•wort** plant
**few**
**few•ness**
**fey** whimsical; *compare* **fay**
**fez** (*plural* **fez•zes**)
**Fez•zan** Libyan region
**fezzed**
**fia•cre** carriage
**fi•an•cé** (*fem* **•cée**)
**Fi•an•na Fail** Irish political party
**fi•as•co** (*plural* **•cos** *or* **•coes**)
**Fiat** (*Trademark*)
**fiat** decree
**fib** (**fibbed, fib•bing**)
**fib•ber**
**fi•bre** (*US* **•ber**)
**fibre•board** (*US* **fiber•**)
**fi•bred** (*US* **•bered**)
**fibre•fill** (*US* **fiber•**)
**fibre•glass** (*US* **fiber•**)
**fibre-optic** (*adj*; *US* **fiber-**)
**fibre optics** (*noun*; *US* **fiber optics**)
**fibre•scope** (*US* **fiber•**)
**fi•bri•form**

**fi•bril** (*or* **•bril•la**; *plural* **•brils** *or* **•bril•lae)** small fibre
**fi•bri•lar** (*or* **•bril•lar, •bril•lose)**
**fi•bril•la•tion** muscle twitching
**fi•bril•li•form**
**fi•brin** blood-clotting protein
**fi•brino•gen**
**fi•brino•gen•ic** (*or* **•ous)**
**fi•brino•geni•cal•ly**
**fi•bri•noly•sin** enzyme
**fi•bri•noly•sis**
**fi•bri•no•lyt•ic**
**fi•brin•ous**
**fi•bro•blast** tissue cell
**fi•bro•blas•tic**
**fi•bro•cement**
**fi•broid**
**fi•bro•in** protein
**fi•bro•ma** (*plural* **•ma•ta** *or* **•mas)** tumour
**fi•broma•tous**
**fi•bro•sis**
**fi•bro•si•tis**
**fi•brot•ic**
**fi•brous**
**fi•brous•ness**
**fi•bro•vas•cu•lar** botany term
**fibu•la** (*plural* **•lae** *or* **•las)** leg bone
**fibu•lar**
**fiche** *short for* **microfiche**
**fichu** scarf
**fick•le**
**fick•le•ness**
**fic•tile** moulded from clay
**fic•tion**
**fic•tion•al**
**fic•tion•ali•za•tion** (*or* **•sa•tion)**
**fic•tion•al•ize** (*or* **•ise)**
**fic•tion•al•ly**
**fic•tion•ist** (*or* **fic•tion•eer)**
**fic•ti•tious** not genuine; *compare* **factitious**
**fic•ti•tious•ness**
**fic•tive** of fiction
**fid** nautical term
**fid•dle**
**fiddle-de-dee**
**fiddle-faddle**
**fiddle•head** (*or* **•neck)** nautical term
**fid•dler**
**fiddle•stick** violin bow
**fiddle•sticks** nonsense
**fiddle•wood**
**fid•dling**
**fid•dly** **(•dli•er, •dli•est)**
**fid•ei•com•mis•sary** (*plural* **•saries)** legal term
**fid•ei•com•mis•sum** (*plural* **•sa)**
**fi•deism**
**fi•deist**
**fi•deis•tic**
**fi•del•ity** (*plural* **•ities)**
**fidg•et**
**fidg•et•ing•ly**
**fidg•ety**
**fi•du•cial**
**fi•du•ci•ary** trustee
**fie** exclamation
**fief** (*or* **feoff)** property granted to vassal
**field**
**field•er**
**field•fare** bird
**field-holler** African-American singing style
**field•mouse**
**field•piece** gun
**fields•man** (*plural* **•men)**
**field•stone**
**field•work**
**fiend**
**fiend•ish**
**fiend•ish•ness**
**fierce**
**fierce•ly**
**fierce•ness**
**fi•eri fa•ci•as** legal term
**fiery**
**Fie•so•le** Italian town
**fi•es•ta**
**Fife** Scottish region
**fife**
**fif•er**
**fif•teen**
**fif•teenth**
**fifth**
**fif•ti•eth**
**fif•ty** (*plural* **•ties)**
**fifty-fifty**
**fig**
**fight (fight•ing, fought)**
**fight•er**
**fighter-bomber**
**fight•ing**
**fig•ment**
**figu•ral**
**figu•rant** (*fem* **•rante)** dancer
**fig•ur•ate** musical term
**fig•ura•tion**
**fig•ura•tive**
**fig•ura•tive•ly**
**fig•ura•tive•ness**
**fig•ure**
**fig•ured**
**figure-ground** psychology term
**figure•head**
**fig•ur•er**
**figu•rine** statuette
**fig•wort**
**Fiji**
**Fi•jian**
**fil** *variant of* **fils**
**fila•gree** *variant spelling of* **filigree**
**fila•ment**
**fila•men•tary** (*or* **•tous)**
**fi•lar** of thread
**fi•laria** (*plural* **•lariae)** worm
**fi•lar•ial** (*or* **•ian)**
**fila•ria•sis**
**fila•ture** silk spinning
**fil•bert** nut
**filch**
**filch•er**
**file**
**file•card**
**file•fish** (*plural* **•fish** *or* **•fishes)**
**fil•er**
**fi•let** lace; meat fillet
**fi•let mi•gnon** (*plural* **fi•lets mi•gnons)** beef cut
**fil•ial**
**fil•ial•ly**
**fil•ial•ness**
**fili•ate** legal term
**fili•ation** lineage
**fili•beg** (*or* **fil•li•, phili•)** kilt
**fili•bus•ter**
**fili•bus•ter•er**
**fili•bus•ter•ism**
**fili•cid•al**

**fili•cide** killing son or daughter
**fili•form** threadlike
**fili•gree** (*or* **fila•**, **filla•**; **•gree•ing**, **•greed**)
**fil•ings**
**Fili•pi•no** (*plural* **•nos**) inhabitant of Philippines
**fill**
**filla•gree** *variant spelling of* **filigree**
**filled**
**fill•er**
**fil•let**
**fill•ing**
**fil•lip**
**fil•lis•ter** (*or* **fil•is•ter**, **fil•les•ter**) wood plane
**fil•ly** (*plural* **•lies**)
**film**
**film•ic**
**filmi•ly**
**filmi•ness**
**fil•mog•ra•phy** (*plural* **•phies**)
**film•set** (**•setting**, **•set**)
**film•setter**
**film•setting**
**filmy** (**filmi•er**, **filmi•est**)
**filo** thin pastry
**filo•plume** feather
**fi•lose** threadlike
**filo•selle** thread
**fils** (*or* **fil**; *plural* **fils**) Middle Eastern coin
**fil•ter** separating device; *compare* **philtre**
**fil•ter•abil•ity** (*or* **•able•ness**)
**fil•ter•able** (*or* **fil•trable**)
**filter-tipped**
**filth**
**filthi•ly**
**filthi•ness**
**filthy** (**filthi•er**, **filthi•est**)
**fil•trat•able** *variant of* **filterable**
**fil•trate**
**fil•tra•tion**
**fi•lum** (*plural* **•la**) anatomy term
**fim•ble** plant
**fim•bria** (*plural* **•briae**) anatomy term
**fim•brial**
**fim•bri•ate** (*or* **•bri•at•ed**, **•bril•late**) fringed
**fim•bria•tion**
**fin** (**fin•ning**, **finned**)
**fin•able** (*or* **fine•**)
**fi•na•gle** use trickery
**fi•na•gler**
**fi•nal**
**fi•na•le**
**fi•nal•ism** philosophical doctrine
**fi•nal•ist**
**fi•nal•ity** (*plural* **•ities**)
**fi•na•li•za•tion** (*or* **•sa•tion**)
**fi•nal•ize** (*or* **•ise**)
**fi•nal•ly**
**fi•nals**
**fi•nance**
**fi•nan•cial**
**fi•nan•cial•ly**
**fi•nan•ci•er**
**fin•back** whale
**finch**
**find** (**find•ing**, **found**)
**find•able**
**find•er**
**fin de siè•cle** *French* end of 19th century
**find•ing**
**fine**
**fine•able** *variant spelling of* **finable**
**fine-cut**
**fine-draw** (**-drawing**, **-drew**, **-drawn**)
**Fine Gael** Irish political party
**fine-grain**
**fine-grained**
**fine•ly**
**fine•ness**
**fin•ery** (*plural* **•eries**)
**fine•spun**
**fi•nesse**
**fine-tooth** (*or* **-toothed**) comb
**fin•foot** (*plural* **•foots**) bird
**Fin•gal's Cave**
**fin•ger**
**finger•board**
**fin•gered**
**fin•ger•er**
**fin•ger•ing**
**fin•ger•ling** young fish
**finger•mark**
**finger•nail**
**finger•print**
**finger•stall**
**finger•tip**
**Fin•go** (*plural* **•go** *or* **•gos**) African people
**fi•nial**
**fi•ni•aled**
**fin•icky** (*or* **•ick•ing**)
**fin•ing** clarifying liquid
**fin•is** the end
**fin•ish**
**fin•ish•er**
**Fin•is•tère** French department
**Fin•is•terre** Spanish headland
**fi•nite**
**fi•nite•ly**
**fi•nite•ness**
**fink** *Slang* blackleg
**Fin•land**
**Finn**
**fin•nan had•dock** (*or* **Fin•nan had•die**)
**finned**
**fin•ner** whale
**Finn•ic** language group
**fin•ning**
**Finn•ish**
**Finn•mark** Norwegian county
**Finno-Ugric** (*or* **-Ugrian**) language group
**fin•ny** (**•ni•er**, **•ni•est**)
**fino** sherry
**fi•nochio** (*or* **•noc•chio**) fennel
**Fin•ster•aar•horn** Swiss mountain
**fiord** *variant spelling of* **fjord**
**fio•rin** grass
**fip•ple** mouthpiece
**fir**
**fire**
**fire•able**
**fire-and-brimstone**
**fire•arm**
**fire•back**
**fire•ball**
**fire•bird**
**fire•boat**
**fire•bomb**
**fire•box**
**fire•brand**

**fire•brat** insect
**fire•break**
**fire•brick**
**fire•bug** arsonist
**fire•cracker**
**fire•crest** bird
**fire•damp**
**fire•dog**
**fire•drake** dragon
**fire-eater**
**fire-eating**
**fire-extinguish•er**
**fire•fly** (*plural* **•flies**) beetle
**fire•guard**
**fire•man** (*plural* **•men**)
**fire•pan**
**fire•place**
**fire•proof**
**fir•er**
**fire•side**
**fire•stone**
**fire•thorn**
**fire•trap**
**fire•warden**
**fire•water** whisky
**fire•weed**
**fire•wood**
**fire•work**
**fir•ing**
**fir•kin** barrel
**firm**
**fir•ma•ment**
**fir•ma•men•tal**
**fir•mer** chisel
**firm•ness**
**firm•ware** computer term
**first**
**first-born**
**first-class** (*adj*)
**first-foot** (*or* **•footer**)
**first-footing**
**first-hand**
**first•ling** first offspring
**first-nighter**
**first-rate**
**firth** (*or* **frith**)
**fis•cal**
**fish** (*plural* **fish** *or* **fishes**)
**fish•able**
**fish•bolt**
**fish•bowl**
**fish•er**
**fisher•man** (*plural* **•men**)
**fish•ery** (*plural* **•eries**)
**fish-eye** camera lens
**fish•finger**
**fish•gig** pole for impaling fish
**fish-hook**
**fishi•ly**
**fishi•ness**
**fish•ing**
**fish•monger**
**fish•net**
**fish•plate** metal joint
**fish•tail** dance step
**fish•wife** (*plural* **•wives**)
**fishy** (**fishi•er, fishi•est**)
**fis•sile** physics term
**fis•sil•ity**
**fis•sion**
**fis•sion•abil•ity**
**fis•sion•able**
**fis•si•pal•mate** ornithology term
**fis•sipa•rous** reproducing by fission
**fis•si•ped** (*or* **•sip•edal**) zoology term
**fis•si•ros•tral** ornithology term
**fis•sure**
**fist**
**fist•ic** of boxing
**fisti•cuffs**
**fist•mele** archery term
**fis•tu•la** (*plural* **•las** *or* **•lae**) medical term
**fis•tu•lous** (*or* **•lar, •late**)
**fit** (*verb* **fit•ting, fit•ted**; *adj* **fit•ter, fit•test**)
**fitch** (*or* **fitch•et**) polecat
**fit•ful**
**fit•ful•ly**
**fit•ful•ness**
**fit•ment**
**fit•ness**
**fit•table**
**fit•ted**
**fit•ter**
**fit•ting**
**fit•ting•ly**
**fit•ting•ness**
**five**
**five-finger** plant
**five•fold**
**five•penny**
**five•pins**
**fiv•er**
**fives** ball game
**five-star** (*adj*)
**fix**
**fix•able**
**fix•ate**
**fixa•tion**
**fixa•tive**
**fixed**
**fix•ed•ly**
**fix•ed•ness**
**fix•er**
**fix•ity** (*plural* **•ities**) stability
**fix•ture**
**fiz•gig**
**fizz**
**fizz•er**
**fizzi•ness**
**fiz•zle**
**fizzy** (**fizzi•er, fizzi•est**)
**fjeld** (*or* **field**) rocky plateau
**fjord** (*or* **fiord**)
**flab**
**flab•ber•gast**
**flab•bi•ly**
**flab•bi•ness**
**flab•by** (**•bi•er, •bi•est**)
**fla•bel•late** (*or* **•bel•li•form**) fan-shaped
**fla•bel•lum** (*plural* **•la**)
**flac•cid**
**flac•cid•ity** (*or* **•ness**)
**flac•on** bottle
**flag** (**flag•ging, flagged**)
**flag•el•lant** (*or* **•la•tor**)
**flag•el•lant•ism**
**fla•gel•lar**
**flag•el•late**
**flag•el•lat•ed**
**flag•el•la•tion**
**fla•gel•li•form**
**fla•gel•lum** (*plural* **•la** *or* **•lums**) whiplike part
**flageo•let** musical instrument
**flagged**
**flag•ger**
**flag•ging**
**flag•gy** (**•gi•er, •gi•est**) limp
**fla•gi•tious** wicked
**flag•man** (*plural* **•men**)
**flag•on**
**flag•pole**
**fla•gran•cy** (*or* **•grance**)
**fla•grant**
**fla•gran•te de•lic•to** red-handed

**flag•ship**
**flag•staff** (*plural* **•staffs** *or* **•staves)**
**flag•stone**
**flag-waver**
**flag-waving**
**flail**
**flair** talent; *compare* **flare**
**flak** (*or* **flack)**
**flake**
**flak•er**
**flaki•ly**
**flaki•ness**
**flaky (flaki•er, flaki•est)**
**flam (flam•ming, flammed)** *Dialect* deceive
**flam•bé** (*or* **•bée**) cookery term
**flam•beau** (*plural* **•beaux** *or* **•beaus)** torch
**Flam•bor•ough Head** English promontory
**flam•boy•ance** (*or* **•an•cy)**
**flam•boy•ant**
**flame**
**flame•like**
**fla•men** (*plural* **•mens** *or* **fla•mi•nes)** Roman priest
**fla•men•co** (*plural* **•cos)**
**flame-of-the-forest** tree
**flame•out**
**flame•proof**
**flam•er**
**flame-thrower**
**flam•ing**
**fla•min•go** (*plural* **•gos** *or* **•goes)**
**flam•mabil•ity**
**flam•mable**
**flamy (flami•er, flami•est)**
**flan**
**Flan•ders**
**flâne•rie** idleness
**flâ•neur**
**flange**
**flang•er**
**flank**
**flank•er**
**flan•nel (•nel•ling, •nelled;** *US* **•nel•ing, •neled)**
**flan•nel•ette**
**flan•nel•ly**
**flap (flap•ping, flapped)**
**flap•doodle** *Slang* nonsense
**flap•jack**
**flap•per**
**flare** flame; widen; *compare* **flair**
**flare-up** (*noun*)
**flash**
**flash•back**
**flash•board**
**flash•bulb**
**flash•cube**
**flash•er**
**flashi•ly**
**flashi•ness**
**flash•ing**
**flash•light**
**flash•over** electric discharge
**flashy (flashi•er, flashi•est)**
**flask**
**flask•et** basket
**flat (flat•ter, flat•test)**
**flat•boat**
**flat•fish** (*plural* **•fish** *or* **•fishes)**
**flat•foot**
**flat-footed**
**flat-footed•ly**
**flat-footed•ness**
**flat•head** (*plural* **•head** *or* **•heads)** fish
**flat•iron**
**flat•let**
**flat•mate**
**flat•ness**
**flat•ten**
**flat•ten•er**
**flat•ter**
**flat•ter•able**
**flat•ter•er**
**flat•ter•ing**
**flat•ter•ing•ly**
**flat•tery** (*plural* **•teries)**
**flat•ting** metallurgy term
**flat•tish**
**flat•top** *US* aircraft carrier
**flatu•lence** (*or* **•len•cy)**
**flatu•lent**
**fla•tus** (*plural* **•tuses)**
**flat•ways**
**flat•worm**
**flaunch** (*or* **flaunch•ing)** slope round chimney
**flaunt**
**flaunt•er**
**flaunt•ing•ly**
**flaunty (flaunti•er, flaunti•est)**
**flau•tist** (*US* **flut•ist)**
**fla•ves•cent** turning yellow
**fla•vin** (*or* **•vine)** pigment
**fla•vone** plant pigment
**fla•vo•pro•tein** enzyme
**fla•vo•pur•pu•rin** dye
**fla•vor•ous**
**fla•vour** (*US* **•vor)**
**fla•vour•er** (*US* **•vor•)**
**fla•vour•ful** (*US* **•vor•)**
**fla•vour•ing** (*US* **•vor•)**
**fla•vour•less** (*US* **•vor•)**
**fla•vour•some** (*US* **•vor•)**
**flaw**
**flaw•less**
**flaw•less•ness**
**flawy** squally
**flax**
**flax•en** (*or* **flaxy)**
**flax•seed**
**flay**
**flay•er**
**flea**
**flea•bag**
**flea•bane** plant
**flea•bite**
**flea-bitten**
**fleam** lancet
**flea•pit**
**flea•wort** plant
**flèche** spire
**flé•chette** missile
**fleck**
**flec•tion** *variant spelling* (*esp. US*) *of* **flexion**
**fled**
**fledge**
**fledg•ling** (*or* **fledge•)**
**fledgy (fledgi•er, fledgi•est)** feathered
**flee (flee•ing, fled)**
**fleece**
**fleeci•ly**
**fleeci•ness**
**fleecy (fleeci•er, fleeci•est)**
**fle•er** one who flees
**fleer** sneer
**fleet**
**fleet•ing**
**fleet•ness**
**Fleet•wood** Lancashire port
**Flem•ing** native of Flanders
**Flem•ish**
**flense** (*or* **flench, flinch)** strip blubber from whale

**flens•er** (*or* **flench•**, **flinch•**)
**flesh**
**flesh•er** *Scot* butcher
**fleshi•ness**
**flesh•ings** tights
**flesh•li•ness**
**flesh•ly** (**•li•er**, **•li•est**)
**flesh•pots**
**fleshy** (**fleshi•er**, **fleshi•est**)
**fletch**
**fletch•er** arrow maker
**Fletch•er•ism** chewing food thoroughly
**fletch•ings** arrow feathers
**fleur-de-lis** (*or* **-lys**; *plural* **fleurs-de-lis** *or* **-lys**)
**fleu•rette** (*or* **•ret**) ornament
**fleur•on** ornament
**fleu•ry** *variant of* **flory**
**flew**
**flews** bloodhound's lip
**flex**
**flexi•bil•ity** (*or* **•ible•ness**)
**flex•ible**
**flex•ibly**
**flex•ile**
**flex•ion** (*or esp. US* **flection**)
**flex•ion•al**
**flexi•time**
**flex•or** muscle
**flexu•ous** (*or* **•ose**) having many bends
**flex•ur•al**
**flex•ure**
**fley** *Dialect* be afraid
**flib•ber•ti•gib•bet**
**flick**
**flick•er**
**flick•er•ing•ly**
**flick•ery**
**fli•er** (*or* **fly•**)
**flies**
**flight**
**flighti•ly**
**flighti•ness**
**flight•less**
**flighty** (**flighti•er**, **flighti•est**)
**flim•flam** (**•flam•ming**, **•flammed**)
**flim•si•ly**
**flim•si•ness**
**flim•sy** (**•si•er**, **•si•est**)
**flinch**
**flinch•er**
**flinch•ing•ly**
**fling** (**fling•ing**, **flung**)
**fling•er**
**Flint** Welsh town
**flint** quartz
**flinti•ly**
**flinti•ness**
**flint•lock** firearm
**Flint•shire** Welsh county
**flinty** (**flinti•er**, **flinti•est**)
**flip** (**flip•ping**, **flipped**)
**flip-flop** (**-flopping**, **-flopped**)
**flip•pan•cy**
**flip•pant**
**flip•per**
**flip•ping**
**flirt**
**flir•ta•tion**
**flir•ta•tious**
**flir•ta•tious•ness**
**flirt•er**
**flirt•ing•ly**
**flit** (**flit•ting**, **flit•ted**)
**flitch** pork
**flite** (*or* **flyte**) *Scot* scold
**flit•ter**
**flitter•mouse** (*plural* **•mice**) *Dialect* bat
**fliv•ver** old car
**float**
**float•abil•ity**
**float•able**
**float•age** *variant spelling of* **flotage**
**floata•tion** *variant spelling of* **flotation**
**float•er**
**float•ing**
**floaty** (**floati•er**, **floati•est**) light
**floc** *variant of* **floccule**
**floc•cose** tufted
**floc•cu•lant** anticoagulant; *compare* **flocculent**
**floc•cu•late** aggregate
**floc•cu•la•tion**
**floc•cule** (*or* **floc•cu•lus**, **flock**, **floc**) mass of particles
**floc•cu•lence** (*or* **•len•cy**)
**floc•cu•lent** fleecy; *compare* **flocculent**
**floc•cu•lus** (*plural* **•li**) marking on sun
**floc•cus** (*plural* **•ci**) down
**flock**
**flocky**
**Flod•den** battlefield
**floe** ice; *compare* **flow**
**flog** (**flog•ging**, **flogged**)
**flog•ger**
**flog•ging**
**flong** printing term
**flood**
**flood•able**
**flood•er**
**flood•gate**
**flood•light** (**•light•ing**, **•lit**)
**floor**
**floor•age**
**floor•board**
**floor•ing**
**floo•zy** (*or* **•zie**, **•sy**; *plural* **•zies** *or* **•sies**)
**flop** (**flop•ping**, **flopped**)
**flop•pi•ly**
**flop•pi•ness**
**flop•py** (**•pi•er**, **•pi•est**)
**Flora** Roman goddess
**flo•ra** (*plural* **•ras** *or* **•rae**) plant life
**flo•ral**
**flo•ral•ly**
**Flor•ence** Italian city
**Flor•en•tine**
**flo•res•cence** flowering; *compare* **fluorescence**
**flo•ret**
**Flo•ria•nópo•lis** Brazilian port
**flo•ri•at•ed** (*or* **•reated**) architectural term
**flo•ri•bun•da** rose
**flo•ri•cul•tur•al**
**flo•ri•cul•ture**
**flo•ri•cul•tur•ist**
**flor•id**
**Flori•da**
**flo•rid•ity** (*or* **•ness**)
**flo•ri•gen** hormone
**flo•ri•legium** (*plural* **•legia**) book about flowers
**flor•in**
**flo•rist**
**flo•ris•tic**
**flo•ris•ti•cal•ly**
**flo•ris•tics** branch of botany
**flo•ru•it** *Latin* flourished

**flo•ry** (*or* **fleu•**) heraldic term
**flos fer•ri** mineral
**floss**
**flossy** (**flossi•er, flossi•est**)
**flo•tage** (*or* **float•age**)
**flo•ta•tion** (*or* **floata•tion**)
**flo•til•la**
**flot•sam**
**flounce**
**flounc•ing**
**floun•der** (*plural* **•der** *or* **•ders**) fish; to struggle; *compare* **founder**
**flour**
**flour•ish**
**flour•ish•er**
**floury**
**flout**
**flout•er**
**flout•ing•ly**
**flow** liquid movement; *compare* **floe**
**flow•age**
**flow•er**
**flow•er•age**
**flower•bed**
**flow•ered**
**flow•er•er**
**flow•er•et**
**flow•eri•ness**
**flow•er•ing**
**flow•er•less**
**flower-like**
**flower-of-an-hour** plant
**flower•pot**
**flow•ery**
**flown**
**flu** illness; *compare* **flue**
**fluc•tu•ant**
**fluc•tu•ate**
**fluc•tua•tion**
**flue** pipe; *compare* **flu**
**flued**
**flu•en•cy**
**flu•ent**
**fluff**
**fluffi•ly**
**fluffi•ness**
**fluffy** (**fluffi•er, fluffi•est**)
**flu•gel•horn** musical instrument
**flu•id**
**flu•id•al**
**fluid•extract** pharmaceutical term
**flu•id•ic**
**flu•id•ics**
**flu•id•ity** (*or* **•ness**)
**flu•idi•za•tion** (*or* **•sa•tion**)
**flu•id•ize** (*or* **•ise**)
**flu•id•iz•er** (*or* **•is•er**)
**flu•id•ly** (*or* **flu•id•al•ly**)
**fluke**
**fluki•ness**
**fluky** (*or* **fluk•ey; fluki•er, fluki•est**)
**flume** ravine
**flum•mery** (*plural* **•meries**)
**flum•mox**
**flung**
**flunk** *Slang* fail
**flunky** (*or* **flunk•ey;** *plural* **flunkies** *or* **•eys**) servant
**flu•or** *variant of* **fluorspar**
**fluo•rene** chemical compound; *compare* **fluorine**
**fluo•resce**
**fluo•res•cein** (*or* **•ceine**) chemical compound
**fluo•res•cence** radiation emission; *compare* **florescence**
**fluo•res•cent**
**flu•or•ic** of fluorine
**fluori•date**
**fluori•da•tion**
**fluo•ride**
**fluo•rim•eter** *variant of* **fluorometer**
**fluori•nate** treat with fluorine
**fluori•na•tion**
**fluo•rine** (*or* **•rin**) chemical element; *compare* **fluorene**
**fluo•ro•car•bon**
**fluo•rom•eter** (*or* **•rim•**)
**fluo•ro•met•ric** (*or* **•ri•**)
**fluo•rom•etry** (*or* **•rim•**)
**fluoro•scope** X-ray instrument
**fluoro•scop•ic**
**fluoro•scopi•cal•ly**
**fluor•os•co•py**
**fluo•ro•sis**
**flu•or•spar** (*or* **flu•or**) mineral
**flur•ry** (*noun, plural* **•ries;** *verb* **•ries, •ry•ing, •ried**)
**flush**
**flush•er**
**Flush•ing** Dutch port
**flus•ter**
**flute**
**flut•ed**
**flut•er**
**flut•ing**
**flut•ist** *US* flautist
**flut•ter**
**flut•ter•er**
**flut•ter•ing•ly**
**flut•tery**
**fluty** (**fluti•er, fluti•est**)
**flu•vial** (*or* **•via•tile**) of a river
**flu•vio•ma•rine** of sea and river
**flux**
**flux•ion** change
**flux•ion•al** (*or* **•ary**)
**flux•meter**
**fly** (*noun, plural* **flies;** *verb* **flies, fly•ing, flew, flown**)
**fly•able**
**fly•away**
**fly•back** physics term
**fly•blow** (**•blow•ing, •blew, •blown**)
**fly•boat**
**fly•book** angler's fly case
**fly•by** (*plural* **•bys**)
**fly-by-night**
**fly•catcher**
**fly•er** *variant spelling of* **flier**
**fly-fish**
**fly-fisher**
**fly-fishing**
**fly•ing**
**fly•leaf** (*plural* **•leaves**)
**fly•over**
**fly•paper**
**fly-past**
**Flysch** Alpine rock
**fly•speck**
**flyte** *variant spelling of* **flite**
**fly•trap**
**fly•weight**
**fly•wheel**
**foal**
**foam**
**foam•flower**
**foami•ly**

**foami•ness**
**foam•like**
**foamy (foami•er, foami•est)**
**fob (fob•bing; fobbed)**
**fo•cal**
**fo•cali•za•tion** (*or* **•sa•tion)**
**fo•cal•ize** (*or* **•ise)** focus
**fo•cal•ly**
**fo'c's'le** (*or* **fo'c'sle)** *variant spellings of* **forecastle**
**fo•cus** (*noun, plural* **•cuses** *or* **•ci**; *verb* **•cuses, •cus•ing, •cused)**
**fo•cus•able**
**fo•cus•er**
**fod•der**
**foe**
**foehn** *variant spelling of* **föhn**
**foe•man**
**foe•tal** *variant spelling of* **fetal**
**foe•ta•tion** *variant spelling of* **fetation**
**foe•ti•cide** *variant spelling of* **feticide**
**foet•id** *variant spelling of* **fetid**
**foe•tipa•rous** *variant spelling of* **fetiparous**
**foe•tor** *variant spelling of* **fetor**
**foe•tus** *variant spelling of* **fetus**
**fog (fog•ging, fogged)**
**fog•bound**
**fog•bow** light in fog
**fog•dog** white spot in fog
**fogged**
**Fog•gia** Italian city
**fog•gi•ly**
**fog•gi•ness**
**fog•ging**
**fog•gy (•gi•er, •gi•est)**
**fog•horn**
**fogy** (*or* **fo•gey**; *plural* **fogies** *or* **•geys)**
**fo•gy•ish** (*or* **•gey•)**
**föhn** (*or* **foehn)** wind
**foi•ble**
**foil**
**foil•able**
**foils•man** (*plural* **•men)**
**Fo•ism** Chinese Buddhism
**foi•son** plentiful supply
**Fo•ist**
**foist**
**fola•cin** folic acid
**fold**
**fold•able**
**fold•away**
**fold•boat**
**fold•ed**
**fold•er**
**fol•derol** *variant spelling of* **falderal**
**fold•ing**
**fold•out** printing term
**fo•lia•ceous**
**fo•li•age**
**fo•li•ar** of leaves
**fo•li•ate**
**fo•li•at•ed**
**fo•lia•tion**
**fo•lic acid** vitamin
**fo•lio** (*noun, plural* **•lios**; *verb* **•lios, •lio•ing, •lioed)**
**fo•lio•late** botany term
**fo•li•ose** leafy
**fo•lium** (*plural* **•lia)** geometrical curve
**folk**
**Folke•stone**
**folk•ish**
**folk•lore**
**folk•lor•ic**
**folk•lor•ist**
**folk•lor•is•tic**
**folk•moot** medieval assembly
**folk-rock**
**folk•si•ness**
**folk•sy (•si•er, •si•est)**
**folk•ways** sociology term
**fol•li•cle**
**fol•licu•lar**
**fol•licu•late** (*or* **•lat•ed)**
**fol•licu•lin** hormone
**fol•low**
**fol•low•able**
**fol•low•er**
**fol•low•ing**
**follow-on** (*noun*)
**follow-through** (*noun*)
**follow-up** (*noun*)
**fol•ly** (*plural* **•lies)**
**Fol•som man** early man
**Fo•mal•haut** star
**fo•ment** instigate; *compare* **ferment**
**fo•men•ta•tion**
**fo•ment•er**
**fond**
**fon•dant**
**fon•dle**
**fon•dler**
**fon•dling•ly**
**fond•ness**
**fon•due** cookery term
**font** baptismal bowl; *variant spelling* (*esp. US*) *of* **fount**
**Fon•taine•bleau** French town
**font•al**
**fon•ta•nelle** (*or* **•nel)** anatomy term
**Foo•chow** (*or* **Fu-chou)** Chinese port
**food**
**food•stuff**
**fool**
**fool•ery** (*plural* **•eries)**
**fool•har•di•ness**
**fool•hardy (•hardi•er, hardi•est)**
**fool•ish**
**fool•ish•ness**
**fool•proof**
**fools•cap**
**fool's-parsley**
**foot** (*plural* **feet)**
**foot•age**
**foot-and-mouth disease**
**foot•ball**
**foot•ball•er**
**foot•board**
**foot•boy**
**foot•bridge**
**foot-candle** unit
**foot•er**
**foot•fall**
**foot•gear**
**foot•hill**
**foot•hold**
**footie** *variant spelling of* **footy**
**foot•ing**
**foot-lambert** unit
**foot•le** potter
**foot•lights**
**foot•ling** trivial
**foot•loose**
**foot•man** (*plural* **•men)**

**foot•mark**
**foot•note**
**foot•pace** platform before altar
**foot•pad** highwayman
**foot•path**
**foot•plate**
**foot-pound** unit
**foot-poundal** unit
**foot•print**
**foot•rest**
**foot•rope**
**foots** dregs
**foot•sie**
**foot•slog** (**•slog•ging, •slogged**)
**foot•sore**
**foot•stalk**
**foot•stall** base of column
**foot•step**
**foot•stool**
**foot-ton** unit
**foot•wall** geology term
**foot•way**
**foot•wear**
**foot•work**
**foot•worn**
**footy** (*or* **footie**) *Slang* football
**foo yong** (*or* **foo yoong, foo yung, fu yung**) Chinese omelette
**foo•zle** bungle golf shot
**foo•zler**
**fop**
**fop•pery** (*plural* **•peries**)
**fop•pish**
**fop•pish•ness**
**for**
**for•age**
**for•ag•er**
**fo•ra•men** (*plural* **•rami•na** *or* **•ra•mens**) hole in bone
**fo•rami•nal**
**fora•mini•fer** protozoan
**fo•rami•nif•er•al** (*or* **•ous**)
**for•as•much as**
**for•ay**
**for•ay•er**
**for•bade** (*or* **•bad**)
**for•bear** (**•bear•ing, •bore, •borne**) to refrain; *variant spelling of* **forebear**
**for•bear•ance**
**for•bear•er**
**for•bear•ing•ly**
**for•bid** (**•bid•ding, •bade** *or* **•bad, •bid•den** *or* **•bid**)
**for•bid•dance**
**for•bid•den**
**for•bid•der**
**for•bid•ding•ly**
**for•bore**
**for•borne**
**for•by** *Scot* besides
**force**
**force•able**
**forced**
**forc•ed•ly**
**forc•ed•ness**
**force-feed** (**-feeding, -fed**)
**force•ful**
**force•ful•ly**
**force•ful•ness**
**force ma•jeure**
**force•meat**
**for•ceps** (*plural* **•ceps** *or* **•ci•pes**)
**forc•er**
**for•cible**
**for•cible•ness** (*or* **•cibil•ity**)
**for•cibly**
**forc•ing•ly**
**ford**
**ford•able**
**fore**
**fore-and-aft** (*adj*)
**fore-and-after** vessel
**fore•arm**
**fore•bear** (*or* **for•**) ancestor; *compare* **forbear**
**fore•bode**
**fore•bod•er**
**fore•bod•ing**
**fore•brain**
**fore•cast** (**•cast•ing, •cast** *or* **•cast•ed**)
**fore•cast•er**
**fore•cas•tle** (*or* **fo'c's'le, fo'c'sle**)
**fore•clos•able**
**fore•close**
**fore•clo•sure**
**fore•course** boat's sail
**fore•court**
**fore•deck**
**fore•doom**
**fore•father**
**fore•finger**
**fore•foot** (*plural* **•feet**)
**fore•front**
**fore•gather** *variant spelling of* **forgather**
**fore•go** (**•goes, •go•ing, •went, •gone**) precede; *variant spelling of* **forgo**
**fore•go•er**
**fore•going**
**fore•gone**
**fore•gone•ness**
**fore•ground**
**fore•gut**
**fore•hand**
**fore•handed**
**fore•head**
**fore•hock** bacon
**for•eign**
**for•eign•er**
**for•eign•ism**
**for•eign•ness**
**fore•judge** prejudge; *variant spelling of* **forjudge**
**fore•judg•ment** (*or* **•judg•**)
**fore•know** (**•know•ing, •knew, •known**)
**fore•know•able**
**fore•know•ing•ly**
**fore•knowl•edge**
**fore•land**
**fore•leg**
**fore•limb**
**fore•lock**
**fore•man** (*plural* **•men**)
**fore•man•ship**
**fore•mast**
**fore•most**
**fore•name**
**fore•named**
**fore•noon**
**fo•ren•sic** of the law; *compare* **forensics**
**fo•ren•si•cal•ity**
**fo•ren•si•cal•ly**
**fo•ren•sics** debating; *compare* **forensic**
**fore•or•dain**
**fore•or•dain•ment** (*or* **•di•na•tion**)
**fore•part**
**fore•paw**
**fore•peak** nautical term
**fore•play**
**fore•quar•ter**
**fore•reach** nautical term

**fore•run** (**•run•ning, •ran, •run**)
**fore•run•ner**
**fore•sail**
**fore•see** (**•see•ing, •saw, •seen**)
**fore•see•able**
**fore•seen**
**fore•seer**
**fore•shad•ow**
**fore•shad•ow•er**
**fore•shank**
**fore•sheet** nautical term
**fore•shock** *US* minor earthquake
**fore•shore**
**fore•short•en**
**fore•side**
**fore•sight**
**fore•sighted**
**fore•sighted•ness**
**fore•skin**
**for•est**
**for•est•al** (*or* **fo•res•tial**)
**fore•stall**
**fore•stall•er**
**fore•stal•ment**
**for•esta•tion**
**fore•stay** nautical term
**forestay•sail**
**for•est•ed**
**for•est•er**
**forest-like**
**for•est•ry**
**fore•taste**
**fore•tell** (**•tell•ing, •told**)
**fore•tell•er**
**fore•thought**
**fore•thought•ful**
**fore•time** the past
**fore•to•ken** foreshadow
**fore•told**
**fore•tooth** (*plural* **•teeth**)
**fore•top** platform on foremast
**fore-topgal•lant** nautical term
**fore-topmast**
**fore-topsail**
**fore•tri•an•gle** nautical term
**for•ever**
**for•ever•more**
**fore•warn**
**fore•warn•er**
**fore•warn•ing•ly**
**fore•went**
**fore•wind**
**fore•wing**
**fore•word**
**fore•yard** nautical term
**for•feit**
**for•feit•able**
**for•feit•er**
**for•fei•ture**
**for•fend** *US* protect; *Archaic* prevent
**for•fi•cate** forked
**for•gath•er** (*or* **fore•**) assemble
**for•gave**
**forge**
**forge•able**
**forg•er**
**for•gery** (*plural* **•geries**)
**for•get** (**•get•ting, •got, •got•ten**)
**for•get•ful**
**for•get•ful•ly**
**for•get•ful•ness**
**forget-me-not**
**for•get•table**
**for•get•ter**
**forg•ing**
**for•giv•able**
**for•giv•ably**
**for•give** (**•giv•ing, •gave, •giv•en**)
**for•give•ness**
**for•giv•er**
**for•giv•ing•ly**
**for•giv•ing•ness**
**for•go** (*or* **fore•**; **•goes, •go•ing, •went, •gone**) give up; *compare* **forego**
**for•go•er** (*or* **fore•**)
**for•got**
**for•got•ten**
**for•judge** (*or* **fore•**) legal term; *compare* **forejudge**
**for•judg•ment** (*or* **fore•**)
**fork**
**forked**
**fork•ed•ly**
**fork•ed•ness**
**fork•ful**
**fork-lift truck**
**For•lì** Italian city
**for•lorn**
**form** shape, etc.; *US spelling of* **forme**
**form•able**
**for•mal**
**for•mal•de•hyde**
**for•ma•lin** (*or* **for•mol**)
**for•mal•ism**
**for•mal•ist**
**for•mal•is•tic**
**for•mal•ity** (*plural* **•ities**)
**for•mali•za•tion** (*or* **•sa•tion**)
**for•mal•ize** (*or* **•ise**)
**for•mal•iz•er** (*or* **•is•er**)
**for•mal•ly** in a formal way; *compare* **formerly**
**for•mal•ness**
**for•mant** acoustics term
**for•mat** (**•mat•ting, •mat•ted**)
**for•mate** chemistry term
**for•ma•tion**
**for•ma•tion•al**
**forma•tive**
**forma•tive•ly**
**forma•tive•ness**
**forme** (*US* **form**) printing term; *compare* **form**
**for•mer**
**for•mer•ly** in the past; *compare* **formally**
**for•mic** of ants; acid
**For•mi•ca** (*Trademark*)
**for•mi•cary** (*or* **•car•ium**; *plural* **•caries** *or* **•caria**) ant hill
**for•mi•ca•tion** skin sensation
**for•mi•dabil•ity** (*or* **•dable•ness**)
**for•mi•dable**
**for•mi•dably**
**form•less**
**form•less•ness**
**for•mol** *variant of* **formalin**
**For•mo•sa** *former name of* **Taiwan**
**for•mu•la** (*plural* **•las** *or* **•lae**)
**for•mu•laic**
**for•mu•lari•za•tion** (*or* **•sa•tion**)
**for•mu•lar•ize** (*or* **•ise**)
**for•mu•lar•iz•er** (*or* **•is•er**)
**for•mu•lary** (*plural* **•laries**)
**for•mu•late**
**for•mu•la•tion**
**for•mu•la•tor**

**for•mu•lism**
**for•mu•list**
**for•mu•lis•tic**
**form•work** concrete mould
**for•myl** chemistry term
**For•nax** constellation
**for•nenst** *Scot* situated against
**for•ni•cal** of a fornix
**for•ni•cate**
**for•ni•ca•tion**
**for•ni•ca•tor**
**for•nix** (*plural* **•ni•ces**) body structure
**for•sake** (**•sak•ing, •sook, •sak•en**)
**for•sak•en**
**for•sak•en•ness**
**for•sak•er**
**for•sook**
**for•sooth**
**for•ster•ite** mineral
**for•swear** (**•swear•ing, •swore, •sworn**)
**for•swear•er**
**for•sworn**
**for•sythia**
**fort**
**For•ta•leza** Brazilian port
**for•ta•lice** small fort
**Fort-de-France** Martinican capital
**forte** strength
**for•te** musical term
**forte-piano** musical term
**forte•piano** piano
**Forth** Scottish river
**forth** forward; *compare* **fourth**
**forth•com•ing**
**forth•com•ing•ness**
**forth•right**
**forth•right•ness**
**forth•with**
**for•ti•eth**
**for•ti•fi•able**
**for•ti•fi•ca•tion**
**for•ti•fi•er**
**for•ti•fy** (**•fies, •fy•ing, •fied**)
**for•tis** (*plural* **•tes**) phonetics term
**for•tis•si•mo** (*plural* **•mos** *or* **•mi**)
**for•ti•tude**
**for•ti•tu•di•nous**
**Fort Knox**
**fort•night**
**fort•night•ly**
**Fortran** computer language
**for•tress**
**for•tui•tism** philosophy term
**for•tui•tist**
**for•tui•tous** unplanned; *compare* **fatuitous**
**for•tui•tous•ness**
**for•tu•ity** (*plural* **•ities**)
**Fortuna** Roman goddess
**for•tu•nate**
**for•tu•nate•ly**
**for•tu•nate•ness**
**for•tune**
**fortune-hunter**
**fortune-teller**
**fortune-telling**
**for•ty** (*plural* **•ties**)
**forty-niner** prospector
**fo•rum** (*plural* **•rums** *or* **•ra**)
**for•ward** (*adj*)
**for•ward•er** (*noun*)
**for•ward•ness**
**for•wards** (*adv*)
**for•went**
**for•zan•do** musical term
**fos•sa** (*plural* **•sae**) anatomical depression
**fosse** (*or* **foss**) ditch
**fos•sette** bone depression
**fos•sil**
**fos•sil•if•er•ous**
**fos•sil•iz•able** (*or* **•is•able**)
**fos•sili•za•tion** (*or* **•sa•tion**)
**fos•sil•ize** (*or* **•ise**)
**fos•so•rial** used for burrowing
**fos•ter**
**fos•ter•age**
**fos•ter•er**
**fos•ter•ing•ly**
**fos•ter•ling** foster child
**fou•droy•ant** sudden
**fou•et•té** ballet step
**fought**
**foul** bad; *compare* **fowl**
**fou•lard** fabric
**foul•ly**
**foul-mouthed**
**Foul•ness** Essex island
**foul•ness**
**found**
**foun•da•tion**
**foun•da•tion•al**
**foun•da•tion•ary**
**found•er** one who founds; to sink; *compare* **flounder**
**found•ing**
**found•ling**
**found•ry** (*plural* **•ries**)
**fount** fountain; source
**fount** (*or esp. US* **font**) printing term
**foun•tain**
**fountain•head**
**four**
**four-ball** golfing term
**four•chette** anatomy term
**four-colour** (*US* **-color**) photography term
**four-dimension•al**
**Four•drini•er** paper-making machine
**four•fold**
**four-handed**
**Fou•ri•er•ism** social system
**Fou•ri•er•ist** (*or* **•ite**)
**Fou•ri•er•is•tic**
**four-in-hand** carriage
**four-leaf** (*or* **-leaved**) **clover**
**four•pence**
**four•penny**
**four-poster**
**four•ra•gère** ornamental cord
**four•score**
**four•some**
**four•square**
**four-stroke en•gine**
**four•teen**
**four•teenth**
**fourth** 4th; *compare* **forth**
**four-way** (*adj*)
**four-wheel drive**
**fo•vea** (*plural* **•veae**) anatomy term
**fo•veal**
**fo•veate** (*or* **•veat•ed**)
**fo•veo•la** (*plural* **•lae**) small fovea
**fo•veo•lar**
**fo•veo•late** (*or* **•lat•ed**)
**Fowey** Cornish village
**fowl** chicken; *compare* **foul**
**fowl•er** bird hunter

**Fow•liang** (*or* **Fou-liang**) Chinese city
**fowl•ing**
**fox** (*plural* **foxes** *or* **fox**)
**fox•fire** glow
**fox•glove**
**fox•hole**
**fox•hound**
**fox-hunter**
**fox-hunting**
**foxi•ly**
**foxi•ness**
**fox•ing** part of shoe
**fox•like**
**fox•tail** grass
**fox•trot** (**•trot•ting, •trot•ted**)
**foxy** (**foxi•er, foxi•est**)
**foy•er**
**Fra** monk's title
**fra•cas** (*plural* **•cas;** *US* **•cases**) uproar
**frac•tion**
**frac•tion•al** (*or* **•ary**)
**frac•tion•al•ly**
**frac•tion•ate**
**frac•tiona•tion**
**frac•tiona•tor**
**frac•tioni•za•tion** (*or* **•sa•tion**)
**frac•tion•ize** (*or* **•ise**)
**frac•tious**
**frac•to•cu•mu•lus** (*plural* **•li**)
**frac•to•stra•tus** (*plural* **•ti**)
**frac•tura•ble**
**frac•tur•al**
**frac•ture**
**frae** *Scot* from
**frae•num** (*or* **fre•**; *plural* **•na**) fold
**frag** (**frag•ging, fragged**) US military slang term
**frag•ile**
**frag•ile•ly**
**fra•gil•ity** (*or* **•gile•ness**)
**frag•ment**
**frag•men•tal**
**frag•men•tal•ly**
**frag•men•tari•ly**
**frag•men•tari•ness**
**frag•men•tary**
**frag•men•ta•tion**
**fra•grance** (*or* **•gran•cy;** *plural* **•grances** *or* **•gran•cies**)
**fra•grant**
**frail**
**frail•ly**
**frail•ness**
**frail•ty** (*plural* **•ties**)
**fraise** tool; neck ruff; rampart
**Frak•tur** typeface
**fram•able** (*or* **frame•**)
**fram•boe•sia** (*US* **•be•**) disease
**fram•boise** liqueur
**frame**
**frame•less**
**fram•er**
**frame-up**
**frame•work**
**fram•ing**
**franc**
**France**
**Franche-Comté** French region
**fran•chise**
**fran•chise•ment**
**Fran•cis•can**
**fran•cium** chemical element
**fran•co•lin** partridge
**Fran•co•nian** language group
**Fran•co•phile** (*or* **•phil**)
**Fran•co•phobe**
**Fran•co•pho•bia**
**Fran•co•phone** native French speaker
**frang•er** *Austral* condom
**fran•gibil•ity** (*or* **•gible•ness**)
**fran•gible** breakable
**fran•gi•pane** almond pastry
**fran•gi•pani** (*plural* **•panis** *or* **•pani**) shrub
**Frang•lais** French with English words
**frank**
**frank•able**
**frank•al•moign** legal term
**Frankenstein**
**frank•er**
**Frank•furt**
**frank•fur•ter**
**frank•in•cense**
**Frank•ish**
**Frank•lin** Canadian district
**frank•lin** medieval landowner
**frank•lin•ite** mineral
**frank•ness**
**frank•pledge** medieval tithing system
**fran•tic**
**fran•ti•cal•ly** (*or* **fran•tic•ly**)
**frap** (**frap•ping, frapped**) nautical term
**frap•pé** *French* chilled
**frass** insect excrement
**fratchy** quarrelsome
**fra•ter** friar
**fra•ter•nal**
**fra•ter•nal•ly**
**fra•ter•nal•ism**
**fra•ter•nity** (*plural* **•nities**)
**frat•er•ni•za•tion** (*or* **•sa•tion**)
**frat•er•nize** (*or* **•nise**)
**frat•er•niz•er** (*or* **•nis•er**)
**frat•ri•cid•al**
**frat•ri•cide**
**Frau** (*plural* **Frau•en** *or* **Fraus**) *German* woman; Mrs
**fraud**
**fraudu•lence** (*or* **•len•cy**)
**fraudu•lent**
**fraught**
**Fräu•lein** (*plural* **•lein** *or* **•leins**) *German* young woman; Miss
**fraxi•nel•la** plant
**fray**
**fra•zil** ice spikes
**fraz•zle**
**freak**
**freaki•ly**
**freaki•ness**
**freak•ish**
**freak•ish•ness**
**freaky** (**freaki•er, freaki•est**)
**freck•le**
**freck•led** (*or* **•ly**)
**Fred•er•iks•berg** Danish city
**free** (*adj* **fre•er, fre•est;** *verb* **free•ing, freed**)
**free•bie** *Slang* free gift
**free•board**
**free•boot**
**free•booter**
**free•born**
**freed•man** (*plural* **•men**)
**free•dom**

**freed•woman** (*plural* **•women)**
**free-floater** uncommitted person
**free-floating**
**free-for-all**
**free-handed**
**free-hearted**
**free•hold**
**free•holder**
**free•lance**
**free•lancer**
**free-liver**
**free-living**
**free•load** *US* be a sponger
**free•ly**
**free•man** (*plural* **•men)**
**free•martin** female twin calf
**Free•mason** member of secret order
**free•mason** stonemason
**Free•masonic**
**free•masonic**
**Free•masonry**
**free•masonry**
**free-range**
**free•sheet** free newspaper
**free•sia**
**free-spoken**
**free•standing**
**free•stone**
**free•style**
**free-swimmer**
**free-swimming**
**free•thinker**
**free•thinking**
**Free•town** capital of Sierra Leone
**free-trader**
**free•way**
**free•wheel**
**free•wheeling**
**freez•able**
**freeze (freez•ing, froze, fro•zen)**
**freeze-dry (-dries, -drying, -dried)**
**freez•er**
**freeze-up**
**freez•ing**
**Frei•burg** German city
**freight**
**freight•age**
**freight•er**
**freight•liner**
**Fre•man•tle** Australian port
**fremi•tus** (*plural* **•tus)** medical term
**Fre•mont** US city
**French**
**Frenchi•fy (•fies, •fy•ing, •fied)**
**French•man** (*plural* **•men)**
**French•woman** (*plural* **•women)**
**fre•net•ic**
**fre•neti•cal•ly**
**frenu•lum** (*plural* **•la)** zoology term
**fre•num** *variant spelling of* **fraenum**
**fren•zied**
**fren•zy** (*noun, plural* **•zies;** *verb* **•zies, •zy•ing, •zied)**
**Fre•on** (*Trademark*)
**fre•quen•cy** (*plural* **•cies)** physics and statistics term
**fre•quen•cy** (*or* **fre•quence)** frequent occurrence
**fre•quent**
**fre•quent•able**
**fre•quen•ta•tion**
**fre•quen•ta•tive** linguistics term
**fre•quent•er**
**fre•quent•ly**
**fres•co** (*plural* **•coes** *or* **•cos)**
**fresh**
**fresh•en**
**fresh•en•er**
**fresh•er** (*or* **•man;** *plural* **•ers** *or* **•men)**
**fresh•et** river overflowing
**fresh•man** *variant of* **fresher**
**fresh•ness**
**fresh•water** (*adj*)
**fres•nel** unit
**Fres•no** US city
**fret (fret•ting, fret•ted)**
**fret•board**
**fret•ful**
**fret•ful•ly**
**fret•ful•ness**
**fret•less**
**fret•ted**
**fret•work**
**Freud•ian**
**Freudi•an•ism**
**Frey** Norse god
**Freya** Norse goddess
**fri•abil•ity** (*or* **•able•ness)**
**fri•able**
**fri•ar**
**friar•bird**
**fri•ary** (*plural* **•aries)**
**frib•ble** fritter away
**frib•bler**
**Fri•bourg** Swiss town
**fric•an•deau** (*or* **•do;** *plural* **•deaus, deaux,** *or* **•does)** cookery term
**fric•as•see (•see•ing, •seed)** cookery term
**frica•tive** phonetics term
**fric•tion**
**fric•tion•al**
**Fri•day**
**fridge**
**fried**
**friend**
**friend•less**
**friend•less•ness**
**friend•li•ly**
**friend•li•ness**
**friend•ly (•li•er, •li•est)**
**friend•ship**
**fri•er** *variant spelling of* **fryer**
**fries**
**Frie•sian** cattle; *variant spelling of* **Frisian**
**Fries•land** Dutch province
**frieze** decorative strip
**frig (frig•ging, frigged)**
**frig•ate**
**frig•ging**
**fright**
**fright•en**
**fright•en•able**
**fright•en•er**
**fright•en•ing**
**fright•en•ing•ly**
**fright•ful**
**fright•ful•ly**
**frig•id**
**Frig•id•aire** (*Trademark*)
**fri•gid•ity** (*or* **frig•id•ness)**
**fri•jol** (*plural* **•joles)** French bean
**frill**
**frilled**
**frilli•ness**
**frilly (frilli•er, frilli•est)**
**fringe**
**frin•gil•line** (*or* **•lid)** ornithology term

**fringy**
**frip•pery** (*plural* **•peries**)
**frip•pet** frivolous woman
**Fris•bee** (*Trademark*)
**Fris•co** *Slang* San Francisco
**fri•sé** fabric
**fri•sette** (*or* **•zette**) fringe
**fri•seur** *French* hairdresser
**Fri•sian** (*or* **Frie•**) language; of Friesland
**Fri•sian Is•lands**
**frisk**
**frisk•er**
**frisk•et** printing term
**friski•ly**
**friski•ness**
**frisky** (**friski•er, friski•est**)
**fris•son** shiver
**frit** (*or* **fritt; frit•ting, frit•ted**) glassy material
**frith** *variant of* **firth**
**fri•til•lary** (*plural* **•laries**) butterfly; plant
**fritt** *variant spelling of* **frit**
**frit•ter**
**frit•ter•er**
**Friu•li** European region
**Friu•lian**
**Friuli-Venezia Giu•lia** Italian region
**friv•ol** (**•ol•ling, •olled**)
**fri•vol•ity** (*plural* **•ities**)
**friv•ol•ler**
**frivo•lous**
**frivo•lous•ness**
**fri•zette** *variant spelling of* **frisette**
**frizz**
**frizz•er**
**friz•zi•ness** (*or* **•zli•ness**)
**friz•zle**
**friz•zler**
**friz•zy** (*or* **•zly; •zi•er, •zi•est** *or* **•zli•er, •zli•est**)
**fro** from; *compare* **froe**
**frock**
**frock•ing** coarse material
**froe** (*or* **frow**) tool; *compare* **fro**
**frog** (**frog•ging, frogged**)
**frog-bit** plant
**frog•fish** (*plural* **•fish** *or* **•fishes**)
**frogged**
**frog•ging**
**frog•gy**
**frog•hopper** insect
**frog•man** (*plural* **•men**)
**frog•march**
**frog•mouth** bird
**frog•spawn**
**frol•ic** (**•ick•ing, •icked**)
**frol•ick•er**
**frol•ic•some** (*or* **frol•icky**)
**from**
**fro•men•ty** *variant of* **frumenty**
**frond**
**Fronde** French rebellion
**frond•ed**
**fron•des•cence** botany term
**fron•des•cent** (*or* **fron•dose, fron•dous**)
**Fron•deur** French rebel
**frons** (*plural* **fron•tes**) entomology term
**front**
**front•age**
**front•al**
**fron•tal•ity**
**fron•tal•ly**
**front•bencher**
**fron•tier**
**fron•tiers•man** (*plural* **•men**)
**fron•tis•piece**
**front•let** forehead decoration
**fron•to•gen•esis** meteorology term
**fron•toly•sis** meteorology term
**front•runner**
**front•wards** (*or esp. US* **•ward**)
**frost**
**frost•bite**
**frost•bitten**
**frost•ed**
**frosti•ly**
**frosti•ness**
**frost•ing**
**frost•work**
**frosty** (**frosti•er, frosti•est**)
**froth**
**frothi•ly**
**frothi•ness**
**frothy** (**frothi•er, frothi•est**)
**frott•age** rubbing
**frou•frou** swishing sound
**frow** *variant spelling of* **froe**
**fro•ward** obstinate
**frown**
**frown•er**
**frown•ing•ly**
**frowst**
**frows•ty** stale
**frowzi•ness** (*or* **frowsi•**)
**frowzy** (*or* **frowsy; frowzi•er, frowzi•est** *or* **frowsi•er, frows•iest**) shabby
**froze**
**fro•zen**
**fro•zen•ness**
**fruc•tif•er•ous** fruit-bearing
**fruc•ti•fi•ca•tion**
**fruc•ti•fi•er**
**fruc•ti•fy** (**•fies, •fy•ing, •fied**)
**fruc•tose** sugar
**fruc•tu•ous**
**fru•gal**
**fru•gal•ly**
**fru•gal•ity** (*or* **•ness**)
**fru•giv•or•ous** fruit-eating
**fruit**
**fruit•age**
**frui•tar•ian**
**fruit•cake**
**fruit•er** fruit grower
**fruit•er•er** fruit seller
**fruit•ful**
**fruit•ful•ly**
**fruit•ful•ness**
**fruiti•ness**
**frui•tion**
**fruit•less**
**fruit•less•ness**
**fruity** (**fruiti•er, fruiti•est**)
**fru•men•ta•ceous** resembling wheat
**fru•men•ty** (*or* **fro•, fur•**) porridge
**frump**
**frump•ish** (*or* **frumpy**)
**frump•ish•ness** (*or* **frumpi•ness**)
**Frun•ze** *former name of* **Bishkek**
**frus•trate**
**frus•trat•er**
**frus•tra•tion**
**frus•tule** botany term

**frus•tum** (*plural* **•tums** *or* **•ta**) geometric solid
**fru•tes•cence**
**fru•tes•cent** (*or* **•ti•cose**) shrublike
**fry** (*noun, plural* **fries**; *verb* **fries, fry•ing, fried**)
**fry•er** (*or* **fri•**)
**fry•ing**
**Fu-chou** *variant spelling of* **Foochow**
**fuch•sia** shrub
**fuch•sin** (*or* **•sine**) dye
**fuck**
**fuck•er**
**fuck•ing**
**fu•coid**
**fu•coid•al** (*or* **fu•cous**)
**fu•cus** (*plural* **•ci** *or* **•cuses**) seaweed
**fud•dle**
**fuddy-duddy** (*plural* **-duddies**)
**fudge**
**Fueh•rer** *variant spelling of* **Führer**
**fuel** (**fuel•ling, fuelled**; *US* **fuel•ing, fueled**)
**fuel•ler** (*US* **fuel•er**)
**fug**
**fu•ga•cious** fleeting
**fu•gac•ity**
**fu•gal** of a fugue
**fu•gal•ly**
**fu•ga•to** musical term
**fu•gi•tive**
**fu•gi•tive•ly**
**fugle•man** (*plural* **•men**) one used as example
**fugue**
**fu•guist**
**Füh•rer** (*or* **Fueh•**) *German* leader
**Fuji** (*or* **Fujiyama, Fuji-san**) Japanese mountain
**Fu•kien** Chinese province
**Fu•kuo•ka** Japanese city
**Fu•ku•shi•ma** Japanese city
**Fula** (*or* **Fu•lah**; *plural* **Fula** *or* **Fulas** *or* **Fu•lah, Fu•lahs**) African people
**Fu•la•ni** language
**ful•crum** (*plural* **•crums** *or* **•cra**)
**ful•fil** (*US* **•fill**; **•fil•ling, •filled**)
**ful•fil•ler**
**ful•fil•ment** (*US* **•fill•**)
**ful•gent** (*or* **•gid**) resplendent
**ful•gu•rant**
**ful•gu•rate** flash like lightning
**ful•gu•rat•ing** painful
**ful•gu•ra•tion** surgical procedure
**ful•gu•rite** mineral
**ful•gu•rous**
**Ful•ham**
**fu•ligi•nous** smoky
**full**
**full•back**
**full-blooded**
**full-blown**
**full-bodied**
**full•er**
**full-faced**
**full-frontal** (*adj*)
**full-length**
**full-mouthed**
**full•ness**
**full-rigged**
**full-sailed**
**full-scale**
**full-time** (*adj*)
**full-timer**
**ful•ly**
**fully-fledged**
**ful•mar** bird
**ful•mi•nant** sudden
**ful•mi•nate**
**ful•mi•na•tion**
**ful•mi•na•tor**
**ful•mi•na•tory**
**ful•min•ic acid**
**ful•some**
**ful•some•ly**
**ful•some•ness**
**ful•vous** tawny
**fu•mar•ic acid**
**fu•ma•role** volcano vent
**fu•ma•rol•ic**
**fu•ma•to•rium** (*or* **•tory**; *plural* **•riums, •ria**, *or* **•tories**) fumigation chamber
**fu•ma•tory** of fumigation; *compare* **fumitory**
**fum•ble**
**fum•bler**
**fum•bling•ly**
**fum•bling•ness**
**fume**
**fume•less**
**fum•er**
**fu•mi•gant**
**fu•mi•gate**
**fu•mi•ga•tion**
**fu•mi•ga•tor**
**fum•ing**
**fu•mi•tory** (*plural* **•tories**) plant; *compare* **fumatory**
**fumy** (**fumi•er, fumi•est**)
**fun** (**fun•ning, funned**)
**Fu•na•fu•ti** capital of Tuvalu
**fu•nam•bu•lism**
**fu•nam•bu•list** tightrope walker
**Fun•chal** capital of Madeira
**func•tion**
**func•tion•al**
**func•tion•al•ism**
**func•tion•al•ist**
**func•tion•al•ly**
**func•tion•ary** (*plural* **•aries**)
**fund**
**fun•da•ment**
**fun•da•men•tal**
**fun•da•men•tal•ism**
**fun•da•men•tal•ist**
**fun•da•men•tal•is•tic**
**fun•da•men•tal•ity** (*or* **•ness**)
**fun•da•men•tal•ly**
**fund•ed**
**fun•di** mechanic
**fun•dic**
**fun•dus** (*plural* **•di**) anatomy term
**Fun•dy** Canadian bay
**fu•ner•al**
**fu•ner•ary**
**fu•nereal**
**fun•fair**
**fun•gal**
**fun•gi** *plural of* **fungus**
**fun•gibil•ity**
**fun•gible** legal term
**fun•gic**
**fun•gi•cid•al**
**fun•gi•cide**
**fun•gi•form**
**fun•gi•stat**
**fun•gi•stat•ic**

**fun•goid**
**fun•gous** (*adj*)
**fun•gus** (*noun*; *plural* **•gi** *or* **•guses**)
**fu•ni•cle** botany term
**fu•nicu•lar**
**fu•nicu•late**
**fu•nicu•lus** (*plural* **•li**) anatomy term
**funk**
**funk•er**
**funky** (**funki•er, funki•est**)
**fun•nel** (**•nel•ling, •nelled**; *US* **•nel•ing, •neled**)
**fun•ni•ly**
**fun•ni•ness**
**fun•ny** (**•ni•er, •ni•est**)
**fur** (**fur•ring, furred**)
**fur•al•de•hyde**
**fu•ran** (*or* **fur•fu•ran**) chemical compound
**fur•below** ornamental trim
**fur•bish**
**fur•bish•er**
**fur•cate** fork
**fur•cat•ed**
**fur•ca•tion**
**fur•cu•la** (*or* **•lum**; *plural* **•lae** *or* **•la**) forklike organ
**fur•fur** (*plural* **•fures**) scaling of skin
**fur•fu•ra•ceous** of bran
**fur•fur•al•de•hyde**
**fur•fu•ran** *variant of* **furan**
**fu•rio•so** musical term
**fu•ri•ous**
**fu•ri•ous•ness**
**furl**
**furl•able**
**furl•er**
**fur•long** unit
**fur•lough** *US* leave
**fur•men•ty** *variant of* **frumenty**
**fur•nace**
**Fur•ness** Cumbrian peninsula
**fur•nish**
**fur•nish•er**
**fur•nish•ings**
**fur•ni•ture**
**fu•ro•re** (*or esp. US* **fu•ror**)
**fur•phy** (*plural* **•phies**) *Austral* rumour
**furred**
**fur•ri•er** fur dealer; more furry
**fur•ri•ery** (*plural* **•eries**)
**fur•ri•ly**
**fur•ri•ness**
**fur•ring**
**fur•row**
**fur•row•er**
**fur•rowy**
**fur•ry** (**•ri•er, •ri•est**)
**fur•ther** additional; *variant of* **farther**
**fur•ther•ance**
**fur•ther•er**
**further•more**
**further•most**
**fur•thest**
**fur•tive**
**fur•tive•ly**
**fur•tive•ness**
**fu•run•cle** boil
**fu•run•cu•lar** (*or* **•lous**)
**fu•run•cu•lo•sis** skin condition
**fury** (*plural* **furies**)
**furze** gorse
**furzy**
**fu•sain** charcoal
**fus•cous** brownish
**fuse**
**fu•see** (*or* **•zee**) clock part; match
**fu•sel oil**
**fu•selage**
**(fushia)** *incorrect spelling of* **fuchsia**
**Fu•shun** Chinese city
**fu•sibil•ity** (*or* **fusible•ness**)
**fu•sible**
**fu•sibly**
**fu•si•form** spindle-shaped
**fu•sil** musket
**fu•sile** (*or* **•sil**) easily melted
**fu•si•lier**
**fu•sil•lade** rapid gunfire
**fu•sion**
**fu•sion•ism**
**fu•sion•ist**
**fuss**
**fuss•er**
**fussi•ly**
**fussi•ness**
**fuss•pot**
**fussy** (**fussi•er, fussi•est**)
**fus•ta•nel•la** (*or* **•nelle**) Greek skirt
**fus•tian** fabric
**fus•tic** tree
**fus•ti•ly**
**fus•ti•ness**
**fus•ty** (**•ti•er, •ti•est**)
**fu•thark** (*or* **•tharc, •thork, •thorc**) phonetic alphabet
**fu•tile**
**fu•tile•ly**
**fu•tili•tar•ian**
**fu•tili•tari•an•ism**
**fu•til•ity** (*plural* **•ities**)
**fut•tock** part of boat
**fu•ture**
**fu•tur•ism**
**fu•tur•ist**
**fu•tur•is•tic**
**fu•tur•is•ti•cal•ly**
**fu•tur•ity** (*plural* **•ities**)
**fu•tur•olo•gist**
**fu•tur•ol•ogy**
**fu yung** *variant of* **foo yong**
**fu•zee** *variant spelling of* **fusee**
**fuzz**
**fuzzi•ly**
**fuzzi•ness**
**fuzzy** (**fuzzi•er, fuzzi•est**)
**fyke** *US* fishing net
**Fylde** region of Lancashire
**fyrd** Anglo-Saxon militia
**Fyza•bad** (*or* **Faiza•**) Indian city; *compare* **Faizabad**

# G

**Ga** (*or* **Gã**; *plural* **Ga, Gas** *or* **Gã, Gãs**) African people
**gab** (**gab•bing, gabbed**)
**gab•ar•dine** *variant spelling of* **gaberdine**
**gab•ber**
**gab•ble**
**gab•bler**
**gab•bro** (*plural* **•bros**) rock
**gab•bro•ic** (*or* **•it•ic**)
**gab•by** (**•bi•er, •bi•est**) talkative
**ga•belle** French salt tax
**gab•er•dine** fabric
**gab•er•dine** (*or* **•ar•**) cloak
**Ga•bès** Tunisian port
**gab•fest** *US* gathering
**ga•bi•on** stone-filled cylinder
**ga•bi•on•ade** (*or* **•on•nade**)
**ga•ble**
**ga•bled**
**ga•blet** small gable
**Ga•bon**
**Gabo•nese**
**Gabo•ro•ne** Botswanan capital
**gaby** (*plural* **gabies**) simpleton
**gad** (**gad•ding, gad•ded**)
**gad•about**
**gad•der**
**gad•fly** (*plural* **•flies**)
**gadg•et**
**gadg•eteer** lover of gadgetry
**gadg•et•ry**
**gadg•ety**
**Gad•hel•ic** Gaelic language
**ga•did** fish
**ga•doid**
**gado•lin•ic**
**gado•lin•ite** mineral
**gado•lin•ium** chemical element
**ga•droon** (*or* **go•**) decorative moulding
**ga•drooned** (*or* **go•**)
**gad•wall** (*plural* **•walls** *or* **•wall**) duck
**Gael** Gaelic speaker
**Gael•ic**
**gaff** angling pole; nautical boom; *Slang* home
**gaffe** blunder
**gaf•fer**
**gaff-rigged**
**gaff•sail**
**gaff-topsail**
**gag** (**gag•ging, gagged**)
**gaga** *Slang* senile
**Ga•gau•zi** Russian language
**gage** pledge; greengage; *US spelling of* **gauge**
**gagged**
**gag•ger**
**gag•ging**
**gag•gle**
**gahn•ite** mineral
**gai•ety** (*plural* **•eties**)
**gail•lar•dia** plant
**gai•ly**
**gain**
**gain•able**
**gain•er**
**gain•ful**
**gain•ful•ly**
**gain•ful•ness**
**gain•li•ness**
**gain•ly**
**gain•say** (**•say•ing, •said**)
**gain•say•er**
**gait** walk
**gait•er**
**gal** *Slang* girl; unit
**gala**
**ga•lac•ta•gogue** inducing milk secretion
**ga•lac•tic**
**gal•ac•tom•eter**
**gal•ac•tom•etry**
**ga•lac•to•poi•esis** milk production
**ga•lac•to•poi•etic**
**ga•lac•tose** sugar
**ga•la•go** (*plural* **•gos**) bushbaby
**ga•lah** bird
**Galahad**
**ga•lan•gal** plant
**gal•an•tine** glazed pressed meat
**Ga•lá•pa•gos Is•lands**
**Gala•shiels** Scottish town
**Ga•la•ta** Turkish port
**Galatea** mythological character
**gala•tea** fabric
**Ga•laţi** Romanian port
**Ga•la•tia** ancient Asian region
**Ga•la•tians** New Testament book
**Gal•axy** solar system
**gal•axy** (*plural* **•axies**) any star system; distinguished gathering
**gal•ba•num** gum resin
**gale**
**ga•lea** (*plural* **•leae**) helmet-shaped structure
**ga•leate** (*or* **•leat•ed**)
**ga•lei•form**
**ga•lena** (*or* **•lenite**) mineral
**Ga•len•ic** of Galen's medical system
**ga•leni•cal** pharmacology term
**Ga•len•ism**
**Ga•len•ist**
**ga•lère** *French* undesirable people
**Ga•li•bi** (*plural* **•bi** *or* **•bis**) American Indian
**Ga•li•cia** European region
**Ga•li•cian**
**Gali•lean** of Galilee; of Galileo
**Gali•lee** Israeli region
**gali•lee** church porch
**gal•in•gale** (*or* **ga•lan•gal**) plant
**gali•ot** (*or* **gal•li•ot**) small galley
**gali•pot** (*or* **gal•li•pot**) pine resin
**gall**
**Gal•la** (*plural* **•las** *or* **•la**) African people
**gal•lant**
**gal•lant•ness**
**gal•lant•ry** (*plural* **•ries**)
**gall blad•der**
**Gal•le** Sri Lankan port

**gal•leass** (*or* **•li•ass**) warship
**gal•leon**
**gal•ler•ied**
**gal•lery** (*plural* **•leries**)
**gal•ley**
**gall•fly** (*plural* **•flies**)
**gal•li•am•bic** verse metre
**gal•liard** dance
**Gal•lic** of France or Gaul
**gal•lic** chemistry term; of galls
**Gal•li•can**
**Gal•li•can•ism** French Catholic movement
**Gal•lice** *Latin* in French
**Gal•li•cism**
**Gal•li•ci•za•tion** (*or* **•sa•tion**)
**Gal•li•cize** (*or* **•cise**)
**Gal•li•ciz•er** (*or* **•cis•er**)
**gal•li•gas•kins** men's breeches
**gal•li•mau•fry** (*plural* **•fries**) *US* hotchpotch
**gal•li•na•cean**
**gal•li•na•ceous** ornithology term
**gall•ing**
**gal•li•nule** bird
**gal•li•ot** *variant spelling of* **galiot**
**Gal•lipo•li** Turkish port
**gal•li•pot** earthenware pot; *variant spelling of* **galipot**
**gal•lium** chemical element
**gal•li•vant** (*or* **gali•vant, gala•vant**)
**gal•li•wasp** lizard
**gall•nut** (*or* **gall-apple**)
**gal•lo•glass** (*or* **•low•**) Irish military retainer
**gal•lon**
**gal•lon•age**
**gal•loon** decorative cord
**gal•lop** horse's gait; *compare* **galop**
**gal•lop•er**
**gal•lous** chemistry term
**Gal•lo•way** Scottish area
**gal•lows** (*plural* **•lowses** *or* **•lows**)
**gall•stone**
**gal•luses** *Dialect* braces
**ga•loot** *US* clumsy person
**gal•op** dance; *compare* **gallop**
**ga•lore**
**ga•loshes** (*or* **go•**)
**ga•lumph**
**gal•van•ic** (*or* **•vani•cal**)
**gal•vani•cal•ly**
**gal•va•nism**
**gal•va•ni•za•tion** (*or* **•sa•tion**)
**gal•va•nize** (*or* **•nise**)
**gal•va•niz•er** (*or* **•nis•er**)
**gal•va•nom•eter**
**gal•va•no•met•ric** (*or* **•ri•cal**)
**gal•va•nom•etry**
**gal•va•no•scope**
**gal•va•no•scop•ic**
**gal•va•nos•co•py**
**gal•va•no•trop•ic**
**gal•va•not•ro•pism** botany term
**gal•vo** (*plural* **•vos**) *short for* **galvanometer**
**Gal•way** Irish county
**Gal•we•gian**
**gal•yak** (*or* **•yac**) fur
**gam** school of whales
**gam•ba•do** (*plural* **•dos** *or* **•does**) leather stirrup
**gam•beson** medieval garment
**Gam•bia**
**Gam•bian**
**gam•bier** (*or* **•bir**) astringent
**Gam•bier Is•lands**
**gam•bit**
**gam•ble** bet; *compare* **gambol**
**gam•bler**
**gam•bling**
**gam•boge** gum resin
**gam•bo•gian**
**gam•bol** (**•bol•ling, •bolled**; *US* **•bol•ing, •boled**) frolic; *compare* **gamble**
**gam•brel** horse's hock; type of roof
**game**
**game•cock**
**game•keeper**
**game•keeping**
**gam•elan** oriental orchestra
**game•ly**
**game•ness**
**games•man** (*plural* **•men**)
**games•man•ship**
**game•some** merry
**game•ster**
**ga•met•al** (*or* **•ic**)
**gam•etan•gial**
**gam•etan•gium** (*plural* **•gia**)
**gam•ete** reproductive cell
**ga•meto•cyte**
**gam•eto•gen•esis** (*or* **•etog•eny**)
**gam•eto•gen•ic** (*or* **•etog•enous**)
**ga•meto•phore** plant part
**ga•meto•phor•ic**
**ga•meto•phyte** plant producing gametes
**gam•eto•phyt•ic**
**gam•ey** *variant spelling of* **gamy**
**gam•ic** biology term
**gam•in** street urchin
**gam•ine** boyish girl
**gami•ness**
**gam•ing**
**gam•ma** Greek letter
**gam•ma•di•on** (*plural* **•dia**) swastika
**gam•mer** *Dialect* old woman
**gam•mon**
**gam•mon•er** *Slang* deceiver
**gam•my** (**•mi•er, •mi•est**) *Slang* lame
**gamo•gen•esis** biology term
**gamo•genet•ic** (*or* **•geneti•cal**)
**gamo•pet•al•ous** botany term
**gamo•phyl•lous**
**gamo•sep•al•ous**
**gamp** umbrella
**gam•ut**
**gamy** (*or* **gam•ey; gami•er, gami•est**)
**gan** (**gan•ning, ganned**) *Dialect* to go
**Gan•da** (*plural* **•das** *or* **•da**) African people
**gan•der**
**Gan•dhian**
**Gan•dhi•ism** (*or* **•dhism**)
**Gand•zha** Azerbaijani city
**ga•nef** *US* opportunist
**gang**

**gang•bang**
**ganged**
**gang•er** labourers' foreman
**Gan•ges** Indian river
**gang•land**
**gan•glial** (*or* **gan•gli•ar**)
**gan•gling** (*or* **•gly**)
**gan•gli•on** (*plural* **•glia** *or* **•gli•ons**) nerve tissue; cyst
**gan•gli•on•ic** (*or* **•at•ed**)
**gang•plank** (*or* **•way**)
**gan•grene**
**gan•gre•nous**
**gang•ster**
**Gang•tok** Indian city
**gangue** (*or* **gang**) worthless ore
**gang•way**
**gan•is•ter** (*or* **gan•nis•**) rock
**gan•ja** cannabis
**gan•net**
**gan•oid** zoology term
**gan•sey** *Dialect* pullover
**gant•let** rail track; *variant spelling of* **gauntlet**
**gant•line** nautical term
**gan•try** (*or* **gaun•**; *plural* **•tries**)
**Gany•mede** satellite of Jupiter
**Ganymede** mythological character
**gaol** *variant spelling of* **jail**
**gaol•er** *variant spelling of* **jailer**
**gap** (**gap•ping, gapped**)
**gape**
**gap•er**
**gapes** fowl disease
**gape•worm**
**gap•ing•ly**
**gapped**
**gap•ping** grammar term
**gar** (*plural* **gar** *or* **gars**) fish
**gar•age**
**Gara•mond** typeface
**garb**
**gar•bage**
**gar•ble**
**gar•bler**
**garb•less**
**gar•board** nautical term
**gar•çon** *French* waiter
**Gard** French department
**Gar•da** Italian lake
**gar•den**
**gar•den•er**
**gar•denia**
**gar•den•ing**
**gar•fish** (*plural* **•fish** *or* **•fishes**)
**gar•ga•ney** duck
**gar•gan•tuan**
**gar•get** cattle disease
**gar•gety**
**gar•gle**
**gar•gler**
**gar•goyle**
**gar•goyled**
**gar•ial** *variant of* **gavial**
**gari•bal•di** blouse; biscuit
**gar•ish**
**gar•ish•ness**
**gar•land**
**gar•lic**
**gar•licky**
**gar•ment**
**gar•ner**
**gar•net**
**gar•ni•er•ite** mineral
**gar•nish**
**gar•nishee** (**•nishee•ing, •nisheed**) legal term
**gar•nish•er**
**gar•nish•ment** legal notice
**gar•ni•ture** decoration
**Ga•ronne** French river
**ga•rotte** *variant spelling of* **garrotte**
**gar•pike** fish
**gar•ret**
**gar•ri•son**
**gar•rotte** (*or* **gar•rote, ga•rotte**) execution
**gar•rott•er** (*or* **gar•rot•er, ga•rott•er**)
**gar•ru•lous**
**gar•ru•lous•ness** (*or* **gar•ru•lity**)
**gar•rya** shrub
**gar•ter**
**garth** cloistered courtyard
**Gary** US port
**gas** (*noun, plural* **gases** *or* **gas•ses**; *verb* **gases** *or* **gas•ses, gas•sing, gassed**)
**gas•bag**
**Gas•con** of Gascony
**gas•con•ade** boastful talk
**Gas•co•ny**
**gas•eous**
**gas•eous•ness**
**gases** (*or* **gas•ses**)
**gash**
**gas•holder**
**gasi•fi•able**
**gasi•fi•ca•tion**
**gasi•fi•er**
**gasi•form**
**gasi•fy** (**•fies, •fy•ing, •fied**)
**gas•ket**
**gas•kin** part of horse's thigh
**gas•light**
**gas•man** (*plural* **•men**)
**gas•olier** (*or* **•elier**) fitting for gaslights
**gaso•line** (*or* **•lene**) *US* petrol
**gaso•lin•ic**
**gas•om•eter**
**gaso•met•ric** (*or* **•ri•cal**)
**gas•ometry**
**gasp**
**Gas•pé** Canadian peninsula
**gasp•er**
**gasp•ing•ly**
**gassed**
**gas•ser**
**gas•si•ness**
**gas•sing**
**gas•sy** (**•si•er, •si•est**)
(**gasteropod**) *incorrect spelling of* **gastropod**
**gas•tight**
**gas•tight•ness**
**gas•tral•gia** stomach pain
**gas•tral•gic**
**gas•trec•to•my** (*plural* **•mies**)
**gas•tric**
**gas•trin** hormone
**gas•trit•ic**
**gas•tri•tis**
**gas•tro•en•ter•ic**
**gas•tro•en•terit•ic**
**gas•tro•en•teri•tis**
**gas•tro•en•te•rolo•gist**
**gas•tro•en•ter•ol•ogy** (*or* **gas•trol•ogy**)
**gas•tro•en•ter•os•to•my** (*plural* **•mies**) operation
**gas•tro•in•tes•ti•nal**
**gas•tro•lith** stomach stone
**gas•trol•ogy** *variant of* **gastroenterology**

**gas•tro•nome** (*or* **•trono•mer, •trono•mist)**
**gas•tro•nom•ic** (*or* **•nomi•cal)**
**gas•tro•nomi•cal•ly**
**gas•trono•mist**
**gas•trono•my** cooking
**gas•tro•pod** mollusc
**gas•tropo•dan**
**gas•tropo•dous**
**gas•tro•scope** medical instrument
**gas•tro•scop•ic**
**gas•tros•co•pist**
**gas•tros•co•py**
**gas•tros•to•my** (*plural* **•mies)** artificial stomach opening
**gas•tro•to•my** (*plural* **•mies)** stomach operation
**gas•tro•trich** aquatic animal
**gastro•vas•cu•lar**
**gas•tru•la** (*plural* **•las** *or* **•lae)** embryology term
**gas•tru•lar**
**gas•tru•la•tion**
**gas•works**
**gate**
**gâ•teau** (*or* **ga•**; *plural* **•teaux)**
**gate-crash**
**gate-crasher**
**gated**
**gate•fold** folded oversize page
**gate•house**
**gate•keeper**
**gate-leg** (*or* **-legged) table**
**gate•post**
**Gates•head**
**gate•way**
**Gath** biblical city
**gath•er**
**gath•er•able**
**gath•er•er**
**gath•er•ing**
**Gatling gun**
**gauche**
**gauche•ly**
**gauche•ness**
**gau•cherie**
**gau•cho** (*plural* **•chos)** cowboy
**gaud** trinket
**gaud•ery** (*plural* **•eries)**
**gaudi•ly**
**gaudi•ness**
**gaudy (gaudi•er, gaudi•est)**
**gauf•fer** *variant spelling of* **goffer**
**gauge** (*US also* **gage)** measure; *compare* **gage**
**gauge•able** (*US also* **gage•)**
**gauge•ably** (*US also* **gage•)**
**gaug•er** (*US also* **gag•)**
**Gau•ha•ti** Indian city
**Gaul** Roman province
**Gau•lei•ter** German governor
**Gaul•ish**
**Gaull•ism** policies of de Gaulle
**Gaull•ist**
**gaul•theria** shrub
**gaunt**
**gaunt•let** (*or* **gant•)**
**gaunt•ness**
**gaun•try** *variant spelling of* **gantry**
**gaur** cattle
**gauss** (*plural* **gauss)** unit
**gauss•meter**
**Gau•teng** South African province
**gauze**
**gauzi•ly**
**gauzi•ness**
**gauzy (gauzi•er, gauzi•est)**
**ga•vage** forced feeding
**gave**
**gav•el** hammer
**gav•el•kind** land tenure
**ga•vial** (*or* **ghar•ial, gar•ial)** crocodile
**Gäv•le** Swedish port
**ga•votte** (*or* **•vot)**
**gawk**
**gawki•ly** (*or* **gawk•ish•)**
**gawki•ness** (*or* **gawk•ish•)**
**gawky** (*or* **gawk•ish; gawki•er, gawki•est)**
**gawp**
**gay**
**Gay Gor•dons** dance
**Gaza** Palestinian city in Israel
**gaze**
**ga•zebo** (*plural* **•zebos** *or* **•zeboes)**
**gaze•hound**
**ga•zelle** (*plural* **•zelles** *or* **•zelle)**
**gaz•er**
**ga•zette**
**gaz•et•teer**
**Ga•zi•an•tep** Turkish city
**gaz•pa•cho** soup
**ga•zump**
**ga•zump•er**
**Gdańsk** Polish port
**Gdy•nia** Polish port
**gean** cherry
**ge•anti•cli•nal**
**ge•anti•cline** geology term
**gear**
**gear•box**
**gear•ing**
**gear•shift** *US* gear lever
**gear•wheel**
**gecko** (*plural* **geckos** *or* **geckoes)**
**ge•dact** (*or* **•deckt)** organ pipe
**gee (gee•ing, geed)**
**gee-gee**
**geek** sideshow performer
**Gee•long** Australian port
**gee•pound** unit
**geese**
**geest** German heathland
**gee•zer** *Slang* old man; *compare* **geyser**
**ge•gen•schein** glow in sky
**Ge•hen•na** place of torment
**geh•len•ite** mineral
**Geiger count•er**
**gei•sha** (*plural* **•sha** *or* **•shas)**
**gel (gel•ling, gelled)** jelly-like substance; form gel; *variant spelling of* **jell**
**ge•la•da** baboon
**ge•län•de•sprung** ski jump
**gela•tin** (*or* **•tine)**
**ge•lati•ni•za•tion** (*or* **•sa•tion)**
**ge•lati•nize** (*or* **•nise)**
**ge•lati•niz•er** (*or* **•nis•er)**
**ge•lati•noid**
**ge•lati•nous**
**ge•la•tion** freezing
**geld (geld•ing, geld•ed** *or* **gelt)**
**Gel•der•land** (*or* **Guel•)** Dutch province
**gel•id** very cold

**ge•lid•ity** (*or* **•ness**)
**gel•ig•nite**
**gelled**
**gel•ling**
**gel•se•mium** (*plural* **•miums** *or* **•mia**) shrub
**Gel•sen•kir•chen** German city
**gelt** *Slang* money
**gem** (**gem•ming, gemmed**)
**gemi•nate** in pairs
**gemi•na•tion**
**Gemi•ni** constellation; sign of zodiac
**gem•ma** (*plural* **•mae**) plant structure
**gem•ma•ceous**
**gem•mate**
**gem•ma•tion**
**gemmed**
**gem•ming**
**gem•mipa•rous** reproducing by gemmae
**gem•mu•la•tion**
**gem•mule** reproductive body
**gemo•logi•cal** (*or* **gem•mo•**)
**gem•olo•gist** (*or* **gem•molo•**)
**gem•ol•ogy** (*or* **gem•mol•**) study of gems
**ge•mot** Anglo-Saxon assembly
**gems•bok** (*or* **•buck**; *plural* **•bok, •boks** *or* **•buck, •bucks**) antelope
**gem•stone**
**ge•müt•lich** *German* cosy
**gen** *Slang* information
**ge•nappe** worsted
**gen•darme**
**gen•dar•me•rie** (*or* **•ry**)
**gen•der**
**gene**
**ge•nea•logi•cal** (*or* **•log•ic**)
**ge•nealo•gist**
**ge•neal•ogy** (*plural* **•ogies**)
**gen•era** *plural of* **genus**
**gen•er•able** able to be generated
**gen•er•al**
**gen•er•al•is•si•mo** (*plural* **•mos**)
**gen•er•al•ist**
**gen•er•al•ity** (*plural* **•ities**)
**gen•er•ali•za•tion** (*or* **•sa•tion**)
**gen•er•al•ize** (*or* **•ise**)
**gen•er•al•iz•er** (*or* **•is•er**)
**gen•er•al•ly**
**gen•er•al•ness**
**gen•er•al•ship**
**gen•er•ate**
**gen•era•tion**
**gen•era•tive**
**gen•era•tor**
**gen•era•trix** (*plural* **•tri•ces**) geometry term
**ge•ner•ic** (*or* **•neri•cal**)
**ge•neri•cal•ly**
**gen•er•os•ity** (*plural* **•ities**)
**gen•er•ous**
**gen•er•ous•ness**
**Gen•esis** Old Testament book
**gen•esis** (*plural* **•eses**) beginning
**gen•et** (*or* **ge•nette**) catlike animal; *variant spelling of* **jennet**
**ge•net•ic** (*or* **•neti•cal**)
**ge•neti•cal•ly**
**ge•neti•cist**
**ge•net•ics**
**Ge•neva**
**Ge•nevan** (*or* **Gen•evese**; *plural* **•evans** *or* **•evese**)
**gen•ial** cheerful
**ge•nial** of the chin
**ge•ni•al•ity** (*or* **gen•ial•ness**)
**ge•ni•al•ly**
**gen•ic** of a gene
**ge•nicu•late** bending sharply
**ge•nicu•la•tion**
**ge•nie** (*plural* **ge•nies** *or* **ge•nii**)
**geni•pap** (*or* **gen•ip**) fruit
**geni•tal**
**geni•tal•ic**
**geni•tals** (*or* **•ta•lia**)
**geni•ti•val**
**geni•tive** grammar term
**geni•tor** biological father
**genito•uri•nary**
**ge•ni•us** (*plural* **ge•ni•uses**)
**ge•ni•zah** synagogue storeroom
**Genoa** Italian city
**genoa** yacht sail
**geno•cid•al**
**geno•cide**
**Geno•ese** (*or* **•vese**; *plural* **•ese** *or* **•vese**)
**ge•nome** (*or* **•nom**) genetics term
**geno•type** genetics term
**geno•typ•ic** (*or* **•typi•cal**)
**geno•ty•pic•ity**
**gen•re**
**gens** (*plural* **gen•tes**) Roman aristocratic family
**gent**
**gen•teel**
**gen•teel•ly**
**gen•teel•ness**
**gen•tian** plant
**gen•tia•na•ceous**
**gen•tian•el•la** plant
**Gen•tile** not Jewish
**gen•tile** grammar term
**gen•til•ity** (*plural* **•ities**)
**gen•tle**
**gentle•folk**
**gentle•man** (*plural* **•men**)
**gen•tleman-at-arms** (*plural* **•tlemen-**)
**gentle•man•li•ness**
**gentle•man•ly**
**gen•tle•ness**
**gentle•woman** (*plural* **•women**)
**gen•tly**
**gen•tri•fi•ca•tion**
**gen•tri•fy** (**•fies, •fy•ing, •fied**)
**gen•try**
**genu** (*plural* **genua**) knee
**genu•flect**
**genu•flec•tion** (*or* **•flex•ion**)
**genu•flec•tor**
**genu•ine**
**genu•ine•ly**
**genu•ine•ness**
**ge•nus** (*plural* **gen•era** *or* **ge•nuses**)
**geo•cen•tric**
**geo•cen•tri•cal•ly**
**geo•chemi•cal**
**geo•chem•ist**
**geo•chem•is•try**
**geo•chrono•logi•cal**
**geo•chro•nol•ogy**
**ge•ode** rock cavity
**geo•des•ic**

**ge•od•esist**
**geod•esy** (*or* **geo•det•ics**) measurement of earth
**geo•det•ic**
**ge•od•ic**
**geo•dy•nam•ic**
**geo•dy•nami•cist**
**geo•dy•nam•ics**
**ge•og•nos•tic**
**ge•og•no•sy** study of earth's structure
**ge•og•ra•pher**
**geo•graphi•cal** (*or* **•graph•ic)**
**geo•graphi•cal•ly**
**ge•og•ra•phy** (*plural* **•phies)**
**ge•oid** shape of earth
**geo•logi•cal** (*or* **•log•ic)**
**geo•logi•cal•ly**
**ge•olo•gist** (*or* **•ger)**
**ge•olo•gize** (*or* **•gise)**
**ge•ol•ogy**
**geo•mag•net•ic**
**geo•mag•ne•tism**
**geo•man•cer**
**geo•man•cy** prophecy
**geo•man•tic**
**geo•mechan•ics**
**ge•om•eter** (*or* **ge•om•etri•cian)**
**geo•met•ric** (*or* **•ri•cal)**
**geo•met•ri•cal•ly**
**ge•om•etrid** moth
**ge•om•etrize** (*or* **•etrise)**
**ge•om•etry**
**geo•mor•phic** of earth's surface
**geo•mor•pho•logi•cal** (*or* **•log•ic)**
**geo•mor•pho•logi•cal•ly**
**geo•mor•pholo•gy** (*or* **•phog•eny)**
**ge•opha•gist**
**ge•opha•gous**
**ge•opha•gy** (*or* **geo•pha•gia, ge•opha•gism)** eating soil
**geo•physi•cal**
**geo•physi•cist**
**geo•phys•ics**
**geo•phyte** botany term
**geo•phyt•ic**
**geo•po•liti•cal**
**geo•poli•ti•cian**
**geo•poli•tics**
**geo•pon•ic**
**geo•pon•ics** agricultural science
**Geor•die** Tynesider
**George•town** capital of Guyana
**geor•gette** fabric
**Geor•gia** US state; Central Asian country
**Geor•gian**
**geor•gic** poem
**geo•sci•ence**
**geo•stat•ic**
**geo•stat•ics** geology term
**geo•strat•egy**
**geo•stroph•ic** meteorology term
**geo•syn•chro•nous**
**geo•syn•cli•nal**
**geo•syn•cline** geology term
**geo•tac•tic**
**geo•tac•ti•cal•ly**
**geo•tax•is** biology term
**geo•tec•ton•ic** of earth's crust
**geo•ther•mal** (*or* **•mic)**
**geo•trop•ic**
**geo•tropi•cal•ly**
**ge•ot•ro•pism** botany term
**ge•rah** Hebrew weight
**ge•ra•nia•ceous** botany term
**ge•ra•nial** chemistry term
**ge•ra•ni•ol** chemical compound
**ge•ra•nium**
**gera•to•log•ic**
**gera•tol•ogy** study of elderly
**ger•bil** (*or* **•bille, jer•bil)**
**ger•ent** manager
**ger•enuk** antelope
**ger•fal•con** *variant spelling of* **gyrfalcon**
**geri•at•ric**
**geria•tri•cian** (*or* **geri•at•rist)**
**geri•at•rics**
**germ**
**ger•man** of close relationship; *compare* **germen**
**Ger•man**
**ger•man•der** plant
**ger•mane** relevant
**ger•mane•ly**
**ger•mane•ness**
**Ger•man•ic** of Germany
**ger•man•ic** chemistry term
**Ger•man•ism**
**ger•man•ite** mineral
**ger•ma•nium** chemical element
**Ger•mani•za•tion** (*or* **•sa•tion)**
**Ger•man•ize** (*or* **•ise)**
**Ger•man•iz•er** (*or* **•is•er)**
**Ger•mano•phile** (*or* **•phil)**
**Ger•mano•philia**
**Ger•mano•phobe**
**Ger•mano•pho•bia**
**ger•man•ous** chemistry term
**Ger•ma•ny**
**ger•men** (*plural* **•mens** *or* **•mi•na)** biology term; *compare* **german**
**ger•mi•cid•al**
**ger•mi•cide**
**ger•mi•nable** (*or* **•na•tive)**
**ger•mi•nal** embryonic
**ger•mi•nal•ly**
**ger•mi•nant**
**ger•mi•nate**
**ger•mi•na•tion**
**ger•mi•na•tor**
**Ger•mis•ton** South African city
**ger•on•toc•ra•cy** (*plural* **•cies)** government by old men
**ge•ron•to•crat•ic**
**ger•on•to•logi•cal**
**ger•on•tolo•gist**
**ger•on•tol•ogy** study of ageing
**ger•ry•man•der**
**ger•und** grammar term
**ge•run•dial**
**ger•un•di•val**
**ge•run•dive** grammar term
**ges•so** (*plural* **•soes)** white plaster
**ge•stalt** (*plural* **•stalts** *or* **•stal•ten)** overall structure
**Ge•sta•po**
**ges•tate**
**ges•ta•tion**
**ges•ta•tion•al** (*or* **•tive)**
**ges•ta•to•ry**
**ges•ticu•late**
**ges•ticu•la•tion**

**ges•ticu•la•tive**
**ges•ticu•la•tor**
**ges•tur•al**
**ges•ture**
**ges•tur•er**
**get** (**get•ting, got**)
**get•able** (*or* **get•table**)
**get-at-able**
**get•away** (*noun*)
**Geth•sema•ne**
**get-out** (*noun*)
**get•ter**
**get-together**
**Get•tys•burg** US town
**get-up** (*noun*)
**geum** plant
**gew•gaw** showy trinket
**gey•ser** hot spring; water heater; *compare* **geezer**
**gey•ser•ite** mineral
**Ge•zi•ra** Sudanese region
**Gha•na**
**Gha•na•ian** (*or* **Gha•nian**)
**ghar•ial** *variant of* **gavial**
**ghar•ry** (*or* **•ri**; *plural* **•ries**) Indian vehicle
**ghast•li•ness**
**ghast•ly** (**•li•er, •li•est**)
**ghat** steps to river
**Ghats** Indian mountains
**gha•zi** Muslim fighter
**ghee** butter
**Ghent** Belgian port
**gher•kin** pickled cucumber; *compare* **jerkin**
**ghet•to** (*plural* **•tos** *or* **•toes**)
**Ghib•el•line** political faction
**Ghib•el•lin•ism**
**ghib•li** (*or* **gib•**) hot wind
**ghil•lie** laced shoe; *variant spelling of* **gillie**
**ghost**
**ghost•like**
**ghost•li•ness**
**ghost•ly** (**•li•er, •li•est**)
**ghost•write** (**•writ•ing, •wrote, •writ•ten**)
**ghost•writ•er**
**ghoul**
**ghoul•ish**
**gi•ant**
**gi•ant•ess**
**gi•ant•ism** *variant of* **gigantism**
**giaour** non-Muslim
**gib** (**gib•bing, gibbed**)
**gib•ber**
**gib•ber•el•lin** plant hormone
**gib•ber•ish**
**gib•bet**
**gib•bing**
**gib•bon**
**gib•bous** (*or* **•bose**)
**gib•bous•ness**
**gibbs•ite** mineral
**gibe** (*or* **jibe**) taunt; *compare* **gybe**
**Gib•eon** Palestinian town
**gib•er** (*or* **jib•**)
**gib•ing•ly** (*or* **jib•**)
**gib•lets**
**gib•li** *variant spelling of* **ghibli**
**Gi•bral•tar**
**Gi•bral•tar•ian**
**Gib•son** Australian desert; US cocktail
**gid** sheep disease
**gid•di•ly**
**gid•di•ness**
**gid•dy** (*adj* **•di•er, •di•est**; *verb* **•dies, •dy•ing, •died**)
**giddy-up**
**gidgee** (*or* **gidjee**) tree
**gie** *Scot* give
**gift**
**gift•ed**
**gift•ed•ness**
**gift•wrap** (**•wrap•ing, •wrapped**)
**gig** (**gig•ging, gigged**)
**gi•ga•hertz** (*plural* **•hertz**) physics term
**gi•gan•tesque**
**gi•gan•tic**
**gi•gan•ti•cal•ly**
**gi•gan•tic•ness**
**gi•gan•tism** (*or* **gi•ant•ism**)
**gi•gan•toma•chy** battle of giants
**gig•gle**
**gig•gler**
**gig•gly**
**gigo•lo** (*plural* **•los**)
**gi•got** leg of mutton
**gigue** music
**Gi•jón** Spanish port
**gil•bert** unit
**Gil•ber•tian** of W. S. Gilbert
**Gil•bert Is•lands** *former name of* **Kiribati**
**gild** (**gild•ing, gild•ed** *or* **gilt**) cover with gold; *compare* **guild**
**gild•er** one who gilds; *variant spelling of* **guilder**
**gild•ing**
**Gil•ead** mountain region; biblical character
**gi•let** bodice
**gil•gai** *Austral* water hole
**Gilgamesh** legendary king
**gill**
**gilled**
**gil•lie** (*or* **ghil•lie, gil•ly**; *plural* **•lies**) huntsman's attendant; *compare* **ghillie**
**Gil•ling•ham** towns in Kent and Dorset
**gil•lion** one thousand million
**gill-less**
**gil•ly•flower** (*or* **•li•**)
**Gil•son•ite** (*Trademark*) asphalt
**gilt** covered in gold; gilding substance; pig; *compare* **guilt**
**gilt-edged**
**gilt•head** fish
**gim•bals** suspension device
**gim•crack**
**gim•let**
**gim•mal** mechanical joint
**gim•me** *Slang* give me
**gim•mick**
**gim•mick•ry**
**gim•micky**
**gimp** (*or* **guimpe**) fabric trimming
**gin** (**gin•ning, ginned**)
**gin•ger**
**ginger•bread**
**gin•ger•li•ness**
**gin•ger•ly**
**gin•gery**
**ging•ham**
**gin•gi•li** (*or* **•gel•li, •gel•ly**) sesame oil
**gin•gi•va** (*plural* **•vae**) gum
**gin•gi•val**
**gin•gi•vi•tis**

**gin•gly•mus** (*plural* **•mi**) anatomy term
**gink** *Slang* man or boy
**gink•go** (*or* **ging•ko**; *plural* **•goes** *or* **•koes**) tree
**gin•nel** *Dialect* passageway
**gin•seng**
**gip•py** (*plural* **•pies**) *Slang* an Egyptian; gipsy
**gip•sy** (*or* **gyp•**; *plural* **•sies**)
**gipsy•wort**
**gi•raffe** (*plural* **•raffes** *or* **•raffe**)
**gir•an•dole** (*or* **gi•ran•do•la**) candle-holder
**gira•sol** (*or* **giro•sol, gira•sole**) opal
**gird** (**gird•ing, gird•ed** *or* **girt**)
**gird•er**
**gir•dle**
**gir•dler**
**girl**
**girl•friend**
**girl•hood**
**girlie**
**girl•ish**
**girl•ish•ness**
**giro** (*plural* **•ros**) credit transfer; *compare* **gyro**
**gi•ron** (*or* **gy•**) heraldic term
**Gi•ronde** French river
**Gi•ron•dism**
**Gi•ron•dist** French revolutionary
**gi•ron•ny** (*or* **gy•**) heraldic term
**girt**
**girth**
**gi•sarme** battle-axe
**Gis•borne** New Zealand port
**gist**
**git**
**git•tern** ancient guitar
**giu•sto** musical term
**giv•able** (*or* **give•able**)
**give** (**giv•ing, gave, giv•en**)
**give•away** (*noun*)
**giv•en**
**giv•er**
**giz•mo**
**giz•zard**
**gla•bel•la** (*plural* **•lae**) anatomy term
**gla•bel•lar**
**gla•brous** (*or* **•brate**) smooth-skinned
**gla•brous•ness**
**gla•cé** (**•cé•ing, •céed**)
**gla•cial**
**gla•ci•al•ist**
**gla•ci•al•ly**
**gla•ci•ate**
**gla•cia•tion**
**glaci•er**
**glacio•logi•cal** (*or* **•log•ic**)
**glaci•olo•gist** (*or* **gla•ci•al•ist**)
**glaci•ol•ogy**
**glac•is** (*plural* **•ises** *or* **•is**) slope
**glad** (**glad•der, glad•dest**)
**glad•den**
**glad•den•er**
**glade**
**gladi•ate** sword-shaped
**gladia•tor**
**gladia•to•rial**
**gladio•lus** (*plural* **•li** *or* **•luses**)
**glad•ly**
**glad•ness**
**glad•some**
**Glago•lit•ic** Slavic alphabet
**glair** bookbinding glaze
**glairi•ness**
**glairy** (*or* **glair•eous**)
**Gla•mor•gan**
**glam•ori•za•tion** (*or* **•sa•tion**)
**glam•or•ize** (*or* **•ise**; *US also* **•our•**)
**glam•or•iz•er** (*or* **•is•er**)
**glam•or•ous** (*or* **•our•**)
**glam•or•ous•ness** (*or* **•our•**)
**glam•our** (*US also* **glam•or**)
**glance**
**glanc•ing•ly**
**gland**
**glan•dered**
**glan•der•ous**
**glan•ders** disease
**glan•du•lar** (*or* **•lous**)
**glan•dule** small gland
**glans** (*plural* **glan•des**) anatomy term
**glare**
**glar•ing**
**glar•ing•ly**
**glar•ing•ness**
**glary**
**Glas•gow**
**glass**
**glass-blower**
**glass-blowing**
**glasses**
**glass•house**
**glassi•ly**
**glass•ine** book covering
**glassi•ness**
**glass•like**
**glass-maker**
**glass-making**
**glass•man** (*plural* **•men**)
**glass•ware**
**glass•work**
**glass-worker**
**glass•works**
**glass•wort** plant
**glassy** (**glassi•er, glassi•est**)
**Glas•ton•bury**
**Glas•we•gian** of Glasgow
**Glauce** mythological character
**glau•co•ma** eye disease
**glau•co•ma•tous**
**glau•co•nite** mineral
**glau•co•nit•ic**
**glau•cous** waxy
**glaze**
**glaz•er**
**gla•zi•er**
**gla•zi•ery**
**glaz•ing**
**gleam**
**gleam•ing•ly**
**glean**
**glean•able**
**glean•er**
**glean•ings**
**glebe** clergyman's benefice
**glee**
**glee•ful**
**glee•ful•ly**
**glee•ful•ness**
**gleet** medical term
**gleety**
**glen**
**Glen•coe** Scottish massacre
**Glen•dale** US city
**glen•gar•ry** (*plural* **•ries**) Scottish cap
**gle•noid** anatomy term
**Glen•roth•es** Scottish town
**gley** soil

**glia•din** (*or* **•dine**) protein
**glib** **(glib•ber, glib•best)**
**glib•ness**
**glide**
**glid•er**
**glid•ing**
**glid•ing•ly**
**glim** *Slang* lamp
**glim•mer**
**glim•mer•ing**
**glimpse**
**glimps•er**
**glint**
**glio•ma** (*plural* **•ma•ta** *or* **•mas**) tumour
**glio•ma•tous**
**glis•sade** ballet step
**glis•sad•er**
**glis•san•do** (*plural* **•di**) musical term
**glis•ten**
**glis•ten•ing•ly**
**glis•ter** glitter
**glit•ter**
**glit•ter•ing**
**glit•tery**
**Gli•wi•ce** Polish city
**gloam•ing** dusk
**gloat**
**gloat•er**
**gloat•ing•ly**
**glob**
**glob•al**
**glo•bal•ize**
**glob•al•ly**
**glo•bate** (*or* **•bat•ed**)
**globe**
**globe•flower**
**globe•trotter**
**globe•trotting**
**glo•big•eri•na** (*plural* **•nas** *or* **•nae**) tiny animal
**glo•bin** protein
**glo•boid**
**glo•bose** (*or* **•bous**) spherical
**glo•bosi•ty** (*or* **•bose•ness**)
**globu•lar** (*or* **•lous**)
**glob•ule**
**globu•lif•er•ous**
**globu•lin** protein
**glo•chidi•ate**
**glo•chid•ium** (*plural* **•chidia**) biology term
**glock•en•spiel**
**glogg** alcoholic drink
**glom•er•ate**
**glom•era•tion** cluster
**glo•meru•lar**
**glo•meru•late**
**glom•er•ule**
**glo•meru•lus** (*plural* **•li**) anatomy term
**gloom**
**gloom•ful**
**gloomi•ly**
**gloomi•ness**
**gloomy** **(gloomi•er, gloomi•est)**
**Glo•ria** hymn
**glo•ria** fabric
**glo•ri•fi•able**
**glo•ri•fi•ca•tion**
**glo•ri•fi•er**
**glo•ri•fy** **(•fies, •fy•ing, •fied)**
**glo•ri•ous**
**glo•ri•ous•ness**
**glo•ry** (*noun, plural* **•ries**; *verb* **•ries, •ry•ing, •ried)**
**glory-of-the-snow** plant
**gloss**
**glos•sa** (*plural* **•sae** *or* **•sas**) tongue
**glos•sal**
**glos•sar•ial**
**glos•sa•rist**
**glos•sa•ry** (*plural* **•ries)**
**glos•sa•tor** gloss writer
**glos•sec•to•my** (*plural* **•mies**) removal of tongue
**gloss•eme** linguistics term
**gloss•er**
**glossi•ly**
**glossi•ness**
**glos•sit•ic**
**glos•si•tis** inflammation of tongue
**glos•sog•ra•pher**
**glos•sog•ra•phy**
**glos•so•la•lia** gift of tongues
**glossy** (*adj* **glossi•er, glossi•est**; *noun, plural* **glossies)**
**glot•tal**
**glot•tic**
**glot•tide•an**
**glot•tis** (*plural* **•tises** *or* **•ti•des)**
**glot•to•chro•nol•ogy** branch of linguistics
**Glouces•ter**
**Glouces•ter•shire**
**glove**
**glov•er**
**glow**
**glow•er**
**glow•er•ing•ly**
**glow-worm**
**glox•inia** plant
**glu•ca•gon** hormone
**glu•ci•num** (*or* **•cin•ium)** beryllium
**glu•co•cor•ti•cord** biochemistry term
**glu•co•gen•esis** biochemistry term
**glu•co•genet•ic**
**glu•co•neo•gen•esis**
**glu•co•pro•tein** *variant of* **glycoprotein**
**glu•cose**
**glu•cos•ic**
**glu•co•sid•al** (*or* **•ic)**
**glu•co•side**
**glu•co•su•ria** *variant of* **glycosuria**
**glue** **(glu•ing, glued)**
**glu•er**
**gluey** **(glui•er, glui•est)**
**glum** **(glum•mer, glum•mest)**
**glu•ma•ceous**
**glume** botany term
**glum•ness**
**glu•on** hypothetical physics particle
**glut** **(glut•ting, glut•ted)**
**glu•ta•mate**
**glu•ta•mine** amino acid
**glu•ta•thi•one** biochemical compound
**glu•teal** (*or* **•taeal)**
**glu•telin** protein
**glu•ten** protein
**glu•tenous** of gluten; *compare* **glutinous**
**glu•teus** (*or* **•taeus**; *plural* **•tei** *or* **•taei**) buttock muscle
**glu•ti•nous** sticky; *compare* **glutenous**
**glu•ti•nous•ness** (*or* **•nos•ity)**
**glut•ton**
**glut•ton•ous**

**glut•tony** (*plural* **•tonies)**
**gly•cer•ic** of glycerol
**glyc•er•ide** chemical compound
**glyc•er•in** (*or* **•ine)**
**glyc•er•ol** syrupy liquid
**glyc•er•yl** chemistry term
**gly•cine** amino acid
**gly•co•gen** biochemical compound
**gly•co•gen•esis**
**gly•co•genet•ic**
**gly•co•gen•ic**
**gly•col** antifreeze
**gly•col•ic** (*or* **•col•lic)**
**gly•coly•sis** breakdown of glucose
**gly•co•pro•tein** (*or* **glu•co•)**
**gly•co•side** biochemical compound
**gly•co•sid•ic**
**gly•co•su•ria** (*or* **glu•)** sugar in urine
**gly•co•su•ric** (*or* **glu•)**
**glyph** groove on frieze
**glyph•ic**
**glypho•graph**
**gly•phog•ra•pher**
**glypho•graph•ic** (*or* **•graphi•cal)**
**gly•phog•ra•phy** printing process
**glyp•tic**
**glyp•tics** engraving gems
**glyp•to•dont** extinct mammal
**glyp•tog•ra•pher**
**glyp•to•graph•ic** (*or* **•graphi•cal)**
**glyp•tog•ra•phy** engraving gems
**gnarl**
**gnarled** (*or* **gnarly)**
**gnash**
**gnash•ing•ly**
**gnat**
**gnat•catcher** bird
**gnath•ic** (*or* **•al)** of the jaw
**gna•thi•on** anatomy term
**gna•thite** zoology term
**gna•thon•ic** deceitfully flattering
**gnaw (gnaw•ing, gnawed, gnawed** *or* **gnawn)**
**gnaw•able**
**gnaw•er**
**gneiss** rock
**gneiss•ic** (*or* **•oid, •ose)**
**gnoc•chi** dumplings
**gnome**
**gno•mic** (*or* **•mi•cal)** of aphorisms
**gno•mi•cal•ly**
**gnom•ish**
**gno•mon** part of sundial
**gno•mon•ic**
**gno•moni•cal•ly**
**gno•sis** (*plural* **•ses)** spiritual knowledge
**gnos•tic** (*or* **•ti•cal)**
**Gnos•ti•cism**
**Gnos•ti•cize** (*or* **•cise)**
**gno•to•bi•oti•cal•ly**
**gno•to•bi•ot•ics** biology term
**gnu** (*plural* **gnus** *or* **gnu)**
**go** (*verb* **goes, go•ing, went, gone;** *noun, plural* **goes)**
**Goa** Indian district
**goa** gazelle
**goad**
**go-ahead** (*noun, adj*)
**goal**
**goalie**
**goal•keeper**
**goal•keeping**
**goal•less**
**goal•mouth**
**go•an•na** lizard
**goat**
**goatee** beard
**goat•eed**
**goat•herd**
**goat•ish**
**goats•beard** (*or* **goat's-)** plant
**goat•skin**
**goat's-rue** plant
**goat•sucker** bird
**gob (gob•bing, gobbed)**
**gob•bet**
**gob•ble**
**gob•ble•de•gook** (*or* **•dy•)**
**gob•bler**
**Go•belin** tapestry
**go-between**
**Gobi** desert; *compare* **goby**
**Go•bian**
**go•bi•oid** zoology term
**gob•let**
**gob•lin**
**gobo** (*plural* **gobos** *or* **goboes)** microphone shield
**gob•stopper**
**gobu•lar•ity** (*or* **•ness)**
**goby** (*plural* **goby** *or* **gobies)** fish; *compare* **Gobi**
**god**
**god•child** (*plural* **•children)**
**god•damn**
**god•daughter**
**god•dess**
**go•detia** plant
**god•father**
**god-fearing**
**god•forsaken**
**god•head**
**god•hood**
**god•less**
**god•less•ness**
**god•like**
**god•li•ness**
**god•ly (•li•er, •li•est)**
**god•mother**
**go•down** warehouse
**god•parent**
**go•droon** *variant spelling of* **gadroon**
**god•send**
**god•son**
**God•speed**
**Godt•haab** capital of Greenland
**god•wit** bird
**goer**
**goe•thite** (*or* **gö•)** mineral
**gof•fer** (*or* **gauf•)** to crimp; *compare* **gopher**
**Gog** biblical character
**go-getter**
**gog•gle**
**goggle•box**
**goggle-eyed**
**gog•gles**
**Goiâ•nia** Brazilian city
**Goi•ás** Brazilian state
**Goi•del** Gaelic-speaking Celt
**Goi•del•ic** (*or* **Goi•dhel•ic, Ga•dhel•ic)**
**go•ing**
**goi•tre** (*US* **•ter)** thyroid swelling
**goi•trous**

**go-kart**
**Gol•con•da** ruined Indian town
**gold**
**gold-beater**
**gold-beating**
**gold•crest** bird
**gold-dig•ger**
**gold-digging**
**gold•en**
**golden•eye** (*plural* **•eyes** *or* **•eye**) duck
**golden•rod** plant
**golden•seal** plant
**gold•eye** (*plural* **•eyes** *or* **•eye**) fish
**gold•finch**
**gold•fish** (*plural* **•fish** *or* **•fishes**)
**goldi•locks** plant
**gold-miner**
**gold-mining**
**gold-of-pleasure** plant
**gold-plate** (*verb*)
**gold•smith**
**gold•thread** plant
**go•lem** resurrected being
**golf**
**golf•er**
**gol•iard** medieval scholar
**gol•iard•ery**
**Goliath**
**gol•li•wog** (*or* **•wogg**)
**gol•lop** to eat greedily
**gol•lop•er**
**gol•ly** (*plural* **•lies**)
**go•loshes** *variant spelling of* **galoshes**
**gom•broon** pottery
**Go•mel** Belarus city
**Go•mor•rah**
**gom•pho•sis** (*plural* **•ses**) anatomy term
**go•mu•ti** palm tree
**gon•ad** sex organ
**gon•ad•al** (*or* **go•na•dial, go•nad•ic**)
**gon•ado•troph•ic** (*US* **•trop•ic**)
**gon•ado•tro•phin** (*US* **•tro•pin**) hormone
**Gond** tribal Indian
**Gon•dar** Ethiopian city
**Gon•di** Gond language
**gon•do•la**
**gon•do•lier**
**Gond•wa•na•land** ancient continent
**gone**
**gon•er** *Slang* one beyond help; *compare* **gonna**
**gon•fa•lon** (*or* **•non**) banner
**gon•fa•lon•ier** magistrate
**gong**
**Gon•go•rism** literary style
**go•nia•tite** fossil
**go•nid•ial** (*or* **•nid•ic**)
**go•nid•ium** (*plural* **•ia**) botany term
**go•ni•om•eter** angle measurer
**go•nio•met•ric** (*or* **•ri•cal**)
**go•ni•om•etry**
**go•ni•on** (*plural* **•nia**) anatomy term
**gonk** toy
**gon•na** *Slang* going to; *compare* **goner**
**gono•coc•cal** (*or* **•cic**)
**gono•coc•coid**
**gono•coc•cus** (*plural* **•coc•ci**) bacterium
**gono•cyte**
**gono•phore** biology term
**gono•phor•ic** (*or* **go•nopho•rous**)
**gono•pore** zoology term
**gon•or•rhoea** (*US* **•rhea**)
**gon•or•rhoeal** (*or* **•rhoe•ic**; *US* **•rheal** *or* **•rhe•ic**)
**goo**
**goo•ber** peanut
**good** (**bet•ter, best**)
**good•bye**
**good-for-nothing**
**good-humoured**
**good-humoured•ly**
**good•ish**
**good•li•ness**
**good-looking**
**good•ly** (**•li•er, •li•est**)
**good•man** (*plural* **•men**) *Archaic* husband
**good-natured**
**good-natured•ly**
**good•ness**
**good-night**
**goods**
**good-sized**
**good•wife** (*plural* **•wives**)
**Good•win Sands**
**goody** (*plural* **goodies**)
**goody-goody** (*plural* **-goodies**)
**goo•ey** (**gooi•er, gooi•est**)
**goof**
**goofi•ly**
**goofi•ness**
**goofy** (**goofi•er, goofi•est**)
**goog•ly** (*plural* **•lies**) cricket term
**goo•gol** large number
**goo•gol•plex** large number
**Goole** Humberside port
**goon**
**goop** *US* rude person
**goos•an•der** duck
**goose** (*plural* **geese**)
**goose•berry** (*plural* **•berries**)
**goose•foot** (*plural* **•foots**) plant
**goose•gog** *Dialect* gooseberry
**goose•grass**
**goose•neck** nautical term
**goose-step** (**-stepping, -stepped**)
**goosi•ness**
**goosy** (*or* **goos•ey; goosi•er, goosi•est**)
**go•pak** dance
**go•pher** animal; *compare* **goffer**
**Go•rakh•pur** Indian city
**go•ral** antelope
**Gor•bals** Glaswegian suburb
**gor•cock** male grouse
**gore**
**go•reng pi•sang** Malaysian dish
**gorge**
**gorge•able**
**gor•geous**
**gor•geous•ness**
**gorg•er**
**gor•ger•in** architectural term
**Gor•gon** mythological monster
**gor•go•nian** coral
**Gor•gon•zo•la** cheese
**go•ril•la** ape; *compare* **guerrilla**
**go•ril•lian** (*or* **•line**)
**go•ril•loid**

**gori•ly**
**gori•ness**
**Gor•ki** (*or* **•ky**) *former name of* **Nizhni Novgorod**
**Gor•lov•ka** Ukrainian city
**gor•mand•ize** (*or* **•ise**) eat greedily; *compare* **gourmandise**
**gor•mand•iz•er** (*or* **is•er**)
**gorm•less**
**Gorno-Altai** Russian region
**Gorno-Badakh•shan** Tadzhik region
**gorse**
**Gor•sedd** bardic institution
**gory** (**gori•er, gori•est**)
**gosh**
**gos•hawk**
**Go•shen** biblical region
**gos•ling**
**go-slow**
**Gos•pel** New Testament book
**gos•pel** truth; doctrine
**gos•pel•ler** (*US* **•pel•er**)
**Gos•plan** former Soviet commission
**gos•po•din** (*plural* **•po•da**) Russian title of address
**Gos•port**
**gos•sa•mer**
**gos•sip**
**gos•sip•er**
**gos•sip•ing•ly**
**gossip•monger**
**gos•sipy**
**gos•soon** *Irish* servant
**gos•ter** *Dialect* laugh
**got**
**Gö•teborg** (*or* **Goth•en•burg**) Swedish port
**Goth** Germanic people
**Goth•ic**
**Gothi•cal•ly**
**Gothi•cism**
**Got•land** Swedish island
**got•ten**
**Göt•tin•gen** German city
**gouache** art term
**Gou•da** cheese
**gouge**
**goug•er**
**gou•lash**
**gou•ra•mi** (*plural* **•mi** *or* **•mis**) fish
**gourd**
**gour•mand** (*or* **gor•**) greedy person; *compare* **gourmet**
**gour•man•dise** love of food; *compare* **gormandize**
**gour•mand•ism**
**gour•met** epicure; *compare* **gourmand**
**gout**
**gouti•ness**
**gout•weed**
**gouty**
**gov•ern**
**gov•ern•abil•ity** (*or* **•able•ness**)
**gov•ern•able**
**gov•ern•ance**
**gov•er•ness**
**gov•ern•ment**
**gov•ern•men•tal**
**gov•er•nor**
**gov•er•nor•ship**
**gow•an** *Scot* daisy
**Gower** Welsh peninsula
**gown**
**grab** (**grab•bing, grabbed**)
**grab•ber**
**grab•ble** grope
**grab•bler**
**gra•ben** trough of land
**grace**
**grace-and-favour**
**grace•ful**
**grace•ful•ly**
**grace•ful•ness**
**grace•less**
**Graces** Greek goddesses
**grac•ile** slender
**gra•cil•ity** (*or* **grac•ile•ness**)
**gra•cious**
**gra•cious•ness**
**grack•le** bird
**grad** *Slang* graduate
**grad•abil•ity** (*or* **•able•ness**)
**grad•able**
**gra•date** to cause to change
**gra•da•tion**
**gra•da•tion•al**
**grade**
**grad•er**
**gra•di•ent**
**gra•din** (*or* **•dine**) step or ledge
**grad•ual**
**gradu•al•ism**
**gradu•al•ist**
**gradu•al•is•tic**
**gradu•al•ly**
**gradu•al•ness**
**gradu•and** person about to graduate
**gradu•ate**
**gradua•tion**
**gradua•tor**
**gra•dus** (*plural* **•dus•es**) book of musical exercises
**Grae•cism** (*or esp. US* **Gre•**)
**Grae•cize** (*or esp. US* **Gre•**)
**Graeco-Roman** (*or esp. US* **Greco•**)
**graf•fi•ti** (*sing.* **•to**)
**graft**
**graft•er**
**graft•ing**
**Grail** legendary bowl
**grain**
**grain•er**
**graini•ness**
**grain•ing**
**grainy** (**graini•er, graini•est**)
**gral•la•to•rial** ornithology term
**gram** plant
**gram** (*or* **gramme**) unit
**gra•ma** pasture grass
**grama•rye** magic
**gra•mer•cy** *Archaic* thanks
**grami•ci•din** antibiotic
**gra•min•eous** (*or* **•mina•ceous**) of grasses
**grami•nivo•rous** grass-eating
**gram•mar**
**gram•mar•ian**
**gram•mati•cal**
**gram•mati•cal•ly**
**gram•ma•tolo•gist**
**gram•ma•tol•ogy** study of writing systems
**gramme** *variant spelling of* **gram**
**gram-molecu•lar** (*or* **-molar**)
**Gram-negative** bacteriology term
**gramo•phone**

**Gram•pian** Scottish mountains and region
**Gram-positive** bacteriology term
**gram•pus** (*plural* **•puses)** dolphin
**Gra•na•da** Spanish city
**grana•dil•la** fruit
**grana•ry** (*plural* **•ries)**
**grand**
**grand•aunt** *variant of* **great-aunt**
**grand•child** (*plural* **•children)**
**Grand Cou•lee** US dam
**grand•dad**
**grand•daughter**
**gran•dee**
**gran•deur**
**grand•father**
**gran•dilo•quence**
**gran•dilo•quent**
**gran•di•ose**
**gran•di•ose•ly**
**gran•di•os•ity**
**grandio•so** musical term
**grand•ma** (*or* **•mama)**
**grand mal** epilepsy
**grand•master**
**grand•mother**
**grand•nephew** *variant of* **great-nephew**
**grand•niece** *variant of* **great-niece**
**grand•pa** (*or* **•papa)**
**grand•parent**
**grand•son**
**grand•stand**
**grange**
**grang•er•ism**
**grang•eri•za•tion** (*or* **•sa•tion)**
**grang•er•ize** (*or* **•ise)** illustrate with borrowed pictures
**grang•er•iz•er** (*or* **•is•er)**
**gran•ite**
**granite•ware**
**gra•nit•ic** (*or* **gran•it•oid)**
**gran•it•ite** type of granite
**grani•vore**
**gra•nivo•rous** grain-eating
**gran•ny** (*or* **•nie;** *plural* **•nies)**
**grano•dio•rite** rock
**grano•lith** paving material
**grano•lith•ic**
**grano•phyre** rock
**grano•phyr•ic**
**grant**
**Gran•ta** River Cam
**grant•able**
**grantee** legal term
**grant•er**
**grant-in-aid** (*plural* **grants-)**
**gran•tor**
**gran tur•is•mo** touring car
**granu•lar**
**granu•lar•ity**
**granu•late**
**granu•la•tion**
**granu•la•tive**
**granu•la•tor** (*or* **•lat•er)**
**gran•ule**
**granu•lite** rock
**granu•lit•ic**
**granu•lo•cyte**
**granu•lo•cyt•ic**
**granu•lo•ma** (*plural* **•mas** *or* **•ma•ta)** tumour
**granu•loma•tous**
**grape**
**grape•fruit** (*plural* **•fruit** *or* **•fruits)**
**grapes** veterinary term
**grape•shot**
**grape•vine**
**grap•ey** (*or* **grapy)**
**graph**
**graph•eme** linguistics term
**gra•phemi•cal•ly**
**graph•ic** (*or* **graphi•cal)**
**graphi•cal•ly**
**graphi•cal•ness** (*or* **graph•ic•ness)**
**graph•ics**
**graph•ite**
**gra•phit•ic**
**graphi•ti•za•tion** (*or* **•sa•tion)**
**graphi•tize** (*or* **•tise)** convert into graphite
**grapho•log•ic** (*or* **•logi•cal)**
**graph•olo•gist**
**graph•ol•ogy** study of handwriting
**grapho•mo•tor**
**grap•nel**
**grap•pa** grape spirit
**grap•ple**
**grap•pler**
**grap•pling**
**grap•to•lite** fossil
**grapy** *variant spelling of* **grapey**
**Gras•mere** Cumbrian village
**grasp**
**grasp•able**
**grasp•er**
**grasp•ing**
**grass**
**grass•finch**
**grass•hook** sickle
**grass•hopper**
**grassi•ness**
**grass•land**
**grass•quit** bird
**grassy** **(grassi•er, grassi•est)**
**grate**
**grate•ful**
**grate•ful•ly**
**grate•ful•ness**
**grat•er**
**grati•cule** grid
**grati•fi•ca•tion**
**grati•fi•er**
**grati•fy** **(•fies, •fy•ing, •fied)**
**grati•fy•ing•ly**
**gra•tin** cookery term
**grat•ing**
**grat•ing•ly**
**gra•tis** free
**grati•tude**
**gra•tui•tous**
**gra•tu•ity** (*plural* **•ities)**
**Grau•bün•den** Swiss canton
**grau•pel** hail
**grav** unit
**gra•va•men** (*plural* **•vami•na)** legal term
**grave** burial place; accent; serious; engrave
**gra•ve** musical term
**grav•el** **(•el•ling, •elled;** *US* **•el•ing, •eled)**
**grav•el•ish**
**grav•el•ly**
**grav•en**
**grave•ly**
**grave•ness**
**grav•er** engraving tool
**Graves** wine
**Graves•end**
**grave•stone**

**Gra•vett•ian** Palaeolithic culture
**grave•yard**
**grav•id** pregnant
**gra•vid•ity** (*or* **•ness**)
**gra•vim•eter**
**gravi•met•ric** (*or* **•ri•cal**)
**gra•vim•etry**
**gra•vi•tas**
**gravi•tate**
**gravi•tat•er**
**gravi•ta•tion**
**gravi•ta•tion•al**
**gravi•ta•tion•al•ly**
**gravi•ta•tive**
**gravi•ton** physics term
**grav•ity** (*plural* **•ities**)
**gra•vure** printing method
**gra•vy** (*plural* **•vies**)
**gray** *US spelling of* **grey**; unit
**gray•back** *US spelling of* **greyback**
**gray•beard** *US spelling of* **greybeard**
**gray•ling** (*plural* **•ling** *or* **•lings**) fish
**gray•wacke** *US spelling of* **greywacke**
**graze**
**graz•er** animal
**gra•zi•er** farmer
**graz•ing**
**grease**
**grease•paint**
**greas•er**
**grease•wood** (*or* **•bush**)
**greasi•ly**
**greasi•ness**
**greasy** (**greasi•er, greasi•est**)
**great**
**great-aunt** (*or* **grand•**)
**great•coat**
**great•est**
**great•ly**
**great-nephew** (*or* **grand•**)
**great•ness**
**great-niece** (*or* **grand•**)
**Greats** course at Oxford University
**great-uncle** (*or* **grand•**)
**greave** armour
**greaves** tallow residue
**grebe**
**Gre•cian**
**Gre•cism** *variant spelling (esp. US) of* **Graecism**
**Gre•cize** *variant spelling (esp. US) of* **Graecize**
**Greco-Roman** *variant spelling (esp. US) of* **Graeco-Roman**
**Greece**
**greed**
**greedi•ly**
**greedi•ness**
**greedy** (**greedi•er, greedi•est**)
**Greek**
**green**
**green•back** *US* currency note
**green•bottle** fly
**green•brier**
**green•ery** (*plural* **•eries**)
**green•finch**
**green•fly** (*plural* **•flies**)
**green•gage**
**green•grocer**
**green•grocery** (*plural* **•groceries**)
**green•head** male mallard
**green•heart** tree
**green•horn**
**green•house**
**green•ing** cooking apple
**green•ish**
**Green•land**
**Green•land•er**
**green•let** bird
**green•ling** fish
**green•ness**
**Green•ock** Scottish port
**green•ock•ite** mineral
**green•room**
**green•sand**
**Greens•boro** US city
**green•shank** bird
**green•stick** fracture
**green•stone**
**green•stuff**
**green•sward** turf
**Green•wich**
**green•wood**
**greet**
**greet•er**
**greet•ing**
**grega•rine** zoology term
**gre•gari•ous**
**gre•gari•ous•ness**
**Gre•go•rian**
**greige** undyed
**grei•sen** rock
**gre•mi•al** bishop's cloth
**grem•lin**
**Gre•na•da** West Indian state
**gre•nade**
**grena•dier**
**grena•dine** fabric; syrup
**Grena•dines** West Indian islands
**Grendel** legendary monster
**Gre•no•ble** French city
**gres•so•rial** (*or* **•ri•ous**) ornithology term
**Gret•na Green**
**grew**
**grey** (*US* **gray**) colour; *compare* **gray**
**grey•back** (*US* **gray•**) animal
**grey•beard** (*US* **gray•**)
**grey•hen** female black grouse
**grey•hound**
**grey•ish** (*US* **gray•**)
**grey•lag** goose
**grey•ness** (*US* **gray•**)
**grey-state** undyed
**grey•wacke** (*US* **gray•**) rock
**grib•ble** wood-boring animal
**grid**
**grid•dle**
**griddle•cake**
**gride** grate
**grid•iron**
**grief**
**griev•ance**
**grieve**
**griev•er**
**griev•ing**
**griev•ous**
**griev•ous•ness**
**griffe** architectural ornament
**grif•fin** (*or* **grif•fon, gryph•on**) winged monster
**grif•fon** dog; vulture; *variant spelling of* **griffin**
**grig**
**gri•gri** (*or* **gris-gris, gree•gree**; *plural* **•gris** *or* **•grees**) talisman

**grill** cooking senses; *compare* **grille**
**gril•lage** building term
**grille** (*or* **grill**) metal screen; *compare* **grill**
**grilled**
**grill•er**
**grill•room**
**grilse** (*plural* **grilses** *or* **grilse**) salmon
**grim** (**grim•mer, grim•mest**)
**gri•mace**
**gri•mac•er**
**gri•mac•ing•ly**
**Gri•mal•di** moon crater
**gri•mal•kin** old cat
**grime**
**grim•ness**
**Grims•by**
**grimy** (**grim•ier, grim•iest**)
**grin** (**grin•ning, grinned**)
**grind** (**grind•ing, ground**)
**grin•de•lia** plant
**Grin•del•wald** Swiss valley
**grind•er**
**grind•ery** (*plural* **•eries**)
**grind•stone**
**grin•go** (*plural* **•gos**)
**grin•ner**
**grip** (**grip•ping, gripped**)
**gripe**
**grip•er** complainer; *compare* **gripper**
**grip•ing•ly**
**grippe** influenza
**grip•per** one that grips; *compare* **griper**
**grip•ping**
**grip•ping•ly**
**gri•saille** painting term
**gris•eous** greyish
**gri•sette** French girl
**gris•kin** pork cut
**gris•li•ness**
**gris•ly** (**•li•er, •li•est**) gruesome; *compare* **gristly; grizzly**
**gri•son** animal
**grist**
**gris•tle**
**gris•tli•ness**
**gris•tly** having gristle; *compare* **grisly; grizzly**
**grist•mill**
**grit** (**grit•ting, grit•ted**)
**grith** place of safety
**grits** coarsely ground grain
**grit•ti•ly**
**grit•ti•ness**
**grit•ty** (**•ti•er, •ti•est**)
**griv•et** monkey
**griz•zle** become grey; *Slang* whine
**griz•zled**
**griz•zler**
**griz•zly** (*adj* **•zli•er, •zli•est**; *noun, plural* **•zlies**) grey-haired; bear; *compare* **grisly; gristly**
**groan**
**groan•er**
**groan•ing•ly**
**groat** old coin
**groats** crushed grain
**gro•cer**
**gro•cery** (*plural* **•ceries**)
**grock•le** *Dialect* tourist
**Grod•no** Belarussian city
**grog**
**grog•gi•ly**
**grog•gi•ness**
**grog•gy** (**•gi•er, •gi•est**)
**grog•ram** fabric
**groin** abdominal region; vault; *compare* **groyne**
**Gro•li•er** bookbinding style
**grom•met** (*or* **grum•**)
**grom•well** plant
**Gro•ning•en** Dutch province
**groom**
**groom•er**
**groom•ing**
**grooms•man** (*plural* **•men**)
**groove**
**groovy** (**groovi•er, groovi•est**)
**grope**
**grop•er**
**grop•ing•ly**
**gros•beak** bird
**gro•schen** (*plural* **•schen**) Austrian coin
**gros•grain** fabric
**gross**
**gross•ness**
**gros•su•lar•ite** gemstone
**grot** grotto
**gro•tesque**
**gro•tesque•ly**
**gro•tesque•ness**
**gro•tes•query** (*or* **•querie**; *plural* **•queries**)
**grot•to** (*plural* **•toes** *or* **•tos**)
**grouch**
**grouchi•ly**
**grouchi•ness**
**grouchy** (**grouch•ier, grouch•iest**)
**ground**
**ground•age** anchorage fee
**ground•ing**
**ground•less**
**ground•ling**
**ground•mass**
**ground•nut**
**ground•sel**
**ground•sheet**
**ground•sill** joist
**grounds•man** (*plural* **•men**)
**ground•speed**
**ground•work**
**group**
**group•er** (*plural* **•er** *or* **•ers**) fish
**groupie**
**group•ing**
**grouse** (*plural* **grouse** *or* **grouses**)
**grous•er** complainer
**grout**
**grout•er**
**grouts** coffee grounds
**grouty** (**grouti•er, grouti•est**) *Dialect* muddy
**grove**
**grov•el** (**•el•ling, •elled**; *US* **•el•ing, •eled**)
**grov•el•ler** (*US* **•el•er**)
**grov•el•ling•ly** (*US* **•el•ing•ly**)
**grow** (**grow•ing, grew, grown**)
**grow•able**
**grow•er**
**growl**
**growl•er**
**grown**
**grown-up**
**growth**
**groyne** jetty; *compare* **groin**
**Groz•ny** Russian (Chechen) city
**grub** (**grub•bing, grubbed**)

**grub•ber**
**grub•bi•ly**
**grub•bi•ness**
**grub•by** (**grub•bi•er, grub•bi•est**)
**grudge**
**grudg•er**
**grudg•ing**
**grudg•ing•ly**
**gru•el**
**gru•el•ling** (*US* **•el•ing**)
**grue•some** (*or* **grew•**)
**gruff**
**gruff•ish**
**gruff•ness**
**gru•gru** palm tree
**grum•ble**
**grum•bler**
**grum•bling•ly**
**grum•bly**
**grum•met** *variant spelling of* **grommet**
**gru•mous** (*or* **•mose**) botany term
**grump**
**grumpi•ly** (*or* **grump•ish•ly**)
**grumpi•ness** (*or* **grump•ish•ness**)
**grumpy** (*or* **grump•ish; grumpi•er, grumpi•est**)
**Grun•dy** narrow-minded critical person
**grun•ion** fish
**grunt**
**grunt•er**
**grunt•ing•ly**
**grun•tled** contented
**Grus** constellation
**Gru•yère** cheese
**gryph•on** *variant spelling of* **griffin**
**grys•bok** antelope
**gua•ca•mo•le** (*or* **•cha•**) avocado dish
**gua•co** (*plural* **•cos**) plant
**Gua•dal•ca•nal** Pacific island
**Gua•dal•qui•vir** Spanish river
**Gua•de•loupe**
(**guage**) *incorrect spelling of* **gauge**
**guaia•col** medicinal liquid
**guaia•cum** (*or* **guaio•**) tree or resin
**Guam** Pacific island
**guan** bird
**Gua•na•ba•ra** former Brazilian state
**gua•na•co** (*plural* **•cos**) animal
**Gua•na•jua•to** Mexican state
**gua•nase** enzyme
**guani•dine** (*or* **•din**) biochemical compound
**gua•nine** biochemical compound
**gua•no** (*plural* **•nos**) bird excrement
**gua•no•sine** biochemical compound
**Guan•ta•na•mo** Cuban city
**Gua•ra•ni** (*plural* **•ni** *or* **•nis**) Paraguayan people
**gua•ra•ni** (*plural* **•ni** *or* **•nis**) currency
**guar•an•tee** (**•tee•ing, •teed**)
**guar•an•tor**
**guar•an•ty** (*plural* **•ties**) legal term
**guard**
**guard•able**
**guar•dant** (*or* **gar•**) heraldic term
**guard•ed**
**guard•ed•ly**
**guard•ed•ness**
**guard•er**
**guard•house**
**guard•ian**
**guardi•an•ship**
**guard•rail**
**guard•room**
**Guards** regiment
**guards•man** (*plural* **•men**)
**Gua•te•ma•la**
**gua•va** fruit
**Gua•ya•quil** Ecuadorian port
**gua•yu•le** shrub
**gub•bins**
**gu•ber•na•to•rial** of a governor
**guck** slimy substance
**gudg•eon** fish
**guelder-rose**
**Guelph** (*or* **Guelf**) political faction
**Guelph•ic** (*or* **Guelf•**)
**Guelph•ism** (*or* **Guelf•**)
**gue•non** monkey
**guer•don** reward
**Guer•ni•ca** Spanish town
**Guern•sey** Channel island
**guern•sey** sweater
**Guer•rero** Mexican state
**guer•ril•la** (*or* **gue•ril•la**) fighter; *compare* **gorilla**
**guer•ril•la•ism** (*or* **gue•**)
**guess**
**guess•able**
**guess•er**
**guess•ti•mate**
**guess•work**
**guest**
**guest•house**
**guff** *Slang* ridiculous talk
**guf•faw**
**Gui•ana** South American region
**Guia•nese** (*or* **Gui•an•an**)
**guid•able**
**guid•ance**
**guide**
**guide•line**
**guide•post**
**guid•er**
**guid•ing**
**guid•ing•ly**
**gui•don** flag
**Gui•enne** (*or* **Guy•enne**) former French province
**guild** (*or* **gild**) organization; *compare* **gild**
**guil•der** (*or* **gild•er, gul•den**; *plural* **•ders, •der** *or* **•dens, •den**) currency; *compare* **gilder**
**Guild•ford**
**guild•hall** (*or* **gild•**)
**guilds•man** (*or* **gilds•**; *plural* **•men**)
**guile**
**guile•ful**
**guile•ful•ly**
**guile•ful•ness**
**guile•less**
**guil•lemot**
**guil•loche** architectural border
**guil•lo•tine**
**guil•lo•tin•er**
**guilt** guiltiness; remorse; *compare* **gilt**

**guilti•ly**
**guilti•ness**
**guilt•less**
**guilty (guilti•er, guilti•est)**
**guimpe** blouse; *variant spelling of* **gimp**
**Guinea** African republic
**guinea** coin
**Guinea-Bissau** African republic
**Guin•ean**
**guinea pig**
**Guinevere** legendary queen
**gui•pure** lace
**guise**
**gui•tar**
**guitar•fish** (*plural* **•fish** *or* **•fishes**)
**gui•tar•ist**
**Gu•ja•rat** (*or* **•je•**) Indian state
**Gu•ja•ra•ti** (*or* **•je•**)
**Guj•ran•wa•la** Pakistani city
**Gu•lag** former Soviet administrative department
**gu•lar** of the throat
**gulch** *US* ravine
**gul•den** *variant of* **guilder**
**gules** heraldic term
**gulf**
**gulf•weed**
**gull**
**Gul•lah** (*plural* **•lahs** *or* **•lah**) African-American people
**gul•let**
**gul•li•bil•ity** (*or* **•la•**)
**gul•lible** (*or* **•lable**)
**gul•li•bly** (*or* **•la•**)
**gull-wing**
**gul•ly** (*noun, plural* **•lies**; *verb* **•lies, •ly•ing, •lied**)
**gulp**
**gulp•er**
**gulp•ing•ly**
**gum (gum•ming, gummed)**
**Gum•bo** French patois
**gum•bo** (*or* **gom•**; *plural* **•bos**) thick stew
**gum•boil**
**gum•boot**
**gum•bo•til** clay
**gum•drop**
**gum•ma** (*plural* **•mas** *or* **•ma•ta**) tumour
**gum•ma•tous**
**gum•mi•ly**
**gum•mi•ness**
**gum•mite** mineral
**gum•mo•sis** plant disease
**gum•my (•mi•er, •mi•est)**
**gump•tion**
**gum•shield**
**gum•shoe**
**gum•tree**
**gun (gun•ning, gunned)**
**gun•boat**
**gun•cotton**
**gun•fight**
**gun•fighter**
**gun•fire**
**gun•flint**
**gunge**
**gun•gy**
**gunk** *Slang* slimy substance
**gun•lock**
**gun•man** (*plural* **•men**)
**gun•metal**
**gunned**
**gun•nel** fish; *variant spelling of* **gunwale**
**gun•ner**
**gun•nery**
**gun•ning**
**gun•ny** (*plural* **•nies**) *US* fabric
**gun•paper**
**gun•play**
**gun•point**
**gun•powder**
**gun•runner**
**gun•running**
**gun•shot**
**gun-shy**
**gun•slinger**
**gun•smith**
**gun•smithing**
**gun•stock**
**Gun•tur** Indian city
**gun•wale** (*or* **gun•nel**) nautical term
**gun•yah** *Austral* bush hut
**Guo•min•dang** *variant spelling of* **Kuomintang**
**gup•py** (*plural* **•pies**) fish
**Gur** language
**gurd•wa•ra** Sikh place of worship
**gur•gi•ta•tion** surging movement
**gur•gle**
**gur•gling•ly**
**gur•jun** tree
**Gur•kha** (*plural* **•khas** *or* **•kha**)
**Gur•kha•li** language
**Gur•mu•khi** Punjabi script
**gur•nard** (*or* **gur•net**; *plural* **•nard, •nards** *or* **•net, •nets**) fish
**guru** (*plural* **gurus**)
**gush**
**gush•er**
**gush•ing•ly**
**gushy**
**gus•set**
**gust**
**gus•ta•tion** tasting
**gus•ta•tory** (*or* **•tive**)
**gusti•ly**
**gusti•ness**
**gus•to**
**gusty (gusti•er, gusti•est)**
**gut (gut•ting, gut•ted)**
**gut•bucket** jazz
**gut•less**
**gutsy (gutsi•er, gutsi•est)**
**gut•ta** (*plural* **•tae**) drop
**gutta-percha**
**gut•tate** (*or* **•tat•ed**) biology term
**gut•ted**
**gut•ter**
**gut•ter•ing**
**gutter•snipe**
**gut•ting**
**gut•tur•al**
**gut•tur•ali•za•tion** (*or* **•sa•tion**)
**gut•tur•al•ize** (*or* **•ise**)
**gut•tur•al•ly**
**gut•tur•al•ness** (*or* **•ity, •ism**)
**gut•ty** (*plural* **•ties**) *Irish* urchin
**guv** *Slang* governor
**guy**
**Guy•ana** South American republic
**Guya•nese** (*or* **Guy•an•an**)
**Guy•enne** *variant spelling of* **Guienne**
**guy•ot** submerged mountain
**guz•zle**
**guz•zler**
**Gwa•li•or** Indian city

**Gwe•lo** Zimbabwean town
**Gwent** former Welsh county
**Gwyn•edd** Welsh county
**gwyni•ad** fish
**gybe** (*or* **jibe**) nautical term; *compare* **gibe**
**gym**
**gym•kha•na**
**gym•na•si•arch** Greek magistrate
**gym•na•si•ast**
**gym•na•sium** (*plural* **•siums** *or* **•sia**)
**gym•nast**
**gym•nas•tic**
**gym•nas•ti•cal•ly**
**gym•nas•tics**
**gym•noso•phist** Indian ascetic
**gym•no•sperm** conifer
**gym•no•sper•mous**
**gym•slip**
**gy•nae•ceum** (*plural* **•cea**) women's apartments; *compare* **gynoecium**
**gy•nae•cium** *variant spelling of* **gynoecium**
**gy•nae•coc•ra•cy** (*US* **•ne•** *plural* **•cies**) government by women
**gy•nae•co•crat•ic** (*US* **•ne•**)
**gy•nae•coid** (*US* **•ne•**)
**gy•nae•co•logi•cal** (*or* **•log•ic**; *US* **•ne•**)
**gy•nae•co•logi•cal•ly** (*US* **•ne•**)
**gy•nae•colo•gist** (*US* **•ne•**)
**gy•nae•col•ogy** (*US* **•ne•**)
**gy•nae•co•mas•tia** (*US* **•ne•**) male breast development
**gy•nan•dro•morph** biology term
**gy•nan•dro•mor•phic** (*or* **•phous**)
**gy•nan•dro•morph•ism** (*or* **•mor•phy**)
**gy•nan•drous** botany term
**gy•nan•dry** (*or* **•drism**)
**gy•narch•ic**
**gyn•ar•chy** (*plural* **•chies**) gynaecocracy
**gy•noe•cium** (*or* **•nae•**; *US* **•ne•**; *plural* **•cia**) part of flower; *compare* **gynaeceum**
**gy•no•phore** botany term
**gy•no•phor•ic**
**gyp** *Slang* pain
**gyp•se•ous**
**gyp•sif•er•ous**
**gyp•sophi•la** plant
**gyp•sum**
**gyp•sy** *variant spelling of* **gipsy**
**gy•ral** rotating
**gy•rate**
**gy•ra•tion**
**gy•ra•tor**
**gy•ra•tory**
**gyre** circular movement
**gyr•fal•con** (*or* **ger•**)
**gyro** (*plural* **gyros**) gyrocompass; gyroscope; *compare* **giro**
**gy•ro•com•pass**
**gy•ro•mag•net•ic**
**gy•ro•plane**
**gy•ro•scope** (*or* **•stat**)
**gy•ro•scop•ic**
**gy•ro•scop•ics**
**gy•rose** botany term
**gy•ro•sta•bi•liz•er** (*or* **•lis•er**)
**gy•ro•stat•ic** of rotating bodies
**gy•ro•stat•ics**
**gy•rus** (*plural* **gyri**) anatomy term
**gyve** *Archaic* fetter

# H

**ha** (*or* **hah**) exclamation
**haaf** fishing ground
**Haar•lem** Dutch city; *compare* **Harlem**
**haar** fog
**Habakkuk** prophet
**Ha•ba•na** *Spanish* Havana
**ha•ba•nera** dance
**ha•beas cor•pus**
**hab•er•dash•er**
**hab•er•dash•ery**
**hab•er•geon** (*or* **hau•ber•geon**) coat of mail
**hab•ile** skilful
**ha•bili•ment** dress
**ha•bili•tate**
**ha•bili•ta•tion**
**ha•bili•ta•tor**
**hab•it**
**hab•it•abil•ity** (*or* **•able•ness**)
**hab•it•able**
**hab•it•ably**
**hab•it•ant**
**habi•tat**
**habi•ta•tion**
**habi•ta•tion•al**
**hab•it•ed**
**ha•bitu•al**
**ha•bitu•al•ly**
**ha•bitu•al•ness**
**ha•bitu•ate**
**ha•bitu•a•tion**
**habi•tude**
**habi•tu•di•nal**
**ha•bitué**
**habi•tus** (*plural* **•tus**) physical state
**Habsburg** (*or* **Hapsburg**) royal dynasty
**habu** snake
**há•ček** phonetic symbol
**ha•chure** shading
**haci•en•da**
**hack**
**hacka•more** *US* rope halter
**hack•berry** (*plural* **•berries**)
**hack•but** (*or* **hag•**) gun
**hack•but•eer** (*or* **hag•**)
**hack•er**
**hack•ing**
**hack•le**
**hack•ler**
**hack•les**
**Hack•ney** London borough
**hack•ney** carriage; make banal
**hack•neyed**

**hack•ney•ism**
**hack•saw**
**had**
**ha•dal** of ocean depths
**hada•way** *Dialect* hurry
**had•dock**
**hade** geology term
**Ha•de•an**
**Ha•des** underworld
**Ha•dhra•maut** Arabian plateau
**Had•ith** Mohammedan tradition
**hadj** *variant spelling of* **hajj**
**hadj•i** *variant spelling of* **hajji**
**hadn't**
**had•ron** elementary particle
**had•ron•ic**
**had•ro•saur** (*or* **•saur•us**)
**hadst** *Archaic* had
**hae** *Scot* have
**haec•ce•ity** (*plural* **•ities**) philosophy term
**Haeck•elian** of Haeckel
**haem** (*US* **heme**) organic pigment
**haema•chrome** *variant spelling of* **haemochrome**
**haema•cy•tom•eter** (*US* **hema•**)
**hae•mag•glu•tin•ate** (*US* **he•**)
**hae•mag•glu•ti•nin** (*US* **he•**) antibody
**haema•gogue** (*US* **hema•gogue** *or* **•gog**)
**hae•mal** (*US* **he•**)
**haema•tein** (*US* **hema•**) biological stain
**haema•tem•esis** (*US* **hema•**)
**hae•mat•ic** (*US* **he•**)
**haema•tin** (*US* **hema•**) dark pigment
**haema•tin•ic** (*US* **hema•**) medicinal drug
**haema•tite** (*US* **hema•**) mineral
**haema•tit•ic** (*US* **hema•**)
**hae•mato•blast** (*US* **he•**)
**hae•mato•blas•tic** (*US* **he•**)
**haema•to•cele** (*US* **hema•**)
**haema•to•crit** (*US* **hema•**) medical term
**haema•to•cry•al** (*US* **hema•**) zoology term
**haema•to•gen•esis** (*US* **hema•**)
**haema•to•gen•ic** (*US* **hema•**)
**haema•tog•enous** (*US* **hema•**)
**haema•toid** (*or* **hae•moid**; *US* **hema•** *or* **he•**)
**haema•to•log•ic** (*or* **•logi•cal**; *US* **hema•**)
**haema•tolo•gist** (*US* **hema•**)
**haema•tol•ogy** (*US* **hema•**)
**haema•toly•sis** *variant of* **haemolysis**
**haema•to•ma** (*US* **hema•**; *plural* **•mas** *or* **•mata**) blood tumour
**haema•to•poi•esis** (*or* **haemo•poi•esis**; *US* **hema•** *or* **hemo•**)
**haema•to•poi•et•ic** (*or* **haemo•poi•et•ic**; *US* **hema•** *or* **hemo•**)
**haema•to•sis** (*US* **hema•**)
**haema•to•ther•mal** (*US* **hema•**) warm-blooded
**haema•toxy•lin** (*US* **hema•**) dye
**haema•toxy•lon** tree
**haema•to•zo•on** (*US* **hema•**; *plural* **•zoa**)
**haema•tu•ria** (*US* **hema•**)
**haema•tu•ric**
**hae•mic** (*US* **he•**)
**hae•min** (*US* **he•**)
**haemo•chrome** (*or* **haema•**; *US* **hemo•** *or* **hema•**)
**haemo•coel** (*US* **hemo•**) zoology term
**haemo•cya•nin** (*US* **hemo•**)
**haemo•cyte** (*US* **hemo•**)
**haemo•cy•tom•eter** (*US* **hemo•**)
**haemo•di•aly•sis** (*US* **hemo•**)
**haemo•flag•el•late** (*US* **hemo•**) protozoan
**haemo•glo•bin** (*US* **hemo•**)
**haemo•glo•bi•nu•ria** (*US* **hemo•**)
**hae•moid** *variant of* **haematoid**
**haemo•ly•sin** (*US* **hemo•**)
**hae•moly•sis** (*or* **haema•toly•sis**; *US* **he•** *or* **hema•**; *plural* **•ses**)
**haemo•lyt•ic** (*US* **hemo•**)
**haemo•phile** (*US* **hemo•**)
**haemo•philia** (*US* **hemo•**)
**haemo•phili•ac** (*US* **hemo•**)
**haemo•phil•ic** (*US* **hemo•**)
**haemo•poi•esis** *variant of* **haematopoiesis**
**haemo•poi•et•ic** *variant of* **haematopoietic**
**haem•op•ty•sis** (*US* **hem•**) coughing blood
**haem•or•rhage** (*US* **hem•**)
**haem•or•rhag•ic** (*US* **hem•**)
**haem•or•rhoid** (*US* **hem•**)
**haem•or•rhoi•dal** (*US* **hem•**)
**haem•or•rhoid•ec•to•my** (*US* **hem•**; *plural* **•mies**)
**haemo•sta•sis** (*or* **•sia**; *US* **hemo•**)
**haemo•stat** (*US* **hemo•**)
**haemo•stat•ic** (*US* **hemo•**)
**hae•re•mai** Maori welcome
**hae•res** *variant spelling of* **heres**
**Ha-erh-pin** *variant spelling of* **Harbin**
**ha•fiz** Islamic title
**haf•nium** chemical element
**haft**
**Haf•ta•rah** (*or* **Haph•ta•rah**; *plural* **•ta•roth** *or* **•ta•rahs**) biblical reading
**haft•er**
**hag**
**Hagar** biblical character
**hag•but** *variant spelling of* **hackbut**
**Ha•gen** German city
**Hagen** legendary character
**hag•fish** (*plural* **•fish** *or* **•fishes**)
**Hag•ga•dah** (*or* **•da**; *plural* **•dahs, •das,** *or* **•doth**) Jewish literature
**hag•gad•ic** (*or* **•gadi•cal**)
**hag•ga•dist**
**hag•ga•dist•ic**
**Haggai** biblical prophet
**hag•gard**
**hag•gard•ness**
**hag•gis**

**hag•gish**
**hag•gish•ness**
**hag•gle**
**hag•gler**
**hagi•archy** (*plural* **•archies**) government by saints
**hagi•oc•ra•cy** (*plural* **•cies**)
**Hagi•og•ra•pha** Old Testament section
**hagi•og•ra•pher** (*or* **•phist**)
**hagi•o•graph•ic** (*or* **•graphi•cal**)
**hagi•og•ra•phy** (*plural* **•phies**)
**hagi•ola•ter**
**hagi•ola•trous**
**hagi•ola•try** veneration of saints
**hagi•o•log•ic** (*or* **•logi•cal**)
**hagi•olo•gist**
**hagi•ol•ogy** (*plural* **•ogies**) writings about saints
**hagi•o•scope** architectural term
**hagi•o•scop•ic**
**hag•like**
**Hague**
**hah** *variant spelling of* **ha**
**ha-ha** (*or* **haw-haw**) sunken fence
**Hai•da** (*plural* **•da** *or* **•das**) American Indian
**Hai•dan**
**Hai•duk** (*or* **Hey•duck, Hei•duc**) brigand
**Hai•fa** Israeli port
**haik** (*or* **haick**) Arabian garment
**hai•ku** (*or* **hok•ku**; *plural* **•ku**) Japanese verse
**hail** frozen rain; greet; *compare* **hale**
**hail•er**
**hail•stone**
**hail•storm**
**Hai•nan** (*or* **Hai•nan Tao**) Chinese island
**Hai•naut** (*or* **•nault**) Belgian province
**Hai•phong** Vietnamese port
**hair**
**hair•ball**
**hair•brush**
**hair•cloth**
**hair•cut**
**hair•do** (*plural* **•dos**)
**hair•dresser**
**hair•dressing**
**hair•grip**
**hair•if** plant
**hairi•ness**
**hair•less**
**hair•like**
**hair•line**
**hair•net**
**hair•piece**
**hair•pin**
**hair-raising**
**hair's-breadth**
**hair•splitter**
**hair•splitting**
**hair•spring**
**hair•streak** butterfly
**hair•style**
**hair•stylist**
**hair•tail** fish
**hair•weaving**
**hair•worm**
**hairy** (**hairi•er, hairi•est**)
**Hai•ti**
**Hai•tian**
**hajj** (*or* **hadj**; *plural* **hajjes** *or* **hadjes**) Muslim pilgrimage
**haj•ji** (*or* **hadji, haji**)
**hake** (*plural* **hake** *or* **hakes**)
**ha•kea** shrub
**ha•kim** (*or* **•keem**) Muslim judge or physician
**Ha•ko•da•te** Japanese port
**Ha•la•fian** Neolithic culture
**Ha•la•kah** (*or* **•cha**) Jewish literature
**Ha•lak•ic** (*or* **•lach•ic**)
**hal•al** (*or* **hall•al**) Muslim custom
**ha•la•tion** photography term
**ha•la•vah** *variant of* **halvah**
**hal•berd** (*or* **•bert**)
**hal•ber•dier**
**hal•cy•on**
**Halcyone** *variant of* **Alcyone**
**hale** healthy; to haul; *compare* **hail**
**Ha•lea•ka•la** Hawaiian volcano
**hale•ness**
**ha•ler** (*plural* **•lers** *or* **•leru**) Czech coin
**Hales•ow•en** English town
**half** (*plural* **halves**)
**half•back**
**half-baked**
**half•beak** fish
**half-caste**
**half-day**
**half-hearted**
**half-hearted•ly**
**half-hearted•ness**
**half-life**
**half-light**
**half-mast**
**half-naked**
**half-open**
**half•penny** (*plural* **•pennies** *or* **•pence**)
**half•penny•worth**
**half-price**
**half-shut**
**half-time**
**half•tone**
**half•way**
**half•wit**
**half•witted**
**half•witted•ly**
**half•witted•ness**
**hali•but** (*plural* **•but** *or* **•buts**)
**Ha•liç** *Turkish* Golden Horn
**Hali•car•nas•si•an**
**Hali•car•nas•sus** ancient Greek city
**hal•ide** (*or* **•id**) chemical compound
**hali•dom** *Archaic* holy thing
**Hali•fax** Canadian port; British town
**hal•ite** mineral
**hali•to•sis**
**hall**
**hal•lah** *variant spelling of* **challah**
**hall•al** *variant spelling of* **halal**
**Hal•lel** Jewish chant
**hal•le•lu•jah** *variant of* **alleluia**
**hal•liard** *variant spelling of* **halyard**
**hall•mark**
**hal•lo** *variant spelling of* **halloo** *or* **hello**
**hal•loo** (*or* **•lo**; *noun, plural* **•loos** *or* **•los**; *verb* **•loos, •loo•ing, •looed**; *or* **•los,**

**•loing, •loed)** shout; *compare* **hello**
**hal•low**
**hal•lowed**
**hal•lowed•ness**
**Hal•low•e'en** (*or* **Hal•low•een)**
**hal•low•er**
**Hal•low•mas** (*or* **•mass)**
**Hall•statt** archaeology term
**Hall•stat•tian**
**hal•lu•ci•nate**
**hal•lu•ci•na•tion**
**hal•lu•ci•na•tion•al** (*or* **•na•tive)**
**hal•lu•ci•na•tor**
**hal•lu•ci•na•tory**
**hal•lu•cino•gen** drug
**hal•lu•ci•no•gen•ic**
**hal•lu•ci•no•sis** mental disorder
**hal•lux** (*plural* **•luces)** first digit on foot
**hall•way**
**halm** *variant spelling of* **haulm**
**hal•ma**
**Hal•ma•he•ra** Indonesian island
**halo** (*noun, plural* **haloes** *or* **halos;** *verb* **haloes** *or* **halos, halo•ing, haloed)**
**ha•lo•bi•ont** salt-water organism
**halo•gen**
**halo•gen•ate**
**halo•gen•a•tion**
**halo•gen•oid**
**ha•log•enous**
**hal•oid**
**halo-like**
**halo•phyte** plant
**halo•phyt•ic**
**halo•phyt•ism**
**halo•thane**
**halt**
**Hal•tem•price** Hull suburb
**hal•ter**
**hal•tere** zoology term
**halter-like**
**halt•ing**
**halt•ing•ness**
**hal•vah** (*or* **hal•va, ha•la•vah)** sweetmeat
**halve**
**hal•yard** (*or* **hal•liard)**
**ham (ham•ming, hammed)**
**Hama** Syrian city
**Hama•dān** (*or* **Ham•edān)** Iranian city
**hama•dry•ad** nymph
**hama•dry•as** baboon
**ha•mal** (*or* **ham•mal, ha•maul)** Oriental servant
**Ha•ma•ma•tsu** Japanese city
**hama•meli•da•ceous** botany term
**ha•mate** hook-shaped
**Ham•ble•to•nian** horse
**Ham•burg**
**ham•burg•er**
**hame** harness attachment
**Ham•elin** (*or* **Ha•meln)** German town
**Ham•ers•ley** Australian mountain range
**Ham•il•ton** Canadian port
**Ham•il•to•ni•an** maths term
**Ham•ite** African people
**Ham•it•ic**
**ham•let**
**ham•mer**
**ham•mer•er**
**hammer•head** animal
**hammer•headed**
**ham•mer•less**
**hammer-like**
**Ham•mer•smith**
**hammer•toe**
**ham•mock**
**hammock-like**
**Ham•mond** US city
**ham•my (ham•mi•er, ham•mi•est)**
**ham•per**
**ham•pered•ness**
**ham•per•er**
**Hamp•shire**
**Hamp•stead**
**Hamp•ton** US city
**ham•shack•le** fetter a horse
**ham•ster**
**ham•string (•string•ing, •strung)**
**hamu•lar**
**hamu•lus** (*plural* **•li)** hooklike projection
**ham•za** (*or* **•zah)** Arabic phonetic sign
**Han** Chinese dynasty; river
**hana•per** wickerwork basket
**hance** (*or* **haunch)** architectural term
**hand**
**hand•bag**
**hand•ball**
**hand•baller**
**hand•barrow**
**hand•bell**
**hand•bill**
**hand•book**
**hand•brake**
**hand•breadth**
**hand•cart**
**hand•clasp**
**hand•craft**
**hand•cuff**
**hand•fast** *Archaic* agreement
**hand•fasting**
**hand•feed (•feed•ing, •fed)**
**hand•ful**
**hand•grip**
**hand•gun**
**hand•hold**
**handi•cap (•cap•ping, •capped)**
**handi•cap•per**
**handi•craft**
**handi•crafts•man** (*plural* **•men)**
**handi•ly**
**handi•ness**
**handi•work**
**hand•ker•chief**
**han•dle**
**han•dle•able**
**handle•bar**
**han•dled**
**han•dle•less**
**han•dler**
**hand•less**
**hand•like**
**han•dling**
**hand•made**
**hand•maiden** (*or* **•maid)**
**hand-me-down**
**hand-out** (*noun*)
**hand•rail**
**hand•saw**
**hand•sel** (*or* **han•)** *Dialect* new year gift
**hand•set**
**hand•shake**
**hand•some** good-looking; *compare* **hansom**

**hand•some•ly**
**hand•some•ness**
**hand•spike** lever
**hand•spring**
**hand•stand**
**hand•stroke** bell-ringing term
**hand•writing**
**hand•written**
**handy (handi•er, handi•est)**
**handy•man** (*plural* **•men**)
**hang (hang•ing, hung** *or* **hanged)**
**hang•ar** aircraft shed; *compare* **hanger**
**hang•bird**
**Hang•chow** (*or* **Hang-chou**) Chinese port
**hang•dog**
**hanged** killed; *compare* **hung**
**hang•er** support; one that hangs; *compare* **hangar**
**hanger-on** (*plural* **hangers-on**)
**hang•man** (*plural* **•men**)
**hang•nail**
**hang•over**
**hang-up** (*noun*)
**hank**
**hank•er**
**(hankerchief)** *incorrect spelling of* **handkerchief**
**hank•er•er**
**Han•kow** (*or* **Han-k'ou**) former Chinese city
**hanky** (*or* **hankie**; *plural* **hankies**)
**hanky-panky**
**Ha•noi** Vietnamese capital
**Hano•ver**
**Hano•verian**
**Han•sard** parliamentary report
**Hanse** (*or* **Han•sa**) medieval guild
**Han•seat•ic**
**han•sel** *variant spelling of* **handsel**
**han•som** cab; *compare* **handsome**
**Ha•nuk•kah** Jewish festival
**Hanu•man** monkey god
**hanu•man** monkey

**Han•yang** former Chinese city
**hap (hap•ping, happed)** *Archaic* happen; luck
**ha•pax le•go•menon** (*plural* **ha•pax le•go•mena**) nonce word
**ha'•penny** (*plural* **•pennies**)
**hap•haz•ard**
**hap•haz•ard•ness**
**Haph•ta•rah** *variant spelling of* **Haftarah**
**hap•less**
**hap•less•ness**
**hap•lite** *variant spelling of* **aplite**
**hap•lit•ic** *variant spelling of* **aplitic**
**hap•log•ra•phy** (*plural* **•phies**) omission of letter in writing
**hap•loid** biology term
**hap•loidy**
**hap•lo•log•ic**
**hap•lol•ogy** (*plural* **•ogies**) omission of syllable in speech
**hap•lo•sis** biology term
**hap•ly**
**ha'•p'orth**
**hap•pen**
**hap•pen•ing**
**hap•pen•stance**
**hap•pi•ly**
**hap•pi•ness**
**hap•py (•pi•er, •pi•est)**
**happy-go-lucky**
**Hapsburg** *variant spelling of* **Habsburg**
**hap•ten** (*or* **•tene**) medical term
**hap•ter•on** botany term
**hap•tic** of touch
**hap•to•trop•ism** botany term
**ha•ra•ki•ri** (*or* **ha•ri•ka•ri**) Japanese suicide
**ha•ram•bee** African chant
**ha•rangue**
**ha•rangu•er**
**Ha•rap•pa** Pakistani city
**Ha•rap•pan**
**Ha•rar** (*or* **Har•rar**) Ethiopian city
**Ha•rare** Zimbabwean capital

**har•ass**
**har•ass•er**
**har•ass•ing•ly**
**har•ass•ment**
**Har•bin** (*or* **Ha-erh-pin**) Chinese city
**har•bin•ger**
**har•bour** (*US* **•bor**)
**har•bour•age** (*US* **•bor•**)
**har•bour•er** (*US* **•bor•**)
**har•bour•less** (*US* **•bor•**)
**hard**
**hard•back**
**hard•bake** almond toffee
**hard•board**
**hard•en**
**hard•ened**
**hard•en•er**
**hard•en•ing**
**hard•hack** plant
**hard-headed**
**hard-headed•ly**
**hard-headed•ness**
**hard•heads** plant
**hard•hearted**
**hard•hearted•ly**
**hard•hearted•ness**
**har•di•hood**
**har•di•ly**
**har•di•ness**
**hard•ly**
**hard•ness**
**hard•pan** clay layer
**hards** (*or* **hurds**) coarse fibres
**hard•ship**
**hard•tack**
**hard•top**
**hard•ware**
**hard•wood**
**har•dy (•di•er, •di•est)**
**hare**
**hare•bell**
**hare•brained**
**hare•like**
**hare•lip**
**hare•lipped**
**har•em** (*or* **•eem**)
**Har•gei•sa** Somalian city
**hari•cot**
**(haridan)** *incorrect spelling of* **harridan**
**Ha•ri•jan** Indian untouchable

**ha•ri•ka•ri** *variant spelling of* **harakiri**
**Ha•rin•gey** London borough
**hark**
**hark•en** *US variant spelling of* **hearken**
**harl** *variant spelling of* **herl**
**Har•lem** New York district; *compare* **Haarlem**
**har•lequin**
**har•lequin•ade**
**Har•ley Street**
**har•lot**
**har•lot•ry**
**Har•low** Essex town
**harm**
**har•mat•tan** Saharan wind
**harm•er**
**harm•ful**
**harm•ful•ly**
**harm•ful•ness**
**harm•less**
**harm•less•ness**
**har•mon•ic**
**har•moni•ca**
**har•moni•cal•ly**
**har•mon•ics**
**har•mo•ni•ous**
**har•mo•nist**
**har•mo•nis•tic**
**har•mo•nis•ti•cal•ly**
**har•mo•nium**
**har•mo•niz•able**
**har•mo•ni•za•tion**
**har•mo•nize** (*or* **•nise**)
**har•mo•niz•er**
**har•mo•ny** (*plural* **•nies**)
**har•mo•tome**
**har•ness**
**har•ness•er**
**har•ness•less**
**harness-like**
**Har•ney** US mountain
**harp**
**harp•er**
**harp•ings** (*or* **•ins**) nautical term
**har•poon**
**har•poon•er**
**har•poon-like**
**harp•si•chord**
**harp•si•chord•ist**
**har•py** (*plural* **•pies**)
**har•que•bus** *variant spelling of* **arquebus**
**Har•rar** Ethiopian city
**(harrass)** *incorrect spelling of* **harass**
**har•ri•dan**
**har•ri•er**
**Har•ris** Scottish island
**Har•ris•burg** US city
**Har•ro•gate** Yorkshire town
**Har•ro•vian**
**Har•row** London borough
**har•row** tool
**har•row•er**
**har•row•ing**
**har•row•ment**
**har•rumph**
**har•ry** (**•ries, •ry•ing, •ried**)
**harsh**
**harsh•ly**
**harsh•ness**
**hars•let** *variant spelling of* **haslet**
**hart** (*plural* **hart** *or* **harts**)
**har•tal**
**har•te•beest** (*or* **hart•beest**) antelope
**Hart•ford** US port
**Har•tle•pool**
**harts•horn**
**harum-scarum**
**ha•rus•pex** (*plural* **ha•rus•pi•ces**) Roman priest
**ha•rus•pi•cal**
**ha•rus•pi•cy**
**Har•vard**
**har•vest**
**har•vest•er**
**har•vest•ing**
**har•vest•less**
**harvest•man** (*plural* **•men**)
**Har•wich** Essex port
**Har•ya•na** Indian state
**Harz** German mountain range
**has**
**Ha•sa** Saudi Arabian province
**has-been**
**hash**
**Hash•e•mite** descendant of Mohammed
**hash•ish**
**Ha•sid•ic** (*or* **Has•sid•ic**)
**Hasi•dim** (*or* **Has•si•dim**) Jewish sect
**Has•id•ism** (*or* **Has•sid•ism**)
**hask** *Dialect* cough
**has•let** (*or* **hars•**) meat loaf
**hasn't**
**hasp**
**has•sle**
**has•sock** kneeling cushion; *compare* **cassock**
**hast**
**has•tate** botany term
**haste**
**haste•ful**
**haste•ful•ly**
**has•ten**
**has•ten•er**
**hasti•ly**
**hasti•ness**
**Hast•ings**
**has•ty** (**•ti•er, •ti•est**)
**hat** (**hat•ting, hat•ted**)
**hat•able** *variant spelling of* **hateable**
**hat•band**
**hat•box**
**hatch**
**hatch•able**
**hatch•back**
**hatch•el** (**•el•ling, •elled;** *US* **•el•ing, •eled**) comb flax
**hatch•el•ler** (*US* **•el•er**)
**hatch•er**
**hatch•ery** (*plural* **•eries**)
**hatch•et**
**hatchet-like**
**hatch•ing**
**hatch•ment** heraldic term
**hatch•way**
**hate**
**hate•able** (*or* **hat•**)
**hate•ful**
**hate•ful•ly**
**hate•ful•ness**
**hater**
**Hat•field** Hertfordshire town
**hath**
**Hath•or** Egyptian goddess
**Ha•thor•ic**
**hat•less**
**hat•like**
**hat•pin**
**ha•tred**
**hat•ter**
**Hat•ter•as** US cape

**hau•ber•geon** *variant spelling of* **habergeon**
**hau•berk** coat of mail
**haugh** *Dialect* flat valley base
**haugh•ti•ly**
**haugh•ti•ness**
**haugh•ty (•ti•er, •ti•est)**
**haul**
**haul•age**
**haul•er** (*or* **•ier)**
**haulm** (*or* **halm)** plant stem
**haunch**
**haunched**
**haunt**
**haunt•ed**
**haunt•er**
**haunt•ing**
**Hau•ra•ki** New Zealand gulf
**Hau•sa** (*plural* **•sas** *or* **•sa)** African people
**haus•frau**
**haus•tel•late**
**haus•tel•lum** (*plural* **•la)** entomology term
**haus•to•ri•al**
**haus•to•rium** (*plural* **•ria)** plant organ
**haut•boy** strawberry
**haute cou•ture**
**haute cui•sine**
**hau•teur**
**Ha•vana** Cuban capital
**Hav•ant** Hampshire town
**have (has, hav•ing, had)**
**have•lock** protective cap cover
**ha•ven**
**ha•ven•less**
**have-not** (*noun*)
**haven't**
**ha•ver** dither
**Ha•ver•ing** London borough
**hav•er•sack**
**Ha•ver•sian** anatomy term
**hav•er•sine** maths term
**hav•il•dar** Indian NCO
**hav•ing**
**hav•oc (•ock•ing, •ocked)**
**hav•ock•er**
**haw**
**Ha•waii**
**Ha•wai•ian**
**Hawes** English lake
**haw•finch**
**Haw•ick** Scottish town
**hawk**
**hawk•bit** plant
**hawk•er**
**hawk•ing**
**hawk•ish**
**hawk•like**
**hawks•bill** turtle
**hawk•weed**
**Ha•worth** Yorkshire village
**hawse** nautical term
**hawse•hole**
**hawse•pipe**
**haws•er**
**haw•thorn**
**hay**
**hay•box**
**hay•cock** pile of hay
**hay•fork**
**hay•maker**
**hay•making**
**hay•mow**
**hay•rack**
**hay•rick**
**hay•seed**
**hay•stack**
**hay•ward** *Obsolete* parish officer
**hay•wire**
**haz•ard**
**haz•ard•able**
**haz•ard-free**
**haz•ard•ous**
**haz•ard•ous•ness**
**haze**
**ha•zel**
**hazel•hen**
**hazel•nut**
**haz•er** nautical term
**ha•zi•ly**
**ha•zi•ness**
**hazy (ha•zi•er, ha•zi•est)**
**he**
**head**
**head•ache**
**head•achy**
**head•band**
**head•board**
**head•cheese** *US* brawn
**head•dress**
**head•ed**
**head•er**
**head•fast** mooring rope
**head•first**
**head•gear**
**head-hunt**
**head-hunter**
**head-hunting**
**headi•ly**
**headi•ness**
**head•ing**
**head•less**
**head•light** (*or* **•lamp)**
**head•like**
**head•line**
**head•lin•er**
**head•lock**
**head•long**
**head•man** (*plural* **•men)**
**head•master** (*fem* **•mistress)**
**head•master•ship** (*fem* **•mistress•)**
**head•most**
**head-on**
**head•phones**
**head•piece**
**head•pin**
**head•quarters**
**head•race**
**head•rail** billiards term
**head•reach** nautical term
**head•rest**
**head•room**
**head•sail**
**head•scarf** (*plural* **•scarves)**
**head•set**
**head•ship**
**head•shrinker**
**heads•man** (*plural* **•men)** executioner
**head•spring**
**head•square**
**head•stall**
**head•stand**
**head•stock** part of machine tool
**head•stone**
**head•stream**
**head•strong**
**head•strong•ness**
**head•wards** (*or esp. US* **•ward)**
**head•waters**
**head•way**
**head•wind**
**head•word**
**head•work**
**head•worker**
**heady (head•ier, head•iest)**
**heal** cure; *compare* **heel**

**heal•able**
**heal•er**
**heal•ing•ly**
**health**
**health•ful**
**health•ful•ly**
**health•ful•ness**
**healthi•ly**
**healthi•ness**
**healthy** (**health•ier,** **health•iest)**
**heap**
**heap•er**
**heap•ing**
**hear (hear•ing, heard)**
**hear•able**
**hear•er**
**heark•en** (*US also* **hark•)**
**heark•en•er**
**hear•say**
**hearse**
**heart**
**heart•ache**
**heart•beat**
**heart•break**
**heart•breaker**
**heart•breaking**
**heart•breaking•ly**
**heart•broken**
**heart•broken•ly**
**heart•broken•ness**
**heart•burn**
**heart•en**
**heart•en•ing•ly**
**heart•felt**
**hearth**
**hearth•stone**
**hearti•ly**
**hearti•ness**
**heart•land**
**heart•less**
**heart•less•ness**
**heart-rending**
**hearts•ease** wild pansy
**heart•sick**
**heart•sickness**
**heart•some**
**heart•some•ly**
**heart•some•ness**
**heart•strings**
**heart•wood**
**heart•worm**
**hearty (heart•ier,** **hearti•est)**
**heat**
**heat•ed**
**heat•ed•ly**
**heat•ed•ness**
**heat•er**
**heath**
**heath•berry** (*plural* **•berries)**
**hea•then** (*plural* **•thens** *or* **•then)**
**hea•then•dom**
**hea•then•ish**
**hea•then•ish•ness**
**hea•then•ism**
**hea•then•ize**
**hea•then•ness**
**heath•er**
**heath•ered**
**heath•ery**
**heath•fowl**
**heath•like**
**heathy**
**heat•ing**
**heat•less**
**heat•stroke**
**heaume** medieval helmet
**heave (heav•ing, heaved** *or* **hove)**
**heav•en**
**heav•en•li•ness**
**heav•en•ly**
**heav•en•ward** (*adj*)
**heav•en•wards** (*adv*)
**heav•er**
**heaves** horse disease
**heavi•ly**
**heavi•ness**
**heavy** (*adj* **heavi•er,** **heavi•est;** *noun, plural* **heavies)**
**heavy-handed**
**heavy-handed•ly**
**heavy-handed•ness**
**heavy•weight**
**heb•do•mad** *Obsolete* seven
**heb•doma•dal** (*or* **•da•ry)** weekly
**heb•doma•dal•ly**
**Hebe** Greek goddess
**he•be•phre•nia** schizophrenia
**he•be•phren•ic**
**heb•etate** blunt
**heb•eta•tion**
**he•bet•ic** of puberty
**heb•e•tude** lethargy
**heb•etu•di•nous**
**He•bra•ic** (*or* **•brai•cal)**
**He•bra•i•cal•ly**
**He•bra•ism**
**He•bra•ist**
**He•bra•is•tic**
**He•bra•is•ti•cal•ly**
**He•bra•i•za•tion**
**He•bra•ize**
**He•bra•iz•er**
**He•brew**
**Heb•ri•dean**
**Heb•ri•des**
**Heb•ron** Jordanian city
**Heca•te** (*or* **Heka•te)** Greek goddess
**heca•tomb** sacrifice
**heck**
**heck•el•phone** oboe
**heck•le**
**heck•ler**
**hec•tare**
**hec•tic**
**hec•ti•cal•ly**
**hec•to•coty•lus** zoology term
**hec•to•gram**
**hec•to•graph** copying process
**hec•to•graph•ic**
**hec•to•graphi•cal•ly**
**hec•tog•ra•phy**
**hec•tor**
**Hec•u•ba** mythological character
**he'd**
**hed•dle** part of loom
**hedge**
**hedge•hog**
**hedge•hop (•hop•ping,** **•hopped)**
**hedge•hop•per**
**hedg•er**
**hedge•row**
**hedgy**
**He•djaz** Saudi Arabian region
**he•don•ic**
**he•don•ics** branch of psychology
**he•don•ism**
**he•don•ist**
**heebie-jeebies**
**heed**
**heed•er**
**heed•ful**

**heed•ful•ly**
**heed•ful•ness**
**heed•less**
**heed•less•ly**
**heed•less•ness**
**hee•haw**
**heel** part of foot; *compare* **heal**
**heel•ball**
**heeled**
**heel•er**
**heel•less**
**heel•piece**
**heel•post**
**heel•tap**
**Heer•len** Dutch city
**heft**
**heft•er**
**hefti•ly**
**hefti•ness**
**hefty (hefti•er, hefti•est)**
**He•geli•an**
**He•geli•an•ism** school of philosophy
**heg•emon•ic**
**he•gemo•ny**
**Hegi•ra** (*or* **Heji•ra**) flight of Mohammed
**he•gu•men** (*or* **•menos**) Eastern Church leader
**heh** exclamation
**Hei•del•berg** German city
**Hei•duc** *variant spelling of* **Haiduk**
**heif•er**
**heigh-ho**
**height** tallness; *compare* **hight**
**height•en**
**height•en•er**
**Hei•lung•kiang** Chinese province
**Heim•dall** (*or* **Heim•dal, Heim•dallr**) Norse god
**hei•nous**
**hei•nous•ness**
**heir**
**heir•dom**
**heir•ess**
**heir•less**
**heir•loom**
**heir•ship**
**heist**
**heist•er**
**hei•ti•ki** Maori ornament
**He•jaz** (*or* **Hi•jaz**) Saudi Arabian province
**Heji•ra** *variant spelling of* **Hegira**
**Heka•te** *variant spelling of* **Hecate**
**Hek•la** Icelandic volcano
**Hel** (*or* **Hela**) Norse goddess
**held**
**Hel•ena** US city
**Hel•go•land** *variant spelling of* **Heligoland**
**he•li•a•cal** astronomy term; *compare* **helical**
**he•li•an•thus** (*plural* **•thuses**) sunflower
**heli•cal** spiral; *compare* **heliacal**
**heli•cal•ly**
**heli•ces** *plural of* **helix**
**heli•chrysum** plant
**heli•cline** spiral ramp
**heli•co•graph**
**heli•coid**
**heli•coi•dal•ly**
**heli•con** tuba
**Heli•con** Greek mountain
**heli•cop•ter**
**Heli•go•land** (*or* **Hel•go•**) North Sea island
**helio•cen•tric**
**helio•cen•tri•cal•ly**
**helio•cen•tric•i•ty** (*or* **helio•cen•tri•cism**)
**Helio•chrome** (*Trademark*)
**helio•chro•mic**
**helio•graph**
**he•li•og•ra•pher**
**helio•graph•ic**
**heliog•ra•phy**
**helio•gra•vure** printing term
**he•li•ola•ter**
**he•li•ola•trous**
**he•li•ola•try** sun worship
**he•lio•lith•ic**
**he•li•om•eter** telescope
**helio•met•ric**
**helio•met•ri•cal•ly**
**he•li•om•etry**
**He•li•opo•lis** ancient Egyptian city
**Helios** sun god
**helio•stat**
**helio•stat•ic**
**helio•tac•tic**
**helio•tax•is** biology term
**helio•thera•py**
**helio•trope** plant
**helio•trop•ic** growing towards sunlight
**helio•trop•i•cal•ly**
**he•li•ot•ro•pin** chemical compound
**he•li•ot•ro•pism**
**helio•type** printing process
**helio•typ•ic**
**helio•zo•an** biology term
**heli•port**
**he•lium** chemical element
**he•lix** (*plural* **heli•ces** *or* **he•lixes**)
**hell**
**he'll** he will; he shall
**Hel•ladic** archaeology term
**Hel•las** ancient Greece
**hell•bender**
**hell•bent**
**hell•box**
**hell•cat**
**hell•diver** bird
**Hel•le** mythological character
**hel•le•bore** plant
**hel•le•bor•ine** orchid
**Hel•len** legendary king
**Hel•lene** (*or* **Hel•le•nian**) Greek
**Hel•len•ic**
**Hel•leni•cal•ly**
**Hel•len•ism**
**Hel•len•ist**
**Hel•len•is•tic**
**Hel•len•is•ti•cal•ly**
**Hel•leni•za•tion** (*or* **•sa•tion**)
**Hel•len•ize** (*or* **•ise**)
**Hel•len•iz•er** (*or* **•is•er**)
**hel•ler** (*plural* **•ler**) German coin
**hell•ery** wild behaviour
**Hel•les** Turkish cape
**Hel•les•pont** Dardanelles
**hell•fire**
**hell•gram•mite** insect larva
**hell•hole**
**hell•hound**
**hel•lion**
**hell•ish**
**hell•ish•ness**

**hel•lo** (*or* **hal•lo, hul•lo;** *plural* **•los)**
**helm**
**Hel•mand** Asian river
**hel•met**
**hel•met•ed**
**helmet-like**
**hel•minth** parasitic worm
**hel•min•thia•sis**
**hel•min•thic**
**hel•min•thoid**
**hel•min•tho•logi•cal**
**hel•min•tholo•gist**
**hel•min•thol•ogy**
**helm•less**
**helms•man** (*plural* **•men)**
**Helot** ancient Greek class
**helot** serf
**hel•ot•ism**
**hel•ot•ry**
**help**
**help•able**
**help•er**
**help•ful**
**help•ful•ly**
**help•ful•ness**
**help•ing**
**help•less**
**help•less•ness**
**help•mate**
**help•meet** *Archaic* helpmate
**Hel•sin•ki**
**helter-skelter**
**helve** tool handle
**Hel•vel•lyn** English mountain
**Hel•ve•tia** Switzerland
**Hel•ve•tian**
**Hel•vet•ic**
**Hel•vetii** Celtic tribe
**hem (hem•ming, hemmed)**
**hema•** (*or* **hemato•)** *US spelling of words beginning with* **haemo•** *or* **haemato•**
**he•mal** *US spelling of* **haemal**
**he-man** (*plural* -**men)**
**heme** *US spelling of* **haem**
**Hem•el Hemp•stead**
**hem•ely•tron** (*or* **hemi•;** *plural* **•tra)** zoology term
**hem•era•lo•pia** day blindness
**hem•era•lop•ic**
**hemi•al•gia** pain on one side
**hemi•an•ops•ia** sight defect
**he•mic** *US spelling of* **haemic**
**hemi•cel•lu•lose**
**hemi•chor•date** zoology term
**hemi•cy•cle**
**hemi•cy•clic**
**hemi•demi•semi•qua•ver**
**hemi•ely•tron** *variant spelling of* **hemelytron**
**hemi•he•dral** crystallography term
**hemi•hy•drate**
**hemi•hy•drat•ed**
**hemi•mor•phic** crystallography term
**hemi•mor•phism** (*or* **•phy)**
**hemi•mor•phite** mineral
**he•min** *US spelling of* **haemin**
**hemio•la** musical term
**hemi•ol•ic**
**hemi•para•site**
**hemi•plegia**
**hemi•ple•gic**
**hemi•pode** (*or* **•pod)** bird
**he•mip•ter•an** (*or* **•on)** insect
**he•mip•ter•ous**
**hemi•sphere**
**hemi•spher•ic** (*or* **•spheri•cal)**
**hemi•spher•oid**
**hemi•spher•oi•dal**
**hemi•stich** half line of verse
**hemi•ter•pene** chemistry term
**hemi•trope** chemistry term
**hemi•trop•ic**
**hemi•tro•pism** (*or* **he•mit•ro•py)**
**hem•line**
**hem•lock**
**hem•mer**
**hemo•** *US spelling of words beginning with* **haemo•**
**hemp**
**hemp•en**
**hem•stitch**
**hem•stitch•er**
**hen**
**hen•bane** plant
**hen•bit** plant
**hence**
**hence•forth**
**hence•forward**
**hench•man** (*plural* **•men)**
**hen•coop**
**hen•deca•gon**
**hen•de•cago•nal**
**hen•deca•he•dron**
**hen•deca•syl•lab•ic**
**hen•deca•syl•la•ble**
**hen•dia•dys** rhetorical device
**hen•equen** (*or* **hen•equin, heni•quen)** fibre
**henge** archaeology term
**Heng-yang** Chinese city
**hen•house**
**Hen•ley** Oxfordshire town
**hen•na**
**hen•nery** (*plural* **•neries)** poultry house
**heno•theism** worship of one deity
**heno•theist**
**heno•theis•tic**
**hen•peck**
**hen•pecked**
**hen•ry** (*plural* **•ry, •ries,** *or* **•rys)** unit
**hent** *Archaic* seize
**hep**
**hepa•rin** biochemical substance
**he•pat•ic** of liver
**he•pati•ca** plant
**hepa•ti•tis**
**hep•cat**
**Hephaestus** (*or* **Hephaistos)** Greek god
**hep•tad**
**hep•ta•deca•no•ic acid**
**hep•ta•gon**
**hep•tago•nal**
**hep•ta•he•dral**
**hep•ta•he•dron**
**hep•tam•er•ous**
**hep•tam•eter** type of verse line
**hep•ta•met•ri•cal**
**hep•tane** chemical compound
**hep•tan•gu•lar**
**hep•tarch**
**hep•tar•chic**
**hep•tar•chy** (*plural* **•chies)**

**hep•ta•stich**
**Hep•ta•teuch** Old Testament books
**hep•tava•lent**
**hep•tose**
**her**
**Hera** (*or* Here) Greek goddess
**Hera•clea** ancient Greek colony
**Hera•clean**
**Heracles** (*or* **Herakles**) *variants of* **Hercules**
**Hera•cli•dan**
**Hera•clid** (*or* **•klid**) descendant of Hercules
**her•ald**
**he•ral•dic**
**he•ral•di•cal•ly**
**her•ald•ist**
**her•ald•ry**
**He•rat** Afghan city
**herb**
**her•ba•ceous**
**herb•age**
**herb•al**
**herb•al•ist**
**her•bar•ial**
**her•bar•ium** (*plural* **•iums** *or* **•ia**)
**her•bi•cid•al**
**herbi•cide**
**her•bi•vore**
**her•bivo•rous**
**her•bivo•rous•ness**
**herb•like**
**herby** (**herbi•er, herbi•est**)
**Her•cego•vi•na** (*or* **•zego•**) region of Bosnia-Hercegovina
**Her•cu•la•neum** ancient Italian city
**her•cu•lean**
**Her•cu•les** constellation
**Hercules** (*or* **Heracles, Herakles**) mythological hero
**Her•cyn•ian** geology term
**herd**
**herd•er**
**her•dic** *US* small carriage
**herds•man** (*plural* **•men**)
**Herd•wick** sheep
**here**
**here•abouts**
**here•after**
**here•at**
**here•by**
**he•redes** *plural of* **heres**
**he•redi•tabil•ity**
**he•redi•table**
**he•redi•tably**
**her•edita•ment** legal term
**he•redi•tari•an•ism** psychology term
**he•redi•tari•ly**
**he•redi•tari•ness**
**he•redi•tary**
**he•redi•tist**
**he•red•ity** (*plural* **•ities**)
**Her•eford**
**here•in**
**here•in•after**
**here•in•before**
**here•into**
**here•of**
**here•on**
**He•rero** (*plural* **•rero** *or* **•reros**) African people
**he•res** (*or* **hae•**; *plural* **•redes**) heir
**he•resi•arch** heretical leader
**her•esy** (*plural* **•esies**)
**her•etic**
**he•reti•cal**
**he•reti•cal•ly**
**here•to**
**here•to•fore**
**here•under**
**here•unto**
**here•upon**
**here•with**
**heri•ot** medieval death duty
**her•it•abil•ity**
**her•it•able**
**her•it•ably**
**her•it•age**
**heri•tor** (*fem* **•tress**)
**herl** (*or* **harl**) angling term
**herm**
**her•maph•ro•dite**
**her•maph•ro•dit•ic**
**her•maph•ro•diti•cal•ly**
**her•maph•ro•dit•ism**
**Hermaphroditus** mythological character
**her•meneu•tic**
**her•meneu•ti•cal•ly**
**her•meneu•tics**
**her•meneu•tist**
**Hermes** Greek god
**Her•mes** asteroid
**her•met•ic** air-tight; *compare* **hermitic**
**her•meti•cal•ly**
**her•mit**
**her•mit•age**
**Her•mit•ian** maths term
**her•mit•ic** hermit-like; *compare* **hermetic**
**her•miti•cal•ly**
**her•mit•like**
**Her•mon** mountain
**Her•mou•po•lis** Greek port
**hern** *Dialect* heron
**her•nia**
**her•nial**
**her•ni•at•ed**
**her•ni•or•rha•phy** (*plural* **•phies**) hernia surgery
**Hero** mythological character
**hero** (*plural* **heroes**)
**Herodias** mother of Salome
**he•ro•ic**
**he•roi•cal•ly**
**he•ro•ics**
**hero•in** drug
**hero•ine** heroic female
**hero•ism**
**her•on**
**her•on•ry** (*plural* **•ries**)
**her•pes**
**her•pes sim•plex**
**her•pes zos•ter**
**her•pet•ic**
**her•pe•to•log•ic** (*or* **•logi•cal**)
**her•pe•to•logi•cal•ly**
**her•pe•tolo•gist**
**her•pe•tol•ogy** study of reptiles
**Herr** (*plural* **Her•ren**) German title of address
**her•ring** (*plural* **•rings** *or* **•ring**)
**herring•bone**
**hers** of her
**her•self**
**Herst•mon•ceux** (*or* **Hurst•**)
**Hert•ford**
**Hert•ford•shire**
**hertz** (*plural* **hertz**) unit
**Hertz•ian** physics term
**Hertzsprung-Russell diagram**

**Her•zego•vi•na** *variant spelling of* **Hercegovina**
**he's** he is; he has
**Hesi•od•ic** of Hesiod
**Hesione** mythological princess
**hesi•tan•cy**
**hesi•tant**
**hesi•tant•ly**
**hesi•tate**
**hesi•tat•er**
**hesi•tat•ing•ly**
**hesi•ta•tion**
**hesi•ta•tive**
**Hes•per•ia** western land
**Hes•pe•rian**
**Hesperides** mythological characters
**Hes•per•id•ian** (*or* **•ean**)
**hes•peri•din** biochemical compound
**hes•per•id•ium** botany term
**Hes•per•us** evening star
**Hesse** German state
**Hes•sian** of Hesse
**hes•sian** fibre
**hes•site** mineral
**hes•so•nite** gemstone
**hest** behest
**Hestia** Greek goddess
**Hesy•chast** Greek Orthodox mystic
**Hesy•chast•ic**
**het** *Archaic* heated
**he•tae•ra** (*or* **•tai•**; *plural* **•tae•rae** *or* **•tai•rai**) Greek prostitute
**he•tae•ric** (*or* **•tai•**)
**he•tae•rism** (*or* **•tai•**)
**he•tae•rist** (*or* **•tai•**)
**he•tae•ris•tic** (*or* **•tai•**)
**hetero•cer•cal** zoology term
**hetero•chro•mat•ic**
**hetero•chro•ma•tin**
**hetero•chro•ma•tism**
**hetero•chro•mo•some**
**hetero•chro•mous**
**hetero•clite** grammar term
**hetero•clit•ic**
**hetero•cy•clic**
**hetero•dac•tyl** ornithology term
**hetero•dont** zoology term
**hetero•dox**
**hetero•doxy**
**hetero•dyne** electronics term
**het•er•oecious** botany term
**het•er•oecism**
**hetero•gam•ete**
**heteroga•mous**
**het•er•oga•my** botany term
**hetero•geneity**
**hetero•geneous** of different parts; *compare* heterogenous
**hetero•gen•esis**
**hetero•genet•ic**
**hetero•genetical•ly**
**hetero•gen•ous** of different origin; *compare* heterogeneous
**heter•ogeny**
**het•er•ogo•nous**
**heter•ogo•ny** biology term
**hetero•graft**
**hetero•graph•ic**
**het•er•og•ra•phy** grammar term
**het•er•ogy•nous**
**hetero•leci•thal**
**het•er•olo•gous**
**het•er•ol•ogy**
**het•er•oly•sis**
**hetero•lyt•ic**
**het•er•om•er•ous**
**hetero•mor•phic**
**hetero•mor•phism**
**het•er•ono•mous**
**het•er•ono•my**
**hetero•nym** grammar term
**het•er•ony•mous**
**Hetero•ousian** Christian sect
**het•er•opho•ny** musical term
**hetero•phyl•lous**
**hetero•phyl•ly**
**hetero•phyte**
**hetero•plas•tic**
**hetero•plas•ty** (*plural* **•ties**) surgical transplant
**hetero•po•lar**
**hetero•po•larity**
**het•er•op•ter•ous** zoology term
**hetero•scedas•tic•ity** statistics term
**hetero•sex•ism**
**hetero•sex•ist**
**hetero•sex•ual**
**hetero•sexu•al•ity**
**hetero•sex•ual•ly**
**hetero•sis**
**het•er•os•po•rous**
**het•er•os•po•ry**
**hetero•sty•lous**
**hetero•sty•ly** botany term
**hetero•tac•tic**
**hetero•tax•is**
**hetero•thal•lic** botany term
**hetero•to•pia** (*or* **het•er•oto•py**) displacement of body part
**hetero•top•ic**
**hetero•troph•ic** biology term
**hetero•typ•ic** (*or* **•typi•cal**) biology term
**hetero•zy•go•sis**
**hetero•zy•gote**
**hetero•zy•gous** genetics term
**heth** (*or* **cheth**) Hebrew letter
**het•man** (*plural* **•men**) Cossack leader
**heu•land•ite** mineral
**heu•ris•tic**
**heu•ris•ti•cal•ly**
**hew** (**hew•ing, hewed, hewed** *or* **hewn**) cut; *compare* **hue**
**hew•er**
**hex** *US* bewitch
**hexa•chloro•cyclo•hex•ane**
**hexa•chloro•ethane**
**hexa•chloro•phene**
**hexa•chord** musical term
**hexa•co•sa•no•ic acid**
**hex•ad** six
**hexa•decane**
**hexa•deci•mal**
**hex•adic**
**hexa•em•er•ic**
**hexa•em•er•on** (*or* **•hem•er•on**) the Creation
**hexa•gon**
**hex•ago•nal**
**hex•ag•o•nal•ly**
**hexa•gram**
**hexa•gram•moid**
**hexa•he•dral**
**hexa•he•dron**
**hexa•hy•drate**

**hexa•hy•drat•ed**
**hex•am•er•ism**
**hex•am•er•ous** (*or* **•eral**)
**hex•am•eter**
**hexa•methylene•tetramine**
**hexa•met•ric**
**hex•ane**
**hex•an•gu•lar**
**hexa•no•ic acid**
**hexa•pla** Old Testament edition
**hexa•plar** (*or* **•plar•ic**)
**hexa•pod** insect
**hexa•pod•ic**
**hex•apo•dy** (*plural* **•dies**) verse form
**hexa•stich** (*or* **hex•as•ti•chon**) six-line poem
**hexa•stich•ic**
**hexa•style** architecture term
**Hexa•teuch** Old Testament books
**Hexa•teu•chal**
**hexa•va•lent**
**hex•one** chemical compound
**hexo•san** biochemical compound
**hex•ose** sugar
**hex•yl**
**hexyl•resor•cin•ol**
**hey** exclamation
**hey•day**
**Hey•duck** *variant spelling of* **Haiduk**
**Hey•sham** Lancashire port
**Hey•wood** English town
**Hezekiah** biblical character
**hi**
**Hia•leah** US city
**hia•tal**
**hia•tus** (*plural* **•tuses** *or* **•tus**)
**hi•ba•chi** brazier
**hi•ber•nacu•lum** (*or* **•nac•le**; *plural* **•ula** *or* **•les**)
**hi•ber•nal**
**hi•ber•nate**
**hi•ber•na•tion**
**hi•ber•na•tor**
**Hi•ber•nia** Ireland
**Hi•ber•nian**
**Hi•ber•ni•an•ism**
**Hi•ber•ni•cism**
**hi•bis•cus**
**hic•cup** (**•cup•ing, •cuped** *or* **•cup•ping, •cupped**)
**hick**
**hick•ey** *US* gadget
**hicko•ry** (*plural* **•ries**)
**hid**
**hid•able**
**hi•dal•go** (*plural* **•gos**) Spanish nobleman
**Hi•dal•go** Mexican state
**hid•den**
**hid•den•ite** gemstone
**hid•den•ness**
**hide** (**hid•ing, hid, hid•den** *or* **hid**)
**hide-and-seek**
**hide•away**
**hide•bound**
**hide•less**
**hid•eous**
**hid•eous•ly**
**hid•eous•ness** (*or* **hid•eos•ity**)
**hid•er**
**hid•ing**
**hi•dro•sis** sweating
**hi•drot•ic**
**hie** (**hie•ing** *or* **hy•ing, hied**) hurry
**hie•land** *Scot* easily tricked
**hi•emal** of winter
**hi•era•co•sphinx** (*plural* **•sphinxes** *or* **•sphin•ges**)
**hi•er•arch**
**hi•er•ar•chal**
**hi•er•ar•chi•cal**
**hi•er•ar•chi•cal•ly**
**hi•er•arch•ism**
**hi•er•ar•chy** (*plural* **•chies**)
**hi•er•at•ic** of priests
**hi•er•ati•cal•ly**
**hi•er•oc•ra•cy** (*plural* **•cies**)
**hi•ero•crat•ic**
**hi•ero•dule** Greek slave
**hi•ero•du•lic**
**hi•ero•glyph**
**hi•ero•glyph•ic**
**hi•ero•glyphi•cal•ly**
**hi•ero•glyph•ics**
**hi•ero•glyph•ist**
**hi•ero•gram** sacred symbol
**hi•ero•log•ic**
**hi•er•olo•gist**
**hi•er•ol•ogy** (*plural* **•ogies**) sacred literature
**hi•ero•phant** ancient Greek priest
**hi•ero•phant•ic**
**hi•ero•phan•ti•cal•ly**
**hi•fa•lu•tin** *variant spelling of* **highfalutin**
**hi-fi**
**hig•gle**
**higgledy-piggle•dy**
**high**
**high•ball**
**high•bind•er** *US* gangster
**high•born**
**high•boy** *US* tallboy
**high•brow**
**high•chair**
**high•fa•lu•tin** (*or* **hi•**)
**high-flier** (*or* **-flyer**)
**high-flown**
**high-handed**
**high-handed•ly**
**high-handed•ness**
**high•jack** *less common spelling of* **hijack**
**high•jack•er** *less common spelling of* **hijacker**
**High•land** of Scottish Highlands
**high•land**
**high•land•er**
**High•lander**
**High•lands**
**high•life**
**high•light**
**high•ly**
**highly-strung**
**high-minded**
**high-minded•ness**
**high•ness** high condition
**High•ness** title for royalty
**high-rise**
**high•road**
**high-spirit•ed**
**high-spirit•ed•ness**
**hight** *Archaic* named; *compare* **height**
**high•tail**
**high-tech** (*or* **hi-**)
**High•veld** South African region
**high•way**
**highway•man** (*plural* **•men**)
**High Wy•combe**
**hi•jack** (*or* **high•**)
**hi•jack•er** (*or* **high•**)

**Hi•jaz** *variant spelling of* **Hejaz**
**hike**
**hik•er**
**hi•lar** anatomy term
**hi•lari•ous**
**hi•lari•ous•ness**
**hi•lar•ity**
**hill**
**Hil•la** Iraqi town
**hill•bil•ly** (*plural* **•lies**)
**hill•er**
**hill•fort**
**Hil•ling•don** London borough
**hill•ock**
**hill•ocked** (*or* **•ocky**)
**hill•side**
**hilly** (**hilli•er, hilli•est**)
**hilt**
**hi•lum** (*plural* **•la**) botany term
**hi•lus** (*plural* **•li**) anatomy term
**Hil•ver•sum** Dutch city
**him**
**Hi•ma•chal Pra•desh** Indian state
**Hima•la•yan**
**Hima•la•yas**
**hi•mati•on** (*plural* **•matia**) Greek cloak
**Hi•meji** Japanese city
**Hims** *variant of* **Homs**
**him•self**
**Him•yar•ite** Arabian people
**Him•yar•it•ic** language group
**hin** Hebrew unit
**Hi•na•ya•na** Buddhism
**Hi•na•ya•nist**
**Hi•na•ya•nis•tic**
**Hinck•ley** English town
**hind** (*adj* **hind•er, hind•most** *or* **hinder•most**; *noun, plural* **hinds** *or* **hind**)
**hind•brain**
**hin•der** obstruct
**hind•er** at the rear
**hin•der•er**
**hin•der•ing•ly**
**hind•gut**
**Hin•di** language; *compare* **Hindu**
**hind•most** (*or* **hinder•most**)
**Hin•doo** *former spelling of* **Hindu**
**Hin•doo•ism** *former spelling of* **Hinduism**
**hind•quarter**
**hin•drance**
**hind•sight**
**Hin•du** (*plural* **•dus**) people; *compare* **Hindi**
**Hin•du•ism**
**Hin•du Kush** Asian mountains
**Hin•du•stan**
**Hin•du•sta•ni**
**hinge**
**hinge•like**
**hing•er**
**hin•ny** (*noun, plural* **•nies**; *verb* **•nies, •ny•ing, •nied**)
**hint**
**hint•er**
**hinter•land**
**hip**
**hip•bone**
**hip•less**
**hip•like**
**hip•parch** ancient Greek cavalry commander
**Hip•par•chus** moon crater
**hip•pe•as•trum** plant
**hipped**
**hip•pie** (*or* **•py**; *plural* **•pies**)
**hip•po** (*plural* **•pos**)
**hippo•campal**
**hippo•campus** (*plural* **•campi**)
**hip•po•cras** wine
**Hip•po•crat•ic** of Hippocrates
**Hip•po•crene** ancient Greek spring
**Hip•po•crenian**
**hippo•drome**
**hip•po•griff** mythological monster
**Hippolyta** (*or* **Hippolyte**) Amazonian queen
**Hippolytus** son of Theseus
**Hippomenes** mythological character
**hippo•pota•mus** (*plural* **•muses** *or* **•mi**)
**Hip•po Re•gius** ancient African city
**hip•py** *variant spelling of* **hippie**
**hip•sters** trousers
**hir•able** (*or* **hire•**)
**hi•ra•ga•na** Japanese writing
**Hi•ram** biblical character
**hir•cine** lascivious
**hire**
**hire•ling**
**hir•er**
**Hi•ro•shi•ma**
**hir•sute**
**hir•sute•ness**
**hiru•din** anticoagulant
**hi•run•dine** of swallows
**his**
**His•pania** Iberia
**His•pan•ic**
**His•pani•cism**
**His•pani•cist**
**His•pani•ci•za•tion** (*or* **•sa•tion**)
**His•pani•cize** (*or* **•cise**)
**His•panio•la** West Indian island
**his•pid** bristly
**his•pid•ity**
**hiss**
**hiss•er**
**hist**
**his•tami•nase** enzyme
**his•ta•mine**
**his•ta•min•ic**
**his•ti•dine** amino acid
**his•tio•cyte**
**his•tio•cyt•ic**
**his•to•chemi•cal**
**his•to•chem•is•try**
**his•to•gen** plant tissue
**his•to•gen•esis** (*or* **his•tog•eny**)
**his•to•genet•ic** (*or* **•gen•ic**)
**his•to•geneti•cal•ly** (*or* **•geni•cal•ly**
**his•to•gram**
**his•toid**
**his•to•logi•cal** (**his•to•log•ic**)
**his•to•logi•cal•ly**
**his•tolo•gist**
**his•tol•ogy** study of tissues
**his•toly•sis**
**his•to•lyt•ic**
**his•to•lyti•cal•ly**
**his•tone** protein

**his•to•patho•logi•cal**
**his•to•pa•thol•ogy**
**his•to•plas•mo•sis**
**his•to•rian**
**his•to•ri•at•ed** decorated
**his•tor•ic**
**his•tori•cal**
**his•tori•cal•ly**
**his•tor•i•cal•ness**
**his•tori•cism**
**his•tori•cist**
**his•to•ric•ity**
**his•to•ri•og•ra•pher**
**his•to•rio•graph•ic**
**his•to•ri•og•ra•phy**
**his•to•ry** (*plural* **•ries)**
**his•tri•on•ic** (*or* **•oni•cal)**
**his•tri•oni•cal•ly**
**histrionics**
**hit (hit•ting, hit)**
**hitch**
**hitch•er**
**hitch•hike**
**hitch•hik•er**
**hi-tech** *variant spelling of* **high-tech**
**hith•er**
**hither•most**
**hither•to**
**Hit•ler•ism**
**hit•ter**
**Hit•tite**
**hive**
**hive•like**
**hives** nettle rash
**ho** exclamation; *compare* **hoe**
**ho•act•zin** *variant spelling of* **hoatzin**
**hoar**
**hoard** store; *compare* **horde**
**hoard•er**
**hoard•ing**
**hoar•frost**
**hoar•hound** *variant spelling of* **horehound**
**hoari•ly**
**hoari•ness**
**hoarse** grating; *compare* **horse**
**hoarse•ly**
**hoars•en**
**hoarse•ness**
**hoary (hoari•er, hoari•est)**
**hoatch•ing** *Scot* infested
**ho•at•zin** (*or* **•act•)** bird
**hoax**
**hoax•er**
**hob (hob•bing, hobbed)**
**Ho•bart** Tasmanian capital
**Hobbes•ian**
**Hob•bism** political philosophy
**Hob•bist**
**hob•ble**
**hobble•dehoy**
**hob•bler**
**hob•by** (*plural* **•bies)**
**hobby•horse**
**hob•byist**
**hob•goblin**
**hob•like**
**hob•nail**
**hob•nailed**
**hob•nob (•nob•bing, •nobbed)**
**hobo** (*plural* **hobos** *or* **hoboes)** vagrant
**hobo•ism**
**Ho•bo•ken** Belgian city
**hobson-jobson** folk etymology
**Hoch•hei•mer** wine
**hock**
**hock•er**
**hock•ey**
**Hock•tide** former festival
**ho•cus (•cus•ing, cused,** *or* **•cus•sing, •cussed)**
**hocus-pocus (-pocusing, -pocused** *or* **-pocussing, -pocussed)**
**hod**
**hod•den** coarse cloth
**hod•din**
**Ho•dei•da** Yemeni port
**hodge•podge** *US* hotchpotch
**hod•man** (*plural* **•men)**
**ho•dom•eter** *variant of* **odometer**
**hodo•scope**
**hoe (hoe•ing, hoed)** gardening tool; *compare* **ho**
**hoe•down** dance
**Hoek van Hol•land** Hook of Holland
**hoe•like**
**hoer**
**Ho•fei** Chinese city
**hog (hog•ging, hogged)**
**ho•gan** American Indian dwelling
**Ho•garth•ian**
**hog•back** narrow ridge
**hog•fish** *plural* **•fish** *or* **•fishes**
**hogged**
**hog•ger**
**hog•ging**
**hog•gish**
**hog•gish•ly**
**hog•gish•ness**
**hog•like**
**Hog•ma•nay**
**hog•nose** snake
**hog•nut**
**hogs•head**
**hog•tie (•ty•ing, •tied)** *US* tie limbs
**hog•wash**
**hog•weed**
**hoick**
**hoi•den** *variant spelling of* **hoyden**
**hoi pol•loi**
**hoist**
**hoist•er**
**hoity-toity**
**hoke** overact
**hokey cokey** song and dance
**ho•key-pokey** hocus-pocus
**Hok•kai•do** Japanese island
**hok•ku** *variant spelling of* **haiku**
**ho•kum**
**Hol•arc•tic** zoogeographical term
**hold (hold•ing, held)**
**hold•able**
**hold•all**
**hold•er**
**hold•er•ship**
**hold•fast**
**hold•ing**
**hole**
**holey**
**holi•day**
**ho•li•ly**
**Ho•li•ness** pope's title
**ho•li•ness**
**ho•lism**
**ho•lis•tic**
**ho•lis•ti•cal•ly**

**hol•la** *variant of* **hollo**
**hol•land** cloth
**Hol•land**
**hol•lan•daise** sauce
**Hol•land•er**
**Hol•lands** Dutch gin
**hol•ler** *Slang* shout
**hol•lo** (*or* **•la**; *plural* **•los** *or* **•las**) shout
**hol•low**
**hol•low•ly**
**hol•low•ness**
**hol•ly** (*plural* **•lies**)
**hol•ly•hock**
**Hol•ly•wood**
**holm** *Dialect* river island
**hol•mic**
**hol•mium** chemical element
**holo•blas•tic**
**holo•blas•ti•cal•ly**
**holo•caust**
**hol•o•caus•tal** (*or* **•caus•tic**)
**Holo•cene** geological period
**holo•crine** physiology term
**holo•en•zyme**
**holo•gram** handwritten document
**holo•graph** three-dimensional image
**holo•graph•ic**
**hol•o•graphi•cal•ly**
**ho•log•ra•phy**
**holo•he•dral**
**holo•he•drism**
**holo•mor•phic**
**holo•phras•tic**
**holo•phyte**
**holo•phyt•ic**
**holo•plank•ton**
**holo•thu•rian** zoology term
**holo•type**
**holo•typ•ic**
**holo•zo•ic**
**hol•pen** *Archaic* helped
**Hol•stein** German region; cattle
**hol•ster**
**hol•stered**
**holt** *Archaic* woodland
**holus-bolus** *Slang* all at once
**holy** (*adj* **ho•li•er, ho•li•est**; *noun, plural* **holies**)
**Holy•head**
**ho•ly•stone**
**holy•tide**
**hom** (*or* **homa**) sacred plant
**hom•age**
**hom•bre** *US* man
**hom•burg** hat
**home**
**home•bred**
**home•coming**
**home•land**
**home•less**
**home•less•ness**
**home•like**
**home•li•ness**
**home•ly** (**•li•er, •li•est**) unpretentious; *US* ugly; *compare* **homy**
**home•mak•ing**
**homeo•mor•phic** (*or* **homoeo•**)
**homeo•mor•phism** (*or* **homoeo•**)
**homeo•path•ic** (*or* **homoeo•**)
**homeo•pathi•cal•ly** (*or* **homoeo•**)
**homeopa•thist** (*or* **homoepa•**)
**homeopa•thy** (*or* **homoeopa•**)
**homeo•sta•sis** (*or* **homoeo•**)
**homeo•stat•ic** (*or* **homoeo•**)
**homeo•typ•ic** (*or* **•typi•cal, homoeo•**) biology term
**home•own•er**
**home•own•er•ship**
**hom•er**
**Ho•merian**
**Ho•mer•ic**
**Ho•meri•cal•ly**
**home•sick**
**home•sick•ness**
**home•spun**
**home•stead**
**home•stead•er**
**home•ward** (*adj*)
**home•wards** (*adv*)
**home•work**
**homey** *variant spelling of* **homy**
**homey•ness** *variant spelling of* **hominess**
**homi•ci•dal**
**homi•ci•dal•ly**
**homi•cide**
**homi•let•ic** (*or* **homi•leti•cal**)
**homi•leti•cal•ly**
**homi•let•ics** art of preaching sermons
**homi•list**
**homi•ly** (*plural* **•lies**)
**homi•ness** (*or* **homey•ness**)
**hom•ing**
**homi•nid**
**homi•noid**
**homi•ny** *US* ground maize
**homo** (*plural* **homos**) *Slang* homosexual
**homo•cen•tric**
**homo•cen•tri•cal•ly**
**homo•cer•cal** zoology term
**homo•chro•mat•ic**
**homo•chro•ma•tism**
**homo•chro•mous**
**homo•cy•clic**
**homo•dont**
**homoeo•** *variant spelling of words beginning* **homeo•**
**homo•erotic**
**homo•eroti•cism**
**homo•ero•tism**
**ho•moga•mous**
**ho•moga•my** botany term
**ho•mog•enate**
**homo•genei•ty**
**homo•geneous** uniform; *compare* **homogenous**
**homo•geneous•ness**
**ho•mog•eni•za•tion** (*or* **•sa•tion**)
**ho•mog•enize** (*or* **•enise**)
**ho•mog•eniz•er** (*or* **•enis•er**)
**ho•mog•enous** similar through common ancestry; *compare* **homogeneous**
**ho•mog•eny**
**ho•mogo•nous**
**ho•mog•ony** botany term
**homo•graft**
**homo•graph**
**homo•graph•ic**
**ho•moio•ther•mic** warm-blooded
**ho•moio•ther•my**
**Ho•moi•ou•sian**
**Ho•moi•ou•si•an•ism** Christian sect

**homo•log** *US variant spelling of* **homologue**
**ho•molo•gate** ratify
**ho•molo•ga•tion**
**homo•logi•cal** homologous
**homo•logi•cal•ly**
**ho•molo•gize** (*or* **•gise**)
**ho•molo•giz•er** (*or* **•gis•er**)
**ho•molo•gous**
**ho•molo•graph•ic**
**homo•logue** (*US also* **•log**)
**ho•mol•ogy** (*plural* **•ogies**)
**ho•mol•o•sine** cartography term
**ho•moly•sis**
**homo•lyt•ic**
**homo•mor•phic** (*or* **•phous**)
**homo•mor•phism**
**homo•nym**
**homo•nym•ic**
**homo•nym•ity**
**Homo•ou•sian**
**Homo•ou•si•an•ism** Christian sect
**homo•phile**
**homo•phone**
**homo•phon•ic**
**homo•phoni•cal•ly**
**ho•mopho•nous**
**ho•mopho•ny** linguistics term
**homo•phyl•lic**
**ho•mophy•ly** biology term
**homo•plas•tic**
**homo•plas•ti•cal•ly**
**homo•plas•ty**
**homo•po•lar** chemistry term
**homo•po•lar•ity**
**ho•mop•ter•ous** entomology term
**ho•mor•gan•ic** linguistics term
**Homo sa•pi•ens**
**homo•scedas•tic•ity** statistics term
**homo•sex•ual**
**homo•sex•ual•ity**
**homo•sex•ual•ly**
**ho•mos•po•rous** botany term
**ho•mos•po•ry**
**homo•taxi•al•ly**
**homo•tax•ic**
**homo•tax•is**
**homo•thal•lic**
**homo•thal•lism** botany term
**homo•zy•go•sis**
**homo•zy•gote**
**homo•zy•got•ic**
**homo•zy•gous** genetics term
**Homs** (*or* **Hims, Hums**) Syrian city
**ho•mun•cu•lar**
**ho•mun•cu•lus** (*plural* **•li**) miniature man
**homy** (*or* **homey; homi•er, homi•est**) cosy; *compare* **homely**
**ho•nan** fabric
**Honda** (*Trademark*)
**Hon•do** *variant of* **Honshu**
**Hon•du•ran**
**Hon•du•ras**
**hone**
**hon•est**
**hon•est•ly**
**hon•est•ness**
**hon•es•ty** (*plural* **•ties**)
**hone•wort** plant
**hon•ey**
**honey•bee**
**honey•bunch**
**honey•comb**
**honey•dew**
**hon•ey•dewed**
**honey-eater** bird
**hon•eyed** (*or* **•ied**)
**hon•eyed•ly** (*or* **•ied•**)
**honey-like**
**honey•moon**
**honey•moon•er**
**honey•sucker** bird
**honey•suckle**
**hong** Chinese factory
**Hong Kong**
**Ho•nia•ra** capital of Solomon Islands
**hon•ied** *variant spelling of* **honeyed**
**Honi•ton** lace
**honk**
**honk•er**
**honky** (*plural* **honkies**) *US slang* white man
**honky-tonk**
**Hono•lu•lu**
**hon•or** *US spelling of* **honour**
**hono•rar•ium** (*plural* **•rar•iums** *or* **•raria**)
**hon•or•ary**
**hon•or•if•ic**
**hon•or•ifi•cal•ly**
**hon•our** (*US* **•or**)
**Hon•our•able** title of respect
**hon•our•able** (*US* **•or•**)
**hon•our•able•ness** (*US* **•or•**)
**hon•our•ably** (*US* **•or•**)
**hon•our•er** (*US* **•or•**)
**hon•our•less** (*US* **•or•**)
**Hon•shu** (*or* **Hon•do**)
**hooch**
**hood**
**hood•ed**
**hoodie** crow
**hood•less**
**hood•like**
**hood•lum**
**hood•lum•ism**
**hoo•doo** (*plural* **•doos**)
**hoo•doo•ism**
**hood•wink**
**hood•wink•er**
**hoo•ey**
**hoof** (*plural* **hoofs** *or* **hooves**)
**hoof•bound** veterinary term
**hoofed**
**hoof•er**
**hoof•less**
**hoof•like**
**Hoogh•ly** Indian river
**hoo-ha**
**hook**
**hook•ah** oriental pipe
**hooked**
**hook•ed•ness**
**hook•er**
**hook•less**
**hook•like**
**hook•nose**
**hook•nosed**
**hook•worm**
**hooky** (*or* **hookey**)
**hoo•li•gan**
**hoo•li•gan•ism**
**hoop**
**hooped**
**hoop•er**
**hoop•la**
**hoop•like**
**hoo•poe** bird

**hoo•rah** (*or* **•ray**) *variants of* **hurrah**
**hoose•gow** *US* jail
**hoot**
**hoot•en•an•ny** (*or* **hoot•nan•ny**; *plural* **•nies**) *US* folksinging
**hoot•er**
**Hoo•ver** (*Trademark*)
**hoo•ver** (*verb*)
**hooves**
**hop** (**hop•ping, hopped**)
**hope**
**hope•ful**
**hope•ful•ly**
**hope•ful•ness**
**Ho•peh** Chinese province
**hope•less**
**hope•less•ly**
**hope•less•ness**
**hop•er**
**hop•head** *Slang* drug addict
**Hopi** (*plural* **Hopis** *or* **Hopi**) American Indian
**hop•lite** Greek soldier
**hop•lit•ic**
**hop•lol•ogist**
**hop•lol•ogy** study of weapons
**hop•per**
**hop•ping**
**hop•ple** hobble
**hop•pler**
**Hop•pus foot** unit
**hop•sack**
**hop•scotch**
**hora** dance
**Horae** Roman goddesses
**ho•ral** hourly
**ho•ra•ry** *Archaic* hourly
**Ho•ra•tian** of the poet Horace
**Horatius** legendary Roman hero
**horde** mob; *compare* **hoard**
**hor•dein** protein
**Ho•reb** biblical mountain
**hore•hound** (*or* **hoar•**) plant
**ho•ri•zon**
**ho•ri•zon•less**
**hori•zon•tal**
**hori•zon•tal•ly**
**hori•zon•tal•ness**
**hor•me** psychology term
**hor•mic**
**hor•mo•nal**
**hor•mone**
**Hor•muz** (*or* **Or•muz**) Iranian island
**horn**
**horn•beam**
**horn•bill**
**horn•blende** mineral
**horn•blen•dic**
**horn•book**
**horned**
**horn•ed•ness**
**hor•net**
**horn•fels** rock
**horni•ly**
**horni•ness**
**horn•less**
**horn•like**
**horn•pipe**
**horn-rimmed**
**horn•stone**
**horns•wog•gle** *Slang* cheat
**horn•tail** insect
**horn•wort** plant
**horny** (**horni•er, horni•est**)
**horo•loge** timepiece
**horo•log•ic**
**ho•rol•o•gist** (*or* **ho•rolo•ger**)
**horo•lo•gium** (*plural* **•gia**) clock tower
**ho•rol•ogy**
**horo•scope**
**horo•scop•ic**
**ho•ros•co•py** (*plural* **•pies**)
**hor•ren•dous**
**hor•ri•ble**
**hor•ri•ble•ness**
**hor•ri•bly**
**hor•rid**
**hor•rid•ness**
**hor•rif•ic**
**hor•rifi•cal•ly**
**hor•ri•fi•ca•tion**
**hor•ri•fy** (**•fies, •fy•ing, •fied**)
**hor•ri•fy•ing•ly**
**hor•ripi•la•tion** gooseflesh
**hor•ror**
**horror-stricken** (*or* **-struck**)
**hors de com•bat** *French* injured
**hors d'oeu•vre** (*plural* **hors d'oeu•vre** *or* **hors d'oeu•vres**)
**horse** animal; *compare* **hoarse**
**horse•back**
**horse•box**
**horse•flesh**
**horse•fly** (*plural* **•flies**)
**horse•hair**
**horse•hide**
**horse•leech**
**horse•less**
**horse•like**
**horse•man** (*plural* **•men**)
**horse•man•ship**
**horse•mint**
**horse•play**
**horse•power** (*plural* **horse•power**) unit
**horse•radish**
**horse•shoe** (**•shoe•ing, •shoed**)
**horse•tail** plant
**horse•weed**
**horse•whip** (**•whip•ping, •whipped**)
**horse•whip•per**
**horse•woman** (*plural* **•women**)
**horsi•ly**
**horsi•ness**
**horst** ridge
**horsy** (*or* **horsey; horsi•er, horsi•est**)
**hor•ta•to•ri•ly**
**hor•ta•tory** (*or* **•tive**) urging
**hor•ti•cul•tur•al**
**hor•ti•cul•tur•al•ly**
**hor•ti•cul•ture**
**hor•ti•cul•tur•ist**
**hor•tus sic•cus** collection of dried plants
**Horus** Egyptian god
**ho•san•na**
**hose**
**Hosea** biblical character
**ho•sier**
**ho•siery**
**hos•pice**
**hos•pi•table**
**hos•pi•table•ness**
**hos•pi•tably**
**hos•pi•tal**
**hos•pi•tal•ity**
**hos•pi•tali•za•tion** (*or* **•sa•tion**)
**hos•pi•tal•ize** (*or* **•ise**)

**Hos•pi•tal•ler** religious knight
**hos•pi•tal•ler** (*US* **•tal•er)** hospital worker
**hos•pit•ium** (*plural* **•ia)** travellers' refuge
**hos•po•dar** Ottoman ruler
**host**
**hos•ta** plant
**hos•tage**
**hos•tel**
**hos•tel•ler** (*US* **•tel•er)**
**hos•tel•ling** (*US* **•tel•ing)**
**hos•tel•ry** (*plural* **•ries)**
**host•ess**
**hos•tile**
**hos•tile•ly**
**hos•til•ity** (*plural* **•ities)**
**host•ler** *variant of* **ostler**
**hot** (*adj* **hot•ter, hot•test;** *verb* **hot•ting, hot•ted)**
**hot•bed**
**hot-blooded**
**hot-blooded•ness**
**hotch•pot** legal term
**hotch•potch** (*US* **hodge•podge)**
**ho•tel**
**ho•tel•ier**
**hot•foot**
**hot•head**
**hot-headed**
**hot-headed•ly**
**hot-headed•ness**
**hot•house**
**Ho•tien** (*or* **Ho-t'ien, Kho-tan)** Chinese oasis
**hot•ly**
**hot•ness**
**hot•plate**
**hot•pot**
**hot•spur** impetuous person
**Hot•ten•tot** (*plural* **•tot** *or* **•tots)**
**hot•tish**
**Hou•dan** fowl
**hough** hock
**Houghton-le-Spring** Tyneside town
**hou•mous** (*or* **•mus)** *variant of* **hummus**
**hound**
**hound•er**
**Houns•low**
**hour**
**hour•glass**
**hou•ri** (*plural* **•ris)** Muslim nymph
**hour•ly**
**house**
**house•boat**
**house•bound**
**house•boy**
**house•break•er**
**house•break•ing**
**house•carl** medieval servant
**house•coat**
**house•fath•er**
**house•fly** (*plural* **•flies)**
**house•hold**
**house•holder**
**house•holder•ship**
**house•keeper**
**house•keeping**
**hou•sel** *Archaic* Eucharist
**house•leek**
**house•less**
**house•line** nautical term
**house•maid**
**house•man** (*plural* **•men)**
**house•master**
**house•mistress**
**house•moth•er**
**house-proud**
**house•room**
**house•top**
**house•wife** (*plural* **•wives)**
**house•wife•li•ness**
**house•wife•ly**
**house•wif•ery**
**house•work**
**house•worker**
**housey-housey**
**hous•ing**
**Hou•ston** Texan port
**hous•to•nia** plant
**hout•ing** fish
**hove**
**Hove** Sussex town
**hov•el** (**•el•ling, •elled;** *US* **•el•ing, •eled)**
**hov•er**
**hover•craft**
**hov•er•er**
**hov•er•ing•ly**
**hover•port**
**hover•train**
**how**
**how•be•it**
**how•dah** seat on elephant
**how•dy** *US* hello
**howe'er**
**how•ever**
**howf** *Scot* public house
**how•itz•er**
**howl**
**How•land** Pacific island
**howl•er**
**how•let** owl
**howl•ing**
**How•rah** Indian city
**how•so•ever**
**how•tow•die** Scottish chicken dish
**hoy**
**hoya** plant
**hoy•den** (*or* **hoi•)**
**hoy•den•ish** (*or* **hoi•)**
**hoy•den•ish•ness** (*or* **hoi•)**
**Hoy•lake** English town
**Hsi** *variant spelling of* **Si**
**Hsian** *variant spelling of* **Sian**
**Hsiang** *variant spelling of* **Siang**
**Hsin-hai-lien** *variant spelling of* **Sinhailien**
**Hsi•ning** *variant spelling of* **Sining**
**Hsü-chou** *variant spelling of* **Süchow**
**Huai-nan** Chinese city
**Huang Hai** *variant spelling of* **Hwang Hai**
**Huang Ho** *variant spelling of* **Hwang Ho**
**hub**
**hubble-bubble**
**hub•bub**
**hub•by** (*plural* **•bies)**
**hub•cap**
**Hub•li** Indian city
**hu•bris** (*or* **hy•bris)**
**hu•bris•tic**
**hucka•back** fabric
**huck•le**
**huckle•berry** (*plural* **•berries)**
**huck•le•bone** *Archaic* anklebone
**huck•ster**
**huck•ster•ism**
**Hud•ders•field**
**hud•dle**
**hud•dler**
**hu•di•bras•tic** mock-heroic

**Hud•son** Canadian bay; US river
**hue** colour; *compare* **hew**
**hued**
**huff**
**huffi•ly**
**huffi•ness**
**huff•ish**
**huffy** **(huffi•er, huffi•est)**
**hug** **(hug•ging, hugged)**
**huge**
**huge•ly**
**huge•ness**
**hug•gable**
**hug•ger**
**hug•ger•mug•ger**
**Hu•guenot**
**Hu•guenot•ic**
**Hu•guenot•ism**
**huh** exclamation
**Hu•he•hot** (*or* **Hu-ho-hao-t'e)** Chinese town
**hula** (*or* **hula-hula)** Hawaiian dance
**hulk**
**hulk•ing**
**hull**
**Hull** English port; Canadian city
**hul•la•ba•loo** (*or* **•bal•loo;** *plural* **•loos)**
**hull•er**
**hull-less**
**hul•lo** *variant spelling of* **hello**
**hum** **(hum•ming, hummed)**
**hu•man**
**hu•mane**
**hu•mane•ly**
**hu•mane•ness**
**hu•man•ism**
**hu•man•ist**
**hu•man•ist•ic**
**hu•mani•tar•ian**
**hu•mani•tari•an•ism**
**hu•mani•tari•an•ist**
**hu•man•ity** (*plural* **•ities)**
**hu•mani•za•tion** (*or* **•sa•tion)**
**hu•man•ize** (*or* **•ise)**
**hu•man•iz•er** (*or* **•is•er)**
**human•kind**
**hu•man-like**
**hu•man•ly**
**hu•man•ness**
**hu•man•oid**
**Hum•ber**
**Humber•side**
**hum•ble**
**hum•ble•bee**
**hum•ble•ness**
**hum•bler**
**hum•bling•ly**
**hum•bly**
**Hum•boldt cur•rent**
**hum•bug** **(•bug•ging, •bugged)**
**hum•bug•ger**
**hum•bug•gery**
**hum•ding•er**
**hum•drum**
**hum•drum•ness**
**hu•mec•tant**
**hu•mer•al**
**hu•mer•us** (*plural* **•meri)** arm bone; *compare* **humorous**
**hu•mic**
**hu•mid**
**hu•midi•fi•ca•tion**
**hu•midi•fi•er**
**hu•midi•fy** **(•fies, •fy•ing, •fied)**
**hu•midi•stat**
**hu•mid•ity**
**hu•mid•ness**
**hu•mi•dor** tobacco container
**hu•mili•ate**
**hu•mili•at•ing•ly**
**hu•milia•tion**
**hu•mil•ia•tive**
**hu•mili•a•tor**
**hu•mil•ia•tory**
**hu•mil•ity** (*plural* **•ities)**
**hummed**
**hum•mel** *Scot* hornless
**hum•mer**
**hum•ming**
**humming•bird**
**hum•mock**
**hum•mocky**
**hum•mus** (*or* **hou•mus, •mous)** Middle Eastern food
**hu•mor** *US spelling of* **humour**
**hu•mor•al** of body fluids
**hu•mor•esque**
**hu•mor•ist**
**hu•mor•is•tic**
**hu•mor•ous** funny; *compare* **humerus**
**hu•mor•ous•ness**
**hu•mour** **(***US* **•mor)**
**hu•mour•ful** **(***US* **•mor•)**
**hu•mour•less** **(***US* **•mor•)**
**hu•mour•less•ness** **(***US* **•mor•)**
**hu•mour•some** **(***US* **•mor•)**
**hump**
**hump•back**
**hump•backed**
**humph**
**humpi•ness**
**hump•like**
**hump•ty** (*plural* **•ties)** padded seat
**humpy** **(humpi•er, humpi•est)**
**Hums** *variant of* **Homs**
**hu•mus**
**Hun**
**Hu•nan** Chinese province
**hunch**
**hunch•back**
**hunch•backed**
**hun•dred** (*plural* **•dreds** *or* **•dred)**
**hun•dredth**
**hundred•weight** (*plural* **•weights** *or* **•weight)**
**hung** suspended; *compare* **hanged**
**Hun•gar•ian**
**Hun•ga•ry**
**hun•ger**
**Hung•nam** North Korean port
**hun•gri•ly**
**hun•gri•ness**
**hun•gry** **(•gri•er, •gri•est)**
**hunk**
**hunk•ers** *Dialect* haunches
**hunky-dory**
**Hun•like**
**Hun•nish**
**Hun•nish•ly**
**Hun•nish•ness**
**hunt**
**hunt•ed**
**hunt•er**
**hunt•ing**

**Hun•ting•don** Cambridgeshire town
**Hun•ting•don•shire** former English county
**hunts•man** (*plural* **•men**)
**Hunts•ville** US city
**Huon** Tasmanian river
**Hu•peh** (*or* **•pei**) Chinese province
**hup•pah** Jewish wedding ceremony
**hur•dle**
**hur•dler**
**hurds** *variant of* **hards**
**hurdy-gurdy** (*plural* **-gurdies**)
**hurl**
**hurl•er**
**hur•ley** hurling stick
**hurl•ing**
**hurly-burly** (*plural* **-burlies**)
**Hu•ron** (*plural* **•rons** *or* **•ron**) American Indian
**Hu•ron (Lake)**
**hur•rah** (*or* **hoo•ray, hoo•rah**)
**hur•ri•cane**
**hur•ried**
**hur•ried•ly**
**hur•ried•ness**
**hur•ry** (*verb* **•ries, •ry•ing, •ried**; *noun, plural* **•ries**)
**hur•ry•ing•ly**
**hurst** *Archaic* wood
**Hurst•mon•ceux** *variant spelling of* **Herstmonceux**
**hurt (hurt•ing, hurt)**
**hur•ter**
**hurt•ful**
**hurt•ful•ly**
**hurt•ful•ness**
**hurt•le**
**hus•band**
**hus•band•er**
**hus•band•less**
**husband•man** (*plural* **•men**)
**hus•band•ry**
**hush**
**husha•by**
**husk**
**husk•er**
**huski•ly**
**huski•ness**
**husk•like**
**husky** (*adj* **huski•er, huski•est**; *noun, plural* **huskies**)
**huss** dogfish
**hus•sar**
**Huss•ism** (*or* **Huss•it•ism**)
**Huss•ite** heretical Christian
**hus•sy** (*plural* **•sies**)
**hus•tings**
**hus•tle**
**hus•tler**
**hut**
**hutch**
**hut•like**
**hut•ment**
**Hu•tu** (*plural* **•tu** *or* **•tus**) African people
**huz•zah** *Archaic* hurrah
**hwan** *variant of* **won**
**Hwang Hai** (*or* **Huang Hai**) Chinese sea
**Hwang Ho** (*or* **Huang Ho**) Chinese river
**hwyl** poetic fervour
**hya•cinth**
**hya•cin•thine**
**Hyacinthus** mythological character
**Hya•des** (*or* **Hy•ads**) star cluster
**hy•aena** *variant spelling of* **hyena**
**hya•lin** biochemical substance
**hya•line** translucent
**hya•lite** variety of opal
**hya•loid** transparent
**hya•lu•ron•ic acid**
**hya•lu•roni•dase** enzyme
**hy•brid**
**hy•brid•ism**
**hy•brid•ity**
**hy•brid•iz•able** (*or* **•is•able**)
**hy•bridi•za•tion** (*or* **•sa•tion**)
**hy•brid•ize** (*or* **•ise**)
**hy•brid•iz•er** (*or* **•is•er**)
**hy•bris** *variant spelling of* **hubris**
**hy•dan•to•in** crystalline substance
**hy•da•thode** botany term
**hy•da•tid** tapeworm cyst
**Hyde** English town
**Hy•dera•bad**
**hyd•no•car•pate**
**hyd•no•car•pic acid**
**hy•dra** (*plural* **•dras** *or* **•drae**) marine animal
**Hy•dra** mythological character
**hy•drac•id** acid without oxygen
**hy•dran•gea**
**hy•drant**
**hy•dranth** zoology term
**hy•drar•gy•ric**
**hy•drar•gy•rum** mercury
**hy•dras•tine** biochemical compound
**hy•dras•ti•nine** biochemical compound
**hy•dras•tis** plant
**hy•drate**
**hy•drat•ed**
**hy•dra•tion**
**hy•dra•tor**
**hy•drau•lic**
**hy•drau•li•cal•ly**
**hy•drau•lics**
**hy•dra•zine**
**hy•dra•zo•ic acid**
**hy•dria** ancient Greek jar
**hy•dric**
**hy•dride**
**hy•dri•od•ic**
**hy•dro** (*plural* **•dros**)
**hydro•bro•mic**
**hydro•car•bon**
**hydro•cele** pathology term
**hydro•cel•lu•lose**
**hydro•cephal•ic**
**hydro•cepha•lus** (*or* **•cephaly**)
**hydro•chlo•ric**
**hydro•chlo•ride**
**hy•dro•cor•al** (*or* **•cor•al•line**) zoology term
**hydro•cor•ti•sone**
**hydro•cy•an•ic**
**hydro•dy•nam•ic**
**hydro•dy•nami•cal•ly**
**hydro•dy•nam•ics**
**hydro•elec•tric**
**hydro•elec•tric•ity**
**hydro•flu•or•ic**
**hydro•foil**
**hydro•gen**
**hydro•gen•ate**
**hydro•gena•tion**

**hydro•gena•tor**
**hydro•geni•za•tion** (*or* **•sa•tion**)
**hydro•gen•ize** (*or* **•ise**)
**hydro•gen•oly•sis**
**hy•drog•enous**
**hydro•graph**
**hy•drog•ra•pher**
**hydro•graph•ic** (*or* **•graphi•cal**)
**hydro•graphi•cal•ly**
**hy•drog•ra•phy** mapping oceans and rivers
**hy•droid**
**hydro•ki•net•ic** (*or* **•neti•cal**)
**hydro•ki•net•ics**
**hydro•log•ic** (*or* **•logi•cal**)
**hydro•logi•cal•ly**
**hy•drolo•gist**
**hy•drol•ogy**
**hydro•lys•able** (*US* **•lyz•**)
**hy•droly•sate**
**hydro•ly•sa•tion** (*US* **•za•tion**)
**hydro•lyse** (*US* **•lyze**)
**hydro•lys•er** (*US* **•lyz•er**)
**hy•droly•sis**
**hydro•lyte**
**hydro•lyt•ic**
**hydro•mag•net•ics**
**hydro•manc•er**
**hydro•man•cy** divination by water
**hydro•man•tic**
**hydro•mechani•cal**
**hydro•mechan•ics**
**hydro•medu•sa** (*plural* **•sas** *or* **•sae**) zoology term
**hydro•medu•san**
**hydro•mel** mead
**hydro•met•al•lur•gi•cal**
**hydro•met•al•lur•gy**
**hydro•meteor**
**hydro•meteoro•logi•cal**
**hydro•meteor•ol•ogy**
**hy•drom•eter**
**hydro•met•ric** (*or* **•met•ri•cal**)
**hy•drom•etry**
**hydro•path•ic** (*or* **•pathi•cal**)
**hy•dropa•thist** (*or* **hydro•path**)
**hy•dropa•thy** water cure
**hydro•phane** variety of opal
**hydro•phil•ic**
**hy•drophi•lous** botany term
**hy•drophi•ly**
**hydro•pho•bia**
**hydro•pho•bic**
**hydro•phone** underwater microphone
**hydro•phyte**
**hydro•plane**
**hydro•poni•cal•ly**
**hydro•pon•ics**
**hydro•pow•er**
**hydro•scope**
**hydro•ski** hydrofoil on seaplane
**hydro•sphere**
**hydro•stat**
**hydro•stat•ic**
**hydro•stat•ics**
**hydro•sul•phide** (*US* **•fide**)
**hydro•thera•peu•tic**
**hydro•thera•pist**
**hydro•thera•py**
**hydro•trop•ic** growing towards water
**hy•drous**
**hy•drox•ide**
**hy•droxy** chemistry term
**hy•droxyl**
**hydro•zoan** zoology term
**Hy•drus** constellation
**hy•ena** (*or* **•aena**)
**hy•eto•graph** rainfall chart
**hy•eto•graph•ic** (*or* **•graphi•cal**)
**hy•eto•graphi•cal•ly**
**hy•etog•ra•phy**
**Hygeia** Greek goddess
**hy•giene**
**hy•gien•ic**
**hy•gieni•cal•ly**
**hy•gien•ics**
**hy•gien•ist**
**hygro•graph**
**hy•grom•eter** humidity measurer
**hygro•met•ric**
**hygro•met•ri•cal•ly**
**hy•grom•etry**
**hygro•phi•lous** botany term
**hygro•scope**
**hygro•scop•ic**
**hygro•scopi•cal•ly**
**Hyk•sos** (*plural* **•sos**) Asian nomad
**hyla** tree frog
**hy•lo•zo•ism** philosophical doctrine
**hy•lo•zo•ist**
**Hymen** god of marriage
**hy•men** anatomical membrane
**hy•men•al** of the hymen
**hy•meneal** of marriage
**hy•menium** (*plural* **•menia**) fungal tissue
**hy•menop•ter•an** (*plural* **•ter•ans** *or* **•tera**) insect
**hymn**
**hym•nal**
**hym•nic**
**hym•nist** (*or* **hym•no•dist**)
**hym•no•dy**
**hym•nolo•gist**
**hym•nol•ogy**
**hy•oid** bone
**hy•os•cine**
**hy•os•cya•mine**
**hype**
**hyper•ac•id** (*adj*)
**hyper•acid•ity**
**hyper•ac•tive**
**hyper•ac•tiv•ity**
**hyper•aemia** (*US* **•emia**) pathology term
**hyper•aemic** (*US* **•emic**)
**hyper•aes•the•sia** (*US* **•es•**) increased sensitivity
**hyper•aes•thet•ic** (*US* **•es•**)
**hyper•bar•ic** of high pressure
**hyper•ba•ton** reversed word order
**hyper•bo•la** (*plural* **•las** *or* **•lae**) geometrical curve
**hyper•bo•le** exaggeration
**hyper•bol•ic** (*or* **•boli•cal**)
**hyper•bo•lize** (*or* **•lise**) exaggerate
**hyper•bo•loid**
**Hyper•bo•rean** mythological character
**hyper•bo•rean** of extreme north
**hyper•charge**
**hyper•criti•cal**
**hyper•criti•cal•ly**
**hyper•criti•cism**

**hyper•du•lia** veneration for Virgin Mary
**hyper•du•lic** (*or* **hyper•du•li•cal)**
**hyper•gly•cae•mia** (*US* **•cemia)** excess blood sugar
**hyper•gly•cae•mic** (*US* **•cemic)**
**hyper•gol•ic** spontaneously flammable
**hyper•icum** plant
**hyper•in•fla•tion**
**hyper•in•su•lin•ism**
**Hyperion** Greek god
**hyper•ki•nesia** (*or* **•nesis)**
**hyper•ki•net•ic**
**hyper•mar•ket**
**hyper•meter** verse line
**hyper•met•ric** (*or* **•metri•cal)**
**hyper•metro•pia** (*US* **hyper•opia)** long-sightedness
**hyper•metrop•ic**
**hy•perm•ne•sia** psychology term
**hyper•on** elementary particle
**hyper•opia** *US* hypermetropia
**hyper•plasia** enlargement of body part
**hyper•plas•tic**
**hy•perp•noea** (*US* **•nea)** increased breathing rate
**hyper•py•rexia** high fever
**hyper•sen•si•tive**
**hyper•sen•si•tiv•ity**
**hyper•sen•si•tize** (*or* **•tise)** photography term
**hyper•son•ic**
**hyper•space**
**hyper•spa•tial**
**hyper•ten•sion**
**hyper•ten•sive**
**hyper•ther•mia** (*or* **•ther•my)**
**hyper•thy•roid**
**hyper•thy•roid•ism**
**hyper•ton•ic**
**hyper•troph•ic**
**hyper•tro•phy** (*noun, plural* **•phies;** *verb* **•phies, •phy•ing, •phied)**
**hyper•ven•ti•la•tion**
**hyper•vita•mi•no•sis**
**hy•pha** (*plural* **•phae)** part of fungus
**hy•phen**
**hy•phen•ate**
**hy•phena•tion**
**hyp•na•gog•ic** psychology term
**hyp•noid**
**hyp•nol•ogy** study of sleep
**hyp•no•pae•dia**
**hyp•no•sis** (*plural* **•ses)**
**hyp•no•thera•py**
**hyp•not•ic**
**hyp•noti•cal•ly**
**hyp•no•tism**
**hyp•no•tist**
**hyp•no•tize** (*or* **•tise)**
**hypo** (*plural* **hypos)** photographic fixer; syringe
**hypo•acid•ity**
**hypo•caust** Roman heating system
**hypo•cen•tre** (*US* **•ter)**
**hypo•chlor•ite**
**hypo•chlor•ous**
**hypo•chon•dria**
**hypo•chon•dri•ac**
**hypo•chon•dria•cal•ly**
**hypo•chon•drium** (*plural* **•dria)** anatomy term
**hy•poco•rism** pet name
**hy•poc•ri•sy** (*plural* **•sies)**
**hypo•crite**
**hypo•criti•cal**
**hypo•criti•cal•ly**
**hypo•cy•cloid** geometric curve
**hypo•cy•cloi•dal**
**hypo•der•mic**
**hypo•der•mis** biology term
**Hy•po•do•rian** musical term
**hypo•gas•tric**
**hypo•gas•trium** (*plural* **•tria)** anatomy term
**hypo•geal** (*or* **•geous)** botany term
**hypo•gene** geology term
**hy•pog•enous** botany term
**hypo•gen•ic**
**hypo•geum** (*plural* **•gea)** burial vault
**hypo•glos•sal** anatomy term
**hypo•gly•cae•mia** (*US* **•cemia)** low blood sugar
**hypo•gly•caem•ic** (*US* **•cemic)**
**hy•poid**
**hypo•lim•nion** bottom layer in lake
**hypo•ma•nia**
**hypo•man•ic**
**hypo•nas•tic**
**hypo•nas•ty** botany term
**hypo•phys•eal**
**hy•pophy•sis** (*plural* **•ses)** pituitary gland
**hypo•plasia** (*or* **•plas•ty)**
**hypo•sen•si•tize** (*or* **•tise)**
**hypo•stat•ic**
**hypos•ta•sis** (*plural* **•ses)**
**hy•pos•ta•tize** (*or* **•tise)**
**hypo•style** architectural term
**hypo•ten•sion**
**hypo•ten•sive**
**hy•pot•enuse**
**hypo•thala•mus** (*plural* **•mi)**
**hy•poth•ecate** legal term
**hy•poth•eca•tion**
**hy•poth•eca•tor**
**hypo•ther•mia**
**hy•poth•esis** (*plural* **•eses)**
**hy•poth•esize** (*or* **•esise)**
**hypo•theti•cal**
**hypo•theti•cal•ly**
**hypo•thy•roid**
**hypo•thy•roid•ism**
**hypo•ton•ic**
**hy•poxia** oxygen deficiency
**hy•pox•ic**
**hyp•so•met•ric** (*or* **•ri•cal)**
**hyp•som•etry** altitude measurement
**hy•rax** animal
**hy•son** Chinese tea
**hys•sop** herb
**hys•ter•ec•to•my** (*plural* **•mies)**
**hys•te•re•sis** physics term
**hys•te•ria**
**hys•ter•ic**
**hys•teri•cal**
**hys•teri•cal•ly**
**hys•ter•ics**
**hys•tero•gen•ic**
**hys•ter•oid** (*or* **•teroi•dal)**
**hys•ter•oto•my** (*plural* **•mies)** incision into uterus
**hys•tri•co•morph** rodent

# I

**iamb**
**iamb** (*or* **iam•bus**; *plural* **iambs, iam•bi**, *or* **iam•buses**) metrical foot
**iam•bic**
**iam•bi•cal•ly**
**Iap•etus** satellite of Saturn
**iat•ric** (*or* **•ri•cal**) of medicine
**iat•ro•gen•ic**
**iat•ro•genic•ity**
**Iba•dan** Nigerian city
**Iba•gué** Colombian city
**I-beam** girder
**Iberia**
**Iberian**
**ibex** (*plural* **ibexes, ibi•ces**, *or* **ibex**) goat
**Ibibio** (*plural* **Ibibio** *or* **Ibibios**) Nigerian people
**ibis** (*plural* **ibises** *or* **ibis**) bird
**Ibi•za** (*or* **Ivi•za**) Spanish island
**Ibo** (*or* **Igbo**; *plural* **Ibos, Ibo** *or* **Igbos, Igbo**) African people
**Icaria** Greek island
**Icar•ian**
**Icarus** mythological character
**ice**
**ice•berg**
**ice•blink**
**ice•bound**
**ice•box**
**ice•breaker**
**ice•cap**
**ice cream**
**ice•fall**
**Ice•land**
**Ice•land•er**
**Ice•land•ic**
**Iceni** ancient British tribe
**Ichang** (*or* **I-ch'ang**) Chinese port
**I Ching** Chinese book of divination
**Ichi•no•mi•ya** Japanese town
**ich•neu•mon** mongoose; insect
**ich•nite** (*or* **•no•lite**) fossil footprint
**ich•no•graph•ic** (*or* **•graphi•cal**)
**ich•no•graphi•cal•ly**
**ich•nog•ra•phy** ground-plan drawing
**ich•no•logi•cal**
**ich•nol•ogy** study of fossil footprints
**ichor**
**ichor•ous**
**ich•thy•ic** of fishes
**ich•thy•oid** (*or* **•oid•al**)
**ich•thyo•log•ic** (*or* **•logi•cal**)
**ich•thyo•logi•cal•ly**
**ich•thy•olo•gist**
**ich•thy•ol•ogy**
**ich•thy•opha•gous**
**ich•thy•opha•gy**
**ich•thy•or•nis** extinct bird
**ich•thyo•saur** (*or* **•saur•us**; *plural* **•saurs, •saur•uses**, *or* **•sau•ri**)
**ich•thyo•sis** skin disease
**ich•thy•ot•ic**
**ici•cle**
**ici•cled**
**ici•ly**
**ici•ness**
**ic•ing**
**icon** (*or* **ikon**)
**icon•ic** (*or* **iconi•cal**)
**icono•clasm**
**icono•clast**
**icono•clas•tic**
**icono•clas•ti•cal•ly**
**ico•nog•ra•pher**
**icono•graph•ic** (*or* **•graphi•cal**)
**ico•nog•ra•phy** (*plural* **•phies**)
**ico•nola•ter**
**ico•nola•trous**
**ico•nola•try**
**icono•logi•cal**
**ico•nolo•gist**
**ico•nol•ogy**
**icono•mat•ic** representing sounds with pictures
**icono•mati•cism**
**icono•scope**
**ico•sa•he•dral**
**ico•sa•he•dron** (*plural* **•drons** *or* **•dra**)
**ic•ter•ic**
**ic•ter•us** jaundice
**ic•tus** (*plural* **•tuses** *or* **•tus**) poetry term
**icy** (**ici•er, ici•est**)
**I'd** I had; I would
**id**
**Ida** Cretan mountain
**Ida•ho**
**ide** fish
**idea**
**ideal**
**ideal•ism**
**ideal•ist**
**ideal•is•tic**
**ideal•is•ti•cal•ly**
**ideal•ity** (*plural* **•ities**)
**ideali•za•tion** (*or* **•sa•tion**)
**ideal•ize** (*or* **•ise**)
**ideal•iz•er** (*or* **•is•er**)
**ideal•ly**
**ideate** imagine
**idea•tion**
**idea•tion•al**
**idea•tive**
**idea•tum** (*plural* **•ta**) philosophy term
**idée fixe** (*plural* **idées fixes**)
**idem•po•tent** maths term
**iden•tic** diplomacy term
**iden•ti•cal**
**iden•ti•cal•ly**
**iden•ti•cal•ness**
**iden•ti•fi•able**
**iden•ti•fi•able•ness**
**iden•ti•fi•ca•tion**
**iden•ti•fi•er**
**iden•ti•fy** (**•fies, •fy•ing, •fied**)
**Iden•ti•kit** (*Trademark*)
**iden•tity** (*plural* **•tities**)
**ideo•gram** (*or* **•graph**) symbol
**id•eog•ra•phy**

**ideo•logi•cal** (*or* **•log•ic**)
**ideo•logi•cal•ly**
**ideolo•gist** (*or* **ideo•logue**)
**ideol•ogy** (*plural* **•ogies**)
**ideo•mo•tor** physiology term
**ides** day in Roman calendar
**idio•blast** plant cell
**idio•blas•tic**
**idio•cy** (*plural* **•cies**)
**idio•graph•ic**
**idio•lect** individual's language
**idio•lect•al** (*or* **•ic**)
**idi•om**
**idio•mat•ic** (*or* **•mati•cal**)
**idio•mati•cal•ly**
**idio•mor•phic** mineralogy term
**idio•mor•phi•cal•ly**
**idio•mor•phism**
**idio•path•ic**
**idi•opa•thy** (*plural* **•thies**) disease of unknown cause
**idio•phone** musical instrument
**idio•phon•ic**
**idio•syn•cra•sy** (*plural* **•sies**)
**idio•syn•crat•ic**
**idio•syn•crati•cal•ly**
**idi•ot**
**idi•ot•ic**
**idi•oti•cal•ly**
**idle** lazy; *compare* **idol**
**idle•ness**
**idler**
**idly**
**idol** image; *compare* **idle**
**idola•ter** (*fem* **•tress**)
**idola•trize** (*or* **•trise**)
**idola•triz•er** (*or* **•tris•er**)
**idola•trous**
**idola•try**
**idoli•za•tion** (*or* **•sa•tion**)
**idol•ize** (*or* **•ise**)
**idol•iz•er** (*or* **•is•er**)
**idyll** (*or* **idyl**)
**idyl•lic**
**idyl•li•cal•ly**
**idyl•list**
**if**
**Ife** Nigerian town
**Igbo** *variant spelling of* **Ibo**
**ig•loo** (*or* **iglu**; *plural* **•loos** *or* **iglus**)
**ig•ne•ous** geology term
**ig•nes•cent** giving off sparks
**ig•nit•abil•ity** (*or* **•ibil•ity**)
**ig•nit•able** (*or* **•ible**)
**ig•nite**
**ig•nit•er**
**ig•ni•tion**
**ig•ni•tron** physics term
**ig•no•bil•ity** (*or* **•ble•ness**)
**ig•no•ble**
**ig•no•bly**
**ig•no•mini•ous**
**ig•no•miny** (*plural* **•minies**)
**ig•nor•able**
**ig•no•ra•mus** (*plural* **•muses**)
**ig•no•rance**
**ig•no•rant**
**ig•no•ra•tio elen•chi** logic term
**ig•nore**
**ig•nor•er**
**Igraine** (*or* **Ygerne**) King Arthur's mother
**Igua•çú** (*or* **Iguas•sú**) South American river
**igua•na** lizard
**igua•nian**
**iguano•don** dinosaur
**ih•ram** Muslim pilgrim's robes
**IJs•sel•meer** (*or* **Ys•**) Dutch lake
**ikeba•na** Japanese flower arranging
**ikon** *variant spelling of* **icon**
**il•eac** (*or* **•eal**) of ileum; *compare* **iliac**
**Île-de-France**
**il•ei•tis** intestinal disorder
**il•eos•to•my** (*plural* **•mies**) abdominal operation
**Ilesha** Nigerian town
**il•eum** small intestine; *compare* **ilium**
**il•eus** intestinal obstruction
**ilex** tree
**ili•ac** of ilium; *compare* **ileac**
**Ili•ad**
**Ili•ad•ic**
**Il•ium** Troy
**il•ium** (*plural* **•ia**) hip bone; *compare* **ileum**
**ilk**
**Il•kes•ton** Derbyshire town
**I'll** I will; I shall
**ill**
**ill-advised**
**ill-assorted**
**il•la•tive** linguistics term
**Il•la•war•ra** Australian district
**ill-bred**
**ill-breed•ing**
**ill-considered**
**Ille-et-Vilaine** French department
**il•legal**
**il•legal•ity** (*plural* **•ities**)
**il•legali•za•tion** (*or* **•sa•tion**)
**il•legal•ize** (*or* **•ise**)
**il•legal•ly**
**il•leg•ibil•ity** (*or* **•ible•ness**)
**il•leg•ible**
**il•leg•ibly**
**il•legiti•ma•cy** (*or* **•mate•ness**)
**il•legiti•mate**
**il•legiti•mate•ly**
**ill-fated**
**ill-favoured** (*US* **-favored**)
**ill-gotten**
**il•lib•er•al**
**il•lib•er•al•ity** (*or* **•ness, •ism**)
**il•lic•it** illegal; *compare* **elicit**
**il•lim•it•abil•ity** (*or* **•able•ness**)
**il•lim•it•able**
**Il•li•nois**
**Il•li•nois•an** (*or* **•noian, •nois•ian**)
**il•liq•uid**
**il•lit•era•cy** (*plural* **•cies**)
**il•lit•er•ate**
**ill-mannered**
**ill-natured**
**ill•ness**
**il•locu•tion** philosophy term
**il•lo•cu•tion•ary**
**il•logi•cal**
**il•logi•cal•ity** (*or* **•ness**)
**il•logi•cal•ly**
**ill-omened**
**ill-starred**
**ill-timed**
**ill-treat**
**ill-treatment**

**il•lude** deceive; *compare* **allude; elude**
**il•lume**
**il•lu•mi•nance**
**il•lu•mi•nant**
**il•lu•mi•nate**
**il•lu•mi•na•ti** (*sing.* **•to**) enlightened people
**il•lu•mi•na•tion**
**il•lu•mi•na•tive**
**il•lu•mi•na•tor**
**il•lu•mine**
**il•lu•mi•nism** belief in enlightenment
**il•lu•mi•nist**
**ill-use** (*verb*)
**ill-use** (*or* **-usage**)
**il•lu•sion** delusion; *compare* **allusion**
**il•lu•sion•ary** (*or* **•al**)
**il•lu•sion•ism**
**il•lu•sion•ist**
**il•lu•sion•is•tic**
**il•lu•sive** illusory; *compare* **elusive**
**il•lu•so•ri•ly**
**il•lu•so•ri•ness**
**il•lu•sory**
**il•lus•trat•able**
**il•lus•trate**
**il•lus•tra•tion**
**il•lus•tra•tion•al**
**il•lus•tra•tive**
**il•lus•tra•tor**
**il•lus•tri•ous**
**il•lu•via•tion**
**Il•lyria** Adriatic region
**Il•lyr•ian**
**il•men•ite** mineral
**Iloi•lo** Philippine port
**Ilor•in** Nigerian city
**I'm**
**(imaculate)** *incorrect spelling of* **immaculate**
**im•age**
**im•age•ry** (*plural* **•ries**)
**im•agi•nable**
**im•agi•nably**
**im•agi•nal** of an image or imago
**im•agi•nari•ly**
**im•agi•nary**
**im•agi•na•tion**
**im•agi•na•tive**
**im•ag•ine**
**im•ag•in•er**
**im•ag•ism** poetic movement
**im•ag•ist**
**im•ag•is•tic**
**im•ag•is•ti•cal•ly**
**ima•go** (*plural* **•gos, •goes,** *or* **•gi•nes**) adult insect; psychiatry term
**imam** (*or* **imaum**) Islamic priest
**imam•ate**
**ima•ret** Turkish hospice
**im•bal•ance**
**im•becile**
**im•becil•ity** (*plural* **•ities**)
**im•bed** *less common spelling of* **embed**
**im•bibe**
**im•bib•er**
**im•bi•bi•tion**
**im•bri•cate** (*or* **•cat•ed**)
**im•bri•ca•tion**
**im•bro•glio** (*plural* **•glios**)
**im•brue** (*or* **em•**; **•bru•ing, •brued**) to stain; *compare* **imbue**
**im•bue** (**•bu•ing, •bued**) instil; *compare* **imbrue**
**im•id•az•ole**
**im•ide** chemistry term
**im•id•ic**
**(imigrate)** *incorrect spelling of* **immigrate**
**imine** chemistry term
**imi•tabil•ity** (*or* **•table•ness**)
**imi•table**
**imi•tate**
**imi•ta•tion**
**imi•ta•tion•al**
**imi•ta•tive**
**imi•ta•tor**
**im•macu•la•cy** (*or* **•late•ness**)
**im•macu•late**
**im•ma•nence** (*or* **•nen•cy**)
**im•ma•nent** existing within; *compare* **eminent; imminent**
**im•ma•nent•ism** religious belief
**im•ma•terial**
**im•ma•teri•al•ism**
**im•ma•teri•al•ist**
**im•ma•terial•ity** (*or* **•teri•al•ness**)
**im•ma•teri•al•ize** (*or* **•ise**)
**im•ma•ture**
**im•ma•tu•rity** (*or* **•ture•ness**)
**im•meas•ur•abil•ity** (*or* **•able•ness**)
**im•meas•ur•able**
**im•meas•ur•ably**
**im•media•cy** (*or* **im•medi•ate•ness**)
**im•medi•ate**
**im•medi•ate•ly**
**im•medi•cable**
**im•memo•ri•able**
**im•memo•rial**
**im•memo•ri•al•ly**
**im•mense**
**im•mense•ly**
**im•men•si•ty** (*plural* **•ties**)
**im•men•su•rable**
**im•merse**
**im•mers•ible**
**im•mer•sion** immersing; *compare* **emersion**
**im•mer•sion•ism** Christian doctrine
**im•mer•sion•ist**
**im•methodi•cal**
**im•methodi•cal•ly**
**im•mi•grant**
**im•mi•grate** enter country; *compare* **emigrate**
**im•mi•gra•tion**
**im•mi•gra•tory**
**im•mi•gra•tor**
**im•mi•nence**
**im•mi•nent** impending; *compare* **eminent; immanent**
**Im•ming•ham** Humberside port
**im•mis•cibil•ity**
**im•mis•cible**
**im•mis•cibly**
**im•mo•bile**
**im•mo•bil•ism** political policy
**im•mo•bil•ity**
**im•mo•bi•li•za•tion** (*or* **•sa•tion**)
**im•mo•bi•lize** (*or* **•lise**)
**im•mo•bi•liz•er** (*or* **•lis•er**)
**im•mo•der•ate**
**im•mo•der•ate•ly**

**im•mod•era•tion** (*or* **•er•ate•ness)**
**im•mod•est**
**im•mod•es•ty**
**im•mo•late** sacrifice
**im•mo•la•tion**
**im•mo•la•tor**
**im•mor•al** morally bad; *compare* **amoral**
**im•mor•al•ist**
**im•mo•ral•ity** (*plural* **•ities)**
**im•mor•al•ly**
**im•mor•tal**
**im•mor•tal•ity**
**im•mor•tali•za•tion** (*or* **•sa•tion)**
**im•mor•tal•ize** (*or* **•ise)**
**im•mor•tal•iz•er** (*or* **•is•er)**
**im•mor•tal•ly**
**im•mor•telle** everlasting flower
**im•mo•tile**
**im•mo•til•ity**
**im•mov•abil•ity** (*or* **•mov•able•ness)**
**im•mov•able** (*or in legal contexts* **•move•)**
**im•mov•ably**
**im•mune**
**im•mu•nity** (*plural* **•nities)**
**im•mu•ni•za•tion** (*or* **•sa•tion)**
**im•mu•nize** (*or* **•nise)**
**im•mu•niz•er** (*or* **•nis•er)**
**im•mu•no•as•say**
**im•mu•no•chem•is•try**
**im•mu•no•com•pro•mised**
**im•mu•no•genet•ic** (*or* **•geneti•cal)**
**im•mu•no•genet•ics**
**im•mu•no•gen•ic**
**im•mu•no•geni•cal•ly**
**im•mu•no•globu•lin**
**im•mu•no•log•ic** (*or* **•logi•cal)**
**im•mu•no•logi•cal•ly**
**im•mu•nolo•gist**
**im•mu•nol•ogy**
**im•mu•no•reac•tion**
**im•mu•no•sup•pres•sion**
**im•mu•no•sup•pres•sive**
**im•mu•no•thera•py**
**im•mure**
**im•mu•tabil•ity** (*or* **•table•ness)**
**im•mu•table**
**im•mu•tably**
**Imo** Nigerian state
**imp**
**im•pact**
**im•pact•ed**
**im•pac•tion**
**im•pair**
**im•pair•er**
**im•pair•ment**
**im•pa•la** (*plural* **•las** *or* **•la)** antelope
**im•pale**
**im•pale•ment**
**im•pal•er**
**im•pal•pa•bil•ity**
**im•pal•pable**
**im•pal•pably**
**im•pa•na•tion** Christian ritual
**im•pan•el** *US spelling of* empanel
**im•pari•pin•nate** botany term
**im•pari•syl•la•bic**
**im•par•ity** (*plural* **•ities)** disparity
**im•part**
**im•par•ta•tion** (*or* **•part•ment)**
**im•part•er**
**im•par•tial**
**im•par•ti•al•ity** (*or* **•ness)**
**im•par•tial•ly**
**im•part•ibil•ity**
**im•part•ible** legal term
**im•pass•abil•ity** (*or* **•able•ness)**
**im•pass•able**
**im•pass•ably**
**im•passe**
**im•pas•sion**
**im•pas•sioned**
**im•pas•sioned•ly**
**im•pas•sive**
**im•pas•sive•ness** (*or* **•siv•ity)**
**im•pas•ta•tion**
**im•paste** paint thickly
**im•pas•to** paint applied thickly
**im•pa•tience**
**im•pa•ti•ens** (*plural* **•ens)** plant
**im•pa•tient**
**im•peach**
**im•peach•abil•ity**
**im•peach•able**
**im•peach•er**
**im•peach•ment**
**im•pearl**
**im•pec•cabil•ity**
**im•pec•cable**
**im•pec•cably**
**im•pec•cant** sinless
**im•pecu•ni•ous**
**im•pecu•ni•ous•ness** (*or* **•os•ity)**
**im•ped•ance** physics term
**im•pede**
**im•ped•er**
**im•pedi•ment**
**im•pedi•men•ta** impeding objects
**im•pedi•men•tal** (*or* **•tary)**
**im•ped•ing•ly**
**im•pel** **(•pel•ling, •pelled)**
**im•pel•lent**
**im•pel•ler**
**im•pend**
**im•pend•ence** (*or* **•en•cy)**
**im•pend•ing**
**im•pen•etrabil•ity**
**im•pen•etrable**
**im•pen•etrably**
**im•peni•tence** (*or* **•ten•cy, •tent•ness)**
**im•peni•tent**
**im•pera•tive**
**im•pera•tor**
**im•per•cep•tibil•ity** (*or* **•tible•ness)**
**im•per•cep•tible**
**im•per•cep•tibly**
**im•per•cep•tion**
**im•per•cep•tive**
**im•per•cep•tiv•ity** (*or* **•tive•ness)**
**im•per•cipi•ent**
**im•per•cipi•ence**
**im•per•fect**
**im•per•fec•tion**
**im•per•fec•tive**
**im•per•fo•rate**
**im•per•fo•ra•tion**
**im•perial**
**im•peri•al•ism**
**im•peri•al•ist**
**im•peri•al•is•tic**
**im•peri•al•is•ti•cal•ly**

**im•peri•al•ly**
**im•per•il** (**•il•ling, •illed**; *US also* **•il•ing, •iled**)
**im•peri•ous**
**im•per•ish•abil•ity** (*or* **•able•ness**)
**im•per•ish•able**
**im•perium** (*plural* **•peria**) ancient Roman supreme power
**im•per•ma•nence** (*or* **•nen•cy**)
**im•per•ma•nent**
**im•per•meabil•ity** (*or* **•meable•ness**)
**im•per•meable**
**im•per•mis•sibil•ity**
**im•per•mis•sible**
**im•per•son•al**
**im•per•son•al•ity**
**im•per•son•ali•za•tion** (*or* **•sa•tion**)
**im•per•son•al•ize** (*or* **•ise**)
**im•per•son•al•ly**
**im•per•son•ate**
**im•per•sona•tion**
**im•per•sona•tor**
**im•per•ti•nence** (*or* **•nen•cy**)
**im•per•ti•nent**
**im•per•turb•abil•ity** (*or* **•able•ness**)
**im•per•turb•able**
**im•per•turb•ably**
**im•per•tur•ba•tion**
**im•per•vi•ous**
**im•petigi•nous**
**im•peti•go** skin disease
**im•petrate** obtain by prayer
**im•petra•tion**
**im•petra•tive**
**im•petra•tor**
**im•petu•os•ity** (*or* **•ous•ness**)
**im•petu•ous**
**im•petus** (*plural* **•petuses**)
**Im•phal** Indian city
**impi** (*plural* **impi** *or* **impies**) Bantu warrior group
**im•pi•ety** (*plural* **•eties**)
**im•pinge**
**im•pinge•ment**
**im•ping•er**
**im•pi•ous**
**imp•ish**
**im•plac•abil•ity** (*or* **•able•ness**)
**im•plac•able**
**im•plac•ably**
**im•plant**
**im•plan•ta•tion**
**im•plant•er**
**im•plau•sibil•ity** (*or* **•sible•ness**)
**im•plau•sible**
**im•plau•sibly**
**im•plead** prosecute
**im•plead•able**
**im•plead•er**
**im•ple•ment** tool; to carry out
**im•ple•men•tal**
**im•ple•men•ta•tion**
**im•ple•ment•er** (*or* **•or**)
**im•pli•cate**
**im•pli•ca•tion**
**im•plica•tive**
**im•plic•it**
**im•plic•it•ness** (*or* **•plic•ity**)
**(impliment)** *incorrect spelling of* **implement**
**im•plode**
**im•plo•ra•tion**
**im•plo•ra•tory**
**im•plore**
**im•plor•er**
**im•plor•ing•ly**
**im•plo•sion**
**im•plo•sive** phonetics term
**im•ply** (**•plies, •ply•ing, •plied**)
**im•poli•cy** (*plural* **•cies**)
**im•po•lite**
**im•po•lite•ness**
**im•poli•tic**
**im•poli•tic•ly**
**im•pon•dera•bilia**
**im•pon•der•abil•ity** (*or* **•able•ness**)
**im•pon•der•able**
**im•pon•der•ably**
**im•po•nent**
**im•port**
**im•port•able**
**im•por•tance**
**im•por•tant**
**im•por•ta•tion**
**im•port•er**
**im•por•tu•nate**
**im•por•tune**
**im•por•tun•er**
**im•por•tu•nity** (*plural* **•nities**)
**im•pos•able**
**im•pose**
**im•pos•er**
**im•pos•ing**
**im•pos•ing•ly**
**im•po•si•tion**
**im•pos•sibil•ity** (*plural* **•ities**)
**im•pos•sible**
**im•pos•sibly**
**im•post** customs duty
**im•pos•tor** (*or* **•post•er**)
**im•pos•trous** (*or* **•tur•ous**)
**im•pos•ture**
**im•po•tence** (*or* **•ten•cy, •tent•ness**)
**im•po•tent**
**im•pound**
**im•pound•age** (*or* **•ment**)
**im•pound•er**
**im•pov•er•ish**
**im•pov•er•ish•er**
**im•pov•er•ish•ment**
**im•prac•ti•cabil•ity** (*or* **•cable•ness**)
**im•prac•ti•cable** not feasible
**im•prac•ti•cably**
**im•prac•ti•cal** not practical
**im•prac•ti•cal•ity** (*or* **•ness**)
**im•prac•ti•cal•ly**
**im•pre•cate**
**im•pre•ca•tion**
**im•pre•ca•tory**
**im•pre•cise**
**im•pre•ci•sion** (*or* **•cise•ness**)
**im•preg•nabil•ity** (*or* **•nable•ness**)
**im•preg•nable** (*or* **im•preg•na•table**)
**im•preg•nate**
**im•preg•na•tion**
**im•preg•na•tor**
**im•pre•sa** (*or* **im•prese**) emblem
**im•pre•sa•rio** (*plural* **•rios**)
**im•pre•scrip•tibil•ity**
**im•pre•scrip•tible** legal term
**im•press**
**im•press•er**

**im•press•ible**
**im•pres•sion**
**im•pres•sion•abil•ity** (*or* **•able•ness**)
**im•pres•sion•able**
**im•pres•sion•al**
**im•pres•sion•al•ly**
**im•pres•sion•ism**
**im•pres•sion•ist**
**im•pres•sion•is•tic**
**im•pres•sive**
**im•pres•sive•ness**
**im•press•ment** conscription
**im•prest**
**im•pri•ma•tur** sanction
**im•print**
**im•print•er**
**im•print•ing**
**im•pris•on**
**im•pris•on•er**
**im•pris•on•ment**
**im•prob•abil•ity** (*or* **•able•ness**)
**im•prob•able**
**im•pro•bity** (*plural* **•bities**)
**im•promp•tu**
**im•prop•er**
**im•pro•pri•ate** transfer to laity
**im•pro•pria•tion**
**im•pro•pria•tor**
**im•pro•pri•ety** (*plural* **•eties**)
**im•prov•abil•ity** (*or* **•able•ness**)
**im•prov•able**
**im•prove**
**im•prove•ment**
**im•prov•er**
**im•provi•dence**
**im•provi•dent**
**im•prov•ing•ly**
**im•provi•sa•tion**
**im•provi•sa•tion•al**
**im•pro•vise**
**im•pro•vis•er**
**im•pru•dence**
**im•pru•dent** unwise; *compare* **impudent**
**im•pu•dence** (*or* **•den•cy**)
**im•pu•dent** impertinent; *compare* **imprudent**
**im•pugn**
**im•pug•na•tion** (*or* **•pugn•ment**)
**im•pugn•er**
**im•pu•is•sance**
**im•pu•is•sant**
**im•pulse**
**im•pul•sion**
**im•pul•sive**
**im•pul•sive•ness**
**im•pu•nity** (*plural* **•nities**)
**im•pure**
**im•pu•rity** (*plural* **•rities**)
**im•put•abil•ity** (*or* **•able•ness**)
**im•put•able**
**im•pu•ta•tion**
**im•pu•ta•tive**
**im•pute**
**im•put•er**
**in**
**in•abil•ity** (*plural* **•ities**)
**in ab•sen•tia** *Latin* in the absence of
**in•ac•ces•sibil•ity** (*or* **•sible•ness**)
**in•ac•ces•sible**
**in•ac•ces•sibly**
**in•ac•cu•ra•cy** (*plural* **•cies**)
**in•ac•cu•rate**
**in•ac•tion**
**in•ac•ti•vate**
**in•ac•ti•va•tion**
**in•ac•tive**
**in•ac•tiv•ity** (*or* **•tive•ness**)
**in•ad•equa•cy** (*plural* **•cies**)
**in•ad•equate**
**in•ad•mis•sibil•ity**
**in•ad•mis•si•ble**
**in•ad•mis•sibly**
**in•ad•vert•ence** (*or* **•en•cy**)
**in•ad•vert•ent**
**in•ad•vis•abil•ity** (*or* **•able•ness**)
**in•ad•vis•able**
**in•ad•vis•ably**
**in•al•ien•abil•ity** (*or* **•able•ness**)
**in•al•ien•able**
**in•al•ien•ably**
**in•al•ter•abil•ity** (*or* **•able•ness**)
**in•al•ter•able**
**in•al•ter•ably**
**in•amo•ra•ta** (*masc* **•to**; *plural* **•tas** *or* **•tos**) lover
**in•ane**
**in•ani•mate**
**ina•ni•tion**
**in•ani•mate•ness** (*or* **•ma•tion**)
**in•an•ity** (*plural* **•ities**)
**in•ap•pli•cabil•ity** (*or* **•cable•ness**)
**in•ap•pli•cable**
**in•ap•po•site**
**in•ap•pre•ciable**
**in•ap•pre•cia•tive**
**in•ap•pre•hen•sive**
**in•ap•proach•abil•ity**
**in•ap•proach•able**
**in•ap•pro•pri•ate**
**in•ap•pro•pri•ate•ness**
**in•apt** inappropriate; *compare* **inept**
**in•ap•ti•tude** (*or* **•apt•ness**)
**in•arch** botany term
**in•ar•ticu•late**
**in•ar•tis•tic**
**in•ar•tis•ti•cal•ly**
**in•as•much**
**in•at•ten•tion** (*or* **•tive•ness**)
**in•at•ten•tive**
**in•audibil•ity** (*or* **•audible•ness**)
**in•audible**
**in•audibly**
**in•augu•ral**
**in•augu•rate**
**in•augu•ra•tion**
**in•augu•ra•tor**
**in•augu•ra•tory**
**in•aus•pi•cious**
**in•board**
**in•born**
**in•bound**
**in•bred**
**in•breed** (**•breed•ing**, **•bred**)
**Inca** (*plural* **Inca** *or* **Incas**)
**In•caic**
**in•cal•cu•labil•ity** (*or* **•lable•ness**)
**in•cal•cu•lable**
**in•cal•cu•lably**
**in•ca•les•cence**
**in•ca•les•cent** chemistry term
**in cam•era** *Latin* in private
**In•can**
**in•can•desce**
**in•can•des•cence** (*or* **•cen•cy**)
**in•can•des•cent**
**in•can•ta•tion**

**in•can•ta•tion•al** (*or* **•ta•tory**)
**in•ca•pabil•ity** (*plural* **•ities**)
**in•ca•pable**
**in•ca•pably**
**in•ca•paci•tate**
**in•ca•paci•ta•tion**
**in•ca•pac•ity** (*plural* **•ities**)
**in•cap•su•late** *less common spelling of* **encapsulate**
**in•car•cer•ate**
**in•car•cera•tion**
**in•car•cera•tor**
**in•car•di•nate**
**in•car•di•na•tion**
**in•car•nate**
**in•car•na•tion**
**in•cau•tious**
**in•cau•tious•ness** (*or* **•cau•tion**)
**in•cen•dia•rism**
**in•cen•di•ary** (*plural* **•aries**)
**in•cense**
**in•cen•so•ry** (*plural* **•ries**) incense-burner
**in•cen•tive**
**in•cept**
**in•cep•tion**
**in•cep•tive**
**in•cept•or**
**in•cer•ti•tude**
**in•ces•san•cy** (*or* **•sant•ness**)
**in•ces•sant**
**in•cest**
**in•ces•tu•ous**
**inch**
**inch•meal** inch by inch
**in•cho•ate**
**in•choa•tion**
**in•choa•tive**
**In•chon** (*or* **•cheon**) South Korean port
**inch•worm**
**in•ci•dence**
**in•ci•dent**
**in•ci•den•tal**
**in•ci•den•tal•ly**
**in•cin•er•ate**
**in•cin•era•tion**
**in•cin•era•tor**
**in•cipi•ence** (*or* **•en•cy**)
**in•cipi•ent**
**in•ci•pit** *Latin* here begins
**in•cise**
**in•ci•sion**
**in•ci•sive**
**in•ci•sor**
**in•ci•sur•al**
**in•ci•sure**
**in•ci•ta•tion**
**in•cite**
**in•cite•ment**
**in•cit•er**
**in•cit•ing•ly**
**in•ci•vil•ity** (*plural* **•ities**)
**in•clem•en•cy** (*or* **•ent•ness**)
**in•clem•ent**
**in•clin•able**
**in•cli•na•tion**
**in•cli•na•tion•al**
**in•cline**
**in•clin•er**
**in•cli•nom•eter**
**in•close** *less common spelling of* **enclose**
**in•clos•ure** *less common spelling of* **enclosure**
**in•clud•able** (*or* **•ible**)
**in•clude**
**in•clu•sion**
**in•clu•sive**
**in•co•er•cible**
**in•cog•ni•to** (*fem* **•ta**; *plural* **•tos** *or* **•tas**)
**in•cog•ni•zance**
**in•cog•ni•zant**
**in•co•her•ence** (*or* **•en•cy, •ent•ness**)
**in•co•her•ent**
**in•com•bus•tibil•ity** (*or* **•tible•ness**)
**in•com•bus•tible**
**in•com•bus•tibly**
**in•come**
**in•com•ing**
**in•com•men•su•rabil•ity** (*or* **•rable•ness**)
**in•com•men•su•rable**
**in•com•men•su•rably**
**in•com•men•su•rate**
**in•com•mode**
**in•com•mo•di•ous**
**in•com•mod•ity** (*plural* **•ities**)
**in•com•mu•ni•cabil•ity** (*or* **•cable•ness**)
**in•com•mu•ni•cable**
**in•com•mu•ni•cably**
**in•com•mu•ni•ca•do**
**in•com•mu•ni•ca•tive**
**in•com•mut•abil•ity** (*or* **•able•ness**)
**in•com•mut•able**
**in•com•mut•ably**
**in•com•pa•rabil•ity** (*or* **•rable•ness**)
**in•com•pa•rable**
**in•com•pa•rably**
**in•com•pat•ibil•ity** (*or* **•ible•ness**)
**in•com•pat•ible**
**in•com•pat•ibly**
**in•com•pe•tence** (*or* **•ten•cy**)
**in•com•pe•tent**
**in•com•plete**
**in•com•plete•ness** (*or* **•ple•tion**)
**in•com•pli•ance** (*or* **•an•cy**)
**in•com•pli•ant**
**in•com•pre•hen•sibil•ity** (*or* **•sible•ness**)
**in•com•pre•hen•sible**
**in•com•pre•hen•sibly**
**in•com•pre•hen•sion**
**in•com•pre•hen•sive**
**in•com•press•ibil•ity** (*or* **•ible•ness**)
**in•com•press•ible**
**in•com•press•ibly**
**in•com•put•abil•ity**
**in•com•put•able**
**in•con•ceiv•abil•ity** (*or* **•able•ness**)
**in•con•ceiv•able**
**in•con•ceiv•ably**
**in•con•clu•sive**
**in•con•den•sabil•ity** (*or* **•sibil•**)
**in•con•den•sable** (*or* **•sible**)
**in•con•form•ity**
**in•con•gru•ity** (*plural* **•ities**)
**in•con•gru•ous** (*or* **•ent**)
**in•con•gru•ous•ness** (*or* **•gru•ence**)
**in•con•sequence** (*or* **•sequent•ness**)
**in•con•sequen•tial** (*or* **•sequent**)
**in•con•sequen•ti•al•ity** (*or* **•tial•ness**)
**in•con•sequen•tial•ly**
**in•con•sid•er•able**
**in•con•sid•er•ate**
**in•con•sid•era•tion**

**in•con•sist•en•cy** (*plural* **•cies**)
**in•con•sist•ent**
**in•con•sol•abil•ity** (*or* **•able•ness**)
**in•con•sol•able**
**in•con•sol•ably**
**in•con•so•nance**
**in•con•so•nant**
**in•con•spicu•ous**
**in•con•stan•cy** (*plural* **•cies**)
**in•con•stant**
**in•con•sum•able**
**in•con•sum•ably**
**in•con•test•abil•ity** (*or* **•able•ness**)
**in•con•test•able**
**in•con•test•ably**
**in•con•ti•nence** (*or* **•nen•cy**)
**in•con•ti•nent**
**in•con•tro•vert•ibil•ity** (*or* **•ible•ness**)
**in•con•tro•vert•ible**
**in•con•tro•vert•ibly**
**in•con•ven•ience**
**in•con•ven•ient**
**in•con•vert•ibil•ity** (*or* **•ible•ness**)
**in•con•vert•ible**
**in•con•vert•ibly**
**in•con•vin•cibil•ity** (*or* **•cible•ness**)
**in•con•vin•cible**
**in•co•ordi•nate**
**in•co•ordi•na•tion**
**in•cor•po•rable**
**in•cor•po•rate**
**in•cor•po•rat•ed**
**in•cor•po•ra•tion**
**in•cor•po•ra•tive**
**in•cor•po•ra•tor**
**in•cor•po•real**
**in•cor•po•real•ly**
**in•cor•po•reity** (*or* **•real•ity**)
**in•cor•rect**
**in•cor•rect•ness**
**in•cor•ri•gibil•ity** (*or* **•gible•ness**)
**in•cor•ri•gible**
**in•cor•ri•gibly**
**in•cor•rupt**
**in•cor•rupt•ibil•ity** (*or* **•ible•ness**)
**in•cor•rupt•ible**
**in•cor•rupt•ibly**
**in•cras•sate** (*or* **•sat•ed**) thickened
**in•cras•sa•tion**
**in•creas•able**
**in•crease**
**in•creas•ing•ly**
**in•creas•er**
**in•cred•ibil•ity** (*or* **•ible•ness**)
**in•cred•ible**
**in•cred•ibly**
**in•cre•du•lity**
**in•credu•lous**
**in•cre•ment**
**in•cre•men•tal**
**in•cres•cent**
**in•cre•tion** secretion into bloodstream
**in•cre•tion•ary** (*or* **•tory**)
**in•crimi•nate**
**in•crimi•na•tion**
**in•crimi•na•tor**
**in•crimi•na•tory**
**in•cross** inbreed
**in•crust** *variant spelling of* **encrust**
**in•cu•bate**
**in•cu•ba•tion**
**in•cu•ba•tion•al**
**in•cu•ba•tive** (*or* **•tory**)
**in•cu•ba•tor**
**in•cu•bus** (*plural* **•bi** *or* **•buses**) male demon
**in•cu•date** (*or* **•dal**) of incus
**in•cul•cate**
**in•cul•ca•tion**
**in•cul•ca•tor**
**in•cul•pabil•ity** (*or* **•pable•ness**)
**in•cul•pable**
**in•cul•pate**
**in•cul•pa•tion**
**in•cul•pa•tive** (*or* **in•cul•pa•to•ry**)
**in•cum•ben•cy** (*plural* **•cies**)
**in•cum•bent**
**in•cu•nabu•la** (*sing.* **•lum**) early books
**in•cu•nabu•lar**
**in•cur** (**•cur•ring, •curred**)
**in•cur•abil•ity** (*or* **•able•ness**)
**in•cur•able** not curable; *compare* **incurrable**
**in•cu•ri•os•ity** (*or* **•ous•ness**)
**in•cu•ri•ous**
**in•cur•rable** liable to incur; *compare* **incurable**
**in•cur•rence**
**in•cur•rent**
**in•cur•sion**
**in•cur•sive**
**in•cur•vate**
**in•cur•va•tion**
**in•cur•va•ture**
**in•curve**
**in•cus** (*plural* **•cu•des**) ear bone
**in•cuse** design on coin
**Ind** India
**in•da•mine** chemical compound
**in•debt•ed**
**in•debt•ed•ness**
**in•de•cen•cy** (*plural* **•cies**)
**in•de•cent**
**in•de•cidu•ous**
**in•de•ci•pher•abil•ity** (*or* **•able•ness**)
**in•de•ci•pher•able**
**in•de•ci•sion**
**in•de•ci•sive**
**in•de•clin•able**
**in•deco•rous**
**in•de•co•rum**
**in•deed**
**in•de•fati•gabil•ity** (*or* **•gable•ness**)
**in•de•fati•gable**
**in•de•fati•gably**
**in•de•fea•sibil•ity** (*or* **•sible•ness**)
**in•de•fea•sible**
**in•de•fea•sibly**
**in•de•fen•sibil•ity** (*or* **•sible•ness**)
**in•de•fen•sible**
**in•de•fin•able**
**in•de•fin•ably**
**in•defi•nite**
**in•de•his•cence**
**in•de•his•cent** botany term
**in•del•ibil•ity** (*or* **•ible•ness**)
**in•del•ible**
**in•del•ibly**
**in•deli•ca•cy** (*plural* **•cies**)
**in•deli•cate**
**in•dem•ni•fi•ca•tion**
**in•dem•ni•fi•er**

**in•dem•ni•fy** (•fies, •fy•ing, •fied)
**in•dem•nity** (*plural* •nities)
**in•de•mon•strable**
**in•dene** chemical compound
**in•dent**
**in•den•ta•tion**
**in•dent•er** (*or* **den•tor**)
**in•den•tion** indentation
**in•den•ture**
**in•den•ture•ship**
**in•de•pend•ence**
**in•de•pend•en•cy** (*plural* •cies)
**in•de•pend•ent**
**in•de•scrib•abil•ity** (*or* •able•ness)
**in•de•scrib•able**
**in•de•scrib•ably**
**in•de•struct•ibil•ity** (*or* •ible•ness)
**in•de•struct•ible**
**in•de•struct•ibly**
**in•de•ter•mi•nable**
**in•de•ter•mi•na•cy** (*or* •na•tion, •nate•ness)
**in•de•ter•mi•nate**
**in•de•ter•min•ism** philosophy term
**in•de•ter•min•ist**
**in•de•ter•min•is•tic**
**in•dex** (*plural* •dexes *or esp. in mathematical contexts* •di•ces)
**in•dex•er**
**in•dexi•cal**
**index-linked**
**In•dia**
**In•dian**
**In•di•ana** US state
**In•di•an•apo•lis** US city
**In•dic** language group
**in•di•can** chemical compound
**in•di•cant**
**in•di•cat•able**
**in•di•cate**
**in•di•ca•tion**
**in•dica•tive**
**in•di•ca•tor**
**in•dica•tory**
**in•di•ces** *plural of* **index**
**in•di•cia** (*sing.* •cium) distinguishing markings
**in•di•cial**
**in•dict** accuse; *compare* indite
**in•dict•able**
**in•dictee**
**in•dict•er** (*or* •dic•tor)
**in•dict•ment**
**In•dies**
**in•dif•fer•ence**
**in•dif•fer•ent**
**in•dif•fer•ent•ism** indifference to religion
**in•dif•fer•ent•ist**
**in•di•gence**
**in•di•gene** (*or* •gen) a native
**in•dig•enous**
**in•dig•enous•ness** (*or* in•di•gen•ity)
**in•di•gent**
**in•di•gest•ibil•ity** (*or* •ible•ness)
**in•di•gest•ible**
**in•di•ges•tion**
**in•di•ges•tive**
**in•dign** undeserving
**in•dig•nant**
**in•dig•na•tion**
**in•dig•nity** (*plural* •nities)
**in•di•go** (*plural* •gos *or* •goes)
**in•di•goid**
**in•di•got•ic**
**in•di•rect**
**in•di•rec•tion**
**in•di•rect•ness**
**in•dis•cern•ible**
**in•dis•cern•ibly**
**in•dis•ci•pline**
**in•dis•creet** tactless
**in•dis•crete** undivided
**in•dis•cre•tion**
**in•dis•cre•tion•ary**
**in•dis•crimi•nate**
**in•dis•crimi•na•tion**
**in•dis•crimi•na•tive**
**in•dis•pen•sabil•ity** (*or* •sable•ness)
**in•dis•pen•sable**
**in•dis•pen•sably**
**in•dis•pose**
**in•dis•posed**
**in•dis•po•si•tion**
**in•dis•put•abil•ity** (*or* •able•ness)
**in•dis•put•able**
**in•dis•put•ably**
**in•dis•sol•ubil•ity** (*or* •uble•ness)
**in•dis•sol•uble**
**in•dis•sol•ubly**
**in•dis•tinct**
**in•dis•tinc•tive**
**in•dis•tin•guish•abil•ity** (*or* •able•ness)
**in•dis•tin•guish•able**
**in•dis•tin•guish•ably**
**in•dite** *Archaic* write; *compare* **indict**
**in•dium** chemical element
**in•di•vid•ual**
**in•di•vidu•al•ism**
**in•di•vidu•al•ist**
**in•di•vidu•al•is•tic**
**in•di•vidu•al•is•ti•cal•ly**
**in•di•vidu•al•ity** (*plural* •ities)
**in•di•vidu•ali•za•tion** (*or* •sa•tion)
**in•di•vidu•al•ize** (*or* •ise)
**in•di•vidu•al•iz•er** (*or* •is•er)
**in•di•vid•ual•ly**
**in•di•vidu•ate**
**in•di•vidu•ation**
**in•di•vid•ua•tor**
**in•di•vis•ibil•ity** (*or* •ible•ness)
**in•di•vis•ible**
**in•di•vis•ibly**
**Indo•china** (*or* **Indo-China**)
**Indo•chinese** (*or* **Indo-Chinese**)
**in•do•cile**
**in•do•cil•ity**
**in•doc•tri•nate**
**in•doc•tri•na•tion**
**in•doc•tri•na•tor**
**Indo-European**
**in•dole** (*or* •dol) chemical compound
**in•dole•acetic acid**
**in•dole•bu•tyr•ic acid**
**in•do•lence**
**in•do•lent**
**In•dolo•gist**
**In•dol•ogy**
**in•do•metha•cin**
**in•domi•tabil•ity** (*or* •table•ness)
**in•domi•table**
**in•domi•tably**

**In•do•nesia**
**In•do•nesian**
**in•door** (*adj*)
**in•doors** (*adv*)
**Indo-Pacific**
**in•do•phenol**
**In•dore** Indian city
**in•dorse** *variant spelling of* endorse
**in•dox•yl** chemical compound
**in•draught** (*US* **•draft**)
**in•drawn**
**Indre** French department
**Indre-et-Loire** French department
**in•dris** (*or* **•dri**) animal
**in•du•bi•tabil•ity** (*or* **•table•ness**)
**in•du•bi•table**
**in•du•bi•tably**
**in•duce**
**in•duce•ment**
**in•duc•er**
**in•duc•ible**
**in•duct**
**in•duct•ance** electrical property
**in•duc•tee** *US* military conscript
**(inducter)** *incorrect spelling of* **inductor**
**in•duc•tile** not pliant
**in•duc•til•ity**
**in•duc•tion**
**in•duc•tion•al**
**in•duc•tive**
**in•duc•tor**
**in•dulge**
**in•dul•gence**
**in•dul•gent**
**in•dulg•er**
**in•dulg•ing•ly**
**in•du•line** (*or* **•lin**) dye
**in•dult** Catholic dispensation
**in•du•pli•cate** (*or* **•cat•ed**)
**in•du•pli•ca•tion**
**in•du•rate**
**in•du•ra•tion**
**in•du•ra•tive**
**In•dus** Asian river
**in•du•sial**
**in•du•sium** (*plural* **•sia**) membrane
**in•dus•trial**
**in•dus•tri•al•ism**
**in•dus•tri•al•ist**
**in•dus•tri•ali•za•tion** (*or* **•sa•tion**)
**in•dus•tri•al•ize** (*or* **•ise**)
**in•dus•tri•al•ly**
**in•dus•tri•ous**
**in•dus•try** (*plural* **•tries**)
**in•dwell** (**•dwell•ing, •dwelt**)
**in•earth** bury
**in•ebri•ant**
**in•ebri•ate**
**in•ebri•at•ed**
**in•ebria•tion**
**in•ebri•ety**
**in•ed•ibil•ity**
**in•ed•ible**
**in•ed•it•ed**
**in•edu•cabil•ity**
**in•edu•cable**
**in•ef•fabil•ity** (*or* **•fable•ness**)
**in•ef•fable**
**in•ef•fably**
**in•ef•face•abil•ity**
**in•ef•face•able**
**in•ef•fec•tive**
**in•ef•fec•tual**
**in•ef•fec•tu•al•ity** (*or* **•ness**)
**in•ef•fec•tual•ly**
**in•ef•fi•ca•cious**
**in•ef•fi•ca•cy** (*or* **•ca•cious•ness**)
**in•ef•fi•cien•cy**
**in•ef•fi•cient**
**in•elas•tic**
**in•elas•tic•al•ly**
**in•elas•tic•ity**
**in•el•egance** (*or* **•egan•cy**)
**in•el•egant**
**in•eli•gibil•ity** (*or* **•gible•ness**)
**in•eli•gible**
**in•elo•quence**
**in•elo•quent**
**in•eluc•tabil•ity**
**in•eluc•table**
**in•eluc•tably**
**in•ept** incompetent; *compare* inapt
**in•epti•tude**
**in•equal•ity** (*plural* **•ities**)
**in•equi•table**
**in•equi•tably**
**in•equi•ty** (*plural* **•ties**)
**in•eradi•cable**
**in•eradi•cably**
**in•ert**
**in•er•tia**
**in•er•tial**
**in•es•cap•able**
**in•es•cap•ably**
**in•es•cutch•eon** heraldic term
**in esse** *Latin* actually existing
**in•es•sen•tial**
**in•es•sen•ti•al•ity**
**in•es•sive** linguistics term
**in•es•ti•mabil•ity** (*or* **•mable•ness**)
**in•es•ti•mable**
**in•es•ti•mably**
**in•evi•tabil•ity** (*or* **•table•ness**)
**in•evi•table**
**in•evi•tably**
**in•ex•act**
**in•ex•acti•tude**
**in•ex•cus•abil•ity** (*or* **•able•ness**)
**in•ex•cus•able**
**in•ex•cus•ably**
**in•ex•haust•ibil•ity** (*or* **•ible•ness**)
**in•ex•haust•ible**
**in•ex•haust•ibly**
**in•ex•ist•ence** (*or* **•en•cy**)
**in•ex•ist•ent**
**in•exo•rabil•ity** (*or* **•rable•ness**)
**in•exo•rable**
**in•exo•rably**
**in•ex•pe•di•ence** (*or* **•en•cy**)
**in•ex•pe•di•ent**
**in•ex•pen•sive**
**in•ex•pe•ri•ence**
**in•ex•pe•ri•enced**
**in•ex•pert**
**in•ex•pi•able**
**in•ex•pi•ably**
**in•ex•pli•cabil•ity** (*or* **•cable•ness**)
**in•ex•pli•cable**
**in•ex•pli•cably**
**in•ex•plic•it**
**in•ex•press•ibil•ity** (*or* **•ible•ness**)

**in•ex•press•ible**
**in•ex•press•ibly**
**in•ex•pres•sive**
**in•ex•ten•sibil•ity**
**in•ex•ten•sible**
**in•ex•tin•guish•able**
**in•ex•tir•pable**
**in ex•tre•mis** *Latin* in extremity
**in•ex•tri•cabil•ity** (*or* **•cable•ness**)
**in•ex•tri•cable**
**in•ex•tri•cably**
**in•fal•libil•ity** (*or* **•lible•ness**)
**in•fal•lible**
**in•fal•libly**
**in•fam•ize** (*or* **•ise**) make infamous
**in•fa•mous**
**in•fa•my** (*plural* **•mies**)
**in•fan•cy** (*plural* **•cies**)
**in•fant**
**in•fan•ta** Spanish princess
**in•fan•te** Spanish prince
**in•fan•ti•cid•al**
**in•fan•ti•cide**
**in•fan•tile**
**in•fan•ti•lism**
**in•fan•til•ity**
**in•fan•try** (*plural* **•tries**)
**in•fantry•man** (*plural* **•men**)
**in•farct** dead tissue
**in•farct•ed**
**in•farc•tion**
**in•fare** *Dialect* wedding reception
**in•fatu•ate**
**in•fatu•at•ed**
**in•fatu•at•ed•ly**
**in•fat•ua•tion**
**in•fect**
**in•fec•tion**
**in•fec•tious**
**in•fec•tious•ness**
**in•fec•tive**
**in•fec•tive•ness** (*or* **•tiv•ity**)
**in•fec•tor** (*or* **•fect•er**)
**in•fe•cund**
**in•fe•cun•dity**
**in•fe•lici•tous**
**in•fe•lic•ity** (*plural* **•ities**)
**in•fer** (**•fer•ring, •ferred**)
**in•fer•able** (*or* **•ible, •rable, •rible**)
**in•fer•ence**
**in•fer•en•tial**
**in•fe•ri•or**
**in•fe•ri•or•ity**
**in•fer•nal**
**in•fer•nal•ity**
**in•fer•nal•ly**
**in•fer•no** (*plural* **•nos**)
**in•ferred**
**in•fer•rer**
**in•fer•ring**
**in•fer•tile**
**in•fer•til•ity**
**in•fest**
**in•fes•ta•tion**
**in•fest•er**
**in•fi•del**
**in•fi•del•ity** (*plural* **•ities**)
**in•field**
**in•fielder**
**in•fighter**
**in•fighting**
**in•fil•trate**
**in•fil•tra•tion**
**in•fil•tra•tive**
**in•fil•tra•tor**
**in•fi•nite**
**in•fi•nite•ly**
**in•fini•tesi•mal**
**in•fini•tesi•mal•ly**
**in•fini•ti•val**
**in•fini•tive**
**in•fini•tude**
**in•fin•ity** (*plural* **•ities**)
**in•firm**
**in•fir•ma•ry** (*plural* **•ries**)
**in•fir•mity** (*plural* **•mities**)
**in•fix**
**in•fix•ion**
**in•flame**
**in•flam•er**
**in•flam•ing•ly**
**in•flam•mabil•ity** (*or* **•mable•ness**)
**in•flam•mable**
**in•flam•ma•tion**
**in•flam•ma•to•ri•ly**
**in•flam•ma•tory**
**in•flat•able**
**in•flate**
**in•flat•ed•ly**
**in•flat•er** (*or* **•fla•tor**)
**in•fla•tion**
**in•fla•tion•ary**
**in•fla•tion•ism**
**in•fla•tion•ist**
**in•flect**
**in•flect•ed•ness**
**in•flec•tion** (*or* **•flex•ion**)
**in•flec•tion•al** (*or* **•flex•ion•**)
**in•flec•tive**
**in•flec•tor**
**in•flexed** botany term
**in•flex•ibil•ity** (*or* **•ible•ness**)
**in•flex•ible**
**in•flex•ibly**
**in•flex•ion** *variant spelling of* **inflection**
**in•flict**
**in•flict•er** (*or* **•flic•tor**)
**in•flic•tion**
**in•flic•tive**
**in•flo•res•cence**
**in•flo•res•cent**
**in•flow**
**in•flu•ence**
**in•flu•ence•able**
**in•flu•enc•er**
**in•flu•ent** flowing in
**in•flu•en•tial**
**in•flu•en•tial•ly**
**in•flu•en•za**
**in•flu•en•zal**
**in•flux**
**info** *Slang* information
**in•fold** *variant spelling of* **enfold**
**(inforce)** *incorrect spelling of* **enforce**
**in•form**
**in•for•mal**
**in•for•mal•ity** (*plural* **•ities**)
**in•for•mal•ly**
**in•form•ant**
**in•for•ma•tion**
**in•for•ma•tion•al**
**in•forma•tive** (*or* **•tory**)
**in•forma•tive•ly**
**in•form•ed•ly**
**in•form•er**
**in•form•ing•ly**
**infra•cos•tal** anatomy term
**in•fract** violate
**in•frac•tion**
**in•frac•tor**
**in•fra dig**
**infra•lap•sar•ian** theology term
**infra•lap•sari•an•ism**

**in•fran•gibil•ity** (*or* **•gible•ness**)
**in•fran•gible**
**infra•red**
**infra•son•ic**
**infra•soni•cal•ly**
**infra•sound**
**infra•struc•ture**
**in•fre•quen•cy** (*or* **•quence**)
**in•fre•quent**
**in•fringe**
**in•fringe•ment**
**in•fring•er**
**in•fu•lae** (*sing.* **•la**) ribbons on bishop's mitre
**in•fun•dibu•lar** (*or* **•late**)
**in•fun•dibu•li•form**
**in•fun•dibu•lum** (*plural* **•la**) anatomical part
**in•furi•ate**
**in•furi•at•ing•ly**
**in•furia•tion**
**in•fus•cate** (*or* **•cat•ed**) tinged with brown
**in•fuse**
**in•fus•er**
**in•fu•sibil•ity** (*or* **•sible•ness**)
**in•fu•sible**
**in•fu•sion**
**in•fu•sion•ism** theology term
**in•fu•sion•ist**
**in•fu•sive**
**in•fu•so•rial**
**in•gath•er**
**in•gen•ious** skilful; *compare* **ingenuous**
**in•gé•nue** naive girl
**in•genu•ity** (*plural* **•ities**)
**in•genu•ous** naive; *compare* **ingenious**
**in•gest**
**in•ges•ta** (*plural*) food
**in•gest•ible**
**in•ges•tion**
**in•ges•tive**
**in•gle**
**ingle•nook**
**in•glo•ri•ous**
**in•go•ing**
**in•got**
**in•graft** *variant spelling of* **engraft**
**in•grain** (*or* **en•**)
**in•grained** (*or* **en•**)
**in•grain•ed•ly** (*or* **en•**)
**in•grain•ed•ness** (*or* **en•**)
**in•grate**
**in•gra•ti•ate**
**in•gra•ti•at•ing** (*or* **in•gra•tia•tory**)
**in•gra•tia•tion**
**in•grati•tude**
**in•gra•ves•cence**
**in•gra•ves•cent** becoming worse
**in•gre•di•ent**
**in•gress**
**in•gres•sion**
**in•gres•sive**
**in-group**
**in•grow•ing**
**in•grown**
**in•growth**
**in•gui•nal** of the groin
**in•gur•gi•tate** to gorge
**in•gur•gi•ta•tion**
**In•gush** (*plural* **•gushes** *or* **•gush**) Russian people
**in•hab•it**
**in•hab•it•abil•ity**
**in•hab•it•able**
**in•hab•it•an•cy** (*or* **•ance**)
**in•hab•it•ant**
**in•habi•ta•tion**
**in•hal•ant**
**in•ha•la•tion**
**in•ha•la•tor** device aiding breathing
**in•hale**
**in•hal•er**
**in•har•mon•ic**
**in•har•mo•ni•ous**
**in•har•mo•ny**
**in•haul** (*or* **•haul•er**) nautical term
**in•here**
**in•her•ence** (*or* **•en•cy**)
**in•her•ent**
**in•her•it**
**in•her•it•abil•ity** (*or* **•able•ness**)
**in•her•it•able**
**in•her•it•ance**
**in•heri•tor** (*fem* **•tress** *or* **•trix**; *plural* **•tors, •tresses,** *or* **•tri•ces**)
**in•he•sion** inherence
**in•hib•it**
**in•hib•it•able**
**in•hib•it•er** (*or* **•hibi•tor**)
**in•hi•bi•tion**
**in•hibi•tive** (*or* **•tory**)
**in•hibi•tor**
**in•hos•pi•table**
**in•hos•pi•tably**
**in•hos•pi•tal•ity**
**in-house**
**in•hu•man**
**in•hu•mane**
**in•hu•man•ity** (*plural* **•ities**)
**in•hu•ma•tion**
**in•hume** inter
**in•hum•er**
**in•imi•cal**
**in•imi•cal•ly**
**in•imi•cal•ness** (*or* **•ity**)
**in•imi•tabil•ity** (*or* **•table•ness**)
**in•imi•table**
**in•imi•tably**
**ini•on** anatomy term
**in•iqui•tous**
**in•iquity** (*plural* **•iquities**)
**ini•tial** (**•tial•ling, •tialled**; *US* **•tial•ing, •tialed**)
**ini•tial•er** (*or* **•tial•ler**)
**ini•tiali•za•tion** (*or* **•sa•tion**)
**ini•tial•ize** (*or* **•ise**) computer term
**ini•tial•ly**
**ini•ti•ate**
**ini•tia•tion**
**ini•tia•tive**
**ini•tia•tor**
**ini•tia•tory**
**ini•tia•tress** (*or* **•trix**)
**in•ject**
**in•ject•able**
**in•jec•tion**
**in•jec•tive**
**in•jec•tor**
**in•ju•di•cious**
**In•jun** *US* American Indian
**in•junc•tion**
**in•junc•tive**
**in•jur•able**
**in•jure**
**in•jur•er**
**in•ju•ri•ous**
**in•ju•ry** (*plural* **•ries**)
**in•jus•tice**
**ink**
**ink•berry** (*plural* **•berries**)

**ink•blot**
**ink-cap** fungus
**In•ker•man** Crimean battle
**ink•horn**
**inki•ness**
**in•kle** linen tape
**ink•ling**
**ink•stand**
**ink•well**
**inky** (**inki•er, inki•est**)
**in•laid**
**in•land**
**in•land•er**
**in-law**
**in•lay** (**•lay•ing, •laid**)
**in•lay•er**
**in•let** (**•let•ting, •let**)
**in•li•er** geology term
**in loco pa•ren•tis**
**in•mate**
**in me•mo•ri•am**
**in•mi•grant** immigrant
**in•most**
**inn**
**in•nards**
**in•nate**
**in•ner**
**inner•most**
**in•ner•vate** supply with nerves; *compare* **enervate; innovate**
**in•ner•va•tion**
**in•nerve** stimulate
**in•ning** baseball term
**in•nings** (*plural* **•nings**)
**inn•keeper**
**in•no•cence**
**in•no•cent**
**(innoculate)** *incorrect spelling of* **inoculate**
**in•nocu•ous**
**in•nomi•nate**
**in nomi•ne** musical term
**in•no•vate** introduce new ideas; *compare* **enervate; innervate**
**in•no•va•tion**
**in•no•va•tion•al**
**in•no•va•tion•ist**
**in•no•va•tive** (*or* **•tory**)
**in•no•va•tor**
**in•nox•ious** harmless
**Inns•bruck** Austrian city
**in•nu•en•do** (*plural* **•dos** *or* **•does**)
**In•nu•it** (*or* **Inu•it**; *plural* **•it** *or* **•its**) Eskimo
**in•nu•mer•abil•ity** (*or* **•able•ness**)
**in•nu•mer•able** (*or* **•ous**)
**in•nu•mer•ably**
**in•nu•mer•ate**
**in•nu•tri•tion**
**in•nu•tri•tious**
**in•ob•serv•ance**
**in•ob•serv•ant**
**in•ocu•labil•ity**
**in•ocu•lable**
**in•ocu•late**
**in•ocu•la•tion**
**in•ocu•la•tive**
**in•ocu•la•tor**
**in•ocu•lum** (*or* **•lant**; *plural* **•la** *or* **•lants**)
**in•odor•ous**
**in•of•fen•sive**
**in•of•fi•cious** contrary to moral duty
**in•op•er•abil•ity** (*or* **•able•ness**)
**in•op•er•able**
**in•op•era•tive**
**in•op•por•tune**
**in•op•por•tune•ness** (*or* **•tun•ity**)
**in•or•di•na•cy** (*or* **•nate•ness**)
**in•or•di•nate**
**in•or•gan•ic**
**in•or•gani•cal•ly**
**in•os•cu•late**
**in•os•cu•la•tion**
**ino•si•tol** chemical compound
**ino•trop•ic** physiology term
**in•pa•tient**
**in per•pe•tuum**
**in pos•se** *Latin* possible
**in•put** (**•put•ting, •put**)
**in•qi•lab** Indian revolution
**in•quest**
**in•qui•et**
**in•qui•etude**
**in•qui•line** biology term
**in•qui•lin•ism** (*or* **•ity**)
**in•qui•li•nous**
**in•quire** formally investigate; *US spelling of* **enquire**
**in•quir•er**
**in•quiry** (*plural* **•quiries**) formal investigation; *US spelling of* **enquiry**
**in•qui•si•tion**
**in•qui•si•tion•al**
**in•qui•si•tion•ist**
**in•quisi•tive**
**in•quisi•tive•ness**
**in•quisi•tor**
**in•quisi•to•rial**
**in•quisi•to•rial•ly**
**in re** legal term
**in rem** legal term
**in•road**
**in•rush**
**in•sali•vate**
**in•sali•va•tion**
**in•sa•lu•bri•ous**
**in•sa•lu•bri•ty**
**in•sane**
**in•sani•tari•ness** (*or* **•ta•tion**)
**in•sani•tary**
**in•san•ity** (*plural* **•ities**)
**in•sa•tiabil•ity** (*or* **•tiable•ness, •ti•ate•ness**)
**in•sa•tiable** (*or* **•ti•ate**)
**in•sa•tiably** (*or* **•ti•ate•ly**)
**in•scape** person's nature
**in•scrib•able**
**in•scribe**
**in•scrib•er**
**in•scrip•tion**
**in•scrip•tion•al**
**in•scrip•tive**
**in•scru•tabil•ity** (*or* **•table•ness**)
**in•scru•table**
**in•sect**
**in•sec•tar•ium** (*or* **•tary**; *plural* **•tar•iums, •tar•ia,** *or* **•taries**)
**in•sec•tean** (*or* **•tan, •tile**)
**in•sec•ti•cid•al**
**in•sec•ti•cide**
**in•sec•ti•vore**
**in•sec•tivo•rous**
**in•secure**
**in•secu•rity** (*plural* **•rities**)
**in•sel•berg** rocky hill
**in•semi•nate**
**in•semi•na•tion**
**in•semi•na•tor**

**in•sen•sate**
**in•sen•sibil•ity** (*or* **•sible•ness)**
**in•sen•sible**
**in•sen•sibly**
**in•sen•si•tive**
**in•sen•si•tiv•ity**
**in•sen•ti•ence** (*or* **•en•cy)**
**in•sen•ti•ent**
**in•sepa•rabil•ity** (*or* **•rable•ness)**
**in•sepa•rable**
**in•sepa•rably**
**in•sert**
**in•sert•able**
**in•sert•er**
**in•ser•tion**
**in•ser•tion•al**
**in•ses•so•rial** ornithology term
**in•set (•set•ting, •set)**
**in•set•ter**
**in•shore**
**in•side**
**in•sid•er**
**in•sidi•ous**
**in•sight**
**in•sight•ful**
**in•sig•nia** (*plural* **•nias** *or* **•nia)**
**in•sig•nifi•cance** (*or* **•can•cy)**
**in•sig•nifi•cant**
**in•sin•cere**
**in•sin•cere•ly**
**in•sin•cer•ity** (*plural* **•ities)**
**in•sinu•ate**
**in•sin•ua•tion**
**in•sinua•tive** (*or* **•tory)**
**in•sinua•tor**
**in•sip•id**
**in•si•pid•ity** (*or* **•ness)**
**in•sist**
**in•sist•ence** (*or* **•en•cy)**
**in•sist•ent**
**in•sist•er**
**in situ**
**in•so•bri•ety**
**in so far** (*US* **in•so•far)**
**in•so•late** expose to sun; *compare* **insulate**
**in•so•la•tion**
**in•sole**
**in•so•lence**
**in•so•lent**
**in•sol•ubil•ity** (*or* **•uble•ness)**
**in•sol•uble**
**in•sol•ubly**
**in•solv•abil•ity**
**in•solv•able**
**in•sol•ven•cy**
**in•sol•vent**
**in•som•nia**
**in•som•ni•ac**
**in•som•ni•ous**
**in•so•much**
**in•sou•ci•ance**
**in•sou•ci•ant**
**in•span (•span•ning, •spanned)** harness
**in•spect**
**in•spect•able**
**in•spec•tion**
**in•spec•tion•al**
**in•spec•tive**
**in•spec•tor**
**in•spec•to•ral** (*or* **•rial)**
**in•spec•tor•ate**
**in•spec•tor•ship**
**in•spir•able**
**in•spi•ra•tion**
**in•spi•ra•tion•al**
**in•spira•tive**
**in•spira•tory**
**in•spire**
**in•spir•er**
**in•spir•ing**
**in•spir•it**
**in•spir•it•er**
**in•spir•it•ing•ly**
**in•spir•it•ment**
**in•stabil•ity** (*plural* **•ities)**
**in•stall** (*or* **•stal; •stall•ing, •stalled** *or* **•stal•ling, •stalled)**
**in•stal•la•tion**
**in•stall•er**
**in•stal•ment** (*US* **•stall•)**
**in•stance**
**in•stant**
**in•stan•ta•neous**
**in•stan•ta•neous•ness** (*or* **•neity)**
**in•stan•ter** without delay
**in•stan•ti•ate** represent by example
**in•stant•ly**
**in•star** zoology term
**in•state**
**in•state•ment**
**in•stead**
**in•step**
**in•sti•gate**
**in•sti•ga•tion**
**in•sti•ga•tive**
**in•sti•ga•tor**
**in•stil** (*or* **•still; •stil•ling, •stilled** *or* **•still•ing, •stilled)**
**in•stil•la•tion**
**in•still•er**
**in•stil•ment** (*or* **•still•)**
**in•stinct**
**in•stinc•tive** (*or* **•tual)**
**in•sti•tute**
**in•sti•tu•tion**
**in•sti•tu•tion•al**
**in•sti•tu•tion•al•ism**
**in•sti•tu•tion•al•ist**
**in•sti•tu•tion•ali•za•tion** (*or* **•sa•tion)**
**in•sti•tu•tion•al•ize** (*or* **•ise)**
**in•sti•tu•tion•ary**
**in•sti•tu•tive**
**in•sti•tu•tor** (*or* **•tut•er)**
**in•struct**
**in•struct•ible**
**in•struc•tion**
**in•struc•tion•al**
**in•struc•tive**
**in•struc•tor**
**in•struc•tor•ship**
**in•struc•tress**
**in•stru•ment**
**in•stru•men•tal**
**in•stru•men•tal•ism** philosophy term
**in•stru•men•tal•ist**
**in•stru•men•tal•ity**
**in•stru•men•tal•ly**
**in•stru•men•ta•tion**
**in•sub•or•di•nate**
**in•sub•or•di•na•tion**
**in•sub•stan•tial**
**in•sub•stan•ti•al•ity**
**in•sub•stan•tial•ly**
**in•suf•fer•able**
**in•suf•fer•ably**
**in•suf•fi•cien•cy** (*or* **•cience)**
**in•suf•fi•cient**
**in•suf•flate**
**in•suf•fla•tion**
**in•suf•fla•tor**

**in•su•la** (*plural* **•lae**) anatomy term
**in•sul•ant**
**in•su•lar**
**in•su•lar•ity** (*or* **•ism**)
**in•su•late** isolate; *compare* **insolate**
**in•su•la•tion**
**in•su•la•tor**
**in•su•lin** hormone; *compare* **inulin**
**in•sult**
**in•sult•er**
**in•su•per•abil•ity** (*or* **•able•ness**)
**in•su•per•able**
**in•su•per•ably**
**in•sup•port•able**
**in•sup•port•ably**
**in•sup•press•ible**
**in•sur•abil•ity**
**in•sur•able**
**in•sur•ance** financial protection; *insurance against death is* **life assurance**
**in•sure** protect against loss; *compare* **ensure**
**in•sured**
**in•sur•er**
**in•sur•gence**
**in•sur•gen•cy** (*plural* **•cies**)
**in•sur•gent**
**in•sur•mount•abil•ity** (*or* **•able•ness**)
**in•sur•mount•able**
**in•sur•mount•ably**
**in•sur•rec•tion**
**in•sur•rec•tion•al**
**in•sur•rec•tion•ary**
**in•sur•rec•tion•ism**
**in•sur•rec•tion•ist**
**in•sus•cep•tibil•ity**
**in•sus•cep•tible**
**in•swing** cricket term
**in•swinger**
**in•tact**
**in•tag•li•at•ed**
**in•tag•lio** (*plural* **•lios** *or* **•li**) engraving
**in•take**
**in•tan•gibil•ity** (*or* **•gible•ness**)
**in•tan•gible**
**in•tan•gibly**
**in•tar•sia** mosaic of wood
**in•te•ger**
**in•te•gral**
**in•te•gral•ly**
**in•te•grand** maths term
**in•te•grant** part of whole
**in•te•grate**
**in•te•gra•tion**
**in•te•gra•tion•ist**
**in•te•gra•tive**
**in•te•gra•tor**
**in•teg•rity**
**in•tegu•ment**
**in•tegu•men•tary** (*or* **•men•tal**)
**in•tel•lect**
**in•tel•lec•tion** thought
**in•tel•lec•tive**
**in•tel•lec•tual**
**in•tel•lec•tu•al•ism**
**in•tel•lec•tu•al•ist**
**in•tel•lec•tu•al•is•tic**
**in•tel•lec•tu•al•is•ti•cal•ly**
**in•tel•lec•tu•al•ity** (*or* **•ness**)
**in•tel•lec•tu•ali•za•tion** (*or* **•sa•tion**)
**in•tel•lec•tu•al•ize** (*or* **•ise**)
**in•tel•lec•tu•al•iz•er** (*or* **•is•er**)
**in•tel•lec•tu•al•ly**
**in•tel•li•gence**
**in•tel•li•gent**
**in•tel•li•gent•sia**
**in•tel•li•gibil•ity** (*or* **•gible•ness**)
**in•tel•li•gi•ble**
**in•tel•li•gibly**
**In•tel•sat** communications satellite
**in•tem•per•ance**
**in•tem•per•ate**
**in•tend**
**in•tend•ance** French public department
**in•tend•an•cy**
**in•tend•ant** provincial official
**in•tend•ed**
**in•tend•er**
**in•tend•ment** legal term
**in•ten•er•ate** make tender
**in•tense**
**in•ten•si•fi•ca•tion**
**in•ten•si•fi•er**
**in•ten•si•fy** (**•fies**, **•fy•ing**, **•fied**)
**in•ten•sion** logic term; *compare* **intention**
**in•ten•sion•al**
**in•ten•sity** (*plural* **•sities**)
**in•ten•sive**
**in•tent**
**in•ten•tion** purpose; *compare* **intension**
**in•ten•tion•al**
**in•ten•tion•al•ity**
**in•ten•tion•al•ly**
**in•tent•ly**
**in•ter** (**•ter•ring**, **•terred**)
**inter•act**
**inter•ac•tion**
**inter•ac•tion•al**
**inter•ac•tive**
**in•ter•ac•tiv•ity**
**in•ter alia** *Latin* among other things
**in•ter ali•os** *Latin* among other people
**inter•atom•ic**
**inter•bed•ded**
**inter•brain**
**inter•breed** (**•breed•ing**, **•bred**)
**inter•ca•lari•ly**
**inter•ca•lary**
**inter•ca•late**
**inter•ca•la•tion**
**inter•ca•la•tive**
**inter•cede**
**inter•ced•er**
**inter•cel•lu•lar**
**inter•cept**
**inter•cep•tion**
**inter•cep•tive**
**inter•cep•tor** (*or* **•cept•er**)
**inter•ces•sion**
**inter•ces•sion•al** (*or* **inter•ces•sory**)
**inter•ces•sor**
**inter•ces•so•ri•al**
**inter•change**
**inter•change•abil•ity** (*or* **•able•ness**)
**inter•change•able**
**inter•change•ably**
**inter•city**
**inter•clavi•cle**
**inter•cla•vicu•lar**
**inter•col•legi•ate**

**inter•co•lum•nar**
**inter•co•lum•nia•tion**
**inter•com**
**inter•com•mu•ni•cabil•ity**
**inter•com•mu•ni•cable**
**inter•com•mu•ni•cate**
**inter•com•mu•ni•ca•tion**
**inter•com•mu•ni•ca•tive**
**inter•com•mu•ni•ca•tor**
**inter•com•mun•ion**
**inter•con•nect**
**inter•con•nec•tion**
**inter•con•ti•nen•tal**
**inter•cos•tal** anatomy term
**inter•course**
**inter•crop** (**•crop•ping, •cropped**)
**inter•cross** crossbreed
**inter•cur•rence**
**inter•cur•rent**
**inter•denomi•na•tion•al**
**inter•denomi•na•tion•al-ism**
**inter•den•tal**
**inter•de•part•men•tal**
**inter•de•pend•ence** (*or* **•en•cy**)
**inter•de•pend•ent**
**inter•dict**
**inter•dic•tion**
**inter•dic•tive** (*or* **•tory**)
**inter•dic•tor**
**inter•dis•ci•pli•nary**
**in•ter•est**
**in•ter•est•ed**
**in•ter•est•ed•ly**
**in•ter•est•ing**
**inter•face**
**inter•fa•cial**
**inter•fa•cial•ly**
**inter•fac•ing**
**inter•fere**
**inter•fer•ence**
**inter•feren•tial**
**inter•fer•er**
**inter•fer•ing**
**inter•fer•om•eter** physics instrument
**inter•fero•met•ric**
**inter•fero•met•ri•cal•ly**
**inter•fer•om•etry**
**inter•fer•on** biochemical substance
**inter•fer•tile**
**inter•fer•til•ity**
**inter•file**
**inter•flu•ent** flowing together
**inter•fluve** land between rivers
**inter•flu•vial**
**inter•fuse**
**inter•fu•sion**
**inter•ga•lac•tic**
**inter•gla•cial**
**inter•gov•ern•men•tal**
**inter•gra•da•tion**
**inter•gra•da•tion•al**
**inter•grade**
**inter•gra•di•ent**
**inter•group**
**in•ter•im**
**in•te•ri•or**
**inter•ject**
**inter•jec•tion**
**inter•jec•tion•al** (*or* **•tion•ary, •tur•al**)
**inter•jec•tor**
**inter•jec•tory**
**inter•lace**
**inter•lace•ment**
**In•ter•la•ken** Swiss town
**inter•lami•nar**
**inter•lami•nate**
**inter•lami•na•tion**
**inter•lard**
**inter•lay** (**•lay•ing, •laid**)
**inter•leaf** (*noun; plural* **•leaves**)
**inter•leave** (*verb*)
**inter•line**
**inter•lin•ear** (*or* **•eal**)
**inter•lin•eate**
**inter•line•ation**
**inter•lin•er**
**Inter•lin•gua** language
**inter•lin•ing**
**inter•link**
**inter•lock**
**inter•lock•er**
**inter•lo•cu•tion**
**inter•locu•tor**
**inter•locu•to•ri•ly**
**inter•locu•tory**
**inter•locu•tress** (*or* **•trice, •trix**)
**inter•lope**
**inter•lop•er**
**inter•lude**
**inter•lu•nar**
**inter•lu•na•tion** period of moon's invisibility
**inter•mar•riage**
**inter•mar•ry** (**•ries, •ry•ing, •ried**)
**inter•media•cy**
**inter•medi•ary** (*plural* **•aries**)
**inter•medi•ate**
**inter•media•tor**
**in•ter•ment** burial; *compare* **internment**
**inter•mez•zo** (*plural* **•zos** *or* **•zi**)
**inter•mi•gra•tion**
**in•ter•mi•nable**
**in•ter•mi•nable•ness** (*or* **•nabil•ity**)
**in•ter•mi•nably**
**inter•min•gle**
**inter•mis•sion**
**inter•mis•sive**
**inter•mit** (**•mit•ting, •mit•ted**)
**inter•mit•tence** (*or* **•ten•cy**)
**inter•mit•tent** sporadic; *compare* **intromittent**
**inter•mit•tor**
**inter•mix**
**inter•mix•able**
**inter•mix•ture**
**inter•mo•lecu•lar**
**in•tern**
**in•ter•nal**
**in•ter•nal•ity** (*or* **•ness**)
**in•ter•nali•za•tion** (*or* **•sa•tion**)
**in•ter•nal•ize** (*or* **•ise**)
**in•ter•nal•ly**
**inter•na•tion•al**
**inter•na•tion•al•ism**
**inter•na•tion•al•ist**
**inter•na•tion•al•ity**
**inter•na•tion•ali•za•tion** (*or* **•sa•tion**)
**inter•na•tion•al•ize** (*or* **•ise**)
**inter•na•tion•al•ly**
**inter•necine**
**in•ternee**
**In•ter•net**
**inter•neu•rone** (*or* **•ron**)
**in•tern•ist**
**in•tern•ment** confinement; *compare* **interment**
**inter•nod•al**

**inter•node** part of plant stem
**in•tern•ship**
**inter•nun•cial**
**inter•nun•cio** (*plural* **•cios**) papal ambassador
**intero•cep•tive**
**intero•cep•tor** physiology term
**inter•os•cu•late** biology term
**inter•os•cu•la•tion**
**inter•page**
**inter•pel•lant**
**inter•pel•late** question in parliament; *compare* **interpolate**
**in•ter•pel•la•tion**
**in•ter•pel•la•tor**
**inter•pen•etrable**
**inter•pen•etrant**
**inter•pen•etrate**
**inter•pen•etra•tion**
**inter•pen•etra•tive**
**inter•per•son•al**
**inter•phase**
**inter•phone**
**inter•plan•etary**
**inter•play**
**inter•plead** (**•plead•ing, •plead•ed, •plead** *or* **•pled**) legal term
**inter•plead•er**
**Inter•pol**
**in•ter•po•late** insert; *compare* **interpellate**
**in•ter•po•lat•er** (*or* **•la•tor**)
**in•ter•po•la•tion**
**in•ter•po•la•tive**
**inter•pos•able**
**inter•pos•al**
**inter•pose**
**inter•pos•er**
**inter•po•si•tion**
**in•ter•pret**
**in•ter•pret•abil•ity** (*or* **•able•ness**)
**in•ter•pret•able**
**in•ter•pre•ta•tion**
**in•ter•pre•ta•tion•al**
**in•ter•pre•ta•tive**
**in•ter•pret•er**
**in•ter•pre•tive**
**inter•ra•cial**
**inter•ra•cial•ly**
**inter•ra•di•al**
**inter•reg•nal**
**inter•reg•num** (*plural* **•nums** *or* **•na**)
**inter•re•late**
**inter•re•la•tion**
**inter•re•la•tion•ship**
**inter•rex** (*plural* **•re•ges**) interim ruler
**in•ter•ro•bang** (*or* **•tera•bang**) punctuation mark
**in•ter•ro•gate**
**in•ter•ro•gat•ing•ly**
**in•ter•ro•ga•tion**
**in•ter•ro•ga•tion•al**
**in•ter•rogative**
**in•ter•ro•ga•tor**
**in•ter•roga•to•ri•ly**
**in•ter•roga•tory** (*plural* **•tories**)
**in•ter•rupt**
**in•ter•rupt•er** (*or* **•rup•tor**)
**in•ter•rupt•ible**
**in•ter•rup•tion**
**in•ter•rup•tive**
**inter•scho•las•tic**
**inter•sect**
**inter•sec•tion**
**inter•sec•tion•al**
**inter•sex**
**inter•sex•ual**
**inter•sexu•al•ity** (*or* **•ism**)
**inter•sex•ual•ly**
**inter•space**
**inter•spa•tial**
**inter•sperse**
**inter•sper•sion** (*or* **•sal**)
**inter•sta•dial** interglacial
**inter•state**
**inter•stel•lar**
**in•ter•stice**
**in•ter•sti•tial**
**inter•strati•fi•ca•tion**
**inter•strati•fy** (**•fies, •fy•ing, •fied**) geology term
**inter•tex•ture**
**inter•tid•al**
**inter•trib•al**
**inter•tri•go** (*plural* **•gos**) chafed skin
**inter•tropi•cal**
**inter•twine**
**in•ter•val**
**inter•vene**
**inter•ven•er** (*or* **•ve•nor**)
**inter•ven•tion**
**inter•ven•tion•al**
**inter•ven•tion•ism**
**inter•ven•tion•ist**
**inter•view**
**inter•viewee**
**inter•view•er**
**in•ter vivos** legal term
**inter•vo•cal•ic** between vowels
**inter•vo•cali•cal•ly**
**inter•weave** (**•weav•ing, •wove** *or* **•weaved, •woven** *or* **•weaved**)
**inter•weav•er**
**inter•wind** (**•wind•ing, •wound**)
**inter•woven**
**in•tes•ta•cy**
**in•tes•tate**
**in•tes•ti•nal**
**in•tes•tine**
**in•ti•ma** (*plural* **•mae**) anatomy term
**in•ti•ma•cy** (*plural* **•cies**)
**in•ti•mal**
**in•ti•mate**
**in•ti•ma•tion**
**in•timi•date**
**in•timi•da•tion**
**in•timi•da•tor**
**in•tinc•tion** part of Communion
**in•tine** botany term
**into**
**in•tol•er•abil•ity** (*or* **•able•ness**)
**in•tol•er•able**
**in•tol•er•ably**
**in•tol•er•ance**
**in•tol•er•ant**
**in•to•nate**
**in•to•na•tion**
**in•to•na•tion•al**
**in•tone**
**in•ton•er**
**in•tor•sion** botany term
**in toto** *Latin* entirely
**in•toxi•cable**
**in•toxi•cant**
**in•toxi•cate**
**in•toxi•cat•ing•ly**
**in•toxi•ca•tion**
**in•toxi•ca•tive**

**in•toxi•ca•tor**
**intra-atomic**
**intra•car•di•ac**
**intra•cel•lu•lar**
**intra•cos•tal** anatomy term
**intra•cra•nial**
**in•trac•tabil•ity** (*or* **•table•ness)**
**in•trac•table**
**in•trac•tably**
**intra•cu•ta•neous**
**intra•der•mal** (*or* **•mic)**
**in•tra•dos** (*plural* **•dos** *or* **•doses)** inner curve of arch
**intra•mo•lecu•lar**
**intra•mu•ral**
**intra•mus•cu•lar**
**in•tran•si•gence** (*or* **•gen•cy)**
**in•tran•si•gent**
**in•tran•si•gent•ist**
**in•tran•si•tive**
**intra•nu•clear**
**intra•state**
**intra•tel•lu•ric**
**intra•uter•ine**
**in•trava•sa•tion**
**intra•venous**
**(intravert)** *incorrect spelling of* **introvert**
**in•treat** *Archaic* **entreat**
**in•trench** *less common spelling of* **entrench**
**in•trep•id**
**in•tre•pid•ity** (*or* **•trep•id•ness)**
**in•tri•ca•cy** (*plural* **•cies)**
**in•tri•cate**
**in•tri•cate•ness**
**in•trigue (•trigu•ing, •trigued)**
**in•tri•guer**
**intrigu•ing**
**in•trin•sic** (*or* **•si•cal)**
**in•trin•si•cal•ly**
**in•tro** (*plural* **•tros)**
**intro•duce**
**intro•duc•er**
**intro•duc•ible**
**intro•duc•tion**
**intro•duc•to•ri•ly**
**intro•duc•tory**
**in•tro•gres•sion**
**in•troit** prayer
**in•troi•tal**
**intro•ject**
**intro•jec•tion** psychology term
**intro•jec•tive**
**intro•mis•sion** insertion
**intro•mit•tent** insertable; *compare* **intermittent**
**in•trorse** turned inwards
**intro•spect**
**intro•spec•tion**
**intro•spec•tion•al**
**intro•spec•tion•ist**
**intro•spec•tive**
**intro•ver•sion**
**intro•ver•sive** (*or* **•tive)**
**intro•vert**
**in•trude**
**in•trud•er**
**in•trud•ing•ly**
**in•tru•sion**
**in•tru•sion•al**
**in•tru•sive**
**in•trust** *less common spelling of* **entrust**
**in•tu•bate**
**in•tu•ba•tion**
**in•tu•it**
**in•tu•it•able**
**in•tui•tion**
**in•tui•tion•al**
**in•tui•tion•ism** (*or* **•tion•al•ism)**
**in•tui•tion•ist** (*or* **tion•al•ist)**
**in•tui•tive**
**in•tui•tiv•ism**
**in•tui•tiv•ist**
**in•tu•mesce**
**in•tu•mes•cence** (*or* **•cen•cy)**
**in•tu•mes•cent**
**in•tus•sus•cept**
**in•tus•sus•cep•tion** medical and biology term
**in•tus•sus•cep•tive**
**in•twine** *less common spelling of* **entwine**
**inu•lin** plant compound; *compare* **insulin**
**in•unc•tion**
**in•un•dant** (*or* **•da•tory)**
**in•un•date**
**in•un•da•tion**
**in•un•da•tor**
**in•ure** (*or* **en•)**
**in•ur•ed•ness** (*or* **en•)**
**in•urn**
**in ut•ero** *Latin* in the womb
**in•utile**
**in•util•ity**
**in va•cuo** *Latin* in a vacuum
**in•vad•able**
**in•vade**
**in•vad•er**
**in•vagi•nable**
**in•vagi•nate**
**in•vagi•na•tion**
**in•va•lid** disabled person
**in•val•id** not valid
**in•vali•date**
**in•vali•da•tion**
**in•vali•da•tor**
**in•va•lid•ism** being an invalid
**in•va•lid•ity** (*or* **•val•id•ness)** being not valid
**in•valu•able**
**in•valu•ably**
**In•var** (*Trademark*)
**in•vari•abil•ity** (*or* **•able•ness)**
**in•vari•able**
**in•vari•ably**
**in•vari•ance** (*or* **•an•cy)**
**in•vari•ant**
**in•va•sion**
**in•va•sive**
**in•vec•tive**
**in•veigh** rail against
**in•veigh•er**
**in•vei•gle** cajole
**in•vei•gle•ment**
**in•vei•gler**
**in•vent**
**in•vent•ible** (*or* **•able)**
**in•ven•tion**
**in•ven•tion•al**
**in•ven•tive**
**in•ven•tive•ness**
**in•ven•tor**
**in•ven•to•ri•able**
**in•ven•to•ri•al**
**in•ven•tory** (*noun, plural* **•tories;** *verb* **•tories, •tory•ing, •toried)**
**in•ve•rac•ity** (*plural* **•ities)**
**In•ver•car•gill** New Zealand city
**In•ver•ness**

**in•verse**
**in•ver•sion**
**in•ver•sive**
**in•vert**
**in•vert•ase** enzyme
**in•ver•te•bra•cy** (*or* **•tebrate•ness)**
**in•ver•te•bral**
**in•ver•tebrate**
**in•vert•er** (*or* **•ver•tor)**
**in•vert•ibil•ity**
**in•vert•ible**
**in•vest**
**in•vest•able** (*or* **•ible)**
**in•ves•ti•gable**
**in•ves•ti•gate**
**in•ves•ti•ga•tion**
**in•ves•ti•ga•tion•al**
**in•ves•ti•gative** (*or* **•ga•tory)**
**in•ves•ti•ga•tor**
**in•ves•ti•tive**
**in•ves•ti•ture**
**in•vest•ment**
**in•ves•tor**
**in•vet•era•cy** (*or* **•er•ate•ness)**
**in•vet•er•ate**
**in•vi•abil•ity** (*or* **•able•ness)**
**in•vi•able**
**in•vidi•ous**
**in•vigi•late**
**in•vigi•la•tion**
**in•vigi•la•tor**
**in•vig•or•ate**
**in•vig•or•at•ing•ly**
**in•vig•ora•tion**
**in•vig•ora•tive**
**in•vig•ora•tor**
**in•vin•cibil•ity** (*or* **•cible•ness)**
**in•vin•cible**
**in•vin•cibly**
**in•vio•labil•ity** (*or* **•lable•ness)**
**in•vio•lable**
**in•vio•lably**
**in•vio•la•cy** (*or* **•late•ness)**
**in•vio•late**
**in•vis•ibil•ity** (*or* **•ible•ness)**
**in•vis•ible**
**in•vis•ibly**
**in•vi•ta•tion**
**in•vi•ta•tory**
**in•vite**
**in•vit•er**
**in•vit•ing**
**in vi•tro** outside the body
**in vivo** within the body
**in•vo•cable**
**in•vo•ca•tion**
**in•vo•ca•tion•al**
**in•voca•tory**
**in•voice**
**in•voke**
**in•vok•er**
**in•volu•cel** (*or* **•cel•lum;** *plural* **•cels** *or* **•cel•la)** botany term
**in•volu•cel•ate** (*or* **•at•ed)**
**in•vo•lu•cral**
**in•vo•lu•crate**
**in•vo•lu•cre** (*or* **•crum;** *plural* **•cres** *or* **•cra)** botany term
**in•vol•un•tari•ly**
**in•vol•un•tari•ness**
**in•vol•un•tary**
**in•vo•lute** (*or* **lut•ed)**
**in•vo•lu•tion**
**in•vo•lu•tion•al**
**in•volve**
**in•volved**
**in•volve•ment**
**in•volv•er**
**in•vul•ner•abil•ity** (*or* **•able•ness)**
**in•vul•ner•able**
**in•vul•ner•ably**
**in•vul•tua•tion** making images for witchcraft
**in•ward** (*adj*)
**in•ward•ly**
**in•wards** (*adv*)
**in•weave** (**•weav•ing, •wove** *or* **•weaved, •wo•ven** *or* **•weaved)**
**in•wrought**
**Io** satellite of Jupiter
**iodate** chemistry term
**ioda•tion**
**iod•ic** chemistry term
**iodide**
**iodine**
**iodism** iodine poisoning
**iodi•za•tion** (*or* **•sa•tion)**
**iodize** (*or* **iodise)**
**iodiz•er** (*or* **iodis•)**
**iodo•form** antiseptic
**iodo•met•ric** (*or* **•ri•cal)**
**iodo•met•ri•cal•ly**
**iodom•etry** chemistry term
**iodop•sin** retinal pigment
**iodous** chemistry term
**ion**
**Io•na** Scottish island
**Ionia** Aegean region
**Ionian**
**Ion•ic** architecture term
**ion•ic** of ions
**ioni•za•tion** (*or* **•sa•tion)**
**ion•ize** (*or* **•ise)**
**ionone** plant extract
**iono•pause**
**iono•sphere**
**iono•spher•ic**
**ion•to•pho•resis** biochemical technique
**iota**
**iota•cism**
**IOU** (*plural* **IOUs)**
**Iowa**
**ip•ecac** (*or* **•ecacu•an•ha)** purgative
**Ipoh** Malaysian city
**ipo•moea** plant
**ipso facto**
**Ips•wich**
**ira•cund** easily angered
**Irá•kli•on** Cretan port
**Iran**
**Ira•nian**
**Iraq**
**Ira•qi**
**iras•cibil•ity** (*or* **•cible•ness)**
**iras•cible**
**iras•cibly**
**irate**
**Ir•bid** Jordanian town
**ire**
**Ire•land**
**iren•ic** (*or* **ireni•cal)** conciliatory
**ireni•cal•ly**
**iren•ics** branch of theology
**iri•da•ceous** botany term
**iri•dec•to•my** (*plural* **•mies)** eye surgery
**iri•des•cence**
**iri•des•cent**
**irid•ic**
**irid•ium** chemical element
**iri•doto•my** (*plural* **•mies)** eye surgery
**iris** (*plural* **irises)** flowers

**iris** (*plural* **iri•des** *or* **irises**) part of eye
**Irish**
**Irish•ism**
**Irish•man** (*plural* **•men**)
**Irish•woman** (*plural* **•women**)
**irit•ic**
**iri•tis** eye disease
**irk**
**irk•some**
**Ir•ku•tsk** Russian city
**iron**
**iron•bark** tree
**iron•bound** unyielding
**iron•clad**
**iron•er**
**iron•ic** (*or* **ironi•cal**)
**ironi•cal•ly**
**iron•ing**
**iro•nist**
**iro•nize** indulge in irony
**iron•monger**
**iron•mongery**
**Ironsides** Cromwell's cavalry
**iron•stone**
**iron•ware**
**iron•wood**
**iron•work**
**iro•ny** (*plural* **•nies**) sarcasm
**irony** containing iron
**Iro•quoi•an**
**Iro•quois** (*plural* **•quois**) American Indian
**ir•ra•di•ance**
**ir•ra•di•ant**
**ir•ra•di•ate**
**ir•ra•dia•tion**
**ir•ra•dia•tive**
**ir•ra•dia•tor**
**ir•ra•tion•al**
**ir•ra•tion•al•ity** (*or* **•ism**)
**ir•ra•tion•al•ly**
**Ir•ra•wad•dy** Burmese river
**ir•re•claim•abil•ity** (*or* **•able•ness**)
**ir•re•claim•able**
**ir•re•claim•ably**
**ir•rec•on•cil•abil•ity** (*or* **•able•ness**)
**ir•rec•on•cil•able**
**ir•rec•on•cil•ably**
**ir•re•cov•er•able**
**ir•re•cov•er•ably**
**ir•re•cu•sable** unable to be rejected
**ir•re•deem•abil•ity** (*or* **•able•ness**)
**ir•re•deem•able**
**ir•re•deem•ably**
**ir•re•den•tism**
**ir•re•den•tist** territorial claimant
**ir•re•duc•ibil•ity** (*or* **•ible•ness**)
**ir•re•duc•ible**
**ir•re•duc•ibly**
**ir•ref•ra•gabil•ity** (*or* **•gable•ness**)
**ir•ref•ra•gable** indisputable
**ir•ref•ra•gably**
**ir•re•fran•gibil•ity** (*or* **•gible•ness**)
**ir•re•fran•gible** inviolable
**ir•refu•tabil•ity** (*or* **•table•ness**)
**ir•refu•table**
**ir•refu•tably**
**ir•regu•lar**
**ir•regu•lar•ity** (*plural* **•ities**)
**ir•rela•tive** unrelated
**ir•rel•evance** (*or* **•evan•cy**; *plural* **•evances** *or* **•cies**)
**ir•rel•evant**
**ir•re•liev•able**
**ir•re•li•gion**
**ir•re•li•gion•ist**
**ir•re•li•gious**
**ir•re•medi•able**
**ir•re•medi•ably**
**ir•re•mis•sibil•ity** (*or* **•sible•ness**)
**ir•re•mis•sible**
**ir•re•mis•sibly**
**ir•re•mov•abil•ity** (*or* **•able•ness**)
**ir•re•mov•able**
**ir•re•mov•ably**
**ir•repa•rabil•ity** (*or* **•rable•ness**)
**ir•repa•rable**
**ir•repa•rably**
**ir•re•place•able**
**ir•re•plevi•able** (*or* **•sable**) legal term
**ir•re•press•ibil•ity** (*or* **•ible•ness**)
**ir•re•press•ible**
**ir•re•press•ibly**
**ir•re•proach•abil•ity** (*or* **•able•ness**)
**ir•re•proach•able**
**ir•re•proach•ably**
**ir•re•sist•ibil•ity** (*or* **•ible•ness**)
**ir•re•sist•ible**
**ir•re•sist•ibly**
**ir•reso•lubil•ity**
**ir•reso•luble**
**ir•reso•lute**
**ir•reso•lu•tion**
**ir•re•solv•abil•ity** (*or* **•able•ness**)
**ir•re•solv•able**
**ir•re•spec•tive**
**ir•re•spir•able**
**ir•re•spon•sibil•ity** (*or* **•sible•ness**)
**ir•re•spon•sible**
**ir•re•spon•sibly**
**ir•re•spon•sive**
**ir•re•ten•tive**
**ir•re•triev•abil•ity** (*or* **•able•ness**)
**ir•re•triev•able**
**ir•re•triev•ably**
**ir•rev•er•ence**
**ir•rev•er•ent** (*or* **•eren•tial**)
**ir•re•vers•ibil•ity** (*or* **•ible•ness**)
**ir•re•vers•ible**
**ir•re•vers•ibly**
**ir•revo•cabil•ity** (*or* **•cable•ness**)
**ir•revo•cable**
**ir•revo•cably**
**(irridescent)** *incorrect spelling of* **iridescent**
**ir•ri•gable**
**ir•ri•gate**
**ir•ri•ga•tion**
**ir•ri•ga•tion•al**
**ir•ri•ga•tive**
**ir•ri•ga•tor**
**ir•ri•tabil•ity**
**ir•ri•table**
**ir•ri•tably**
**ir•ri•tant**
**ir•ri•tate**
**ir•ri•ta•tion**
**ir•ri•ta•tive**
**ir•ri•ta•tor**
**ir•rupt** enter or increase suddenly; *compare* **erupt**

**ir•rup•tion**
**ir•rup•tive**
**Ir•tysh** (*or* **Ir•tish**) Asian river
**Ir•vine** Scottish town
**is**
**isa•go•ge**
**isa•gog•ic**
**isa•gog•ics** introductory studies
**is•al•lo•bar** line on map
**Isar** European river
**isa•tin** (*or* **•tine**)
**isa•tin•ic**
**Iscariot** biblical character
**is•chae•mia** (*US* **•che•**) inadequate blood supply
**is•chaem•ic** (*US* **•chem•**)
**Is•chia** Mediterranean island
**is•chial**
**is•chium** (*plural* **•chia**) hip bone
**is•en•trop•ic** physics term
**Isère** French river
**Is•fa•han** (*or* **Es•**) Iranian city
**Ishmael** biblical character
**isin•glass**
**Isis** Thames at Oxford; Egyptian goddess
**Is•ken•de•run** Turkish port
**Is•lam**
**Is•lama•bad** Pakistani capital
**Is•lam•ic**
**Is•lam•ist**
**Is•lam•ize**
**is•land**
**is•land•er**
**Is•lay** Scottish island
**isle**
**Isle of Wight**
**is•let**
**Is•ling•ton**
**ism**
**Is•mai•li** Muslim sect
**Is•mai•lia** Egyptian city
**isn't**
**iso•ag•glu•ti•na•tion**
**iso•ag•glu•ti•na•tive**
**iso•ag•glu•ti•nin**
**iso•anti•gen**
**iso•bar**
**iso•bar•ic**
**iso•bar•ism**
**iso•bath** line on map
**iso•bath•ic**
**iso•cheim** (*or* **•chime**) line on map
**iso•chei•mal** (*or* **•menal**, **•chi•mal**)
**iso•chor** (*or* **•chore**) line on graph
**iso•chor•ic**
**iso•chro•mat•ic**
**isoch•ro•nal** (*or* **•nous**)
**isoch•ro•nize** (*or* **•nise**)
**isoch•ro•ous** of uniform colour
**iso•cli•nal** (*or* **•clin•ic**)
**iso•cline** geology term
**isoc•ra•cy** (*plural* **•cies**) political equality
**iso•crat•ic**
**iso•cya•nide**
**iso•dia•met•ric**
**iso•dia•phere** physics term
**iso•di•mor•phism** chemistry term
**iso•di•mor•phous** (*or* **•phic**)
**iso•dy•nam•ic**
**iso•elec•tric**
**iso•elec•tron•ic**
**iso•gam•ete** biology term
**iso•ga•met•ic**
**isoga•mous**
**isoga•my**
**isog•enous** genetically uniform
**isog•eny**
**iso•geo•therm**
**iso•geo•ther•mal** (*or* **•mic**)
**iso•gloss** linguistics term
**iso•glos•sal**
**iso•glot•tic**
**iso•gon** maths term
**iso•gon•ic** (*or* **isogo•nal**)
**iso•hel** line on map
**iso•hy•et** line on map
**iso•labil•ity**
**iso•lable**
**iso•late**
**iso•la•tion**
**iso•la•tion•ism**
**iso•la•tion•ist**
**iso•la•tive**
**iso•la•tor**
**iso•leci•thal** biology term
**iso•leu•cine** amino acid
**iso•lex** linguistics term
**iso•line** isopleth
**isolo•gous** chemistry term
**iso•logue**
**iso•mag•net•ic**
**iso•mer**
**iso•mer•ic**
**isom•er•ism**
**isom•eri•za•tion** (*or* **•sa•tion**)
**isom•er•ize** (*or* **•ise**)
**isom•er•ous**
**iso•met•ric**
**iso•met•ri•cal**
**iso•met•rics** exercises
**iso•metro•pia** physiology term
**isom•etry** maths term
**iso•morph**
**iso•mor•phic** (*or* **•phous**)
**iso•mor•phism**
**iso•nia•zid** medicinal drug
**isono•my** equality before the law
**iso•octane** chemical compound
**iso•phone** linguistics term
**iso•pi•es•tic** having equal atmospheric pressure
**iso•pi•es•ti•cal•ly**
**iso•pleth** line on map
**iso•pod** crustacean
**isopo•dan** (*or* **•dous**)
**iso•prene** chemical compound
**iso•pro•pyl**
**iso•rhyth•mic** musical term
**isos•celes** geometry term
**iso•seis•mal**
**is•os•mot•ic**
**iso•spon•dy•lous** zoology term
**isos•ta•sy** (*plural* **•sies**) geological theory
**iso•stat•ic**
**iso•ster•ic** chemistry term
**iso•tac•tic**
**isoth•er•al**
**iso•there** line on map
**iso•therm**
**iso•ther•mal**
**iso•tone** chemistry term
**iso•ton•ic**
**iso•to•nic•ity**
**iso•tope**
**iso•top•ic**

**iso•topi•cal•ly**
**isoto•py**
**iso•tron** physics apparatus
**iso•trop•ic**
**iso•tropi•cal•ly**
**isot•ro•pous**
**isot•ro•py**
**Is•ra•el**
**Is•rae•li** (*plural* **•lis** *or* **•li**)
**Is•rael•ite**
**Is•ra•fil** Islamic archangel
**is•su•able**
**is•su•ance**
**is•su•ant**
**is•sue** (**•su•ing, •sued**)
**is•su•er**
**Is•sus** battle
**Is•tan•bul**
**isth•mi•an**
**isth•moid**
**isth•mus** (*plural* **•muses** *or* **•mi**)
**is•tle** (*or* **ix•**) fibre
**Is•tria** Adriatic peninsula
**Is•trian**
**it**
**ita•colu•mite** sandstone
**Ital•ian**
**Ital•ian•ate**
**Ital•ian•esque**
**Ital•ian•ism**
**Ital•ian•ize**
**Ital•ic** language
**ital•ic** type or print
**Itali•cism**
**itali•ci•za•tion** (*or* **•sa•tion**)
**itali•cize** (*or* **•cise**)
**Ita•ly**
**itch**
**itchi•ness**
**itch•ing**
**itchy** (**itchi•er, itchi•est**)
**item**
**itemi•za•tion** (*or* **•sa•tion**)
**item•ize** (*or* **•ise**)
**it•er•ant**
**it•er•ate**
**it•era•tion** (*or* **•er•ance**)
**it•era•tive**
**Itha•ca** Greek island
**Itha•can**
**ithy•phal•lic** poetry term
**itin•er•an•cy** (*or* **•era•cy**; *plural* **•cies**)
**itin•er•ant**
**itin•er•ary** (*plural* **•aries**)
**itin•er•ate** travel about
**itin•era•tion**
**it'll** it will; it shall
**its** of it
**it's** it is
**it•self**
**Iva•no•vo** Russian city
**I've** I have
**ivied**
**ivo•ry** (*plural* **•ries**)
**ivy** (*plural* **ivies**)
**Iwo Jima** Pacific island
**ixia** plant
**ix•tle** *variant spelling of* **istle**
**izard** chamois
**Izhevsk** Russian city
**Iz•mir** Turkish port
**Iz•mit** Turkish town

# J

**jab** (**jab•bing, jabbed**)
**Jab•al•pur** (*or* **Jub•bul•pore**) Indian city
**jabbed**
**jab•ber**
**jab•ber•er**
**jab•ber•wocky** nonsense verse
**jab•bing**
**jabi•ru** bird
**jabo•ran•di** shrub
**ja•bot** frill
**jaca•mar** bird
**ja•ça•na** bird
**jaca•ran•da** tree
**ja•cinth** gemstone
**jack**
**jack•al**
**jacka•napes**
**jack•ass**
**jack•boot**
**jack•daw**
**jack•eroo** (*or* **jacka•roo**; *plural* **•roos**) *Austral* trainee sheep-station manager
**jack•et**
**jack•et•ed**
**jack•fish** (*plural* **•fish** *or* **•fishes**)
**jack•fruit**
**jack•hammer**
**jack•knife** (*plural* **•knives**)
**jack•pot**
**jacks** game
**jack•shaft**
**jack•smelt** (*plural* **•smelts** *or* **•smelt**) fish
**jack•snipe** (*plural* **•snipe** *or* **•snipes**) bird
**Jack•son** US city
**Jack•son•ville** US port
**jack•stay** nautical term
**jack•straws** game
**Jaco•bean** of James I
**Ja•co•bian** maths term
**Jaco•bin** French radical
**Jaco•bin•ic** (*or* **•bini•cal**)
**Jaco•bin•ism**
**Jaco•bite** of James II
**Jaco•bit•ic**
**Jaco•bit•ism**
**ja•co•bus** (*plural* **•buses**) coin
**jaco•net** fabric
**Jac•quard** fabric; loom
**jac•ti•ta•tion** boasting
**Ja•cuzzi** (*Trademark*)
**jade**
**jad•ed**
**jade•ite** mineral
**jae•ger** marksman; bird
**Jael** biblical character
**Jaf•fa** Israeli port
**Jaff•na** Sri Lankan port
**jag** (**jag•ging, jagged**)
**jag•ged**
**jag•ged•ly**
**jag•ged•ness**
**jag•gery** (*or* **•gary, •ghery**) date sugar
**jag•ging**
**jag•gy** (**•gi•er, •gi•est**)
**jagu•ar**
**ja•gua•ron•di** (*or* **•run•**; *plural* **•dis**) feline

**jai alai** Spanish game
**jail** (*or* **gaol**)
**jail•bird** (*or* **gaol•**)
**jail•break** (*or* **gaol•**)
**jail•er** (*or* **•or, gaol•er**)
**jail•house**
**Jain** (*or* **Jai•na**) Hindu
**Jain•ism**
**Jain•ist**
**Jai•pur** Indian city
**Ja•ja•pu•ra** (*or* **Dja•**) Indonesian port
**Ja•kar•ta** (*or* **Dja•**) Indonesian capital
**jal•ap** (*or* **•op**) purgative
**ja•lap•ic**
**Ja•lis•co** Mexican state
**ja•lopy** (*or* **•lop•py**; *plural* **•lopies** *or* **•lop•pies**)
**jalou•sie** shutter
**jam** (**jam•ming, jammed**) crowd; preserve; *compare* **jamb**
**Ja•mai•ca**
**Ja•mai•can**
**jamb** (*or* **jambe**) part of frame; *compare* **jam**
**jam•ba•laya** Creole dish
**jam•bart** (*or* **jam•beau, jam•ber**; *plural* **•barts, •beaux,** *or* **•bers**) armour
**Jam•bi** (*or* **Djam•**) Indonesian port
**jam•bo•ree**
**jammed**
**jam•mer**
**jam•ming**
**Jam•mu** Indian city
**jam•my** (**•mi•er, •mi•est**)
**Jam•na•gar** Indian city
**jam•pan** sedan chair
**Jam•shed•pur** Indian city
**Jamshid** (*or* **Jamshyd**) mythological king
**Ja•na•ta** Indian political party
**jan•gle**
**jan•gler**
**Ja•nicu•lum** Roman hill
**jan•is•sary** (*or* **jani•zary**; *plural* **•saries** *or* **•zaries**) Turkish guard
**jani•tor** (*fem* **•tress**)
**jani•to•ri•al**
**Jan•sen•ism** Catholic doctrine
**Jan•sen•ist**
**Jan•sen•is•tic** (*or* **•ti•cal**)
**Janu•ary** (*plural* **•aries**)
**Janus** Roman god
**Ja•pan**
**ja•pan** (**•pan•ning, •panned**) lacquer
**Japa•nese**
**jape**
**jap•er**
**jap•ery**
**Japheth** biblical character
**jap•ing•ly**
**ja•poni•ca** shrub
**Ja•pu•rá** South American river
**jar** (**jar•ring, jarred**)
**jar•di•nière** plant holder
**jar•ful**
**jar•gon** language
**jar•gon** (*or* **•goon**) gemstone
**jar•goni•za•tion** (*or* **•sa•tion**)
**jar•gon•ize** (*or* **•ise**)
**jarl** Scandinavian chieftain
**jaro•site** mineral
**jarp** (*or* **jaup**) *Dialect* to smash
**jar•rah** tree
**jarred**
**jar•ring**
**jar•ring•ly**
**Jar•row** English port
**jar•vey** (*or* **•vie**) coachman
**jas•mine**
**jas•pé** variegated
**jas•per**
**Jat** (*plural* **Jat** *or* **Jats**) Indo-European people
**jato** (*plural* **•tos**) jet-assisted takeoff
**jaun•dice**
**jaunt**
**jaun•ti•ly**
**jaun•ty** (**•ti•er, •ti•est**)
**Java**
**Java•nese** (*or* **Ja•van**)
**jave•lin**
**jaw**
**Ja•wan** Indian soldier
**jaw•bone**
**jaw•breaker**
**jay**
**Jaya** (*or* **Dja•ja**) Indonesian mountain
**jay•walk**
**jay•walk•er**
**jay•walk•ing**
**jazz**
**jazzi•ly**
**jazzi•ness**
**jazzy** (**jazzi•er, jazzi•est**)
**jeal•ous**
**jeal•ous•ly**
**jeal•ousy** (*plural* **•ousies**)
**jeans**
**jeb•el** (*or* **djeb•**) Arab hill
**Jeb•el Musa** Moroccan mountain
**Jed•da** *variant spelling of* **Jidda**
**jeep**
**jeer**
**jeer•er**
**jeer•ing•ly**
**je•had** *variant spelling of* **jihad**
**Je•hol** Chinese region
**Je•ho•vah**
**Je•ho•vian** (*or* **•vic**)
**je•ju•nal**
**je•june** naive
**je•june•ly**
**je•june•ness** (*or* **je•jun•ity**)
**je•ju•num** small intestine
**Jekyll and Hyde**
**jell** (*or* **gel**; **jel•ling, jelled** *or* **gel•ling, gelled**) congeal; *compare* **gel**
**jel•laba** (*or* **•lab•ah**) cloak
**jel•lied**
**jel•li•fi•ca•tion**
**jel•li•fy** (**•fies, •fy•ing, •fied**)
**jello** *US* jelly
**jel•ly** (*noun, plural* **•lies**; *verb* **•lies, •ly•ing, •lied**)
**jelly•bean**
**jelly•fish** (*plural* **•fish** *or* **•fishes**)
**jem•my** (*noun, plural* **•mies**; *verb* **•mies, •my•ing, •mied**)
**jen•net** (*or* **gen•et, gen•net**) female donkey; *compare* **genet**
**jen•ny** (*plural* **•nies**) machine; female animal
**jeop•ard•ize** (*or* **•ise**)

**jeop•ardy**
**je•quir•ity** (*or* **•quer•**; *plural* **•ties**) plant
**jer•bil** *variant spelling of* **gerbil**
**jer•boa**
**jer•emi•ad** lamentation
**Je•rez** Spanish town
**Jeri•cho**
**je•rid** javelin
**jerk**
**jerk•er**
**jerki•ly**
**jer•kin** jacket; *compare* **gherkin**
**jerky** (**jerki•er, jerki•est**)
**jero•bo•am** wine bottle
**Jer•ry** (*plural* **•ries**) *Slang* German
**jer•ry** (*plural* **•ries**) *Slang* chamber pot
**jerry-build** (**-building, -built**)
**Jer•sey** island; cattle
**jer•sey** garment
**Je•ru•sa•lem**
**jess** falconry term
**jes•sa•mine** *Archaic* jasmine
**jest**
**jes•ter**
**Jesu**
**Jesu•it**
**Jesu•it•ic** (*or* **•iti•cal**)
**Jesu•it•ism** (*or* **•it•ry**)
**Jesus**
**jet** (**jet•ting, jet•ted**)
**jeté** ballet step
**jet•liner**
**jet•port**
**jet-propelled**
**jet•sam** (*or* **•som**)
**jet•setter**
**jet•ti•ness**
**jet•ti•son**
**jet•ton** gambling token
**jet•ty** (*plural* **•ties**)
**Jew**
**jew•el** (**•ell•ing, •elled**; *US* **•el•ing, •eled**)
**jewel•fish** (*plural* **•fish** *or* **•fishes**)
**jew•el•ler** (*US* **•el•er**)
**jew•el•lery** (*US* **•el•ry**)
**Jew•ess**
**jew•fish** (*plural* **•fish** *or* **•fishes**)
**Jew•ish**
**Jew•ish•ness**
**Jew•ry** (*plural* **•ries**)
**jew's-ear** fungus
**jew's-harp**
**Jezebel** biblical character
**jezebel** shameless woman
**Jhan•si** Indian city
**jib** (**jib•bing, jibbed**)
**jib•ber**
**jib•bons** *Dialect* spring onions
**jibe** *variant spelling of* **gibe** *or* **gybe**
**jib-headed**
**Ji•bou•ti** *variant spelling of* **Djibouti**
**Jid•da** (*or* **•dah, Jed•**) Saudi Arabian port
**jif•fy** (*or* **jiff**; *plural* **jif•fies** *or* **jiffs**)
**jig** (**jig•ging, jigged**)
**jig•ger**
**jig•gered**
**jigger•mast**
**jiggery-pokery**
**jig•ging**
**jig•gle**
**jig•gly**
**jig•saw**
**ji•had** (*or* **je•**) Islamic holy war
**jil•lion** large number
**jil•lionth**
**jilt**
**jilt•er**
**jin•gle**
**jin•gler**
**jin•gly** (**•gli•er, •gli•est**)
**jin•go** (*plural* **•goes**)
**jin•go•ism**
**jin•go•ist**
**jin•go•is•tic**
**jin•go•is•ti•cal•ly**
**Jin•ja** Ugandan town
**jink**
**jinks** high spirits; *compare* **jinx**
**jin•ni** (*or* **•nee, djin•ni, djin•ny**; *plural* **jinn** *or* **djinn**) Muslim spirit
**jinx** bad luck; *compare* **jinks**
**ji•pi•ja•pa** plant
**jit•ter**
**jitter•bug** (**•bug•ging, •bugged**)
**jit•tery**
**jive**
**Joab** biblical character
**Job** biblical character
**job** (**job•bing, jobbed**)
**job•ber**
**job•bery** corruption
**job•bing**
**Job•cen•tre**
**job•less**
**job•less•ness**
**Jocasta** mother of Oedipus
**Jock** *Slang* Scot
**jock•ey**
**jock•strap**
**jo•cose**
**jo•cose•ly**
**jo•cose•ness** (*or* **jo•cos•ity**)
**jocu•lar**
**jocu•lar•ity**
**joc•und**
**jo•cun•dity** (*or* **joc•und•ness**)
**Jodh•pur** Indian city
**jodh•purs** riding trousers
**Jodo** Buddhist sect
**joey** *Austral* young kangaroo
**jog** (**jog•ging, jogged**)
**jog•ger**
**jog•gle**
**jog•gler**
**Jog•ja•kar•ta** *variant spelling of* **Yokyakarta**
**jog-trot** (**-trot•ting, -trot•ted**)
**jo•han•nes** (*or* **•an•**; *plural* **•nes**) Portuguese coin
**Jo•han•nes•burg**
**John Dory** fish
**john•ny** (*plural* **•nies**) *Slang* man; condom
**John o'Groats**
**John•so•nian** of Samuel Johnson
**Jo•hore** Malaysian state
**joie de vivre**
**join**
**join•der** legal term
**join•er**
**join•ery**
**joint**
**joint•ed**

**joint•er**
**joint•ly**
**joint•ress** legal term
**join•ture** legal term
**joint•worm**
**joist**
**jo•joba** tree; oil
**joke**
**jok•er**
**jok•ey** (*or* **joky; joki•er, joki•est)**
**jok•ing•ly**
**jol•li•fi•ca•tion**
**jol•li•fy (•fies, •fy•ing, •fied)**
**jol•lity** (*plural* **•lities)**
**jol•ly** (*adj* **•li•er, •li•est;** *verb* **•lies, •ly•ing, •lied)**
**Jolo** Philippine island
**jolt**
**jolt•er**
**jolt•ing•ly**
**jolty**
**Jön•kö•ping** Swedish city
**jon•nock** *Dialect* genuine
**jon•quil**
**Jop•pa** biblical Jaffa
**Jor•dan**
**Jor•da•nian**
**jo•rum** drinking bowl
**Jos** Nigerian city
**josh** *US* tease
**joss** Chinese deity
**jos•tle**
**jos•tler**
**jot (jot•ting, jot•ted)**
**jot•ter**
**joual** Canadian French dialect
**joule** unit of energy
**jounce** jolt
**jour•nal**
**jour•nal•ese**
**jour•nal•ism**
**jour•nal•ist**
**jour•nal•is•tic**
**jour•nal•is•ti•cal•ly**
**jour•nali•za•tion** (*or* **•sa•tion)**
**jour•nal•ize** (*or* **•ise)** record in journal
**jour•nal•iz•er** (*or* **•is•er)**
**jour•ney**
**jour•ney•er**
**journey•man** (*plural* **•men)** craftsman
**journo** (*plural* **journos)** *Austral* journalist
**joust**
**joust•er**
**Jove** Roman god
**jo•vial**
**jo•vi•al•ity** (*or* **•ness)**
**jo•vi•al•ly**
**Jo•vian**
**jowl**
**joy**
**joy•ful**
**joy•ful•ly**
**joy•ful•ness**
**joy•less**
**joy•less•ness**
**joy•ous**
**joy•ous•ness**
**joy•pop (•pop•ping, •popped)** *Slang* take drugs
**joy-ride (-riding, -rode, -ridden)**
**joy•rider**
**Juan de Fuca** US–Canadian strait
**juba** African-American dance
**Ju•bal** biblical character
**Jub•bul•pore** *variant spelling of* **Jabalpur**
**jube** church gallery
**ju•bi•lance** (*or* **•lan•cy)**
**ju•bi•lant**
**ju•bi•late**
**ju•bi•la•tion**
**ju•bi•lee**
**Ju•daea** (*or* **•dea)**
**Ju•daean** (*or* **•dean)**
**Ju•da•ic** (*or* **•dai•cal)**
**Ju•dai•ca** Jewish literature
**Ju•da•ism**
**Ju•da•ist**
**Ju•da•is•tic**
**Ju•dai•za•tion** (*or* **•sa•tion)**
**Ju•da•ize** (*or* **•ise)**
**Ju•da•iz•er** (*or* **•is•er)**
**Judas** traitor
**ju•das** peephole
**jud•der**
**judge**
**judge•able**
**judg•er**
**judge•ship**
**judg•ing•ly**
**judg•ment** (*or* **judge•)**
**judg•men•tal** (*or* **judge•)**
**ju•di•cable**
**ju•di•ca•tive**
**ju•di•ca•tor** judge
**ju•di•ca•to•rial**
**ju•di•ca•tory**
**ju•di•ca•ture**
**ju•di•cial**
**ju•di•cial•ly**
**ju•di•ci•ary** (*plural* **•aries)**
**ju•di•cious**
**ju•di•cious•ly**
**ju•di•cious•ness**
**judo**
**ju•do•gi** judo costume
**ju•do•ist**
**ju•do•ka** judo expert
**Judy** (*or* **judy;** *plural* **Judies** *or* **judies)** *Slang* girl
**jug (jug•ging, jugged)**
**ju•gal** cheekbone
**ju•gate** botany term
**jug•ful** (*plural* **•fuls)**
**jugged**
**Jug•ger•naut** Hindu idol
**jug•ger•naut** vehicle; destructive force
**jug•ging**
**jug•gins** silly fellow
**jug•gle**
**jug•gler**
**jug•glery**
**jug•gling**
**ju•glan•da•ceous** botany term
**Ju•go•sla•via** *variant spelling of* **Yugoslavia**
**jugu•lar**
**ju•gum** biology term
**juice**
**juici•ly**
**juici•ness**
**juicy (juici•er, juici•est)**
**ju•jit•su** (*or* **ju•jut•su, jiu•)**
**juju** African fetish
**ju•ju•ism**
**ju•ju•ist**
**ju•jube** plant; sweet
**juke•box**
**ju•lep** drink
**Jul•ian** of Julius Caesar
**ju•li•enne** cookery term
**Jul•lun•dur** Indian city
**July** (*plural* **Julies)**
**jum•ble**

**jum•bler**
**jum•bly** (**•bli•er, •bli•est**)
**jum•bo** (*plural* **•bos**)
**jum•buck** *Austral* sheep
**Jum•na** Indian river
**jump**
**jump•able**
**jump•er**
**jumpi•ly**
**jumpi•ness**
**jump-off** (*noun*)
**jump-start**
**jumpy** (**jumpi•er, jumpi•est**)
**jun•ca•ceous** botany term
**jun•co** (*plural* **•cos**) bird
**junc•tion**
**junc•tion•al**
**junc•ture**
**Jun•diaí** Brazilian city
**June**
**Ju•neau** Alaskan capital
**Jung•frau** Swiss mountain
**Jung•ian** psychiatry term
**jun•gle**
**jun•gly** (**•gli•er, •gli•est**)
**jun•ior**
**ju•ni•per**
**junk**
**Jun•ker** Prussian landowner
**jun•ket**
**jun•ket•er** (*or* **•ket•ter, •ke•teer**)
**junkie** (*or* **junky**; *plural* **junkies**)
**junk•yard**
**Juno** Roman goddess; asteroid
**Ju•no•esque**
**jun•ta**
**Ju•pi•ter** planet
**Jupiter** Roman god
**ju•pon** garment
**Jura** European mountains; Scottish island
**jura** *plural of* **jus**
**ju•ral** of the law
**Ju•ras•sic** geological period
**ju•rat** legal term
**ju•ra•tory**
**ju•rel** fish
**ju•ridi•cal** (*or* **•rid•ic**)
**ju•ris•con•sult** legal advisor
**ju•ris•dic•tion**
**ju•ris•dic•tion•al**
**ju•ris•dic•tion•al•ly**
**ju•ris•dic•tive**
**ju•ris•pru•dence**
**ju•ris•pru•dent**
**ju•ris•pru•den•tial**
**ju•ris•pru•den•tial•ly**
**ju•rist**
**ju•ris•tic** (*or* **•ti•cal**)
**ju•ror**
**Ju•ruá** South American river
**jury** (*plural* **juries**)
**jury•man** (*plural* **•men**)
**jury-rigged** nautical term
**jury•woman** (*plural* **•women**)
**jus** (*plural* **jura**) legal right
**jus ci•vi•le** civil law
**jus di•vi•num** divine law
**jus na•tu•ra•le** natural law
**jus•sive** grammar term
**jus soli** legal term
**just**
**jus•tice**
**jus•tice•ship**
**jus•ti•ci•abil•ity**
**jus•ti•ci•able** subject to jurisdiction
**jus•ti•ci•ar** medieval legal officer
**jus•ti•ci•ar•ship**
**jus•ti•ci•ary** (*plural* **•aries**)
**jus•ti•fi•abil•ity** (*or* **•able•ness**)
**jus•ti•fi•able**
**jus•ti•fi•ably**
**jus•ti•fi•ca•tion**
**jus•ti•fi•ca•tory** (*or* **•tive**)
**jus•ti•fi•er**
**jus•ti•fy** (**•fies, •fy•ing, •fied**)
**jus•ti•fy•ing•ly**
**jus•tle** jostle
**just•ly**
**just•ness**
**jut** (**jut•ting, jut•ted**)
**Jute** Germanic tribe
**jute** fibre
**Jut•ish**
**Jut•land** Danish peninsula
**Jut•land•er**
**jut•ted**
**jut•ting**
**ju•venes•cence** youth
**ju•venes•cent**
**ju•venile**
**ju•venilia**
**ju•venil•ity** (*plural* **•ities**)
**jux•ta•pose**
**jux•ta•po•si•tion**
**jux•ta•po•si•tion•al**

# K

**kab•ba•la** (*or* **ka•ba•la**) *variant spellings of* **cabbala**
**ka•ba•ra•go•ya** lizard
**Ka•bardino-Balkar** Russian republic
**ka•bu•ki** Japanese drama
**Ka•bul** Afghan capital
**Ka•byle** (*plural* **•byles** *or* **•byle**) Berber people
**ka•chang pu•teh** Malaysian dish
**ka•chi•na** American Indian spirit
**Kad•dish** (*plural* **kad•di•shim**) Jewish prayer
**Ka•di•yev•ka** *former name of* **Stakhanov**
**Ka•du•na** Nigerian state
**Kaf•fir** (*plural* **•firs** *or* **•fir**)
**kaf•fir** sorghum
**Kaf•ir** (*plural* **•irs** *or* **•ir**) Afghan people
**kaf•tan** (*or* **caf•**)
**Ka•gera** African river
**Ka•go•shi•ma** Japanese port
**kai•ak** *variant spelling of* **kayak**
**Kai•feng** Chinese city
**kail** *variant spelling of* **kale**
**kai•nite** mineral
**kai•no•gen•esis** *variant spelling of* **caenogenesis**
**Kai•ser**
**kai•ser•dom** (*or* **•ism**)

**Kai•sers•lau•tern** German city
**kaka** parrot
**ka•ka•po** (*plural* **•pos**) parrot
**ka•kemo•no** (*plural* **•nos**) Japanese wall hanging
**kaki** (*plural* **kakis**) fruit
**kala-azar** disease
**Ka•la•ha•ri** African desert
**Kala•ma•zoo** US city
**Ka•lat** (*or* **Khe•**) Pakistani region
**kale** (*or* **kail**) cabbage
**ka•lei•do•scope**
**ka•lei•do•scop•ic**
**ka•lei•do•scopi•cal•ly**
**kal•ends** *variant spelling of* **calends**
**kale•yard** (*or* **kail•**) *Scot* vegetable garden
**Kal•goor•lie** Australian city
**Kali** Hindu goddess
**kali** plant
**kal•ian** hookah
**ka•lif** (*or* **kha•**) *variant spellings of* **caliph**
**Ka•li•nin** *former name of* **Tver**
**Ka•li•nin•grad** Russian port
**kal•mia** shrub
**Kal•muck** (*or* **•myk**; *plural* **•mucks, •muck** *or* **•myks, •myk**) Mongoloid people
**ka•long** fruit bat
**kal•so•mine** *variant spelling of* **calcimine**
**Ka•lu•ga** Russian city
**Kama** Russian river; Hindu god
**kama•cite** alloy
**Kama•ku•ra** Japanese city
**ka•ma•la** tree
**Ka•ma•su•tra** Hindu text
**Kam•chat•ka** Russian peninsula
**kame** mound
**Kamensk-Uralski** Russian city
**Ka•met** Indian mountain
**kami** (*plural* **kami**) Japanese spirit
**ka•mi•ka•ze**
**Kam•pa•la** Ugandan capital
**kam•pong** Malaysian village
**Kampuchea**
**Kampuchean**
**kana** Japanese writing
**kana•my•cin** antibiotic
**Ka•nan•ga** city in the Democratic Republic of Congo
**Ka•na•ra** (*or* **Ca•**) Indian region
**Ka•na•rese** (*or* **Ca•**; *plural* **•rese**)
**Kana•za•wa** Japanese port
**Kan•chi•pu•ram** Indian city
**Kan•da•har** Afghan city
**Kan•dy** Sri Lankan city
**kan•ga** (*or* **khan•**) African garment
**kan•ga•roo** (*plural* **•roos**)
**Kang•chen•jun•ga** (*or* **Kan•chen•**) Himalayan mountain
**Kan•na•da** Indian language
**Kano** Nigerian state
**Kan•pur** Indian city
**Kan•sas**
**Kan•su** Chinese province
**kan•tar** unit of weight
**Kant•ian**
**Kant•ian•ism** (*or* **Kant•ism**) philosophy
**Kao•hsiung** (*or* **Kao-hsiung**) Chinese port
**kao•li•ang** sorghum
**kao•lin** (*or* **•line**)
**kao•lin•ic**
**kao•lin•ite** mineral
**kaon** physics particle
**ka•pell•meis•ter** (*plural* **•ter**)
**ka•pok**
**kap•pa** Greek letter
**ka•put** *Slang* not functioning; *compare* **caput**
**kara•bi•ner** mountaineering clip
**Karachai-Cherkess** Russian region
**Ka•ra•chi** Pakistani city
**Ka•ra•gan•da** Kazakh city
**Kara•ite** Jewish sect
**Kara-Kalpak** Uzbek republic
**Ka•ra•ko•ram** mountain range
**Ka•ra•ko•rum** Mongolian city
**kara•kul** (*or* **cara•**) sheep; *compare* **caracul**
**ka•ra•te**
**Kar•ba•la** (*or* **Ker•be•**) Iraqi town
**Ka•relia** Russian republic
**Ka•relian**
**Ka•ren** (*plural* **•rens** *or* **•ren**) Thai language and people
**Ka•ri•ba** African lake and dam
**Karl-Marx-Stadt** *former name of* **Chemnitz**
**Karls•ruhe** German city
**kar•ma** destiny
**kar•mic**
**Kar•na•taka** Indian state
**Ka•roo** (*or* **Kar•roo**) South African plateau
**ka•roo** (*or* **kar•roo**; *plural* **•roos**) plateau
**ka•ross** African garment
**kar•ri** tree
**karst** limestone scenery
**karst•ic**
**karyo•gam•ic**
**kary•oga•my** biology term
**karyo•ki•nesis**
**karyo•ki•net•ic**
**karyo•lymph**
**kary•oly•sis**
**karyo•lyt•ic**
**karyo•plasm**
**karyo•plas•mic** (*or* **•mat•ic**)
**karyo•some**
**karyo•type**
**karyo•typ•ic** (*or* **•typi•cal**)
**Ka•sai** African river
**kas•bah** (*or* **cas•**)
**ka•sher** *variant spelling of* **kosher**
**Kash•gar** Chinese city
**Kash•mir**
**Kash•miri** (*plural* **•miris** *or* **•miri**)
**Kash•mir•ian**
**Kas•sa•la** Sudanese city
**Kas•sel** German city
**kat** (*or* **khat**) narcotic
**kata•bat•ic** meteorology term
**ka•ta•ka•na** Japanese writing
**Ka•tan•ga** *former name of* **Shaba**

**Kat•an•gese**
**Ka•thia•war** Indian peninsula
**Kat•mai** Alaskan volcano
**Kat•man•du** (*or* **Kath•**) Nepalese capital
**Ka•to•wi•ce** Polish city
**Kat•si•na** Nigerian city
**Kat•te•gat** Scandinavian strait
**ka•ty•did** insect
**Ka•uai** Hawaiian island
**Kau•nas** Lithuanian city
**kau•ri** (*or* **•ry**; *plural* **•ris** *or* **•ries**) tree
**kava** drink
**Ka•wa•sa•ki** Japanese port
**kay•ak** (*or* **kai•**) canoe
**Kay•seri** Turkish city
**ka•za•chok** dance
**Ka•zakh** (*or* **•zak**; *plural* **•zakhs** *or* **•zaks**)
**Ka•zakh•stan** Central Asian country
**Ka•zan** Russian city
**Kaz•bek** Georgian volcano
**ka•zoo** (*plural* **•zoos**) musical instrument
**ke•bab**
**keck** retch
**Ked•ah** Malaysian state
**ked•dah** *variant spelling of* **kheda**
**kedge** nautical term
**ked•geree**
**Ke•di•ri** Indonesian city
**keek** *Scot* peep
**keel**
**keel•haul**
**keel•son** (*or* **kel•**)
**keen**
**keen•ness**
**keep** (**keep•ing, kept**)
**keep•er**
**keep•net**
**keep•sake**
**kees•hond** (*plural* **•honds** *or* **•honden**) dog
**Kee•wa•tin** Canadian district
**keg**
**Keigh•ley** Yorkshire town
**keis•ter** (*or* **kees•**) *US* buttocks
**keit•loa** rhinoceros
**Ke•lan•tan** Malaysian state
**ke•loid** (*or* **che•**) scar tissue
**ke•loi•dal** (*or* **che•**)
**kelp** seaweed
**kel•pie** (*or* **•py**; *plural* **•pies**) sheepdog
**kel•son** *variant spelling of* **keelson**
**Kelt** *variant spelling of* **Celt**
**kelt** salmon
**kel•ter** (*or esp. US* **kil•**)
**Kelt•ic** *variant spelling of* **Celtic**
**kel•vin** unit
**Ke•mero•vo** Russian city
**kempt** tidy
**ken** (**ken•ning, kenned** *or* **kent**)
**ke•naf** fibre
**Ken•dal** Cumbrian town
**ken•do** Japanese sport
**Ken•il•worth** Warwickshire town
**kenned** (*or* **kent**)
**ken•nel** (**•nel•ling, •nelled**; *US* **•nel•ing, •neled**)
**ke•no** (*or* **kee•no, ki•no, qui•no**) US game
**ke•no•sis** theology term
**ke•not•ic**
**Ken•sing•ton**
**ken•speckle** *Scot* easily recognized
**Kent**
**ken•te** fabric
**Kent•ish**
**kent•ledge** ship's ballast
**Ken•tuck•ian**
**Ken•tucky**
**Ken•ya**
**Ken•yan**
**Keos** Greek island
**kep** *Dialect* to catch
**kepi** (*plural* **kepis**) military cap
**kept**
**Kera•la** Indian state
**kera•tin** protein
**ke•rat•ini•za•tion** (*or* **•sa•tion**)
**ke•rat•in•ize** (*or* **•ise**)
**kera•ti•tis** eye disease
**kera•tog•enous**
**kera•toid** horny
**kera•to•plas•tic**
**kera•to•plas•ty** (*plural* **•ties**) eye surgery
**kera•tose** zoology term
**kera•to•sis** skin condition
**kerb** (*US* **curb**) pavement edge; *compare* **curb**
**Ker•be•la** *variant spelling of* **Karbala**
**kerb•ing** (*US* **curb•**)
**kerb•stone** (*US* **curb•**)
**Kerch** Ukrainian port
**ker•chief**
**ker•chiefed**
**kerf** saw cut
**ker•fuf•fle**
**Ker•gue•len Is•lands**
**Ker•man** Iranian city
**Ker•man•shah** Iranian city
**ker•mes** insect; dye
**ker•mis** Dutch carnival
**kern** (*or* **kerne**) printing term
**ker•nel**
**ker•nite** mineral
**kero•sene** (*or* **•sine**)
**Ker•ry** Irish county
**Ker•ry** (*plural* **•ries**) cattle
**ker•sey** woollen cloth
**ker•sey•mere** woollen cloth
**Kes•te•ven** Lincolnshire region
**kes•trel**
**Kes•wick**
**ketch** sailing vessel
**ketch•up** (*US also* **catch•up, cat•sup**)
**ke•tene** toxic gas
**keto** chemistry term
**ke•tone**
**ke•ton•ic**
**ke•to•nu•ria**
**ke•tose** sugar
**ke•to•sis** medical term
**ke•tox•ime**
**Ket•ter•ing** Northamptonshire town
**ket•tle**
**kettle•drum**
**kettle•drummer**
**kettle•ful**
**kev•el** nautical term
**Kew**
**kex** plant
**key**
**key•board**

**key•hole**
**Keynes•ian•ism** economic theory
**key•note**
**key•stone**
**key•stroke**
**key•way**
**Kha•ba•rovsk** Russian port
**khad•dar** (*or* **kha•di**) Indian cloth
**Kha•kass** Russian region
**kha•ki** (*plural* **•kis**)
**Khal•kha** Mongolian language
**kham•sin** (*or* **kam•seen, •sin**) wind
**khan**
**khan•ate**
**khan•ga** *variant spelling of* **kanga**
**kha•rif** Indian crop
**Khar•kov** Ukrainian city
**Khar•toum** (*or* **•tum**)
**khat** *variant spelling of* **kat**
**kha•yal** Indian music
**kheda** (*or* **khed•ah, ked•dah**) elephant enclosure
**khe•dive** viceroy of Egypt
**Kher•son** Ukrainian port
**Khmer** Cambodian people
**Khmer•ian**
**Kho•dzhent** Tadzhik city
**Khoi•khoi** language group
**Khoi•san** language
**Kho•tan** *variant of* **Hotien**
**Khul•na** Bangladeshi city
**khus•khus** grass
**Khy•ber Pass**
**ki•aat** tree
**ki•ang** wild ass
**Kiang•si** Chinese province
**Kiang•su** Chinese province
**Kiao•chow** Chinese territory
**kib•ble**
**kib•butz** (*plural* **•but•zim**)
**kib•butz•nik**
**kibe** chilblain
**kib•itz** *US* interfere
**kib•lah** (*or* **•la**) direction of Mecca
**ki•bosh**
**kick**
**kick•able**
**kick•back**
**kick•er**
**kick•off**
**kick•shaw** trinket
**kick•sorter** physics apparatus
**kick•stand**
**kick-start**
**kid** (**kid•ding, kid•ded**)
**kid•der**
**Kid•der•min•ster**
**kid•ding**
**kid•dle** device for catching fish
**Kid•dush** Jewish blessing
**kid•dy** (*or* **•die**; *plural* **•dies**)
**kid•nap** (**•nap•ping, •napped**; *US* **•nap•ing, •naped**)
**kid•nap•per** (*US* **•nap•er**)
**kid•ney**
**kid•skin**
**Kiel** German port
**Kiel•ce** Polish city
**kier** bleaching vat
**kie•sel•guhr** soft rock
**kie•ser•ite** mineral
**Kiev**
**kif** (*or* **kaif, keef, kef, kief**) marijuana
**Ki•ga•li** capital of Rwanda
**ki•koi** cloth
**kiku•mon** Japanese emblem
**Ki•ku•yu** (*plural* **•yus** *or* **•yu**) African people
**Kil•dare**
**Kili•man•ja•ro**
**Kil•ken•ny**
**kill**
**Kil•lar•ney**
**kill•deer** (*plural* **•deer** *or* **•deers**) bird
**kill•er**
**kil•lick** (*or* **•lock**) anchor
**Kil•lie•cran•kie** Scottish battle site
**kil•li•fish** (*plural* **•fish** *or* **•fishes**)
**kill•ing**
**kill•ing•ly**
**kill-joy**
**Kil•mar•nock**
**kiln**
**kilo** (*plural* **kilos**)
**kilo•calo•rie**
**kilo•cycle**
**kilo•gram** (*or* **•gramme**)
**kilo•hertz**
**kilo•metre** (*US* **•meter**)
**kilo•met•ric** (*or* **•ri•cal**)
**kilo•ton**
**kilo•volt**
**kilo•watt**
**kilowatt-hour**
**kilt**
**kilt•ed**
**kil•ter** *variant spelling* (*esp. US*) *of* **kelter**
**Kim•ber•ley** South African city
**kim•ber•lite** rock
**ki•mo•no** (*plural* **•nos**)
**ki•mo•noed**
**kin**
**Kina•ba•lu** Malaysian mountain
**kin•aes•the•sia** (*or* **•sis**; *US* **•es•**) physiology term
**kin•aes•thet•ic** (*US* **•es•**)
**ki•nase** biochemical agent
**Kin•car•dine** (*or* **Kin•car•dine•shire**) former Scottish county
**kin•cob** fabric
**kind**
**kin•der•gar•ten**
**kin•der•gar•ten•er**
**kind-hearted**
**kind-hearted•ly**
**kind-hearted•ness**
**kin•dle**
**kin•dler**
**kind•less** *Archaic* heartless
**kind•li•ness**
**kin•dling**
**kind•ly** (**•li•er, •li•est**)
**kind•ness**
**kin•dred**
**kin•dred•ness** (*or* **kin•dred•ship**)
**kine** cattle
**kin•emat•ic**
**kin•emati•cal•ly**
**kin•emat•ics** branch of physics
**ki•nesics** study of body language
**ki•net•ic**
**ki•neti•cal•ly**
**ki•net•ics** branch of mechanics

**ki•neto•nu•cle•us**
**ki•neto•plast**
**king**
**king•bird**
**king•bolt**
**king•cup**
**king•dom**
**king•fish** (*plural* **•fish** *or* **•fishes**)
**king•fisher**
**king•let**
**king•li•ness**
**king•ly**
**king•maker**
**king-of-arms** (*plural* **kings-**)
**king•pin**
**king•ship**
**king-size** (*or* **-sized**)
**King's Lynn**
**King•ston** Jamaican capital; Canadian port
**Kingston upon Thames**
**Kings•town** capital of St Vincent and the Grenadines
**King•wa•na** African language
**king•wood**
**ki•nin** protein
**kink**
**kin•ka•jou** animal
**kinki•ly**
**kinki•ness**
**kinky** (**kinki•er, kinki•est**)
**kin•ni•kin•nick** (*or* **•ki•nic**) mixture for smoking
**kino** resin
**Kin•ross** former Scottish county
**kins•folk**
**Kin•sha•sa** capital of the Democratic Republic of Congo
**kin•ship**
**kins•man** (*plural* **•men**)
**kins•woman** (*plural* **•women**)
**ki•osk**
**kip** (**kip•ping, kipped**)
**kip•per**
**Kir•ghiz** (*or* **•giz**; *plural* **•ghiz** *or* **•giz**) *variant spelling of* **Kyrgyz**
**Kir•ghi•zia** (*or* **•gi•**) *variant spelling of* **Kyrgyzstan**
**Ki•ri•ba•ti** island republic
**kiri•gami** paper cutting
**Ki•rin** Chinese province
**kirk**
**Kirk•by** Merseyside town
**Kirk•cal•dy** Scottish port
**Kirk•cud•bright** Scottish county
**kirk•man** (*plural* **•men**) *Scot* church member
**Kirk•patrick** Antarctic mountain
**Kir•kuk** Iraqi city
**Kirk•wall** Scottish town
**Kir•man** Persian carpet
**Ki•rov** Russian city
**Ki•ro•va•bad** *former name of* **Gandzha**
**Ki•ro•vo•grad** Ukrainian city
**Kirsch** (*or* **Kirsch•was•ser**) cherry brandy
**Ki•run•di** African language
**Kis•an•ga•ni** city in the Democratic Republic of Congo
**kish** graphite
**Ki•shi•nev** *Russian name of* **Chişinău**
**kis•met**
**kiss**
**kiss•able**
**kis•sel** Russian dessert
**kiss•er**
**kiss•ing**
**kist** *Dialect* large coffer
**kit** (**kit•ting, kit•ted**)
**Ki•ta•kyu•shu** Japanese port
**kit•bag**
**kitch•en**
**Kitch•ener** Canadian town
**kitch•en•ette** (*or* **•et**)
**kitchen•ware**
**kite**
**kith**
**kitsch**
**kit•ten**
**kit•ten•ish**
**kit•ten•ish•ness**
**kit•ti•wake**
**kit•tle** *Scot* capricious
**kit•ty** (*plural* **•ties**)
**Kit•we** Zambian city
**kiva** underground room
**Ki•wa•nis** US organization
**kiwi** (*plural* **kiwis**)
**Klai•pe•da** Lithuanian port
**klang•far•be** musical term
**Klans•man** (*plural* **•men**) Ku Klux Klan member
**klax•on**
**Kleen•ex** (*Trademark*; *plural* **•ex** *or* **•exes**)
**klepht** Greek brigand
**kleph•tic**
**klep•to•ma•nia** (*or* **clep•**)
**klep•to•ma•ni•ac** (*or* **clep•**)
**klip•spring•er** antelope
**Klon•dike** Canadian region
**kloof** mountain pass
**klys•tron** electronics apparatus
**knack**
**knack•er**
**knack•ery**
**knack•wurst** (*or* **knock•**) sausage
**knag** knot in wood
**knap** (**knap•ping, knapped**) *Dialect* hill crest; to hit
**knap•per**
**knap•sack**
**knap•weed**
**knar** *variant spelling of* **knur**
**knave**
**knav•ery** (*plural* **•eries**)
**knav•ish**
**knav•ish•ness**
**knaw•el** plant
**knead**
**knead•er**
**knee** (**knee•ing, kneed**)
**knee•cap** (**•cap•ping, •capped**)
**knee-deep**
**knee•hole**
**kneel** (**kneel•ing, knelt** *or* **kneeled**)
**kneel•er**
**knee•pad**
**knee•pan** kneecap
**knees-up**
**knell**
**knelt**
**Knes•set** Israeli parliament
**knew**
**Knickerbocker** *US* New Yorker
**knick•er•bock•ers**

**knick•ers**
**knick•knack** (*or* **nick•nack**)
**knick•point**
**knife** (*plural* **knives**)
**knif•er**
**knife•rest**
**knight**
**knight-errant** (*plural* **knights-**)
**knight-errantry**
**knight•head** nautical term
**knight•hood**
**knight•li•ness**
**knight•ly**
**knish** dumpling
**knit** (**knit•ting, knit•ted** *or* **knit**)
**knit•table**
**knit•ter**
**knit•ting**
**knit•wear**
**knob** (**knob•bing, knobbed**) projection; *compare* **nob**
**knob•bly** (**•bli•er, •bli•est**)
**knob•by** (**•bi•er, •bi•est**)
**knob•ker•rie** stick
**knock**
**knock•down** (*adj*)
**knock•er**
**knock-kneed**
**knock-on**
**knock•out**
**knoll**
**Knos•sos** (*or* **Cnos•sus**) Cretan city
**knot** (**knot•ting, knot•ted**)
**knot•grass**
**knot•hole**
**knot•ted**
**knot•ter**
**knot•ti•ly**
**knot•ti•ness**
**knot•ting**
**knot•ty** (**•ti•er, •ti•est**)
**knot•weed**
**knout** whip
**know** (**know•ing, knew, known**)
**know•able**
**know-all**
**know•er**
**know-how**
**know•ing**
**know•ing•ly**
**know•ing•ness**
**knowl•edge**
**knowl•edge•able** (*or* **•edg•able**)
**knowl•edge•ably**
**known**
**Knox•ville** US city
**knuck•le**
**knuckle•bone**
**knuckle-duster**
**knuckle•head**
**knuck•ly**
**knur** (*or* **knurr, knar**) knot in wood
**knurl** (*or* **nurl**) ridge
**knurled**
**KO** (*verb* **KO's, KO'ing, KO'ed**; *noun, plural* **KO's**)
**koa** tree
**koa•la**
**koan** Buddhist riddle
**kob** antelope
**Kobe** Japanese port
**Ko•blenz** (*or* **Co•**) German city
**kob•old** mythological spirit
**Ko•chi** Japanese port
**Kodak** (*Trademark*)
**Ko•di•ak** bear; Alaskan island
**Ko•dok** Sudanese town
**kof•ta** Indian food
**koft•gar** Indian goldsmith
**Ko•hi•ma** Indian city
**Kohi•noor** (*or* **•nor, •nur**) diamond
**kohl** cosmetic
**kohl•ra•bi** (*plural* **•bies**) cabbage
**Ko•hou•tek** comet
**koi•ne** common language
**Ko•kand** Uzbek city
**ko•kanee** salmon
**Koko Nor** (*or* **Kuka Nor**) Chinese lake
**kola** *variant spelling of* **cola**
**Kol•ha•pur** Indian city
**ko•lin•sky** (*plural* **•skies**) mink
**kol•khoz** (*or* **•khos, •koz**) collective farm
**Kol Ni•dre** Jewish prayer
**kolo** (*plural* **kolos**) dance
**Ko•lom•na** Russian city
**Ko•lo•ni•a** capital of Micronesia
**Ko•ly•ma** Russian river
**Ko•ma•ti** African river
**ko•mat•ik** Eskimo sledge
**Komi** (*plural* **•mi** *or* **•mis**) Finnish people
**Kom•mu•narsk** *former name of* **Alchevsk**
**Ko•mo•do** Indonesian island
**Kom•so•mol** former Soviet association
**Kom•so•molsk** Russian city
**Kon•go** (*plural* **•gos** *or* **•go**) African people
**kon•go•ni** animal
**ko•ni•ol•ogy** (*or* **co•**)
**Kon•stanz** *variant spelling of* **Constance**
**Kon•ya** (*or* **Konia**) Turkish city
**koo•doo** *variant spelling of* **kudu**
**kook** *US* eccentric person
**kooka•bur•ra**
**kooky** (*or* **kookie; kooki•er, kooki•est**) *US* crazy
**Koo•te•nay** (*or* **•nai**) US river
**kop** hill
**ko•peck** (*or* **•pek, co•peck**) Russian coin
**Ko•peisk** (*or* **•peysk**) Russian city
**kop•je** (*or* **•pie**) hill
**Ko•ran**
**Ko•ran•ic**
**Kor•do•fan** Sudanese province
**Ko•rea**
**Ko•rean**
**kor•ma** food
**Kor•or** capital of Belau
**ko•ru•na** Czech coin
**Kos** Greek island
**kos** (*plural* **kos**) Indian unit of distance
**Kos•ci•us•ko** Australian mountain
**ko•sher** (*or* **ka•**)
**Ko•ši•ce** Czech city
**Kosovo-Metohi•ja** region in Serbia
**Ko•stro•ma** Russian city

**Kota** (*or* **Ko•tah**) Indian city
**koto** (*plural* **kotos**) musical instrument
**kou•li•bia•ca** (*or* **cou•**) food
**kou•mis** (*or* **•miss**) *variant spellings of* **kumiss**
**Kov•rov** Russian city
**kow•hai** tree
**Kow•loon** part of Hong Kong
**kow•tow**
**kow•tow•er**
**Ko•zhi•kode** Indian port
**Kra** Thai isthmus
**kraal** (*or* **craal**) African village
**kraft** wrapping paper; *compare* **craft**
**krait** snake
**Kra•ka•toa** (*or* **•tau**) Indonesian island
**kra•ken** sea monster
**Kra•ma•torsk** Ukrainian city
**kra•meria** shrub
**Kras•no•dar** Russian city
**Kras•no•yarsk** Russian city
**Kre•feld** German city
**Kre•men•chug** Ukrainian city
**Krem•lin**
**krieg•spiel** war game
**krill** (*plural* **krill**)
**krim•mer** (*or* **crim•**) lambswool
**Krio** African language
**kris** knife
**Krish•na**
**Krish•naism**
**Kriss Krin•gle** *US* Santa Claus
**Kris•tian•sand** Norwegian port
**Kris•tian•stad** Swedish town
**kro•mes•ky** savoury dish
**kró•na** (*plural* **•nur**) Icelandic or Swedish coin
**kro•ne** (*plural* **•ner**) Danish or Norwegian coin
**Kron•stadt** Russian port
**kroon** (*plural* **kroons** *or* **krooni**) Estonian coin
**Kru•gers•dorp** South African city
**kryp•ton**
**Kua•la Lum•pur**
**Ku•ching** Malaysian port
**ku•dos** prestige
**kudu** (*or* **koo•doo**) antelope
**kud•zu** plant
**Ku•fic** (*or* **Cu•**) Arabic script
**Kui•by•shev** (*or* **Kuy•**) *former name of* **Samara**
**Ku Klux Klan**
**Ku Klux•er** (*or* **Ku Klux Klan•ner**)
**kuk•ri** (*plural* **•ris**) Gurkha knife
**kula** Pacific island ceremony
**ku•lak** wealthy Russian peasant
**Ku•ma•mo•to** Japanese city
**Ku•masi** Ghanaian city
**kum•ba•loi** worry beads
**ku•miss** (*or* **kou•miss, kou•mis, kou•myss**) drink
**küm•mel** German liqueur
**kum•quat** (*or* **cum•**) fruit
**kung fu**
**Kun•gur** Chinese mountain
**Kun•lun** (*or* **Kuen•, Kwen•**) Chinese mountains
**Kun•ming** (*or* **K'un-ming**) Chinese city
**kunz•ite** gemstone
**Kuo•min•tang** (*or* **Guo•min•dang**) political party
**Ku•ra** Asian river
**Kurd** Turkic people
**Kurd•ish**
**Kur•di•stan** (*or* **Kur•destan, Kor•destan**)
**Kure** Japanese port
**Kur•gan** Russian city
**Ku•ril Is•lands**
**kur•ra•jong** (*or* **cur•**) tree
**kur•saal** building at health resort
**Kursk** Russian city
**kur•to•sis** statistics term
**Kus•ko•kwim** Alaskan river
**Ku•tai•si** Georgian city
**Kutch** (*or* **Cutch**) former Indian state
**Ku•wait**
**Ku•wai•ti**
**Kuz•netsk Ba•sin** Russian region
**kvass** (*or* **kvas, quass**) drink
**Kwa** language group
**kwa•cha** Zambian currency
**Kwa•ja•lein** Pacific atoll
**Kwa•ki•utl** (*plural* **•utl** *or* **•utls**) American Indian
**Kwang•chow•an** Chinese region
**Kwang•ju** Korean city
**Kwangsi-Chuang** Chinese region
**Kwang•tung** Chinese province
**kwan•za** Angolan currency
**kwashi•or•kor** protein deficiency
**Kwa•Zu•lu/Na•tal** South African province
**Kwei•chow** (*or* **Kuei•chou**) Chinese province
**Kwei•lin** (*or* **Kuei-lin**) Chinese city
**Kwei•yang** (*or* **Kuei-yang**) Chinese city
**kwe•la** African music
**ky•ani•za•tion** (*or* **•sa•tion**)
**ky•an•ize** (*or* **•ise**) treat timber
**kyat** Burmese currency
**kyle** *Scot* narrow strait
**ky•lix** (*or* **cy•lix**; *plural* **•li•kes**) drinking vessel
**ky•loe** cattle
**ky•mo•graph** (*or* **cy•**) medical instrument
**ky•mo•graph•ic** (*or* **cy•**)
**Kyo•to** (*or* **Kio•**) Japanese city
**ky•pho•sis** (*plural* **•ses**) spinal curvature
**ky•phot•ic**
**Kyr•gyz** (*plural* **•gyz**)
**Kyr•gyz•stan** Central Asian country
**Kyrie elei•son**
**kyu** judo grade
**Kyu•shu** (*or* **Kiu•**) Japanese island

# L

**laa•ger** (*or* **la•**) African camp; *compare* **lager**
**lab**
**laba•rum** (*plural* **•ra**) Christian banner
**lab•da•num** (*or* **la•**) plant resin
**la•bel** (**•bel•ling, •belled**; *US* **•bel•ing, •beled**)
**la•bel•ler** (*US* **•bel•er**)
**la•bel•loid**
**la•bel•lum** (*plural* **•la**) biology term
**la•bia** *plural of* **labium**
**la•bial**
**la•bi•al•ism**
**la•bi•al•ity**
**la•bi•ali•za•tion** (*or* **•sa•tion**)
**la•bi•al•ize** (*or* **•ise**)
**la•bial•ly**
**la•bi•ate** plant
**la•bile**
**la•bil•ity**
**la•bio•den•tal**
**la•bio•na•sal**
**la•bio•velar**
**la•bium** (*plural* **•bia**)
**lab•lab** bean
**la•bora•tory** (*plural* **•tories**)
**La•bor** Australian political party
**la•bor** *US spelling of* **labour**
**la•bo•ri•ous**
**la•bo•ri•ous•ly**
**la•bo•ri•ous•ness**
**La•bour** British political party
**la•bour** (*US* **•bor**)
**la•boured** (*US* **•bored**)
**la•boured•ly** (*US* **•bored•**)
**la•bour•er** (*US* **•bor•**)
**la•bour•ism** (*US* **•bor•**)
**la•bour•ist** (*US* **•bor•**)
**La•bour•ite** Labour Party supporter
**Lab•ra•dor** Canadian peninsula; dog
**lab•ra•dor•ite** mineral
**la•bret** lip ornament
**lab•roid** (*or* **•rid**) fish
**la•brum** (*plural* **•bra**) lip
**La•buan** Malaysian island
**la•bur•num**
**Laby•rinth** mythological maze
**laby•rinth**
**laby•rin•thi•cal•ly**
**laby•rin•thine** (*or* **•thian, •thic**)
**lac** resin; *variant spelling of* **lakh**
**lac•co•lith** (*or* **•lite**) geology term
**lac•co•lith•ic** (*or* **•lit•ic**)
**lace**
**Lac•edae•mon** Sparta
**Lac•edae•mo•nian**
**lac•er**
**lac•er•abil•ity**
**lac•er•able**
**lac•er•ant** distressing
**lac•er•ate**
**lac•era•tion**
**lac•era•tive**
**La•cer•ta** constellation
**lac•er•til•ian** lizard
**lace-up** (*adj, noun*)
**lace•wing** insect
**(lacey)** *incorrect spelling of* **lacy**
**lach•es** (*sing.*) legal term
**lach•ry•mal** *variant spelling of* **lacrimal**
**lach•ry•ma•tory** (*plural* **•tories**) vessel; *variant spelling of* **lacrimatory**
**lach•ry•mose**
**lach•ry•mose•ly**
**lach•ry•mos•ity**
**laci•ly**
**laci•ness**
**lac•ing**
**la•cini•ate** (*or* **•cinia•ted**) jagged
**la•cinia•tion**
**lack**
**lacka•dai•si•cal**
**lacka•dai•si•cal•ly**
**lacka•dai•si•cal•ness**
**lack•ey**
**lack•lustre** (*US* **•luster**)
**La•co•nia** ancient Greek country
**La•co•nian**
**la•con•ic** (*or* **•coni•cal**) of few words
**la•coni•cal•ly**
**La Co•ru•ña** (*or* **Co•run•na**) Spanish port
**lac•quer**
**lac•quer•er**
**lac•ri•mal** (*or* **lach•ry•, lac•ry•**)
**lac•ri•ma•tion**
**lac•ri•ma•tor** (*or* **lach•ry•, lac•ry•**) substance causing tear flow
**lac•ri•ma•tory** (*or* **lach•ry•, lac•ry•**; *adj*) of tears; *compare* **lachrymatory**
**la•crosse**
**lac•tal•bu•min**
**lac•tam** chemical group
**lac•ta•ry** of milk
**lac•tase** enzyme
**lac•tate**
**lac•ta•tion**
**lac•ta•tion•al**
**lac•ta•tion•al•ly**
**lac•teal**
**lac•teal•ly**
**lac•tes•cence**
**lac•tes•cent**
**lac•tic**
**lac•tif•er•ous**
**lac•to•ba•cil•lus** (*plural* **•li**)
**lac•to•gen•ic**
**lac•tom•eter**
**lac•tone** chemical compound
**lac•ton•ic**
**lac•to•pro•tein**
**lac•to•scope**
**lac•tose** milk sugar
**la•cu•na** (*plural* **•nae** *or* **•nas**)
**la•cu•nar** (*plural* **•nars** *or* **•nar•ia**) ceiling panel; of lacunae
**la•cu•nose** (*or* **•nal, •nary**)
**lacu•nos•ity**
**la•cus•trine**
**lacy** (**laci•er, laci•est**)

**lad**
**lad•der**
**lad•die**
**lad•dish**
**lade (lad•ing, lad•ed, lad•en** *or* **lad•ed)** load cargo; *compare* **laid**
**lad•er**
**la-di-da** (*or* **lah-di-dah)**
**la•dies** *plural of* **lady**
**la•dies' man**
**lad•ing** cargo
**La•di•no** language
**la•di•no** (*plural* **•nos)** clover
**la•dle**
**ladle•ful**
**la•dler**
**lady** (*plural* **la•dies)**
**lady•bird**
**la•dy•fy** (*or* **•di•; •fy•ing, •fied)**
**lady-in-waiting** (*plural* **ladies-)**
**lady-killer**
**lady•like**
**lady•love**
**la•dy•ship**
**lady's maid** (*plural* **la•dies' maids)**
**La•dy•smith** South African city
**lady's-slipper** orchid
**lady's-smock** plant
**Laertes** mythological character
**lae•vo•ro•ta•tion** (*US* **le•)**
**lae•vo•ro•ta•tory** (*or* **•ro•ta•ry;** *US* **le•)**
**laevu•lin** (*US* **levu•)**
**laevu•lose** (*US* **levu•)** a sugar
**lag (lag•ging, lagged)**
**lag•an** (*or* **li•gan)** wreckage
**la•gena** bottle
**la•ger** beer; *compare* **laager**
**lag•gard**
**lag•gard•ly**
**lag•gard•ness**
**lagged**
**lag•ging**
**la•gniappe** (*or* **•gnappe)** *US* small gift
**lago•morph** type of mammal
**lago•mor•phic** (*or* **•phous)**
**la•goon**
**La•gos** Nigerian port
**lah** musical note
**lah-di-dah** *variant spelling of* **la-di-da**
**Lahn•da** language
**La•hore** Pakistani city
**Lah•ti** Finnish town
**laic** (*or* **lai•cal)** secular
**lai•cal•ly**
**lai•cism**
**lai•ci•za•tion** (*or* **•sa•tion)**
**lai•cize** (*or* **•cise)**
**laid** *past tense and past participle of* **lay**; *compare* **lade; lain**
**laik** *Dialect* to play
**lain** *past participle of* **lie**; *compare* **laid**
**lair**
**laird**
**lairy (lairi•er, lairi•est)** *Austral* gaudy
**lais•sez faire** (*or* **lais•ser faire)**
**laissez-faireism** (*or* **laisser-)**
**lais•sez pas•ser**
**la•ity**
**lake**
**Lake•land** the Lake District
**lak•er** lake cargo boat
**lakh** (*or* **lac)** 100 000 Indian rupees
**Lak•shad•weep** Indian islands
**laky (laki•er, laki•est)** reddish
**Lala** Indian form of address
**la•lang** grass
**Lal•lans** (*or* **•lan)** Scottish dialect
**lal•la•tion** speech defect
**lal•ly•gag (•gag•ging, •gagged)** *US* loiter
**lam (lam•ming, lammed)**
**lama** Tibetan priest; *compare* **llama**
**La•ma•ism** form of Buddhism
**La•ma•ist**
**La•ma•is•tic**
**La•marck•ian**
**La•marck•ism** theory of evolution
**la•ma•sery** (*plural* **•series)**
**lamb**
**lam•baste** (*or* **•bast)** *Slang* beat severely
**lamb•da** Greek letter
**lamb•da•cism** phonetics term
**lamb•doid** (*or* **•doi•dal)**
**lam•ben•cy**
**lam•bent**
**lam•bert** unit of illumination
**Lam•beth**
**lamb•kin**
**lam•bre•quin** ornamental hanging
**lamb•skin**
**lamé** fabric
**lame**
**la•mel•la** (*plural* **•lae** *or* **•las)** thin layer
**la•mel•lar** (*or* **lam•el•late, la•mel•lose)**
**lam•el•lat•ed**
**lam•el•la•tion**
**la•mel•li•branch** mollusc
**la•mel•li•bran•chi•ate**
**la•mel•li•corn** beetle
**la•mel•li•form**
**la•mel•li•ros•tral** (*or* **•trate)** zoology term
**lam•el•los•ity**
**lame•ly**
**lame•ness**
**la•ment**
**lam•en•table**
**lam•en•table•ness**
**lam•en•tably**
**la•men•ta•tion**
**La•men•ta•tions** biblical book
**la•ment•ed**
**la•ment•er**
**la•mia** (*plural* **•mias** *or* **•miae)** mythological monster
**lami•na** (*plural* **•nae** *or* **•nas)** thin plate
**lami•nable**
**lami•nar** (*or* **•nose)**
**lami•naria** seaweed
**lami•nate**
**lami•na•ted**
**lami•na•tion**
**lami•na•tor**
**lami•ni•tis** horse disease
**Lam•mas** religious feast

**lam•mer•gei•er** (*or* **•gey•er**) vulture
**lamp**
**lam•pas** animal disease; fabric
**lamp•black**
**Lam•pedu•sa** Mediterranean island
**lam•pern** lamprey
**lam•pion** oil lamp
**lamp•lighter**
**lam•poon**
**lam•poon•er** (*or* **•ist**)
**lam•poon•ery**
**lamp•post**
**lam•prey**
**lam•pro•phyre** rock
**La•nai** Hawaiian island
**la•nai** veranda
**Lan•ark** Scottish town
**la•nate** (*or* **•nose**) woolly
**Lan•ca•shire**
**Lan•cas•ter**
**Lan•cas•trian**
**lance**
**lance•let** tiny animal
**lan•ceo•late** tapering
**lanc•er**
**lan•cers** dance
**lan•cet** surgical knife
**lan•cet•ed** architectural term
**lance•wood**
**Lan•chow** (*or* **Lan-chou**) Chinese city
**lan•cin•ate**
**lan•ci•na•tion**
**Land** (*plural* **Län•der**) German state
**land**
**land•am•mann** Swiss official
**lan•dau**
**lan•dau•let** (*or* **•lette**)
**land•ed**
**Landes** French region
**Lan•des•haupt•mann** Austrian governor
**land•fall**
**land•form**
**land•grave** German ruler
**land•gra•vine** landgrave's wife
**land•ing**
**land•lady** (*plural* **•ladies**)
**land•locked**
**land•lop•er** *Scot* vagrant
**land•lord**
**land•lub•ber**
**land•mark**
**land•mass**
**land•owner**
**land•owner•ship**
**land•owning**
**land•race** pig breed
**land•scape**
**land•scap•ist**
**Land's End**
**land•shark** land profiteer
**land•side** part of plough
**lands•knecht** a mercenary
**land•slide**
**lands•man** (*plural* **•men**)
**Land•tag** German assembly
**land•ward**
**lane**
**lang** *Scot* long
**lang•lauf** cross-country skiing
**lang•läuf•er**
**lan•gouste** spiny lobster
**lang•syne** *Scot* long ago; *compare* **auld lang syne**
**lan•guage**
**langue** linguistics term
**langue de chat** biscuit
**Langue•doc** French region
**langue d'oc** language
**lan•guid**
**lan•guid•ness**
**lan•guish**
**lan•guish•er**
**lan•guish•ment**
**lan•guor** weariness; *compare* langur
**lan•guor•ous**
**lan•guor•ous•ness**
**lan•gur** monkey; *compare* languor
**lan•iard** *variant spelling of* lanyard
**la•ni•ary** (*plural* **•aries**) tooth
**la•nif•er•ous** (*or* **•nig•**) wool-bearing
**lank**
**lanki•ly**
**lanki•ness**
**lank•ly**
**lank•ness**
**lanky** (**lanki•er, lanki•est**)
**lan•ner** falcon
**lan•ner•et** male lanner
**lano•lat•ed**
**lano•lin** (*or* **•line**)
**Lan•sing** US city
**lans•que•net** gambling game
**lan•ta•na** shrub
**lan•tern**
**lan•tha•nide** (*or* **•non**) chemistry term
**lan•tha•num** chemical element
**la•nu•go** (*plural* **•gos**) fine hair
**lan•yard** (*or* **•iard**)
**Lao** (*plural* **Lao** *or* **Laos**) Asian people
**Laoag** Philippine city
**Laocoon** mythological priest
**La•odi•cea** ancient Greek city
**La•odi•cean**
**la•odi•cean** indifferent
**Laoigh•is** Irish county
**Laos**
**Lao•tian**
**lap** (**lap•ping, lapped**)
**lapa•rot•omy** (*plural* **•omies**) abdominal surgery
**La Paz** Bolivian capital
**lap•board**
**lap-chart**
**la•pel**
**la•pelled**
**lapi•dar•ian**
**lapi•dary** (*plural* **•daries**)
**lapi•date** to stone
**lapi•da•tion**
**la•pidi•fy** (**•fy•ing, •fied**) change into stone
**la•pil•lus** (*plural* **•li**) piece of lava
**lap•is lazu•li**
**Lap•land**
**Lap•land•er**
**Lapp**
**lapped**
**lap•per**
**lap•pet**
**lap•pet•ed**
**lap•ping**
**Lapp•ish**

**laps•able** (*or* **•ible**)
**lapse**
**laps•er**
**lap•strake** nautical term
**lap•sus** (*plural* **•sus**) error
**lap•wing**
**lar•board**
**lar•cenist** (*or* **•cener**)
**lar•cenous**
**lar•ceny** (*plural* **•cenies**)
**larch**
**lard**
**lar•der**
**lar•don** (*or* **•doon**) strip of fat
**lardy**
**lares** Roman gods
**large**
**large•ly**
**large-minded**
**larg•en**
**large•ness**
**large-scale**
**lar•gess** (*or* **•gesse**)
**lar•ghet•to** (*plural* **•tos**) music term
**larg•ish**
**lar•go** (*plural* **•gos**)
**lari•at** lasso
**lar•ine** of gulls
**Lá•ri•sa** (*or* **La•ris•sa**) Greek city
**lark**
**lark•er**
**lark•ish•ness**
**lark•some**
**lark•spur**
**lar•nax** terracotta coffin
**La Ro•chelle** French port
**lar•ri•gan** leather boot
**lar•ri•kin** *Austral* hooligan
**lar•rup** *Dialect* to beat
**lar•va** (*plural* **•vae**) preadult animal; *compare* **lava**
**lar•val**
**lar•vi•cid•al**
**lar•vi•cide**
**lar•yn•geal** (*or* **la•ryn•gal**)
**la•ryn•ges** *plural of* **larynx**
**lar•yn•git•ic**
**lar•yn•gi•tis**
**la•ryn•go•logi•cal** (*or* **•log•ic**)
**lar•yn•golo•gist**
**lar•yn•gol•ogy**
**la•ryn•go•scope**
**la•ryn•go•scop•ic**
**la•ryn•gos•co•pist**
**la•ryn•gos•co•py**
**lar•yn•got•omy** (*plural* **•omies**)
**lar•ynx** (*plural* **la•ryn•ges** *or* **lar•ynxes**)
**la•sa•gne** (*or* **•gna**)
**La Salle** Canadian city
**las•car** (*or* **lash•kar**) East Indian sailor
**Las•caux** French cave
**las•civi•ous**
**las•civi•ous•ly**
**las•civi•ous•ness**
**lase** act as laser
**la•ser**
**lash**
**lash•er**
**lash•ing**
**Lashio** Burmese town
**lash•kar** *variant spelling of* **las•car**
**lash-up** (*noun*)
**las•ket** nautical term
**Las Pal•mas**
**La Spe•zia** Italian port
**lass**
**Las•sa fe•ver**
**las•sie**
**las•si•tude**
**las•so** (*noun, plural* **•sos** *or* **•soes**; *verb* **•sos** *or* **•soes, •so•ing, •soed**)
**las•so•er**
**last**
**last•er**
**last•ing**
**last•ing•ly**
**last•ly**
**Las Ve•gas**
**Lata•kia** Syrian port
**latch**
**latch•et** *Archaic* shoelace
**latch•key**
**late**
**late•comer**
**la•teen** nautical term
**lateen•rigged**
**(lateish)** *incorrect spelling of* **latish**
**late•ly**
**la•ten•cy**
**late•ness**
**la•tent**
**lat•er**
**lat•er•al**
**lat•er•al•ly**
**Lat•er•an** Roman palace
**lat•er•ite** clay
**lat•er•it•ic**
**lat•ero•ver•sion**
**lat•est**
**la•tex** (*plural* **•texes** *or* **lati•ces**)
**lath** (*plural* **laths**) wood strip
**lathe** machine
**lath•er**
**lath•ery**
**la•thi** Indian stick
**lati•cif•er•ous** botany term
**lati•meria** fish
**Lat•in**
**Lat•in•ate**
**Lat•in•ism**
**Lat•in•ist**
**La•tin•ity**
**Lat•ini•za•tion** (*or* **•sa•tion**)
**Lat•in•ize** (*or* **•ise**)
**Lat•in•iz•er** (*or* **•is•er**)
**La•ti•no** (*plural* **•nos**) *US* Latin American
**lat•ish**
**lati•tude**
**lati•tu•di•nal**
**lati•tu•di•nal•ly**
**lati•tu•di•nar•ian**
**lati•tu•di•nari•an•ism**
**La•tium** Italian region
**la•tria** Catholic worship
**la•trine**
**lats** (*plural* **latu**, *or* **lati**) Latvian currency
**lat•ten** sheet metal
**lat•ter**
**latter-day**
**lat•ter•ly**
**latter•most**
**lat•tice**
**lat•ticed**
**Lat•via**
**Lat•vian**
**laud**
**laud•abil•ity** (*or* **•able•ness**)
**laud•able**
**laud•ably**
**lau•da•num**
**lau•da•tion** praise

**lauda•tory** (*or* **•tive**)
**laud•er**
**laugh**
**laugh•able**
**laugh•able•ness**
**laugh•ably**
**laugh•er**
**laugh•ing•ly**
**laugh•ter**
**launch**
**launch•er**
**laun•der**
**laun•der•er**
**Laun•der•ette** (*Trademark*)
**laun•dress**
**Laun•dro•mat** (*Trademark*)
**laun•dry** (*plural* **•dries**)
**laundry•man** (*plural* **•men**)
**laundry•woman** (*plural* **•women**)
**lau•ra•ceous** botany term
**Laura•sia** ancient continent
**lau•reate**
**lau•reate•ship**
**lau•rea•tion**
**lau•rel** (**•rel•ling, •relled;** *US* **•rel•ing, •reled**)
**Lau•ren•tian** of St Lawrence river; *compare* **Lawrentian**
**lau•rus•ti•nus** shrub
**Lau•sanne**
**lav** *short for* lavatory
**lava** molten rock; *compare* **larva**
**lava•bo** (*plural* **•boes** *or* **•bos**)
**lav•age** medical procedure
**La•val** Canadian city
**la•va•tion** washing
**la•va•tion•al**
**lava•tory** (*plural* **•tories**)
**lav•en•der**
**la•ver** seaweed; font
**lav•er•ock** *Dialect* skylark
**lav•ish**
**lav•ish•er**
**lav•ish•ly**
**lav•ish•ness**
**law**
**law-abiding**
**law•breaker**
**law•breaking**
**law•ful**
**law•ful•ly**
**law•ful•ness**
**law•giver**
**law•giving**
**law•less**
**law•less•ly**
**law•less•ness**
**law•man** (*plural* **•men**)
**lawn**
**lawny**
**law•ren•cium** chemical element
**Law•ren•tian** of D. H. Lawrence; *compare* **Laurentian**
**law•suit**
**law•yer**
**lax**
**laxa•tion** defecation
**laxa•tive**
**lax•ity** (*or* **lax•ness**)
**lax•ly**
**lay** (**lay•ing, laid**)
**lay•about**
**lay-by**
**(layed)** *incorrect spelling of* **laid**
**lay•er**
**lay•er•ing**
**lay•ette**
**lay•ing**
**lay•man** (*plural* **•men**)
**lay•shaft**
**lay•woman** (*plural* **•women**)
**laz•ar** leper
**laza•ret•to** (*or* **•ret, •rette;** *plural* **•tos, •rets, •rettes**) ship's locker; leper hospital
**laze**
**la•zi•ly**
**la•zi•ness**
**lazu•lite** mineral
**lazu•rite** lapis lazuli
**lazy** (**la•zi•er, la•zi•est**)
**lazy•bones**
**L-dopa**
**lea** meadow; unit of length; *compare* **lee; ley**
**leach** percolate; *compare* **leech**
**leach•er**
**lead** (**lead•ing, led**) guide
**lead** (**lead•ing, lead•ed**) metal
**lead•en**
**lead•en•ly**
**lead•en•ness**
**lead•er**
**lead•er•ship**
**lead-in** (*noun*)
**lead•ing**
**leads•man** (*plural* **•men**)
**lead•wort** shrub
**leady**
**leaf** (*plural* **leaves**)
**leaf•age**
**leaf climber**
**leaf•cutter** ant
**leaf-hopper** insect
**leafi•ness**
**leaf•let**
**leaf•stalk**
**leafy** (**leafi•er, leafi•est**)
**league** (**leagu•ing, leagued**)
**leak** hole; escape; *compare* **leek**
**leak•age**
**leak•er**
**leaki•ness**
**leaky** (**leaki•er, leaki•est**)
**leal** *Scot* loyal
**Leam•ing•ton**
**lean** (**lean•ing, leant** *or* **leaned**)
**Leander** mythological character
**lean•ness**
**leant**
**lean-to** (*plural* **-tos**)
**leap** (**leap•ing, leapt** *or* **leaped**)
**leap•er**
**leap•frog** (**•frog•ging, •frogged**)
**leapt**
**learn** (**learning, learnt** *or* **learned**)
**learn•able**
**learn•ed** wise
**learn•ed•ly**
**learn•ed•ness**
**learn•er**
**learn•ing**
**learnt**
**leary** *variant spelling of* **leery**
**leas•able**
**lease**
**lease•back** property transaction
**lease•hold**
**lease•holder**
**leas•er**
**leash**

**least**
**least•ways**
**leat** trench
**leath•er**
**leather•back** turtle
**Leath•er•ette** (*Trademark*)
**Leath•er•head** Surrey town
**leather•head** bird
**leath•eri•ness**
**leather•jacket** fish; insect
**leath•ern**
**leather•neck** *Slang* US marine
**leather•wood**
**leath•ery**
**leave (leav•ing, left)**
**leaved** with leaves
**leav•en**
**leav•en•ing**
**leav•er**
**leaves** *plural of* **leaf** *or* **leave**; *present tense of* **leave**
**leave-taking**
**leav•ing**
**Leba•nese**
**Leba•non**
**leb•en** curdled milk
**Le•bens•raum** *German* territory
**leb•ku•chen** (*plural* **•chen**) biscuit
**Lech** European river
**lech** lust
**lech•er**
**lech•er•ous**
**lech•ery** (*plural* **•eries**)
**leci•thin** biochemical compound
**le•cithi•nase** enzyme
**lec•tern**
**lec•tion** variant reading
**lec•tion•ary** (*plural* **•aries**) book of church readings
**lec•tor** lecturer
**lec•tor•ate** (*or* **•ship**)
**lec•ture**
**lec•tur•er**
**lec•ture•ship**
**lecy•thus** (*plural* **•thi**) Greek vase
**led**
**Leda** mythological character
**le•der•ho•sen** leather shorts
**ledge**
**ledged**
**ledg•er**
**ledg•er line** (*or* **leg•**) musical term
**ledgy**
**lee** sheltered side; *compare* **lea; ley**
**lee•board**
**leech** bloodsucker; *compare* **leach**
**leech** (*or* **leach**) nautical term; *compare* **leach**
**Leeds**
**leek** vegetable; *compare* **leak**
**leer**
**leer•ing•ly**
**leery** (*or* **leary; leeri•er, leeri•est** *or* **leari•er, leari•est)**
**lees** sediment
**leet** manorial court
**lee•ward**
**Lee•ward Is•lands**
**lee•way**
**left**
**left-hand** (*adj*)
**left-handed**
**left-handed•ly**
**left-handed•ness**
**left-hander**
**left•ism**
**left•ist**
**left•over**
**left•wards**
**left-winger**
**lefty** (*plural* **lefties)**
**leg (leg•ging, legged)**
**lega•cy** (*plural* **•cies)**
**le•gal**
**le•gal•ese** legal jargon
**le•gal•ism**
**le•gal•ist**
**le•gal•is•tic**
**le•gal•is•ti•cal•ly**
**le•gal•ity** (*plural* **•ities)**
**le•gali•za•tion** (*or* **•sa•tion)**
**le•gal•ize** (*or* **•ise)**
**le•gal•ly**
**leg•ate** envoy
**lega•tee** recipient of legacy
**leg•ate•ship**
**lega•tine**
**le•ga•tion**
**le•ga•tion•ary**
**le•ga•to** (*plural* **•tos)** music term
**lega•tor** bequeather
**lega•to•rial**
**leg•end**
**leg•end•ary** (*adj*)
**leg•end•ry** (*noun*)
**leg•er•demain**
**leg•er•demain•ist**
**leg•er line** *variant spelling of* **ledger line**
**legged** *past tense of* **leg**
**leg•ged** having legs
**leg•gi•ness**
**leg•ginged**
**leg•gings**
**leg•gy (•gi•er, •gi•est)**
**Leg•horn** Livorno; domestic fowl
**leg•horn** straw hat
**leg•ibil•ity** (*or* **•ible•ness)**
**leg•ible**
**leg•ibly**
**le•gion**
**le•gion•ary** (*plural* **•aries)**
**le•gion•naire**
**leg•is•late**
**leg•is•la•tion**
**leg•is•la•tive**
**leg•is•la•tor**
**leg•is•la•to•rial**
**leg•is•la•tress**
**leg•is•la•ture**
**le•gist** legal expert
**le•git** *Slang* legitimate
**le•giti•ma•cy** (*or* **•mate•ness)**
**le•giti•mate**
**le•giti•mate•ly**
**le•giti•ma•tion**
**le•giti•ma•ti•za•tion** (*or* **•sa•tion)** legitimization
**le•giti•ma•tize** (*or* **•tise)** legitimize
**le•giti•mism**
**le•giti•mist** supporter of legitimate ruler
**le•giti•mis•tic**
**le•giti•mi•za•tion** (*or* **•sa•tion)**
**le•giti•mize** (*or* **•mise)**
**leg•less**
**leg•man** (*plural* **•men)** *US* newspaper reporter
**leg•room**

**leg•ume** pod
**le•gu•min** protein
**le•gu•mi•nous** botany term
**leg•work**
**Le Ha•vre** French port
**lei** Hawaiian garland
**Leices•ter**
**Leices•ter•shire**
**Lei•den** (*or* **Ley•**) Dutch city
**Leigh** English town
**Lein•ster** Irish province
**Leip•zig** German city
**leish•ma•nia** protozoan
**leish•mania•sis** (*or* **•ma•nio•sis**) infection
**leis•ter** fishing spear
**lei•sure**
**lei•sured**
**lei•sure•li•ness**
**lei•sure•ly**
**Leith** Scottish port
**leit•mo•tiv** (*or* **•tif**)
**Lei•trim** Irish county
**lek** Albanian currency
**Le Mans** French city
**lem•ma** (*plural* **•mas** *or* **•ma•ta**) logic term
**lem•ming**
**lem•nis•cate** maths term
**lem•nis•cus** (*plural* **•nis•ci**) anatomy term
**Lem•nos** (*or* **Lím•**) Greek island
**lem•on**
**lem•on•ade**
**lem•ony**
**lem•pi•ra** Honduran currency
**le•mur**
**lemu•roid** (*or* **•rine**)
**Lena** Russian river
**lend** (**lend•ing, lent**)
**lend•er**
**lend-lease**
**length**
**length•en**
**length•en•er**
**lengthi•ly**
**lengthi•ness**
**length•ways** (*or* **•wise**)
**lengthy** (**lengthi•er, lengthi•est**)
**le•ni•en•cy** (*or* **•ni•ence**)
**le•ni•ent**
**le•ni•ent•ly**
**Le•ni•na•bad** *former name of* **Khodzhent**
**Le•ni•na•kan** Armenian city
**Le•nin•grad**
**Len•in•ism** political theory
**Len•in•ist** (*or* **•ite**)
**le•nis** (*plural* **le•nes**) linguistics term
**leni•tive** soothing pain
**len•ity** (*plural* **•ities**)
**leno** (*plural* **lenos**) fabric weave
**lens**
**Lent**
**lent**
**len•ta•men•te** musical term
**Len•ten** of Lent
**len•tic** ecology term
**len•ti•cel** botany term
**len•ti•cel•late**
**len•ticu•lar** (*or* **•ti•form**)
**len•ti•form**
**len•tigi•nous** (*or* **•nose**)
**len•ti•go** (*plural* **•tigi•nes**) freckle
**len•til**
**len•tis•si•mo** music term
**len•to** (*plural* **•tos**) music term
**Leo** constellation
**León** cities in Spain, Mexico, and Nicaragua
**Leo•nid** (*plural* **Leo•nids** *or* **Le•oni•des**) meteor shower
**leo•nine**
**leop•ard**
**leop•ard•ess**
**leopard's-bane** plant
**leo•tard**
**lep•er**
**le•pido•lite** mineral
**lepi•dop•ter•an** (*plural* **•ter•ans** *or* **•tera**)
**lepi•dop•ter•ist**
**lepi•dop•ter•ous**
**lepi•do•si•ren** fish
**lepi•dote** biology term
**lepo•rid** hare
**lepo•rine** of hares
**lep•re•chaun**
**lep•ro•sar•ium** (*plural* **•ia**) leper hospital
**lep•rose**
**lep•ro•sy**
**lep•rous**
**lep•rous•ness**
**lep•to•cepha•lus** (*plural* **•li**) eel larva
**lep•ton** (*plural* **•ta**) Greek currency
**lep•ton** (*plural* **•tons**) physics particle
**lep•to•phyl•lous** botany term
**lep•tor•rhine** zoology term
**lep•to•some** slender person
**lep•to•so•mic** (*or* **•mat•ic**)
**lep•to•spi•ro•sis** disease
**lep•to•tene** biology term
**le•quear** ceiling panel
**Ler•wick** Scottish town
**Les•bian** of Lesbos
**les•bian** female homosexual
**les•bi•an•ism**
**Les•bos** Greek island
**Les Cayes** Haitian port
**lese-majesty** (*or* **lèse-majesté**)
**le•sion**
**Le•so•tho** African kingdom
**less**
**les•see** one to whom lease is granted
**les•see•ship**
**less•en**
**less•er** less great; *compare* lessor
**les•son**
**les•sor** one who grants lease; *compare* **lesser**
**lest**
**let** (**let•ting, let**)
**le•thal**
**le•thal•ity**
**le•thal•ly**
**le•thar•gic** (*or* **•gi•cal**)
**le•thar•gi•cal•ly**
**leth•ar•gy** (*plural* **•gies**)
**Leth•bridge** Canadian city
**Le•the** mythological river
**Leto** mother of Apollo
**let's**
**Lett** a Latvian
**let•ter**
**let•tered**
**let•ter•er**
**letter•head**
**let•ter•ing**
**letter•press**
**let•ter•set**

**let•ting**
**Let•tish** Latvian
**let•tuce**
**leu•cine** (*or* **•cin**) amino acid
**leu•cite** mineral
**leu•cit•ic**
**leu•co•crat•ic** geology term
**leu•co•cyte** (*US* **•ko•**)
**leu•co•cyt•ic** (*US* **•ko•**)
**leu•co•cy•to•sis** (*US* **•ko•**)
**leu•co•cy•tot•ic** (*US* **•ko•**)
**leu•co•der•ma** (*US* **•ko•**) unpigmented skin
**leu•co•der•mal** (*or* **•mic**; *US* **•ko•**)
**leu•co•ma** corneal scar
**leu•co•maine** biochemical compound
**leu•co•penia** (*US* **•ko•**)
**leu•co•penic** (*US* **•ko•**)
**leu•co•plast** (*or* **•plas•tid**) structure in plant cell
**leu•co•poi•esis** (*US* **•ko•**)
**leu•co•poi•et•ic** (*US* **•ko•**)
**leu•cor•rhoea** (*US* **•kor•rhea**) vaginal discharge
**leu•cor•rhoeal** (*US* **•kor•rheal**)
**leu•cot•omy** brain surgery
**leu•kae•mia** (*US* **•ke•mia**)
**leuko** *US spelling of some words beginning with* **leuco•**
**lev** (*plural* **leva**) Bulgarian currency
**Le•val•loi•sian** (*or* **•lois**) Palaeolithic culture
**Le•vant** Middle Eastern region
**le•vant** leather
**le•vant•er** wind
**Le•van•tine** of Levant
**le•van•tine** silk cloth
**le•va•tor**
**levee**
**lev•el** (**•el•ling**, **•elled**; *US* **•el•ing**, **•eled**)
**level-headed**
**level-headed•ly**
**level-headed•ness**
**Lev•el•ler** radical Parliamentarian
**lev•el•ler** (*US* **•el•er**)
**lev•el•ly**
**Le•ven** Scottish loch
**lev•er**
**lev•er•age**
**lev•er•et** young hare
**Le•ver•ku•sen** German town
**levi•able**
**le•via•than** biblical monster
**levi•er**
**levi•gate** grind into powder
**levi•ga•tion**
**levi•ga•tor**
**levi•rate** marrying brother's widow
**Le•vis** (*Trademark*) jeans
**levi•tate**
**levi•ta•tion**
**levi•ta•tor**
**Le•vite** priest
**Le•viti•cal** (*or* **Le•vit•ic**)
**Le•viti•cus** biblical book
**lev•ity** (*plural* **•ities**)
**le•vo•ro•ta•tion** *US spelling of* **laevorotation**
**le•vo•ro•ta•tory** *US spelling of* **laevorotatory**
**levu•lin** *US spelling of* **laevulin**
**levu•lose** *US spelling of* **laevulose**
**levy** (*verb* **levies**, **levy•ing**, **levied**; *noun*, *plural* **levies**)
**lewd**
**lewd•ly**
**lewd•ness**
**Lew•es** Sussex town
**Lew•is** Scottish island
**lew•is** (*or* **lew•is•son**) lifting device
**Lewi•sham**
**lew•is•ite** war gas
**lex** (*plural* **leges**) body of laws
**lex•eme** linguistics term
**lexi•cal**
**lexi•cal•ity**
**lexi•cal•ly**
**lexi•cog•ra•pher**
**lexi•co•graph•ic** (*or* **•graphi•cal**)
**lexi•co•graphi•cal•ly**
**lexi•cog•ra•phy**
**lexi•co•logi•cal**
**lexi•co•logi•cal•ly**
**lexi•colo•gist**
**lexi•col•ogy**
**lexi•con**
**lexi•co•sta•tis•tics**
**lexi•gra•phy**
**Lex•ing•ton** US city
**lex•is** vocabulary
**lex loci** law of the place
**ley** prehistoric track; *compare* **lea**; **lee**
**Ley•den** *variant spelling of* **Leiden**
**Ley•te** Philippine island
**Lha•sa** Tibetan capital
**li** unit of length
**lia•bil•ity** (*plural* **•ities**)
**lia•ble**
**li•aise**
**liai•son**
**lia•na** (*or* **li•ane**) plant
**lia•noid**
**Liao•ning** Chinese province
**Liao•tung** (*or* **•dong**) Chinese peninsula
**Liao•yang** Chinese city
**liar**
**Li•ard** Canadian river
**li•ard** coin
**Lias** rock series
**lias** blue limestone
**Li•as•sic**
**lib** *Slang* liberation
**li•ba•tion**
**li•ba•tion•al** (*or* **•ary**)
**li•bec•cio** (*or* **•chio**) Corsican wind
**li•bel** (**•bel•ling**, **•belled**; *US* **•bel•ing**, **•beled**)
**li•bel•lant** (*US* **•bel•ant**)
**li•bel•lee** (*US* **•bel•ee**)
**li•bel•ler** (*or* **li•bel•ist**; *US* **•bel•er** *or* **•bel•ist**)
**li•bel•lous** (*US* **•bel•ous**)
**Lib•er•al** political party
**lib•er•al** progressive; abundant
**lib•er•al•ism**
**lib•er•al•ist**
**lib•er•al•is•tic**
**lib•er•al•ity** (*plural* **•ities**)
**lib•er•ali•za•tion** (*or* **•sa•tion**)
**lib•er•al•ize** (*or* **•ise**)
**lib•er•al•iz•er** (*or* **•is•er**)
**lib•er•al•ly**
**lib•er•al•ness**
**lib•er•ate**
**lib•era•tion**

**lib•era•tor** (*fem* **•tress**)
**Li•beria**
**Li•berian**
**lib•er•tar•ian** freethinker; *compare* **libertine**
**lib•er•tari•an•ism**
**li•ber•ti•cid•al**
**li•ber•ti•cide** destruction of freedom
**lib•er•tine** dissolute person; *compare* **libertarian**
**lib•er•tin•ism** (*or* **•age**)
**lib•er•ty** (*plural* **•ties**)
**li•bidi•nal**
**li•bidi•nous**
**li•bi•do** (*plural* **•dos**)
**Li•bra** constellation; sign of zodiac
**Lib•ran**
**li•brar•ian**
**li•brar•ian•ship**
**li•brary** (*plural* **•braries**)
**li•brate** waver
**li•bra•tion**
**li•bra•tion•al**
**li•bra•tory**
**li•bret•tist**
**li•bret•to** (*plural* **•tos** *or* **•ti**)
**Li•breville** Gabonese capital
**li•bri•form** botany term
**Lib•rium** (*Trademark*)
**Libya**
**Liby•an**
**lice**
**li•cence** (*US* **•cense**) a permit
**li•cens•able**
**li•cense** to grant licence; *US spelling of* **licence**
**li•cen•see**
**li•cens•er** (*or* **•cen•sor**)
**li•cen•ti•ate** licence holder; *compare* **licentious**
**li•cen•ti•ate•ship**
**li•cen•tia•tion**
**li•cen•tious** promiscuous; *compare* **licentiate**
**li•cen•tious•ness**
**li•chee** (*or* **•chi**) *variant spelling of* **litchi**
**li•chen**
**li•chen•in** chemical compound
**li•chen•oid**
**li•chen•ol•ogy**
**li•chen•ous** (*or* **•ose**)
**Lich•field** Staffordshire city
**lich gate** (*or* **lych gate**)
**lic•it** lawful
**lick**
**lick•er**
**lick•er•ish** *Archaic* lustful; *compare* **liquorice**
**lickety-split** *US* very quickly
**lick•ing**
**lick•spit•tle**
**lico•rice** *US spelling of* **liquorice**
**lic•tor** Roman official
**lid**
**lid•ded**
**lid•less**
**lido** (*plural* **lidos**)
**lie** (**ly•ing, lied**) tell untruth; *compare* **lye**
**lie** (**ly•ing, lay, lain**) recline; *compare* **lye**
**Lieb•frau•milch** (*or* **•frau•en•milch**) wine
**Liech•ten•stein**
**lied** (*plural* **lied•er**) song
**lief** *Archaic* willingly
**Li•ège** Belgian city
**liege** owed allegiance
**liege•man** (*plural* **•men**)
**lien** legal term
**lien•al**
**li•en•ter•ic**
**li•en•tery** medical term
**li•erne** architectural term
**Li•etu•va** Lithuania
**lieu**
**lieu•ten•an•cy**
**lieu•ten•ant**
**life** (*plural* **lives**)
**life•blood**
**life•boat**
**life•guard**
**life•less**
**life•less•ly**
**life•less•ness**
**life•like**
**life•line**
**life•long** for life; *compare* **livelong**
**lif•er**
**life-saver**
**life-saving**
**life-size** (*or* **-sized**)
**life•time**
**Lif•fey** Irish river
**lift**
**lift•able**
**lift•boy**
**lift•er**
**lift•off**
**liga•ment**
**liga•men•tous** (*or* **•tal, •ta•ry**)
**li•gan** *variant spelling of* **lagan**
**lig•and** chemistry term
**li•gate** constrict with ligature
**li•ga•tion**
**liga•tive**
**liga•ture**
**li•ger** animal
**light** (**light•ing, light•ed** *or* **lit**)
**light•en**
**light•en•er**
**light•en•ing** making lighter; *compare* **lightning**
**light•er**
**light•er•age**
**lighter•man** (*plural* **•men**)
**light-fast**
**light-fingered**
**light-footed**
**light-headed**
**light-headed•ly**
**light-headed•ness**
**light-hearted**
**light-hearted•ly**
**light-hearted•ness**
**light•house**
**light•ing**
**light•ish**
**light•ly**
**light•ness**
**light•ning** light flash; *compare* **lightening**
**light•ship**
**light•some**
**light•weight**
**lign•al•oes** tree
**lig•ne•ous**
**lig•ni•fi•ca•tion**
**lig•ni•form**
**lig•ni•fy** (**•fies, •fy•ing, •fied**) make woody
**lig•nin** plant tissue
**lig•nite** brown coal
**lig•nit•ic**

**lig•no•caine** anaesthetic
**lig•no•cel•lu•lose**
**lig•num vi•tae** wood
**lig•ro•in** chemical compound
**ligu•la** (*plural* **•lae** *or* **•las**) part of insect's lip
**ligu•lar**
**ligu•late**
**lig•ule** plant part
**ligu•loid**
**lig•ure** biblical gem
**Li•gu•ria** Italian region
**Li•gu•ri•an**
**lik•able** (*or* **like•**)
**lik•able•ness** (*or* **like•**)
**Li•ka•si** city in the Democratic Republic of Congo
**like**
**like•li•hood** (*or* **•ness**)
**like•ly** (**•li•er, •li•est**)
**like-minded**
**like-minded•ly**
**like-minded•ness**
**lik•en**
**like•ness**
**like•wise**
**lik•ing**
**li•lac**
**lilia•ceous**
**lil•ied**
**Lilith** biblical demon
**Lille** French city
**Lil•li•pu•tian** tiny person
**lilly-pilly** tree
**Lilo** (*Trademark*; *plural* **Lilos**)
**Li•long•we** Malawian capital
**lilt**
**lilting**
**lily** (*plural* **lilies**)
**lily-livered**
**Lima** Peruvian capital
**lima** bean
**lima•cine** of slugs
**li•ma•çon** maths term
**Li•mas•sol** Cypriot port
**limb**
**lim•bate** botany term
**lim•ber**
**lim•bic** anatomy term
**limb•less**
**lim•bo** (*plural* **•bos**)
**Lim•burg** (*or* **•bourg**) Belgian or Dutch province
**Lim•burg•er** cheese
**lim•bus** (*plural* **•bi**) anatomy term
**lime**
**lime•ade**
**lime•kiln**
**lime•light**
**li•men** (*plural* **•mens** *or* **limi•na**) psychology term
**Lim•er•ick** Irish port and county
**lim•er•ick** comic verse
**li•mes** (*plural* **limi•tes**) boundary of Roman empire
**lime•stone**
**lime•water**
**lim•ey** *US* Briton; *compare* **limy**
**li•mico•line** ornithology term
**li•mico•lous** living in mud
**limi•nal** psychology term
**limi•ness**
**lim•it**
**lim•it•able**
**limi•tar•ian**
**limi•tary**
**limi•ta•tion**
**lim•it•ed**
**lim•it•er**
**lim•it•less**
**lim•it•less•ly**
**lim•it•less•ness**
**limi•trophe** near a frontier
**limn** to draw
**lim•ner**
**lim•net•ic** ecology term
**lim•no•logi•cal** (*or* **•log•ic**)
**lim•nolo•gist**
**lim•nol•ogy** study of lakes
**Lím•nos** *variant spelling of* **Lemnos**
**Li•moges** French city
**limo•nene** chemical compound
**li•mo•nite** mineral
**Li•mou•sin** French region
**lim•ou•sine** car
**limp**
**limp•er**
**lim•pet**
**lim•pid**
**lim•pid•ity** (*or* **•ness**)
**limp•ing•ly**
**limp•kin** bird
**limp•ness**
**Lim•po•po** African river
**limu•lus** (*plural* **•li**) crab
**limy** (**limi•er, limi•est**) of lime; *compare* **limey**
**lin•able** (*or* **line•**)
**lin•age** (*or* **line•**) number of lines; *compare* **lineage**
**lin•alo•ol** (*or* **•alol**)
**linch•pin** pin for wheel; *compare* **lynch**
**Lin•coln**
**Lin•coln•shire**
**lin•crus•ta** embossed wallpaper
**linc•tus** (*plural* **•tuses**)
**lin•dane** pesticide
**lin•den**
**Lin•dis•farne**
**line** (**lin•ing, lined**)
**lin•eage** descent from ancestor; *variant spelling of* **linage**
**lin•eal**
**lin•eal•ly** directly; *compare* **linearly**
**linea•ment** facial feature; *compare* **liniment**
**linea•men•tal**
**lin•ear**
**lin•ear•ity**
**lin•ear•ly** in a line; *compare* **lineally**
**lin•eate** (*or* **•eat•ed**)
**lin•ea•tion**
**line•caster**
**line-engrav•er**
**line-engrav•ing**
**line•man** (*plural* **•men**) *US* footballer; rail worker; *compare* **linesman**
**lin•en** fabric; *compare* **linin**
**lineo•late** (*or* **•lat•ed**)
**line-out**
**lin•er**
**lines•man** (*plural* **•men**) sporting official; rail worker; *compare* **lineman**
**line-up** (*noun*)
**ling** heather
**ling** (*plural* **ling** *or* **lings**) fish

**ling•cod** (*plural* **•cod** *or* **•cods**) fish
**lin•ger**
**lin•ger•er**
**lin•gerie**
**lin•ger•ing•ly**
**lin•go** (*plural* **•goes**)
**lin•gua** (*plural* **•guae**) the tongue
**lin•gua fran•ca** (*plural* **lin•gua fran•cas** *or* **lin•guae fran•cae**) common language
**lin•gual**
**lin•gual•ly**
**lin•gui•form**
**lin•gui•ni** pasta
**lin•guist**
**lin•guis•tic**
**lin•guis•ti•cal•ly**
**lin•guis•tics**
**lin•gu•late** (*or* **•lat•ed**)
**lin•hay** *Dialect* farm building
**lini•ment** topical medicine; *compare* **lineament**
**li•nin** biology term; *compare* **linen**
**lin•ing**
**link**
**link•able**
**link•age**
**link•boy** torch carrier
**link•man** (*plural* **•men**) broadcaster
**Lin•kö•ping** Swedish city
**link-up** (*noun*)
**link•work**
**Lin•lith•gow** Scottish town
**linn** *Scot* waterfall
**Lin•nean** (*or* **•naean**) of Linnaeus; *note* **Linnean Society**
**lin•net**
**Lin•nhe** Scottish loch
**lino** (*plural* **linos**)
**li•no•cut**
**li•no•leate**
**li•no•leum**
**Li•no•type** (*Trademark*)
**Li•no•typ•er** (*or* **•ist**)
**lin•sang** animal
**lin•seed**
**linsey-woolsey** fabric
**lin•stock**
**lint**
**lin•tel**
**lin•telled** (*US* **•teled**)
**lint•er**
**lint•white** *Scot* linnet
**linty**
**Linz** Austrian port
**lion**
**li•on•ess**
**lion•fish** (*plural* **•fish** *or* **•fishes**)
**lion-hearted**
**li•oni•za•tion** (*or* **•sa•tion**)
**li•on•ize** (*or* **•ise**)
**li•on•iz•er** (*or* **•is•er**)
**lip** (**lip•ping, lipped**)
**li•pase** enzyme
**Li•petsk** Russian city
**li•pid**
**lip•oid** fatty
**lip•oi•dal**
**li•poly•sis**
**lipo•lyt•ic**
**li•po•ma** (*plural* **•mas** *or* **•mata**) tumour
**li•poma•tous**
**lipo•phil•ic** (*or* **lipo•trop•ic**) chemistry term
**lipo•pro•tein**
**Lip•pe** German river
**Lip•pi•zan•er** horse
**lip•py** (**•pi•er, •pi•est**) *US* insolent
**lip-read** (**-reading, -read**)
**lip-reader**
**lip•stick**
**li•quate** separate by melting
**li•qua•tion**
**liq•ue•fa•cient**
**liq•ue•fac•tion** (*or* **•ui•**)
**liq•ue•fac•tive** (*or* **•ui•**)
**liq•ue•fi•able** (*or* **•ui•**)
**liq•ue•fi•er** (*or* **•ui•**)
**liq•ue•fy** (*or* **•ui•**; **•fies, •fy•ing, •fied**)
**li•quesce**
**li•ques•cence** (*or* **•cen•cy**)
**li•ques•cent**
**li•queur**
**liq•uid**
**liq•uid•am•bar** balsam
**liq•ui•date**
**liq•ui•da•tion**
**liq•ui•da•tor**
**li•quid•ity**
**liq•uid•ize** (*or* **•ise**)
**liq•uid•iz•er** (*or* **•is•er**)
**liq•ui•fy** *variant spelling of* **liquefy**
**liq•uor**
**liquo•rice** (*US* **lico•**) confectionery; *compare* **lickerish**
**lira** (*plural* **lire** *or* **liras**)
**lirio•den•dron** (*plural* **•drons** *or* **•dra**) tree
**liri•pipe** (*or* **•poop**) tip of graduate's hood
**Lis•bon**
**lisle**
**lisp**
**lis pen•dens** legal term
**lisp•er**
**lis•som** (*or* **•some**)
**lis•som•ness** (*or* **•some•**)
**list**
**list•able**
**list•ed**
**lis•tel** architectural term
**lis•ten**
**lis•ten•er**
**lis•ter** plough
**lis•teri•osis** food poisoning
**list•ing**
**list•less**
**list•less•ness**
**lit**
**lita•ny** (*plural* **•nies**)
**li•tchi** (*or* **•chee, •chi, ly•chee**; *plural* **•tchis, •chees, •chis,** *or* **•chees**)
**li•ter** *US spelling of* **litre**
**lit•era•cy**
**lit•er•al** of words or letters; *compare* **littoral**
**lit•er•al•ism**
**lit•er•al•ist**
**lit•er•al•is•tic**
**lit•er•al•is•ti•cal•ly**
**lit•er•al•ly**
**lit•er•al•ness** (*or* **•ity**)
**lit•er•ari•ly**
**lit•er•ari•ness**
**lit•er•ary**
**lit•er•ate**
**lit•era•ti** scholarly people
**lit•era•tim** letter for letter
**lit•era•tion**
**lit•era•tor** *variant of* **littérateur**

**lit•era•ture**
**lith•arge** lead compound
**lithe**
**lithe•ly**
**lithe•ness**
**lithe•some**
**lithia** lithium compound
**li•thia•sis** medical term
**lith•ic** of stone
**lith•ium**
**li•tho** (*plural* **•thos**) lithograph
**litho•graph**
**li•thog•ra•pher**
**litho•graph•ic** (*or* **•graphi•cal**)
**litho•graphi•cal•ly**
**li•thog•ra•phy**
**lith•oid** (*or* **li•thoi•dal**)
**litho•log•ic** (*or* **•logi•cal**)
**litho•logi•cal•ly**
**li•tholo•gist**
**li•thol•ogy** study of rocks
**litho•marge** kaolin
**litho•meteor**
**litho•phyte**
**litho•phyt•ic**
**litho•pone** pigment
**litho•sol** soil
**litho•sphere**
**litho•tom•ic** (*or* **•tomi•cal**)
**li•thoto•mist**
**li•thoto•my** (*plural* **•mies**) removal of bladder stone
**li•thot•rity** (*plural* **•rities**) crushing of bladder stone
**Lithua•nia**
**Lithua•nian**
**liti•gable**
**liti•gant**
**liti•gate**
**liti•ga•tion**
**liti•ga•tor**
**li•ti•gious**
**lit•mus**
**li•to•tes** (*plural* **•tes**) understatement
**li•tre** (*US* **•ter**)
**lit•ter**
**lit•té•ra•teur** (*or* **lit•era•tor**) professional writer
**litter•bug**
**lit•tle**
**lit•to•ral** of the shore; *compare* **literal**
**li•tur•gi•cal** (*or* **•gic**)
**li•tur•gi•cal•ly**
**li•tur•gics** study of liturgies
**lit•ur•gism**
**lit•ur•gist**
**lit•ur•gis•tic**
**lit•ur•gy** (*plural* **•gies**)
**liv•abil•ity** (*or* **live•**)
**liv•able** (*or* **live•**)
**liv•able•ness** (*or* **live•**)
**live**
**live•able** *variant spelling of* livable
**live•li•hood**
**live•li•ness**
**live•long** very long; entire; *compare* **lifelong**
**live•ly** (**•li•er, •li•est**)
**liv•en**
**liv•en•er**
**liv•er**
**liv•er•ied**
**liv•er•ish**
**liv•er•ish•ness**
**Liv•er•pool**
**Liv•er•pud•lian**
**liver•wort** plant
**liver•wurst** sausage
**liv•ery** (*plural* **•eries**)
**liv•ery•man** (*plural* **•men**)
**live•stock**
**live•trap** (**•trap•ping, •trapped**)
**live•ware** computer workers
**liv•id**
**liv•id•ly**
**liv•id•ness** (*or* **li•vid•ity**)
**liv•ing**
**Li•vo•nia** former Russian province; US city
**Li•vo•nian**
**Li•vor•no** Italian port
**lix•ivi•ate** chemistry term
**lix•ivia•tion**
**lix•iv•ium** (*plural* **•iums** *or* **•ivia**) alkaline solution
**liz•ard**
**Lju•blja•na** Slovenian capital
**lla•ma** animal; *compare* **lama**
**Llan•daff** Cardiff suburb
**Llan•dud•no** Welsh town
**Llan•elli** (*or* **•elly**) Welsh town
**lla•no** (*plural* **•nos**) grassland
**Lla•no Es•ta•ca•do** Texan region
**Lloyd's** underwriters
**lo** exclamation
**loach**
**load** burden, etc.; *compare* **lode**
**load•ed**
**load•er**
**load•ing**
**load•star** *variant spelling of* **lodestar**
**load•stone** *variant spelling of* **lodestone**
**loaf** (*plural* **loaves**)
**loaf•er**
**loam**
**loami•ness**
**loamy** (**loami•er, loami•est**)
**loan**
**loan•able**
**loan•er**
**loath** (*or* **loth**) reluctant
**loathe** to hate
**loath•er**
**loath•ing**
**loath•ly**
**loath•some**
**loath•some•ness**
**loaves** *plural of* **loaf**
**lob** (**lob•bing, lobbed**)
**lo•bar**
**lo•bate** (*or* **•bat•ed**)
**lobbed**
**lob•bing**
**lob•by** (*noun, plural* **•bies**; *verb* **•bies, •by•ing, •bied**)
**lob•by•er**
**lob•by•ism**
**lob•by•ist**
**lobe**
**lo•bec•to•my** (*plural* **•mies**)
**lo•belia**
**lo•beline** alkaloid
**Lo•bi•to** Angolan port
**lob•lol•ly** (*plural* **•lies**) tree
**lo•boto•my** (*plural* **•mies**)
**lob•scouse** sailor's stew
**lob•ster** (*plural* **•sters** *or* **•ster**)
**lobu•lar** (*or* **•late, •lat•ed, •lose**)
**lobu•la•tion**
**lob•ule**

**lo•cal**
**lo•cale** (*noun*)
**lo•cal•ism**
**lo•cal•ist**
**lo•cal•is•tic**
**lo•cal•ity** (*plural* **•ities**)
**lo•cal•iz•able** (*or* **•is•able**)
**lo•cali•za•tion** (*or* **•sa•tion**)
**lo•cal•ize** (*or* **•ise**)
**lo•cal•iz•er** (*or* **•is•er**)
**lo•cal•ly**
**lo•cat•able**
**lo•cate**
**lo•cat•er**
**lo•ca•tion**
**loca•tive**
**loch**
**lochia** vaginal discharge
**loch•ial**
**loci** *plural of* **locus**
**lock**
**lock•able**
**lock•age** canal locks
**lock•er**
**lock•et**
**lock•jaw**
**lock•nut**
**lock•out** (*noun*)
**lock•smith**
**lock•smithery** (*or* **•smithing**)
**lock•up** (*noun*)
**loco** (*plural* **locos**) *Slang* locomotive; *US* insane
**lo•co•ism** cattle disease
**lo•co•man** (*plural* **•men**) engine driver
**lo•co•mo•tion**
**lo•co•mo•tive**
**lo•co•mo•tor** of locomotion
**lo•co•weed**
**locu•lar** (*or* **•late**) biology term
**locu•la•tion**
**loc•ule** (*or* **locu•lus**; *plural* **•ules** *or* **•li**) biology term
**lo•cum** *short for* **locum tenens**
**lo•cum te•nens** (*plural* **lo•cum te•nen•tes**) professional stand-in
**lo•cus** (*plural* **loci**)
**lo•cust**
**lo•cu•tion**
**Lod** Israeli town
**lode** ore deposit; *compare* **load**
**lo•den** wool
**lode•star** (*or* **load•**)
**lode•stone** (*or* **load•**)
**lodge**
**lodge•able**
**lodg•er**
**lodg•ing**
**lodg•ings**
**lodg•ment** (*or* **lodge•**)
**lodi•cule** botany term
**Łódź** Polish city
**lo•ess** soil
**lo•ess•ial** (*or* **•al**)
**Lo•fo•ten Is•lands**
**loft**
**loft•er** golf club
**lofti•ly**
**lofti•ness**
**lofty** (**lofti•er, lofti•est**)
**log** (**log•ging, logged**)
**Lo•gan** Canadian mountain
**logan•berry** (*plural* **•berries**)
**lo•ga•nia•ceous** botany
**lop-eared**
**lop•er**
**lo•pho•branch** fish
**lopho•bran•chi•ate**
**lo•pho•phor•ate**
**lo•pho•phore** zoology term
**lop•ing**
**loga•oedic** verse form
**loga•rithm**
**loga•rith•mic** (*or* **•mi•cal**)
**loga•rith•mi•cal•ly**
**log•book**
**loge** theatre box
**logged**
**log•ger**
**log•ger•head**
**log•gia** (*plural* **•gias** *or* **•gie**) roofed gallery; *compare* **logia**
**log•ging**
**logia** *plural of* **logion**; *compare* **loggia**
**log•ic**
**logi•cal**
**logi•cal•ity** (*or* **•ness**)
**logi•cal•ly**
**lo•gi•cian**
**logi•cism**
**logi•on** (*plural* **logia**) saying of Christ
**lo•gis•tic**
**lo•gis•ti•cal**
**lo•gis•ti•cal•ly**
**log•is•ti•cian**
**lo•gis•tics**
**log•log** maths term
**logo** (*plural* **logos**)
**logo•gram** (*or* **•graph**)
**logo•gram•mat•ic** (*or* **•graph•ic, •graphi•cal**)
**logo•gram•mati•cal•ly** (*or* **•graphi•cal•ly**)
**lo•gog•ra•pher**
**lo•gog•ra•phy**
**logo•griph** word puzzle
**logo•griph•ic**
**lo•goma•chist**
**lo•goma•chy** (*plural* **•chies**) word argument
**logo•paedic** (*US* **•pedic**)
**logo•paedics** (*US* **•pedics**) speech therapy
**log•or•rhoea** (*US* **•rhea**) talkativeness
**Log•os** second person of Trinity
**log•os** reason
**logo•type** printing term
**lo•go•typy**
**log•wood**
**logy** (**logi•er, logi•est**) *US* dull or listless
**Lohengrin** legendary character
**loin**
**loin•cloth**
**Loire** French river
**Loire-Atlantique** French department
**Loi•ret** French department
**Loir-et-Cher** French department
**loi•ter**
**loi•ter•er**
**loi•ter•ing•ly**
**Loki** Norse god
**loll**
**Lol•lard**
**Lol•lardy** (*or* **•lard•ry, •lard•ism**)
**loll•er**
**loll•ing•ly**

**lol•li•pop**
**lol•lop**
**lol•ly** (*plural* **•lies**)
**Lom•bard**
**Lom•bar•dic**
**Lom•bardy**
**Lom•bok** Indonesian island
**Lomé** capital of Togo
**lo•ment** (*or* **•men•tum;** *plural* **•ments** *or* **•men•ta**) plant pod
**lo•men•ta•ceous**
**Lo•mond** Scottish lake
**Lon•don**
**Lon•don•der•ry**
**Lon•don•er**
**Lon•dri•na** Brazilian city
**lone**
**lone•li•ness**
**lone•ly** (**•li•er, •li•est**)
**lone•ness**
**lon•er**
**lone•some**
**lone•some•ly**
**lone•some•ness**
**long**
**lon•gan** fruit
**lon•ga•nim•ity** patience
**lon•gani•mous**
**long•boat**
**long•bow**
**long•cloth**
**long-distance** (*adj*)
**long-drawn-out**
**lon•geron** part of aircraft
**lon•gev•ity**
**lon•gevous**
**Long•ford** Irish county
**long-haired**
**long•hand**
**long-headed** shrewd
**long•horn** cattle
**lon•gi•corn** beetle
**long•ing**
**long•ing•ly**
**long•ish**
**lon•gi•tude**
**lon•gi•tu•di•nal**
**long johns** underpants
**long-lived**
**long-range** (*adj*)
**long•ship**
**long•shore**
**long•shore•man** (*plural* **•men**)
**long-sighted**
**long-sighted•ly**
**long-sighted•ness**
**long•spur** bird
**long-standing**
**long-suffer•ance**
**long-suffer•ing**
**long-term**
**long•time** (*adj*)
**Lon•gueuil** Canadian city
**lon•gueur** *French* boredom
**long•ways** (*US* **•wise**)
**long-winded**
**long-winded•ly**
**long-winded•ness**
**Long•year•byen** Norwegian village
**lo•nic•era** honeysuckle
**loo** (*plural* **loos**)
**loo•by** (*plural* **•bies**) fool
**loo•fah** (*US also* **•fa, luf•fa**)
**look**
**look•alike**
**look•er**
**looker-on** (*plural* **lookers-**)
**look-in** (*noun*)
**look•out**
**loom**
**loom-state** undyed
**loon**
**looni•ness**
**loony** (*or* **looney;** *adj* **looni•er, looni•est;** *noun, plural* **loonies**)
**loop**
**loop•er** caterpillar
**loop•hole**
**loopi•ness**
**loopy** (**loopi•er, loopi•est**)
**loose**
**loose•box**
**loose-jointed**
**loose-leaf** (*adj*)
**loose•ly**
**loos•en**
**loos•en•er**
**loose•ness**
**loose•strife** plant
**loose-tongued**
**loos•ish**
**loot**
**loot•er**
**lop** (**lop•ping, lopped**)
**lope**
**lopped**
**lop•per**
**lop•ping**
**lop•sided**
**lop•sided•ly**
**lop•sided•ness**
**lo•qua•cious**
**lo•quac•ity** (*or* **lo•qua•cious•ness**)
**lo•quat** fruit
**lo•qui•tur** *Latin* he or she speaks
**lor** exclamation
**lo•ran** navigation system
**Lord** God
**lord** nobleman
**lord•li•ness**
**lord•ling**
**lord•ly** (**•li•er, •li•est**)
**lor•do•sis** spinal curvature
**lor•dot•ic**
**lord•ship**
**lordy** exclamation
**lore** knowledge; zoology term; *compare* law
**Lo•relei** siren
**lor•gnette**
**lor•gnon**
**lo•ri•ca** (*plural* **•cae**) shell
**lori•cate** (*or* **•cat•ed**)
**lori•keet** parrot
**lori•mer** (*or* **•ner**) metalworker
**lo•ris** (*plural* **•ris**) animal
**lorn** forsaken
**Lor•raine**
**lor•ry** (*plural* **•ries**) vehicle
**lory** (*plural* **lories**) parrot
**los•able**
**Los An•ge•les**
**lose** (**los•ing, lost**)
**lo•sel** *Dialect* worthless person
**los•er**
**los•ing**
**loss**
**los•sy** dissipating energy
**lost**
**lot** (**lot•ting, lot•ted**)
**lota** (*or* **lo•tah**) water container
**Lot-et-Garonne** French department
**loth** *variant spelling of* **loath**
**Lo•thario** (*plural* **•tharios**) libertine

**Lo•thian** former Scottish region
**lo•tic** ecology term
**lo•tion**
**lot•ted**
**lot•tery** (*plural* **•teries**)
**lot•ting**
**lot•to**
**lo•tus** (*or* **lo•tos**)
**lotus-eater**
**louche** shifty
**loud**
**loud•en**
**loud-hailer**
**loud•ish**
**loud•ly**
**loud•mouth**
**loud•ness**
**loud•speaker**
**lough**
**Lough•bor•ough** Leicestershire town
**lou•is** (*or* **lou•is d'or;** *plural* **lou•is** *or* **lou•is d'or**) coin
**Lou•is•burg** (*or* **•bourg**) Canadian fortress
**Loui•si•ana**
**Lou•is•ville** US port
**lounge**
**loung•er**
**loupe** magnifying glass
**lour** (*or* **low•er**) look menacing
**Lourdes** French town
**lour•ing•ly** (*or* **low•er•**)
**louse** (*plural* **lice**)
**louse•wort**
**lousi•ly**
**lousi•ness**
**lousy** (**lousi•er, lousi•est**)
**lout**
**Louth** Irish county
**lout•ish**
**lout•ish•ly**
**lout•ish•ness**
**Lou•vain** Belgian town
**lou•var** fish
**Lou•vre** French museum
**lou•vre** (*US* **•ver**) slat
**lou•vred** (*US* **•vered**)
**lov•abil•ity** (*or* **love•**)
**lov•able** (*or* **love•**)
**lov•ably** (*or* **love•**)
**lov•age** plant
**lov•at** fabric
**love**
**love•bird**
**love•less**
**love•li•ness**
**love•lock**
**love•lorn**
**love•ly** (*adj* **•li•er, •li•est;** *noun, plural* **•lies**)
**love•making**
**lov•er**
**love•sick**
**love•sick•ness**
**lov•ey**
**lovey-dovey**
**lov•ing**
**lov•ing•ly**
**lov•ing•ness**
**low**
**low•an** bird
**low•born** (*or* **•bred**)
**low•boy** *US* table with drawers
**low•bred**
**low•brow**
**low•brow•ism**
**low•down** (*noun*)
**low-down** (*adj*)
**low•er** less high; *variant spelling of* **lour**
**low•er•able**
**low•er•ing•ly** *variant spelling of* **louringly**
**lower•most**
**low•est**
**Lowes•toft**
**low-key** (*or* **-keyed**)
**Low•land** of Lowlands
**low•land** flat ground
**Low•land•er**
**low•land•er**
**Low•lands** Scottish region
**low•li•ness**
**low•ly** (**•li•er, •li•est**)
**low-minded**
**low•ness**
**low-pitched**
**low-rise** (*adj*)
**low-spirit•ed**
**lox** smoked salmon
**loxo•drom•ic** (*or* **•dromi•cal**)
**loxo•dromi•cal•ly**
**loxo•drom•ics** (*or* **lox•od•ro•my**) navigation technique
**loy•al**
**loy•al•ism**
**Loy•al•ist** Northern Irish Protestant
**loy•al•ist**
**loy•al•ly**
**loy•al•ty** (*plural* **•ties**)
**Lo•yang** Chinese city
**loz•enge**
**loz•engy** heraldic term
**Lo•zère** French department
**Lozi** Zambian language
**Lu•an•da** Angolan capital
**Luba** (*plural* **Luba**) African people
**lub•ber** clumsy person
**Lub•bock** Texan city
**Lü•beck** German port
**Lu•blin** Polish city
**lub•ri•cant**
**lu•bri•cate**
**lu•bri•ca•tion**
**lu•bri•ca•tion•al**
**lu•bri•ca•tive**
**lu•bri•ca•tor**
**lu•bric•ity** lewdness
**lu•bri•cous** (*or* **•cious**)
**Lu•bum•ba•shi** city in the Democratic Republic of Congo
**lu•carne** dormer window
**lu•cen•cy**
**lu•cent**
**Lu•cerne** Swiss town
**lu•cerne** plant
**lu•cid**
**lu•cid•ity** (*or* **•cid•ness**)
**Lu•ci•fer**
**lu•cif•er•in** biochemical compound
**Lucina** Roman goddess
**luck**
**lucki•ly**
**lucki•ness**
**luck•less**
**luck•less•ness**
**Luck•now** Indian city
**lucky** (**lucki•er, lucki•est**)
**luc•ra•tive**
**lu•cra•tive•ly**
**lu•cre**
**lu•cu•brate** to study
**lu•cu•bra•tion**
**lu•cu•bra•tor**
**Lud•dite**

**Lu•dhia•na** Indian city
**lu•di•crous**
**Lud•low** Shropshire town
**ludo**
**Lud•wigs•ha•fen** German city
**luff** nautical term
**luf•fa** *US variant spelling of* **loofah**
**Luft•waf•fe** German Air Force
**lug (lug•ging, lugged)**
**Lu•gan•da** African language
**Lu•gansk** Ukrainian city
**luge** toboggan
**Lu•ger** (*Trademark*)
**lug•gage**
**lugged**
**lug•ger**
**lug•ging**
**lug•sail**
**lu•gu•bri•ous**
**lug•worm**
**luke•warm**
**lull**
**lulla•by** (*noun, plural* **•bies;** *verb* **•bies, •by•ing, •bied)**
**lull•ing•ly**
**lulu** *US* wonderful person or thing
**lum•ba•go**
**lum•bar** of loin
**lum•ber** timber; move awkwardly
**lum•ber•er**
**lum•ber•ing**
**lum•ber•ing•ly**
**lumber•jack**
**lumber•jacket**
**lumber•yard**
**lum•bri•cal**
**lum•bri•ca•lis** muscle
**lum•bri•coid** wormlike
**lu•men** (*plural* **•mens**) unit
**lu•men** (*plural* **•mina**) anatomical duct
**lu•men•al** (*or* **•min•**)
**lu•mi•nance**
**lu•mi•nary** (*plural* **•naries**)
**lu•mi•nesce**
**lu•mi•nes•cence**
**lu•mi•nes•cent**
**lu•mi•nos•ity** (*plural* **•ities**)
**lu•mi•nous**
**lu•mi•nous•ly**
**lu•mis•te•rol** biochemical compound
**lum•me** exclamation
**lum•mox** clumsy person
**lump**
**lump•en** stupid
**lum•pen•pro•le•tari•at**
**lum•per** *US* stevedore
**lump•fish** (*plural* **•fish** *or* **•fishes)**
**lumpi•ly**
**lumpi•ness**
**lump•ish**
**lumpy (lumpi•er, lumpi•est)**
**Luna** Roman goddess
**luna** moth; *compare* **lunar**
**lu•na•cy** (*plural* **•cies)**
**lu•nar** of the moon; *compare* **luna**
**lu•nate** (*or* **•nat•ed)**
**lu•na•tic** (*or* **lu•nati•cal)**
**lu•na•tion** lunar month
**lunch**
**lunch•eon**
**lunch•eon•ette** *US* café
**lunch•er**
**Lund** Swedish city
**Lun•dy** island
**lune** maths term
**Lü•ne•burg** German city
**lu•nette**
**lung**
**lunge**
**lung•er**
**lung•fish** (*plural* **•fish** *or* **•fishes)**
**lung•ful**
**lun•gi** (*or* **•gee**) Indian cloth
**lung•worm**
**lung•wort** plant
**lu•ni•so•lar**
**lu•ni•tid•al**
**lu•nu•la** (*or* **•nule;** *plural* **•lae** *or* **•nules)**
**lu•nu•late** (*or* **•lat•ed)**
**luny** (*adj* **luni•er, luni•est;** *noun, plural* **lunies)**
**Lu•per•ca•lia** (*plural* **•lia** *or* **•lias**) Roman festival
**lu•pin** (*US* **•pine**) plant
**lu•pine** wolflike; *US spelling of* **lupin**
**lu•pu•lin** sedative
**Lu•pus** constellation
**lu•pus** skin disease
**lur** (*or* **lure;** *plural* **lures)** musical horn
**lurch**
**lurch•er**
**lurch•ing•ly**
**lur•dan** stupid
**lure**
**lur•er**
**Lu•rex** (*Trademark*)
**lu•rid**
**lu•rid•ness**
**lur•ing•ly**
**lurk**
**lurk•er**
**lurk•ing•ly**
**Lu•sa•ka** Zambian capital
**Lu•sa•tia** German region
**Lu•sa•tian**
**lus•cious**
**lus•cious•ness**
**lush**
**lush•ly**
**lush•ness**
**Lü•shun** Chinese port
**Lu•si•ta•nia** ship
**lust**
**lus•ter** *US spelling of* **lustre**
**lust•ful**
**lust•ful•ly**
**lust•ful•ness**
**lusti•ly**
**lusti•ness**
**lus•tral**
**lus•trate** purify
**lus•tra•tion**
**lus•tra•tive**
**lus•tre** (*US* **•ter)**
**lus•tre•less** (*US* **•ter•)**
**lustre•ware** (*US* **luster•)**
**lus•trous**
**lus•trum** (*plural* **•trums** *or* **•tra**) five years
**lusty (lusti•er, lusti•est)**
**lute**
**lu•teal** biology term
**lu•tein•iz•ing hor•mone**
**lu•tenist** lute player
**lu•teo•lin** plant compound
**lu•teous** greenish-yellow
**Lu•tetia** *Latin* Paris
**lu•tetium** (*or* **•tecium)** chemical element
**Lu•ther•an**
**Lu•ther•an•ism**

**Lu•ther•ism**
**lu•thern** dormer window
**Lu•tine bell**
**Lu•ton**
**lux** (*plural* **lux**) unit
**lux•ate** dislocate
**luxa•tion**
**Lux•em•bourg**
**Lux•or** Egyptian town
**lux•ulia•nite** (*or* **•ul•lia•nite**) granite
**luxu•ri•ance**
**luxu•ri•ant**
**luxu•ri•ate**
**luxu•ria•tion**
**luxu•ri•ous**
**luxu•ry** (*plural* **•ries**)
**Lu•zon** Philippine island
**Ly•all•pur** Pakistani city
**ly•can•thrope** werewolf
**ly•can•thro•py**
**ly•cée** (*plural* **•cées**) French school
**Ly•ceum** Athenian school
**ly•ceum** public building
**ly•chee** *variant spelling of* **litchi**
**lych gate** *variant spelling of* **lich gate**
**lych•nis** plant
**ly•co•pod** club moss
**ly•co•po•dium** type of club moss
**lydd•ite** explosive
**Lydia** ancient Asian region
**Lyd•ian**
**lye** alkaline solution; *compare* **lie**
**ly•ing**
**lying-in** (*plural* **lyings-in**)
**lyke-wake** vigil over corpse
**Lyme Re•gis**
**Lym•ing•ton** Hampshire town
**lymph**
**lym•phad•eni•tis**
**lym•phan•gial**
**lym•phan•git•ic**
**lym•phan•gi•tis** (*plural* **•gi•des**)
**lym•phat•ic**
**lym•phati•cal•ly**
**lym•pho•blast** blood cell
**lym•pho•blas•tic**
**lym•pho•cyte** blood cell
**lym•pho•cyt•ic**
**lym•pho•cy•to•sis**
**lym•pho•cy•tot•ic**
**lym•phoid**
**lym•pho•ma** (*plural* **•ma•ta** *or* **•mas**) tumour
**lym•pho•ma•toid**
**lym•pho•poi•esis** (*plural* **•eses**)
**lym•pho•poi•et•ic**
**lyn•cean** resembling a lynx
**lynch** kill; *compare* **linchpin**
**lynch•er**
**lynch•ing**
**lynx** (*plural* **lynxes** *or* **lynx**)
**Lyon** French city
**Lyon•nais** former French province
**ly•on•naise** cookery term
**Ly•on•nesse** legendary place
**lyo•phil•ic**
**ly•ophi•lize** (*or* **•lise**) freeze-dry
**lyo•pho•bic**
**Lyra** constellation
**ly•rate** (*or* **rat•ed**)
**lyre**
**lyre•bird**
**lyr•ic**
**lyri•cal**
**lyri•cal•ly**
**lyri•cism**
**lyri•cist**
**lyr•ist**
**lyse** biology term
**ly•ser•gic acid**
**ly•sim•eter**
**ly•sin** substance that destroys cells
**ly•sine** amino acid
**ly•sis** (*plural* **•ses**) biology term
**Ly•sol** (*Trademark*)
**ly•so•so•mal**
**ly•so•some** cell particle
**ly•so•zyme** enzyme
**Lyth•am St. Anne's**
**lyth•ra•ceous** botany term
**lyt•ic** biology term
**lyt•ta** (*plural* **•tas** *or* **•tae**) zoology term

# M

**ma** *Slang* mother
**Ma'am** title of address for royalty
**maar** (*plural* **maars** *or* **maare**) volcanic crater
**Maas•tricht** (*or* **Maes•**) Dutch city
**Mab** fairy queen
**ma•bela** ground corn
**mac**
**ma•ca•bre**
**ma•ca•co** (*plural* **•cos**) lemur; *compare* **macaque**
**mac•ad•am** road surface
**maca•da•mia** tree
**mac•ad•ami•za•tion** (*or* **•sa•tion**)
**mac•ad•am•ize** (*or* **•ise**)
**mac•ad•am•iz•er** (*or* **•is•er**)
**Ma•cao** Chinese city
**ma•caque** monkey; *compare* **macaco**
**maca•ro•ni** (*plural* **•nis**) pasta
**maca•ro•ni** (*plural* **•nies**) dandy
**maca•ron•ic** type of verse
**maca•roni•cal•ly**
**maca•roon**
**Ma•cas•sar** *variant spelling of* **Makassar**
**ma•caw**
**Mac•ca•bean**
**Mac•ca•bees** Apocryphal book
**mac•ca•boy** (*or* **•co•boy, •ca•baw**) snuff
**Mac•cles•field**
**mace**
**mace•bearer**
**ma•cedoine** diced vegetables

**Mac•edon** (*or* **•edo•nia**) former kingdom
**Mac•edo•nia** S European country; division of Greece
**Mac•edo•nian**
**Ma•ceió** Brazilian port
**mac•er** macebearer
**mac•er•ate**
**mac•er•at•er** (*or* **•era•tor**)
**mac•era•tion**
**mac•era•tive**
**ma•chan** tiger-hunting platform
**ma•chete**
**Machia•vel•lian** (*or* **•vel•ian**)
**ma•chico•late** fortifications term
**ma•chico•la•tion**
**ma•chin•abil•ity**
**ma•chin•able** (*or* **•chine•**)
**machi•nate**
**machi•na•tion**
**machi•na•tor**
**ma•chine**
**machine-gun** (*verb*; **-gunning, -gunned**)
**ma•chin•ery** (*plural* **•eries**)
**ma•chin•ist**
**ma•chis•mo**
**Mach•meter** physics term
**Mach num•ber** physics term
**macho**
**ma•chree** *Irish* my dear
**Ma•chu Pic•chu** Incan city
**Ma•cí•as Ngue•ma** Guinean island
**Mac•kay** Australian port
**Mac•ken•zie** Canadian district or river
**macke•rel** (*plural* **•rel** *or* **•rels**)
**Macki•naw coat**
**mack•in•tosh** (*or* **mac•in•**)
**mack•le** (*or* **mac•ule**) printing term; *compare* **macle**
**Maclaurin's se•ries** maths term
**ma•cle** mineral; *compare* **mackle**
**Mâ•con** French city; wine
**mac•ra•mé**
**mac•ren•cepha•ly** (*or* **•lia**) abnormally large brain
**macro•bi•ot•ic**
**macro•cephal•ic** (*or* **mega•**, **mega•lo•**)
**macro•cepha•ly** (*or* **mega•**, **mega•lo•**) abnormally large head
**macro•cli•mate**
**macro•cli•mat•ic**
**macro•cli•mati•cal•ly**
**macro•cosm**
**macro•cos•mic**
**macro•cos•mi•cal•ly**
**macro•cyst**
**macro•cyte** blood cell
**macro•cyt•ic**
**macro•cy•to•sis**
**macro•eco•nom•ic**
**macro•eco•nom•ics**
**macro•evo•lu•tion**
**macro•evo•lu•tion•ary**
**macro•gam•ete** (*or* **mega•**)
**macro•graph**
**macro•graph•ic**
**macro•mo•lecu•lar**
**macro•mol•ecule**
**mac•ron** phonetic symbol
**macro•nu•cleus** (*plural* **•clei**)
**macro•nu•tri•ent**
**macro•phage** cell
**macro•phag•ic**
**macro•phys•ics**
**mac•rop•ter•ous** having large wings
**macro•scop•ic** (*or* **•scopi•cal**)
**macro•scopi•cal•ly**
**macro•spo•ran•gium** (*plural* **•gia**) botany term
**macro•spore**
**ma•cru•ral** (*or* **•roid, •rous**)
**ma•cru•ran** crustacean
**macu•la** (*or* **mac•ule**; *plural* **•lae** *or* **•ules**) anatomy term
**macu•la lu•tea** (*plural* **macu•lae lu•teae**) spot on retina
**macu•lar**
**macu•la•tion**
**mac•ule** *variant of* **mackle** *or* **macula**
**mad** (**mad•der, mad•dest**)
**Mada•gas•can**
**Mada•gas•car**
**mad•am** term of address; conceited girl; brothel keeper
**mad•ame** (*plural* **mes•dames**) *French* lady; Mrs
**mad•cap**
**mad•den**
**mad•den•ing**
**mad•der** plant; dye; more mad
**mad•dest**
**mad•ding** *Archaic* mad or maddening
**made**
**Ma•dei•ra**
**mad•eleine** cake
**mad•emoi•selle** (*plural* **mes•de•moi•selles**)
**mad•house**
**Madh•ya Pra•desh** Indian state
**Madi•son** US city and avenue
**mad•ly**
**mad•man** (*plural* **•men**)
**mad•ness**
**Ma•don•na** Virgin Mary
**Ma•dras** Indian port
**mad•ras** fabric
**mad•re•por•al** (*or* **•por•ic, •por•it•ic, •po•rian**)
**mad•re•pore** coral
**Ma•drid**
**mad•ri•gal**
**mad•ri•gal•esque**
**mad•ri•gal•ian**
**mad•ri•gal•ist**
**mad•ri•lène** consommé
**ma•dro•ña** (*or* **•ño, •ne**; *plural* **•ñas, •ños,** *or* **•nes**) tree
**Ma•du•ra** Indonesian island
**Ma•du•rai** Indian city
**Ma•du•rese** of Madura
**ma•du•ro** cigar
**mad•woman** (*plural* **•women**)
**mad•wort** plant
**Ma•eba•shi** Japanese city
**Mael•strom** Norwegian whirlpool
**mael•strom** whirlpool; confusion
**mae•nad** (*or* **me•nad**)

**mae•nad•ic**
**maes•to•so** musical term
**maes•tro** (*plural* **•tros** *or* **•tri**)
**Maf•eking** South African town
**Ma•fia** (*or* **Maf•fia**)
**ma•fio•so** (*plural* **•sos** *or* **•si**)
**mag**
**maga•zine**
**mag•da•len** reformed prostitute
**Mag•da•lena** Colombian river
**Mag•da•lenian** Palaeolithic culture
**Mag•de•burg** German city
**Ma•gel•lan** strait
**ma•gen•ta**
**mag•got** fly larva; *compare* **magot**
**mag•goti•ness**
**mag•goty**
**Ma•ghreb** (*or* **•ghrib**)
**Ma•ghre•bi** (*or* **•ghri•**)
**Magi** (*sing.* **Magus**) biblical wise men
**magi** *plural of* **magus**
**ma•gian**
**mag•ic** (**•ick•ing, •icked**)
**magi•cal**
**magi•cal•ly**
**ma•gi•cian**
**ma•gilp** *variant spelling of* **megilp**
**Ma•gi•not line**
**mag•is•te•rial**
**mag•is•te•rial•ly**
**mag•is•tery** (*plural* **•teries**) alchemical substance
**mag•is•tra•cy** (*or* **•ture**; *plural* **•cies** *or* **•tures**)
**mag•is•tral** pharmacology term
**mag•is•tral•ly** (*or* **mag•is•trati•cal•ly**)
**mag•is•trate**
**mag•is•trate•ship**
**mag•is•tra•ture** *variant of* **magistracy**
**Mag•le•mo•sian** (*or* **•sean**) Mesolithic culture
**mag•ma** (*plural* **•mas** *or* **•ma•ta**) molten rock
**mag•mat•ic**
**mag•ma•tism**
**Mag•na Car•ta** (*or* **Char•ta**)
**mag•na•nim•ity** (*plural* **•ities**)
**mag•nani•mous**
**mag•nani•mous•ness**
**mag•nate**
**mag•ne•sia** magnesium oxide
**mag•ne•sian** (*or* **•ne•sic, •ne•sial**)
**mag•ne•site** mineral
**mag•ne•sium**
**mag•net**
**mag•net•ic**
**mag•neti•cal•ly**
**mag•net•ics**
**mag•net•ism**
**mag•net•ite** mineral
**mag•net•it•ic**
**mag•net•iz•able** (*or* **•is•able**)
**mag•neti•za•tion** (*or* **•sa•tion**)
**mag•net•ize** (*or* **•ise**)
**mag•net•iz•er** (*or* **•is•er**)
**mag•ne•to** (*plural* **•tos**)
**mag•ne•to•chemi•cal**
**mag•ne•to•chem•is•try**
**mag•ne•to•elec•tric** (*or* **•tri•cal**)
**mag•ne•to•elec•tric•ity**
**mag•ne•to•graph**
**mag•ne•to•hy•dro•dy•nam•ic**
**mag•ne•to•hy•dro•dy•nam•ics**
**mag•ne•tom•eter**
**mag•ne•to•met•ric**
**mag•ne•tom•etry**
**mag•ne•to•mo•tive**
**mag•ne•ton** physics unit; *compare* **magnetron**
**mag•ne•to•sphere**
**mag•ne•to•stric•tion**
**mag•ne•to•stric•tive**
**mag•ne•tron** microwave generator; *compare* **magneton**
**mag•ni•fi•able**
**Mag•nifi•cat** canticle
**mag•ni•fi•ca•tion**
**mag•nifi•cence**
**mag•nifi•cent**
**mag•nifi•co** (*plural* **•coes**) grandee
**mag•ni•fi•er**
**mag•ni•fy** (**•fies, •fy•ing, •fied**)
**mag•nilo•quence**
**mag•nilo•quent**
**Mag•ni•to•gorsk** Russian city
**mag•ni•tude**
**mag•ni•tu•di•nous**
**mag•no•lia**
**mag•no•lia•ceous**
**mag•num** (*plural* **•nums**) wine bottle
**mag•num opus**
**mag•nus** hitchknot
**Magog** biblical character
**ma•got** oriental figurine; *compare* **maggot**
**mag•pie**
**mag•uey** fibre
**Magus** (*sing. of* **Magi**)
**magus** (*plural* **magi**) Zoroastrian priest; sorcerer
**Mag•yar** Hungarian
**Ma•ha•bha•ra•ta** (*or* **•tam, •tum**) Indian poem
**Ma•hal•la el Ku•bra** Egyptian city
**Ma•ha•na•di** Indian river
**ma•ha•ra•jah** (*or* **•ja**)
**ma•ha•ra•ni** (*or* **•nee**) maharajah's wife
**Ma•ha•rash•tra** Indian state
**ma•ha•ri•shi** Hindu teacher
**ma•hat•ma** Brahman sage
**Ma•ha•ya•na** Buddhist school
**Mahé** Seychelles island
**Ma•hi•can** (*or* **Mo•**; *plural* **•cans** *or* **•can**) American Indian
**mah•jong** (*or* **mah-jongg**)
**mahl•stick** *variant spelling of* **maulstick**
**ma•hoga•ny** (*plural* **•nies**)
**Ma•hom•etan** Muslim
**ma•ho•nia** shrub
**ma•hout** elephant keeper
**Mah•rat•ta** *variant spelling of* **Maratha**
**mah•seer** fish
**Maia** mythological character
**maid**
**mai•dan** meeting place
**maid•en** young girl
**maiden•hair** fern

**Maid•en•head** S English town
**maid•en•head** virginity
**maid•en•hood**
**maid•en•li•ness**
**maid•en•ly**
**maid•servant**
**Maid•stone** Kent town
**maieu•tic** (*or* **•ti•cal**) philosophy term
**Mai•kop** Russian city
**mail**
**mail•able**
**mail•bag**
**mail•box**
**mail•coach**
**mail•er**
**mail•sack**
**mail•shot**
**maim**
**maim•er**
**main**
**main•brace**
**Maine** US state
**Maine-et-Loire** French department
**Main•land** Scottish island
**main•land**
**main•line** (*adj, verb*)
**main•ly**
**main•mast**
**main•sail**
**main•sheet**
**main•spring**
**main•stay**
**main•stream**
**main•tain**
**main•tain•able**
**main•tain•er**
**main•te•nance**
**main•top**
**main-topmast**
**main•top•sail**
**Mainz** German port
**ma•ioli•ca** *variant spelling of* **majolica**
**mai•son•ette** (*or* **•son•nette**)
**maî•tre d'hô•tel** (*plural* **maî•tres d'hô•tel**)
**maize** cereal; *compare* **maze**
**ma•jes•tic** (*or* **•ti•cal**)
**ma•jes•ti•cal•ly**
**Maj•es•ty** (*plural* **•ties**) title for royalty
**maj•es•ty** dignity
**ma•joli•ca** (*or* **•ioli•**) pottery
**ma•jor**
**Ma•jor•ca**
**major-domo** (*plural* **-domos**)
**ma•jor•ette**
**ma•jor•ity** (*plural* **•ities**)
**Ma•juro** capital of the Marshall Islands
**ma•jus•cu•lar**
**ma•jus•cule** printing term
**Ma•ka•lu** Himalayan mountain range
**Ma•kas•ar** (*or* **•kas•sar, •cas•sar**) Indonesian port
**make** (**mak•ing, made**)
**make-believe** (*noun*)
**make•fast**
**mak•er**
**make•shift**
**make-up** (*noun*)
**make•weight** (*noun*)
**Ma•ke•yev•ka** Ukrainian city
**Ma•khach•ka•la** Russian port
**mak•ing**
**mako** (*plural* **makos**) shark; tree
**Ma•kur•di** Nigerian port
**Mala•bar** Indian region
**Ma•la•bo** capital of Equatorial Guinea
**mal•ab•sorp•tion**
**Ma•lac•ca** Malaysian state
**ma•lac•ca** walking stick
**mala•chite** mineral
**mala•co•logi•cal**
**mala•colo•gist**
**mala•col•ogy** study of molluscs
**mala•coph•yl•lous** having fleshy leaves
**mala•cop•te•ryg•ian** fish
**mala•cos•tra•can** crustacean
**mala•cos•tra•cous**
**mal•ad•dress** awkwardness
**mal•ad•just•ed**
**mal•ad•just•ment**
**mal•ad•min•is•ter**
**mal•ad•min•is•tra•tion**
**mal•ad•min•is•tra•tor**
**mala•droit**
**mala•droit•ness**
**mala•dy** (*plural* **•dies**)
**mala fide** *Latin* in bad faith
**Má•la•ga** Spanish port; wine
**Mala•gasy** Madagascan language
**ma•la•gueña** dance
**ma•laise**
**mala•mute** (*or* **mal•emute**) Eskimo dog
**mal•an•ders** (*or* **mal•lan•, mal•len•**) horse disease
**Ma•lang** Indonesian city
**mala•pert** saucy
**mala•prop•ian**
**mala•prop•ism**
**mal•ap•ro•pos**
**ma•lar** of the cheek
**ma•laria**
**ma•lar•ial** (*or* **•lar•ian, •lari•ous**)
**ma•lar•key** (*or* **•ky**)
**mal•as•simi•la•tion**
**mal•ate** chemistry term
**Mala•thi•on** (*Trademark*)
**Ma•la•tya** Turkish city
**Ma•la•wi**
**Ma•la•wian**
**Ma•lay**
**Ma•laya**
**Mala•ya•lam** (*or* **•laam**) language
**Ma•lay•an**
**Ma•lay•sia**
**Ma•lay•sian**
**mal•con•tent**
**mal de mer** *French* sea sickness
**Mal•dives**
**Mal•div•ian** (*or* **•di•van**)
**male**
**Malé** capital of the Maldives
**ma•leate** chemistry term
**mal•edict**
**mal•edic•tion**
**mal•edic•tive** (*or* **•tory**)
**mal•efac•tion**
**mal•efac•tor** (*fem* **•tress**)
**ma•lef•ic**
**ma•lefi•cence**
**ma•lefi•cent**
**ma•leic acid**
**male•ness**
**ma•levo•lence**
**ma•levo•lent**
**mal•fea•sance** illegal act
**mal•fea•sant**

**mal•for•ma•tion**
**mal•formed**
**mal•func•tion**
**mal•gré lui** *French* in spite of himself
**Mali** African republic
**Malian**
**mal•ic acid**
**mal•ice**
**ma•li•cious**
**ma•li•cious•ness**
**ma•lign**
**ma•lig•nan•cy** (*plural* **•cies**)
**ma•lig•nant**
**ma•lign•er**
**ma•lig•nity** (*plural* **•nities**)
**mal•im•print•ed**
**mal•im•print•ing**
**ma•lines** fabric
**ma•lin•ger**
**ma•lin•ger•er**
**Ma•lin•ke** (*or* **•nin•ke**; *plural* **•ke** *or* **•kes**) African people
**mali•son** curse
**mall**
**mal•lam** (*or* **mal•am**) Islamic scholar
**mal•lard** (*plural* **•lard** *or* **•lards**)
**mal•le•abil•ity** (*or* **•able•ness**)
**mal•le•able**
**mal•lee** tree
**mal•le•muck** bird
**mal•leo•lar**
**mal•leo•lus** (*plural* **•li**) ankle bone
**mal•let**
**mal•le•us** (*plural* **•lei**) ear bone
**mal•low**
**malm** limestone
**Malmö** Swedish port
**malm•sey** wine
**mal•nour•ished**
**mal•nu•tri•tion**
**mal•oc•clud•ed**
**mal•oc•clu•sion** dentistry term
**mal•odor•ous**
**ma•lo•nic acid**
**mal•pighia•ceous** botany. term
**Mal•pigh•ian** anatomy term
**mal•posed**
**mal•po•si•tion**
**mal•prac•tice**
**mal•prac•ti•tion•er**
**malt**
**Mal•ta**
**malt•ase** enzyme
**malt•ed**
**Mal•tese** (*plural* **•tese**)
**mal•tha** mineral tar
**Mal•thu•sian**
**Mal•thu•si•an•ism** population theory
**malti•ness**
**malt•ing**
**malt•ose** sugar
**mal•treat**
**mal•treat•er**
**mal•treat•ment**
**malt•ster**
**malty** (**malti•er, malti•est**)
**mal•va•ceous** botany term
**mal•va•sia** wine
**Mal•vern**
**mal•voi•sie** wine
**mam** *Slang* mother
**mama** (*or* **mam•ma**) mother; *compare* **mamma**
**mam•ba** snake
**mam•bo** (*plural* **•bos**) dance
**mam•elon** hillock
**Mam•eluke** (*or* **Mama•luke**) Egyptian ruler
**ma•mey** (*or* **mam•mee**) fruit; *compare* **mammy**
**ma•mil•la** (*US* **mam•mil•**; *plural* **•lae**) nipple
**ma•mil•lary** (*US* **mam•mil•**)
**ma•mil•late** (*or* **•lat•ed**; *US* **mam•mil•**)
**mam•ma** (*plural* **•mae**) breast; *compare* **mama**
**mam•ma** *variant spelling of* **mama**
**mam•mal**
**mam•ma•lian**
**mam•ma•logi•cal**
**mam•malo•gist**
**mam•mal•ogy**
**mam•ma•ry**
**mam•mee** *variant spelling of* **mamey**
**mam•mif•er•ous**
**mam•mil•la** *US spelling of* **mamilla**
**mam•mock** *Dialect* shred
**mam•mo•gram**
**mam•mog•ra•phy**
**mam•mon**
**mam•mon•ism**
**mam•mon•ist** (*or* **•ite**)
**mam•mon•is•tic**
**mam•moth**
**mam•my** (*or* **•mie**; *plural* **•mies**) mother; *compare* **mamey**
**Man (Isle of)**
**man** (*noun, plural* **men**; *verb* **man•ning, manned**)
**mana** power; *compare* **manna**
**mana•cle**
**Ma•na•do** *variant spelling of* **Menado**
**man•age**
**man•age•abil•ity** (*or* **•able•ness**)
**man•age•able**
**man•age•ably**
**man•age•ment**
**man•ag•er**
**man•ag•er•ess**
**mana•gerial**
**mana•geri•al•ly**
**man•ag•ing**
**Ma•na•gua** Nicaraguan capital
**mana•kin** bird; *compare* **manikin; mannequin**
**Ma•na•ma** capital of Bahrain
**ma•ña•na** *Spanish* tomorrow
**Ma•nas•sas** US town
**man-at-arms** (*plural* **men-**)
**mana•tee** sea mammal
**mana•toid**
**Ma•naus** (*or* **Ma•náos**) Brazilian port
**Manche** French department
**Man•ches•ter**
**man•chi•neel** tree
**Man•chu** (*plural* **•chus** *or* **•chu**) Chinese dynasty
**Man•chu•ria**
**Man•chu•rian**
**man•ci•ple** steward
**Man•cu•nian** native of Manchester
**Man•daean**
**Man•dae•an•ism** Iraqi sect
**Man•da•lay** Burmese city

**man•da•mus** (*plural* **•muses**) legal term
**Man•da•rin** language
**man•da•rin** official; fruit; duck
**man•da•tary** *variant spelling of* **mandatory** (*noun*)
**man•date**
**man•da•to•ri•ly**
**man•da•tory** obligatory
**man•da•tory** (*or* **•tary**; *plural* **•tories** *or* **•taries**) mandate holder
**Man•de** (*plural* **•de** *or* **•des**) language group
**man•di** Indian market
**man•di•ble**
**man•dibu•lar**
**man•dir** Hindu temple
**man•do•la** mandolin
**man•do•lin** (*or* **•line**)
**man•do•lin•ist**
**man•dor•la** art term
**man•drake** (*or* **man•drago•ra**)
**man•drel** (*or* **•dril**) spindle
**man•drill** monkey
**man•du•cate** eat or chew
**mane**
**man-eater**
**maned**
**ma•nège** (*or* **•nege**) riding school; compare **ménage**
**ma•nes** Roman deities
**ma•neu•ver** *US spelling of* **manoeuvre**
**man•ful**
**man•ful•ly**
**man•ful•ness**
**man•ga•bey** monkey
**Man•ga•lore** Indian port
**man•ga•nate**
**man•ga•nese**
**man•gan•ic**
**Man•gan•in** (*Trademark*)
**man•ga•nite** mineral
**man•ga•nous**
**mange** skin disease
**man•gel-wur•zel** (*or* **•gold-**)
**man•ger**
**mange-tout** pea
**man•gi•ly**
**man•gi•ness**
**man•gle**
**man•gler**
**man•go** (*plural* **•goes** *or* **•gos**)
**man•go•nel** war engine
**man•go•steen** fruit
**man•grove**
**man•gy** (*or* **•gey**; **•gi•er, •gi•est**)
**man•handle**
**Man•hat•tan**
**man•hole**
**man•hood**
**man-hour**
**man•hunt**
**man•hunter**
**ma•nia**
**ma•ni•ac**
**ma•nia•cal**
**ma•nia•cal•ly**
**man•ic**
**manic-depres•sive**
**Mani•chae•ism** (*or* **•che•**) religion
**Mani•chee**
**ma•ni•cot•ti** stuffed noodles
**mani•cure**
**mani•cur•ist**
**mani•fest**
**mani•fest•able**
**mani•fes•ta•tion**
**mani•fes•ta•tion•al**
**mani•fes•to** (*plural* **•toes** *or* **•tos**)
**mani•fold**
**mani•fold•er**
**mani•kin** (*or* **mana•kin, man•ni•kin**) dwarf; *compare* **manakin; mannequin**
**Ma•nila** Philippine port
**ma•nil•la** African currency
**ma•nille** card trump
**mani•oc** (*or* **manio•ca**) plant
**mani•ple**
**ma•nipu•labil•ity**
**ma•nipu•lar**
**ma•nipu•lat•able** (*or* **•lable**)
**ma•nipu•late**
**ma•nipu•la•tion**
**ma•nipu•la•tive**
**ma•nipu•la•tor**
**ma•nipu•la•tory**
**Ma•ni•pur** Indian region
**Ma•ni•sa** Turkish city
**Mani•to•ba** Canadian province
**mani•tou** (*or* **•tu**; *plural* **•tous, tou,** *or* **•tus, •tu**) American Indian spirit
**Mani•tou•lin** Canadian island
**Mani•za•les** Colombian city
**man•kind**
**manky** (**manki•er, manki•est**) *Scot* dirty
**man•like**
**man•li•ness**
**man•ly** (**•li•er, •li•est**)
**man-made**
**man•na** celestial food; *compare* **mana**
**manned**
**man•ne•quin** model; *compare* **manakin; manikin**
**man•ner**
**man•nered**
**man•ner•ism**
**man•ner•ist**
**man•ner•is•tic** (*or* **•ti•cal**)
**man•ner•is•ti•cal•ly**
**man•ner•less**
**man•ner•less•ness**
**man•ner•li•ness**
**man•ner•ly**
**Mann•heim** German city
**man•nish**
**man•nish•ness**
**man•nit•ic**
**man•ni•tol** plant compound
**man•nose** sugar
**ma•noeu•vrabil•ity** (*US* **•neu•**)
**ma•noeu•vrable** (*US* **•neu•**)
**ma•noeu•vre** (*US* **•neu•ver**)
**ma•noeu•vrer** (*US* **•neu•ver•er**)
**man-of-war** (*plural* **men-**)
**ma•nom•eter**
**mano•met•ric** (*or* **•ri•cal**)
**mano•met•ri•cal•ly**
**ma•nom•etry**
**man•or**
**ma•no•rial**
**man•power**
**man•qué** unfulfilled
**man•rope** ship railing
**man•sard** roof
**manse**

**man•servant** (*plural* **men•servants)**
**Mans•field** Nottinghamshire town
**man•sion**
**man-sized**
**man•slaughter**
**man•sue•tude** gentleness
**man•ta** fish; fabric
**man•teau** (*plural* **•teaus** *or* **•teaux)** cloak
**man•tel** (*or* **•tle)** frame round fireplace; *compare* **mantle**
**man•tel•et** woman's mantle
**man•tel•let•ta** vestment
**mantel•piece**
**mantel•shelf** (*plural* **•shelves)**
**mantel•tree** lintel over fireplace
**man•tic** of prophecy
**man•ti•cal•ly**
**man•til•la** Spanish scarf
**man•tis** (*plural* **•tises** *or* **•tes)**
**man•tis•sa** maths term
**man•tle** cloak; *compare* **mantel**
**man•tling**
**man•tra** Hindu psalm
**man•trap**
**Man•tua** Italian city
**man•tua** gown
**manu•al**
**manu•al•ly**
**ma•nu•brial**
**ma•nu•brium** (*plural* **•bria** *or* **•briums)** zoology term
**manu•fac•tory** (*plural* **•tories)**
**manu•fac•tur•able**
**manu•fac•tur•al**
**manu•fac•ture**
**manu•fac•tur•er**
**manu•fac•tur•ing**
**ma•nu•ka** tree
**Ma•nu•kau** New Zealand city
**manu•mis•sion**
**manu•mit (•mit•ting, •mit•ted)** free from slavery
**ma•nure**
**ma•nur•er**
**ma•nus** (*plural* **•nus)** hand
**manu•script**
**Manx**
**Manx•man** (*plural* **•men)**
**many**
**many•plies** cow's stomach
**many-sided**
**many-sided•ness**
**man•za•nil•la** sherry
**Mao•ism**
**Mao•ist**
**Mao•ri** (*plural* **•ris** *or* **•ri)**
**map (map•ping, mapped)**
**ma•ple**
**map•pable**
**Ma•pu•to** capital of Mozambique
**ma•quette** sculptor's model
**Ma•quis** French Resistance
**ma•quis** (*plural* **•quis)** shrubby vegetation
**mar (mar•ring, marred)**
**mara** rodent
**mara•bou** stork
**mara•bout** Muslim holy man
**ma•ra•bun•ta** wasp
**ma•raca** percussion instrument
**Mara•cai•bo** Venezuelan port and lake
**Ma•ra•cay** Venezuelan city
**mar•ag•ing steel**
**Ma•ra•nhão** Brazilian state
**ma•ras•ca** cherry tree
**mara•schi•no** (*plural* **•nos)** liqueur; cherry
**ma•ras•mic**
**ma•ras•mus**
**Ma•ra•tha** (*or* **Mah•rat•ta)** Indian people
**Ma•ra•thi** (*or* **Mah•rat•ti)**
**Mara•thon** Greek plain
**mara•thon** race
**ma•raud**
**ma•raud•er**
**mara•vedi** (*plural* **•vedis)** coin
**mar•ble**
**mar•bled**
**mar•bler**
**mar•bling**
**mar•bly**
**Mar•burg** German city
**marc** brandy
**mar•ca•site** mineral
**mar•ca•siti•cal**
**mar•cel (•cel•ling, •celled)** hair style
**mar•ces•cence**
**mar•ces•cent** botany term
**March** month; *compare* **Marche**
**march**
**Marche** former French province; *compare* **March**
**march•er**
**Marches** border country
**mar•che•sa** (*plural* **•se)** wife of marchese
**mar•che•se** (*plural* **•si)** Italian nobleman
**mar•chion•ess** wife of marquis or marquess
**Mar del Pla•ta** Argentine city
**Mar•di Gras** Shrove Tuesday
**mardy** *Dialect* spoilt or irritable
**mare** (*plural* **mares)** female horse
**mare** (*plural* **ma•ria)** lunar plain
**mare clau•sum** legal term
**mare li•be•rum** legal term
**ma•rem•ma** (*plural* **•me)** marsh
**mare's-tail** cloud; plant
**marg** (*or* **marge)** *short for* **margarine**
**mar•gar•ic** (*or* **•it•ic)** of pearl
**mar•ga•rine** (*or* **•rin)**
**mar•ga•ri•ta** cocktail
**mar•ga•rite** mineral; *compare* **marguerite**
**Mar•gate**
**Mar•gaux** wine
**mar•gay** animal
**mar•gin**
**mar•gin•al**
**mar•gi•na•lia**
**mar•gin•al•ity**
**mar•gin•al•ly**
**mar•gin•ate**
**mar•gina•tion**
**mar•gra•vate**
**mar•grave** German nobleman
**mar•gra•vine** wife of margrave
**mar•gue•rite** flower; *compare* **margarite**

**mari•achi** Mexican street musicians
**Mar•ian** of the Virgin Mary
**Ma•ria•nao** Cuban city
**Ma•ri•bor** Slovenian city
**mari•cul•ture**
**mari•gold**
**ma•ri•jua•na** (*or* **•hua•**)
**ma•rim•ba** percussion instrument
**ma•ri•na**
**mari•nade** (*noun, verb*)
**mari•nate** (*verb*)
**mari•na•tion**
**Ma•rin•du•que** Philippine island
**ma•rine**
**Mari•ner** US space probe
**mari•ner** seaman
**Mari•ola•try** (*or* **Mary•**) veneration of Virgin Mary
**Mari•ol•ogy** (*or* **Mary•**)
**mari•on•ette**
**mari•po•sa** plant
**Mar•ist** member of Christian sect
**mar•it•age** feudal right
**mari•tal**
**mari•time**
**Mari•time** Alps; Provinces
**Mari•tim•er**
**Ma•ri•u•pol** Ukrainian city
**mar•jo•ram**
**mark**
**mark•down** (*noun*)
**marked**
**mark•ed•ly**
**mark•ed•ness**
**mark•er**
**mar•ket**
**mar•ket•abil•ity** (*or* **•able•ness**)
**mar•ket•able**
**mar•ket•ably**
**mar•ket•er**
**mar•ket•ing**
**market•place**
**mar•khor** (*or* **•khoor**; *plural* **•khors, •khor** *or* **•khoors, •khoor**) goat
**mark•ing**
**mark•ka** (*plural* **•kaa**) Finnish currency
**marks•man** (*plural* **•men**)
**marks•man•ship**
**marks•woman** (*plural* **•women**)
**mark-up** (*noun*)
**marl**
**mar•la•cious** (*or* **marly**)
**Marl•bor•ough**
**mar•lin** (*plural* **•lin** *or* **•lins**) fish
**mar•line** (*or* **•lin, •ling**) nautical rope
**mar•line•spike** (*or* **•lin•, •ling•**)
**mar•lite** (*or* **marl•stone**)
**marly**
**mar•ma•lade**
**Mar•ma•ra** (*or* **•mo•**) Turkish sea
**Mar•mite** (*Trademark*) food
**mar•mite** cooking pot
**mar•mo•real** (*or* **•rean**) of marble
**mar•mo•set**
**mar•mot** animal
**Marne** French river
**maro•cain** fabric
**Maro•nite** Syrian Christian
**ma•roon**
**ma•rooned**
**maro•quin** leather
**Marprelate tracts**
**marque** brand of car
**mar•quee**
**mar•quess** British nobleman
**mar•quess•ate**
**mar•que•try** (*or* **•que•te•rie**; *plural* **•tries** *or* **•ries**)
**mar•quis** (*plural* **•quises** *or* **•quis**) foreign nobleman
**mar•quis•ate**
**mar•quise** gemstone; wife of marquis
**mar•qui•sette** fabric
**Mar•ra•kech** (*or* **•kesh**) Moroccan city
**mar•ram** grass
**Mar•ra•no** (*plural* **•nos**) Iberian Jew
**marred**
**mar•rer**
**mar•riage**
**mar•riage•abil•ity** (*or* **•able•ness**)
**mar•riage•able**
**mar•ried**
**mar•ri•er**
**mar•ring**
**mar•ron** chestnut
**mar•ron gla•cé** (*plural* **mar•rons gla•cés**) glazed chestnut
**mar•row**
**marrow•bone**
**marrow•fat** pea
**mar•ry** (**•ries, •ry•ing, •ried**)
**Mars**
**Mar•sa•la** Sicilian port; wine
**Mar•seil•laise** French national anthem
**Mar•seille** (*or* **•seilles**) French port
**mar•seille** (*or* **•seilles**) fabric
**marsh**
**mar•shal** (**•shal•ling, •shalled**; *US* **•shal•ling, •shaled**)
**mar•shal•cy** (*or* **•shal•ship**)
**Mar•shall Is•lands** Pacific Ocean country
**mar•shal•ler** (*US* **•shal•er**)
**Mar•shal•sea** former prison
**marshi•ness**
**marsh•land**
**marsh•mal•low** sweet
**marsh mal•low** plant
**marshy** (**marshi•er, marshi•est**)
**mar•su•pial**
**mar•su•pia•lian** (*or* **•su•pian**)
**mar•su•pium** (*plural* **•pia**) pouch
**mart**
**mar•ta•gon** lily
**mar•tel•la•to** (*or* **•lan•do**) music term
**Mar•tel•lo** tower
**mar•ten** (*plural* **•tens** *or* **•ten**) mammal; *compare* **martin**
**mar•ten•site** metallurgy term
**mar•ten•sit•ic**
**mar•tial**
**mar•tial•ism**
**mar•tial•ist**
**mar•tial•ly**
**Mar•tian**
**mar•tin** bird; *compare* **marten**
**mar•ti•net**

**mar•ti•net•ish**
**mar•ti•net•ism**
**mar•tin•gale**
**Mar•ti•ni** (*Trademark*) vermouth
**mar•ti•ni** (*plural* **•nis**) cocktail
**Mar•ti•ni•can**
**Mar•ti•nique**
**Mar•tin•mas**
**mart•let** heraldic swallow
**mar•tyr**
**mar•tyr•dom**
**mar•tyr•ize** (*or* **•ise**)
**mar•tyri•za•tion** (*or* **•sa•tion**)
**mar•tyro•logi•cal** (*or* **•log•ic**)
**mar•tyr•olo•gist**
**mar•tyr•ol•ogy** (*plural* **•ogies**)
**mar•tyry** (*plural* **•tyries**) martyr's shrine
**mar•vel** (**•vel•ling, •velled;** *US* **•vel•ing, •veled**)
**mar•vel•lous** (*US* **•vel•ous**)
**mar•vel•ment**
**Marx•ian**
**Marxi•an•ism**
**Marx•ism**
**Marxism-Leninism**
**Marx•ist**
**Marxist-Leninist**
**Mary•land**
**mar•zi•pan**
**Ma•sai** (*plural* **•sais** *or* **•sai**) African people
**Ma•san** Korean port
**Mas•ba•te** Philippine island
**mas•cara**
**mas•cle** heraldic term
**mas•con** lunar region
**mas•cot**
**mas•cu•line**
**mas•cu•lin•ity** (*or* **•line•ness**)
**mas•cu•li•ni•za•tion** (*or* **•sa•tion**)
**mas•cu•lin•ize** (*or* **•ise**)
**ma•ser** microwave laser; *compare* **mazer**
**Ma•se•ru** capital of Lesotho
**mash**
**mash•er**
**Mash•had** (*or* **Me•shed**) Iranian city
**mashie** (*or* **mashy;** *plural* **mashies**) golf club
**mas•jid** (*or* **mus•**) mosque
**mask** face covering, etc.; *variant spelling of* **masque**
**mas•ka•nonge** (*or* **•ki•**) *variants of* **muskellunge**
**masked**
**mask•er**
**maso•chism**
**maso•chist**
**maso•chis•tic**
**Ma•son** freemason
**ma•son** stone worker
**Mason-Dixon Line**
**Ma•son•ic**
**ma•son•ic**
**ma•soni•cal•ly**
**ma•son•ry** (*plural* **•ries**)
**Ma•so•ra** (*or* **Ma•so•rah, Mas•so•ra, Mas•so•rah**) Hebrew text
**Maso•rete** (*or* **Mas•so•rete, Maso•rite**) Hebrew scholar
**masque** (*or* **mask**) entertainment; *compare* **mask**
**mas•quer** (*or* **mask•er**)
**mas•quer•ade**
**mas•quer•ad•er**
**Mass** church service
**mass**
**Mas•sa•chu•set** (*or* **•setts;** *plural* **•sets, •set,** *or* **•setts**) American Indian
**Mas•sa•chu•setts** US state
**mas•sa•cre**
**mas•sa•crer**
**mas•sage**
**mas•sag•er** (*or* **•ist**)
**mas•sa•sau•ga** snake
**mas•sé** billiards stroke
**mass•edly**
**mas•se•ter** muscle
**mas•se•ter•ic**
**mas•seur** (*fem* **•seuse**)
**mas•si•cot** mineral
**mas•sif** landform; *compare* **massive**
**Mas•sif Cen•tral** French plateau
**mas•sive** huge; *compare* **massif**
**mas•sive•ness** (*or* **•siv•ity**)
**Mas•so•ra** (*or* **•rah**) *variant spellings of* **Masora**
**mas•so•thera•peu•tic**
**mas•so•thera•pist**
**mas•so•thera•py** massage
**mass-produce**
**mass-produc•er**
**mass pro•duc•tion**
**massy** (**massi•er, massi•est**) massive
**mast**
**mas•ta•ba** (*or* **•bah**) pyramid prototype
**mas•tec•to•my** (*plural* **•mies**)
**mas•ter**
**master-at-arms** (*plural* **masters-**)
**mas•ter•dom**
**mas•ter•ful**
**mas•ter•ful•ly**
**mas•ter•ful•ness**
**mas•ter•hood**
**mas•ter•li•ness**
**mas•ter•ly**
**master•mind**
**master•piece**
**mas•ter•ship**
**master•stroke**
**master•work**
**mas•tery** (*plural* **•teries**)
**mast•head**
**mas•tic** resin
**mas•ti•cable** chewable
**mas•ti•cate**
**mas•ti•ca•tion**
**mas•ti•ca•tor**
**mas•ti•ca•tory** (*plural* **•tories**)
**mas•tiff**
**mas•ti•gopho•ran** (*or* **•go•phore**) protozoan
**mas•ti•tis** breast inflammation
**mas•to•don** extinct elephant
**mas•toid** ear bone
**mas•toid•ec•to•my** (*plural* **•mies**)
**mas•toid•itis** ear inflammation
**mas•tur•bate**
**mas•tur•ba•tion**
**mas•tur•ba•tor**

**Ma•su•ria** Polish region
**Ma•su•rian**
**mat (mat•ting, mat•ted)** floor covering; tangle; *compare* **matte**
**mat** (*or* **matt, matte; mat•ting, mat•ted**) lacking gloss; *compare* **matte**
**Mata•be•le** (*plural* **•les** *or* **•le**) African people
**Mata•be•le•land**
**Ma•ta•di** port in the Democratic Republic of Congo
**mata•dor**
**Mata•mo•ros** Mexican port
**Mata•pan** Greek cape
**match**
**match•board**
**match•box**
**match•less**
**match•less•ness**
**match•maker**
**match•mark**
**match•stick**
**match•wood**
**mate**
**maté** (*or* **mate**) tea
**matelas•sé** embossed
**mate•lot** (*or* **•lo, •low**) *Slang* sailor
**mat•elote** (*or* **•elotte**) fish stew
**ma•ter** *Slang* mother
**ma•ter•fa•mili•as**
**ma•terial**
**ma•teri•al•ism**
**ma•teri•al•ist**
**ma•teri•al•is•tic**
**ma•teri•al•ity** (*plural* **•ities**)
**ma•teri•ali•za•tion** (*or* **•sa•tion**)
**ma•teri•al•ize** (*or* **•ise**)
**ma•teri•al•iz•er** (*or* **•is•er**)
**ma•teri•al•ly**
**ma•teria medi•ca** study of drugs
**ma•teri•el** (*or* **•téri•**) materials and equipment
**ma•ter•nal**
**ma•ter•nal•ism**
**ma•ter•nal•is•tic**
**ma•ter•nal•ly**
**ma•ter•nity**
**matey (mati•er, mati•est)**
**matey•ness** (*or* **mati•ness**)
**math•emati•cal** (*or* **•emat•ic**)
**math•emati•cal•ly**
**math•ema•ti•cian**
**math•emat•ics**
**Ma•thu•ra** Indian city
**mati•er**
**mati•est**
**Ma•til•da** *Austral* bushman's swag
**mat•in** (*or* **mat•tin, mat•in•al**) of matins
**mati•née**
**mati•ness** *variant spelling of* **mateyness**
**mat•ins** (*or* **mat•tins**)
**Mat•lock** Derbyshire town
**Mato Gros•so** (*or* **Mat•to Gros•so**) Brazilian plateau
**ma•tri•arch**
**ma•tri•ar•chal** (*or* **•chic**)
**ma•tri•ar•chate**
**ma•tri•ar•chy** (*plural* **•chies**)
**ma•tri•ces** *plural of* **matrix**
**mat•ri•cid•al**
**mat•ri•cide**
**mat•ri•cli•nous** (*or* **mat•ro•cli•nous, mat•ro•cli•nal**) biology term
**ma•tricu•lant**
**ma•tricu•late**
**ma•tricu•la•tion**
**ma•tricu•la•tor**
**mat•ri•lin•eal**
**mat•ri•lin•eal•ly**
**mat•ri•lo•cal** living with wife's family
**mat•ri•lo•cal•ity**
**mat•ri•mo•nial**
**mat•ri•mo•nial•ly**
**mat•ri•mo•ny** (*plural* **•nies**)
**ma•trix** (*plural* **•tri•ces**)
**mat•ro•cli•nous** (*or* **•nal**) *variants of* **matriclinous**
**ma•tron**
**ma•tron•age**
**ma•tron•al**
**ma•tron•li•ness**
**ma•tron•ly**
**mat•ro•nym•ic** *variant spelling of* **metronymic**
**Ma•tsu•ya•ma** Japanese port
**matt** *variant spelling of* **mat**
**mat•ta•more** subterranean storehouse
**matte** smelting material; *variant spelling of* **mat**
**mat•ted**
**mat•ter**
**Mat•ter•horn**
**matter-of-fact** (*adj*)
**mat•ting**
**mat•tock** agricultural tool
**mat•tress**
**matu•rate**
**matu•ra•tion**
**matu•ra•tion•al**
**ma•tura•tive**
**ma•ture**
**ma•tur•ity**
**ma•tu•ti•nal** of morning
**(maty)** *incorrect spelling of* **matey**
**mat•zo** (*or* **•zoh;** *plural* **•zos, •zohs,** *or* **•zoth**) Jewish biscuit
**mat•zoon** (*or* **mad•**) fermented milk
**maud** plaid shawl
**maud•lin**
**maud•lin•ism**
**maud•lin•ness**
**maul**
**maul•er**
**maul•stick** (*or* **mahl•**) artist's stick
**Mau Mau** (*plural* **Mau Maus** *or* **Mau Mau**) Kenyan terrorist
**Mau•na Kea** Hawaiian volcano
**Mau•na Loa** Hawaiian volcano
**maund** unit of weight
**maun•der** behave aimlessly
**maun•der•er**
**Maun•dy** money; Thursday
**Mau•rist** French monk
**Mau•ri•ta•nia** African republic
**Mau•ri•ta•nian**
**Mau•ri•tian**
**Mau•ri•tius** island state
**Mau•ser** (*Trademark*) gun
**mau•so•lean**
**mau•so•leum** (*plural* **•leums** *or* **•lea**)

**mauve**
**mav•er•ick**
**ma•vis** *Dialect* thrush
**ma•vour•neen** Irish term of endearment
**maw**
**mawk•ish**
**mawk•ish•ness**
**maw•sie** *Scot* jersey
**maxi** (*plural* **maxis**) long garment
**max•il•la** (*plural* **•lae**) upper jaw
**max•il•lar** (*or* **•lary**)
**max•il•li•ped** (*or* **•pede**) zoology term
**max•il•li•ped•ary**
**max•im**
**maxi•ma** (*plural of* **maximum**)
**maxi•mal**
**Maxi•mal•ist** Russian revolutionary
**maxi•mal•ist** activist
**maxi•mal•ly**
**maxi•min** maths term
**maxi•mi•za•tion** (*or* **•sa•tion**)
**max•im•ize** (*or* **•ise**)
**maxi•miz•er** (*or* **•mis•er**)
**maxi•mum** (*plural* **•mums** *or* **•ma**)
**maxi•mus** bell-ringing term
**maxi•sin•gle**
**ma•xixe** dance
**max•well** unit
**May**
**may** (**might**)
**Maya** (*plural* **Maya** *or* **Mayas**) American Indian
**maya** Hindu concept
**Ma•yan**
**may•be** (*adv*)
**May•day** signal
**May Day** 1 May
**Ma•yenne** French department
**May•fair**
**May•flower** ship
**may•flower** plant
**may•fly** (*plural* **•flies**)
**may•hem** (*or* **mai•**)
**May•ing** May Day celebration
**mayn't** may not
**Mayo** Irish county
**Ma•yon** Philippine volcano
**may•on•naise**
**mayor**
**mayor•al**
**mayor•al•ty** (*plural* **•ties**)
**mayor•ess**
**mayor•ship**
**may•pole**
**may•weed**
**Ma•zat•lán** Mexican port
**Maz•da•ism** (*or* **Maz•deism**) religion
**maze** confusing network; *compare* **maize**
**ma•zer** (*or* **•zard, maz•zard**) bowl; *compare* **maser**
**ma•zi•ly**
**ma•zi•ness**
**ma•zu•ma** *US* money
**ma•zur•ka** (*or* **•zour•**)
**mazy** (**•zi•er, •zi•est**) perplexing
**maz•zard** (*or* **ma•zard**) *variants of* **mazer**
**Mba•ba•ne** capital of Swaziland
**Mbu•ji•ma•yi** city in the Democratic Republic of Congo
**McCar•thy•ism** anticommunism
**McCoy** *Slang* genuine thing
**McNaughten Rules** (*or* **McNaghten Rules**)
**me** pronoun; *variant spelling of* **mi**
**mea cul•pa** *Latin* my fault
**mead** drink; *compare* **meed**
**mead•ow**
**meadow•lark**
**meadow•sweet**
**mea•gre** (*US* **•ger**)
**meal**
**meal•worm**
**mealy** (**meali•er, meali•est**)
**mealy-mouthed**
**mean** (**mean•ing, meant**) intend; miserly; midpoint; *compare* **mien**
**me•ander**
**me•ander•er**
**me•ander•ing•ly**
**me•androus**
**mean•ing**
**mean•ing•ful**
**mean•ing•ful•ly**
**mean•ing•ful•ness**
**mean•ing•less**
**mean•ing•less•ness**
**mean•ness**
**means** (*plural* **means**) method
**meant**
**mean•time**
**mean•while**
**meany** (*plural* **meanies**) *Slang* miserly person
**mea•sled**
**mea•sles**
**mea•sly** (**•sli•er, •sli•est**)
**meas•ur•abil•ity** (*or* **•able•ness**)
**meas•ur•able**
**meas•ur•ably**
**meas•ure**
**meas•ured**
**meas•ured•ly**
**meas•ure•less**
**meas•ure•ment**
**meas•ur•er**
**meas•ur•ing**
**meat**
**meat•ball**
**Meath** Irish county
**meati•ly**
**meati•ness**
**mea•tus** (*plural* **•tuses** *or* **•tus**) anatomy term
**meaty** (**meati•er, meati•est**)
**Mec•ca**
**Mec•ca•no** (*Trademark*)
**me•chan•ic**
**me•chani•cal**
**me•chani•cal•ly**
**mecha•ni•cian**
**me•chan•ics**
**mecha•nism**
**mecha•nist**
**mecha•nis•tic**
**mecha•nis•ti•cal•ly**
**mecha•ni•za•tion** (*or* **•sa•tion**)
**mecha•nize** (*or* **•nise**)
**mecha•niz•er** (*or* **•nis•er**)
**mecha•no•thera•py**
**Mech•elen** (*or* **•lin**) Belgian city
**meck** *Dialect* small coin

**Meck•len•burg** German region
**me•co•nium**
Med *short for* **Mediterranean**
**med•al** (*verb* **•al•ling, •alled;** *US* **•al•ing, •aled**) award; *compare* **meddle**
**me•dal•lic**
**me•dal•lion**
**me•dal•lion•ist**
**med•al•list** (*US* **•al•ist**)
Me•dan Indonesian city
**med•dle** interfere; *compare* **medal**
**med•dler** interferer; *compare* **medlar**
**med•dle•some**
**med•dle•some•ness**
**med•dling•ly**
Mede inhabitant of Media
Medea mythological princess
Me•del•lín Colombian city
Me•dia ancient country
**me•dia** *plural of* **medium,** *esp. in communications sense*
**me•dia** (*plural* **•diae**) anatomy and phonetics term
**me•dia•cy**
**me•di•aeval** *variant spelling of* **medieval**
**me•dial**
**me•dial•ly**
Me•dian of Medes or Media
**me•dian**
**me•di•ant** music term
**me•di•as•ti•nal**
**me•di•as•ti•num** (*plural* **•na**) anatomy term
**me•di•ate**
**me•dia•tion**
**me•dia•tive** (*or* **•tory, •to•rial**)
**me•dia•ti•za•tion** (*or* **•sa•tion**)
**me•dia•tize** (*or* **•tise**) annex a state
**me•dia•tor**
**me•dia•to•ri•al•ly**
**me•dia•trix** (*or* **•trice**)
**med•ic** *Slang* doctor; *US spelling of* **medick**
**medi•cable**
**medi•ca•bly**
Medi•caid US health assistance
**medi•cal**
**medi•cal•ly**
**me•dica•ment**
**medi•ca•men•tal** (*or* **•tary**)
Medi•care US health insurance
**medi•cate**
**medi•ca•tion**
**medi•ca•tive**
**me•dici•nal**
**me•dici•nal•ly**
**medi•cine**
**med•ick** (*US* **•ic**) plant; *compare* **medic**
**medi•co** (*plural* **•cos**)
**me•di•eval** (*or* **•aeval**)
**me•di•eval•ism** (*or* **•aeval•**)
**me•di•eval•ist** (*or* **•aeval•**)
**me•di•eval•is•tic** (*or* **•aeval•**)
**me•di•eval•ly** (*or* **•aeval•**)
Me•di•na Saudi Arabian city
**me•dio•cre**
**me•di•oc•rity** (*plural* **•rities**)
**medi•tate**
**medi•tat•ing•ly**
**medi•ta•tion**
**medi•ta•tive**
**medi•ta•tive•ness**
**medi•ta•tor**
Medi•ter•ra•nean
**me•dium** (*plural* **•dia** *or* **•diums**)
**med•lar** fruit; *compare* **meddler**
**med•ley**
Mé•doc French region; wine
**me•dul•la** (*plural* **•las** *or* **•lae**)
**me•dul•lary** (*or* **•lar**)
**med•ul•lat•ed**
Medusa mythological character
**me•du•sa** (*plural* **•sas** *or* **•sae**) jellyfish
**me•du•san**
**me•du•soid**
Med•way
**mee** Malaysian noodles
**meed** *Archaic* reward; *compare* **mead**
**meek**
**meek•ly**
**meek•ness**
**meer•kat** mongoose
**meer•schaum**
Mee•rut Indian city
**meet** (**meet•ing, met**) come together; *compare* **mete**
**meet** (*adj*) *Archaic* fitting; *compare* **mete**
**meet•er**
**meet•ing**
**mega•cephal•ic** *variant of* **macrocephalic**
**mega•cepha•ly** *variant of* **macrocephaly**
**mega•cy•cle**
**mega•death**
**mega•ga•mete** *variant of* **macrogamete**
**mega•lith**
**mega•lith•ic**
**mega•lo•blast** blood cell
**mega•lo•blast•ic**
**mega•lo•car•dia** abnormally large heart
**mega•lo•cephal•ic** *variant of* **macrocephalic**
**mega•lo•cepha•ly** *variant of* **macrocephaly**
**mega•lo•ma•nia**
**mega•lo•ma•ni•ac**
**mega•lo•ma•nia•cal**
**mega•lopo•lis**
**mega•lo•poli•tan**
**mega•lo•saur** dinosaur
**mega•phone**
**mega•phon•ic**
**mega•phoni•cal•ly**
**mega•pode** bird
Mega•ra Greek town
**mega•ron** (*plural* **•ra**) room
**mega•spore** botany term
**mega•spor•ic**
**mega•spo•ro•phyll**
**me•gass** (*or* **•gasse**) paper
**mega•there** (*or* **•ther•ium;** *plural* **•theres** *or* **•ther•ia**) extinct sloth
**mega•ton**
**mega•volt**
**mega•watt**
**me•gil•lah** (*plural* **•lahs** *or* **•loth**) Hebrew scroll
**me•gilp** (*or* **ma•**) oil-painting medium

**meg•ohm**
**me•grim** *Archaic* migraine
**Mei•ji** period in Japanese history
**meio•sis** (*plural* **•ses**) cell division; rhetorical device; *compare* **miosis**
**mei•ot•ic**
**mei•oti•cal•ly**
**Meis•sen** German town
**Meis•ter•sing•er** (*plural* **•er** *or* **•ers**)
**Mek•nès** Moroccan city
**Me•kong** Asian river
**mel** honey
**mela•leu•ca** shrub
**mela•mine**
**mel•an•cho•lia**
**mel•an•cho•li•ac**
**mel•an•chol•ic**
**mel•an•choli•cal•ly**
**mel•an•choli•ly**
**mel•an•choli•ness**
**mel•an•choly** (*plural* **•cholies**)
**Mela•nesia**
**Mela•nesian**
**mé•lange** *French* mixture
**me•lan•ic**
**mela•nin** pigment
**mela•nism** dark pigmentation; *variant of* **melanosis**
**mela•nis•tic**
**mela•nite** gemstone
**mela•no•cyte** melanin cell
**mela•noid**
**mela•no•ma** (*plural* **•mas** *or* **•ma•ta**) tumour
**mela•no•sis** (*or* **•nism**) skin disease
**mela•nos•ity**
**mela•not•ic**
**mela•nous**
**mela•phyre** rock
**mela•to•nin** hormone
**Melba** sauce; toast
**Mel•bourne**
**Mel•bur•nian**
**Mel•chite** Eastern Church member
**meld**
**me•lee** (*or* **mê•lée**)
**me•lia•ceous** botany term
**mel•ic** to be sung
**meli•lot** plant
**meli•nite** explosive
**me•lio•rate** ameliorate
**me•lio•ra•tion**
**me•lio•rism**
**me•lis•ma** (*plural* **•ma•ta** *or* **•mas**) musical term
**mel•is•mat•ic**
**Me•li•to•pol** Ukrainian city
**mel•lif•er•ous** (*or* **•lif•ic**) producing honey
**mel•lif•lu•ous** (*or* **•lu•ent**) sweet-sounding
**mel•lif•lu•ous•ness** (*or* **•lu•ence**)
**mel•lo•phone** brass instrument
**mel•low**
**mel•low•ness**
**me•lo•deon** accordion
**me•lod•ic**
**me•lodi•cal•ly**
**me•lo•dious**
**me•lo•di•ous•ness**
**melo•dist**
**melo•dize** (*or* **•dise**)
**melo•diz•er** (*or* **•dis•er**)
**melo•dra•ma**
**melo•dra•mat•ic**
**melo•dra•mati•cal•ly**
**melo•drama•tist**
**melo•drama•tize** (*or* **•tise**)
**melo•dy** (*plural* **•dies**)
**mel•oid** beetle
**mel•on**
**Me•los** Greek island
**melt** (**melt•ing, melt•ed, melt•ed** *or* **mol•ten**)
**melt•abil•ity**
**melt•able**
**melt•age**
**melt•down**
**melt•er**
**melt•ing•ly**
**mel•ton** fabric
**Mel•ton Mow•bray**
**melt•water**
**Mem•ber** an MP
**mem•ber**
**mem•ber•ship**
**mem•brane**
**mem•bra•nous** (*or* **•bra•na•ceous**)
**me•men•to** (*plural* **•tos** *or* **•toes**)
**me•men•to mori**
**memo** (*plural* **memos**)
**mem•oir**
**memo•ra•bilia** (*sing.* **•rabi•le**)
**memo•rabil•ity** (*or* **•rable•ness**)
**memo•rable**
**memo•rably**
**memo•ran•dum** (*plural* **•dums** *or* **•da**)
**me•mo•rial**
**me•mo•ri•al•ist**
**me•mo•ri•ali•za•tion** (*or* **•sa•tion**)
**me•mo•ri•al•ize** (*or* **•ise**)
**me•mo•ri•al•iz•er** (*or* **•is•er**)
**memo•riz•able** (*or* **•ris•able**)
**memo•ri•za•tion** (*or* **•sa•tion**)
**memo•rize** (*or* **•rise**)
**memo•riz•er** (*or* **•ris•er**)
**memo•ry** (*plural* **•ries**)
**Mem•phis**
**Mem•phre•ma•gog** North American lake
**mem•sa•hib**
**men**
**men•ace**
**men•ac•er**
**men•ac•ing•ly**
**me•nad** *variant spelling of* **maenad**
**mena•di•one** vitamin
**Me•na•do** (*or* **Ma•**) Indonesian port
**mé•nage** household; *compare* **manège**
**mé•nage à trois** (*plural* **mé•nage à trois**)
**me•nag•erie**
**Menai Strait**
**Me•nam** Thai river
**mena•qui•none** vitamin
**men•ar•che** start of menstruation
**men•ar•cheal** (*or* **•chial**)
**mend**
**mend•able**
**men•da•cious**
**men•da•cious•ness**
**men•dac•ity** (*plural* **•ities**) untruthfulness; *compare* **mendicancy**

**men•de•levium** chemical element
**Men•de•lian**
**Men•del•ism** (*or* **•de•li•an•ism**) science of heredity
**mend•er**
**men•di•can•cy** (*or* **men•dic•ity**) begging; *compare* **mendacity**
**men•di•cant**
**mend•ing**
**Men•dips**
**Men•do•za** Argentine city
**Menelaus** mythological king
**men•folk**
**men•ha•den** (*plural* **•den**) fish
**men•hir** Bronze Age stone
**me•nial**
**me•nial•ly**
**me•nin•geal**
**me•nin•ges** (*sing.* **me•ninx**) brain membranes
**men•in•git•ic**
**men•in•gi•tis**
**me•nis•coid**
**me•nis•cus** (*plural* **•ci** *or* **•cuses**)
**meni•sper•ma•ceous** botany term
**meno** musical term
**me•nol•ogy** (*plural* **•ogies**) ecclesiastical calendar
**meno•pau•sal** (*or* **•sic**)
**meno•pause**
**me•no•rah** Jewish candelabrum
**men•or•rha•gia** excessive menstruation
**men•or•rhag•ic**
**Men•sa** constellation
**men•ses** (*plural* **•ses**) menstruation
**Men•she•vik** Russian socialist
**mens rea** legal term
**men•strual**
**men•stru•ate**
**men•strua•tion**
**men•struous**
**men•struum** (*plural* **•struums** *or* **•strua**) solvent
**men•sur•able**
**men•su•ral**
**men•su•ra•tion** measuring; *compare* **menstruation**
**men•su•ra•tion•al**
**men•su•ra•tive**
**mens•wear**
**men•tal**
**men•tal•ism** philosophy term
**men•tal•is•tic**
**men•tal•is•ti•cal•ly**
**men•tal•ity** (*plural* **•ities**)
**men•tal•ly**
**men•tha•ceous** botany term
**men•thol**
**men•tho•la•ted**
**men•tion**
**men•tion•able**
**men•tion•er**
**Men•ton** French town
**men•tor**
**men•to•rial**
**menu**
**meow** (*or* **miaou, miaow**)
**mepa•crine** drug
**Meph•is•to•phelean** (*or* **•phelian**)
**Mephistopheles** (*or* **Mephisto**)
**me•phit•ic** (*or* **•phiti•cal**) poisonous
**me•phiti•cal•ly**
**me•phi•tis** foul stench
**me•pro•ba•mate** tranquillizer
**mer•bro•min** antiseptic
**mer•can•tile**
**mer•can•til•ism**
**mer•can•til•ist**
**mer•cap•tan** chemical compound
**mer•cap•tide** chemical compound
**mer•cap•to•pu•rine** drug
**mer•ce•nari•ly**
**mer•ce•nari•ness**
**mer•ce•nary** (*plural* **•naries**)
**mer•cer**
**mer•ceri•za•tion** (*or* **•sa•tion**)
**mer•cer•ize** (*or* **•ise**)
**mer•chan•dise**
**mer•chan•dis•er**
**mer•chant**
**mer•chant•able**
**mer•chant•man** (*plural* **•men**) ship
**Mer•cia** Anglo-Saxon kingdom
**Mer•cian**
**mer•ci•ful**
**mer•ci•ful•ly**
**mer•ci•ful•ness**
**mer•ci•less**
**mer•ci•less•ness**
**mer•cu•rate** treat with mercury
**mer•cu•ra•tion**
**mer•cu•rial**
**mer•cu•ri•al•ism** mercury poisoning
**mer•cu•ri•ali•za•tion** (*or* **•sa•tion**)
**mer•cu•ri•al•ize** (*or* **•ise**)
**mer•cu•rial•ly**
**mer•cu•ri•al•ness** (*or* **•ri•al•ity**)
**mer•cu•ric**
**Mer•cu•ro•chrome** (*Trademark*)
**mer•cu•rous**
**Mer•cu•ry** planet
**Mercury** Roman god
**mer•cu•ry** (*or* **•ries**)
**mer•cy** (*plural* **•cies**)
**mere**
**mere•ly**
**me•ren•gue** dance
**mer•etri•cious** insincere; *compare* **meritorious**
**mer•gan•ser** (*plural* **•sers** *or* **•ser**) duck
**merge**
**mer•gence**
**mer•ger**
**me•rid•ian**
**me•ridio•nal**
**me•ringue**
**me•ri•no** (*plural* **•nos**)
**Meri•on•eth•shire** former Welsh county
**me•ri•stem** plant tissue
**meri•ste•mat•ic**
**me•ris•tic** biology term
**mer•it**
**mer•it•ed•ly**
**mer•it•less**
**meri•toc•ra•cy** (*plural* **•cies**)
**meri•to•ri•ous** praiseworthy; *compare* **meretricious**

**mer•kin** pubic wig
**merle** *Scot* blackbird
**mer•lin** falcon
**mer•lon** part of battlement
**mer•maid**
**mer•man** (*plural* **•men**)
**mero•blas•tic** biology term
**mero•blas•ti•cal•ly**
**mero•crine** physiology term
**Meroë** ancient Sudanese city
**mero•plank•ton**
**Mero•vin•gian** Frankish dynasty
**mero•zo•ite** biology term
**mer•ri•ly**
**mer•ri•ment**
**mer•ri•ness**
**mer•ry** (**•ri•er, •ri•est**)
**merry-go-round**
**merry•maker**
**merry•making**
**merry•thought** wishbone
**Merse** Scottish area
**Mer•se•burg** German city
**Mer•sey**
**Mer•sey•side**
**Mer•sin** Turkish port
**Mer•thyr Tyd•fil**
**Mer•ton** London borough
**mesa** tableland
**mé•sal•li•ance** *French* unsuitable marriage; *compare* **misalliance**
**mes•arch** botany term
**Mesa Verde** Colorado plateau
**mes•cal** cactus; alcohol
**mes•ca•line** (*or* **•lin**) drug
**mes•dames** *plural of* **madame**
**mes•de•moi•selles** *plural of* **mademoiselle**
**mes•em•bry•an•themum** plant
**mes•en•cephal•ic**
**mes•en•cepha•lon** part of brain
**mes•en•chy•mal** (*or* **•chyma•tous**)
**mes•en•chyme** embryology term
**mes•en•ter•ic**
**mes•en•teri•tis**
**mes•en•ter•on** (*plural* **•tera**) zoology term
**mes•en•ter•on•ic**
**mes•en•tery** (*plural* **•teries**)
**mesh**
**Meshach** biblical character
**Me•shed** *variant spelling of* **Mashhad**
**meshy**
**me•sial** anatomy term
**me•sial•ly**
**me•sic** ecology term; of a meson
**mesi•cal•ly**
**me•sity•lene** chemical compound
**mes•mer•ic**
**mes•meri•cal•ly**
**mes•mer•ism**
**mes•mer•ist**
**mes•meri•za•tion** (*or* **sa•tion**)
**mes•mer•ize** (*or* **•ise**)
**mes•mer•iz•er** (*or* **•is•er**)
**mesne** legal term
**meso•ben•thos**
**meso•blast** embryonic tissue
**meso•carp** botany term
**meso•ce•phal•ic**
**meso•ceph•aly**
**meso•crat•ic** geology term
**meso•derm**
**meso•der•mal** (*or* **•mic**)
**meso•gas•tric**
**meso•gas•trium**
**meso•glea** (*or* **•gloea**)
**me•sog•na•thism** (*or* **•thy**)
**me•sog•na•thous**
**Meso•lith•ic** archaeological period
**meso•morph**
**meso•mor•phic** of muscular build
**meso•mor•phism**
**meso•mor•phous**
**meso•mor•phy**
**me•son** elementary particle
**meso•neph•ric**
**meso•neph•ros**
**meso•pause** meteorology term
**meso•phyll**
**meso•phyl•lic** (*or* **•lous**)
**meso•phyte**
**meso•phyt•ic**
**Meso•po•ta•mia**
**Meso•po•ta•mian**
**meso•sphere**
**meso•spher•ic**
**meso•thelial**
**meso•thelium**
**meso•tho•rac•ic**
**meso•tho•rax** (*plural* **•raxes** *or* **•races**)
**Meso•zo•ic** geological period
**mes•quite** (*or* **•quit**) tree
**mess**
**mes•sage**
**mes•sa•line** fabric
**Mes•sene** ancient Greek city
**mes•sen•ger**
**Mes•senia** Greek region
**Mes•si•ah**
**mes•si•an•ic** (*or* **Mes•**)
**mes•sieurs** *plural of* **monsieur**
**messi•ly**
**Mes•si•na** Sicilian port
**messi•ness**
**mess•mate**
**Messrs** *plural of* **Mr**
**mes•suage** legal term
**messy** (**messi•er, messi•est**)
**mes•ter** *Dialect* master
**mes•ti•zo** (*fem* **•za**; *plural* **•zos** *or* **•zoes, •zas**) one of mixed parentage
**mes•tra•nol** synthetic hormone
**met**
**Meta** Colombian river
**meta•bol•ic**
**meta•boli•cal•ly**
**me•tabo•lism**
**me•tabo•lite**
**me•tabo•liz•abil•ity** (*or* **•lis•abil•ity**)
**me•tabo•liz•able** (*or* **•lis•able**)
**me•tabo•lize** (*or* **•lise**)
**meta•car•pal**
**meta•car•pus** (*plural* **•pi**) hand bones; *compare* **metatarsus**
**meta•cen•tre** (*US* **•ter**) physics term
**meta•cen•tric**
**meta•chro•mat•ic**
**meta•chro•ma•tism**
**meta•cin•nab•a•rite** mercury ore

**meta•female** genetics term
**meta•ga•lac•tic**
**meta•gal•axy** (*plural* **•axies**)
**met•age** official measuring of goods
**meta•gen•esis**
**meta•ge•net•ic** (*or* **•gen•ic**)
**meta•geneti•cal•ly**
**me•tag•na•thism**
**me•tag•na•thous**
**met•al** (*verb* **•al•ling, •alled;** *US* **•al•ing, •aled**) substance; *compare* **mettle**
**meta•lan•guage**
**me•tal•lic**
**me•tal•li•cal•ly**
**met•al•lif•er•ous**
**met•al•line** of metals
**met•al•list** (*US* **•al•ist**)
**met•al•li•za•tion** (*or* **•sa•tion;** *US* **met•ali•za•tion**)
**met•al•lize** (*or* **•lise;** *US* **•al•ize**)
**me•tal•lo•cene** chemical compound
**met•al•log•ra•pher** (*or* **•phist**)
**me•tal•lo•graph•ic**
**me•tal•lo•graphi•cal•ly**
**met•al•log•ra•phy**
**met•al•loid**
**met•al•loi•dal**
**met•al•lur•gic** (*or* **•gi•cal**)
**met•al•lur•gi•cal•ly**
**met•al•lur•gist**
**met•al•lur•gy**
**metal•work**
**metal•worker**
**metal•working**
**meta•male** genetics term
**meta•math•emati•cal**
**meta•math•ema•ti•cian**
**meta•math•emat•ics**
**meta•mer** chemistry term
**me•tam•er•al**
**meta•mere** zoology term
**meta•mer•ic**
**meta•meri•cal•ly**
**me•tam•er•ism**
**meta•mor•phic** (*or* **•phous**)
**meta•mor•phism** geology term
**meta•mor•phose**
**meta•mor•pho•sis** (*plural* **•ses**)
**meta•neph•ros**
**meta•phase** biology term
**meta•phor**
**meta•phor•ic** (*or* **•phori•cal**)
**meta•phori•cal•ly**
**meta•phori•cal•ness**
**meta•phos•phate**
**meta•phrase** literal translation
**meta•phrast**
**meta•phras•tic** (*or* **•ti•cal**)
**meta•phras•ti•cal•ly**
**meta•phys•ic**
**Meta•physi•cal** denoting poetic group
**meta•physi•cal** of metaphysics
**meta•physi•cal•ly**
**meta•phy•si•cian** (*or* **•physi•cist**)
**meta•phys•ics**
**meta•pla•sia**
**meta•plasm**
**meta•plas•mic**
**meta•psy•cho•logi•cal**
**meta•psy•chol•ogy**
**meta•so•ma•tism** (*or* **•ma•to•sis**) geology term
**meta•sta•bil•ity**
**meta•sta•ble**
**me•tas•ta•sis** (*plural* **•ses**) medical term
**me•tas•ta•size** (*or* **•sise**)
**meta•stat•ic**
**meta•stati•cal•ly**
**meta•tar•sal**
**meta•tar•sus** (*plural* **•si**) foot bones; *compare* **meta carpus**
**meta•theo•ry** study of philosophy
**meta•therian** marsupial
**me•tath•esis** (*plural* **•eses**) linguistics term
**me•tath•esize** (*or* **•esise**)
**meta•thet•ic** (*or* **•theti•cal**)
**meta•tho•rac•ic**
**meta•tho•rax** (*plural* **•raxes** *or* **•races**)
**meta•xy•lem**
**meta•zo•an**
**meta•zo•ic**
**mete** allot; *compare* **meet**
**met•em•piri•cal** (*or* **•pir•ic**)
**met•em•piri•cist**
**met•em•pir•ics**
**me•tem•psy•cho•sis** (*plural* **•ses**)
**met•en•cephal•ic**
**met•en•cepha•lon** (*plural* **•lons** *or* **•la**) embryology term
**me•teor**
**me•teor•ic**
**me•teori•cal•ly**
**me•teor•ite**
**me•teor•it•ic**
**me•teoro•graph**
**me•teoro•graph•ic** (*or* **•graphi•cal**)
**me•teor•oid**
**me•teoro•logi•cal** (*or* **•log•ic**)
**me•teoro•logi•cal•ly**
**me•teor•olo•gist**
**me•teor•ol•ogy** study of weather; *compare* **metrology**
**me•ter** instrument; *US spelling of* **metre**
**met•es•trus** *US spelling of* **metoestrus**
**meth•ac•ry•late**
**metha•done** (*or* **•don**) drug
**met•haemo•glo•bin** (*US* **•hemo•**)
**me•thane**
**metha•nol**
**me•thinks**
**me•thio•nine** amino acid
**meth•od**
**me•thodi•cal** (*or* **•thod•ic**)
**me•thodi•cal•ly**
**me•thodi•cal•ness**
**Meth•od•ism**
**Meth•od•ist**
**Meth•od•is•ti•cal•ly**
**meth•odi•za•tion** (*or* **•sa•tion**)
**meth•od•ize** (*or* **•ise**)
**meth•od•iz•er** (*or* **•is•er**)
**meth•odo•logi•cal**
**meth•odo•logi•cal•ly**
**meth•od•olo•gist**
**meth•od•ol•ogy** (*plural* **•ogies**)
**metho•trex•ate** drug
**me•thought**

**meth•ox•ide**
**Me•thu•se•lah**
**me•thyl**
**meth•yl•al** chemical compound
**me•thyla•mine**
**meth•yl•ate**
**meth•yla•tion**
**meth•yla•tor**
**me•thyl•do•pa**
**meth•yl•ene**
**me•thyl•ic**
**me•thyl•naph•tha•lene**
**met•ic** ancient Greek alien
**me•ticu•lous**
**me•ticu•lous•ness** (*or* **•los•ity**)
**mé•ti•er** profession
**Mé•tis** (*or* **•tif**; *plural* **•tis** *or* **•tifs**) one of mixed parentage
**met•oes•trus** (*US* **•es•**)
**me•tol** chemical compound
**Me•ton•ic cy•cle**
**meto•nym**
**meto•nymi•cal** (*or* **•nym•ic**)
**me•tony•my** (*plural* **•mies**) linguistics term
**met•ope** architectural term
**me•top•ic** of the forehead
**me•tral•gia** womb pain
**me•tre** (*US* **•ter**) unit; verse rhythm; *compare* **meter**
**met•ric**
**met•ri•cal**
**met•ri•cal•ly**
**met•ri•cate**
**met•ri•ca•tion**
**met•rics** use of poetic metre
**met•ri•fi•er**
**met•ri•fy** (**•fies, •fy•ing, •fied**)
**met•rist**
**me•tri•tis** inflammation of womb
**met•ro** (*or* **mét•**; *plural* **•ros**)
**met•ro•logi•cal**
**me•trolo•gist**
**me•trol•ogy** (*plural* **•ogies**) study of measurement; *compare* **meteorology**
**met•ro•ni•da•zole**
**met•ro•nome**
**met•ro•nom•ic** of a metronome
**met•ro•nym•ic** (*or* **mat•**) maternal name
**me•tropo•lis** (*plural* **•lises**)
**met•ro•poli•tan**
**met•ro•poli•tan•ism**
**me•tror•rha•gia** abnormal bleeding from womb
**met•tle** courage; *compare* **metal**
**met•tle•some**
**Metz** French city
**meu** plant
**meu•nière** cookery term
**Meurthe-et-Moselle** French department
**Meuse** European river
**mew**
**mewl**
**mewl•er**
**mews** (*plural* **mews**)
**Mexi•cali** Mexican city
**Mexi•can**
**Mexi•co**
**me•zereon** shrub
**me•zereum** (*or* **•zereon**) drug
**Me•zières** French town
**me•zu•zah** (*plural* **•zahs** *or* **•zoth**)
**mez•za•nine**
**mez•zo** (*plural* **•zos**) musical term
**mezzo-relievo** (*or* **-rilievo**; *plural* **-relievos** *or* **-rilievos**)
**mezzo-soprano** (*plural* **-sopranos**)
**mez•zo•tint**
**mi** (*or* **me**) musical term
**Mi•ami**
**miaou** (*or* **miaow**) *variant spellings of* **meow**
**mi•as•ma** (*plural* **•ma•ta** *or* **•mas**)
**mi•as•mal** (*or* **•mat•ic, •mati•cal, •mic**)
**mica**
**mi•ca•ceous**
**Mi•caw•ber** feckless person
**Mi•caw•ber•ish**
**mice**
**mi•cel•lar**
**mi•celle** (*or* **•cell, •cel•la**)
**Mich•ael•mas**
**Michi•gan**
**Michi•gan•der**
**Michi•gan•ite**
**Mi•choa•cán** Mexican state
**mick•ery** pool in river bed
**mick•ey** (*or* **micky**; *as in* **take the mickey**)
**Mick•ey Finn**
**mick•le** *Dialect* much
**Mic•mac** (*plural* **•macs** *or* **•mac**) American Indian
**micro•analy•sis** (*plural* **•ses**)
**micro•ana•lyst**
**micro•ana•lyt•ic** (*or* **•lyti•cal**)
**micro•bal•ance**
**micro•baro•graph**
**mi•crobe**
**mi•cro•bial** (*or* **•bic, •bian**)
**micro•bio•logi•cal** (*or* **•log•ic**)
**micro•bi•olo•gist**
**micro•bi•ol•ogy**
**micro•cephal•ic**
**micro•cepha•lous**
**micro•cepha•ly** abnormally small skull
**micro•chemi•cal**
**micro•chem•is•try**
**micro•chip**
**micro•cir•cuit**
**micro•cir•cuit•ry**
**micro•cli•mate**
**micro•cli•mat•ic**
**micro•cli•mati•cal•ly**
**micro•cli•ma•to•log•ic** (*or* **•logi•cal**)
**micro•cli•ma•tolo•gist**
**micro•cli•ma•tol•ogy**
**micro•cline** mineral
**micro•coc•cus** (*plural* **•coc•ci**)
**micro•com•put•er**
**micro•copy** (*plural* **•copies**) reduced photographic copy
**micro•cosm** (*or* **•cos•mos**)
**micro•cos•mic** (*or* **•cos•mi•cal**)
**micro•crys•tal•line**
**micro•cyte** blood cell
**micro•cyt•ic**
**micro•detec•tor**
**micro•dont** (*or* **•don•tous**)
**micro•dot**
**micro•eco•nom•ic**
**micro•eco•nom•ics**

**micro•elec•tron•ic**
**micro•elec•tron•ics**
**micro•fiche**
**micro•film**
**micro•gam•ete**
**micro•graph**
**mi•crog•ra•pher**
**micro•graph•ic**
**micro•graphi•cal•ly**
**mi•crog•ra•phy**
**micro•groove**
**micro•habi•tat**
**micro•light**
**micro•lith**
**micro•meteor•ite**
**micro•meteor•ol•ogy**
**mi•crom•eter** measuring instrument
**micro•metre** (*US* **•meter)** unit of length
**micro•met•ric** (*or* **•ri•cal)**
**mi•crom•etry**
**micro•minia•turi•za•tion** (*or* **•sa•tion)**
**mi•cron** (*plural* **•crons** *or* **•cra)** unit of length
**Micro•nesia**
**Micro•nesian**
**micro•nu•cleus** (*plural* **•clei)**
**micro•nu•tri•ent**
**micro•or•gan•ism**
**micro•palae•on•to•logi•cal** (*or* **•log•ic;** *US* **•pale•)**
**micro•palae•on•tolo•gist** (*US* **•pale•)**
**micro•palae•on•tol•ogy** (*US* **•pale•)**
**micro•para•site**
**micro•para•sit•ic**
**micro•phone**
**micro•phon•ic**
**micro•pho•to•graph**
**micro•pho•to•graph•ic**
**micro•pho•tog•ra•phy**
**micro•physi•cal**
**micro•phys•ics**
**micro•phyte** microscopic plant
**micro•phyt•ic**
**micro•print**
**micro•pro•ces•sor**
**micro•py•lar**
**micro•pyle** biology term
**micro•py•rom•eter**
**micro•read•er**
**micro•scope**
**micro•scop•ic** (*or* **•scopi•cal)**
**micro•scopi•cal•ly**
**mi•cros•co•pist**
**mi•cros•co•py**
**micro•sec•ond**
**micro•seism**
**micro•seis•mic** (*or* **•mi•cal)**
**micro•so•mal** (*or* **•so•mial, •so•mic)**
**micro•some** biology term
**micro•spo•ran•gium** (*plural* **•gia)**
**micro•spore**
**micro•spor•ic** (*or* **•spo•rous)**
**micro•sporo•phyll**
**micro•stoma•tous** (*or* **mi•cros•to•mous)** having small mouth
**micro•struc•ture**
**micro•tome** cutting instrument
**micro•tom•ic** (*or* **•tomi•cal)**
**mi•croto•mist**
**mi•croto•my** (*plural* **•mies)**
**micro•ton•al**
**micro•to•nal•ity**
**micro•tone** musical term
**micro•wave**
**mi•crurgy** microscopy technique
**mic•tu•rate**
**mic•tu•ri•tion**
**mid** *Archaic* amid
**mid-** *prefix denoting* middle
**mid•air**
**Midas** legendary king
**mid•brain**
**mid•day**
**Mid•del•burg** Dutch city
**mid•den**
**mid•dle**
**middle-aged**
**middle•brow**
**middle•browism**
**middle-class** (*adj*)
**middle-distance** (*adj*)
**middle•man** (*plural* **•men)**
**Mid•dles•brough**
**Mid•dle•sex**
**Mid•dle•ton** English town
**middle•weight**
**mid•dling**
**mid•dy** (*plural* **•dies)** midshipman
**mid•field**
**Mid•gard** Norse mythological place
**midge**
**midg•et**
**Mid Gla•mor•gan** former Welsh county
**mid•gut**
**Mid•heav•en** astrology term
**Midi** S France
**midi** skirt length
**Mid•ian** biblical character
**Midi•an•ite**
**midi•nette** Parisian salesgirl
**mid•iron** golf club
**mid•land** inland region
**Mid•lands** central England
**mid•line**
**Mid•lo•thian** Scottish council area
**mid•most**
**mid•night**
**mid-off**
**mid-on**
**mid•point**
**mid•rash** (*plural* **•ra•shim)** Jewish biblical commentaries
**mid•rib** leaf vein
**mid•riff**
**mid•sec•tion**
**mid•ship**
**mid•ship•man** (*plural* **•men)**
**mid•ships**
**midst**
**mid•sum•mer**
**mid•term**
**mid•town** *US* town centre
**mid•way**
**mid•week**
**Mid•west** (*or* **Mid•dle West)** US region
**Mid•west•ern**
**Mid•west•ern•er**
**mid-wicket**
**mid•wife** (*plural* **•wives)**
**mid•wife•ry**
**mid•win•ter**
**mid•year**
**mien** bearing; *compare* **mean**
**miff** *Slang* take offence
**mif•fi•ness**

**mif•fy** (**•fi•er, •fi•est**)
**might**
**mighti•ly**
**mighti•ness**
**mighty** (**mighti•er, mighti•est**)
**mi•gnon** *French* dainty
**mi•gnon•ette** plant
**mi•graine**
**mi•grain•ous**
**mi•grant**
**mi•grate**
**mi•gra•tion**
**mi•gra•tion•al**
**mi•gra•tor**
**mi•gra•tory**
**mih•rab** niche in mosque
**mi•ka•do** (*plural* **•dos**)
**mike** *Slang* microphone
**mil** unit of length
**mi•la•dy** (*or* **•la•di**; *plural* **•dies**)
**mil•age** *variant spelling of* **mileage**
**Mi•lan**
**Mil•an•ese** (*plural* **•ese**)
**milch**
**mild**
**mil•dew**
**mil•dewy**
**mild•ness**
**mile**
**mile•age** (*or* **mil•age**)
**mile•om•eter** (*or* **mi•lom•eter**)
**mile•post**
**mil•er**
**Mi•lesian**
**mile•stone**
**Mi•letus** old Asian city
**mil•foil** plant
**mili•aria** heat rash
**mil•iary**
**mi•lieu** (*plural* **•lieus** *or* **•lieux**)
**mili•tan•cy** (*or* **•tant•ness**)
**mili•tant**
**mili•tari•ly**
**mili•ta•rism**
**mili•ta•rist**
**mili•ta•ris•tic**
**mili•ta•ris•ti•cal•ly**
**mili•ta•ri•za•tion** (*or* **•sa•tion**)
**mili•ta•rize** (*or* **•rise**)
**mili•tary** (*plural* **•taries**)
**mili•tate**
**mili•ta•tion**
**mi•li•tia**
**mi•li•tia•man** (*plural* **•men**)
**mil•ium** (*plural* **milia**) skin nodule
**milk**
**milk•er**
**milk•fish** (*plural* **•fish** *or* **•fishes**)
**milki•ly**
**milki•ness**
**milk•maid**
**milk•man** (*plural* **•men**)
**milko** *Austral* milkman
**milk•sop**
**milk•weed**
**milk•wort**
**milky** (**milki•er, milki•est**)
**Milky Way**
**mill**
**mill•able**
**mill•board**
**mill•dam**
**milled**
**mille•feuille** pastry
**mille•fleurs** textile design
**mil•le•nar•ian** (*or* **•nary**)
**mil•le•nari•an•ism** Christian belief
**mil•le•nary** (*plural* **•naries**) a thousand; *compare* **millinery**
**mil•len•nial**
**mil•len•ni•al•ist**
**mil•len•nium** (*plural* **•niums** *or* **•nia**)
**mil•le•pede** *variant spelling of* **millipede**
**mil•le•pore** coral-like organism
**mil•ler**
**mil•ler•ite** mineral
**mil•lesi•mal** denoting a thousandth
**mil•let**
**mil•li•ard** thousand million
**mil•liary** denoting Roman mile
**mil•li•bar**
**mil•lieme** Tunisian coin
**mil•li•gram** (*or* **•gramme**)
**mil•li•li•tre** (*US* **•ter**)
**mil•li•metre** (*US* **•meter**)
**mil•line** unit of advertising copy
**mil•li•ner**
**mil•li•nery** hat making; *compare* **millenary**
**mill•ing**
**mil•lion** (*plural* **•lions** *or* **•lion**)
**mil•lion•aire** (*or* **•lion•naire**)
**mil•lion•air•ess**
**mil•lionth**
**mil•li•pede** (*or* **•le•pede, •le•ped**)
**mil•li•sec•ond**
**mill•pond**
**mill•race**
**mill•run**
**mill•stone**
**mill•stream**
**mill•wheel**
**mill•wright**
**mi•lord**
**mi•lom•eter** *variant spelling of* **mileometer**
**milque•toast** *US* timid person
**milt**
**mil•ter**
**Mil•ton•ic** (*or* **•to•nian**) of John Milton
**Mil•ton Keynes**
**Mil•wau•kee** US port
**mim** *Dialect* prim
**Mi•mas** satellite of Saturn
**mime**
**Mimeo•graph** (*Trademark*)
**mim•er**
**mi•mesis**
**mi•met•ic**
**mi•meti•cal•ly**
**mim•etite** mineral
**mim•ic** (**•ick•ing, •icked**)
**mim•ick•er**
**mim•ic•ry** (*plural* **•ries**)
**miminy-piminy** *variant of* **niminy-piminy**
**Mimir** Norse giant
**mi•mo•sa**
**mimo•sa•ceous**
**Min** Chinese dialect
**mina** (*plural* **minae** *or* **minas**) ancient unit
**mina** *variant spelling of* **myna**

**min•able** (*or* **mine•able**)
**mi•na•cious** threatening
**mi•nac•ity**
**Mina Has•san Tani** Moroccan port
**mina•ret**
**mina•ret•ed**
**Mi•nas Ge•rais** Brazilian state
**mina•to•ri•ly** (*or* **•ri•al•ly**)
**mina•tory** (*or* **•to•rial**)
**mince**
**mince•meat**
**minc•er**
**Minch** Atlantic channel
**minc•ing**
**minc•ing•ly**
**mind**
**Min•dan•ao** Philippine island
**mind•ed**
**Min•del** glaciation period
**mind•er**
**mind•ful**
**mind•ful•ly**
**mind•ful•ness**
**mind•less**
**mind•less•ness**
**mind-reader**
**mind-reading**
**mine**
**mine•field**
**mine•lay•er**
**min•er** one who mines; *compare* **minor**
**min•er•al**
**min•er•ali•za•tion** (*or* **•sa•tion**)
**min•er•al•ize** (*or* **•ise**)
**min•er•al•iz•er** (*or* **•is•er**)
**min•er•alo•cor•ti•coid** hormone
**min•er•al•ogi•cal** (*or* **•og•ic**)
**min•er•alo•gist**
**min•er•al•ogy**
**min•estro•ne**
**mine•sweeper**
**mine•sweeping**
**Ming**
**min•gle**
**Min•gre•lian** (*or* **Min•grel**) Georgian people
**min•gy** (**•gi•er, •gi•est**)
**mini** (*plural* **minis**)
**minia•ture**
**minia•tur•ist**
**minia•turi•za•tion** (*or* **•sa•tion**)
**minia•tur•ize** (*or* **•ise**)
**mi•ni•bar**
**mini•bus**
**mini•cab**
**mini•com•put•er**
**mini•dress**
**mini•fi•ca•tion**
**mini•fy** (**•fies, •fy•ing, •fied**)
**min•im**
**mini•ma** (*plural of* **minimum**)
**mini•mal**
**Mini•mal•ist** Russian revolutionary
**mini•mal•ist** advocate of minimal policy
**mini•mal•ly**
**mini•max** maths term
**mini•mi•za•tion** (*or* **•sa•tion**)
**mini•mize** (*or* **•mise**)
**mini•miz•er** (*or* **•mis•er**)
**mini•mum** (*plural* **•mums** *or* **•ma**)
**mini•mus** youngest
**min•ing**
**min•ion**
**mini•pill**
**(miniscule)** *incorrect spelling of* **minuscule**
**mini•skirt**
**mini•skirted**
**min•is•ter**
**min•is•terial**
**min•is•terial•ly**
**min•is•te•rium** (*plural* **•ria**) Lutheran ministers
**min•is•trant**
**mini•stra•tion**
**min•is•tra•tive**
**min•is•try** (*plural* **•tries**)
**Mini•track** (*Trademark*)
**(miniture)** *incorrect spelling of* **miniature**
**min•ium** red lead
**mini•ver** fur
**mini•vet** bird
**mink**
**minke** whale
**Min•na** Nigerian city
**Min•ne•apo•lis**
**min•neo•la** hybrid fruit
**min•ne•sing•er** German minstrel
**Min•ne•so•ta**
**Min•ne•so•tan**
**min•now** (*plural* **•nows** *or* **•now**)
**Mi•no•an** of Cretan culture
**mi•nor** lesser; *compare* **miner**
**Mi•nor•ca**
**Mi•nor•can**
**Mi•no•rite** friar
**mi•nor•ity** (*plural* **•ities**)
**Minos** legendary king
**Minotaur** legendary monster
**Minsk** Belarussian capital
**min•ster**
**min•strel**
**min•strel•sy** (*plural* **•sies**)
**mint**
**mint•age**
**mint•er**
**Min•ton** porcelain
**minty** (**minti•er, minti•est**)
**minu•end** maths term
**minu•et**
**mi•nus**
**mi•nus•cu•lar**
**mi•nus•cule**
**min•ute** 60 seconds
**mi•nute** very small
**min•ute•ly** every minute
**mi•nute•ly** in great detail
**Min•ute•man** (*plural* **•men**)
**mi•nute•ness**
**min•utes** record of proceedings
**mi•nu•tiae** (*sing.* **•tia**) trifling details
**minx**
**minx•ish**
**Mio•cene** geological period
**mio•sis** (*or* **myo•**) constriction of pupil; *compare* **meiosis**
**mi•ot•ic** (*or* **my•**)
**Mi•que•lon** French island
**mi•ra•bi•le dic•tu** *Latin* wonderful to relate
**Mira Ceti** star
**mi•ra•cid•ial**
**mi•ra•cid•ium** (*plural* **•iia**) fluke larva
**mira•cle**

**mi•racu•lous**
**mira•dor** balcony or turret
**mi•rage**
**Mi•ran•da** satellite of Uranus
**mire**
**mire•poix** vegetable mixture
**mir•ky** *variant spelling of* **murky**
**mir•ror**
**mirth**
**mirth•ful**
**mirth•ful•ly**
**mirth•ful•ness**
**mirth•less**
**mirth•less•ness**
**miry**
**mis•ad•ven•ture**
**mis•ad•vise**
**mis•align•ment**
**mis•al•li•ance** unsuitable alliance; *compare* **mésalliance**
**mis•an•thrope** (*or* **•thro•pist)**
**mis•an•throp•ic** (*or* **•thropi•cal)**
**mis•an•thropi•cal•ly**
**mis•an•thro•pist** *variant of* **misanthrope**
**mis•an•thro•py**
**mis•ap•pli•ca•tion**
**mis•ap•ply (•plies, •ply•ing, •plied)**
**mis•ap•pre•hend**
**mis•ap•pre•hend•ing•ly**
**mis•ap•pre•hen•sion**
**mis•ap•pre•hen•sive**
**mis•ap•pro•pri•ate**
**mis•ap•pro•pria•tion**
**mis•be•come (•com•ing, •came)** be unsuitable for
**mis•be•got•ten**
**mis•be•have**
**mis•be•hav•er**
**mis•be•hav•iour** (*US* **•ior)**
**mis•be•lief**
**mis•cal•cu•late**
**mis•cal•cu•la•tion**
**mis•call**
**mis•car•riage**
**mis•car•ry (•ries, •ry•ing, •ried)**
**mis•cast (•cast•ing, •cast)**
**mis•ce•gena•tion** interbreeding
**mis•ce•genet•ic**
**mis•cel•la•nea** (*plural*)
**mis•cel•la•neous**
**mis•cel•la•nist**
**mis•cel•la•ny** (*plural* **•nies)**
**mis•chance**
**mis•chief**
**mis•chie•vous**
**mis•chiev•ous•ness**
**misch met•al**
**mis•cibil•ity**
**mis•cible** capable of mixing; *compare* **missable**
**mis•con•ceive**
**mis•con•ceiv•er**
**mis•con•cep•tion**
**mis•con•duct**
**mis•con•struc•tion**
**mis•con•strue (•stru•ing, •strued)**
**mis•copy (•copies, •copy•ing, •cop•ied)**
**mis•count**
**mis•cre•ance** (*or* **•an•cy)**
**mis•cre•ant** wrongdoer
**mis•cre•ate** create badly
**mis•crea•tion**
**mis•cue (•cu•ing, •cued)**
**mis•date**
**mis•deal (•deal•ing, •dealt)**
**mis•deal•er**
**mis•deed**
**mis•de•mean•ant**
**mis•de•mean•our** (*US* **•or)**
**mis•di•rect**
**mis•di•rec•tion**
**mis•doubt**
**mise** legal term
**mise en scène** scenery
**mi•ser**
**mis•er•able**
**mis•er•able•ness**
**mis•er•ably**
**mi•sère** call in solo whist
**Mis•erere** 51st psalm
**mis•erere** misericord
**mis•eri•cord** (*or* **•corde)** part of church
**mi•ser•li•ness**
**mi•ser•ly**
**mis•ery** (*plural* **•eries)**
**mis•fea•sance** legal term
**mis•file**
**mis•fire**
**mis•fit (•fit•ting, •fit•ted)**
**mis•for•tune**
**mis•give (•giv•ing, •gave, •giv•en)**
**mis•giv•ing**
**mis•gov•ern**
**mis•gov•ern•ment**
**mis•gov•er•nor**
**mis•guid•ance**
**mis•guide**
**mis•guid•ed**
**mis•guid•er**
**mis•han•dle**
**mis•hap**
**mis•hear (•hear•ing, •heard)**
**mis•hit (•hit•ting, •hit)**
**mish•mash**
**Mish•nah** (*or* **•na)** Jewish precepts
**Mish•na•ic**
**mis•in•form**
**mis•in•form•ant** (*or* **•form•er)**
**mis•in•for•ma•tion**
**mis•in•ter•pret**
**mis•in•ter•pre•ta•tion**
**mis•in•ter•pret•er**
**mis•join•der** legal term
**mis•judge**
**mis•judg•er**
**mis•judg•ment** (*or* **•judge•)**
**Mis•kolc** Hungarian city
**mis•lay (•lay•ing, •laid)**
**mis•lay•er**
**mis•lead (•lead•ing, •led)**
**mis•lead•er**
**mis•man•age**
**mis•man•age•ment**
**mis•man•ag•er**
**mis•match**
**mis•no•mer**
**mi•soga•mist** marriage hater
**mi•soga•my**
**mi•sogy•nist** woman hater
**mi•sogy•nous**
**mi•sogy•ny**
**mi•solo•gist**
**mi•sol•ogy** hatred of reasoning
**miso•neism** hatred of anything new
**miso•neist**
**miso•neis•tic**

**mis•pick•el** mineral
**mis•place**
**mis•place•ment**
**mis•play**
**mis•plead** (**•plead•ing, •plead•ed, •plead,** *or* **•pled**)
**mis•plead•ing**
**mis•print**
**mis•pri•sion** concealment of treason
**mis•prize** (*or* **•prise**) undervalue
**mis•pro•nounce**
**mis•pro•nun•cia•tion**
**mis•pro•por•tion**
**mis•quo•ta•tion**
**mis•quote**
**mis•read** (**•read•ing, •read**)
**mis•re•mem•ber**
**mis•re•port**
**mis•rep•re•sent**
**mis•rep•re•sen•ta•tion**
**mis•rep•re•sen•ta•tive**
**mis•rep•re•sent•er**
**mis•rule**
Miss title of address
**miss**
**miss•able** able to be missed; *compare* **miscible**
**mis•sal** prayer book
**mis•sel thrush** *variant spelling of* **mistle thrush**
**mis•shape** (**•shap•ing, •shaped** *or* **•shap•en**)
**mis•sile**
**mis•sile•ry** (*or* **•sil•ry**)
**mis•sing**
**mis•sion**
**mis•sion•ary** (*plural* **•aries**)
**mis•sion•er**
**mis•sis**
**miss•ish**
**Mis•sis•sau•ga** Canadian town
**Mis•sis•sip•pi**
**Mis•sis•sip•pian**
**mis•sive**
**Mis•souri**
**Mis•sou•rian**
**mis•spell** (**•spell•ing, •spelt** *or* **•spelled**)
**mis•spend** (**•spend•ing, •spent**)
**mis•state**
**mis•state•ment**
**mis•sup•pose**
**missy** (*plural* **missies**)
**mist**
**mis•tak•able** (*or* **•take•**)
**mis•tak•ably** (*or* **•take•**)
**mis•take** (**•tak•ing, •took** *or* **•tak•en**)
**mis•tal** *Scot* cowshed
**Mis•tas•si•ni** Canadian lake
**mis•teach** (**•teach•ing, •taught**)
**mis•ter**
**mis•ti•gris** joker in poker
**misti•ly**
**mis•time**
**misti•ness**
**mis•tle thrush** (*or* **mis•sel thrush**)
**mis•tle•toe**
**mis•took**
**mis•tral** wind; *compare* **mistrial**
**mis•treat**
**mis•treat•ment**
**mis•tress**
**mis•tri•al** void trial; *compare* **mistral**
**mis•trust**
**mis•trust•er**
**mis•trust•ful**
**mis•trust•ful•ly**
**mis•trust•ful•ness**
**mis•trust•ing•ly**
**misty** (**misti•er, misti•est**)
**mis•under•stand** (**•stand•ing, •stood**)
**mis•us•age**
**mis•use**
**mis•us•er**
**mitch** *Dialect* play truant
**mite**
**mi•ter** *US spelling of* **mitre**
**Mith•ra•ic**
**Mith•ra•ism** (*or* **•rai•cism**)
**Mith•ra•ist**
**Mith•ras** (*or* **•ra**) Persian god
**mith•ri•dat•ic**
**mith•ri•da•tism** immunity to poison
**miti•cid•al**
**miti•cide** mite-killer
**miti•gable**
**miti•gate**
**miti•gat•ing**
**miti•ga•tion**
**miti•ga•tive** (*or* **•tory**)
**miti•ga•tor**
**mi•tis** malleable iron
**mi•to•chon•drial**
**mi•to•chon•drion** (*plural* **•dria**) biology term
**mi•to•sis** (*plural* **•ses**) cell division
**mi•tot•ic**
**mi•toti•cal•ly**
**mi•trail•leuse** machine gun
**mi•tral**
**mi•tre** (*US* **•ter**)
**mitre•wort** (*US* **miter•**) plant
**mitt**
**mit•ten**
**mit•ti•mus** (*plural* **•muses**) legal term
**mitz•vah** (*plural* **•vahs** *or* **•voth**)
**mix**
**mix•abil•ity**
**mix•able**
**mixed**
**mix•er**
**mix•ing**
**mixo•lyd•ian** music term
**Mix•tec** (*plural* **•tecs** *or* **•tec**) American Indian
**mix•ture**
**mix-up** (*noun*)
**Mi•zar** star
**Mi•zo•ram** Indian state
**miz•zen** (*or* **miz•en**) nautical term
**miz•zen•mast** (*or* **miz•en•**)
**miz•zle** *Dialect* drizzle
**m'lud**
**mne•mon•ic** memory aid
**mne•moni•cal•ly**
**mne•mon•ics**
**Mnemosyne** Greek goddess
**mo** (*plural* **mos**) *Slang* moment
**moa** extinct bird
**Moab** biblical kingdom
**Mo•ab•ite**
**moan**
**moan•er**
**moan•ing•ly**
**moat** ditch; *compare* **mote**
**mob** (**mob•bing, mobbed**)
**mob•ber**

**mob•cap**
**Mo•bile** US port
**mo•bile**
**mo•bil•ity**
**mo•bi•liz•able** (*or* **•lis•able**)
**mo•bi•li•za•tion** (*or* **•sa•tion**)
**mo•bi•lize** (*or* **•lise**)
**mob•oc•ra•cy** (*plural* **•cies**)
**mobo•crat**
**mobo•crat•ic** (*or* **•crati•cal**)
**mob•ster**
**Mo•bu•tu** *former name of* **Albert**
**moc•ca•sin**
**Mo•cha** Yemeni port
**mo•cha** coffee
**mock**
**mock•able**
**mock•er**
**mock•ery** (*plural* **•eries**)
**mock-heroic**
**mock-heroical•ly**
**mocking•bird**
**mock•ing•ly**
**mock-up** (*noun*)
**mod**
**mod•al**
**mo•dal•ity**
**mo•dal•ly**
**mode**
**mod•el** (**•el•ling, •elled;** *US* **•el•ing, •eled**)
**mod•el•ler** (*US* **•el•er**)
**mo•dem** computer term
**Mo•dena** Italian city
**mod•er•ate**
**mod•er•ate•ly**
**mod•er•ate•ness**
**mod•era•tion**
**mod•era•to** music term
**mod•era•tor**
**mod•era•tor•ship**
**mod•ern**
**mo•derne** architectural style
**mod•ern•ism**
**mod•ern•ist**
**mod•ern•is•tic**
**mod•ern•is•ti•cal•ly**
**mo•der•nity** (*plural* **•nities**)
**mod•erni•za•tion** (*or* **•sa•tion**)
**mod•ern•ize** (*or* **•ise**)
**mod•ern•iz•er** (*or* **•is•er**)
**mod•ern•ness**
**mod•est**
**mod•est•ly**
**mod•es•ty** (*plural* **•ties**)
**modge** *Dialect* to botch
**modi•cum**
**modi•fi•abil•ity** (*or* **•able•ness**)
**modi•fi•able**
**modi•fi•ca•tion**
**modi•fi•ca•tory** (*or* **•tive**)
**modi•fi•er**
**modi•fy** (**•fies, •fy•ing, •fied**)
**mo•dil•lion** architectural ornament
**mo•dio•lus** (*plural* **•li**) anatomy term
**mod•ish**
**mod•ish•ness**
**mo•diste** (*plural* **•distes**) fashionable dressmaker
**modu•la•bil•ity**
**modu•lar**
**modu•late**
**modu•la•tion**
**modu•la•tive** (*or* **•tory**)
**modu•la•tor**
**mod•ule**
**modu•lus** (*plural* **•li**) physics term
**mo•dus op•eran•di** (*plural* **modi op•eran•di**) method of working
**mo•dus vi•ven•di** (*plural* **modi vi•ven•di**) practical compromise
**mo•fette** opening in volcano
**mog** *Slang* cat
**Moga•dishu** (*or* **•discio**) Somali capital
**Moga•don** (*Trademark*) drug
**Moga•dor** Moroccan port
**mog•gy** (*or* **•gie;** *plural* **•gies**) *Slang* cat
**Mo•gi•lev** (*or* **•hi•**) Belarussian city
**Mo•gul** Muslim ruler
**mo•gul** important person
**mo•hair**
**Mo•ham•med•an** Muslim
**Mo•ha•ve** (*or* **•ja•;** *plural* **•ves** *or* **•ve**) American Indian
**Mo•ha•ve Des•ert** (*or* **Mo•ja•ve Des•ert**)
**Mo•hawk** (*plural* **•hawks** *or* **•hawk**) American Indian
**Mo•hi•can** *variant spelling of* **Mahican**
**Mo•hock** ruffian
**Mo•hole** geological project
**moi•der** *Dialect* to bother
**moi•dore** coin
**moi•ety** (*plural* **•eties**) half
**moire** (*noun*) fabric
**moi•ré** (*adj*) having watered pattern
**moist**
**mois•ten**
**moist•en•er**
**moist•ness**
**mois•ture**
**mois•tur•ize** (*or* **•ise**)
**mois•tur•iz•er** (*or* **•is•er**)
**Mo•ja•ve** *variant spelling of* **Mohave**
**moke** *Slang* donkey
**Mok•po** South Korean port
**mola** (*plural* **mola** *or* **molas**) fish
**mo•lal**
**mo•lal•ity** (*plural* **•ities**) chemistry term
**mo•lar** tooth; chemistry term
**mo•lar•ity**
**mo•las•ses**
**mold** *US spelling of* **mould**
**Mol•da•via**
**Mol•da•vian**
**mol•da•vite** glass
**mold•er** *US spelling of* **moulder**
**Mol•do•va** E European country
**mole**
**mo•lecu•lar**
**mol•ecule**
**mole•hill**
**mole•skin**
**mo•lest**
**mo•les•ta•tion**
**mo•lest•er**
**mo•line** heraldic term
**Mo•li•se** Italian region
**moll**
**mol•li•fi•able**
**mol•li•fi•ca•tion**
**mol•li•fi•er**

**mol•li•fy** (**•fies, •fy•ing, •fied**)
**mol•li•fy•ing•ly**
**mol•lusc** (*US* **•lusk**)
**mol•lus•can** (*US* **•kan**)
**mol•lus•coid** (*or* **•coi•dal**) zoology term
**mol•ly** (*plural* **•lies**) fish
**molly•coddle**
**molly•coddler**
**Molly Maguire** Irish secret society member
**Mo•loch** Semitic god
**mo•loch** lizard
**Mo•lo•kai** Hawaiian island
**molt** *US spelling of* **moult**
**mol•ten**
**mol•to** musical term
**Mo•luc•cas** Indonesian islands
**moly** (*plural* **molies**) mythological herb; flower
**mo•lyb•date**
**mo•lyb•de•nite** mineral
**mo•lyb•de•nous**
**mo•lyb•de•num** chemical element
**mo•lyb•dic**
**mo•lyb•dous**
**mom** *US* mother
**Mom•ba•sa** Kenyan port
**mo•ment**
**mo•men•tari•ly**
**mo•men•tary**
**mo•men•tous**
**mo•men•tum** (*plural* **•ta** *or* **•tums**)
**Momus** Greek god
**mona** monkey
**Mona•can**
**mona•chal** monastic
**mona•chism**
**Mona•co**
**mon•ad** (*plural* **•ads** *or* **mona•des**)
**mona•del•phous** botany term
**mo•nad•ic** (*or* **•nadi•cal**)
**mon•ad•ism** (*or* **•ad•ol•ogy**) philosophy
**mon•ad•is•tic**
**mo•nad•nock** hill
**mon•ad•ol•ogy** *variant of* **monadism**
**Mona•ghan** Irish county
**mon•al** (*or* **•aul**) pheasant
**mo•nan•drous** botany term
**mo•nan•dry**
**mo•nan•thous** botany term
**mon•arch**
**mo•nar•chal** (*or* **•chi•al**)
**mo•nar•chic** (*or* **•chi•cal**)
**mon•ar•chism**
**mon•ar•chist**
**mon•ar•chis•tic**
**mon•ar•chy** (*plural* **•chies**)
**mo•nar•da** plant
**mon•as•te•rial**
**mon•as•tery** (*plural* **•teries**)
**mo•nas•tic** (*or* **•ti•cal**)
**mo•nas•ti•cal•ly**
**mo•nas•ti•cism**
**mon•atom•ic** (*or* **mono•**)
**mon•aural**
**mona•zite** mineral
**Mönchen-Gladbach** German city
**Mon•day**
**mondi•al** of the world
**Mon•egasque** citizen of Monaco
**Monel metal** (*Trademark*)
**mon•etar•ism**
**mon•etar•ist**
**mon•etary**
**mon•eti•za•tion** (*or* **•sa•tion**)
**mon•etize** (*or* **•etise**)
**mon•ey** (*plural* **•eys** *or* **•ies**)
**money•changer**
**mon•eyed** (*or* **mon•ied**)
**money•lender**
**money•lending**
**money•maker**
**money•making**
**money-spinner**
**money•wort**
**mon•ger**
**mon•ger•ing**
**mon•go** (*or* goe; *plural* **•gos** *or* **•goes**) Mongolian currency
**Mon•gol**
**Mon•go•lia**
**Mon•go•lian**
**Mon•gol•ic**
**mon•go•lism** *former name of* **Down's syndrome**
**Mon•gol•oid**
**mon•goose** (*plural* **•gooses**)
**mon•grel**
**mon•grel•ism** (*or* **•ness**)
**mon•greli•za•tion** (*or* **•sa•tion**)
**mon•grel•ize** (*or* **•ise**)
**mon•grel•ly**
**moni•ker** (*or* **mon•ick•er**) *Slang* nickname
**mo•nili•form**
**mon•ism**
**mon•ist**
**mo•nis•tic**
**mo•nis•ti•cal•ly**
**mo•ni•tion** warning
**moni•tor**
**moni•to•rial**
**moni•tor•ship**
**moni•tory** (*or* **•to•rial**) warning
**moni•tress**
**monk**
**mon•key**
**monkey•pot** tree
**monk•fish** (*plural* **•fish** *or* **•fishes**)
**Mon-Khmer** language
**monk•hood** being a monk
**monk•ish**
**monks•hood** plant
**Mon•mouth**
**Mon•mouth•shire** Welsh county
**mono** (*plural* **monos**)
**mono•ac•id** (*or* **mon•ac•id, mono•acid•ic, mona•cid•ic**)
**mono•atom•ic** *variant of* **monatomic**
**mono•ba•sic**
**mono•carp** botany term
**mono•car•pel•lary**
**mono•car•pic** (*or* **•pous**)
**Mo•noc•er•os** constellation
**mono•cha•sial**
**mono•cha•sium** (*plural* **•sia**) botany term
**mono•chlo•ride**
**mono•chord** acoustic instrument
**mono•chro•mat** (*or* **•mate**)
**mono•chro•mat•ic** (*or* **mono•chro•ic**)
**mono•chro•mati•cal•ly**
**mono•chro•ma•tism** visual defect

**mono•chrome**
**mono•chro•mic** (*or* **•mi•cal**)
**mono•chrom•ist**
**mono•cle**
**mono•cli•nal**
**mono•cline** geology term
**mono•clin•ic** crystallography term
**mono•cli•nism** botany term
**mono•cli•nous**
**mono•coque** car or aircraft body
**mono•coty•ledon** botany term
**mono•coty•ledon•ous**
**mo•noc•ra•cy** (*plural* **•cies**)
**mono•crat**
**mono•crat•ic**
**mo•nocu•lar**
**mono•cul•ture**
**mono•cy•clic**
**mono•cyte** blood cell
**mono•cyt•ic**
**mo•nod•ic** (*or* **•nodi•cal**)
**mono•dist**
**mono•dra•ma**
**mono•dra•mat•ic**
**mono•dy** (*plural* **•dies**)
**mo•noecious** (*or* **•necious, •noi•cous**) botany term
**mono•fila•ment** (*or* **•fil**)
**mo•noga•mist**
**mo•noga•mis•tic**
**mo•noga•mous**
**mo•noga•my** having one spouse; *compare* monogyny
**mono•gen•esis** biology term
**mono•genet•ic**
**mono•gen•ic** genetics term
**mo•nog•enous**
**mo•nog•eny**
**mono•gram**
**mono•gram•matic**
**mono•grammed**
**mono•graph**
**mo•nog•ra•pher**
**mono•graph•ic**
**mono•graphi•cal•ly**
**mo•nogy•nist**
**mo•nogy•nous**
**mo•nogy•ny** having one female partner; *compare* monogamy
**mono•hull**
**mono•hy•brid**
**mono•hy•drate**
**mono•hy•droxy**
**mo•nola•ter** (*or* **•trist**)
**mo•nola•trous**
**mo•nola•try** worship of one god
**mono•lay•er**
**mono•lin•gual**
**mono•lith**
**mono•lith•ic**
**mono•lithi•cal•ly**
**mono•log•ic** (*or* **•logi•cal**)
**mono•log•ist**
**mono•logue** (*US also* **•log**)
**mo•nol•ogy**
**mono•ma•nia**
**mono•ma•ni•ac**
**mono•ma•nia•cal**
**mono•mark**
**mono•mer** chemistry term
**mono•mer•ic**
**mo•nom•er•ous** botany term
**mono•me•tal•lic**
**mono•met•al•lism**
**mono•met•al•list**
**mo•nom•eter** verse line
**mono•met•ri•cal** (*or* **•met•ric**)
**mo•no•mial**
**mono•mo•lecu•lar**
**mono•mor•phic** (*or* **•phous**)
**mono•mor•phism**
**mono•nu•clear**
**mono•nu•cleo•sis**
**mono•pet•al•ous**
**mo•nopha•gous**
**mo•nopha•gy**
**mono•pho•bia**
**mono•pho•bic**
**mono•phon•ic**
**mo•nopho•ny**
**mon•oph•thong**
**mon•oph•thon•gal**
**mono•phy•let•ic** genetics term
**mono•phyl•lous** botany term
**mono•plane**
**mono•plegia**
**mono•plegic**
**mono•po•dial**
**mono•po•dium** (*plural* **•dia**) botany term
**mo•nopo•lism**
**mo•nopo•list**
**mo•nopo•lis•tic**
**mo•nopo•lis•ti•cal•ly**
**mo•nopo•li•za•tion** (*or* **•sa•tion**)
**mo•nopo•lize** (*or* **•lise**)
**mo•nopo•liz•er** (*or* **•lis•er**)
**Mo•nopo•ly** (*Trademark*) game
**mo•nopo•ly** (*plural* **•lies**)
**mono•pro•pel•lant**
**mo•nop•so•nis•tic**
**mo•nop•so•ny** (*plural* **•nies**) economics term
**mon•op•te•ros** (*or* **•ron**; *plural* **•roi** *or* **•ra**) architectural term
**mono•rail**
**mono•sac•cha•ride**
**mono•semy** having only one meaning
**mono•sepa•lous**
**mono•so•dium glu•ta•mate**
**mono•some** chromosome
**mono•so•mic**
**mono•sper•mous** (*or* **•sper•mal**)
**mono•stich** single-line poem
**mono•stich•ic**
**mono•stich•ous** botany term
**mono•stome** (*or* **mo•nos•to•mous**) having one mouth
**mo•nos•tro•phe** poem
**mono•stroph•ic**
**mono•sty•lous** botany term
**mono•syl•lab•ic**
**mono•syl•labi•cal•ly**
**mono•syl•la•bism**
**mono•syl•la•ble**
**mono•theism**
**mono•theist**
**mono•theis•tic**
**mono•theis•ti•cal•ly**
**mono•tint**
**mono•tone**
**mono•ton•ic**
**mo•noto•nous**
**mo•noto•ny** (*plural* **•nies**)
**mono•trema•tous**
**mono•treme** mammal

**mo•no•tri•chous** (*or* **•trich•ic**) bacteriology term
**Mono•type** (*Trademark*) typesetting machine
**mono•type**
**mono•typ•ic**
**mono•va•lence** (*or* **•len•cy**)
**mono•va•lent**
**mon•ox•ide**
**Mon•ro•via** Liberian capital
**Mons** Belgian town
**mons** (*plural* **mon•tes**) anatomy term
**Mon•sei•gneur** (*plural* **Mes•sei•gneurs**) French title
**mon•sieur** (*plural* **mes•sieurs**) *French* gentleman; Mr
**Mon•sig•nor** (*plural* **•nors** *or* **•nori**) ecclesiastical title
**mon•soon**
**mon•ster**
**mon•strance** receptacle for consecrated Host
**mon•stros•ity** (*plural* **•ities**)
**mon•strous**
**mon•strous•ness**
**mon•tage**
**Mon•ta•gnard** (*plural* **•gnards** *or* **•gnard**) mountain people
**Mon•tana**
**mon•tane** of mountainous regions
**Mon•tau•ban** French city
**Mont Blanc**
**mont•bre•tia** plant
**mon•te** gambling game
**Mon•te Car•lo**
**Mon•te•go Bay** Jamaican port
**mon•teith** bowl for cooling wineglasses
**Mon•te•ne•grin**
**Mon•te•ne•gro** Yugoslav republic
**Mon•te•rey** Californian city
**mon•te•ro** (*plural* **•ros**) hunting cap
**Mon•ter•rey** Mexican city
**Montessori meth•od**
**Mon•te•vi•deo** Uruguayan capital
**mont•gol•fier** hot-air balloon
**Mont•gom•ery** US city
**month**
**month•ly** (*plural* **•lies**)
**mon•ti•cule** small hill
**Mont•mar•tre**
**Mont•par•nasse**
**Mont•pel•lier**
**Mon•treal**
**Mon•treuil** Parisian suburb
**monu•ment**
**monu•men•tal**
**monu•men•tal•ly**
**monu•men•tal•ity**
**Mon•za** Italian city
**mon•zo•nite** rock
**mon•zo•nit•ic**
**moo**
**mooch**
**mooch•er**
**mood**
**moodi•ly**
**moodi•ness**
**moody** (**moodi•er**, **moodi•est**)
**Moog syn•the•siz•er** (*Trademark*)
**moo•lah** *Slang* money
**mool•vie** (*or* **•vi**) Muslim learned man
**moon**
**moon•beam**
**moon•calf** (*plural* **•calves**)
**moon•eye** fish
**moon-faced**
**moon•fish** (*plural* **•fishes** *or* **•fish**)
**moon•flower**
**mooni•ly**
**mooni•ness**
**moon•less**
**moon•light**
**moon•lighter**
**moon•light•ing**
**moon•lit**
**moon•quake**
**moon•raker** sail
**moon•rise**
**moon•scape**
**moon•seed**
**moon•set**
**moon•shine**
**moon•shiner** *US* whisky smuggler
**moon•shot**
**moon•stone**
**moon•struck** (*or* **•stricken**)
**moon•wort**
**moony** (**mooni•er**, **mooni•est**)
**Moor** African Muslim
**moor** open ground; attach boat; *compare* **more**
**moor•age**
**moor•cock**
**moor•fowl**
**moor•hen**
**moor•ing**
**moor•ings**
**Moor•ish**
**moor•land**
**moor•wort** shrub
**moose** (*plural* **moose**)
**moot**
**moot•er**
**mop** (**mop•ping, mopped**)
**mope**
**moped** *past tense of* **mope**
**mo•ped** motorcycle
**mop•er**
**mop•ing•ly**
**mo•poke** owl
**mopped**
**mop•pet**
**mop•ping**
**mo•quette** fabric
**mor** humus
**mora** (*plural* **morae** *or* **moras**) prosody term
**mo•ra•ceous** botany term
**Mo•ra•da•bad** Indian city
**mo•rain•al** (*or* **•ic**)
**mo•raine** glacier debris; *compare* **murrain**
**mor•al**
**mo•rale** confidence
**mor•al•ism**
**mor•al•ist**
**mor•al•is•tic**
**mor•al•is•ti•cal•ly**
**mo•ral•ity** (*plural* **•ities**)
**mor•ali•za•tion** (*or* **•sa•tion**)
**mor•al•ize** (*or* **•ise**)
**mor•al•iz•er** (*or* **•is•er**)
**mor•al•iz•ing•ly** (*or* **•is•ing•ly**)
**mor•al•ly**
**Mor•ar** Scottish loch
**mo•rass**

**mora•to•rium** (*plural* **•ria** *or* **•riums)**
**mora•tory**
**Mo•ra•va** Czech river
**Mo•ra•via**
**Mo•ra•vian**
**Mo•ra•vi•an•ism** religious movement
**Mor•ay** Scottish council area
**mo•ray** (*plural* **•rays)** eel
**mor•bid**
**mor•bid•ity**
**mor•bid•ness**
**mor•bif•ic** causing disease
**mor•bifi•cal•ly**
**Mor•bi•han** French department
**mor•bil•li** measles
**mor•ceau** (*plural* **•ceaux)** *French* morsel
**mor•cha** Indian demonstration
**mor•da•cious** sarcastic
**mor•dac•ity** (*or* **•da•cious•ness)**
**mor•dan•cy**
**mor•dant** sarcastic; dye fixer
**mor•dent** musical ornament
**Mord•vin** (*plural* **•vin** *or* **•vins)** Finnish people
**Mor•dvin•ian**
**more** *comparative of* **much;** *compare* **moor**
**More•cambe** Lancashire town
**mo•reen** fabric
**more•ish** (*or* **mor•ish)**
**mo•rel** edible fungus
**Mo•relia** Mexican city
**mo•rel•lo** (*plural* **•los)** cherry
**Mo•relos** Mexican state
**more•over**
**mo•res** customs
**Mo•res•co** *variant spelling of* **Morisco**
**Mo•resque** Moorish
**Mor•gan** horse
**mor•ga•nat•ic**
**mor•ga•nati•cal•ly**
**mor•gan•ite** gemstone
**Morgan le Fay** legendary character
**morgue**
**mori•bund**
**mori•bun•dity**
**mo•ri•on** helmet
**Mo•ris•co** (*or* **•res•;** *plural* **•coes** *or* **•cos)** Spanish Moor
**mor•ish** *variant spelling of* **moreish**
**Mor•mon**
**Mor•mon•ism**
**morn** morning; *compare* **mourn**
**mor•nay** cookery term
**morn•ing**
**morning-glory** (*plural* **-glories)**
**Moro** (*plural* **Moros** *or* **Moro)** Muslim people
**Mo•roc•can**
**Mo•roc•co**
**mo•roc•co** leather
**mor•on**
**Mo•ro•ni** capital of Comoro Islands
**mo•ron•ic**
**mo•roni•cal•ly**
**mo•ron•ism** (*or* **•ity)**
**mo•rose**
**mo•rose•ly**
**mo•rose•ness**
**morph** linguistics term
**mor•phal•lax•is** (*plural* **•laxes)** zoology term
**mor•pheme** grammatical unit
**mor•phem•ic**
**mor•phemi•cal•ly**
**Morpheus** Greek god
**mor•phine** (*or* **•phia)**
**mor•phin•ism**
**mor•pho•gen•esis**
**mor•pho•genet•ic** (*or* **•gen•ic)**
**mor•pho•log•ic** (*or* **•logi•cal)**
**mor•pho•logi•cal•ly**
**mor•pholo•gist**
**mor•phol•ogy**
**mor•pho•pho•neme** linguistics term
**mor•pho•pho•nemic**
**mor•pho•pho•nemics**
**mor•pho•sis** (*plural* **•ses)** biology term
**mor•ris dance**
**mor•ro** (*plural* **•ros)** hill
**mor•row**
**Mors** Roman god
**Morse** code
**morse** cloak fastening
**mor•sel**
**mort** hunting term
**mor•tal**
**mor•tal•ity** (*plural* **•ities)**
**mor•tal•ly**
**mor•tar**
**mortar•board**
**mort•gage**
**mort•gage•able**
**mort•ga•gee**
**mort•gag•or** (*or* **•er)**
**mor•tice** *variant spelling of* **mortise**
**mor•ti•cian** *US* undertaker
**mor•ti•fi•ca•tion**
**mor•ti•fi•er**
**mor•ti•fy (•fies, •fy•ing, •fied)**
**mor•ti•fy•ing•ly**
**mor•tise** (*or* **•tice)**
**mor•tis•er**
**mort•main** legal term
**mor•tu•ary** (*plural* **•aries)**
**moru•la** (*plural* **•las** *or* **•lae)** biology term
**moru•lar**
**mor•wong** fish
**Mo•sa•ic** (*or* **•sai•cal)** of Moses
**mo•sa•ic (•ick•ing, •icked)**
**mo•sai•cist**
**mos•cha•tel** plant
**Mos•cow**
**Mo•selle** European river; wine
**mo•sey**
**Mos•lem** *variant spelling of* **Muslim**
**Mo•so•tho** (*plural* **•tho** *or* **•thos)** African people
**mosque**
**mos•qui•to** (*plural* **•toes** *or* **•tos)**
**moss**
**moss•back** *US* conservative
**moss•bunk•er** fish
**Mos•si** (*plural* **•sis** *or* **•si)** African people
**mos•sie** bird
**mossi•ness**
**mos•so** musical term
**moss•trooper**

**mossy (mossi•er, mossi•est)**
**most**
**most•ly**
**Mosul** Iraqi city
**mote** tiny speck; *compare* **moat**
**mo•tel**
**mo•tet**
**moth**
**moth•ball**
**moth-eaten**
**moth•er**
**moth•er•hood**
**mother-in-law** (*plural* **mothers-)**
**mother•land**
**moth•er•less**
**moth•er•li•ness**
**moth•er•ly**
**mother-of-pearl**
**mother•wort** plant
**moth•proof**
**mothy (mothi•er, mothi•est)**
**mo•tif** theme; *compare* **motive**
**mo•tile**
**mo•til•ity**
**mo•tion**
**mo•tion•er**
**mo•tion•less**
**mo•tion•less•ness**
**mo•ti•vate**
**mo•ti•va•tion**
**mo•ti•va•tion•al**
**mo•ti•va•tive**
**mo•tive** reason; causing motion; *compare* **motif**
**mo•tive•less**
**mo•tive•less•ness**
**mo•tiv•ity**
**mot juste** (*plural* **mots justes)**
**mot•ley**
**mot•mot** bird
**mo•to•cross** motorcycle race
**mo•to•neu•ron** nerve cell
**mo•tor**
**motor•bike**
**motor•boat**
**motor•bus**
**motor•cade**
**motor•car**
**motor•coach**
**motor•cycle**
**motor•cyclist**
**mo•tor•ist**
**mo•tori•za•tion** (*or* **•sa•tion)**
**mo•tor•ize** (*or* **•ise)**
**motor•man** (*plural* **•men)**
**motor•way**
**motte** castle mound
**mott•le**
**mot•to** (*plural* **•toes** *or* **•tos)**
**mouf•lon** (*or* **mouf•flon)** wild sheep
**mouil•lé** phonetics term
**mould** (*US* **mold)**
**mould•abil•ity** (*US* **mold•)**
**mould•able** (*US* **mold•)**
**mould•board** (*US* **mold•)** curved blade of plough
**mould•er** (*US* **mold•)** crumble; one who moulds
**mouldi•ness** (*US* **moldi•)**
**mould•ing** (*US* **mold•)**
**mould•warp** *Dialect* mole
**mouldy** (*US* **moldy; mouldi•er, mouldi•est,** *US* **moldi•er, moldi•est)**
**mou•lin** glacier shift
**Moul•mein** (*or* **Maul•main)** Burmese port
**moult** (*US* **molt)**
**moult•er** (*US* **molt•)**
**mound**
**mount**
**mount•able**
**moun•tain**
**moun•tain•eer**
**moun•tain•eer•ing**
**moun•tain•ous**
**mountain•top**
**moun•tebank**
**moun•tebank•ery**
**mount•ed**
**mount•er**
**Mountie** Canadian policeman
**mount•ing**
**Mount Rush•more**
**mourn** grieve; *compare* **morn**
**mourn•er**
**mourn•ful**
**mourn•ful•ly**
**mourn•ful•ness**
**mourn•ing**
**mouse** (*plural* **mice)**
**mous•er**
**mouse•tail** plant
**mouse•trap**
**mousi•ness**
**mous•ing** nautical term
**mous•sa•ka** (*or* **mou•sa•)**
**mousse**
**mousse•line** fabric; cookery term
**mous•tache** (*US* **mus•)**
**mousy** (*or* **mous•ey; mousi•er, mousi•est)**
**mouth**
**mouth•brooder** (*or* **•breeder)** fish
(**mouthe**) *incorrect spelling of* **mouth** (*verb*)
**mouth•er**
**mouth•ful** (*plural* **•fuls)**
**mouth•part**
**mouth•piece**
**mouth-to-mouth**
**mouth•wash**
**mouth•water•ing**
**mou•ton** processed sheepskin
**mov•abil•ity** (*or* **•able•ness)**
**mov•able** (*or in legal contexts* **move•)**
**mov•ably**
**move (mov•ing, moved)**
**move•ables** legal term
**move•ment**
**mov•er**
**movie**
**Movie•tone** (*Trademark*)
**mov•ing**
**mov•ing•ly**
**Mo•vio•la** (*Trademark*)
**mow (mow•ing, mowed, mowed** *or* **mown)**
**mow•burnt** agricultural term
**mow•er**
**moxa** medicinal substance
**moxie** *US* courage
**Mo•zam•bi•can**
**Mo•zam•bique** (*or* **Mo•çam•)**
**moz•za•rel•la** cheese
**moz•zet•ta** (*or* **mo•zet•ta)** clerical cape
**Mpu•ma•lan•ga** South African province
**Mr** (*plural* **Messrs)**
**Mrs**

**Ms**
**much (more, most)**
**much•ness**
**mu•cic acid**
**mu•cid** mouldy
**mu•ci•lage**
**mu•ci•lagi•nous**
**mu•cin** biochemical compound
**mu•cin•ous**
**muck**
**muck•er**
**mucki•ly**
**mucki•ness**
**muck•le** *Scot* much
**muck•rake**
**muck•rak•er**
**muck•worm**
**mucky (mucki•er, mucki•est)**
**mu•coid** (*or* **•coi•dal)**
**mu•co•mem•bra•nous**
**mu•co•poly•sac•cha•ride**
**mu•co•pro•tein**
**mu•co•pu•ru•lent**
**mu•co•sa** (*plural* **•sae)** mucous membrane
**mu•cos•ity**
**mu•cous** (*or* **•cose;** *adj***)**
**mu•cro** (*plural* **mu•cro•nes)** biology term
**mu•cro•nate** (*or* **•nat•ed)**
**mu•cro•na•tion**
**mu•cus** (*noun*)
**mud (mud•ding, mud•ded)**
**mud•cat** fish
**mud•died**
**mud•di•ly**
**mud•di•ness**
**mud•dle**
**mud•dled•ness**
**muddle•headed**
**muddle•headed•ness**
**mud•dle•ment**
**mud•dler**
**mud•dling•ly**
**mud•dy** (*adj* **•di•er, •di•est;** *verb* **•dies, •dy•ing, •died)**
**mud•fish** (*plural* **•fish** *or* **•fishes)**
**mud•guard**
**mu•dir** governor
**mud•lark**
**mud•pack**
**mu•dra** Hindu dance movement
**mud•skipper** fish
**mud•slinger**
**mud•slinging**
**mud•stone**
**muen•ster** cheese
**mues•li**
**mu•ez•zin** mosque official
**muff**
**muf•fin**
**muf•fle**
**muf•fler**
**Muf•ti** (*plural* **•tis)** Muslim legal adviser
**muf•ti** (*plural* **•tis)** civilian dress
**Mu•fu•li•ra** Zambian town
**mug (mug•ging, mugged)**
**mug•ger** street robber
**mug•ger** (*or* **•gar, •gur)** crocodile
**mug•gi•ly**
**mug•gi•ness**
**mug•gins**
**mug•gy (•gi•er, •gi•est)**
**mug•wort**
**mug•wump** politically neutral person
**Mu•ham•mad•an** Muslim
**Mühl•hau•sen** German city
**muk•luk** Eskimo boot
**mu•lat•to** (*plural* **•tos** *or* **•toes)**
**mul•berry** (*plural* **•berries)**
**mulch** soil enricher
**mulct** cheat
**mule**
**mu•leta** matador's cape
**mu•leteer** mule driver
**mul•ey** (*or* **mul•ley)** hornless cattle
**mul•ga** tree
**Mül•heim an der Ruhr** German city
**mu•li•eb•rity** womanhood
**mul•ish**
**mul•ish•ness**
**Mull** Scottish island
**mull**
**mul•lah** (*or* **mul•la)** Muslim leader
**mul•lein** (*or* **•len)** plant
**mul•ler**
**mul•let**
**mul•ley** *variant spelling of* **muley**
**mul•li•gan** stew
**mul•li•ga•taw•ny**
**mul•li•on**
**mul•li•oned**
**mul•lite** mineral
**mul•lock** *Dialect* mess
**mullo•way** fish
**Mul•tan** Pakistani city
**mul•tan•gu•lar** (*or* **multi•an•)**
**mul•teity** manifoldness
**multi•birth**
**multi•cel•lu•lar**
**multi•chan•nel**
**multi•cide** mass murder
**multi•col•lin•ear•ity** statistics term
**multi•col•oured** (*US* **•ored)**
**multi•di•rec•tion•al**
**multi•dis•ci•pli•nary**
**multi•fac•et•ed**
**multi•fac•to•rial**
**multi•fari•ous**
**multi•fid** (*or* **mul•tifi•dous)**
**multi•foil** looped design
**multi•fold**
**multi•fo•li•ate**
**multi•form**
**multi•for•mity**
**multi•gravi•da** obstetrics term
**multi•hull**
**multi•lami•nar**
**multi•lat•er•al**
**multi•lin•gual**
**multi•media**
**multi•mil•lion•aire**
**multi•na•tion•al**
**multi•no•mial**
**multi•nu•clear** (*or* **•cleate)**
**mul•tipa•ra** (*plural* **•rae)** obstetrics term
**multi•par•ity**
**mul•tipa•rous**
**multi•par•tite**
**multi•plane** multi-winged aircraft
**multi•ple**
**multiple-choice**
**multiple•poind•ing** Scottish legal term
**multi•plet** physics term
**multi•plex** electronics term

**multi•plex•er**
**multi•pli•able**
**multi•pli•cand** number multiplied
**multi•pli•cate** manifold
**multi•pli•ca•tion**
**multi•pli•ca•tion•al**
**multi•pli•ca•tive**
**multi•plic•ity** (*plural* **•ities**)
**multi•pli•er**
**multi•ply** (**•plies, •ply•ing, •plied**)
**multi•pro•gram•ming**
**multi•pur•pose**
**multi•racial**
**multi•role**
**multi•screen**
**multi•stage**
**multi•sto•rey**
**multi•tude**
**multi•tu•di•nous**
**multi•va•len•cy**
**multi•va•lent**
**multi•vi•bra•tor**
**mul•ture** miller's fee
**mum** mother; silent
**mum** (*or* **mumm; mum•ming, mummed**) act in mummer's play
**Mum•bai** *Indian name of* **Bombay**
**mum•ble**
**mum•bler**
**mum•bling•ly**
**mum•bo jum•bo** (*plural* **mum•bo jum•bos**)
**mum•chance** dumbstruck
**mum•mer**
**mum•mery** (*plural* **•meries**)
**mum•mi•fi•ca•tion**
**mum•mi•fy** (**•fies, •fy•ing, •fied**)
**mum•my** (*plural* **•mies**)
**mumps**
**munch**
**munch•er**
**mun•dane**
**mun•dane•ness**
**mung** bean
**munga** *Austral* food
**mun•go** (*or* **mon•go, mon•goe;** *plural* **•gos** *or* **•goes**) fabric
**Mu•nich**
**mu•nici•pal**
**mu•nici•pal•ity** (*plural* **•ities**)
**mu•nici•pali•za•tion** (*or* **•sa•tion**)
**mu•nici•pal•ize** (*or* **•ise**)
**mu•nici•pal•ly**
**mu•nifi•cence** (*or* **•cent•ness**)
**mu•nifi•cent**
**mu•ni•ment** means of defence
**mu•ni•ments** title deeds
**mu•ni•tion**
**Mun•ster** Irish province
**Mün•ster** German city
**munt•jac** (*or* **•jak**) deer
**muon** elementary particle
**mu•ral**
**mu•ral•ist**
**mur•der**
**mur•der•er** (*fem* **•ess**)
**mur•der•ous**
**mur•der•ous•ness**
**Mu•reş** European river
**mu•rex** (*plural* **mu•ri•ces**) mollusc
**mu•ri•cate** (*or* **•cat•ed**) biology term
**mu•rine** of rats and mice
**murk** (*or* **mirk**)
**murki•ly** (*or* **mirki•**)
**murki•ness** (*or* **mirki•**)
**murky** (*or* **mirky; murki•er, murki•est** *or* **mirki•er, mirki•est**)
**Mur•mansk** Russian port
**mur•mur**
**mur•mur•er**
**mur•mur•ing**
**mur•mur•ous**
**mur•phy** (*plural* **•phies**) *Dialect* potato
**mur•rain** cattle disease; *compare* **moraine**
**Mur•ray** Australian river
**murre** guillemot
**murre•let** bird
**mur•rhine** (*or* **•rine**) Roman vase material
**Mur•rum•bidgee** Australian river
**mur•ther** *Archaic* murder
**mu•sa•ceous** botany term
**Mus•ca** constellation
**mus•ca•del** (*or* **•delle**) *variants of* **muscatel**
**mus•ca•dine** US grape
**mus•ca•rine** poisonous alkaloid
**Mus•cat** capital of Oman
**mus•cat** grape
**mus•ca•tel** (*or* **•del, •delle**) wine
**mus•cid** fly
**mus•cle**
**muscle-bound**
**mus•cle•man** (*plural* **•men**)
**mus•cly**
**mus•co•va•do** (*or* **mus•ca•**) raw sugar
**Mus•co•vite** native of Moscow
**mus•co•vite** mineral
**Mus•co•vy** Russian principality; duck
**mus•cu•lar**
**mus•cu•lar•ity**
**mus•cu•la•ture**
**muse**
**muse•ful**
**mus•eol•ogy** museum organization; *compare* **musicology**
**mus•er**
**mu•sette** bagpipe
**mu•seum**
**mush**
**mushi•ly**
**mushi•ness**
**mush•room**
**mushy** (**mushi•er, mushi•est**)
**mu•sic**
**mu•si•cal**
**mu•si•cale** *US* musical evening
**mu•si•cal•ly**
**mu•si•cal•ness** (*or* **•ity**)
**mu•si•cian**
**mu•si•cian•ship**
**mu•si•co•logi•cal**
**mu•si•colo•gist**
**mu•si•col•ogy** study of music; *compare* **museology**
**mus•jid** *variant spelling of* **masjid**
**musk**
**mus•keg** bog

**mus•kel•lunge** (*or* **mas•ka•nonge, •ki•**) fish
**mus•ket**
**mus•ket•eer**
**mus•ket•ry**
**muski•ness**
**musk•melon**
**musk•rat** (*plural* **•rats** *or* **•rat**)
**musky** (**muski•er, muski•est**)
**Mus•lim** (*or* **Mos•lem**; *plural* **•lims, •lim** *or* **•lems, •lem**)
**Mus•lim•ism** (*or* **Mos•lem•**)
**mus•lin**
**muso** *Austral* musician
**mus•quash**
**muss** *US* rumple
**mus•sel** mollusc; *compare* **muscle**
**must**
**mus•tache** *US spelling of* **moustache**
**mus•ta•chio** (*plural* **•chi•os**)
**mus•ta•chi•oed**
**mus•tang**
**mus•tard**
**mus•tee** (*or* **mes•**) person of mixed parentage
**mus•te•line** of badger family
**mus•ter**
**musth** (*or* **must**) sexual heat in animals
**musti•ly**
**musti•ness**
**mus•ty** (**•ti•er, •ti•est**)
**mu•tabil•ity** (*or* **•table•ness**)
**mu•table**
**mu•tably**
**mu•ta•gen** substance causing mutation
**mu•ta•gen•ic**
**mu•tant**
**mu•tate**
**mu•ta•tion**
**mu•ta•tion•al**
**mu•ta•tis mu•tan•dis**
**mutch** linen cap
**mute**
**mute•ness**
**mu•ti•cous** botany term
**mu•ti•late**
**mu•ti•la•tion**
**mu•ti•la•tive**
**mu•ti•la•tor**
**mu•ti•neer**
**mu•ti•nous**
**mu•ti•ny** (*noun, plural* **•nies**; *verb* **•nies, •ny•ing, •nied**)
**mut•ism**
**mutt** *Slang* fool; cur
**mut•ter**
**mut•ter•er**
**mut•ter•ing•ly**
**mut•ton**
**mutton•chops** side whiskers
**mut•tony**
**mu•tu•al**
**mu•tu•al•ity** (*or* **•ness**)
**mu•tu•al•ize** (*or* **•ise**)
**mu•tu•al•ly**
**mu•tule** architecture term
**Mu•zak** (*Trademark*)
**mu•zhik** (*or* **mou•jik, mu•jik**) Russian peasant
**muzz** make muzzy
**muz•zi•ly**
**muz•zi•ness**
**muz•zle**
**muz•zler**
**muz•zy** (**•zi•er, •zi•est**)
**my**
**my•al•gia** muscle pain
**my•al•gic**
**mya•lism** witchcraft
**my•all** tree
**My•an•mar** *official name of* **Burma**
**my•as•thenia** muscular weakness
**my•as•then•ic**
**my•celial**
**my•celium** (*plural* **•celia**) fungal body
**my•celoid**
**My•cenae** ancient Greek city
**My•cenaean**
**my•ceto•ma** (*plural* **•mas** *or* **•ma•ta**) fungal infection
**my•ceto•zoan** fungus
**my•co•bac•te•rium** (*plural* **•ria**)
**my•co•logi•cal** (*or* **•log•ic**)
**my•colo•gist**
**my•col•ogy** study of fungi
**my•cor•rhi•za** (*or* **•co•rhi•**; *plural* **•zae** *or* **•zas**) botany term
**my•cor•rhi•zal** (*or* **•co•rhi•**)
**my•co•sis** fungal disease
**my•cot•ic**
**my•dria•sis** pupil dilation
**myd•ri•at•ic**
**my•elen•cephal•ic**
**my•elen•cepha•lon** (*plural* **•lons** *or* **•la**) embryology term
**my•elin** (*or* **•eline**) nerve sheath
**my•elin•ic**
**my•eli•tis**
**my•eloid**
**my•elo•ma** tumour
**my•elo•ma•toid**
**myia•sis** (*plural* **•ses**) infestation by fly larvae
**my•lo•nite** rock
**myna** (*or* **my•nah, mina**) bird
**Myn•heer** Dutch title of address
**myo•car•dial**
**myo•car•dio•graph**
**myo•car•di•tis**
**myo•car•dium** (*plural* **•dia**) heart muscle
**myo•gen•ic**
**myo•glo•bin** protein
**myo•graph**
**myo•graph•ic**
**myo•graphi•cal•ly**
**my•og•ra•phy**
**myo•log•ic** (*or* **•logi•cal**)
**my•olo•gist**
**my•ol•ogy** study of muscle diseases
**myo•ma** (*plural* **•mas** *or* **•ma•ta**) tumour
**my•ope**
**myo•pia**
**my•op•ic**
**my•opi•cal•ly**
**myo•sin** protein
**myo•sis** *variant spelling of* **miosis**
**myo•so•tis** (*or* **•sote**) plant
**myo•tome** anatomy term
**myo•to•nia** lack of muscle tone
**myo•ton•ic**
**myri•ad**
**myria•pod** invertebrate
**myri•apo•dan**
**myri•apo•dous**

**my•ri•ca** medicinal bark
**myr•meco•logi•cal**
**myr•mecolo•gist**
**myr•mecol•ogy** study of ants
**myr•mecopha•gous**
**myr•meco•phile**
**myr•mecophi•lous**
**Myr•mi•don** (*plural* **mi•dons** *or* **mido•nes**) mythological race
**my•roba•lan** fruit
**myrrh**
**myr•ta•ceous**
**myr•tle**
**my•self**
**My•sore** Indian city
**mys•ta•gog•ic** (*or* **•gogi•cal**)
**mys•ta•gogi•cal•ly**
**mys•ta•gogue** mystic teacher
**mys•ta•go•gy**
**mys•teri•ous**
**mys•teri•ous•ness**
**mys•tery** (*plural* **•teries**)
**mys•tic**
**mys•ti•cal**
**mys•ti•cal•ly**
**mys•ti•cism**
**mys•ti•fi•ca•tion**
**mys•ti•fi•er**
**mys•ti•fy** (**•fies, •fy•ing, •fied**)
**mys•ti•fy•ing•ly**
**mys•tique**
**myth**
**mythi•cal**
**mythi•cal•ly**
**mythi•cist** (*or* **•ciz•er, •cis•er**)
**mythi•ci•za•tion** (*or* **•sa•tion**)
**mythi•cize** (*or* **•cise**)
**mytho•logi•cal**
**my•tholo•gist**
**my•tholo•gi•za•tion** (*or* **•sa•tion**)
**my•tholo•gize** (*or* **•gise**)
**my•tholo•giz•er** (*or* **•gis•er**)
**my•thol•ogy** (*plural* **•ogies**)
**mytho•ma•nia** psychiatric term
**mytho•ma•ni•ac**
**mytho•poeia** (*or* **•po•esis**) myth making
**mytho•poe•ic**
**mytho•poe•ism**
**mytho•poe•ist**
**my•thos** (*plural* **•thoi**) group of beliefs
**(myxamatosis)** *incorrect spelling of* **myxomatosis**
**myx•oedema** (*US* **•edema**) thyroid disease
**myx•oedem•ic** (*US* **•edem•**)
**myxo•ma** (*plural* **•mas** *or* **•ma•ta**) tumour
**myxo•ma•to•sis**
**myx•oma•tous**
**myxo•my•cete** fungus
**myxo•my•cetous**
**myxo•vi•rus**

# N

**Naafi** (*or* **NAAFI**)
**nab** (**nab•bing, nabbed**)
**Na•blus** (*or* **Nabu•lus**) Jordanian town
**na•bob**
**na•bob•ery** (*or* **•ism**)
**Nabonidus** biblical character
**Naboth** biblical character
**na•celle** part of aircraft
**na•cre** mother-of-pearl
**na•cred**
**na•cre•ous**
**Na-Dene** (*or* **-Déné**) language group
**na•dir**
**nae** *Scot* no
**nae•void** (*US* **ne•**)
**nae•vus** (*US* **ne•**; *plural* **•vi**) birthmark
**nag** (**nag•ging, nagged**)
**Naga** (*plural* **Nagas** *or* **Naga**) Indian people
**Na•ga•land**
**na•ga•na** (*or* **n'ga•na**) animal disease
**Na•ga•no** Japanese city
**Na•ga•ri** Indian script
**Na•ga•sa•ki** Japanese port
**nagged**
**nag•ger**
**nag•ging**
**na•gor** antelope
**Nagorno-Karabakh** Azerbaijani autonomous region
**Na•go•ya** Japanese city
**Nag•pur** Indian city
**Na•huatl** (*plural* **•huatl** *or* **•huatls**) American Indian
**Na•hua•tlan**
**nai•ad** (*plural* **•ads** *or* **•ades**)
**na•ïf** *variant spelling of* **naive**
**nail**
**nail•brush**
**nail•er**
**nail•file**
**nail•head** decorative device
**nain•sook** fabric
**nai•ra** Nigerian currency
**Nairn** former Scottish county
**Nai•ro•bi**
**nais•sant** heraldry term
**na•ive** (*or* **•ïve, •if**)
**na•ive•ty** (*or* **•ive•té, •ïve•té**)
**Najd** *variant spelling of* **Nejd**
**na•ked**
**na•ked•ness**
**na•ker** kettledrum
**Na•khi•che•van** Azerbaijani autonomous region
**Nal•chik** Russian city
**Nama** (*or* **Na•ma•qua**; *plural* **Nama, Namas** *or* **•qua, •quas**) Khoikhoi people
**nam•able** (*or* **name•**)
**Na•man•gan** Uzbek city
**namby-pamby** (*plural* **-pambies**)
**nam•dah** *variant spelling of* **numdah**
**name**
**name-dropper**
**name-dropping**
**name•less**
**name•ly**
**name•plate**

**name•sake**
**name•tape**
**Nam•hoi** Chinese city
**Na•mibia**
**Na•mib•ian**
**Na•mur** Belgian province
**nan** (*or* **nanna**) *Slang* grandmother
**Nan•chang** (*or* **Nan-ch'ang**) Chinese city
**Nan•cy** French city
**nan•cy** (*plural* **•cies**) effeminate man
**Nan•da Devi** Himalayan mountain
**Nan•ga Par•bat** Himalayan mountain
**nan•keen** (*or* **•kin**) fabric
**Nan•king** (*or* **Nan-ching**) Chinese port
**nanna** *variant of* **nan**
**Nan•ning** (*or* **Nan-ning**) Chinese port
**nan•ny** (*plural* **•nies**)
**na•no•metre** (*US* **•meter**)
**na•no•plank•ton** (*or* **nan•no•**)
**na•no•sec•ond**
**Nan Shan** Chinese mountain range
**Nantes** French port
**Nan•tuck•et** US island
**Nan•tung** Chinese city
**Naoise** Irish mythological character
**nap** (**nap•ping, napped**)
**na•palm**
**nape**
**naph•tha**
**naph•tha•lene** (*or* **•line, •lin**)
**naph•thene**
**naph•thol**
**naph•thyl**
**Na•pier** New Zealand port
**Na•pier•ian loga•ri•thm**
**na•pi•form** turnip-shaped
**nap•kin**
**Na•ples**
**na•po•le•on** coin
**Na•po•leon•ic**
**nap•pa** leather
**nappe** rock fold
**napped**
**nap•per** *Slang* head
**nap•pi•ness**
**nap•ping**
**nap•py** (*noun, plural* **•pies**; *adj* **•pi•er, •pi•est**)
**Nara** Japanese city
**Na•ra•yan•ganj** Bangladeshi city
**nar•ceine** (*or* **•ceen**) alkaloid
**nar•cis•sism** (*or* **nar•cism**)
**nar•cis•sist**
**nar•cis•sis•tic**
**nar•cis•sus** (*plural* **•si** *or* **•suses**)
**nar•co•analy•sis**
**nar•co•lep•sy**
**nar•co•lep•tic**
**nar•co•sis** (*plural* **•ses**)
**nar•co•syn•thesis** medical treatment
**nar•cot•ic**
**nar•coti•cal•ly**
**nar•co•tism**
**nar•co•ti•za•tion** (*or* **•sa•tion**)
**nar•co•tize** (*or* **•tise**)
**nard** medicinal plant
**nar•es** (*sing.* **•is**) nostrils
**nar•ghi•le** hookah
**nar•ial** (*or* **•ine**)
**nark**
**Nar•ra•gan•set** (*or* **•sett**; *plural* **•set, •sets** *or* **•sett, •setts**) American Indian
**nar•rat•able**
**nar•rate**
**nar•ra•tion**
**nar•ra•tive**
**nar•ra•tor** (*or* **•rat•er**)
**nar•row**
**narrow-minded**
**narrow-minded•ness**
**nar•row•ness**
**nar•thex** church portico
**Nar•vik** Norwegian port
**nar•whal** (*or* **•wal, •whale**) whale
**nary** *Dialect* not
**na•sal**
**na•sal•ity**
**na•sali•za•tion** (*or* **•sa•tion**)
**na•sal•ize** (*or* **•ise**)
**na•sal•ly**
**nas•cence** (*or* **•cen•cy**)
**nas•cent**
**Nash•ville** US city
**na•sial**
**na•si•on** anatomy term
**na•so•fron•tal**
**na•so•pha•ryn•geal**
**na•so•phar•ynx** (*plural* **•pha•ryn•ges** *or* **•phar•ynxes**)
**Nas•sau** German region; Bahamian capital
**nas•tic** botany term
**nas•ti•ly**
**nas•ti•ness**
**na•stur•tium**
**nas•ty** (*adj* **•ti•er, •ti•est**; *noun, plural* **•ties**)
**Na•tal** Brazilian port; former South African province
**na•tal** of birth
**na•tal•ity**
**na•tant** floating
**na•ta•tion** swimming
**na•ta•tion•al**
**na•ta•tory**
**na•tes** (*sing.* **•tis**) buttocks
**na•tion**
**na•tion•al**
**na•tion•al•ism**
**na•tion•al•ist**
**na•tion•al•is•tic**
**na•tion•al•ity** (*plural* **•ities**)
**na•tion•ali•za•tion** (*or* **•sa•tion**)
**na•tion•al•ize** (*or* **•ise**)
**na•tion•al•ly**
**na•tion•hood**
**nation•wide**
**na•tive**
**na•tiv•ism**
**na•tiv•ist**
**na•tiv•is•tic**
**Na•tiv•ity** Christ's birth
**na•tiv•ity** (*plural* **•ities**) birth or origin
**NATO**
**nat•ro•lite** mineral
**na•tron** mineral
**nat•ter**
**nat•ter•jack** toad
**nat•ti•ly**
**nat•ti•ness**
**nat•ty** (**•ti•er, •ti•est**)
**natu•ral**
**natu•ral•ism** artistic movement; *compare* **naturism**

**natu•ral•ist**
**natu•ral•is•tic**
**natu•ral•is•ti•cal•ly**
**natu•rali•za•tion** (*or* **•sa•tion)**
**natu•ral•ize** (*or* **•ise)**
**natu•ral•ly**
**natu•ral•ness**
**na•ture**
**na•tur•ism** nudism; *compare* **naturalism**
**na•tur•ist**
**na•turo•path**
**na•turo•path•ic**
**na•tur•opa•thy** nature cure
**naught** *Archaic* nothing; *US spelling of* **nought**
**naugh•ti•ly**
**naugh•ti•ness**
**naugh•ty (•ti•er, •ti•est)**
**nau•plius** (*plural* **•plii)** crustacean larva
**Nau•ru** island republic
**Nau•ruan**
**nau•sea**
**nau•seate**
**nau•sea•tion**
**nau•seous**
**nau•seous•ness**
**nautch** (*or* **nauch)** Indian dance
**nau•ti•cal**
**nau•ti•cal•ly**
**nau•ti•loid**
**nau•ti•lus** (*plural* **•luses** *or* **•li)** mollusc
**Nava•ho** (*or* **•jo;** *plural* **•ho, •hos** *or* **•jo, •jos)** American Indian
**na•val** of ships; *compare* **navel**
**na•val•ly**
**nav•ar** navigation system
**nava•rin** mutton stew
**Na•varre**
**nave**
**na•vel** umbilicus; *compare* **naval**
**navi•cert** cargo certificate
**na•vicu•lar** boat-shaped
**navi•gabil•ity** (*or* **•gable•ness)**
**navi•gable**
**navi•gably**
**navi•gate**
**navi•ga•tion**
**navi•ga•tion•al**
**navi•ga•tor**
**nav•vy** (*plural* **•vies)** labourer
**navy** (*plural* **navies)**
**na•wab** Indian prince
**Nax•os** Greek island
**nay** no; *compare* **neigh**
**Na•ya•rit** Mexican state
**Naza•rene** inhabitant of Nazareth; Syrian Christian
**Naza•reth**
**Naza•rite** (*or* **Nazi•)** Old Testament ascetic
**Naze** Essex headland
**Nazi** (*plural* **Nazis)**
**Na•zi•fy (•fies, •fy•ing, •fied)**
**Na•zism**
**Ndja•me•na** capital of Chad
**Ndo•la** Zambian city
**Neagh** Northern Irish lake
**Ne•an•der•thal**
**neap** tide
**Nea•poli•tan**
**near**
**near•by**
**Ne•arc•tic** zoogeographical term
**near•ly**
**near•ness**
**near•side**
**near-sighted**
**near-sighted•ness**
**neat**
**neat•en**
**neath** *Archaic* beneath
**neat•ness**
**neat's-foot oil**
**neb** *Dialect* projecting part
**Ne•bras•ka**
**nebu•chad•nez•zar** wine bottle
**nebu•la** (*plural* **•lae** *or* **•las)**
**nebu•lar**
**nebu•li•za•tion** (*or* **•sa•tion)**
**nebu•lize** (*or* **•lise)** atomize
**nebu•liz•er** (*or* **•lis•er)**
**nebu•los•ity** (*plural* **•ities)**
**nebu•lous**
**nebu•lous•ness**
**ne•ces•saries**
**nec•es•sari•ly**
**nec•es•sary**
**ne•ces•si•tar•ian** (*or* **nec•es•sar•ian)**
**ne•ces•si•tari•an•ism** (*or* **nec•es•sari•an•ism)** philosophy term
**ne•ces•si•tate**
**ne•ces•sita•tion**
**ne•ces•si•ta•tive**
**ne•ces•si•tous**
**ne•ces•sity** (*plural* **•sities)**
**neck**
**Neck•ar** German river
**neck•band**
**neck•cloth**
**neck•er**
**neck•er•chief**
**neck•lace**
**neck•line**
**neck•piece**
**neck•tie**
**neck•wear**
**nec•ro•bio•sis** death of cells
**nec•ro•bi•ot•ic**
**ne•crola•try** worship of the dead
**nec•ro•logi•cal**
**ne•crolo•gist**
**ne•crol•ogy** (*plural* **•ogies)** list of dead people
**nec•ro•man•cer**
**nec•ro•man•cy**
**nec•ro•man•tic**
**nec•ro•philia** (*or* **ne•crophi•lism)**
**nec•ro•phili•ac** (*or* **•phile)**
**nec•ro•phil•ic**
**nec•ro•phobe**
**nec•ro•pho•bia**
**nec•ro•pho•bic**
**ne•cropo•lis** (*plural* **•lises** *or* **•leis)**
**nec•rop•sy** (*plural* **•sies)**
**ne•crose** (*verb*)
**ne•cro•sis**
**ne•crot•ic**
**ne•croto•my** (*plural* **•mies)** dissection of corpse
**nec•tar**
**nec•tar•eous** (*or* **•ous)**
**nec•tar•ine**
**nec•ta•ry** (*plural* **•ries)**
**ned•dy** (*plural* **•dies)**
**née** (*or* **nee)** indicating maiden name

**need**
**need•ful**
**need•ful•ness**
**needi•ness**
**nee•dle**
**needle•cord**
**needle•craft**
**needle•fish** (*plural* **•fish** *or* **•fishes**)
**needle•ful**
**needle•point**
**need•less**
**need•less•ness**
**needle•woman** (*plural* **•women**)
**needle•work**
**need•ments**
**needn't**
**needy** (**needi•er, needi•est**)
**neep** *Dialect* turnip
**ne'er**
**ne'er-do-well**
**ne•fari•ous**
**nefari•ous•ness**
**ne•gate**
**ne•ga•tion**
**nega•tive**
**nega•tive•ness**
**negative-raising** grammar term
**nega•ti•vism**
**nega•tiv•ist**
**nega•tiv•is•tic**
**nega•tiv•ity**
**ne•ga•tor** (*or* **•gat•er**)
**ne•ga•to•ry**
**Neg•ev** (*or* **•eb**) Israeli desert
**ne•glect**
**ne•glect•er** (*or* **•glec•tor**)
**ne•glect•ful**
**ne•glect•ful•ly**
**ne•glect•ful•ness**
**neg•li•gee** (*or* **•gée, •gé**)
**neg•li•gence**
**neg•li•gent**
**neg•li•gibil•ity** (*or* **•gible•ness**)
**neg•li•gible**
**neg•li•gibly**
**ne•go•tiabil•ity**
**ne•go•tiable**
**ne•go•ti•ant**
**ne•go•ti•ate**
**ne•go•tia•tion**
**ne•go•tia•tor**
**Ne•gress**
**Ne•gril•lo** (*plural* **•los** *or* **•loes**) African Negroid people
**Neg•ri Sem•bi•lan** Malaysian state
**Ne•grit•ic** of Negroes or Negritos
**Ne•gri•to** (*plural* **•tos** *or* **•toes**) Asian Negroid people
**ne•gri•tude**
**Ne•gro** (*plural* **•groes**)
**Ne•groid**
**Ne•gro•ism**
**Ne•gro•phile** (*or* **•phil**)
**Ne•gro•phobe**
**Ne•gro•pho•bia**
**Neg•ro•pont** Greek island
**Ne•gros** Philippine island
**ne•gus** (*plural* **•guses**) spiced drink
**neigh** sound of a horse; *compare* **nay**
**neigh•bour** (*US* **•bor**)
**neigh•bour•hood** (*US* **•bor•**)
**neigh•bour•ing** (*US* **•bor•**)
**neigh•bour•li•ness** (*US* **•bor•**)
**neigh•bour•ly** (*US* **•bor•**)
**Neis•se** Polish river
**nei•ther**
**Nejd** (*or* **Najd**) Saudi Arabian province
**nek** mountain pass
**nek•ton** minute marine organisms
**nek•ton•ic**
**nel•ly** (*plural* **•lies**)
**Nel•son** Lancashire town; New Zealand port
**nel•son** wrestling hold
**ne•lum•bo** (*plural* **•bos**) plant
**nema•thel•minth** worm
**ne•mat•ic** chemistry term
**nema•to•cyst**
**nema•to•cys•tic**
**nema•tode**
**Nem•bu•tal** (*Trademark*)
**Ne•mea** ancient Greek valley
**Ne•mean**
**ne•mer•tean** (*or* **nem•er•tine**) marine worm
**ne•mesia** plant
**Nemesis** Greek goddess
**nem•esis** (*plural* **•eses**) retribution
**(nemonic)** *incorrect spelling of* **mnemonic**
**nene** goose
**neo•an•throp•ic**
**neo•ars•phena•mine**
**Neo•cene** geological term
**neo•clas•si•cal** (*or* **•sic**)
**neo•clas•si•cism**
**neo•clas•si•cist**
**neo•co•lo•nial**
**neo•co•lo•ni•al•ism**
**neo•co•lo•ni•al•ist**
**neo•dym•ium** chemical element
**Neo•gaea** zoogeographical area
**Neo•gaean**
**Neo•gene** geological term
**neo•im•pres•sion•ism**
**neo•lith**
**Neo•lith•ic**
**neo•logi•cal**
**neo•logi•cal•ly**
**ne•olo•gism** (*or* **ne•ol•ogy**; *plural* **•gisms** *or* **•ogies**)
**ne•olo•gist**
**ne•olo•gis•tic** (*or* **•ti•cal**)
**ne•olo•gis•ti•cal•ly**
**ne•olo•gize** (*or* **•gise**)
**ne•ol•ogy** *variant of* **neologism**
**neo•my•cin** antibiotic
**neon**
**neo•na•tal**
**neo•nate** newborn child
**neo•phyte** novice
**neo•phyt•ic**
**neo•plasm** tumour
**neo•plas•tic**
**neo•plas•ti•cism** style of painting
**neo•plas•ty** plastic surgery
**Neo-Platonism** philosophy
**Neo-Platonist**
**neo•prene** synthetic rubber
**ne•ot•enous**
**ne•ot•eny** zoology term
**neo•ter•ic** modern

**neo•teri•cal•ly**
**Neo•tropi•cal** zoogeographical term
**neo•type**
**Neo•zo•ic** geological term
**Ne•pal**
**Nepa•lese** (*plural* **•lese**)
**Ne•pali**
**ne•pen•the**
**ne•pen•thean**
**ne•per** unit
**neph•eline** (*or* **•elite**) mineral
**neph•elin•ite** rock
**neph•elom•eter** chemistry apparatus
**neph•elom•etry**
**neph•ew**
**nepho•gram**
**nepho•graph**
**nepho•logi•cal**
**ne•pholo•gist**
**ne•phol•ogy** study of clouds
**nepho•scope**
**ne•phral•gia** kidney pain
**ne•phral•gic**
**ne•phrec•to•my** (*plural* **•mies**) removal of kidney
**ne•phrid•ial**
**ne•phrid•ium** (*plural* **•phridia**) excretory organ
**neph•rite** mineral
**ne•phrit•ic** of the kidneys
**ne•phri•tis**
**ne•phrol•ogy**
**neph•ron**
**ne•phro•sis**
**ne•phrot•ic**
**ne•phroto•my** (*plural* **•mies**)
**ne plus ul•tra** *Latin* the perfect state
**ne•pot•ic** (*or* **•tis•tic**)
**nepo•tism**
**nepo•tist**
**Nep•tune** planet
**Neptune** Roman god
**Nep•tu•nian**
**nep•tu•nium** chemical element
**ne•ral** chemistry term
**Ne•reid** (*plural* **•rei•des**) Greek nymph
**ne•reis** worm
**ne•rit•ic** ecology term
**nero•li** oil
**ner•vate** having leaf veins
**nerve**
**nerve•less**
**nerve•less•ness**
**nerve-racking** (*or* **-wracking**)
**nervi•ly**
**nerv•ine** soothing the nerves
**nervi•ness**
**nerv•ous**
**nerv•ous•ness**
**ner•vure** biology term
**nervy** (**nervi•er, nervi•est**)
**nes•ci•ence** ignorance
**nes•ci•ent**
**nesh** *Dialect* timid
**Ness** Scottish lake
**ness** promontory
**nes•sel•rode** pudding
**nest**
**nest•er**
**nes•tle**
**nes•tler**
**nest•ling**
**Nestor** mythological character
**Nes•to•ri•an•ism** theological doctrine
**net** (**net•ting, net•ted**) mesh
**net** (*or* **nett; net•ting, net•ted**) remaining; earn as profit
**net•ball**
**neth•er**
**Neth•er•land•er**
**Neth•er•lands**
**nether•most**
**net•su•ke**
**nett** *variant spelling of* **net**
**net•ted**
**net•ting**
**net•tle**
**net•tle•some** causing irritation
**net•tly**
**net•ty** *Dialect* lavatory
**net•work**
**Neu•châ•tel** Swiss city and lake
**Neuf•châ•tel** French town; cheese
**neume** (*or* **neum**) musical symbol
**neu•ral**
**neu•ral•gia**
**neu•ral•gic**
**neu•ras•the•nia**
**neu•ras•then•ic**
**neu•ras•theni•cal•ly**
**neu•rec•to•my** (*plural* **•mies**)
**neu•rit•ic**
**neu•ri•tis**
**neu•ro•blast** embryonic cell
**neu•ro•coele** embryology term
**neu•ro•fi•bril**
**neu•ro•fi•bril•lar**
**neu•ro•gen•ic**
**neu•rog•lia** nerve tissue
**neu•ro•hy•pophy•sis** (*plural* **•ses**)
**neu•ro•lem•ma** (*or* **neu•ri•**) nerve sheath
**neu•ro•logi•cal**
**neu•rolo•gist**
**neu•rol•ogy**
**neu•ro•ma** (*plural* **•ma•ta** *or* **•mas**) tumour
**neu•roma•tous**
**neu•ro•mus•cu•lar**
**neu•rone** (*or* **•ron**) nerve cell
**neu•ron•ic**
**neu•ro•path** person with nervous disorder
**neu•ro•path•ic**
**neu•ro•pathi•cal•ly**
**neu•ro•pa•tholo•gist**
**neu•ro•pa•thol•ogy**
**neu•ropa•thy** disease of nervous system
**neu•ro•physio•logi•cal**
**neu•ro•physio•logi•cal•ly**
**neu•ro•physi•olo•gist**
**neu•ro•physi•ol•ogy**
**neu•ro•psy•chi•at•ric**
**neu•ro•psy•chia•trist**
**neu•ro•psy•chia•try**
**neu•rop•ter•an** (*or* **•on;** *plural* **•ter•ans** *or* **•tera**) insect
**neu•rop•ter•ous** (*or* **•ter•an**)
**neu•ro•sci•ence**
**neu•ro•sis** (*plural* **•ses**)
**neu•ro•sur•geon**
**neu•ro•sur•gery**
**neu•ro•sur•gi•cal**
**neu•ro•sur•gi•cal•ly**
**neu•rot•ic**

**neu•roti•cal•ly**
**neu•roti•cism**
**neu•roto•mist**
**neu•roto•my** (*plural* **•mies**) nerve surgery
**neu•ro•vas•cu•lar**
**Neuss** German city
**neu•ter**
**neu•tral**
**neu•tral•ism**
**neu•tral•ist**
**neu•tral•ity**
**neu•trali•za•tion** (*or* **•sa•tion**)
**neu•tral•ize** (*or* **•ise**)
**neu•tral•iz•er** (*or* **•is•er**)
**neu•tral•ly**
**neu•tret•to** (*plural* **•tos**) physics term
**neu•tri•no** (*plural* **•nos**) elementary particle
**neu•tron**
**neu•tro•phil** (*or* **•phile**) blood cell
**Neva** Russian river
**Ne•va•da**
**névé** mass of ice
**nev•er**
**never•more**
**never-never**
**never•the•less**
**Ne•vis** West Indian island
**ne•vus** *US spelling of* **naevus**
**new**
**New•ark** English town; US port
**new•born**
**New Bruns•wick**
**New•burg** cookery term
**New•bury**
**New•cas•tle** Australian port
**New•castle-under-Lyme**
**New•castle-upon-Tyne**
**new•comer**
**new•el**
**new•fan•gled**
**New•fie** *Slang* inhabitant of Newfoundland
**New•found•land**
**New•found•land•er**
**New•gate** former prison
**New•ham** London borough
**New•ha•ven**
**new•ish**
**new•ly**
**newly•wed**
**New•mar•ket**
**new•mar•ket** gambling game; riding coat
**new•ness**
**New Or•le•ans**
**New•port** Isle of Wight town; Welsh port
**news**
**news•agent**
**news•cast** *US* news broadcast
**news•caster**
**news•hawk**
**newsi•ness**
**news•letter**
**news•paper**
**news•paper•man** (*plural* **•men**)
**new•speak**
**news•print**
**news•reel**
**news•stand**
**news•worthi•ness**
**news•worthy**
**newsy** (**newsi•er, newsi•est**)
**newt**
**New•ton** Welsh town
**new•ton** unit
**Newton•abbey** Northern Irish town
**New•to•nian** of Isaac Newton
**New Zea•land**
**New Zea•land•er**
**next**
**next-door** (*adj*)
**nex•us** (*plural* **nex•us** *or* **nex•uses**)
**ngaio** (*plural* **ngaios**) tree
**ngo•ma** African drum
**Ngu•ni** language
**ngwee** Zambian coin
**nia•cin** vitamin
**Ni•aga•ra**
**Nia•mey** capital of Niger
**nib** (**nib•bing, nibbed**)
**nib•ble**
**nib•bler**
**nib•lick** golf club
**Nica•ra•gua**
**Nica•ra•guan**
**nic•co•lite** mineral
**Nice** French city
**nice**
**Ni•cene Creed**
**nice•ness**
**ni•cety** (*plural* **•ceties**)
**niche**
**Ni•chrome** (*Trademark*)
**nic•ish**
**nick**
**nick•el** (**•el•ling, •elled**; *US* **•el•ing, •eled**)
**nick•el•ic**
**nick•el•if•er•ous**
**nickel•odeon**
**nick•el•ous**
**nick•er**
**nick•nack** *variant spelling of* **knickknack**
**nick•name**
**Nico•bar** Indian islands
**Nicol prism**
**Nico•sia** Cypriot capital
**ni•co•tia•na** plant
**nico•tina•mide** vitamin
**nico•tine**
**nico•tin•ic**
**nico•tin•ism**
**nic•ti•tate** (*or* **nic•tate**) to blink
**nic•ti•ta•tion** (*or* **nic•ta•tion**)
**ni•dal**
**niddle-noddle** nod rapidly
**nide** *variant of* **nye**
**ni•dico•lous** ornithology term
**nidi•fi•cate** build nest
**nidi•fi•ca•tion**
**ni•difu•gous** ornithology term
**nidi•fy** (**•fies, •fy•ing, •fied**) build nest
**nid-nod** (**-nod•ding, -nod•ded**)
**ni•dus** (*plural* **•di**)
**niece**
**ni•el•list**
**ni•el•lo** (*noun, plural* **•li** *or* **•los**; *verb* **•lo•ing, •loed**) engraving term
**Nier•stein•er** wine
**Nie•tzschean**
**Nie•tzsche•ism** (*or* **•tzschean•ism**) philosophy
**nieve** *Dialect* fist
**Niè•vre** French department

**niff**
**niffy (niffi•er, niffi•est)**
**nif•ti•ly**
**nif•ti•ness**
**nif•ty (•ti•er, •ti•est)**
**Ni•ger**
**Ni•geria**
**Ni•gerian**
**nig•gard**
**nig•gard•li•ness**
**nig•gard•ly**
**nig•ger**
**nig•gle**
**nig•gler**
**nig•gling**
**nig•gly**
**nigh**
**night**
**night•cap**
**night•club**
**night•dress**
**night•fall**
**night•gown**
**night•hawk**
**nightie** (*or* **nighty**; *plural* **nighties)**
**night•in•gale**
**night•jar**
**night•life**
**night-light**
**night•long**
**night•ly**
**night•mare**
**night•mar•ish**
**night•rider**
**night•shade**
**night•shirt**
**night•spot**
**night-time**
**night•wear**
**ni•gres•cence**
**ni•gres•cent** blackish
**ni•gro•sine** (*or* **•sin)** pigment
**ni•hil** *Latin* nothing
**ni•hil•ism**
**ni•hil•ist**
**ni•hil•is•tic**
**ni•hil•ity**
**Nii•ga•ta** Japanese port
**Nij•megen** Dutch town
**Nik•ko** Japanese town
**Ni•ko•la•yev** Ukrainian city
**nil**
**nil de•spe•ran•dum** *Latin* never despair
**Nile**
**nil•gai** (*or* **•ghau**; *plural* **•gai, •gais,** *or* **•ghau, •ghaus)** antelope
**Ni•lot•ic**
**nim** game
**nim•ble**
**nim•ble•ness**
**nimble•wit** *US* clever person
**nim•bly**
**nim•bo•stra•tus** (*plural* **•ti)**
**nim•bus** (*plural* **•bi** *or* **•buses)**
**Nîmes** French city
**niminy-piminy** (*or* **miminy-)**
**Nimrod** biblical hunter
**nin•com•poop**
**nine**
**nine•fold**
**nine•pins**
**nine•teen**
**nine•teenth**
**nine•ti•eth**
**nine•ty** (*plural* **•ties)**
**Ni•neveh** Assyrian capital
**Ning•po** Chinese port
**Ning•sia Hui** Chinese region
**nin•ny** (*plural* **•nies)**
**ni•non** fabric
**ninth**
**nio•bic**
**nio•bite**
**nio•bium** chemical element
**nio•bous**
**nip (nip•ping, nipped)**
**nipa** palm tree
**Nipi•gon** Canadian lake
**Nip•is•sing** Canadian lake
**nip•per**
**nip•pi•ly**
**nip•ple**
**nipple•wort** plant
**Nip•pon**
**Nip•pon•ese** (*plural* **•ese)**
**Nip•pur** Babylonian city
**nip•py (•pi•er, •pi•est)**
**nir•va•na**
**nir•va•nic**
**Niš** Yugoslav town
**Ni•sha•pur** Iranian town
**Ni•shi•no•mi•ya** Japanese city
**nisi** legal term
**nisi pri•us** legal term
**ni•sus** (*plural* **•sus)** striving
**nit**
**ni•ter** *US spelling of* **nitre**
**Ni•terói** Brazilian port
**ni•tid** bright
**ni•tra•mine**
**ni•trate**
**ni•tra•tion**
**ni•tre** (*US* **•ter)**
**ni•tric** containing nitrogen
**ni•tride** chemical compound
**ni•trid•ing** metallurgy term
**ni•tri•fi•able**
**ni•tri•fi•ca•tion**
**ni•tri•fy (•fies, •fy•ing, •fied)**
**ni•trile**
**ni•trite**
**ni•tro•bac•te•ria** (*sing.* **•rium)**
**ni•tro•ben•zene**
**ni•tro•cel•lu•lose**
**ni•tro•chlo•ro•form**
**ni•tro•gen**
**ni•trog•eni•za•tion** (*or* **•sa•tion)**
**ni•trog•en•ize** (*or* **•ise)**
**ni•trog•enous**
**ni•tro•glyc•er•in** (*or* **•ine)**
**ni•trom•eter**
**ni•tro•methane**
**ni•tro•met•ric**
**ni•tro•par•af•fin**
**ni•trosa•mine**
**ni•tro•so** (*or* **•syl)**
**ni•trous**
**nit•ty (•ti•er, •ti•est)**
**nitty-gritty**
**nit•wit**
**Niue** Pacific island
**ni•val** of snow
**ni•va•tion** geology term
**niv•eous** resembling snow
**Ni•ver•nais** former French province
**nix** (*fem* **nixie)** water sprite
**nix•er** *Irish* spare-time job
**Ni•zam** Indian title
**ni•zam** former Turkish soldier

**Nizh•ni** (*or* **•nii) Nov•go•rod** Russian city
**Njord** (*or* **Njorth**) Norse god
**no** (*plural* **noes** *or* **nos**)
**No** (*or* **Noh**) Japanese drama
**Noa•chian** (*or* **No•ach•ic**) of Noah
**nob** *Slang* wealthy person; cribbage term; *compare* **knob**
**no-ball**
**nob•ble**
**nob•bler**
**nob•but** *Dialect* nothing but
**no•belium** chemical element
**no•bili•ary**
**no•bil•ity** (*plural* **•ities**)
**no•ble**
**no•ble•man** (*plural* **•men**)
**no•ble•ness**
**no•blesse oblige** *French* nobility obliges
**noble•woman** (*plural* **•women**)
**no•bly**
**no•body** (*plural* **•bodies**)
**no•ci•cep•tive** causing pain
**nock** notch on arrow
**noc•tam•bu•lism** (*or* **•la•tion**)
**noc•tam•bu•list**
**noc•ti•lu•ca** (*plural* **•cae**) protozoan
**noc•ti•lu•cence**
**noc•ti•lu•cent**
**noc•tu•id** moth
**noc•tule** bat
**noc•turn** part of Catholic matins; *compare* **nocturne**
**noc•tur•nal**
**noc•tur•nal•ity**
**noc•tur•nal•ly**
**noc•turne** musical piece; *compare* **nocturn**
**nocu•ous**
**nod** (**nod•ding, nod•ded**)
**no•dal**
**no•dal•ity**
**nod•dle**
**nod•dy** (*plural* **•dies**) bird; fool
**node**
**nodi•cal** astronomy term
**no•dose** (*or* **•dous**)
**no•dos•ity**
**nodu•lar** (*or* **•lose, •lous**)
**nod•ule**
**no•dus** (*plural* **•di**) problematic situation
**Noel** (*or* **Noël**)
**no•esis** intellectual functioning
**no•et•ic**
**nog**
**nog•gin** measure of spirits
**nog•ging** building term
**Noh** *variant spelling of* **No**
**noil** textile fibres
**noise**
**noise•less**
**noise•less•ness**
**noi•sette**
**noisi•ly**
**noisi•ness**
**noi•some** offensive
**noi•some•ness**
**noisy** (**noisi•er, noisi•est**)
**no•lens vo•lens** *Latin* willing or unwilling
**noli-me-tangere** warning; plant
**nol•le pros•equi** legal term
**nolo con•ten•de•re** legal term
**noma** medical term
**no•mad**
**no•mad•ic**
**no•madi•cal•ly**
**no•mad•ism**
**no-man's-land**
**nom•arch**
**nom•ar•chy** (*or* **nome**; *plural* **•chies** *or* **nomes**) Greek province
**nom•bril** heraldic term
**nom de guerre** (*plural* **noms de guerre**) assumed name
**nom de plume** (*plural* **noms de plume**) pen name
**nome** *variant of* **nomarchy**
**no•men** (*plural* **nomi•na**) ancient Roman's name
**no•men•cla•tor** inventor of names
**no•men•cla•ture**
**nomi•nal**
**nomi•nal•ism**
**nomi•nal•ist**
**nomi•nal•is•tic**
**nomi•nal•ly**
**nomi•nate**
**nomi•na•tion**
**nomi•na•tive**
**nomi•na•tor**
**nomi•nee**
**no•mism** theology term
**no•mis•tic**
**no•moc•ra•cy** (*plural* **•cies**) government based on law
**nomo•gram** (*or* **•graph**) type of graph
**no•mog•ra•pher**
**nomo•graph•ic**
**nomo•graphi•cal**
**no•mo•graphi•cal•ly**
**no•mog•ra•phy** (*plural* **•phies**)
**no•mo•logi•cal**
**no•mo•logi•cal•ly**
**no•molo•gist**
**no•mol•ogy** science of law
**nomo•thet•ic** (*or* **•theti•cal**) giving laws
**no•nage**
**no•na•genar•ian**
**nona•gon**
**non•ago•nal**
**non•aligned**
**non•ap•pear•ance**
**non•at•tend•ance**
**non•at•tribu•tive**
**nonce**
**non•cha•lance**
**non•cha•lant**
**non-com** *Slang* noncommissioned officer
**non•com•bat•ant**
**non•com•mis•sioned**
**non•com•mit•tal**
**non•com•mit•tal•ly**
**non•com•pli•ance**
**non com•pos men•tis** *Latin* of unsound mind
**non•con•cur•rent**
**non•con•duc•tor**
**non•con•form•ism**
**Non•con•form•ist** dissenting Protestant
**non•con•form•ist** one who does not conform
**Non•con•form•ity** (*or* **•ism**)
**non•con•form•ity**
**non•con•sti•tu•tion•al**
**non•con•ta•gious**

**non•con•tribu•ting**
**non•con•tribu•tory**
**non•co•op•era•tion**
**non•co•op•era•tive**
**non•co•op•era•tor**
**non•cor•rod•ing**
**non•crea•tive**
**non•de•nomi•na•tion•al**
**non•de•script**
**non•dis•junc•tion**
**non•drink•er**
**none**
**non•ed•ible**
**non•ego** philosophy term
**non•en•tity** (*plural* **•tities**)
**non•equiva•lence**
**nones** Roman date; canonical hour
**non•es•sen•tial**
**none•such** (*or* **non•**)
**non•et**
**none•the•less**
**non•ethi•cal**
**non•event**
**non•ex•ist•ence**
**non•ex•ist•ent**
**non•ex•plo•sive**
**non•fac•tual**
**non•fea•sance** legal term
**non•fer•rous**
**non•fic•tion**
**non•fic•tion•al**
**non•flam•mable**
**nong** *Austral* stupid person
**non•har•mon•ic**
**non•iden•ti•cal**
**non•idio•mat•ic**
**no•nil•lion** $10^{54}$
**no•nil•lionth**
**non•in•dus•trial**
**non•in•fec•tious**
**non•in•flam•mable**
**non•inter•ven•tion**
**non•inter•ven•tion•al**
**non•inter•ven•tion•ist**
**non•in•toxi•cat•ing**
**non•ir•ri•tant**
**non•join•der** legal term
**non•judg•men•tal** (*or* **•judge•**)
**non•ju•ror** one refusing to take oath
**non li•cet** *Latin* unlawful
**non•ma•lig•nant**
**non•medi•cal**
**non•mem•ber**
**non•met•al**
**non•met•al•lic**
**non•op•er•able**
**non•op•era•tive**
**non•pa•reil** unsurpassed
**non•par•ous** never having given birth
**non•par•tici•pat•ing**
**non•par•ti•san** (*or* **•zan**)
**non•par•ty**
**non•plus** (*noun, plural* **•pluses**; *verb* **•plusses, •plus•sing, •plussed**; *US* **•pluses, •plus•ing, •plused**)
**non•poi•son•ous**
**non•po•liti•cal**
**non•pro•duc•tive**
**non•pro•duc•tive•ness**
**non•pro•duc•tiv•ity**
**non•pro•gres•sive**
**non•pro•lif•era•tion**
**non-pros** (**-prosses, -prossing, -prossed**) legal term
**non pro•sequi•tur** legal term
**non•rep•re•sen•ta•tion•al**
**non•resi•dence** (*or* **•den•cy**)
**non•resi•dent**
**non•resi•den•tial**
**non•re•sis•tant**
**non•re•stric•tive**
**non•re•turn•able**
**non•rig•id**
**non•sched•uled**
**non•sec•ta•rian**
**non•sense**
**non•sen•si•cal**
**non•sen•si•cal•ly**
**non•sen•si•cal•ness** (*or* **•ity**)
**non se•qui•tur**
**non•slip**
**non•smok•er**
**non•spe•cif•ic**
**non•stand•ard**
**non•stand•ard•ized** (*or* **•ised**)
**non•start•er**
**non•sta•tive** linguistics term
**non•stick**
**non•stimu•lat•ing**
**non•stop**
**non•stra•te•gic**
**non-striker**
**non•such** *variant spelling of* **nonesuch**
**non•suit**
**non•swim•mer**
**non•tech•ni•cal**
**non•tox•ic**
**non•typi•cal**
**non-U**
**non•un•ion**
**non•un•ion•ism**
**non•ver•bal**
**non•vio•lence**
**non•vio•lent**
**non•vot•er**
**non-White**
**noo•dle**
**nook**
**noon**
**noon•day**
**no-one** (*or* **no one**)
**noon•ing** *US* midday break
**noon•time** (*or* **•tide**)
**noose**
**no•pal** cactus
**no-par** (*adj*)
**nope** *Slang* no
**nor**
**nor•adrena•line**
**Nor•dic**
**Nor•folk**
**no•ria** waterwheel
**Nori•cum** Celtic Alpine kingdom
**nor•ite** rock
**nork** *Austral* breast
**norm**
**Nor•ma** constellation
**nor•mal**
**nor•mal•ity** (*or esp. US* **•cy**)
**nor•mali•za•tion** (*or* **•sa•tion**)
**nor•mal•ize** (*or* **•ise**)
**nor•mal•ly**
**Nor•man**
**Nor•man•dy**
**nor•ma•tive**
**Norn** Norse goddess
**Norr•kö•ping** Swedish port
**Norse**
**Norse•man** (*plural* **•men**)
**north**
**North•al•ler•ton** Yorkshire town
**North•amp•ton**

**North•amp•ton•shire**
**north•bound**
**north•country•man** (*plural* **•men**)
**north•east**
**north•easter**
**north•easter•ly** (*plural* **•lies**)
**north•eastern**
**north•eastward**
**nor•ther•ly** (*plural* **•lies**)
**north•ern**
**north•ern•er**
**north•ern•most**
**north•ing** navigation term
**north-northeast**
**north-northwest**
**North Pole**
**North•um•ber•land** county
**North•um•bria** region
**North•um•brian**
**north•ward** (*adj*)
**north•wards** (*adv*)
**north•west**
**north•wester**
**north•wester•ly** (*plural* **•lies**)
**north•western**
**north•westward**
**North•wich** Cheshire town
**Nor•way**
**Nor•we•gian**
**Nor•wich**
**nose**
**nose•bag**
**nose•band**
**nose•bleed**
**nose-dive** (*verb*)
**nose•gay**
**nos•ey** *variant spelling of* **nosy**
**nosh**
**no-side** rugby term
**nosi•ly**
**nosi•ness**
**nos•ing**
**no•so•co•mial** medical term
**no•sog•ra•pher**
**no•so•graph•ic**
**no•sog•ra•phy** written description of disease
**noso•logi•cal**
**noso•logi•cal•ly**
**no•solo•gist**
**no•sol•ogy** classification of diseases
**nos•tal•gia**
**nos•tal•gic**
**nos•tal•gi•cal•ly**
**nos•toc** alga
**nos•to•log•ic**
**nos•tol•ogy** study of senility
**nos•tril**
**nos•trum** quack medicine
**nosy** (*or* **nos•ey**, **nosi•er**, **nosi•est**)
**nosy-parker**
**not**
**nota bene** *Latin* note well
**no•tabil•ity** (*plural* **•ities**)
**no•table**
**no•table•ness**
**no•tably**
**no•tar•ial**
**no•ta•rize** (*or* **•rise**)
**no•ta•ry** (*plural* **•ries**)
**no•tate**
**no•ta•tion**
**no•ta•tion•al**
**notch**
**note**
**note•book**
**note•case**
**not•ed**
**note•let**
**note•paper**
**note•worthi•ly**
**note•worthi•ness**
**note•worthy**
**noth•ing**
**noth•ing•ness**
**no•tice**
**no•tice•abil•ity**
**no•tice•able**
**no•tice•ably**
**no•ti•fi•able**
**no•ti•fi•ca•tion**
**no•ti•fi•er**
**no•ti•fy** (**•fies**, **•fy•ing**, **•fied**)
**no-tillage** farming system
**not•ing**
**no•tion**
**no•tion•al**
**no•tion•al•ly**
**no•titia** ecclesiastical register
**no•to•chord** zoology term
**no•to•chord•al**
**No•to•gaea** zoogeographical term
**No•to•gaean**
**no•to•ri•ety** (*or* **no•to•ri•ous•ness**)
**no•to•ri•ous**
**no•tor•nis** bird
**no•to•ther•ium** (*plural* **•theria**) extinct marsupial
**no•tour** legal term
**No•tre Dame**
**no trump** bridge term
**Not•ting•ham**
**Not•ting•ham•shire**
**no•tum** (*plural* **•ta**) entomology term
**No•tus** mythological wind
**not•with•stand•ing**
**Nou•ak•chott** capital of Mauritania
**nou•gat**
**nought** (*US* **naught**) zero; *compare* **naught**
**nou•menon** (*plural* **•mena**) philosophy term
**noun**
**noun•al**
**nour•ish**
**nour•ish•er**
**nour•ish•ing•ly**
**nour•ish•ment**
**nous** *Slang* common sense
**nou•veau riche** (*plural* **nou•veaux riches**)
**nova** (*plural* **novae** *or* **novas**) star
**no•vacu•lite** rock
**No•va•ra** Italian city
**Nova Sco•tia**
**no•va•tion** legal term
**nov•el**
**nov•el•ese**
**nov•el•ette**
**nov•el•et•tish**
**nov•el•ist**
**nov•el•is•tic**
**nov•eli•za•tion** (*or* **•sa•tion**)
**nov•el•ize** (*or* **•ise**)
**no•vel•la** (*plural* **•las** *or* **•le**)
**nov•el•ty** (*plural* **•ties**)
**No•vem•ber**
**no•vena** (*plural* **•venae**) Catholic devotion
**Nov•go•rod** Russian city
**nov•ice**
**no•vi•ti•ate** (*or* **•ci•ate**)
**No•vo•caine** (*Trademark*)

**No•vo•kuz•netsk** Russian city
**No•vo•si•birsk** Russian city
**now**
**nowa•days**
**no•way**
**Now•el** (*or* **•ell**) *Archaic* Noel
**no•where**
**nowt** *Dialect* nothing
**Nox** Roman goddess
**nox•ious**
**nox•ious•ness**
**no•yade** execution by drowning
**noy•au** (*plural* **•aux**) liqueur
**noz•zle**
**nth**
**nu•ance**
**nub**
**Nuba** (*plural* **Nubas** *or* **Nuba**) Sudanese people
**nub•bin** *US* undeveloped fruit
**nub•ble**
**nub•bly** (*or* **•by**)
**nu•becu•la** (*plural* **•lae**) small galaxy
**Nu•bia**
**Nu•bian**
**nu•bile**
**nu•bil•ity**
**nu•cel•lar**
**nu•cel•lus** (*plural* **•li**) botany term
**nu•cha** (*plural* **•chae**) nape of neck
**nu•chal**
**nu•clear**
**nu•clease** enzyme
**nu•cleate**
**nu•clea•tion**
**nu•clea•tor**
**nu•clei** *plural of* **nucleus**
**nu•cleic**
**nu•clein** protein
**nu•cleo•lar** (*or* **•late, •lat•ed, •loid**)
**nu•cleo•lus** (*plural* **•li**) part of cell nucleus
**nu•cleon**
**nu•cleon•ic**
**nu•cleoni•cal•ly**
**nu•cleon•ics** branch of physics
**nu•cleo•phile**
**nu•cleo•phil•ic**
**nu•cleo•plasm**
**nu•cleo•plas•mic** (*or* **•mat•ic**)
**nu•cleo•pro•tein**
**nu•cleo•side** biochemical compound
**nu•cleo•tide** biochemical compound
**nu•cleus** (*plural* **•clei** *or* **•cleuses**)
**nu•clide** type of atom
**nude**
**nude•ness**
**nudge**
**nudg•er**
**nu•di•branch** mollusc
**nu•di•caul** (*or* **•cau•lous**) botany term
**nud•ism**
**nud•ist**
**nu•dity** (*plural* **•dities**)
**Nue•vo León** Mexican state
**nu•ga•tory**
**nug•gar** sailing boat
**nug•get**
**nug•gety**
**nui•sance**
**nuke** *Slang* nuclear bomb
**Nu•ku'a•lo•fa** Tongan capital
**null**
**nul•lah** Indian stream
**nulla-nulla** Aboriginal club
**nul•li•fi•ca•tion**
**nul•li•fi•ca•tion•ist**
**nul•li•fid•ian** sceptic
**nul•li•fi•er**
**nul•li•fy** (**•fies, •fy•ing, •fied**)
**nul•lipa•ra** (*plural* **•rae**) obstetrics term
**nul•lipa•rous**
**nul•li•pore** seaweed
**nul•lity** (*plural* **•lities**)
**Nu•man•tia** ancient Spanish city
**numb**
**num•bat** marsupial
**num•ber** numeral
**numb•er** more numb
**num•ber•less**
**number•plate**
**numb•fish** (*plural* **•fish** *or* **•fishes**)
**numb•ness**
**numb•skull** *variant spelling of* **numskull**
**num•dah** (*or* **nam•**) Indian fabric
**nu•men** (*plural* **•mi•na**) Roman deity
**nu•mer•able**
**nu•mer•ably**
**nu•mera•cy**
**nu•mer•al**
**nu•mer•ary** of numbers; *compare* **nummary**
**nu•mer•ate**
**nu•mera•tion**
**nu•mera•tive**
**nu•mera•tor**
**nu•meri•cal** (*or* **•mer•ic**)
**nu•meri•cal•ly**
**nu•mero•logi•cal**
**nu•mer•ol•ogy** divination by numbers
**nu•mer•ous**
**nu•mer•ous•ness**
**Nu•midia** ancient African country
**Nu•mid•ian**
**nu•mi•nous** awe-inspiring
**nu•mis•mat•ic**
**nu•mis•mat•ics** (*or* **•ma•tol•ogy**)
**nu•mis•ma•tist** (*or* **•tolo•gist**)
**num•ma•ry** of coins; *compare* **numerary**
**num•mu•lar**
**num•mu•lite** fossil
**num•mu•lit•ic**
**num•skull** (*or* **numb•**)
**nun**
**nuna•tak** mountain peak
**Nunc Di•mit•tis** canticle
**nun•cia•ture**
**nun•cio** (*plural* **•cios**)
**nun•cle** *Dialect* uncle
**nun•cu•pa•tive** legal term
**Nun•eaton**
**nun•hood**
**nun•like**
**nun•nery** (*plural* **•neries**)
**Nupe** (*plural* **Nupe** *or* **Nupes**) Nigerian people
**nup•tial**
**Nu•rem•berg**

**Nuri** (*plural* **Nuris** *or* **Nuri**) Indo-European people
**Nu•ri•stan** Afghan region
**nurse**
**nurse•maid**
**nurse•ry** (*plural* **•ries**)
**nursery•man** (*plural* **•men**)
**nurs•ing**
**nurs•ling** (*or* **nurse•**) nursed child
**nur•tur•able**
**nur•ture**
**nur•tur•er**
**nut** (**nut•ting, nut•ted**)
**nu•tant** botany term
**nu•ta•tion**
**nu•ta•tion•al**
**nut•brown**
**nut•case**
**nut•cracker**
**nut•gall**
**nut•hatch**
**nut•let**
**nut•meg**
**nu•tria** coypu fur
**nu•tri•ent**
**nu•tri•ment**
**nu•tri•tion**
**nu•tri•tion•al** (*or* **•ary**)
**nu•tri•tion•ist**
**nu•tri•tious**
**nu•tri•tious•ness**
**nu•tri•tive**
**nut•shell**
**nut•ted**
**nut•ter**
**nut•ti•ly**
**nut•ti•ness**
**nut•ting**
**nut•ty** (**•ti•er, •ti•est**)
**nut•wood**
**nux vomi•ca**
**nuz•zle**
**nya•la** (*plural* **•la** *or* **•las**) antelope
**Nyan•ja** (*plural* **•ja** *or* **•jas**) African people
**Ny•asa•land** *former name of* **Malawi**
**nyc•ta•gi•na•ceous** botany term
**nyc•ta•lo•pia** night blindness
**nyc•ti•nas•tic**
**nyc•ti•nas•ty** botany term
**nyc•ti•trop•ic**
**nyc•tit•ro•pism** botany term
**nyc•to•pho•bia**
**nyc•to•pho•bic**
**nye** (*or* **nide**) flock of pheasants
**ny•lon**
**nymph**
**nym•pha** (*plural* **•phae**) anatomy term
**nym•phaea•ceous** botany term
**nym•phal** (*or* **•phean**)
**nym•pha•lid** butterfly
**nymph•et**
**nymph•like**
**nym•pho** (*plural* **•phos**)
**nym•pho•lep•sy** (*plural* **•sies**) violent emotion
**nym•pho•lept**
**nym•pho•lep•tic**
**nym•pho•ma•nia**
**nym•pho•ma•ni•ac**
**nym•pho•ma•nia•cal**
**nys•tag•mic**
**nys•tag•mus** eye condition
**nys•ta•tin** antibiotic
**Nyx** Greek goddess

# O

**O** exclamation; *used chiefly in religious and poetic contexts*
**oaf** (*plural* **oafs**)
**oaf•ish**
**oaf•ish•ness**
**oak**
**oak•en**
**Oak•ham** Leicestershire town
**Oak•land** US port
**oakum** fibre
**oar**
**oared**
**oar•fish** (*plural* **•fish** *or* **•fishes**)
**oar•lock**
**oars•man** (*plural* **•men**)
**oars•man•ship**
**oasis** (*plural* **oases**)
**oast**
**oast•house**
**oat**
**oat•cake**
**oat•en**
**oath** (*plural* **oaths**)
**oat•meal**
**Oaxa•ca** Mexican state
**oba** African chief
**Oban** Scottish port
**ob•bli•ga•to** (*or* **ob•li•**; *plural* **•tos** *or* **•ti**) musical term
**ob•con•ic** botany term
**ob•cor•date** botany term
**ob•du•ra•cy** (*or* **•rate•ness**)
**ob•du•rate**
**obeah** *variant of* **obi**
**obedi•ence**
**obedi•ent**
**obedi•en•tia•ry** (*plural* **•ries**) holder of monastic office
**obei•sance**
**obei•sant**
**ob•elis•cal**
**ob•elisk**
**ob•elis•koid**
**ob•elize** (*or* **•elise**)
**ob•elus** (*plural* **•eli**) text symbol
**Ober•am•mer•gau** German village
**Ober•hau•sen** German city
**Ober•land** Swiss region
**Ober•on** satellite of Uranus
**Oberon** fairy king
**obese**
**obesity** (*or* **obese•ness**)
**obey**
**obey•er**
**ob•fus•cate**
**ob•fus•ca•tion**
**ob•fus•ca•tory**
**obi** (*plural* **obis** *or* **obi**) Japanese sash
**obi** (*or* **obeah**; *plural* **obis** *or* **obeahs**) witchcraft

**obit** obituary; memorial service
**obi•ter dic•tum** (*plural* **obi•ter dic•ta**) *Latin* something said in passing
**obi•tu•ar•ist**
**obi•tu•ary** (*plural* **•aries**)
**ob•ject**
**ob•jec•ti•fi•ca•tion**
**ob•jec•ti•fy** (**•fies, •fy•ing, •fied**)
**ob•jec•tion**
**ob•jec•tion•abil•ity** (*or* **•able•ness**)
**ob•jec•tion•able**
**ob•jec•tion•ably**
**ob•jec•tive**
**ob•jec•tiv•ism**
**ob•jec•tiv•ist**
**ob•jec•tiv•is•tic**
**ob•jec•tiv•is•ti•cal•ly**
**ob•jec•tiv•ity** (*or* **•tive•ness**)
**ob•jet d'art** (*plural* **ob•jets d'art**)
**ob•jet trou•vé** (*plural* **ob•jets trou•vés**) *French* object considered aesthetically
**ob•jur•gate** scold
**ob•jur•ga•tion**
**ob•jur•ga•tor**
**ob•jur•ga•tory** (*or* **•tive**)
**ob•lan•ceo•late** botany term
**ob•last** Russian administrative division
**ob•late**
**ob•la•tion**
**ob•la•tory** (*or* **•tion•al**)
**ob•li•gable**
**ob•li•gate**
**ob•li•ga•tion**
**ob•li•ga•tion•al**
**ob•liga•tive**
**ob•li•ga•to** *variant spelling of* **obbligato**
**ob•li•ga•tor**
**ob•liga•to•ri•ly**
**ob•liga•tory**
**oblige**
**ob•li•gee** creditor
**oblig•er**
**oblig•ing**
**ob•li•gor** debtor
**oblique**
**oblique•ness**
**obliqui•tous**
**obliqui•ty** (*plural* **•ties**)
**oblit•erate**
**oblit•era•tion**
**oblit•era•tive**
**oblit•era•tor**
**oblivi•on**
**oblivi•ous**
**ob•livi•ous•ness**
**ob•long**
**ob•lo•quy** (*plural* **•quies**)
**ob•nox•ious**
**ob•nox•ious•ness**
**ob•nu•bil•ate** to darken
**oboe**
**obo•ist**
**obo•lus** (*or* **obol**; *plural* **•li** *or* **obols**) Greek unit; coin
**ob•ovate** botany term
**ob•ovoid** botany term
**ob•rep•tion** obtaining by deceit
**ob•scene**
**ob•scen•ity** (*plural* **•ities**)
**ob•scur•ant**
**ob•scu•rant•ism**
**ob•scu•rant•ist**
**ob•scu•ra•tion**
**ob•scure**
**ob•scu•rity** (*plural* **•rities**)
**ob•se•quent**
**ob•se•quies** (*sing.* **•quy**)
**ob•se•qui•ous**
**ob•se•qui•ous•ness**
**ob•serv•able**
**ob•serv•able•ness** (*or* **•abil•ity**)
**ob•serv•ably**
**ob•ser•vance**
**ob•ser•vant**
**ob•ser•va•tion**
**ob•ser•va•tion•al**
**ob•ser•va•tion•al•ly**
**ob•ser•va•tory** (*plural* **•tories**)
**ob•serve**
**ob•serv•er**
**ob•sess**
**ob•ses•sion**
**ob•ses•sion•al**
**ob•ses•sive**
**ob•ses•sive•ness**
**ob•sid•ian**
**ob•so•lesce**
**ob•so•les•cence**
**ob•so•les•cent**
**ob•so•lete**
**ob•so•lete•ness**
**ob•sta•cle**
**ob•stet•ric** (*or* **•ri•cal**)
**ob•stet•ri•cal•ly**
**ob•ste•tri•cian**
**ob•stet•rics**
**ob•sti•na•cy** (*plural* **•cies**)
**ob•sti•nate**
**ob•sti•pa•tion**
**ob•strep•er•ous**
**ob•strep•er•ous•ness**
**ob•struct**
**ob•struct•er** (*or* **•struc•tor**)
**ob•struc•tion**
**ob•struc•tion•al**
**ob•struc•tion•ism**
**ob•struc•tion•ist**
**ob•struc•tive**
**ob•struc•tive•ness**
**ob•stru•ent** medical term
**ob•tain**
**ob•tain•abil•ity**
**ob•tain•able**
**ob•tain•er**
**ob•tain•ment**
**ob•tect** entomology term
**ob•trude**
**ob•trud•er**
**ob•tru•sion**
**ob•tru•sive**
**ob•tru•sive•ness**
**ob•tund** deaden
**ob•tu•rate** block up
**ob•tu•ra•tion**
**ob•tu•ra•tor**
**ob•tuse**
**ob•tuse•ness**
**ob•verse**
**ob•ver•sion**
**ob•vert** logic term
**ob•vi•ate**
**ob•via•tion**
**ob•vi•ous**
**ob•vi•ous•ly**
**ob•vi•ous•ness**
**ob•vo•lute**
**ob•vo•lu•tion**
**ob•vo•lu•tive**
**oca** plant
**oca•ri•na** musical instrument
**oc•ca•sion**
**oc•ca•sion•al**

**oc•ca•sion•al•ism** philosophical theory
**oc•ca•sion•al•ly**
**Oc•ci•dent** Europe and America
**oc•ci•dent** the west
**Oc•ci•den•tal** (*noun*)
**oc•ci•den•tal** (*or* **Oc•**; *adj*)
**Oc•ci•den•tal•ism**
**Oc•ci•den•tal•ist**
**oc•ci•den•tali•za•tion** (*or* **Oc•**, **•sa•tion**)
**oc•ci•den•tal•ize** (*or* **Oc•**, **•ise**)
**oc•ci•den•tal•ly** (*or* **Oc•**)
**oc•cipi•tal**
**oc•ci•put** (*plural* **•puts** *or* **•cipi•ta**) anatomy term
**oc•clude**
**oc•clud•ent**
**oc•clu•sal**
**oc•clu•sion**
**oc•clu•sive**
**oc•clu•sive•ness**
**oc•cult**
**oc•cul•ta•tion** astronomy term
**oc•cult•ism**
**oc•cult•ist**
**oc•cu•pan•cy** (*plural* **•cies**)
**oc•cu•pant**
**oc•cu•pa•tion**
**oc•cu•pa•tion•al**
**oc•cu•pi•er**
**oc•cu•py** (**•pies**, **•py•ing**, **•pied**)
**oc•cur** (**•cur•ring**, **•curred**)
**oc•cur•rence**
**oc•cur•rent**
**ocean**
**ocean•ar•ium** (*plural* **•ar•iums** *or* **•aria**)
**ocean-going**
**Oceania** Pacific islands
**Oce•an•ian**
**Ocean•ic** of Oceania
**ocean•ic** of the ocean
**Ocea•nid** (*plural* **Ocea•nids** *or* **Oceani•des**) Greek nymph
**ocean•og•ra•pher**
**oceano•graph•ic** (*or* **•graphi•cal**)
**oceano•graphi•cal•ly**
**ocean•og•ra•phy**
**ocean•ol•ogy**
**ocel•lar**
**oc•el•late** (*or* **•lated**) having ocelli; *compare* **oscillate**; **osculate**
**oc•el•la•tion**
**ocel•lus** (*plural* **•li**) simple eye
**oc•elot**
**och** *Scot* exclamation
**ocher** *US spelling of* **ochre**
**och•loc•ra•cy** (*plural* **•cies**) mob rule
**och•lo•crat**
**och•lo•crat•ic**
**och•lo•pho•bia** fear of crowds
**ochre** (*US* **ocher**)
**ochre•ous** (*or* **ochrous**, **ochry**; *US* **ocher•ous** *or* **ochery**)
**ochroid**
**ock•er** *Austral* boorish person
**o'clock**
**oco•til•lo** (*plural* **•los**) tree
**oc•rea** (*or* **och•**; *plural* **•reae**) sheath
**oc•re•ate**
**oc•ta•chord** musical instrument
**oc•tad**
**oc•tad•ic**
**oc•ta•gon** (*or* **•tan•gle**)
**oc•tago•nal**
**oc•tago•nal•ly**
**oc•ta•he•dral**
**oc•ta•he•drite**
**oc•ta•he•dron** (*plural* **•drons** *or* **•dra**)
**oc•tal** number system
**oc•tam•er•ous**
**oc•tam•eter**
**oc•tane**
**oc•tan•gu•lar**
**Oc•tans** constellation
**oc•tant** eighth part of circle
**oc•tar•chy** (*plural* **•chies**)
**(octaroon)** *incorrect spelling of* **octoroon**
**oc•ta•va•lent**
**oc•tave**
**oc•ta•vo** (*plural* **•vos**) book size
**oc•ten•nial**
**oc•ten•nial•ly**
**oc•tet**
**oc•til•lion** $10^{48}$
**oc•til•lionth**
**Oc•to•ber**
**oc•to•deci•mo** (*plural* **•mos**)
**oc•to•genar•ian** (*or* **oc•tog•enary**; *plural* **•ians** *or* **•enaries**)
**(octogon)** *incorrect spelling of* **octagon**
**(octohedral)** *incorrect spelling of* **octahedral**
**oc•to•pod**
**oc•to•pus** (*plural* **•puses**)
**oc•to•roon**
**oc•to•syl•lab•ic**
**oc•to•syl•la•ble**
**oc•troi** duty on goods
**oc•tu•ple**
**ocu•lar**
**ocu•lar•ist** artificial-eye maker
**ocu•list** ophthalmologist
**ocu•lo•mo•tor**
**oda•lisque** (*or* **•lisk**)
**odd**
**odd•ball**
**odd•ity** (*plural* **•ities**)
**odd•ly**
**odd•ment**
**odd•ness**
**odd-pinnate** botany term
**odds-on**
**ode**
**Oden•se** Danish port
**Oder** European river
**Odes•sa** Ukrainian port
**odeum** (*plural* **odea**) (building for musical performances; *compare* **odium**; **oidium**
**Odin** (*or* **Othin**) Norse god
**odi•ous**
**odi•ous•ness**
**odium** hatred; *compare* **odeum**; **oidium**
**odom•eter** (*or* **ho•dom•**) *US* mileometer
**od•on•tal•gia** toothache
**od•on•tal•gic**
**odon•to•blast**
**odon•to•blas•tic**
**odon•to•glos•sum** orchid

**odon•to•graph** gear-tooth marking aid
**odon•to•graph•ic**
**od•on•tog•ra•phy**
**odon•toid**
**odon•to•logi•cal**
**od•on•tolo•gist**
**od•on•tol•ogy** science of teeth
**od•on•topho•ral** (*or* **•toph•or•ous**)
**odon•to•phore** zoology term
**odor** *US spelling of* **odour**
**odor•if•er•ous**
**odor•ous**
**odor•ous•ness**
**odour** (*US* **odor**)
**odour•less** (*US* **odor•**)
**Od•ys•sean**
**Odysseus** mythological hero
**Od•ys•sey** poem
**oede•ma** (*US* **ede•**; *plural* **•ma•ta**)
**oedema•tous** (*or* **•tose**; *US* **edema•**)
**oedi•pal** (*or* **•pean**)
**Oedipus** mythological character
**oeil•lade** suggestive glance
**oeno•logi•cal** (*US* **eno•**)
**oenolo•gist** (*US* **enolo•**)
**oenol•ogy** (*US* **enol•**) study of wine
**oeno•mel** drink
**Oenone** Greek nymph
**o'er** over
**oer•sted** unit
**oesopha•geal** (*US* **esopha•**)
**oesopha•gus** (*US* **esopha•**; *plural* **•gi**)
**oes•tra•di•ol** (*US* **es•**) hormone
**oes•tri•ol** (*US* **es•**) hormone
**oes•tro•gen** (*US* **es•**)
**oes•tro•gen•ic** (*US* **es•**)
**oes•tro•geni•cal•ly** (*US* **es•**)
**oes•trone** (*US* **es•**) hormone
**oes•trous** (*adj*; *US* **es•**)
**oes•trus** (*noun*; *US* **es•**)
**oeuvre** work of art
**of**
**off**
**of•fal**
**Of•fa•ly** Irish county
**off•beat**
**off-centre**
**off•drive** (**•driving, •drove, •driven**)
**Of•fen•bach** German city
**of•fence** (*US* **•fense**)
**of•fend**
**of•fend•er**
**of•fen•sive**
**of•fen•sive•ness**
**of•fer**
**of•fer•er** (*or* **•fe•ror**)
**of•fer•ing**
**of•fer•tory** (*plural* **•tories**)
**off-glide**
**off•hand**
**off•handed**
**off•handed•ly**
**off•hand•ed•ness**
**of•fice**
**of•fic•er**
**of•fi•cial**
**of•fi•cial•dom**
**of•fi•cial•ese**
**of•fi•cial•ly**
**of•fi•ci•ant**
**of•fi•ci•ary** (*plural* **•aries**) body of officials
**of•fi•ci•ate**
**of•fi•cia•tion**
**of•fi•cia•tor**
**of•fi•cious**
**of•fi•cious•ness**
**of•fing**
**of•fish**
**off-key** (*adj*)
**off-licence**
**off-line** (*adj*)
**off-load**
**off-peak**
**off•print**
**off-putting**
**off-season** (*adj*)
**off•set** (**•set•ting, •set**)
**off•shoot**
**off•shore**
**off•side**
**off•spring**
**off•stage**
**off-white**
**oft**
**of•ten**
**Oga•den** Ethiopian region
**Og•bo•mo•sho** Nigerian city
**og•do•ad** group of eight
**ogee** architectural moulding
**og•ham** (*or* **ogam**) ancient writing
**ogiv•al**
**ogive** architectural term
**ogle**
**ogler**
**Ogo•oué** (*or* **•we**) African river
**ogre** (*fem* **ogress**)
**ogre•ish**
**Ogyg•ian** prehistoric
**oh**
**Ohio**
**ohm**
**ohm•age**
**ohm•meter**
**oid•ium** (*plural* **•ia**) fungal spore
**oil**
**oil•bird**
**oil•can**
**oil•cloth**
**oil•cup**
**oil•er**
**oil•field**
**oil•fired**
**oili•ly**
**oili•ness**
**oil•man** (*plural* **•men**)
**oil•skin**
**oil•stone**
**oily** (**oili•er, oili•est**)
**oint•ment**
**Oi•reach•tas** Irish parliament
**Oita** Japanese city
**OK** (*or* **okay**; *noun, plural* **OK's** *or* **okays**; *verb* **OK'ing, OK'ed** *or* **okay•ing, okayed**)
**oka** (*or* **oke**) Turkish weight
**oka•pi** (*plural* **•pis** *or* **•pi**)
**okay** *variant of* **OK**
**Oka•ya•ma** Japanese city
**Okee•cho•bee** Florida lake
**okey-doke** (*or* **-dokey**)
**Oki•na•wa** Japanese island
**Ok•la•ho•ma**
**Okla•ho•man**
**okra** vegetable
**okta** meteorological unit
**old**
**Old Bai•ley**
**old•en**

**Ol•den•burg** German city
**old•er**
**old•fangled**
**old-fashioned**
**Old•ham** English town
**oldie**
**old•ness**
**old-time**
**old-timer**
**Ol•du•vai** Tanzanian gorge
**old•wife** (*plural* **•wives**) duck; fish
**old-world**
**olé** Spanish exclamation
**olea•ceous** botany term
**oleagi•nous** oily
**olean•der** shrub
**oleas•ter** shrub
**oleate** chemistry term
**olec•ra•nal**
**olec•ra•non** anatomy term
**olefine** (*or* **olefin**)
**olefin•ic**
**oleic acid**
**oleo•graph**
**oleo•graph•ic**
**oleog•ra•phy**
**oleo•res•in**
**oleo•res•in•ous**
**oleum** (*plural* **olea** *or* **oleums**) chemistry term
**ol•fac•tion**
**ol•fac•tory** (*plural* **•tories**)
**oliba•num** frankincense
**olid** foul-smelling
**oli•garch**
**oli•gar•chic** (*or* **•chi•cal**)
**oli•gar•chi•cal•ly**
**oli•gar•chy** (*plural* **•chies**)
**Oli•go•cene** geological period
**oli•go•chaete** worm
**oli•go•clase** mineral
**oli•gopo•lis•tic**
**oli•gopo•ly** (*plural* **•lies**) economics term
**oli•gop•so•nis•tic**
**oli•gop•so•ny** (*plural* **•nies**) economics term
**oli•go•sac•cha•ride**
**oli•go•troph•ic** ecology term
**oli•got•ro•phy**
**oli•gu•ret•ic**
**oli•gu•ria** (*or* **•resis**) medical term
**olio** (*plural* **olios**) miscellany
**oli•va•ceous**
**oli•vary**
**ol•ive**
**oliv•en•ite** mineral
**oli•vine** mineral
**olla** cooking pot
**olla po•dri•da** Spanish stew
**ol•ogy** (*plural* **•ogies**) *Slang* branch of knowledge
**olo•ro•so** (*plural* **•sos**) sherry
**Olym•pia**
**Olym•pi•ad**
**Olym•pian**
**Olym•pic**
**Olym•pus** Greek mountain
**Om** Hindu syllable
**oma•dhaun** *Irish* fool
**Omagh** Irish town
**Oma•ha** US city
**Oman** Arabian sultanate
**Omani**
**oma•sum** (*plural* **•sa**) cow's stomach
**Omay•yad** (*or* **Umay•**; *plural* **•yads** *or* **•ya•des**) caliph
**om•bre** (*US* **•ber**) card game
**om•buds•man** (*plural* **•men**)
**Om•dur•man** Sudanese city
**omega**
**ome•lette** (*or esp. US* **ome•let**)
**omen**
**omen•tal**
**omen•tum** (*plural* **•ta**) anatomy term
**omer** Hebrew unit
**omi•cron** Greek letter
**omi•nous**
**omi•nous•ness**
**omis•sible**
**omis•sion**
**omit** (**omit•ting, omit•ted**)
**omit•ter**
**om•ma•tid•ial**
**om•ma•tid•ium** (*plural* **•tidia**) zoology term
**om•mato•phore** zoology term
**om•ma•topho•rous**
**om•ni•bus** (*plural* **•buses**)
**om•ni•com•pe•tence**
**om•ni•com•pe•tent**
**om•ni•di•rec•tion•al**
**om•ni•fari•ous** of all sorts
**om•nif•ic** (*or* **om•nifi•cent**)
**om•nipo•tence**
**om•nipo•tent**
**om•ni•pres•ence**
**om•ni•pres•ent**
**om•ni•range** navigation system
**om•nis•ci•ence**
**om•nis•ci•ent**
**omnium-gather•um** assortment
**om•ni•vore**
**om•niv•or•ous**
**omo•pha•gia** (*or* **omoph•agy**) eating raw food
**omo•phag•ic** (*or* **omopha•gous**)
**Omphale** mythological queen
**om•pha•los** sacred object
**Omu•ta** Japanese city
**on**
**ona•ger** (*plural* **•gri** *or* **•gers**) wild ass
**ona•gra•ceous** botany term
**onan•ism**
**onan•ist**
**once**
**once-over**
**onco•gene**
**on•co•gen•ic** (*or* **on•cog•enous**)
**on•co•logi•cal**
**on•colo•gist**
**on•col•ogy** study of tumours
**on•coming**
**on•cost**
**on•do•gram**
**on•do•graph**
**on•dom•eter**
**one**
**Onei•da** (*plural* **•das** *or* **•da**) US city and lake; American Indian
**onei•ric** of dreams
**onei•ro•crit•ic**
**onei•ro•criti•cal**
**one•ness**
**one-off**
**oner** *Slang* something outstanding

**on•er•ous**
**on•er•ous•ness**
**one•self**
**one-sided**
**one-sidedness**
**one-step**
**one-time**
**one-to-one**
**one-track**
**one-upmanship**
**one-way**
**on-glide**
**on•going**
**on•ion**
**onion•skin** paper
**on•iony**
**Onit•sha** Nigerian port
**on•looker**
**on•looking**
**only**
**ono•ma•si•ol•ogy**
**ono•mas•tic**
**ono•mas•tics** study of proper names
**ono•mato•poeia**
**ono•mato•poe•ic** (*or* **•po•et•ic**)
**ono•mato•poei•cal•ly** (*or* **•po•eti•cal•ly**)
**on•rush**
**on•set**
**on•shore**
**on•side** sports term
**on•slaught**
**on•stage**
**On•tario**
**onto**
**on•to•gen•ic** (*or* **•ge•net•ic**)
**on•to•geni•cal•ly** (*or* **•ge•neti•cal•ly**)
**on•tog•eny** (*or* **•to•gen•esis**) biology term
**on•to•logi•cal**
**on•to•logi•cal•ly**
**on•tol•ogy** philosophy term
**onus** (*plural* **onuses**)
**onus pro•ban•di** burden of proof
**on•ward**
**on•wards**
**ony•chopho•ran** zoology term
**ony•mous** bearing author's name
**onyx** gemstone; *compare* **oryx**
**oocyte** biology term
**oodles**
**oof** *Slang* money
**ooga•mous**
**oog•amy** biology term
**oogen•esis**
**ooge•net•ic**
**oogo•nial**
**oogo•nium** (*plural* **•nia** *or* **•niums**) biology term
**ooh** exclamation
**oolite** rock
**oolit•ic**
**oologi•cal**
**oolo•gist**
**ool•ogy** study of birds' eggs
**oolong** tea
**oomi•ak** *variant spelling of* **umiak**
**oom•pah**
**oopho•rec•to•my** (*plural* **•mies**) removal of ovary
**oopho•rit•ic**
**oopho•ri•tis**
**oophyte** botany term
**oophyt•ic**
**oosperm**
**oosphere** botany term
**oospore**
**oo•spor•ic** (*or* **•ous**)
**ootheca** (*plural* **oothecae**) zoology term
**oothecal**
**ootid** zoology term
**ooze**
**oozi•ly**
**oozi•ness**
**oozy** (**oozi•er, oozi•est**)
**opac•ity** (*plural* **•ities**)
**opah** fish
**opal**
**opa•lesce**
**opal•es•cence**
**opal•es•cent**
**opal•ine**
**opaque** (**opaqu•ing, opaqued**)
**opaque•ness**
**open**
**open-and-shut**
**open•cast**
**open-ended**
**open•er**
**open-eyed**
**open-faced**
**open•handed**
**open•handed•ness**
**open•hearted**
**open•hearted•ness**
**open•ing**
**open-minded**
**open-minded•ness**
**open-mouthed**
**open•ness**
**open•work**
**op•era**
**op•er•abil•ity**
**op•er•able**
**op•er•and** maths term
**op•er•ant**
**op•er•ate**
**op•er•at•ic**
**op•er•ati•cal•ly**
**op•er•at•ics**
**op•era•tion**
**op•era•tion•al**
**op•era•tion•al•ism** (*or* **•tion•ism**) science term
**op•era•tion•al•ist•ic**
**op•era•tion•al•ly**
**op•era•tive**
**op•era•tive•ness** (*or* **•tiv•ity**)
**op•era•tize** (*or* **•tise**) make into an opera
**op•era•tor**
**oper•cu•lar** (*or* **•late**)
**oper•cu•lum** (*plural* **•la** *or* **•lums**) biology term
**op•er•et•ta**
**op•er•et•tist**
**op•er•on** genetics term
**ophi•cleide** musical instrument
**ophid•ian**
**ophio•logi•cal**
**ophi•olo•gist**
**ophi•ol•ogy** study of snakes
**Ophir** biblical region
**ophite** rock
**ophit•ic**
**Ophiu•chus** constellation
**oph•thal•mia**
**oph•thal•mic**
**oph•thal•mi•tis**
**oph•thal•mo•logi•cal**
**oph•thal•molo•gist**
**oph•thal•mol•ogy**
**oph•thal•mo•scope**

**oph•thal•mo•scop•ic**
**oph•thal•mos•co•py**
**opi•ate**
**opine**
**opin•ion**
**opin•ion•at•ed** (*or* **opin•iona•tive**)
**opin•ion•at•ed•ness**
**opis•tho•branch** zoology term
**op•is•thog•na•thism**
**op•is•thog•na•thous**
**opium**
**opi•um•ism**
**Opor•to** Portuguese port
**opos•sum** (*plural* **•sums** *or* **•sum**)
**op•pi•dan** urban
**op•pi•late** to block
**op•pi•la•tion**
**op•po•nen•cy**
**op•po•nent**
**op•por•tune**
**op•por•tune•ness**
**op•por•tun•ism**
**op•por•tun•ist**
**op•por•tun•is•tic**
**op•por•tu•nity** (*plural* **•nities**)
**op•pos•abil•ity**
**op•pos•able**
**op•pos•ably**
**op•pose**
**op•pos•er**
**op•pos•ing•ly**
**op•po•site** on the other side of; *compare* **apposite**
**op•po•site•ness**
**Op•po•si•tion** parliamentary party
**op•po•si•tion**
**op•po•si•tion•al**
**op•po•si•tion•ist**
**op•press**
**op•pres•sing•ly**
**op•pres•sion**
**op•pres•sive**
**op•pres•sive•ness**
**op•pres•sor**
**op•pro•bri•ous**
**op•pro•brium**
**op•pugn** to dispute
**op•pug•nant**
**op•pugn•er**
**Ops** Roman goddess
**op•son•ic**
**op•so•nin**
**op•so•ni•za•tion** (*or* **•sa•tion, •soni•fi•ca•tion**)
**op•so•nize** (*or* **•nise, •soni•fy**) medical term
**opt**
**op•ta•tive** expressing a wish
**(opthalmic)** *incorrect spelling of* **ophthalmic**
**(opthalmology)** *incorrect spelling of* **ophthalmology**
**op•tic**
**op•ti•cal**
**op•ti•cal•ly**
**op•ti•cian**
**op•tics**
**op•ti•mal**
**op•ti•mal•ly**
**op•ti•mism**
**op•ti•mist**
**op•ti•mis•tic** (*or* **•ti•cal**)
**op•ti•mis•ti•cal•ly**
**op•ti•mi•za•tion** (*or* **•sa•tion**)
**op•ti•mize** (*or* **•mise**)
**op•ti•mum** (*plural* **•ma** *or* **•mums**)
**op•tion**
**op•tion•al**
**op•tion•al•ly**
**op•tom•eter**
**op•to•met•ric**
**op•tom•etrist** ophthalmic optician
**op•tom•etry**
**opu•lence** (*or* **•len•cy**)
**opu•lent**
**opun•tia** plant
**opus** (*plural* **opuses** *or* **opera**)
**or**
**or•ache** (*or esp. US* **or•ach**) plant
**ora•cle**
**oracu•lar**
**ora•cy**
**Ora•dea** Romanian city
**oral** of the mouth; *compare* **aural**
**oral•ly**
**Oran** Algerian port
**or•ange**
**or•ange•ade**
**Or•ange•ism**
**Orange•man** (*plural* **•men**) Irish Protestant
**or•ang•ery** (*plural* **•eries**)
**orange•wood**
**orang-utan** (*or* **-outang**)
**orate**
**ora•tion**
**ora•tor**
**ora•tori•cal**
**ora•to•rio** (*plural* **•rios**)
**ora•tory** (*plural* **•tories**)
**orb**
**or•bicu•lar** (*or* **•late, •lat•ed**)
**or•bicu•lar•ity**
**or•bit**
**or•bit•al**
**orc** whale
**Or•cad•ian** of the Orkneys
**or•cein** dye
**or•chard**
**or•ches•tra**
**or•ches•tral**
**or•ches•tral•ly**
**or•ches•trate**
**or•ches•tra•tion**
**or•ches•tra•tor**
**or•ches•tri•na** (*or* **•on**) musical instrument
**or•chid**
**or•chi•da•ceous**
**or•chil** (*or* **ar•**) lichen; dye
**or•chis** orchid
**or•chit•ic**
**or•chi•tis** inflammation of testicle
**or•ci•nol** (*or* **or•cin**) chemical compound
**Or•cus** Roman god
**or•dain**
**or•dain•er**
**or•dain•ment**
**or•deal**
**or•der**
**or•der•er**
**or•der•li•ness**
**or•der•ly** (*plural* **•lies**)
**or•di•nal**
**or•di•nance** decree; *compare* **ordnance; ordonnance**
**or•di•nand**
**or•di•nari•ly**
**or•di•nari•ness**
**or•di•nary** (*plural* **•naries**)
**or•di•nate**
**or•di•na•tion**

**ord•nance** weaponry; *compare* **ordinance; ordonnance**
**or•don•nance** systematic arrangement; *compare* **ordnance; ordinance**
**Or•do•vi•cian** geological period
**or•dure** excrement
**Or•dzho•ni•ki•dze** (*or* **Or•jo•**) *former name of* **Vladikavkas**
**ore** mineral
**öre** (*plural* **öre**) Swedish currency
**øre** (*plural* **øre**) Danish or Norwegian currency
**oread** Greek nymph
**Örebro** Swedish town
**orec•tic** of desire
**orega•no**
**Or•egon**
**Oren•burg** Russian city
**Orestes** mythological character
**orfe** fish
**or•fray** *variant spelling of* **orphrey**
**or•gan**
**or•gan•die** (*US* **•dy**; *plural* **•dies**)
**or•ga•nelle**
**or•gan•ic**
**or•gani•cal•ly**
**or•gani•cism** biological theory
**or•gani•cist**
**or•gani•cis•tic**
**or•gan•ism**
**or•gan•is•mal** (*or* **•mic**)
**or•gan•ist**
**or•gani•za•tion** (*or* **•sa•tion**)
**or•gani•za•tion•al** (*or* **•sa•tion•al**)
**or•gan•ize** (*or* **•ise**)
**or•gan•iz•er** (*or* **•is•er**)
**or•gano•gen•esis**
**or•gano•genet•ic**
**or•gano•geneti•cal•ly**
**or•gano•graph•ic** (*or* **•graphi•cal**)
**or•gan•og•ra•phist**
**or•gan•og•ra•phy**
**or•gano•lep•tic**
**or•gano•logi•cal**
**or•gan•olo•gist**
**or•gan•ol•ogy**
**or•gano•metal•lic**
**or•ga•non** (*or* **•num**; *plural* **•na**, **•nons**, *or* **•nums**) philosophy term
**or•gano•phos•phate**
**or•gano•thera•peu•tic**
**or•gano•thera•py**
**or•ga•num** (*plural* **•na** *or* **•nums**) music; *variant spelling of* **organon**
**or•gan•za** fabric
**or•gan•zine** silk thread
**or•gasm**
**or•gas•mic** (*or* **•tic**)
**or•geat** barley drink
**or•gi•as•tic**
**orgy** (*plural* **orgies**)
**ori•bi** (*plural* **•bi** *or* **•bis**) antelope
**ori•el** window; *compare* **oriole**
**Ori•ent** eastern countries
**ori•ent** the east; *variant of* **orientate**
**Ori•en•tal** (*noun*)
**ori•en•tal** (*or* **Ori•**; *adj*)
**Ori•en•tal•ism**
**Ori•en•tal•ist**
**ori•en•tali•za•tion** (*or* **Ori•**, **•sa•tion**)
**ori•en•tal•ize** (*or* **Ori•**, **•ise**)
**ori•en•tal•ly** (*or* **Ori•**)
**ori•en•tate** (*or* **ori•ent**)
**ori•en•ta•tion**
**ori•en•ta•tion•al**
**Ori•en•te** Cuban province
**ori•en•teer•ing**
**ori•fice**
**ori•flamme** flag
**ori•ga•mi** paper folding
**ori•ga•num** marjoram or oregano
**ori•gin**
**origi•nal**
**origi•nal•ity** (*plural* **•ities**)
**origi•nal•ly**
**origi•nate**
**origi•na•tion**
**origi•na•tor**
**ori•na•sal** phonetics term; *compare* **oronasal**
**Ori•no•co** South American river
**ori•ole** bird; *compare* **oriel**
**Ori•on** constellation
**Orion** mythological character
**ori•son** prayer
**Oris•sa** Indian state
**Ori•ya** (*plural* **•ya**) Indian people
**Ori•za•ba** Mexican city
**Ork•ney Is•lands** (*or* **Ork•neys**)
**orle** heraldic term
**Or•lé•ans** French city
**Or•lon** (*Trademark*)
**or•lop** nautical term
**Orly** Parisian suburb
**or•mer** mollusc
**or•mo•lu** decoration
**Or•muz** *variant spelling of* **Hormuz**
**or•na•ment**
**or•na•men•tal**
**or•na•men•tal•ly**
**or•na•men•ta•tion**
**or•nate**
**or•nate•ness**
**or•nith•ic** of birds
**or•ni•thine** amino acid
**or•ni•this•chian** zoology term
**or•ni•tho•logi•cal**
**or•ni•tho•logi•cal•ly**
**or•ni•tholo•gist**
**or•ni•thol•ogy**
**or•ni•tho•man•cy** divination from bird behaviour
**or•ni•tho•pod** dinosaur
**or•ni•thop•ter** (*or* **or•thop•ter**) aircraft
**or•ni•tho•rhyn•chus** platypus
**or•ni•thos•co•py** divination by bird observation
**or•ni•tho•sis**
**oro•ban•cha•ceous** botany term
**oro•gen•ic** (*or* **•ge•net•ic**)
**oro•geni•cal•ly** (*or* **•geneti•cal•ly**)
**orog•eny** (*or* **oro•gen•esis**) mountain formation
**orog•ra•pher** (*or* **orolo•gist**)
**oro•graph•ic** (*or* **oro•logi•cal**)

**oro•graphi•cal•ly** (*or* **oro•logi•cal•ly**)
**orog•ra•phy** (*or* **orol•ogy**) mapping mountain relief
**oro•ide** alloy
**orom•eter**
**Oron•tes** Asian river
**oro•tund** resonant; pompous; *compare* **rotund**
**or•phan**
**or•phan•age**
**or•phari•on** lute
**Or•phean**
**Orpheus**
**Or•phic**
**Or•phism** ancient Greek religion
**or•phrey** (*or* **•fray**) border on vestment
**or•pi•ment** mineral
**or•pine** (*or* **•pin**) plant
**or•re•ry** (*plural* **•ries**) model of solar system
**or•ris** (*or* **•rice**) plant
**or•ta•nique** fruit
**or•thi•con** electronic device
**ortho•cen•tre** (*US* **•ter**) maths term
**ortho•cephal•ic** (*or* **•cepha•lous**) anatomy term
**ortho•cepha•ly**
**ortho•chro•mat•ic**
**ortho•chro•ma•tism**
**ortho•clase** mineral
**ortho•don•tic**
**ortho•don•tics** (*or* **•don•tia**)
**or•tho•don•tist**
**Ortho•dox** religion
**ortho•dox** conforming
**ortho•doxy** (*plural* **•doxies**)
**ortho•ep•ic**
**ortho•epi•cal•ly**
**ortho•epy** correct pronunciation
**ortho•gen•esis**
**ortho•ge•net•ic**
**ortho•geneti•cal•ly**
**ortho•gen•ic** medical term
**ortho•geni•cal•ly**
**or•thog•na•thism** (*or* **•thy**)
**or•thog•na•thous** anatomy term
**or•thogo•nal**
**or•thogo•nal•ly**
**or•thog•ra•pher** (*or* **•phist**)
**ortho•graph•ic** (*or* **•graphi•cal**)
**ortho•graphi•cal•ly**
**or•thog•ra•phy** (*plural* **•phies**)
**ortho•hy•dro•gen**
**ortho•mor•phic**
**ortho•paedic** (*US* **•pedic**)
**ortho•paedics** (*US* **•pedics**)
**ortho•paedist** (*US* **•pedist**)
**ortho•phos•phate**
**ortho•psy•chi•at•ric**
**ortho•psy•chia•trist**
**ortho•psy•chia•try**
**or•thop•ter** *variant of* **ornithopter**
**or•thop•ter•an** (*or* **•on**; *plural* **•ans** *or* **•tera**) insect
**or•thop•ter•ous** (*or* **•an**)
**or•thop•tic**
**or•thop•tics**
**or•thop•tist**
**ortho•rhom•bic** crystallography term
**ortho•scop•ic**
**or•thos•ti•chous**
**or•thos•ti•chy** (*plural* **•chies**) botany term
**ortho•trop•ic**
**or•thot•ro•pism**
**or•thot•ro•pous** botany term
**or•to•lan** bird
**orts** *Dialect* scraps
**Oru•ro** Bolivian city
**Or•vie•to** Italian town; wine
**Or•wel•lian**
**oryx** (*plural* **or•yxes** *or* **oryx**) antelope; *compare* **onyx**
**os** (*plural* **ossa**) bone
**os** (*plural* **ora**) mouth
**Osage** (*plural* **Osages** *or* **Osage**) American Indian
**Osa•ka** Japanese port
**Os•car** film award
**os•cil•late** fluctuate regularly; *compare* **ocellate**; **osculate**
**os•cil•la•tion**
**os•cil•la•tor**
**os•cil•la•tory**
**os•cil•lo•gram**
**os•cil•lo•graph**
**os•cil•lo•graph•ic**
**os•cil•log•ra•phy**
**os•cil•lo•scope**
**os•cine** ornithology term
**os•ci•tan•cy** (*or* **•tance**; *plural* **•tan•cies** *or* **•tances**)
**os•ci•tant** drowsy
**os•cu•lant** biology term
**os•cu•lar**
**os•cu•late** kiss; maths term; *compare* **ocellate; oscillate**
**os•cu•la•tion**
**os•cu•la•tory**
**os•cu•lum** (*plural* **•la**) mouthlike part
**Osha•wa** Canadian city
**Oshog•bo** Nigerian city
**osier** willow tree
**Osiris** Egyptian god
**Oslo**
**Os•man•li** of Ottoman Empire
**os•mic**
**os•mi•ous** *variant of* **osmous**
**os•mi•rid•ium** alloy
**os•mium** metal
**os•mom•eter**
**os•mo•met•ric**
**os•mo•met•ri•cal•ly**
**os•mom•etry**
**os•mose** undergo osmosis
**os•mo•sis** (*plural* **•ses**)
**os•mot•ic**
**os•moti•cal•ly**
**os•mous** (*or* **•mi•ous**)
**os•mun•da** (*or* **•mund**) fern
**Os•na•brück** German city
**os•na•burg** fabric
**os•prey**
**Ossa** Greek mountain
**os•sein** protein
**os•seous** bony
**Os•setia** Georgian and Russian region
**Os•set•ic** (*or* **•se•tian**)
**Ossian** legendary Irish bard
**os•si•cle** small bone
**os•sicu•lar**
**os•sif•er•ous**
**os•si•fi•ca•tion**
**os•si•fi•er**
**os•si•frage** bird
**os•si•fy** (**•fies, •fy•ing, •fied**)
**os•su•ary** (*plural* **•aries**) urn for bones
**os•teal**

**os•tei•tic**
**os•tei•tis**
**Os•tend** Belgian port
**os•ten•sibil•ity**
**os•ten•sible**
**os•ten•sibly**
**os•ten•sive**
**os•ten•sory** (*plural* **•sories**) container for Host
**os•ten•ta•tion**
**os•ten•ta•tious**
**os•teo•ar•thrit•ic**
**os•teo•ar•thri•tis**
**os•teo•blast** bone cell
**os•teo•blas•tic**
**os•teoc•la•sis** medical term
**os•teo•clast**
**os•teo•clas•tic**
**os•teo•gen•esis**
**os•teoid**
**os•teo•logi•cal**
**os•teo•logi•cal•ly**
**os•teolo•gist**
**os•teol•ogy** study of bones
**os•teo•ma** (*plural* **•ma•ta** *or* **•mas**) tumour
**os•teo•ma•la•cia**
**os•teo•ma•la•cial** (*or* **•lac•ic**)
**os•teo•my•eli•tis**
**os•teo•path** (*or* **•teopa•thist**)
**os•teo•path•ic**
**os•teo•pathi•cal•ly**
**os•teopa•thy**
**os•teo•phyte** bony outgrowth
**os•teo•phyt•ic**
**os•teo•plas•tic**
**os•teo•plas•ty** (*plural* **•ties**) bone grafting
**os•teo•por•o•sis**
**os•teo•tome** surgical instrument
**os•teoto•my** (*plural* **•mies**)
**Os•tia** ancient Italian town
**os•ti•ary** (*plural* **•aries**) Catholic official
**os•ti•na•to** (*plural* **•tos**) musical term
**os•tio•lar**
**os•ti•ole** pore
**os•tium** (*plural* **•tia**) biology term
**ost•ler** (*or* **host•ler**)
**ost•mark** former East German currency
**os•to•sis** formation of bone
**os•tra•cism**
**os•tra•ciz•able** (*or* **•cis•**)
**os•tra•cize** (*or* **•cise**)
**os•tra•ciz•er** (*or* **•cis•er**)
**os•tra•cod** tiny animal
**os•tra•co•dan** (*or* **•dous**)
**os•tra•co•derm** extinct fish
**Os•tra•va** Czech city
**os•trich** (*plural* **•triches** *or* **•trich**)
**Os•tro•goth**
**otal•gia** earache
**oth•er**
**other-direct•ed**
**other•gates** *Archaic* otherwise
**oth•er•ness**
**other•where** *Archaic* elsewhere
**other•wise**
**other•worldli•ness**
**other•worldly**
**otic** of the ear
**oti•ose** futile
**oti•os•ity** (*or* **•ose•ness**)
**oti•tis**
**oto•cyst**
**oto•cys•tic**
**oto•la•ryn•go•logi•cal**
**oto•lar•yn•golo•gist**
**oto•lar•yn•gol•ogy**
**oto•lith**
**oto•lith•ic**
**oto•logi•cal**
**otolo•gist**
**otol•ogy**
**oto•scope**
**oto•scop•ic**
**ot•ta•va** octave
**Ot•ta•wa**
**ot•ter** (*plural* **•ters** *or* **•ter**)
**Ot•to•man** (*or* **Oth•man**; *plural* **•mans**) Turk; Turkish
**ot•to•man** (*plural* **•mans**) sofa
**oua•ba•in** drug
**Ouachi•ta** (*or* **Washi•ta**) US river
**Oua•ga•dou•gou** capital of Burkina Faso
**oua•na•niche** salmon
**oubli•ette** dungeon
**ouch**
**Oudh** Indian region
**ought** should; *variant spelling of* **aught**
**Oui•ja** (*Trademark*)
**Ouj•da** Moroccan city
**ounce**
**our**
**ours** of us
**our•selves**
**Ouse** English river
**ousel** *variant spelling of* **ouzel**
**oust**
**out**
**out•age** missing goods
**out-and-out**
**out•back**
**out•bal•ance**
**out•bid** (**•bid•ding, •bid, •bid•den** *or* **•bid**)
**out•bluff**
**out•board**
**out•bound**
**out•brave**
**out•break**
**out•breed** (**•breed•ing, •bred**)
**out•build•ing**
**out•burst**
**out•cast** one cast out
**out•caste** one with no caste
**out•class**
**out•come**
**out•crop** (**•crop•ping, •cropped**)
**out•cross**
**out•cry** (*noun, plural* **•cries**; *verb* **•cries, •cry•ing, •cried**)
**out•date**
**out•dat•ed**
**out•dis•tance**
**out•do** (**•does, •do•ing, •did, •done**)
**out•door** (*adj*)
**out•doors** (*adv*)
**out•er**
**outer•most**
**out•face**
**out•fall**
**out•field**
**out•field•er**
**out•fit** (**•fit•ting, •fit•ted**)
**out•fit•ter**
**out•flank**

**out•flow**
**out•foot**
**out•fox**
**out•gas** (**•gas•ses, •gas•sing, •gassed**)
**out•go** (**•goes, •go•ing, •went, •gone**)
**out•go•ing** (*adj*)
**out•go•ings**
**out-group**
**out•grow** (**•grow•ing, •grew, •grown**)
**out•growth**
**out•gun** (**•gun•ning, •gunned**)
**out•haul**
**out•house**
**out•ing**
**out•jockey**
**out•land•er**
**out•land•ish**
**out•last**
**out•law**
**out•law•ry** (*plural* **•ries**)
**out•lay** (**•lay•ing, •laid**)
**out•let**
**out•li•er**
**out•line**
**out•live**
**out•look**
**out•ly•ing**
**out•man** (**•man•ning, •manned**)
**out•ma•noeu•vre** (*US* **•ver**)
**out•match**
**out•mod•ed**
**out•num•ber**
**out-of-doors**
**out-of-the-way**
**out•pa•tient**
**out•point**
**out•port**
**out•post**
**out•pour**
**out•pour•ing**
**out•put** (**•put•ting, •put** *or* **•put•ted**)
**out•rage**
**out•ra•geous**
**out•ra•geous•ness**
**out•rank**
**ou•tré** unconventional
**out•reach**
**out•ride** (**•rid•ing, •rode, •rid•den**)
**out•rid•er**
**out•rig•ger**
**out•right**
**out•ri•val** (**•val•ling, •valled;** *US* **•val•ing, •valed**)
**out•run** (**•run•ning, •ran, •run**)
**out•run•ner**
**out•rush**
**out•sell** (**•sell•ing, •sold**)
**out•sert** printing term
**out•set**
**out•shine** (**•shin•ing, •shone**)
**out•shoot** (**•shoot•ing, •shot**)
**out•side**
**out•sid•er**
**out•size**
**out•skirts**
**out•smart**
**out•sole**
**out•spo•ken**
**out•spread** (**•spread•ing, •spread**)
**out•stand** (**•stand•ing, •stood**)
**out•stand•ing** (*adj*)
**out•stare**
**out•sta•tion**
**out•stay**
**out•stretch**
**out•strip** (**•strip•ping, •stripped**)
**out•swing**
**out•swing•er**
**out•talk**
**out•think** (**•think•ing, •thought**)
**out•vote**
**out•ward** (*adj*)
**out•ward•ly**
**out•wards** (*adv*)
**out•wash** glacial deposit
**out•wear** (**•wear•ing, •wore, •worn**)
**out•weigh**
**out•wit** (**•wit•ting, •wit•ted**)
**out•work** (**•work•ing, •worked** *or* **•wrought**)
**out•work•er**
**ouzel** (*or* ousel) bird
**ouzo** (*plural* ouzos) drink
**ova** *plural of* ovum
**oval**
**oval•ness** (*or* **•ity**)
**ovar•ian**
**ovari•ec•to•my**
**ovari•oto•my** (*plural* **•mies**)
**ova•ri•tis**
**ova•ry** (*plural* **•ries**)
**ovate**
**ova•tion**
**ova•tion•al**
**oven**
**oven•bird**
**oven-ready**
**oven•ware**
**over**
**over•abun•dance**
**over•achieve**
**over•act**
**over•ac•tive**
**over•age**
**over•all**
**over•alls**
**over•am•bi•tious**
**over•anx•ious**
**over•arch**
**over•arm**
**over•awe**
**over•bal•ance**
**over•bear** (**•bear•ing, •bore, •borne**)
**over•bear•ing•ly**
**over•bid** (**•bid•ding, •bid, •bid•den** *or* **•bid**)
**over•blown**
**over•board**
**over•book**
**over•boot**
**over•build** (**•build•ing, •built**)
**over•bur•den**
**over•call**
**over•came**
**over•ca•pac•ity**
**over•capi•tali•za•tion** (*or* **•sa•tion**)
**over•capi•tal•ize** (*or* **•ise**)
**over•cast**
**over•cau•tious**
**over•charge**
**over•check**
**over•cloud**
**over•coat**
**over•come** (**•com•ing, •came, •come**)
**over•com•pen•sate**

**over•com•pen•sa•tion**
**over•com•pen•sa•tory**
**over•con•fi•dent**
**over•cook**
**over•criti•cal**
**over•criti•cize** (*or* **•cise**)
**over•crop** (**•crop•ping, •cropped**)
**over•crowd**
**over•crowd•ing**
**over•cul•ti•vate**
**over•devel•op**
**over•devel•op•ment**
**over•do** (**•does, •do•ing, •did, •done**)
**over•dos•age**
**over•dose**
**over•draft** money
**over•draught** air current
**over•draw** (**•draw•ing, •drew, •drawn**)
**over•dress**
**over•drive** (**•driv•ing, •drove, •driv•en**)
**over•due**
**over•dye**
**over•eat** (**•eat•ing, •ate, •eat•en**)
**over•elabo•rate**
**over•em•pha•size** (*or* **•sise**)
**over•em•phat•ic**
**over•en•thu•si•asm**
**over•en•thu•si•as•tic**
**over•es•ti•mate**
**over•es•ti•ma•tion**
**over•ex•cite**
**over•ex•pose**
**over•ex•po•sure**
**over•feed** (**•feed•ing, •fed**)
**over•fill**
**over•flight**
**over•flow** (**•flow•ing, •flowed, •flown**)
**over•fly** (**•flies, •fly•ing, •flew, •flown**)
**over•fold** geology term
**over•gar•ment**
**over•gen•er•ous**
**over•glaze**
**over•ground**
**over•grow** (**•grow•ing, •grew, •grown**)
**over•growth**
**over•hand**
**over•hang** (**•hang•ing, •hung**)
**over•haul**
**over•head**
**over•heads**
**over•hear** (**•hear•ing, •heard**)
**over•heat**
**over•hung**
**Over•ijs•sel** Dutch province
**over•in•dulge**
**over•in•dul•gence**
**over•in•dul•gent**
**over•is•sue** (**•sues, •su•ing, •sued**)
**over•joyed**
**over•kill**
**over•land**
**over•lap** (**•lap•ping, •lapped**)
**over•lay** (**•lay•ing, •laid**)
**over•leaf**
**over•lie** (**•ly•ing, •lay, •lain**)
**over•load**
**over•long**
**over•look**
**over•lord**
**over•ly**
**over•man** (**•man•ning, •manned**)
**over•man•tel**
**over•master**
**over•mat•ter**
**over•much**
**over•nice**
**over•night**
**over•pass** (**•pas•sing, •passed, •past**)
**over•pay** (**•pay•ing, •paid**)
**over•pitch**
**over•play**
**over•plus** excess
**over•popu•late**
**over•popu•la•tion**
**over•pow•er**
**over•pow•er•ing**
**over•print**
**over•pro•duce**
**over•pro•duc•tion**
**over•pro•tect**
**over•pro•tec•tion**
**over•pro•tec•tive**
**over•quali•fied**
**over•ran**
**over•rate**
**over•reach**
**over•react**
**over•reac•tion**
**over•ride** (**•rid•ing, •rode, •rid•den**)
**over•rid•er**
**over-riding** (*adj*)
**over•ripe**
**over•rode**
**over•rule**
**over•run** (**•run•ning, •ran, •run**)
**over•score** cross out
**over•seas**
**over•see** (**•see•ing, •saw, •seen**)
**over•seer**
**over•sell** (**•sell•ing, •sold**)
**over•set** (**•set•ting, •set**) disturb
**over•sew** (**•sew•ing, •sewed, •sewn**)
**over•sexed**
**over•shad•ow**
**over•shoe**
**over•shoot** (**•shoot•ing, •shot**)
**over•side**
**over•sight**
**over•sim•pli•fi•ca•tion**
**over•sim•pli•fy** (**•fies, •fy•ing, •fied**)
**over•size**
**over•sized**
**over•skirt**
**over•slaugh** military term
**over•sleep** (**•sleep•ing, •slept**)
**over•soul** spiritual essence
**over•spend** (**•spend•ing, •spent**)
**over•spill** (**•spill•ing, •spilt** *or* **•spilled**)
**over•staff**
**over•state**
**over•state•ment**
**over•stay**
**over•steer**
**over•step** (**•step•ping, •stepped**)
**over•strung**
**over•stuff**
**over•sub•scribe**
**overt**

**over•take** (**•tak•ing, •took, •tak•en**)
**over•task**
**over•tax**
**over-the-counter** (*adj*)
**over•throw** (**•throw•ing, •threw, •thrown**)
**over•thrust** geological fault
**over•time**
**over•tire**
**over•tired**
**over•tone**
**over•took**
**over•top** (**•top•ping, •topped**)
**over•trade**
**over•trick** bridge term
**over•trump**
**over•ture**
**over•turn**
**over•use**
**over•view**
**over•watch**
**over•ween•ing**
**over•weigh**
**over•weight**
**over•whelm**
**over•whelm•ing**
**over•wind** (**•wind•ing, •wound**)
**over•win•ter**
**over•word** repeated word
**over•work**
**over•write** (**•writ•ing, •wrote, •writ•ten**)
**over•wrought**
**ovi•du•cal** (*or* **•duc•tal**)
**ovi•duct**
**Ovie•do** Spanish city
**ovif•er•ous**
**ovi•form** egg-shaped
**ovine** sheeplike
**ovi•par•ity**
**ovipa•rous** egg-laying
**ovi•pos•it**
**ovi•po•si•tion**
**ovi•posi•tor**
**ovi•sac** egg sac
**ovoid**
**ovo•lo** (*plural* **•li**) architectural term
**ovo•tes•tis** (*plural* **•tes**)
**ovo•vi•vi•par•ity**
**ovo•vi•vipa•rous**
**ovu•lar**
**ovu•late**
**ovu•la•tion**
**ovule**
**ovum** (*plural* **ova**)
**ow** exclamation
**owe**
**ow•el•ty** (*plural* **•ties**) legal term
**Ower•ri** Nigerian town
**ow•ing**
**owl**
**owl•et**
**owl•ish**
**own**
**own•er**
**owner-occupier**
**own•er•ship**
**owt** *Dialect* anything
**ox** (*plural* **oxen**)
**oxa•late** chemistry term
**ox•al•ic acid**
**oxa•lis** plant
**oxa•zine**
**ox•blood**
**ox•bow** lake
**Ox•bridge**
**oxen** *plural of* **ox**
**ox•eye** plant
**Ox•fam**
**Ox•ford**
**Ox•ford•shire**
**ox•heart** cherry
**ox•hide**
**oxi•dant**
**oxi•dase** enzyme
**oxi•date** oxidize
**oxi•da•tion**
**oxi•da•tion•al**
**oxi•da•tion-reduction**
**oxi•da•tive**
**ox•ide**
**oxi•di•met•ric**
**oxi•dim•etry**
**oxi•diz•able** chemistry term
**oxi•di•za•tion** (*or* **•sa•tion**)
**oxi•dize** (*or* **•dise**)
**oxi•diz•er** (*or* **•dis•er**)
**ox•ime** chemical compound
**ox•lip** plant
**Oxo•nian**
**ox•pecker** bird
**ox•tail**
**ox•tongue**
**oxy•acety•lene**
**oxy•acid**
**oxy•cephal•ic** (*or* **•cepha•lous**) anatomy term
**oxy•cepha•ly**
**oxy•gen**
**oxy•gen•ate** (*or* **•ize, •ise**)
**oxy•gena•tion**
**oxy•gen•ic** (*or* **ox•yg•enous**)
**oxy•gen•iz•able** (*or* **•is•able**)
**oxy•ge•niz•er** (*or* **•is•er**)
**oxy•hae•mo•glo•bin** (*US* **•he•**)
**oxy•hy•dro•gen**
**oxy•mo•ron** (*plural* **•mo•ra**) rhetoric term
**oxy•salt**
**oxy•sul•phide** (*US* **•fide**)
**oxy•tet•ra•cy•cline**
**oxy•to•cic**
**oxy•to•cin** hormone
**oxy•tone** linguistics term
**oyer** legal term
**oyez** (*or* **oyes**) interjection
**Oyo** Nigerian state
**oys•ter**
**oyster•catcher**
**Oz** *Austral* Australia
**Oza•lid** (*Trademark*)
**ozo•cerite** (*or* **•kerite**) wax
**ozone**
**ozon•ic** (*or* **ozo•nous**)
**ozo•nif•er•ous**
**ozo•ni•za•tion** (*or* **•sa•tion**)
**ozo•nize** (*or* **•nise**)
**ozo•niz•er** (*or* **•nis•er**)
**ozo•noly•sis**
**ozo•no•sphere** ozone layer

# P

**pa** *Slang* father
**paca** animal
**pace**
**pace•maker**
**pac•er**
**pace•setter**
**pace•way** *Austral* racecourse
**pa•cha** *variant spelling of* **pasha**
**pa•chi•si** board game
**pachy•derm** animal
**pachy•der•ma•tous**
**pachy•tene** genetics term
**Pa•cif•ic** ocean, etc.
**pa•cif•ic** conciliatory
**pa•cifi•cal•ly**
**paci•fi•ca•tion**
**paci•fi•er**
**paci•fism**
**paci•fist**
**paci•fy** (**•fies, •fy•ing, •fied**)
**pack**
**pack•able**
**pack•age**
**pack•ag•er**
**pack•ag•ing**
**pack•er**
**pack•et**
**pack•horse**
**pack•ing**
**pack•saddle**
**pack•thread**
**pact**
**pad** (**pad•ding, pad•ded**)
**pa•dang** Malaysian field
**pa•dauk** (*or* **•douk**) tree
**pad•ding**
**pad•dle**
**paddle•fish** (*plural* **•fish** *or* **•fishes**)
**pad•dler**
**pad•dock**
**Pad•dy** (*plural* **•dies**) *Slang* Irishman
**pad•dy** (*plural* **•dies**) rice field; temper
**pad•dy•whack**
**pad•emel•on** (*or* **pad•dy•mel•on**) wallaby
**pad•lock**
**pa•dre**
**pa•dro•ne** Italian innkeeper
**Pad•ua**
**padua•soy** fabric
**paean** (*US also* **pean**) song of praise; *compare* **paeon; pean; peon**
**pae•di•at•ric** (*US* **pe•**)
**pae•dia•tri•cian** (*US* **pe•**)
**pae•di•at•rics** (*US* **pe•**)
**pae•do•gen•esis** biology term
**pae•do•genet•ic** (*or* **•gen•ic**)
**pae•do•logi•cal** (*US* **pe•**)
**pae•dolo•gist** (*US* **pe•**)
**pae•dol•ogy** (*US* **pe•**)
**pae•do•mor•pho•sis** biology term
**pae•do•phile** (*US* **pe•**)
**pae•do•philia** (*US* **pe•**)
**pa•el•la** (*plural* **•las**)
**pae•on** metrical foot; *compare* **paean; pean; peon**
(**paeony**) *incorrect spelling of* **peony**
**pa•gan**
**pa•gan•ism**
**pa•gan•ist**
**pa•gan•ist•ic**
**pa•gan•isti•cal•ly**
**pa•gani•za•tion** (*or* **•sa•tion**)
**pa•gan•ize** (*or* **•ise**)
**pa•gan•iz•er** (*or* **•is•er**)
**page**
**pag•eant**
**pag•eant•ry** (*plural* **•ries**)
**page•boy**
**pagi•nal**
**pagi•nate**
**pagi•na•tion**
**pa•go•da**
**pa•gu•rian** (*or* **•rid**) zoology term
**Pa•hang** Malaysian state
**Pa•ha•ri** language group
**Pah•la•vi** Persian language
**paid**
**pai•gle** *Dialect* cowslip
**Paign•ton**
**pail** bucket; *compare* **pale**
**pail•lette** sequin
**pain** hurt; *compare* **pane**
**pained**
**pain•ful**
**pain•ful•ly**
**pain•ful•ness**
**pain•killer**
**pain•less**
**pain•less•ness**
**pains•taking**
**pains•taking•ness**
**paint**
**paint•box**
**paint•brush**
**paint•er**
**paint•er•ly**
**paint•ing**
**paint•work**
**painty**
**pair** two similar things; *compare* **pare**
**pair-oar**
**pai•sa** (*plural* **•se**) Indian coin
**Pais•ley** Scottish town
**pais•ley** fabric; pattern
**pa•jam•as** *US spelling of* **pyjamas**
**pa•keha** non-Maori
**Pa•ki•stan**
**Pa•ki•stani**
**pal** (**pal•ling, palled**) *Slang* friend; to befriend; *compare* **pall**
**pal•ace**
**pala•din**
**palae•an•throp•ic** (*US* **pale•**)
**Palae•arc•tic** zoogeographical region
**palae•eth•no•logi•cal** (*US* **pale•**)
**palae•eth•nolo•gist** (*US* **pale•**)
**palae•eth•nol•ogy** (*US* **pale•**)
**palaeo•an•thro•pol•ogy** (*US* **paleo•**)
**palaeo•bo•tani•cal** (*or* **•tan•ic;** *US* **paleo•**)
**palaeo•bota•nist** (*US* **paleo•**)
**palaeo•bota•ny** (*US* **paleo•**)

**Palaeo•cene** (*US* **Paleo•**) geological epoch
**palaeo•cli•ma•tol•ogy** (*US* **paleo•**)
**palaeo•eth•no•bota•ny** (*US* **paleo•**)
**Palaeo•gene** (*US* **Paleo•**) geology term
**palaeo•graph•ic** (*US* **paleo•**)
**palaeo•graphi•cal** (*US* **paleo•**)
**palae•og•ra•phy** (*US* **paleo•**) study of ancient handwriting
**palaeo•lith** (*US* **paleo•**)
**Palaeo•lith•ic** (*US* **Paleo•**)
**palae•on•to•graph•ic** (*or* **•graphi•cal**; *US* **pale•**)
**palae•on•tog•ra•phy** (*US* **pale•**) description of fossils
**palae•on•to•logi•cal** (*US* **pale•**)
**palae•on•tolo•gist** (*US* **pale•**)
**palae•on•tol•ogy** (*US* **pale•**)
**Palaeo•zo•ic** (*US* **Paleo•**) geological era
**palaeo•zoo•logi•cal** (*US* **paleo•**)
**palaeo•zo•olo•gist** (*US* **paleo•**)
**palaeo•zo•ol•ogy** (*US* **paleo•**)
**pal•aes•tra** (*plural* **•tras** *or* **•trae**)
**pal•ais** dance
**pal•an•quin** (*or* **•keen**)
**pal•at•abil•ity** (*or* **•able•ness**)
**pal•at•able**
**pal•at•ably**
**pala•tal**
**pala•tali•za•tion** (*or* **•sa•tion**)
**pala•tal•ize** (*or* **•ise**) phonetics term
**pal•ate** roof of mouth; *compare* **palette**; **pallet**
**pa•la•tial**
**pa•la•tial•ly**
**pa•la•tial•ness**
**Pa•lati•nate** German region
**pa•lati•nate** territory of palatine prince
**Pala•tine** of the Palatinate; Roman hill
**pala•tine**
**Pa•lau** *former name of* **Belau**
**pa•la•ver**
**pale** lacking colour; wooden post; *compare* **pail**
**pa•lea** (*plural* **•leae**) botany term
**pa•lea•ceous**
**pale•face**
**pale•ly** in a pale way; *compare* **paly**
**Pa•lem•bang** Indonesian port
**pale•ness**
**paleo•** *US spelling of words beginning with* **palaeo•**
**Pa•ler•mo** Sicilian capital
**Pal•es•tine**
**Pal•es•tin•ian**
**pal•ette** (*or* **pal•let**) artist's board; *compare* **palate**; **pallet**
**pal•ette knife** (*plural* **pal•ette knives**)
**pal•frey**
**pal•imp•sest** manuscript
**pal•in•drome**
**pal•in•drom•ic**
**pal•ing**
**pal•in•gen•esis** (*plural* **•eses**) theology term
**pal•in•genet•ic**
**palin•geneti•cal•ly**
**pali•node** poem
**pali•sade**
**pal•ish**
**pall** coffin cover; to be boring; *compare* **pal**; **pawl**
**Pal•la•dian** architectural term
**pal•lad•ic** chemistry term
**Pal•la•dium** statue of Athena
**pal•la•dium** chemical element
**pal•la•dous** chemistry term
**Pallas** Athena; asteroid
**pall•bearer**
**palled** *past tense of* **pal** *or* **pall**
**pal•let** straw bed; potter's knife; machine part; *variant spelling of* **palette**; *compare* **palate**
**pal•leti•za•tion** (*or* **•sa•tion**)
**pal•let•ize** (*or* **•ise**)
**pal•li•asse** (*or* **pail•lasse**)
**pal•li•ate**
**pal•lia•tion**
**pal•lia•tive**
**pal•lia•tor**
**pal•lid**
**pal•lium** (*plural* **•lia** *or* **•liums**) vestment; anatomy term
**Pall Mall**
**pal•lor**
**pal•ly** (**•li•er**, **•li•est**)
**palm**
**Pal•ma** Spanish resort; *compare* **Parma**
**pal•ma•ceous** botany term
**pal•mar**
**pal•mate** (*or* **•mat•ed**)
**pal•ma•tion**
**palm•er** pilgrim
**pal•mette** archaeological ornament
**pal•met•to** (*plural* **•tos** *or* **•toes**) palm tree
**Pal•mi•ra** Colombian city
**palm•ist**
**palm•is•try**
**pal•mi•tate** chemistry term
**pal•mi•tin** chemical compound
**palmy** (**palmi•er**, **palmi•est**)
**pal•my•ra** palm tree
**pa•lo•lo** (*plural* **•los**) worm
**Palo•mar** Californian mountain
**palo•mi•no** (*plural* **•nos**) horse
**pa•loo•ka** *US* clumsy person
**palp** (*or* **pal•pus**; *plural* **palps** *or* **pal•pi**)
**pal•pabil•ity** (*or* **•pable•ness**)
**pal•pable**
**pal•pably**
**pal•pate** examine medically; of palps; *compare* **palpitate**
**pal•pa•tion**
**pal•pe•bral** of the eyelid
**pal•pe•brate**

**pal•pi•tate** beat rapidly; *compare* **palpate**
**pal•pi•ta•tion**
**pal•sied**
**pal•stave** archaeology term
**pal•sy** (*noun, plural* **•sies;** *verb* **•sies, •sy•ing, •sied)**
**pal•ter** be insincere
**pal•ter•er**
**pal•tri•ly**
**pal•tri•ness**
**pal•try (•tri•er, •tri•est)**
**paly** heraldic term; *compare* **palely**
**paly•no•logi•cal**
**paly•nolo•gist**
**paly•nol•ogy** study of pollen
**Pa•mirs** Asian mountains
**pam•pas**
**pam•pean**
**pam•per**
**pam•per•er**
**pam•pero** (*plural* **•peros)** wind
**pam•phlet**
**pam•phlet•eer**
**Pam•phylia** ancient Asian region
**Pam•plo•na** Spanish city
**Pan** Greek god
**pan (pan•ning, panned)**
**pana•cea**
**pana•cean**
**pa•nache**
**pa•na•da** thick sauce
**Pana•ma**
**pana•ma**
**Pana•ma•nian**
**Pan-Ameri•can**
**Pan-Ameri•can•ism**
**Pan-Arab** (*or* **-Arabic)**
**Pan-Arabism**
**pana•tela** (*or* **pana•tel•la)**
**Pa•nay** Philippine island
**pan•cake**
**pan•chax** fish
**Pan•chen Lama**
**pan•chro•mat•ic**
**pan•chro•ma•tism**
**pan•cre•as**
**pan•cre•at•ic**
**pan•crea•tin**
**pan•da** animal; *compare* **pander**
**(pandamonium)** *incorrect spelling of* **pandemonium**
**pan•da•na•ceous** botany term
**pan•da•nus** (*plural* **•nuses)** plant
**Pandarus** mythological character
**Pan•dean** of Pan
**pan•dect** treatise
**pan•dem•ic**
**pan•de•mo•ni•ac** (*or* **•mon•ic)**
**pan•de•mo•nium**
**pan•der** gratify weakness; pimp; *compare* **panda**
**pan•der•er**
**pan•dit** *less common spelling of* **pundit** *except as Indian title, as in* **Pandit Nehru**
**Pandora** mythological character
**pan•dora** *variant of* **bandora**
**pan•dour** Croatian soldier
**pan•dow•dy** (*plural* **•dies)** *US* fruit pie
**pan•du•rate** (*or* **•du•ri•form)** botany term
**pan•dy** (*plural* **•dies)** school punishment
**pane** sheet of glass; *compare* **pain**
**pan•egyr•ic** praise; *compare* **paregoric**
**pan•egyri•cal**
**pan•egyr•ist**
**pan•egy•rize** (*or* **•rise)**
**pan•el (•el•ling, •elled;** *US* **•el•ing, •eled)**
**pan•el•list**
**pan•et•to•ne** spiced bread
**pan•ful** (*plural* **•fuls)**
**pang**
**pan•ga** knife
**Pan•gaea** ancient continent
**pan•gen•esis** heredity theory
**pan•genet•ic**
**pan•geneti•cal•ly**
**pan•go•lin** animal
**pan•han•dle**
**Pan•hel•len•ic**
**Pan•hel•len•ism**
**Pan•hel•len•ist**
**Pan•hel•len•is•tic**
**pan•ic (•ick•ing, •icked)**
**pan•icky**
**pani•cle** botany term
**pani•cled**
**panic-stricken** (*or* **-struck)**
**pa•nicu•late** (*or* **•lat•ed)**
**pan•jan•drum**
**pan•mix•is** (*or* **•mixia)** genetics term
**Pan•mun•jom** Korean village
**pan•nage** pig pasturage
**panne** fabric
**pan•ni•er**
**pan•ni•kin**
**pa•no•cha** (*or* **pe•nu•che)** sugar
**pano•plied**
**pano•ply** (*plural* **•plies)**
**pan•op•tic** (*or* **•ti•cal)**
**pan•op•ti•cal•ly**
**pano•ra•ma**
**pano•ram•ic**
**pano•rami•cal•ly**
**pan•pipes**
**pan•soph•ic** (*or* **•sophi•cal)**
**pan•sophi•cal•ly**
**pan•so•phy** universal knowledge
**pan•sy** (*plural* **•sies)**
**pant**
**pan•ta•lets** (*or* **•lettes)** women's drawers
**pan•ta•loon** pantomime character
**pan•ta•loons** men's trousers
**pan•tech•ni•con**
**pan•theism**
**pan•theist**
**pan•theis•tic** (*or* **•ti•cal)**
**pan•theis•ti•cal•ly**
**Pan•the•on** Roman temple
**pan•the•on** temple to all gods
**pan•ther** (*plural* **•thers** *or* **•ther)**
**panties**
**pan•ti•hose**
**pan•tile**
**pan•ti•soc•ra•cy** community ruled by all
**pan•to** (*plural* **•tos)** *Slang* pantomime
**pan•to•graph**
**pan•tog•ra•pher**

**pan•to•graph•ic**
**pan•to•graphi•cal•ly**
**pan•tog•ra•phy**
**pan•to•mime**
**pan•to•mim•ic**
**pan•to•mim•ist**
**pan•to•then•ic acid**
**pan•toum** verse form
**pan•try** (*plural* **•tries**)
**pants**
**pant•suit** *US* trouser suit
**panty•waist** *US* childish person
**pan•zer**
**Pao•ting** (*or* **Pao-ting**) Chinese city
**Pao•tow** Chinese city
**pap**
**papa**
**pa•pa•cy** (*plural* **•cies**)
**pa•pa•in** enzyme
**pa•pal**
**pa•pal•ly**
**pa•pa•vera•ceous** botany term
**pa•pa•ver•ine** alkaloid
**pa•paw** (*or* **paw•**) American fruit
**pa•pa•ya** West Indian fruit
**Pa•pe•ete** Tahitian capital
**pa•per**
**paper•back**
**paper•bark** tree
**paper•board**
**paper•boy**
**paper•clip**
**paper-cutter**
**pa•per•er**
**paper•girl**
**paper•hanger**
**paper•hanging**
**pa•peri•ness**
**paper•knife** (*plural* **•knives**)
**paper•weight**
**paper•work**
**pa•pery**
**pap•eterie** box for papers
**Paph•la•go•nia** Roman province
**Pa•phos** Cypriot village
**papier-mâché**
**pa•pil•la** (*plural* **•lae**)
**pa•pil•lary** (*or* **•late**, **•lose**)
**pap•il•lo•ma** (*plural* **•ma•ta** *or* **•mas**) tumour
**pap•il•lo•ma•to•sis**
**pap•il•lo•ma•tous**
**pap•il•lon** dog
**pap•il•lote** paper frill in cookery
**pa•pist**
**pa•pis•ti•cal** (*or* **•pis•tic**)
**pa•pist•ry**
**pa•poose** (*or* **pap•poose**) American Indian baby
**pap•pose** (*or* **•pous**)
**pap•pus** (*plural* **•pi**) plant hairs
**pap•py** (**•pi•er**, **•pi•est**) mushy
**pap•ri•ka**
**Pa•puan**
**Pa•pua New Guinea**
**papu•lar**
**pap•ule** (*or* **papu•la**; *plural* **•ules** *or* **•lae**)
**papu•lif•er•ous**
**papy•ra•ceous**
**papy•rolo•gist**
**papy•rol•ogy**
**pa•py•rus** (*plural* **•ri** *or* **•ruses**)
**par** accepted standard; *compare* **parr**
**para** (*plural* **paras** *or* **para**) coin
**para** (*plural* **paras**) paratrooper; paragraph
**Pará** Brazilian state
**pa•raba•sis** (*pluras* **•ses**) speech of Greek chorus
**para•bio•sis** (*plural* **•ses**) union of two individuals
**para•bi•ot•ic**
**para•blast** biology term
**para•blas•tic**
**para•ble** religious story
**pa•rabo•la** maths term
**para•bol•ic** of a parabola
**para•bol•ic** (*or* **•boli•cal**) of parables
**para•boli•cal•ly**
**pa•rabo•list**
**pa•rabo•li•za•tion** (*or* **•sa•tion**)
**pa•rabo•lize** (*or* **•lise**)
**pa•rabo•loid** maths term
**pa•rabo•loi•dal**
**para•brake**
**pa•ra•ceta•mol**
**pa•rach•ro•nism** error in dating
**para•chute**
**para•chut•ist**
**Para•clete** Holy Ghost
**para•clete** mediator
**pa•rade**
**pa•rad•er**
**para•digm**
**para•dig•mat•ic**
**para•dise**
**para•di•sia•cal** (*or* **•disi•ac**)
**para•dos** bank behind trench
**para•dox**
**para•doxi•cal**
**para•doxi•cal•ly**
**para•drop**
**par•aes•thesia** (*US* **•es•**; *plural* **•thesiae**) medical term
**par•aes•thet•ic** (*US* **•es•**)
**par•af•fin** (*or* **•fine**)
**para•form•al•de•hyde** (*or* **para•form**)
**para•gen•esis** (*or* **•genesia**) geology term
**para•genet•ic**
**para•geneti•cal•ly**
**para•go•ge** (*or* **para•gogue**) linguistics term
**para•gog•ic** (*or* **•gogi•cal**)
**para•gogi•cal•ly**
**para•gon**
**para•graph**
**para•graphia** psychiatric term
**para•graph•ic** (*or* **•graphi•cal**)
**para•graphi•cal•ly**
**Para•guay**
**Para•guay•an**
**para•hy•dro•gen**
**Pa•raí•ba** Brazilian state
**para•keet** (*or* **par•ra•keet**)
**para•lan•guage**
**par•al•de•hyde**
**para•leip•sis** (*or* **•lip•sis**; *plural* **•ses**) rhetorical device
**pa•ra•li•pom•ena** supplementary writings
**par•al•lac•tic**
**par•al•lac•ti•cal•ly**
**par•al•lax**

**par•al•lel** (**•lel•ing, •leled**)
**par•al•lel•epi•ped** (*or* **•lelo•pi•ped**)
**par•al•lel•ism**
**par•al•lel•ist**
**par•al•lelo•gram**
**pa•ralo•gism** invalid argument
**pa•ralo•gist**
**pa•ralo•gis•tic**
**para•ly•sa•tion** (*US* **•za•tion**)
**para•lyse** (*US* **•lyze**)
**para•lys•er** (*US* **•lyz•er**)
**pa•raly•sis** (*plural* **•ses**)
**para•lyt•ic**
**para•lyti•cal•ly**
**para•mag•net•ic**
**para•mag•net•ism**
**Para•mari•bo** capital of Surinam
**para•mat•ta** (*or* **par•ra•mat•ta**) fabric
**para•mecium** (*plural* **•mecia**) protozoan
**para•med•ic**
**para•medi•cal**
**para•ment** (*plural* **•ments** *or* **•men•ta**) vestment
**pa•ram•eter**
**para•met•ric** (*or* **•ri•cal**)
**para•mili•tary**
**par•am•ne•sia**
**para•mo** (*plural* **•mos**) Andean plateau
**para•morph** mineralogy term
**para•mor•phic** (*or* **•phous**)
**para•mor•phism**
**para•mount**
**par•amour**
**Pa•ra•ná** Brazilian state, river, and city
**pa•rang** knife
**para•noia**
**para•noi•ac**
**para•noid**
**para•nor•mal**
**para•pet**
**para•pet•ed**
**par•aph** flourish after signature
**para•pher•na•lia**
**para•phrase**
**para•phras•tic**
**pa•raphy•sis** (*plural* **•ses**) botany term
**para•plegia**
**para•plegic**
**para•po•dium** (*plural* **•dia**) zoology term
**para•prax•is** psychology term
**para•psy•chol•ogy**
**Para•quat** (*Trademark*)
**para•sang** Persian unit
**para•sele•ne** (*plural* **•nae**) astronomy term
**Pa•ra•shah** (*plural* **•shoth**) synagogue reading
**para•site**
**para•sit•ic**
**para•siti•cal•ly**
**para•siti•cid•al**
**para•siti•cide**
**para•sit•ism**
**para•si•tize** (*or* **•tise**)
**para•si•to•logi•cal**
**para•sit•olo•gist**
**para•sit•ol•ogy**
**para•sol**
**pa•ras•ti•chy** (*plural* **•chies**) botany term
**para•sym•pa•thet•ic**
**para•syn•the•sis** linguistics term
**para•syn•the•ton** (*plural* **•ta**)
**para•tac•tic**
**para•tac•ti•cal•ly**
**para•tax•is** linguistics term
**para•thi•on** insecticide
**para•thy•roid**
**para•troop•er**
**para•troops**
**para•ty•phoid**
**para•vane** device on minesweeper
**par avion** *French* by plane
**para•zo•an** (*plural* **•zoans** *or* **•zoa**) zoology term
**par•boil**
**par•buck•le** rope sling
**par•cel** (**•cel•ling, •celled**; *US* **•cel•ing, •celed**)
**par•cenary** joint heirship
**par•cener**
**parch**
**parch•ment**
**par•close** church screen
**pard** *Archaic* leopard
**par•da•lote** bird
**pard•ner** *US* partner
**par•don**
**par•don•able**
**par•don•ably**
**par•don•er**
**pare** trim; *compare* **pair**
**par•egor•ic** medicine; *compare* **panegyric**
**pa•rei•ra** medicinal root
**pa•ren•chy•ma** tissue
**par•en•chyma•tous**
**par•ent**
**par•ent•age**
**pa•ren•tal**
**par•en•ter•al** medical term
**par•en•ter•ally**
**pa•ren•thesis** (*plural* **•theses**)
**pa•ren•thesize** (*or* **•thesise**)
**par•en•thet•ic** (*or* **•theti•cal**)
**par•en•theti•cal•ly**
**par•ent•hood**
**par•er**
**par•er•gon** (*plural* **•ga**) additional work
**pa•resis** paralysis
**par•es•thesia** *US spelling of* **paraesthesia**
**pa•ret•ic**
**par ex•cel•lence** *French* beyond comparison
**par•fait** dessert
**par•fleche** rawhide
**par•get**
**par•get•ing**
**par•he•lic** (*or* **•he•lia•cal**)
**par•he•li•on** (*plural* **•lia**) astronomy term
**pa•ri•ah**
**Parian** marble
**pari•es** (*plural* **pa•ri•etes**) anatomy term
**pa•ri•etal**
**pari-mutuel** (*plural* **pari-mutuels** *or* **paris-mutuels**) betting system
**par•ing**
**pari pas•su** *Latin* legal term
**pari•pin•nate** botany term
**Par•is** French capital
**Paris** mythological character
**par•ish**
**pa•rish•ion•er**

**Pa•ris•ian**
**Pa•risi•enne** Parisian woman
**pari•son** glass mass
**pari•syl•lab•ic**
**par•ity** (*plural* **•ities**)
**park**
**par•ka** coat
**par•kin** cake
**park•ing**
**par•kin•son•ism**
**park•land**
**park•way**
**parky** (**parki•er, parki•est**)
**par•lance**
**par•lan•do** music term
**par•lay** *US* double up in betting
**par•ley** discuss
**par•ley•er**
**par•lia•ment** (*or* **Par•**)
**Par•lia•men•tar•ian** parliamentary supporter in Civil War
**par•lia•men•tar•ian**
**par•lia•men•tari•an•ism** (*or* **•tar•ism**)
**par•lia•men•ta•ry**
**par•lour** (*US* **•lor**)
**par•lous** dangerous
**Par•ma** Italian city; *compare* **Palma**
**Par•men•tier** cookery term
**Par•me•san** cheese
**Par•nas•sian**
**Par•nas•sus**
**pa•ro•chial**
**pa•ro•chi•al•ism**
**pa•ro•chi•al•ly**
**pa•rod•ic** (*or* **•rodi•cal**)
**paro•dy** (*noun, plural* **•dies**; *verb* **•dies, •dy•ing, •died**)
**pa•roi•cous** (*or* **•roe•cious**) botany term
**pa•rol** oral
**pa•rol•able**
**pa•role** conditional release
**pa•rolee**
**paro•no•ma•sia** play on words
**paro•no•mas•ti•cal•ly**
**paro•nym** linguistics term
**paro•nym•ic** (*or* **pa•rony•mous**)
**Pár•os** Greek island
**pa•rot•ic** near the ear
**pa•rot•id** gland
**paro•ti•tis** (*or* **pa•roti•di•tis**) mumps
**pa•ro•toid** poison gland on toad
**par•ox•ysm**
**par•ox•ys•mal** (*or* **•mic**)
**par•quet**
**par•quet•ry**
**parr** (*plural* **parrs** *or* **parr**) salmon; *compare* **par**
**par•rel** (*or* **•ral**) nautical term
**par•ri•cid•al**
**par•ri•cide** killing of parent; *compare* **patricide**
**par•rot**
**parrot-fashion**
**parrot•fish** (*plural* **•fish** *or* **•fishes**)
**par•ry** (*verb* **•ries, •ry•ing, •ried**; *noun, plural* **•ries**)
**pars•able**
**parse**
**par•sec** unit
**Par•see**
**Par•see•ism** Indian religion
**pars•er**
**par•si•mo•ni•ous**
**par•si•mo•ny**
**pars•ley**
**pars•nip**
**par•son**
**par•son•age**
**part**
**par•take** (**•tak•ing, •took, •tak•en**)
**par•tak•er**
**par•tan** *Scot* crab
**part•ed**
**par•terre** garden
**par•theno•car•pic** (*or* **•pous**)
**par•theno•car•py** botany term
**par•theno•genesis**
**par•theno•genet•ic**
**par•theno•geneti•cal•ly**
**Par•the•non** Greek temple
**Parthenope** mythological character
**Par•thia** ancient Asian country
**Par•thian**
**par•tial**
**par•tial•ity** (*plural* **•ities**)
**par•tial•ly**
**par•tial•ness**
**part•ible**
**par•tici•pant**
**par•tici•pate**
**par•tici•pa•tion** (*or* **•tici•pance**)
**par•tici•pa•tor**
**par•ti•cipi•al**
**par•ti•ci•ple**
**par•ti•cle**
**parti-coloured** (*US* **-colored**)
**par•ticu•lar**
**par•ticu•lar•ism**
**par•ticu•lar•ist**
**par•ticu•lar•is•tic**
**par•ticu•lar•ity** (*plural* **•ities**)
**par•ticu•lari•za•tion** (*or* **•sa•tion**)
**par•ticu•lar•ize** (*or* **•ise**)
**par•ticu•lar•iz•er** (*or* **•is•er**)
**par•ticu•late** (*adj*)
**part•ing**
**par•ti pris** *French* preconceived opinion
**par•ti•san** (*or* **•zan**)
**par•ti•san•ship** (*or* **•zan•ship**)
**par•ti•ta** musical piece
**par•tite** divided
**par•ti•tion**
**par•ti•tion•er** (*or* **•ist**)
**par•ti•tive**
**part•let** shawl
**part•ly**
**part•ner**
**part•ner•ship**
**par•ton** physics term
**par•took**
**par•tridge** (*plural* **•tridges** *or* **•tridge**)
**part-time** (*adj*)
**part-timer**
**par•tu•ri•ent** of childbirth
**par•tu•ri•fa•cient**
**par•tu•ri•tion**
**par•ty** (*plural* **•ties**)
**pa•ru•lis** (*plural* **•li•des**) gumboil
**pa•rure** set of jewels
**par•venu** (*fem* **•venue**)

**par•vis** (*or* **•vise**) church porch
**Pasa•dena** US city
**Pa•sar•ga•dae** ancient Persian city
**Pa•say** Philippine city
**pas•cal** unit
**pas•chal** of Easter
**Pas-de-Calais** French department
**pas de deux** (*plural* **pas de deux**) ballet sequence
**pash** *Slang* infatuation
**Pa•sha** Turkish title
**pa•sha** (*or* **•cha**) Ottoman governor
**pa•sha•lik** (*or* **•lic**) province of pasha
**Pash•to** (*or* **Push•tu**) language
**paso do•ble** (*plural* **paso do•bles** *or* **pasos do•bles**) dance
**pasque•flow•er**
**pas•quin•ade** (*or* **pas•quil**) satire
**pas•quin•ad•er**
**pass**
**pass•able** able to be passed; *compare* **passible**
**pass•ably**
**pas•sa•ca•glia** musical piece
**pas•sade** dressage term
**pas•sage**
**passage•way**
**pas•sant** heraldic term
**pass•book**
**pas•sé** out-of-date
**passed** *past tense of* **pass**; *compare* **past**
**passe•men•terie** decorative trimming
**pas•sen•ger**
**passe-partout** picture mounting
**passe•pied** dance
**passer-by** (*plural* **passers-by**)
**pas•ser•ine** ornithology term
**pas seul** dance sequence
**pas•sibil•ity**
**pas•sible** sensitive; *compare* **passable**
**pas•si•flo•ra•ceous** botany term
**pas•sim** *Latin* throughout
**pass•ing**
**Pas•sion** Christ's sufferings
**pas•sion**
**pas•sion•al**
**pas•sion•ate**
**pas•sion•ate•ness**
**passion•flower**
**pas•sion•less**
**pas•sion•less•ness**
**Passion•tide**
**pas•sive**
**pas•sive•ness** (*or* **pas•siv•ity**)
**pas•siv•ism**
**pas•siv•ist**
**pass•key**
**Pass•over**
**pass•port**
(passtime) *incorrect spelling of* **pastime**
**pas•sus** (*plural* **•sus** *or* **•suses**) part of poem
**pass•word**
**past**
**pas•ta**
**paste**
**paste•board**
**pas•tel** drawing crayon; *compare* **pastille**
**pas•tel•list** (*or* **•tel•ist**)
**pas•tern** part of horse's foot
**paste-up**
**pas•teur•ism** rabies treatment
**pas•teuri•za•tion** (*or* **•sa•tion**)
**pas•teur•ize** (*or* **•ise**)
**pas•teur•iz•er** (*or* **•is•er**)
**pas•tic•cio** (*plural* **•cios**) pastiche
**pas•tiche** artistic medley; *compare* **postiche**
**pas•tille** (*or* **•til**) lozenge; *compare* **pastel**
**pasti•ly**
**pas•time**
**pasti•ness**
**pas•tis** alcoholic drink
**pas•tor**
**pas•to•ral** of shepherds or pastors
**pas•to•rale** (*plural* **•rales** *or* **•ra•li**) musical piece
**pas•to•ral•ly**
**pas•tor•ate**
**pas•tra•mi** smoked beef
**pas•try** (*plural* **•tries**)
**pas•tur•age**
**pas•ture**
(pasturize) *incorrect spelling of* **pasteurize**
**pasty** (*noun, plural* **pasties**; *adj* **pasti•er, pasti•est**) a pastry; pale
**pat** (**pat•ting, pat•ted**)
**pa•ta•gium** (*plural* **•gia**) zoology term
**Pata•go•nia** South American region
**patch**
**patch•able**
**patch•er**
**patchi•ly**
**patchi•ness**
**patchou•li** (*or* **pachou•li patchou•ly**) perfume
**patch•work**
**patchy** (**patchi•er, patchi•est**)
**pate** the head
**pâté** food; *compare* **pattée**
**pâté de foie gras** (*plural* **pâtés de foie gras**)
**pa•tel•la** (*plural* **•lae**) kneecap
**pa•tel•lar**
**pa•tel•late**
**pa•tel•li•form**
**pat•en** (*or* **•in, •ine**) plate for Eucharist; *compare* **patten**
**pa•ten•cy**
**pa•tent**
**pa•tent•able**
**pa•tentee**
**pa•tent•ly**
**pa•ten•tor**
**pa•ter** *Slang* father
**pa•ter•fa•mili•as** (*plural* **pa•tres•fa•mili•as**) male head of family
**pa•ter•nal**
**pa•ter•nal•ism**
**pa•ter•nal•ist**
**pa•ter•nal•is•tic**
**pa•ter•nal•is•ti•cal•ly**
**pa•ter•nal•ly**
**pa•ter•nity**
**Pat•er•nos•ter** Lord's Prayer
**pat•er•nos•ter** rosary beads; fishing tackle; lift

**Pat•er•son** US city
**path**
**Pa•than** Afghan or Pakistani Muslim
**pa•thet•ic**
**pa•theti•cal•ly**
**path•finder**
**path•finding**
**patho•gen** (*or* **•gene**)
**patho•gen•esis** (*or* **pa•thog•eny**)
**patho•genet•ic** of disease
**patho•gen•ic** causing disease
**path•og•no•mon•ic** indicating disease
**path•og•no•moni•cal•ly**
**path•og•no•my** study of emotions
**patho•logi•cal** (*or* **•log•ic**)
**patho•logi•cal•ly**
**pa•tholo•gist**
**pa•thol•ogy** (*plural* **•ogies**)
**pa•thos**
**path•way**
**Pa•tia•la** Indian city
**pa•tience**
**pa•tient**
**pa•tient•ly**
**pati•na**
**pa•tio** (*plural* **•tios**)
**pa•tis•serie**
**Pat•mos** Greek island
**Pat•na** Indian city; rice
**pat•ois** (*plural* **pat•ois**) dialect
**Pa•tras** Greek port
**pa•trial**
**pa•tri•arch**
**pa•tri•ar•chal**
**pa•tri•ar•chate**
**pa•tri•ar•chy** (*plural* **•chies**)
**pa•tri•cian**
**pa•tri•ci•ate** rank of patrician
**pat•ri•cid•al**
**pat•ri•cide** killing one's father; *compare* **parricide**
**pat•ri•cli•nous** (*or* **•ro•cli•nous, •ro•cli•nal**) resembling male parent
**pat•ri•lin•eal** (*or* **•ear**)
**pat•ri•lo•cal** living with husband's family
**pat•ri•mo•nial**
**pat•ri•mo•ny** (*plural* **•nies**)
**pa•tri•ot**
**pat•ri•ot•ic**
**pat•ri•ot•ism**
**pa•tris•tic** (*or* **•ti•cal**)
**pa•tris•ti•cal•ly**
**pa•trol** (**•trol•ling, •trolled**)
**pa•trol•ler**
**patrol•man** (*plural* **•men**)
**pa•trol•ogy** writings of Church Fathers
**pa•tron**
**pat•ron•age**
**pa•tron•al**
**pa•tron•ess**
**pat•ron•ize** (*or* **•ise**)
**pat•ron•iz•er** (*or* **•is•er**)
**pat•ron•iz•ing•ly** (*or* **•is•ing•ly**)
**pat•ro•nym•ic**
**pat•ted**
**pat•tée** type of cross; *compare* **pâté**
**pat•ten** wooden clog; *compare* **paten**
**pat•ter**
**pat•tern**
**pat•ting**
**pat•ty** (*plural* **•ties**)
**patu•lous**
**paua** shellfish
**pau•cal** linguistics term
**pau•city**
**paul•dron** armour plate
**Paul•ine** of St Paul
**pau•low•nia** tree
**paunch**
**paunchi•ness**
**paunchy** (**paunchi•er, paunchi•est**)
**pau•per**
**pau•per•ism**
**pau•per•ize** (*or* **•ise**)
**pause**
**paus•er**
**paus•ing•ly**
**pav•age** paving tax
**pa•vane** (*or* **pa•van**) dance
**pave**
**pavé** paved surface
**pave•ment**
**pa•vil•ion**
**pav•ing**
**pav•ior** (*or* **•iour**) one who paves
**pav•is** (*or* **•ise**) shield
**Pav•lo•va** meringue cake
**pavo•nine** of peacocks
**paw**
**pawky** (**pawki•er, pawki•est**) *Scot* drily witty
**pawl** part of ratchet; *compare* **pall**
**pawn**
**pawn•age**
**pawn•broker**
**pawn•broking**
**Paw•nee** (*plural* **•nees** *or* **•nee**) American Indian
**pawn•shop**
**paw•paw** *variant spelling of* **papaw**
**pax**
**pax•wax** *Dialect* ligament
**pay** (**pay•ing, paid**)
**pay•able**
**pay•day**
**payee**
**pay•er**
**pay•load**
**pay•master**
**pay•ment**
**pay•nim** *Archaic* heathen
**pay-off** (*noun*)
**pay•ola** *US* bribe
**pay•phone**
**pay•roll**
**pea**
**peace**
**peace•able**
**peace•able•ness**
**peace•ful**
**peace•ful•ly**
**peace•ful•ness**
**peace•maker**
**peace•time**
**peach**
**peachi•ness**
**peachy** (**peachi•er, peachi•est**)
**pea•cock** (*plural* **•cocks** *or* **•cock**)
**pea•fowl** (*plural* **•fowls** *or* **•fowl**)
**pea•hen**
**peak** summit; to sicken; *compare* **peek; peke**
**peaked**
**peaky** (**peaki•er, peaki•est**)

**peal** loud sound; *compare* **peel**
**pean** heraldic term; *US variant spelling of* **paean**; *compare* **paeon; peon**
**pea•nut**
**pear**
**pearl** jewel; *compare* **purl**
**pearl•er**
**pearl•ite** steel constituent; *variant spelling of* **perlite**
**pearl•it•ic**
**pearl•ized** (*or* **•ised**)
**pearly** (*adj* **pearli•er, pearli•est**; *noun, plural* **pearlies**)
**pear•main** apple
**peas•ant**
**peas•ant•ry**
**pease** *Dialect* pea
**pea•shooter**
**pea•soup•er** *Slang* fog
**peat**
**peaty**
**peau de soie** fabric
**peb•ble**
**pebble-dash**
**peb•bling**
**peb•bly**
**pe•can** nut; *compare* **pekan**
**pec•ca•bil•ity**
**pec•cable** liable to sin
**pec•ca•dil•lo** (*plural* **•los** *or* **•loes**)
**pec•can•cy**
**pec•cant**
**pec•ca•ry** (*plural* **•ries** *or* **•ry**) piglike animal
**pec•ca•vi** (*plural* **•vis**) confession of guilt
**peck**
**peck•er**
**peck•ing**
**peck•ish**
**pec•tase** enzyme
**pec•tate**
**pec•ten** (*plural* **•tens** *or* **•ti•nes**) zoology term; *compare* **pectin**
**pec•tic** of pectin; *compare* **peptic**
**pec•tin** gelling substance; *compare* **pecten**
**pec•ti•nate** (*or* **•nat•ed**) comb-shaped
**pec•ti•na•tion**
**pec•tin•ous**
**pec•tiz•able** (*or* **•tis•able**)
**pec•ti•za•tion** (*or* **•sa•tion**)
**pec•tize** (*or* **•tise**) jellify
**pec•to•ral**
**pecu•late** embezzle
**pecu•la•tion**
**pecu•la•tor**
**pe•cu•liar**
**pe•cu•li•ar•ity** (*plural* **•ities**)
**pe•cu•ni•ari•ly**
**pe•cu•ni•ary**
**peda•gog•ic** (*or* **•gogi•cal**)
**peda•gogi•cal•ly**
**peda•gog•ics**
**peda•gog•ism** (*or* **•gogu•ism**)
**peda•gogue** (*or* **•gog**)
**peda•go•gy**
**ped•al** (**•al•ling, •alled**; *US* **•dal•ing, •daled**) foot lever; operate pedals; *compare* **peddle**
**pe•dal** of the foot
**pe•dal•fer** soil
**ped•al•ler** (*US* **•al•er**) one who pedals; *compare* **peddler; pedlar**
**peda•lo** (*plural* **•los** *or* **•loes**) pedal boat
**ped•ant**
**pe•dan•tic**
**ped•ant•ry** (*plural* **•ries**)
**ped•ate** biology term
**pe•dati•fid** botany term
**ped•dle** sell; *compare* **pedal**
**ped•dler** drugs seller; *US spelling of* **pedlar**
**ped•er•ast** (*or* **paed•**)
**ped•er•as•tic** (*or* **paed•**)
**ped•er•as•ty** (*or* **paed•**)
**ped•es•tal**
**pe•des•trian**
**pe•des•tria•ni•za•tion** (*or* **•sa•tion**)
**pe•des•tri•an•ize** (*or* **•ise**)
**Pedi** African people
**pe•di•at•rics** *US spelling of* **paediatrics**
**pedi•cab** tricycle cab
**pedi•cel** flower stalk
**pedi•cle** small stalk
**pe•dicu•lar** of lice or pedicles
**pe•dicu•late** zoology term
**pe•dicu•lo•sis** infestation with lice
**pe•dicu•lous**
**pedi•cure**
**pedi•form**
**pedi•gree**
**pedi•greed**
**pedi•ment**
**pedi•ment•al**
**pedi•palp** zoology term
**ped•lar** (*US* **ped•dler**) hawker; *compare* **peddler**
**pedo•cal** soil
**pe•do•logi•cal**
**pe•dolo•gist**
**pe•dol•ogy** study of soils
**pe•dom•eter**
**pe•dun•cle** flower stalk
**pe•dun•cu•lar**
**pe•dun•cu•late** (*or* **•lat•ed**)
**pe•dun•cu•la•tion**
**pee** (**pee•ing, peed**)
**Pee•bles** former Scottish county
**peek** peep; *compare* **peak; peke**
**peeka•boo**
**peel** rind; to be shed; fortified tower; *compare* **peal**
**peel•er**
**peelie-wally** *Scot* unwell
**peel•ing**
**peen** part of hammer
**peep**
**peep•er**
**peep•hole**
**peep•show**
**pee•pul** (*or* **pi•pal**) sacred tree
**peer** a noble; an equal; to look; *compare* **pier**
**peer•age**
**peer•ess**
**peer•less**
**peeve** *Slang* irritate
**peev•ers** *Scot* hopscotch
**peev•ish**
**peev•ish•ness**
**pee•wee** *variant spelling of* **pewee**
**pee•wit** (*or* **pe•wit**) lapwing
**peg** (**peg•ging, pegged**)

**Pega•sus** mythological horse; constellation
**peg•board**
**peg•ma•tite** rock
**peg•ma•tit•ic**
**peign•oir**
**pejo•ra•tion**
**pe•jo•ra•tive**
**pek•an** animal; *compare* pecan
**peke** *Slang* Pekingese dog; *compare* **peak; peek**
**Pe•kin** duck
**Pe•king** *variant spelling of* **Beijing**
**Pe•king•ese** (*or* **•kin•**) dog; of Peking
**pe•koe** tea
**pel•age**
**Pe•la•gi•an•ism** Christian doctrine
**pe•lag•ic** of open sea
**pel•ar•go•nium**
**Pe•lée** West Indian volcano
**pel•er•ine** cape
**Peleus** mythological character
**pelf** *Slang* money
**pel•ham** horse's bit
**peli•can**
**Pe•li•on** Greek mountain
**pe•lisse**
**pe•lite** rock
**pe•lit•ic**
**Pel•la** ancient Greek city
**pel•la•gra**
**pel•la•grous**
**pel•let**
**pel•li•cle**
**pel•licu•lar**
**pel•li•tory** (*plural* **•tories**) plant
**pell-mell**
**pel•lu•cid**
**pel•lu•cid•ity** (*or* **•ness**)
**Pel•man•ism** memory training
**pel•man•ism** card game
**pel•met**
**Pelo•pon•nese**
**Pelo•pon•ne•sian**
**Pelops** mythological character
**pe•lo•ria** botany term
**pe•lo•rus** (*plural* **•ruses**) gyrocompass
**pe•lo•ta** ball game
**Pe•lo•tas** Brazilian port
**pelt**
**pel•tast** ancient Greek soldier
**pel•tate** botany term
**pel•ta•tion**
**pelt•er**
**Peltier ef•fect**
**pelt•ry** (*plural* **•ries**) animal pelts
**pel•vic**
**pel•vis** (*plural* **•vises** *or* **•ves**)
**Pem•ba** Tanzanian island
**Pem•broke**
**Pem•broke•shire** Welsh county
**pem•mi•can** (*or* **pemi•can**) food
**pem•phi•gus** skin disease
**pen** (**pen•ning, penned**) writing tool; write
**pen** (**pen•ning, penned** *or* **pent**) enclosure; enclose
**pe•nal**
**pe•nali•za•tion** (*or* **•sa•tion**)
**pe•nal•ize** (*or* **•ise**)
**pen•al•ty** (*plural* **•ties**)
**pen•ance**
**Pe•nang** Malaysian state
**pe•na•tes** Roman gods
**pence**
**pen•cel** (*or* **•sel, •sil**) small flag; *compare* **pencil**
**pen•chant**
**Pen•chi** (*or* **•ki**) Chinese city
**pen•cil** (**•cil•ling, •cilled**; *US* **•cil•ing, •ciled**) writing tool, etc.; *compare* **pencel**
**pen•cil•ler** (*US* **•cil•er**)
**pend**
**pen•dant** necklace
**pen•dent** dangling
**pen•den•te lite** legal term
**pen•den•tive** architectural term
**pend•ing**
**pen•dragon** leader of ancient Britons
**pen•du•lous**
**pen•du•lum**
**pe•neplain** (*or* **•neplane**) flat land
**pe•ne•pla•na•tion**
**pen•etrabil•ity**
**pen•etrable**
**pen•etra•lia** innermost parts
**pen•etra•lian**
**pen•etrance**
**pen•etrant**
**pen•etrate**
**pen•etra•tion**
**pen•etra•tor**
**Peng•pu** (*or* **Pang-fou**) Chinese city
**pen•guin**
**peni•cil•late** biology term
**peni•cil•la•tion**
**peni•cil•lin** antibiotic
**peni•cil•lium** (*plural* **•liums** *or* **•lia**) mould
**pe•nile** of the penis
**pe•nil•li•on** (*sing.* **pe•nill**) Welsh sung poetry
**pen•in•su•la**
**pen•in•su•lar**
**pe•nis** (*plural* **•nises** *or* **•nes**)
**peni•tence**
**peni•tent**
**peni•ten•tial**
**peni•ten•tia•ry** (*plural* **•ries**)
**pen•knife** (*plural* **•knives**)
**pen•man** (*plural* **•men**)
**pen•man•ship**
**pen•na** (*plural* **•nae**) feather
**pen•nant** ship's flag; *compare* **pennon**
**pen•nate** (*or* **•nat•ed**)
**penned**
**pen•nies**
**pen•ni•less**
**pen•ni•less•ness**
**Pen•nine**
**Pen•nines**
**pen•ning**
**pen•ni•nite** mineral
**pen•non** long flag; *compare* **pennant**
**Penn•syl•va•nia**
**Penn•syl•va•nian**
**pen•nul•ti•mate**
**pen•ny** (*plural* **pen•nies** *or* **pence**)
**pen•ny•cress**
**penny-pincher**
**penny-pinching**
**penny•royal** plant
**penny•weight**

**penny-wise**
**penny•wort** plant
**penny•worth**
**pe•no•logi•cal** (*or* **poe•**)
**pe•nolo•gist** (*or* **poe•**)
**pe•nol•ogy** (*or* **poe•**)
**Pen•rith** Cumbrian town
**pen•sile** ornithology term
**pen•sil•ity** (*or* **•sile•ness**)
**pen•sion**
**pen•sion•able**
**pen•sion•ary** (*plural* **•aries**)
**pen•sion•er**
**pen•sive**
**pen•sive•ness**
**pen•stock** water channel
**pent**
**pen•ta•chlo•ro•phe•nol**
**pen•ta•cle** *variant of* **pentagram**
**pen•tad** group of five
**pen•ta•dac•tyl**
**Pen•ta•gon** US defence headquarters
**pen•ta•gon** five-sided polygon
**pen•tago•nal**
**pen•ta•gram** (*or* **•cle**) magical symbol
**pen•ta•he•dron** (*plural* **•drons** *or* **•dra**)
**pen•tam•er•ous** botany term
**pen•tam•eter** verse line
**pen•tane** organic compound
**pen•tan•gu•lar**
**pen•ta•no•ic acid**
**pen•ta•prism**
**pen•ta•quine** drug
**pen•tar•chi•cal**
**pen•tar•chy** (*plural* **•chies**) government by five
**pen•ta•stich** five-line poem
**Pen•ta•teuch** Old Testament books
**pen•tath•lete**
**pen•tath•lon**
**pen•ta•ton•ic** musical term
**pen•ta•va•lent**
**Pen•tecost**
**Pen•tecos•tal**
**pen•tene** organic compound
**pent•house**
**pen•ti•men•to** (*plural* **•ti**) art term
**pent•land•ite** mineral
**pen•to•bar•bi•tone** (*US* **•tal**)
**pen•tode** electronic valve
**pen•tom•ic** military term
**pen•to•san** biochemical compound
**pen•tose** sugar
**Pen•to•thal** (*Trademark*)
**pent•ox•ide**
**pent•ste•mon** (*or* **pen•ste•mon**) plant
**pent-up**
**pen•tyl** chemistry term
**pentylene•tetrazol**
**pe•nu•che** *variant of* **panocha**
**pen•ult** (*or* **pe•nul•ti•ma**)
**pe•nul•ti•mate**
**pe•num•bra** (*plural* **•brae** *or* **•bras**)
**pe•num•bral** (*or* **•brous**)
**pe•nu•ri•ous**
**penu•ry**
**Pen•za** Russian city
**Pen•zance**
**peon** Indian worker; debtor; *compare* **paean**; **paeon**; **pean**
**pe•on•age** (*or* **pe•on•ism**)
**peo•ny** (*plural* **•nies**)
**peo•ple**
**Peo•ria** US port
**pep** (**pep•ping, pepped**)
**pep•lum** (*plural* **•lums** *or* **•la**) ruffle
**pepo** (*plural* **pepos**) botany term
**pep•per**
**pepper•corn**
**pepper•grass**
**pepper•mint**
**pepper•wort**
**pep•pery**
**pep•py** (**•pi•er, •pi•est**)
**pep•sin** (*or* **•sine**) enzyme
**pep•si•nate**
**pep•sino•gen** enzyme
**pep•tic** of digestion; *compare* **pectic**
**pep•ti•dase** enzyme
**pep•tide** protein
**pep•tiz•able** (*or* **•tis•able**)
**pep•ti•za•tion** (*or* **•sa•tion**)
**pep•tize** (*or* **•tise**)
**pep•tiz•er** (*or* **•tis•er**)
**pep•tone** product of digestion
**pep•to•ni•za•tion** (*or* **•sa•tion**)
**pep•to•nize** (*or* **•nise**)
**pep•to•niz•er** (*or* **•nis•er**)
**Pe•quot** (*plural* **•quot** *or* **•quots**) American Indian
**per**
**per•acid**
**pera•cid•ity**
**per•ad•ven•ture** *Archaic* by chance
**Pe•raea** ancient Palestinian region
**Pe•rak** Malaysian state
**per•am•bu•late**
**per•am•bu•la•tion**
**per•am•bu•la•tor**
**per•am•bu•la•tory**
**per an•num**
**per•bo•rate** chemistry term
**per•cale** sheet fabric
**per•ca•line** lining fabric
**per capi•ta**
**per•ceiv•abil•ity**
**per•ceiv•able**
**per•ceive**
**per•ceiv•er**
**per cent**
**per•cent•age**
**per•cen•tile**
**per•cept** object of perception
**per•cep•tibil•ity** (*or* **•tible•ness**)
**per•cep•tible**
**per•cep•tibly**
**per•cep•tion**
**per•cep•tion•al**
**per•cep•tive**
**per•cep•tivi•ty** (*or* **•tive•ness**)
**per•cep•tual**
**perch** (*plural* **(for fish) perch** *or* **perches**)
**per•chance**
**perch•er**
**Per•cheron** horse
**per•chlo•rate**
**per•chlo•ride**
**per•cipi•ence**
**per•cipi•ent**
**per•coid** (*or* **•coi•dean**) zoology term

**per•co•late**
**per•co•la•tion**
**per•co•la•tive**
**per•co•la•tor**
**per•cuss**
**per•cus•sion**
**per•cus•sion•ist**
**per•cus•sive**
**per•cus•sor**
**per•cu•ta•neous**
**per diem** *Latin* every day
**per•di•tion**
**per•egri•nate**
**per•egri•na•tion**
**per•egri•na•tor**
**per•egrine**
**Pe•rei•ra** Colombian city
**pe•rei•ra** medicinal bark
**per•emp•to•ri•ly**
**per•emp•to•ri•ness**
**per•emp•tory**
**pe•ren•nate** botany term
**pe•ren•na•tion**
**per•en•nial**
**per•en•nial•ly**
**per•fect**
**per•fect•er**
**per•fect•ibil•ity**
**per•fect•ible**
**per•fec•tion**
**per•fec•tion•ism**
**per•fec•tion•ist**
**per•fec•tive**
**per•fec•to** (*plural* **•tos**) cigar
**per•fer•vid** ardent
**per•fidi•ous**
**per•fidi•ous•ness**
**per•fi•dy** (*plural* **•dies**)
**per•fo•li•ate** botany term
**per•fo•li•a•tion**
**per•fo•rable**
**per•fo•rate**
**per•fo•ra•tion**
**per•fo•ra•tive** (*or* **•tory**)
**per•fo•ra•tor**
**per•force**
**per•form**
**per•form•able**
**per•for•mance**
**per•for•ma•tive**
**per•form•er**
**per•form•ing**
**per•fume**
**per•fum•er**
**per•fum•ery** (*plural* **•eries**)
**per•func•to•ri•ly**
**per•func•to•ri•ness**
**per•func•tory**
**per•fuse**
**per•fu•sion**
**per•fu•sive**
**Per•ga•mum** ancient Asian city
**per•go•la**
**per•haps**
**peri** (*plural* **peris**) fairy
**peri•anth** petals of flower
**peri•apt** amulet
**peri•blem** plant tissue
**peri•car•dit•ic**
**peri•car•di•tis**
**peri•car•dium** (*plural* **•dia**)
**peri•carp** botany term
**peri•car•pial** (*or* **•pic**)
**peri•chon•drium** (*plural* **•dria**) anatomy term
**peri•clase** mineral
**peri•clas•tic**
**peri•cli•nal** botany term
**peri•cline** mineral
**pe•rico•pe** church reading
**peri•cra•nial**
**peri•cra•nium** (*plural* **•nia**)
**peri•cy•cle** plant tissue
**peri•cy•clic**
**peri•cyn•thi•on** point in lunar orbit
**peri•derm** botany term
**peri•derm•al** (*or* **•ic**)
**pe•rid•ium** (*plural* **•ridia**) botany term
**peri•dot** gemstone
**peri•do•tite** rock
**peri•do•tit•ic**
**peri•gean** (*or* **•geal**)
**peri•gee** point in lunar orbit
**peri•gon** maths term
**Peri•gor•dian** Palaeolithic culture
**pe•rigy•nous** botany term
**pe•rigy•ny**
**peri•he•lion** (*plural* **•lia**) point in planet's orbit
**per•il**
**peri•lous**
**peri•lous•ness**
**peri•lune** point in lunar orbit
**peri•lymph** anatomy term
**pe•rim•eter**
**peri•met•ric** (*or* **•ri•cal, pe•rim•etral**)
**peri•met•ri•cal•ly**
**pe•rim•etry**
**peri•morph** mineralogy term
**peri•mor•phic** (*or* **•phous**)
**peri•mor•phism**
**peri•mys•ium** anatomy term
**peri•na•tal**
**peri•neal**
**peri•neph•rium** (*plural* **•ria**) anatomy term
**peri•neum** (*plural* **•nea**) vaginal area
**peri•neu•ri•tic**
**peri•neu•ri•tis**
**peri•neu•rium** nerve tissue
**pe•ri•od**
**pe•rio•date** chemistry term
**pe•ri•od•ic**
**peri•od•ic acid**
**pe•ri•odi•cal**
**pe•ri•odi•cal•ly**
**pe•rio•dic•ity** (*plural* **•ities**)
**perio•don•tal**
**perio•don•tic**
**perio•don•ti•cal•ly**
**perio•don•tics**
**perio•don•tol•ogy** branch of dentistry
**peri•onych•ium** (*plural* **•onychia**) anatomy term
**peri•os•teum** (*plural* **•tea**) bone tissue
**peri•os•tit•ic**
**peri•os•ti•tis**
**peri•otic** around the ear
**peri•pa•tet•ic**
**peri•pa•teti•cal•ly**
**peri•peteia** (*or* **•petia, pe•rip•ety**) drama term
**peri•peteian** (*or* **•petian**)
**pe•riph•er•al**
**pe•riph•er•al•ly**
**pe•riph•ery** (*plural* **•eries**)
**pe•riph•ra•sis** (*plural* **•ses**) circumlocution
**peri•phras•tic**
**peri•phras•ti•cal•ly**
**pe•riphy•ton** aquatic organisms
**pe•rip•teral**
**pe•rique** tobacco

**peri•sarc** zoology term
**peri•sar•cal** (*or* **•cous**)
**peri•scope**
**peri•scop•ic**
**peri•scopi•cal•ly**
**per•ish**
**per•ish•abil•ity** (*or* **•able•ness**)
**per•ish•able**
**per•ish•er**
**per•ish•ing**
**peri•sperm** botany term
**peri•sperm•al**
**peri•spo•menon** linguistics term
**pe•ris•so•dac•tyl** (*or* **•tyle**) zoology term
**pe•ris•so•dac•ty•lous**
**peri•stal•sis** (*plural* **•ses**)
**peri•stal•tic**
**peri•stal•ti•cal•ly**
**peri•sto•mal** (*or* **•mial**)
**peri•stome** botany term
**peri•sty•lar**
**peri•style** colonnade
**peri•thecium** (*plural* **•thecia**) botany term
**peri•to•neal**
**peri•to•neum** (*plural* **•nea** *or* **•niums**)
**peri•to•nit•ic**
**peri•to•ni•tis**
**peri•track** taxiway
**pe•rit•ri•cha** (*sing.* **peri•trich**) biology term
**pe•rit•ri•chous**
**peri•wig**
**peri•win•kle**
**(perjorative)** *incorrect spelling of* **pejorative**
**per•jure**
**per•jur•er**
**per•jury** (*plural* **•juries**)
**perk**
**perki•ly**
**perki•ness**
**perky** **(perki•er, perki•est)**
**Per•lis** Malaysian state
**per•lite** (*or* **pearl•**) filler and soil-conditioner; *compare* **pearlite**
**per•lit•ic** (*or* **pearl•**)
**per•lo•cu•tion**
**per•lo•cu•tion•ary**
**Perm** Russian port
**perm**
**per•ma•frost**
**perm•al•loy**
**per•ma•nence**
**per•ma•nen•cy** (*plural* **•cies**)
**per•ma•nent**
**per•man•ga•nate**
**per•me•abil•ity** (*plural* **•ities**)
**per•me•able**
**per•me•ance**
**per•me•ant**
**per•me•ate**
**per•mea•tion**
**per•mea•tive**
**per•mea•tor**
**per men•sem** *Latin* every month
**Per•mian** geological period
**per•mis•sibil•ity**
**per•mis•sible**
**per•mis•sion**
**per•mis•sive**
**per•mis•sive•ness**
**per•mit** **(•mit•ting, •mit•ted)**
**per•mit•ter**
**per•mit•tiv•ity** (*plural* **•ities**) physics term
**per•mu•ta•tion**
**per•mu•ta•tion•al**
**per•mute**
**Per•nam•bu•co** Brazilian state
**per•ni•cious**
**per•ni•cious•ness**
**per•nick•eti•ness**
**per•nick•ety**
**Per•nod** (*Trademark*)
**pe•ro•neal** of the outer leg
**pero•rate**
**pero•ra•tion**
**pe•roxi•dase** enzyme
**per•ox•ide**
**per•pend** (*or* **•pent**) wall stone
**per•pen•dicu•lar**
**per•pen•dicu•lar•ity**
**per•pe•trate**
**per•pe•tra•tion**
**per•pe•tra•tor**
**per•pet•ual**
**per•pet•ual•ly**
**per•petu•ate**
**per•petua•tion**
**per•pe•tu•ity** (*plural* **•ities**)
**Per•pi•gnan** French town
**per•plex**
**per•plex•ity** (*plural* **•ities**)
**per•qui•site**
**Per•rier** (*Trademark*)
**per•ron** flight of steps
**per•ry** (*plural* **•ries**) pear wine
**per•salt** chemical compound
**per se** *Latin* in itself
**perse** greyish-blue
**per•secute**
**per•secu•tion**
**per•secu•tive** (*or* **•tory**)
**per•secu•tor**
**Per•seid** meteor shower
**Persephone** mythological character
**Per•sepo•lis** capital of ancient Persia
**Perseus** mythological character
**Per•seus** constellation
**per•sever•ance**
**per•se•ver•ant**
**per•sev•era•tion** psychology term
**per•severe**
**Per•sia**
**Per•sian**
**per•si•caria** plant
**per•si•ennes** Persian blinds
**per•si•flage**
**per•sim•mon** fruit
**Per•sis** ancient Persian region
**per•sist**
**per•sis•tence** (*or* **•ten•cy**)
**per•sis•tent**
**per•sist•er**
**per•son** (*plural* **•sons**)
**per•so•na** (*plural* **•nae**)
**per•son•able**
**per•son•able•ness**
**per•son•age**
**per•so•na gra•ta** (*plural* **per•so•nae gra•tae**)
**per•son•al**
**per•son•al•ism**
**per•son•al•ist**
**per•son•al•is•tic**
**per•son•al•ity** (*plural* **•ities**)

**per•son•ali•za•tion** (*or* **•sa•tion)**
**per•son•al•ize** (*or* **•ise)**
**per•son•al•ly**
**per•son•al•ty** (*plural* **•ties)** personal property
**per•so•na non gra•ta** (*plural* **per•so•nae non gra•tae)**
**per•son•ate**
**per•sona•tion**
**per•sona•tive**
**per•sona•tor**
**per•soni•fi•able**
**per•soni•fi•ca•tion**
**per•soni•fy (•fies, •fy•ing, •fied)**
**per•son•nel**
**per•spec•tive**
**Per•spec•tiv•ism** philosophical doctrine
**Per•spex** (*Trademark*)
**per•spi•ca•cious** perceptive; *compare* **perspicuous**
**per•spi•cac•ity** (*or* **•ca•cious•ness)**
**per•spi•cu•ity** (*or* **•spicu•ous•ness)**
**per•spicu•ous** lucid; *compare* **perspicacious**
**per•spi•ra•tion**
**per•spir•atory**
**per•spire**
**per•spir•ing•ly**
**per•suad•abil•ity** (*or* **per•sua•si•bil•ity)**
**per•suad•able** (*or* **per•sua•sible)**
**per•suade**
**per•suad•er**
**per•sua•sion**
**per•sua•sive**
**per•sua•sive•ness**
**(persue)** *incorrect spelling of* **pursue**
**pert**
**per•tain**
**Perth**
**per•ti•na•cious**
**per•ti•nac•ity** (*or* **•na•cious•ness)**
**per•ti•nence**
**per•ti•nent**
**pert•ness**
**per•turb**
**per•turb•able**
**per•turb•ably**
**per•tur•ba•tion**
**per•turb•ing•ly**
**per•tus•sis** whooping cough
**Peru**
**Pe•ru•gia** Italian city
**pe•ruke** wig
**pe•rus•al**
**pe•ruse**
**pe•rus•er**
**Pe•ru•vian**
**per•vade**
**per•vad•er**
**per•va•sion**
**per•va•sive**
**per•va•sive•ness**
**per•verse**
**per•verse•ness**
**per•ver•sion**
**per•ver•sity** (*plural* **•sities)**
**per•ver•sive**
**per•vert**
**per•vert•ed**
**per•vert•ed•ly**
**per•vert•ed•ness**
**per•vert•er**
**per•ver•tible**
**per•vi•ous**
**per•vi•ous•ness**
**pes** (*plural* **pedes)** foot
**Pe•sach** (*or* **•sah)** Passover
**pe•sade** dressage term
**Pe•sca•ra** Italian city
**pe•seta** Spanish currency
**pe•sewa** Ghanaian currency
**Pesha•war** Pakistani city
**Pe•shit•ta** (*or* **•shi•to)** Syriac Bible
**pesky (peski•er, peski•est)**
**peso** (*plural* **pesos)** coin
**pe•soni•fi•er**
**pes•sa•ry** (*plural* **•ries)**
**pes•si•mism**
**pes•si•mist**
**pes•si•mis•tic** (*or* **•ti•cal)**
**pes•si•mis•ti•cal•ly**
**pest**
**pes•ter**
**pes•ter•er**
**pes•ter•ing•ly**
**pest•hole**
**pes•ti•cid•al**
**pes•ti•cide**
**pes•tif•er•ous**
**pes•ti•lence**
**pes•ti•lent**
**pes•ti•len•tial**
**pes•tle**
**pet (pet•ting, petted)**
**pet•al**
**pet•al•if•er•ous** (*or* **•al•ous)**
**pet•al•ine**
**pet•alled** (*US* **•aled)**
**petal-like**
**peta•lod•ic**
**pet•alo•dy** botany term
**pet•al•oid**
**pe•tard**
**pet•cock** valve on steam boiler
**pe•techia** (*plural* **•techiae)** red spot on skin
**pe•techial**
**pe•ter**
**Pe•ter•bor•ough**
**Pe•ter•lee** Durham town
**Pe•ter•loo** massacre
**peter•man** (*plural* **•men)** *Slang* safe-breaker
**Pe•ters•burg** US city; *compare* **St Petersburg**
**pe•ter•sham** ribbon
**pethi•dine**
**petio•late** (*or* **•la•ted)**
**peti•ole** leaf stalk
**pe•tio•lule**
**pet•it** of lesser importance; small; *compare* **petite**
**pe•tit bour•geois** (*plural* **pe•tits bour•geois)**
**pe•tite** small and dainty; *compare* **petit**
**pet•ite bour•geoisie**
**pet•it four** (*plural* **pet•its fours)** small cake
**pe•ti•tion**
**pe•ti•tion•ary**
**pe•ti•tion•er**
**pet•it mal** epilepsy
**pet•it point** needlework stitch
**pe•tits pois** *French* peas
**Pet•ra** ancient city
**pet•rel** bird; *compare* **petrol**
**Pe•tri dish**
**pet•ri•fac•tion** (*or* **pet•ri•fi•ca•tion)**
**pe•tri•fi•er**
**pet•ri•fy (•fies, •fy•ing, •fied)**

**Pe•trine** of St Peter
**pet•ro•chemi•cal**
**pet•ro•chem•is•try**
**pet•ro•dol•lar**
**pet•ro•glyph** prehistoric rock carving
**Pet•ro•grad** *former name of* **Leningrad**
**pe•trog•ra•pher**
**pet•ro•graph•ic** (*or* **•graphi•cal**)
**pet•ro•graphi•cal•ly**
**pe•trog•ra•phy** classification of rocks
**pet•rol** fuel; *compare* **petrel**
**pet•ro•la•tum** petroleum jelly
**pe•tro•leum**
**pe•trol•ic** of petroleum
**pet•ro•logi•cal**
**pe•trolo•gist**
**pe•trol•ogy** (*plural* **•ogies**) study of rocks
**pet•ro•nel** firearm
**Pe•tro•pav•lovsk** Kazakh city
**Pe•tró•po•lis** Brazilian city
**pe•tro•sal** anatomy term
**pet•rous**
**Pe•tro•za•vodsk** Russian city
**pet•ter**
**pet•ti•coat**
**pet•ti•fog** (**•fog•ging, •fogged**)
**pet•ti•fog•ger**
**pet•ti•fog•gery**
**pet•ti•ly**
**pet•ting**
**pet•tish**
**pet•tish•ness**
**pet•ti•toes** pigs' trotters
**pet•ty** (**•ti•er, •ti•est**)
**petu•lance** (*or* **•lan•cy**)
**petu•lant**
**pe•tu•nia**
**pe•tun•tse** (*or* **•tze**) mineral
**pew**
**pe•wee** (*or* **pee•**) bird
**pe•wit** *variant spelling of* **peewit**
**pew•ter**
**pew•ter•er**
**pe•yo•te** cactus
**pfen•nig** (*plural* **•nigs** *or* **•ni•ge**) German coin
**Pforz•heim** German city
**Phaedra** wife of Theseus
**Phaëthon** mythological character
**phae•ton** horse-drawn carriage
**phage** virus
**phag•edae•na** (*or esp. US* **•edena**) ulcer
**phago•cyte**
**phago•cyt•ic**
**phago•cy•to•sis**
**phago•ma•nia** compulsive eating
**phago•ma•ni•ac**
**phago•pho•bia**
**phago•pho•bic**
**phal•ange** *variant of* **phalanx**
**pha•lan•geal** anatomy term
**pha•lan•ger** marsupial
**pha•lan•ges** *plural of* **phalanx**
**phal•an•stery** (*plural* **•steries**)
**phal•anx** (*plural* **phal•anxes** *or* **pha•lan•ges**) battle formation; compact group
**phal•anx** (*or* **•ange**; *plural* **pha•lan•ges**) finger or toe bone
**phala•rope** bird
**phal•lic**
**phal•li•cism** (*or* **phal•lism**)
**phal•li•cist** (*or* **phal•list**)
**phal•lus** (*plural* **•li** *or* **•luses**)
**phan•ero•crys•tal•line**
**phan•ero•gam** botany term
**phan•ero•gam•ic** (*or* **•er•oga•mous**)
**pha•nero•phyte** botany term
**Pha•nero•zo•ic** biology term
**phan•tasm**
**phan•tas•ma•go•ria** (*or* **•gory**)
**phan•tas•ma•go•ric** (*or* **•ri•cal**)
**phan•tas•ma•go•ri•cal•ly**
**phan•tas•mal** (*or* **•mic**)
**phan•tom**
**phar•aoh** (*or* **Phar•**)
**phar•aon•ic** (*or* **Phar•**)
**Phari•sa•ic** (*or* **•sai•cal**)
**Phari•see**
**phar•ma•ceu•ti•cal** (*or* **•tic**)
**phar•ma•ceu•tics**
**phar•ma•cist** (*or* **•ma•ceu•tist**)
**phar•ma•co•dy•nam•ic**
**phar•ma•co•dy•nam•ics**
**phar•ma•cog•no•sist**
**phar•ma•cog•nos•tic**
**phar•ma•cog•no•sy** branch of pharmacology
**phar•ma•co•logi•cal**
**phar•ma•colo•gist**
**phar•ma•col•ogy**
**phar•ma•co•poeia**
**phar•ma•co•poe•ial** (*or* **•poe•ic**)
**phar•ma•co•poe•ist**
**phar•ma•cy** (*plural* **•cies**)
**Pha•ros** Greek lighthouse
**phar•yn•geal** (*or* **pha•ryn•gal**)
**phar•yn•gi•tis**
**phar•yn•go•logi•cal**
**phar•yn•golo•gist**
**phar•yn•gol•ogy**
**pha•ryn•go•scope**
**pha•ryn•go•scop•ic**
**phar•yn•gos•co•py**
**phar•yn•goto•my** (*plural* **•mies**)
**phar•ynx** (*plural* **pha•ryn•ges** *or* **phar•ynxes**)
**phase**
**pha•sic** (*or* **phaseal**)
**phas•mid** insect
**phat•ic** of conversation
**pheas•ant**
**phel•lem**
**phel•lo•derm**
**phel•lo•der•mal**
**phel•lo•gen**
**phel•lo•genet•ic** (*or* **•gen•ic**)
**phe•na•caine** anaesthetic
**phe•nac•etin** analgesic
**phena•cite** (*or* **•kite**) mineral
**phe•nan•threne**
**phena•zine**
**phe•net•ic** biology term
**phe•neti•dine**
**phen•etole**
**phen•for•min** drug
**phe•no•bar•bi•tone** (*US* **•tal**)

**phe•no•copy** (*plural* **•copies**) biology term
**phe•no•cryst** geology term
**phe•nol**
**phe•no•late** disinfect
**phe•nol•ic**
**phe•no•logi•cal**
**phe•nolo•gist**
**phe•nol•ogy** study of phenomena
**phenol•phthalein**
**phe•nom•ena** *plural of* phenomenon
**phe•nom•enal**
**phe•nom•enal•ism**
**phe•nom•enal•ist**
**phe•nom•enal•is•ti•cal•ly**
**phe•nom•enal•ly**
**phe•nom•eno•logi•cal**
**phe•nom•enol•ogy**
**phe•nom•enon** (*plural* **•ena** *or* **•enons**)
**phe•no•thia•zine**
**phe•no•type** biology term
**phe•no•typ•ic** (*or* **•typi•cal**)
**phe•no•typi•cal•ly**
**phe•nox•ide**
**phe•nyl**
**phenyl•alanine**
**phenyl•keton•uria**
**phero•mone** chemical in animals
**phew**
**phial**
**Phi Beta Kap•pa** US academic society
**Phila•del•phia**
**phila•del•phus** shrub
**Phi•lae** Egyptian island
**phi•lan•der**
**phi•lan•der•er**
**phil•an•throp•ic** (*or* **•thropi•cal**)
**phi•lan•thro•pist** (*or* **phil•an•thrope**)
**phi•lan•thro•py** (*plural* **•pies**)
**phil•an•thropi•cal•ly**
**phila•tel•ic**
**phila•teli•cal•ly**
**phi•lat•elist**
**phi•lat•ely**
**phil•har•mon•ic**
**phil•hel•lene** (*or* **•len•ist**) lover of Greece
**phil•hel•len•ism**
**Phi•lip•pi** ancient Macedonian city
**phi•lip•pic** bitter speech
**Phil•ip•pine**
**Phil•ip•pines**
**Phil•is•tine**
**Phil•is•tin•ism**
**phil•lu•men•ist** collector of matchbox labels
**philo•den•dron** (*plural* **•drons** *or* **•dra**) plant
**phi•logy•ny** fondness for women
**philo•logi•cal**
**phi•lolo•gist** (*or* **•ger**)
**phi•lol•ogy**
**philo•mel** (*or* **•mela**) nightingale
**Philomela** mythological princess
**phi•loso•pher**
**philo•soph•ic**
**philo•sophi•cal** (*or* **•soph•ic**)
**philo•sophi•cal•ly**
**philo•sophi•cal•ness**
**phi•loso•phi•za•tion** (*or* **•sa•tion**)
**phi•loso•phize** (*or* **•phise**)
**phi•loso•phiz•er** (*or* **•phis•er**)
**phi•loso•phy** (*plural* **•phies**)
**phil•tre** (*US* **•ter**) love potion; *compare* **filter**
**phi•mo•sis** medical term
**phi-phenom•enon** (*plural* **•ena**) psychology term
**phiz** *Slang* face
**phle•bit•ic**
**phle•bi•tis**
**phlebo•scle•ro•sis**
**phlebo•tom•ic** (*or* **•tomi•cal**)
**phle•boto•mist**
**phle•boto•mize**
**phle•boto•my** (*plural* **•mies**) incision into vein
**phlegm**
**phleg•mat•ic** (*or* **•mati•cal**)
**phleg•mati•cal•ly**
**phleg•mati•cal•ness** (*or* **•mat•ic•ness**)
**phlo•em** plant tissue
**phlo•gis•tic**
**phlo•gis•ton**
**phlogo•pite** mineral
**phlox** (*plural* **phlox** *or* **phloxes**)
**phlyc•ten** (*or* **•te•na**; *plural* **•tens** *or* **•nae**) blister
**Phnom Penh** (*or* **Pnom Penh**) Cambodian capital
**pho•bia**
**pho•bic**
**Pho•bos** satellite of Mars
**pho•cine** of seals
**Pho•cis** region of ancient Greece
**pho•co•melia** (*or* **•com•ely**)
**Phoe•be** satellite of Saturn
**phoe•be** bird
**Phoebus** Apollo
**Phoe•ni•cia**
**Phoe•ni•cian**
**Phoe•nix** US city
**phoe•nix** legendary bird
**phon** unit
**pho•nate** utter speech
**pho•na•tion**
**pho•na•tory**
**phone**
**phone-in** (*noun*)
**pho•neme** linguistics term
**pho•nemic**
**pho•nemi•cal•ly**
**pho•nemics**
**pho•net•ic**
**pho•neti•cal•ly**
**pho•neti•cian**
**pho•net•ics**
**pho•net•ist**
**pho•ney** (*or* **•ny**; *adj* **•ni•er, •ni•est**; *noun, plural* **•neys** *or* **•nies**)
**pho•ney•ness** (*or* **•ni•**)
**phon•ic**
**phoni•cal•ly**
**phon•ics** teaching method
**pho•ni•ness** *variant spelling of* phoneyness
**pho•no•gram**
**pho•no•gram•ic** (*or* **•gram•mic**)
**pho•no•graph**
**pho•nog•ra•pher** (*or* **•phist**)
**pho•nog•ra•phy**
**pho•no•lite** rock
**pho•no•lit•ic**
**pho•no•logi•cal**

**pho•nolo•gist**
**pho•nol•ogy** (*plural* **•ogies**)
**pho•nom•eter**
**pho•no•met•ric** (*or* **•ri•cal**)
**pho•non** physics term
**pho•no•scope**
**pho•no•tac•tics** branch of linguistics
**pho•no•type**
**pho•no•typ•ic** (*or* **•typi•cal**)
**pho•no•typ•ist** (*or* **•typ•er**)
**pho•no•typy** phonetic transcription
**pho•ny** *variant spelling of* **phoney**
**phoo•ey**
**phos•gene** poisonous gas
**phos•ge•nite** mineral
**phos•pha•tase** enzyme
**phos•phate**
**phos•phat•ic**
**phos•pha•tide** biochemical compound
**phos•pha•ti•za•tion** (*or* **•sa•tion**)
**phos•pha•tize** (*or* **•tise**)
**phos•pha•tu•ria**
**phos•pha•tu•ric**
**phos•phene** physiology term; *compare* **phosphine**
**phos•phide**
**phos•phine** gas; *compare* **phosphene**
**phos•phite**
**phos•pho•crea•tine** (*or* **•tin**)
**phos•pho•lip•id**
**phos•pho•pro•tein**
**phos•phor**
**phos•pho•rate**
**phos•pho•resce**
**phos•pho•res•cence**
**phos•pho•res•cent**
**phos•phor•ic**
**phos•pho•rism**
**phos•pho•rite** mineral
**phos•pho•rit•ic**
**phos•phoro•scope**
**phos•pho•rous** (*adj*)
**phos•pho•rus** (*noun*)
**phos•phory•lase** enzyme
**phot** unit
**pho•tic** of light
**pho•to** (*plural* **•tos**)
**photo•ac•tin•ic**
**photo•ac•tive**
**photo•auto•troph•ic** biology term
**photo•bath•ic** biology term
**photo•cath•ode**
**photo•cell**
**photo•chemi•cal**
**photo•chem•ist**
**photo•chem•is•try**
**photo•com•pose**
**photo•com•pos•er**
**photo•com•po•si•tion**
**photo•con•duc•tion**
**photo•con•duc•tiv•ity**
**photo•con•duc•tor**
**photo•copi•er**
**photo•copy** (*noun, plural* **•copies;** *verb* **•copies, •copy•ing, •cop•ied**)
**photo•cur•rent**
**photo•dis•in•te•gra•tion**
**photo•dy•nam•ic**
**photo•dy•nam•ics**
**photo•elas•tic•ity**
**photo•elec•tric** (*or* **•tri•cal**)
**photo•elec•tri•cal•ly**
**photo•elec•tric•ity**
**photo•elec•tron**
**photo•elec•tro•type**
**photo•emis•sion**
**photo•emis•sive**
**photo•en•grave**
**photo•en•grav•er**
**photo•en•grav•ing**
**Photo•fit** (*Trademark*)
**photo•flash**
**photo•flood** tungsten lamp
**photo•fluo•rog•ra•phy**
**photo•gen•ic**
**photo•geni•cal•ly**
**photo•geol•ogy**
**photo•gram** type of photograph
**photo•gram•met•ric**
**photo•gram•metrist**
**photo•gram•metry**
**photo•graph**
**pho•tog•ra•pher**
**photo•graph•ic**
**photo•graphi•cal•ly**
**pho•tog•ra•phy**
**photo•gra•vure**
**photo•jour•nal•ism**
**photo•jour•na•list**
**photo•jour•na•lis•tic**
**photo•ki•nesis**
**photo•ki•net•ic**
**photo•ki•neti•cal•ly**
**photo•litho•graph**
**photo•li•thog•ra•pher**
**photo•li•thog•ra•phy**
**pho•to•lu•mi•nes•cence**
**pho•to•lu•mi•nes•cent**
**pho•toly•sis**
**photo•lyt•ic**
**photo•map** (**•map•ping, •mapped**)
**photo•mechani•cal**
**pho•tom•eter**
**photo•met•ric**
**photo•met•ri•cal•ly**
**pho•tom•etrist**
**pho•tom•etry**
**photo•micro•graph**
**photo•mi•crog•ra•pher**
**photo•micro•graph•ic**
**photo•micro•graphi•cal•ly**
**photo•mi•crog•ra•phy**
**photo•mon•tage**
**photo•multi•pli•er**
**photo•mu•ral**
**pho•ton**
**photo•nas•tic**
**photo•nas•ty** botany term
**photo•neu•tron**
**photo•nu•cle•ar**
**photo-offset**
**photo•peri•od**
**photo•peri•od•ic**
**photo•peri•odi•cal•ly**
**photo•peri•od•ism** biology term
**pho•tophi•lous** botany term
**pho•tophi•ly**
**photo•pho•bia**
**photo•pho•bic**
**photo•phore** light-producing organ
**photo•pia** day vision
**pho•top•ic**
**photo•poly•mer**
**photo•recep•tor**
**photo•recon•nais•sance**
**photo•sen•si•tive**
**photo•sen•si•tiv•ity**
**photo•sen•si•ti•za•tion** (*or* **•sa•tion**)
**photo•sen•si•tize** (*or* **•tise**)
**photo•set** (**•set•ting, •set**)
**photo•set•ter**
**photo•sphere** surface of sun

**photo•spher•ic**
**Photo•stat** (*Trademark*) machine
**photo•stat** (*noun, verb*) photocopy
**photo•stat•ic**
**photo•syn•the•sis**
**photo•syn•the•size**
**photo•syn•thet•ic**
**photo•syn•theti•cal•ly**
**photo•tac•tic**
**photo•tax•is** (*or* **•taxy**) biology term
**photo•tele•graph•ic**
**photo•tele•graphi•cal•ly**
**photo•teleg•ra•phy**
**photo•thera•peu•tic**
**photo•thera•peu•ti•cal•ly**
**photo•thera•py** (*or* **•peu•tics**)
**photo•ther•mic** (*or* **•mal**)
**photo•ther•mi•cal•ly** (*or* **•mal•ly**)
**photo•ton•ic**
**pho•toto•nus** botany term
**photo•to•pog•ra•phy**
**photo•tran•sis•tor**
**photo•trop•ic**
**pho•tot•ro•pism** botany term
**photo•tube**
**photo•type**
**photo•type•set•ting**
**photo•typ•ic**
**photo•typi•cal•ly**
**photo•ty•pog•ra•phy**
**photo•vol•ta•ic**
**photo•zin•co•graph**
**photo•zin•cog•ra•phy**
**phras•al**
**phrase**
**phra•seo•gram** symbol
**phra•seo•graph** phrase
**phra•seo•graph•ic**
**phra•seog•ra•phy**
**phra•seo•logi•cal**
**phra•seolo•gist**
**phra•seol•ogy** (*plural* **•ogies**)
**phras•ing**
**phra•tric** anthropology term
**phra•try** (*plural* **•tries**)
**phre•at•ic** geography term
**phren•ic** of the diaphragm
**phre•net•ic** *obsolete spelling of* **frenetic**
**phreno•logi•cal**
**phre•nolo•gist**
**phre•nol•ogy** study of head bumps
**Phrygia** ancient Asian country
**Phryg•ian**
**phtha•lein**
**phthal•ic acid**
**phthalo•cya•nine**
**phthi•ria•sis** infestation with lice; *compare* **pthisis**
**phthi•sic**
**phthisi•cal**
**phthi•sis** wasting disease; *compare* **phthiriasis**
**phut**
**phy•co•logi•cal**
**phy•colo•gist**
**phy•col•ogy** study of algae
**phy•co•my•cete** fungus
**phy•co•my•cetous**
**phy•lac•tery** (*plural* **•teries**) case for Hebrew texts
**phy•le** (*plural* **•lae**) ancient Greek tribe
**phy•let•ic** (*or* **phy•lo•genet•ic**) biology term
**phy•leti•cal•ly** (*or* **phy•lo•geneti•cal•ly**)
**phyl•lite** rock
**phyl•lit•ic**
**phyl•lo•clade** (*or* **•clad**) botany term
**phyl•lode** botany term
**phyl•lo•dial**
**phyl•loid** leaflike
**phyl•lome** botany term
**phyl•lom•ic**
**phyl•lo•qui•none** vitamin
**phyl•lo•tax•is** (*or* **•taxy**; *plural* **•taxes** *or* **taxies**)
**phyl•lox•era** (*plural* **•erae** *or* **•eras**) vine pest
**phy•lo•gen•ic** (*or* **•genet•ic**)
**phy•log•eny** (*or* **•lo•gen•esis**; *plural* **•nies** *or* **•eses**) biology term
**phylo•tac•tic**
**phy•lum** (*plural* **•la**)
**physi•at•ric** (*or* **•ri•cal**)
**physi•at•rics** *US* physiotherapy
**phys•ic** (**•ick•ing, •icked**)
**physi•cal**
**physi•cal•ism** philosophical doctrine
**physi•cal•ist**
**physi•cal•is•tic**
**physi•cal•ly**
**physi•cal•ness**
**phy•si•cian**
**physi•cist**
**physi•co•chemi•cal**
**phys•ics**
**physio•crat**
**physio•crat•ic**
**physi•og•nom•ic** (*or* **•nomi•cal**)
**physi•og•nomi•cal•ly**
**physi•og•no•mist**
**physi•og•no•my** (*plural* **•mies**)
**physi•og•ra•pher**
**physio•graph•ic** (*or* **•graphi•cal**)
**physi•og•ra•phy** physical geography
**physio•logi•cal**
**physio•logi•cal•ly**
**physi•olo•gist**
**physi•ol•ogy**
**(physionomy)** *incorrect spelling of* **physiognomy**
**physio•thera•pist**
**physio•thera•py**
**phy•sique**
**phy•so•clis•tous** zoology term
**phy•so•stig•mine** (*or* **•min**) drug
**phy•sos•to•mous** zoology term
**phyto•gen•esis** (*or* **phy•tog•eny**) botany term
**phyto•genet•ic**
**phyto•geneti•cal•ly**
**phyto•gen•ic**
**phyto•geog•ra•pher**
**phyto•geog•ra•phy**
**phy•tog•ra•phy**
**phyto•hor•mone**
**phy•tol•ogy**
**phy•ton** botany term
**phyto•patho•logi•cal**
**phyto•pa•tholo•gist**
**phyto•pa•thol•ogy**
**phy•topha•gous**
**phy•topha•gy**

**phyto•plank•ton**
**phyto•plank•ton•ic**
**phyto•so•cio•logi•cal**
**phyto•so•ci•olo•gist**
**phyto•so•ci•ol•ogy**
**phyto•tox•in**
**phyto•tron** botanical apparatus
**pi** (*plural* **pis**) Greek letter
**Pia•cen•za** Italian town
**pi•acu•lar** making atonement
**pi•affe** dressage term
**pia ma•ter** brain membrane
**pia•nism**
**pia•nis•si•mo**
**pia•nist**
**pia•nis•tic**
**pi•ano** (*plural* **•anos**)
**pi•ano•for•te**
**Pia•no•la** (*Trademark*)
**pi•as•sa•va** (*or* **•ba**) palm tree
**pi•as•tre** (*or esp. US* **•ter**) currency
**Piauí** Brazilian state
**pi•az•za**
**pi•broch** bagpipe music
**pica** printer's measure; eating dirt; *compare* **pika**
**pica•dor**
**Pic•ar•dy** French region
**pica•resque** of type of fiction; *compare* **picturesque**
**pica•roon** (*or* **picka•**) adventurer
**pica•yune** *US* of little value
**Pic•ca•dil•ly**
**pic•ca•lil•li** pickle
**pic•ca•nin•ny** (*or* **picka•**; *plural* **•nies**)
**pic•co•lo** (*plural* **•los**)
**pice** (*plural* **pice**) coin
**pic•eous** of pitch
**pichi•ci•ego** (*plural* **•egos**) animal
**pick**
**picka•back** *variant of* **piggyback**
**pick•able**
**pick•axe** (*US* **•ax**)
**pick•er**
**pick•er•el** (*plural* **•el** *or* **•els**) fish
**pickerel•weed**
**pick•et**
**pick•et•er**
**pick•et•ing**
**pick•ings**
**pick•le**
**pick•led**
**pick•ler**
**pick•lock**
**pick-me-up**
**pick•pocket**
**pick-up** (*noun*)
**Pick•wick•ian**
**picky**
**pic•nic** (**•nick•ing**, **•nicked**)
**pic•nick•er**
**pico•line** chemical compound
**pico•lin•ic**
**pi•cot** pattern of loops
**pico•tee** carnation
**pic•rate** chemistry term
**pic•ric acid**
**pic•rite** rock
**pic•ro•tox•in**
**Pict**
**Pict•ish**
**pic•to•graph**
**pic•to•rial**
**pic•to•rial•ly**
**pic•ture**
**pic•tur•esque** strikingly pleasing; *compare* **picaresque**
**pic•tur•esque•ness**
**pic•ul** unit
**pid•dle**
**pid•dling**
**pid•dock** mollusc
**pidg•in** language; *compare* **pigeon**
**pie**
**pie•bald**
**piece**
**pièce de ré•sis•tance** (*plural* **pièces de ré•sis•tance**)
**piece-dyed**
**piece•meal**
**piec•er**
**piece•work**
**pie•crust**
**pied** multi-coloured
**pied-à-terre** (*plural* **pieds-à-terre**)
**Pied•mont** Italian region
**pied•mont** at mountain base
**pied•mont•ite** mineral
**pie-eyed**
**pie•man** (*plural* **•men**)
**pier** landing place; pillar; *compare* **peer**
**pierc•able**
**pierce**
**pierc•er**
**pierc•ing**
**pierc•ing•ly**
**Pi•erian**
**Pi•eri•des** Muses
**pi•eri•dine** zoology term
**Pi•er•rot** pantomime clown
**pi•età** religious painting
**Pie•ter•mar•itz•burg** South African city
**pi•ety** (*plural* **•eties**)
**pi•ezo•chem•is•try**
**pi•ezo•elec•tric**
**pi•ezo•elec•tri•cal•ly**
**pi•ezo•elec•tric•ity**
**pi•ezom•eter**
**pi•ezo•met•ric**
**pi•ezo•met•ri•cal•ly**
**pif•fle**
**pig** (**pig•ging**, **pigged**)
**pi•geon** bird; *compare* **pidgin**
**pigeon•hole**
**pigeon-toed**
**pig•face** plant
**pig•fish** (*plural* **•fish** *or* **•fishes**)
**pig•gery** (*plural* **•geries**)
**pig•gin** small bucket
**pig•gish**
**pig•gish•ness**
**pig•gy** (*noun, plural* **•gies**; *adj* **•gi•er**, **•gi•est**)
**piggy•back** (*or* **picka•back**)
**pig-headed**
**pig-headed•ness**
**pig•let**
**pig•like**
**pig•meat**
**pig•ment**
**pig•men•tary**
**pig•men•ta•tion**
**pig•ment•ed**
**pig•my** *variant spelling of* **pygmy**
**pig•nut**

**pig•skin**
**pig•stick**
**pig•stick•er**
**pig•stick•ing**
**pig•sty** (*plural* **•sties**)
**pig•swill**
**pig•tail**
**pig•tailed**
**pig•weed**
**pika** animal; *compare* pica
**pike**
**pike•let** crumpet
**pike•perch** (*plural* **•perch** *or* **•perches**) fish
**pik•er**
**pike•staff**
**pil•af** (*or* **•aff**) *variant of* **pilau**
**pi•las•ter**
**pi•lau** (*or* **pil•af, pil•aff**) rice dish
**pilch** *Archaic* infant's garment
**pil•chard**
**pile**
**pi•leate** (*or* **•leat•ed**) biology term
**pile-driver**
**pi•leous** of hair
**piles**
**pi•leum** (*plural* **•lea**) top of bird's head
**pile-up** (*noun*)
**pi•leus** (*plural* **•lei**) mushroom cap
**pile•wort**
**pil•fer**
**pil•fer•age**
**pil•fer•er**
**pil•garlic** *Dialect* pitiful person
**pil•grim**
**pil•grim•age**
**pili** (*plural* **pilis**) tree
**pi•li** *plural of* **pilus**
**pi•lif•er•ous**
**pili•form**
**pil•ing**
**pill**
**pil•lage**
**pil•lag•er**
**pil•lar**
**pill•box**
**pil•lion**
**pil•li•winks** instrument of torture
**pil•lo•ry** (*noun, plural* **•ries**; *verb* **•ries, •ry•ing, •ried**)
**pil•low**
**pillow•case** (*or* **•slip**)
**pi•lo•car•pine** (*or* **•pin**) drug
**pi•lose** biology term
**pi•lot**
**pi•lot•age**
**Pils•ner** (*or* **Pil•sen•er**) beer
**Pilt•down man**
**pilu•lar**
**pil•ule**
**pi•lus** (*plural* **•li**) a hair
**pi•men•to** (*plural* **•tos**) spice
**pi•mien•to** (*plural* **•tos**) sweet pepper
**pimp**
**pim•per•nel**
**pim•ple**
**pim•pled**
**pim•pli•ness**
**pim•ply** (**•pli•er, •pli•est**)
**pin** (**pin•ning, pinned**)
**pi•na•ceous** botany term
**pina•fore**
**pi•nas•ter** pine tree
**pin•ball**
**pince-nez** (*plural* **pince-nez**)
**pin•cer**
**pin•cers** tool
**pinch**
**pinch•beck** imitation gold
**pinch•cock** clamp
**pinch•penny** (*plural* **•pennies**)
**pin•cushion**
**Pin•dar•ic** ode
**pind•ling** *Dialect* peevish
**Pin•dus** Greek mountain range
**pine**
**pin•eal gland**
**pine•apple**
**pi•nene** chemical compound
**pi•nery** (*plural* **•neries**)
**pi•netum** (*plural* **•neta**) plantation
**pin•feather**
**pin•fish** (*plural* **•fish** *or* **•fishes**)
**pin•fold**
**ping**
**ping•er**
**pin•go** (*plural* **•gos**) landform
**Ping-Pong** (*Trademark*) (*or* **ping-pong**)
**pin•guid** fatty
**pin•guid•ity** (*or* **•ness**)
**pin•head**
**pin•hole**
**pin•ion**
**pin•ite** mineral
**pink**
**pink•eye**
**pinkie** (*or* **pinky**) *US* little finger
**pink•ish**
**pink•root**
**pinky** pinkish; *variant spelling of* **pinkie**
**pin•na** (*plural* **•nae** *or* **•nas**) biology term
**pin•nace** boat
**pin•na•cle**
**pin•nate** (*or* **•nat•ed**) feather-like
**pin•nati•fid** botany term
**pin•na•tion**
**pin•nati•par•tite** botany term
**pin•nati•ped** ornithology term
**pin•nati•sect** botany term
**pinned**
**pin•ner**
**pin•ning**
**pin•ni•ped** (*or* **•pedian**) zoology term
**pin•nu•lar**
**pin•nule** (*or* **•nu•la**; *plural* **•nules** *or* **•nu•lae**)
**pin•ny** (*plural* **•nies**) *Slang* pinafore
**pi•noch•le** (*or* **•nuch•le, •noc•le**) card game
**pi•no•le** flour
**pin•point**
**pin•prick**
**pin•stripe**
**pint**
**pin•ta** skin disease
**pin•ta•dera** Neolithic stamp
**pin•tail** (*plural* **•tails** *or* **•tail**) duck
**pin•tle** hinge pin

**pin•to** (*plural* **•tos**) piebald horse
**pin-up** (*noun*)
**pin•wheel**
**pin•work**
**pin•worm**
**pinx•it** *Latin* painted (*inscription on painting*)
**piny** (*or* **piney; pini•er, pini•est**)
**pio•let** ice axe
**pion** physics term
**pio•neer**
**pi•ous**
**pi•ous•ness**
**pip** (**pip•ping, pipped**)
**pipa** toad
**pip•age**
**pi•pal** *variant spelling of* **peepul**
**pipe**
**pipe•clay**
**pipe•fish** (*plural* **•fish** *or* **•fishes**)
**pipe•fitting**
**pipe•line**
**pip•er**
**pip•era•ceous** botany term
**pi•pera•zine** drug
**pi•peri•dine** organic compound
**pip•er•ine** alkaloid
**pip•ero•nal** fragrant compound
**pipe•stone**
**pi•pette**
**pipe•wort**
**pip•ing**
**pipi•strelle** bat
**pip•it** bird
**pip•kin** small pot
**pipped**
**pip•pin** apple
**pip•ping**
**pip•sis•sewa** plant
**pip•squeak**
**pi•quan•cy** (*or* **•quant•ness**)
**pi•quant**
**pique** (**piqu•ing, piqued**)
**pi•qué** fabric
**pi•quet** card game
**pi•ra•cy** (*plural* **•cies**)
**Pi•rae•us** (*or* **Pei•**) Greek port
**pi•ra•nha** (*or* **•na**)
**pi•rate**
**pi•rat•ic** (*or* **•rati•cal**)
**pi•rati•cal•ly**
**pirn** fishing rod
**pi•rog** (*plural* **•ro•gi**) pie
**pi•rogue** (*or* **pi•ra•gua**) canoe
**pirou•ette**
**Pisa**
**pis al•ler** *French* a last resort
**pis•ca•ry** (*plural* **•ries**) fishing place
**pis•ca•to•rial** (*or* **•tory**)
**Pi•sces** constellation; sign of zodiac
**pis•ci•cul•tur•al**
**pis•ci•cul•ture**
**pis•ci•cul•tur•ist**
**pis•ci•na** (*plural* **•nae** *or* **•nas**) basin in church
**pis•cine**
**pis•civo•rous**
**pi•shogue** *Irish* sorcery
**pisi•form** pealike
**pis•mire** *Dialect* ant
**pi•so•lite** rock
**piss**
**pis•ta•chio** (*plural* **•chios**)
**pis•ta•reen** coin
**piste** skiing slope
**pis•til** flower part; *compare* **pistol**
**pis•til•late**
**pis•tol** (**•tol•ling, •tolled;** *US* **•tol•ing, •toled**) gun; *compare* **pistil**
**pis•tole** coin
**pis•to•leer** soldier
**pis•ton**
**pit** (**pit•ting, pit•ted**)
**pita** fibre; *compare* **pitta**
**pita•pat** (**•pat•ting, •pat•ted**)
**Pit•cairn** Pacific island
**pitch**
**pitch-black**
**pitch•blende** mineral
**pitch-dark**
**pitch•er**
**pitch•fork**
**pitchi•ness**
**pitch•om•eter** nautical term
**pitch•stone**
**pitchy** (**pitchi•er, pitchi•est**)
**pit•eous**
**pit•eous•ness**
**pit•fall**
**pith**
**pit•head**
**pith•ecan•thro•pine** (*or* **•poid**)
**pith•ecan•thro•pus** (*plural* **•pi**) apelike man
**pithi•ly**
**pithi•ness**
**pi•thos** (*plural* **•thoi**) oil container
**pithy** (**pithi•er, pithi•est**)
**piti•able**
**piti•able•ness**
**piti•ably**
**piti•ful**
**piti•ful•ly**
**piti•ful•ness**
**piti•less**
**piti•less•ness**
**pit•man** (*plural* **•men**)
**pi•ton** mountaineering spike
**pit•saw**
**pit•ta** flat bread; *compare* **pita**
**pit•tance**
**pitter-patter**
**Pitts•burgh** US port
**pi•tui•tary** (*plural* **•taries**)
**pitu•ri** shrub
**pity** (*noun, plural* **pities;** *verb* **pities, pity•ing, pit•ied**)
**pity•ing•ly**
**pity•ria•sis** (*plural* **•ses**) skin disease
**Piu•ra** Peruvian city
**piv•ot**
**piv•ot•al**
**pix** *Slang* pictures; *compare* **pyx**
**pix•el** component of digitized picture
**pix•el•ate** video technique
**pix•el•a•tion**
**pixie** (*or* **pixy;** *plural* **pixies**)
**pixi•lat•ed** *US* eccentric
**pize** *Dialect* to hit
**piz•za**
**piz•ze•ria**
**piz•zi•ca•to** (*plural* **•ti** *or* **•tos**)
**plac•abil•ity** (*or* **•able•ness**)

**plac•able** easily placated; *compare* **placeable**
**plac•ard**
**pla•cate**
**pla•ca•tion**
**placa•tory** (*or* **•tive)**
**place** position; *compare* **plaice**
**place•able** easily placed; *compare* **placable**
**pla•cebo** (*plural* **•cebos** *or* **•ceboes)**
**place•ment**
**pla•cen•ta** (*plural* **•tas** *or* **•tae)**
**pla•cen•tal** (*or* **•tate)**
**plac•en•ta•tion**
**plac•er**
**pla•cet** vote of assent
**plac•id**
**pla•cid•ity** (*or* **•ness)**
**plac•ing**
**plack•et** dressmaking term
**placo•derm** extinct fish
**plac•oid** platelike
**(plad)** *incorrect spelling of* **plaid**
**pla•fond** ceiling; card game
**pla•gal** musical term
**plage** astronomy term
**pla•gia•rism**
**pla•gia•rist**
**pla•gia•ris•tic**
**pla•gia•rize** (*or* **•rise)**
**pla•gia•riz•er** (*or* **•ris•er)**
**pla•gio•clase** mineral
**pla•gio•cli•max** ecology term
**pla•gi•ot•ro•pism** botany term
**plague (plagu•ing, plagued)**
**plagu•er**
**pla•gui•ly**
**pla•guy** (*or* **•guey)**
**plaice** (*plural* **plaice** *or* **plaices)** fish; *compare* **place**
**plaid** tartan cloth
**plain** simple; unattractive; treeless region; *compare* **plane**
**plain•chant**
**plain•ish** rather plain; *compare* **planish**
**plain-laid** describing rope
**plain•ness**
**plains•man** (*plural* **•men)**
**plain•song**
**plain-spoken**
**plaint**
**plain•tiff** legal term
**plain•tive** melancholy
**plain•tive•ness**
**plait** braid; *compare* **plat**
**plan (plan•ning, planned)**
**pla•nar**
**pla•nar•ian** flatworm
**pla•na•tion** erosion of land
**planch•et** blank coin
**plan•chette** board for spirit messages
**plane** aircraft; level; tool; tree; *compare* **plain**
**plan•er**
**plan•et**
**plan•etar•ium** (*plural* **•iums** *or* **•taria)**
**plan•etary** (*plural* **•etaries)**
**plan•etesi•mal** small planetary body
**plan•et•oid** asteroid
**plan•etoid•al**
**plan•form** silhouette
**plan•gen•cy**
**plan•gent**
**pla•nim•eter**
**pla•ni•met•ric** (*or* **•ri•cal)**
**pla•nim•etry**
**plan•ish** to smooth; *compare* **plainish**
**plan•ish•er**
**plani•sphere**
**plani•spher•ic**
**plank**
**plank•ing**
**plank-sheer** nautical term
**plank•ton**
**plank•ton•ic**
**planned**
**plan•ner**
**plan•ning**
**plano-concave**
**plano-convex**
**plano•gam•ete**
**pla•no•graph•ic**
**pla•no•graphi•cal•ly**
**pla•nog•ra•phy** printing process
**pla•nom•eter**
**pla•no•met•ric**
**pla•nom•etry**
**pla•no•sol** soil
**plant**
**plant•able**
**plan•tain** weed; cooking banana
**plan•tar** of sole of foot
**plan•ta•tion**
**plant•er**
**plan•ti•grade** zoology term
**planu•la** (*plural* **•lae)** larva
**planu•lar**
**plaque**
**plash**
**plashy (plashi•er, plashi•est)**
**plasm** protoplasm
**plas•ma** blood fluid; physics term
**plas•ma•gel** jelly-like protoplasm
**plas•ma•gene**
**plas•ma•gen•ic**
**plas•ma•sol** fluid protoplasm
**plas•min** enzyme
**plas•mo•des•ma** (*or* **•desm;** *plural* **•des•ma•ta** *or* **•desms)** botany term
**plas•mo•dium** (*plural* **•dia)** biology term; malaria parasite
**plas•mo•lyse** (*US* **•lyze)**
**plas•moly•sis**
**plas•mo•lyt•ic**
**plas•mo•lyti•cal•ly**
**plas•mon** biology term
**plas•mo•some**
**Plas•sey** Indian battle site
**plas•ter**
**plaster•board**
**plas•tered**
**plas•ter•er**
**plas•ter•ing**
**plas•tic**
**plas•ti•cal•ly**
**Plas•ti•cine** (*Trademark*)
**plas•tic•ity**
**plas•ti•ci•za•tion** (*or* **•sa•tion)**
**plas•ti•cize** (*or* **•cise)**
**plas•ti•ciz•er** (*or* **•cis•er)**
**plas•tid** cell structure

**plas•tom•eter** plasticity measurer
**plas•to•met•ric**
**plas•tom•etry**
**plas•tral**
**plas•tron**
**plat** small plot; *compare* **plait**
**plat•an** plane tree; *compare* **platen**
**plat du jour** (*plural* **plats du jour**)
**plate**
**plat•eau** (*plural* **•eaus** *or* **•eaux**)
**plat•ed**
**plate•ful** (*plural* **•fuls**)
**plate•layer**
**plate•let**
**plate•mark** hallmark
**plat•en** printing plate; typewriter roller; *compare* **platan**
**plat•er**
**plat•form**
**plati•na** alloy
**plat•ing**
**pla•tin•ic**
**plati•nif•er•ous**
**plat•ini•rid•ium** alloy
**plati•ni•za•tion** (*or* **•sa•tion**)
**plati•nize** (*or* **•nise**)
**plati•no•cya•nide**
**plati•noid**
**plati•no•type** photographic process
**plati•nous**
**plati•num**
**platinum-blond** (*fem* **-blonde**)
**plati•tude**
**plati•tu•di•nize** (*or* **•nise**)
**plati•tu•di•niz•er** (*or* **•nis•er**)
**plati•tu•di•nous**
**Pla•ton•ic** of Plato
**pla•ton•ic** nonerotic
**pla•toni•cal•ly**
**Pla•to•nism**
**Pla•to•nize** (*or* **•nise**)
**pla•toon**
**Platte** US river
**plat•ter**
**platy** (**plati•er, plati•est**)
**platy** (*plural* **platy, platys,** *or* **platies**) fish
**platy•hel•minth** flatworm
**platy•hel•min•thic**
**platy•pus** (*plural* **•puses**)
**plat•yr•rhine** (*or* **•rhin•ian**) zoology term
**plau•dit**
**plau•sibil•ity** (*or* **•sible•ness**)
**plau•sible**
**plau•sibly**
**plau•sive** approving
**play**
**pla•ya** lake
**play•able**
**play-act**
**play-actor**
**play•back**
**play•bill**
**play•boy**
**play•er**
**play•fellow**
**play•ful**
**play•ful•ly**
**play•ful•ness**
**play•goer**
**play•ground**
**play•group**
**play•house**
**play•let**
**play•mate**
**play-off** (*noun*)
**play•pen**
**play•room**
**play•school**
**play•suit**
**play•thing**
**play•time**
**play•wright**
**pla•za**
**plea**
**pleach** make hedge
**plead** (**plead•ing, plead•ed, plead** *or* **pled**)
**plead•able**
**plead•er**
**pleas•able**
**pleas•ance** secluded garden
**pleas•ant**
**pleas•ant•ness**
**pleas•ant•ry** (*plural* **•ries**)
**please**
**pleased**
**pleas•ed•ly**
**pleas•er**
**pleas•ing**
**pleas•ing•ness**
**pleas•ur•able**
**pleas•ur•able•ness**
**pleas•ur•ably**
**pleas•ure**
**pleas•ure•ful**
**pleas•ure•less**
**pleat**
**pleat•er**
**pleb**
**pleb•by** (**•bi•er, •bi•est**)
**ple•beian**
**ple•beian•ism**
**plebi•scite**
**plec•tog•nath** fish
**plec•trum** (*or* **•tron**; *plural* **•tra, •trums,** *or* **•trons**)
**pledge**
**pledgee**
**pledg•er** (*or esp. in legal contexts* **•or**)
**pledg•et** bandaging pad
**plei•ad** talented group
**Pleia•des** constellation
**Pleiades** (*sing.* **Pleiad**) mythological characters
**plein-air** art term
**plei•ot•ro•pism** genetics term
**Pleis•to•cene** geological epoch
**ple•na•ri•ly**
**ple•na•ry**
**ple•nipo•tent**
**pleni•po•ten•ti•ary** (*plural* **•aries**)
**pleni•tude** abundance
**plen•teous**
**plen•teous•ness**
**plen•ti•ful**
**plen•ti•ful•ly**
**plen•ti•ful•ness**
**plen•ty** (*plural* **•ties**)
**ple•num** (*plural* **•nums** *or* **•na**)
**pleo•chro•ic**
**ple•och•ro•ism** chemistry term
**pleo•mor•phic**
**pleo•mor•phism** (*or* **•phy**) biology term
**pleo•nasm** use of superfluous words
**pleo•nas•tic**
**pleo•nas•ti•cal•ly**

**ple•sio•saur**
**ples•sor** *variant of* **plexor**
**plethо•ra**
**ple•thys•mo•graph**
**pleu•ra** (*plural* **•rae**) membrane round lungs; *plural of* **pleuron**
**pleu•ral**
**pleu•ri•sy**
**pleu•rit•ic**
**pleu•ro•dont** zoology term
**pleu•ro•dy•nia** pain between ribs
**pleu•ron** (*plural* **•ra**) zoology term; *compare* **pleura**
**pleu•ro•pneu•mo•nia**
**pleu•roto•my** (*plural* **•mies**)
**pleus•ton** floating algae
**plew** (*or* **plue, plu**) beaver skin
**plexi•form**
**Plexi•glass** (*Trademark*)
**plex•or** (*or* **ples•sor**) medical hammer
**plex•us** (*plural* **•uses** *or* **•us**) network
**pli•abil•ity** (*or* **able•ness**)
**pli•able**
**pli•an•cy** (*or* **•ant•ness**)
**pli•ant**
**pli•ca** (*plural* **•cae**) anatomy term
**pli•cal**
**pli•cate** (*or* **•cat•ed**) pleated
**pli•cate•ness**
**pli•ca•tion** (*or* **plica•ture**)
**plié** ballet posture
**pli•er** (*or* **ply•**) one who plies
**pli•ers** tool
**plight**
**plight•er**
**plim•soll** (*or* **•sole**)
**Plim•soll line**
**plinth**
**Plio•cene** (*or* **Pleio•cene**) geological epoch
**plis•sé** fabric with wrinkled finish
**ploat** *Dialect* thrash
**plod** (**plod•ding, plod•ded**)
**plod•der**
**plod•ding•ly**
**plod•ding•ness**
**plodge** *Dialect* wade
**Plo•eşti** Romanian city
**plonk**
**plonk•er** *Slang* idiot
**plonko** *Austral* alcoholic
**plop** (**plop•ping, plopped**)
**plo•sion** phonetics term
**plo•sive** phonetics term
**plot** (**plot•ting, plot•ted**)
**plot•ter**
**Plough** group of stars
**plough** (*US* **plow**)
**plough•boy** (*US* **plow•**)
**plough•er** (*US* **plow•**)
**plough•man** (*US* **plow•**; *plural* **•men**)
**plough•man•ship** (*US* **plow•**)
**plough•share** (*US* **plow•**)
**plough•staff** (*US* **plow•**)
**Plov•div** Bulgarian city
**plov•er**
**plow** *US spelling of* **plough**
**ploy**
**pluck**
**pluck•er**
**plucki•ly**
**plucki•ness**
**plucky** (**plucki•er, plucki•est**)
**plug** (**plug•ging, plugged**)
**plug•board**
**plum** fruit; *compare* **plumb**
**plum•age**
**plu•mate** (*or* **•mose**)
**plumb** work as plumber; experience misery; *compare* **plum**
**plumb•able**
**plum•bagi•na•ceous** botany term
**plum•ba•go** (*plural* **•gos**) graphite; plant
**plum•beous** of lead
**plumb•er**
**plumb•ery** (*plural* **•eries**)
**plum•bic** chemistry term
**plum•bi•con** TV camera tube
**plum•bif•er•ous**
**plumb•ing**
**plum•bism** lead poisoning
**plum•bous** chemistry term
**plum•bum** lead
**plume**
**plum•met**
**plum•my** (**•mi•er, •mi•est**)
**plump**
**plump•er**
**plump•ness**
**plu•mule**
**plumy** (**plumi•er, plumi•est**)
**plun•der**
**plun•der•able**
**plun•der•age**
**plun•der•er**
**plun•der•ous**
**plunge**
**plung•er**
**plunk**
**plu•per•fect** grammar term
**plu•ral**
**plu•ral•ism**
**plu•ral•ist**
**plu•ral•ity** (*plural* **•ities**)
**plu•rali•za•tion** (*or* **•sa•tion**)
**plu•ral•ize** (*or* **•ise**)
**plu•ral•iz•er** (*or* **•is•er**)
**plu•ral•ly**
**plus**
**plush**
**plush•ness**
**plushy** (**plushi•er, plushi•est**)
**Pluto** Greek god
**Plu•to** planet
**plu•toc•ra•cy** (*plural* **•cies**)
**plu•to•crat**
**plu•to•crat•ic** (*or* **•crati•cal**)
**plu•to•crati•cal•ly**
**plu•ton** geology term
**Plu•to•nian** infernal
**plu•ton•ic** geology term
**plu•to•nium**
**plu•vial** of rain
**plu•vi•om•eter**
**plu•vio•met•ric**
**plu•vio•met•ri•cal•ly**
**plu•vi•om•etry**
**plu•vi•ous** (*or* **•ose**)
**ply** (*verb* **plies, ply•ing, plied**; *noun, plural* **plies**)
**ply•er** *variant spelling of* **plier**
**Plym•outh**
**ply•wood**
**Plzeň** Czech city
**pneu•ma** philosophy term
**pneu•mat•ic**
**pneu•mati•cal•ly**

**pneu•mat•ics** branch of physics
**pneu•ma•tol•ogy** branch of theology
**pneu•ma•toly•sis** geology term
**pneu•ma•tom•eter**
**pneu•ma•tom•etry**
**pneu•mato•phore** biology term
**pneu•mo•ba•cil•lus** (*plural* **•li**)
**pneu•mo•coc•cus** (*plural* **•coc•ci**)
**pneu•mo•co•nio•sis**
**pneu•mo•dy•nam•ics** pneumatics
**pneu•mo•en•cepha•lo•gram**
**pneu•mo•gas•tric**
**pneu•mo•graph**
**pneu•mo•nec•to•my** (*or* **pneu•mec•to•my**; *plural* **•mies**)
**pneu•mo•nia**
**pneu•mon•ic**
**pneu•mon•it•is**
**pneu•mo•tho•rax**
**Po** Italian river
**po** (*plural* **pos**) chamber pot
**poa•ceous** botany term
**poach**
**poach•er**
**poach•ing**
**po•chard** (*plural* **•chards** *or* **•chard**) duck
**pock**
**pock•et**
**pock•et•able**
**pocket•book**
**pock•et•ful** (*plural* **•fuls**)
**pocket•knife** (*plural* **•knives**)
**pock•mark**
**poco** musical term
**po•co•cu•ran•te** indifferent
**pod** (**pod•ding, pod•ded**)
**po•dag•ra** gout
**po•dag•ral** (*or* **•ric, •ri•cal, •rous**)
**pod•dy** (*plural* **•dies**) *Austral* hand-fed calf
**po•des•ta** Italian magistrate
**podgi•ly**
**podgi•ness**
**Pod•go•ri•ca** capital of Montenegro
**podgy** (**podgi•er, podgi•est**)
**po•dia•try** *US* chiropody
**po•dium** (*plural* **•diums** *or* **•dia**)
**Po•dolsk** Russian city
**podo•phyl•lin** medicinal resin
**pod•zol** (*or* **•sol**)
**pod•zol•ic** (*or* **•sol•ic**)
**poem**
**po•esy** (*plural* **•esies**)
**poet**
**po•et•as•ter** inferior poet
**po•et•ess**
**po•et•ic** (*or* **•eti•cal**)
**po•eti•cal•ly**
**po•eti•cize** (*or* **po•et•ize, po•eti•cise, po•et•ise**)
**po•et•ics**
**poet lau•reate** (*plural* **poets lau•reate**)
**po•et•ry**
**po-faced**
**pogge** fish
**po•go•nia** orchid
**pog•rom**
**Po•hai** inlet of Yellow Sea
**poi** Hawaiian food
**poign•an•cy**
**poign•ant**
**poi•ki•lo•ther•mic** (*or* **•mal**) cold-blooded
**poi•ki•lo•ther•mism** (*or* **•my**)
**poi•lu** French soldier
**poin•cia•na** tree
**poin•set•tia** house plant
**point**
**point-blank**
**pointe** ballet term
**point•ed**
**point•ed•ly**
**point•ed•ness**
**Pointe-Noire** Congolese port
**point•er**
**poin•til•lism** painting technique
**poin•til•list**
**point•ing**
**point•less**
**point•less•ness**
**points•man** (*plural* **•men**)
**point-to-point**
**poise**
**poised**
**poi•son**
**poi•son•er**
**poi•son•ous**
**poi•son•ous•ness**
**Poi•tiers** French town
**Poi•tou** former French province
**poke**
**poke•berry** (*plural* **•berries**)
**pok•er**
**poke•weed**
**poki•ly**
**poki•ness**
**poky** (**poki•er, poki•est**)
**Po•land**
**po•lar**
**po•lar•im•eter**
**po•lari•met•ric**
**po•lar•im•etry**
**Po•la•ris** North Star; missile
**po•lari•scope**
**po•lar•ity** (*plural* **•ities**)
**po•lar•iz•able** (*or* **•is•able**)
**po•lari•za•tion** (*or* **•sa•tion**)
**po•lar•ize** (*or* **•ise**)
**po•lar•iz•er** (*or* **•is•er**)
**po•lar•og•ra•phy**
**Po•lar•oid** (*Trademark*)
**pol•der** reclaimed land
**Pole** Polish native; star
**pole**
**pole•axe** (*US* **•ax**)
**pole•cat** (*plural* **•cats** *or* **•cat**)
**pol•emarch** ancient Greek official
**po•lem•ic**
**po•lemi•cal**
**po•lemi•cal•ly**
**po•lemi•cist** (*or* **•emist**)
**po•lem•ics**
**pol•emo•nia•ceous** botany term
**po•len•ta** Italian porridge
**pol•er**
**pole-vault** (*verb*)
**po•leyn** armour
**po•lice**
**police•man** (*plural* **•men**)
**police•woman** (*plural* **•women**)
**poli•cy** (*plural* **•cies**)
**policy•holder**

**po•lio**
**po•lio•my•eli•tis**
**pol•is** (*plural* **•eis**) Greek city-state
**Po•lish**
**pol•ish**
**pol•ish•er**
**Pol•it•bu•ro**
**po•lite**
**po•lite•ness**
**poli•tesse** *French* formal politeness
**poli•tic** shrewd
**po•liti•cal** of politics
**po•liti•cal•ly**
**poli•ti•cian**
**po•liti•cize** (*or* **•cise**)
**poli•tick•ing** political canvassing
**po•liti•co** (*plural* **•cos**) *Slang* politician
**poli•tics**
**pol•ity** (*plural* **•ities**)
**pol•je** geography term
**pol•ka** (*noun, plural* **•kas**; *verb* **•kas, •ka•ing, •kaed**)
**poll**
**pol•lack** (*or* **•lock**; *plural* **•lacks, •lack** *or* **•locks, •lock**) fish
**pol•lan** fish; *compare* **pollen**
**pol•lard**
**polled**
**pol•len** plant product; *compare* **pollan**
**pol•lex** (*plural* **•li•ces**) thumb
**pol•li•cal**
**pol•li•nate** (*or* **•lenate**)
**pol•li•na•tion** (*or* **•lena•tion**)
**pol•li•na•tor** (*or* **•lena•tor**)
**poll•ing**
**pol•lin•ic** of pollen
**pol•li•nif•er•ous** (*or* **•lenif•er•ous**)
**pol•lin•ium** (*plural* **•linia**)
**pol•lino•sis** (*or* **•leno•**) hay fever
**pol•li•wog** (*or* **•ly•**) *Slang* sailor; tadpole
**poll•ster**
**pol•lu•cite** mineral
**pol•lu•tant**
**pol•lute**
**pol•lut•er**
**pol•lu•tion**
**Pollux** star; mythological character
**polo**
**polo•naise**
**po•lo•nium** radioactive element
**po•lo•ny** (*plural* **•nies**) sausage
**Pol•ta•va** Ukrainian city
**pol•ter•geist**
**pol•troon**
**poly** (*plural* **polys**) *Slang* polytechnic
**polya•del•phous** botany term
**poly•am•ide**
**poly•an•drous**
**poly•an•dry**
**poly•an•thus** (*plural* **•thuses**)
**poly•atom•ic**
**poly•ba•sic**
**poly•ba•site** mineral
**poly•car•pel•lary**
**poly•car•pic** (*or* **•pous**) botany term
**poly•carpy**
**poly•cen•trism** political theory
**poly•chaete** worm
**poly•chae•tous**
**poly•cha•sium** (*plural* **•sia**) botany term
**poly•chro•mat•ic** (*or* **•mic, •mous**)
**poly•chro•ma•tism**
**poly•chrome**
**poly•chro•my**
**poly•clin•ic** hospital
**poly•con•ic** maths term
**poly•coty•ledon**
**poly•coty•ledon•ous**
**poly•cy•clic**
**poly•cy•thae•mia** (*US* **•themia**)
**poly•dac•tyl**
**poly•dac•ty•lous**
**poly•dem•ic** ecology term
**poly•dip•sia**
**poly•dip•sic**
**poly•em•bry•on•ic**
**poly•em•bry•ony**
**poly•es•ter**
**po•lyga•la** plant
**poly•ga•la•ceous**
**po•lyga•mist**
**po•lyga•mous**
**po•lyga•my**
**poly•gene** genetics term
**poly•gen•ic**
**poly•gen•esis** biology term
**poly•genet•ic**
**poly•geneti•cal•ly**
**poly•glot**
**poly•glot•ism** (*or* **•glot•tism**)
**poly•gon**
**poly•go•naceous** botany term
**po•lygo•nal**
**po•lygo•num** plant
**poly•graph** lie detector
**poly•graph•ic**
**poly•graphi•cal•ly**
**po•lygy•nist**
**po•lygy•nous**
**po•lygy•ny**
**poly•he•dral**
**poly•he•dron** (*plural* **•drons** *or* **•dra**)
**poly•hy•droxy** (*or* **•dric**)
**poly•iso•prene**
**poly•math**
**poly•math•ic**
**poly•mer**
**poly•mer•ic**
**po•lym•er•ism**
**po•lym•eri•za•tion** (*or* **•sa•tion**)
**poly•mer•ize** (*or* **•ise**)
**po•lym•er•ous**
**poly•morph**
**poly•mor•phism**
**poly•mor•pho•nu•clear**
**poly•mor•phous** (*or* **•phic**)
**poly•myx•in** antibiotic
**Poly•nesia**
**Poly•nesian**
**poly•neu•ri•tis**
**Polynices** mythological character
**poly•no•mial**
**poly•nu•clear** (*or* **•cleate**)
**poly•nu•cleo•tide**
**po•lyn•ya** arctic water
**poly•ony•mous** having several names
**pol•yp**

**poly•pary** (*or* **•par•ium;** *plural* **•paries** *or* **•paria)** zoology term
**poly•pep•tide**
**poly•pet•al•ous**
**poly•pha•gia**
**pol•ypha•gous**
**poly•phase**
**poly•phone** linguistics term
**poly•phon•ic**
**poly•phoni•cal•ly**
**po•lypho•nous**
**po•lypho•ny** (*plural* **•nies)** musical term
**poly•phy•let•ic** biology term
**poly•phy•leti•cal•ly**
**poly•phyo•dont** zoology term
**poly•ploid** genetics term; *compare* **polypoid**
**poly•ploi•dal** (*or* **•dic)**
**poly•ploi•dy**
**poly•pod** many-legged animal
**po•lypo•dous**
**poly•po•dy** (*plural* **•dies)** fern
**poly•poid** of a polyp; *compare* **polyploid**
**poly•pro•pyl•ene**
**poly•pro•to•dont** zoology term
**pol•yp•tych** altarpiece
**poly•pus** (*plural* **•pi)** pathological polyp
**poly•rhythm**
**poly•rhyth•mic**
**poly•sac•cha•ride** (*or* **•rose)**
**poly•semous**
**poly•semy** ambiguity
**poly•sep•al•ous**
**poly•so•mic** genetics term
**poly•sty•rene**
**poly•sul•phide** (*US* **•fide)**
**poly•syl•lab•ic** (*or* **•labi•cal)**
**poly•syl•labi•cal•ly**
**poly•syl•la•ble**
**poly•syl•lo•gism**
**poly•syn•deton** grammar term
**poly•syn•the•sis**
**poly•syn•the•sism**
**poly•syn•thet•ic**
**poly•tech•nic**
**poly•tet•ra•fluo•ro•ethy-lene**
**poly•theism**
**poly•theist**
**poly•theis•tic**
**poly•theis•ti•cal•ly**
**poly•thene**
**poly•to•nal**
**poly•to•nal•ist**
**poly•to•nal•ity** (*or* **•ism)**
**poly•troph•ic** biology term
**poly•typ•ic** (*or* **•typi•cal)**
**poly•un•satu•rat•ed**
**poly•urethane** (*or* **•urethan)**
**poly•uria**
**poly•ur•ic**
**poly•va•len•cy**
**poly•va•lent**
**poly•vi•nyl**
**Polyxena** mythological princess
**poly•zoan** aquatic organism
**poly•zo•ar•ium** (*plural* **•aria)**
**poly•zo•ic**
**pom** *short for* **pommy**
**pom•ace** pulped apples
**po•ma•ceous** botany term
**po•made** hair oil
**po•man•der**
**pome** fruit of apple
**pom•egran•ate**
**pom•elo** (*plural* **•elos)** grapefruit
**Pom•era•nia** European region
**Pom•era•nian**
**pom•fret** liquorice sweet
**pomi•cul•ture**
**pom•if•er•ous**
**pom•mel** part of saddle; *less common spelling of* **pummel**
**pom•my** (*plural* **•mies)** *Austral* English person
**pomo•logi•cal**
**pom•olo•gist**
**pom•ol•ogy** fruit cultivation
**Po•mo•na** Roman goddess
**pomp**
**pom•pa•dour** hairstyle
**pom•pa•no** (*plural* **•no** *or* **•nos)** fish
**Pom•peii**
**Pom•pei•ian**
**Pom•pey** *Slang* Portsmouth
**pom-pom** cannon
**pom•pon** (*or* **•pom)** globular tuft, flower, etc.
**pom•pos•ity** (*plural* **•ities)**
**pomp•ous**
**pomp•ous•ness**
**Pon•ce** Puerto Rican port
**ponce**
**pon•cho** (*plural* **•chos)**
**pond**
**pon•der**
**pon•der•abil•ity**
**pon•der•able**
**pon•der•er**
**pon•der•ous**
**Pon•di•cher•ry** Indian territory
**Pon•do•land** South African region
**pond-skater** insect
**pond•weed**
**pone** maize bread
**pong**
**pon•gee** fabric
**pon•gid** ape
**pon•iard** dagger
**pons** (*plural* **pon•tes)** anatomy term
**pons asi•no•rum** geometry theorem
**pons Va•ro•lii** (*plural* **pon•tes Va•ro•lii)** part of brain
**pont** river ferry
**Pont•char•train** US lake
**Pon•te•fract**
**Pon•tia•nak** Indonesian port
**Pon•tic** of the Black Sea
**pon•ti•fex** (*plural* **•tifi•ces)**
**pon•tiff**
**pon•tifi•cal**
**pon•tifi•cals** bishop's robes
**pon•tifi•cate**
**pon•tine** of bridges
**pon•to•nier** bridge builder
**pon•toon**
**Pon•ty•pool** Welsh town
**Pon•ty•pridd** Welsh town
**pony** (*plural* **ponies)**
**pony•tail**
**pooch**
**pood** unit of weight
**poo•dle**

**poof** (*or* **poove**) *Slang* homosexual; *compare* **pouf**
**pooh**
**Pooh-Bah** pompous official
**pooh-pooh**
**pool**
**Poole** Dorset port
**pools** gambling system
**poon** tree
**Poo•na** (*or* **Pune**) Indian city
**poop**
**poor** needy; unfortunate; *compare* **pore**; **pour**
**poor•house**
**poor•ly**
**poor•ness**
**pop** (**pop•ping, popped**)
**pop•corn**
**pope**
**pope•dom**
**pop•ery**
**pop•eyed**
**pop•gun**
**pop•in•jay**
**pop•ish**
**pop•ish•ness**
**pop•lar**
**pop•lin**
**pop•lit•eal** anatomy term
**Po•po•ca•té•petl** Mexican volcano
**pop•over**
**pop•pa•dom** (*or* **•dum**) Indian bread
**popped**
**pop•per**
**pop•pet**
**pop•ping**
**pop•ple**
**pop•py** (*plural* **•pies**)
**poppy•cock**
**poppy•head**
**Pop•si•cle** (*Trademark*)
**pop•sy** (*plural* **•sies**)
**popu•lace**
**popu•lar**
**popu•lar•ity**
**popu•lari•za•tion** (*or* **•sa•tion**)
**popu•lar•ize** (*or* **•ise**)
**popu•lar•iz•er** (*or* **•is•er**)
**popu•late**
**popu•la•tion**
**popu•lism**
**popu•list**
**Popu•list** member of US political party
**popu•lous**
**popu•lous•ness**
**por•bea•gle** shark
**porce•lain**
**por•cel•la•neous**
**porch**
**por•cine**
**por•cu•pine**
**pore** examine; small hole; *compare* **poor**; **pour**
**por•gy** (*plural* **•gy** *or* **•gies**) fish
**po•rif•er•an** a sponge
**po•rif•er•ous**
**Po•ri•rua** New Zealand city
**po•rism** mathematical proposition
**pork**
**pork•er**
**porki•ness**
**pork•pie**
**porky** (**porki•er, porki•est**)
**por•noc•ra•cy** (*plural* **•cies**) government by prostitutes
**por•nog•ra•pher**
**por•no•graph•ic**
**por•no•graphi•cal•ly**
**por•nog•ra•phy**
**poro•mer•ic** chemistry term
**po•ros•ity** (*plural* **•ities**)
**po•rous**
**po•rous•ness**
**por•phy•ria** disease
**por•phy•rin** pigment
**por•phy•rit•ic** geology term
**por•phy•rog•enite** prince
**por•phy•roid** geology term
**por•phy•rop•sin** pigment
**por•phy•ry** (*plural* **•ries**) rock
**por•poise** (*plural* **•poise** *or* **•poises**)
**por•ridge**
**por•rin•ger** dish
**Porsena** legendary king
**port**
**port•abil•ity** (*or* **•able•ness**)
**port•able**
**Por•ta•down** Northern Irish town
**por•tage**
**por•tal**
**por•ta•men•to** (*plural* **•ti**) musical term
**por•ta•tive** portable
**Port-au-Prince** Haitian capital
**port•cul•lis**
**porte-cochere** covered entrance
**por•tend**
**por•tent**
**por•ten•tous**
**por•ten•tous•ness**
**por•ter**
**por•ter•age**
**porter•house**
**port•fire**
**port•fo•lio** (*plural* **•lios**)
**Port Har•court** Nigerian port
**port•hole**
**por•ti•co** (*plural* **•coes** *or* **•cos**)
**por•ti•ère** door curtain
**por•tion**
**Port•land**
**Port•laoise** Irish town
**port•li•ness**
**Port Louis** capital of Mauritius
**port•ly** (**•li•er, •li•est**)
**port•man•teau** (*plural* **•teaus** *or* **•teaux**)
**Port Mores•by** capital of New Guinea
**Pôr•to Ale•gre** Brazilian port
**Port of Spain** capital of Trinidad and Tobago
**Por•to Novo** capital of Benin
**por•trait**
**por•trait•ist**
**por•trai•ture**
**por•tray**
**por•tray•able**
**por•tray•al**
**por•tray•er**
**port•ress**
**Port Said** Egyptian port
**Port-Salut** cheese
**Ports•mouth**
**Port Tal•bot** Welsh port
**Por•tu•gal**
**Por•tu•guese** (*plural* **•guese**)
**por•tu•laca** plant
**por•tu•la•ca•ceous**

**pose**
**Poseidon** Greek god
**pos•er** one who poses; problem
**po•seur** affected person
**posh**
**pos•it** postulate; *compare* **posset**
**posi•tif** organ keyboard
**po•si•tion**
**po•si•tion•al**
**posi•tive**
**posi•tive•ly**
**posi•tive•ness**
**posi•tiv•ism**
**posi•tiv•ist**
**posi•tiv•is•tic**
**posi•tiv•is•ti•cal•ly**
**posi•tron** physics term
**posi•tro•nium** physics term
**po•sol•ogy** branch of medicine
**pos•se**
**pos•sess**
**pos•sessed**
**pos•ses•sion**
**pos•ses•sive**
**pos•ses•sive•ness**
**pos•ses•sor**
**pos•ses•so•ry**
**pos•set** hot drink; *compare* **posit**
**pos•sibil•ity** (*plural* **•ities)**
**pos•sible**
**pos•sibly**
**pos•sum** *Slang* opossum; phalanger
**post**
**post•age**
**post•al**
**post•ax•ial**
**post•bag**
**post-bellum** after war
**post•box**
**post•boy**
**post•card**
**post•ca•val** anatomy term
**post chaise**
**post•code**
**post•coit•al**
**post•date**
**post•di•lu•vial**
**post•di•lu•vian**
**post•doc•tor•al**
**post•er**
**poste res•tante**
**pos•teri•or**
**pos•ter•ity**
**pos•tern**
**post•fix** add to the end
**post-free**
**post•gla•cial**
**post•gradu•ate**
**post•haste**
**post•hu•mous**
**post•hyp•not•ic**
**pos•tiche** architectural term; *compare* **pastiche**
**pos•ti•cous** posterior
**pos•til** marginal note
**pos•til•ion** (*or* **•til•lion)**
**post•im•pres•sion•ism**
**post•im•pres•sion•ist**
**post•ing**
**post•limi•ny** (*or* **•li•min•ium**; *plural* **•nies** *or* **•minia)** legal term
**post•lude** concluding music
**post•man** (*plural* **•men)**
**post•mark**
**post•master**
**post•me•rid•ian** (*adj*)
**post me•rid•iem** *Latin* after noon
**post•mil•len•nial**
**post•mod•ern**
**post•mod•ern•ism**
**post•mod•ern•ist**
**post•mor•tem**
**post•na•tal**
**post•nup•tial**
**post-obit** legal term
**post•op•era•tive**
**post•paid**
**post•par•tum** after childbirth
**post•pon•able**
**post•pone**
**post•pone•ment**
**post•pon•er**
**post•po•si•tion**
**post•po•si•tion•al**
**post•posi•tive**
**post•pran•dial**
**post•script**
**pos•tu•lan•cy** (*or* **•lant•ship)**
**pos•tu•lant**
**pos•tu•late**
**pos•tu•la•tion**
**pos•tu•la•tor**
**pos•tur•al**
**pos•ture**
**pos•tur•er**
**post•war**
**posy** (*plural* **posies)**
**pot (pot•ting, pot•ted)**
**pot•abil•ity** (*or* **•able•ness)**
**po•table** drinkable
**po•tage** *French* soup; *compare* **pottage**
**po•tam•ic**
**po•ta•mol•ogy** study of rivers
**pot•ash**
**po•tas•sic**
**po•tas•sium**
**po•ta•tion** drinking
**po•ta•to** (*plural* **•toes)**
**pot-au-feu** French stew
**pot•bel•lied**
**pot•belly** (*plural* **•bellies)**
**pot•boiler**
**pot•boy** (*or* **pot•man**; *plural* **•boys** *or* **•men)**
**potch** *Austral* inferior opal
**po•teen** *Irish* illicit whiskey
**po•ten•cy** (*or* **•tence**; *plural* **•ten•cies** *or* **•tences)**
**po•tent**
**po•ten•tate** ruler; *compare* **potentiate**
**po•ten•tial**
**po•ten•ti•al•ity** (*plural* **•ities)**
**po•ten•tial•ly**
**po•ten•ti•ate** increase effectiveness; *compare* **potentate**
**po•ten•til•la**
**po•ten•ti•om•eter**
**po•tent•ness**
**pot•ful** (*plural* **•fuls)**
**pot•head** *Slang* cannabis user
**poth•er**
**pot•herb**
**pot•hole**
**pot•holer**
**pot•hol•ing**
**pot•hook**
**pot•house**
**pot•hunter**
**po•tiche** (*plural* **•tiches)** tall vase
**po•tion**

**Potiphar** biblical character
**pot•latch** ceremonial feast
**pot•luck**
**Po•to•mac** US river
**pot•pie** stew pie
**pot•pour•ri** (*plural* **•ris**)
**Pots•dam** German city
**pot•sherd** (*or* **•shard**)
**pot•stone**
**pot•tage** thick soup; *compare* **potage**
**pot•ted**
**pot•ter**
**pot•ter•er**
**Pot•teries** Staffordshire region
**pot•tery** (*plural* **•teries**)
**pot•ting**
**pot•to** (*plural* **•tos**) animal
**pot•ty** (*adj* **•ti•er, •ti•est;** *noun, plural* **•ties**)
**pouch**
**pouched**
**pouchy**
**pouf** (*or* **pouffe**) cushion seat; *compare* **poof**
**pou•lard** (*or* **•larde**) spayed hen
**poult** young chicken
**poul•ter•er**
**poul•tice**
**poul•try**
**poultry•man** (*plural* **•men**)
**pounce**
**pound**
**pound•age**
**pound•al** unit
**pound•er**
**pour** flow; *compare* **poor; pore**
**pour•boire** *French* tip
**pour•er**
**pour•par•ler** *French* informal conference
**pour•point** doublet
**pous•sette** country dance
**pous•sin** spring chicken
**pout**
**pout•er**
**pout•ing•ly**
**pov•er•ty**
**poverty-stricken**
**pow** exclamation
**pow•an** fish
**pow•der**
**pow•der•er**
**pow•dery**
**pow•er**
**power•boat**
**pow•er•ful**
**pow•er•ful•ly**
**pow•er•ful•ness**
**power•house**
**pow•er•less**
**pow•er•less•ness**
**pow•wow**
**Pow•ys** Welsh county
**pox**
**poxy**
**Po•yang** Chinese lake
**Poz•nań** Polish city
**poz•zuo•la•na** (*or* **•zo•**) volcanic ash
**prac•ti•cabil•ity** (*or* **•cable•ness**)
**prac•ti•cable**
**prac•ti•cably**
**prac•ti•cal**
**prac•ti•cal•ity** (*or* **•cal•ness**)
**prac•ti•cal•ly**
**prac•tice** (*noun*)
**prac•tise** (*US* **•tice**; *verb*)
**prac•tised** (*US* **•ticed**)
**prac•ti•tion•er**
**prae•dial** (*or* **pre•**) of land
**prae•di•al•ity** (*or* **pre•**)
**prae•mu•ni•re** legal term
**prae•no•men** Roman's first name
**Prae•se•pe** star cluster
**prae•sid•ium** *variant spelling of* **presidium**
**prae•tor** (*or* **pre•**) Roman magistrate
**prag•mat•ic**
**prag•mati•cal•ly**
**prag•mat•ics** (*sing.*)
**prag•ma•tism**
**prag•ma•tist**
**prag•ma•tis•tic**
**Prague**
**Praia** capital of Cape Verde
**prai•rie**
**praise** acclaim; *compare* **prase**
**prais•er**
**praise•worthi•ly**
**praise•worthi•ness**
**praise•worthy**
**pra•line**
**prall•triller** musical term
**pram**
**prance**
**pranc•er**
**pranc•ing•ly**
**pran•dial**
**prang**
**prank**
**prank•ish**
**prank•ster**
**prase** quartz; *compare* **praise**
**pra•seo•dym•ium** chemical element
**prat** *Slang* idiot
**prate** chatter
**prat•er**
**prat•in•cole** bird
**prat•ing•ly**
**pra•tique** permission to use port
**Pra•to** Italian city
**prat•tle**
**prat•tler**
**prat•tling•ly**
**prau** *variant of* **proa**
**prawn**
**prawn•er**
**prax•is** (*plural* **prax•ises** *or* **praxes**) practice
**pray** utter prayer; *compare* **prey**
**prayer** petition
**pray•er** one who prays
**prayer•ful**
**prayer•ful•ly**
**preach**
**preach•er**
**preachi•fi•ca•tion**
**preachi•fy** (**•fies, •fy•ing, •fied**)
**preach•ment**
**pre•ad•am•ite**
**pre•ad•ap•ta•tion**
**pre•ado•les•cence**
**pre•ado•les•cent**
**pre•am•ble**
**pre•am•bu•lar** (*or* **•la•tory, •lary**)
**pre•am•pli•fi•er**
**pre•ar•range**
**pre•ar•ranged**
**pre•ar•range•ment**
**pre•ar•rang•er**
**pre•ax•ial**
**preb•end**

**pre•ben•dal**
**preb•en•dary** (*plural* **•daries**)
**Pre•cam•brian** geological term
**pre•can•cel** (**•cel•ling, •celled**; *US* **•cel•ing, •celed**)
**pre•can•cel•la•tion**
**pre•cari•ous**
**pre•cari•ous•ness**
**pre•cast** (**•cast•ing, •cast**)
**preca•tory** (*or* **•tive**)
**pre•cau•tion**
**pre•cau•tion•ary** (*or* **•tion•al**)
**pre•cau•tious**
**pre•cede** come before; *compare* **proceed**
**prec•edence**
**prec•edent**
**prec•eden•tial**
**pre•ced•ing**
**pre•cen•tor** cleric; *compare* **preceptor**
**pre•cen•to•rial**
**pre•cept**
**pre•cep•tive**
**pre•cep•tor** teacher; *compare* **precentor**
**pre•cep•tor•ate**
**pre•cep•to•rial** (*or* **•to•ral**)
**pre•cep•tor•ship**
**pre•cep•tress**
**pre•cess**
**pre•ces•sion** rotation; motion of equinoxes; *compare* **procession**
**pre•ces•sion•al**
**pre•cinct**
**pre•ci•os•ity** (*plural* **•ities**) affectation
**pre•cious**
**pre•cious•ness**
**preci•pice**
**preci•piced**
**pre•cipi•tance** (*or* **•tan•cy**)
**pre•cipi•tant**
**pre•cipi•tate**
**pre•cipi•ta•tion**
**pre•cipi•ta•tive**
**pre•cipi•ta•tor**
**pre•cipi•tin** antibody
**pre•cipi•tous**
**pre•cipi•tous•ness**
**pre•cis** (*or* **pré•**; *plural* **•cis**)
**pre•cise**
**pre•cise•ness**
**pre•ci•sian** strict observer of rules; *compare* **precision**
**pre•ci•sian•ism**
**pre•ci•sion** accuracy; *compare* **precisian**
**pre•ci•sion•ism**
**pre•ci•sion•ist**
**pre•clini•cal**
**pre•clud•able**
**pre•clude**
**pre•clu•sion**
**pre•clu•sive**
**pre•co•cial** ornithology term
**pre•co•cious**
**pre•co•cious•ness** (*or* **pre•coc•ity**)
**pre•cog•ni•tion**
**pre•cog•ni•tive**
**pre•con•ceive**
**pre•con•cep•tion**
**pre•con•cert**
**pre•con•demn**
**pre•con•di•tion**
**pre•co•ni•za•tion** (*or* **•sa•tion**)
**pre•co•nize** (*or* **•nise**) announce publicly
**pre•con•scious**
**pre•con•scious•ness**
**pre•con•tract**
**pre•cook**
**pre•criti•cal**
**pre•cur•sor**
**pre•cur•sory** (*or* **•sive**)
**pre•da•cious** (*or* **•ceous**) predatory
**pre•da•cious•ness** (*or* **•ceous•ness, pre•dac•ity**)
**pre•date** precede
**pre•da•tion** predatory action
**preda•tor**
**preda•to•ri•ly**
**preda•to•ri•ness**
**preda•tory**
**pre•de•cease**
**pre•de•ces•sor**
**pre•del•la** (*plural* **•le**) altar platform; painting
**pre•des•ti•nar•ian**
**pre•des•ti•nari•an•ism**
**pre•des•ti•nate** predestined; *variant of* **predestine**
**pre•des•ti•na•tion**
**pre•des•tine** (*or* **•ti•nate**)
**pre•de•ter•mi•nate**
**pre•de•ter•mi•na•tion**
**pre•de•ter•mi•na•tive**
**pre•de•ter•mine**
**pre•de•ter•min•er**
**pre•dial** *variant spelling of* **praedial**
**predi•cabil•ity** (*or* **•cable•ness**)
**predi•cable** affirmable
**pre•dica•ment**
**predi•cant** of preaching
**predi•cate**
**predi•ca•tion**
**pre•dica•tive**
**predi•ca•tory** of preaching
**pre•dict**
**pre•dict•abil•ity** (*or* **•able•ness**)
**pre•dict•able**
**pre•dict•ably**
**pre•dic•tion**
**pre•dic•tive**
**pre•dic•tive•ly**
**pre•dic•tor**
**pre•di•gest**
**pre•di•ges•tion**
**pre•di•lec•tion**
**pre•dis•pos•al**
**pre•dis•pose**
**pre•dis•po•si•tion**
**pred•ni•sone** drug
**pre•domi•nance** (*or* **•nan•cy**)
**pre•domi•nant**
**pre•domi•nate**
**pre•domi•na•tion**
**pre•domi•na•tor**
**pre-eclamp•sia**
**pree•mie** (*or* **pre•mie**) *US* premature baby
**pre-eminence**
**pre-eminent**
**pre-empt**
**pre-emption**
**pre-emptive**
**pre-emptor**
**pre-emptory**
**preen**
**preen•er**
**pre-exist**

**pre-exist•ence**
**pre•fab**
**pre•fab•ri•cate**
**pre•fab•ri•ca•tion**
**pre•fab•ri•ca•tor**
**pref•ace**
**pref•ac•er**
**prefa•to•ri•ly** (*or* **•ri•al•ly**)
**prefa•tory** (*or* **•to•rial**)
**pre•fect**
**pre•fec•to•rial**
**pre•fec•tur•al**
**pre•fec•ture**
**pre•fer** (**•fer•ring, •ferred**)
**pref•er•abil•ity** (*or* **•able•ness**)
**pref•er•able**
**pref•er•ably**
**pref•er•ence**
**pref•er•en•tial**
**pref•er•en•tial•ly**
**pref•er•en•ti•al•ity**
**pre•fer•ment**
**pre•fer•rer**
**pre•figu•ra•tion**
**pre•figu•ra•tive**
**pre•figu•ra•tive•ness**
**pre•fig•ure**
**pre•fig•ure•ment**
**pre•fix**
**pre•fix•al**
**pre•flight**
**pre•form**
**pre•for•ma•tion**
**pre•fron•tal** anatomy term
**pre•gla•cial**
**preg•nabil•ity**
**preg•nable**
**preg•nan•cy** (*plural* **•cies**)
**preg•nant**
**pre•heat**
**pre•hen•sile**
**pre•hen•sion**
**pre•his•to•rian**
**pre•his•tor•ic** (*or* **•tori•cal**)
**pre•his•tori•cal•ly**
**pre•his•to•ry** (*plural* **•ries**)
**pre•homi•nid**
**pre-ignition**
**pre•judge**
**pre•judg•er**
**pre•judg•ment** (*or* **•judge•ment**)
**preju•dice**
**preju•di•cial**
**prela•cy** (*plural* **•cies**)
**prel•ate**
**pre•lat•ic**
**prela•tism**
**prela•tist**
**prela•ture**
**pre•lect** to lecture
**pre•lec•tion**
**pre•lec•tor**
**pre•lexi•cal** grammar term
**pre•limi•nari•ly**
**pre•limi•nary** (*plural* **•naries**)
**pre•lims** front matter of book; first exams
**pre•lit•era•cy**
**pre•lit•er•ate**
**prel•ude**
**pre•lud•er**
**pre•lu•di•al**
**pre•lu•sion**
**pre•lu•sive** (*or* **•so•ry**)
**pre•mari•tal**
**prema•ture**
**prema•tur•ity** (*or* **•ture•ness**)
**pre•max•il•la** (*plural* **•lae**) bone
**pre•max•il•lary**
**pre•med** *short for* **premedical; premedication**
**pre•medi•cal**
**pre•medi•ca•tion**
**pre•medi•tate**
**pre•medi•tat•ed•ly**
**pre•medi•ta•tion**
**pre•medi•ta•tive**
**pre•medi•ta•tor**
**pre•men•stru•al**
**prem•ier** first in importance
**premi•ere** first performance
**prem•ier•ship**
**prem•ise** state as premiss; *variant spelling of* **premiss**
**prem•ises** land and buildings
**prem•iss** (*or* **•ise**) logical statement
**pre•mium**
**pre•mo•lar**
**premo•ni•tion**
**pre•moni•tory**
**pre•morse** biology term
**pre•mu•ni•tion** immunity
**pre•na•tal**
**pre•nomi•nal**
**pre•oc•cu•pa•tion** (*or* **•pan•cy**)
**pre•oc•cu•py** (**•pies, •py•ing, •pied**)
**pre•or•dain**
**pre•or•di•na•tion**
**prep** *Slang* homework; preparatory school
**pre•pack**
**pre•pack•age**
**prepaid**
**prepa•ra•tion**
**pre•para•tive**
**pre•para•to•ri•ly**
**pre•para•tory**
**pre•pare**
**pre•par•ed•ly**
**pre•par•ed•ness**
**pre•pay** (**•pay•ing, •paid**)
**pre•pay•able**
**pre•pay•ment**
**pre•pense** premeditated
**pre•pon•der•ance** (*or* **•an•cy**)
**pre•pon•der•ant**
**pre•pon•der•ate**
**pre•pon•der•at•ing•ly**
**pre•pon•dera•tion**
**prepo•si•tion**
**prepo•si•tion•al**
**pre•posi•tive** linguistics term
**pre•posi•tor** (*or* **•pos•tor**) prefect
**pre•pos•sess**
**pre•pos•sess•ing**
**pre•pos•sess•ing•ness**
**pre•pos•ses•sion**
**pre•pos•ter•ous**
**pre•pos•ter•ous•ness**
**pre•po•ten•cy**
**pre•po•tent**
**pre•puce** foreskin
**pre•pu•tial**
**Pre-Raphael•ite**
**pre•re•cord**
**pre•requi•site**
**pre•roga•tive**
**pre•sa** (*plural* **•se**) musical term
**pres•age**
**pre•sage•ful**
**pre•sag•er**

**pres•byo•pia**
**pres•by•op•ic**
**pres•by•ter** church elder
**pres•by•ter•al**
**pres•byt•er•ate**
**pres•by•ter•ial**
**Pres•by•ter•ian** Church
**pres•by•ter•ian** of government by presbyters
**Pres•by•teri•an•ism**
**pres•by•teri•an•is•tic**
**pres•by•tery** (*plural* **•teries**)
**pre•school**
**pres•ci•ence** foreknowledge
**pres•ci•ent**
**pre•scribe** give ruling; order use of drug; *compare* **proscribe**
**pre•scrib•er**
**pre•script**
**pre•scrip•tibil•ity**
**pre•scrip•tible**
**pre•scrip•tion**
**pre•scrip•tive**
**pre•scrip•tiv•ism**
**pres•ence**
**pres•ent** the time now; in existence now
**pre•sent** gift; to give
**pre•sent•able**
**pre•sent•ably**
**pre•sent•able•ness** (*or* **•abil•ity**)
**pres•en•ta•tion**
**pres•en•ta•tion•al**
**pres•en•ta•tion•ism** philosophy term
**pres•en•ta•tion•ist**
**pre•senta•tive**
**pre•senta•tive•ness**
**present-day** (*adj*)
**pres•en•tee**
**pre•sent•er**
**pre•sen•tient**
**pre•sen•ti•ment**
**pres•ent•ly**
**pre•sent•ment**
**pre•serv•abil•ity**
**pre•serv•able**
**pres•er•va•tion**
**pre•serva•tive**
**pre•serve**
**pre•serv•er**
**pre•set** (**•set•ting, •set**)
**pre•set•ter**
**pre•shrunk**
**pre•side**
**presi•den•cy** (*plural* **•cies**)
**presi•dent**
**president-elect**
**presi•den•tial**
**pre•sid•er**
**pre•sidio** (*plural* **•sidios**) military establishment
**pre•sid•ium** (*or* **prae•**; *plural* **•iums** *or* **•ia**) Communist committee
**pre•sig•ni•fy** (**•fies, •fy•ing, •fied**)
**press**
**press•er** one that presses; *compare* **pressor**
**press-gang** (*verb*)
**press•ing**
**press•ing•ness**
**press•man** (*plural* **•men**)
**press•mark** code on library book
**pres•sor** (*adj*) increasing blood pressure; *compare* **presser**
**press•room**
**press-up** (*noun*)
**pres•sure**
**pres•suri•za•tion** (*or* **•sa•tion**)
**pres•sur•ize** (*or* **•ise**)
**pres•sur•iz•er** (*or* **•is•er**)
**press•work**
**pres•ti•digi•ta•tion**
**pres•ti•digi•ta•tor**
**pres•tige**
**pres•tig•ious**
**pres•tig•ious•ness**
**pres•tis•si•mo** (*plural* **•mos**) musical term
**pres•to** (*plural* **•tos**)
**Pres•ton** Lancashire town
**Pres•ton•pans** Scottish battle site
**pre•stress**
**Prest•wich** Scottish town
**pre•sum•able**
**pre•sum•ably**
**pre•sume**
**pre•sum•ed•ly**
**pre•sum•er**
**pre•sum•ing•ly**
**pre•sump•tion**
**pre•sump•tive**
**pre•sump•tive•ness**
**pre•sump•tu•ous**
**pre•sump•tu•ous•ness**
**pre•sup•pose**
**pre•sup•po•si•tion**
**pre•tence** (*US* **•tense**)
**pre•tend**
**pre•tend•ed•ly**
**pre•tend•er**
**pre•ten•sion**
**pre•ten•tious**
**pre•ten•tious•ness**
**pret•er•ite** (*or* **•it**) grammar term
**pret•eri•tion** act of omitting
**pre•teri•tive** grammar term
**pre•ter•natu•ral**
**pre•ter•natu•ral•ism**
**pre•ter•natu•ral•ness** (*or* **•ral•ity**)
**pre•test**
**pre•text**
**Pre•to•ria**
**pret•ti•fy** (**•fies, •fy•ing, •fied**)
**pret•ti•ly**
**pret•ti•ness**
**pret•ty** (*adj* **•ti•er, •ti•est**; *verb* **•ties, •ty•ing, •tied**)
**pret•zel** biscuit
**pre•vail**
**pre•vail•er**
**pre•vail•ing**
**pre•vail•ing•ly**
**preva•lence** (*or* **•lent•ness**)
**preva•lent**
**pre•vari•cate**
**pre•vari•ca•tion**
**pre•vari•ca•tor**
**pre•ve•ni•ent** preceding
**pre•vent**
**pre•vent•able**
**pre•vent•ably**
**pre•ven•ta•tive** *variant of* **preventive**
**pre•vent•er**
**pre•ven•tion**
**pre•ven•tive** (*or* **•ta•tive**)
**pre•ven•tive•ness** (*or* **•ta•tive•ness**)
**pre•view** (*or* **•vue**)
**pre•vi•ous**
**pre•vi•ous•ly**
**pre•vi•ous•ness**
**pre•vi•sion**

**pre•vo•cal•ic** coming before a vowel
**pre•war**
**prey** victim; to hunt; victimize; *compare* **pray**
**prey•er**
**Priam** mythological king
**pri•ap•ic** of Priapus
**pria•pism** medical term
**Priapus** fertility god
**price**
**price•less**
**price•less•ness**
**pricey** (*or* **pricy; prici•er, prici•est)**
**prick**
**prick•er**
**prick•et**
**prick•le**
**prick•li•ness**
**prick•ly (•li•er, •li•est)**
**pricy** *variant spelling of* **pricey**
**pride**
**pride•ful**
**prie-dieu** kneeling desk
**pri•er** (*or* **pry•**) one who pries; *compare* **prior**
**priest**
**priest•craft**
**priest•ess**
**priest-hole**
**priest•hood**
**priest•li•ness**
**priest•ly (•li•er, •li•est)**
**priest-ridden**
**prig**
**prig•gery** (*or* **prig•gish•ness)**
**prig•gish**
**prig•gism**
**prill**
**prim** (*adj* **prim•mer, prim•mest;** *verb* **prim•ming, primmed)**
**pri•ma bal•leri•na**
**pri•ma•cy** (*plural* **•cies)**
**pri•ma don•na** (*plural* **pri•ma don•nas)**
**pri•mae•val** *variant spelling of* **primeval**
**pri•ma fa•cie**
**pri•mal**
**pri•ma•quine** drug
**pri•mari•ly**
**pri•ma•ry** (*plural* **•ries)**
**pri•mate**
**pri•ma•tial**
**pri•ma•tol•ogy** branch of zoology
**prime**
**prime•ness**
**pri•mer** introductory text
**prim•er** one that primes
**pri•mero** card game
**pri•meval** (*or* **•mae•val)**
**pri•meval•ly**
**primi•gravi•da** (*plural* **•das** *or* **•dae)** obstetrics term
**pri•mine** botany term
**prim•ing**
**pri•mipa•ra** (*or* **uni•**; *plural* **•ras** *or* **•rae)** obstetrics term
**primi•par•ity**
**pri•mipa•rous**
**primi•tive**
**primi•tive•ness**
**primi•tiv•ism**
**primi•tiv•ist**
**primi•tiv•is•tic**
**prim•ness**
**pri•mo** (*plural* **•mos** *or* **•mi)**
**pri•mo•geni•tary**
**pri•mo•geni•tor**
**pri•mo•geni•ture**
**pri•mor•dial**
**pri•mor•dium** (*plural* **•dia)**
**primp**
**prim•rose**
**primu•la**
**primu•la•ceous**
**pri•mum mo•bi•le** *Latin* prime mover
**Pri•mus** (*Trademark*) stove
**pri•mus** presiding bishop
**prince**
**prince•dom**
**prince•li•ness**
**prince•ling**
**prince•ly (•li•er, •li•est)**
**prin•cess**
**Prince•ton** US town
**prin•ci•pal** foremost; head person; *compare* **principle**
**prin•ci•pal•ity** (*plural* **•ities)**
**prin•ci•pal•ly**
**Prín•ci•pe** island
**prin•cip•ium** (*plural* **•cipia)** fundamental principle
**prin•ci•ple** standard; *compare* **principal**
**prin•ci•pled**
**prink**
**prink•er**
**print**
**print•abil•ity** (*or* **•able•ness)**
**print•able**
**print•er**
**print•ing**
**print•maker**
**print•out**
**pri•on**
**pri•or** abbot's deputy; *compare* **prier**
**pri•or•ate**
**pri•or•ess**
**pri•or•ity** (*plural* **•ities)**
**pri•ory** (*plural* **•ories)**
**pris•age** duty on wine
**prise** (*or* **prize)** force open; *compare* **prize**
**prism**
**pris•mat•ic**
**pris•ma•toid** geometric solid
**pris•ma•toid•al**
**pris•moid**
**pris•moid•al**
**pris•on**
**pris•on•er**
**pris•si•ly**
**pris•si•ness**
**pris•sy (•si•er, •si•est)**
**pris•tine**
**prithee**
**pri•va•cy** (*plural* **•cies)**
**pri•vate**
**pri•va•teer**
**pri•va•tion**
**priva•tive**
**priv•et**
**privi•lege**
**privi•leged**
**privi•ly**
**priv•ity** (*plural* **•ities)** legal relationship
**privy** (*noun, plural* **privies;** *adj* **privi•er, privi•est)** lavatory; secret
**prize** award; *variant spelling of* **prise**
**prize•fight**
**prize•fighter**
**pro** (*plural* **pros)**
**proa** (*or* **prau)** boat
**pro•ac•tive**

**pro-am** professional and amateur
**proba•bil•ism**
**prob•abil•ist**
**prob•abil•is•tic**
**prob•abil•ity** (*plural* **•ities**)
**prob•able**
**prob•ably**
**pro•band** person in genealogical study
**pro•bang** surgical instrument
**pro•bate**
**pro•ba•tion**
**pro•ba•tion•al** (*or* **•tion•ary**)
**pro•ba•tion•er**
**pro•ba•tive** (*or* **•tory**)
**probe**
**probe•able**
**prob•er**
**pro•bity**
**prob•lem**
**prob•lem•at•ic** (*or* **•ati•cal**)
**prob•lem•ati•cal•ly**
**pro bono pub•li•co** *Latin* for the public good
**pro•bos•cid•ean** (*or* **•ian**) zoology term
**pro•bos•cis** (*plural* **•cises** *or* **•ci•des**)
**pro•caine**
**pro•cam•bial**
**pro•cam•bium** botany term
**pro•carp** botany term
**pro•ca•thedral** church
**pro•cedur•al**
**pro•cedure**
**pro•ceed** carry on; *compare* **precede**
**pro•ceed•er**
**pro•ceed•ing**
**pro•ceed•ings**
**pro•ceeds** (*noun*)
**proc•eleus•mat•ic** prosody term
**pro•cephal•ic** anatomy term
**pro•cess**
**pro•ces•sion**
**pro•ces•sion•al**
**pro•ces•sor**
**process-server**
**pro•chro•nism** dating error
**pro•claim**
**proc•la•ma•tion**
**pro•clama•tory**
**pro•clit•ic** linguistics term
**pro•cliv•ity** (*plural* **•ities**)
**Procne** mythological princess
**pro•con•sul**
**pro•con•su•lar**
**pro•con•su•late** (*or* **•sul•ship**)
**pro•cras•ti•nate**
**pro•cras•ti•na•tion**
**pro•cras•ti•na•tor**
**pro•creant** (*or* **•crea•tive**)
**pro•cre•ate**
**pro•crea•tion**
**pro•crea•tor**
**Pro•crus•tean**
**Procrustes** mythological robber
**pro•cryp•tic** zoology term
**pro•cryp•ti•cal•ly**
**proc•to•logi•cal**
**proc•tolo•gist**
**proc•tol•ogy** branch of medicine
**proc•tor**
**proc•to•rial**
**proc•to•scope**
**proc•to•scop•ic**
**proc•tos•co•py**
**pro•cum•bent**
**pro•cur•able**
**procu•ra•tion**
**procu•ra•tor**
**procu•ra•tor fis•cal** Scottish legal officer
**procu•ra•tory**
**pro•cure**
**pro•cure•ment** (*or* **•cur•ance, •cur•al**)
**pro•cur•er** (*fem* **•ess**)
**prod** (**prod•ding, prod•ded**)
**prod•der**
**prodi•gal**
**prodi•gal•ity** (*plural* **•ities**)
**prodi•gal•ly**
**pro•di•gious**
**pro•di•gious•ness**
**prodi•gy** (*plural* **•gies**)
**pro•dro•mal** (*or* **•drom•ic**)
**pro•drome** symptom of disease
**pro•duce**
**pro•duc•er**
**pro•duc•ibil•ity**
**pro•duc•ible**
**prod•uct**
**pro•duc•tion**
**pro•duc•tion•al**
**pro•duc•tive**
**prod•uc•tiv•ity** (*or* **•tive•ness**)
**pro•em** preface
**pro•emial**
**prof** *Slang* professor
**profa•na•tion**
**pro•fana•to•ry**
**pro•fane**
**pro•fane•ness**
**pro•fan•er**
**pro•fan•ity** (*plural* **•ities**)
**pro•fess**
**pro•fess•ed•ly**
**pro•fes•sion**
**pro•fes•sion•al**
**pro•fes•sion•al•ism**
**pro•fes•sion•al•ist**
**pro•fes•sion•al•ly**
**pro•fes•sor**
**prof•es•so•rial**
**prof•es•sor•iate** (*or* **•so•rate**)
**pro•fes•sor•ship**
**prof•fer**
**prof•fer•er**
**pro•fi•cien•cy** (*plural* **•cies**)
**pro•fi•cient**
**pro•file**
**prof•it**
**prof•it•abil•ity**
**prof•it•able**
**prof•it•ably**
**profi•teer**
**prof•it•er**
**pro•fit•er•ole**
**prof•it•less**
**profit-sharing**
**prof•li•ga•cy**
**prof•li•gate**
**prof•lu•ent** flowing smoothly
**pro-form** grammar term
**pro for•ma** *Latin* as prescribed
**pro•found**
**pro•found•ly**
**pro•found•ness**
**pro•fun•dity** (*plural* **•dities**)
**pro•fuse**
**pro•fuse•ly**
**pro•fuse•ness**
**pro•fu•sion**

**prog** **(prog•ging, progged)** *Slang* prowl
**pro•geni•tive**
**pro•geni•tive•ness**
**pro•geni•tor**
**prog•eny** (*plural* **•enies)**
**pro•ges•ta•tion•al** before pregnancy
**pro•ges•ter•one** hormone
**pro•ges•to•gen** (*or* **pro•ges•tin)** synthetic progesterone
**pro•glot•tis** (*or* **•tid;** *plural* **•glot•ti•des)** tapeworm segment
**prog•na•thism**
**prog•na•thous** (*or* **•nath•ic)**
**prog•no•sis** (*plural* **•ses)**
**prog•nos•tic**
**prog•nos•ti•cate**
**prog•nos•ti•ca•tion**
**prog•nos•ti•ca•tive**
**prog•nos•ti•ca•tor**
**pro•gram** *US spelling of* programme
**pro•gram** **(•gram•ming, •grammed)** computer term
**pro•gram•ma•ble**
**pro•gram•mat•ic**
**pro•gramme** (*US* **•gram; •gram•ming, •grammed;** *US* **•gram•ing, •gramed)**
**pro•gram•mer**
**pro•gress**
**pro•gres•sion**
**pro•gres•sion•al**
**Pro•gres•sive** political party
**pro•gres•sive**
**pro•gres•sive•ness**
**pro•gres•siv•ism**
**pro•gres•siv•ist**
**pro•hib•it**
**pro•hib•it•er** (*or* **•hibi•tor)**
**pro•hi•bi•tion**
**pro•hi•bi•tion•ary**
**pro•hi•bi•tion•ism**
**pro•hi•bi•tion•ist**
**pro•hibi•tive** (*or* **•tory)**
**pro•hibi•tive•ness**
**proj•ect**
**pro•jec•tile**
**pro•jec•tion**
**pro•jec•tion•al**
**pro•jec•tion•ist**
**pro•jec•tive**
**pro•jec•tor**
**pro•jet** draft treaty
**Pro•kop•yevsk** Russian city
**pro•lac•tin** hormone
**pro•la•mine** plant protein
**pro•lapse**
**pro•late** spheroidal
**pro•late•ness**
**prole**
**pro•leg** zoology term
**pro•legom•enal**
**pro•legom•enon** (*plural* **•ena)** critical introduction
**pro•lep•sis** (*plural* **•ses)** rhetorical device
**pro•lep•tic**
**pro•lep•ti•cal•ly**
**pro•letar•ian** (*or* **•letary;** *plural* **•ians** *or* **•letaries)**
**pro•letar•ian•ism**
**pro•letar•ian•ness**
**pro•letari•at**
**pro•lif•er•ate**
**pro•lif•era•tion**
**pro•lif•era•tive**
**pro•lif•er•ous**
**pro•lif•ic**
**pro•lifi•cal•ly**
**pro•lif•ic•ness** (*or* **•lifi•ca•cy)**
**pro•line** amino acid
**pro•lix** long-winded
**pro•lix•ity** (*or* **•ness)**
**pro•locu•tor** Anglican official
**pro•logue** (*US also* **•log; •logu•ing, •logued;** *US also* **•log•ing, •loged)**
**pro•long**
**pro•lon•ga•tion**
**pro•long•er**
**pro•long•ment**
**pro•lu•sion** preliminary essay
**pro•lu•so•ry**
**prom**
**prom•enade**
**prom•enad•er**
**Pro•methean**
**Prometheus** mythological character
**pro•methium** radioactive element
**promi•nence**
**promi•nent**
**promi•nent•ness**
**promis•cu•ity** (*plural* **•ities)**
**pro•mis•cu•ous**
**pro•mis•cu•ous•ness**
**prom•ise**
**promi•see**
**prom•is•er** (*or in legal contexts* **promi•sor)**
**prom•is•ing**
**prom•is•sory**
**prom•on•tory** (*plural* **•tories)**
**pro•mot•able**
**pro•mote**
**pro•mot•er**
**pro•mo•tion**
**pro•mo•tion•al**
**pro•mo•tive**
**pro•mo•tive•ness**
**prompt**
**prompt•book**
**prompt•er**
**promp•ti•tude**
**prompt•ness**
**prom•ul•gate**
**prom•ul•ga•tion**
**prom•ul•ga•tor**
**pro•my•celium** (*plural* **•celia)** botany term
**pro•nate**
**pro•na•tion**
**pro•na•tor** muscle
**prone**
**prone•ness**
**pro•neph•ric**
**pro•neph•ros** (*plural* **•roi** *or* **•ra)** zoology term
**prong**
**prong•horn** deer
**pro•nomi•nal** of a pronoun
**pro•nomi•nali•za•tion** (*or* **•sa•tion)**
**pro•nomi•nal•ize** (*or* **•ise)**
**pro•noun**
**pro•nounce**
**pro•nounce•able**
**pro•nounced**
**pro•nounc•ed•ly**
**pro•nounce•ment**
**pro•nounc•er**
**pron•to**
**pro•nu•clear**
**pro•nu•cleus** (*plural* **•clei)**
**pro•nun•cia•men•to** (*plural* **•tos)** manifesto

**pro•nun•cia•tion**
**pro-oestrus** (*US* **pro•es•trus**)
**proof**
**proof•read** (**•read•ing, •read**)
**proof•reader**
**prop** (**prop•ping, propped**)
**pro•pae•deu•tic** preparatory instruction
**pro•pae•deu•ti•cal**
**propa•gabil•ity** (*or* **•gable•ness**)
**propa•gable**
**propa•gan•da**
**propa•gan•dism**
**propa•gan•dist**
**propa•gan•dize** (*or* **•dise**)
**propa•gate**
**propa•ga•tion**
**propa•ga•tion•al**
**propa•ga•tive**
**propa•ga•tor**
**propa•gule** (*or* **pro•pagu•lum**; *plural* **•gules** *or* **•la**) botany term
**pro•pane**
**pro•pa•roxy•tone** grammar term
**pro pa•tria** *Latin* for one's country
**pro•pel** (**•pel•ling, •pelled**)
**pro•pel•lant** (*or* **•lent**; *noun*)
**pro•pel•lent** (*adj*)
**pro•pel•ler**
**pro•pene** chemical compound
**pro•pen•sity** (*plural* **•sities**)
**prop•er**
**prop•er•ly**
**prop•er•ness**
**prop•er•tied**
**prop•er•ty** (*plural* **•ties**)
**pro•phage** virus
**pro•phase** biology term
**proph•ecy** (*plural* **•ecies**)
**proph•esi•able**
**proph•esi•er**
**proph•esy** (**•esies, •esy•ing, •esied**)
**proph•et** (*fem* **•et•ess**)
**pro•phet•ic**
**pro•pheti•cal•ly**
**prophy•lac•tic**
**prophy•lax•is**
**pro•pin•quity**
**pro•pio•nate**
**pro•pi•on•ic acid**
**pro•pi•ti•able**
**pro•pi•ti•ate**
**pro•pi•tia•tion**
**pro•pi•tia•tious** appeasing; *compare* **propitious**
**pro•pi•tia•tive**
**pro•pi•tia•tor**
**pro•pi•tious** favourable; *compare* **propipiatious**
**pro•pi•tious•ness**
**prop•jet**
**propo•lis** substance collected by bees
**pro•po•nent**
**pro•por•tion**
**pro•por•tion•abil•ity**
**pro•por•tion•able**
**pro•por•tion•al**
**pro•por•tion•al•ity**
**pro•por•tion•al•ly**
**pro•por•tion•ate**
**pro•por•tion•ate•ness**
**pro•por•tion•ment**
**pro•po•sable**
**pro•po•sal**
**pro•pose**
**pro•pos•er**
**propo•si•tion**
**propo•si•tion•al**
**pro•posi•tus** (*plural* **•ti**) legal term
**pro•pound**
**pro•pound•er**
**pro•prae•tor** provincial praetor
**pro•prano•lol**
**pro•pri•etari•ly**
**pro•pri•etary**
**pro•pri•etor** (*fem* **•etress**)
**pro•pri•etor•ial**
**pro•pri•ety** (*plural* **•eties**)
**pro•prio•cep•tive**
**pro•prio•cep•tor** nerve ending
**prop•to•sis** (*plural* **•ses**) medical term
**pro•pul•sion**
**pro•pul•sive** (*or* **•sory**)
**pro•pyl** chemistry term
**propy•laeum** (*or* **•lon**; *plural* **•laea** *or* **•lons, •la**) temple portico
**pro•pyl•ene** propene
**propy•lite** geology term
**pro rata**
**pro•rate**
**pro•ra•tion**
**pro•ro•ga•tion**
**pro•rogue**
**pro•sa•ic**
**pro•sai•cal•ly**
**pro•sa•ic•ness**
**pro•sa•ism** (*or* **•sai•cism**) prosaic style
**pro•scenium** (*plural* **•scenia** *or* **•sceniums**)
**pro•sciut•to** Italian ham
**pro•scribe** prohibit; *compare* **prescribe**
**pro•scrip•tion**
**pro•scrip•tive**
**pro•scrip•tive•ness**
**prose**
**pro•sec•tor** dissector
**pros•ecut•able**
**pros•ecute**
**pros•ecu•tion**
**pros•ecu•tor**
**pros•elyte**
**pros•elyt•ic**
**pros•elyt•ism**
**pros•elyti•za•tion** (*or* **•sa•tion**)
**pros•elyt•ize** (*or* **•ise**)
**pros•elyt•iz•er** (*or* **•is•er**)
**pros•en•cepha•lon** (*plural* **•la**) anatomy term
**pros•en•chy•ma** plant tissue
**pros•en•chy•ma•tous**
**Proserpina** Roman goddess
**prosi•ly**
**pro•sim•ian** zoology term
**prosi•ness**
**pro•sod•ic**
**proso•dist**
**proso•dy**
**proso•po•poeia** (*or* **•peia**) rhetorical device
**proso•po•poeial** (*or* **•peial**)
**pros•pect**
**pro•spec•tive**
**pro•spec•tor**
**pro•spec•tus** (*plural* **•tuses**)
**pros•per**
**pros•per•ity** (*plural* **•ities**)
**pros•per•ous**
**pros•per•ous•ness**

**pros•ta•glan•din** hormone-like compound
**pros•tate** gland; *compare* **prostrate**
**pros•ta•tec•to•my** (*plural* **•mies**)
**pros•tat•ic**
**pros•ta•ti•tis**
**pros•the•sis** (*plural* **•ses**) artificial body part; *compare* **prothesis**
**pros•thet•ic**
**pros•theti•cal•ly**
**pros•thet•ics**
**pros•tho•don•tics** branch of dentistry
**pros•tho•don•tist**
**pros•ti•tute**
**pros•ti•tu•tion**
**pros•ti•tu•tor**
**pro•sto•mium** (*plural* **•mia**) zoology term
**pros•trate** face down; *compare* **prostate**
**pros•tra•tion**
**pro•style** architectural term
**prosy** (**prosi•er, prosi•est**)
**pro•tac•tin•ium** radioactive element
**pro•tago•nism**
**pro•tago•nist**
**pro•ta•mine** protein
**pro•tan•drous** botany term
**pro•tan•dry**
**pro•ta•no•pia** red blindness
**pro•ta•nop•ic**
**prota•sis** (*plural* **•ses**) conditional clause
**pro•tea** shrub
**pro•tean** variable
**pro•tease** enzyme
**pro•tect**
**pro•tec•tion**
**pro•tec•tion•ism**
**pro•tec•tion•ist**
**pro•tec•tive**
**pro•tec•tive•ness**
**pro•tec•tor**
**pro•tec•to•ral**
**pro•tec•tor•ate**
**pro•tec•tory** (*plural* **•tories**) institution for children
**pro•tec•tress**
**pro•té•gé** (*fem* **•gée**)
**pro•tein**
**pro•teina•ceous** (*or* **•tein•ic, •tei•nous**)
**pro•tein•ase** enzyme
**pro tem** (*or* **pro tem•po•re**) temporarily
**pro•teoly•sis**
**pro•teo•lyt•ic**
**pro•teose** biochemical compound
**Pro•tero•zo•ic** geology term
**pro•test**
**Prot•es•tant** religion
**pro•test•ant** protester
**Prot•es•tant•ism**
**pro•tes•ta•tion**
**pro•test•er**
**pro•test•ing•ly**
**Proteus** Greek god
**pro•tha•la•mi•on** (*or* **•mium**; *plural* **•mia**) marriage song
**pro•thal•lic** (*or* **•lial**)
**pro•thal•lus** (*or* **•lium**; *plural* **•li** *or* **•lia**) botany term
**proth•esis** linguistics term; *compare* **prosthesis**
**pro•thet•ic**
**pro•theti•cal•ly**
**pro•thono•tar•ial** (*or* **pro•tono•**)
**pro•tho•no•tary** (*or* **proto•no•tary**; *plural* **•taries**)
**pro•tho•rax** (*plural* **•raxes** *or* **•ra•ces**)
**pro•throm•bin**
**pro•tist** microscopic organism
**pro•tium** isotope of hydrogen
**proto•chor•date** zoology term
**proto•col**
**pro•togy•nous**
**pro•togy•ny** biology term
**proto•his•tor•ic**
**proto•his•to•ry**
**proto•hu•man**
**proto•lan•guage**
**proto•lith•ic** of the Stone Age
**proto•mor•phic** primitive
**pro•ton**
**proto•nema** (*plural* **•ne•ma•ta**) botany term
**proto•ne•mal** (*or* **•nema•tal**)
**proto•path•ic**
**pro•topa•thy** physiology term
**proto•plasm**
**proto•plas•mic** (*or* **•mal, •mat•ic**)
**proto•plast**
**proto•plas•tic**
**Proto•semit•ic** language
**proto•star**
**proto•stele** botany term
**proto•stelic**
**proto•therian** zoology term
**proto•troph•ic** biology term
**proto•ty•pal** (*or* **•typ•ic, •typi•cal**)
**proto•type**
**pro•tox•ide**
**proto•xy•lem**
**proto•zoan** (*or* **•zo•on**; *plural* **•zoans** *or* **•zoa**)
**proto•zoo•logi•cal**
**proto•zo•olo•gist**
**proto•zo•ol•ogy**
**pro•tract**
**pro•tract•ed•ly**
**pro•tract•ed•ness**
**pro•trac•tile** (*or* **•tract•ible**)
**pro•trac•tion**
**pro•trac•tive**
**pro•trac•tor**
**pro•trud•able**
**pro•trude**
**pro•tru•dent**
**pro•tru•sile**
**pro•tru•sion**
**pro•tru•sive**
**pro•tru•sive•ness**
**pro•tu•ber•ance** (*or* **•an•cy**; *plural* **•ances** *or* **•an•cies**)
**pro•tu•ber•ant**
**pro•tyle** (*or* **•tyl**) chemistry term
**proud**
**proud•ness**
**proust•ite** mineral
**prov•abil•ity**
**prov•able**
**prove** (**prov•ing, proved, proved** *or* **prov•en**)
**prov•enance** (*or* **•veni•ence**)
**Pro•ven•çal** of Provence
**Pro•ven•çale** cookery term
**Pro•vence**

**prov•en•der**
**prov•en•ly**
**pro•ven•tricu•lar**
**pro•ven•tricu•lus** (*plural* **•li**) zoology term
**prov•erb**
**pro•ver•bial**
**pro•ver•bial•ly**
**pro•vide**
**Provi•dence** US port
**provi•dence**
**provi•dent**
**provi•den•tial**
**provi•den•tial•ly**
**pro•vid•er**
**prov•ince**
**pro•vin•cial**
**pro•vin•cial•ism**
**pro•vin•ci•al•ity**
**pro•virus**
**pro•vi•sion**
**pro•vi•sion•al** (*or* **•ary**)
**pro•vi•sion•al•ly**
**pro•vi•sion•er**
**pro•vi•sions**
**pro•vi•so** (*plural* **•sos** *or* **•soes**)
**pro•vi•so•ri•ly**
**pro•vi•sory**
**pro•vita•min**
**Pro•vo** (*plural* **•vos**) Provisional IRA member
**provo•ca•tion**
**pro•voca•tive**
**pro•voca•tive•ness**
**pro•voke**
**pro•vok•ing•ly**
**pro•vo•lo•ne** cheese
**prov•ost**
**prow**
**prow•ess**
**prowl**
**prowl•er**
**Proxi•ma** star
**proxi•mal** anatomy term
**proxi•mal•ly**
**proxi•mate** nearest
**proxi•mate•ness**
**proxi•ma•tion**
**prox•im•ity**
**proxi•mo** next month
**proxy** (*plural* **proxies**)
**prude**
**pru•dence**
**pru•dent**
**pru•den•tial**
**pru•dent•ness**
**prud•ery** (*plural* **•eries**)
**prud•ish**
**prud•ish•ness**
**prui•nose** botany term
**prun•able**
**prune**
**pru•nel•la** (*or* **•nelle, •nel•lo**) fabric
**pru•nelle** liqueur
**prun•er**
**pru•ri•ence**
**pru•ri•ent** lewd; *compare* **purulent**
**pru•ri•go** skin disease
**pru•rit•ic**
**pru•ri•tus** itching
**Prus•sia**
**Prus•sian**
**prus•si•ate** cyanide
**prus•sic acid**
**pry** (*verb* **pries, pry•ing, pried**; *noun, plural* **pries**)
**pry•er** *variant spelling of* **prier**
**pryta•neum** (*plural* **•nea**) ancient Greek town hall
**psalm**
**psalm•ic**
**psalm•ist**
**psalm•od•ic**
**psalmo•dist**
**psalmo•dy** (*plural* **•dies**)
**Psalms** Old Testament book
**Psal•ter** (*or* **psal•**) psalm book
**psal•ter•ium** (*plural* **•teria**) cow's stomach
**psal•tery** (*plural* **•teries**) musical instrument
**pse•phite** rock
**pse•phit•ic**
**psepho•logi•cal**
**psepho•logi•cal•ly**
**pse•pholo•gist**
**pse•phol•ogy** study of elections
**pseud** *Slang* pretentious person
**pseud•axis** botany term
**Pseud•epig•ra•pha** Jewish writings
**pseu•do** *Slang* pretended
**pseudo•carp** botany term
**pseudo•morph** geology term
**pseudo•mor•phic** (*or* **•phous**)
**pseudo•mor•phism**
**pseudo•mu•tu•al•ity** (*plural* **•ities**) psychology term
**pseudo•nym**
**pseudo•nym•ity**
**pseu•dony•mous**
**pseudo•po•dium** (*plural* **•dia**) biology term
**pshaw** exclamation
**psi** Greek letter
**psilo•cy•bin** hallucinogen
**psi•lom•elane** mineral
**psit•ta•cine** of parrots
**psit•ta•co•sis**
**Pskov** Russian city
**pso•as** muscle
**pso•ra•lea** plant
**pso•ria•sis** skin disease
**pso•ri•at•ic**
**psych** *Slang* deduce; prepare
**Psyche** mythological character
**psy•che** human mind
**psychedelia**
**psychedel•ic** (*or* **psycho•**)
**psychedeli•cal•ly** (*or* **psycho•deli•**)
**psy•chi•at•ric**
**psy•chi•at•ri•cal•ly**
**psy•chia•trist**
**psy•chia•try**
**psy•chic** telepathic
**psy•chi•cal**
**psy•cho** (*plural* **•chos**) *Slang* psychopath
**psycho•acous•tics**
**psycho•ac•tive**
**psycho•ana•lyse** (*US* **•lyze**)
**psycho•analy•sis**
**psycho•ana•lyst**
**psycho•ana•lyt•ic** (*or* **•lyti•cal**)
**psycho•ana•lyti•cal•ly**
**psycho•bio•logi•cal**
**psycho•bi•olo•gist**
**psycho•bi•ol•ogy**
**psycho•chemi•cal**
**psycho•dra•ma**
**psycho•dra•mat•ic**
**psycho•dy•nam•ic**
**psycho•dy•nami•cal•ly**

**psycho•dy•nam•ics**
**psycho•gen•esis**
**psycho•genet•ic**
**psycho•geneti•cal•ly**
**psycho•gen•ic**
**psycho•geni•cal•ly**
**psy•chog•no•sis**
**psy•chog•nos•tic**
**psycho•graph**
**psycho•graph•ic**
**psy•chog•ra•phy**
**psycho•his•to•ry** (*plural* **•ries**)
**psycho•ki•nesis**
**psycho•ki•net•ic**
**psycho•lin•guist**
**psycho•lin•guis•tic**
**psycho•lin•guis•tics**
**psycho•logi•cal**
**psycho•logi•cal•ly**
**psy•cholo•gism** belief in psychology
**psy•cholo•gist**
**psy•cholo•gist•ic**
**psy•cholo•gize** (*or* **•gise**)
**psy•chol•ogy** (*plural* **•ogies**)
**psycho•met•ric** (*or* **•ri•cal**)
**psycho•met•ri•cal•ly**
**psycho•metri•cian** (*or* **psy•chom•etrist**)
**psycho•met•rics** (*or* **psy•chom•etry**) testing mental processes
**psycho•mo•tor**
**psycho•neu•ro•sis** (*plural* **•ses**)
**psycho•neu•rot•ic**
**psycho•path**
**psycho•path•ic**
**psycho•path•ical•ly**
**psycho•patho•logi•cal**
**psycho•pa•tholo•gist**
**psycho•pa•thol•ogy**
**psy•chopa•thy**
**psycho•phar•ma•co•logi•cal**
**psycho•phar•ma•colo•gist**
**psycho•phar•ma•col•ogy**
**psycho•physi•cal**
**psycho•phys•ics**
**psycho•physio•logi•cal**
**psycho•physi•olo•gist**
**psycho•physi•ol•ogy**
**psycho•sex•ual**
**psycho•sexu•al•ity**
**psy•cho•sis** (*plural* **•ses**)
**psycho•so•cial**
**psycho•so•mat•ic**
**psycho•sur•gery**
**psycho•sur•gi•cal**
**psycho•tech•ni•cal**
**psycho•tech•ni•cian**
**psycho•tech•nics**
**psycho•thera•peu•tic**
**psycho•thera•peu•ti•cal•ly**
**psycho•thera•pist**
**psycho•thera•py**
**psycho•trop•ic**
**psy•chot•ic**
**psy•choti•cal•ly**
**psy•choto•mi•met•ic**
**psy•chrom•eter** humidity meter
**psy•chro•phil•ic** biology term
**psyl•lid** (*or* **•la**) insect
**Ptah** Egyptian god
**ptar•mi•gan** (*plural* **•gans** *or* **•gan**) bird
**pteri•do•logi•cal**
**pteri•dolo•gist**
**pteri•dol•ogy** study of ferns
**pteri•do•phyte**
**pteri•do•phyt•ic** (*or* **•dophy•tous**)
**pteri•do•sperm** extinct plant
**ptero•dac•tyl**
**ptero•pod** mollusc
**ptero•saur**
**ptery•goid** anatomy term
**ptery•la** (*plural* **•lae**) ornithology term
**pti•san** grape juice
**pto•choc•ra•cy** (*plural* **•cies**) government by the poor
**Ptol•emae•us** moon crater
**Ptol•ema•ic**
**Ptol•ema•ist**
**pto•maine** (*or* **•main**) chemical compound
**pto•sis** (*plural* **•ses**) drooping of eyelid
**ptya•lin** enzyme
**ptya•lism** excessive salivation
**pub** (**pub•bing, pubbed**)
**pu•ber•ty**
**pu•beru•lent** downy
**pu•bes** (*plural* **•bes**) pubic region; *plural of* **pubis**
**pu•bes•cence**
**pu•bes•cent**
**pu•bic**
**pu•bis** (*plural* **•bes**) hip bone
**pub•lic**
**pub•li•can**
**pub•li•ca•tion**
**pub•li•cist**
**pub•lic•ity**
**pub•li•cize** (*or* **•cise**)
**pub•lic•ly**
**public-spirit•ed**
**pub•lish**
**pub•lish•able**
**pub•lish•er**
**puc•coon** plant
**puce**
**puck**
**puck•er**
**puck•ish**
**puck•ish•ness**
**pud•ding**
**pud•dle**
**pud•dler**
**pud•dling**
**pud•dly**
**pu•den•cy** modesty
**pu•den•dal**
**pu•den•dum** (*plural* **•da**)
**pudgi•ly**
**pudgi•ness**
**pudgy** (**pudgi•er, pudgi•est**)
**Pue•bla** Mexican city
**Pueb•lo** (*plural* **•lo** *or* **•los**) American Indian
**pueb•lo** (*plural* **•los**) village
**pu•er•ile**
**pu•er•il•ism**
**pu•er•il•ity** (*plural* **•ities**)
**pu•er•per•al**
**pu•er•per•ium** period after childbirth
**Puer•to Ri•can**
**Puer•to Rico**
**puff**
**puff•ball**
**puff•bird**
**puff•er**
**puff•ery** (*plural* **•eries**) exaggerated praise
**puffi•ly**
**puf•fin**
**puffi•ness**

**puffy** **(puffi•er, puffi•est)**
**pug** **(pug•ging, pugged)** dog; knead clay
**pug•gish**
**pu•gi•lism**
**pu•gi•list**
**pu•gi•lis•tic**
**pu•gi•lis•ti•cal•ly**
**pug•na•cious**
**pug•nac•ity** (*or* **•na•cious•ness)**
**pug-nosed**
**puis•ne** legal term
**pu•is•sance** *Archaic* power; showjumping event
**pu•is•sant**
**puke**
**puk•ka**
**pul** (*plural* **puls** *or* **puli)** Afghan coin
**pul•chri•tude**
**pul•chri•tudi•nous**
**pule** to whimper
**pul•er**
**pull**
**pul•let**
**pul•ley**
**pull-in** (*noun*)
**Pull•man** (*plural* **•mans)** rail coach
**pull-out** (*noun*)
**pull•over**
**pul•lu•late** breed rapidly
**pul•lu•la•tion**
**pul•mo•nary**
**pul•mo•nate**
**pul•mon•ic**
**Pul•motor** (*Trademark*)
**pulp**
**pulpi•ness**
**pul•pit**
**pulp•wood**
**pulpy** **(pulpi•er, pulpi•est)**
**pul•que** alcoholic drink
**pul•sar** star
**pul•sate**
**pul•sa•tile**
**pul•sa•til•ity**
**pul•sa•tion**
**pul•sa•tive**
**pul•sa•tor**
**pul•sa•tory**
**pulse**
**pulse•jet**
**pul•sim•eter** (*or* **•som•)**
**pul•ver•able**
**pul•veri•za•tion** (*or* **•sa•tion)**
**pul•ver•ize** (*or* **•ise)**
**pul•ver•iz•er** (*or* **•is•er)**
**pul•veru•lence**
**pul•veru•lent** of dust
**pul•vil•lus** (*plural* **•li)** zoology term
**pul•vi•nate** (*or* **•nat•ed)**
**pul•vi•nus** (*plural* **•ni)** botany term
**puma**
**pum•ice**
**pu•mi•ceous**
**pum•mel** (*or* **pom•**; **•mel•ling, •melled;** *US* **•mel•ing, •meled)** to pound; *compare* **pommel**
**pump**
**pum•per•nick•el**
**pump•kin**
**pumpkin•seed**
**pun** **(pun•ning, punned)**
**punce** *Dialect* kick
**punch**
**punch•ball**
**punch•board**
**punch•bowl**
**punch-drunk**
**pun•cheon**
**punch•er**
**Pun•chi•nel•lo** (*plural* **•los** *or* **•loes)** clown
**punch-up** (*noun*)
**punchy** **(punchi•er, punchi•est)**
**punc•tate** (*or* **•tat•ed)**
**punc•ta•tion**
**punc•tilio** (*plural* **•tilios)** etiquette
**punc•tili•ous**
**punc•tili•ous•ness**
**punc•tu•al**
**punc•tu•al•ity**
**punc•tu•al•ly**
**punc•tu•ate**
**punc•tua•tion**
**punc•tua•tor**
**punc•tum** (*plural* **•ta)** anatomy term
**punc•tur•able**
**punc•ture**
**punc•tur•er**
**pun•dit** (*or* **pan•)** expert; learned Hindu; *compare* **pandit**
**pung** *US* sleigh
**pun•gen•cy**
**pun•gent**
**Pu•nic** of Carthage
**puni•ness**
**pun•ish**
**pun•ish•abil•ity**
**pun•ish•able**
**pun•ish•er**
**pun•ish•ing•ly**
**pun•ish•ment**
**pu•ni•tive** (*or* **•tory)**
**pu•ni•tive•ness**
**Pun•jab**
**Pun•ja•bi** (*or* **Pan•)**
**punk**
**pun•ka** (*or* **•kah)** palm-leaf fan
**punned**
**pun•ner**
**pun•net**
**pun•ning**
**pun•ster**
**punt**
**punt•er**
**pun•ty** (*plural* **•ties)** glass-blowing rod
**puny** **(pu•ni•er, pu•ni•est)**
**pup** **(pup•ping, pupped)**
**pupa** (*plural* **pupae** *or* **pupas)**
**pu•pal**
**pu•par•ial**
**pu•par•ium** (*plural* **•paria)**
**pu•pate**
**pu•pa•tion**
**pu•pil**
**pu•pil•lage** (*US* **•pil•age)**
**pu•pil•lary** (*or* **•pi•lary)**
**pu•pipa•rous** entomology term
**pup•pet**
**pup•pet•eer**
**pup•pet•ry**
**pup•ping**
**Pup•pis** constellation
**pup•py** (*plural* **•pies)**
**pup•py•hood**
**pup•py•ish**
**Pu•ra•na** Sanskrit writings
**Pur•beck** Dorset peninsula; marble

**pur•blind**
**pur•chasa•bil•ity**
**pur•chas•able**
**pur•chase**
**pur•chas•er**
**pur•dah** (*or* **pur•da, par•dah**)
**pure**
**pure•bred**
**pu•ree** (*or* **puri**) Indian bread
**pu•rée** (**•rée•ing, •réed**) pulped food
**pure•ly**
**pure•ness**
**pur•fle** ornamental band
**pur•ga•tion**
**pur•ga•tive**
**pur•ga•to•rial**
**pur•ga•tory**
**purge**
**purg•er**
**Puri** Indian port
**pu•ri•fi•ca•tion**
**pu•ri•fi•ca•tor** Communion cloth
**pu•rifi•ca•tory**
**pu•ri•fi•er**
**pu•ri•fy** (**•fies, •fy•ing, •fied**)
**Pu•rim** Jewish holiday
**pu•rine** (*or* **•rin**) biochemical compound
**pur•ism**
**pur•ist**
**pu•rist•ic**
**pu•ris•ti•cal•ly**
**Pu•ri•tan** extreme Protestant
**pu•ri•tan** strictly moral person
**pu•ri•tani•cal** (*or* **•tan•ic**)
**pu•ri•tani•cal•ness**
**Pu•ri•tan•ism**
**pu•ri•tan•ism**
**pu•rity**
**purl** knitting stitch; *compare* **pearl**
**pur•ler** headlong fall
**pur•lieu** outlying area
**pur•lin** (*or* **•line**) roof beam
**pur•loin**
**pur•loin•er**
**pur•ple**
**pur•ple•ness**
**pur•plish**
**pur•port**
**pur•pose**
**pur•pose•ful**
**pur•pose•ful•ly** determinedly; *compare* **purposely**
**pur•pose•ful•ness**
**pur•pose•less**
**pur•pose•less•ness**
**pur•pose•ly** intentionally; *compare* **purposefully**
**pur•pos•ive**
**pur•pos•ive•ness**
**pur•pu•ra** disease
**pur•pure** heraldic purple
**pur•pu•rin** biological dye
**purr**
**purse**
**purs•er**
**purs•lane** plant
**pur•su•ance**
**pur•su•ant**
**pur•sue** (**•su•ing, •sued**)
**pur•su•er**
**pur•suit**
**pur•sui•vant** heraldic officer
**pursy** short-winded
**pu•ru•lence** (*or* **•len•cy**)
**pu•ru•lent** of pus; *compare* **prurient**
**pur•vey**
**pur•vey•ance**
**pur•vey•or**
**pur•view** scope
**pus** matter from wound; *compare* **puss**
**Pu•san** South Korean port
**push**
**push•chair**
**push•er**
**pushi•ly**
**pushi•ness**
**push•ing**
**push•ing•ly**
**push•ing•ness**
**push•over**
**push-pull**
**push•rod**
**Push•tu** *variant of* **Pashto**
**push-up** *US* press-up
**pushy** (**pushi•er, pushi•est**)
**pu•sil•la•nim•ity**
**pu•sil•lani•mous**
**puss** *Slang* cat; *compare* **pus**
**pus•sy** (**•si•er, •si•est**) full of pus
**pussy** (*or* **pussy•cat**; *plural* **pussies** *or* **•cats**)
**pussy•foot**
**pus•tu•lant**
**pus•tu•lar**
**pus•tu•late**
**pus•tu•la•tion**
**pus•tule**
**put** (**put•ting, put**) to place, etc.; *compare* **putt**
**pu•ta•men** (*plural* **•tami•na**) botany term
**pu•ta•tive**
**put-down** (*noun*)
**put•log** (*or* **•lock**) scaffold beam
**put-on** (*noun*)
**pu•tre•fac•tion**
**pu•tre•fac•tive** (*or* **•fa•cient**)
**pu•tre•fi•able**
**pu•tre•fi•er**
**pu•tre•fy** (**•fies, •fy•ing, •fied**)
**pu•tres•cence**
**pu•tres•cent**
**pu•tres•cine** organic compound
**pu•trid**
**pu•trid•ity** (*or* **•trid•ness**)
**(putrify)** *incorrect spelling of* **putrefy**
**Putsch** *German* uprising
**putt** golf stroke; *compare* **put**
**put•tee** (*or* **•ty**; *plural* **•tees** *or* **•ties**) leg cloth
**putt•er** golf club
**put•ter** placer
**putt•ing** golf stroke
**put•ting** placing
**put•to** (*plural* **•ti**) boy cupid
**put•ty** (*noun, plural* **•ties**; *verb* **•ties, •ty•ing, •tied**)
**putty•root**
**put-up** (*adj*)
**Puy de Dôme** French department
**puz•zle**
**puz•zle•ment**
**puz•zler**
**puz•zling•ly**
**pya** Burmese coin
**py•aemia** (*US* **•emia**) blood poisoning

**py•aemic** (*US* **•emic**)
**pyc•nid•ium** (*plural* **•nidia**) botany term
**pyc•nom•eter** density measurer
**pyc•no•met•ric**
**Pyd•na** ancient Macedonian town
**pye-dog** (*or* **pie-**)
**py•elit•ic**
**py•eli•tis** kidney disease
**py•elo•gram**
**py•elo•graph•ic**
**py•elog•ra•phy**
**py•elo•nephri•tis**
**py•emia** *US spelling of* **pyaemia**
**py•gid•ial**
**py•gid•ium** (*plural* **•gidia**) zoology term
**Pygmalion** mythological king
**Pyg•my** (*or* **Pig•**; *plural* **•mies**) African race
**pyg•my** (*or* **pig•**; *plural* **•mies**) dwarf
**py•ja•ma** (*US* **pa•**; *adj*)
**py•ja•mas** (*US* **pa•**)
**pyk•nic** squat
**py•lon**
**py•lo•rec•to•my** (*plural* **•mies**)
**py•lo•ric**
**py•lo•rus** (*plural* **•ri**) stomach opening
**pyo•der•ma** skin disease
**pyo•gen•esis**
**pyo•gen•ic** causing pus; *compare* **pyrogenic**
**py•oid**
**Pyong•yang** capital of North Korea
**py•or•rhoea** (*US* **•rhea**) gum disease
**py•or•rhoeal** (*or* **•rhoe•ic**; *US* **•rheal** *or* **•rhe•ic**)
**pyo•sis** pus formation
**py•ra•can•tha** shrub
**pyra•lid** moth
**pyra•mid**
**py•rami•dal** (*or* **pyra•midi•cal, pyra•mid•ic**)
**Pyramus** legendary lover
**py•ran** chemical compound
**py•ra•nom•eter** solarimeter
**py•rar•gy•rite** mineral
**py•ra•zole** chemical compound
**pyre**
**py•rene** chemical compound; botany term
**Pyr•enean**
**Pyr•enees**
**Py•ré•nées At•lan•tiques** French department
**Py•ré•nées-Orientales** French department
**pyr•enoid** protein granule
**py•rethrin** insecticide
**py•rethrum** plant
**py•ret•ic** of fever
**Py•rex** (*Trademark*)
**py•rexia** fever
**py•rex•ial** (*or* **•rex•ic**)
**pyr•he•li•om•eter**
**pyr•he•lio•met•ric**
**pyri•dine** chemical compound
**pyri•dox•al** biochemical compound
**pyri•doxa•mine**
**pyri•dox•ine**
**pyri•form** pear-shaped
**py•rimi•dine** biochemical compound
**py•rite** mineral
**py•ri•tes** (*plural* **•tes**) mineral
**py•rit•ic** (*or* **•ti•tous**)
**pyro•cat•echol** (*or* **•echin**)
**pyro•chemi•cal**
**pyro•clas•tic** geology term
**pyro•con•duc•tiv•ity**
**pyro•elec•tric**
**pyro•elec•tric•ity**
**pyro•gal•late**
**pyro•gal•lic**
**pyro•gal•lol**
**pyro•gen**
**pyro•gen•ic** (*or* **py•rog•enous**) causing heat or fever; *compare* **pyogenic**
**py•rog•nos•tics**
**py•rog•ra•pher**
**pyro•graph•ic**
**py•rog•ra•phy** (*plural* **•phies**) design by burning
**pyro•lig•ne•ous** (*or* **•lig•nic**)
**pyro•lit•ic**
**pyro•lu•site** mineral
**py•roly•sis** chemical reaction
**pyro•man•cer**
**pyro•man•cy** divination by fire
**pyro•ma•nia**
**pyro•ma•ni•ac**
**pyro•ma•nia•cal**
**pyro•man•tic**
**pyro•met•al•lur•gy**
**py•rom•eter**
**pyro•met•ric** (*or* **•met•ri•cal**)
**pyro•met•ri•cal•ly**
**py•rom•etry**
**pyro•mor•phite** mineral
**py•rone** chemical compound
**py•rope** garnet
**pyro•phor•ic**
**pyro•phos•phate**
**pyro•pho•tom•eter**
**pyro•pho•tom•etry**
**pyro•phyl•lite** mineral
**pyro•sis** heartburn
**pyro•stat**
**pyro•stat•ic**
**pyro•sul•phate** (*US* **•fate**)
**pyro•tech•nic** (*or* **•ni•cal**)
**pyro•tech•nics**
**py•rox•ene** mineral
**py•rox•en•ic**
**py•rox•enite** rock
**py•roxy•lin** constituent of plastics
**Pyrrha** mythological character
**Pyr•rhic** of Pyrrhus
**pyr•rhic** prosody term
**pyr•rho•tite** (*or* **•tine**) mineral
**pyr•rhu•loxia** bird
**pyr•role** biochemical compound
**pyr•rol•ic**
**pyr•roli•dine**
**pyr•ru•vic acid**
**Py•thago•rean**
**Pythia** mythological priestess

**Pyth•ian**
**py•thon**
**py•thon•ess** female soothsayer
**py•thon•ic**
**pyu•ria** medical term
**pyx** container for Eucharist; *compare* **pix**
**pyx•id•ium** (*plural* **•idia**) botany term
**pyxie** shrub
**pyx•is** (*plural* **pyxi•des**) box

# Q

**Qair•wan** Tunisian city
**Qa•tar** Arabian state
**Qa•ta•ri**
**Qeshm** (*or* **Qishm**) Iranian island
**qin•tar** (*or* **•dar**) Albanian coin
**qua** in the capacity of
**quack**
**quack•ery** (*plural* **•eries**)
**quack•sal•ver** quack doctor
**quad** quadrangle; quadruplet; *compare* **quod**
**quad•ra•ge•nar•ian**
**Quad•ra•gesi•ma**
**Quad•ra•gesi•mal**
**quad•ran•gle**
**quad•ran•gu•lar**
**quad•rant**
**quad•ran•tal**
**quad•ra•phon•ic** (*or* **•ro•**)
**quad•ra•phon•ics** (*or* **•ro•**)
**quad•rat** ecology term
**quad•rate** cube; bone
**quad•rat•ic**
**quad•rat•ics** branch of algebra
**quad•ra•ture** maths term
**quad•ren•nial**
**quad•ren•nial•ly**
**quad•ren•nium** (*plural* **•niums** *or* **•nia**)
**quad•ric** maths term
**quad•ri•cen•ten•nial**
**quad•ri•ceps** (*plural* **•cepses**) muscle
**quad•ri•cipi•tal**
**quad•ri•fid** botany term
**quad•ri•ga** (*plural* **•gas** *or* **•gae**) chariot
**quad•ri•lat•er•al**
**quad•rille** dance
**quad•ril•lion** $10^{24}$
**quad•ril•lionth**
**quad•ri•no•mial**
**quad•ri•par•tite**
**quad•ri•plegia**
**quad•ri•plegic**
**quad•ri•sect**
**quad•ri•sec•tion**
**quad•ri•va•len•cy** (*or* **•lence**)
**quad•ri•va•lent**
**quad•riv•ial** having four roads meeting
**quad•riv•ium** medieval branch of learning
**quad•roon**
**quad•ru•ma•nous** zoology term
**quad•ru•ped**
**quad•ru•ped•al**
**quad•ru•ple**
**quad•ru•plet**
**quad•ru•plex** fourfold
**quad•ru•pli•cate**
**quad•ru•pli•ca•tion**
**quad•ru•plic•ity** (*plural* **•ities**)
**quaes•tor** (*or* **ques•**) Roman magistrate
**quaff**
**quaff•er**
**quag•ga** (*plural* **•gas** *or* **•ga**) extinct horse
**quag•gy** (**•gi•er**, **•gi•est**) marshy
**quag•mire**
**qua•hog** clam
**quail** (*plural* **quails** *or* **quail**)
**quaint**
**quaint•ness**
**quake**
**Quak•er**
**Quak•er•ism**
**quaki•ly**
**quaki•ness**
**quaky** (**quaki•er**, **quaki•est**)
**qua•le** (*plural* **•lia**) philosophy term
**quali•fi•able**
**quali•fi•ca•tion**
**quali•fi•ca•tory**
**quali•fied**
**quali•fi•er**
**quali•fy** (**•fies**, **•fy•ing**, **•fied**)
**quali•fy•ing•ly**
**quali•ta•tive**
**qual•ity** (*plural* **•ities**)
**qualm**
**qualm•ish**
**quam•ash** plant
**quan•da•ry** (*plural* **•ries**)
**quan•dong** (*or* **•dang**, **•tong**) fruit tree
**quango** (*plural* **quangos**)
**quant** punting pole
**quan•tal**
**quan•tic** maths term
**quan•ti•fi•able**
**quan•ti•fi•ca•tion**
**quan•ti•fi•er**
**quan•ti•fy** (**•fies**, **•fy•ing**, **•fied**)
**quan•ti•ta•tive** (*or* **quan•ti•tive**)
**quan•tity** (*plural* **•tities**)
**quan•ti•za•tion** (*or* **•sa•tion**)
**quan•tize** (*or* **•tise**)
**quan•tum** (*plural* **•ta**)
**qua•qua•ver•sal** geology term
**quar•an•tine**
**quare** *Irish* remarkable
**quark**
**quar•rel** (**•rel•ling**, **•relled**; *US* **•rel•ing**, **•reled**)
**quar•rel•ler** (*US* **•rel•er**)
**quar•rel•some**
**quar•rian** bird
**quar•ri•er** (*or* **quarry•man**; *plural* **•ers** *or* **•men**)
**quar•ry** (*noun*, *plural* **•ries**; *verb* **•ries**, **•ry•ing**, **•ried**)
**quart**
**quar•tan** every third day
**quar•ter**

**quar•ter•age** quarterly payment
**quarter•back**
**quarter-bound**
**quarter•deck**
**quar•tered**
**quarter•final**
**quarter-hour**
**quar•ter•ing**
**quarter•light** window
**quar•ter•ly** (*plural* **•lies**)
**quarter•master**
**quar•tern** measure of weight
**quar•ters**
**quarter•saw** (**•saw•ing, •sawed, •sawed** *or* **•sawn**)
**quarter•staff** (*plural* **•staves**)
**quar•tet** (*or* **•tette**)
**quar•tic** maths term
**quar•tile**
**quar•to** (*plural* **•tos**)
**quartz**
**quartz•if•er•ous**
**quartz•ite**
**qua•sar**
**quash**
**quas•sia** tree
**qua•ter•cen•te•nary** (*plural* **•naries**)
**Qua•ter•nary** geological period
**qua•ter•nary** (*plural* **•naries**) of four; fourth
**qua•ter•ni•on** maths term
**qua•ter•ni•ty** (*plural* **•ties**) group of four
**quat•rain**
**qua•tre** playing card
**quatre•foil**
**quat•tro•cen•to** 15th century
**qua•ver**
**qua•ver•er**
**qua•ver•ing•ly**
**qua•very** (*or* **•ver•ous**)
**quay**
**quay•age**
**quay•side**
**quea•si•ly**
**quea•si•ness**
**quea•sy** (**•si•er, •si•est**)
**Que•bec**
**Qué•be•cois** (*plural* **•cois**)
**que•bra•cho** (*plural* **•chos**) tree
**Quech•ua** (*or* **Kech•ua**; *plural* **•uas** *or* **•ua**) American Indian
**Quech•uan** (*or* **Kech•**)
**queen**
**queen•cake**
**queen•dom**
**queen•li•ness**
**queen•ly** (**•li•er, •li•est**)
**Queens** New York borough
**Queens•ber•ry rules**
**Queens•land**
**queer**
**queer•ness**
**quell**
**quell•er**
**quel•que•chose** insignificant thing
**quench**
**quench•able**
**quench•er**
**que•nelle** dumpling
**quer•cetin** (*or* **•ci•tin**) pigment
**quer•cine** of the oak
**Que•réta•ro** Mexican state
**que•rist** questioner
**quern** stone hand mill
**queru•lous**
**queru•lous•ness**
**que•ry** (*noun, plural* **•ries**; *verb* **•ries, •ry•ing, •ried**)
**quest**
**quest•er**
**quest•ing•ly**
**ques•tion**
**ques•tion•able**
**ques•tion•able•ness** (*or* **•abil•ity**)
**ques•tion•ably**
**ques•tion•ary**
**ques•tion•er**
**ques•tion•ing**
**ques•tion•less**
**ques•tion•naire**
**Quet•ta** Pakistani city
**quet•zal** bird
**Quet•zal•coa•tl** Aztec god
**queue** (**queu•ing, queued**) line; pigtail; *compare* **cue**
**Que•zon City** Philippine capital
**quib•ble**
**quib•bler**
**quib•bling•ly**
**Qui•beron** French peninsula
**quiche**
**quick**
**quick•en**
**quick-freeze** (**-freezing, -froze, -frozen**)
**quickie**
**quick•lime**
**quick•ly**
**quick•ness**
**quick•sand**
**quick•set** hedge
**quick•silver**
**quick•step** (**•step•ping, •stepped**)
**quick-tempered**
**quick-witted**
**quick-witted•ness**
**quid**
**quid•dity** (*plural* **•dities**)
**quid•nunc** gossipmonger
**quid pro quo** (*plural* **quid pro quos**)
**qui•es•cence** (*or* **•cen•cy**)
**qui•es•cent**
**qui•et**
**qui•et•en**
**qui•et•ism** form of mysticism
**qui•et•ness**
**qui•etude**
**qui•etus** (*plural* **•etuses**)
**quiff**
**quill**
**quil•lai** tree
**quill•wort**
**Quil•mes** Argentine city
**quilt**
**quilt•er**
**quilt•ing**
**quin**
**qui•na•ry** (*noun, plural* **•ries**) consisting of five
**qui•nate** composed of five parts
**quince**
**quin•cen•te•nary** (*plural* **•naries**)
**quin•cun•cial**
**quin•cunx** arrangement of five
**quin•deca•gon** 15-sided figure
**quin•deca•plet** group of 15
**quin•de•cen•nial**

**Qui Nhong** Vietnamese port
**quini•dine**
**qui•nine**
**quin•ol**
**quino•line**
**qui•none**
**quino•noid** (*or* **quin•oid**)
**quin•qua•genar•ian**
**Quin•qua•gesi•ma**
**quin•que•fo•li•ate**
**quin•quen•nial**
**quin•quen•nial•ly**
**quin•quen•nium** (*plural* **•nia**)
**quin•que•par•tite**
**quin•que•reme** ship
**quin•que•va•len•cy** (*or* **•lence**)
**quin•que•va•lent**
**quin•sy**
**quint** organ stop; piquet term
**quin•tain** tilting target
**quin•tal** unit of weight
**quin•tan** recurring every fourth day
**quin•tes•sence**
**quin•tes•sen•tial**
**quin•tes•sen•tial•ly**
**quin•tet** (*or* **•tette**)
**quin•tic** maths term
**quin•tile** astrology term
**quin•til•lion** (*plural* **•lions** *or* **•lion**) $10^{30}$
**quin•til•lionth**
**quin•tu•ple**
**quin•tu•plet**
**quin•tu•pli•cate**
**quin•tu•pli•ca•tion**
**quip** (**•quip•ping, •quipped**)
**quip•ster**
**quire** set of paper; *compare* choir
**Quiri•nal** Roman hill
**Quirinus** Roman god
**quirk**
**quirki•ly**
**quirki•ness**
**quirky** (**quirki•er, quirki•est**)
**quirt** whip
**quis•ling**
**quist** *Dialect* wood pigeon
**quit** (**quit•ting, quit•ted** *or* **quit**)
**quitch** grass
**quit•claim** legal term
**quite**
**Qui•to** Ecuadorian capital
**quits**
**quit•tance**
**quit•ter** one that quits
**quit•tor** horse's foot infection
**quiv•er**
**quiv•er•er**
**quiv•er•ful**
**quiv•er•ing•ly**
**quiv•ery**
**qui vive** *French* attentive
**quix•ot•ic** (*or* **•oti•cal**)
**quix•oti•cal•ly**
**quixo•tism**
**quiz** (*noun, plural* **quiz•zes**; *verb* **quiz•zes, quiz•zing, quizzed**)
**quiz•master**
**quiz•zer**
**quiz•zi•cal**
**quiz•zi•cal•ity**
**quiz•zi•cal•ly**
**quod** *Slang* jail; *compare* quad
**quod erat de•mon•stran•dum** *Latin* which was to be proved
**quod•li•bet** piece of music
**quod•li•beti•cal**
**quod•li•beti•cal•ly**
**quoin** (*or* **coign, coigne**) cornerstone
**quoit**
**quoits**
**quok•ka** wallaby
**quon•dam** former
**quor•um**
**quo•ta**
**quot•abil•ity**
**quot•able**
**quo•ta•tion**
**quote**
**quoth** *Archaic* said
**quo•tid•ian** daily
**quo•tient**
**quo war•ran•to** legal term

# R

**Ra** (*or* **Re**) Egyptian god
**Ra•bat** Moroccan capital
**ra•ba•to** (*or* **re•**; *plural* **•tos**) collar
**rab•bet** *variant of* **rebate**
**rab•bi** (*or* **•bin**; *plural* **•bis** *or* **•bins**)
**rab•bin•ate** office of rabbi
**Rab•bin•ic** language
**rab•bini•cal** (*or* **•bin•ic**)
**rab•bin•ism**
**rab•bit** *note* **Welsh rabbit** (*or* **rarebit**)
**rab•bit•er**
**rabbit•fish** (*plural* **•fish** *or* **•fishes**)
**rab•bit•ry** (*plural* **•ries**)
**rab•bity**
**rab•ble**
**rab•bler**
**rabble-rouser**
**rabble-rousing**
**Rab•elai•sian**
**rabi** Indian crop
**rab•id**
**ra•bid•ity** (*or* **rab•id•ness**)
**ra•bies**
**rac•coon** (*or* **ra•coon**)
**race**
**race•card**
**race•course**
**race•go•er**
**race•horse**
**ra•ceme** botany term
**ra•cemic** chemistry term
**rac•emism**
**rac•emi•za•tion** (*or* **•sa•tion**)
**rac•emize**
**rac•emose** (*or* **•emous**) botany term
**rac•er**
**race•track**

**ra•chial** (*or* **•chid•ial, rha•**)
**ra•chis** (*or* **rha•**; *plural* **•chises** *or* **•chi•des**) biology term
**ra•chit•ic**
**ra•chi•tis** rickets
**Rach•man•ism** exploitation of tenants
**ra•cial**
**ra•cial•ly**
**raci•ly**
**raci•ness**
**rac•ing**
**rac•ism** (*or* **ra•cial•ism**)
**rac•ist** (*or* **ra•cial•ist**)
**rack** frame; toothed bar; to strain; etc.; *compare* **wrack**
**rack** (*or* **wrack**) destruction, *esp. in* **rack and ruin**
**rack-and-pinion**
**rack•er**
**rack•et** disturbance; dishonest practice
**rack•et** (*or* **rac•quet**) bat
**rack•et•eer**
**rack•ets** game
**rack•ety**
**rack-rent**
**rack-renter**
**rac•on•teur**
**ra•coon** *variant spelling of* **raccoon**
**rac•quet** *variant spelling of* **racket**
**racy** (**raci•er, raci•est**)
**rad** unit
**ra•dar**
**radar•scope**
**rad•dle**
**rad•dled**
**ra•dial**
**ra•dial•ly**
**radial-ply**
**ra•dian** unit
**ra•di•ance** (*or* **•an•cy**; *plural* **•ances** *or* **•an•cies**)
**ra•di•ant**
**ra•di•ate**
**ra•dia•tion**
**ra•dia•tion•al**
**ra•dia•tive** (*or* **•tory**)
**ra•dia•tor**
**radi•cal** basic; extreme; chemistry term; *compare* **radicle**
**radi•cal•ism**
**radi•cal•is•tic**
**radi•cal•is•ti•cal•ly**
**radi•cal•ly**
**radi•cal•ness**
**radi•cand** maths term
**radi•cel** tiny root
**radi•ces** *plural of* **radix**
**radi•cle** embryonic plant root; *compare* **radical**
**ra•dii** *plural of* **radius**
**ra•dio** (*noun, plural* **•dios**; *verb* **•dios, •dio•ing, •di•oed**)
**radio•ac•ti•vate**
**radio•ac•ti•va•tion**
**radio•ac•tive**
**radio•ac•tiv•ity**
**radio•bio•logi•cal**
**radio•bi•olo•gist**
**radio•bi•ol•ogy**
**radio•car•bon**
**radio•chemi•cal**
**radio•chem•ist**
**radio•chem•is•try**
**radio•com•mu•ni•ca•tion**
**radio•el•ement**
**radio•gen•ic**
**radio•gram**
**radio•graph**
**ra•di•og•ra•pher**
**radio•graph•ic**
**ra•di•og•ra•phy**
**radio•iso•tope**
**radio•iso•top•ic**
**radio•lar•ian** marine organism
**radio•lo•ca•tion•al**
**radio•logi•cal**
**ra•di•olo•gist**
**ra•di•ol•ogy**
**radio•lu•cent**
**radio•lu•mi•nes•cence**
**radio•lu•mi•nes•cent**
**ra•di•oly•sis**
**ra•di•om•eter**
**radio•met•ric**
**ra•di•om•etry**
**ra•dio•mi•crom•eter**
**radio•nu•clide**
**radio•pac•ity** (*or* **radio-opacity**)
**radio•paque** (*or* **radio-opaque**) impervious to X-rays
**radio•phone**
**radio•phon•ic**
**radio•phoni•cal•ly**
**ra•di•opho•ny**
**radio•scope**
**radio•scop•ic**
**radio•scopi•cal•ly**
**ra•di•os•co•py**
**radio•sen•si•tive**
**radio•sen•si•tiv•ity**
**radio•sonde** meteorological device
**radio•tele•gram**
**radio•tele•graph**
**radio•tele•graph•ic**
**radio•tele•graphi•cal•ly**
**radio•teleg•ra•phy**
**radio•telem•etry**
**radio•tele•phone**
**radio•tele•phon•ic**
**radio•telepho•ny**
**radio•tele•type**
**radio•thera•peu•tic**
**radio•thera•peu•ti•cal•ly**
**radio•thera•pist**
**radio•thera•py**
**radio•thermy**
**radio•tox•ic**
**rad•ish**
**ra•dium** radioactive element
**ra•dius** (*plural* **•dii** *or* **•di•uses**)
**ra•dix** (*plural* **•di•ces** *or* **•dixes**) maths or biology term
**Rad•nor•shire** former Welsh county
**Ra•dom** Polish city
**ra•dome** radar antenna's housing
**ra•don** radioactive element
**radu•la** (*plural* **•lae**) zoology term
**radu•lar**
**raff** *Dialect* rubbish
**raf•fia** (*or* **raphia**)
**raf•fi•nate** chemistry term
**raf•fi•nose** sugar
**raff•ish**
**raff•ish•ness**
**raf•fle**
**raf•fler**
**raf•fle•sia** plant
**raft**
**raft•er**

**rag** (**rag•ging, ragged**)
**raga** musical term
**raga•muf•fin**
**rag•bag**
**rage**
**ragged** teased
**rag•ged** tattered
**rag•ged•ness**
**rag•gedy**
**raggle-taggle**
**ragi** (*or* **rag•gee, rag•gy**) cereal
**rag•lan**
**rag•man** (*plural* **•men**)
**ra•gout** stew
**rag•tag**
**rag•time**
**rag•weed**
**rag•worm**
**rag•wort**
**raid**
**raid•er**
**rail**
**rail•car**
**rail•er**
**rail•head**
**rail•ing**
**rail•lery** (*plural* **•leries**)
**rail•road**
**rail•way**
**rail•way•man** (*plural* **•men**)
**rai•ment**
**rain**
**rain•band**
**rain•bird**
**rain•bow**
**rain•check**
**rain•coat**
**rain•drop**
**rain•fall**
**Rai•ni•er** US mountain
**raini•ly**
**raini•ness**
**rain•maker**
**rain•making**
**rain•out** radioactive fallout
**rain•proof**
**rain•storm**
**rain•water**
**rain•wear**
**rainy** (**raini•er, raini•est**)
**rais•able** (*or* **raise•**)
**raise** elevate; *compare* **raze**
**rais•er**
**rai•sin**
**rais•ing**
**rai•siny**
**rai•son d'être** (*plural* **rai•sons d'être**)
**raj**
**ra•jah** (*or* **raja**)
**Ra•ja•sthan** Indian state
**Raj•kot** Indian city
**Raj•put** (*or* **•poot**) Indian clan
**Ra•jya Sa•bha** chamber of Indian parliament
**rake**
**rake-off** (*noun*)
**rak•er**
**raki** (*or* **ra•kee**) drink
**rak•ish**
**rak•ish•ly**
**rak•ish•ness**
**rale** (*or* **râle**) medical term
**Ra•leigh** US city
**ral•len•tan•do** musical term
**ral•li•er**
**ral•line** ornithology term
**ral•ly** (*verb* **•lies, •ly•ing, •lied**; *noun, plural* **•lies**)
**ral•ly•cross**
**ram** (**ram•ming, rammed**)
**Rama** Hindu hero
**Ramachandra** mythological character
**Rama•dan** (*or* **Rhama•dhan, Rama•zan**) period in Muslim year
**Ra•mat Gan** Israeli city
**ram•ble**
**ram•bler**
**ram•bling**
**Ram•bouil•let** sheep
**ram•bunc•tious** *Slang* boisterous
**ram•bu•tan** fruit
**ram•ekin** (*or* **•equin**)
**ram•en•ta•ceous**
**ra•men•tum** (*plural* **•ta**) fern scale
**ramie** (*or* **ramee**) fibre
**rami•fi•ca•tion**
**rami•form**
**rami•fy** (**•fies, •fy•ing, •fied**)
**Ra•mil•lies** Belgian battle site
**ram•jet**
**rammed**
**ram•mer**
**ram•ming**
**ram•mish** (*or* **ram•my**)
**ra•mose** (*or* **•mous**) branched
**ra•mos•ity**
**ramp**
**ram•page**
**ram•pa•geous**
**ram•pa•geous•ness**
**ram•pag•er**
**ram•pan•cy**
**ram•pant**
**ram•part**
**ram•pi•on** plant
**Ram•pur** Indian city
**ram•rod**
**Rams•gate**
**ram•shack•le**
**ram•sons** plant
**ram•til** plant
**ramu•lose** (*or* **•lous**)
**ra•mus** (*plural* **rami**) biology term
**ran**
**rance** marble
**ranch**
**ranch•er**
**ran•che•ro** (*plural* **•ros**) US rancher
**Ran•chi** Indian city
**ran•cid**
**ran•cid•ness** (*or* **•ity**)
**ran•cor•ous**
**ran•cor•ous•ness**
**ran•cour** (*US* **•cor**)
**rand**
**ran•dan** boat
**randi•ly**
**randi•ness**
**ran•dom**
**ran•domi•za•tion** (*or* **•sa•tion**)
**ran•dom•ize** (*or* **•ise**)
**ran•dom•ness**
**randy** (**randi•er, randi•est**)
**rang**
**range**
**range•finder**
**Rang•er** senior Guide
**rang•er**
**rangi•ly**
**rangi•ness**
**Ran•goon** Burmese capital
**rangy** (**rangi•er, rangi•est**)

**rani** (*or* **ra•nee**) Indian queen or princess
**rank**
**rank•er**
**Rankine scale**
**rank•ing**
**ran•kle**
**rank•ness**
**ran•sack**
**ran•sack•er**
**ran•som**
**ran•som•er**
**rant**
**rant•er**
**rant•ing•ly**
**ra•nun•cu•la•ceous** botany term
**ra•nun•cu•lus** (*plural* **•luses** *or* **•li**) plant
**rap** (**rap•ping, rapped**) strike; *compare* **wrap**
**ra•pa•cious**
**ra•pac•ity** (*or* **•pa•cious•ness**)
**Rapa Nui** Easter Island
**rape**
**rape•seed**
**Rapha•el•esque**
**ra•phe** (*plural* **•phae**) botany term
**raphia** *variant spelling of* **raffia**
**ra•phide** (*or* **ra•phis**; *plural* **raphi•des**) botany term
**rap•id**
**ra•pid•ity** (*or* **rap•id•ness**)
**rap•ids**
**ra•pi•er**
**rap•ine** (*noun*)
**rap•ist**
**rap•pa•ree** Irish soldier
**rapped** *past tense of* **rap**; *compare* **rapt**
**rap•pee** snuff
**rap•pel** (**•pel•ling, •pelled**) mountaineering technique
**rap•per**
**rap•ping**
**rap•port** harmony
**rap•por•teur** preparer of report
**rap•proche•ment**
**rap•scal•lion**
**rapt** engrossed; *compare* **rapped**
**rap•tor** bird of prey
**rap•to•rial**
**rap•ture**
**rap•tur•ous**
**rap•tur•ous•ness**
**rara avis** (*plural* **ra•rae aves**) *Latin* unusual person or thing
**rare**
**rare•bit** *variant of* **(Welsh) rabbit**
**rar•efac•tion** (*or* **•efi•ca•tion**)
**rar•efac•tion•al** (*or* **•efac•tive**)
**rar•efi•able**
**rar•efi•er**
**rar•efy** (**•fies, •fy•ing, •fied**)
**rare•ly**
**rare•ripe** *US* ripening early
**rar•ing**
**rar•ity** (*plural* **•ities**)
**Ra•ro•ton•ga** Pacific island
**ras•bo•ra** fish
**ras•cal**
**ras•cal•ity** (*plural* **•ities**)
**ras•cal•ly**
**rase** *variant spelling of* **raze**
**rash**
**rash•er**
**rash•ness**
**Rasht** (*or* **Resht**) Iranian city
**ra•so•rial** zoology term
**rasp**
**ras•pa•tory** (*plural* **•tories**) surgical instrument
**rasp•berry** (*plural* **•berries**)
**rasp•er**
**rasp•ing** (*or* **raspy**)
**rasse** civet; *compare* **wrasse**
**Ras•ta•far•ian** (*or* **Ras•ta**)
**ras•ter** electronics term
**rat** (**rat•ting, rat•ted**)
**ra•ta** tree
**rat•abil•ity** (*or* **•able•ness, rate•**)
**rat•able** (*or* **rate•**)
**rat•ably** (*or* **rate•**)
**rata•fia** (*or* **•fee**) liqueur; biscuit
**ra•tal** ratable value
**ra•tan** *variant spelling of* **rattan**
**rata•tat-tat** (*or* **rata•tat**)
**ra•ta•touille** vegetable stew
**rat•bag**
**ratch•et**
**rate**
**rate•able** *variant spelling of* **ratable**
**ra•tel** animal
**rate•payer**
**rat•fink**
**rat•fish** (*plural* **•fish** *or* **•fishes**)
**rathe** (*or* **rath**) *Archaic* blossoming early
**ra•ther**
**rati•fi•able**
**rati•fi•ca•tion**
**rati•fi•er**
**rati•fy** (**•fies, •fy•ing, •fied**)
**ra•tine** (*or* **ra•teen, rat•teen, rati•né**) cloth
**rat•ing**
**ra•tio** (*plural* **•tios**)
**ra•ti•oci•nate** argue logically
**ra•ti•oci•na•tion**
**ra•ti•oci•na•tor**
**ra•tion**
**ra•tion•al** using reason
**ra•tion•ale** basis
**ra•tion•al•ism**
**ra•tion•al•ist**
**ra•tion•al•is•tic**
**ra•tion•al•is•ti•cal•ly**
**ra•tion•al•ity** (*plural* **•ities**)
**ra•tion•ali•za•tion** (*or* **•sa•tion**)
**ra•tion•al•ize** (*or* **•ise**)
**ra•tion•al•iz•er** (*or* **•is•er**)
**ra•tion•al•ly**
**ra•tions**
**Rat•is•bon** Regensburg
**rat•ite** flightless bird
**Rat•lam** Indian city
**rat•line** (*or* **•lin**) nautical term
**ra•toon** (*or* **rat•toon**) new shoot
**rats•bane**
**rat-tail** fish; horse; file
**rat•tan** (*or* **ra•tan**)
**rat•ted**
**rat•ter**
**rat•ti•ly**
**rat•ti•ness**
**rat•ting**
**rat•tish**
**rat•tle**

**rattle•box**
**rat•tler**
**rattle•snake**
**rattle•trap**
**rat•tling**
**rat•tly** (**•tli•er, •tli•est**)
**rat•trap**
**rat•ty** (**•ti•er, •ti•est**)
**rau•cous**
**rau•cous•ness** (*or* **rau•city**)
**raun•chy** (**•chi•er, •chi•est**)
**rau•wol•fia** drug
**rav•age**
**rav•age•ment**
**rav•ag•er**
**rave**
**rav•el** (**•el•ling, •elled;** *US* **•el•ing, •eled**)
**rave•lin** fortification
**rav•el•ler** (*US* **•el•er**)
**rav•el•ly**
**ra•ven** bird
**rav•en** to plunder
**rav•en•er**
**rav•en•ing**
**Ra•ven•na** Italian city
**rav•en•ous**
**rav•en•ous•ness**
**rav•er**
**rave-up**
**ra•vine**
**rav•ing**
**ra•vio•li**
**rav•ish**
**rav•ish•er**
**rav•ish•ing**
**rav•ish•ment**
**raw**
**Ra•wal•pin•di**
**raw•boned**
**raw•hide**
**ra•win•sonde** meteorological balloon
**raw•ness**
**ray**
**ray•less**
**ray•let**
**ray•on**
**raze** (*or* **rase**) destroy; *compare* **raise**
**razee** ship
**raz•er** (*or* **ras•**) demolisher; *compare* **razor**
**ra•zoo** *Austral* small sum of money
**ra•zor** shaver; *compare* **razer**
**razor•back** whale
**razor•bill**
**razor-cut** (**-cutting, -cut**)
**razz** *Slang* deride
**razz•ma•tazz** (*or* **razzle-dazzle**)
**re** concerning
**re•ab•sorb**
**reach**
**reach•able**
**reach•er**
**re•act** act in response
**re-act** act again
**re•ac•tance** physics term
**re•ac•tant**
**re•ac•tion**
**re•ac•tion•al**
**re•ac•tion•ary** (*plural* **•aries**)
**re•ac•tion•ism**
**re•ac•ti•vate**
**re•ac•ti•va•tion**
**re•ac•tive**
**re•ac•tiv•ity** (*or* **•tive•ness**)
**re•ac•tor**
**read** (**read•ing, read**)
**read•abil•ity** (*or* **•able•ness**)
**read•able**
**read•ably**
**re•ad•dress**
**read•er**
**read•er•ship**
**read•ily**
**readi•ness**
**Read•ing**
**re•adjust**
**re•adjust•able**
**re•adjust•er**
**re•adjust•ment**
**re•admis•sion**
**re•admit** (**•admit•ting, •admit•ted**)
**re•admit•tance**
**read-out** (*noun*)
**ready** (*adj* **readi•er, readi•est;** *verb* **readies, ready•ing, readied**)
**ready-made**
**ready-mix**
**ready-to-wear**
**ready-witted**
**re•affirm**
**re•affir•ma•tion** (*or* **•affirm•ance**)
**re•affor•est** (*or* **•for•est**)
**re•affor•esta•tion** (*or* **•for•esta•tion**)
**re•agent**
**real** actual
**real** (*plural* **reals** *or* **rea•les**) Spanish coin
**real** (*plural* **reis**) Portuguese coin
**re•al•gar** mineral
**re•align**
**re•align•ment**
**re•al•ism**
**re•al•ist**
**re•al•is•tic**
**re•al•is•ti•cal•ly**
**re•al•ity** (*plural* **•ities**)
**re•al•iz•able** (*or* **•is•able**)
**re•al•iz•ably** (*or* **•is•ably**)
**re•ali•za•tion** (*or* **•sa•tion**)
**re•al•ize** (*or* **•ise**)
**re•al•iz•er** (*or* **•is•er**)
**re•allo•cate**
**re•allo•ca•tion**
**re•al•ly**
**realm**
**Re•al•po•li•tik** *German* opportunistic politics
**re•al•tor** *US* estate agent
**re•al•ty** real property
**ream**
**ream•er**
**re•ani•mate**
**re•ani•ma•tion**
**reap**
**reap•able**
**reap•er**
**re•appear**
**re•appear•ance**
**re•apply** (**•applies, •apply•ing, •applied**)
**re•appoint**
**re•appoint•ment**
**re•appor•tion**
**re•apprais•al**
**re•appraise**
**rear**
**rear•er**
**rear•guard**
**re•arm**
**rear•most**
**re•arrange**
**re•arrange•ment**
**re•arrang•er**
**rear•ward** (*adj*)
**rear•wards** (*adv*)

**rea•son**
**rea•son•able**
**rea•son•able•ness** (*or* **•abil•ity**)
**rea•son•ably**
**rea•soned**
**rea•son•er**
**rea•son•ing**
**re•as•sem•ble**
**re•assur•ance**
**re•assure**
**re•assur•er**
**re•assur•ing**
**rea•ta** *variant spelling of* **riata**
**re•awak•en**
**reb** *US* Confederate soldier
**re•bar•ba•tive**
**re•bat•able** (*or* **•bate•**)
**re•bate** refund
**re•bate** (*or* **rab•bet**) carpentry term
**re•bat•er**
**re•bec** (*or* **•beck**) musical instrument
**re•bel** (**•bel•ling, •belled**)
**re•bel•lion**
**re•bel•lious**
**re•bel•lious•ness**
**re•birth**
**re•born**
**re•bound**
**re•buff**
**re•build** (**•build•ing, •built**)
**re•buk•able**
**re•buke**
**re•buk•er**
**re•buk•ing•ly**
**re•bus** (*plural* **•buses**) picture puzzle
**re•but** (**•but•ting, •but•ted**)
**re•but•table**
**re•but•tal**
**re•but•ter**
**rec** *Slang* recreation ground
**re•cal•ci•trance** (*or* **•tran•cy**)
**re•cal•ci•trant**
**re•cal•esce**
**re•ca•les•cence** chemistry term
**re•ca•les•cent**
**re•call**
**re•call•able**
**re•cant**
**re•can•ta•tion**
**re•cant•er**
**re•cap** (**•cap•ping, •capped**)
**re•capi•tali•za•tion** (*or* **•sa•tion**)
**re•capi•tal•ize** (*or* **•ise**)
**re•ca•pitu•late**
**re•ca•pitu•la•tion**
**re•ca•pitu•la•tive** (*or* **•tory**)
**re•cap•tion** legal term
**re•cap•ture**
**re•cast** (**•cast•ing, •cast**)
**rec•ce** (**•ce•ing, •ced** *or* **•ceed**) *Slang* reconnoitre; reconnaissance
**re•cede** withdraw
**re-cede** restore
**re•ceipt**
**re•ceipt•or**
**re•ceiv•able**
**re•ceive**
**re•ceiv•er**
**re•ceiv•er•ship**
**re•cen•sion** literary revision
**re•cent**
**re•cent•ness** (*or* **•cen•cy**)
**re•cept** psychology term
**re•cep•ta•cle**
**re•cep•tion**
**re•cep•tion•ist**
**re•cep•tive**
**re•cep•tiv•ity** (*or* **•tive•ness**)
**re•cep•tor**
**re•cess**
**re•ces•sion**
**re•ces•sion•al**
**re•ces•sive**
**re•ces•sive•ness**
**Rech•abite** teetotaller
**re•charge**
**ré•chauf•fé** warmed-up food
**re•cher•ché** exquisite; rare
**re•chris•ten**
**re•cidi•vism**
**re•cidi•vist**
**re•cidi•vis•tic** (*or* **•cidi•vous**)
(recieve) *incorrect spelling of* **receive**
**Re•ci•fe** Brazilian port
**reci•pe**
**re•cipi•ence**
**re•cipi•ent**
**re•cip•ro•cal**
**re•cip•ro•cal•ity** (*or* **•ness**)
**re•cip•ro•cal•ly**
**re•cip•ro•cate**
**re•cip•ro•ca•tion**
**re•cip•ro•ca•tive** (*or* **•tory**)
**re•cip•ro•ca•tor**
**reci•proc•ity**
**re•ci•sion** cancellation
**re•cit•able**
**re•cit•al**
**reci•ta•tion**
**reci•ta•tive** (*or* **•ta•ti•vo**)
**re•cite**
**re•cit•er**
**reck•less**
**reck•less•ness**
**Reck•ling•hau•sen** German city
**reck•on**
**reck•on•er**
**reck•on•ing**
**re•claim**
**re•claim•able**
**re•claim•ant** (*or* **•er**)
**rec•la•ma•tion**
**ré•clame** acclaim
**re•clin•able**
**rec•li•nate** bent backwards
**rec•li•na•tion**
**re•cline**
**re•clin•er**
**re•clothe**
**re•cluse**
**re•clu•sion**
**re•clu•sive**
**rec•og•ni•tion**
**rec•og•ni•tion•al** (*or* **•ni•tive, •ni•tory**)
**rec•og•niz•abil•ity** (*or* **•nis•**)
**rec•og•niz•able** (*or* **•nis•**)
**rec•og•niz•ably** (*or* **•nis•**)
**re•cog•ni•zance** (*or* **•sance**)
**rec•og•nize** (*or* **•nise**)
**rec•og•ni•zee** (*or* **•see**)
**rec•og•niz•er** (*or* **•nis•er** *or in legal contexts* **•ni•zor, •ni•sor**)
**re•coil**
**re•coil•er**
**re•coil•ing•ly**
**re•coil•less**
**rec•ol•lect**
**rec•ol•lec•tion**
**rec•ol•lec•tive**
**re•com•bi•nant**
**re•com•bi•na•tion**
**re•com•bine**
**re•com•mence**

**re•com•mence•ment**
**rec•om•mend**
**rec•om•mend•able**
**rec•om•men•da•tion**
**rec•om•menda•tory**
**rec•om•mend•er**
**re•com•mit** (**•mit•ting, •mit•ted**)
**re•com•mit•ment** (*or* **•mit•tal**)
**rec•om•pen•sable**
**rec•om•pense**
**rec•om•pens•er**
**re•com•pose**
**re•com•po•si•tion**
**rec•on•cil•abil•ity** (*or* **•able•ness**)
**rec•on•cil•able**
**rec•on•cil•ably**
**rec•on•cile**
**rec•on•cile•ment**
**rec•on•cil•er**
**rec•on•cilia•tion**
**rec•on•cilia•tory**
**rec•on•cil•ing•ly**
**re•con•dite**
**re•con•dite•ness**
**re•con•di•tion**
**re•con•di•tion•er**
**re•con•nais•sance** (*or* **•nois•sance**)
**rec•on•noi•tre** (*US* **•ter**)
**rec•on•noi•trer** (*US* **•ter•er**)
**re•con•sid•er**
**re•con•sid•era•tion**
**re•con•stitu•ent**
**re•con•sti•tute**
**re•con•sti•tut•ed**
**re•con•sti•tu•tion**
**re•con•struct**
**re•con•struc•tible**
**re•con•struc•tion**
**re•con•struc•tive** (*or* **•tion•al**)
**re•con•struc•tor**
**re•con•vene**
**re•con•ver•sion**
**re•con•vert**
**rec•ord** (*noun*)
**re•cord** (*verb*)
**re•cord•able**
**record-changer**
**re•cord•er**
**re•cord•ing**
**record-player**
**re•count** relate
**re-count** count again
**re•count•al**
**re•coup**
**re•coup•able**
**re•coup•ment**
**re•course**
**re•cov•er** regain
**re-cover** cover again
**re•cov•er•abil•ity**
**re•cov•er•able**
**re•cov•er•er**
**re•cov•ery** (*plural* **•eries**)
**re-create**
**re-creation** new creation
**rec•rea•tion** enjoyment
**rec•rea•tion•al**
**re-creator**
**rec•re•ment** waste matter
**rec•re•men•tal**
**re•crimi•nate**
**re•crimi•na•tion**
**re•crimi•na•tive** (*or* **•tory**)
**re•crimi•na•tor**
**re•cru•desce**
**re•cru•des•cence**
**re•cruit**
**re•cruit•able**
**re•cruit•er**
**re•cruit•ment**
**re•crys•tal•li•za•tion** (*or* **•sa•tion**)
**re•crys•tal•lize** (*or* **•lise**)
**rec•ta** *plural of* **rectum**
**rec•tal**
**rec•tan•gle**
**rec•tan•gu•lar**
**rec•tan•gu•lar•ity**
**rec•ti** *plural of* **rectus**
**rec•ti•fi•able**
**rec•ti•fi•ca•tion**
**rec•ti•fi•er**
**rec•ti•fy** (**•fies, •fy•ing, •fied**)
**rec•ti•lin•ear** (*or* **•eal**)
**rec•ti•tude**
**rec•to** (*plural* **•tos**) right-hand page
**rec•to•cele** hernia
**rec•tor**
**rec•tor•ate**
**rec•tor•ial**
**rec•tor•ship**
**rec•tory** (*plural* **•tories**)
**rec•trix** (*plural* **•tri•ces**) tail feather
**rec•tum** (*plural* **•tums** *or* **•ta**) part of intestine
**rec•tus** (*plural* **•ti**) muscle
**re•cum•bence** (*or* **•ben•cy**)
**re•cum•bent**
**re•cu•per•ate**
**re•cu•pera•tion**
**re•cu•pera•tive**
**re•cu•pera•tor**
**re•cur** (**•cur•ring, •curred**)
**re•cur•rence**
**re•cur•rent**
**re•cur•ring•ly**
**re•cur•sion** returning
**re•curve**
**recu•sance** (*or* **•san•cy**)
**recu•sant** insubordinate
**re•cy•cle**
**red** (**red•der, red•dest**) colour; *variant spelling of* **redd**
**re•dact** prepare for publication
**re•dac•tion**
**re•dac•tion•al**
**re•dac•tor**
**re•dan** fortification
**red-blooded**
**red•breast**
**red•brick**
**red•bud** tree
**red•bug**
**red•cap**
**red•coat**
**red•cur•rant**
**redd** (*or* **red; red•ding, redd** *or* **red•ded**) *Dialect* to tidy
**red•den**
**red•dish**
**Red•ditch**
**red•dle** *variant spelling of* **ruddle**
**re•deco•rate**
**re•deem**
**re•deem•abil•ity**
**re•deem•able** (*or* **re•demp•tible**)
**re•deem•ably**
**re•deem•er**
**re•deem•ing**
**re•deliv•er**
**re•deliv•ery**
**re•demand**

**re•demand•able**
**re•demp•tion**
**re•demp•tion•al** (*or* **•tive, •tory**)
**re•demp•tion•er** emigrant to America
**Re•demp•tor•ist** Catholic missionary
**re•deploy**
**re•deploy•ment**
**re•de•sign**
**re•devel•op**
**re•devel•op•er**
**re•devel•op•ment**
**red•eye**
**red-faced**
**red•fin** fish
**red•fish** (*plural* **•fish** *or* **•fishes**)
**red-handed**
**red•head**
**red-headed**
**red-hot**
**re•dia** (*plural* **•diae**) zoology term
**re•dial** (**•dial•ling, •dialled;** *US* **•dial•ing, •dialed**)
**Re•dif•fu•sion** (*Trademark*)
**red•in•gote** overcoat
**red•in•te•grate** renew
**red•in•te•gra•tion**
**red•in•te•gra•tive**
**re•di•rect**
**re•di•rec•tion**
**re•dis•count**
**re•dis•cov•er**
**re•dis•cov•ery** (*plural* **•eries**)
**re•dis•trib•ute**
**re•dis•tri•bu•tion**
**red•neck**
**red•ness**
**redo** (**re•does, •do•ing, •did, •done**)
**redo•lence** (*or* **•len•cy**)
**redo•lent**
**re•dou•ble**
**re•doubt** fortification
**re•doubt•able**
**re•doubt•able•ness**
**re•doubt•ably**
**re•dound** affect
**redo•wa** folk dance
**re•dox** chemistry term
**red•poll** bird
**re•draft**
**re•draw** (**•drawing, •drew, •drawn**)
**re•dress** put right
**re-dress** dress again
**re•dress•able** (*or* **•ible**)
**re•dress•er** (*or* **•dres•sor**)
**red•root** plant
**red•shank** bird
**red•skin**
**red•start** bird
**re•duce**
**re•duc•er**
**re•duc•ibil•ity**
**re•duc•ible**
**re•duc•tase** enzyme
**re•duc•tio ad ab•sur•dum**
**re•duc•tion**
**re•duc•tion•al** (*or* **•tive**)
**re•dun•dan•cy** (*plural* **•cies**)
**re•dun•dant**
**re•du•pli•cate**
**re•du•pli•ca•tion**
**re•du•pli•ca•tive**
**re•du•vi•id** insect
**red•ware** seaweed
**red•wing** bird
**red•wood**
**re-echo** (**-echoes, -echoing, -echoed**)
**reed**
**reed•buck** (*plural* **•bucks** *or* **•buck**) antelope
**reedi•ness**
**reed•ing** moulding
**reed•ling** bird
**re-educate**
**re-education**
**reedy** (**reedi•er, reedi•est**)
**reef**
**reef•er**
**reek**
**reek•ing•ly**
**reeky**
**reel**
**reel•able**
**reel•ably**
**re-elect**
**re-election**
**reel•er**
**re-em•ploy**
**re-em•ploy•ment**
**reen** (*or* **rean**) *Dialect* ditch
**re-enact**
**re-enforce** enforce again; *compare* **reinforce**
**re-enforce•ment**
**re-enforc•er**
**re-enter**
**re-entrance**
**re-entrant**
**re-entry** (*plural* **-entries**)
**reeve** (**reev•ing, reeved** *or* **rove**) nautical term; bird; medieval official
**re-examin•able**
**re-examina•tion**
**re-examine**
**re-examin•er**
**re-export**
**re-exporta•tion**
**re-export•er**
**ref** *Slang* referee
**re•face**
**re•fash•ion**
**re•fec•tion**
**re•fec•tory** (*plural* **•tories**)
**re•fer** (**•fer•ring, •ferred**)
**ref•er•able** (*or* **re•fer•rable**)
**ref•eree** (**•eree•ing, •ereed**)
**ref•er•ence**
**ref•er•enc•er**
**ref•er•en•dum** (*plural* **•dums** *or* **•da**)
**ref•er•ent**
**ref•er•en•tial** of a reference; *compare* **reverential**
**re•fer•ral**
**re•fer•rer**
**re•fill**
**re•fill•able**
**re•fin•able**
**re•fi•nance**
**re•fine**
**re•fined**
**re•fine•ment**
**re•fin•er**
**re•fin•ery** (*plural* **•eries**)
**re•fin•ish**
**re•fin•ish•er**
**re•fit** (**•fit•ting, •fit•ted**)
**re•flate**
**re•fla•tion**
**re•flect**
**re•flec•tance**
**re•flect•ing•ly**
**re•flec•tion** (*or* **•flex•ion**)
**re•flec•tion•al** (*or* **•flex•ion•al**)

**re•flec•tive** contemplative; able to reflect; *compare* **reflexive**
**re•flec•tive•ness** (*or* **•tiv•ity**)
**re•flec•tor**
**re•flet** lustre
**re•flex**
**re•flex•ion** *variant spelling of* **reflection**
**re•flex•ive** grammar term; *compare* **reflective**
**re•flex•ive•ness** (*or* **•iv•ity**)
**re•flex•ol•ogy** therapy
**re•flux**
**re•form** improve
**re-form** form again
**re•form•able**
**Ref•or•ma•tion** religious movement
**ref•or•ma•tion**
**re-formation**
**ref•or•ma•tion•al**
**re•forma•tive**
**re•forma•tory** (*plural* **•tories**)
**re•formed**
**re•form•er**
**re•form•ism**
**re•form•ist**
**re•fract**
**re•fract•able**
**re•frac•tion**
**re•frac•tion•al**
**re•frac•tive**
**re•frac•tive•ness** (*or* **•tiv•ity**)
**re•frac•tom•eter**
**re•frac•to•met•ric**
**re•frac•tom•etry**
**re•frac•tor**
**re•frac•to•ri•ly**
**re•frac•to•ri•ness**
**re•frac•tory** (*plural* **•tories**)
**re•frain**
**re•frain•er**
**re•frain•ment**
**re•fran•gibil•ity** (*or* **•gible•ness**)
**re•fran•gible**
**re•freeze** (**•freez•ing**, **•froze**, **•fro•zen**)
**re•fresh** (*or* **•fresh•en**)
**re•fresh•er**
**re•fresh•ful**
**re•fresh•ing**
**re•fresh•ment**
**re•frig•er•ant**
**re•frig•er•ate**
**re•frig•era•tion**
**re•frig•era•tive** (*or* **•tory**)
**re•frig•era•tor**
**re•frin•gen•cy** (*or* **•gence**)
**re•frin•gent**
**re•froze**
**re•fu•el** (**•el•ling**, **•elled**; *US* **•el•ing**, **•eled**)
**ref•uge**
**refu•gee**
**refu•gee•ism**
**re•fu•gium** (*plural* **•gia**)
**re•ful•gence** (*or* **•gen•cy**)
**re•ful•gent** shining
**re•fund** give back money
**re-fund** replace bond issue
**re•fund•able**
**re•fund•er**
**re•fur•bish**
**re•fur•bish•ment**
**re•fus•able**
**re•fus•al**
**re•fuse** decline
**ref•use** rubbish
**re•fus•er**
**refu•tabil•ity**
**refu•table**
**refu•ta•tion**
**re•fute**
**re•fut•er**
**re•gain**
**re•gain•able**
**re•gain•er**
**re•gal** royal
**re•gale** amuse
**re•gale•ment**
**re•ga•lia**
**re•gal•ity** (*plural* **•ities**)
**re•gal•ly**
**re•gard**
**re•gard•able**
**re•gar•dant** heraldic term
**re•gard•ful**
**re•gard•ing**
**re•gard•less**
**re•gards**
**re•gat•ta**
**re•ge•late**
**re•ge•la•tion** physics term
**Re•gen•cy** historical period
**re•gen•cy** (*plural* **•cies**) rule by regent
**re•gen•er•able**
**re•gen•era•cy**
**re•gen•er•ate**
**re•gen•era•tion**
**re•gen•era•tive**
**re•gen•era•tor**
**Re•gens•burg** German city
**re•gent**
**re•gent•al**
**re•gent•ship**
**reg•gae**
**Reg•gio di Ca•la•bria** Italian port
**Reg•gio nell'Emilia** Italian city
**regi•cid•al**
**regi•cide**
**re•gime** (*or* **ré•gime**) administration
**regi•men** course of treatment
**regi•ment**
**regi•men•tal**
**regi•men•tals** military dress
**regi•men•ta•tion**
**Re•gi•na** the queen; Canadian city
**re•gion**
**re•gion•al**
**re•gion•al•ism**
**re•gion•al•ist**
**re•gion•al•ly**
**reg•is•ter**
**reg•is•ter•er**
**reg•is•trable**
**reg•is•trant**
**reg•is•trar**
**reg•is•trar•ship**
**reg•is•tra•tion**
**reg•is•tra•tion•al**
**reg•is•try** (*plural* **•tries**)
**Re•gius pro•fes•sor**
**reg•let**
**reg•nal** of a sovereign
**reg•nant** reigning
**rego•lith**
**re•gorge**
**rego•sol** soil
**re•grate** buy up for profit
**re•grat•er**
**re•gress**
**re•gres•sion**
**re•gres•sive**
**re•gres•sive•ness**
**re•gres•sor**

**re•gret** (**•gret•ting, •gret•ted**)
**re•gret•ful**
**re•gret•ful•ly**
**re•gret•ful•ness**
**re•gret•table**
**re•gret•tably**
**re•gret•ter**
**re•group**
**re•growth**
**regu•lable**
**regu•lar**
**regu•lar•ity** (*plural* **•ities**)
**regu•lari•za•tion** (*or* **•sa•tion**)
**regu•lar•ize** (*or* **•ise**)
**regu•late**
**regu•la•tion**
**regu•la•tive** (*or* **•tory**)
**regu•la•tor**
**regu•line**
**regu•lus** (*plural* **•luses** *or* **•li**) impure metal
**re•gur•gi•tant**
**re•gur•gi•tate**
**re•gur•gi•ta•tion**
**re•ha•bili•tate**
**re•ha•bili•ta•tion**
**re•ha•bili•ta•tive**
**re•hash**
**re•hear** (**•hear•ing, •heard**)
**re•hears•al**
**re•hearse**
**re•hears•er**
**re•heat**
**re•heat•er**
**re•ho•bo•am** wine bottle
**re•house**
**Reich** *German* kingdom or republic
**Reichs•mark** (*plural* **•marks** *or* **•mark**) currency
**Reichs•tag** German assembly
**rei•fi•ca•tion**
**rei•fier**
**rei•fy** (**•fies, •fy•ing, •fied**) make real
**Rei•gate**
**reign** rule; *compare* **rein**
**re•im•burs•able**
**re•im•burse**
**re•im•burse•ment**
**re•im•burs•er**
**re•im•port**
**re•im•por•ta•tion**
**re•im•pose**
**re•im•po•si•tion**
**re•im•pres•sion**
**Reims** (*or* **Rheims**) French city
**rein** long strap; *compare* **reign**
**re•incar•nate**
**re•incar•na•tion**
**re•incar•na•tion•ist**
**rein•deer** (*plural* **•deer** *or* **•deers**)
**re•inforce** strengthen; *compare* **re-enforce**
**re•inforce•ment**
**re•install**
**re•in•stal•la•tion**
**re•instate**
**re•instate•ment**
**re•insta•tor**
**re•insur•ance**
**re•insure**
**re•insur•er**
**re•intro•duce**
**re•intro•duc•tion**
**re•invest**
**re•invest•ment**
**re•issu•able**
**re•issue** (**•issu•ing, •issued**)
**re•issu•er**
**re•it•er•ant**
**re•it•er•ate**
**re•it•era•tion**
**re•it•era•tive**
**re•ject**
**re•ject•able**
**re•ject•er** (*or* **•jec•tor**)
**re•jec•tion**
**re•jec•tive**
**re•jig** (**•jig•ging, •jigged**) re-equip
**re•joice**
**re•joic•er**
**re•joic•ing**
**re•join**
**re•join•der**
**re•ju•venate** (*or* **•venize, •venise**)
**re•ju•vena•tion**
**re•ju•vena•tor**
**re•ju•venesce**
**re•ju•venes•cence**
**re•ju•venes•cent**
**re•kin•dle**
**re•la•bel** (**•bel•ling, •belled;** *US* **•bel•ing, •beled**)
**re•lapse**
**re•laps•er**
**re•lat•able**
**re•late**
**re•lat•ed**
**re•lat•ed•ness**
**re•lat•er** one that relates; *compare* **relator**
**re•la•tion**
**re•la•tion•al**
**re•la•tion•ship**
**rela•tive**
**rela•tive•ly**
**rela•tiv•ism**
**rela•tiv•ist**
**rela•tiv•is•tic**
**rela•tiv•is•ti•cal•ly**
**rela•tiv•ity**
**re•la•tor** legal term; *compare* **relater**
**re•la•tum** (*plural* **•ta**) logic term
**re•lax**
**re•lax•able**
**re•lax•ant**
**re•laxa•tion**
**re•lax•ed•ly**
**re•lax•er**
**re•lax•in** hormone
**re•lay** convey
**re-lay** (**-laying, -laid**) lay again
**re•lease**
**re•leas•er**
**rel•ega•table**
**rel•egate**
**rel•ega•tion**
**re•lent**
**re•lent•less**
**re•lent•less•ness**
**re•let** (**•let•ting, •let**)
**rel•evance** (*or* **•evan•cy**)
**rel•evant**
**re•li•abil•ity** (*or* **•able•ness**)
**re•li•able**
**re•li•ably**
**re•li•ance**
**re•li•ant**
**rel•ic** object from past
**rel•ict** biology term; widow
**re•lief**
**re•liev•able**
**re•lieve**

**re•liev•er**
**re•li•gion**
**re•li•gion•ism**
**re•ligi•ose**
**re•ligi•os•ity**
**re•li•gious**
**re•li•gious•ness**
**re•linc**
**re•lin•quish**
**re•lin•quish•er**
**re•lin•quish•ment**
**reli•quary** (*plural* **•quaries**)
**re•liquiae** fossil remains
**rel•ish**
**rel•ish•able**
**rel•ish•ing•ly**
**re•liv•able**
**re•live**
**re•load**
**re•lo•cate**
**re•lo•ca•tion**
**re•luc•tance** (*or* **•tan•cy**)
**re•luc•tant**
**rel•uc•tiv•ity** (*plural* **•ities**) physics term
**rely** (**re•lies, rely•ing, re•lied**)
**re•made**
**re•main**
**re•main•der**
**remainder•man** (*plural* **•men**) legal term
**re•mains**
**re•make** (**•mak•ing, •made**)
**re•mand**
**re•mand•ment**
**rema•nence** physics term
**re•mark**
**re•mark•able**
**re•mark•able•ness** (*or* **•abil•ity**)
**re•mark•ably**
**re•mark•er**
**re•marque** (*or* **•mark**) mark on engraved plate
**re•mar•riage**
**re•mar•ry** (**•ries, •ry•ing, •ried**)
**re•match**
**re•medi•able**
**re•medi•ably**
**re•medial**
**re•medial•ly**
**rem•edi•less**
**rem•edy** (*noun, plural* **•edies**; *verb* **•edies, •edy•ing, •edied**)
**re•mem•ber**
**re•mem•ber•er**
**re•mem•brance**
**Re•mem•branc•er** Exchequer official
**re•mex** (*plural* **remi•gcs**) flight feather
**re•mig•ial**
**re•mind**
**re•mind•er**
**re•mind•ful**
**remi•nisce**
**remi•nis•cence**
**remi•nis•cent**
**re•mise** legal term
**re•miss** negligent
**re•mis•sibil•ity** (*or* **•sible•ness**)
**re•mis•sible**
**re•mis•sion** (*or* **•mit•tal**)
**re•mis•sive**
**re•miss•ness**
**re•mit** (**•mit•ting, •mit•ted**)
**re•mit•table**
**re•mit•tal**
**re•mit•tance** payment
**re•mit•tee**
**re•mit•tence** (*or* **•ten•cy**) diminution
**re•mit•tent**
**re•mit•ter** (*or* **•tor**)
**rem•nant**
**re•mod•el** (**•el•ling, •elled**)
**re•mod•el•ler**
**re•mon•eti•za•tion** (*or* **•sa•tion**)
**re•mon•etize** (*or* **•etise**)
**re•mon•strance**
**re•mon•strant**
**re•mon•strate**
**re•mon•stra•tion**
**re•mon•stra•tive**
**re•mon•stra•tor**
**re•mon•tant**
**rem•on•toir** (*or* **•toire**) device in clock
**remo•ra** fish
**re•morse**
**re•morse•ful**
**re•morse•ful•ly**
**re•morse•ful•ness**
**re•morse•less**
**re•morse•less•ness**
**re•mote**
**remote-controlled**
**re•mote•ness**
**re•mould** (*US* **•mold**)
**re•mount**
**re•mov•abil•ity** (*or* **•able•ness**)
**re•mov•able**
**re•mov•ably**
**re•mov•al**
**re•mov•al•ist** *Austral* furniture remover
**re•move**
**re•mov•er**
**Rem•scheid** German city
**re•mu•ner•abil•ity**
**re•mu•ner•able**
**re•mu•ner•ate**
**re•mu•nera•tion**
**re•mu•nera•tive**
**re•mu•nera•tor**
**Re•nais•sance** historical period
**re•nais•sance** (*or* **•nas•cence**) revival
**re•nal**
**re•name**
**re•nas•cent**
**Ren•ault** (*Trademark*)
**rend** (**rend•ing, rent**)
**rend•er** (*noun*)
**ren•der** (*verb*)
**rend•er•able** submittable; *compare* **rendible**
**rend•er•er**
**ren•der•ing**
**ren•dez•vous** (*plural* **•vous**)
**rend•ible** tearable; *compare* **renderable**
**ren•di•tion**
**ren•dzi•na** soil
**ren•egade**
**re•nege** (*or* **•negue**)
**re•neg•er** (*or* **•negu•er**)
**re•nego•ti•able**
**re•nego•ti•ate**
**re•nego•tia•tion**
**re•new**
**re•new•abil•ity**
**re•new•able**
**re•new•al**
**re•new•edly**
**re•new•er**
**Ren•frew** Scottish town

**reni•form** kidney-shaped
**re•nin** kidney enzyme; *compare* **rennin**
**Rennes** French city
**ren•net**
**ren•nin** milk-coagulating enzyme; *compare* **renin**
**Reno** US city
**re•nounce**
**re•nounce•ment**
**re•nounc•er**
**reno•vate**
**reno•va•tion**
**reno•va•tive**
**reno•va•tor**
**re•nown**
**re•nowned**
**re•nown•edly**
**rens•selaer•ite** mineral
**rent**
**rent•abil•ity**
**rent•able**
**rent•al**
**rente** *French* type of income
**rent•er**
**rent-free**
**ren•tier** one living on rentes
**rent-roll**
**re•num•ber**
**re•nun•cia•tion**
**re•nun•cia•tive** (*or* **•tory**)
**ren•voi** legal term
**re•oc•cu•pa•tion**
**re•oc•cu•py** (**•pies, •py•ing, •pied**)
**re•open**
**re•or•der**
**re•or•gani•za•tion** (*or* **•sa•tion**)
**re•or•gan•ize** (*or* **•ise**)
**re•or•gan•iz•er** (*or* **•is•er**)
**rep** *Slang* representative; repertory
**rep** (*or* repp) fabric
**re•paint**
**re•pair**
**re•pair•able** able to be repaired; *compare* reparable
**re•pair•er**
**re•pair•man** (*plural* **•men**)
**re•pand** having a wavy margin
**repa•rabil•ity**
**repa•rable** able to be made good; *compare* **repairable**
**repa•rably**
**repa•ra•tion**
**re•para•tive** (*or* **•tory**)
**rep•ar•tee**
**rep•ar•ti•tion**
**re•past**
**re•pat•ri•ate**
**re•pat•ria•tion**
**re•pay** (**•pay•ing, •paid**)
**re•pay•able**
**re•pay•ment**
**re•peal**
**re•peal•able**
**re•peal•er**
**re•peat**
**re•peat•abil•ity**
**re•peat•able**
**re•peat•ed**
**re•peat•ed•ly**
**re•peat•er**
**rep•echage** contest for runners-up
**re•pel** (**•pel•ling, •pelled**)
**re•pel•lence** (*or* **•len•cy**)
**re•pel•lent**
**re•pel•ler**
**re•pel•ling•ly**
**re•pel•ling•ness**
**re•pent**
**re•pent•ance**
**re•pent•ant**
**re•pent•er**
**re•peo•ple**
**re•per•cus•sion**
**re•per•cus•sive**
**rep•er•toire**
**rep•er•to•rial**
**rep•er•tory** (*plural* **•tories**)
**rep•etend** repeated digit
**ré•pé•ti•teur** opera-singer coach
**rep•eti•tion**
**rep•eti•tious**
**rep•eti•tious•ness**
**re•peti•tive**
**re•peti•tive•ness**
**re•phrase**
**re•pine**
**re•place**
**re•place•abil•ity**
**re•place•able**
**re•place•ment**
**re•plac•er**
**re•plan** (**•plan•ning, •planned**)
**re•plant**
**re•play**
**re•plen•ish**
**re•plen•ish•er**
**re•plen•ish•ment**
**re•plete**
**re•plete•ness**
**re•ple•tion**
**re•ple•tive**
**re•plevi•able** (*or* **•plev•is•able**)
**re•plev•in** legal term
**re•plevy** (*verb* **•plevies, •plevy•ing, •plev•ied;** *noun, plural* **•plevies**) legal term
**rep•li•ca**
**rep•li•cate**
**rep•li•ca•tion**
**rep•li•ca•tive**
**re•pli•er**
**re•ply** (*verb* **•plies, •ply•ing, •plied;** *noun, plural* **•plies**)
**re•point**
**re•pone** legal term
**re•port**
**re•port•able**
**re•port•age**
**re•port•ed•ly**
**re•port•er**
**re•pos•al**
**re•pose**
**re•pos•ed•ly**
**re•pose•ful**
**re•pose•ful•ly**
**re•pose•ful•ness**
**re•pos•er**
**re•pos•it** put away
**re•po•si•tion**
**re•posi•tory** (*plural* **•tories**)
**re•pos•sess**
**re•pos•ses•sion**
**re•pos•ses•sor**
**re•pot** (**•pot•ting, •pot•ted**)
**re•pous•sé** raised design
**repp** *variant spelling of* **rep**
**rep•re•hend**
**rep•re•hend•able**
**rep•re•hend•er**
**rep•re•hen•sibil•ity** (*or* **•sible•ness**)
**rep•re•hen•sible**
**rep•re•hen•sibly**

**rep•re•hen•sion**
**rep•re•hen•sive**
**rep•re•hen•sory**
**rep•re•sent** correspond to
**re-present** present again
**rep•re•sent•abil•ity**
**rep•re•sent•able**
**rep•re•sen•ta•tion**
**rep•re•sen•ta•tion•al**
**rep•re•sen•ta•tion•al•ism** philosophy term
**rep•re•sen•ta•tion•al•is•tic**
**rep•re•senta•tive**
**rep•re•senta•tive•ness**
**re•press** restrain
**re-press** press again
**re•press•er** (*or* **•pres•sor**)
**re•press•ible**
**re•pres•sion**
**re•pres•sive**
**re•pres•sive•ness**
**re•priev•able**
**re•prieve**
**re•priev•er**
**rep•ri•mand**
**rep•ri•mand•er**
**rep•ri•mand•ing•ly**
**re•print**
**re•print•er**
**re•pris•al**
**re•prise**
**re•pro** (*plural* **•pros**)
**re•proach**
**re•proach•able**
**re•proach•ably**
**re•proach•er**
**re•proach•ful**
**re•proach•ful•ly**
**re•proach•ful•ness**
**re•proach•ing•ly**
**rep•ro•ba•cy** (*or* **•bate•ness**)
**rep•ro•bate**
**rep•ro•bat•er**
**rep•ro•ba•tion**
**rep•ro•ba•tive** (*or* **•tion•ary**)
**re•pro•duce**
**re•pro•duc•er**
**re•pro•duc•ibil•ity**
**re•pro•duc•ible**
**re•pro•duc•tion**
**re•pro•duc•tive**
**re•pro•duc•tive•ness**
**rep•ro•graph•ic**
**re•prog•ra•phy**
**re•proof** rebuke
**re-proof** renew texture
**re•prov•able**
**re•prov•al**
**re•prove**
**re•prov•er**
**re•prov•ing•ly**
**re•pro•vi•sion**
**rep•tant**
**rep•tile**
**rep•til•ian**
**rep•ti•loid**
**re•pub•lic**
**Re•pub•li•can** political party
**re•pub•li•can** of a republic
**re•pub•li•can•ism**
**re•pub•li•cani•za•tion** (*or* **•sa•tion**)
**re•pub•li•can•ize** (*or* **•ise**)
**re•pub•li•ca•tion**
**re•pub•lish**
**re•pub•lish•able**
**re•pub•lish•er**
**re•pu•di•able**
**re•pu•di•ate**
**re•pu•dia•tion**
**re•pu•dia•tive**
**re•pu•dia•tor**
**re•pu•dia•tory**
**re•pugn** oppose
**re•pug•nance** (*or* **•nan•cy**; *plural* **•nances** *or* **•nan•cies**)
**re•pug•nant**
**re•pulse**
**re•puls•er**
**re•pul•sion**
**re•pul•sive**
**re•pul•sive•ness**
**repu•tabil•ity** (*or* **•table•ness**)
**repu•table**
**repu•tably**
**repu•ta•tion**
**re•pute**
**re•put•ed**
**re•put•ed•ly**
**re•quest**
**re•quest•er**
**requi•em**
**requi•es•cat** prayer
**re•quir•able**
**re•quire**
**re•quire•ment**
**re•quir•er**
**requi•site**
**requi•si•tion**
**requi•si•tion•ary**
**requi•si•tion•er** (*or* **•ist**)
**re•quit•able**
**re•quit•al**
**re•quite**
**re•quite•ment**
**re•quit•er**
**re•ra•dia•tion**
**re•read** (**•read•ing**, **•read**)
**rere•dos**
**rere•mouse** *Dialect* bat
**re•route** (**•route•ing** *or* **•rout•ing**, **•routed**)
**re•run** (**•run•ning**, **•ran**, **•run**)
**re•sal•able** (*or* **•sale•**)
**re•sale**
**re•scind**
**re•scind•able**
**re•scind•er**
**re•scind•ment**
**re•scis•sible** rescindable
**re•scis•sion**
**re•scis•sory** able to rescind
**re•script**
**res•cu•able**
**res•cue** (**•cu•ing**, **•cued**)
**res•cu•er**
**re•search**
**re•search•able**
**re•search•er**
**re•seat**
**re•seau** (*plural* **•seaux** *or* **•seaus**) lace mesh
**re•sect** remove surgically
**re•sec•tion**
**re•sec•tion•al**
**res•eda** plant
**re•sell** (**•sell•ing**, **•sold**)
**re•sem•blance**
**re•sem•blant**
**re•sem•ble**
**re•sem•bler**
**re•sent**
**re•sent•ful**
**re•sent•ful•ly**
**re•sent•ful•ness**
**re•sent•ment**
**re•ser•pine** drug
**re•serv•able**
**re-servable**
**res•er•va•tion**
**re•serve** set aside, etc.
**re-serve** serve again

**re•served**
**re•serv•ed•ly**
**re•serv•ed•ness**
**re•serv•er**
**re•serv•ist**
**res•er•voir**
**re•set** (**•set•ting, •set**)
**re•set•ter**
**re•set•tle**
**re•set•tle•ment**
**re•shape**
**re•ship** (**•ship•ping, •shipped**)
**re•ship•ment**
**Resht** *variant spelling of* **Rasht**
**re•shuf•fle**
**re•side**
**resi•dence**
**resi•den•cy** (*plural* **•cies**)
**resi•dent**
**resi•den•tial**
**resi•den•tiary** (*plural* **•tiaries**)
**resi•dent•ship**
**re•sid•er**
**re•sid•ual**
**re•sidu•ary**
**resi•due**
**re•sid•uum** (*plural* **•sidua**)
**re•sign** give up
**re-sign** sign again
**res•ig•na•tion**
**re•signed**
**re•sign•ed•ly**
**re•sign•ed•ness**
**re•sign•er**
**re•sile** spring back
**re•sile•ment**
**re•sili•ence** (*or* **•en•cy**)
**re•sili•ent**
**res•in** gumlike substance; *compare* **rosin**
**res•in•ate**
**res•in•if•er•ous**
**res•in•oid**
**res•in•ous**
**res•in•ous•ness**
**resi•pis•cence** acknowledgment of error
**re•sist**
**Re•sist•ance** French organization
**re•sist•ance**
**re•sist•ant** (*or* **•sis•tive**)
**Re•sis•ten•cia** Argentine city
**re•sist•er** opposer; *compare* **resistor**
**re•sist•ibil•ity** (*or* **•ible•ness**)
**re•sist•ible**
**re•sist•ibly**
**re•sist•ing•ly**
**re•sis•tive•ness** (*or* **•tiv•ity**)
**re•sis•tiv•ity** electrical property
**re•sist•less**
**re•sis•tor** electrical component; *compare* **resister**
**re•sit** (**•sit•ting, •sat**)
**res•na•tron** electronic valve
**re•sole**
**re•sol•ubil•ity** (*or* **•uble•ness**)
**re•sol•uble** resolvable
**re-soluble** able to be dissolved again
**reso•lute**
**reso•lute•ness**
**reso•lu•tion**
**reso•lu•tion•er** (*or* **•ist**)
**re•solv•abil•ity** (*or* **•able•ness**)
**re•solv•able**
**re•solve**
**re•solved**
**re•solv•ed•ness**
**re•sol•vent**
**re•solv•er**
**reso•nance**
**reso•nant**
**reso•nate**
**reso•na•tion**
**reso•na•tor**
**re•sorb**
**re•sorb•ent**
**res•or•cin•ol** chemical compound
**re•sorp•tion**
**re•sorp•tive**
**re•sort** holiday town; to use
**re-sort** sort again
**re•sort•er**
**re•sound** echo
**re-sound** sound again
**re•sound**
**re•sound•ing**
**re•sound•ing•ly**
**re•source**
**re•source•ful**
**re•source•ful•ly**
**re•source•ful•ness**
**re•source•less**
**re•spect**
**re•spect•abil•ity** (*plural* **•ities**)
**re•spect•able**
**re•spect•ably**
**re•spect•er**
**re•spect•ful**
**re•spect•ful•ly**
**re•spect•ful•ness**
**re•spect•ing**
**re•spec•tive**
**re•spec•tive•ly**
**re•spir•abil•ity**
**res•pir•able**
**res•pi•ra•tion**
**res•pi•ra•tion•al**
**res•pi•ra•tor**
**re•spira•tory**
**re•spire**
**res•pite**
**re•splend•ence** (*or* **•en•cy**)
**re•splend•ent**
**re•spond**
**re•spond•ence** (*or* **•en•cy**)
**re•spond•ent** legal term
**re•spond•er**
**re•sponse**
**re•spons•er** (*or* **•spon•sor**) radio receiver
**re•spon•sibil•ity** (*plural* **•ities**)
**re•spon•sible**
**re•spon•sible•ness**
**re•spon•sibly**
**re•spon•sive**
**re•spon•sive•ly**
**re•spon•sive•ness**
**re•spon•so•ry** (*plural* **•ries**)
**re•spray**
**res pu•bli•ca** *Latin* the state
**rest**
**re•state**
**re•state•ment**
**res•tau•rant**
**res•tau•ra•teur**
**rest•er**
**rest•ful**
**rest•ful•ly**
**rest•ful•ness**
**rest•harrow** plant
**res•ti•form**
**rest•ing**

**res•ti•tu•tion**
**res•ti•tu•tive** (*or* **•tory**)
**res•tive**
**res•tive•ly**
**res•tive•ness**
**rest•less**
**rest•less•ly**
**rest•less•ness**
**re•stock**
**re•stor•able**
**Res•to•ra•tion** historical period
**res•to•ra•tion**
**res•to•ra•tion•ism** theological belief
**re•stora•tive**
**re•store**
**re•stor•er**
**re•strain**
**re•strain•able**
**re•strain•ed•ly**
**re•strain•er**
**re•strain•ing•ly**
**re•straint**
**re•strict**
**re•strict•ed•ly**
**re•strict•ed•ness**
**re•stric•tion**
**re•stric•tion•ist**
**re•stric•tive**
**re•stric•tive•ly**
**re•stric•tive•ness**
**re•struc•ture**
**re•style**
**re•sult**
**re•sult•ant**
**re•sum•able**
**re•sume** restart
**ré•su•mé** summary
**re•sump•tion**
**re•sump•tive**
**re•su•pi•nate** botany term
**re•su•pi•na•tion**
**re•sur•face**
**re•surge**
**re•sur•gence**
**re•sur•gent**
**res•ur•rect**
**Res•ur•rec•tion** rising of Christ
**res•ur•rec•tion** revival
**res•ur•rec•tion•al**
**res•ur•rec•tion•ary**
**res•ur•rec•tion•ism**
**res•ur•rec•tion•ist**
**re•sus•ci•table**
**re•sus•ci•tate**
**re•sus•ci•ta•tion**
**re•sus•ci•ta•tive**
**re•sus•ci•ta•tor**
**ret** (**ret•ting, ret•ted**) soak fibre
**re•ta•ble** altar screen
**re•tail**
**re•tail•er**
**re•tain**
**re•tain•abil•ity** (*or* **•able•ness**)
**re•tain•able**
**re•tain•er**
**re•tain•ment**
**re•take** (**•tak•ing, •took, •tak•en**)
**re•tak•er**
**re•tali•ate**
**re•talia•tion**
**re•talia•tive** (*or* **•tory**)
**re•talia•tor**
**re•tard**
**re•tard•ant**
**re•tard•ate** retarded person
**re•tar•da•tion** (*or* **•tard•ment**)
**re•tarda•tive** (*or* **•tory**)
**re•tard•ed**
**re•tard•er**
**re•tard•ing•ly**
**retch** vomit; *compare* **wretch**
**rete** (*plural* **re•tia**) anatomy term
**re•tell** (**•tell•ing, •told**)
**re•tene** chemical compound
**re•ten•tion**
**re•ten•tive**
**re•ten•tive•ly**
**re•ten•tive•ness**
**re•ten•tiv•ity**
**re•think** (**•think•ing, •thought**)
**re•tial** of a rete
**re•ti•ar•ius** (*plural* **•arii**) gladiator
**reti•cence**
**reti•cent**
**reti•cle** (*or* **•cule**) grid; *compare* **reticule**
**re•ticu•lar**
**re•ticu•late**
**re•ticu•la•tion**
**reti•cule** woman's bag; *variant of* **reticle**
**re•ticu•lo•cyte**
**re•ticu•lo•en•do•the•lial** anatomy term
**re•ticu•lum** (*plural* **•la**) network; cow's stomach
**reti•na** (*plural* **•nas** *or* **•nae**)
**reti•nacu•lar**
**reti•nacu•lum** (*plural* **•la**) biology term
**reti•nal**
**reti•nene** biochemical compound
**reti•nite** resin
**reti•ni•tis**
**reti•nol** biochemical compound
**reti•no•scop•ic**
**reti•no•scopi•cal•ly**
**reti•nos•co•pist**
**reti•nos•co•py** ophthalmic procedure
**reti•nue**
**reti•nued**
**re•tire**
**re•tire•ment**
**re•tir•er**
**re•tir•ing**
**re•tir•ing•ly**
**re•tool**
**re•tor•sion** reprisal
**re•tort**
**re•tort•er**
**re•tor•tion** retorting
**re•touch**
**re•touch•able**
**re•touch•er**
**re•trace**
**re•trace•able**
**re•trace•ment**
**re•tract**
**re•tract•abil•ity** (*or* **•ibil•**)
**re•tract•able** (*or* **•ible**)
**re•trac•tile**
**re•trac•til•ity**
**re•trac•tion**
**re•trac•tive**
**re•trac•tor**
**re•train**
**re•tread** (**•tread•ing, •tread•ed**) remould
**re-tread** (**-tread•ing, -trod, -trod•den** *or* **-trod**) tread again

**re•treat**
**re•treat•al**
**re•trench**
**re•trench•able**
**re•trench•ment**
**re•tri•al**
**ret•ri•bu•tion**
**re•tribu•tive** (*or* **•tory)**
**re•tribu•tive•ly**
**re•triev•abil•ity**
**re•triev•able**
**re•triev•ably**
**re•triev•al**
**re•trieve**
**re•triev•er**
**ret•ro** (*plural* **•ros)** *Slang* retrorocket
**retro•act**
**retro•ac•tion**
**retro•ac•tive**
**retro•ac•tive•ly**
**retro•ac•tiv•ity** (*or* **•tive•ness)**
**retro•cede** give back
**retro•ces•sion** (*or* **•ced•ence)**
**retro•ces•sive** (*or* **•ced•ent)**
**retro•choir** space behind altar
**retro•fire**
**retro•fit** (**•fit•ting, •fit•ted**) equip with extra parts
**retro•flex** (*or* **•flexed)**
**retro•flex•ion** (*or* **•flec•tion)**
**retro•gra•da•tion**
**retro•gra•da•tory**
**retro•grade**
**retro•gress**
**retro•gres•sion**
**retro•gres•sive**
**retro•gres•sive•ly**
**retro•ject** throw backwards
**retro•len•tal** anatomy term
**retro-operative**
**retro•pack**
**retro•rock•et**
**re•trorse** pointing backwards
**retro•spect**
**retro•spec•tion**
**retro•spec•tive**
**retro•spec•tive•ly**
**retro•spec•tive•ness**
**re•trous•sé**
**retro•verse**
**retro•ver•sion**
**retro•vert•ed**
**re•try** (**•tries, •try•ing, •tried)**
**ret•si•na**
**re•tune**
**re•tuner**
**re•turn**
**re•turn•abil•ity**
**re•turn•able**
**re•turn•er**
**re•tuse** botany term
**re•type**
**re•uni•fi•ca•tion**
**re•uni•fy** (**•fies, •fy•ing, •fied)**
**Réu•nion** French island
**re•union**
**re•union•ism**
**re•union•ist**
**re•union•is•tic**
**re•unit•able**
**re•unite**
**re•unit•er**
**re•up•hol•ster**
**re•us•abil•ity** (*or* **•able•ness)**
**re•us•able**
**re•use**
**re•uti•li•za•tion** (*or* **•sa•tion)**
**re•uti•lize** (*or* **•lise)**
**rev** (**rev•ving, revved)**
**re•val•ori•za•tion** (*or* **•sa•tion)**
**re•val•or•ize** (*or* **•ise)** revalue
**re•valua•tion**
**re•value** (**•valu•ing, •valued)**
**re•vamp**
**re•vamp•er**
**re•vamp•ing**
**re•vanch•ism** foreign policy
**re•vanch•ist**
**re•veal**
**re•veal•abil•ity**
**re•veal•able**
**re•veal•ed•ly**
**re•veal•er**
**re•veal•ing**
**re•veal•ing•ly**
**re•veal•ment**
**re•veg•etate** grow again
**re•veg•eta•tion**
**re•veil•le**
**rev•el** (**•el•ling, •elled;** *US* **•el•ing, •eled)**
**rev•ela•tion**
**rev•ela•tion•al**
**rev•ela•tion•ist** believer in divine revelation
**rev•el•ler** (*US* **•el•er)**
**rev•el•ment**
**rev•el•rous**
**rev•el•ry** (*plural* **•ries)**
**rev•enant**
**re•venge**
**re•venge•ful**
**re•venge•ful•ly**
**re•veng•er**
**re•veng•ing•ly**
**rev•enue**
**rev•enued**
**rev•enu•er** *US* revenue officer
**re•ver•able**
**re•ver•ber•ant**
**re•ver•ber•ate**
**re•ver•bera•tion**
**re•ver•bera•tive**
**re•ver•bera•tor**
**re•ver•bera•tory** (*plural* **•tories)**
**re•vere**
**rev•er•ence**
**rev•er•enc•er**
**rev•er•end** deserving reverence; clergyman
**rev•er•ent** feeling reverence
**rev•er•en•tial** showing reverence; *compare* **referential**
**rev•er•en•tial•ly**
**rev•er•ent•ly**
**rev•er•ent•ness**
**re•ver•er**
**rev•erie** (*or* **•ery;** *plural* **•eries)**
**re•vers** (*plural* **•vers)** lapel
**re•ver•sal**
**re•verse**
**re•vers•er**
**re•ver•si** board game
**re•vers•ibil•ity** (*or* **•ible•ness)**
**re•vers•ible**
**re•vers•ibly**
**re•ver•sion**
**re•ver•sion•ary** (*or* **•al)**
**re•ver•sion•er** legal term
**re•vert**
**re•vert•er**
**re•vert•ible**

**re•ver•tive**
**re•vest** restore power
**re•vet** (**•vet•ting, •vet•ted**) face with stones
**re•vet•ment**
**re•view** survey; critical opinion; *compare* **revue**
**re•view•able**
**re•view•al**
**re•view•er**
**re•vile**
**re•vile•ment**
**re•vil•er**
**re•vil•ing•ly**
**re•vis•abil•ity**
**re•vis•able**
**re•vis•al**
**re•vise**
**re•vis•er** (*or* **•or**)
**re•vi•sion**
**re•vi•sion•al** (*or* **•ary**)
**re•vi•sion•ism**
**re•vi•sion•ist**
**re•vi•so•ry**
**re•vi•tali•za•tion** (*or* **•sa•tion**)
**re•vi•tal•ize** (*or* **•ise**)
**re•viv•abil•ity**
**re•viv•able**
**re•viv•ably**
**re•viv•al**
**re•viv•al•ism**
**re•viv•al•ist**
**re•viv•al•is•tic**
**re•vive**
**re•viv•er**
**re•vivi•fi•ca•tion**
**re•vivi•fy** (**•fies, •fy•ing, •fied**)
**re•viv•ing•ly**
**revi•vis•cence** revival
**revi•vis•cent**
**revo•cabil•ity** (*or* **•cable•ness**)
**revo•cable** (*or* **re•vok•able**)
**revo•cably**
**revo•ca•tion**
**re•voca•tive** (*or* **revo•ca•tory**)
**re•voice**
**re•vok•able** *variant spelling of* **revocable**
**re•voke**
**re•vok•er**
**re•vok•ing•ly**
**re•volt**
**re•volt•er**
**re•volt•ing**
**re•volt•ing•ly**
**revo•lute** botany term
**revo•lu•tion**
**revo•lu•tion•ari•ly**
**revo•lu•tion•ary** (*plural* **•aries**)
**revo•lu•tion•ist**
**revo•lu•tion•ize** (*or* **•ise**)
**revo•lu•tion•iz•er** (*or* **•is•er**)
**re•volv•able**
**re•volve**
**re•volv•er**
**re•volv•ing**
**re•volv•ing•ly**
**re•vue** entertainment; *compare* **review**
**re•vul•sion**
**re•vul•sion•ary**
**re•vul•sive**
**re•ward**
**re•ward•able**
**re•ward•er**
**re•ward•ing**
**re•wind** (**•wind•ing, •wound**)
**re•wind•er**
**re•wir•able**
**re•wire**
**re•word**
**re•work**
**re•write** (**•writ•ing, •wrote, •writ•ten**)
**Rex** the king
**Rey•kja•vik** Icelandic capital
**Rey•no•sa** Mexican city
**rhab•do•man•cy** water divining
**rhab•do•man•tist** (*or* **•man•cer**)
**rhab•do•myo•ma** (*plural* **•mas** *or* **•ma•ta**) tumour
**Rhae•tia** Roman province
**Rhae•tian**
**Rhae•tic** (*or* **Rhe•tic**) geology term
**rham•na•ceous** botany term
**rhap•sod•ic**
**rhap•sodi•cal•ly**
**rhap•so•dist**
**rhap•so•dis•tic**
**rhap•so•dize** (*or* **•dise**)
**rhap•so•dy** (*plural* **•dies**)
**rhata•ny** (*plural* **•nies**) shrub
**rhea** bird
**rhe•bok** (*or* **ree•**; *plural* **•boks** *or* **•bok**) antelope
**Rheims** *variant spelling of* **Reims**
**Rhe•mish** of Reims
**Rhen•ish** of the Rhine
**rhe•nium** chemical element
**rheo•base** physiology term
**rheo•logi•cal**
**rhe•olo•gist**
**rhe•ol•ogy** branch of physics
**rhe•om•eter**
**rheo•met•ric**
**rhe•om•etry**
**rheo•stat**
**rheo•stat•ic**
**rheo•tac•tic**
**rheo•tax•is** biology term
**rheo•trop•ic**
**rhe•ot•ro•pism** botany term
**rhe•sus**
**rhe•tor** teacher of rhetoric
**rheto•ric**
**rhe•tori•cal**
**rhe•tori•cal•ly**
**rhe•tori•cian**
**rheum**
**rheu•mat•ic**
**rheu•mati•cal•ly**
**rheu•mat•ics**
**rheu•ma•tism**
**rheu•ma•toid** (*or* **•toi•dal**)
**rheu•ma•tolo•gist**
**rheu•ma•tol•ogy**
**rheumy**
**Rheydt** German town
**rhigo•lene** anaesthetic
**rhi•nal** of the nose
**Rhine**
**Rhine•land**
**Rhineland-Palati•nate** German state
**rhi•nen•cephal•ic**
**rhi•nen•cepha•lon** (*plural* **•lons** *or* **•la**) anatomy term
**rhine•stone**
**rhi•ni•tis**
**rhi•no** (*plural* **•nos** *or* **•no**)
**rhi•noc•er•os** (*plural* **•oses** *or* **•os**)
**rhi•no•cerot•ic**
**rhi•no•logi•cal**

**rhi•nolo•gist**
**rhi•nol•ogy** branch of medicine
**rhi•no•plas•tic**
**rhi•no•plas•ty** plastic surgery of nose
**rhi•no•scop•ic**
**rhi•nos•co•py**
**rhi•zo•bium** (*plural* **•bia**) bacterium
**rhi•zo•car•pous** botany term
**rhi•zo•cepha•lan** zoology term
**rhi•zo•cepha•lous**
**rhi•zo•gen•ic** (*or* **•zo•genet•ic, •zog•enous)**
**rhi•zoid** rootlike part
**rhi•zoi•dal**
**rhi•zoma•tous**
**rhi•zome**
**rhi•zo•morph**
**rhi•zo•mor•phous**
**rhi•zo•pod** protozoan
**rhi•zopo•dan**
**rhi•zopo•dous**
**rhi•zo•pus** fungus
**rhi•zo•sphere**
**rhi•zoto•my** (*plural* **•mies**) surgery
**rho** Greek letter
**rho•da•mine** dye
**Rhode Is•land**
**Rhodes**
**Rho•desia**
**Rho•desian**
**Rho•dian** of Rhodes
**rho•dic**
**rho•di•nal** oil
**rho•dium** chemical element
**rho•do•chro•site** mineral
**rho•do•den•dron**
**rhodo•lite** gemstone
**rhodo•nite** mineral
**rho•dop•sin** retinal pigment
**rhomb** rhombus; *compare* **rhumb**
**rhom•ben•cepha•lon** anatomy term
**rhom•bic** (*or* **•bi•cal)**
**rhom•bo•he•dral**
**rhom•bo•he•dron** (*plural* **•drons** *or* **•dra)**
**rhom•boid**
**rhom•boi•dal**
**rhom•bus** (*plural* **•buses** *or* **•bi)** geometric figure
**rhon•chal** (*or* **•chial)**
**rhon•chus** (*plural* **•chi)** breathing sound
**Rhon•dda**
**Rhône**
**rho•ta•cism** phonetics term
**rho•ta•cist**
**rho•ta•cis•tic**
**rho•tic**
**rhu•barb**
**rhumb** navigation term; *compare* **rhomb; rum**
**rhum•ba** *variant spelling of* **rumba**
**rhum•ba•tron**
**rhyme** identical-sounding word; verse; *compare* **rime**
**rhyme•ster** (*or* **rhym•er)**
**rhyn•cho•cephal•ian** zoology term
**rhyo•lite** rock
**rhyo•lit•ic**
**rhythm**
**rhyth•mic** (*or* **•mi•cal)**
**rhyth•mi•cal•ly**
**rhyth•mic•ity**
**rhyth•mics**
**rhy•ton** (*plural* **•ta)** drinking vessel
**ria** inlet
**rial** currency
**Ri•al•to** Venetian island
**ri•al•to** (*plural* **•tos)** market
**ria•ta** (*or* **rea•ta)** lasso
**rib (rib•bing, ribbed)**
**rib•ald**
**rib•ald•ry**
**rib•and** (*or* **rib•band)** award
**Rib•ble** English river
**rib•bon**
**ribbon•fish** (*plural* **•fish** *or* **•fishes)**
**ribbon•wood**
**Ri•bei•rão Pré•to** Brazilian city
**ri•bo•fla•vin** (*or* **•vine)** vitamin
**ri•bo•nu•clease** enzyme
**ri•bo•nu•cleic acid**
**ri•bose** sugar
**ri•bo•so•mal**
**ri•bo•some** part of cell
**rib•wort**
**rice**
**rice•bird**
**ric•er** *US* sieve
**ri•cer•ca•re** (*or* **ri•cer•car;** *plural* **•ca•ri** *or* **•cars)** musical term
**rich**
**riches**
**Rich•mond**
**rich•ness**
**Richter scale**
**ri•cin** protein
**ric•ino•leic acid**
**rick**
**rick•eti•ness**
**rick•ets**
**rick•ett•sia** (*plural* **•siae** *or* **•sias)** pathogenic microorganism
**rick•ett•sial**
**rick•ety**
**rick•rack** (*or* **ric•rac)** braid
**rick•shaw** (*or* **•sha)**
**rico•chet (•chet•ing, •chet•ed** *or* **•chet•ting, •chet•ted)**
**ri•cot•ta** cheese
**ric•tal**
**ric•tus** (*plural* **•tus** *or* **•tuses)** gape
**rid (rid•ding, rid** *or* **rid•ded)**
**rid•able** (*or* **ride•)**
**rid•dance**
**rid•den**
**rid•der**
**rid•dle**
**rid•dler**
**ride (rid•ing, rode, rid•den)**
**ride•able** *variant spelling of* **ridable**
**rid•er**
**rid•er•less**
**ridge**
**ridge•ling** (*or* **ridg•ling, rid•gel)** veterinary term
**ridge•pole** (*or* **•tree)** roof timber
**ridge•way**
**ridgy**
**ridi•cule**
**ridi•cul•er**
**ri•dicu•lous**
**ri•dicu•lous•ly**
**ri•dicu•lous•ness**
**rid•ing**

**ri•dot•to** (*plural* **•tos**) musical entertainment
**ries•ling** wine
**Rif** (*or* **Riff**; *plural* **Rifs, Riffs, Rifis** *or* **Rif, Riff**) Moroccan people
**rife**
**rife•ness**
**riff** jazz term
**rif•fle**
**rif•fler**
**riff•raff**
**ri•fle**
**rifle•bird**
**rifle•man** (*plural* **•men**)
**ri•fler**
**ri•fle•ry**
**ri•fling**
**rift**
**rig** (**rig•ging, rigged**)
**Riga** Latvian port
**riga•doon** (*or* **ri•gau•don**) dance
**ri•ga•to•ni** pasta
**rig•ger**
**rig•ging**
**right**
**right•able**
**right-angled**
**right•en**
**right•eous**
**right•eous•ly**
**right•eous•ness**
**right•er**
**right•ful**
**right•ful•ly**
**right•ful•ness**
**right-hand** (*adj*)
**right-handed**
**right-handed•ness**
**right-hander**
**right•ish**
**right•ism**
**right•ist**
**right•ly**
**right-minded**
**right-minded•ly**
**right-minded•ness**
**right•ness**
**right•ward** (*adj*)
**right•wards** (*adv*)
**right-winger**
**rig•id**
**ri•gidi•fy** (**•fy•ing, •fied**)
**ri•gid•ity** (*or* **•ness**)
**rig•id•ly**
**rig•ma•role** (*or* **riga•**)
**ri•gor** medical term; *compare* **rigour**
**rig•or** *US spelling of* **rigour**
**rig•or•ism**
**rig•or•ist**
**rig•or•is•tic**
**rig•or mor•tis**
**rig•or•ous**
**rig•or•ous•ly**
**rig•or•ous•ness**
**rig•our** (*US* **•or**) harshness; *compare* **rigor**
**Rig-Veda** Hindu poetry
**Ri•je•ka** Croatian port
**Rijks•museum**
**rile**
**rill** stream; channel
**rill** (*or* **rille**) moon valley
**ril•let**
**rim** (**rim•ming, rimmed**)
**rime** frost; *less common spelling of* **rhyme**
**rim-fire**
**Ri•mi•ni**
**rimmed**
**rim•ming**
**ri•mose** botany term
**ri•mos•ity**
**rim•rock**
**rimy** (**rimi•er, rimi•est**)
**rind**
**rinder•pest**
**ring** (**ring•ing, rang, rung**) produce sound
**ring** (**ring•ing, ringed**) circular band; to encircle
**ring•bolt**
**ring•bone**
**ring•dove**
**ring-dyke**
**rin•gent** botany term
**ring•er**
**ring•git** Malaysian currency
**ring•hals** (*plural* **•hals** *or* **•halses**) snake
**ring•ing**
**ring•leader**
**ring•let**
**ring•master**
**ring-necked**
**ring•side**
**ring•tail** animal
**ring-tailed**
**ring•worm**
**rink**
**rins•abil•ity** (*or* **•ibil•ity**)
**rins•able** (*or* **•ible**)
**rinse**
**rins•er**
**Rio de Ja•nei•ro**
**Rio Grande**
**Rio Gran•de do Nor•te** Brazilian state
**Rio Gran•de do Sul** Brazilian state
**riot**
**ri•ot•er**
**ri•ot•ous**
**ri•ot•ous•ly**
**ri•ot•ous•ness**
**rip** (**rip•ping, ripped**)
**ri•par•ian** of a river bank
**rip•cord**
**ripe**
**ripe•ly**
**rip•en**
**rip•en•er**
**ripe•ness**
**ri•pieno** (*plural* **•pienos**) musical term
**rip-off** (*noun*)
**Rip•on**
**ri•poste** (*or* **•post**)
**rip•pable**
**ripped**
**rip•per**
**rip•ping**
**rip•ple**
**rip•pler**
**rip•plet**
**rip•pling•ly**
**rip•ply**
**rip-roaring**
**rip•saw**
**rip•snorter**
**rip•tide**
**rise** (**ris•ing, rose, ris•en**)
**ris•er**
**ris•ibil•ity** (*plural* **•ities**)
**ris•ible** laughable
**ris•ibly**
**ris•ing**
**risk**
**risk•er**
**risk•ily**
**riski•ness**

**risky** (**riski•er, riski•est**) involving risk; *compare* **risqué**
**Ri•sor•gi•men•to** political movement
**ri•sot•to** (*plural* **•tos**)
**ris•qué** improper; *compare* **risky**
**Riss** glaciation
**ris•sole**
**ri•tar•dan•do** musical term
**rite**
**ri•tenu•to** musical term
**ri•tor•nel•lo** musical term
**ritu•al**
**ritu•al•ism**
**ritu•al•ist**
**ritu•al•is•tic**
**ritu•al•is•ti•cal•ly**
**ritu•al•ize** (*or* **•ise**)
**ritu•al•ly**
**ritzy** (**ritzi•er, ritzi•est**)
**ri•val** (**•val•ling, •valled;** *US* **•val•ing •valed**)
**ri•val•rous**
**ri•val•ry** (*plural* **•ries**)
**rive** (**riv•ing, rived, rived** *or* **riv•en**)
**riv•er**
**river•bed**
**river•head**
**riv•er•ine**
**River•side** US city
**river•side**
**riv•et**
**riv•et•er**
**Rivi•era**
**ri•vi•ère** necklace
**rivu•let**
**rix-dollar**
**Ri•yadh** Saudi Arabian capital
**ri•yal** currency
**roach** nautical term; *Slang* cockroach
**roach** (*plural* **roach** *or* **roaches**) fish
**road**
**road•bed**
**road•block**
**road•holding**
**road•house**
**road•roller**
**road•runner** bird
**road•stead**
**road•ster**
**road•way**
**road•work** sports training
**road•works** road repairs
**road•worthi•ness**
**road•worthy**
**roam**
**roam•er**
**roan**
**Roa•noke** US island
**roar**
**roar•er**
**roar•ing**
**roast**
**roast•er**
**roast•ing**
**rob** (**rob•bing, robbed**)
**roba•lo** (*plural* **•los** *or* **•lo**) fish
**rob•and** (*or* **rob•bin**) nautical term
**rob•ber**
**rob•bery** (*plural* **•beries**)
**rob•bin** *variant of* **roband**; *compare* **robin**
**rob•bing**
**robe**
**rob•in** bird; *compare* **robbin**
**ro•binia** tree
**ro•ble** oak
**ro•bor•ant** fortifying
**ro•bot**
**ro•bot•ics**
**ro•bot•ism** (*or* **•bot•ry**)
**ro•bust**
**ro•bust•ness**
**roc** legendary bird; *compare* **rock**
**ro•caille** decorative work
**roc•am•bole** plant
**Roch•dale** Lancashire town
**Roch•es•ter** Kent city; US city
**roch•et** bishop's surplice
**rock** hard mass; sway; *compare* **roc**
**rocka•bil•ly**
**rock-and-roll** (*or* **rock-'n'-roll**)
**rock-and-roller** (*or* **rock-'n'-roller**)
**rock-bottom** (*adj*)
**rock-bound**
**rock•er**
**rock•ery** (*plural* **•eries**)
**rock•et**
**rock•et•eer** (*or* **•er**) rocket engineer
**rock•et•ry**
**rock•fish** (*plural* **•fish** *or* **•fishes**)
**Rock•ford** US city
**Rockies** Rocky Mountains
**rocki•ly**
**rocki•ness**
**rock•like**
**rock•ling** (*plural* **•lings** *or* **•ling**) fish
**rock•oon** exploratory rocket
**rock•rose**
**rock•shaft**
**rock•weed**
**rocky** (**rocki•er, rocki•est**)
**Rocky Moun•tains**
**ro•co•co**
**rod**
**rode**
**ro•dent**
**ro•denti•cide**
**ro•deo** (*plural* **•deos**)
**rod•like**
**rodo•mon•tade** boastful talk
**roe** fish ovary or testis; deer; *compare* **row**
**roe•buck** (*plural* **•bucks** *or* **•buck**)
**roent•gen** (*or* **rönt•**) radiation unit
**roent•geno•gram** (*or* **•graph, rönt•**) *US* X-ray photograph
**roent•gen•ol•ogy** (*or* **rönt•**) radiology
**ro•ga•tion**
**roga•tory**
**rog•er**
**rogue**
**ro•guery** (*plural* **•gueries**)
**ro•guish**
**ro•guish•ly**
**ro•guish•ness**
**roil**
**roily** (**roili•er, roili•est**) cloudy
**rois•ter**
**roist•er•er**
**roist•er•ous**
**role** (*or* **rôle**)
**role-playing**
**roll**

**roll•away** mounted on rollers
**roll•bar**
**roll•er**
**rol•lick**
**rol•lick•ing**
**rol•lick•some** (*or* **•licky**)
**roll•ing**
**roll•mop**
**roll•neck**
**roll-on** (*noun, adj*)
**Rolls Royce** (*Trademark*)
**roll-top**
**roll•way**
**roly-poly** (*plural* **-polies**)
**Rom** (*plural* **Roma**) male gipsy
**Ro•ma•gna** Italian region
**Ro•ma•ic** language
**ro•maine** *US* cos lettuce
**ro•ma•ji** alphabet
**Ro•man** of Rome
**ro•man** type style
**Ro•mance** language
**ro•mance** love affair
**Roma•nes** Romany language
**Ro•man•esque** art style
**Ro•ma•nia** (*or* **Ru•**)
**Ro•ma•nian** (*or* **Ru•**)
**Ro•man•ism** Roman Catholicism
**Ro•man•ist**
**Ro•man•ize** (*or* **•ise**)
**Ro•ma•no** cheese
**Romanov** Russian dynasty
**Ro•mansch** (*or* **•mansh**) Swiss language
**ro•man•tic**
**ro•man•ti•cal•ly**
**ro•man•ti•cism**
**ro•man•ti•cist**
**ro•man•ti•ci•za•tion** (*or* **•sa•tion**)
**ro•man•ti•cize** (*or* **•cise**)
**Roma•ny** (*or* **Rom•ma•ny**; *plural* **•nies**)
**Rome**
**Romeo** (*plural* **Romeos**)
**romp**
**romp•er**
**romp•ers** baby garment
**romp•ing•ly**
**ron•deau** (*plural* **•deaux**) poem; *compare* **rondo**
**ron•del** (*or* **roun•del**) poem
**ron•delet** poem
**ron•do** (*plural* **•dos**) musical work; *compare* **rondeau**
**ron•dure** curvature
**rone** *Scot* drainpipe
**Ro•neo** (*Trademark*; *verb* **•neos, •neo•ing, •neod**; *noun, plural* **•neos**)
**rong•geng** Malay dance
**rönt•gen** *variant spelling of* **roentgen**
**roo** *Austral* kangaroo
**rood**
**Roo•depoort** South African city
**roof** (*plural* **roofs**)
**roof•ing**
**roof•less**
**roof•tree**
**rook**
**rook•ery** (*plural* **•eries**)
**rookie** *Slang* new recruit
**room**
**room•er**
**room•ette** *US* rail sleeper
**room•ful** (*plural* **•fuls**)
**roomi•ly**
**roomi•ness**
**room•mate**
**roomy** (**roomi•er, roomi•est**)
**roor•back** *US* false report
**roose** *Dialect* to praise
**roost**
**roost•er**
**root**
**root•age**
**root•er**
**rooti•ness**
**root•le**
**root•less**
**root•let**
**root•like**
**root•stock**
**rooty**
**rop•able** (*or* **rope•**)
**rope**
**rope•walk**
**ropi•ly**
**ropi•ness**
**ropy** (**ropi•er, ropi•est**)
**roque** US game
**Roque•fort** cheese
**roque•laure** cloak
**ro•quet** croquet term
**ror•qual** whale
**Rorschach test**
**rort** *Austral* party
**rorty**
**ros•ace** rose window
**ro•sa•ceous** botany term
**ro•sani•line** (*or* **•lin**) dye
**ro•sar•ian** rose grower
**Ro•sa•rio** Argentine port
**ro•sar•ium** (*plural* **•sar•iums** *or* **•saria**) rose garden
**ro•sary** (*plural* **•saries**) prayer beads; *compare* **rosery**
**Ros•com•mon** Irish county
**rosé** wine
**rose**
**ro•seate**
**Ros•eau** capital of Dominica
**rose•bay** plant
**rose•bud**
**rose•bush**
**rose•fish** (*plural* **•fish** *or* **•fishes**)
**rose•hip**
**ro•sel•la** parrot
**ro•sema•ling** decoration
**rose•mary** (*plural* **•maries**)
**ro•seo•la** skin rash
**ro•seo•lar**
**rose-root** plant
**ro•sery** (*plural* **•series**) rose garden; *compare* **rosary**
**Ro•set•ta** Egyptian town
**ro•sette**
**rose•wood**
**Rosh Ha•sha•nah** (*or* **Rosh Ha•sha•na**) Jewish New Year
**Ro•si•cru•cian**
**Ro•si•cru•cian•ism**
**rosi•ly**
**ros•in** type of resin
**Ros•in•ante** old horse
**rosi•ness**
**rosin•weed**
**ros•iny**
**ros•tel•late** (*or* **•lar**)
**ros•tel•lum** (*plural* **•la**) biology term
**ros•ter**
**Ros•tock** German port
**Ros•tov** Russian port
**ros•tral** (*or* **•trate, •trat•ed**)

**ros•trum** (*plural* **•trums** *or* **•tra**)
**rosy** (**rosi•er, rosi•est**)
**rot** (**rot•ting, rot•ted**)
**rota**
**Ro•ta•me•ter** (*Trademark*)
**Ro•tar•ian**
**Ro•ta•ry** association
**ro•ta•ry** (*plural* **•ries**)
**ro•tat•able**
**ro•tate**
**ro•ta•tion**
**ro•ta•tion•al**
**ro•ta•tive**
**ro•ta•tor**
**ro•ta•tory**
**rote**
**ro•tenone** insecticide
**rot•gut**
**Roth•er•ham** Yorkshire town
**Rothe•say** Scottish town
**roti** bread
**ro•ti•fer** minute organism
**ro•tif•er•al** (*or* **•ous**)
**ro•tis•serie**
**rotl** (*plural* **rotls** *or* **ar•tal**) unit of weight
**ro•to•gra•vure** printing process
**ro•tor**
**Ro•to•rua** New Zealand city
**rot•ted**
**rot•ten**
**rot•ten•ly**
**rot•ten•ness**
**rotten•stone**
**rot•ter**
**Rot•ter•dam**
**rot•ting**
**Rott•wei•ler** dog
**ro•tund** stout; *compare* **orotund**
**ro•tun•da** building
**ro•tun•dity** (*or* **•tund•ness**)
**Rou•baix** French city
**rou•ble** (*or* **ru•**)
**rouche** *variant spelling of* **ruche**
**roué**
**Rou•en** French city
**rouge**
**rouge et noir** card game
**rough**
**rough•age**
**rough-and-readi•ness**
**rough-and-ready**
**rough-and-tumble**
**rough•cast** (**cast•ing, •cast**)
**rough•cast•er**
**rough-dry** (**-dries, -dry•ing, -dried**)
**rough•en**
**rough-hew** (**-hewing, -hewed, -hewed** *or* **-hewn**)
**rough•house**
**rough•ish**
**rough•ly**
**rough•neck**
**rough•ness**
**rough•rider**
**rough•shod**
**rough-spoken**
**rou•lade**
**rou•leau** (*plural* **•leaux** *or* **•leaus**)
**rou•lette**
**round**
**round•about** (*noun, adj*)
**round-arm** cricketing term
**round•ed**
**round•ed•ness**
**roun•del**
**roun•de•lay** dance
**round•er**
**round•ers**
**Round•head** Parliamentarian
**round•house**
**round•ish**
**round•ly**
**round•ness**
**round-shouldered**
**rounds•man** (*plural* **•men**)
**round•up** (*noun*)
**round•worm**
**roup** *Dialect* auction; bird disease
**roupy**
**rouse**
**rous•edness**
**rous•er**
**rous•ing**
**rous•ing•ly**
**Rous•sil•lon** former French province
**roust**
**roust•about**
**rout** defeat
**route** road; course
**route•march**
**rout•er**
**rou•tine**
**rou•tine•ly**
**rou•tin•ism**
**rou•tin•ist**
**roux** (*plural* **roux**) fat-and-flour paste; *compare* **rue**
**rove**
**rove-over** prosody term
**rov•er**
**row** line; propel boat; *compare* **roe**
**ro•wan**
**row•boat**
**row•di•ly**
**row•di•ness** (*or* **•dy•ism**)
**row•dy** (**•di•er, •di•est**)
**row•el** (**•el•ling, •elled;** *US* **•el•ing, •eled**) spur wheel
**row•er**
**row•lock**
**roy•al**
**roy•al•ism**
**roy•al•ist**
**roy•al•is•tic**
**roy•al•ly**
**roy•al•ty** (*plural* **•ties**)
**roz•zer** *Slang* policeman
**rub** (**rub•bing, rubbed**)
**ru•bái•yát** Persian verse form
**Rub' al Kha•li** Arabian desert
**ru•ba•to** (*plural* **•tos**) musical term
**rubbed**
**rub•ber**
**rub•ber•ize** (*or* **•ise**)
**rubber•neck** *Slang* inquisitive person
**rubber-stamp** (*verb*)
**rub•bery**
**rub•bing**
**rub•bish**
**rub•bishy**
**rub•ble**
**rubble•work**
**rub•bly**
**rube** *US* country bumpkin
**ru•befa•cient**
**ru•befac•tion**
**ru•befy** (**•befies, •befy•ing, •befied**) make red

**ru•bel•la** German measles; *compare* **rubeola**
**ru•bel•lite** gemstone
**ru•beo•la** measles; *compare* **rubella**
**ru•beo•lar**
**ru•bes•cence**
**ru•bes•cent**
**ru•bia•ceous** botany term
**Ru•bi•con**
**ru•bi•cund**
**ru•bi•cun•dity**
**ru•bid•ic**
**ru•bid•ium** radioactive element
**ru•bigi•nous** (*or* **•nose**) rust-coloured
**ru•bi•ous** dark red
**ru•bric**
**ru•bri•cal**
**ru•bri•cate**
**ru•bri•ca•tion**
**ru•bri•ca•tor**
**ru•bri•cian**
**ruby** (*plural* **rubies**)
**ruche** (*or* **rouche**)
**ruch•ing**
**ruck**
**ruck•sack**
**ruck•us** (*plural* **•uses**) uproar
**ruc•tion**
**ru•da•ceous** geology term
**rud•beckia** plant
**rudd** (*plural* **rudd** *or* **rudds**) fish
**rud•der**
**rudder•head**
**rudder•less**
**rudder•post**
**rud•di•ly**
**rud•di•ness**
**rud•dle** (*or* **rad•**, **red•**) red dye
**rud•dock** *Dialect* robin
**rud•dy** (**•di•er**, **•di•est**)
**rude**
**rude•ly**
**rude•ness** (*or* **ru•dery**)
**ru•deral** botany term
**Ru•des•heim•er** wine
**ru•di•ment**
**ru•di•men•ta•ril•ly** (*or* **•men•tal•ly**)
**ru•di•men•ta•ry** (*or* **•men•tal**)
**rud•ish**
**rue** (**ru•ing, rued**) regret; plant; *compare* **roux**
**rue•ful**
**rue•ful•ly**
**rue•ful•ness**
**ru•fes•cence**
**ru•fes•cent**
**ruff** raised collar; bird; cards term
**ruffe** (*or* **ruff**) fish
**ruf•fian**
**ruf•fi•an•ism**
**ruf•fi•an•ly**
**ruf•fle**
**ruf•fler**
**ruf•fly**
**ru•fous**
**rug**
**ruga** (*plural* **rugae**) anatomy term
**Rug•by** Warwickshire town
**rug•by** football
**rug•ged**
**rug•ged•ize** (*or* **•ise**) make durable
**rug•ged•ly**
**rug•ged•ness**
**rug•ger**
**ru•gose** (*or* **•gous**, **•gate**)
**ru•gos•ity**
**Ruhr** German river
**ruin**
**ru•in•able**
**ru•ina•tion**
**ru•in•er**
**ru•ing**
**ru•in•ous**
**Ruis•lip**
**rul•able**
**rule**
**rul•er**
**rul•ing**
**rum** (**rum•mer, rum•mest**) spirit; *Slang* odd; *compare* **rhumb**
**Ru•ma•nia** *variant spelling of* Romania
**rum•ba** (*or* **rhum•**)
**rum•ble**
**rum•bler**
**rum•bling•ly**
**rum•bly**
**rum•bus•tious**
**rum•bus•tious•ly**
**rum•bus•tious•ness**
**Ru•melia** part of Ottoman empire
**ru•men** (*plural* **•mens** *or* **•mi•na**) cow's stomach
**ru•mi•nant**
**ru•mi•nate**
**ru•mi•nat•ing•ly**
**ru•mi•na•tion**
**ru•mi•na•tive**
**ru•mi•na•tor**
**rum•mage**
**rum•mag•er**
**rum•mer** drinking glass
**rum•my**
**ru•mour** (*US* **•mor**)
**rump**
**rum•ple**
**rum•ply**
**rum•pus** (*plural* **•puses**)
**run** (**run•ning, ran, run**)
**run•about** (*noun*)
**run•away** (*noun, adj*)
**runch** plant
**run•ci•nate** botany term
**Run•corn** Cheshire town
**run•dle** ladder rung
**run•down** (*noun*)
**run-down** (*adj*)
**rune**
**rung**
**ru•nic**
**run•nel** (*or* **•let**)
**run•ner**
**runner-up** (*plural* **runners-up**)
**run•ning**
**run•ny** (**•ni•er**, **•ni•est**)
**Run•ny•mede**
**run•off** (*noun*)
**run-of-the-mill**
**run-on** (*noun*)
**runt**
**runti•ness**
**runt•ish**
**runt•ish•ness**
**runty**
**run-up** (*noun*)
**run•way**
**ru•pee**
**ru•pi•ah** (*plural* **•ah** *or* **•ahs**) Indonesian currency
**rup•tur•able**
**rup•ture**
**ru•ral**

**ru•ral•ism**
**ru•ral•ist** (*or* **•ite**)
**ru•ral•ity**
**ru•rali•za•tion** (*or* **•sa•tion**)
**ru•ral•ize** (*or* **•ise**)
**ru•ral•ly**
**Ru•ri•ta•nia** fictional kingdom
**Ru•ri•ta•nian**
**Ruse** Bulgarian city
**ruse**
**rush**
**rush•er**
**rushi•ness**
**rushy** (**rushi•er, rushi•est**)
**rusk**
**rus•set**
**rus•set•ish** (*or* **•sety**)
**Rus•sia**
**Rus•sian**
**Rus•sian•ize** (*or* **•ise**)
**Russ•ky** (*or* **•ki**; *plural* **•kies** *or* **•kis**) *Slang* a Russian
**Rus•so•phile** (*or* **•phil**)
**Rus•so•phobe**
**Rus•so•pho•bia**
**Rus•so•pho•bic**
**rust**
**rus•tic**
**rus•ti•cal•ly**
**rus•ti•cate**
**rus•ti•ca•tion**
**rus•ti•ca•tor**
**rus•tic•ity**
**rusti•ly**
**rusti•ness**
**rus•tle**
**rus•tler**
**rus•tling•ly**
**rust•proof**
**rusty** (**rusti•er, rusti•est**)
**rut** (**rut•ting, rut•ted**)
**ru•ta•ba•ga** *US* swede
**ru•ta•ceous** botany term
**Ru•the•nia** Ukrainian region
**Ru•the•nian**
**ru•then•ic**
**ru•the•nious**
**ru•the•nium** chemical element
**ruth•er•ford** unit
**ruth•ful**
**ruth•less**
**ruth•less•ly**
**ruth•less•ness**
**ru•ti•lat•ed** mineralogy term
**ru•tile** mineral
**Rut•land** English county
**rut•ted**
**rut•ti•ly**
**rut•ti•ness**
**rut•ting**
**rut•tish** of an animal in rut
**rut•tish•ness**
**rut•ty** (**•ti•er, •ti•est**) full of ruts
**Ru•wen•zo•ri** African mountains
**Rwan•da** African republic
**Rya•zan** Russian city
**Ry•binsk** Russian city
**Ry•dal** Cumbrian village
**rye**
**rye-brome** plant
**rye•grass**
**ryo•kan** Japanese inn
**ryot** Indian peasant

# S

**Saab** (*Trademark*)
**Saar** European river
**Saar•brück•en** German city
**Saar•land** German state
**Saba** West Indian island
**Sa•ba•dell** Spanish town
**saba•dil•la** plant
**Sa•bah** Malaysian state
**sa•ba•yon** dessert
**Sab•ba•tar•ian** observer of Sabbath
**Sab•bath** seventh day
**sab•bath** (*or* **•bat**) rest period
**Sab•bati•cal** (*or* **•bat•ic**) of the Sabbath
**sab•bati•cal** (*noun*) academic leave
**Sa•bel•lian** language
**sa•ber** *US spelling of* **sabre**
**sa•bin** unit
**Sab•ine**
**sa•ble** (*plural* **•bles** *or* **•ble**)
**sab•ot**
**sabo•tage**
**sabo•teur**
**sa•bra** Israeli-born Jew
**sa•bre** (*US* **•ber**)
**sa•bre•tache** (*US* **•ber•**) leather case
**sabu•los•ity**
**sabu•lous** (*or* **•lose**) gritty
**sac** biological pouch; *compare* **sack**
**saca•ton** grass
**sac•cate**
**sac•cha•rase** enzyme
**sac•cha•rate** chemical compound
**sac•cha•ride** sugar
**sac•chari•fi•ca•tion**
**sac•chari•fy** (**•fies, •fy•ing, •fied**)
**sac•cha•rim•eter**
**sac•cha•rin** sugar
**sac•cha•rine** sugary
**sac•cha•rin•ity**
**sac•cha•ri•za•tion** (*or* **•sa•tion**)
**sac•cha•rize** (*or* **•rise**)
**sac•cha•roid** (*or* **•roi•dal**) geology term
**sac•cha•rom•eter**
**sac•cha•rose**
**sac•cu•late** (*or* **•lat•ed, •lar**)
**sac•cu•la•tion**
**sac•cule** (*or* **•cu•lus**)
**sac•er•do•tal**
**sac•er•do•tal•ism**
**sa•chet**
**sack** bag; to plunder, etc.; *compare* **sac**
**sack•but**
**sack•cloth**
**sack•er**
**sack•ful** (*plural* **•fuls**)
**sack•ing**
**sack•like**
**sa•cral** of sacred rites or the sacrum
**sac•ra•ment**

**sac•ra•men•tal**
**sac•ra•men•tal•ism**
**sac•ra•men•tal•ist**
**sac•ra•men•tal•ity** (*or* **•ness**)
**sac•ra•men•tal•ly**
**Sac•ra•men•tar•ian** theology term
**Sac•ra•men•to** US port
**sa•crar•ium** (*plural* **•craria**) church sanctuary
**sa•cred**
**sa•cred•ness**
**sac•ri•fice**
**sac•ri•fice•able**
**sac•ri•fic•er**
**sac•ri•fi•cial**
**sac•ri•fi•cial•ly**
**sac•ri•fic•ing**
**sac•ri•lege**
**sac•ri•legious**
**sac•ri•legious•ness**
**sac•ri•legist**
**sac•ris•tan** (*or* **sac•rist**)
**sac•ris•ty** (*plural* **•ties**)
**sa•cro•ili•ac** anatomy term
**sac•ro•sanct**
**sac•ro•sanc•tity** (*or* **•sanct•ness**)
**sa•crum** (*plural* **•cra**) bone
**sad** (**sad•der, sad•dest**)
**sad•den**
**sad•den•ing**
**sad•der**
**sad•dest**
**sad•dle**
**saddle•back**
**saddle•bag**
**saddle•bill**
**saddle•bow**
**saddle•cloth**
**sad•dler**
**sad•dlery** (*plural* **•dleries**)
**saddle•tree** saddle frame
**Sad•du•cean**
**Sad•du•cees**
**sad•iron** heavy iron
**sad•ism**
**sad•ist**
**sa•dis•tic**
**sa•dis•ti•cal•ly**
**sad•ly**
**sad•ness**
**sado•maso•chism**
**sado•maso•chist**
**sado•maso•chis•tic**
**Sa•do•wa** battle site
**sa•fa•ri** (*plural* **•ris**)
**safe**
**safe-conduct**
**safe-deposit** (*or* **safety-**)
**safe•guard**
**safe•keeping**
**safe•light** photography term
**safe•ness**
**safe•ty** (*plural* **•ties**)
**saf•fian** tanned leather
**saf•flow•er**
**saf•fron**
**Sa•fid Rud** Iranian river
**saf•ra•nine** (*or* **•nin**) dye
**saf•role** plant oil
**sag** (**sag•ging, sagged**)
**saga**
**sa•ga•cious**
**sa•ga•cious•ness**
**sa•gac•ity**
**saga•more** American Indian chief
**sage**
**sage•brush** shrub
**sag•gar** (*or* **•ger**) pottery-firing box
**sagged**
**sag•ging**
**Sa•git•ta** constellation
**sag•it•tal**
**Sag•it•ta•rian**
**Sag•it•ta•rius**
**sag•it•tate** (*or* **sa•git•ti•form**)
**sago** (*plural* **sagos**)
**Sa•guache** US mountain range
**sa•gua•ro** (*or* **•hua•**; *plural* **•ros**) cactus
**Sa•hap•tin** (*or* **•tan**; *plural* **•tins, •tin** *or* **•tans, •tan**) American Indian
**Sa•ha•ra**
**Sa•har•an**
**Sa•ha•ran•pur** Indian town
**Sa•hel** African region
**sa•hib** (*or* **•heb**)
**said**
**Sai•da** Lebanese port
**sai•ga** antelope
**Sai•gon**
**sail**
**sail•able**
**sail•cloth**
**sail•er** sailing vessel; *compare* **sailor**
**sail•fish** (*plural* **•fish** *or* **•fishes**)
**sail•ing**
**sail•or** seaman; *compare* **sailer**
**sail•or•ly**
**sail•plane**
**sain•foin** plant
**saint**
**St Al•bans**
**St An•drews**
**St Aus•tell** Cornish town
**St Ber•nard** dog
**saint•ed**
**Sainte Foy** suburb of Quebec
**Saint-Émilion** wine
**St-Étienne** French town
**St Gall** Swiss town
**St George's** capital of Grenada
**St He•le•na** Atlantic island
**St Hel•ens** Merseyside town
**St Hel•ier** Jersey town
**saint•hood**
**St Ives**
**St John** Canadian city
**St John's** Canadian city; Antiguan port
**St Kil•da** Hebridean island
**St Kitts** West Indian country
**St Law•rence** North American river
**St Leg•er** horse race
**saint•li•ly**
**saint•li•ness**
**St Lou•is** US city
**St Lu•cia** West Indian country
**saint•ly**
**St Mo•ritz** Swiss resort
**St Paul** US city
**saint•pau•lia** plant
**St Pe•ters•burg** Russian city
**St Vitus's dance**
**Sai•pan** Pacific island
**Saïs** Egyptian city
**saithe** fish
**Sai•va** Hindu
**Sa•kai** Japanese port
**sake** benefit
**sake** (*or* **saké, saki**) Japanese liquor; *compare* **saki**

**sa•ker** falcon
**Sa•kha•lin** (*or* **•ghal•ien)** Russian island
**saki** monkey; *compare* **sake**
**Sak•tas** Hindu sect
**Sa•kya•mu•ni** title of Buddha
**sal** salt
**sa•laam** Muslim greeting
**sal•able** *variant spelling* (*esp. US*) *of* **saleable**
**sa•la•cious**
**sa•la•cious•ness** (*or* **•lac•ity)**
**sal•ad**
**Sala•man•ca** Spanish city
**sala•man•der** amphibian
**sala•man•drine**
**Sa•lam•bria** Greek river
**sa•la•mi** sausage; *compare* **salmi**
**Sala•mis** Greek island
**sala•ried**
**sala•ry** (*noun, plural* **•ries;** *verb* **•ries, •ry•ing, •ried)**
**sal•chow** ice-skating jump
**sale**
**sale•abil•ity** (*or* **•able•ness)**
**sale•able** (*or esp. US* **sal•able)**
**sale•ably**
**Sa•lem** Indian city; US city
**sal•ep** dried orchid tuber
**sal•era•tus** sodium bicarbonate
**Sa•ler•no** Italian port
**sale•room**
**sales•clerk**
**sales•man** (*plural* **•men)**
**sales•man•ship**
**sales•room**
**sales•woman** (*plural* **•women)**
**Sal•ford**
**Sa•lian** Frankish
**Sal•ic** of Frankish law
**sal•ic** geology term
**sali•ca•ceous** botany term
**sa•li•cin** (*or* **•cine)** drug
**sa•li•cion•al** (*or* **sa•li•cet)** organ stop
**sali•cor•nia** plant
**sa•licy•late**
**sali•cyl•ic acid**
**sa•li•ence** (*or* **•en•cy)**
**sa•li•ent**
**sa•li•en•tian** amphibian
**sa•li•ent•ness**
**sa•lif•er•ous** containing salt
**sali•fi•able**
**sali•fi•ca•tion**
**sali•fy** **(•fies, •fy•ing, •fied)** mix with salt
**sal•im•eter**
**sali•met•ric**
**sal•im•etry**
**sa•lina** salt lake
**sa•line** containing salt
**sa•lin•ity**
**sali•nom•eter**
**sali•no•met•ric**
**sali•nom•etry**
**Salis•bury**
**Sa•lish** (*or* **•lish•an)** language
**sa•li•va**
**sali•vary**
**sali•vate**
**sali•va•tion**
**sal•lee** tree
**sal•let** (*or* **sal•et, sa•lade)** helmet
**sal•li•er**
**sal•low**
**sal•low•ness**
**sal•ly** (*noun, plural* **•lies;** *verb* **•lies, •ly•ing, •lied)**
**Sal•ly Lunn** cake
**sal•ma•gun•di** salad
**sal•ma•naz•ar** wine bottle
**sal•mi** (*or* **•mis;** *plural* **•mis)** French stew; *compare* **salami**
**salm•on** (*plural* **•ons** *or* **•on)**
**salmon•berry** (*plural* **•berries)**
**sal•mo•nel•la** (*plural* **•lae)** bacterium
**sal•mo•nel•lo•sis**
**sal•mo•noid**
**sal•ol** chemical compound
**sa•lon** reception room; beauty establishment, etc.; *compare* **saloon**
**Sa•lo•ni•ka** Greek port
**sa•loon** large room; pub bar; *compare* **salon**
**sa•loop** aromatic infusion
**salo•pette** skiing garment
**sal•pa** (*plural* **•pas** *or* **•pae)** marine organism
**sal•pi•con** chopped food
**sal•pi•form**
**sal•pi•glos•sis** plant
**sal•pin•gec•to•my** (*plural* **•mies)**
**sal•pin•gian**
**sal•pin•gi•tic**
**sal•pin•git•is**
**sal•pinx** (*plural* **•pin•ges)** Fallopian tube
**sal•si•fy** (*plural* **•fies)** vegetable
**salt**
**Sal•ta** Argentine city
**sal•tant** biology term
**sal•ta•rel•lo** (*plural* **•li** *or* **•los)** dance
**sal•ta•tion** biology term
**sal•ta•to•rial** (*or* **sal•ta•tory)** adapted for jumping
**salt•box**
**salt•bush**
**salt•cellar**
**salt•ed**
**salt•er**
**salt•ern** saltworks
**salt•fish**
**sal•ti•grade** moving by jumps
**Sal•til•lo** Mexican state
**salti•ly**
**salti•ness**
**sal•tire** (*or* **•tier)** heraldic term
**salt•ness**
**salt•pan**
**salt•pe•tre** (*US* **•ter)**
**salt•pot**
**sal•tus** (*plural* **•tuses)** break in sequence
**salt•water**
**salt•works**
**salt•wort**
**salty** **(salti•er, salti•est)**
**sa•lu•bri•ous**
**sa•lu•bri•ous•ness** (*or* **•bri•ty)**
**Sa•lu•ki** dog
**salu•tari•ly**
**salu•tari•ness**
**salu•tary** beneficial; *compare* **salutatory**
**salu•ta•tion**
**sa•lu•ta•to•ri•ly**

**sa•lu•ta•tory** welcoming; *compare* **salutary**
**sa•lute**
**sa•lut•er**
**sal•vabil•ity** (*or* **•vable•ness**)
**salv•able**
**sal•vably**
**Sal•va•dor** Brazilian port
**Sal•va•do•rian**
**sal•vage** rescue; *compare* selvage
**sal•vage•able**
**sal•vag•er**
**sal•va•tion**
**sal•va•tion•al**
**sal•va•tion•ism**
**sal•va•tion•ist** member of evangelical sect
**salve**
**sal•ver** tray; *compare* **salvor**
**sal•ver•form** botany term
**sal•via** plant
**sal•vo** (*plural* **•vos** *or* **•voes**) gun fire
**sal•vo** (*plural* **•vos**) provisos
**sal vola•ti•le**
**sal•vor** one who salvages; *compare* **salver**
**Sal•ween** Asian river
**Sal•yut** Soviet space station
**Salz•burg**
**Salz•git•ter** German city
**Sa•ma•ra** Russian city
**sa•ma•ra** botany term
**Sa•maria** Palestinian region
**Sa•mari•tan**
**Sa•mari•tan•ism**
**sa•mar•ium** chemical element
**Sa•mar•kand**
**sa•mar•skite** mineral
**sam•ba** (*plural* **•bas**) dance
**sam•bar** (*or* **•bur**; *plural* **•bars**, **•bar** *or* **•burs**, **•bur**) deer
**same**
**same•ness**
**Sa•mian** of Samos
**sami•sen** musical instrument
**sam•ite** fabric
**sa•mi•ti** (*or* **•thi**) Indian political association
**Sam•nite**
**Sam•ni•um** ancient Italian city
**Sa•moa** Pacific island country
**Sa•mo•an**
**Sa•mos** Greek island
**Samo•thrace** Greek island
**samo•var**
**Samo•yed** (*plural* **•yed** *or* **•yeds**) Siberian people; dog
**sam•pan** boat
**sam•phire** plant
**sam•ple**
**sam•pler**
**sam•pling**
**Sam•sun** Turkish port
**samu•rai** (*plural* **•rai**)
**San** language group
**San'a** (*or* **Sa•naa**) capital of Yemen
**San An•to•nian**
**San An•to•nio** US city
**sana•to•rium** (*US* **sani•ta•**; *plural* **•riums** *or* **•ria**)
**san•be•ni•to** (*plural* **•tos**) garment
**San Ber•nar•di•no** US city
**sanc•ti•fi•able**
**sanc•ti•fi•ca•tion**
**sanc•ti•fi•er**
**sanc•ti•fy** (**•fies**, **•fy•ing**, **•fied**)
**sanc•ti•mo•ni•ous**
**sanc•ti•mo•ni•ous•ness**
**sanc•ti•mo•ny**
**sanc•tion**
**sanc•tion•able**
**sanc•tion•er**
**sanc•ti•tude**
**sanc•tity** (*plural* **•tities**)
**sanc•tu•ary** (*plural* **•aries**)
**sanc•tum** (*plural* **•tums** *or* **•ta**)
**Sanc•tus** hymn
**sand**
**san•dal**
**san•dalled** (*US* **•daled**)
**sandal•wood**
**san•da•rac** (*or* **•rach**) tree
**sand•bag** (*verb* **•bag•ging**, **•bagged**)
**sand•bag•ger**
**sand•bank**
**sand•blast**
**sand•blast•er**
**sand-blind**
**sand-blindness**
**sand•box**
**sand-cast** (**-casting**, **-cast**)
**sand•er**
**sand•er•ling** bird
**sand•fly** (*plural* **•flies**)
**sand•grouse**
**san•dhi** (*plural* **•dhis**) linguistics term
**sand•hog** *US* underground worker
**Sand•hurst**
**San Di•ego** US port
**sandi•ness**
**sand•man** (*plural* **•men**)
**sand•paper**
**sand•piper**
**sand•pit**
**San•dring•ham**
**sand•soap**
**sand•stone**
**sand•storm**
**sand•wich**
**sand•worm**
**sand•wort**
**sandy** (**sandi•er**, **sandi•est**)
**sane**
**sane•ness**
**San Fernando** Trinidadian port
**San•for•ize** (*or* **•ise**; *Trademark*)
**San Fran•cis•can**
**San Fran•cis•co**
**sang**
**san•ga•ree** spiced drink
**sang-froid**
**San•graal** (*or* **•greal**) Holy Grail
**san•gria** drink
**san•gui•naria** drug; plant
**san•gui•nari•ly**
**san•gui•nari•ness**
**san•gui•nary**
**san•guine**
**san•guine•ness** (*or* **•guin•ity**)
**san•guin•eous**
**san•guino•len•cy**
**san•guino•lent** containing blood
**San•hed•rin** Jewish tribunal
**sani•cle** plant

**sa•ni•es** discharge from wound
**sani•tar•ian** of sanitation
**san•itari•ly**
**sani•tari•ness**
**sani•ta•rium** *US spelling of* **sanatorium**
**sani•tary**
**sani•ta•tion**
**sani•tize** (*or* **•tise**)
**san•ity**
**San Jose** Californian city
**San José** Costa Rican capital
**San Juan** Puerto Rican capital
**sank**
**San Luis Po•to•sí** Mexican state
**San Mari•nese** (*or* **Sam•mari•nese**)
**San Ma•ri•no** European republic
**sann•ya•si** Brahman mendicant
**San Sal•va•dor** capital of El Salvador
**sans-culotte**
**San Se•bas•tián** Spanish port
**san•ser•if** (*or* **sans serif**)
**san•se•vieria** plant
**San•skrit**
**San•skrit•ic**
**San•skrit•ist**
**sans ser•if** *variant spelling of* **san•ser•if**
**San Ste•fa•no** Turkish village
**San•ta Ana** El Salvador city; Californian city
**San•ta Ca•ta•ri•na** Brazilian state
**San•ta Cla•ra** Cuban city
**Santa Claus**
**San•ta Cruz** Argentine province; Bolivian city
**San•ta Cruz de Te•ne•rife** Tenerife port
**San•ta Fe** Mexican city; Argentine port
**san•ta•la•ceous** botany term
**San•ta Maria** Brazilian city
**San•ta Mar•ta** Colombian port
**San•tan•der** Spanish port
**San•ta•rém** Brazilian port
**San•tee** US river
**San•tia•go** Chilean capital
**San•tia•go de Cuba** Cuban port
**San•tia•go del Es•te•ro** Argentine city
**San•to Do•min•go** capital of Dominican Republic
**san•toni•ca** plant
**san•to•nin**
**San•tos** Brazilian port
**São Luís** (*or* **São Luíz**) Brazilian port
**Saône-et-Loire** French department
**São Pau•lo** Brazilian port
**São Tomé e Prín•ci•pe** island republic
**sap** (**sap•ping, sapped**)
**sapa•jou** monkey
**sa•pele** tree
**sa•phe•na** (*plural* **•nae**) vein
**sa•phe•nous**
**(saphire)** *incorrect spelling of* **sapphire**
**sap•id** palatable
**sa•pid•ity** (*or* **•ness**)
**sa•pi•ence** (*or* **•en•cy**) wisdom
**sa•pi•ent**
**sa•pi•en•tial**
**sap•in•da•ceous** botany term
**sap•less**
**sap•ling**
**sapo•dil•la** fruit
**sapo•na•ceous** soapy
**sa•poni•fi•able**
**sa•poni•fi•ca•tion**
**sa•poni•fi•er**
**sa•poni•fy** (**•fies, •fy•ing, •fied**)
**sapo•nin** plant compound
**sapo•nite** mineral
**sa•po•ta** fruit
**sapo•ta•ceous**
**sap•pan•wood** (*or* **sap•an•**)
**sapped**
**sap•per**
**Sap•phic** verse form; of Sappho
**sap•phire**
**sap•phir•ine** mineral
**sap•pi•ly**
**sap•pi•ness**
**sap•ping**
**Sap•po•ro** Japanese city
**sap•py** (**•pi•er, •pi•est**)
**sa•prae•mia** (*US* **•pre•**) blood poisoning
**sa•prae•mic** (*US* **•pre•**)
**sap•robe** organism inhabiting foul water
**sap•ro•bic**
**sap•ro•gen•ic** (*or* **•ous**)
**sap•ro•genic•ity**
**sap•ro•lite** geological deposit
**sap•ro•lit•ic**
**sap•ro•pel** sludge
**sap•ro•pel•ic**
**sa•propha•gous** feeding on decaying matter
**sap•ro•phyte**
**sap•ro•phyt•ic**
**sap•ro•phyti•cal•ly**
**sap•ro•zo•ic**
**sap•sa•go** cheese
**sap•sucker** bird
**sap•wood**
**sara•band** (*or* **•bande**)
**Sara•cen**
**Sara•cen•ic** (*or* **•ceni•cal**)
**Sara•gos•sa** Spanish city
**Sa•ra•jevo** (*or* **Se•**) Bosnia-Hercegovinan capital
**sa•ran** resin
**Sa•ransk** Russian city
**Sa•ra•tov** Russian city
**Sa•ra•wak** Malaysian state
**sar•casm**
**sar•cas•tic**
**sar•cas•ti•cal•ly**
**sar•co•carp** botany term
**sar•coid**
**sar•co•ma** (*plural* **•mas** *or* **•ma•ta**)
**sar•co•ma•toid** (*or* **•tous**)
**sar•co•ma•to•sis**
**sar•copha•gus** (*plural* **•gi** *or* **•guses**)
**sar•cous** muscular or fleshy
**sard** gemstone
**sar•dine** (*plural* **•dine** *or* **•dines**)
**Sar•dinia**
**Sar•din•ian**

**Sar•dis** (*or* **•des**) ancient Asian city
**sar•di•us** biblical gemstone
**sar•don•ic**
**sar•doni•cal•ly**
**sar•doni•cism**
**sar•don•yx** gemstone
**Sar•gas•so** sea
**sar•gas•so** (*plural* **•sos**) seaweed
**sar•gas•sum** seaweed
**sarge** *Slang* sergeant
**Sar•go•dha** Pakistani city
**sari** (*plural* **•ris**)
**Sark** Channel island
**sar•men•tose** (*or* **•tous, •ta•ceous**) botany term
**Sar•nia** Canadian port
**sa•rong**
**sa•ron•ic**
**sa•ros** cycle of eclipses
**sar•panch** Indian leader
**sar•ra•cenia** plant
**sar•ra•cenia•ceous**
**sar•sa•pa•ril•la**
**sar•sen** boulder
**Sarthe** French department
**sar•tor** tailor
**sar•to•rial**
**sar•to•rius** (*plural* **•to•rii**) muscle
**Sar•um** Salisbury
**Sa•sebo** Japanese port
**sash**
**Sas•katch•ewan**
**Sas•ka•toon** Canadian city
**sas•ka•toon** fruit
(**sarsparilla**) *incorrect spelling of* **sarsaparilla**
**sass** *US* insolent
**sas•sa•by** (*plural* **•bies**) antelope
**sas•sa•fras** tree; oil
**Sas•sa•nid** (*plural* **•sa•nids** *or* **•sani•dae**) member of Persian dynasty
**Sas•sa•ri** Sardinian city
**Sas•se•nach**
**sas•si•ly**
**sas•si•ness**
**sas•sy** (**•si•er, •si•est**) saucy
**sas•sy** (*or* **sass•wood, sas•sy wood**) tree
**sa•stru•ga** (*or* **zas•tru•**) ridge on snowfield
**sat**
**sa•tai** (*or* **•tay**) Indonesian food
**Satan**
**sa•tang** (*plural* **•tang**) Thai coin
**sa•tan•ic** (*or* **•tani•cal**)
**sa•tani•cal•ly**
**sa•tani•cal•ness**
**Sa•tan•ism**
**Sa•tan•ist**
**satch•el**
**sate**
**sa•teen** imitation satin
**sat•el•lite**
**sat•el•lit•ium** astrology term
**sa•tem** linguistics term
**sa•ti•abil•ity** (*or* **•able•ness**)
**sa•ti•able**
**sa•ti•ably**
**sa•ti•ate**
**sa•tia•tion**
**sa•ti•ety**
**sat•in**
**sati•net** (*or* **•nette**) imitation satin
**satin•wood**
**sat•iny**
**sat•ire** parody; *compare* **satyr**
**sa•tir•ic**
**sa•tiri•cal** (*or* **•tir•ic**)
**sa•tiri•cal•ly**
**sa•tiri•cal•ness**
**sati•rist**
**sati•ri•za•tion** (*or* **•sa•tion**)
**sati•rize** (*or* **•rise**)
**sati•riz•er** (*or* **•ris•er**)
**sat•is•fac•tion**
**sat•is•fac•tion•al**
**sat•is•fac•to•ri•ly**
**sat•is•fac•to•ri•ness**
**sat•is•fac•tory**
**sat•is•fi•able**
**sat•is•fi•er**
**sat•is•fy** (**•fies, •fy•ing, •fied**)
**sat•is•fy•ing•ly**
**sa•trap** Persian governor
**sa•trapy** (*plural* **•trapies**)
**Sa•tsu•ma** Japanese province; porcelain
**sat•su•ma** fruit
**satu•rabil•ity**
**satu•rable**
**satu•rant**
**satu•rate**
**satu•rat•ed**
**satu•rat•er** (*or* **•ra•tor**)
**satu•ra•tion**
**Sat•ur•day**
**Sat•urn** planet
**Saturn** Roman god
**Sat•ur•na•lia** (*plural* **•lia** *or* **•lias**) ancient festival
**Sa•tur•nian**
**sa•tur•ni•id** moth
**sat•ur•nine**
**sat•ur•nine•ness** (*or* **•nin•ity**)
**sat•ur•nism** lead poisoning
**sat•ya•gra•hi** nonviolent protester
**sa•tyr** goatlike deity; lustful man; *compare* **satire**
**saty•ria•sis** (*or* **sa•tyro•ma•nia**)
**sa•tyr•ic** (*or* **•tyri•cal**)
**sa•ty•rid** butterfly
**sauce**
**sauce•pan**
**sau•cer**
**sau•cer•ful** (*plural* **•fuls**)
**sau•ci•ly**
**sau•ci•ness**
**saucy** (**•ci•er, •ci•est**)
**Sau•di** (*or* **Sau•di Ara•bian**)
**Sau•di Ara•bia**
**sau•er•bra•ten** beef dish
**sau•er•kraut**
**sau•ger** fish
**Sault Ste Ma•rie** Canadian city; US city
**sau•na**
**saun•ter**
**saun•ter•er**
**sau•rian** lizard-like
**saur•is•chian** dinosaur
**sau•ro•pod** dinosaur
**sau•ropo•dous**
**sau•ry** (*plural* **•ries**) fish
**sau•sage**
**sau•té** (**•té•ing** *or* **•tée•ing, •téed**)
**Sau•ternes** wine
**Sava** (*or* **Save**) Yugoslav river
**sav•able** (*or* **save•able**)
**sav•able•ness** (*or* **save•**)
**sav•age**
**sav•age•ness**

**sav•age•ry** (*plural* **•ries**)
**Sa•vaii** Samoan island
**sa•van•na** (*or* **•nah**)
**Sa•van•nah** US port
**sa•vant** (*fem* **•vante**) learned person
**sa•vate** form of boxing
**save**
**save•able** *variant spelling of* **savable**
**save-all**
**sav•eloy**
**sav•er**
**sav•in** (*or* **•ine**) shrub
**sav•ing**
**sav•ings**
**Sav•iour** (*US* **•ior**) Christ
**sav•iour** (*US* **•ior**) rescuer
**Sa•voie** French department
**savoir-faire**
**sa•vor•ous**
**sa•vory** (*plural* **•vories**) plant; *US spelling of* **savoury**
**sa•vour** (*US* **•vor**)
**sa•vouri•ness** (*US* **•vori•**)
**sa•vour•ing•ly** (*US* **•vor•**)
**sa•voury** (*US* **•vory**; *plural* **•vouries**)
**Sa•voy** French region
**sa•voy** cabbage
**Sa•voy•ard** of Savoy
**sav•vy** (**•vies, •vy•ing, •vied**)
**saw** (**saw•ing, sawed, sawed** *or* **sawn**)
**saw•bill**
**saw•bones**
**saw•der** flatter
**saw•dust**
**sawed**
**saw•er** one that saws; *compare* **sawyer**
**saw•fish** (*plural* **•fish** *or* **•fishes**)
**saw•fly** (*plural* **•flies**)
**saw•horse**
**saw•ing**
**saw•mill**
**sawn**
**sawn-off**
**saw•tooth**
**saw•yer** professional timber sawer; *compare* **sawer**
**sax** axe
**saxe blue**
**sax•horn**
**sax•ico•lous** (*or* **saxa•tile**) biology term
**saxi•fra•ga•ceous**
**saxi•frage**
**Sax•on**
**Saxo•ny** German state
**saxo•ny** yarn
**Saxo•ny-An•halt** German state
**saxo•phone**
**saxo•phon•ic**
**sax•opho•nist**
**sax•tuba**
**say** (**say•ing, said**)
**say•er**
**say-so**
**say•yid** (*or* **say•id, said**) Muslim title
**saz•erac** cocktail
**scab** (**scab•bing, scabbed**)
**scab•bard**
**scab•bi•ly**
**scab•bi•ness**
**scab•ble** shape roughly
**scab•by** (**•bi•er, •bi•est**)
**sca•bies**
**sca•bi•et•ic**
**sca•bi•ous** scabby; plant
**sca•brous** scaly; salacious
**scad** fish
**scads** *US* many
**Sca•fell Pike** Cumbrian mountain
**scaf•fold**
**scaf•fold•er**
**scaf•fold•ing**
**scag** (**scag•ging, scagged**) *Dialect* to tear
**scaglio•la** imitation marble
**scal•able**
**scal•able•ness**
**scal•ably**
**scal•age** *US* price reduction
**sca•lar** maths term; *compare* **scaler**
**sca•lare** fish
**sca•lari•form**
**scala•wag** *variant spelling of* **scallywag**
**scald**
**scald•fish** (*plural* **•fish** *or* **•fishes**)
**scale**
**scale•board** veneer
**sca•lene** maths term
**sca•lenus** (*plural* **•leni**) muscle
**scal•er** one that scales; *compare* **scalar**
**scales**
**scali•ness**
**scall** scalp disease
**scal•lion** small onion
**scal•lop**
**scal•lop•er**
**scal•ly•wag** (*or* **scala•wag**)
**sca•lop•pi•ne** (*or* **•ni**) Italian dish
**scalp**
**scal•pel**
**scal•pel•lic**
**scalp•er**
**scalp•ing**
**scaly** (**scali•er, scali•est**)
**scam•mo•ni•ate**
**scam•mo•ny** (*plural* **•nies**) plant; medicinal resin
**scamp**
**scamp•er**
**scam•per•er**
**scam•pi**
**scamp•ish**
**scan** (**scan•ning, scanned**)
**scan•dal**
**scan•dali•za•tion** (*or* **•sa•tion**)
**scan•dal•ize** (*or* **•ise**)
**scan•dal•iz•er** (*or* **•is•er**)
**scandal•monger**
**scan•dal•ous**
**scan•dal•ous•ness**
**Scan•da•roon** pigeon
**scan•dent** climbing
**Scan•dian** Scandinavian
**scan•dic** of scandium
**Scan•di•na•via**
**Scan•di•na•vian**
**scan•dium** chemical element
**scan•ner**
**scan•sion**
**scan•so•rial** adapted for climbing
**scant**
**scanti•ly**
**scanti•ness**
**scant•ling** rafter
**scant•ness**

**scanty** (**scanti•er, scanti•est**)
**Scapa Flow** naval base
**scape** biology term
**scape•goat**
**scape•grace**
**scapho•pod** mollusc
**scapo•lite** mineral
**scap•ose** botany term
**scapu•la** (*plural* **•lae** *or* **•las**) shoulder bone
**scapu•lar** of scapula; part of monk's habit
**scar** (**scar•ring, scarred**)
**scar•ab** beetle
**scara•bae•id** (*or* **•baean**)
**scara•bae•oid** (*or* **scara•boid**)
**scara•bae•us** (*plural* **•bae•uses** *or* **•baei**) scarab
**Scar•borough**
**scarce**
**scarce•ly**
**scarce•ment** wall ledge
**scarce•ness**
**scar•city** (*plural* **•cities**)
**scare**
**scare•crow**
**scare•monger**
**scar•er**
**scarf** (*plural* **scarfs** *or* **scarves**)
**scarf•skin** outer skin layer
**scari•fi•ca•tion**
**scari•fi•ca•tor** surgical instrument
**scari•fi•er**
**scari•fy** (**•fies, •fy•ing, •fied**)
**scar•ing•ly**
**scari•ous** (*or* **•ose**) botany term
**scar•la•ti•na** scarlet fever
**scar•la•ti•nal** (*or* **•nous**)
**scar•let**
**scarp**
**scarp•er**
**scary** (**scari•er, scari•est**)
**scat** (**scat•ting, scat•ted**)
**scathe**
**scath•ing**
**scato•logi•cal** (*or* **•log•ic**)
**sca•tolo•gist**
**sca•tol•ogy** study of excrement
**scat•ter**
**scat•ter•able**
**scatter•brain**
**scatter•brained**
**scat•ter•er**
**scatter-gun**
**scat•ter•ing**
**scat•ti•ly**
**scat•ti•ness**
**scat•ty** (**•ti•er, •ti•est**)
**scaup** duck
**scav•enge**
**scav•en•ger**
**sce•nario** (*plural* **•narios**)
**sce•nar•ist**
**scend** (*or* **send; scend•ing, scend•ed** *or* **send•ing, sent**) nautical term
**scene**
**scen•ery** (*plural* **•eries**)
**sce•nic**
**sce•ni•cal•ly**
**sce•nog•raph•er**
**sce•no•graph•ic** (*or* **•graphi•cal**)
**sce•no•graphi•cal•ly**
**sce•nog•ra•phy** depicting in perspective
**scent**
**scented**
**scent•less**
**scep•tic** (*US* **skep•**) doubter; *compare* **septic**
**scep•ti•cal** (*US* **skep•**)
**scep•ti•cal•ly** (*US* **skep•**)
**scep•ti•cal•ness** (*US* **skep•**)
**scep•ti•cism** (*US* **skep•**)
**scep•tre** (*US* **•ter**)
**scep•tred** (*US* **•tered**)
**Schaer•beek** Belgian city
**Schaff•hau•sen** Swiss town
**schap•pe** yarn or fabric
**schedu•lar**
**sched•ule**
**scheel•ite** mineral
**Scheldt** European river
**sche•ma** (*plural* **•ma•ta**)
**sche•mat•ic**
**sche•mati•cal•ly**
**sche•ma•tism**
**sche•ma•ti•za•tion** (*or* **•sa•tion**)
**sche•ma•tize** (*or* **•tise**)
**scheme**
**schem•er**
**schem•ing**
**schem•ing•ly**
**scher•zan•do** (*plural* **•di** *or* **•dos**) musical term
**scher•zo** (*plural* **•zos** *or* **•zi**)
**schil•ler** metallic lustre
**schil•ling** Austrian currency
**schip•per•ke** dog
**schism**
**schis•mat•ic** (*or* **•mati•cal**)
**schis•mati•cal•ly**
**schis•mati•cal•ness**
**schist** rock
**schis•tose**
**schis•tos•ity**
**schis•to•some** blood parasite
**schis•to•so•mia•sis**
**schizo** (*plural* **schizos**)
**schizo•carp** botany term
**schizo•car•pous** (*or* **•pic**)
**schizo•gen•esis** biology term
**schizo•genet•ic**
**schi•zogo•ny** zoology term
**schiz•oid**
**schizo•my•cete** biology term
**schizo•my•cet•ic**
**schizo•my•cetous**
**schi•zont** zoology term
**schizo•phre•nia**
**schizo•phren•ic**
**schizo•phy•ceous**
**schizo•phyte**
**schizo•phyt•ic**
**schizo•pod** crustacean
**schizo•thy•mia** psychology term
**schizo•thy•mic**
**schle•miel** *US* clumsy
**schlep** (**schlep•ping, schlepped**) *US* drag
**Schleswig-Holstein** German state
**schlie•ren** physics term
**schlie•ric**
**schlock** *US* inferior goods
**schmaltz** (*or* **schmalz**) sentimentality
**schmaltzy**
**schmooze** *US* chat
**schnapps** (*or* **schnaps**)
**schnau•zer** dog
**schnecke** (*plural* **schneck•en**) *US* bread roll

**schnit•zel**
**schnook** *US* stupid person
**schnor•rer** *US* professional beggar
**schnoz•zle** *Slang* nose
**scho•la can•to•rum** (*plural* **schol•ae can•to•rum)** choir
**schol•ar**
**schol•ar•li•ness**
**schol•ar•ly**
**schol•ar•ship**
**scho•las•tic**
**scho•las•ti•cal**
**scho•las•ti•cal•ly**
**scho•las•ti•cate** Jesuit's probation period
**scho•las•ti•cism**
**scho•li•ast**
**scho•li•as•tic**
**scho•lium** (*plural* **•lia)** marginal note
**school**
**school•boy**
**school•child** (*plural* **•children)**
**school•girl**
**school•fellow**
**school•house**
**schoolie** *Austral* schoolteacher
**school•ing**
**school•marm**
**school•marm•ish**
**school•master**
**school•master•ship**
**school•mate**
**school•mistress**
**school•mistressy**
**school•teacher**
**schoon•er**
**schorl** mineral
**schor•la•ceous**
**schot•tische** dance
**schuss** ski run
**schwa** (*or* **shwa)** unstressed vowel sound
**Schwa•ben** German region
**Schwe•rin** German city
**Schwyz** Swiss town
**sci•aenid** (*or* **•aenoid)** fish
**sci•ama•chy** (*or* **•oma•, ski•)** fight with imaginary enemy
**sci•at•ic**
**sci•ati•ca**
**sci•ence**
**sci•en•ter** legal term
**sci•en•tial** knowledgeable
**sci•en•tif•ic**
**sci•en•tifi•cal•ly**
**sci•en•tism**
**sci•en•tist**
**sci•en•tis•tic**
**Sci•en•tolo•gist**
**Sci•en•tol•ogy** religious cult
**sci-fi**
**scili•cet** that is
**scil•la** plant
**Scil•lo•nian**
**Scil•ly Isles** (*or* **Scil•lies)**
**scimi•tar** (*or* **simi•)**
**scin•coid** (*or* **•coid•ian)** skinklike
**scin•tig•ra•phy** medical technique
**scin•til•la** minute amount
**scin•til•late**
**scin•til•lat•ing•ly**
**scin•til•la•tion**
**scin•til•la•tor** physics term
**scin•til•lom•eter**
**scio•man•cer**
**scio•man•cy** divination through ghosts
**scio•man•tic**
**sci•on** descendant; plant graft
**scir•rhoid**
**scir•rhos•ity**
**scir•rhous** (*adj*)
**scir•rhus** (*plural* **•rhi** *or* **•rhuses)** cancerous growth; *compare* **cirrus**
**scis•sel** waste metal
**scis•sile** divisible
**scis•sion**
**scis•sor**
**scis•sors**
**sciu•rine** of squirrels
**sciu•roid**
**sclaff** golf stroke
**sclaff•er**
**scle•ra** eyeball covering
**scle•ren•chy•ma** plant tissue
**scle•ren•chyma•tous**
**scle•rite** zoology term
**scle•rit•ic**
**scle•ri•tis** (*or* **•ro•ti•tis)** eye inflammation
**scle•ro•der•ma** skin disease
**scle•ro•der•ma•tous**
**scle•roid**
**scle•ro•ma** (*plural* **•ma•ta)** hard tissue
**scle•rom•eter** geology apparatus
**sclero•met•ric**
**scle•ro•phyll** botany term
**scle•ro•pro•tein**
**scle•ro•sal**
**scle•rosed**
**scle•ro•sis** (*plural* **•ses)**
**scle•rot•ic**
**scle•ro•ti•oid** (*or* **•ro•tial)**
**scle•ro•tium** (*plural* **•tia)** fungal tissue
**scle•roto•my** (*plural* **•mies)** eye surgery
**scle•rous**
**scoff**
**scoff•er**
**scoff•ing•ly**
**scoff•law** *US* habitual lawbreaker
**scold**
**scold•able**
**scold•er**
**scold•ing**
**scold•ing•ly**
**scol•ecite** mineral
**sco•lex** (*plural* **sco•leces** *or* **scoli•ces)** tapeworm head
**sco•lio•sis** (*or* **•lio•ma)** spinal curvature
**sco•li•ot•ic**
**(scollop)** *incorrect spelling of* **scallop**
**scolo•pen•drid** centipede
**scolo•pen•drine**
**scom•broid** fish
**sconce**
**Scone** Scottish site of coronation stone
**scone** cake
**scoop**
**scoop•er**
**scoot**
**scoot•er**
**scop** Anglo-Saxon minstrel
**scope**
**sco•pola•mine** drug
**sco•po•line** sedative
**scopu•la** (*plural* **•las** *or* **•lae)** zoology term

**scopu•late**
**scor•bu•tic** (*or* **•ti•cal**) having scurvy
**scorch**
**scorch•er**
**scorch•ing**
**score**
**score•board**
**score•card**
**scor•er**
**sco•ria** (*plural* **•riae**) solid lava; slag
**sco•ria•ceous**
**sco•ri•fi•ca•tion**
**sco•ri•fi•er**
**sco•ri•fy** (**•fies, •fy•ing, •fied**)
**scorn**
**scorn•er**
**scorn•ful**
**scorn•ful•ly**
**scorn•ful•ness**
**scorn•ing•ly**
**scor•pae•nid** fish
**scor•pae•noid**
**scor•per** (*or* **scau•**) chisel
**Scor•pi•an** of Scorpio
**Scor•pio** sign of zodiac
**scor•pi•oid**
**Scor•pi•on** Scorpius
**scor•pi•on** arachnid
**Scor•pius** constellation
**Scot**
**Scotch** whisky; eggs; broth; *its use as a synonym for* **Scottish** *or* **Scots** *is regarded as incorrect*
**scotch**
**sco•ter** (*plural* **•ters** *or* **•ter**) duck
**scot-free**
**sco•tia** architectural moulding
**Scot•land**
**sco•to•ma** (*plural* **•mas** *or* **•ma•ta**) visual defect
**sco•toma•tous**
**sco•to•pia** night vision
**sco•top•ic**
**Scots**
**Scots•man** (*plural* **•men**)
**Scots•woman** (*plural* **•women**)
**Scot•ti•cism**
**Scot•tie** (*or* **Scot•ty**; *plural* **•ties**)
**Scot•tish**
**scoun•drel**
**scoun•drel•ly**
**scour**
**scour•er**
**scourge**
**scourg•er**
**scourg•ing•ly**
**Scouse** Liverpudlian
**scouse** *Dialect* stew
**scout**
**scout•er**
**scout•master**
**scow** boat
**scowl**
**scowl•er**
**scowl•ing•ly**
**Scrab•ble** (*Trademark*) game
**scrab•ble**
**scrab•bler**
**scrag** (**scrag•ging, scragged**)
**scrag•gi•ly**
**scrag•gi•ness**
**scrag•gly** (**•gli•er, •gli•est**) untidy
**scrag•gy** (**•gi•er, •gi•est**) scrawny
**scram** (**scram•ming, scrammed**)
**scramb** (*or* **scram**) *Dialect* scratch
**scram•ble**
**scram•bler**
**scran** *Slang* food
**Scran•ton** US city
**scrap** (**scrap•ping, scrapped**)
**scrap•able**
**scrap•book**
**scrape**
**scrap•er**
**scrap•er•board**
**scrap•heap**
**scrap•pi•ly**
**scrap•pi•ness**
**scrap•py** (**•pi•er, •pi•est**)
**scratch**
**scratch•card**
**scratch•er**
**scratchi•ly**
**scratchi•ness**
**scratchy** (**scratchi•er, scratchi•est**)
**scrawl**
**scrawl•er**
**scrawly**
**scrawni•ly**
**scrawni•ness**
**scrawny** (**scrawni•er, scrawni•est**)
**screak** *Dialect* screech
**scream**
**scream•er**
**scree**
**screech**
**screech•er**
**screechy**
**screed**
**screen**
**screen•able**
**screen•er**
**screen•ings** sifted refuse
**screen•play**
**screw**
**screw•ball**
**screw•driver**
**screw•er**
**screw•worm**
**screwy** (**screwi•er, screwi•est**)
**scrib•al** of scribes
**scrib•ble**
**scrib•bler**
**scrib•bly**
**scribe**
**scrib•er** tool
**scrim** fabric
**scrim•mage** struggle; *compare* **scrummage**
**scrim•mag•er**
**scrimp**
**scrimpi•ly**
**scrimpi•ness**
**scrimpy** (**scrimpi•er, scrimpi•est**)
**scrim•shank** *Slang* shirk work
**scrim•shaw** sailors' carving
**scrip** certificate
**script**
**scrip•to•rium** (*plural* **•riums** *or* **•ria**)
**scrip•tur•al**
**scrip•ture** sacred book
**Scrip•tures** Bible
**script•writer**
**script•writing**
**scrive•ner**

**scro•bicu•late** (*or* **•lat•ed**) biology term
**scrod** *US* young cod
**scrofu•la**
**scrofu•lous**
**scroll**
**scroll•work**
**scroop** *Dialect* creak
**scrophu•laria•ceous** botany term
**scro•tal**
**scro•tum** (*plural* **•ta** *or* **•tums)**
**scrouge** *Dialect* to crowd
**scrounge**
**scroung•er**
**scrub (scrub•bing, scrubbed)**
**scrub•ber**
**scrub•bi•ness**
**scrub•by (•bi•er, •bi•est)**
**scrub•land**
**scruff**
**scruffi•ly**
**scruffi•ness**
**scruffy (scruffi•er, scruffi•est)**
**scrum (scrum•ming, scrummed)**
**scrum•mage** rugby scrum; *compare* **scrimmage**
**scrum•mag•er**
**scrump** *Dialect* steal apples
**scrump•tious**
**scrump•tious•ness**
**scrumpy** cider
**scrunch**
**scru•ple**
**scru•pu•lous**
**scru•pu•lous•ness**
**scru•ta•tor** examiner
**scru•ti•neer**
**scru•ti•nize** (*or* **•nise)**
**scru•ti•niz•er** (*or* **•nis•er)**
**scru•ti•niz•ing•ly** (*or* **•nis•ing•ly)**
**scru•ti•ny** (*plural* **•nies)**
**scry (scry•ing, scried)** crystal-gaze
**scu•ba**
**scud (scud•ding, scud•ded)**
**scuff**
**scuf•fle**
**scull** oar; *compare* **skull**
**scull•er**
**scul•lery** (*plural* **•leries)**
**scul•lion**
**scul•pin** (*plural* **•pin** *or* **•pins)** fish
**sculp•sit** *Latin* sculptured (*inscription on sculpture*)
**sculpt**
**sculp•tor** (*fem* **•tress)**
**sculp•tur•al**
**sculp•tur•al•ly**
**sculp•ture**
**sculp•tur•esque**
**scum (scum•ming, scummed)**
**scum•ble** art term
**scum•mer**
**scum•my (•mi•er, •mi•est)**
**scun•cheon** part of door jamb; *compare* **scutcheon**
**scunge** *Austral* borrow
**scungy (scungi•er, scungi•est)** *Austral* miserable
**scun•ner** *Scot* aversion
**Scun•thorpe**
**scup** fish
**scup•per** ship's drain
**scup•per•nong** wine
**scurf**
**scurfy**
**scur•ril•ity**
**scur•ril•ous**
**scur•ri•lous•ness**
**scur•ry** (*verb* **•ries, •ry•ing, •ried**; *noun, plural* **•ries)**
**scur•vi•ly**
**scur•vi•ness**
**scur•vy (•vi•er, •vi•est)**
**scut** tail
**scu•tage** feudal payment
**Scu•ta•ri** Albanian town; Turkish town
**scu•tate** biology term
**scu•ta•tion**
**scutch** separate fibres
**scutch•eon** escutcheon; *compare* **scuncheon**
**scute** zoology term
**scu•tel•lar**
**scu•tel•late**
**scu•tel•la•tion**
**scu•tel•lum** (*plural* **•la)** biology term
**scu•ti•form** shield-shaped
**scut•ter**
**scut•tle**
**scuttle•butt** ship's drinking fountain
**scu•tum** (*plural* **•ta)** zoology term; Roman shield
**Scylla** sea monster
**scy•phi•form** cup-shaped
**scy•phis•to•ma** (*plural* **•mae** *or* **•mas)** zoology term
**scy•pho•zo•an** jellyfish
**scy•phus** (*plural* **•phi)** drinking cup
**scythe**
**Scythia** ancient Asian region
**Scyth•ian**
**sea**
**sea•bed**
**sea•board**
**sea•borne**
**sea•coast**
**sea•cock**
**sea•dog**
**sea•farer**
**sea•faring**
**sea•food**
**sea•front**
**sea•girt**
**sea•going**
**sea•gull**
**seal** device; to close; animal; *compare* **seel**
**seal•able**
**sea-lane**
**seal•ant**
**sealed-beam**
**seal•er**
**seal•ery** (*plural* **•eries)**
**sea•lion**
**seal-point** Siamese cat
**seal•skin**
**Sealy•ham** terrier
**seam**
**sea•man** (*plural* **•men)** sailor; *compare* **semen**
**sea•man•ly**
**sea•man•ship**
**sea•mark**
**seam•er**
**seami•ness**
**seam•less**
**sea•mount** underwater mountain
**seam•stress** (*or* **semp•)**
**seamy (seami•er, seami•est)**

**Sean•ad Éire•ann** Irish parliament
**se•ance**
**sea•plane**
**sea•port**
**sea•quake**
**sear** scorch; gun part; *compare* **seer; sere**
**search**
**search•able**
**search•er**
**search•ing**
**search•ing•ly**
**search•light**
**sear•ing**
**sea•scape**
**sea•shell**
**sea•shore**
**sea•sick**
**sea•sick•ness**
**sea•side**
**sea•son**
**sea•son•able**
**sea•son•able•ness**
**sea•son•ably**
**sea•son•al**
**sea•son•al•ly**
**sea•son•al•ness**
**sea•soned•ly**
**sea•son•er**
**sea•son•ing**
**seat**
**seat•ed**
**seat•er**
**seat•ing**
**Se•at•tle**
**sea•wan** (*or* **se•wan**) shell beads
**sea•ward** (*adj*)
**sea•wards** (*adv*)
**sea•ware** seaweed
**sea•water**
**sea•way**
**sea•weed**
**sea•worthiness**
**sea•worthy**
**se•ba•ceous**
**Se•bas•to•pol** *variant spelling of* **Sevastopol**
**se•bif•er•ous** biology term
**seb•or•rhoea** (*US* **•rhea**)
**seb•or•rhoeal** (*or* **•rhoe•ic;** *US* **•rheal** *or* **•rhe•ic**)
**se•bum** oily secretion
**sec** *short for* **second** *or* **secant**; dry (*of wine*)
**se•cant**
**seca•teurs**
**sec•co** (*plural* **•cos**) wall painting
**se•cede** withdraw
**se•ced•er**
**se•ces•sion**
**se•ces•sion•al**
**se•ces•sion•ism**
**se•ces•sion•ist**
**se•clude**
**se•clud•ed** sheltered; *compare* **seclusive**
**se•clud•ed•ness**
**se•clu•sion**
**se•clu•sive** reclusive; *compare* **secluded**
**se•clu•sive•ness**
**sec•ond** unit of time; following first
**se•cond** transfer
**sec•ond•ari•ly**
**sec•ond•ari•ness**
**sec•ond•ary** (*plural* **•aries**)
**second-best** (*adj*)
**second-class** (*adj*)
**se•conde** fencing position
**sec•ond•er**
**second-floor** (*adj*)
**second-hand**
**se•cond•ment**
**se•con•do** (*plural* **•di**) part in piano duet
**second-rate**
**second-rater**
**second-sighted**
**se•cre•cy** (*plural* **•cies**)
**se•cret**
**sec•re•taire** writing desk
**sec•re•tar•ial**
**sec•re•tari•at**
**sec•re•tary** (*plural* **•taries**)
**sec•retary-general** (*plural* **sec•re•taries-general**)
**sec•re•tary•ship**
**se•crete**
**se•cre•tin** hormone
**se•cre•tion**
**se•cre•tion•ary**
**se•cre•tive**
**se•cre•tive•ness**
**se•cre•tory**
**sect**
**sec•tar•ian**
**sec•tari•an•ism**
**sec•tary** (*plural* **•taries**) member of sect
**sec•tile** easily sliced
**sec•til•ity**
**sec•tion**
**sec•tion•al**
**sec•tion•al•ism**
**sec•tion•al•ist**
**sec•tion•ali•za•tion** (*or* **•sa•tion**)
**sec•tion•al•ize** (*or* **•ise**)
**sec•tion•al•ly**
**sec•tor**
**sec•tor•al**
**sec•to•rial**
**secu•lar**
**secu•lar•ism**
**secu•lar•ist**
**secu•lar•is•tic**
**secu•lar•ity** (*plural* **•ities**)
**secu•lari•za•tion** (*or* **•sa•tion**)
**secu•lar•ize** (*or* **•ise**)
**secu•lar•iz•er** (*or* **•is•er**)
**se•cund** botany term
**sec•un•dine** botany term
**sec•un•dines** (*plural*) afterbirth
**se•cur•able**
**se•cure**
**se•cure•ment**
**se•cure•ness**
**se•cur•er**
**se•cu•rity** (*plural* **•rities**)
**se•dan**
**se•date**
**se•date•ness**
**se•da•tion**
**seda•tive**
**sed•en•tari•ly**
**sed•en•tari•ness**
**sed•en•tary**
**Se•der** Jewish meal
**sedge**
**Sedge•moor** English battle site
**sedgy**
**se•di•lia** (*sing.* **•le**) church seats
**sedi•ment**
**sedi•men•tari•ly**
**sedi•men•tary** (*or* **•tal**)
**sedi•men•ta•tion**

**sedi•men•tol•ogy**
**sedi•men•tous**
**se•di•tion**
**se•di•tion•ary** (*plural* **•aries**)
**se•di•tious**
**se•di•tious•ness**
**se•duce**
**se•duc•er**
**se•duc•ible** (*or* **•duce•able**)
**se•duc•ing•ly**
**se•duc•tion**
**se•duc•tive**
**se•duc•tive•ness**
**se•duc•tress**
**se•du•lity**
**sedu•lous**
**sedu•lous•ness**
**se•dum** plant
**see** (**see•ing, saw, seen**)
**see•able**
**See•beck** philately term
**seed**
**seed•bed**
**seed•cake**
**seed•case**
**seed•er**
**seedi•ly**
**seedi•ness**
**seed•less**
**seed•ling**
**seedy** (**seedi•er, seedi•est**)
**see•ing**
**seek** (**seek•ing, sought**)
**seek•er**
**seel** falconry term; *compare* seal
**seem**
**seem•er**
**seem•ing**
**seem•ing•ly**
**seem•li•ness**
**seem•ly** (**•li•er, •li•est**)
**seen**
**seep**
**seep•age**
**seer** prophet; *compare* sear; sere
**seer•sucker**
**see•saw**
**seethe**
**seeth•ing•ly**
**Sef•ton** area of Merseyside
**seg•ment**
**seg•men•tal**
**seg•men•tary**
**seg•men•ta•tion**
**se•gno** (*plural* **•gni**) musical term
**Se•go•via** Spanish town
**seg•re•gable**
**seg•re•gate**
**seg•re•ga•tion**
**seg•re•ga•tion•al**
**seg•re•ga•tion•ist**
**seg•re•ga•tive**
**seg•re•ga•tor**
**se•gui•dil•la** dance
**seiche** water movement
(**seige**) *incorrect spelling of* siege
**sei•gneur**
**sei•gneu•rial**
**sei•gneury** (*plural* **•gneuries**)
**sei•gnior•age**
**Seine** French river
**seine** fishing net
**Seine-et-Marne** French department
**Seine-Maritime** French department
**Seine-Saint-Denis** French department
**seis•able**
**seise** legal term; *compare* seize
**seis•er**
**sei•sin** legal term
**seism** earthquake
**seis•mic** (*or* **•mal, •mi•cal**)
**seis•mi•cal•ly**
**seis•mism**
**seis•mo•gram**
**seis•mo•graph**
**seis•mog•ra•pher**
**seis•mo•graph•ic**
**seis•mog•ra•phy**
**seis•mo•log•ic** (*or* **•logi•cal**)
**seis•molo•gist**
**seis•mol•ogy**
**seis•mo•scope**
**seis•mo•scop•ic**
(**seive**) *incorrect spelling of* sieve
**seiz•able**
**seize** grasp; *compare* seise
**seiz•er**
**seiz•ing**
**sei•zure**
**se•jant** (*or* **•jeant**) heraldic term
**Sejm** Polish legislature
**Sek•on•di** Ghanaian port
**se•la•chian** zoology term
**sela•gi•nel•la** moss
**Se•lan•gor** Malaysian state
**sel•dom**
**se•lect**
**se•lec•tion**
**se•lec•tive**
**se•lec•tive•ness**
**se•lec•tiv•ity**
**se•lect•ness**
**se•lec•tor**
**sel•enate**
**se•lenic**
**se•leni•ous** (*or* **•lenous**)
**sel•enite** mineral
**se•lenium** chemical element
**se•leno•graph**
**se•lenog•ra•pher** (*or* **•phist**)
**se•leno•graph•ic** (*or* **•graphi•cal**)
**se•leno•graphi•cal•ly**
**se•lenog•ra•phy** mapping moon's surface
**se•lenolo•gist**
**se•lenol•ogy** study of moon
**se•leno•mor•phol•ogy**
**Se•leu•cid** (*plural* **•cids** *or* **•cidae**) member of Hellenistic dynasty
**self** (*plural* **selves**)
**self-abasement**
**self-abnega•tion**
**self-absorbed**
**self-absorp•tion**
**self-abuse**
**self-action**
**self-actuali•za•tion**
**self-addressed**
**self-aggran•dize•ment**
**self-analy•sis**
**self-analyti•cal**
**self-anneal•ing**
**self-annihi•la•tion**
**self-appoint•ed**
**self-assertion**
**self-assertive**
**self-assurance**
**self-assured**
**self-aware**
**self-aware•ness**
**self-cater•ing**
**self-centred** (*US* **-centered**)

**self-centred•ness** (*US* **-centered•ness)**
**self-coloured** (*US* **-colored)**
**self-concept**
**self-confessed**
**self-confidence**
**self-confident**
**self-conscious**
**self-conscious•ness**
**self-contained**
**self-contra•dic•tion**
**self-contra•dic•tory**
**self-control**
**self-controlled**
**self-deception** (*or* **-deceit)**
**self-deceptive**
**self-defence**
**self-denial**
**self-denying**
**self-discipline**
**self-disciplined**
**self-educat•ed**
**self-employed**
**self-efface•ment**
**self-effacing**
**self-esteem**
**self-evident**
**self-evidence**
**self-feeder**
**self-fertile**
**self-fertili•za•tion** (*or* **•sa•tion)**
**self-fertilized** (*or* **-fertilised)**
**self-govern•ment**
**self•heal** plant
**self-help**
**self•hood**
**self-image**
**self-import•ance**
**self-import•ant**
**self-imposed**
**self-improve•ment**
**self-induced**
**self-induct•ance**
**self-induction**
**self-inductive**
**self-indulgence**
**self-indulgent**
**self-inflict•ed**
**self-inflic•tion**
**self-interest**
**self•ish**
**self•ish•ness**
**self-justifi•ca•tion**
**self-justify•ing**
**self-knowledge**
**self•less**
**self•less•ness**
**self-liquidat•ing**
**self-loading**
**self-made**
**self-opin•ion•at•ed** (*or* **-opinioned)**
**self-pity**
**self-pitying**
**self-pollinat•ed**
**self-pollina•tion**
**self-portrait**
**self-possessed**
**self-posses•sion**
**self-preser•va•tion**
**self-propelled**
**self-protec•tion**
**self-raising**
**self-regard**
**self-reliance**
**self-reliant**
**self-reproach**
**self-reproach•ful**
**self-respect**
**self-respect•ing**
**self-restraint**
**self-righteous**
**self-righteous•ness**
**self-rule**
**self-sacrifice**
**self-sacrific•ing**
**self•same**
**self-satisfac•tion**
**self-satisfied**
**self-sealing**
**self-seeker**
**self-seeking**
**self-service**
**self-starter**
**self-styled**
**self-sufficiency**
**self-sufficient** (*or* **-suffic•ing)**
**self-taught**
**self-willed**
**self-winding**
**Sel•juk** (*or* **•ju•kian)** member of Turkish dynasty
**Sel•kirk** former Scottish county
**sell (sell•ing, sold)**
**sell•er**
**selling-plater** type of racehorse
**Sel•lo•tape** (*Trademark*)
**sell•out** (*noun*)
**Selt•zer** mineral water
**sel•va** forest
**sel•vage** (*or* **•vedge)** edge of fabric; *compare* **salvage**
**selves** *plural of* **self**
**se•man•tic**
**se•man•ti•cal•ly**
**se•man•ti•cist**
**se•man•tics**
**sema•phore**
**sema•phor•ic** (*or* **•phori•cal)**
**sema•phori•cal•ly**
**Se•ma•rang** (*or* **Sa•)** Indonesian port
**se•ma•sio•logi•cal**
**se•ma•sio•logi•cal•ly**
**se•ma•si•olo•gist**
**se•ma•siol•ogy** semantics
**se•mat•ic** zoology term
**sema•tol•ogy** semantics
**sem•blance**
**semé** (*or* **se•mée)** heraldry term
**sem•eme** linguistics term
**se•men** ejaculated fluid; *compare* **seaman**
**se•mes•ter**
**se•mes•tral**
**semi** (*plural* **semis)**
**semi•an•nual**
**semi•an•nu•al•ly**
**semi•aquat•ic**
**semi•ar•id**
**semi•arid•ity**
**semi•auto•mat•ic**
**semi•auto•mati•cal•ly**
**Semi-Bantu** African language
**semi•bold** printing term
**semi•breve**
**semi•cen•ten•nial**
**semi•cir•cle**
**semi•cir•cu•lar**
**semi•co•lon**
**semi•con•duc•tion**
**semi•con•duc•tor**
**semi•con•scious**
**semi•con•scious•ness**
**semi•de•tached**
**semi•di•am•eter**
**semi•di•ur•nal**

**semi•dome**
**semi•el•lip•ti•cal**
**semi•fi•nal**
**semi•fi•nal•ist**
**semi•flu•id**
**semi•flu•id•ic**
**semi•flu•id•ity**
**semi•lit•er•ate**
**semi•lu•nar**
**semi•month•ly**
**semi•nal**
**semi•nal•ity**
**semi•nal•ly**
**semi•nar**
**semi•nar•ial**
**semi•nar•ian** student at seminary
**semi•nary** (*plural* **•naries**)
**semi•nif•er•ous** transporting semen
**Semi•nole** (*plural* **•noles** *or* **•nole**) American Indian
**se•mi•ol•ogy** (*or* **•mei•**)
**se•mi•ot•ic** (*or* **•mei•**)
**se•mi•ot•ics** (*or* **•mei•**) study of symbols
**Se•mi•pa•la•tinsk** Kazakh city
**semi•pal•mate** (*or* **•mat•ed**) zoology term
**semi•para•sit•ic**
**semi•para•sit•ism**
**semi•per•meabil•ity**
**semi•per•meable**
**semi•porce•lain**
**semi•precious**
**semi•pro** (*plural* **•pros**)
**semi•pro•fes•sion•al**
**semi•qua•ver**
**Se•mira•mis** legendary queen
**semi•rig•id**
**semi•skilled**
**semi•sol•id**
**Se•mite** (*or* **Shem•ite**)
**Se•mit•ic** (*or* **She•**)
**Se•mit•ics** study of Semitic languages
**Semi•tist**
**semi•ton•al•ly**
**semi•tone**
**semi•ton•ic**
**semi•trail•er**
**semi•tropi•cal**
**semi•trop•ics**
**semi•vit•reous**
**semi•vo•cal** (*or* **•cal•ic**)
**semi•vow•el**
**semi•week•ly**
**semi•year•ly**
**semo•li•na**
**sem•per fi•de•lis** *Latin* always faithful
**sem•per pa•ra•tus** *Latin* always prepared
**sem•pi•ter•nal** everlasting
**sem•pi•ter•nity**
**sem•pli•ce** musical term
**sem•pre** musical term
**semp•stress** *variant spelling of* **seamstress**
**sen** (*plural* **sen**) Oriental currency
**sen•ar•mon•tite** mineral
**sen•ary** of six
**Sen•ate** senate of USA, ancient Rome, etc.
**sen•ate** legislative body
**sena•tor**
**sena•to•rial**
**send** (**send•ing, sent**)
**send•able**
**Sen•dai** Japanese city
**sen•dal** fabric
**send•er**
**send•off**
**send-up** (*noun*)
**Sen•eca** (*plural* **•ecas** *or* **•eca**) American Indian
**sen•ega** plant
**Sen•egal**
**Sen•ega•lese**
**Sen•egam•bia** African region
**se•nes•cence**
**se•nes•cent**
**sen•eschal** medieval steward
**sen•hor** (*plural* **•hors** *or* **•hores**) *Portuguese* man; Mr
**sen•hora** *Portuguese* woman; Mrs
**sen•hor•ita** *Portuguese* young woman; Miss
**se•nile**
**se•nil•ity**
**sen•ior**
**sen•ior•ity** (*plural* **•ities**)
**Sen•lac** battle site
**sen•na**
**Sen•nar** Sudanese region
**sen•net** fanfare
**sen•nit** braided cordage
**se•ñor** (*plural* **•ñors** *or* **•ñores**) *Spanish* man; Mr
**se•ño•ra** *Spanish* woman; Mrs
**se•ño•ri•ta** *Spanish* young woman; Miss
**sen•sate** (**•sat•ed**)
**sen•sa•tion**
**sen•sa•tion•al**
**sen•sa•tion•al•ly**
**sen•sa•tion•al•ism**
**sen•sa•tion•al•ist**
**sen•sa•tion•al•is•tic**
**sense**
**sense•less**
**sense•less•ness**
**sen•si•bilia** what can be sensed
**sen•sibil•ity** (*plural* **•ities**)
**sen•sible**
**sen•sible•ness**
**sen•sibly**
**sen•sil•lum** (*plural* **•la**) zoology term
**sen•si•tive**
**sen•si•tive•ness**
**sen•si•tiv•ity** (*plural* **•ities**)
**sen•si•ti•za•tion** (*or* **•sa•tion**)
**sen•si•tize** (*or* **•tise**)
**sen•si•tiz•er** (*or* **•tis•er**)
**sen•si•tom•eter**
**sen•si•tom•etry**
**sen•sor** sensing device; *compare* **censor**
**sen•so•ri•mo•tor** (*or* **sen•so•mo•tor**) physiology term
**sen•so•rium** area of brain
**sen•so•ry** (*or* **•rial**)
**sen•sual** gratifying the senses; *compare* **censual**; **sensuous**
**sen•su•al•ism**
**sen•su•al•ist**
**sen•su•al•ity** (*plural* **•ities**)
**sen•su•al•ly**
**sen•su•al•ness**
**sen•su•ous** pleasing to the senses; *compare* **sensual**
**sen•su•ous•ness**
**sent**
**sen•tence**

**sen•ten•tial**
**sen•ten•tious**
**sen•ten•tious•ness**
**sen•tience** (*or* **•tien•cy)**
**sen•ti•ent**
**sen•ti•ment**
**sen•ti•ment•al**
**sen•ti•men•tal•ism**
**sen•ti•men•tal•ist**
**sen•ti•men•tal•ity** (*plural* **•ities)**
**sen•ti•men•tali•za•tion** (*or* **•sa•tion)**
**sen•ti•men•tal•ize** (*or* **•ise)**
**sen•ti•men•tal•ly**
**sen•ti•nel**
**sen•try** (*plural* **•tries)**
**Se•nus•si** (*or* **•nu•si**; *plural* **•sis)** member of Muslim sect
**sen•za** musical term
**Seoul** capital of South Korea
**sep•al**
**se•palled** (*or* **•pal•ous)**
**se•pa•loid** (*or* **•line)**
**sepa•rabil•ity** (*or* **•rable•ness)**
**sepa•rable**
**sepa•rate**
**sepa•rate•ness**
**sepa•ra•tion**
**sepa•ra•tism**
**sepa•ra•tist** (*or* **•ra•tion•ist)**
**sepa•ra•tis•tic**
**sepa•ra•tive**
**sepa•ra•tive•ness**
**sepa•ra•tor**
**sepa•ra•trix** (*plural* **•trices)** oblique stroke
**Se•phar•di** (*plural* **•dim)** Iberian Jew
**Se•phar•dic**
**se•pia**
**se•pio•lite** mineral
**se•poy** Indian soldier
**sep•sis**
**sept** clan
**sep•ta** *plural of* **septum**
**sep•tal**
**sep•tar•ian**
**sep•tar•ium** (*plural* **•ia)** geology term
**sep•tate**
**sep•ta•va•lent** *variant spelling of* **septivalent**
**Sep•tem•ber**
**Sep•tem•brist** French revolutionary
**sep•te•nary** (*plural* **•naries)**
**sep•ten•nial**
**sep•ten•nium** (*plural* **•niums** *or* **•nia)**
**sep•tet** (*or* **•tette)**
**sep•tic** putrefying; *compare* **sceptic**
**sep•ti•cae•mia** (*US* **•cemia)**
**sep•ti•cae•mic** (*US* **•cemic)**
**sep•ti•cal•ly**
**sep•ti•cid•al** botany term
**sep•tic•ity**
**sep•tif•ra•gal** botany term
**sep•ti•lat•er•al**
**sep•til•lion** (*plural* **•lion** *or* **•lions)** $10^{42}$
**sep•til•lionth**
**sep•time** fencing position
**sep•ti•va•lent** (*or* **•ta•)**
**sep•tua•genar•ian**
**Sep•tua•gesi•ma** third Sunday before Lent
**Sep•tua•gint** Greek Old Testament
**sep•tum** (*plural* **•ta)**
**sep•tu•ple**
**sep•tup•let**
**sep•tu•pli•cate**
**se•pul•chral**
**se•pul•chral•ly**
**sep•ul•chre** (*US* **•cher)**
**sep•ul•ture** burial
**se•qua•cious** in sequence
**se•quac•ity**
**se•quel**
**se•quela** (*plural* **•quelae)** medical term
**se•quence**
**se•quenc•er** electronic device
**se•quent**
**se•quen•tial**
**se•quen•ti•al•ity**
**se•quen•tial•ly**
**se•ques•ter**
**se•ques•trable**
**se•ques•tral**
**se•ques•trant**
**se•ques•trate**
**se•ques•tra•tion**
**se•ques•tra•tor**
**se•ques•trum** (*plural* **•tra)** medical term
**se•quin**
**se•quined**
**se•quoia**
**ser** (*or* **seer)** Indian unit
**sera** *plural of* **serum**
**sé•rac** ice pinnacle
**se•ra•glio** (*plural* **•glios)**
**se•rail** harem
**Se•rang** Indonesian island
**ser•aph** (*plural* **•aphs** *or* **•aphim)** angel; *compare* **serif**
**se•raph•ic** (*or* **•raphi•cal)**
**Sera•pis** Egyptian god
**Serb** a Serbian
**Ser•bia** Yugoslav republic
**Ser•bian**
**Serbo-Croat** (*or* **-Croa•tian)** language
**ser•dab** chamber in Egyptian tomb
**sere** ecology term; *compare* **cere; sear; seer**
**sere** (*or* **sear)** withered; *compare* **cere; sear; seer**
**se•rein** tropical rain
**ser•enade**
**ser•enad•er**
**se•rena•ta** cantata
**ser•en•dip•ity**
**se•rene**
**se•rene•ness**
**se•ren•ity** (*plural* **•ities)**
**serf** medieval peasant; *compare* **surf**
**serf•dom** (*or* **•hood)**
**serge** fabric; *compare* **surge**
**ser•gean•cy** (*or* **•geant•ship)**
**ser•geant**
**Ser•gi•pe** Brazilian state
**se•rial** story in instalments; in series; *compare* **cereal**
**se•rial•ism**
**se•riali•za•tion** (*or* **•sa•tion)**
**se•rial•ize** (*or* **•ise)**
**se•rial•ly**
**se•ri•ate**
**se•ria•tim** in a series
**se•ri•ceous**
**seri•cin** protein in silk
**seri•cul•tur•al**

**seri•cul•ture** silkworm rearing
**seri•cul•tur•ist**
**seri•ema** bird
**se•ries** (*plural* **•ries**)
**series-wound** electrical term
**ser•if** (*or* **•iph**) printing term; *compare* **seraph**
**seri•graph** silk-screen print
**se•rig•ra•phy**
**ser•in** bird
**ser•ine** amino acid
**se•rin•ga** rubber tree; *compare* **syringa**
**se•rio•com•ic** (*or* **•comi•cal**)
**se•rio•comi•cal•ly**
**se•ri•ous** grave; *compare* **serous**
**se•ri•ous•ly**
**se•ri•ous•ness**
**ser•jeant at law**
**ser•mon**
**ser•mon•ic**
**ser•moni•cal**
**ser•mon•ize** (*or* **•ise**)
**ser•mon•iz•er** (*or* **•is•er**)
**se•ro•log•ic** (*or* **•logi•cal**)
**se•rolo•gist**
**se•rol•ogy** study of serums
**se•ro•sa** membrane
**se•rosi•ty** (*or* **•rous•ness**)
**se•roti•nal** (*or* **•nous**)
**sero•tine** bat
**sero•to•nin** biochemical compound
**se•rous** of serum; *compare* **serious**
**ser•ow** antelope
**ser•pent**
**ser•pen•tine**
**ser•pigi•nous**
**ser•pi•go** skin disease
**ser•pu•lid** worm
**ser•ra•nid** (*or* **•noid**) fish
**ser•rate**
**ser•rat•ed**
**ser•ra•tion** (*or* **•ture**)
**ser•ried**
**ser•ri•form**
**ser•ru•late** (*or* **•lat•ed**)
**ser•ru•la•tion** notch
**ser•tu•lar•ian** zoology term
**se•rum** (*plural* **•rums** *or* **•ra**)
**serv•able** (*or* **serve•**)
**ser•val** (*plural* **•vals** *or* **•val**) animal
**serv•ant**
**serve**
**serv•er**
**serv•ery** (*plural* **•eries**)
**ser•vice**
**ser•vice•abil•ity** (*or* **•able•ness**)
**ser•vice•able**
**ser•vice•ably**
**ser•vice•berry** (*plural* **•berries**)
**ser•vice•man** (*plural* **•men**)
**ser•vi•ette**
**ser•vile**
**ser•vil•ity** (*or* **•vile•ness**)
**serv•ing**
**ser•vi•tor**
**ser•vi•tude**
**ser•vo** (*plural* **•vos**)
**ser•vo•mechani•cal**
**ser•vo•mecha•nism**
**ser•vo•mo•tor**
**sesa•me**
**sesa•moid** bone
**Se•so•tho** language
**ses•qui•al•te•ra** organ stop
**ses•qui•car•bon•ate**
**ses•qui•cen•ten•nial**
**ses•qui•ox•ide**
**ses•qui•peda•lian** (*or* **•quip•edal**) using long words
**ses•qui•peda•li•an•ism**
**ses•sile**
**ses•sil•ity**
**ses•sion** meeting; *compare* **cession**
**ses•sion•al**
**ses•sion•al•ly**
**ses•terce** (*or* **•ter•tius**; *plural* **•terces** *or* **•tia**) Roman coin
**ses•ter•tium** (*plural* **•tia**) Roman coin
**ses•tet** six-line verse; *compare* **sextet**
**ses•ti•na** verse form
**Ses•tos** ancient Turkish town
**set** (**set•ting, set**)
**seta** (*plural* **setae**) small bristle
**se•ta•ceous**
**se•tal**
**set•back**
**se•ti•form**
**set•line**
**set-off** printing term
**se•tose** bristly
**set•screw**
**sett** (*or* **set**) paving slab; badger's den
**set•tee**
**set•ter**
**set•ting**
**set•tle**
**set•tle•able**
**set•tle•ment**
**set•tler** (*or in legal contexts* **•tlor**)
**set-to** (*noun, plural* **-tos**)
**set-up** (*noun*)
**Se•van** Armenian lake
**Se•vas•to•pol** (*or* **•bas•**) Ukrainian port
**sev•en**
**sev•en•fold**
**sev•en•teen**
**sev•en•teenth**
**sev•enth**
**sev•en•ti•eth**
**sev•en•ty** (*plural* **•ties**)
**sev•er**
**sev•er•able**
**sev•er•al**
**sev•er•al•ly**
**sev•er•al•ty** (*plural* **•ties**) separateness
**sev•er•ance**
**se•vere**
**se•vere•ness**
**se•ver•ity** (*plural* **•ities**)
**Sev•ern** British river
**Se•ville** Spanish port
**Sèvres** porcelain
**sew** (**sew•ing, sewed, sewn** *or* **sewed**) to stitch; *compare* **sow**
**sew•age** waste matter
**sew•er** sewage drain; one who sews; *compare* **suer**
**sew•er•age** system of sewers
**sew•ing**
**sewn**
**sex**
**sexa•genar•ian**
**sex•ag•enary** (*plural* **•enaries**)

**Sexa•gesi•ma** second Sunday before Lent
**sexa•gesi•mal** of 60
**sex•cen•te•nary** (*plural* **•naries)**
**sex•en•nial**
**sexi•ly**
**sexi•ness**
**sex•ism**
**sex•ist**
**sexi•va•lent** (*or* **sexa•)**
**sex•less**
**sex•less•ness**
**sex•olo•gist**
**sex•ol•ogy**
**sex•par•tite**
**sex•pot**
**sext** canonical hour
**sex•tant**
**sex•tet** (*or* **•tette)** group of six; *compare* **sestet**
**sex•tile**
**sex•til•lion** (*plural* **•lions** *or* **•lion)** $10^{36}$
**sex•til•lionth**
**sex•to•deci•mo** (*plural* **•mos)**
**sex•ton**
**sex•tu•ple**
**sex•tup•let**
**sex•tu•pli•cate**
**sex•ual**
**sexu•al•ity**
**sex•ual•ly**
**sexy** (**sexi•er, sexi•est)**
**Sey•chelles**
**Sfax** Tunisian port
**sfor•zan•do** (*or* **•za•to)** musical term
**sfu•ma•to** art term
**sgraf•fi•to** (*plural* **•ti)** art term
**Sha•ba** region of the Democratic Republic of Congo
**shab•bi•ly**
**shab•bi•ness**
**shab•by** (**•bi•er, •bi•est)**
**shack**
**shack•le**
**shack•ler**
**shad** (*plural* **shad** *or* **shads)** fish
**shad•bush**
**shad•dock** fruit
**shade**
**shadi•ly**
**shadi•ness**
**shad•ing**
**sha•doof** (*or* **•duf)** water-raising device
**shad•ow**
**shadow-box**
**shadow-boxing**
**shad•ow•er**
**shad•ow•graph**
**shad•owi•ness**
**shad•owy**
**Shadrach** biblical character
**shady** (**shadi•er, shadi•est)**
**shaft**
**shaft•ing**
**shag** (**shag•ging, shagged)**
**shag•bark** (*or* **shell•bark)**
**shag•gi•ly**
**shag•gi•ness**
**shag•gy** (**•gi•er, •gi•est)**
**sha•green**
**shah**
**shah•dom**
**Shah•ja•han•pur** Indian city
**shak•able** (*or* **shake•)**
**shake** (**shak•ing, shook, shak•en)**
**shake•down** (*noun*)
**shak•er**
**Shak•ers** US sect
**Shake•spear•ean** (*or* **•ian)**
**Shake•spear•ea•na**
**shake-up** (*noun*)
**Shakh•ty** Russian city
**shaki•ly**
**shaki•ness**
**shako** (*or* **shacko**; *plural* **shakos** *or* **shackos)** military headdress
**shaky** (**shaki•er, shaki•est)**
**shale**
**shall** (**should)**
**shal•loon** fabric
**shal•lop** boat
**shal•lot**
**shal•low**
**shal•low•ness**
**sha•lom** Jewish greeting; *compare* **slalom**
**shalt**
**shaly**
**sham** (**sham•ming, shammed)**
**sham•able** (*or* **shame•)**
**sham•an** priest
**sham•an•ism**
**Sha•mash** Assyrian god
**sham•ble**
**sham•bles**
**sham•bol•ic**
**shame**
**shame•faced**
**shame•faced•ness**
**shame•ful**
**shame•ful•ly**
**shame•ful•ness**
**shame•less**
**shame•less•ness**
**sham•mer**
**sham•my** (*plural* **•mies)** leather
**sham•poo** (*noun, plural* **•poos**; *verb* **•poos, •poo•ing, •pooed)**
**sham•poo•er**
**sham•rock**
**Shan** (*plural* **Shans** *or* **Shan)** Mongoloid people
**shan•dry•dan** cart
**shan•dy** (*plural* **•dies)**
**shan•dy•gaff** *US* shandy
**Shang** Chinese dynasty
**Shang•hai** Chinese port
**shang•hai** (**•hais, •hai•ing, •haied)** kidnap
**Shangri-la**
**shank**
**Shan•non** Irish river
**shan•ny** (*plural* **•nies)** fish
**Shan•si** Chinese province
**shan't** shall not
**Shan•tung** Chinese province
**shan•tung** silk
**shan•ty** (*plural* **•ties)** hut
**shan•ty** (*or* **shan•tey, chan•ty**; *US* **chan•tey**; *plural* **•ties** *or* **•teys)** sea song
**shanty•town**
**shap•able** (*or* **shape•)**
**shape**
**shape•less**
**shape•less•ness**
**shape•li•ness**
**shape•ly** (**•li•er, •li•est)**
**shap•er**
**shar•able** (*or* **share•)**

**shard** (*or* **sherd**)
**share**
**share•crop** (**•crop•ping, •cropped**)
**share•crop•per**
**share•holder**
**share-out** (*noun*)
**shar•er**
**sha•ria** (*or* **she•**) Islamic doctrines
**shark**
**shark•skin**
**Sha•ron** Israeli plain
**sharp**
**sharp•en**
**sharp•en•er**
**sharp•er**
**sharp-eyed**
**sharp•ish**
**sharp•ness**
**sharp-set**
**sharp•shooter**
**sharp-sighted**
**sharp-sighted•ness**
**sharp-tongued**
**sharp-witted**
**sharp-witted•ness**
**shash•lik** (*or* **•lick**) kebab
**shat•ter**
**shat•ter•er**
**shat•ter•ing•ly**
**shatter•proof**
**shav•able** (*or* **shave•**)
**shave** (**shav•ing, shaved, shaved** *or* **shav•en**)
**shav•er**
**Sha•vian** of G. B. Shaw
**shav•ing**
**shawl**
**shawm** musical instrument
**Shaw•nee** (*plural* **•nees** *or* **•nee**) American Indian
**she**
**shea** tree
**shead•ing** Manx region
**sheaf** (*plural* **sheaves**)
**shear** (**shear•ing, sheared, sheared** *or* **shorn**) cut; deformation; *compare* **sheer**
**shear•er**
**shear•legs** *variant spelling of* **sheerlegs**
**shear•ling**
**shears**
**shear•water** bird
**sheat•fish** (*plural* **•fish** *or* **•fishes**)
**sheath** (*noun; plural* **sheaths**)
**sheath•bill**
**sheathe** (*verb*)
**sheath•ing**
**sheave** bind in sheaves; grooved wheel
**She•ba** ancient kingdom
**she•bang** *Slang* situation
**she•been** (*or* **•bean**) illegal drinking place
**She•chem** ancient Jordanian town
**shed** (**shed•ding, shed**)
**she'd** she had; she would
**shed•able** (*or* **shed•dable**)
**shed•der**
**sheen**
**sheeny**
**sheep** (*plural* **sheep**)
**sheep•cote**
**sheep-dip**
**sheep•dog**
**sheep•fold**
**sheep•ish**
**sheep•ish•ness**
**sheep•shank** knot
**sheeps•head** (*plural* **•head** *or* **•heads**) fish
**sheep•shearer**
**sheep•shearing**
**sheep•skin**
**sheep•walk** grazing land
**sheer** steep; transparent; absolutely; deviate; *compare* **shear**
**sheer•legs** (*or* **shear•**) lifting device
**Sheer•ness** English port
**sheer•ness**
**sheet**
**sheet•ing**
**Shef•field**
**sheik** (*or* **sheikh**)
**sheik•dom** (*or* **sheikh•**)
**shei•la** *Austral* girl
**shek•el**
**shel•duck** (*or* **•drake**; *plural* **•ducks, •duck** *or* **•drakes, •drake**)
**shelf** (*plural* **shelves**)
**shell**
**she'll** she will
**shel•lac** (**•lack•ing, •lacked**)
**shell•back** experienced sailor
**shell•fire**
**shell•fish** (*plural* **•fish** *or* **•fishes**)
**shell-less**
**shell-like**
**shell•proof**
**shell-shocked**
**Shel•ta** tinkers' language
**shel•ter**
**shel•ter•er**
**shel•tie** (*or* **•ty**; *plural* **•ties**) dog; pony
**shelve** (*verb*)
**shelv•er**
**shelv•ing**
**She•ma** Jewish doctrine
**she•moz•zle**
**Shen•an•do•ah** US river; national park
**she•nani•gan**
**Shen•si** Chinese province
**Shen•yang** Chinese city
**She•ol** abode of the dead
**shep•herd**
**shep•herd•ess**
**shepherd's-purse**
**Shep•pey (Isle of)**
**sher•ardi•za•tion** (*or* **•sa•tion**)
**sher•ard•ize** (*or* **•ise**)
**Sheraton** furniture
**sher•bet**
**Sher•brooke** Canadian city
**sherd** *variant spelling of* **shard**
**she•rif** (*or* **•reef**) Muslim ruler
**sher•iff** officer
**Sher•pa** (*plural* **•pas** *or* **•pa**)
**sher•ry** (*plural* **•ries**)
**sher•wa•ni** Indian coat
**she's** she is
**Shet•land**
**shew•bread** (*or* **show•**) biblical bread
**Shi•ah** Muslim sect
**shiai** judo contest
**shib•bo•leth**
**shick•er** *Austral* alcoholic drink
**shied**

**shield**
**shield•er**
**shiel•ing** *Scot* hut; pasture
**shi•er** (*adj*) *variant spelling of* **shyer**
**shi•est** *variant spelling of* **shyest**
**shift**
**shift•er**
**shifti•ly**
**shifti•ness**
**shift•ing•ly**
**shift•less**
**shift•less•ness**
**shifty** (**shifti•er, shifti•est**)
**shi•gel•la** bacterium
**Shih•chia•chuang** (*or* **•kia•chwang**) Chinese city
**shih-tzu** dog
**Shi•ism**
**Shi•ite** adherent of Shiah
**shi•kar** (**•kar•ring, •karred**) hunt game
**shi•ka•ri** (*or* **•ree**; *plural* **•ris** *or* **•rees**) hunter
**Shi•ko•ku** Japanese island
**shil•lelagh** (*or* **shil•la•la**) Irish cudgel
**shil•ling**
**Shil•long** Indian city
**shilly•shalli•er**
**shilly•shally** (**•shallies, •shally•ing, •shallied**)
**Shi•loh** biblical city
**shi•ly** *less common spelling of* **shyly**
**shim** (**shim•ming, shimmed**)
**shim•mer**
**shim•mer•ing•ly**
**shim•mery**
**shim•my** (*noun, plural* **•mies**; *verb* **•mies, •my•ing, •mied**) dance
**Shi•mo•no•seki** Japanese port
**shin** (**shin•ning, shinned**)
**shin•bone**
**shin•dig** (*or* **•dy**; *plural* **•digs** *or* **•dies**)
**shine** (**shin•ing, shone**)
**shin•er**
**shin•gle**
**shin•gler**
**shin•gles**
**shin•gly**
**shini•ness**
**Shin•to** Japanese religion
**Shin•to•ism**
**Shin•to•ist**
**shin•ty** (*US* **•ny**; *plural* **•ties** *or* **•nies**) hockey
**shiny** (**shini•er, shini•est**)
**ship** (**ship•ping, shipped**)
**ship•able**
**ship•board**
**ship•builder**
**ship•building**
**ship•load**
**ship•master** (*or* **•man**; *plural* **•masters** *or* **•men**)
**ship•mate**
**ship•ment**
**ship•owner**
**ship•per**
**ship•ping**
**ship-rigged**
**ship•shape**
**ship•way**
**ship•worm**
**ship•wreck**
**ship•wright**
**ship•yard**
**shi•ra•lee** *Austral* swagman's bundle
**Shi•raz** Iranian city
**Shi•ré** African river
**shire**
**shirk**
**shirk•er**
**shirr**
**shirr•ing**
**shirt**
**shirti•ly**
**shirti•ness**
**shirt•ing**
**shirt•sleeve**
**shirt-tail**
**shirt•waister**
**shirty** (**shirti•er, shirti•est**)
**shit** (**shit•ting, shit•ted** *or* **shit**)
**shit•tah** (*plural* **•tim** *or* **•tahs**) biblical tree
**Shit•tim** biblical place
**shit•ty**
**Shiva** *variant spelling of* **Siva**
**shive** cork
**shiv•er**
**shiv•er•er**
**shiv•er•ing•ly**
**shiv•ery**
**Shi•zuo•ka** Japanese city
**Shluh** (*plural* **Shluhs** *or* **Shluh**) African people
**shoal**
**shoali•ness**
**shoaly**
**shoat** (*or* **shote**) weaned piglet
**shock**
**shock•abil•ity**
**shock•able**
**shock•er**
**shock•headed**
**shock•ing**
**shock•ing•ness**
**shock•proof**
**shod**
**shod•di•ly**
**shod•di•ness**
**shod•dy** (**•di•er, •di•est**)
**shoe** (**shoe•ing, shod**) footwear; *compare* **shoo**
**shoe•bill**
**shoe•black**
**shoe•horn**
**shoe•lace**
**shoe•maker**
**shoe•making**
**shoe•shine**
**shoe•string**
**shoe•tree**
**sho•far** (*or* **•phar**; *plural* **•fars, •phars** *or* **•froth, •phroth**) Jewish horn
**sho•gun** Japanese leader
**sho•gun•ate**
**sho•ji** (*plural* **•ji** *or* **•jis**) paper screen
**Sho•la•pur** Indian city
**Sho•na** (*plural* **•na** *or* **•nas**) African people
**shone**
**shoo** (**shoos, shoo•ing, shooed**) chase off; *compare* **shoe**
**shook**
**shoon** *Scot* shoes
**shoot** (**shoot•ing, shot**)
**shoot•er**
**shoot-out** (*noun*)
**shop** (**shop•ping, shopped**)
**shop•girl**
**shop•keeper**

**shop•keeping**
**shop•lifter**
**shop•lifting**
**shop•per**
**shop•ping**
**shop•soiled** (*US* **•worn**)
**shop•talk**
**shop•walker**
**shop•worn** *US* shopsoiled
**shor•an** radar system
**shore**
**shore•less**
**shore•line**
**shore•ward** (*adj*)
**shore•wards** (*adv*)
**shor•ing**
**shorn**
**short**
**short•age**
**short•bread**
**short•cake**
**short-change**
**short-changer**
**short-circuit** (*verb*)
**short•coming**
**short•en**
**short•en•er**
**short•en•ing**
**short•fall**
**short-haired**
**short•hand**
**short-handed**
**short-handed•ness**
**short•horn** cattle
**shortie** (*or* **shorty**; *plural* **shorties**)
**short•ish**
**short-list** (*verb*)
**short-lived**
**short•ly**
**short•ness**
**short-range**
**shorts**
**short-sighted**
**short-sighted•ness**
**short-spoken**
**short-tempered**
**short-term** (*adj*)
**short-waisted**
**short-winded**
**shorty** *variant spelling of* shortie
**Sho•sho•ne** (*or* **•ni**; *plural* **•nes, •ne** *or* **•nis, •ni**) American Indian
**Sho•sho•nean** (*or* **•nian**)
**shot**
**shote** *variant spelling of* shoat
**shot•gun** (**•gun•ning, •gunned**)
**shot-putter**
**shott** (*or* **chott**) salt lake
**shot•ten** recently spawned
**should**
**shoul•der**
**shouldn't**
**shouse** *Austral* lavatory
**shout**
**shout•er**
**shove**
**shov•el** (**•el•ling, •elled**; *US* **•el•ing, •eled**)
**shov•el•er** duck; *compare* shoveller
**shovel•ful** (*plural* **•fuls**)
**shovel•head** shark
**shov•el•ler** (*US* **•el•er**) one who shovels; *compare* shoveler
**shovel•nose** fish
**shov•er**
**show** (**show•ing, showed, shown** *or* **showed**)
**show•biz**
**show•boat**
**show•case**
**showd** *Scot* rock
**show•down**
**show•er**
**shower•proof**
**show•ery**
**show•girl**
**showi•ly**
**showi•ness**
**show•ing**
**show•jumper**
**show•jumping**
**show•man** (*plural* **•men**)
**show•man•ship**
**shown**
**show-off** (*noun*)
**show•piece**
**show•place**
**show•room**
**showy** (**showi•er, showi•est**)
**shrank**
**shrap•nel**
**shred** (**shred•ding, shred•ded** *or* **shred**)
**shred•der**
**Shreve•port** US city
**shrew**
**shrewd**
**shrewdie** *Austral* shrewd person
**shrewd•ness**
**shrew•ish**
**shrew•ish•ness**
**Shrews•bury**
**shriek**
**shriek•er**
**shrie•val** of a sheriff
**shriev•al•ty** (*plural* **•ties**)
**shrift**
**shrike**
**shrill**
**shrill•ness**
**shrilly**
**shrimp**
**shrimp•er**
**shrine**
**shrink** (**shrink•ing, shrank** *or* **shrunk, shrunk** *or* **shrunk•en**)
**shrink•able**
**shrink•age**
**shrink•er**
**shrink•ing•ly**
**shrink-wrap** (**-wrapping, -wrapped**)
**shrive** (**shriv•ing, shrove** *or* **shrived, shriv•en** *or* **shrived**)
**shriv•el** (**•el•ling, •elled**; *US* **•el•ing, •eled**)
**shriv•er**
**shroff** detector of counterfeit money
**Shrop•shire**
**shroud**
**shroud-laid**
**shrove**
**Shrove•tide**
**shrub**
**shrub•bery** (*plural* **•beries**)
**shrub•bi•ness**
**shrub•by** (**•bi•er, •bi•est**)
**shrug** (**shrug•ging, shrugged**)
**shrunk**
**shrunk•en**
**shuck**

**shuck•er**
**shucks** exclamation
**shud•der**
**shud•der•ing•ly**
**shud•dery**
**shuf•fle**
**shuffle•board**
**shuf•fler**
**shug•gy** (*plural* **•gies**) *Dialect* swing
**shul** (*or* **schul**; *plural* **shuln** *or* **schuln**) synagogue
**shun** (**shun•ning, shunned**)
**shun•nable**
**shun•ner**
**shunt**
**shunt•er**
**shunt-wound** electrical term
**shush**
**shut** (**shut•ting, shut**)
**shut•down** (*noun*)
**shut•eye**
**shut-off** (*noun*)
**shut•out** (*noun*)
**shut•ter**
**shut•ter•ing**
**shut•tle**
**shuttle•cock**
**shy** (*adj* **shy•er, shy•est** *or* **shi•er, shi•est**; *verb* **shies, shy•ing, shied**; *noun, plural* **shies**)
**shy•er** (*noun*)
**Shy•lock** heartless creditor
**shy•ly**
**shy•ness**
**shy•ster**
**Si** (*or* **Hsi**) Chinese river
**sial** part of earth's crust
**si•ala•gog•ic** (*or* **•alo•**) stimulating salivation
**si•ala•gogue** (*or* **•alo•**)
**si•al•ic**
**Si•al•kot** Pakistani city
**sia•loid** saliva-like
**Siam** *former name of* **Thailand**
**sia•mang** ape
**Sia•mese** (*plural* **•mese**)
**Sian** (*or* **Hsian**) Chinese city
**Siang** (*or* **Hsiang**) Chinese river
**Siang•tan** Chinese city
**sib** (*or* **sibb**) kin
**Si•beria**
**Si•berian**
**sibi•lance** (*or* **•lan•cy**)
**sibi•lant**
**sibi•late**
**sibi•la•tion**
**Si•biu** Romanian town
**sib•ling**
**sib•yl** prophetess
**sib•yl•line** (*or* **si•byl•lic**)
**sic** *Latin* thus; *indicates the deliberate inclusion of a questionable word in text*
**sic•ca•tive** drying agent
**sice** *variant spelling of* **syce**
**Si•cil•ian**
**Sici•ly**
**sick**
**sick•bay**
**sick•bed**
**sick•en**
**sick•en•er**
**sick•en•ing**
**sick•en•ing•ly**
**sick•le**
**sickle•bill**
**sick•li•ness**
**sick•ly** (**•li•er, •li•est**)
**sick•ness**
**sic pas•sim** *Latin* thus everywhere; *indicates a word in text is the same throughout*
**Sicy•on** ancient Greek city
**side**
**side•band** electronics term
**side•board**
**side•boards** (*or esp. US* **•burns**)
**side•car**
**side-dress**
**side•kick**
**side•light**
**side•line**
**side•long**
**si•dereal** of stars
**si•der•ite** mineral
**si•der•it•ic**
**si•dero•lite** meteorite
**si•der•osis** disease
**si•dero•stat** astronomical instrument
**si•dero•stat•ic**
**sid•er•ot•ic**
**side-saddle**
**side•show**
**side•slip** (**•slip•ping, •slipped**)
**sides•man** (*plural* **•men**)
**side-splitting**
**side•step** (**•step•ping, •stepped**)
**side•step•per**
**side•stroke**
**side•swipe**
**side•swip•er**
**side•track**
**side•walk** *US* pavement
**side•wall**
**side•ward** (*adj*)
**side•wards** (*adv*)
**side•ways**
**side•wheel**
**side•wheeler** boat
**side•winder** snake
**Sidi-bel-Abbès** Algerian city
**sid•ing**
**si•dle**
**si•dler**
**Si•don** Phoenician city
**siè•cle** *French* century
**siege**
**sie•mens** (*plural* **•mens**) unit
**Si•ena** Italian city
**si•en•na** pigment
**si•er•ra**
**Si•er•ra Leo•ne**
**Si•er•ra Le•on•ean**
**Si•er•ra Ma•dre** Mexican mountains
**si•er•ran**
**Si•er•ra Ne•va•da** US mountains
**si•es•ta**
**sieve**
**(sieze)** *incorrect spelling of* **seize**
**si•fa•ka** animal
**sift**
**sift•er**
**sift•ings**
**sigh**
**sigh•er**
**sight** vision; *compare* **site**
**sight•able**
**sight•ed**
**sight•er**
**sight•less**
**sight•less•ness**
**sight•li•ness**

**sight•ly** (**•li•er, •li•est**)
**sight-read** (**-reading, -read**)
**sight-reader**
**sight•screen**
**sight•see** (**•see•ing, •saw, •seen**)
**sight•seer**
**sig•la** list of symbols
**sig•los** (*plural* **•loi**) coin
**sig•ma** Greek letter
**sig•mate**
**sig•ma•tion**
**sig•moid** (*or* **•moi•dal**)
**sig•moido•scope** medical instrument
**sig•moido•scop•ic**
**sig•moid•os•co•py**
**sign**
**sig•nal** (**•nal•ling, •nalled;** *US* **•nal•ling, •naled**)
**sig•nal•ize** (*or* **•ise**)
**sig•nal•ler** (*US* **•nal•er**)
**sig•nal•ly**
**sig•nal•man** (*plural* **•men**)
**sig•na•tory** (*plural* **•tories**)
**sig•na•ture**
**sign•board**
**sign•er**
**sig•net** seal on ring; *compare* **cygnet**
**sig•ni•fi•able**
**sig•nifi•cance**
**sig•nifi•cant**
**sig•nifi•cant•ly**
**sig•ni•fi•ca•tion**
**sig•nifi•ca•tive**
**sig•nifi•ca•tive•ness**
**sig•ni•fi•er**
**sig•ni•fy** (**•fies, •fy•ing, •fied**)
**si•gnor** (*plural* **•gnors** *or* **•gnori**) *Italian* man; Mr
**si•gno•ra** (*plural* **•ras** *or* **•re**) *Italian* woman; Mrs
**si•gno•re** (*plural* **•ri**) *Italian* man; Sir
**si•gnori•na** (*plural* **•nas** *or* **•ne**) *Italian* young woman; Miss
**sign•post**
**Sigurd** Norse hero
**sika** deer
**sike** *Dialect* small stream
**Sikh**
**Sikh•ism**
**Sik•kim** Indian state
**Sik•ki•mese**
**si•lage**
**Si•las•tic** (*Trademark*)
**sild** fish
**sile** *Dialect* rain
**si•lence**
**si•lenc•er**
**si•lent**
**si•lent•ly**
**si•lent•ness**
**Silenus** Greek satyr
**Si•lesia** European region
**si•lesia** fabric
**si•lex** heat-resistant glass
**sil•hou•ette**
**sili•ca** mineral; *compare* **silicon; silicone**
**sili•cate**
**si•li•ceous** (*or* **•cious**)
**si•lic•ic**
**sili•cide** chemical compound
**sili•cif•er•ous**
**si•lici•fi•ca•tion**
**si•lici•fy** (**•fies, •fy•ing, •fied**)
**sili•cle** (*or* **si•licu•la, sili•cule**) botany term
**sili•con** chemical element; *compare* **silica; silicone**
**sili•cone** polymer; *compare* **silica; silicon**
**sili•co•sis** disease
**si•licu•lose**
**si•li•qua** (*or* **•lique;** *plural* **•li•quae, •li•quas,** *or* **•liques**) botany term
**sili•qua•ceous**
**silk**
**silka•line** (*or* **•lene**) fabric
**silk•en**
**silki•ly**
**silki•ness**
**silk•worm**
**silky** (**silki•er, silki•est**)
**sill**
**sil•la•bub** *variant spelling of* **syllabub**
**sil•li•ly**
**sil•li•ma•nite** mineral
**sil•li•ness**
**sil•ly** (*adj* **•li•er, •li•est;** *noun, plural* **•lies**)
**silo** (*plural* **silos**)
**si•lox•ane**
**silt**
**sil•ta•tion**
**silty**
**Si•lu•res** ancient Britons
**Si•lu•rian** geological period; of Silures
**si•lu•rid** fish
**sil•va** *variant spelling of* **sylva**
**sil•van** *variant spelling of* **sylvan**
**Silvanus** (*or* **Sylvanus**) Roman god
**sil•ver**
**sil•ver•er**
**silver•fish** (*plural* **•fish** *or* **•fishes**)
**sil•veri•ness**
**sil•ver•ing**
**silver•point** drawing technique
**silver•side**
**silver•smith**
**silver•ware**
**silver•weed**
**sil•very**
**sil•vi•cul•tur•al**
**sil•vi•cul•ture** tree cultivation
**sil•vi•cul•tur•ist**
**s'il vous plaît** *French* please
**sima** layer of earth's crust
**sima•rou•ba** (*or* **•ru•**) tree
**sima•rou•ba•ceous** (*or* **•ru•**)
**Sim•birsk** Russian city
**Sim•fero•pol** Ukrainian city
**sim•ian** (*or* **simi•ous**)
**simi•lar**
**simi•lar•ity** (*plural* **•ities**)
**simi•lar•ly**
**simi•le** (*plural* **•les**)
**si•mili•tude**
**simi•ous** *variant of* **simian**
**sim•mer**
**sim•mer•ing•ly**
**sim•nel** cake
**si•mo•ni•ac** practiser of simony
**si•mo•nia•cal**
**si•mo•nia•cal•ly**
**si•mon•ist**
**si•mo•ny**
**si•moom** (*or* **•moon**) wind
**simp** *US* simpleton

**sim•pa•ti•co**
**sim•per**
**sim•per•er**
**sim•per•ing•ly**
**sim•ple**
**simple-minded**
**simple-minded•ly**
**simple-minded•ness**
**sim•ple•ness**
**sim•ple•ton**
**sim•plex**
**sim•pli•ci•den•tate** zoology term
**sim•plic•ity** (*plural* **•ities**)
**sim•pli•fi•ca•tion**
**sim•pli•fi•ca•tive**
**sim•pli•fi•er**
**sim•pli•fy** (**•fies, •fy•ing, •fied**)
**sim•plism**
**sim•plis•tic**
**sim•plis•ti•cal•ly**
**Sim•plon Pass**
**simp•ly**
**Simp•son** Australian desert
**simu•la•crum** (*plural* **•cra**)
**simu•lant**
**simu•lar**
**simu•late**
**simu•lated**
**simu•la•tion**
**simu•la•tive**
**simu•la•tor**
**sim•ul•cast** radio–TV broadcast
**sim•ul•ta•neous**
**sim•ul•ta•neous•ly**
**sim•ul•ta•neous•ness** (*or* **•ta•neity**)
**sin** (**sin•ning, sinned**)
**Si•nai** Egyptian peninsula
**Si•na•it•ic** (*or* **Si•na•ic**)
**Si•na•loa** Mexican state
**sin•an•thro•pus** primitive man
**sina•pism** mustard plaster
**Sin•ar•quist** Mexican fascist
**since**
**sin•cere**
**sin•cere•ly**
**sin•cer•ity** (*or* **•cere•ness**)
**sin•cipi•tal**
**sin•ci•put** (*plural* **•ci•puts** *or* **•cipi•ta**) part of skull
**Sind** Pakistani province
**Sin•dhi** (*plural* **•dhi** *or* **•dhis**)
**sine** trigonometry term; *Latin* without
**si•necure**
**si•necur•ism**
**si•necur•ist**
**sine die** *Latin* without a day fixed
**sine qua non** *Latin* essential requirement
**sin•ew**
**sin•ewi•ness**
**sin•ewy**
**sin•fo•nia** (*plural* **•nie**) symphony
**sin•fo•niet•ta**
**sin•ful**
**sin•ful•ly**
**sin•ful•ness**
**sing** (**sing•ing, sang, sung**)
**sing•able**
**Sin•ga•pore**
**Sin•ga•po•rean**
**singe** (**singe•ing, singed**)
**sing•er**
**sing•ing•ly**
**sin•gle**
**single-acting**
**single-action**
**single-blind**
**single-breasted**
**single-cross**
**single-decker**
**single-handed**
**single-minded**
**single-minded•ness**
**single•ness**
**single-phase**
**sin•gles** tennis match
**single-space** (*verb*)
**single•stick** wooden sword
**sin•glet**
**sin•gle•ton**
**single-track** (*adj*)
**sin•gly**
**sing•song**
**sin•gu•lar**
**sin•gu•lar•ity** (*plural* **•ities**)
**sin•gu•lari•za•tion** (*or* **•sa•tion**)
**sin•gu•lar•ize** (*or* **•ise**)
**sin•gu•lar•ly**
**sin•gu•lar•ness**
**sin•gul•tus** hiccup
**sinh** trigonometry term
**Sin•hai•lien** (*or* **Hsin-hai-lien**) Chinese city
**Sin•ha•lese** (*or* **•gha•**; *plural* **•leses** *or* **•lese**) Sri Lankan
**Si•ning** (*or* **Hsi•ning**) Chinese city
**sin•is•ter**
**sin•is•ter•ly**
**sin•is•ter•ness**
**sin•is•tral** of the left side
**sin•is•tral•ly**
**sin•is•tro•dex•tral**
**sin•is•tror•sal**
**sin•is•trorse** spiralling right to left
**sin•is•trous**
**Si•nit•ic** language group
**sink** (**sink•ing, sank** *or* **sunk, sunk** *or* **sunk•en**)
**sink•able**
**sink•er**
**sink•hole**
**Sinkiang-Uighur** Chinese region
**sink•ing**
**sin•less**
**sin•less•ness**
**sinned**
**sin•ner**
**Sinn Fein**
**Sinn Fein•er**
**Sinn Fein•ism**
**sin•ning**
**Si•no•logi•cal**
**Si•nolo•gist**
**Si•no•logue**
**Si•nol•ogy** study of Chinese
**Sino-Tibetan**
**sin•ter** silicaceous deposit
**sinu•ate** (*or* **•at•ed**) botany term
**Si•nŭi•ju** North Korean port
**sinu•os•ity** (*or* **sinua•tion**; *plural* **•ities** *or* **•tions**)
**sinu•ous**
**sinu•ous•ly**
**sinu•ous•ness**
**si•nus** (*plural* **•nuses**)
**si•nusi•tis**
**si•nus•oid** maths term
**si•nusoi•dal**
**Siouan**
**Sioux** (*plural* **Sioux**)
**sip** (**sip•ping, sipped**)

**si•phon** (*or* **sy•**)
**si•phon•age**
**si•phon•al** (*or* **•ic**)
**si•pho•no•phore** marine animal
**si•pho•nopho•rous**
**si•phono•stele** botany term
**si•pho•no•stelic**
**Si•ple** Antarctic mountain
**sipped**
**sip•per**
**sip•pet** small piece
**sip•ping**
**sir**
**sir•dar** leader
**sire**
**si•ren**
**si•renian** zoology term
**Si•ret** European river
**Sir•ius** star
**sir•loin**
**si•roc•co** (*plural* **•cos**) wind
**sir•rah** archaic term of address
**sir•ree** US exclamation
**sir•up** *US variant spelling of* **syrup**
**sir•vente** verse form
**sis**
**si•sal**
**Sisera** biblical character
**sis•kin** bird
**sis•sy** (*plural* **•sies**)
**sis•sy•ish**
**sis•ter**
**sis•ter•hood**
**sister-in-law** (*plural* **sisters-**)
**sis•ter•li•ness**
**sis•ter•ly**
**Sis•tine** chapel
**sis•troid** maths term
**sis•trum** (*plural* **•tra**) musical instrument
**Sisy•phean**
**Sisyphus** mythological king
**sit** (**sit•ting, sat**)
**si•tar** musical instrument
**si•tar•ist**
**sit•com**
**site** place; *compare* **sight**
**sit•fast** sore on horse
**sit-in** (*noun*)
**si•tol•ogy** study of nutrition
**si•tos•ter•ol** soya-bean extract
**sit•ter**
**sit•ting**
**situ•ated** (*or esp. in legal contexts* **•ate**)
**situa•tion**
**situa•tion•al**
**situ•la** (*plural* **•lae**) Iron Age container
**si•tus** (*plural* **•tus**) anatomical location
**sitz•kreig**
**sitz•mark** skiing term
**Siva** (*or* **Shiva**) Hindu god
**Si•va•ism**
**Si•va•ist**
**Si•vas** Turkish city
**si•wash** Canadian sweater
**six**
**six•ain** six-line poem
**six•fold**
**six-footer**
**six•mo** (*plural* **•mos**) book size
**six•pence**
**six•penny**
**sixte** fencing position
**six•teen**
**six•teen•mo** (*plural* **•mos**) book size
**six•teenth**
**sixth**
**sixth-former**
**six•ti•eth**
**six•ty** (*plural* **•ties**)
**siz•able** (*or* **size•**)
**siz•able•ness** (*or* **size•**)
**siz•ably** (*or* **size•**)
**siz•ar** maintained student
**si•zar•ship**
**size**
**sized**
**siz•er**
**siz•zle**
**siz•zler**
**sjam•bok** whip
**Ska•gen** *variant of* **Skaw**
**Skag•er•rak** Scandinavian channel
**skald** (*or* **scald**) Scandinavian bard
**skat** card game
**skate** (*noun, verb*) sport
**skate** (*plural* **skate** *or* **skates**) fish
**skate•board**
**skate•board•er**
**skat•er**
**skat•ing**
**skat•ole** organic compound
**Skaw** (*or* **Ska•gen**) Danish cape
**skean** dagger
**ske•dad•dle**
**skeet** clay-pigeon shooting
**skeg** nautical term
**skein**
**skel•etal**
**skel•etal•ly**
**skel•eton**
**skel•eton•ize** (*or* **•ise**)
**skelf** *Dialect* wood splinter
**skel•ly** (*plural* **•lies**) fish
**Skel•mers•dale** Merseyside town
**skelp** *Dialect* slap; metal tube
**sken** (**sken•ing, skenned**) *Dialect* squint
**skep** beehive
**skep•tic** *US spelling of* **sceptic**
**sker•rick** *US* small fragment
**sker•ry** (*plural* **•ries**) *Scot* small island
**sket** (**sket•ting, sket•ted**) *Welsh* splash
**sketch**
**sketch•able**
**sketch•book**
**sketch•er**
**sketchi•ly**
**sketchi•ness**
**sketchy** (**sketchi•er, sketchi•est**)
**skew**
**skew•back**
**skew•bald**
**skew•er** long pin; *compare* **skua**
**skew•ness**
**skew•whiff**
**ski** (*verb* **skis, ski•ing, skied** *or* **ski'd**; *noun, plural* **skis**)
**ski•able**
**skia•scope** eye-examining instrument
**ski•as•co•py**
**ski•bob**
**ski•bob•ber**
**ski•bob•bing**

**skid** (**skid•ding, skid•ded**)
**skid•lid** *Slang* crash helmet
**skid•pan**
**skid•proof**
**skid•way** *US* platform for logs
**skied**
**ski•er** one who skis; *compare* **skyer**
**skiff**
**skif•fle**
**ski•ing**
**ski•jor•er**
**ski•jor•ing** snow sport
**skil•ful** (*US* **skill•**)
**skil•ful•ly** (*US* **skill•**)
**skil•ful•ness** (*US* **skill•**)
**skill**
**skilled**
**skil•let**
**skill•ful** *US spelling of* **skilful**
**skil•ling** coin
**skil•lion** *Austral* lean-to
**skil•ly** thin soup
**skim** (**skim•ming, skimmed**)
**skim•mer**
**skim•mia** shrub
**skim•mings**
**skimp**
**skimpi•ly**
**skimpi•ness**
**skimpy** (**skimpi•er, skimpi•est**)
**skin** (**skin•ning, skinned**)
**skin-deep**
**skin-diver**
**skin•flint**
**skin•ful**
**skin•head**
**skink** lizard
**skin•less**
**skinned**
**skin•ner**
**skin•ni•ness**
**skin•ning**
**skin•ny** (**•ni•er, •ni•est**)
**skint**
**skin•tight**
**skip** (**skip•ping, skipped**)
**skip•jack** (*plural* **•jacks** *or* **•jack**) fish
**ski•plane**
**skip•per**
**skip•pet** box for document
**skip•ping**
**skipping-rope**
**Skip•ton** Yorkshire town
**skirl** *Dialect* play bagpipes
**skir•mish**
**skir•mish•er**
**skirr** move rapidly
**skir•ret** plant
**skirt**
**skirt•er** *Austral* fleece trimmer
**skirt•ing**
**skit**
**skite** *Austral* boast
**skit•ter**
**skit•tish**
**skit•tish•ly**
**skit•tish•ness**
**skit•tle**
**skive**
**skiv•er**
**skiv•vy** (*noun, plural* **•vies**; *verb* **•vies, •vy•ing, •vied**)
**skoal** drinking toast
**skoki•aan** South African liquor
**Skop•je** Macedonian capital
(**skrimshank**) *incorrect spelling of* **scrimshank**
**skua** bird; *compare* **skewer**
**skul•dug•gery**
**skulk**
**skulk•er**
**skull** head bones; *compare* **scull**
**skull•cap**
**skunk** (*plural* **skunk** *or* **skunks**)
**sky** (*noun, plural* **skies**; *verb* **skies, sky•ing, skied**)
**sky•dive** (**•div•ing, •dived** (*US* **dove**), **dived**)
**sky•div•er**
**Skye** Scottish island
**sky•er** one who skies; *compare* **skier**
**sky-high**
**sky•jack**
**sky•jack•er**
**Sky•lab** US space station
**sky•lark**
**sky•lark•er**
**sky•light**
**sky•line**
**sky•rocket**
**Sky•ros** (*or* **Scy•**) Greek island
**sky•sail**
**sky•scape**
**sky•scraper**
**sky•wards** (*or esp. US* **•ward**)
**sky•writer**
**sky•writing**
**slab** (**slab•bing, slabbed**)
**slab•ber** *Dialect* slobber
**slack**
**slack•en**
**slack•er**
**slack•ness**
**slacks**
**slag** (**slag•ging, slagged**)
**slag•gy**
**slain**
**slais•ter** *Scot* confused mess
**slak•able** (*or* **slake•**)
**slake**
**slak•er**
**sla•lom** skiing race; *compare* **shalom**
**slam** (**slam•ming, slammed**)
**slan•der**
**slan•der•er**
**slan•der•ous**
**slan•der•ous•ness**
**slang**
**slangi•ly**
**slangi•ness**
**slangy**
**slant**
**slant•ing**
**slant•ing•ly** (*or* **slant•ly**)
**slant•wise** (*or* **•ways**)
**slap** (**slap•ping, slapped**)
**slap-bang**
**slap•dash**
**slap•happy** (**•happier, •happiest**)
**slap•jack** card game
**slap•per**
**slap•shot** ice hockey shot
**slap•stick**
**slap-up** (*adj*)
**slash**
**slash•er**
**slash•ing•ly**
**slat** (**slat•ting, slat•ted**)
**slate**
**slat•er**
**slath•er** *Slang* large quantity

**slati•ness**
**slat•ing**
**slat•tern**
**slat•tern•li•ness**
**slat•tern•ly**
**slaty** (**slati•er, slati•est**)
**slaugh•ter**
**slaugh•ter•er**
**slaughter•house**
**slaughter•man** (*plural* **•men**)
**slaugh•ter•ous**
**Slav**
**slave**
**slave-drive** (**-driving, -drove, -driven**)
**slave-driver**
**slav•er**
**slav•er•er**
**slav•ery**
**slav•ey** servant
**Slav•ic** *variant of* **Slavonic**
**slav•ish**
**slav•ish•ly**
**slav•ish•ness**
**slav•oc•ra•cy** (*plural* **•cies**) domination by slaveholders
**Sla•vo•nia** Croatian region
**Sla•vo•nian**
**Sla•von•ic** (*or* **Slav•ic**) language
**Slavo•phile** (*or* **•phil**)
**Sla•vophi•lism**
**slay** (**slay•ing, slew, slain**) kill; *compare* **sleigh**
**slay•er**
**sleave** tangled thread; *compare* **sleeve**
**slea•zi•ly**
**slea•zi•ness**
**slea•zy** (**•zi•er, •zi•est**)
**sled** (**sled•ding, sled•ded**) *variant* (*esp. US*) *of* **sledge**
**sled•der**
**sledge** (*or esp. US* **sled**)
**sledge•hammer**
**sleek**
**sleek•ness**
**sleep** (**sleep•ing, slept**)
**sleep•er**
**sleepi•ly**
**sleepi•ness**
**sleep•less**
**sleep•less•ly**
**sleep•less•ness**
**sleep•walk**
**sleep•walk•er**
**sleep•walk•ing**
**sleepy** (**sleepi•er, sleepi•est**)
**sleepy•head**
**sleet**
**sleety**
**sleeve** covering; *compare* **sleave**
**sleeve•less**
**sleev•ing** wire insulation
**sleigh** sledge; *compare* **slay**
**sleigh•er**
**sleight** trick; *compare* **slight**
**slen•der**
**slen•der•ize** (*or* **•ise**)
**slen•der•ness**
**slept**
**sleuth**
**sleuth•hound**
**slew** *past tense of* **slay**
**slew** (*US also* **slue**) twist
**slice**
**slice•able**
**slic•er**
**slick**
**slick•en•side** geology term
**slick•er**
**slick•ly**
**slick•ness**
**slid**
**slid•able**
**slide** (**slid•ing, slid** *or* **slid•den**)
**slide-action**
**slid•er**
**slid•ing**
**sli•er** *variant spelling of* **slyer**
**sli•est** *variant spelling of* **slyest**
**slight** small; snub; *compare* **sleight**
**slight•ing**
**slight•ing•ly**
**slight•ly**
**slight•ness**
**Sli•go** Irish county
**sli•ly** *variant spelling of* **slyly**
**slim** (*adj* **slim•mer, slim•mest**; *verb* **slim•ming, slimmed**)
**slime**
**slimi•ly**
**slimi•ness**
**slim•mer**
**slim•ming**
**slim•ness**
**slim•sy** *US* frail
**slimy** (**slimi•er, slimi•est**)
**sling** (**sling•ing, slung**)
**sling•back**
**sling•er**
**sling•shot**
**slink** (**slink•ing, slunk**)
**slinki•ly**
**slinki•ness**
**slink•ing•ly**
**slinky** (**slinki•er, slinki•est**)
**slip** (**slip•ping, slipped**)
**slip•case**
**slip•knot**
**slip•noose**
**slip-on** (*adj, noun*)
**slip•over**
**slip•page**
**slip•per**
**slip•pered**
**slip•peri•ness**
**slipper•wort**
**slip•pery**
**slip•pi•ness**
**slip•ping•ly**
**slip•py** (**•pi•er, •pi•est**)
**slip•sheet**
**slip•shod**
**slip•shoddi•ness** (*or* **•shod•ness**)
**slip•slop**
**slip•stream**
**slip-up** (*noun*)
**slip•way**
**slit** (**slit•ting, slit**)
**slith•er**
**slith•ery**
**slit•ter**
**sliv•er**
**sliv•er•er**
**slivo•vitz** plum brandy
**slob**
**slob•ber**
**slob•ber•er**
**slob•bery**
**sloe** fruit; *compare* **slow**
**sloe-eyed**
**slog** (**slog•ging, slogged**)
**slo•gan**
**slo•gan•eer**
**slog•ger**
**sloop**

**sloop-rigged**
**sloot** ditch
**slop** (**slop•ping, slopped**)
**slope**
**slop•er**
**slop•ing**
**slop•ing•ly**
**slop•pi•ly**
**slop•pi•ness**
**slop•py** (**•pi•er, •pi•est**)
**slops**
**slop•work**
**slop•worker**
**slosh**
**sloshy**
**slot** (**slot•ting, slot•ted**)
**sloth**
**sloth•ful**
**sloth•ful•ly**
**sloth•ful•ness**
**slot•ter**
**slouch**
**slouch•er**
**slouchi•ly**
**slouchi•ness**
**slouch•ing•ly**
**slouchy**
**Slough** Berkshire town
**slough** bog; to shed
**sloughy**
**Slo•vak** (*or* **•vak•ian**)
**Slo•vakia** E European country
**slov•en**
**Slo•vene** (*or* **•venian**)
**Slo•venia** SE European country
**slov•en•li•ness**
**slov•en•ly**
**slow** not fast, etc.; *compare* **sloe**
**slow•coach**
**slow•down**
**slow•ly**
**slow•ness**
**slow•poke** *US* slowcoach
**slow-witted**
**slow•worm**
**slub** (**slub•bing, slubbed**) lump in yarn; twist fibre
**slub•ber•de•gul•lion** slovenly person
**sludge**
**sludgy**
**slue** (**slu•ing, slued**) *US variant spelling of* **slew**
**slug** (**slug•ging, slugged**)
**sluga•bed**
**slug•gard**
**slug•gard•li•ness**
**slug•gard•ly**
**slug•ger**
**slug•gish**
**slug•gish•ness**
**sluice**
**sluice•gate**
**slum** (**slum•ming, slummed**)
**slum•ber**
**slum•ber•er**
**slum•ber•ing•ly**
**slum•ber•less**
**slum•ber•ous**
**slum•ber•ous•ness**
**slum•mer**
**slum•my** (**•mi•er, •mi•est**)
**slump**
**slung**
**slunk**
**slur** (**slur•ring, slurred**)
**slurp**
**slur•ry** (*plural* **•ries**)
**slush**
**slushi•ness**
**slushy**
**slut**
**slut•tish**
**slut•tish•ness**
**sly** (**sly•er, sly•est** *or* **sli•er, sli•est**)
**sly•ly** (*or* **sli•**)
**sly•ness**
**slype** passageway in cathedral
**smack**
**smack•er**
**small**
**small•boy** steward's assistant
**small•holder**
**small•holding**
**small•ish**
**small-minded**
**small-minded•ly**
**small-minded•ness**
**small•ness**
**small•pox**
**smalls** underwear
**small-scale**
**smalt** blue glass; pigment
**smalt•ite** mineral
**smal•to** (*plural* **•tos** *or* **•ti**) mosaic pieces
**sma•rag•dite** mineral
**smarm**
**smarmy** (**smarmi•er, smarmi•est**)
**smart**
**smart•en**
**smartie** clever person
**smart•ing•ly**
**smart•ish**
**smart•ness**
**smash**
**smash•able**
**smash•er**
**smash•ing**
**smash-up** (*noun*)
**smat•ter**
**smat•ter•er**
**smat•ter•ing**
**smaze** *US* smoky haze
**smear**
**smear•er**
**smeari•ness**
**smeary** (**smeari•er, smeari•est**)
**smec•tic** chemistry term
**smeg•ma** sebum
**smell** (**smell•ing, smelt** *or* **smelled**)
**smelli•ness**
**smelly** (**smelli•er, smelli•est**)
**smelt** (*plural* **smelt** *or* **smelts**) extract metal; fish
**smel•ter**
**smelt•ery** (*plural* **•eries**)
**smew** duck
**smid•gen** (*or* **•gin**)
**smi•la•ca•ceous** botany term
**smi•lax** shrub
**smile**
**smil•er**
**smil•ing•ly**
**smil•ing•ness**
**smirch**
**smirch•er**
**smirk**
**smirk•er**
**smirk•ing•ly**
**smit** (*or* **smit•tle**) *Dialect* infection

**smite** (**smit•ing, smote, smit•ten** *or* **smit**)
**smit•er**
**smith**
**smith•er•eens**
**smith•ery** (*plural* **•eries**)
**Smith•so•nian** US museum
**smith•son•ite** mineral
**smithy** (*plural* **smithies**)
**smit•ten**
**smock**
**smock•ing**
**smog**
**smog•gy**
**smok•able** (*or* **smoke•**)
**smoke**
**smoke•house**
**smoke•jack** spit-turning device
**smoke•less**
**smok•er**
**smoke•stack**
**smoki•ly**
**smoki•ness**
**smok•ing**
**smo•ko** (*or* **smoke•ho**; *plural* **•kos** *or* **•hos**) *Austral* teabreak
**smoky** (**smoki•er, smoki•est**)
**smol•der** *US spelling of* **smoulder**
**Smo•lensk** Russian city
**smolt** young salmon
**smooch**
**smoodge** *Austral* smooch
**smooth**
**smooth•able**
**smooth•bore**
**smooth•en**
**smooth•er**
**smooth-faced**
**smoothie**
**smooth•ness**
**smooth-spoken**
**smooth-tongued**
**smor•gas•bord** Scandinavian hors d'oeuvres
**smote**
**smoth•er**
**smoth•ery**
**smoul•der** (*US* **smol•**)
**smri•ti** Hindu literature
**smudge**
**smudgi•ly** (*or* **smudg•ed•ly**)
**smudgi•ness**
**smudgy** (**smudgi•er, smudgi•est**)
**smug** (**smug•ger, smug•gest**)
**smug•gle**
**smug•gler**
**smug•gling**
**smug•ly**
**smug•ness**
**smut** (**smut•ting, smut•ted**)
**smutch** smudge
**smutchy**
**smut•ti•ly**
**smut•ti•ness**
**smut•ty** (**•ti•er, •ti•est**)
**Smyr•na** ancient Asian city
**snack**
**snack•ette** snack bar
**snaf•fle**
**sna•fu** (**•fues, •fu•ing, •fued**) *US* chaos; make chaotic
**snag** (**snag•ging, snagged**)
**snaggle•tooth** (*plural* **•teeth**)
**snag•gy**
**snail**
**snail-like**
**snake**
**snake•bite**
**snake•like**
**snake•mouth** orchid
**snake•root**
**snake•skin**
**snaki•ly**
**snaki•ness**
**snaky** (**snaki•er, snaki•est**)
**snap** (**snap•ping, snapped**)
**snap•back**
**snap•dragon**
**snap•pable**
**snap•per**
**snap•pi•ly**
**snap•pi•ness**
**snap•ping•ly**
**snap•py** (**•pi•er, •pi•est**)
**snap•shot**
**snare**
**snar•er**
**snar•ing•ly**
**snarl**
**snarl•er**
**snarl•ing•ly**
**snarl-up** (*noun*)
**snarly**
**snatch**
**snatch•er**
**snatchi•ly**
**snatchy** (**snatchi•er, snatchi•est**) spasmodic
**snath** (*or* **snathe**) scythe handle
**snaz•zi•ly**
**snaz•zi•ness**
**snaz•zy** (**•zi•er, •zi•est**)
**sneak**
**sneak•ers** shoes
**sneaki•ly**
**sneaki•ness**
**sneak•ing**
**sneak•ing•ly**
**sneak•ing•ness**
**sneaky** (**sneaki•er, sneaki•est**)
**sneck** wall stone; latch
**sned** (**sned•ding, sned•ded**) *Dialect* to prune
**sneer**
**sneer•er**
**sneer•ing**
**sneer•ing•ly**
**sneeze**
**sneez•er**
**sneeze•wort**
**sneezy**
**snib** *Scot* door fastening
**snick**
**snick•er**
**snick•et** *Dialect* passageway
**snide**
**snide•ness**
**sniff**
**sniff•er**
**sniffi•ly**
**sniffi•ness**
**sniff•ing•ly**
**snif•fle**
**snif•fler**
**snif•fy** (**•fi•er, •fi•est**)
**snif•ter**
**snig•ger**
**snig•ger•ing•ly**
**snig•gle** catch eels
**snig•gler**
**snip** (**snip•ping, snipped**)
**snipe** (*plural* **snipe** *or* **snipes**) bird; to attack
**snipe•fish** (*plural* **•fish** *or* **•fishes**)
**snip•er**

**sniper•scope**
**snip•pet**
**snip•pi•ly**
**snip•pi•ness** (*or* **•peti•ness**)
**snip•py** (**•pi•er, •pi•est**)
**snips** shears
**snitch**
**sniv•el** (**•el•ling, •elled;** *US* **•el•ing, •eled**)
**sniv•el•ler** (*US* **•el•er**)
**sniv•el•ly**
**snob**
**snob•bery**
**snob•bish**
**snob•bish•ness** (*or* **•bism**)
**Sno-Cat** (*Trademark*)
**snog** (**snog•ging, snogged**)
**snood**
**snook** rude gesture
**snook** (*plural* **snook** *or* **snooks**) fish
**snook•er**
**snoop**
**snoop•er**
**snooper•scope**
**snoopy**
**snoot** *Slang* nose
**snooti•ly**
**snooti•ness**
**snooty** (**snooti•er, snooti•est**)
**snooze**
**snooz•er**
**snoozy**
**snore**
**snor•er**
**snor•kel**
**snort**
**snort•er**
**snort•ing•ly**
**snot**
**snot•ti•ly**
**snot•ti•ness**
**snot•ty** (*noun, plural* **•ties;** *adj* **•ti•er, •ti•est**)
**snout**
**snout•ed**
**snout•like**
**snow**
**snow•ball**
**snow•ball•ing**
**snow•berry** (*plural* **•berries**)
**snow•bird**
**snow-blind**
**snow-blind•ness**
**snow•blink** reflection from snow
**snow•bound**
**snow•cap**
**snow•capped**
**Snow•don**
**Snow•donia**
**snow•drift**
**snow•drop**
**snow•fall**
**snow•field**
**snow•flake**
**snowi•ly**
**snowi•ness**
**snow•man** (*plural* **•men**)
**snow•mobile**
**snow•plough**
**snow•shed**
**snow•shoe** (**•shoe•ing, •shoed**)
**snow•sho•er**
**snow•storm**
**snow-white**
**snowy** (**snowi•er, snowi•est**)
**snub** (**snub•bing, snubbed**)
**snub•ber**
**snub•bing•ly**
**snub•by**
**snub-nosed**
**snuff**
**snuff•box**
**snuf•fer**
**snuffi•ness**
**snuff•ing•ly**
**snuf•fle**
**snuf•fler**
**snuf•fly**
**snuffy** (**snuffi•er, snuffi•est**) unpleasant
**snug** (*adj* **snug•ger, snug•gest;** *verb* **snug•ging, snugged**)
**snug•gery** (*plural* **•geries**)
**snug•gle**
**snug•ness**
**snye** river channel
**so**
**soak**
**soak•age**
**soak•er**
**soak•ing**
**soak•ing•ly**
**so-and-so** (*plural* **so-and-sos**)
**soap**
**soap•bark**
**soap•berry** (*plural* **•berries**)
**soap•box**
**soapi•ly**
**soapi•ness**
**soap•less**
**soapo•lal•lie** drink
**soap•stone** (*or* **•rock**)
**soap•suds**
**soap•sudsy**
**soap•wort**
**soapy** (**soapi•er, soapi•est**)
**soar**
**soar•er**
**soar•ing•ly**
**sob** (**sob•bing, sobbed**)
**sob•ber**
**sob•bing•ly**
**so•beit** *Archaic* provided that
**so•ber**
**so•ber•ing•ly**
**so•ber•ness**
**so•bri•ety**
**so•bri•quet** (*or* **sou•**)
**soc•age** legal term
**soc•ag•er**
**so-called** (*adj*)
**soc•cer**
**So•che** (*or* **So-ch'e**) Chinese town
**So•chi** Russian city
**so•cia•bil•ity** (*or* **•ble•ness**)
**so•cia•ble**
**so•cia•bly**
**so•cial**
**so•cial•ism**
**so•cial•ist**
**so•cial•is•tic**
**so•cial•is•ti•cal•ly**
**so•cial•ite**
**so•ci•al•ity** (*plural* **•ities**)
**so•cial•iz•able** (*or* **•is•able**)
**so•ciali•za•tion** (*or* **•sa•tion**)
**so•cial•ize** (*or* **•ise**)
**so•cial•iz•er** (*or* **•is•er**)
**so•cial•ly**
**so•cial•ness**
**so•ci•etal**
**so•ci•ety** (*plural* **•eties**)
**So•cin•ian**
**So•cini•an•ism** religious doctrine
**so•cio•biolo•gy**

**so•cio•eco•nom•ic**
**so•cio•eco•nomi•cal•ly**
**so•cio•lin•guist**
**so•cio•lin•guis•tic**
**so•cio•lin•guis•tics**
**so•cio•logi•cal**
**so•ci•olo•gist**
**so•ci•ol•ogy**
**so•cio•met•ric**
**so•ci•om•etrist**
**so•ci•om•etry**
**so•cio•path**
**so•cio•path•ic**
**so•ci•opa•thy**
**so•cio•po•liti•cal**
**sock**
**sock•dolo•ger** (*or* **•dola•**) *US* decisive blow
**sock•et**
**sock•eye** salmon
**so•cle** plinth
**soc•man** (*or* **soke•**; *plural* **•men**) tenant
**So•crat•ic** (*or* **•crati•cal**)
**sod** (**sod•ding, sod•ded**)
**soda**
**so•da•lite** mineral
**so•dal•ity** (*plural* **•ities**) Catholic society
**so•da•mide** chemical compound
**sod•den**
**sod•den•ness**
**sod•ding**
**so•dium**
**Sod•om** biblical city
**sodo•mite**
**sodo•mize** (*or* **•mise**)
**sodo•my**
**so•ever**
**sofa**
**so•far** marine locating system
**sof•fit** architectural term
**So•fia** Bulgarian capital
**soft**
**sof•ta** Muslim student
**soft•ball**
**soft-boiled**
**sof•ten**
**sof•ten•er**
**soft-finned**
**soft-headed**
**soft•hearted**
**soft•hearted•ness**
**softie** *variant spelling of* **softy**
**soft•ness**
**soft-pedal** (**-pedalling, -pedalled**; *US* **-pedaling, -pedaled**)
**soft-soap** (*verb*)
**soft-spoken**
**soft•ware**
**soft•wood**
**softy** (*or* **softie**; *plural* **softies**)
**sog•gi•ly**
**sog•gi•ness**
**sog•gy** (**•gi•er, •gi•est**)
**soh** (*or* **so**) musical note
**Soho**
**soi-disant** *French* so-called
**soi•gné** (*fem* **•gnée**) well-groomed
**soil**
**soil•age** green fodder
**soil•less**
**soi•ree**
**so•journ**
**so•journ•er**
**soke** legal term
**sol** colloid
**sol** (*plural* **sols** *or* **so•les**) Peruvian currency
**sol•ace**
**sol•ac•er**
**sola•na•ceous** botany term
**so•lan•der** botanical box
**so•la•num** plant
**so•lar**
**so•lar•im•eter**
**so•lar•ium** (*plural* **•laria** *or* **•lar•iums**)
**so•lari•za•tion** (*or* **•sa•tion**)
**so•lar•ize** (*or* **•ise**)
**sold**
**sol•dan** *Archaic* sultan
**sol•der**
**sol•der•able**
**sol•der•er**
**sol•dier**
**sol•dier•li•ness**
**sol•dier•ly**
**sol•diery** (*plural* **•dieries**)
**sole** only; underside of foot or shoe; *compare* **soul**
**sole** (*plural* **sole** *or* **soles**) fish; *compare* **soul**
**sol•ecism**
**sol•ecist**
**sol•ecis•tic** (*or* **•ti•cal**)
**sole•ly**
**sol•emn**
**so•lem•ni•fi•ca•tion**
**so•lem•ni•fy** (**•fies, •fy•ing, •fied**)
**so•lem•nity** (*plural* **•nities**)
**sol•em•ni•za•tion** (*or* **•sa•tion**)
**sol•em•nize** (*or* **•nise**)
**sol•em•niz•er** (*or* **•nis•er**)
**sol•emn•ness** (*or* **•em•ness**)
**so•leno•don** animal
**so•lenoid**
**so•lenoi•dal**
**So•lent** English strait
**sol-fa** musical system
**sol•fa•ta•ra** volcanic vent
**sol•fa•ta•ric**
**sol•feg•gio** (*or* **•fège**; *plural* **•feg•gi, •feg•gios,** *or* **•fèges**) musical term
**sol•fe•ri•no** reddish-purple
**soli** musical term
**so•lic•it**
**so•lici•ta•tion**
**so•lici•tor**
**So•lici•tor Gen•er•al** (*plural* **So•lici•tors Gen•er•al**)
**so•lici•tor•ship**
**so•lici•tous**
**so•lici•tous•ly**
**so•lici•tous•ness**
**so•lici•tude**
**sol•id**
**soli•da•go** (*plural* **•gos**) plant
**soli•dar•ity** (*plural* **•ities**)
**soli•dary** united by interests
**so•lidi•fi•able**
**so•lidi•fi•ca•tion**
**so•lidi•fi•er**
**so•lidi•fy** (**•fies, •fy•ing, •fied**)
**so•lid•ity**
**sol•id•ness**
**solid-state** (*adj*)
**soli•dus** (*plural* **•di**) oblique stroke in text
**soli•fid•ian** religious term
**soli•fluc•tion** (*or* **•flux•ion**) soil movement
**So•li•hull** English town
**so•lilo•quist** (*or* **•quiz•er, •quis•er**)
**so•lilo•quize** (*or* **•quise**)

**so•lilo•quy** (*plural* **•quies**)
**So•ling•en** German city
**sol•ip•sism**
**sol•ip•sist**
**sol•ip•sis•tic**
**soli•taire** game; gem
**soli•tari•ly**
**soli•tari•ness**
**soli•tary** (*plural* **•taries**)
**soli•tude**
**soli•tu•di•nous**
**sol•ler•et** part of armour
**sol•mi•za•tion** (*or* **•sa•tion**) musical term
**solo** (*plural* **solos** *or* **soli**)
**so•lo•ist**
**Solo•mon Is•lands**
**sol•on•chak** soil
**solo•netz** (*or* **•nets**) soil
**So•lo•thurn** Swiss town
**sol•stice**
**sol•sti•tial**
**sol•ubil•ity** (*plural* **•ities**)
**solu•bil•ize** (*or* **•ise**)
**sol•uble**
**sol•uble•ness**
**sol•ubly**
**so•lum** (*plural* **•lums** *or* **•la**) soil layer
**so•lute**
**so•lu•tion**
**So•lu•trean** Palaeolithic culture
**solv•abil•ity** (*or* **•able•ness**)
**solv•able**
**solv•ate**
**solva•tion**
**Solvay pro•cess**
**solve**
**sol•ven•cy**
**sol•vent**
**solv•er**
**sol•voly•sis** chemistry term
**Sol•way Firth**
**soma** (*plural* **soma•ta** *or* **somas**) biology term
**So•ma•li** (*plural* **•lis** *or* **•li**)
**So•ma•lia** African republic
**So•ma•lian**
**So•ma•li•land** former African region
**so•mat•ic** of the body
**so•mati•cal•ly**
**so•ma•to•log•ic** (*or* **•logi•cal**)
**so•ma•tolo•gist**
**so•ma•tol•ogy**
**so•ma•to•plasm**
**so•ma•to•plas•tic**
**so•ma•to•pleu•ral** (*or* **•ric**)
**so•ma•to•pleure** embryonic tissue
**so•ma•to•type**
**som•bre** (*US* **•ber**)
**som•bre•ly** (*US* **•ber•**)
**som•bre•ness** (*US* **•ber•**)
**som•brero** (*plural* **•breros**)
**som•brous**
**some**
**some•body** (*plural* **•bodies**)
**some•day**
**some•how**
**some•one**
**some•place**
**som•er•sault** (*or* **sum•mer•sault**)
**Som•er•set**
**some•thing**
**some•time** (*adv, adj*)
**some•times**
**some•way**
**some•what**
**some•where**
**some•wise** somehow
**so•mi•tal** (*or* **•mit•ic**)
**so•mite** embryonic tissue
**Somme** French river
**som•melier** wine steward
**som•nam•bu•lance**
**som•nam•bu•lant**
**som•nam•bu•late**
**som•nam•bu•la•tion**
**som•nam•bu•la•tor**
**som•nam•bu•lism**
**som•nam•bu•list**
**som•nam•bu•lis•tic**
**som•nilo•quy** (*plural* **•quies**) talking in one's sleep
**som•no•lence** (*or* **•len•cy**)
**som•no•lent**
**son**
**so•nance**
**so•nant** phonetics term
**so•nant•al** (*or* **•nan•tic**)
**so•nar**
**so•na•ta**
**sona•ti•na**
**son•dage** archaeological trench
**sonde** observing device
**sone** unit
**son et lu•mi•ère**
**song**
**song•bird**
**song•ful**
**song•ful•ly**
**song•ful•ness**
**Son•ghai** (*plural* **•ghai** *or* **•ghais**) African people
**song•ster** (*fem* **•stress**)
**song•writer**
**son•ic**
**so•nif•er•ous**
**son-in-law** (*plural* **sons-**)
**son•net**
**son•net•eer**
**son•ny** (*plural* **•nies**)
**so•no•buoy**
**So•no•ra** Mexican state
**son•or•ant** phonetics term
**so•nor•ity**
**so•no•rous**
**so•no•rous•ness**
**Soo•chow** (*or* **Su-chou**) Chinese city
**sook** *Dialect* coward
**soon**
**soon•er**
**soot**
**sooth** *Archaic* truth
**soothe**
**sooth•er**
**sooth•ing**
**sooth•ing•ly**
**sooth•say** (**•say•ing, •said**)
**sooth•say•er**
**sooti•ly**
**sooti•ness**
**sooty** (**sooti•er, sooti•est**)
**sop** (**sop•ping, sopped**)
**soph•ism**
**soph•ist**
**soph•ist•er** second-year undergraduate
**so•phis•tic** (*or* **•ti•cal**)
**so•phis•ti•cal•ly**
**so•phis•ti•cate**
**so•phis•ti•cat•ed**
**so•phis•ti•ca•tion**
**so•phis•ti•ca•tor**
**soph•ist•ry** (*plural* **•ries**)
**sopho•more** *US* second-year student

**So•phy** (*or* **So•phi**; *plural* **•phies**) title of Persian kings
**so•por** stupor
**sopo•rif•er•ous**
**sopo•rif•ic**
**sopo•rifi•cal•ly**
**sopped**
**sop•pi•ly**
**sop•pi•ness**
**sop•ping**
**sop•py** (**•pi•er, •pi•est**)
**so•pra•ni•no** (*plural* **•nos**)
**so•pra•no** (*plural* **•nos** *or* **•ni**)
**sora** bird
**sorb** tree
**sor•befa•cient** causing absorption
**sor•bet**
**sorb•ic acid**
**sor•bi•tol**
**Sor•bonne** French university
**sor•bose** sugar
**sor•cer•er** (*fem* **•ess**)
**sor•cer•ous**
**sor•cery** (*plural* **•ceries**)
**sor•did**
**sor•did•ness**
**sor•di•no** (*plural* **•ni**) musical term
**sore**
**so•redium** (*plural* **•redia**) botany term
**sore•head** *US* peevish person
**sore•ly**
**sore•ness**
**sor•ghum** cereal crop
**sor•go** (*or* **•gho**; *plural* **•gos** *or* **•ghos**) fodder crop
**sori** *plural of* **sorus**
**sori•cine** shrewlike
**so•ri•tes** logic term
**so•riti•cal** (*or* **•rit•ic**)
**sorn** *Scot* scrounge hospitality
**So•ro•ca•ba** Brazilian city
**so•ror•ate** marriage custom
**so•rori•cid•al**
**so•rori•cide**
**so•ror•ity** (*plural* **•ities**)
**so•ro•sis** (*plural* **•ses**) botany term
**sorp•tion** adsorption or absorption
**sor•rel**
**Sor•ren•to** Italian port
**sor•ri•ly**
**sor•ri•ness**
**sor•row**
**sor•row•er**
**sor•row•ful**
**sor•row•ful•ly**
**sor•row•ful•ness**
**sor•ry** (**•ri•er, •ri•est**)
**sort**
**sort•able**
**sort•er**
**sor•tie** (**•tie•ing, •tied**)
**sor•ti•lege** divination by drawing lots
**sor•ti•tion** casting lots
**so•rus** (*plural* **•ri**) spore-producing structure
**Sos•no•wiec** Polish town
**so-so**
**sos•te•nu•to** musical term
**sot**
**so•te•ri•ol•ogy** doctrine of salvation
**So•thic** of Sirius
**So•tho** (*plural* **•tho** *or* **•thos**) African people
**sot•tish**
**sot•to voce**
**sou** coin
**sou•bise** onion sauce
**sou•brette** pert girl
**sou•bri•quet** *variant spelling of* **sobriquet**
**sou•chong** tea
**Sou•dan** *French* Sudan
**souf•fle** medical term
**souf•flé** light dish
**sough** sighing sound
**sought**
**soul** spirit; *compare* **sole**
**soul-destroy•ing**
**soul•ful**
**soul•ful•ly**
**soul•ful•ness**
**soul•less**
**soul•less•ly**
**soul•less•ness**
**soul-searching**
**sound**
**sound•able**
**sound•box**
**sound•er**
**sound•ing**
**sound•less**
**sound•less•ness**
**sound•ly**
**sound•ness**
**sound•post** musical term
**sound•proof**
**sound•track**
**soup**
**soup•çon** *French* slight amount
**soup•fin** shark
**soupy** (**soupi•er, soupi•est**)
**sour**
**source**
**sour•dine** organ stop
**sour•ish**
**sour•ly**
**sour•ness**
**sour•puss**
**sour•sop** fruit
**sou•sa•phone**
**sou•sa•phon•ist**
**souse**
**sous•lik** (*or* **sus•**) animal
**Sousse** Tunisian port
**sou•tache** braid
**sou•tane** cassock
**sout•er** *Scot* cobbler
**sou•ter•rain** underground chamber
**south**
**South•amp•ton**
**south•bound**
**South•down** sheep
**south•east**
**south•easter**
**south•easter•ly** (*plural* **•lies**)
**south•eastern**
**south•eastern•most**
**south•eastward** (*adj*)
**south•eastwards** (*adv*)
**South•end-on-Sea** Essex town
**south•er**
**south•er•li•ness**
**south•er•ly** (*plural* **•lies**)
**south•ern**
**south•ern•er**
**south•ern•most**
**southern•wood**
**south•ing** navigation term
**south•paw**
**South Pole**
**South•port**
**south-southeast**
**south-southwest**

**south•ward** (*adj*)
**south•wards** (*adv*)
**South•wark** London borough
**south•west**
**south•wester** strong wind
**south•wester•ly** (*plural* **•lies**)
**south•western**
**south•western•most**
**south•westward** (*adj*)
**south•westwards** (*adv*)
**sou•venir**
**sou'•west•er** hat
**sov•er•eign**
**sov•er•eign•ty** (*plural* **•ties**)
**So•vetsk** Russian town
**So•vi•et** of the former USSR
**so•vi•et** a former Soviet council
**so•vi•et•ism**
**so•vi•et•ist**
**so•vi•et•is•tic**
**so•vi•eti•za•tion** (*or* **•sa•tion**)
**so•vi•et•ize** (*or* **•ise**)
**sov•khoz** (*plural* **•kho•zy**) state farm
**sov•ran** *Poetic* sovereign
**sow** female pig
**sow** (**sow•ing, sowed, sown** *or* **sowed**) plant seed; *compare* **sew**
**sow•bread** plant
**sow•er**
**So•we•to** South African suburb
**sow•ing**
**sown**
**soya bean** (*US* **soy•bean**)
**soy sauce**
**So•yuz** Russian spacecraft
**soz•zled**
**spa** mineral spring; *compare* **spar**
**space**
**space•band** printing term
**space-bar**
**space•craft**
**space•less**
**space•man** (*plural* **•men**)
**space•port**
**spac•er**
**space•ship**
**space•suit**
**space-time** physics term
**space•walk**
**space•woman** (*plural* **•women**)
**spac•ing**
**spa•cious** roomy; *compare* **specious**
**spa•cious•ness**
**spade**
**spade•fish** (*plural* **•fish** *or* **•fishes**)
**spade•ful** (*plural* **•fuls**)
**spad•er**
**spade•work**
**spa•di•ceous**
**spa•dix** (*plural* **•di•ces**) botany term
**spae** *Scot* foretell
**spa•ghet•ti**
**Spain**
**spake**
**spall** rock splinter
**spalla•tion** nuclear reaction
**spal•peen** *Irish* rascal
**Spam** (*Trademark*)
**span** (**span•ning, spanned**)
**span•cel** (**•cel•ling, •celled;** *US* **•cel•ing, •celed**) fettering rope
**span•drel** (*or* **•dril**) architectural term
**spang** *US* exactly
**span•gle**
**span•gly**
**Span•iard**
**span•iel**
**Span•ish**
**Spanish-American**
**spank**
**spank•er**
**spank•ing**
**span•ner**
**spar** (**spar•ring, sparred**) fight; nautical gear; mineral; *compare* **spa**
**spar•able** small nail
**spare**
**spare•ly**
**spare•ness**
**spar•er**
**spare•rib**
**sparge** sprinkle
**spar•id** (*or* **•oid**) fish
**spar•ing** frugal; *compare* **sparring**
**spar•ing•ly**
**spar•ing•ness**
**spark**
**spar•kle**
**spar•kler**
**spar•ling** (*plural* **•lings** *or* **•ling**) fish
**spar•ring** fighting; *compare* **sparing**
**spar•row**
**sparrow•grass** *Dialect* asparagus
**sparrow•hawk**
**spar•ry** geology term
**sparse**
**sparse•ly**
**sparse•ness** (*or* **spar•sity**)
**Spar•ta**
**Spar•tan**
**Spar•tan•ism**
**spar•teine** alkaloid
**spasm**
**spas•mod•ic** (*or* **•modi•cal**)
**spas•modi•cal•ly**
**spas•tic**
**spas•ti•cal•ly**
**spat** *past tense of* **spit**
**spat** (**spat•ting, spat•ted**) quarrel
**spatch•cock**
**spate**
**spa•tha•ceous**
**spathe** botany term
**spathed**
**spath•ic** (*or* **•ose**) mineralogy term
**spa•tial** (*or* **•cial**)
**spa•ti•al•ity**
**spa•tial•ly**
**spa•tio•tem•por•al**
**spat•ter**
**spatu•la**
**spatu•lar**
**spatu•late**
**spav•in**
**spav•ined**
**spawn**
**spawn•er**
**spay**
**speak** (**speak•ing, spoke, spo•ken**)
**speak•able**
**speak•easy** (*plural* **•easies**)
**speak•er**
**speak•er•ship**
**speak•ing**

**spear**
**spear•er**
**spear•head**
**spear•mint**
**spear•wort**
**spec** speculation
**spe•cial**
**spe•cial•ism**
**spe•cial•ist**
**spe•cial•is•tic**
**spe•ci•al•ity** (*US* **•ty**; *plural* **•ities**) special skill; *compare* **specialty**
**spe•ciali•za•tion** (*or* **•sa•tion**)
**spe•cial•ize** (*or* **•ise**)
**spe•cial•ly**
**spe•cial•ness**
**spe•cial•ty** (*plural* **•ties**) legal term; medical speciality; *US spelling of* **speciality**
**spe•cia•tion** biology term
**spe•cie** coin money
**spe•cies** (*plural* **•cies**)
**speci•fi•able**
**spe•cif•ic**
**spe•cifi•cal•ly**
**speci•fi•ca•tion**
**speci•fi•ca•tive**
**speci•fic•ity**
**speci•fi•er**
**speci•fy** (**•fies**, **•fy•ing**, **•fied**)
**speci•men**
**spe•ci•os•ity** (*plural* **•ities**)
**spe•cious** deceptively plausible; *compare* **spacious**
**spe•cious•ly**
**spe•cious•ness**
**speck**
**speck•le**
**specs** *Slang* spectacles
**spec•ta•cle**
**spec•ta•cled**
**spec•ta•cles**
**spec•tacu•lar**
**spec•tacu•lar•ly**
**spec•ta•tor**
**spec•tra** *plural of* **spectrum**
**spec•tral**
**spec•tral•ity** (*or* **•tral•ness**)
**spec•tral•ly**
**spec•tre** (*US* **•ter**)
**spec•tro•bo•lom•eter**
**spec•tro•bolo•met•ric**
**spec•tro•graph**
**spec•tro•graph•ic**
**spec•tro•graphi•cal•ly**
**spec•trog•ra•phy**
**spec•tro•he•lio•graph**
**spec•tro•he•lio•graph•ic**
**spec•tro•he•lio•scope**
**spec•tro•he•lio•scop•ic**
**spec•trom•eter**
**spec•tro•met•ric**
**spec•trom•etry**
**spec•tro•pho•tom•eter**
**spec•tro•photo•met•ric**
**spec•tro•pho•tom•etry**
**spec•tro•scope**
**spec•tro•scop•ic** (*or* **•scopi•cal**)
**spec•tro•scopi•cal•ly**
**spec•tros•co•pist**
**spec•tros•co•py**
**spec•trum** (*plural* **•tra**)
**specu•lar**
**specu•late**
**specu•la•tion**
**specu•la•tive**
**specu•la•tive•ly**
**specu•la•tive•ness**
**specu•la•tor**
**specu•lum** (*plural* **•la** *or* **•lums**)
**sped**
**speech**
**speechi•fi•ca•tion**
**speechi•fi•er**
**speechi•fy** (**•fies**, **•fy•ing**, **•fied**)
**speech•less**
**speech•less•ly**
**speech•less•ness**
**speed** (**speed•ing**, **sped** *or* **speed•ed**)
**speed•boat**
**speed•er**
**speedi•ly**
**speedi•ness**
**speedo** (*plural* **speedos**) *Slang* speedometer
**speed•om•eter**
**speed•ster**
**speed•way**
**speed•well**
**Speed•writing** (*Trademark*)
**speedy** (**speedi•er**, **speedi•est**)
**speel** *Dialect* wood splinter; *compare* **spiel**
**speiss** smelting term
**spe•laean** (*or* **•lean**) of caves
**spe•leo•logi•cal** (*or* **•laeo•**)
**spe•leolo•gist** (*or* **•laeolo•**)
**spe•leol•ogy** (*or* **•laeol•**) study of caves
**spelk** *Dialect* wood splinter
**spell** (**spell•ing**, **spelt** *or* **spelled**)
**spell•able**
**spell•bind** (**•bind•ing**, **•bound**)
**spell•bind•er**
**spell•bound**
**spell•er**
**spell•ing**
**spelt** wheat; *past tense of* **spell**
**spel•ter** impure zinc
**spe•lunk•er** cave explorer
**spe•lunk•ing**
**spence** *Dialect* larder
**spen•cer** short coat; vest
**Spen•cer Gulf**
**spend** (**spend•ing**, **spent**)
**spend•able**
**spend•er**
**spend•thrift**
**Spen•serian** of the poet Spenser
**spent**
**spe•os** temple
**sperm** (*plural* **sperm** *or* **sperms**)
**sper•ma•ceti** waxy substance
**sper•mary** (*plural* **•maries**) sperm-producing organ
**sper•ma•the•ca**
**sper•ma•the•cal**
**sper•mat•ic**
**sper•ma•tid** immature sperm
**sper•ma•tium** (*plural* **•tia**)
**sper•mato•cyte**
**sper•mato•gen•esis**
**sper•ma•to•genet•ic**
**sper•mato•go•nial**
**sper•mato•go•nium** (*plural* **•nia**)
**sper•ma•topho•ral**
**sper•mato•phore**

**sper•ma•to•phyte** seed plant
**sper•ma•to•phyt•ic**
**sper•ma•tor•rhoea** (*US* **•rhea)**
**sper•ma•to•zo•al** (*or* **•an, •ic)**
**sper•ma•to•zo•id** botany term
**sper•ma•to•zo•on** (*plural* **•zoa)**
**sper•mic**
**sper•mi•ci•dal**
**sper•mi•cide**
**sperm•ine** biochemical compound
**sper•mio•gen•esis**
**sper•mio•genet•ic**
**sper•mo•go•nium** (*plural* **•nia)**
**sper•mo•phile** animal
**sper•mous**
**sperry•lite** mineral
**spes•sar•tite** mineral
**spew**
**spew•er**
**Spey** Scottish river
**sphag•nous**
**sphag•num**
**sphal•er•ite** mineral
**sphene** mineral
**sphe•nic** wedge-shaped
**sphe•no•don** lizard
**sphe•noid** (*noun*) bone
**sphe•noid** (*or* **•noi•dal**; *adj*) wedge-shaped
**spher•al**
**sphere**
**spheri•cal** (*or* **spher•ic)**
**spheri•cal•ly**
**spheri•cal•ness**
**sphe•ric•ity**
**spher•ics** (*US* **sfer•ics)** atmospherics
**sphe•roid**
**sphe•roi•dal**
**sphe•roi•dic•ity**
**sphe•rom•eter**
**spheru•lar**
**spher•ule** tiny sphere
**spheru•lite** geology term
**spheru•lit•ic**
**sphery** *Poetic* spherelike; starlike
**sphinc•ter**
**sphinc•ter•al**
**sphin•go•my•elin**
**sphin•go•sine**
**Sphinx** mythological monster
**sphinx** (*plural* **sphinxes** *or* **sphin•ges)** Egyptian statue
**sphra•gis•tic**
**sphra•gis•tics** study of seals
**sphyg•mic** of the pulse
**sphyg•mo•graph**
**sphyg•mo•graph•ic**
**sphyg•mog•ra•phy**
**sphyg•moid**
**sphyg•mo•ma•nom•eter**
**Spi•ca** star
**spi•ca** (*plural* **•cae** *or* **•cas)** spiral bandage
**spi•cate** botany term
**spic•ca•to** musical term
**spice**
**spice•berry** (*plural* **•berries)**
**spice•bush**
**spic•er**
**spic•ery** (*plural* **•eries)**
**spici•ly**
**spici•ness**
**spick-and-span** (*or* **spic-)**
**spicu•late**
**spic•ule**
**spicu•lum** (*plural* **•la)**
**spicy** **(spici•er, spici•est)**
**spi•der**
**spider•man** (*plural* **•men)**
**spider•wort**
**spi•dery**
**spied**
**spie•gelei•sen** pig iron
**spiel** *Slang* glib talk; *compare* speel
**spiel•er**
**spif•fing**
**spif•fy** **(•fi•er, •fi•est)** *US* smart
**spif•li•cate** *Slang* destroy
**spig•nel** plant
**spig•ot** cask stopper
**spike**
**spike•let** grass flower
**spike•nard** plant
**spike-rush** plant
**spiki•ly**
**spiki•ness**
**spiky** **(spiki•er, spiki•est)**
**spile** heavy stake
**spill** **(spill•ing, spilt** *or* **spilled)**
**spill•age**
**spill•er**
**spil•li•kin** (*or* **spili•)** thin strip
**spil•li•kins** game
**spill•way**
**spilt**
**spin** **(spin•ning, spun)**
**spi•na bi•fi•da**
**spin•ach**
**spi•nal**
**spi•nal•ly**
**spin•dle**
**spin•dling**
**spin•dly** **(•dli•er, •dli•est)**
**spin•drift** (*or* **spoon•)** sea spray
**spin-dry** **(-dries, -drying, -dried)**
**spin-dryer**
**spine**
**spine-chiller**
**spine-chilling**
**spi•nel** mineral
**spine•less**
**spine•less•ness**
**spi•nes•cence**
**spi•nes•cent**
**spin•et**
**spi•nif•er•ous** (*or* **•nig•)**
**spini•fex** plant
**spini•ness**
**spin•na•ker** racing sail
**spin•ner**
**spin•ner•et** zoology term
**spin•ney**
**spin•ning**
**spin-off**
**spi•nose**
**spi•nos•ity**
**spi•nous**
**Spi•no•zism** philosophical system
**spin•ster**
**spin•ster•hood**
**spin•ster•ish**
**spin•tha•ri•scope** physics apparatus
**spi•nule**
**spi•nu•lose**
**spiny** **(spini•er, spini•est)**
**spiny-finned**

**spira•cle** respiratory aperture
**spi•racu•lar**
**spi•racu•late**
**spi•raea** shrub
**spi•ral** (**•ral•ling, •ralled;** *US* **•ral•ing, •ralled**)
**spi•ral•ly**
**spi•rant** phonetics term
**spire**
**spi•reme** cytology term
**spi•rif•er•ous**
**spi•ril•lar**
**spi•ril•lum** (*plural* **•la**) bacterium
**spir•it**
**spir•it•ed**
**spir•it•ed•ly**
**spir•it•ed•ness**
**spir•it•less**
**spir•it•less•ness**
**spi•ri•to•so** musical term
**spiri•tous** *variant of* **spirituous**
**spir•itu•al**
**spir•itu•al•ism**
**spir•itu•al•ist**
**spir•itu•al•ity** (*plural* **•ities**)
**spir•itu•ali•za•tion** (*or* **•sa•tion**)
**spir•itu•al•ize** (*or* **•ise**)
**spir•itu•al•iz•er** (*or* **•is•er**)
**spir•itu•al•ly**
**spir•itu•al•ness**
**spir•itu•el** (*fem* **•elle**) witty
**spir•itu•os•ity** (*or* **•ous•ness**)
**spir•itu•ous** (*or* **spiri•tous**) alcoholic
**spir•ket•ting** nautical term
**spi•ro•chaete** bacterium
**spi•ro•chae•to•sis**
**spi•ro•graph** medical apparatus
**spi•ro•graph•ic**
**spi•ro•gy•ra** alga
**spi•roid**
**spi•rom•eter**
**spi•ro•met•ric**
**spi•rom•etry**
**spi•ro•no•lac•tone** drug
**spirt** *variant spelling of* **spurt**
**spiru•la** mollusc
**spiry**
**spit** (**spit•ting, spat** *or* **spit**) expectorate
**spit** (**spit•ting, spit•ted**) pointed rod; pierce
**spitch•cock**
**spite**
**spite•ful**
**spite•ful•ly**
**spite•ful•ness**
**spit•fire**
**Spit•head**
**spit•sticker** wood-engraving tool
**spit•ter**
**spit•tle**
**spittle•bug**
**spit•toon**
**spitz** dog
**spiv**
**spiv•vy**
**splake** trout
**splanch•nic** visceral
**splash**
**splash•back**
**splash•board**
**splash•down**
**splash•er**
**splashi•ly**
**splashi•ness**
**splashy** (**splashi•er, splashi•est**)
**splat**
**splat•ter**
**splay**
**splay•foot**
**splay•footed•ly**
**spleen**
**spleen•ish** (*or* **spleeny**)
**spleen•wort**
**splen•did**
**splen•did•ness**
**splen•dif•er•ous**
**splen•dor•ous** (*or* **•drous**)
**splen•dour** (*US* **•dor**)
**sple•nec•to•my** (*plural* **•mies**) removal of spleen
**sple•net•ic** (*or* **•neti•cal**) peevish
**sple•neti•cal•ly**
**sple•nial** of the splenius
**splen•ic** of the spleen
**sple•ni•tis**
**sple•nius** (*plural* **•nii**) muscle
**sple•no•mega•ly**
**splice**
**splic•er**
**spline** machine part
**splint**
**splin•ter**
**splin•tery**
**Split** Croatian port
**split** (**split•ting, split**)
**split-level**
**splits** gymnastic act
**split•ter**
**split•ting**
**splodge**
**splodgy**
**splore** *Scot* revel
**splotch**
**splotchy**
**splurge**
**splut•ter**
**splut•ter•er**
**splut•tery**
**spode** porcelain
**spodu•mene** mineral
**spoil** (**spoil•ing, spoilt** *or* **spoiled**)
**spoil•age**
**spoil•er**
**spoil•five** card game
**spoils**
**spoil•sport**
**Spo•kane** US city
**spoke**
**spo•ken**
**spoke•shave**
**spokes•man** (*plural* **•men**)
**spokes•woman** (*plural* **•women**)
**spo•li•ate** despoil
**spo•lia•tion**
**spo•lia•tory**
**spon•da•ic** (*or* **•dai•cal**)
**spon•dee** metrical foot
**spon•du•lix** (*or* **•licks**) *Slang* money
**spon•dy•li•tis** spinal disorder
**sponge**
**sponge•able**
**spong•er**
**spon•gi•ly**
**spon•gin**
**spon•gi•ness**
**spon•gio•blast** nerve cell
**spon•gio•blas•tic**
**spon•gy** (**•gi•er, •gi•est**)
**spon•sion** sponsorship
**spon•son** support on boat

**spon•sor**
**spon•so•rial**
**spon•sor•ship**
**spon•ta•neity** (*plural* **•neities**)
**spon•ta•neous**
**spon•ta•neous•ly**
**spon•ta•neous•ness**
**spon•toon** short pike
**spoof**
**spoof•er**
**spook**
**spooki•ly**
**spooki•ness**
**spook•ish**
**spooky** (**spooki•er, spooki•est**)
**spool**
**spoon**
**spoon•bill**
**spoon•er•ism**
**spoon-feed** (**-feeding, -fed**)
**spoon•ful** (*plural* **•fuls**)
**spoony** (**spooni•er, spooni•est**) amorous
**spoor** animal trail; *compare* **spore**
**spoor•er**
**Spora•des** Greek islands
**spo•rad•ic** (*or* **•radi•cal**)
**spo•radi•cal•ly**
**spo•radi•cal•ness**
**spo•ran•gial**
**spo•ran•gium** (*plural* **•gia**)
**spore** reproductive body; *compare* **spoor**
**spo•ro•carp**
**spo•ro•cyst**
**spo•ro•cyte**
**spo•ro•gen•esis**
**spo•rog•enous**
**spo•ro•go•nial**
**spo•ro•go•nium** (*plural* **•nia**)
**spo•rogo•ny**
**spo•ro•phore**
**spo•ro•phyll** (*or* **•phyl**)
**spo•ro•phyte**
**spo•ro•phyt•ic**
**spo•ro•zo•an**
**spo•ro•zo•ite**
**spor•ran**
**sport**
**sport•er**
**sporti•ly**
**sporti•ness**
**sport•ing**
**sport•ing•ly**
**spor•tive**
**spor•tive•ly**
**spor•tive•ness**
**sports•cast**
**sports•caster**
**sports•man** (*plural* **•men**)
**sportsman-like**
**sports•man•ly**
**sports•man•ship**
**sports•wear**
**sports•woman** (*plural* **•women**)
**sporty** (**sporti•er, sporti•est**)
**sporu•late** produce spores
**sporu•la•tion**
**spor•ule**
**spot** (**spot•ting, spot•ted**)
**spot•less**
**spot•less•ness**
**spot•light** (**•light•ing, •lit** *or* **•light•ed**)
**spot-on**
**spot•table**
**spot•ted**
**spot•ter**
**spot•ti•ly**
**spot•ti•ness**
**spot•ty** (**•ti•er, •ti•est**)
**spot-weld**
**spot-welder**
**spous•al** marriage ceremony
**spouse**
**spout**
**spout•er**
**sprag**
**sprain**
**sprang**
**sprat**
**sprawl**
**sprawl•er**
**sprawl•ing**
**sprawly**
**spray**
**spray•er**
**spread** (**spread•ing, spread**)
**spread•able**
**spread-eagle**
**spread•er**
**sprech•stimme** *German* musical term
**spree**
**sprig** (**sprig•ging, sprigged**)
**sprig•ger**
**sprig•gy**
**spright•li•ness**
**spright•ly** (**•li•er, •li•est**)
**spring** (**spring•ing, sprang** *or* **sprung, sprung**)
**spring•board**
**Spring•bok** South African athlete
**spring•bok** (*or* **•buck**; *plural* **•bok, boks** *or* **•buck, •bucks**) antelope
**spring-clean**
**spring-cleaning**
**springe** snare
**spring•er**
**Spring•field** US city
**spring•haas** (*plural* **•haas, •ha•se**) animal
**spring•head**
**springi•ly**
**springi•ness**
**spring•ing**
**spring•let**
**Springs** South African city
**spring•tail**
**spring•time**
**spring•wood**
**springy** (**springi•er, springi•est**)
**sprin•kle**
**sprin•kler**
**sprin•kling**
**sprint**
**sprint•er**
**sprit** nautical term
**sprite**
**sprit•sail**
**sprock•et**
**sprout**
**spruce**
**spruce•ly**
**spruce•ness**
**sprue** disease
**spru•ik** *Austral* speak in public
**sprung**
**spry** (**spri•er, spri•est**)
**spry•ly**
**spry•ness**
**spud** (**spud•ding, spud•ded**)
**spume** froth
**spu•mes•cence**
**spu•mes•cent**
**spu•mo•ne** (*or* **•ni**; *plural* **•ni**) ice cream

**spu•mous** (*or* **spumy**)
**spun**
**spunk**
**spunki•ly**
**spunki•ness**
**spunky** (**spunki•er, spunki•est**)
**spur** (**spur•ring, spurred**)
**spurge** plant
**spu•ri•ous**
**spu•ri•ous•ly**
**spu•ri•ous•ness**
**spurn**
**spurn•er**
**spur•ri•er** spur maker
**spur•ry** (*or* **•rey**; *plural* **•ries**) plant
**spurt** (*or* **spirt**)
**sput•nik** Soviet satellite
**sput•ter**
**sput•ter•er**
**spu•tum** (*plural* **•ta**)
**spy** (*noun, plural* **spies**; *verb* **spies, spy•ing, spied**)
**spy•glass**
**spy•ing**
**squab** (*plural* **squabs** *or* **squab**) young pigeon
**squab•ble**
**squab•bler**
**squab•by** (**•bi•er, •bi•est**)
**squac•co** (*plural* **•cos**) heron
**squad**
**squad•die** (*or* **•dy**; *plural* **•dies**) *Slang* soldier
**squad•ron**
**squa•lene** biochemical compound
**squal•id**
**squa•lid•ity** (*or* **squal•id•ness**)
**squall**
**squall•er**
**squal•ly**
**squal•or**
**squa•ma** (*plural* **•mae**) scale
**squa•mate**
**squa•ma•tion**
**squa•mo•sal** bone
**squa•mous** (*or* **•mose**)
**squa•mous•ness** (*or* **•mose**)
**squamu•lose** covered with small scales
**squan•der**
**squan•der•er**
**squan•der•ing•ly**
**square**
**square•ly**
**square•ness**
**squar•er**
**square-rigger**
**squar•ish**
**squar•rose** biology term
**squash**
**squash•er**
**squashi•ly**
**squashi•ness**
**squashy** (**squashi•er, squashi•est**)
**squat** (**squat•ting, squat•ted**)
**squat•ness**
**squat•ter**
**squat•toc•ra•cy** *Austral* rich farmers
**squaw**
**squawk**
**squawk•er**
**squeak**
**squeak•er**
**squeaki•ly**
**squeaki•ness**
**squeaky**
**squeal**
**squeal•er**
**squeam•ish**
**squeam•ish•ness**
**squee•gee** (*or* **squil•**; **•gee•ing, •geed**)
**squeez•able**
**squeeze**
**squeez•er**
**squelch**
**squelch•er**
**squelch•ing•ly**
**sque•teague** (*plural* **•teague** *or* **•teagues**) fish
**squib** (**squib•bing, squibbed**)
**squid** (*plural* **squid** *or* **squids**)
**squif•fy** (**•fi•er, •fi•est**)
**squig•gle**
**squig•gler**
**squig•gly**
**squill** plant
**squil•la** (*plural* **•las** *or* **•lae**) shrimp
**squinch** architectural support
**squint**
**squint•er**
**squinty**
**squire**
**squire•ar•chy** (*or* **squir•ar•chy**; *plural* **•chies**)
**squirm**
**squirm•er**
**squirm•ing•ly**
**squirmy**
**squir•rel**
**squirrel•fish** (*plural* **•fish** *or* **•fishes**)
**squirt**
**squirt•er**
**squish**
**squishy** (**squishi•er, squishi•est**)
**squit** *Slang* insignificant person
**squiz** (*plural* **squizzes**) *Austral* inquisitive glance
**Sri Lan•ka**
**Sri Lan•kan**
**Sri•na•gar** Indian city
**St** *abbrev. for* **Saint**; *all entries preceded by* **St** *are listed in the section of this dictionary following the entry* **saint**
**stab** (**stab•bing, stabbed**)
**Sta•bat Ma•ter** hymn
**stab•ber**
**sta•bile** arts term
**sta•bil•ity** (*plural* **•ities**)
**sta•bi•li•za•tion** (*or* **•sa•tion**)
**sta•bi•lize** (*or* **•lise**)
**sta•bi•li•zer** (*or* **•ser**)
**sta•ble**
**stable•boy**
**stable•man** (*plural* **•men**)
**sta•ble•ness**
**sta•bling**
**sta•bly**
**stac•ca•to**
**stack**
**stack•er**
**stac•te** biblical spice
**stad•dle** prop
**staddle•stone**
**stad•hold•er** (*or* **stadt•**) Dutch ruler
**sta•di•om•eter**
**sta•dium** (*plural* **•diums** *or* **•dia**)

**staff** (*plural* **staffs**) personnel
**staff** (*plural* **staffs** *or* **staves**) pole
**staff** (*or* **stave**; *plural* **staffs** *or* **staves**) musical term
**Staf•fa** Scottish island
**staff•er** *Slang* staff member
**staff•man** (*plural* **•men**)
**Staf•ford**
**Staf•ford•shire**
**stag**
**stage**
**stage•coach**
**stage•craft**
**stage•hand**
**stage-manage**
**stag•er**
**stag•fla•tion** economics term
**stag•gard** deer
**stag•ger**
**stagger•bush**
**stag•ger•er**
**stag•ger•ing**
**stag•ger•ing•ly**
**stag•gers** horse disease
**stag•hound**
**stagi•ly**
**stagi•ness**
**stag•ing**
**Sta•gi•ra** ancient Macedonian city
**stag•nan•cy** (*or* **•nance**)
**stag•nant**
**stag•nate**
**stag•na•tion**
**stagy** (**stagi•er, stagi•est**) theatrical
**staid** sedate; *compare* **stayed**
**staid•ness**
**stain**
**stain•abil•ity**
**stain•able**
**stain•er**
**Staines** Surrey town
**stain•less**
**stair** step; *compare* **stare**
**stair•case**
**stair•head**
**stairs**
**stair•way**
**stair•well**
**stake** stick; money; *compare* **steak**
**stake•hold•er**
**stake•out**
**Stak•han•ov** Ukrainian city
**sta•lac•ti•form**
**stal•ac•tite** downward projection in cave
**stal•ac•tit•ic** (*or* **•titi•cal**)
**sta•lag** German prison camp
**stal•ag•mite** upward projection in cave
**stal•ag•mit•ic** (*or* **•miti•cal**)
**stale**
**stale•ly**
**stale•mate**
**stale•ness**
**Sta•lin•ism**
**Sta•lin•ist**
**stalk**
**stalked**
**stalk•er**
**stalki•ly**
**stalki•ness**
**stalk•like**
**stalky** (**stalki•er, stalki•est**)
**stall**
**stall-feed** (**-feeding, -fed**)
**stal•lion**
**stal•wart**
**stal•wart•ness**
**Stam•bul** (*or* **•boul**) part of Istanbul
**sta•men** (*plural* **sta•mens** *or* **stami•na**)
**Stam•ford** US city
**stami•na**
**stami•nal**
**stami•nate** having stamens
**stami•nif•er•ous**
**stami•node** (*or* **•no•dium**; *plural* **•nodes** *or* **•no•dia**) botany term
**stami•no•dy**
**stam•mel** fabric
**stam•mer**
**stam•mer•er**
**stam•mer•ing•ly**
**stamp**
**stam•pede**
**stam•ped•er**
**stamp•er**
**stance**
**stanch** (*or* **staunch**) check blood flow; *compare* **staunch**
**stanch•able** (*or* **staunch•**)
**stanch•er** (*or* **staunch•**)
**stan•chion**
**stand** (**stand•ing, stood**)
**stand•ard**
**standard-bearer**
**stand•ardi•za•tion** (*or* **•sa•tion**)
**stand•ard•ize** (*or* **•ise**)
**stand•ard•iz•er** (*or* **•is•er**)
**stand-by** (*noun*; *plural* **-bys**)
**standee** one who stands
**stand•er**
**stand-in** (*noun*)
**stand•ing**
**stand•ish** inkstand
**stand•offish**
**stand•pipe**
**stand•point**
**stand•still**
**stang** *Dialect* throb with pain
**stan•hope** carriage
**stank**
**Stan•ley** capital of Falkland Islands
**Stan•na•ries** English district
**stan•na•ry** (*plural* **•ries**) tin mine
**stan•nic** chemistry term
**stan•nif•er•ous**
**stan•nite** mineral
**stan•nous** chemistry term
**stan•za**
**stan•zaed**
**stan•za•ic**
**sta•pedial**
**sta•pelia** plant
**sta•pes** (*plural* **•pes** *or* **•pedes**) ear bone
**staphy•lo•coc•cal**
**staphy•lo•coc•cus** (*plural* **•coc•ci**)
**staphy•lo•plas•tic**
**staphy•lo•plas•ty** palate surgery
**staphy•lor•rhaph•ic**
**staphy•lor•rha•phy** repair of cleft palate
**sta•ple**
**sta•pler**
**star** (**star•ring, starred**)
**star-apple**
**Sta•ra Za•go•ra** Bulgarian city
**star•board**

**starch**
**starch•er**
**starchi•ly**
**starchi•ness**
**starch-reduced**
**starchy (starchi•er, starchi•est)**
**star-crossed**
**star•dom**
**star•dust**
**stare** look at; *compare* **stair**
**star•er**
**star•fish** (*plural* **•fish** *or* **•fishes**)
**star•flower**
**star•gaze**
**star•gaz•er**
**star•gaz•ing**
**stark**
**stark•ness**
**star•less**
**star•let**
**star•light**
**star•like**
**star•ling**
**star•lit**
**star-of-Bethlehem** plant
**starred**
**star•ri•ly**
**star•ri•ness**
**star•ry (•ri•er, •ri•est)**
**starry-eyed**
**star-spangled**
**start**
**start•er**
**star•tle**
**star•tler**
**star•tling**
**star•tling•ly**
**star•va•tion**
**starve**
**starve•ling**
**starv•er**
**starv•ing**
**star•wort**
**stash**
**sta•sis** stagnation
**stat•able** (*or* **state•**)
**sta•tant** heraldic term
**state**
**state•craft**
**state•hood**
**State•house** *US* state capitol
**state•less**
**state•less•ness**
**state•li•ness**
**state•ly (•li•er, •li•est)**
**state•ment**
**Stat•en Is•land**
**sta•ter** one who states; ancient coin; *compare* **stator**
**state•room**
**States** the USA
**state•side**
**states•man** (*plural* **•men**)
**statesman-like** (*or* **states•man•ly**)
**states•man•ship**
**states•woman** (*plural* **•women**)
**stat•ic**
**stati•cal**
**stati•cal•ly**
**stat•ice** plant
**stat•ics**
**sta•tion**
**sta•tion•ari•ly**
**sta•tion•ari•ness**
**sta•tion•ary** not moving; *compare* **stationery**
**sta•tion•er**
**sta•tion•ery** writing materials; *compare* **stationary**
**station•master**
**stat•ism** state control
**stat•ist**
**sta•tis•tic**
**sta•tis•ti•cal**
**sta•tis•ti•cal•ly**
**stat•is•ti•cian**
**sta•tis•tics**
**sta•tive** linguistics term
**stato•blast** zoology term
**stato•cyst** zoology term
**stato•lith** biology term
**stato•lith•ic**
**sta•tor** part of machine; *compare* **stater**
**stato•scope** aircraft instrument
**statu•ary** (*plural* **•aries**)
**statue**
**stat•ued**
**statu•esque**
**statu•esque•ly**
**statu•esque•ness**
**statu•ette**
**stat•ure**
**sta•tus** (*plural* **•tuses**)
**sta•tus quo**
**statu•table**
**stat•ute**
**statu•to•ri•ly**
**statu•tory**
**staunch** loyal; *variant spelling of* **stanch**
**staunch•ness**
**stau•ro•lite** mineral
**stau•ro•lit•ic**
**stau•ro•scope**
**stau•ro•scopi•cal•ly**
**Sta•vang•er** Norwegian port
**stave (stav•ing, staved** *or* **stove)** wooden strip; to crush; *variant spelling of* **staff**
**staves** (*noun*) *plural of* **staff** *or* **stave**
**staves•acre** plant
**Stav•ro•pol** Russian city
**stay**
**stayed** *past tense of* **stay**; *compare* **staid**
**stay•er**
**stays** boned corsets
**stay•sail**
**stead**
**stead•fast** (*or* **sted•**)
**stead•fast•ness** (*or* **sted•**)
**steadi•ly**
**steadi•ness**
**steady** (*adj* **steadi•er, steadi•est**; *verb* **stead•ies, steady•ing, stead•ied**)
**steady•ing•ly**
**steak** meat; *compare* **stake**
**steak•house**
**steal (steal•ing, stole, sto•len)**
**steal•er**
**stealth**
**stealth•ful**
**stealthi•ly**
**stealthi•ness**
**stealthy (stealthi•er, stealthi•est)**
**steam**
**steam•boat**
**steam-boiler**
**steam-chest**
**steam-engine**
**steam•er**

**steamie** *Scot* public washhouse
**steami•ly**
**steami•ness**
**steam•roller**
**steam•ship**
**steam-shovel**
**steam•tight**
**steam•tight•ness**
**steamy** (**steami•er, steami•est**)
**ste•ap•sin** enzyme
**stea•rate**
**ste•aric**
**stea•rin** (*or* **•rine**) biochemical compound
**stea•rop•tene**
**stea•tite** mineral
**stea•tit•ic**
**stea•toly•sis** digestive process
**stea•to•py•gia** (*or* **•ga**) excessively fat buttocks
**stea•to•pyg•ic** (*or* **•py•gous**)
**stea•tor•rhoea** (*US* **•rhea**)
**steed**
**steel** alloy; *compare* **stele**
**steel•head** (*plural* **•heads** *or* **•head**) fish
**steeli•ness**
**steel•work**
**steel•worker**
**steel•working**
**steel•works**
**steely** (**steeli•er, steeli•est**)
**steel•yard**
**steen•bok** *variant spelling of* **steinbok**
**steep**
**steep•en**
**steep•er**
**steep•ish**
**stee•ple**
**steeple•chase**
**steeple•chas•er**
**steeple•jack**
**steep•ness**
**steer** guide; bullock; *compare* **stere**
**steer•able**
**steer•age**
**steer•age•way**
**steer•er**
**steer•ing**
**steers•man** (*plural* **•men**)
**steeve** nautical term
**stego•don** (*or* **•dont**) extinct mammal
**stego•myia** mosquito
**stego•saur** (*or* **•saur•us**)
**stein** beer mug
**stein•bok** (*or* **steen•**; *plural* **•boks** *or* **•bok**) antelope
**ste•lar** of a stele; *compare* **stellar**
**ste•le** (*or* **•la**; *plural* **•lae** *or* **•les**) stone slab
**stele** plant tissue; *compare* **steel**
**stel•lar** of stars; *compare* **stelar**
**stel•lara•tor** physics apparatus
**stel•late** (*or* **•lat•ed**)
**stel•lif•er•ous**
**stel•li•form**
**stel•li•fy** (**•fies, •fy•ing, •fied**) change into a star
**Stel•lite** (*Trademark*)
**stel•lu•lar**
**stem** (**stem•ming, stemmed**)
**stem•head**
**stem•ma** family tree
**stem•mer**
**stem•son** nautical term
**stem•ware** stemmed glasses
**stem-winder**
**stench**
**sten•cil** (**•cil•ling, •cilled**; *US* **•cil•ing, •ciled**)
**sten•cil•ler** (*US* **•cil•er**)
**Sten gun**
**steno** (*plural* **stenos**) *US* shorthand typist
**steno•graph**
**ste•nog•ra•pher** *US* shorthand typist
**steno•graph•ic** (*or* **•graphi•cal**)
**ste•nog•ra•phy**
**steno•ha•line**
**steno•pet•al•ous**
**ste•nopha•gous**
**steno•phyl•lous**
**ste•no•sis** (*plural* **•ses**)
**steno•ther•mal**
**ste•not•ic**
**steno•trop•ic** (*or* **•top•**) ecology term
**Steno•type** (*Trademark*)
**steno•typ•ic**
**steno•typ•ist**
**steno•typy** form of shorthand
**sten•tor** loud person; microscopic animal
**sten•to•rian**
**step** (**step•ping, stepped**) motion of foot; stage; etc.; *compare* **steppe**
**step•brother**
**step•child** (*plural* **•children**)
**step•daughter**
**step•father**
**stepha•no•tis**
**step•ladder**
**step•mother**
**step-parent**
**steppe** grassy plain; *compare* **step**
**step•per**
**Steppes** Eurasian grasslands
**step•sister**
**step•son**
**step•wise**
**ste•ra•dian** unit
**ster•co•ra•ceous** of dung
**ster•co•rico•lous**
**ster•cu•lia•ceous** botany term
**stere** unit; *compare* **steer**
**ste•reo** (*plural* **•reos**)
**ste•reo•bate** foundation of building
**ste•reo•chem•is•try**
**ste•reo•chrome**
**ste•reo•chro•my** wall painting
**ste•reo•gram**
**ste•reo•graph**
**ste•reo•graph•ic** (*or* **•graphi•cal**)
**ste•reog•ra•phy**
**ste•reo•iso•mer**
**ste•reo•isom•er•ism**
**ste•reo•iso•met•ric**
**ste•reo•met•ric**
**ste•reo•met•ri•cal**
**ste•reom•etry**
**ste•reo•phon•ic**
**ste•reo•phoni•cal•ly**
**ste•reoph•ony**
**ste•reop•sis** stereoscopic vision

**ste•reop•ti•con** type of projector
**ste•reo•scope**
**ste•reo•scop•ic** (*or* **•scopi•cal)**
**ste•reo•scopi•cal•ly**
**ste•reos•co•pist**
**ste•reos•co•py**
**ste•reo•spe•cif•ic**
**ste•reo•tac•tic** (*or* **•ti•cal)**
**ste•reo•tac•ti•cal•ly**
**ste•reo•tax•is** biology term
**ste•reot•omy**
**ste•reo•trop•ic**
**ste•reot•ro•pism** botany term
**ste•reo•type**
**ste•reo•typ•er** (*or* **•ist)**
**ste•reo•typ•ic** (*or* **•typi•cal)**
**ste•reo•typy**
**ste•reo•vi•sion**
**ste•ric** (*or* **•ri•cal)** chemistry term
**ste•ri•cal•ly**
**ster•ig•ma** (*plural* **•ma•ta)** botany term
**steri•lant**
**ster•ile**
**ste•ril•ity**
**steri•liz•able** (*or* **•lis•able)**
**steri•li•za•tion** (*or* **•sa•tion)**
**steri•lize** (*or* **•lise)**
**steri•liz•er** (*or* **•lis•er)**
**ster•let** fish
**ster•ling**
**stern**
**ster•nal** of the sternum
**stern•most**
**stern•ness**
**stern•post**
**stern•son** nautical term
**ster•num** (*plural* **•na** *or* **•nums)** breastbone
**ster•nu•ta•tion** sneezing
**ster•nu•ta•tive**
**ster•nu•ta•tor**
**ster•nu•ta•tory** (*plural* **•tories)**
**stern•wards** (*or esp. US* **•ward)**
**stern•way**
**ster•oid**
**ster•oi•dal**
**ster•ol** biochemical compound
**ster•tor** noisy breathing
**ster•to•rous**
**ster•to•rous•ness**
**stet (stet•ting, stet•ted)**
**stetho•scope**
**stetho•scop•ic**
**ste•thos•co•py**
**stet•son**
**ste•vedore**
**Ste•ven•age** Hertfordshire town
**Ste•ven•graph** (*or* **•vens•)** silk picture
**stew**
**stew•ard**
**stew•ard•ess**
**stew•ard•ship**
**stewed**
**sthen•ic** strong
**stib•ine** poisonous gas
**stib•nite** mineral
**stich** line of poetry; *compare* **stitch**
**stich•ic**
**stichi•cal•ly**
**sticho•met•ric** (*or* **•ri•cal)**
**sti•chom•etry**
**sticho•mythia** (*or* **sti•chomy•thy)** drama term
**stick (stick•ing, stuck)**
**stick•er**
**stick•ful** (*plural* **•fuls)**
**sticki•ly**
**sticki•ness**
**stick•le** argue
**stickle•back**
**stick•ler**
**stick•seed**
**stick•tight** plant
**stick-up** (*noun*)
**stick•weed**
**sticky (sticki•er, sticki•est)**
**sticky•beak** *Austral* inquisitive person
**stiff**
**stiff•en**
**stiff•en•er**
**stiff•ness**
**sti•fle**
**sti•fler**
**sti•fling**
**sti•fling•ly**
**stig•ma** (*plural* **•mas)** mark; flower part
**stig•ma** (*plural* **•ma•ta)** crucifixion mark
**stig•mas•ter•ol** biochemical compound
**stig•mat•ic** (*or* **•mati•cal)**
**stig•ma•tism**
**stig•ma•tist**
**stig•ma•ti•za•tion** (*or* **•sa•tion)**
**stig•ma•tize** (*or* **•tise)**
**stig•ma•tiz•er** (*or* **•tis•er)**
**stil•bene**
**stil•bite** mineral
**stil•boes•trol** (*US* **•bes•)**
**stile** steps over fence; *compare* **style**
**sti•let•to** (*noun, plural* **•tos;** *verb* **•toes, •toe•ing, •toed)**
**still**
**stil•lage** platform
**still•birth**
**still•born**
**still life** (*plural* **still lifes)** picture
**stil•li•cide** legal term
**still•ness**
**stilt**
**stilt•ed**
**stilt•ed•ness**
**Stil•ton** cheese
**stimu•lable**
**stimu•lant**
**stimu•late**
**stimu•lat•ing•ly**
**stimu•la•tion**
**stimu•la•tive**
**stimu•la•tor** (*or* **•lat•er)**
**stimu•lus** (*plural* **•li)**
**sting (sting•ing, stung)**
**sting•er**
**stin•gi•ly**
**stin•gi•ness**
**sting•ing•ly**
**stin•go** beer
**sting•ray**
**stin•gy (•gi•er, •gi•est)**
**stink (stink•ing, stank** *or* **stunk)**
**stink•er**
**stink•horn** fungus
**stink•ing•ly**
**stink•ing•ness**
**stink•pot**
**stink•stone**
**stink•weed**

**stink•wood**
**stint**
**stint•er**
**stipe** plant stalk
**sti•pel** small leaflike structure; *compare* **stipple**
**sti•pel•late**
**sti•pend**
**sti•pen•di•ary** (*plural* **•aries**)
**sti•pes** (*plural* **stipi•tes**) zoology term
**sti•pi•form** (*or* **stipi•ti•**)
**stipi•tate**
**stip•ple** dot or fleck; *compare* **stipel**
**stip•pler**
**stip•pling**
**stipu•lable**
**stipu•lar**
**stipu•late**
**stipu•la•tion**
**stipu•la•tor**
**stipu•la•tory**
**stip•ule** leaflike structure
**stir** (**stir•ring, stirred**)
**stirk** heifer
**Stir•ling** Scottish town
**stirps** (*plural* **stir•pes**) line of descendants
**stir•rable**
**stir•rer**
**stir•ring**
**stir•ring•ly**
**stir•rup**
**stitch** needlework link; *compare* **stich**
**stitch•er**
**stitch•ing**
**stitch•wort**
**stithy** (*plural* **stithies**) *Dialect* forge
**sti•ver** coin
**stoa** (*plural* **stoae** *or* **stoas**) covered walk
**stoat**
**stob** *Dialect* stump
**sto•chas•tic** statistics term
**sto•chas•ti•cal•ly**
**stock**
**stock•ade**
**stock•breeder**
**stock•breeding**
**stock•broker**
**stock•bro•ker•age** (*or* **•broking**)
**stock•er**
**stock•fish** (*plural* **•fish** *or* **•fishes**)
**stock•holder**
**stock•holding**
**Stock•holm**
**stocki•ly**
**stocki•ness**
**stocki•net**
**stock•ing**
**stock•inged**
**stock•ish** stupid
**stock•ist**
**stock•jobber**
**stock•jobbery** (*or* **•jobbing**)
**stock•man** (*plural* **•men**)
**stock•pile**
**stock•pil•er**
**Stock•port** English town
**stock•pot**
**stock•room**
**stocks** instrument of punishment
**stock-still**
**stock•taking**
**Stock•ton** English town; US port
**stocky** (**stocki•er, stocki•est**)
**stock•yard**
**stodge**
**stodgi•ly**
**stodgi•ness**
**stodgy** (**stodgi•er, stodgi•est**)
**sto•gy** (*or* **sto•gey**; *plural* **•gies**) *US* cigar
**Sto•ic** philosopher
**sto•ic** self-controlled person
**stoi•cal**
**stoi•cal•ly**
**stoi•cal•ness**
**stoi•chio•logi•cal**
**stoi•chi•ol•ogy** branch of biology
**stoi•chio•met•ric**
**stoi•chi•om•etry** branch of chemistry
**stoi•cism**
**stoke**
**stoke•hold**
**stoke•hole**
**Stoke Mandeville** Buckinghamshire town
**stok•er**
**stokes** (*or* **stoke**; *plural* **stokes**) unit
**stole** long shawl; *past tense of* **steal**
**stol•en**
**stol•id**
**sto•lid•ity** (*or* **stol•id•ness**)
**stol•len** bread
**sto•lon** stem
**sto•loni•fer•ous**
**sto•ma** (*plural* **•ma•ta**)
**stom•ach**
**stomach•ache**
**stom•ach•er**
**sto•mach•ic**
**sto•machi•cal**
**stom•achy**
**sto•ma•tal** (*or* **stoma•tous**)
**sto•mat•ic** of the mouth
**sto•ma•ti•tic**
**sto•ma•ti•tis**
**sto•ma•tol•ogy**
**stoma•to•plas•ty**
**stoma•to•pod** crustacean
**sto•mo•daeal** (*or* **•deal**)
**sto•mo•daeum** (*or* **•deum**) embryonic mouth cavity
**stomp**
**stomp•er**
**ston•able** (*or* **stone•**)
**stone**
**stone-blind**
**stone•chat** bird
**stone•crop** plant
**stone•cutter**
**stone•cutting**
**stoned**
**stone•fish** (*plural* **•fish** *or* **•fishes**)
**stone•fly** (*plural* **•flies**)
**stone•ground**
**Stone•henge**
**stone•less**
**stone-lily** fossil
**stone•mason**
**stone•mason•ry**
**ston•er**
**stone•wall**
**stone•wall•er**
**stone•ware**
**stone•work**
**stone•worker**
**stone•wort** alga
**stoni•ly**
**stoni•ness**

**stonk** bombard with artillery
**stony** (*or* **stoney; stoni•er, stoni•est**)
**stony-broke**
**stony-hearted**
**stony-hearted•ness**
**stood**
**stooge**
**stook**
**stook•er**
**stool**
**stoop** bend body; *compare* **stoup; stupe**
**stoop•er**
**stoop•ing•ly**
**stop** (**stop•ping, stopped**)
**stop•cock**
**stope** mine excavation
**stop•gap**
**stop-go** economics term
**stop•ing** geology term
**stop•light**
**stop•over** (*noun*)
**stop•pable**
**stop•page**
**stop•per**
**stop•ping**
**stops** card game
**stop•watch**
**stor•able**
**stor•age**
**sto•rax** plant; drug
**store**
**store•house**
**store•keeper**
**store•keeping**
**store•room**
**sto•rey** (*plural* **•reys** *or* **•ries**) level; *compare* **story**
**sto•reyed** multilevelled
**sto•ried** recorded
**stork**
**storks•bill** plant
**storm**
**storm•bound**
**stormi•ly**
**stormi•ness**
**storm•proof**
**storm-trooper**
**stormy** (**stormi•er, stormi•est**)
**Stor•no•way** Scottish port
**Stor•ting** (*or* **•thing**) Norwegian parliament
**sto•ry** (*plural* **•ries**) tale; *compare* **storey**
**story•book**
**story•teller**
**story•telling**
**stoss** geology term
**stot** (**stot•ting, stot•ted**) *Scot* bounce
**sto•tin•ka** (*plural* **•ki**) Bulgarian coin
**sto•tious** *Irish* drunk
**stot•ter** *Scot* good-looking woman
**stound** *Dialect* short period
**stoup** basin for holy water; drinking mug; *compare* **stoop; stupe**
**stour** *Dialect* turmoil
**Stour•bridge** English town
**stout**
**stout•hearted**
**stout•hearted•ness**
**stout•ish**
**stout•ness**
**stove**
**stove•pipe**
**stove•pipes** tight trousers
**stov•er**
**stow**
**stow•age**
**stow•away**
**stra•bis•mal** (*or* **•mic, •mi•cal**)
**stra•bis•mus** squint
**strad•dle**
**strad•dler**
**Stradi•var•ius** violin
**strafe**
**straf•er**
**strag•gle**
**strag•gler**
**strag•gling•ly**
**strag•gly** (**•gli•er, •gli•est**)
**straight** not curved; directly; *compare* **strait**
**straight•away**
**straight•edge**
**straight•en** put straight; *compare* **straiten**
**straight•en•er**
**straight-faced**
**straight•forward**
**straight•forward•ness**
**straight•ness**
**strain**
**strained**
**strained•ness**
**strain•er**
**strain•ing•ly**
**strait** sea channel; difficulty; *compare* **straight**
**strait•en** embarrass financially; *compare* **straighten**
**strait•jacket** (*or* **straight•**)
**strait-laced** (*or* **straight-**)
**strait•ness**
**strake** metal part of wheel
**stra•mo•nium** drug
**Strand** London street
**strand**
**stranded**
**strange**
**strange•ness**
**stran•ger**
**stran•gle**
**strangle•hold**
**stran•gler**
**stran•gles** horse disease
**stran•gu•late**
**stran•gu•la•tion**
**stran•gu•ry** painful urination
**Stran•raer** Scottish port
**strap** (**strap•ping, strapped**)
**strap•hanger**
**strap•hanging**
**strap•less**
**strap•pa•do** (*plural* **•does**) torture
**strap•per**
**strap•ping**
**Stras•bourg** French city
**strass** imitation gem
**stra•ta** *plural of* **stratum**
**strata•gem**
**stra•tal**
**stra•tegic** (*or* **•tegi•cal**)
**stra•tegi•cal•ly**
**stra•tegics** military strategy
**strat•egist**
**strat•egy** (*plural* **•egies**)
**Stratford-on-Avon**
**strath** *Scot* glen
**Strath•clyde** former Scottish region
**strath•spey** dance
**stra•ticu•late** geology term
**stra•ticu•la•tion**
**strati•fi•ca•tion**

**strati•form**
**strati•fy** (**•fies, •fy•ing, •fied**)
**stra•tig•ra•pher** (*or* **•phist**)
**strati•graph•ic** (*or* **•graphi•cal**)
**stra•tig•ra•phy** study of rock strata
**stra•toc•ra•cy** (*plural* **•cies**) military rule
**strato•crat**
**strato•crat•ic**
**strato•cu•mu•lus** (*plural* **•li**)
**strato•pause** meteorology term
**strato•sphere**
**strato•spher•ic** (*or* **•spheri•cal**)
**stra•tum** (*plural* **•ta** *or* **•tums**) layer
**stra•tus** (*plural* **•ti**) cloud
**stra•vaig** *Scot* wander
**straw**
**straw•berry** (*plural* **•berries**)
**straw•board**
**straw•flower**
**strawy**
**stray**
**stray•er**
**strays** electronics term
**streak**
**streaked**
**streak•er**
**streaki•ly**
**streaki•ness**
**streak•ing**
**streaky** (**streaki•er, streaki•est**)
**stream**
**stream•er**
**stream•line**
**stream•lined**
**street**
**street•car**
**street•light** (*or* **•lamp**)
**street•walker**
**street•walking**
**stre•lit•zia** plant
**strength**
**strength•en**
**strength•en•er**
**strenu•os•ity** (*or* **•ous•ness**)
**strenu•ous**
**strep•to•coc•cal** (*or* **•cic**)
**strep•to•coc•cus** (*plural* **•coc•ci**)
**strep•to•ki•nase** drug
**strep•to•my•cin** antibiotic
**strep•to•thri•cin** antibiotic
**stress**
**stress•ful**
**stress•ful•ly**
**stretch**
**stretch•abil•ity**
**stretch•able**
**stretch•er**
**stretcher-bearer**
**stretchi•ness**
**stretchy** (**stretchi•er, stretchi•est**)
**stret•to** (*plural* **•tos** *or* **•ti**) musical term
**streu•sel** pastry topping
**strew** (**strew•ing, strewed, strewn** *or* **strewed**)
**strew•er**
**strewth** exclamation
**stria** (*plural* **striae**)
**stri•ate** (*or* **•at•ed**)
**stria•tion**
**strick** textile fibres
**strick•en**
**strick•le**
**strict**
**strict•ness**
**stric•ture**
**stride** (**strid•ing, strode, strid•den**)
**stri•dence** (*or* **•den•cy**)
**stri•dent**
**stri•dor** wheezing sound
**stridu•late** zoology term
**stridu•la•tion**
**stridu•la•tor**
**stridu•la•tory**
**stridu•lous** (*or* **•lant**)
**stridu•lous•ness** (*or* **stridu•lance**)
**strife**
**strigi•form** ornithology term
**strig•il** body scraper
**stri•gose** biology term
**strik•able**
**strike** (**strik•ing, struck**)
**strike•bound**
**strike•breaker**
**strike•breaking**
**strik•er**
**strik•ing**
**strik•ing•ness**
**string** (**string•ing, strung**)
**string•board**
**stringed**
**strin•gen•cy**
**strin•gen•do** musical term
**strin•gent**
**string•er**
**string•halt** veterinary term
**stringi•ly**
**stringi•ness**
**string•piece**
**stringy** (**stringi•er, stringi•est**)
**strip** (**strip•ping, stripped**)
**stripe**
**strip•er**
**strip•ling** lad
**strip•per**
**strip•tease**
**stripy** (**stripi•er stripi•est**)
**strive** (**striv•ing, strove, striv•en**)
**striv•er**
**strobe** lighting
**stro•bic** spinning
**stro•bi•la** (*plural* **•lae**) body of tapeworm
**stro•bi•la•ceous**
**stro•bi•la•tion**
**stro•bi•lus** (*or* **stro•bile**; *plural* **•li, •luses** *or* **•biles**) plant cone
**stro•bo•scope**
**stro•bo•scop•ic** (*or* **•scopi•cal**)
**stro•bo•scopi•cal•ly**
**strode**
**stroga•noff**
**stroke**
**stroll**
**stroll•er**
**stro•ma** (*plural* **•ma•ta**) biology term
**stro•mat•ic** (*or* **•ma•tous**)
**stro•mato•lite** rock
**stro•mato•lit•ic**
**Strom•bo•li** volcanic island
**strong**
**strong-arm**
**strong•box**
**strong•hold**
**strong•ly**
**strong•man** (*plural* **•men**)

**strong-minded**
**strong-minded•ness**
**strong•ness**
**strong•room**
**strong-willed**
**stron•gyle** (*or* **•gyl**) parasitic worm
**strontia** strontium compound
**stron•ti•an•ite** (*or* **stron•tian**) mineral
**stron•tium** chemical element
**strop** (**strop•ping, stropped**)
**stro•phan•thin** drug
**stro•phan•thus** tree
**stro•phe** prosody term
**stroph•ic** (*or* **strophi•cal**)
**strop•pi•ly**
**strop•pi•ness**
**strop•py** (**•pi•er, •pi•est**)
**Stroud** English town
**stroud** fabric
**strove**
**struck**
**struc•tur•al**
**struc•tur•al•ism**
**struc•tur•al•ist**
**struc•tur•al•ly**
**struc•ture**
**struc•ture•less**
**stru•del**
**strug•gle**
**strug•gler**
**strug•gling•ly**
**strum** (**strum•ming, strummed**)
**stru•ma** (*plural* **•mae**) swelling
**stru•mat•ic** (*or* **stru•mous, stru•mose**)
**strum•mer**
**strum•pet**
**strung**
**strut** (**strut•ting, strut•ted**)
**stru•thi•ous** ostrich-like
**strut•ter**
**strut•ting•ly**
**strych•nic**
**strych•nine**
**strych•nin•ism**
**stub** (**stub•bing, stubbed**)
**stub•bi•ly**
**stub•bi•ness**
**stub•ble**
**stub•bled**
**stub•bly**
**stub•born**
**stub•born•ness**
**stub•by** (**•bi•er, •bi•est**)
**stuc•co** (*noun, plural* **•coes** *or* **•cos**; *verb* **•coes** *or* **•cos, •co•ing, •coed**)
**stuck**
**stud** (**stud•ding, stud•ded**)
**stud•book**
**stud•ding**
**studding•sail**
**stu•dent**
**stu•dent•ship**
**stud•horse**
**stud•ied**
**stud•ied•ly**
**stud•ied•ness**
**stu•dio** (*plural* **•dios**)
**stu•di•ous**
**stu•di•ous•ness**
**stud•work**
**study** (*noun, plural* **studies**, *verb* **stud•ies, study•ing, stud•ied**)
**stuff**
**stuffed**
**stuff•er**
**stuf•fi•ly**
**stuffi•ness**
**stuff•ing**
**stuffy** (**stuffi•er, stuffi•est**)
**stull** mining prop
**stul•ti•fi•ca•tion**
**stul•ti•fi•er**
**stul•ti•fy** (**•fies, •fy•ing, •fied**)
**stum** (**stum•ming, stummed**) wine-making term
**stum•ble**
**stum•bler**
**stum•bling•ly**
**stu•mer** *Slang* forgery
**stump**
**stump•er**
**stumpi•ness**
**stumpy** (**stumpi•er, stumpi•est**)
**stun** (**stun•ning, stunned**)
**stung**
**stunk**
**stun•ner**
**stun•ning**
**stun•ning•ly**
**stunt**
**stunt•ed**
**stunt•ed•ness**
**stupe** medical compress; *compare* **stoop; stoup**
**stu•pefa•ci•ent** (*or* **•pefac•tive**)
**stu•pefac•tion**
**stu•pefi•er**
**stu•pefy** (**•pefies, •pefy•ing, •pefied**)
**stu•pefy•ing•ly**
**stu•pen•dous**
**stu•pen•dous•ness**
**stu•pid**
**stu•pid•ity** (*plural* **•ities**)
**stu•pid•ness**
**stu•por**
**stu•por•ous**
**stur•di•ly**
**stur•di•ness**
**stur•dy** (**•di•er, •di•est**)
**stur•geon**
**Stur•mer** apple
**stut•ter**
**stut•ter•er**
**stut•ter•ing•ly**
**Stutt•gart** German city
**sty** (*noun, plural* **sties**, *verb* **sties, sty•ing, stied**) pig's pen
**sty** (*or* **stye**; *plural* **sties** *or* **styes**) inflamed eye spot
**Styg•ian** of the Styx
**stylar**
**style** form; elegance; flower part; *compare* **stile**
**style•book**
**styl•er**
**sty•let**
**sty•li•form**
**styl•ish**
**styl•ish•ness**
**styl•ist**
**sty•lis•tic**
**sty•lis•ti•cal•ly**
**sty•lite** recluse
**styli•za•tion** (*or* **•sa•tion**)
**styl•ize** (*or* **•ise**)
**styl•iz•er** (*or* **•is•er**)
**sty•lo•bate** architectural term
**sty•lo•graph**

**sty•lo•graph•ic** (*or* **•graphi•cal**)
**sty•lo•graphi•cal•ly**
**sty•log•ra•phy** engraving
**sty•loid**
**sty•lo•lite** geology term
**sty•lo•lit•ic**
**sty•lo•pize** (*or* **•pise**) parasitize with stylops
**sty•lo•po•dium** (*plural* **•dia**) botany term
**sty•lops** (*plural* **•lo•pes**) insect
**sty•lo•stix•is** acupuncture
**sty•lus** (*plural* **•li** *or* **•luses**)
**sty•mie** (*or* **•my**; *verb* **•mies, •mie•ing, •mied** *or* **•mies, •my•ing, •mied**; *noun, plural* **•mies**)
**styp•sis**
**styp•tic**
**styp•ti•cal**
**styp•tic•ity**
**sty•ra•ca•ceous**
**sty•rax** tree
**sty•rene** organic compound
**Styria** Austrian province
**Styx** mythological river
**su•abil•ity**
**su•able**
**Sua•kin** Sudanese port
**suave**
**suave•ly**
**suav•ity** (*or* **suave•ness**)
**sub** (**sub•bing, subbed**)
**sub•ac•etate**
**sub•acid**
**sub•acid•ity** (*or* **•acid•ness**)
**sub•acute** medical term
**sub•acute•ly**
**sub•agent**
**su•bah** Mogul province
**sub•al•pine**
**sub•al•tern**
**sub•al•ter•nate** botany term
**sub•al•ter•na•tion**
**sub•ant•arc•tic**
**sub•aquat•ic**
**sub•aque•ous**
**sub•arc•tic**
**sub•ar•id**
**sub•as•sem•bly** (*plural* **•blies**)
**sub•atom•ic**
**sub•audi•tion**
**sub•auricu•lar**
**sub•ax•il•la•ry**
**sub•base** pedestal base
**sub•base•ment**
**sub•bass** (*or* **•base**) organ stop
**sub•cali•bre**
**sub•car•ti•lagi•nous**
**sub•ce•les•tial**
**sub•cep•tion** subliminal perception
**sub•chlo•ride**
**sub•class**
**sub•cla•vian**
**sub•cli•mac•tic**
**sub•cli•max**
**sub•com•mit•tee**
**sub•con•scious**
**sub•con•scious•ness**
**sub•con•ti•nent**
**sub•con•ti•nen•tal**
**sub•con•tract**
**sub•con•trac•tor**
**sub•con•tra•ry** (*plural* **•ries**)
**sub•cor•tex** (*plural* **•tices**)
**sub•cor•ti•cal**
**sub•cul•tur•al**
**sub•cul•ture**
**sub•cu•ta•neous**
**sub•dea•con**
**sub•dea•con•ate**
**sub•de•lir•ium** (*plural* **•lir•iums** *or* **•liria**)
**sub•di•aco•nal**
**sub•di•aco•nate** subdeacon's rank
**sub•di•vide**
**sub•di•vid•er**
**sub•di•vi•sion**
**sub•di•vi•sion•al**
**sub•domi•nant**
**sub•du•able**
**sub•du•al**
**sub•duct**
**sub•duc•tion**
**sub•due** (**•dues, •du•ing, •dued**)
**sub•dued•ly**
**sub•dued•ness**
**sub•edit**
**sub•edi•tor**
**sub•equa•to•rial**
**su•ber•in** plant substance
**su•beri•za•tion** (*or* **•sa•tion**)
**su•ber•ize** (*or* **•ise**)
**su•ber•ose** (*or* **•bereous, •ber•ic**) of cork
**sub•fami•ly** (*plural* **•lies**)
**sub•floor**
**sub•fusc** drab; academic dress
**sub•ge•ner•ic**
**sub•ge•nus** (*plural* **•gen•era** *or* **•ge•nuses**)
**sub•gla•cial**
**sub•gla•cial•ly**
**sub•group**
**sub•head•ing** (*or* **•head**)
**sub•hu•man**
**sub•in•dex** (*plural* **•dices** *or* **•dexes**)
**sub•in•feu•date**
**sub•in•feu•da•tion**
**sub•in•feu•da•tory** (*plural* **•tories**)
**sub•ir•ri•gate**
**sub•ir•ri•ga•tion**
**su•bi•to** musical term
**sub•ja•cen•cy**
**sub•ja•cent**
**sub•ject**
**sub•ject•abil•ity**
**sub•ject•able**
**sub•jec•ti•fi•ca•tion**
**sub•jec•ti•fy** (**•fies, •fy•ing, •fied**)
**sub•jec•tion**
**sub•jec•tive**
**sub•jec•tive•ly**
**sub•jec•tiv•ism**
**sub•jec•tiv•ist**
**sub•jec•ti•vis•tic**
**sub•jec•ti•vis•ti•cal•ly**
**sub•jec•tiv•ity** (*or* **•tive•ness**)
**subject-raising**
**sub•join**
**sub•join•der**
**sub ju•di•ce**
**sub•ju•gable**
**sub•ju•gate**
**sub•ju•ga•tion**
**sub•ju•ga•tor**
**sub•junc•tion**
**sub•junc•tive**
**sub•king•dom**
**sub•lease**
**sub•les•see**
**sub•les•sor**
**sub•let** (**•let•ting, •let**)

**sub•lieu•ten•an•cy**
**sub•lieu•ten•ant**
**sub•li•mable**
**sub•li•mate**
**sub•li•ma•tion**
**sub•lime**
**sub•lime•ly**
**sub•limi•nal**
**sub•limi•nal•ly**
**sub•lim•ity** (*plural* **•ities**)
**sub•lin•gual**
**sub•lit•to•ral** near seashore
**sub•lu•nary** between moon and earth
**sub-machine-gun**
**sub•mar•gin•al**
**sub•ma•rine**
**sub•ma•rin•er**
**sub•max•il•lary** of lower jaw
**sub•me•di•ant** musical term
**sub•men•tal** beneath the chin
**sub•merge** (*or* **•merse**)
**sub•mers•ibil•ity** (*or* **•merg•**)
**sub•mers•ible** (*or* **•merg•**)
**sub•mer•sion** (*or* **•merg•ence**)
**sub•micro•scop•ic**
**sub•micro•scopi•cal•ly**
**sub•miss** *Archaic* docile
**sub•mis•sion**
**sub•mis•sive**
**sub•mis•sive•ly**
**sub•mis•sive•ness**
**sub•mit** (**•mit•ting, •mit•ted**)
**sub•mit•table** (*or* **•mis•sible**)
**sub•mit•tal**
**sub•mit•ter**
**sub•mit•ting•ly**
**sub•mon•tane**
**sub•mu•co•sa** (*plural* **•sae**)
**sub•mul•ti•ple**
**sub•nor•mal**
**sub•nor•mal•ity**
**sub•nor•mal•ly**
**sub•ocean•ic**
**sub•or•bi•tal**
**sub•or•der**
**sub•or•di•nal**
**sub•or•di•nary** (*plural* **•naries**) heraldic term
**sub•or•di•nate**
**sub•or•di•nate•ly**
**sub•or•di•nate•ness**
**sub•or•di•na•tion**
**sub•or•di•na•tive**
**sub•orn**
**sub•or•na•tion**
**sub•or•na•tive**
**sub•orn•er**
**sub•ox•ide**
**sub•phy•lar**
**sub•phy•lum** (*plural* **•la**)
**sub•plot**
**sub•poe•na** (**•nas, •na•ing, •naed**)
**sub•popu•la•tion**
**sub•prin•ci•pal**
**sub•re•gion**
**sub•re•gion•al**
**sub•rep•tion** concealment of facts
**sub•rep•ti•tious**
**sub•ro•gate** legal term
**sub•ro•ga•tion**
**sub rosa** *Latin* in secret
**sub•rou•tine**
**sub•scapu•lar**
**sub•scribe**
**sub•scrib•er**
**sub•script**
**sub•scrip•tion**
**sub•scrip•tive**
**sub•sec•tion**
**sub•se•quence**
**sub•se•quent**
**sub•serve**
**sub•ser•vience** (*or* **•vi•en•cy**)
**sub•ser•vi•ent**
**sub•set**
**sub•shrub**
**sub•side**
**sub•sid•ence**
**sub•sid•er**
**sub•sidi•ari•ly**
**sub•sidi•ari•ness**
**sub•sidi•ary** (*plural* **•aries**)
**sub•si•diz•able** (*or* **•dis•able**)
**sub•si•di•za•tion** (*or* **•sa•tion**)
**sub•si•dize** (*or* **•dise**)
**sub•si•diz•er** (*or* **•dis•er**)
**sub•si•dy** (*plural* **•dies**)
**sub•sist**
**sub•sist•ence**
**sub•sist•ent**
**sub•sist•er**
**sub•sist•ing•ly**
**sub•so•cial**
**sub•soil**
**sub•soil•er**
**sub•so•lar**
**sub•son•ic**
**sub•soni•cally**
**sub•spe•cies** (*plural* **•cies**)
**sub•spe•cif•ic**
**sub•spe•cifi•cal•ly**
**sub•stage**
**sub•stance**
**sub•stand•ard**
**sub•stan•tial**
**sub•stan•tial•ism**
**sub•stan•tial•ist**
**sub•stan•ti•al•ity** (*or* **•tial•ness**)
**sub•stan•tial•ly**
**sub•stan•ti•ate**
**sub•stan•tia•tion**
**sub•stan•tia•tive**
**sub•stan•tia•tor**
**sub•stan•ti•val** grammar term
**sub•stan•ti•val•ly**
**sub•stan•tive**
**sub•stan•tive•ly**
**sub•stan•tive•ness**
**sub•stan•ti•vi•za•tion** (*or* **•sa•tion**)
**sub•stan•tiv•ize** (*or* **•ise**)
**sub•sta•tion**
**sub•stitu•ent**
**sub•sti•tuta•bil•ity**
**sub•sti•tut•able**
**sub•sti•tute**
**sub•sti•tu•tion**
**sub•sti•tu•tive**
**sub•strate**
**sub•stra•tive** (*or* **•tal**)
**sub•stra•tum** (*plural* **•stra•ta**)
**sub•struc•tur•al** (*or* **•tion•al**)
**sub•struc•ture** (*or* **•tion**)
**sub•sum•able**
**sub•sume**
**sub•sump•tion**
**sub•sump•tive**
**sub•tan•gent**
**sub•tem•per•ate**
**sub•ten•an•cy** (*plural* **•cies**)
**sub•ten•ant**
**sub•tend**
**sub•ter•fuge**

**sub•ter•ra•nean**
**sub•ter•res•trial**
**sub•tili•za•tion** (*or* **•sa•tion**)
**sub•til•ize** (*or* **•ise**) refine
**sub•til•iz•er** (*or* **•is•er**)
**sub•ti•tle**
**sub•titu•lar**
**sub•tle**
**sub•tle•ness**
**sub•tler** more subtle; *compare* **sutler**
**sub•tle•ty** (*plural* **•ties**)
**sub•tly**
**sub•ton•ic** musical note
**sub•tor•rid**
**sub•to•tal** (**•tal•ling, •talled;** *US* **•tal•ing, •taled**)
**sub•tract**
**sub•tract•er**
**sub•trac•tion**
**sub•trac•tive**
**sub•tra•hend** number subtracted
**sub•tropi•cal**
**sub•trop•ics**
**sub•type**
**sub•typi•cal**
**su•bu•late** awl-shaped
**sub•urb**
**sub•ur•ban**
**sub•ur•ban•ite**
**sub•ur•bani•za•tion** (*or* **•sa•tion**)
**sub•ur•ban•ize** (*or* **•ise**)
**sub•ur•bia**
**sub•vene**
**sub•ven•tion**
**sub•ven•tion•ary**
**sub•ver•sion**
**sub•ver•sive**
**sub•ver•sive•ly**
**sub•ver•sive•ness**
**sub•vert**
**sub•vert•er**
**sub•way**
**sub•zero**
**suc•ce•da•neous**
**suc•ce•da•neum** (*plural* **•nea**) substitute drug
**suc•ceed**
**suc•ceed•able**
**suc•ceed•er**
**suc•ceed•ing•ly**
**suc•cen•tor** cathedral cleric
**suc•cess**
**suc•cess•ful**
**suc•cess•ful•ly**
**suc•cess•ful•ness**
**suc•ces•sion**
**suc•ces•sion•al**
**suc•ces•sive**
**suc•ces•sive•ly**
**suc•ces•sive•ness**
**suc•ces•sor**
**suc•ces•sor•al**
**suc•cin•ate** chemical compound
**suc•cinct**
**suc•cinct•ness**
**suc•cin•ic** of amber; chemistry term
**suc•cory** (*plural* **•cories**) chicory
**suc•co•tash** *US* mixed vegetables
**suc•cour** (*US* **•cor**)
**suc•cour•able** (*US* **•cor•**)
**suc•cour•er** (*US* **•cor•**)
**suc•cu•bus** (*plural* **•bi**) female demon
**suc•cu•lence** (*or* **•len•cy**)
**suc•cu•lent**
**suc•cumb**
**suc•cumb•er**
**suc•cur•sal** subsidiary
**suc•cuss**
**suc•cus•sion**
**suc•cus•sive**
**such**
**such•like**
**Su•chou** *variant spelling of* **Soochow**
**Sü•chow** (*or* **Hsü-chou**) Chinese city
**suck**
**suck•er**
**sucker•fish** (*or* **suck•fish;** *plural* **•fish** *or* **•fishes**)
**suck•le**
**suck•ler**
**suck•ling**
**su•crase** enzyme
**su•crose** sugar
**suc•tion**
**suc•tion•al**
**suc•to•rial**
**Su•dan**
**Su•da•nese** (*plural* **•nese**)
**Su•dan•ic**
**su•dar•ium** (*plural* **•daria**) face cloth
**su•da•to•rium** (*or* **•tory;** *plural* **•to•ria** *or* **•tories**) steam-bath room
**Sud•bury** Canadian city
**sudd** water weed
**sud•den**
**sud•den•ness**
**Su•deten•land** Czech region
**Su•detes** (*or* **Su•deten**) European mountains
**su•dor** sweat
**su•dor•al**
**su•dor•if•er•ous**
**su•dor•if•ic**
**suds**
**sudsy**
**sue** (**su•ing, sued**)
**(sueable)** *incorrect spelling of* **suable**
**suede**
**suer** one who sues; *compare* **sewer**
**suet**
**su•ety**
**Suez**
**suf•fer**
**suf•fer•able**
**suf•fer•ance**
**suf•fer•er**
**suf•fer•ing**
**suf•fice**
**suf•fic•er**
**suf•fi•cien•cy** (*plural* **•cies**)
**suf•fi•cient**
**suf•fix**
**suf•fix•al**
**suf•fix•ion**
**suf•fo•cate**
**suf•fo•cat•ing•ly**
**suf•fo•ca•tion**
**suf•fo•ca•tive**
**Suf•folk**
**suf•fra•gan** assistant bishop
**suf•fra•gan•ship**
**suf•frage**
**suf•fra•gette**
**suf•fra•get•tism**
**suf•fra•gism**
**suf•fra•gist**
**suf•fru•ti•cose** botany term
**suf•fu•mi•gate**
**suf•fu•mi•ga•tion**
**suf•fuse**

**suf•fu•sion**
**suf•fu•sive**
**Sufi** (*plural* **Sufis**) Muslim mystic
**Su•fic**
**Su•fism**
**Su•fis•tic**
**sug•ar**
**sug•ari•ness**
**sugar•plum**
**sug•ary**
**sug•gest**
**sug•gest•er**
**sug•gest•ibil•ity**
**sug•gest•ible**
**sug•gest•ible•ness**
**sug•gest•ing•ly**
**sug•ges•tion**
**sug•ges•tive**
**sug•ges•tive•ly**
**sug•ges•tive•ness**
**sui•cid•al**
**sui•cid•al•ly**
**sui•cide**
**sui gen•eris** unique
**su•int** substance in fleece
**suit** clothes; set of cards; petition; to be appropriate; *compare* **suite**
**suit•abil•ity** (*or* **•able•ness**)
**suit•able**
**suit•ably**
**suit•case**
**suite** set of rooms; furniture; musical piece; *compare* **suit**
**suit•ing**
**suit•or**
**Su•khu•mi** Georgian port
**su•ki•ya•ki** Japanese dish
**Su•la•we•si** Indonesian island
**sul•cate**
**sul•ca•tion**
**sul•cus** (*plural* **•ci**) groove
**sul•fur** *US spelling of* **sulphur**; *note all words starting* **sulph-** *have the US spelling* **sulf-**
**sulk**
**sulk•er**
**sulki•ly**
**sulki•ness**
**sulky** (*adj* **sulki•er, sulki•est**; *noun, plural* **sulkies**) sullen; vehicle
**sul•lage** sewage
**sul•len**
**sul•len•ness**
**sul•li•able**
**sul•ly** (**•lies, •ly•ing, •lied**)
**sul•pha** (*US* **•fa**) class of drugs; *compare* **sulphur**
**sul•pha•dia•zine** (*US* **•fa•**)
**sul•pha•nila•mide** (*US* **•fa•**)
**sul•phate** (*US* **•fate**)
**sul•pha•thia•zole** (*US* **•fa•**)
**sul•pha•tion** (*US* **•fa•**)
**sul•phide** (*US* **•fide**)
**sul•phi•soxa•zole** (*US* **•fi•**)
**sul•phite** (*US* **•fite**)
**sul•phit•ic** (*US* **•fit•**)
**sul•phona•mide** (*US* **•fona•**) sulpha drug
**sul•pho•nate** (*US* **•fo•**)
**sul•phone** (*US* **•fone**)
**sul•phon•me•thane** (*US* **•fon•**)
**sul•phur** (*US* **•fur**) chemical element; *compare* **sulpha**
**sul•phur•ate** (*US* **•fur•**)
**sul•phu•ra•tion** (*US* **•fu•**)
**sul•phu•reous** (*US* **•fu•**)
**sul•phu•reous•ness** (*US* **•fu•**)
**sul•phu•ret** (*US* **•fu•**; **•ret•ting, •ret•ted**, *US* **•ret•ing, •ret•ed**)
**sul•phu•ric** (*US* **•fu•**)
**sul•phu•ri•za•tion** (*or* **•sa•tion**; *US* **•fu•ri•za•tion**)
**sul•phu•rize** (*or* **•rise**; *US* **•fu•rize**)
**sul•phur•ous** (*US* **•fur•**)
**sul•phur•ous•ness** (*US* **•fur•**)
**sul•phur•yl** (*US* **•fur•**)
**sul•tan**
**sul•tana**
**sul•tan•ate**
**sul•tan•ic**
**sul•tri•ly**
**sul•tri•ness**
**sul•try** (**•tri•er, •tri•est**)
**Sulu** Philippine archipelago
**sum** (**sum•ming, summed**)
**su•mach** (*or* **•mac**) shrub
**Su•ma•tra**
**Su•ma•tran**
**Su•mer** Babylonian region
**Su•me•rian**
**sum•ma** (*plural* **•mae**) medieval compendium
**sum•ma cum lau•de** highest achievement in examination
**sum•mand** part of a sum
**sum•mari•ly**
**sum•mari•ness**
**sum•ma•riz•able** (*or* **•ris•able**)
**sum•ma•ri•za•tion** (*or* **•sa•tion**)
**sum•ma•rize** (*or* **•rise**)
**sum•ma•riz•er** (*or* **•ris•er**)
**sum•mary** (*plural* **•maries**) brief account; *compare* **summery**
**sum•ma•tion**
**sum•ma•tion•al**
**sum•mer**
**summer•house**
**sum•meri•ness**
**sum•mer•sault** *variant spelling of* **somersault**
**summer•time**
**summer•wood**
**sum•mery** like summer; *compare* **summary**
**summing-up** (*plural* **summings-**)
**sum•mit**
**sum•mit•al**
**sum•mit•ry**
**sum•mon** (*verb*)
**sum•mon•able**
**sum•mons** (*noun, plural* **•monses**; *verb* **•mons, •mons•ing, •monsed**)
**sum•mum bon•um** *Latin* highest good
**Sumo** wrestling
**sump**
**sump•tua•ry**
**sump•tu•ous**
**sump•tu•ous•ness** (*or* **•tu•os•ity**)
**sun** (**sun•ning, sunned**)
**sun•bake** *Austral* sunbathing
**sun•baked**
**sun•bathe**
**sun•bather**
**sun•beam**
**sun•bird**
**sun•bonnet**
**sun•bow**
**sun•burn**

**sun•burnt** (*or* **•burned**)
**sun•burst**
**sun•dae** dessert
**Sun•da Is•lands**
**Sun•day**
**sun•der**
**sun•der•able**
**sun•der•ance**
**sun•der•er**
**Sun•der•land**
**sun•dew**
**sun•dial**
**sun•dog** small rainbow
**sun•down**
**sun•dress**
**sun-dried**
**sun•dry** (*plural* **•dries**)
**sun•fast**
**sun•fish** (*plural* **•fish** *or* **•fishes**)
**sun•flower**
**sung**
**Sun•ga•ri** Chinese river
**sun•glass** burning glass
**sun•glasses** spectacles
**sun•glow**
**sun-god**
**sun•grebe** bird
**sun•hat**
**sunk**
**sunk•en**
**sun•less**
**sun•less•ness**
**sun•light**
**sun•lit**
**sunn** fibre
**Sun•na** Islamic law
**sunned**
**Sun•ni** (*plural* **•ni**) Muslim sect
**sun•ni•ly**
**sun•ni•ness**
**sun•ning**
**Sun•nite** Muslim
**sun•ny** (**•ni•er, •ni•est**)
**sun•ray** pleats
**sun•rise**
**sun•roof**
**sun•set**
**sun•shade**
**sun•shine**
**sun•shiny**
**sun•spot**
**sun•spotted**
**sun•star** starfish
**sun•stroke**
**sun•suit**
**sun•tan**
**sun•tanned**
**sun•trap**
**sun•wards** (*or esp. US* **•ward**)
**sun•wise**
**sup** (**sup•ping, supped**)
**su•per**
**super•abil•ity** (*or* **•able•ness**)
**super•able**
**super•ably**
**super•abound**
**super•abun•dance**
**supera•bun•dant**
**super•add**
**super•ad•di•tion**
**super•ad•di•tion•al**
**super•an•nu•ate**
**super•an•nu•at•ed**
**super•an•nua•tion**
**su•perb**
**super•ba•zaar** Indian store
**su•perb•ness**
**super•cal•en•der**
**super•car•go** (*plural* **•goes**)
(**supercede**) *incorrect spelling of* **supersede**
**super•charge**
**super•char•ger**
**super•cili•ary** of the eyebrow
**super•cili•ous**
**super•cili•ous•ness**
**super•class**
**super•co•lum•nar**
**super•con•duc•tion**
**super•con•duc•tive** (*or* **•duct•ing**)
**super•con•duc•tiv•ity**
**super•con•duc•tor**
**super•cool** (*verb*)
**super-duper**
**super•ego** (*plural* **•egos**)
**super•el•eva•tion**
**super•emi•nence**
**super•emi•nent**
**super•eroga•tory** superfluous
**super•fami•ly** (*plural* **•lies**)
**super•fe•cun•da•tion**
**super•fe•tate**
**super•fe•ta•tion** physiology term
**super•fi•cial**
**super•fi•ci•al•ity** (*or* **•cial•ness**)
**super•fi•cial•ly**
**super•fine**
**super•fix** linguistics term
**super•fluid**
**super•flu•id•ity**
**super•flu•ity**
**super•flu•ous**
**super•flu•ous•ness**
**super•gi•ant**
**super•gla•cial**
**super•heat** (*verb*)
**super•he•ro** (*plural* **•roes**)
**super•het•ero•dyne** radio receiver
**super•high•way** *US* fast dual carriageway
**super•hu•man**
**super•hu•man•ity** (*or* **•man•ness**)
**super•im•pose**
**super•im•po•si•tion**
**super•in•cum•bence** (*or* **•ben•cy**)
**super•in•cum•bent**
**super•in•duce**
**super•induce•ment**
**super•in•duc•tion**
**super•in•tend**
**super•in•tend•ence**
**super•in•tend•en•cy** (*plural* **•cies**) office of superintendent
**super•in•ten•dent**
**Su•peri•or** US lake
**su•peri•or**
**su•peri•or•ity**
**super•ja•cent**
**super•la•tive**
**super•la•tive•ly**
**super•la•tive•ness**
**super•lun•ar**
**super•lun•ary**
**super•man** (*plural* **•men**)
**super•mar•ket**
**super•nal** celestial
**super•nal•ly**
**super•na•tant**
**super•na•ta•tion**
**super•natu•ral**
**super•natu•ral•ism**
**super•natu•ral•ist**
**super•natu•ral•is•tic**

**super•natu•ral•ly**
**super•natu•ral•ness**
**super•nor•mal**
**super•nor•mal•ity** (*or* **•ness**)
**super•nor•mal•ly**
**super•no•va** (*plural* **•vae** *or* **•vas**)
**super•nu•mer•ary** (*plural* **•aries**)
**super•or•der**
**super•ordi•nal**
**super•or•di•nate**
**super•ox•ide**
**super•phos•phate**
**super•physi•cal**
**super•pos•able**
**super•pose**
**super•po•si•tion**
**super•pow•er**
**super•satu•rat•ed** chemistry term
**super•satu•ra•tion**
**super•scribe**
**super•script**
**super•scrip•tion**
**super•sed•able**
**super•sede**
**super•sed•ence**
**super•sed•er**
**super•se•dure**
**super•sen•sible** (*or* **•sory**)
**super•ses•sion**
**super•sex** genetics term
**super•son•ic**
**super•soni•cal•ly**
**super•son•ics**
**super•star**
**super•sti•tion**
**super•sti•tious**
**super•sti•tious•ness**
**super•store**
**super•stra•tum** (*plural* **•ta** *or* **•tums**)
**super•struct** build on another structure
**super•struc•tur•al**
**super•struc•ture**
**super•tank•er**
**super•tax**
**super•ton•ic** musical note
**super•vene**
**super•veni•ent**
**super•ven•tion** (*or* **•veni•ence**)
**super•vise**
**super•vi•sion**
**super•vi•sor**
**super•vi•sory**
**su•pi•nate**
**su•pi•na•tion**
**su•pi•na•tor** muscle
**su•pine**
**su•pine•ly**
**su•pine•ness**
**su•plex** wrestling hold
**supped**
**sup•per**
**sup•ping**
**sup•plant**
**sup•plan•ta•tion**
**sup•plant•er**
**sup•ple**
**supple•jack** plant
**sup•ple•ly** *variant spelling of* supply
**sup•plement**
**sup•plemen•tal**
**sup•ple•men•ta•ri•ly** (*or* **•tal•ly**)
**sup•plemen•ta•ry** (*plural* **•ries**)
**sup•plemen•ta•tion**
**sup•plement•er**
**sup•ple•ness**
**sup•pletion** linguistics term
**sup•pletive**
**sup•pleto•ri•ly**
**sup•pletory**
**sup•pli•able**
**sup•pli•ance** (*or* **•an•cy**)
**sup•pli•ant**
**sup•pli•cant** (*or* **•pli•ant**)
**sup•pli•cate**
**sup•pli•ca•tion**
**sup•pli•ca•tory**
**sup•pli•er**
**sup•ply** (*noun, plural* **•plies**; *verb* **•plies, •ply•ing, •plied**)
**sup•ply** (*or* **sup•ple•ly**) in a supple way
**sup•port**
**sup•port•abil•ity** (*or* **•able•ness**)
**sup•port•ably**
**sup•port•able**
**sup•port•er**
**sup•port•ing**
**sup•port•ive**
**sup•pos•able**
**sup•pose**
**sup•posed**
**sup•pos•ed•ly**
**sup•pos•er**
**sup•po•si•tion**
**sup•po•si•tion•al**
**sup•po•si•tious** (*or* **•posi•ti•tious**)
**sup•po•si•tious•ness** (*or* **•posi•ti•tious•ness**)
**sup•posi•tive** involving supposition
**sup•posi•tory** (*plural* **•tories**)
**sup•press**
**sup•press•ible**
**sup•pres•sion**
**sup•pres•sive**
**sup•pres•sor** (*or* **•press•er**)
**sup•pu•rate**
**sup•pu•ra•tion**
**sup•pu•ra•tive**
**su•pra** above
**supra•glot•tal**
**supra•lap•sar•ian** theology term
**supra•limi•nal**
**supra•mo•lecu•lar**
**supra•na•tion•al**
**supra•na•tion•al•ism**
**supra•or•bit•al**
**supra•re•nal**
**supra•seg•men•tal**
**su•prema•cist**
**su•prema•cy**
**Su•prema•tism** cubist art
**su•prema•tism**
**Su•prema•tist**
**su•preme**
**su•prême** cookery term
**su•preme•ly**
**su•preme•ness**
**su•prem•ity**
**su•pre•mo** (*plural* **•mos**)
**sura** Koran chapter
**Su•ra•ba•ya** (*or* **•ja, Soe•ra•ba•ja**) Indonesian port
**su•rah** fabric
**Su•ra•kar•ta** Indonesian town
**su•ral** anatomy term
**Su•rat** Indian port
**su•rat** fabric
**sur•base** architectural term
**sur•base•ment**

**sur•cease**
**sur•charge**
**sur•charg•er**
**sur•cin•gle** horse's girth; cassock belt
**sur•coat**
**sur•cu•lose** bearing suckers
**surd** maths term
**sure**
**sure-fire**
**sure-footed**
**sure-footed•ly**
**sure-footed•ness**
**sure•ly**
**sure•ness**
**sure•ty** (*plural* **•ties**)
**surf** breaking waves; *compare* **serf**
**surf•able**
**sur•face**
**surface-active**
**sur•fac•er**
**sur•fac•tant**
**surf•bird**
**surf•board**
**surf•boat**
**surf•caster**
**surf•casting** shore-fishing
**sur•feit**
**sur•feit•er**
**surf•er**
**surfie** *Austral* surfer
**surf•ing**
**surf•like**
**surf•perch** fish
**surf•rider**
**surfy**
**surge** rush; *compare* **serge**
**sur•geon**
**sur•geon•cy** (*plural* **•cies**)
**surgeon•fish** (*plural* **•fish** *or* **•fishes**)
**surg•er**
**sur•gery** (*plural* **•geries**)
**sur•gi•cal**
**sur•gi•cal•ly**
**su•ri•cate** animal
**Su•ri•nam** South American republic
**sur•jec•tion**
**sur•jec•tive**
**sur•li•ly**
**sur•li•ness**
**sur•ly** (**•li•er, •li•est**)
**sur•mis•able**
**sur•mise**
**sur•mis•ed•ly**
**sur•mis•er**
**sur•mount**
**sur•mount•able**
**sur•mount•able•ness**
**sur•mount•er**
**sur•name**
**sur•pass**
**sur•pass•able**
**sur•pas•sing**
**sur•pass•ing•ly**
**sur•pass•ing•ness**
**sur•plice** vestment
**sur•pliced**
**sur•plus** (*plural* **•pluses**) excess
**sur•plus•age**
**sur•print** overprint
**sur•prise**
**sur•pris•ed•ly**
**sur•pris•er**
**sur•pris•ing**
**sur•pris•ing•ly**
**sur•pris•ing•ness**
**sur•ra** animal disease
**sur•re•al**
**sur•re•al•ism**
**sur•re•al•ist**
**sur•re•al•is•tic**
**sur•re•al•is•ti•cal•ly**
**sur•re•but•tal**
**sur•re•but•ter**
**sur•re•join•der**
**sur•ren•der**
**sur•ren•der•er**
**sur•rep•ti•tious**
**sur•rep•ti•tious•ness**
**Sur•rey** English county
**sur•rey** carriage
**sur•ro•gate**
**sur•ro•gate•ship**
**sur•ro•ga•tion**
**sur•round**
**sur•round•ing**
**sur•round•ings**
**sur•tax**
**sur•tout** overcoat
**sur•veil•lance**
**sur•veil•lant**
**sur•vey**
**sur•vey•able**
**sur•vey•ing**
**sur•vey•or**
**sur•vey•or•ship**
**sur•viv•abil•ity**
**sur•viv•able**
**sur•viv•al**
**sur•vive**
**sur•vi•vor**
**Susa** ancient Persian city
**sus•cep•tance** magnetic property
**sus•cep•tibil•ity** (*plural* **•ities**)
**sus•cep•tible**
**sus•cep•tibly**
**sus•cep•tible•ness**
**sus•cep•tive**
**sus•cep•tiv•ity** (*or* **•tive•ness**)
**su•shi** Japanese food
**sus•lik** *variant spelling of* **souslik**
**sus•pect**
**sus•pect•er**
**sus•pend**
**sus•pend•er**
**sus•pend•ibil•ity**
**sus•pend•ible** (*or* **•pens•**)
**sus•pense**
**sus•pense•ful**
**sus•pen•sion**
**sus•pen•sive**
**sus•pen•sive•ness**
**sus•pen•soid** chemistry term
**sus•pen•sor**
**sus•pen•so•ry** (*plural* **•ries**)
**sus•pi•cion**
**sus•pi•cion•al**
**sus•pi•cious**
**sus•pi•cious•ness**
**sus•pi•ra•tion**
**sus•pire** sigh
**Sus•que•han•na** US river
**suss**
**Sus•sex**
**sus•tain**
**sus•tain•able**
**sus•tain•ed•ly**
**sus•tain•er**
**sus•tain•ing•ly**
**sus•tain•ment**
**sus•te•nance**
**sus•ten•tacu•lar** supporting
**sus•ten•ta•tion** nourishment
**sus•ten•tion**
**su•sur•rant**
**su•sur•rate**

**su•sur•ra•tion** (*or* **su•sur•rus**)
**Suth•er•land** former Scottish county
**Sut•lej** Asian river
**sut•ler** provisioner; *compare* **subtler**
**su•tra** Sanskrit sayings
**sut•tee** Hindu custom
**Sut•ton** London borough
**Sut•ton Cold•field** English town
**su•tur•al**
**su•ture**
**Suva** Fijian capital
**Su•wan•nee** (*or* **Swa•nee**) US river
**su•ze•rain**
**su•ze•rain•ty** (*plural* **•ties**)
**Sval•bard** Norwegian archipelago
**svelte**
**Sverd•lovsk** *former name of* **Yekaterinburg**
**swab** (**swab•bing, swabbed**)
**swab•ber**
**Swa•bia** former German duchy
**Swa•bian**
**swacked** *Slang* intoxicated
**swad•dle**
**swag** (**swag•ging, swagged**)
**swage** tool
**swag•er**
**swag•ger**
**swag•ger•er**
**swag•ger•ing•ly**
**swag•man** (*plural* **•men**)
**Swa•hi•li** (*plural* **•lis** *or* **•li**)
**Swa•hi•lian**
**swain**
**swal•low**
**swal•low•able**
**swal•low•er**
**swallow•tail**
**swallow•wort**
**swam**
**swa•mi** (*plural* **•mies** *or* **•mis**) Hindu title
**swamp**
**swamp•land**
**swampy** (**swampi•er, swampi•est**)
**swan** (**swan•ning, swanned**)
**Swa•nee** *variant spelling of* **Suwannee**
**swan•herd**
**swank**
**swanki•ly**
**swanki•ness**
**swanky** (**swanki•er, swanki•est**)
**swan•like**
**swan•nery** (*plural* **•neries**)
**swan's-down**
**Swan•sea**
**swan•skin**
**swan-upping**
**swap** (*or* **swop; swap•ping, swapped** *or* **swop•ping, swopped**)
**swap•per** (*or* **swop•**)
**swa•raj** Indian self-government
**sward** (*or* **swarth**) turf; *compare* **sword**
**swarf** metal off-cuttings
**swarm**
**swarthi•ly**
**swarthi•ness**
**swarthy** (**swarthi•er, swarthi•est**)
**swash** splash
**swash•buck•ler**
**swash•buck•ling**
**swash•ing•ly**
**swas•ti•ka**
**swat** (**swat•ting, swat•ted**) hit; *compare* **swot**
**swatch**
**swath** (*or* **swathe**; *noun*)
**swath•able** (*or* **swathe•**)
**swathe** (*verb*)
**Swa•tow** Chinese port
**swats** *Dialect* beer
**swat•ter**
**sway**
**sway•able**
**sway-back**
**sway•er**
**sway•ing•ly**
**Swa•zi** (*plural* **•zis** *or* **•zi**)
**Swa•zi•land**
**swear** (**swear•ing, swore, sworn**)
**swear•er**
**swear•ing•ly**
**swear•word**
**sweat** (**sweat•ing, sweat** *or* **sweat•ed**)
**sweat•band**
**sweat•box**
**sweat•er**
**sweati•ly**
**sweati•ness**
**sweat•shop**
**sweaty** (**sweati•er, sweati•est**)
**Swede** native of Sweden
**swede** vegetable
**Swe•den**
**Swe•den•bor•gi•an•ism** (*or* **•bor•gism**) religious movement
**Swe•dish**
**swee•ny** veterinary term
**sweep** (**sweep•ing, swept**)
**sweep•back**
**sweep•er**
**sweep•ing**
**sweep•ing•ly**
**sweep•ing•ness**
**sweep•ings**
**sweep•stake**
**sweet**
**sweet•bread**
**sweet•brier**
**sweet•en**
**sweet•en•er**
**sweet•en•ing**
**sweet•heart**
**sweetie**
**sweetie•wife** (*plural* **•wives**) *Scot* talkative woman
**sweet•ish**
**sweet•meal**
**sweet•meat**
**sweet•ness**
**sweet•shop**
**sweet•sop** fruit
**swell** (**swell•ing, swelled, swol•len** *or* **swelled**)
**swell•fish** (*plural* **•fish** *or* **•fishes**)
**swell•ing**
**swel•ter**
**swel•ter•ing**
**swel•ter•ing•ly**
**swept**
**swept•back**
**swept•wing**
**swerv•able**
**swerve**

**swerv•er**
**swerv•ing•ly**
**swift**
**swift•er** nautical term
**swiftie** *Austral* a trick
**swift•let** bird
**swift•ness**
**swig** **(swig•ging, swigged)**
**swig•ger**
**swill**
**swill•er**
**swim** **(swim•ming, swam, swum)**
**swim•mable**
**swim•mer**
**swim•mer•et** zoology term
**swim•ming•ly**
**swim•suit**
**swin•dle**
**swin•dler**
**swin•dling•ly**
**Swin•don**
**swine** (*plural* **swines)**
**swine•herd**
**swine•pox**
**swing** **(swing•ing, swung)**
**swing•boat**
**swinge** **(swinge•ing, swinged)** punish
**swing•er**
**swing•ing**
**swin•gle** flax-beating instrument
**swing•om•eter**
**swing-wing**
**swin•ish**
**swin•ish•ness**
**swink** *Dialect* toil
**swipe**
**swipes** *Slang* beer
**swip•ple** (*or* **swi•ple)** part of flail
**swirl**
**swirl•ing•ly**
**swirly**
**swish**
**swish•er**
**swish•ing•ly**
**swishy**
**Swiss**
**switch**
**switch•back**
**switch•board**
**switch•er**
**switch•eroo** *US* unexpected change
**switch•girl** *Austral* switchboard operator
**switch-over** (*noun*)
**swith•er** *Scot* hesitate
**Switz•er** a Swiss
**Swit•zer•land**
**swiv•el** **(•el•ling, •elled;** *US* **•el•ing, •eled)**
**swiv•et** *Dialect* excitement
**swizz** *Slang* disappointment
**swiz•zle**
**swol•len**
**swol•len•ness**
**swoon**
**swoon•ing•ly**
**swoop**
**swoosh**
**swop** *variant spelling of* **swap**
**sword** weapon; *compare* **sward**
**sword•bill**
**sword•craft**
**sword•fish** (*plural* **•fish** *or* **•fishes)**
**sword•like**
**sword•play**
**swords•man** (*plural* **•men)**
**swords•man•ship**
**sword•stick**
**sword•tail** fish
**swore**
**sworn**
**swot** **(swot•ting, swot•ted)** study; *compare* **swat**
**swound** *Dialect* swoon
**swum**
**swung**
**swy** *Austral* gambling game
**Syba•ris** ancient Greek colony
**Syba•rite**
**syba•rite** lover of luxury
**syba•rit•ic** (*or* **•riti•cal)**
**syba•riti•cal•ly**
(sybil) *incorrect spelling of* **sibyl**
**syca•mine** mulberry
**syca•more**
**syce** (*or* **sice, saice)** Indian servant
**sy•cee** silver ingots
**sy•co•nium** (*plural* **•nia)** botany term
**syco•phan•cy**
**syco•phant**
**syco•phan•tic**
**syco•phan•ti•cal•ly**
**sy•co•sis** skin disease
**Syd•ney** Australian city; Canadian port
**Sy•ene** ancient Egyptian town
**sy•enite** rock
**sy•enit•ic**
**Syk•tyv•kar** Russian city
**syl•la•bary** (*plural* **•baries)**
**syl•lab•ic**
**syl•labi•cal•ly**
**syl•labi•cate** syllabify
**syl•labi•fi•ca•tion** (*or* **•labi•ca•tion)**
**syl•labi•fy** **(•fies, •fy•ing, •fied)**
**syl•la•bism**
**syl•la•ble**
**syl•labo•gram**
**syl•lab•og•ra•phy**
**syl•la•bub** (*or* **sil•)**
**syl•la•bus** (*plural* **•buses** *or* **•bi)**
**syl•lep•sis** (*plural* **•ses)** linguistics term
**syl•lep•tic**
**syl•lep•ti•cal•ly**
**syl•lo•gism**
**syl•lo•gis•tic**
**syl•lo•gis•ti•cal**
**syl•lo•gis•ti•cal•ly**
**syl•lo•gi•za•tion** (*or* **•sa•tion)**
**syl•lo•gize** (*or* **•gise)**
**syl•lo•giz•er** (*or* **•gis•er)**
**sylph**
**sylph•ic** (*or* **•id)**
**sylph•like** (*or* **•ish)**
**syl•va** (*or* **sil•**; *plural* **•vas** *or* **•vae)** trees
**syl•van** (*or* **sil•)**
**syl•van•ite** mineral
**Sylvanus** *variant spelling of* **Silvanus**
**syl•vat•ic** (*or* **•ves•tral)** occurring in a wood
**syl•vite** (*or* **•vine)** mineral
**sym•bi•ont**
**sym•bi•on•tic**
**sym•bio•sis**
**sym•bi•ot•ic** (*or* **•oti•cal)**

**sym•bi•oti•cal•ly**
**sym•bol** (**•bol•ling, •bolled;** *US* **•bol•ing, •boled**) thing representing something; *compare* **cymbal**
**sym•bol•ic** (*or* **•boli•cal**)
**sym•boli•cal•ly**
**sym•boli•cal•ness**
**sym•bol•ism**
**sym•bol•ist**
**sym•bol•is•tic** (*or* **•ti•cal**)
**sym•bol•is•ti•cal•ly**
**sym•boli•za•tion** (*or* **•sa•tion**)
**sym•bol•ize** (*or* **•ise**)
**sym•bo•logi•cal**
**sym•bolo•gist**
**sym•bol•ogy**
**sym•met•al•lism** economic doctrine
**sym•met•ri•cal**
**sym•met•ri•cal•ly**
**sym•met•ri•cal•ness**
**sym•me•tri•za•tion** (*or* **•sa•tion**)
**sym•me•trize** (*or* **•trise**)
**sym•me•try** (*plural* **•tries**)
**sym•pa•thec•to•my** (*plural* **•mies**) nerve surgery
**sym•pa•thet•ic** (*or* **•theti•cal**)
**sym•pa•theti•cal•ly**
**sym•pa•thin** hormone
**sym•pa•thize** (*or* **•thise**)
**sym•pa•thiz•er** (*or* **•this•er**)
**sym•pa•thiz•ing•ly** (*or* **•this•ing•ly**)
**sym•pa•tho•lyt•ic** pharmacology term
**sym•pa•tho•mi•met•ic** pharmacology term
**sym•pa•thy** (*plural* **•thies**)
**sym•pat•ric** biology term
**sym•pat•ri•cal•ly**
**sym•pet•al•ous**
**sym•phile** entomology term
**sym•phon•ic**
**sym•phoni•cal•ly**
**sym•pho•ni•ous**
**sym•pho•nist**
**sym•pho•ny** (*plural* **•nies**)
**sym•phys•ial** (*or* **•eal**)
**sym•physi•cal•ly** (*or* **•phyti•**)
**sym•phy•sis** (*plural* **•ses**) anatomy term
**sym•phys•tic** (*or* **•phyt•ic**)
**sym•po•dial**
**sym•po•dium** (*plural* **•dia**) botany term
**sym•po•si•ac**
**sym•po•sium** (*plural* **•siums** *or* **•sia**)
**symp•tom**
**symp•to•mat•ic** (*or* **•mati•cal**)
**symp•to•mati•cal•ly**
**symp•toma•tol•ogy**
**syn•aer•esis** *variant spelling of* **syneresis**
**syn•aes•the•sia** (*US* **•es•**) medical term
**syn•aes•thet•ic** (*US* **•es•**)
**syna•gogi•cal** (*or* **•gog•al**)
**syna•gogue**
**syna•lepha** (*or* **•loepha**) linguistics term
**syn•apse** nerve-cell junction
**syn•ap•sis** (*plural* **•ses**) stage of meiosis
**syn•ap•tic** (*or* **•ti•cal**)
**syn•ap•ti•cal•ly**
**syn•ar•chy** (*plural* **•chies**) joint rule
**syn•ar•thro•dial**
**syn•ar•thro•sis** (*plural* **•ses**) anatomy term
**sync** *Slang* synchronize; synchrony
**syn•carp** botany term
**syn•car•pous**
**syn•car•py**
**syn•chro** (*plural* **•chros**) electrical device
**syn•chro•cy•clo•tron**
**syn•chro•flash** camera mechanism
**syn•chro•mesh**
**syn•chron•ic**
**syn•chroni•cal•ly**
**syn•chro•nism**
**syn•chro•nis•tic** (*or* **•ti•cal**)
**syn•chro•nis•ti•cal•ly**
**syn•chro•ni•za•tion** (*or* **•sa•tion**)
**syn•chro•nize** (*or* **•nise**)
**syn•chro•niz•er** (*or* **•nis•er**)
**syn•chro•nous**
**syn•chro•nous•ness**
**syn•chrony**
**syn•chro•scope** (*or* **•chrono•**)
**syn•chro•tron**
**syn•clas•tic** maths term
**syn•cli•nal**
**syn•cline** geology term
**syn•cli•no•rium** (*plural* **•ria**)
**Syn•com** communications satellite
**syn•co•pate**
**syn•co•pa•tion**
**syn•co•pa•tor**
**syn•co•pe**
**syn•cop•ic** (*or* **•co•pal**)
**syn•cret•ic** (*or* **•cre•tis•tic**)
**syn•cre•tism**
**syn•cre•tist**
**syn•cre•ti•za•tion** (*or* **•sa•tion**)
**syn•cre•tize** (*or* **•tise**) combine differing beliefs
**syn•cyt•ial**
**syn•cyt•ium** (*plural* **•cytia**) zoology term
**syn•dac•tyl**
**syn•dac•tyly** (*or* **•tyl•ism**)
**syn•de•sis** linguistics term
**syn•des•mo•sis** (*plural* **•ses**) anatomy term
**syn•des•mot•ic**
**syn•det•ic** (*or* **•deti•cal**)
**syn•deti•cal•ly**
**syn•de•ton**
**syn•dic** business agent
**syn•di•cal**
**syn•di•cal•ism**
**syn•di•cal•ist**
**syn•di•cal•is•tic**
**syn•di•cate**
**syn•di•ca•tion**
**syn•dic•ship**
**syn•dio•tac•tic** chemistry term
**syn•drome**
**syn•drom•ic**
**syne** *Scot* since
**syn•ec•do•che** figure of speech
**syn•ec•doch•ic** (*or* **•dochi•cal**)
**syn•ec•dochi•cal•ly**
**syn•eco•log•ic** (*or* **•logi•cal**)
**syn•eco•logi•cal•ly**
**syn•ecol•ogy**

**syn•ec•tics** problem solving
**syn•er•esis** (*or* **•aer•**) chemistry or phonetics term
**syn•er•get•ic** (*or* **•gis•tic**)
**syn•er•geti•cal•ly** (*or* **•gis•ti•**)
**syn•er•gic**
**syn•er•gism** acting together
**syn•er•gist**
**syn•er•gis•tic**
**syn•er•gy** (*plural* **•gies**)
**syn•esis** linguistics term
**syn•es•the•sia** *US spelling of* **synaesthesia**
**syn•gam•ic** (*or* **•ga•mous**)
**syn•ga•my** (*or* **•gen•esis**) biology term
**syni•zesis** phonetics or biology term
**syn•kary•on** biology term
**syn•kary•on•ic**
**syn•od**
**syn•od•al** (*or* **•odi•cal**)
**syn•od•ic**
**syn•oecious** (*or* **syn•ecious, synoi•cous**) botany term
**syn•oekete** (*or* **•oecete**) zoology term
**syno•nym**
**syno•nym•ic** (*or* **•nymi•cal**)
**syno•nym•ity**
**syn•ony•mize** (*or* **•mise**)
**syn•ony•mous**
**syn•ony•mous•ness**
**syn•ony•my** (*plural* **•mies**)
**syn•op•sis** (*plural* **•ses**)
**syn•op•tic**
**syn•op•ti•cal•ly**
**syn•op•tist**
**syno•via** fluid in joint
**syno•vial**
**syno•vit•ic**
**syno•vi•tis**
**syn•sep•al•ous** botany term
**syn•tac•tic** (*or* **•ti•cal**)
**syn•tac•ti•cal•ly**
**syn•tac•tics** study of symbols
**syn•tag•ma** (*or* **syn•tagm;** *plural* **•tag•ma•ta** *or* **•tagms**) linguistics term
**syn•tax**
**syn•the•sis** (*plural* **•ses**)
**syn•the•sist**
**syn•the•si•za•tion** (*or* **•sa•tion**)
**syn•the•size** (*or* **•sise**)
**syn•the•siz•er** (*or* **•sis•er**)
**syn•thet•ic**
**syn•theti•cal**
**syn•theti•cal•ly**
**syn•the•tism** art term
**syn•the•tist**
**syn•ton•ic** psychology term
**syn•toni•cal•ly**
**sy•pher** woodworking term; *compare* **cipher**
**sy•pher•ing**
**syphi•lis**
**syphi•lit•ic**
**syphi•liti•cal•ly**
**syphi•loid**
**syphi•lolo•gist**
**syphi•lol•ogy**
**syphi•lo•ma** (*plural* **•mas** *or* **•ma•ta**) tumour
**sy•phon** *variant spelling of* **siphon**
**Sy•ra•cuse** Italian port; US city
**Syria**
**Syri•ac**
**Syr•ian**
**sy•rin•ga** ornamental shrub; *compare* **seringa**
**sy•ringe**
**sy•rin•geal**
**sy•rin•go•my•elia** disease
**sy•rin•go•my•el•ic**
**syr•inx** (*plural* **sy•rin•ges** *or* **syr•inx•es**) zoology term
**syr•phid** fly
**syr•up** (*US also* **sir•**)
**syr•upy**
**sys•sar•co•sis** (*plural* **•ses**) anatomy term
**sys•sar•cot•ic**
**sys•tal•tic** of heartbeat
**sys•tem**
**sys•tem•at•ic** methodical; *compare* **systemic**
**sys•tem•ati•cal•ly**
**sys•tem•ati•cal•ness**
**sys•tem•at•ics**
**sys•tema•tism**
**sys•tema•tist**
**sys•tema•ti•za•tion** (*or* **•sa•tion**)
**sys•tema•tize** (*or* **•tise**)
**sys•tema•tiz•er** (*or* **•tis•er**)
**sys•tema•tol•ogy**
**sys•tem•ic** affecting whole body; *compare* **systematic**
**sys•temi•cal•ly**
**sys•temi•za•tion** (*or* **•sa•tion**) systematization
**sys•tem•iz•er** (*or* **•is•er**)
**sys•to•le**
**sys•tol•ic**
**Syz•ran** Russian port
**syzy•geti•cal•ly**
**sy•zyg•ial** (*or* **syzy•get•ic, syzy•gal**)
**syzy•gy** (*plural* **•gies**) astronomy term
**Szcze•cin** Polish port
**Sze•chwan** Chinese province
**Sze•ged** Hungarian city

# T

**ta** *Slang* thank you
**Taal** Philippine volcano
**tab** (**tab•bing, tabbed**)
**taba•nid** fly
**tab•ard**
**taba•ret** fabric
**Ta•bas•co** Mexican state; (*Trademark*) sauce
**tabbed**
**tab•bing**
**tab•by** (*plural* **•bies**)
**tab•er•nac•le**
**tab•er•nacu•lar**
**ta•bes** wasting
**ta•bes•cence**

**ta•bes•cent**
**tab•la•ture** musical notation
**ta•ble**
**tab•leau** (*plural* **•leaux** *or* **•leaus)**
**table•cloth**
**ta•ble d'hôte** (*plural* **ta•bles d'hôte)**
**table•land**
**table•spoon**
**table•spoon•ful** (*plural* **•fuls)**
**tab•let**
**table-turning**
**table•ware**
**tab•loid**
**ta•boo** (*or* **tabu**; *plural* **•boos** *or* **•bus)**
**ta•bor** (*or* **•bour)** drum
**tabo•ret** (*or* **tabou•)** stool
**tabo•rin** (*or* **tabou•)** drum
**Ta•briz** Iranian city
**tabu•lable**
**tabu•lar**
**tabu•lar•ize**
**tabu•late**
**tabu•la•tion**
**tabu•la•tor**
**taca•ma•hac** (*or* **tac•ma•hack)** gum
**ta•cet** musical term
**tache** *Archaic* buckle; *Slang* moustache
**tach•eom•eter** (*or* **ta•chym•)** surveying instrument; *compare* **tachometer**
**tacheo•met•ric** (*or* **•ri•cal, tachy•)**
**tacheo•met•ri•cal•ly** (*or* **tachy•)**
**tach•eom•etry** (*or* **ta•chym•)**
**tachi•na** fly
**ta•chis•to•scope**
**ta•chis•to•scop•ic**
**ta•chis•to•scopi•cal•ly**
**tacho•graph** speed-recording device
**ta•chom•eter** speed-measuring device; *compare* **tacheometer**
**tacho•met•ric** (*or* **•ri•cal)**
**tacho•met•ri•cal•ly**
**ta•chom•etry**
**tachy•car•dia** rapid heartbeat
**tachy•car•di•ac**
**ta•chyg•ra•pher** (*or* **•phist)**
**tachy•graph•ic** (*or* **•graphi•cal)**
**ta•chyg•ra•phy** shorthand
**tachy•lyte** (*or* **•lite)** basalt
**tachy•lyt•ic** (*or* **•lit•)**
**ta•chym•eter** *variant of* **tacheometer**
**ta•chym•etry** *variant of* **tacheometry**
**tachy•on** physics term
**tachy•phy•lax•is** medical term
**tac•it**
**tac•it•ness**
**taci•turn**
**taci•tur•nity**
**tack**
**tack•er**
**tack•et** *Dialect* hobnail
**tacki•ly**
**tacki•ness**
**tack•le**
**tack•ler**
**tacky (tacki•er, tacki•est)**
**tac•node** maths term
**taco** (*plural* **tacos)** Mexican food
**Ta•co•ma** US port
**taco•nite** rock
**tact**
**tact•ful**
**tact•ful•ly**
**tact•ful•ness**
**tac•tic**
**tac•ti•cal**
**tac•ti•cal•ly**
**tac•ti•cian**
**tac•tics**
**tac•tile**
**tac•til•ity**
**tact•less**
**tact•less•ness**
**tac•tual**
**tad** *US* boy
**tad•pole**
**Ta•dzhik** (*plural* **•dzhiks** *or* **•dzhik)** Muslim people
**Ta•dzhiki•stan** Central Asian republic
**Tae•gu** South Korean city
**Tae•jon** South Korean city
**tae•nia** (*or esp. US* **te•**; *plural* **•niae)** band; architectural term; *compare* **tinea**
**tae•nia** (*US also* **te•**; *plural* **•niae)** tapeworm; *compare* **tinea**
**tae•nia•cide** (*US also* **te•)**
**tae•nia•fuge** (*US also* **te•)**
**tae•nia•sis** (*US also* **te•)**
**taf•fe•ta**
**taff•rail** ship's rail
**Taf•fy** (*plural* **•fies)** *Slang* Welshman
**taf•fy** (*plural* **•fies)** *US* sweet
**tafia** (*or* **taf•fia)** rum
**Ta•fi•lelt** (*or* **Ta•fi•la•let)** oasis
**tag (tag•ging, tagged)**
**Ta•ga•log** (*plural* **•logs** *or* **•log)** Philippine people
**Ta•gan•rog** Russian port
**tag•gers** tin-coated iron sheet
**tag•ging**
**ta•glia•tel•le** pasta
**tag•meme** linguistics term
**tag•mem•ic**
**tag•mem•ics**
**Ta•gus** European river
**ta•hi•na** sesame paste
**Ta•hi•ti**
**Ta•hi•tian**
**tahr** animal
**tah•sil•dar** Indian tax collector
**Tai•chung** (*or* **T'ai-chung)** Chinese city
**tai•ga** subarctic forests
**tail** appendage; compare **tale**
**tail•back**
**tail•board**
**tail-ender**
**tail•gate**
**tail•ing**
**taille** (*plural* **tailles)** French tax
**tail•less**
**tail•light** (*or* **•lamp)**
**tail-like**
**tai•lor**
**tailor•bird**
**tailor-made**
**tail•piece**
**tail•pipe**

**tail•plane**
**tail•race**
**tails** tail coat
**tail•skid**
**tail•spin**
**tail•stock**
**tail•wind**
**tain** mirror backing
**Tai•nan** (*or* **T'ai-nan**) Chinese city
**taint**
**tai•pan** snake
**Tai•pei** (*or* **T'ai-pei**) Taiwanese capital
**Tai•wan**
**Tai•wan•ese**
**Tai•yuan** (*or* **T'ai-yüan**) Chinese city
**taj** Muslim cap
**Taj Ma•hal**
**taka** Bangladeshi currency
**tak•able** (*or* **take•able**)
**ta•ka•he** bird
**Taka•mat•su** Japanese port
**take** (**tak•ing, took, tak•en**)
**take•away**
**tak•en**
**take•off**
**take•over**
**tak•er**
**tak•in** animal
**tak•ing**
**tak•ing•ness**
**tak•ings**
**Ta•ko•ra•di** Ghanaian port
**tala•poin** monkey
**ta•laria** winged sandals
**talc** (**talck•ing, talcked** *or* **talc•ing, talced**)
**Tal•ca•hua•no** Chilean city
**talc•ose** (*or* **tal•cous**)
**tal•cum**
**tale** story; *compare* **tail**
**tal•ent**
**tal•ent•ed**
**ta•les** legal term
**ta•les•man** (*plural* **•men**)
**tali•grade** zoology term
**tali•on** legal term
**tali•ped**
**tali•pes** club foot
**tali•pot** palm tree
**tal•is•man** (*plural* **•mans**)
**tal•is•man•ic**
**talk**
**talka•bil•ity**
**talk•able**
**talka•tive**
**talka•tive•ly**
**talka•tive•ness**
**talk•er**
**talkie**
**talking to** (*plural* **-tos**)
**tall**
**tal•lage** historical tax
**Tal•la•has•see** US city
**tall•boy**
**tal•li•er**
**Tal•linn** (*or* **•lin**) Estonian capital
**tall•ish**
**tal•lith** (*plural* **•lai•sim, •lithes** *or* **•li•toth**) prayer shawl
**tall•ness**
**tal•low**
**tal•ly** (*verb* **•lies, •ly•ing, •lied**; *noun, plural* **•lies**)
**tally-ho** (*verb* **-hos, -hoing, -hoed**; *noun, plural* **-hos**)
**tally•man** (*plural* **•men**)
**Tal•mud** Jewish literature
**Tal•mud•ic** (*or* **•mudi•cal**)
**Tal•mud•ism**
**Tal•mud•ist**
**tal•on**
**ta•loned**
**ta•luk** (*or* **•lu•ka, •loo•ka**) Indian district
**ta•lus** (*plural* **•li**) anklebone
**ta•lus** (*plural* **•luses**) scree
**tam•abil•ity** (*or* **tame•**)
**tam•able** (*or* **tame•**)
**tam•able•ness** (*or* **tame•**)
**ta•ma•le** Mexican food
**ta•man•dua** (*or* **•du**) animal
**tama•rack** tree
**ta•ma•rau** (*or* **•rao**) cattle
**tama•rin** monkey
**tama•rind** (*or* **•rin•do**; *plural* **•rinds** *or* **•rin•dos**) tree, fruit
**tama•risk** tree
**ta•ma•sha** Indian entertainment
**Ta•mau•li•pas** Mexican state
**Tam•bo•ra** Indonesian volcano
**tam•bour**
**tam•boura** musical instrument
**tam•bou•rin** dance
**tam•bou•rine** musical instrument
**tam•bou•rin•ist**
**Tam•bov** Russian city
**tame**
**tame•able** *variant spelling of* **tamable**
**tame•ness**
**tam•er**
**Tame•side** area of Greater Manchester
**Tam•il** (*plural* **•ils** *or* **•il**) Asian people
**Tam•il Nadu** Indian state
**tam•is** (*plural* **•ises**) straining cloth
**Tam•ma•ny Hall** US political party organization
**tam•my** (*plural* **•mies**)
**tam-o'-shanter**
**tam•ox•i•fen**
**tamp**
**Tam•pa** Florida resort
**tam•per**
**Tam•pe•re** Finnish city
**tam•per•er**
**Tam•pi•co** Mexican port
**tamp•ing** *Welsh* angry
**tam•pi•on** (*or* **tom•**) gun plug
**tam•pon** medical plug
**tam•pon•ade**
**tam-tam** gong; *compare* **tom-tom**
**tan** (**tan•ning, tanned**)
**Tana** Ethiopian lake
**tana** lemur
**tana•ger** bird
**Tana•na** Alaskan river
**tan•bark**
**tan•dem**
**tan•doori**
**Tang** Chinese dynasty
**tang**
**Tan•ga** Tanzanian port
**Tan•gan•yi•ka** African lake
**tan•ge•lo** (*plural* **•los**) hybrid fruit
**tan•gen•cy**
**tan•gent**
**tan•gen•tial**

**tan•gen•ti•al•ity**
**tan•gen•tial•ly** (*or* **•tal•ly**)
**Tan•ge•rine** of Tangier
**tan•ge•rine** fruit
**tan•gibil•ity** (*or* **•gible•ness**)
**tan•gible**
**Tan•gier** Moroccan port
**tangi•ness**
**tan•gle**
**tan•gle•ment**
**tan•gler**
**tan•gly**
**tan•go** (*noun, plural* **•tos**; *verb* **•goes, •go•ing, •goed**)
**tan•go•ist**
**tan•gram** puzzle
**Tang•shan** Chinese city
**tangy** (**tangi•er, tangi•est**)
**tanh** maths term
**Ta•nis** ancient Egyptian city
**tan•ist** heir of Celtic chieftain
**Tan•jore** Indian city
**tank**
**tan•ka** (*plural* **•kas** *or* **•ka**) Japanese verse
**tank•age**
**tank•ard**
**tank•er**
**tank•ful** (*plural* **•fuls**)
**tan•nage**
**tan•nate**
**tanned**
**tan•ner**
**tan•nery** (*plural* **•neries**)
**tan•nic**
**tan•nin**
**tan•ning**
**Tan•noy** (*Trademark*)
**tan•sy** (*plural* **•sies**) plant
**Tan•ta** Egyptian city
**tan•ta•late**
**tan•tal•ic**
**tan•ta•lite** mineral
**tan•ta•li•za•tion** (*or* **•sa•tion**)
**tan•ta•lize** (*or* **•lise**)
**tan•ta•liz•er** (*or* **•lis•er**)
**tan•ta•liz•ing•ly** (*or* **•lis•ing•ly**)
**tan•ta•lous** chemistry term; *compare* **tantalus**
**tan•ta•lum** chemical element
**Tantalus** mythological king
**tan•ta•lus** case for bottles; *compare* **tantalous**
**tan•ta•mount**
**tan•ta•ra** fanfare
**tan•tivy** (*plural* **•tivies**) hunting cry
**tan•to** musical term
**Tan•tra** Sanskrit books
**Tan•tric**
**Tan•trism**
**Tan•trist**
**tan•trum**
**Tan•za•nia**
**Tan•za•nian**
**Tao•ism** Chinese philosophy
**Tao•ist**
**tap** (**tap•ping, tapped**)
**tapa** mulberry bark
**tap-dance** (*verb*)
**tap-dancer**
**tapa•der•a** stirrup covering
**tape**
**ta•per**
**ta•per•er**
**ta•per•ing•ly**
**tap•es•tried**
**tap•es•try** (*plural* **•tries**)
**ta•petal**
**ta•petum** (*plural* **•peta**) biology term
**tape•worm**
**tap•hole**
**tapio•ca**
**ta•pir** (*plural* **•pirs** *or* **•pir**) animal
**tap•is** (*plural* **tap•is**) carpet
**tap•pable**
**tapped**
**tap•per**
**tap•pet**
**tap•ping**
**tappit-hen**
**tap•room**
**tap•root**
**tap•ster**
**tar** (**tar•ring, tarred**)
**ta•ra•did•dle** *variant spelling of* **tarradiddle**
**ta•ra•ma•sa•la•ta**
**ta•ran•tass** Russian carriage
**tar•an•tel•la** dance; *compare* **tarantula**
**tar•ant•ism** nervous disorder
**Ta•ran•to** Italian port
**ta•ran•tu•la** (*plural* **•las** *or* **•lae**) spider; *compare* **tarantella**
**ta•raxa•cum** plant
**tar•boosh** (*or* **•bush, •bouche**) Muslim cap
**Tar•de•noi•sian** Mesolithic culture
**tar•di•grade** minute animal
**tar•di•ly**
**tar•di•ness**
**tar•dy** (**•di•er, •di•est**)
**tare** plant; weight of goods container; *compare* **tear**
**tar•get**
**tar•iff**
**Ta•rim** Chinese river
**tar•la•tan** fabric
**tar•mac** (**•mack•ing, •macked**)
**tarn** lake
**tar•nal** *US* damned
**tar•na•tion**
**Tarn-et-Garonne** French department
**tar•nish**
**tar•nish•able**
**tar•nish•er**
**taro** (*plural* **taros**) plant
**ta•rot** card
**tarp** *Austral* tarpaulin
**tar•pan** extinct horse
**tar•pau•lin**
**Tar•pe•ian Rock**
**tar•pon** (*plural* **•pons** *or* **•pon**) fish
**tar•ra•did•dle** (*or* **ta•ra•**)
**tar•ra•gon**
**Tar•ra•sa** Spanish city
**tarred**
**tar•ri•ness**
**tar•ring**
**tar•ry** (*verb* **•ries, •ry•ing, •ried**; *adj* **•ri•er, •ri•est**)
**tar•sal**
**tar•si•er** animal
**tar•so•meta•tar•sal**
**tar•so•meta•tar•sus** (*plural* **•si**)
**Tar•sus** Turkish city
**tar•sus** (*plural* **•si**) ankle bones
**tart**
**tar•tan**

**Tar•tar** *variant spelling of* **Tatar**
**tar•tar** deposit on teeth; fearsome person; sauce; chemical substance
**tar•tar•ic**
**tar•tari•za•tion** (*or* **•sa•tion**)
**tar•tar•ize** (*or* **•ise**)
**tar•tar•ous** of tartar
**Tar•ta•rus** Hades
**Tar•ta•ry** *variant spelling of* **Tatary**
**tart•let**
**tart•ness**
**tar•trate**
**tarty**
**Tar•zan**
**Tash•kent** Uzbek capital
**ta•sim•eter** temperature-change measurer
**tasi•met•ric**
**ta•sim•etry**
**task**
**task•er**
**task•master** (*fem* **•mistress**)
**task•work**
**Tas•ma•nia**
**Tas•ma•nian**
**Tas•man Sea**
**Tass** former Soviet news agency
**tass** *Dialect* cup
**tas•sel** (**•sel•ling, •selled;** *US* **•sel•ing, •seled**)
**tas•sel•ly**
**tas•set** piece of armour
**tast•able**
**taste**
**taste•ful**
**taste•ful•ly**
**taste•ful•ness**
**taste•less**
**taste•less•ness**
**tast•er**
**tasti•ly**
**tasti•ness**
**tasty** (**tasti•er, tasti•est**)
**tat** (**tat•ting, tat•ted**)
**ta-ta** *Slang* goodbye
**Ta•tar** (*or* **Tar•tar**) Mongoloid people
**Ta•tar•ian** (*or* **Tar•tar•ian, Ta•tar•ic, Tar•tar•ic**)
**Ta•ta•ry** (*or* **Tar•ta•ry**) historical region
**ta•ter** *Dialect* potato
**Tat•ler** journal; *compare* **tattler**
**tatou•ay** armadillo
**Ta•tra** mountain range
**tat•ted**
**tat•ter**
**tat•ter•de•mal•ion**
**tat•ter•sall** fabric
**tat•ting**
**tat•tle**
**tat•tler** one who tattles; *compare* **Tatler**
**tattle•tale**
**tat•tling•ly**
**tat•too** (*noun, plural* **•toos;** *verb* **toos, •too•ing, •tooed**)
**tat•too•ist** (*or* **•er**)
**tat•ty** (**•ti•er, •ti•est**)
**tatty-peelin** *Scot* pretentious
**tau** Greek letter; *compare* **taw**
**taught** past tense of teach; *compare* **taut**
**taunt**
**taunt•er**
**taunt•ing•ly**
**Taun•ton** Somerset town
**taupe** brownish grey
**Tau•ranga** New Zealand port
**Tau•rean**
**tau•rine** bull-like; biochemical compound
**tau•ro•ma•chian**
**tau•roma•chy** bullfighting
**Tau•rus** constellation; sign of zodiac
**taut** tight; *compare* **taught**
**taut•en**
**taut•ness**
**tau•tog** fish
**tau•to•logi•cal** (*or* **•to•log•ic, •tolo•gous**)
**tau•to•logi•cal•ly**
**tau•tolo•gize** (*or* **•gise**)
**tau•tol•ogy** (*plural* **•gies**)
**tau•to•mer** chemistry term
**tau•to•mer•ic**
**tau•tom•er•ism**
**tau•to•nym** biology term
**tau•to•nym•ic** (*or* **•tony•mous**)
**tau•tony•my**
**Ta•vel** wine
**tav•ern**
**tav•ern•er**
**taw** marble; tanning term; *compare* **tau**
**taw•dri•ly**
**taw•dri•ness**
**taw•dry** (**•dri•er, •dri•est**)
**taw•er**
**taw•ny** (*or* **•ney**)
**tawse** (*or* **taws**) leather strap
**tax**
**tax•abil•ity** (*or* **•able•ness**)
**tax•able**
**taxa•ceous** botany term
**taxa•tion**
**taxa•tion•al**
**tax-deduct•ible**
**tax•eme** linguistics term
**tax•er**
**taxi** (*noun, plural* **taxis** *or* **taxies;** *verb* **taxies, taxi•ing, tax•ied**)
**taxi•cab**
**taxi•der•mal** (*or* **•mic**)
**taxi•der•mist**
**taxi•der•my**
**taxi•meter**
**tax•ing•ly**
**taxi•plane**
**tax•is** biology term; surgical process
**taxis** (*or* **taxies**) *plural of* **taxi**
**taxi•way**
**tax•man** (*plural* **•men**)
**tax•on** (*plural* **taxa**) biology term
**taxo•nom•ic** (*or* **•nomi•cal**)
**taxo•nomi•cal•ly**
**tax•ono•mist** (*or* **•mer**)
**tax•ono•my**
**tax•payer**
**tax•paying**
**Tay** Scottish river
**tay** *Irish* tea
**tay•ra** animal
**Tay•side** former Scottish region
**taz•za** wine cup
**Tbi•li•si** (*or* **Tif•lis**) Georgian capital

**te** (*or* **ti**) musical term; *compare* **tea; tee**
**tea** beverage; *compare* **te; tee**
**tea•berry** (*plural* **•berries**)
**tea•cake**
**tea•cart**
**teach** (**teach•es, teach•ing, taught**)
**teach•able**
**teach•er**
**teach-in**
**teach•ing**
**tea•cup**
**tea•cup•ful** (*plural* **•fuls**)
**tea•house**
**teak**
**tea•kettle**
**teal** (*plural* **teals** *or* **teal**) duck
**team** group; *compare* **teem**
**tea-maker**
**team-mate**
**team•ster**
**team•work**
**tea•pot**
**tea•poy** table with tripod base
**tear** (**tear•ing, tore, torn**) rip; *compare* **tare**
**tear** drop from eye; *compare* **tier**
**tear•able**
**tear•er**
**tear•ful**
**tear•ful•ly**
**tear•ful•ness**
**tear•ing**
**tear•ing•ly**
**tear-jerker**
**tear•less**
**tea•room**
**tease**
**tea•sel** (*or* **•zel, •zle; •sel•ling, •selled;** *US* **•sel•ing, •seled**)
**teas•er**
**tea•shop**
**teas•ing•ly**
**tea•spoon**
**tea•spoon•ful** (*plural* **•fuls**)
**teat**
**techi•ly** *variant spelling of* **tetchily**
**techi•ness** *variant spelling of* **tetchiness**
**tech•ne•tium** chemical element
**tech•nic** *variant of* **technique**
**tech•ni•cal**
**tech•ni•cal•ity** (*plural* **•ities**)
**tech•ni•cal•ly**
**tech•ni•cian**
**Tech•ni•col•or** (*Trademark*)
**tech•nics** study of industry
**tech•nique** (*or* **•nic**)
**tech•noc•ra•cy** (*plural* **•cies**)
**tech•no•crat**
**tech•no•crat•ic**
**tech•nog•ra•phy**
**tech•no•logi•cal**
**tech•no•logi•cal•ly**
**tech•nolo•gist**
**tech•nol•ogy** (*plural* **•ogies**)
**tech•no•struc•ture**
**techy** *variant spelling of* **tetchy**
**tec•ton•ic**
**tec•toni•cal•ly**
**tec•ton•ics**
**tec•tri•cial**
**tec•trix** (*plural* **•tri•ces**) feather
**ted** (**ted•ding, ted•ded**) shake out hay
**ted•der**
**ted•dy** (*plural* **•dies**)
**Te De•um**
**te•di•ous**
**te•di•ous•ness**
**te•dium**
**tee** (**tee•ing, teed**) golf term; T-shaped part; *compare* **te; tea**
**teem** abound; *compare* **team**
**teem•ing**
**teen**
**teen•age**
**teen•aged**
**teen•ager**
**tee•ny** (**•ni•er, •ni•est**)
**teeny•bopper**
**Tees** English river
**Tees•side**
**tee•ter**
**teeth** *plural of* **tooth**
**teethe** (*verb*)
**teeth•ing**
**tee•to•tal**
**tee•to•tal•ism**
**tee•to•tal•ler** (*US* **•tal•er**)
**tee•to•tum** spinning top
**tef** (*or* **teff**) grass
**Tef•lon** (*Trademark*)
**teg** sheep
**teg•men** (*plural* **•mi•na**) zoology term
**teg•mi•nal**
**Te•gu•ci•gal•pa** Honduran capital
**tegu•lar** of a tile
**tegu•lar•ly**
**Teh•ran** (*or* **Te•he•ran**)
**Te•huan•tepec** Mexican region
**tek•tite**
**tela** (*plural* **telae**) weblike structure
**tel•aes•the•sia** (*US* **•es•**) paranormal perception
**tel•aes•thet•ic** (*US* **•es•**)
**tela•mon** (*plural* **•mones**) supporting pillar
**tel•an•gi•ec•ta•sis** (*or* **•sia;** *plural* **•ses**) medical term
**tel•an•gi•ec•tat•ic**
**Tel•auto•graph** (*Trademark*)
**tel•auto•graph•ic**
**tel•autog•ra•phy**
**Tel Aviv**
**tele•cast** (**•cast•ing, •cast** *or* **•cast•ed**)
**tele•cast•er**
**tele•com•mu•ni•ca•tion**
**tele•com•mu•ni•ca•tions**
**tele•con•fer•ence**
**tele•con•fer•en•cing**
**tel•edu** badger
**te•le•ga** cart
**tele•gen•ic**
**tel•eg•no•sis** parapsychology term
**tel•eg•nos•tic**
**tel•egon•ic**
**Telegonus** son of Odysseus
**te•lego•ny** genetics term
**tele•gram**
**tele•graph**
**te•leg•ra•pher** (*or* **•phist**)
**tele•graph•ic**
**tele•graphi•cal•ly**
**te•leg•ra•phy**
**tele•ki•ne•sis**
**tele•ki•net•ic**

**Telemachus** son of Odysseus
**tel•emark** skiing term
**tele•me•di•cine**
**te•lem•eter**
**tele•met•ric** (*or* **•ri•cal**)
**tele•met•ri•cal•ly**
**te•lem•etry**
**tel•en•cephal•ic**
**tel•en•cepha•lon** anatomy term
**teleo•logi•cal** (*or* **•log•ic**)
**teleo•logi•cal•ly**
**tele•olo•gism**
**tele•olo•gist**
**tele•ol•ogy**
**tel•eost** fish
**tele•path•ic**
**tele•pathi•cal•ly**
**te•lepa•thist**
**te•lepa•thize** (*or* **•thise**)
**te•lepa•thy**
**tele•phone**
**tele•phon•er**
**tele•phon•ic**
**te•lepho•nist**
**te•lepho•ny**
**tele•photo•graph•ic**
**tele•pho•tog•ra•phy**
**tele•photo**
**tele•play**
**tele•print•er**
**tele•prompt•er**
**Tele•ran** (*Trademark*) navigational aid
**tele•scope**
**tele•scop•ic**
**tele•scopi•cal•ly**
**te•les•co•py**
**tele•script**
**tele•sis**
**tele•spec•tro•scope**
**tele•ste•reo•scope**
**tel•es•the•sia** *US spelling of* telaesthesia
**te•les•tich** poem
**tele•thon**
**tele•tran•scrip•tion**
**tele•tube** *short for* television tube
**Tele•type** (*Trademark*)
**Tele•type•set•ter** (*Trademark*)
**tele•type•set•ting**
**te•leu•to•spore**
**te•leu•to•spor•ic**
**tele•vise**
**tele•vi•sion**
**tele•vi•sion•al**
**tele•vi•sion•ary**
**tele•writ•er**
**tel•ex**
**Tel•ford** Shropshire town
**tel•geni•cal•ly**
**te•lial**
**tel•ic** purposeful
**te•lio•spore**
**te•lium** (*plural* **•lia**) fungal structure
**tell** (**tell•ing, told**)
**tell•able**
**Tell el Amar•na** Egyptian ruins
**tell•er**
**tell•ing**
**tell•ing•ly**
**tell•tale**
**tel•lu•rate** chemistry term
**tel•lu•rian** of the earth
**tel•lu•ric**
**tel•lu•ride** chemical compound
**tel•lu•ri•on** (*or* **•lu•rian**) model of earth
**tel•lu•rite**
**tel•lu•rium** chemical element
**tel•lu•rize** (*or* **•rise**)
**tel•lu•rom•eter** surveying instrument
**tel•lu•rous**
**tel•ly** (*plural* **tel•lies**)
**telo•phase** biology term
**telo•pha•sic**
**tel•pher** (*or* **•fer**)
**tel•pher•age** (*or* **•fer•**) transport system
**tel•pher•ic** (*or* **•fer•**)
**tel•son** zoology term
**tel•son•ic**
**Tel•star** satellite
**Te•luk•be•tung** (*or* **Te•loek•be•toeng**) Indonesian port
**Tema** Ghanaian port
**tem•er•ari•ous**
**te•mer•ity**
**temp**
**tem•per**
**tem•pera** painting medium
**tem•per•abil•ity**
**tem•per•able**
**tem•pera•ment**
**tem•pera•men•tal**
**tem•pera•men•tal•ly**
**tem•per•ance**
**tem•per•ate**
**tem•per•ate•ly**
**tem•per•ate•ness**
**tem•pera•ture**
**tem•per•er**
**tem•pest**
**tem•pes•tu•ous**
**tem•pes•tu•ous•ness**
**Tem•plar** member of religious order
**tem•plate** (*or* **•plet**)
**tem•ple**
**tem•po** (*plural* **•pos** *or* **•pi**)
**tem•po•ral** of time or the temples
**tem•po•ral•ity**
**tem•po•ral•ly** of time
**tem•po•rari•ly** not permanently
**tem•po•rari•ness**
**tem•po•rary** (*plural* **•raries**)
**tem•po•ri•za•tion** (*or* **•sa•tion**)
**tem•po•rize** (*or* **•rise**)
**tem•po•riz•er** (*or* **•ris•er**)
**tempt**
**tempt•able**
**temp•ta•tion**
**tempt•er**
**tempt•ing**
**tempt•ing•ly**
**tempt•ress**
**tem•pu•ra** Japanese food
**Te•mu•co** Chilean city
**ten**
**ten•abil•ity** (*or* **•able•ness**)
**ten•able**
**ten•ably**
**ten•ace** bridge term
**te•na•cious**
**te•na•cious•ness**
**te•nac•ity**
**te•nacu•lum** (*plural* **•la**) surgical instrument
**te•naille** fortification
**ten•an•cy** (*plural* **•cies**)
**ten•ant**
**ten•ant•able**
**ten•ant•ry**

**tench** (*plural* **tench**)
**tend**
**ten•den•cy** (*plural* **•cies**)
**ten•den•tious** (*or* **•cious**)
**ten•den•tious•ness** (*or* **•cious•**)
**ten•der**
**ten•der•able**
**ten•der•er**
**tender•foot** (*plural* **•foots** *or* **•feet**)
**tender•hearted**
**tender•hearted•ness**
**ten•deri•za•tion** (*or* **•sa•tion**)
**ten•der•ize** (*or* **•ise**)
**ten•der•iz•er** (*or* **•is•er**)
**ten•der•loin**
**ten•der•ness**
**ten•din•itis** inflammation of tendon
**ten•di•nous** of tendons
**ten•don**
**ten•dril**
**ten•dril•lar** (*or* **•ous**)
**ten•ebrism** style of painting
**ten•ebrist**
**ten•ebros•ity**
**ten•ebrous** (*or* **te•neb•ri•ous**)
**Ten•edos** Greek island
**ten•ement**
**ten•emen•tal** (*or* **•tary**)
**ten•ement•ed**
**Ten•erife**
**te•nes•mic**
**te•nes•mus** medical term
**ten•et** belief
**ten•fold**
**Ten•gri Nor** Chinese lake
**te•nia** *variant spelling* (*esp. US*) *of* **taenia**
**ten•ner**
**Ten•nes•sean**
**Ten•nes•see**
**ten•nis**
**ten•no** (*plural* **•no** *or* **•nos**) Japanese emperor
**ten•on**
**ten•on•er**
**ten•or**
**teno•rite** mineral
**te•nor•rha•phy** (*plural* **•phies**) tendon surgery
**te•noto•mist**
**te•noto•my** (*plural* **•mies**) incision into tendon
**ten•pin**
**ten•pins**
**ten•rec** animal
**tense**
**tense•ly**
**tense•ness**
**ten•sibil•ity** (*or* **•sible•ness**)
**ten•sible**
**ten•sile**
**ten•sil•ity** (*or* **•sile•ness**)
**ten•sim•eter** device measuring vapour pressure
**ten•si•om•eter** device measuring tensile strength
**ten•sion**
**ten•sion•al**
**ten•sive**
**ten•sor**
**ten•so•rial**
**tent**
**ten•ta•cle**
**ten•ta•cled**
**ten•tacu•lar**
**tent•age** tents
**ten•ta•tion** mechanical process
**ten•ta•tive**
**ten•ta•tive•ness**
**tent•ed**
**ten•ter**
**tenter•hook**
**tenth**
**tenu•ity**
**tenu•ous**
**tenu•ous•ness**
**ten•ure**
**tenu•rial**
**te•nu•to** musical term
**teo•cal•li** (*plural* **•lis**) Aztec pyramid
**teo•sin•te** grass
**te•pal** botany term
**te•pee** (*or* **tee•**) tent
**tep•efac•tion**
**tep•efy** (**•efies**, **•efy•ing**, **•efied**) make tepid
**teph•rite** rock
**teph•rit•ic**
**Te•pic** Mexican city
**tep•id**
**te•pid•ity** (*or* **tep•id•ness**)
**te•qui•la**
**Te•rai** Indian marshland
**ter•aph** (*plural* **•aphim**) biblical god
**tera•tism** malformed fetus
**tera•to•gen**
**tera•to•gen•ic** causing fetal deformity
**tera•toid**
**tera•to•log•ic** (*or* **•logi•cal**)
**tera•tolo•gist**
**tera•tol•ogy** study of fetal abnormalities
**tera•to•ma** (*plural* **•mas** *or* **•ma•ta**)
**ter•bic**
**ter•bium** chemical element
**terce** (*or* **tierce**) canonical hour
**ter•cel** (*or* **tier•cel**) male falcon
**ter•cen•te•nary** (*or* **•cen•ten•nial**; *plural* **•naries** *or* **•nials**)
**ter•cet** verse
**ter•ebene**
**te•reb•ic acid**
**ter•ebinth** tree
**ter•ebin•thine**
**te•re•do** (*plural* **•dos** *or* **•di•nes**) mollusc
**Te•re•si•na** Brazilian port
**te•rete** botany term
**ter•gal**
**ter•gi•ver•sate**
**ter•gi•ver•sa•tion**
**ter•gi•ver•sa•tor** (*or* **•ver•sant**)
**ter•gi•ver•sa•tory**
**ter•gum** (*plural* **•ga**) zoology term
**teri•ya•ki** Japanese food
**term**
**ter•ma•gan•cy**
**ter•ma•gant**
**ter•mi•nabil•ity** (*or* **•nable•ness**)
**ter•mi•nable**
**ter•mi•nal**
**ter•mi•nal•ly**
**ter•mi•nate**
**ter•mi•na•tion**
**ter•mi•na•tion•al**
**ter•mi•na•tive**
**ter•mi•na•tor**
**ter•mi•na•tory**
**ter•mi•no•logi•cal**

**ter•mi•nolo•gist**
**ter•mi•nol•ogy** (*plural* **•ogies**)
**ter•mi•nus** (*plural* **•ni** *or* **•nuses**)
**ter•mi•tar•ium** (*plural* **•taria**) termite nest
**ter•mite**
**ter•mit•ic**
**term•less**
**ter•mor** (*or* **•mer**) legal term
**tern** bird; compare **terne**; **turn**
**ter•na•ry** (*plural* **•ries**)
**ter•nate** botany term
**terne** alloy; *compare* **tern**; **turn**
**Ter•ni** Italian city
**ter•pene**
**ter•pe•nic**
**ter•pin•eol**
**Terpsichore** Greek Muse
**Terp•si•cho•rean** (*or* **•real**)
**ter•ra** land
**ter•race**
**ter•ra•cot•ta**
**ter•ra fir•ma**
**ter•rain** surroundings; *compare* **terrane**
**Ter•ra•my•cin** (*Trademark*)
**ter•rane** rock formation; *compare* **terrain**
**ter•ra•pin**
**ter•rar•ium** (*plural* **•rar•iums** *or* **•raria**) biological container
**ter•raz•zo**
**ter•rene** earthly; *compare* **terrine; tureen**
**terre•plein** top of rampart
**ter•res•trial**
**ter•res•tri•al•ly**
**ter•ret** harness ring
**terre-verte** painting pigment
**ter•ri•ble**
**ter•ri•ble•ness**
**ter•ri•bly**
**ter•rico•lous** living in soil
**ter•ri•er**
**ter•rif•ic**
**ter•rifi•cal•ly**
**ter•ri•fi•er**
**ter•ri•fy** (**•fies, •fy•ing, •fied**)
**ter•ri•fy•ing•ly**
**ter•rig•enous** of the earth
**ter•rine** dish; food; *compare* **terrene; tureen**
**ter•ri•to•rial**
**ter•ri•to•ri•al•ism**
**ter•ri•to•ri•al•ist**
**ter•ri•to•ri•al•ity**
**ter•ri•to•ri•ali•za•tion** (*or* **•sa•tion**)
**ter•ri•to•ri•al•ize** (*or* **•ise**)
**ter•ri•to•rial•ly**
**ter•ri•tory** (*plural* **•tories**)
**ter•ror**
**ter•ror•ful**
**ter•ror•ism**
**ter•ror•ist**
**ter•ror•is•tic**
**ter•rori•za•tion** (*or* **•sa•tion**)
**ter•ror•ize** (*or* **•ise**)
**ter•ror•iz•er** (*or* **•is•er**)
**terror-stricken** (*or* **-struck**)
**ter•ry** (*plural* **•ries**) towelling
**terse**
**terse•ly**
**terse•ness**
**ter•tial** ornithology term
**ter•tian** recurring every other day
**Ter•tiary** geological period
**ter•tiary** (*plural* **•tiaries**)
**ter•tium quid** a third unknown thing
**ter•va•lent** *variant of* **trivalent**
**Tery•lene** (*Trademark*)
**ter•zet•to** (*plural* **•tos** *or* **•ti**) vocal trio
**tes•la** unit; coil
**tes•sel•late**
**tes•sel•la•tion**
**tes•sera** (*plural* **•serae**) mosaic tile
**tes•ser•act** four-dimensional figure
**tes•ser•al**
**tes•si•tu•ra** musical term
**test**
**tes•ta** (*plural* **•tae**) seed coat
**test•abil•ity**
**test•able**
**tes•ta•ceous**
**tes•ta•cy**
**tes•ta•ment**
**tes•ta•men•tal**
**tes•ta•men•tary**
**tes•tate**
**tes•ta•tor** (*fem* **•trix**)
**test-drive** (*verb* **-driving, -drove, -driven**)
**test•er** one who tests
**tes•ter** canopy; coin
**tes•tes** *plural of* **testis**
**tes•ti•cle**
**tes•ticu•lar**
**tes•ticu•late**
**tes•ti•fi•ca•tion**
**tes•ti•fi•er**
**tes•ti•fy** (**•fies, •fy•ing, •fied**)
**testi•ly**
**tes•ti•mo•nial**
**tes•ti•mo•ny** (*plural* **•nies**)
**testi•ness**
**test•ing**
**test•ing•ly**
**tes•tis** (*plural* **•tes**)
**tes•ton** (*or* **•toon**) coin
**tes•tos•ter•one** hormone
**tes•tu•di•nal** (*or* **•nary**) of tortoises
**tes•tu•do** (*plural* **•di•nes**) Roman military manoeuvre
**tes•ty** (**•ti•er, •ti•est**)
**te•tan•ic**
**te•tani•cal•ly**
**teta•ni•za•tion** (*or* **•sa•tion**)
**teta•nize** (*or* **•nise**)
**teta•nus**
**teta•ny**
**te•tar•to•he•dral•ism** (*or* **te•to•he•drism**)
**te•tar•to•he•dral**
**tetchi•ly** (*or* **techi•**)
**tetchi•ness** (*or* **techi•**)
**tetchy** (*or* **techy; tetchi•er, tetchi•est** *or* **techi•er, techi•est**)
**tête-à-tête** (*plural* **-têtes** *or* **-tête**)
**tête-bêche** philately term
**teth•er**
**tet•ra** (*plural* **•ra** *or* **•ras**) fish
**tetra•ba•sic**
**tetra•ba•sic•ity**
**tetra•brach** metrical foot
**tetra•bran•chi•ate** zoology term
**tetra•chlo•ride**
**tetra•chord** musical term
**tetra•chor•dal**

**te•trac•id** chemistry term
**tetra•cy•cline**
**tet•rad**
**te•trady•mite** mineral
**tetra•dy•na•mous** botany term
**tetra•ethyl**
**te•trago•nal**
**tetra•gram**
**tetra•he•dral**
**tetra•he•drite** mineral
**tetra•he•dron** (*plural* **•drons** *or* **•dra)**
**te•tral•ogy** (*plural* **•ogies)** set of four
**te•tram•er•ism**
**te•tram•er•ous** biology term
**tetra•methyl•diar•sine**
**tetra•ple•gia**
**tetra•ploid** genetics term
**tetra•ploidy**
**tetra•pod**
**tetra•pod•ic**
**te•trapo•dy** (*plural* **•dies)** metrical unit
**te•trap•ter•ous** four-winged
**te•trarch**
**te•trarch•ate**
**te•trar•chic** (*or* **•chi•cal)**
**te•trar•chy** (*plural* **•chies)**
**tetra•spore**
**tetra•spor•ic** (*or* **•ous)**
**tetra•stich** four-line poem
**tetra•stich•ic** (*or* **tetras•ti•chal)**
**te•tras•ti•chous** botany term
**tetra•syl•lab•ic** (*or* **•labi•cal)**
**tetra•syl•la•ble**
**tetra•tom•ic**
**tetra•va•len•cy**
**tetra•va•lent**
**tet•rode** electronic valve
**te•trox•ide**
**tet•ryl**
**tet•ter** skin eruption
**Te•tuán** Moroccan city
**Teucer** mythological character
**Teu•ton** ancient German
**Teu•ton•ic**
**Teu•ton•ism**
**Teu•ton•ize** (*or* **•ise)**
**Tewkes•bury**
**Tex•an**
**Tex•as**
**text**
**text•book**
**tex•tile**
**tex•tu•al** of text; *compare* **textural**
**tex•tu•al•ism**
**tex•tu•al•ist**
**tex•tu•al•ly**
**tex•tu•ary** (*plural* **•aries)**
**tex•tur•al** of texture; *compare* **textual**
**tex•tur•al•ly**
**tex•ture**
**Thai** (*plural* **Thais** *or* **Thai)**
**Thai•land**
**thala•men•cephal•ic**
**thala•men•cepha•lon** (*plural* **•lons** *or* **•la)** anatomy term
**tha•lam•ic**
**tha•lami•cal•ly**
**thala•mus** (*plural* **•mi)** part of brain
**tha•las•sic** of the sea
**thal•as•soc•ra•cy** (*or* **•at•toc•)**
**tha•ler** (*or* **ta•**; *plural* **•ler** *or* **•lers)** coin
**tha•lido•mide**
**thal•lic**
**thal•lium** chemical element
**thal•loid**
**thal•lo•phyte**
**thal•lo•phyt•ic**
**thal•lous** of thallium
**thal•lus** (*plural* **•li** *or* **•luses)** botany term
**thal•weg** (*or* **tal•)** geography term
**Thames**
**than**
**thana•top•sis**
**Thanatos** personification of death
**thane** (*or* **thegn)**
**Than•et**
**Than•ja•vur** Indian city
**thank**
**thank•ful**
**thank•ful•ly**
**thank•ful•ness**
**thank•less**
**thank•less•ness**
**thanks•giving**
**Thap•sus** battle site
**Thá•sos** Greek island
**that**
**thatch**
**thatch•er**
**Thatch•er•ism**
**Thatch•er•ite** supporter of Margaret Thatcher
**thatch•ing**
**thau•ma•tol•ogy** study of miracles
**thau•ma•trope**
**thau•ma•tropi•cal**
**thau•ma•turge** miracle performer
**thau•ma•tur•gic**
**thau•ma•tur•gy**
**thaw**
**thaw•er**
**thea•ceous** botany term
**the•an•throp•ic**
**the•an•thro•pism**
**the•an•thro•pist**
**the•ar•chic**
**the•ar•chy** (*plural* **•chies)** government by gods
**thea•tre** (*US* **•ter)**
**theatre•goer** (*US* **theater•)**
**the•at•ri•cal**
**the•at•ri•cal•ity** (*or* **•cal•ness)**
**the•at•ri•cal•ly**
**the•at•ri•cals** dramatic entertainments
**the•at•rics** exaggerated mannerisms
**the•ba•ine** drug
**The•ban**
**Thebes**
**the•ca** (*plural* **•cae)** biology term
**the•cal** (*or* **•cate)**
**the•co•dont** extinct reptile
**thee**
**theft**
**thegn** *variant spelling of* **thane**
**the•ine** stimulant in tea
**their** of them; *compare* **there; they're**
**theirs**
**the•ism**
**the•ist**
**the•is•tic** (*or* **•ti•cal)**
**the•is•ti•cal•ly**
**them**

**the•mat•ic**
**the•mati•cal•ly**
**theme**
**Themis** Greek goddess
**them•selves**
**then**
**the•nar** palm of hand
**the•nard•ite** mineral
**thence**
**thence•forth**
**thence•forward** (*or* **•forwards)**
**theo•bro•mine**
**theo•cen•tric** theology term
**theo•cen•tric•ity**
**theo•cen•trism** (*or* **•tri•cism)**
**the•oc•ra•cy** (*plural* **•cies)**
**the•oc•ra•sy** mingling of deities
**theo•crat**
**theo•crat•ic** (*or* **•crati•cal)**
**theo•crati•cal•ly**
**the•odi•cy** (*plural* **•cies)** branch of theology
**the•odo•lite**
**the•odo•lit•ic**
**the•ogo•ny** (*plural* **•nies)** origin of the gods
**theo•lo•gian**
**theo•logi•cal**
**theo•logi•cal•ly**
**the•olo•gist**
**the•olo•gi•za•tion** (*or* **•sa•tion)**
**the•olo•gize** (*or* **•gise)**
**the•olo•giz•er** (*or* **•gis•er)**
**the•ol•ogy** (*plural* **•ogies)**
**the•oma•chy** (*plural* **•chies)** battle among the gods
**theo•man•cy**
**theo•ma•nia**
**theo•ma•niac**
**the•ono•my** being governed by God
**the•opa•thy** religious emotion
**the•opha•gy** (*plural* **•gies)**
**the•opha•ny** (*plural* **•nies)** manifestation of deity
**Theophi•lus** moon crater
**theo•pho•bia**
**theo•pho•bi•ac**
**theo•phyl•line**
**the•or•bo** (*plural* **•bos)** musical instrument
**theo•rem**
**theo•remat•ic** (*or* **•rem•ic)**
**theo•remati•cal•ly**
**theo•reti•cal** (*or* **•ret•ic)**
**theo•reti•cal•ly**
**theo•reti•cian**
**theo•ret•ics**
**theo•rist**
**theo•ri•za•tion** (*or* **•sa•tion)**
**theo•rize** (*or* **•rise)**
**theo•riz•er** (*or* **r•is•er)**
**theo•ry** (*plural* **•ries)**
**theo•soph•ic** (*or* **•sophi•cal)**
**theo•sophi•cal•ly**
**the•oso•phism**
**the•oso•phist**
**the•oso•phy**
**thera•peu•tic**
**thera•peu•ti•cal•ly**
**thera•peu•tics**
**thera•pist**
**the•rap•sid** extinct reptile
**thera•py** (*plural* **•pies)**
**there** in that place; *compare* **their; they're**
**there•abouts** (*or* **•about)**
**there•after**
**there•at**
**there•by**
**there•fore**
**there•from**
**there•in**
**there•in•after**
**there•into**
**there•of**
**there•on**
**there•to**
**there•to•fore**
**there•under**
**there•upon**
**there•with** (*or* **•with•al)**
**the•ri•an•throp•ic** part animal, part human
**the•rian•thro•pism**
**the•rio•morph**
**the•rio•mor•phic** (*or* **•phous)** in animal form
**therm** unit
**ther•mae** public baths
**therm•aes•the•sia** (*US* **•es•)** sensitivity to temperature
**ther•mal**
**ther•mal•ly**
**ther•mal•ize** (*or* **•ise)**
**ther•mic**
**ther•mi•on**
**ther•mi•on•ic**
**ther•mi•on•ics**
**ther•mis•tor**
**Ther•mit** (*or* **•mite;** *Trademark*)
**ther•mite pro•cess**
**ther•mo•baro•graph**
**ther•mo•chemi•cal**
**ther•mo•chemi•cal•ly**
**ther•mo•chem•ist**
**ther•mo•chem•is•try**
**ther•mo•cline**
**ther•mo•cou•ple**
**ther•mo•dy•nam•ic** (*or* **•nami•cal)**
**ther•mo•dy•nami•cal•ly**
**ther•mo•dy•nam•ics**
**ther•mo•elec•tric** (*or* **•tri•cal)**
**ther•mo•elec•tri•cal•ly**
**ther•mo•elec•tric•ity**
**ther•mo•elec•tron**
**ther•mo•gen•esis**
**ther•mog•enous** (*or* **•mo•genet•ic)**
**ther•mo•gram**
**ther•mo•graph**
**ther•mog•ra•pher**
**ther•mo•graph•ic**
**ther•mog•ra•phy**
**ther•mo•junc•tion**
**ther•mo•la•bile**
**ther•mo•lu•mi•nes•cence**
**ther•mo•lu•mi•nes•cent**
**ther•moly•sis**
**ther•mo•lyt•ic**
**ther•mo•mag•net•ic**
**ther•mom•eter**
**ther•mo•met•ric** (*or* **•ri•cal)**
**ther•mo•met•ri•cal•ly**
**ther•mom•etry**
**ther•mo•nu•clear**
**ther•mo•phile** (*or* **•phil)** organism thriving in warmth
**ther•mo•phil•ic** (*or* **•phil•ous)**
**ther•mo•pile** radiant-energy detector
**ther•mo•plas•tic**
**ther•mo•plas•tic•ity**
**Ther•mopy•lae** battle site

**Ther•mos** (*Trademark*)
**ther•mo•scope**
**ther•mo•scop•ic** (*or* **•scopi•cal**)
**ther•mo•scopi•cal•ly**
**ther•mo•set•ting**
**ther•mo•si•phon**
**ther•mo•sphere** atmospheric layer
**ther•mo•sta•bil•ity**
**ther•mo•stable**
**ther•mo•stat**
**ther•mo•stat•ic**
**ther•mo•stati•cal•ly**
**ther•mo•stat•ics**
**ther•mo•tac•tic**
**ther•mo•tax•is** biology term
**ther•mo•ten•sile**
**ther•mo•thera•py**
**ther•mo•trop•ic**
**ther•mo•tro•pism** botany term
**the•roid** beastlike
**the•ro•pod** dinosaur
**the•ropo•dan**
**the•sau•rus** (*plural* **•ri** *or* **•ruses**)
**these**
**Theseus** mythological character
**the•sis** (*plural* **•ses**)
**Thespian**
**Thes•sa•li•an**
**Thes•sa•lo•nian**
**Thes•sa•lo•ni•ca** ancient Thessaloníki
**Thes•sa•lo•ní•ki** Greek port
**Thes•sa•ly** Greek region
**the•ta**
**thet•ic** of metrical stress
**theti•cal•ly**
**Thetis** Greek goddess
**the•urg•ic** (*or* **•ur•gi•cal**)
**the•ur•gi•cal•ly**
**the•ur•gist**
**the•ur•gy** (*plural* **•gies**) divine intervention
**thew** muscle
**they**
**they'd** they would; they had
**they'll** they will; they shall
**they're** they are; *compare* **their; there**
**they've** they have
**thia•mine** (*or* **•min**) vitamin
**thia•zine**
**thia•zole** (*or* **•zol**)
**thick**
**thick-and-thin**
**thick•en**
**thick•en•er**
**thick•en•ing**
**thick•et**
**thick•head**
**thick•headed•ness**
**thick•leaf** (*plural* **•leaves**) plant
**thick•ly**
**thick•ness**
**thick•set**
**thick-skinned**
**thick-witted**
**thick-witted•ness**
**thief** (*plural* **thieves**)
**thieve**
**thiev•ery** (*plural* **•eries**)
**thiev•ing**
**thiev•ing•ly**
**thiev•ish**
**thiev•ish•ness**
**thigh**
**thigh•bone**
**thig•mo•tac•tic**
**thig•mo•tax•is** biology term
**thig•mo•trop•ic**
**thig•mot•ro•pism** botany term
**thim•ble**
**thim•ble•ful** (*plural* **•fuls**)
**thimble•rig** game
**thimble•weed**
**thimble•wit** *US* dunce
**thi•mero•sal** antiseptic
**thin** (*adj* **thin•ner, thin•nest;** *verb* **thin•ning, thinned**)
**thine**
**thin-film** electronics term
**thing**
**thingu•ma•bob** (*or* **thinga•**)
**thingu•ma•jig** (*or* **thinga•**)
**think** (**think•ing, thought**)
**think•able**
**think•er**
**think•ing**
**think-tank**
**thin•ner**
**thin•ness**
**thin•nish**
**thin-skinned**
**thio•cya•nate**
**thio•cy•an•ic acid**
**thio-ether**
**thiol**
**thi•on•ic** of sulphur
**thio•nine** (*or* **•nin**)
**thio•nyl**
**thio•pen•tone** (*US* **•tal**)
**thio•phen** (*or* **•phene**)
**thio•sina•mine**
**thio•sul•phate** (*US* **•fate**)
**thio•sul•phur•ic acid** (*US* **•fur•**)
**thio•ura•cil**
**thio•urea**
**third**
**third-rate**
**third•stream** jazz
**thirl** *Dialect* to drill
**Thirl•mere** Cumbrian lake
**thirst**
**thirst•er**
**thirsti•ly**
**thirsti•ness**
**thirsty** (**thirsti•er, thirsti•est**)
**thir•teen**
**thir•teenth**
**thir•ti•eth**
**thir•ty** (*plural* **•ties**)
**this**
**this•tle**
**thistle•down**
**this•tly**
**thith•er** (*or* **•er•ward**)
**thither•to**
**thixo•trop•ic**
**thix•ot•ro•py** chemistry term
**thole** (*or* **thole•pin**)
**tho•los** (*plural* **•loi**) tomb
**Tho•mism** doctrine of Thomas Aquinas
**Tho•mist**
**Thon•bu•ri** Thai city
**thong**
**Thor** Norse god
**tho•rac•ic** (*or* **•ra•cal**)
**tho•ra•co•plas•ty** (*plural* **•ties**) surgery
**thora•coto•my** (*plural* **•mies**)
**thor•ax** (*plural* **thor•axes** *or* **tho•ra•ces**)
**tho•ria** chemical compound

**tho•ria•nite** mineral
**tho•ric**
**tho•rite** mineral
**tho•rium** radioactive element
**thorn**
**thorn•back** fish
**thorn•bill**
**thorni•ly**
**thorni•ness**
**thorny** (**thorni•er, thorni•est**)
**tho•ron** radioisotope of radon
**thor•ough**
**Thorough•bred** horse
**thorough•bred** purebred
**thorough•fare**
**thorough•going**
**thor•ough•ly**
**thor•ough•ness**
**thorough•paced**
**thorough•pin** swollen hock
**those**
**Thoth** Egyptian god
**thou**
**though**
**thought**
**thought•ful**
**thought•ful•ly**
**thought•ful•ness**
**thought•less**
**thought•less•ness**
**thought-out**
**thou•sand**
**thou•sandth**
**Thrace** Balkan region
**thrall**
**thrall•dom**
**thrash**
**thrash•er**
**thrash•ing**
**thrawn** *Dialect* crooked
**thread**
**thread•bare**
**thread•er**
**thread•fin** (*plural* **•fin** *or* **•fins**) fish
**threadi•ness**
**Thread•needle Street**
**thread•worm**
**thready** (**threadi•er, threadi•est**)
**threap** (*or* **threep**) *Dialect* to scold
**threat**
**threat•en**
**threat•en•er**
**threat•en•ing**
**three**
**three-dimension•al**
**three•fold**
**three-legged**
**three-phase**
**three-piece**
**three-ply**
**three-quarter** (*adj*)
**three-quarters**
**three•score**
**three•some**
**three-wheeler**
**threm•ma•tol•ogy** science of breeding
**threno•dy** (*or* **thre•node**; *plural* **•dies** *or* **•nodes**) ode of lamentation
**threo•nine** amino acid
**thresh**
**thresh•er**
**thresh•old**
**threw**
**thrice**
**thrift**
**thrifti•ly**
**thrifti•ness**
**thrift•less**
**thrift•less•ness**
**thrifty** (**thrifti•er, thrifti•est**)
**thrill**
**thrill•er**
**thrill•ing**
**thrips** (*plural* **thrips**) insect
**thrive** (**thriv•ing, thrived** *or* **throve, thrived** *or* **thriv•en**)
**throat**
**throati•ly**
**throati•ness**
**throat•lash** (*or* **•latch**) bridle strap
**throaty** (**throati•er, throati•est**)
**throb** (**throb•bing, throbbed**)
**throe** violent pang; *compare* throw
**throm•bin** enzyme
**throm•bo•cyte**
**throm•bo•cyt•ic**
**throm•bo•em•bo•lism**
**throm•bo•gen** protein
**throm•bo•phle•bi•tis**
**throm•bo•plas•tic**
**throm•bo•plas•tin**
**throm•bose** (*verb*)
**throm•bo•sis**
**throm•bot•ic**
**throm•bus** (*plural* **•bi**) blood clot
**throne**
**throng**
**thros•tle** thrush
**throt•tle**
**throt•tler**
**through**
**through•out**
**through•put**
**through•way**
**throw** (**throw•ing, threw, thrown**) cast; *compare* throe
**throw•away** (*adj, noun*)
**throw•back**
**throw•er**
**thrown**
**throw•ster** yarn spinner
**thrum** (**thrum•ming, thrummed**)
**thrum•mer**
**thrush**
**thrust**
**thrust•er**
**thud** (**thud•ding, thud•ded**)
**Thug** Indian assassin
**thug**
**thug•gee** practices of Thugs
**thug•gery**
**thug•gish**
**thu•ja** (*or* **•ya**) tree
**Thule** ancient northern land; Eskimo settlement
**thu•lium** chemical element
**thumb**
**thumb•nail**
**thumb•nut**
**thumb•print**
**thumb•screw**
**thumb•stall**
**thumb•tack** *US* drawing pin
**thump**
**thump•er**
**thump•ing**
**thun•der**

**thunder•bird**
**thunder•bolt**
**thunder•clap**
**thunder•cloud**
**thun•der•er**
**thunder•head** cloud
**thun•der•ing**
**thun•der•ous**
**thunder•shower**
**thunder•stone**
**thunder•storm**
**thunder•struck** (*or* **•stricken)**
**thun•dery**
**Thur•gau** Swiss canton
**thu•ri•ble** incense container
**thu•ri•fer** thurible carrier
**Thu•rin•gia** German state
**Thu•rin•gian**
**Thur•rock** area of Essex
**Thurs•day**
**thus**
**thwack**
**thwack•er**
**thwart**
**thwart•er**
**thy**
**Thyestes** mythological character
**thy•la•cine** animal
**thyme** herb
**thym•elaea•ceous** botany term
**thym•ic**
**thy•mi•dine**
**thy•mine**
**thy•mol**
**thy•mus** (*plural* **•muses** *or* **•mi)**
**thymy** of thyme
**thy•ra•tron**
**thy•ris•tor**
**thy•ro•cal•ci•ton•in** hormone
**thy•roid**
**thy•roid•ec•to•my** (*plural* **•mies)**
**thy•roidi•tis**
**thy•ro•toxi•co•sis**
**thy•ro•tro•pin** (*or* **•phin)** hormone
**thy•rox•ine** (*or* **•in)** hormone
**thyrse** (*plural* **therses)** botany term
**thyr•soid**
**thyr•sus** (*plural* **•si)** Bacchus' staff
**thysa•nu•ran** insect
**thy•self**
**ti** plant; *variant spelling of* **te**
**Tia Ma•ria** (*Trademark*)
**ti•ara**
**ti•ar•aed**
**Ti•ber**
**Ti•bes•ti** African mountains
**Ti•bet**
**Ti•bet•an**
**tibia** (*plural* **tibiae** *or* **tibias)**
**tib•ial**
**tic** twitch; *compare* **tick**
**ti•cal** (*plural* **•cals** *or* **•cal)**
**tic dou•lou•reux** neuralgia
**Ti•ci•no** Swiss canton; river
**tick** parasite; *compare* **tic**
**tick•er**
**tick•et**
**tick•ing**
**tick•le**
**tick•ler**
**tick•lish**
**tick•lish•ness**
**tick•ly**
**tick•tack**
**tick-tack-toe** *US* noughts and crosses
**tick•tock**
**Ti•con•dero•ga** US battle site
**tid•al**
**tid•al•ly**
**tid•bit** *US spelling of* **titbit**
**tid•dler**
**tid•dly**
**tiddly•winks**
**tide**
**tide•mark**
**tide•water**
**tide•way**
**ti•di•ly**
**ti•di•ness**
**tid•ings**
**tidy** (*adj* **tidi•er, tidi•est;** *verb* **ti•dies, tidy•ing, ti•died;** *noun, plural* **ti•dies)**
**tie (ty•ing, tied)**
**tie•back** *US* curtain fastening
**tie•breaker** (*or* **•break)**
**tied**
**tie-dyeing**
**tie-dyed**
**tie•man•nite** mineral
**Tien•tsin** (*or* **T'ien-ching)** Chinese city
**tie•pin**
**tier** layer; *compare* **tear**
**tierce** fencing position; *variant spelling of* **terce**
**tiered**
**Tier•ra del Fue•go** South American archipelago
**tiff**
**tif•fa•ny** (*plural* **•nies)** fabric
**tif•fin** meal
**Tif•lis** *variant spelling of* **Tbilisi**
**ti•ger**
**ti•ger•ish**
**tiger's-eye** (*or* **tiger•eye)** gemstone
**tight**
**tight•en**
**tight•en•er**
**tight•fisted**
**tight•knit**
**tight-lipped**
**tight•ness**
**tight•rope**
**tights**
**tight•wad**
**tig•lic acid**
**ti•gon** (*or* **tig•lon)** animal
**Ti•gré** Ethiopian region
**ti•gress**
**Ti•gri•nya** Ethiopian language
**Ti•gris** Asian river
**Ti•jua•na** Mexican city
**tike** *variant spelling of* **tyke**
**tiki** Maori amulet
**ti•lapia** fish
**Til•burg** Dutch city
**Til•bury** Essex region
**til•bury** (*plural* **•buries)** carriage
**til•de** phonetic symbol
**tile**
**tile•fish** (*plural* **•fish** *or* **•fishes)**
**til•er**
**tilia•ceous** botany term
**til•ing**
**till**

**till•able**
**till•age**
**til•land•sia** plant
**till•er**
**til•li•cum** *US* friend
**Til•sit** *former name of* **Sovetsk**
**tilt**
**tilt•er**
**tilth**
**tilt•yard**
**Tima•ru** New Zealand port
**tim•bal** (*or* **tym•**) kettledrum
**tim•bale** pie
**tim•ber** wood; *compare* **timbre**
**timber•head**
**tim•ber•ing**
**timber•land**
**timber•work**
**timber•yard**
**tim•bre** tone quality; *compare* **timber**
**tim•brel** tambourine
**Tim•buk•tu** Malian town
**time**
**time•able**
**time•card**
**time-consum•ing**
**time-honoured**
**time•keeper**
**time•keeping**
**time-lag**
**time•less**
**time•less•ness**
**time•li•ness**
**time•ly** (**•li•er, •li•est**)
**time•ous** *Scot* timely
**time•piece**
**tim•er**
**time•saver**
**time•saving**
**time•server**
**time•serving**
**time•table**
**time•work**
**time•worker**
**time•worn**
**tim•id**
**ti•mid•ity** (*or* **tim•id•ness**)
**tim•ing**
**Ti•mi•şoa•ra** Romanian city
**ti•moc•ra•cy** (*plural* **•cies**) political system
**Ti•mor** Indonesian island
**tim•or•ous**
**tim•or•ous•ness**
**timo•thy** grass
**tim•pa•ni** (*or* **tym•**; *sing.* **•no**) kettledrums; *compare* **tympanum**
**tim•pa•nist** (*or* **tym•**)
**timps** *short for* **timpani**
**tin** (**tin•ning, tinned**)
**tina•mou** bird
**tin•cal** borax
**tinct** tinted
**tinc•to•rial** of dyeing
**tinc•ture**
**tin•der**
**tinder•box**
**tin•dery**
**tine**
**tinea** ringworm; *compare* **taenia**
**tin•eal**
**tin•eid** moth
**tin•foil**
**ting**
**ting-a-ling**
**tinge** (**tinge•ing** *or* **ting•ing, tinged**)
**tin•gle**
**tin•gler**
**tin•gling•ly**
**tin•gly**
**ti•ni•ly**
**ti•ni•ness**
**tink•er**
**tink•er•er**
**tin•kle**
**tin•kling**
**tin•kly**
**tin liz•zie** *Slang* decrepit car
**tinned**
**tin•ni•ly**
**tin•ni•ness**
**tin•ning**
**tin•ni•tus** ringing in ears
**tin•ny** (**•ni•er, •ni•est**)
**tin-plate** (*verb*)
**tin•pot** *Slang* inferior
**tin•sel** (**•sel•ling, •selled;** *US* **•sel•ing, •seled**)
**tin•smith**
**tint**
**Tin•tag•el**
**tint•ed**
**tin•tin•nabu•lar** (*or* **•lary, •lous**)
**tin•tin•nabu•la•tion**
**tin•tin•nabu•lum** (*plural* **•la**) bell
**tin•type** photographic print
**tin•ware**
**tin•work**
**tiny** (**tini•er, tini•est**)
**tip** (**tip•ping, tipped**)
**tip•cat** game
**tip-off** (*noun*)
**tip•pable**
**tipped**
**tip•per**
**Tip•per•ary**
**tip•pet** cape
**tip•ping**
**tip•ple**
**tip•pler**
**tip•si•ly**
**tip•si•ness**
**tip•staff**
**tip•ster**
**tip•sy** (**•si•er, •si•est**)
**tip•toe** (**•toe•ing, •toed**)
**tip•top**
**ti•rade**
**Ti•ra•na** (*or* **•në**) Albanian capital
**tire** exhaust; *US spelling of* **tyre**
**tire•less**
**tire•less•ness**
**tire•some**
**tire•some•ness**
**Ti•rich Mir** Pakistani mountain
**tir•ing**
**tiro** *variant spelling of* **tyro**
**Ti•rol** *variant spelling of* **Tyrol**
**Ti•ros** US satellite
**Ti•ru•nel•veli** Indian city
**'tis**
**ti•sane**
**tis•sue**
**tit**
**Ti•tan** Greek god; satellite of Saturn
**ti•tan•ate** chemistry term
**Ti•tan•esque**
**Ti•ta•nia** satellite of Uranus
**ti•tan•ic** huge; chemistry term

**ti•tani•cal•ly**
**ti•tan•if•er•ous**
**Ti•tan•ism** spirit of rebellion
**ti•tan•ite** mineral
**ti•ta•nium** chemical element
**ti•tano•saur**
**ti•tano•there** extinct mammal
**ti•tan•ous**
**tit•bit** (*US* **tid•**)
**ti•ter** *US spelling of* **titre**
**tith•able**
**tithe**
**tith•er**
**tith•ing**
**Tithonus** mythological character
**titi** (*plural* **titis**) monkey
**tit•il•late**
**tit•il•lat•ing**
**tit•il•la•tion**
**tit•il•la•tive**
**titi•vate** (*or* **tit•ti•**)
**titi•va•tion** (*or* **tit•ti•**)
**titi•va•tor** (*or* **tit•ti•**)
**tit•lark**
**ti•tle**
**ti•tled**
**title•holder**
**tit•man** (*plural* **•men**) small piglet
**tit•mouse** (*plural* **•mice**)
**Ti•to•grad** *former name of* **Podgorica**
**Ti•to•ism**
**Ti•to•ist**
**ti•trant** chemistry term
**ti•trat•able**
**ti•trate**
**ti•tra•tion**
**ti•tre** (*US* **•ter**)
**tit•ter**
**tit•ter•er**
**tit•tle**
**tittle-tattle**
**tittle-tattler**
**tit•tup** (**•tup•ping, •tupped**)
**titu•ba•tion** medical term
**titu•lar** (*or* **•lary**; *plural* **•lars** *or* **•laries**)
**Tiv** (*plural* **Tivs** *or* **Tiv**) African people
**Tivo•li** Italian town
**tiz•zy** (*plural* **•zies**)
**Tlax•ca•la** Mexican state
**Tlin•git** (*plural* **•gits** *or* **•git**) American Indian
**tme•sis** linguistics term
**to**
**toad**
**toad•fish** (*plural* **•fish** *or* **•fishes**)
**toad•flax**
**toad•ish** (*or* **•like**)
**toad•stone**
**toad•stool**
**toady** (*noun, plural* **toadies**; *verb* **toadies, toady•ing, toad•ied**)
**toady•ism**
**to-and-fro** (*adj*)
**toast**
**toast•er**
**toast•master** (*fem* **•mistress**)
**to•bac•co** (*plural* **•cos** *or* **•coes**)
**to•bac•co•nist**
**To•ba•go** West Indian island
**to•bog•gan**
**to•bog•gan•er** (*or* **•ist**)
**To•bruk** Libyan port
**toby jug**
**toc•ca•ta**
**To•char•ian** (*or* **•khar•**) language
**to•col•ogy** (*or* **•kol•**) obstetrics
**to•coph•er•ol** vitamin
**toc•sin** alarm bell; *compare* **toxin**
**tod**
**to•day**
**tod•dle**
**tod•dler**
**tod•dy** (*plural* **•dies**)
**to-do** (*plural* **-dos**)
**tody** (*plural* **todies**) bird
**toe** (**toe•ing, toed**)
**toea** coin
**toe•cap**
**toed**
**toe•hold**
**toe-in**
**toe•ing**
**toe•nail**
**toey** *Austral* nervous
**toff**
**tof•fee** (*or* **•fy**; *plural* **•fees** *or* **•fies**)
**toft** homestead
**tog** (**tog•ging, togged**)
**toga**
**to•geth•er**
**to•geth•er•ness**
**togged**
**tog•gery** clothes
**tog•ging**
**tog•gle**
**Tog•li•at•ti** Russian city
**Togo** African republic
**To•go•lese**
**to•he•roa** mollusc
**toil**
**toile** fabric
**toil•er**
**toi•let** lavatory
**toi•let•ry** (*plural* **•ries**)
**toi•lette** act of dressing
**toil•some** (*or* **•ful**)
**toil•some•ness**
**To•kay** wine
**to•kay** lizard
**to•ken**
**to•ken•ism**
**toko•loshe** mythical creature
**To•kyo**
**tola** unit of weight
**to•lan** (*or* **•lane**) organic compound
**tol•bu•ta•mide** drug
**told**
**tole** metal ware
**To•ledo** Spanish city; US city
**tol•er•able**
**tol•er•able•ness** (*or* **•abil•ity**)
**tol•er•ably**
**tol•er•ance**
**tol•er•ant**
**tol•er•ate**
**tol•era•tion**
**tol•era•tion•ism**
**tol•era•tion•ist**
**tol•era•tive**
**tol•era•tor**
**toli•dine**
**toll**
**toll•booth** (*or* **tol•**)
**toll•gate**
**toll•house**
**Tol•pud•dle** Dorset town; martyrs

**Tol•tec** (*plural* **•tecs** *or* **•tec**) American Indian
**tolu•ate** chemical compound
**To•lu•ca** Mexican city
**tolu•ene**
**to•lu•ic acid**
**to•lui•dine**
**tolu•yl**
**tol•yl**
**tom** male animal
**toma•hawk**
**tom•al•ley** lobster liver
**to•man** coin
**to•ma•to** (*plural* **•toes**)
**tomb**
**tom•bac** (*or* **tam•**) alloy
**tomb•like**
**tom•bo•la** lottery
**tom•bo•lo** (*plural* **•los**) sand bar
**tom•boy**
**tom•boy•ish**
**tomb•stone**
**tom•cat**
**tome** book
**to•men•tose**
**to•men•tum** (*plural* **•ta**) biology term
**tom•fool**
**tom•fool•ery** (*plural* **•eries**)
**tom•my** (*plural* **•mies**)
**tommy•rot**
**tomo•gram**
**to•mog•ra•phy** X-ray technique
**to•mor•row**
**tom•pi•on** *variant spelling of* **tampion**
**Tomsk** Russian city
**tom•tit**
**tom-tom** drum; *compare* **tam-tam**
**ton** imperial weight; *compare* **tonne; tun**
**ton•al**
**to•nal•ity** (*plural* **•ities**)
**ton•al•ly**
**Ton•bridge** Kent town; *compare* **Tunbridge Wells**
**ton•do** (*plural* **•di**) circular painting
**tone**
**tone-deaf**
**tone•less**
**tone•less•ness**
**ton•eme** linguistics term
**ton•er**
**to•net•ic** linguistics term
**tong**
**Tonga** Pacific kingdom
**Ton•ga** (*plural* **•gas** *or* **•ga**) African people
**Tong•an**
**tongs**
**tongue** (**tongu•ing, tongued**)
**tongue-tied**
**ton•ic**
**toni•cal•ly**
**to•nic•ity**
**to•night**
**ton•ing**
**tonk** *Austral* effeminate man
**ton•ka** tree; bean
**Ton•kin** (*or* **Tong•king**) Chinese gulf
**Ton•le Sap** Cambodian lake
**ton•nage** (*or* **tun•**)
**tonne** metric weight; *compare* **ton; tun**
**ton•neau** (*plural* **•neaus** *or* **•neaux**)
**to•nom•eter**
**tono•met•ric**
**to•nom•etry**
**ton•sil**
**ton•sil•lar** (*or* **•lary**)
**ton•sil•lec•to•my** (*plural* **•mies**)
**ton•sil•lit•ic**
**ton•sil•li•tis**
**ton•sil•loto•my** (*plural* **•mies**)
**ton•so•rial**
**ton•sure**
**ton•tine** annuity scheme
**to•nus** muscle tone
**too**
**toodle-oo**
**took**
**tool**
**tool•er**
**tool•ing**
**tool•less**
**tool-maker**
**tool-making**
**toon** tree
**toot**
**toot•er**
**tooth** (*plural* **teeth**)
**tooth•ache**
**tooth•brush**
**toothed**
**toothi•ly**
**toothi•ness**
**tooth•less**
**tooth•paste**
**tooth•pick**
**tooth•some**
**tooth•some•ness**
**tooth•wort**
**toothy** (**tooth•ier, toothi•est**)
**too•tle**
**too•tler**
**toots** (*or* **toot•sie**) term of endearment
**toot•sy** (*or* **tootsy-wootsy**; *plural* **•sies** *or* **-•wootsies**) *Slang* foot
**top** (**top•ping, topped**)
**top•arch** ruler
**top•ar•chy**
**to•paz**
**to•pazo•lite** gemstone
**top•coat**
**top-dress** (*verb*)
**tope**
**to•pee** (*or* **topi**; *plural* **•pees** *or* **topis**) tropical helmet
**To•pe•ka** US city
**top•er**
**top-flight** (*adj*)
**top•gal•lant** ship's mast
**top-heavily**
**top-heaviness**
**top-heavy**
**To•phet** (*or* **•pheth**) biblical place
**to•phus** (*plural* **•phi**) gout stone
**topi** *variant spelling of* **topee**
**to•pi•ar•ian**
**to•pia•rist**
**to•pi•ary**
**top•ic**
**topi•cal**
**topi•cal•ity**
**topi•cal•ly**
**top•knot**
**top•less**
**top•less•ness**
**top-level** (*adj*)
**top•lofty** haughty

**top•mast**
**top•min•now** (*plural* **•now** *or* **•nows**) fish
**top•most**
**top•notch**
**top•notcher**
**to•pog•ra•pher**
**topo•graph•ic** (*or* **•graphi•cal**)
**topo•graphi•cal•ly**
**to•pog•ra•phy** (*plural* **•phies**) mapping; *compare* **topology**
**topo•logic** (*or* **•logi•cal**)
**topo•logi•cal•ly**
**to•polo•gist**
**to•pol•ogy** branch of geometry; *compare* **topography**
**topo•nym**
**topo•nym•ic** (*or* **•nymi•cal**)
**to•pony•my**
**top•os** (*plural* **•oi**) basic concept
**topo•type**
**topped**
**top•per**
**top•ping**
**top•ple**
**top•sail**
**top-secret** (*adj*)
**top-shell** mollusc
**top•side**
**top•soil**
**top•spin**
**topsy-turvy**
**toque** (*or* **to•quet**) hat
**tor** hill; *compare* **torr**
**To•rah** Jewish writings
**Tor•bay** Devon town
**tor•bern•ite** mineral
**torch**
**torch•bearer**
**tor•chère** candelabrum stand
**tor•chier** (*or* **•chiere**) lamp
**torch•light**
**torch•lit**
**tor•chon** lace
**torch•wood**
**tore**
**torea•dor**
**to•re•ro** (*plural* **•ros**) bullfighter
**to•reu•tic**
**to•reu•tics** metalworking
**Tor•faen** Welsh county borough
**tori** *plural of* **torus**
**tor•ic**
**to•rii** (*plural* **•rii**) gateway
**tor•ment**
**tor•ment•ed•ly**
**tor•men•til** plant
**tor•ment•ing•ly**
**tor•men•tor** (*or* **•ment•er**)
**torn**
**tor•nad•ic**
**tor•na•do** (*plural* **•does** *or* **•dos**) storm; *compare* **tournedos**
**to•roid** geometry term
**to•roi•dal**
**to•roi•dal•ly**
**To•ron•to**
**To•ron•to•nian**
**to•rose** (*or* **•rous**) biology term
**tor•pe•do** (*noun, plural* **•does**; *verb* **•does, •do•ing, •doed**)
**tor•pid**
**tor•pid•ity** (*or* **•ness**)
**tor•por**
**tor•por•if•ic**
**tor•quate**
**Tor•quay**
**torque** metal collar; mechanical force
**tor•ques** zoology term
**torr** unit; *compare* **tor**
**Tor•rance** US city
**tor•re•fac•tion** (*or* **•ri•**)
**tor•re•fy** (*or* **•ri•**; **•fies, •fy•ing, •fied**) roast
**tor•rent**
**tor•ren•tial**
**tor•ren•tial•ly**
**Tor•re•ón** Mexican city
**Tor•ri•cel•lian** physics term
**tor•rid**
**tor•rid•ity** (*or* **•ness**)
**tor•sade** ornament on hat
**tor•si•bil•ity**
**tor•sion**
**tor•sion•al**
**torsk** (*plural* **torsks** *or* **torsk**) fish
**tor•so** (*plural* **•sos** *or* **•si**)
**tort** legal term
**torte** cake
**tor•tel•li•ni** pasta
**tort•feasor** legal term
**tor•ti•col•lar**
**tor•ti•col•lis** wryneck
**tor•til•la** Mexican pancake
**tor•tious** legal term; *compare* **tortuous; torturous**
**tor•toise**
**tortoise•shell**
**tor•to•ni** ice cream
**tor•tri•cid** moth
**tor•tu•os•ity** (*plural* **•ities**)
**tor•tu•ous** twisting; devious; *compare* **tortious; torturous**
**tor•tu•ous•ness**
**tor•ture**
**tor•tured•ly**
**tor•tur•er**
**tor•ture•some**
**tor•tur•ing•ly**
**tor•tur•ous** causing pain; *compare* **tortious; tortuous**
**To•ruń** Polish city
**to•rus** (*plural* **•ri**)
**Tory** (*plural* **Tories**)
**To•ry•ism**
**tosh**
**toss**
**toss•er**
**toss•pot** *Archaic* drinker
**tot** (**tot•ting, tot•ted**)
**to•tal** (**•tal•ling, •talled**; *US* **•tal•ing,•taled**)
**to•tali•tar•ian**
**to•tali•tar•ian•ism**
**to•tal•ity** (*plural* **•ities**)
**to•tali•za•tion** (*or* **•sa•tion**)
**to•tali•za•tor** (*or* **•sa•tor**) betting machine
**to•tal•ize** (*or* **•ise**)
**to•tal•iz•er** (*or* **•is•er**)
**to•tal•ly**
**to•ta•quine** drug
**tote**
**to•tem**
**to•tem•ic**
**to•temi•cal•ly**
**to•tem•ism**
**to•tem•ist**
**to•tem•is•tic**
**tot•er**
**to•ti•pal•mate**
**to•ti•pal•ma•tion**

**to•tipo•ten•cy**
**to•tipo•tent** zoology term
**tot•ted**
**tot•ter**
**tot•ter•er**
**tot•tery**
**tot•ting**
**tou•can**
**touch**
**touch•able**
**touch•down**
**tou•ché** acknowledgment
**touch•er**
**touchi•ly**
**touchi•ness**
**touch•ing**
**touch•ing•ly**
**touch•line**
**touch•mark**
**touch•stone**
**touch-type**
**touch-typist**
**touch•wood**
**touchy (touchi•er, touchi•est)**
**tough**
**tough•en**
**tough•en•er**
**toughie**
**tough•ish**
**tough•ness**
**Tou•lon** French town
**Tou•louse** French city
**tou•pee** hairpiece
**tour**
**tou•ra•co** (*or* **tu•**; *plural* **•cos**) bird
**Tou•raine** French region
**Tou•rane** Vietnamese port
**tour•bil•lion** whirlwind
**tour de force** (*plural* **tours de force)**
**tour•er**
**tour•ism**
**tour•ist**
**tour•is•tic**
**tour•isty**
**tour•ma•line**
**tour•ma•lin•ic**
**tour•na•ment**
**tour•nedos** (*plural* **•nedos)** steak; *compare* **tornado**
**tour•ney**
**tour•ni•quet**
**Tours** French town
**tou•sle**
**tous-les-mois** plant
**tout** *Slang* solicit
**tout à fait** *French* completely
**tout en•sem•ble** *French* all in all
**tout le monde** *French* everyone
**to•va•risch (•rich** *or* **•rish)** Russian term of address
**tow**
**tow•age**
**to•ward** (*adj*)
**to•wards** (*prep.*)
**tow•bar**
**tow•boat**
**tow•el (•el•ling, •elled;** *US* **•el•ing, •eled)**
**tow•el•ling** (*US* **•el•ing)**
**tow•er**
**Tow•er Ham•lets** London borough
**tow•er•ing**
**tow-haired**
**tow•head**
**tow•hee** bird
**tow•line**
**town**
**townee**
**town•hall**
**town•scape**
**town•ship**
**towns•man** (*plural* **•men)**
**towns•people** (*or* **•folk)**
**towns•woman** (*plural* **•women)**
**tow•path**
**tow•rope**
**tox•aemia** (*US* **•emia)**
**tox•aemic** (*US* **•emic)**
**tox•al•bu•min**
**toxa•phene**
**tox•ic**
**toxi•cal•ly**
**toxi•cant** poison
**tox•ic•ity**
**toxi•co•gen•ic**
**toxi•co•logi•cal** (*or* **•log•ic)**
**toxi•co•logi•cal•ly**
**toxi•colo•gist**
**toxi•col•ogy**
**toxi•co•sis**
**tox•in** poison; *compare* tocsin
**tox•oid**
**tox•ophi•lite** archer
**tox•ophi•lit•ic**
**tox•ophi•ly**
**toxo•plas•mic**
**toxo•plas•mo•sis**
**toy**
**To•ya•ma** Japanese city
**toy•er**
**tra•beated** (*or* **•beate)** architectural term
**tra•bea•tion**
**tra•becu•la** (*plural* **•lae)** anatomy term
**tra•becu•lar** (*or* **•late)**
**Trab•zon** Turkish port
**trace**
**trace•abil•ity** (*or* **•able•ness)**
**trace•able**
**trace•less**
**trac•er**
**trac•ery** (*plural* **•eries)**
**tra•chea** (*plural* **•cheae)**
**tra•cheal**
**tra•cheate**
**tra•che•id** (*or* **•ide)** plant cell
**tra•chei•dal**
**tra•che•itis**
**tra•cheo•phyte** botany term
**tra•che•osto•my** (*plural* **•mies)**
**tra•che•oto•mist**
**tra•che•oto•my** (*plural* **•mies)**
**tra•cho•ma** eye disease
**tra•choma•tous**
**tra•chyte** rock
**tra•chyt•ic**
**trachy•toid**
**trac•ing**
**track**
**track•able**
**track•er**
**track•less**
**track•suit**
**tract**
**trac•tabil•ity** (*or* **•table•ness)**
**trac•table**
**trac•tably**
**Trac•tar•ian**
**Trac•tari•an•ism** religious movement
**trac•tate** treatise
**trac•tile** ductile

**trac•til•ity**
**trac•tion**
**trac•tion•al**
**trac•tive**
**trac•tor**
**trad** *Slang* traditional jazz
**trad•able** (*or* **trade•**)
**trade**
**trade-in** (*noun*)
**trade•mark**
**trade-off** (*noun*)
**trad•er**
**trad•es•can•tia** plant
**trades•man** (*plural* **•men**)
**trades•people** (*or* **•folk**)
**trades•woman** (*plural* **•women**)
**trade union** (*plural* **trade unions**) *note* **Trades Union Congress**
**trad•ing**
**tra•di•tion**
**tra•di•tion•al**
**tra•di•tion•al•ism**
**tra•di•tion•al•ist**
**tra•di•tion•al•is•tic**
**tra•di•tion•ally**
**tra•di•tion•ist**
**tradi•tor** (*plural* **•to•res** *or* **•tors**) Christian betrayer
**tra•duce**
**tra•duce•ment**
**tra•duc•er**
**tra•du•cian•ism** theology term
**tra•du•cian•ist** (*or* **•du•cian**)
**tra•du•cian•is•tic**
**tra•duc•ible**
**Tra•fal•gar**
**traf•fic** (**•fick•ing, •ficked**)
**traf•fi•ca•tor** car indicator
**traf•fick•er**
**Traf•ford** area of Greater Manchester
**traga•canth** plant
**tra•gal**
**tra•gedian** (*fem* **•gedi•enne**)
**trag•edy** (*plural* **•edies**)
**trag•ic** (*or* **tragi•cal**)
**tragi•cal•ly**
**tragi•com•edy** (*plural* **•edies**)
**tragi•com•ic** (*or* **•comi•cal**)
**tragi•comi•cal•ly**
**trago•pan** bird
**tra•gus** (*plural* **•gi**) part of ear
**trail**
**trail•blazer**
**trail•blazing**
**trail•er**
**trail•ing•ly**
**trail•less**
**train**
**train•able**
**train•band** English militia
**train•bearer**
**trainee**
**train•er**
**train•ing**
**traipse**
**trait** characteristic
**trai•tor**
**trai•tor•ous**
**trai•tor•ous•ness**
**trai•tress**
**tra•ject** *Archaic* transport
**tra•jec•tile**
**tra•jec•tion**
**tra•jec•tory** (*plural* **•tories**)
**tra-la**
**Tra•lee** Irish town
**tram** (**tram•ming, trammed**)
**tram•car**
**tram•line**
**tram•mel** (**•el•ling, •elled**; *US* **•el•ing, •eled**)
**tram•mel•ler** (*US* **•mel•er**)
**tram•mie** *Austral* tram driver
**tra•mon•tane** (*or* **trans•**) across mountains
**tramp**
**tramp•er**
**tramp•ish**
**tramp•ish•ness**
**tram•ple**
**tram•pler**
**tram•po•line**
**tram•po•lin•er** (*or* **•ist**)
**tram•way**
**trance**
**trance•like**
**tranche**
**tran•nie** *Slang* transistor radio
**tran•quil**
**tran•quil•lity**
**tran•quil•li•za•tion** (*or* **•sa•tion**; *US* **•quili•za•tion**)
**tran•quil•lize** (*or* **•lise**; *US* **•quil•ize**)
**tran•quil•liz•er** (*US* **•quil•iz•er**)
**tran•quil•ly**
**tran•quil•ness**
**trans•act**
**trans•ac•ti•nide**
**trans•ac•tion**
**trans•ac•tion•al**
**trans•ac•tor**
**trans•al•pine**
**trans•at•lan•tic**
**Trans•cau•ca•sia** Central Asian region
**Trans•cau•ca•sian**
**trans•ceiv•er**
**trans•cend**
**tran•scend•ence** (*or* **•en•cy**)
**trans•cend•ent**
**tran•scen•den•tal**
**tran•scen•den•tal•ism**
**tran•scen•den•tal•ist**
**tran•scen•den•tal•ity**
**tran•scen•den•tal•ly**
**tran•scend•ent•ness**
**trans•con•ti•nen•tal**
**trans•con•ti•nen•tal•ly**
**tran•scrib•able**
**tran•scribe**
**tran•scrib•er**
**tran•script**
**tran•scrip•tion**
**tran•scrip•tion•al** (*or* **•scrip•tive**)
**trans•cul•tura•tion**
**trans•cur•rent**
**trans•duc•er**
**trans•duc•tion**
**tran•sect**
**tran•sec•tion**
**tran•sept**
**tran•sep•tal**
**trans•eunt** philosophy term
**trans•fer** (**•fer•ring, •ferred**)
**trans•fer•abil•ity**
**trans•fer•able** (*or* **•fer•rable**)
**trans•fer•ase** enzyme
**trans•feree**
**trans•fer•ence**
**trans•fer•en•tial**
**trans•fer•rer** (*or in legal contexts* **•fer•or**)

**trans•fer•rin** biochemical compound
**trans•figu•ra•tion**
**trans•fig•ure**
**trans•fig•ure•ment**
**trans•fi•nite**
**trans•fix** (**•fix•ing, fixed** *or* **•fixt**)
**trans•fix•ion**
**trans•form**
**trans•form•able**
**trans•for•ma•tion**
**trans•for•ma•tion•al**
**trans•forma•tive**
**trans•form•er**
**trans•form•ism** evolutionary theory
**trans•form•ist**
**trans•fuse**
**trans•fus•er**
**trans•fus•ible** (*or* **•able**)
**trans•fu•sion**
**trans•fu•sive**
**trans•gress**
**trans•gress•ible**
**trans•gress•ing•ly**
**trans•gres•sion**
**trans•gres•sive**
**trans•gres•sor**
**tran•ship** *variant spelling of* **transship**
**trans•hu•mance** migration of livestock
**trans•hu•mant**
**tran•si•ence** (*or* **•en•cy, •ent•ness**)
**tran•si•ent**
**trans•il•lu•mi•nate**
**trans•il•lu•mi•na•tion**
**trans•il•lu•mi•na•tor**
**tran•sis•tor**
**tran•sis•tori•za•tion** (*or* **•sa•tion**)
**tran•sis•tor•ize** (*or* **•ise**)
**trans•it**
**tran•sit•able**
**tran•si•tion**
**tran•si•tion•al** (*or* **•ary**)
**tran•si•tion•al•ly**
**tran•si•tive**
**tran•si•tive•ness** (*or* **•tiv•ity**)
**tran•si•to•ri•ly**
**tran•si•to•ri•ness**
**tran•si•tory**
**Trans-Jordan**
**Trans-Jordanian**
**Trans•kei** former South African province
**Trans•kei•an**
**trans•lat•abil•ity** (*or* **•able•ness**)
**trans•lat•able**
**trans•late**
**trans•la•tion**
**trans•la•tion•al**
**trans•la•tor**
**trans•la•to•rial**
**trans•lit•er•ate**
**trans•lit•era•tion**
**trans•lit•era•tor**
**trans•lo•cate**
**trans•lo•ca•tion**
**trans•lu•cence** (*or* **•cen•cy**)
**trans•lu•cent**
**trans•lu•nar** (*or* **•nary**)
**trans•mi•grant**
**trans•mi•grate**
**trans•mi•gra•tion**
**trans•mi•gra•tion•al**
**trans•mi•gra•tive**
**trans•mi•gra•tor**
**trans•mi•gra•tory**
**trans•mis•sibil•ity**
**trans•mis•sible**
**trans•mis•sion**
**trans•mis•sive**
**trans•mis•sive•ness**
**trans•mis•siv•ity**
**trans•mit** (**•mit•ting, •mit•ted**)
**trans•mit•table** (*or* **•tible**)
**trans•mit•tal**
**trans•mit•tance**
**trans•mit•tan•cy** physics term
**trans•mit•ter**
**trans•mog•ri•fi•ca•tion**
**trans•mog•ri•fy** (**•fies, •fy•ing, •fied**)
**trans•mon•tane** *variant of* **tramontane**
**trans•mun•dane** beyond this world
**trans•mut•able**
**trans•mut•ably**
**trans•mu•ta•tion**
**trans•mu•ta•tion•al** (*or* **•ta•tive**)
**trans•mu•ta•tion•ist**
**trans•mute**
**trans•mut•er**
**trans•ocean•ic**
**tran•som**
**tran•son•ic** of the sound barrier
**trans•pa•cif•ic**
**trans•pa•dane**
**trans•par•en•cy** (*plural* **•cies**)
**trans•par•ent**
**trans•par•ent•ness**
**tran•spicu•ous** transparent
**trans•pierce**
**tran•spir•able**
**tran•spi•ra•tion**
**tran•spira•tory**
**tran•spire**
**trans•plant**
**trans•plant•able**
**trans•plan•ta•tion**
**trans•plant•er**
**trans•po•lar**
**tran•spond•er** (*or* **•spon•dor**)
**trans•pon•tine** across a bridge
**trans•port**
**trans•port•abil•ity**
**trans•port•able**
**trans•por•ta•tion**
**trans•port•ed•ly**
**trans•port•er**
**trans•port•ive**
**trans•pos•abil•ity**
**trans•pos•able**
**trans•pos•al**
**trans•pose**
**trans•pos•er**
**trans•po•si•tion**
**trans•po•si•tion•al** (*or* **•posi•tive**)
**trans•sexu•al**
**trans•sex•ual•ism**
**trans•ship** (*or* **tran•ship; •ship•ping, •shipped**)
**trans•ship•ment** (*or* **tran•ship•**)
**Trans-Siberian Rail•way**
**tran•sub•stan•tial**
**tran•sub•stan•ti•ate**
**tran•sub•stan•tia•tion**
**tran•sub•stan•tia•tion•al•ist**
**tran•su•date**
**tran•su•da•tion**
**tran•su•da•tory**

**tran•sude**
**transu•ran•ic** (*or* **ra•nian, •ra•nium**) chemistry term
**Trans•vaal**
**Trans•vaal•er**
**Trans•vaal•ian**
**trans•valu•ation**
**trans•value** (**•valu•ing, •valued**)
**trans•valu•er**
**trans•ver•sal**
**trans•ver•sal•ly**
**trans•verse**
**trans•verse•ly**
**trans•verse•ness**
**trans•ves•tism** (*or* **•ti•tism**)
**trans•ves•tite**
**Transylvania**
**Transylvanian**
**trap** (**trap•ping, trapped**)
**tra•peze**
**tra•pezial**
**tra•pezium** (*plural* **•peziums** *or* **•pezia**)
**tra•pezius** (*plural* **•peziuses**) muscle
**tra•pezo•he•dral**
**tra•pezo•he•dron** (*plural* **•drons** *or* **•dra**)
**trap•ezoid**
**trap•per**
**trap•pings**
**Trap•pist** monk
**trap•rock**
**traps** belongings
**trap•shooter**
**trap•shooting**
**tra•pun•to** (*plural* **•tos**) quilting
**trash**
**trashi•ly**
**trashi•ness**
**trashy** (**trashi•er, trashi•est**)
**trass** rock
**trat•to•ria**
**trau•ma** (*plural* **•mas, •ma•ta**)
**trau•mat•ic**
**trau•mati•cal•ly**
**trau•ma•tism**
**trau•ma•ti•za•tion** (*or* **•sa•tion**)
**trau•ma•tize** (*or* **•tise**)
**trav•ail**
**trave** horse-shoeing cage; crossbeam
**trav•el** (**•el•ling, •elled**; *US* **•el•ing, •eled**)
**trav•el•ler** (*US* **•el•er**)
**trav•elogue** (*US also* **•elog**)
**tra•vers•able**
**tra•vers•al**
**trav•erse**
**tra•vers•er**
**trav•er•tine** (*or* **•tin**) rock
**trav•es•ty** (*noun, plural* **•ties**; *verb* **•ties, •ty•ing, •tied**)
**tra•vois** (*plural* **•vois**) sledge
**trawl**
**trawl•er**
**tray** receptacle; *compare* **trey**
**tray•mobile** *Austral* trolley
**treach•er•ous**
**treach•er•ous•ness**
**treach•ery** (*plural* **•eries**)
**trea•cle**
**trea•cli•ness**
**trea•cly**
**tread** (**tread•ing, trod, trod•den** *or* **trod**)
**tread•er**
**trea•dle**
**trea•dler**
**tread•mill**
**trea•son**
**trea•son•able** (*or* **•ous**)
**trea•son•able•ness**
**trea•son•ably**
**treas•ur•able**
**treas•ure**
**treas•ur•er**
**treas•ur•er•ship**
**treasure-trove**
**Treas•ury** government department
**treas•ury** (*plural* **•uries**)
**treat**
**treat•able**
**treat•er**
**trea•tise**
**treat•ment**
**trea•ty** (*plural* **•ties**)
**Trebi•zond** *former name of* **Trabzon**
**tre•ble**
**Tre•blin•ka** concentration camp
**tre•bly**
**trebu•chet** (*or* **tre•buck•et**) weapon
**tre•cen•tist**
**tre•cen•to** 14th century
**tree** (**tree•ing, treed**)
**tree•hopper** insect
**tree•less**
**tree•less•ness**
**tre•en** wooden
**tree•nail** (*or* **tre•nail, trun•nel**) dowel
**treen•ware**
**tre•foil**
**tre•ha•la** sugary substance
**tre•ha•lose**
**treil•lage** trellis
**trek** (**trek•king, trekked**)
**trek•ker**
**trel•lis**
**trellis•work**
**trema•tode** parasite
**trem•ble**
**trem•bler**
**trem•bling•ly**
**trem•bly**
**tre•men•dous**
**tre•men•dous•ness**
**tremo•lite** mineral
**tremo•lo** (*plural* **•los**)
**trem•or**
**trem•or•ous**
**tremu•lant** musical term
**tremu•lous**
**tremu•lous•ness**
**trench**
**trench•an•cy**
**trench•ant**
**trench•er**
**trencher•man** (*plural* **•men**) hearty eater
**trend**
**trendi•ly**
**trendi•ness**
**trendy** (*adj* **trendi•er, trendi•est**; *noun, plural* **trendies**)
**Treng•ga•nu** Malaysian state
**Trent** English river
**Trentino-Alto Adi•ge** Italian region
**Tren•ton** US city
**tre•pan** (**•pan•ning, panned**) surgical instrument

**tre•pang** sea cucumber
**trephi•na•tion**
**tre•phine** surgical instrument
**trepi•da•tion**
**trepo•nema** (*or* **•neme**; *plural* **•nemas, •nema•ta,** *or* **•nemes**) bacterium
**trepo•nema•tous**
**tres•pass**
**tres•pass•er**
**tress**
**tres•sure** heraldic term
**tressy**
**tres•tle**
**trestle•tree**
**trestle•work**
**tret** commerce term
**tre•val•ly** fish
**trews** trousers
**trey** card or dice thrown; *compare* **tray**
**tri•able**
**tri•able•ness**
**tri•ac•id**
**Tri•ad** Chinese secret society
**tri•ad**
**tri•ad•ic**
**tri•ad•ism**
**tri•age**
**tri•al**
**tri•an•gle**
**tri•an•gu•lar**
**tri•an•gu•lar•ity**
**tri•an•gu•late**
**tri•an•gu•la•tion**
**Tri•an•gu•lum** constellation
**tri•ar•chy** (*plural* **•chies**)
**Trias** geology term
**Tri•as•sic**
**tri•ath•lon**
**tri•atom•ic**
**tri•atomi•cal•ly**
**tri•ax•ial**
**tria•zine** (*or* **•zin**)
**tria•zole**
**tria•zol•ic**
**trib•ade** lesbian
**tri•bad•ic**
**trib•ad•ism**
**trib•al**
**trib•al•ism**
**trib•al•ist**
**trib•al•ly**
**tri•ba•sic**
**tribe**
**tribes•man** (*plural* **•men**)
**trib•let** spindle
**tri•bo•elec•tric**
**tri•bo•elec•tric•ity**
**tri•bol•ogy** study of friction
**tri•bo•lu•mi•nes•cence**
**tri•bo•lu•mi•nes•cent**
**tri•brach** metrical foot
**tri•brach•ic** (*or* **•brach•ial**)
**tri•bro•mo•etha•nol**
**tribu•la•tion**
**tri•bu•nal**
**tribu•nary**
**tribu•nate** (*or* **trib•une•ship**)
**trib•une**
**tribu•tari•ly**
**tribu•tary** (*plural* **•taries**)
**trib•ute**
**trice**
**tri•cen•ten•ary** (*plural* **•aries**)
**tri•cen•ten•nial**
**tri•ceps** (*plural* **•cepses** *or* **•ceps**)
**tri•cera•tops**
**tri•chia•sis** eye condition
**tri•chi•na** (*plural* **•nae**) parasite
**trichi•nia•sis** *variant of* **trichinosis**
**trichi•ni•za•tion** (*or* **•sa•tion**)
**trichi•nize** (*or* **•nise**)
**Trichi•nopo•ly** Indian city
**trichi•no•sis** (*or* **•nia•**) parasitic disease
**trichi•nous**
**trich•ite** crystal
**tri•chit•ic**
**tri•chlo•ride**
**tri•chlo•ro•acetic acid**
**tri•chlo•ro•phenoxy•acetic acid**
**tricho•cyst** zoology term
**tricho•cys•tic**
**tricho•gyne** botany term
**tricho•gyn•ial** (*or* **•ic**)
**trich•oid**
**tri•cholo•gist**
**tri•chol•ogy** study of hair
**tri•chome** plant structure
**tri•chom•ic**
**tricho•mon•ad** parasite
**tricho•mona•dal** (*or* **•mon•al**)
**tricho•mo•nia•sis**
**tri•chop•ter•an** insect
**tri•cho•sis** hair disease
**tricho•tom•ic** (*or* **•choto•mous**)
**tri•choto•my** (*plural* **•mies**)
**tri•chro•ic**
**tri•chro•ism** crystallography term
**tri•chro•mat**
**tri•chro•mat•ic** (*or* **•chro•mic**)
**tri•chro•ma•tism**
**trick**
**trick•er**
**trick•ery** (*plural* **•eries**)
**tricki•ly**
**tricki•ness**
**trick•ing•ly**
**trick•le**
**trick•ling•ly**
**trick•ly**
**trick•si•ness**
**trick•ster**
**trick•sy** (**•si•er, •si•est**) mischievous
**tricky** (**tricki•er, tricki•est**)
**tri•clin•ic** crystallography term
**tri•clin•ium** (*plural* **•ia**) Roman dining room
**tri•col•our** (*US* **•or**)
**tri•col•oured** (*US* **•ored**)
**tri•corn** (*or* **•corne**) hat
**tri•cos•tate** biology term
**tri•cot** fabric
**tri•co•tine** fabric
**tri•crot•ic** medical term
**tri•crot•ism**
**tric•trac** (*or* **trick•track**) board game
**tri•cus•pid**
**tri•cus•pi•dal**
**tri•cy•cle**
**tri•cy•clic** chemistry term
**tri•cy•clist**
**tri•dac•tyl** (*or* **•tyl•ous**)
**tri•dent**
**tri•den•tate** (*or* **•tal**)
**Tri•den•tine** of Council of Trent
**tri•di•men•sion•al**
**tri•di•men•sion•al•ity**

**trid•uum** prayer days
**tried**
**tri•en•nial**
**tri•en•nial•ly**
**tri•en•nium** (*plural* **•niums** *or* **•nia)**
**Trier** German city
**tri•er** one who tries
**tri•er•ar•chy (•chies)**
**Tri•este** Italian port
**trif•fid** fictional plant
**tri•fid** three-lobed
**tri•fle**
**tri•fler**
**tri•fling**
**tri•fo•cal**
**tri•fo•li•ate** (*or* **•at•ed)**
**tri•fo•lium** plant
**tri•fo•rial**
**tri•fo•rium** (*plural* **•ria)** part of church
**tri•fur•cate** (*or* **•cat•ed)**
**tri•fur•ca•tion**
**trig (trig•ging, trigged)** *Dialect* neat; wedge
**tri•gemi•nal** anatomy term
**trig•ger**
**trigger•fish** (*plural* **•fish** *or* **•fishes)**
**tri•glyc•er•ide**
**tri•glyph** architectural term
**tri•glyph•ic**
**tri•gon** harp
**trigo•nal** crystallography term
**trigo•no•met•ric** (*or* **•ri•cal)**
**trigo•no•met•ri•cal•ly**
**trigo•nom•etry**
**trigo•nous** botany term
**tri•graph** phonetics term
**tri•graph•ic**
**tri•he•dral**
**tri•he•dron** (*plural* **•drons** *or* **•dra)**
**tri•hy•drate**
**tri•hy•dric** (*or* **•droxy)**
**tri•io•do•thy•ro•nine**
**trike** *Slang* tricycle
**tri•lat•er•al**
**tri•lat•er•al•ly**
**tri•lat•era•tion** surveying method
**tril•by** (*plural* **•bies)**
**tri•lem•ma**
**tri•lin•ear**
**tri•lin•gual**
**tri•lin•gual•ism**
**tri•lin•gual•ly**
**tri•lit•er•al**
**tri•lith•ic**
**tri•lith•on** (*or* **tri•lith)**
**trill**
**tril•lion**
**tril•lionth**
**tril•lium** plant
**tri•lo•bate** three-lobed
**tri•lo•bite** fossil
**tri•locu•lar**
**tril•ogy** (*plural* **•gies)**
**trim** (*adj* **trim•mer, trim•mest**; *verb* **trim•ming, trimmed)**
**tri•ma•ran**
**tri•mer** chemistry term
**trim•er•ous**
**tri•mes•ter**
**tri•mes•tral** (*or* **•trial)**
**trim•eter** verse line
**tri•metha•di•one**
**tri•met•ric** (*or* **•ri•cal)**
**tri•met•ro•gon** aerial photography
**trim•ly**
**trim•mer**
**trim•ming**
**trim•ness**
**tri•mo•lecu•lar**
**tri•month•ly**
**tri•morph**
**tri•mor•phic** (*or* **•phous)**
**tri•mor•phism**
**Tri•mur•ti** Hindu gods
**tri•nal**
**tri•na•ry** consisting of three
**Trin•co•ma•lee** Sri Lankan port
**trine** astrology term
**Trini•dad**
**Trini•dad•ian**
**Trini•tar•ian** believer in the Trinity
**Trini•tar•ian•ism**
**tri•ni•tro•ben•zene**
**tri•ni•tro•cre•sol**
**tri•ni•tro•glyc•er•in**
**tri•ni•tro•phe•nol**
**tri•ni•tro•tolu•ene** (*or* **•ol)**
**Trin•ity** God
**trini•ty** (*plural* **•ities)**
**trin•ket**
**trin•ket•ry**
**tri•nocu•lar**
**tri•no•mial**
**trio** (*plural* **trios)**
**tri•ode** electronic valve
**tri•oecious** (*or* **•ecious)** botany term
**trio•elein**
**tri•ol**
**trio•let** verse form
**tri•ose**
**tri•ox•ide**
**trip (trip•ping, tripped)**
**tri•pal•mi•tin**
**tri•par•tite**
**tri•par•tite•ly**
**tri•par•ti•tion**
**tripe**
**trip•hammer**
**tri•phe•nyl•me•thane**
**tri•phibi•ous**
**triph•thong** vowel sound
**triph•thong•al**
**triphy•lite** mineral
**tri•pin•nate** botany term
**tri•plane**
**tri•ple**
**tri•plet**
**triple•tail** (*plural* **•tail** *or* **•tails)** fish
**triple-tongue** musical term
**Tri•plex** (*Trademark*)
**trip•li•cate**
**trip•li•ca•tion**
**tri•plic•ity** (*plural* **•ities)** group of three
**trip•lo•blas•tic**
**trip•loid** biology term
**trip•loidy**
**triply**
**tri•pod**
**tripo•dal**
**tripo•dy** (*plural* **•dies)** metrical unit
**Tripo•li** Libyan capital
**tripo•li** rock
**Tripo•li•ta•nia** Libyan region
**Tripo•li•ta•nian**
**tri•pos**
**trip•per**
**trip•pet**
**trip•ping•ly**
**trip•tane**
**trip•ter•ous**

**Triptolemus** mythological character
**trip•tych** altarpiece; *compare* **tryptic**
**trip•tyque** customs permit
**Tripu•ra** Indian state
**trip•wire**
**tri•que•trous**
**tri•ra•di•ate**
**tri•reme**
**tri•sac•cha•ride**
**tri•sect**
**tri•sec•tion**
**tri•sec•tor**
**tri•se•rial**
**tris•kai•deka•pho•bia** fear of number 13
**tris•kai•deka•pho•bic**
**tris•keli•on** (*or* **•kele**) symbol
**tris•mic**
**tris•mus** lockjaw
**tris•oc•ta•he•dral**
**tris•oc•ta•he•dron** (*plural* **•drons** *or* **•dra**)
**tri•some** genetics term
**tri•so•mic**
**tri•somy**
**Tris•tan da Cu•nha** South Atlantic islands
**tris•tich** three-line poem
**tris•tich•ic**
**tris•ti•chous**
**tri•sul•phide**
**tri•syl•la•ble**
**tri•syl•lab•ic** (*or* **•labi•cal**)
**tri•tano•pia** blue blindness
**tri•tan•op•ic**
**trite**
**trite•ly**
**trite•ness**
**tri•the•ism** belief in Trinity
**tri•the•ist**
**triti•ate** chemistry term
**tritia•tion**
**triti•ca•le** hybrid cereal
**triti•cum** cereal grass
**trit•ium** isotope of hydrogen
**Tri•ton** satellite of Neptune
**Triton** Greek god
**tri•ton** mollusc
**tri•tone** musical term
**tritu•rable**
**tritu•rate** grind
**tritu•ra•tion**
**tritu•ra•tor**
**tri•umph**
**tri•um•phal**
**tri•um•phal•ly**
**tri•um•phant**
**tri•umph•er**
**tri•um•vir** (*plural* **•virs** *or* **•vi•ri**)
**tri•um•vi•ral**
**tri•um•vi•rate**
**tri•une** three in one
**tri•unity**
**tri•va•len•cy**
**tri•va•lent** (*or* **ter•**)
**Tri•van•drum** Indian city
**triv•et**
**trivia** (*plural*)
**triv•ial**
**trivi•al•ity** (*plural* **•ities**)
**trivi•ali•za•tion** (*or* **•sa•tion**)
**trivi•al•ize** (*or* **•ise**)
**trivi•al•ly**
**trivi•al•ness**
**tri•week•ly** (*plural* **•lies**)
**Tro•as** Trojan region
**troat** bellow
**tro•car** surgical instrument
**tro•cha•ic** of a trochee
**tro•chai•cal•ly**
**tro•chal** zoology term
**tro•chan•ter** anatomy term
**troche** lozenge
**tro•chee** metrical foot
**trochi•lus** hummingbird
**troch•lea** (*plural* **•leae**) anatomy term
**troch•le•ar**
**tro•choid**
**tro•choi•dal**
**trocho•phore** (*or* **•sphere**) zoology term
**trod**
**trod•den**
**trog** (**trog•ging, trogged**) stroll
**trog•lo•dyte**
**trog•lo•dyt•ic** (*or* **•dyti•cal**)
**tro•gon** bird
**troi•ka**
**Troilus** mythological character
**Tro•jan**
**troll**
**trol•ley**
**trol•lop**
**trom•bi•dia•sis** mite infestation
**trom•bone**
**trom•bon•ist**
**trom•mel**
**trompe** forge apparatus
**trompe l'oeil** (*plural* **trompe l'oeils**) painting illusion
**tro•na** mineral
**Trond•heim** Norwegian port
**troop** large group; move in group; *compare* **troupe**
**troop•er**
**troops**
**troop•ship**
**troost•ite** mineral
**tro•paeo•lin**
**tro•paeo•lum** (*plural* **•lums** *or* **•la**) plant
**trope** figure of speech; liturgical interpolation
**troph•al•lac•tic**
**troph•al•lax•is**
**troph•ic** of nutrition
**trophi•cal•ly**
**tropho•blast** embryonic membrane
**tropho•blas•tic**
**tropho•zo•ite** zoology term
**tro•phy** (*plural* **•phies**)
**trop•ic** line of latitude
**tro•pic** of a tropism
**tropi•cal**
**tropi•cal•ity**
**tropi•cali•za•tion** (*or* **•sa•tion**)
**tropi•cal•ize** (*or* **•ise**)
**tropi•cal•ly**
**tropic•bird**
**trop•ics**
**tro•pism** biology term
**tropo•log•ic** (*or* **•logi•cal**)
**tro•pol•ogy** (*plural* **•ogies**) use of tropes
**tropo•pause** atmospheric layer
**tro•pophi•lous**
**tropo•phyte**
**tropo•phyt•ic**
**tropo•sphere** atmospheric layer
**tropo•spher•ic**
**trop•po** musical term

**Tros•sachs** Scottish valley
**trot** (**trot•ting, trot•ted**)
**troth**
**trot•line**
**Trot•sky•ism**
**Trot•sky•ite** (*or* **•ist**)
**trot•ter**
**tro•tyl** TNT
**trou•ba•dour**
**trou•ble**
**trou•bled•ly**
**trouble•maker**
**trouble•making**
**trou•bler**
**trouble•shooter**
**trou•ble•some**
**trou•ble•some•ness**
**trou•bling•ly**
**trou•blous**
**trou-de-loup** (*plural* **trous-de-loup**) pit for defence
**trough**
**trounce**
**troupe** group of performers; *compare* **troop**
**troup•er**
**trou•pial** bird
**trouse** Irish breeches
**trou•sered**
**trou•sers**
**trous•seau** (*plural* **•seaux** *or* **•seaus**)
**trout** (*plural* **trout** *or* **trouts**)
**trou•vère** (*or* **•veur**) medieval poet
**trove**
**tro•ver** legal term
**Trow•bridge** Wiltshire town
**trow•el** (**•el•ling, •elled**; *US* **•el•ing, •eled**)
**trow•el•ler** (*US* **•el•er**)
**Troy**
**tru•an•cy**
**tru•ant**
**truce**
**Tru•cial States**
**truck**
**truck•age** *US* conveyance by lorry
**truck•er**
**truckie** *Austral* truck driver
**truck•ing**
**truck•le**
**truck•ler**
**truck•load**
**trucu•lence** (*or* **•len•cy**)
**trucu•lent**
**trudge**
**trudg•en** swimming stroke
**trudg•er**
**true** (*adj* **tru•er, tru•est**; *verb* **tru•ing, trued**)
**true-blue**
**true-born**
**true-life** (*adj*)
**true•love**
**true•ness**
**truf•fle**
**trug**
**tru•ism**
**tru•is•tic** (*or* **•ti•cal**)
**Trujillo** Peruvian city
**tru•ly**
**tru•meau** (*plural* **•meaux**) architectural term
**trump**
**trump•ery** (*plural* **•eries**)
**trum•pet**
**trum•pet•er**
**trumpet•weed**
**trun•cate**
**trun•cat•ed**
**trun•ca•tion**
**trun•cheon**
**trun•dle**
**trunk**
**trunk•fish** (*plural* **•fish** *or* **•fishes**)
**trunk•ful** (*plural* **•fuls**)
**trunks**
**trun•nion** pivot
**Tru•ro** Cornish town
**truss**
**truss•er**
**truss•ing**
**trust**
**trust•abil•ity**
**trust•able**
**trus•tee** (**•tee•ing, •teed**)
**trus•tee•ship**
**trust•er**
**trust•ful** (*or* **•ing**)
**trust•ful•ly** (*or* **•ing•ly**)
**trust•ful•ness** (*or* **•ing•**)
**trusti•ly**
**trusti•ness**
**trust•worthi•ly**
**trust•worthi•ness**
**trust•worthy**
**trusty** (**trusti•er, trusti•est**)
**truth**
**truth•ful**
**truth•ful•ly**
**truth•ful•ness**
**truth-function** logic term
**truth-value** logic term
**try** (*verb* **tries, try•ing, tried**; *noun, plural* **tries**)
(**tryer**) *incorrect spelling of* **trier**
**try•ing•ly**
**try•ing•ness**
**try•ma** (*plural* **•ma•ta**) botany term
**try-on** (*noun*)
**try-out** (*noun*)
**trypa•no•so•mal** (*or* **•som•ic**)
**trypa•no•some** parasite
**trypa•no•so•mia•sis** sleeping sickness
**try•par•sa•mide**
**tryp•sin** enzyme
**tryp•sino•gen** enzyme
**tryp•tic** of trypsin; *compare* **triptych**
**tryp•to•phan** amino acid
**try•sail**
**tryst**
**tryst•er**
**tsar** (*or* **czar**)
**tsar•dom** (*or* **czar•**)
**tsar•evitch** (*or* **czar•**)
**tsa•ri•na** (*or* **•rit•sa, cza•**)
**tsar•ism** (*or* **czar•**)
**tsar•ist** (*or* **czar•**)
**Tse•li•no•grad** *former name of* Astana
**tset•se** (*or* **tzet•ze**)
**Tshi•lu•ba** African language
**Tsi•nan** (*or* **Chi•nan, Chi-nan**) Chinese city
**Tsing•hai** (*or* **Ching•hai, Ch'ing-hai**) Chinese province
**Tsing•tao** (*or* **Ching•tao, Ch'ing-tao**) Chinese port
**Tson•ga** (*plural* **•ga** *or* **•gas**) African people
**tsu•na•mi** tidal wave
**Tsu•shi•ma** Japanese islands
**tsu•tsu•ga•mu•shi dis•ease**
**Tswa•na** (*plural* **•na** *or* **•nas**) African people

**Tua•reg** (*plural* **•reg** *or* **•regs**) Berber people
**tuart** tree
**tua•ta•ra** reptile
**tub** (**tub•bing, tubbed**)
**tuba** (*plural* **tubas** *or* **tubae**) musical instrument; *compare* **tuber**
**tu•bal**
**Tubal-cain** biblical character
**tu•bate**
**tubbed**
**tub•bi•ness**
**tub•bing**
**tub•by** (**•bi•er, •bi•est**)
**tube**
**tube•less**
**tu•ber** underground plant stem; *compare* **tuba**
**tu•ber•cle**
**tu•ber•cu•lar**
**tu•ber•cu•late** covered with nodules
**tu•ber•cu•la•tion**
**tu•ber•cu•lin**
**tu•ber•cu•lo•sis**
**tu•ber•cu•lous**
**tu•ber•ose** plant; *compare* **tuberous**
**tu•ber•os•ity** (*plural* **•ities**)
**tu•ber•ous** (*or* **•ose**) having tubers; *compare* **tuberose**
**tu•bi•fex** (*plural* **•fex** *or* **•fexes**) worm
**tu•bi•form**
**tub•ing**
**tub-thumper**
**tubu•lar**
**tu•bu•lar•ity**
**tu•bu•late**
**tu•bu•la•tion**
**tu•bu•la•tor**
**tu•bule**
**tu•bu•li•flo•rous** botany term
**tu•bu•lous**
**Tu•ca•na** constellation
**tu•chun** Chinese governor
**tuck**
**tuck•er**
**tuck•et** flourish on trumpet
**tu•co•tu•co** (*or* **tu•cu•tu•cu**) animal
**Tuc•son** US city
**Tu•cu•mán** Argentine city
**Tu•dor**
**Tues•day**
**tufa** soft rock
**tuff** hard rock
**tuffa•ceous**
**tuf•fet**
**tuft**
**tuft•ed**
**tuft•er**
**tufty**
**tug** (**tug•ging, tugged**)
**tug•ger**
**tu•grik** (*or* **•ghrik**) Mongolian currency
**tui** bird
**Tui•ler•ies** French palace
**tui•tion**
**tui•tion•al** (*or* **•ary**)
**tu•la•rae•mia** (*US* **•re•**) disease
**tu•la•rae•mic** (*US* **•remic**)
**tu•lip**
**tulip•wood**
**tulle** fabric
**Tul•sa** US city
**tum** *Slang* stomach
**tum•ble**
**tumble-down**
**tumble-drier**
**tumble•home** nautical term
**tum•bler**
**tum•bler•ful** (*plural* **•fuls**)
**tumble•weed**
**tum•brel** (*or* **•bril**)
**tu•mefa•ci•ent**
**tu•mefac•tion**
**tu•mefy** (**•mefies, •mefy•ing, •mefied**) swell
**tu•mes•cence**
**tu•mes•cent**
**tu•mid**
**tu•mid•ity** (*or* **•ness**)
**tum•my** (*plural* **•mies**)
**tu•mor•ous** (*or* **•mor•al**)
**tu•mour** (*US* **•mor**)
**tump** *Dialect* small mound
**tu•mu•lar**
**tu•mu•lose** (*or* **•lous**)
**tu•mu•los•ity**
**tu•mult**
**tu•mul•tu•ous**
**tu•mul•tu•ous•ness**
**tu•mu•lus** (*plural* **•li**) burial mound
**tun** (**tun•ning, tunned**) cask; *compare* **ton; tonne**
**tuna** (*plural* **tuna** *or* **tunas**)
**tun•able** (*or* **tune•**)
**Tun•bridge Wells** Kent town; *compare* **Tonbridge**
**tun•dra**
**tune**
**tune•ful**
**tune•ful•ly**
**tune•ful•ness**
**tune•less**
**tune•less•ness**
**tun•er**
**tune•smith**
**tung•sten**
**tung•stic**
**tung•stite** mineral
**Tun•gus** (*plural* **•guses** *or* **•gus**) Mongoloid people
**Tun•gu•sian**
**Tun•gus•ic** language
**tu•nic**
**tu•ni•ca** (*plural* **•cae**) anatomy term
**tu•ni•cate** marine animal
**tu•ni•cle** vestment
**tun•ing** musical term
**Tu•nis** Tunisian capital
**Tu•ni•sia**
**Tu•ni•sian**
**tun•nage** *variant spelling of* **tonnage**
**tun•nel** (**•nel•ling, •nelled;** *US* **•nel•ing, •neled**)
**tun•nel•ler** (*US* **•nel•er**)
**tun•ny** (*plural* **•nies** *or* **•ny**) tuna fish
**tup** (**tup•ping, tupped**)
**tu•pelo** (*plural* **•pelos**) tree
**Tupi** (*plural* **•pis** *or* **•pi**) South American Indian
**tupped**
**tup•pence** *variant spelling of* **twopence**
**tup•pen•ny** *variant spelling of* **twopenny**
**tup•ping**
**tuque** cap
**tur•ban**
**tur•baned**
**tur•ba•ry** (*plural* **•ries**) peat-cutting area
**tur•bel•lar•ian** flatworm

**tur•bid** opaque; muddy; *compare* **turgid**
**tur•bi•dim•eter**
**tur•bid•ity** (*or* **•ness**)
**tur•bi•nate** (*or* **•nal**) scroll-shaped
**tur•bi•na•tion**
**tur•bine**
**tur•bit** pigeon
**tur•bo•car**
**tur•bo•charg•er**
**turbo-electric**
**tur•bo•fan**
**tur•bo•gen•era•tor**
**tur•bo•jet**
**tur•bo•prop**
**tur•bo•super•charg•er**
**tur•bot** (*plural* **•bot** *or* **•bots**)
**tur•bu•lence** (*or* **•len•cy**)
**tur•bu•lent**
**turd**
**tur•dine** of thrushes
**tu•reen** soup dish; *compare* **terrene; terrine**
**turf** (*plural* **turfs** *or* **turves**)
**turfi•ness**
**turfy** (**turfi•er, turfi•est**)
**tur•ges•cence** (*or* **•cen•cy**)
**tur•ges•cent**
**tur•gid** swollen; pompous; *compare* **turbid**
**tur•gid•ity** (*or* **•ness**)
**tur•gite** mineral
**tur•gor** biology term
**Tu•rin** Italian city
**Turing ma•chine**
**turi•on** plant bud
**Turk**
**Tur•ke•stan** *variant spelling of* **Turkistan**
**Tur•key**
**tur•key** (*plural* **•keys** *or* **•key**)
**Tur•ki** of Turkic
**Tur•kic** language
**Turk•ish**
**Tur•ki•stan** (*or* **•ke•**) Asian region
**Turk•men** language
**Turk•meni•stan** Central Asian country
**Turko•man** (*or* **Turk•man**; *plural* **•mans** *or* **•men**) Asian people
**Tur•ku** Finnish city
**tur•mer•ic**
**tur•moil**
**turn** move; *compare* **tern; terne**
**turn•able**
**turn•about**
**turn•around**
**turn•buckle**
**turn•coat**
**turn•er**
**turn•ery** (*plural* **•eries**) lathe work
**turn•ing**
**tur•nip**
**turn•key**
**turn-off** (*noun*)
**turn-on** (*noun*)
**turn-out** (*noun*)
**turn•over** (*noun*)
**turn•pike**
**turn-round** (*noun*)
**turn•sole** plant
**turn•stile**
**turn•stone** bird
**turn•table**
**turn-up** (*noun*)
**tur•pen•tine**
**tur•peth** plant
**tur•pi•tude**
**turps** turpentine
**tur•quoise**
**tur•ret**
**tur•ret•ed**
**tur•ricu•late** (*or* **•la•ted**)
**tur•tle**
**turtle•back** part of ship
**turtle•dove**
**turtle•neck**
**tur•tler**
**Tus•can**
**Tus•ca•ny**
**Tus•ca•ro•ra** (*plural* **•ras** *or* **•ra**) American Indian
**tusche** lithographic substance
**Tus•cu•lum** ancient city
**tush**
**tusk**
**tusk•er**
**tusk•like**
**tus•sah** (*or* **tus•sore**) silk
**tus•sal**
**tus•sis** cough
**tus•sive**
**tus•sle**
**tus•sock**
**tus•socky**
**tus•sore** *variant spelling of* **tussah**
**tut** (**tut•ting, tut•ted**)
**tu•tee**
**tu•telage**
**tu•telary** (*or* **•telar**; *plural* **•telaries** *or* **•telars**)
**tu•ti•or•ism** Catholic doctrine
**tu•ti•or•ist**
**tu•tor**
**tu•tor•age** (*or* **•ship**)
**tu•to•rial**
**tu•to•rial•ly**
**tut•san** shrub
**tut•ti** musical term
**tutti-frutti** ice cream
**tut•ty** polishing powder
**tutu** ballet skirt
**Tuvalu** Pacific state
**tu-whit tu-whoo**
**tux•edo** (*plural* **•dos**)
**tu•yère** (*or* **twy•er**) blast-furnace nozzle
**Tver** Russian city
**twad•dle**
**twad•dler**
**twain**
**twang**
**twangy**
**'twas**
**tway•blade** orchid
**tweak**
**twee**
**Tweed** Scottish river
**tweed** fabric
**tweedy** (**tweedi•er, tweedi•est**)
**tweeny** (*plural* **tweenies**) *Slang* maid
**tweet**
**tweet•er** loudspeaker
**tweeze**
**twee•zers**
**twelfth**
**Twelfth•tide** Epiphany
**twelve**
**twelve•mo** (*plural* **•mos**) paper size
**twelve•month**
**twelve-tone** musical term
**twen•ti•eth**
**twen•ty** (*plural* **•ties**)
**'twere**

**twerp**
**Twi** (*plural* **Twi** *or* **Twis**) language or people
**twi•bill** (*or* **•bil**) tool
**twice**
**twice-laid**
**Twick•en•ham**
**twid•dle**
**twid•dler**
**twig** (**twig•ging, twigged**)
**twig•gy** (**•gi•er, •gi•est**)
**twi•light**
**twi•lit**
**twill**
**twin** (**twin•ning, twinned**)
**twine**
**twin•er**
**twin•flower**
**twinge** (**twinge•ing** *or* **twing•ing, twinged**)
**twink**
**twin•kle**
**twin•kler**
**twin•kling•ly**
**twirl**
**twirl•er**
**twist**
**twist•abil•ity**
**twist•able**
**twist•ed•ly**
**twist•er**
**twist•ing•ly**
**twisty** (**twisti•er, twisti•est**)
**twit** (**twit•ting, twit•ted**)
**twitch**
**twitch•er**
**twitchi•ly**
**twitchi•ness**
**twitch•ing•ly**
**twitchy** (**twitchi•er, twitchi•est**)
**twite** bird
**twit•ter**
**twit•ter•er**
**twit•tery**
**twixt**
**two** (*plural* **twos**)
**two-by-four**
**two-dimen•sion•al**
**two-dimen•sion•al•ity**
**two-dimen•sion•al•ly**
**two-edged**
**two-faced**
**two-facedly**
**two-facedness**
**two•fold**
**two-handed**
**two-handed•ly**
**two•pence** (*or* **tup•pence**)
**two•pen•ny** (*or* **tup•pen•ny**)
**two-phase**
**two-piece**
**two-ply** (*plural* **-plies**)
**two-seater**
**two-sided**
**two•some**
**two-step**
**two-stroke**
**two-time**
**two-timer**
**two-tone**
**two-way**
**Ty•burn**
**Tyche** Greek goddess
**tych•ism** philosophy term
**Ty•cho** moon crater
**ty•coon**
**ty•ing**
**tyke** (*or* **tike**)
**ty•lo•pod** zoology term
**ty•lo•sis** botany term
**tym•pan** printing term
**tym•pa•ni** *variant spelling of* **timpani**
**tym•pan•ic**
**tym•pa•nist** *variant spelling of* **timpanist**
**tym•pa•ni•tes** (*or* **•pa•ny**) abdominal distension
**tym•pa•nit•ic**
**tym•pa•ni•tis**
**tym•pa•num** (*plural* **•nums** *or* **•na**) part of ear; architectural term; *compare* **timpani**
**tym•pa•ny** *variant of* **tympanites**
**Tyne** English river
**Tyne and Wear** former English county
**Tyne•side**
**Tyn•wald** Manx Parliament
**type**
**type•bar**
**type•case**
**type•cast** (**•cast•ing, •cast**)
**type•cast•er**
**type•face**
**type-high**
**type•script**
**type•set** (**•set•ting, •set**)
**type•set•ter**
**type•write** (**•writ•ing, •wrote, •writ•ten**)
**type•writ•er**
**typh•li•tic**
**typh•li•tis** intestinal disorder
**typh•lol•ogy** study of blindness
**ty•pho•gen•ic** causing typhoid
**ty•phoid**
**ty•phoi•dal**
**ty•phoi•din**
**ty•phon•ic**
**ty•phoon**
**ty•phous** (*adj*)
**ty•phus** (*noun*)
**typi•cal** (*or* **typ•ic**)
**typi•cal•ly**
**typi•cal•ness** (*or* **•ity**)
**typi•fi•ca•tion**
**typi•fi•er**
**typi•fy** (**•fies, •fy•ing, •fied**)
**typ•ing**
**typ•ist**
**typo** (*plural* **typos**)
**ty•pog•ra•pher**
**ty•po•graphi•cal** (*or* **•graph•ic**)
**ty•po•graphi•cal•ly**
**ty•pog•ra•phy**
**ty•po•logi•cal** (*or* **•log•ic**)
**ty•polo•gist**
**ty•pol•ogy** theology term
**ty•poth•etae** *US* printers
**ty•ra•mine**
**ty•ran•ni•cal** (*or* **ran•nic**)
**ty•ran•ni•cal•ly**
**ty•ran•ni•cal•ness**
**ty•ran•ni•cid•al**
**ty•ran•ni•cide**
**tyr•an•nize** (*or* **•nise**)
**tyr•an•niz•er** (*or* **•nis•er**)
**tyr•an•niz•ing•ly** (*or* **•nis•ing•ly**)
**ty•ran•no•saur** (*or* **•saur•us**)
**tyr•an•nous**
**tyr•an•nous•ness**
**tyr•an•ny** (*plural* **•nies**)
**ty•rant**
**Tyre** Lebanese port

**tyre** (*US* **tire**) wheel ring; *compare* **tire**
**Tyr•ian**
**tyro** (*or* **tiro**; *plural* **tyros** *or* **tiros**) novice
**ty•ro•ci•dine** antibiotic
**Ty•rol** (*or* **Ti•**) Austrian province
**Tyro•lese** (*or* **•lean**)
**Ty•ro•li•enne** dance
**Ty•rone** Irish county
**ty•ron•ic** (*or* **ti•**)
**ty•ro•si•nase** enzyme
**ty•ro•sine** amino acid
**ty•ro•thri•cin** antibiotic
**Tyr•rhe•nian Sea**
**Tyu•men** Russian port
**tzar** *less common spelling of* **tsar**
**Tzi•gane** gipsy
**tzet•ze** variant spelling of **tsetse**
**Tzu-po** (*or* **Tze•po**) Chinese city

# U

**ubi•ety** being in particular place
**ubiqui•tar•ian** Lutheran
**ubiqui•tous**
**ubiquity** (*or* **ubiqui•tous•ness**)
**ubi su•pra** *Latin* where mentioned above
**U-boat**
**Udai•pur** Indian city
**udal** legal term
**ud•der**
**Udi•ne** Italian city
**udo** (*plural* **udos**) plant
**Uf•fizi** Italian art gallery
**UFO** (*plural* **UFOs**)
**ufol•ogy** study of UFOs
**Ugan•da**
**Ugan•dan**
**Uga•rit•ic** language
**ugli** (*plural* **uglis** *or* **uglies**) fruit
**ug•li•fi•ca•tion**
**ug•li•fi•er**
**ug•li•fy** (**•fies, •fy•ing, •fied**)
**ug•li•ly**
**ug•li•ness**
**ugly** (**ug•li•er, ug•li•est**)
**Ugrian** Asian people
**Ugric** language
**uh•lan** Polish lancer
**uhu•ru** African national independence
**Uigur** (*or* **Uighur**; *plural* **Uigur, Uigurs** *or* **Uighur, Uighurs**) Mongoloid people
**Uigu•rian** (*or* **•ric, Uighu•**)
**uin•ta•there** extinct mammal
**uit•land•er** *South African* foreigner
**Uj•jain** Indian city
**ukase** tsar's edict
**uke•lele** *variant spelling of* **ukulele**
**uki•yoe** (*or* **ukiyo-e**) Japanese art
**Ukraine**
**Ukrain•ian**
**uku•lele** (*or* **uke•**)
**Ulan Ba•tor** Mongolian capital
**Ulan-Ude** Russian city
**ul•cer**
**ul•cer•ate**
**ul•cera•tion**
**ul•cera•tive**
**ul•cer•ous**
**ulema** Muslim scholar
**ul•lage**
**ul•laged**
**Ulls•wa•ter**
**ul•ma•ceous** botany term
**ulna** (*plural* **ulnae** *or* **ulnas**) arm bone
**ul•nar**
**ulot•ri•chous** curly haired
**ulot•ri•chy**
**Ul•ster** Northern Ireland
**ul•ster** overcoat
**Ul•ster•man** (*plural* **•men**)
**ul•te•ri•or**
**ul•ti•ma** final syllable
**ul•ti•mate**
**ul•ti•mate•ly**
**ul•ti•ma•tum** (*plural* **•tums** *or* **•ta**)
**ul•ti•mo** last month
**ul•ti•mo•geni•ture** legal term
**ul•tra**
**ultra•cen•trifu•gal**
**ultra•cen•trifu•ga•tion**
**ultra•cen•tri•fuge**
**ultra•con•ser•va•tive**
**ultra•fiche**
**ultra•fil•ter**
**ultra•fil•tra•tion**
**ultra•high**
**ultra•ism** extreme philosophy
**ultra•ist**
**ultra•is•tic**
**ultra•ma•rine** colour
**ultra•mi•crom•eter**
**ultra•micro•scope**
**ultra•micro•scop•ic**
**ultra•mi•cros•co•py**
**ultra•mod•ern**
**ultra•mod•ern•ism**
**ultra•mod•ern•ist**
**ultra•mod•ern•is•tic**
**ultra•mon•tane** beyond the mountains
**ultra•mon•ta•nism** religious doctrine
**ultra•mon•tan•ist**
**ultra•mun•dane** beyond this world
**ultra•na•tion•al**
**ultra•na•tion•al•ism**
**ultra•na•tion•al•ist**
**ultra•na•tion•al•is•tic**
**ultra•short**
**ultra•son•ic**
**ultra•soni•cal•ly**
**ultra•son•ics**
**ultra•sound**
**ultra•struc•tur•al**
**ultra•struc•ture**
**ultra•vio•let**
**ul•tra vi•res** legal term
**ultra•vi•rus**
**ulu•lant**
**ulu•late** wail

**ulu•la•tion**
**Ul•ya•novsk** *former name of* **Simbirsk**
**Umay•yad** *variant spelling of* **Omayyad**
**um•bel** botany term
**um•bel•late** (*or* **•lar, •lat•ed**)
**um•bel•lif•er•ous**
**um•bel•lu•late**
**um•bel•lule**
**um•ber** pigment
**um•bili•cal**
**um•bili•cate**
**um•bili•ca•tion**
**um•bili•cus** (*plural* **•ci**) navel
**um•bili•form**
**umbo** (*plural* **um•bo•nes** *or* **umbos**) small hump
**um•bo•nate** (*or* **•bo•nal, •bon•ic**)
**um•bra** (*plural* **•brae**) shadow
**um•brage**
**um•bra•geous** shady
**um•bral**
**um•brel•la**
**Um•bria** Italian region
**Um•brian**
**Um•bri•el** satellite of Uranus
**umi•ak** (*or* **oomi•**) Eskimo boat
**um•laut**
**um•pire**
**um•pire•ship** (*or* **•pir•age**)
**ump•teen**
**ump•teenth**
**Um•ta•li** Zimbabwean city
**un•abashed**
**un•abat•ed**
**un•able**
**un•abridged**
**un•ab•sorbed**
**un•ac•cent•ed**
**un•ac•cep•table**
**un•ac•claimed**
**un•ac•com•mo•dat•ed**
**un•ac•com•mo•dat•ing**
**un•ac•com•pa•nied**
**un•ac•com•plished**
**un•ac•count•able**
**un•ac•count•able•ness** (*or* **•abil•ity**)
**un•ac•count•ably**
**un•ac•count•ed**
**un•ac•counted-for**
**un•ac•cus•tomed**
**un•ack•nowl•edged**
**un•ac•quaint•ed**
**un•ad•mit•ted**
**un•adopt•ed**
**un•adorned**
**un•adul•ter•at•ed**
**un•ad•ven•tur•ous**
**un•ad•vised**
**un•ad•vis•ed•ly**
**un•ad•vis•ed•ness**
**un•af•fect•ed**
**un•afraid**
**un•aid•ed**
**un•aimed**
**un•aired**
**un•al•loyed** pure
**un•al•ter•able**
**un•al•ter•ably**
**un•al•tered**
**un•am•bigu•ous**
**un•am•bi•tious**
**un-Ameri•can**
**una•nim•ity** (*or* **unani•mous•ness**)
**unani•mous**
**un•an•nounced**
**un•an•swer•able**
**un•an•swered**
**un•ap•peal•able** legal term
**un•ap•peased**
**un•ap•pre•ciat•ed**
**un•ap•pre•cia•tive**
**un•ap•proach•able**
**un•ap•pro•pri•at•ed**
**un•apt** inapt
**un•apt•ness**
**un•argu•able**
**un•arm**
**un•armed**
**unary** consisting of single element
**un•ashamed**
**un•asham•ed•ly**
**un•asham•ed•ness**
**un•asked**
**un•as•sail•able**
**un•as•sist•ed**
**un•as•sumed**
**un•as•sum•ing**
**un•atoned**
**un•at•tached**
**un•at•tain•able**
**un•at•tend•ed**
**un•at•test•ed**
**un•at•trac•tive**
**un•authen•ti•cat•ed**
**un•author•ized**
**un•avail•able**
**un•avail•ing**
**un•avoid•abil•ity** (*or* **•able•ness**)
**un•avoid•able**
**un•avoid•ably**
**un•aware**
**un•aware•ness**
**un•awares** (*adv*)
**un•backed**
**un•bal•ance**
**un•bal•anced**
**un•bal•las•ted**
**un•bar** (**•bar•ring, •barred**)
**un•bear•able**
**un•bear•able•ness**
**un•bear•ably**
**un•beat•able**
**un•beat•en**
**un•be•com•ing**
**un•be•com•ing•ness**
**un•be•fit•ting**
**un•be•known** (*or* **•knownst**)
**un•be•lief**
**un•be•liev•abil•ity** (*or* **•able•ness**)
**un•be•liev•able**
**un•be•liev•ably**
**un•be•liev•er**
**un•be•liev•ing**
**un•be•liev•ing•ly**
**un•belt**
**un•bend** (**•bend•ing, •bent**)
**un•bend•able**
**un•bend•ing**
**un•bend•ing•ness**
**un•bent**
**un•bi•ased** (*or* **•assed**)
**un•bi•ased•ly** (*or* **•assed•**)
**un•bi•ased•ness** (*or* **•assed•**)
**un•bid•den**
**un•bind** (**•bind•ing, •bound**)
**un•birth•day**
**un•blem•ished**
**un•blessed**
**un•bless•ed•ness**
**un•blink•ing**
**un•block**
**un•blush•ing**

**un•bolt**
**un•bolt•ed**
**un•boned**
**un•bon•net** remove hat
**un•born**
**un•bos•om** relieve by disclosing
**un•bound** released
**un•bound•ed** unlimited
**un•bowed**
**un•brace** relax
**un•break•able**
**un•bred**
**un•bri•dle**
**un•bri•dled**
**un-Brit•ish**
**un•bro•ken**
**un•brushed**
**un•buck•le**
**un•bur•den**
**un•bur•ied**
**un•but•ton**
**un•caged**
**uncalled-for**
**un•can•ni•ly**
**un•can•ny (•ni•er, •ni•est)**
**un•cap (•cap•ping, •capped)**
**uncared-for**
**un•car•ing**
**un•ceas•ing**
**un•ceas•ing•ness**
**un•cer•emo•ni•ous**
**un•cer•emo•ni•ous•ness**
**un•cer•tain**
**un•cer•tain•ness**
**un•cer•tain•ty** (*plural* **•ties)**
**un•chain**
**un•chal•lenge•able**
**un•chal•lenged**
**un•changed**
**un•chang•ing**
**un•chap•er•oned**
**un•charged**
**un•chari•table**
**un•chari•tably**
**un•chari•table•ness**
**un•chart•ed** not mapped
**un•char•tered** not authorized
**un•chaste**
**un•chaste•ness** (*or* **•chas•tity)**
**un•checked**
**un•chris•tian**
**un•church** excommunicate
**un•cial** type of capital letter
**un•ci•form** hook-shaped
**un•ci•na•ria•sis** hookworm disease
**un•ci•nate**
**un•ci•nus** (*plural* **•ni)** small hook
**un•cir•cum•cised**
**un•civ•il**
**un•ci•vil•ity** (*or* **•civ•il•ness)**
**un•civi•lized** (*or* **•lised)**
**un•civil•ly**
**un•clad**
**un•claimed**
**un•clasp**
**un•clas•si•fied**
**un•cle**
**un•clean**
**un•cleaned**
**un•clean•li•ness**
**un•clean•ly**
**un•clean•ness**
**un•clear**
**un•clench**
**un•clip (•clip•ping, •clipped)**
**un•cloak**
**un•clog (•clog•ging, •clogged)**
**un•close**
**un•clothe (•cloth•ing, •clothed** *or* **•clad)**
**un•clothed**
**un•cloud•ed**
**un•clut•tered**
**unco** *Scot* strange
**un•coil**
**un•coined**
**un•com•fort•able**
**un•com•fort•ably**
**un•com•mer•cial**
**un•com•mit•ted**
**un•com•mon**
**un•com•mon•ly**
**un•com•mon•ness**
**un•com•mu•ni•ca•tive**
**un•com•pen•sat•ed**
**un•com•peti•tive**
**un•com•plain•ing**
**un•com•plet•ed**
**un•com•pli•cat•ed**
**un•com•pli•men•ta•ry**
**un•com•pro•mis•ing**
**un•com•pro•mis•ing•ness**
**un•con•cealed**
**un•con•cern**
**un•con•cerned**
**un•con•cern•ed•ly**
**un•con•cern•ed•ness**
**un•con•clud•ed**
**un•con•di•tion•al**
**un•con•di•tion•al•ly**
**un•con•di•tion•al•ness** (*or* **•ity)**
**un•con•di•tioned**
**un•con•fined**
**un•con•firmed**
**un•con•form•abil•ity** (*or* **•able•ness)**
**un•con•form•able**
**un•con•form•ity** (*plural* **•ities)**
**un•con•gen•ial**
**un•con•gen•ial•ly**
**un•con•nect•ed**
**un•con•nect•ed•ness**
**un•con•quer•able**
**un•con•quered**
**un•con•scion•able** unscrupulous; excessive
**un•con•scious**
**un•con•scious•ness**
**un•con•sent•ing**
**un•con•sti•tu•tion•al**
**un•con•sti•tu•tion•al•ity**
**un•con•sti•tu•tion•al•ly**
**un•con•strained**
**un•con•sum•mat•ed**
**un•con•tami•nat•ed**
**un•con•test•ed**
**un•con•trol•labil•ity** (*or* **•lable•ness)**
**un•con•trol•lable**
**un•con•trol•lably**
**un•con•ven•tion•al**
**un•con•ven•tion•al•ity**
**un•con•ven•tion•al•ly**
**un•con•vert•ed**
**un•con•vinced**
**un•con•vinc•ing**
**un•cooked**
**un•co•opera•tive**
**un•co•ordi•nat•ed**
**un•cork**
**un•cor•rected**
**un•cor•robo•rat•ed**
**un•cor•rupt•ed**
**un•count•able**
**un•count•ed**

**un•cou•ple**
**un•couth**
**un•cov•enant•ed**
**un•cov•er**
**un•cov•ered**
**un•criti•cal**
**un•criti•cal•ly**
**un•cross**
**un•crowned**
**unc•tion**
**unc•tu•os•ity** (*or* **•tu•ous•ness)**
**unc•tu•ous**
**un•cul•ti•vat•ed**
**un•curbed**
**un•cured**
**un•curl**
**un•curt•ained**
**un•cus** (*plural* unci) hooked structure
**un•cut**
**un•dam•aged**
**un•damped**
**un•dat•ed**
**un•daunt•ed**
**un•deca•gon** eleven-sided polygon
**un•de•ceiv•able**
**un•de•ceive**
**un•de•ceiv•er**
**un•de•cid•ed**
**un•de•cid•ed•ness**
**un•de•clared**
**un•de•feat•ed**
**un•de•fend•ed**
**un•de•filed**
**un•de•mand•ing**
**un•demo•crat•ic**
**un•demo•crati•cal•ly**
**un•de•mon•stra•tive**
**un•de•ni•able**
**un•de•ni•ably**
**un•der**
**under•achieve**
**under•achieve•ment**
**under•achiev•er**
**under•act**
**under•age**
**under•arm**
**under•belly** (*plural* **•bellies)**
**under•bid (•bid•ding, •bid)**
**under•bid•der**
**under•body** (*plural* **•bodies)**
**under•bred**
**under•breeding**
**under•brush** *US* undergrowth
**under•buy (•buy•ing, •bought)**
**under•capi•tal•ize** (*or* **•ise)**
**under•carriage**
**under•cart** undercarriage
**under•charge**
**under•clay**
**under•clothes** (*or* **•cloth•ing)**
**under•coat**
**under•cook**
**under•cov•er**
**under•croft** underground chamber
**under•cur•rent**
**under•cut (•cut•ting, •cut)**
**under•de•vel•op**
**under•de•vel•op•ment**
**under•do (•does, •do•ing, •did, •done)**
**under•dog**
**under•done**
**under•drain**
**under•drain•age**
**under•dressed**
**under•em•ployed**
**under•em•ploy•ment**
**under•es•ti•mate**
**under•es•ti•ma•tion**
**under•ex•pose**
**under•ex•po•sure**
**under•feed (•feed•ing, •fed)**
**under•felt**
**under•floor**
**under•foot**
**under•fur**
**under•gar•ment**
**under•gird (•gird•ing, •gird•ed** *or* **•girt)** strengthen from below
**under•glaze**
**under•go (•goes, •go•ing, •went, •gone)**
**under•go•er**
**under•gone**
**under•gradu•ate**
**under•ground**
**under•grown**
**under•growth**
**under•hand**
**under•hand•ed**
**under•hand•ed•ly**
**under•hand•ed•ness**
**under•hung**
**under•laid**
**under•lain**
**under•lay (•lay•ing, •laid)** to place under
**under•let (•let•ting, •let)**
**under•let•ter**
**under•lie (•ly•ing, •lay, •lain)** to lie under
**under•li•er**
**under•line**
**under•ling**
**under•ly•ing**
**under•manned**
**under•men•tioned**
**under•mine**
**under•min•er**
**under•min•ing•ly**
**under•most**
**under•named**
**under•neath**
**under•nour•ish**
**under•nour•ished**
**under•nour•ish•ment**
**under•paid**
**under•paint•ing**
**under•pants**
**under•pass**
**under•pay (•pay•ing, •paid)**
**under•pay•ment**
**under•pin (•pin•ning, •pinned)**
**under•pin•nings**
**under•play**
**under•plot** subplot
**under•price**
**under•privi•leged**
**under•pro•duc•tion**
**under•proof** less than proof spirit
**under•prop (•prop•ping, •propped)**
**under•quote**
**under•rate**
**under•ripe**
**under•score**
**under•sea**
**under•seal**
**under•sec•re•tary** (*plural* **•taries)**
**under•sec•re•tary•ship**
**under•sell (•sel•ling, •sold)**
**under•sell•er**
**under•set (•set•ting, •set)**
**under•sexed**

**under•sher•iff**
**under•shirt**
**under•shoot** (**•shoot•ing, •shot**)
**under•side**
**under•signed**
**under•sized**
**under•skirt**
**under•slung**
**under•soil**
**under•sold**
**under•spend** (**•spend•ing, •spent**)
**under•staffed**
**under•stand** (**•stand•ing, •stood**)
**under•stand•able**
**under•stand•ably**
**under•stand•ing**
**under•stand•ing•ly**
**under•state**
**under•state•ment**
**under•stock**
**under•stood**
**under•study** (*noun, plural* **•studies**; *verb* **•studies, •study•ing, •stud•ied**)
**under•sur•face**
**under•take** (**•tak•ing, •took, •tak•en**)
**under•tak•er**
**under•tak•ing**
**under•thrust** geological fault
**under•tint**
**under•tone**
**under•took**
**under•tow**
**under•trick** bridge term
**under•trump**
**under•valu•ation**
**under•value** (**•valu•ing, •val•ued**)
**under•valu•er**
**under•vest**
**under•wa•ter**
**under•wear**
**under•weight**
**under•went**
**under•wing** moth
**under•world**
**under•write** (**•writ•ing, •wrote, •writ•ten**)
**under•writ•er**
**un•des•cend•ed**
**un•de•served**
**un•de•serv•ing**
**un•de•sign•ing**
**un•de•sir•abil•ity** (*or* **•able•ness**)
**un•de•sir•able**
**un•de•sir•ably**
**un•de•sired**
**un•de•tect•ed**
**un•de•ter•mined**
**un•de•terred**
**un•de•vel•oped**
**un•de•vi•at•ing**
**un•di•ag•nosed**
**un•did**
**un•dies**
**un•dif•fer•en•ti•at•ed**
**un•di•gest•ed**
**un•dig•ni•fied**
**un•di•lut•ed**
**un•dim•in•ished**
**un•dimmed**
**un•dine** water spirit
**un•di•rect•ed**
**un•dis•ci•plined**
**un•dis•closed**
**un•dis•cov•ered**
**un•dis•crimi•nat•ing**
**un•dis•guised**
**un•dis•put•ed**
**un•dis•solved**
**un•dis•tin•guished**
**un•dis•trib•ut•ed** logic term
**un•dis•turbed**
**un•di•vid•ed**
**undo** (**un•does, un•do•ing, un•did, un•done**)
**un•do•er**
**un•do•ing**
**un•done**
**un•doubt•ed**
**un•doubt•ed•ly**
**un•dreamed** (*or* **•dreamt**)
**un•dress**
**un•drink•able**
**un•due**
**un•du•lance**
**un•du•lant**
**un•du•late**
**un•du•la•tion**
**un•du•la•tor**
**un•du•la•tory**
**un•du•ly**
**un•dy•ing**
**un•earned**
**un•earth**
**un•earth•li•ness**
**un•earth•ly**
**un•ease**
**un•easi•ly**
**un•easi•ness**
**un•easy**
**un•eat•able**
**un•eat•en**
**un•eco•nom•ic**
**un•eco•nomi•cal**
**un•eco•nomi•cal•ly**
**un•ed•it•ed**
**un•edu•cat•ed**
**un•elect•able**
**un•emo•tion•al**
**un•emo•tion•al•ly**
**un•em•ploy•abil•ity**
**un•em•ploy•able**
**un•em•ployed**
**un•em•ploy•ment**
**un•end•ing**
**un•en•gaged**
**un-Eng•lish**
**un•en•light•ened**
**un•en•ter•pris•ing**
**un•en•thu•si•as•tic**
**un•en•thu•si•asti•cal•ly**
**un•en•vi•able**
**un•equal**
**un•equalled** (*US* **•equaled**)
**un•equal•ly**
**un•equivo•cal**
**un•equivo•cal•ly**
**un•equivo•cal•ness**
**un•err•ing**
**un•err•ing•ly**
**un•es•sen•tial** *less common word for* **inessential**
**un•ethi•cal**
**un•ethi•cal•ly**
**un•even**
**un•even•ness**
**un•event•ful**
**un•event•ful•ly**
**un•ex•am•pled**
**un•ex•cep•tion•able** beyond criticism
**un•ex•cep•tion•able•ness** (*or* **•abil•ity**)
**un•ex•cep•tion•al** ordinary
**un•ex•cit•ing**
**un•ex•pec•ted**
**un•ex•pec•ted•ly**
**un•ex•pect•ed•ness**

**un•ex•pe•ri•enced**
**un•ex•pired**
**un•ex•plain•able** *less common word for* **inexplicable**
**un•ex•plained**
**un•ex•plod•ed**
**un•ex•plored**
**un•ex•posed**
**un•ex•pressed**
**un•ex•pres•sive**
**un•ex•pres•sive•ness**
**un•ex•pur•gat•ed**
**un•fad•ing**
**un•fail•ing**
**un•fair**
**un•fair•ness**
**un•faith•ful**
**un•faith•ful•ly**
**un•faith•ful•ness**
**un•fa•mil•iar**
**un•fa•mili•ar•ity**
**un•fash•ion•able**
**un•fash•ion•ably**
**un•fas•ten**
**un•fa•thered**
**un•fath•om•able**
**un•fath•omed**
**un•fa•vour•able** (*US* **•vor•**)
**un•fa•vour•able•ness** (*US* **•vor•**)
**un•fa•vour•ably** (*US* **•vor•**)
**un•fed**
**un•feel•ing**
**un•feel•ing•ness**
**un•feigned**
**un•feigned•ly**
**un•femi•nine**
**un•fenced**
**un•fer•til•ized** (*or* **•ised**)
**un•fet•ter**
**un•fil•ial**
**un•filled**
**un•fin•ished**
**un•fit**
**un•fit•ness**
**un•fit•ted**
**un•fit•ting**
**un•fix**
**un•flag•ging**
**un•flap•pabil•ity** (*or* **•pable•ness**)
**un•flap•pable**
**un•flat•ter•ing**
**un•fledged**
**un•flinch•ing**
**un•flinch•ing•ness**
**un•flust•ered**
**un•fo•cused**
**un•fold**
**un•fold•er**
**un•forced**
**un•fore•see•able**
**un•fore•seen**
**un•for•get•table**
**un•for•giv•able**
**un•for•giv•en**
**un•for•giv•ing**
**un•for•got•ten**
**un•formed**
**un•for•tu•nate**
**un•for•tu•nate•ly**
**un•for•tu•nate•ness**
**un•found•ed**
**un•found•ed•ness**
**un•framed**
**un•freeze** (**•freez•ing, •froze, •fro•zen**)
**un•fre•quent•ed**
**un•friend•li•ness**
**un•friend•ly** (**•li•er, •li•est**)
**un•frock**
**un•froze**
**un•fro•zen**
**un•fruit•ful**
**un•fruit•ful•ly**
**un•fruit•ful•ness**
**un•ful•filled**
**un•furl**
**un•fur•nished**
**un•gain•li•ness**
**un•gain•ly** (**•li•er, •li•est**)
**Un•ga•va** Canadian region
**un•gen•er•ous**
**un•gen•tle•man•ly**
**un-get-at-able**
**un•glazed**
**un•god•li•ness**
**un•god•ly** (**•li•er, •li•est**)
**un•gov•ern•able**
**un•gov•ern•able•ness**
**un•gov•ern•ably**
**un•grace•ful**
**un•grace•ful•ly**
**un•gra•cious**
**un•gram•mati•cal**
**un•grate•ful**
**un•grate•ful•ly**
**un•grate•ful•ness**
**un•grudg•ing**
**un•gual** (*or* **•gu•lar**) of finger- or toenails
**un•guard•ed**
**un•guard•ed•ness**
**un•guent** ointment
**un•guen•tary**
**un•guicu•late** biology term
**un•gui•nous** greasy
**un•guis** (*plural* **•gues**) claw or hoof
**un•gu•la** (*plural* **•lae**) maths term
**un•gu•lar**
**un•gu•late** hoofed mammal
**un•gu•li•grade** walking on hooves
**un•hair**
**un•hal•lowed**
**un•ham•pered**
**un•hand**
**un•hand•some**
**un•hand•some•ness**
**un•hap•pi•ly**
**un•hap•pi•ness**
**un•hap•py** (**•pi•er, •pi•est**)
**un•harmed**
**un•har•ness**
**un•healthi•ly**
**un•healthi•ness**
**un•healthy** (**•healthi•er, •healthi•est**)
**un•heard**
**unheard-of**
**un•heed•ed**
**un•heed•ing**
**un•helm** remove the helmet of
**un•help•ful**
**un•help•ful•ly**
**un•her•ald•ed**
**un•hesi•tat•ing**
**un•hid•den**
**un•hinge**
**un•ho•li•ness**
**un•ho•ly** (**•li•er, •li•est**)
**un•hon•oured** (*US* **•ored**)
**un•hook**
**unhoped-for**
**un•horse**
**un•hur•ried**
**un•hurt**
**un•hy•gien•ic**
**un•hy•gieni•cal•ly**
**un•hy•phen•at•ed**
**uni** *Austral* university

**Uni•at** (*or* **•ate**) Eastern Church
**Uni•at•ism**
**uni•ax•ial**
**uni•cam•er•al**
**uni•cam•er•al•ism**
**uni•cam•er•al•ist**
**uni•cel•lu•lar**
**uni•cel•lu•lar•ity**
**uni•col•our** (*or* **•oured**; *US* **•or** *or* **•ored**)
**uni•corn**
**uni•cos•tate** having one rib
**uni•cy•cle**
**uni•cy•clist**
**un•iden•ti•fi•able**
**un•iden•ti•fied**
**uni•di•rec•tion•al**
**uni•fi•able**
**uni•fi•ca•tion**
**uni•fied**
**uni•fi•er**
**uni•fo•li•ate** botany term
**uni•fo•lio•late** botany term
**uni•form**
**uni•formi•tar•ian**
**uni•formi•tari•an•ism** geological theory
**uni•form•ity** (*plural* **•ities**)
**uni•form•ly**
**uni•form•ness**
**uni•fy** (**•fies, •fy•ing, •fied**)
**uni•ju•gate** botany term
**uni•lat•er•al**
**uni•lat•er•al•ism** (*or* **•ity**)
**uni•lat•er•al•ly**
**un•il•lus•trat•ed**
**uni•locu•lar** botany term
**un•im•agi•nable**
**un•im•agi•nably**
**un•im•agi•na•tive**
**un•im•ag•ined**
**un•im•paired**
**un•im•peach•abil•ity** (*or* **•able•ness**)
**un•im•peach•able**
**un•im•ped•ed**
**un•im•por•tant**
**un•im•pos•ing**
**un•im•pressed**
**un•im•pres•sive**
**un•im•proved**
**un•in•cor•po•ra•ted**
**un•in•flu•enced**
**un•in•formed**
**un•in•hab•it•able**
**un•in•hab•it•ed**
**un•in•hib•it•ed**
**un•in•jured**
**un•in•spired**
**un•in•spir•ing**
**un•in•sur•able**
**un•in•sured**
**un•in•tel•li•gence**
**un•in•tel•li•gent**
**un•in•tel•li•gible**
**un•in•tel•li•gibly**
**un•in•tend•ed**
**un•in•ten•tion•al**
**un•in•ten•tion•ally**
**un•in•ter•est•ed** not interested; *compare* disinterested
**un•in•ter•est•ed•ly**
**un•in•ter•est•ed•ness**
**un•in•ter•est•ing**
**un•in•ter•rupt•ed**
**uni•nu•cleate**
**un•in•vit•ed**
**un•in•vit•ing**
**un•ion**
**un•ion•ism**
**un•ion•ist**
**un•ion•is•tic**
**un•ioni•za•tion** (*or* **•sa•tion**)
**un•ion•ize** (*or* **•ise**) join trade union
**un-ionized** not ionized
**uni•para** *variant of* primipara
**unip•ar•ous** biology term
**uni•per•son•al**
**uni•per•son•al•ity**
**uni•pla•nar**
**uni•pod** one-legged support
**uni•po•lar**
**uni•po•lar•ity**
**unique**
**unique•ly**
**unique•ness**
**uni•ra•mous** undivided
**uni•sep•tate** biology term
**uni•sex**
**uni•sexu•al**
**uni•sexu•al•ity**
**uni•son**
**uniso•nous** (*or* **•nal, •nant**)
**unit**
**Uni•tar•ian**
**uni•tar•ian**
**Uni•tari•an•ism** Christian belief
**uni•tari•an•ism** centralized government
**uni•tary**
**unite**
**unit•ed**
**unit•ed•ly**
**unit•ed•ness**
**unit•er**
**uni•tive**
**unity** (*plural* **unities**)
**uni•va•len•cy**
**uni•va•lent**
**uni•valve** zoology term
**uni•ver•sal**
**uni•ver•sal•ism**
**uni•ver•sal•ist**
**uni•ver•sal•is•tic**
**uni•ver•sal•ity** (*plural* **•ities**)
**uni•ver•sali•za•tion** (*or* **•sa•tion**)
**uni•ver•sal•ize** (*or* **•ise**)
**uni•ver•sal•ly**
**uni•ver•sal•ness**
**uni•verse**
**uni•ver•sity** (*plural* **•sities**)
**uni•vo•cal** unambiguous
**un•just**
**un•jus•ti•fi•able**
**un•jus•ti•fied**
**un•just•ness**
**un•kempt**
**un•kempt•ness**
**un•kenned** *Dialect* unknown
**un•ken•nel** (**•nel•ling, •nelled**; *US* **•nel•ing, •neled**)
**un•kind**
**un•kind•li•ness**
**un•kind•ness**
**un•knit** (**•knit•ting, •knit•ted** *or* **•knit**)
**un•know•able**
**un•know•able•ness** (*or* **•abil•ity**)
**un•know•ing**
**un•know•ing•ly**
**un•known**
**un•known•ness**
**un•la•belled** (*US* **•beled**)
**un•lace**
**un•lade** unload
**un•la•den**

**un•lady•like**
**un•laid**
**un•lam•ent•ed**
**un•lash**
**un•latch**
**un•law•ful**
**un•law•ful•ly**
**un•law•ful•ness**
**un•lay (•lay•ing, •laid)** untwist
**un•lead** printing term
**un•lead•ed**
**un•learn (•learn•ing, •learnt** *or* **•learned)**
**un•learn•ed** ignorant
**un•leash**
**un•leav•ened**
**un•less**
**un•let•tered**
**un•li•censed**
**un•like**
**un•like•li•ness (*or* •li•hood)**
**un•like•ly**
**un•lim•ber** prepare for use
**un•lim•it•ed**
**un•lined**
**un•list•ed**
**un•lit**
**un•live**
**un•lived-in**
**un•load**
**un•load•er**
**un•lock**
**un•lock•able**
**unlooked-for**
**un•loose (*or* •loos•en)**
**un•lov•able**
**un•loved**
**un•love•ly**
**un•lov•ing**
**un•lucki•ly**
**un•lucki•ness**
**un•lucky (•lucki•er, •lucki•est)**
**un•made**
**un•make (•mak•ing, •made)**
**un•mak•er**
**un•man (•man•ning, •manned)**
**un•man•age•able**
**un•man•li•ness**
**un•man•ly**
**un•manned**
**un•man•nered**
**un•man•ner•li•ness**
**un•man•ner•ly**
**un•marked**
**un•mar•riage•able**
**un•mar•ried**
**un•mask**
**un•mask•er**
**un•matched**
**un•mean•ing**
**un•meant**
**un•meas•ur•able** unable to be measured; *compare* **immeasurable**
**un•meas•ured**
**un•meet** unsuitable
**un•men•tion•able**
**un•men•tion•ables**
**un•mer•ci•ful**
**un•mer•ci•ful•ly**
**un•mer•it•ed**
**un•mind•ful**
**un•mis•tak•able (*or* •take•)**
**un•mis•tak•ably (*or* •take•)**
**un•miti•gat•ed**
**un•mixed**
**un•mo•lest•ed**
**un•moor**
**un•mor•al** amoral
**un•mo•ral•ity**
**un•mount•ed**
**un•mourned**
**un•moved**
**un•mu•si•cal**
**un•mu•si•cal•ly**
**un•mu•si•cal•ness**
**un•muz•zle**
**un•name•able**
**un•named**
**un•natu•ral**
**un•natu•ral•ly**
**un•natu•ral•ness**
**un•navi•gable**
**un•nec•es•sari•ly**
**un•nec•es•sary**
**un•neigh•bour•ly (*US* •bor•)**
**un•nerve**
**un•nerv•ing**
**un•no•ticed**
**un•num•bered**
**un•ob•jec•tion•able**
**un•ob•scured**
**un•ob•ser•vant**
**un•ob•served**
**un•ob•struct•ed**
**un•ob•tain•able**
**un•ob•tru•sive**
**un•ob•tru•sive•ly**
**un•ob•tru•sive•ness**
**un•oc•cu•pied**
**un•of•fend•ing**
**un•of•fi•cial**
**un•of•fi•cial•ly**
**un•opened**
**un•op•posed**
**un•or•gan•ized (*or* •ised)**
**un•origi•nal**
**un•ortho•dox**
**un•owned**
**un•pack**
**un•pack•er**
**un•paged**
**un•paid**
**un•paint•ed**
**un•pained**
**un•pal•at•able**
**un•par•al•leled**
**un•par•don•able**
**un•par•lia•men•ta•ry**
**un•pat•ent•ed**
**un•pat•ri•ot•ic**
**un•paved**
**un•peeled**
**un•peg (•peg•ging, •pegged)**
**un•peo•ple (*verb*)**
**un•per•ceived**
**un•per•fo•rat•ed**
**un•per•son**
**un•per•turbed**
**un•pick**
**un•pin (•pin•ning, •pinned)**
**un•pity•ing**
**un•place•able**
**un•placed**
**un•planned**
**un•play•able**
**un•pleas•ant**
**un•pleas•ant•ness**
**un•pleas•ing**
**un•plug (•plug•ging, •plugged)**
**un•plumbed**
**un•poli•tic**
**un•po•liti•cal**
**un•polled**
**un•pol•lut•ed**
**un•popu•lar**
**un•popu•lar•ity**
**un•posed**

**un•prac•ti•cal** impractical
**un•prac•ti•cal•ity** (*or* **•ness**)
**un•prac•tised** (*US* **•ticed**)
**un•prec•edent•ed**
**un•pre•dict•abil•ity** (*or* **•able•ness**)
**un•pre•dict•able**
**un•pre•dict•ably**
**un•preju•diced**
**un•pre•medi•tat•ed**
**un•pre•medi•ta•tion**
**un•pre•pared**
**un•pre•par•ed•ness**
**un•pre•pos•sess•ing**
**un•pre•sent•able**
**un•pre•ten•tious**
**un•pre•ten•tious•ness**
**un•pre•vent•able**
**un•priced**
**un•prin•ci•pled**
**un•print•able**
**un•pro•duc•tive**
**un•pro•fessed**
**un•pro•fes•sion•al**
**un•pro•fes•sion•al•ly**
**un•prof•it•abil•ity** (*or* **•able•ness**)
**un•prof•it•able**
**un•prof•it•ably**
**un•prom•is•ing**
**un•prompt•ed**
**un•pro•nounce•able**
**un•pro•tect•ed**
**un•prov•able**
**un•proved**
**un•prov•en**
**un•pro•vid•ed**
**un•pub•lished**
**un•punc•tual**
**un•pun•ished**
**un•put•down•able**
**un•quali•fi•able**
**un•quali•fied**
**un•quench•able**
**un•ques•tion•abil•ity** (*or* **•able•ness**)
**un•ques•tion•able**
**un•ques•tion•ably**
**un•ques•tioned**
**un•ques•tion•ing**
**un•qui•et**
**un•quote**
**un•rav•el** (**•el•ling, •elled;** *US* **•el•ing, •eled**)
**un•rav•el•ler** (*US* **•el•er**)
**un•rav•el•ment**
**un•reach•able**
**un•re•ac•tive**
**un•read**
**un•read•abil•ity** (*or* **•able•ness**)
**un•read•able**
**un•readi•ness**
**un•ready**
**un•real**
**un•re•al•is•tic**
**un•re•al•isti•cal•ly**
**un•re•al•ity**
**un•re•al•ized** (*or* **•ised**)
**un•rea•son**
**un•rea•son•able**
**un•rea•son•able•ness**
**un•rea•son•ably**
**un•rea•son•ing**
**un•reck•on•able**
**un•rec•og•niz•able** (*or* **•nis•able**)
**un•rec•og•nized** (*or* **•nised**)
**un•rec•on•ciled**
**un•re•con•struct•ed**
**un•re•cord•ed**
**un•reeve** (**•reev•ing, •rove** *or* **•reeved**) nautical term
**un•re•fined**
**un•re•flect•ed**
**un•re•flec•tive**
**un•re•gard•ed**
**un•re•gen•era•cy**
**un•re•gen•er•ate** unrepentant
**un•reg•is•tered**
**un•re•hearsed**
**un•re•lat•ed**
**un•re•lent•ing**
**un•re•li•abil•ity** (*or* **•able•ness**)
**un•re•li•able**
**un•re•li•ably**
**un•re•mit•ting**
**un•re•paired**
**un•re•peat•able**
**un•re•pent•ant**
**un•re•port•ed**
**un•rep•re•senta•tive**
**un•rep•re•sent•ed**
**un•re•quit•ed**
**un•re•served**
**un•re•serv•ed•ly**
**un•re•serv•ed•ness**
**un•re•sist•ing**
**un•re•solved**
**un•re•spon•sive**
**un•rest**
**un•re•strained**
**un•re•strict•ed**
**un•re•ward•ed**
**un•re•ward•ing**
**un•rhymed**
**un•rid•able**
**un•rid•dle** solve
**un•rid•dler**
**un•ri•fled**
**un•rig** (**•rig•ging, •rigged**)
**un•right•eous**
**un•rip** (**•rip•ping, •ripped**)
**un•ripe** (*or* **•rip•ened**)
**un•ri•valled** (*US* **•valed**)
**un•roll**
**un•root**
**un•round•ed**
**un•rove** nautical term
**un•ruf•fled**
**un•ruf•fled•ness**
**un•ruled**
**un•ru•li•ness**
**un•ru•ly** (**•li•er, •li•est**)
**un•sad•dle**
**un•safe**
**un•said**
**un•sale•able** (*US* **•sal•able**)
**un•salt•ed**
**un•sanc•tioned**
**un•sani•tary**
**un•sat•is•fac•tori•ly**
**un•sat•is•fac•tory**
**un•sat•is•fied**
**un•sat•is•fy•ing**
**un•satu•rat•ed**
**un•satu•ra•tion**
**un•saved**
**un•sa•vouri•ly** (*US* **•vori•**)
**un•sa•vouri•ness** (*US* **•vori•**)
**un•sa•voury** (*US* **•vory**)
**un•say** (**•say•ing, •said**)
**un•scal•able**
**un•scarred**
**un•scathed**
**un•scent•ed**
**un•sched•uled**
**un•schooled**
**un•sci•en•tif•ic**
**un•sci•en•tifi•cal•ly**
**un•scram•ble**
**un•scram•bler**
**un•scratched**

**un•screened**
**un•screw**
**un•script•ed**
**un•scru•pu•lous**
**un•scru•pu•lous•ness** (*or* **•los•ity)**
**un•seal**
**un•seal•able**
**un•seam**
**un•search•able**
**un•sea•son•able**
**un•sea•son•ably**
**un•sea•soned**
**un•seat**
**un•sea•worthy**
**un•secured**
**un•seed•ed**
**un•seem•li•ness**
**un•seem•ly**
**un•seen**
**un•seg•re•gat•ed**
**un•self•con•scious**
**un•self•ish**
**un•self•ish•ness**
**un•sepa•rat•ed**
**un•ser•vice•able**
**un•set**
**un•set•tle**
**un•set•tled**
**un•set•tle•ment**
**un•sex**
**un•shack•le**
**un•shad•ed**
**un•shak•able** (*or* **•shake•)**
**un•shak•en**
**un•shap•en**
**un•shav•en**
**un•sheathe**
**un•shed**
**un•ship (•ship•ping, •shipped)**
**un•shock•able**
**un•sight•ed**
**un•sight•li•ness**
**un•sight•ly**
**un•signed**
**un•sink•able**
**un•skil•ful** (*US* **•skill•ful)**
**un•skilled**
**un•slaked**
**un•sling (•sling•ing, •slung)**
**un•smil•ing**
**un•smoked**
**un•snap (•snap•ping, •snapped)**
**un•snarl**
**un•so•ciabil•ity** (*or* **•ciable•ness)**
**un•so•ciable**
**un•so•ciably**
**un•so•cial**
**un•sold**
**un•so•lic•it•ed**
**un•solv•able**
**un•solved**
**un•so•phis•ti•cat•ed**
**un•so•phis•ti•cat•ed•ness** (*or* **•ca•tion)**
**un•sort•ed**
**un•sought**
**un•sound**
**un•spar•ing**
**un•speak•able**
**un•speak•ably**
**un•spe•cif•ic**
**un•speci•fied**
**un•spent**
**un•spoiled** (*or* **•spoilt)**
**un•spo•ken**
**un•sport•ing**
**un•spot•ted**
**un•sta•ble**
**un•stamped**
**un•steadi•ly**
**un•steadi•ness**
**un•steady** (*adj* **•steadi•er, •steadi•est;** *verb* **•steadies, •steady•ing, •stead•ied)**
**un•step (•step•ping, •stepped)** nautical term
**un•stick (•stick•ing, •stuck)**
**un•stint•ing**
**un•stop (•stop•ping, •stopped)**
**un•stop•pable**
**un•stopped**
**un•strained**
**un•strap (•strap•ping, •strapped)**
**un•strati•fied**
**un•stressed**
**un•stri•at•ed**
**un•string (•string•ing, •strung)**
**un•striped**
**un•struc•tured**
**un•strung**
**un•stuck**
**un•stud•ied**
**un•sub•stan•tial**
**un•sub•stan•ti•al•ity**
**un•sub•stan•ti•at•ed**
**un•suc•cess•ful**
**un•suc•cess•ful•ly**
**un•sug•ared**
**un•suit•abil•ity** (*or* **•able•ness)**
**un•suit•able**
**un•suit•ably**
**un•suit•ed**
**un•sul•ied**
**un•sung**
**un•sure**
**un•sur•passed**
**un•sus•pect•ed**
**un•sus•pect•ing**
**un•swathe**
**un•swear (•swear•ing, •swore, •sworn)** retract
**un•sweet•ened**
**un•swept**
**un•swerv•ing**
**un•sym•pa•thet•ic**
**un•sym•pa•theti•cal•ly**
**un•sys•tem•at•ic**
**un•taint•ed**
**un•tame•able**
**un•tamed**
**un•tan•gle**
**un•tapped**
**un•tast•ed**
**un•taught**
**un•teach (•teach•ing, •taught)**
**un•teach•able**
**un•tear•able**
**un•ten•abil•ity** (*or* **•able•ness)**
**un•ten•able**
**un•ten•ant•ed**
**Un•ter•wal•den** Swiss canton
**un•test•ed**
**un•thanked**
**un•thank•ful**
**un•thank•ful•ness**
**un•think (•think•ing, •thought)**
**un•think•abil•ity** (*or* **•able•ness)**
**un•think•able**
**un•think•ably**
**un•think•ing**

**un•thought-of**
**un•thread**
**un•ti•di•ly**
**un•ti•di•ness**
**un•ti•dy** (*adj* **•di•er, •di•est**; *verb* **•dies, •dy•ing, •died**)
**un•tie** (**•ty•ing, •tied**)
**un•til**
**un•time•ly**
**un•tinged**
**un•tir•ing**
**un•tit•led**
**unto**
**un•told**
**un•touch•abil•ity**
**un•touch•able**
**un•touched**
**un•to•ward**
**un•trace•able**
**un•trained**
**un•tram•melled** (*US* **•meled**)
**un•trans•lat•able**
**un•trav•elled** (*US* **•eled**)
**un•treat•able**
**un•treat•ed**
**un•tried**
**un•trod•den**
**un•true**
**un•truss**
**un•trust•worthy**
**un•truth**
**un•truth•ful**
**un•truth•ful•ly**
**un•truth•ful•ness**
**un•tuck**
**un•turned**
**un•tu•tored**
**un•typi•cal**
**un•us•able**
**un•used**
**un•usual**
**un•usu•al•ly**
**un•ut•ter•able**
**un•ut•tered**
**un•val•ued**
**un•var•ied**
**un•var•nished**
**un•vary•ing**
**un•veil**
**un•veil•ing**
**un•versed**
**un•voice** phonetics term
**un•voiced**
**un•want•ed**
**un•war•rant•able**
**un•war•rant•ed**
**un•wari•ly**
**un•wari•ness**
**un•wary**
**un•washed**
**un•watched**
**un•wat•ered**
**un•wa•ver•ing**
**un•wear•able**
**un•wea•ried**
**un•weary•ing**
**un•wed**
**un•weighed**
**un•wel•come**
**un•well**
**un•wept**
**un•whole•some**
**un•whole•some•ly**
**un•whole•some•ness**
**un•wieldi•ly** (*or* **•wield•li•ly**)
**un•wieldi•ness** (*or* **•wield•li•ness**)
**un•wieldy** (*or* **•wield•ly**)
**un•willed**
**un•will•ing**
**un•will•ing•ness**
**un•wind** (**•wind•ing, •wound**)
**un•wind•able**
**un•wind•er**
**un•wink•ing**
**un•wise**
**un•wise•ly**
**un•wish**
**un•wished**
**un•wit•nessed**
**un•wit•ting**
**un•wont•ed**
**un•work•able**
**un•world•li•ness**
**un•world•ly**
**un•worn**
**un•worthi•ly**
**un•worthi•ness**
**un•wor•thy** (**•thi•er, thi•est**)
**un•wound**
**un•wrap** (**•wrap•ping, •wrapped**)
**un•writ•ten**
**un•yield•ing**
**un•yoke**
**un•zip** (**•zip•ping, •zipped**)
**up** (**up•ping, upped**)
**up-anchor**
**up-and-coming**
**up-and-under**
**Upani•shad** Hindu treatise
**upas** tree
**up•beat**
**up-bow** musical term
**up•braid**
**up•braid•er**
**up•bring•ing**
**up•build** (**•build•ing, •built**)
**up•build•er**
**up•cast** (**•cast•ing, •cast**)
**up•country**
**up•date**
**up•dat•er**
**up•draught** (*US* **•draft**)
**up•end**
**up•grade**
**up•grad•er**
**up•growth**
**up•heav•al**
**up•heave** (**•heav•ing, •heaved** *or* **•hove**)
**up•held**
**up•hill**
**up•hold** (**•hold•ing, •held**)
**up•hold•er**
**up•hol•ster**
**up•hol•ster•er**
**up•hol•stery** (*plural* **•steries**)
**up•hove** *variant of* **upheaved**
**uphroe** *variant spelling of* **euphroe**
**up•keep**
**up•land**
**up•lift**
**up•lift•er**
**up•lift•ing**
**up•most** *variant of* **uppermost**
**upon**
**up•per**
**upper-case** (*adj, verb*)
**upper-class** (*adj*)
**upper•cut** (**•cut•ting, •cut**)
**upper•most** (*or* **up•most**)
**up•pish**
**up•pish•ness**

**up•pi•ty**
**Upp•sa•la** (*or* **Up•sa•la**) Swedish city
**up•raise**
**up•rais•er**
**up•rear**
**up•right**
**up•right•ness**
**up•rise** (**•ris•ing, •rose, •ris•en**)
**up•ris•er**
**up•ris•ing**
**up•river**
**up•roar**
**up•roari•ous**
**up•root**
**up•root•er**
**up•rose**
**up•rush**
**Up•sa•la** *variant spelling of* **Uppsala**
**up•set** (**•set•ting, •set**)
**up•set•table**
**up•set•ter**
**up•set•ting**
**up•shot**
**up•side**
**upside-down**
**upside-downness**
**up•si•lon** Greek letter
**up•stage**
**up•stairs**
**up•stand•ing**
**up•stand•ing•ness**
**up•start**
**up•state**
**up•stream**
**up•stretched**
**up•stroke**
**up•surge**
**up•sweep** (**•sweep•ing, •swept**)
**up•swing** (**•swing•ing, •swung**)
**upsy-daisy**
**up•take**
**up•throw**
**up•thrust**
**up•tight**
**up•tilt**
**up-to-date**
**up-to-dateness**
**up•town**
**up•turn**
**up•ward** (*adj*)
**up•ward•ly**
**up•ward•ness**
**up•wards** (*adv*)
**up•wind**
**Ur** Sumerian city
**ura•cil** biochemical compound
**urae•mia** (*US* **ure•**)
**urae•mic** (*US* **ure•**)
**urae•us** (*plural* **•uses**) sacred serpent
**Ural** Russian river
**Ural-Altaic** language group
**Ural•ic** (*or* **Ura•lian**)
**ural•ite** mineral
**ural•it•ic**
**Urals** Russian mountains
**ura•naly•sis** *variant of* **urinalysis**
**Ura•nian** of Uranus; celestial
**uran•ic** chemistry term
**ura•nide** chemical element
**urani•nite** mineral
**ura•nite** mineral
**ura•nit•ic**
**ura•nium**
**ura•nog•ra•pher** (*or* **•phist**)
**ura•no•graph•ic** (*or* **•graphi•cal**)
**ura•nog•ra•phy** star mapping
**ura•nous** chemistry term
**Ura•nus** planet
**Uranus** Greek god
**ura•nyl** chemical group
**ura•nyl•ic**
**urate**
**urat•ic**
**ur•ban**
**ur•bane**
**ur•bane•ly**
**ur•bane•ness**
**ur•ban•ite**
**ur•ban•ity** (*plural* **•ities**)
**ur•bani•za•tion** (*or* **•sa•tion**)
**ur•ban•ize** (*or* **•ise**)
**urbi et orbi** papal blessing
**ur•ceo•late** pitcher-shaped
**ur•chin**
**urd** bean plant
**urdé** heraldic term
**Urdu**
**urea**
**ureal** (*or* **ureic**)
**urease** enzyme
**ure•dial**
**uredium** (*or* **uredin•ium**; *plural* **uredia** *or* **uredinia**) fungal structure
**uredo** (*plural* **uredi•nes**) urticaria
**uredo•so•rus** (*plural* **•so•ri**) uredium
**uredo•spore**
**ureic** *variant of* **ureal**
**ureide** chemical compound
**ure•mia** *US spelling of* **uraemia**
**ureter**
**ureter•al** (*or* **•ic**)
**urethane** (*or* **urethan**) chemistry term
**urethra** (*plural* **urethrae** *or* **urethras**)
**urethral**
**urethrit•ic**
**urethri•tis**
**urethro•scope**
**urethro•scop•ic**
**urethros•co•py**
**uret•ic** of urine
**urge**
**ur•gen•cy**
**ur•gent**
**urg•er**
**urg•ing•ly**
**uric**
**uri•dine** biochemical compound
**uri•nal**
**uri•naly•sis** (*or* **ura•**; *plural* **•ses**)
**uri•nant** heraldic term
**uri•nary** (*plural* **•naries**)
**uri•nate**
**uri•na•tion**
**uri•na•tive**
**urine**
**uri•nif•er•ous** transporting urine
**uri•no•geni•tal** *variant of* **urogenital**
**uri•nous** (*or* **•nose**)
**Ur•mia** Iranian lake
**urn**
**urn•field** cemetery
**urn•like**
**uro•chord** zoology term

**uro•chor•dal**
**uro•chor•date** marine animal
**uro•chrome** pigment
**uro•dele** type of amphibian
**uro•geni•tal** (*or* **uri•no•**)
**urog•enous** producing urine
**uro•lith** stone in urinary tract
**uro•lith•ic**
**uro•log•ic** (*or* **•logi•cal**)
**urolo•gist**
**urol•ogy** branch of medicine
**uro•pod** crustacean appendage
**uropo•dal** (*or* **•dous**)
**uro•pyg•ial**
**uro•pyg•ium** base of bird's tail
**uro•scop•ic**
**uros•co•pist**
**uros•co•py** examination of urine
**uro•style** zoology term
**ur•sine** of bears
**Ur•su•line** nun
**Ur•text** *German* original text
**ur•ti•ca•ceous** botany term
**ur•ti•caria** nettle rash
**ur•ti•car•ial** (*or* **•cari•ous**)
**ur•ti•cate** medical term
**ur•ti•ca•tion**
**Urua•pan** Mexican city
**Uru•guay**
**Uru•guay•an**
**Urum•chi** (*or* **Wu-lu-mu-ch'i**) Chinese city
**uru•shi•ol** poisonous liquid
**us**
**us•abil•ity** (*or* **•able•ness, use•**)
**us•able** (*or* **use•**)
**us•age**
**us•ance** commerce term
**use**
**use•abil•ity** (*or* **•able•ness**) *variants of* **usability**
**use•able** *variant spelling of* **usable**
**used**
**use•ful**
**use•ful•ly**
**use•ful•ness**
**use•less**
**use•less•ness**
**user**
**Ush•ant** French island
**ush•er**
**ush•er•ette**
**Usk** Welsh river
**Üs•kü•dar** Turkish town
**us•que•baugh** Irish liqueur
**Usta•shi** terrorist organization
**Ust-Kameno•gorsk** Kazakh city
**us•tu•la•tion** burning
**usu•al**
**usu•al•ly**
**usu•al•ness**
**usu•fruct** legal term
**usu•fruc•tu•ary** (*plural* **•aries**)
**usu•rer**
**usu•ri•ous**
**usu•ri•ous•ness**
**usurp**
**usur•pa•tion**
**usur•pa•tive** (*or* **•tory**)
**usurp•er**
**usurp•ing•ly**
**usu•ry** (*plural* **•ries**)
**Utah**
**Utah•an**
**Ute** (*plural* **Utes** *or* **Ute**) American Indian
**uten•sil**
**uter•ine**
**uter•us** (*plural* **uteri**)
**Ut•gard** Norse mythological place
**Uti•ca** ancient African city
**utili•tar•ian**
**utili•tari•an•ism**
**util•ity** (*plural* **•ities**)
**uti•liz•able** (*or* **•lis•able**)
**uti•li•za•tion** (*or* **•sa•tion**)
**uti•lize** (*or* **•lise**)
**uti•liz•er** (*or* **•lis•er**)
**ut in•fra** *Latin* as below
**uti pos•si•detis** legal term
**ut•most** (*or* **utter•**)
**Uto-Aztecan** language
**Uto•pia**
**Uto•pian** (*or* **uto•**)
**Uto•pi•an•ism** (*or* **uto•**)
**Utrecht** Dutch province
**utri•cle** (*or* **utricu•lus**; *plural* **utri•cles** *or* **utricu•li**) part of ear
**utricu•lar** (*or* **•late**)
**utricu•li•tis**
**ut su•pra** *Latin* as above
**Ut•tar Pra•desh** Indian state
**ut•ter**
**ut•ter•able**
**ut•ter•able•ness**
**ut•ter•ance**
**ut•ter•er**
**ut•ter•ly**
**utter•most** *variant of* **utmost**
**U-turn**
**uva•rov•ite** green garnet
**uvea** part of eye
**uveal** (*or* **uveous**)
**uveit•ic**
**uveitis**
**uvu•la** (*plural* **•las** *or* **•lae**)
**uvu•lar**
**uvu•li•tis**
**Ux•bridge**
**uxo•rial** wifely
**uxo•ri•cid•al**
**uxo•ri•cide**
**uxo•ri•ous** wife-loving
**uxo•ri•ous•ness**
**Uz•bek** (*plural* **•beks** *or* **•bek**)
**Uz•beki•stan** Central Asian country

# V

**Vaal** South African river
**vac** *Slang* vacation
**va•can•cy** (*plural* **•cies**)
**va•cant**
**va•cant•ness**
**va•cat•able**
**va•cate**
**va•ca•tion**
**va•ca•tion•ist** (*or* **•er**)
**vac•ci•nal**
**vac•ci•nate**
**vac•ci•na•tion**
**vac•ci•na•tor**
**vac•cine**
**vac•cinia** cowpox
**vac•cin•ial**
**vac•il•lant**
**vac•il•late**
**vac•il•lat•ing**
**vac•il•lat•ing•ly**
**vac•il•la•tion**
**vac•il•la•tor**
**vacua** *plural of* **vacuum**
**va•cu•ity** (*plural* **•ities**)
**vacuo•lar**
**vacuo•late**
**vacuo•la•tion**
**vacu•ole** cell cavity
**vacu•ous**
**vacu•ous•ness**
**vacuum** (*plural* **vacuums** *or* **vacua**)
**vacuum-packed**
**vade me•cum** handbook
**Va•do•da•ra** Indian city
**va•dose** geology term
**Va•duz** Liechtenstein capital
**vag** *Austral* vagrant
**vaga•bond**
**vaga•bond•age**
**vaga•bond•ism**
**va•gal** of the vagus
**va•gary** (*plural* **•garies**)
**va•gi•na** (*plural* **•nas** *or* **•nae**)
**vagi•nal**
**vagi•nate** botany term
**vagi•nec•tomy** (*plural* **•tomies**)
**vagi•nis•mus** vaginal spasm
**vagi•ni•tis**
**va•goto•my** (*plural* **•mies**) surgery of the vagus
**va•go•to•nia** overactivity of the vagus
**va•go•trop•ic** affecting the vagus
**va•gran•cy** (*plural* **•cies**)
**va•grant**
**va•grant•ness**
**vague**
**vague•ly**
**vague•ness**
**va•gus** (*plural* **•gi**) nerve
**va•hana** mythological vehicle
**vain** conceited; *compare* **vane**
**vain•glo•ri•ous**
**vain•glo•ry**
**vain•ly**
**vain•ness**
**vair** fur trimming
**Va•lais** Swiss canton
**val•ance** drapery; *compare* **valence**
**val•anced**
**Val-de-Marne** French department
**Val-d'Oise** French department
**vale** *Latin* farewell
**vale** valley; *compare* **veil**
**val•edic•tion**
**val•edic•tory** (*plural* **•tories**)
**va•lence** (*or* **•len•cy**; *plural* **•lences** *or* **•cies**) chemistry term; *compare* **valance**
**Va•len•cia** Spanish port
**Va•len•ci•ennes** French town; lace
**va•len•cy** *variant of* **valence**
**val•en•tine**
**va•lerian** plant
**va•leria•na•ceous**
**va•ler•ic**
**val•et**
**va•leta** *variant spelling of* **veleta**
**Va•let•ta** *variant spelling of* **Valletta**
**val•etu•di•nar•ian** (*or* **•nary**; *plural* **•ians** *or* **•naries**)
**val•etu•di•nar•ian•ism**
**val•gus** medical term
**Val•hal•la**
**val•iance** (*or* **•ian•cy, •iant•ness**)
**val•iant**
**val•id**
**vali•date**
**vali•da•tion**
**vali•da•tory**
**va•lid•ity**
**val•id•ness**
**va•line** amino acid
**va•lise**
**Valium** (*Trademark*)
**Val•kyrie** (*or* **Wal•kyrie, Val•kyr**)
**Va•lla•do•lid** Spanish city
**val•la•tion** building fortifications
**val•lecu•la** (*plural* **•lae**) biology term
**val•lecu•lar** (*or* **•late**)
**Val•le d'Ao•sta** Italian region
**Val•let•ta** (*or* **Va•let•ta**) Maltese capital
**val•ley**
**va•lo•nia** acorns used in tanning
**val•ori•za•tion** (*or* **•sa•tion**)
**val•or•ize** (*or* **•ise**) fix price for
**val•or•ous**
**val•our** (*US* **•or**)
**Val•pa•rai•so** Chilean port
**valse** *French* waltz
**valu•able**
**valu•able•ness**
**valu•ably**
**valu•ate**
**valua•tion**
**valua•tion•al**
**valua•tor**
**value** (**valu•ing, valued**)
**value•less**
**value•less•ness**
**valu•er**

**valu•ta** currency exchange rate
**val•vate**
**valve**
**valve•less**
**val•vu•lar**
**val•vule** (*or* **valve•let**)
**val•vu•li•tis** heart-valve inflammation
**vam•brace** armour
**va•moose**
**vamp**
**vam•pire**
**vam•pir•ic** (*or* **•ish**)
**vam•pir•ism**
**Van** Turkish city
**van**
**vana•date** chemical compound
**va•nad•ic**
**va•nadi•nite** mineral
**va•na•dium** chemical element
**vana•dous**
**va•na•spa•ti** vegetable fat
**Van•cou•ver**
**van•da** orchid
**Van•dal** Germanic invader
**van•dal** destroyer
**van•dal•ism**
**van•dal•is•tic** (*or* **•dal•ish**)
**van•dal•ize** (*or* **•ise**)
**Van•dyke** beard; collar
**vane** flat blade; *compare* **vain**
**vang** nautical term
**van•guard**
**va•nil•la**
**va•nil•lic**
**van•il•lin**
**van•ish**
**van•ish•er**
**van•ish•ing•ly**
**van•ish•ment**
**van•ity** (*plural* **•ities**)
**van•quish**
**van•quish•able**
**van•quish•er**
**van•quish•ment**
**van•tage**
**Vanu•atu** island republic
**van•ward**
**vap•id**
**va•pid•ity**
**vap•id•ness**
**va•por•es•cence**
**va•por•es•cent**
**va•po•ret•to** (*plural* **•ti** *or* **•tos**) steamboat
**va•por•if•ic**
**va•por•im•eter**
**va•por•iz•able** (*or* **•is•able**)
**va•pori•za•tion** (*or* **•sa•tion**)
**va•por•ize** (*or* **•ise**)
**va•por•iz•er** (*or* **•is•er**)
**va•por•ous**
**va•por•ous•ness** (*or* **•os•ity**)
**va•pour** (*US* **•por**)
**va•pour•abil•ity** (*US* **•por•**)
**va•pour•able** (*US* **•por•**)
**va•pour•er** (*US* **•por•**)
**va•pour•ish** (*US* **•por•**)
**va•pour•ish•ness** (*US* **•por•**)
**var** unit of power
**vara** unit of length
**va•rac•tor** electronic device
**Va•ra•na•si** Indian city
**Va•ran•gian** medieval Scandinavian
**var•ec** seaweed
**varia** literary miscellany
**vari•abil•ity** (*or* **•able•ness**)
**vari•able**
**vari•ably**
**vari•ance**
**vari•ant**
**vari•ate** a random variable
**vari•ation**
**vari•ation•al** (*or* **•ative**)
**vari•cel•la** chickenpox
**vari•cel•lar**
**vari•cel•late** ridged
**vari•cel•loid**
**vari•ces** *plural of* **varix**
**vari•co•cele** medical term
**vari•col•oured** (*US* **•ored**)
**vari•cose**
**vari•co•sis**
**vari•cos•ity** (*plural* **•ities**)
**vari•coto•my** (*plural* **•mies**) varicose-vein surgery
**var•ied**
**var•ied•ness**
**varie•gate**
**varie•gat•ed**
**varie•ga•tion**
**va•ri•etal**
**va•ri•ety** (*plural* **•eties**)
**vari•form**
**va•rio•la** smallpox
**va•rio•lar**
**va•rio•late** inoculate
**va•rio•la•tion**
**vari•ole** geology term
**vari•olite** rock
**vario•lit•ic**
**vario•loid** mild smallpox
**va•rio•lous** of smallpox
**vari•om•eter**
**vario•rum** annotated text
**vari•ous**
**vari•ous•ly**
**vari•ous•ness**
**var•is•cite** mineral
**var•is•tor** electronic component
**vari•type**
**Vari•typ•er** (*Trademark*) justifying typewriter
**vari•typ•ist**
**var•ix** (*plural* **vari•ces**) varicose vein
**var•let**
**var•mint**
**Var•na** Bulgarian port
**var•na** Hindu caste
**var•nish**
**var•nish•er**
**var•sity** (*plural* **•sities**) *Slang* university
**var•us** medical term
**varve** geology term
**vary** (**varies, vary•ing, var•ied**)
**vary•ing•ly**
**vas•al** of vas deferens; *compare* **vassal**
**vas•cu•lar** conducting fluids
**vas•cu•lar•ity**
**vas•cu•lari•za•tion** (*or* **•sa•tion**) medical term
**vas•cu•lum** (*plural* **•la** *or* **•lums**) plant-specimen container
**vas de•fe•rens** (*plural* **vasa de•fe•ren•tia**) anatomy term
**vase**
**vas•ec•to•mize** (*or* **•mise**)
**vas•ec•to•my** (*plural* **•mies**)
**Vas•eline** (*Trademark*)
**vaso•active** affecting blood vessels
**vaso•con•stric•tion**
**vaso•con•stric•tive**

**vaso•con•stric•tor**
**vaso•di•la•tion**
**vaso•di•la•tor**
**vaso•in•hibi•tor**
**vaso•in•hibi•tory**
**vaso•mo•tor**
**vaso•pres•sin** hormone
**vas•sal** feudal tenant; *compare* **vasal**
**vas•sal•age**
**vas•sal•ize** (*or* **•ise**)
**vast**
**Väs•ter•ås** Swedish city
**vas•tity**
**vast•ness**
**vasty** (**vasti•er, vasti•est**) *Archaic* vast
**vat** (**vat•ting, vat•ted**)
**vat•ic** of a prophet
**Vati•can**
**Vati•can•ism**
**Vau•cluse** French department
**Vaud** Swiss canton
**vau•de•ville**
**vau•de•vil•lian**
**vau•de•vil•list**
**Vau•dois** (*plural* **•dois**) of Vaud; Waldenses
**vault**
**vault•ed**
**vault•er**
**vault•ing**
**vaunt**
**vaunt•er**
**vaunt•ing•ly**
**vava•sor** (*or* **•sour**) vassal
**veal**
**veal•er** veal calf
**vec•tor**
**vec•to•rial**
**Veda** Hindu scriptures
**ve•da•lia** ladybird
**Ve•dan•ta** Hindu school of philosophy
**Ve•dan•tic**
**Ved•da** (*or* **•dah**; *plural* **•da, •das** *or* **•dah, •dahs**) Sri Lankan people
**Ved•doid**
**ve•dette**
**Ve•dic** of the Veda
**veer**
**veer•ing•ly**
**veery** (*plural* **veeries**) bird
**veg** *Slang* vegetables
**Vega** star
**ve•gan**
**veg•eta•ble**
**veg•etal** of plants; nonsexual
**veg•etar•ian**
**veg•etari•an•ism**
**veg•etate**
**veg•eta•tion**
**veg•eta•tion•al**
**veg•eta•tive**
**veg•eta•tive•ness**
**ve•he•mence**
**ve•he•ment**
**ve•hi•cle**
**ve•hicu•lar**
**Veii** Etruscan city
**veil** head covering; *compare* **vale**
**veiled**
**veil•ed•ly**
**veil•er**
**veil•ing**
**vein**
**vein•ing**
**vein•let**
**vein•stone** ore material
**veiny** (**veini•er, veini•est**)
**ve•la•men** (*plural* **•lami•na**) biology term
**ve•lar** biology or phonetics term
**ve•lar•ium** (*plural* **•laria**) awning in Roman theatre
**ve•lari•za•tion** (*or* **•sa•tion**)
**ve•lar•ize** (*or* **•ise**) phonetics term
**ve•late** biology term
**Vel•cro** (*Trademark*)
**veld** (*or* **veldt**)
**ve•leta** (*or* **va•**) dance
**veli•ger** mollusc larva
**ve•li•tes** Roman troops
**vel•le•ity** (*plural* **•ities**) a wish
**Vel•lore** Indian town
**vel•lum** parchment; *compare* **velum**
**ve•lo•ce** musical term
**ve•loci•pede** early bicycle
**ve•loc•ity** (*plural* **•ities**)
**ve•lo•drome** cycle-racing arena
**ve•lours** (*or* **•lour**) fabric
**ve•lou•té** sauce
**ve•lum** (*plural* **•la**) biology term; *compare* **vellum**
**ve•lure** velvet
**ve•lu•ti•nous** covered with hairs
**vel•vet**
**vel•vet•een**
**vel•vety**
**vena** (*plural* **venae**) vein
**vena cava** (*plural* **venae cavae**)
**ve•nal** open to bribery; *compare* **venial**
**ve•nal•ity**
**ve•nal•ly**
**ve•nat•ic** (*or* **•nati•cal**) of hunting
**ve•na•tion** arrangement of veins; *compare* **vernation**
**ve•na•tion•al**
**vend**
**Ven•da** (*plural* **•da** *or* **•das**) African people
**ven•dace** (*plural* **•daces** *or* **•dace**) fish
**Ven•dée** French department
**ven•dee** buyer
**vend•er** *variant spelling of* **vendor**
**ven•det•ta**
**ven•det•tist**
**vend•ibil•ity** (*or* **•ible•ness**)
**vend•ible**
**vend•ing**
**ven•di•tion**
**ven•dor** (*or* **vend•er**)
**ven•due** *US* public sale
**ve•neer**
**ve•neer•er**
**ve•neer•ing**
**ven•epunc•ture** *variant spelling of* **venipuncture**
**ven•er•abil•ity** (*or* **•able•ness**)
**ven•er•able**
**ven•er•ably**
**ven•er•ate**
**ven•era•tion**
**ven•era•tion•al** (*or* **•era•tive**)
**ven•era•tor**
**ve•nereal**
**ve•nere•olo•gist**
**ve•nere•ol•ogy**

**ven•ery** hunting; sexual gratification
**ven•esec•tion** incision into vein
**Ve•netia** ancient Italian region
**Ve•netian**
**Ve•net•ic** language
**Ve•neto** Italian region
**Ven•ezue•la**
**Ven•ezue•lan**
**venge•ance**
**venge•ful**
**venge•ful•ly**
**venge•ful•ness**
**ve•nial** easily forgiven; *compare* **venal**
**ve•ni•al•ity** (*or* **•al•ness**)
**ve•nial•ly**
**Ven•ice**
**ven•in** poison
**veni•punc•ture** (*or* **ven•epunc•ture**)
**ve•ni•re fa•ci•as** legal term
**veni•son**
**Ve•ni•te** 95th psalm
**Venn dia•gram**
**ven•om**
**ven•om•ous**
**ve•nose**
**ve•nos•ity**
**ve•nous**
**ve•nous•ness**
**vent**
**vent•age** small hole
**ven•tail** armour
**ven•ter** biology or legal term
**ven•ti•lable**
**ven•ti•late**
**ven•ti•la•tion**
**ven•ti•la•tive**
**ven•ti•la•tor**
**ven•ti•la•tory**
**ven•tral**
**ven•tral•ly**
**ven•tri•cle**
**ven•tri•cose** biology term
**ven•tri•cos•ity**
**ven•tricu•lar**
**ven•tricu•lus** (*plural* **•li**) zoology term
**ven•tri•lo•quial** (*or* **•qual**)
**ven•trilo•quism** (*or* **•quy**)
**ven•trilo•quist**
**ven•trilo•quis•tic**
**ven•trilo•quize** (*or* **•quise**)
**ven•trilo•quy** *variant of* **ventriloquism**
**ven•ture**
**ven•tur•er**
**ven•ture•some** (*or* **•tu•rous**)
**ven•ture•some•ness**
**Venturi tube**
**venue**
**venu•lar**
**ven•ule** small vein
**Ve•nus** planet
**Venus** Roman goddess
**Ve•nu•sian**
**ve•ra•cious** truthful; *compare* **voracious**
**ve•ra•cious•ness**
**ve•rac•ity** (*plural* **•ities**)
**Vera•cruz** Mexican state
**ve•ran•da** (*or* **•dah**)
**ve•ran•daed** (*or* **•dahed**)
**ve•ra•tri•dine** chemical compound
**vera•trine** (*or* **•trin**) former medicine
**verb**
**ver•bal**
**ver•bal•ism**
**ver•bal•ist**
**ver•bali•za•tion** (*or* **•sa•tion**)
**ver•bal•ize** (*or* **•ise**)
**ver•bal•iz•er** (*or* **•is•er**)
**ver•bal•ly**
**ver•ba•tim**
**ver•be•na**
**ver•be•na•ceous** botany term
**ver•bi•age**
**ver•bid** linguistics term
**ver•bi•fi•ca•tion**
**ver•bi•fy** (**•fies, •fy•ing, •fied**)
**ver•bose**
**ver•bose•ly**
**ver•bos•ity** (*or* **•bose•ness**)
**ver•bo•ten** *German* forbidden
**ver•dan•cy**
**ver•dant**
**ver•der•er**
**ver•dict**
**ver•di•gris**
**ver•din** bird
**ver•dure**
**ver•dur•ous**
**Ve•ree•ni•ging** South African city
**verge**
**ver•ger**
**ver•glas** (*plural* **•glases**) thin ice
**ve•ridi•cal** truthful
**ve•ridi•cal•ity**
**veri•fi•able**
**veri•fi•ca•tion**
**veri•fi•ca•tive** (*or* **•tory**)
**veri•fi•er**
**veri•fy** (**•fies, •fy•ing, •fied**)
**veri•ly**
**veri•simi•lar** likely
**veri•si•mili•tude**
**ver•ism** extreme realism
**ve•ris•mo** type of opera
**ver•ist**
**ve•ris•tic**
**veri•table**
**veri•table•ness**
**veri•tably**
**ver•ity** (*plural* **•ities**)
**ver•juice**
**ver•kramp•te** Afrikaner nationalist
**ver•lig•te** South African liberal
**ver•meil** gilded metal
**ver•mi•cel•li**
**ver•mi•cid•al**
**ver•mi•cide**
**ver•micu•lar** wormlike
**ver•micu•late**
**ver•micu•la•tion**
**ver•micu•lite** mineral
**ver•mi•form**
**ver•mi•fuge** worm-expelling drug
**ver•mil•ion** (*or* **•mil•lion**)
**ver•min**
**ver•mi•na•tion** infestation with vermin
**ver•mi•nous**
**ver•min•ous•ness**
**ver•mis** (*plural* **•mes**) part of brain
**ver•mivo•rous** worm-eating
**Ver•mont**
**Ver•mont•er**
**ver•mouth**
**ver•nacu•lar**
**ver•nacu•lar•ism**
**ver•nal**

**ver•nali•za•tion** (*or* **•sa•tion**)
**ver•nal•ize** (*or* **•ise**) botany term
**ver•nal•ly**
**ver•na•tion** leaf arrangement in bud; *compare* **venation**
**ver•ni•er** measuring scale
**ver•nis•sage** opening of art exhibition
**Ve•ro•na** Italian city
**Vero•nal** (*Trademark*) drug
**ve•roni•ca** shrub
**ver•ru•ca** (*plural* **•cae** *or* **•cas**)
**ver•ru•cose** (*or* **•cous**)
**ver•ru•cos•ity**
**Ver•sailles**
**ver•sant** mountain side
**ver•sa•tile**
**ver•sa•til•ity** (*or* **•tile•ness**)
**verse**
**versed**
**ver•si•cle**
**ver•si•col•our** (*US* **•or**)
**ver•si•fi•ca•tion**
**ver•si•fi•er**
**ver•si•fy** (**•fies, •fy•ing, •fied**)
**ver•sion**
**ver•sion•al**
**vers li•bre** *French* free verse
**ver•so** (*plural* **•sos**) left-hand page
**ver•sus** against
**vert** heraldry term
**ver•te•bra** (*plural* **•brae** *or* **•bras**)
**ver•te•bral**
**ver•te•brate**
**ver•te•bra•tion**
**ver•tex** (*plural* **•texes** *or* **•tices**) apex; *compare* **vortex**
**ver•ti•cal**
**ver•ti•cal•ity** (*or* **•ness**)
**ver•ti•cal•ly**
**ver•ti•ces** *plural of* **vertex**
**ver•ti•cil** biology term
**ver•ti•cil•las•ter** botany term
**ver•ti•cil•las•trate**
**ver•tic•il•late**
**ver•tic•il•la•tion**
**ver•tigi•nous** of vertigo
**ver•tigi•nous•ness**
**ver•ti•go** (*plural* **•ti•goes** *or* **•tigi•nes**)
**ver•tu** *variant spelling of* **virtu**
**Vertumnus** Roman god
(**verucca**) *incorrect spelling of* **verruca**
**Veru•la•mium** *Latin* St Albans
**ver•vain** plant
**verve**
**ver•vet** monkey
**very**
**Very light**
**vesi•ca** (*plural* **•cae**) bladder
**vesi•cal** of the bladder; *compare* **vesicle**
**vesi•cant** (*or* **•ca•tory**; *plural* **•cants** *or* **•ca•tories**) blistering substance
**vesi•cate**
**vesi•ca•tion**
**vesi•cle** small cavity; *compare* **vesical**
**ve•sicu•lar**
**ve•sicu•late**
**ve•sicu•la•tion**
**ves•per** evening prayer
**ves•per•al** prayer book
**ves•pers** canonical hour
**ves•per•tilio•nid** zoology term
**ves•per•tilio•nine**
**ves•per•tine** occurring in the evening
**ves•pi•ary** (*plural* **•aries**) wasps' nest
**ves•pid** entomology term
**ves•pine** of wasps
**ves•sel**
**vest**
**Ves•ta** asteroid
**Vesta** Roman goddess
**ves•ta** wooden match
**ves•tal** virgin
**vest•ed**
**ves•ti•ary** (*plural* **•aries**) room for clothes
**ves•tibu•lar**
**ves•ti•bule**
**ves•tige**
**ves•tig•ial**
**vest•ment**
**vest•ment•al**
**vest•ment•ed**
**ves•tral**
**ves•try** (*plural* **•tries**)
**vestry•man** (*plural* **•men**)
**ves•tur•al**
**ves•ture** garment
**ve•su•vi•an•ite** mineral
**Ve•su•vi•us**
**vet** (**vet•ting, vet•ted**)
**vetch**
**vetch•ling**
**vet•er•an**
**vet•eri•nar•ian**
**vet•eri•nary**
**veti•ver** a grass
**veto** (*noun, plural* **vetoes**; *verb* **vetoes, ve•to•ing, ve•toed**)
**ve•to•er**
**vet•ted**
**vet•ting**
**vex**
**vexa•tion**
**vexa•tious**
**vexa•tious•ness**
**vex•ed•ly**
**vex•ed•ness**
**vex•er**
**vex•il•lary** (*or* **•lar**)
**vex•il•late**
**vex•il•lolo•gist**
**vex•il•lol•ogy** study of flags
**vex•il•lum** (*plural* **•la**) biology term
**vex•ing•ly**
**via**
**vi•abil•ity**
**vi•able**
**Via Dolo•ro•sa** road to Calvary
**via•duct**
**Vi•ag•ra** (*Trademark*)
**vial** *less common spelling of* **phial**
**via me•dia** *Latin* compromise
**vi•and** a food
**vi•ands** provisions
**vi•ati•cum** (*plural* **•ca** *or* **•cums**)
**vibes** *Slang* vibrations; vibraphone
**vib•ist** vibraphone player
**vi•bracu•lar**

**vi•bracu•loid**
**vi•bracu•lum** (*plural* **•la**) zoology term
**vi•bra•harp** musical instrument
**vi•bran•cy**
**vi•brant**
**vi•bra•phone**
**vi•bra•phon•ist**
**vi•brate**
**vi•bra•tile**
**vi•bra•til•ity**
**vi•brat•ing•ly**
**vi•bra•tion**
**vi•bra•tion•al**
**vi•bra•tive**
**vi•bra•to** (*plural* **•tos**)
**vi•bra•tor**
**vi•bra•tory**
**vib•rio** (*plural* **•rios**) bacterium
**vib•ri•oid**
**vi•bris•sa** (*plural* **•sae**) whisker
**vi•bris•sal**
**vi•bron•ic** physics term
**vi•bur•num**
**vic•ar**
**vic•ar•age**
**vi•car•ial**
**vi•cari•ate** (*or* **vic•ar•ship**)
**vi•cari•ous**
**vi•cari•ous•ness**
**vice** sin; deputy; in place of
**vice** (*US* **vise**) tool
**vice ad•mi•ral**
**vice-admiral•ty**
**vice-chairman** (*plural* **-chairmen**)
**vice-chairman•ship**
**vice chan•cel•lor**
**vice-chancellor•ship**
**vice•ge•ral**
**vice•ge•ren•cy** (*plural* **•cies**)
**vice•ge•rent** deputy
**vice•like** (*US* **vise•**)
**vic•enary** of 20
**vi•cen•nial** 20 years
**Vi•cen•za** Italian city
**vice-presiden•cy** (*plural* **•cies**)
**vice presi•dent**
**vice-presiden•tial**
**vice•re•gal** of viceroy
**vice•reine** viceroy's wife
**vice•roy**
**vice•roy•al•ty** (*plural* **•ties**)
**vice•roy•ship**
**vice ver•sa**
**Vi•chy** French town
**vi•chy•ssoise** soup
**vici•nal**
**vi•cin•ity** (*plural* **•ities**)
**vi•cious**
**vi•cious•ness**
**vi•cis•si•tude**
**vi•cis•si•tu•di•nary** (*or* **•di•nous**)
**Vicks•burg** US city
**vi•comte** (*fem* **•com•tesse**) French noble
**vic•tim**
**vic•timi•za•tion** (*or* **•sa•tion**)
**vic•tim•ize** (*or* **•ise**)
**vic•tim•iz•er** (*or* **•is•er**)
**vic•tor**
**Vic•to•ria** place name
**vic•to•ria** carriage; plum; water lily
**Vic•to•rian**
**Vic•to•ri•ana**
**Vic•to•ri•an•ism**
**vic•to•ri•ous**
**vic•to•ri•ous•ness**
**vic•to•ry** (*plural* **•ries**)
**vict•ual** (**•ual•ling, •ualled;** *US* **•ual•ing, •ualed**)
**vict•ual•ler** (*US also* **•ual•er**)
**vict•uals**
**vi•cu•ña**
**vide** *Latin* see
**vi•deli•cet** *Latin* namely
**video** (*noun, plural* **videos**; *verb* **videos, video•ing, videoed**)
**vid•eo•phone**
**vid•eo•phon•ic**
**video-tape** (*verb*)
**vidi•con** small television camera tube
**vie** (**vying, vied**)
**Vi•en•na** Austrian capital
**Vienne** French river; department
**Vi•en•nese** (*plural* **•nese**)
**Vien•ti•ane** Laotian capital
**Vi•et•cong** (*or* **Viet Cong**)
**Vi•et•minh** (*or* **Viet Minh**)
**Vi•et•nam**
**Vi•et•nam•ese** (*plural* **•ese**)
**view**
**view•able**
**view•er**
**view•finder**
**view•ing**
**view•less**
**view•point**
**vi•gesi•mal** of 20
**vig•il**
**vigi•lance**
**vigi•lant**
**vigi•lan•te**
**vi•gnette**
**vi•gnet•ting** photography term
**vi•gnet•tist**
**Vigo** Spanish port
**vi•go•ro•so** musical term
**vig•or•ous**
**vig•or•ous•ness**
**vig•our** (*US* **•or**)
**Vi•jaya•wa•da** Indian town
**Vi•king**
**vi•la•yet** Turkish administrative division
**vile**
**vile•ly**
**vile•ness**
**vili•fi•ca•tion**
**vili•fi•er**
**vili•fy** (**•fies, •fy•ing, •fied**)
**vili•pend** treat with contempt
**vil•la**
**vil•lage**
**vil•lag•er**
**Vil•la•her•mo•sa** Mexican town
**vil•lain** (*fem* **•lain•ess**) wicked person; *compare* **villein**
**vil•lain•ous**
**vil•lain•ous•ness**
**vil•lainy** (*plural* **•lainies**)
**vil•la•nel•la** (*plural* **•las**) song
**vil•la•nelle** verse form
**Vil•la•no•van** archaeology term
**vil•lat•ic** rustic
**vil•lein** serf; *compare* **villain**
**Ville•ur•banne** French town
**vil•li** *plural of* **villus**
**vil•li•form**

**vil•los•ity** (*plural* **•ities**)
**vil•lous**
**vil•lus** (*plural* **•li**)
**Vil•ni•us** (*or* **•ny•**) Lithuanian capital
**vim** *Slang* vigour
**vi•men** (*plural* **vimi•na**) plant shoot
**Vimi•nal** Roman hill
**vi•min•eous**
**vina** musical instrument
**vi•na•ceous**
**Viña del Mar** Chilean city
**vinai•grette**
**vi•nasse** residue in a still
**vin•cible**
**vin•cu•lum** (*plural* **•la**) maths symbol; anatomy term
**vin•di•cabil•ity**
**vin•di•cable**
**vin•di•cate**
**vin•di•ca•tion**
**vin•di•ca•tor**
**vin•di•ca•tory**
**vin•dic•tive**
**vin•dic•tive•ly**
**vin•dic•tive•ness**
**vine**
**vine•dresser**
**vin•egar**
**vin•egar•roon** arachnid
**vin•egary**
**vin•ery** (*plural* **•eries**) place for growing grapes
**vine•yard**
**vine•yard•ist**
**vingt-et-un** card game
**vi•nic** of wine
**vini•cul•tur•al**
**vini•cul•ture**
**vini•cul•tur•ist**
**vi•nif•er•ous**
**vi•nifi•ca•tion**
**vi•nifi•ca•tor** wine-making apparatus
**Vin•land** *Viking name for* NE America
**Vin•ni•tsa** Ukrainian city
**vino** (*plural* **vinos**) *Slang* wine
**vin or•di•naire** (*plural* **vins or•di•naires**)
**vi•nos•ity**
**vi•nous**
**vin•tage**
**vin•tag•er** grape harvester
**vint•ner**
**viny**
**(vinyard)** *incorrect spelling of* **vineyard**
**vi•nyl**
**vi•nyli•dene** chemistry term
**viol**
**vio•la**
**vio•labil•ity** (*or* **•lable•ness**)
**vio•lable**
**vio•la•ceous** botany term
**vio•la da gam•ba**
**vio•la d'amo•re**
**vio•late**
**vio•la•tion**
**vio•la•tive**
**vio•la•tor** (*or* **•lat•er**)
**vio•lence**
**vio•lent**
**vio•let**
**vio•lin**
**vio•lin•ist**
**vi•ol•ist**
**vio•lon•cel•list**
**vio•lon•cel•lo** (*plural* **•los**) cello
**vio•lone** musical instrument
**vi•per**
**vi•per•ine**
**vi•per•ous** (*or* **•ish**)
**vi•ragi•nous**
**vi•ra•go** (*plural* **•goes** *or* **•gos**)
**vi•ral**
**vir•elay** poem
**vireo** (*plural* **vireos**) bird
**vi•res•cence**
**vi•res•cent** becoming green
**vir•ga** meteorology term
**vir•gate** rod-shaped; obsolete land measure
**vir•gin**
**vir•gin•al**
**vir•gin•al•ly**
**Vir•ginia**
**Vir•gin•ian**
**vir•gin•ity**
**virgin's-bower** plant
**Vir•go** constellation; sign of zodiac
**Vir•goan**
**vir•go in•tac•ta** virgin
**vir•gu•late** rod-shaped
**vir•gule** printing term
**viri•des•cence**
**viri•des•cent** becoming green
**vi•rid•ian** green pigment
**vi•rid•ity** greenness
**vir•ile**
**viri•lism** medical term
**vi•ril•ity**
**vi•ro•logi•cal**
**vi•rolo•gist**
**vi•rol•ogy**
**vir•tu** (*or* **ver•**) connoisseurship
**vir•tual**
**vir•tu•al•ity**
**vir•tu•al•ly**
**vir•tue**
**vir•tu•os•ic**
**vir•tu•os•ity**
**vir•tuo•so** (*plural* **•sos** *or* **•si**)
**vir•tu•ous**
**vir•tu•ous•ness**
**viru•lence**
**viru•lent**
**vi•rus** (*plural* **•ruses**)
**visa** (**vi•sa•ing, vi•saed**)
**vis•age**
**Vi•sa•kha•pat•nam** *variant of* **Vishakhapatnam**
**vis-à-vis**
**Vi•sa•yan** (*plural* **•yans** *or* **•yan**) Philippine people
**vis•ca•cha** (*or* **viz•**) animal
**vis•cera** (*sing.* **•cus**) internal organs
**vis•cer•al**
**vis•ce•ro•mo•tor** physiology term
**vis•cid**
**vis•cid•ity** (*or* **•ness**)
**vis•coid** (*or* **•coi•dal**)
**vis•com•eter** (*or* **•co•sim•eter**)
**vis•co•met•ric** (*or* **•ri•cal**)
**vis•com•etry**
**vis•cose**
**vis•cos•ity** (*plural* **•ities**)
**vis•count**
**vis•count•cy** (*or* **•county**; *plural* **•cies** *or* **•counties**)
**vis•count•ess**
**vis•cous** thick; *compare* **viscus**
**vis•cous•ness**

**vis•cus** *sing. of* **viscera;** *compare* **viscous**
**vise** *US spelling of* **vice**
**Vi•sha•kha•pat•nam** (*or* **Vi•sa•kha•pat•nam, Vi•za•ga•pa•tam)** Indian port
**Vishnu** Hindu god
**vis•ibil•ity**
**vis•ible**
**vis•ible•ness**
**vis•ibly**
**Visi•goth**
**vi•sion**
**vi•sion•al**
**vi•sion•ari•ness**
**vi•sion•ary** (*plural* **•aries)**
**vis•it**
**vis•it•able**
**visi•tant**
**vis•ita•tion**
**vis•ita•tion•al**
**vis•ita•to•rial** of official visitation
**visi•tor**
**visi•to•rial**
**vi•sor** (*or* **•zor)**
**vi•sored** (*or* **•zored)**
**vis•ta**
**vis•taed**
**Vis•tu•la** Polish river
**vis•ual**
**visu•ali•za•tion** (*or* **•sa•tion)**
**visu•al•ize** (*or* **•ise)**
**visu•al•iz•er** (*or* **•is•er)**
**visu•al•ly**
**vi•ta•ceous** botany term
**vi•tal**
**vi•tal•ism** philosophical doctrine
**vi•tal•ist**
**vi•tal•is•tic**
**vi•tal•ity** (*plural* **•ities)**
**vi•tali•za•tion** (*or* **•sa•tion)**
**vi•tal•ize** (*or* **•ise)**
**vi•tal•iz•er** (*or* **•is•er)**
**vi•tal•ly**
**vi•tals**
**vita•min**
**vita•min•ic**
**Vi•tebsk** Belarussian city
**vi•tel•lin** protein
**vi•tel•line** of egg yolk
**vi•ti•able**
**vi•ti•ate**
**vi•tia•tion**
**vi•tia•tor**
**viti•cul•tur•al**
**viti•cul•ture** grape cultivation
**viti•cul•tur•er** (*or* **•ist)**
**viti•li•go** unpigmented skin
**Vi•to•ria** Spanish city
**Vi•tó•ria** Brazilian port
**vit•rain** coal
**vit•re•ous**
**vit•re•ous•ness** (*or* **•os•ity)**
**vi•tres•cence**
**vi•tres•cent**
**vit•ric** of glass
**vit•ri•fi•abil•ity**
**vit•ri•fi•able**
**vit•ri•fi•ca•tion**
**vit•ri•form**
**vit•ri•fy** (**•fies, •fy•ing, •fied)**
**vit•rine** glass display case
**vit•ri•ol** (**•ol•ing, •oled** *or* **•ol•ling, •olled)**
**vit•ri•ol•ic**
**vit•ri•oli•za•tion** (*or* **•sa•tion)**
**vit•ri•ol•ize** (*or* **•ise)**
**vit•ta** (*plural* **•tae)** biology term
**vit•tate**
**vi•tu•line** of calves
**vi•tu•per•ate**
**vi•tu•pera•tion**
**vi•tu•pera•tive**
**vi•tu•pera•tor**
**viva** (**vi•va•ing, vi•vaed)** *short for* **viva voce**
**vi•va•ce** musical term
**vi•va•cious**
**vi•va•vious•ly**
**vi•va•cious•ness**
**vi•vac•ity** (*plural* **•ities)**
**vi•var•ium** (*plural* **•iums** *or* **•ia)**
**viva voce** oral exam
**vi•ver•rine** zoology term
**viv•id**
**viv•id•ness**
**vivi•fi•ca•tion**
**vivi•fi•er**
**vivi•fy** (**•fies, •fy•ing, •fied)**
**vivi•par•ity** (*or* **vi•vipa•rism, vi•vipa•rous•ness)**
**vi•vip•ar•ous**
**vivi•sect**
**vivi•sec•tion**
**vivi•sec•tion•al**
**vivi•sec•tion•ist**
**vivi•sec•tor**
**vix•en**
**vix•en•ish**
**vix•en•ish•ness**
**Vi•yel•la** (*Trademark*)
**Vi•za•ga•pa•tam** *variant spelling of* **Vishakhapatnam**
**viz•ard** mask
**viz•ca•cha** *variant spelling of* **viscacha**
**vi•zier**
**vi•zier•ate**
**vi•zor** *variant spelling of* **visor**
**Vlach** (*or* **Wa•lach)** medieval European people
**Vla•di•mir** Russian port
**Vla•di•vos•tok** Russian port
**vo•cab** *short for* **vocabulary**
**vo•cable** vocal sound
**vo•cabu•lary** (*plural* **•laries)**
**vo•cal**
**vo•cal•ic**
**vo•cal•ise** vocal exercise; *variant spelling of* **vocalize**
**vo•cal•ism**
**vo•cal•ist**
**vo•cal•ity** (*or* **•ness)**
**vo•cali•za•tion** (*or* **•sa•tion)**
**vo•cal•ize** (*or* **•ise)**
**vo•cal•iz•er** (*or* **•is•er)**
**vo•cal•ly**
**vo•ca•tion**
**vo•ca•tion•al**
**voca•tive**
**vo•cif•er•ance**
**vo•cif•er•ant**
**vo•cif•er•ate**
**vo•cif•era•tion**
**vo•cif•era•tor**
**vo•cif•er•ous**
**vo•cif•er•ous•ness**
**vod•ka**
**vogue**
**voguish**
**Vo•gul** (*plural* **•gul** *or* **•guls)** Siberian people
**voice**
**voiced**
**voice•ful**

**voice•less**
**voice•less•ness**
**voice-over**
**voice•print**
**voic•er**
**void**
**void•able**
**void•able•ness**
**void•ance** annulment
**void•ed**
**void•er**
**voile** fabric
**Voio•tia** Greek department
**voir dire** legal term
**Voj•vo•di•na** (*or* **Voi•**) Yugoslav region
**Vo•lans** constellation
**vo•lant**
**Vola•puk** artificial language
**Vola•puk•ist**
**vo•lar** anatomy term
**vola•tile**
**vola•til•ity**
**vo•lati•liz•able** (*or* **•lis•able**)
**vo•lati•liza•tion** (*or* **•lisa•tion**)
**vo•lati•lize** (*or* **•lise**)
**vol-au-vent**
**vol•can•ic**
**vol•cani•cal•ly**
**vol•can•ic•ity**
**vol•can•ism** (*or* **vul•**)
**vol•cani•za•tion** (*or* **•sa•tion**)
**vol•can•ize** (*or* **•ise**)
**vol•ca•no** (*plural* **•noes** *or* **•nos**)
**vol•cano•logi•cal** (*or* **vul•**)
**vol•can•olo•gist** (*or* **vul•**)
**vol•can•ol•ogy** (*or* **vul•**)
**vole**
**Vol•ga** Russian river
**Vol•go•grad** Russian port
**voli•tant** moving rapidly
**vo•li•tion**
**vo•li•tion•al** (*or* **•ary**)
**voli•tive** of the will
**vol•ley**
**volley•ball**
**vol•ley•er**
**Vo•log•da** Russian city
**vo•lost** peasant community
**vol•plane** glide without power
**Vol•sci** Latin people
**volt**
**Vol•ta** African river or lake
**vol•ta** (*plural* **•te**) dance
**volt•age**
**vol•ta•ic**
**vol•ta•ism**
**vol•tam•eter** instrument measuring electric charge; *compare* **voltmeter**
**volt•am•meter** instrument measuring volts or amperes; *compare* **voltmeter**
**volt-ampere** unit
**Vol•ta Re•don•da** Brazilian city
**volte-face** (*plural* **volte-face**) reversal of opinion
**volt•me•ter** instrument measuring volts; *compare* **voltameter; voltammeter**
**vol•ubil•ity** (*or* **•uble•ness**)
**vol•uble**
**vol•ubly**
**vol•ume**
**vol•umed**
**vo•lu•meter**
**volu•met•ric**
**volu•met•ri•cal•ly**
**vo•lu•metry**
**vo•lu•mi•nos•ity** (*or* **•nous•ness**)
**vo•lu•mi•nous**
**vol•un•tar•ily**
**vol•un•tari•ness**
**vol•un•ta•rism** (*or* **•tary•**)
**vol•un•ta•rist** (*or* **•tary•**)
**vol•un•ta•ris•tic**
**vol•un•tary** (*plural* **•aries**)
**vol•un•teer**
**vo•lup•tu•ary** (*plural* **•aries**)
**vo•lup•tu•ous**
**vo•lup•tu•ous•ness** (*or* **•os•ity**)
**vol•ute**
**vo•lu•tion**
**vol•va** (*plural* **•vae** *or* **•vas**) mushroom sheath; *compare* **vulva**
**vol•vate**
**Volvo** (*Trademark*)
**vol•vox** microscopic animal
**vol•vu•lus** (*plural* **•luses**) intestinal disorder
**vo•mer** bone
**vo•mer•ine**
**vom•it**
**vom•it•er**
**vomi•tive**
**vomi•tory** (*plural* **•tories**)
**vomi•tu•ri•tion** retching
**vomi•tus** (*plural* **•tuses**) vomited matter
**voo•doo** (*noun, plural* **•doos**; *verb* **•doos, •doo•ing, •dooed**)
**voo•doo•ism**
**voo•doo•ist**
**voo•doo•is•tic**
**Voor•trek•ker** Afrikaner settler
**vo•ra•cious** greedy; *compare* **veracious**
**vo•rac•ity** (*or* **•ra•cious•ness**)
**Vor•arl•berg** Austrian province
**vor•la•ge** skiing position
**Vo•ro•nezh** Russian city
**Vo•ro•shi•lov•grad** *former name of* **Lugansk**
**vor•tex** (*plural* **•texes** *or* **•ti•ces**) whirling mass; *compare* **vertex**
**vor•ti•cal**
**vor•ti•cel•la** (*plural* **•lae**) protozoan
**vor•ti•ces** *plural of* **vortex**
**vor•ti•cism** art movement
**vor•ti•cist**
**vor•tigi•nous**
**Vosges** French mountain range
**Vos•tok** Soviet spacecraft
**vot•able** (*or* **vote•**)
**vo•tar•ess** (*or* **vo•tress**)
**vo•ta•rist**
**vo•ta•ry** (*plural* **•ries**)
**vote**
**vote•able** *variant spelling of* **votable**
**vot•er**
**vo•tive**
**vo•tive•ness**
**vo•tress** *variant of* **votaress**
**Vo•ty•ak** (*plural* **•aks** *or* **•ak**) Finnish people
**vouch**
**vouch•er**
**vouch•safe**

**vouch•safe•ment**
**vouge** weapon
**vous•soir** wedge-shaped stone
**Vou•vray** wine
**vow**
**vow•el**
**vow•eli•za•tion** (*or* **•sa•tion)**
**vow•el•ize** (*or* **•ise)**
**vowel•less**
**vow•er**
**vox** (*plural* **vo•ces)** voice
**vox hu•ma•na** organ stop
**vox po•pu•li** public opinion
**voy•age**
**voy•ag•er**
**vo•ya•geur** Canadian woodsman
**vo•yeur**
**vo•yeur•ism**
**vo•yeur•is•tic**
**vo•yeur•is•ti•cal•ly**
**vrai•sem•blance** verisimilitude
**vroom** exclamation
**vug** mining term
**Vulcan** Roman god
**vul•ca•nian** volcanic
**vul•can•ism** *variant spelling of* **volcanism**
**vul•can•ite** hard rubber
**vul•can•iz•able** (*or* **•is•able)**
**vul•cani•za•tion** (*or* **•sa•tion)**
**vul•can•ize** (*or* **•ise)**
**vul•can•iz•er** (*or* **•is•er)**
**vul•can•ol•ogy** *variant spelling of* **volcanology**
**vul•gar**
**vul•gar•ian**
**vul•gar•ism**
**vul•gar•ity** (*plural* **•ities)**
**vul•gari•za•tion** (*or* **•sa•tion)**
**vul•gar•ize** (*or* **•ise)**
**vul•gar•iz•er** (*or* **•is•er)**
**vul•gar•ness**
**Vul•gate** Latin Bible
**vul•gate** commonly accepted text
**vul•ner•abil•ity** (*or* **•able•ness)**
**vul•ner•able**
**vul•ner•ably**
**vul•ner•ary** (*plural* **•aries)** wound-healing drug
**Vul•pecu•la** constellation
**vul•pine** (*or* **•pecu•lar)** of foxes
**vul•ture**
**vul•tur•ine**
**vul•tur•ous**
**vul•va** (*plural* **•vae** *or* **•vas)** female external genitals; *compare* **volva**
**vul•val** (*or* **•var, •vate)**
**vul•vi•form**
**vul•vi•tis**
**vul•vo•vagi•ni•tis**
**vy•ing**

# W

**Wa•bash** US river
**wacky (wacki•er, wacki•est)**
**wad (wad•ding, wad•ded)**
**wad•able** (*or* **wade•)**
**wad•ding**
**wad•dle**
**wad•dler**
**wad•dling•ly**
**wad•dy** (*noun, plural* **•dies;** *verb* **•dies, •dy•ing, •died)** Aboriginal club; *compare* **wadi**
**wade**
**wade•able** *variant spelling of* **wadable**
**wad•er**
**wad•ers**
**wadi** (*or* **wady;** *plural* **wadis** *or* **wa•dies)** watercourse; *compare* **waddy**
**Wadi Hal•fa** Sudanese town
**Wad Me•da•ni** Sudanese town
**wad•set (•set•ting, •set•ted)** *Scot* mortgage
**wady** *variant spelling of* **wadi**
**wae** *Dialect* woe
**wa•fer**
**wa•fery**
**waff** *Dialect* gust
**waf•fle**
**waft**
**waft•age**
**waft•er**
**wag (wag•ging, wagged)**
**wage**
**wa•ger**
**wa•ger•er**
**wages**
**wag•ga** *Austral* blanket
**Wag•ga Wag•ga** Australian city
**wagged**
**wag•gery**
**wag•ging**
**wag•gish**
**wag•gish•ness**
**wag•gle**
**wag•gling•ly**
**wag•gly**
**Wag•ne•rian**
**wag•on** (*or* **wag•gon)**
**wag•on•er** (*or* **wag•gon•)**
**wag•on•ette** (*or* **wag•gon•)**
**wagon-lit** (*plural* **wagons-lits)** sleeping car
**wagon•load** (*or* **waggon•)**
**wag•tail**
**Wah•ha•bi** (*or* **Wa•ha•bi;** *plural* **•bis)** conservative Muslim
**wa•hi•ne** Polynesian woman
**wa•hoo** (*plural* **•hoos)** tree; fish
**waif**
**Wai•ka•to** New Zealand river
**Wai•ki•ki** Hawaiian resort
**wail**
**wail•er**
**wail•ful**
**wail•ing•ly**
**wain** farm wagon; *compare* **wane**

**wain•scot**
**wain•scot•ed**
**wain•scot•ing** (*or* **•scot•ting**)
**wain•wright**
**waist**
**waist•band**
**waist•coat**
**waist•ed**
**waist•less**
**waist•line**
**wait**
**wait•er**
**wait•ress**
**waive** relinquish; *compare* **wave**
**waiv•er** relinquishment; *compare* **waver**
**Wa•kash•an** American Indian language
**Wa•ka•ya•ma** Japanese city
**wake** (**wak•ing, woke, wok•en**)
**Wake•field**
**wake•ful**
**wake•ful•ly**
**wake•ful•ness**
**wake•less**
**wak•en**
**wak•en•er**
**wak•er**
**wake•rife** *Dialect* wakeful
**wake-robin** plant
**wak•ing**
**Wa•lach** *variant of* **Vlach**
**Wa•la•chia** (*or* **Wal•la•chia**) former European principality
**Wał•brzych** Polish city
**Wal•che•ren** Dutch island
**Wal•den•ses** Catholic sect
**wald•grave** medieval German forest officer
**Wal•dorf sal•ad**
**wale** weal; ridge
**Wa•ler** horse; *compare* **whaler**
**Wales**
**walk**
**walk•able**
**walk•about**
**walk•er**
**walkie-talkie** (*or* **walky-talky**; *plural* **-talkies**)
**walk-in** (*adj*)
**walk•ing**
**walk-on** (*noun, adj*)
**walk•out** (*noun*)
**walk•over** (*noun*)
**walk•way**
**Wal•kyrie** *variant spelling of* **Valkyrie**
**walky-talky** *variant spelling of* **walkie-talkie**
**wall**
**wal•la•by** (*plural* **•bies** *or* **•by**)
**Wal•la•chia** *variant spelling of* **Walachia**
**wal•lah** (*or* **wal•la**) *Slang* person in charge
**wal•la•roo** (*plural* **•roos** *or* **•roo**) large kangaroo
**Wal•la•sey** Merseyside town
**wall•board**
**walled**
**wal•let**
**wall•eye** (*plural* **•eyes** *or* **•eye**)
**wall•eyed**
**wall•flower**
**wall-like**
**Wal•loon** French-speaking Belgian
**wal•lop**
**wal•lop•er**
**wal•lop•ing**
**wal•low**
**wal•low•er**
**wall•paper**
**Walls•end** English town
**wall-to-wall**
**wal•ly** *Slang* idiot; *Scot* made of china
**wal•nut**
**Wal•pur•gis Night**
**wal•rus** (*plural* **•ruses** *or* **•rus**)
**Wal•sall**
**Wal•tham For•est** London borough
**waltz**
**waltz•er**
**wame** *Dialect* belly; womb
**wam•pum** shell money
**wan** (*adj* **wan•ner, wan•nest**; *verb* **wan•ning, wanned**)
**wand**
**wan•der**
**wan•der•er**
**wan•der•ing**
**wan•der•ing•ly**
**wan•der•lust**
**wan•deroo** (*plural* **•deroos**) monkey
**wan•doo** (*plural* **•doos**) tree
**Wands•worth**
**wane** decrease; *compare* **wain**
**waney** (*or* **wany**; **wani•er, wani•est**)
**Wan•ga•nui** New Zealand port
**wan•gle**
**wan•gler**
**wank**
**wan•na** *Slang* want to
**wanned**
**wan•ner**
**wan•nest**
**wan•ning**
**want**
**want•er**
**want•ing**
**wan•ton**
**wan•ton•ness**
**wap•en•take** former county division
**wapi•ti** (*plural* **•tis**) deer
**wap•pen•shaw** gathering of clans
**war** (**war•ring, warred**)
**Wa•ran•gal** Indian city
**wa•ra•tah** shrub
**warb** *Austral* dirty person
**war•ble**
**war•bler**
**ward**
**ward•ed**
**war•den**
**war•den•ry**
**war•der** (*fem* **•dress**)
**ward•robe**
**ward•room**
**ward•ship**
**ware** *Archaic* beware
**ware•house**
**ware•house•man** (*plural* **•men**)
**wares** goods
**war•fare**
**war•fa•rin**
**war•head**

**war•horse**
**wari•ly**
**wari•ness**
**wari•son** bugle note
**War•ley** English town
**war•like**
**war•lock**
**war•lord**
**warm**
**warm-blooded**
**warm-blooded•ness**
**warm•er**
**warm-hearted**
**warm-hearted•ness**
**warm•ish**
**warm•ness**
**war•monger**
**warmth**
**warm-up** (*noun*)
**warn**
**warn•er**
**warn•ing**
**warp**
**warp•age**
**war•path**
**warp•er**
**war•plane**
**war•rant**
**war•rant•abil•ity**
**war•rant•able**
**war•rant•ably**
**war•rant•ee**
**war•rant•er** one who warrants
**war•ran•tor** warranty giver
**war•ran•ty** (*plural* **•ties**)
**warred**
**war•ren**
**war•rig•al** *Austral* dingo
**war•ring**
**War•ring•ton** Cheshire town
**war•ri•or**
**War•saw**
**war•ship**
**war•sle** *Dialect* wrestle
**wart**
**wart•ed**
**war•time**
**warty** (**warti•er, warti•est**)
**War•wick**
**War•wick•shire**
**wary** (**wari•er, wari•est**)
**was**
**wash**
**wash•abil•ity**
**wash•able**
**wash•basin**
**wash•board**
**wash•bowl**
**wash•day**
**wash•er**
**washer•man** (*plural* **•men**)
**washer•woman** (*or* **wash•woman**; *plural* **•women**)
**wash•ery** (*plural* **•eries**)
**wash-house**
**washi•ly**
**wash•in** aeronautics term
**washi•ness**
**wash•ing**
**Wash•ing•ton**
**Wash•ing•to•nian**
**washing-up**
**wash•out** (*noun*)
**wash•rag** *US* face cloth
**wash•room**
**wash•stand**
**wash•tub**
**wash•woman** *variant of* **washerwoman**
**washy** (**washi•er, washi•est**)
**wasn't**
**wasp**
**waspi•ly**
**waspi•ness**
**wasp•ish**
**wasp•ish•ness**
**waspy**
**was•sail**
**was•sail•er**
**wast•able**
**wast•age**
**waste**
**waste•ful**
**waste•ful•ly**
**waste•ful•ness**
**waste•land**
**waste•paper**
**wast•er**
**waste•weir** water channel
**wast•rel**
**wat** Thai monastery
**wa•tap** American Indian thread
**watch**
**watch•case**
**watch•dog**
**watch•er**
**watch•ful**
**watch•ful•ly**
**watch•ful•ness**
**watch-glass**
**watch•maker**
**watch•making**
**watch•man** (*plural* **•men**)
**watch•strap**
**watch•tower**
**watch•word**
**wa•ter**
**wa•ter•age** transportation by ship
**water•bed**
**water•borne**
**water•buck** antelope
**water•colour** (*US* **•color**)
**water•colour•ist** (*US* **•color•**)
**water-cool**
**water-cooled**
**water•course**
**water•craft**
**water•cress**
**wa•ter•er**
**water•fall**
**Wa•ter•ford**
**water•fowl**
**water•front**
**Water•gate**
**wa•teri•ness**
**wa•ter•less**
**water•logged**
**Wa•ter•loo**
**water•man** (*plural* **•men**)
**water•man•ship**
**water•mark**
**water•melon**
**water•proof**
**water•proof•ness**
**water-repellent**
**water-resistant**
**water•scape**
**water•shed**
**water-sick** excessively irrigated
**water•side**
**water-ski** (*noun, plural* **•skis**; *verb* **-skis, -skiing, -skied** *or* **ski'd**)
**water-skier**
**water•spout**
**water•tight**
**water•tightness**
**water•way**

**water•weed**
**water•works**
**water•worn**
**wa•tery**
**Wat•ford**
**watt** unit
**watt•age**
**watt-hour**
**wat•tle**
**wattle•bird**
**watt•meter**
**Wa•tu•si** (*or* **•tut•**; *plural* **•sis** *or* **•si**) African people
**waul** (*or* **wawl**) wail
**wave** undulation, etc.; move to and fro; *compare* **waive**
**wave•band**
**wave•form** physics term
**wave•guide** electronics term
**wave•length**
**wave•let**
**wave•like**
**wa•vell•ite** mineral
**wave•meter**
**wave•off** signal to aircraft
**wa•ver** hesitate; one who waves; *compare* **waiver**
**wa•ver•er**
**wa•ver•ing•ly**
**wavi•ly**
**wavi•ness**
**wavy** (**wavi•er, wavi•est**)
**wawl** *variant spelling of* **waul**
**wax**
**wax•berry** (*plural* **•berries**)
**wax•bill** bird
**wax•en**
**wax•er**
**waxi•ly**
**waxi•ness**
**wax•like**
**wax•plant**
**wax•wing** bird
**wax•work** object
**wax•work•er**
**wax•works** exhibition
**waxy** (**waxi•er, waxi•est**)
**way**
**way•bill** document
**way•farer**
**way•faring**
**Way•land** legendary smith
**way•lay** (**•lay•ing, •laid**)
**way•lay•er**
**way-out**
**way•side**
**way•ward**
**way•ward•ness**
**wayz•goose** printers' annual outing
**Wa•ziri•stan** Asian region
**we**
**weak**
**weak•en**
**weak•en•er**
**weak•fish** (*plural* **•fish** *or* **•fishes**)
**weak•kneed**
**weak•li•ness**
**weak•ling**
**weak•ly** (**•li•er, •li•est**)
**weak-minded**
**weak-minded•ness**
**weak•ness**
**weak-willed**
**weal** prosperity
**weal** (*or* **wheal**) mark on skin
**Weald** English region
**weald** open country; *compare* **wield**
**wealth**
**wealthi•ly**
**wealthi•ness**
**wealthy** (**wealthi•er, wealthi•est**)
**wean**
**wean•er**
**wean•ling**
**weap•on**
**weap•oned**
**weap•on•eer**
**wea•pon•ry**
**Wear** English river
**wear** (**wear•ing, wore, worn**)
**wear•abil•ity**
**wear•able**
**wear•er**
**wea•ri•ful** *variant of* **wearisome**
**wea•ri•less**
**wea•ri•ly**
**wea•ri•ness**
**wear•ing**
**wear•ing•ly**
**wea•ri•some** (*or* **•ful**)
**wea•ri•some•ness** (*or* **•ful•ness**)
**wear•proof**
**wea•ry** (*adj* **•ri•er, •ri•est**; *verb* **•ries, ry•ing, •ried**)
**wea•ry•ing•ly**
**wea•sand** *Dialect* windpipe
**wea•sel** (*plural* **•sel** *or* **•sels**)
**wea•sel•ly**
**weath•er** climatic conditions; *compare* **wether; whether**
**weath•er•abil•ity**
**weather-beaten**
**weather•board**
**weather•boarding**
**weather-bound**
**weather•cock**
**weath•er•er**
**weather•glass**
**weath•er•ing**
**weath•er•ly** nautical term
**weather•man** (*plural* **•men**)
**weather•proof**
**weather-wise**
**weather•worn**
**weave** (**weav•ing, wove** *or* **weaved, wo•ven** *or* **weaved**)
**weav•er** one who weaves; *compare* **weever**
**weaver•bird**
**weav•ing**
**web** (**web•bing, webbed**)
**web•bing**
**web•by** (**•bi•er, •bi•est**)
**we•ber** unit
**web•foot**
**web-footed**
**web•site** Internet location
**web-toed**
**wed** (**wed•ding, wed•ded** *or* **wed**)
**we'd** we had; we would
**wed•ding**
**wed•el•ing** skiing turn
**wedge**
**Wedg•wood** (*Trademark*) pottery
**wedgy**
**wed•lock**
**Wednes•day**
**wee** (**wee•ing, wee'd**) *Slang* tiny; to urinate
**weed**
**weed•er**
**weedi•ly**
**weedi•ness**

**weed•killer**
**weedy** (**weedi•er, weedi•est**)
**week**
**week•day**
**week•end**
**week•end•er**
**week•ly** (*plural* **•lies**)
**week•night**
**wee•ny** (*or* **ween•sy; •ni•er, •ni•est** *or* **•si•er, •si•est**)
**weep** (**weep•ing, wept**)
**weep•er**
**weepi•ness**
**weep•ing**
**weep•ing•ly**
**weepy** (*adj* **weepi•er, weepi•est**; *noun, plural* **weepies**)
**wee•ver** fish; *compare* **weaver**
**wee•vil**
**wee•vily**
**weft**
**Wehr•macht** German armed service
**wei•ge•la** shrub
**weigh**
**weigh•able**
**weigh•bridge**
**weigh•er**
**weight**
**weight•er**
**weighti•ly**
**weighti•ness**
**weight•ing**
**weight•less**
**weight•less•ness**
**weight•lifter**
**weight•lifting**
**weighty** (**weighti•er, weighti•est**)
**Wei•hai** Chinese port
**Wei•mar** German city
**Wei•mar•an•er** dog
(**Weir**) *incorrect spelling of* **Wear**
**weir**
**weird**
**weir•die** (*or* **•do**; *plural* **•dies** *or* **•dos**)
**weird•ness**
**Weis•mann•ism** biological theory
**weka** bird
**Welch** *variant spelling of* **Welsh**, *now obsolete except in regimental names, esp.* **Royal Welch Fusiliers**
**welch** *variant spelling of* **welsh**
**wel•come**
**wel•come•ly**
**wel•come•ness**
**wel•com•er**
**weld**
**weld•abil•ity**
**weld•able**
**weld•er** (*or* **wel•dor**)
**wel•fare**
(**welk**) *incorrect spelling of* **whelk**
**Wel•kom** South African town
**well**
**we'll** we will; we shall
**well-accustomed**
**well-acquaint•ed**
**well-acted**
**well-adapted**
**well-advised**
**well-appoint•ed**
**well-argued**
**well-assort•ed**
**well-attend•ed**
**well-aware**
**well-balanced**
**well-behaved**
**well•being**
**well-bred**
**well-built**
**well-connect•ed**
**well-construct•ed**
**well-defined**
**well-deserved**
**well-developed**
**well-disposed**
**well-document•ed**
**well-done**
**well-dressed**
**well-educat•ed**
**well-endowed**
**well-equipped**
**well-established**
**well-favoured** (*US* **•favored**)
**well-fed**
**well-found**
**well-founded**
**well-groomed**
**well-grounded**
**well•head**
**well-heeled**
**well-hung**
**wel•lies** *Slang* Wellington boots
**well-informed**
**Wel•ling•ton** New Zealand capital; boot
**well-intentioned**
**well-judged**
**well-knit**
**well-known**
**well-mannered**
**well-matched**
**well-meaning**
**well-nigh**
**well-off**
**well-oiled**
**well-organized** (*or* **-organised**)
**well-paid**
**well-pleased**
**well-preserved**
**well-propor•tioned**
**well-provid•ed**
**well-qualified**
**well-read**
**well-received**
**well-rounded**
**Wells** Somerset city
**well-situat•ed**
**well-spent**
**well-spoken**
**well•spring**
**well-support•ed**
**well-tempered**
**well-thought-of**
**well-timed**
**well-to-do**
**well-tried**
**well-turned**
**well-wisher**
**well-wishing**
**well-worded**
**well-worn**
**Welsh**
**welsh** (*or* **welch**) fail in obligation
**Welsh•man** (*plural* **•men**)
**Welsh•woman** (*plural* **•women**)
**welt**
**wel•ter**
**wel•ter•weight**
**wel•witschia** plant

**Wel•wyn Gar•den City**
**Wem•bley**
**wen** cyst
**wench**
**wench•er**
**Wend** Slavonic people
**wend**
**Wend•ish**
**Wen•dy house**
**Wens•ley•dale** Yorkshire town; cheese
**went**
**wen•tle•trap** mollusc
**wept**
**were**
**we're** we are
**weren't** were not
**were•wolf** (*plural* **•wolves)**
**wer•gild** (*or* **were•gild, wer•geld)** price on life
**wer•ner•ite** mineral
**Wes•ley•an**
**Wes•ley•an•ism**
**Wes•sex**
**west**
**west•bound**
**West Brom•wich**
**west•er** to move towards west
**west•er•ing**
**west•er•li•ness**
**west•er•ly** (*plural* **•lies)**
**west•ern**
**west•ern•er**
**west•ern•ism**
**west•erni•za•tion** (*or* **•sa•tion)**
**west•ern•ize** (*or* **•ise)**
**west•ern•most**
**West Ger•many** former country
**West In•dian**
**West In•dies**
**west•ing** westerly movement
**West•meath** Irish county
**West•min•ster**
**West•mor•land** former English county
**west-northwest**
**Weston-super-Mare**
**West•pha•lia**
**West•pha•lian**
**west-southwest**
**west•ward** (*adj*)
**west•wards** (*adv*)
**wet** (*adj* **wet•ter, wet•test;** *verb* **wet•ting, wet** *or* **wet•ted)** not dry; make wet; *compare* **whet**
**weth•er** male sheep; *compare* **weather; whether**
**wet•lands**
**wet•ness**
**wet-nurse** (*verb*)
**wet•tabil•ity**
**wet•table**
**wet•ted**
**wet•ter**
**wet•test**
**wet•ting**
**wet•tish**
**we've** we have
**Wex•ford** Irish county
**Wey•mouth**
**whack**
**whack•er**
**whack•ing**
**whacko** exclamation
**whale** (*plural* **whales** *or* **whale)**
**whale•boat**
**whale•bone**
**whal•er** whale catcher; whaleboat; *compare* **Waler**
**whal•ing**
**wham (wham•ming, whammed)**
**whang**
**Whan•ga•rei** New Zealand port
**whangee** bamboo grass
**whare** Maori hut
**wharf** (*plural* **wharves** *or* **wharfs)**
**wharf•age**
**wharf•in•ger**
**wharve** flywheel; pulley
**what**
**what•ev•er**
**what•not**
**what•sit**
**what•so•ev•er**
**whaup** *Scot* curlew
**wheal** *variant spelling of* **weal**
**wheat**
**wheat•ear** bird
**wheat•en**
**wheat•worm**
**whee•dle**
**whee•dler**
**whee•dling•ly**
**wheel**
**wheel•bar•row**
**wheel•base**
**wheel•chair**
**wheel•er**
**wheeler-dealer**
**wheel•house**
**wheelie** skateboarding manoeuvre
**wheel•less**
**wheel•work**
**wheel•wright**
**wheen** *Dialect* few
**wheeze**
**wheez•er**
**wheezi•ly**
**wheezi•ness**
**wheez•ing•ly**
**wheezy (wheezi•er, wheezi•est)**
**whelk**
**whelp**
**when**
**whence**
**whence•so•ev•er**
**whene'er**
**when•ever**
**when•so•ever**
**where**
**where•abouts**
**where•as**
**where•at**
**where•by**
**where'er**
**where•fore**
**where•from**
**where•in**
**where•into**
**where•of**
**where•on**
**where•so•ever**
**where•to**
**where•upon**
**wher•ever**
**where•with**
**where•with•al**
**wher•rit** worry
**wher•ry** (*plural* **•ries)** boat
**wherry•man** (*plural* **•men)**
**whet (whet•ting, whet•ted)** sharpen; stimulate; *compare* **wet**

**wheth•er** (*conj.*) *compare* **weather; wether**
**whet•stone**
**whet•ter**
**whey** watery liquid
**whey•ey** (*or* **•ish, •like)**
**whey•face**
**whey•faced**
**which**
**which•ever**
**whick•er** whinny; *compare* **wicker**
**whid•ah** *variant spelling of* **whydah**
**whiff**
**whiff•er**
**whif•fle**
**whif•fler**
**whif•fle•tree** crossbar in harness
**Whig** political party
**Whig•gery** (*or* **•gism)**
**Whig•gish**
**Whig•gish•ness**
**while** during; *note* **while away;** *compare* **wile**
**whilst**
**whim**
**whim•brel** bird
**whim•per**
**whim•per•er**
**whim•per•ing•ly**
**whim•si•cal**
**whim•si•cal•ity** (*plural* **•ities)**
**whim•si•cal•ly**
**whim•si•cal•ness**
**whim•sy** (*or* **•sey;** *noun, plural* **•sies** *or* **•seys;** *adj* **•si•er, •si•est)**
**whin** gorse
**whin•chat** bird
**whine**
**whin•er**
**whinge**
**whin•ing•ly**
**whin•ny** (*verb* **•nies, •ny•ing, •nied;** *noun, plural* **•nies)**
**whin•stone**
**whiny (whini•er, whini•est)** peevish; *compare* **winy**
**whip (whip•ping, whipped)**
**whip•cord**
**whip•lash**
**whip•like**
**whip•per**
**whipper-in** (*plural* **whippers-in)**
**whip•per•snap•per**
**whip•pet**
**whip•ping**
**whip•poor•will**
**whippy (whip•pier, whip•piest)**
**whip-round** (*noun*)
**whip•saw**
**whip•stall** aeronautics term
**whip•stitch**
**whip•stock** whip handle
**whip•worm**
**whir** (*or* **whirr; whir•ring, whirred)**
**whirl** spin; confusion; *compare* **whorl**
**whirl•about**
**whirl•er**
**whirli•gig**
**whirl•ing•ly**
**whirl•pool**
**whirl•wind**
**whirly•bird**
**whirr** *variant spelling of* **whir**
**whish** swish
**whisk**
**whisk•er**
**whisk•ered**
**whisk•ers**
**whisk•ery**
**whis•key** Irish or US whisky
**whis•ky** (*plural* **•kies)**
**whis•per**
**whis•per•er**
**whist**
**whis•tle**
**whis•tler**
**whis•tling**
**Whit** Christian festival
**whit** iota
**white**
**white•bait**
**white•beam** tree
**white•cap** white-crested wave
**White•chapel**
**white-collar** (*adj*)
**white•damp** mine gas
**whit•ed sep•ul•chre**
**white-eye** bird
**white•fish** (*plural* **•fish** *or* **•fishes)**
**white•fly** (*plural* **•flies)**
**White•hall**
**white-hot**
**white-livered**
**whit•en**
**whit•en•er**
**white•ness**
**whit•en•ing**
**white•out**
**whites**
**white-slaver**
**white•smith** metal polisher
**white•throat** bird
**white•wall** tyre
**white•wash**
**white•wash•er**
**white•wood**
**whit•ey** (*or* **wity;** *plural* **•eys** *or* **wities)**
**whith•er**
**whit•ing** (*plural* **•ing** *or* **•ings)** fish
**whit•ing** (*or* **•en•ing)** ground chalk
**whit•ish**
**whit•low**
**Whit•sun**
**Whit•sun•tide**
**whit•tle**
**whit•tler**
**whit•tlings** wood shavings
**whity** whitish; *variant spelling of* **whitey**
**whiz** (*or* **whizz; whiz•zing, whizzed)**
**whiz-bang** (*or* **whizz-)**
**whiz•zer**
**who**
**whoa**
**who'd** who had; who would
**who•dun•it** (*or* **•dun•nit)**
**who•ever**
**whole**
**whole•food**
**whole•hearted**
**whole•hearted•ness**
**whole•meal**
**whole•ness**
**whole•sale**
**whole•sal•er**

**whole•some**
**whole•some•ly**
**whole•some•ness**
**who'll** who will; who shall
**whol•ly**
**whom**
**whom•ever**
**whom•so•ever**
**whoop**
**whoo•pee**
**whoop•er** swan
**whoop•ing cough**
**whoops** exclamation
**whoosh** (*or* **woosh**)
**whop** (*or* **wop; whop•ping, whopped** *or* **wop•ping, wopped**) hit
**whop•per**
**whop•ping**
**whore**
**whore•dom**
**whore•house**
**whore•monger**
**whore•son**
**whor•ish**
**whorl** spiral pattern or arrangement; *compare* **whirl**
**whorled**
**whortle•berry** (*plural* **•berries**)
**who's** who is
**whose** of who
**who•so•ever** (*or* **who•so**)
**why** (*plural* **whys**)
**Why•al•la** Australian port
**whyd•ah** (*or* **whid•**) bird
**Wichi•ta** US city
**Wick** Scottish town
**wick**
**wick•ed**
**wick•ed•ness**
**wick•er** flexible twig; *compare* **whicker**
**wicker•work**
**wick•et**
**wicket•keeper**
**wick•ing**
**wicki•up** American Indian hut
**Wick•low** Irish county
**wico•py** plant
**wid•der•shins** *variant spelling of* **withershins**
**wide**
**wide-awake**
**wide-awakeness**
**wide-eyed**
**wide•ly**
**wid•en**
**wid•en•er**
**wide•ness**
**wide-open**
**wide-ranging**
**wide-screen** (*adj*)
**wide•spread**
**widg•eon** *variant spelling of* **wigeon**
**widg•et**
**widgie** *Austral* unruly woman
**wid•ish**
**Wid•nes** Cheshire town
**wid•ow**
**wid•ow•er**
**wid•ow•hood**
**width**
**width•wise** (*or* **•ways**)
**wield** manipulate; *compare* **weald**
**wield•able**
**wield•er**
**wieldy** (**wieldi•er, wieldi•est**)
**Wie•ner schnit•zel**
**(wier)** *incorrect spelling of* **weir**
**(wierd)** *incorrect spelling of* **weird**
**Wies•ba•den** German city
**wife** (*plural* **wives**)
**wife•li•ness**
**wife•ly**
**wig** (**wig•ging, wigged**)
**Wig•an**
**wig•eon** (*or* **widg•**) duck
**wigged**
**wig•ging**
**wig•gle**
**wig•gler**
**wig•gly**
**Wight (Isle of)**
**wig•wag** (**•wag•ging, •wagged**)
**wig•wag•ger**
**wig•wam**
**wil•co** signalling expression
**wild**
**wild•cat** (**•cat•ting, •cat•ted**)
**wild•cat•ter**
**wil•de•beest** (*plural* **•beests** *or* **•beest**)
**wil•der•ness**
**wild-eyed**
**wild•fire**
**wild•fowl**
**wild•fowl•er**
**wild•fowl•ing**
**wild-goose chase**
**wild•ing** (*or* **•ling**)
**wild•life**
**wild•ness**
**wile** craftiness; trick; *compare* **while**
**wil•ful** (*US* **will•**)
**wil•ful•ly** (*US* **will•**)
**wil•ful•ness** (*US* **will•**)
**Wil•helms•ha•ven** German port
**wili•ly**
**wili•ness**
**will**
**will•able**
**wil•lem•ite** mineral
**will•er**
**wil•let** bird
**will•ful** *US spelling of* **wilful**
**Wil•liams•burg** US city
**wil•lies** *Slang* fright
**will•ing**
**will•ing•ness**
**wil•li•waw** *US* turmoil
**will-o'-the-wisp**
**wil•low**
**wil•low•herb**
**wil•lowy**
**will•power**
**willy-nilly**
**wilt**
**Wil•ton** carpet
**Wilt•shire**
**wily** (**wili•er, wili•est**)
**wim•ble** tool
**Wim•ble•don**
**wimp**
**wimp•ish**
**wim•ple**
**Wim•py** (*Trademark*) hamburger
**win** (**win•ning, won**)
**wince**
**winc•er**
**win•cey** fabric
**win•cey•ette**

**winch**
**winch•er**
**Win•ches•ter** English city; rifle
**win•ches•ter** large bottle
**winc•ing•ly**
**wind (wind•ing, wound)** coil
**wind (wind•ing, wind•ed)** air current, etc.
**wind•able**
**wind•age**
**wind•bag**
**wind•blown**
**wind-borne**
**wind•bound**
**wind•break**
**wind-broken** asthmatic
**wind•burn**
**wind•burnt** (*or* **•burned)**
**wind•cheater**
**wind•ed**
**wind•er**
**Win•der•mere**
**wind•fall**
**wind•flower**
**wind•gall** fetlock swelling
**wind•galled**
**Wind•hoek** Namibian capital
**wind•hover** *Dialect* kestrel
**windi•ly**
**windi•ness**
**wind•ing**
**wind•ing•ly**
**wind•jam•mer**
**wind•lass**
**win•dle•straw** *Dialect* dried grass
**wind•mill**
**win•dow**
**window-dresser**
**window-dressing**
**window•pane**
**window-shop (-shopping, -shopped)**
**window-shopper**
**window•sill**
**wind•pipe**
**wind-pollinat•ed**
**wind-pollina•tion**
**wind•row** line of hay
**wind•row•er**
**wind•sail**
**wind•screen**
**wind•shield**
**wind•sock**
**Wind•sor**
**wind•storm**
**wind•sucker**
**wind-sucking**
**wind•swept**
**wind-up** (*noun*)
**wind•ward**
**windy (windi•er, windi•est)**
**wine**
**wine•bibber**
**wine•bibbing**
**wine•glass**
**wine•glass•ful**
**wine•press**
**win•ery** (*plural* **•eries)**
**wine•skin**
**wing**
**wing•ding** *US* party
**winged**
**wing•er**
**wing•less**
**wing•less•ness**
**wing•let**
**wing•like**
**wing•over** aircraft manoeuvre
**wing•span** (*or* **•spread)**
**wink**
**wink•er**
**win•kle**
**win•nable**
**Win•ne•ba•go** (*plural* **•gos** *or* **•go)** US lake; American Indian
**win•ner**
**win•ning**
**win•ning•ness**
**win•nings**
**Win•ni•peg**
**Win•ni•peg•ger**
**Win•ni•pego•sis** Canadian lake
**win•now**
**win•now•er**
**wino** (*plural* **winos)** *Slang* wine drinker
**win•some**
**win•some•ly**
**win•some•ness**
**Winston-Salem** US city
**win•ter**
**winter•bourne** stream
**win•ter•er**
**winter•feed (•feeding, •fed)**
**winter•green** shrub
**winter•kill**
**winter•time**
**win•tri•er**
**win•tri•est**
**win•tri•ly**
**win•tri•ness** (*or* **•teri•ness)**
**win•try** (*or* **•tery; •tri•er, •tri•est)**
**winy (wini•er, wini•est)** like wine; *compare* **whiny**
**winze** mining shaft
**wipe**
**wipe-out** (*noun*)
**wip•er**
**wire**
**wire•draw (•draw•ing, •drew, •drawn)**
**wire-gauge**
**wire-haired**
**wire•less**
**wire•man** (*plural* **•men)** *US* electrician
**wir•er**
**wire•work**
**wire•worker**
**wire•works**
**wire•worm**
**wire-wove**
**wiri•ly**
**wiri•ness**
**wir•ing**
**wir•ra** Irish exclamation
**Wir•ral** English peninsula
**wiry (wiri•er, wiri•est)**
**Wis•con•sin**
**Wis•con•sin•ite**
**wis•dom**
**wise**
**wisea•cre**
**wise•crack**
**wise•crack•er**
**wise•ly**
**wise•ness**
**wi•sent** European bison
**wish**
**wish•bone**
**wish•er**
**wish•ful**
**wish•ful•ly**
**wish•ful•ness**
**wishy-washy**
**wisp**

**wispi•ly**
**wispi•ness**
**wispy** (**wispi•er, wispi•est**)
**wis•te•ria**
**wist•ful**
**wist•ful•ly**
**wist•ful•ness**
**wit**
**wit•an** Anglo-Saxon council
**witch**
**witch•craft**
**witch elm** *variant spelling of* **wych elm**
**witch•ery** (*plural* **•eries**)
**witch•et•ty** edible grub
**witch ha•zel** (*or* **wych hazel**)
**witch-hunt**
**witch-hunter**
**witch-hunting**
**witch•ing**
**witch•like**
**wite** *Scot* blame
**wit•ena•gamot** witan
**with**
**with•al**
**with•draw** (**•draw•ing, •drew, •drawn**)
**with•draw•able**
**with•draw•al**
**with•draw•er**
**with•drawn**
**with•drawn•ness**
**with•drew**
**withe** (*or* **withy**; *plural* **withes** *or* **withies**) flexible twig
**with•er**
**with•ered•ness**
**with•er•er**
**with•er•ing•ly**
**with•er•ite** mineral
**with•ers**
**with•er•shins** (*or* **wid•der•**)
**with•hold** (**•hold•ing, •held**)
**with•hold•er**
**with•in**
**with•out**
**with•stand** (**•stand•ing, •stood**)
**with•stand•er**
**with•stood**
**withy** (*plural* **withies**) willow tree; *variant spelling of* **withe**
**wit•less**
**wit•less•ness**
**wit•loof** Belgian chicory
**wit•ness**
**wit•ness•able**
**wit•ness•er**
**wits**
**wit•ter**
**wit•ti•cism**
**wit•ti•ly**
**wit•ti•ness**
**wit•ting•ly** intentional
**wit•ty** (**•ti•er, •ti•est**)
**Wit•wa•ters•rand** South African region
**wive** *Archaic* to marry
**wi•vern** *variant spelling of* **wyvern**
**wives** *plural of* **wife**
**wiz•ard**
**wiz•ard•ry**
**wiz•en**
**wiz•ened**
**woad**
**woad•ed**
**wob•be•gong** shark
**wob•ble**
**wob•bler**
**wob•bli•ness**
**wob•bly** (**•bli•er, •bli•est**)
**Woden** (*or* **Wodan**) Anglo-Saxon god
**wodge**
**woe**
**woe•be•gone**
**woe•ful**
**woe•ful•ly**
**woe•ful•ness**
**wog•gle**
**wok**
**woke**
**wok•en**
**Wo•king**
**wold** upland
**wolf** (*plural* **wolves**)
**wolf•bane** (*or* **wolfs•bane, wolf's-bane**) plant
**wolf•er** *variant of* **wolver**
**wolf•fish** (*plural* **•fish** *or* **•fishes**)
**wolf•hound**
**wolf•ish**
**wolf•ish•ness**
**wolf•like**
**wolf•ram** tungsten
**wolf•ram•ite** mineral
**wolfs•bane** (*or* **wolf's-bane**) *variants of* **wolfbane**
**wolf-whistle** (*verb*)
**wol•las•ton•ite** mineral
**Wol•lon•gong** Australian city
**wol•ly** (*plural* **•lies**) *Dialect* pickled cucumber; *compare* **wally**
**Wol•of** (*plural* **•of** *or* **•ofs**) African people
**wolv•er** (*or* **wolf•**) wolf hunter
**Wol•ver•hamp•ton**
**wol•ver•ine** animal
**wolves** *plural of* **wolf**
**wom•an** (*plural* **•en**)
**wom•an•hood**
**wom•an•ish**
**wom•an•ish•ness**
**wom•an•ize** (*or* **•ise**)
**wom•an•iz•er** (*or* **•is•er**)
**wom•an•kind**
**woman-like**
**wom•an•li•ness**
**wom•an•ly**
**womb**
**wom•bat**
**womb•like**
**wom•en**
**women•folk**
**wom•era** *variant spelling of* **woomera**
**won** *past tense of* **win**
**won** (*or* **hwan**; *plural* **won** *or* **hwan**) North Korean currency
**won•der**
**won•der•er**
**won•der•ful**
**won•der•ful•ly**
**won•der•ful•ness**
**wonder•land**
**won•der•ment**
**wonder•work** miracle
**wonder-worker**
**wonder-working**
**won•drous**
**won•drous•ness**
**won•ky** (**•ki•er, •ki•est**)
**Won•san** North Korean port

**wont** accustomed; custom
**won't** will not
**wont•ed**
**won ton** Chinese food
**woo** (**woos, woo•ing, wooed**)
**wood**
**wood•bine**
**wood•borer** beetle larva
**wood•carver**
**wood•carving**
**wood•chat** bird
**wood•chuck**
**wood•cock**
**wood•craft**
**wood•crafts•man** (*plural* **•men**)
**wood•cut**
**wood•cut•ter**
**wood•cutting**
**wood•ed**
**wood•en**
**wooden•head**
**wood•en•ness**
**wood•grouse**
**woodi•ness**
**wood•land**
**wood•lander**
**wood•lark**
**wood•louse** (*plural* **•lice**)
**wood•man** (*plural* **•men**)
**wood•note** natural song
**wood•pecker**
**wood•pile**
**wood•print**
**wood•ruff** plant
**wood•rush**
**wood•screw**
**wood•shed**
**wood•sia** fern
**woods•man** (*plural* **•men**)
**wood•wind**
**wood•work**
**wood•worker**
**wood•working**
**wood•worm**
**woody** (**woodi•er, woodi•est**)
**wooed**
**woo•er**
**woof** weft; bark of dog
**woof•er** loudspeaker
**woo•ing**
**wool**
**wool•gather•er**
**wool•gather•ing**
**wool•grower**
**wool•growing**
**wool•len** (*US* **wool•en**)
**wool•li•ly**
**wool•li•ness**
**wool•ly** (*US also* **wooly**; *adj* **•li•er, •li•est**; *noun, plural* **•lies**)
**wool•pack**
**wool•sack**
**Woom•era** Australian town
**woom•era** (*or* **wom•era**) Aboriginal spear thrower
**Woop Woop** *Austral* remote town
**woosh** *variant spelling of* **whoosh**
**woozi•ly**
**woozi•ness**
**woozy** (**woozi•er, woozi•est**)
**wop** *variant spelling of* **whop**; *Slang* Italian
**Worces•ter**
**Worces•ter•shire** former county; *note* **Worcestershire sauce**
**word**
**word•age**
**word-blind**
**word•book**
**word•break**
**word-deaf**
**wordi•ly**
**wordi•ness**
**word•ing**
**word•less**
**word•less•ness**
**word-perfect**
**word•play**
**word•smith**
**wordy** (**wordi•er, wordi•est**)
**wore**
**work**
**work•abil•ity** (*or* **•able•ness**)
**work•able**
**worka•day**
**worka•hol•ic**
**work•bag**
**work•bench**
**work•book**
**work•box**
**work•day**
**work•er**
**worker-priest**
**work•folk**
**work-harden**
**work-harden•ing**
**work•horse**
**work•house**
**work-in** (*noun*)
**work•ing**
**work•load**
**work•man** (*plural* **•men**)
**work•man•like**
**work•man•ly**
**work•man•ship**
**work-out** (*noun*)
**work•people**
**work•piece**
**work•room**
**works**
**work•shop**
**work•shy**
**Work•sop** English town
**work•table**
**work-to-rule** (*noun*)
**world**
**world-beater**
**world-beating**
**world•li•ness**
**world•ling**
**world•ly** (**•li•er, •li•est**)
**worldly-wise**
**world-shaking**
**world-weariness**
**world-weary**
**world•wide**
**worm**
**worm•cast**
**worm-eaten**
**worm•er**
**worm•hole**
**worm•like** (*or* **•ish**)
**worm•seed**
**worm•wood**
**wormy** (**wormi•er, wormi•est**)
**worn**
**worn-out**
**wor•ri•er**
**wor•ri•ment**
**wor•ri•some**
**wor•rit** *Dialect* tease
**wor•ry** (*verb* **•ries, •ry•ing, •ried**; *noun, plural* **•ries**)
**wor•ry•wart** worrier
**worse**

**wors•en**
**wor•ship** (**•ship•ping, •shipped**; *US* **•ship•ing, •shiped**)
**wor•ship•able**
**wor•ship•ful**
**wor•ship•ful•ly**
**wor•ship•ful•ness**
**wor•ship•per**
**wor•ship•ping•ly**
**worst**
**wor•sted** fabric
**worst•ed** defeated
**wort** soaked malt
**worth**
**wor•thi•ly**
**wor•thi•ness**
**Wor•thing**
**worth•less**
**worth•less•ly**
**worth•less•ness**
**worth•while**
**worth•while•ness**
**wor•thy** (*adj* **•thi•er, •thi•est**; *noun, plural* **•thies**)
**Wotan** Germanic god
**would**
**would-be**
**wouldn't**
**wouldst**
**wound**
**wound•able**
**wound•ed**
**wound•er**
**wound•ing•ly**
**wound•wort**
**wove**
**wo•ven**
**wow**
**wow•ser** *Austral* puritanical person
**wrack** seaweed; *variant spelling of* **rack**
**wraith**
**wraith•like**
**wran•gle**
**wran•gler**
**wrap** (**wrap•ping, wrapped**)
**wrap•over** (*or* **•around, •round**)
**wrap•per**
**wrap•ping**
**wrasse** fish; *compare* **rasse**
**wrath** anger; *compare* **wroth**
**wrath•ful**
**wrath•ful•ly**
**wrath•ful•ness**
**wreak**
**wreak•er**
**wreath** (*noun, plural* **wreaths**)
**wreathe** (*verb*)
**wreck**
**wreck•age**
**wreck•er**
**wreck•fish** (*plural* **•fish** *or* **•fishes**)
**Wre•kin** English hill
**Wren** member of WRNS
**wren** bird
**wrench**
**wrest**
**wrest•er**
**wres•tle**
**wres•tler**
**wres•tling**
**wretch** miserable person; *compare* **retch**
**wretch•ed**
**wretch•ed•ness**
**Wrex•ham**
**wried** contorted
**wri•er** *variant spelling of* **wryer**
**wri•est** *variant spelling of* **wryest**
**wrig•gle**
**wrig•gler**
**wrig•gling•ly**
**wrig•gly** (**•gli•er, •gli•est**)
**wright** maker or repairer
**wring** (**wring•ing, wrung**)
**wring•er**
**wrin•kle**
**wrin•kly**
**wrist**
**wrist•band**
**wrist•let** bracelet
**wrist•lock**
**wrist•watch**
**writ**
**writ•able**
**write** (**writ•ing, wrote, writ•ten**)
**write-off** (*noun*)
**writ•er**
**writhe**
**writh•er**
**writh•ing•ly**
**writ•ing**
**writ•ten**
**Wro•cław** Polish city
**wrong**
**wrong•doer**
**wrong•doing**
**wrong•er**
**wrong-foot** (*verb*)
**wrong•ful**
**wrong•ful•ly**
**wrong•ful•ness**
**wrong-headed**
**wrong-headed•ness**
**wrong•ly**
**wrong•ness**
**wrote**
**wroth** *Archaic* angry; *compare* **wrath**
**wrought**
**wrought-up**
**wrung**
**wry** (*adj* **wry•er, wry•est** *or* **wri•er, wri•est**; *verb* **wries, wry•ing, wried**)
**wry•bill** bird
**wry•ing**
**wry•ly**
**wry•neck**
**wry•ness**
**Wu** Chinese dialect
**Wu•han** Chinese city
**Wu-hsi** *variant spelling of* **Wusih**
**Wuhu** Chinese port
**wul•fen•ite** mineral
**Wu-lu-mu-ch'i** *variant of* **Urumchi**
**wun•der•kind** (*plural* **•kinds** *or* **•kind•er**) child prodigy
**Wup•per•tal** German city
**wurley** (*or* **wurlie**) Aboriginal hut
**wurst** German sausage
**Würt•tem•berg** former German state
**Würz•burg** German city
**wus** Welsh term of address
**Wu•sih** (*or* **Wu-hsi**) Chinese city
**Wy•an•dotte** domestic fowl
**wych elm** (*or* **witch elm**)
**wych hazel** *variant spelling of* **witch hazel**
**Wyc•lif•fite** (*or* **Wyc•lif•ite**)
**Wye** British river

**Wyke•ham•ist** member of Winchester College
**wynd** *Scot* lane
**Wyo•ming**
**wy•vern** (*or* **wi•**) heraldic beast

# X

**xan•thate** chemical compound
**xan•tha•tion**
**xan•the•in** plant pigment
**xan•thene** chemical compound
**xan•thic** chemistry or botany term
**xan•thin** plant pigment
**xan•thine** chemical compound
**xan•thoch•ro•ism** animal skin condition
**xan•tho•ma** (*plural* **•mas** *or* **•ma•ta**) skin nodule
**xan•tho•phyll** plant pigment
**xan•tho•phyll•ous**
**xan•thous** having yellowish hair
**Xan•thus** ancient Asian city
**x-axis**
**X-chromosome**
**xe•bec** (*or* **ze•bec, ze•beck**) ship
**xe•nia** botany term
**xe•nial**
**xeno•cryst**
**xe•noga•mous**
**xe•noga•my** cross-fertilization
**xeno•gen•esis** botany term
**xeno•genet•ic** (*or* **•gen•ic**)
**xeno•glos•sia** language ability
**xeno•lith** geology term
**xeno•lith•ic**
**xeno•mor•phic** geology term
**xeno•mor•phi•cal•ly**
**xen•on** chemical element
**xeno•phile**
**xeno•phobe**
**xeno•pho•bia**
**xeno•pho•bic**
**xeno•trans•plant** surgical procedure
**xeno•trans•plan•ta•tion**
**xer•arch** ecology term
**xe•ric** of dry conditions
**xe•ri•cal•ly**
**xe•ro•der•ma** (*or* **•mia**) dry skin
**xe•ro•der•mat•ic** (*or* **•ma•tous**)
**xe•rog•ra•pher**
**xe•ro•graph•ic**
**xe•ro•graphi•cal•ly**
**xe•rog•ra•phy** photocopying
**xe•ro•mor•phic** botany term
**xe•ro•phile**
**xe•rophi•lous** living in dry conditions
**xe•rophi•ly**
**xe•roph•thal•mia** (*or* **xe•ro•ma**) eye disease
**xe•roph•thal•mic**
**xe•ro•phyte**
**xe•ro•phyt•ic**
**xe•ro•phyti•cal•ly**
**xe•ro•phyt•ism**
**xe•ro•sere** ecology term
**xe•ro•sis** dryness of tissues
**xe•rot•ic**
**Xer•ox** (*Trademark*)
**Xho•sa** (*plural* **•sa** *or* **•sas**) African people
**Xho•san**
**xi** (*plural* **xis**) Greek letter
**xiphi•ster•num** (*plural* **•na**) part of breastbone
**xiph•oid** anatomy or biology term
**xipho•su•ran** zoology term
**Xmas**
**X-radiation**
**X-ray** (*or* **x-ray**)
**xy•lan** biochemistry term
**xy•lem** plant tissue
**xy•lene** chemical compound
**xy•li•dine** chemical compound
**xy•lo•carp** botany term
**xy•lo•car•pous**
**xy•lo•graph** wood engraving
**xy•log•ra•pher**
**xy•lo•graph•ic** (*or* **•graphi•cal**)
**xy•log•ra•phy**
**xy•loid** woody
**xy•lol** chemical compound
**xy•lopha•gous** wood-eating
**xy•lo•phone**
**xy•lo•phon•ic**
**xy•lopho•nist**
**xy•lose** sugar
**xy•loto•mist**
**xy•loto•mous** wood-boring
**xy•loto•my** preparing wood for microscopy
**xy•lyl** chemistry term
**xyst** (*or* **xys•tus, xys•tos**) portico
**xys•ter** surgical file

# Y

**yacht**
**yacht•ing**
**yachts•man** (*plural* **•men**)
**yachts•man•ship** (*or* **yacht•**)
**yachts•woman** (*plural* **•women**)
**ya•hoo** (*plural* **•hoos**) coarse person
**ya•hoo•ism**
**yak** (**yak•king, yakked**)
**Ya•kut** (*plural* **•kuts** *or* **•kut**) Russian people
**Ya•kutsk** Russian port
**Yale** US university; (*Trademark*) lock
**Yal•ta** Ukrainian port
**yam**
**yam•mer**
**yam•mer•er**
**yang** Chinese masculine principle; *compare* **yin**
**Yang•tze**
**yank** tug
**Yank** (*or* **Yan•kee**) *Slang* American
**Yan•kee•ism**
**Ya•oun•dé** (*or* **Ya•un•de**) Cameroon capital
**yap** (**yap•ping, yapped**)
**ya•pok** animal
**ya•pon** *variant spelling of* **yaupon**
**yapped**
**yap•per**
**yap•ping**
**yap•py**
**yar•bor•ough** bridge or whist term
**yard•age**
**yard•arm**
**yard•stick**
**Yar•mouth**
**yar•mul•ke** skullcap
**yarn**
**yarn-dyed**
**Ya•ro•slavl** Russian city
**yar•row**
**yash•mak** (*or* **•mac**)
**yata•ghan** sword
**Ya•un•de** *variant spelling of* **Yaoundé**
**yau•pon** (*or* **ya•pon**) shrub
**yau•tia** plant
**yaw**
**yawl**
**yawn**
**yawn•er**
**yawn•ing•ly**
**yaws** disease
**y-axis**
**Y-chromosome**
**ye**
**yea**
**yean•ling** goat's or sheep's young
**year**
**year•book**
**year•ling**
**year•long**
**year•ly** (*plural* **•lies**)
**yearn**
**yearn•er**
**yearn•ing**
**yeast**
**yeasti•ly**
**yeasti•ness**
**yeasty** (**yeasti•er, yeasti•est**)
**Ye•ka•te•rin•burg** Russian city
**yell**
**yell•er**
**yel•low**
**yellow•bark**
**yellow-belly** (*plural* **-bellies**)
**yellow•bird**
**yellow•hammer**
**yel•low•ish**
**yellow•legs** bird
**yel•lows** disease
**Yellow•stone**
**yellow•tail** (*plural* **•tails** *or* **•tail**) fish
**yellow•weed**
**yellow•wood**
**yel•lowy**
**yelp**
**yelp•er**
**Yem•en**
**Yem•eni**
**yen** (**yen•ning, yenned**)
**yen** (*plural* **yen**) Japanese currency
**Ye•ni•sei** Russian river
**Yen•tai** (*or* **Yen-t'ai**) Chinese port
**yeo•man** (*plural* **•men**)
**yeo•man•ry** (*plural* **•ries**)
**Yeo•vil**
**yer•ba** beverage
**Ye•re•van** Armenian capital
**yes**
**yes-man** (*plural* **-men**)
**yes•ter•day**
**yes•ter•year**
**yeti**
**yew**
**Ygg•dra•sil** mythological tree
**Yid•dish**
**yield**
**yield•able**
**yield•er**
**yield•ing•ly**
**yield•ing•ness**
**yin** Chinese feminine principle; *compare* **yang**
**Ying•kow** (*or* **Ying-k'ou**) Chinese port
**yip•pee**
**ylang-ylang** (*or* **ilang-ilang**) tree
**ylem** original matter of universe
**yob** (*or* **yob•bo**; *plural* **yobs** *or* **yob•bos**)
**yo•del** (**•del•ling, •delled**; *US* **•del•ing, •deled**)
**yo•del•ler** (*US* **•del•er**)
**yoga**
**yo•ghurt** (*or* **•gurt**)
**yogi** (*plural* **yo•gis** *or* **yo•gin**) yoga master
**yo•gic**
**yo•gism**
**yo•gurt** *variant spelling of* **yoghurt**
**yo•him•bine** medicinal substance
**yoicks** huntsman's exclamation
**yoke** frame; burden; link; part of garment; *compare* **yolk**

**yo•kel**
**yo•kel•ish**
**Yo•ko•ha•ma** Japanese city
**Yok•ya•kar•ta** (*or* **Jog•ja•**) Indonesian city
**yolk** part of egg; *compare* **yoke**
**yolky**
**Yom Kip•pur**
**yon** (*or* **yond**)
**yon•der**
**yoni** female genitalia
**Yon•kers** US city
**Yonne** French department and river
**yon•nie** *Austral* stone
**yoo-hoo**
**yore**
**York**
**york•er** cricket term
**York•ist**
**York•shire**
**Yorkshire•man** (*plural* **•men**)
**Yo•ru•ba** (*plural* **•bas** *or* **•ba**) African people
**Yo•ru•ban**
**Yo•semi•te** US national park
**Yoshkar-Ola** Russian city
**you**
**you'd** you would; you had
**you'll** you will; you shall
**young**
**young•berry** (*plural* **•berries**)
**young•ish**
**young•ster**
**Youngs•town** US city
**your** of you
**you're** you are
**yours**
**your•self** (*plural* **•selves**)
**youth**
**youth•ful**
**youth•ful•ly**
**youth•ful•ness**
**you've** you have
**yowl**
**yowl•er**
**yo-yo** (*plural* **-yos**)
**Ypres**
**Yquem** French vineyard
**yt•ter•bia** chemical compound
**yt•ter•bite** mineral
**yt•ter•bium** chemical element
**yt•tria** chemical compound
**yt•tric**
**yt•trif•er•ous**
**yt•trium** chemical element
**yuan** (*plural* **yuan**) Chinese currency
**Yu•ca•tán** Mexican state
**yuc•ca**
**Yuga** Hindu age
**Yu•go•slav** (*or* **Ju•**)
**Yu•go•sla•via** (*or* **Ju•**)
**Yu•go•sla•vian** (*or* **Ju•**)
**yuk**
**yuk•ky**
**Yu•kon**
**Yu•kon•er**
**yu•lan** tree
**yule**
**yule•tide**
**Yu•man** language group
**yum•my** (**•mi•er, •mi•est**)
**Yün•nan** Chinese province
**yup** *Slang* yes
**yup•pie**
**Yve•lines** French department

# Z

**za•ba•glio•ne**
**Za•brze** Polish city
**Za•ca•te•cas** Mexican state
**zaf•fer** (*or* **zaf•fre**) pigment
**Zaga•zig** (*or* **Zaqa•ziq**) Egyptian city
**Za•greb**
**zai•bat•su** Japanese wealthy families
**Za•ïre** *former name of* the Democratic Republic of Congo
**Za•ïr•ese**
**Za•ïr•ian**
**Zama** ancient African city
**Zam•be•zi** (*or* **•se**)
**Zam•be•zian**
**Zam•bia**
**Zam•bian**
**Zam•bo•an•ga** Philippine port
**za•mia** plant
**za•min•dar** (*or* **ze•**) Indian landowner
**za•min•dari** (*or* **ze•**; *plural* **•daris**) estate
**za•ni•ly**
**za•ni•ness**
**Zan•te** Greek island
**zan•thoxy•lum** tree
**zany** (*adj* **zani•er, zani•est**; *noun, plural* **zanies**)
**Zan•zi•bar**
**Zan•zi•ba•ri**
**zap** (**zap•ping, zapped**)
**za•pa•dea•do** (*plural* **•dos**) dance
**Za•po•rozh•ye** Ukrainian city
**Za•po•tec** (*plural* **•tecs** *or* **•tec**) American Indian
**Zapo•tec•an**
**Zaqa•ziq** *variant of* **Zagazig**
**Za•ra•go•za** Spanish city
**zara•tite** mineral
**za•reba** (*or* **•ree•ba**) African enclosure
**zarf** coffee-cup holder
**Zar•ga** (*or* **Sar•ka**) Jordanian town
**Za•ria** Nigerian city
**zar•zue•la** Spanish opera
**z-axis**
**zeal**
**Zea•land** Danish island; *compare* **Zeeland**
**zeal•ot**
**zeal•ot•ry**
**zeal•ous**
**zeal•ous•ness**
**ze•bec** (*or* **•beck**) *variant spellings of* **xebec**
**Zebedee** biblical character
**zeb•ra** (*plural* **•ras** *or* **•ra**)
**zebra-like** (*or* **ze•bra•ic**)
**zebra•wood**

**ze•brine** (*or* **•broid**)
**zebu** ox
**zec•chi•no** (*plural* **•ni**) coin
**zed**
**zedo•ary** condiment
**zee** *US* zed
**Zee•brug•ge**
**Zee•land** Dutch province; *compare* **Zealand**
**Zee•land•er**
**zein** protein
**Zeist** Dutch city
**Zeit•geist** *German* spirit of the age
**ze•min•dar** *variant spelling of* **zamindar**
**ze•min•dari** *variant spelling of* **zamindari**
**Zen**
**ze•na•na** women's part of house
**Zen•ic**
**Zen•ist**
**zen•ith**
**zen•ith•al**
**zeo•lite** mineral
**zeo•lit•ic**
**zeph•yr** breeze; fabric
**Zephyrus** Greek god
**zep•pe•lin**
**zero** (*noun, plural* **zeros** *or* **zeroes**; *verb* **zeroes, ze•ro•ing, ze•roed**)
**zero-rated**
**zeroth**
**zest**
**zest•ful**
**zest•ful•ly**
**zest•ful•ness**
**zesty**
**zeta** Greek letter
**zeug•ma** figure of speech
**zeug•mat•ic**
**zeug•mati•cal•ly**
**Zeus**
**Zhda•nov** *former name of* **Mariupol**
**Zhi•to•mir** Ukrainian city
**zho** *variant spelling of* **zo**
**zib•el•ine** fur
**zib•et** animal
**ziff** *Austral* beard
**zig•gu•rat** (*or* **zik•ku•rat, ziku•rat**) temple tower
**zig•zag** (**•zag•ging, •zagged**)
**zig•zag•ged•ness**
**zig•zag•ger**
**zila** (*or* **zil•la, zil•lah**) Indian administrative district
**zilch**
**zil•lion** (*plural* **•lions** *or* **•lion**)
**Zim•ba•bwe**
**Zim•ba•bwe•an**
**zinc**
**zin•cate**
**zinc•ic** (*or* **•ous, •oid**)
**zinc•if•er•ous**
**zinc•ite** mineral
**zinck•en•ite** *variant spelling of* **zinkenite**
**zincky** (*or* **zincy, zinky**)
**zin•co** (*plural* **•cos**) *short for* **zincograph**
**zin•co•graph** zinc printing-plate
**zin•cog•ra•pher**
**zin•co•graph•ic** (*or* **•graphi•cal**)
**zin•cog•ra•phy**
**zincy** *variant spelling of* **zincky**
**Zin•fan•del** wine grape
**zing**
**zin•ga•ro** (*fem* **•ra**; *plural* **•ri** *or* **•re**) gipsy
**zin•gi•bera•ceous** botany term
**zingy**
**zin•jan•thro•pus** fossil hominid
**zin•ken•ite** (*or* **zinck•en•ite**) mineral
**zinky** *variant spelling of* **zincky**
**zin•nia** plant
**Zion** (*or* **Sion**)
**Zi•on•ism**
**Zi•on•ist**
**Zi•on•is•tic**
**zip** (**zip•ping, zipped**)
**zip•per**
**zip•py** (**•pi•er, •pi•est**)
**zirc•al•loy**
**zir•con**
**zir•co•nia** chemical compound
**zir•con•ic**
**zir•co•nium** chemical element
**zith•er**
**zith•er•ist**
**Zla•to•ust** Russian town
**zlo•ty** (*plural* **•tys** *or* **•ty**) Polish currency
**zo** (*or* **zho, dzo**; *plural* **zos, zhos, dzos** *or* **zo, zho, dzo**) cattle
**zo•di•ac**
**zo•dia•cal**
**Zo•har** Jewish text
**zois•ite** mineral
**Zom•ba** Malawian city
**zom•bie** (*or* **•bi**; *plural* **•bies** *or* **•bis**)
**zom•bi•ism**
**zon•al** (*or* **zona•ry**)
**zon•ate** (*or* **zo•nat•ed**)
**zo•na•tion**
**Zond** Soviet spacecraft
**zone**
**zone•time**
**zonu•lar**
**zon•ule**
**zoo** (*plural* **zoos**)
**zoo•chemi•cal**
**zoo•chem•is•try**
**zoo•chore** botany term
**zoo•geog•ra•pher**
**zoo•geo•graph•ic** (*or* **•graphi•cal**)
**zoo•geo•graphi•cal•ly**
**zoo•geog•ra•phy**
**zoo•gloea** (*US* **•glea**; *plural* **•gloeas** *or* **•gloeae**, *US* **•gleas** *or* **•gleae**) bacterial mass
**zoo•gloeal** (*US* **•gleal**)
**zo•og•ra•pher**
**zoo•graph•ic** (*or* **•graphi•cal**)
**zo•og•ra•phy**
**zo•oid**
**zo•ol•at•er**
**zo•ola•trous**
**zo•ola•try** worship of animals
**zoo•logi•cal**
**zo•olo•gist**
**zo•ol•ogy** (*plural* **•ogies**)
**zoom**
**zoo•met•ric** (*or* **•ri•cal**)
**zo•om•etry**
**zoo•mor•phic**
**zoo•mor•phism**

**zo•ono•sis** (*plural* **•ses**) pathology term
**zo•opha•gous** feeding on animals
**zoo•phile**
**zoo•philia** fondness for animals
**zoo•phil•ic**
**zo•ophi•lism** sexual attraction to animals
**zo•ophi•lous** pollinated by animals
**zoo•pho•bia**
**zo•opho•bous**
**zoo•phyte**
**zoo•phyt•ic** (*or* **•phyti•cal**)
**zoo•plank•ton**
**zoo•plas•tic**
**zoo•plas•ty** surgical transplantation
**zoo•sperm**
**zoo•sper•mat•ic**
**zoo•spo•ran•gial**
**zoo•spo•ran•gium** (*plural* **•gia**)
**zoo•spore**
**zoo•spor•ic** (*or* **zo•os•por•ous**)
**zo•os•ter•ol** biochemical compound
**zoo•tech•nics**
**zoo•tom•ic** (*or* **•tomi•cal**)
**zoo•tomi•cal•ly**
**zo•oto•mist**
**zo•oto•my** animal dissection
**zoo•tox•ic**
**zoo•tox•in**
**zo•ril•la** (*or* **zo•rille**) animal
**Zo•ro•as•trian**
**Zo•ro•as•tri•an•ism**
**zos•ter** shingles
**Zou•ave** French infantryman
**zounds** archaic exclamation
**zoy•sia** grass
**zuc•chet•to** (*plural* **•tos**) skullcap
**zuc•chi•ni** (*plural* **•ni** *or* **•nis**)
**zug•zwang** chess position
**Zui•der Zee** (*or* **Zuy•**)
**Zulu** (*plural* **Zulus** *or* **Zulu**)
**Zu•lu•land**
**Zü•rich**
**Zwickau** German city
**zwie•back** toasted rusk
**Zwing•lian** denoting religious movement
**zwit•teri•on**
**zwit•teri•on•ic**
**zyg•apo•phys•eal** (*or* **•ial**)
**zyga•pophy•sis** (*plural* **•ses**) part of vertebra
**zy•go•dac•tyl** ornithology term
**zy•go•dac•tyl•ism**
**zy•go•dac•ty•lous**
**zy•go•ma** (*plural* **•ma•ta**) bone
**zy•go•mat•ic**
**zy•go•mor•phic** (*or* **•phous**) botany term
**zy•go•mor•phy** (*or* **•phism**)
**zy•go•phyl•la•ceous** botany term
**zy•go•phyte**
**zy•gose**
**zy•go•sis** (*plural* **•ses**) biology term
**zy•go•spore**
**zy•go•spor•ic**
**zy•gote** fertilized egg cell
**zy•go•tene** stage of cell division
**zy•got•ic**
**zy•goti•cal•ly**
**zy•mase** enzyme
**zy•mo•gen** enzyme precursor
**zy•mo•gen•esis**
**zy•mo•gen•ic**
**zy•mo•log•ic** (*or* **•logi•cal**)
**zy•molo•gist**
**zy•mol•ogy**
**zy•moly•sis** fermentation
**zy•mo•lyt•ic**
**zy•mom•eter**
**zy•mo•sis** (*plural* **•ses**) disease
**zy•mot•ic**
**zy•moti•cal•ly**
**zy•mur•gy** branch of chemistry
**Zyr•ian** language

# First Names

Aaron
Abbey (*or* Abbie, Abby)
Abe
Abel
Abigail
Abner
Abraham
Abram
Absalom
Ada
Adah
Adair
Adam
Adamina
Adamnan
Addie (*or* Addy)
Adela
Adelaide
Adele
Adelheid
Adelina
Adeline
Adlai
Adolf (*or* Adolph, Adolphe)
Adolphus
Adrian
Adriana
Adrianne (*or* Adrienne)
Aeneas
Afra
Agacia
Agatha
Aggie
Agnes
Agneta
Aidan
Aileen
Ailie
Ailis
Ailith
Ailsa
Aimee
Aine
Ainslie (*or* Ainsley)
Aisling
Aislinn
Aithne
Al
Alain
Alan (*or* Allan, Allen, Alun)
Alana (*or* Alanna)
Alaric
Alasdair (*or* Alastair) *variant spellings of* Alistair
Alban
Albany
Alberic
Albert
Alberta
Albertina
Albertine
Albin
Albina
Albinia
Albreda
Alda
Alden
Aldhelm
Aldis
Aldith
Aldo
Aldous (*or* Aldus)
Aldred
Aldreda
Aldwyn (*or* Aldwin)
Alec
Aled
Aledwen
Alethea
Alex
Alexa
Alexander
Alexandra
Alexandria
Alexandrina
Alexia
Alexis
Alf
Alfie
Alfonso *variant spelling of* Alphonso
Alfred
Alfreda
Algar
Alger
Algernon
Algie (*or* Algy)
Alice (*or* Alys)
Alicia
Alick
Alina
Aline
Alison (*or* Allison)
Alistair (*or* Alasdair, Alastair)
Alix
Allan *variant spelling of* Alan
Allegra
Allen *variant spelling of* Alan
Ally (*or* Allie)
Alma
Alonso (*or* Alonzo)
Aloysia (*or* Aloisia)
Aloysius
Alphonse
Alphonsine
Alphonso (*or* Alfonso)
Alphonsus
Althea
Alun *variant spelling of* Alan
Alured
Alva (*or* Alvah)
Alvar
Alvie
Alvin
Alvina
Alvis
Alwyn
Alys *variant spelling of* Alice
Amabel
Amalia
Amalie
Amanda
Amaryllis
Amata
Amber
Ambrose
Ambrosina
Ambrosine
Ambrosius
Amelia
Amias *variant spelling of* Amyas
Amice
Amicia
Aminta
Amos
Amy
Amyas (*or* Amias)
Anastasia
Ancel
André
Andrea

**Andreas**
**Andrée**
**Andrew**
**Andy**
**Aneira**
**Aneurin** (*or* **Aneirin**)
**Angel**
**Angela**
**Angelica**
**Angelina**
**Angeline**
**Angelique**
**Angelo**
**Angharad**
**Angie**
**Angus**
**Anis** (*or* **Annis, Annice**)
**Anita**
**Ann** *variant spelling of* **Anne**
**Anna**
**Annabel** (*or* **Annabelle**)
**Annabella**
**Annalisa**
**Annaple**
**Anne** (*or* **Ann**)
**Anneliese**
**Annette**
**Annice** *variant spelling of* **Anis**
**Annie**
**Annika**
**Annis**
**Annora**
**Anona**
**Anouska**
**Ansel** (*or* **Ansell**)
**Anselm**
**Anselma**
**Anstey**
**Anstice**
**Anthea**
**Anthony** (*or* **Antony**)
**Antoine**
**Antoinette**
**Anton**
**Antonia**
**Antonina**
**Antonio**
**Antony** *variant spelling of* **Anthony**
**Anwen**
**Anya**
**Aphra**
**Apollonia**
**Appolina**
**Appoline**
**April**
**Aquila**
**Arabella**
**Araminta**
**Archelaus**
**Archer**
**Archibald**
**Archie** (*or* **Archy**)
**Ariadne**
**Ariane**
**Arianna**
**Arlene** (*or* **Arleen**) *variant spellings of* **Arline**
**Arletta**
**Arlette**
**Arline** (*or* **Arlene, Arleen**)
**Armand**
**Armin**
**Armina**
**Armine**
**Arnaud**
**Arnold**
**Art**
**Artemas** (*or* **Artemus**)
**Artemisia**
**Arthur**
**Arthuretta**
**Arthurina**
**Arthurine**
**Artie** (*or* **Arty**)
**Asa**
**Asher**
**Ashley**
**Aspasia**
**Astra**
**Astrid**
**Athelstan**
**Athene**
**Athol**
**Auberon**
**Aubert**
**Aubrey**
**Aud**
**Audra**
**Audrey**
**August**
**Augusta**
**Augustina**
**Augustine** (*or* **Augustin**)
**Augustus**
**Aulay**
**Aurea**
**Aurelia**
**Aurelian**
**Aureola**
**Aureole**
**Auriel**
**Auriol**
**Aurora**
**Aurore**
**Austen**
**Austin**
**Ava**
**Aveline**
**Averil**
**Avery**
**Avis** (*or* **Avice**)
**Avril**
**Axel**
**Aylmer**
**Aylwin**
**Azariah**
**Bab**
**Babette**
**Babs**
**Baldie**
**Baldwin**
**Balthasar** (*or* **Balthazar**)
**Barbara** (*or* **Barbra**)
**Barbary**
**Barbie**
**Barclay** *variant spelling of* **Berkeley**
**Bardolph**
**Barnabas**
**Barnaby**
**Barnard**
**Barnet**
**Barney**
**Baron** (*or* **Barron**)
**Barrett**
**Barrington**
**Barry** (*or* **Barrie**)
**Bart**
**Bartholomew**
**Bartle**
**Bartlett** (*or* **Bartlet**)
**Basie**
**Basil**
**Basilia**
**Basilie**
**Basilla**
**Bastian**
**Bathsheba**
**Baubie**
**Bea** (*or* **Bee**)
**Beata**
**Beatrice**
**Beatrix**

**Beattie** (*or* **Beatty**)
**Beau**
**Becky**
**Bedelia**
**Bedford**
**Bee** *variant spelling of* **Bea**
**Belinda**
**Bella**
**Belle** (*or* **Bell, Bel**)
**Ben**
**Benedict** (*or* **Benedick**)
**Benedicta**
**Benet** *variant spelling of* **Bennet**
**Benita**
**Benito**
**Benjamin**
**Benjy**
**Bennet** (*or* **Bennett, Benet**)
**Benny**
**Bentley**
**Berengaria**
**Berenger**
**Berenice**
**Berkeley** (*or* **Barclay**)
**Bernadette**
**Bernadina**
**Bernadine**
**Bernard**
**Bernardina**
**Bernardine**
**Bernhard**
**Bernice**
**Bernie** (*or* **Berny**)
**Berry**
**Bert**
**Berta**
**Bertha**
**Berthold**
**Bertie**
**Bertram**
**Bertrand**
**Beryl**
**Bess**
**Bessie** (*or* **Bessy**)
**Beta**
**Beth**
**Bethan**
**Bethany**
**Bethel** (*or* **Bethell**)
**Bethia**
**Betsy**
**Bette**
**Bettina**
**Bettrys**
**Betty**
**Beulah**
**Beverley** (*or* **Beverly**)
**Bevis**
**Bianca**
**Biddy**
**Bill**
**Billy** (*or* **Billie**)
**Bina**
**Bing**
**Birdie**
**Birgit**
**Birgitta**
**Bjorn**
**Blaine** (*or* **Blane**)
**Blair**
**Blaise** (*or* **Blase**)
**Blake**
**Blanche** (*or* **Blanch**)
**Blane** *variant spelling of* **Blaine**
**Blodwen**
**Blodyn**
**Blossom**
**Blythe**
**Boaz**
**Bob**
**Bobby** (*or* **Bobbie**)
**Bonamy**
**Bonar**
**Boniface**
**Bonita**
**Bonnie** (*or* **Bonny**)
**Boris**
**Botolph** (*or* **Botolf, Botulf**)
**Boyce**
**Boyd**
**Brad**
**Bradley**
**Bram**
**Brandon** (*or* **Brandan**)
**Branwen**
**Brenda**
**Brendan**
**Brent**
**Brett** (*or* **Bret**)
**Brian** (*or* **Bryan**)
**Brice** *variant spelling of* **Bryce**
**Bride**
**Bridget** (*or* **Brigit, Brigitte**)
**Bridie**
**Brighid** (*or* **Brigid**)
**Brigitta**
**Briony** *variant spelling of* **Bryony**
**Brita**
**Britannia**
**Britt**
**Brock**
**Broderick**
**Bronwen** (*or* **Bronwyn**)
**Bruce**
**Brunetta**
**Bruno**
**Bryan** *variant spelling of* **Brian**
**Bryce** (*or* **Brice**)
**Bryn**
**Bryony** (*or* **Briony**)
**Bud**
**Burt**
**Buster**
**Byron**
**Cadel** (*or* **Cadell**)
**Caesar**
**Cai**
**Caitlin**
**Caius**
**Caleb**
**Calum** (*or* **Callum**)
**Calvin**
**Cameron**
**Camilla**
**Camille**
**Camillus**
**Campbell**
**Candace**
**Candice**
**Candida**
**Candy**
**Canice**
**Cara** (*or* **Kara**)
**Caradoc** (*or* **Caradog**)
**Carey** *variant spelling of* **Cary**
**Carina** (*or* **Karina**)
**Carita**
**Carl** (*or* **Karl**)
**Carla**
**Carleen** (*or* **Carlene**)
**Carlo**
**Carlos**
**Carlotta**
**Carlton** (*or* **Carleton**)
**Carly**
**Carmel**
**Carmela**
**Carmelita**
**Carmen**
**Carol** (*or* **Carole**)
**Carola**

**Carolina**
**Caroline**
**Carolus**
**Carolyn**
**Carrie**
**Carter**
**Carthach**
**Carthage**
**Cary** (*or* **Carey**)
**Caryl**
**Carys**
**Casey**
**Casimir**
**Caspar**
**Cass**
**Cassandra**
**Cassie**
**Cath** (*or* **Kath**)
**Catherine** (*or* **Katherine, Katharine, Catharine**)
**Cathleen** *variant spelling of* **Kathleen**
**Cathy** (*or* **Kathy**)
**Catrin**
**Catriona**
**Cecil**
**Cecile**
**Cecilia**
**Cecily** (*or* **Cecilie**)
**Cedric** (*or* **Cedrych**)
**Ceinwen**
**Celeste**
**Celestina**
**Celestine**
**Celia**
**Celina** *variant spelling of* **Selina**
**Celine**
**Cerdic**
**Ceri**
**Ceridwen**
**Cerys**
**Chad**
**Charis**
**Charissa**
**Charity**
**Charlene**
**Charles**
**Charlie** (*or* **Charley**)
**Charlotte**
**Charlton**
**Charmaine**
**Charmian**
**Chas**
**Chattie**
**Chauncey** (*or* **Chauncy**)
**Chay**
**Cherie** (*or* **Sherry, Sherri**)
**Cherry**
**Cheryl**
**Chester**
**Chloe**
**Chris**
**Chrissie** (*or* **Chrissy**)
**Christabel**
**Christian**
**Christiana**
**Christiania**
**Christie** (*or* **Christy**)
**Christina** (*or* **Kristina**)
**Christine** (*or* **Kristine**)
**Christmas**
**Christopher**
**Christy** *variant spelling of* **Christie**
**Chrystal** *variant spelling of* **Crystal**
**Chuck**
**Cicely**
**Cilla**
**Cinderella**
**Cindy**
**Cis** (*or* **Ciss**)
**Cissy** (*or* **Cissie, Sissy, Sissie**)
**Claire** (*or* **Clare**)
**Clara**
**Clarence**
**Claribel**
**Clarice**
**Clarinda**
**Clarissa**
**Clark**
**Clarrie**
**Claud** (*or* **Claude**)
**Claudette**
**Claudia**
**Claudine**
**Claudius**
**Clayton**
**Cledwyn**
**Clem**
**Clemence**
**Clemency**
**Clement**
**Clementia**
**Clementina**
**Clementine**
**Cleo**
**Cleopatra**
**Cliff**
**Clifford**
**Clifton**
**Clint**
**Clinton**
**Clive**
**Clodagh**
**Clotilda**
**Clyde**
**Colette**
**Colin**
**Colina**
**Colleen**
**Colley**
**Colm**
**Colum**
**Columba**
**Columbina**
**Columbine**
**Conan**
**Concepta**
**Concetta**
**Conn**
**Connie**
**Connor** (*or* **Conor**)
**Conrad**
**Constance**
**Constancy**
**Constant**
**Constantia**
**Constantine**
**Cora**
**Coral**
**Coralie**
**Cordelia**
**Corinna**
**Corinne**
**Cormac**
**Cornelia**
**Cornelius**
**Corney**
**Cosimo**
**Cosmo**
**Courtney** (*or* **Courtenay**)
**Craig**
**Cressida**
**Crispian**
**Crispin**
**Crystal** (*or* **Chrystal**)
**Cuddy** (*or* **Cuddie**)
**Curt** *variant spelling of* **Kurt**
**Curtis**
**Cuthbert**
**Cy**
**Cynthia**

**Cyprian**
**Cyril**
**Cyrus**
**Cytherea**
**Daff** *variant spelling of* **Daph**
**Dafydd**
**Dagmar**
**Dai**
**Daisy**
**Dale**
**Damaris**
**Damian** (*or* **Damien**)
**Damon**
**Dan**
**Dana**
**Dane**
**Danette**
**Daniel**
**Daniella**
**Danielle**
**Danita**
**Danny**
**Dante**
**Danuta**
**Daph** (*or* **Daff**)
**Daphne**
**Darby** (*or* **Derby**)
**Darcy** (*or* **D'Arcy**)
**Darlene**
**Darren**
**Darryl** (*or* **Darrell, Daryl, Darrel**)
**Dave**
**David**
**Davida**
**Davina**
**Davinia**
**Davy**
**Dawn**
**Dean**
**Deanna**
**Deanne**
**Deb**
**Debbie**
**Deborah**
**Debra**
**Decima**
**Decimus**
**Declan**
**Dee**
**Deirdre**
**Del**
**Delia**
**Delilah**
**Della**
**Delphine**
**Delwyn** (*or* **Delwen**)
**Delyth**
**Demelza**
**Denholm**
**Denise**
**Dennie** (*or* **Denny**)
**Dennis** (*or* **Denis, Denys**)
**Denzil**
**Derby** *variant spelling of* **Darby**
**Derek** (*or* **Derrick, Deryck, Deryk**)
**Dermot**
**Derry**
**Deryn**
**Des**
**Desdemona**
**Desiree**
**Desmond**
**Dewi**
**Dexter**
**Diamond**
**Diana**
**Diane** (*or* **Dianne**)
**Diarmuid** (*or* **Diarmait**)
**Dick**
**Dickie** (*or* **Dicky**)
**Dickon**
**Digby**
**Diggory**
**Dillon**
**Dilys**
**Dinah**
**Dion**
**Dione** (*or* **Dionne**)
**Dionysia**
**Dionysius**
**Dirk**
**Dodie**
**Doll**
**Dolly**
**Dolores**
**Dominic** (*or* **Dominick**)
**Dominica**
**Dominique**
**Don**
**Donal**
**Donald**
**Donalda**
**Donaldina**
**Donna**
**Donny**
**Donovan**
**Dora**
**Doran**
**Dorcas**
**Doreen**
**Dorette**
**Doria**
**Dorian**
**Dorinda**
**Doris** (*or* **Dorice**)
**Dorita**
**Dorothea**
**Dorothy**
**Dorrie**
**Dot**
**Dottie**
**Doug**
**Dougal**
**Dougie** (*or* **Duggie**)
**Douglas**
**Dowsabel**
**Dreda**
**Drew**
**Drogo**
**Drusilla**
**Duane** (*or* **Dwayne**)
**Dudley**
**Dugald**
**Duggie** *variant spelling of* **Dougie**
**Duke**
**Dulce**
**Dulcibella**
**Dulcie**
**Duncan**
**Dunstan**
**Durand**
**Dustin**
**Dwayne** *variant spelling of* **Duane**
**Dwight**
**Dylan**
**Dymphna**
**Dympna**
**Eamon** (*or* **Eamonn**)
**Earl** (*or* **Erle**)
**Earnest** *variant spelling of* **Ernest**
**Eartha**
**Easter**
**Eben**
**Ebenezer**
**Ed**
**Eda**
**Eddie** (*or* **Eddy**)
**Eden**
**Edgar**

**Edie**
**Edith**
**Edmund** (*or* **Edmond**)
**Edna**
**Edom**
**Edward**
**Edwin** (*or* **Edwyn**)
**Edwina**
**Effie**
**Egbert**
**Egidia**
**Egidius**
**Eileen**
**Eiluned** *variant spelling of* **Eluned**
**Eilwen**
**Eily**
**Eira**
**Eirian**
**Eithne**
**Elain**
**Elaine**
**Eldon**
**Eldred**
**Eldreda**
**Eleanor** (*or* **Elinor**)
**Eleanora**
**Eleazar**
**Elena**
**Eleonora**
**Elfreda** (*or* **Elfrida**)
**Eli**
**Elias**
**Elihu**
**Elijah**
**Elined** *variant spelling of* **Eluned**
**Elinor** *variant spelling of* **Eleanor**
**Eliot** *variant spelling of* **Elliott**
**Elisabeth** *variant spelling of* **Elizabeth**
**Elise**
**Elisha**
**Elissa**
**Eliza**
**Elizabeth** (*or* **Elisabeth**)
**Elkanah**
**Ella**
**Ellen**
**Ellery**
**Ellie**
**Elliott** (*or* **Elliot, Eliot**)
**Ellis**
**Elma**
**Elmer**
**Eloisa**
**Eloise**
**Elroy**
**Elsa**
**Elsie**
**Elspeth**
**Elspie**
**Elton**
**Eluned** (*or* **Elined, Eiluned**)
**Elvie**
**Elvin**
**Elvina**
**Elvira**
**Elvis**
**Elwyn**
**Emanuel** (*or* **Emmanuel**)
**Emanuela** (*or* **Emmanuela**)
**Emblem**
**Emblyn**
**Emeline** *variant spelling of* **Emmeline**
**Emelyn**
**Emerald**
**Emery**
**Emil** (*or* **Emile**)
**Emilia**
**Emily**
**Emlyn**
**Emma**
**Emmanuel** *variant spelling of* **Emanuel**
**Emmanuela** *variant spelling of* **Emanuela**
**Emmeline** (*or* **Emeline**)
**Emmie**
**Emrys**
**Ena**
**Enid**
**Enoch**
**Enos**
**Eoghan**
**Ephraim**
**Eppie**
**Erasmus**
**Eric** (*or* **Erik**)
**Erica** (*or* **Erika**)
**Erin**
**Erle** *variant spelling of* **Earl**
**Ermintrude** (*or* **Ermyntrude**)
**Ernest** (*or* **Earnest**)
**Ernestine**
**Ernie**
**Errol**
**Erwin** *variant spelling of* **Irwin**
**Esau**
**Esme** (*or* **Esmee**)
**Esmeralda**
**Esmond**
**Essie**
**Estella**
**Estelle**
**Esther**
**Ethan**
**Ethel**
**Ethelbert**
**Etheldreda**
**Ethelinda**
**Ethelred**
**Ethne**
**Etta**
**Ettie** (*or* **Etty**)
**Eugene**
**Eugenia**
**Eugenie**
**Eulalia**
**Eulalie**
**Eunice**
**Euphemia**
**Eustace**
**Eustacia**
**Eva**
**Evadne**
**Evan**
**Evangelina**
**Evangeline**
**Eve**
**Eveleen**
**Evelina**
**Eveline**
**Evelyn**
**Everard**
**Everild**
**Evie**
**Evita**
**Evonne** *variant spelling of* **Yvonne**
**Ewan** (*or* **Ewen**)
**Ezekiel**
**Ezra**
**Fabian**
**Fabiana**
**Faith**
**Fanny**
**Farquhar**
**Farran** (*or* **Farren, Faron**)
**Faustina**

**Fay** (*or* **Faye**)
**Feargus** *variant spelling of* **Fergus**
**Fedora**
**Felice**
**Felicia**
**Felicity**
**Felix**
**Fenella**
**Feodora**
**Ferdinand**
**Fergie**
**Fergus** (*or* **Feargus**)
**Fern**
**Fernando**
**Fidel**
**Fidelia**
**Fifi**
**Finlay**
**Finola**
**Fiona**
**Fionnuala** (*or* **Fionnghuala**)
**Fitzroy**
**Flavia**
**Fletcher**
**Fleur**
**Flora**
**Florence**
**Floretta**
**Florette**
**Florian**
**Florinda**
**Florrie**
**Floss**
**Flossie**
**Flower**
**Floy**
**Floyd**
**Fluellen**
**Flurry**
**Fortunatus**
**Fortune**
**Foster**
**Franca**
**Frances** (*fem*)
**Francesca**
**Francesco**
**Francie**
**Francine**
**Francis** (*masc*)
**Francisca**
**Francisco**
**Franco**
**Frank**
**Frankie**
**Franklin**
**Frannie** (*or* **Franny**)
**Fraser** (*or* **Frazer**)
**Fred**
**Freda**
**Freddie** (*or* **Freddy**)
**Frederica** (*or* **Frederika, Fredrica, Fredrika**)
**Frederick** (*or* **Frederic, Fredrick, Fredric**)
**Freya**
**Frieda**
**Fulbert**
**Gabby** (*or* **Gabbie, Gabi, Gaby**)
**Gabriel**
**Gabriella**
**Gabrielle**
**Gaenor** *variant spelling of* **Gaynor**
**Gail** (*or* **Gayle, Gale**)
**Gaius**
**Gamaliel**
**Gareth**
**Garfield**
**Garnet**
**Garret** (*or* **Garrett**)
**Garrick**
**Garth**
**Gary** (*or* **Garry**)
**Gaspar**
**Gavin**
**Gawain**
**Gay** (*or* **Gaye**)
**Gayle** *variant spelling of* **Gail**
**Gaylord**
**Gaynor** (*or* **Gaenor**)
**Gemma** (*or* **Jemma**)
**Gene**
**Genevieve**
**Genevra** *variant spelling of* **Ginevra**
**Geoff** (*or* **Jeff**)
**Geoffrey** (*or* **Jeffrey, Jeffery**)
**Geordie**
**George**
**Georgette**
**Georgia**
**Georgiana**
**Georgie**
**Georgina**
**Geraint**
**Gerald**
**Geraldine**
**Gerard** (*or* **Gerrard**)
**Gerda**
**Germaine** (*or* **Germain**)
**Gerontius**
**Gerry** (*or* **Jerry**)
**Gershom**
**Gert**
**Gertie**
**Gertrude**
**Gervase** (*or* **Gervais**)
**Gerwyn**
**Gethin**
**Ghislaine**
**Gideon**
**Gil**
**Gilbert**
**Gilberta**
**Gilbertine**
**Gilda**
**Giles** (*or* **Gyles**)
**Gill** (*or* **Jill**)
**Gillian** (*or* **Jillian, Gillean**)
**Gilroy**
**Gina**
**Ginette**
**Ginevra** (*or* **Genevra**)
**Ginger**
**Ginny**
**Gisela**
**Giselle**
**Glad**
**Gladys**
**Glen** (*or* **Glenn**)
**Glenda**
**Glenna**
**Glenys** (*or* **Glenis**)
**Gloria**
**Glyn**
**Glynis** (*or* **Glinys**)
**Godfrey**
**Godwin**
**Goldie**
**Goldwin** (*or* **Goldwyn**)
**Gordon**
**Grace**
**Gracie**
**Graham** (*or* **Graeme, Grahame**)
**Grainne**
**Grania**
**Grant**
**Granville**
**Greg** (*or* **Gregg**)
**Gregor**
**Gregory**
**Grenville**

**Greta**
**Gretchen**
**Gretel**
**Griffith**
**Griselda**
**Grizel** (*or* **Grizzel**)
**Grover**
**Guendolen** *variant spelling of* **Gwendoline**
**Guido**
**Guinevere**
**Gulielma**
**Gunter** (*or* **Gunther**)
**Gus**
**Gussie**
**Gusta**
**Gustave** (*or* **Gustav, Gustaf**)
**Gustavus**
**Guy**
**Gwen**
**Gwenda**
**Gwendoline** (*or* **Gwendolyn, Gwendolen, Guendolen**)
**Gwenllian**
**Gwilym** (*or* **Gwylim**)
**Gwladys**
**Gwyn**
**Gwyneth** (*or* **Gwynneth, Gwynedd**)
**Gwynfor**
**Gyles** *variant spelling of* **Giles**
**Hadassah**
**Hadrian**
**Hagar**
**Haidee**
**Hal**
**Halcyon**
**Ham**
**Hamilton**
**Hamish**
**Hamlet**
**Hamlyn**
**Hammond**
**Hamnet**
**Hamo**
**Hamon**
**Hank**
**Hannah**
**Hannibal**
**Hans**
**Hardy**
**Harley**
**Harold**
**Harriet** (*or* **Harriette**)
**Harriot**
**Harrison**
**Harry**
**Hartley**
**Harvey**
**Hattie** (*or* **Hatty**)
**Haydn** (*or* **Haydon, Hayden**)
**Hayley**
**Hazel**
**Heath**
**Heather**
**Hebe**
**Heber**
**Hector**
**Hedda**
**Hedley**
**Hedwig**
**Hedy**
**Heidi**
**Helen**
**Helena**
**Helene**
**Helewise**
**Helga**
**Héloïse**
**Hennie** (*or* **Henny**)
**Henri**
**Henrietta**
**Henriette**
**Henry**
**Hephzibah**
**Hepsie** (*or* **Hepsey, Hepsy**)
**Hepzibah**
**Herb**
**Herbert**
**Herbie**
**Hereward**
**Herman** (*or* **Hermann**)
**Hermia**
**Hermione**
**Hervé**
**Hervey**
**Hester**
**Hetty**
**Heulwen**
**Hew** *variant spelling of* **Hugh**
**Hezekiah**
**Hieronymus**
**Hilary** (*or* **Hillary**)
**Hilda** (*or* **Hylda**)
**Hildebrand**
**Hildegard** (*or* **Hildegarde**)
**Hillary** *variant spelling of* **Hilary**
**Hippolyta**
**Hippolytus**
**Hiram**
**Hob**
**Hobart**
**Holden**
**Holly**
**Homer**
**Honor** (*or* **Honour**)
**Honora**
**Honoria**
**Hope**
**Horace**
**Horatia**
**Horatio**
**Horry**
**Hortense**
**Hortensia**
**Howard**
**Howell** (*or* **Howel**) *variant spellings of* **Hywel**
**Hubert**
**Hugh** (*or* **Huw, Hew**)
**Hughie** (*or* **Huey**)
**Hugo**
**Huldah, Hulda**
**Humbert**
**Humph**
**Humphrey**
**Huw** *variant spelling of* **Hugh**
**Hyacinth**
**Hyacintha**
**Hylda** *variant spelling of* **Hilda**
**Hyman**
**Hymie**
**Hypatia**
**Hywel** (*or* **Howell, Howel**)
**Iago**
**Ian** (*or* **Iain**)
**Ianthe**
**Ibbie** (*or* **Ibby**)
**Ichabod**
**Ida**
**Idonea**
**Idris**
**Ifor**
**Ignatius**
**Igor**
**Ike**
**Ilma**
**Ilona**
**Ilse**
**Immy**
**Imogen**

**Ina**
**Inez**
**Inga**
**Inge**
**Ingeborg**
**Ingram**
**Ingrid**
**Ingvar**
**Inigo**
**Iola**
**Iolanthe**
**Iolo**
**Iona**
**Iorwerth**
**Ira**
**Irene**
**Iris**
**Irma**
**Irvin** (*or* **Irvine**)
**Irving**
**Irwin** (*or* **Erwin**)
**Isa**
**Isaac** (*or* **Izaak**)
**Isabel** (*or* **Isabelle**)
**Isabella**
**Isadora**
**Isaiah**
**Iseult**
**Ishbel**
**Isidora**
**Isidore**
**Isla**
**Ismay**
**Isobel**
**Isolda**
**Isolde**
**Israel**
**Issy** (*or* **Izzy**)
**Ita**
**Ithel**
**Ivah**
**Ivan**
**Ives**
**Ivo**
**Ivor**
**Ivy**
**Izaak** *variant spelling of* **Isaac**
**Izzy** *variant spelling of* **Issy**
**Jabez**
**Jacinta**
**Jacinth**
**Jack**
**Jackie** (*or* **Jacky, Jacqui**)
**Jacob**
**Jacoba**
**Jacobina**
**Jacqueline** (*or* **Jacquelyn**)
**Jacques**
**Jacquetta**
**Jacqui** *variant spelling of* **Jackie**
**Jade**
**Jael**
**Jago**
**Jake**
**James**
**Jamesina**
**Jamie**
**Jan**
**Jane** (*or* **Jayne**)
**Janet**
**Janetta**
**Janette**
**Janice** (*or* **Janis**)
**Janie** (*or* **Janey**)
**Janine**
**Japheth**
**Jarrod** (*or* **Jarred, Jared**)
**Jarvis**
**Jasmine**
**Jason**
**Jasper**
**Jay**
**Jayne** *variant spelling of* **Jane**
**Jean**
**Jeanette** (*or* **Jeannette**)
**Jeanne**
**Jeannie** (*or* **Jeanie**)
**Jeannine**
**Jed**
**Jedidiah**
**Jeff** *variant spelling of* **Geoff**
**Jefferson**
**Jeffrey** (*or* **Jeffery**) *variant spellings of* **Geoffrey**
**Jehane**
**Jem**
**Jemima**
**Jemma** *variant spelling of* **Gemma**
**Jemmy**
**Jenna**
**Jennifer** (*or* **Jenifer**)
**Jenny** (*or* **Jennie**)
**Jephthah**
**Jeremiah**
**Jeremias**
**Jeremy**
**Jermaine**
**Jerome**
**Jerry** *variant spelling of* **Gerry**
**Jess**
**Jessamine** (*or* **Jessamyn**)
**Jesse**
**Jessica**
**Jessie**
**Jesus**
**Jethro**
**Jewel**
**Jill** *variant spelling of* **Gill**
**Jillian** *variant spelling of* **Gillian**
**Jim**
**Jimmy**
**Jinny**
**Jo**
**Joachim**
**Joan**
**Joanna**
**Joanne**
**Job**
**Jocasta**
**Jocelyn** (*or* **Joscelin**)
**Jock**
**Jodie** (*or* **Jodi, Jody**)
**Joe**
**Joel**
**Joey**
**Johanna**
**Johannes**
**John** (*or* **Jon**)
**Johnny** (*or* **Johnnie**)
**Jolene** (*or* **Joleen**)
**Jolyon**
**Jonah**
**Jonas**
**Jonathan**
**Jonquil**
**Jordan**
**Joscelin** *variant spelling of* **Jocelyn**
**José**
**Joseph**
**Josepha**
**Josephine**
**Josette**
**Josh**
**Joshua**
**Josiah**
**Josias**
**Josie**
**Joss**
**Jotham**
**Joy**
**Joyce**

**Juan**
**Juanita**
**Judah**
**Judas**
**Judd**
**Jude**
**Judith**
**Judoc**
**Judy** (*or* **Judi**)
**Jules**
**Julia**
**Julian**
**Juliana**
**Julianne**
**Julie**
**Julienne**
**Juliet** (*or* **Juliette**)
**Julitta**
**Julius**
**June**
**Junior**
**Juno**
**Justin**
**Justina**
**Justine**
**Kane**
**Kara** *variant spelling of* **Cara**
**Karel**
**Karen**
**Karin**
**Karina** *variant spelling of* **Carina**
**Karl** *variant spelling of* **Carl**
**Karol**
**Kate**
**Kath** *variant spelling of* **Cath**
**Katherine** (*or* **Katharine**) *variant spellings of* **Catherine**
**Kathleen** (*or* **Cathleen**)
**Kathryn**
**Kathy** *variant spelling of* **Cathy**
**Katie** (*or* **Katy**)
**Katrina**
**Katrine**
**Kay**
**Keeley**
**Keir**
**Keith**
**Kelda**
**Kelly** (*or* **Kellie**)
**Kelvin**
**Ken**
**Kendal** (*or* **Kendall**)
**Kendra**
**Kenelm**
**Kenneth**
**Kenny**
**Kenrick**
**Kent**
**Kentigern**
**Kenton**
**Keren**
**Kerenhappuch**
**Kerry** (*or* **Kerrie, Kerri, Keri**)
**Kester**
**Keturah**
**Kevin**
**Keziah** (*or* **Kezia**)
**Kieran**
**Kim**
**Kimball**
**Kimberly** (*or* **Kimberley**)
**Kinborough**
**King**
**Kingsley**
**Kirby**
**Kirk**
**Kirsten**
**Kirsty**
**Kit**
**Kitty**
**Kris**
**Kristen** (*or* **Kristin**)
**Kristina** *variant spelling of* **Christina**
**Kristine** *variant spelling of* **Christine**
**Kurt** (*or* **Curt**)
**Kyle**
**Kylie**
**Laban**
**Lachlan**
**Laetitia** (*or* **Letitia**)
**Lalage**
**Lambert**
**Lana**
**Lance**
**Lancelot**
**Lanty**
**Laraine** (*or* **Larraine**)
**Larissa**
**Larry**
**Lars**
**Launce**
**Launcelot**
**Laura** (*or* **Lora**)
**Lauraine**
**Laureen** (*or* **Loreen**)
**Laurel**
**Lauren**
**Laurence** (*or* **Lawrence**)
**Laurencia** (*or* **Laurentia**)
**Lauretta** *variant spelling of* **Loretta**
**Laurette** (*or* **Lorette**)
**Laurie** (*or* **Lauri, Lori**)
**Laurina**
**Laurinda** *variant spelling of* **Lorinda**
**Laverne**
**Lavina** (*or* **Lavena**)
**Lavinia**
**Lawrence** *variant spelling of* **Laurence**
**Lawrie**
**Layton** *variant spelling of* **Leighton**
**Lazarus**
**Leah**
**Leander**
**Leanne** (*or* **Lianne**)
**Lee** (*or* **Leigh**)
**Leighton** (*or* **Layton**)
**Leila** (*or* **Leilah, Lela**)
**Lelia**
**Lemmy**
**Lemuel**
**Lena**
**Lennox**
**Lenny** (*or* **Lennie**)
**Lenore**
**Leo**
**Leofric**
**Leoline**
**Leon**
**Leona**
**Leonard**
**Leonie**
**Leonora**
**Leopold**
**Leroy**
**Lesley** (*fem*)
**Leslie** (*masc or fem*)
**Lester**
**Leta**
**Letitia** (*or* **Laetitia**)
**Lettice**
**Letty** (*or* **Lettie**)
**Levi**
**Lew**
**Lewis**
**Liam**
**Liana**

**Lianne** *variant spelling of* **Leanne**
**Libby**
**Liddy**
**Liesl** (*or* **Liesel**)
**Lila**
**Lilac**
**Lili**
**Lilian** (*or* **Lillian**)
**Lilias** (*or* **Lillias**)
**Lilith**
**Lilla** (*or* **Lillah**)
**Lily** (*or* **Lillie**)
**Lina**
**Lincoln**
**Linda** (*or* **Lynda**)
**Lindsay** (*masc or fem*)
**Lindsey** (*fem*)
**Lindy**
**Linette** *variant spelling of* **Lynette**
**Linnet**
**Lionel**
**Lisa**
**Lisbeth** *variant spelling of* **Lizbeth**
**Lise**
**Lisette**
**Lita**
**Liz**
**Liza**
**Lizanne**
**Lizbeth** (*or* **Lisbeth**)
**Lizzie** (*or* **Lizzy**)
**Llewellyn** (*or* **Llewelyn**)
**Llinos**
**Lloyd**
**Lois**
**Lola**
**Lolita**
**Lolly**
**Lonnie**
**Lora** *variant spelling of* **Laura**
**Loraine** *variant spelling of* **Lorraine**
**Loreen** *variant spelling of* **Laureen**
**Loren** (*or* **Lorin**)
**Lorenzo**
**Loretta** (*or* **Lauretta**)
**Lorette** *variant spelling of* **Laurette**
**Lori** *variant spelling of* **Laurie**
**Lorin**
**Lorinda** (*or* **Laurinda**)

**Lorna**
**Lorne** (*or* **Lorn**)
**Lorraine** (*or* **Loraine**)
**Lottie** (*or* **Lotty**)
**Lou**
**Louella** (*or* **Luella**)
**Louie**
**Louis**
**Louisa**
**Louise**
**Loveday**
**Lovell**
**Lowell**
**Lucas**
**Lucasta**
**Luce**
**Lucetta**
**Lucette**
**Lucia**
**Lucian** (*or* **Lucien**)
**Luciana**
**Lucie**
**Lucienne**
**Lucilla**
**Lucille**
**Lucina**
**Lucinda**
**Lucius**
**Lucky**
**Lucrece**
**Lucretia**
**Lucrezia**
**Lucy**
**Ludo**
**Ludovic**
**Luella** *variant spelling of* **Louella**
**Luke**
**Lulu**
**Luther**
**Lydia**
**Lyle**
**Lyn** *variant spelling of* **Lynn**
**Lynda** *variant spelling of* **Linda**
**Lyndon**
**Lynette** (*or* **Lynnette, Linette**)
**Lynn** (*or* **Lynne, Lyn**)
**Lynsey**
**Lyra**
**Lyulf** (*or* **Lyulph**)
**Mabel** (*or* **Mable**)
**Mabella**
**Mabelle**

**Maddie** (*or* **Maddy**)
**Madeleine** (*or* **Madeline**)
**Madelina**
**Madge**
**Madoc**
**Madonna**
**Mae**
**Maeve** (*or* **Meave**)
**Magda**
**Magdalena**
**Magdalene** (*or* **Magdalen**)
**Maggie**
**Magnolia**
**Magnus**
**Mahala** (*or* **Mahalah**)
**Mahalia**
**Maidie**
**Mair**
**Maire**
**Mairin**
**Maisie**
**Malachi** (*or* **Malachy**)
**Malcolm**
**Malise**
**Mallory** (*or* **Malory**)
**Malvin**
**Malvina**
**Mamie**
**Manasseh**
**Manasses**
**Mandy**
**Manfred**
**Manley**
**Manny**
**Mansel** (*or* **Mansell**)
**Manuel**
**Manuela**
**Manus**
**Mara** (*or* **Marah**)
**Marc**
**Marcel**
**Marcella**
**Marcelle**
**Marcellus**
**Marcia**
**Marcie** (*or* **Marcy**)
**Marco**
**Marcus**
**Margaret**
**Margareta** (*or* **Margaretta**)
**Margarita** (*or* **Marguerita**)
**Marge**
**Margery** *variant spelling of* **Marjorie**
**Margie**

**Margot** (*or* **Margo**)
**Marguerite**
**Maria**
**Mariabella**
**Mariam** (*or* **Mariamne**)
**Marian** *variant spelling of* **Marion**
**Marianne**
**Marie**
**Mariel**
**Marietta** (*or* **Mariette**)
**Marigold**
**Marilyn**
**Marina**
**Mario**
**Marion** (*or* **Marian**)
**Marisa** (*or* **Marissa**)
**Marita**
**Marius**
**Marjorie** (*or* **Margery**)
**Mark**
**Marla**
**Marlene**
**Marlin** (*or* **Marlyn**)
**Marmaduke**
**Marnie** (*or* **Marni**)
**Marsha**
**Marshall** (*or* **Marshal**)
**Marta**
**Martha**
**Marti** (*or* **Martie**)
**Martin** (*or* **Martyn**)
**Martina**
**Martine**
**Marty**
**Marvin** (*or* **Marvyn**)
**Mary**
**Matilda**
**Matt** (*or* **Mat**)
**Matthew**
**Matthias**
**Mattie** (*or* **Matty**)
**Maud** (*or* **Maude**)
**Maudie**
**Maura** *variant spelling of* **Moira**
**Maureen**
**Maurice** (*or* **Morris**)
**Mavis**
**Max**
**Maximilian**
**Maxine**
**Maxwell**
**May**
**Maynard**
**Meave** *variant spelling of* **Maeve**
**Meg**
**Megan** (*or* **Meghan**)
**Meggie** (*or* **Meggy**)
**Mehala** (*or* **Mehalah, Mehalia**)
**Mehetabel** (*or* **Mehitabel**)
**Meirion** (*or* **Merrion**)
**Mel**
**Melania**
**Melanie** (*or* **Melloney**)
**Melba**
**Melicent** (*or* **Melisent**)
**Melinda**
**Meliora**
**Mélisande**
**Melissa**
**Melody** (*or* **Melodie**)
**Melva**
**Melville**
**Melvin** (*or* **Melvyn**)
**Melvina**
**Mercedes**
**Mercia**
**Mercy**
**Meredith**
**Meriel**
**Merilyn** (*or* **Merrilyn**)
**Merle**
**Merlin**
**Merrion** *variant spelling of* **Meirion**
**Merry**
**Merton**
**Merv**
**Mervyn** (*or* **Mervin**)
**Meryl**
**Meta**
**Mia**
**Micah**
**Michael**
**Michaela**
**Michelle** (*or* **Michele**)
**Mick**
**Mickey** (*or* **Micky**)
**Mignon**
**Mike**
**Milborough**
**Milburn**
**Mildred**
**Miles** (*or* **Myles**)
**Millicent**
**Millie** (*or* **Milly**)
**Milo**
**Milton**
**Mima**
**Mimi**
**Mina**
**Minerva**
**Minna**
**Minnie**
**Minty**
**Mira** *variant spelling of* **Myra**
**Mirabel** (*or* **Mirabelle**)
**Mirabella**
**Miranda**
**Miriam**
**Mitch**
**Mitchell**
**Mitzi**
**Modesty**
**Moira** (*or* **Moyra, Maura**)
**Moll**
**Molly**
**Mona**
**Monica**
**Monique**
**Montague** (*or* **Montagu**)
**Montgomery**
**Monty** (*or* **Monte**)
**Morag**
**Moray**
**Mordecai**
**Morgan**
**Morna**
**Morris** *variant spelling of* **Maurice**
**Mort**
**Mortimer**
**Morty**
**Morwenna**
**Moses**
**Moshe**
**Moss**
**Moyna**
**Moyra** *variant spelling of* **Moira**
**Muir**
**Mungo**
**Murdoch**
**Muriel**
**Murray**
**Murtagh**
**Myfanwy**
**Myles** *variant spelling of* **Miles**
**Myra** (*or* **Mira**)
**Myrna**
**Myron**

**Myrtilla**
**Myrtle**
**Mysie**
**Nada**
**Nadia**
**Nadine**
**Nahum**
**Nan**
**Nance**
**Nancy**
**Nanette**
**Nanny**
**Naomi**
**Napoleon**
**Narcissus**
**Nat**
**Natalia**
**Natalie**
**Natasha**
**Nathan**
**Nathaniel** (*or* **Nathanael**)
**Neal** *variant spelling of* **Neil**
**Ned**
**Neddie** (*or* **Neddy**)
**Nehemiah**
**Neil** (*or* **Neill, Neal, Niall**)
**Nell**
**Nellie** (*or* **Nelly**)
**Nelson**
**Nerina**
**Nerissa**
**Nerys**
**Nessa**
**Nessie**
**Nest**
**Nesta**
**Netta**
**Nettie**
**Neva**
**Neville** (*or* **Nevil**)
**Newton**
**Niall** *variant spelling of* **Neil**
**Nichola** *variant spelling of* **Nicola**
**Nicholas** (*or* **Nicolas**)
**Nick**
**Nicky** (*or* **Nikki**)
**Nicodemus**
**Nicol**
**Nicola** (*or* **Nichola**)
**Nicolas** *variant spelling of* **Nicholas**
**Nicole**
**Nicolette**
**Nigel**
**Nikki** *variant spelling of* **Nicky**
**Nina**
**Ninette**
**Ninian**
**Nita**
**Noah**
**Noel** (*or* **Nowell**)
**Noeleen** (*or* **Noeline**)
**Noelle** (*or* **Noele**)
**Nola**
**Nolan**
**Nona**
**Nora** (*or* **Norah**)
**Norbert**
**Noreen**
**Norm**
**Norma**
**Norman**
**Norris**
**Norton**
**Nova**
**Nowell** *variant spelling of* **Noel**
**Nuala**
**Nye**
**Nyree**
**Obadiah**
**Oberon**
**Octavia**
**Octavian**
**Octavius**
**Odette**
**Odile**
**Odilia**
**Odo**
**Ogden**
**Olaf**
**Olave** (*or* **Olav**)
**Olga**
**Oliff**
**Oliva**
**Olive**
**Oliver**
**Olivet**
**Olivia**
**Olivier**
**Ollie**
**Olwen** (*or* **Olwyn**)
**Olympia**
**Omar**
**Ona**
**Onuphrius**
**Oonagh** (*or* **Oona**)
**Opal**
**Ophelia**
**Oriana**
**Oriel**
**Orlando**
**Orrell**
**Orson**
**Orval**
**Orville**
**Osbert**
**Osborn** (*or* **Osborne**)
**Oscar**
**Osmond** (*or* **Osmund**)
**Ossy** (*or* **Ossie**)
**Oswald**
**Oswin**
**Otho**
**Otis**
**Ottilia**
**Ottilie**
**Otto**
**Owen** (*or* **Owain**)
**Owena**
**Ozzy** (*or* **Ozzie**)
**Pablo**
**Paddy**
**Padraig**
**Palmer**
**Pam**
**Pamela**
**Pamelia**
**Pandora**
**Pansy**
**Paolo**
**Parker**
**Parnel** (*or* **Parnell**)
**Parry**
**Parthenia**
**Pascal**
**Pascale**
**Pascoe**
**Pat**
**Patience**
**Patricia**
**Patrick**
**Patsy**
**Patti** (*or* **Patty, Pattie**)
**Paul**
**Paula**
**Paulette**
**Pauline**
**Peace**
**Pearl**
**Pearlie**
**Pedro**
**Peg**

**Peggy**
**Pelham**
**Penelope**
**Penny**
**Pepin**
**Pepita**
**Perce**
**Percival** (*or* **Perceval**)
**Percy**
**Perdita**
**Peregrine**
**Peronel**
**Perpetua**
**Perry**
**Peta**
**Pete**
**Peter**
**Petra**
**Petrina**
**Petronella**
**Petronilla**
**Petula**
**Phebe** *variant spelling of* **Phoebe**
**Phemie**
**Phil**
**Philadelphia**
**Philemon**
**Philibert**
**Philip** (*or* **Phillip**)
**Philippa** (*or* **Phillipa, Phillippa**)
**Phillida** *variant spelling of* **Phyllida**
**Phillis** *variant spelling of* **Phyllis**
**Philomena**
**Phineas** (*or* **Phinehas**)
**Phoebe** (*or* **Phebe**)
**Phyllida** (*or* **Phillida**)
**Phyllis** (*or* **Phillis**)
**Pia**
**Pierre**
**Piers**
**Pip**
**Pippa**
**Piran**
**Pleasance**
**Poldie**
**Poll**
**Polly**
**Pollyanna**
**Poppy**
**Portia**
**Preston**
**Primrose**
**Prince**
**Prisca**
**Priscilla**
**Prissy**
**Pru** (*or* **Prue**)
**Prudence**
**Prunella**
**Queena**
**Queenie** (*or* **Queeny**)
**Quentin** (*or* **Quintin**)
**Quincy**
**Quinn**
**Quintin** *variant spelling of* **Quentin**
**Rab**
**Rabbie**
**Rachel** (*or* **Rachael**)
**Radcliff** (*or* **Radcliffe**)
**Rae**
**Raelene**
**Rafael** *variant spelling of* **Raphael**
**Rafaela** *variant spelling of* **Raphaela**
**Rafe**
**Raina**
**Raine**
**Rainer** *variant spelling of* **Rayner**
**Ralph**
**Ramon**
**Ramona**
**Ramsay** (*or* **Ramsey**)
**Ranald**
**Randall** (*or* **Randal**)
**Randolph**
**Randy**
**Raoul**
**Raphael** (*or* **Rafael**)
**Raphaela** (*or* **Rafaela**)
**Ray**
**Raymond** (*or* **Raymund**)
**Raymonde**
**Rayner** (*or* **Raynor, Rainer**)
**Rebecca** (*or* **Rebekah**)
**Redvers**
**Reg**
**Reggie**
**Regina**
**Reginald**
**Reine**
**Rena** (*or* **Rina**)
**Renata**
**René** (*masc*)
**Renée** (*fem*)
**Renie** (*or* **Rene**)
**Reuben**
**Rex**
**Reynard**
**Reynold**
**Rhea** (*or* **Ria**)
**Rhiannon**
**Rhoda**
**Rhona**
**Rhonda**
**Rhonwen**
**Rhys**
**Ria** *variant spelling of* **Rhea**
**Rica** (*or* **Rika**)
**Ricarda**
**Ricardo**
**Rich**
**Richard**
**Richenda**
**Richie**
**Richmal**
**Rick**
**Ricky** (*or* **Ricki, Rikki**)
**Rika** *variant spelling of* **Rica**
**Rina** *variant spelling of* **Rena**
**Rita**
**Roald**
**Rob**
**Robbie**
**Robert**
**Roberta**
**Robin**
**Robina**
**Robyn**
**Rochelle**
**Rod**
**Roddy**
**Roderick**
**Rodge**
**Rodger** *variant spelling of* **Roger**
**Rodney**
**Rodolph**
**Rodrigo**
**Roger** (*or* **Rodger**)
**Roisin**
**Roland** (*or* **Rowland**)
**Rolf** (*or* **Rolph**)
**Rollo**
**Rolly**
**Rolph** *variant spelling of* **Rolf**
**Roly**
**Roma**
**Romaine**

**Ron**
**Rona**
**Ronald**
**Ronalda**
**Ronna**
**Ronnette**
**Ronnie**
**Rory**
**Ros**
**Rosa**
**Rosabel** (*or* **Rosabelle**)
**Rosabella**
**Rosaleen**
**Rosalia**
**Rosalie**
**Rosalind**
**Rosalinda**
**Rosaline** (*or* **Rosalyn**)
**Rosamund** (*or* **Rosamond**)
**Rosanna** (*or* **Roseanna**)
**Rosanne** (*or* **Roseann, Roseanne**)
**Rose**
**Roseline** (*or* **Roselyn**)
**Rosemary** (*or* **Rosemarie**)
**Rosetta**
**Rosie**
**Rosina**
**Rosita**
**Roslyn** (*or* **Rosslyn**)
**Ross**
**Rowan**
**Rowena**
**Rowland** *variant spelling of* **Roland**
**Roxana**
**Roxane** (*or* **Roxanne**)
**Roxanna**
**Roxy**
**Roy**
**Royal**
**Royston**
**Rubina**
**Ruby**
**Rudolph** (*or* **Rudolf**)
**Rudy** (*or* **Rudi**)
**Rufus**
**Rupert**
**Ruperta**
**Russ**
**Russell** (*or* **Russel**)
**Ruth**
**Ruthie**
**Ryan**
**Sabina**
**Sabrina**
**Sacha**
**Sacheverell**
**Sadie**
**Saffron**
**Sal**
**Salamon**
**Salena** (*or* **Salina**)
**Sally**
**Salome**
**Salvador**
**Salvatore**
**Sam**
**Samantha**
**Sammy**
**Samson** (*or* **Sampson**)
**Samuel**
**Sanchia**
**Sandra**
**Sandy** (*or* **Sandie**)
**Sapphira**
**Sapphire**
**Sarah** (*or* **Sara, Sarra**)
**Sarai**
**Saranna**
**Sarina**
**Sarita**
**Sarra** *variant spelling of* **Sarah**
**Saul**
**Saxon**
**Scarlett** (*or* **Scarlet**)
**Scott**
**Seamus** (*or* **Shamus**)
**Sean** (*or* **Shaun, Shawn**)
**Seb**
**Sebastian**
**Sefton**
**Selby**
**Selina** (*or* **Selena, Celina**)
**Selma**
**Selwyn**
**Senga**
**Septima**
**Septimus**
**Seraphina**
**Serena**
**Serge**
**Sergei**
**Sergio**
**Sergius**
**Seth**
**Seumas**
**Seward**
**Sextus**
**Seymour**
**Shamus** *variant spelling of* **Seamus**
**Shane**
**Shani**
**Shannon**
**Shari**
**Sharon** (*or* **Sharron**)
**Shaun** *variant spelling of* **Sean**
**Shauna**
**Shaw**
**Shawn** *variant spelling of* **Sean**
**Sheba**
**Sheena** (*or* **Shena**)
**Sheila** (*or* **Shelagh, Sheelagh, Sheilah**)
**Sheldon**
**Shelley** (*or* **Shelly**)
**Shem**
**Shena** *variant spelling of* **Sheena**
**Sheridan**
**Sherry** (*or* **Sherri**) *variant spellings of* **Cherie**
**Sheryl**
**Shirl**
**Shirley**
**Sholto**
**Shona**
**Shushana** (*or* **Shushanna**)
**Sian**
**Sibbie** (*or* **Sibby**)
**Sibella**
**Sibilla**
**Sibyl**
**Sibylla**
**Sid** (*or* **Syd**)
**Sidney** (*or* **Sydney**)
**Sidonia**
**Sidony** (*or* **Sidonie**)
**Siegfried**
**Sigismund**
**Sigmund**
**Silas**
**Síle**
**Silvana**
**Silvanus** (*or* **Sylvanus**)
**Silvester**
**Silvia**
**Sim**
**Simeon**
**Simon**
**Simona**
**Simone**

**Sinclair**
**Sìne**
**Sinead**
**Siobhan**
**Sisley**
**Sissy** (*or* **Sissie**) *variant spellings of* **Cissy**
**Solly**
**Solomon**
**Sonia** (*or* **Sonya, Sonja**)
**Sophia**
**Sophie** (*or* **Sophy**)
**Sophronia**
**Sorcha**
**Spencer**
**Stacey** (*or* **Stacy**)
**Stafford**
**Stan**
**Stanford**
**Stanislas** (*or* **Stanislaus**)
**Stanley**
**Steenie**
**Stella**
**Stephanie** (*or* **Stefanie**)
**Stephen** (*or* **Steven**)
**Steve**
**Stevie**
**Stewart** *variant spelling of* **Stuart**
**Stirling**
**St John**
**Stuart** (*or* **Stewart**)
**Sue**
**Sukey**
**Susan**
**Susannah** (*or* **Susanna, Suzanna**)
**Susie** (*or* **Suzy**)
**Suzanne** (*or* **Susanne**)
**Suzette**
**Suzy**
**Swithin**
**Sybella**
**Sybil** (*or* **Sibyl**)
**Sybilla**
**Syd** *variant spelling of* **Sid**
**Sydney** *variant spelling of* **Sidney**
**Sylvanus** *variant spelling of* **Silvanus**
**Sylvester** (*or* **Silvester**)
**Sylvia** (*or* **Silvia**)
**Sylvie**
**Tabitha**
**Tacey** (*or* **Tacy**)
**Taffy**
**Talbot**
**Taliesin**
**Talitha**
**Tallulah**
**Tam**
**Tamar**
**Tamara**
**Tamasine**
**Tammy**
**Tamsin**
**Tancred**
**Tania** *variant spelling of* **Tanya**
**Tanith**
**Tansy**
**Tanya** (*or* **Tania**)
**Tara**
**Tarquin**
**Tatiana**
**Taylor**
**Ted**
**Teddy** (*or* **Teddie**)
**Tegan**
**Tegwen**
**Temperance**
**Terence** (*or* **Terrence**)
**Teresa** (*or* **Theresa**)
**Terry** (*or* **Terri**)
**Tertius**
**Tess**
**Tessa**
**Tessie**
**Tetty**
**Tex**
**Thaddeus**
**Thea**
**Thekla** (*or* **Thecla**)
**Thelma**
**Theo**
**Theobald**
**Theodora**
**Theodore**
**Theodoric**
**Theodosia**
**Theophania**
**Theophila**
**Theophilus**
**Theresa** *variant spelling of* **Teresa**
**Thérèse**
**Theresia**
**Thirza** (*or* **Thirsa**)
**Thom**
**Thomas**
**Thomasin**
**Thomasina**
**Thomasine**
**Thora**
**Thorley**
**Thornton**
**Thurstan** (*or* **Thurston**)
**Thyra**
**Tibby**
**Tiffany**
**Tilda**
**Tilly**
**Tim**
**Timmy**
**Timothea**
**Timothy**
**Tina**
**Tirzah**
**Tisha**
**Titus**
**Tobias**
**Toby**
**Todd**
**Tolly**
**Tom**
**Tommy**
**Toni**
**Tonia** (*or* **Tonya**)
**Tony**
**Topsy**
**Torquil**
**Totty**
**Tracy** (*or* **Tracey**)
**Travers**
**Travis**
**Trevor** (*or* **Trefor**)
**Tricia** (*or* **Trisha**)
**Trina**
**Trissie**
**Tristan**
**Tristram**
**Trix**
**Trixie**
**Troy**
**Trudy** (*or* **Trudie, Trudi**)
**Tryphena**
**Tudor**
**Turlough**
**Tybalt**
**Tyra**
**Tyrone**
**Ulric**
**Ulrica**
**Ulysses**

**Una**
**Unity**
**Upton**
**Urban**
**Uriah**
**Ursula**
**Val**
**Valda**
**Valentina**
**Valentine**
**Valeria**
**Valerie**
**Vanda**
**Vanessa**
**Vashti**
**Vaughan** (*or* **Vaughn**)
**Velda**
**Velma**
**Venetia**
**Venus**
**Vera**
**Vere**
**Verena**
**Verity**
**Verna**
**Vernon**
**Verona**
**Veronica**
**Véronique**
**Vic** (*or* **Vick**)
**Vicky** (*or* **Vicki, Vickie, Vikki**)
**Victor**
**Victoria**
**Victorine**
**Vida**
**Vilma**
**Vin**
**Vina**
**Vince**
**Vincent**
**Vincentia**
**Vinnie** (*or* **Vinny**)
**Vinny**
**Viola**
**Violet**
**Violetta**
**Violette**
**Virgil**
**Virginia**
**Vita**
**Vitus**
**Viv**
**Viva**
**Vivia**
**Vivian** (*or* **Vivien, Vyvyan**)
**Viviana**
**Vivienne**
**Wade**
**Wal**
**Walburga**
**Waldo**
**Wallace** (*or* **Wallis**)
**Wally**
**Walt**
**Walter**
**Wanda**
**Ward**
**Warner**
**Warren**
**Warwick**
**Washington**
**Wat**
**Wayne**
**Wenda**
**Wendell**
**Wendy**
**Wesley**
**Wilbert**
**Wilbur**
**Wilf**
**Wilfred** (*or* **Wilfrid**)
**Wilfrida** (*or* **Wilfreda**)
**Wilhelmina**
**Will**
**Willa**
**Willard**
**William**
**Williamina**
**Willie** (*or* **Willy**)
**Willis**
**Willoughby**
**Wilma**
**Wilmer**
**Wilmot**
**Win**
**Windsor**
**Winfred** (*or* **Winfrid**)
**Winifred** (*or* **Winnifred, Winefred**)
**Winnie**
**Winston**
**Winthrop**
**Woodrow**
**Wyatt**
**Wybert**
**Wyndham**
**Wynford**
**Wynn** (*or* **Wynne**)
**Wystan**
**Xanthe**
**Xavier**
**Xenia**
**Yasmin**
**Yehudi**
**Yolanda**
**Yolande**
**Yves**
**Yvette**
**Yvonne** (*or* **Evonne**)
**Zacchaeus**
**Zachariah**
**Zacharias**
**Zachary**
**Zak** (*or* **Zack**)
**Zana**
**Zandra**
**Zane**
**Zara**
**Zechariah**
**Zedekiah**
**Zelda**
**Zelma**
**Zena**
**Zenobia**
**Zephaniah**
**Zillah**
**Zinnia**
**Zita**
**Zoë** (*or* **Zoe**)
**Zola**
**Zora** (*or* **Zorah**)
**Zuleika**

# Biographical Names

Aalto, Alvar
Aaltonen, Wäinö
Abbado, Claudio
Abbas
Abbas, Ferhat
Abd Allah (*known as* the Khalifa)
'Abd al-Malik ibn Marwan
'Abd ar-Rahman III an-Nasir
Abdelkader
Abdulhamid
Abdullah
Abdul Rahman, Tunku
Abel, Sir Frederick Augustus
Abel, Niels Henrik
Abelard, Peter
Abercrombie, Sir (Leslie) Patrick
Abercromby, Sir Ralph
Aberdeen, George Hamilton-Gordon, 4th Earl of
Absalom son of King David
Absalon 12th-century Danish statesman
Abu al-Wafa
Abu Bakar sultan of Johore
Abu Bakr first caliph
Abu Hanifah
Abu Nuwas
Accius, Lucius
Accoramboni, Vittoria
Achard, Franz Karl
Achebe, Chinua
Acheson, Dean (Gooderham)
Acton, John Emerich Edward Dalberg-Acton, 1st Baron
Adalbert
Adam, Adolphe-Charles
Adam, James
Adam, Robert
Adam, William
Adamnan, St
Adamov, Arthur
Adams, Charles Francis
Adams, Gerry
Adams, Henry
Adams, John
Adams, John Couch
Adams, John Quincy
Adams, Richard
Adams, Samuel
Adamson, Robert
Addington, Henry, 1st Viscount Sidmouth
Addinsell, Richard
Addison, Joseph
Addison, Thomas
Adenauer, Konrad
Ader, Clément
Adler, Alfred
Adler, Felix
Adler, Larry
Adrian, Edgar Douglas, 1st Baron
Aelfric
Aeneas Silvius
Aeschines
Aeschylus
Aesop
Aetius, Flavius
Afghani, Jamal ad-Din al-
Aga Khan
Agassiz, Alexander
Agassiz, Jean Louis Rodolphe
Agathocles
Agee, James
Agesilaus
Agha Mohammad Khan
Agnesi, Maria Gaetana
Agnew, Spiro T(heodore)
Agnon, Shmuel Yosef
Agostini, Giacomo
Agricola, Georgius
Agricola, Gnaeus Julius
Agricola, Johann
Agrippa, Marcus Vipsanius
Agrippina
Ahad Ha'am
Ahern, Bertie
Ahmad Khan, Sir Sayyid
Ahmad Shah Durrani
Ahmed
Ahmose
Aiken, Howard Hathaway
Ailred of Rievaulx, St
Ainsworth, W(illiam) Harrison
Airy, Sir George Biddell
Aistulf
Akbar
Akhenaton (*or* Ikhnaton)
Akhmatova
Akiba ben Joseph
Akihito
Alain-Fournier
Alanbrooke, Alan Francis Brooke, 1st Viscount
Alarcón, Pedro Antonio de
Alarcón y Mendoza, Juan Ruiz de
Alba, Fernando Alvarez de Toledo, Duke of
Albee, Edward
Albéniz, Isaac Manuel Francisco
Alberoni, Giulio
Albers, Josef
Alberti, Leon Battista
Alberti, Raphael
Albertus Magnus, St
Albinoni, Tomaso
Alboin
Albuquerque, Alfonso de
Alcaeus
Alcibiades
Alcmaeon
Alcock, Sir John (William)
Alcoforado, Marianna
Alcott, Louisa May
Alcuin
Aldanov, Mark
Aldhelm, St
Aldington, Richard
Aldiss, Brian W(ilson)
Aldrich, Thomas Bailey
Aldridge, Ira Frederick
Alegría, Ciro
Alekhine, Alexander
Alemán, Mateo
Alexander, Sir William, 1st Earl of Stirling
Alexander of Tunis, Harold, 1st Earl
Alexius Comnenus
al-Farabi, Mohammed ibn Tarkhan

Fabre, Jean Henri
Fabricius ab Aquapendente, Hieronymus
Fabritius, Carel
Fabry, Charles
Fadden, Sir Arthur William
Fahd Ibn Abdul Aziz
Fa-hsien *variant spelling of* Fa Xian
Faidherbe, Louis (Léon César)
Fairbanks, Douglas
Fairfax, Thomas, 3rd Baron
Faisal
Faisal Ibn Abdul Aziz
Fakhr ad-Din II
Falla, Manuel de
Fallopius, Gabriel
Fangio, Juan Manuel
Fa Ngum
Fantin-Latour, (Ignace) Henri (Joseph Théodore)
Faraday, Michael
Farel, Guillaume
Fargo, William
Farnaby, Giles
Farnese, Alessandro, Duke of Parma
Farouk
Farquhar, George
Fassbinder, Rainer Werner
Fateh Singh, Sant
Fatimah
Faulkner, William
Fauré, Gabriel (Urbain)
Fawcett, Henry
Fawcett, Dame Millicent Garrett
Fawkes, Guy
Fa Xian (*or* Fa-hsien)
Fechner, Gustav Theodor
Feininger, Lyonel (Charles Adrian)
Fellini, Federico
Fénelon, François de Salignac de la Mothe
Ferlinghetti, Lawrence
Fermat, Pierre de
Fermi, Enrico
Fernandel
Ferrar, Nicholas
Ferrier, Kathleen
Ferrier, Susan Edmonstone
Feuchtwanger, Lion
Feuerbach, Ludwig Andreas
Feuillère, Edwige
Feydeau, Georges
Feynman, Richard Phillips
Fibonacci, Leonardo
Fichte, Johann Gottlieb
Ficino, Marsilio
Field, Cyrus West
Field, John
Fielding, Henry
Fields, Gracie
Fields, W. C.
Fife, Duncan *variant spelling of* Phyfe, Duncan
Filarete
Fillmore, Millard
Finlay, Carlos Juan
Finney, Albert
Finsen, Niels Ryberg
Firbank, (Arthur Annesley) Ronald
Firdausi
Firth, J(ohn) R(upert)
Fischer, Bobby
Fischer, Emil Hermann
Fischer-Dieskau, Dietrich
Fischer von Erlach, Johann Bernhard
Fisher, Andrew
Fisher, John Arbuthnot, 1st Baron
Fisher, St John
Fitzgerald, Edward
Fitzgerald, Ella
Fitzgerald, F(rancis) Scott (Key)
Fitzgerald, George Francis
Fitzsimmons, Bob
Flagstad, Kirsten Malfrid
Flaherty, Robert (Joseph)
Flamininus, Titus Quinctius
Flaminius, Gaius
Flamsteed, John
Flaubert, Gustave
Flaxman, John Henry
Flecker, (Herman) James Elroy
Flémalle, Master of
Fleming, Sir Alexander
Fleming, Ian (Lancaster)
Fleming, Sir John Ambrose
Fleming, Paul
Fletcher, John
Fleury, André Hercule de, Cardinal
Flinders, Matthew
Flood, Henry
Florey, Howard Walter, Baron
Florio, John
Floris, Cornelis
Floris, Frans
Flotow, Friedrich von
Fludd, Robert
Flynn, Errol
Fo, Dario
Foch, Ferdinand
Fokine, Michel
Fokker, Anthony Hermann Gerard
Foley, John Henry
Fonda, Henry
Fonda, Jane
Fonda, Peter
Fontana, Domenico
Fontane, Theodor
Fontanne, Lyn
Fontenelle, Bernard le Bovier de
Fonteyn, Dame Margot
Foot, Michael (Mackintosh)
Forbes, George William
Ford, Ford Madox
Ford, Gerald R(udolph)
Ford, Harrison
Ford, Henry
Ford, John
Foreman, George
Forester, C(ecil) S(cott)
Forman, Miloš
Forster, E(dward) M(organ)
Fortescue, Sir John
Foscolo, Ugo
Foster, Jodie
Foster, Sir Norman
Foster, Stephen Collins
Fothergill, John
Foucault, Jean Bernard Léon
Fouché, Joseph, Duc d'Otrante
Fouqué, Friedrich Heinrich Karl, Baron de la Motte
Fouquet, Jean
Fouquet, Nicolas
Fourier, (François Marie) Charles
Fourier, Jean Baptiste Joseph, Baron
Fourneyron, Benoît

Gibbons, Orlando
Gibbs, James
Gibbs, Josiah Willard
Gibran, Khalil
Gibson, Mel
Gide, André
Gielgud, Sir (Arthur) John
Gierek, Edward
Gigli, Beniamino
Gilbert, Sir Humphrey
Gilbert, William
Gilbert, Sir William Schwenk
Giles, Carl Ronald
Gill, (Arthur) Eric (Rowton)
Gillespie, Dizzy
Gillray, James
Ginkel, Godert de, 1st Earl of Athlone
Ginsberg, Allen
Giordano, Luca
Giorgione
Giotto
Giraldus Cambrensis
Giraudoux, Jean
Girtin, Thomas
Giscard d'Estaing, Valéry
Gish, Dorothy
Gish, Lillian
Gislebertus
Gissing, George Robert
Giulini, Carlo Maria
Giulio Romano
Gladstone, W(illiam) E(wart)
Glanville, Ranulf de
Glaser, Donald Arthur
Glass, Philip
Glazunov, Aleksandr Konstantinovich
Glendower, Owen
Glinka, Mikhail Ivanovich
Gluck, Christoph Willibald
Gneisenau, August (Wilhelm Anton), Graf Neithardt von
Gobbi, Tito
Gobind Singh (*or* Govind Singh)
Gobineau, Joseph Arthur, Comte de
Godard, Jean-Luc
Goddard, Robert Hutchings
Gödel, Kurt
Goderich, George Frederick Samuel Robinson, Viscount
Godiva, Lady
Godolphin, Sidney, Earl of
Godoy, Manuel de
Godunov, Boris (Fedorovich)
Godwin, William
Goebbels, (Paul) Joseph
Goes, Hugo van der
Goethe, Johann Wolfgang von
Gogol, Nikolai Vasilievich
Gold, Thomas
Golding, Sir William
Goldoni, Carlo
Goldschmidt, Richard Benedict
Goldsmith, Oliver
Goldwyn, Samuel
Golgi, Camillo
Gollancz, Victor
Golovkin, Gavril Ivanovich, Count
Gómez, Juan Vicente
Gomułka, Władysław
Goncharov, Ivan Aleksandrovich
Goncourt, Edmond de
Goncourt, Jules de
Gondomar, Diego Sarmiento de Acuña, Conde de
Góngora y Argote, Luis de
González de Mendoza, Pedro
Goodman, Benny
Goodyear, Charles
Goolagong, Evonne *maiden name of* Evonne Cawley
Goossens, Sir Eugene
Goossens, Leon
Gorbachov, Mikhail Sergeevich
Gordon, Charles George
Gore, Al(bert)
Górecki, Henryk
Göring, Hermann Wilhelm
Gorki, Maksim
Gorky, Arshile
Gorton, Sir John Grey
Gossaert, Jan (*known as* Mabuse)
Gosse, Sir Edmund
Gottfried von Strassburg
Gottsched, Johann Christoph
Goujon, Jean
Gounod, Charles François
Govind Singh *variant spelling of* Gobind Singh
Gower, John
Gowon, Yakubu
Goya(y Lucientes), Francesco (Jose) de
Goyen, Jan Josephszoon van
Gozzi, Carlo
Gozzoli, Benozzo
Gracchus, Gaius Sempronius
Gracchus, Tiberius Sempronius
Grace, W(illiam) G(ilbert)
Graf, Steffi
Graham, Billy
Graham, Martha
Graham, Thomas
Grahame, Kenneth
Grainger, Percy Aldridge
Gramsci, Antonio
Granados, Enrique
Granby, John Manners, Marquess of
Grant, Cary
Grant, Duncan James Corrowr
Grant, Ulysses S(impson)
Granville, Granville George Leveson-Gower, 2nd Earl
Granville, John Carteret, 1st Earl
Granville-Barker, Harley
Grappelli, Stephane
Grass, Günter
Gratian(us), Flavius
Grattan, Henry
Graves, Robert (Ranke)
Gray, Asa
Gray, Thomas
Greeley, Horace
Green, Henry
Greenaway, Kate
Greenaway, Peter
Greene, (Henry) Graham
Greene, Nathaneal
Greene, Robert
Greenough, Horatio
Greenwood, Walter

Newcomen, Thomas
Ne Win
Newman, John Henry, Cardinal
Newman, Paul
Newton, Sir Isaac
Nexø, Martin Andersen
Ney, Michel, Prince of Moscow
Ngo Dinh Diem
Niarchos, Stavros Spyros
Nicholson, Ben
Nicholson, Jack
Nicholson, William
Nicias
Nicklaus, Jack William
Nicolai, Otto Ehrenfried
Nicolson, Sir Harold (George)
Niebuhr, Barthold Georg
Nielsen, Carl (August)
Niemeyer, Oscar
Niemöller, Martin
Nietzsche, Friedrich
Nightingale, Florence
Nijinsky, Vaslav
Nikisch, Arthur
Nilsson, Birgit Marta
Nimitz, Chester W(illiam)
Nirenberg, Marshall Warren
Nithsdale, William Maxwell, 5th Earl of
Niven, David
Nixon, Richard Milhous
Nizam al-Mulk
Nkomo, Joshua
Nkrumah, Kwame
Nobel, Alfred Bernhard
Nobile, Umberto
Noble, Sir Andrew
Nobunaga Oda
Noel-Baker, Philip John
Noguchi, Hideyo
Nolan, Sir Sidney
Nolde, Emil
Nollekens, Joseph
Nono, Luigi
Nordenskjöld, Nils Adolf Erik, Baron
Norfolk, Thomas Howard, Duke of
Noriega, Manuel
North, Frederick, Lord
North, Sir Thomas
Northcliffe, Alfred Charles William Harmsworth, 1st Viscount
Northrop, John Howard
Northumberland, John Dudley, Duke of
Nostradamus
Novalis
Novello, Ivor
Novotný Antonín
Noyes, Alfred
Nu, U
Nuffield, William Richard Morris, 1st Viscount
Nureyev, Rudolf
Nurhachi
Nurmi, Paavo Johannes
Nyerere, Julius (Kambarage)
Nyssa, St Gregory of
Oakley, Annie
Oastler, Richard
Oates, Lawrence Edward Grace
Oates, Titus
Obote, (Apollo) Milton
O'Brien, Conor Cruise
O'Brien, Flann
O'Brien, William
O'Brien, William Smith
O'Casey, Sean
Ockham, William of
O'Connell, Daniel
O'Connor, Feargus
O'Connor, Frank
Oda Nobunaga
Odets, Clifford
Odoacer
Oë, Kenzaburo
Oehlenschläger, Adam (Gottlob)
Oersted, Hans Christian
Offa
Offenbach, Jacques
O'Flaherty, Liam
Ogden, C(harles) K(ay)
Ogdon, John
Oglethorpe, James Edward
O'Hara, John (Henry)
O'Higgins, Bernardo
Ohm, Georg Simon
Oistrakh, David
Oistrakh, Igor
O'Keeffe, Georgia
Okeghem, Jean d'
Olbers, Heinrich Wilhelm Matthäus
Oldcastle, Sir John
Oldenbarneveldt, Johan van
Oldenburg, Claes (Thure)
Oliphant, Sir Mark Laurence Elwin
Olivares, Gaspar de Guzmán, Conde-Duque de
Oliver, Isaac
Olivier, Laurence (Kerr), Baron
Omar Khayyam
Onassis, Aristotle Socrates
Oñate, Juan de
O'Neill, Eugene
O'Neill, Terence, Baron
Onsager, Lars
Ophüls, Max
Opie, John
Opitz (von Boberfeld), Martin
Oppenheimer, J. Robert
Orcagna, Andrea
Orczy, Baroness Emmusca
Oresme, Nicole d'
Orff, Carl
Origen
Orlando, Vittorio Emanuele
Orléans, Charles, Duc d'
Orléans, Louis Philippe Joseph, Duc d'
Orlov, Aleksei Grigorievich
Orlov, Grigori Grigorievich, Count
Ormandy, Eugene
Ormonde, James Butler, 1st Duke of
Orozco, José
Ortega (Saavedra), Daniel
Ortega y Gasset, José
Ortelius, Abraham
Ortoli, François Xavier
Orwell, George
Osborne, Dorothy
Osborne, John
O'Shea, Katherine Page
Osler, Sir William
Osman
Ossian
Ossietsky, Carl von

Ostade, Adrian van
Ostrovskii, Aleksandr Nikolaevich
Ostwald, (Friedrich) Wilhelm
Oswald, Lee Harvey
Oswiu
Otis, Elisha Graves
Otto, Nikolaus August
Otway, Thomas
Oudry, Jean-Baptiste
Ouida
Ouspensky, Peter
Outram, Sir James
Ovid
Owen, Alun Davies
Owen, David (Anthony Llewellyn), Baron
Owen, Robert
Owen, Wilfred
Owens, Jesse
Oxenstierna, Axel, Count
Pabst, G(eorge) W(ilhelm)
Pachomius, St
Pachymeres, Georgius
Pacino, Al
Paderewski, Ignacy (Jan)
Páez, José Antonio
Paganini, Niccolò
Page, Sir Earle (Christmas Grafton)
Page, Sir Frederick Handley
Pahlavi, Mohammed Reza
Pahlavi, Reza Shah
Paine, Thomas
Paisley, Ian
Palaeologus, Michael
Palestrina, Giovanni Pierluigi da
Paley, William
Palgrave, Francis Turner
Palissy, Bernard
Palladio, Andrea
Palma Vecchio, Jacopo
Palmer, Arnold
Palmer, Samuel
Palmerston, Henry John Temple, 3rd Viscount
Pandit, Vijaya Lakshmi
Pan Gu (*or* P'an Ku)
Panini
Pankhurst, Dame Christabel
Pankhurst, Emmeline
Pankhurst, Sylvia
Papadopoulos, George
Papen, Franz von
Pappus of Alexandria
Paracelsus
Paré, Ambroise
Pareto, Vilfredo
Paris, Matthew
Park, Mungo
Park Chung Hee
Parker, Charlie (Christopher)
Parker, Dorothy Rothschild
Parker, Matthew
Parkes, Sir Henry
Parkinson, (Cyril) Northcote
Parkman, Francis
Parmenides
Parmigianino
Parnell, Charles Stewart
Parr, Catherine
Parry, Sir Hubert
Parry, Sir William Edward
Parsons, Sir Charles Algernon
Partridge, Eric Honeywood
Pascal, Blaise
Pašić, Nicola
Pasionaria, La *see* Ibarruri, Dolores
Pasmore, Victor
Pasolini, Pier Paolo
Passy, Frédéric
Pasternak, Boris
Pasteur, Louis
Pater, Walter (Horatio)
Paterson, William
Patinir, Joachim
Patmore, Coventry
Paton, Alan
Patti, Adelina
Patton, George S(mith)
Pauli, Wolfgang
Pauling, Linus Carl
Paulinus of Nola, St
Paulus, Friedrich
Pausanias
Pavarotti, Luciano
Pavese, Cesare
Pavlov, Ivan Petrovich
Pavlova, Anna
Paxinou, Katina
Paxton, Sir Joseph
Paz, Octavio
Peacock, Thomas Love
Peake, Mervyn
Pears, Sir Peter
Pearse, Patrick Henry
Pearson, Lester B(owles)
Peary, Robert Edwin
Peckinpah, Sam
Peel, Sir Robert
Peele, George
Péguy, Charles
Peirce, Charles Sanders
Pelagius
Pelé
Pelham, Henry
Pelletier, Pierre Joseph
Penda
Penderecki, Krzysztof
Pendlebury, John Devitt Stringfellow
Penn, William
Penney, William George, Baron
Penrose, Sir Roger
Pepys, Samuel
Perceval, Spencer
Percy, Sir Henry (*known as* Harry Hotspur)
Percy, Bishop Thomas
Perelman, S(idney) J(oseph)
Peres, Shimon
Pérez de Cuéllar, Javier
Pérez Galdós, Benito
Pergolesi, Giovanni (Battista)
Pericles
Perkin, Sir William Henry
Perón, Evita
Perón, Isabel
Perón, Juan (Domingo)
Pérotin
Perrault, Charles
Perrin, Jean-Baptiste
Perry, Fred(erick John)
Perry, Matthew C(albraith)
Perse, Saint-John
Pershing, John J(oseph)
Perugino
Perutz, Max Ferdinand
Pestalozzi, Johann Heinrich
Pétain, (Henri) Philippe
Peterson, Oscar Emmanuel
Petipa, Marius
Petit, Roland
Petöfi, Sándor
Petrarch

Petrie, Sir (William Matthew) Flinders
Petronius Arbiter
Petrosian, Tigran Vartanovich
Pevsner, Antoine
Pevsner, Sir Nikolaus (Bernhard Leon)
Phaedrus
Phalaris
Phidias
Phidippides
Philadelphus, Ptolomy
Philby, Harold Adrian Russell
Philby, H(arry) St John (Bridge)
Philemon
Philidor, André Danican
Philidor, François André Danican
Phillip, Arthur
Philo Judaeus
Phiz *see* Browne, Hablot Knight
Phryne
Phyfe (*or* Fife), Duncan
Piaf, Edith
Piaget, Jean
Picabia, Francis
Picasso, Pablo
Piccard, Auguste
Piccard, Jacques
Piccard, Jean-Félix
Pickford, Mary
Pico della Mirandola, Giovanni, Conte
Pieck, Wilhelm
Piero della Francesca
Piero di Cosimo
Piggott, Lester Keith
Pilate, Pontius
Piłsudski, Józef Klemens
Pinckney, Charles
Pinckney, Charles Cotesworth
Pinckney, Thomas
Pindar
Pinero, Sir Arthur Wing
Pinkerton, Allan
Pinochet, Augusto
Pinter, Harold
Pinturicchio
Piozzi, Hester Lynch (*married name* Thrale)
Piper, John
Pirandello, Luigi
Piranesi, Giambattista
Pisanello
Pisano, Andrea
Pisano, Giovanni
Pisano, Nicola
Pisistratus
Pissarro, Camille
Pissarro, Lucien
Pitman, Sir Isaac
Pitt, William
Pitt-Rivers, Augustus Henry Lane Fox
Pius pope
Pizarro, Francisco
Place, Francis
Planck, Erwin
Planck, Max Karl Ernst Ludwig
Plantagenet surname of English kings 1154–1485
Plath, Sylvia
Plato
Plautus, Titus Maccius
Pleasence, Donald
Plekhanov, Georgi Valentinovich
Pliny
Plomer, William
Plotinus
Plowright, Joan
Plunket, St Oliver
Plutarch
Pocahontas
Po Chü-i *variant spelling of* Bo Zhu Yi
Podgorny, N(ikolai) V(iktorovich)
Poe, Edgar Allan
Poggio Bracciolini, Giovanni Francesco
Poincaré, Jules Henri
Poincaré, Raymond
Poisson, Siméon Dénis
Poitiers, Diane de, Duchesse de Valentinois
Polanski, Roman
Pole, Reginald, Cardinal
Polignac, Auguste Jules Armand Marie, Prince de
Poliziano
Polk, James K(nox)
Pollaiuolo, Antonio
Pollaiuolo, Piero
Pollock, Jackson
Polo, Marco
Polybius
Polycarp, St
Polyclitus
Polycrates
Pombal, Sebastião José de Carvalho e Mello, Marquês de
Pompadour, Mme de
Pompey
Pompidou, Georges (Jean Raymond)
Ponce de Leon, Juan
Poniatowski, Józef
Poniatowski, Stanisław
Pontiac
Pontormo, Jacopo da
Pope, Alexander
Popov, Aleksandr Stepanovich
Popov, Oleg Konstantinovich
Popper, Sir Karl Raimund
Porphyriogenitus, Constantine
Porphyry
Porter, Cole (Albert)
Porter, Katherine Anne
Porter, Peter
Portland, William Henry Cavendish Bentinck, 3rd Duke of
Potemkin, Grigori Aleksandrovich
Potter, Beatrix
Potter, Paul
Potter, Stephen
Poulenc, Francis
Pound, Ezra
Poussin, Nicolas
Powell, Anthony
Powell, Cecil Frank
Powell, (John) Enoch
Powys, John Cowper
Powys, Theodore Francis
Praetorius, Michael
Prandtl, Ludwig
Prasad, Rajendra
Praxiteles
Preminger, Otto (Ludwig)
Prescott, John (Leslie)
Prescott, William Hickling
Presley, Elvis (Aaron)

Prester John
Pretorius, Andries (Wilhelmus Jacobus)
Pretorius, Marthinus Wessel
Prévert, Jacques
Previn, André
Prévost d'Exiles, Antoine François, Abbé
Pride, Thomas
Priestley, J(ohn) B(oynton)
Priestley, Joseph
Primo de Rivera, José Antonio
Primo de Rivera, Miguel
Prior, Matthew
Priscian
Pritchett, Sir V(ictor) S(awden)
Proclus
Procopius
Prokofiev, Sergei
Prokop
Propertius, Sextus
Protagoras
Proudhon, Pierre Joseph
Proust, Joseph-Louis
Proust, Marcel
Prout, William
Prud'hon, Pierre Paul
Prynne, William
Psamtik
Pseudo-Dionysius the Areopagite
Ptolemy
Puccini, Giacomo
Pucelle, Jean
Pudovkin, Vsevolod
Pufendorf, Samuel von
Pugachov, Yemelyan Ivanovich
Pugin, Augustus Welby Northmore
Pulci, Luigi
Pullman, George Mortimer
Purcell, Edward Mills
Purcell, Henry
Purchas, Samuel
Pusey, Edward Bouverie
Pushkin, Aleksandr
Puttnam, Sir David (Terence)
Puvis de Chavannes, Pierre (Cécile)
Pu Yi, Henry
Pym, John
Pynchon, Thomas
Pyrrhon
Pyrrhus
Pythagoras
Pytheas
Qaboos ibn Sa'id
Qaddafi, Moammar al-
Qian Long (*or* Ch'ien-lung)
Quant, Mary
Quasimodo, Salvatore
Queneau, Raymond
Quercia, Jacopo della
Quesnay, François
Quesnel, Pasquier
Quiller-Couch, Sir Arthur Thomas
Quine, Willard van Orman
Quintilian
Quisling, Vidkun (Abraham Lauritz Jonsson)
Qu Qiu Bai (*or* Ch'ü Ch'iu-pai)
Rabelais, François
Rabi, Isidor Isaac
Rachmaninov, Sergei
Racine, Jean
Rackham, Arthur
Radcliffe, Ann (Ward)
Radcliffe-Brown, Alfred Reginald
Radek, Karl
Radić, Stjepan
Radiguet, Raymond
Raeburn, Sir Henry
Raeder, Erich
Raffles, Sir Thomas Stamford
Rafsanjani, Hojatoleslam Ali Akbar Hashemi
Raglan, FitzRoy James Henry Somerset, 1st Baron
Raikes, Robert
Raine, Kathleen
Rainier, Prince
Rais, Gilles de
Rákóczy, Ferenc
Raleigh, Sir Walter
Ramakrishna
Raman, Sir Chandrasekhara Venkata
Ramanuja
Rambert, Dame Marie
Rameau, Jean Philippe
Ramón y Cajal, Santiago
Ramsay, Allan
Ramsay, Sir William
Ramses
Ramsey, Sir Alf
Ram Singh
Ramus, Petrus
Ranjit Singh, Maharaja
Ranjitsinhji Vibhaji, Kumar Shri, Maharajah Jam Sahib of Nawanagar
Rank, J(oseph) Arthur, 1st Baron
Rank, Otto
Ranke, Leopold von
Ransom, John Crowe
Ransome, Arthur Mitchell
Raphael
Rashi
Rasmussen, Knud Johan Victor
Rasputin, Grigori Yefimovich
Rathenau, Walther
Rattigan, Sir Terence
Rattle, Sir Simon
Ratushinskaya, Irina
Rauschenberg, Robert
Ravel, Maurice
Rawlinson, Sir Henry Creswicke
Rawsthorne, Alan
Ray, John
Ray, Man
Ray, Satyajit
Rayleigh, John William Strutt, 3rd Baron
Rayleigh, Robert John Strutt, 4th Baron
Razi, ar-
Razin, Stenka
Read, Sir Herbert
Reade, Charles
Reading, Rufus Daniel Isaacs, 1st Marquess of
Reagan, Ronald
Réaumur, René-Antoine Ferchault de
Reber, Grote
Recamier, Jeanne Françoise Julie Adelaide
Redford, Robert
Redgrave, Corin
Redgrave, Lynn
Redgrave, Sir Michael

Redgrave, Vanessa
Redmond, John Edward
Redon, Odilon
Redouté, Pierre Joseph
Reed, Sir Carol
Reed, John
Reed, Lou
Reed, Walter
Reeves, William Pember
Reger, Max
Regiomontanus
Regnier, Henri François Joseph de
Regulus, Marcus Attilus
Rehoboam
Reich, Wilhelm
Reid, Sir George Houston
Reid, Thomas
Reinhardt, Django
Reinhardt, Max
Reith, John Charles Walsham, 1st Baron
Remarque, Erich Maria
Rembrandt (Harmenszoon) van Rijn
Remington, Eliphalet
Renan, (Joseph) Ernest
Rendell, Ruth (Barbara), Baroness
Reni, Guido
Rennie, John
Renoir, Jean
Renoir, Pierre Auguste
Resnais, Alain
Respighi, Ottorino
Retz, Jean François Paul de Gondi, Cardinal de
Reuter, Paul Julius, Baron von
Revere, Paul
Reynaud, Paul
Reynolds, Albert
Reynolds, Sir Joshua
Rhee, Syngman
Rheticus
Rhine, Joseph Banks
Rhodes, Cecil (John)
Rhodes, Wilfred
Rhys, Jean
Ribbentrop, Joachim von
Ribera, José de
Ricardo, David
Ricci, Marco
Ricci, Matteo
Ricci, Sebastiano
Riccio, David
Rich, Richard, 1st Baron
Richard, Sir Cliff
Richards, Frank
Richards, Sir Gordon
Richards, I(vor) A(rmstrong)
Richardson, Henry Handel
Richardson, Henry Hobson
Richardson, Sir Ralph
Richardson, Samuel
Richelieu, Armand Jean du Plessis, Cardinal de
Richler, Mordecai
Richter, Hans
Richter, Johann Paul Friedrich.
Richter, Sviatoslav (Teofilovitch)
Richthofen, Manfred, Freiherr von
Ridley, Nicholas
Ridolfi, Roberto
Riebeeck, Jan van
Riefensthal, Leni
Riel, Louis
Riemann, Georg Friedrich Bernhard
Rienzo, Cola di
Riesman, David
Riley, Bridget Louise
Rilke, Rainer Maria
Rimbaud, Arthur
Rimsky-Korsakov, Nikolai
Rivera, Diego
Rizzio, David
Roach, Hal
Robbe-Grillet, Alain
Robbins, Frederick Chapman
Robbins, Jerome
Roberts, Frederick Sleigh, 1st Earl
Roberts, Tom
Robeson, Paul
Robespierre, Maximilien François Marie Isidore de
Robey, Sir George
Robinson, Edward G.
Robinson, Edwin Arlington
Robinson, John (Arthur Thomas)
Robinson, Mary
Robinson, Sir Robert
Robinson, Sugar Ray
Robinson, William Heath
Robson, Dame Flora
Rochester, John Wilmot, 2nd Earl of
Rockefeller, John D(avison)
Rockefeller, Nelson A(ldrich)
Rockingham, Charles Watson-Wentworth, 2nd Marquess of
Roderic Irish king
Rodgers, Richard Charles
Rodin, Auguste
Rodney, George Brydges, 1st Baron
Rodrigo, Joaquín
Roebling, John Augustus
Roebling, Washington Augustus
Roentgen, Wilhelm Konrad
Rogers, Ginger
Rogers, John
Rogers, Sir Richard
Roget, Peter Mark
Röhm, Ernst
Rokitansky, Karl, Freiherr von
Rolfe, Frederick William
Rolland, Romain
Rolls, Charles Stewart
Romains, Jules
Rommel, Erwin
Romney, George
Romulus Augustulus
Ronsard, Pierre de
Roon, Albrecht, Graf von
Roosevelt, Eleanor
Roosevelt, Franklin D(elano)
Roosevelt, Theodore
Root, Elihu
Rory O'Connor
Rosa, Salvator
Roscelin
Roscius, Quintus
Rosebery, Archibald Philip Primrose, 5th Earl of
Rosenberg, Ethel
Rosenberg, Julius
Rosewall, Ken(neth Ronald)
Ross, Sir James Clark
Ross, Sir Ronald
Rosse, William Parsons, 3rd Earl of

Rossellini, Roberto
Rossetti, Christina Georgina
Rossetti, Dante Gabriel
Rossini, Gioacchino Antonio
Rostand, Edmond
Rostropovich, Mstislav
Roth, Philip
Rothermere, Harold Sydney Harmsworth, 1st Viscount
Rothko, Mark
Rothschild, James
Rothschild, Karl Mayer
Rothschild, Lionel Nathan
Rothschild, Mayer Amschel
Rothschild, Nathan Mayer
Rothschild, Nathaniel Mayer Victor, 3rd Baron
Rothschild, Salomon Mayer
Rouault, Georges (Henri)
Roubillac, Louis François
Rouget de l'Isle, Claude Joseph
Rousseau, Henri
Rousseau, Jean Jacques
Rousseau, (Pierre Étienne) Théodore
Roussel, Albert
Roussel, Raymond
Roux, Pierre Paul Emile
Rowe, Nicholas
Rowlandson, Thomas
Rowley, Thomas
Rowse, A(lfred) L(eslie)
Royce, Sir (Frederick) Henry
Royce, Josiah
Rubbra, Edmund
Rubens, Peter Paul
Rubinstein, Anton
Rubinstein, Artur
Rublyov, Andrey
Ruggles, Carl
Ruisdael, Jacob van
Ruysdael, Salomon van
Ruiz, Juan
Rumford, Benjamin Thompson, Count
Runcie, Robert Alexander Kennedy, Baron
Rundstedt, (Karl Rudolf) Gerd von
Runeberg, Johan Ludvig
Runyon, Damon
Rurik
Rushdie, Salman
Rusk, (David) Dean
Ruskin, John
Russell, Bertrand Arthur William, 3rd Earl
Russell, John, 1st Earl
Russell, Ken
Russell, Lord William
Russell, Sir William Howard
Rutherford, Ernest, 1st Baron
Rutherford, Dame Margaret
Rutherford, Mark
Ruyter, Michiel Adriaanszoon de
Ryder, Sue, Baroness
Rykov, Aleksei Ivanovich
Ryle, Gilbert
Ryle, Sir Martin
Saarinen, Eero
Sabatier, Paul
Sachs, Hans
Sachs, Nelly (Leonie)
Sackville, Thomas, 1st Earl of Dorset
Sadat, Anwar
Sade, Donatien Alphonse François, Marquis de
Sa'di
Sagan, Françoise
Saigo Takamori
Sainte-Beuve, Charles-Augustin
Saint-Exupéry, Antoine de
Saint-Just, Louis (Antoine Léon) de
Saint-Laurent, Yves
Saint-Saëns, Camille
Saint-Simon, Claude Henri de Rouvroy, Comte de
Saint-Simon, Louis de Rouvroy, Duc de
Sakharov, Andrei Dimitrievich
Saki *pen name of* H(ector) H(ugh) Munro
Saladin
Salam, Abdus
Salazar, António de Oliveira
Sales, St Francis of
Salieri, Antonio
Salinger, J(erome) D(avid)
Salisbury, Robert Arthur Talbot Gascoyne-Cecil, 3rd Marquess of
Salisbury, Robert Cecil, 1st Earl of
Sallust
Sampras, Pete
Samudra Gupta
Samuel, Herbert Louis, 1st Viscount
Sand, George
Sandage, Allan Rex
Sandburg, Carl
Sandwich, John Montagu, 4th Earl of
Sanger, Frederick
Sankara
San Martin, José de
Santa Anna, Antonio López de
Santayana, George
Santer, Jacques
Sapir, Edward
Sapper *pen name of* H(erman) C(yril) McNeile
Sappho
Sardou, Victorien
Sargent, John Singer
Sargent, Sir Malcolm
Sargon
Saroyan, William
Sarraute, Nathalie
Sarto, Andrea del
Sartre, Jean-Paul
Sassetta
Sassoon, Siegfried
Satie, Erik
Sato Eisaku
Saud
Saussure, Ferdinand de
Savage, Michael Joseph
Savage, Richard
Savery, Thomas
Savonarola, Girolamo
Saxe, Maurice, Comte de
Saxe-Weimar, Duke Bernhard of
Saxo Grammaticus
Sayers, Dorothy L(eigh)
Scaliger, Joseph Justus
Scaliger, Julius Caesar
Scarfe, Gerald
Scargill, Arthur
Scarlatti, Alessandro

**Scarlatti, Domenico**
**Scarron, Paul**
**Schacht, Hjalmar**
**Scheel, Walter**
**Scheele, Carl Wilhelm**
**Schelling, Friedrich**
**Schiaparelli, Elsa**
**Schiele, Egon**
**Schiller, (Johann Christoph) Friedrich(von)**
**Schlegel, August Wilhelm von**
**Schegel, (Carl Wilhelm) Friedrich von**
**Schleiden, Matthias Jakob**
**Schlesinger, John**
**Schlick, Moritz**
**Schlieffen, Alfred, Graf von**
**Schliemann, Heinrich**
**Schmeling, Max**
**Schmidt, Helmut**
**Schnabel, Artur**
**Schnitzler, Arthur**
**Schoenberg, Arnold**
**Schopenhauer, Arthur**
**Schreiner, Olive**
**Schrödinger, Erwin**
**Schubert, Franz (Peter)**
**Schumacher, Michael**
**Schuman, Robert** French statesman; *compare* Schumann, Robert
**Schuman, William (Howard)**
**Schumann, Clara**
**Schumann, Elisabeth**
**Schumann, Robert (Alexander)** German composer; *compare* Schuman, Robert
**Schuschnigg, Kurt von**
**Schütz, Heinrich**
**Schwann, Theodor**
**Schwarzenberg, Felix, Fürst zu**
**Schwarzkopf, Dame Elisabeth**
**Schweitzer, Albert**
**Schwitters, Kurt**
**Scipio Aemilianus Africanus** grandson of Scipio Africanus
**Scipio Africanus**
**Scofield, (David) Paul**
**Scorsese, Martin**
**Scott, Sir George Gilbert**
**Scott, Sir Giles Gilbert**
**Scott, Sir Peter Markham**
**Scott, Robert Falcon**
**Scott, Ronnie**
**Scott, Sir Walter**
**Scriabin, Alexander**
**Scullin, James Henry**
**Seaborg, Glenn Theodore**
**Searle, Ronald William Fordham**
**Seddon, Richard John**
**Seeger, Pete**
**Seferis, George**
**Seghers, Hercules Pieterzoon**
**Segovia, Andrés**
**Segrè, Emilio**
**Selden, John**
**Seleucus I Nicator**
**Selkirk, Alexander**
**Sellers, Peter**
**Selwyn Lloyd, John, Baron**
**Selznick, David O(liver)**
**Semiramis**
**Sempringham, St Gilbert of**
**Senanayake, D(on) S(tephen)**
**Senanayake, Dudley**
**Seneca**
**Senefelder, Aloys**
**Senghor, Léopold Sédar**
**Sennacherib**
**Sennett, Mack**
**Sergius of Radonezh, St**
**Servetus, Michael**
**Sesostris**
**Sesshu**
**Sessions, Roger**
**Seth, Vikram**
**Seton, Ernest Thompson**
**Seurat, Georges**
**Severini, Gino**
**Severus, Lucius Septimius**
**Severus Alexander**
**Sévigné, Marie de Rabutin-Chantal, Marquise de**
**Seymour, Jane**
**Shackleton, Sir Ernest Henry**
**Shadwell, Thomas**
**Shaffer, Anthony**
**Shaffer, Peter**
**Shaftesbury, Anthony Ashley Cooper, Earl of**
**Shah Jahan**
**Shahn, Ben**
**Shaka**
**Shakespeare, William**
**Shamir, Yitzhak**
**Shankar, Ravi**
**Shapur**
**Sharp, Cecil (James)**
**Shastri, Shri Lal Bahadur**
**Shaw, Artie**
**Shaw, George Bernard**
**Shaw, (Richard) Norman**
**Sheene, Barry**
**Shelburne, William Petty Fitzmaurice, 2nd Earl of**
**Shelley, Mary Wollstonecraft**
**Shelley, Percy Bysshe**
**Shenstone, William**
**Shepard, Ernest Howard**
**Shepard, Allan Bartlett**
**Sheppard, Jack**
**Sheraton, Thomas**
**Sheridan, Philip H(enry)**
**Sheridan, Richard Brinsley**
**Sherman, John**
**Sherman, William Tecumseh**
**Sherrington, Sir Charles Scott**
**Shevardnadze, Eduard**
**Shockley, William Bradfield**
**Sholes, Christopher Latham**
**Sholokhov, Mikhail**
**Shostakovich, Dmitri**
**Shostakovich, Maxim**
**Shovell, Sir Cloudesley**
**Shrapnel, Henry**
**Shute, Nevil**
**Sibelius, Jean**
**Sica, Vittoria De**
**Sickert, Walter Richard**
**Siddons, Sarah**
**Sidgwick, Henry**
**Sidmouth, Henry Addington, 1st Viscount**
**Sidney, Algernon**
**Sidney, Sir Philip**
**Siemens, Ernst Werner von**
**Siemens, Friedrich**
**Siemens, Karl**

Siemens, Sir William
Sienkiewicz, Henryk
Sieyès, Emmanuel Joseph
Siger of Brabant
Signac, Paul
Signorelli, Luca
Sigurdsson *variant spelling of* Sverrir
Sihanouk, Norodim, Prince
Sikorski, Władysław Polish statesman
Sikorsky, Igor Ivan US engineer
Sillitoe, Alan
Silone, Ignazio
Si-ma Qian (*or* Ssu-ma Ch'ien)
Simenon, Georges
Simeon Stylites, St
Simms, William Gilmore
Simnel, Lambert
Simon, John Allsebrook, 1st Viscount
Simon, (Marvin) Neil
Simon, Paul
Simonov, Konstantin
Simpson, George Gaylord
Simpson, N(orman) F(rederick)
Sinatra, Frank
Sinclair, Upton
Singer, Isaac Bashevis
Singer, Isaac Merrit
Siqueiros, David Alfaro
Sisley, Alfred
Sitwell, Edith
Sitwell, Sir Osbert
Sitwell, Sacheverell
Sivaji
Sixtus pope
Skalkottas, Nikos
Skanderbeg
Skelton, John
Skinner, Burrhus Frederic
Slade, Felix
SlánskýRudolf
Slim, William Joseph, 1st Viscount
Sloane, Sir Hans
Sluter, Claus
Smart, Christopher
Smetana, Bedřich
Smiles, Samuel
Smith, Adam
Smith, Bessie
Smith, Harvey
Smith, Ian (Douglas)
Smith, John
Smith, Joseph
Smith, Sir Keith Macpherson
Smith, Dame Maggie
Smith, Sir Ross Macpherson
Smith, Stevie
Smithson, Alison
Smithson, Peter
Smollett, Tobias (George)
Smuts, Jan (Christiaan)
Smythe, Pat
Snefru
Snow, C(harles) P(ercy), Baron
Snowdon, Antony Armstrong-Jones, Earl of
Snyders, Frans
Soames, (Arthur) Christopher (John), Baron
Soane, Sir John
Soares, Mario
Sobers, Sir Garry
Sobieski, John
Socinus, Faustus
Socinus, Laelius
Socrates
Soddy, Frederick
Söderblom, Nathan
Solon
Soloviov, Vladimir Sergevich
Solti, Sir Georg
Solzhenitsyn, Aleksandr
Somers, John, Baron
Somerset, Edward Seymour, 1st Duke of
Somerset, Robert Carr, Earl of
Sommerfeld, Arnold Johannes Wilhelm
Sondheim, Stephen (Joshua)
Song (*or* Sung), T. V.
Song Qing-ling (*or* Sung Ch'ing-ling)
Song Mei-ling (*or* Sung Mei-ling)
Sophocles
Sopwith, Sir Thomas Octave Murdoch
Soranus of Ephesus
Sorel, Georges
Sosigenes of Alexandria
Soter, Ptolomy
Soto, Hernando de
Soufflot, Jacques Germain
Soult, Nicolas Jean de Dieu, Duc de Dalmatie
Souphanouvong, Prince
Sousa, John Philip
Soustelle, Jacques (Émile)
Southampton, Henry Wriothesley, 3rd Earl of
Southcott, Joanna
Southey, Robert
Soutine, Chaim
Soyinka, Wole
Spaak, Paul Henri
Spallanzani, Lazzaro
Spark, Dame Muriel
Spartacus
Spassky, Boris
Spearman, Charles Edward
Speke, John Hanning
Spence, Sir Basil
Spencer, Herbert
Spencer, Sir Stanley
Spencer, Thomas
Spender, Sir Stephen
Spengler, Oswald
Spenser, Edmund
Speranski, Mikhail Mikhailovich
Spielberg, Steven
Spillane, Mickey
Spinoza, Benedict
Spitz, Mark (Andrew)
Spock, Benjamin McLane
Spohr, Louis
Spooner, William Archibald
Ssu-ma Ch'ien *variant spelling of* Si-ma Qian
Staël, Anne Louise Germaine Necker, Madame de
Stahl, Georg Ernst
Stainer, Sir John
Stalin, Joseph
Stamitz, Johann
Standish, Myles
Stanford, Sir Charles (Villiers)
Stanhope, Charles, 3rd Earl
Stanhope, James, 1st Earl
Stanislavsky, Konstantin

Stanisław, St
Stanley, Sir Henry Morton
Stanton, Elizabeth Cady
Stark, Dame Freya (Madeline)
Starr, Ringo
Staudinger, Hermann
Stauffenberg, Claus, Graf von
Steel, Sir David (Martin Scott)
Steele, Sir Richard
Steen, Jan
Stefan Dušan
Stein, Sir (Marc) Aurel
Stein, Gertrude
Stein, Karl, Freiherr vom
Steinbeck, John
Steiner, Rudolf
Steinmetz, Charles Proteus
Steinway, Henry (Engelhard)
Stendhal
Steno, Nicolaus
Stephen, Sir Leslie
Stephenson, George
Stephenson, Robert British civil engineer; *compare* Stevenson, Robert Louis
Stern, Isaac
Sternberg, Josef von
Sterne, Laurence
Stevens, Wallace
Stevenson, Adlai E(wing)
Stevenson, Frances
Stevenson, Robert Louis Scottish novelist; *compare* Stephenson, Robert
Stewart, Jackie
Stewart, James (Maitland)
Stewart, Rod
Stieglitz, Alfred
Stiernhielm, Georg Olofson
Stilicho, Flavius
Stilwell, Joseph W(arren)
Stirling, Sir James
Stockhausen, Karlheinz
Stoker, Bram
Stokes, Sir George Gabriel
Stokowski, Leopold
Stolypin, Petr Arkadievich
Stopes, Marie Charlotte Carmichael
Stoppard, Miriam
Stoppard, Tom
Storey, David
Storm, (Hans) Theodor Woldsen
Stoss, Veit
Stowe, Harriet Beecher
Strabo
Strachey, (Giles) Lytton
Stradivari, Antonio
Strafford, Thomas Wentworth, 1st Earl of
Stratton, Charles (*known as* Tom Thumb)
Strauss, Johann
Strauss, Richard
Stravinsky, Igor
Strawson, Sir Peter Frederick
Streep, Meryl
Streicher, Julius
Streisand, Barbra
Stresemann, Gustav
Strindberg, August
Stroheim, Erich von
Strong, Sir Roy (Colin)
Struve, Otto
Stuart surname of Scottish and English monarchs
Stuart, John McDouall
Stubbs, George
Stubbs, William
Sturluson, Snorri
Sturt, Charles
Stuyvesant, Peter
Suárez (Gonzalez), Adolfo, Duke of
Suarez, Francisco de
Suckling, Sir John
Sucre, Antonio José de
Su Dong Po (*or* Su Tung-p'o)
Sue, Eugène
Suetonius
Suger of Saint-Denis
Suharto
Sukarno
Suleiman
Sulla, Lucius Cornelius
Sullivan, Sir Arthur
Sullivan, John Lawrence
Sullivan, Louis Henry
Sully, Maximilien de Béthune, Duc de
Sully-Prudhomme, René François Armand
Sunderland, Robert Spencer, 2nd Earl of
Sun Yat-sen (*or* Sun Zhong Shan)
Suppiluliumas
Surrey, Henry Howard, Earl of
Surtees, John
Surtees, Robert Smith
Suslov, Mikhail
Sutcliffe, Herbert
Sutherland, Graham Vivian
Sutherland, Dame Joan
Sutton, Walter Stanborough
Suvorov, Aleksandr Vasilievich, Count
Sverrir (*or* Sigurdsson)
Svevo, Italo
Swammerdam, Jan
Swan, Sir Joseph Wilson
Swedenborg, Emanuel
Sweyn Forkbeard
Swift, Jonathan
Swinburne, Algernon Charles
Swithin, St
Symonds, John Addington
Symons, Arthur (William)
Synge, John Millington
Szabó, Istvan
Szell, George
Szent-Györgyi, Albert(von Nagyrapolt)
Szewinska, Irena
Szilard, Leo
Szymanowski, Karol
Tabari, Muhammad ibn Jarir al-
Tacitus, Cornelius
Taft, Robert Alphonso
Taft, William Howard
Tagore, Debendranath
Tagore, Rabindranath
Taine, Hippolyte Adolphe
Talbot, William Henry Fox
Taliesin
Talleyrand
Tallien, Jean Lambert
Tallis, Thomas
Tamerlane *variant of* Timur
Tancred
Tange Kenzo
Tanguy, Yves
Tanizaki Jun-ichiro

Tannhäuser
Tasman, Abel Janszoon
Tasso, Torquato
Tate, Allen
Tate, Harry
Tate, Nahum
Tati, Jacques
Tattersall, Richard
Tatum, Art(hur)
Tatum, Edward Lawrie
Tavener, John 20th-century British composer
Taverner, John 16th-century English composer
Tawney, R(ichard) H(enry)
Taylor, A(lan) J(ohn) P(ercivale)
Taylor, Brook
Taylor, Elizabeth
Taylor, Frederick Winslow
Taylor, Jeremy
Taylor, Zachary
Tchaikovsky, Peter Ilich
Teach, Edward
Tebaldi, Renata
Teck, Mary of
Tecumseh
Tedder, Arthur William, 1st Baron
Teilhard de Chardin, Pierre
Te Kanawa, Dame Kiri
Telemann, Georg Philipp
Telesio, Bernardino
Telford, Thomas
Teller, Edward
Temple, Frederick
Temple, Shirley
Temple, William
Teng Hsiao-p'ing *variant spelling of* Deng Xiao Ping
Teniers, David
Tenniel, Sir John
Tennyson, Alfred, Lord
Tenzing Norgay
Terborch, Gerard
Terbrugghen, Hendrik
Terman, Lewis Madison
Terry, Dame Ellen (Alice)
Tertullian(us), Quintus Septimius Florens
Tesla, Nikola
Tetrazzini, Luisa
Tetzel, Johann
Teyte, Dame Maggie
Thackeray, William Makepeace
Thais
Thales
Thatcher, Margaret (Hilda), Baroness
Themistocles
Thenard, Louis-Jacques
Theocritus
Theodorakis, Mikis
Theodoric
Theodosius
Theophrastus
Thespis
Thibaud, Jacques
Thiers, Louis Adolphe
Thistlewood, Arthur
Thomas, Dylan
Thomas, Edward
Thompson, Emma
Thompson, Francis
Thomson, Sir George Paget
Thomson, James
Thomson, Sir Joseph John
Thomson, Kenneth Roy, 2nd Baron
Thomson, Virgil
Thomson, William, 1st Baron Kelvin
Thomson of Fleet, Roy Herbert, 1st Baron
Thoreau, Henry David
Thorndike, Dame Sybil
Thornhill, Sir James
Thorpe, (John) Jeremy
Thorvaldsen, Bertel
Thrale, Hester Lynch (*maiden name* Piozzi)
Throckmorton, Francis
Throckmorton, Sir Nicholas
Thucydides
Thurber, James
Thutmose
Tibaldi, Pellegrino
Tiberius
Tibullus, Albius
Tieck, (Johann) Ludwig
Tiepolo, Giovanni Battista
Tiepolo, Giovanni Domenico
Tiglath-pileser
Tilak, Bal Gangadhar
Tillett, Benjamin
Tilley, Vesta
Tillich, Paul (Johannes)
Tilly, Johan Tserclaes, Graf von
Timoshenko, Semyon Konstantinovich
Timur (*or* Tamerlane)
Tinbergen, Jan
Tinbergen, Niko(laas)
Tintoretto
Tippett, Sir Michael
Tipu Sahib
Tirpitz, Alfred von
Tirso de Molina
Tissot, James Joseph Jacques
Titian
Tito
Titus (Flavius Vespasianus)
Tobey, Mark
Tocqueville, Alexis de
Todd, Alexander Robertus, Baron
Toghril Beg
Togliatti, Palmiro
Togo Heihachiro
Tojo Hideki
Tokugawa Ieyasu
Tolkien, J(ohn) R(onald) R(euel)
Toller, Ernst
Tolstoy, Leo (Nikolaevich), Count
Tom Thumb *see* Stratton, Charles
Tone, (Theobald) Wolfe
Tong Zhi (*or* T'ung-chih)
Tooke, John Horne
Torquemada, Tomás de
Torricelli, Evangelista
Tortelier, Paul
Toscanini, Arturo
Tostig
Totila
Toulouse-Lautrec, Henri (Marie Raymond) de
Touré, (Ahmed) Sékou
Tournefort, Joseph Pitton de
Tourneur, Cyril
Tours, St Gregory of
Toussaint-L'Ouverture, François Dominique
Townes, Charles Hard
Townshend, Charles, 2nd Viscount

Townshend, Pete
Toynbee, Arnold (Joseph)
Toynbee, (Theodore) Philip
Tracy, Spencer
Traherne, Thomas
Trajan(us), Marcus Ulpius
Traven, B(en) US novelist
Travers, Ben(jamin) British dramatist
Tree, Sir Herbert (Draper) Beerbohm
Trenchard, Hugh Montague, 1st Viscount
Trevelyan, George Macaulay
Trevelyan, Sir George Otto
Trevino, Lee
Trevithick, Richard
Trevor-Roper, Hugh Redwald, Baron Dacre
Trilling, Lionel
Trimble, David
Trollope, Anthony
Tromp, Cornelis (Martenszoon)
Tromp, Maarten (Harpertszoon)
Trotsky, Leon
Trudeau, Pierre Elliott
Trueman, Freddy
Truffaut, François
Trujillo (Molina), Rafael (Leónidas)
Truman, Harry S.
Truth, Sojourner
Tryggvason, Olaf
Ts'ao Chan *variant spelling of* Cao Chan
Tshombe, Moise (Kapenda)
Tsiolkovski, Konstantin Eduardovich
Tsvetaeva, Marina
Tubman, Harriet
Tubman, William V(acanarat) S(hadrach)
Tudjman, Franjo
Tu Fu *variant spelling of* Du Fu
Tull, Jethro
Tulsidas
T'ung-chih *variant spelling of* Tong Zhi
Tunney, Gene
Tupac Amarú
Tupolev, Andrei Niklaievich
Turenne, Henri de la Tour d'Auvergne, Vicomte de
Turgenev, Ivan
Turgot, Anne Robert Jacques, Baron de l'Aulne
Turishcheva, Ludmilla
Turner, Joseph Mallord William
Turner, Nat
Turpin, Dick
Tussaud, Marie
Tutankhamen
Tutu, Desmond
Tutuola, Amos
Twain, Mark
Tyler, John
Tyler, Wat
Tylor, Sir Edward Burnett
Tyndale, William
Tyndall, John
Tzimisces, John
Tz'u-hsi *variant spelling of* Zi Xi
Uccello, Paolo
Udall, Nicholas
Uhland, (Johann) Ludwig
Ulanova, Galina
Ulbricht, Walter
Umberto
Unamuno y Jugo, Miguel de
Undset, Sigrid
Ungaretti, Giuseppe
Updike, John (Hoyer)
Urban pope
Urey, Harold Clayton
Urfé, Honoré d'
Ussher, James
Ustinov, Sir Peter (Alexander)
Utagawa Kuniyoshi
Utamaro, Kitagawa
Utrillo, Maurice
Valdemar (*or* Waldemar)
Valens
Valentinian
Valentino, Rudolf
Valera, Eamon De
Valéry, Paul
Valla, Lorenzo
Valois, Dame Ninette de
Valois, Margaret of
Van Allen, James Alfred
Vanbrugh, Sir John
Van Buren, Martin
Vance, Cyrus
Vancouver, George
Vanderbilt, Cornelius
Van der Post, Sir Laurens
Van der Waals, Johannes Diderik
van de Velde, Adriaen
van de Velde, Esaias
van de Velde, Henry
van de Velde, Willem
van Dieman, Anthony
Van Dyck, Sir Anthony
Vane, Sir Henry
van Eyck, Hubert
van Eyck, Jan
Van Gogh, Vincent
Vansittart, Robert Gilbert, 1st Baron
Van't Hoff, Jacobus Henricus
Vardhamana *see* Mahavira
Varèse, Edgard
Vargas, Getúlio
Vargas Llosa, (Jorge) Mario (Pedro)
Varro, Marcus Terentius
Vasarely, Victor
Vasari, Giorgio
Vauban, Sébastian Le Prestre de
Vaughan, Henry
Vaughan Williams, Ralph
Vavilov, Nikolai Ivanovich
Vega (Carpio), Lope Félix de
Velázquez, Diego Rodriguez de Silva
Vendôme, Louis Joseph, Duc de
Venizélos, Eleuthérios
Ventris, Michael
Vercingetorix
Verdi, Giuseppe
Verhaeren, Émile
Verlaine, Paul
Vermeer, Jan
Verne, Jules
Vernon, Edward
Veronese, Paolo
Verrocchio, Andrea del
Versace, Gianni
Verwoerd, Hendrik Frensch
Vesalius, Andreas

**Vespasian**
**Vespucci, Amerigo**
**Vicente, Gil**
**Vicky** *pen name of* **Victor Weisz**
**Vico, Giambattista**
**Victor Emmanuel** Italian king
**Victoria, Tomás Luis de**
**Vidal, Gore**
**Vidal de la Blache, Paul**
**Vignola, Giacomo da**
**Vigny, Alfred de**
**Villa, Pancho**
**Villa-Lobos, Heitor**
**Villars, Claude Louis Hector, Duc de**
**Villehardouin, Geoffroi de**
**Villeneuve, Pierre**
**Villiers de l'Isle-Adam, Philippe Auguste, Comte de**
**Villon, François**
**Vincent de Paul, St**
**Viollet-le-Duc, Eugène Emmanuel**
**Virchow, Rudolf**
**Viren, Lasse Artturi**
**Visconti, Luchino**
**Vitruvius**
**Vittorini, Elio**
**Vittorino da Feltre**
**Vivaldi, Antonio**
**Vivekananda, Swami**
**Vivés, Juan Luis**
**Vladimir, St**
**Vlaminck, Maurice de**
**Volta, Alessandro Giuseppe Antonio Anastasio, Count**
**Voltaire**
**Vondel, Joost van den**
**Vonnegut, Kurt**
**Voroshilov, Kliment Yefremovich**
**Vorster, Balthazar Johannes**
**Voysey, Charles Francis Annesley**
**Voznesenskii, Andrei**
**Vuillard, (Jean) Édouard**
**Vyshinskii, Andrei Yanuareevich**
**Wace**
**Wade, Virginia**
**Wagner, (Wilhelm) Richard**
**Wagner, Siegfried**
**Wagner, Wieland**
**Wagner von Jauregg, Julius**
**Wain, John** British novelist; *compare* **Wayne, John**
**Wajda, Andrzej**
**Wakefield, Edward Gibbon**
**Waksman, Selman Abraham**
**Walafrid Strabo**
**Walburga, St**
**Walcott, Derek**
**Waldemar** *variant spelling of* **Valdemar**
**Waldheim, Kurt**
**Wałęsa, Lech**
**Waley, Arthur**
**Walker, Alice**
**Wallace, Alfred Russel**
**Wallace, Edgar**
**Wallace, Lew(is)**
**Wallace, Sir William**
**Wallenstein, Albrecht Wenzel von**
**Waller, Edmund**
**Waller, (Thomas) Fats**
**Wallis, Sir Barnes (Neville)**
**Walpole, Horace 4th Earl of Orford**
**Walpole, Sir Hugh (Seymour)**
**Walpole, Sir Robert, 1st Earl of Orford**
**Walsingham, Sir Francis**
**Walter, Bruno**
**Walter, Hubert**
**Walter, John**
**Walther von der Vogelweide**
**Walton, Ernest Thomas Sinton**
**Walton, Izaak**
**Walton, Sir William (Turner)**
**Wang An Shi** (*or* **Wang An-shih)**
**Wang Jing Wei** (*or* **Wang Ching-wei)**
**Warbeck, Perkin**
**Ward, Artemus**
**Ward, Barbara, Baroness Jackson**
**Ward, Mrs Humphry**
**Ward, Sir Joseph George**
**Ward, Sir Leslie**
**Warhol, Andy**
**Warlock, Peter**
**Warren, Earl**
**Warton, Joseph**
**Warton, Thomas**
**Warwick, Richard Neville, Earl of**
**Washington, Booker T(aliaferro)**
**Washington, George**
**Wasserman, August von**
**Waterhouse, Alfred**
**Watson, James Dewey**
**Watson, John Broadus**
**Watson, John Christian**
**Watson-Watt, Sir Robert Alexander**
**Watt, James**
**Watteau, (Jean) Antoine**
**Watts, George Frederick**
**Waugh, Alec (Raban)**
**Waugh, Auberon**
**Waugh, Evelyn (Arthur St John)**
**Wavell, Archibald Percival, 1st Earl**
**Wayne, John** US actor; *compare* **Wain, John**
**Webb, Beatrice (Potter)**
**Webb, Mary**
**Webb, Sidney (James), Baron Passfield**
**Weber, Carl Maria von**
**Weber, Ernst Heinrich**
**Weber, Max**
**Weber, Wilhelm Eduard**
**Webern, Anton von**
**Webster, John**
**Webster, Noah**
**Wedekind, Frank**
**Wedgwood, Dame Cicely Veronica**
**Wedgwood, Josiah**
**Weelkes, Thomas**
**Wegener, Alfred Lothar**
**Weil, Simone**
**Weill, Kurt**
**Weir, Peter (Lindsay)**
**Weismann, August Friedrich Leopold**
**Weiss, Peter**
**Weissmuller, Johnny**
**Weisz, Victor** (*pen name* **Vicky)**
**Weizmann, Chaim (Azriel)**

Weldon, Fay
Welensky, Sir Roy
Welles, (George) Orson
Wellesley, Richard Colley, Marquess
Wellesz, Egon
Wellington, Arthur Wellesley, 1st Duke of
Wells, Henry
Wells, H(erbert) G(eorge)
Wenceslas
Wentworth, Thomas, 1st Earl of Strafford
Wentworth, William Charles
Werfel, Franz
Wergeland, Henrik Arnold
Wesker, Arnold
Wesley, Charles
Wesley, John
Wesley, Samuel
Wesley, Samuel Sebastian
West, Benjamin
West, Mae
West, Nathanael
West, Dame Rebecca
Westwood, Vivienne
Weyden, Rogier van der
Wharton, Edith (Newbold)
Wheatstone, Sir Charles
Wheeler, Sir (Robert Eric) Mortimer
Whistler, James (Abbott) McNeill
Whistler, Laurence
Whistler, Rex
White, Gilbert
White, Patrick
White, T(erence) H(anbury)
Whitefield, George
Whitehead, A(lfred) N(orth)
Whitelaw, William (Stephen Ian), 1st Viscount
Whitgift, John
Whitlam, (Edward) Gough
Whitman, Walt
Whitney, Eli
Whittier, John Greenleaf
Whittington, Dick
Whittle, Sir Frank
Whorf, Benjamin Lee
Whymper, Edward
Widor, Charles Marie
Wieland, Christoph Martin
Wiener, Norbert
Wiesenthal, Simon
Wigner, Eugene Paul
Wilberforce, William
Wilde, Oscar
Wilder, Billy
Wilder, Thornton
Wilkes, John
Wilkie, Sir David
Wilkins, Sir George Hubert
Wilkins, Maurice Hugh Frederick
Williams, John
Williams, J(ohn) P(eter) R(hys)
Williams, Roger
Williams, Shirley (Vivien Teresa Brittain)
Williams, Tennessee
Williams, William Carlos
Williams-Ellis, Sir Clough
Williamson, Henry
Williamson, Malcolm
Willis, Ted
Wills (Moody), Helen
Wilson, Sir Angus
Wilson, Charles Thomson Rees
Wilson, Colin
Wilson, Edmund US critic
Wilson, Edmund Beecher US biologist
Wilson, (James) Harold, Baron
Wilson, Sir Henry Hughes
Wilson, Henry Maitland, 1st Baron
Wilson, Richard
Wilson, (Thomas) Woodrow
Winckelmann, Johann Joachim
Wingate, Orde Charles
Winkler, Hans Günter
Winstanley, Gerrard
Winterhalter, Franz Xavier
Winthrop, John
Wise, Thomas James
Wiseman, Nicholas Patrick Stephen
Wishart, George
Wissler, Clark
Witt, Johan de
Witte, Sergei Yulievich
Wittgenstein, Ludwig
Wodehouse, Sir P(elham) G(renville)
Woffington, Peg
Wöhler, Friedrich
Wolf, Hugo
Wolfe, Charles
Wolfe, James
Wolfe, Thomas
Wolfenden, John Frederick, Baron
Wolf-Ferrari, Ermanno
Wölfflin, Heinrich
Wolfit, Sir Donald
Wolfram von Eschenbach
Wolfson, Sir Isaac
Wollstonecraft, Mary
Wolseley, Garnet Joseph, 1st Viscount
Wolsey, Thomas, Cardinal
Wood, Aaron
Wood, Enoch
Wood, Sir Henry (Joseph)
Wood, John
Wood, Ralph
Woodville, Elizabeth
Woodward, Robert Burns
Woolf, Leonard (Sidney)
Woolf, (Adeline) Virginia
Woollett, William
Woolley, Sir Leonard
Woolworth, F(rank) W(infield)
Wootton, Barbara, Baroness
Wordsworth, William
Wotton, Sir Henry
Wouwerman, Jan
Wouwerman, Philips
Wouwerman, Pieter
Wrangel, Ferdinand Petrovich, Baron von
Wrangel, Peter Nikolaievich, Baron
Wren, Sir Christopher
Wren, P(ercival) C(hristopher)
Wright, Frank Lloyd
Wright, Judith
Wright, Orville
Wright, Richard
Wright, Wilbur
Wu Hou
Wundt, Wilhelm